COMMONWEALTH UNIVERSITIES YEARBOOK 2008

A Directory to the
Universities of the Commonwealth
and the Handbook of their Association

Volume 2

Association of Commonwealth Universities
Woburn House, 20-24 Tavistock Square, London WC1H 9HF
Tel: +44(0) 20 7380 6700 Fax: +44(0) 20 7387 2655 E-mail: info@acu.ac.uk
Website: http://www.acu.ac.uk

INSTITUTIONS IN THIS VOLUME

Principal features of the ACU Yearbook

University profiles

Facts and figures cover:
- foundation date
- history and location
- library holdings
- academic year: term/semester dates
- statistics: staff/student figures
- recurrent income levels

Courses and enrolment

Detailed entries help students to find out about opportunities overseas:
- entry to first degree courses: application procedures and basic education requirements
- first and higher degrees: titles, course lengths and general admission requirements
- language of instruction
- academic awards: scholarships, bursaries, etc.

Study options

Specially compiled national guides identify degree options in many countries including Australia, Bangladesh, Canada, Ghana, Hong Kong, India, Kenya, Malaysia, New Zealand, Nigeria, Pakistan, South Africa, Sri Lanka and the United Kingdom. The guides focus on broad subject areas and indicate which universities offer facilities for study and/or research at undergraduate, postgraduate and doctoral level. These detailed tables appear at the beginning of country sections. In Canada, for example, it is easy to see that Chinese features at eight institutions, to first degree level at six, to master's at one and to doctoral level at another.

Higher education systems

Short introductions to higher education systems set the scene in the larger countries, and normally cover: the university system, academic year, language of instruction, pre-university education, admission to first degree courses, method of application, university finance, student finance, staff and student numbers. In countries where there are multiple universities, **maps** pinpoint the location of institutions.

150,000 key academics and managers

These extensive listings are a much used part of the Yearbook and form the core of each university's entry. Full entries include:
- executive head and other senior management officers listed by name in order of seniority
- deans and secretaries of faculties/schools
- heads of departments
- alphabetical listing by department of all senior teaching and research staff
- directors of research and other centres
- administrative contact officers
- heads of campuses/constituent colleges
- degree qualifications with awarding institutions for all staff
- phone/fax numbers and e-mail addresses for faculties, departments, special centres and, separately, for service managers

Research strengths

Summaries of the general areas of research currently undertaken by academic units and special centres complement the detailed staff lists and provide an overview of each academic section's work. The many and wide-ranging interests are all traceable through the extensive index system which extends to over 29,000 entries.

Central services

Up to 45 areas of special organisational responsibility are identified in most institutions and the contact officer named. Included are: academic affairs, accommodation, admissions, alumni, careers, computing services, conferences/corporate hospitality, credit transfer, distance education, estates and buildings, finance, industrial liaison, language training for international students, marketing, public relations, quality assurance and accreditation, sport and recreation, strategic planning, student welfare *et al.*

Affiliated colleges in Asia

In Bangladesh, India and Pakistan, where teaching often takes place in colleges affiliated to a university, the colleges are listed alphabetically by location.

Four substantial indexes complete the scope of the Yearbook:

- to the **2,700** university institutions, their constituent colleges and selected centres, and the location of affiliated colleges
- to subjects of study offered by the **21,000** academic departments and subdepartments
- to the **29,000** departmental research entries
- to the **150,000** academic and managerial staff listed in the university chapters

CONTENTS

PAKISTAN

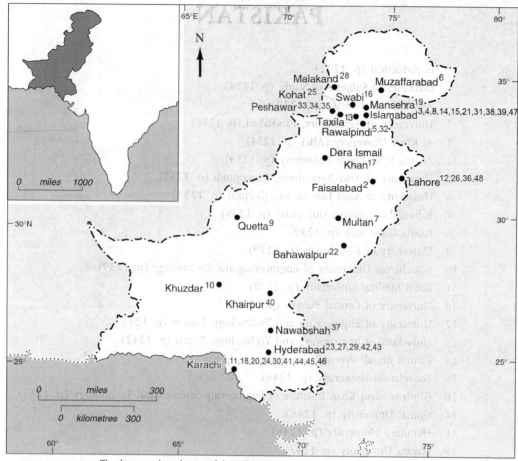

The places named are the seats of the university institutions numbered on the previous page

THE UNIVERSITIES OF PAKISTAN

Information compiled by the Higher Education Commission, Pakistan as at 18 March 2008

The University System

At present there are 65 public sector and 57 private sector universities/degree-awarding institutions in Pakistan.

Although fully autonomous, the universities' affairs are subject to a certain amount of governmental control, due to provisions in their acts of incorporation relating to the appointment of vice-chancellors and pro-vice-chancellors by the chancellor, the President of Pakistan or the provincial governors as *ex-officio* chancellors, and nominations by the government to university senates and syndicates. Internal governance of the universities is generally through the senate, syndicate, academic council, board of faculties and studies, selection boards, advanced studies and research board, finance and planning committee, affiliation committee, and the discipline committee. The vice-chancellor is the principal executive officer and academic head of the university.

The Higher Education Commission (HEC), established on 11 September 2002 is empowered to carry out the evaluation, improvement and promotion of higher education, research and development; to formulate policies, guiding principles and priorities for higher education institutions; and to prescribe conditions under which institutions, including those that are not part of the state educational system, may be opened and operated. The mandate of the HEC encompasses all degree-awarding universities and institutions, both in the public and private sectors, and supports the attainment of quality education by facilitating and co-ordinating self-assessment of academic programmes and their external review by national and international experts. The HEC also supervises the planning, development and accreditation of public and private sector institutions of higher education. Its goal is to facilitate the reform process.

The higher education sector through HEC activities has adopted a pivotal role in the production of human capital, and the generation and transmission of knowledge, in order to achieve a competitive position in the global knowledge economy. The renewed financial commitment of the government of Pakistan towards higher education has resulted in a dramatic renaissance in the sector. In its role of facilitating the transformation of Pakistan into a knowledge economy, the HEC is now endeavouring to strengthen the systems and the institutions of which it is comprised—where the creation of knowledge takes place—and to develop and consolidate mechanisms for accelerated advancement in sciences, engineering and technology while ensuring relevance to national development objectives and international trends and requirements.

A few of the initiatives undertaken by the HEC in this respect are: PhD local and foreign scholarships (in technologically advanced countries); postdoctoral facilities for existing faculty; funding to attend and/or present papers at local and foreign conferences; training in teaching skills; accelerated revision of curricula; improvement in infrastructure for teaching and research, including digital library access and video conferencing facilities; the introduction of tenure track system and other incentives for faculty; increase in benchmark criteria for appointing faculty; instituting quality assurance mechanism; establishment of accreditation councils; stringent criteria for admission to and award of MPhil/PhD degrees; definition of HEC-recognised research journals; launch of four-year bachelor degree programmes across all universities/institutes; development of affiliation criteria; improvement of examination and testing systems and services; and the promotion and strengthening of the semester system.

Academic Year

The academic year generally begins in early September or January and ends in August or December, respectively; the long vacation is in July–August.

Language of Instruction

English and Urdu.

Pre-University Education

Primary education lasts for five years. Secondary education is divided into three cycles: three years' middle school, two years' secondary and two years' higher secondary schooling. On completion of the second cycle, pupils take the secondary school certificate. Pupils may then study for a further two years or three years in the case of technical education, specialising in science, arts or technical and vocational studies. At the end of this period, pupils take the examinations for the intermediate certificate/higher secondary school certificate/diploma of associate engineering. Vocational secondary courses lead to the higher secondary school certificate or a diploma in technical/vocational subjects.

Admission to First Degree Courses

The basic entrance requirement is the intermediate or higher secondary school certificate, or its equivalent. Admission to professional colleges and universities is based on performance in the entry test as well as in the public examinations at higher secondary level conducted by the boards of intermediate and secondary education. Entry tests are also being progressively introduced through independent testing and assessment agencies specialising in accurate performance evaluation of students at various educational institutions at different levels. Places are not available to all who qualify and desire to enter. There is a high demand for professional courses in medicine, dentistry, engineering and business, etc, as a result of which admission to these courses is much more difficult than admission to general university education. Competition for admission to the general universities is not as keen since the wide network of affiliated colleges enables a large portion of students to gain admission. Special quotas are reserved for students from federally administrated Tribal and Northern Areas, who live in remote regions of Pakistan with limited access to quality higher education facilities, as well as for foreign students. However, apart from these exceptions, all universities and degree-awarding institutes are open, based on merit, to all persons of either gender, irrespective of religion, race, creed, class, colour or domicile, and no person is denied admission on these grounds.

Method of application. Direct to the university.

Length of course. Formerly, the universities offered two-year bachelor degree courses in arts, commerce and some other general subjects. However, these programmes have recently been upgraded to four-year courses. Bachelor honours degrees in basic science subjects and degrees in IT, engineering, pharmacy, veterinary medicine, agriculture, etc, have always been four-year courses, and five years in the case of architecture and medicine.

Frameworks/templates for four-year integrated bachelor degree programs in basic, social, natural and applied sciences have been developed as a minimum baseline for the review and revision of curricula at undergraduate level. The majority of the private as well as public sector universities have initiated four-year undergraduate degree programs in various disciplines to bring them on a par with international standards.

Finance

Before 1979, recurring grants for universities were provided by the provincial governments and development grants by the federal government. Since 1979, the Federal Government has taken sole responsibility for all university funding. With the establishment of the HEC in 2002, there has been a substantial growth in the level of funding provided by the federal government, which has promised to increase proportionately grants for the universities year after year until funding to the higher education sector attains a level of 1% of GNP.

The recurring grant to the universities/institutes has grown from Rs3.486 billion in 2002–2003 to Rs15.766 billion in 2007–2008, showing a percentage increase of 352% during the past four years. Similarly, the development allocation to these institutions expanded from Rs4.265 billion in 2002–2003 to Rs18.00 billion in 2007–2008, showing an increase of 322% during the same period. This has permitted development activities on the universities' campuses to proceed with great speed.

HEC has provided substantial funds to the universities for the promotion of academic and research activities, seminars, conferences, travel grants, faculty exchange programmes, institutional strengthening, partial PhD programmes, postdoctoral fellowships and teaching/research support programmes for young PhD students.

Prior to 2002, university activities were generally under-funded. To counteract the lack of funding, many universities started to admit students on a self-financing basis, particularly in demand-oriented subjects, such as business and management sciences, computer studies and engineering. Some public sector universities followed by launching programmes on a full-cost basis, with enhanced rates of tuition fees and service charges. With the establishment of the HEC and the unprecedented increase in university funding, this practice is being discouraged.

Nevertheless, recurring expenditure remains skewed in favour of salary and allowance as only 5–7% of the allocation is actually spent on research, libraries, equipment, chemicals and glassware, while 65–80% is consumed by salaries and allowances. However, the problem of research is being ameliorated in a different way wherein grants for research projects in the universities are funded directly by the HEC. These grants are available up to the Rs6 million for each research project, mainly for scientific research. Numerous other initiatives have been taken for the promotion of research and to instil an environment conducive to research, exploration and reasoning.

Student finance. For master's degrees, tuition fees range from Rs13,000–15,000 per annum on average for social sciences, Rs20,000–25,000 for applied and basic sciences, while engineering and medical studies cost Rs50,000 per annum. Under the self-financed scheme, engineering and medical fees are approximately Rs200,000.

Staff and Student Numbers
In 2003–2004, the total number of teaching staff in Pakistan's universities was 37,405, of which 31,250 were at public, and 6155 at private, institutions. Of the 31,250 staff at public universities, 10,653 were full-time and 20,597 were part-time. 3938 were full-time and 2217 were part-time in the private sector.

During the same period, a total of 521,473 students were enrolled, of which 308,476 were male and 212,997 were female.

Further Information
Government of Pakistan. Finance Division. *Economic survey of Pakistan 2006–2007.* Islamabad (www.finance.gov.pk).
————. Planning Commission. *Pakistan medium term development framework 2005–2010.* Islamabad (www.pc.gov.pk).
Higher Education Commission, Islamabad. *Education policy 1998–2010* (www.moe.gov.pk/edupolicy.htm).
Ministry of Education. *Pakistan education statistics 2005–2006.*
————. *Handbook to universities/institutes of Pakistan 2005.* Islamabad (ISBN: 969-417-090-7).
World Bank. Human Development Sector, South Asia Region. *Pakistan—Higher education policy note, report #37247,* 28 June 2006.

The Pakistan Directory to Subjects of Study follows on p. 1224

The table below shows which of the institutions indicated provide facilities for study and/or research in the subjects named. In the case of related subject areas which have been grouped together (eg Agronomy/Soil Science), it should be borne in mind that one or more of the subjects may be offered by the institution concerned.

Subject	Aga Khan	Al-Khair U. (AJK)	Arid Agric., Rawalpindi	Azad Jammu & Kashmir	Fatima Jinnah Women	Foundation	Ghulam Ishaq Khan	Islamia, Bahawalpur	Lahore, Management	Mehran	N.-W.F.P. U.E.T.	N.E.D. Eng. & Tech.	National U.S.T.	Quaid-e-Awam	Riphah Internat.	S. Zulfikar Ali Bhutto	Sindh	Sir Syed U.E.T.	U.E.T., Lahore
Aboriginal Studies								MD											
Accountancy/Accounting		U	UM	X		UM						U	X		UM		U		
Administration/Administrative Studies				UM		U							X				UM		
Advertising			UM			UM									M				
Agriculture/Agricultural Science				X				UM											
Agronomy/Soil Science			X	MD															
American Studies								U											
Anaesthesia/Anaesthesiology															UM				
Anatomical Science/Anatomy	U												X		X				
Ancient Indian History and Culture																	UM		
Anthropology/Folklore			M					U											
Applied Chemistry															U		M		
Applied Physics				M									MD		U		M		
Aquaculture/Fisheries/Marine Science																	X		
Arabic								X	U								X		
Architecture									U	UD			UM						UM
Area Studies																	D		
Art Theory																	U		
Art, Fine		U		X	UM												UM		
Art, History of																	U		
Arts General																	U		
Asian/Pacific Studies								U											
Banking/Finance		U				UM			UM			U	X		UM	X	UM		
Behavioural Sciences				MD		U		U							U	D			
Biochemistry	U	MD	M			U		X					X		U		X		
Bioengineering															U				
Biology			M					U							UM				
Biology Molecular															X				
Biomedical Sciences												U			X				
Biophysics															U	D			
Biostatistics	M					U									U				
Biotechnology																	X		
Botany/Plant Science			M	MD				UM									X		
Building/Built Environment/Construction												U							
Business Administration		UM	UM	X	M				M			U	X		UM	X	UM		
Business Computing												U			UM				

TO SUBJECTS OF STUDY

For further information about the individual subjects taught at each institution, please refer to the *Index to Subjects of Study* at the end of the Yearbook, but for full details about subjects/courses offered at universities in the Commonwealth each institution's own official publications must be consulted. U = may be studied for first degree course; M = may be studied for master's degree course; D = research facilities to doctoral level; X = all three levels (UMD). **Note**—The table only includes information provided by institutions currently in membership of the Association of Commonwealth Universities.

	Aga Khan	Al-Khair U. (AJK)	Arid Agric., Rawalpindi	Azad Jammu & Kashmir	Fatima Jinnah Women	Foundation	Ghulam Ishaq Khan	Islamia, Bahawalpur	Lahore, Management	Mehran	N.-W.F.P. U.E.T.	N.E.D. Eng. & Tech.	National U.S.T.	Quaid-e-Awam	Riphah Internat.	S. Zulfikar Ali Bhutto	Sindh	Sir Syed U.E.T.	U.E.T., Lahore
Business Economics													UM						
Business/Commerce		UM	U	X				UM	UM			U	X				X	X	
Catholicism																	X		
Chemistry			UM	MD				X				U			U		X		M
Child Health						U													
Child Welfare						U													
Communication Sciences					M						MD	UM				D			
Communication/Journalism/Media Studies						U						U					X	X	
Communications/Information Management						UM						U				D			
Community Education	U																		
Community Health	U					U													
Community Medicine	U					U									U				
Computer Science		UM	UM	UM	M	U		M	X				X	X	UM	X	X	U	M
Consumer Studies						UM			M						M				
Creative Writing									U						U				
Criminology																	M		
Crop Science/Production			X																
Defence Studies					M														
Dentistry	U												U		U				
Dermatology													U		U				
Design				U								UM					U		
Design, Industrial												UM							
Development Studies						UM			U			U					M		
E-Business												M	X		M	UM			
E-Commerce				UM								M	X		M	UM	M		
Economic History									U										
Economic Planning and Development																M			
Economics			M	M	X	UM		X	UM			U	UM			UM	X	X	
Economics Agricultural/Agribusiness			M						M								D		
Education	M	UM	X	UM	X	X		X								D	X		
Education Distance																	U		
Educational Psychology						X													
Electronics													X				U	UM	
Energy Studies													M	X					
Engineering			X					X			X	UM	X	U					
Engineering Aeronautical/Aerospace													U						

	Aga Khan	Al-Khair U. (AJK)	Arid Agric., Rawalpindi	Azad Jammu & Kashmir	Fatima Jinnah Women	Foundation	Ghulam Ishaq Khan	Islamia, Bahawalpur	Lahore, Management	Mehran	N.-W.F.P. U.E.T.	N.E.D. Eng. & Tech.	National U.S.T.	Quaid-e-Awam	Riphah Internat.	S. Zulfikar Ali Bhutto	Sindh	Sir Syed U.E.T.	U.E.T., Lahore
Engineering Agricultural/Fisheries											X								
Engineering Architectural												U							
Engineering Biomedical										U		U			U				
Engineering Business												UM			U				
Engineering Chemical/Petrochemical/Process										X	U		MD						UM
Engineering Civil/Environmental/Structural										X	X	UM	X	X				UM	UM
Engineering Communications/Telecommunications			U			U				X	U	UM	X				X		
Engineering Computer		U	U				X			X	X	UM	X	UM	U			U	M
Engineering Construction													X						
Engineering Electrical/Electronic			X				X			X	X	UM	X	X	U			U	X
Engineering Geological												UM							
Engineering Industrial										X		UM							
Engineering Information Technology										MD			X						
Engineering Instrumentation												UM							
Engineering Management													M		U				
Engineering Manufacturing										MD		UM	UM						
Engineering Marine												UM	U						
Engineering Materials/Mineral Resources/Petroleum							X				X								UM
Engineering Mathematical													MD	U					
Engineering Mechanical/Production			U				X			X	X	UM	X	X					X
Engineering Metallurgical/Mining							X				U	UM	U						UM
Engineering Nuclear												UM							
Engineering Software				U	U	U				X		UM	X		UM		UM		
English	U	M	U	X	X	UM			UM			U			U		X		
Entomology			X			U											UM		
Entrepreneurship						UM									M				
Environmental Health						U							UM						
Environmental Science/Studies				X					U				UM			D	MD	M	
Epidemiology						U													
Ergonomics						U													
Ethics						U									UM				
Ethics, Law and Governance						UM													
European Studies									U										
Food Science/Nutrition/Home Science/Dietetics																	M		
Forensic Science															U				
Forestry			UM																

	Aga Khan	Al-Khair U. (AJK)	Arid Agric., Rawalpindi	Azad Jammu & Kashmir	Fatima Jinnah Women	Foundation	Ghulam Ishaq Khan	Islamia, Bahawalpur	Lahore, Management	Mehran	N.-W.F.P. U.E.T.	N.E.D. Eng. & Tech.	National U.S.T.	Quaid-e-Awam	Riphah Internat.	S. Zulfikar Ali Bhutto	Sindh	Sir Syed U.E.T.	U.E.T., Lahore
French/French Studies									U										
Genetics																	U		
Genetics and Plant Breeding				MD															
Geographic Information Systems/Geomatics													MD				U		
Geography								UM									UM		
Geology/Earth Sciences/Atmospheric Studies				UM													X		
Geophysics																	M		
Health Education							U						UM				X		
Health Sciences/Studies	MD																		
Health/Hospital Administration													U		U				
History			M					X	UM			U					X		
Horticulture			X	MD															
Housing/Real Estate													U						
Human Resource Economics													M						
Immunology/Infection/Immunity							U												
Industrial Relations/Personnel/HRM		UM		UM					UM						U				
Information Science/Studies/Systems			UM						M			UM	U		U	X	M		
Information Technology		UM		UM									X		U		X		
International Business				UM															
International Marketing													MD		M				
International Relations/Studies									U							D	X		
Islamic/Middle Eastern Studies	U			M	M	U		X	UM						U		X	U	
Land Resource Science													M						
Law Business/Commercial/Economic/Industrial															U				
Law/Legal Studies		U	UM					U	M				UM				U	U	
Library/Information Science		UM							M								MD		
Logic/Computation															U				
Management			M				X		UM			U			UM	X			
Maritime Studies												UM							
Marketing		M	UM	UM					UM				UM		UM	X	M		
Materials Science							X						UM						
Mathematics			UM	MD			U	X	UD			U	MD		U	D	X	U	M
Mechatronics													X						
Medical Ethics															U	U			
Medical Physics																M			
Medicine, Obstetrics and Gynaecology	U												U		UM				

	Aga Khan	Al-Khair U. (AJK)	Arid Agric., Rawalpindi	Azad Jammu & Kashmir	Fatima Jinnah Women	Foundation	Ghulam Ishaq Khan	Islamia, Bahawalpur	Lahore, Management	Mehran	N.-W.F.P. U.E.T.	N.E.D. Eng. & Tech.	National U.S.T.	Quaid-e-Awam	Riphah Internat.	S. Zulfikar Ali Bhutto	Sindh	Sir Syed U.E.T.	U.E.T., Lahore
Medicine, Orthopaedic													U		U				
Medicine, Otorhinolaryngology/Otolaryngology						U							U		U				
Medicine, Paediatric	U														X				
Medicine, Palliative													U						
Medicine/Surgery	U												U		UM			U	
Microbiology/Medical Microbiology	U												UM		U		UM		
Mobile Communications/Telecommunications													X						
Multimedia									M			UM					M		
Natural Resource Studies									U								U		
Network Technology/Security										MD									
Nursing/Midwifery	UM														U				
Occupational Health/Therapy						U													
Ophthalmology													U		U				
Pakistan Studies	U	U				U		U	UM				U		U		MD	U	
Palaeontology/Palaeobiology																	D		
Parasitology																	MD		
Pathology	U														U				
Persian								UM									M		
Pharmacology	U												X		X		MD		
Pharmacy/Pharmaceutical Science								X							U		UM		
Philosophy						U			U						U	MD	U		
Physical Education/Sports Science		UM															UM		
Physics			MD				X	U			U		UM		U		X	U	
Physiology	U												X		U		X		
Physiotherapy													U						
Planning/Landscape Studies												M							UM
Plant Pathology			X	MD															
Politics/Political Science/Government							X	U									X		
Polymer Science												U							
Population Studies/Demography																	MD		
Project Management															M				
Psychiatry	U												U		U				
Psychology	U					UM		U							U	MD	X		
Psychology Clinical						UM													
Public Administration				MD	M												X		
Public Health/Population Health						U							U						

	Aga Khan	Al-Khair U. (AJK)	Arid Agric., Rawalpindi	Azad Jammu & Kashmir	Fatima Jinnah Women	Foundation	Ghulam Ishaq Khan	Islamia, Bahawalpur	Lahore, Management	Mehran	N.-W.F.P. U.E.T.	N.E.D. Eng. & Tech.	National U.S.T.	Quaid-e-Awam	Riphah Internat.	S. Zulfikar Ali Bhutto	Sindh	Sir Syed U.E.T.	U.E.T., Lahore
Punjabi								U											
Religion/Theology									U										
Robotics													U						
Rural Studies/Development									U							MD			
Social Work/Studies																MD	UM		
Sociology			M		U				U				U		U	MD	X		
Statistics/Actuarial Science			M	UM					X	UM			M	MD			D	X	
Taxation						U									M				
Teacher Training		UM	X					UM							M		UM		
Textiles/Fibre Science/Technology			U								UD		U						U
Toxicology														U	U				
Transport Studies													UM					U	
Urdu			M					X	U								X	U	
Vedas/Vedic																	MD		
Women's/Gender Studies					MD				U								M		
Zoology			M	MD					U								X		

AGA KHAN UNIVERSITY

Founded 1983

Member of the Association of Commonwealth Universities

Postal Address: Stadium Road, PO Box 3500, Karachi 74800, Pakistan
Telephone: (021) 493 0051 **Fax:** (021) 493 4294 **E-mail:** president@aku.edu
URL: http://www.aku.edu

PRESIDENT AND CHIEF EXECUTIVE OFFICER*—Rasul, Firoz, BSc *Herts.*, MBA *McG.*, Hon. LLD *S.Fraser*
PROVOST—Doe, Prof. William, MB BS *Syd.*, MSc *Lond.*, MA *Lond.*, PhD *Lond.*
VICE PRESIDENT, HEALTH SERVICES—Ariotti, Dallas, BA *Macq.*, MPsych *Syd.*
DIRECTOR GENERAL, PLANNING AND DEVELOPMENT OF CAMPUSES—Nurmohamed, Karim, BArch *Manc.*
DIRECTOR GENERAL/CHIEF FINANCIAL OFFICER‡—Haji, Al-Karim, BCom *Br.Col.*
DIRECTOR GENERAL, RESOURCE DEVELOPMENT AND PUBLIC AFFAIRS—Fancy, Asif B., BA *Lanc.*
CHIEF ACADEMIC OFFICER FOR EAST AFRICA—King, Prof. Laetitia J., BACur *S.Af.*, MACur *S.Af.*, DLitt&Phil *S.Af.*

GENERAL INFORMATION

History. The university was established in 1983 as the first private university in Pakistan. Its faculty of Health Sciences, comprising a medical college and school of nursing, is co-located with Aga Khan University Hospital. The Institute for Educational Development is located at another campus in Karachi, while the Institute for the Study of Muslim Civilizations is based in London.

The headquarters of the university are based in Karachi but it has programmes and campuses in Pakistan, United Kingdom, Kenya, Tanzania, Uganda and Afghanistan, as well as capacity building initiatives in Syria and Egypt.

Admission to first degree courses (see also Pakistan Introduction). Information on admission to specific courses can be obtained from the student affairs department (student.affairs@aku.edu).

First Degrees (see also Pakistan Directory to Subjects of Study). BScN, MB BS.
Length of course. Full-time: BScN: 4 years; MB BS: 5 years.

Higher Degrees (see also Pakistan Directory to Subjects of Study).
Master's. MEd, MSc.
Length of course. Full-time: MEd, MSc: 2 years.
Doctoral. PhD.
Length of course. Full-time: PhD: 4 years.

Libraries. Volumes: 51,814. Periodicals subscribed to: 636. Other holdings: large collection of audio-visual material.

Statistics. Staff (2007): 7368 (589 academic, 6779 non-academic). Students (2007): full-time 1022 (357 men, 665 women); part-time 5 (5 women); international 32 (10 men, 22 women); undergraduate 884 (282 men, 602 women); master's 123 (68 men, 55 women); doctoral 20 (9 men, 11 women).

FACULTIES/SCHOOLS

Medical College
Tel: (021) 486 4402
Dean: Khurshid, Prof. Mohammad, MB BS *Karachi*, FRCPath, FRCP

Nursing, School of
Tel: (021) 486 5400
Dean: Amarsi, Prof. Yasmin, BScN *McM.*, MScN *Arizona*, PhD *McM.*

ACADEMIC UNITS
Anaesthesiology
Tel: (021) 486 4639
Afshan, Gauhar, MB BS *Karachi*   Assoc. Prof.

Ahmed, Aliya, MB BS *Karachi*, FFARCSI   Asst. Prof.
Chohan, Ursula, MB BS *Karachi*, FFARCS   Prof.†
Hamid, Mohammad, MB BS *Karachi*   Asst. Prof.
Hoda, M. Qamarul, MB BS *Karachi*, FFARCSI   Prof.
Hussain, Aziza M., MB BS *Karachi*   Asst. Prof.
Ismail, Samina, MB BS *Karachi*   Asst. Prof.
Kamal, Rehana S., MB BS *Punjab*, FRCA, FFARCSI   Prof.†
Khan, Fauzia A., MB BS *Punjab*, FRCA   Tajdin H. Jaffer Prof.; Chairperson*
Khan, Fazal H., MB BS *Karachi*   Prof.
Khan, Mansoor A., MB BS *Karachi*   Asst. Prof.
Khan, Mueenullah, MB BS *Punjab*   Assoc. Prof.
Minai, Fawzia Nasim, MB BS *Karachi*   Asst. Prof.
Monem, Abdul, MB BS *Sindh*   Asst. Prof.
Naqvi, Hamid Iqil, MB BS *Punjab*   Assoc. Prof.
Saleemullah, Hameedullah, MB BS *Karachi*   Assoc. Prof.
Samad, Khalid, MB BS *Karachi*   Asst. Prof.
Siddiqui, Shahla, MB BS *Karachi*   Asst. Prof.
Other Staff: 3 Sr. Instrs.; 5 Instrs.; 2 Fellows; 1 Sr. Lectr.†; 1 Lectr.†; 1 Clin. Asst.†; 1 Hon. Physician

Biological and Biomedical Sciences
Tel: (021) 486 4541
E-mail: biomedical@aku.edu
Ali, Syed, MSc *Karachi*, MA *N.Y.*, PhD *N.Y.*   Asst. Prof.
Chaudhry, Bushra, MSc *Punjab*, PhD *Punjab*   Asst. Prof.
Enam, S. Ather, MD *Northwestern*, PhD *Northwestern*, FRCSCan, FRCSI, FACS   Assoc. Prof.
Frossard, Philippe M., MSc *Stras.*, MPhil *Stras.*, PhD *Stras.*, DSc *Stras.*   Abdulaziz Hussainali Sharif Prof.; Chairman*
Gilani, Anwar H., MSc *Faisalabad*, PhD *Syd.*   Noor Mohammed Shamji Prof.
Iqbal, Mohammad Perwaiz, MSc *Punjab*, MS *N.Y.*, PhD *N.Y.*   Kurban Nagji Prof.
Khan, A. N., MB BS *Lahore*, MPhil *Karachi*, PhD *Indiana*   Prof.†
Khan, Shagufta, MSc *Karachi*, MPhil *Karachi*, PhD *Karachi*   Asst. Prof.
Mehdi, Syed Yawar, MB BS *Karachi*, FRCSI   Asst. Prof.
Qureshi, Sohail, MSc *Quaid-i-Azam*, PhD *Maine(USA)*   Assoc. Prof.
Rohra, Dileep Kumar, MB BS *Karachi*, MPhil *Karachi*, PhD *Tohoku*   Assoc. Prof.
Saeed, Sheikh Abdul, BSc *Karachi*, MSc *Quaid-i-Azam*, MPhil *Quaid-i-Azam*, PhD *Aberd.*   Assoc. Prof.
Saeed, Sheikh Arshad, PhD *Newcastle(UK)*, FIBiol   Prof.†
Siddiqui, Anwar A., MSc *Karachi*, MPhil *Quaid-i-Azam*, PhD *Belf.*   Akbar Ali Habib Bandeali Prof.

Siddiqui, Arif, MSc *Karachi*, MPhil *Quaid-i-Azam*, PhD *Glas.*   Assoc. Prof.
Sultana, Taranum, MSc *Karachi*, PhD *Karolinska*   Asst. Prof.
Other Staff: 9 Sr. Instrs.; 2 Instrs.; 1 Hon. Lectr.

Community Health Sciences
E-mail: chs@aku.edu
Abid, Fauziah Rabbani, MB BS *Karachi*, MPH *Alabama*   Assoc. Prof.
Ali, Tazeen Saeed, BScN *Aga Khan(P'stan.)*, MSc *Aga Khan(P'stan.)*   Asst. Prof.
Azam, Syed Iqbal, BSc *Karachi*, MSc *Karachi*   Asst. Prof.
Bryant, John H., MD *Col.*   Prof. Emer.
Fatmi, S. Zafar Ahmed, MB BS *Karachi*   Asst. Prof.
Iqbal, Bilal, MB BS *Pesh.*, MSc *Aga Khan(P'stan.)*   Asst. Prof. (on leave)
Israr, Syed Muhammad, MB BS *Sindh*, MSc *Heidel.*   Asst. Prof.; Acting Head, Health Systems
Jafar, Tazeen, MB BS *Aga Khan(P'stan.)*, MPH *Harv.*   Assoc. Prof.
Jehan, Imtiaz, MB BS *Karachi*, MSc *McG.*   Asst. Prof.
Jokhio, Abdul Hakeem, MB BS *Sindh*, MSc *Birm.*, PhD *Birm.*   Assoc. Prof.
Kadir, M. Masood, MB BS *Karachi*, MPH *Hawaii*   Assoc. Prof.; Head, Public Health Practice
Karim, Mehtab S., MA *Chic.*, PhD *Cornell*   Noormahomed Pirmahomed Sheriff Prof.; Head, Population and Reproductive Health Programme
Karmaliani, Rozina, BScN *Aga Khan(P'stan.)*, MPH *Minn.*, MScN *Minn.*, PhD *Minn.*   Khatijabai Mohan Manji Dharolia Assoc. Prof.
Khan, Kausar S., MA *Karachi*, MA *McM.*   Assoc. Prof.
Khoja, Shariq, MB BS *Karachi*, MSc *Calg.*, PhD *Calg.*   Asst. Prof.
Khuwaja, Ali Khan, MB BS *Sindh*   Asst. Prof.
Mahmud, Sadia, MSc *Quaid-i-Azam*, MS *Indiana*, PhD *Indiana*   Asst. Prof.
Pappas, Gregory, MD *Case W.Reserve*, PhD *Case W.Reserve*   Noordin M. Thobani Prof.; Chairman*
Pasha, Omrana, MB BS *Aga Khan(P'stan.)*, MSPH *Alabama*   Asst. Prof.
Rizvi, Narjis, MB BS *Karachi*, MSc *Heidel.*   Asst. Prof. (on leave)
Saleem, Sarah, MB BS *Karachi*, MSc *Aga Khan(P'stan.)*   Asst. Prof.
Siddiqui, Amna Rehana, MB BS *Karachi*, MSPH *Alabama*, PhD *Calif.*   Asst. Prof.
Walraven, Gijs, MD MPH *Leeds*, PhD   Visiting Prof.
Other Staff: 15 Sr. Instrs.; 4 Instrs.; 1 Visiting Prof.†; 2 Visiting Asst. Profs.†; 1 Lectr.†; 8 Hon. Lectrs.

Educational Development

within Health Sciences

Tel: (021) 486 4501 E-mail: ded@aku.edu

Saeed, Sheikh Abdul, BSc Karachi, MSc Quaid-i-Azam, MPhil Quaid-i-Azam, PhD Aberd.   Assoc. Prof.

Zuberi, Rukhsana W., MB BS Punjab, MPHE Chic.   Prof.; Head*

Other Staff: 1 Sr. Lectr.; 1 Lectr.; 1 Visiting Fac.; 1 Sr. Instr.; 1 Instr.

English Language, Centre of

Tel: (021) 486 5434 E-mail: cel@aku.edu

Ahmed, Shabana, MA Karachi   Asst. Prof.

Ali, Zubeda Kasim, MPhil Karachi, MA Karachi   Asst. Prof.

Cane, Graeme A., BA Brad., MA Newcastle(UK), MA Leeds, PhD Strath.   Head*

Hussain, Nasreen, BEd Karachi, MEd Manc.   Assoc. Prof.

Noorali, Dilshad, BEd A.Iqbal Open, MA A.Iqbal Open   Asst. Prof.

Sikander, Aliya, MA Karachi   Asst. Prof.

Zafar, Mohammad, MA Baloch., MA Warw.   Asst. Prof.

Other Staff: 5 Sr. Instrs.; 2 Lectrs.†

Educational Development, Institute for (Eastern Africa)

Tel: (022) 2150051 Fax: (0745) 067 534

Farah, Iffat, MA Karachi, MA Kent, PhD Penn.   Prof.; Head, Res. and Policy Studies

MacLeod, Gordon, MA Edin., MSc Stir., PhD Stir.   Prof.; Dir.*

Oyoo, Samuel, BEd Nott., MEd Leeds, PhD Monash   Asst. Prof.

Rarieya, Jane F. A., MEd Aga Khan(P'stan.), EdD Keele   Asst. Prof.; Head, Programmes

Other Staff: 6 Lectrs.; 3 Asst. Lectrs.; 3 Tutors

Educational Development, Institute for (Karachi)

Tel: (021) 634 7611 Fax: (021) 634 7617 E-mail: ied@aku.edu

Ashraf, Dilshad, MEd Aga Khan(P'stan.), PhD Tor.   Asst. Prof.

Bashiruddin, Ayesha, MA Pesh., MA Durh., PhD Tor.   Asst. Prof.; Head, Academic Programmes

Dean, Bernadette L., MSc Karachi, MEd Aga Khan(P'stan.), PhD Alta.   Assoc. Prof.; Head, Academics and Student Affairs

Halai, Anjum, MEd Aga Khan(P'stan.), DPhil Oxf.   Assoc. Prof.; Head, Res. and Policy Studies

Halai, Nelofer, MSc S.Mississippi, PhD Tor.   Assoc. Prof.

Hussain, Rana, MEd Tor.   Asst. Prof.

Khaki, Jan-e-Alam, MA Karachi, MA Lond., PhD Tor.   Asst. Prof.

Memon, Muhammad, MA Karachi, MEd Karachi, MA Islam., PhD Sur.   Prof.; Dir.*

Mohammad, Razia Fakir, MA Karachi, MEd Aga Khan(P'stan.), DPhil Oxf.   Asst. Prof.

Pardhan, Sadrudin, MBA Alta., MSc Uppsala, PhD Uppsala   Prof.; Dir., Outreach

Qureshi, Rashida, MA Pesh., MA Kansas State, PhD Kansas State   Asst. Prof.

Rizvi, Meher, MEd Karachi, PhD Qld.   Asst. Prof.

Shafa, Moladad Mohammad, MEd Aga Khan(P'stan.), PhD Tor.   Asst. Prof.; Head, Professnl. Devel. Centre, Northern Areas

Tajik, Mir Afzal, MEd Aga Khan(P'stan.), PhD Tor.   Asst. Prof.; Head, Professnl. Devel. Centre, Chitral

Vazir, Nilofar, MEd Aga Khan(P'stan.), PhD Tor.   Asst. Prof.

Other Staff: 13 Sr. Instrs.; 9 Instrs.; 2 Assoc. Profs.†

Family Medicine

Tel: (021) 486 4843 E-mail: family.medicine@aku.edu

Ali, Niloufer Sultan, MB BS Karachi   Assoc. Prof.

Andrades, Marie, MB BS Karachi   Asst. Prof.

Dhanani, Raheem H., MB BS Karachi   Asst. Prof.

Jiwani, Aziz A. Rehman, MB BS Aga Khan(P'stan.)   Asst. Prof.

Khuwaja, Ali Khan, MB BS Sindh   Asst. Prof.

Pasha, Omrana, MB BS Aga Khan(P'stan.), MSPH Alabama   Asst. Prof.

Qidwai, Waris, MB BS Karachi   Assoc. Prof.

Qureshi, Riaz H., MB BS Karachi, FRCGP   Noor Mohammed E. Mewawalla Prof.; Chairman*

Sabzwari, Saniya, MB BS Karachi   Asst. Prof.

Zuberi, Rukhsana W., MB BS Punjab, MPHE Chic.   Prof.

Other Staff: 1 Sr. Lectr.; 4 Sr. Instrs.; 10 Lectrs.†; 1 Hon. Lectr.

Islamic and Pakistan Studies

Tel: (021) 486 4445

1 Lectr.†

Medicine

Tel: (021) 486 4661

Abid, Shahab, MB BS Karachi, FRCPEd   Assoc. Prof.

Adil, Salman Naseem, MB BS Karachi   Assoc. Prof.; Head, Oncol.

Akhter, Jaweed, MB BS Newcastle(UK), FRCPEd, FACP   Assoc. Prof.; Head, Internal Med.

Azharuddin, Muhammad, MB BS Karachi   Asst. Prof.

Baqir, Syed Muhammad, MB BS Karachi   Asst. Prof.

Bhatti, Maqsood Ahmed, MB BS Sindh   Asst. Prof.

Dhakam, Sajid, MB BS Aga Khan(P'stan.), FACC   Assoc. Prof.; Head, Cardiol.

Hameed, Aamir, MB BS Punjab   Asst. Prof.

Hamid, Saeed Sadiq, MB BS Punjab, FRCP, FACP, FRCPI   Prof.

Haque, Ahmed Suleman, MB BS Karachi   Asst. Prof.

Hassan, Mushtaq, MB BS Punjab, MD Punjab, FRCPEd   Hon. Prof.

Husain, Javed, MB BS Punjab   Asst. Prof.

Islam, Najmul, MB BS Karachi, FRCP   Prof.

Jabbar, Abdul, MB BS Karachi, FRCP   Prof.; Head, Endocrinol., Diabetes and Metabolism

Jafar, Tazeen, MB BS Aga Khan(P'stan.), MPH Harv.   Assoc. Prof.; Head, Nephrol.

Jafary, Fahim H., MB BS Aga Khan(P'stan.), FACC   Assoc. Prof.

Jafri, S. M. Wasim, MB BS Karachi, FRCP, FRCPEd, FACP, FRCPGlas   Ibn-e-Sina Prof.; Chairman*

Jamil, Bushra, MB BS Karachi   Asst. Prof.

Kakepoto, Ghulam Nabi, MB BS Sindh, PhD Lond.   Assoc. Prof.

Kamal, Ayeesha, MB BS Aga Khan(P'stan.), FAHA   Asst. Prof.

Kashif, Waqaruddin, MB BS Karachi, MD   Asst. Prof.

Khan, Javaid A., MB BS Karachi, FRCPEd   Nizar Noor Mohammed E. Mewawalla Prof.

Khan, M. Aslam, MB BS Karachi   Assoc. Prof.

Khan, M. Attaullah, MB BS Sindh, FRCP, FACP   Karim Jiwa Prof.

Khan, Nadeem Ullah, MB BS Aga Khan(P'stan.)   Asst. Prof.

Khan, Sohail Abrar Ahmed, MB BS Karachi   Asst. Prof.

Khealani, Bhojo Asumal, MB BS Sindh   Asst. Prof.

Masood, Nehal, MB BS Karachi   Asst. Prof.

Mazhar, Abdur Rauf, MB BS Aga Khan(P'stan.)   Asst. Prof.

Nadeem, Syed Muhammad Najaf Ali, MB BS Karachi   Asst. Prof.

Razzak, Junaid A., MB BS Aga Khan(P'stan.)   Assoc. Prof.; Head, Emergency Med.

Salahuddin, Nawal, MB BS Aga Khan(P'stan.)   Assoc. Prof.

Shafqat, Saad, MB BS Aga Khan(P'stan.), PhD Duke   Assoc. Prof.

Shah, S. Hasnain Ali, MB BS Punjab, MD, FRCPEd   Prof.

Sheerani, Mughis, MB BS Karachi, MD Utah   Asst. Prof.

Smythe, Cheves M., MD Harv., FACP   Prof. Emer.

Sultan, Fateh Ali Tipoo, MB BS Karachi   Asst. Prof.

Syed, Nadir Ali, MB BS Aga Khan(P'stan.)   Assoc. Prof.; Head, Neurol.

Syed, Shaukat Ali, MB BS Punjab, FRCPEd, FRCPGlas   Hon. Prof.

Tai, Javed Majid, MB BS Karachi   Asst. Prof.

Tariq, Muhammad, MB BS Karachi   Asst. Prof.

Vellani, Camer W., MB BCh Wales, MD Wales, FRCP   Distinguished Univ. Prof. Emer.

Wasay, Mohammad S., MB BS Karachi, FRCPEd   Assoc. Prof.

Zubairi, Ali Bin S., MB BS Karachi   Asst. Prof.

Zuberi, Lubna, MB BS Aga Khan(P'stan.)   Asst. Prof.

Other Staff: 10 Sr. Instrs.; 2 Visiting Fac.; 1 Sr. Lectr.†; 40 Lectrs.†

Muslim Civilizations, Institute for the Study of (London)

Tel: (0207) 907 1020 Fax: (0207) 907 1030 E-mail: ismc.uk@aku.edu

Ben Abdeljelil, Moncef, Doctorat Tunis   Prof.

Filali-Ansary, Abdou, BA Mohammed V, PhD Dijon   Prof.*; Dir.*

Sadria, Modjtaba, MA Paris, PhD Paris, PhD Queb.   Prof.

Savant, Sarah B., MA Chic., PhD Harv.   Asst. Prof.

Weber, Stefan, MA Bonn, PhD   Asst. Prof.

Other Staff: 2 Sr. Lectrs.

Nursing, School of

Ali, Asho, BSc Karachi, MSc Karachi   Asst. Prof.

Ali, Fauziya, BScN Aga Khan(P'stan.), MEd Wales, PhD Alta.   Asst. Prof.; Dir., BScN Programme

Ali, Nadia M., BScN Aga Khan(P'stan.), MScN Arizona   Asst. Prof. (on leave)

Ali, Tazeen Saeed, BScN Aga Khan(P'stan.), MSc Aga Khan(P'stan.)   Asst. Prof.

Amarsi, Yasmin, BScN McM., MScN Arizona, PhD McM.   Shakur Jamal Prof.

Asad, Nargis, MA Karachi, PhD Karachi   Asst. Prof.

Barolia, Rubina, BScN Aga Khan(P'stan.), MScN Aga Khan(P'stan.)   Asst. Prof.

Dias, Jacqueline Maria, BScN McM., MEd Wales   Asst. Prof.

Gul, Raisa Begum, BScN McM., MHA NSW   Asst. Prof.

Herberg, Paula, MS Maryland, PhD Utah   Prof. Emer.

Jan, Rafat, BScN Aga Khan(P'stan.), MScN S.Carolina, PhD Iowa   Ali Saju Assoc. Prof.

Karmaliani, Rozina, BScN Aga Khan(P'stan.), MPH Minn., MScN Minn., PhD Minn.   Khatijabai Mohan Manji Dharolia Assoc. Prof.; Dir., MScN Programme

Khalid, Farida, BScN Aga Khan(P'stan.), MSN Villanova   Asst. Prof.

Khan, Shehla Yasmin, BSc Karachi, MSc Karachi   Asst. Prof.

Khowaja, Khurshid, BScN Aga Khan(P'stan.), PhD Ballarat   Asst. Prof.

Rehan, Seema, BScN Aga Khan(P'stan.), MScN Aga Khan(P'stan.)   Asst. Prof.

Rizvi, Qudsia Khatoon, BScN Aga Khan(P'stan.), MES Karachi   Asst. Prof.

Saeed, Tanveer, BSc Punjab, MSc Quaid-i-Azam, MPhil Quaid-i-Azam   Asst. Prof.

Other Staff: 1 Sr. Instr./Dir., Diploma Programmes; 26 Sr. Instrs.; 31 Instrs.; 1 Asst. Prof.†

Academic Centre (Kenya)

Koronjo, Jane M., MCH Nair., MPH Atlanta   Sr. Lectr.

Loefler, Martha, MSc Wales   Sr. Lectr.; Academic Head*

Mureithi, Connie, MEd Cardiff   Sr. Lectr.

Mwenda, James, MCommH Liv.   Sr. Lectr.

Other Staff: 3 Lectrs.; 3 Asst. Lectrs.

Academic Centre (Tanzania)

Chiza, Brighton, MSc Dar.   Sr. Lectr.
Sande, Leah, MPH Tumaini   Sr. Lectr.
Yengo, Mavis L., BA S.Af.   Lectr.; Academic Head*
Other Staff: 1 Lectr.; 3 Asst. Lectrs.

Academic Centre (Uganda)

Lematia, Ruth M. O., MSc Case W.Reserve   Academic Head*
Other Staff: 3 Lectrs.; 2 Asst. Lectrs.

Regional Office (Kenya)

Arudo, John, BScN MSc MSc   Regional Res. Co-ordinator
Ganga-Limando, Makombo, BScN Kinshasa, MSc Natal, MACur Natal, PhD Natal   Regional Programme Co-ordinator*
King, Laetit... J., BACur S.Af., MACur S.Af., DLitt&Phil S.Af.   Firoz Kassam Prof.; Assoc. Dean, Nursing
Mabalhin, Myrla, BScN Philippines, MA Philippines, EdD Philippines   Regional Curriculum Co-ordinator

Obstetrics and Gynaecology

Tel: (021) 486 4641 E-mail: obgyn@aku.edu
Begum, Aliya, MB BS Karachi   Asst. Prof.
Chaudhury, Nasreen, MB BS Karachi, FRCOG   Assoc. Prof.
Jokhio, Abdul Hakeem, MB BS Sindh, MSc Birm., PhD Birm.   Assoc. Prof.
Khan, Zeenat Eva, MB BS Karachi   Asst. Prof.
Mohsin, Raheela, MB BS Punjab   Asst. Prof.
Munim, Shama, MB BS Karachi   Asst. Prof.
Naru, Tahira Yasmeen, MD Düsseldorf   Assoc. Prof.
Pal, Brig. (Retd.) Jahan Ara, MB BS Karachi, FRCOG   Hon. Prof
Qureshi, Rahat Najam, MB BS Karachi, FRCOG   Shiraz Habib Kassam Assoc. Prof.
Rizvi, Javed H., MB BS Karachi, FACS, FRCOG   Puribai Kanji Jamal Prof.; Chairman*
Sikander, Rozina, MB BS Karachi   Asst. Prof.
Zuberi, Nadeem, MB BS Sindh   Asst. Prof.
Other Staff: 6 Sr. Lectrs.; 5 Sr. Instrs.

Paediatrics

Tel: (021) 486 4782
Ahmed, Shakeel, MB BS Karachi   Asst. Prof.
Atiq, Mehnaz, MB BS Marath.   Assoc. Prof.
Bhutta, Z. A., MB BS Pesh., PhD Karolinska, FRCPEd, FRCPCH   Husein Laljee Dewraj Prof.; Chairman*
Billoo, Abdul Gaffar, MB BS Karachi, FRCPEd   Prof.
Fadoo, Zehra, MB BS Aga Khan(P'stan.), FAAPA   Asst. Prof.
Haque, Anwar Ul, MB BS Karachi, MD   Asst. Prof.
Ibrahim, Shahnaz H., MB BS Karachi   Assoc. Prof.
Khan, Iqtidar A., MB BS Pesh., FRCPI   Prof.
Linblad, Bo S., MD Karolinska, PhD Karolinska   Prof. Emer.
Nizami, Shaikh Qamaruddin, MB BS Pesh.   Abdul Sultan Jamal Prof.
Salat, M. Sohail, MB BS Karachi, FAAPA   Asst. Prof.
Shah, Uzma, MB BS Karachi, FAAPA   Assoc. Prof.
Zaidi, Anita, MB BS Aga Khan(P'stan.), MS Harv.   Assoc. Prof.
Other Staff: 8 Sr. Instrs.; 1 Instr.; 7 Fellows; 1 Sr. Lectr.†; 5 Lectrs.†; 14 Hon. Fac.†

Pathology and Microbiology

Tel: (021) 486 4531
Adil, Salman Naseem, MB BS Karachi   Assoc. Prof.; Head, Haematol.
Ahmed, Rashida, MB BS Karachi, MHPE Maastricht   Assoc. Prof., Histopathology
Ahmed, Zubair, MB BS Karachi   Asst. Prof.
Ahsan, Aamir, MB BS Karachi   Asst. Prof.
Azad, Najamul Sahar, MB BS Baloch.   Asst. Prof.
Bashir, Zahid, MB BS Punjab   Asst. Prof.

Beg, M. Asim, MB BS Punjab, PhD Manc.   Assoc. Prof.
Ghani, Farooq, MB BS Karachi, MS Boston, PhD Boston   Assoc. Prof.
Hasan, Rumina, MB BS Lond., MSc Lond., PhD Lond., FRCPath   Prof.; Chairperson*
Hasan, Sheema H., MB BS Punjab, FRCPath   Prof.
Hasan, Zahra, BSc Lond., PhD Lond.   Assoc. Prof.
Hussain, Rabia, MSc Karachi, PhD W.Ont., FRCPath   Gulamali Hirji Prof.
Irfan, Seema, MB BS Karachi   Asst. Prof.
Jabeen, Kausar, MB BS Karachi   Asst. Prof.
Jamil, Bushra, MB BS Karachi   Assoc. Prof.
Kakepoto, Ghulam Nabi, MB BS Sindh, PhD Lond.   Assoc. Prof.
Kayani, Naila, MB BS Punjab   Prof.
Khan, Ayesha Habib, MB BS Karachi   Asst. Prof.
Khan, Erum, MB BS Karachi   Asst. Prof.
Khurshid, Mohammad, MB BS Karachi, FRCPath, FRCP   Haiderali R. Charania Prof.
Moatter, Tariq, MSc Karachi, MPhil Karachi, PhD N.Y.   Assoc. Prof.
Moiz, Bushra, MB BS Karachi   Asst. Prof.
Pervez, Shahid, MB BS Baloch., PhD Lond.   Prof.; Head, Histopathol.
Qazi, Romena, MSc Pesh., MPhil Quaid-i-Azam, PhD Glas.   Asst. Prof.
Shaikh, M. Usman, MB BS Punjab   Asst. Prof.
Siddiqui, Imran, MB BS Karachi, FRCPath   Assoc. Prof.; Head, Clin. Pathol.
Zafar, Afia, MB BS Karachi, FRCP   Assoc. Prof.; Head, Microbiol.
Zaman, Viqar, MB BS Karachi, PhD Edin., FRCPath   Hon. Prof.
Other Staff: 5 Sr. Instrs.; 5 Lectrs.; 7 Instrs.

Postgraduate Medical Education (East Africa)

Abdullah, M. S., MMEd Nair., MB ChB   Prof.†
Adala, Henry S., MB ChB Kampala, MMEd   Prof.†
Ahmed, Mushtaq, MB BS Karachi, FRCS   Prof.; Assoc. Dean*
Amata, Andrew, MB BS Nigeria, DA Nigeria   Assoc. Prof.; Chairman, Anaesthesiol.
Chauhan, Rajendra, MB BS MS   Hon. Prof.
Jiwani, Azim H., MB ChB Mak.   Assoc. Prof.
Macharia, William M., MB ChB MMEd MSc   Prof.; Chairman, Paediatrics
Malik, Saleem, MB BS DMRD Brist.   Asst. Prof.; Chairman, Radiol.
Matuja, William B., MB ChB   Prof.†
Mkony, Charles, MD Dar., MMEd Dar.   Hon. Prof.†
Odhiambo, Peter A., MB BS Calc., MMEd Nair., FRCSEd   Hon. Prof.†
Ojwang, Peter J., MB ChB, FRCPath, FCPath   Prof.; Chairman, Pathol.
Poenaru, Dan, BSc Tor., MD Tor.   Hon. Prof.†
Premji, Zulfiqarali, MD Dar., MSc Lond., PhD Karolinska   Hon. Prof.†
Raja, Asad J., MB BS Karachi, MHSc Tor., FRCSEd   Prof.; Chairman, Surgery
Rana, Farzana, MB ChB Nair., MMEd Nair.   Asst. Prof.
Rees, Jeffrey, MB ChB Edin., DMRD Edin., FRCPCan, FRCR   Prof.; Dir., Postgrad. Medical Educn. (East Africa)
Riyat, Malkit, MB ChB Nair.   Asst. Prof.
Roelofse, James A., MB ChB Stell., MMEd Stell., PhD Stell.   Visiting Prof.†
Samnakay, Saeed, MB ChB   Asst. Prof.
Sande, Gerishom M., MB ChB MMEd   Hon. Prof.†
Stones, William, MB BS MD, FRCOG   Prof.; Chairman, Obstet. and Gynaecol.
Vinayak, Sudhir, MB ChB Nair., MMEd Nair.   Asst. Prof.
Yonga, Gerald, MMEd MBA   Assoc. Prof.; Chairman, Med.
Other Staff: 4 Sr. Lectrs.†; 1 Hon. Sr. Lectr.

Postgraduate Medical Education (Karachi)

Tel: (021) 486 4407 E-mail: pgme@aku.edu
Syed, Nadir Ali, MB BS Aga Khan(P'stan.)   Assoc. Prof.; Assoc. Dean*

Psychiatry

Tel: (021) 486 4692   E-mail: psychiatry.department@aku.edu
Ahmer, Syed, MB BS Karachi   Asst. Prof.
Khan, Murad M., MB BS Karachi   Prof.; Chairman*
Khan, Saiqa, MA Karachi, PhD Karachi   Asst. Prof.
Naqvi, Haider Ali, MB BS Punjab   Asst. Prof.
Syed, Ehsan Ullah, MB BS Karachi   Asst. Prof.
Zaman, Riffat M., MA Karachi, MA Mich.State, PhD Mich.State   Prof.
Other Staff: 2 Visiting Asst. Profs.; 1 Instr.; 1 Hon. Sr. Lectr.; 3 Hon. Lectrs.

Radiology

Tel: (021) 486 2020 E-mail: radiology@aku.edu
Ahmad, Muhammad Nadeem, MB BS Karachi   Karim Kurji Assoc. Prof.; Chairman*
Ahsan, Humera, MB BS Karachi, FRCR   Assoc. Prof.
Azeemuddin, M., MB BS Karachi   Asst. Prof.
Bari, Vaqar, MB BS Punjab, DMRD Punjab   Asst. Prof.
Haider, Zishan, MB BS Punjab   Asst. Prof.
Haq, Tanveer Ul, MB BS Karachi, FRCR   Assoc. Prof.
Husen, Yousuf, MB BS Karachi, FRCR   Assoc. Prof.
Hussain, Riffat Parveen, MB BS Karachi, MS Quaid-i-Azam   Asst. Prof.
Karsan, Farrok, MD, FRCPCan   Asst. Prof.
Khan, Dawar Burhan A., MB BS Karachi   Asst. Prof.
Masroor, Imrana, MB BS Karachi   Asst. Prof.
Memon, Wasim Ahmed, MB BS Karachi   Asst. Prof.
Nadeem, Naila, MB BS Punjab   Asst. Prof.
Sajjad, Zafar, MB BS Karachi, FRCR   Assoc. Prof.
Other Staff: 6 Sr. Instrs.; 4 Lectrs.; 2 Instrs.; 1 Med. Physicist

Surgery

Tel: (021) 486 4754   E-mail: surgery.aku@aku.edu
Abbas, Farhat, MB BS Karachi, FRCSEd, FRCSGlas   Hussein Cumber Assoc. Prof.
Ali, Azam, MB BS Aga Khan(P'stan.), FRCSEd, FRCSGlas   Ibn-e-Haithem Assoc. Prof.; Head, Ophthalmol.
Alvi, Abdul R., MB BS Punjab, FRCSGlas   Asst. Prof.
Amanullah, Muneer, MB BS Karachi, FRCSEd, FRCSGlas   Asst. Prof.
Ather, M. Hammad, MB BS Karachi   Assoc. Prof.
Awan, M. Sohail, MB BS Punjab   Asst. Prof.
Azami, Rizwan, MB BS Karachi   Hassanali Sajan Assoc. Prof.
Bari, M. Ehsan, MB BS Punjab, FRCSI   Asst. Prof.
Biyabani, S. Raziuddin, MB BS Punjab   Assoc. Prof.; Head, Urol.
Chaudhry, Tanveer Anjum, MB BS Karachi, FRCSEd   Asst. Prof.
Chawla, Tabish, MB BS Punjab, FRCSGlas   Asst. Prof.
Enam, S. Ather, MD Northwestern, PhD Northwestern, FRCSCan, FRCSI, FACS   Assoc. Prof.; Head, Neurosurgery
Fatimi, Saulat, MB BS Aga Khan(P'stan.)   Assoc. Prof.
Fida, Mubassar, MB BS Punjab   Asst. Prof.
Hameed, Khalid, MB BS Karachi, FRCSI   Assoc. Prof.; Head, General Surg.
Hashmi, Pervaiz Mehmood, MB BS Islamia, Bahawal.   Asst. Prof.
Ikram, Mubasher, MB BS Punjab   Asst. Prof.
Khan, M. Arif Mateen, MB BS Karachi, FRCSGlas   Assoc. Prof.

Khan, Mumtaz J., MB BS *Aga Khan(P'stan.)*, FACS
Assoc. Prof.; Head, Otolaryngol.
Khan, Rizwan, MB BS, FRCSEd, FRCSGlas
Asst. Prof.
Khan, Sadaf M., MB BS *Aga Khan(P'stan.)*, FACS
Asst. Prof.
Khan, Shaista M., MB BS *Karachi*, FRCSEd
Abdulali D. Charolia Prof.
Lakdawala, Riaz H., MB BS *Karachi* Assoc.
Prof.; Head, Orthop.
Memon, Amanullah, MB BS *Karachi*, FRCSEd
Quaid-e-Azam Prof.; Chairman*
Nazir, Zafar, MB BS *Punjab*, FRCSEd, FRCSGlas
Assoc. Prof.; Head, Paed. Surg.
Pal, Inam, MB BS *Karachi*, MSc *Lond.*, FRCS
Assoc. Prof.
Pishori, Turab I., MB BS *Karachi*, FRCSGlas
Assoc. Prof.
Sami, Shahid A., MB BS *Karachi*, FRCSEd
Assoc. Prof.; Head, Cardiothoracic Surg.
Shah, Mahnaz Naveed, MD *Baylor* Asst. Prof.
Sharif, Hasanat, MB BS *Karachi*, FRCS, FRCSEd,
FRCSGlas Asst. Prof.
Siddiqui, Azfar Aftab, BDS *Punjab*, MSc Assoc.
Prof.; Head, Dentistry
Siddiqui, Khurram M., MB BS *Karachi*, FRCSGlas
Asst. Prof.
Suhail, Anwar, MB BS *Karachi*, FRCSEd Asst.
Prof.
Talati, Jamsheer, MB BS *Karachi*, FRCSEd
Habiba Sabjaali Jiwa Prof.
Umer, Masood, MB BS *Aga Khan(P'stan.)* Asst.
Prof.
Wajid, Muhammed A., MB BS *Punjab*, FRCS,
FRCSEd Asst. Prof.
Zafar, Hasnain, MB BS *Aga Khan(P'stan.)*,
FRCSGlas Asst. Prof.
Other Staff: 10 Sr. Instrs.; 1 Lectr.; 5 Instrs.; 1
Fellow

SPECIAL CENTRES, ETC

Human Development Programme

Tel: (021) 496 9811 Fax: (021) 924 4321
E-mail: human.development@aku.edu
Rafique, Ghazala, MB BS *Sindh*, MPH *Quaid-e-Awam UEST* Asst. Prof.; Deputy Dir.*
Other Staff: 1 Sr. Instr.; 1 Instr.

CONTACT OFFICERS

Accommodation. Senior Manager: Akbarali,
Laila, MBA *Karachi*, MA(EducMgt) *Warw.*
(E-mail: student.affairs@aku.edu)
Admissions (first degree). Senior Manager:
Akbarali, Laila, MBA *Karachi*, MA(EducMgt)
Warw. (E-mail: student.affairs@aku.edu)
Admissions (higher degree). Senior Manager:
Akbarali, Laila, MBA *Karachi*, MA(EducMgt)
Warw. (E-mail: student.affairs@aku.edu)
Alumni. Co-ordinator, Alumni Affairs:
Wahedna, Abdul Haq, BBA *Florida Atlantic*,
MBA *Karachi* (E-mail: alumni@aku.edu)
Computing services. Acting Director,
Information Technology: Deshmukh,
Jawed, BE *Karachi*, MS *Wash.State*, MSCS *New Br.* (E-mail: jawed.deshmukh@aku.edu)
Development/fund-raising. Senior Director,
Resource Development and Public Affairs:
Fancy, Asif B., BA *Lanc.*
(E-mail: resource.development@aku.edu)
Estates and buildings/works and services.
Director General, Planning and
Development of Campuses: Nurmohamed,
Karim, BArch *Manc.*
(E-mail: karim.nurmohamed@aku.edu)
Examinations. Senior Manager: Akbarali, Laila,
MBA *Karachi*, MA(EducMgt) *Warw.*
(E-mail: student.affairs@aku.edu)
Finance. Chief Financial Officer: Haji, Al-
Karim, BCom *Br.Col.*
(E-mail: alkarim.haji@aku.edu)
General enquiries. President and Chief
Academic Officer: Rasul, Firoz, BSc *Herts.*,
MBA *McG.*, Hon. LLD *S.Fraser*
(E-mail: president@aku.edu)
General enquiries. Provost: Doe, Prof.
William, MB BS *Syd.*, MSc *Lond.*, MA *Lond.*,
PhD *Lond.* (E-mail: provost@aku.edu)
Health services. Medical Director and
Associate Dean, Clinical Affairs: Hamid,
Prof. Saeed Sadiq, MB BS *Punjab*, FRCP,
FACP, FRCPI (E-mail: saeed.hamid@aku.edu)
International office. Senior Manager: Akbarali,
Laila, MBA *Karachi*, MA(EducMgt) *Warw.*
(E-mail: international.office@aku.edu)
Library (chief librarian). Librarian: Demers,
Normand, BA *McG.*, MLIS *McG.*
(E-mail: normand.demers@aku.edu)
Marketing. Director General and Chief
Executive Officer, Aga Khan University

Hospital: Khan, Nadeem M., BA *Pesh.*, BSc
Lond., FCA (E-mail: marketing@aku.edu)
Personnel/human resources. Director,
Human Resources: Surani, Navroz, LLB
Karachi, MBA *Karachi*, MIR *Qu.*
(E-mail: navroz.surani@aku.edu)
Public relations. Director, General Resource
Development and Public Affairs: Fancy, Asif
B., BA *Lanc.* (E-mail: public.affairs@aku.edu)
Publications. Director, Public Affairs: Tyabji,
Talaat, MA *Karachi*
(E-mail: talaat.tyabji@aku.edu)
Purchasing. Director, Material Management:
Merchant, Javed, FCA
(E-mail: javed.merchant@aku.edu)
Safety. Manager, Safety and Security: Rehman,
Salim-ur, BSc *Pesh.*
(E-mail: salim.rehman@aku.edu)
Scholarships, awards, loans. Senior Manager:
Akbarali, Laila, MBA *Karachi*, MA(EducMgt)
Warw. (E-mail: student.affairs@aku.edu)
Schools liaison. Senior Manager: Akbarali,
Laila, MBA *Karachi*, MA(EducMgt) *Warw.*
(E-mail: student.affairs@aku.edu)
Security. Manager, Safety and Security:
Rehman, Salim-ur, BSc *Pesh.*
(E-mail: salim.rehman@aku.edu)
Sport and recreation. Manager/Contractor:
Riaz Akbar, BCom *Karachi*
(E-mail: sports.centre@aku.edu)
Staff development and training. Director,
Human Resources: Surani, Navroz, LLB
Karachi, MBA *Karachi*, MIR *Qu.*
(E-mail: navroz.surani@aku.edu)
Strategic planning. Provost: Doe, Prof.
William, MB BS *Syd.*, MSc *Lond.*, MA *Lond.*,
PhD *Lond.* (E-mail: provost@aku.edu)
Student welfare/counselling. Student
Counsellor, Student Affairs: Mahmood,
Amynah, MPhil *Karachi*
(E-mail: student.affairs@aku.edu)
Students from other countries. Senior
Manager: Akbarali, Laila, MBA *Karachi*,
MA(EducMgt) *Warw.*
(E-mail: international.office@aku.edu)
Students with disabilities. Senior Manager:
Akbarali, Laila, MBA *Karachi*, MA(EducMgt)
Warw. (E-mail: student.affairs@aku.edu)

[*Information supplied by the institution as at 22
November 2007, and edited by the ACU*]

UNIVERSITY OF AGRICULTURE, FAISALABAD

Founded 1961

Postal Address: Faisalabad 38040, Punjab, Pakistan
Telephone: (041) 920 0200 **Fax:** (041) 920 0764 **E-mail:** vc_uaf@yahoo.com
URL: www.uaf.edu.pk

VICE-CHANCELLOR*—Khan, Iqrar A., BSc(Agr) *W.Pak.Ag.*, MS *Calif.*, MSc *W.Pak.Ag.*,
PhD *Calif.*
REGISTRAR‡—Hussain, Muhammad, BA *Punjab*, MA *Islamia, Bahawal.*, MBA *Agric.*,
Faisalabad

AL-KHAIR UNIVERSITY (AJK)

Founded 1994

Member of the Association of Commonwealth Universities

Postal Address: 88-W, Fazal-ul-Haq Road, Blue Area, Islamabad, Pakistan
Street address: Mirpur, Azad Kashmir, Pakistan
Telephone: (051) 287 9907-8 **Fax:** (051) 287 9906 **E-mail:** alkhairuniversityajk@yahoo.com

VICE-CHANCELLOR*—Goraya, Prof. Khan A., LLB *Punjab*, MA *Punjab*, MSc *Quaid-i-Azam*
PRO-VICE-CHANCELLOR—Goraya, Muhammad I. A.
REGISTRAR‡—Aslam Asghar, M.
CONTROLLER OF EXAMINATIONS—Bashir, Muhammad
TREASURER—Swati, Shahnawaz K.
DEPUTY TREASURER—Maqddus, Khudija

GENERAL INFORMATION

First Degrees (see also Pakistan Directory to Subjects of Study) (* = with honours). BA, BBA, BCom, BCS, BEd, BIT, BLS, BPEd, BSc, BS(CS), BS(IT), BTech, BTech*, LLB.

Higher Degrees (see also Pakistan Directory to Subjects of Study).
Master's. MA, MBA, MCom, MCS, MEd, MIT, MLS, MPEd, MSc.

Libraries. Volumes: 5000.

FACULTIES/SCHOOLS

Arts

Dean: Huda, A. S.

Computer Science

Dean: Huda, A. S.

Education

Dean: Huda, A. S.

Management Sciences

Dean: Huda, A. S.

AFFILIATED COLLEGES

[Institutions listed by location below provide courses leading to degrees, etc. of the university]

Abbottobad. College of Business Administration and Education
Bagh. College of Education
Bahawalnagar. Educare College of Information Technology
Bahawalpur. U. K. College of Technology
Bhimber. College of Education
D. I. Khan. Jinnah Institute of Information Technology and Management Sciences
Faisalabad. Institute of Management Sciences
Gujurat. Chenab College of Information Technology
Islamabad. College of Business Administration; College of Computer Sciences; College of Professional Studies
Karachi. College of Business Administration and Computer Science; Institute of Scientific Management; Pakistan Institute of Professional Sciences; SPIRIT Institute of Management and Computer Sciences
Karak. Institute of Education and Research
Kohar. Institute of Education and Research
Kotli. College of Education
Lahore. Centre for Health and Population Studies; College of Business Administration; College of Information Technology; College of Technical Education; Institute of Computer Technology; Matrix Institute of Emerging Sciences; Modern College of Commerce; Proceed Institute of Management and Information Technology
Multan. College of Professional Studies; National College
Pallandri. College of Education
Peshawar City. Institute of Education and Research
Quetta. College of Law, Education and Information Technology
Rawalkot. College of Education, Law and Management Science
Rawalpindi. College of Global Technologies; College of Information Technology; Jinnah Islamia College of Commerce; South Asian Institute of Management and Information Technology; University College
Sadiqabad. Sadiq Abad Polytechnic Institute
Sargodha. College of Business Administration; Iqra Girl's College
Sheikhupura. College of Management Sciences
Sukkur. College of Education, Management Sciences and Information Technology
Swabi. Institute of Education and Research
Wah. College of Management and Information Technology

[Information supplied by the institution as at 4 February 2005, and edited by the ACU]

ALLAMA IQBAL OPEN UNIVERSITY

Founded 1974

Postal Address: Sector H-8, Islamabad, Pakistan
Telephone: (051) 925 0111 **Fax:** (051) 925 0026 **E-mail:** aiou@paknet.ptc.pk

VICE-CHANCELLOR*—Butt, Prof. Mahmood H., MA *Punjab*, MS *Indiana*, PhD *Indiana*
REGISTRAR‡—Ilyas, Ahmad, MA *Punjab*

UNIVERSITY OF ARID AGRICULTURE, RAWALPINDI

Founded 1994

Member of the Association of Commonwealth Universities

Postal Address: Murree Road, Shamsabad, Rawalpindi 46300, Pakistan
Telephone: (051) 929 0151 **Fax:** (051) 929 0160 **E-mail:** uaar@yahoo.com
URL: http://www.uaar.edu.pk

VICE-CHANCELLOR*—Khan, Prof. Khalid Mahmood, MSc Punjab, PhD Edin., BSc
REGISTRAR‡—Butt, Aslam Farooq
CONTROLLER OF EXAMINATIONS—Nisar, Muhammad, BSc Agric., Faisalabad, MPhil Arid Ag.
TREASURER—Mubarak Shah, Syed, MA Punjab

GENERAL INFORMATION

History. Originally founded as Barani Agricultural College, Rawalpindi, in 1979, the university gained its present name and status in 1994.

It is located at the centre of the twin cities of Islamabad and Rawalpindi.

Admission to first degree courses (see also Pakistan Introduction). Home students: intermediate secondary certificate, with second division or higher in appropriate subjects; age limit: 23 years. International students: equivalent qualification. Applicants whose first language is not English are required to pass an English language test.

First Degrees (see also Pakistan Directory to Subjects of Study) (* = with honours). BBA*, BCS*, BEd, BIT*, BScAgri*.

Length of course. Full-time: BEd: 1–1½ years; BBA*: 3 years; BCS*, BIT*, BScAgri*: 4 years.

Higher Degrees (see also Pakistan Directory to Subjects of Study).

Master's. MBA, MCS, MEd, MIT, MPhil(Edu), MSc, MScAgri, MSc(Edu).

Admission. Applicants for admission to master's courses must hold at least a second division first degree in an appropriate subject.

MBA (professional): 2 years; MBA (executive): 1–1½ years.

Length of course. Full-time: MEd: 1–1½ years; MBA, MCS, MIT, MPhil(Edu), MSc, MSc(Edu), MScAgri: 2 years.

Doctoral. PhD.

Admission. PhD: applicants should have an appropriate master's degree.

Length of course. Full-time: PhD: 3 years.

Libraries. 12,400 books; 15 serial titles.

FACULTIES/SCHOOLS

Crop and Food Sciences
Tel: (051) 929 0153
Dean: Ahmad, Prof. Shahbaz, MSc Agric., Faisalabad, PhD Oregon

Sciences
Tel: (051) 929 0467
E-mail: afsarmianpk@yahoo.com
Dean: Mian, Prof. Afsar, MSc Punjab, PhD Punjab

ACADEMIC UNITS

Agronomy
Ansar, Muhammad, PhD   Asst. Prof.
Ashraf, Muhammad, MSc Agric., Faisalabad, PhD Oregon   Assoc. Prof.
Aziz, Irfan, MSc   Asst. Prof.
Fayyaz-ul-Hassan, PhD   Assoc. Prof.
Mahmood, Tariq, PhD   Assoc. Prof.
Malik, Muhammad Azim, PhD   Prof.; Chairman*
Razzaq, Abdul, PhD   Asst. Prof.
Zammurad Iqbal Ahmed, M., PhD   Assoc. Prof.

Other Staff: 4 Lectrs.

Animal Science
Tel: (051) 929 0467
E-mail: afsarmianpk@yahoo.com
1 Lectr.

Biochemistry
Tel: (051) 445 1772
E-mail: azrakhanum@uaar.edu.pk
Gulfaraz, Muhammad, PhD   Assoc. Prof.
Kaukab, Ghazala, PhD   Asst. Prof.
Khanum, Azra, MSc Karachi, MPhil Islam., PhD Islam.   Assoc. Prof.; Chairperson*
Naqvi, Syed M. S., MSc Islam., MPhil Islam., PhD Middle East Tech.   Assoc. Prof.
Other Staff: 2 Lectrs.
Research: biotechnology; environmental biology; ethnobotany; molecular biology; stress physiology

Botany
Akram, Abida, MSc   Asst. Prof.
Arshad, Muhammad, PhD   Assoc. Prof.
Asghar, Rehana, MSc Baloch., MS Calif., PhD Calif.   Assoc. Prof.; Chairperson*
Waheed, Abdul, PhD   Asst. Prof.
Other Staff: 1 Lectr.

Economics
Ahmad, Sarfraz, MSc Agric., Faisalabad, PhD Tennessee   Assoc. Prof.; Chairman*
Malik, Ikram A., MSc   Asst. Prof.
Mohsin, Abdul Q., PhD   Asst. Prof.
Zahid, Saeed A., MSc   Asst. Prof.
Other Staff: 3 Lectrs.
Research: agricultural credit; agricultural marketing; farm management and production economics; farming systems

Engineering, Agricultural
Nisar, Muhammad, BSc Agric., Faisalabad, MPhil Arid Ag.   Asst. Prof.; Chairman*

English and Humanities
Tel: (051) 929 0467
Iqbal, Yasir, MA Punjab   Lectr.; Head*

Entomology
Aslam, Muhammad, MSc Agric., Faisalabad, PhD Georgia   Assoc. Prof.
Humayun Javed, MSc   Asst. Prof.
Khaliq, Abdul, MSc Agric., Faisalabad, PhD Agric., Faisalabad   Prof.; Chairman*
Naeem, Muhammad A., PhD   Asst. Prof.
Other Staff: 3 Lectrs.

Food Technology
Ali, Muhammad, MSc   Asst. Prof.
Masud, Tariq, MSc Islam., MPhil Islam., PhD Islam.   Assoc. Prof.; Chairman*
Other Staff: 3 Lectrs.
Research: biotechnology; cereal technology; food microbiology; meat technology; product development

Forestry
Khan, Irshad Ahmed, PhD   Asst. Prof.; Chairman*
Mirza, Sarwat N., PhD   Assoc. Prof.
Other Staff: 1 Lectr.

Horticulture
Abbasi, Nadeem Akhtar, PhD   Assoc. Prof.; Chairman*
Hafiz, Ishfaq Ahmad, PhD   Asst. Prof.
Other Staff: 2 Lectrs.
Research: floriculture; vegetable seed production

Plant Breeding and Genetics
Akram, Zahid, MSc   Asst. Prof.
Khan, Saif Ullah Ajmal, PhD   Assoc. Prof.
Minhas, Nasir M., MSc   Asst. Prof.
Munir, Muhammad, MSc Agric., Faisalabad, PhD Liv.   Prof.; Chairman*
Other Staff: 2 Lectrs.

Plant Pathology
Irfan-Ul-Haque, MSc Karachi, PhD Missouri   Prof.; Chairman*
Khan, Muhammad Shahid A., PhD   Assoc. Prof.
Rauf, Abdul, PhD   Asst. Prof.
Riaz, Abid, MSc   Asst. Prof.
Other Staff: 3 Lectrs.

Soil Science
Ali, Safdar, MSc Agric., Faisalabad, PhD Oregon   Assoc. Prof.
Ghulam Jilani, PhD   Asst. Prof.
Khan, Khalid S., PhD   Assoc. Prof.
Lone, Muhammad Iqbal, MSc Agric., Faisalabad, PhD   Assoc. Prof.
Naeem, Muhammad A., PhD   Assoc. Prof.
Yousaf, Muhammad, MSc Agric., Faisalabad, PhD Calif.   Assoc. Prof.; Chairman*
Other Staff: 2 Lectrs.

Statistics, Mathematics and Computer Sciences
Azam, Muhammad, MSc   Asst. Prof.
Shakoor, Abdush, MSc Agric., Faisalabad   Asst. Prof.; Chairman*
Other Staff: 4 Lectrs.

Zoology
Akhtar, Shsmim, MSc   Asst. Prof.
Mian, Afsar, MSc Punjab, PhD Punjab   Prof.
Mussaddeq, Yasmin, MSc Punjab, PhD Birm.   Assoc. Prof.; Chairman*
Qayyum, Mazhar, PhD   Assoc. Prof.

SPECIAL CENTRES, ETC

Continuing Education, Home Economics and Women Development, Division of
Tel: (051) 929 0467
Kayyani, Almas, MSc   Asst. Prof.
Mian, Afsar, MSc Punjab, PhD Punjab   Prof.; Dir.*
Other Staff: 1 Lectr.

Education and Research, University Institute of

Tel: (051) 929 0413

Iqbal, Ch. Muhammad, MEd *Punjab*, MA *Islam.*, MA *Punjab*, PhD *Punjab*   Dir.*

Information Technology, Centre for

Tel: (051) 929 0154 Fax: (051) 929 0113

Afzal, Muhammad, PhD   Prof.; Dir.*
Ahmad, Muneeb, MSc   Asst. Prof.
Chaudhary, Jamil M., MSc   Asst. Prof.
Hafeez, Yasir, MSc   Asst. Dir.
Other Staff: 2 Lectrs.; 7 Res. Assocs.; 1 Network Administrator

Management Sciences, University Institute of

Tel: (051) 929 0155

Ajmal, Javaria, MBA *Arid Ag.*   Asst. Dir.
Akhtar, Zaheer M., PhD   Prof.; Dir.*
Ayaz Elahi, MBA *Arid Ag.*   Asst. Dir.
Nasreen, Bushra, MBA   Asst. Prof.
Rehman, Abdul, MBA   Asst. Prof.

Other Staff: 3 Lectrs.; 1 Career Planning Officer

CONTACT OFFICERS

Admissions (first degree). Registrar: Butt, Aslam Farooq
Admissions (higher degree). Registrar: Butt, Aslam Farooq
Estates and buildings/works and services. Estate Care Officer: Ghulam Sarwar, Major (Retd.)
Examinations. Controller of Examinations: Nisar, Muhammad, BSc *Agric., Faisalabad*, MPhil *Arid Ag.*
Finance. Deputy Treasurer: Batool, Iram S., MBA *Gomal*
Finance. Treasurer: Mubarak Shah, Syed, MA *Punjab*
Library (chief librarian). In-charge, Library: Ahmad, M. Zammurad I., MSc *Agric., Faisalabad*, PhD *Agric., Faisalabad*
Library (enquiries). Deputy Librarian: Masood, Shahid, MA *Baloch.*
Purchasing. Store Officer: Rajpoot, Latif

Research. Director, Research: Lone, Iqbal M., PhD (E-mail: lone@uaar.edu.pk)
Research. Director, Advanced Studies and Research: Mahmood, Tariq, PhD
Scholarships, awards, loans. Deputy Treasurer: Batool, Iram S., MBA *Gomal*
Security. Security Officer: Ghulam Sarwar, Major (Retd.)
Sport and recreation. Assistant Director (Sport and recreation): Khigi, Saleem
Strategic planning. Deputy Director (Planning): (vacant)
Student welfare/counselling. Director, Students' Affairs: Naeem, Azhar, PhD
Students from other countries. Director, Students' Affairs: Naeem, Azhar, PhD
Students with disabilities. Director, Students' Affairs: Naeem, Azhar, PhD
Women. Acting Director (Women): Mian, Prof. Afsar, MSc *Punjab*, PhD *Punjab* (E-mail: afsarmianpk@yahoo.com)

[Information supplied by the institution as at 27 May 2005, and edited by the ACU]

UNIVERSITY OF AZAD JAMMU AND KASHMIR

Founded 1980

Member of the Association of Commonwealth Universities

Postal Address: Camp Office NISTE, H/8-1, Faiz Ahmed Faiz Road, Islamabad, Pakistan
Telephone: (051) 925 9151 **Fax:** (051) 925 9152 **E-mail:** info@ajku.edu.pk
URL: http://www.ajku.edu.pk

VICE-CHANCELLOR*—Khan, Prof. Manzoor H., BSc *B'desh.Engin.*, MSc *Birm.*, PhD *Birm.*
REGISTRAR‡—Akhtar, Prof. R. N., MA *Punjab*, PhD *Essex*
DIRECTOR OF FINANCE AND PLANNING—Ghous, Ghulam, MA *Multan*, MBA *Quaid-i-Azam*, MS *Salf.*, PhD *Hull*
CONTROLLER OF EXAMINATIONS—Malik, Prof. Z. H., MPhil *Pesh.*, PhD *Pesh.*
DIRECTOR, ACADEMICS, EDUCATION PLANNING AND RESEARCH—Ahmad, Prof. K. F., MSc *Pesh.*, PhD *Newcastle(UK)*
DIRECTOR OF WORKS—Khan, Aurangzeb, BScEngg(Civil) *Lahore UET*
CHIEF LIBRARIAN—Yaqoob, Ch. Muhammad, MLS *Karachi*

GENERAL INFORMATION

History. The university was founded by the promulgation of the University of Azad and Kashmir ordinance in July 1980.

Admission to first degree courses (see also Pakistan Introduction). Intermediate or Higher Secondary Certificate.

First Degrees (see also Pakistan Directory to Subjects of Study). BA, BSc, LLB.
Length of course. Full-time: BA, BSc: max. 2 years; LLB: max. 3 years. Part-time: BA, BSc: max. 2 years; LLB: max. 3 years. By distance learning: BA, BSc: max. 2 years; LLB: max. 3 years.

Higher Degrees (see also Pakistan Directory to Subjects of Study).
Master's. MA, MPhil, MSc.
Admission. Applicants for admission to master's degrees must hold an appropriate first degree with at least second class honours.
Length of course. Full-time: MA, MPhil, MSc: max. 2 years. Part-time: MA, MPhil, MSc: max. 2 years. By distance learning: MA, MPhil, MSc: max. 2 years.
Doctoral. PhD.
Admission. Applicants for admission to PhD must have completed MPhil.
Length of course. Full-time: PhD: max. 4 years. Part-time: PhD: max. 4 years. By distance learning: PhD: max. 4 years.

Language of Instruction. English and Urdu.

Libraries. Volumes: 150,000. Periodicals subscribed to: 35. Other holdings: 200,000 digital library (online research journals). Special collections: Allama Iqbal; Kashmir; conflict resolution; Quaid-e-Azam.

Income (2005–2006). Total, Rs262,344,000.

Statistics. Staff (2005–2006): 1189 (288 academic, 901 non-academic). Students (2005–2006): full-time 3773 (2434 men, 1339 women); undergraduate 2254 (1680 men, 574 women); master's 1512 (750 men, 762 women); doctoral 7 (4 men, 3 women).

FACULTIES/SCHOOLS

Administrative Sciences (Kotli), University College of
Tel: (058660) 42972 Fax: (058660) 45814
   E-mail: uck_it2002@yahoo.com
Dean: Sajid, M. A., MA *Punjab*, PhD *Strath.*

Agriculture (Rawalakot), University College of
Tel: (051) 442 5724 Fax: (051) 442 5724
   E-mail: dryusufali@yahoo.com
Dean: Choudhary, A. Y., MSc *Agric., Faisalabad*, PhD *Zhejiang*

Arts
Tel: (051) 925 8344
Dean: Khan, M. S., MA *Punjab*, PhD *Karachi*

Engineering, University College of
Tel: (058610) 42612 Fax: (058610) 44156
   E-mail: riazdat@yahoo.com
Dean: Mughal, Prof. M. R., MSc *Wayne State*, PhD *Lahore UET*

Home Economics, University College of
Tel: (058610) 43681 Fax: (058610) 44849
Dean: Nayyer, Prof. S., MA *Punjab*

Quality Enhancement Cell
Tel: (051) 925 8970
   E-mail: drhabib56@yahoo.com
Dean: Rehman, Prof. H., MSc *Karachi*, PhD *Karachi*

ACADEMIC UNITS

Agriculture, Rawalakot
Tel: (051) 442 5724 Fax: (051) 442 5724
Abbasi, M. K., MSc *Agric., Faisalabad*, PhD *Wales*   Prof.; Chairman*
Ahmad, K. F., MSc *Pesh.*, PhD *Newcastle(UK)*   Prof.
Ahmad, M. J., MSc *Agric., Faisalabad*, PhD *Agric., Faisalabad*   Assoc. Prof.; Chairman*
Anjum, M. S., MSc *Agric., Faisalabad*, PhD *Agric., Faisalabad*   Assoc. Prof.
Awan, M. S., MSc *Agric., Faisalabad*   Asst. Prof.
Choudhary, A. Y., MSc *Agric., Faisalabad*, PhD *Zhejiang*   Prof.; Dean*
Choudhary, M. A., MSc *Agric., Faisalabad*   Asst. Prof.

Choudhry, M. B., MSc *Agric.*, *Faisalabad*, PhD *Reading*   Prof.
Gardezi, D. N. A., MSc *Agric.*, *Faisalabad*, PhD *Wales*   Prof.
Hamid, A., MSc *Agric.*, *Faisalabad*, PhD *P.F.U.*, *Moscow*   Prof.
Hussain, M., MSc *Agric.*, *Faisalabad*, PhD *Agric.*, *Faisalabad*   Assoc. Prof.
Hussain, T., MSc *Pesh.*   Assoc. Prof.
Iqbal, M., MSc *Agric.*, *Faisalabad*   Asst. Prof.
Javed, A., MSc *Agric.*, *Faisalabad*   Asst. Prof.
Kazmi, M. A., MSc *Agric.*, *Faisalabad*, PhD *Halle*   Prof.
Khan, K. M., MSc *Agric.*, *Faisalabad*, PhD *Agric.*, *Faisalabad*   Assoc. Prof.
Khan, M. F., MSc *Pesh.*, PhD *Wales*   Prof.; Chairman*
Khan, M. Q., MSc *Agric.*, *Faisalabad*, PhD *Wales*   Assoc. Prof.
Khan, M. R., MSc *Karachi*, PhD *Newcastle(UK)*   Prof.; Chairman*
Khan, M. R., MSc *Pesh.*, PhD *Putra*   Asst. Prof.
Khan, M. S., MA *Punjab*, PhD *Karachi*   Prof.
Khan, S. A., MScAgric *Pesh.*   Asst. Prof.
Majeed, A., MSc *Agric.*, *Faisalabad*, PhD *Agric.*, *Faisalabad*   Assoc. Prof.
Qureshi, M. A., MSc *Agric.*, *Faisalabad*, PhD *Agric.*, *Faisalabad*   Assoc. Prof.
Rathore, H. A., MSc *Agric.*, *Faisalabad*   Assoc. Prof.
Saleem, A., MSc *Agric.*, *Faisalabad*, MPhil *Agric.*, *Faisalabad*   Asst. Prof.
Shah, S. R. A., MSc *Agric.*, *Faisalabad*, PhD *Quaid-i-Azam*   Assoc. Prof.
Shah, Z. A., MSc *Agric.*, *Faisalabad*   Asst. Prof.
Siddiqui, M. H., MSc *Agric.*, *Faisalabad*   Asst. Prof.
Zafar, M. A., MA *Punjab*, PhD *Karachi*   Prof.
Other Staff: 13 Lectrs.
Research: agronomy; food technology; horticulture; plant breeding and genetics; soil science

Art and Design
Tel: (058610) 46101
Ali, S. R., MA *Pesh.*   Prof.; Chairperson*
Dar, S., MA *Punjab*   Assoc. Prof.
Naqvi, F., MA *Lahore*   Assoc. Prof.
Qadir, Z., MA *Punjab*   Asst. Prof.
Riaz, N., MA *Punjab*, MPhil *Punjab*   Asst. Prof.
Saddiqui, R. A., MFA *Punjab*   Asst. Prof.
Shahzadi, F., MA *Ban.Vid.*   Asst. Prof.
Other Staff: 3 Lectrs.; 1 Librarian

Botany
Tel: (0300) 986 3095
Akhtar, T., MSc *Punjab*, MPhil *Quaid-i-Azam*   Asst. Prof.
Choudhry, A. H., MSc *Punjab*, MPhil *Sheff.*   Assoc. Prof.
Gorsi, M. S., MSc *Karachi*, MPhil   Assoc. Prof.; Chairman*
Khattak, T. M., MSc *Pesh.*, MPhil *Karachi*   Assoc. Prof.
Majid, A. S., MSc *Agric.*, *Faisalabad*, MPhil *Quaid-i-Azam*, PhD   Asst. Prof.
Malik, Z. H., MPhil *Pesh.*, PhD *Pesh.*   Prof.
Murtaza, G., MSc *Punjab*, MPhil *Quaid-i-Azam*   Asst. Prof.
Shafiq-ur-Rehman, MSc *Punjab*   Assoc. Prof.
Other Staff: 2 Lectrs.
Research: cell biology; ethnobotany; microbiology; plant physiology; tissue culture

Business Administration
Tel: (058660) 42972 Fax: (058660) 42972
Farooqi, M. A., PhD   Assoc. Prof.
Ghous, Ghaulam, MSc *Multan*, PhD *Hull*   Prof.
Khan, M. S., MBA *Azad J&K*   Asst. Prof.; Chairman*
Kiani, N. A., MBA *Azad J&K*   Asst. Prof.
Sajid, M. A., MA *Punjab*, PhD *Strath.*   Prof.
Zafar, A., MBA *Azad J&K*   Asst. Prof.
Other Staff: 1 Lectr.
Research: customer relationship management; emotional intelligence of professional managers in Azad Jammu and Kashmir;

implementation of total quality management (TQM) in hotel management; leadership development; pre- and post-privatisation performance of selected industries in Pakistan

Chemistry
Tel: (0334) 512 8606
Aziz, A. K., MSc *Punjab*   Assoc. Prof.
Aziz, M. Ch., MSc *Pesh.*, PhD *Quaid-i-Azam*   Assoc. Prof.
Khan, M. H., MSc *Punjab*, PhD *Punjab*   Prof.; Chairman*
Khan, M. R., MSc *Karachi*   Asst. Prof.
Khan, M. S., MSc *Gomal*, MPhil *Pesh.*, PhD *Pesh.*   Assoc. Prof.
Rehman, H., MSc *Karachi*, PhD *Karachi*   Prof.
Sadiq-ur-Rehman, MSc *Pesh.*, MPhil *Quaid-i-Azam*, PhD *Quaid-i-Azam*   Assoc. Prof.
Tahseen, G., MSc *Islamia, Bahawal.*, PhD *Hull*   Asst. Prof.
Yasin, A. K., MSc *Quaid-i-Azam*, MPhil *Quaid-i-Azam*   Asst. Prof.
Other Staff: 8 Lectrs.
Research: environmental chemistry; natural product chemistry; organic synthesis; organometallics; solvent extraction

Commerce
Tel: (058660) 42972 Fax: (058660) 42972
Ahmed, I, MBA *Azad J&K*   Asst. Prof.
Akram, S., MSc *Azad J&K*   Asst. Prof.
Arshad, M., MSc *Agric.*, *Faisalabad*, MPhil *Agric.*, *Faisalabad*   Assoc. Prof.
Chaudhary, M. S., MBA *Gomal*   Asst. Prof.; Chairman*
Hussain, S., MA *Karachi*   Asst. Prof.
Hussain, S., MBA *Azad J&K*   Asst. Prof.
Khan, M. A., MBA *Pesh.*   Asst. Prof.
Other Staff: 4 Lectrs.
Research: banking efficiency and measurement of leading commercial banks of Pakistan

Computer Sciences and Information Technology, Kotli
Tel: (058660) 45266 Fax: (058660) 42972
Choudhary, M. A., MSc *Gomal*   Coordinator*
Other Staff: 7 Lectrs.

Computer Sciences and Information Technology, Mirpur
Tel: (058610) 46377 Fax: (058610) 46377
Eng. Khalid, M., MS   Prof.
Islam, K., MSc *NSW*, PhD *NSW*   Prof.
Khalid, M., MSc *Agric.*, *Faisalabad*   Asst. Prof.
Mughal, M. R., MSc *Wayne State*, PhD *Lahore UET*   Prof.; Chairman*
Qasim, M., MSc *Quaid-i-Azam*, MPhil *Quaid-i-Azam*   Asst. Prof.
Other Staff: 13 Lectrs.

Computer Sciences and Information Technology, Muzaffarabad
Tel: (0301) 567 8456
Khan, M. W., MSc *Punjab*   Assoc. Prof.; Chairman*
Other Staff: 17 Lectrs.
Research: artificial intelligence (AI); databases; distributed systems; networking; web development techniques

Computer Sciences (Rawalakot), Centre for
Tel: (051) 442 5724 Fax: (051) 442 5724
Khan, M. R., MSc *Karachi*, PhD *Newcastle(UK)*   Prof.; Chairman*
Other Staff: 8 Lectrs.

Engineering and Technology, Mirpur
Tel: (058610) 42612 Fax: (058610) 44156
E-mail: riazdat@yahoo.com
Ahmad, M. S., MSc *Taxila UET*, PhD *Cracow*   Prof.
Ahmad, M., MA *Karachi*   Assoc. Prof.
Amin, S., BSc *Lahore UET*   Asst. Prof.
Dar, S. H., BE *Karachi*   Asst. Prof.

Hussain, N., MSc *Howard*   Prof.; Chairman*
Khan, M. Q., MSc *Agric.*, *Faisalabad*, PhD *Wales*   Assoc. Prof.
Masood, K., BSc *Natnl.Coll.Arts(Lahore)*   Asst. Prof.
Mirza, M. S., BSc *Lahore UET*   Asst. Prof.
Nusarullah, M., MSEE *Houston*   Prof.
Qureshi, M. A., BE *Pesh.*   Asst. Prof.; Coordinator*
Qureshi, W. K., BSc *Lahore UET*   Asst. Prof.
Ratial, N. I., BSc *Azad J&K*   Asst. Prof.
Waris, M., MSc *Taxila UET*   Assoc. Prof.
Yasmin, Z., MSc *Quaid-i-Azam*, MPhil *Pesh.*   Assoc. Prof.
Other Staff: 10 Lectrs.
Research: computer engineering; electronics; power engineering; telecommunications engineering

English
Tel: (051) 925 9153
E-mail: nhb67@hotmail.com
Abbasi, A. W. M., MA *Islam.*   Asst. Prof.
Akhtar, R. N., MA *Punjab*, PhD *Essex*   Prof.; Chairman*
Bukhari, N. H.   Asst. Prof.
Gillani, K. T., MA *Punjab*, MPhil *Glas.*   Asst. Prof.
Haroon-ur-Rashid, MA *Azad J&K*   Asst. Prof.
Jan, M., MA *Pesh.*   Asst. Prof.
Other Staff: 2 Lectrs.
Research: linguistics (morphology, semantics, socio-linguistics, syntax)

Geology, Institute of
Tel: (0300) 836 0841
Andrabi, B., MSc *Punjab*   Asst. Prof.
Awan, A., MS *Purdue*, PhD *Purdue*   Prof.
Baig, M. S., MSc *Punjab*, PhD *Oregon*   Prof.
Farooq, A., MSc *Azad J&K*, MPhil *Azad J&K*   Asst. Prof.
Ikram-ul-Rashid, MA *Punjab*   Asst. Prof.
Jaral, A. W., MSc *Punjab*   Asst. Prof.
Khan, M. A., MSc *Karachi*, PhD *Karachi*   Prof.; Dir.*
Khan, M. R., MSc *Punjab*, PhD *Quaid-i-Azam*   Prof.
Khan, M. S., MSc *Pesh.*, PhD *Punjab*   Prof.
Munir, M., MSc *Punjab*   Assoc. Prof.
Qureshi, M. A., MSc *Punjab*   Assoc. Prof.
Qureshi, M. S., MSc *Punjab*   Asst. Prof.
Qureshi, Z., MSc *Punjab*   Prof.
Raja, M. K., MSc *Punjab*   Assoc. Prof.
Saeed, Z., MSc *Punjab*   Prof.
Saleem, M., MSc *Punjab*   Asst. Prof.
Saraf, T. Y., MSc *Punjab*   Asst. Prof.
Siddiqui, I., MSc *Punjab*   Asst. Prof.
Other Staff: 1 Lectr.; 2 Sr. Res. Officers
Research: economic geology; engineering geology; environment; geophysics and seismology; structure tectonics

Home Economics
Tel: (058610) 43681
Arshad, W., MSc *Punjab*   Asst. Prof.
Bukshi, R. A., MA *Punjab*   Asst. Prof.
Fatima, K., MSc *Punjab*   Asst. Prof.
Gul, T., MSc *Pesh.*   Asst. Prof.
Jabeen, M., MA *Punjab*   Assoc. Prof.
Khanum, R., MSc *Quaid-i-Azam*   Asst. Prof.
Nayyar, S., MA *Punjab*   Assoc. Prof.; Dean*
Rafique, N., MSc *Punjab*   Assoc. Prof.
Shah, Saeeda J. A., MA *Manc.*, PhD *Nott.*   Prof.
Other Staff: 5 Lectrs.

Islamic Studies, Institute of
Tel: (058610) 44849 Fax: (058610) 44849
Anjum, N., MA *Punjab*   Assoc. Prof.
Khaliq, A., MA *Karachi*, PhD *Karachi*   Assoc. Prof.; Dir.*
Mussadiq, M., MA *Punjab*   Asst. Prof.
Pirzada, H. A., MA *Punjab*, PhD *Leeds*   Assoc. Prof.
Rajorvi, M. S., MA *Punjab*   Assoc. Prof.
Other Staff: 5 Lectrs.

Mathematics

Tel: (0300) 484 6438

Baig, M. S., MSc Punjab, MPhil Quaid-i-Azam, PhD Ankara   Prof.; Chairman*
Hussain, Z., MSc Quaid-i-Azam, MPhil Quaid-i-Azam   Asst. Prof.
Khan, M. S., MSc Quaid-i-Azam, MPhil Quaid-i-Azam   Asst. Prof.
Khan Aman Ullah, MSc Punjab, PhD Kiev   Prof.
Qureshi, M. N., MSc Quaid-i-Azam, MPhil Quaid-i-Azam, PhD Quaid-i-Azam   Asst. Prof.
Qureshi, S. M., MSc Punjab, MPhil Quaid-i-Azam   Asst. Prof.
Other Staff: 2 Lectrs.
Research: differential equation; differential geometry; fluid mechanics; group symmetry; topology

Physics

Tel: (0300) 952 2842

Attaka, A., MSc Pesh.   Asst. Prof.
Hussain, A. B., MSc Azad J&K   Asst. Prof.
Iqbal, A., MSc Pesh., PhD Nott.   Prof.; Chairman*
Jabeen, S., MSc Punjab   Asst. Prof.
Khan, G. A., MSc Punjab, MPhil Punjab, PhD Brun.   Prof.
Khazir-ul-Haq, MSc Azad J&K, MPhil Quaid-i-Azam   Asst. Prof.
Mahmood, S., MSc Azad J&K, MPhil Quaid-i-Azam   Asst. Prof.
Majid, A., MSc Pesh.   Assoc. Prof.
Rathore, B. A., MSc Punjab, PhD Belgrade   Prof.
Other Staff: 2 Lectrs.
Research: electronics; materials science; plasma physics; solid-state nuclear track detector (SSNTD)/nuclear track detector (NTD); thin films

Public Administration

Tel: (058660) 44150 Fax: (058660) 42972

Chaudhary, M. A., MPA Gomal   Asst. Prof.
Hussain, S., MA Karachi   Asst. Prof.
Malik, M. A., MA Punjab, PhD Pesh.   Assoc. Prof.; Chairman*
Other Staff: 4 Lectrs.
Research: managerial talent and efficiency of professional verses non-professional managers in banking sector; role of public and private sector in development of small and medium-sized enterprises (SMEs) in Azad Jammu and Kashmir

Statistics

Tel: (051) 925 9158

Choudhary, M. A., MPhil Faisalabad   Assoc. Prof.; Chairman*
Other Staff: 4 Lectrs.

Zoology

Tel: (0333) 506 7909

Anwar, K. K., MSc Punjab, PhD Sur.   Prof.
Awan, S. M., MPhil Azad J&K, MSc Punjab   Assoc. Prof.
Chaudhary, B. A., MSc Punjab   Assoc. Prof.

Khan, M. N., MSc Quaid-i-Azam, MPhil Quaid-i-Azam   Assoc. Prof.
Malik, M. A., MSc Quaid-i-Azam, MPhil Quaid-i-Azam, PhD Lond.   Prof.; Chairman*
Nayyar, A. Q., MSc Punjab   Assoc. Prof.
Rafique, M., MSc Pesh., MPhil Azad J&K   Assoc. Prof.
Shafi, Nuzhat, MSc Azad J&K, MPhil Azad J&K   Asst. Prof.
Other Staff: 1 Lectr.
Research: biotechnology; fisheries; microbiology; molecular biology; wildlife

SPECIAL CENTRES, ETC

Economics, Kashmir Institute of

Tel: (0333) 576 7704

Iqbal, J., MSc Azad J&K, MPhil Karachi   Assoc. Prof.
Qureshi, E., MA Punjab   Assoc. Prof.; Dir.*
Shah, H. N. S., MSc Quaid-i-Azam, MPhil Quaid-i-Azam, PhD Quaid-i-Azam   Assoc. Prof.
Other Staff: 5 Lectrs.
Research: conventional economics; disaster economics; divine economics

CONTACT OFFICERS

Academic affairs. Director, Academics, Education Planning and Research: Ahmad, Prof. K. F., MSc Pesh., PhD Newcastle(UK)
(E-mail: kfarooqahmed@yahoo.com)
Accommodation. Director, Students' Affairs: Khan, M. R., MSc Punjab, PhD Quaid-i-Azam
Admissions (first degree). Director, Students' Affairs: Khan, M. R., MSc Punjab, PhD Quaid-i-Azam
Admissions (higher degree). Director, Students' Affairs: Khan, M. R., MSc Punjab, PhD Quaid-i-Azam
Careers. Registrar: Akhtar, Prof. R. N., MA Punjab, PhD Essex
(E-mail: nasimakhtarraja@hotmail.com)
Computing services. Programmer: Naqvi, T. H., MCS Islam.
(E-mail: tanvirhussain@hotmail.com)
Consultancy services. Director of Finance and Planning: Ghous, Ghulam, MA Multan, MBA Quaid-i-Azam, MS Salf., PhD Hull
Development/fund-raising. Deputy Director, Academics, Education Planning and Research: Khawaja, Z. U., MSc Faisalabad
Equal opportunities. Director, Students' Affairs: Khan, M. R., MSc Punjab, PhD Quaid-i-Azam
Estates and buildings/works and services. Director of Works: Khan, Aurangzeb, BScEngg(Civil) Lahore UET
Examinations. Controller of Examinations: Malik, Prof. Z. H., MPhil Pesh., PhD Pesh.
(E-mail: zhmalik51@hotmail.com)
Finance. Director of Finance: Ghous, Ghulam, MA Multan, MBA Quaid-i-Azam, MS Salf., PhD Hull
General enquiries. Registrar: Akhtar, Prof. R. N., MA Punjab, PhD Essex
(E-mail: nasimakhtarraja@hotmail.com)

Health services. Medical Officer: Haider, Waqar, MB BS
International office. Director, Academics, Education Planning and Research: Ahmad, Prof. K. F., MSc Pesh., PhD Newcastle(UK)
(E-mail: kfarooqahmed@yahoo.com)
Library (chief librarian). Chief Librarian: Yaqoob, Ch. Muhammad, MLS Karachi
Marketing. Director of Finance: Ghous, Ghulam, MA Multan, MBA Quaid-i-Azam, MS Salf., PhD Hull
Minorities/disadvantaged groups. Director, Students' Affairs: Khan, M. R., MSc Punjab, PhD Quaid-i-Azam
Ombudsman. Assistant Registrar, Academic: Gillani, S. Shafait, BA LLB
Personnel/human resources. Registrar: Akhtar, Prof. R. N., MA Punjab, PhD Essex
(E-mail: nasimakhtarraja@hotmail.com)
Public relations. Public Relations Officer: Iqbal, Z., MA Azad J&K
(E-mail: zafariqbalpro@gmail.com)
Publications. Director, Academics, Education Planning and Research: Ahmad, Prof. K. F., MSc Pesh., PhD Newcastle(UK)
(E-mail: kfarooqahmed@yahoo.com)
Purchasing. Director of Finance: Ghous, Ghulam, MA Multan, MBA Quaid-i-Azam, MS Salf., PhD Hull
Quality assurance and accreditation. Dean: Rehman, Prof. H., MSc Karachi, PhD Karachi
(E-mail: drhabib56@yahoo.com)
Research. Director, Academics, Education Planning and Research: Ahmad, Prof. K. F., MSc Pesh., PhD Newcastle(UK)
(E-mail: kfarooqahmed@yahoo.com)
Safety. Project Director (Safety): Ghous, Ghulam, MA Multan, MBA Quaid-i-Azam, MS Salf., PhD Hull
Scholarships, awards, loans. Director, Academics, Education Planning and Research: Ahmad, Prof. K. F., MSc Pesh., PhD Newcastle(UK)
(E-mail: kfarooqahmed@yahoo.com)
Security. Director, Estate: Samid, A. K., BSc Punjab
Sport and recreation. Director, Sports: Abdin, Z., MA Punjab
Staff development and training. Registrar: Akhtar, Prof. R. N., MA Punjab, PhD Essex
(E-mail: nasimakhtarraja@hotmail.com)
Student union. Director, Students' Affairs: Khan, M. R., MSc Punjab, PhD Quaid-i-Azam
Student welfare/counselling. Director, Students' Affairs: Khan, M. R., MSc Punjab, PhD Quaid-i-Azam
Students from other countries. Director, Students' Affairs: Khan, M. R., MSc Punjab, PhD Quaid-i-Azam
Students with disabilities. Director, Students' Affairs: Khan, M. R., MSc Punjab, PhD Quaid-i-Azam
Women. Director, Students' Affairs: Khan, M. R., MSc Punjab, PhD Quaid-i-Azam

[Information supplied by the institution as at 31 May 2006, and edited by the ACU]

BAHAUDDIN ZAKARIYA UNIVERSITY

Founded 1975

Postal Address: Multan, Punjab 60800, Pakistan
Telephone: (061) 921 0071-5 **Fax:** (061) 921 0098 **E-mail:** regbzu@brain.net.pk
URL: http://www.bzu.edu.pk

VICE-CHANCELLOR*—Zafarullah, Prof. Muhammad, PhD Strath., MBA
REGISTRAR‡—Chaudhry, Prof. Muhammad A., PhD Lond., MSc MPhil

BAHRIA UNIVERSITY

Founded 2000

Postal Address: Shangrila Road, Sector E-8, Islamabad, Pakistan
Telephone: (051) 926 0002 **Fax:** (051) 926 0885
URL: http://www.bahria.edu.pk

RECTOR*—Farooq Rashid, Vice-Admiral, BSc MSc *Quaid-i-Azam*
REGISTRAR‡—Raza, Cdre. Mumtaz, BSc *Karachi*, MSc *Karachi*, MSc *Manc.*

UNIVERSITY OF BALOCHISTAN

Founded 1970

Postal Address: Sariab Road, Quetta, Balochistan, Pakistan
Telephone: (081) 921 1288 **Fax:** (081) 921 1277 **E-mail:** university_balochistan@yahoo.com
URL: http://www.uob.edu.pk

VICE-CHANCELLOR*—Gul, Brig. Agha A.
REGISTRAR‡—Shaif-ur-Rehman, PhD *Baloch.*

BALOCHISTAN UNIVERSITY OF ENGINEERING AND TECHNOLOGY

Founded 1994

Postal Address: Khuzdar, Balochistan, Pakistan
Telephone: (0848) 412834 **Fax:** (0848) 413197 **E-mail:** registrar@buetk.edu.pk
URL: http://www.buetk.edu.pk

VICE-CHANCELLOR*—Khan, Brig. (Retd.) Mukhtar A., SIM, MSc(Physics)
REGISTRAR‡—Qambrani, Sher A., MA(PolSc)

BAQAI MEDICAL UNIVERSITY

Founded 1996

Postal Address: 51 Deh Tor, Gadap Road, Super Highway, Karachi 74600, Pakistan
Telephone: (021) 4410293 **Fax:** (021) 4410317 **E-mail:** info@baqai.edu.pk
URL: http://www.baqai.edu.pk

VICE-CHANCELLOR*—Ahmad, Lt.-Gen. (Retd.) Prof. Syed A., MB BS *Lond.*, PhD *Lond.*, FRCPath
REGISTRAR‡—Khan, Prof. Khursheed A., MSc *Karachi*, PhD *Karachi*

UNIVERSITY OF CENTRAL PUNJAB

Founded 2002

Member of the Association of Commonwealth Universities

Postal Address: 31 Main Gulberg, Lahore 54660, Pakistan
Telephone: (042) 575 5314-7 **Fax:** (042) 571 0881
URL: http://www.ucp.edu.pk

RECTOR*—Mahmood, Mian A.

UNIVERSITY OF ENGINEERING AND TECHNOLOGY, LAHORE

Founded 1961

Member of the Association of Commonwealth Universities

Postal Address: Grand Trunk Road, Lahore 54890, Pakistan
Telephone: (042) 682 2012 **Fax:** (042) 682 2566 **E-mail:** registrar@edu.uet.pk
URL: http://www.uet.edu.pk

VICE-CHANCELLOR*—Khan, Lt.-Gen. (Retd.) Muhammad A., MSc
SENIOR DEAN—Hassan, Prof. Faizul, PhD *Manc.*, BScEngg
PRO-VICE-CHANCELLOR—(vacant)
REGISTRAR‡—Hussain, Prof. Majid
CONTROLLER OF EXAMINATIONS—(vacant)
TREASURER/DEPUTY REGISTRAR (PLANNING AND DEVELOPMENT)—(vacant)
LIBRARIAN—(vacant)
CONVENOR—Tahir, Prof. M. Akram, PhD
PROJECT DIRECTOR—(vacant)
ASSISTANT REGISTRAR (ACADEMIC)—Butt, Ghulam Suchiyar

GENERAL INFORMATION

History. The university was originally established as the Maclegon Technical College, Lahore in 1923, its name being changed in 1924 to Maclegon Engineering College. In 1931, it was renamed the Punjab Engineering and Technical College, and the Government College of Engineering and Technology, Lahore, in 1956. In 1961 it became the West Pakistan University of Engineering and Technology.

Admission to first degree courses (see also Pakistan Introduction). Intermediate or Higher Secondary Certificate.

First Degrees (see also Pakistan Directory to Subjects of Study). BArch, BSc.
   Length of course. Full-time: BSc: 4 years; BArch: 5 years.

Higher Degrees (see also Pakistan Directory to Subjects of Study).
   Master's. MArch, MPhil, MSc.
   Length of course. Full-time: MPhil, MSc: 2 years.
   Part-time: MPhil, MSc: 3 years.
   Doctoral. PhD.
   Length of course. Part-time: PhD: 4 years.

Libraries. Volumes: 125,000. Other holdings: 16,500 bound serials.

Academic Awards. 23 awards ranging in value from Rs550 to Rs9000.

FACULTIES/SCHOOLS

Architecture and Planning
Tel: (042) 682 9250
Dean: Zaidi, S. Shabih ul Hassan

Chemical, Mineral and Metallurgical Engineering
Tel: (042) 682 9230
Dean: Hassan, Prof. Faizul, PhD *Manc.*, BScEngg

Civil Engineering
Tel: (042) 682 9222
Dean: Ali, Prof. Waris, BScEngg MS PhD

Electrical Engineering
Tel: (042) 682 9234
Dean: (vacant)

Mechanical Engineering
Tel: (042) 682 9221
Dean: Qureshi, Prof. A. H., PhD

Natural Sciences, Humanities and Islamic Studies
Tel: (042) 682 9215
Dean: Shah, Prof. Nawazish Ali, PhD

ACADEMIC UNITS

Architecture and Design, School of
Tel: (042) 682 9223
Ahmad, T., PhD   Asst. Prof.
Akbar, S., BArch PhD   Prof.
Arshad, M., PhD   Assoc. Prof.
Awan, M. Y., BArch PhD   Prof.
Butt, A. Q., MSc *Asian I.T.*, *Bangkok*, PhD *Lond.*, BSc BArch   Prof.
Gelani, I. A. S., MSc *Asian I.T.*, *Bangkok*, BArch   Prof.
Jamal, S., BArch   Asst. Prof.
Malik, R. A., PhD *Sheff.*, BArch   Prof.; Chairman*
Mir, Naeem, BArch   Assoc. Prof.
Naz, Neelum, BArch PhD   Prof.
Rehman, A., PhD   Prof.

Chemistry
Tel: (042) 682 9239
Ahmad, Saeed   Assoc. Prof.
Akbar, Erum   Asst. Prof.
Ansari, Zamir A., MSc *Punjab*   Asst. Prof.
Gillani, S. Rubina   Asst. Prof.
Haq, I., MSc *Punjab*, PhD   Prof.
Qureshi, M. Naseem   Asst. Prof. (on leave)
Tahira, Fazeelat, MSc *Punjab*, PhD *Curtin*   Prof.

City and Regional Planning
Tel: (042) 682 9203
Ahmad, Ijaz, MSc   Asst. Prof.
Anjum, Ghulam A., BSc PhD   Prof.
Bajwa, E. U., PhD *Glas.*, BSc MPhil   Prof.
Farooqi, N. H., BSc   Assoc. Prof.
Hameed, R.   Assoc. Prof.
Malik, T. H., PhD *C.England*, BSc   Prof.
Mayo, S. M.   Asst. Prof.
Nadeem, Obaidullah   Asst. Prof.
Qamar-ul-Islam, MPhil *Edin.*, MSc PhD   Prof.
Shabih-ul-Hassan Zaidi, S., MSc *Asian I.T.*, *Bangkok*, PhD   Prof.; Chairman*

Computer Science
Tel: (042) 682 9260
Afzal, Muhammad   Asst. Prof.
Ahmed, Tauqir   Asst. Prof.
Ahsan, S. M.   Asst. Prof.
Arshad, Shazia   Asst. Prof.
Asif, K. Hussain   Asst. Prof.
Farooq, Amjad   Asst. Prof.
Farooq, Tahir   Asst. Prof.
Haq, Shaiq A., PhD   Prof.; Chairman*
Shah, Abad Ali, PhD   Prof.
Shoaib, Muhammad   Asst. Prof.

Engineering, Architecture and Design
Tel: (042) 682 9419
Alamgir, S., MArch   Asst. Prof.
Ali, H., MSc   Asst. Prof.
Chaudhry, F., MSc   Asst. Prof.
Chishti, F. A., PhD   Asst. Prof.
Hayat, K., PhD   Asst. Prof.
Khan, M. A., MArch   Assoc. Prof.

Mian, Zua ud Din   Prof.
Sheikh, A. S., PhD   Prof.
Tahir, M. A., PhD   Prof.

Engineering, Chemical
Tel: (042) 682 9488
Agha, Hamid R., PhD   Asst. Prof.
Ahmad, M. Mahmood, PhD   Prof.; Chairman*
Bashir, S., MScEng *Akron*, PhD *Akron*, BScEngg   Assoc. Prof.
Feroze, N., BScEngg PhD   Prof.
Hussain, M., MScEngg   Assoc. Prof.
Jafri, T. M., PhD   Asst. Prof. (on leave)
Khan, J. R., MScEngg PhD   Prof.
Mamoor, G. M., BScEngg PhD   Prof.
Naqvi, S. H. J., BScEngg   Assoc. Prof.
Naveed, S., MScEngg PhD   Prof.
Noon, M. Z., PhD *Leeds*, BScEngg   Assoc. Prof.
Qazi, Zaka ur Rehman, MSc   Asst. Prof.
Ramzan, N.   Asst. Prof.
Rasool, S., BScEngg PhD   Prof.
Saleemi, A. R., PhD   Prof.
Shah Muhammad, BScEngg   Assoc. Prof.

Engineering, Civil
Tel: (042) 682 9202
Ahmad, Kafeel   Asst. Prof.
Akbar, A., PhD   Prof.
Akhtar, M. N., BScEngg   Asst. Prof.
Ali, Z., BScEngg PhD   Prof.
Amir, M., MScEng *Rice*, BSc   Asst. Prof. (on leave)
Ashiq, M., PhD   Assoc. Prof. (on leave)
Ashraf, M., MSc *Sur.*, PhD *Sur.*   Prof.; Chairman*
Bakht, Bilal   Asst. Prof. (on leave)
Chishti, S., BScEngg   Asst. Prof. (on leave)
Farooq, K.   Assoc. Prof.
Goroya, R. A.   Assoc. Prof.
Hameed, Asif   Asst. Prof.
Ilyas, M., BScEngg PhD   Prof.
Javed, M. A., BScEngg MSc   Prof.
Khan, N. M.   Asst. Prof.
Khan, S. B., BScEngg   Assoc. Prof.
Mirza, Waseem, PhD   Assoc. Prof.
Mobin, Sajjad   Asst. Prof. (on leave)
Muneeb, Anwar ul Haq   Asst. Prof.
Qayyum, T. I., BScEngg MSc PhD   Prof.
Qazi, A. U.   Asst. Prof.
Rahman, Habib, MScEngg PhD   Assoc. Prof.
Rashid, Imtiaz   Asst. Prof.
Rehman, A., MSc   Assoc. Prof.
Rizwan, S. A., MSc *Sur.*   Prof.
Saleem, Imran, MScEngg   Asst. Prof. (on leave)
Shakir, A. S., BScEngg PhD   Prof.
Sharif, M. B.   Asst. Prof.
Siddiqi, Jamal ur Rehman, MScEngg *Lahore UET*   Asst. Prof.
Siddiqui, Z. A., BScEngg   Prof.
Tahir, M. A., BScEngg MSc PhD   Prof.

Engineering, Electrical

Tel: (042) 682 9229

Ahmad, M., MScEngg *Texas*, BScEngg   Assoc. Prof.
Ali, H., MScEngg *Lahore UET*, BScEngg   Asst. Prof.
Ali, M.   Asst. Prof. (on leave)
Aslam, M. F., MScEngg *Lahore UET*, BScEngg   Assoc. Prof.
Awan, F. G., MSc   Asst. Prof.
Ayyaz, M. N., MScEngg   Assoc. Prof.
Goraya, I. A., BScEngg *NED Eng.*, MScEngg *Lahore UET*   Asst. Prof.
Hashim, Ghulam Murtaza   Assoc. Prof. (on leave)
Hassan, H. T., MSc   Assoc. Prof.
Hayat, K., PhD   Asst. Prof.
Hussain, A., MScEngg   Assoc. Prof.
Iqbal, J., MSc   Assoc. Prof.
Izhar, T., BScEngg MScEngg PhD   Prof.
Javed, Kashif   Asst. Prof. (on leave)
Kamran, M.   Asst. Prof. (on leave)
Khan, M. A., PhD   Assoc. Prof.
Khan, M. Zubair A., MScEng *Manc.*, PhD *Manc.*   Prof.
Khan, W. M., MScEngg   Assoc. Prof.
Mahmood ul Hassan, K., BScEngg PhD   Prof.
Mohsin, S. A.   Asst. Prof.
Qureshi, S. A., MSc *Manc.*, PhD *Manc.*, BScEngg   Prof.
Rehman, Ch. M. Asad   Asst. Prof. (on leave)
Saeed, M., BScEngg MSc   Assoc. Prof.
Saleem, M., BScEngg MSc PhD   Prof.
Salman, M.   Asst. Prof. (on leave)
Shah, A. H., MScEngg PhD   Prof.
Shami, U. T.   Asst. Prof.
Sheikh, M. I., PhD   Assoc. Prof.
Sheikh, N. M., PhD   Prof.; Chairman*
Suleman, M., MScEngg   Assoc. Prof.
Tahir, Ahsan   Asst. Prof.
Tahir, Muhammad   Asst. Prof. (on leave)
Usman, M., MSc   Asst. Prof.
Yousaf, M., MScEngg *Lahore UET*, BScEngg   Asst. Prof.

Engineering, Mechanical

Tel: (042) 682 9208

Abid, J.   Asst. Prof.
Ahmad, Naseer   Asst. Prof.
Aized, T. A.   Assoc. Prof.
Anwar, J.   Asst. Prof.
Arif, K. M.   Asst. Prof.
Aslam, M. A., MScEngg   Assoc. Prof.
Bhutta, M. M. A.   Asst. Prof.
Chaudhry, I. A., MScEngg *Asian I.T., Bangkok*, PhD   Prof.
Cheema, J. M. I., BSc MScEngg   Assoc. Prof. (on leave)
Hassan, I.   Asst. Prof.
Hayat, N., PhD   Assoc. Prof.
Hussain, Shabbir   Asst. Prof.
Inayat, Samsoon   Asst. Prof.
Jamal, Y., MScEngg *Asian I.T., Bangkok*, BScEngg PhD   Assoc. Prof.
Kaleem, A., BScEngg   Asst. Prof.
Kausar, Zareena   Asst. Prof.
Malik, S. M.   Asst. Prof.
Mirza, A. R., MSc   Assoc. Prof.
Mirza, M. R., MSc *Manc.*, PhD *Newcastle(UK)*, BSc   Prof.; Chairman*
Mufti, N. A., PhD   Prof.
Mughal, Hameed U., MScEngg PhD   Prof.
Piracha, J. L., BScEngg   Prof.
Qureshi, A. H., PhD   Prof.
Qureshi, A. M.   Asst. Prof.
Qureshi, N. A., BScEngg MSc   Assoc. Prof. (on leave)
Raza, Ali   Asst. Prof.
Rehman, A.   Asst. Prof.
Saleem, M. Q.   Asst. Prof.
Shah, A. N.   Asst. Prof.
Shah, F. H., PhD   Prof.
Shahid, Ijaz M., MScEngg   Assoc. Prof.
Shaikh, A. A., MScEngg   Assoc. Prof.
Siddique, Z., BScEngg   Asst. Prof.
Tabassum, S. A., BScEngg PhD   Prof.

Waheed, A., BScEngg   Asst. Prof. (on leave)
Zaidi, M. H.   Asst. Prof.

Engineering, Metallurgical, and Material Science

Tel: (042) 682 9207

Ahmad, A., PhD *Birm.*, MScEngg   Prof.
Ahmad, Shabbir   Asst. Prof. (on leave)
Ajmal, M., MSc *Manc.*, PhD *Manc.*   Prof.
Akhtar, Fareed   Asst. Prof. (on leave)
Ali, L., PhD   Prof.
Anwar, M. Y., MScEngg PhD   Prof.
Ashraf, M., MSc   Assoc. Prof.
Awan, G. H.   Assoc. Prof.
Ghauri, K. M., PhD *Strath.*, MScEngg   Prof.
Hassan, Faizul, PhD *Manc.*, BScEngg   Prof.
Iqbal, J., MSc *Manc.*, PhD *Manc.*   Prof.
Zaidi, S. Q. H., MSc   Prof.; Chairman*

Engineering, Mining

Tel: (042) 682 9212

Aadil, N., PhD   Prof.
Chattha, N. H., BSc MScEngg   Prof.
Chaudhry, M. A., BSc PhD   Prof.; Chairman*
Gillani, S. T. A., BScEngg PhD   Assoc. Prof.
Iqbal, M. M.   Asst. Prof.
Khan, M. S., PhD   Assoc. Prof.
Saqib, S.   Asst. Prof.
Sheikh, Ibrat Anwar   Asst. Prof.
Tariq, S. M., PhD   Prof.
Yaqub, BScEngg PhD   Asst. Prof.

Engineering, Petroleum and Gas

Tel: (042) 682 9471

Afzal, J., BScEngg   Assoc. Prof.
Ali, M., BScEngg   Assoc. Prof.
Bhatti, A. A., BScEngg MSc   Asst. Prof.
Inamullah, M., BScEngg   Asst. Prof.
Khan, A. S., MScEngg   Prof.; Chairman*
Khan, A.   Asst. Prof.
Zahoor, M. K.   Asst. Prof.

Humanities and Social Sciences

Tel: (042) 682 9493

Zaidi, S. M. H., MA *Punjab*, MSc   Assoc. Prof.; Chairman*
Zaidi, S. Q.   Asst. Prof.

Islamic Studies

Tel: (042) 682 9246

Farooqi, H. M. I., PhD   Assoc. Prof.
Malik, M. K., PhD   Asst. Prof.

Mathematics

Tel: (042) 682 9210

Ahmad, M. O., MSc MPhil PhD   Prof.; Chairman*
Ahmad, S., MSc *Punjab*   Assoc. Prof.
Chaudhry, M. A., MSc *Punjab*   Asst. Prof.
Chaudhry, N. A., MSc *Punjab*   Asst. Prof.
Gul, M. N., MSc *Punjab*, MPhil *Lahore UET*, PhD   Asst. Prof.
Mushtaq, M.   Asst. Prof.
Naeem, M.   Asst. Prof.
Shafique, M.   Asst. Prof.
Shah, N. A., BEd *Punjab*, MSc *Punjab*, PhD   Prof.
Shahid, N. A., MSc *Punjab*   Asst. Prof.

Physics

Tel: (042) 682 9204

Iqbal, M., PhD   Asst. Prof.
Khaleeq-ur-Rehman, M., MSc *Punjab*, PhD *Manc.*   Prof.; Chairman*
Latif, A., MSc *Punjab*, MPhil   Asst. Prof.
Malik, J. S., MPhil   Asst. Prof.
Rafique, M. S., PhD   Asst. Prof.

SPECIAL CENTRES, ETC

Environmental Engineering and Research, Institute of

Tel: (042) 682 9248

Ali, Waris, BScEngg MS PhD   Prof.
Bari, A. J., MEngg *Asian I.T., Bangkok*, BScEngg   Prof.; Dir.*
Haider, H.   Asst. Prof.

Hayder, S.   Assoc. Prof.
Qureshi, T. A., MSEng PhD   Prof.

CONTACT OFFICERS

Academic affairs. Director, Student Affairs: Bari, Prof. A. J., MEngg *Asian I.T., Bangkok*, BScEngg
Accommodation. Resident Officer: (vacant)
Admissions (first degree). Deputy Registrar (Students Section): Bajwa, M. Ashraf, BA LLB
Admissions (higher degree). (Contact chairman of department concerned)
Alumni. Resident Officer: (vacant)
Careers. Director, Students Finance Assistance Bureau: Naveed, Shahid, PhD *Newcastle(UK)*
Computing services. Chairman, Computer Science Department: Haq, Prof. Shaiq A., PhD
Development/fund-raising. Treasurer/Deputy Registrar (Planning and Development): (vacant)
Estates and buildings/works and services. Project Director: (vacant), MScEngg
Examinations. Controller of Examinations: (vacant)
Finance. Treasurer: (vacant)
General enquiries. Registrar: Hussain, Prof. Majid
Health services. Chief Medical Officer: Amin, Muhammad, MB BS *Punjab*
Industrial liaison. Director, Research: Durrani, Prof. K. E., MScEngg PhD
International office. Deputy Registrar (Students Section): Bajwa, M. Ashraf, BA LLB
Library (chief librarian). Librarian: (vacant)
Personnel/human resources. Registrar: Hussain, Prof. Majid
Public relations. Public Relations Officer: Irfan, M., MA
Publications. Head, Publications: Zaidi, Saiyada Q., MA
Purchasing. Treasurer: (vacant)
Research. Director, Research: Durrani, Prof. K. E., MScEngg PhD
Safety. Resident Officer: (vacant)
Scholarships, awards, loans. Director, Placement Bureau: Naveed, Shahid, PhD *Newcastle(UK)*
Security. Security Officer: Anjum, A. M.
Sport and recreation. Director, Physical Education: Tanveer, M.
Staff development and training. Registrar: Hussain, Prof. Majid
Student welfare/counselling. Director, Student Affairs: Bari, Prof. A. J., MEngg *Asian I.T., Bangkok*, BScEngg
Students from other countries. Director, Student Affairs: Bari, Prof. A. J., MEngg *Asian I.T., Bangkok*, BScEngg

AFFILIATED COLLEGES

[Institutions listed by location below provide courses leading to degrees, etc. of the university]

Bahawalpur. Government College of Technology, Bahawalpur
Faisalabad. Government College of Technology, Faisalabad; N.F.C. Institute of Engineering and Fertilizer Research, Faisalabad
Gujranwala. Rachna College of Engineering and Technology, Gujranwala
Lahore. Garrison Science Degree College for Boys, Lahore; Government College of Technology, Lahore; Himayat-I-Islam Postgraduate Institute, Lahore
Rasul. Government College of Technology, Rasul

[Information supplied by the institution as at 3 May 2006, and edited by the ACU]

UNIVERSITY OF ENGINEERING AND TECHNOLOGY, TAXILA

Founded 1993

Postal Address: Taxila 47050, Pakistan
Telephone: (051) 904 7405 **Fax:** (051) 904 7420 **E-mail:** registrar@uettaxila.edu.pk
URL: http://www.uettaxila.edu.pk/

VICE-CHANCELLOR*—Jamal, Prof. Habibullah, BScEngg *Lahore UET*, MASc *Tor.*, PhD
Tor., FIE(P)
REGISTRAR‡—Bhatti, Aslam, MPA *A.Iqbal Open*, MAEPM *Quaid-i-Azam*

FATIMA JINNAH WOMEN UNIVERSITY

Founded 1998

Member of the Association of Commonwealth Universities

Postal Address: The Mall, Rawalpindi, Pakistan
Telephone: (051) 927 0050 **Fax:** (051) 927 1168 **E-mail:** fjwuvc@comsats.net.pk
URL: http://www.fjwu.edu.pk/

VICE-CHANCELLOR*—Khan, Prof. Saeeda A., MA *Edinboro State*, PhD *Bowling Green*
REGISTRAR‡—Rab, Maryam, MA *Lond.*, MA *Pesh.*
CONTROLLER OF EXAMINATIONS—Sheikh, Mussarrat A., MS *Indiana*, MEd *Pesh.*, MA
Pesh., PhD *Indiana*
TREASURER—Maqbool, Col., BSc *Dhaka Eng.&Tech.*

GENERAL INFORMATION

History. The university was established in 1998 in the Old Presidency under the Fatima Jinnah Women University Act.

It is located in Rawalpindi, approximately 25km from the capital.

Admission to first degree courses (see also Pakistan Introduction). To qualify for the Software Engineering entrance test, candidates must hold 60% marks in FSC (pre-engineering or A levels in maths/physics). For Computer Arts and other higher degree programs 45% marks are required.

First Degrees (see also Pakistan Directory to Subjects of Study) (* = with honours). BA, BA*, BBA, BBus, BCA, BCommSc, BCS, BDDS, BEcon, BEng, BEnvSc, BFA, BGenderSt, BIsL, BMath, BPA, BSc, BSc*, BSE.

Length of course. Full-time: BA, BA*, BCA, BEcon, BEng, BEnvSc, BFA, BSc, BSc*, BSE: 4 years.

Higher Degrees (see also Pakistan Directory to Subjects of Study).

Master's. MA, MBA, MCommSc, MCS, MDDS, MEcon, MEdu, MEng, MEnvSc, MFA, MGenderSt, MIsL, MPA, MS, MSc.

Length of course. Full-time: MA, MBA, MCommSc, MCS, MDDS, MEcon, MEdu, MEng, MEnvSc, MFA, MGenderSt, MIsL, MPA, MSc: 2½ years.

Doctoral. PhD.

Length of course. Full-time: PhD: 4–6 years.

Language of Instruction. Urdu and English.

Libraries. Volumes: 20,705. Other holdings: 18,000 periodicals; 979 audio-visual.

Academic Year (2007–2008). Two semesters: 6 February–15 June; 12 September–25 January.

Income (2007–2008). Total, Rs513,097,000.

Statistics. Staff (2006–2007): 143 (102 academic, 41 non-academic). Students (2006–

2007): undergraduate 1777; master's 3089; doctoral 28.

FACULTIES/SCHOOLS

Arts and Social Sciences
Fax: (051) 927 1169
    E-mail: fjwueng@isb.comsats.net.pk
Dean: Qadir, Prof. Samina A., MEd *Wales*, PhD *Lanc.*

Education
Dean: Khan, Prof. Saeeda A., MA *Edinboro State*, PhD *Bowling Green*

Islamic and Oriental Learning
Dean: Khan, Prof. Saeeda A., MA *Edinboro State*, PhD *Bowling Green*

Law, Commerce and Management and Administrative Sciences
E-mail: fjwueco@isb.comsats.net.pk
Dean: Khan, Prof. Naheed Zia, MA *Punjab*, MPhil *Glas.*, PhD *Strath.*

Science and Technology
E-mail: r.kausar@fjwu.edu.pk
Dean: Kausar, Prof. Rukhsana, MA *Punjab*, PhD *Sur.*

ACADEMIC UNITS

Behavioural Sciences
E-mail: bhs@fjwu.edu.pk
Kausar, Rukhsana, MA *Punjab*, PhD *Sur.*   Prof.; Chairperson*
Other Staff: 2 Profs.; 1 Assoc. Prof.; 5 Lectrs.; 13 Adjunct Fac.
Research: advanced counselling skills and practicum; children with developmental deficit/difficulties; health psychology; industrial organisational psychology; neuropsychological assessment

Business Administration
E-mail: mba_mpa@fjwu.edu.pk
Chaudhry, Ali Mohd., PhD *Hawaii*   Prof.; Chairperson*
Other Staff: 1 Prof.; 3 Asst. Profs.; 5 Lectrs.; 15 Adjunct Fac.

Research: finance; information technology; management; marketing

Communication Sciences
E-mail: comm@fjwu.edu.pk
Zaidi, M. Shamim, PhD *Tehran*   Chairperson*
Other Staff: 3 Lectrs.; 9 Adjunct Fac.
Research: electronic media; media management; print media; telecommunication

Computer Arts
E-mail: bca@fjwu.edu.pk
Gul, Zarin, MA *Kingston(UK)*   Chairperson*
Other Staff: 1 Asst. Prof.; 2 Lectrs.; 12 Adjunct Fac.
Research: computer animation; graphic design; textile design; video production

Computer Sciences
E-mail: mcs@fjwu.edu.pk
Sohail, Rashid A., MS *Ill.*   In-Charge*
Other Staff: 1 Prof.; 3 Asst. Profs.; 5 Lectrs.; 1 Adjunct Fac.
Research: computer graphics; database management systems; network programming; operating systems

Defence and Diplomatic Studies
E-mail: fjwudds@mail.comsats.net.pk
Kiyani, Saima, MA *Quaid-i-Azam*, MPhil *Quaid-i-Azam*, PhD *Taxila UET*   In-Charge*
Other Staff: 5 Lectrs.; 6 Adjunct Fac.
Research: defence; diplomacy

Economics
E-mail: fjwueco@mail.comsats.net.pk
Khan, Naheed Zia, MA *Punjab*, MPhil *Glas.*, PhD *Strath.*   Prof.; Chairperson*
Other Staff: 3 Profs.; 5 Lectrs.; 6 Adjunct Fac.
Research: demography; gender and development; human resources development; money and finance; public finance

Education
E-mail: fjwuedu@isb.comsats.net.pk
Sheikh, Mussarrat A., MS *Indiana*, MEd *Pesh.*, MA *Pesh.*, PhD *Indiana*   Assoc. Prof.; Program Co-ordinator*
Other Staff: 1 Assoc. Prof.; 5 Lectrs.; 6 Adjunct Fac.

Research: counselling; education technology; educational leadership and management; learning disabilities; teacher education

Engineering, Software

E-mail: fjwubse@mail.comsats.net.pk
Hussein, Muneer, MPhil Brad.   Asst. Prof.; In-Charge*
Other Staff: 5 Lectrs.; 1 Visiting Fac.
Research: artificial intelligence; databases; networking; software designing

English

E-mail: fjwueng@comsats.net.pk
Qadir, Samina A., MEd Wales, PhD Lanc.   Prof.; Chairperson*
Other Staff: 1 Prof.; 1 Assoc. Prof.; 1 Asst. Prof.; 10 Adjunct Fac.
Research: drama; linguistics; novel; poetry; teaching English as a foreign language

Environmental Sciences

E-mail: fjwuenv@mail.comsats.net.pk
Rafique, Uzaira, MPhil Quaid-e-Awam UEST, PhD Quaid-e-Awam UEST   Asst. Prof.; Chairperson*
Other Staff: 4 Profs.; 6 Asst. Profs.
Research: environmental biology (biodegradation and bioremediation); environmental chemistry; geographic information systems (GIS) and spatial referencing systems (SRS); social environment

Fine Arts

E-mail: fjwu_finearts@yahoo.com
Shaheen, Tabassum, PhD Hacettepe   Asst. Prof.; Chairperson*
Other Staff: 1 Asst. Prof.; 7 Lectrs.; 20 Adjunct Fac.
Research: computer graphics; oil painting/miniature painting; photography; textile designing; videography/documentary production

Gender Studies

E-mail: fjwuwrrc@isb.comsats.net.pk
Hasan, Rukhsana, MA Pesh., MA N.Y.State, PhD N.Y.State   Asst. Prof.; Chairperson*
Other Staff: 1 Asst. Prof.; 2 Lectrs.; 9 Adjunct Fac.
Research: community development; economic contribution of men and women (paid and unpaid work); gender, planning and development; gender-based project planning and implementation; human resource development

Islamic Studies

E-mail: fjwisl@mail.comsats.net.pk
Rafiq, Aayesha, LLB IIU(P'stan.)   In-Charge*
Other Staff: 2 Lectrs.; 6 Visiting Fac.
Research: criminal law of Islam; Islamic banking and finance; Islamic law of war and peace; legal study of Quran and Sunnah; political thought in Islam

Public Administration

E-mail: mba_mpa@fjwu.edu.pk
Akhtar, Shoaib, MA Punjab, MCom W'gong.   Asst. Prof.; Chairperson*
Other Staff: 3 Asst. Profs.; 5 Lectrs.; 1 Visiting Fac.
Research: public finance; public human resource management; public management; public marketing; public policy

SPECIAL CENTRES, ETC

Canadian Studies Resource, Centre for (CSRC)

Qadir, Samina A., MEd Wales, PhD Lanc.   Prof.; Dir.*

Research: Canadian culture/history; Canadian literature; English language teaching (ELT) in Canada; multiculturalism

Collaboration and Linkages, Centre for

E-mail: uzairaiqbal@yahoo.com
Rafique, Uzaira, MPhil Quaid-e-Awam UEST, PhD Quaid-e-Awam UEST   Dir.*

Higher Education Leadership and Management Studies, Centre for

Khan, Saeeda A., MA Edinboro State, PhD Bowling Green   Dir.*

Information Technology, Centre for

E-mail: sheri@isb.paknet.com.pk
Sheri, Brig. Kaleem, BA Punjab, BScEng Lahore UET, MSc Lahore UET   Dir.*

Peace, Democracy and Conflict Resolution in South Asia, Centre for

E-mail: mba_mpa@fjwu.edu.pk
Akhtar, Shoaib, MA Punjab, MCom W'gong.   Asst. Prof.; Dir.*
Research: conflict resolution in South Asia with gender perspective

Psychological Research, Centre for (CPR)

E-mail: r.kausar@fjuw.edu.pk
Kausar, Rukhsana, MA Punjab, PhD Sur.   Prof.; Dir.*
Other Staff: 2 Res. Officers
Research: career counselling; measuring attitude and public opinion; personnel selection; psychological assessment; psychological test construction

Women's Research and Resource Centre

E-mail: fjwuwrrc@isb.comsats.net.pk
Qadir, Samina A., MEd Wales, PhD Lanc.   Prof.
Other Staff: 1 Res. Officer
Research: gender and social issues affecting the academic and professional development of women

CONTACT OFFICERS

Academic affairs. Registrar: Rab, Maryam, MA Lond., MA Pesh.
(E-mail: fjwudreg@comsats.net.pk)
Accommodation. Deputy Controller of Examinations: Raja, Bushra Inayat, MA Punjab (E-mail: fjwudexam@comsats.net.pk)
Admissions (first degree). Deputy Director, Admissions: Raza, Nighat, MA Punjab, MA A.Iqbal Open (E-mail: nighat.reza@gmail.com)
Admissions (higher degree). Dean, Faculty of Arts and Social Sciences: Qadir, Prof. Samina A., MEd Wales, PhD Lanc.
(E-mail: fjwueng@comsats.net.pk)
Adult/continuing education. (Contact the Admission Office)
(E-mail: fjwuadm@comsats.net.pk)
Alumni. Alumni Officer: Ahmed, Sarah, MBA FJ Women (E-mail: ahmedsarah@gmail.com)
Computing services. Director, Computer Sciences: Sheri, Brig. Kaleem, BA Punjab, BScEng Lahore UET, MSc Lahore UET
(E-mail: sheri@isb.paknet.com.pk)
Conferences/corporate hospitality. Dean, Faculty of Arts and Social Sciences: Qadir, Prof. Samina A., MEd Wales, PhD Lanc.
(E-mail: fjwuwrrc@isb.comsats.net.pk)
Credit transfer. Yasmin, Azra, PhD Punjab
(E-mail: azrayasmin@fjwu.edu.pk)
Development/fund-raising. Registrar: Rab, Maryam, MA Lond., MA Pesh.
(E-mail: fjwudreg@comsats.net.pk)

Equal opportunities. Vice-Chancellor: Khan, Prof. Saeeda A., MA Edinboro State, PhD Bowling Green
Estates and buildings/works and services. Mahmood, Lt. Col. Naveed, BSc MBA
(E-mail: ue@fjwu.edu.pk)
Examinations. Deputy Controller of Examinations: Raja, Bushra Inayat, MA Punjab (E-mail: fjwudexam@comsats.net.pk)
Finance. Deputy Treasurer: Akhtar, Shoaib, MA Punjab, MCom W'gong.
(E-mail: fjwutres@comsats.net.pk)
General enquiries. Registrar: Rab, Maryam, MA Lond., MA Pesh.
(E-mail: fjwudreg@comsats.net.pk)
Health services. Central Medical Officer: Shabbir, Saadia, MSc Glas., MB BS
(E-mail: fjwumed@mail.comsats.edu.pk)
Industrial liaison. Associate Dean: Khan, Prof. Naheed Zia, MA Punjab, MPhil Glas., PhD Strath. (E-mail: fjwueco@comsats.net.pk)
International office. Registrar: Rab, Maryam, MA Lond., MA Pesh.
(E-mail: fjwudreg@comsats.net.pk)
Language training for international students. Dean, Faculty of Arts and Social Sciences: Qadir, Prof. Samina A., MEd Wales, PhD Lanc. (E-mail: fjwueng@comsats.net.pk)
Library (chief librarian). In-charge Librarian: Rashid, Julie Ann, MA Emporia State
(E-mail: library@fjwu.edu.pk)
Library (enquiries). Akhtar, Gulnaz, MLIS
Marketing. (Contact the Registrar's Office)
(E-mail: fjwudre@comsats.net.pk)
Ombudsman. Ombudsman: Bashir, Raja
Personnel/human resources. Deputy Treasurer: Akhtar, Shoaib, MA Punjab, MCom W'gong.
(E-mail: placement@fjwu.edu.pk)
Public relations. Registrar: Rab, Maryam, MA Lond., MA Pesh.
(E-mail: fjwudreg@comsats.net.pk)
Publications. Dean, Faculty of Arts and Social Sciences: Qadir, Prof. Samina A., MEd Wales, PhD Lanc.
(E-mail: fjwuwrrc@isb.comsats.net.pk)
Purchasing. Director: Sheri, Brig. Kaleem, BA Punjab, BScEng Lahore UET, MSc Lahore UET
(E-mail: sheri@isb.paknet.com.pk)
Research. Director: Qadir, Prof. Samina A., MEd Wales, PhD Lanc.
(E-mail: fjwuwrrc@isb.comsats.net.pk)
Safety. Ahmad, Lt. Col. Ijaz, BSc Lahore UET
(E-mail: ijazsaleem@gmail.com)
Scholarships, awards, loans. Bano, Saira, MA FJ Women (E-mail: fjwuadm@comsats.net.pk)
Security. Ahmad, Lt. Col. Ijaz, BSc Lahore UET
(E-mail: ijazsaleem@gmail.com)
Sport and recreation. Deputy Treasurer: Zafar, Sheeba, MA Quaid-e-Awam UEST
(E-mail: fjwutres@comsats.net.pk)
Staff development and training. Vice-Chancellor: Khan, Prof. Saeeda A., MA Edinboro State, PhD Bowling Green
(E-mail: fjwu@isb.comsats.net.pk)
Student welfare/counselling. Assistant Registrar: Akhtar, Farzana, MA FJ Women
Students from other countries. Registrar: Rab, Maryam, MA Lond., MA Pesh.
(E-mail: fjwudreg@comsats.net.pk)
University press. Dean, Faculty of Arts and Social Sciences: Qadir, Prof. Samina A., MEd Wales, PhD Lanc.
(E-mail: fjwuwrrc@isb.comsats.net.pk)

[Information supplied by the institution as at 11 October 2007, and edited by the ACU]

FOUNDATION UNIVERSITY

Founded 2002

Member of the Association of Commonwealth Universities

Postal Address: 198 Street No. 50, F-10/4, Islamabad, Pakistan
Telephone: (051) 210 0280 **Fax:** (051) 210 0282 **E-mail:** registrar@fui.edu.pk
URL: http://www.fui.edu.pk

RECTOR*—Khan, Prof. Manzoor H.
REGISTRAR‡—Tanwir-ul-Islam, Air Cdre (Retd)
GENERAL MANAGER, FINANCE—Mazhar-ul-Haq

GENERAL INFORMATION

History. Established in October 2002, Foundation University is a federal university which is sponsored by the Fauji Foundation.
It is located in Islamabad and Rawalpindi.

First Degrees (see also Pakistan Directory to Subjects of Study) (* = with honours). BA*, BBA, BS, MB BS.
Length of course. Full-time: BA, BBA, BS: 4 years; MB BS: 5 years.*

Higher Degrees (see also Pakistan Directory to Subjects of Study).
Master's. MA, MBA, MPhil, MS.
Length of course. Full-time: MA, MBA, MPhil, MS: 2 years.
Doctoral. PhD.
Length of course. Full-time: PhD: 3–5 years.

Language of Instruction. English and Urdu.

Libraries. Volumes: 14,500. Periodicals subscribed to: 70.

Income (2006–2007). Total, Rs257,981,789.

Statistics. Staff (2006–2007): 439 (187 academic, 252 non-academic). Students (2006–2007): total 1368.

FACULTIES/SCHOOLS
Education
Tel: (051) 581 2346 Fax: (051) 552 7069
E-mail: maqsud_bukhari@yahoo.com
Principal: Bukhari, Prof. Muhammad M. A., PhD *Dhaka*

Engineering and Information Technology
Tel: (051) 551 6094 Fax: (051) 558 4574
E-mail: aftab_ff@hotmail.com
Dean: Ahmad, Aftab, MPhil PhD

Liberal Arts and Sciences, Foundation University College of
Tel: (051) 581 2346 Fax: (051) 552 7069
E-mail: fuclas@fui.edu.pk
Head: Bukhari, Prof. Muhammad M. A., PhD *Dhaka*

Management Sciences
Tel: (051) 579 0361-2 Fax: (051) 558 4574
E-mail: drmisaif@hotmail.com
Professor: Saif, Muhammad I., PhD *Ankara*

Medical Sciences
Tel: (051) 578 8252 Fax: (051) 578 8582
E-mail: deanfmcrwp@isb.paknet.com.pk
Principal: Mallhi, Prof. Ashraf A, MB BS, FRCS, FICS

ACADEMIC UNITS
Anaesthesiology
Dur-i-Shahwar, MB BS   Asst. Prof.
Hussain, Brig. (Retd.) Noor, MB BS   Prof.
Mansoor-ul-Haq, MB BS   Asst. Prof.

Anatomy
Ahmad, Anis, MB BS   Asst. Prof.
Chaudry, Shabbir A., MB BS MPhil   Prof.; Head*
Khan, Huma M., MB BS   Asst. Prof.
Qamar, Muhammad A., MB BS   Asst. Prof.
Siddiqi, Najam A., PhD   Assoc. Prof.

Biochemistry
Malik, Abdur R., MB BS   Asst. Prof.
Rauf, Shahid, MB BS MPhil   Assoc. Prof.
Saiyed, Nadeem H., MSc PhD   Prof.; Head*
Wahid, Maryam, MB BS MPhil   Asst. Prof.

Community Medicine
Ahmad, Mahmood, MB BS   Prof.; Head*
Hussain, Col. (Retd.) Ashiq, MB BS MSc   Assoc. Prof.
Khan, Muhammad H., MB BS   Assoc. Prof.
Khan, Muhammad W., MBS MSc   Assoc. Prof.
Siddique, Waqar A., MB BS MPH   Asst. Prof.
Zaidi, Nosheen, MB BS MPH   Asst. Prof.

Dermatology
Farid-ur-Rehman, MB BS   Asst. Prof.
Other Staff: 1 Sr. Registrar

Education
Bukhari, Muhammad M. A., PhD *Dhaka*   Prof.; Head*
Other Staff: 1 Asst. Prof.; 3 Lectrs.

English
Khan, Muhammad A., MA   Prof.; Head*
Other Staff: 1 Asst. Prof.; 3 Lectrs.

Forensic Medicine
Hanif, Muhammad, MB BS   Asst. Prof.
Rasheed, Mian A., MB BS   Prof.; Head*

Gynaecology/Obstetrics
Dawood, Nasira S.   Assoc. Prof.
Hayat, Zartaj   Asst. Prof.
Mallhi, Saeeda A., MB BS MS   Prof.
Naeem, Fareeha   Asst. Prof.
Sohail, Irum   Assoc. Prof.

Medicine and Allied Subjects
Abbasi, Shahid, MB BS   Asst. Prof.
Durrani, A. A., MB BS, FRCP   Asst. Prof.
Khan, M. Saeed, MB BS, FRCP   Assoc. Prof.
Malik, Javaid M., MB BS   Asst. Prof.
Moin, Shaheen, MB BS, FRCP   Prof.; Head*
Nasim, Amjad, MB BS   Asst. Prof.
Saneed, Azhar, MB BS
Shahzad, Aamir, MB BS   Assoc. Prof.
Siddiq, Masood, MB BS   Prof.
Yaqoob, Nayyer, MB BS   Asst. Prof.

Neurosurgery
Miraj-us-Siraj, MB BS   Asst. Prof.

Ophthalmology
Ahmed, Brig. (Retd.) Tahir, MB BS   Prof.; Head*
Ahmed, Zafar, MB BS   Asst. Prof.
Aslam, Muhammad A., MB BS   Asst. Prof.
Iftikhar, Shahzad, MB BS, FRCS   Asst. Prof.
Naeem, B. A., MB BS   Asst. Prof.

Orthopaedics
Iqbal, Brig. (Retd.) Amjad, MB BS MSc   Prof.; Head*
Maqbool, Nauman   Asst. Prof.

Paediatrics
Firdous, Akhtar, MB BS   Prof.; Head*
Hussain, Gul, MB BS   Asst. Prof.
Malik, Faisal R., MB BS   Asst. Prof.
Shabbir, Asma, MB BS   Asst. Prof.

Pathology
Aftab, Irum, MB BS MPhil   Asst. Prof.
Alvi, Ehsan A., MB BS MPhil   Assoc. Prof.
Kazi, Faiza, MB BS MPhil   Prof.
Khan, Masood A., MB BS MPhil   Asst. Prof.
Khan, Mumtaz A., MB BS   Asst. Prof.
Luqman, Muhammad, MB BS MPhil   Prof.
Masood, Kamran, MB BS   Asst. Prof.
Mumtaz, Shahim, MB BS MPhil   Assoc. Prof.
Saeed, Sammi, PhD   Asst. Prof.
Sajid, S. D., PhD   Assoc. Prof.
Zafar, Lubna, MB BS   Assoc. Prof.

Pharmacology and Therapeutics
Gondal, Ghulam M., MB BS   Assoc. Prof.
Khan, Amna, MB BS   Asst. Prof.
Shah, Mahbood A., PhD *Lond.*   Asst. Prof.

Physiology
Ahmed, Owais, MB BS   Asst. Prof.
Khan, Saadat A., MB BS MPhil   Prof.; Head*
Malik, Abdur R., MB BS   Asst. Prof.
Razaq, Zubia, MB BS   Asst. Prof.

Psychiatry
Abbas, Nadeem, MB BS   Assoc. Prof.
Azad, Nadia, MB BS   Asst. Prof.

Radiology
Mufti, M. Mudassir, MB BS   Asst. Prof.
Qureshi, Ishtiaq A., MB BS   Prof.; Head*

Research and Development
Arif, Mansoor, PhD *Lahore*   Assoc. Prof.
Ehsan-ur-Rehman, PhD *Pesh.*   Assoc. Prof.
Other Staff: 2 Asst. Profs.; 15 Lectrs.

Surgery and Allied Subjects
Ahmed, Ishtiaq, MB BS   Assoc. Prof.
Hussain, Malik A., MB BS   Asst. Prof.
Khan, Basharat A., MB BS, FRCSEd, FRCS   Assoc. Prof.
Kiani, Shahnaz B., MB BS   Asst. Prof.
Mallhi, Ashraf A, MB BS, FRCS, FICS   Prof.; Head*
Masood, Rehan, MB BS   Asst. Prof.
Ullah, Samu, MB BS   Asst. Prof.

Undergraduate Studies
Ehsan-ur-Rehman, PhD *Pesh.*   Assoc. Prof.
Other Staff: 1 Asst. Prof.; 10 Lectrs.

Urology
Farouk, Khalid, MB BS   Asst. Prof.; Head*

CONTACT OFFICERS
Academic affairs. Registrar: Tanwir-ul-Islam, Air Cdre (Retd)
(E-mail: registrar@fui.edu.pk)

Accommodation. Administrator: Qamar-uz-Zaman, Lt. Col. (Retd)

Admissions (first degree). Deputy Registrar: Alam, Lt. Col. (Retd) Muhammad
(E-mail: dr1@fui.edu.pk)

Admissions (higher degree). Deputy Registrar: Alam, Lt. Col. (Retd) Muhammad
(E-mail: dr1@fui.edu.pk)

Alumni. Deputy Registrar: Alam, Lt. Col. (Retd) Muhammad(E-mail: dr1@fui.edu.pk)

Careers. (contact the relevant college)

Conferences/corporate hospitality. Deputy Registrar-II: Raja, Lt. Col. (Retd) Javed Akhtar

Consultancy services. (contact the relevant college)

Development/fund-raising. Administrator: Qamar-uz-Zaman, Lt. Col. (Retd)

Equal opportunities. (contact the relevant college)

Examinations. Controller of Examinations: Qamar-uz-Zaman, Lt. Col. (Retd)

Finance. General Manager, Finance: Mazhar-ul-Haq(E-mail: gmf@fui.edu.pk)

General enquiries. Registrar: Tanwir-ul-Islam, Air Cdre (Retd)
(E-mail: registrar@fui.edu.pk)

Industrial liaison. Registrar: Tanwir-ul-Islam, Air Cdre (Retd)
(E-mail: registrar@fui.edu.pk)

International office. Registrar: Tanwir-ul-Islam, Air Cdre (Retd)
(E-mail: registrar@fui.edu.pk)

Library (chief librarian). Librarian, FUCLAS: Bibi, Shagufta
(E-mail: shawspk@hotmail.com)

Library (chief librarian). Librarian, FUIMCS: Naseer, Mirza Muhammad
(E-mail: mmnaseer@gmail.com)

Marketing. (contact the relevant college)

Personnel/human resources. Deputy Registrar-II: Raja, Lt. Col. (Retd) Javed Akhtar

Public relations. Public Relations Officer: Qazi, Qaiser Mahmood
(E-mail: pro@fui.edu.pk)

Publications. Public Relations Officer: Qazi, Qaiser Mahmood(E-mail: pro@fui.edu.pk)

Purchasing. Administrator: Qamar-uz-Zaman, Lt. Col. (Retd)

Quality assurance and accreditation. Director of Studies: Ahmed, Maj. Gen. (Retd) Mehmood

Research. (contact the relevant college)

Safety. (contact the relevant college)

Scholarships, awards, loans. Principal, FUMC: Malhi, Ashraf Ali
(E-mail: deanfmcrwp@isb.paknet.com.pk)

Schools liaison. Public Relations Officer: Qazi, Qaiser Mahmood(E-mail: pro@fui.edu.pk)

Sport and recreation. Public Relations Officer: Qazi, Qaiser Mahmood
(E-mail: pro@fui.edu.pk)

Staff development and training. Deputy Registrar-II: Raja, Lt. Col. (Retd) Javed Akhtar

Strategic planning. Director, Strategic Planning: Uppal, Brig. (Retd) Muhammad Ayub(E-mail: director@fui.edu.pk)

Student welfare/counselling. (contact the relevant college)

Students from other countries. (contact the relevant college)

University press. Public Relations Officer: Qazi, Qaiser Mahmood
(E-mail: pro@fui.edu.pk)

Women. Principal, FUCLAS: Bukhari, Prof. Muhammad M. A., PhD Dhaka
(E-mail: maqsud_bukhari@yahoo.com)

[Information supplied by the institution as at 10 October 2007, and edited by the ACU]

GHULAM ISHAQ KHAN INSTITUTE OF ENGINEERING SCIENCES AND TECHNOLOGY

Founded 1992

Additional Member of the Association of Commonwealth Universities

Postal Address: Topi 23460, District Swabi, North-West Frontier Province, Pakistan
Telephone: (0938) 271858 **Fax:** (0938) 271862 **E-mail:** rector@giki.edu.pk
URL: http://www.giki.edu.pk

RECTOR*—Sadiq, Abdullah, PhD
PRO-RECTOR (ACADEMIC)—Tirmizi, Prof. S. Ikram A., PhD Brun.
DEAN (STUDENT AFFAIRS)—Jameel-Un-Nabi, PhD Heidel.
DIRECTOR (FINANCE)—Ismail, Muhammad, MBA
DEPUTY DIRECTOR (ADMINISTRATION)‡—Shah, M. Yousaf, MPA

GENERAL INFORMATION

History. The institute was established in 1992.
It is located 110km from Islamabad.

Admission to first degree courses (see also Pakistan Introduction). Applicants must take the institute's own admissions test. International applicants may take Scholastic Aptitude Test (SAT) II in physics and mathematics.

First Degrees (see also Pakistan Directory to Subjects of Study). BE.

Higher Degrees (see also Pakistan Directory to Subjects of Study).
Master's. MS.
Admission. Applicants for admission to master's degree courses must hold an appropriate first degree.
Doctoral. PhD.
Admission. Applicants for admission to PhD degree courses must hold an appropriate first degree and a master's degree.

Libraries. Volumes: 23,000. Periodicals subscribed to: 63.

Academic Year (2006–2007). Two semesters: August–December; January–May.

Income (2005–2006). Total, Rs234,434,000.

FACULTIES/SCHOOLS

Computer System/Software Engineering
Fax: (0938) 271878 E-mail: asif@giki.edu.pk
Dean: Gilani, S. A. Mahmood, PhD

Electronic Engineering
Fax: (0938) 272950 E-mail: junaid@giki.edu.pk
Dean: Mughal, Junaid M., PhD Birm.

Engineering Sciences
Fax: (0938) 271890
E-mail: tirmizi@giki.edu.pk
Dean: Tirmizi, Prof. S. Ikram A., PhD Brun.

Mechanical Engineering
Fax: (0938) 271889
E-mail: chattha@giki.edu.pk
Dean: Chattha, Prof. Javed A., PhD Birm.

Metallurgy and Materials Engineering
Fax: (0938) 271880 E-mail: khalid@giki.edu.pk
Dean: Khalid, Prof. Fazal A., DPhil Oxf.

ACADEMIC UNITS
Arranged by Faculties

Engineering, Computer System/ Software Engineering
Ahmad, Mushtaq, PhD Manc. Foreign Prof.
Bangash, M. Ajmal K., PhD Sur. Asst. Prof.

Gilani, S. A. Mahmood, PhD Asst. Prof.; Acting Head*
Kavokin, Alex A., PhD Prof.
Vigneras, Pierre, PhD Bordeaux Asst. Prof.
Other Staff: 13 Res. Assocs.
Research: artificial intelligence and neural networks; databases, graphics, multimedia and human computer interaction; programming languages; software engineering; software quality assurance and testing

Engineering, Electronic
Ahmad, Nisar, PhD Lond. Asst. Prof.
Bazzaz, A. Shafa'at, PhD I.N.S.A.Toulouse Foreign Prof.
Karimov, Khasan S., PhD St.Petersburg, DSc Tashkent Foreign Prof.
Khan, Laiq, PhD Strath. Asst. Prof.
Mughal, Junaid M., PhD Birm. Assoc. Prof.; Interim Head*
Muhammad, Noor, PhD Syd. Asst. Prof.
Shafiq, Muhammad, PhD Chiba Foreign Prof.
Other Staff: 3 Res. Assocs.
Research: communication and signal processing; electric power and control systems; microelectronics and ASIC design

Engineering, Mechanical
Fax: (0938) 271889
E-mail: chattha@giki.edu.pk
Abid, Muhammad, PhD Strath. Assoc. Prof.
Asim, M. Farooqi, PhD Tokyo I.T. Asst. Prof.

Bannikov, Mykola, PhD Prof.
Chattha, Javed A., PhD Birm. Prof.; Head*
Khan, M. Sultan, PhD Br.Col. Asst. Prof.
Kharlamov, Yuriy A., PhD Prof.
Mughal, M. Pervez, PhD Wash.State Assoc.
  Prof.
Other Staff: 4 Res. Assocs.
Research: computational mechanics; design and
  manufacturing; thermal fluid engineering

Engineering, Metallurgy and Materials

Fax: (0938) 271880 E-mail: khalid@giki.edu.pk
Draper, H. Peter, PhD Lond. Foreign Prof.
Ejaz, Muhammad, PhD Kyoto Asst. Prof.
Khalid, Fazal A., DPhil Oxf. Prof.; Head*
Shahid, Muhammad, PhD UMIST Assoc. Prof.
Other Staff: 4 Res. Assocs.
Research: corrosion; phase transformation;
  processing and characterisation of advanced
  steels; structure-property relationship; super
  alloys

Engineering Sciences

Bukhari, Syed J. H., PhD Brad. Visiting Prof.
Haq, Siraj, PhD Liv. Asst. Prof.
Irgaziev, Bakhadir F., PhD Moscow Foreign
  Prof.
Mirakhmedov, Sherzod, PhD Tashkent, DSc
  Tashkent Foreign Prof.
Nabi, Jameel Un, PhD Heidel. Assoc. Prof.
Qazi, Ibrahim, PhD Sheff. Asst. Prof.
Sayyad, M. Hassan, PhD Assoc. Prof.
Shabbir, Ghulam, PhD Aberd. Assoc. Prof.
Tirmizi, S. Ikram A., PhD Brun. Prof.; Head*
Other Staff: 2 Res. Assocs.
Research: lasers and electro-optics; modelling
  and simulations; semiconductors and super-
  conducting devices

CONTACT OFFICERS

Academic affairs. Pro-Rector (Academics):
  Tirmizi, Prof. S. Ikram A., PhD Brun.
Admissions (first degree). Pro-Rector
  (Academics): Tirmizi, Prof. S. Ikram A.,
  PhD Brun.
Admissions (higher degree). Pro-Rector
  (Academics): Tirmizi, Prof. S. Ikram A.,
  PhD Brun.
Adult/continuing education. Pro-Rector
  (Academics): Tirmizi, Prof. S. Ikram A.,
  PhD Brun.
Alumni. Dean (Student Affairs): Jameel-Un-
  Nabi, PhD Heidel.
Archives. Secretary to the Rector: Ahmad,
  Sajjad
Careers. Careers Officer: Shahid, Muhammad,
  PhD UMIST
Computing services. Dean (Computer System/
  Software Engineering: Gilani, S. A.
  Mahmood, PhD
Conferences/corporate hospitality. Deputy
  Director (Administration): Shah, M. Yousaf,
  MPA
Consultancy services. Dean (Student Affairs):
  Jameel-Un-Nabi, PhD Heidel.
Credit transfer. Controller of Examinations:
  Akhtar, Faheem, MS Rensselaer
Development/fund-raising. Rector: Sadiq,
  Abdullah, PhD
Estates and buildings/works and services.
  Deputy Director (Maintenance): Baig, M.
  Afzal
Examinations. Controller of Examinations:
  Akhtar, Faheem, MS Rensselaer
Finance. Director (Finance): Ismail,
  Muhammad, MBA

General enquiries. Dean (Student Affairs):
  Jameel-Un-Nabi, PhD Heidel.
Health services. In-Charge Medical Centre:
  Yasmin, Samia
Industrial liaison. Dean (Student Affairs):
  Jameel-Un-Nabi, PhD Heidel.
International office. International Students'
  Counsellor: Jameel-Un-Nabi, PhD Heidel.
Library (enquiries). Librarian: Iqbal, Salim
Personnel/human resources. Director,
  Establishment: Yousaf, Muhammad
Public relations. Public Relations Officer:
  Khan, Muqaddam
Purchasing. Deputy Director (Procurement):
  Khan, Latifullah
Quality assurance and accreditation. Rector:
  Sadiq, Abdullah, PhD
Research. Rector: Sadiq, Abdullah, PhD
Scholarships, awards, loans. Pro-Rector
  (Academics): Tirmizi, Prof. S. Ikram A.,
  PhD Brun.
Schools liaison. Pro-Rector (Academics):
  Tirmizi, Prof. S. Ikram A., PhD Brun.
Security. Deputy Director (Administration):
  Shah, M. Yousaf, MPA
Sport and recreation. Dean (Student Affairs):
  Jameel-Un-Nabi, PhD Heidel.
Staff development and training. Pro-Rector
  (Academics): Tirmizi, Prof. S. Ikram A.,
  PhD Brun.
Student welfare/counselling. Dean (Student
  Affairs): Jameel-Un-Nabi, PhD Heidel.

[Information supplied by the institution as at 19 October
2006, and edited by the ACU]

GOMAL UNIVERSITY

Founded 1974

Postal Address: Dera Ismail Khan, North-West Frontier Province, Pakistan
Telephone: (0961) 750279, 750266 **Fax:** (0961) 750255 **E-mail:** vc@gu.edu.pk
URL: http://www.gu.edu.pk

VICE-CHANCELLOR*—Khan, Prof. Muhammad F.
REGISTRAR‡—Khan, Mohammad J., BA Pesh., LLB Gomal

HAMDARD UNIVERSITY

Founded 1991

Postal Address: Shahrah-e-Madina-tal-Hikmat, Muhammad Bin Qasim Avenue, Karachi 74600, Pakistan
Telephone: (021) 644 0017 **Fax:** (021) 644 0066 **E-mail:** huvc@hamdard.net.pk
URL: http://www.hamdard.edu.pk/

VICE-CHANCELLOR*—Khan, Prof. Nasim A., PhD
REGISTRAR‡—Ali, Ameer H., MSA

HAZARA UNIVERSITY

Founded 2001

Postal Address: Dhodial, Mansehra, N.W.F.P., Pakistan
Telephone: (0997) 530732 **Fax:** (0997) 530046 **E-mail:** hazara_university@yahoo.com
URL: http://www.hu.edu.pk

VICE-CHANCELLOR*—Ali, Prof. Ihsan, MA Pesh., MA Lond., PhD Camb.
REGISTRAR‡—Khan, Prof. Sher Ali, MA A.Iqbal Open, MSc Pesh.

INSTITUTE OF BUSINESS ADMINISTRATION

Founded 1955

Postal Address: Karachi University Campus, Karachi 75270, Pakistan
Telephone: (021) 924 3090-5 **Fax:** (021) 924 3421 **E-mail:** iba@iba.edu.pk
URL: http://www.iba.edu.pk/

DEAN AND DIRECTOR*—Danishmand, BA MBA
DIRECTOR ADMINISTRATION‡—Zaidi, Col. (Retired) Saiyed M.

INSTITUTE OF BUSINESS MANAGEMENT

Founded 1998

Member of the Association of Commonwealth Universities

Postal Address: Main Ibrahim Hyderi Road, Korangi Creek, Karachi 75190, Pakistan
Telephone: (021) 111002 **Fax:** (021) 509 0968 **E-mail:** jahangir@cbm.edu.pk
URL: http://www.cbm.edu.pk/

PRESIDENT*—Karim, Shahjehan S., BA
EXECUTIVE DIRECTOR ACADEMICS—Karim, Talib S., BS MA
EXECUTIVE DIRECTOR, ADMINISTRATION, ADMISSIONS AND FINANCE‡—Mohsin, Sabina, BBA MS

GENERAL INFORMATION

History. The institute was established in 1998.

Admission to first degree courses (see also Pakistan Introduction). Applicants should hold Higher Secondary Certificate (HSE) or A level.

First Degrees (* = with honours). BBA*, BS.
Length of course. Full-time: BBA*, BS: 4 years.

Higher Degrees.
Master's. MBA, MCS, MPhil.
Admission. Applicants to master's degrees should hold a first degree or equivalent.
MBA (Executive) for working students: 2 years.
Length of course. Full-time: MBA, MCS: 1–2 years; MPhil: 2 years.

Libraries. Volumes: 23,300. Periodicals subscribed to: 62. Other holdings: 716 audiovisual items. Special collections: government documents; World Bank publications.

Academic Year (2007–2008). 3 terms: 18 June–31 August; 10 September–6 January; 14 January–1 May.

Income (2006–2007). Total, Rs173,000,000.

Statistics. Staff (2006–2007): 302 (78 academic, 224 non-academic). Students (2006–2007): undergraduate 2361.

FACULTIES/SCHOOLS
Business Management, College of
E-mail: dean@cbm.edu.pk
Dean: Janjua, Muhammad A., BA Lahore, MA Lahore, MA
Secretary: Dastagir, Ghulam, BA

Computer Science and Information Systems, College of
E-mail: eahmed@cbm.edu.pk
Advisor: Karim, Ahmer S., PhD
Secretary: Majid, Abdul, BCom

Economics and Social Development, College of
E-mail: cesd@cbm.edu.pk
Director: Ansari, Javed, PhD
Secretary: Rizvi, Khadim H., MA

ACADEMIC UNITS
Accounting and Finance
E-mail: jz275@yahoo.com
Ayubi, Sharique, MBA MA   Asst. Prof.
Maqbool ur Rehman, Syed, MBA   Asst. Prof.
Zubairi, Hamid J., BE MBA   Head*
Other Staff: 1 Sr. Lectr.; 2 Lectrs.; 1 Sr. Res.
Fellow; 1 Sr. Fellow; 1 Instr.
Research: banking; corporate finance; risk management

Commerce
Alam, Maqsood, MA
Other Staff: 2 Instrs.

Communication
E-mail: dr.larik@cbm.edu.pk
Habib, Zehra, MA MATESOL   Assoc. Prof.
Larik, K. M., MPhil PhD   Sr. Fellow; Head*
Other Staff: 1 Sr. Lectr.; 3 Lectrs.; 1 Sr. Fellow; 3 Instrs.
Research: gender issues in the lighthouse; testing in English language teaching

Computer Sciences
E-mail: eahmed@cbm.edu.pk
Ahmed, Ejaz, MSc PhD   Prof.; Head*
Alam, Abu T.
Amin, Farrukh, MCS MA   Asst. Prof.
Other Staff: 1 Sr. Lectr.; 5 Lectrs.; 2 Instrs.
Research: decision sciences; information and management; rating of IT software houses in Karachi

Economics
E-mail: jz275@yahoo.com
3 Lectrs.; 1 Sr. Fellow; 2 Instrs.
Research: aggregate import demand function for Pakistan; exchange rate volatility; imports and real output determinants in Pakistan

Engineering, Industrial

E-mail: mikhan@cbm.edu.pk

Iqbal, Asif, BE MS   Asst. Prof.
Khan, Muhammad I., PhD   Prof.
Mirza, Mufaddal, PhD   Assoc. Prof.
Other Staff: 1 Sr. Fellow
Research: mixing and segregation of particulate
solids of different particle size

General Science

E-mail: akhtarzee200@yahoo.com

Zaman, Akhter   Co-ordinator*
Other Staff: 2 Sr. Fellows

Health and Hospital Management

E-mail: fawzia.hoodbhoy@cbm.edu.pk

Hoodbhoy, Fawzia, MHS Tor.   Assoc. Prof.;
Head*

Humanities

Shaheen, Shagufta, MA
Other Staff: 2 Instrs.

Management and Human Resources Management

E-mail: javaid_ahmed@cbm.edu.pk

Ahmed, Javaid, BScEng Lond., BA Lanc., MBus
Lanc.   Assoc. Prof.; Head*

Molvi, Abdul Q., BSc Karachi, MBA Karachi
Assoc. Prof.
Other Staff: 1 Sr. Lectr.; 1 Sr. Res. Fellow; 1
Sr. Fellow
Research: combating contemporary management
challenges; structural scenario of human
resources in Pakistan

Marketing

E-mail: meghani53@yahoo.com

Ahmed, Syed M., MBA Calif.   Asst. Prof.
Khairi, Baber S., MBA   Asst. Prof.
Meghani, Shahnaz, MBA   Assoc. Prof.; Head*
Other Staff: 2 Sr. Lectrs.; 1 Lectr.
Research: employee motivation; influence of
chemists on end users; organisational
culture; product failure

Social Sciences

1 Lectr.; 1 Sr. Fellow; 2 Instrs.
Research: community health sciences; politics

Statistics and Mathematics

E-mail: syed_iftikhar_ali@hotmail.com

Ali, Syed I., MS PhD   Prof.
Other Staff: 4 Lectrs.; 2 Instrs.

CONTACT OFFICERS

Academic affairs. Executive Director
Academics: Karim, Talib S., BS MA
(E-mail: t-karim@cyber.net.pk)
Admissions (first degree). Manager,
Admissions: Hoodbhoy, Nargis, BEd Karachi,
MA Karachi (E-mail: admissions@cbm.edu.pk)
Admissions (higher degree). Executive
Director, Admissions: Mohsin, Sabina, BBA
MS (E-mail: sabina@cbm.edu.pk)
Examinations. Controller, Examinations:
Soomro, Naz, LLB MA
(E-mail: naz@cbm.edu.pk)
Finance. Manager, Finance: Ali, Aslam Q.
(E-mail: aslam.ali@cbm.edu.pk)
General enquiries. Senior Manager, Internal
Audit and Corporate Affairs: Jahangir, M.
W. (E-mail: jahangir@cbm.edu.pk)
Library (chief librarian). Librarian: Iqbal,
Anila, MPhil Lond.
(E-mail: anila@cbm.edu.pk)

[Information supplied by the institution as at 6 December
2007, and edited by the ACU]

INTERNATIONAL ISLAMIC UNIVERSITY

Founded 1980

Postal Address: PO Box 1243, Islamabad 44000, Pakistan
Telephone: (051) 926 1910 **Fax:** (051) 225 0821 **E-mail:** president@iiu.edu.pk

PRESIDENT*—Ghazi, Mahmood A., BA Punjab, MA Punjab, PhD Punjab
DIRECTOR (PRESIDENT SECRETARIAT)‡—Khwaja, Gulzar A., MSc A.Bello

ISLAMIA UNIVERSITY, BAHAWALPUR

Founded 1975

Member of the Association of Commonwealth Universities

Postal Address: Bahawalpur, Pakistan
Telephone: (0621) 925 0235 **Fax:** (0621) 925 0232 **E-mail:** vciub@mul.paknet.com.pk
URL: http://www.iub.edu.pk

VICE-CHANCELLOR*—Khan, Prof. Belal A., BA Government Coll.Univ.(Lahore), MPA Beirut,
PhD S.Illinois
SECRETARY TO THE VICE-CHANCELLOR—Ali, Liaquat, MA Islamia, Bahawal.
REGISTRAR‡—Malik, Zain A.
TREASURER—Dahir, Ghulam H., MA
ACTING LIBRARIAN—Rashid, Abdul

GENERAL INFORMATION

History. The university was originally
established in 1925 as Jamia Abbasia, an
institution for higher education in religious
science. It was renamed Jamia Islamia in 1963
and became a university under its present
name in 1975.

First Degrees (see also Pakistan Directory to
Subjects of Study). BA, BSc.

Higher Degrees (see also Pakistan Directory
to Subjects of Study).
Master's. MA, MPhil, MSc.
Admission. Applicants for admission to
master's degree courses must hold a first

degree with at least second class division, or
equivalent qualification.
Doctoral. PhD.

Language of Instruction. English and Urdu.

Libraries. Volumes: 125,000. Periodicals
subscribed to: 162.

FACULTIES/SCHOOLS

Arts

Tel: (0621) 925 0332
Dean: (vacant)

Islamic Learning

Tel: (0621) 925 0319
Dean: Rehmat, Prof. A. R., MA Punjab, PhD
Lond.

Science

Tel: (0621) 925 0321
Dean: (vacant)

ACADEMIC UNITS

Arabic

Tel: (0621) 925 0328

Dar, Surrya, MA Punjab, PhD Punjab   Assoc.
Prof.
Khalid Rahila, MA Islamia, Bahawal., PhD Islamia,
Bahawal.   Asst. Prof.
Khan, S. T., MA Punjab, PhD Punjab   Prof.;
Head*
Other Staff: 2 Lectrs.

Business Administration

Tel: (0621) 925 0258
Ali, Muhammad Walaua, MBA B.Zak.   Asst. Prof.
Other Staff: 7 Lectrs.

Chemistry

Tel: (0621) 925 0343
Abdul Wadood, MSc Punjab, PhD Glas.   Assoc. Prof.
Chohan, Z., MSc Karachi, MSc Glas., PhD Aberd. Asst. Prof.
Ghouri, M. S., MSc Punjab, PhD Wales   Assoc. Prof.
Khan, Z. F., MSc Punjab, PhD Glas.   Prof.
Makshoof Athar, MSc Quaid-i-Azam, PhD Islamia, Bahawal.   Assoc. Prof.
Mehmood, K., MSc Punjab, PhD Punjab   Assoc. Prof.
Mirza, M. L., MSc Islam., PhD Glas.   Prof.; Head*
Moazzam, M., MSc Punjab, PhD Brun.   Prof.
Nasim, Faizul H., MSc Islamia, Bahawal., PhD Brown   Assoc. Prof.
Sheikh, Q. I., MSc Agric., Faisalabad   Asst. Prof. (on leave)
Other Staff: 4 Lectrs.
Research: analytical, inorganic, organic and physical chemistry; biochemistry

Computer Science

Tel: (0621) 925 0336
Muhammad, Dost, MSc B.Zak.   Lectr.; Head*
Other Staff: 6 Lectrs.
Research: database management system; Java

Economics

Tel: (0621) 925 0329
Basit, Amir B., MA Islamia, Bahawal., MPhil Quaid-i-Azam, PhD Quaid-i-Azam   Asst. Prof.
Kausar, Tasnim, MA Punjab   Asst. Prof.; Head*
Other Staff: 4 Lectrs.
Research: agricultural economics; foreign aid; international economics; public finance; rural development

Education

Tel: (0621) 925 0348
Adeeb, M. A., MA B.Zak., PhD Brad.   Prof.; Head*
Lubna, Waheed, MA B.Zak.   Asst. Prof.
Muhammad, Akhtar, MA B.Zak.   Asst. Prof.
Other Staff: 7 Lectrs.
Research: curriculum development; educational research; health education; teaching strategies; traffic education

Educational Training

Tel: (0621) 925 0340
Hashmi, Nighat, MA Punjab   Asst. Prof.
Muhammad, Waheed, MA B.Zak.   Asst. Prof.; Head*
Other Staff: 3 Lectrs.

English

Tel: (0621) 925 0335
Jajja, M. Ayub, MA Islamia, Bahawal.   Asst. Prof.
Khattak, Zahir J., MA Karachi, PhD Tufts   Prof.; Head*
Salahuddin, Shahnaz, MA Islamia, Bahawal.   Asst. Prof.
Other Staff: 4 Lectrs.
Research: African writers; Afro-American writers

Geography

Tel: (0621) 925 0327
Abdul Sattar, MSc Punjab   Asst. Prof.
Khan, Asad A., MSc Punjab   Asst. Prof.
Malik, M. K., MSc Punjab, PhD Lond.   Assoc. Prof. (on leave)
Other Staff: 4 Lectrs.
Research: environment; population; resources; urban geography

History and Pakistan Studies

Tel: (0621) 925 0331
Bhatti, Abdul J., MA Punjab   Asst. Prof.
Rashid, I. A.   Asst. Prof.
Rizvi, M. A., MA PhD   Prof.; Head*
Rizvi, Shahid Hassan, PhD Islamia, Bahawal.   Asst. Prof.
Shahid, Abdul R., MA Islamia, Bahawal., MPhil Quaid-i-Azam   Asst. Prof.
Other Staff: 1 Lectr.
Research: South Asian history

Islamic Studies

Tel: (0621) 925 0319
Ahmed, M., MA   Asst. Prof.
Akram, M. Rana, PhD   Prof.
Farooqi, M. Y., Fazil Dars-e-Nizami Punjab, MA Punjab, PhD Exe.   Prof. (on deputation)
Khan, M. G., MA Islamia, Bahawal., PhD Islamia, Bahawal.   Assoc. Prof.
Khan, S. B., LLB Karachi, MA Karachi, PhD St And.   Asst. Prof.
Mohiuddin, Abrar, MA Islamia, Bahawal.   Asst. Prof.
Rehmat, A. R., MA Punjab, PhD Lond.   Prof.; Head*
Syed, I. H., MA   Asst. Prof.
Zafar, A. R., PhD Glas., MA   Prof.
Other Staff: 3 Lectrs.
Research: Hadith; Islamic law and jurisprudence; Tafseer and Seerat

Law

Tel: (0621) 925 0261
Butt, M. N., LLB Punjab, MCL Emory   Asst. Prof. (on leave)
Sial, A. Q., LLB Islamia, Bahawal.   Asst. Prof.; Head*
Other Staff: 2 Lectrs.

Library and Information Science

Tel: (0621) 925 0371
Abbas, G., MLS Karachi   Asst. Prof.
Bukhari Syed Abdul Rehman   Asst. Prof.
Hashmi, Fouzia, MLS Sindh   Asst. Prof.
Khalid, H. M., MLS Karachi, PhD Manc.Met.   Asst. Prof. (on leave)
Other Staff: 2 Lectrs.
Research: university libraries in Pakistan

Mass Communication

Tel: (0621) 925 0317
Ahmed, S., MA Gomal   Asst. Prof.
Shamsuddin, Muhammad, MA Karachi, PhD Lond.   Prof.; Head*
Other Staff: 5 Lectrs.
Research: communication research; development journalism; media in developing countries

Mathematics

Tel: (0621) 925 0326
Abbasi, G. Q., MSc Punjab, PhD Moscow   Prof. (on deputation)
Akhtar, K. P., MSc Punjab, PhD Manc.   Asst. Prof.
Hafiz, A. M., MSc Punjab, MPhil Islam.   Asst. Prof.
Mahmood, T., MSc Punjab, PhD Manc.   Assoc. Prof.; Head*
Other Staff: 7 Lectrs.
Research: algebra (group theory); computer software; financial analysis; fluid mechanics; numerical analysis

Persian

Tel: (0621) 925 0328
Ahmad, M., MA MPhil   Asst. Prof.; Head*
Muhammad Iqbal, MA Punjab, PhD Tehran   Asst. Prof.
Other Staff: 2 Lectrs.

Pharmacy

Tel: (0621) 876318
Ahmed, Mehmood, PhD Punjab   Assoc. Prof.
Ashraf, Mahmmad, MSc Islamia, Bahawal., PhD Manc.   Assoc. Prof.
Nisar-ur-Rehman, MPhil Punjab, MSc   Asst. Prof.
Riffat, Zaman, MPhil   Asst. Prof.
Shafique, M. K., MSc Punjab, PhD Lond.   Prof.; Head*
Other Staff: 5 Lectrs.
Research: drug formulation; drug instruction; enzymology; ethnobotany; natural products

Physics

Tel: (0621) 925 0330
Ahmad, K., MSc Islam., MPhil Islam., PhD   Assoc. Prof.
Asghar, M., MPhil Quaid-i-Azam, PhD Quaid-i-Azam, MSc   Assoc. Prof.
Chaudhry, M. A., MSc Punjab, PhD Sur.   Assoc. Prof.; Head*
Khan, M. Afzal, MSc Punjab, PhD Dund.   Assoc. Prof.
Muhammad, J., MSc Punjab, PhD Sur.   Asst. Prof.
Naveed, S., PhD Dund., MSc   Asst. Prof.
Shaheen, M. H., MSc B.Zak., PhD Manc.   Asst. Prof.
Sheikh, A. A., MSc Punjab, PhD Sur.   Prof.
Other Staff: 2 Lectrs.
Research: computer simulation of defects in metals; materials; plasma electronics

Political Science

Tel: (0621) 925 0332
Abbasi, Hina Q., MA Karachi, PhD Moscow   Prof.
Hussain, Musawar, MA B.Zak.   Asst. Prof.
Musarrat, Razia, PhD Islamia, Bahawal., MA   Assoc. Prof.; Head*
Server, Gulam, MA PhD   Asst. Prof.
Other Staff: 3 Lectrs.
Research: cause and effect of amendments to the constitution of Islamic Republic of Pakistan; politics of aliens in Pakistan

Saraki

Tel: (0621) 925 0328
Chandio, J. H., MA Islamia, Bahawal.   Lectr.; Head*
Other Staff: 2 Lectrs.

Statistics

Tel: (0621) 925 0321
Akhtar, Munir, MSc Punjab, PhD S'ton.   Prof.; Head*
Aleem, M., MSc Islamia, Bahawal., PhD B.Zak.   Asst. Prof.
Aziz Muhammed Uousaf   Asst. Prof.
Malik, M. A., MSc Punjab, MA Punjab, PhD   Prof.
Rasool, M., MSc Punjab, PhD Sur.   Prof.
Shah, A. M., MSc Islamia, Bahawal.   Asst. Prof.
Shah, M. A. A., MSc Islamia, Bahawal.   Asst. Prof.
Other Staff: 3 Lectrs.
Research: design of experiments; missing observations

Urdu and Iqbaliyat

Tel: (0621) 925 0345
Ahmad, S., MA Punjab, PhD Punjab   Prof.; Head*
Najeeb-Ud-Din, Jamal, PhD Karachi   Prof.
Rao, Roshan A., BEd Punjab, MA Punjab, PhD Punjab   Assoc. Prof.
Shaheen, Aqeela, MA B.Zak., PhD Karachi   Assoc. Prof.
Other Staff: 3 Lectrs.
Research: criticism; personality; poetry

SPECIAL CENTRES, ETC

Desert Studies, Cholistan Institute of

Tel: (0621) 925 0341
Arshad Ch. Muhammad, PhD   Deputy Dir.
Iqbal, R. M., PhD Wales   Jt. Dir.*
Shafiq Ch. Muhammad, PhD   Deputy Dir.
Other Staff: 2 Res. Officers

Pakistan Gallery
No staff at present

CONTACT OFFICERS

Development/fund-raising. Project Director: Saleem, Muhammad C.
Examinations. Controller of Examinations: Safique, Muhammad, MA
Finance. Treasurer: Dahir, Ghulam H., MA
General enquiries. Registrar: Ahmad, Nazir C., MA *Islamia, Bahawal.*, MAEPM *A.Iqbal Open*

Health services. Senior Medical Officer: (vacant)
Library (chief librarian). Acting Librarian: Rashid, Abdul
Marketing. Deputy Registrar (Public Relations): Hassan Shahid Rizvi
Public relations. Deputy Registrar (Public Relations): Hassan Shahid Rizvi
Purchasing. Administrative Officer, Store and Purchase: Iqbal, Hussain
Scholarships, awards, loans. Registrar: Ahmad, Nazir C., MA *Islamia, Bahawal.*, MAEPM *A.Iqbal Open*

Sport and recreation. Director, Physical Education (acting): Sattar Abdul
Strategic planning. Project Director: Sadiq, Muhammad C.
Student welfare/counselling. Director, Student Office: Arshad, Muhammad, MSc *Punjab*, PhD *Sur.*

[*Information supplied by the institution as at 24 March 2005, and edited by the ACU*]

ISRA UNIVERSITY

Founded 1997

Postal Address: Hala Road, PO Box 313, Hyderabad, Sindh, Pakistan
Telephone: (0221) 203 0181-4 **Fax:** (0221) 203 0180 **E-mail:** info@isra.edu.pk
URL: http://www.isra.edu.pk

VICE-CHANCELLOR*—Kazi, Asadullah, MSc *Lond.*, PhD *Lond.*
REGISTRAR‡—Qureshi, M. Nawaz, LLB *Sindh*, MA *Sindh*

UNIVERSITY OF KARACHI

Founded 1951

Member of the Association of Commonwealth Universities

Postal Address: Karachi, Sindh 75270, Pakistan
Telephone: (021) 926 1300-6 **Fax:** (021) 926 1340 **E-mail:** registrar@ku.edu.pk
URL: http://www.uok.edu.pk

VICE-CHANCELLOR*—Siddiqui, Prof. Pirzada Q. R., MSc *Karachi*, PhD *Newcastle(UK)*
PRO-VICE-CHANCELLOR—Ahmed, Prof. Akhlaq, MSc *Karachi*, PhD *Exe.*, FRSChem
REGISTRAR‡—Alvi, Prof. Muhammad R.
DIRECTOR OF FINANCE—Khalid, S. M., MBA
CONTROLLER OF EXAMINATIONS—Qureshi, Naeemuddin A.

GENERAL INFORMATION

History. The university was established in June 1951 by the Karachi University Act.

Admission to first degree courses (see also Pakistan Introduction). Intermediate or Higher Secondary Certificate.

First Degrees (* = with honours). BA*, BBA*, BLIS, BPA*, BPharm, BS, BSc*.

Higher Degrees.
Master's. MA, MBA, MCom, MCS, MLIS, MPA, MPhil, MSc.
Doctoral. DLitt, DSc, PhD.

Language of Instruction. English and Urdu.

Libraries. Volumes: 300,000.

FACULTIES/SCHOOLS
Arts
Fax: (021) 924 3171
Dean: Shamsuddin, Prof. M.

Business Administration and Commerce
Fax: (021) 924 3171
Dean: Shamsuddin, Prof. M.

Islamic Studies
Fax: (021) 924 3220
Dean: Noori, Prof. Jalaluddin A., MA *Punjab*, PhD *Karachi*

Law
Tel: (021) 923 2002
Dean: Hassan, Prof. S. Mamoon

Medicine
Tel: (021) 662 8353
Dean: Karim, Prof. Sadiya A.

Pharmacy
Fax: (021) 924 3173
Dean: Sultana, Prof. Najma, MSc *Karachi*, PhD *Karachi*

Science
Fax: (021) 924 3206
Dean: Rasool, Prof. Sheikh A., MSc *Karachi*, PhD *Moscow*

ACADEMIC UNITS
Agriculture
Shehzad, Saleem   Chairperson*

Arabic
Ihsan-ul-haq, MA *Karachi*, PhD *Karachi*   Prof.
Ishaq, Muhammad, MA *Karachi*, PhD *Karachi*   Assoc. Prof.

Numani, M. Abdush S.   Prof.; Chairperson*
Shaheed, Abdul, MA *Karachi*, PhD *Karachi*   Prof.
Other Staff: 3 Lectrs.

Bengali
Khan, M. Abu Tayyab   Chairperson (In-charge)*
Other Staff: 1 Lectr.

Biochemistry
Akhtar, Naheed, MSc *Karachi*, MPhil *Karachi*, PhD *Karachi*   Prof.
Azhar, Abid, MSc *Karachi*, PhD *Canberra*   Prof.
Bano, Samina, MSc *Karachi*, PhD *Wales*   Assoc. Prof.
Batool, Farhat   Asst. Prof.
Haider, Saida, MSc *Karachi*   Assoc. Prof.
Haleem, Darakshan J., MSc *Karachi*, MPhil *Karachi*, PhD *Lond.*   Prof.; Chairperson*
Jahangir, Shakila, MSc *Karachi*, PhD *Warw.*   Prof.
Jamall, Siddiqa   Asst. Prof.
Khanam, Aziza, MSc *Karachi*, MPhil *Karachi*, PhD *Karachi*   Prof.
Mahboob, Tabassum, MSc *Karachi*, MPhil *Karachi*, PhD *Karachi*   Prof.
Naz, Hajra   Asst. Prof.
Parveen, Tahira, MSc *Karachi*, MPhil *Karachi*, PhD *Karachi*   Assoc. Prof.
Qidwai, Iqbal M., MSc *Karachi*   Prof.
Qureshi, Shamim A.   Asst. Prof.
Siddiqi, Nikhat, MSc *Karachi*, PhD *Sur.*   Prof.

Sultana, Viqar, MSc Karachi, PhD Karachi Prof.
Zarina, Shamshad, MSc Karachi, PhD Karachi
Assoc. Prof.
Other Staff: 6 Lectrs.

Biotechnology

Kamal, Mustafa Asst. Prof.; Chairperson (In-charge)*
Siddiqua, Syeda M. Asst. Prof.
Other Staff: 6 Lectrs.

Botany

Abid, Rubina Asst. Prof.
Ajmal Khan, M., MSc Karachi, PhD Ohio Prof.
Dawar, Shahnaz Asst. Prof.
Gul, Bilquees Asst. Prof.
Haq, Ihteshamul, MSc Karachi, PhD Karachi
Assoc. Prof.
Iqbal, M. Zafar, MSc Karachi, PhD Lanc. Prof.;
Chairperson*
Ismail, Shoaib, MSc Karachi, PhD Karachi Assoc.
Prof.
Khatoon, Khalida, MSc Karachi, PhD Bath Prof.
Khatoon, Surayya, MSc Karachi, PhD Karachi
Prof.
Perveen, Anjum Asst. Prof.
Qadri, Raiha Asst. Prof.
Rehman, Aliya, MA Calif., MSc Karachi, PhD
Karachi Asst. Prof.
Shahzad, Saleem, MSc Karachi, PhD Karachi
Assoc. Prof.
Usman, Mubina, MSc Karachi, PhD Auck. Prof.
Zaki, Javed, MSc Karachi, PhD Karachi Prof.
Other Staff: 4 Lectrs.

Business Administration

Baloch, Shahnaz Asst. Prof.
Zaki, S. A. R. Z., MCom Karachi Assoc. Prof.;
Chairman*
Other Staff: 5 Lectrs.

Chemical Technology/Engineering

Jabbar, Athar Asst. Prof.
Khan, Fasiullah Prof.; Chairperson*
Other Staff: 2 Lectrs.

Chemistry

see also Special Centres, etc
Ali, Kazim, MSc Karachi Asst. Prof.
Ali, Syed A., MSc Karachi, MPhil Quaid-i-Azam
Prof.
Anis, Itrat Asst. Prof.
Arayne, M. Saeed, MSc Karachi, MPhil Karachi
Prof.
Begum, Saeedan, MSc Karachi, MPhil Quaid-i-
Azam, DrRerNat Bonn Prof.
Fatima, Nasreen Asst. Prof.
Firdous, Sadiqa, MSc Karachi, PhD Karachi Prof.
Ifzal, Rehana, MSc Karachi, MPhil Karachi, PhD
Karachi Prof.
Jabeen, Shaista, MSc Karachi, MPhil Karachi
Prof.
Khalid, Zahida, MSc Karachi, MPhil Karachi
Prof.
Khan, Bushra, MSc Karachi, MPhil Karachi Prof.
Khan, Nasirudin, MSc MPhil Asst. Prof.
Maqsood, Zahida, MSc Karachi, PhD Karachi
Prof.
Moinuddin, Shaikh Asst. Prof.
Mumtaz, Majid, MSc Karachi, MPhil Karachi
Assoc. Prof.
Nizami, Shaikh Sirajuddin, MSc Karachi, MPhil
Karachi, PhD Aberd. Prof.
Qadri, Masooda, MSc Karachi, MPhil Karachi
Asst. Prof.
Rashid, Munawwa Asst. Prof.
Rehman, Mutiur, MSc Karachi Asst. Prof.
Rehmani, Fauzia S. Assoc. Prof.
Saeed, Rehana Asst. Prof.
Siddiqui, Azhar Asst. Prof.
Sultata Rahat, MSc Karachi, PhD Karachi Assoc.
Prof.
Tahir Hajira, MSc Karachi, PhD Islam. Asst.
Prof.
Uddin, Fahim Prof.; Chairperson*
Waqar, Dilshad Prof.

Other Staff: 7 Lectrs.

Chemistry, Applied

Afaq, Shagufta Asst. Prof.
Ahmed, Riaz, MSc Karachi, PhD Karachi Asst.
Prof.
Ali, Syed I., MSc Karachi, PhD Strath. Prof.;
Chairperson*
Kamal, Muhammad A. Asst. Prof.
Kazmi, Mehdi Hasan, MSc Karachi, PhD Karachi
Assoc. Prof.
Naqvi, Mumtaz D. Asst. Prof.
Rasheed, Abdur, MSc Karachi, MPhil Karachi
Asst. Prof.
Shaista, Amtul R., MSc Karachi Asst. Prof.
Other Staff: 5 Lectrs.

Commerce

Ali, Tahir Asst. Prof.
Zafar, Dilshad, MCom Karachi Assoc. Prof.;
Chairperson*
Other Staff: 6 Lectrs.

Computer Science

Burney, S. M. Aqil, MSc Karachi, MPhil Karachi,
PhD Strath. Prof.
Ezamuddin, M. M., MSc T.U.Berlin, MSc Karachi
Assoc. Prof.; Chairperson*
Hussain, Syed Jamal, MSc Karachi Asst. Prof.
Khan, Sadiq Ali Asst. Prof.
Mahmood, Nadeem Asst. Prof.
Sami, Bader, MSc Karachi Asst. Prof.
Touheed, Nasir Assoc. Prof.
Other Staff: 11 Lectrs.

Economics

Ahsanuddin, Muhammad Asst. Prof.
Ali, Muhammad Asst. Prof.
Arshad, Rabia, MA Brist., MA Karachi Asst.
Prof.
Husain, S. Waqar, MSc Karachi Asst. Prof.
Mujahid, Nooreen Asst. Prof.
Mustafa, Khalid, MSc Quaid-i-Azam Asst. Prof.
Safdar, Rubina, MSc Karachi Asst. Prof.
Shafiq-ur-Rehman, MA Wat., MA Karachi
Prof.; Chairperson*
Shehzad, Mirza M. Asst. Prof.
Waheed, Abdul Asst. Prof.
Zaheer, Rumana Asst. Prof.
Other Staff: 6 Lectrs.

Education

Memon, Ghulam R., MEd Karachi Assoc. Prof.;
Chairperson*
Other Staff: 3 Lectrs.

English

Bano, Dilshat, MA Karachi Asst. Prof.
Kazi, Amberina M., MA Karachi Prof.
Khalid, Fouzia S., MA Karachi, PhD Leeds Prof.
Khan, Farhana W. Asst. Prof.
Khan, Kaleem R., MA Karachi, MA Lanc. Prof.;
Chairperson*
Moosvi, Naushaba, MA Karachi Asst. Prof.
Shafi, Iftikhar Asst. Prof.
Shaheen, Lubna Asst. Prof.
Shakir, Huma Asst. Prof.
Wasim, Nishat Asst. Prof.
Wasti, S. Munir, MA Karachi, MPhil Karachi
Prof.
Zaidi, S. M. Tayyab Asst. Prof.
Other Staff: 4 Lectrs.

Food Science and Technology

Abid Hasnain, M., MSc Karachi, MPhil Karachi
Assoc. Prof.; Chairperson*
Ara, Jehan Asst. Prof.
Asad Sayeed, S., MSc Karachi, PhD Karachi
Assoc. Prof.
Naz, Shahina Asst. Prof.
Siddiqui, Rahmanullah Asst. Prof.
Other Staff: 4 Lectrs.

Genetics

Ansari, Maqsood A., MSc Karachi, MS Calif.
Asst. Prof.

Farooqi, Shakeelur R., MSc Karachi, PhD Kansas
State Asst. Prof.
Haider, Talat, MSc Karachi, MPhil Karachi Prof.
Khan, Obaid Yusuf, MSc Karachi, PhD Karachi
Assoc. Prof.; Chairperson*
Mansoor, Simeen Asst. Prof.
Mohsin, Tazeen Asst. Prof.
Naqvi, Farzana N., MSc Karachi, MPhil Karachi
Prof.
Qureshi, Fauad M. Asst. Prof.
Other Staff: 3 Lectrs.

Geography

Afsar, Sheeba Asst. Prof.
Akhtar, Shamshad Asst. Prof.
Ali, S. Shahid, MSc Karachi Asst. Prof.
Azad, Azra Parveen, MSc Punjab Prof.
Burke, Farkhanda, MA Calc., MPhil Alig., PhD
Alig. Prof.
Kazmi, Jamil H. Chairperson*
Mahmood, Khalida Prof.
Rehmani, Shakeela A. Assoc. Prof.
Other Staff: 2 Lectrs.

Geology

Adil, Tayyaba S. Asst. Prof.
Ahmed, Mujeeb Assoc. Prof.
Bashir, Erum Asst. Prof.
Bilal, Muhammad Asst. Prof.
Hamid, Gulraiz, MSc Karachi Assoc. Prof.
Khan, Athar A. Prof.
Khan, Nadeem A., MSc Karachi Assoc. Prof.
Naseem, Shahid, MSc Karachi, PhD Karachi
Prof.
Niamatullah, M., MSc Baloch., PhD Kiel Prof.
Shaikh, Shamim A., MSc Karachi Prof.
Viqar Hussain, MSc MPhil Prof.;
Chairperson*
Other Staff: 3 Lectrs.

Health and Physical Education

Rehman, Muti-ur Chairperson (Co-
ordinator)*
Other Staff: 3 Lectrs.

History, General

Afzal, Nasreen, MA Karachi Asst. Prof.
Beg, Tania Asst. Prof.
Habeeb, Shama, MA Karachi Assoc. Prof.
Hussain, Javed, MA Pesh., PhD Camb. Prof.
Khan, Hina Asst. Prof.
Rasheed, Nargis, MA Karachi Assoc. Prof.;
Chairperson*
Siddiqui, Asrar A., MA Karachi Asst. Prof.
Taha, S. M. Asst. Prof.
Other Staff: 5 Lectrs.

History, Islamic

Farnaz, Soofia Asst. Prof.
Jabeen, Farzana Asst. Prof.
Siddiqi, M. Shakeel, MA Karachi Asst. Prof.
Sohail, Farah N. Asst. Prof.
Zaheer, Nigar S., MA Karachi, PhD Karachi
Assoc. Prof.; Chairperson*
Zubair, Muhammad Asst. Prof.
Other Staff: 2 Lectrs.

International Relations

Ahmed, Shaikh M. Asst. Prof.
Ahmer, Moonis, MSc Islam., MPhil Karachi, PhD
Karachi Prof.
Ghous, Khalida, MA Karachi, PhD Karachi Prof.
Hameed, Syed A. Asst. Prof.
Mehdi, S. Sikander, MA Dacca Prof.
Siddiqui, Huma N. Asst. Prof.
Tabassum, Shaista Asst. Prof.
Wizarat, Talat A., MA S.Carolina, MA Karachi
Prof.; Chairperson*
Other Staff: 5 Lectrs.

Islamic Learning

see also Hist., Islamic
Akhtar, Nasir Ahmed, MA Karachi, PhD Karachi
Asst. Prof.
Ali, Zahid Asst. Prof.

Auj, M. Shakeel, MA Karachi, PhD Karachi   Asst. Prof.
Firdous, Rehana, MA Karachi, PhD Karachi   Asst. Prof.
Khan, Obaid A.   Asst. Prof.
Mehdi, Ghulam, MA Karachi   Prof.; Chairperson*
Nasiruddin   Asst. Prof.
Noori, Jalaluddin A., MA Punjab, PhD Karachi   Prof.
Other Staff: 2 Lectrs.

Karachi University Business School

Tel: (021) 482 3541
Zaki, S. A. R. Z., MCom Karachi   Chairperson*

Library and Information Science

Khan, Anwar S., MLS Karachi   Asst. Prof.
Khan, Farhat H.   Asst. Prof.
Nasreen, Munira A., MLS Karachi   Asst. Prof.
Naveed-e-Sehar   Asst. Prof.
Sherwani, Malahat K., MLS Karachi   Prof.; Chairperson*
Siddiqi, Rafat P.   Asst. Prof.
Siddique, Muhammad, MLS Karachi   Asst. Prof.
Other Staff: 3 Lectrs.

Mass Communication

Bari Jafri, M. Inam, MA Karachi   Assoc. Prof.
Ghaznavi, Mehmood, MA Karachi, PhD Karachi   Prof.; Chairperson*
Jafri, Fouzia R.   Prof.
Masood, Tahir, MA Karachi, PhD Karachi   Prof.
Naseem, Sarwar, MA Karachi   Assoc. Prof.
Naz, Fouzia   Asst. Prof.
Qureshi, Samina   Asst. Prof.
Shamsuddin, M., MA Karachi, PhD Lond.   Prof.
Taj, Rafia, MA Karachi   Assoc. Prof.
Other Staff: 1 Lectr.

Mathematics

Ahmed, Mushtaq   Asst. Prof.
Ansari, Javed   Asst. Prof.
Aziz, Akhtar Jehan, MSc Karachi   Asst. Prof.
Fahim, Rashida, MSc Islam., MPhil Islam.   Asst. Prof.
Iqbal, Muhammad J.   Asst. Prof.
Jahan Abbasi, Sarwar, MA Karachi, PhD Edin.   Asst. Prof.
Jamil, Muhammad, MSc Karachi, MS W.Illinois   Asst. Prof.
Kamal, S. Arif, MSc Karachi, MS Indiana, MA Johns H., PhD Karachi   Prof.
Khan, Nasiruddin, MSc Bucharest, MSc Karachi, PhD Karachi   Prof.
Naeem, Rana K., MSc Windsor, MSc Karachi, PhD Windsor   Prof.; Chairperson*
Qamar, Naveda, MSc Karachi, MPhil Karachi   Asst. Prof.
Qureshi, Muhammad S., MSc Karachi, MPhil Karachi   Asst. Prof.
Shakeel, Rehana, MSc Karachi, MPhil Karachi   Asst. Prof.
Zaidi, Syed A. A.   Assoc. Prof.
Other Staff: 5 Lectrs.

Microbiology

Abbas, Tanveer   Asst. Prof.
Ahmed, Aqeel, MSc Karachi, PhD Karachi   Prof.
Ahmed, Samia   Asst. Prof.
Ahmed, Zaid   Asst. Prof.
Ali, Tasneem A., MSc Karachi, PhD Sheff.   Prof.
Ansari, Fasihuddin A., MSc Karachi, MPhil Karachi, PhD Lond.   Prof.
Baqai, Rukhshana   Prof.
Hiader, Fouzia   Asst. Prof.
Jahan, Nayyar F., MSc Karachi   Assoc. Prof.
Jamil, Nusrat, MSc Karachi, PhD Lond.   Prof.; Chairperson*
Kazmi, Shahana U., MSc Karachi, PhD Maryland   Prof.
Khalid, Syed M., MSc Karachi   Prof.
Khan, Shakeel Ahmed, MSc Karachi, PhD   Prof.
Mahmood, Nayyar   Asst. Prof.
Mujahid, Talat Yasmeen, MSc Karachi   Assoc. Prof.

Rasool, Sheikh A., MSc Karachi, PhD Moscow   Prof.
Shahnaz Naseem, MSc Karachi   Assoc. Prof.
Siddiqui, Ruquaya, MSc Karachi, PhD Lond.   Prof.
Siddiqui, Shameem A., MSc Karachi, MPhil Karachi   Prof.
Subhan, Syed A.   Asst. Prof.
Wahab, Abdul   Asst. Prof.
Other Staff: 9 Lectrs.

Natural Science

Haleem, Darakshan J., MSc Karachi, MPhil Karachi, PhD Lond.   Prof.; Chairperson (Co-ordinator)*

Persian

Afsar, Rehana, MA Karachi   Assoc. Prof.; Chairperson*
Noori, Salim N., MA Karachi   Asst. Prof.
Other Staff: 2 Lectrs.

Petroleum Technology

Qadri, Majeedullah, MSc Karachi, PhD Karachi   Prof.; Chairman*
Siddiqi, Shamim A.   Prof.

Pharmaceutical Chemistry

Ahmed, Mansoor   Asst. Prof.
Akhter, Shamim   Asst. Prof.
Ali, Farzana H.   Asst. Prof.
Arif, Muhammad, MSc Karachi, PhD Karachi   Prof.
Chishti, Kamran A., MPharm   Asst. Prof.
Hasan, Sohail   Asst. Prof.
Mushtaq, Nousheen   Asst. Prof.
Siddiqui, Afaq A.   Asst. Prof.
Sultana, Najma, MSc Karachi, PhD Karachi   Prof.
Vaid, Fiyaz H. M.   Asst. Prof.; Chairperson*

Pharmaceutics

Baqir Shyum Naqvi, Syed, MSc Karachi, PhD Karachi   Prof.
Hamid, Shaista   Asst. Prof.
Hasan, Fauzia, MPharm Karachi, MPhil Karachi, PhD   Prof.
Razvi, Nighat, MPharm Karachi, MPhil Karachi, PhD Karachi   Prof.; Chairperson*
Shoaib, M. Harris   Asst. Prof.
Other Staff: 6 Lectrs.

Pharmacognosy

Ahmed, Mansoor, MSc Karachi, PhD E.T.H.Zürich   Prof.
Ahmed, Waseemuddin S., MPharm Karachi, PhD Karachi   Prof.
Azhar, Iqbal   Asst. Prof.
Mazhar, Farah   Asst. Prof.
Rizwani, Ghazala H., BPharm Karachi, MPharm Karachi, PhD Karachi   Prof.; Chairperson*
Siddiqui, Shahida, MSc Sindh, PhD Sindh   Prof.
Other Staff: 1 Lectr.

Pharmacology

Afriz, Syeda   Asst. Prof.
Ahmed, Shahida P., MSc Karachi, MPhil Karachi, PhD Karachi   Prof.
Khan, Rafeeq A., MPharm Karachi, PhD Karachi   Assoc. Prof.; Chairperson*
Najam, Raheela   Asst. Prof.
Rehman, Asif B., MSc Karachi, MPhil Karachi, MD   Prof.
Sajid, Tasneem M.   Asst. Prof.
Takween, Shamoona   Asst. Prof.
Other Staff: 2 Lectrs.

Philosophy

Ameeri, Javed I.   Asst. Prof.
Babar, Zahoor-ul-Hassan   Asst. Prof.; Chairperson (In-charge)*
Husan Zahoorul, MA Karachi   Asst. Prof.
Shabbir, Ahsan, MA Karachi, PhD Karachi   Asst. Prof.
Soori, Abdul W.   Asst. Prof.
Other Staff: 2 Lectrs.

Physics

Akhter, S. Kaab, MSc Karachi, MSc Laur., PhD Sing.   Prof.
Altaf Husain, M., MSc Karachi, MPhil Karachi   Assoc. Prof.
Anis, Muhammad Khalid, MSc CNAA, MSc Karachi, PhD CNAA   Prof.
Ayub, Birjees N., MSc Karachi, PhD Lond.   Asst. Prof.
Bano, Naquiba, MSc Karachi, MPhil Karachi, PhD Lond.   Prof.
Jamila, Sajida, MSc Karachi, PhD Nott.   Assoc. Prof.
Khan, Iqbal A., MSc Karachi, PhD Kent State   Prof.; Chairperson*
Mahmood, Shahid   Asst. Prof.
Manzoor, Sadia   Asst. Prof.
Naseeruddin, MSc Karachi, MPhil Karachi   Assoc. Prof.
Qidwai, Ansar A., MSc Karachi, MPhil Karachi, PhD Durh.   Prof.
Rahim, Tehseen, PhD Lond.   Asst. Prof.
Rizvi, Shabana   Asst. Prof.
Rizvi, Syed D. H., MSc Karachi   Prof.
Ulfat, Intikhab   Asst. Prof.
Zahiruddin   Asst. Prof.
Other Staff: 6 Lectrs.

Physics, Applied

Farrukh, Fairda   Asst. Prof.
Hussain, Abid   Asst. Prof.
Hussain, Arshad   Asst. Prof.
Qadeer, Abdul, MSc Karachi, MSc Laur., PhD Hull   Prof.
Siddiqui, Najeeb, MSc Karachi, PhD Lond.   Assoc. Prof.
Yousufzai, M. Ayub Khan   Prof.
Zaidi, S. Shahid H., MSc Karachi, PhD Lond.   Prof.; Chairperson*
Other Staff: 2 Lectrs.

Physiology

Amer, Shehla, MSc Karachi, PhD Exe.   Prof.
Amin, Qamar, MSc Karachi   Prof.; Chairperson*
Azeem, Muhammad A., MSc Karachi, PhD Karachi   Prof.
Fatima, Habib, MSc Karachi   Asst. Prof.
Hasain, Zaheer, MSc Karachi, PhD Karachi   Asst. Prof.
Hasan, Ruqayya, MSc Karachi   Asst. Prof.
Javaid, Ayesha, MSc Karachi   Asst. Prof.
Naeem, Tazeen, MSc Karachi   Asst. Prof.
Savanur, Arifa   Asst. Prof.
Other Staff: 12 Lectrs.

Political Science

Idrees, Nusrat, MA Karachi   Asst. Prof.
Khalid, Tanweer, MA Karachi   Prof.
Qadri, Hafiz M. A., MA Karachi, PhD Karachi   Assoc. Prof.; Chairperson*
Qadri, Muhammad A., MA Karachi, MPhil Karachi, PhD Karachi   Assoc. Prof.
Saeed, Samina, MA Karachi, PhD Karachi   Asst. Prof.
Sultana, Summer, MA Karachi   Asst. Prof.
Other Staff: 1 Lectr.

Psychology

Faheem, Anwar   Asst. Prof.
Feroz, Rubina   Assoc. Prof.
Iqbal, Farah   Asst. Prof.
Jehangir, Anjum A., MA Patna, PhD Patna   Assoc. Prof.
Khan, Jawaid F.   Asst. Prof.
Malik, Anila A.   Asst. Prof.
Raees, Sohaila, MA Karachi, PhD Karachi   Assoc. Prof.
Rizvi, Haider A., MSc Karachi   Assoc. Prof.; Chairperson*
Tariq, Qudsia   Asst. Prof.
Other Staff: 2 Lectrs.

Public Administration

Baloch, Akhtar, MA Karachi   Asst. Prof.
Humayun, Syed, MA Karachi, PhD Karachi   Prof.; Chairperson*

Iraqi, Khalid M., MA Karachi Asst. Prof.
Wajdi, M. Abuzar, MA Karachi, PhD Karachi Prof.
Other Staff: 5 Lectrs.

Quran and Sunnah

Ghazi, Shehnaz Asst. Prof.
Haque, Mufti I. Asst. Prof.
Haroon, Zeenat Asst. Prof.
Jahan, Mussarat Asst. Prof.; Chairperson (In-charge)*

Sindhi

Abbasi, Khurshid, MA Karachi Prof.
Hussain, Fahmida, MA Sindh, PhD Karachi Prof.
Memon, Abdul G. Asst. Prof.
Memon, M. Saleem, MA Karachi Prof.; Chairperson*
Parveen, Naheed Asst. Prof.
Shah, Muhammad A. Asst. Prof.
Other Staff: 1 Lectr.

Social Work

Ara Shafi, Hunas, MA Karachi Asst. Prof.
Aziz, Shama, MA Karachi, PhD Karachi Assoc. Prof.
Farman, Najma, MA Karachi Assoc. Prof.
Huda, Fakhrul, MA Karachi, MPhil Karachi Asst. Prof.
Husain, Anzar, MA Karachi Asst. Prof.
Kazi, Kulsoom, MA Karachi Assoc. Prof.; Chairperson*
Shah, Nasreen A. Assoc. Prof.
Shahid, M., MA Karachi Assoc. Prof.
Other Staff: 2 Lectrs.

Sociology

Burfat, Fateh M. Prof.; Chairperson*
Faridi, Farhat, MA Karachi Assoc. Prof.
Iqbal, Mussarat, LLB Karachi, MA Karachi, PhD Karachi Assoc. Prof.
Khan, Shahana Asst. Prof.
Shehzad, Sobia A. Asst. Prof.
Sultan, Saba Rana, MA Karachi, PhD Karachi Asst. Prof.
Zaigham, Farzana Asst. Prof.
Zubairi, Nabeel A. Asst. Prof.
Other Staff: 1 Lectr.

Special Education

Tel: (021) 924 3216
Begum, Zohra Asst. Prof.
Fatema, Kaniz Asst. Prof.
Kazimi, Anjum B. Asst. Prof.
Khatoon, Aqeela Asst. Prof.
Sajjad, Shahida Asst. Prof.
Shahzadi, Shagufta Assoc. Prof.; Chairperson*
Sulman, Nasir Asst. Prof.
Vaqar, Kaniz F. Asst. Prof.

Statistics

Ahmed, Ejaz, MSc Karachi, PhD Strath. Prof.
Ahmed, S. Afrozuddin, MSc Karachi Prof.
Akram, Muhammad Asst. Prof.
Ali, Tasneem, MSc Karachi Asst. Prof.
Aslam, Muhammad, MSc Karachi, MPhil Karachi Assoc. Prof.
Hussain, Ehtesham, MSc Karachi, MPhil Karachi Assoc. Prof.
Hussain, Ghulam, MSc Karachi Prof.
Khurshid, Anwer, MSc Karachi, PhD Exe. Prof.
Shafi, Rafia Asst. Prof.
Siddiqui, Asim J., MSc McG., MSc Karachi Prof.; Chairperson*
Siddiqui, Junaid, MSc Karachi, PhD Exe. Prof.
Uddin, Mudassir, MSc Oxf., MPhil Karachi, PhD Aberd. Assoc. Prof.
Yasmeen, Farah Asst. Prof.
Other Staff: 6 Lectrs.

Urdu

Afshan, Rahat Asst. Prof.
Ahmed, Zulqarnain Asst. Prof.
Farman, Uzma, MA Karachi, PhD Karachi Asst. Prof.
Farooqi, Sohaila Asst. Prof.
Firdous, Tanzeemul Asst. Prof.

Iqbal, Zafar, MA Sindh, PhD Sindh Prof.
Mir, Masooma R. Asst. Prof.
Shameel, Suraiya Asst. Prof.
Shamsuddin, M. Prof.; Chairperson (In-charge)*
Zaidi, Mehjabeen, MA Karachi, PhD Karachi Asst. Prof.

Usool-ud-Din

Mansoori, Hissamuddin Prof.; Chairperson*
Rashid, Abdul, MA Karachi, PhD Karachi Prof.

Visual Studies

Kazi, Durriya Chairperson (Project Dir.)*

Zoology

Akhtar, Kahkashan Asst. Prof.
Azmi, Arshad M., MSc Karachi, MPhil Karachi, PhD Karachi Prof.
Barkati, Sohail, MSc Karachi, PhD Karachi Prof.
Begum, Farida, MSc Karachi, PhD Karachi Prof.
Ghani, Naseem A. Assoc. Prof.
Khan, Afshan J. Asst. Prof.
Khan, Farhanullah Prof.
Khan, M. Zaheer Asst. Prof.
Khan, Muhammad Atiqullah Assoc. Prof.
Khatoon, Nasira Assoc. Prof.
Muhammad, Fatima A., MSc Karachi, PhD Karachi Asst. Prof.
Rehana Farooq, Yasmeen, MSc Karachi, MPhil Karachi Asst. Prof.
Rizvi, Sayed Anser, MSc Karachi, PhD Karachi Asst. Prof.
Saqib, Tasneem A., MSc Karachi, MPhil Karachi Prof.
Siddiqui, Nikhat Y., MSc Karachi, PhD Karachi Prof.; Chairperson*
Yasmeen, Rehana Assoc. Prof.
Yousuf, Masarrat Asst. Prof.
Zaidi, Raees H., MSc Karachi, PhD Karachi Asst. Prof.
Other Staff: 3 Lectrs.

SPECIAL CENTRES, ETC

Applied Economics Research Centre

Ahmad, Nuzhat Prof.
Aqeel, Anjum Asst. Prof.
Bilgrami, Samina Assoc. Prof.
Butt, Muhammad Sabihuddin Assoc. Prof.
Hai, Akhtar A. Assoc. Prof.
Wasti, Syed A. Asst. Prof.
Wizarat, Shahida Prof.; Dir.*

Bio-Technology and Genetic Engineering, Dr. A. Q. Khan Institute of (KIBGE)

Naqvi, S. H. Mujtaba Dir.*

Business Administration, Institute of (IBA)

Danishmand Dir.*

Chemical Sciences, H. E. J. International Centre for

Tel: (021) 498 3591 Fax: (021) 496 3373
Abbasi, Atiya, MSc Karachi, PhD Karachi Prof.
Ahmed, Vaqar U. Prof.
Ahmed, Zaheer Asst. Prof.
Ali, Muhammad Shaiq, MSc Karachi, PhD Karachi Assoc. Prof.
Ali, Syed A. Asst. Prof.
Anjum, Shazia Asst. Prof.
Atta-ur-Rehman, MSc Karachi, PhD Camb., ScD Camb. Prof.; Dir.*
Begum, Sabira, MSc Karachi, PhD Karachi Assoc. Prof.
Choudhry, M. Iqbal, MSc Karachi, PhD Karachi Prof.
Dar, Ahsana, MSc Karachi, MPhil Karachi, MS St.Louis, PhD Karachi Prof.
Faizi, Shaheen, MSc Karachi, PhD Karachi Prof.
Khan, Khalid M. Assoc. Prof.
Khan, Saifullah Asst. Prof.
Malik, Abdul, MSc Karachi, PhD Karachi Prof.
Qasmi, Zaheer-ul-Haq Asst. Prof.
Raza, Mahsin Asst. Prof.
Shaheen, Farzana Asst. Prof.

Siddiqi, Bina, MSc Karachi, MPhil Karachi, PhD Karachi Prof.

Clinical Psychology, Institute of

Ahmed, Riaz Asst. Prof.
Ali, Uzma Asst. Prof.
Bano, S. Tahira Asst. Prof.
Shamsuddin, M. Prof.; Dir.*

Environmental Studies, Institute of

Tel: (021) 474843
Khan, Moazzam A. Asst. Prof.; Dir. (In-charge)*
Omm-e-Hany Asst. Prof.
Other Staff: 3 Lectrs.

Europe, Area Study Centre for

Hasan, Rubab Asst. Prof.
Shah, Syed I. Assoc. Prof.
Tahir, Naveed A., MA Prof.; Dir.*

Halophytes, Institute of

Khan, M. Ajmal Dir.*

Information Technology, Umair Bhasha Institute of (UBIT)

Burney, S. M. Aqil, MSc Karachi, MPhil Karachi, PhD Strath. Dir.*

Languages, Institute of

Sabir, Muhammad Prof.; Dir.*

M. A. H. Qadri Biological Research Centre

Khan, Shakeel Ahmed, MSc Karachi, PhD Dir.*

Marine Biology, Centre of Excellence in

Tel: (021) 470572
Ayub, Zarrien Asst. Prof.
Hussain, S. Makhadoom Prof.
Khan, Sabahat A. Asst. Prof.
Mustaquim, Javed Prof.; Dir.*
Qari, Rashida Asst. Prof.
Qureshi, Naureen A. Asst. Prof.
Siddiqui, Ghazala Asst. Prof.
Siddiui, Pirzada J. A. Asst. Prof.
Zehra, Itrat Assoc. Prof.
Other Staff: 2 Lectrs.

Marine Reference Collection and Resource Centre

Kazmi, Quddusi B., MSc Karachi, PhD Karachi Prof.; Dir.*

Marine Sciences, Institute of

Fatima, Meher, MSc Karachi, PhD Karachi Assoc. Prof.; Dir.*

Mass Communication, Dr Firoz Ahmed Institute of

Nasim, Sarwar Dir.*

Molecular Genetics, Centre for

Ahmed, Nuzhat Prof.; Dir.*

Molecular Medicine and Drug Research, Dr Nadra Panjwani Centre for

Chaudhry, Iqbal Dir.*

National Nematological Research Centre (NNRC)

Tel: (021) 496 9019
Fayyaz, Shahina Dir.*

Pakistan Agriculture and Research Centre (PARC)

Khatoon, Suraiya Dir.*

Pakistan Study Centre

Tel: (021) 496 2497
Ahmed, Syed J. Dir.*
Haider, Navin G. Asst. Prof.
Shaheen, Anwar Asst. Prof.

Pharmaceutical Sciences, Research Institute of

Sultana, Najma, MSc Karachi, PhD Karachi Prof.; Dir.*

Shaikh Zayed Islamic Research Centre

Rehman, Khalil ur Prof.; Dir.*
Other Staff: 5 Lectrs.

Space and Planetary Physics, Institute of

Rasool, Sheikh A., MSc *Karachi*, PhD *Moscow*
  Prof.; Dir.*

Women Studies, Centre of Excellence for

Shah, Nasreen A. Dir.*

CONTACT OFFICERS

Examinations. Controller of Examinations:
  Qureshi, Naeemuddin A.
Finance. Director of Finance: Khalid, S. M.,
  MBA
Library (chief librarian). Librarian: Akhtar,
  Mukhtar, MA *Karachi*
Marketing. Public Relations Officer: (vacant)
Public relations. Public Relations Officer:
  (vacant)

AFFILIATED COLLEGES

[Institutions listed by location below provide
  courses leading to degrees, etc. of the
  university]
Bahadurabad. Askary Degree College
Gizri. Govt. Degree Girls' College
Gulistan-e-Jauhar. Jauhar Degree College;
  Liaquat Ali Khan College of Dentistry;
  Shaheen Public College
Gulshan-e-Iqbal. College of Banking and
  Finance; College of Digital and
  Management Sciences; College of
  Management and Information Technology;
  D. E. W. A. Academy; Govt. College; Govt.
  Degree Girls College; Hashmat Memorial
  College of Education; Hayat ul Islam Degree
  Girls' College; Ideal College for Girls; Indus
  Institute; University College
Islamabad. Systems Research Institute
Karachi. ABSA College for Deaf; Adamson
  Institute of Business Administration and
  Technology; Al-Hamd College of
  Professional Education; Al-Noor Degree
  Science College; Altamash Institute of
  Dental Medicine; Arab Foundation College;
  B. A. M. M. PECHS Govt. College for
  Women; Bahria Foundation College; Bright
  Star Degree Girls' College; C. A. M. S.
  College of Business Administration; College
  of Accounting and Management Sciences;
  Defence Authority Degree College for Boys;

Defence Authority Degree College for
Women; Defence School of Business
Education; Elite's College; F. I. R. S. T.
College of Business and Science; Fatima
Jinnah Dental College; Govt. Adamjee
Science College; Govt. Allama Iqbal College;
Govt. City College; Govt. College of
Commerce and Economics; Govt. College of
Education; Govt. College of Physical
Education; Govt. D. J. Science College;
Govt. Degree Arts/Science/Commerce
College; Govt. Degree Boys' and Girls'
College; Govt. Degree College for Boys and
Girls; Govt. Degree College for Men; Govt.
Degree College for Men (Bufferzone); Govt.
Degree College for Women (Korangi No.
4); Govt. Degree College for Women
(Korangi No. 6); Govt. Degree Girls'
College; Govt. Degree Girls' College (P. I. B.
Colony); Govt. Degree Girls' Commerce
College; Govt. Degree Science College;
Govt. H. I. Osmania Girls' College; Govt. H.
R. H. Aga Khan Girls' College; Govt. Haji
Abdullah Haroon College; Govt. Islamia
Arts/Commerce College; Govt. Islamia
College for Women; Govt. Islamia Law
College; Govt. Islamia Science College;
Govt. Karachi College for Women; Govt.
Khatoon-e-Pakistan College for Women;
Govt. Khurshid Girls' College; Govt.
National College; Govt. PECHS Education
Foundation Science College; Govt. Raunaq-
e-Islam College for Women; Govt. S. M.
Arts and Commerce College; Govt. S. M.
Law College; Govt. Superior Science
College; Ida Rieu Poor Welfare Association;
Institute of Air Safety; Institute of Business
Education; Institute of Computer Science;
Institute of Management and Computer
Science; Jinnah Medical College; Jinnah
Postgraduate Medical Centre; K. M. A.
Degree Girls' College; Kulsoom Bai Valika
Social Security Hospital; Kursheed Govt.
Girls' College; Liaquat College of
Management Sciences; Liaquat National
Hospital; MA Ayesha Institute of Education
and Allied Health Sciences; Mehran Degree
Girls' College; Mid Asia Institute of
Information Technology; Modern College;
Modern Degree College; National Institute
of Cardiovascular Diseases; Ojha Institute of
Chest Diseases; Orthopaedic and Medical
Institute; P. A. F. College of Education;
Pakistan Marine Academy; Rana Liaquat Ali
Khan Govt. College of Home Economics;
Rehan College of Education; S. M. B. Fatima

Jinnah Govt. Girls' College; S. S. A. T.
Degree College; School of Army Air
Defence; School of Ordnance; Shah Latif
Boys' College; Shaheen College of
Computers; Sindh Institute of Urology and
Transplantation; Sir Admjee Institute of
Technology; Sir Syed College of Medical
Science for Girls; St. Lawrence Govt. Degree
Girls' College; Tec College
Karimabad. Govt. A. P. W. A. College; Govt.
  Sirajuddullah College
Liaquataba/Qasimabad. Govt. Degree Science
  College
Liaqutabad. Govt. Quaid-e-Millat College
Lyari. Allama I. I. Kazi College of Education;
  Govt. Degree Science/Commerce College
Malir. Govt. Degree College for Women; Govt.
  Degree Science College; Govt. Degree
  Science/Arts College; Govt. Jamia Millia
  College; Govt. Jamia Millia College of
  Education; Govt. Liaquat College
Manora. Pakistan Naval Academy
Nazimabad. Abbasi Shaheed Hospital; Govt.
  Jinnah College; Govt. Sir Syed Girls'
  College; Sir Syed Govt. Girls' College
Nazimabad Chowrangi. Govt. Degree College
  for Women
North Karachi. Govt. College for Boys; Govt.
  Degree Girls' College; Mid Asia Institute of
  Information Technology
North Nazimabad. Govt. Abdullah College for
  Women; Govt. Degree Girls' College; Govt.
  Premier College; Karachi Medical and
  Dental College; Pakistan Shipowners' Govt.
  College; Progressive Degree Girls' College
Orangi Town. Maulana Adbul Hamid
  Badayuni Govt. Science/Commerce College
Saddar. Govt. St. Joseph's College for Women;
  Notre Dame Institute of Education; Trinity
  Girls College
Shahra-e-Faisal. Govt. Aisha Bawani College
Shahra-e-Liaquat. Govt. Degree College for
  Women; Govt. S. M. Science College
Shahrah-e-Faisal. P. A. F. Air War College;
  Pakistan Navy Staff College
Shara-e-Faisal. Fazzia Degree College
Zulfiqarabad. Madar-e-Millat Degree Girls'
  College

[Information supplied by the institution as at 4 October
2006, and edited by the ACU]

KOHAT UNIVERSITY OF SCIENCE AND TECHNOLOGY

Founded 2001

Postal Address: Bannu Road, off Jerma Kohat, N.W.F.P., Pakistan
Telephone: (0922) 554565 **Fax:** (0922) 554556 **E-mail:** kust@psh.pknet.com.pk
URL: http://www.kust.edu.pk

ACTING VICE-CHANCELLOR*—Khan, Prof. Abdus S., BSc MSc PhD
REGISTRAR‡—Khan, Prof. Abdus S., BSc MSc PhD

LAHORE UNIVERSITY OF MANAGEMENT SCIENCES

Founded 1985

Member of the Association of Commonwealth Universities

Postal Address: Sector U, Lahore Defence Housing Authority, Lahore 54792, Pakistan
Telephone: (042) 572 2670-9 **Fax:** (042) 572 2591 **E-mail:** admissions@lums.edu.pk
URL: http://www.lums.edu.pk

VICE-CHANCELLOR*—Durrani, Ahmad J., BSc LahoreUET, MBA Houston, PhD Mich.,
    FASCE
DEAN, GRADUATE SCHOOL OF BUSINESS—Haque, Ehsan ul, BSc Lahore UET, MBA Penn.,
    PhD Texas
DEAN, SCHOOL OF ARTS AND SCIENCES—Khurshid, Prof. Anwar, MSc Lahore UET, MS
    N.Y.State, MBA Ohio State, PhD Mich.State
GENERAL MANAGER (STUDENT AND ALUMNI AFFAIRS)—Khan, Mohammad A., MS Ill.
MANAGER (FINANCE AND ACCOUNTS)—Butt, Asim
GENERAL MANAGER (ADMINISTRATION AND SERVICES)‡—Khan, Azmatullah, BSc NED
    Eng., BE NED Eng.

GENERAL INFORMATION

History. The university was established in
1985.
    It is located 8km south of Lahore airport.

Admission to first degree courses (see also
Pakistan Introduction). Applicants should have
General Certificate of Education (GCE) A level,
US Scholastic Aptitude Test (SAT I and II), or
equivalent qualifications.

First Degrees (see also Pakistan Directory to
Subjects of Study) (* = with honours). BA/
LLB*, BSc*.
    Length of course. Full-time: BSc*: 4 years; BA/
LLB*: 5 years.

Higher Degrees (see also Pakistan Directory
to Subjects of Study).
    Master's. EMBA, MBA, MS, MSc.
    Admission. Admission to MBA is via the
Graduate Management Admission Test (GMAT)
plus interview. Admission to MS is via the
Graduate Record Exam (GRE) plus interview.
Applicants must have a minimum of 16 years
of education.
    Length of course. Full-time: MS, MSc: 1–2 years;
EMBA, MBA: 2 years.
    Doctoral. PhD.
    Admission. Admission to PhD is via the
Graduate Record Exam (GRE) plus interview.
Applicants must have a minimum of 16 years
of education.
    Length of course. Full-time: PhD: 3–8 years.

Libraries. Volumes: 40,000. Periodicals
subscribed to: 330. Other holdings: 7500
annual reports on around 745 listed companies
in Pakistan; 6800 pamphlets. Special
collections: World Bank; Asian Development
Bank; United Nations; Government of Pakistan.

Income (2005–2006). Total, £2,404,692.

Statistics. Staff (2005–2006): 323 (74
academic, 249 non-academic). Students
(2005–2006): full-time 1378 (923 men, 455
women); international 2; undergraduate 1060
(645 men, 415 women); master's 308 (269
men, 39 women); doctoral 12 (11 men, 1
woman).

FACULTIES/SCHOOLS

Arts and Sciences, School of (SOAS)
E-mail: soasfaculty@mail.lums.edu.pk
Dean: Khurshid, Prof. Anwar, MSc Lahore UET,
    MS N.Y.State, MBA Ohio State, PhD Mich.State

Business, Suleman Dawood School of
E-mail: gsbafaculty@mail.lums.edu.pk
Dean: Haque, Ehsan ul, BSc Lahore UET, MBA
    Penn., PhD Texas

ACADEMIC UNITS

Arts and Sciences
Aziz, Sadaf, LLB Br.Col., MSc Lond.   Asst. Prof.
Cheema, H. Moeen, LLB Lond., LLM Harv.
    Asst. Prof.
Shah, A. Sikandar, BA Mich., JD Mich.
Siddique, Osama, MA Oxf., LLM Harv.   Asst.
    Prof.; Head*
Wilson, Joseph, LLM McG., DCL McG.   Asst.
    Prof.
Other Staff: 2 Adjunct Fac.

Business, Graduate School of
Afghan, Nasir, MBA Maastricht, PhD T.H.Twente
    Asst. Prof.
Ali, Imran, MSc Lahore UET, MS N.Y.State, MBA
    Ohio State, PhD ANU   Jamil Nishtar Prof.,
    Agribusiness, Business History and Business
    Policy
Amir, Irfan, MBA Punjab, PhD Manc.   Assoc.
    Prof.
Anwar, M. Farooq, MSc Buffalo, PhD Buffalo
    Asst. Prof.
Ashraf, M. Junaid   Asst. Prof.
Butt, Arif N., MSc Georgia I.T., MBA Lahore MS
    Asst. Prof.
Chaudhry, Wasique W., MBA Asian I.T., Bangkok
    Asst. Prof.
Ghani, Jawaid, SB M.I.T., PhD Penn.   Prof.
Ghaznavi, Dawood, MSc(Engg) Moscow Steel &
    Alloys, MPPM Yale   Assoc. Prof.
Haque, Ehsan ul, BSc Lahore UET, MBA Penn.,
    PhD Texas   Assoc. Prof.; Dean*
Hassan, Syed Z., MS Stan., MSEM Stan., PhD
    Stan.   Prof.
Khan, Jamshed H., BSME Texas, MBA Texas,
    MSIE Texas, PhD Texas   Assoc. Prof.; Assoc.
    Dean, MBA and EMBA Programmes
Khan, Wasif M., BSc Lahore UET, MSc Oregon
    State, MPPM Yale   Assoc. Prof.
Malik, Azmat, MBA Calif.   Assoc. Prof.
Mubashir Ali, S., PhD Manc.   Assoc. Prof.
Rafi Khan, F., MPhil Camb., PhD McG.   Asst.
    Prof.
Rana, Arif I., MS Purdue, PhD Rensselaer   Assoc.
    Prof.
Rashid, Kamran   Asst. Prof.
Sipra, Naim, MBA Texas, PhD Texas   Prof.
Other Staff: 3 Visiting Fac.; 5 Adjunct Fac.
Research: corporate governance; family business;
    marketing, finance, leadership; non-profit
    management, small enterprises; supply-
    chain management

Computer Science
Awais, Mian M., MSc Lond., PhD Lond.   Asst.
    Prof.
Baqai, M. Shahab, MSEE S.Calif., PhD Purdue
    Asst. Prof.
Ikram, Jahanghir, MSc Manc., MA S.Fraser, PhD
    S.Fraser   Asst. Prof.
Ikram, Mohammad Z., MEngSc Melb., MSCECE
    Georgia I.T., PhD Georgia I.T.   Asst. Prof. (on
    leave)
Iqbal, M. Ashraf, MSc Lahore UET, PhD Lahore
    UET   Prof.
Jadoon, Tariq, MSc Strath., PhD Strath.   Asst.
    Prof.
Karim, Asim, BSc Lahore UET, MS Ohio State, PhD
    Ohio State   Asst. Prof.
Khan, Nadeem A., MEE Philips'(Eindhoven), MTD
    T.U.Eindhoven, PhD T.U.Eindhoven   Asst. Prof.
Khan, Sohaib, PhD Central Flor.   Asst. Prof.
Khurshid, Anwar, MSc Lahore UET, MS N.Y.State,
    MBA Ohio State, PhD Mich.State   Prof.
Lone, Asim, MS S.Calif., PhD S.Calif.   Asst.
    Prof.
Masud, Shahid, MEngSc NSW, PhD Belf.   Asst.
    Prof.
Shah, Syed I. A., MSc Ott., PhD Col.   Assoc.
    Prof. (on leave)
Shamail, Shafay, MSc Wales, PhD Bath   Head*
Tariq, Salim, MS Arizona State, PhD Arizona State
Uzmi, Zartash A., MS Stan., PhD Stan.
Zaman, Arif, MA Claremont, PhD Stan.   Prof.
Other Staff: 2 Teaching Fellows (1 on leave);
    3 Visiting Fac.; 8 Adjunct Fac.
Research: artificial intelligence (AI); digital signal
    processing; distributed systems in computer
    networks; software engineering; theoretical
    computer science

Economics
Bari, Faisal, MA Oxf., PhD McG.   Assoc. Prof.
Burki, A. Abid, PhD Kansas State   Assoc. Prof.
Cheema, Ali, MPhil Camb., PhD Camb.   Asst.
    Prof.; Head*
Hussain, S. Turrab, MA Essex, PhD Essex   Asst.
    Prof.
Khan, Mushtaq, MSc Quaid-i-Azam, PhD Kansas
    State   Asst. Prof.
Nasim, Anjum, BSc Lond., MA Essex, PhD Essex
    Prof.
Zaman, Asad, MA Stan., PhD Stan.   Prof.
Other Staff: 2 Teaching Fellows; 3 Visiting Fac.
Research: agricultural policy and the World
    Trade Organisation (WTO); governance and
    decentralisation; public finance issues;
    theoretical econometrics

Mathematics
Beg, Ismet, MSc Punjab, PhD Bucharest   Prof.
Hussain, Wasiq, MSc Quaid-i-Azam, MPhil Quaid-
    i-Azam, PhD Glas.   Asst. Prof.
Jafri, Zaeem, MSc Lahore UET, PhD Sur.   Assoc.
    Prof.; Head*
Tariq, Nessim, BSc Lond., MSc Lond., PhD New
    Br.   Assoc. Prof. (on leave)
Other Staff: 1 Teaching Fellow; 1 Visiting Fac.;
    3 Adjunct Fac.
Research: applied mathematics relativity;
    functional analysis; fuzzy set theory;
    microelectronics/device physics; wave
    motion

Social Sciences

Ahsen, M. Shabbir, MA *Karachi*, PhD *Karachi* Asst. Prof.

Irfan, Ghazala, PhD *Punjab* Assoc. Prof.

Khan, Furrukh A., MA *Kent*, PhD *Kent* Asst. Prof.

Rais, R. Baksh, PhD *Calif.* Prof.; Head*

Shah, H. Gulzar, MSS *Utah State*, PhD *Utah State* Asst. Prof.

Sherazi, Saima N., MA *Punjab* Asst. Prof.; Co-ordinator (on leave)

Zaheer, Khalid, MBA *Punjab*, PhD *Wales* Asst. Prof.

Zubair, Sara, EdM *Harv.*, MA

Other Staff: 1 Lectr.; 8 Teaching Fellows (3 on leave); 1 Visiting Fac.; 15 Adjunct Fac.

CONTACT OFFICERS

Academic affairs. Dean, Graduate School of Business: Haque, Ehsan ul, BSc *Lahore UET*, MBA *Penn.*, PhD *Texas*

Academic affairs. Dean, School of Arts and Sciences: Khurshid, Prof. Anwar, MSc *Lahore UET*, MS *N.Y.State*, MBA *Ohio State*, PhD *Mich.State*

Accommodation. Assistant Manager, Administration: Raza, Mubashara

Admissions (first degree). Deputy Manager, Admissions and Financial Aid: Hafeez,

Samina, MA *Punjab* (E-mail: admission@lums.edu.pk)

Admissions (higher degree). Deputy Manager, Admissions and Financial Aid: Hafeez, Samina, MA *Punjab* (E-mail: admission@lums.edu.pk)

Alumni. Manager, Marketing and External Relations: Kamran, Nuzhat, MA *Punjab*, MBA *Lahore MS* (E-mail: alumni@lums.edu.pk)

Archives. Chief Librarian: Ramzan, Muhammad, MLS

Careers. Manager, Career Development Office: Kanwal, Shumaila

Computing services. Manager, Information Technology Support Centre: Qureshi, Waqar

Credit transfer. Deputy Manager, Admissions: Hafeez, Samina, MA *Punjab*

Development/fund-raising. General Manager, Student and Alumni Affairs: Khan, Mohammad A., MS *Ill.*

Equal opportunities. Senior Manager, Human Resource: Malik, Shazi, MBusEd *Punjab*

Estates and buildings/works and services. General Manager, Administration and Services: Khan, Azmatullah, BSc *Lahore UET*, BE *Lahore UET*

Examinations. Manager, Student Services: Haq, Naheed, MBA *San Francisco State*

Finance. Manager (Finance and Accounts): Butt, Asim

Library (chief librarian). Chief Librarian: Ramzan, Muhammad, MLS

Library (enquiries). Chief Librarian: Ramzan, Muhammad, MLS

Marketing. Manager, Marketing and External Relations: Kamran, Nuzhat, MA *Punjab*, MBA *Lahore MS*

Personnel/human resources. Senior Manager, Human Resource: Malik, Shazi, MBusEd *Punjab*

Public relations. General Manager, Student and Alumni Affairs: Khan, Mohammad A., MS *Ill.*

Scholarships, awards, loans. Deputy Manager, Admissions: Hafeez, Samina, MA *Punjab*

Sport and recreation. Manager, Student Services: Haq, Naheed, MBA *San Francisco State*

Staff development and training. Senior Manager, Human Resource: Malik, Shazi, MBusEd *Punjab*

Student welfare/counselling. Student Counsellor: Khan, Nashi

[*Information supplied by the institution as at 21 May 2005, and edited by the ACU*]

LIAQUAT UNIVERSITY OF MEDICAL AND HEALTH SCIENCES

Founded 2001

Postal Address: Jamshoro, Sindh, Pakistan
Telephone: (0221) 771239 **Fax:** (0221) 772389 **E-mail:** lumhs@hyd.paknet.com.pk
URL: http://www.lumhs.edu.pk

VICE-CHANCELLOR*—Shaikh, Prof. Noshad A.
REGISTRAR‡—Memon, Afzal

MALAKAND UNIVERSITY

Postal Address: Chakdara, Distt. Dir, Malakand Division, Pakistan
Telephone: (0936) 761446
URL: http://www.uom.edu.pk/

VICE-CHANCELLOR*—Shah, Prof. Jahandar

MEHRAN UNIVERSITY OF ENGINEERING AND TECHNOLOGY

Founded 1963

Member of the Association of Commonwealth Universities

Postal Address: Jamshoro 76062, Sindh, Pakistan
Fax: (22) 277 1382
URL: http://www.muet.edu.pk

VICE-CHANCELLOR*—Rajput, Prof. Abdul Q. K., BE Sindh, MSc Leeds, PhD Pitt.
REGISTRAR‡—Uqaili, Prof. Mohammad A., BE NED Eng., MA Sindh, PhD Leeds
DIRECTOR, FINANCE—Shaikh, Muneer A., BE Mehran, MBA Sindh, MA Sindh
DIRECTOR, PLANNING AND DEVELOPMENT—Kazi, Abdul Razak, BA Sindh, MA Sindh

GENERAL INFORMATION

History. The university was founded in 1963 as Sindh University Engineering College, a constituent college of the University of Sindh. In March 1977 it achieved university status and was renamed Mehran University of Engineering and Technology.

Admission to first degree courses (see also Pakistan Introduction). Intermediate (pre-engineering) exam with at least division 2 (subject to clearance of an entry test) is required. International applicants, nominated by the Ministry of Finance and Economic Affairs, may be admitted under a cultural exchange programme.

First Degrees (see also Pakistan Directory to Subjects of Study). BArch, BCRP, BEngg.
   Length of course. Full-time: BCRP, BEngg: 4 years; BArch: 5 years.

Higher Degrees (see also Pakistan Directory to Subjects of Study).
   Master's. MEngg, MPhil.
   Admission. Applicants for admission to master's degree, MPhil (research) courses should hold BEngg in first class.
   Length of course. Full-time: MEngg: 1½ years; MPhil: 2 years. Part-time: MEngg: 2 years; MPhil: 3 years.
   Doctoral. PhD.
   Admission. Applicants for admission to PhD should hold MEngg in first class.
   Length of course. Full-time: PhD: 2 years.

Libraries. Volumes: 100,000. Other holdings: 15,000 E-journals.

FACULTIES/SCHOOLS

Architecture, Planning, Arts and Design
Tel: (022) 277 1638 E-mail: dali@usa.com
Dean: Khowaja, Prof. Dost A., BE Mehran, PhD Strath.

Electrical, Electronics and Computer Engineering
Tel: (022) 277 2268
Dean: Abro, Prof. M. Rafique, BE Sindh, PhD Sheff.

Engineering
Tel: (022) 277 1312
Dean: Suhag, Prof. Riaz A., BE Sindh, PhD Acad.Romania

Science, Technology and Humanities
Tel: (022) 277 1352
Dean: Panhwar, Prof. M. Ibrahim, BE Sindh, PhD Sheff.

ACADEMIC UNITS
Architecture
Tel: (022) 277 2293
Brohi, M. Afzal, BArch Mehran, LLB Sindh, MA Sindh   Asst. Prof.

Halephota, A. R., BArch Mehran, MA Sindh   Asst. Prof.
Irfan, Arain N., BArch Sindh   Assoc. Prof.; Chairman*
Jokhio, M. H., BArch Mehran   Asst. Prof.
Khan, Nadeemullah, BArch Lahore UET   Asst. Prof.
Memon, Irfan Ahmed, BArch Mehran   Asst. Prof.
Pathan, Moazim A., BArch Mehran   Asst. Prof.
Serhandi, M. Hafeez J., BArch Mehran   Asst. Prof.
Shar, B. K., BArch Mehran, PhD Newcastle(UK)   Prof.
Soomro, A. R., BArch Mehran, MArch Tongji, PhD Tongji   Assoc. Prof. (on lien)

Basic Sciences and Related Studies
supporting department
Tel: (022) 277 1409
Abro, Saifullah, MSc Sindh   Asst. Prof.
Baloch, Ahsanullah, BSc Sindh, MSc Sindh, PhD Wales   Prof.
Bhutto, Ghulam Y., BSc Sindh, MSc Sindh   Asst. Prof.
Chajro, K. M., MSc Sindh   Asst. Prof.
Ghanghro, Abdul R., MA Sindh, PhD Sindh   Prof.
Jamali, Yasmin Z., MA Sindh   Asst. Prof.
Pathan, A. N., MSc Sindh   Assoc. Prof.
Shah, Syed F., MSc Sindh, MPhil Sindh   Asst. Prof.
Shaikh, Asif A., BSc Sindh, MSc Sindh, MPhil Sindh   Asst. Prof.
Shaikh, M. U., MSc Cran.   Prof.; Chairman*
Solangi, M. Anwar, MSc Sindh   Asst. Prof. (on leave)

City and Regional Planning
Tel: (022) 277 2294
Dahri, M. A., BE Mehran   Assoc. Prof.; Chairman*
Khowaja, Dost A., BE Mehran, PhD Strath.   Prof.
Memon, Noor M., BE NED Eng., MCP Penn., MS Penn.   Visiting Prof.
Shaikh, Masood M., BSc Lahore UET, MSc Asian I.T., Bangkok   Asst. Prof.

Engineering, Biomedical
Tel: (022) 277 1334
Chowdhry, B. S., BE Mehran, PhD S'ton.   Prof.; Chairman*
Chowdhry, N. P., BE Mehran, ME Brun.   Asst. Prof.
Herchandani, Pardeep K., MB BS Sindh   Visiting Prof.
Khan, Badaruddja, MB BS Sindh   Visiting Prof.
Memon, M. Saleh, PhD Sindh   Visiting Prof.
Qureshi, Shugafta, MB BS Sindh   Visiting Prof.
Shah, Inayatullah, PhD Brun.   Visiting Prof.
Shaikh, Mohsin A., BE Mehran, ME Strath.   Asst. Prof.
Syed Faisal Ali, BE Mehran   Visiting Prof.

Engineering, Chemical
Tel: (022) 277 1642
Ansari, A. K., BE Sindh, MSc Wales, PhD Wales   Prof.
Bhatti Inamullah, BE Mehran   Asst. Prof.

Memon, Munawar A., BE Sindh, MSc Sheff.   Prof.; Chairman*
Pirzada, A. H., MA Sindh, BE   Asst. Prof. (on deputation)
Qureshi Khadija, BE Mehran, ME Mehran   Asst. Prof. (on leave)
Shaikh, Shaheen A., BE Mehran, ME Mehran   Asst. Prof.
Soomro, Suhail A., BE Mehran, MSc Brad.   Asst. Prof.
Syed, Farman A. S., BE Mehran, ME Mehran   Asst. Prof. (on leave)
Talpur, Abdul K., MSc Sindh, PhD Sindh   Prof.

Engineering, Civil
Tel: (022) 277 1269
Ansari, Javed K., BE Mehran, ME Mehran   Asst. Prof.
Ansari, Kamran, BE Mehran, ME Asian I.T., Bangkok   Asst. Prof.
Baloch, Tauha H. A., BE Mehran, MSc Sing., PhD Griff.   Assoc. Prof.
Gugarman, M. M., BE Mehran, PhD Huazhong U.S.T.   Prof.
Hindu, Aneel K., BE Mehran, ME Asian I.T., Bangkok   Asst. Prof.
Khaskheli, G. B., MEng Sheff., PhD Glas.   Prof.
Khatri, M. S., BE Sindh, MSc Glas.   Prof.; Chairman*
Kumbhar, M. Y., BE(Agri) Sindh, ME Mehran   Prof.
Lashari, Abdul N., BE NED Eng., MS King Fahd   Asst. Prof. (on leave)
Leghari, Khalifa Q., BE Sindh, ME Sindh   Asst. Prof.
Mahar, Rasool B., BE Mehran, MSc Sindh, PhD Tsinghua   Asst. Prof.
Mahesar, Ghulam H., MSc Sindh   Asst. Prof.
Memon, Prof. Abdul R., BE NED Eng., ME Brun.   Assoc. Prof.
Memon, Ali A., BE Sindh, MPhil Brad.   Prof.
Memon, Allah B., BE Roor., ME Roor.   Assoc. Prof
Memon, Arshad A., BE Mehran   Asst. Prof.
Memon, Ashfaque A., BE Mehran, ME Mehran   Asst. Prof.
Memon, Gul H., BE Sindh, MSc Glas.   Prof.
Memon, Hizbullah, BE Mehran   Asst. Prof.
Memon, M. Ali, BE Mehran, ME Mehran   Asst. Prof.
Memon, Muhammad S., BE Sindh, ME   Assoc. Prof
Memon, Mumtaz A., BE Sindh, ME Asian I.T., Bangkok   Prof.
Memon, Rizwan A., BE Mehran, ME Mehran   Asst. Prof.
Memon, Zubair A., BE Mehran, MSc PhD   Asst. Prof.
Pathan, Ashfaque A., BE Mehran   Asst. Prof.
Phul, Atta M., BE Mehran   Assoc. Prof.
Qureshi, Abdul S., BE Mehran, PhD T.U.Dresden   Prof.
Shaikh, Pervez A., BE Mehran, ME Mehran   Asst. Prof.

Engineering, Computer Systems and Software
Tel: (022) 277 1206
Akram, Shaikh M., BE Mehran, ME Karachi   Asst. Prof. (on leave)

Hafiz, Tahseen H., BE Mehran, ME Mehran
Assoc. Prof.
Hashmani, Manzoor A., BE Mehran, ME PhD
Foreign Prof.
Jaffery, Naveed A., BE Mehran, ME Mehran   Asst.
Prof.
Memon, Nasrullah, MSc Sindh, ME Karachi
Asst. Prof. (on leave)
Rai, Meheshwari P., BE Sindh, MSc Lough.   Asst.
Prof. (on leave)
Rajput, Abdul Q. K., BE Sindh, MSc Leeds, PhD
Pitt.   Visiting Prof.
Samejo, Arbab A., BE Mehran, ME Mehran, PhD
Mehran   Asst. Prof.
Shaikh, Muhammad Z., BE Mehran, ME Mehran
Assoc. Prof.; Chairman*
Thebo, L. A., BE Mehran, ME Mehran   Asst. Prof.
Unar, M. H., BE Mehran, MSc Wayne State
Assoc. Prof. (on leave)
Unar, Mukhtiar A., BE Mehran, MSc Glas., PhD
Glas.   Prof.

Engineering, Electrical

Tel: (022) 277 1351
Abro, M. Rafique, BE Sindh, PhD Sheff.   Prof.
Baloch, B. H., BE Sindh, ME Kumamoto   Assoc.
Prof.
Burdi, M. K., BE Sindh, MSc Lough., PhD Bath
Prof.
Chang, A. Q., BE Sindh, ME Mehran   Prof.
Hashmani, Ashfaque A., BE Mehran, ME NU
Singapore   Asst. Prof. (on leave)
Memon, Ali A., BE Mehran, ME Mehran   Asst.
Prof. (on leave)
Memon, Anwar A., BE Sindh   Asst. Prof.
Memon, Zubair A., BE Mehran, MSc PhD   Asst.
Prof.
Mirani, M. A., BE Sindh, MA Sindh   Assoc.
Prof.; Chairman*
Pathan, A. Z., BE Sindh, MSc T.H.Dresden   Prof.
Shaikh, Noor N., BE Mehran, ME Mehran   Asst.
Prof.
Uqaili, Mohammad A., BE NED Eng., MA Sindh,
PhD Leeds   Prof.

Engineering, Electronics

Tel: (022) 277 1334
Abro, Farzana R., BE NED Eng., ME Mehran
Asst. Prof.
Ahmed, Yousfani N., BE Mehran, ME Mehran
Asst. Prof. (on lien)
Ansari, Abdul S., BE NED Eng.   Asst. Prof.
Baloch, A. K., BE Sindh, MPhil S'ton., PhD Brad.
Prof.
Chowdhry, B. S., BE Mehran, PhD S'ton.   Prof.;
Chairman*
Dayo, Khalil-ur-Rehman, BE Mehran, ME Mehran,
PhD Mehran   Asst. Prof.
Khowaja, Mehboob, BE Mehran, ME Mehran
Asst. Prof.
Memon, Farida, BE Mehran, ME Mehran   Asst.
Prof.
Palijo, Tania, BE Mehran, ME Mehran   Asst. Prof.
Waseer, Tufail A., BE Mehran, ME Mehran   Asst.
Prof.

Engineering, Industrial

Tel: (022) 277 1247
Abbasi, Aitbar A., BE Mehran   Assoc. Prof.
Abbasi, Siraj A., BE Mehran   Asst. Prof.
Korai, Mukhtiar A., BE Mehran   Asst. Prof.
Lakhair, A. Qayoom, BE Mehran   Asst. Prof.
Maree, H. B., BE Mehran, PhD Brun.   Prof.;
Chairman*
Nebhwani, M., BE Mehran, ME Mehran   Assoc.
Prof.
Shah, Aijaz A., LLB Sindh, MA Sindh   Asst. Prof.
Shah, Rashdi Pir R., BE Mehran, MSc Nott., PhD
Nott.   Prof.
Shaikh, Ghulam Y., BE Mehran, ME Mehran, MBA
Sindh   Asst. Prof.
Sohag, R. A., BE Sindh, PhD Acad.Romania   Prof.
Tanwari, A., BE Mehran, PhD Brad.   Prof.

Engineering, Mechanical

Tel: (022) 277 1275
Abbasi, A. F., BE Mehran, ME Mehran   Asst.
Prof.

Brohi, K. M., BE Mehran, MA Sindh, PhD Nagoya
Assoc. Prof.
Durani, H. A., BE Mehran   Assoc. Prof.
Jamali, M. Sharif, BE Mehran   Asst. Prof.
Khowaja, J. H., BE Mehran   Assoc. Prof.
Khowaja, Nadir A., BE Mehran   Assoc. Prof.
Memon, Abdul S., BE Mehran, ME Mehran   Asst.
Prof.
Memon, Ashfaque A., BE Sindh, MPhil Mehran
Assoc. Prof.
Memon, Mujeebuddin, BE Mehran, DPhil Sus.
Prof.
Memon, Mushtaque A., ME Hiroshima   Prof.
Memon, Shoukat A., BE Mehran, ME Mehran
Asst. Prof.
Mughal, Ghulam Y., BE Mehran   Asst. Prof.
Nizamani, R. A., BE Mehran   Assoc. Prof.
Panhwar, M. Ibrahim, BE Sindh, PhD Sheff.
Prof.
Qaimkhani, M. Atif, BE Mehran, ME Mehran
Asst. Prof.
Sangi, Muhammad J., BE Mehran   Asst. Prof.
Shaikh, Nazimuddin, BE Sindh, MEng Sheff.
Prof.; Chairman*

Engineering, Metallurgy and Materials

Tel: (022) 277 1425
Abro, M. Ishaque A., BE Mehran, ME Mehran
Asst. Prof.
Ansari, Baqar A., BE Mehran, ME Mehran   Asst.
Prof.
Essani, Ashfaque A., BE Mehran, ME Mehran
Asst. Prof.
Jokhio, M. H., BE NED Eng., ME Mehran   Assoc.
Prof.
Mallah, Abdul H., BE Mehran, PhD Sheff.   Prof.;
Chairman*
Memon, Ali N., BE Mehran   Asst. Prof.
Memon, Riaz A., BE Mehran   Asst. Prof.
Memon, Sikandar A., BE Mehran   Asst. Prof.
Memon, Sultan A., BE Mehran   Asst. Prof.

Engineering, Mining

Tel: (022) 277 1327 Fax: (022) 277 1327
Halepota, G. R., BE Sindh, MPhil Nott.   Prof.
Memon, Ahsan A., BE Mehran   Asst. Prof.
Memon, Saeed A., BE Mehran   Asst. Prof.
Pathan, A. G., BE Mehran, PhD Nott.   Prof.
Pathan, Pervez A., MSc Sindh   Assoc. Prof.
Rind, Muhammad H., BE Mehran   Asst. Prof.
Shah, Mohammad A., BEng Nott., LLB Nott.,
PhD Nott.   Prof.; Chairman*
Sherazi, M. A., BE Mehran   Asst. Prof.
Yakoob, Behan M., BE Mehran   Asst. Prof.

Engineering, Telecommunication

Tel: (022) 277 2277
Khanzada, Tariq J., BE Mehran, ME Mehran
Asst. Prof. (on leave)
Memon, Aftab A., BE Mehran, ME Louisiana State,
PhD   Prof.; Chairman*
Shah, Asif A., BE Mehran, ME Mehran   Asst.
Prof. (on leave)
Shah, Wajiha, BE Mehran, ME Mehran   Asst.
Prof. (on leave)
Shaikh, Faisal K., BE Mehran, ME Mehran   Asst.
Prof. (on leave)
Umrani, Abdul W., BE Mehran, ME NU Singapore,
PhD NU Singapore   Assoc. Prof.
Ursani, Ahsan A., BE Mehran, ME Mehran
Asst. Prof. (on leave)
Zaki, Nafeesa, BE Mehran, ME Mehran   Asst.
Prof. (on leave)

Engineering, Textile

Tel: (022) 277 1565
Arain, Farooq A., BE Mehran   Asst. Prof.
Khiani, Raj K., BSc Lahore UET   Asst. Prof.;
Incharge Chairman*
Rafique, Jathial M., BE Mehran, PhD Manc.
Prof.
Samo, Abdul R., MSc Sindh, MSc Leeds   Visiting
Prof.
Soomro, Noorullah, BE NED Eng. (on leave)

Petroleum and Natural Gas Engineering, Institute of

Tel: (022) 277 1241 Fax: (022) 277 2453
Arbani, S. A., BE Mehran, MSc U.S.S.R.Acad.Sc.
Prof.; Director*
Baladi, Shahzad A., BE Mehran   Asst. Prof.
Memon, H. R., BEng Leeds, PhD Leeds   Prof.
Memon, M. Khan, BE Mehran   Asst. Prof.
Qazi, Rafique A., BEng Salf., PhD Salf.   Prof.
(on lien)
Sahito, M. H., BE Mehran   Asst. Prof.
Samoon, A. D., BE Mehran   Asst. Prof.
Soomro, Zulekha, MSc Sindh   Assoc. Prof.
Tunio, Abdul H., BE Mehran, ME Mehran   Asst.
Prof.

SPECIAL CENTRES, ETC

English Language Development Centre

Tel: (022) 277 1286
Bodlo, Muhammed H., MA Sindh, MA Edin.
Prof.; Dir.*
Chandio, Tasneem S., MA Sindh   Asst. Prof.
(on leave)
Pathan, Rosy I., MA Sindh, MEd Leeds   Asst.
Prof.

Environmental Engineering and Management, Institute of

Tel: (022) 277 1182
Ansari, A. K., BE Sindh, MSc Wales, PhD Wales
Prof.
Memon, A. Rasheed, BE NED Eng., ME Brun.
Dir.*

Information and Communication Technologies, Institute of

Tel: (022) 277 1558
Baloch, A. K., BE Sindh, MPhil S'ton., PhD Brad.
Prof.; Dir.*
Chowdhry, B. S., BE Mehran, PhD S'ton.   Prof.;
Co-Dir.
Hafiz, Tahseen H., BE Mehran, ME Mehran
Assoc. Prof.
Hashmani, Manzoor A., BE Mehran, ME PhD
Foreign Prof.
Khanzada, Tariq J., BE Mehran, ME Mehran
Asst. Prof. (on leave)
Memon, Aftab A., BE Mehran, ME Louisiana State,
PhD   Prof.
Shah, Asif A., BE Mehran, ME Mehran   Asst.
Prof. (on leave)
Shah, Wajiha, BE Mehran, ME Mehran   Asst.
Prof. (on leave)
Shaikh, Faisal K., BE Mehran, ME Mehran   Asst.
Prof. (on leave)
Shaikh, Muhammad Z., BE Mehran, ME Mehran
Assoc. Prof.
Thebo, L. A., BE Mehran, ME Mehran   Asst. Prof.
Umrani, Abdul W., BE Mehran, ME NU Singapore,
PhD NU Singapore   Assoc. Prof.
Uqaili, Mohammad A., BE NED Eng., MA Sindh,
PhD Leeds   Prof.
Ursani, Ahsan A., BE Mehran, ME Mehran   Asst.
Prof. (on leave)
Zaki, Nafeesa, BE Mehran, ME Mehran   Asst.
Prof. (on leave)

Irrigation and Drainage Engineering, Institute of

Tel: (022) 277 1226
Babar, M. M., BE Nanjing, ME Mehran, PhD Kyoto
Prof.
Kori, Shafi M., BE Mehran, ME Mehran   Assoc.
Prof.
Lashari, B. K., BE(Agri) Sindh Ag., ME Mehran,
PhD Cracow Agric.   Prof.; Dir.*
Memon, H. M., BE NED Eng., PhD Lond.   Emer.
Prof.
Qureshi, A. L., BE Mehran, ME Mehran, PhD
Mehran   Assoc. Prof.
Shaikh, A. Hadi, BE NED Eng., PhD   Eminent
Scholar and Prof.

Science and Technology Development, Institute of

Tel: (022) 277 2430 Fax: (022) 277 2433

Chowdhry, B. S., BE Mehran, PhD S'ton.   Prof.
Khaskhely, G. Hussain, MA Sindh, MSc Glas.   Visiting Prof.
Larik, Noor M., PhD S'ton.   Visiting Prof.
Memon, Hafeezur R., BE NED Eng., PhD Leeds   Prof.
Panhwar, M. Ibrahim, BE Sindh, PhD Sheff.   Prof.
Qureshi, S. M., BE NED Eng., ME Asian I.T., Bangkok, PhD Sheff.   Prof. Emer.; Hon. Dir.*
Shah, Rashdi Pir R., BE Mehran, MSc Nott., PhD Nott.   Prof.; Co-Dir.
Uqaili, Mohammad A., BE NED Eng., MA Sindh, PhD Leeds   Prof.
Other Staff: 5 Teaching Res. Assocs.

CONTACT OFFICERS

Academic affairs. Dean, Engineering: Rajput, Prof. Abdul Q. K., BE Sindh, MSc Leeds, PhD Pitt. (E-mail: aqkrajput@hotmail.com)
Accommodation. Provost, Hotels: Sehrai, Prof. Mujeebuddin, BE Mehran, PhD Sus.
Admissions (higher degree). (Please contact the Director of the Special Centre concerned.)
Computing services. Computing Services Director Incharge: Pathan, Abdul J., MSc Sindh
Consultancy services. Consultancy Services Officer: (vacant)
Development/fund-raising. Director, Finance (fund raising): Shaikh, Muneer A., BE Mehran, MBA Sindh, MA Sindh

Development/fund-raising. Director, Planning and Development: Kazi, Abdul Razak, BA Sindh, MA Sindh
Distance education. Registrar: Uqaili, Prof. Mohammad A., BE NED Eng., MA Sindh, PhD Leeds
Estates and buildings/works and services. Project Director: Kandhir, Ghulam S., BE Sindh, ME Lough.
Examinations. Controller of Examinations: Rajput, Abdul A., BE Sindh, LLB Sindh
Finance. Director, Finance: Shaikh, Muneer A., BE Mehran, MBA Sindh, MA Sindh
General enquiries. Registrar: Uqaili, Prof. Mohammad A., BE NED Eng., MA Sindh, PhD Leeds
Health services. Registrar: Uqaili, Prof. Mohammad A., BE NED Eng., MA Sindh, PhD Leeds
Industrial liaison. Director (Industrial liaison): Baloch, Prof. Abdul K., BE Sindh, MPhil S'ton., PhD S'ton. (E-mail: ak_baloch@yahoo.com)
International office. Registrar: Uqaili, Prof. Mohammad A., BE NED Eng., MA Sindh, PhD Leeds
Library (enquiries). Library Enquiries Officer: Munshey, Mumtaz I., MA Sindh, MSc Hawaii (E-mail: lmuetj@hyd.paknet.com.pk)
Marketing. Assistant Registrar (Public Relations): Baloch, Mushtaque A., MA Sindh
Public relations. Assistant Registrar (Public Relations): Baloch, Mushtaque A., MA Sindh
Publications. Division (Incharge): Rajput, Prof. Abdul Q. K., BE Sindh, MSc Leeds, PhD Pitt. (E-mail: aqkrajput@hotmail.com)
Purchasing. Director, Finance: Shaikh, Muneer A., BE Mehran, MBA Sindh, MA Sindh

Research. Incharge (Research): Rajput, Prof. Abdul Q. K., BE Sindh, MSc Leeds, PhD Pitt. (E-mail: aqkrajput@hotmail.com)
Safety. Registrar: Uqaili, Prof. Mohammad A., BE NED Eng., MA Sindh, PhD Leeds
Sport and recreation. Director (Sport and recreation): Channa, Najeeb-ur-Rehman, BE Mehran
Staff development and training. Director, Planning and Development: Kazi, Abdul Razak, BA Sindh, MA Sindh
Student welfare/counselling. Director, Student Affairs: Memon, Atta-ur-Rehman, MA Sindh, LLB Sindh (E-mail: atta_pirson@hotmail.com)
Students from other countries. Director, Student Affairs: Memon, Atta-ur-Rehman, MA Sindh, LLB Sindh (E-mail: atta_pirson@hotmail.com)
Students with disabilities. Director, Student Affairs: Memon, Atta-ur-Rehman, MA Sindh, LLB Sindh (E-mail: atta_pirson@hotmail.com)

AFFILIATED COLLEGES

[Institutions listed by location below provide courses leading to degrees, etc. of the university]

Hyderabad. Agha Taj Muhammad Institute of Information Technology; Government College of Technology; Hyderabad Institute of Arts, Science and Technology
Karachi. Dawood College of Engineering and Technology

[Information supplied by the institution as at 10 November 2007, and edited by the ACU]

MOHAMMAD ALI JINNAH UNIVERSITY

Founded 1998

Member of the Association of Commonwealth Universities

Postal Address: Islamabad Campus, Jinnah Avenue, Blue Area, Islamabad 44000, Pakistan
Telephone: (051) 111 878787 **Fax:** (051) 282 2743 **E-mail:** info@jinnah.edu.pk
URL: http://www.jinnah.edu.pk

EXECUTIVE VICE-PRESIDENT*—Ahmed, Muhammad M., MSc Quaid-i-Azam, MPhil Punjab, PhD Camb., FIEE
REGISTRAR‡—Kashif, Jahangir, BBA Central Arkansas

GENERAL INFORMATION

First Degrees. BS.
Length of course. Full-time: BS: 4 years. Part-time: BS: 7 years.

Higher Degrees.
Master's. MS.
Length of course. Full-time: MS: $1\frac{1}{2}$–2 years. Part-time: MS: 4 years.
Doctoral. PhD.
Length of course. Full-time: PhD: 3 years. Part-time: PhD: 6 years.

Statistics. Students (2008): undergraduate 1499 (1499 men; master's 375 (375 men); doctoral 35 (35 men).

FACULTIES/SCHOOLS
Engineering and Applied Sciences

Dean: Qadar, Prof. Muhammad A., MSc Quaid-i-Azam, PhD Sur.

Management and Social Sciences

Dean: Butt, Prof. Safdar A., MCom Karachi, PhD

ACADEMIC UNITS
Computer Sciences and Bioinformatics

Dar, Nayyer M., MSc Quaid-i-Azam, PhD Brad.   Assoc. Prof.; Head*

Electronic Engineering

Fazal ur Rehman, Prof., MEng McG., PhD McG.   Prof.; Head*

Management Sciences

Rajput, Ansir A., BS N.Y.State, MBA Babson   Assoc. Prof.

Social Sciences

Akbar, Ayesha, MPhil A.Iqbal Open, PhD A.Iqbal Open   Assoc. Prof.; Head*

N. E. D. UNIVERSITY OF ENGINEERING AND TECHNOLOGY

Founded 1977

Member of the Association of Commonwealth Universities

Postal Address: Karachi 75270, Pakistan
Telephone: (021) 926 1261-8 **Fax:** (021) 926 1255 **E-mail:** registrar@neduet.edu.pk
URL: http://www.neduet.edu.pk

VICE-CHANCELLOR*—Kalam, Abul, BSc *Madr.*, MA *Madr.*, FIEE, FIMechE, FCILT
PRO-VICE-CHANCELLOR—Haque, Prof. Shamsul, BSc *Karachi*, MSc *Karachi*, MPhil
    Karachi, PhD *Aberd.*
REGISTRAR‡—Khan, J. Aziz, BE(Civil) NED *Eng.*, MEngg *Asian I.T., Bangkok*
DIRECTOR OF FINANCE—Sajeeruddin, Muhammad
RESIDENT AUDITOR—Quasim, Abul
CONTROLLER OF EXAMINATIONS—Ahmed, Afaq, BSc MSc
DIRECTOR, PLANNING AND PROJECTS—Khan, A. A., BE(Civil)
CONTROLLER OF SERVICES—Wasiuddin, S., BE(Civil) NED *Eng.*, MS NED *Eng.*
CHIEF LIBRARIAN—Mehar, Yasmin, BA *Karachi*, MLS *Karachi*, DLS *Karachi*

GENERAL INFORMATION

History. The university was established in 1977.
    It is situated about 12km east of Karachi.

Admission to first degree courses (see also Pakistan Introduction). Higher Secondary Certificate (HSC) of the Board of Intermediate Examination or equivalent qualification, such as USA 12th grade exam or General Certificate of Education (GCE) A levels in chemistry, mathematics and physics.

First Degrees (see also Pakistan Directory to Subjects of Study). BArch, BCST, BE.
    Length of course. Full-time: BCST, BE: 4 years; BArch: 5 years.

Higher Degrees (see also Pakistan Directory to Subjects of Study).
    Master's. MEngg, MSc(CompSc), MSc(UrbanPlanning).
    Admission. Applicants for admission to master's degrees must normally hold a BE from any recognised university.
    Length of course. Full-time: MSc(CompSc), MSc(UrbanPlanning): $1\frac{1}{2}$ years; MEngg: $2\frac{1}{2}$ years.
    Doctoral. PhD.

Libraries. Volumes: 94,500. Periodicals subscribed to: 225.

FACULTIES/SCHOOLS

Engineering, Civil and Architecture
E-mail: deancea@neduet.edu.pk
Dean: Rafeeqi, Prof. S. F. A., BE(Civil) *King Fahd*, MS *King Fahd*, PhD *H-W*
Secretary: Ismail, M.

Engineering, Electrical and Computer
E-mail: deanece@neduet.edu.pk
Dean: Mirza, Prof. Shahid H., BE(EE) *Oklahoma*, MS(EE) *Oklahoma*, PhD *Birm.*
Secretary: Waseem

Engineering, Mechanical and Manufacturing
E-mail: deanmme@neduet.edu.pk
Dean: Qureshi, Prof. N., BSc *Karachi*, BE(Mech) NED *Eng.*, MS *Detroit*, PhD *Detroit*
Secretary: Hameed, A. M.

Science, Technology and Humanities
E-mail: deansth@neduet.edu.pk
Dean: Pathan, Prof. M. K., LLB MSc MA PhD
Secretary: Ahmed, Saeed

ACADEMIC UNITS

Architecture and Planning
Tel: (021) 921 3058
    E-mail: coccd@neduet.edu.pk

Ahmed, N., BArch *Harv.*, MCP *Middle East Tech.*, PhD *Lough.*   Prof.; Chairman*
Hasan, Salman M., BArch *Lahore*   Asst. Prof.
Mumtaz, S. N., BArch MUD   Asst. Prof.
Naeem, Anila, MS *Middle East Tech.*, BArch   Assoc. Prof.
Ravi, R. K., BArch MUD   Asst. Prof.
Sadiq, Asiya, BArch *Leuven*, MArch *Leuven*   Assoc. Prof.
Sheikh, F. B., BArch *Mehran*, MSc(UrbanPlanning) NED *Eng.*   Asst. Prof.
Ubaid, F. A., BArch *Middle East Tech.*, MCPUD *Middle East Tech.*   Assoc. Prof.
Other Staff: 3 Lectrs.
Research: alternative arrangements for water supply in urban areas

Computer Sciences and Information Technology
E-mail: chaircsit@neduet.edu.pk
Ahmed, Z. N., MCS *Karachi*   Asst. Prof.
Haque, S. I., BSc *Manc.*, MPhil *Manc.*   Asst. Prof.
Khan, Jawaid A., BSc *Karachi*, MSc(Maths) *Karachi*, MSc NED *Eng.*   Assoc. Prof.
Khan, M. M., MSc NED *Eng.*, MCIT NED *Eng.*   Assoc. Prof.
Khan, N. A., MSc(CompSc) NED *Eng.*, MSc *Karachi*   Asst. Prof.
Khan, S. N., MSc *Karachi*, MPhil *Quaid-i-Azam*, DPhil *Sus.*   Prof.; Chairperson*
Nizami, S. T., BSc NED *Eng.*, MSc(CompSc) NED *Eng.*   Assoc. Prof.
Sattar, S. A., BE(Mech) NED *Eng.*, MSc(CompSc) NED *Eng.*, MCS NED *Eng.*   Asst. Prof.
Usmani, M., BE NED *Eng.*, MSc(CompSc) NED *Eng.*, PhD NED *Eng.*   Assoc. Prof.
Other Staff: 4 Lectrs.; 1 Res. Fellow
Research: formalisation of software development process

Engineering, Automative and Marine
Tamimi, A. A., BE(Mech) MS   Assoc. Prof.
Tufail, M., BE(Mech) MSc PhD   Prof.; Chairman*
Zafar, Amber F., BE(Mech) NED *Eng.*, MS(Mech) NUST(P'stan.)   Asst. Prof.
Other Staff: 3 Lectrs.

Engineering, Biomedical
E-mail: mukhtar@neduet.edu.pk
Ahmed, M., BSc BE(Mech) MS   Assoc. Prof.; Acting Chairman*
Bari, A. Z., BE(Mech) ME   Asst. Prof.
Maheshwari, H. K., BE(Electronics) *Mehran*, MS NU *Singapore*   Asst. Prof.
Master, N., BS BSc MS   Assoc. Prof.; Co-Chairperson
Yasmin, F., PhD *Karachi*   Assoc. Prof., Biochemistry
Other Staff: 8 Lectrs.

Engineering, Civil
E-mail: civilchr@neduet.edu.pk
Adnan, M., BE(Civil) NED *Eng.*, MEngg(Civil) NED *Eng.*   Asst. Prof. (on leave)
Ahsan, P. F., BSc(Engg) *Alig.*, MSc *Leeds*   Prof. Emer.
Ali, M. S., BE(Civil) NED *Eng.*, MS *Oklahoma*, PhD *Birm.*   Prof.
Ali, W., BE(Civil) NED *Eng.*, MEngg(Civil) NED *Eng.*   Asst. Prof.
Batool, F., BE(Civil) NED *Eng.*, MEngg(Civil) NED *Eng.*   Asst. Prof.
Bukhary, S., BE(Civil) NED *Eng.*, MEngg(Civil) NED *Eng.*   Asst. Prof.
Farooqi, Aftab A., BE(Civil) NED *Eng.*, MEngg(Civil) NED *Eng.*   Assoc. Prof.
Farooqui, R. H., BE(Civil) NED *Eng.*, MS NU *Singapore*   Asst. Prof. (on leave)
Jafri, S. M. K., BE(Civil) NED *Eng.*, MSc NED *Eng.*   Asst. Prof.
Khalid, H., BE(Civil) NED *Eng.*, MSc NED *Eng.*   Asst. Prof.
Khan, A. M., BSc *Seoul*, MSc *Seoul*, PhD *Seoul*   Assoc. Prof.
Khan, R. A., BE(Civil) NED *Eng.*, MSc(Civil) NED *Eng.*   Asst. Prof. (on leave)
Khan, S. A., BE(Civil) MS(Civil)   Prof.
Kumar, M., BE(Civil) NED *Eng.*, ME(Civil) NED *Eng.*   Asst. Prof. (on leave)
Lodi, S. H., BE(Civil) NED *Eng.*, MS *Oregon*, PhD *H-W*   Prof.; Chairman*
Marri, A., BE(Civil) *Quaid-e-Awam UEST*, MEngg *Asian I.T., Bangkok*   Asst. Prof. (on leave)
Masood, A., BE(Civil) NED *Eng.*, MEngg(Env) NED *Eng.*   Asst. Prof.
Memon, A. Q., BE(Civil) NED *Eng.*, ME *Asian I.T., Bangkok*   Asst. Prof. (on leave)
Mirza, M. T., BE(Civil) NED *Eng.*, MSc(Civil) NED *Eng.*   Assoc. Prof.
Mooben, S. S., BE(Civil) NED *Eng.*, MSc *Alta.*   Asst. Prof.
Qadeer, A., BE(Civil) *Asian I.T., Bangkok*, MEngg *Asian I.T., Bangkok*   Asst. Prof. (on leave)
Qadir, A., BE(Civil) NED *Eng.*, MSc(Civil) NED *Eng.*   Assoc. Prof. (on leave)
Qasim, S., BE(Civil) NED *Eng.*, MEngg(Civil) NED *Eng.*   Asst. Prof.
Rafi, M. M., BE(Civil) NED *Eng.*, MSc(Civil) NED *Eng.*   Asst. Prof. (on leave)
Rehman, A., BE(Civil) NED *Eng.*, MS *King Fahd*, PhD *King Fahd*   Prof.
Saleem, F., BE(Civil) NED *Eng.*, MSc *Karachi*   Asst. Prof. (on leave)
Sangi, A. J., BE(Civil) NED *Eng.*, MEngg(Civil) NED *Eng.*   Asst. Prof.
Siddiqui, S. H., BE(Civil) NED *Eng.*, MSc(Civil) NED *Eng.*   Asst. Prof.
Other Staff: 11 Lectrs.; 1 Sr. Res. Fellow

Engineering, Computer and Information Systems
E-mail: chaircsd@neduet.edu.pk
Ali, A., BE(CompSys) NED *Eng.*, MEngg(CompSys) NED *Eng.*   Asst. Prof.

Ali, S. A., BE(CompSys) NED Eng., MEng Asst. Prof.

Ali, S. M. U., BE(Electr) MS Asst. Prof.

Haider, S. A., BSEE MEngg(CompSys) Asst. Prof.

Ilyas, M. Saqib, BE(CompSys) MS(EE) Asst. Prof. (on leave)

Inayat, Q. A., BE(CompSys) NED Eng., MEngg(CompSys) NED Eng. Asst. Prof. (on leave)

Khan, M. A. A., BE(CompSys) MSc(CompSc) Asst. Prof. (on leave)

Khurram, M., BE(CompSys) MEngg(CompSys) Asst. Prof.

Mirza, Shahid H., BE(EE) Oklahoma, MS(EE) Oklahoma, PhD Birm. Prof.

Noor, H., BE(CompSys) NED Eng., MS NED Eng. Asst. Prof.

Qasim, S. Z., BE(CompSys) MBA Asst. Prof.

Siddiqui, A. A., MSEE Penn.State, BE(Elect) Prof.; Chairman*

Tahzeeb, Shahab, BE(CompSys) MEngg(CompSys) Asst. Prof.

Other Staff: 19 Lectrs.

Engineering, Electrical

E-mail: ced@neduet.edu.pk

Ahmed, I., BE(Elect) NED Eng., MEngg NED Eng. Asst. Prof.

Ahmed, N., BE(Elec) MEngg Asst. Prof.

Ahmed, S., MSc(ElecEng) Chalmers U.T. Asst. Prof.

Altaf, T., BSc(Engg) Alig., MSc(Engg) Alig., PhD Brad. Prof.; Chairman*

Ansari, I. A., MSc(EE) NED Eng., BE(Elect) Asst. Prof.

Aslam, M. I., BE(Elect) MEngg Asst. Prof.

Athar, S., BE(Elect) MEngg Asst. Prof.

Khawaja, Attaullah, MSc(EE) NED Eng., BE(Elect) Asst. Prof. (on leave)

Larik, R. M., BE(Elect) MEngg Asst. Prof.

Memon, M. A., BE(Elect) MEngg Asst. Prof.

Nadyme, M., BS(Elect) Middle East Tech., MS(Elect) Middle East Tech. Assoc. Prof.

Qadir, A., BE(Elec) NED Eng., MSc(EE) NED Eng., PhD NED Eng. Prof.

Qazi, S. A., MSc Lanc., BE(Elect) PhD Asst. Prof.

Qureshi, M. I. A., BE(Elect) MEngg Assoc. Prof.

Shoaib, S., BE(Elect) NED Eng., MEngg(EE) NED Eng. Asst. Prof.

Sultan, U., BE(Elect) MEngg Asst. Prof.

Tabassum, S., MEngg NED Eng., BE(Elect) Asst. Prof.

Zeb, A., BE(Elect) MEngg Asst. Prof.

Other Staff: 19 Lectrs.

Research: realisation and study of current mode filters and oscillators for integrated circuit implementation

Engineering, Electronic

E-mail: cld@neduet.edu.pk

Bakhsh, Ghous, BE(Electronics) NED Eng., MEngg(Elec) NED Eng. Asst. Prof.

Faraz, S., BE(Elect) NED Eng., MEngg(Elec) NED Eng. Asst. Prof.

Hussain, S. I., BE(Elect) NED Eng., MSc Asst. Prof. (on leave)

Javed, M., BE(Elect) NED Eng., MSc(Elect) NED Eng. Asst. Prof.

Khambaty, A. M., MSCIS New Jersey I.T., BE(Electronics) Asst. Prof.

Nauman, Mohammad, BE(Elect) NED Eng., MS(EE) N.Carolina State Assoc. Prof.

Qadir, A., BE(Elect) NED Eng., MSc(EE) NED Eng., PhD NED Eng. Prof.; Chairman*

Raza, Hashim, BE(Elect) MSc(CommEng) Asst. Prof.

Razi, A., BE(Elect) MSc(CommEng) Asst. Prof.

Siddiqi, Shahzad, BE(Elect) NED Eng., MEngg(Comm) NED Eng. Asst. Prof.

Other Staff: 9 Lectrs.

Engineering, Environmental

E-mail: chenv@neduet.edu.pk

Ali, M., BE(Mech) NED Eng., MEngg NED Eng. Asst. Prof.

Chakrabarti, H. M., BEngg Lond., MEngg Lond., PhD Manc. Asst. Prof.

Ejaz, M. S., BE(Civil) NED Eng., MSc(Civil) NED Eng., PhD Utah State Prof.; Chairman*

Ibrahim, F., BE(Civil) MEngg

Iqbal, S. M., BE(Civil) NED Eng., MS Cinc. Assoc. Prof. (on deputation)

Mehdi, M. R., BE(Civil) NED Eng., PhD Karachi, MS Assoc. Prof. (on deputation)

Mustafa, A., BE(Civil) NED Eng., MEngg NED Eng. Asst. Prof. (on leave)

Siddiqui, Z., BE(Civil) Asian I.T., Bangkok, MEngg Asian I.T., Bangkok Asst. Prof. (on leave)

Engineering, Industrial and Manufacturing

E-mail: cid@neduet.edu.pk

Hasan, S. M., BE MS

Iqbal, S. A., BE(Mech) NED Eng., MEngg NED Eng. Assoc. Prof. (on leave)

Irfan, Syed M., BE(Civil) NED Eng., MEngg NED Eng. Assoc. Prof.

Islam, S. H., BE(Mech) MEngg Asst. Prof. (on leave)

Jafri, A. R., BE(Mech) NED Eng., MEngg Asst. Prof. (on leave)

Khan, M. A., BE(Mech) MEngg Asst. Prof.

Qureshi, N. U., BSc BE(Mech) MS PhD Prof.

Riza, Syed H., BE(Mech) NED Eng. Assoc. Prof.

Shoaib, M., BE(Mech) NED Eng., MEngg Asst. Prof.

Siddiqui, M. Ali, BE NED Eng., MSc Wayne State Asst. Prof. (on leave)

Tufail, M., BA Karachi, BE(Mech) NED Eng., MSc Nott., PhD Nott. Prof.; Chairman*

Zaheer, A., BE(Mech) MS

Zulqarnain, A., BE(Mech) NED Eng., MEngg Asst. Prof.

Other Staff: 7 Lectrs.

Research: computer aided design for manufacturing systems for machined components; design of remote controlled navigation system for mobile robots; mechanical properties of braided commingled glass/polypropene composites

Engineering, Mechanical

E-mail: cmed@neduet.edu.pk

Ahmed, Aftab, BE(Mech) NED Eng. Assoc. Prof.

Akhlaque, M., BSc Karachi, BE(Mech) NED Eng., MSc(Env) NED Eng. Asst. Prof. (on deputation)

Ansari, M. N., BE(Mech) NED Eng., MSc(Nuclear) Islam. Assoc. Prof.

Azeem, S. M. Rizwan, BE(Mech) NED Eng., MSc Oxf. Assoc. Prof.

Hasani, S. M. Fakhir, BE(Mech) NED Eng., MS King Fahd, PhD Akron Prof.; Chairman*

Hashmi, S. Mushahid Hussain, BE(Mech) NED Eng., MSc NED Eng. Asst. Prof. (on leave)

Khalid, A., BE NED Eng., MSc Glas. Assoc. Prof.

Khan, J. A., BE Prof. Emer.

Khan, Khalil Ahmad, BSc(Engg) Alig., MS Case W.Reserve, PhD Maryland Prof.

Mahmood, Khursheed, MSc Cran., PhD Cran., BE(Mech) Prof.

Mahmood, M., BE NED Eng., MSc Beds., PhD Beds. Prof.

Mustafa, Ibrahim, BE(Chemical) Wash.(Mo.), MEng Wash.(Mo.), DSc(Chemical) Wash.(Mo.) Assoc. Prof.

Naseemuddin, BE(Mech) NED Eng., MEngg NED Eng. Asst. Prof. (on leave)

Pasha, M. Kamal, BE(Mech) NED Eng., MSc NED Eng. Asst. Prof.

Shakaib, M., BE(Mech) NED Eng., MSc(Mech) NED Eng. Asst. Prof.

Sultan, M. Sarwar, BE(Mech) NED Eng., MS Asst. Prof.

Engineering, Petroleum

Haneef, Javed, BE(Mech) NED Eng., MSc Karachi, MCS Karachi Asst. Prof.

Khan, Afzal A., BSc Karachi, MSc Karachi Asst. Prof.

Lodi, S. H., BE(Civil) NED Eng., MS Oregon, PhD H-W Prof.; Acting Chairman*

Siddqi, S. H.

Other Staff: 3 Lectrs.

Engineering, Textile

E-mail: ctd@neduet.edu.pk

Ahmed, Fariduddin, BSc MSc Asst. Prof.

Farooq, Salma, BSc Lahore UET Asst. Prof.

Hashmi, Syed Badar, BSc Assoc. Prof. (on leave)

Hussain, Deedar, BSc Asst. Prof.

Mehmood, M., BE NED Eng., MSc Beds., PhD Beds. Prof.

Pasha, Khalid, BSc Manc., MSc Manc., PhD Manc. Assoc. Prof.; Chairman*

Qureshi, N. U., BSc BE(Mech) MS PhD Prof.

Siddique, B. Z. Asst. Prof.

Siddique, S. Hussain, BE Mehran, MSc Asst. Prof.

Other Staff: 6 Lectrs.

Research: effects of cationisation of cotton fabric on colour fastness properties of pigment prints; textile pigment printing

Humanities and Management

E-mail: chd@neduet.edu.pk

Ahsan, Nasreen M., BA Dacca, MA Dacca, MEd Leeds Assoc. Prof. (on leave)

Azhar, Afifa Z., MA Karachi, MSc A.Iqbal Open Assoc. Prof.

Ghous, Muhammad Ali, MA Karachi Asst. Prof.

Hasan, Farooq, PhD Karachi Asst. Prof.

Jalil, Sima Z., MA Karachi Assoc. Prof.

Khadija, Tahira, MA Karachi Asst. Prof.

Khan, Raza A., MA MPhil Assoc. Prof.

Shaikh, Muhammad Ali, LLB Karachi, BE(Mech) MBA Prof.; Chairman*

Shakoor, Farzana, MA Karachi, MPhil Karachi Asst. Prof.

Usmani, S. F., LLB Karachi, MA Karachi Assoc. Prof.

Zaki, Sajida, MA PhD Assoc. Prof.

Other Staff: 5 Lectrs.

Mathematics and Basic Sciences

E-mail: chms@neduet.edu.pk

Afridi, Musarrat U. K., MSc B.Zak., PhD Nihon Prof.

Baig, M. M., MSc(CompSc) NED Eng., MSc(Maths) Karachi Asst. Prof.

Faryaz, U., MSc(Maths) Karachi, MSc(CompSc) NED Eng. Asst. Prof.

Fatemi, M., MSc Karachi Assoc. Prof.

Hussain, Athar, MSc Karachi Assoc. Prof.

Hussain, M., MSc(Maths) Islam., MSc(CompSc) NED Eng. Asst. Prof.

Khan, Muhammad Z., MSc Karachi, MPhil Karachi Asst. Prof.

Khan, Saghirun-Nisa, MSc MPhil PhD Prof.; Chairperson*

Nouman, S. M., MSc Karachi, MSc(CompSc) NED Eng. Asst. Prof.

Praveen, Shaista, MSc Karachi, PhD Karachi Asst. Prof.

Rafique, M., MSc Sindh, MPhil S'ton., BSc Assoc. Prof.

Shaheen, R., BSc MSc MPhil MEd Asst. Prof.

Siddiqi, J. A., MSc(Maths) Karachi Asst. Prof.

Other Staff: 5 Lectrs.

CONTACT OFFICERS

Academic affairs. Acting Registrar (Academic): Hassan, S. A., BA MA (E-mail: dracad@neduet.edu.pk)

Accommodation. Controller of Services: Wasi Uddin, S., BE(Civil) NED Eng., MEngg(Env) NED Eng. (E-mail: cos@neduet.edu.pk)

Admissions (first degree). Chairman, Admissions Committee: Mahmood, Prof. Muzzaffar, BE(Mech) Cran.IT, MSc Cran.IT, PhD Cran.IT (E-mail: deanengg@neduet.edu.pk)

Admissions (higher degree). (Contact the chairman of the relevant department) (E-mail: deanengg@neduet.edu.pk)

Archives. Director, Planning and Projects: Khan, A. A., BE(Civil)
(E-mail: pd@neduet.edu.pk)

Careers. Manager, Industrial Liaison: Ghafoor, F. H., BE(Mech) NED Eng.
(E-mail: dil@neduet.edu.pk)

Computing services. Managing Senior Executive: Yunus, M. E., BE Karachi, MSc Karachi

Consultancy services. Director, Planning and Projects: Khan, A. A., BE(Civil)
(E-mail: pd@neduet.edu.pk)

Credit transfer. (contact relevant Dean)
(E-mail: deancea@neduet.edu.pk)

Development/fund-raising. Director of Finance: Sajeeruddin, Muhammad
(E-mail: df@neduet.edu.pk)

Development/fund-raising. Director of Finance: Saeed, A., BCom MA(Econ)
(E-mail: df@neduet.edu.pk)

Estates and buildings/works and services. Controller of Services: Wasi Uddin, S., BE(Civil) NED Eng., MEngg(Env) NED Eng.
(E-mail: cos@neduet.edu.pk)

Examinations. Controller of Examinations: Ahmed, Afaq, BSc MSc
(E-mail: contexam@neduet.edu.pk)

Finance. Director of Finance: Sajeeruddin, Muhammad (E-mail: df@neduet.edu.pk)

Finance. Director of Finance: Saeed, A., BCom MA(Econ) (E-mail: df@neduet.edu.pk)

General enquiries. Registrar: Khan, J. Aziz, BE(Civil) NED Eng., MEngg Asian I.T., Bangkok
(E-mail: registrar@neduet.edu.pk)

Health services. Senior Medical Officer: Kamal, J., MB BS
(E-mail: smo@neduet.edu.pk)

Industrial liaison. Manager, Industrial Liaison: Ghafoor, F. H., BE(Mech) NED Eng.
(E-mail: dil@neduet.edu.pk)

Library (chief librarian). Chief Librarian: Mehar, Yasmin, BA Karachi, MLS Karachi, DLS Karachi (E-mail: libadmin@neduet.edu.pk)

Marketing. Manager, Industrial Liaison: Ghafoor, F. H., BE(Mech) NED Eng.
(E-mail: dil@neduet.edu.pk)

Ombudsman. Vice-Chancellor: Kalam, Abul, BSc Madr., MA Madr., FIEE, FIMechE, FCILT
(E-mail: vc@neduet.edu.pk)

Personnel/human resources. Deputy Registrar (Establishment): Larik, M. Aslam, BA LLB MA(PolSc) MA(Econ)
(E-mail: registrar@neduet.edu.pk)

Public relations. Personal Secretary to Vice-Chancellor: Haque, Shamsul, BA
(E-mail: vc@neduet.edu.pk)

Publications. Co-Editor, Editorial Board: Mahmood, Prof. Muzzaffar, BE(Mech) Cran.IT, MSc Cran.IT, PhD Cran.IT
(E-mail: deanmee@neduet.edu.pk)

Purchasing. Assistant Director Finance (Purchase): Imtiaz, Syed S., MBA East(Manila) (E-mail: df@neduet.edu.pk)

Safety. Controller of Services: Wasi Uddin, S., BE(Civil) NED Eng., MEngg(Env) NED Eng.
(E-mail: cos@neduet.edu.pk)

Scholarships, awards, loans. Assistant Registrar (Co-ordination Section): Bhutto, M. A., BE(Civil) MA
(E-mail: registrar@neduet.edu.pk)

Schools liaison. Registrar: Khan, J. Aziz, BE(Civil) NED Eng., MEngg Asian I.T., Bangkok
(E-mail: registrar@neduet.edu.pk)

Security. Assistant Registrar (Security and General): Akhtar, J., BA Karachi
(E-mail: registrar@neduet.edu.pk)

Sport and recreation. Acting Manager, Physical Education: Latif, A., BA Karachi, MSc Karachi
(E-mail: deanstud@neduet.edu.pk)

Staff development and training. Registrar: Khan, J. Aziz, BE(Civil) NED Eng., MEngg Asian I.T., Bangkok
(E-mail: registrar@neduet.edu.pk)

Student welfare/counselling. Controller, Student Affairs: Usmani Suhail, Fazil, LLB Karachi, MA (E-mail: csa@neduet.edu.pk)

Students from other countries. Registrar: Khan, J. Aziz, BE(Civil) NED Eng., MEngg Asian I.T., Bangkok
(E-mail: registrar@neduet.edu.pk)

Students with disabilities. Senior Medical Officer: Kamal, J., MB BS
(E-mail: smo@neduet.edu.pk)

AFFILIATED COLLEGES

[Institutions listed by location below provide courses leading to degrees, etc. of the university]

Karachi. Institute of Aviation Technology; Institute of Industrial Electronic Engineering; KANUPP Institute of Nuclear Power Engineering

[Information supplied by the institution as at 23 August 2007, and edited by the ACU]

NATIONAL UNIVERSITY OF MODERN LANGUAGES

Postal Address: Sector H-9, Islamabad, Pakistan
Telephone: (051) 925 7638 **Fax:** (051) 445042
URL: http://www.numl.edu.pk/

RECTOR*—Khan, Brig. Aziz A.
REGISTRAR‡—Ahmed, Syed J.

NATIONAL UNIVERSITY OF SCIENCES AND TECHNOLOGY

Founded 1991

Member of the Association of Commonwealth Universities

Postal Address: Tamiz-ud-Din Road, PO Box 297, Rawalpindi Cantonment 46000, Pakistan
Telephone: (051) 923 7415 **Fax:** (051) 927 1577 **E-mail:** dqa@nust.edu.pk
URL: http://www.nust.edu.pk

RECTOR*—Asghar, Muhammad, MS *Quaid-i-Azam*, BE(Civil)
PRO-RECTOR—Mushtaq, Muhammad, MS
PROJECT ADVISOR—Ahmad, Sheikh Mahmood, MS
REGISTRAR‡—Nasrullah Khan, Muhammad, PhD
DIRECTOR GENERAL (FINANCE)—Saeed, Tahir, MA
DIRECTOR GENERAL (PROJECT DEVELOPMENT AND CO-ORDINATION)—Siddiqui, Arif
 Mahmud, BS
DIRECTOR (EXAMS AND ACADEMICS)—Khan, Zuhr, MS
DIRECTOR (RESEARCH AND DEVELOPMENT)—Absar, Salman, MS
DIRECTOR (MANAGEMENT INFORMATION SYSTEMS)—ul Hasan, Shabih, MS
DIRECTOR (PLANNING AND DEVELOPMENT)—Sheikh, Ashfaq, MS
DIRECTOR (HUMAN RESOURCE MANAGEMENT)—Kakar, Tariq Javed, MS
DIRECTOR (QUALITY ASSURANCE)—Ismail, Muhammad, MS
DIRECTOR (PROJECT)—Akhtar, Muhammad, MS

GENERAL INFORMATION

History. The university was founded in 1991.
 It is based in Rawalpindi, with campuses in
Rawalpindi, Islamabad, Risalpur and Karachi.

Admission to first degree courses (see also
Pakistan Introduction). Candidates should have
a minimum of 60% aggregate marks in
matriculation and intermediate (FSc pre-
engineering for BE, FSc pre-medical for MB
BS/BDS, FSc pre-engineering/computer science
for BIT and FSc/FA for BBA) from a Board of
Intermediate and Secondary Education.
Equivalent qualifications are also accepted.

First Degrees (see also Pakistan Directory to
Subjects of Study) (* = with honours). BBA*,
BDS, BE, BIT, MB BS.
 Length of course. Full-time: BBA*, BDS, BE, BIT:
4 years; MB BS: 5 years.

Higher Degrees (see also Pakistan Directory
to Subjects of Study).
 Master's. MBA, MIT, MS.
 Admission. MS (engineering): first division BE
or BSc in relevant discipline. MS
(environmental engineering): BE, BSc or MSc
in a relevant discipline. Practical experience is
also highly desirable for all engineering
degrees. MBA: first degree with minimum
60% marks; preference given to applicants
with a high score in GMAT, TOEFL and with
sixteen years of education. MIT: first or
master's degree or postgraduate diploma in a
relevant discipline, preferably with a
cumulative grade point average (CGPA) of 2.5
out of 4.
 Length of course. Full-time: MIT, MS: $1\frac{1}{2}$ years;
MBA: 2 years. *Part-time:* MIT, MS: $4\frac{1}{2}$ years.
 Doctoral. PhD.
 Admission. PhD: relevant first or master's
degree. Engineering, information technology,
computer science: CGPA of 3 out of 4. Work
experience with a reputable organisation is
preferred.
 Length of course. Full-time: PhD: 3–4 years.

Libraries. Volumes: 325,213. Periodicals
subscribed to: 409. Other holdings: IEEE/EEE;
Pro-Quest; Medical Library; JSTOR data; Digital
Library; 1430 CD-ROMS on proceedings of
international conferences.

Income (2006–2007). Total, Rs955,333,000.

Statistics. Staff (2006–2007): 1870 (634
academic, 1236 non-academic). Students
(2006–2007): full-time 5446 (4436 men,
1010 women); international 102 (69 men, 33
women); undergraduate 4639 (3748 men,
891 women); master's 640 (563 men, 77
women); doctoral 65 (56 men, 9 women).

ACADEMIC UNITS
Aeronautical Engineering, College of

Tel: (051) 928 0513 Fax: (0923) 73294

Afzal, Mian Muhammad, MS   Assoc. Prof.
Ahmad, Fareed, MS   Asst. Prof.
Ahmad, Jamil, MS   Asst. Prof.
Ain, Mirat Ul, MPhil   Asst. Prof.
Ali, Syed Talat, MS   Asst. Prof.
Amin, Omer, MPhil   Asst. Prof.
Amin, Sadiq, MS   Asst. Prof.
Anwar, Muhammad, MS   Asst. Prof.
Ashraf, Ehsan Ellahi, MPhil   Asst. Prof.
Chaudhry, Imran Ali, PhD   Assoc. Prof.
Dad, Hassan, MS   Asst. Prof.
Dar, Hasan Jamil, MS   Asst. Prof.
Hanif, Muhammad, MS   Asst. Prof.
Hassan, Aamir, PhD   Asst. Prof.
Hussain, Mushtaq, MS   Asst. Prof.
Ikram, Asad, MS   Asst. Prof.
Imanaliev, Talaibek, PhD   Asst. Prof.
Iqbal, Shahzada, MS   Asst. Prof.
Javed, Nasir, MS   Asst. Prof.
Junaid, Ahmad, MS   Asst. Prof.
Khalil, Muhammad Aamir, MS   Asst. Prof.
Khan, Abdul Munem, PhD   Asst. Prof.
Khan, Abdul Naeem, MS   Asst. Prof.
Khan, Anila Ishaque, MS   Asst. Prof.
Khan, Fida Muhammad, PhD   Assoc. Prof.
Khan, Hamid M., MS   Asst. Prof.
Khan, Ishaat Saboor, MS   Asst. Prof.
Khan, Muhammad Sarfraz, MS   Asst. Prof.
Mansoor, Atif Bin, MS   Asst. Prof.
Masood, Ammar, PhD   Asst. Prof.
Masud, Jehanzeb, PhD   Assoc. Prof.
Mateen, Abdul, MS   Asst. Prof.
Nadeem, Ahmed Ejaz, PhD   Asst. Prof.
Naeem, Muhammad, PhD   Asst. Prof.
Naqvi, Mesam Abbas, PhD   Asst. Prof.
Naqvi, Muhammad Ali, MS   Asst. Prof.
Nusrat, Murtaza, MS   Asst. Prof.
Parvez, Khalid, PhD   Asst. Prof.; Dean*
Qureshi, Taimur, MS   Asst. Prof.
Rehman, Atiq ur, MPhil   Asst. Prof.
Shahid, Muhammad, MS   Asst. Prof.
Shami, Muiz ud Din, PhD   Assoc. Prof.
Sheikh, M. Ashfaq, PhD   Asst. Prof.
Sheikh, Shakil, PhD   Asst. Prof.
Tehami, Ahmad Waqar, MS   Asst. Prof.
Ul Mulk, Shafqat, MS   Asst. Prof.
Ur Rehman, Khair, MPhil   Asst. Prof.
Other Staff: 9 Lectrs.
Research: communication and microwave and
 millimetre technologies; flow analysis and
 heat transfer; modelling and simulation IT;
 neural network; structural analysis materials

Civil Engineering, College of

Tel: (0923) 631127 Fax: (0923) 631127
Ahad, Memon Abdul, MS   Asst. Prof.
Ahmad, Basharat, MS   Asst. Prof.
Ahmad, Hafeez, MS   Asst. Prof.
Ahmad, Shakil, MS   Asst. Prof.
Ahmad, Zahid Tauqeer, MS   Asst. Prof.
Ahmed, Malik Muhammad Tanseer, MS   Asst.
 Prof.
Ahmed, Shabbir, MS   Asst. Prof.
Akram, Tayyab, PhD   Prof.
Bhatti, Adbul Qadir, MS   Asst. Prof.
Bhatti, Mukhtar Ahmed, MS   Asst. Prof.
Gabril, H. F., MSc MPhil   Asst. Prof.
Ghani, Imtiaz, MS   Asst. Prof.
Gilbert, Baladi Y., PhD   Assoc. Prof.
Haider, Sajjad, PhD   Assoc. Prof.
Iqbal, Muhammad, MS   Asst. Prof.
Jamil, Awais, MS   Asst. Prof.
Javed, Farhat, PhD   Assoc. Prof.
Khan, Ehsan Ullah, MS   Asst. Prof.
Khan, Marwat, MS   Asst. Prof.
Khan, Muhammad Nuasruallah, PhD   Assoc.
 Prof.
Khan, Sardar, MS   Asst. Prof.
Khan, Shaukat Ali, MS   Asst. Prof.
Khan, Zulfiqar Ali, MS   Asst. Prof.
Mahmood, Malik Azhar, MS   Asst. Prof.
Malik, Adnan Rauf, MS   Asst. Prof.
Memon, Shazim Ali, MS   Asst. Prof.
Mushtaq, Kamran, MS   Asst. Prof.
Qureshi, Intikhab Ahmed, PhD   Asst. Prof.;
 Dean*
Rafiq, Choudhry Muhammad, MS   Asst. Prof.
Rehman, Habib-Ur, MS   Asst. Prof.
Safdar, Sohail, MS   Asst. Prof.
Taylor, William C., PhD   Assoc. Prof.
Other Staff: 5 Lectrs.
Research: concrete and geotech analysis;
 hydraulic and hydro informatics; public
 health engineering; structural engineering;
 survey and mapping

Electrical and Mechanical Engineering, College of

Tel: (051) 5613 2720 Fax: (051) 547 4306
Ahmed, Riaz, MS   Asst. Prof.
Ali, Syed Irshad, MS   Asst. Prof.
Ashiq, Muhammad, MS   Asst. Prof.
Ashraf, Muhammad, PhD   Asst. Prof.
Azim, Raja Amer, MS   Asst. Prof.
Bhatti, Farooq Ahmed, PhD   Assoc. Prof.
Bhatti, Kamran Aziz, MS   Asst. Prof.
Chaudhry, Salman, MS   Asst. Prof.
Dar, Amir Hanif, PhD   Asst. Prof.
Ejaz, Arif, MS   Asst. Prof.
Farooq, Mudassar, PhD   Asst. Prof.
Fatima, Shahnaz, MS   Asst. Prof.
Ghafoor, Abdul, PhD   Prof.; Dean*
Hanif, Muhammad, PhD   Asst. Prof.

Hassan, Dure Shahwar, MS   Asst. Prof.
Hayee, Sobia, MS   Asst. Prof.
Hussain, Akhtar, MS   Asst. Prof.
Hussain, Tahir, MS   Asst. Prof.
Ihsan, Mohjeeb Bin, PhD   Assoc. Prof.
Imran, Tajammal, PhD   Prof.
Iqbal, Javaid, PhD   Asst. Prof.
Iqbal, Tauseef, MS   Asst. Prof.
Ismail, Muhammad, MS   Asst. Prof.
Israr, Adeel, MS   Asst. Prof.
Jamal, Arshad, MS   Asst. Prof.
Jauhar, Ajmal, MS   Asst. Prof.
Javed, M. Younus, PhD   Prof.
Javed, Muhammad Saqib, MS   Asst. Prof.
Kaleem, Muhammad, MS   Asst. Prof.
Karim, Abdul, MS   Asst. Prof.
Kashif, Abdul Rehman, PhD   Asst. Prof.
Kazmi, Syed Muhammad Raza, MS   Asst. Prof.
Khan, Hamid Ullah   Asst. Prof.
Khan, M. Riaz, MS   Asst. Prof.
Khan, Mahmood Anwar, PhD   Assoc. Prof.
Khan, Muhammad Farooq, MA   Asst. Prof.
Khan, Nawar, PhD   Assoc. Prof.
Khan, Rehan Ahmed, MS   Asst. Prof.
Khan, Shoaib A, PhD   Asst. Prof.
Khanum, Assia, MS   Asst. Prof.
Khurshid, Akhtar, MS   Asst. Prof.
Mahmood, Maryam, MA   Asst. Prof.
Malik, Akhtar Nawaz, PhD   Prof.
Malik, Basharat Ullah, PhD   Assoc. Prof.
Malik, Ijaz A., PhD   Prof.
Malik, M. Afzaal, PhD   Prof.
Malik, Muhammad Bilal, PhD   Asst. Prof.
Malik, Sabeen, MS   Asst. Prof.
Malik, Shahzad A., PhD   Asst. Prof.
Muhammad, Ejaz, PhD   Asst. Prof.
Munawar, Khalid, PhD   Assoc. Prof.
Nasir, Saleha, MS   Asst. Prof.
Qadir, Asghar, PhD   Prof.
Qazalbash, Arfakhshand Ali, MS   Asst. Prof.
Qureshi, Bilal Ahmed, MS   Asst. Prof.
Qureshi, Fareed Uddin F., MS   Asst. Prof.
Rafiq, Muhammad, PhD   Prof.
Riaz, Adil, MPhil   Asst. Prof.
Rizvi, Tafazzul Mehdi, MS   Asst. Prof.
Shabbir, Ghulam, MS   Asst. Prof.
Shah, Syed Hussain, MS   Asst. Prof.
Shah, Syed Tasweer H., MS   Asst. Prof.
Shaikh, Shahzad Amin, MS   Asst. Prof.
Sharief, Khalid, MPhil   Asst. Prof.
Sheriff, Samreen, MS   Asst. Prof.
Siddiqui, Ahmed Saeed, MPhil   Asst. Prof.
Siddiqui, Azad Akhter, PhD   Asst. Prof.
Sohail, Ahmed, MS   Asst. Prof.
Sohail, Shaleeza, PhD   Asst. Prof.
Ul Ain, Qurat, MPhil   Asst. Prof.
Ullah, Himayat, MA   Asst. Prof.
Umbreen, Saima, MA   Asst. Prof.
Yaqub, Ejaz, MS   Asst. Prof.
Other Staff: 1 Visiting Assoc. Prof.; 19 Lectrs.
Research: artificial intelligence; flow-induced
    vibrations; hardware/software co-design;
    modern control; signal processing

Environmental Science and Engineering, Institute of

Tel: (051) 927 1597 Fax: (051) 927 1597
    E-mail: piese@isb.paknet.com.pk
Aslam, Irfan, PhD   Asst. Prof.
Aslam, Muhammad Rizwan, MS   Asst. Prof.
Awan, Muhammad Ali, MPhil   Asst. Prof.
Baig, Muhammad Anwar, PhD   Assoc. Prof.;
    Dean*
Farooq, Shaukat, PhD   Asst. Prof.
Hashmi, Imran, PhD   Asst. Prof.
Khan, Sher Jamal, MS   Asst. Prof.
Khan, Zahiuddin, PhD   Assoc. Prof.
Qazi, Ishtiaq A., PhD   Asst. Prof.
Sajjad, Muhammad, MS   Asst. Prof.
Other Staff: 2 Visiting Asst. Profs.; 4 Lectrs.
Research: disposal/treatment of refinery waste

Geographic Information Systems, Institute of

Hussain, Mubashar, PhD   Asst. Prof.
Khattak, M. Umar K., PhD   Prof.; Dean*
Malik, Mansoor, MS   Asst. Prof.
Mehdi, Muhammad Raza, PhD   Asst. Prof.

Minhas, Bushra Naseem, MS   Asst. Prof.
Mumtaz, Salman Ali, MS   Asst. Prof.
Rabab, Uzma, MS   Asst. Prof.
Saeed, Osama Bin, MS   Asst. Prof.
Other Staff: 1 Project Manager
Research: contaminated sites remediation;
    environmental analysis and analytical
    techniques; water treatment and resources
    management

Information Technology, Institute of

Tel: (051) 928 0443 Fax: (051) 928 0782
    E-mail: niit@isb.paknet.com.pk
Abbasi, Uzma Tariq, MS   Asst. Prof.
Ahmed, Ejaz, MS   Asst. Prof.
Ahmed, Hafiz Farooq, PhD   Asst. Prof.
Ahmed, Nadeem, MS   Asst. Prof.
Ahmed, Naseer, MS   Asst. Prof.
Ahmed, Rizwan, MS   Asst. Prof.
Ahmed, Tauqeer, MS   Asst. Prof.
Ali, Altaf, MS   Asst. Prof.
Ali, Arshad, PhD   Prof.
Atif, Muhammad, MS   Asst. Prof.
Aziz, Asim, PhD   Asst. Prof.
Aziz, Saqib, MS   Asst. Prof.
Baig, Samiullah, MS   Asst. Prof.
Bazmi, Aslam, MA   Asst. Prof.
Bilal, Muhammad, MS   Asst. Prof.
Ch, Ahsan Ahmed, MS   Asst. Prof.
Daud, Imran, MS   Asst. Prof.
Ghafoor, Abdul, MS   Asst. Prof.
Gohr, N. D., PhD   Assoc. Prof.
Haider, Syed Ali, MS   Asst. Prof.
Hayat, Amir, MS   Asst. Prof.
Jabeen, Fakhra, MS   Asst. Prof.
Jelani, Aamir, MS   Asst. Prof.
Kalim, Umar, MS   Asst. Prof.
Kamal, Atif, MS   Asst. Prof.
Kayani, Shamila, MS   Asst. Prof.
Khan, Maqsudul Hassan, MS   Asst. Prof.
Khan, Sharifullah, PhD   Assoc. Prof.
Khan, Tashfeen, MS   Asst. Prof.
Khan, Zaheer Abbas, MIT   Asst. Prof.
Khattak, Shahrzad, MS   Asst. Prof.
Khawer, Usman, MA   Asst. Prof.
Kiayani, Saad Liaqat, MS   Asst. Prof.
Mahmood, Nasir, MS   Asst. Prof.
Mir, Saqib, MS   Asst. Prof.
Mirza, Fauzan, PhD   Asst. Prof.
Munir, Kamran, MIT   Asst. Prof.
Murtaza, Saeed, PhD   Asst. Prof.
Nazir, Arshad, MS   Asst. Prof.
Niazi, Muaz Ahmed K., MS   Asst. Prof.
Qureshi, Nauman Ahmed, MS   Asst. Prof.
Ramzan, Muhammad, MS   Asst. Prof.
Rao, Imran, MS   Asst. Prof.
Raza, Jamil, PhD   Asst. Prof.
Ruhullah, MS   Asst. Prof.
Saghir, Muhammad, PhD   Asst. Prof.
Sajjad, Ali, MS   Asst. Prof.
Shafique, Sara, MBA   Asst. Prof.
Shams, Muniba, MS   Asst. Prof.
Shaukat, Mansoor, MS   Asst. Prof.
Shibli, Awais, MS   Asst. Prof.
Tufail, Ali, MS   Asst. Prof.
Umer, Muhammad, MS   Asst. Prof.
Usman, Ayesha, MS   Asst. Prof.
Zaidi, Kamran Hussain, MS
Zaidi, S. Muhammad Hassan, PhD   Assoc.
    Prof.; Dean*
Other Staff: 19 Lectrs.
Research: computer software engineering (object
    orientated database in a wide area network
    environment); distributed computing; grid
    analysis; multi-agent system semantic grid;
    optoelectronics

Management Sciences, Institute of

Tel: (051) 927 1610 Fax: (051) 927 1610
    E-mail: nims@nims.edu.pk
Ahmad, Muhammad Raza, MS   Asst. Prof.
Ahmed, Afshan, MBA   Asst. Prof.
Durrani, Tahir Khan, PhD   Asst. Prof.
Hanif, Atiya, MPA   Asst. Prof.
Hussain, Muhammad, PhD   Assoc. Prof.
Idrees, Khurram, MBA   Asst. Prof.
Jabbar, Zeenat, MBA   Asst. Prof.
Jafri Sabir, Hussain, MS   Asst. Prof.

Kazmi, Saeed Haider, MBA   Asst. Prof.
Khan, Dilawar Ali, PhD   Prof.; Dean*
Nazir, Imran, MPA   Asst. Prof.
Obaid, Asfia, MPA   Asst. Prof.
Pervaiz, Ayesha, MPA   Asst. Prof.
Rahman, Asif Ali, MBA   Asst. Prof.
Rashid, Syed Haroon, MBA   Asst. Prof.
Sarwar, Muhammad Saad, MBA   Asst. Prof.
Sarwar, Naukhez, MBA   Asst. Prof.
Shaheen, Rozina, MBA   Asst. Prof.
Syed, Zahid Hussain, MS   Asst. Prof.
Taslim, Muhammad, MS   Asst. Prof.
Other Staff: 2 Lectrs.
Research: econometrics; global marketing;
    human resource management (HRM) and
    organisational behaviour; micro
    development economics

Marine Engineering, College of

Tel: (021) 924 0152 Fax: (021) 924 0112
    E-mail: co@pnec.edu.pk
Ahmad, Aijaz, MS   Asst. Prof.
Ahmed, Afzal, PhD   Assoc. Prof.
Ahmed, Fawad, MS   Asst. Prof.
Ahmed, Intesar, MS   Asst. Prof.
Ahmed, Saeed, MS   Asst. Prof.
Ahmed, Shoib, MS   Asst. Prof.
Ahmed, Zamir, MS   Asst. Prof.
Ahmed, Zeeshan, MS   Asst. Prof.
Akhtar, Pervez, PhD   Assoc. Prof.
Alam, Syed Nazeer, MS   Asst. Prof.
Ali, Mirza Ahmed, MS   Asst. Prof.
Amin, Khalid Mohammad, MS   Asst. Prof.
Arshed, Ghulam Mushed, MS   Asst. Prof.
Askari, Syed Jawid, MS   Asst. Prof.
Ayub, Muhammad, MS   Asst. Prof.
Aziz, Arshad, MS   Asst. Prof.
Beg, Omar Ali, MS   Asst. Prof.
Butt, Shahid Ikraullah, MS   Asst. Prof.
Danish, Syed Noman, MS   Asst. Prof.
Fahad, Muhammad, MS   Asst. Prof.
Farooqi, Sohail Zaki, PhD   Asst. Prof.
Farooqui, Johar Khurshid, MS   Asst. Prof.
Haider, Tarique, MS   Asst. Prof.
Hamid, R. Q., PhD   Asst. Prof.
Hasan, Syed Ali, PhD   Assoc. Prof.
Hashmi, Khurram Jamal, MS   Asst. Prof.
Hussain, Nusrat, MS   Asst. Prof.
Hussain, Sarfraz, PhD   Asst. Prof.
Hussain, Tanweer, MS   Asst. Prof.
Imran, Muhammad, MS   Asst. Prof.
Iqbal, Najeeb, MS   Asst. Prof.
Jaffri, Rajub Ali, MS   Asst. Prof.
Jamshed, M. Azeem, MS   Asst. Prof.
Jan, Mustafa, MS   Asst. Prof.
Janjua, Naem-ul-Hasan, MS   Asst. Prof.
Javed, Amjid, MS   Asst. Prof.
Khaliq, Adnan, MS   Asst. Prof.; Dean*
Khan, Imran Ahmed, MS   Asst. Prof.
Khan, M. Farhan, MS   Asst. Prof.
Khan, M. Safeer, MS   Asst. Prof.
Khan, M. Yasir, MPhil   Asst. Prof.
Khwaja, Asim Ali, MS   Asst. Prof.
Koraishy, Babar Masood, MS   Asst. Prof.
Kuhrram, Farhan, MS   Asst. Prof.
Mahboob, Iram, MS   Asst. Prof.
Mahmud, Riaz, MS   Asst. Prof.
Marchant, Ali Imran, MS   Asst. Prof.
Mehboob, Athar, PhD   Asst. Prof.
Moin, Lubna, MS   Asst. Prof.
Qureshi, Ikram Rasool, MS   Asst. Prof.
Rahi, M. A. Akhtar, PhD   Asst. Prof.
Rasheed, Haroon, MS   Asst. Prof.
Raza, Munawar, MS   Asst. Prof.
Rizvi, Sahir Mehdi, MS   Asst. Prof.
Samiah, Abdul, MS   Asst. Prof.
Shaikh, Abdul Rashid, MS   Asst. Prof.
Shakeel, Muhammad, MS   Asst. Prof.
Shakoor, Abdul, PhD   Asst. Prof.
Sohail, Muhammad, MS   Asst. Prof.
Ul Hasnain, S. Khursheed, MS   Asst. Prof.
Ur Rehman, Khatib, MS   Asst. Prof.
Waheed, Abdul, MS   Asst. Prof.
Waheed, M., MS   Asst. Prof.
Yahya, Ashraf, MS   Asst. Prof.
Yasin, Azra, MCS   Asst. Prof.
Zaidi, S. K. N., PhD   Assoc. Prof.
Zia-ul-Haq, Muhammad, MS   Asst. Prof.

Other Staff: 13 Lectrs.
Research: efficient hardware implementation of elliptic curve cryptography; multi-variable linear control system; network security through cryptology; non-linear control systems; simulated study of the synchronised electricity generation in a grid connected wind form

Medical Sciences, College of

Tel: (051) 927 0257 Fax: (051) 558 1085
Abbas, Asad, BDS   Asst. Prof.
Ahmad, Ijaz, MB BS MPhil   Asst. Prof.
Ahmad, Muhammad, MB BS   Assoc. Prof.
Ahmed, Naseem Saud, MB BS MPhil   Asst. Prof.
Ali, Salman, MB BS   Assoc. Prof.
Aslam, Muhammad, MB BS PhD   Prof.; Dean*
Awan, Zubair Ahmed, MB BS MPhil   Asst. Prof.
Azad, Azad Ali, BDS   Asst. Prof.
Baig, Mushtaq Ahmed, MB BS   Prof.
Butt, Idrees Farooq, MB BS MPhil   Assoc. Prof.
Butt, Shadab Ahmed, MB BS   Asst. Prof.
Chaudhry, Ahmed Khan, MB BS   Assoc. Prof.
Chaudhry, Muhammad Parwez, BDS   Assoc. Prof.
Choudhry, Muhammad Ashraf, MB BS   Asst. Prof.
Choudhry, Naseer Ahmed, MB BS MPhil   Asst. Prof.
Hafeez, Sohail, MB BS   Asst. Prof.
Haleem, Abdul, MB BS   Asst. Prof.
Hassan, Ayub, BDS   Asst. Prof.
Hussain, Muhammad Mazhar, MB BS MPhil   Assoc. Prof.
Hussain, Safdar, MB BS   Asst. Prof.
Ibrahim, Muhammad Wasim, BDS   Asst. Prof.
Iqbal, Muhammad, MB BS   Asst. Prof.
Ishaq, Mazhar, MB BS   Assoc. Prof.
Jamal, Shahid, MB BS   Asst. Prof.
Jan, Hameed Ullah, BDS   Asst. Prof.
Kakar, Salik Javed, MB BS MPhil   Asst. Prof.
Kaleem, Muhammad, BDS MS   Asst. Prof.
Khalid, Mehmood Raja, MB BS   Asst. Prof.
Khan, Aslam, MB BS
Khan, Bushra Tayyaba, BPharm MPhil   Asst. Prof.
Khan, Dilshad Ahmed, MB BS PhD   Assoc. Prof.
Khan, Iqbal Ahmad, MB BS MBA   Assoc. Prof.
Khan, Muhammad Naeem, MB BS   Prof.
Khan, Munir Ahmad, MB BS MPhil   Assoc. Prof.
Mahmood, Nasir, MB BS MPhil   Asst. Prof.
Manzoor, Manzoor Ahmed, BDS   Assoc. Prof.
Minhas, Liaqat, MB BS
Mishwani, Muhammad Hussain, MB BS
Mubarik, Azhar, MB BS
Muzaffar, Sultan, MB BS   Prof.
Najam, Zahida, BDS
Najmi, M. H., MB BS PhD   Prof.
Naveed, Abdul Khaliq, MB BS MPhil   Prof.
Nuri, Muhammad Masudul H., MB BS   Prof.
Qamar, Khadija, MB BS MPhil   Asst. Prof.
Qazi, Shahid Shuja, BDS   Prof.
Rana, Mowadat Hussain, MB BS PhD   Prof.
Rashid, Mamoon, MB BS   Assoc. Prof.
Riaz, Muhammad Adeel, BDS MS   Assoc. Prof.
Shah, Irfan, BDS   Asst. Prof.
Shukar, Irfan, MB BS   Asst. Prof.
Sultana, Abida, MB BS   Asst. Prof.
Syeda, Iffat Batool, BDS   Assoc. Prof.
Tarin, Bilal Ahmed, MB BS   Assoc. Prof.
Tariq, Ghulam Rasool, MB BS   Asst. Prof.
Ud Din, Muhammad Shahab, BDS MS   Assoc. Prof.
Ul Hassan, Najm, MB BS   Asst. Prof.
Ul Majid, Nasim, MB BS   Asst. Prof.
Uraizy, Syed Mustafa H., MB BS   Asst. Prof.
Waheed, Akbar, MB BS MPhil   Assoc. Prof.
Zafar, Lubna, MB BS   Asst. Prof.
Other Staff: 26 Lectrs.
Research: anti-diabetic role of medical plants; anti-oxidant role of polyphenoles from medicinal plants; development of interheptic perebaliary glands in human liver; dynamics of chloroquine-resistance in Plasmodium falciparum in Pakistan; effect of ultrasound

Telecommunication Engineering, College of

Tel: (051) 927 1501 Fax: (051) 927 1502
Abid, Muhammad Amjad, MS   Asst. Prof.
Ahmad, Farooq, MS   Asst. Prof.
Ahmed, Attiq, MS   Asst. Prof.
Ahmed, Fazal, MS   Asst. Prof.
Akbar, Muhammed, PhD   Prof.; Dean*
Akbar, Salim, PhD   Prof.
Akram, Muhammad, MA   Asst. Prof.
Ali, Irtaza, MS   Asst. Prof.
Ali, Muzaffar, MS   Asst. Prof.
Amjad, Muhammad Faisal, MS   Asst. Prof.
Arsalan, Qamar Hamayun, MS   Asst. Prof.
Bilal, Muhammad Bashir, MS   Asst. Prof.
Cheema, Hammad Mehmood, MS   Asst. Prof.
Farooq, Umar, MS   Asst. Prof.
Faryad, Muhammad, MS   Asst. Prof.
Habib, Yousaf, MPhil   Asst. Prof.
Haq, Nasrul, MS   Asst. Prof.
Hussain, Mukhtar, PhD   Assoc. Prof.
Hussain, Shahzad, PhD   Assoc. Prof.
Hussain, Syed Javed, MS   Asst. Prof.
Iqbal, Raja, MS   Asst. Prof.
Irshad, Muhammad, MS   Asst. Prof.
Jafri, Muhammad Noman, PhD   Prof.
Kakar, Tariq Javed, MS   Asst. Prof.
Khan, Muhammad Fayyaz, MS
Khan, Muhammad, MS   Asst. Prof.
Khan, Muhasmad Asadullah, MS   Asst. Prof.
Khattak, Naveed Sarfraz, MS   Asst. Prof.
Khokhar, Imtiaz Ahmed, MS   Asst. Prof.
Maqsood, Tariq, MPhil   Asst. Prof.
Masood, Ashraf, PhD   Assoc. Prof.
Masood, Talib Hussain, MS   Asst. Prof.
Mori, Kinji, PhD   Asst. Prof.
Murtaza, Saeed, PhD   Asst. Prof.
Murtaza, Zeeshan, MS   Asst. Prof.
Naeem, Muhammad, MS   Asst. Prof.
Obaid, Atiya, MS   Asst. Prof.
Rana, Tauseef Ahmed, MS   Asst. Prof.
Rao, Muhammad Khalid, MS   Asst. Prof.
Rashid, Imran, MS   Asst. Prof.
Rauf, Abdul, MS   Asst. Prof.
Raza, Arif, MS   Asst. Prof.
Rehman, Abdul, MS   Asst. Prof.
Saleem, Muhammad, MS   Asst. Prof.
Sheikh, Tariq Hussain, MS   Asst. Prof.
Siddiqui, Kaleem Iqbal, MS   Asst. Prof.
Ul Haq, Mofassir, MS   Asst. Prof.
Ul Mustafa, Zaka, MS   Asst. Prof.
Zaidi, Syed Ather Mohsin, MS   Asst. Prof.
Zia, Jamil Ahmed, MS   Asst. Prof.
Other Staff: 13 Lectrs.
Research: computer architecture; digital signal processing; digital system; information security; very large scale integration (VLSI) design

Transportation, National Institute of

Tel: (0923) 631 211 Fax: (0923) 631 211
Ahad, Memon Abdul, MS   Asst. Prof.
Ahmad, Hafeez, MS   Asst. Prof.
Ahmad, Shakil, MS   Asst. Prof.
Ahmad, Zahid Tauqeer, MS   Asst. Prof.
Ahmed, Masood, MS   Asst. Prof.
Akram, Tayyab, PhD   Prof.; Dean*
Ali, Liaqat, PhD   Assoc. Prof.
Amir, Shahzad Ul Hassan, MS   Asst. Prof.
Bhatti, Adbul Qadir, MS   Asst. Prof.
Gabril, H. F., MSc MPhil   Asst. Prof.
Gilbert, Baladi Y., PhD   Assoc. Prof.
Haider, Sajjad, PhD   Asst. Prof.
Iqbal, Muhammad Naveed, MS   Asst. Prof.
Iqbal, Muhammad, MS   Asst. Prof.
Javed, Farhat, PhD   Asst. Prof.
Kayani, M. Khaliq ur Rashid, PhD   Prof.
Khan, Marwat, MS   Asst. Prof.
Khan, Muhabat, MS   Asst. Prof.
Khan, Muhammad Nuasruallah, PhD   Assoc. Prof.
Khan, Sardar, MS   Asst. Prof.
Khan, Shaukat Ali, MS   Asst. Prof.
Khan, Zulfiqar Ali, MS   Asst. Prof.
Mahmood, Malik Azhar, MS   Asst. Prof.
Mahmood, Tariq, PhD   Prof.
Mahmood, Zafar, MS   Asst. Prof.
Malik, Adnan Rauf, MS   Asst. Prof.
Maqsood, Tariq, MS   Asst. Prof.
Memon, Shazim Ali, MS   Asst. Prof.
Mushtaq, Kamran, MS   Asst. Prof.
Rafiq, Choudhry Muhammad, MS   Asst. Prof.
Rao, Shafqat Ali, MS   Asst. Prof.
Rehman, Habib-Ur, MS   Asst. Prof.
Riaz, Muhammad, MS   Asst. Prof.
Safdar, Sohail, MS   Asst. Prof.
Shaikh, Muhammad Ali, MS   Asst. Prof.
Taylor, William C., PhD   Assoc. Prof.
Ul Hasan, Syed Waqar, MS   Asst. Prof.
Ullah, Imran, MPhil   Asst. Prof.
Zahid, Arshad, MS   Asst. Prof.
Other Staff: 26 Lectrs.
Research: city planning; dynamics architecture; pavement material evaluation; soil stabilisation; transportation engineering

SPECIAL CENTRES, ETC

Applied Mathematics and Physics, Centre for

Ali, Rahmat, PhD   Asst. Prof.
Kamran, Tayyab, PhD   Asst. Prof.
Mermanov, Anvarbek, PhD   Asst. Prof.
Qadir, Asghar, PhD   Asst. Prof.
Rafiq, Muhammad, PhD   Prof.; Dean*
Rashid, Muneer Ahmad, PhD   Asst. Prof.
Saifullah, Khalid, PhD   Asst. Prof.
Sazhenkov, Sergei, PhD   Asst. Prof.
Other Staff: 2 Lectrs.
Research: differential equations; mathematical physics; relativity

Chemical Engineering and Material Sciences, Centre for

Ahmad, Sheikh Mahmood, MS   Asst. Prof.
Elahi, Fazal, MBA   Asst. Prof.
Hussain, Arshad, PhD   Asst. Prof.
Khan, Amir Azam, PhD   Prof.
Malik, Abdul Qadeer, PhD   Assoc. Prof.
Sanaullah, Khairuddin, PhD   Prof.; Dean*
Shariq, Ahmad, PhD   Asst. Prof.
Research: ceramics materials and surface treatments; fluid mechanics; petroleum engineering; physical chemistry

Cyber Technology and Spectrum Management, Centre for

Ahmad, Habeel, ME   Asst. Prof.
Baig, Muhammad Shamim, PhD   Prof.; Dean*
Khaliq, Samin, MS   Asst. Prof.
Saqib, Nazar Abbas, PhD   Assoc. Prof.
Tariq, Saleem, MS   Prof.
Toor, Yasser Sarfaraz, MS   Asst. Prof.
Other Staff: 1 Lectr.
Research: hardwares and systems; information security embedded design

Technology Incubation, Centre for

Ali, Mansoor, MBA   Asst. Prof.
Farooq, Umar, MBA   Assoc. Prof.
Ghuman, Abid Parvez, PhD   Prof.; Dean*
Khan, Muhammad Raza A., MS   Asst. Prof.
Other Staff: 1 Lectr.
Research: capacity building management; consultancy and management of product; incubates embodiment; industrial linkages

CONTACT OFFICERS

Admissions (first degree). Deputy Director, Registration (Undergraduate): Razi, S. M. (E-mail: info@nust.edu.pk)
Admissions (higher degree). Deputy Director, Registration (Postgraduate): Hussain, Lt. Col. (Rtd.) Tahir (E-mail: regn_pg@nust.edu.pk)

[Information supplied by the institution as at 9 October 2007, and edited by the ACU]

NORTH-WEST FRONTIER PROVINCE AGRICULTURAL UNIVERSITY

Founded 1981

Postal Address: PO Pakistan Forest Institute, Peshawar, North-West Frontier Province, Pakistan
Telephone: (091) 921 6532 Fax: (091) 921 6520 E-mail: mafzaldt@yahoo.com
URL: http://www.aup.edu.pk/

VICE-CHANCELLOR*—Khalil, Prof. Said K., MSc N-WFP Ag., PhD Prague Agric.
REGISTRAR‡—Khan, Dilawar, MA Gomal

NORTH-WEST FRONTIER PROVINCE UNIVERSITY OF ENGINEERING AND TECHNOLOGY

Founded 1980

Member of the Association of Commonwealth Universities

Postal Address: University PO Box 814, Peshawar, North-West Frontier Province, Pakistan
Telephone: (091) 921 6493 Fax: (091) 921 6494
URL: http://www.nwfpuet.edu.pk

VICE-CHANCELLOR*—Gilani, Imtiaz H., BSc(Engg) Pesh., MScEngg Asian I.T., Bangkok,
MBA Rutgers
REGISTRAR‡—Khan, Lt. Col.(Retd.) Imtiaz A., MSc(ElectEng)
DIRECTOR OF FINANCE AND PLANNING—Khan, Muhammad S., MCom

GENERAL INFORMATION

History. Originally established in 1952 as the faculty of engineering, University of Peshawar, the university achieved independent status in 1980.

The university's main campus is in Peshawar, and the other three campuses are in Abbottabad, Mardan and Bannu.

Admission to first degree courses (see also Pakistan Introduction). Intermediate (pre-engineering) exam from a Board of Intermediate and Secondary Education in Pakistan (or other recognised equivalent qualification); or BTech (pass) degree; or 3-year post-matriculation diploma in engineering. A minimum 60% pass mark is required in all cases. All applicants must take the university's entrance test.

First Degrees (see also Pakistan Directory to Subjects of Study). BScEngg.
Length of course. Full-time: BScEngg: 4 years.

Higher Degrees (see also Pakistan Directory to Subjects of Study).
Master's. MScEngg.
Admission. Applicants must hold a first degree in a relevant discipline of engineering and must pass an entrance test.
Length of course. Full-time: MScEngg: 2 years. Part-time: MScEngg: 4 years.
Doctoral. PhD.
Length of course. Full-time: PhD: 3 years. Part-time: PhD: 4 years.

Libraries. Volumes: 100,000.

Income (2005–2006). Total, Rs308,933,000.

Statistics. Staff (2005–2006): 1288 (298 academic, 990 non-academic). Students (2005–2006): full-time 3275 (3113 men, 162 women); international 68 (67 men, 1 woman); master's 291 (291 men); doctoral 35 (35 men).

FACULTIES/SCHOOLS
Engineering
Tel: (091) 921 6495 Fax: (091) 921 8160
E-mail: dean@nwfpuet.edu.pk
Dean: Khan, Prof. M. Mansoor, BE Pesh., PhD Nott.

ACADEMIC UNITS
Basic Sciences and Islamiat
Tel: (091) 921 6502
Ali, Amjad, MSc   Asst. Prof.
Ali, Sardar, MSc Pesh., MPhil Quaid-i-Azam Assoc. Prof.
Atiq, Md. Tahir, MPhil Quaid-i-Azam, MSc Pesh. Asst. Prof.
Iqbal, Javed, LLB Pesh., MA Pesh., MPhil Punjab Asst. Prof.
Jehan, Shah, MSc Pesh., MPhil Quaid-i-Azam Assoc. Prof.
Kamal, Md. Mustafa, BEd Pesh., MSc Punjab Asst. Prof.
Khan, Mumtaz, MSc Pesh., MPhil Strath.   Assoc. Prof.
Khurshid-ul-Wahab, MSc Pesh., MPhil Quaid-i-Azam   Assoc. Prof.
Muhammad, Ali, MSc Pesh., MPhil Quaid-i-Azam Asst. Prof.
Pervez, Khalid, MSc Pesh., MPhil Strath.   Assoc. Prof.
Qasim, Ghulam, MSc Gomal, PhD Shanghai Prof.
Raza-ur-Rehman, Qazi, MSc   Asst. Prof.
Saeed-ur-Rehman, Hafiz, MSc Pesh., MPhil Pesh., PhD Pesh.   Prof.; Chairman*
Shah, Wahid A., BEd Pesh., MA Pesh., PhD Pesh. Prof.
Siraj-ul-Islam, MSc Pesh., MPhil Quaid-i-Azam, PhD Ghulam IKIST   Asst. Prof.
Ullah, Kifayat, MSc Quaid-i-Azam   Asst. Prof.
Other Staff: 7 Lectrs.

Computer Science and Information Technology
Tel: (091) 921 8423
E-mail: babar@nwfpuet.edu.pk

Babar, M. Inayatullah K., PhD   Chairman*
Other Staff: 6 Lectrs.

Engineering, Agricultural
Tel: (091) 921 6852
E-mail: mahmood33@yahoo.com
Alamgir, Muhammad, BScEngg Pesh., MSc McG. Assoc. Prof.
Ashraf, Saadat, BScEngg Pesh., MSc Strath., PhD Curtin   Asst. Prof.
Ibrahim, Muhammad, BScEngg Pesh., MSc Pesh. Asst. Prof.
Khan, Daulat, BScEngg Pesh., MSc Strath., PhD George Washington   Assoc. Prof.
Khan, Mahmood A., BSc Pesh., MSc Pesh.   Asst. Prof.
Khan, Taj A., BScEngg Pesh., MScEngg Pesh., MSc Strath., PhD Strath.   Assoc. Prof.
Khattak, Muhammad S. K., BSc Pesh., MSc Pesh. Asst. Prof.
Mahmood, Zahid, BScEngg Pesh., MSc Philippines, PhD Iowa State   Prof.; Chairman*
Syed-ul-Abrar, BScEngg Pesh., MS Utah, MPhil Strath.   Prof.
Zia-ul-Haq, BSc Pesh., MSc Pesh.   Asst. Prof.
Other Staff: 3 Lectrs.
Research: farm machinery and power; hydrology; irrigation and drainage; soil and water conservation

Engineering, Chemical
Tel: (091) 921 8180
Ahmad, Farooq, BSc Pesh., MSc Punjab   Asst. Prof.
El-Dessouky, Hisham T., PhD   Prof.; Chairman*
Gul, Saeed, BSc Pesh., MSc Punjab   Asst. Prof.
Swati, Imran K., BSc Pesh., MSc Punjab   Asst. Prof.
Younas, Muhammad, BSc Pesh., MSc Punjab Asst. Prof.
Other Staff: 8 Lectrs.

Engineering, Civil
Tel: (091) 921 6775
E-mail: drakhtarnaeem@hotmail.com

Ahmad, Irshad, BSc Pesh., MSc Pesh., PhD Pesh. Asst. Prof.

Ahmad, Naveed, BScEngg Pesh., MSc *George Washington* Asst. Prof.

Ali, Amjad, BScEngg Pesh., MSc *Colorado*, MPhil *Strath.* Prof.

Ali, Qaiser, BSc Pesh., MSc Pesh., PhD Pesh. Prof.

Ali, Syed M., BSc Pesh., MSc Pesh. Asst. Prof.

Ashraf, Muhammad, BSc Pesh., MSc Pesh. Asst. Prof.

Durrani, M. A. Q. Jehangir, BScEngg Pesh., MSc *Punjab*, PhD *Birm.* Prof.

Javed, Muhammad, BSc Pesh., MSc Pesh. Asst. Prof.

Khaliq, Fazal, BE Pesh., MSc *Punjab* Prof.

Khan, Akhtar N., BSc Pesh., MScEngg Pesh., MS *Ill.*, PhD *Ill.* Prof.; Chairman*

Naseer, Amjad, BSc Pesh., MSc Pesh. Asst. Prof.

Other Staff: 4 Lectrs.

Engineering, Computer System

Tel: (091) 921 6590 Fax: (091) 921 6589
E-mail: yahya.khawaja@nwfpuet.edu.pk

Awan, Faryal A., BSc Pesh., MSc Pesh. Asst. Prof.

Hassan, Laiq, BSc Pesh., MSc Pesh. Asst. Prof.

Khan, Sheraz A., BSc Pesh., MSc *Islam.* Asst. Prof.

Mufti, Zahid W., BSc Pesh., MSc Pesh. Asst. Prof.

ul Haq, Ihsan, BSc Pesh., MSc Pesh. Asst. Prof.

Usman, Muhammad, BSc Pesh., MSc *Islam.* Asst. Prof.

Yahya, Khawaja M., BScEngg Pesh., MS *Mich.*, PhD *Mich.* Prof.; Chairman*

Zafar, Haseeb, MSc *George Washington* Asst. Prof.

Other Staff: 8 Lectrs.

Engineering, Electrical

Tel: (091) 921 6498
E-mail: amk@nwfpuet.edu.pk

Ahmad, Gulzar, BSc Pesh., MSc *George Washington* Asst. Prof.

Akhtar, Javed, BScEngg Pesh., MSc *New Jersey I.T.* Asst. Prof.

Arbab, M. Naeem, BScEngg Pesh., MSc *Manc.*, PhD *Manc.* Prof.

Azzam-ul-Asar, BScEngg Pesh., MSc *Strath.*, PhD *Strath.* Prof.

Babar, Inayatullah K., BSc Pesh., MSc *George Washington*, PhD *George Washington* Assoc. Prof.

Khan, Iftikhar A., PhD *Colorado* Prof.

Khan, M. Zahir, BSc *Karachi*, MSc *Strath.* Prof.

Khan, Syed M. M. A., BSc Pesh., MSc Pesh., MScEngg Asst. Prof.

Mutalib, Abdul, BE Pesh., MSc *Strath.* Prof.; Chairman*

Noor, S. Fayyaz, BScEngg Pesh., MSc Pesh., MEd *Oregon*, PhD *Strath.* Prof.

Shafi, Mohsin A., BSc Pesh., MSc Pesh., MSc *Kansai* Assoc. Prof.

Shah, Syed W., BSc *Azad J&K*, MSc Pesh., PhD *Strath.* Assoc. Prof.

Ullah, Amjad, BScEngg Pesh., MScEngg *George Washington* Assoc. Prof.

Yahya, Khawaja M., BScEngg Pesh., MS *Mich.*, PhD *Mich.* Prof.

Yousaf, Faqir Z., BSc Pesh., MScEngg Pesh., MSc *George Washington* Asst. Prof.

Other Staff: 9 Lectrs.

Engineering, Industrial

Tel: (091) 921 6465

Hussain, Iftikhar, BSc Pesh., MSc *Taxila UET*, PhD *Brad.* Prof.; Chairman*

Maqsood, Shahid, BSc Pesh., MSc *Hudd.* Asst. Prof.

Other Staff: 3 Lectrs.

Engineering, Mechanical

Tel: (091) 921 6499
E-mail: mirfana@brain.net.pk

Ahmad, Iftikhar, BScEngg Pesh., MSc *Punjab* Assoc. Prof.

Ahmad, Muhammad M., BSc Pesh., MSc Pesh. Assoc. Prof.

Arif, M. Ali, BSc Pesh., MSc *Nott.* Asst. Prof.

Azam, Khizar, BSc Pesh., MSc *George Washington* Asst. Prof.

Baseer, M. Abdul, BScEngg Pesh., MSc *Shiraz*, PhD *Bath* Prof.

Hadi, Abdul, BScEngg Pesh., MS *Shiraz* Assoc. Prof.

Hafeez-ur-Rehman, BSc Pesh., MScEngg *George Washington* Asst. Prof.

Irfan Mufti, M. A. A., BSc Pesh., MScEngg *Punjab*, PhD *Case W.Reserve* Prof.; Chairman*

Irfanullah, BScEngg Pesh., MS *Mich.*, PhD *Mich.* Prof.

Khan, Haji S. F. U., BSc Pesh. Asst. Prof.

Khan, M. Tahir, BSc Pesh., MSc Asst. Prof.

Khattak, M. Naeem, BScEngg Pesh., MSc *Strath.* Assoc. Prof.

Noor, Sahar, BSc Pesh., MSc *Karachi*, PhD *Brad.* Asst. Prof.

Pervez, Muhammad, BScEngg Pesh., MSc *Punjab* Prof.

Shah, Shoukat A., BScEngg Pesh., MSc Pesh. Asst. Prof.

Shah, Syed R. A., BScEngg Pesh., MSc *Wash.*, PhD *George Washington* Asst. Prof.

Shakoor, Abdul, BSc Pesh., MSc *Hudd.* Asst. Prof.

Tajik, Saeed J., BScEngg Pesh., MPhil *City(UK)* Prof.

Ullah, Hamid, BSc Pesh., MSc Pesh. Asst. Prof.

Other Staff: 8 Lectrs.

Engineering, Mechatronics

Tel: (091) 921 6499

Irfanullah, BScEngg Pesh., MS *Mich.*, PhD *Mich.* Prof.; Chairman*

Other Staff: 1 Lectr.

Engineering, Mining

Tel: (091) 921 6501
E-mail: kgjadoon@yahoo.com

Ahmed, Ishaq, BSc Pesh., MSc Pesh. Asst. Prof.

Akbar, Siddique, BScEngg Pesh., MSc Pesh. Asst. Prof.

Aman-ul-Mulk, BSc Pesh., MScEngg Pesh., MSc *George Washington* Assoc. Prof.

Asad, M. Waqar A., BScEngg Pesh., MSc *Colorado Sch.of Mines*, PhD *Colorado Sch.of Mines* Assoc. Prof.

Din, Feroz, BScEngg Pesh., MScEngg Pesh. Assoc. Prof.

Jadoon, Khan G., BScEngg Pesh., PhD *Nott.* Prof.

Khan, Etesham Ullah, BScEngg Pesh., MSc(Eng) *Lond.* Asst. Prof.

Khan, Muhammad M., BScEng *Punjab*, PhD *Nott.* Prof.; Chairman*

Muhammad, Nisar, BSc Pesh., MSc Pesh. Asst. Prof.

Muhammad, Noor, BScEngg Pesh., MSc *McG.*, PhD *Nott.* Prof.

Naseem, Tariq, BScEngg Pesh., MPhil *Nott.* Assoc. Prof.

Raza, Salim, BSc Pesh., MSc Pesh. Asst. Prof.

Research: computer applications in mining; mine design; minerals processing; safety and mine environment

ABOTTABAD

Tel: (0992) 381700 Fax: (0992) 383627

Architecture, City and Regional Planning

Ahmad, Sameeta, MArch *Texas* Asst. Prof.

Ali, Arshad, PhD Prof.; Chairman*

Izhar-ul-Hassan, BArch *Lahore UET*, MSc Pesh. Asst. Prof.

Jamil, Salman, MSc(Arch) *Georgia* Asst. Prof.

Qureshi, Shabirullah, BArch *NED Eng.* Asst. Prof.

Other Staff: 9 Lectrs.

Electronics

Riaz-ul-Hassnain, Syed, BSc Pesh., MSc Pesh. Asst. Prof.

Shah, Syed M., BSc Pesh., MSc Prof.

Other Staff: 3 Lectrs.

BANNU

Tel: (0928) 927 0008 Fax: (0928) 927 0009

Basic Sciences

4 Lectrs

Engineering, Civil

Badrashi, Yasir I., BSc Pesh., MSc Pesh. Asst. Prof.

Noor-ul-Amin, PhD Chairman*

Rehan, Rashid, BSc Pesh., MSc Asst. Prof.

Shah, Mohib A., BSc Pesh., MSc Pesh.

Other Staff: 6 Lectrs.

Engineering, Electrical

4 Lectrs.

MARDAN

Tel: (0937) 923 0295 Fax: (0937) 923 0296

Basic Sciences

4 Lectrs.

Engineering, Computer Software

Babar, Mehmood J., MSc Pesh.

Jan, Sadaqat, BSc *Philippines*, MSc Pesh. Asst. Prof.

Other Staff: 7 Lectrs.

Engineering, Telecommunication

5 Lectrs.

CONTACT OFFICERS

Academic affairs. Dean, Faculty of Engineering: Khan, Prof. M. Mansoor, BE Pesh., PhD *Nott.*
(E-mail: dean@nwfpuet.edu.pk)

Academic affairs. Deputy Registrar: Ullah, Sami (E-mail: dean@nwfpuet.edu.pk)

Accommodation. Provost: Sayyed-ul-Abrar, Prof., MPhil

Admissions (first degree). Dean, Faculty of Engineering: Khan, Prof. M. Mansoor, BE Pesh., PhD *Nott.*
(E-mail: dean@nwfpuet.edu.pk)

Admissions (higher degree). Director, Postgraduate Studies: Muhammad, Prof. Noor, BScEngg Pesh., MSc *McG.*, PhD *Nott.*
(E-mail: noormohd.pk@yahoo.com)

Adult/continuing education. Dean, Faculty of Engineering: Khan, Prof. M. Mansoor, BE Pesh., PhD *Nott.*
(E-mail: dean@nwfpuet.edu.pk)

Consultancy services. (Contact the chairman of the relevant department)

Development/fund-raising. Director of Finance and Planning: Khan, Muhammad S., MCom
(E-mail: msarwarkhan@yahoo.com)

Distance education. Director, Postgraduate Studies: Muhammad, Prof. Noor, BScEngg Pesh., MSc *McG.*, PhD *Nott.*
(E-mail: noormohd.pk@yahoo.com)

Estates and buildings/works and services. Director of Works: Siddique, Mohammad

Examinations. Controller of Examinations: Nisar, Mohammad

Finance. Director of Finance and Planning: Khan, Muhammad S., MCom
(E-mail: msarwarkhan@yahoo.com)

General enquiries. Registrar: Khan, Lt. Col.(Retd.) Imtiaz A., MSc(ElectEng)
(E-mail: registrar@nwfpuet.edu.pk)

Health services. Medical Officer, Islamia College, Peshawar: Rehman, Sher

Industrial liaison. Secretary, Board of Advanced Studies and Research: Jadoon, Prof. Khan G., BScEngg Pesh., PhD *Nott.*
(E-mail: kgjadoon@yahoo.com)

International office. Assistant Registrar: Murad, Ahmad

Library (chief librarian). Librarian: Rashid, Abdur, LLB Gomal, MLSc Punjab

Minorities/disadvantaged groups. In-Charge, Students' Affairs: Mehmood, Prof. Zahid, PhD (E-mail: mehmood333@yahoo.com)

Ombudsman. Registrar: Khan, Lt. Col.(Retd.) Imtiaz A., MSc(ElectEng) (E-mail: registrar@nwfpuet.edu.pk)

Publications. Chief Editor: Farooq, Shumaila, MA(Jour)

Publications. Chief Editor: Jadoon, Prof. Khan G., BScEngg Pesh., PhD Nott. (E-mail: kgjadoon@yahoo.com)

Purchasing. Director of Finance and Planning: Khan, Muhammad S., MCom (E-mail: msarwarkhan@yahoo.com)

Research. Secretary, Board of Advanced Studies and Research: Jadoon, Prof. Khan G., BScEngg Pesh., PhD Nott. (E-mail: kgjadoon@yahoo.com)

Safety. Administrative Officer: Aftab Ahmad, Abbasi

Scholarships, awards, loans. Registrar: Khan, Lt. Col.(Retd.) Imtiaz A., MSc(ElectEng) (E-mail: registrar@nwfpuet.edu.pk)

Schools liaison. Director of Finance and Planning: Khan, Muhammad S., MCom (E-mail: msarwarkhan@yahoo.com)

Security. Administrative Officer: Aftab Ahmad, Abbasi

Sport and recreation. Assistant Director of Sports: Ali, Muhammad

Staff development and training. Registrar: Khan, Lt. Col.(Retd.) Imtiaz A., MSc(ElectEng) (E-mail: registrar@nwfpuet.edu.pk)

Student welfare/counselling. In-Charge, Students' Affairs: Mehmood, Prof. Zahid, PhD (E-mail: mehmood333@yahoo.com)

Students from other countries. Foreign Students' Advisor: Jehangir Durrani, Prof. M. A. Q., PhD

Students with disabilities. In-Charge, Students' Affairs: Mehmood, Prof. Zahid, PhD (E-mail: mehmood333@yahoo.com)

University press. Registrar: Khan, Lt. Col.(Retd.) Imtiaz A., MSc(ElectEng) (E-mail: registrar@nwfpuet.edu.pk)

CAMPUS/COLLEGE HEADS

Abottabad, Abottabad, Pakistan. (Tel: (0992) 381700; Fax: (0992) 383627) Co-ordinator: Shah, Prof. Syed M., BSc Pesh., MSc

Bannu, Bannu, Pakistan. (Tel: (0928) 927 0008; Fax: (0928) 927 0009) Co-ordinator: Shah, Mohib A., BSc Pesh., MSc Pesh.

Mardan, Mardan, Pakistan. (Tel: (0937) 923 0295; Fax: (0937) 923 0296) Co-ordinator: Babar, Mehmood J., MSc Pesh.

AFFILIATED COLLEGES

[Institutions listed by location below provide courses leading to degrees, etc. of the university]

Islamabad. Institute of Communication Technology

Peshawar. Gandhara Institute of Science and Technology; Government College of Technology; Peshawar College of Engineering and Technology

[Information supplied by the institution as at 12 October 2007, and edited by the ACU]

UNIVERSITY OF PESHAWAR

Founded 1950

Postal Address: Peshawar, North-West Frontier Province, Pakistan
Telephone: (091) 921 6471 **Fax:** (091) 921 6470 **E-mail:** vice-chancellor@upesh.edu.pk
URL: http://www.upesh.edu

VICE-CHANCELLOR*—Rashid, Prof. Haroon, PhD
REGISTRAR‡—Bahadar, Sher, LLB MA(PolSc)

UNIVERSITY OF THE PUNJAB, LAHORE

Founded 1882

Member of the Association of Commonwealth Universities

Postal Address: Quaid-e-Azam Campus, Lahore, Punjab, Pakistan
Telephone: (055) 920 0985 **Fax:** (055) 920 1223 **E-mail:** unipunjab@wol.net.pk
URL: http://www.pu.edu.pk

VICE-CHANCELLOR*—Kamran, Prof. Mujahid, MSc PhD
PRO-VICE-CHANCELLOR—(vacant)
REGISTRAR‡—Khan, Muhammad N., MSc Punjab, LLB Punjab, PhD Guelph
TREASURER—Bhatti, Jamil
CONTROLLER OF EXAMINATIONS—Malik, Prof. Ehsan M., PhD
CHIEF LIBRARIAN—Hanif, Muhammad
RESIDENT OFFICER I—Farooq, Prof. Umar, MSc Lond., MSc Punjab
RESIDENT OFFICER II—Malik, Zaheer Muhammad
RESIDENT AUDITOR—Hussain, Sajid

QUAID-E-AWAM UNIVERSITY OF ENGINEERING SCIENCE AND TECHNOLOGY

Founded 1996

Member of the Association of Commonwealth Universities

Postal Address: Sakrand Road, Nawabshah 67480, Sindh, Pakistan
Telephone: (0244) 937 0373 **Fax:** (0244) 937 0367 **E-mail:** registrar@quest.edu.pk
URL: http://www.quest.edu.pk

VICE-CHANCELLOR*—Junejo, Prof. Anwar A., BE *Sindh*, PhD *Wales*, FIE(P)
REGISTRAR‡—Shah, Syed Ghulam K.
CONTROLLER OF EXAMINATIONS—Durani, Nazir A., BE *Mehran*
DIRECTOR (FINANCE)—Bughio, Sikander M., LLB BCom MA(Econ)
LIBRARIAN—Mughal, Mohammad R., BCom *Sindh*, MLSc *Sindh*, MA *Sindh*
RESIDENT AUDITOR—Memon, Rab D., LLB MA(Econ)
DIRECTOR (PLANNING AND DEVELOPMENT)—Soomro, Prof. Wahid B., BE *Sindh*, ME *Toyohashi*, PhD *Kobe*

GENERAL INFORMATION

History. Initially founded in 1974 and renamed in 1980, the institution became a university in 1996.

It is located in central Sindh province, about 300km north-east of Karachi.

Admission to first degree courses (see also Pakistan Introduction). Intermediate Science or Higher Secondary School Certificate or pre-engineering examination.

First Degrees (see also Pakistan Directory to Subjects of Study). BSc.
Length of course. Full-time: BSc: 4 years.

Higher Degrees (see also Pakistan Directory to Subjects of Study).
Master's. Admission. Facilities are available for research leading to postgraduate degrees in some fields of civil and mechanical engineering.

Libraries. Volumes: 30,000.

FACULTIES/SCHOOLS

Engineering
Dean: Soomro, Prof. Ali B., BE *Sindh*, PhD *Sheff*.

Technology
Dean: Sheikh, Prof. Sadaruddin, BE *Sindh*, PhD *S'ton*.

ACADEMIC UNITS

Basic Sciences and Related Studies
Tel: (0241) 937 0378
Ansari, I. A., MSc *Sindh*   Asst. Prof.
Bhutto, K. H., MSc *Sindh*   Prof.
Jatoi, H. B., LLB *Sindh*, MSc *Sindh*   Asst. Prof.
Korai, M. A., MSc *Sindh*   Asst. Prof.
Shah, A. H., MA *Sindh*   Asst. Prof.
Umrani, Abdul A., MA *Sindh*, PhD *Sindh*   Prof.; Chairman*
Other Staff: 4 Lectrs.

Energy and Environment
Memon, Mueenuddin   Prof.; Chairman*
Other Staff: 1 Prof.; 2 Asst. Profs.; 2 Lectrs.

Engineering, Civil
Tel: (0241) 937 0375
    E-mail: dccquest@yahoo.com
Ansari, A. A., BE *Mehran*, LLB *Sindh*, ME *Mehran*, MA *Sindh*   Assoc. Prof.

Buller, G. S., BE *Mehran*, MSc *Tennessee*   Assoc. Prof.
Durrani, N. A., BE *Mehran*   Assoc. Prof.
Jamali, Azizullah, BE *Mehran*   Asst. Prof.
Jokhio, Sirajuddin, BE *NED Eng.*   Asst. Prof.
Kazi, A. R., BE *Mehran*   Asst. Prof.
Keerio, N. S., BE *Mehran*   Asst. Prof.
Lakho, N. A., BE *Mehran*   Asst. Prof.
Memon, B. A., BE *Mehran*, ME   Asst. Prof.
Memon, M. A., BE *Mehran*, MPhil *Mehran*   Assoc. Prof.
Memon, M. A., BE *Sindh*   Asst. Prof.
Memon, Mehmood, BE *NED Eng.*, PhD *Glas.*   Prof.
Memon, N. A., BE *Mehran*   Asst. Prof.
Memon, N. A., BE *NED Eng.*   Asst. Prof.
Saand, Abdullah, BE *Mehran*, ME *Mehran*   Assoc. Prof.
Shaikh, A. M., BE *Sindh*, MPhil *Mehran*   Prof.
Wagan, Ghulam H., BE *Mehran*, ME *Mehran*   Prof.; Chairman*
Other Staff: 2 Lectrs.

Engineering, Computer Systems, and Information Technology
Tel: (0241) 937 0369
Khaskheli, N. A., BE *Sindh*   Asst. Prof.
Memon, M. S., BE *Mehran*   Asst. Prof.
Memon, Niaz A., BE *Mehran*   Asst. Prof.; Chairman*
Sheikh, Sadaruddin, BE *Sindh*, PhD *S'ton*.   Prof.
Soomro, M. A., BE *Mehran*   Asst. Prof.
Other Staff: 11 Lectrs.

Engineering, Electrical
Tel: (0241) 937 0369
Keerio, J. M., BE *Sindh*, ME *Chiba*   Prof.
Keerio, M. U., BE *Mehran*   Asst. Prof.
Khooharo, Khalilullah, BE *Mehran*   Asst. Prof.
Larik, G. S., BE *Mehran*   Asst. Prof.
Memon, M. D., BE *Sindh*, MSc *Lond.*   Prof.
Memon, N. D., BE *NED Eng.*   Assoc. Prof.
Sheikh, Sadaruddin, BE *Sindh*, PhD *S'ton*.   Prof.; Chairman*
Siddiqui, R. A., BE *Mehran*   Asst. Prof. (on leave)
Soomro, M. I., BE *Mehran*   Asst. Prof.
Tanwani, N. K., BE *Mehran*   Asst. Prof.
Other Staff: 2 Lectrs.

Engineering, Electronic
Memon, Mueenuddin   Prof.; Chairman*
Other Staff: 1 Prof.; 2 Asst. Profs.; 2 Lectrs.

Engineering, Mechanical
Tel: (0241) 937 0380
    E-mail: ahameed_@hotmail.com

Abro, Z. A., BE *Mehran*   Asst. Prof.
Akhound, M. A., BE *Mehran*   Asst. Prof.
Manganhar, A. L., BE *Mehran*   Asst. Prof.
Memon, A. G., BE *Mehran*   Asst. Prof.
Memon, A. H., BE *Mehran*, PhD *Sheff*.   Prof.
Memon, A. S., BE *Sindh*   Assoc. Prof.
Memon, L. A., BE *Mehran*   Asst. Prof.
Memon, Zaheeruddin, BE *Mehran*, LLB *Sindh*, MA *Sindh*, ME *Mehran*   Asst. Prof.
Samo, Saleem R., BE *Mehran*, ME *Asian I.T., Bangkok*, PhD *UMIST*   Prof.; Chairman*
Soomro, Ali B., BE *Sindh*, PhD *Sheff*.   Prof.
Soomro, W. B., BE *Sindh*, ME *Toyohashi*, PhD *Kobe*   Prof.
Soomro, Z. A., BE *Mehran*, ME *NUST(P'stan.)*   Asst. Prof.
Talpur, M. H., BE *Sindh*, LLB *Sindh*   Assoc. Prof.
Tunio, N. A., BE *Mehran*, MSc   Assoc. Prof.
Wadho, J. M., BE *Mehran*   Assoc. Prof.
Other Staff: 3 Lectrs.

CONTACT OFFICERS

Academic affairs. Vice-Chancellor: Junejo, Prof. Anwar A., BE *Sindh*, PhD *Wales*, FIE(P)
    (E-mail: anwarjunejo@hotmail.com)
Admissions (first degree). Chairman, Admissions Committee and Dean, Faculty of Technology: Sheikh, Prof. Sadaruddin, BE *Sindh*, PhD *S'ton*.
Admissions (higher degree). Chairman, Admissions Committee and Dean, Faculty of Technology: Sheikh, Prof. Sadaruddin, BE *Sindh*, PhD *S'ton*.
Examinations. Controller of Examinations: Durani, Nazir A., BE *Mehran*
Finance. Director (Finance): Bughio, Sikander M., LLB BCom MA(Econ)
General enquiries. Registrar: Shah, Syed Ghulam K.
    (E-mail: information@quest.edu.pk)
Library (chief librarian). Librarian: Mughal, Mohammad R., BCom *Sindh*, MLSc *Sindh*, MA *Sindh*

AFFILIATED COLLEGES

[Institutions listed by location below provide courses leading to degrees, etc. of the university]

Khairpur. Government College of Technology
Nawabshah. Habib College of Technology

[*Information supplied by the institution as at 26 April 2006, and edited by the ACU*]

QUAID-I-AZAM UNIVERSITY

Founded 1965

Postal Address: Islamabad 45320, Pakistan
Telephone: (051) 921 9877 **Fax:** (051) 921 9888
URL: http://www.qau.edu.pk

VICE-CHANCELLOR*—Jan, M. Qasim, PhD *Lond.*
REGISTRAR‡—Sohail, Sajid, MSc
REGISTRAR‡—Hasan, Aurangzeb, MSc *Pesh.*, MPhil *Lyons I*, PhD *Lyons I*

RIPHAH INTERNATIONAL UNIVERSITY

Founded 2002

Member of the Association of Commonwealth Universities

Postal Address: Street No. 48, Sector G-6/1-1, Islamabad 44000, Pakistan
Telephone: (051) 287 7390-5 **Fax:** (051) 282 8189 **E-mail:** infodesk@riphah.edu.pk
URL: http://www.riphah.edu.pk

VICE-CHANCELLOR*—Ahmad, Prof. Anis, MA *Temple*, PhD *Temple*
REGISTRAR‡—Akbar, Col. (Retd.) Sajjad, MSc *Lahore UET*, PhD
CONTROLLER OF EXAMINATIONS—Lodhi, P. N. M. Farooq K., BSc *Baloch.*, MA *Baloch.*
FINANCE CONTROLLER—Nasir, Muhammad B., BCom

GENERAL INFORMATION

Admission to first degree courses (see also Pakistan Introduction). Higher Secondary School Certificate or equivalent (as certified by the Inter Board Committee of Chairmen) and good academic standing.

First Degrees (see also Pakistan Directory to Subjects of Study). BDS, BSc, BSEE, MB BS.
Length of course. Full-time: BDS, BSc, BSEE: 4 years; MB BS: 5 years.

Higher Degrees (see also Pakistan Directory to Subjects of Study).
Master's. MBA, MSEE.
Admission. First degree or equivalent (as determined by the Higher Education Commission) and good academic standing.
Length of course. Full-time: MBA, MSEE: 2 years.
Doctoral. DPharm, PhD.
Admission. Higher degree and good academic standing; additional criteria may be set by the Higher Education Commission.
Length of course. Full-time: PhD: 2 years; DPharm: 5 years.

Libraries. Volumes: 12,000. Periodicals subscribed to: 52.

FACULTIES/SCHOOLS

Computing
E-mail: naveedikram@riphah.edu.pk
Dean: Ikram, Naveed, MSc *Salf.*, PhD *Salf.*

Engineering and Applied Sciences
E-mail: sharifbhatti@riphah.edu.pk
Dean: Bhatti, Prof. M. Sharif, BSc *Punjab*, PhD *Lond.*

Health and Medical Sciences
Tel: (051) 556 5981 Fax: (051) 556 7527
E-mail: principal@iimc.edu.pk
Dean: Khan, Lt. Gen. (Retd.) Najam, MB BS

Management Sciences
Dean: Seyal, Faiez H.

Pharmaceutical Sciences
Tel: (051) 556 5981 Fax: (051) 5567527
E-mail: miana@riphah.edu.pk
Dean: Miana, Prof. G. A., MSc *Calg.*, PhD *Calg.*

ACADEMIC UNITS

Anaesthesiology
Mustafa, Ghulam, MB BS, FACS   Asst. Prof.
Salim, Muhammad, MB BS *Dhaka*, PhD *Colombo*, FRCA, FACS   Prof.

Anatomy
Hashmi, Ramiz I., MB BS MPhil   Prof.
Javed, Arshad, MB BS *Punjab*   Asst. Prof.
Khan, Sikandar H., MB BS *Punjab*   Asst. Prof.
Shakoor, Nuzhat, MB BS   Asst. Prof.

Biochemistry
Haroon, Sadia, MPhil *NUST(P'stan.)*, MB BS   Asst. Prof.
Jehan, Zaib, BSc *Pesh.*, MSc *Pesh.*, MPhil *Quaid-i-Azam*   Asst. Prof.
Nizam-ul-Haq, MPhil *Karachi*, MB BS   Prof.
Sadiq, Muhammad, BSc MB BS MPhil   Prof.

Community Medicine
Bhatti, Muhammad A., MB BS MPH MSc   Asst. Prof.
Inam-ul-Haq, MB BS *Punjab*, MPH *Punjab*   Asst. Prof.
Khan, Sana U., MSc *Quaid-i-Azam*, MB BS   Prof.
Khan, Shabbir A., MSc *Karachi*, MB BS   Prof.

Computing
Kamran, Sarwar, BSc *Punjab*, MA *Punjab*, PhD *Quaid-i-Azam*   Prof.
Mateen, Abdul, BA *Punjab*, MSc *Sund.*   Asst. Prof.
Qamar, M. Sabir, BSc *B.Zak.*, MSc *Quaid-i-Azam*, MS *IIU Malaysia*   Asst. Prof.
Qureshi, Atif, BS MS   Asst. Prof.

Dentistry
Ahmed, Kabir, BDS   Assoc. Prof.
Aqeel, Ijaz, BDS, FDSRCS   Prof.
Arshad, Noeen, BDS   Asst. Prof.
Bashir, Ulfat, BDS   Asst. Prof.
Butt, Rafik A., BDS MDS   Prof.
Hussain, Ayub, BDS   Asst. Prof.

Hyder, Pakeeza R., BDS MPhil   Asst. Prof.
Irfanullah, BDS   Asst. Prof.
Khadim, Muhammad I., BDS MPhil   Prof.
Rafique, Mohammad, BDS, FDSRCS   Asst. Prof.
Rashid, Farida, BDS PhD   Assoc. Prof.
Rehmatullah, BDS   Asst. Prof.
Younus, Muhammad, BDS MDS   Assoc. Prof.

Ear, Nose and Throat
Ahmad, Ashfaq, MB BS   Asst. Prof.
Mahmood, Khalid, MB BS *Punjab*, FRCP   Prof.
Qureshi, M. Ishaq, MB BS, FRCS   Asst. Prof.

Engineering, Electrical
Ahmad, Fazal-Din, BSc *Punjab*, BE *Karachi*, MSc *Punjab*, MSc *S'ton.*   Asst. Prof.
Ahmad, Mushtaq, BSc MSc   Asst. Prof.
Akbar, Sajjad, MBA *Al-Khair*, PhD *Louisiana State*, BSc MSc   Assoc. Prof.
Anwar, Muhammad, BSc *Pesh.*, MSc *Lahore UET*   Assoc. Prof.
Anwar, Shahid, MSc *Alabama*, BSc   Asst. Prof.
Hafeez, Muhammad   Asst. Prof.
Hameedullah, Hafiz, PhD *Arid Ag.*   Asst. Prof.
Ibraheem, Muhammad, BSc *Punjab*, MSc *Punjab*, MSc *Belf.*   Asst. Prof.
Owais, Syed M., BScMath *Pesh.*, BScEngg *Pesh.*, MS *Tennessee*   Asst. Prof.
Rushdi, Javed, BSc MSc   Asst. Prof.
Saleem, Tariq, BE MSc   Asst. Prof.
Tahir, Abdul H., BSc *Punjab*, MSc *Punjab*, PhD *Punjab*   Assoc. Prof.
Yusuf, S. M., BSc *Punjab*, MSc *Punjab*, PhD *Tennessee*   Prof.

Forensic Medicine
Chughtai, Baber R., BSc MB BS   Assoc. Prof.
Uraizy, S. M. H., MB BS   Prof.

Management Sciences
Ahmad, Tehsin, BBA *Pitt.*, MBA *N.Y.State*   Sr. Lectr.
Jan, Mian A., BSc *Pesh.*, MBA *IIU(P'stan.)*, MPhil *NU Mod.Langs.*   Asst. Prof.

Medicine
Baqai, Tariq, MB BS   Assoc. Prof.
Hussain, Arshad, MB BS   Prof.
Khan, Hamza R., MB BS *Quaid-i-Azam*   Assoc. Prof.

Saima, Kausar, MB BS *Punjab* Asst. Prof.
Sattar, Shah, MB BS *Pesh.* Asst. Prof.
Sharif-uz-Zaman, MB BS Prof.
Toori, Kaleemullah, MB BS Asst. Prof.

Obstetrics and Gynaecology

Amber, Shamsun N., MB BS
Awan, Azra S., MB BS *Quaid-i-Azam* Assoc. Prof.
Javed, Rubina, MB BS *Karachi* Asst. Prof.
Khan, Yasmeen, MB BS *Al-Khair* Asst. Prof.
Nasir, Razia, MB BS *Punjab*, FRCOG Prof.
Waqar, Fareesa, MB BS *Punjab* Assoc. Prof.
Zafar, Shamsa, MB BS *Punjab* Assoc. Prof.

Ophthalmology

Butt, Imran, MB BS Asst. Prof.
Durrani, M. Yasin K., MB BS *Karachi*, FRCP Prof.
Ghani, Naheed, MB BS
Hafeez-ur-Rehman, MB BS Asst. Prof.
Mirza, Aneequllah B., MB BS Asst. Prof.

Paediatrics

Kundi, Zafarullah, MB BS Prof.
Najam, Yawar, MB BS *Punjab* Asst. Prof.
Rafiq, Shahid, MB BS Asst. Prof.
Tahir, Muhammad, MB BS *Punjab* Asst. Prof.

Pathology

Bari, Abdul, MB BS *Punjab*, MPhil *Quaid-i-Azam* Asst. Prof.
Iqbal, Waseem, MPhil *Karachi*, MB BS Prof.
Khan, Masood A., MB BS *B.Zak.*, MPhil *Quaid-i-Azam* Asst. Prof.
Mahmood-ur-Rehman, MB BS MPhil Prof.
Masood-ul-Hassan, MB BS *Sindh*, MPhil *Quaid-i-Azam* Assoc. Prof.
Muzaffar, M., MB BS, FRCP, FRCPI Prof.

Pharmacology

Ali, Asad, MB BS Asst. Prof.
Mateen, Abdul, MB BS MPhil Prof.
Sial, Ahmad Y., MB BS MPhil Prof.
Turabi, Aftab, MPhil *Quaid-i-Azam*, MB BS Assoc. Prof.

Pharmacy

Inam-ul-Haq, BScPharm *Punjab*, PhD *Rome* Prof.
Jehan, Zaib, BSc *Pesh.*, MSc *Pesh.*, MPhil *Quaid-i-Azam* Asst. Prof.
Khan, Naeem H., BPharm *Punjab*, MPharm *Punjab* Prof.
Saeed-ul-Haq, Rafiuzzaman, BPharm *Punjab*, PhD *Lond.*, MSc Prof.
Shah, Syed I. H., BSc MSc Assoc. Prof.

Physiology

Hameed, M. Amjid, MB BS MPhil Prof.
Khan, Umar A., MB BS MPhil Prof.

Radiology

Ahmad, Munawwar, MB BS *Punjab*
Akhtar, Fahmida, MB BS Asst. Prof.
Manzoor, Shahid, MB BS *Punjab*, MPhil *Punjab* Asst. Prof.

Surgery

Chaudry, Abdul R., MB BS *Punjab* Prof.
Danish, Khalid F., MB BS *Punjab* Asst. Prof.
Khan, M. Iqbal, MB BS *Tashkent*, MD *Tashkent*, FRCS, FRCSGlas Assoc. Prof.
Nazir, Muhammad, MB BS *B.Zak.*, FRCS Asst. Prof.
Nurus-Sami, Ahmad, MB BS *Punjab* Asst. Prof.
Perveen, MB BS MS
Rasheed, Danial, MB BS, FRCS Prof.
Tasadaq, Tariq, MB BS, FRCS

CONTACT OFFICERS

Admissions (first degree). Deputy Registrar (Admissions): Khan, Lt. Col. (Retd.) Purvez J.(E-mail: jamal@riphah.edu.pk)
Admissions (higher degree). Deputy Registrar (Admissions): Khan, Lt. Col. (Retd.) Purvez J.(E-mail: jamal@riphah.edu.pk)
Examinations. Controller of Examinations: Lodhi, P. N. M. Farooq K., BSc *Baloch.*, MA *Baloch.* (E-mail: farooq@riphah.edu.pk)
Finance. Finance Controller: Nasir, Muhammad B., BCom (E-mail: nasir@riphah.edu.pk)
General enquiries. Registrar: Akbar, Col. (Retd.) Sajjad, MSc *Lahore UET*, PhD (E-mail: sajjad@riphah.edu.pk)
Library (chief librarian). Librarian: Ramazan, Mian (E-mail: ramzan@iimc.edu.pk)

AFFILIATED COLLEGES

[Institutions listed by location below provide courses leading to degrees, etc. of the university]

Faisalabad. Informatics Computer Institute
Islamabad. National Institute of Science and Technical Education; Women's Institute of Science and Humanities
Lahore. Allied College of Textile Management and Administration; TIU Institute

[Information supplied by the institution as at 1 July 2005, and edited by the ACU]

SHAH ABDUL LATIF UNIVERSITY

Founded 1987

Postal Address: Khairpur, Sindh, Pakistan
Telephone: (0243) 928 0061 **Fax:** (0243) 928 0060 **E-mail:** nilofer12@yahoo.com
URL: www.salu.edu.pk

VICE-CHANCELLOR*—Shaikh, Prof. Nilofer, BA *Sindh*, MA *Sindh*, MA *Camb.*, PhD *Camb.*
REGISTRAR‡—Palijo, Ali N., MA

SHAHEED ZULFIKAR ALI BHUTTO INSTITUTE OF SCIENCE AND TECHNOLOGY

Founded 1995

Additional Member of the Association of Commonwealth Universities

Postal Address: 90 and 100 Clifton, Karachi 75600, Pakistan
Telephone: (021) 111 922 478 **Fax:** (021) 583 0446 **E-mail:** info@szabist.edu.pk
URL: http://www.szabist.edu.pk

PRESIDENT*—Laghari, Javaid R., BE Sindh, MS Middle East Tech., PhD N.Y.State
ADMINISTRATIVE CONTROLLER‡—Azeem, Mohammad, MPA Karachi
FINANCIAL CONTROLLER—Hanif, Mohammad, MBA Bhutto IST
PUBLIC RELATIONS OFFICER—Haq, Anwar Ul, BSc Karachi
LIBRARIAN—Ruqayia, Khatoon, MLib&InfSc Karachi

GENERAL INFORMATION

History. The institute was established by an act of the Sindh Assembly in 1995.
It is located in Karachi, the provincial capital of Sindh, and has three other campuses in Islamabad, Larkana and Dubai.

Admission to first degree courses (see also Pakistan Introduction). Pakistani applicants: Higher School Certificate (HSC). International applicants: certificates/diplomas satisfying matriculation requirements in country of origin are generally accepted. All candidates must demonstrate ability in English (eg by TOEFL/IELTS scores).

First Degrees (see also Pakistan Directory to Subjects of Study). BBA, BS, BSc(Dev&Econ), BS(MediaSc), LLB.
Length of course. Full-time: BSc(Dev&Econ), LLB: 3 years; BBA, BS, BS(MediaSc): 4 years.

Higher Degrees (see also Pakistan Directory to Subjects of Study).
Master's. MBA, MS.
Admission. Applicants for admission to master's degrees (MBA, MCS) should hold a first degree (4 years of university education).
Length of course. Full-time: MBA, MS: 1–2 years.
Doctoral. PhD.
Admission. Applicants for admission to postgraduate programmes (MS, PhD) should have a second degree (4–5 years of university education).
Length of course. Full-time: PhD: 2 years.

Libraries. Volumes: 5073. Periodicals subscribed to: 82. Other holdings: 532 other holdings; CD collection.

Statistics. Staff (2005–2006): 270 (205 academic, 65 non-academic).

ACADEMIC UNITS

Accounting

Asaf, Nabila, MBA Miami(Fla.)
Aslam, Javed M., MBA Lond.
Mehar, Ayub, MPhil Karachi
Siddiqui, S. A., MBA Inst.Bus.Ad.(P'stan.)
Siddiqui, Ziaullah

Computer Science

Abbasi, Hafeez, MSc Quaid-i-Azam
Abidi, Syed Sajjad Raza, MCS Bhutto IST
Ahmed, Feroz, MLS W.Ont.
Ahmed, Munira, MES Syd.
Ahmed, Tanzeem, MBA C'dia.
Aijazuddin, MSc Karachi
Akhter, Nadeem, MS W.Chester
Akram, Asif, MSc NED Eng.
Ali, Asaf M., MS King Fahd
Ali, Nadeem, MCS Karachi
Arshad, Syed Z., MS Bhutto IST
Bhutto, Kashif A., MCS Bhutto IST
Daudpota, Nadeem, PhD Beijing

Haider, Najmi, PhD Brun.
Hanif, Mohammad, MS C.U.N.Y.
Haque, Syed N., MSc Karachi
Hashmi, Nouman F., MCS Bhutto IST
Hashmi, Qutubuddin, MSc Karachi
Hussain, Syed Azhar, MSc Punjab
Iqbal, Maryam, BE NED Eng.
Jafri, Atiya, MBA Wales
Jamil, Mazhar, MCS Karachi
Karamat, Perwaiz, MBA W.Coast
Kazi, Asif, MSc Sindh
Khalid, Syed M., MSc Karachi
Khan, Mohammad A., MCS Bhutto IST
Khan, Rao A. M., BE NED Eng.
Khan, Wajeehuddin, MS Bhutto IST
Khawaja, Muhammad A., MS Bhutto IST
Memon, Aslam P., MSc Sindh
Mighal, Muhammad Y., PhD Ankara
Muhammad, Ali, PhD Nott.
Nadeem, Mohammad, MSc E.Lond.
Pathan, Amir H., PhD Strath.
Quraishi, Shuja M., MPhil Karachi
Qureshi, Faheem J., MCS Bahria
Rajput, A. Q. K., PhD Pitt.
Rana, Muhammad B., MCS Bhutto IST
Raza, S. A., MPhil E.Lond.
Riaz, Asim, MCS Bhutto IST
Rizvi, Syed A. I., MS NED Eng.
Sangi, A. Aziz, MSc Ill.
Shah, Mubarak A., PhD Wayne State
Shahzad, Amer, MS W.Mich.
Shaikh, Zubair A., PhD N.Y.Polytech.
Shakir, Hina, BE NED Eng.
Siddiqui, M. Irfan, MSc Newcastle(UK)
Tahir, Rizwan, MCS Bhutto IST
Unar, Manzoor H., MS Wayne State
Uqaili, Ayaz, MS Asian I.T., Bangkok
Usman, Muhammad A., MSc UMIST
Yousuf, Syed, MSc Karachi
Zaidi, Hasan M., MCS Bhutto IST

Economics

Abbas, Ghulam, MSc Karachi
Dhakan, Ali A., PhD Sindh
Ejaz, Muhammad, MBA Inst.Bus.Ad.(P'stan.)
Ghayas Uddin, MSc Karachi
Hussain, Syed A., MA Vanderbilt
Isani, Muzaffar A., PhD Georgetown
Ishaque, Qasim, PhD C.U.N.Y.
Khan, Waqas A., MBA Bhutto IST
Memon, Naheed, MSc Lond.
Panhwer, Iqbal, PhD Sindh Ag.
Shaheen, Rozina, MAS Karachi
Zia-ur-Reham, MBA Inst.Bus.Ad.(P'stan.)

Finance

Ahmed, Syed J., MBA Oklahoma State
Amir, Shaheena S., MBA Lahore MS
Carapiet, Saadia, MPhil Camb.
Faysal, Abdullah, MBA Alabama
Fazli, Fakhre A., MBA Inst.Bus.Ad.(P'stan.)
Haq, Zia U., MBA Bhutto IST
Jamal, Kashif, MAF Monash
Jilani, M. Khalid
Kamran, Shahid, MSc Wales
Khan, M. Tariq, MBA Inst.Bus.Ad.(P'stan.)
Khatri, Siddik, MBA Inst.Bus.Ad.(P'stan.)

Mehar, Ayub, MPhil Karachi
Mustaqim, Asif, MBA Inst.Bus.Ad.(P'stan.)
Nawaz, Sarvat K., MBA Inst.Bus.Ad.(P'stan.)
Samad, Imran, MBA Pesh.
Shabbir, Amama, MPhil Cran.
Sheikh, Muhammad A., MBA Inst.Bus.Ad.(P'stan.)
Siddiqui, Kamran, MBA Inst.Bus.Ad.(P'stan.)
Sultan, Shahab, MBA Bhutto IST
Termezy, Syed M., MBA Inst.Bus.Ad.(P'stan.)
Waheed, Amjad, PhD S.Illinois
Yousfani, Abdul M., MBA Col.
Zia, Muhammad A., MBA Bhutto IST
Zia-ur-Rahman, MBA Inst.Bus.Ad.(P'stan.)

Law

Ahmad, Nausheen, LLM Lond.
Ahmed, Sheeza, LLM Col.
Kadir, Irshad A., MA Camb.
Sarki, Shaista, LLM Temple
Shaikh, Ali M., LLM Warw.
Shaikh, Farrukh Z., LLB Wales
Siddiqui, Ali A. M., LLB Wolv.
Soomro, Muhammad O., BSc Lond.
Walliullah, Agha S., LLB Lond.

Management

Abbasy, Hafsa, MBA Inst.Bus.Ad.(P'stan.)
Afghan, Nasir, PhD T.H.Twente
Alam, Faisal, MBA Inst.Bus.Ad.(P'stan.)
Baig, Mirza A., PhD Kharagpur
Baig, Mirza D. F., MBA F.Dickinson
Choudhry, Mohammad A., PhD Sindh
Hameed, Azhar, MSc Lond.
Huda, Zainul, PhD Brun.
Ismail, Muneer, MBA Inst.Bus.Ad.(P'stan.)
Jalbani, Amanat A., PhD Edin.
Kamal, Ahsan, MBA Inst.Bus.Ad.(P'stan.)
Kazi, Aftab, PhD Pitt.
Larik, Ghulam S., PhD New Haven Coll.
Majdul-Ahsan, Syed, MBA New Mexico State
Manzoor, Raja A., MBA Bhutto IST
Maqsood, Azra, MS Bhutto IST
Murad, Hasnain, MBA Liv.
Rashid, Bilal, MSc Cran.
Raza, Syed M. R., MBA Bhutto IST
Saeed, Kanwer A., MBA Lahore MS
Shah, Masood A., MPA Punjab
Shehla, Najib S., MBA Bhutto IST
Siddiqui, Arshad, MS Bhutto IST
Siddiqui, Muhammad A., MS Bhutto IST

Marketing

Effendi, Qashif, MBA Inst.Bus.Ad.(P'stan.)
Ejaz, Meesha, MBA Inst.Bus.Ad.(P'stan.)
Hameed, Muhammad F., MBA Bhutto IST
Hasan, Tania, MBA Inst.Bus.Ad.(P'stan.)
Hashmi, Shahida T., MBA Asian Inst.Management
Jalees, Tariq, MBA La Verne
Kamal, Sajid, MBA Central State(Okla.)
Khan, Mansoor A., MBA Inst.Bus.Ad.(P'stan.)
Khan, Shariq H., MBA Calif.
Kohati, Kiran, MBA Inst.Bus.Ad.(P'stan.)
Mapara, Shakeel, MBA Quaid-i-Azam
Memon, Muhammad K., MBA Sur.
Naqvi, Asad M., MBA Inst.Bus.Ad.(P'stan.)
Noor, Ayesha F., MBA Inst.Bus.Ad.(P'stan.)
Qadri, Yasir, MBA Oklahoma

Riaz, Yasir, MBA *Oklahoma*
Sattar, Irfan, MBA *Inst.Bus.Ad.(P'stan.)*
Sharih, Saba, MBA *Inst.Bus.Ad.(P'stan.)*
Siddiqui, Shoaib A., MBA *Inst.Bus.Ad.(P'stan.)*

Mathematics and Statistics
Asif, Zaheeruddin, MBA *Inst.Bus.Ad.(P'stan.)*
Hanfi, Wajid, MBA *Inst.Bus.Ad.(P'stan.)*
Ismail, Abbas, MBA *Inst.Bus.Ad.(P'stan.)*
Kamal, Syed A., PhD *Karachi*
Khan, M. Sohail, MBA *Inst.Bus.Ad.(P'stan.)*
Khan, M. Tariq, MBA *Inst.Bus.Ad.(P'stan.)*
Mahesri, Sajjad, MS *Penn.State*
Maqsood, Haris B., MBA *Bhutto IST*
Nadeem-ud-din, M., MBA *Inst.Bus.Ad.(P'stan.)*
Naz, Farah, MSc *Karachi*
Samiuddin, Mohammad, PhD *Wales*

CONTACT OFFICERS

Academic affairs. Deputy Director (Academic affairs): Maqsood, Azra, MS *Bhutto IST* (E-mail: azra@szabist.edu.pk)
Admissions (first degree). Administrative Controller: Azeem, Mohammad, MPA *Karachi* (E-mail: azeem@szabist.edu.pk)
Admissions (higher degree). Administrative Controller: Azeem, Mohammad, MPA *Karachi* (E-mail: azeem@szabist.edu.pk)

Alumni. Executive Development Officer: Shah, Bisma, BBA *Bhutto IST* (E-mail: bisma@szabist.edu.pk)
Computing services. System Administrator: Kazi, Asif, MSc *Sindh* (E-mail: asif@szabist.edu.pk)
Consultancy services. Co-ordinator (Consultancy Services): Jalbani, Amanat A., PhD *Edin.* (E-mail: jalbani@szabist.edu.pk)
Examinations. Academic Controller: Siddique, Mohammad, MBA *Sindh* (E-mail: siddique@szabist.edu.pk)
Finance. Financial Controller: Hanif, Mohammad, MBA *Bhutto IST* (E-mail: hanif@szabist.edu.pk)
General enquiries. Administrative Controller: Azeem, Mohammad, MPA *Karachi* (E-mail: azeem@szabist.edu.pk)
International office. Public Relations Officer: Haq, Anwar Ul, BSc *Karachi* (E-mail: anwar@szabist.edu.pk)
Library (chief librarian). Librarian: Ruqayia, Khatoon, MLib&InfSc *Karachi* (E-mail: ruqayia@szabist.edu.pk)
Marketing. Public Relations Officer: Haq, Anwar Ul, BSc *Karachi* (E-mail: anwar@szabist.edu.pk)
Public relations. Public Relations Officer: Haq, Anwar Ul, BSc *Karachi* (E-mail: anwar@szabist.edu.pk)

Research. Deputy Director (Research): Maqsood, Azra, MS *Bhutto IST* (E-mail: azra@szabist.edu.pk)
Students from other countries. Public Relations Officer: Haq, Anwar Ul, BSc *Karachi* (E-mail: anwar@szabist.edu.pk)

CAMPUS/COLLEGE HEADS

Dubai Campus, Knowledge Village, Block 4B, PO Box 500230, Dubai, United Arab Emirates. (Tel: (04) 366 4601-6; Fax: (04) 366 4607; E-mail: info@szabist.ac.ae) Administrative Officer: Lasrado, Flavy, MA *Karachi*
Islamabad Campus, SZABIST Islamabad Campus, Block 3-D, Markaz, Sector F-8, Islamabad, Pakistan. (Tel: (051) 285 5151-2; Fax: (051) 285 6984) Deputy Director: Hussain, Syed A., MA *C.U.N.Y.*
Larkana Campus, SZABIST Larkana Campus, Opposite GPO, Larkana, Sindh, Pakistan. (Tel: (0741) 444760; Fax: (0741) 60780; E-mail: info@lrk.szabist.edu.pk) Deputy Director: Memon, Pervaiz A., MS *Bhutto IST*

[Information supplied by the institution as at 28 June 2005, and edited by the ACU]

UNIVERSITY OF SINDH

Founded 1947

Member of the Association of Commonwealth Universities

Postal Address: Jamshoro, Sindh, Pakistan
Telephone: (022) 277 1363 **Fax:** (022) 277 1372 **E-mail:** registrar@usindh.edu.pk
URL: http://www.usindh.edu.pk

VICE-CHANCELLOR*—Siddiqui, Mazharul Haq, BA *Sindh*, MSc *Quaid-i-Azam*
REGISTRAR‡—Soomro, Prof. Saeed A., MSc *Sindh*, PhD *Wales*
ADVISOR, PLANNING AND DEVELOPMENT—Shaikh, Muhammad H., MA
CONTROLLER OF EXAMINATIONS—Pathan, Prof. Parvez A., MBA *Sindh*, MSc *Lond.*, PhD *Lond.*
DIRECTOR OF FINANCE—Hingoro, Faiz M., LLB *Sindh*, MA *Sindh*
CONSULTANT ON HIGHER EDUCATION—Ahmed, Prof. M. Rais, MSc *Karachi*, PhD *Sheff.*
INSPECTOR OF COLLEGES—Chachar, A. Khalique, LLB *Sindh*, MA *Sindh*, MSc *Quaid-i-Azam*
DEPUTY REGISTRAR—Bhatti, Noor A., MCom *Sindh*

GENERAL INFORMATION

History. The university was established in 1947 under a charter granted by the Sindh Provincial Assembly. It was initially based at Karachi, moved to Hyderabad in 1951 and to its present site in 1961.

It is located at Jamshoro, approximately 160km from Karachi and 18km from Hyderabad, and has a second campus at Hyderabad.

Admission to first degree courses (see also Pakistan Introduction). Higher Secondary Certificate (HSC) or equivalent qualification and rating in the pre-entry written test.

First Degrees (see also Pakistan Directory to Subjects of Study) (* = with honours). BA, BA*, BBA*, BCom, BCom*, BPA*, BS*, BSc, BS(CS)*, BS(IT)*.
Length of course. Full-time: BA, BCom, BSc: 2 years; BA*, BBA*, BCom*, BPA*: 3 years; BS(CS)*, BS(IT)*, BS*: 4 years.

Higher Degrees (see also Pakistan Directory to Subjects of Study) (* = with honours).
Master's. BEd, BHPEd*, LLB, MA, MBA, MCIT, MCom, MCS, MEd, MHPEd, MLIS, MPA, MPhil, MS, MSc.

Admission. Applicants for admission to master's or second bachelor's degree courses must normally hold a relevant first degree.
Length of course. Full-time: BEd, BHPEd*, MHPEd, MLIS: 1 year; MA, MBA, MCIT, MCom, MEd, MPA, MSc: 1–2 years; MCS, MPhil, MS: 2 years; LLB: 3 years. By *distance learning:* BEd, LLB, MEd: 1 year.
Doctoral. PhD.
Admission. Applicants should normally hold an MPhil or MS.
Length of course. Full-time: PhD: 3 years.

Libraries. Volumes: 255,862. Periodicals subscribed to: 60. Special collections: Allama I. I. Kazi; Sindhology.

Income (2005–2006). Total, Rs679,370,000.

Statistics. Staff (2005–2006): 2242 (642 academic, 1600 non-academic). Students (2006): full-time 16,512 (11,765 men, 4747 women); part-time 1981 (1722 men, 259 women); international 128 (110 men, 18 women); distance education/external 929 (373 men, 556 women); undergraduate 47,834; master's 11,902; doctoral 44 (28 men, 16 women).

FACULTIES/SCHOOLS
Arts
Tel: (022) 277 1681
Dean: Bughio, Prof. M. Qasim, LLB *Sindh*, MA *Sindh*, PhD *Essex*

Commerce and Business Administration
Tel: (022) 277 1474
Dean: Syed, Prof. Shah A. A. G., LLB *Sindh*, MCom *Sindh*, MBA *Leeds*, PhD *Wales*

Education
Tel: (022) 920 0158
Dean: Panhwar, Prof. Iqbal A., MA *Sindh*, MSc *Sindh Ag.*, MA *Windsor*, PhD *Sindh*

Islamic Studies
Tel: (022) 277 1119
Dean: Bhutto, Prof. Sanaullah, MA *Sindh*, MA *Medina*, PhD *Sindh*

Law
Tel: (022) 920 0161
Dean: Shaikh, Ahmed A., BCom *Sindh*, LLB *Sindh*

Natural Sciences
Tel: (022) 277 1443
Dean: Khuhawar, Prof. M. Yar, MSc *Sindh*, PhD *Birm.*, DSc *Birm.*

Pharmacy

Tel: (022) 277 2486

Acting Dean: Khuhawar, Prof. M. Yar, MSc
Sindh, PhD Birm., DSc Birm.

Social Sciences

Tel: (022) 277 2039

Dean: Sheikh, Prof. Rafia A., MA Sindh, MA
Lough., PhD Lond.

ACADEMIC UNITS

Arts and Design, Institute of

Bhatti, Muhammad A., MA Punjab, MFA Edinboro
State, PhD Ohio   Prof.; Dir.*
Khaskheli, G. Qasim, MA Sindh   Asst. Prof.
Khilji, Naimatullah, MA Sindh   Asst. Prof.
Pirzada, Anjum J., MA Punjab   Asst. Prof.
Other Staff: 2 Lectrs.; 1 Res. Assoc.

Biochemistry, Institute of

Fax: (022) 277 1517

Ghanghro, A. B., MSc Sindh, PhD Sindh   Asst.
Prof.
Khan, M. Yakoob, MSc Sindh, PhD Sindh   Asst.
Prof.
Memon, Allahnawaz, MSc Sindh, MPhil Sindh,
PhD Sindh   Prof.; Dir.*
Other Staff: 5 Lectrs.

Biotechnology and Genetic Engineering, Institute of

Tel: (022) 277 2359

Choudhary, Rehmatullah, MSc Sindh, MPhil
Sindh, PhD Moscow   Visiting Prof.
Dahot, Muhammad U., MSc Sindh, PhD Sindh
Prof.; Dir.*
Other Staff: 3 Lectrs.; 2 Res. Assocs.
Research: enzymes and fermentation; plant
biotechnology

Botany, Institute of

Abro, Hidayatullah, MSc Sindh, PhD Sindh   Prof.
Arain, Basir A., MSc Sindh, MPhil Sindh, PhD
Sindh   Prof.
Hassany, Syeda S., MSc Sindh, MSc Syd., PhD
Sindh   Prof.
Khoja, Ashraf B., MSc Sindh   Asst. Prof.
Mangrio, Sher M., MSc Sindh, PhD Sindh
Assoc. Prof.
Memon, Abdul H., MSc Sindh, PhD Karachi
Prof.
Memon, Mahjabeen, MSc Sindh, MPhil Sindh
Asst. Prof.
Pirzada, A. Jabbar, MSc SA Latif   Asst. Prof.
Rajput, M. A., MSc Sindh, MPhil Sindh, PhD Sindh
Visiting Prof.
Rajput, M. Tahir, MSc Sindh, MPhil Sindh, PhD
Syd.   Prof.; Dir.*
Sahito, Mushtaque A., MSc Sindh, MPhil Sindh,
PhD Sindh   Prof.
Shah, Syed A. G., MSc Sindh, MPhil Sindh
Assoc. Prof.
Shahani, Pirsumal H., MSc Sindh   Asst. Prof.
Shaikh, Wazir, MSc Sindh, MPhil Sindh, PhD
Karachi   Prof.
Soomro, Shamshad, MSc Sindh, MPhil Sindh,
PhD Sindh   Prof.
Tirmizi, S. A. Saeeduddin, MSc Sindh, MPhil
Sindh, PhD Sindh   Prof.
Other Staff: 2 Lectrs.; 3 Res. Assocs.
Research: bacteriology; genetics; mycology;
phycology; plant taxonomy

Business Administration, Institute of

Tel: (022) 277 2005

Gopang, Nazir A., MBA Sindh   Asst. Prof.
Kazi, Ferozuddin, MCom   Prof.; Dir.*
Kazi, Zahid H., MBA Sindh   Asst. Prof.
Memon, M. Mian, MBA Sindh   Asst. Prof. (on
leave)
Pathan, Muhammad A., MBA Sindh   Asst. Prof.
Shah, Abdul S., MBA Sindh   Asst. Prof.
Syed, Shah A. A. G., LLB Sindh, MCom Sindh,
MBA Leeds, PhD Wales   Prof.
Zardari, Khair M., LLB Sindh, MCom Sindh, MBA
Leeds   Assoc. Prof.

Other Staff: 13 Lectrs.; 5 Res. Assocs.
Research: human resource management and
industrial relations; marketing

Chemistry, M. A. Kazi Institute of

Tel: (022) 277 1704

Abbasi, Ubedullah M., MSc Sindh, MSc Salf.,
PhD Salf.   Prof.; Dir.*
Arain, M. Rafi, MSc Sindh, PhD Moscow   Prof.,
Analytical Chemistry
Bhatti, Abdul G., MSc Sindh, PhD Sindh   Prof.
Bozdar, Rasool B., MSc Sindh, PhD Sindh   Prof.,
Inorganic Chemistry
Bughio, Muhammad N., MSc Sindh, MPhil Sindh
Asst. Prof., Inorganic Chemistry
Burdi, Dadu K., MSc Sindh, PhD Quaid-i-Azam
Assoc. Prof., Organic Chemistry
Khaskhelly, Ghulam Q., MSc Sindh, PhD Sindh
Prof., Organic Chemistry
Khuhawar, M. Yar, MSc Sindh, PhD Birm., DSc
Birm.   Prof., Analytical Chemistry
Mangrio, Niaz A., MSc Sindh, PhD Glas.   Prof.
Mastoi, G. Murtaza, MSc Sindh, PhD Sindh
Assoc. Prof.
Memon, Muhammad A., MSc Sindh, MPhil
Sindh, PhD Sindh   Prof., Inorganic Chemistry
Memon, Saifullah, MSc Sindh, PhD Moscow
Visiting Prof.
Memon, Sikandar A., MSc Sindh, PhD Lond.
Prof., Analytical Chemistry
Qureshi, Abdul S., MSc Sindh, PhD Leip.   Prof.,
Inorganic Chemistry
Qureshi, Attaur R., MSc Sindh, PhD Sindh
Visiting Prof., Organic Chemistry
Qureshi, Muhammad S., MSc   Asst. Prof.
Shaikh, Muhammad S., MSc Sindh, PhD Moscow
Prof., Physical Chemistry
Tanwari, Zafarullah, MSc Sindh   Asst. Prof.,
Organic Chemistry
Vasandani, Abdul G., MSc Sindh, PhD Sindh
Assoc. Prof., Physical Chemistry
Other Staff: 7 Lectrs.; 1 Chem. Analyst
Research: analytical chemistry; inorganic
chemistry; organic chemistry; physical
chemistry

Commerce, Institute of

Abro, Muhammad H., MCom Sindh   Asst. Prof.
Agha, Riaz H., MCom Sindh   Assoc. Prof.;
Dir.*
Chandio, J. A., MCom Sindh   Asst. Prof.
Jamali, Ghulam R., LLB Sindh, MCom Sindh
Asst. Prof.
Jamali, Noor M., MCom Sindh   Asst. Prof.
Kanasro, Hakim A., MCom Sindh   Asst. Prof.
Kazi, N. F., MCom Sindh   Asst. Prof.
Shaikh, Khalid H., MCom Sindh, PhD Karachi
Asst. Prof. (on lien)
Shaikh, M. Ayoob, MCom Sindh, PhD SA Latif
Assoc. Prof. (on lien)
Shaikh, Manzoor A., MCom Sindh   Assoc. Prof.
Soomro, Muneeruddin, LLB Sindh, MCom Sindh
Asst. Prof. (on leave)
Other Staff: 6 Lectrs.; 1 Res. Assoc.

Comparative Religion and Islamic Culture

Bhutto, Sanaullah, MA Sindh, MA Medina, PhD
Sindh   Prof.; Chairman*
Khan, Hafiz Munir, MA Sindh, PhD Sindh   Asst.
Prof.
Khan, M. Anwar, MA Sindh, PhD Sindh   Assoc.
Prof.
Usman, Najama, MA Sindh   Asst. Prof.
Other Staff: 2 Visiting Profs.; 3 Lectrs.
Research: comparative religion; Islamic culture;
Muslim history

Curriculum Development and Special Education

Tel: (022) 920 0158

Kamboh, M. Aslam, MA Sindh, MEd Sindh
Asst. Prof.; Chairman-in-Charge*
Khan, Saleha Parven, MA Sindh   Asst. Prof.
Shah, Syed G. A., BEd Sindh, MA Sindh, MEd
Sindh   Asst. Prof.
Other Staff: 2 Lectrs.
Research: curriculum studies

Economics

Jamali, Khalida, MA Sindh, PhD Sindh   Prof.
Jamali, Sobho K., MA Sindh   Asst. Prof.
Kazi, Iqbal H., LLB Sindh, MA Sindh   Prof.;
Chairman*
Khawaja, Seema, MA Sindh   Asst. Prof.
Mirza, Albeena, MA Sindh   Asst. Prof.
Panhwar, Murad K., MA Sindh   Prof.
Pirzada, Imtiaz A., MSc Quaid-i-Azam   Asst.
Prof.
Qasmi, Merhab, MA Sindh, PhD Sindh   Prof.
Rajar, Wasayo, LLB Sindh, MA Sindh   Prof.
Ram Nanik, MA   Asst. Prof.
Shaikh, Najma, MA Sindh
Soomro, Sikander H., MA Sindh
Umrani, Anwar H., MA Sindh   Assoc. Prof.
Other Staff: 1 Lectr.; 2 Res. Assocs.
Research: banking and finance; human resource
development and management; marketing

Educational Management and Supervision

Tel: (022) 920 0158

Almani, A. Sattar, MA Sindh, MEd Sindh, MBA
Sindh, PhD Hamdard   Asst. Prof.
Channa, Din M., MA Sindh, MEd Sindh   Asst.
Prof.; Chairman-in-Charge*
Khuwaja, Mumtaz, MSc Sindh, MEd Sindh   Asst.
Prof.
Messo, M. Shafi, MEd Sindh   Asst. Prof.
Panhwar, Iqbal A., MA Sindh, MSc Sindh Ag., MA
Windsor, PhD Sindh   Prof.
Other Staff: 2 Lectrs.
Research: educational management and planning

English

Ansari, Arifa, MA Sindh   Assoc. Prof.
Baloch, Ghulam H., MA Sindh   Asst. Prof.
Buriro, G. Ali, MA Sindh   Asst. Prof.
Memon, Rafique A., MA Sindh   Asst. Prof.
Palli, A. Aziz, MA Sindh   Asst. Prof.
Panhwar, Farida Y., MA Sindh   Asst. Prof.;
Chairperson-in-Charge*
Panhwar, M. Murad, MA Sindh   Asst. Prof.
Sangi, M. Khan, MA Sindh   Asst. Prof.
Shah, S. Sharaf A., MA Sindh, MA Nott.   Asst.
Prof. (on lien)
Shah, Syed Ismail, BEd Sindh, MA Sindh   Asst.
Prof.
Suhag, Asif A., MA Sindh   Assoc. Prof.
Other Staff: 8 Lectrs.; 4 Res. Assocs.

Freshwater Biology and Fisheries

Tel: (022) 277 1681

Abbasi, Abdul R., MSc Sindh, PhD Wales   Prof.
Baloch, Wazir A., MSc Sindh, MS Kagoshima, PhD
Kagoshima   Prof.
Daudpota, Naeemuddin, MSc Sindh   Asst. Prof.
Leghari, Sultan M., MSc Sindh, PhD Sindh
Prof.; Chairman*
Narejo, Naeem T., MSc Sindh, MPhil Sindh, PhD
B'desh.Ag.   Prof.
Sahito, Gulshan A., MSc Sindh, PhD Sindh   Prof.
Other Staff: 1 Emer. Prof.; 3 Lectrs.

Geography

Tel: (022) 277 1681

Baloch, Nargis A., MSc   Asst. Prof.
Dhanani, M. Rafique, MSc Karachi, MSc Asian
I.T., Bangkok   Assoc. Prof.; Chairman*
Kazi, Shahnaz, MSc Sindh   Assoc. Prof.
Other Staff: 4 Lectrs.
Research: hydrogeography; land-use surveys;
physical geography; political geography;
urban and population geography

History, General

Lakho, Ghulam M., MA Sindh, PhD Sindh
Assoc. Prof.
Soomro, M. Qasim, MA Sindh, MPhil Quaid-i-
Azam, PhD Sindh   Prof.; Chairman*
Other Staff: 1 Lectr.; 1 Res. Assoc.

History, Muslim

Bughio, Mir M., MA Sindh   Prof.; Chairman*
Other Staff: 1 Lectr.; 1 Res. Assoc.

Information Technology, Institute of

Tel: (022) 277 1609
Ansari, Abdul W., MSc Sindh, PhD Brun. Prof.; Dir.*
Bhutto, Arifa, MSc Sindh Asst. Prof.
Ismaili, Imdad A., MSc Sindh, PhD Lond. Prof.
Khoumbati, R. Khalil, MSc Sindh Asst. Prof. (on leave)
Kumbhar, M. A., MSc Asst. Prof.
Lachman Das, MSc Sindh Asst. Prof.
Larik, Shahid H., MSc Sindh Asst. Prof.
Mirbhar, G. Qadir, MSc Sindh Asst. Prof. (on lien)
Seehar, Lubna M., MSc Sindh Asst. Prof.
Shaikh, Asad A., MSc Clarkson, MSc Sindh Assoc. Prof.
Shoro, G. M., MSc Sindh Asst. Prof.
Syed, Azhar A. S., MSc Asst. Prof.
Syed, Raza H., MSc Sindh Asst. Prof.
Ujjan, M. H. I., BE Mehran Asst. Prof.
Other Staff: 4 Lectrs.; 8 Res. Assocs.

International Relations

Kandhar, Azra, LLB Sindh, MA Sindh, PhD Sindh Assoc. Prof.
Mangi, Lutfullah, MA Sindh, MA Wat., PhD Lond. Prof.; Chairman*
Mangrio, Naghma, MA Sindh Asst. Prof.
Shah, Mehtab A., MA Sindh, MA Warw., PhD Lond. Prof.
Shaikh, Inamullah, MA Sindh Asst. Prof. (on deputation)
Tunio, Abdul L., MA Sindh, PhD Quaid-i-Azam Assoc. Prof.
Other Staff: 5 Lectrs.; 1 Res. Assoc.; 2 Adjunct Staff

Language, Institute of

Jalbani, Attaullah, MA Sindh Assoc. Prof., Arabic
Shaikh, H. A. Ghani, LLB Sindh, MA Sindh, PhD Sindh Prof.; Dir.*
Other Staff: 2 Lectrs.; 1 Res. Assoc.; 1 Adjunct Staff Member
Research: Arabic languages and literature

Law

Leghari, M. Y., LLB Chairman*

Library and Information Science and Archive Studies

Ansari, Khadija, MA Sindh, MLIS Sindh Asst. Prof.
Baloch, H. Akhtar, MA Sindh, MLIS Sindh Asst. Prof.
Hajano, Manzoor A., MA Sindh, MLIS Sindh, PhD Sindh Asst. Prof.
Sheikh, Rafia A., MA Sindh, MA Lough., PhD Lond. Prof.
Soomro, Sheerin G., MA Sindh, MLIS Sindh Asst. Prof.; Chairperson-in-Charge*
Other Staff: 1 Lectr.

Management Sciences

E-mail: pa_usindh_pk@hotmail.com
Abbasi, Zarin, MPA Sindh Asst. Prof.
Burdi, M. Bux, MPA Sindh, PhD Karachi Asst. Prof.
Kandhro, S. H., MPA Sindh, MSc Asst. Prof. (on leave)
Lalani, Farah, MPA Sindh Asst. Prof. (on leave)
Mangi, Aftab, MPA Sindh Asst. Prof.
Panhwar, Khalid N., MPA Sindh Asst. Prof.
Pardesi, M. Yousif, MA Sindh, MA Edinboro State, MPA Penn.State Prof.; Chairman*
Shaikh, Ghulam S., MPA Quaid-i-Azam Asst. Prof.
Siddiqui, Siraj J., MA Edinboro State, MA Sindh, PhD Sindh Assoc. Prof.
Other Staff: 7 Lectrs.; 4 Res. Assocs.

Mass Communication

Agha, Rafique A., MA Sindh Asst. Prof.; Chairman-in-Charge*
Chang, Rizwana, MA Sindh Asst. Prof.

Jaffery, Fouzia R., MA Karachi, PhD Sindh Prof. (on lien)
Makhijani, Har B., LLB Sindh, MA Sindh Asst. Prof.
Qureshi, Z. A., MA Sindh Asst. Prof.
Rashdi, Ibadullah, MA Sindh Assoc. Prof.
Soomro, Badaruddin, MA Sindh Asst. Prof.
Other Staff: 3 Lectrs.; 2 Res. Assocs.

Mathematics and Computer Science, Institute of

Tel: (022) 277 1551
E-mail: imcs@usindh.edu.pk
Brohi, Abdul W., MSc Sindh Asst. Prof.
Brohi, M. Nawaz, MSc Quaid-i-Azam Asst. Prof. (on lien)
Chandio, Muhammad S., MSc Sindh, PhD Wales Prof.
Jalbani, Shamsuddin, MSc Sindh Asst. Prof.
Keerio, Hayat A., MSc Sindh Asst. Prof.
Kundnani, Doulat R., MSc Sindh Asst. Prof.
Maree, M. Rehman, MSc Sindh Asst. Prof. (on leave)
Memon, Abdul G., MSc Sindh Asst. Prof.
Memon, Ali A., MSc Sindh Asst. Prof.
Memon, Kamaluddin, MSc Sindh Asst. Prof.
Memon, Manzoor A., MSc Sindh, MPhil Islamia, Bahawal. Assoc. Prof.
Memon, Riaz A., MSc Sindh, PhD Shanghai Prof.
Memon, Sirajuddin, MSc Sindh Assoc. Prof.
Shaikh, A. Wasim, MSc Sindh Asst. Prof. (on leave)
Shaikh, Noor A., MSc Sindh, MPhil Quaid-i-Azam, PhD Sindh Prof.; Dir.*
Soomro, A. Sattar, MSc Sindh, PhD Shanghai U.S.T. Prof.
Soomro, Abdul K., MSc Sindh Asst. Prof.
Other Staff: 21 Lectrs.; 12 Res. Assocs.

Microbiology

Agha, Asad N., MSc SA Latif, MPhil Quaid-i-Azam Asst. Prof.
Channar, Bashir A., MSc Aberd., MSc Sindh Assoc. Prof.; Chairman*
Porgar, Abdul S., MSc Sindh Asst. Prof.
Other Staff: 6 Lectrs.; 2 Res. Assocs.

Pharmaceutical Chemistry

Leghari, M. Yousif, BPharm Sindh, MPharm Punjab Assoc. Prof.; Chairman*
Memon, M. Usman, MSc Sindh, PhD Kobe Prof.
Panhwar, Fouzia, BPharm Sindh, MPharm Sindh Asst. Prof.
Rind, Mehboob Ali, MSc Sindh Assoc. Prof.
Other Staff: 1 Res. Assoc.

Pharmaceutics

Almani, Khalida F., BPharm Sindh, MPharm Sindh, PhD Sindh Asst. Prof.
Bhatti, Abdul R., BPharm Sindh, MPhil B.Zak. Asst. Prof.
Dayo, Abdullah, BPharm Sindh, PhD Nanjing Prof.; Chairman*
Maka, Ghulam A., MSc SA Latif, PhD Assoc. Prof.
Memon, Naheed, BPharm Sindh, MPharm Sindh Asst. Prof.
Other Staff: 1 Lectr.; 1 Res. Assoc.

Pharmacognosy

Gilal, Roshan A., BPharm Sindh, MPhil B.Zak. Asst. Prof.; Chairman-in-Charge*
Other Staff: 1 Lectr.

Pharmacology

Bhatti, Shoukat Ali, BPharm Sindh, MSc B.Zak. Asst. Prof.
Mughal, Mahmoodul Hassan, MB BS Sindh Asst. Prof.
Ozra, Ahsan, BPharm Dhaka, MPharm Dhaka Assoc. Prof.; Chairperson*
Soomro, A. Muhammad, MSc Sindh Asst. Prof.
Other Staff: 1 Lectr.; 1 Res. Assoc.

Philosophy

Leghari, Salma, MA Sindh Lectr.; Chairperson-in-Charge*
Other Staff: 2 Lectrs.; 1 Res. Assoc.

Physics, Institute of

Kalhoro, M. Siddique, MSc Sindh, PhD Brun. Prof.
Khushk, Muhammad M., MSc Sindh Prof.; Dir.*
Mughal, Akhtar H., MSc Sindh, PhD Brun. Prof.
Shah, S. Gulsher, MSc Sindh Asst. Prof.
Shah, S. Inayatullah, MSc Sindh, MSc Sur., PhD Lond. Assoc. Prof. (on lien)
Other Staff: 6 Lectrs.; 1 Res. Assoc.

Physiology

Bhatti, Rashida, MSc Sindh Asst. Prof.
Chughatai, Latafat A., MSc Sindh Asst. Prof.
Jokhio, Rukhsana, MSc Sindh, PhD Sindh Asst. Prof.
Mahesar, Hidayatullah, MSc Sindh Asst. Prof.
Memon, Fehmida, MSc Sindh Asst. Prof.
Seehar, Ghulam M., MSc Sindh, PhD Glas. Prof.; Chairman*
Shaikh, Bilquees B., MSc Sindh, MPhil Quaid-i-Azam Assoc. Prof.
Shaikh, Jiando, MSc Sindh Asst. Prof.
Shaikh, M. Akbar, MSc Sindh Asst. Prof.
Soomro, A. Latif, MSc Sindh Asst. Prof.
Other Staff: 2 Lectrs.; 3 Res. Assocs.

Political Science

Bukhari, Syed M. S., LLB Sindh, MA Sindh Prof.
Jalbani, Din M., MA Sindh Assoc. Prof.
Mehranvi, Abdul A., LLB Sindh, MA Sindh Assoc. Prof. (on lien)
Memon, Aslam P., LLB Sindh, MA Sindh Asst. Prof. (on lien)
Pardesi, Yasmeen Y., LLB Sindh, MA Sindh Asst. Prof.
Phul, Gul M., MA Sindh Prof.
Rashdi, Razia S., MA Sindh Prof.; Chairperson*
Shaikh, Bashir A., LLB Sindh, MA Sindh Prof.
Shaikh, Munawar S., LLB Sindh, MA Sindh Asst. Prof.
Shaikh, Zahida, MA Sindh Asst. Prof.
Other Staff: 4 Lectrs.

Psychological Testing, Guidance and Research

Jafri, S. Iftikhar H., LLB Sindh, MSc Sindh, MA(Ed) Sindh Asst. Prof.
Mughal, Farzana, MA Sindh, MEd Sindh Asst. Prof.
Munshi, Parveen, MA Sindh, MEd Sindh, PhD Hamdard Assoc. Prof.; Chairperson*
Soomro, Nazar H., MA Sindh, MEd Edinboro Asst. Prof.
Other Staff: 1 Lectr.

Psychology

Fatima, Zohra, MA Sindh, PhD Aegean Asst. Prof.
Qureshi, Misbah B., MSc Sindh, MPhil Sindh Asst. Prof. (on leave)
Shah, Irfana, MA Sindh Asst. Prof.
Thaheem, Nagina P., MA Sindh, PhD Sindh Assoc. Prof.; Chairperson*
Other Staff: 3 Lectrs.; 4 Res. Assocs.
Research: cross-cultural studies

Science and Technical Education

Siyal, Nabi B., MSc Sindh, MEd Sindh Asst. Prof.
Solangi, Sultana, MA MEd Asst. Prof.; Chairperson-in-Charge*
Other Staff: 2 Lectrs.

Sindhi

Bughio, M. Qasim, LLB Sindh, MA Sindh, PhD Essex Prof.
Hakro, M. Anwar F., MA Sindh, PhD Sindh Asst. Prof.
Imdad, Sahar, MA Sindh, PhD Sindh Prof.

Khuwaja, Noor A., MA Sindh, PhD Sindh   Prof.;
Chairperson*
Mirza, Qamar J., MA Sindh, PhD Sindh   Prof.
Mufti, Tehmina, MA Sindh, PhD Sindh   Prof.
Other Staff: 3 Lectrs.

Social Work

Bhanbhan, Shamim A., MA Sindh   Asst. Prof.
Dahri, Ghulam R., MA Sindh   Asst. Prof. (on
leave)
Nizamani, M. Zahid, LLB Sindh, MA Sindh
Assoc. Prof.; Chairman*
Other Staff: 2 Lectrs.; 2 Res. Assocs.

Sociology

Jakhrani, Ghulam M., MA Sindh, PhD Sindh
Assoc. Prof.
Junejo, Tanvir S., MA Sindh, PhD Sindh   Prof.
Kakepoto Hamadullah, MA Sindh   Asst. Prof.
(on leave)
Khowaja, Izzat K., LLB Sindh, MA Sindh, MEd
Sindh, MA Keele   Prof.
Shaikh, Khalida, MA Sindh   Prof.; Chairperson*
Talpur, Fakhrunnisa, BEd Sindh, MA Sindh
Assoc. Prof.
Other Staff: 6 Lectrs.; 2 Res. Assocs.

Statistics

Junejo, Ishtique A., MSc Sindh   Asst. Prof.
Memon, Azizullah, MSc Sindh   Assoc. Prof.
Mirza, Anis A., MSc Sindh   Assoc. Prof.
Rajput, Ilyas M., LLB Sindh, MSc Sindh   Assoc.
Prof.; Chairman*
Sabhayo, Rahim B., MSc Sindh   Assoc. Prof.
Shah, S. A. Nawaz H., MSc Sindh   Asst. Prof.
Shah, Syed M. A., MSc Sindh, PhD Bucharest
Prof.
Soomro, Imdad H., MSc Sindh   Asst. Prof.
Talpur, Ghulam H., MSc Sindh, PhD Shanghai
U.S.T.   Prof.
Other Staff: 4 Lectrs.; 1 Res. Assoc.
Research: demographic studies; operations
research; probability analysis

Urdu

Jilani, Atiq A., MA Sindh   Asst. Prof.
Mirza, Saleem B., MA Sindh   Asst. Prof.
Sartaj, Naseem A., MA Sindh, PhD Sindh   Prof.
Syed, Javed I., MA Sindh, MPhil Sindh, PhD Sindh
Prof.; Chairperson*
Other Staff: 1 Lectr.

Zoology

Ashok, Kumar, MSc Sindh, MPhil Sindh   Assoc.
Prof.
Baloch, Naheed, MSc Sindh, PhD Sindh   Asst.
Prof.
Dharejo, Ali M., MSc Sindh   Prof.
Gachal, Ghulam S., MSc Sindh, PhD Wales
Assoc. Prof.
Kehar, Aijaz A., MSc Sindh   Assoc. Prof.
Khan, Muhammad M., MSc Sindh, PhD Sing.
Visiting Prof.
Memon, Nasreen, MSc Sindh, PhD Karachi   Prof.
Memon, Tahira J., MSc Sindh, MPhil Sindh
Asst. Prof.
Mughal, Mufarrah, MSc Sindh   Assoc. Prof.
Pitafi, Karim D., MSc Sindh, PhD Nott.   Prof.
Shah, Syed Anwar A., MSc Sindh   Assoc. Prof.
Shaikh, Azra A., MSc Tuskegee, MSc Sindh, PhD
Sindh   Prof.
Shaikh, Ghulam S., MSc Sindh   Asst. Prof.
Shaikh, Shamsuddin A., MSc Sindh, MPhil Quaid-
i-Azam, PhD Quaid-i-Azam   Prof.
Sindhi, Mehtab, MSc Sindh, MPhil Quaid-i-Azam
Asst. Prof.
Soomro, Mahmoodul H., MSc Sindh   Asst.
Prof.
Soomro, Naheed S., MSc Sindh, PhD Sindh
Prof.
Wagan, M. Saeed, MSc Sindh, PhD Sindh   Prof.;
Chairman*
Other Staff: 2 Lectrs.; 1 Museum Curator
Research: endocrinology; entomology; genetics;
parasitology; vertebrate biology

SPECIAL CENTRES, ETC

Allama I. I. Kazi Chair

Tel: (022) 278 3654
Baloch, N. A., MA Alig., PhD Col.   Prof. Emer.
Research: life and work of Allama I. I. Kazi

Analytical Chemistry, Centre of Excellence in

Tel: (022) 277 1379 Fax: (022) 277 1560
E-mail: deac@hyd.paknet.com.pk
Bhangar, M. Iqbal, MSc Sindh, PhD Lond.   Prof.;
Dir.*
Kazi, Tasneem G., MSc Sindh, PhD Sindh   Prof.
Shah, Waliullah, MSc Sindh, PhD Sindh   Assoc.
Prof. (on lien)
Sherazi, S. Tufail H., MSc Punjab, PhD Sindh
Asst. Prof.
Sirajuddin, MSc Pesh., PhD Pesh.   Asst. Prof.
Other Staff: 5 Res. Assocs.
Research: analytical techniques; environmental
studies; instrumental specialisation

Environmental Science, Centre of

Baloch, Mushtaque A., MSc Sindh, PhD Sur.
Prof.; Dir.*

Far East and South East Asia Study Centre

Tel: (022) 277 1207 Fax: (022) 277 1208
E-mail: esasc@hyd.pknet.com.pk
Firdous, Nilofer, LLB Sindh, MA Sindh   Assoc.
Prof.
Ghaloo, Raza H., MA Sindh   Assoc. Prof.
Jarwar, Jamila, MA Sindh   Asst. Prof.
Mangi, Lutfullah, MA Sindh, MA Wat., PhD Lond.
Prof.; Dir.*
Shah, Deedar H., MA Sindh, PhD Moscow   Prof.
Soomro, Hidayat A., MA Sindh   Assoc. Prof.
Other Staff: 3 Lectrs.; 1 Asst. Librarian

Geology, Pure and Applied, Centre for

Tel: (022) 277 2408
Ansari, Qudsia, MSc Sindh   Asst. Prof.
Bablani, Saeed A., MSc Quaid-i-Azam, MPhil
Trondheim   Asst. Prof.
Brohi, Imdad A., MSc Sindh, PhD Hiroshima
Prof.
Leghari, Amanullah, MSc Sindh, PhD Pesh.
Museum Curator
Pathan, Mushtaque A., MSc Sindh   Asst. Prof.
Siddique, Imdadullah, MSc Sindh, MPhil Pesh.
Asst. Prof.
Solangi, Sarfraz H., MSc Sindh, PhD Wales
Prof.
Usmani, Parveen A., MSc Sindh, MPhil Sindh,
PhD Sindh   Prof.; Chairperson*
Other Staff: 6 Lectrs.; 1 Res. Assoc.; 1 Adjunct
Prof.
Research: biostratigraphy; foraminiferal
micropalaeontology; hydrogeology;
sedimentology

Health and Physical Education, Centre for

Ansari, M. Akram, MHPEd Sindh   Asst. Prof.
Qureshi, Yasmeen I., MA Sindh, MHPEd Sindh,
PhD Sindh   Assoc. Prof.; Dir.*
Shah, Akhtar A., MB BS Sindh   Asst. Prof. (on
leave)
Other Staff: 3 Lectrs.; 1 Res. Assoc.

Pakistan Study Centre

Tel: (022) 277 2335
E-mail: pscjamshoro@hotmail.com
Baloch, Farzana, MA Sindh   Asst. Prof.
Sahar, Ghulam N., MA Sindh   Asst. Prof.
Sheikh, Rafia A., MA Sindh, MA Lough., PhD
Lond.   Acting Dir.*
Other Staff: 1 Lectr.; 1 Adjunct Staff Member

Rural Development Communication

Tel: (022) 277 2383 Fax: (022) 277 2224
E-mail: crdcpk@yahoo.com
Rashdi, Ibadullah, MA Sindh   Assoc. Prof.; Dir.
(Addtnl. Charge)*

Soomro, Badaruddin, MA Sindh   Asst. Prof.
(Addtnl. Charge)
Other Staff: 1 Consultant

Sindh Development Studies Centre

Tel: (022) 277 1223 Fax: (022) 277 1297
Jariko, Ghulam A., MA Sindh, MSc Sindh, MPA
Sindh   Asst. Prof.
Mughal, Shahabuddin, MA Sindh   Asst. Prof.
Pathan, Parvez A., MBA Sindh, MSc Lond., PhD
Lond.   Prof.
Rind, Zareen K., MBA Sindh, MSc Lond.   Asst.
Prof.
Taherani, Abida, MA Sindh, MA Lond., PhD
Colorado State   Prof.; Dir.*
Talpur, Mushraf A., MSc Quaid-i-Azam, MSc Lond.
Asst. Prof.
Other Staff: 2 Staff Economists; 1 Lectr.; 2 Res.
Assocs.; 1 Adjunct Staff Member

Sindhology, Institute of

Tel: (022) 277 1386
E-mail: sindhology-1@hotmail.com
Aysha Madad, MA Sindh   Deputy Dir. (Res.)
Bughio, Razia Q., MA Sindh   Deputy Dir.
(Publications)
Maka, Muhammad Q., MA(SW) Sindh   Deputy
Dir. (Musicology)
Shoro, Shoukat H., MA Sindh   Dir.*
Other Staff: 1 Addtnl. Dir.; 1 Librarian; 1
Display Officer
Research: sindhological studies

Women's Development, Institute of

Shah, Parveen, MA Sindh, MPhil Sindh, PhD Sindh
Prof.; Dir.*
Other Staff: 2 Lectrs.; 5 Res. Assocs.

CONTACT OFFICERS

Academic affairs. Deputy Registrar: Qureshi,
M. Ally, BCom Sindh, LLB Sindh
Accommodation. Provost, Hostels: Kalhoro,
Prof. M. Siddique, MSc Sindh, PhD Brun.
Admissions (first degree). Director,
Admissions: Rajar, M. Saleh, MA Sindh
(E-mail: dir_admissions@usindh.edu.pk)
Admissions (higher degree). Director,
Graduate Studies: Ahmed, Prof. M. Rais,
MSc Karachi, PhD Sheff.
(E-mail: consultantonh_ed@yahoo.com)
Distance education. Director, Distance
Education (Non-formal): Memon, A. Sattar,
MSc Sindh
Examinations. Controller of Examinations:
Pathan, Prof. Parvez A., MBA Sindh, MSc
Lond., PhD Lond.
(E-mail: p_pathan@usindh.edu.pk)
General enquiries. Registrar: Soomro, Prof.
Saeed A., MSc Sindh, PhD Wales
Library (chief librarian). Librarian (In-
Charge), Allama I. I. Kazi Central Library:
Roonjho, M. Azam, MLIS Sindh
Public relations. Public Relations Officer:
Panhwar, A. Majeed, MA Sindh
(E-mail: majeed.panwhar@usindh.edu.pk)
Sport and recreation. Director, Sports (Boys):
Ansari, M. Akram, MHPEd Sindh
Sport and recreation. Director, Sports (Girls):
Bhatti, Mukhtiar
Student welfare/counselling. Advisor: Kazi,
Prof. Iqbal H., LLB Sindh, MA Sindh
(E-mail: iqbal_kazi@usindh.edu.pk)
Student welfare/counselling. Director,
Admissions: Rajar, M. Saleh, MA Sindh
(E-mail: dir_admissions@usindh.edu.pk)
University press. Manager, University Press:
Bhutto, Allahbachayo, MA Sindh

AFFILIATED COLLEGES

[Institutions listed by location below provide
courses leading to degrees, etc. of the
university]

Badin. Government Boys' College, Matli;
Government Girls' College; Government
Girls' College, Matli; Government Islamia
College

Dadu. Government Boys' College; Government Boys' College, Khairpur N. Shah; Government Girls' College; Pir Illahi Bux Government Law College

Hyderabad. College of Modern Sciences, Latifabad; Dr. I. H. Zuberi Girls' College of Home Economics; Federal Government College; Government Boys' College; Government Boys' College, Matiari; Government Boys' College, Tando Muhammad Khan; Government City College; Government Degree College and Postgraduate Centre, Latifabad; Government Ghazali College of Arts and Commerce, Latifabad; Government Girls' College; Government Girls' College, Hala; Government Girls' College, Qasimabad; Government Girls' College, Tando Muhammad Khan; Government Jinnah Law College; Government K. B. M. S. Girls' College; Government M. B. and G. F. Girls' College; Government S. M. Arts College, Tando Allahyar; Government Sachal Sarmast Arts College; Government Sachal Sarmast

Commerce College; Government Sarwary Islamia College, Hala; Government Shah Latif Girls' College, Latifabad; Government Sindh College of Commerce; Government Sindh Law College; Institute of Modern Sciences and Arts; Institute of Science and Management; Jinnah Girls' College, Latifabad; Net Institute of Information Technology; Noor College of Professional Education, Sultanabad; Noor Shah Bukhari Boys' College; SAM Institute of Computer and Management Sciences, Latifabad; Shah Waliullah Degree College, Mansoorah; Western Graduate College

Jamshoro. Centre of Excellence for Arts and Design; Government Boys' College, Kotri; Government Boys' College, Sehwan Sharif; Government Girls' College; Government Girls' College, Kotri

Mirpurkhas. Government College, Tando Jan; Government Ibne Rushid Girls' College; Government Model College; Government Shah Abdul Latif Boys' College; Muhammad Institute of Science and Technology

Nawabsah. Government Boys' College; Government Boys' College, Sakrand; Government Girls' College; Govenment Sachal Sarmast College; Quaid-e-Azam Law College

Sanghar. Government Boys' College; Government Degree College, Khipro; Government Degree College, Shadadpur; Government Girls' College; Government Girls' College, Tando Adam; Government New Aligarh College, Tando Adam

Sukkar. Sukkar Institute of Science and Technology

Thar. Government Boys' College, Mithi

Thatta. Government Boys' College; Government Girls' College

Umerkot. Government Boys' College; M. D. Oriental and Degree College

[Information supplied by the institution as at 15 May 2006, and edited by the ACU]

SINDH AGRICULTURE UNIVERSITY

Founded 1977

Postal Address: Tandojam, Sindh 70060, Pakistan
Telephone: (0221) 276 5869 **Fax:** (0221) 276 5300 **E-mail:** info@sau.edu.pk
URL: http://www.sau.edu.pk

VICE-CHANCELLOR*—Sheikh, Bashir A., MSc Agric., Faisalabad, PhD Iowa State
REGISTRAR‡—Soomro, Fateh M., MSc Sindh Ag., PhD Iowa State

SIR SYED UNIVERSITY OF ENGINEERING AND TECHNOLOGY

Founded 1993

Member of the Association of Commonwealth Universities

Postal Address: Gulshan-e-Iqbal University Road, Karachi 75300, Pakistan
Telephone: (021) 498 8000 **Fax:** (021) 498 2393 **E-mail:** registrar@ssuet.edu.pk
URL: http://www.ssuet.edu.pk

VICE-CHANCELLOR*—Ahmad, Prof. Saiyid N., BSc(Engg) Alig., PhD Lond.
REGISTRAR‡—Syed, Shah Mahmood H., LLB Karachi, MA Karachi
CONTROLLER OF EXAMINATIONS—Jaffri, Adil Akhtar, MSc Karachi
DIRECTOR, FINANCE—Hussain, Munawwar, BCom Sindh, MAEcon Karachi
DIRECTOR, PLANNING AND DEVELOPMENT—Khan, Abdul J., BSc Alig.
LIBRARIAN—Siddiqui, Maqsood Alam, MLS Karachi

GENERAL INFORMATION

History. The university, sponsored by Aligarh Muslim University Old Boys' Association of Pakistan, was established in 1993 by a provincial government ordinance.

Admission to first degree courses (see also Pakistan Introduction). Higher Secondary Certificate (intermediate, pre-engineering) with minimum 60% or equivalent.

First Degrees (see also Pakistan Directory to Subjects of Study). BS.
Length of course. Full-time: BS: 4 years.

Higher Degrees (see also Pakistan Directory to Subjects of Study).
Master's. MS.
Length of course. Full-time: MS: 2 years.

Libraries. Volumes: 60,000. Periodicals subscribed to: 90.

Academic Awards (2005–2006). 1135 awards ranging in value from Rs10,000 to Rs18,000.

Income (2005–2006). Total, Rs200,580,000.

Statistics. Students (2005–2006): full-time 2329 (2064 men, 265 women).

FACULTIES/SCHOOLS
Basic and Applied Sciences
E-mail: jawaidrizvi@hotmail.com
Dean: Rizvi, Prof. Jawaid Hassan, MA W.Ont., PhD W.Ont.
Secretary: (vacant)

Engineering
Dean: Siddiqui, Prof. Najeeb, MSc Karachi, PhD Lond.
Secretary: Imtiaz-un-Nisa

ACADEMIC UNITS
Engineering, Biomedical
E-mail: mahaleem@ssuet.edu.pk
Bhatti, Iqbal A., BE NED Eng., MSc Karachi, MBA A.Iqbal Open   Asst. Prof.
Haleem, Abdul Muhammad, PhD Leeds   Prof.; Chairman*
Iqbal, Javed, BE NED Eng., MS   Asst. Prof.
Syeda, Shahnaz, BSc Punjab, MB BS Punjab   Asst. Prof.
Other Staff: 9 Lectrs.; 5 Asst. Profs.
Research: artificial limbs fabrication; biomedical engineering systems; medical equipment

Engineering, Civil

E-mail: dr_makhdumi@hotmail.com
Makhdumi, S. M., MSc *UMIST*, PhD *Nott.*
  Prof.; Chairman*
Rizvi, Syed S. A., BSc *Alig.*   Asst. Prof.
Tayyab, Muhammad, BE *NED Eng.*, MTM *Karachi*
  Asst. Prof.
Other Staff: 5 Asst. Profs.; 7 Lectrs.

Engineering, Computer

E-mail: tasadduq@gmail.com
Mumtazul, Imam, MSc *Sindh*, PhD *Lond.*   Prof.
Tasadduq, Imran A., MS *Pet.& Min.*, *Saudi Arabia*,
  PhD *W.Ont.*   Chairman*
Other Staff: 1 Assoc. Prof.; 14 Asst. Profs.; 34
  Lectrs.

Engineering, Electronic

E-mail: najeeb@ssuet.edu.pk
Askari, M. Suleman, BE *Karachi*   Asst. Prof.
Azhar, Saeed, MSc *NED Eng.*   Asst. Prof.
Baig, M. Siddiqi, MS *Mich.State*   Asst. Prof.
Sharif, Muhammad, BScEngg *Lahore UET*   Asst.
  Prof.
Siddiqui, Najeeb, MSc *Karachi*, PhD *Lond.*   Prof.;
  Chairman*
Other Staff: 1 Prof.; 14 Asst. Profs.; 30 Lectrs.
Research: high speed analog to digital converter
  (ADC); solar board systems; transbotics

Mathematics, Applied

E-mail: jawaidrizvi@hotmail.com
Ahmed, Naeem, MA *Karachi*, MA *Manit.*, MA
  Flor.   Asst. Prof.
Durrani, Naeem K., BSc *Alig.*, MSc *Alig.*   Asst.
  Prof.
Rizvi, Jawaid Hassan, MA *W.Ont.*, PhD *W.Ont.*
  Prof.; Chairman*
Other Staff: 1 Assoc. Prof.; 8 Lectrs.; 2 Visiting
  Fellows

Physics, Applied

E-mail: jawaidrizvi@hotmail.com
Ahmed, Akhlaq, MSc *Karachi*, MSc *Leeds*   Asst.
  Prof.
Rizvi, Jawaid Hassan, MA *W.Ont.*, PhD *W.Ont.*
  Prof.; Chairman*
Other Staff: 1 Asst. Prof.; 1 Lectr.

SPECIAL CENTRES, ETC

Human Settlements and Environment, Institute of

E-mail: mahimam@ssuet.edu.pk
Mansoor Imam   Deputy Dir.

CONTACT OFFICERS

Academic affairs. Dean, Engineering: Siddiqui,
  Prof. Najeeb, MSc *Karachi*, PhD *Lond.*
  (E-mail: najeeb@ssuet.edu.pk)
Accommodation. Director, Students' Affairs:
  Fasihuddin, Syed, BSc *Karachi*, LLB *Karachi*,
  MPA *Karachi*

Admissions (first degree). Registrar: Syed,
  Shah Mahmood H., LLB *Karachi*, MA *Karachi*
  (E-mail: registrar@ssuet.edu.pk)
Admissions (higher degree). Dean,
  Engineering: Siddiqui, Prof. Najeeb, MSc
  Karachi, PhD *Lond.*
  (E-mail: najeeb@ssuet.edu.pk)
Adult/continuing education. In-Charge
  (Adult/continuing education): Naqvi
  Mukhtar, BSc *Punjab*, MSc *Cant.*
Alumni. Honorary Secretary General, Aligarh
  Muslim Old Boys' Association: Khan, Zakir
  A.
Careers. Associate Professor (Careers): Ali
  Abrar (E-mail: abrarkarachi@yahoo.com)
Computing services. Systems Manager:
  Ghulam Nabi, BSc *Sindh*, MSc *Sindh*
Conferences/corporate hospitality. Registrar:
  Syed, Shah Mahmood H., LLB *Karachi*, MA
  Karachi
Consultancy services. Dean, Engineering:
  Siddiqui, Prof. Najeeb, MSc *Karachi*, PhD
  Lond. (E-mail: najeeb@ssuet.edu.pk)
Credit transfer. Dean, Engineering: Siddiqui,
  Prof. Najeeb, MSc *Karachi*, PhD *Lond.*
  (E-mail: najeeb@ssuet.edu.pk)
Development/fund-raising. Honorary
  Treasurer: Munif, M. Afzal
Development/fund-raising. Director, Finance:
  Hussain, Munawwar, BCom *Sindh*, MAEcon
  Karachi
Distance education. Dean, Engineering:
  Siddiqui, Prof. Najeeb, MSc *Karachi*, PhD
  Lond. (E-mail: najeeb@ssuet.edu.pk)
Estates and buildings/works and services.
  Director, Planning and Development: Khan,
  Abdul J., BSc *Alig.*
Examinations. Controller of Examinations:
  Jaffri, Adil Akhtar, MSc *Karachi*
Finance. Director, Finance: Hussain,
  Munawwar, BCom *Sindh*, MAEcon *Karachi*
General enquiries. Deputy Registrar: Soomro,
  A. G. (E-mail: nahmereen@ssuet.edu.pk)
Health services. Medical Advisor: Iftikhar,
  Syed
Industrial liaison. Chairman, Biomedical
  Engineering: Haleem, Prof. Abdul
  Muhammad, PhD *Leeds*
  (E-mail: mahaleem@ssuet.edu.pk)
International office. Deputy Secretary to the
  Chancellor: Zaman, Mubarak
  (E-mail: mzaman@ssuet.edu.pk)
Language training for international students.
  Dean, Basic and Applied Sciences: Rizvi,
  Prof. Jawaid Hassan, MA *W.Ont.*, PhD
  W.Ont. (E-mail: jawaidrizvi@hotmail.com)
Library (chief librarian). Librarian: Siddiqui,
  Maqsood Alam, MLS *Karachi*
  (E-mail: njafri@ssuet.edu.pk)
Library (enquiries). Cataloguer: Bano,
  Shamim
Marketing. Deputy Secretary to the Chancellor:
  Zaman, Mubarak
  (E-mail: muhaq@ssuet.edu.pk)
Minorities/disadvantaged groups. Director,
  Students' Affairs: Fasihuddin, Syed, BSc

  Karachi, LLB *Karachi*, MPA *Karachi*
  (E-mail: amnaqui786@hotmail.com)
Personnel/human resources. Registrar: Syed,
  Shah Mahmood H., LLB *Karachi*, MA *Karachi*
  (E-mail: registrar@ssuet.edu.pk)
Public relations. Deputy Secretary to the
  Chancellor: Zaman, Mubarak
  (E-mail: muhaq@ssuet.edu.pk)
Publications. Deputy Secretary to the
  Chancellor: Zaman, Mubarak
  (E-mail: muhaq@ssuet.edu.pk)
Purchasing. Purchase Office: Syed,
  Muhammad Shoaib
Quality assurance and accreditation. Dean,
  Engineering: Siddiqui, Prof. Najeeb, MSc
  Karachi, PhD *Lond.*
  (E-mail: najeeb@ssuet.edu.pk)
Research. Dean, Engineering: Siddiqui, Prof.
  Najeeb, MSc *Karachi*, PhD *Lond.*
  (E-mail: najeeb@ssuet.edu.pk)
Safety. Chief Security Officer: Ahmed,
  Chaudhry R.
Scholarships, awards, loans. Honorary
  Secretary General, Aligarh Muslim Old Boys'
  Association: Khan, Zakir A.
Security. Chief Security Officer: Ahmed,
  Chaudhry R.
Sport and recreation. Sports Officer: Ali Abrar
  (E-mail: abrarkarachi@yahoo.com)
Sport and recreation. Honorary Sports
  Adviser: (vacant)
Staff development and training. Vice-
  Chancellor: Ahmad, Prof. Saiyid N.,
  BSc(Engg) *Alig.*, PhD *Lond.*
  (E-mail: vc@ssuet.edu.pk)
Student welfare/counselling. Director,
  Students' Affairs: Fasihuddin, Syed, BSc
  Karachi, LLB *Karachi*, MPA *Karachi*
  (E-mail: amnaqui786@hotmail.com)
Students from other countries. Director,
  Students' Affairs: Fasihuddin, Syed, BSc
  Karachi, LLB *Karachi*, MPA *Karachi*
  (E-mail: amnaqui786@hotmail.com)
Students with disabilities. Chairman,
  Biomedical Engineering: Haleem, Prof.
  Abdul Muhammad, PhD *Leeds*
  (E-mail: mahaleem@ssuet.edu.pk)
University press. Proprietor of the Press, Sir
  Syed University Press: Hassan, Khawaja Q.
  (E-mail: kwanh85@hotmail.com)

AFFILIATED COLLEGES

[Institutions listed by location below provide
  courses leading to degrees, etc. of the
  university]
Karachi. Aligarh Institute of Technology; Sir
  Syed College of Medical Sciences for Girls
Lahore. Overseas Pakistanis Science and
  Technology City (OPSTEC) College of
  Computer Science
Rawalpindi. Sir Syed Science College,
  Rawalpindi

[*Information supplied by the institution as at 18 May
  2006, and edited by the ACU*]

ZIAUDDIN UNIVERSITY

Founded 1995

Postal Address: 4/B, Shahra-e-Ghalib, Block-6, Clifton, Karachi 75600, Pakistan
Telephone: (021) 586 2937-9 **Fax:** (021) 586 2940 **E-mail:** info@zu.edu.pk
URL: http://www.zu.edu.pk

VICE-CHANCELLOR*—Siddiqi, Shahid A., MA *Karachi*
REGISTRAR‡—Yousaf, Muhammad, BA *Sindh*

PAPUA NEW GUINEA

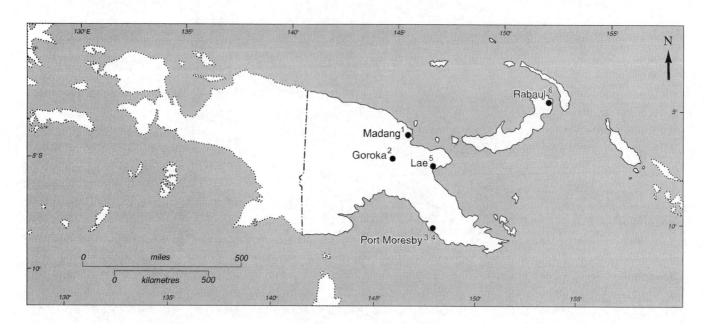

The places named are the seats of the university institutions numbered above

DIVINE WORD UNIVERSITY

Founded 2000

Postal Address: PO Box 483, Madang, Papua New Guinea
Telephone: 852 2937 **Fax:** 852 2812 **E-mail:** jjczuba@global.net.pg
URL: http://www.dwu.ac.pg

PRESIDENT*—Czuba, Fr. Jan
VICE-PRESIDENT (ACADEMIC)‡—Gesch, Fr. Patrick, PhD *Syd.*

UNIVERSITY OF GOROKA

Founded 1997

Member of the Association of Commonwealth Universities

Postal Address: PO Box 1078, Goroka, Eastern Highlands Province, Papua New Guinea
Telephone: 731 1700 **Fax:** 732 2620
URL: http://www.uog.ac.pg/

ACTING VICE-CHANCELLOR*—Mel, Michael, BEd *Victoria Coll.(Aust.)*, PhD *Flin.*
PRO-VICE-CHANCELLOR (ADMINISTRATION)‡—Musawe, Sinebare, BEd *PNG*, MEd *Birm.*, MInfoTech *W'gong.*, PhD *W'gong.*
PRO-VICE-CHANCELLOR (ACADEMIC AND DEVELOPMENT)—Kata, Joseph, BEd *PNG*, MBA *W'gong.*

PACIFIC ADVENTIST UNIVERSITY

Founded 1997

Postal Address: Private Mail Bag, Boroko, NCD, Papua New Guinea
Telephone: 328 1112 **Fax:** 328 1257
URL: http://www.pau.ac.pg/

VICE-CHANCELLOR*—Schubert, Branimir

UNIVERSITY OF PAPUA NEW GUINEA

Founded 1965

Member of the Association of Commonwealth Universities

Postal Address: PO Box 320, University, NCD, Papua New Guinea
Telephone: 326 7200 **Fax:** 326 7187 **E-mail:** vcoffice@upng.ac.pg
URL: http://www.upng.ac.pg

VICE-CHANCELLOR*—Hynes, Prof. Ross A., BA *NE*, MSc *PNG*, PhD *Lond.*, FAIM
PRO-VICE-CHANCELLOR—Kavana, Andrew, BA *PNG*, MA *Syd.*, PhD *Qld.*
REGISTRAR‡—Malaibe, Vincent, BSc *PNG*, MSc *Auck.*, MSc *Arizona*
BURSAR—Croake, Edward, BBus *Mitchell C.A.E.*

PAPUA NEW GUINEA UNIVERSITY OF TECHNOLOGY

Founded 1973

Member of the Association of Commonwealth Universities

Postal Address: Private Mail Bag, Lae 411, Morobe Province, Papua New Guinea
Telephone: 473 4999 **Fax:** 475 7667
URL: http://www.unitech.ac.pg/

VICE-CHANCELLOR*—Baloiloi, Misty, BA *PNG Tech.*, MSc *NSW*
PRO-VICE-CHANCELLOR (ACADEMIC)—Satter, Prof. M. A., BTech *Lough.*, MBA *H-W*, PhD *Lough.*
PRO-VICE-CHANCELLOR (ADMINISTRATION)—Tovirika, Wilson, BSc *Vudal*, MEd *Philippines*
DIRECTOR, PLANNING AND DEVELOPMENT—Wandau, Peter, BA *PNG*, MEd(Admin) *NE*
REGISTRAR‡—Sako, Allan, BA *PNG*, MPP *Well.*
BURSAR—Imbok, Jimmy, BA *PNG*
ACTING UNIVERSITY LIBRARIAN—Topagur, Raphael, BA *PNG*, BEd *PNG*, MES *Wales*

GENERAL INFORMATION

History. The university was first established in 1965 as Papua New Guinea Institute of Higher Technical Education. Its name was changed to Papua New Guinea Institute of Technology in 1970, and in 1973 it became a university under its present name.

It is located about 9km from the centre of Lae.

First Degrees. BACH, BAFT, BArc, BBld, BCAC, BCar, BCBE, BCIT, BCMA, BECV, BEEL, BEME, BEMN, BEMP, BFTE, BLST, BSAg, BSAP, BScF, BScS, BSFM, BTCD, BTCV, BTSR.

Length of course. Full-time: BACH, BAFT, BCAC, BCar, BCBE, BCIT, BCMA, BECV, BEEL, BEME, BEMN, BEMP, BFTE, BLST, BSAg, BSAP, BScF, BScS, BSFM, BTCD, BTCV, BTSR: 4 years; BArc, BBld: 5 years.

Higher Degrees.
Master's. MPhil.
Length of course. Full-time: MPhil: 2 years. *Part-time:* MPhil: 4 years.
Doctoral. PhD.
Length of course. Full-time: PhD: 5 years. *Part-time:* PhD: 8 years.

Libraries. Volumes: 103,000. Periodicals subscribed to: 100. Special collections: rare Papua New Guinea books.

ACADEMIC UNITS

Agriculture

Tel: 473 4451 Fax: 473 4477
    E-mail: ahalim@ag.unitech.ac.pg
Akanda, S. I., BSC *B'desh.Ag.*, MSc *B'desh.Ag.*, PhD *Oregon*   Sr. Lectr.
Danbaro, G., BSc *Cape Coast*, MPhil PhD *Kobe*   Sr. Lectr.
Halim, A.   Prof.; Head*
Nath, S., BSc *Alld.*, MTech *IIT Delhi*, PhD *Kansas*   Visiting Prof.
Pal, U. R., BSc *Gorak.*, MSc *Kanpur*, PhD *GBP*   Sr. Lectr.
Other Staff: 4 Lectrs.
Research: animal traction and training; earthworm farming, research and development; genetic improvement of quils; genotypic variation on sweet potato; PGR - based detection of viruses infecting sweet potato

Architecture and Building

Tel: 473 4501 Fax: 473 4520
    E-mail: rmilani@arch-bld.unitech.ac.pg
Gonduan, C. K., BArch *PNG Tech.*, MA *Stuttgart*, PhD *James Cook*   Assoc. Prof.
Milani, R. B., BEnvDes *Minn.*, MArch *Minn.*   Prof.; Head*
Pathre, P. S., BE *Mys.*, ME *IIT Delhi*   Sr. Lectr.
Sariman, A. C., BArch *PNG Tech.*, MSc *H-W*, PhD *James Cook*   Sr. Lectr.
Other Staff: 2 Lectrs.; 3 Sr. Tech. Instrs.; 1 Principal Tech. Instr.; 1 Tech. Instr.

Business Studies

Tel: 473 4401 Fax: 473 4433
    E-mail: hod@dbs.unitech.ac.pg
Corbin, T. P., BSc *Mich.*, JD *Mich.*   Sr. Lectr.
Mainardi, S., BSc *PNG Tech.*, MSc *Tokyo Agric.& Technol.*, PhD *Tokyo Agric.& Technol.*   Assoc. Prof.
Raymond, H. A., BA *Col.*, PhD *Brun.*   Prof.; Head*
Other Staff: 7 Lectrs.; 2 Sr. Tech. Instrs.; 4 Tech. Instrs.
Vacant Posts: 3 Assoc. Profs.; 5 Sr. Lectrs.; 1 Lectr.

Engineering, Civil

Tel: 473 4621 Fax: 473 4633
    E-mail: ckobal@civil.unitech.ac.pg
Kobal, C., BE *PNG Tech.*, BE *Cant.*, MSc *Cant.*   Acting Head*
Puvanachandran, V. M., MSc *Brad.*, PhD *Warw.*   Assoc. Prof.
Rajapakse, J. P., MSc *P.F.U., Moscow*   Sr. Lectr.
Telue, Y. K., BEng *PNG Tech.*, BEng *Qld.UT*, PhD *Qld.UT*   Sr. Lectr.
Other Staff: 2 Lectrs.; 1 Sr. Tech. Instr.; 1 Tech. Instr.
Vacant Posts: 1 Prof.; 1 Assoc. Prof.; 2 Sr. Lectrs.; 1 Lectr.
Research: identification and recommendation for black-spot improvements

Engineering, Electrical and Communication

Tel: 473 4701 Fax: 473 4733
    E-mail: wkostecki@ee.unitech.ac.pg
Kostecki, W., MSc *T.U.Lodz*, PhD *T.U.Lodz*   Sr. Lectr.; Acting Head*
Other Staff: 5 Lectrs.; 2 Sr. Tech. Instrs.
Vacant Posts: 1 Prof.; 2 Assoc. Profs.; 1 Sr. Lectr.; 1 Lectr.; 1 Chief Tech. Instr.

Engineering, Mechanical

Tel: 473 4851 Fax: 473 4868
    E-mail: jpumwa@mech.unitech.ac.pg
Luo, Z. C., BSc *Quaid-e-Awam UEST*, MSc *Huazhong U.S.T.*, PhD *Huazhong U.S.T.*   Sr. Lectr.
Pumwa, J., BE *PNG Tech.*, MEng *Wolv.*, PhD *Texas*   Assoc. Prof.; Acting Head*
Other Staff: 6 Lectrs.; 1 Sr. Tech. Instr.
Vacant Posts: 1 Prof.; 1 Assoc. Prof.; 1 Sr. Lectr.
Research: solar radiation measurement

Engineering, Mining

Tel: 473 4671 Fax: 473 4699
    E-mail: kpathak@mining.unitech.ac.pg
Afenya, P. M., BSc *Ghana*, MSc *Lond.*, PhD *Lond.*   Assoc. Prof.
Pathak, D. K., BTech MTech PhD *Lond.*   Prof.; Head*
Other Staff: 2 Lectrs.; 1 Sr. Tech. Instr.
Vacant Posts: 1 Assoc. Prof.; 1 Sr. Lectr.
Research: seabed (international research cruise)

Forestry

Tel: 473 4651 Fax: 473 4669
    E-mail: rturia@fo.unitech.ac.pg
Turia, R., BSc *PNG Tech.*, MSSc *RMIT*   Lectr.; Acting Head*
Other Staff: 3 Lectrs.; 1 Lectr.†
Vacant Posts: 1 Prof.; 1 Assoc. Prof.; 1 Sr. Lectr.
Research: impact of effective communication in traditional agro-forestry

Language and Communication Studies

Tel: 473 4751 Fax: 473 4766
    E-mail: jkalu@lcs.unitech.ac.pg
Kalu, J., BA *Jos*, MA *Ib.*, MA *Lagos*, MSc *Aston*   Sr. Lectr.; Acting Head*
Yarapea, A., BA *Vudal*, MA *Syd.*, MPhil *Syd.*   Sr. Lectr.
Other Staff: 1 Sr. Lectrs.; 4 Lectrs.; 4 Lectrs.†; 2 Temp. Lectrs.
Vacant Posts: 1 Prof.; 1 Assoc. Prof.
Research: impact of effective communication in traditional agro-forestry

Mathematics and Computer Science

Tel: 473 4801 Fax: 473 4820
    E-mail: rmisra@cms.unitech.ac.pg
Misra, R., MSc *Lucknow*, PhD *Alld.*   Prof.; Head*
Moshi, A., BSc *Dar.*, MSc *Car.*, PhD *Car.*   Sr. Lectr.
Wilkins, C. W., BSc *Adel.*, PhD *Adel.*   Sr. Lectr.
Other Staff: 2 Sr. Lectrs.; 3 Lectrs.; 2 Sr. Tech. Instrs.; 3 Tech. Instrs.; 5 Lectrs.†
Vacant Posts: 1 Assoc. Pof.

Physics, Applied

Tel: 473 4901 Fax: 473 4920
    E-mail: rsoto@ap.unitech.ac.pg
Dey, S. C., BSc *Chitt.*, MSc *Chitt.*, MAppSc *NSW*, PhD *ANU*   Sr. Lectr.
Ghosh, G., BSc *Burd.*, MSc *Burd.*, PhD *Burd.*   Sr. Lectr.
Sam, R., BEng *PNG Tech.*, MSc *Manc.*, PhD *James Cook*   Assoc. Prof.
Soto, R., BSEE MSEE *Houston*   Lectr.; Acting Head*
Other Staff: 1 Sr. Tech. Instr.; 1 Tech. Instr.†
Vacant Posts: 1 Prof.; 1 Sr. Lectr.; 2 Lectrs.

Sciences, Applied

Tel: 473 4551 Fax: 473 4558
    E-mail: bamoa@appsci.unitech.ac.pg
Amoa, B., BSc *Ghana*, PhD *Leeds*   Sr. Lectr.; Acting Head*
Other Staff: 4 Lectrs.; 1 Sr. Tech. Instr.; 1 Tech. Instr.; 3 Lectrs.†; 2 Temp. Lectrs.
Vacant Posts: 1 Prof.; 2 Assoc. Profs.; 1 Sr. Lectrs.
Research: PNG vanilla

Surveying and Land Studies

Tel: 473 4951 Fax: 473 4977
    E-mail: dkpal@survey.unitech.ac.pg
Pal, D.. K., BSc *Calc.*, MSc *Calc.*, PhD *Delhi*   Head*

Suat, J. K., BTech PNG Tech., MA Qld.   Sr. Lectr.
Other Staff: 5 Lectrs.; 4 Sr. Tech. Instrs.; 1 Principal Tech. Instrs.; 1 Chief Tech. Instr.
Vacant Posts: 1 Sr. Lectr.; 1 Lectr.

CONTACT OFFICERS

Academic affairs. Registrar: Sako, Allan, BA PNG, MPP Well.
(E-mail: asako@admin.unitech.ac.pg)
Accommodation. Pro-Vice-Chancellor (Administration): Tovirika, Wilson, BSc Vudal, MEd Philippines
(E-mail: wtovirika@admin.unitech.ac.pg)
Adult/continuing education. Head of Open and Distance Learning: Bopi, George
(E-mail: gbopi@dodl.unitech.ac.pg)
Careers. Career Development Officer: Wakana, Anna
(E-mail: awakana@admin.unitech.ac.pg)
Computing services. Computer and Electronic Services Unit Manager: Amol, Berry
(E-mail: bamol@its.unitech.ac.pg)
Consultancy services. Executive Manager, University Development Company: Juju, Jeffery (E-mail: jj@udc.unitech.ac.pg)

Development/fund-raising. Executive Manager, University Development Company: Juju, Jeffery
(E-mail: jj@udc.unitech.ac.pg)
Distance education. Head of Open and Distance Learning: Bopi, George
Estates and buildings/works and services. Head of Buildings and Grounds: Tzilu, B.
(E-mail: btzilu@maint.unitech.ac.pg)
Examinations. Senior Assistant Registrar (Academic): Thomas, Veronica
(E-mail: vthomas@admin.unitech.ac.pg)
Finance. Bursar: Imbok, Jimmy, BA PNG
(E-mail: jimbok@admin.unitech.ac.pg)
General enquiries. Registrar: Sako, Allan, BA PNG, MPP Well.
Health services. Medical Officer: Das, P. Lal
Industrial liaison. Executive Manager, University Development Company: Juju, Jeffery
International office. Director, Student Services: Maip, Simon
Library (chief librarian). Acting University Librarian: Topagur, Raphael, BA PNG, BEd PNG, MES Wales

Personnel/human resources. Deputy Registrar (Administration): Fainame, John
Publications. Information Officer: (vacant)
Purchasing. Stores and Transport Manager: Micah, Danny
Safety. Director, Security Service: Nabao, Joe
Scholarships, awards, loans. Scholarships Officer: Fugre, Leo
Schools liaison. Admissions Officer: Laskam, John
Security. Director, Security Service: Nabao, Joe
Sport and recreation. Student Representative Council Executive Officer: Maha, William
Staff development and training. Career Development Officer: Wakana, Anna
Student welfare/counselling. Director, Student Services: Maip, Simon
Students from other countries. Director, Student Services: Maip, Simon
Students with disabilities. Director, Student Services: Maip, Simon

[Information supplied by the institution as at 23 October 2007, and edited by the ACU]

UNIVERSITY OF VUDAL

Founded 1997

Postal Address: Private Mail Bag, Rabaul, East New Britain Province, Papua New Guinea
Telephone: 983 9144 **Fax:** 983 9166 **E-mail:** ntali@daltron.com.pg

VICE-CHANCELLOR*—Siaguru, Prof. Philip, MBE

SIERRA LEONE

DIRECTORY TO SUBJECTS OF STUDY

The table below shows which subjects are available for study and/or research at the universities in Sierra Leone.
U = may be studied for first degree course; M = may be studied for master's degree course;
D = research facilities to doctoral level; X = all three levels (UMD).

	Njala	Sierra Leone: Fourah Bay
Accountancy/Accounting		UM
Agriculture/Agricultural Science	U	
Botany/Plant Science		UM
Chemistry	X	UM
Crop Science/Production	X	
Development Studies	M	
Economics	UM	UM
Education	UM	
Education Primary	U	
Education Secondary	U	
Educational Administration	M	
Energy Studies	M	
Engineering Civil/Environmental/Structural		UM
Engineering Electrical/Electronic		UM
Engineering Mechanical/Production		UM
English		UM
Environmental Management	M	

	Njala	Sierra Leone: Fourah Bay
Environmental Science/Studies	U	
Food Science/Nutrition/Home Science/Dietetics	UM	
Geography		UM
Geology/Earth Sciences/Atmospheric Studies		UM
History		UM
Languages, Modern		UM
Law/Legal Studies		U
Linguistics/Translation		UM
Mathematics		UM
Peace/War Studies	M	
Philosophy		UM
Physical Education/Sports Science	UM	
Physics		UM
Politics/Political Science/Government		UM
Religion/Theology		UM
Sociology		UM
Wood Science	U	

NJALA UNIVERSITY

Founded 1964

Member of the Association of Commonwealth Universities

Postal Address: Private Mail Bag, Freetown, Sierra Leone
Telephone: (022) 226851 **E-mail:** njaluv@yahoo.com
URL: http://www.nu-online.com/

VICE-CHANCELLOR AND PRINCIPAL*—Alghali, Prof. Aliyageen M., BSc S.Leone, MSc Ib., PhD Ib.
PRO-VICE-CHANCELLOR (NJALA CAMPUS)—Gbamanja, Prof. Sahr P. T., BSc S.Leone, MSc Howard, PhD Ill.
DEPUTY VICE-CHANCELLOR (BO CAMPUS)—Manasaray, Prof. Abdulla, BA S.Leone, MEd Ib., PhD Ib.
REGISTRAR‡—Bongay, F. P., BA S.Leone, MEd S.Leone
FINANCE DIRECTOR—Saboleh, A. T.
DIRECTOR OF PHYSICAL AND PLANT SERVICES—Manyeh, A. J., BSc Reading
DIRECTOR OF PLANNING, RESEARCH AND DEVELOPMENT—Thompson, Prof. Ekundayo J. D., BA S.Leone, BAEd Hull, MEd Hull, DEd S.Af.

GENERAL INFORMATION

History. Njala University College was incorporated in 1964 and became a constituent college of the University of Sierra Leone in 1966. It became Njala University on 1 August 2005.
It is located about 200km east of Freetown.

Admission to first degree courses. General Certificate of Education (GCE) with O level passes (minimum grade 6 in not more than 2 sittings) in 5 approved subjects including English language.

First Degrees (see also Sierra Leone Directory to Subjects of Study) (* = with honours). BA, BEd, BScAgric, BScAgricEcons*, BScAgricEd, BScAgricEd*, BScAgricExtn*.
Length of course. Full-time: BA, BEd, BScAgric, BScAgricEcons*, BScAgricEd, BScAgricEd*, BScAgricExtn*: 4 years.

Higher Degrees (see also Sierra Leone Directory to Subjects of Study).
Master's. MA, MAEd, MALing, MBA, MPA, MPH, MPhil, MPhilAgricExtn, MPhilEd, MSc, MScAgricEd, MScAgricExtn, MScChem, MScCropSci, MScDevStds, MScEcon, MScEd, MScEd, MScEnvBio, MScRuralDev.
Length of course. Full-time: MPhil, MPhilAgricExtn, MPhilEd: 1 year; MA, MAEd, MALing, MPA, MSc, MScAgricEd, MScAgricExtn, MScChem, MScCropSci, MScDevStds, MScEcon, MScEd, MScEnvBio, MScRuralDev: $1\frac{1}{4}$ years; MBA, MPH: $1\frac{1}{2}$ years.
Doctoral. PhD.
Admission. Master's degree with at least 4.2 GPA (grade point average).
Length of course. Full-time: PhD: 3 years.

Libraries. Volumes: 50,000.

Academic Year (2007–2008). Two semesters: 13 October–15 February; 16 February–30 September.

Statistics. Staff (2007): 484 (239 academic, 245 non-academic).

FACULTIES/SCHOOLS

Agriculture
Dean: Lakoh, A. K., BSc S.Leone, MPhil Ife, PhD Cornell

Community Health Sciences
Dean: Robert, G. M. T., BSc S.Leone, PhD Paris, Drd'État Paris

Education
Dean: Saidu, P. K., BA Durh., MEd Wales, MA Lough.

Environmental Sciences
Dean: Bomah, A. K., BA S.Leone, MA Clark, PhD Clark

Forestry and Horticulture
Dean: Ikotun, Prof. Babatunde, BSc Ib., PhD Lond., FIBiol

Postgraduate Studies Board
Dean: Gbamanja, Prof. Sahr P. T., BSc S.Leone, MSc Howard, PhD Ill.

Social Sciences
Dean: Conteh, Bob K., BScAgricEd S.Leone, MA Leeds, PhD Leeds

Technology
Dean: Bockari-Gevao, S. M., MSc(AgriEngg) PhD

ACADEMIC UNITS

Agricultural Economics and Extension
Josiah, B. P., PhD Reading, BA   Lectr.; Head*
Vacant Posts: 1 Prof.; 1 Sr. Lectr.

Agricultural Education
Vacant Posts: 1 Prof.

Agricultural Engineering
Vacant Posts: 1 Sr. Lectr.

Animal Science
Kanu Saidu, BScAgric S.Leone, MSc PhD   Lectr.; Head*
Vacant Posts: 1 Prof.; 2 Sr. Lectrs.; 1 Lectr.

Biological Sciences
Sundufu Abu James, BScEd S.Leone, PhD   Lectr.; Acting Head*
Vacant Posts: 1 Prof.

Chemistry
Koroma, B. M., BScAgric S.Leone, MSc PhD   Head*
Vacant Posts: 1 Sr. Lectr.; 2 Lectrs.

Crop Protection
Koroma, J. P. C., BScAgric S.Leone, MScAgric PhD   Acting Head*

Crop Science
Lahai, M. T., BScAgric S.Leone, MScAgric S.Leone   Head*
Vacant Posts: 1 Prof.; 2 Sr. Lectrs.

Geography and Rural Development
Winnebah, T. R. A.   Head*
Vacant Posts: 1 Lectr.

Home Economics
Tijani, R. S., BSc S.Leone, MSc S.Leone   Acting Head*
Vacant Posts: 1 Prof.; 1 Lectr.

Language Education
Manyeh, M. K., PhD Leeds, BAEd   Lectr.; Head*
Vacant Posts: 2 Lectrs.

Mathematics
Fofanah, R., BSc S.Leone, MSc S.Leone   Acting Head*
Other Staff: 1 Lectr.
Vacant Posts: 1 Prof.; 1 Sr. Lectr.

Physical Education
Laggao, S., MSc PhD   Head*

Physics
Fofanah, I., BScEd S.Leone, MSc PhD   Acting Head*
Vacant Posts: 1 Prof.

Soil Science
Momoh, E. J. J., BScAgricEd S.Leone, MScAgric PhD   Head*

Teacher Education
Saidu, P. K., BA Durh., MEd Wales, MA Lough. Head*

SPECIAL CENTRES, ETC

Continuing Education, Centre for
Kaikai, C. M., BScEd S.Leone, MA Kent State, PhD Kent State   Dir.*

Educational Services Centre
Saidu, P. K., BA Durh., MEd Wales, MA Lough. Dir.*

Environmental Management and Quality Control, Institute of
Bah, O. M., BAEd S.Leone, MSc Lond., PhD Lond. Dir.*

Geography and Development Studies, Institute of
Bomah, A. K., BA S.Leone, MA Clark, PhD Clark Dir.*
Vacant Posts: 1 Lectr.

National Agricultural Training Centre
Lakoh, A. K., BSc S.Leone, MPhil Ife, PhD Cornell Dir.*

Science Curriculum Development Centre
Gbamanja, Sahr P. T., BSc S.Leone, MSc Howard, PhD Ill.   Prof.; Head*

CONTACT OFFICERS

General enquiries. Registrar: Bongay, F. P., BA S.Leone, MEd S.Leone

[Information supplied by the institution as at 1 September 2007, and edited by the ACU]

UNIVERSITY OF SIERRA LEONE

Founded 1967

Member of the Association of Commonwealth Universities

Postal Address: Private Mail Bag, Freetown, Sierra Leone
Telephone: (022) 226859

VICE-CHANCELLOR AND PRINCIPAL*—Gbakima, Aiah A., PhD
PRO-VICE-CHANCELLOR—Taqi, Prof. A. M., MMEd Mak., MD Moscow
UNIVERSITY SECRETARY AND REGISTRAR‡—Thomas, J. A. G., MEd Manc., BA

COLLEGE OF MEDICINE AND ALLIED HEALTH SCIENCES

Founded 1988

Postal Address: Private Mail Bag, Freetown, Sierra Leone
Telephone: (022) 240884

PRINCIPAL*—Taqi, Prof. A. M., MMEd Mak., MD Moscow
DEPUTY REGISTRAR‡—Campbell, M. A., MA Reading, FCIS
ESTATE OFFICER (ACTING)—Davies, F. C. O.

FOURAH BAY COLLEGE

Founded 1827

Postal Address: PO Box 87, Mount Aureol, Freetown, Sierra Leone
Telephone: (022) 27260

DEPUTY VICE-CHANCELLOR*—Redwood-Sawyerr, J. A. S., BEng S.Leone, MSc(Eng) Essex, PhD Essex
ASSISTANT TO DEPUTY VICE-CHANCELLOR—Fode, Daniel V. A., BSc Louvain, MSc Louvain, PhD Louvain
DEPUTY REGISTRAR‡—Dumbuya, S. N., BA S.Leone, MBA S.Leone, MEd Manc.
SENIOR ASSISTANT FINANCE OFFICER—Lansana, A. M., BSc S.Leone, MSc Birm.
SENIOR MEDICAL OFFICER—Dumbuya, M. E. M.
ESTATE OFFICER—Thomas, C. J.

GENERAL INFORMATION

History. The college was founded by the Church Missionary Society in 1827. It became affiliated to the University of Durham in 1876, and in 1967, a constituent college of the University of Sierra Leone.
It is located on Mt. Auzeol, on the outskirts of Freetown.

Admission to first degree courses. General Certificate of Education (GCE) with O level passes/WASSCE credits in not more than 2 sittings) in 5 approved subjects including English language. There are also individual faculty and departmental requirements.

First Degrees (see also Sierra Leone Directory to Subjects of Study) (* = with honours). BA*, BA, BEng*, BEng(Gen), BSc*, LLB*.
Length of course. Full-time: BA, BA*, BEng(Gen), BSc*, LLB*: 4 years; BEng*: 5 years.

Higher Degrees (see also Sierra Leone Directory to Subjects of Study).
Master's. MA, MEng, MSc, MSc(Econ).
Admission. A good first degree, as determined by the board of postgraduate studies.
Length of course. Full-time: MA, MEng, MSc, MSc(Econ): 2 years. Part-time: MA, MEng, MSc, MSc(Econ): 3 years.

Doctoral. PhD.
Length of course. Full-time: PhD: 3–4 years.

Libraries. Volumes: 120,000.

FACULTIES/SCHOOLS

Arts
Dean: Ali, Joe A. D., BA S.Leone, MA S.Leone, PhD Wis.

Engineering
Dean: Savage, A. B., BEng S.Leone, MS Arizona

Pure and Applied Science
Dean: Ndomahina, Ernest T., BSc S.Leone, MSc Wales, PhD Kiel

Social Sciences and Law
Dean: Ashley, Dominic T. J., BA Livingston, MA Ohio, PhD Wis.

ACADEMIC UNITS

Accounting and Finance
Bendu, D. A., BSc S.Leone, MSc S.Leone, MA S.Leone, PhD S.Leone   Lectr.; Head*
Other Staff: 1 Assoc. Lectr.; 1 Sr. Teaching Fellow

Biological Sciences
Karim, A. B., BSc S.Leone, MSc S.Leone, DPhil Oxf.   Sr. Lectr.; Head*
Other Staff: 4 Lectrs.
Research: agroforestry systems and practices; biodiversity in tropical ecosystems; biology of the spiral whitefly; conservation of bird life in Sierra Leone; environmental concerns in Africa

Chemistry
Kormoh, M. K., BSc S.Leone, MSc S.Leone, PhD Lond.   Sr. Lectr.
Yormah, Thomas B. R., BSc Birm., MSc Birm., PhD Birm.   Sr. Lectr.; Head*
Vacant Posts: 3 Lectrs.
Research: food and nutrition studies; human nutrition; medicinal plants; natural products; soil physical fertility studies

Economics and Commerce
Thula, D., BA Harv., DLitt MA   Teaching Fellow; Head*
Other Staff: 6 Lectrs.; 1 Staff Member

Educational Studies. Division of
Jones, B. B., BAEd Indiana, MSc Indiana, PhD Indiana   Sr. Lectr.; Head*
Other Staff: 3 Lectrs.; 1 Sr. Teaching Fellow
Research: historical development of adult education in West Africa; motivational

dynamics affecting participation in literacy; needs assessment survey for distance education; planning and management of university distance education; women in literacy

Engineering, Civil

Savage, A. B., BEng *S.Leone*, MS *Arizona*
Teaching Fellow; Head*
Other Staff: 2 Lectrs.
Research: timber structures and low cost materials for housing

Engineering, Electrical and Electronic

Bah, M., BEng *S.Leone*, MPhil *Wales*, PhD *Wales*
Lectr.; Head*
Redwood-Sawyerr, J. A. S., BEng *S.Leone*,
MSc(Eng) *Essex*, PhD *Essex*   Assoc. Prof.
Other Staff: 3 Lectrs.
Research: communications; electrical machines; electronics; energy studies; engineering education and training

Engineering, Mechanical and Maintenance

Davidson, Ogunlade R., BEng *S.Leone*, MSc
Manc., PhD *Salf.*   Prof.
Squire, C., BSc MPhil   Sr. Lectr.; Head*
Other Staff: 3 Lectrs.

Extra-Mural Studies, Division of

Turay, E. D. A., BA *Birm.*, MA *Birm.*, MEd *S'ton.*
Sr. Lectr.; Head*
Other Staff: 1 Tutor; 3 Staff Members

Geography

Johnson, R. G., BSc MSc PhD   Sr. Lectr.
Tengbeh, Paul B., BA *Ife*, MSc *Ife*, PhD *Ife*   Sr.
Lectr.; Head*
Other Staff: 2 Lectrs.
Research: coastal and marine environmental studies; environmental problems and urban household studies; sustainable development; transport network development; urban transport

Geology

Fode, Daniel V. A., BSc *Louvain*, MSc *Louvain*,
PhD *Louvain*   Sr. Lectr.
Other Staff: 4 Lectrs.
Research: deformation styles in Archaean greenstone belts in Sierra Leone and Liberia; gold mineralisation in Archaean greenstone belts of Sierra Leone, structural controls and geochemistry; ground water potential and use in Sierra Leone; petrology of basic igneous rocks; urban geology in town planning and land use

History and African Studies

Alie, J. A. D., BA *S.Leone*, MA *S.Leone*, PhD *Wis.*
Sr. Lectr.

Harleston, K. A. L., BFA *De Mont.*, MFA *Benin*
Sr. Lectr.
Other Staff: 2 Lectrs.; 1 Sr. Teaching Fellow
Research: analysis of the liberated African registers deposited in the National Archives, Freetown; civic and human rights education; conflict and conflict resolution/peace education; retrievals and outreaches in the diaspora: the case of Sierra Leone; urbanisation and social change in the East End of Freetown since the early nineteenth century

Language Studies

Osho, K. O., BA *S.Leone*   Lectr.; Head*
Other Staff: 12 Lectrs.; 1 Assoc. Lectr.
Research: a sociolinguistic survey of the roles of Krio in the changing context of contemporary times; generative phonology; new grammar of the Themne language; research into a generative syntax; voices in Krio

Law

Halloway, E. A., BA *Oxf.*, MA *Oxf.*, LLM *Lond.*
Lectr.; Head*
Other Staff: 4 Lectrs.; 1 Staff Member

Mathematics

Bockarie, Alex, BScEd *S.Leone*, MSc *Mich.*, PhD
Mich.   Sr. Lectr.; Head*
Other Staff: 4 Lectrs.

Philosophy and Religious Studies

Foullah, Rev. L. A., BTh *Liberia*, MDiv *Nair.*,
MTh *Nair.*, PhD *Leeds*   Sr. Lectr.; Head*
Labor, Rev. Fr. A. B., BA *Louvain*, MA *Indiana*,
PhD *Duquesne*   Sr. Lectr.
Shyllon, Rev. Dr. Leslie E. T., MTh *St And.*, PhD
Aberd., LDiv   Sr. Lectr.
Other Staff: 1 Assoc. Lectr.
Research: biblical languages; bioethics; influence of missionaries in the educational development of Sierra Leone; New Testament textual criticism; the church in Sierra Leone

Physics

Aruna, S. A., BSc MEd PhD   Sr. Lectr.
Godwin, V. E., BSc *Durh.*, MSc *Oregon*, PhD
Missouri   Assoc. Prof.
Other Staff: 1 Assoc. Lectr.; 1 Staff Member
Research: condensed matter (heterastructures and superlattices); electromagnetic theory; group theory; noise pollution, optoelectronics, investigation of silicon carbide as an optoelectronic material; seismic prospecting techniques, analysis and interpretations

Political Science

incorporates the Peace and Conflict Studies Unit

Gbla, P., BA *S.Leone*, MSc   Sr. Lectr.; Head*
Pratt, M.   Co-ordinator, Peace and Conflict Studies
Other Staff: 5 Lectrs.
Research: governance; leadership and democracy in Sierra Leone; local government; public sector reform; social anthropology

Sociology

Ashley, Dominic T. J., BA *Livingston*, MA *Ohio*,
PhD *Wis.*   Lectr.; Head*
Myers, R. G., BA *Penn.*, MA *Penn.*   Lectr./Sr.
Lectr.

SPECIAL CENTRES, ETC

Educational and Extra-Mural Studies, Institute of

Joof, A., BA *Montana*, MA *Colorado*, MEd *Colorado*,
MPhil *Colorado*, PhD *Colorado*   Prof.; Head*

Library Archives, Information and Communication Studies, Institute of (INSLICS)

Cole, B. P.   Sr. Lectr.; Dir.*
Kargbo, J. A.   Sr. Lectr.

Marine Biology and Oceanography, Institute of

Johnson, R. G., BSc MSc PhD   Sr. Lectr.
Ndomahina, Ernest T., BSc *S.Leone*, MSc *Wales*,
PhD *Kiel*   Sr. Lectr.
Other Staff: 2 Lectrs.
Vacant Posts: 1 Lectr.; 1 Res. Fellow
Research: bioeconomic analysis of the shrimp fishery in Sierra Leone; environmental effects of port extension activities in Freetown; fish discards from the trawl fishery of Sierra Leone; food and feeding inter-relationship of demersal species of Sierra Leone; investigation of organo-chlorine levels in four commercially exploited fish species in Sierra Leone

Population Studies, Institute for

Thomas, Armand C., BA *Durh.*, MA *Ghana*, PhD
Lond.   Sr. Lectr.; Dir.*
Other Staff: 2 Lectrs.

CONTACT OFFICERS

General enquiries. Deputy Registrar:
Dumbuya, S. N., BA *S.Leone*, MBA *S.Leone*,
MEd *Manc.*

[Information supplied by the institution as at 12 July 2006, and edited by the ACU]

SINGAPORE

Directory to Subjects of Study (p. 1288)

Nanyang Technological University (p. 1291) National University of Singapore (p. 1304)

DIRECTORY TO SUBJECTS OF STUDY

The table below shows which subjects are available for study and/or research at the universities in Singapore. U = may be studied for first degree course; M = may be studied for master's degree course; D = research facilities to doctoral level; X = all three levels (UMD).

	Nanyang Technol.	National, Singapore
Accountancy/Accounting	X	UM
Advertising	UM	
Anaesthesia/Anaesthesiology		MD
Anatomical Science/Anatomy	U	X
Animal Science/Husbandry/Production		U
Animatronics/Computer Arts	UM	
Applied Chemistry	X	M
Applied Physics	X	M
Aquaculture/Fisheries/Marine Science		X
Architecture		X
Art Theory	MD	
Art, Fine	X	
Art, History of	MD	MD
Artificial Intelligence	X	
Arts General	X	
Arts Management	U	
Arts and Culture	MD	
Arts, Graphic	UM	
Aviation	MD	
Banking/Finance	X	X
Behavioural Sciences	X	MD
Biochemistry	X	X
Bioengineering	UD	MD
Bioethics	U	
Bioinformatics	X	
Biology	X	X
Biology Molecular	X	X
Biomedical Sciences	X	X
Biophysics	X	U
Biotechnology	X	MD
Botany/Plant Science	X	X
Building/Built Environment/Construction		X
Business Administration	X	UM
Business Economics	U	
Business/Commerce	X	UM
Chemistry	U	X
Child and Family Psychology	X	

	Nanyang Technol.	National, Singapore
Child/Youth Studies	D	
Chinese Language and Literature	X	
Chinese/Chinese Studies	X	X
Cognitive Science	X	
Communication Sciences	X	
Communication/Journalism/Media Studies	X	
Communications/Information Management	X	X
Community Education	MD	
Community Health		MD
Computer Science	X	X
Conservation Studies		UM
Consumer Studies	MD	
Counselling	X	
Curriculum and Assessment Studies	MD	
Defence Studies	MD	
Dentistry		X
Design	UM	
Design, Industrial	UM	U
Development Studies	MD	
Drama/Theatre/Dance/Performing Arts	X	U
E-Business	X	
E-Commerce		X
Ecology	X	MD
Economic History	UD	
Economic Planning and Development	UD	
Economics	X	X
Economics Agricultural/Agribusiness	X	
Education	X	
Education Primary	MD	
Education Secondary	MD	
Education Special	MD	
Education Tertiary	MD	
Educational Administration	MD	
Educational Psychology	X	
Electronics	X	
Emergency/Trauma Care Technology	U	

	Nanyang Technol.	National, Singapore
Energy Studies	U	
Engineering	X	X
Engineering Aeronautical/Aerospace	U	
Engineering Automobile	U	
Engineering Biomedical	X	
Engineering Business	U	
Engineering Chemical/Petrochemical/Process	UD	X
Engineering Civil/Environmental/Structural	X	X
Engineering Communications/Telecommunications	X	
Engineering Computer	X	X
Engineering Design	U	
Engineering Electrical/Electronic	X	UM
Engineering Environmental Geophysics	U	
Engineering Fire		M
Engineering Geological	MD	M
Engineering Industrial	U	U
Engineering Information Technology	U	
Engineering Instrumentation	U	
Engineering Management	X	
Engineering Manufacturing	UM	
Engineering Marine	U	
Engineering Materials/Mineral Resources/Petroleum	U	
Engineering Mathematical	U	
Engineering Mechanical/Production	X	U
Engineering Metallurgical/Mining	U	
Engineering Polymer	U	
Engineering Software	X	X
English	X	X
English as a Second Language	MD	
Entrepreneurship	U	
Environmental Management	U	
Environmental Science/Studies	U	
Ergonomics	U	
Estate Management		UM
Ethics, Law and Governance	X	
European Studies		U
Film/Photography/Television/Animation	UM	
Food Science/Nutrition/Home Science/Dietetics	U	X
Forensic Science	U	

	Nanyang Technol.	National, Singapore
Genetics	U	
Geography	X	X
Hindi	X	
History		X
History/Philosophy of Science	MD	
Horticulture	U	
Housing/Real Estate		X
Human Biology	U	
Human Genetics	U	
Human Movement/Kinesiology/Biomechanics	MD	
Human Resource Development	U	
Industrial Chemistry	U	
Industrial Relations/Personnel/HRM	UM	
Information Science/Studies/Systems		X
Information Technology	X	
Insurance	U	
International Finance	U	
International Finance Economics	U	
International Marketing	U	
International Relations/Studies	U	M
Internet Computing/Technologies	D	
Japanese/Japanese Studies		X
Laboratory Science Technology	U	
Language Teaching/Learning	MD	
Language and Communication	MD	
Languages, Modern	U	
Law Environmental	U	
Law Intellectual Property/Copyright	U	M
Law International/Comparative/Trade		M
Law/Legal Studies	U	X
Library/Information Science	MD	
Literature, Comparative	X	
Logic/Computation	U	
Logistics	M	
Malay Language/Studies		X
Management	X	UM
Maritime Studies	UM	MD
Marketing	X	UM
Materials Science	X	X

	Nanyang Technol.	National, Singapore
Mathematics	X	X
Mechatronics	X	U
Medicine, Chinese	U	
Medicine, Obstetrics and Gynaecology		MD
Medicine, Orthopaedic		MD
Medicine, Paediatric		MD
Medicine/Surgery		UM
Meteorology	X	
Microbiology/Medical Microbiology	X	U
Military Science	U	
Mobile Communications/Telecommunications	MD	
Multimedia	X	X
Music	X	U
Music Education	X	
Nanotechnology	U	
Network Technology/Security	MD	
Nursing Education/Administration		UM
Occupational Health/Therapy		U
Ophthalmology		MD
Optics/Photonics	U	
Pathology		MD
Pharmacology		X
Pharmacy/Pharmaceutical Science		X
Philosophy	MD	X
Physical Education/Sports Science	X	
Physics	X	X
Physiology	U	X
Physiotherapy		U
Planning/Landscape Studies		UM

	Nanyang Technol.	National, Singapore
Politics/Political Science/Government		X
Polymer Science	X	
Product Design and Technology	U	
Project Management	U	MD
Psychiatry		MD
Psychology	X	X
Psychology Clinical	X	
Public Administration	M	MD
Public Health/Population Health		M
Public Relations	X	
Radiography/Diagnostic Technology/MRI		U
Robotics	X	
Social Work/Studies	MD	X
Sociology	X	X
Speech Science/Pathology/Therapy		U
Statistics/Actuarial Science	X	X
Surveying/Quantity Surveying		U
Tamil	MD	
Taxation	U	
Teacher Training	X	
Textiles/Fibre Science/Technology	U	
Tourism/Hospitality/Leisure/Recreation	M	
Transport Studies	MD	
Visual Arts	UM	
Women's/Gender Studies	U	
Zoology	MD	MD

NANYANG TECHNOLOGICAL UNIVERSITY

Founded 1991

Member of the Association of Commonwealth Universities

Postal Address: Nanyang Avenue, Singapore 639798
Telephone: 6791 1744 **Fax:** 6791 1604
URL: http://www.ntu.edu.sg

PRESIDENT*—Su Guaning, Prof., BScEE *Alta.*, MSEE *Cal.Tech.*, MSc(Stats) *Stan.*, PhD *Stan.*, PMD *Harv.*, FIE(Sing)
PROVOST—Andersson, Prof. Bertil, BSc *Umeå*, MSc *Umeå*, PhD *Lund*, DSc *Lund*
ASSOCIATE PROVOST—Er, Prof. Meng Hwa, BEng *NU Singapore*, PhD *Newcastle(NSW)*, FIE(Sing)
SECRETARY TO THE UNIVERSITY‡—Teo, Anthony, BA *NU Singapore*, MBA *Harv.*
CHIEF PLANNING OFFICER/REGISTRAR—Pek, Siok Ching, BSc *NU Singapore*, MSc *Lond.*
CHIEF FINANCIAL OFFICER—Goh Boon Huat, LLB *Lond.*
CHIEF HUMAN RESOURCE OFFICER—Yu, Sau Ting (Angela), BA *Sing.*, BSocSci *Sing.*
UNIVERSITY LIBRARIAN—Choy, Fatt Cheong, BSc *Newcastle(UK)*, MS *Ill.*

GENERAL INFORMATION

History. The university was founded in 1991, having been originally established as Nanyang Technological Institute in 1981.

It is situated in the south-western part of Singapore in Jurong, 25km from the city centre.

Admission to first degree courses. Singapore applicants: General Certificate of Education (GCE) with: passes in at least 2 subjects at A level; a pass in the general paper (waived in special cases); minimum grade D7 in a second language; and relevant project work. For certain courses special entry requirements must also be fulfilled. Candidates with relevant diplomas from a polytechnic in Singapore may also apply, but for admission to related courses only. International students: qualifications which satisfy matriculation requirements in the student's home country may be considered.

First Degrees (see also Singapore Directory to Subjects of Study) (* = with honours).
BA*, BAcc, BAEd, BBus, BCommStudies*, BEng(Aero), BEng(Bioeng), BEng(Chem&BiomolEng), BEng(Civil), BEng(CompEng), BEng(CompSc), BEng(Elect), BEng(EnvEng), BEng(MatlsEng), BEng(Mech), BFA*, BSc*, BSc(BMS), BSc(BMS)*, BSc(Ed), BSc(Maritime).

Length of course. Full-time: BAcc, BBus: 3 years; BA*, BAEd, BCommStudies*, BEng(Aero), BEng(Bioeng), BEng(Chem&BiomolEng), BEng(Civil), BEng(CompEng), BEng(CompSc), BEng(Elect), BEng(EnvEng), BEng(MatlsEng), BEng(Mech), BFA*, BSc(Ed), BSc(Maritime), BSc*: 4 years; BSc(BMS), BSc(BMS)*: 5 years.
Part-time: BEng(Elect), BEng(Mech): 5 years.

Higher Degrees (see also Singapore Directory to Subjects of Study).
Master's. MA, MA(ApplLing), MA(ApplPsy), MAcc, MA(EdMgt), MA(InstructionalDesign&Technology), MA(SocialStudies), MBA, MBA(Acc), MBA(B&F), MBA(InternationalBusiness), MBA(Marketing), MBA(StratMgt), MBA(Technol), MBus, MCommStudies, MEA, MEd, MEng, MHospMgt, MMassComm, M(PublicAdmin), MSc, MSc(Bioinformatics), MSc(BiomedicalEng), MSc(BusinessSpecialisation), MSc(CIM), MSc(CivilEng), MSc(CommEng), MSc(CommSoftware&Networks), MSc(CompContr&Autom), MSc(DigitalMediaTech), MSc(EmbeddedSys), MSc(EnvironmentalEng), MSc(ESS), MSc(Finance), MSc(FinEng), MSc(HumanFactorsEng), MSc(IndustrialEcol), MSc(InfoStudies), MSc(InfoSys), MSc(IntegratedCircuitDesign), MSc(InternationalRelations), MSc(IntlConstrMgt), MSc(IntPolEcon), MSc(KnowledgeManagement), MSc(LifeSc),

MSc(Log), MSc(ManagerialEcons), MSc(Maritime), MSc(MechEng), MSc(Mech&ProcofMatl), MSc(Microelectronics), MSc(OffshoreEng), MSc(Photonics), MSc(PowerEng), MSc(PrecEng), MSc(SP), MSc(SPD), MSc(StrategicStudies), MSc(Technopreneurship&Innov).

Admission. Applicants for admission to master's degrees by coursework must normally hold an appropriate first degree and, for most courses, have relevant work experience. Master's degrees by research (MA, MAcc, MASc, MBus, MCommStudies, MEng, MSc): a first degree with at least upper second class honours and the ability to pursue research in the proposed field.

Executive MBA course lasts from 16 to 32 months. Basic MSc as shown is from the School of Biological Sciences.

Length of course. Full-time: MEA: 1 year; MBA, MBA(Acc), MBA(B&F), MBA(InternationalBusiness), MBA(Marketing), MBA(StratMgt), MBA(Technol), MHospMgt, MSc(BiomedicalEng), MSc(BusinessSpecialisation), MSc(CIM), MSc(Finance), MSc(FinEng), MSc(HumanFactorsEng), MSc(InfoStudies), MSc(Log), MSc(ManagerialEcons), MSc(Mech&ProcofMatl), MSc(MechEng), MSc(PrecEng), MSc(SPD): 1–2 years; M(PublicAdmin), MA, MAcc, MBus, MCommStudies, MEng, MSc, MSc(CivilEng), MSc(CommEng), MSc(CommSoftware&Networks), MSc(CompContr&Autom), MSc(EnvironmentalEng), MSc(IntegratedCircuitDesign), MSc(InternationalRelations), MSc(IntlConstrMgt), MSc(IntPolEcon), MSc(Maritime), MSc(Microelectronics), MSc(OffshoreEng), MSc(Photonics), MSc(PowerEng), MSc(SP), MSc(StrategicStudies), MSc(Technopreneurship&Innov): 1–3 years; MMassComm: 1–4 years; MSc(IndustrialEcol): 1½–3 years; MA(ApplPsy): 2–4 years. *Part-time:* MSc(Technopreneurship&Innov): 0½–3 years; MBus, MCommStudies: 1–3 years; MA, MAcc, MEng, MMassComm, MSc: 1–4 years; MSc(BusinessSpecialisation), MSc(IntegratedCircuitDesign): 1½–3 years; MBA, MBA(Acc), MBA(B&F), MBA(InternationalBusiness), MBA(Marketing), MBA(StratMgt), MBA(Technol): 1½–5 years; MSc(ManagerialEcons): 2–3 years; M(PublicAdmin), MA(ApplLing), MA(EdMgt), MA(InstructionalDesign&Technology), MA(SocialStudies), MEd, MSc(Bioinformatics), MSc(BiomedicalEng), MSc(CIM), MSc(CivilEng), MSc(CommEng), MSc(CommSoftware&Networks), MSc(CompContr&Autom), MSc(DigitalMediaTech), MSc(EmbeddedSys), MSc(EnvironmentalEng), MSc(ESS), MSc(FinEng), MSc(HumanFactorsEng),

MSc(InfoStudies), MSc(InfoSys), MSc(InternationalRelations), MSc(IntlConstrMgt), MSc(IntPolEcon), MSc(KnowledgeManagement), MSc(Log), MSc(Maritime), MSc(Mech&ProcofMatl), MSc(MechEng), MSc(Microelectronics), MSc(OffshoreEng), MSc(Photonics), MSc(PowerEng), MSc(PrecEng), MSc(SP), MSc(SPD), MSc(StrategicStudies): 2–4 years; MA(ApplPsy): 3–4 years.

Doctoral. PhD.

Admission. Applicants for PhD must have a bachelor's degree with at least second class upper honours and/or a master's degree and the ability to pursue research in the proposed field.

Length of course. Full-time: PhD: 2–5 years. Part-time: PhD: 2–7 years.

Libraries. Volumes: 976,256. Other holdings: 59,050 AV/multimedia; 182 databases. Special collections: National Institute of Education (education and teacher training); Media Resource Library (audio-visual and multimedia resources).

Academic Awards (2006–2007). 277 awards ranging in value from S$100 to S$1500.

Income (2005–2006). Total, S$499,805,000.

Statistics. Staff (2006–2007): 4580 (2513 academic, 2067 non-academic). Students (2006–2007): full-time 23,870 (13,008 men, 10,862 women); part-time 4407 (2805 men, 1602 women); international 7074 (4603 men, 2471 women); undergraduate 19,739 (10,782 men, 8957 women); master's 4989 (3074 men, 1915 women); doctoral 1882 (1268 men, 614 women).

FACULTIES/SCHOOLS

Art, Design and Media
Tel: 6316 8821 Fax: 6795 3140
E-mail: d-adm@ntu.edu.sg
Chair: Kerlow, Prof. Isaac V., BFA *N.Y.Sch.Visual Arts*, MS *Pratt*
Personal Assistant: Aw Lee Ting

Biological Sciences
Tel: 6316 2800 Fax: 6791 3856
E-mail: d-sbs@ntu.edu.sg
Chair: Tam, Prof. James P., BSc *Wis.*, PhD *Wis.*
Secretary: Yee Lee Choo

Chemical and Biomedical Engineering
Tel: 6790 6731 Fax: 6794 9220
E-mail: d-scbe@ntu.edu.sg
Chair: Ching, Prof. Chi Bun, BSc *Aston*, PhD *Aston*, FIE(Sing)
Secretary: Ang Shiou Ching

Civil and Environmental Engineering

Tel: 6790 5264 Fax: 6791 0676
E-mail: d-cee@ntu.edu.sg
Acting Chair: Teh, Cee Ing, BE *Malaya*, DPhil *Oxf.*
Secretary: Chim-Ng Phui Har, Janet

Communication and Information

Tel: 6790 6109 Fax: 6794 3662
E-mail: d-sci@ntu.edu.sg
Chair: Ang, Peng Hwa, LLB *NU Singapore*, MA *S.Calif.*, PhD *Mich.State*
Secretary: Yanti bte Aris

Computer Engineering

Tel: 6790 5788 Fax: 6791 9414
E-mail: d-sce@ntu.edu.sg
Acting Chair: Goh, Prof. Eck Soong (Angela), BSc *UMIST*, MSc *UMIST*, PhD *UMIST*, FBCS
Secretary: Kum, Jolene

Education, National Institute of

Tel: 6790 3088 Fax: 6896 9423
E-mail: director@nie.edu.sg
Director: Lee, Prof. Sing Kong, BHortSc *Cant.*, PhD *NU Singapore*
Secretary: Goh Hui Kat, Charmaine

Electrical and Electronic Engineering

Tel: 6790 5402 Fax: 6791 2687
E-mail: d-eee@ntu.edu.sg
Chair: Kam, Prof. Chan Hin, BEng *Sing.*, MSc *Nan.*, MSEE *S.Calif.*, PhD *NU Singapore*
Secretary: Tan, Elaine

Engineering, College of

Tel: 6790 6708 Fax: 6791 2523
E-mail: d-coe@ntu.edu.sg
Dean: Pan, Prof. Tso-Chien, BS *Cheng Kung*, MS *Calif.*, PhD *Calif.*

Hospitality Management, Cornell-Nanyang Institute of

Tel: 6790 6480 Fax: 6794 9796
E-mail: d-cni@ntu.edu.sg
Dean: Siguaw, Prof. Judy A., BBA *Lamar*, MBA *Louisiana Tech*, DBA *Louisiana Tech*
Secretary: Zareena Binte Hussain

Humanities and Social Sciences

Tel: 6790 6983 Fax: 6794 2830
E-mail: d-hss@ntu.edu.sg
Chair: Wong, Prof. W. C. (Lawrence), BA *HK*, MPhil *HK*, PhD *Lond.*
Secretary: Chiam-Lim, Shirley

Materials Science and Engineering

Tel: 6790 5609 Fax: 6790 0921
E-mail: d-mse@ntu.edu.sg
Chair: Boey, Prof. Yin Chiang (Freddy), BE *Monash*, PhD *NU Singapore*, FIMMM, FIE(Sing)
Secretary: Chua, Jane

Mechanical and Aerospace Engineering

Tel: 6790 5486 Fax: 6791 1859
E-mail: d-mae@ntu.edu.sg
Chair: Lam, Prof. Khin Yong, BSc *Lond.*, SM *M.I.T.*, PhD *M.I.T.*
Secretary: Lim, Jesamine

Nanyang Business School

Tel: 6790 5697 Fax: 6791 3697
E-mail: d-nbs@ntu.edu.sg
Chair: Singh, Prof. Jitendra, BS *Lucknow*, MA *Stan.*, PhD *Stan.*, MBA
Secretary: Ang, Sabrina

Physical and Mathematical Sciences

Tel: 6790 3754 Fax: 6316 6984
E-mail: spms-v1@ntu.edu.sg
Chair: Lee, Prof. Soo-Ying, BSc *Malaya*, PhD *Chic.*, FRSChem
Secretary: Lin, Claire Jiaying

ACADEMIC UNITS
Arranged by Schools

Art, Design and Media

Tel: 6790 6667 Fax: 6790 3140
E-mail: adm-info@ntu.edu.sg
Kerlow, Isaac V., BFA *N.Y.Sch.Visual Arts*, MS *Pratt* Prof.; Chair*
Sethi, Suresh Assoc. Prof.; Assoc. Chair
Other Staff: 2 Visiting Profs.; 28 Asst. Profs.; 2 Lectrs.

Biological Sciences

Tel: 6316 2800 Fax: 6791 3856
E-mail: d-sbs@ntu.edu.sg
Tam, James P., BSc *Wis.*, PhD *Wis.* Prof.; Chair*
Other Staff: 1 Prof.; 1 Sr. Tutor
Research: cell signalling; genetic diseases; immunology; protein chemistry; structural biology

Chemical Biology and Biotechnology

E-mail: h-dcbb@ntu.edu.sg
Bose, Salil K., BSc *Calc.*, MS *Roch.*, MSc *Jad.*, PhD *Roch.* Visiting Prof.
Liu, Chuan Fa, BSc *Nanjing Pharm.*, PhD *Montpellier II* Assoc. Prof.
Nordenskiold, Lars, BSc *Stockholm*, PhD *Stockholm* Prof.; Acting Head*
Shochat, Susana, BSc *Jerusalem*, MSc *Jerusalem*, PhD *Ley.* Assoc. Prof.
Tam, James P., BSc *Wis.*, PhD *Wis.* Prof.
Other Staff: 8 Asst. Profs.; 2 Lectrs.; 2 Sr. Fellows; 9 Res. Fellows; 1 Adjunct Assoc. Prof.; 2 Adjunct Asst. Profs.
Research: biochemistry; biophysics; drug design; enzymology; photobiology and plant physiology

Genomics and Genetics

Tel: 6316 2809
Chen, Ken Shiung, BS *Texas*, MA *Texas*, PhD *Texas* Assoc. Prof.
Dieter, Christian S., PhD *Tübingen* Assoc. Prof.
Dröge, Peter, PhD *Constance* Assoc. Prof.; Head*
Kambadur, Ravi, BSc *S.Venkat.*, MSc *S.Venkat.*, PhD *Pg.IMER* Assoc. Prof.
Karjalainen, Klaus E., MD *Helsinki*, PhD *Helsinki* Prof.
Preiser, Peter R., BA *Delaware*, PhD *Delaware* Assoc. Prof.
Other Staff: 3 Asst. Profs.; 5 Res. Fellows; 1 Adjunct Prof.; 3 Adjunct Assoc. Profs.; 2 Adjunct Asst. Profs.
Research: biochemistry and biophysical chemistry; gene expression; malaria; molecular biology; molecular parasitology

Molecular and Cell Biology

Tel: 6316 2809
Dröge, Peter, PhD *Constance* Assoc. Prof.; Acting Head*
Featherstone, Mark S., PhD *McG.* Prof.
Konishi, Shiro, BS *Toyama*, MS *Toyama*, PhD *Tokyo* Visiting Prof.
Law, Sai-Kit (Alex), BSc *Cal.Tech.*, PhD *Harv.* Prof.
Ruedl, Christine, PhD *Innsbruck* Assoc. Prof.
Sugrue, Richard J., BSc *Lond.*, PhD *Kent* Assoc. Prof.
Other Staff: 8 Asst. Profs.; 5 Res. Fellows; 3 Adjunct Asst. Profs.; 1 Adjunct Assoc. Prof.
Research: genetics; molecular biology; molecular immunology; protein biochemistry; protein chemistry

Structural and Computational Biology

Tel: 6316 2812 E-mail: h-dscb@ntu.edu.sg
Grüber, Gerhard, DrNatSc *Mainz* Assoc. Prof.
Lescar, Julien, MSc *Paris XI* PhD *Paris XI*, BSc *Paris XI* Assoc. Prof.
Nordenskiöld, Lars, BSc *Stockholm*, PhD *Stockholm* Prof.; Head*
Pervushin, Konstantin, MSc *Moscow Phys.& Technol.Inst.*, PhD *Russian Acad.Sc.* Assoc. Prof.

Torres, Jaume, BSc *A.U.Barcelona*, PhD *Barcelona* Assoc. Prof.
Yoon, Ho Sup, BSc *Seoul*, MS *Korea A.I.S.T.*, PhD *Chic.* Assoc. Prof.
Other Staff: 4 Asst. Profs.; 1 Sr. Res. Fellow; 15 Res. Fellows; 1 Adjunct Prof.; 1 Adjunct Assoc. Prof.
Research: biocomputing collodial chemistry; biomacromolecular chemistry; biophysical chemistry; biostatistics; medical informatics

Chemical and Biomedical Engineering, School of

Tel: 6790 6731 Fax: 6794 9220
E-mail: d-scbe@ntu.edu.sg
Ching, Chi Bun, BSc *Aston*, PhD *Aston*, FIE(Sing) Prof.; Chair*

Bioengineering

Tel: 6790 6086 Fax: 6791 1761
E-mail: h-bioe-coe@ntu.edu.sg
Cheang, Hong Ning (Philip), BE *Monash*, PhD *Monash* Assoc. Prof.
Fuss, Franz K., MD *Vienna*, PhD *Vienna* Assoc. Prof.
James, Morley A. Visiting Prof.
Kim, Kyong Tai, BS *Seoul*, MS *Korea A.I.S.T.*, PhD *Mass.* Visiting Prof.
Li, Changming, BS *China U.S.T.*, MS *Wuhan*, PhD *Wuhan* Assoc. Prof.
Liao, Kin, BS *Virginia Polytech.*, MS *Virginia Polytech.*, PhD *Virginia Polytech.* Assoc. Prof.
Luong, John H. T., BEng *Mass.*, PhD *McG.*, PhD *W.Ont.* Prof.; Head*
Wang, Joseph Nanyang Prof.
Other Staff: 9 Asst. Profs.; 12 Res. Fellows; 8 Res. Assocs.
Research: bioelectronics; bioimaging; biomaterials; biomechanics; bio-nanotechnology

Bioinformatics Research Centre

Tel: 6790 6609 Fax: 6316 2780
E-mail: birc@ntu.edu.sg
Rajapakse, Jagath C., BSc(Eng) *Moratuwa*, MSc *N.Y.State*, PhD *N.Y.State* Assoc. Prof.; Dir.*
Other Staff: 1 Deputy Dir.; 4 Res. Fellows; 1 Singapore-MIT Alliance Res. Fellow; 32 Affiliated Acad. Staff
Research: chemoinformatics; computational biology; functional genomics; structural genomics and proteomics; systems biology

Biomedical Engineering Research, Centre for

Tel: 6790 6420 Fax: 6791 2274
E-mail: d-bme@ntu.edu.sg
Venkatraman, Subbu S., BSc *B'lore.*, MSc IIT *Madras*, PhD *Carnegie-Mellon* Assoc. Prof.; Dir.*
Other Staff: 7 Res. Fellows; 1 Singapore Millennium Foundation Res. Fellow; 20 Academic Staff; 2 Deputy Dirs.; 1 Centre Manager
Research: bioimaging; biomaterials; biophotonics and biosensors; medical imaging and signal processing; medical instrumentation/telemedicine

Chemical and Biomolecular Engineering

Tel: 6790 6743 Fax: 6794 7553
E-mail: h-cbe@ntu.edu.sg
Chan, Mary B. E., BEng *NU Singapore*, PhD *M.I.T.* Assoc. Prof.; Assoc. Chair (Res. and Grad. Studies)
Li, Changming, BS *China U.S.T.*, MS *Wuhan*, PhD *Wuhan* Assoc. Prof.
Ng, Siu Choon, BA *Oxf.*, DPhil *Oxf.* Assoc. Prof.; Head*
Other Staff: 6 Visiting Profs.; 7 Assoc. Profs.; 33 Asst. Profs.; 1 Sr. Fellow; 1 Sr. Tutor
Research: biosensors, bioanalytics and bioimaging (bioelectronics, microbial fuel cell, microfluidics, electrochemistry, MRI, ultrasonics, positron emission tomography); chiral and pharmaceutical engineering (large-scale separations, materials, process analytical technologies (PAT), synthesis); industrial chemistry and green technology

(bioprocess engineering, colloids, enzyme processing, flavour and fragrances, generation of 'bio-fuels' using bio-feedstocks, renewable resources, speciality chemicals); multiscale process systems engineering: multiscale modelling, molecular simulation, entropic lattice boltzmann, control of particulate process, plant-wide control and optimisation, sonochemical systems engineering; nanotechnology, catalysis and reaction engineering (molecular tailoring of materials for catalysis/reaction and medicine)

Civil and Environmental Engineering

Tel: 6790 5265 Fax: 6791 0676
   E-mail: d-cee@ntu.edu.sg
Teh, Cee Ing, BE Malaya, DPhil Oxf.   Assoc. Prof.; Acting Chair*

Environmental and Water Resources Engineering

Tel: 6790 5308 E-mail: ewre@ntu.edu.sg
Chang, Niansheng, BS Wuhan, MS Nanjing, PhD Nan.Tech.   Assoc. Prof.
Chiew, Yee Meng, BE Auck., PhD Auck. Temasek Prof.
Chui, Peng Cheong, BEng NU Singapore, MSc NU Singapore, DEng Kyoto   Assoc. Prof.
Gin, Yew-Hoong (Karina), BEng Melb., MEng NU Singapore, ScD M.I.T.   Assoc. Prof.
Ivanov, Volodymyr   Assoc. Prof.
Law, W.-K. (Adrian), BSc(Eng) HK, MS Calif., PhD Calif.   Assoc. Prof.
Lim, Siow Yong, BEng Liv., PhD Liv.   Assoc. Prof.
Liu, Yu, BE N.W.Inst.of Light Industry, MEng I.N.S.A.Toulouse, PhD I.N.S.A.Toulouse   Assoc. Prof.
Lo, Y.-M. (Edmund), BSc Cal.Tech., MSc Cal.Tech., PhD M.I.T.   Assoc. Prof.; Head*
Shuy, Eng Ban, BE W.Aust., MSc Sing., PhD Qld.   Assoc. Prof.
Sun, D. (Darren), MSc NSW, PhD NSW   Assoc. Prof.
Tan, Soon Keat, BE Auck., ME Auck., PhD Auck.   Assoc. Prof.
Tay, Joo Hwa, BS Natnl.Taiwan, MS Cinc., PhD Tor.   Prof.
Wang, Jing-Yuan, BS Natnl.Chung Hsing, MCE N.Carolina State, PhD N.Carolina State   Assoc. Prof.
Wong, S. W. (Tommy), BSc Leeds, MSc Birm., PhD NU Singapore, FASCE   Assoc. Prof.
Other Staff: 7 Asst. Profs.; 12 Res. Fellows; 1 Teaching Fellow; 2 Adjunct Assoc. Profs.
Research: coastal and offshore processes; emerging contaminants and advanced chemical processes; environmental bioprocesses and biotechnology; membrane science and technology; watershed, rivers and lakes

Infrastructure Systems and Maritime Studies

Tel: 6790 5307 E-mail: h-isms@ntu.edu.sg
Chew, A. S. (David), BEng Sing., MASc Wat., MBA Oklahoma City, DBA S.Qld.   Assoc. Prof.
Chu, Jian, BE Chongqing Archit.& Engin., PhD NSW   Assoc. Prof.
Fan, S. L. (Henry), BS Natnl.Taiwan, MS Idaho, PhD Calif.   Prof.
Goh, Pong Chai, BSurv NSW, MSurv NSW   Assoc. Prof.
Goh, T. C. (Anthony), BEng Monash, PhD Monash   Assoc. Prof.
Koo, Tsai Kee, BSurv NSW, MSc Lond., MPhil Lond.   Assoc. Prof. (on leave)
Lam, Soi Hoi, BS Natnl.Taiwan, MSE Texas, PhD Texas   Assoc. Prof.
Leong, Eng Choon, BEng NU Singapore, MEng NU Singapore, PhD W.Aust.   Assoc. Prof.; Head*
Low, Bak Kong, BS M.I.T., MS M.I.T., PhD Calif., FASCE   Assoc. Prof.
Lum, Kit Meng, BEng NU Singapore, MSc NU Singapore, MSE Texas, PhD Nan.Tech.   Assoc. Prof.

Rahardjo, Harianto, MSc Sask., PhD Sask.   Prof.
Tan, Yan Weng, BE Monash, MEngSc Monash   Assoc. Prof.
Teh, Cee Ing, BE Malaya, DPhil Oxf.   Assoc. Prof.
Ting, Seng Kiong, BE Monash, MEng Monash, SM M.I.T., ScD M.I.T.   Assoc. Prof.
Tiong, L. K. (Robert), BSc Glas., ME Calif., PhD Nan.Tech.   Assoc. Prof.
Tor, Yam Khoon, BSurv NSW, MSurv NSW, PhD Nan.Tech.   Assoc. Prof.
Wong, Kai Sin, BSCE Ill., MS Calif., PhD Calif.   Assoc. Prof.
Wong, Yiik Diew, BE Cant., PhD Cant.   Assoc. Prof.
Other Staff: 1 Visiting Prof.; 2 Asst. Profs.; 1 Assoc. Professorial Fellow; 1 Res. Fellow; 3 Teaching Fellows; 1 Adjunct Prof.; 2 Adjunct Assoc. Profs.
Research: geotechnical engineering; maritime studies; project management and finance; spatial information; transportation engineering

Infrastructure Systems, Centre for

Tel: 6790 5328 Fax: 6792 3886
   E-mail: d-cis@ntu.edu.sg
Fan, S. L. (Henry), BS Natnl.Taiwan, MS Idaho, PhD Calif.   Prof.; Dir.*
Research: project management; transportation engineering

Structures and Mechanics

Tel: 6790 5306 E-mail: h-dsm@ntu.edu.sg
Ang, T. C. (Paul), BEng Sing., MSc NU Singapore   Assoc. Prof.
Chiew, Sing Ping, BSc Wales, MSc Wales, PhD NU Singapore, FIStructE   Assoc. Prof.
Chuang, Poon-Hwei, BEng Sing., MSc S'ton., PhD Lond.   Assoc. Prof.
Fan, Sau Cheong, BSc(Eng) HK, PhD HK, FIStructE, FICE, FHKIE   Prof.
Fung, Tat Ching, BSc(Eng) HK, PhD HK   Assoc. Prof.; Head*
Lee, Chi King, BSc(Eng) HK, MPhil HK, PhD Lond.   Assoc. Prof.
Lee, Sai Cheng, BEng Sing., MSc Lond., PhD Nan.Tech.   Assoc. Prof.
Li, Bing, BE Tongji, PhD Cant.   Assoc. Prof.
Lie, Seng Tjhen, BSc(Eng) Lond., MSc Lond., PhD UMIST   Assoc. Prof.
Lok, Tat Seng, BSc Aston, PhD Warw.   Assoc. Prof.
Pan, Tso-Chien, BS Cheng Kung, MS Calif., PhD Calif.   Prof.
Soh, Chee Kiong, BEng C'dia., SM M.I.T., PhD Wales   Prof.
Tan, Kang Hai, BSc Manc., PhD Manc.   Assoc. Prof.
Tan, Teng Hooi, BEng Sing., MSc NU Singapore, PhD Nan.Tech.   Assoc. Prof.
Teng, Susanto, BSCE Iowa, MSCE Iowa, PhD Iowa   Assoc. Prof.
Yip, Woon Kwong, BEng Sing., MSc NU Singapore, PhD NU Singapore   Assoc. Prof.
Zhao, Zhiye, BS Tsinghua, MSc Lond., PhD CNAA   Assoc. Prof.
Other Staff: 1 Visiting Prof.; 6 Asst. Profs.; 11 Res. Fellows; 1 Teaching Fellow; 1 Adjunct Assoc. Prof
Research: computational mechanics; concrete, building technology and fire engineering; protective technology; structural connections; structural dynamics and seismic engineering

Communication and Information

Tel: 6790 6108 Fax: 6794 3662
   E-mail: wwwsci@ntu.edu.sg
Ang, Peng Hwa, LLB NU Singapore, MA S.Calif., PhD Mich.State   Assoc. Prof.; Chair*

Communication Research

Tel: 6790 4108 Fax: 6792 4329
   E-mail: h-dcr@ntu.edu.sg
Choi, S. K. (Alfred), BA York(Can.), MA York(Can.), PhD York(Can.)   Assoc. Prof.

Detenber, Benjamin H., BA Stan., PhD Stan.   Assoc. Prof.; Head*
Kuo, C. Y. (Eddie), BA Natnl.Chengchi, MA Hawaii, PhD Minn.   Prof.
Other Staff: 6 Asst. Profs.; 1 Sr. Tutor; 1 Lectr.
Research: communication policy and regulation; culture and communication; internet studies and media psychology; media economics and management; political communication

Electronic and Broadcast Media

Tel: 6790 5769 Fax: 6792 7526
   E-mail: h-debm@ntu.edu.sg
Hao, Xiaoming, BA Beijing Teachers', MA Chinese Acad.Soc.Sc., MA Missouri, PhD Missouri   Assoc. Prof.; Head*
Other Staff: 4 Asst. Profs.; 2 Lectrs.
Research: Asian cinema studies; impact of information and communication technologies for human development; media and cultural studies in Asia-Pacific; media issues and regulations in Southeast Asia; social impact of broadcast media

Information Studies

Tel: 6790 4608 Fax: 6792 5214
   E-mail: h-dis@ntu.edu.sg
Chaudhry, Abdus S., BA Punjab, MA Punjab, MS Hawaii, PhD Ill.   Assoc. Prof.; Head*
Foo, S. B. (Schubert), BSc Strath., MBA Strath., PhD Strath., FBCS, FIMechE   Prof.
Goh, H. L. (Dion), BA NU Singapore, MSc Florida State, PhD Texas A.& M.   Assoc. Prof.
Khoo, S. G., BA Harv., MSc Ill., PhD Syr.   Assoc. Prof.
Majid, Shaheen M., BSc Punjab, MSc W.Ont., MLIS W.Ont., MSc Punjab, PhD City(UK)   Assoc. Prof.
Ravi, S. Sharma, BSc Bran., MSc Regina, PhD Wat.   Assoc. Prof.
Tan, J. Y. (Margaret), BCom Newcastle(NSW), MBA Adel., PhD Qld.   Assoc. Prof.
Theng, Yin Leng, BSc NU Singapore, MSc UMIST, PhD Middx.   Assoc. Prof.
Other Staff: 4 Asst. Profs.; 1 Lectr.; 1 Sr. Fellow; 1 Adjunct Asst. Prof.
Research: digital libraries and information retrieval; information and knowledge management; knowledge organisation and discovery; users and usability studies

Journalism and Publishing

Tel: 6790 5769 Fax: 6792 7526
   E-mail: h-djp@ntu.edu.sg
George, Cherian, BA Camb., MSc Col., PhD Stan.   Asst. Prof.; Acting Head*
Other Staff: 5 Asst. Profs.; 1 Lectr.; 2 Adjunct Assoc. Profs.
Research: conflict reporting; information control and censorship; media law and ethics; online journalism; press cultures and norms

Public and Promotional Communication

Tel: 6790 4108/6669 Fax: 6792 4329
   E-mail: h-dppc@ntu.edu.sg
Karan, Kavita, BSc AP Ag., BCJ Osm., MCJ Osm., MPhil Osm., PhD Lond.   Assoc. Prof.
Lee, Chun Wah, BS Portland, MA Colorado, PhD Ohio   Assoc. Prof.
Lwin, May O., BA NU Singapore, MBA NU Singapore, PhD NU Singapore   Acting Head*
Other Staff: 5 Asst. Profs.; 1 Sr. Fellow; 1 Adjunct Assoc. Prof.; 1 Adjunct Asst. Prof.
Research: advertising management; corporate communication strategies; health and social communications; Internet and interactive communications; public communications campaigns

Computer Engineering

Tel: 6790 5788 Fax: 6791 9414
   E-mail: d-sce@ntu.edu.sg
Goh, Eck Soong (Angela), BSc UMIST, MSc UMIST, PhD UMIST, FBCS   Prof.; Acting Chair*

Advanced Information Systems, Centre for

Tel: 6790 6929 Fax: 6790 6559
E-mail: assourav@ntu.edu.sg
Bhowmick, Sourav S., BEng Nag., MComp
Griff., PhD Nan.Tech. Assoc. Prof.; Dir.*
Other Staff: 22 Fac. Members; 1 Res. Fellow
Research: information and knowledge grid (data
mining, extensible markup language
(XML), grid-based data warehousing,
information retrieval, stream data analysis;
information security (access control,
intrusion detection, security protocol,
trends analysis); Internet and mobile
computing (e-learning, mobile commerce,
pervasive computing, software agents);
simulation and decision support (large-scale
complex learning)

Computational Intelligence, Centre for

Tel: 6790 4926 Fax: 6792 6559
E-mail: ashcquek@ntu.edu.sg
Quek, Hiok Chai, BSc H-W, PhD H-W Assoc.
Prof.; Dir.*
Other Staff: 1 Lee Kuan Yew Postdoctoral
Fellow; 1 Res. Assoc.
Research: adaptive and autonomous systems;
decision support systems; knowledge
engineering and discovery; nature-inspired
systems

Computer Communications

Tel: 6790 6241 Fax: 6792 6559
E-mail: h-dcc@ntu.edu.sg
Chan, Syin, BEng NU Singapore, PhD Kent
Assoc. Prof.
Chia, Liang Tien (Clement), BSc Lough., PhD
Lough. Assoc. Prof.; Head*
Das, Amitabha, BTech Kharagpur, MS Calif., PhD
Calif. Assoc. Prof.
Lau, Chiew Tong, BEng Lakehead, MASc Br.Col.,
PhD Br.Col. Assoc. Prof.
Lee, Bu Sung, BSc Lough., PhD Lough. Assoc.
Prof.
Lee, Keok Kee, BEng NU Singapore, MEE Rice
Assoc. Prof.
Leong, Peng Chor, BSc Essex, MS Calif. Assoc.
Prof.
Lin, Weisi, BSc Zhongshan, MSc Zhongshan, PhD
Lond. Assoc. Prof.
Madhukumar, A. S., BTech Kerala, MTech
Cochin, PhD IIT Madras Assoc. Prof.
Vun, Nicholas C. H., BE Monash, MEngSc Monash
Assoc. Prof.
Wong, Kin Keong, BEng Monash, MEngSc
Monash Assoc. Prof.
Yeo, Chai Kiat, BEng NU Singapore,
MSc(ElectEng) NU Singapore Assoc. Prof.
Yow, Kin Choong, BEng NU Singapore, PhD
Camb. Assoc. Prof.
Other Staff: 1 Visiting Prof.; 8 Asst. Profs.; 2
Lectrs.; 1 Sr. Tutor; 1 Adjunct Assoc. Prof.;
1 Adjunct Asst. Prof.
Research: advanced networking; grid computing;
parallel and distributed simulation;
processing of multimedia data; wireless and
ad hoc network

Computer Science

Tel: 6790 4600 Fax: 6792 6559
E-mail: h-dcsc@ntu.edu.sg
Ayani, Rassul, MSc T.U.Vienna, MSc(CompSc)
Stockholm, PhD R.I.T.Stockholm Visiting Prof.
Cai, Wentong, BS Nankai, MS Nankai, PhD Exe.
Assoc. Prof.; Head*
Hsu, Wen Jing, BS Natnl.Chiao Tung(Taiwan), MS
Natnl.Chiao Tung(Taiwan), PhD Natnl.Chiao
Tung(Taiwan) Assoc. Prof.
Huang, Shell Ying, BSc Lond., PhD Lond.
Assoc. Prof.
Leung, Maylor K., BS Natnl.Taiwan, BSc Sask.,
MSc Sask., PhD Sask. Assoc. Prof.
Loh, K. K. (Peter), BEng NU Singapore,
MSc(ElectEng) NU Singapore, MSc Manc., PhD
Nan.Tech. Assoc. Prof.
Muller-Wittig, Wolfgang K., DrIng
T.U.Darmstadt Assoc. Prof.
Ng, Geok See, BMath Wat., MASc Wat., PhD
Nan.Tech. Assoc. Prof.

Pasquier, Michel B., DrIng Inst.Nat.Poly.Grenoble,
PhD Inst.Nat.Poly.Grenoble Assoc. Prof.
Quek, Hiok Chai, BSc H-W, PhD H-W Assoc.
Prof.
Sourin, Alexei, MSc Moscow Phys.& Technol.Inst.,
PhD Moscow Phys.& Technol.Inst. Assoc. Prof.
Sun, Chengzheng, MPhil E.China Inst.Technol.,
PhD Changsha I.T. Prof.
Turner, Stephen J., BA Camb., MA Camb., MSc
Manc., PhD Manc. Assoc. Prof.
Other Staff: 12 Asst. Profs.; 2 Lectrs.; 1
Teaching Fellow; 1 Adjunct Assoc. Prof.; 1
Adjunct Asst. Prof.
Research: computational intelligence; computer
algorithms; parallel and distributed
computing; visual computing and digital
media

Computing Systems

Tel: 6790 4611 Fax: 6792 6559
E-mail: h-dcs@ntu.edu.sg
Abdul Wahab Bin Abdul Rahman, BSc Essex,
MSc(ElectEng) NU Singapore, PhD Nan.Tech.
Assoc. Prof.
Annamalai, Benjamin P., BE IISc., BSc IISc., MS
N.Dakota State, PhD Idaho Assoc. Prof.
Cham, Tat Jen, BA Camb., PhD Camb. Assoc.
Prof.
Fong, Cheuk Ming, BEng Lond., MSc Lond., PhD
Auck. Assoc. Prof.
Goh, Wooi Boon, BSc Birm., MPhil Warw.
Assoc. Prof.; Head*
Man, Zhihong, BE Shanghai Jiaotong, MS Chinese
Acad.Sc., PhD Melb. Assoc. Prof.
Maskell, Douglas L., BE James Cook, MEng James
Cook, PhD James Cook Assoc. Prof.
McLoughlin, Ian V., BEng Birm., PhD Birm.
Assoc. Prof.
Sluzek, Andrzej, MSc Warsaw U.T., PhD Warsaw
U.T., DSc Warsaw U.T. Assoc. Prof.
Srikanthan, Thambipillai, BSc CNAA, PhD CNAA
Assoc. Prof.
Other Staff: 10 Asst. Profs.; 2 Lectrs.; 2 Sr.
Fellows; 1 Sr. Tutor; 1 Adjunct Assoc. Prof.
Research: computer architecture and digital
systems; computer graphics and computer
vision; forensic and security systems; high
performance embedded systems; image and
signal processing

Information Systems

Tel: 6790 4802 Fax: 6792 6559
E-mail: h-disy@ntu.edu.sg
Bhowmick, Sourav S., BEng Nag., MComp
Griff., PhD Nan.Tech. Assoc. Prof.
Chaudhari, N. S., BTech IIT Bombay, MTech IIT
Bombay, PhD IIT Bombay, FIETE Assoc. Prof.
Goh, E. S. (Angela), BSc Manc., MSc Manc., PhD
Manc., FBCS Prof.
Hui, Siu Cheung, BSc Sus., DPhil Sus. Assoc.
Prof.
Khong, Chooi Peng, BA Malaya, MA Birm., MEd
Pitt., PhD Malaya Assoc. Prof.
Kwoh, Chee Keong, BEng NU Singapore,
MSc(IndEng) NU Singapore, PhD Lond. Assoc.
Prof.
Lim, Ee Peng, BSc NU Singapore, PhD Minn.
Assoc. Prof.; Head*
Lin, Feng, BEng Zhejiang, MEng Zhejiang, PhD
Nan.Tech. Assoc. Prof.
Ng, Wee Keong, BSc NU Singapore, MS Mich.,
PhD Mich. Assoc. Prof.
Rajapakse, Jagath C., BSc(Eng) Moratuwa, MSc
N.Y.State, PhD N.Y.State Assoc. Prof.
Tan, Ah Hwee, BSc NU Singapore, MSc NU
Singapore, PhD Boston Assoc. Prof.
Tan, Eng Chong, BSc Nan., MSc Auck., PhD
Melb. Assoc. Prof.
Other Staff: 12 Asst. Profs.; 1 Sr. Fellow; 1
Adjunct Prof.; 5 Adjunct Assoc. Profs.; 1
Adjunct Asst. Prof.
Research: bio-informatics; database and
knowledge engineering (data warehousing/
mining database); digital libraries
(information retrieval, knowledge
management, text/web mining); Internet/
mobile information systems (agents, e-
services, mobile databases, m-services)

Multimedia and Network Technology, Centre for

Tel: 6790 6578 Fax: 6792 6559
E-mail: astjcham@ntu.edu.sg
Cham, Tat Jen, BA Camb., PhD Camb. Assoc.
Prof.; Dir.*
Other Staff: 3 Res. Fellows; 25 Fac. Members
Research: asynchronous transfer mode (ATM)
and multiprotocol label switching (MPLS);
mobile computing; network simulation;
quality of service (QoS) of network and
application; software radio

Parallel and Distributed Computing, Centre for

Tel: 6790 4054 Fax: 6792 6559
E-mail: assjturner@ntu.edu.sg
Turner, Stephen J., BA Camb., MA Camb., MSc
Manc., PhD Manc. Assoc. Prof.; Dir.*
Other Staff: 2 Res. Assocs.; 21 Fac. Members
Research: multi-agent systems; parallel and
computer architecture; parallel and
distributed algorithms and applications;
parallel and distributed simulation; system
support for grid computing

Education, National Institute of

Tel: 6790 3888 Fax: 6896 9033
E-mail: niepr@nie.edu.sg

Asian Language and Culture

Tel: 6790 3559
Abdullah, Kamsiah, BA Lond., MEd Malaya, PhD
Lond. Assoc. Prof.
Chan, Chiu Ming, BA HK, MA Wis., PhD Wis.
Assoc. Prof.
Chew, Cheng Hai, BA Nan., MA Chinese HK, PhD
NU Singapore Prof.
Goh Yeng Seng, BA Natnl.Taiwan, PhD Lond.
Assoc. Prof.; Head*
Guo, Xi, MA Nanjing Visiting Prof.
Hadijah, Bte Rahmat, BA Sing., MA NU Singapore,
PhD Lond. Assoc. Prof.
Koh, Hock Kiat, BA Natnl.Taiwan, MEd Nan.Tech.,
MA Nan.Tech., PhD Nan.Tech. Assoc. Prof.
Lim, Buan Chay, BA Nan., PhD NU
Singapore Assoc. Prof.
Paitoon, Masmintra C., BEd Sri Nakharinwirot,
MA Malaya, PhD Malaya Assoc. Prof.
Woon, Wee Lee, BA Nan., MA Nan., PhD Leeds
Assoc. Prof.
Yan, Shoucheng, BA Shanghai 2nd Med.Coll., MA
E.China Normal, PhD Indiana Assoc. Prof.
Other Staff: 17 Asst. Profs.; 6 Lectrs.; 2 Sr.
Fellows; 5 Teaching Fellows
Research: bilingualism and teaching of Chinese,
Tamil and Malay; Chinese, Tamil and Malay
linguistics; Chinese, Tamil and Malay
literature and culture; pedagogy in Chinese,
Tamil and Malay

Early Childhood and Special Needs Education

Tel: 6790 3309 Fax: 6896 9152
Lim, Heng Fook (Levan), BA Guelph, MEd
N.Texas, PhD Lehigh Assoc. Prof.
Wright, Susan K., BEd Alta., MEd Alta., PhD
Newcastle(UK) Assoc. Prof.; Head*
Other Staff: 9 Asst. Profs.; 2 Lectrs.; 2
Teaching Fellows
Research: early childhood education; education
of mainstream students with diverse
abilities; education of students with high
ability; education of students with
learning/behavioural difficulties; parental
involvement in education

English Language and Literature

Tel: 6790 3513 Fax: 6896 9149
Chandrasegaran, Antonia, BA Malaya, MA Sing.,
PhD NU Singapore Assoc. Prof.
Chew, Ghim Lian (Phyllis), BA Sing., MA
Hawaii, PhD Macq. Assoc. Prof.
Goh, Chuen Meng (C.), BA Malaya, MA Birm.,
PhD Lanc. Assoc. Prof.
Kramer-Dahl, Anneliese, BA Mainz, MA Mich.,
PhD Mich. Assoc. Prof.
Low, Ee Ling, BA NU Singapore, MPhil Camb.,
PhD Camb. Assoc. Prof.

Lubna, Alsagoff, BA NU *Singapore*, MA NU *Singapore*, PhD *Stan.*   Assoc. Prof.; Head*

Seow, Thiam Chew A., BA *Lanc.*, MA *Syd.*, PhD *Monash*   Assoc. Prof.

Wee, Wang Ling (C. J.), BA NU *Singapore*, MA NU *Singapore*, PhD *Chic.*   Assoc. Prof.

Wong Yeang Lam, R., BA *Sing.*, MEd NU *Singapore*, PhD *Tor.*   Assoc. Prof.

Other Staff: 16 Asst. Profs.; 1 Asst. Prof. Fellow; 12 Lectrs.; 2 Sr. Fellows; 7 Teaching Fellows; 1 Teaching Assoc.

Humanities and Social Studies Education

Tel: 6790 3429 Fax: 6896 9135

Ang, Cheng Guan, BA NU *Singapore*, MA *Lond.*, PhD *Lond.*   Assoc. Prof.; Head*

Blackburn, Kevin, BA *Qld.*, PhD *Qld.*   Assoc. Prof.

Bui, Elisabeth N., BA *Col.*, MS *Cornell*, PhD *Texas A.& M.*   Assoc. Prof.

Chatterjea, Kalyani, BA *Calc.*, MA *Calc.*, PhD NU *Singapore*   Assoc. Prof.

Goh, Kim Chuan, BA *Malaya*, MA *Malaya*, PhD *Leeds*   Prof.

Goh Chor Boon, BSc *Lond.*, MA *Oregon*, PhD *NSW*   Assoc. Prof.

Hack Karl, BA *Oxf.*, MA *Oxf.*, DPhil *Oxf.*   Assoc. Prof.

Lee, Christine, BA *Sing.*, MA *Col.*, MEd *Col.*, EdD *Col.*   Assoc. Prof.

Ooi Giok Ling, BA *Malaya*, MA *Malaya*, PhD *ANU*   Assoc. Prof.

Wang, Zhenping, MA *Prin.*, PhD *Prin.*   Assoc. Prof.

Wong, Shuang Yann, BA *Sci.U.Malaysia*, MA *Hiroshima*, PhD *Wat.*   Assoc. Prof.

Wong Tai Chee, BA *Paris*, MA *Paris*, PhD *ANU*   Assoc. Prof.

Other Staff: 7 Asst. Profs.; 5 Lectrs.; 1 Sr. Fellow; 7 Teaching Fellows

Research: citizenship education; co-operative learning; ethnic relations and multicultural education; Singapore history; use of technology in education and web-based learning

Information Technology in Education, Centre for

Tel: 6790 3077 Fax: 6896 9365

Wettasinghe, Cyraine M., BA NU *Singapore*, MA *George Washington*, EdD *George Washington*   Asst. Prof.; Head*

Learning Sciences and Technologies

Tel: 6790 3310 Fax: 6896 8038

Chee, Yam San, BSc *Lond.*, PhD *Qld.*   Assoc. Prof.

Chen, Der-Thang (Victor), BSc *Natnl.Taiwan*, MSc *Oregon*, PhD *Oregon*   Assoc. Prof.

Cheung, Wing Sum, BS *N.Illinois*, MS *N.Illinois*, EdD *N.Illinois*   Assoc. Prof.

Hung, Wei Loong (David), BS *Car.*, MComp *Monash*, PhD NU *Singapore*   Assoc. Prof.; Head*

Jacobson, Michael J., BA *Col.*, MA *Col.*, PhD *Ill.*   Assoc. Prof.

Looi, Chee Kit, BSc *Nan.*, MSc *Br.Col.*, PhD *Edin.*   Assoc. Prof.

Tan, Seng Chee, BSc NU *Singapore*, MEd *Nan.Tech.*, PhD *Penn.State*   Assoc. Prof.

Williams, Michael D., BS *Minn.*, MA *Minn.*, PhD *Minn.*   Assoc. Prof.

Wong, Angela, BSc *Sing.*, MEd *Hawaii*, PhD *Curtin*   Assoc. Prof.

Wong Siew Koon, P., BSc *Malaya*, MS(Ed) *Indiana*, PhD *Minn.*   Assoc. Prof.

Other Staff: 12 Asst. Profs.; 3 Lectrs.; 4 Teaching Fellows

Research: classroom environment; engaged learning; pedagogic models of IT integration; reflective thinking and practices among teachers; technology infusion to promote thinking

Mathematics and Mathematics Education

Tel: 6790 3926 Fax: 6896 9417
E-mail: chweetee.low@nie.edu.sg

Ang, Keng Cheng, BSc *Adel.*, PhD *Adel.*   Assoc. Prof.

Edge, Douglas R. M., BSc *McG.*, MEd *McG.*, PhD *Maryland*   Assoc. Prof.

Fan, Lianghua, MS *E.China Normal*, PhD *Chic.*   Assoc. Prof.

Foong, Pui Yee, BSc *Sing.*, MEdSt *Monash*, PhD *Monash*   Assoc. Prof.

Kaur, Berinderjeet, BSc *Sing.*, MEd *Nott.*, PhD *Monash*   Assoc. Prof.

Koay, Phong Lee, BSc *Malaya*, BEd *Monash*, MEd *Monash*, PhD *Qld.*   Assoc. Prof.

Lim, Keng Suan, BSc *Nan.*, MSc *Manc.*, PhD *Manc.*   Assoc. Prof.

Lim-Teo, Suat Khoh, BSc *Sing.*, MSc *Qld.*, PhD NU *Singapore*   Assoc. Prof.

Ng, Swee Fong, BSc *Malaya*, MEd *Birm.*, PhD *Birm.*   Assoc. Prof.

Phang, Lay Ping R., BSc *Manc.*, MSc *Manc.*, PhD *Manc.*   Assoc. Prof.

Teo, Beng Chong, BSc NU *Singapore*, MS *Iowa*, PhD *Iowa*   Assoc. Prof.

Wong, Khoon Yoong, BSc *Tas.*, PhD *Qld.*   Assoc. Prof.; Head*

Yap, Sook Fwe, BSc *Sing.*, MSc *Auck.*, PhD *Wis.*   Assoc. Prof.

Zhao, Dongsheng, BS *Shaanxi Normal*, MS *Shaanxi Normal*, PhD *Camb.*   Assoc. Prof.

Other Staff: 1 Assoc. Prof. Fellow; 14 Asst. Profs.; 5 Lectrs.; 5 Teaching Fellows

Research: algebra and analysis; integrated circuit technology (ICT) in mathematics education; international comparative studies in mathematics education; mathematical modelling and statistics; mathematics curriculum and instruction

Natural Sciences and Science Education

Tel: 6790 3976 Fax: 896 9414

Boo, Hong Kwen, BSc *Sing.*, MEd *Harv.*, PhD *Lond.*   Assoc. Prof.

Cheah, Horn Mun, BA *Camb.*, MA *Camb.*, MPhil *Camb.*, PhD *Camb.*   Assoc. Prof.

Chen, Lai Keat, BSc *Malaya*, MSc *Sci.U.Malaysia*, PhD NU *Singapore*   Assoc. Prof.

Chew, Shit Fun, BSc NU *Singapore*, PhD NU *Singapore*   Assoc. Prof.

Chia, Tet Fatt, BSc NU *Singapore*, MSc NU *Singapore*, PhD NU *Singapore*   Assoc. Prof.

Chin, Hui Li (Christine), BSc NU *Singapore*, MSc *Tor.*, MA *Br.Col.*, PhD *Ill.*   Assoc. Prof.

Diong, Cheong Hoong, BSc *Malaya*, MS *Hawaii*, PhD *Hawaii*   Assoc. Prof.

Foong, See Kit, BSc *Malaya*, PhD *Texas*   Assoc. Prof.

Gan, Leong Huat, BSc *Well.*, MSc *Well.*, PhD *Qu.*   Prof.

Gan, Yik Yuen (alias Yap Y. Y.), BSc *Nan.*, PhD *Aberd.*   Assoc. Prof.

Goh, Ngoh Khang, BSc *Nan.*, MSc *Mün.*, PhD *Mün.*   Assoc. Prof.

He, Jie, BS *S.China Normal Coll.*, MS *Chinese Acad.Sc.*, PhD *Macq.*   Assoc. Prof.

Joseph, Phillip R., II, BSEd *Salem State*, MEd *Penn.State*, PhD *Colorado*   Assoc. Prof.

Koh, Chong Lek, BSc *Malaya*, MSc *Malaya*, PhD *Lond.*   Assoc. Prof.

Koh, Thiam Seng, BSc NU *Singapore*, MSc *Massey*, PhD *Monash*   Assoc. Prof.

Kwek, Leong Chuan, BSc *Otago*, MSc NU *Singapore*, PhD NU *Singapore*   Assoc. Prof.

Lee, Choon Keat (Paul), BSc *Lond.*, PhD *Lond.*   Assoc. Prof.

Lee, Kam Wah L., BSc *Nan.*, MSc *E.Anglia*, PhD *Monash*   Assoc. Prof.

Lim Siew-Lee, S., BSc *Sing.*, MSc NU *Singapore*, PhD *W.Ont.*   Assoc. Prof.; Head*

Rawat, Rajdeep S., BSc *Delhi*, MSc *Delhi*, PhD *Delhi*   Assoc. Prof.

Springham, Stuart V., BSc *Strath.*, PhD *Edin.*   Assoc. Prof.

Subramaniam, Ramanathan, BSc NU *Singapore*, MSc *Salf.*, PhD *Salf.*   Assoc. Prof.

Tan, Kim Chwee (Daniel), BSc *Curtin*, MSc *Curtin*, PhD *Curtin*   Assoc. Prof.

Tan, Swee Ngin, BSEd *Ag.U.Malaysia*, PhD *Deakin*   Assoc. Prof.

Tan, Tuck Lee (Augustine), BSc NU *Singapore*, MSc NU *Singapore*, PhD NU *Singapore*   Assoc. Prof.

Tan, Wee Hin Leo, BBM *Sing.*, BSc *Sing.*, PhD *Sing.*, Hon. DSc   Prof.

Teng, Piang-Siong (Paul), BAgrSc *Cant.*, PhD *Cant.*   Prof.

Teo, Khay Chuan, BSc *Nan.*, PhD *W.Ont.*   Assoc. Prof.

Tham, Foong Yee, BSc NU *Singapore*, MSc NU *Singapore*, PhD *Nott.*   Assoc. Prof.

Toh, Kok Aun, BSc *Malaya*, MA *Stan.*, DPhil *Oxf.*   Assoc. Prof.

Xu, Shuyan, BSc *Nanjing*, PhD *Flin.*   Prof.

Yan, Yaw Kai, BSc NU *Singapore*, MSc NU *Singapore*, PhD *Lond.*   Assoc. Prof.

Yap, Kueh Chin, BSc *Malaya*, MSc *Sur.*, PhD *Georgia*   Assoc. Prof.

Other Staff: 3 Assoc. Prof. Fellows; 15 Asst. Profs.; 2 Asst. Prof. Fellows; 5 Lectrs.; 1 Sr. Fellow; 7 Teaching Fellows; 1 Adjunct Prof.

Research: agrosociotechnology; creativity in science education; environmental biology, ecology and physiology; molecular genomic technology and bio-informatics; plasma physics and processing

Physical Education and Sports Science

Tel: 6790 3682 Fax: 6896 9260

Chia, Yong Hwa (Michael), BSc *Lough.*, PhD *Exe.*   Assoc. Prof.; Head*

Fry, Joan M., BAppSc *Preston I.T.*, MSc *Melb.*, PhD *Georgia*   Assoc. Prof.

McNeill, Michael C., MSc *Lough.*, PhD *Lough.*   Assoc. Prof.

Nicholas, Giles A., BEd *Lough.*, MSc *Lough.*, PhD *Nan.Tech.*   Assoc. Prof.

Quek, Jin Jong, BS *Oregon*, MS *Oregon*, PhD *Qld.*   Assoc. Prof.

Tan, Kwang San (Steven), BS *Oregon*, MS *Oregon*, PhD *Georgia*   Assoc. Prof.

Teo-Koh, Sock Miang, BPE *Alta.*, MSc *Alta.*, PhD *Oregon*   Assoc. Prof.

Wang, Chee Keng (John), BSc *Lough.*, PhD *Lough.*   Assoc. Prof.

Other Staff: 14 Asst. Profs.; 1 Lectr.; 4 Teaching Fellows

Research: children with learning difficulties and the motor performance of school children; inter-generational coronary risk factors in school children and their families; military experience and the teaching of secondary physical education; physical activity and physical fitness in overweight children; teaching psychological skills to school-age athletes

Policy and Leadership Studies

Tel: 6790 3237 Fax: 6896 9151

Chew Oon Ai, J., BA *Sing.*, BSocSci *Sing.*, MSocSci *Sing.*, PhD *Monash*   Assoc. Prof.

Lee Ong Kim, BSc *Malaya*, MEd *Pitt.*, PhD *Chic.*   Assoc. Prof.; Head*

Low, Guat Tin, BEd *Adelaide C.A.E.*, BA *Flin.*, BEd *Flin.*, MEd *Flin.*, MA *Mich.*, EdD *Mich.*   Assoc. Prof.

Saravanan, Gopinathan, BA *Sing.*, MEd *Sing.*, PhD *N.Y.State*   Prof.

Tan, Eng Thye (Jason), BSc NU *Singapore*, MEd *HK*, PhD *N.Y.State*   Assoc. Prof.

Zhang, Yenming, MSc *S.Connecticut*, MEd *Harv.*, EdD *Harv.*   Assoc. Prof.

Other Staff: 2 Assoc. Prof. Fellows; 12 Asst. Profs.; 1 Lectr.; 3 Teaching Fellows; 1 Adjunct Asst. Prof.

Research: impact of globalisation on Singapore education; marketisation of education in Singapore; school-community partnerships; teacher professional development in Singapore; values education in Singapore

Psychological Studies

Tel: 6790 3199 Fax: 6896 9410

Chang Shook Cheong, A., BSc *Sing.*, MEd *Sing.*, PhD *Macq.*   Assoc. Prof.

D'Rozario, Vilma, BA *Sing.*, MS(Ed) *Indiana*, PhD *Minn.*   Assoc. Prof.

Khoo, Angeline, BA *Sing.*, MEd NU *Singapore*, PhD *ANU*   Assoc. Prof.

Lui Hah Wah, E., BSocSci Chinese HK, MA Mich.State, EdS Mich.State, PhD Mich.State Assoc. Prof.

Neihart, Maureen F., BA Car., MA N.Colorado, PhD N.Colorado Assoc. Prof.

Seng, Seok Hoon, BA Sing., MEd Colorado State, PhD Hawaii Assoc. Prof.

Tan, Ai Girl, BSc(Ed) Ag.U.Malaysia, MEng Tokyo I.T., PhD Munich Assoc. Prof.

Tan, Oon Seng, BSc NU Singapore, MEd NU Singapore, PhD Nan.Tech. Assoc. Prof.; Head*

Tay-Koay, Siew Luan, BA Malaya, MA Col., MEd Col., MEd Philippines, PhD Oregon Assoc. Prof.

Other Staff: 17 Asst. Profs.; 4 Lectrs.; 2 Teaching Fellows; 1 Adjunct Assoc. Prof.

Research: assessment and educational measurement; cognitive and education psychology; issues in counselling; metacognition, problem-based learning and cognitive coaching; psychosocial development and behavioural problems

Visual and Performing Arts

Tel: 6790 3554 Fax: 6896 9143

Chia, Wei Khuan, BA Nan., BMus Ohio, MMus Cinc., DMA Cinc. Assoc. Prof.; Head*

Chong, Nguik Yin (Sylvia), BMus S.Illinois, MMus Ill., EdD Ill. Assoc. Prof.

Matthews, John S., MPhil Lond., PhD Lond. Prof.

Tang, Yap Ming (Kelly), BA York(Can.), MMus Northwestern, PhD Mich.State Assoc. Prof.

Other Staff: 7 Asst. Profs.; 9 Lectrs.; 3 Adjunct Assoc. Profs.

Research: art in early childhood; composition of orchestral, choral and chamber music; development of visual representation; psychology of creative musical processes; visual literacy

Electrical and Electronic Engineering

Tel: 6790 5402 Fax: 6791 2687
E-mail: d-eee@ntu.edu.sg

Heng, Michael S. H., BA Sing., BSocSc Sing., MSc Lond. Assoc. Prof.

Kam, Chan Hin, BEng Sing., MSc Nan., MSEE S.Calif., PhD NU Singapore Prof.; Chair*

Lim, Jessica J. P., BA Sing., LLB Lond., LLM Lond., MBT NSW Assoc. Prof.

Other Staff: 1 Assoc. Prof. Fellow; 1 Asst. Prof.; 2 Adjunct Profs.; 2 Adjunct Assoc. Profs.

Circuits and Systems

Tel: 6790 5630 Fax: 6792 0415
E-mail: h-eee2@ntu.edu.sg

Chan, Pak Kwong, BSc Essex, MSc Manc., PhD Plym. Assoc. Prof.

Chang, Chip Hong, BEng NU Singapore, MEng Nan.Tech., PhD Nan.Tech. Assoc. Prof.

Chang, Joseph S., BEng Monash, PhD Melb. Assoc. Prof.

Do, Manh Anh, BSc Saigon, BE Cant., PhD Cant. Prof.

Goh, Wang Ling, BEng Belf., PhD Belf. Assoc. Prof.

Gwee, Bah Hwee, BEng Aberd., MEng Nan.Tech., PhD Nan.Tech. Assoc. Prof.

Ho, Duan Huat, BEng Sing., MSEE N.Y.State Assoc. Prof.

Jong, Ching Chuen, BSc(Eng) Lond., PhD Lond. Assoc. Prof.

Koh, Liang Mong, BSc Salf., PhD UMIST Assoc. Prof.

Lam, Yvonne Y. H., BSc Aston, MSc S'ton., PhD S'ton. Assoc. Prof.

Lau, Kim Teen, BSEE Cornell, MEng Cornell Assoc. Prof.

Lim, Meng Hiot, BS S.Carolina, MS S.Carolina, PhD S.Carolina Assoc. Prof.

Ng, Lian Soon, BEng NU Singapore, MSc S'ton. Assoc. Prof.

Ong, K. S. (Vincent), BEng NU Singapore, MEng NU Singapore, PhD NU Singapore Assoc. Prof.

See, K. Y., BEng NU Singapore, PhD Lond. Assoc. Prof.

Siek, L. (alias Hsueh L.), BASc Ott., MEngSc NSW Assoc. Prof.

Tan, Cher Ming, BEng NU Singapore, MASc Tor., PhD Tor. Assoc. Prof.

Yeo, Kiat Seng, BEng Nan.Tech., PhD Nan.Tech. Assoc. Prof.; Head*

Zhang, Yue Ping, BE Taiyuan U.T., ME Taiyuan U.T., PhD Chinese HK, FCIC Assoc. Prof.

Other Staff: 4 Assoc. Prof. Fellows; 4 Asst. Profs.; 3 Res. Fellows; 1 Teaching Fellow; 1 Adjunct Assoc. Prof.

Research: low-power integrated circuit (IC) design; mixed-signal integrated circuit (IC) design; radio frequency (RF) IC and systems design; very large scale integration (VLSI) and embedded systems

Communication Engineering

Tel: 6790 4534 Fax: 6793 3318
E-mail: h-eee5@ntu.edu.sg

Aditya, Sheel, BTech IIT Delhi, PhD IIT Delhi, FIETE Assoc. Prof.

Alphones, A., BSc Madr., BTech Anna, MTech Kharagpur, PhD Kyoto Assoc. Prof.

Bose, Sanjay K., BTech IIT Kanpur, MS N.Y.State, PhD N.Y.State, FIETE Assoc. Prof.

Cheng, Tee Hiang, BEng Strath., PhD Strath. Assoc. Prof.; Head*

Dubey, Vimal K., BSc Raj., BE IISc., ME IISc., PhD McM. Assoc. Prof.

Guan, Yong Liang, BEng NU Singapore, PhD Lond. Assoc. Prof.

Gunawan, Erry, BSc Leeds, MBA Brad., PhD Brad. Assoc. Prof.

Koh, Soo Ngee, BEng Sing., BSc Lond., MSc Lough., PhD Lough., FIE(Sing) Prof.

Law, Choi Look, BSc(Eng) Lond., PhD Lond. Assoc. Prof.

Lee, C. K., BSc Kent, PhD Kent Assoc. Prof.

Li, Kwok Hung, BSc Chinese HK, MS Calif., PhD Calif. Assoc. Prof.

Lu, Yilong, BE Harbin, ME Tsinghua, PhD Lond. Assoc. Prof.

Ng, Chee Hock, BEng NU Singapore, MS(CompEng) S.Calif. Assoc. Prof.

Ser, Wee, BSc Lough., PhD Lough. Assoc. Prof.

Shen, Zhongxiang, BE China U.S.T., MS Southeast(Nanjing), PhD Wat. Assoc. Prof.

Shum, Ping, BEng Birm., PhD Birm. Assoc. Prof.

Soong, Boon Hee, BE Auck., PhD Newcastle(NSW) Assoc. Prof.

Tan, Soon Hie, BE Auck., PhD Auck. Assoc. Prof.

Tan, Soon Yim, BEng Malaya, PhD Nan.Tech. Assoc. Prof.

Teh, Kah Chan, BEng Nan.Tech., PhD Nan.Tech. Assoc. Prof.

Zhong, Wende, BE Beijing Posts & Telecommunicns., ME Tokyo Electro-Communicns., PhD Tokyo Electro-Communicns. Assoc. Prof.

Zhu, Lei, BE Nanjing I.T., ME Southeast(Nanjing), PhD Tokyo Electro-Communicns. Assoc. Prof.

Other Staff: 2 Assoc. Prof. Fellows; 9 Asst. Profs.; 10 Res. Fellows; 1 Singapore Millennium Foundation Res. Fellow; 1 Adjunct Prof.; 5 Adjunct Assoc. Profs.; 7 Adjunct Asst. Profs.

Research: microwave circuits, antennas and propagation; modulation, coding and signal processing; radar systems and microwave imaging

Control and Instrumentation Engineering

Tel: 6790 4174 Fax: 6792 3318
E-mail: h-eee4@ntu.edu.sg

Adams, Martin D., BA Oxf., MA Oxf., DPhil Oxf. Assoc. Prof.

Cai, Wenjian, BS Harbin, MS Harbin, PhD Oakland Assoc. Prof.

Chan, John C. Y., BE Cant., ME Cant., PhD Cant. Assoc. Prof.

Cheah, Chien Chern, BEng NU Singapore, MEng Nan.Tech., PhD Nan.Tech. Assoc. Prof.

Chin, Teck Chai, BSc Strath., MSc(IndEng) NU Singapore, MEng Sheff., PhD S.Aust. Assoc. Prof.

Chu, Yun Chung, BSc Chinese HK, MPhil Chinese HK, PhD Camb. Assoc. Prof.

Chua, Chin Seng, BEng NU Singapore, PhD Monash Assoc. Prof.

Er, Meng Joo, BEng NU Singapore, MEng NU Singapore, PhD ANU Assoc. Prof.

Koh, Tong San, BSc NU Singapore, PhD NU Singapore Assoc. Prof.

Lee, Peng Hin, BEng NU Singapore, MSEE S.Calif., MSc(IndEng) NU Singapore, PhD Tokyo Assoc. Prof.

Ling, Keck Voon, BEng NU Singapore, DPhil Oxf. Assoc. Prof.

Low, Kay Soon, BEng NU Singapore, PhD NSW Assoc. Prof.

Mao, Kezhi, BEng Shandong, MEng Northeastern, PhD Sheff. Assoc. Prof.

Saratchandran, Paramasivan, BSc(Eng) Kerala, MTech Kharagpur, MSc City(UK), DPhil Oxf. Assoc. Prof.

Sim, Siong Leng, MSc Lond., PhD Nan.Tech. Assoc. Prof.

Soh, Cheong Boon, BE Monash, PhD Monash Assoc. Prof.

Soh, Yeng Chai (William), BE Cant., PhD Newcastle(NSW) Prof.

Song, Qing, BS Harbin Shipbldg.Engin., MS Dalian Maritime, PhD Strath. Assoc. Prof.

Suganthan, Ponnuthurai N., BA Camb., MA Camb., PhD Nan.Tech. Assoc. Prof.

Sundararajan, Narasimhan, BE Madr., MTech IIT Madras, PhD Ill., FIEEE, FIE(Sing) Prof.

Sung, Eric, BEng Sing., MSEE Wis., PhD Nan.Tech. Assoc. Prof.

Teoh, Eam Khwang, BE Auck., ME Auck., PhD Newcastle(NSW) Assoc. Prof.

Wang, Dan Wei, BE S.China Tech., MSE Mich., PhD Mich. Assoc. Prof.; Head*

Wang, Han, BE N.E.Heavy Machinery Inst., Qiqihaer, PhD Leeds Assoc. Prof.

Wang, Jianliang, BE Beijing I.T., MS Johns H., PhD Johns H. Assoc. Prof.

Wen, Changyun, BE Xi'an Jiaotong, PhD Newcastle(NSW) Assoc. Prof.

Wijesoma, Wijerupage S., BSc(Eng) Moratuwa, PhD Camb. Assoc. Prof.

Wong, Patricia J. Y., BSc NU Singapore, MSc(FinEng) NU Singapore, PhD NU Singapore Assoc. Prof.

Xie, Lihua, BE E.China Inst.Eng., ME E.China Inst.Technol., PhD Newcastle(NSW), FIEEE, FIE(Sing) Prof.

Zhang, Cishen, BE Tsinghua, PhD Newcastle(NSW) Assoc. Prof.

Zhu, Kuanyi, BS N.E.Tech.(Shenyang), ME Louvain, PhD Louvain Assoc. Prof.

Other Staff: 1 Asst. Prof.; 5 Res. Fellows; 3 Adjunct Assoc. Profs.; 2 Adjunct Asst. Profs.

Research: biomedical engineering; computer vision and machine intelligence; control theory and applications; intelligent instrumentation systems; robotics and automation

Information Communication Institute of Singapore

Tel: 6790 6368 Fax: 6792 2971
E-mail: d-icis@ntu.edu.sg

Ang, Yew Hock, BSc Strath., PhD Strath. Assoc. Prof.

Feng, Gang, BE China U.Electronic S.T., ME China U.Electronic S.T., PhD Chinese HK Assoc. Prof.

Lin, Qingping, BE Shanghai Maritime, ME Shanghai Maritime, PhD Strath. Assoc. Prof.

Low, Chor Ping, BSc NU Singapore, MSc NU Singapore, PhD NU Singapore Assoc. Prof.; Head*

Siew, C. K., BEng Sing., MSc Lond., PhD Nan.Tech. Assoc. Prof.

Tan, Hee Beng Kuan, BSc Nan., MSc NU Singapore, PhD NU Singapore Assoc. Prof.

Other Staff: 1 Professorial Fellow; 1 Assoc. Prof. Fellow; 4 Asst. Profs.; 1 Res. Fellow; 2 Teaching Fellows; 2 Adjunct Assoc. Profs.

Research: networking; soft computing; software engineering

Information Engineering

Tel: 6790 5872 Fax: 6793 3318
E-mail: h-eee3@ntu.edu.sg

Abeysekera, Saman S., BS Peradeniya, MEE Philips'(Eindhoven), PhD Qld.   Assoc. Prof.

Bi, Guoan, BS Dalian I.T., MSc Essex, PhD Essex   Assoc. Prof.

Chan, Chee Keong, BEng NU Singapore, MSc Lond., PhD Nan.Tech.   Assoc. Prof.

Chan, Choong Wah, BSc CNAA, MSc Manc., PhD UMIST   Assoc. Prof.

Chan, Kap Luk, BEng Lond., PhD Lond.   Assoc. Prof.

Chau, Lap Pui, BEng Oxf.Brookes, PhD HKPU   Assoc. Prof.

Chen, Lihui, BE Zhejiang, PhD St And.   Assoc. Prof.

Chiam, Tee Chye, BSc Monash, PhD Monash   Assoc. Prof.

Chong, Y. K., BEng NU Singapore, MScEng S.Calif.   Assoc. Prof.

Chua, Hock Chuan, BEng NU Singapore, MSc Purdue   Assoc. Prof.

Er, Meng Hwa, BEng NU Singapore, PhD Newcastle(NSW), FIE(Sing)   Prof.

Falkowski, Bogdan J., MgrInz T.U.Warsaw, PhD Portland State   Assoc. Prof.

Foo, Say Wei, BEng Newcastle(NSW), MSc Sing., PhD Lond., FIEE, FIE(Sing)   Assoc. Prof.

Gan, Woon Seng, BEng Strath., PhD Strath.   Assoc. Prof.

Kot, Alex C., BSEE Roch., MBA Roch., MS Rhode I., PhD Rhode I., FIEEE   Prof.

Lew, Henry, BEng Melb., BSc Melb., PhD Melb.   Assoc. Prof.

Lim, Yong Ching, BSc Lond., PhD Lond., FIEEE, FIE(Sing)   Prof.

Lin, Zhiping, BE S.China Tech., PhD Camb.   Assoc. Prof.

Ma, Kai Kuang, BE Chung Yuan, MSEE Duke, PhD N.Carolina State   Prof.

Makur, Anamitra, BTech Kharagpur, MS Cal.Tech., PhD Cal.Tech.   Assoc. Prof.

Ng, Boon Poh, BEng NU Singapore, MSc Lond., PhD Nan.Tech.   Assoc. Prof.

Rahardja, Susanto, BEng NU Singapore, MEng Nan.Tech., PhD Nan.Tech.   Assoc. Prof.

Siyal, Mohammed Yakoob, BE Mehran, MSc Manc., MBA Sur., PhD UMIST   Assoc. Prof.

Soon, Ing Yann, BEng NU Singapore, MSc(ElectEng) NU Singapore, PhD Nan.Tech.   Assoc. Prof.

Tan, Boon Tiong, BEng NU Singapore, MSEE Wis.   Assoc. Prof.

Tan, Yap Peng, BS Natnl.Taiwan, MA Prin., PhD Prin.   Assoc. Prof.; Head*

Toh, Guan Nge, BEng NU Singapore, MSc Manc.   Assoc. Prof.

Wang, Lipo, BSc Natnl.U.Defence Technol., PhD Louisiana State   Assoc. Prof.

Xue, Ping, BS Harbin, MA Prin., MSE Prin., PhD Prin.   Assoc. Prof.

Zhu, Ce, BSc Sichuan, MS Southeast(Nanjing), PhD Southeast(Nanjing)   Assoc. Prof.

Other Staff: 1 Assoc. Prof. Fellow; 7 Asst. Profs.; 4 Res. Fellows; 1 Teaching Fellow; 3 Adjunct Assoc. Profs.; 1 Adjunct Asst. Prof.

Research: information security; multimedia signal processing; signal processing for communication; soft computing

Integrated Circuits and Systems, Centre for

Tel: 6790 5439 Fax: 6792 0415
E-mail: emado@ntu.edu.sg

Do, Manh Anh, BSc Saigon, BE Cant., PhD Cant.   Prof.; Dir.*

Other Staff: 1 Prof.; 12 Assoc. Profs.; 4 Asst. Profs.; 2 Adjunct Assoc. Profs.

Research: mixed-signal integrated circuits (IC) and applications; radio frequency (RF) integrated circuits (IC) and systems; very large scale integration (VLSI) and embedded systems

Intelligent Machines, Centre for

Tel: 6790 4524 Fax: 6793 3318
E-mail: elhxie@ntu.edu.sg

Xie, Lihua, BE E.China Inst.Eng., ME E.China Inst.Technol., PhD Newcastle(NSW), FIEEE, FIE(Sing)   Prof.; Dir.*

Research: control systems technologies; machine learning; mobile robotics; real-time and embedded information systems; surveillance technology

Microelectronics

Tel: 6790 6371 Fax: 6793 3318
E-mail: h-eee6@ntu.edu.sg

Au, Yeung Tin Cheung, BSc HK, MPhil HK, PhD HK   Assoc. Prof.

Chan, Y. C., BEng Tokyo, MEng Tokyo, PhD Tokyo   Assoc. Prof.

Chen, Tupei, BS Zhongshan, MS Zhongshan, PhD HK   Assoc. Prof.

Chin, Mee Koy, BS M.I.T., BS(Phys) M.I.T., MS(Phys) Calif., PhD Calif.   Assoc. Prof.

Fan, Weijun, BE Natnl.U.Defence Technol., MS Chinese Acad.Sc., PhD NU Singapore   Assoc. Prof.

Hu, Jun Hui, BE Zhejiang, ME Zhejiang, PhD Tokyo I.T.   Assoc. Prof.

Lau, S. P. (Daniel), BSc Lond., PhD Wales(Swansea)   Assoc. Prof.

Lau, W. S., BSc HK, MPhil Chinese HK, PhD Penn.State   Assoc. Prof.

Liu, Ai-Qun, BE Xi'an Jiaotong, MS Beijing, PhD NU Singapore   Assoc. Prof.

Mei Ting, BE Zhejiang, ME Zhejiang, PhD NU Singapore   Assoc. Prof.

Ng, Geok Ing, BSE Mich., MSE Mich., PhD Mich.   Assoc. Prof.

Ngo, Q. N. (John), BE Monash, PhD Monash   Assoc. Prof.

Pey, Kin Leong, BEng NU Singapore, PhD NU Singapore   Assoc. Prof.; Head*

Pita, Kantisara, BSc Lond., MSc Lond., PhD Lond.   Assoc. Prof.

Radhakrishnan, K., BSc Madr., MSc Madr., MTech IIT Kanpur, PhD NU Singapore   Assoc. Prof.

Rusli, BEng NU Singapore, MEng NU Singapore, PhD Camb.   Assoc. Prof.

Sun, Changqing, BS Wuhan, MSc Tianjin, PhD Murd., FIP, FRSCan   Assoc. Prof.

Sun, Xiaowei, BE Tianjin, ME Tianjin, PhD HKUST, PhD Tianjin   Assoc. Prof.

Tan, Ooi Kiang, BEng NU Singapore, MSc Edin., PhD Nan.Tech.   Assoc. Prof.

Tang, Dingyuan, BS Wuhan, MS Chinese Acad.Sc., PhD Hanover   Assoc. Prof.

Tay, Beng Kang, BEng NU Singapore, MSc(ElectEng) NU Singapore, PhD Nan.Tech.   Assoc. Prof.

Tjin, Swee Chuan, BSc NE, PhD Tas.   Assoc. Prof.

Tse, Man Siu, BSc HK, MPhil Chinese HK   Assoc. Prof.

Wong, Terence K. S., BA Camb., PhD Camb.   Assoc. Prof.

Yoon, Soon Fatt, BEng Wales, PhD Wales   Prof.

Yu, Siu Fung, BEng Lond., PhD Camb.   Assoc. Prof.

Yuan, Xiaocong, BE Tianjin, ME Tianjin, PhD Lond.   Assoc. Prof.

Zhang, Dao Hua, BS Shandong, MS Shandong, PhD NSW   Assoc. Prof.

Zhang, Qing, BS Lanzhou, MS Chinese Acad.Sc., PhD Kanazawa   Assoc. Prof.

Zhou, Xing, BE Tsinghua, MS Roch., PhD Roch.   Assoc. Prof.

Zhu, Weiguang, BS Shanghai Jiaotong, MS Shanghai Jiaotong, PhD Purdue, FIE(Sing)   Prof.

Other Staff: 2 Assoc. Prof. Fellows; 7 Asst. Profs.; 1 Sr. Res. Fellow; 39 Res. Fellows; 1 Adjunct Prof.; 2 Adjunct Assoc. Profs.; 5 Adjunct Asst. Profs.

Research: compound semiconductor materials and devices; micro-electro-mechanical systems (MEMS) and integrated microsystems technology; nanoelectronics and devices; sensors, actuators and smart materials; silicon technology

Microelectronics Centre

Tel: 6790 6371 Fax: 6792 0415
E-mail: eklpey@ntu.edu.sg

Pey, Kin Leong, BEng NU Singapore, PhD NU Singapore   Assoc. Prof.; Dir.*

Research: compound semiconductor materials and devices; micro-electro-mechanical systems (MEMS) and integrated microsystems technology; nanoelectronics and devices; sensors, actuators and smart materials; silicon technology

Modelling and Control of Complex Systems, Centre for

Tel: 6790 5423 Fax: 6792 0415
E-mail: eycsoh@ntu.edu.sg

Soh, Yeng Chai (William), BE Cant., PhD Newcastle(NSW)   Prof.; Dir.*

Research: computational electromagnetics; computational nano-electronics; modelling and control of networks; modelling of biological systems; modelling, optimisation and control techniques

Photonics Research Centre

Tel: 6790 4845 Fax: 6791 0415
E-mail: esctjin@ntu.edu.sg

Tjin, Swee Chuan, BSc NE, PhD Tas.   Assoc. Prof.; Dir.*

Research: bio-photonics; fibre and laser optics; photonic materials and devices

Power Engineering

Tel: 6790 4542 Fax: 6793 3318
E-mail: h-eee1@ntu.edu.sg

Chen, Shiun, BEng Cant., PhD Cant.   Assoc. Prof.

Choi, San Shing, BE Cant., PhD Cant.   Prof.

Choo, Fook Hoong, BSc Leeds, MSc UMIST   Assoc. Prof.

Goel, Lalit K., BTech Kakatiya, MSc Sask., PhD Sask.   Assoc. Prof.; Head*

Gooi, Hoay Beng, BS Natnl.Taiwan, MScE New Br., PhD Ohio State   Assoc. Prof.

Haque, Mohammed H., BSc B'desh.Engin., MSc B'desh.Engin., PhD King Fahd, FIEAust   Assoc. Prof.

Lie, Tek Tjing, BS Oklahoma State, MS Mich.State, PhD Mich.State   Assoc. Prof.

Luo, Fang Lin, BS Sichuan, PhD Camb.   Assoc. Prof.

Maswood, Ali I., BEng Moscow Power Inst., MEng Moscow Power Inst., PhD C'dia.   Assoc. Prof.

Shrestha, Govinda B., BEE Jad., MBA Hawaii, MS Rensselaer, PhD Virginia Polytech.   Assoc. Prof.

So, Ping Lam, BEng Warw., PhD Lond.   Assoc. Prof.

Tan, Yoke Lin, BEng NU Singapore, MSc Lond., PhD Nan.Tech.   Assoc. Prof.

Tseng, King Jet, BEng NU Singapore, MEng NU Singapore, PhD Camb.   Assoc. Prof.

Vilathgamuwa, D. M., BSc Moratuwa, PhD Camb.   Assoc. Prof.

Wang, Peng, BS Xi'an Jiaotong, MS Taiyuan U.T., MSc Sask., PhD Sask.   Assoc. Prof.

Wang, Youyi, BE Beijing U.S.T., ME Tsinghua, PhD Newcastle(NSW)   Assoc. Prof.

Other Staff: 2 Assoc. Prof. Fellows; 3 Asst. Profs.; 1 Res. Fellow; 2 Res. Engineers

Research: electrical energy conversion systems; flexible transmission-distribution systems; power market; power quality analysis and enhancement; protection and condition monitoring

Signal Processing, Centre for

Tel: 6790 5951 Fax: 6791 2383
E-mail: d-csp@ntu.edu.sg

Ser, Wee, BSc Lough., PhD Lough.   Assoc. Prof.; Dir.*

Other Staff: 6 Res. Fellows; 11 Researchers

Research: adaptive and statistical signal processing; bio-signal processing; digital signal processing system development; multimedia signal processing

Humanities and Social Sciences, School of

Tel: 6790 6983 Fax: 6794 2830
E-mail: d-hss@ntu.edu.sg
Wong, W. C. (Lawrence), BA HK, MPhil HK, PhD Lond. Prof.; Chair*
Other Staff: 2 Asst. Profs.; 1 Res. Fellow
Research: Chinese; economics; English; psychology; sociology

Chinese

Tel: 6790 6715 Fax: 6792 2334
E-mail: h-dch@ntu.edu.sg
Crossland-Guo, Shuyun, BA Iowa, MA Iowa, PhD Hawaii Assoc. Prof.
Lee, Guan Kin, BA Nan., MA Nan., PhD HK Assoc. Prof.; Head*
Quah, Sy Ren, BA Natnl.Taiwan, MA NU Singapore, MPhil Camb., PhD Camb. Assoc. Prof.; Deputy Head
Yuan, Xing Pei, BA Peking Prof.
Other Staff: 2 Profs.; 4 Assoc. Profs.; 6 Asst. Profs.; 4 Teaching Fellows; 1 Adjunct Assoc. Prof.; 1 Adjunct Asst. Prof.
Research: linguistics and Chinese linguistics; literature, history and thought (pre-modern China); modern Chinese literature, history and culture; studies of ethnic Chinese; translation studies

Economics

Tel: 6790 6073 Fax: 6794 6303
E-mail: h-dae@ntu.edu.sg
Alba, Joseph D., BS Philippines, MA Wichita, MBA Philippines, PhD Houston Assoc. Prof.
Chen, Kang, BS Xiamen, MS Ohio, PhD Maryland Assoc. Prof.
Chew, S. L. (Rosalind), BSocSci Sing., MA W.Ont., PhD NU Singapore Assoc. Prof.
Chew, Soon Beng, BCom Nan., MSocSci Sing., PhD W.Ont. Prof.
Hsiao, Cheng, BA Natnl.Taiwan, BPhil Oxf., MSc Stan., PhD Stan. Nanyang Prof.
Huang, Weihong, BE Shandong Mining, MSc Tianjin, MA S.Calif., PhD S.Calif. Assoc. Prof.
Leu, Mike G.-J., BS Natnl.Taiwan, MA Calif., MS Nebraska, PhD Calif. Assoc. Prof.
Lim, Chong Yah, BBM, PJG, BA Malaya, MA Malaya, DPhil Oxf. Prof.
Liu Yunhua, BS New Eng.IT, MA Ohio State, MS New Eng.IT, PhD Ohio State Assoc. Prof.; Head*
Low, Chan Kee, BEc Monash, PhD Monash Assoc. Prof.
Ng, Beoy Kui, BEc Malaya, MSc Lond. Assoc. Prof.
Park, Donghyun, BA Virginia, MA Calif., PhD Calif. Assoc. Prof.
Quah, T. E. (Euston), BA S.Fraser, MA Vic.(BC), PhD NU Singapore Assoc. Prof.; Head*
Rahman, Shahidur, BSc Dhaka, MEc NE, MSc Dhaka, PhD Monash Assoc. Prof.
Reisman, David A., BSc(Econ) Lond., MSc Lond., DSc(Econ) Lond., PhD Sur. Prof.
Sakellariou, Christos, BA Athens Sch.Econ., MA Windsor, PhD Ott. Assoc. Prof.
Soon, Lee Ying, BA Malaya, MEc Malaya, MA Penn., PhD Penn. Assoc. Prof.
Tan, Khye Chong, BSc Cant., MSocSc Sci.U.Malaysia, PhD Lond. Assoc. Prof.
Tan, Kim Heng, BE Adel., MCom NSW, PhD Syd. Assoc. Prof.
Tan, Kong Yam, BA Prin., PhD Stan. Prof.
Yao, Shuntian, BS Zhongshan, MA Calif., MS Zhongshan, PhD Calif. Assoc. Prof.
Yip, S. L. (Paul), BSocSc HK, MSc Lond., PhD Lond. Assoc. Prof.
Other Staff: 4 Profs.; 16 Assoc. Profs.; 8 Asst. Profs.; 2 Lectrs.; 2 Sr. Fellows; 1 Adjunct Prof.
Research: applied econometrics; economics of social policy; economies of East Asia (especially China); environmental economics and management; international trade and finance

English

Tel: 6790 4631 Fax: 6794 6303
E-mail: h-deng@ntu.edu.sg
Koh, Tai Ann, BA Sing., PhD Sing. Prof., English
Murphy, Cornelius A., BA N.U.I., MA N.U.I., PhD N.U.I. Assoc. Prof.; Acting Head*
Other Staff: 2 Assoc. Profs.; 9 Asst. Profs.; 1 Prof.†
Research: Asian-American and Southeast Asian literature and culture; British literature; contemporary literature and film studies; cultural studies/gender studies; Irish literature

Psychology

Tel: 6790 6705 Fax: 6794 6303
E-mail: h-dpsy@ntu.edu.sg
Ang, P. H. (Rebecca), BA NU Singapore, BSocSc NU Singapore, MComm Nan.Tech., PhD Texas A.& M. Assoc. Prof.
Chang, Weining C., LLB Natnl.Taiwan, MA Houston, PhD Houston Assoc. Prof.; Head*
Chay, Yue Wah, BSc Wales, DPhil Oxf. Assoc. Prof.
Other Staff: 2 Assoc. Profs.; 8 Asst. Profs.; 1 Lectr.; 1 Teaching Fellow; 2 Adjunct Assoc. Profs.; 1 Adjunct Asst. Prof.
Research: brain mapping, cognition and language; child and adolescent psychology and psychopathology; cultural and social psychology; industrial-organisation psychology (personnel selection, work satisfaction, turnover, psychometrics); psychology in the Asian context (personality resilience, achievement motivation)

Sociology

Tel: 6316 8730 Fax: 6794 6303
E-mail: h-dsoc@ntu.edu.sg
Benjamin, Geoffrey, MA Camb., PhD Camb. Assoc. Prof.
Cheung, Paul, BA Sing., MA Hawaii, PhD Mich. Assoc. Prof.
Kwok, K. W. (Anthony), BA NU Singapore, MA Calif., PhD Calif. Assoc. Prof.; Head*
Other Staff: 3 Assoc. Profs.; 6 Asst. Profs.; 1 Prof.†
Research: economic sociology (development social change, post-socialist); political sociology (state, civil society, social movements, nationalism); social institutions and organisational change (East Asian and Southeast Asian societies); social policy and planning (health, education and cultural policies); sociology of culture (family, gender, ethnicity, religion, transnationalism)

Materials Science and Engineering

Tel: 6790 5609 Fax: 6792 0921
E-mail: d-mse@ntu.edu.sg
Boey, Yin Chiang (Freddy), BE Monash, PhD NU Singapore, FIMMM, FIE(Sing) Prof.; Chair*
Other Staff: 4 Teaching Fellows

Energetic Materials Research Centre

Tel: 6790 4066 Fax: 6792 7173
E-mail: hgang@ntu.edu.sg
Ang, How Ghee, BSc Malaya, MA Camb., PhD Camb., PhD Monash, DSc NU Singapore, FRSChem, FRACI, FTWAS Res. Prof.; Dir.*
Other Staff: 4 Res. Fellows

Materials Science

Tel: 6790 4586 Fax: 6790 9081
E-mail: h-dms@ntu.edu.sg
Chen, Zhong, BE China Inst.Mining Technol., ME Hefei Technol., PhD Reading Assoc. Prof.
Kloc, Christian, MEng Gliwice, PhD Polish Acad.Sc. Prof.
Klooster, Wim T., MSc T.H.Twente, PhD T.H.Twente Assoc. Prof.
Liang, Meng Heng, BEng Liv., PhD Liv., FIMMM Assoc. Prof.

Oh, Joo Tien, BSc(Eng) Lond., MEng NU Singapore, MMet Sheff., PhD Nan.Tech. Assoc. Prof.
Ramanujan, Raju V., BTech IIT Bombay, ME Carnegie-Mellon, PhD Carnegie-Mellon Assoc. Prof.
Seow, Hong Pheow, BEng Qld., MEngSc Qld. Assoc. Prof.
Sritharan, Thirumany, BScEngin Peradeniya, PhD Sheff. Assoc. Prof.; Head*
White, Timothy J., BSc NE, PhD ANU Assoc. Prof.
Other Staff: 6 Asst. Profs.; 4 Res. Fellows; 4 Teaching Fellows; 2 Adjunct Assoc. Profs.; 2 Adjunct Asst. Profs.
Research: advanced characterisation of materials; computational materials science; ecomaterials, catalysis and photocatalysis; interfaces and barrier layers; nanomaterials and multifunctional materials

Materials Technology

Tel: 6790 4626 Fax: 6790 9081
E-mail: h-dmt@ntu.edu.sg
Hu, Xiao, BE Tsinghua, MSc Manc., PhD Manc. Assoc. Prof.
Lu, Xuehong, BE Tsinghua, ME Tsinghua, PhD Camb. Assoc. Prof.
Ma, Jan, BEng NU Singapore, MEng NU Singapore, PhD Camb. Assoc. Prof.
Mhaisalkar, Subodh G., BTech IIT Bombay, MS Ohio State, PhD Ohio State Assoc. Prof.; Head*
Venkatraman, Subbu S., BSc B'lore., MSc IIT Madras, PhD Carnegie-Mellon Assoc. Prof.
Wong, Chee Cheong, BS M.I.T., PhD M.I.T. Assoc. Prof.
Other Staff: 1 Nanyang Prof.; 6 Assoc. Profs.; 9 Asst. Profs.; 1 Visiting Sr. Res. Fellow; 16 Res. Fellows; 4 Adjunct Assoc. Profs.; 2 Adjunct Asst. Profs.
Research: biomaterials; defence materials; nanoelectronics and interconnects; organic/polymer electronics; rare earth nanomaterials

Mechanical and Aerospace Engineering

Tel: 6790 5486 Fax: 6791 1859
E-mail: d-mae@ntu.edu.sg
Hoon, Kay Hiang, BSc Strath., PhD Strath. Assoc. Prof.
Lam, Khin Yong, BSc Lond., SM M.I.T., PhD M.I.T. Prof.; Chair*
Leong, Kai Choong, BEng NU Singapore, MSME Calif., PhD Qld. Assoc. Prof.
Lim, Lennie E. N., BSc Sur., PhD Sur., FIE(Sing) Prof.
Lye, Sun Woh, BSc Bath, PhD Bath Prof.
Research: advanced electronics and manufacturing processes; biomedical and biomaterials engineering; engineering design and modelling; intelligent systems, logistics and engineering management; nanotechnology and microsystems

Advanced Design and Modelling Laboratory

Tel: 6790 4004 Fax: 6792 4062
E-mail: mgeorg@ntu.edu.sg
Thimm, Georg L., PhD Inst.Technol., Lausanne Asst. Prof.; Dir.*
Other Staff: 1 Deputy Dir.
Research: computer-aided design (CAD), computer-aided manufacturing (CAM) and computer-assisted education (CAE); product life-cycle management; product realisation; rapid prototyping; virtual reality/visualisation

Aerospace Engineering, Division of

Tel: 6790 4040 Fax: 6791 3502
E-mail: h-dase@ntu.edu.sg
Lin, Rongming, BS Zhejiang, PhD Lond. Assoc. Prof.
Liu, Yong, BS Beijing Aeron.& Astron., DrTechn T.U.Helsinki, PhD T.U.Helsinki Assoc. Prof.
Low, Eicher, BS Wash., MS Minn., PhD Minn. Assoc. Prof.

Ng, Teng Yong, BEng NU Singapore, MEng NU Singapore, PhD NU Singapore   Assoc. Prof.

Shang, Huai Min, BEng Sing., MSc Aston, PhD Aston, FIE(Sing)   Prof.; Acting Head*

Wong, Brian S., BSc Manc., MSc Manc., PhD UMIST   Assoc. Prof.

Other Staff: 5 Asst. Profs.; 1 Assoc. Prof. Fellow

Research: aerodynamics, aerovehicle design, computational fluid dynamics, turbulent reacting flows; aerospace design and analysis, computational mechanics, multi-scale modelling, novel and emerging engineered materials, condition monitoring, ultra light cellular materials; aircraft/spacecraft dynamics and control, flight modelling/simulation, unmanned aerial vehicles, human-machine interactions; composites manufacturing and process modelling, gelation mechanisms for hydrogels, fibre reinforced composites, thermal controls for micro-satellites; fluid power, machine design, fault diagnosis, manufacturing automation

Engineering Mechanics

Tel: 6790 5521 Fax: 6795 4630
E-mail: h-dem@ntu.edu.sg

Ang, Hock Eng, BSc Wales, MSc Lond.   Assoc. Prof.

Ang, Whye Teong, BSc Adel., PhD Adel.   Assoc. Prof.

Asundi, Anand K., BTech IIT Bombay, MTech IIT Bombay, PhD N.Y.State, FIE(Sing)   Prof.

Chai, Gin Boay, BSc Strath., PhD Strath.   Assoc. Prof.

Chollet, Franck A., BSc Franche-Comté-Besançon   Assoc. Prof.

Chou, Siaw Meng, BEng Strath., PhD Strath.   Assoc. Prof.

Du, Hejun, BE Nanjing Aeron.Inst., ME Nanjing Aeron.Inst., PhD Lond.   Assoc. Prof.

Fan, Hui, BS Tsinghua, MS Tsinghua, PhD Ill.   Assoc. Prof.

Guo, Ningqun, BS Nanjing Aeron.Inst., PhD Lond.   Assoc. Prof.

Hoon, Kay Hiang, BSc Strath., PhD Strath.   Assoc. Prof.

Huang Weimin, BS Southeast(Nanjing), MS Southeast(Nanjing), PhD Camb.   Assoc. Prof.

Lam, Khin Yong, BSc Lond., SM M.I.T., PhD M.I.T.   Assoc. Prof.

Li Chuan, BSc Natnl.Cheng Kung, MS Mich., PhD Mich.   Assoc. Prof.

Lim, Geok Hian, BSc(Eng) Lond., MSc Lond., PhD Aston, FIMechE   Assoc. Prof.

Lim, Mong King, BEng Sing., MSc Maine(France), DrSc Maine(France), FIE(Sing)   Prof.

Ling, Shih Fu, BS Cheng Kung, MSME Purdue, PhD Purdue   Prof.

Liu, Bo, BEng Huazhong U.S.T., MEng Huazhong U.S.T., PhD Manc.   Assoc. Prof.

Lu, Guoxing, BEng Jilin, MSc Cran., PhD Camb.   Assoc. Prof.

Miao, Jianmin, BEng Tongji, DrIng T.U.Darmstadt   Assoc. Prof.

Ng, Heong Wah, BEng Liv., PhD Liv.   Assoc. Prof.

Ong, Lin Seng, BSc Strath., PhD Strath., FIMechE   Assoc. Prof.

Pang, John H. L., BSc Strath., PhD Strath.   Assoc. Prof.; Head*

Rajendran, Sellakkulti, BSc Madr., BTech Anna, MEng IISc., PhD IISc.   Assoc. Prof.

Seah, Leong Keey, BSc Strath., PhD Strath.   Assoc. Prof.

Shang, Huai Min, BEng Sing., MSc Aston, PhD Aston, FIE(Sing)   Prof.

Shu, Dongwei, BS Beijing, MS Beijing, PhD Camb.   Assoc. Prof.

Tai, Kang, BEng NU Singapore, PhD Lond.   Assoc. Prof.

Tan, Soon Huat, BEng Strath., PhD Strath.   Assoc. Prof.

Teo, Ee Chon, BSc Nott., MSc Nott., PhD Strath.   Assoc. Prof.

Vahdati, Nader, BSME Portland, MSME Portland, PhD Calif.   Assoc. Prof.

Wang, Shao, BS Chongqing, MS Ill., PhD Ill.   Assoc. Prof.

Wu, Mao See, BSc Lond., SM M.I.T., PhD M.I.T.   Assoc. Prof.

Xiao, Zhongmin, BS China U.S.T., ME Chinese Acad.Sc., MS Rutgers, PhD Rutgers   Assoc. Prof.

Xu, Daolin, ME Dalian U.T., PhD Lond., BE   Assoc. Prof.

Other Staff: 1 Assoc. Prof. Fellow; 1 Asst. Prof.; 12 Res. Fellows; 1 Adjunct Prof.; 4 Adjunct Assoc. Profs.; 2 Adjunct Asst. Profs.

Research: biomechanics and biosensing; engineering computations and modelling; mechanical and micro system; mechanics of materials and structures

Human Factors and Ergonomics, Centre for

Tel: 6790 5894

Lim, Kee Yong, BSc Lond., MSc Lond., PhD Lond., FErgS   Assoc. Prof.; Dir.*

Other Staff: 1 Asst. Prof.; 1 Deputy Dir.

Research: ergonomics (biomechanics, design methods, environmental design, safety engineering, workstation design); human computer interaction (e- and m-commerce, infocomm applications, mobile computing, virtual reality applications); human factors engineering (cognitive and systems ergonomics, mental model, socio-technical design, teamwork); product design (affective and socio-cultural design, collaborative design, interaction design, user interfaces, military systems and applications)

Manufacturing Engineering

Tel: 6790 4818 Fax: 6795 3482
E-mail: h-dmer@ntu.edu.sg

Chian, Kerm Sin, BSc Manc., PhD UMIST   Assoc. Prof.

Jiang San Ping, BS S.China U.T., PhD City(UK)   Assoc. Prof.

Khor, Khiam Aik, BSc Monash, PhD Monash, FIMMM   Prof.

Lam, Yee Cheong, BE Melb., PhD Melb., FIEAust   Prof.

Lee, S. G. (Stephen), BEng Sing., MSc Manc., PhD Nan.Tech.   Assoc. Prof.; Head*

Li, Lin, BS Beijing I.C.T., MS Kyoto, PhD Kyoto   Assoc. Prof.

Lim, Lennie E. N., BSc Sur., PhD Sur., FIE(Sing)   Prof.

Liu, Erjia, BE Harbin, MS Harbin, PhD Leuven   Assoc. Prof.

Loh, Nee Lam, BEng Liv., PhD Liv., FIMMM   Assoc. Prof.

Loh, Ngiap Hiang, BSc Aston, PhD Aston   Assoc. Prof.

Lye, Sun Woh, BSc Bath, PhD Bath   Prof.

Murukeshan Vaddkke Matham, BSc CNAA, PhD CNAA   Assoc. Prof.

Ong, Nan Shing, BSc Manc., MSc NU Singapore, PhD Nan.Tech.   Assoc. Prof.

Shearwood, Christopher, BSc Leeds, PhD Leeds   Assoc. Prof.

Sivashanker Sathiamoorthy, BEng NU Singapore, PhD Camb.   Assoc. Prof.

Tan, Ming Jen, BSc(Eng) Lond., PhD Lond.   Assoc. Prof.

Tay, Meng Leong, BEng Sing., MSc Lond.   Assoc. Prof.

Tor, Shu Beng, BSc CNAA, PhD CNAA   Assoc. Prof.

Yeo, Swee Hock, BSc(Eng) Lond., MEng NU Singapore, PhD NU Singapore   Assoc. Prof.

Yue Chee Yoon, BE Monash, PhD Monash, FIE(Sing)   Prof.

Zhang, S. (Sam), BE Northeastern, ME Central Iron & Steel Res.Inst., Beijing, PhD Wis.   Assoc. Prof.

Zhou, Wei, BEng Tsinghua, PhD Camb.   Assoc. Prof.

Other Staff: 1 Nanyang Prof.; 4 Asst. Profs.; 13 Res. Fellows; 1 Adjunct Assoc. Prof.; 1 Adjunct Asst. Prof.

Research: advanced materials modelling and processes; advanced measurement, metrology and non-destructive testing; solid oxide fuel cell; tissue engineering; ultra-precision engineering

Mechanics of Micro-Systems, Centre for

Tel: 6790 6204 Fax: 6791 1975

Du, Hejun, BE Nanjing Aeron.Inst., ME Nanjing Aeron.Inst., PhD Lond.   Assoc. Prof.; Dir.*

Other Staff: 4 Res. Fellows

Research: dynamics and vibration of HDDs and microsystems; mechanics in manufacturing of miniaturised micro-systems; mechanics of micro-electrical mechanical systems; mechanics of miniaturised sensors and actuators; processing and characterisation of thin films for micro-devices

Mechatronics and Design

Tel: 6790 5600 Fax: 6791 3712
E-mail: h-dmd@ntu.edu.sg

Cai, Yiyu, BSc Nanjing, MSc Zhejiang, PhD NU Singapore   Assoc. Prof.

Chauhan, Sunita, BSc MDU, MSc Kuruk., MTech Kuruk., PhD Lond.   Assoc. Prof.

Chen, Chun-Hsien, BS Natnl.Cheng Kung, MS Missouri, PhD Missouri   Assoc. Prof.

Chen, Guang, BE Tsinghua, MS Tsinghua, PhD Georgia I.T.   Assoc. Prof.

Chen, I-Ming, BS Natnl.Taiwan, MS Cal.Tech., PhD Cal.Tech.   Assoc. Prof.

Gan, G. K. (Jacob), BEng Sing., MSE Mich., PhD Mich.   Assoc. Prof.

Khoo, Li Pheng, BEng Tokyo, MSc NU Singapore, PhD Wales, FIE(Sing)   Prof.

Lau, W. S. (Michael), BEng Sing., MSc NU Singapore, PhD Aston   Assoc. Prof.

Lee, Yong Tsui, BSc Leeds, MS Roch., PhD Leeds   Assoc. Prof.

Leong, Kah Fai, BEng NU Singapore, MSE Stan., MSME Stan.   Assoc. Prof.

Lim, Tau Meng, BSc Strath., PhD Strath.   Assoc. Prof.

Low, Kin Huat, BS Cheng Kung, MASc Wat., PhD Wat.   Assoc. Prof.

Ma, Yongsheng, BE Tsinghua, MSc Manc., PhD Manc.   Assoc. Prof.

Ng, Wan Sing, BEng NU Singapore, MEng NU Singapore, PhD Lond., FIMechE   Assoc. Prof.

Phung, Viet, BE Qld., MEngSc Monash   Assoc. Prof.

Seet, G. L. (Gerald), BSc CNAA, MSc Dund., PhD Aston, FIMechE   Assoc. Prof.; Head*

Woo, Cheng Hsiang (Tony), BSEE Ill., MSEE Ill., PhD Ill.   Prof.

Xie, Ming, BE China Textile, PhD Rennes   Assoc. Prof.

Yap, Fook Fah, BA Camb., PhD Camb.   Assoc. Prof.

Yeo, Song Huat, BSc Birm., PhD Birm.   Assoc. Prof.

Zhong, Zhaowei, ME Tohoku, PhD Tohoku, BE   Assoc. Prof.

Other Staff: 1 Nanyang Prof.; 7 Asst. Profs.; 4 Res. Fellows; 1 Sr. Fellow; 1 Adjunct Assoc. Prof.; 1 Adjunct Asst. Prof.

Research: bio-informatics and manufacturing informatics; design (biomedical product, collaboration product development, customer-oriented design, product lifecycle management (PLM), smart product design, deployable structures); dynamics and vibration (mechanics of micro-systems, modular re-configurable machines, parallel flexure mechanism, vehicle technology and vibration control); mechatronics and control (autonomous robots and vehicles, biomechatronics, intelligent machines, medical robots, underwater robotic vehicles, machine vision)

Micromachines Centre

Tel: 6790 6994 Fax: 6790 6995

Miao, Jianmin, BEng Tongji, DrIng T.U.Darmstadt   Assoc. Prof.; Dir.*

Other Staff: 1 Deputy Dir.

Research: biochip fabrication; MEMS training/education; micro-electrical-mechanical systems (MEMS)/nano-electrical-mechanical systems (NEMS) technology and research; nanotechnology

Project Management and Advancement, Centre for

Tel: 6790 4333 Fax: 6792 4062
Yeo, Khim Teck, BEng Sing., MBA Strath., MSc Manc., PhD UMIST   Assoc. Prof.; Dir.*
Research: management of complex product systems projects; project risk management/ capability maturity models; research and development (R&D) and new product development (NPD) project management; systems thinking and project management

Robotics Research Centre

Tel: 6790 5568 Fax: 6793 5921
    E-mail: d-rrc@ntu.edu.sg
Seet, G. L. (Gerald), BSc CNAA, MSc Dund., PhD Aston, FIMechE   Assoc. Prof.; Dir.*
Other Staff: 6 Res. Fellows; 4 Project Officers
Research: biomedical robotics and rehabilitation; entertainment robotic systems; intelligent vehicles and adaptive locomotion systems; mixed multi agent collaborative robotics; underwater robotics inspection and manipulation

Supply Chain Management, Centre for

Tel: 6790 4333
Piplani, Rajesh, BSc Alig., MS Arizona State, PhD Purdue   Assoc. Prof.; Dir.*
Other Staff: 1 Deputy Dir.
Research: closed loop supply chain management (reverse logistics); supply chain capability and reliability analysis; supply chain contracts (supplier-owned inventory); supply chain management applications (health care supply chain management); supply chain management modelling and analysis

Systems and Engineering Management

Tel: 6790 4364 Fax: 6795 7329
    E-mail: h-dsem@ntu.edu.sg
Chua, Chee Kai, BEng NU Singapore, MSc NU Singapore, PhD Nan.Tech.   Assoc. Prof.; Head*
Foo, Check Teck, LLB Lond., MBA City(UK), PhD St And., FCIM   Assoc. Prof.
Helander, Martin E. G., MEng Chalmers U.T., PhD Chalmers U.T., FIEAust, FErgS   Prof.
Khong, Poh Wah, BSc Strath., PhD Strath.   Assoc. Prof.
Kumar, Arun, BTech I.Sch.Mines, MS S.Illinois, PhD Virginia Polytech.   Assoc. Prof.
Lim, Choon Seng, BSc Strath., MSc Manc., PhD UMIST   Assoc. Prof.
Lim, Kee Yong, BSc Lond., MSc Lond., PhD Lond., FErgS   Assoc. Prof.
Lim, Y. E. (Samuel), BSc Strath., PhD Strath.   Assoc. Prof. (on leave)
Piplani, Rajesh, BSc Alig., MS Arizona State, PhD Purdue   Assoc. Prof.
Pokharel, Shaligram, BE Kashmir, MASc Wat., PhD Wat.   Assoc. Prof.
Sim, Siang Kok, BSc Newcastle(UK), MSc Essex, PhD Strath.   Assoc. Prof.
Sivakumar, Appa I., BEng Brad., PhD Brad.   Assoc. Prof.
Wu, Zhang, BS Huazhong U.S.T., MEng McM., PhD McM.   Assoc. Prof.
Yeo, Khim Teck, BEng Sing., MBA Strath., MSc Manc., PhD UMIST   Assoc. Prof.
Other Staff: 6 Asst. Profs.; 1 Assoc. Prof. Fellow; 1 Sr. Fellow; 1 Res. Fellow
Research: engineering management (project management, quality management, strategic management, risk management, medical systems); human factors and ergonomics (human-computer interaction); product lifecycle management (mass customisation, operations research, optimisation); supply chain and logistics networks (reverse logistics, supply chain design and optimisation); systems engineering (systems thinking, system design and methodologies)

Thermal and Fluids Engineering

Tel: 6790 5497 Fax: 6795 4623
    E-mail: h-dtfe@ntu.edu.sg
Chai, C. K. (John), BSc Windsor, MS Wis., PhD Minn.   Assoc. Prof.
Chan, Siew Hwa, BS Natnl.Taiwan, MSc Birm., PhD Lond.   Assoc. Prof.
Chan, Weng Kong, BEng NU Singapore, DrIng École Nat.Sup.d'Arts & Métiers, Paris   Assoc. Prof.; Head*
Chua, Leok Poh, BE Newcastle(NSW), PhD Newcastle(NSW)   Assoc. Prof.
Damodaran, Murali, BTech IIT Kanpur, MS Cornell, PhD Cornell   Assoc. Prof.
Gong, H. (Thomas), BE Wuhan Water Transportation Eng., MS Delaware, PhD Delaware   Assoc. Prof.
Ho, Hiang Kwee, BSc Newcastle(UK), SM M.I.T.   Assoc. Prof.
Huang, Xiaoyang, BS Nanjing, MS Chinese Acad.Sc., PhD Camb.   Assoc. Prof.
Kulish, Vladimir V., BSc Moscow Power Inst., MSc Moscow Power Inst., PhD Russian Acad.Sc., PhD S.Methodist   Assoc. Prof.
Lam, Chung Yau, BSc(Eng) Lond., PhD Lond.   Assoc. Prof.
Leong, Kai Choong, BEng NU Singapore, MSME Calif., PhD Qld.   Assoc. Prof.; Assoc. Chair, Acad.
Low, Seow Chay, BEng Sing., MSc Manc., PhD UMIST   Assoc. Prof.
Lua, Aik Chong, BEng Sheff., PhD Sheff.   Prof.
Ng, Yin Kwee, BEng Newcastle(UK), PhD Camb.   Assoc. Prof.
Nguyen, Nam-Trung, DrIng DrIngHabil   Assoc. Prof.
Ooi, Kim Tiow, BEng Strath., PhD Strath.   Assoc. Prof.
Shu, Jian Jun, BS Fudan, PhD Keele   Assoc. Prof.
Tan, Fock Lai, BEng NU Singapore, MSME Rensselaer   Assoc. Prof.
Toh, Kok Chuan, BE Auck., MSME Stan.   Assoc. Prof.
Wong, Teck Neng, BEng Strath., PhD Strath.   Assoc. Prof.
Wong, Yew Wah, BEng Sing., MSc NU Singapore   Assoc. Prof.
Yang, C. (Charles), BS Tsinghua, MSc China U.S.T., PhD Alta.   Assoc. Prof.
Yeo, Joon Hock, BSc Strath., PhD Lond.   Assoc. Prof.
Yeung, W. H. (William), BASc Br.Col., MASc Br.Col., PhD Br.Col.   Assoc. Prof.
Yu, C. M. (Simon), BEng Lond., PhD Lond.   Assoc. Prof.
Zhao, Yong, BS Xi'an Jiaotong, MSc Manc., PhD UMIST   Assoc. Prof.
Other Staff: 1 Assoc. Prof. Fellow; 1 Asst. Prof.; 3 Res. Fellows
Research: applied thermofluids (aerodynamics, aircraft propulsion, computational fluid dynamics (CFD), flow visualisation); biomedical engineering; energy and environment (fuel cell, fuel reforming, pollution control); microscale transport phenomena (microscale pumping, mixing and flow visualisation)

Nanyang Business School

Tel: 6790 5683-4 Fax: 6791 3697
    E-mail: d-nbs@ntu.edu.sg
Chen, Y. F. (Geraldine), BA NU Singapore, BSocSci NU Singapore, MSc Lond., PhD Lond.   Assoc. Prof.
Hong, Hai, BE Cant., ME Cant., MPA Harv., PhD Carnegie-Mellon   Prof.
Singh, Jitendra, BS Lucknow, MA Stan., PhD Stan., MBA   Prof.; Dean*
Other Staff: 1 Adjunct Assoc. Prof.

Accounting

Tel: 6790 4819 Fax: 6793 7956
    E-mail: ahttan@ntu.edu.sg
Choo, Teck Min, BAcc NU Singapore, PhD Pitt.   Assoc. Prof.
Chung, Lai Hong, BAcc NU Singapore, PhD Pitt.   Assoc. Prof.

Foo, See Liang, BCom NSW, PhD Hull, FCA   Assoc. Prof.
Goh, Chye Tee, BCom Nan., MCom NSW   Assoc. Prof.
Hossain, Mahmud, BCom Rajsh., MCom Rajsh., MBA Denver, PhD Massey   Assoc. Prof.
Kwok, C. H. (Branson), BCom W.Aust., MBA W.Aust., FCPA   Assoc. Prof.
Lee, Lip Nyean, BEc Malaya, MBA Strath.   Assoc. Prof.
Lee-Chin, F. T. (Marina), BCom Nan., MBA Melb., FCPA   Assoc. Prof.
Ng, Eng Juan, BEc Malaya, MBA S.Calif.   Assoc. Prof.
Tan, Hun Tong, BAcc NU Singapore, MA Mich., PhD Mich.   Prof.
Tan, K. G. (Clement), BAcc NU Singapore, MSc(Econ) Lond.   Assoc. Prof.
Tan, M. S. (Patricia), BAcc NU Singapore, PhD Br.Col.   Assoc. Prof.; Head*
Yeo, H. H. (Gillian), BAcc Sing., MS Ill., PhD Ill.   Prof.; Dean, Degree Programme; Exec. Vice-Dean
Other Staff: 14 Asst. Profs.; 3 Lectrs.; 1 Sr. Fellow; 3 Sr. Tutors; 6 Adjunct Assoc. Profs.
Research: accounting and security prices/ valuation; corporate governance; determinants of analyst forecasts; determinants of auditor performance; strategic production/disclosure of accounting information

Banking and Finance

Tel: 6790 4927 E-mail: akyding@ntu.edu.sg
Balasooriya, Uditha, BA S.Lanka, MA W.Ont., PhD W.Ont.   Assoc. Prof.
Cao, Yong, BEc Sichuan, MEc Chinese Acad.Soc.Sc., MEcDev ANU, PhD ANU   Assoc. Prof.
Charoenwong, Charlie, BE Chulalongkorn, MBA Memphis State, PhD Memphis State   Assoc. Prof.
Chong, Beng Soon, BS S.Illinois, MA Wash., MS S.Illinois, PhD Wash.   Assoc. Prof.
Ding, K. Y. (David), BCom Windsor, MBA Tennessee, PhD Memphis State   Assoc. Prof.
Dufey, Gunter, BA Würzburg, MA Wash., DBA Wash.   Prof.
Fock, Siew Tong, BA Sing., BSocSci Sing., MSc NU Singapore, PhD Bath   Assoc. Prof.; Vice-Dean, Undergrad. Programmes
Ho, Kim Wai, BSc Lond., MFin RMIT, PhD Nan.Tech., FCA   Assoc. Prof.
Hwang, Chuan Yang, BS Natnl.Cheng Kung, MBA Chic., MS Natnl.Cheng Kung, PhD Calif.   Prof.
Kang, C. S. (Joseph), BA Kon-Kuk, MA S.Methodist, MPA Seoul, PhD S.Methodist   Assoc. Prof.
Lau, Sie Ting, BS(BusAdmin) Clarion, MBA Clarion, PhD Texas   Assoc. Prof.; Head*
Low, Buen Sin, BAcc NU Singapore, MBA Tor., PhD Manc.   Assoc. Prof.
Saw, L. C. (Sutiap), BSc Monash, MA Penn., PhD Penn.   Assoc. Prof.
Sen, Nilanjan, BA Jad., MA Virginia Polytech., PhD Virginia Polytech.   Assoc. Prof.
Shrestha, Keshab M., BSc Tribhuvan, MA N.Y.State, MS N.Y.State, PhD N.Y.State   Assoc. Prof.
Sun, Qian, BS(Econ) Beijing, MBA Wm.Paterson, PhD Arizona State   Assoc. Prof.
Tan, Khee Giap, BA CNAA, MA E.Anglia, PhD E.Anglia   Assoc. Prof.
Tan, Kok Hui, BA Minn., PhD Arizona State   Assoc. Prof.
Tan-Ooi, Lee Lee, BSc Malaya, MS Northeastern   Assoc. Prof.
Wang, Peiming, BS Shanghai 2nd Polytech., MA York(Can.), MS Shanghai Inst.Mech.Engin., PhD Br.Col.   Assoc. Prof.
Wong, Yoke Wai, BSc City(UK), MBA City(UK), FSA   Assoc. Prof.
Yee, Wah Chin, BBA Sing., MBA Strath., FCIS   Assoc. Prof.
Yuan, Wu, BS Wuhan, MStats NSW, PhD NSW   Assoc. Prof.
Other Staff: 7 Asst. Profs.; 2 Lectrs.; 2 Sr. Tutors; 3 Adjunct Assoc. Profs.
Research: asset pricing and investments; Chinese financial market; corporate finance and

corporate governance; derivatives, financial engineering and risk management; market microstructure

Business Law

Tel: 6790 5657 Fax: 6793 5189
E-mail: acsyeo@ntu.edu.sg
Ang, B. W. (Steven), LLB NU Singapore, LLM Lond. Assoc. Prof.
Goh-Low, S. Y. (Erin), LLB NU Singapore, LLM Lond. Assoc. Prof.; Head*
Leow, Chye Sian, LLB NU Singapore, LLM Camb. Assoc. Prof.
Ong, C. S. (Dennis), LLB Lond., LLM Lond. Assoc. Prof.
Samtani, Anilkumar K., LLB NU Singapore, LLM NU Singapore Assoc. Prof.
Tan, How Teck, BEc Adel., MTax Syd. Assoc. Prof.
Tan, Lay Hong, LLB Sing., LLM Lond. Assoc. Prof.
Tan, S. K. (Harry), BSocSc Keele, LLB Melb. Assoc. Prof.
Tan-Chua, P. N. (Angela), BAcc Sing., MBA NU Singapore Assoc. Prof.
Tan-Khaw, P. G. (Moira), LLB NU Singapore, LLM NU Singapore Assoc. Prof.
Teo, C. C. (Jack), LLB NU Singapore, LLM NU Singapore Assoc. Prof.
Yeo, C. S. (Victor), LLB NU Singapore, LLM Melb. Assoc. Prof.
Other Staff: 4 Asst. Profs.; 1 Adjunct Assoc. Prof.
Research: consumer and marketing law; corporate and securities law; corporate governance; e-business and IT law; intellectual property law

Cornell-Nanyang Institute of Hospitality Management

Tel: 6316 6760 Fax: 6794 9796
Siguaw, Judy A., BBA Lamar, MBA Louisiana Tech, DBA Louisiana Tech Prof.; Dean*
Smith, Russell A., BArch Qld., MArch Qld., DDes Harv., FRAIA Assoc. Prof.; Vice-Dean
Other Staff: 1 Sr. Tutor

Information Technology and Operations Management

Tel: 6790 5699 Fax: 6792 2313
E-mail: asksia@ntu.edu.sg
Bhatnagar, Rohit, BTech Ban., PhD McG. Assoc. Prof.
Chen Shaoxiang, BS Nanjing, MBA Leuven, DrScEc Leuven Assoc. Prof.
Das, Amit, BTech Kharagpur, PhD Minn. Assoc. Prof.
Li, Z.-F. (Michael), BS Beijing Normal, PhD Br.Col., PhD Regina Assoc. Prof.
Neo, Boon Siong, BAcc NU Singapore, MBA Pitt., PhD Pitt. Prof.
Periasamy, Kanapaty P., MSc Aston, DPhil Oxf. Assoc. Prof.
Sethi, Vijay, BTech IIT Delhi, MBA Ohio, PhD Pitt. Prof.
Sia, Siew Kien, BAcc NU Singapore, MInfmSystems Qld., PhD Nan.Tech. Assoc. Prof.; Head*
Soh, W. L. (Christina), BAcc NU Singapore, PhD Calif. Assoc. Prof.
Tung, Lai Lai, BAcc NU Singapore, MBA Indiana, PhD Indiana Assoc. Prof.
Viswanathan, S., BTech IIT Madras, MS Case W.Reserve, PhD Case W.Reserve Assoc. Prof.
Wang, Qinan, BS Hunan Normal, MBA Nankai, PhD McM. Assoc. Prof.
Other Staff: 6 Asst. Profs.; 2 Lectrs.; 2 Sr. Tutors; 2 Adjunct Assoc. Profs.; 1 Adjunct Asst. Prof.
Research: e-government and public sector IT; enterprise systems implementation; operation and supply chain management; outsourcing and IT personnel management; strategic IT-enabled organisation/industry transformation

Marketing and International Business

Tel: 6790 5682 E-mail: akemurali@ntu.edu.sg
Chan, Geraldine Y. F., BA NU Singapore, BSocSci NU Singapore, MSc Lond., PhD Lond. Assoc. Prof.
Contractor, Farok J., BSE Bom., MBA Penn., MS Mich., PhD Penn. Nanyang Prof.
Erramilli, Murali K., BSc Poona, MSc Poona, MBA Poona, PhD Arkansas Assoc. Prof.
Gupta, Vivek, BCom Alld., LLB Lucknow, MBA Rhode I. Assoc. Prof.
Henderson, Joan F., BSc Wales, MSc Strath., PhD Edin. Assoc. Prof.
Hooi, Den Huan, BSc Brad., PhD Manc. Assoc. Prof.
Kannan, Srinivasan, BE Madr., PhD Calif., MBA Canon Visiting Prof.
Leong, Choon Chiang, BBA Hawaii, MS Wash., FCMI Assoc. Prof.
McGovern, Ian, BA Manc., MBA City HK, PhD Manc. Assoc. Prof.
Sangwan, Sunanda, BA Kuruk., MA Inst.Soc.Stud.(The Hague), MA Punjab, PhD Rotterdam Assoc. Prof.
Wan, Chew Yoong, MBA Lausanne Assoc. Prof.; Head*
Other Staff: 7 Asst. Profs.; 1 Sr. Fellow; 3 Sr. Tutors; 1 Adjunct Assoc. Prof.
Research: consumer behaviour and communication (cross cultural, online user behaviour); international business (entry strategies, multinationals, regionalisation); marketing strategy (customer satisfaction, loyalty, market expansion); quantitative modelling (modelling applications, virtual communication); tourism and hospitality management (social impacts, sustainable urban tourism)

Strategy, Management and Organisation

Tel: 6790 4717 E-mail: asang@ntu.edu.sg
Ang, Soon, BAcc NU Singapore, MCom NSW, PhD Minn. Prof.
Cascio, Wayne F., MA Emory, PhD Roch. Goh Tjoei Kok Prof.
Chan, Teng Heng, BSc Malaya, MBA Aston, PhD Lond. Assoc. Prof.
Chew, K. H. (Irene), BA Sing., MA Leeds, PhD NSW Assoc. Prof.
Das, Shobha S., BA Delhi, PhD Minn. Assoc. Prof.
Ho, Mian Lian, BA Sing., MA Monash, PhD Monash Assoc. Prof.
Lall, Ashish, BA Delhi, MA Delhi, MA Car., PhD Car. Assoc. Prof.
Ng, Kok Yee, BAcc Nan.Tech., PhD Mich.State Assoc. Prof.
Osman-Gani, Aahad M., MA Ohio State, PhD Ohio State Assoc. Prof.
Quazi, Hesan A., BSc(Engin) B'desh.Engin., MSc(Engin) B'desh.Engin., MBA Indiana, DPhil Sus. Assoc. Prof.
Rogers, Priscilla S., BS W.Mich., PhD Mich. Visiting Prof.
Tan, Joo Seng, BA Malaya, MMLS Malaya, PhD Malaya Assoc. Prof.
Templer, Klaus-Jurgen, PhD Hamburg Assoc. Prof.
Tsui-Auch, Lai Si, BSc HK, MA Mich.State, PhD Mich.State Assoc. Prof.
Wee, Beng Geok, BBA Sing., MBA Cran.IT, PhD Hull Assoc. Prof.
Wee, Chow Hou, BBA Sing., MBA W.Ont., PhD W.Ont. Prof.; Head*
Wong, F. H. (Irene), BA Malaya, MA Malaya, PhD Alta. Assoc. Prof.
Other Staff: 4 Asst. Profs.; 9 Lectrs.; 2 Sr. Fellows; 3 Sr. Tutors; 1 Teaching Fellow; 1 Adjunct Prof.; 3 Adjunct Assoc. Profs.
Research: business communication strategies and methods; cultural intelligence (effective cross-cultural individual interactions), leadership assessments and development; human resource management (HRM) in Asia (compensation and benefits, human resource metrics, knowledge management, training and development); social network analysis, individual performance and team

learning; strategic management and effective organisation of small and medium enterprises

Physical and Mathematical Sciences

Tel: 6790 3754 Fax: 6316 6984
E-mail: spms-v1@ntu.edu.sg
Lee, Soo-Ying, BSc Malaya, PhD Chic., FRSChem Prof.; Chair*
Other Staff: 6 Profs.; 1 Visiting Prof.; 6 Assoc. Profs.; 39 Asst. Profs.; 7 Lectrs.; 2 Sr. Fellows; 2 Teaching Fellows; 2 Adjunct Profs.; 10 Adjunct Assoc. Profs.; 5 Adjunct Asst. Profs.
Research: chemistry and biological chemistry; mathematical and economics sciences; physics and applied physics

Chemistry and Biological Chemistry, Division of

Tel: 6316 8911 Fax: 6791 1961
Lee, Soo-Ying, BSc Malaya, PhD Chic., FRSChem Prof.
Leung, Pak Hing, BSc CNAA, PhD ANU Prof.; Assoc. Chair (Academics)
Loh, Teck Peng, BEng Tokyo, MEng Tokyo, PhD Harv. Prof.; Head*
Narasaka, Koichi, BSc Tokyo, MSc Tokyo, PhD Tokyo Nanyang Prof.
Zhong GuoFu, BSc Nanjing Sci. & Tech., MSc Shanghai, PhD Scripps Assoc. Prof.
Other Staff: 3 Profs.; 13 Asst. Profs.; 2 Lectrs.; 2 Sr. Fellows; 2 Adjunct Profs.; 8 Adjunct Assoc. Profs.; 2 Adjunct Asst. Profs.
Research: biological chemistry; catalysis; natural product synthesis; synthetic methodology; theoretical and physical chemistry

Mathematical Sciences, Division of

Tel: 6316 3747 Fax: 6316 6984
Ling, San, BA Camb., MA Camb., PhD Calif. Prof.; Head*
Schmidt, Bernhard, BSc Giessen, MS(Math) Giessen, PhD Augsburg Assoc. Prof.
Tai, Xue Cheng, Lic Jyväskylä, PhD Jyväskylä Assoc. Prof.
Wang, Huaxiong, BSc Fujian Normal, MSc Fujian Normal, PhD Haifa, PhD W'gong. Assoc. Prof.
Xing, Chaoping, BS Anhui, MS Northwest Telecommunicns.Engin.Inst., PhD Shanghai U.S.T. Prof.
Other Staff: 2 Profs.; 4 Assoc. Profs.; 13 Asst. Profs.; 1 Lectrs.; 2 Teaching Fellows; 1 Adjunct Assoc. Prof.; 2 Adjunct Asst. Profs.
Research: algebra; algebraic geometry; computational mathematics; convex analysis; discrete mathematics

Physics and Applied Physics, Division of

Tel: 6316 3747 Fax: 6316 6984
Huan, Cheng Hon (Alfred), BA Oxf., DPhil Oxf. Prof.; Head*
Qiu, Zi Qiang, BS Beijing, PhD Johns H. Visiting Prof.
Shen, Zexiang, BS Jilin, PhD Lond. Assoc. Prof.; Assoc. Chair (Res. and Grad.)
Other Staff: 1 Prof.; 1 Visiting Prof.; 1 Assoc. Prof.; 13 Asst. Profs.; 2 Lectrs.; 1 Adjunct Assoc. Prof.; 2 Adjunct Asst. Profs.
Research: atmospheric physics; biophysics and soft condensed matter; computational and theoretical physics; condensed matter physics and nanomaterials; laser spectroscopy and photonics

SPECIAL CENTRES, ETC

Advanced Materials Research, Centre for

Tel: 6790 4626 Fax: 6790 9081
E-mail: d-amrc@ntu.edu.sg
Subodh Mhaisalkar, BTech IIT Bombay, PhD Ohio State Assoc. Prof.; Dir.*
Other Staff: 25 Res. Staff
Research: biomaterials (body pumps including heart pumps and pumps for renal functionality, biodegradable stents and therapeutic targeting); defence materials (functionally graded nano composite

materials); energy and catalysis (energy
harnessing, generation and catalysis for
environmental applications); nano- and
organic electronics (organic thin film
transistors, advanced Si based
nanoelectronics and advanced interconnect
applications); nanophotonics and magnetics
(integrated transceiver modules and polymer
based waveguides/photonic crystals,
spintronic materials to rare earth materials)

Advanced Media Technology, Centre for

Tel: 6790 6988 Fax: 6792 8123
E-mail: askwmwittig@ntu.edu.sg
Muller-Wittig, Wolfgang K., DrIng
T.U.Darmstadt   Assoc. Prof.; Dir.*
Other Staff: 1 Lee Kuan Yew Postdoctoral
Fellow; 3 Res. Assocs.; 1 Fac. Member
Research: medical and scientific visualisation;
next generation learning environments for
life science; three-dimensional modelling
and reconstruction of incident scenes;
virtual and augmented environments for
medical applications; virtual engineering and
manufacturing

Advanced Studies, Institute of

Tel: 6790 6491 Fax: 6794 4941
E-mail: d-ias@ntu.edu.sg
Phua, Kok Khoo   Prof.; Dir.*
Other Staff: 1 Adjunct Prof.

Chinese Language and Culture, Centre for

Tel: 6790 6301 Fax: 6792 2334
E-mail: d-cclc@ntu.edu.sg
Lee, Guan Kin, BA Nan., MA Nan., PhD HK
Assoc. Prof.; Dir.*
Other Staff: 1 Assoc. Prof.; 1 Res. Fellow; 1
Res. Assoc.
Research: Chinese education in Southeast Asia;
Chinese language and dialects in Asia;
Chinese literature in Asia; Chinese migration
and networks (global and local issues);
Chinese traditional and pop cultures in Asia

Continuing Education, Centre for

Tel: 6790 4221 Fax: 6774 2911
E-mail: d-cce@ntu.edu.sg
Seah, Ben Hun, BBA NU Singapore, MBA
Nan.Tech.   Dir.*

Emerging Research Lab (ER Lab)

Tel: 6790 6965 Fax: 6792 6559
E-mail: asahtan@ntu.edu.sg
Tan, Ah Hwee, BSc NU Singapore, MSc NU
Singapore, PhD Boston   Assoc. Prof.; Dir.*
Other Staff: 1 Res. Fellows; 1 Res. Assoc.; 8
Fac. Members
Research: cognitive and neural systems; DNA
chip design; evolutionary and complex
systems; intelligent media

Environmental Engineering Research, Centre for

Tel: 6790 4100 Fax: 6792 7319
E-mail: d-eerc@ntu.edu.sg
Wang, Jing-Yuan, BS Natnl.Chung Hsing, MCE
N.Carolina State, PhD N.Carolina State   Assoc.
Prof.; Dir.*
Other Staff: 5 Res. Fellows; 1 Singapore
Millennium Foundation Res. Fellow
Research: clean water management;
environmental biotechnology; environmental
remediation; waste to resources

Financial Engineering and Risk Management, Centre for

Tel: 6790 4758 Fax: 6793 7440
E-mail: mfe@ntu.edu.sg
Low, Buen Sin, BAcc NU Singapore, MBA Tor.,
PhD Manc. Assoc. Prof.; Dir.*
Research: asset management and capital markets;
computational finance; corporate finance
and financial engineering; financial
technology; risk management

Forensics and Security Lab (ForSe Lab)

Tel: 6790 5491 Fax: 6792 6559
E-mail: assycho@ntu.edu.sg
Cho, Siu Yeung (David), BEng City HK, PhD
City HK   Asst. Prof.; Dir.*
Other Staff: 8 Fac. Members
Research: biometric techniques using infrared
imaging; EEG signal processing for brain
computer interface; facial analysis using
emotion and expression; facial, fingerprint
and palmprint recognition; intelligent video
surveillance and monitoring for suspicious
human action

gameLAB

Tel: 6790 6124 Fax: 6792 6559
E-mail: ckwong@ntu.edu.sg
Wong Chee Kien, Gabriel, BEng Nan.Tech.,
MEng Nan.Tech.   Lectr.; Dir.*
Other Staff: 5 Res./Project Staff; 10 Fac.
Members
Research: advanced gaming platforms (game
engines, ubiquitous gaming); artificial
intelligence for games and simulation;
serious games (applications for education,
healthcare, training)

High-Performance Embedded Systems, Centre for

Tel: 6790 6638 Fax: 6792 0774
E-mail: chipes@ntu.edu.sg
Srikanthan, Thambipillai, BSc CNAA, PhD CNAA
Assoc. Prof.; Dir.*
Other Staff: 1 Res. Fellow
Research: algorithms to architectures; computer
arithmetic; embedded signal processing;
embedded software; reconfigurable
computing

Humanities and Social Sciences Research Centre

Tel: 6514 8364 E-mail: d-hssrc@ntu.edu.sg
Wong, W. C. (Lawrence), BA HK, MPhil HK,
PhD Lond.   Prof.; Dir.*
Research: gender studies (feminist and
masculinity studies); global studies
(development and social change); language
and literacy studies (multiculturalism and
multilingualism); Singapore studies (social
and economic indicators, religion and social
change); urban studies (contemporary cities,
metropolitan, global and cosmopolitan)

Innovation and Technology Transfer Office

Tel: 6790 5533 Fax: 6792 1737
E-mail: d-itto@ntu.edu.sg
Yu, Hou Cheong (Alex), BEng McM., PhD Tor.
Dir.*
Other Staff: 9 Staff Members

Intelligent Systems Centre

Tel: 6790 6678 Fax: 6316 4480
E-mail: d-intellisys@ntu.edu.sg
Chen, I-Ming, BS Natnl.Taiwan, MS Cal.Tech.,
PhD Cal.Tech.   Assoc. Prof.; Dir.*
Other Staff: 6 Res. Fellows; 7 Res. Assocs.; 5
Project Officers
Research: cognitive information systems;
computational intelligence algorithms for
problem solving; cyber sensor
infrastructures; robotics and haptics
interfaces; wireless sensor networks

Managed Computing Competency Centre

Tel: 6790 5405 Fax: 6793 3318
E-mail: d-aspc@ntu.edu.sg
Gay, Robert K. L., BEng Sheff., MEng Sheff., PhD
Sheff.   Prof.; Dir.*
Other Staff: 1 Sr. Res. Fellow
Research: e-business technology; e-learning; grid
computing; knowledge management; service
management

Maritime Research Centre

Tel: 6790 5321 Fax: 6790 6620
E-mail: d-mrc@ntu.edu.sg
Tan, Soon Keat, BE Auck., ME Auck., PhD Auck.
Assoc. Prof.; Dir.*
Other Staff: 5 Res. Fellows
Research: marine environment and resources;
maritime IT and communications; maritime
transport and logistics; offshore and
maritime engineering and port operations
and security; port and maritime technology

Nanyang Technopreneurship Centre

Tel: 6790 5892 Fax: 6792 0467
E-mail: ntc@ntu.edu.sg
Tan, Teng Kee, BCom Nan., MBA Northwestern,
PhD Camb.   Assoc. Prof.; Dir.*
Other Staff: 2 Adjunct Assoc. Profs.

Network Technology Research Centre

Tel: 6790 5019 Fax: 6792 6894
E-mail: d-ntrc@ntu.edu.sg
Shum, Ping, BEng Birm., PhD Birm.   Assoc.
Prof.; Dir.*
Other Staff: 8 Res. Fellows
Research: mobile network technology; network
control and engineering; optical
communications; power line
communications

Pedagogy and Practice, Centre for Research in

Tel: 6790 3321 Fax: 6896 9845
Albright, James J., BA Trent, BEd Dal., MA
Mt.St.Vin., PhD Penn.State
Hogan, David J., BEd Syd., BA Syd., MEd Ill.,
PhD Ill.   Prof.; Dean*
McInerney, Dennis, BA Macq., BEd NE, MEd NE,
PhD Syd.   Prof.
Other Staff: 8 Asst. Profs.; 1 Sr. Fellow; 2
Teaching Fellows
Research: home and school studies in mother
tongue; information technology classrooms;
language and literacy; multiliteracies and
learning artefacts; qualitative and
quantitative descriptions of classroom
practices

Positioning and Wireless Technology Centre

Tel: 6791 7326 Fax: 6793 3318
E-mail: d-pwtc@ntu.edu.sg
Law, Choi Look, BSc(Eng) Lond., PhD Lond.
Assoc. Prof.; Dir.*
Other Staff: 4 Res. Fellows
Research: applications of global positioning
systems; differential global positioning
systems; pseudolites and indoor positioning
systems; radio frequency identification;
wireless networks

Precision Engineering and Nanotechnology Centre

Tel: 6790 6336 Fax: 6790 4674
E-mail: d-pen@ntu.edu.sg
Zhou, Wei, BEng Tsinghua, PhD Camb.   Assoc.
Prof.; Dir.*
Other Staff: 4 Res. Fellows
Research: nanofabrication; nanometrology; nano-
processes; ultra-precision machining

Protective Technology Research, Centre for

Tel: 6790 5285 Fax: 6791 0046
E-mail: ptrc@ntu.edu.sg
Pan Tso-Chien, BS Cheng Kung, MS Calif., PhD
Calif.   Prof.; Dir.*
Other Staff: 7 Res. Fellows; 2 Deputy Dirs.; 8
Project Officers
Research: blast effect mitigation; ground shock
effects; reinforced concrete material
modelling; structural damage assessment;
underground space development

Satellite Engineering Centre

Tel: 6790 5390 Fax: 6792 0415
E-mail: eshtan@ntu.edu.sg
Tan, Soon Hie, BE *Auck.*, PhD *Auck.*   Assoc. Prof.; Dir.*
Other Staff: 3 Res. Fellows
Research: ground-station and mobile ground terminal development; low earth orbit satellite payloads and applications; low earth orbit satellite space bus and systems

Temasek Laboratories

Tel: 6790 5910 Fax: 6790 0215
E-mail: temasek-labs@ntu.edu.sg
Shang, Huai Min, BEng *Sing.*, MSc *Aston*, PhD *Aston*, FIE(Sing)   Prof.; Dir.*
Other Staff: 1 Sr. Res. Scientist; 16 Res. Scientists; 11 Assoc. Scientists
Research: advanced materials for protection; advanced radar systems; monolithic microwave integrated circuits (MMIC); signal processing system on chip; tropical weather

4G Research Laboratory

Tel: 6790 4287 Fax: 6792 6559
E-mail: ascpfu@ntu.edu.sg
Fu, Chengpeng (Franklin), BEng *Shanghai U.S.T.*, MPhil *Shanghai U.S.T.*, PhD *City HK*   Asst. Prof.; Dir.*
Other Staff: 5 Res. Staff; 10 Fac. Members
Research: next generation internet; next generation networks; 4G protocol, architecture, chip and embedded systems

CONTACT OFFICERS

Academic affairs. Divisional Director, Office of Academic Services: Lim, Paik Suan, BA *NU Singapore* (E-mail: oas-query@ntu.edu.sg)
Academic affairs. Head, Foundation Programmes Administration (National Institute of Education): Koh, Sou Keaw, BSc *Nan.*, MSc *Auck.*
Accommodation. Deputy Director, Student Affairs Office: Shang, Angela L. P., BA *NU Singapore*
Accommodation. Head, Foundation Programmes Administration (National Institute of Education): Koh, Sou Keaw, BSc *Nan.*, MSc *Auck.*
Admissions (first degree). Assistant Director, Office of Admissions and Financial Aid: Low, R. Louis, BSc *Lond.* (E-mail: adm-intnl@ntu.edu.sg)
Admissions (first degree). Deputy Director, Office of Admissions and Financial Aid: Tai, Kian Heng, BSocSci *NU Singapore* (E-mail: adm_local@ntu.edu.sg)
Admissions (first degree). Head, Foundation Programmes Administration (National Institute of Education): Koh, Sou Keaw, BSc *Nan.*, MSc *Auck.* (E-mail: nieadmtp@nie.edu.sg)
Admissions (higher degree). Assoc. Dean, Graduate Programmes and Research (National Institute of Education): Subramaniam, Ramanathan, BSc *NU Singapore*, MSc *Salf.*, PhD *Salf.* (E-mail: nieadmpp@nie.edu.sg)
Admissions (higher degree). Deputy Director, Graduate Studies Office: Grace, Leong, BCom *Dal.* (E-mail: gradstudies@ntu.edu.sg)
Adult/continuing education. Director, Centre for Continuing Education: Seah, Ben Hun, BBA *NU Singapore*, MBA *Nan.Tech.* (E-mail: d-cce@ntu.edu.sg)
Adult/continuing education. Associate Dean, Graduate Programmes and Research (National Institute of Education): Tan, Tuck Lee (Augustine), BSc *NU Singapore*, MSc *NU Singapore*, PhD *NU Singapore* (E-mail: augustine.tan@nie.edu.sg)
Alumni. Head, Public, International and Alumni Relations (National Institute of Education): Campbell, Patricia E. A., BA *Curtin* (E-mail: niepr@nie.edu.sg)

Alumni. Assistant Director, Alumni Affairs Office: Teo, Chin Kwei (Jimmy), BIT *Qld.UT*
Careers. Director, Career and Attachment Office: Ng, B. H., BE *Malaya*, MSc *Sing.* (E-mail: wwopa@ntu.edu.sg)
Careers. Head, Foundation Programmes Administration (National Institute of Education): Koh, Sou Keaw, BSc *Nan.*, MSc *Auck.*
Computing services. Head, Computer Services Centre (National Institute of Education): Koh-Goh, H. C., BSc *Nan.* (E-mail: servicedesk@nie.edu.sg)
Computing services. Director, IT Operations: Goh, T. C., BSc *Nan.*, MSc *N.Y.State* (E-mail: helpdesk@ntu.edu.sg)
Consultancy services. Assistant Head, Human Resource Department (National Institute of Education): Neo, G. K., BEng *Lough.*
Consultancy services. Assistant Director, Office of Human Resources: Ang, Yee Chay, BA *NU Singapore*, MSc *Nan.Tech.*
Credit transfer. Divisional Director, Office of Academic Services: Lim, Paik Suan, BA *NU Singapore* (E-mail: oas-query@ntu.edu.sg)
Credit transfer. Head, Foundation Programmes Administration (National Institute of Education): Koh, Sou Keaw, BSc *Nan.*, MSc *Auck.*
Development/fund-raising. Director, Development Office: Harper, Marina T., BMusic *Ball*, MMusic *Cinc.*, MBA *Cinc.*, MA *Cinc.*
Estates and buildings/works and services. Head, Development and Estate Department (National Institute of Education): Selvaratnam, Selvarajan, BSc *H-W* (E-mail: nieded@nie.edu.sg)
Estates and buildings/works and services. Chief Building and Infrastructure Officer, Office of Facilities Planning and Management: Chia, Oi Leng, BEng *NU Singapore*, MSc(Civil) *NU Singapore*
Examinations. Divisional Director, Office of Academic Services: Lim, Paik Suan, BA *NU Singapore*
Examinations. Head, Foundation Programmes Administration (National Institute of Education): Koh, Sou Keaw, BSc *Nan.*, MSc *Auck.*
Finance. Head, Finance (National Institute of Education): Choong, A. L. (Michelle), BAcc *Sing.* (E-mail: niefin@nie.edu.sg)
Finance. Financial Controller, Office of Finance: Ang, Kah Kin (Edwin), BAcc *NU Singapore*, MBA *Leic.*
General enquiries. Divisional Director, Office of Academic Services: Lim, Paik Suan, BA *NU Singapore*
General enquiries. Divisional Director (Corporate Planning and Development) (National Institute of Education): Sim, C. T., BA *Sing.*
Industrial liaison. Director, Career and Attachment Office: Ng, B. H., BE *Malaya*, MSc *Sing.* (E-mail: wwopa@ntu.edu.sg)
International office. Assistant Director, International Relations Office: Jain, Amit, BCom *Bom.*, MA *J.Nehru U.* (E-mail: amit@ntu.edu.sg)
Language training for international students. Associate Professor (National Institute of Education): Lubna, Alsagoff, BA *NU Singapore*, MA *NU Singapore*, PhD *Stan.* (E-mail: lubna.alsagoff@nie.edu.sg)
Language training for international students. Director, Language and Communication Centre: Lai, Phooi Ching, BA *Wellesley*, EdM *Harv.*, EdD *Hawaii* (E-mail: d-oa@ntu.edu.sg)
Library (chief librarian). Librarian: Choy, Fatt Cheong, BSc *Newcastle(UK)*, MS *Ill.* (E-mail: lib@ntu.edu.sg)
Library (enquiries). Head, Library and Information Services Centre (National Institute of Education): Yeo-Tang, I.-S. (Isabel), BSc *Sing.* (E-mail: servicedesk@nie.edu.sg)

Marketing. Head, Public, International and Alumni Relations (National Institute of Education): Campbell, Patricia E. A., BA *Curtin* (E-mail: niepr@nie.edu.sg)
Marketing. Director, Corporate Communications Office: Tan, Su Yuen, BSc *NU Singapore*
Ombudsman. Vice-President, Office of Human Resources: Yu, Sau Ting (Angela), BA *Sing.*, BSocSci *Sing.*
Personnel/human resources. Head, Human Resource Department (National Institute of Education): Ko, Y. H. (Jacklyn), BAcc *NU Singapore* (E-mail: niehrd@nie.edu.sg)
Personnel/human resources. Vice-President, Office of Human Resources: Yu, Sau Ting (Angela), BA *Sing.*, BSocSci *Sing.*
Public relations. Head, Public, International and Alumni Relations (National Institute of Education): Campbell, Patricia E. A., BA *Curtin* (E-mail: niepr@nie.edu.sg)
Public relations. Director, Corporate Communications Office: Tan, Su Yuen, BSc *NU Singapore*
Publications. Deputy Director, Office of Academic Services: Tan, Sock Leng, BA *NU Singapore*
Publications. Head, Foundation Programmes Administration (National Institute of Education): Koh, Sou Keaw, BSc *Nan.*, MSc *Auck.*
Purchasing. Divisional Director, Office of Finance: Chew, H. S., BCom *Nan.*
Purchasing. Head, Finance (National Institute of Education): Choong, A. L. (Michelle), BAcc *Sing.* (E-mail: niefin@nie.edu.sg)
Quality assurance and accreditation. Head, Foundation Programmes Administration (National Institute of Education): Koh, Sou Keaw, BSc *Nan.*, MSc *Auck.*
Research. Associate Dean, Graduate Programmes and Research (National Institute of Education: Tan, Tuck Lee (Augustine), BSc *NU Singapore*, MSc *NU Singapore*, PhD *NU Singapore* (E-mail: augustine.tan@nie.edu.sg)
Research. Director of Research: Khor, Prof. Khiam Aik, BSc *Monash*, PhD *Monash*, FIMMM
Safety. Head, Development and Estate Department (National Institute of Education): Selvaratnam, Selvarajan, BSc *H-W* (E-mail: nieded@nie.edu.sg)
Safety. Chief Building and Infrastructure Officer, Office of Facilities Planning and Management: Chia, Oi Leng, BEng *NU Singapore*, MSc(Civil) *NU Singapore*
Scholarships, awards, loans. Assistant Director, Office of Admissions and Financial Aid: Ho, Diana, MA *James Cook* (E-mail: ug_scholarships@ntu.edu.sg)
Scholarships, awards, loans. Senior Assistant Director, Office of Admissions and Financial Aid: Truong, May Lin (Jasmine), BBA *S.Fraser* (E-mail: finaid@ntu.edu.sg)
Scholarships, awards, loans. Head, Foundation Programmes Administration (National Institute of Education): Koh, Sou Keaw, BSc *Nan.*, MSc *Auck.*
Security. Head, Development and Estate Department (National Institute of Education): Selvaratnam, Selvarajan, BSc *H-W* (E-mail: nieded@nie.edu.sg)
Security. Chief Building and Infrastructure Officer, Office of Facilities Planning and Management: Chia, Oi Leng, BEng *NU Singapore*, MSc(Civil) *NU Singapore*
Sport and recreation. Associate Professor, Academic (National Institute of Education): Chia, Yong Hwa (Michael), BSc *Lough.*, PhD *Exe.* (E-mail: yhmchia@nie.edu.sg)
Sport and recreation. Deputy Director, Sports and Recreation Centre, Student Affairs Office: Loh-Low, Sheryl C. G., MBA *S.Cross*
Staff development and training. Head, Human Resource Department (National Institute of Education): Ko, Y. H. (Jacklyn), BAcc *NU Singapore*

Staff development and training. Vice-President, Office of Human Resources: Yu, Sau Ting (Angela), BA *Sing.*, BSocSci *Sing.*

Student union. Divisional Director, Student Affairs Office: Seah, Wai Choo, BA *Nan.*, MSS *U.S.Sports Acad.*

Student welfare/counselling. Student Counsellor, Student Counselling Centre: Hamid, Mariam, BA *W.Aust.*, MPsych *Monash*

Student welfare/counselling. Head, Foundation Programmes Administration (National Institute of Education): Koh, Sou Keaw, BSc *Nan.*, MSc *Auck.*

Students from other countries. Divisional Director, International Student Centre: Chua, Poh Gek, BA *Malaya*

Students from other countries. Head, Foundation Programmes Administration (National Institute of Education): Koh, Sou Keaw, BSc *Nan.*, MSc *Auck.*

Students with disabilities. Divisional Director, Office of Academic Services: Lim, Paik Suan, BA NU *Singapore*

Students with disabilities. Head, Foundation Programmes Administration (National Institute of Education): Koh, Sou Keaw, BSc *Nan.*, MSc *Auck.*

University press. Head, Public, International and Alumni Relations (National Institute of Education): Campbell, Patricia E. A., BA *Curtin* (E-mail: niepr@nie.edu.sg)

University press. Director, Corporate Communications Office: Tan, Su Yuen, BSc NU *Singapore*

[*Information supplied by the institution as at 13 November 2007, and edited by the ACU*]

NATIONAL UNIVERSITY OF SINGAPORE

Founded 1905

Member of the Association of Commonwealth Universities

Postal Address: 21 Lower Kent Ridge Road, Singapore 119077
Telephone: 6516 6666 **Fax:** 6775 7630
URL: http://www.nus.edu.sg

PRESIDENT*—Shih, Prof. Choon-Fong, MS *Harv.*, PhD *Harv.*
PROVOST—Tan, Prof. Chorh Chuan, MB BS *Sing.*, MMed(IntMed) NU *Singapore*, PhD NU *Singapore*, FACP, FRACP, FRCP, FRCPEd
DEPUTY PRESIDENT (ADMINISTRATION)‡—Mullinix, Joseph P., BA *Georgetown*, MBA *Chic.*
CHIEF EXECUTIVE OFFICER, NUS ENTERPRISE—Chan, Lily, BA *Agnes Scott*, PhD *Ill.*
VICE-PRESIDENT (CAMPUS INFRASTRUCTURE)—Yong, Prof. K. Y., PBM, BEng *Sheff.*, PhD *Sheff.*
VICE PRESIDENT (RESEARCH/LIFE SCIENCES)—Wong, Prof. E. L. John, MB BS, FRCPEd
VICE-PRESIDENT (UNIVERSITY AND GLOBAL RELATIONS)—Loh, Y. K. Lawrence, BBA NU *Singapore*, PhD *M.I.T.*
VICE-PRESIDENT (HUMAN RESOURCES)—Cho, Daniel, BSc NU *Singapore*
VICE PROVOST (ACADEMIC PERSONNEL)—Lai, Prof. C. H., BA *Chic.*, MS *Chic.*, PhD *Chic.*
VICE PROVOST (EDUCATION)—Kong, Prof. L. L. Lily, BA NU *Singapore*, MA NU *Singapore*, PhD *Lond.*
DIRECTOR (FINANCE)—Prasad, Ajith, BSc *Sing.*, MSc *Lond.*

GENERAL INFORMATION

History. The university traces its roots to 1905, when Singapore's first centre of higher education, King Edward VII College of Medicine, was established.

The main campus at Kent Ridge is located about 12km from the city centre.

Admission to first degree courses. Singapore–Cambridge General Certificate of Education (GCE) A level exam, or GCE A level/Higher School Certificate (HSC) exam, conducted by UK, Brunei, Hong Kong, Maldivian or Mauritius examination boards, or HSC exam (conducted by the Malaysian Examinations Syndicate in collaboration with the Cambridge Local Examinations Syndicate), or Sijil Tinggi Persekolahan Malaysia (STPM) (conducted by the Malaysian Examinations Council). Other qualifications which satisfy matriculation requirements in the student's home country are usually acceptable.

First Degrees (see also Singapore Directory to Subjects of Study) (* = with honours). BA*, BA, BA(Arch), BA(ID), BApplSc*, BApplSc, BBA*, BBA, BComp, BComp*, BDS, BEng, BSc*, BSc, BSc(Bldg), BSc(Pharm), BSc(Pharm)*, BSc(RealEst), BSocSci*, BTech*, LLB, MB BS.

Length of course. Full-time: BA: 2–5 years; BComp: 3 years; BApplSc, BBA*, BComp*, BSc(Pharm)*, BSc*, LLB: 4 years; BA(Arch), BA*, BApplSc*, BBA, BSc, BSc(Pharm), BSocSci*: 5 years; MB BS: 5–8 years; BA(ID), BEng: 6 years; BDS, BSc(Bldg), BSc(RealEst): 7 years. *Part-time:* BTech*: 4 years.

Higher Degrees (see also Singapore Directory to Subjects of Study). *Master's.* LLM, MA, MA(ApplLing), MA(ChineseStud), MA(EngStud), MArch, MA(SEAsianStud), MA(UrbanDesign), MBA,

MCL, MClinEmbry, MComp, MDS(Endodontics), MDS(Oral&MaxillofacialSurg), MDS(Orthodontics), MDS(Periodontology), MDS(Prosthodontics), MEng, MMed(Anaesth), MMed(DiagnosticRadiology), MMed(FamilyMed), MMed(IntMed), MMed(ObstandGynae), MMed(OM), MMed(Ophthalmology), MMed(Orl), MMed(OrthSurg), MMed(Paed), MMed(PH), MMed(Psychiatry), MMed(Surg), MNursing, MPA, MPharm(ClinPharm), MPM, MPP, MSc, MSc(ApplFin), MSc(AppliedPhysics), MSc(Bldg), MSc(BldgSc), MSc(ChemEng), MSc(CivilEng), MSc(Computing), MSc(ConstructionLaw&Arbitration), MSc(ElectEng), MSc(EnvEng), MSc(EnvironmentalMgt), MSc(EstMgt), MSc(FinEng), MSc(Ind&SysEng), MSc(Maths), MSc(MatSciEng), MSc(Mechatronics), MSc(MechEng), MSc(MgtofTech), MSc(Mktg), MSc(Pharm), MSc(Physics), MSc(ProjectMgt), MSc(RealEst), MSc(SHE), MSc(Stats), MSc(TranspSys&Mgt), MSocSci, MSocSci(ApplEcons), MSocSci(Econs), MSocSci(IntStud), MSocSci(SocialWork), MTech.

Admission. Applicants for admission to coursework programmes must hold a good bachelor's degree in the relevant discipline and, in some cases, should also have a period of relevant work experience. Research programmes: a relevant bachelor's degree with at least second class honours and the ability to pursue research in the proposed field.

Length of course. Full-time: MA(UrbanDesign), MArch, MBA, MCL, MClinEmbry, MDS(Endodontics), MDS(Oral&MaxillofacialSurg), MDS(Orthodontics), MDS(Periodontology), MDS(Prosthodontics), MMed(OM), MMed(PH), MPA, MPharm(ClinPharm), MPM, MSc(ApplFin), MSc(BldgSc), MSc(Computing), MSc(EnvironmentalMgt), MSc(FinEng),

MSc(Ind&SysEng), MSc(Maths), MSc(MgtofTech), MSc(Mktg), MSc(Physics), MSc(ProjectMgt), MSc(RealEst), MSc(Stats), MTech: 1 year; MSc(ChemEng), MSc(CivilEng), MSc(ElectEng), MSc(EnvEng), MSc(MatSciEng), MSc(Mechatronics), MSc(MechEng), MSc(SHE): 1–2 years; LLM, MA, MA(ApplLing), MA(ChineseStud), MA(EngStud), MA(SEAsianStud), MComp, MEng, MSc, MSc(Bldg), MSc(EstMgt), MSc(Pharm), MSc(TranspSys&Mgt), MSocSci, MSocSci(ApplEcons), MSocSci(Econs), MSocSci(IntStud), MSocSci(SocialWork): 1–3 years; MSc(AppliedPhysics): 1–4 years; MNursing: 1½ years; MPP, MSc(ConstructionLaw&Arbitration): 2 years. *Part-time:* MSc(Physics), MSc(Stats): 1–4 years; MSc(Maths): 1½–3 years; MSc(FinEng): 1½–4 years; MSc(EnvironmentalMgt): 2 years; MBA, MPA, MPharm(ClinPharm), MPM, MSc(ChemEng), MSc(CivilEng), MSc(ElectEng), MSc(EnvEng), MSc(MatSciEng), MSc(Mechatronics), MSc(MechEng), MSc(SHE), MSc(TranspSys&Mgt): 2–4 years; MArch, MDS(Endodontics), MDS(Oral&MaxillofacialSurg), MDS(Orthodontics), MDS(Periodontology), MDS(Prosthodontics): 3 years; MA(ApplLing), MA(ChineseStud), MA(EngStud), MA(SEAsianStud), MSocSci(ApplEcons), MSocSci(Econs), MSocSci(IntStud), MSocSci(SocialWork): 4 years.

Doctoral. DSurg, PhD.

DLitt, DSc, LLD: based on published work. *Length of course.* Full-time: DSurg, PhD: 2–5 years.

Libraries. Volumes: 2,372,172. Periodicals subscribed to: 12,976. Other holdings: 11,171 electronic journals; 27,423 media programmes; 13,631 microfilms; 11,542 microfiches; 25,772 electronic resource titles. Special collections: Singapore company reports; Singapore/Malaysia.

Statistics. Students (2005–2006): full-time 22,108 (10,781 men, 11,327 women); part-time 986 (691 men, 295 women); undergraduate 22,751 (11,109 men, 11,642 women); master's 5607 (3585 men, 2022 women); doctoral 2605 (1687 men, 918 women).

FACULTIES/SCHOOLS

Arts and Social Sciences
Tel: 6516 3986 Fax: 6777 0751
    E-mail: fasdean@nus.edu.sg
Dean: Tan, Tai Yong, BA *NU Singapore*, MA *NU Singapore*, PhD *Camb.*

Business
Tel: 6516 3075 Fax: 6779 1365
    E-mail: bizdean@nus.edu.sg
Dean: Earley, Prof. Christopher P., BA *Knox(Ill.)*, MA *Ill.*, PhD *Ill.*

Computing
Tel: 6516 4782 Fax: 6775 7451
    E-mail: comdean@nus.edu.sg
Dean: Joxan, Prof. Jaffar, BSc *Melb.*, MSc *Melb.*, PhD *Monash*

Dentistry
Tel: 6772 4988 Fax: 6778 5742
    E-mail: dendox2@nus.edu.sg
Dean: Tan, Keson B. C., BDS *Sing.*, MSD *Wash.*, FDSRCSEd, FAMS

Design and Environment
Tel: 6516 3475 Fax: 6777 3953
    E-mail: sdedean@nus.edu.sg
Dean: Cheong, Prof. H. F., BEng *Sing.*, MS *Cinc.*, PhD *Colorado State*

Engineering
Tel: 6516 2142 Fax: 6775 0120
    E-mail: engdean@nus.edu.sg
Dean: Ramakrishna, Prof. Seeram, BEng *And.*, MTech *IIT Madras*, PhD *Camb.*, FIMMM, FIE(Sing), FIMechE

Integrative Sciences and Engineering, NUS Graduate School for
Tel: 6516 1480 Fax: 6464 1148
    E-mail: bchbh@nus.edu.sg
Executive Director: Halliwell, Prof. Barry, BA *Oxf.*, DPhil *Oxf.*, DSc *Lond.*

Law
Tel: 6516 3631 Fax: 6779 0979
    E-mail: lawdean@nus.edu.sg
Dean: Tan, Prof. C. H., LLB *NU Singapore*, LLM *Camb.*

Medicine
Tel: 6516 8745 Fax: 6778 5743
    E-mail: medbox5@nus.edu.sg
Dean: Wong, Prof. John E. L., MB BS, FRCPEd

Music, Yong Siew Toh Conservatory of
Tel: 6516 1107 Fax: 6872 6915
    E-mail: conservatory@nus.edu.sg
Director: Aitken, Eugene A., PhD *Oregon*

Public Policy, Lee Kuan Yew School of
Tel: 6516 3500 Fax: 6777 7020
    E-mail: kishore_mahbubani@nus.edu.sg
Dean: Mahbubani, Kishore, BA *Sing.*, MA *Dal.*, Hon. PhD *Dal.*

Science
Tel: 6516 3333 Fax: 6777 4279
    E-mail: scidean@nus.edu.sg
Dean: Tan, Prof. E. C., BSc *NU Singapore*, MS *Yale*, PhD *Yale*

University Scholars Programme
Tel: 6516 4613 Fax: 6773 1012
    E-mail: uspdir@nus.edu.sg
Director: Pang, Peter Y. H., BSc *Tor.*, PhD *Ill.*

ACADEMIC UNITS

Architecture
Tel: 6516 3452 Fax: 6779 3078
    E-mail: akisec@nus.edu.sg
Bonollo, Elivio, BE *Melb.*, MEngSc *Melb.*, PhD *Melb.*   Visiting Prof.
Boucharenc, Christian, MA *Kobe*, PhD *Kobe*   Asst. Prof.
Bozovic-Stamenovic, Ruzica, MSci *Belgrade*, DrSci *Belgrade*   Asst. Prof.
Chan, Yew Lih, MA *York(UK)*   Assoc. Prof.; Deputy Head (Admin. and Finance)
Cheah, Kok Ming, BArch *NU Singapore*, BA(ArchStud) *NU Singapore*   Sr. Lectr.
Hee, Limin, BArch *NU Singapore*, BA(ArchStud) *NU Singapore*, MA(Architecture) *Harv.*, DDes *Harv.*   Asst. Prof.
Heng, Chye Kiang, PhD *Calif.*   Prof.; Head*
Lai, Chee Kien, BArch *NU Singapore*, BA(ArchStud) *NU Singapore*, MArch *NU Singapore*, PhD *Calif.*   Asst. Prof.
Lim, Joseph Ee Man, BArch *NU Singapore*, MSc *Strath.*, PhD *H-W*   Assoc. Prof.; Deputy Head (Academic)
Low, Boon Liang, BArch *NU Singapore*, MSc *Pratt*   Sr. Lectr.; Dir., MAUD Programme
Ong, Boon Lay, BArch *Auck.*, MArch *Auck.*, PhD *Camb.*   Sr. Lectr.
Sakamoto, Tsuto, BE *Tokyo Sci.*, ME *Waseda*, MS *Col.*   Asst. Prof.
Tan, Beng Kiang, BArch *NU Singapore*, MArch *Calif.*, PhD *Harv.*   Asst. Prof.
Tan, Boon Thor, BArch *NU Singapore*, BA(ArchStud) *NU Singapore*   Asst. Prof.
Tan, Milton, BA *Nott.*, BArch *Nott.*, PhD *Harv.*   Assoc. Prof.
Tay, Kheng Soon   Prof.†
Teh, Kem Jin, BSc *Belf.*, MSc *Belf.*   Assoc. Prof.; Dir., BAID Programme
Tse, Swee Ling   Assoc. Prof.
Viray, Erwin J. S., BS *Philippines*, ME *Kyoto I.T.*, PhD *Tokyo*   Asst. Prof.
Widodo, Johannes, MArch *Leuven*, PhD *Tokyo*   Asst. Prof.
Wittkopf, Stephen K., DrIng *T.U.Darmstadt*   Asst. Prof.
Wong, Bobby Chong Thai, MDesSt *Harv.*   Assoc. Prof.; Deputy Head (Res.)
Wong, Yunn Chii, AB *Wash.*, BS *Wash.*, MArch *Wash.*, PhD *M.I.T.*   Assoc. Prof.
Yang, Perry Pei-Ju, MS *M.I.T.*, MSc *Natnl.Taiwan*, PhD *Natnl.Taiwan*   Asst. Prof.
Yen Ching-Chiuan, PhD *C.England*, MA *Manc.Met.*   Asst. Prof.
Other Staff: 2 Fellows; 3 Sr. Tutors; 5 Adjunct Assoc. Profs.†; 6 Adjunct Asst. Profs.†
Research: Asian cities; Asian modernity; furniture design; industrial design; sustainable urban development and ecology

Bioengineering
Tel: 6516 1610 Fax: 6872 3069
    E-mail: biesec@nus.edu.sg
Buist, M. L., BEng *Auck.UT*, PhD *Auck.UT*   Asst. Prof.
Chen, N. G., BS *Hunan*, MS *Peking*, PhD *Tsinghua*   Asst. Prof.
Feng, S. S., MEng *Tsinghua*, PhD *Col.*   Assoc. Prof.
Goh, J. C. H., BSc *Strath.*, PhD *Strath.*   Assoc. Prof.
Han, Ming-Yong, BSc *Jilin*, MSc *Jilin*, PhD *Jilin*   Asst. Prof.
Huang, Z. W., BS *Fujian Normal*, MS *Fujian Normal*, PhD *Nan.Tech.*   Asst. Prof.
Hutmacher, D. W., BA *T.H.Aachen*, MS *T.H.Aachen*, MBA *Henley*, PhD *NU Singapore*   Asst. Prof.
Lee, Taeyong, MS *Wis.*, PhD *Wis.*, BS   Asst. Prof.
Li, J., BS *Sichuan*, MS *Osaka*, PhD *Osaka*   Asst. Prof.
Li, X. P., BEng *Guangxi*, MEng *Guangxi*, PhD *NSW*   Assoc. Prof.
Lim, C. T., BEng *NU Singapore*, PhD *Camb.*   Assoc. Prof.
Lim, K. M., BEng *NU Singapore*, MEng *NU Singapore*, MS *Stan.*, PhD *Stan.*   Asst. Prof.

Low, Hong Tong, BEng *Sheff.*, MEng *McG.*, PhD *McG.*   Assoc. Prof.
Ong, S. H., BE *W.Aust.*, PhD *Syd.*   Assoc. Prof.
Phan, T. T., PhD *NU Singapore*, MD   Asst. Prof.
Raghunath, Michael, MD *Mainz*, DrHabil *Mün.*   Assoc. Prof.
Roy, R., BEng *W.Bengal UT*, MSc *Oklahoma*, PhD *N.Y.State*   Asst. Prof.
Schantz, Jan-Thorsten, MD *Freib.*, PhD *NU Singapore*   Asst. Prof.
Sheppard, C. J. R., BA *Camb.*, MA *Camb.*, PhD *Camb.*   Prof.; Head*
Toh, S. L., BSc *Strath.*, PhD *Strath.*   Assoc. Prof.
Tong, Y. W., BSc *Qu.*, PhD *Tor.*   Asst. Prof.
Trau, D. W., MSc *Aix-la-Chapelle*, PhD *HKUST*   Asst. Prof.
Zhang, Y., BS *Zhejiang*, PhD *Zhejiang*   Asst. Prof.
Other Staff: 26 Res. Staff; 1 Adjunct Prof.; 1 Adjunct Assoc. Prof.; 2 Adjunct Asst. Profs.

Biological Sciences
Tel: 6516 2692 Fax: 6779 2486
    E-mail: dbsleesc@nus.edu.sg
Anand, G. S., BPharm *BITS*, MS *BITS*, PhD *Rutgers*   Asst. Prof.
Chan, W. K., BSc *NU Singapore*, PhD *NU Singapore*   Assoc. Prof.
Chew, F. T., BSc *Ag.U.Malaysia*, PhD *NU Singapore*   Asst. Prof.
Chou, L. M., BSc *Sing.*, PhD *Sing.*   Prof.
Chung, Maxey C. M., BSc *Well.*, MSc *Well.*, PhD *Well.*   Assoc. Prof.
Ding, Jeak Ling, BSc *Wales*, PhD *Lond.*   Prof.
Ge, R., BSc *Nankai*, PhD *Penn.*   Assoc. Prof.
Gong, Z., BSc *Qingdao Oceanol.*, PhD *McG.*   Assoc. Prof.
Han, J. H., BSc *Beijing*, PhD *Wash.*   Asst. Prof.
He, Y., BSc *Hunan Agric.*, MSc *Chinese Acad.Sc.*, PhD *Kentucky*   Asst. Prof.
Hew, C. L., MSc *S.Fraser*, PhD *Br.Col.*   Prof.; Head*
Hong, Y., BSc *Wuhan*, PhD *Gött.*   Assoc. Prof.
Ip, Y. K., BSc *Minn.*, MA *Rice*, PhD *Rice*   Prof.
Kini, M. R., BSc *Mys.*, MSc *Mys.*, PhD *Mys.*   Prof.
Kumar, P. P., BSc *Mys.*, MSc *Madr.*, PhD *Calg.*   Assoc. Prof.
Lam, T. J., BSc *Br.Col.*, PhD *Br.Col.*   Emer. Prof.
Leung, K. Y., BSA *Sask.*, MSc *Sask.*, PhD *Guelph*   Assoc. Prof.
Li, D., BSc *Hubei*, MSc *Huazhong Agric.*, PhD *Cant.*   Assoc. Prof.
Lim, T. M., BSc *NU Singapore*, PhD *Camb.*   Assoc. Prof.
Liou, Y. C., BSc *Natnl.Taiwan*, MSc *Natnl.Taiwan*, PhD *Qu.*   Asst. Prof.
Loh, C. S., BSc *Nan.*, MSc *Sing.*, PhD *Camb.*   Assoc. Prof.
Low, B. C., BSc *Otago*, PhD *Otago*   Assoc. Prof.
Meier, R., MSc *New Orleans*, PhD *Cornell*   Assoc. Prof.
Melamed, P., MSc *Tel-Aviv*, PhD *Tel-Aviv*   Asst. Prof.
Mok, Y. K., BSc *HK Baptist*, MPhil *Chinese HK*, PhD *Camb.*   Asst. Prof.
Ng, H. H., BSc *Sing.*, PhD *Edin.*   Asst. Prof.
Ng, P. K. L., BSc *NU Singapore*, PhD *NU Singapore*   Prof.
Ong, Bee Lian, BSc *Sing.*, MSc *NU Singapore*, DrRerNat *T.H.Darmstadt*   Asst. Prof.
Pan, S. Q., BSc *Wuhan*, MSc *Beijing*, PhD *Kentucky*   Assoc. Prof.
Sheu, F. S., BS *Natnl.Taiwan*, MS *Northwestern*, PhD *Northwestern*   Assoc. Prof.
Sivaraman, J., BSc *B'thidasan.*, MSc *B'thidasan.*, PhD *Anna*   Asst. Prof.
Sodhi, N., BSc *Panjab*, MSc *Panjab*, PhD *Sask.*   Assoc. Prof.
Song, J., BSc *Southwest Ag.(Beibei)*, MSc *Southwest Ag.(Beibei)*, PhD *Chinese Acad.Sc.*   Asst. Prof.
Swaminathan, K., BSc *Madr.*, MSc *Madr.*, PhD *Bom.*   Assoc. Prof.
Swarup, S., BSc *Punj.Ag.*, MSc *IARI*, PhD *Flor.*   Assoc. Prof.
Tammi, Martti, BSc *Uppsala*, PhD *Uppsala*   Asst. Prof.
Tan, Benito C., BSc *Far Eastern*, MSc *Philippines*, PhD *Br.Col.*   Assoc. Prof.

Tan, H. T. W., BSc Sing., PhD NU Singapore
Assoc. Prof.
Tan, T. K., BSc Sing., PhD NU Singapore   Assoc.
Prof.
Wang, S., BSc Fudan, MSc Zhejiang, PhD
Gothenburg   Assoc. Prof.
Wenk, Markus, BS Basle, PhD Basle   Asst. Prof.
Wong, S. M., BSc Nan., MS Virginia, PhD Cornell
Prof.
Yang, Daiwen, BSc Wuhan, MSc Jilin, PhD
Chinese Acad.Sc.   Assoc. Prof.
Yao, Shaoqin, BSc Ohio, PhD Purdue   Assoc.
Prof.
Yeoh, Hock Hin, BSc Malaya, MSc Malaya, PhD
ANU   Assoc. Prof.
Yu, Hao, BEng Shanghai Jiaotong, MSc Shanghai
Jiaotong, PhD NU Singapore   Asst. Prof.
Other Staff: 1 Lectr.; 45 Res. Fellows; 30
Assoc./Asst./Adjunct Profs.
Research: biodiversity; biotechnology; cell,
molecular and developmental biology;
structural biology and proteomics

Building

Tel: 6516 5150 Fax: 6775 5502
E-mail: bdgsec@nus.edu.sg
Chan, Philip C. F., LLB Lond., LLM Lond., PhD
Lond.   Assoc. Prof.; Deputy Head (Admin.
and Finance); Programme Dir., MSc
(Construcn. Law and Dispute Resolution)
Chan, Swee Lean, BSc(Bldg) Sci.U.Malaysia,
MSc(IndEng) NU Singapore, PhD NU Singapore
Asst. Prof.
Cheong, David K. W., BEng Lough., PhD Nott.
Assoc. Prof.; Programme Dir., BSc(Bldg)
and BSc (Project and Facilities
Management)
Chew, Michael Y. L., BBldg NSW, MEngSc Syd.,
PhD NSW   Assoc. Prof.
Goh, Bee Hua, BSc(Bldg) NU Singapore,
MSc(Bldg) NU Singapore, PhD Lond.   Asst.
Prof.
Lee, Siew Eang, BSc H-W, MSc H-W, PhD H-W
Assoc. Prof.; Head, Energy and
Sustainability Unit
Lim, Guan Tiong, BSc CNAA, PhD Lanc.   Sr.
Lectr.
Ling, Yean Yng (Florence), BSc(Bldg) NU
Singapore, MSc(Int'lConstrMgt) Nan.Tech., PhD
NU Singapore   Assoc. Prof.; Programme Dir.,
BSc(Bldg) (part-time) and BBldg (CME)
Low, Sui Pheng, BSc(Bldg) NU Singapore,
MSc(Eng) Birm., PhD Lond.   Prof.
Ofori, George, BSc Kumasi, MSc Lond., PhD Lond.,
DSc Lond.   Prof.; Head*
Raphael, Benny, BTech IIT Madras, MS IIT
Madras, PhD Strath.   Asst. Prof.
Sekhar, S. C., BE Raj., PhD Adel.   Assoc. Prof.;
Dir. for External Relations
Tan, Willie C. K., BSurv Newcastle(NSW),
MSc(EstMgt) NU Singapore, PhD Syd.   Assoc.
Prof.; Programme Dir., MSc (Project
Management)
Teo, Evelyn A. L., BBldg NSW, PhD NSW
Asst. Prof.
Tham, Kwok Wai, BEng NU Singapore, MBldg
Syd., PhD Syd.   Assoc. Prof.; Deputy Head
(Res.)
Wong, Nyuk Hien, BSc(Bldg) NU Singapore,
MSc(BldgSc) NU Singapore, PhD Carnegie-Mellon
Assoc. Prof.; Deputy Head (Academic);
Programme Dir., MSc(BldgSc)
Other Staff: 2 Adjunct Profs.; 7 Adjunst Assoc.
Profs.; 1 Adjunct Asst. Prof.
Research: construction management and
economics; total building performance

Business Policy

Tel: 6516 3050 Fax: 6779 5059
E-mail: bsphead@nus.edu.sg
Chandran, Ravi, LLB NU Singapore, LLM Camb.
Assoc. Prof.
Chung, Jaiho, BA Seoul, PhD Harv.   Asst. Prof.
Davis, Rachel, BA B'lore., MA J.Nehru U., MBA
Ill., PhD Ill.   Assoc. Prof.
Delios, Andrew, BBA Manit., MBA Manit., PhD
W.Ont.   Assoc. Prof.; Head*

Fang, Christina H. F., BAcc Nan.Tech., PhD Penn.
Asst. Prof.
Hwang, Peter, BA Fujen, MBA Chengchi, PhD
Mich.   Assoc. Prof.
Jo, Seung Gyu, BA Yonsei, MA Yonsei, PhD Penn.
Asst. Prof.
Lan, Luh Luh, LLB NU Singapore, LLM Camb.
Asst. Prof.
Leong, Susanna, LLB NU Singapore, LLM Lond.
Asst. Prof.
Lim, Chin, BAgricSc Malaya, MSc Br.Col., PhD
Qu.   Prof.
Lim, Kwang Hui, BEng NU Singapore, PhD M.I.T.
Asst. Prof.
Loh, Y. K. Lawrence, BBA NU Singapore, PhD
M.I.T.   Assoc. Prof.
Mahmood, Ishtiaq, BA Oberlin, PhD Harv.   Asst.
Prof.
Ouliaris, Sam, BCom Melb., MCom Melb., MA
Yale, MPhil Yale, PhD Yale   Prof.
Pangarkar, Nitin, BE Nag., MBA Delhi, PhD Mich.
Assoc. Prof.
Png, Ivan, BA Camb., PhD Stan.   Prof.
Shachat, Jason, BS Tulane, MA Arizona, PhD
Arizona   Assoc. Prof.
Singh, Kulwant, BBA NU Singapore, MBA NU
Singapore, PhD Mich.   Assoc. Prof.
Tan, Kong Yam, BA Prin., MA Stan., PhD Stan.
Prof.
Tay, Catherine S. K., LLB Lond., LLM Lond.
Assoc. Prof.
Ter, Kah Leng, LLM Brist.   Assoc. Prof.
Toh, Mun Heng, BA Sing., BSocSci Sing., MSc
Lond., PhD Lond.   Assoc. Prof.
Wang, Pien, BL Natnl.Chengchi, MBA U.S.Internat.,
DBA U.S.Internat.   Asst. Prof.
Wong, Poh Kam, BSc M.I.T., BSEE M.I.T., MSc
M.I.T., PhD M.I.T.   Assoc. Prof.
Yayavaram, Sai, BTech IIT Madras, PhD Texas,
MBA   Asst. Prof.
Other Staff: 1 Res. Officer; 1 Instr.

Chemistry

Tel: 6516 2658 Fax: 6779 1691
E-mail: chmsec@nus.edu.sg
Ang, How Ghee, BSc Malaya, MSc Malaya, MA
Camb., PhD Camb., PhD Monash, DSc NU
Singapore   Emer. Prof.
Ang, Siau Gek, BSc NU Singapore, MSc NU
Singapore, PhD Camb.   Assoc. Prof.
Bettens, Ryan P. A., BSc Qld., PhD Monash
Asst. Prof.
Chan, Hardy Sze On, BSc CNAA, PhD Manc.,
FIMMM   Prof.
Chin, Wee Shong, BSc NU Singapore, PhD NU
Singapore   Asst. Prof.
Chuah, Gaik Khuan, BSc NU Singapore, MSc NU
Singapore, PhD Texas A.& M.   Assoc. Prof.
Fan, Wai Yip, BSc Lond., PhD Camb.   Asst. Prof.
Goh, Suat Hong, BSc Nan., MSc Akron, PhD
Akron, DSc NU Singapore, FIMMM   Prof.
Harrison, Leslie J., BSc Glas., PhD Glas.   Assoc.
Prof.
Hor, Andy T. S., BSc Lond., DPhil Oxf., DSc
Lond., FRSChem   Prof.; Head*
Huang, Dejian, BSc Fujian Normal, MSc Chinese
Acad.Sc., PhD Indiana   Asst. Prof.
Huang, Hsing Hua, BSc Malaya, MSc Malaya,
DPhil Oxf., DSc NU Singapore   Emer. Prof.
Jaenicke, Stephan, BSc Cologne, MSc Karlsruhe,
PhD Karlsruhe   Assoc. Prof.
Kang, Hway Chuan, BS Yale, PhD Cal.Tech.
Assoc. Prof.
Kasapis, Stefan, BSc Salonika, MSc Lond., PhD
Cran.   Assoc. Prof.
Khoo, Soo Beng, BSc Sci.U.Malaysia, PhD Alta.
Assoc. Prof.
Khor, Eugene, BSc Lakehead, PhD Virginia Polytech.
Assoc. Prof.
Kiang, Ai Kim, BSc Lond., PhD Camb.   Emer.
Prof.
Lai, Yee Hing, BSc Nan., PhD Vic.(BC)   Assoc.
Prof.
Lam, Yulin, BSc NU Singapore, PhD NU Singapore
Asst. Prof.
Lear, Martin J., BSc Glas., PhD Glas.   Asst. Prof.
Lee, Hian Kee, BSc Cant., PhD Cant.   Prof.

Leong, Weng Kee, BA Camb., MSc NU Singapore,
PhD S.Fraser   Assoc. Prof.
Li, Sam F. Y., BSc Lond., PhD Lond., DSc Lond.
Prof.
Li, Tianhu, BSc Jilin, MSc Beijing I.C.T., PhD N.Y.
Assoc. Prof.
Loh, Kian Ping, BSc NU Singapore, DPhil Oxf.
Assoc. Prof.
Lu, Yixin, BSc Fudan, PhD McG.   Asst. Prof.
Popovich, David G., BSc Tor., MSc Tor., PhD
Br.Col.   Asst. Prof.
Sim, Wee Sun, BSc NU Singapore, PhD Camb.
Asst. Prof.
Siow, Kok Siong, BSc Nan., MSc S.Fraser, PhD
McG.   Assoc. Prof. Fellow
Tan, Choon Hong, BSc NU Singapore, PhD Camb.
Asst. Prof.
Toh, Chee Seng, BSc NU Singapore, MSc NU
Singapore, PhD S'ton.   Asst. Prof.
Valiyaveettil, Suresh, BSc Calicut, MSc Calicut,
MTech IIT Delhi, PhD Vic.(BC)   Asst. Prof.
Vittal, Jagadese J., BSc Madr., MSc Madr., PhD
IISc.   Assoc. Prof.
Wohland, Thorsten, PhD Inst.Technol., Lausanne
Asst. Prof.
Wong, Richard M. W., BSc Newcastle(NSW),
BMath Newcastle(NSW), PhD ANU   Assoc.
Prof.
Xu, Guo Qin, BS Fudan, MA Prin., PhD Prin.
Prof.
Xu, Qing-hua, BSc Zhejiang, MSc Peking, MSc
Chic., PhD Calif.   Asst. Prof.
Xue, Feng, BSc Tsinghua, PhD Chinese HK   Asst.
Prof.
Yao, Shaoqin, BSc Ohio, PhD Purdue   Asst. Prof.
Yip, John H. K., BSc HK, PhD HK   Assoc. Prof.
Zhou, Weibiao, BSc Beijing I.C.T., MEng Chinese
Acad.Sc., PhD Qld.   Assoc. Prof.
Other Staff: 4 Visiting Profs.; 3 Lectrs.; 1 Sr.
Res. Fellow; 3 Res. Fellows; 2 Visiting
Fellows; 1 Instr.; 1 Adjunct Prof.; 7 Adjunct
Assoc. Profs.; 1 Adjunct Sr. Res. Fellow
Research: analytical science; computation,
modelling and spectroscopy; medicinal
chemistry and chemical biology; molecular
design, structure and synthesis; surface,
materials and catalysis

Chinese Studies

Tel: 6516 3900 Fax: 6779 4167
E-mail: chssec@nus.edu.sg
Lee, C. H., BA NU Singapore, MEd Ohio, MA NU
Singapore, PhD NU Singapore   Asst. Prof.
Lee, C. L., BA NU Singapore, MA NU Singapore,
MA Ill., PhD Ill.   Assoc. Prof.
Lee, C. Y., BA HK, MPhil HK, PhD ANU   Assoc.
Prof.; Head*
Lin, P. Y., BA Fujen, MA Lond., MA Kent, MPhil
Camb., PhD Lond.   Asst. Prof.
Liu, H., BA Xiamen, MA Fudan, PhD Ohio
Assoc. Prof.
Lo, Y. K., MA Mich., PhD Mich., MA   Asst.
Prof.
Neo, P. F., BA NU Singapore, MA NU Singapore,
PhD Calif.   Asst. Prof.
Ng, Daisy S. Y., BA HK, MA Chinese HK, MA
Stan., MPhil HK, PhD Harv.   Asst. Prof.
Ong, C. W., BA NU Singapore, MA NU Singapore,
PhD Harv.   Asst. Prof.
Shi, Y. Z., BA Lanzhou, MA Huazhong U.S.T., MA
Calif., PhD Stan.   Asst. Prof.
St. André, J. G., BA Boston, MA Chic., PhD Chic.
Asst. Prof.
Su, J. L., BA Tunghai, MA Wash., PhD Wash.
Assoc. Prof.
Wee, L. H., BA NU Singapore, MA NU Singapore,
PhD Rutgers   Asst. Prof.
Wong, S. K., BA Natnl.Taiwan, MA Indiana, PhD
Indiana   Assoc. Prof.
Wu, Gabriel Y. C., BA NU Singapore, MA NU
Singapore, MA Wash., PhD Wash.   Asst. Prof.
Xiao, C., MA People's, China, MA Wash., PhD
Wash.   Assoc. Prof.
Xu, J., BA Henan, MA Huazhong Normal, MA
Hawaii, PhD Maryland   Assoc. Prof.
Yung, S. S., BA HK, MA Prin., MPhil HK, PhD
Prin.   Assoc. Prof.
Other Staff: 1 Sr. Tutor; 1 Postdoctoral Fellow;
3 Visiting Fellows

Research: Chinese grammar; Chinese intellectual history; classical Chinese literature; history and culture of Southeast Asian Chinese

Communications and New Media Programme

Tel: 6516 4670 Fax: 6779 4911
E-mail: cnmsec@nus.edu.sg
Cho, Hichang, BA Korea, MA Mich.State, PhD Cornell   Asst. Prof.
Chung, Peichi, BA Tunghai, MA Ohio, PhD Indiana   Asst. Prof.
Lim, Sun Sun, BSocSci NU Singapore, MSc Lond., PhD Lond.   Asst. Prof.
Rivera, Milagros, BA Puerto Rico, MA Flor., PhD Flor.   Assoc. Prof.; Head*
Shim, Doobo, BA Korea, MA Wis., PhD Wis.   Asst. Prof.
Sreekumar, T. T., BA Kerala, MA Kerala, MPhil J.Nehru U., PhD HKUST   Asst. Prof.
Other Staff: 1 Visiting Sr. Fellow; 6 Instrs.
Research: Asian new media industry; game studies; ICT development and adoption; ICT regulation and policy; new media studies

Computer Science

Tel: 6516 2726 Fax: 6779 7465
E-mail: tanps@comp.nus.edu.sg
Abhik, Roychoudhury, PhD N.Y.State   Asst. Prof.
Ananda, A. L., BE B'lore., MTech IIT Kanpur, MSc Manc., PhD Manc.   Assoc. Prof.
Bressan, Stephane, MSc Lille, PhD Lille   Sr. Lectr.
Chakraborty, Samarjit, PhD   Asst. Prof.
Chan, Chee Yong, BSc NU Singapore, MSc NU Singapore, PhD   Asst. Prof.
Chan, Mun Choon, BSc Purdue, MSc Col., MPhil Col., PhD Col.   Asst. Prof.
Chang, Ee Chien, BSc NU Singapore, MSc NU Singapore, PhD N.Y.   Asst. Prof.
Cheng Holun, Alan, BSc MPhil PhD   Asst. Prof.
Chin, Wei Ngan, BSc Manc., MSc Manc., PhD Lond.   Assoc. Prof.
Chionh, E. W., BSc Nan., MMath Wat., PhD Wat.   Assoc. Prof.
Chua, Tat Seng, BSc Leeds, PhD Leeds   Prof.
Dong, J. S., BInfTech Qld., PhD Qld.   Assoc. Prof.
Fang Chee Hung, Anthony, BSc NU Singapore, MSc Brown, PhD Brown   Asst. Prof.
Heng, A. K., BSc Nan., MSc Nantes, PhD Toulouse   Sr. Lectr.
Henz, M., MSc N.Y.State, PhD Saar   Assoc. Prof.
Hsu, David, BSc Br.Col., PhD Stan.   Asst. Prof.
Hsu, Wynne, BSc NU Singapore, MS Purdue, PhD Purdue   Assoc. Prof.
Huang Zhiyong, BEng Tsinghua, MEng Tsinghua, PhD E.T.H.Zürich   Asst. Prof.
Jaffar, Joxan, BSc Melb., MSc Melb., PhD Monash   Prof.
Jain, Sanjay, BTech Kharagpur, MSc Roch., PhD Roch.   Prof.; Head*
Jarzabek, S., MSc Warsaw, PhD Warsaw   Assoc. Prof.
Kalnis, Panagiotis, PhD HKUST   Asst. Prof.
Kan Min Yen, BS Col., MS Col., PhD Col.   Asst. Prof.
Kankanhalli, M. S., BTech Kharagpur, MS Rensselaer, PhD Rensselaer   Prof.
Khoo, Siau Cheng, BSc NU Singapore, MSc NU Singapore, MS Yale, MPhil Yale, PhD Yale   Assoc. Prof.
Lee, W. S., BE Qld., PhD ANU   Assoc. Prof.
Lee Wong Li, Janice, BSc NU Singapore, MSc NU Singapore, PhD NU Singapore   Asst. Prof.
Leong, Hon Wai, BSc Malaya, PhD Cornell   Assoc. Prof.
Leong, Tze Yun, PhD M.I.T.   Assoc. Prof.
Leow, W. K., BSc NU Singapore, MSc NU Singapore, PhD Texas   Assoc. Prof.
Ling, T. W., BSc Nan., MMath Wat., PhD Wat.   Prof.
Low, Kok Lim, BSc NU Singapore, MSc NU Singapore, PhD N.Carolina   Asst. Prof.
Mitra, Tulika, PhD N.Y.State   Asst. Prof.

Ng Hwee Tou, BSc Tor., MS Stan., PhD Texas   Assoc. Prof.
Niederreiter, Harald, PhD Vienna   Prof.
Ong Ghim Hwee, BSc Nan., MSc Nan., MSc Lond., PhD Lough.   Sr. Lectr.
Ooi, B. C., BSc Monash, PhD Monash   Prof.
Ooi Wei Tsang, BSc NU Singapore, PhD Cornell   Asst. Prof.
Pazhamaneri Subramanian, Thiagarajan, PhD Rice   Prof.
Pung, H. K., BSc Kent, PhD Kent   Assoc. Prof.
Sim Mong Cheng, Terence, SB M.I.T., MSc Stan., PhD Carnegie-Mellon   Asst. Prof.
Sulzmann, Martin, PhD Yale   Asst. Prof.
Sung Wing Kin, Ken, BSc HK, PhD HK   Asst. Prof.
Tan, C. L., BSc NU Singapore, MSc Sur., PhD Virginia   Assoc. Prof.
Tan, K. L., BSc NU Singapore, MSc NU Singapore, PhD NU Singapore   Assoc. Prof.
Tan, S. H. G., BSc NU Singapore, MSc Manc., PhD Manc.   Sr. Lectr.
Tan Sun Teck, BSc Nan., MSc Essex, PhD Essex   Sr. Lectr.
Tan Tiow Seng, PhD Ill.   Assoc. Prof.
Tay, Yong Chiang, BSc Sing., MS Harv., PhD Harv.   Prof.
Teh, H. C., BSc Natnl.Taiwan, MSc Wat., PhD McM.   Assoc. Prof.
Teo, Y. M., BTech Brad., MSc Manc., PhD Manc.   Assoc. Prof.
Tung Kum Hoe, Anthony, BSc NU Singapore, MSc NU Singapore, PhD S.Fraser   Asst. Prof.
Wang Ye, BEng S.China U.T., MSc T.U.Berlin, DrIng Tampere   Asst. Prof.
Wong, Lim Soon, BSc Lond., MSc Penn., PhD Penn.   Prof.
Wong, Weng Fai, BSc NU Singapore, MSc NU Singapore, DrEngSc Tsukuba   Assoc. Prof.
Xing Chaoping, BSc Anhui, MSc, PhD China U.S.T.   Assoc. Prof.
Yap, Hock Chuan Roland, BSc Monash, MSc Monash, PhD Monash   Assoc. Prof.
Yuen, C. K., BSc Alta., MSc Tor., PhD Syd.   Prof.
Other Staff: 4 Visiting Profs.; 3 Lectrs.; 2 Sr. Tutors; 2 Sr. Fellows; 16 Res. Fellows; 1 Instr.
Research: algorithms; computational learning theory; database; graphics; medical informatics

Decision Sciences

Tel: 6516 3067 Fax: 6779 2621
E-mail: dscsec@nus.edu.sg
Ang, James S. K., BSc Sing., MASc Wat., PhD Wat.   Assoc. Prof.
Brah, Shaukat A., BSc Lahore UET, MSc Iowa, PhD Houston   Assoc. Prof.
Chou, Fee Seng, BSc Cant., PhD Cant.   Assoc. Prof.; Head*
Chou, Mabel Cheng-Feng, BSc Natnl.Taiwan, MSc Northwestern, PhD Northwestern   Asst. Prof.
Chu-Chun-Lin, Singfat, BSc Qu., PhD Br.Col.   Assoc. Prof.
Goh, Mark K. H., BSc Adel., MBA Deakin, PhD Adel.   Assoc. Prof.
Hsiao, Rueylin, BSc Natnl.Taiwan I.T., MSc Warw., MPhil Cran., PhD Warw.   Asst. Prof.
Hui, Tak Kee, BSc Nan., MMath Wat., PhD Tor.   Assoc. Prof.
Hum, Sin Hoon, BCom Newcastle(NSW), BE Newcastle(NSW), PhD Calif.   Assoc. Prof.
Hwarng, Brian H., BS Tunghai, MS Missouri, PhD Arizona State   Assoc. Prof.
Ou, Jihong, BS Zhengzhou I.T., MS Chinese Acad.Sc., MS Mass., PhD M.I.T.   Assoc. Prof.
Quek, Ser Aik, BSc Manc., MS M.I.T., PhD Calif.   Assoc. Prof.
Sim, Melvyn S. S., BEng NU Singapore, MEng NU Singapore, PhD M.I.T.   Asst. Prof.
Sok, Pek Hooi, BSc Lond., MSc Lond., MSc NU Singapore, PhD M.I.T.   Asst. Prof.
Sum, Chee Chuong, BEng NU Singapore, PhD Minn.   Assoc. Prof.
Sun, Jie, BS Tsinghua, MS Chinese Acad.Sc., MS Wash., PhD Wash.   Prof.

Teo, Chung Piaw, BSc NU Singapore, PhD M.I.T.   Assoc. Prof.
Teo, Thompson S. H., BEng NU Singapore, MSc NU Singapore, PhD Pitt.   Assoc. Prof.
Ye, Hengqing, BSc S.China U.T., MSc S.China U.T., PhD HKUST   Asst. Prof.
Other Staff: 1 Visiting Prof.; 1 Res. Fellow; 3 Adjunct Assoc. Profs.

Economics

Tel: 6516 3941 Fax: 6775 2646
E-mail: ecssec@nus.edu.sg
Abeysinghe, T., BA Ceyl., MSc Colombo, MA Thammasat, PhD Manit.   Assoc. Prof.
Blomqvist, A. G., PhD Prin.   Prof.
Chakraborty, I., PhD Ill.   Assoc. Prof.
Chander, P., PhD I.Stat.I.   Prof.; Head*
Chang, Youngho, BAgricSc Seoul, MA Yonsei, PhD Hawaii   Asst. Prof.
Chia, Ngee Choon, BA NU Singapore, BSocSci NU Singapore, MA W.Ont., PhD W.Ont.   Assoc. Prof.
Chin, A. T. H., BA CNAA, MA Leeds, PhD Macq.   Assoc. Prof.
Chung, W., BA Seoul, PhD Texas A.& M.   Asst. Prof.
Cremers, E. T., BA Kentucky, PhD Minn.   Asst. Prof.
Donoghue, Mark, BA Auck., MA Auck., PhD Syd.   Asst. Prof.
Hu, Albert Guangzhou, BA Nankai, PhD Brandeis   Assoc. Prof.
Hui, Weng Tat, BEc Tas., MEc ANU, PhD ANU   Assoc. Prof.
Hur, J., BA Songang, MA Songang, MSc Wis., PhD Wis.   Asst. Prof.
In, Y., BA Seoul, PhD Brown   Asst. Prof.
Kang, C. H., BA Seoul, MA Seoul, PhD Cornell   Asst. Prof.
Kapur, B. K., BSocSci Sing., MA Stan., PhD Stan.   Prof.
Kim, J., PhD Yale   Asst. Prof.
Lee, J., BA Seoul, MA Seoul, PhD Cornell   Asst. Prof.
Lim, B. T., BA Sing., BSc Sing., MPhil Oxf., PhD Calif.   Sr. Lectr.
Lim, K. L., BA Sing., BSocSci Sing., MA Car., PhD Sing.   Sr. Lectr.
Lin, Mau-Ting, PhD Boston   Asst. Prof.
Liu, Haoming, BEc Beijing, MA W.Ont., PhD W.Ont.   Asst. Prof.
Lu, Jingfeng, PhD S.Calif.   Asst. Prof.
Park, Cheolbeom, BA Seoul, MA Seoul, PhD Mich.   Asst. Prof.
Park, Cheolsung, BA Yonsei, MA Yonsei, PhD Penn.   Asst. Prof.
Poddar, Sougata, BStat I.Stat.I., MStat I.Stat.I., PhD Louvain   Asst. Prof.
Premaratne, H. A. G., BSc Colombo, MSc Ill., PhD Ill.   Asst. Prof.
Riyanto, Y. E., BSc Gadjah Mada, MA Leeds, MSc Leuven, PhD Leuven   Asst. Prof.
Saha, Souresh, BStat I.Stat.I., MStat I.Stat.I., PhD Minn.   Asst. Prof.
Seevaratnam, V., PhD Lond.   Asst. Prof.
Shin, Jang-Sup, BA Seoul, MPhil Camb., PhD Camb.   Assoc. Prof.
Sun, Y., PhD Ill.   Prof.
Tay, B. N., BCom Nan., MA Tor., PhD Hawaii   Assoc. Prof.
Thangavelu, S. M., BA Winn., MA Qu., PhD Qu.   Assoc. Prof.
Tong, Sarah, PhD Calif.   Asst. Prof.
Tongzon, J. L., BA Manila, MA Manila, PhD Tas.   Assoc. Prof.
Tsui, A. K. C., BSSc Chinese HK, MS Kentucky, PhD Kentucky   Assoc. Prof.
Wilson, P. R. D., BA Exe., PhD Warw.   Assoc. Prof.
Wong, W. K., BSc Chinese HK, MSc Wis., PhD Wis.   Assoc. Prof.
Wong, Wei K., BSocSci NU Singapore, PhD Calif.   Asst. Prof.
Wright, J., PhD Stan.   Assoc. Prof.
Xing, X., BA Beijing, MA Pitt., PhD Pitt.   Assoc. Prof.
Zeng, J., BSc Xiamen, MA Xiamen, PhD W.Ont.   Assoc. Prof.

Zhang, J., PhD W.Ont. Assoc. Prof.
Other Staff: 1 Emer. Prof.; 1 Visiting Prof.; 1 Visiting Assoc. Prof.; 1 Sr. Tutor; 1 Sr. Fellow; 4 Res. Fellows; 2 Visiting Fellows; 1 Postdoctoral Fellow
Research: education; financial economics; growth theory and development (Asia); labour economics; microeconomics, macroeconomics and econometrics (core areas, game theory, industrial organisation)

Engineering, Chemical and Biomolecular

Tel: 6516 2186 Fax: 6779 1936
E-mail: chehead@nus.edu.sg
Birgersson, K. E., MSc R.I.T.Stockholm, PhD R.I.T.Stockholm Asst. Prof.
Chen, S. B., BSc Tsinghua, MSc Natnl.Taiwan, PhD Cornell Assoc. Prof.
Chiu, M. S., BSc Natnl.Taiwan, PhD Georgia I.T. Assoc. Prof.
Chung, N. T. S., BSc Chung Yuan, MSc Natnl.Taiwan, PhD N.Y.State Prof.
Farooq, S., BSc B'desh.Engin., MSc B'desh.Engin., PhD New Br. Prof.
Favelukis, M., BSc Haifa(Technion), MS Haifa(Technion), DSc Haifa(Technion) Asst. Prof.
Feng, S., BSc Peking, MSc Tsinghua, PhD Col. Assoc. Prof.
Foo, S. C., BSc Cheng Kung, MSc Cinc., MEng Asian I.T., Bangkok, PhD Qld. Assoc. Prof. Fellow
Garland, M. V., BSc Penn.State, MSc Northwestern, PhD E.T.H.Zürich Assoc. Prof.
Hidajat, K., BSc UMIST, PhD Camb. Assoc. Prof.
Hong, L., BSc Xiamen, MSc Xiamen, PhD N.Y.State Assoc. Prof.
Jiang, J. W., BEng E.China U.S.T., PhD E.China U.S.T. Asst. Prof.
Kang, E. T., BA Nebraska, BSc Wis., MSc N.Y.State, PhD N.Y.State Prof.
Karimi, I. A., BTech IIT Bombay, MSc Purdue, PhD Purdue Assoc. Prof.
Kawi, S., BSc Texas, MSc Ill., PhD Delaware Assoc. Prof.
Krantz, W. B., BSc Ill., PhD Calif., BA Isaac M. Meyer Prof.
Krishnaswamy, P. R., BSc Ban., PhD New Br. Assoc. Prof. Fellow
Lee, D. Y., BSc Yonsei, MSc Korea A.I.S.T., PhD Korea A.I.S.T. Asst. Prof.
Lee, J. Y., BSc Sing., MSE Mich., PhD Mich. Prof.
Li, Z., BSc Nanjing, MEng Nanjing, PhD Vienna Assoc. Prof.
Liu, B., BSc Nanjing, MSc Nanjing, PhD NU Singapore Asst. Prof.
Loh, K. C., BEng NU Singapore, MEng NU Singapore, MSCEP M.I.T., PhD M.I.T. Assoc. Prof.
Neoh, Koon Gee, BSc M.I.T., ScD M.I.T. Prof.
Rajagopalan, R., BTech IIT Madras, MSc Syr., PhD Syr. Prof.; Head*
Rangaiah, G. P., BTech And., MTech IIT Kanpur, PhD Monash Assoc. Prof.
Saeys, M., BEng Ghent, MEng Ghent, PhD Ghent Asst. Prof.
Samavedham, L., BEng BITS, MSc IIT Madras, PhD Alta. Asst. Prof.
Srinivasan, M. P., BTech Madr., MS Calif., PhD Calif. Assoc. Prof.
Srinivasan, R., BTech IIT Madras, PhD Purdue Assoc. Prof.
Tan, R. B. H., BSc Lond., MEng NU Singapore, PhD Camb. Assoc. Prof.
Tan, T. C., BE Otago, PhD UMIST Prof. Fellow
Ti, H. C., BSc Natnl.Cheng Kung, PhD Leeds Sr. Lectr.
Ting, Y. P., BSc UMIST, MSc UMIST, PhD Monash Assoc. Prof.
Tong, Y. W., BSc Qu., PhD Tor. Asst. Prof.
Trau, D. W., MSc Aix-la-Chapelle, PhD HKUST Asst. Prof.
Uddin, M. S., BSc B'desh.Engin., MSc UMIST, PhD UMIST Assoc. Prof.
Wang, C. H., BSc Natnl.Taiwan, MSc Johns H., MA Prin., PhD Prin. Assoc. Prof.

Yang, K. L., BSc Natnl.Taiwan, MSc Natnl.Taiwan, PhD Georgia I.T. Asst. Prof.
Yap, Miranda G. S., BSc Sing., MSc Lond., PhD Tor. Prof.
Yung, L. Y., BEng Minn., PhD Delaware Asst. Prof.
Zeng, H. C., BSc Xiamen, PhD Br.Col. Assoc. Prof.
Zhao, G. X. S., BSc Shandong, PhD Qld. Assoc. Prof.
Other Staff: 15 Res. Fellows; 3 Postdoctoral Fellows; 2 Instrs.; 8 Res. Engineers; 4 Professl. Officers
Research: biomolecular and biomedical engineering; chemical and biological systems engineering; chemical engineering sciences; functionalised and nanostructured materials and devices

Engineering, Civil

Tel: 6516 2149 Fax: 6779 1635
E-mail: cvehgm@nus.edu.sg
Ang, K. K., BEng Sing., MEng NU Singapore, PhD NSW Assoc. Prof.
Babovic, V., MSc T.H.Delft, PhD T.H.Delft Assoc. Prof.
Balendra, T., BSc(Eng) S.Lanka, MEng Asian I.T., Bangkok, PhD Northwestern Prof.
Chan, E. S., BEng Sing., MEng NU Singapore, ScD M.I.T. Prof.; Head*
Chan, W. T., BEng Sing., MEng NU Singapore, MSc Stan., PhD Stan. Assoc. Prof.; Programme Dir., Infrastructure Systems and Management Group
Cheong, H. F., BEng Sing., MS Cinc., PhD Colorado State Prof.
Cheu, R. L., BEng NU Singapore, MEng NU Singapore, PhD Calif. Assoc. Prof.
Chew, S. H., BEng NU Singapore, MEng NU Singapore, MS Calif., PhD Calif. Asst. Prof.
Chin, H. C., BEng Sing., MEng NU Singapore, PhD S'ton. Assoc. Prof.; Deputy Head, Undergrad. Studies
Choo, Y. S., BSc Manc., MSc Manc., PhD Manc., FIMarEST, FRINA, FASCE Assoc. Prof.; Dir., Centre for Offshore Res. and Engin.; Programme Dir., Coastal and Offshore Engin.
Chow, Y. K., BSc Manc., MSc Manc., PhD Manc. Prof.
Chua, D. K. H., BE Adel., MEng NU Singapore, MSc Calif., PhD Calif. Assoc. Prof.
Fwa, T. F., BEng Sing., MASc Wat., PhD Purdue Prof.; Dir., Centre for Transportation Res.
Koh, C. G., BEng Sing., MEng NU Singapore, MS Calif., PhD Calif. Prof.
Lee, D. H., BBA Tamkang, MS Natnl.Central(Taiwan), PhD Ill. Assoc. Prof.
Lee, F. H., BEng Monash, MEng NU Singapore, MPhil Camb., PhD Camb. Assoc. Prof.; Dir., Centre for Protective Technol.; Programme Dir., Geotech. Engin.
Lee, S. L., PBM, BSCE Mapua I.T., Manila, MSc Mich., PhD Calif., FICE Emer. Prof.
Leung, C. F., BEng Liv., PhD Liv. Assoc. Prof.
Liew, Richard J. Y., BEng NU Singapore, MEng NU Singapore, PhD Purdue Assoc. Prof.; Programme Dir., Struct. Engin.
Lin Pengzhi, BEng Tianjin, MS Hawaii, PhD Cornell Assoc. Prof.
Maalej, M., BSc Colorado State, MSc M.I.T., PhD Mich. Assoc. Prof.
Meng, Q., BS E.China Normal, MSc Chinese Acad.Sc., PhD HKUST Asst. Prof.
Ong, G. K. C., BEng Sing., PhD Dund. Assoc. Prof.; Deputy Head, Infrastructure and Resources
Phoon, K. K., BEng NU Singapore, MEng NU Singapore, PhD Cornell Assoc. Prof.; Dir., Centre for Soft Ground Engin.
Quek, S. T., BE Monash, MEng NU Singapore, MS Ill., PhD Ill. Prof.; Deputy Head, Postgrad. Studies
Swaddiwudhipong, S., BEng Chulalongkorn, MEng Asian I.T., Bangkok, PhD HK Prof.
Tan, K. H., BEng Tokyo I.T., MEng NU Singapore, DrEng Tokyo Assoc. Prof.
Tan, S. A., BEng Auck., MEng NU Singapore, MSc Calif., PhD Calif. Assoc. Prof.

Tan, Prof. T. S., BE Cant., MSc Cal.Tech., PhD Cal.Tech. Assoc. Prof.
Wang, C. M., BEng Monash, MEng Monash, PhD Monash Prof.
Wee, T. H., BEng Tokyo I.T., MEng NU Singapore, DrEng Tokyo I.T. Assoc. Prof.
Yong, K. Y., PBM, BEng Sheff., PhD Sheff. Prof.
Zhang, M. H., BSc Tongji, DrIng T.U.Trondheim Assoc. Prof.; Dir., Centre for Construcn. Materials and Technol.
Other Staff: 14 Res. Fellows; 1 Teaching Fellow; 18 Res. Engineers; 4 Professl. Officers; 1 Assoc. Prof.†; 1 Asst. Prof.†
Research: disaster prevention and mitigation; high-strength, lightweight and high-performance materials; novel composite structural systems; offshore and storage systems; protective structural systems

Engineering, Electrical and Computer

Tel: 6516 2109 Fax: 6779 1103
E-mail: elesec@nus.edu.sg
Abdullah, Al Mamum, BTech Kharagpur, PhD NU Singapore Asst. Prof.
Adeyeye, O. Adekunle, BSc Ilorin, MPhil Camb., PhD Camb. Assoc. Prof.
Armand, Marc A., BEng Brist., PhD Brist. Asst. Prof.
Ashraf, A. Kassim, BEng NU Singapore, MEng NU Singapore, PhD Carnegie-Mellon Assoc. Prof.
Attallah, Samir, MSc Bordeaux I, PhD Bordeaux I Asst. Prof.
Bae, Seongtae, BSc Kwangwoon, MSc Kwangwoon, PhD Minn. Asst. Prof.
Bharadwaj, V., BSc Madur., ME IISc., PhD IISc. Assoc. Prof.
Chan, D. S. H., BSc Manc., MSc Manc., PhD Salf. Prof.
Chang, C. S., MSc Manc., PhD Manc. Assoc. Prof.
Chen, Benmei, BS Xiamen, MS Gonzaga, PhD Wash. Prof.
Chen, Nanguang, BS Hunan, MS Peking, PhD Tsinghua Asst. Prof.
Chen, Xudong, BSc Zhejiang, MSc Zhejiang, PhD M.I.T. Asst. Prof.
Cheok, A. D., BE Adel., PhD Adel. Assoc. Prof.
Cheong, L. F., BEng NU Singapore, PhD Maryland Asst. Prof.
Chim, W. K., BEng NU Singapore, PhD NU Singapore Assoc. Prof.
Cho, Byung-Jin, PhD Korea A.I.S.T. Assoc. Prof.
Choi, W. K., BSc Edin., MBA Edin., PhD Edin. Assoc. Prof.
Chong, Tow Chong, BEng Tokyo I.T., MEng NU Singapore, ScD M.I.T. Prof.
Chor, E. F., BEng Sing., MEng NU Singapore, PhD S'ton. Assoc. Prof.
Chua, K. C., BEng Auck., MEng NU Singapore, PhD Auck. Assoc. Prof.
Chua, S. J., BEng Sing., PhD Wales Prof.
Devotta, J. B. X., BSc S.Lanka, PhD Lond. Assoc. Prof.
Garg, H. K., BTech IIT Madras, MEng C'dia., PhD C'dia. Assoc. Prof.
Ge, Suzhi, BTech Beijing Aeron.& Astron., PhD Lond. Prof.
Ha, Yajun, BSc Zhejiang, MEng NU Singapore, PhD Leuven Asst. Prof.
Hang, C. C., BEng Sing., MSc Warw., PhD Warw., FIEE Prof.
Heng, C. H., BEng NU Singapore, MEng NU Singapore, PhD Ill. Asst. Prof.
Ho, W. K., BEng NU Singapore, PhD NU Singapore Assoc. Prof.
Hong, M. H., BSc Xiamen, MSc Xiamen, MEng NU Singapore, PhD NU Singapore Asst. Prof.
Jacob, Carl C., BEng Pret., MEng Pret., PhD Pret. Assoc. Prof.
Kam, P. Y., BS M.I.T., MS M.I.T., PhD M.I.T. Prof.
Khambadkone, M. Ashwin, BE Bom., MTech IIT Kanpur, DrIng Wuppertal Asst. Prof.
Khursheed, A., BSc Edin., PhD Edin. Assoc. Prof.
Ko, C. C., BSc Lough., PhD Lough. Prof.
Kooi, P. S., BSc Natnl.Taiwan, MSc Manc., DPhil Oxf. Prof.

Lee, C. K. (Vincent), MSc Natnl.Tsing Hua, MSc Rutgers, PhD Tokyo Asst. Prof.
Lee, S. J., BEng Seoul, MEng Texas, PhD Texas Asst. Prof.
Lee, T. H., BA Camb., MEng NU Singapore, MSc Yale, PhD Yale Prof.
Leong, M. S., BSc(Eng) Lond., PhD Lond. Prof.
Li, L. W., BSc Xuzhou Normal, PhD Monash, MEng Assoc. Prof.
Li, M. F. Prof.
Lian Yong, PhD NU Singapore, BEng Assoc. Prof.
Liang, Y. C., MEng Natnl.Tsing Hua, PhD Syd. Assoc. Prof.
Liew, Ah Choy, BE Qld., PhD Qld., FIE(Sing) Prof.
Liew, Y. F. (Thomas), BSc NU Singapore, PhD Rensselaer Assoc. Prof.
Lim, K. W., BE Malaya, DPhil Oxf. Assoc. Prof.
Ling, C. H., BSc Lond., PhD Lond. Prof.
Loh, A. P., BEng Malaya, DPhil Oxf. Assoc. Prof.
Low, T. S., BSc S'ton., PhD S'ton. Prof.
Mansoor, A. Jalil, BA Camb., MA Camb., PhD Camb. Asst. Prof.
Mehul, Motani, BSEE Cooper Union, MSEE Syr., PhD Cornell Asst. Prof.
Mohan, G., MTech Kharagpur, PhD IIT Madras, BEng Asst. Prof.
Moorthi, P., BEng NU Singapore, MEng NU Singapore, PhD Calif. Asst. Prof.
Mouthaan, Koenraad, MSc T.H.Delft, PhD T.H.Delft Asst. Prof.
Nallanathan, Arumugam, BSc(Eng) S.Lanka, PhD HK Asst. Prof.
Ng, C. S., BEng Sing., MEng NU Singapore, PhD Wis. Assoc. Prof.
Ng, S. S., BSc Birm., PhD Birm. Assoc. Prof.
Ng, Vivian, BSc Lond., PhD Camb. Assoc. Prof.
Ong, K. K. W., BSc Leeds, PhD Camb. Assoc. Prof.
Ong, S. H., BE W.Aust., PhD Syd. Assoc. Prof.
Ooi, B. L., BEng NU Singapore, PhD NU Singapore Assoc. Prof.
Oruganti, R., BTech IIT Madras, MTech IIT Madras, PhD Virginia Polytech. Assoc. Prof.
Phang, Jacob C. H., BA Camb., MA Camb., PhD Camb. Prof.
Prahlad, V., BTech Calicut, MTech IIT Madras, PhD IIT Madras Asst. Prof.
Ranganath, S., BTech IIT Kanpur, ME IISc., PhD Calif. Assoc. Prof.
Sadasivan, Puthusserypady, BTech Calicut, MTech Calicut, PhD IISc. Asst. Prof.
Samudra, G. S., BSc Nag., MSc IIT Bombay, MS Purdue, PhD Purdue Assoc. Prof.
Sanjib, K. Panda, BE S.Guj., MTech Ban., PhD Camb. Assoc. Prof.
Soh, W. S., BEng NU Singapore, MEng NU Singapore, PhD Carnegie-Mellon Asst. Prof.
Srinivasan, Dipti, MEng NU Singapore, PhD NU Singapore, BE Assoc. Prof.
Srinivasan, Vikram, BSc Madr., ME IISc., PhD Calif. Asst. Prof.
Tan, K. C., BEng Glas., PhD Glas. Assoc. Prof.
Tan, K. K., BEng NU Singapore, PhD NU Singapore Assoc. Prof.
Tan, L. S., BEng Sing., MEng NU Singapore, PhD Hawaii Assoc. Prof.
Tan, W. W., BEng NU Singapore, MEng NU Singapore, DPhil Oxf. Asst. Prof.
Tay, E. B. (Arthur), BEng NU Singapore, PhD NU Singapore Asst. Prof.
Tay, T. T., BEng NU Singapore, PhD ANU Assoc. Prof.
Teo, K. L., BSc Sing., PhD Sing. Assoc. Prof.
Tham, C. K., BA Camb., MA Camb., PhD Camb. Assoc. Prof.
Thong, J. T. L., BA Camb., MA Camb., PhD Camb. Assoc. Prof.
Wang, Q. G., BEng Zhejiang, MEng Zhejiang, PhD Zhejiang Prof.
Winkler, Stefan, PhD Asst. Prof.
Wong, L. W. C., BSc Lough., PhD Lough. Prof.
Wong, W. K., BEng NU Singapore, PhD NU Singapore Asst. Prof.
Wu, Y. H., BSc Shaanxi Normal, MEng Shizuoka, PhD Kyoto Assoc. Prof.

Xiang, C., BSc Fudan, PhD Yale Asst. Prof.
Xiang, N., BSc PhD DTech Asst. Prof.
Xin, Yan, PhD Minn. Asst. Prof.
Xu, J. X., BSc Zhejiang, MEng Tokyo, PhD Tokyo Assoc. Prof.
Xu, Y. P., BSc Nanjing, PhD NSW Assoc. Prof.
Yao, Libin, BSc China U.Electronic S.T., MSc Nanjing, PhD Leuven Asst. Prof.
Yen, Shih-Cheng, BSc Penn., MSc Penn., PhD Penn. Asst. Prof.
Yeo, S. P., BA Camb., MA Camb., MEng NU Singapore, PhD Lond. Prof.; Head*
Yeo, T. S., BEng Sing., MEng NU Singapore, PhD Cant. Prof.
Yeo, Y. C., BEng NU Singapore, MEng NU Singapore, MS Calif., PhD Calif. Asst. Prof.
Yu, C. Y., BSc Tsinghua, PhD S.Calif., MSc Asst. Prof.
Zhu, C. X., BEng Xidian, MEng Xidian, PhD HKUST Asst. Prof.

Engineering, Environmental Science

Tel: 6516 3384 Fax: 6774 4202
E-mail: ese-enquiry@nus.edu.sg
Bai, R. B., BEng Chongqing, MEng Chongqing, PhD Dund. Assoc. Prof.
Balasubramanian, R., BSc Madur., MSc IIT Madras, MTech IIT Delhi, PhD Miami(Fla.) Sr. Lectr.
Chen, J. P., BSc Huaqiao, MSc Tsinghua, PhD Georgia I.T. Assoc. Prof.
He, J., BS Harbin, MS Tsinghua, PhD Georgia I.T. Asst. Prof.
Hu, J. Y., BEng Tsinghua, MEng Tsinghua, PhD Tsinghua Assoc. Prof.
Liu, Wen-Tso, BS Prov.Taipei I.T., Taiwan, MS Rutgers, MS Calif., PhD Tokyo Assoc. Prof.
Ng, H. Y., BEng Sing., MEng Sing., PhD Calif. Asst. Prof.
Ng, W. J., BSc Lond., MSc Birm., PhD Birm. Prof.
Obbard, J. P., BSc Lanc., PhD Lanc. Assoc. Prof.
Ong, S. L., BEng Sing., MESc W.Ont., PhD Tor. Prof.
Pehkonen, S. O., BSc Oregon State, PhD Cal.Tech. Assoc. Prof.
Song, Lianfa, BS Peking, MS Peking, PhD Calif. Assoc. Prof.
Yeo, T. S., BEng Sing., MEng Sing., PhD Cant. Prof.; Head*
Yu, Liya, BSc Natnl.Cheng Kung, MSc Stan., PhD Stan. Asst. Prof.
Other Staff: 1 Visiting Prof.; 8 Res. Fellows; 1 Res. Engineer

Engineering, Industrial and Systems

Tel: 6516 2203 Fax: 6777 1434
E-mail: isesec@nus.edu.sg
Ang, B. W., BSc Nan., PhD Camb. Prof.; Head*
Chai, K. H., BEng Tech.U.Malaysia, MEng S.Aust., PhD Camb. Asst. Prof.
Chew, E. P., BEng NU Singapore, MEng NU Singapore, MS Georgia I.T., PhD Georgia I.T. Assoc. Prof.
Goh, T. N., BE Sask., PhD Wis. Prof.
Huang, H. C., BS Natnl.Taiwan, MA Yale, MS Yale, MPhil Yale, PhD Yale Assoc. Prof.
Ibrahim, Y., BEng Sing., MSc NU Singapore, PhD Stan. Assoc. Prof.
Jaruphongsa, W., BEng Chulalongkorn, MSc S.Calif., PhD Texas A.& M. Asst. Prof.
Lee, C. U., BS Seoul, MS Seoul, PhD Penn.State Asst. Prof.
Lee, L. H., BSc Natnl.Taiwan, MSc Harv., PhD Harv. Assoc. Prof.
Ng, K. M., BSc NU Singapore, MS Stan., PhD Stan. Asst. Prof.
Ng, S. H., BS Mich., MS Mich., PhD Mich. Asst. Prof.
Ong, H. L., BSc Nan., MSc Lakehead, MSc McM., PhD Wat. Assoc. Prof.
Poh, K. L., BEng NU Singapore, MEng NU Singapore, MS Stan., PhD Stan. Assoc. Prof.
Tan, K. C., BS Mass., MS Mass., PhD Virginia Polytech. Assoc. Prof.

Tang, L. C., BEng NU Singapore, MEng NU Singapore, MSc Cornell, PhD Cornell Assoc. Prof.
Xie, M., MSc R.I.T.Stockholm, PhD Linköping Prof.
Yap, C. M., BEng NU Singapore, MSc Pitt., PhD Pitt. Sr. Lectr.
Other Staff: 2 Sr. Fellows; 6 Res. Fellows; 1 Adjunct Prof.; 4 Adjunct Assoc. Profs.; 1 Adjunct Asst. Prof.

Engineering, Mechanical

Tel: 6516 2212 Fax: 6779 1459
E-mail: mpesec@nus.edu.sg
Ang, Marcelo (Jr.) H., BSc De La Salle, MS Hawaii, MS Roch., PhD Roch. Assoc. Prof.
Chau, F. S., BSc Nott., PhD Nott. Assoc. Prof.; Deputy Head, Admin.; Group Head, Applied Mechanics
Cheng, L., BEng Tsinghua, MSc Tsinghua, PhD Tsinghua Assoc. Prof.
Chew, C. H., BEng NU Singapore, MSME Georgia I.T., PhD Georgia I.T. Assoc. Prof.
Chew, C. M., BEng NU Singapore, MEng NU Singapore, SM M.I.T., PhD M.I.T. Asst. Prof.
Chew, Y. T., BE W.Aust., MEngSc W.Aust., PhD Camb., FIE(Sing) Prof.; Deputy Dir., ORE; Group Head, Fluid
Chou, S. K., BEng NU Singapore, DrIng École Nat.Sup.d'Arts & Métiers, Paris, FIE(Sing) Prof.; Vice-Dean, EIR; Group Head, Energy and Biothermal
Fuh, J. Y. H., BSc Natnl.Chiao Tung, MBA Natnl.Taiwan, MSc Calif., PhD Calif. Assoc. Prof.
Gibson, I., BSc Hull, PhD Hull Assoc. Prof.
Gupta, M., BEng Nag., MEng IISc., PhD Calif. Assoc. Prof.; Group Head, Materials Sci.
Hong, G. S., BEng Sheff., PhD Sheff. Assoc. Prof.
Khoo, Boo Cheong, BA Camb., MEng NU Singapore, PhD M.I.T. Prof.
Lai, M. O., BEng Auck., MEng Auck., PhD Auck. Assoc. Prof.
Lee, H. P., BA Camb., MA Camb., MEng NU Singapore, MS Stan., PhD Stan. Assoc. Prof. (on leave)
Lee, K. S., BSc Manc., MSc Manc., PhD Manc. Assoc. Prof.
Lee, T. S., BEng NSW, PhD NSW Assoc. Prof.; Deputy Head, Academic
Leng, G. S. B., BSc Ill., MSc Ill., PhD Ill. Assoc. Prof.
Li, X. P., BEng Guangxi, MEng Guangxi, PhD NSW Assoc. Prof. (Joint appointment with Bioengineering)
Lim, C. T., BEng NU Singapore, PhD Camb. Assoc. Prof. (Joint appointment with Bioengineering)
Lim, Christina Y. H., BEng NU Singapore, PhD NU Singapore Asst. Prof.
Lim, K. B., BEng NU Singapore, DrIng École Centrale des A.& M. Assoc. Prof.; Dir., DSTA/ NUS/SUPELEC ONERA Joint Res. Lab.; Dir., NUS Enterprise
Lim, K. M., BEng NU Singapore, MEng NU Singapore, MS Stan., PhD Stan. Asst. Prof. (Joint appointment with Bioengineering)
Lim, L. C., BSc Nan., MSc Leeds, PhD Cornell Assoc. Prof.
Lim, S. C., BA Oxf., MA Oxf., MEng NU Singapore, PhD Camb., FIMechE, FIMMM Prof.; Head*
Lim, S. P., BSc NU Singapore, MSc S'ton., PhD S'ton. Assoc. Prof.
Lim, T. T., BEng Melb., PhD Melb. Assoc. Prof.
Liu, G. R., BEng Hunan, MEng Beijing Aeron.& Astron., PhD Tohoku Assoc. Prof.; Dir., ACES; President, SACM
Loh, H. T., BEng Adel., MEng NU Singapore, MS Mich., PhD Mich. Assoc. Prof.; Deputy Head, Special Projects
Low, Hong Tong, BEng Sheff., MEng McG., PhD McG. Assoc. Prof. (Joint appointment with Bioengineering)
Lu Li, BEng Tsinghua, MEng Tsinghua, PhD Leuven Prof.

Lu Wenfeng, BS *Tennessee*, MS *N.Y.*, PhD *Minn.* Assoc. Prof.

Luo, S. C., BEng *Melb.*, MEng *NU Singapore*, PhD *Lond.* Assoc. Prof.

Mujumdar, Arun S., BChemEng *Bom.*, MEng *McG.*, PhD *McG.*, FCIC, FASME, FIIChE, FIE(Sing)   Prof.

Nee, Andrew Y. C., MSc *Manc.*, PhD *Manc.*, DEng *UMIST*   Prof.; Dir., ORE

Ng, K. C., BSc *Strath.*, PhD *Strath.*   Prof.

Ong, C. J., BEng *NU Singapore*, MEng *NU Singapore*, MSE *Mich.*, PhD *Mich.*   Assoc. Prof.; Group Head, Control

Ong, S. K., BEng *NU Singapore*, PhD *NU Singapore* Assoc. Prof.

Poo, A. N., BEng *NU Singapore*, MSc *Wis.*, PhD *Wis.*, FIE(Sing)   Prof.; Dir., BTech Programmes

Quan, Chenggen, BEng *Harbin*, MEng *Harbin*, PhD *Warw.*   Assoc. Prof.

Rahman, M., BEng *B'desh.Engin.*, MEng *Tokyo I.T.*, DrEng *Tokyo I.T.*   Prof.

Ramakrishna, Seeram, BEng *And.*, MTech *IIT Madras*, PhD *Camb.*, FIMMM, FIE(Sing), FIMechE   Prof.; Co-Dir., NUSNNI

Seah, K. H. (Major), BSc *S'ton.*, MSc *Qu.*, PhD *Qu.*   Assoc. Prof.; Group Head, Manufacturing

Senthil Kumar, A., BEng *Anna*, MEng *Anna*, PhD *NU Singapore*   Assoc. Prof.

Shah, Dilip A., BSc *Baroda*, BTech *M.I.T.*, MEng *IISc.*, PhD *Newcastle(NSW)*   Sr. Lectr.

Shim, Victor P. W., BE *Auck.*, MEng *NU Singapore*, PhD *Camb.*   Prof.; Deputy Head, Outreach

Shu Chang, BEng *Nanjing Aeron.& Astron.*, MEng *Nanjing Aeron.& Astron.*, PhD *Glas.*   Prof.

Sinha, S. K., BSc *R.I.T.Stockholm*, MSc *IISc.*, PhD *Lond.*   Asst. Prof.

Subramaniam, Velusamy, BEng *NU Singapore*, MEng *NU Singapore*, SM *M.I.T.*, PhD *M.I.T.* Asst. Prof.

Tan, Vincent B. C., BEng *NU Singapore*, MEng *NU Singapore*, PhD *Northwestern*   Asst. Prof.

Tay, Andrew A. O., BEng *NSW*, PhD *NSW*, FIE(Sing), FASME   Prof.

Tay, C. J., BSc *Strath.*, PhD *Strath.*   Assoc. Prof.

Tay, Francis E. H., BEng *NU Singapore*, MEng *NU Singapore*, PhD *M.I.T.*   Assoc. Prof.

Tay, T. E., BEng *Melb.*, PhD *Melb.*   Assoc. Prof.

Teo, C. L., BEng *NU Singapore*, MEng *NU Singapore*, PhD *Calif.*   Assoc. Prof.; Dir., NUS Overseas Coll. (on leave)

Teoh, S. H., BEng *Monash*, PhD *Monash*   Prof.

Thamburaja, P., BEng *Lond.*, SM *M.I.T.*, PhD *M.I.T.*   Asst. Prof.

Thoroddsen, S. T., BSc *Iceland*, MSc *Colorado State*, PhD *Calif.*   Assoc. Prof.

Toh, S. L., BSc *Strath.*, PhD *Strath.*   Assoc. Prof.; Deputy Head, Bioengin.

Vedantam, S., BTech *IIT Madras*, MSc *Penn.State*, ScD *M.I.T.*   Asst. Prof.

Wijeysundera, N. E., BScEng *Ceyl.*, MSc *Birm.*, PhD *Birm.*, FASME   Prof. Fellow†

Winoto, S. H., BSc *Lond.*, MSc *Lond.*, PhD *Lond.* Assoc. Prof.

Wong, Y. S., BEng *NU Singapore*, MEng *NU Singapore*, PhD *UMIST*   Assoc. Prof.

Yap, C., BESc *W.Ont.*, MEng *NU Singapore*, PhD *Manc.*   Assoc. Prof.; Asst. Dean, Undergrad. Programmes

Yeo, K. S., BEng *Auck.*, MEng *NU Singapore*, PhD *Camb.*   Assoc. Prof.; Deputy Head, Res.

Zeng, K. Y., BSc *Hunan*, PhD *R.I.T.Stockholm* Asst. Prof.

Zhang, Y. F., BEng *Shanghai Jiaotong*, PhD *Bath* Assoc. Prof.

Zhou, G. Y., BEng *Zhejiang*, PhD *Zhejiang*   Asst. Prof.

Other Staff: 2 Sr. Tutors; 5 Res. Fellows; 1 Visiting Sr. Fellow; 1 Visiting Sr. Scientist; 2 Adjunct Assoc. Profs.; 10 Adjunct Asst. Profs.; 2 Assoc. Prof. Fellows†

Research: advanced manufacturing; biomechanical engineering; defence; energy; innovative materials

Engineering Science Programme

Tel: 6516 5408 Fax: 6775 4710
   E-mail: engsharm@nus.edu.sg

Baaquie, B. E., BS *Cal.Tech.*, PhD *Cornell*   Assoc. Prof.

Birgersson, K. E., MSc *R.I.T.Stockholm*, PhD *R.I.T.Stockholm*   Asst. Prof.

Goh, S. S., BA *Oxf.*, MS *Mich.*, PhD *Mich.* Assoc. Prof.

Ho, G. W., BSc *NU Singapore*, MSc *NU Singapore*, PhD *Camb.*   Asst. Prof.

Khursheed, A., BSc *Edin.*, PhD *Edin.*   Assoc. Prof.; Deputy Head, Academic

Mujumdar, Arun S., BChemEng *Bom.*, MEng *McG.*, PhD *McG.*, FCIC, FASME, FIIChE, FIE(Sing)   Prof.; Deputy Head, Res.

Pang, S. D., BEng *NU Singapore*, MEng *NU Singapore*, PhD *Northwestern*   Asst. Prof.

Reddy, J. N., BEng *Osm.*, MS *Oklahoma State*, PhD *Alabama*   Prof.; Head*

Sheppard, C. J. R., BA *Camb.*, MA *Camb.*, PhD *Camb.*   Prof.

Wang, C. M., BEng *Monash*, MEng *Monash*, PhD *Monash*   Prof.; Deputy Head, Admin. and Grad. Studies

Watt, F., BSc *Newcastle(UK)*, PhD *Newcastle(UK)* Prof.

Wee, Andrew Thye Shen, BA *Camb.*, MA *Camb.*, DPhil *Oxf.*   Prof.

Wong, M. W., BSc *Newcastle(NSW)*, BMath *Newcastle(NSW)*, PhD *ANU*   Assoc. Prof.

Yeoh, Hock Hin, BSc *Malaya*, MSc *Malaya*, PhD *ANU*   Assoc. Prof.

English Language and Literature

Tel: 6516 3914-5 Fax: 6773 2981
   E-mail: ellbox5@nus.edu.sg

Abraham, Sunita A., BA *NU Singapore*, MA *NU Singapore*, PhD *Birm.*   Asst. Prof.

Ang, Susan W. L., BA *Camb.*, MA *Camb.*, PhD *Camb.*   Asst. Prof.

Bao, Zhiming, PhD *M.I.T.*   Assoc. Prof.

Bishop, Ryan, BA *N.Texas*, MA *N.Texas*, PhD *Rice* Assoc. Prof.

Chng, Huang-Hoon, BA *NU Singapore*, MA *NU Singapore*, PhD *Texas*   Assoc. Prof.

Cruz-Ferreira, Madalena, MA *Manc.*, PhD *Manc.* Sr. Lectr.

Goh, Robbie B. H., BA *NU Singapore*, MA *NU Singapore*, PhD *Chic.*   Assoc. Prof.; Head*

Gwee, Li Sui, BA *NU Singapore*, MA *NU Singapore*, MPhil *Lond.*, PhD *Lond.*   Asst. Prof.

Ho, Chee-Lick, BA *Tianjin Normal*, MA *Kansas*, MPhil *Kansas*, PhD *Kansas*   Sr. Lectr.

Holden, Philip J., BA *Lond.*, MA *Flor.*, PhD *Br.Col.*   Assoc. Prof.

Kim, Chonghyuck, BA *Chonpuk*, MA *Chonpuk*, PhD *Delaware*   Asst. Prof.

Lazar, Michelle M., BA *NU Singapore*, MA *NU Singapore*, PhD *Lanc.*   Asst. Prof.

Lim, Walter S. H., BA *Tor.*, MA *Tor.*, PhD *Tor.* Assoc. Prof.

Loon, Robin, BA *NU Singapore*, MA *NU Singapore*, PhD *Lond.*   Asst. Prof.

Mohanan, K. P., BSc *Kerala*, MA *Meerut*, MS *M.I.T.*, PhD *M.I.T.*   Prof.

Oh, Tomasina S. S., BA *Sci.U.Malaysia*, MPhil *Camb.*, PhD *Camb.*   Asst. Prof.

O'Halloran, Kay L., BEd *W.Aust.*, PhD *Murd.* Assoc. Prof.

Ooi, Vincent B. Y., BA *NU Singapore*, MA *NU Singapore*, PhD *Lanc.*   Assoc. Prof.

Pakir, Anne, BA *Sing.*, MA *Calif.*, PhD *Hawaii* Assoc. Prof.

Pan, Daphne, BA *Sing.*, MSc *Sur.*, MA *York(Can.)*, PhD *York(Can.)*   Assoc. Prof.

Patke, Rajeev S., BA *Poona*, MA *Poona*, DPhil *Oxf.* Assoc. Prof.

Philips, John W. P., BA *N.Lond.*, MA *Sus.*, DPhil *Sus.*   Assoc. Prof.

Richardson, John A., BA *E.Anglia*, PhD *Manc.* Assoc. Prof.

Sankaran, Chitra, BA *Madr.*, MA *Madr.*, MPhil *Madr.*, PhD *Lond.*   Asst. Prof.

Seet, K. K., BA *NU Singapore*, MA *Tor.*, PhD *Exe.* Sr. Lectr.

Shen, Grant G. R., MA *Shanghai Normal*, PhD *Hawaii*   Assoc. Prof.

Talib, Ismail S., BA *Sing.*, MA *NU Singapore*, PhD *E.Anglia*   Assoc. Prof.

Tan, Peter K. W., BA *Malaya*, PhD *Edin.*   Sr. Lectr.

Thumboo, Edwin, BBM, BA *Malaya*, PhD *Sing.* Emer. Prof.; Prof. Fellow

Turner, Barnard E., BA *Br.Col.*, MA *E.Anglia*, PhD *Oregon*   Assoc. Prof.

Wee, Lionel H. A., BA *NU Singapore*, MA *NU Singapore*, MA *Calif.*, PhD *Calif.*   Assoc. Prof.

Wee, Valerie, BA *NU Singapore*, MA *NU Singapore*, PhD *Texas*   Asst. Prof.

Whalen-Bridge, John, BA *Conn.*, MA *Calif.*, PhD *S.Calif.*   Assoc. Prof.

Yeo Wei Wei, BA *York(UK)*, PhD *Camb.*   Asst. Prof.

Yeoh Guan Hin, Gilbert, BA *Harv.*, MA *Harv.*, PhD *Harv.*   Asst. Prof.

Yong, Li-Lan, BA *Oxf.*, PhD *Lond.*   Assoc. Prof.

Other Staff: 2 Postdoctoral Fellows; 3 Visiting Fellows; 1 Adjunct Asst. Prof.

Research: language (English in multilingual settings, language contact and change, language planning and policy, language variation); literature (Asian diasporas and cultural transformations, literatures and cultures in the Asia-Pacific context, postcolonial studies, writing and cultural production in English)

Finance and Accounting

Tel: 6516 3066 Fax: 6779 2083
   E-mail: fnbhead@nus.edu.sg

Chen, Renbao, BA *Anhui*, MA *Penn.*, PhD *Penn.* Assoc. Prof.

Cheng, Nam Sang, BSc *Warw.*, MSc *Lond.*, PhD *Brad.*   Asst. Prof.

Chng, Chee Kiong, BAcc *NU Singapore*, PhD *Qld.* Sr. Lectr.

Fong, Wai Mun, BSocSci *NU Singapore*, PhD *Manc.*   Assoc. Prof.

Hameed, Allaudeen, BBA *NU Singapore*, PhD *N.Carolina*   Assoc. Prof.; Head*

Ho, Yew Kee, BEc *Monash*, MSc *Carnegie-Mellon*, MEc *Monash*, PhD *Carnegie-Mellon*   Assoc. Prof.

Kang, Wenjin, BS *Peking*, MA *Calif.*, PhD *Calif.* Asst. Prof.

Kwok, Winston C. C., BBA *NU Singapore*, MBA *W.Ont.*, PhD *W.Ont.*   Asst. Prof.

Lam, Swee-Sum, BAcc *Sing.*, PhD *Wash.*   Assoc. Prof.

Lee, Inmoo, BBA *Korea*, MS *Ill.*, PhD *Ill.*   Assoc. Prof.

Li, Nan, BA *Wuhan*, MA *Wuhan*, PhD *Chic.* Asst. Prof.

Lim, Joseph Y. S., BBA *Sing.*, MBA *Col.*, MPhil *N.Y.*, PhD *N.Y.*   Assoc. Prof.

Loh, Alfred L. C., BAcc *Sing.*, MCom *NSW*, PhD *W.Aust.*   Assoc. Prof.

Low, Chee Kiat, BBA *NU Singapore*, PhD *Yale* Asst. Prof.

Mak Yuen Teen, BCom *Otago*, MCom *Otago*, PhD *Well.*   Assoc. Prof.

Mian, Mujtaba G., BCom *Punjab*, MBA *Lahore* MS, PhD *Syd.*   Asst. Prof.

Naqvi, Syed M. H., BSc *Lond.*, MSc *Lond.*, PhD *Lond.*   Assoc. Prof.

Sankaraguruswamy, Srinivasan, BCom *Osm.*, MCom *Delhi*, PhD *Purdue*   Asst. Prof.

Sequeira, John M., BSc *Ulster*, MSocSci *NU Singapore*, PhD *W.Aust.*   Asst. Prof.

Shih, Sheng-Hua Michael, BS *Natnl.Taiwan*, MS *Akron*, PhD *Minn.*   Assoc. Prof.

Srinivasan, Anand, MS *Cornell*, PhD *N.Y.*, BTech Asst. Prof.

Tan, Ruth S.-K., BAcc *NU Singapore*, MSc *Penn.State*, PhD *Wash.*   Assoc. Prof.

Wilkins, Trevor A., BCom *Qld.*, MCom *NSW*, PhD *Qld.*   Assoc. Prof.

Yamada, Takeshi, BA *Keio*, MA *Keio*, PhD *Calif.* Assoc. Prof.

Yeo, Wee Yong, BBA *NU Singapore*, MB *Indiana*, PhD *Indiana*   Asst. Prof.

Other Staff: 1 Sr. Tutor; 5 Adjunct Assoc. Profs.

Geography

Tel: 6516 3851 Fax: 6777 3091
    E-mail: geosec@nus.edu.sg
Bunnell, Timothy, BA Nott., PhD Nott.   Asst.
    Prof.
Chang Tou Chuang, BA NU Singapore, MA NU
    Singapore, PhD McG.   Assoc. Prof.
Grundy-Warr, Carl E. R., BA Leic., MA Durh.,
    PhD Durh.   Sr. Lectr.
Higgitt, David, BA Oxf., PhD Exe.   Assoc. Prof.
Huang Swee Lian, Shirlena, BA Sing., MA NU
    Singapore, PhD Tor.   Assoc. Prof.; Head*
Kong, L. L. Lily, BA NU Singapore, MA NU
    Singapore, PhD Lond.   Prof.
Lee Yong-Sook, BA Ewha, MA Ewha, PhD Rutgers
    Asst. Prof.
Lu XiXi, BSc Beijing, MSc Nanjing, PhD Durh.
    Assoc. Prof.
Raguraman, K., BA NU Singapore, MA NU
    Singapore, PhD Wash.   Assoc. Prof.
Roth, Matthias, MSc Br.Col., PhD Br.Col.   Assoc.
    Prof.
Savage, Victor R., BA Sing., MA Calif., PhD Calif.
    Assoc. Prof.
Teo Cheok Chin, Peggy, BA Sing., MA NU
    Singapore, MS Penn.State, PhD Penn.State   Assoc.
    Prof.
Wang Yi-Chen, BS Natnl.Taiwan, MS Natnl.Taiwan,
    PhD N.Y.State   Asst. Prof.
Wong Poh Poh, BA Sing., MA Sing., PhD McG.
    Assoc. Prof.
Yeoh, Brenda S. A., BA Camb., MA Camb., DPhil
    Oxf.   Prof.
Yeung Wai Chung, Henry, BA NU Singapore,
    PhD Manc.   Prof.
Other Staff: 1 Sr. Tutor; 2 Visiting Fellows
Research: critical, social and cultural geography
    of Asia (ageing, migration, tourism and
    cultural identity); environmental processes
    and change in the Tropics; implications of
    urbanisation in Asia; political economics of
    transformation in Asia

History

Tel: 6516 3838 Fax: 6774 2528
    E-mail: hissec@nus.edu.sg
Aung-Thwin, Maitrii, BA N.Illinois, PhD Mich.
    Asst. Prof.
Barnard, Timothy, BA Kentucky, MA Ohio, PhD
    Hawaii   Assoc. Prof.
Borschberg, Peter, BA Kent, PhD Camb.   Assoc.
    Prof.
Clancey, Gregory K., BA Bates, MA Boston, PhD
    M.I.T.   Assoc. Prof.
DuBois, Thomas, BA Chic., MA Calif., PhD Calif.
    Asst. Prof.
Farrell, Brian P., BA Car., MA Car., PhD McG.
    Assoc. Prof.; Deputy Head
Feener, Michael, BA Colorado, MA Boston, PhD
    Boston   Assoc. Prof.
Gordon, Ian L., BA Syd., MA Roch., PhD Roch.
    Assoc. Prof.
Huang, Jianli, BA Sing., MA NU Singapore, PhD
    ANU   Assoc. Prof.; Convenor, China
    Studies Minor Programme
Kelly, Michael, BA NE, BA Melb., PhD Melb.
    Asst. Prof.
Kudaisya, Medha M., BA Delhi, MA J.Nehru U.,
    MPhil J.Nehru U., PhD Camb.   Asst. Prof.
Lau, Albert, BA Sing., PhD Lond.   Assoc. Prof.;
    Head*
Lockhart, Bruce, BA Cornell, MA Yale, PhD Cornell
    Asst. Prof.
Murfett, Malcolm H., BA Leeds, DPhil Oxf.,
    FRHistS   Assoc. Prof.
Peleggi, Maurizio, BA Rome, MA ANU, PhD ANU
    Assoc. Prof.
Reid, Anthony, BA Well., MA Well., PhD Camb.
    Prof.
Ricklefs, Merle C., BA Colorado Coll., PhD Cornell
    Prof.
Sai, Siew Min, BA NU Singapore, PhD Mich.
    Asst. Prof.
Tan, Tai Yong, BA NU Singapore, MA NU
    Singapore, PhD Camb.   Assoc. Prof.
Teow, See Heng, BA NU Singapore, PhD Harv.
    Assoc. Prof.

Yang, Bin, BA Renmin, MA Renmin, PhD
    Northeastern   Asst. Prof.
Yong, Mun Cheong, BA Sing., MA Yale, PhD
    Sing.   Assoc. Prof.; Dir., Office of
    Programmes
Other Staff: 1 Lectr.; 1 Sr. Tutor; 1
    Postdoctoral Fellow; 1 Visiting Sr. Fellow; 2
    Visiting Fellows; 1 Adjunct Prof.; 1 Adjunct
    Assoc. Prof.
Research: American history; art history; East
    Asian history; European history; history of
    Southeast Asian

Information Systems

Tel: 6516 4368 Fax: 6779 7365
    E-mail: angcl@comp.nus.edu.sg
Bock Gee Woo, Gilbert, BA Yonsei, MBA S.Calif.,
    PhD Korea A.I.S.T.   Asst. Prof.
Chan, H. C., BA Camb., MA Camb., PhD Br.Col.
    Assoc. Prof.
Goh, Khim Yong, BSc NU Singapore, MSc NU
    Singapore, PhD Chic.   Asst. Prof.
Heng, Cheng Suang, BSc NU Singapore, MSc NU
    Singapore, PhD Stan.   Asst. Prof.
Hui, K. L., BA HKUST, PhD HKUST   Asst. Prof.
Hung, Yu-Ting (Caisy), BA Chung Yuan, MSc
    Maryland, MBA Indiana, PhD Indiana   Asst.
    Prof.
Jiang, Zhenhui (Jack), BEc Tsinghua, BEng
    Tsinghua, MBA Tsinghua, PhD Br.Col.   Asst.
    Prof.
Kankanhalli, Atreyi M., BEng IIT Delhi, MSc
    Rensselaer, PhD NU Singapore   Asst. Prof.
Kim Hee Woong, BSc Korea A.I.S.T., MSc Korea
    A.I.S.T., PhD Korea A.I.S.T.   Asst. Prof.
Lim, L. H. John, BEng NU Singapore, MSc NU
    Singapore, PhD Br.Col.   Assoc. Prof.
Pan, S. L., BSBA S.E.Missouri, MBA Texas, MA
    Lond., PhD Warw.   Asst. Prof.
Png, P. L. I., BA Camb., PhD Stan.   Chair Prof.
Poo, C. C., BSc Manc., MSc Manc., PhD UMIST
    Assoc. Prof.
Setiono, R., BSc E.Mich., MSc Wis., PhD Wis.
    Assoc. Prof.
Tan, C. Y. B., BSc NU Singapore, MSc NU
    Singapore, PhD NU Singapore   Assoc. Prof.;
    Head*
Tan, Swee Lin (Sharon), BSc NU Singapore, MSc
    NU Singapore, MSc Carnegie-Mellon, PhD Carnegie-
    Mellon   Asst. Prof.
Tang, Qian, BEng Tongji, MSc Flor., PhD Flor.
Teo, H. H., BSc NU Singapore, MSc NU Singapore,
    PhD NU Singapore   Asst. Prof.
Wei, K. K., BSc Nan., DPhil York(UK)   Prof.
Woon, Irene, BBA Sing., MSc Aston, PhD Aston
    Sr. Lectr.
Xu, Yunjie, MSc Fudan, PhD Syr.   Asst. Prof.
Yeo, G. K., BSc Sing., MMath Wat., MASc Wat.,
    PhD Wat.   Assoc. Prof.
Other Staff: 1 Chair Prof.; 4 Lectrs./Sr. Lectrs.;
    1 Lectr.; 5 Instrs.; 3 Adjunct Profs.; 1
    Adjunct Assoc. Prof.

Japanese Studies

Tel: 6516 3728 Fax: 6776 1409
    E-mail: jpssec@nus.edu.sg
Avenell, Simon A., BCom Qld., BA
    Internat.Christian(Tokyo), MA Calif., PhD Calif.
    Asst. Prof.
Lim, Beng Choo, BA NU Singapore, MA NU
    Singapore, MA Cornell, PhD Cornell   Asst. Prof.
Maclachlan, Elizabeth, BA Cornell, MA Col., PhD
    Col.   Asst. Prof.
Meyer-Ohle, Hendrik C., MA Marburg, PhD
    Marburg   Assoc. Prof.
Saito, Asato, BA St.Paul's(Tokyo), MA
    Newcastle(UK), PhD Lond.   Asst. Prof.
Terada, Takashi, LLB Doshisha, MA ANU, PhD
    ANU   Asst. Prof.
Thang, Leng Leng, BA NU Singapore, MA NU
    Singapore, PhD Ill.   Assoc. Prof.; Head*
Tsu, Yun Hui (Timothy), BA
    Internat.Christian(Tokyo), MA Prin., PhD Prin.
    Assoc. Prof. (on leave)
Other Staff: 2 Visiting Fellows
Research: Japanese-Chinese studies (Chinese
    community in Japan, cultural interactions);
    Japanese-Southeast Asian studies (mass

media, popular culture, women, work);
    modern Japan (ageing and inter-
    generational relations, civil society)

Law

Tel: 6516 1305 Fax: 6779 0979
Beckman, Robert C., BBA Wis., JD Wis., LLM
    Harv.   Assoc. Prof.
Bell, Gary F., BTh Laval, BCL McG., LLB McG.,
    LLM Col.   Assoc. Prof.
Chan, Wing Cheong, BA Oxf., MA Oxf., LLM
    Cornell   Assoc. Prof.
Chan Weng, Tracey E., LLB NU Singapore, LLM
    Harv.   Asst. Prof.
Chin, Tet Yung, LLB Lond., BCL Oxf.   Assoc.
    Prof.
Crown, Barry C., LLB Jerusalem, LLM Lond., MLitt
    Oxf.   Assoc. Prof.
Ellinger, E. P., MJur Jerusalem, DPhil Oxf.   Emer.
    Prof.
Ewing-Chow, Michael, LLB NU Singapore, LLM
    Harv.   Asst. Prof.
Fordham, Margaret, BA Durh.   Assoc. Prof.
Girvin, Stephen D., BA Natal, LLB Natal, LLM
    Natal, PhD Aberd.   Assoc. Prof.
Ho, Hock Lai, LLB NU Singapore, BCL Oxf., PhD
    Camb.   Assoc. Prof.
Ho, Peng Kee, LLB Sing., LLM Harv.   Assoc.
    Prof. (on leave)
Hor, Michael Y. M., BCL Oxf., LLB NU Singapore,
    LLM Chic.   Prof.
Hsu, Locknie, LLB NU Singapore, LLM Harv.
    Assoc. Prof.
Jayakumar, S., BBM, LLB Sing., LLM Yale   Prof.
    (on leave)
Kaan, Terry S. H., LLB NU Singapore, LLM Harv.
    Assoc. Prof.
Koh, Kheng-Lian, LLB Malaya, LLM Sing., PhD
    Sing.   Prof.
Koh, Tommy T. B., PJG, BBM, DUBC, LLB
    Malaya, LLM Harv., Hon. LLD Yale   Prof. (on
    leave)
Kumaralingam, Amirthalingam, LLB ANU, PhD
    ANU   Assoc. Prof.
Lee Tye Beng, Joel, LLB Well., LLM Harv.
    Assoc. Prof.
Leong, Wai Kum, LLB Malaya, LLM Harv.   Prof.
Li, Mei Qin, LLB Peking, LLM Col.   Assoc. Prof.
Lim, Lei Theng, LLB NU Singapore, LLM Harv.
    Asst. Prof.
Lim Chin Leng, LLB Buckingham, BCL Oxf., PhD
    Nott.   Assoc. Prof.
Loke Fay Hoong, Alexander, LLB NU Singapore,
    LLM Col.   Assoc. Prof.
Lye, Irene L. H., LLB Sing., LLM Lond., LLM
    Harv.   Assoc. Prof.
Neo, Dora S. S., BA Oxf., MA Oxf., LLM Harv.
    Assoc. Prof.
Ng, Siew Kuan, LLB Lond., LLM Camb.   Assoc.
    Prof.
Ng-Loy, Wee Loon, LLB NU Singapore, LLM Lond.
    Assoc. Prof.
Ong, Burton (Tze En), LLB NU Singapore, BCL
    Oxf., LLM Harv.   Asst. Prof.
Ong, Debbie (Siew Ling), LLB NU Singapore,
    LLM Camb.   Assoc. Prof.
Phua, Lye Huat (Stephen), LLB NU Singapore,
    LLM Lond.   Assoc. Prof.
Pinsler, Jeffrey D., LLB Liv., LLM Camb., LLD
    Liv.   Prof.
Poh, Chu Chai, LLB Sing., LLM Lond., LLD Lond.
    Assoc. Prof.
Ramraj, Victor, BA McG., LLB Tor., MA Tor.,
    PhD Tor.   Assoc. Prof.
Seng, Daniel (Kiat Boon), BCL Oxf., LLB NU
    Singapore   Assoc. Prof.
Sornarajah, M., LLB Ceyl., LLM Lond., LLM Yale,
    PhD Lond., LLD Lond.   Prof.
Tan, Alan K. J., LLB NU Singapore, LLM Yale
    Assoc. Prof.
Tan, Prof. C. H., LLB NU Singapore, LLM Camb.
    Assoc. Prof.; Head*
Tan, Seow Hon, LLB NU Singapore, LLM Harv.,
    SJD Harv.   Asst. Prof.
Tan, Terence (Bian Chye), LLB NU Singapore,
    LLM Lond.   Asst. Prof.
Tan, Yock Lin, BSc Lond., BA Oxf., BCL Oxf.
    Prof.

Tang Hang Wu, LLB NU Singapore, LLM Camb.,
PhD Camb. Asst. Prof.

Tay, S. C. Simon, LLB NU Singapore, LLM Harv.
Assoc. Prof.

Teo, Keang Sood, LLB Malaya, LLM Malaya, LLM
Harv. Assoc. Prof.

Thio, Li-Ann, BA Oxf., LLM Harv., PhD Camb.
Assoc. Prof.

Tjio, Hans, BA Camb., MA Camb., LLM Harv.
Assoc. Prof.

Wang, Jiangyu, LLB Chinese Pol.Sci.& Law, LLM
Peking, MJur Oxf., LLM Penn., SJD Penn. Asst.
Prof.

Whalen-Bridge, Helena, LLM NU Singapore, JD
Conn. Asst. Prof.

Winslow, V. S., BA Camb., LLB Camb., MA
Camb. Assoc. Prof.

Wong, Eleanor (Siew Yin), LLB NU Singapore,
LLM N.Y. Assoc. Prof.

Woon, Walter C. M., LLB NU Singapore, LLM
Camb. Prof. (on leave)

Yeo, Hwee Ying, LLB Sing., LLM Lond. Assoc.
Prof.

Yeo, Tiong Min, LLB NU Singapore, BCL Oxf.,
DPhil Oxf. Assoc. Prof.

Other Staff: 13 Tutors; 12 Legal Writing
Instrs.; 9 Adjunct Assoc. Profs.; 4 Adjunct
Asst. Profs.

Malay Studies

Tel: 6516 2635 Fax: 6773 2980
E-mail: mlssec@nus.edu.sg

Noor Aisha bte Abdul Rahman, LLB NU
Singapore, MA NU Singapore, PhD NU Singapore
Asst. Prof.

Shaharuddin, Maaruf, BSocSc Sci.U.Malaysia, MA
NU Singapore, PhD NU Singapore Assoc. Prof.;
Head*

Suriani, Suratman, BA NU Singapore, MA Monash,
PhD Bielefeld Asst. Prof.

van der Putten, Jan, BA Ley., MA Ley., PhD Ley.
Asst. Prof.

Research: Malay family and household; Malay
political culture/Malay elites; Malay/
Indonesian literature; social history of the
Malays; tradition, religion and
modernisation among the Malays

Management and Organisation

Tel: 6516 3187 Fax: 6775 5571
E-mail: obrhead@nus.edu.sg

Arvey, Richard D., BA Occidental, MS Minn., PhD
Minn. Visiting Prof.

Boyle, Elizabeth M., BA C.U.A., MBA N.Y., PhD
N.Y. Asst. Prof.

Chia, Audrey W. Y., BA NU Singapore, PhD Texas
Assoc. Prof.

Chia, Ho Beng, BA NU Singapore, PhD Br.Col.
Sr. Lectr.

Chung Chi-Nien, BSocSci Chinese Culture, MA
Tsinghua, PhD Stan. Asst. Prof.

Earley, Christopher P., BA Knox(Ill.), MA Ill.,
PhD Ill. Prof.

Foo, Maw Der, BBA NU Singapore, PhD M.I.T.
Asst. Prof.

Koh, William L. K., BBA NU Singapore, PhD
Oregon Asst. Prof.

Kowtha, Rao N., BA Osm., MBA Texas A.& M.,
PhD Texas A.& M. Assoc. Prof.

Lim, Ghee Soon, BA NU Singapore, PhD Ill.
Assoc. Prof.; Head*

Lim, Vivien K. G., BSocSci NU Singapore, PhD
Pitt. Assoc. Prof.

McAllister, Daniel J., BA Trin.W., MA Br.Col.,
PhD Calif. Assoc. Prof.

Narayanan, Jayanth, BE B'lore., PhD Lond.Bus.
Asst. Prof.

Song, Zhaoli, BA Sichuan, MS Chinese Acad.Sc., MS
Minn., PhD Minn.

Tan, Chwee Huat, BAcc NU Singapore, MBA Wis.,
MSc Wis., PhD Wis. Prof. Fellow

Teo, Albert C. Y., BA NU Singapore, BSocSci NU
Singapore, MS Calif., PhD Calif. Assoc. Prof.

Wan, David T. W., BCom W.Aust., PhD Manc.
Asst. Prof.; Deputy Head

Wu, Pei Chuan, BBus Tamkang, MBA George
Washington, PhD Manc. Asst. Prof.

Zyphur, Michael J., BSc San Diego State, MSc
Tulane, PhD Tulane Asst. Prof.

Other Staff: 1 Adjunct Assoc. Prof.; 2 Adjunct
Asst. Profs.

Marketing

Tel: 6516 3058 Fax: 6779 5941
E-mail: mkthead@nus.edu.sg

Ang, Swee Hoon, BBA NU Singapore, PhD Br.Col.
Assoc. Prof.

Chong, Juin Kuan, BSc Cant., PhD Calif.
Assoc. Prof.

Chu, Junhong, BA Beijing, MA Beijing, PhD Chic.
Asst. Prof.

Krishnan, Trichy, BE Madr., MA Texas, PhD Texas
Assoc. Prof.; Head*

Lau, Geok Theng, BBA NU Singapore, PhD W.Ont.
Assoc. Prof.; Asst. Dean (Undergrad.
Programme)

Lee, Khai Sheang, BEng Melb., PhD Tor. Assoc.
Prof.

Lee, Yih Hwai, BBA NU Singapore, PhD N.Carolina
Assoc. Prof.

Leong, Siew Meng, BBA NU Singapore, MBA
Wis., PhD Wis. Prof.

Li, Xiuping, BA Dalian U.T., MA Dalian U.T.,
PhD Tor. Asst. Prof.

Lim, Wei Shi, BSc NU Singapore, PhD Lond.
Assoc. Prof.

Rajiv, Surendra, BS Patna, MBA IIITM, MS
Carnegie-Mellon, PhD Carnegie-Mellon Prof.;
Asst. Dean (Res. and PhD Programme)

Shamdasani, Prem, BBA NU Singapore, PhD
S.Calif. Assoc. Prof.; Vice-Dean (Office of
Exec. Educn.)

Tambyah, Siok Kuan, BBA NU Singapore, PhD
Wis. Assoc. Prof.

Tan, Soo Jiuan, BBA Sing., MSc Wash.(Mo.), PhD
Wash.(Mo.) Assoc. Prof.

Wirtz, Jochen, PhD Lond., BBA Assoc. Prof.

Yeung, Catherine, BBA HKUST, PhD HKUST
Asst. Prof.

Other Staff: 2 Lectrs.

Materials Science and Engineering

Tel: 6516 1080 Fax: 6776 3604
E-mail: msesec@nus.edu.sg

Adams, S., MSc Saar, PhD Saar, DrHabil Gött.
Asst. Prof.

Blackwood, D. J., BSc S'ton., MSc S'ton., PhD
S'ton. Assoc. Prof.

Chow, G. M., BS N.Y.State, MSc Conn., PhD Conn.
Prof.; Head*

Chua, H. C. D., BSc NU Singapore, PhD Camb.
Asst. Prof.

Ding, J., BSc Wuppertal, MSc Wuppertal, PhD
Bochum Assoc. Prof.; Deputy Head, Admin.

Gong, H., BSc Yunnan, MSc Yunnan, PhD T.H.Delft
Assoc. Prof.

Li, Y., BEng Huazhong U.S.T., MEng Sheff., PhD
Sheff. Assoc. Prof.; Deputy Head, Academic

Wang, J., BSc N.W.Inst.of Light Industry, MSc Leeds,
PhD Leeds Assoc. Prof.; Deputy Head,
Academic

Xue, J. M., BSc Shanghai U.S.T., MSc Shanghai
U.S.T., PhD Shanghai U.S.T. Sr. Lectr.

Zhang, Y. W., BSc Northwestern P.U.(Xi'an), MSc
Northwestern P.U.(Xi'an), PhD Northwestern
P.U.(Xi'an) Asst. Prof.

Other Staff: 1 Asst. Prof. (joint appointment);
8 Res. Fellows; 3 Res. Engineers

Research: biotechnology; infocom technology;
nanostructures and nanostructured materials
for high density information; specific
intersection of nanotechnology and
biotechnology; sustainable energy

Mathematics

Tel: 6516 2738 Fax: 6779 5452
E-mail: matsec@nus.edu.sg

Aslaksen, H., CandMag Oslo, PhD Calif. Assoc.
Prof.

Bao, W., BSc Tsinghua, MS Tsinghua, PhD Tsinghua
Assoc. Prof.

Berrick, A. J., BSc Syd., DPhil Oxf. Prof.

Chan, H. H., BSc NU Singapore, PhD Ill. Assoc.
Prof.

Chen, L. H.-Y., BSc Sing., MS Stan., PhD Stan.
Prof.

Chew, T. S., BSc Nan., MSc Nan., PhD NU
Singapore Assoc. Prof.

Chin, C. W., BA Calif., PhD Prin. Asst. Prof.

Choi, K. P., BSc HK, MSc Ill., PhD Ill. Assoc.
Prof.

Chong, C. T., BS Iowa State, PhD Yale Prof.

Chu, D., BSc Tsinghua, MSc Tsinghua, PhD
Tsinghua Assoc. Prof.

Chua, S. K., BSc NU Singapore, MSc NU Singapore,
PhD Rutgers Assoc. Prof.

Dai, M., BSc Suzhou, MPhil HK Poly., PhD Fudan
Asst. Prof.

Goh, S. S., BA Oxf., MS Mich., PhD Mich.
Assoc. Prof.

Karthik, N., BEng Natnl.Taiwan, PhD Sing., PhD
M.I.T. Asst. Prof.

Koh, K. M., BSc Nan., MSc Manit., PhD Manit.
Prof.

Kong, Y., BS Tsinghua, MS Chinese Acad.Sc., PhD
Wash. Asst. Prof.

Lang, M. L., PhD Ohio State Assoc. Prof.

Lawton, Wayne M., BA Wesleyan, PhD Wesleyan
Assoc. Prof.

Lee, S. L., BSc Malaya, MSc Malaya, PhD Alta.
Prof.; Head*

Lee, S. T., BSc NU Singapore, PhD Yale Assoc.
Prof.

Leong, Y. K., BSc Sing., PhD ANU Assoc. Prof.

Leung, D. H. H., BS Illinois State, PhD Ill.
Assoc. Prof.

Leung, F. P. F., BA HK, MA York(Can.), MS Notre
Dame(Ind.), PhD Notre Dame(Ind.) Assoc.
Prof.

Leung, K. H., BSc HK, PhD Calif. Assoc. Prof.;
Deputy Head

Leung, M. C., BSc HK, MSc Mich., PhD Mich.
Assoc. Prof.

Lian, B. H., BSc Tor., MPhil Yale, PhD Yale
Prof.

Lin, P., BSc Nanjing, MSc Nanjing, PhD Br.Col.
Assoc. Prof.

Loke, H. Y., BSc NU Singapore, PhD Harv.
Assoc. Prof.

Lou, J. H., BSc Natnl.Taiwan, PhD Cornell Sr.
Lectr.

Ma, L. S. L., BSc HK, PhD HK Assoc. Prof.

McInnes, B. T., BSc Qld., MSc Syd., PhD Syd.
Assoc. Prof.

Ng, T. B., BSc Warw., MSc Br.Col., PhD Warw.
Assoc. Prof.

Niederreiter, Harald, PhD Vienna Prof.

Pang, Peter Y. H., BSc Tor., PhD Ill. Assoc.
Prof.

Poh, R. K. S., BSc Nan., MSc Nan., PhD NU
Singapore Sr. Lectr.

Quek, T. S., BSc Sing., MSc Sing., PhD Sing.
Assoc. Prof.

Shen, Z., BSc Hehai, MSc Alta., PhD Alta. Prof.

Sun, D., BSc Nanjing, MSc Nanjing, PhD Chinese
Acad.Sc. Assoc. Prof.

Sun, Y. N., BS China U.S.T., MS Ill., PhD Ill.
Prof.

Tan, E. C., BSc NU Singapore, MS Yale, PhD Yale
Prof.

Tan, H. H., BSc Adel., PhD Adel. Assoc. Prof.

Tan, K. M., BA Camb., MA Camb., PhD Camb.
Asst. Prof.

Tan, R. C. E., BAppSc RMIT, BSc La Trobe, PhD
La Trobe Assoc. Prof.

Tan, S. P., BA Oxf., MA Calif., PhD Calif.
Assoc. Prof.

Tan, V., BSc NU Singapore, MSc NU Singapore, PhD
Calif. Assoc. Prof.

Tang, W. S., BSc HK, MSc Tor., PhD Tor.
Assoc. Prof.

Tay, T. S., BSc Malaya, MMath Wat., PhD Wat.
Assoc. Prof.

Tay, Yong Chiang, BSc Sing., MS Harv., PhD
Harv. Prof.

To, W. K., BSc HK, MA Col., PhD Col. Assoc.
Prof.

Toh, K. C., BSc NU Singapore, MSc NU Singapore,
PhD Cornell Assoc. Prof.

Wong, Y. L., BSc HK, MPhil HK, PhD Calif. Sr.
Lectr.

Wu, J., MS Nankai, MA Roch., PhD Roch., BS Assoc. Prof.

Xing, C., BSc Anhui, MSc China U.Electronic S.T., PhD China U.S.T.   Assoc. Prof.

Xu, X. W., BSc Nanjing, MSc Nanjing, PhD Conn. Assoc. Prof.

Yang, Yue, BS Beijing, MS Cornell, PhD Cornell Assoc. Prof.

Yip, A. M. H., BSc Chinese HK, MPhil HK, PhD Calif.   Asst. Prof.

Zhang, D. Q., BSc E.China Normal, MSc Osaka, PhD Osaka   Assoc. Prof.

Zhang, L., BSc Lanzhou, MSc Lanzhou, PhD Wat. Assoc. Prof.

Zhao, G. Y., BSc Xiamen, MSc Xiamen, PhD Würzburg   Assoc. Prof.

Zhu, C., BSc Zhejiang, MSc Yale, PhD Yale   Prof.

Other Staff: 2 Lectrs.; 4 Res. Fellows; 4 Visiting Fellows; 6 Res. Staff; 3 Adjunct Staff

NUS Business School

Tel: 6516 4799 Fax: 6872 1438
E-mail: askbiz@nus.edu.sg

Lau, Geok Theng, BBA NU Singapore, PhD W.Ont. Assoc. Prof.; Asst. Dean (Undergrad. Student Affairs)

Lee, Khai Sheang, BEng Melb., PhD Tor.   Assoc. Prof.; Vice-Dean (Undergrad. Studies)

Lim, Chin, BAgricSc Malaya, MSc Br.Col., PhD Qu.   Prof.; Dir.*

Quek, Ser Aik, BSc Manc., MS M.I.T., PhD Calif. Assoc. Prof.; Vice-Dean (Grad. Studies/MBA Programmes)

Rajiv, Surendra, BS Patna, MBA IIITM, MS Carnegie-Mellon, PhD Carnegie-Mellon   Prof.; Asst. Dean (Res. and PhD Programme)

Wilkins, Trevor A., BCom Qld., MCom NSW, PhD Qld.   Assoc. Prof.; Vice-Dean (Finance and Admin.)

Pharmacy

Tel: 6516 2648 Fax: 6779 1554
E-mail: phabox2@nus.edu.sg

Boelsterli, Urs A., MSc Zür., PhD Zür.   Assoc. Prof.

Chan, E. W. Y., BPharm China Med.Coll., PhD Manc.   Assoc. Prof.

Chan, Sui Yung, BSc(Pharm) NU Singapore, MBA NU Singapore, PhD Belf.   Assoc. Prof.; Head*

Chan Chun Yong, Eric, BSc(Pharm) NU Singapore, PhD NU Singapore   Asst. Prof.

Chan Lai Wah, BSc(Pharm) NU Singapore, PhD NU Singapore   Assoc. Prof.

Chen, Yu Zong, BSc Dalian U.T., MSc Chinese Acad.Sc., PhD UMIST   Assoc. Prof.

Chiu, Gigi Ngar Chee, BSc(Pharm) Br.Col., PhD Br.Col.   Asst. Prof.

Chui, Wai Keung, BSc(Pharm) NU Singapore, PhD Aston   Asst. Prof.

Ee, Pui Lai (Rachel), BSc(Pharm) NU Singapore, PhD Ill.   Asst. Prof.

Go, Mei Lin, BSc(Pharm) Sing., PhD NU Singapore Assoc. Prof.

Heng, P. W. S., BSc(Pharm) Sing., PhD NU Singapore   Assoc. Prof.

Ho Chi Lui, Paul, BPharm Qld., PhD Qld. Assoc. Prof.

Koh, Hwee Ling, BSc(Pharm) NU Singapore, MSc(Pharm) NU Singapore, PhD Camb.   Asst. Prof.

Kurup, T. R. R., BPharm Raj., MPharm BITS, MSc Lond., PhD Lond.   Assoc. Prof.

Li, Shu Chuen, BPharm S.Aust.I.T., MAppSc S.Aust.I.T., MBA Deakin, PhD Monash   Assoc. Prof.

Lim, Lee Yong, BSc(Pharm) NU Singapore, PhD Manc.   Assoc. Prof.

Ng, Lawrence Ka-Yun, BSc(Pharm) Wis., MSc Wis., PhD Wis.   Assoc. Prof.

Sklar, Grant E., BSc(Pharm) Manit., PharmD Wayne State   Sr. Lectr.

Zhou, Shu Feng, MB BS Guangzhou, PhD Auck. Asst. Prof.

Other Staff: 1 Lectr.; 1 Instr.

Philosophy

Tel: 6516 3896 Fax: 6777 9514
E-mail: phivdevi@nus.edu.sg

Chan, Alan K. L., BA Winn., MA Manit., PhD Tor.   Prof.

Chong, Chi Tat, BSc Iowa State, PhD Yale   Univ. Prof.

D'Cruz, Mark J., BA NU Singapore, MA NU Singapore, PhD Rutgers   Asst. Prof. (on leave)

Heng, Hock Jiuan, BA Oxf., MPhil Col., PhD Col.   Asst. Prof.

Holbo, John C., BA Calif., BA Chic., MA Calif., PhD Calif.   Asst. Prof.

Kyle, Swan, BA Grove City, MA Grove City, PhD Bowling Green   Asst. Prof.

Lim, Cecilia T. N., BA NU Singapore, MA NU Singapore, PhD Pitt.   Assoc. Prof.

Nuyen, Ann Tuan, BA Qld., BEcon Qld., MA Qld., MEc Monash, PhD Qld.   Assoc. Prof.

Pelczar, Michael W., AB Amherst, MA Virginia, PhD Virginia   Asst. Prof.

Tagore, S. N., BA Oakland, MA Miami(Ohio), MA Purdue, PhD Purdue   Assoc. Prof.

Tan, Sor Hoon, BA Oxf., MA NU Singapore, PhD Hawaii   Assoc. Prof.

Ten, Chin Liew, BA Malaya, MA Lond., FAHA, FASSA   Prof.; Head*

Other Staff: 3 Sr. Tutors; 1 Visiting Fellow

Research: analytic philosophy; Chinese philosophy and religion; European continental philosophy; history of western philosophy (Descartes); Indian philosophy

Physics

Tel: 6516 2603 Fax: 6777 6126
E-mail: physec@nus.edu.sg

Baaquie, B. E., BS Cal.Tech., PhD Cornell   Assoc. Prof.

Berthold-George, Englert, PhD   Prof.

Breese, M. B. H., BSc Manc., PhD Salf.   Assoc. Prof.

Chan, Phil A. H., PhD NU Singapore   Sr. Lectr.

Chowdari, B. V. R., BSc And., MSc Baroda, PhD IIT Kanpur   Assoc. Prof.

Chung, K. Y., BSc Sing., PhD Stan.   Asst. Prof.

Feng, Y. P., BSc Lanzhou, PhD Illinois Tech.Inst. Assoc. Prof.

Ho, Peter K. H., BSc NU Singapore, PhD Camb. Asst. Prof.

Hsu, T. S., BSc Nan., DrIng Inst.Nat.Poly.Toulouse Sr. Lectr.

Ji, W., BSc Fudan, MSc H-W, PhD H-W   Assoc. Prof.

Kaszlikowski, D., MPhys Gdansk, PhD Gdansk Asst. Prof.

Kuok, M. H., BSc Cant., PhD Cant.   Assoc. Prof.

Kurtsiefer, C., PhD Constance   Assoc. Prof.

Lai, C. H., BA Chic., MS Chic., PhD Chic.   Prof.

Lamas Linares, A., BSc Sheff., MSc Lond., DPhil Oxf.   Asst. Prof.

Li, B. W., BSc Nanjing, MSc Chinese Acad.Sc., PhD Oldenburg   Assoc. Prof.

Lim, H. S., BSc NU Singapore, MSc NU Singapore, DPhil Oxf.   Asst. Prof.

Lim, H., BSc Sing., PhD Reading   Prof.

Liu, X. Y., BSc Shandong, MSc Shandong, PhD Nijmegen   Assoc. Prof.

Mahendiran, R., BS Madr., MSc IISc., PhD IISc. Asst. Prof.

Oh, C. H., BSc Otago, PhD Otago   Prof.

Ong, C. K., BSc Nan., MSc Manit., PhD Manit. Prof.

Osipowicz, T., PhD Gött.   Assoc. Prof.

Sow, C. H., BSc NU Singapore, MSc NU Singapore, PhD Chic.   Asst. Prof.

Tan, B. T. G., PBM, PPA, BSc Sing., DPhil Oxf. Prof.

Tang, S. H., BSc Sing., MA N.Y.State, PhD N.Y.State   Prof.

Tay, S. C., BSc NU Singapore, MSc NU Singapore, PhD NU Singapore   Sr. Lectr.

Teo, E. H. K., BSc Flin., PhD Camb.   Assoc. Prof.

Tok, Eng Soon, BSc NU Singapore, PhD Lond. Assoc. Prof.

Van Der Maarel, J. R. C., BSc Ley., MS Ley., PhD Ley.   Assoc. Prof.

Wang, J. S., BSc Jilin, MSc Carnegie-Mellon, PhD Carnegie-Mellon   Prof.

Wang, X. S., BSc Fudan, PhD Maryland   Asst. Prof.

Watt, F., BSc Newcastle(UK), PhD Newcastle(UK) Prof.

Wee, Andrew Thye Shen, BA Camb., MA Camb., DPhil Oxf.   Prof.; Head*

Willeboordse, H. F., BSc Amst., MSc Amst., PhD Tokyo   Sr. Lectr.

Yan, J., BSc Lanzhou, MS Lanzhou, PhD Chinese Acad.Sc.   Asst. Prof.

Zhang, Donghui, BSc Fudan, MSc Chic., PhD N.Y.   Assoc. Prof.

Other Staff: 2 Lectrs.; 2 Visiting Profs.; 2 Sr. Res. Fellows; 2 Res. Fellows; 3 Instrs.; 2 Adjunct Profs.; 4 Adjunct Assoc. Profs.; 1 Adjunct Asst. Prof.

Political Science

Tel: 6516 3970 Fax: 6779 6815
E-mail: polsec@nus.edu.sg

Chan, Heng Chee, BA Sing., MA Sing., MA Cornell, PhD Sing.   Prof. (on leave)

Chen, An, ML Shanghai, MA Yale, MPhil Yale, PhD Yale   Assoc. Prof.

Chong, Chia Siong (Alan), BSocSci NU Singapore, MSc Lond., PhD Lond.   Asst. Prof.

Davidson, Jamie, BA Penn., MA Lond., PhD George Washington   Asst. Prof.

Haque, Shamsul, BSS Dhaka, MSS Dhaka, MPA S.Calif., PhD S.Calif.   Assoc. Prof.

Kyaw, Yin Hlaing, BA Mandalay, MA Cornell, PhD Cornell   Asst. Prof.

Lee, Lai To, BA Chinese HK, MA Calif., PhD Calif. Assoc. Prof.; Deputy Dir., Internat. Relations Office; Academic Convenor, Master of Soc. Scis. (Internat. Studies) Programme; Head*

Li, Peter M., BA Penn., MA Calif., PhD Calif. Asst. Prof.

Lin, Kun-Chin, BA Harv., MA Calif., PhD Calif. Asst. Prof.

Mutalib, M. H., BA NU Singapore, BSocSci NU Singapore, MA ANU, PhD Syd.   Assoc. Prof.

Putterman, Ethan A., BA Colorado, MSc Lond., MA Chic., PhD Chic.   Asst. Prof.

Quah, J. S. T., BSocSci Sing., MSocSci Sing., PhD Florida State   Prof.

Rappa, Antonio L., BSocSci NU Singapore, PhD Hawaii   Asst. Prof.

Singh, B., BSocSci NU Singapore, MA ANU, PhD ANU   Assoc. Prof.

Sridharan, Kripa, BA Baroda, MA Baroda, MSc(Econ) Lond., PhD NU Singapore   Sr. Lectr.

Tan, Kenneth P. A. Sze-Sian, BSc Brist., PhD Camb.   Asst. Prof.

Wang, Cheng-Lung, BA Natnl.Taiwan, MA Natnl.Taiwan, MA N.Y.State, PhD N.Y.State Asst. Prof.

Wong, Yik Pern (Reuben), BSocSci NU Singapore, MPhil Lond., PhD Lond.   Asst. Prof.

Other Staff: 1 Postdoctoral Fellow; 1 Lectr.†

Research: classical, modern and post-modern political thought; comparative politics and government in East Asia and Southeast Asia; international politics in the Asia-Pacific; international relations and communication; public administration and governance in Southeast Asia and South Asia

Psychology

Tel: 6516 3749 Fax: 6773 1843
E-mail: psybox1@nus.edu.sg

Bishop, George D., BA Hope, MS Yale, PhD Yale Prof.; Head*

Cheung, Mike, BSSc Chinese HK, MPhil Chinese HK, PhD Chinese HK   Asst. Prof.

Chua, Fook Kee, BA Well., MA Cant., PhD Calif. Assoc. Prof.

Collinson, Simon, BSc Curtin, MSc Macq., DPhil Oxf.   Asst. Prof.

Elliott, John M., BA Camb., MA Camb., PhD Sheff.   Assoc. Prof. Fellow

Goh, Winston, BA NU Singapore, BSocSci NU Singapore, MSocSci NU Singapore, PhD Indiana Asst. Prof.

Graham, Steven, BSc Manc., PhD Camb.   Asst. Prof.

Hon, Nicholas, BSocSci NU Singapore, PhD Camb.   Asst. Prof.

Penney, Trevor, BSc Nfld., MSc Nfld., PhD Col.   Assoc. Prof.

Rickard Liow, Susan J., BSc Lond., PhD Lond.   Assoc. Prof.

Schirmer, Annett, PhD Leip.   Asst. Prof.

Sim, Tick Ngee, BSocSci NU Singapore, MSc Wis., PhD Wis.   Assoc. Prof.

Singh, Ramadhar, BA Bihar, MA Bihar, MS Purdue, PhD Purdue   Prof.

Tan, L. M. Vicky, BS Minn., MA Minn., PhD Lond.   Asst. Prof.

Tong, Eddie, BSocSci NU Singapore, MSocSci NU Singapore, PhD Mich.   Asst. Prof.

Why, Yong Peng, BSocSci NU Singapore, MSocSci NU Singapore, PhD St And.   Asst. Prof.

Other Staff: 1 Visiting Assoc. Prof.; 1 Sr. Tutor; 1 Instr.; 1 Adjunct Asst. Prof.

Research: cognitive neuroscience (affective neuroscience, brain imaging, executive function); developmental psychology (adolescence, early language learning); health psychology (psychosocial factors in health and disease); psycholinguistics (bilingualism, language disorders, language learning); social psychology (emotion, inter-group attitudes)

Public Policy, Lee Kuan Yew School of

Tel: 6516 6134 Fax: 6778 1020
    E-mail: sppsec@nus.edu.sg

Asher, Mukul G., BA Bom., MA Wash., PhD Wash.   Prof.

Barter, Paul A., BSc Adel., MEnvSt Adel., PhD Murd.   Asst. Prof.

Brassard, Caroline, BSc Montr., MA Tor.   Asst. Prof.

Fritzen, Scott, BA Mich.State, MPA Prin., PhD Prin.   Asst. Prof.

Hui, Weng Tat, BEc Tas., MEc ANU, PhD ANU   Assoc. Prof.; Vice-Dean

Kadir, Suzaina, BA NU Singapore, BS NU Singapore, MA Wis., PhD Wis.   Asst. Prof.

Mutebi, Alex M., BA Macalester, MPA Prin., PhD Prin.   Asst. Prof.

Phua, Kai Hong, AB Harv., SM Harv., PhD Lond.   Assoc. Prof.

Ramesh, M., BA Patna, MA Sask., PhD   Assoc. Prof.

Rethinaraj, T. S. Gopi, BA B'thidasan., MSc B'thidasan., PhD Ill.   Asst. Prof.

Thampapillai, Jesuthason, BScAgri Ceyl., MEcon NE, PhD NE   Assoc. Prof.

Wu, Wenbo, BSc Beijing, MSc Beijing, PhD Carnegie-Mellon   Asst. Prof.

Wu, Xun, BEng Zhejiang, MPA Alaska, PhD N.Carolina   Asst. Prof.

Other Staff: 1 Visiting Prof.; 1 Res. Fellow; 1 Postdoctoral Fellow; 1 English Lang. Teacher; 6 Adjunct Profs.; 2 Adjunct Assoc. Profs.

Research: development studies; economic policy and analysis; international relations and security studies; public management and governance; social policy

Real Estate

Tel: 6516 3414 Fax: 6774 8684
    E-mail: rstsec@nus.edu.sg

Addae-Dapaah, Kwame, BSc Kumasi, MSc Reading, PhD Strath.   Sr. Lectr.; Programme Dir.

Cheng, Fook Jam, MSc Reading   Sr. Lectr.

Chin, Lawrence K. H., BSc(EstateManagement) Sing., PhD Georgia   Sr. Lectr.

Christudason, Alice, LLB Sing., LLM Lond., PhD Lond.   Assoc. Prof.

Chun, Joseph, LLB NU Singapore, PhD Lond.   Asst. Prof.

Fu, Yuming, BEng Shanghai Jiaotong, MSc Br.Col., PhD Br.Col.   Assoc. Prof.; Dir., CRES

Han, Sun Sheng, BEng Tongji, MSc Asian I.T., Bangkok, PhD S.Fraser   Assoc. Prof.; Deputy Head (Academic)

Ho, Kim Hin David, MPhil Camb., PhD Camb.   Assoc. Prof.

Lim, Lan Yuan, BSc(EstMgt) Sing., BSc(Econ) Lond., LLB Lond., MBA Sing., MSc Bath, FRICS, FCIS   Assoc. Prof.

Liow, Kim Hiang, BSc(EstateManagement) NU Singapore, MSc(Prop&MainMgt) NU Singapore, PhD Manc.   Assoc. Prof.

Lum, Sau Kim, BSc(EstateManagement) NU Singapore, MLE Aberd., PhD Calif.   Asst. Prof.

Malone-Lee, Lai Choo, BSc(EstateManagement) Sing., MTCP Syd., PhD Tokyo I.T.   Sr. Lectr.; Programme Dir., MSc (Environmental Management)

Muhammad Faishal, BSc(EstateManagement) NU Singapore, MSc(RealEstate) NU Singapore, PhD UMIST   Asst. Prof.; Programme Dir., MSc (Real Estate)

Ong, Seow Eng, BSc(EstMgt) NU Singapore, MBus Indiana, PhD Indiana   Assoc. Prof.; Deputy Head (Res.)

Ooi, Joseph Thian Leong, BSc(EstateManagement) NU Singapore, MSc(RealEstate) NU Singapore, PhD UMIST   Asst. Prof.; Co-Dir., MBA

Sim, Loo Lee, BA Sing., LLB Lond., MSc Lond., PhD NU Singapore   Assoc. Prof.; Head*

Sing, Tien Foo, BSc(EstMgt) NU Singapore, MPhil Camb., PhD Camb.   Assoc. Prof.; Deputy Head (Admin. and Finance)

Tu, Yong, BSc Nankai, MSc Nankai, PhD Napier   Assoc. Prof.

Wong, Khei Mie, BSc(EstateManagement) NU Singapore, MSc(Prop&MainMgt) NU Singapore, MPhil Camb., PhD Camb.   Asst. Prof.; Programme Dir., BSc (Real Estate)

Yu, Shi Ming, MSc Reading, PhD Reading   Assoc. Prof.

Yuen, Belinda, BA Sing., MA Sheff., PhD Melb.   Assoc. Prof.

Zhu, Jieming, BE Tongji, ME Tongji, PhD Strath.   Assoc. Prof.

Other Staff: 2 Sr. Tutors; 4 Adjunct Assoc. Profs.

Research: corporate and securitised real estate; housing research; institutional and spatial analyses of real estate

Social Work

Tel: 6516 3812 Fax: 6778 1213
    E-mail: swksec@nus.edu.sg

Mehta, Kalyani, BSocSci Sing., MSocSci Sing., PhD Sing.   Assoc. Prof.

Mohd Maliki bin Osman, BA Sing., BSocSci Sing., MSocSci Sing., PhD Ill.   Asst. Prof. (on leave)

Ng, Guat Tin, BA Sing., PhD Wash.   Asst. Prof.

Ngiam, Tee Liang, BSocSci Sing., MSc Wales, PhD Calif.   Assoc. Prof.; Head*

Ow, Rosaleen S. O., BSocSci Sing., MSc Wales, PhD Sing.   Sr. Lectr.

Rowlands, Claire A., PhD Newcastle(NSW), BSW   Sr. Lectr.

Sim, Timothy B. W., BA Sing., MSc Lond., PhD HK   Asst. Prof.

Tan, Ngoh Tiong, BA Sing., MSW Penn., PhD Minn.   Assoc. Prof.

Other Staff: 1 Lectr.; 1 Assoc. Prof. Fellow; 2 Sr. Fellows; 1 Visiting Fellow; 1 Instr.

Research: criminal justice and rehabilitation (addictions, juvenile delinquency, youth issues); family studies (family-based policy and social work practice); non-profit sector excellence (governance, outcome management, programme evaluation); social development (community and social capital developments); social gerontology (macro-micro intervention on ageing issues)

Sociology

Tel: 6516 3822 Fax: 6777 9579
    E-mail: socsec@nus.edu.sg

Alatas, Syed F., BSc Oregon, MA Johns H., PhD Johns H.   Assoc. Prof.

Chan, Wei Ming (Angelique), BA Reed, MA Calif., PhD Calif.   Asst. Prof.

Chua, Beng Huat, BSc Acad., MA York(Can.), PhD York(Can.)   Prof.

Dorairajoo, Saroja, BSocSci Sing., MA Cornell, MA Ohio, PhD Harv.   Asst. Prof.

Erb, Maribeth, BA N.Y.State, MA N.Y.State, PhD N.Y.State   Assoc. Prof.

Goh Pei Siong, Daniel, BSocSci NU Singapore, MSocSci NU Singapore, PhD Mich.   Asst. Prof.

Hadiz, Vedi R., BA Indonesia, PhD Murd.   Assoc. Prof.

Hing, Ai Yun, BSocSci Sing., MSocSci Sing., PhD Aberd.   Assoc. Prof.

Ho, Kong Chong, BSocSci Sing., MSocSci NU Singapore, PhD Chic.   Assoc. Prof.

Jarman, Jennifer, BA Tor., MA Tor., PhD Camb.   Asst. Prof.

Jones, Gavin W., BA Curtin, PhD ANU   Prof.

Leong, Wai Teng (Laurence), BSocSci NU Singapore, MSocSci Calif., PhD Calif.   Sr. Lectr.

Lian, Kwen Fee, BA Sing., BA Well., MA Well., PhD Well.   Assoc. Prof.; Head*

Narayanan, Ganapathy, BA NU Singapore, MA Brun., PhD NU Singapore   Asst. Prof.

Pereira, Alexius A., BSocSci NU Singapore, MSocSci NU Singapore, PhD Lond.   Asst. Prof.

Quah, Stella R., BA Colombia Natnl., MSc Florida State, PhD Sing.   Prof.

Raffin, Anne, BA Lyons II, MA New Sch.Soc.Res.(N.Y.), PhD New Sch.Soc.Res.(N.Y.)   Asst. Prof.

Rajah, Ananda, BSocSci Sing., PhD ANU   Assoc. Prof.

Rupp, Stephanie K., BA Dartmouth, MEd Harv., MPhil Yale, PhD Yale   Asst. Prof.

Safman, Rachel, MA Harv., PhD Cornell   Asst. Prof.

Schmidt, Volker H., MA Bielefeld, PhD Bremen   Assoc. Prof.

Sinha, Vineeta, BSocSci NU Singapore, MSocSci NU Singapore, MSocSci Johns H., PhD Johns H.   Asst. Prof.

Straughan, Paulin, BA NU Singapore, MA Virginia, PhD Virginia   Assoc. Prof.

Tan, Ern Ser, BSocSci Sing., MSocSci NU Singapore, PhD Cornell   Assoc. Prof.

Thompson, Eric C., BA Macalester, MA Wash., PhD Wash.   Asst. Prof.

Tong, Chee Kiong, BSocSci Sing., MA Cornell, PhD Cornell   Assoc. Prof.; Chairman, Grad. Studies

Turner, Bryan S., BA Leeds, MA Camb., DLitt Flin.   Prof.

Waterson, Roxana H., BA Camb., MA Camb., PhD Camb.   Assoc. Prof.

Other Staff: 4 Fellows

Research: ethnicity, nation-state, migration and globalisation; family, ageing and health; gender studies; sociology and anthropology of Southeast Asian societies; studies on religion

South Asian Studies Programme

Tel: 6516 4528 Fax: 6777 0616
    E-mail: sashead@nus.edu.sg

Adnan, Shapan, BA Sus., PhD Camb.   Assoc. Prof.

Kudaisya, Gyanesh, BA Delhi, MA J.Nehru U., MPhil J.Nehru U., PhD Camb.   Asst. Prof.

Niklas, Ulrike, MA Cologne, PhD Cologne   Asst. Prof.

Reeves, Peter, BA Tas., MA Tas., PhD ANU   Visiting Prof.; Head*

Yahya, Faizal, BA Sing., MA Hull, PhD Syd.   Asst. Prof.

Other Staff: 2 Fellows

Research: cultures and cultural development in South Asia; nineteenth- and twentieth-century social, political and economic development of the South Asian states; political economy of the South Asian region and the South Asian states

Southeast Asian Studies Programme

Tel: 6516 6338 Fax: 6777 6608
    E-mail: seasec@nus.edu.sg

Daquila, T. C., BSc Central Luzon, MA Louvain, PhD ANU   Sr. Lectr.

Goh, Beng Lan, BA Sci.U.Malaysia, MA Ochanomizu, PhD Monash   Asst. Prof.

Hamilton-Hart, Natasha E., BA Otago, MA Cornell, PhD Cornell   Asst. Prof.

Ileto, Reynaldo C., BA Ateneo de Manila, MA Cornell, PhD Cornell   Prof.

Johnson, Irving C., BA NU Singapore, PhD Harv.   Asst. Prof.

Miksic, John N., AB Dartmouth, MA Ohio, MA Cornell, PhD Cornell   Assoc. Prof.

Montesano, Michael J., BA Yale, MA Cornell, PhD Cornell   Asst. Prof.

Mrazek, Jan, MA Cornell, PhD Cornell   Asst. Prof.

Pholsena, Vatthana, BA Grenoble, MA Grenoble, PhD Hull   Asst. Prof.

Sulistiyanto, Priyambudi, LLB Indonesia, MA Flin., PhD Adel.   Asst. Prof.

Yeoh, Brenda S. A., BA Camb., MA Camb., DPhil Oxf.   Prof.; Head*

Other Staff: 1 Sr. Tutor; 2 Visiting Fellows

Research: corporate and financial restructuring, regional trade and multilateralism; cultural resource management, historical archaeology; explorations of local/indigenous knowledge and regional scholarship; the arts (music, theatre, visual arts), art history and mass media issues; transnational migration, borderlands, cross-border movements

Statistics and Applied Probability

Tel: 6516 1667 Fax: 6872 3919
E-mail: stasec@nus.edu.sg

Bai, Zhidong, BS China U.S.T., PhD China U.S.T.   Prof.

Biman, Chakraborty, BStat I.Stat.I., MStat I.Stat.I., PhD I.Stat.I.   Asst. Prof.

Chan, Hock Peng, BSc NU Singapore, PhD Stan.   Assoc. Prof.

Chan, Yiu Man, BA HK, MSc Tor., PhD Tor.   Sr. Lectr.

Chaudhuri, Sanjay, BStat I.Stat.I., MStat I.Stat.I., PhD Wash.   Asst. Prof.

Chen, Hsiao Yun (Louis), BSc Sing., MS Stan., PhD Stan.   Prof.

Chen, Zehua, BSc Wuhan, MS Iowa, PhD Wis.   Assoc. Prof.

Chiang Kok Leong, Andy, BA NU Singapore, BSocSci NU Singapore, MS Iowa State, PhD Iowa State   Asst. Prof.

Choi, Kwok Pui, BSc HK, MSc Ill., PhD Ill.   Assoc. Prof.

Chua, Tin Chiu, BSc Nan., MSc Manit., PhD Iowa State   Assoc. Prof.

Gan, Fah Fatt, BScEd Malaya, MS Iowa State, PhD Iowa State   Assoc. Prof.

Guha, Apratim, BStat I.Stat.I., MStat I.Stat.I., MA Calif., PhD Calif.   Asst. Prof.

Ho, Man Wai, BSc HKUST, PhD HKUST   Asst. Prof.

Kuk, Yung Cheng (Anthony), BA Rutgers, PhD Stan.   Prof.; Head*

Kwong, Koon Shing, BBA Northeast Louisiana, MSc Temple, PhD Temple   Assoc. Prof.

Leng, Chenlei, BA E.China U.S.T., PhD Wis.   Asst. Prof.

Lim, Tiong Wee, BSc Lond., PhD Stan.   Asst. Prof.

Loh, Wei Liem, BSc Sing., MSc NU Singapore, MS Stan., PhD Stan.   Assoc. Prof.

Stephenson, Alec G., BSc Warw., MSc Oxf., PhD Lanc.   Asst. Prof.

Wang, Yougan, BSc Zhejiang, MSc(Stat) Peking, DPhil Oxf.   Assoc. Prof.

Xia, Yingcun, BSc Zhongshan, MSc(Stat) Zhejiang, PhD HK   Asst. Prof.

Yannis, Yatracos, BSc Athens, MSc Lond., PhD Calif., Dr Paris VI   Prof.

Yap, Von Bing, BSc NU Singapore, MSc NU Singapore, PhD Calif.   Asst. Prof.

Zhang, Jin Ting, BSc Peking, MSc Chinese Acad.Sc., PhD N.Carolina   Asst. Prof.

Zhou, Wang, BSc Shanghai, MSc Shanghai, PhD HKUST   Asst. Prof.

Other Staff: 1 Visiting Prof.; 3 Visiting Assoc. Profs.

University Scholars Programme

Tel: 6516 4425 Fax: 6773 1012
E-mail: usphelp@nus.edu.sg

Alatas, Syed F., BSc Oregon, MA Johns H., PhD Johns H.   Assoc. Prof.

Chin, Hoong Chor, BEng NU Singapore, MEng NU Singapore, PhD S'ton.   Assoc. Prof.

Chin, Wee Shong, BSc NU Singapore, PhD NU Singapore   Asst. Prof.

Chong, Chi Tat, BSc Iowa State, PhD Yale   Prof.

Favareau, Donald F., BA Calif., PhD Calif.   Asst. Prof.

Geertsema, Johan H., BA Potchef., MA Potchef., PhD Cape Town   Asst. Prof.

Kang, Hway Chuan, BS Yale, PhD Cal.Tech.   Assoc. Prof.; Deputy Dir.

Khursheed, A., BSc Edin., PhD Edin.   Assoc. Prof.

Kudaisya, Medha M., BA Delhi, MA J.Nehru U., MPhil J.Nehru U., PhD Camb.   Asst. Prof.

Lee, C. Y., BA HK, MPhil HK, PhD ANU   Assoc. Prof.

Leng, Andrew, BA Reading, MA Reading, PhD Qld.   Asst. Prof.

Leong, Hon Wai, BSc Malaya, PhD Cornell   Assoc. Prof.

Lim, Wei Shi, BSc NU Singapore, PhD Lond.   Assoc. Prof.

Lo, Mun Hou, AB Prin., MA Harv., PhD Harv.   Asst. Prof.

Maiwald, Michael H., BA Rutgers, MA Duke, PhD Duke   Asst. Prof.

Meier, R., MSc New Orleans, PhD Cornell   Assoc. Prof.

Nerney, Paul R., BA Providence(R.I.), MA Manila   Sr. Lectr.

Ni, Yibin, BA E.China Normal, MA Lond., PhD Lond.   Asst. Prof.

Nuyen, Ann Tuan, BA Qld., BEcon Qld., MA Qld., MEc Monash, PhD Qld.   Assoc. Prof.

Pang Yu Hin, Peter, BSc Tor., PhD Ill.   Assoc. Prof.; Dir.*

Pehkonen, S. O., BSc Oregon State, PhD Cal.Tech.   Assoc. Prof.

Quek, Ser Aik, BSc Manc., MS M.I.T., PhD Calif.   Assoc. Prof.

Rupp, Stephanie K., BA Dartmouth, MEd Harv., MPhil Yale, PhD Yale   Asst. Prof.

Ryan, Barbara T., BA Dartmouth, MA N.Carolina, PhD N.Carolina   Asst. Prof.

Sheu, F. S., BS Natnl.Taiwan, MS Northwestern, PhD Northwestern   Assoc. Prof.

Singh, Kuldip, BSc NU Singapore, MSc NU Singapore, PhD NU Singapore   Sr. Lectr.

Tan, Kenneth P. A. Sze-Sian, BSc Brist., PhD Camb.   Asst. Prof.

Tan, Sor Hoon, BA Oxf., MA NU Singapore, PhD Hawaii   Assoc. Prof.

Teo, Albert C. Y., BA NU Singapore, BSocSci NU Singapore, MS Calif., PhD Calif.   Assoc. Prof.

Wang, S., BSc Fudan, MSc Zhejiang, PhD Gothenburg   Assoc. Prof.

Wee, Thye Shen, BA Camb., MA Camb., DPhil Oxf.   Prof.

Yew, Kong Leong, BA Indiana, MA ANU, PhD Adel.   Assoc. Prof.

Other Staff: 2 Assoc. Prof. Fellows; 1 Lectr.; 1 Sr. Visiting Fellow; 2 Instrs.; 2 Adjuncts

DENTISTRY

Tel: 6772 4988 Fax: 6778 5742
E-mail: dendox2@nus.edu.sg

Dean's Office (Dentistry)

Tel: 6772 4989 E-mail: densec@nus.edu.sg
Cao, Tong, DDS Zhejiang, PhD Showa   Asst. Prof.
Other Staff: 2 Res. Fellows
Research: stem cell research

Oral and Maxillofacial Surgery

Tel: 6772 4932 Fax: 6773 2600
E-mail: omssec@nus.edu.sg

Ho, Kee Hay, BDS Sing., FDSRCPSGlas, FDSRCSEd   Assoc. Prof.

Loh, Hong Sai, BDS Sing., MDS Sing., FDSRCSEd, FDSRCPSGlas   Prof. Fellow†

Yeo, Jinn Fei, BDS Sing., MDS Sing., MSc Lond., FDSRCSEd   Assoc. Prof.; Head*

Other Staff: 1 Visiting Fellow; 1 Dental Instr.; 2 Adjunct Asst. Profs.†

Research: origins and management of orofacial pain

Preventive Dentistry

Tel: 6772 4943 Fax: 6773 2602
E-mail: pndsec@nus.edu.sg

Foong, Kelvin W. C., BDS Sing., MDS Adel., PhD Sing., FDSRCS   Assoc. Prof.; Vice Dean (Res.)

Hsu, Chin Ying (Stephen), MSc Iowa, PhD Iowa, DDS Natnl.Yang Ming Med.   Assoc. Prof.

Lim, Lum Peng, BDS Sing., MSc Lond., PhD HK   Assoc. Prof.

Mohamed Azharashid bin Mohamed Tahir, BDS Sing., MSc Lond.   Asst. Prof.

Mok, Betty Y. Y., BDS Sing., MSc Lond.   Sr. Lectr.

Ong, Grace H. L., BDS Sing., MSc Lond.   Assoc. Prof.; Vice Dean (Academic Affairs); Head*

Soh, Jen, BDS Sing., MDS Sing., PhD Gron.   Asst. Prof.

Teo, Choo Soo, BDS Sing., MSc Lond.   Assoc. Prof.

Other Staff: 1 Visiting Prof.; 1 Visiting Fellow; 1 Adjunct Assoc. Prof.†; 1 Adjunct Asst. Prof.†

Research: aetiology and prevention of craniofacial anomalies

Restorative Dentistry

Tel: 6772 4954 Fax: 6773 2603
E-mail: rsdsec@nus.edu.sg

Anil, Kishen, BDS Madr., MDS Dr MGR, PhD Nan.Tech.

Chang, Willy S. W., BDSc Qld., MS Maryland, MSc Maryland

Chew, Chong Lin, BDS Sing., MSD Indiana, MDS Sing., PhD Sing., FDSRCSEd   Prof.; Dir., Div. of Grad. Dental Studies

Keng, Siong Beng, BDS Sing., MSc Lond., MDS Sing., FFDRCSI, FAMS   Assoc. Prof.; Asst. Dean

Koh, Gerald C. H., MB BS Sing., MMEd

Neo, Jennifer C. L., BDS Sing., MSc Iowa, FAMS   Assoc. Prof.; Head*

Sae-Lim, Varawan, DDS Chulalongkorn   Assoc. Prof.

Tan, Keson B. C., BDS Sing., MSD Wash., FDSRCSEd, FAMS   Assoc. Prof.

Thean, Hilary P. Y., BDS Sing., MSc Lond.   Sr. Lectr.

Other Staff: 2 Visiting Fellows; 1 Adjunct Asst. Prof.†

Research: biomaterials; endodontics and dental traumatology; stress analysis of implants

MEDICINE

Tel: 6516 8745 Fax: 6778 5743
E-mail: medbox5@nus.edu.sg

Anaesthesia

Tel: 6772 4200 Fax: 6777 5702
E-mail: anasec@nus.edu.sg

Chen, Fun Gee Edward, MB BS Sing., MMed(Anaesth) NU Singapore, FANZCA   Assoc. Prof.; Head*

Lee, Tat Leang, MB BS Sing., MMed(Anaesth) NU Singapore, FANZCA   Prof.

Liu Hern Choon, Eugene, MB ChB Leic., MPhil Camb., FRCA   Assoc. Prof.

Ti, Lian Kah, MB BS Sing., MMed(Anaesth) NU Singapore   Asst. Prof.

Other Staff: 1 Sr. Res. Fellow; 2 Res. Fellows

Research: airway equipment; cardiothoracic outcome database; pain

Anatomy

Tel: 6516 3200 Fax: 6778 7643
E-mail: antsec@nus.edu.sg

Bay, Boon Huat, MB BS NU Singapore, PhD NU Singapore   Assoc. Prof.

Dheen, S. T., BSc B'thidasan., MSc Madr., MPhil Madr., PhD NU Singapore   Asst. Prof.

Gopalakrishnakone, P., MB BS Ceyl., PhD Lond., DSc NU Singapore   Prof.

He, Beiping, BM *Shanghai 2nd Med.Coll.*, MMed *Shanghai 2nd Med.Coll.*, PhD *NU Singapore*   Asst. Prof.

Kaur, Charanjit, BSc *Punjab*, MB BS *Punjabi*, PhD *NU Singapore*   Assoc. Prof.

Liang, Fengyi, BM *Henan*, MMed *Peking Union Med.*, PhD *Frib.*   Asst. Prof.

Ling, Eng Ang, BSc *Natnl.Taiwan*, PhD *Camb.*, DSc *NU Singapore*   Prof.; Head*

Ng, Yee Kong, BDS *NU Singapore*, PhD *NU Singapore*   Asst. Prof.

Ong, Wei Yi, BDS *NU Singapore*, PhD *NU Singapore*   Assoc. Prof.

Rajendran, K., MB BS *Sing.*, FRCSEd   Assoc. Prof.

Tay, Samuel S. W., BSc *Sing.*, MSc *Sing.*, PhD *NU Singapore*   Assoc. Prof.

Voon, Frank C. T., MB BS *Malaya*, PhD *Lond.*   Assoc. Prof.

Yip, George W. C., MB BS *NU Singapore*, PhD *Lond.*   Asst. Prof.

Other Staff: 2 Res. Fellows

Research: cancer biology; molecular neurobiology; neuroscience; venoms and toxin

Biochemistry

Tel: 6516 3240 Fax: 6779 1453
E-mail: bchsec@nus.edu.sg

Armstrong, Jeffrey, MSc *Brun.*, PhD *Tulane*   Asst. Prof.

Chang, Chan Fong, BSc *Birm.*, PhD *Lond.*   Assoc. Prof.

Cheung, Nam Sang (Steve), BSc *Natnl.Taiwan*, MSc *Natnl.Taiwan*, PhD *Melb.*   Asst. Prof.

Chua, Kim Lee, BSc *NU Singapore*, PhD *Camb.*   Sr. Lectr.

Chung, Maxey C. M., BSc *Well.*, MSc *Well.*, PhD *Well.*   Assoc. Prof.

Clement, Marie-Veronique, BSc *Paris VI*, MSc *Paris VI*, PhD *Paris VI*   Assoc. Prof.

Deng, Lih Wen, BSc *Natnl.Taiwan*, PhD *Camb.*   Asst. Prof.

Gan, Yunn Hwen, BS *Purdue*, PhD *Wis.*   Asst. Prof.

Halliwell, Barry, BA *Oxf.*, DPhil *Oxf.*, DSc *Lond.*   Prof.; Head*

Jenner, Andrew, BSc *Lond.*, PhD *Lond.*   Asst. Prof.

Jeyaseelan, Kandiah, BSc *Ceyl.*, PhD *Sheff.*, FIBiol   Prof.

Khoo, Hoon Eng, BA *Smith*, PhD *Lond.*   Assoc. Prof.

Lee, G. L. Caroline, BSc *NU Singapore*, MSc *NU Singapore*, PhD *Texas*   Asst. Prof.

Li, Qiu-Tian, BSc *S.China U.T.*, MSc *Natnl.U.Defence Technol.*, PhD *Melb.*   Prof.

Raghunath, Michael, MD *Mainz*, DrHabil *Mün.*   Assoc. Prof.

Sit, Kim Ping, BSc *Sing.*, MSc *McG.*, PhD *McG.*, DSc *NU Singapore*   Prof.; Deputy Head

Song Jianxing, BSc *S.China Agric.*, MSc *S.China Agric.*, PhD *Chinese Acad.Sc.*   Asst. Prof.

Tammi, Martti, BSc *Uppsala*, PhD *Uppsala*   Asst. Prof.

Tan, Chee Hong, BSc *Sing.*, MSc *Tor.*, PhD *Tor.*   Assoc. Prof.

Tan, May Chin (Theresa), BSc *NU Singapore*, PhD *NU Singapore*   Asst. Prof.

Tan, Tin Wee, BA *Camb.*, MSc *Lond.*, PhD *Edin.*   Assoc. Prof.

Tang, Bor Luen, BSc *NU Singapore*, MSc *NU Singapore*, PhD *NU Singapore*   Asst. Prof.

Teo, Tian Seng, BSc *Sing.*, MSc *Sing.*, PhD *Manit.*   Assoc. Prof.

Too, Heng Phon, BSc *Lond.*, PhD *Lond.*   Assoc. Prof.

Wenk, Markus, BS *Basle*, PhD *Basle*   Asst. Prof.

Whiteman, M., BSc *Herts.*, PhD *Lond.*   Assoc. Prof.

Yang, Hongyuan (Robert), BM *Beijing Med.*, MPhil *Col.*, PhD *Col.*   Asst. Prof.

Yeong, Foong May, BSc *NU Singapore*, PhD *Vienna*   Asst. Prof.

Other Staff: 14 Res. Fellows; 20 Adjunct Staff

Research: molecular and cellular mechanisms underlying human diseases; molecular mechanisms of the action of toxic agents; neurobiology

Community, Occupational and Family Medicine

Tel: 6516 4988 Fax: 6779 1489
E-mail: cofsec@nus.edu.sg

Chia, Kee Seng, MB BS *Sing.*, MSc(OccupationalMedicine) *Sing.*, MD *Sing.*, FFOMRCS   Prof.

Chia, Sin Eng, MB BS *Sing.*, MSc(OccupationalMedicine) *Sing.*, MD *Sing.*, FFOMRCS   Assoc. Prof.

Goh, Gerald C. H., MB BS *Sing.*, MMed(FamilyMedicine)   Prof.

Goh, Lee Gan, MB BS *Sing.*, MMed(IntMed) *Sing.*, FRCGP, FRACGP   Assoc. Prof.

Koh, David S. Q., MB BS *Sing.*, MSc(OccupationalMedicine) *Sing.*, PhD *Birm.*, FFOMRCS   Prof.; Head*

Koh, Woon Puay, MB BS *Sing.*, PhD *Syd.*   Asst. Prof.

Lee, Hin Peng, MB BS *Sing.*, MSc(PublicHealth) *Sing.*, FFPHM   Prof.

Lee, Jeannette J. M., BSc(Med) *NSW*, MB BS *NSW*, FRACGP   Asst. Prof.

Lim, Meng Kin, MB BS *Sing.*, MSc(OccupationalMedicine) *Sing.*, MPH *Harv.*, FRCPEd   Assoc. Prof.

Ng, Daniel P. K., BSc *Sing.*, PhD *Melb.*   Asst. Prof.

Ong, Choon Nam, BSc *Nan.*, MSc *Lond.*, PhD *Manc.*   Prof.

Phua, Kai Hong, AB *Harv.*, SM *Harv.*, PhD *Lond.*   Assoc. Prof.

Saw, Seang Mei, MB BS *Sing.*, MPH *Johns H.*, PhD *Johns H.*   Assoc. Prof.

Seow, Adeline L. H., MB BS *Sing.*, MMed(PublicHealth) *Sing.*, MD *Sing.*   Assoc. Prof.

Shankar, Anoop, MB BS MPH MD PhD   Asst. Prof.

Shen, Han Ming, BMed *Zhejiang*, MPH *Zhejiang*, PhD *Sing.*   Asst. Prof.

Wong, Mee Lian, MB BS *Malaya*, MPH *Malaya*, MD *Sing.*   Assoc. Prof.

Other Staff: 3 Res. Fellows

Research: chronic diseases (cancer, cardiovascular diseases, diabetes, myopia); environmental and occupational health (cancer chemoprotectants, reactive oxygen species, salivary biomarkers); health services research

Dermatology and Venereology

National Skin Centre (NSC)

Tel: 6253 4455 Fax: 6253 3225
E-mail: nsc_hrd@nsc.gov.sg

1 Lectr.; 8 Sr. Consultants; 8 Consultants; 6 Assoc. Consultants; 1 Adjunct Assoc. Prof.; 1 Clin. Prof.; 1 Clin. Assoc. Prof.

Diagnostic Radiology

Tel: 6772 4211 Fax: 6773 0190
E-mail: dnrsec@nus.edu.sg

Goh, P. S., MB BS *Melb.*, FRCR   Asst. Prof.

Shuter, B., BSc *Syd.*, PhD *Syd.*   Sr. Lectr.

Tan, Lenny K. A., MB BS *Sing.*, FRCR, FRCPEd, FRANZCR   Prof.

Venkatesh, Sudhakar K., MB BS *B'lore.*, MMed *Sing.*, MD *Delhi*, FRCR   Asst. Prof.

Wang, Shih-chang, BSc(Med) *Syd.*, MB BS *Syd.*, FRANZCR, FAMS   Assoc. Prof.; Chief, Diag. Imaging, Natnl. Univ. Hospital; Head*

Other Staff: 1 Sr. Res. Fellow

Research: applications of multislice computer-aided tomography (CT) for vascular and gastrointestinal pathology; magnetic resonance (MR) and functional magnetic resonance imaging (fMRI) of cognitive function; magnetic resonance (MR) of magnetic nanoparticles for cellular tracking applications; minimally invasive ablation of primary hepatic malignancy; 3-D image processing, registration and quantitation for clinical applications

Medicine

Tel: 6772 4350 Fax: 6779 4112
E-mail: mdcsec@nus.edu.sg

Burgunder, Jean-Marc, MD *Berne*   Prof.

Cheah, Jin Seng, MB BS *Sing.*, MD *Sing.*, FRACP   Prof.

Chen Chien Shing, MD PhD   Assoc. Prof.

Chia, Boon Lock, MB BS *Sing.*, FRACP, FRCPEd   Prof.

Fisher, Dale A., BMedSci *Tas.*, MB BS *Tas.*, FRACP   Assoc. Prof.

Ho, Khek Yu, MB BS *Syd.*, MD *Sing.*, FRACP   Assoc. Prof.; Head*

Kueh, Yan-Koon, BSc *Br.Col.*, MSc *Br.Col.*, MD *Br.Col.*, FRCPCan   Assoc. Prof.

Lam Su Ping, Carolyn, MB BS *Sing.*   Asst. Prof.

Lee, Evan J. C., MB BS *Sing.*, MMed(IntMed) *Sing.*, MD *Sing.*, FRCPEd   Assoc. Prof.

Lee, Kok Onn, BSc *Belf.*, MB BCh BAO *Belf.*, MD *Belf.*, FRCPEd, FRCP, FRCPI, FRACP   Prof.

Lee, Yin Mei, MB ChB *Dund.*   Asst. Prof.

Lim, Chuen Hian (Erle), MB BS *Sing.*, MMed(IntMed) *Sing.*   Asst. Prof.

Lim, Seng Gee, MB BS *Monash*, MD *Monash*, FRACP   Assoc. Prof.

Lim, Tow Keang, MB BS *Malaya*, MMed(IntMed) *Sing.*, FRCPEd   Assoc. Prof.

Lim, Yean Teng, MB BS *Sing.*, MMed(IntMed) *Sing.*, FACC, FRCP   Assoc. Prof.

Lim Hsuen, Elaine, BA *Camb.*, MA *Camb.*, MB BChir *Camb.*, PhD *Camb.*   Asst. Prof.

Lim Pin, PJG, PPA, BA *Camb.*, MB BChir *Camb.*, MD *Camb.*, MA *Camb.*, FRCP, FRACP, FRCPEd, FACP   Prof.

Ling, Lieng Hsi, MB BS *Malaya*, FRCPEd, FRCPGlas   Assoc. Prof.

Liu, Edison, MD   Prof.

Low, Fatt Hoe (Adrian), MB BS *Sing.*   Asst. Prof.

Oh, Vernon M. S., BA *Camb.*, MA *Camb.*, MB BChir *Camb.*, MD *Camb.*, FACP, FRCP, FRCPEd   Prof.

Ong, Benjamin K. C., MB BS *Sing.*, MMed(IntMed) *Sing.*, FRCPGlas, FRCPEd   Assoc. Prof.

Seet, Chee Seong (Raymond), MB BS *Sing.*, MMed(IntMed) *Sing.*   Asst. Prof.

Tambyah, A. Paul, MB BS *Sing.*   Assoc. Prof.

Tan, Chorh Chuan, MB BS *Sing.*, MMed(IntMed) *NU Singapore*, PhD *NU Singapore*, FACP, FRACP, FRCP, FRCPEd   Prof.

Thai, Ah Chuan, MB BS *Sing.*, MMed(IntMed) *Sing.*, FRCPEd   Assoc. Prof.

Wai, Chun Tao (Desmond)

Wilder-Smith, Einar, MB BS *Heidel.*, MD *Heidel.*   Assoc. Prof.

Wong, John E. L., MB BS, FRCPEd   Prof.

Yeoh, Khay Guan, MB BS *Sing.*, MMed(IntMed) *Sing.*   Assoc. Prof.

Other Staff: 1 Visiting Prof.; 1 Sr. Res. Fellow; 2 Res. Scientists; 1 Visiting Fellow; 3 Adjunct Profs.; 7 Adjunct Assoc. Profs.; 5 Adjunct Sr. Fellows; 3 Adjunct Fellows; 1 Adjunct Res. Fellow; 1 Hon. Adjunct Asst. Prof.

Research: cardiology; clinical pharmacology; dermatology; endocrinology; gastroenterology

Microbiology

Tel: 6516 3275 Fax: 6776 6872
E-mail: micsec@nus.edu.sg

Chan, Soh Ha, MB BS *Monash*, PhD *Melb.*, FRCPA, FAMS   Prof.

Chow, Vincent T. K., MB BS *NU Singapore*, MSc *Lond.*, MD *NU Singapore*, PhD *NU Singapore*, FRCPath   Assoc. Prof.

Ho, Bow, BSc *Bom.*, PhD *Wales*   Assoc. Prof.

Kemeny, David M., BSc *Lond.*, PhD *Lond.*, FRCPath   Prof.; Head*

Lee, Yuan Kun, BSc *Nan.*, MSc *Nan.*, PhD *Lond.*   Assoc. Prof.

Lehming, Norbert, DrHabil *Cologne*   Asst. Prof.

Lu, Jinhua, BSc *Hebei*, DPhil *Oxf.*   Asst. Prof.

MacAry, Paul A., BSc PhD   Asst. Prof.

Ng, Mary M. L., BSc Monash, PhD Monash   Assoc. Prof.

Nga, Been Hen, BSc Malaya, PhD Sheff.   Assoc. Prof. Fellow

Poh, Chit Laa, BSc Monash, PhD Monash   Assoc. Prof.

Ren, E. C., BSc Malaya, PhD NU Singapore   Assoc. Prof.

Seah, Geok Teng, MB BS NU Singapore, MSc Lond., PhD Lond.   Asst. Prof.

Sim, Tiow Suan, BSc Lond., PhD Lond.   Assoc. Prof.

Tan, Shyong Wei (Kevin), BSc NU Singapore, PhD NU Singapore   Asst. Prof.

Taylor, Mark B., MA Camb., MB BS Lond., PhD Kent, FRCPath   Asst. Prof.

Wong, Siew Heng, MSc NU Malaysia, PhD NU Singapore   Asst. Prof.

Other Staff: 1 Postdoctoral Fellow; 1 Visiting Fellow; 17 Res. Fellows/Res. Assts.; 8 Adjunct Staff

Research: immunology; infectious diseases; vaccine initiative

Obstetrics and Gynaecology

Tel: 6772 4261 Fax: 6779 4753
    E-mail: obgsec@nus.edu.sg

Adaikan, P. Ganesan, MSc NU Singapore, PhD NU Singapore, FIBiol   Res. Assoc. Prof.

Biswas, Arijit, MB BS Calc., MD All India IMS, MD Sing., FRCOG, FAMS   Assoc. Prof.

Bongso, Ariff, MSc Guelph, PhD Guelph, DSc Sing., DSc S.Lanka, DVM Ceyl., FRCOG, FSLCOG   Res. Prof.

Chan, Jerry Kok Yen, MB BCh BAO Trinity(Dub.), MA Trinity(Dub.)   Asst. Prof.

Chong Yap Seng, MB BS NU Singapore, MMEd(ObstandGynae), FAMS   Asst. Prof.

Fong Chui Yee, BSc NU Singapore, MSc NU Singapore, PhD NU Singapore   Res. Asst. Prof.

Fong Yoke Fai, MB BS NU Singapore, MMEd(ObstandGynae), FRANZCOG   Asst. Prof.

Goh, Victor H. H., BSc NU Singapore, PhD NU Singapore, FRCPath   Res. Prof.

Gong Yinhan, BSc Wuhan, MSc Wuhan, PhD NU Singapore   Res. Asst. Prof.

Ilancheran, A., MB BS MMed MD, FRCOG   Assoc. Prof.

Mahesh Choolani, MB BS NU Singapore, MMEd(ObstandGynae) Lond., PhD Lond., FRANZCOG, FAMS   Asst. Prof.

Rauff, Mary, MB BS NU Singapore, MMEd(ObstandGynae), FRCOG   Assoc. Prof.

Singh, Kuldip, MB BS NU Singapore, MA Exe., MMed NU Singapore, MD NU Singapore, FRCOG   Prof.

Wong, P. C., MB BS Malaya, MMEd(ObstandGynae) NU Singapore, FRCOG   Assoc. Prof.; Head*

Wong, Yee Chee, MB BS NU Singapore, MMed NU Singapore, FRCOG   Assoc. Prof.

Yong, Eu Leong, MB BS NU Singapore, MMed NU Singapore, PhD NU Singapore   Prof.

Other Staff: 1 Sr. Res. Fellow; 1 Res. Fellow; 1 Adjunct Prof.

Research: cell-based therapies and reproductive endocrinology; genomics, proteomics and mechanisms of reproductive diseases; herbal drug discovery and pharmacology; maternal-foetal medicine; reproductive cancer biology

Ophthalmology

Tel: 6772 5316 Fax: 6777 7161
    E-mail: ophsec@nus.edu.sg

Ang, Leonard Pek-Kiang, MB BS NU Singapore, MMEd(Ophthalmology), FRCSEd   Asst. Prof.

Aung, Tin, MB BS NU Singapore, MMed NU Singapore, PhD Lond., FRCSEd, FRCOG   Assoc. Prof.

Chee, Soon Phaik, MB BS NU Singapore, MMEd(Ophthalmology), FRCSGlas, FRCSEd, FRCOG   Assoc. Prof.

Chew, Paul T. K., MB BS NU Singapore, MMed NU Singapore, FRCSEd, FAMS, FRCOG   Assoc. Prof.

Lim, Arthur S. M., BBM, MB BS Sing., Hon. MD, FAMS, FRCS, FRCSEd, FRACS, FICS, FRACOG, FRCOG   Clin. Prof.

Tan, Donald T. H., MB BS NU Singapore, FRCSGlas, FRCSEd, FRCOG, FAMS   Prof.; Head*

Wong, Tien Yin, MB BS NU Singapore, MMed NU Singapore, MPH Johns H., PhD Johns H., FRCSEd   Assoc. Prof.

Other Staff: 1 Visiting Prof.; 2 Jt. Appt. Staff; 1 Adjunct Prof.; 1 Adjunct Assoc. Prof.; 4 Adjunct Asst. Profs.

Research: myopia; ocular surface disease; stem cells

Otolaryngology

Tel: 6772 5370 Fax: 6775 3820
    E-mail: enthead@nus.edu.sg

Chao Siew Shuen, MB BS, FRCS   Asst. Prof.

Lim, Lynne Hsueh Lee, MPH Harv., MB BS, FRCSEd, FAMS   Asst. Prof.

Loh Kwok Seng, MB BS, FRCS   Asst. Prof.

Smith, James D., MD   Visiting Prof.

Tan, Luke Kim Siang, MB BS MMedSci, FRCSEd, FAMS, FRCSGlas   Assoc. Prof.; Head*

Yeoh, Kian Hian, MB BS HK, FRCSEd   Clin. Prof.

Other Staff: 1 Sr. Res. Scientist/Dir. of Res.; 1 Res. Assoc. Prof.

Research: genetic research in hearing loss; head and neck cancer; rhinology and rhinologic immunology

Paediatrics

Tel: 6772 4420 Fax: 6779 7486
    E-mail: paesec@nus.edu.sg

Chong, Siong-Chuan (Samuel), BSc NU Singapore, MSc Br.Col., PhD Baylor Coll.Med.   Assoc. Prof.

Chua, Kaw Yan, BSc Massey, PhD Massey   Prof.

Goh, Li Meng (Denise), MB BS NU Singapore, MMed NU Singapore   Asst. Prof.

Goh, Yam Thiam (Daniel), MB BS Sing., MMed NU Singapore   Assoc. Prof.

Joseph, Roy, MB BS Madr., MMed NU Singapore   Assoc. Prof.

Lee, Yung Seng, MB BS NU Singapore, MMed NU Singapore   Asst. Prof.

Loke, Kah Yin, MB BS NU Singapore, MMed NU Singapore, FRCPEd   Assoc. Prof.

Low, Poh Sim, MB BS Sing., MMed NU Singapore, MD NU Singapore, FRCPEd, FRCPCH, FRACP   Prof.

Ngiam, Siew Pei (Nicola), MB BS NU Singapore, MMed NU Singapore   Asst. Prof.

Quah, Thuan Chong, MB BS Sing., MMed NU Singapore   Assoc. Prof.

Quak, Seng Hock, MB BS Sing., MMed NU Singapore, MD NU Singapore, FRCPGlas, FRCPCH, FAMS   Assoc. Prof.; Head*

Quek, Swee Chye, MB BS NU Singapore, MMed NU Singapore, MD NU Singapore, FACC, FRCPCH, FAMS   Assoc. Prof.

Shek, Pei-Chi (Lynette), MB BS NU Singapore, MMed NU Singapore   Asst. Prof.

Tay, Kiat Hong (Stacey), MB BS NU Singapore, MMed NU Singapore   Asst. Prof.

Van Bever, Hugo P. S., MD Ghent   Prof., Clinical Paediatrics

Yap, Hui Kim, MB BS Sing., MMed NU Singapore, MD NU Singapore, FRCPEd, FRCPCH   Prof.

Yeoh, Eng Juh (Allen), MB BS NU Singapore, MMed NU Singapore   Asst. Prof.

Zubair Amin, MB BS Dhaka   Asst. Prof.

Other Staff: 2 Sr. Res. Fellows; 2 Adjunct Assoc. Profs.

Research: human genetics; immunology and allergy; paediatric oncology

Pathology

Tel: 6772 4300 Fax: 6778 0671
    E-mail: patsec@nus.edu.sg

Chang, Alexander R., MB ChB Otago, MD Otago, DCP Otago, FRCPA, FHKAM   Visiting Prof.

Hewitt, Robert E., BSc Lond., MB BS Lond., PhD Glas.   Asst. Prof.

Koay, Evelyn S. C., BSc Malaya, MSc Lond., PhD Hawaii, FRCPath   Assoc. Prof.

Lee, Yoke Sun, MB BS Sing., MD NU Singapore, FRCPA   Prof.

Lim, Yaw Chyn, MSc Brad., PhD Brad.   Asst. Prof.

Putti, Thomas C., MB BS Osm., MD Osm.

Raju, Gangaraju C., MB BS S.Venkat., MD S.Venkat., FRCPath   Assoc. Prof.

Salto-Tellez, Manuel, LMS Oviedo   Asst. Prof.

Sethi, Sunil K., MB BS NU Singapore, MMed(IntMed) NU Singapore, PhD Sur.   Assoc. Prof.

Shanmugaratnam, K., MD Malaya, PhD Lond., FRCPA, FRCPath   Prof. Fellow

Soong, Richie C. T., BS W.Aust., PhD W.Aust.   Asst. Prof.

Tan, Kong Bing, MB BS Sing., FRCPA   Asst. Prof.

Teh, Ming, BA Yale, MD Johns H., FRCPA, FRCPath   Assoc. Prof.; Head*

Thamboo, Thomas P., MB BS Leeds, FRCPA   Asst. Prof.

Tock, Edward P. C., PPA, MB BS Malaya, MD Sing., PhD Lond., FRCPA, FRCPath   Prof. Fellow

Wee, Aileen, MB BS Sing., FRCPA   Prof.

Other Staff: 1 Sr. Tutor

Research: characterisation of neoplasms using molecular immunohistochemistry and morphological techniques

Pharmacology

Tel: 6516 3264 Fax: 6773 0579
    E-mail: phcsec@nus.edu.sg

Bhatia, Madhav, BSc All India IMS, MSc All India IMS, PhD All India IMS   Assoc. Prof.

Bian, Jin Song, MSc Nanjing Med., PhD HK, MB BS   Asst. Prof.

Boelsterli, Urs A., MSc Zür., PhD Zür.   Assoc. Prof.

Dawe, Gavin S., BSc Edin., PhD Lond.   Asst. Prof.

Gwee, Matthew C. E., BPharm Sing., PhD Sing., MHPEd NSW, FIBiol   Prof.

Lee, Edmund J. D., MB BS Sing., MMed Sing., PhD NSW   Prof.

Lee, How-Sung, BPharm Sing., MPharm Sing., PhD Sing.   Assoc. Prof.

Low, Chian Ming, BSc(Pharm) Sing., MSc Lond., PhD Sing.   Asst. Prof.

Moore, Philip K., BSc Lond., PhD Lond.   Prof.; Head*

Sim, Meng Kwoon, BSc Sing., MSc Syd., PhD Syd., DSc Sing.   Assoc. Prof.

Tan, Benny K. H., MB BS Sing., PhD NU Singapore   Assoc. Prof.

Tan, Chay Hoon, MB BS Sing., MMed NU Singapore, PhD Sing.   Assoc. Prof.

Wong, Peter T. H., BSc Lond., PhD Lond.   Assoc. Prof.

Wong, W. S. Fred, BSPharm St.John's(N.Y.), MS Ohio State, PhD Ohio State   Assoc. Prof.

Other Staff: 1 Sr. Res. Fellow; 8 Res. Fellows

Research: cardiovascular pharmacology; inflammation and asthma; neuropharmacology; pharmacogenomics; pharmacokinetics

Physiology

Tel: 6516 3223 Fax: 6778 8161
    E-mail: phssec@nus.edu.sg

Deng, Yuru, MS N.Y.State, DDS Kaohsiung, PhD N.Y.State   Asst. Prof.

Hande, M. Prakash, BSc M'lore., MSc Mys., PhD M'lore.   Assoc. Prof.

Ho, Ting Fei, MB BS Sing., MMed NU Singapore, MD NU Singapore, FRCPEd   Assoc. Prof.

Hooi, Shing Chuan, MB BS NU Singapore, PhD Harv.   Assoc. Prof.; Head*

Hwang, Peter L. H., MB BS Sing., PhD McG., FRCPCan   Prof.

Khanna, Sanjay, BPharm Delhi, MPharm Panjab, MSc Br.Col., PhD Br.Col.   Assoc. Prof.

Koh, Dow Rhoon, MB BS NU Singapore, MMed NU Singapore, PhD Tor.   Assoc. Prof.

Lee, Chee Wee, BSc McG., MSc McG., PhD Alta.   Assoc. Prof.

Lee, Yiu Wah Alan, BSc HK, PhD HK   Asst. Prof.

Lee Beng Huat, Martin, MB BS NU Singapore, PhD Calif.   Asst. Prof.

Leung Pui Lam, Bernard, BSc Glas., PhD Glas.   Asst. Prof.

Lim, Lina H. K., BSc Lond., PhD Lond.   Asst. Prof.

Lim, Yaw Chyn, MSc Brad., PhD Brad.   Asst. Prof.

Melendez, Alirio J., MB BS Moscow, BSc Glas., PhD Glas.   Asst. Prof.

Pervaiz, Shazib, MB BS Punjab, PhD S.Methodist   Assoc. Prof.

Schwarz, Herbert, PhD Würzburg   Assoc. Prof.

Shen, Shali, MB BS Yuzhou, MD Yuzhou, MSc Brussels, PhD Brussels   Asst. Prof.

Soong, Tuck Wah, BSc NU Singapore, PhD NU Singapore   Assoc. Prof.

Swaminathan, Srividya, BSc Delhi, MSc B'lore., PhD J.Nehru U.   Asst. Prof.; Sr. Res. Scientist

Wang Nai-dy, BA Calif., BSc Calif., PhD Wayne State   Asst. Prof.

Wong, Chong Thim, BSc W.Aust., PhD W.Aust.   Assoc. Prof.

Yap Suen Mei, Celestial, MB BS NU Singapore, PhD Edin.   Asst. Prof.

Yu, Hanry, BSc Mich.State, MSc Wash.(Mo.), PhD Duke   Assoc. Prof.

Other Staff: 21 Res. Fellows; 4 Adjunct Assoc. Profs.; 6 Adjunct Asst. Profs.

Research: apoptosis and cancer biology; cell and tissue engineering; immunology and inflammation; neurobiology

Psychological Medicine

Tel: 6772 4514 Fax: 6777 2191
   E-mail: pcmfslc@nus.edu.sg

Fones, Soon Leng (Calvin), MB BS NU Singapore, MMed NU Singapore   Assoc. Prof.; Head*

Kua, Ee Heok, PBM, MB BS Malaya, MD NU Singapore, FRCPsych   Prof.

Kumar, Rajeev, MB BS ANU, DPM ANU, MD ANU, PhD ANU, FRANZCP   Asst. Prof.

Tan Hao Yang, MB BS NU Singapore, MMed NU Singapore   Asst. Prof.

Other Staff: 3 Adjunct Staff

Research: anxiety disorders; geriatric psychiatry; gerontology; health sciences; psychiatric epidemiology

Surgery

Tel: 6772 4221 Fax: 6777 8427
   E-mail: sursec@nus.edu.sg

Chiong, Edmund, MB BS, FRCSEd, FRCSI   Asst. Prof.

Esuvaranathan, Kesavan, MB BS, FRCSGlas, FRCSEd   Assoc. Prof.

Lee, Chuen Neng, MB BS MMed, FRCSGlas, FRCSEd, FRACS, FACC   Prof.

Leong, Peng Kheong (Adrian), MB BS NU Singapore, MMed NU Singapore, FRCSEd, FAMS   Assoc. Prof.

Lim, Thiam Chye, MB BS Malaya, FRCSEd   Assoc. Prof.

Prabhakaran, K., MB BS Sing., MMed Sing., FRCSEd, FRCSGlas   Assoc. Prof.

Robless, Peter A., MB ChB MD, FRCSEd, FRCS   Assoc. Prof.

Schantz, Jan-Thorsten, MD Freib., PhD NU Singapore   Asst. Prof.

Ti, Thiow Kong, MB BS Sing., MD Malaya, FRCS, FRACS, FRCSEd   Prof. Fellow

Wong, Poo Sing, MB BS, FRCSEd   Assoc. Prof.

Other Staff: 4 Acad. Res. Staff

Research: bladder cancer; breast cancer; prostatic cancer/urinary incontinence; stem cell research in myocardial infarct models; tissue engineering for bone/skin reconstruction

Surgery, Orthopaedic

Tel: 6772 4342 Fax: 6778 0720
   E-mail: dossec@nus.edu.sg

Das De, Shamal, MB BS Calc., MChOrth Liv., MD NU Singapore, FRCSEd, FRCS   Prof.

Goh, Cho Hong (James), BSc Strath., PhD Strath.   Res. Assoc. Prof. (joint appointment with Bioengineering)

Hee, Hwan Tak, MB BS Sing., FRCSEd, FRCSGlas   Asst. Prof.

Hui, Hoi Po (James), MB BS Sing., FRCSEd   Assoc. Prof.

Lee, Eng Hin, PBM, MD, FRCSCan, FRCSGlas, FRCSEd   Prof.

Lim, Yutang A., MB BS Sing., FRCSGlas   Assoc. Prof.

Nather, Abdul A. M., PBM, MB BS Sing., MD NU Singapore, FRCSEd, FRCSGlas   Assoc. Prof.

Pho, Robert W. H., MB BS Syd., MD Syd., FRCSEd   Prof. Fellow

Prem Kumar, V., MB BS Sing., FRCSEd, FRCSGlas   Prof.

Saminathan, Suresh N., MB BS Sing., MMed Sing., FRCSEd, FAMS   Asst. Prof.

Satkunanantham, Kandiah, MB BS Sing., MMed Sing., FRCSEd, FAMS   Prof.

Wang, Wilson E Jan, MB BS Lond., DPhil Oxf., FRCSGlas   Asst. Prof.

Wong, Hee Kit, MB BS Sing., MChOrth Liv., MMed NU Singapore, FRCSGlas   Prof.; Head*

Other Staff: 1 Visiting Prof.; 1 Res. Fellow; 1 Adjunct Prof.; 2 Adjunct Assoc. Profs.; 1 Hon. Adjunct Assoc. Prof.; 1 Hon. Adjunct Asst. Prof.

Research: musculoskeletal tissue engineering including stem cell research; orthopaedic bioengineering; osteoporosis and fractures

SPECIAL CENTRES, ETC

Asia Research Institute

Tel: 6516 3810 Fax: 6779 1428
   E-mail: arisec@nus.edu.sg

Reid, Anthony, BA Well., MA Well., PhD Camb.   Prof.; Dir.*

Other Staff: 2 Asst. Profs.; 7 Sr. Res. Fellows; 15 Visiting Sr. Res. Fellows; 12 Postdoctoral Fellows; 5 Res. Leaders

Research: changing family; cultural studies; migration; religion and globalisation

Corporate Governance and Financial Reporting Centre

Tel: 6516 7609 Fax: 6778 4275
   E-mail: cgfrc@nus.edu.sg

Lan, Luh Luh, LLB NU Singapore, LLM Camb.   Asst. Prof.; Deputy Dir.

Mak Yuen Teen, BCom Otago, MCom Otago, PhD Well.   Assoc. Prof.; Dir.*

Other Staff: 1 Manager; 1 Asst. Manager

Research: corporate governance; financial reporting

E-Business, Centre for

Tel: 6516 6225 Fax: 6779 2621
   E-mail: e-biz@nus.edu.sg

Ang, James S. K., BSc Sing., MASc Wat., PhD Wat.   Assoc. Prof.; Dir.*

Chou, Fee Seng, BSc Cant., PhD Cant.   Assoc. Prof.

Hsiao, Rueylin, BSc Natnl.Taiwan I.T., MSc Warw., MPhil Cran., PhD Warw.   Asst. Prof.

Ou, Jihong, BS Zhengzhou I.T., MS Chinese Acad.Sc., MS Mass., PhD M.I.T.   Assoc. Prof.

Sun, Jie, BS Tsinghua, MS Chinese Acad.Sc., MS Wash., PhD Wash.   Prof.

Teo, Chung Piaw, BSc NU Singapore, PhD M.I.T.   Assoc. Prof.

Teo, Thompson S. H., BEng NU Singapore, MSc NU Singapore, PhD Pitt.   Assoc. Prof.

Ye, Hengqing, BSc S.China U.T., MSc S.China U.T., PhD HKUST   Asst. Prof.

Other Staff: 1 Res. Fellow

Research: e-business innovations and services; Internet traffic congestion; quality of service level; software development for project management

Financial Studies, Saw Centre for

Tel: 6516 5835 Fax: 6874 5834
   E-mail: sawcentre@nus.edu.sg

Lim, Joseph Y. S., BBA Sing., MBA Col., MPhil N.Y., PhD N.Y.   Assoc. Prof.; Dir.*

Saw Swee Hock, BA Sing., MA Sing., PhD Lond.   Prof.; Patron

Yamada, Takeshi, BA Keio, MA Keio, PhD Calif.   Assoc. Prof.

Other Staff: 1 Res. Fellow

Research: corporate finance; financial policy issues; fund management; risk management; wealth management

Language Studies, Centre for

Tel: 6516 6346 Fax: 6777 7736
   E-mail: clssec@nus.edu.sg

Chan, Wai Meng, MA Würzburg, DrPhil Kassel   Asst. Prof.; Dir.*

Chin, Kwee Nyet, BA NU Singapore, MA NU Singapore, PhD HK   Sr. Lectr.

Reeves, Peter, BA Tas., MA Tas., PhD ANU   Visiting Prof.

Suthiwan, Titima, BA Chulalongkorn, PhD Hawaii   Asst. Prof.

Other Staff: 23 Lectrs.; 1 Fellow; 12 Instrs.

Research: foreign language education; second language acquisition

Logistics Institute

Asia Pacific

Tel: 6516 4842 Fax: 6775 3391
   E-mail: tlihead@nus.edu.sg

de Souza, Robert, PhD   Exec. Dir.*

Other Staff: 3 Dirs.; 7 Res. Fellows; 7 Res. Engineers

Research: defence logistics; supply chain intelligence; supply chain optimisation; supply chain technology

Mathematical Sciences, Institute for

Tel: 6516 1897 Fax: 6873 8292
   E-mail: ims@nus.edu.sg

Chen, Hsiao Yun (Louis), BSc Sing., MS Stan., PhD Stan.   Prof.; Dir.*

Other Staff: 1 Deputy Dir.

Research: applied probability; computational biology; Stein's method

Nanoscience and Nanotechnology Initiative

Tel: 6516 4265 Fax: 6872 5563
   E-mail: nnisec@nus.edu.sg

Cho, Byung-Jin, PhD Korea A.I.S.T.   Assoc. Prof.; Deputy Dir.

Ramakrishna, Seeram, BEng And., MTech IIT Madras, PhD Camb., FIMMM, FIE(Sing), FIMechE   Prof.; Co-Dir.*

Wee, Andrew Thye Shen, BA Camb., MA Camb., DPhil Oxf.   Prof.; Co-Dir.*

Other Staff: 20 Principal Investigators; 20 Co-Principal Investigators

Research: nanobiotechnology; nanofibre science and engineering; nanomagnetics and spintronics; nano/micro fabrication; nanophotonics

Project Management and Construction Law, Centre for

Tel: 6516 3437 Fax: 6775 5502
   E-mail: bdgccf@nus.edu.sg

Chan, Philip C. F., LLB Lond., LLM Lond., PhD Lond.   Assoc. Prof.; Co-Dir.*

Tan, Willie C. K., BSurv Newcastle(NSW), MSc(EstMgt) NU Singapore, PhD Syd.   Assoc. Prof.; Co-Dir.*

Research: project management and construction law

Remote Imaging, Sensing and Processing, Centre for

Tel: 6516 6396 Fax: 6775 7717
   E-mail: crisp@nus.edu.sg

Kwoh, L. K., BTech S.Aust., MEngSc NSW   Dir.*

Research: geometric processing; remote sensing of coastal waters; remote sensing of regional environment; synthetic aperture radar (SAR) applications (inteferometric, polarimetric); 3-D mapping

Singapore Synchrotron Light Source

Tel: 6516 1135 Fax: 6773 6734
   E-mail: slsuserdeck@nus.edu.sg

Moser, Herbert O., DrIng   Prof.; Dir.*

Other Staff: 1 Sr. Res. Fellow (Beamline Scientists); 7 Res. Fellows (Beamline and Accelerator Scientists)
Research: generation and application of synchrotron radiation; materials science (hard/soft X-rays, infrared); micro- and nano-fabrication (electromagnetic/photonic/ optical micro- and nano-devices, nanolithography); nanoscience and technology (novel nanomaterials/ applications); supramini-based 4th generation light sources

South Asian Studies, Institute of

Tel: 6516 6179 Fax: 6776 7505
E-mail: isaspt@nus.edu.sg
Tan, Tai Yong, BA NU Singapore, MA NU Singapore, PhD Camb.   Assoc. Prof.; Dir. (Acting)*
Other Staff: 1 Visiting Sr. Res. Fellow; 3 Res. Fellows; 1 Visiting Res. Fellow
Research: economic developments (cold chain management, economic reforms, energy, health economics, information technology and telecommunications, infrastructure, special economic zones); elections and political parties; politics and governance; regional and international developments (South Asia regionalism, South Asia-China relations, South Asia-Southeast Asia relations, South Asia-United States relations); state studies

Temasek Laboratories

Tel: 6516 4029 Fax: 6872 6840
E-mail: tslsec@nus.edu.sg
Lim, Hock, BSc Sing., PhD Reading   Prof.; Dir.*
Other Staff: 4 Principal Res. Scientists; 2 Sr. Res. Scientists; 27 Res. Scientists; 18 Assoc. Scientists; 1 Adjunct Sr. Principal Res. Scientist; 2 Adjunct Principal Res. Scientists; 1 Adjunct Res. Scientist
Research: aerodynamics (aerodynamic devices, flow control, shape optimisation); control and guidance (non-linear robust flight control, tactical guidance); electromagnetics (materials, radiation, scattering); information security (cryptography, quantum cryptography, system security); signal processing (information processing, wavelets)

Total Building Performance, Centre for

Tel: 6516 4082 Fax: 6773 3837
E-mail: bdgtyy@nus.edu.sg
Lee, Siew Eang, BSc H-W, MSc H-W, PhD H-W   Assoc. Prof.; Dir.*
Tham, Kwok Wai, BEng NU Singapore, MBldg Syd., PhD Syd.   Assoc. Prof.; Deputy Dir.

Other Staff: 1 Res. Fellow
Research: total building performance

Tropical Marine Science Institute

Tel: 6774 9656 Fax: 6774 9654
E-mail: tmskampj@nus.edu.sg
Chan, E. S., BEng Sing., MEng NU Singapore, ScD M.I.T.   Prof.; Dir.*
Other Staff: 1 Res. Assoc. Prof.; 1 Principal Res. Fellow; 3 Sr. Res. Fellows; 16 Res. Fellows; 19 Res. Engineers
Research: acoustic research; environmental monitoring; marine biology and aquaculture; marine eco-toxicology and chemistry; physical oceanography

CONTACT OFFICERS

Accommodation. Assistant Manager, Office of Student Affairs: Toh, Chwee Peng, BSc H-W (E-mail: osatohcp@nus.edu.sg)
Admissions (first degree). Dean of Admissions: Tan, Prof. T. S., BE Cant., MSc Cal.Tech., PhD Cal.Tech.
Adult/continuing education. Senior Manager, Operations: Wong Peng Meng, BSc NU Singapore (E-mail: nexquery@nus.edu.sg)
Alumni. Director, Office of Alumni Relations: Teo, Choo Soo, BDS Sing., MSc Lond. (E-mail: oarsec@nus.edu.sg)
Careers. Senior Manager, Office of Student Affairs: Wong, Sing Chee, BSSc NU Singapore, MA Missouri (E-mail: osawsc@nus.edu.sg)
Computing services. Director, Computer Centre: Hor, Tommy, BSc Lond., MPhil HK (E-mail: ccesec@nus.edu.sg)
Conferences/corporate hospitality. Director, Office of Corporate Relations: Toh, Bernard, BA(ArchStud) NU Singapore, MBA Cran. (E-mail: ocrsec@nus.edu.sg)
Development/fund-raising. Director, Development Office: Chew, K. C., BA Harv. (E-mail: dvosec@nus.edu.sg)
Estates and buildings/works and services. Senior Manager, Office of Estate and Development: Tan, Ian, BEng Nan. (E-mail: oedtani@nus.edu.sg)
Finance. Deputy Bursar, Office of Finance: Tay, Sok Kian, BSc Manc., FCA (E-mail: ofntsk@nus.edu.sg)
Health services. Director, University Health, Wellness and Counselling Centre: Chua, Catherine, MB BS NSW, Dr (E-mail: uhssec@nus.edu.sg)
Industrial liaison. Deputy Director, Industry and Technology Relations Office: Kway, Jasmine, BEng NU Singapore, PhD NU Singapore (E-mail: jasminekway@nus.edu.sg)
International office. Director, International Relations Office: Loh, Prof. Hong Sai, BDS

Sing., MDS Sing., FDSRCSEd, FDSRCPSGlas (E-mail: irosec@nus.edu.sg)
Library (chief librarian). Director, NUS Libraries: Yap, Sylvia, BSc Sing. (E-mail: clbsec@nus.edu.sg)
Personnel/human resources. Vice-President (Human Resources): Cho, Daniel, BSc NU Singapore (E-mail: ohrhead@nus.edu.sg)
Public relations. Head, Media Relations: Thayalan, Leila, LLB LLM (E-mail: ocrlt@nus.edu.sg)
Publications. Head, Corporate Information and Identity: Wong, M. L. Mabel, BA NU Singapore (E-mail: ocrwongm@nus.edu.sg)
Quality assurance and accreditation. Acting Director, Office of Quality Management: Tan, K. C., BS Mass., MS Mass., PhD Virginia Polytech. (E-mail: oqmsec@nus.edu.sg)
Research. Director, Office of Research: Nee, Prof. Andrew Y. C., MSc Manc., PhD Manc., DEng UMIST (E-mail: oresec@nus.edu.sg)
Scholarships, awards, loans. Registrar: Ang, Siau Gek, BSc NU Singapore, MSc NU Singapore, PhD Camb. (E-mail: regenquiry@nus.edu.sg)
Security. Senior Manager, Office of Estate and Development: Samynathan, P., BA S.Illinois (E-mail: oedsp@nus.edu.sg)
Sport and recreation. Head, Sports and Recreation Centre: Seetow, Cheng Fave, BA RMIT (E-mail: osascf@nus.edu.sg)
Staff development and training. Vice-President (Human Resources): Cho, Daniel, BSc NU Singapore (E-mail: ohrhead@nus.edu.sg)
Student union. President, NUS Students' Union: Quek Boon Guan, Danny (E-mail: u0201337@nus.edu.sg)
Student welfare/counselling. Acting Head of Counselling Centre, University Health, Wellness and Counselling Centre: Lew, Ann-Marie, PhD Calif. (E-mail: counselling@nus.edu.sg)
Students from other countries. Senior Administrative Officer, International Student Services: Anwar, Reza Shah Mohd, BA NU Singapore (E-mail: rezashah@nus.edu.sg)
Students with disabilities. Co-ordinator, Office of Student Affairs: Pang, Yu Ling, BSc UMIST (E-mail: osapyl@nus.edu.sg)
University press. Director, NUS Publishing: Krastoka, Paul (E-mail: nusbooks@nus.edu.sg)

[Information supplied by the institution as at 31 May 2006, and edited by the ACU]

SOUTH AFRICA

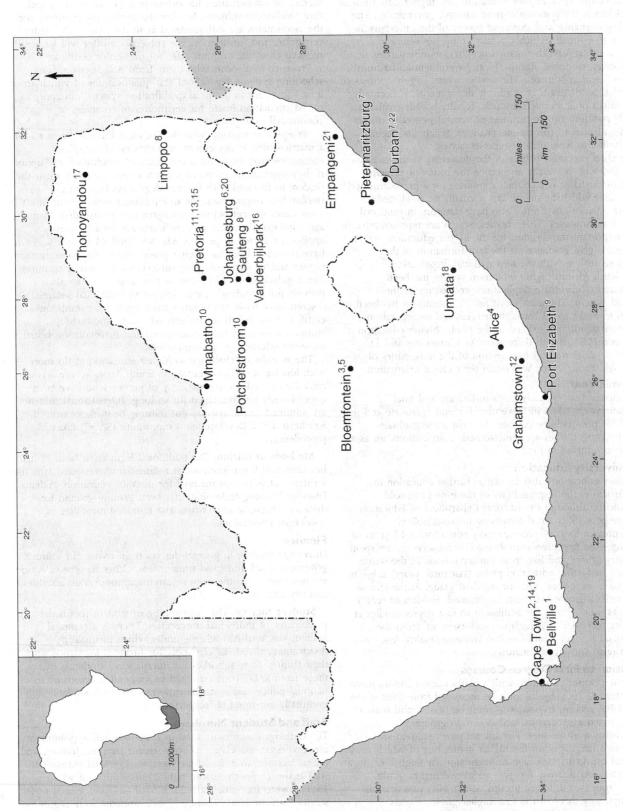

THE UNIVERSITIES OF SOUTH AFRICA

N

Thohoyandou[17]

Limpopo[8]

Pretoria[11,13,15]

Johannesburg[6,20]

Gauteng[8]

Vanderbijlpark[16]

Mmabatho[10]

Potchefstroom[10]

Bloemfontein[3,5]

Empangeni[21]

Pietermaritzburg[7]

Durban[7,22]

Umtata[18]

Alice[4]

Port Elizabeth[9]

Grahamstown[12]

Cape Town[2,14,19]

Bellville[1]

The places named are the seats of the institutions numbered on the previous page

THE UNIVERSITIES OF SOUTH AFRICA

Information compiled by Higher Education South Africa (HESA) as at 30 November 2006

The University System

In terms of the 1997 Higher Education Act, higher education in South Africa is the responsibility of national government. The control, governance and executive power of the university is vested in its council, which typically comprises senior management (at least the vice-chancellor), representatives of staff, donors, students, alumni, local government and a number of government appointees. The senate, which largely consists of full professors or heads of academic departments, is normally the guardian of academic standards. Faculty boards (which are typically standing sub-committees of senate) generally consist of academic staff of the various faculties. Senate and faculty boards will also have student representatives.

The chief executive officer of the university is the vice-chancellor, who is usually also called the rector or principal. The vice-chancellor is a council appointee for a predetermined period, after which he or she can normally be re-elected.

South African universities also have statutory institutional fora on the campuses. These bodies, which are representative of all the important stakeholders for the higher education institutions, give guidance on the transformation of the institutions in line with the new national dispensation.

The South African higher education system has been restructured to eliminate duplications created under the apartheid system. The number of public institutions has been reduced from 32 to 23 through mergers and incorporations. The binary divide that existed in the public higher education system pre-2002, where there were 21 universities and 15 technikons, is blurred by the creation of the universities of technology, though they will retain their career orientation.

Academic Year

The academic year typically starts in January and final examinations are taken in November for undergraduate and in January for postgraduate courses. As most undergraduate university programmes are semesterised, examinations are as a rule also conducted in June.

Pre-University Education

Pre-tertiary education (also known as further education in South Africa) is the responsibility of the nine provincial governments, although the national Department of Education retains responsibility for determining national policy.

The present basis of pre-university education is 12 years of schooling—the first nine years being compulsory—seven spent in primary school and five in secondary school. In the senior secondary or further education phase (last three years) subjects can be taken at higher grade or standard grade. At the end of the 12 years a senior certificate is obtained. Holders of senior certificates who qualify for admission to first degree studies at university receive a 'matriculation endorsement' from the General and Further Education and Training Quality Assurance Council (also known as Umalusi).

Admission to First Degree Courses

To obtain a senior certificate with a matriculation endorsement a minimum of six subjects must be presented from four of the six available groups, five subjects must be passed, and both a predetermined aggregate as well as certain grouping requirements must be met. The subject pass requirements include two languages on the higher grade, one of which must be a local university language of instruction (ie English or, to a lesser extent, Afrikaans), and two additional higher grade subjects from two different groups with a 40% pass mark in the compulsory three of the four higher grade subjects.

As from 2008 the National Senior Certificate will replace the senior certificate. The phasing in of the new programme started as from the tenth grade in 2006. The National Senior Certificate will consist of two compulsory official languages, mathematical literacy or mathematics, life orientation (a half subject) and three additional subjects. Neither the subject programmes nor the assessments are differentiated as in the case of the senior certificate, and furthermore the subjects on offer will be greatly reduced from the ones on offer for the senior certificate.

Prospective students who come from non-South African schooling systems, the school exit qualifications of which are at least equivalent to the local qualification system, can apply to the Matriculation Board for certificates of complete or conditional exemption.

Prospective students who do not meet the requirements for a matriculation endorsement or certificate of complete exemption may apply for a certificate of conditional exemption, if they meet the requirements. Such a certificate will allow the student to proceed with his/her degree studies, but the outstanding requirement, or an equivalent requirement, must in some cases be met before the degree can be awarded. Mature age conditional exemption certificates are on a university's application issued to persons who are aged 23 or over and who have passed at least one higher grade subject and three further higher and/or standard grade subjects for the senior certificate. The regulations for admission to first degree studies also provide for a student's admission on an individual senate's discretionary basis. Universities must apply for exemption certificates on behalf of students who have successfully completed institutionally determined and matriculation board recorded selection programmes/tests.

The worldwide challenge to higher education to do more with less has a special meaning in South Africa where access must be opened up to a majority of people who have been educationally disadvantaged for so long. International students are admitted to the system, but training of students from the Southern Africa Development Community (SADC) takes precedence.

Methods of tuition. The traditional lecturer in front of his/her class is still predominant at residential universities, as is the written text as tuition material for distance education students. Distance learning technology has been gaining ground for distance education universities and removed campuses of residential universities.

Finance

University income in general derives from two main sources: government subsidies and student fees. Other income categories are donations, income from research and innovation activities, and investments.

Student finance. The determining of student fees is the prerogative of individual universities. There is a National Student Financial Aid Scheme under which financially disadvantaged students can apply for financial assistance with their studies. State subsidies for international students, except those from SADC countries, will be suspended according to national policy and it can be expected that such students will eventually become full-fee-paying

Staff and Student Numbers

The rankings customarily used in academic staff appointments are: professor, associate professor, senior lecturer, lecturer and junior lecturer. In 2005, there were 43,336 total permanent staff at the 23 South African public universities, of whom 15,315 were academic staff, 21,375 administrative, and 6646 service staff. In 2005, about 737,472 students were registered at 23 South African universities, of whom 254,877 were registered mainly for courses offered in distance mode, and 115,589 were postgraduates.

SOUTH AFRICA : DIRECTORY TO SUBJECTS OF STUDY

The table below shows which of the institutions indicated provide facilities for study and/or research in the subjects named. In the case of related subject areas which have been grouped together (eg Agronomy/Soil Science), it should be borne in mind that one or more of the subjects may be offered by the institution concerned.

For further information about the individual subjects taught at each institution, please refer to the *Index to Subjects of Study* at the end of the Yearbook, but for full details about subjects/courses offered at universities in the Commonwealth each institution's own official publications must be consulted. U = may be studied for first degree course; M = may be studied for master's degree course; D = research facilities to doctoral level; X = all three levels (UMD). **Note**—The table only includes information provided by institutions currently in membership of the Association of Commonwealth Universities.

	Cape Town	Fort Hare	Johannesburg	KwaZulu-Natal	Nelson Mandela Met.	North-West	Pretoria	Rhodes	Stellenbosch	Venda	Western Cape	Witwatersrand
Accountancy/Accounting	X	X	X	X	X	X	X	X	X		X	X
Administration/Administrative Studies	M	X	X		X	X	X		X			
Advertising			X									
African Languages/Studies	X	X	X	X	X	X	X	X	X		X	X
Afrikaans/Dutch	X	X	X	X	X	X	X	X	X		X	X
Agricultural Extension and Education						X				X		
Agriculture/Agricultural Science		X		U	X	X	X		X	X	X	
Agronomy/Soil Science		UM		X		X	X		X	X		
Agrotechnology							X			X		
Anaesthesia/Anaesthesiology									X			
Anatomical Science/Anatomy		U				X	X		X		UM	X
Animal Nutrition/Animal Physiology									X	X		
Animal Science/Husbandry/Production		X		X		X	X	X	X	X		
Anthropology/Folklore	X	U	X	X	X	U	X	X	MD	X	X	U
Applied Chemistry							MD		X	X		
Applied Physics							X			X		
Aquaculture/Fisheries/Marine Science	X	X			X			X	M		MD	
Arabic	U		X								X	
Archaeology	X	UM		U			X					X
Architectural Design					X		X					
Architecture	X			X	X		X					X
Area Studies							U					
Art, Fine	X	X		X	U		X	X	X			X
Art, History of	X	UM		X	X	X	X	X	X			U
Artificial Intelligence							MD					
Arts General									X			
Arts and Culture									X			
Arts, Graphic						UM	X		UM			
Asian/Pacific Studies									UM			
Astronomy/Astrophysics/Space Science	X					MD						
Audiology							X		UM	X		U
Banking/Finance			X		X	X	X	X	X			
Behavioural Sciences		UM	X	X		X	X	X	X			
Biochemistry	X	X	X	X	X	X	X	X	X		X	X
Bioengineering									M			
Bioethics									MD			
Bioinformatics							X	U			MD	
Biology	X	X	X	X	X	X	X	X	X		X	X
Biology Molecular				MD	X	MD	X		X			

	Cape Town	Fort Hare	Johannesburg	KwaZulu-Natal	Nelson Mandela Met.	North-West	Pretoria	Rhodes	Stellenbosch	Venda	Western Cape	Witwatersrand
Biomedical Sciences	M	U		X	U		X		X		X	
Biophysics					U		U		M			
Biostatistics							X					
Biotechnology		UM			X		X	X	X		X	
Botany/Plant Science	X	X	X	X	X	X	X	X	X		X	
Building/Built Environment/Construction	X			X	X		X		X			X
Business Administration		X		X	X	X	X		X	X		M
Business Computing						X	U					
Business Economics							X		X	X		
Business Information Systems					U		X		X			
Business/Commerce	X	X	X	X	X	X	X	X	X	X		X
Chemistry	X	X	X	X	X	X	X	X	X		X	X
Child Health									X	X		
Child Welfare							X		X	X		
Child and Family Psychology									X	X		
Child/Youth Studies				X	X		X		X	X	M	
Chinese Language and Literature									U			
Chinese/Chinese Studies									U			
Civil Care/Security							X					
Classics/Greek/Latin/Ancient History	X	U	X	X		X	X	X	X			X
Cognitive Science				X			UM					
Communication Sciences		X	X				X			UM		
Communication/Journalism/Media Studies	U	X	X	X	U	X	U	X	X	UM		
Communications/Information Management			X		X		X		MD	UM		
Community Education							M		UM			
Community Health					U		X				X	
Community Medicine							X		UM			
Community Studies				X		X	X		X	X		
Computer Science	X	X	X	X	X	X	X	X	X	U	X	X
Conservation Studies	M			X	X	X	X					
Consumer Studies				MD	X	X	X					
Corporate Governance									UM			
Counselling			MD	MD	X	X	X		X			
Creative Writing	X			MD	UM	U	UM		M			
Criminal Justice/Public Policy					X		X			X		
Criminology		X				X	X				X	X
Crop Science/Production		X		X		X	X		X	X		
Cultural Heritage							X		M			
Cultural Studies		U			U		X		X			

	Cape Town	Fort Hare	Johannesburg	KwaZulu-Natal	Nelson Mandela Met.	North-West	Pretoria	Rhodes	Stellenbosch	Venda	Western Cape	Witwatersrand
Curriculum and Assessment Studies							X		X	X		
Deaf Studies							X					
Defence Studies									UM			
Dentistry							X				X	X
Dermatology									UM			
Design				U			X		UM			
Design, Industrial							X					
Development Studies			X	X	X	X	X	X	X	X	X	
Diplomacy									M			
Disability Studies							U		M			
Drama/Theatre/Dance/Performing Arts	X			X			X	X	X			
E-Business							U		MD			
E-Commerce					U	M	U		M			
Ecology		X			X	X	X		X			
Economic History	X			X	X		X	X	X			X
Economic Planning and Development									X			
Economics	X	X	X	X	X	X	X	X	X	X	X	X
Economics Agricultural/Agribusiness		X		X		X	X		X	X		
Education	X	X	X	X	X	X	X	X	X	X	X	X
Education Adult							X	MD	M	X	X	
Education Distance				MD		X	UM		MD	U		
Education Extension							X					
Education Primary						X	X	X	UM			
Education Secondary						X	X		MD			
Education Special						X	X		X	X		
Education Tertiary							X		MD			
Educational Administration							X					
Educational Psychology							X		X	X		
Egyptology									MD			
Electronics									X			
Emergency/Trauma Care Technology							M					
Engineering			X	X	X		X		X			X
Engineering Aeronautical/Aerospace							X		MD			U
Engineering Agricultural/Fisheries				X			X					
Engineering Automobile									MD			
Engineering Biomedical	MD								MD			
Engineering Chemical/Petrochemical/Process	X			X		X	X		X			X
Engineering Civil/Environmental/Structural	X		X	X	X		X		X			X
Engineering Communications/Telecommunications							X		X			

	Cape Town	Fort Hare	Johannesburg	KwaZulu-Natal	Nelson Mandela Met.	North-West	Pretoria	Rhodes	Stellenbosch	Venda	Western Cape	Witwatersrand
Engineering Computer							X		X			
Engineering Construction							X		X			
Engineering Design							X					
Engineering Electrical/Electronic	X		X	X	X	X	X		X			X
Engineering Geological									X			
Engineering Industrial					X		X		X			X
Engineering Information Technology									MD			
Engineering Instrumentation							X		X			
Engineering Management							MD		M			
Engineering Manufacturing							X		X			
Engineering Materials/Mineral Resources/Petroleum						X	X		X			
Engineering Mathematical									X			
Engineering Mechanical/Production	X		X	X	X	X	X		X			X
Engineering Medical	MD								MD			
Engineering Metallurgical/Mining	X			X		X	X			U		X
Engineering Software							X		X			
English	X	X	X	X	X	X	X	X	X	X	X	X
English as a Second Language							U		M			
Entomology		X				MD	X	X	X			
Entrepreneurship					X		X		X	UM		
Environmental Geosciences									X			
Environmental Health					U		X		M			
Environmental Management						MD				X		
Environmental Science/Studies	X		X	X	X	X	X	X	X	X	X	U
Epidemiology						MD						
Ergonomics							U				U	
Estate Management							UM					
Ethics					UM	X	X		MD		U	
Ethics, Law and Governance						UM						
Ethnicity/Multiculturalism					UM		U					
Ethnomusicology							X			U		
European Studies			X				U					
European Union Studies							U					
Fashion/Clothing					U		X					
Fertility/Embryology							MD			M		
Film/Photography/Television/Animation	X						X	X				
Food Science/Nutrition/Home Science/Dietetics	X			X		X	X		X	X	X	
Forensic Science	MD						MD				U	
Forestry				MD	U		MD		X	X		

	Cape Town	Fort Hare	Johannesburg	KwaZulu-Natal	Nelson Mandela Met.	North-West	Pretoria	Rhodes	Stellenbosch	Venda	Western Cape	Witwatersrand
French/French Studies	X		X	X	X	U	X	X	UM		U	U
Genetics	X	UM		X	X		X		X			X
Genetics and Plant Breeding									X	X		
Geographic Information Systems/Geomatics					X	X	X		X	X		
Geography	X	X	X	X	X	X	X	X	X	X	X	X
Geology/Earth Sciences/Atmospheric Studies	X	U	X	X	X		X	X	X	X	X	X
Geophysics		UM				X	X		M			
German/Germanic Studies	X	U	X	X	X	U	X	X	X		X	U
Global Studies									M			
Greek, Modern/Greek Studies	X			X		X	X					
Health Education							MD			U	MD	
Health Information							MD					
Health Sciences/Studies	X		X	X	X		X		X		X	X
Health/Hospital Administration	UM				M		X		M		X	
Hebrew/Semitic Studies	X		X	U		X	X		X			
Heritage Studies				X			X		UM		U	
History	X	X	X	X	X	X	X	X	X	X	X	U
History/Philosophy of Science					UM	U	X		X			
Horticulture		X		X			X		X	X		
Hotel Management									X			
Housing/Real Estate				MD			X					U
Human Biology							X		X	X		
Human Genetics							X		MD			
Human Movement/Kinesiology/Biomechanics				MD	X	X	X	X	X		X	
Human Resource Development						X						
Human Resource Economics									UM			
Human Rights/Globalisation							X		UM			
Indigenous Knowledge Systems										U		
Industrial Relations/Personnel/HRM	X	X		MD	X	X	X		X		X	
Industrial and Organisation Psychology					X	X			X			
Information Science/Studies/Systems	X	X	X	X	X	UM	X	X	X		X	X
Information Technology							X					
Insurance						UM	X					
International Finance									X			
International Finance Economics									X			
International Marketing									MD			
International Relations/Studies			X		X	X	X	X	X	X		X
Internet Computing/Technologies						U						
Islamic/Middle Eastern Studies	X		X									

	Cape Town	Fort Hare	Johannesburg	KwaZulu-Natal	Nelson Mandela Met.	North-West	Pretoria	Rhodes	Stellenbosch	Venda	Western Cape	Witwatersrand
Italian	X			U								X
Jewish Studies	X								MD			
Kiswahili/Swahili	X											
Labour Studies						UM						
Land Management/Rehabilitation						X	X				M	
Landscape Architecture							X					
Language Teaching/Learning						X	X		M			
Language and Communication						X	X					
Languages, Modern	X		X				X		X			U
Law Business/Commercial/Economic/Industrial					UM	X	MD		X		MD	
Law Civil						X						
Law Employment/Labour						X	X	X	MD		X	
Law Enforcement/Security Management						UM						
Law Environmental						X	UM		M		MD	
Law Intellectual Property/Copyright					UM	X	U		M			
Law International/Comparative/Trade					UM	X	X		X		MD	
Law Legal Practice					UM	X	U			X		
Law Property/Construction/Housing					U	X						
Law Transport							X		M			
Law/Legal Studies	X	X	X	X	UM	X	X	X	X	X	X	X
Library/Information Science	X	X	X	MD			X		X	UM	X	
Linguistics/Translation	X		X	X	X	X	X	X	X	X	X	M
Literature, Comparative							X		X			
Livestock Science						MD			X	X		
Logistics									X			
Management	X		X	X	X	X	X	X	X	X	X	X
Management Information Systems											M	
Management, Hotel and Catering Technology										U		
Maritime Studies				MD					MD			
Marketing	X		MD	X			X		X			
Materials Science						U	X		X			
Mathematics	X	X	X	X	X	X	X	X	X		X	X
Mechatronics	X			U					X			
Medical Ethics							U		M			
Medicine, Alternative											X	
Medicine, Chinese											U	
Medicine, Indian											U	
Medicine, Obstetrics and Gynaecology							MD		X			
Medicine, Orthopaedic									MD			

	Cape Town	Fort Hare	Johannesburg	KwaZulu-Natal	Nelson Mandela Met.	North-West	Pretoria	Rhodes	Stellenbosch	Venda	Western Cape	Witwatersrand
Medicine, Otorhinolaryngology/Otolaryngology									UM			
Medicine, Paediatric							MD		X			
Medicine/Surgery	X			X			X		X			X
Meteorology							X					
Microbiology/Medical Microbiology	X	X		X	X	X	X	X	X	X	X	X
Military Science					X				UM			
Mobile Communications/Telecommunications							X					
Multimedia	X				X		X		UM			
Musculoskeletal Studies							MD					
Museum Studies							UM			M	U	
Music	X	X		X	X	X	X	X	X	X		X
Music Education					X	U	X		X	X		
Music Jazz						U						
Music Technology					UM	U	UM		MD			
Nanotechnology							MD		UM			
Natural Resource Studies						X	MD		X			
Neuroscience							MD					
Nursing/Midwifery	X	UM	X	X	X	X	X		X	X	X	X
Occupational Health/Therapy	X						X		UM		X	X
Oenology/Viticulture/Wine Studies									X			
Operational Research/Operations Management						X			MD			
Ophthalmology									X			
Optometry/Vision Science			X									X
Palaeontology/Palaeobiology							U					X
Parasitology						MD	X					
Pastoral Studies						X	X					
Pathology							MD		X			
Peace/War Studies					X	X	X					
Pharmacology	MD			X	X	X	MD	X	MD		X	X
Pharmacy/Pharmaceutical Science						X	X	X			X	X
Philosophy	X	X	X	X	X	X	X	X	X	X	X	X
Physical Education/Sports Science	X	X	X	MD	X	X	X	X	X	U	X	X
Physics	X	X	X	X	X	X	X	X	X	X	X	X
Physiology	MD	U	U	X	X	X	X	X	X		X	X
Physiotherapy	X					X	X		UM	U	X	X
Planning/Landscape Studies	X		X	MD	X	X	X		MD			X
Plant Pathology						MD	X		X			
Politics/Political Science/Government	X		X	X	X	X	X	X	X	X	X	X
Polymer Science							MD		X			

	Cape Town	Fort Hare	Johannesburg	KwaZulu-Natal	Nelson Mandela Met.	North-West	Pretoria	Rhodes	Stellenbosch	Venda	Western Cape	Witwatersrand
Popular Culture									UM			
Population Studies/Demography				X	X		X		UM		UM	
Portuguese/Portugese Studies												U
Product Design and Technology							U					
Project Management						X	X					
Property						X						
Property Economics						X						
Psychiatry							MD		MD			
Psychology	X	X	X	X	X	X	X	X	X	X	X	X
Psychology Clinical					X	UM	MD		X	X	M	
Psychotherapy					X	X	X			U		
Public Administration	X	X	X		X	X	X	X	X	X	X	X
Public Health/Population Health							X		M	X	MD	
Public Relations						X	U					
Public Sector Management						X	X		X			
Publishing							X					
Radiography/Diagnostic Technology/MRI							X					X
Radiology						MD						
Rehabilitation Medicine/Therapy/Science							X		M			
Religion/Theology	X	X	X	X	X	X	X		X		X	X
Remote Sensing										U		
Risk Management						MD						
Rural Extension							X			X		
Rural Studies/Development				X	X	U	X		UM	X		
Sculpture							X					
Social Policy					X		M		X			
Social Reconstruction					UM							
Social Work/Studies	X	X	X	X	X	X	X		X	X	X	X
Sociology	X	X	X	X	X	X	X	X	X	X	X	X
Sotho						X			MD	X		
Spanish/Hispanic/Latin American Studies							U					
Speech Science/Pathology/Therapy	X						X		UM			X
Statistics/Actuarial Science	X	X	X	X	X	X	X	X	X	X	X	X
Surveying/Quantity Surveying	X			X	X		X					X
Sustainable Communities									MD			
Sustainable Development						UM	MD		MD			
Taxation			X	MD	M	UM	X	X	UM		U	X
Teacher Training	MD		X	X	X	U	X	X	X	U	X	X
Textiles/Fibre Science/Technology					MD	X	U			X		

	Cape Town	Fort Hare	Johannesburg	KwaZulu-Natal	Nelson Mandela Met.	North-West	Pretoria	Rhodes	Stellenbosch	Venda	Western Cape	Witwatersrand
Tourism/Hospitality/Leisure/Recreation			U		X	X	X			X	U	
Toxicology						MD	X					
Transport Studies			X			U	X		X			
Urban Studies						X	X					
Vedas/Vedic										X		
Veterinary Science							X					
Visual Arts	X			MD	UM	X	X					
Wildlife Management		UM			U	X	MD		X			
Women's/Gender Studies	X			U			MD		MD	X	UM	
Wood Science					U							
Youth and Community Development									X			
Zoology	X	X	X	X	X	X	X	X	X	X	X	X
Zulu	X		X	X	X	X	X		MD			X

CAPE PENINSULA UNIVERSITY OF TECHNOLOGY

Founded 2005

Postal Address: PO Box 1906, Bellville, 7535 South Africa
Telephone: (021) 959 6911 **Fax:** (021) 951 5422 **E-mail:** info@cput.ac.za
URL: www.cput.ac.za

VICE-CHANCELLOR*—Mazwi-Tanga, Prof. Lineo V., MSc *Fort Hare*

UNIVERSITY OF CAPE TOWN

Founded 1918

Member of the Association of Commonwealth Universities

Postal Address: Private Bag, Rondebosch, 7701 South Africa
Telephone: (021) 650 9111 **Fax:** (021) 650 2138 **E-mail:** aeshta@bremner.uct.ac.za
URL: http://www.uct.ac.za

VICE-CHANCELLOR DESIGNATE*—Price, Max, MB BCh *Witw.*, BA *Oxf.*, MSc *Lond.*
DEPUTY VICE-CHANCELLOR (INNOVATION AND RES., POSTGRAD. STUDIES, INSTITUTIONAL TRANSFORMATION)—De la
  Rey, Prof. Cheryl, BA *Natal*, MA *Natal*, PhD *Cape Town*
DEPUTY VICE-CHANCELLOR (PLANNING/BUDGETING, REGIONAL COLLABORATION, CHEC/ICTS, QUAL.
  ASSURANCE)—Hall, Prof. Martin J., BA *Camb.*, MA *Camb.*, PhD *Camb.*, FRSSAf
DEPUTY VICE-CHANCELLOR (OVC/OPERATIONAL MGMT. AND COORDINATION, UNI. LIBRARIES, INSTITUTIONAL
  FORUM)—West, Prof. Martin E., BA *Cape Town*, MA *Cape Town*, PhD *Cape Town*
DEPUTY VICE-CHANCELLOR (STUDENT DEVEL. INTERNAT. COOPERATION, GOVT./COMMUNITY RELATIONS, HIV/
  AIDS)—Nhlapo, Prof. Thandabantu, BA *UBLS*, LLB *Glas.*, DPhil *Oxf.*
REGISTRAR‡—Davidse, Brian
FINANCE DIRECTOR—Uliana, Prof. Enrico, MCom *Cape Town*, PhD *Stell.*
EXECUTIVE DIRECTOR, DEPARTMENT OF COMMUNICATION DEVELOPMENT—Kruger, Gerda, BA *Rand Afrikaans*, MBSc
  Cape Town
EXECUTIVE DIRECTOR, UNIVERSITY LIBRARIES—Rapp, Joan, BA *Mary Baldwin*, MA *Wash.*, MLS *Rutgers*, MBA *S.Illinois*
EXECUTIVE DIRECTOR, INFORMATION AND COMMUNICATION TECHNOLOGY SERVICES—Naicker, Pragasen
EXECUTIVE DIRECTOR, DEVELOPMENT AND ALUMNI AFFAIRS—McNamara, James, BA *Georgetown*, MA *Calif.*, PhD *Calif.*,
  Dr *Georgetown*

GENERAL INFORMATION

History. The university was established in 1829 as South African College, and achieved university status in 1918.

Its main campus is located at Groote Schuur, Cape Town, on the slopes of Table Mountain.

Admission to first degree courses (see also South African Introduction). Minimum requirement: senior certificate endorsed for university admission, or certificate from Matriculation Board granting exemption from this endorsement; or matriculation/exemption certificate issued by the Matriculation Board or Joint Matriculation Board. In addition, each faculty has its own minimum requirements. The university's Alternative Admissions Research Project (AARP) administers its own entrance tests, which are open to all applicants on a voluntary basis.

First Degrees (see also South African Directory to Subjects of Study) (* = with honours). BA*, BA, BA(FA), BAS, BATP, BBibl*, BBibl, BBusSc, BCom*, BCom, BEd, BMus*, BMus, BNforRNs, BSc*, BSc, BSc(Audiol), BSc(ConstrStudies)*, BSc(Eng), BSciEd, BSc(Med)*, BSc(Med), BSc(OccTher), BSc(Physio), BSc(PropertyStudies), BSc(Sp-LangPath), BSc(Survey), BSocSc*, BSocSc, BSocSc(SW), LLB, MB ChB.

All courses are full-time and normally last 3 or 4 years. Honours degrees last an additional year. Extended undergraduate degree programmes in engineering, health sciences and science are 1 year longer.

Higher Degrees (see also South African Directory to Subjects of Study).

Master's. BArch, BEd, ChM, LLB, LLM, MA, MA(FA), MArch, MBA, MBibl, MBusSc, MCom, MCPUD, MCRP, MD, MEd, MEngMan, MFA, MFamMed, MIndAdmin, MLA, MMEd, MMus, MPH, MPhil, MPhil(HDM), MPubAd, MSc, MSc(Eng), MSocSc.

Admission. An honours degree or a recognised 4-year bachelor's degree must generally be completed prior to admission to a master's degree programme and subsequent doctoral degree programme.

Master's degrees are offered by dissertation or by taught courses and a minor dissertation, and normally last 1 year. BArch (post BAS): 3 years.

Doctoral. DArch, DEconSc, DEd, DFA, DLitt, DMus, DSc, DSc(Eng), DSc(Med), DSocSc, LLD, MD, PhD.

Doctorates are research degrees and normally last 2 years.

Libraries. Volumes: 824,000. Periodicals subscribed to: 7400.

FACULTIES/SCHOOLS

Commerce
Tel: (021) 650 2695-6 Fax: (021) 650 4369
  E-mail: comsec@commerce.uct.ac.za
Dean: Pitt, Prof. Douglas C., BA *Exe.*, MA *Exe.*,
  PhD *Manc.*, FRSA
Faculty Office Manager (Academic): Maponya,
  Simon, BAdmin *S.Af.*

Engineering and the Built Environment
Tel: (021) 650 2699 Fax: (021) 650 3782
  E-mail: faculty@ebe.uct.ac.za
Dean: O'Connor, Prof. Cyril T., BSc *S.Af.*, BSc
  Cape Town, PhD *Cape Town*, FRSSAf

Faculty Office Manager (Academic): Galvin,
  Jeremy R., BA *Rhodes*, MA *Qu.*

Health Sciences
Tel: (021) 406 6346 Fax: (021) 447 8955
  E-mail: medfac@curie.uct.ac.za
Dean: Jacobs, Prof. Marian E., MB ChB *Cape
  Town*, FCP(SA)
Faculty Office Manager (Academic):
  Klingenberg, Brenda, BA *OFS*

Humanities
Tel: (021) 650 4215-6 Fax: (021) 686 9840
  E-mail: ugrad@humanities.uct.ac.za
Dean: Ensor, Prof. Paula, BSocSc *Natal*, BA *Cape
  Town*, MSc(Ed) *Lond.*, PhD *Lond.*
Faculty Office Manager (Academic): Van
  Heerden, Karen, BA(Ed) *Rand Afrikaans*, MEd
  P.Elizabeth, PhD *Rhodes*

Law
Tel: (021) 650 3086-7 Fax: (021) 650 5608
  E-mail: lawsec@law.uct.ac.za
Dean: Corder, Prof. Hugh M., BCom *Cape Town*,
  LLB *Cape Town*, LLB *Camb.*, DPhil *Oxf.*
Faculty Office Manager (Academic): Fuller,
  Judy

Science
Tel: (021) 650 2712 Fax: (021) 650 2710
  E-mail: scifac@science.uct.ac.za
Dean: Driver, Prof. Kathleen A., BSc *Witw.*,
  MSc *Stan.*, PhD *Witw.*
Faculty Office Manager (Academic): Wienand,
  Karen, MSc *Cape Town*

ACADEMIC UNITS

Accounting

Tel: (021) 650 2269 Fax: (021) 689 7582
E-mail: comsec@commerce.uct.ac.za
Bourne, Peter J. M. Assoc. Prof.
Chamisa, E., BAcc Z'bwe., MA Lanc., PhD Birm.
Sr. Lectr.
Chivaka, R., BCom NUST Bulawayo, MSc Manc.,
PhD Cape Town Sr. Lectr.
Cilliers, A. J., BCom S.Af. Sr. Lectr.
Clayton, Roderick D., MCompt S.Af. Sr. Lectr.
Correia, Carlos, MCom Cape Town Assoc. Prof.
Cramer, P. J., BCompt S.Af., MBA Cape Town
Sr. Lectr.
Everingham, Geoffrey K., BCom P.Elizabeth,
BCom Cape Town, MAS Ill. Prof.
Graham, Mark, BBusSc Cape Town, MCom Cape
Town Assoc. Prof.
Kew, J., BCom Cape Town, MBA Cape Town Sr.
Lectr.
Lomax, A., BSc Wales, BCom Cape Town Sr.
Lectr.
Lubbe, Ilse, BCom Rand Afrikaans Sr. Lectr.
Minter, Marie T., BSc Cape Town Assoc. Prof.
Puttick, George A., BCom Cape Town Sr. Lectr.
Roeleveld, Jennifer, BCompt S.Af., BCom Cape
Town, LLM Cape Town Assoc. Prof.
Smith, Colin C., BSocSc(SW) Cape Town,
BCompt S.Af. Sr. Lectr.
Surtees, Peter, MCom Rhodes Prof.†
Taylor, Josephine, BCom Cape Town Sr. Lectr.
Uliana, Enrico, MCom Cape Town, PhD Stell.
Prof.
Warneke, D., BCom Cape Town Sr. Lectr.
Watson, Alexandra, BCom Cape Town Assoc.
Prof.
West, Craig, MCom Cape Town Sr. Lectr.
Wormald, Michael P., BCom Cape Town Assoc.
Prof.; Head*
Other Staff: 8 Lectrs.
Research: auditing; financial accounting; financial
management; management accounting;
taxation

African Studies, Centre for

Tel: (021) 650 2308 Fax: (021) 689 7560
E-mail: africas@humanities.uct.ac.za
Cooper, Brenda L., MA Birm., DPhil Sus. Prof.;
Dir.* (cross-appointment with Engl. Lang.
and Lit.)
Other Staff: 1 Assoc. Prof.
Research: comparative literature; contemporary
South African art; movements for rights,
justice and state reform; West African
magical realism

Archaeology

Tel: (021) 650 2353 Fax: (021) 650 2352
E-mail: lynn@age.uct.ac.za
Ackermann, Rebecca R., MA Arizona, PhD Wash.
Sr. Lectr.
Hall, Simon L., MA Witw., PhD Stell. Sr. Lectr.
Parkington, John E., MA Camb., PhD Camb.
Prof.
Sealy, Judith C., MSc Cape Town, PhD Cape Town
Assoc. Prof.; Head*
Smith, Andrew B., PhD Calif. Assoc. Prof.
Van der Merwe, Nikolaas J., MA Yale, PhD Yale
Prof.
Other Staff: 1 Chief Sci. Officer; 1 Principal
Sci. Officer
Research: laboratory study of archaeomaterials;
light stable isotopes as environmental and
dietary tracers; paleoenvironmental
research; surveys of selected modern
environments

Architecture, Planning and Geomatics

Tel: (021) 650 2374 Fax: (021) 650 3705
E-mail: archiplan@ebe.uct.ac.za
Carter, Francis, BArch Cape Town Sr. Lectr./
Studiomaster
Coetzer, Nicholas, BArch Pret., MArch Pratt Sr.
Lectr./Studiomaster
De Beer, Pieter F., BArch Pret., MArch Pratt Sr.
Lectr./Studiomaster

Dewar, David, BA Cape Town, MURP Cape Town,
PhD Cape Town BP Prof., Urban and
Regional Planning
Jacobs, Khalied, BArch Cape Town, MArch Leuven
Sr. Lectr./Studiomaster
Le Grange, Lucien P., BArch Cape Town,
MArch(UD) Rice Assoc. Prof.; Dir.*
Low, Iain, BArch Cape Town, MArch(UD)
Assoc. Prof.
Merry, Charles L., BSc(Survey) Cape Town, PhD
New Br. Assoc. Prof.
Noero, Jo, BArch Natal, MPhil Newcastle(UK),
Hon. DSc Brighton Prof.
Oberholzer, Bernard J., BArch Cape Town, MLA
Penn. Sr. Lectr./Studiomaster
Ruther, Heinz, PhD Cape Town Prof.
Steenkamp, Alta, MArch Pret. Sr. Lectr./
Studiomaster
Watson, Vanessa J., BA Natal, MCRP Cape Town,
PhD Witw. Prof.
Whittal, Jennifer F., BSc(Surv) Cape Town,
MSc(Eng) Cape Town Sr. Lectr.
Wilkinson, Peter B., BSc(Eng) Natal, MCRP Cape
Town Assoc. Prof.
Other Staff: 1 Lectr.
Research: city planning and urban design in the
African context; conservation; contemporary
architectural theory and practice; urbanism
and housing

Astronomy

Tel: (021) 650 2391 Fax: (021) 650 3342
E-mail: astro@artemesia.ast.uct.ac.za
Fairall, Anthony P., BSc Cape Town, PhD Texas
Prof.
Feast, Michael W., BSc Lond., PhD Lond.,
Hon. DSc Cape Town, FRSSAf Hon. Prof.
Kraan-Korteweg, C., DPhil Basle Prof.; Head*
Warner, Brian B., BSc Lond., MA Oxf., PhD
Lond., DSc Lond., DSc Oxf., FRSSAf Prof.
Woudt, Patrick A., PhD Cape Town Sr. Lectr.
Research: cataclysmic and degenerate stars;
cepheids and RR lyrae stars; long period
red variables; short period variables; theory
and observation of variable stars

Botany

Tel: (021) 650 2447 Fax: (021) 650 4041
E-mail: botany@botzoo.uct.ac.za
Bolton, John J., BSc Liv., PhD Liv. Prof.
Bond, William J., BSc Exe., MSc Cape Town, PhD
Calif. Harry Bolus Prof.
Cowling, Richard M., BSc Cape Town, PhD Cape
Town Hon. Prof.
Cramer, Michael D., MSc Witw., PhD Cape Town
Assoc. Prof.
February, Ed C., BA Cape Town, PhD Cape Town
Sr. Lectr.
Hendderson, Terry A., MSc Nfld., PhD Reading
Assoc. Prof.
Hoffman, M. T., BSc Cape Town, PhD Cape Town
Leslie Hill Prof.
Huntley, Bryan J., BSc Natal, MSc Pret. Hon.
Prof.; Dir., Natnl. Bot. Inst.
Linder, H. Peter, BSc Natal, PhD Cape Town
Hon. Prof.
Midgley, Jeremy J., BSc Cape Town, PhD Cape
Town Assoc. Prof.; Head*
Other Staff: 1 Emer. Assoc. Prof.
Research: biogeography and evolutionary biology
of Cape flora; floristics; plant population,
community and reproductive ecology;
systematics

Business, Graduate School of

Tel: (021) 406 1911 Fax: (021) 421 5510
E-mail: trbillen@gsb2.uct.ac.za
April, Kurt, BSc(Eng) Cape Town, MSc(Eng) Cape
Town, MBA Cape Town Sr. Lectr.
Burgess, Steve, BSc Ohio State, BA Ohio State, PhD
Witw. Prof.
Donovan, Elspeth, BSc Cape Town, MBA Cape
Town Sr. Lectr.
Eberhard, Anton, BSc(ChemEng) Cape Town, BA
S.Af., PhD Edin. Prof.
Everson, Janine, BA Witw., MBA Cape Town Sr.
Lectr.

Faull, Norman H. B., BSc Stell., BEng Stell., MSc
Cran., MBA Cape Town, PhD Cape Town Prof.
Foster-Pedley, J., MBA Ashridge Sr. Lectr.
Gilbert, Evan, BCom Rhodes, BCom Cape Town,
MCom Witw., PhD Camb. Sr. Lectr.
Horwitz, Frank M., BA(SocSci) Witw., MPM
Witw., PhD Witw. Dir.*
Kaplan, David E., BA Cape Town, BCom Cape
Town, MA Kent, DPhil Sus. Prof.
Keith, Beverley, BA Cape Town, MA Warw., PhD
Warw. Sr. Lectr.
Koelble, Thomas, MA Essex, PhD Calif. Prof.
Marks, Amy S., BA Mt.Holyoke, PhD Northwestern
Sr. Lectr.
Mbabane, Loyiso, BA Witw., MA Witw., MM
Witw. Sr. Lectr.
Parker, Hamieda, BSc(Eng) Cape Town, MBA
Cape Town, PhD Cape Town Sr. Lectr.
Ryan, Tom, BSc(Eng) Cape Town, MIndAdmin
Cape Town, MBA Cape Town Assoc. Prof.
Standish, Barry, BCom Natal, MA Cape Town Sr.
Lectr.
Stewart-Smith, A., BA Cape Town, MA Cape Town,
PhD Cape Town Sr. Lectr.
Stringer, Lance, BSc S.Af., MBA Cape Town,
MCom Cape Town Sr. Lectr.
Sulcas, P., BA Cape Town, MCom Cape Town,
DCom Stell. Prof.
Wood, Eric, BSc(MechEng) Cape Town, MPhil
Camb., PhD Camb. Assoc. Prof.
Other Staff: 4 Lectrs.; 1 Asst. Lectr.; 1 Sr.
Researcher; 4 Researchers
Research: effective manufacturing worldwide;
entrepreneurship; marketing and
management of technology; monitoring
employment equity in South Africa; social
marketing of tobacco products

Chemistry

Tel: (021) 650 2446 Fax: (021) 689 7499
E-mail: burke@science.uct.ac.za
Bourne, Susan A., BSc Cape Town, PhD Cape Town
Assoc. Prof.
Bull, James R., MSc Natal, DPhil Oxf., FRSChem,
FRSSAf Emer. Prof.
Caira, Mino R., MSc Cape Town, MEd Cluj-Napoca
Med.& Pharm., PhD Cape Town Prof.
Chibale, Kelly, BScEd Zambia, PhD Camb.
Assoc. Prof.
Davidowitz, Bette, MSc Cape Town, PhD Cape
Town Sr. Lectr.
Egan, Tim, BSc Witw., PhD Witw. Assoc. Prof.
Gammon, David W., BSc Cape Town, PhD Cape
Town Assoc. Prof.
Hunter, Roger, BSc Lond., PhD Lond. Mally
Prof., Organic Chemistry
Hutton, Alan T., MSc Cape Town, PhD Cape Town
Assoc. Prof.
Jackson, Graham E., BSc Cape Town, PhD Cape
Town, FRSChem Prof.
Linder, Peter W., MSc Natal, PhD Camb. Emer.
Prof.
Moss, John R., BSc Leeds, PhD Leeds, FRSChem
Jamison Prof., Inorganic Chemistry
Naidoo, Kevin J., MSc Cape Town, PhD Mich.
Assoc. Prof.
Nassimbeni, Luigi R., MSc Rhodes, PhD Cape
Town, FRSChem, FRSSAf Emer. Prof.
Ravenscroft, Neil, BSc Cape Town, PhD Cape Town
Sr. Lectr.
Rodgers, Allen L., MSc Cape Town, PhD Cape
Town Prof.; Head*
Stephen, Alistair M., MSc Cape Town, PhD Cape
Town, DPhil Oxf. Emer. Prof.
Other Staff: 1 Lectr.; 4 Sr. Sci. Officers; 7 Hon.
Res. Assocs.
Research: inclusion compounds, polymorphism
and related solid state phenomena;
synthetic studies in organic, organometallic
and co-ordination chemistry

Computer Science

Tel: (021) 650 2663 Fax: (021) 689 9465
E-mail: dept@cs.uct.ac.za
Berman, Sonia, BSc Rhodes, MSc Cape Town, PhD
Cape Town Assoc. Prof.
Blake, Edwin H., BSc Witw., PhD Lond. Prof.

Gain, James E., MSc Rhodes, PhD Camb.   Sr. Lectr.

Kritzinger, Pieter S., MSc(Eng) Witw., PhD Wat.   Prof.

Linck, Michael H., MSc Cape Town, PhD Cape Town   Sr. Lectr.

MacGregor, Kenneth J., BSc Strath., MSc Glas.   Prof.; Head*

Marais, Patrick C., MSc Cape Town, DPhil Oxf.   Sr. Lectr.

Marsden, Gary G., BSc Stir., PhD Stir.   Assoc. Prof.

Potgieter, Anet E., MSc Pret., PhD Pret.   Sr. Lectr.

Suleman, Hussein, MSc Durban-W., PhD Virginia Polytech.   Sr. Lectr.

Other Staff: 4 Lectrs.; 1 Adjunct Prof.

Research: computer experimentation; data network architectures; database systems; interactive computer graphics

Construction Economics and Management

Tel: (021) 650 3443 Fax: (021) 689 7564
E-mail: bowenpa@eng.uct.ac.za

Boaden, Bruce G., BSc(QS) Witw., MBA Br.Col., PhD Witw.   Emer. Prof.

Bowen, Paul, BScQS Natal, BCom Natal, MSc H-W., PhD P.Elizabeth, FRICS   Prof.; Head*

Cattell, Keith S., BSc(QS) P.Elizabeth, MPhil Cape Town   Assoc. Prof.

Evans, Kathleen, BSc(QS) Cape Town, MSSc Cape Town   Sr. Lectr.

Massyn, Mark W., BSc P.Elizabeth   Sr. Lectr.

Michell, Karen A., BSc(QS) Cape Town, MPhil Cape Town   Sr. Lectr.

Root, David, BSc Salf., MSc Bath, PhD Bath   Sr. Lectr.

Shakantu, Winston, BSc Copperbelt, MSc Reading   Sr. Lectr.

Stevens, Alan J., MSc Cape Town, PhD P.Elizabeth, FRICS   Emer. Prof.

Other Staff: 1 Lectr.

Research: computer-based education; effectiveness of building procurement systems; housing development and management; property management; training and human resource management

Criminal Law and Justice

Tel: (021) 650 2672 Fax: (021) 686 2577
E-mail: leeman@law.uct.ac.za

Burchell, Jonathan, BA Natal, LLB Natal, LLM Camb., PhD Witw.   Prof.

Leeman, Israel, BA Stell., LLB Stell.   Emer. Prof.

Schärf, Wilfried, BCom Witw., LLB Witw., MSocSc Cape Town   Assoc. Prof.

Schwikkard, P. J., BA Witw., LLB Natal, LLM Natal, LLD Stell.   Prof.; Head*

Steyn, Esther, BJuris S.Af., LLB W.Cape, LLM Cape Town   Sr. Lectr.

Van der Spuy, Elrena, BA Stell., MA Stell., PhD Cape Town   Sr. Lectr.

Research: adjectival law (criminal procedure, evidence, sentencing and punishment); criminal procedure and refugee law; direct training of legal professionals; practical applications of the legal process

Criminology, Institute of

Tel: (021) 650 2988-9 Fax: (021) 650 3790
E-mail: decibel@protem.uct.ac.za

Schärf, Wilfried, BCom Witw., LLB Witw., MSocSc Cape Town   Assoc. Prof.

Shearing, C. D., BSocSc Natal, MA Tor., PhD Tor.   Prof.

Van der Spuy, Elrena, BA Stell., MA Stell., PhD Cape Town   Sr. Lectr.; Dir.*

Other Staff: 1 Co-ordinator, Soc. Justice Resource Project; 2 Researchers

Research: ecological criminology; gender violence; policing; prisons and punishment; youth justice

Dance, School of

Tel: (021) 650 2398-9 Fax: (021) 650 3524
E-mail: pearsona@protem.uct.ac.za

Cheesman, Dianne, BPhil Durh.   Sr. Lectr.

Fourie, Danie, BMus Cape Town   Sr. Lectr.

Friedman, Sharon, BA Cape Town   Sr. Lectr.

Triegaardt, Elizabeth E., BSc Cape Town   Assoc. Prof.; Head*

Other Staff: 1 Lectr.

Research: African dance; choreography; ethnology; practical teaching; teaching methodology

Drama

Tel: (021) 480 7100 Fax: (021) 424 2355
E-mail: svalley@hiddingh.uct.ac.za

Banning, Yvonne, BA Natal, MA Witw.   Sr. Lectr.

Fleishman, Mark, BA Cape Town, MA Cape Town   Assoc. Prof.; Head*

Hyland, Geoffrey, BA Free State, BA Cape Town, MFA   Sr. Lectr.

Mills, Elizabeth, BA Cape Town, MA Rhodes   Sr. Lectr.

Morris, Gay, BA Cape Town, MA Cape Town   Assoc. Prof.

Weare, C., BA Rhodes   Assoc. Prof.; Dir.*

Other Staff: 4 Lectrs.

Research: scripts and academic writing of cultural relevance to contemporary South African concerns; teaching methods; theatre productions

Economics, School of

Tel: (021) 650 2723 Fax: (021) 650 2854
E-mail: pbassing@commerce.uct.ac.za

Abraham, Haim, MA Tel-Aviv, PhD Jerusalem   Prof.

Ayogu, Melvin, BA Calif.State, PhD Ohio State   Prof.

Bhorat, Haroon, BSocSc Cape Town, MA Stell., PhD Stell.   Assoc. Prof.

Black, Anthony H., BA Cape Town, BA Sus., MSocSc Natal   Assoc. Prof.; Dir.*

Burns, Justine, BCom Natal, MPhil Camb., PhD Mass.   Sr. Lectr.

Conradie, Beatrice, BSc Stell., MSc Stell., PhD Colorado   Sr. Lectr.

Edwards, Lawrence, BA Cape Town, BA Rhodes, MA Lond., MSc Lond., PhD Cape Town   Sr. Lectr.

Fedderke, Johann, BCom Natal, MPhil Camb., PhD Camb.   Prof.

Kaplan, David E., BA Cape Town, BCom Cape Town, MA Kent, DPhil Sus.   Prof.

Keswell, Malcolm, BCom Durban-W., MSocSc Natal, MA Mass., PhD Mass.   Sr. Lectr.

Leibbrandt, Murray V., BSocSc Rhodes, MA Notre Dame(Ind.), PhD Notre Dame(Ind.)   Prof.

Leiman, Anthony, BA Natal, BA S.Af., MA Cape Town   Sr. Lectr.

Muchapondwa, Edwin, BSc Z'bwe., MSc Z'bwe., PhL Gothenburg, PhD Gothenburg   Sr. Lectr.

Muradzikwa, Samson, BSocSc Cape Town, MSocSc Cape Town   Sr. Lectr.

Nathan, Cedric D., BCom Witw., MSc Lond., PhD S.Fraser   Sr. Lectr.

Nattrass, Nicoli J., BA Stell., BSocSc Cape Town, MA Natal, MSc Oxf., DPhil Oxf.   Prof.

Ross, Don, BA W.Ont., MA W.Ont., PhD W.Ont.   Prof.

van Walbeek, Corne, BCom Stell., MCom Stell.   Sr. Lectr.

Wittenberg, Martin, BA Natal, MA Natal, MCom Witw., PhD Natal   Assoc. Prof.

Other Staff: 6 Lectrs.

Research: agricultural economics; health economics; international finance; manpower and labour practices in southern Africa; science and technology policies

Education, School of

Tel: (021) 650 2769 Fax: (021) 650 3489
E-mail: ingrid@humanities.uct.ac.za

Bakker, Nigel, BA Cape Town, BEd Cape Town, MA Cape Town, MPhil Cape Town   Sr. Lectr.

Baxen, Jean, BA S.Af., MEd Leeds   Sr. Lectr.

Breen, Christopher J., BSc(Eng) Cape Town, MEd Exe., MPhil Camb.   Assoc. Prof.

Davis, Zain, BA Cape Town, MPhil Cape Town   Sr. Lectr.

Ensor, Paula, BSocSc Natal, BA Cape Town, MSc(Ed) Lond., PhD Lond.   Prof.

Esterhuyse, Johannes S., BA Cape Town, MA Cape Town   Sr. Lectr.

Gilmour, James D., BBusSc Cape Town, MA Sus.   Sr. Lectr.

Jacklin, Heather J., BA Witw., MEd Witw., PhD Witw.   Sr. Lectr.

Laugksch, Rudiger C., BSc Cape Town, BSc P.Elizabeth, MSc Cape Town, PhD Cape Town   Assoc. Prof.

Muller, Johan P., MA P.Elizabeth, Dr Ley., PhD Cape Town   Prof.

Prinsloo, Mastin H., BA Natal, MEd Lond.   Sr. Lectr.

Rochford, Kevin, BSc Melb., PhD Cape Town   Assoc. Prof.

Siebörger, Robert F., BA Rhodes, BEd Rhodes, MA Rhodes, MPhil Exe.   Assoc. Prof.

Soudien, Crain A., BA Cape Town, BEd S.Af., MA Cape Town, EdM N.Y.State, PhD N.Y.State   Assoc. Prof.; Head*

Other Staff: 2 Lectrs.

Research: knowledge development and transfer; policy evaluation and support; race, culture, identity and language studies; student learning in higher education

Engineering, Chemical

Tel: (021) 650 4036 Fax: (021) 650 5501
E-mail: jills@chemeng.uct.ac.za

Bradshaw, Dee, BSc(Eng) Cape Town, PhD Cape Town   Sr. Lectr.

Burton, Stephanie G., BSc Z'bwe., PhD Rhodes   Assoc. Prof.

Deglon, David A., BSc Witw., PhD Cape Town   Sr. Lectr.

Dry, Mark E., MSc Rhodes, PhD Brist.   Hon. Prof.

Fletcher, Jack C. Q., BSc(Eng) Cape Town, PhD Cape Town   Assoc. Prof.

Fraser, Duncan McK., BSc(Eng) Cape Town, PhD Cape Town   Assoc. Prof.

Hansford, Geoffrey S., BSc(Eng) Cape Town, MSc Cape Town, MSE Penn., PhD Penn.   Prof.

Harrison, Susan T. L., BSc Cape Town, PhD Camb.   Prof.

Lewis, Alison E., MSc(Eng) Cape Town, PhD Cape Town   Assoc. Prof.

Moller, Klaus P., BSc(Eng) Cape Town, PhD Cape Town   Assoc. Prof.

O'Connor, Cyril T., BSc S.Af., BSc Cape Town, PhD Cape Town, FRSSAf   Prof.

Van Steen, Eric W. J., MSc(Eng) T.U.Eindhoven, PhD Karlsruhe   Prof.

von Blottnitz, H. B., BSc Cape Town, BSc S.Af., MSc(Eng) Cape Town, DrIng T.H.Aachen   Prof.; Dir.*

Other Staff: 1 Principal Sci. Officer; 2 Hon. Assoc. Profs.

Research: bacterial leaching of ores; bioprocess engineering; catalysis; environmental process engineering; minerals processing

Engineering, Civil

Tel: (021) 650 2584 Fax: (021) 689 7471
E-mail: civil@engfac.uct.ac.za

Alexander, Mark G., BSc(Eng) Witw., MSc(Eng) Witw., PhD Witw.   Prof.

Armitage, Neil P., BScEng Natal, MSc(Eng) Cape Town   Assoc. Prof.

Del Mistro, Romano, BSc(Eng) Cape Town, MURP Cape Town, PhD Pret.   Assoc. Prof.

Ekama, George A., BSc(Eng) Cape Town, PhD Cape Town, FRSSAf   Prof.; Head*

Loewenthal, Richard E., BSc(Eng) Witw., MSc(Eng) Cape Town, PhD Cape Town   Assoc. Prof.

Marais, Nicholas J., BSc(Eng) Cape Town, PhD Cape Town   Assoc. Prof.

Wentzel, Mark C., BSc Cape Town, PhD Cape Town   Prof.; Principal Res. Officer

Zingoni, Alphose, BSc(Eng) Z'bwe.Open, MSc(Eng) Lond., PhD Lond.   Prof.

Other Staff: 4 Emer. Assoc. Profs.; 6 Sr. Lectrs.†; 2 Lectrs.†; 1 Hon. Res. Assoc.

Research: computer-assisted learning in engineering education; structural materials and geotechnical research; urban and transportation engineering; water

Engineering, Electrical

Tel: (021) 650 2787 Fax: (021) 650 3465
E-mail: aburmei@eng.uct.ac.za
Braae, Martin, MSc(Eng) Cape Town, PhD UMIST Prof.
Chan, Anthony, BSc HK, PhD Maryland Prof.
De Jager, Gerhardus, MSc Rhodes, MBL S.Af., PhD Manc. Prof.
Dlodlo, Mqhele, MSc Kansas, PhD T.H.Delft Assoc. Prof.
Downing, Barry J., MSc Brad., PhD Sheff., F(SA)IEE Prof.
Folly, Komla A., MSc(Eng) Beijing, PhD Hiroshima Assoc. Prof.
Gaunt, Trevor, BSc(Eng) Natal, MBL S.Af., PhD Cape Town, FIEE, F(SA)IEE Assoc. Prof.; Head*
Greene, John R., MSc(Eng) Cape Town Assoc. Prof.
Inggs, Michael R., BSc Rhodes, PhD Lond. Prof.
Jongens, Adrian, MSc(Eng) Cape Town Sr. Lectr.
Mashao, Daniel J., MSc(Eng) Cape Town, PhD Brown Sr. Lectr.
McLaren, S. Glen, BSc(Eng) Cape Town, PhD Cape Town Emer. Prof.
Nicolls, Fred, MSc(Eng) Cape Town, PhD Cape Town Sr. Lectr.
Petroianu, Alexander, DrIng Bucharest Emer. Prof.
Tapson, Jonathan C., BSc Cape Town, BSc(Eng) Cape Town Prof.
Ventura, Manuel J. E., BSc Cape Town, BSc(Eng) Cape Town, BSc Pret. Sr. Lectr.
Wilkinson, Andrew, BSc Cape Town, PhD Lond. Sr. Lectr.
Other Staff: 5 Lectrs.; 1 Sr. Res. Officer
Research: control engineering; digital systems (asynchronous transfer mode (ATM) networks); image processing and vision systems; remote sensing; telecommunications (digital modulation)

Engineering, Mechanical

incorporating Engineering Management, Centre for Research in Computational and Applied Mechanics (CERECAM), Energy Research Institute, Centre for Materials Engineering and Continuing Engineering Education

Tel: (021) 650 3231 Fax: (021) 650 3240
E-mail: meceng@ebe.uct.ac.za
Bennett, Kevin F., BSc(Eng) Cape Town, MSc CNAA, PhD Cape Town, F(SA)IME Prof.
Knutsen, Robert D., BSc Cape Town, PhD Cape Town Assoc. Prof.
Lang, Candace I., BSc Cape Town, PhD Cape Town Assoc. Prof.
Lister, Gordon, BSc(Eng) H-W, BCom S.Af., MSc(Eng) Lond. Sr. Lectr.
Meyer, Chris J., MEng Stell., PhD Stell. Sr. Lectr.
Nurick, Gerald N., MScEng Natal, PhD Cape Town, F(SA)IME Prof.
Pearce, Howard T., BSc(Eng) Cape Town, MS Ill., PhD Ill. Sr. Lectr.
Redelinghuys, Chris, BIng Stell., MS Stan., PhD Stell. Prof.
Reed, B. I., MSc(Eng) Cape Town Sr. Lectr.
Sayers, Anthony T., BSc City(UK), MSc Birm., PhD Cape Town Assoc. Prof.
Tait, Robert B., BSc Rhodes, BSc(Eng) Cape Town, MA Oxf., PhD Cape Town Prof.; Head*
Vicatos, George, BSc Newcastle(UK), MSc Lond., PhD Cape Town Sr. Lectr.
Other Staff: 5 Lectrs.; 1 Adjunct Prof.
Research: fluid mechanics; fracture mechanics; internal combustion engines; manufacturing systems; quality management

English Language and Literature

Tel: (021) 650 2861 Fax: (021) 650 3726
E-mail: buchanan@humanities.uct.ac.za
Beatty, Michael T., BA Witw., MA Dal., PhD Dal. Sr. Lectr.
Brink, André P., MA Potchef., DLitt Rhodes, Hon. DLitt Witw., Hon. DLH Hon. Prof.
Coetzee, John M., MA Cape Town, PhD Texas, Hon. DLitt Strath., Hon. DLitt Buffalo, Hon. DLitt Natal, Hon. DLitt Skidmore, FRSL Emer. Prof.
Cooper, Brenda L., MA Birm., DPhil Sus. Prof.
Distiller, Natasha, BA Cape Town, MA Oxf., PhD Cape Town Prof.
Driver, Dorothy J., MA Rhodes, PhD Rhodes Prof.
Edgecombe, Rodney S., MA Rhodes, PhD Camb. Assoc. Prof.
Fincham, Gail, BA Col., MA Tel-Aviv, DPhil York(UK) Sr. Lectr.
Garuba, Harry, MA Ib., PhD Ib. Assoc. Prof.
Higgins, John A., MA Camb., PhD Cape Town Prof.
Love, Nigel L., MA Oxf., DPhil Oxf. Assoc. Prof.
Marx, Lesley G., MA Cape Town, PhD Cape Town Assoc. Prof.
McCormick, Kay M., BA Natal, MA Lond., PhD Cape Town Prof.
Mesthrie, Rajend, BPaed Cape Town, BA Cape Town, BA S.Af., MA Texas, PhD Cape Town Prof.
Schalkwyk, David J., BA Stell., MA York(UK), DPhil York(UK) Prof.
Sole, Kelwyn, BA Witw., MA Lond., PhD Witw. Prof.
Watson, Stephen, MA Cape Town, PhD Cape Town Prof.; Head*
Other Staff: 6 Lectrs.
Research: autobiography; drama, poetry and prose from the European Middle Ages to contemporary South Africa; media and film; travel writing

Environmental and Geographical Science

Tel: (021) 650 2874 Fax: (021) 650 3791
E-mail: admin@enviro.uct.ac.za
Crush, J., MA Camb., MA W.Laur., PhD Qu. Hon. Prof.
Davies, Ronald J., MSc Rhodes, PhD Lond. Emer. Prof.
Dewar, Neil, MA Cape Town, MCRP Cape Town, PhD Cape Town Sr. Lectr.
Eckardt, Frank, MSc Cran., DPhil Oxf. Sr. Lectr.
Fuggle, Richard F., BSc Natal, MSc Louisiana State, PhD McG. Shell Prof., Environmental Studies
Hewitson, Bruce C., BSc Cape Town, MSc Penn., PhD Penn. Prof.
Meadows, Michael E., BSc Sus., PhD Camb. Prof.; Head*
Oldfield, Sophie E., BA Syr., MA Minn., PhD Minn. Sr. Lectr.
Parnell, Sue M., MA Witw., PhD Witw. Assoc. Prof.
Ramutsindela, Maano, MA North(S.Af.), PhD Lond. Sr. Lectr.
Other Staff: 3 Lectrs.
Research: biogeographical research; hydrodynamics and physical characteristics of estuaries; impact of development projects on biophysical and social environment; regional implications of global climate change, climate modelling, precipitation controls and satellite climatology

Extra Mural Studies, Centre for

Tel: (021) 650 2888 Fax: (021) 650 2893
E-mail: ems@humanities.uct.ac.za
Fiske, Ingrid J., BA Witw., BA Cape Town, MA Qu. Assoc. Prof.
Rall, Medee, MPhil Cape Town Dir.*
Other Staff: 1 Lectr.
Research: communities in development; cultural studies; curriculum development and evaluation; national policy

Fine Art, Michaelis School of

Tel: (021) 480 7103 Fax: (021) 424 2889
E-mail: iwillis@hiddingh.uct.ac.za
Alexander, Jane, MA(FA) Witw. Assoc. Prof.
Grundlingh, Geoffrey P. Assoc. Prof.
Inggs, Stephen C., MAFA Natal Assoc. Prof.
Langerman, Fritha, MFA Cape Town Sr. Lectr.
MacKenny, Virginia, BAFA Natal, MA Natal Sr. Lectr.
Payne, Malcolm J., MFA Cape Town Prof.
Skotnes, Pippa A., MFA Cape Town Prof.; Dir.*
Younge, J. Gavin F., BA S.Af., MA(FA) Cape Town Prof.
Other Staff: 4 Lectrs.
Research: changing notion of monuments; iconographic experimentation; issues of identity, the body, memory; modernist and post-modernist technologies in plastic and time-based arts; visual exegesis through display

Geological Sciences

Tel: (021) 650 2931 Fax: (021) 650 3783
E-mail: whitmore@science.uct.ac.za
Compton, John S., BA San Diego, PhD Harv. Assoc. Prof.
De Wit, Maarten J., BSc Trinity(Dub.), PhD Camb. Philipson-Stow Prof., Mineralogy and Geology
Frimmel, Hartwig E. E., PhD Vienna Assoc. Prof.
Gurney, John J., BSc Cape Town, PhD Cape Town, FRSSAf Emer. Prof.
Harris, Christopher, BA Oxf., DPhil Oxf. Assoc. Prof.; Head*
Le Roex, Anton P., BSc Stell., BSc Cape Town, PhD Cape Town Prof.
Minter, W. E. L., BSc Cape Town, PhD Witw. Emer. Prof.
Reid, David L., MSc Well., PhD Cape Town Assoc. Prof.
Richardson, Stephen H., BSc Cape Town, PhD M.I.T. Assoc. Prof.
Roychoudhury, Alakendra N., MSc I.Sch.Mines, PhD Georgia Sr. Lectr.
Smith, George, BA Camb., MA Camb. Sr. Lectr.
Other Staff: 1 Sr. Res. Officer; 1 Principal Sci. Officer; 2 Sr. Sci. Officers; 2 Sci. Officers
Research: geochemistry; igneous and metamorphic petrology; marine geology; sedimentology; structural geology and tectonics

Historical Studies

Tel: (021) 650 2742 Fax: (021) 689 7581
E-mail: bren@humanities.uct.ac.za
Adhikari, M., PhD Cape Town Assoc. Prof.
Bickford-Smith, Vivian J., PhD Camb. Prof.
Field, Sean, MSocSc Cape Town, PhD Essex Sr. Lectr.
Godby, Michael A. P., BA Trinity(Dub.), MA Birm., PhD Witw. Prof.
Jeppie, S., BA W.Cape, MA W.Cape, PhD Prin. Sr. Lectr.
Mager, Anne, PhD Cape Town Assoc. Prof.
Mendelsohn, Richard, BA Cape Town, PhD Witw. Assoc. Prof.; Head*
Nasson, William R., BA Hull, MA York(UK), PhD Camb. Prof.
Penn, Nigel G., BA Witw., PhD Cape Town Assoc. Prof.
Phillips, Howard, BA Cape Town, MA Lond., PhD Cape Town Prof.
Saunders, Christopher C., BA Cape Town, MA Oxf., DPhil Oxf. Prof.
van Sittert, Lance, PhD Cape Town Sr. Lectr.
Worden, Nigel A., PhD Camb. Prof.
Other Staff: 3 Lectrs.
Research: Cape Town history; environmental history; gendered history; medical, mining, maritime, public and war history; Western Cape oral history

Information and Library Studies

Centre for Higher Education Development (CHED)

Tel: (021) 650 3090 Fax: (021) 650 3489
E-mail: cil@ched.uct.ac.za
De Jager, Karin, BA Rhodes, MA Rhodes, MBibl Cape Town, PhD Cape Town Assoc. Prof.
Nassimbeni, Mary M., BA Rhodes, PhD Cape Town Assoc. Prof.

Smith, Janette G., BSc Stell., MA Cape Town   Sr. Lectr.

Underwood, Peter G., MBA Cran., MIInfSc, FLA   Prof.; Head*

Other Staff: 1 Lectr.

Research: information literacy; information management; information needs analysis; library performance measurement and evaluation

Information Systems

Tel: (021) 650 2261 Fax: (021) 650 2280
E-mail: nsamuels@commerce.uct.ac.za

Brown, Irwin, BScEng Z'bwe., MInfSys Curtin   Sr. Lectr.

Cloete, Eric, MSc Natal, DTech Cape Peninsula UT   Sr. Lectr.

Eccles, Michael G., MCom Cape Town   Sr. Lectr.

Hart, Michael L., BSc Cape Town, MSc Cape Town, PhD Cape Town   Assoc. Prof.

Johnston, Kevin, BSc Rhodes, BSc S.Af., MCom Cape Town   Head*

Kyobe, Michael, MBA Durh., PhD Free State   Assoc. Prof.

Nash, Jane, BA Cape Town, BSc S.Af., MCom Cape Town   Sr. Lectr.

Scott, Elsje, BSc Stell., BSc S.Af., MSc Stell.   Sr. Lectr.

Sewchurran, Kosheek, BSc S.Af., MSc S.Af.   Sr. Lectr.

Seymour, Lisa F., PhD Cape Town   Sr. Lectr.

Smith, Derek C., BTech Brad., MCom Cape Town   Prof.

Stander, Adrie, BSc S.Af., MTech Cape Peninsula UT   Sr. Lectr.

Van Belle, Jean-Paul, LicEcon Ghent, BCom Cape Town, MBA Stell., PhD Cape Town   Assoc. Prof.

Other Staff: 3 Lectrs.

Research: health information systems; management (technological and social aspects); personnel-related issues; systems development approaches

Languages and Literatures, School of

comprising African Languages and Literatures, Afrikaans and Netherlandic Studies, and Linguistics

Tel: (021) 650 2312 Fax: (021) 650 4032

Hambidge, Joan H., BA Stell., MA Pret., PhD Rhodes, PhD Cape Town   Prof.; Dir.*

African Languages and Literatures

Tel: (021) 650 2301 Fax: (021) 650 3726
E-mail: bren@beattie.uct.ac.za

Gxilishe, Sandile, BA Fort Hare, MEd Col., MA Stell., DLitt Stell.   Assoc. Prof.

Nyamende, Abner, BA Transkei, MA Cape Town, PhD Cape Town   Head*

Satyo, Sizwe C., BA Fort Hare, MA S.Af., DLitt&Phil S.Af.   Prof.

Other Staff: 1 Lectr.

Research: historical linguistics; lexicography; oral literature; second language acquisition; sociolinguistics

Afrikaans and Netherlandic Studies

E-mail: eck@beattie.uct.ac.za

Hambidge, Joan H., BA Stell., MA Pret., PhD Rhodes, PhD Cape Town   Prof.

Snyman, Henning, BA Stell., PhD Cape Town, DLitt Cape Town   Prof.

Van der Merwe, Chris N., BA Stell., MA Stell., LittDrs Utrecht, DLitt&Phil Rand Afrikaans   Assoc. Prof.; Head*

Van Heerden, Etienne R., BA Stell., LLB Stell., MA Witw., PhD Rhodes   Prof.

Research: Caribbean Dutch studies; children's literature; historical linguistics; war literature

Law, Commercial

Tel: (021) 650 3065 Fax: (021) 686 2577
E-mail: dorothy@law.uct.ac.za

Emslie, Trevor S., BA Witw., LLB Witw., BCom Cape Town, MBA Cape Town   Assoc. Prof.

Hare, John E., BCom Cape Town, LLB Cape Town, LLM Lond., LLD Cape Town   Prof.

Hofman, Julien, BL Z'bwe.Open, LLB Z'bwe.Open, BTheol Greg., LJC Greg., LPhil Heythrop   Assoc. Prof.

Jooste, Richard D., BA Cape Town, BCom Cape Town, LLB Cape Town, LLM Camb.   Prof.

Kalula, Evance R., LLB Zambia, LLM Lond., PhD Warw.   Prof.

Larkin, M. P., BCom Witw., LLB Witw.   Prof.; Head*

Le Roux, K., BJuris P.Elizabeth, LLB P.Elizabeth, LLM Stell.   Sr. Lectr.

Lehman, Karin, BA Cape Town, LLB Cape Town, LLM Nott.   Sr. Lectr.

Other Staff: 11 Lectrs.

Research: admiralty law and practice; company law; development and labour in southern Africa; revenue law

Law, Private

Tel: (021) 650 3447 Fax: (021) 650 2577
E-mail: hutch@law.uct.ac.za

De Vos, W., BA Stell., LLB Stell., DrsJur Ley., LLD Cape Town   Emer. Prof.

Du Bois, F. G., BA Stell., BA Oxf., LLB Stell., BCL Oxf.   Assoc. Prof.

Fagan, A. G., BA Cape Town, LLB Cape Town, DPhil Oxf.   Assoc. Prof.; Head*

Himonga, Chuma N., LLB Zambia, LLM Lond., PhD Lond.   Prof.

Hutchison, Dale B., BCom Cape Town, LLB Cape Town, PhD Camb.   Prof.

Paleker, Mohamed, BA Cape Town, LLB Rhodes, LLM Cape Town   Sr. Lectr.

Pope, Anne, BA Rhodes, LLB Rhodes   Sr. Lectr.

Visser, Daniel P., BJuris Pret., LLB Pret., LLD Pret., DrJur Ley.   Prof.

Other Staff: 2 Lectrs.

Research: enrichment; historical development of South African law and comparison with law in other systems; law in operation in South Africa (family law); law of contract (overlap between contract and delict); law of persons

Law, Public

Tel: (021) 650 3078 Fax: (021) 689 8546
E-mail: lawlas@law.uct.ac.za

Bennett, Thomas W., BA Rhodes, LLB Rhodes, PhD Cape Town   Prof.

Cheadle, Halton, BA Natal, BProc S.Af., LLB Witw.   Prof.

Chirwa, Danwood, LLB Malawi, LLM Pret., LLD W.Cape   Sr. Lectr.

Corder, Hugh M., BCom Cape Town, LLB Cape Town, LLB Camb., DPhil Oxf.   Prof.

Murray, Christina M., BA Stell., LLB Stell., LLM Mich.   Prof.; Head*

Pillay, Anashri, BA Natal, LLB Natal, LLM Lond.   Sr. Lectr.

Powell, Cathy, BA Cape Town, LLB Cape Town, LLM Humboldt   Sr. Lectr.

van Bueren, Geraldine, LLB Lond., LLM Lond.   Prof.

Other Staff: 1 Lectr.

Research: administrative justice in the context of the Bill of Rights; fiscal powers of government; race and gender discrimination in South African customary law; relationship of national and provincial organs of state; role of the judiciary

Management Studies, School of

Tel: (021) 650 2311 Fax: (021) 689 7570

Bagraim, Jeffrey, BBusSc Cape Town, MA Cape Town   Assoc. Prof.

Cohen, Michael, BCom Witw., MSc(Econ) Lond.   Sr. Lectr.

Dorrington, Robert E., BA S.Af., BCom Natal, BSc Cape Town, MPhil Cape Town, FIA, FASSA   Prof., Actuarial Science

Flynn, Dave, BA Stell., BCom Natal, BEd Cape Town, MBA Cape Town   Assoc. Prof.

Grant, Terry, BA Cape Town, MA Cape Town   Sr. Lectr.

Human, G. J. P., BEcon Free State, MEcon Free State   Sr. Lectr.

Kendal, Shannon, MSc Cape Town, PhD Cape Town, FIA, FASSA   Sr. Lectr.

Louw-Potgieter, J., MA Stell., DPsych Ley., PhD Brist.   Prof.

MacDonald, Iain L., BSc Cape Town, MSc Oxf., PhD Cape Town   Assoc. Prof.

Simpson, John D., BSc Cape Town, MBA Cape Town, PhD Cape Town   John Garlick Prof., Business Science; Head*

Toerien, F., MBA Cape Town, PhD Rand Afrikaans   Sr. Lectr.

van Lill, Burger, MA Stell., PhD S.Af.   Prof.

van Rensburg, Paul, BSocSci Natal, MCom Natal, PhD Natal   Prof.

Other Staff: 15 Lectrs.

Research: finance; human resource management; knowledge organisations; marketing; occupational psychology

Mathematics and Applied Mathematics

Tel: (021) 650 3191 Fax: (021) 650 2334
E-mail: maths@ucthpx.uct.ac.za

Barashenkov, Igor V., MSc Moscow, PhD Jt.Inst.Nuclear Res., Dubna   Prof.

Becker, Ronald I., BSc Cape Town, PhD M.I.T.   Emer. Prof.

Brattka, Vasco, PhD Hagen Open   Assoc. Prof.

Brümmer, Guillaume C. L., MSc Stell., DrMath Amst., PhD Cape Town   Emer. Prof.

Bruyns, Peter V., MA Oxf., MSc Cape Town, DPhil Oxf.   Sr. Lectr.

Butterworth, Douglas S., MSc Cape Town, PhD Lond.   Prof.

Conradie, Jurie J., MSc Stell., PhD Camb.   Sr. Lectr.

Dunsby, Peter K. S., BSc Lond., PhD Lond.   Sr. Lectr.

Ebobisse Bille, Franscois, PhD Pisa   Sr. Lectr.

Ellis, George F. R., BSc Cape Town, BCom Cape Town, PhD Camb., Hon. DSc Natal, FRAS, FIMA   Prof., Complex Systems

Frith, John L., MSc Cape Town, PhD Cape Town   Sr. Lectr.

Gay, David T., AB Harv., PhD Calif.   Sr. Lectr.

Gilmour, Christopher R. A., MSc Cape Town, PhD Cape Town   Assoc. Prof.; Head*

Hardie, Keith A., MSc Natal, PhD Camb.   Emer. Prof.

Hellaby, Charles W., BSc St And., MSc Qu., PhD Qu.   Sr. Lectr.

Hughes, Kenneth R., BSc Cape Town, PhD Cape Town, PhD Warw.   Sr. Lectr.

Janelidze, George, MSc Tbilisi, PhD Tbilisi, DSc St.Petersburg   Prof.

Künzi, Hans-Pieter A., MSc Berne, PhD Berne   Prof.

Laurie, Henri, BA Stell., BSc S.Af., PhD Cape Town   Sr. Lectr.

Myers, Tim G., BSc Leic., PhD Leeds   Assoc. Prof.

Ouwehand, Peter W., MSc Cape Town, PhD Cape Town   Sr. Lectr.

Prince, Robert, BSc W.Cape, MSc Cape Town   Sr. Lectr.

Reddy, Batmanathan D., BSc(Eng) Cape Town, PhD Camb., FRSSAf   Prof., Applied Mathematics

Rynhoud, Alan N., MSc Cape Town   Sr. Lectr.

Schauerte, Anneliese, BSc Natal, MSc Cape Town, PhD McM.   Sr. Lectr.

Webb, John H., BSc Cape Town, PhD Camb.   Prof.

Yanovski, Alexander, MSc Sofia, PhD Jt.Inst.Nuclear Res., Dubna   Assoc. Prof.

Other Staff: 9 Lectrs.; 1 Sr. Res. Officer; 3 Res. Officers; 1 Emer. Assoc. Prof.; 1 Hon. Res. Assoc.

Research: biological modelling; continuum mechanics; general relativity and cosmology; topology, analysis, logic and theoretical computer science

Modern and Classical Languages and Literatures

comprising Arabic, Classics, French Language and Literature, German Language and Literature, Hebrew and Jewish Studies, and Italian Studies

Tel: (021) 650 2895 Fax: (021) 685 5530
E-mail: sonja@humanities.uct.ac.za

Classics

Tel: (021) 650 2607-8
E-mail: leeb@humanities.uct.ac.za

Atkinson, John E., BA Durh., PhD Cape Town Emer. Prof.

Chandler, Clive E., BA Cape Town, MA Cape Town, PhD Cape Town Head*

Wardle, David, MA Oxf., DPhil Oxf. Assoc. Prof.

Whitaker, Richard A., BA Witw., MA Oxf., PhD St And. Prof.

Other Staff: 1 Lectr.

Research: ancient Greek and Roman world; key ideological phenomena in ancient history; modern reflections of and reactions to the ancient world; translation and interpretation of texts

French Language and Literature

Cornille, Jean-Louis, LicPhilRom Angers, MenPhil Angers, Dr Nijmegen Prof., Modern French Literature; Head*

Everson, Vanessa, BA Nott., MA Oxf. Sr. Lectr.

Other Staff: 1 Lectr.

Research: foreign/second language didactics and teaching strategies; francophone and African studies; gay, lesbian and women's studies and the literature of the seventeenth, nineteenth and twentieth centuries; West African cinema

German Language and Literature

Pakendorf, Gunther, MA Witw., PhD Cape Town Assoc. Prof.; Head*

Other Staff: 2 Lectrs.

Research: colonial discourses; literature from 1770 to the present; theory and didactics; women's studies and psychoanalysis

Hebrew and Jewish Studies

Tel: (021) 650 2945 Fax: (021) 650 3062
E-mail: kc@humanities.uct.ac.za

Goldenberg, David, PhD Dropsie Prof.

Reisenberger, Azila, MA Cape Town, PhD Cape Town Sr. Lectr.

Shain, Milton, MA S.Af., MA Leeds, PhD Cape Town Prof.; Head*

Research: Biblical literature and rhetoric; Jewish feminism; modernity and Jewish memory; South African Jewry

Italian Studies

E-mail: leeb@humanities.uct.ac.za

Saxby, Nelia N., BA Lond., MPhil Lond., PhD Cape Town Assoc. Prof.; Head*

Other Staff: 2 Lectrs.

Research: Renaissance dialogue; twentieth-century women's writing; unpublished manuscripts of the fifteenth century

Molecular and Cell Biology

Tel: (021) 650 3270 Fax: (021) 689 7573
E-mail: secmic@molbiol.uct.ac.za

Abratt, Val, BSc Rhodes, PhD Cape Town Assoc. Prof.

Brandt, Wolf F., BSc Cape Town, PhD Cape Town Assoc. Prof.

Coyne, Vernon E., BSc Rhodes, BSc Cape Town, PhD Cape Town Assoc. Prof.

Denby, Katherine, BSc Brist., DPhil Oxf. Sr. Lectr.

Farrant, Jill, BSc Natal, PhD Natal Prof.; Head*

Illing, Nicola, MSc Cape Town, DPhil Oxf. Assoc. Prof.

Klump, Horst H., DrRerNat Freib. Prof., Biochemistry

Lindsey, George, BSc Sus., DPhil Sus. Assoc. Prof.

Mundree, Sagadevan, BPaed Auburn, BSc Auburn, MBA Cape Town, PhD Auburn Assoc. Prof.

O'Ryan, Colleen, BSc Cape Town, PhD Cape Town Sr. Lectr.

Reid, Shenz J., BSc Rhodes, PhD Rhodes Assoc. Prof.

Rybicki, Edward P., MSc Cape Town, PhD Cape Town Prof., Microbiology

Thomson, Jennifer A., BSc Cape Town, MA Camb., PhD Rhodes Prof.

Other Staff: 4 Lectrs.

Research: molecular biology (bacteria and viruses important in industry, agriculture, mariculture and medicine)

Music, South African College of

Tel: (021) 650 2631 Fax: (021) 650 2627
E-mail: staylor@protem.uct.ac.za

Andrews, Darryl, BMus Cape Town Sr. Lectr., Jazz Studies

Bezuidenhout, Morne, DMus S.Af. Sr. Lectr., Musicology

Campbell, Michael I., BMus N.Texas, DMus Cape Town Assoc. Prof., Jazz Studies

Davids, Virginia Assoc. Prof., Singing

Du Toit, Francois, BMus Cape Town, FTCL Assoc. Prof., Piano

Fitch, G., MMus Manhattan Sch. Assoc. Prof., Piano

Gobbato, Angelo M. G., BSc Cape Town, Hon. DMus Cape Town Prof.; Dir., Opera Sch.

Hartman, Sidwill Assoc. Prof.

Herbst, Anri, DPhil Stell. Assoc. Prof.; Deputy Dir.

Hofmeyr, Hendrik, MMus Cape Town, DMus Cape Town Assoc. Prof., Musicology

Kierman, Sean A., BA Antioch, BMus Witw., MA P.Elizabeth Sr. Lectr., Brass

Klatzow, Peter J. L., DMus Cape Town Prof., Composition

Larey, Franklin, BA(Mus) W.Cape, MMus Cinc., DMA Cinc. Assoc. Prof., Piano; Dir.*

Liebl, Brad L., MM Cinc., DMA Cinc. Assoc. Prof., Singing

Lilley, Andrew C. P., BAS Cape Town Sr. Lectr., Jazz Studies

Nixon, Michael, MA Wesleyan Sr. Lectr., Ethnomusicology

Rossi, Michael, DMA New Eng.Cons. Assoc. Prof., Jazz Studies

Other Staff: 4 Lectrs

Research: composition (instrumental, jazz, vocal); ethnomusicology; music of Bruneau, Delius, Schoenberg

Oceanography

Tel: (021) 650 3277 Fax: (021) 650 3979
E-mail: shill@ocean.uct.ac.za

Brundrit, Geoffrey B., BSc Manc., PhD Manc. Prof., Physical Oceanography

Lutjeharms, Johann, MSc Cape Town, DSc Cape Town, PhD Wash., FRSSAf Prof., Ocean Climatology

Reason, Chris, BSc Cape Town, MSc Br.Col., MPhil City(UK), PhD Br.Col. Assoc. Prof.

Shannon, L. Vere, MSc Cape Town, PhD Cape Town Hon. Prof.

Shillington, Frank A., BSc Witw., MSc Cape Town, PhD Cape Town Prof.; Head*

Waldron, Howard, BSc Wales(Swansea), MSc Cape Town, PhD Cape Town Sr. Lectr.

Research: air-sea interaction; coastal meteorology; marine climatology; physical oceanography, ocean modelling; shelf dynamics

Philosophy

Tel: (021) 650 3316 Fax: (021) 650 3490
E-mail: philosophy@humanities.uct.ac.za

Benatar, David, BSocSc Cape Town, PhD Cape Town Assoc. Prof.; Head*

d'Entreves, Passerin, BA Lond., MA Boston, PhD Boston Prof.

Galgut, Elisa, BA Witw., MA Witw., MA Rutgers, PhD Rutgers Sr. Lectr.

Weiss, Bernhard, BSc Durh., PhD St And. Sr. Lectr.

Other Staff: 1 Lectr.

Research: analytical philosophy (aesthetics, cognitive science, logic, moral and political philosophy and jurisprudence, philosophy of economics, philosophy of mind and language, philosophy of religion, philosophy of science)

Physics

Tel: (021) 650 3326 Fax: (021) 650 3342
E-mail: jennings@physci.uct.ac.za

Allie, Muhammed S., MSc Cape Town, PhD Cape Town Assoc. Prof.

Aschman, David G., BSc Cape Town, DPhil Oxf. Prof.

Britton, David T., MSc Lond., PhD Lond. Assoc. Prof.

Brooks, Francis D., DSc Rhodes Emer. Prof.

Buffler, A., MSc Cape Town, PhD Cape Town Assoc. Prof.

Cleymans, Jean W. A., MSc Louvain, DèsSc Louvain, FRSSAf Prof., Theoretical Physics

Comrie, Craig M., MSc Natal, PhD Camb. Assoc. Prof.; Head*

Dominguez, Cesareo A., MSc Buenos Aires, PhD Buenos Aires, FRSSAf Prof.

Fearick, Roger W., BSc Witw., PhD Witw. Sr. Lectr.

Harting, M., DrIng Munich F.A.F. Assoc. Prof.

Juritz, J. W. F., MSc Cape Town Emer. Prof.

Muronga, A. T. M., MSc Cape Town, PhD Minn. Sr. Lectr.

Perez, Sandro M., BSc Witw., DPhil Oxf. Prof.

Robertson, Gerald N. van der H., BSc Cape Town, DPhil Oxf. Emer. Prof.

Spargo, P., BSc(Eng) Witw., MSc Witw., FRSSAf Emer. Prof.

Vilakazi, Z., MA Witw., PhD Witw. Sr. Lectr.

Viollier, Raoul D., DrPhilNat Basle, FRSSAf Prof.

Other Staff: 2 Lectrs.; 1 Sr. Res. Assoc.

Research: applied optics; nuclear physics; physics education; theoretical physics

Political Studies

Tel: (021) 650 3381 Fax: (021) 689 7574
E-mail: politics@humanities.uct.ac.za

Akokpari, John, BA Ghana, MA Internat.(Japan), PhD Dal. Sr. Lectr.

Butler, Anthony, MA Oxf., PhD Camb. Assoc. Prof.

Cameron, Robert, MPubAd Cape Town, PhD Cape Town Prof.; Head*

Mattes, R., MA Delaware, PhD Ill. Assoc. Prof.

Reddy, Thivendren, BSocSc Natal, MA Wash., PhD Wash. Sr. Lectr.

Schrire, Robert A., BCom Cape Town, MA American(D.C.), PhD Calif. Prof.

Seegers, Annette, MA Pret., PhD Loyola(Ill.) Prof.

Simons, Mary, BA Cape Town Sr. Lectr.

Stephan, Harry, BA Calif., PhD Georgetown Sr. Lectr.

Other Staff: 2 Lectrs.

Research: civil-military relations; comparative politics; intellectual history and local government; political ethics; South African politics and policy analysis

Psychology

Tel: (021) 650 3430 Fax: (021) 650 4104
E-mail: heather@humanities.uct.ac.za

Ameen, O., MB ChB Witw. Sr. Lectr.

Bandawe, C., PhD Cape Town Sr. Lectr.

Dowdall, Terry, BA Natal, MA Cape Town Sr. Lectr.

Foster, Donald H., BA Stell., MSc Lond., PhD Camb. Prof.

Gobodo-Madikizela, P., PhD Cape Town Assoc. Prof.

Louw, Johannes, MA Stell., DrsPsy Ley., PhD Amst. Prof.

Schomer, Helgo, PhD Cape Town Sr. Lectr.

Solms, Mark, PhD Witw. Prof.

Swartz, Sally, PhD Cape Town Assoc. Prof.; Head*

Thomas, Kevin, PhD Arizona Sr. Lectr.

Tredoux, Colin G., PhD Cape Town Sr. Lectr.

Other Staff: 6 Lectrs.

Research: child development; gender; intergroup relations; policy development; social change in southern Africa

Religious Studies

Tel: (021) 650 3452 Fax: (021) 689 7575
E-mail: jardienn@humanities.uct.ac.za

Chidester, David S., BA Calif., PhD Calif. Prof.; Head*

Cochrane, J. R., BSc Cape Town, MDiv Chic., PhD Cape Town Prof.

Kwenda, C. W., BTh S.Af., STM Indianapolis, MPhil Syr., PhD Syr. Sr. Lectr.

Mazamisa, Llewellyn W., BD Theol.Sch.Kampen, ThDrs Theol.Sch.Kampen, PhD Theol.Sch.Kampen Sr. Lectr.
Tayob, Abdulkader I., BA Durban-W., BA Cape Town, PhD Temple   Assoc. Prof.
Wanamaker, Charles A., BA Lincoln Christian, MA Ill., MCS Regent Coll.(Br.Col.), PhD Durh. Assoc. Prof.
Other Staff: 3 Lectrs.
Research: contemporary religion; religious education curricula; resource development for schools

Social Anthropology

Tel: (021) 650 3679 Fax: (021) 650 2307
E-mail: socanth@humanities.uct.ac.za
Brokensha, D., BA Rhodes, BLitt Oxf., MA Camb., DPhil Oxf.   Hon. Prof.
Comaroff, J. L., BA Cape Town, PhD Lond.   Hon. Prof.
Fordred-Green, Lesley, BA Cape Town, PhD Cape Town   Sr. Lectr.
Frankental, S., PhD Cape Town   Sr. Lectr.
Levine, Susan, BA Bard, PhD Temple   Sr. Lectr.
Ross, Fiona, MSocSc Cape Town, PhD Cape Town Assoc. Prof.
Sichone, Owen, BA Zambia, MA Sus., PhD Camb. Sr. Lectr.
Spiegel, Andrew D., MA Cape Town, PhD Cape Town   Assoc. Prof.; Head*
West, Martin E., BA Cape Town, MA Cape Town, PhD Cape Town   Prof.
Other Staff: 3 Hon. Res. Assocs.
Research: anthropology of tourism; boundaries; children; domestic dynamics and family violence; urbanisation

Social Development

Tel: (021) 650 3493 Fax: (021) 689 2739
E-mail: halford@humanities.uct.ac.za
Becker, Lily, BA(SW) Stell., BSocSc Cape Town, MSocSc Cape Town   Sr. Lectr.
Booyens, Margaret, BA(SW) P.Elizabeth, MA(SW) P.Elizabeth, DPhil P.Elizabeth   Sr. Lectr.
O'Brien, Connie, BA(SW) Durban-W., BSocSc Cape Town, MA Witw., PhD Brad.   Sr. Lectr.
Smit, Andre De V., BSocSc(SW) Cape Town, BCom Cape Town, MPubAd Cape Town Assoc. Prof.; Head*
Sturgeon, Shona, BSocSc(SW) Cape Town, MSocSc Cape Town   Sr. Lectr.
Taylor, Viviene, BA(SW) Durban-W., BSocSc Cape Town, MSocSc Cape Town   Assoc. Prof.
Other Staff: 3 Lectrs.
Research: cultural diversity; gender studies; mental health; social security systems; substance abuse

Sociology

Tel: (021) 650 3501 Fax: (021) 689 7576
E-mail: socio@humanities.uct.ac.za
Cooper, D. M., BSc(Eng) Cape Town, MSocSc Birm., PhD Birm.   Assoc. Prof.; Head*
Crankshaw, Owen, PhD Witw.   Assoc. Prof.
Erasmus, Zimitri, MSocSc Cape Town, PhD Nijmegen   Sr. Lectr.
Graaff, Johan F. D., BA Stell., LLB Stell., MSc Brist., PhD Stell.   Sr. Lectr.
Grossman, Jonathan, BSocSc Cape Town, PhD Warw.   Sr. Lectr.
Head, Judith, BSocSc Middx., MPH W.Cape, PhD Durh.   Sr. Lectr.
Jubber, Kenneth C., MA Witw., PhD Cape Town Assoc. Prof.
Lincoln, Merwyn D., BA Natal, MA W.Laur., PhD Cape Town   Sr. Lectr.
Maree, Johannes J., BSc Rhodes, MA Oxf., MA Sus., PhD Cape Town   Prof.
Ntsebeza, Lungisile, BA S.Af., MA Natal, PhD Rhodes   Assoc. Prof.
Seekings, Jeremy F., BA Oxf., BA Witw., DPhil Oxf.   Assoc. Prof.
Steyn, Melissa, BA S.Af., MA Arizona, PhD Cape Town   Assoc. Prof.
Other Staff: 1 Lectr.
Research: equity and development; political violence, protest and organisation;

sociology of the body; workplace restructuring

Statistical Sciences

Tel: (021) 650 3219 Fax: (021) 650 4773
E-mail: statdept@maths.uct.ac.za
Barr, Graham D. I., BSc Cape Town, BA Cape Town, MSc Cape Town, PhD Cape Town   Prof.
Bradfield, David J., MSc Cape Town, PhD Cape Town   Prof.
Dunne, Timothy T., BA Natal, BSc Natal, BEd Natal, PhD Cape Town   Prof.; Head*
Guo, Renkuan G., BSc Tsinghua, MSc Iowa State, PhD Iowa State   Assoc. Prof.
Haines, Linda M., BSc Natal, MA Camb., PhD S.Af.   Prof.
Little, F., MSc Cape Town, PhD Cape Town   Sr. Lectr.
Nyirenda, Juwa C., PhD Camb.   Sr. Lectr.
Scott, Leanne D., MSc Cape Town, PhD Cape Town Sr. Lectr.
Stewart, Theodor J., BSc(Eng) Cape Town, MSc S.Af., PhD S.Af.   Prof.
Stielau, Karl, BSc Natal   Sr. Lectr.
Thiart, Christien, MSc Cape Town, PhD Cape Town Assoc. Prof.
Troskie, Casparus G., MSc Pret., PhD S.Af. Emer. Prof.
Underhill, Leslie G., MSc Cape Town, PhD Cape Town   Dir., Avian Demography Unit; Prof., Avian Demography
Other Staff: 6 Lectrs.
Research: biostatistics; decision theory; multiple-criteria decision-making; multivariate analysis; stochastic hydrology and meteorology

Zoology

Tel: (021) 650 3603 Fax: (021) 650 3301
E-mail: lederboer@botzoo.uct.ac.za
Branch, George M., BSc Cape Town, PhD Cape Town, FRSSAf   Prof.
Bronner, G., MSc Natal, PhD Natal   Sr. Lectr.
Chinsamy-Turan, Anusuya, BSc Witw., PhD Witw., FRSSAf   Prof.
Crowe, Timothy M., MSc Chic., PhD Cape Town Prof.
Day, Jennifer A., BSc Cape Town, PhD Cape Town Assoc. Prof.; Head*
Du Plessis, Prof. Morné A., MSc Pret., PhD Cape Town   Prof.
Field, Johannes G., BSc Cape Town, PhD Cape Town, FRSSAf   Prof.
Gäde, Gerd, MS Mün., PhD Mün.   Prof.
Govender, A., MSc Natal, PhD Natal   Sr. Lectr.
Griffiths, Charles L., BSc S'ton., PhD Cape Town Assoc. Prof.
Hockey, Philip A. R., BSc Edin., PhD Cape Town Assoc. Prof.
Hoffman, John H., MSc Rhodes, PhD Rhodes Assoc. Prof.; Chief Res. Officer
Jacobs, D., BSc Cape Town, PhD Hawaii   Assoc. Prof.
Lucas, Mike I., BSc Wales, PhD Wales   Sr. Lectr.
Moloney, C., BSc Cape Town, PhD Cape Town   Sr. Lectr.
O'Riain, J., BSc Cape Town, PhD Cape Town   Sr. Lectr.
Picker, Michael D., BSc Witw., PhD Witw.   Sr. Lectr.
Ryan, Peter G., MSc Cape Town, PhD Cape Town Sr. Lectr.
Other Staff: 1 Lectr.; 2 Emer. Assoc. Profs.
Research: biochemistry; ecology; ethology; physiology

HEALTH SCIENCES

Tel: (021) 406 6346 Fax: (021) 447 8955
E-mail: medfac@curie.uct.ac.za

Anaesthesia

Tel: (021) 404 5001-4 Fax: (021) 447 5206
E-mail: gunst@samiot.uct.ac.za
Bosenberg, A. T., MB ChB Cape Town   Prof.
Butt, A. D., MB ChB Cape Town   Sr. Lectr.
Dyer, Robert A., BSc Stell., MB ChB Cape Town Assoc. Prof.

Falanga, Franca M., MB ChB Cape Town   Sr. Lectr.
Gordon, Peter C., MB ChB Witw., BSc(Chem) Natal   Assoc. Prof.
Heijke, Sylvia A. M., MB ChB Cape Town   Sr. Lectr.
Ing, R. J., MB ChB Witw.   Sr. Lectr.
James, Michael F. M., MB ChB Birm., PhD Witw., FRCA   Prof.; Head*
Llewellyn, R. L., MB ChB Cape Town   Sr. Lectr.
Nieuwveld, Bobby R. W., MB BCh Witw.   Sr. Lectr.
Ruttmann, Thomas G., MB ChB Cape Town Assoc. Prof.
Thomas, J. M., MB ChB Cape Town   Sr. Lectr.
Other Staff: 10 Lectrs.
Research: assessment of new agents in paediatric anaesthesia; coagulation; regional anaesthesia in obstetric patients

Biomedical Sciences, School of

Steyn, L. M., MB ChB Stell., PhD Cape Town, FCPath   Prof.; Dir.*

Anatomical Pathology

Tel: (021) 406 6160 Fax: (021) 448 1789
E-mail: dominica@chempath.uct.ac.za
Bowen, Robert M., MB ChB Cape Town, MMedPath Cape Town, FCPath   Principal Specialist; Head, Surg. Pathol.
Duffield, M. S., MB ChB Rhodes, MMedPath Cape Town   Sr. Lectr.
Govender, Dhirendra, MB ChB Natal, MMed Natal, FCPath   Prof.; Head*
Taylor, D. A., MB ChB Z'bwe.Open, MMedPath(Anat) Cape Town, PhD Manc.   Sr. Lectr.
Wainwright, Helen C., MB ChB Cape Town   Sr. Lectr.
Other Staff: 1 Lectr.
Research: diseases prevalent in local or national communities (tuberculosis, viral infections - HIV, EBV, CMV - and various cancers), particularly those affecting disadvantaged groups

Chemical Pathology

Tel: (021) 406 6185 Fax: (021) 448 8150
E-mail: sweber@chempath.uct.ac.za
Berman, Peter A., MB ChB Cape Town, MMedPath(Chem) Cape Town, PhD Cape Town, DSc(Med) Cape Town   Sr. Lectr.
Henderson, Howard, BSc Cape Town, PhD Cape Town   Prof.; Head*
King, Judy A., BSc Cape Town, MSc Cape Town, PhD Cape Town   Sr. Lectr.
McIntosh, David B., BSc Witw., PhD Cape Town Assoc. Prof.
Owen, Tricia E. P., BSc Lond., PhD Lond.   Sr. Lectr.
Steenkamp, Daan J., BSc Stell., MSc S.Af., PhD Rand Afrikaans   Assoc. Prof.
Vreede, Helena, MB ChB Cape Town, MMedPath(Chem) Cape Town   Sr. Lectr.
Other Staff: 1 Lectr.
Research: biochemical parasitology; G protein-coupled receptor/function; haemoglobin cross-linking; inherited metabolic disorders/molecular evolution; molecular pumps and transporters/anti-malarial drug development

Dermatology

Tel: (021) 406 3376 Fax: (021) 447 8232
E-mail: adhikari@uctgsh1.uct.ac.za
Jessop, Susan J., MB ChB Cape Town   Sr. Lectr.
Todd, Gail, BScAgric Natal, MB ChB Cape Town, PhD Cape Town   Assoc. Prof.; Head*
Research: anti-convulsants; genetics of psoriasis; primary and secondary dermatological care; psychological aspects of skin diseases

Forensic Medicine and Toxicology

Tel: (021) 406 6412 Fax: (021) 448 1249
E-mail: june@curie.uct.ac.za
Liebenberg, Linda, MB ChB Stell., MMedPath Cape Town   Sr. Lectr.

Martin, Lorna J., MB BCh Witw., MMedPath
Cape Town Prof.; Head*
van der Heyde, Yolande, BSc Cape Town, MB
ChB Cape Town, MMedPath Cape Town Sr.
Lectr.
Research: alcohol and unnatural deaths;
community epidemiology network on drug
use; provision of a sustainable database on
violence and injury in the Cape Town
metropole; public policy and health
promotion

Haematology

Tel: (021) 404 3073 Fax: (021) 448 8607
du Toit, Cecile E., MB ChB Free State,
MMed(IntMed) Cape Town Sr. Lectr.
McDonald, Andrew, MB ChB S.Af. Sr. Lectr.
Novitzky, Nicolas, PhD Cape Town, FCP(SA)
Prof.; Head*
Stein, Maureen, MB ChB Cape Town Sr. Lectr.
Research: blood stem cell transplantation;
Hodgkin's disease and malignant
lymphomas; myeloma; the leukaemias and
myelo-dysplastic syndromes

Human Genetics

Tel: (021) 406 6297 Fax: (021) 447 7703
E-mail: avs@cormack.uct.ac.za
Beighton, Peter, MD Lond., PhD Witw., FRCP,
FRCPCH, FRSSAf Emer. Prof.
De Decker, Rik, MB ChB Cape Town, MSc Cape
Town Sr. Lectr.
du Toit, E., MB ChB Cape Town, MD Cape Town
Hon. Prof. Emer.
Greenberg, L. J. H. L., BSc Stell., PhD Cape Town
Assoc. Prof.
Ramesar, Raj S., BSc Natal, MSc Natal, PhD Cape
Town Prof.; Head*
Other Staff: 1 Hon. Prof.; 2 Hon. Sr. Lectrs.
Research: childhood handicap (blindness,
hearing loss, crippling and mental
retardation); colonic cancer; foetal alcohol
syndrome; genetic basis of manic
depressive psychosis

Immunology

Tel: (021) 406 6616 Fax: (021) 448 6116
E-mail: bryffel@uctgsh1.uct.ac.za
Brombacher, Frank, PhD Freib. Assoc. Prof.;
Head*
Brown, Gordon, PhD Cape Town Assoc. Prof.
du Toit, E., MB ChB Cape Town, MD Cape Town
Hon. Prof.
Jacobs, M., PhD Cape Town Assoc. Prof.
Lopata, Andreas, PhD Cape Town Sr. Lectr.
Nurse, Barbara, PhD Cape Town Sr. Lectr.
Potter, Paul C., BSc Cape Town, MB ChB Cape
Town, MD Cape Town, FCP(SA) Assoc. Prof.
Ryffel, Bernhard, MD Berne, PhD Basle Hon.
Prof.
Wilson, Elaine L., PhD Cape Town Hon. Prof.
Research: allergology; clinical immunology;
infectious immunology; transplantation
immunology

Medical Biochemistry

Tel: (021) 406 6335 Fax: (021) 447 7669
E-mail: vkoen@curie.uct.ac.za
Hendricks, Denver T., BSc Cape Town, PhD Cape
Town Sr. Lectr.
Katz, Arieh A., MSc Jerusalem, PhD Jerusalem
Assoc. Prof.
Parker, M. I., BSc Cape Town, PhD Cape Town
Prof.; Head*
Sikakana, Cynthia N. T., BS Wesleyan, PhD Wis.
Sr. Lectr.
Sturrock, Ed D., BSc Cape Town, PhD Cape Town
Assoc. Prof.
Thilo, Lutz R., MSc Pret., DrRerNat Heidel.
Assoc. Prof.
Other Staff: 2 Hon. Sr. Lectrs.
Research: cellular and molecular biology of
breast and oesophageal cancer; endocytic
trafficking and characteristics of the
mycobacterial phagosome; molecular basis
of mycobacterium tuberculosis-host cell
interaction; proteolytic processing of
membrane proteins

Medical Microbiology

Tel: (021) 406 6363 Fax: (021) 448 8153
E-mail: lsteyn@curie.uct.ac.za
Elisha, B. G., BSc Cape Town, PhD Cape Town
Assoc. Prof.
Oliver, S. P., MMedPath Cape Town Sr. Lectr.
Segal, Heidi, BSc Cape Town, PhD Cape Town Sr.
Lectr.
Steyn, L. M., MB ChB Stell., PhD Cape Town,
FCPath Prof.; Head*
Whitelaw, Andrew, MB ChB Witw., MSc Cape
Town Sr. Lectr.
Other Staff: 6 Hon. Lectrs.
Research: clinical microbiology; molecular
medical microbiology; paediatric medical
microbiology; virology

Paediatric Pathology

Tel: (021) 658 6044 Fax: (021) 689 1287
Henderson, Howard, BSc Cape Town, PhD Cape
Town Assoc. Prof.
Shuttleworth, Margaret H. G., BSc Cape Town,
MB ChB Cape Town, MMedPath Cape Town
Sr. Lectr.
Sinclair-Smith, Colin C., MB ChB Cape Town,
MMedPath Cape Town Assoc. Prof.; Head*
Other Staff: 3 Lectrs.

Child and Adolescent Health, School of

Tel: (021) 658 5074 Fax: (021) 689 1287
E-mail: dpower@ich.uct.ac.za
Argent, A., MB BCh Witw., MMed Witw.,
FCP(SA), FRCPCH Assoc. Prof.
Beatty, David W., MB ChB Cape Town, MD Cape
Town, FCP(SA) Prof.
Burgess, J. D., MB ChB Cape Town, FCP(SA)
Sr. Lectr.
Delport, Stephen V., MB ChB Cape Town, MMed
Cape Town, FCP(SA) Assoc. Prof.
Hartley, P. S., MB ChB Cape Town, FCP(SA)
Assoc. Prof.
Henley, L. D., MSocSc Cape Town, PhD Cape Town
Sr. Lectr.
Hussey, Greg D., MB ChB Cape Town, MMed
Cape Town, MSc Lond. Prof.
Ireland, J. D., MB ChB Cape Town, MD Cape
Town, FCP(SA) Assoc. Prof.
Jacobs, Marian E., MB ChB Cape Town, FCP(SA)
Prof., Child Health; Head*
Kibel, M. A., MB BCh Witw., FRCPEd Emer.
Prof.
Klein, Max, MB ChB Cape Town, FCP(SA)
Assoc. Prof.
Mann, Michael D., MB ChB Cape Town,
MMed(Paed) Cape Town, MMed(NucMed)
Cape Town, PhD Cape Town Assoc. Prof.
Moller, G., MB ChB Cape Town, FCP(SA) Sr.
Lectr.
Motala, C., MB ChB Cape Town, FCP(SA)
Assoc. Prof.
Power, David J., MB BS Lond., MD Cape Town
Emer. Prof.
Reynolds, L. G. Von B., MB ChB Cape Town,
FCP(SA) Prof.
Roux, Paul, MB ChB Cape Town, MD Cape Town,
FCP(SA) Sr. Lectr.
Swingler, George H., MB ChB Cape Town, PhD
Cape Town, FCP(SA) Prof.; Head*
Woods, David L., MB ChB Cape Town, MD Cape
Town, FRCP Assoc. Prof.
Other Staff: 2 Emer. Assoc. Profs.; 13 Lectrs.; 9
Sr. Lectrs.†; 18 Lectrs.†; 5 Hon. Sr. Lectrs.;
4 Hon. Lectrs.†
Research: immunology; infectious diseases,
especially HIV and tuberculosis; nutrition-
related disorders

Health and Rehabilitation Sciences, School of

Tel: (021) 406 6534
Amosun, S. L., BSc(Physio) Ib., PhD Ib. Prof.;
Jt. Head*
Mewka, Julia, BScNurs North(S.Af.), BA S.Af.,
MSocSc(Nursing) Free State, PhD Seattle
Prof.; Jt. Head*

Human Biology

Tel: (021) 650 4579 Fax: (021) 686 6213
E-mail: yblomkam@sports.uct.ac.za
Bosch, Andrew N., BSc Natal, BA(PhysEd)
Rhodes, MA Rhodes, PhD Cape Town Sr. Lectr.
Derman, Wayne, BSc(Med) Cape Town, MB ChB
Pret., PhD Cape Town Assoc. Prof.
Douglas, Tania, BSc(Eng) Cape Town, MS
Vanderbilt, PhD Strath. Sr. Lectr.
Kellaway, Laurie A., MSc Cape Town, PhD Cape
Town Sr. Lectr.
Kidson, Sue H., BSc Witw., PhD Witw. Prof.;
Head*
Lambert, Estelle V., BA(PhysEd) S.Carolina, MSc
S.Carolina, PhD Cape Town Prof.
Lambert, Mike I., BSc(Agric) Natal, BA(PhysEd)
Rhodes, MSc S.Carolina, PhD Cape Town Assoc.
Prof.
Lang, Dirk M., DrRerNat Constance Sr. Lectr.
Louw, Graham, BVSc Pret., DVSc Pret. Assoc.
Prof.
Morris, A. G., BSc Wolv., PhD Witw. Assoc.
Prof.
Noakes, Timothy, MB ChB Cape Town, MD Cape
Town Prof.
Ojuka, Edward, BSc(Med) Mak., PhD Brigham
Young Sr. Lectr.
Querido, David, MSc Cape Town, PhD Cape Town
Sr. Lectr.
Russell, Viv, BSc Cape Town, MSc Cape Town, PhD
Stell. Prof.
Schwellnus, Martin P., MB BCh Witw., MSc
Cape Town, MD Cape Town Assoc. Prof.
Slater, C. P., MB ChB Cape Town Sr. Lectr.
Vaughan, Christopher L., BSc Rhodes, PhD Iowa
Prof.
Warton, C. M. R., MB ChB Z'bwe. Sr. Lectr.
Weight, Lindsay M., BSc Natal, BSc S.Af.,
BSc(Med) Cape Town, MSc Cape Town, PhD
Cape Town Sr. Lectr.
Other Staff: 1 Hon. Assoc. Prof.

Medicine

Tel: (021) 406 6198 Fax: (021) 448 6815
E-mail: jbutler@uctgsh1.uct.ac.za
Ainslie, Gillian M., MB ChB Cape Town, FRCP
Assoc. Prof.; Head, Pulmonol.
Bateman, Eric D., MB ChB Cape Town, MD Cape
Town, FRCP Prof.; Head, Respirol.
Benatar, Solomon R., MB ChB Cape Town, FFA,
FRCP, Hon. FACP Prof.; Dir., Centre for
Bio-Ethics
Bryer, Alan, MB BCh Witw., MMed Cape Town,
PhD Cape Town, FCP(SA) Assoc. Prof.; Sr.
Physician
Commerford, Patrick J., MB ChB, FCP(SA),
FACC Helen and Morris Mauerberger
Prof.; Head, Cardiol.
Eastman, R. W., MB ChB Cape Town, FRCP
Assoc. Prof.; Sr. Physician; Head, Neurol.
Halkett, Janet, MB ChB Cape Town, FCP(SA)
Sr. Lectr.; Sr. Physician
Hift, Richard J., MB ChB Cape Town, MMed Cape
Town, FCP(SA) Assoc. Prof.; Sr. Physician
Kalla, Asgar A., MB ChB Cape Town, MD Cape
Town, FCP(SA), FRCPGlas, FRACP, FACP,
FRCPI, FRCP Prof.
Kies, Brian M., MB ChB Cape Town, FCP(SA)
Sr. Lectr.; Sr. Physician
Kirsch, Ralph E., MB ChB Cape Town, MD Cape
Town, DSc(Med) Cape Town, FCP(SA),
FRCPGlas, FRCP, FACP, FRCPI Prof.;
Head*
Lee Pan, Edward B., MB ChB Cape Town, MMed
Stell. Sr. Lectr.; Sr. Physician
Levitt, Naomi S., MB ChB Cape Town, MD Cape
Town Prof.; Head, Endocrinol. and
Diabetol.
Louw, Jacob A., MB ChB Stell., MMed Stell.,
PhD Cape Town, FCP(SA) Prof.; Head,
Gastroenterol.
Maartens, Gary, MB ChB Cape Town, MMed Cape
Town, FCP(SA) Assoc. Prof.; Sr. Physician
Marais, Adrian D., MB ChB Cape Town, FCP(SA)
Assoc. Prof.; Sr. Physician; Head, Lipid
Meissner, P., BSc(Med) Cape Town, PhD Cape
Town Assoc. Prof.; Sr. Physician

Opie, Lionel H., BM BCh Oxf., MD Cape Town, DPhil Oxf., DSc(Med) Cape Town, FRCP, FRSSAf Emer. Prof.†; Dir., Heart Res. Unit

Pascoe, Michael, MB ChB Cape Town, FCP(SA) Sr. Lectr.; Head, Renal

Raine, Richard I., MB ChB Cape Town, MMed Cape Town, FCP(SA) Sr. Lectr.; Sr. Physician

Rayner, Brian L., MB ChB Cape Town, FCP(SA) Sr. Lectr.; Sr. Physician

Ress, Stanley R., MB ChB Pret., FCP(SA) Assoc. Prof.; Sr. Physician; Head, Clin. Immunol. Lab.

Scott-Millar, Robert N., MB BCh Witw., FCP(SA) Assoc. Prof.; Sr. Physician

Seggie, Janet L., BSc Birm., MB ChB Birm., MD Birm., FRCP Assoc. Prof.; Sr. Physician; Head, Gen. Med.

Shephard, Enid, BSc(Med) Cape Town, PhD Cape Town Assoc. Prof.; Sr. Physician

Spearman, Wendy, MB ChB Cape Town, MMed Cape Town, FCP(SA) Sr. Lectr.; Sr. Physician

Stevens, John, MD Lond., FRCP Sr. Lectr.; Sr. Physician

Swanepoel, Charles R., MB ChB Cape Town, FRCP Assoc. Prof.; Sr. Physician

White, Neil W., MB ChB Cape Town, MD Cape Town, FCP(SA) Assoc. Prof.; Sr. Physician

Willcox, Paul A., BSc Birm., MB ChB Birm. Assoc. Prof.; Sr. Physician

Other Staff: 7 Lectrs./Physicians; 11 Sr. Lectrs./Sr. Physicians†; 12 Lectrs./Physicians†; 1 Emer. Assoc. Prof.†; 5 Hon. Sr. Lectrs.; 2 Hon. Lectrs.

Neurosurgery

Tel: (021) 406 6213-4 Fax: (021) 406 6555 E-mail: jcpeter@uctgsh1.uct.ac.za

Fieggen, Graham, BSc Cape Town, MB ChB Cape Town, MSc Lond., FCS(SA) Assoc. Prof.

Peter, Jonathan C., MB ChB Cape Town, FRCSEd Helen and Morris Mauerberger Prof.; Head*

Semple, Patrick, MB ChB Cape Town, MMed Cape Town, FCS(SA) Assoc. Prof.

Taylor, MB BCh Witw., FCS(SA) Sr. Lectr.

Other Staff: 2 Lectrs.; 4 Sr. Lectrs.†; 1 Lectr.†

Research: epilepsy; paediatric, pituitary, spinal and vascular neurosurgery

Nursing and Midwifery

Clow, Sheila E., BSocSc Natal, MSc(Nursing) Cape Town Assoc. Prof.; Acting Head*

Duma, Sinegugu E., BCur S.Af., MCur Natal Sr. Lectr.

Khalil, Doris, BA Ghana, PhD Liv., MA Assoc. Prof.

Mayers, Pat, BA(Nursing) Stell., BCur Cape Town, MSc(Med) Cape Town Sr. Lectr.

Obstetrics and Gynaecology

Tel: (021) 406 6114 Fax: (021) 448 6921 E-mail: jsorrel@uctgsh1.uct.ac.za

Anthony, John, MB ChB Cape Town Assoc. Prof.

Coetzee, Edward J., MB ChB Cape Town, FRCOG Assoc. Prof.

Denny, Lynette A., MB ChB Cape Town, MMed(O&G) S.Af., PhD Cape Town Prof.

Draper, G., MB ChB Pret., MSc Lond. Sr. Lectr.

Dyer, Silke J., MB ChB Munich, MMed Munich Sr. Lectr.

Fawcus, Susan R., MB BS Lond., MA Lond. Sr. Lectr.

Gunston, Keith D., MB ChB Cape Town, FRCOG Sr. Lectr.

Matinde, T., MB ChB Z'bwe., FRANZCOG Sr. Lectr.

Ncayiyana, Daniel J. M. Hon. Prof.

Schoeman, L., MB ChB Cape Town, MMed(O&G) Stell. Sr. Lectr.

Stewart, Chantal J. M., MMed Cape Town Sr. Lectr.

Van der Spuy, Zephne M., MB ChB Stell., PhD Lond., FRCOG Prof.; Head*

Other Staff: 5 Lectrs.; 2 Emer. Assoc. Profs.; 3 Sr. Lectrs.†; 21 Lectrs.†; 10 Hon. Sr. Lectrs.; 10 Hon. Lectrs.

Research: abnormalities of lipid metabolism in black women with pre-eclampsia;

anticonvulsants used in prevention of eclamptic seizures; clinical trials assessing the efficacy of Trilostane; detection of cervical cancer

Occupational Therapy

Tel: (021) 406 6395 Fax: (021) 406 6323 E-mail: tdlakiya@uctgsh1.uct.ac.za

Beeton, H. A., BA S.Af., MSc Cape Town Sr. Lectr.

Duncan, E. Madeleine, BA Durban-W., BOccupationalTherapy OFS Sr. Lectr.

Lorenzo, Theresa, BSc Witw., MSc Lond., PhD Lond. Sr. Lectr.

Van Nierkerk, Lana, BA Free State, BA Cape Town, MSc Cape Town Assoc. Prof.; Head*

Other Staff: 5 Lectrs./Chief Occupnl. Therapists; 3 Hon. Lectrs.

Research: assessment of disabled persons' fitness for work; qualitative research

Ophthalmology

Tel: (021) 406 6215-6 Fax: (021) 406 6218 E-mail: nvuuren@uctgsh1.uct.ac.za

Grotte, R. H., MB BS Newcastle(UK), FRCSEd Sr. Lectr.

Lecuona, K., MB ChB Cape Town Sr. Lectr.

Murray, Anthony D., MB BCh Witw., FRCSEd Morris Mauerberger Prof.; Head*

Other Staff: 16 Sr. Lectrs.†

Research: cataract surgery; corneal disease; glaucoma; ocular tumours; paediatric ophthalmology

Orthopaedic Surgery

Tel: (021) 406 6157-8 Fax: (021) 472709 E-mail: jwalters@uctgsh1.uct.ac.za

Hoffman, E. B., MB ChB Stell., FCS(SA) Assoc. Prof.

Siboto, G., MB ChB Natal, FRCSEd Sr. Lectr.

Solomons, M. M., MB ChB Cape Town, FCS(SA) Sr. Lectr.

Walters, Johan, MB ChB Cape Town, FCS(SA) Pieter Moll and Nuffield Prof.; Head*

Other Staff: 5 Sr. Lectrs.†; 10 Hon. Sr. Lectrs.

Research: arthritis surgery; hand surgery; hip joint replacement surgery; paediatric surgery

Otorhinolaryngology

Tel: (021) 406 6420 Fax: (021) 448 6461 E-mail: jrooyen@uctgsh1.uct.ac.za

Fagan, Johan J., MB ChB Cape Town, MMed Cape Town, FCS(SA) Prof.; Head*

Prescott, Christopher A. J., MB ChB St And., FRCS Assoc. Prof.

Other Staff: 2 Sr. Lectrs.†; 6 Lectrs.†

Research: alaryngeal speech; childhood cholesteatoma; percutaneous tracheostomy; profoundly deaf pre-school children; swallowing disorders

Paediatric Surgery

Tel: (021) 658 5012 Fax: (021) 689 1287 E-mail: hrode@ich.uct.ac.za

Davies, M. R. Q., MB ChB S.Af., MMed S.Af., FRCSEd Prof.

Hoffman, T., MB ChB Stell., FCS(SA) Assoc. Prof.

Hudson, Donald A., MB ChB Cape Town, FCS(SA) Assoc. Prof.

Prescott, Christopher A. J., MB ChB St And., FRCS Assoc. Prof.

Rode, Heinz, MMed Pret., FCS(SA), FRCSEd Charles F. M. Saint Prof.; Head*

Van As, Sebastian A., MBA S.Af., PhD Cape Town, MB ChB Assoc. Prof.

Other Staff: 2 Res. Social Workers

Research: burn therapy; child accident prevention; common diseases of Africa; liver transplantation; surgical care

Pharmacology

Tel: (021) 406 6008 Fax: (021) 448 1989 E-mail: gary@curie.uct.ac.za

Barnes, Karen, MB ChB Cape Town Assoc. Prof.

Blockman, M., MB ChB Cape Town, BPharm Cape Town Sr. Lectr.

Maartens, Gary, MB ChB Cape Town, MMed Cape Town, FCP(SA) Prof.; Head*

Smith, Peter J., BSc Cape Town, PhD Cape Town Assoc. Prof.

Other Staff: 1 Med. Natural Scientist; 1 Hon. Sr. Lectr.

Research: adverse effects of medicines in the body; blood levels of drugs with narrow therapeutic ranges; traditional medicines; use and safety of essential medicines

Physiotherapy

Tel: (021) 404 4407 Fax: (021) 448 8157 E-mail: damosun@uctgsh1.uct.ac.za

Amosun, S. L., BSc(Physio) Ib., PhD Ib. Prof.; Head*

Jelsma, Jennifer, BSc(Physio) Stell., MPhil Z'bwe., PhD Leuven Assoc. Prof.

Other Staff: 5 Lectrs.; 2 Lectrs.†

Research: clinical supervision; ecology theory and changes in physiotherapy practice; role of physiotherapists in sports medicine

Psychiatry and Mental Health

Tel: (021) 406 6566 Fax: (021) 448 8158 E-mail: bh@ray.uct.ac.za

Anderson, R. B. H., BA Cape Town, MSc Cape Town Sr. Lectr./Sr. Clin. Psychologist

Baumann, S. E., MB ChB Cape Town Sr. Lectr.

Berg, Astrid, MB ChB Pret., MPhil Cape Town Assoc. Prof.

Bothwell, Robert A., MB BCh Witw. Sr. Lectr.

De Jager, W., MA P.Elizabeth Sr. Lectr./Sr. Clin. Psychologist

Flisher, Alan, MB ChB Cape Town, MSc Cape Town, MMed Cape Town, MPhil Cape Town, PhD Cape Town Prof.

Gillis, L. S., MD Witw. Emer. Prof.

Hawkridge, S., MB BCh Witw. Sr. Lectr.

Kaliski, Sean Z., BA Witw., MB BCh Witw., MMed Cape Town, PhD Cape Town Assoc. Prof.

Lay, Stephen J., BA Witw., MA Cape Town Sr. Lectr./Sr. Clin. Psychologist

Molteno, Christopher D., BA S.Af., MB ChB Cape Town, MMed Cape Town, MD Cape Town, PhD S.Af. Vera Grover Prof., Mental Handicap

Peter, E., MD Tor. Sr. Lectr.

Robertson, Brian A., MD Cape Town Emer. Prof.

Shorthall, N., MB ChB Cape Town Sr. Lectr.

Soltau, Hans, MA P.Elizabeth Sr. Lectr.

Stein, Dan J., BSc Cape Town, MB ChB Cape Town, PhD Stell. Prof.; Head*

White, D. A., MB ChB Cape Town, MMed Cape Town Assoc. Prof.

Williams-Ashman, P. F., MB ChB Witw. Sr. Lectr.

Wilson, Donald A. B., BSc Cape Town, MB ChB Cape Town Assoc. Prof.

Zabow, Tuviah, MB ChB Cape Town Prof.

Other Staff: 9 Lectrs./Specialists; 10 Lectrs./Clin. Psychologists; 3 Lectrs./Med. Officers; 9 Sr. Lectrs./Sr. Specialists†; 2 Lectrs./Specialists†; 4 Lectrs./Psychologists†; 5 Med. Officers†; 2 Hon. Lectrs.

Research: adolescent mental health in sub-Saharan Africa; epidemiological studies in children and adolescents; genetics in schizophrenia; mental health provision at primary care level; risk-taking behaviour in adolescents

Public Health and Family Medicine, School of

Tel: (021) 406 6306 Fax: (021) 406 6163

Ehrlich, Rodney, BBusSc Cape Town, MB ChB Cape Town, PhD Cape Town Prof.; Dir.*

Hellenberg, Derek, MB ChB Cape Town, MFamMed Stell. Assoc. Prof.

London, Leslie, BSc Witw., MB ChB Cape Town, MMed Cape Town, MD Cape Town Prof.

Myers, Jonathan, BSc Cape Town, MB ChB Cape Town, MD Cape Town Prof.

Radiation Oncology

Tel: (021) 404 4263-5 Fax: (021) 404 5259
E-mail: hazel@ray.uct.ac.za
Abratt, Raymond D., MB ChB Pret., MMed Cape Town Prof.
Beningfield, Stephan J., MB ChB Cape Town Prof.; Head*
Murray, Elizabeth M., MB ChB Cape Town, MMed Cape Town Sr. Lectr.
Parkes, Jeanette, MB ChB Cape Town Sr. Lectr.
Stannard, Clare, BSc Lond., MB BS Sr. Lectr.
Van Wijk, Adrian L., MB ChB Cape Town Sr. Lectr.
Other Staff: 5 Lectrs.; 2 Hon. Lectrs.
Research: drug-related clinical studies; incidence of cancer and epidemiological characteristics; proton and neutron beam radiotherapy; retinoblastoma and ocular malignant melanoma; stereo-photogrammtric patient positioning

Radiology

Tel: (021) 404 6426 Fax: (021) 404 4185
E-mail: steveb@curie.uct.ac.za
Ball, H. S., BSc St And., MB ChB Dund. Sr. Lectr.
Beningfield, Stephan J., MB ChB Cape Town Prof.; Head*
Research: abnormalities of cerebral perfusion in patients with Alzheimer's disease; effects of drugs on renal function; effects of treatments on bone density; gastrointestinal tract; Tc-99m Sestamibi imaging

Surgery

Tel: (021) 406 6229 Fax: (021) 448 6461
E-mail: ypeiser@uctgsh1.uct.ac.za
Bornman, Peter C., MB BCh Pret., MMed OFS, FRCSEd Prof.; Head, Surg. Gastroenterol.
Dent, David M., MB ChB Cape Town, ChM Cape Town, FCS(SA), FRCS, FRCPSGlas Emer. Prof.
Goldberg, Paul, MB ChB Cape Town, MMed Cape Town, FCS(SA) Assoc. Prof.
Immelman, Edward J., MB ChB Cape Town, FCS(SA), FRCS Prof.
Kahn, Delawir, MB ChB Birm., ChM Cape Town, FCS(SA), FRCS Assoc. Prof.; Head, Organ Transplant Unit and Surg. Labs.
Krige, Jacobus E. J., MB ChB Cape Town, FRCSEd, FCS(SA) Assoc. Prof.
Michell, W. Lance, MB ChB Cape Town Assoc. Prof.; Head, Surg. Intensive Care Unit
Terblanche, John, MB ChB Cape Town, ChM Cape Town, FCS(SA), FRCS, FRCPGlas, FRCSGlas, Hon. FACS, Hon. FACP, Hon. FRCSEd Prof.; Co-Dir. UCT/MRC Liver Res. Centre; Head*
Other Staff: 7 Lectrs.; 1 Sr. Med. Nat. Scientist; 23 Sr. Lectrs.†; 1 Lectr.†; 4 Hon. Sr. Lectrs.; 1 Hon. Lectr.
Research: breast, colorectal, hepatobiliary, pancreatic and vascular diseases; critical care medicine; transplantation; trauma

Urology

Tel: (021) 406 6529 Fax: (021) 406 6122
E-mail: jnaude@uctgsh1.uct.ac.za
Barnes, Richard D., MB ChB Cape Town, FRCSEd Sr. Lectr.
Pontin, Alan R., MB ChB Birm., FRCSEd Head*
Other Staff: 5 Sr. Lectrs.†
Research: management of erectile dysfunction; management of female incontinence; metabolic investigation of nephrolithiasis; reconstructive urological surgery; renal transplantion

SPECIAL CENTRES, ETC

Academic Development Programme

Tel: (021) 650 2252 Fax: (021) 685 3793
E-mail: vtwynam@ched.uct.ac.za
Jawitz, Jeffrey, BSc Cape Town, MPhil Cape Town Sr. Lectr.
Scott, Ian R., BA Cape Town Assoc. Prof.; Dir.*

Research: curriculum development; effects of educational disadvantage

Academic Support Programme for Engineering in Cape Town

ASPECT
Tel: (021) 650 3238 Fax: (021) 685 3938
E-mail: htp@engfca.uct.ac.za
Pearce, Howard T., BSc(Eng) Cape Town, MS Ill., PhD Ill. Co-ordinator*
Other Staff: 3 Lectrs.; 1 Lectr.†

African Ornithology, Percy FitzPatrick Institute of

Tel: (021) 650 3290-1 Fax: (021) 650 3295
E-mail: fitz@botzoo.uct.ac.za
Crowe, Timothy M., MSc Chic., PhD Cape Town Prof.
Du Plessis, Prof. Morné A., MSc Pret., PhD Cape Town Dir.*
Hockey, Philip A. R., BSc Edin., PhD Cape Town Assoc. Prof.
Other Staff: 1 Lectr.; 1 Sci. Officer
Research: conservation biology and evolutionary ecology

Bolus Herbarium

Tel: (021) 650 3724 Fax: (021) 650 4041
Midgley, Jeremy J., BSc Cape Town, PhD Cape Town Dir.*
Other Staff: 1 Keeper; 1 Curator; 3 Res. Assocs.; 1 Sr. Sci. Officer
Research: Cape flora; documentary diversity; endemism; revisionary taxonomy

Cape Heart Centre

(including Heart Research Unit and UCT/University College Hatter Institute)
Tel: (021) 406 6358 Fax: (021) 447 8789
Opie, Lionel H., BM BCh Oxf., MD Cape Town, DPhil Oxf., DSc(Med) Cape Town, FRCP, FRSSAf Emer. Prof.; Dir.*
Other Staff: 3 Chief Med. Researchers; 3 Sci. Investigators; 2 Hon. Chief Med. Researchers
Research: molecular mechanisms involved in heart failure and creation of new therapeutic molecules

Electron Microscope Unit

Tel: (021) 650 2818 Fax: (021) 689 1528
E-mail: mwaldron@uctvms.uct.ac.za
Sewell, B. Trevor, MSc Witw., PhD Lond. Assoc. Prof.; Dir.*
Research: computer analysis of gel electrophoretograms; fish ageing; immunolabelling of fibrinogen in neutrophils; predictive autofocusing techniques; studies of chromatic fibre

Higher Education Development, Centre for

Tel: (021) 650 2645 Fax: (021) 685 5743
Hall, Martin J., BA Camb., MA Camb., PhD Camb., FRSSAf Prof.; Dean*

International Labour Resource and Information Group (ILRIG)

Tel: (021) 447 6375 Fax: (021) 448 2282
E-mail: ilrig@worknet.atc.org
Pape, Charles W., PhD Deakin Co-Dir.*
Other Staff: 2 Res. Assocs.
Research: gender and globalisation; impact of globalisation on South African economy

Jewish Studies and Research, Isaac and Jessie Kaplan Centre for

Tel: (021) 650 3062 Fax: (021) 650 3062
E-mail: prince@beattie.uct.ac.za
Shain, Milton, MA S.Af., MA Leeds, PhD Cape Town Dir.*

Lucy Lloyd Archive Resource and Exhibition Centre

Tel: (021) 480 7112 Fax: (021) 480 7112
E-mail: llarec@hiddingh.uct.ac.za
Inggs, Stephen C., MAFA Natal Assoc. Prof.

Payne, Malcolm J., MFA Cape Town Assoc. Prof.
Skotnes, Pippa A., MFA Cape Town Dir.*
Other Staff: 1 Res. Assoc.

Marine and Environmental Law, Institute of

Tel: (021) 650 3074 Fax: (021) 689 8546
E-mail: lawmar@law.uct.ac.za
Devine, Dermott, BA N.U.I., LLB N.U.I., LLB S.Af., LLD Cape Town Dir.*
Glazawski, Jan, BCom Cape Town, LLB Cape Town, MA Cape Town, LLM Lond. Assoc. Prof.
Other Staff: 3 Hon. Consultants
Research: coastal zone law

Marine Studies, Centre for

Tel: (021) 650 3278 Fax: (021) 650 3283
E-mail: cms@physci.uct.ac.za
Brown, Alexander C., MSc Rhodes, PhD Cape Town, DSc Cape Town Emer. Prof.
Other Staff: 1 Operations Manager

Socio-Legal Research, Centre for

Tel: (021) 650 2505 Fax: (021) 685 6826
E-mail: wilkinso@law.uct.ac.za
Burman, Sandra B., BA Cape Town, LLB Cape Town, MA Oxf., DPhil Oxf. Prof.; Dir.*
Other Staff: 2 Res. Assocs.
Research: reform of South Africa's legal and social welfare systems in view of existing legislation regarding women, children and the operation of the family

South African Bird Ringing Unit

Tel: (021) 650 3227 Fax: (021) 650 9111
E-mail: lgu@maths.uct.ac.za
Underhill, Leslie G., MSc Cape Town, PhD Cape Town Dir.*
Research: database of recoveries of southern African birds and re-trap database, directed at movement and survival

Southern Africa Labour and Development Research Unit

Tel: (021) 480 7147 Fax: (021) 423 2456
E-mail: adamshiddingh@uct.ac.za
Wilson, Francis A., BSc Cape Town, MA Camb., PhD Camb. Dir.*
Other Staff: 1 Res. Fellow; 1 Researcher
Research: manpower and labour practices in southern Africa

Urban Problems Research Unit

Tel: (021) 650 3599 Fax: (021) 686 0152
E-mail: arpinfo@centlivres.uct.ac.za
Wilkinson, Peter B., BSc(Eng) Natal, MCRP Cape Town Dir.*
Other Staff: 1 Sr. Scientific Officer; 1 Researcher
Research: housing policy; local government reorganisation; spatial planning in local context; travel behaviour and local area movement network configuration

CONTACT OFFICERS

Academic affairs. Finance and Operations Manager: Davidse, Brian (E-mail: davidseb@bremner.uct.ac.za)
Accommodation. Manager, Student Accommodation: Andrews, Hilda (E-mail: andrewsh@protem.uct.ac.za)
Admissions (first degree). Director, Student Recruitment and Enrolment Management (REMO): Herman, Carl (E-mail: admissions@bremner.uct.ac.za)
Admissions (higher degree). Director, Student Recruitment and Enrolment Management (REMO): Herman, Carl (E-mail: admissions@bremner.uct.ac.za)
Adult/continuing education. Director, Extra-Mural Studies: Rall, Medee, MPhil Cape Town (E-mail: ts@education.uct.ac.za)
Alumni. Director, Alumni Office: McNamara, James, BA Georgetown, MA Calif., PhD Calif., Dr Georgetown (E-mail: alumni@bremner.uct.ac.za)

Archives. Manager, Archives: Hart, Lesley
(E-mail: lesley@uctlib.uct.ac.za)
Careers. Director, Careers Office: Short, Anne
(E-mail: ashort@ched.uct.ac.za)
Computing services. Director, Information
Technology Services: Naicker, Pragasen
(E-mail: pnn@its.uct.ac.za)
Conferences/corporate hospitality. Head,
Event Management: Smit, Judy
(E-mail: smitj@bremner.uct.ac.za)
Consultancy services. Director, UCT
Innovation: Heher, Tony
Credit transfer. Co-ordinator, Student
Administration (SAS): Rich, Sigi M.
(E-mail: fadrec@bremner.uct.ac.za)
Development/fund-raising. Director,
Fundraising: McNamara, James, BA
Georgetown, MA *Calif.*, PhD *Calif.*, Dr *Georgetown*
(E-mail: mcnamaraj@bremner.uct.ac.za)
Equal opportunities. Equal Opportunity
Officer: van Eeden, Dave
(E-mail: vaneeden@bremner.uct.ac.za)

Estates and buildings/works and services.
Executive Director, Properties and Services:
Critien, John J.
(E-mail: hfairwea@forest.uct.ac.za)
Examinations. Examinations Officer:
Abrahams, Michelle
(E-mail: mabrahams@bremner.uct.ac.za)
Finance. Director, Finance Department: Uliana,
Prof. Enrico, MCom *Cape Town*, PhD *Stell.*
(E-mail: euliana@bremner.uct.ac.za)
International office. Director, International
Academic Programmes Office: Shackleton,
Lesley Y., BSc *Cape Town*, MSc *Cape Town*
(E-mail: iapo@education.uct.ac.za)
Library (chief librarian). University Librarian
and Director, University Libraries: Rapp,
Joan, BA *Mary Baldwin*, MA *Wash.*, MLS
Rutgers, MBA *S.Illinois*
(E-mail: selref@uctlib.uct.ac.za)
Marketing. Director, Department of
Communication: Kruger, Gerda, BA *Rand
Afrikaans*, MBSc *Cape Town*
(E-mail: krugerg@bremner.uct.ac.za)

Purchasing. Purchasing Officer: Adams, Trevor
(E-mail: adamst@bremner.uct.ac.za)
Safety. Manager, Risk Services: Tunstall, John
(E-mail: tunstall@forest.uct.ac.za)
Scholarships, awards, loans. Head,
Undergraduate Funding Office: Salasa,
Tasneem (E-mail: tsalasa@icts.uct.ac.za)
Scholarships, awards, loans. Head,
Postgraduate Scholarships Office: Vranas,
Linda J. (E-mail: lvranas@its.uct.ac.za)
Security. Head, Campus Protection Service:
(vacant)
Sport and recreation. Head, Sports
Administration: Donald, John A., BA *Rhodes*
Student union. Executive Director, Student
Affairs: Khan, Moonira

[*Information supplied by the institution as at 28 June
2006, and edited by the ACU*]

CENTRAL UNIVERSITY OF TECHNOLOGY

Founded 1981

Postal Address: Private Bag X20539, Bloemfontein, 9300 South Africa
Telephone: (051) 507 3911 **Fax:** (051) 507 3310
URL: www.cut.ac.za

VICE-CHANCELLOR AND PRINCIPAL*—Mthembu, Prof. Thandwa, BSc *Fort Hare*, MSc *Vanderbilt*, PhD *Witw.*
REGISTRAR‡—Vinger, M. J. G., PhD *Jo'burg.*

DURBAN UNIVERSITY OF TECHNOLOGY

Founded 2002

Member of the Association of Commonwealth Universities

Postal Address: PO Box 1334, Durban, 4000 South Africa
Telephone: (031) 204 2473 **Fax:** (031) 204 2539 **E-mail:** camerons@dut.ac.za
URL: http://www.dut.ac.za

VICE-CHANCELLOR AND PRINCIPAL*—du Pré, Prof. Roy

UNIVERSITY OF FORT HARE

Founded 1916

Member of the Association of Commonwealth Universities

Postal Address: Private Bag X1314, Alice, Eastern Cape, 5700 South Africa
Telephone: (040) 602 2181 **Fax:** (040) 653 2314 **E-mail:** sheena@admin.ufh.ac.za
URL: http://www.ufh.ac.za

VICE-CHANCELLOR*—Tom, Mvuyo, MB ChB *Natal*, MFamMed *Witw.*, MSc *Lond.*
REGISTRAR AND SECRETARY TO SENATE AND COUNCIL‡—Mrwetyana, Nothemba, BA *Fort Hare*, BEd *Fort Hare*, MEd
 Fort Hare, MEd *Rhodes*, PhD *Natal*
CHIEF FINANCIAL OFFICER—Ramoo, C.
CHIEF HUMAN RESOURCES OFFICER—Dweba, Z., BAdmin *S.Af.*

GENERAL INFORMATION

History. The university was originally founded in 1916 as South African Native College.

Admission to first degree courses (see also South African Introduction). Applicants for admission should hold a Matriculation Certificate, a School Leaving Certificate or a Further Education and Training (FET4) Certificate. Alternative qualifications or experience may be accepted. Certain programmes may have specific requirements.

First Degrees (see also South African Directory to Subjects of Study) (* = with honours). BA, BA*, BAcc, BAcc*, BAdmin, BAdmin*, BAgric, BAgric*, BBibl, BCom, BCom*, BCur, BCur(I&A), BEcon, BEcon*, BEd, BFineArt, BJuris, BPed, BProc, BSc, BSc*, BScAgric, BScAgric*, BSocSc, BSocSc*, BSocSc(Com), BSocSc(Com)*, BSocSc(HRM), BSocSc(HRM)*, BSocSc(SW), BSocSc(SW)*, BTh, BTh*, LLB.
 Length of course. Full-time: BAgric*, BTh*: 1–2 years; BAgric, BScAgric, BSocSc, BSocSc(Com), BSocSc(HRM), BTh: 3 years; BPed, LLB: 4 years; BBibl, BSocSc(SW): 4–5 years.

Higher Degrees (see also South African Directory to Subjects of Study).
 Master's. LLM, MA, MAdmin, MAgric, MA(HMS), MBA, MBibl, MCom, MCur, MEd, MFineArt, MPhil, MPS, MSc, MScAgric, MSocSc, MSocSc(Com), MSocSc(CPS), MSocSc(DS), MSocSc(HRM), MSocSc(SW), MSPD, MTh.
 Admission. Applicants must hold a four-year first degree (or a three-year first degree followed by an honours degree) of this university or equivalent qualification.
 Doctoral. DAdmin, DCom, DEd, DLitt&Phil, DSc, DScAgric, DSocSc, DTh, LLD, PhD.
 Admission. Master's degree or equivalent.

Libraries. 140,000 books, periodicals and other material. Special collections: Howard Pim (rare books).

Academic Year (2007–2008).
February–December.

FACULTIES/SCHOOLS
Education
Executive Dean: Zinn, Prof. D., BA *Cape Town*, MEd *Harv.*, DEd *Harv.*
Faculty Manager (Acting): Ndlovu, M.

Law
Executive Dean: Osode, Prof. P. C., LLB *Jos*, LLM *Lagos*, SJD *Tor.*

Management and Commerce
Acting Executive Dean: Tom, Mvuyo, MB ChB *Natal*, MFamMed *Witw.*, MSc *Lond.*
Secretary: Magocoba, N. P.

Science and Agriculture
Tel: (040) 602 2287 Fax: (040) 653 1730
 E-mail: jraats@ufh.ac.za
Executive Dean: Raats, Prof. J. G., MScAgric *OFS*, PhD *Natal*
Faculty Administrative Officer: Smith, M. S., BSocSc *Fort Hare*

Social Science and Humanities
Executive Dean: Hendricks, Prof. J. P., BA *W.Cape*, MA *Mich.*, PhD *Mich.*
Faculty Manager: Nguna, N. N., BA *Fort Hare*, MA *Fort Hare*

ACADEMIC UNITS
Accounting
Bartlett, Gillian, MCom   Prof.; Head*

African Languages
Botha, C. R., DLitt&Phil *Stell.*, MA   Prof.
Lesoetsa, N. P., BA *S.Af.*, BA *Transkei*, MA *Stell.*, PhD *P.Elizabeth*   Sr. Lectr.
Other Staff: 3 Lectrs.

Agricultural Economics, Extension and Rural Development
Belete, A., MSc *Addis Ababa*, PhD *NE*   Prof., Economics
Bester, B. J., PhD(Agric) *Stell.*   Prof., Economics
Fraser, G. C. G., MCom *Rhodes*, PhD(Agric) *Stell.*   Prof., Economics; Head*
Williams, J. L. H., BA *Stell.*, BA *P.Elizabeth*, MAgricExt *Fort Hare*   Sr. Lectr., Extension
Other Staff: 1 Lectr. (Extension)
Vacant Posts: 1 Prof. (Extension); 1 Lectr. (Economics)

Agronomy
Brutsch, M. O., MScAgric *Natal*   Sr. Lectr., Horticultural Science; Head*
de Villiers, J. H. G., MScAgric *Natal*   Sr. Lectr., Genetics
Harry, R. B. A., BScAgric *Natal*, MScAgric *Stell.*   Sr. Lectr., Soil Science
Joubert, A. B. D., BScEngAgric *Natal*   Sr. Lectr., Agricultural Engineering
Mnkeni, P. N. S., BSc(Agric) *Dar.*, PhD *McG.*, MSc   Prof., Soil Science
Other Staff: 3 Lectrs. (1 Crop Science, 1 Horticultural Science, 1 Soil Science)
Vacant Posts: 2 Profs. (Crop Science); 1 Sr. Lectr. (Agricultural Engineering); 2 Lectrs. (1 Horticultural Science, 1 Irrigation)

Biochemistry and Microbiology
Bradley, Graeme   Prof., Biochemistry
Mabinya, L. V., MSc *Fort Hare*   Sr. Lectr., Biochemistry; Head*
Okoh, A.   Prof., Microbiology
Pironcheva, G.   Prof., Biochemistry
Other Staff: 2 Lectrs.; 1 Jr. Lectr.

Botany
Tel: (040) 602 2323 Fax: (040) 602 2323
 E-mail: aafolayan@ufh.ac.za
Afolayan, A. J., MSc *Ib.*, PhD *Pret.*   Prof.; Head*

Grierson, D. S., MSc *P.Elizabeth*, PhD *Fort Hare*   Assoc. Prof.
Magwa, M. L., BSc *S.Af.*, PhD *Fort Hare*   Prof.

Business Management
Tel: (043) 704 7015 Fax: (043) 704 7070
Herbst, G., BCom *OFS*, MCom *OFS*, DCom *Durban-W.*   Sr. Lectr.
Jordaan, B. D., BCom *P.Elizabeth*, MCom *P.Elizabeth*   Sr. Lectr.
Roberts-Lombard, M.   Deputy Head
Rowles, M.   Head*
Wicks, M.   Sr. Lectr.
Other Staff: 3 Lectrs.

Communication
Dube, Jerome
Gayanza, Buli
Oyedemi, Toks
Sehume, Jeffrey M.
Sigila, Pumeza

Computer Science
Chadwick, Jim, BSc *Rhodes*, MSc *N.U.I.*, PhD *ANU*   Prof.; Head*
Muyingi, Hippolyte N., MSc *Kinshasa*, PhD *V.U.Brussels*   Prof.
Other Staff: 1 Lectr.; 1 Jr. Lectr.

Criminology

Crop Science

Curriculum Studies

Development Studies
Tel: (040) 602 2100 Fax: (040) 653 1007
 E-mail: pmonyia@ufh.ac.za
Buthelezi, S., BA MA MSc   Prof.
Mayende, D. P., BA MA PhD   Prof.
Mfono, Z., BA *Fort Hare*, MA *Pret.*, MA *Ohio*, DPhil   Sr. Lectr.
Monyai, P. B., BSc MSc   Head*
Rahim, A., BA MA PhD   Prof.

Economics
Faure, A. P., DPhil *Stell.*, BA MA   Investec Prof., Financial Markets, Money and Banking
Ncube, M., PhD *Gothenburg*, BSc MSc   Assoc. Prof.
Odhiambo, N., PhD *Stell.*, BA MA   Deputy Head
Tsegaye, A., BA *Addis Ababa*, MA *Kent*, PhD *Kent*   Head*
Other Staff: 1 Lectr.; 3 Jr. Lectrs.; 1 Tutor

Education, Faculty of
Fihla, P. M., BEd *Rhodes*, MEd *S.Af.*, BA MA MEd PhD   Prof.
Jiya, M. A. Y., BEd *Fort Hare*, MEd *Rhodes*, MEd *Leeds*, DEd *W.Cape*, BSc   Assoc. Prof.
Lindeque, B. R. G., BA *S.Af.*, BEd *Rand Afrikaans*, MEd *Rand Afrikaans*, DEd *Fort Hare*   Prof.
Pakade, J., BA *Fort Hare*, PhD *Ill.*, MEd   Sr. Lectr.
Rahim, A., MA *Wat.*, PhD *Tor.*   Sr. Lectr.

Zinn, D., BA *Cape Town*, MEd *Harv.*, DEd *Harv.*
    Prof.; Head*
Other Staff: 6 Lectrs.

English

4 Lectrs.

Fine Art

Genetics

Geographic Information Systems

Tel: (046) 622 4314 Fax: (046) 622 4365
    E-mail: grs@imaginet.co.za
du Plessis, Marinda, MSc *Rhodes* Lectr.; Head*
Mallinson, Clyde, MSc *Rhodes* Sr. Lectr.
Tyson, Caryll, MSc *Dund.* Sr. Lectr.
Other Staff: 1 Jr. Lectr.

Geography, Land Use and Environmental Sciences

Tel: (040) 602 2080
Magagula, H. B. Deputy Head
Seethal, C. E. P. Prof.; Head*
Wotshela, L. Sr. Lectr.
Other Staff: 2 Lectrs.; 1 Jr. Lectr.

Geology

Tel: (040) 602 2150 Fax: (040) 626 2917
    E-mail: wkoll@ufh.ac.za
Baojin Zhao, PhD *Witw.*, MSc   Prof.; Head*
Gunter, C. J., MSc *OFS* Sr. Lectr.
Other Staff: 1 Lectr.; 2 Visiting Lectrs.†; 3
    Adjunct Profs.; 1 Hon. Sr. Lectr.

Historical and Contextual Theology

History

Yekela, D. S., BA *Fort Hare*, MA *Rhodes* Sr.
    Lectr.

Horticulture

Industrial Psychology

Tel: (040) 602 2607 Fax: (040) 663 1007
    E-mail: anel@ufh.ac.za
Murugan, Chan Head*
Other Staff: 5 Staff Members

Information Systems

Flowerday, Stephen, MBA *Oxf.Brookes*, BSc Sr.
    Lectr.
Roets, Rinette, BSc *Cape Town*, BA *S.Af.*, MSc
    Lond., MEd *Rhodes* Assoc. Prof.
Vlok, Danie, BA *Stell.*, BA *P.Elizabeth*, MBA *Rhodes*
    Head*
Other Staff: 2 Jr. Lectrs.; 1 Tutor

Law, Nelson R. Mandela School of

Tel: (040) 602 2618 Fax: (040) 602 2618
du Plessis, P. A., LLB *Pret.*, LLM *S.Af.*, BA
    Prof., Mercantile Law
Iya, Phillip F., BA *E.Af.*, LLB *Mak.*, LLM *Yale*,
    PhD *Warw.* Prof., African Law
Maree, D., BA *Rhodes*, LLB *Rhodes* Sr. Lectr.
Osode, P. C., LLB *Jos*, LLM *Lagos*, SJD *Tor.*
    Prof.; Head*
Pienaar, J., BA *Stell.*, LLB *Stell.*, LLM *Natal* Sr.
    Lectr., Private Law

Rembe, N. S., LLB *Dar.*, LLM *Dar.*, PhD *Wales*
    Unesco/Oliver Tambo Prof.; Dir., Human
    Rights Centre
Stewart, S. T., BA *Rhodes*, LLB *Rhodes* Sr. Lectr.,
    African Law
Visser, H. M. P., BJuris *Pret.*, LLB *Pret.*, LLM
    S.Af. Sr. Lectr., Mercantile Law
Welz, D., LLB *S.Af.*, LLM *S.Af.*, MA *Hamburg*,
    DrPhil *Hamburg*, DLitt *Pret.* Sr. Lectr.
Other Staff: 8 Lectrs.; 3 Jr. Lectrs.; 1 Tutor; 1
    Adjunct Prof.; 1 Adjunct Teaching Fellow

Library and Information Science

Livestock and Pasture Science

Chimonyo, Michael, PhD Assoc. Prof.
Dube, S., PhD *Texas A.& M.* Head*
Other Staff: 2 Lectrs. (Animal Science); 1
    Visiting Scientist; 1 Lectr.†

Mathematics (Pure and Applied)

Tel: (040) 602 2369 Fax: (040) 602 2369
    E-mail: bmakamba@ufh.ac.za
Kalinde, A., MSc *Montpellier*, PhD *Brussels* ,
    Functional Analysis
Makamba, B. B., BSc *Fort Hare*, PhD *Rhodes*
    Prof., Algebra; Head*
Okecha, G. E. Prof., Numerical Analysis
Van Dyk, T. J., PhD *Pret.* Prof., Algebra
Other Staff: 3 Staff Members

Movement and Sport Science

Music

Dargie, D. J., PhD *Rhodes*, BA BTh BMus Prof.
Other Staff: 1 Lectr.

New Testament, Practical Theology and Classical Culture

Old Testament Studies and Hebrew

Philosophy

Louw, Tobie J. G., BA *Stell.*, MA *Stell.*,
    DLitt&Phil *Fort Hare* Prof.; Head*
Olivier, Abraham, BA *Stell.*, MA *Stell.*, DPhil
    Tübingen Sr. Lectr.; Postdoctoral Res. Fellow
Other Staff: 1 Undergrad. Tutor

Physics

Psychology

Alberts, Charlie, BA *Stell.*, MA(Psych) *Stell.* Sr.
    Lectr.; Deputy Head
Marx, Jacqui, BA *S.Af.*, MA(Psych) *KwaZulu-Natal*
Ngqangweni, Hlonelwa, BAEd *NUL*, BA *Rhodes*,
    BEd *Rhodes*, MA(Psych) *Natal*
Nichols, Lionel, PhD EdD Prof.; Head*
Ravgee, Champa, MA(Psych) *Rhodes*
Sandlana, Nonkululeko, BCur BSocSci
Van Heerden, Gary, MSocSci *Rhodes*, MTh
Verhage, Herman, MA(Psych) DPhil Prof.
Other Staff: 1 Jr. Lectr.; 1 Tutor

Psychology of Education

Public Administration

Tel: (040) 639 2445 Fax: (040) 639 2447
    E-mail: iile@fhig.ufh.ac.za
Ile, Isioma U., BEd MPA Head*

Mle, T. R., BA MA PhD Sr. Lectr.
Sikakne, B. H., BA *Fort Hare*, MAdmin *OFS*
    Deputy Head
Other Staff: 1 Jr. Lectr.

Social Development

Social Work

Sociology

Soil Science

Statistics

Zoology

SPECIAL CENTRES, ETC

Agricultural and Rural Development Research Institute

Masika, P. J. D., MScAgric DScAgric Dir.*
Other Staff: 2 Agric. Economists; 1 Animal
    Scientist; 1 Agronomist

Agricultural Engineering and Animal Traction Centre

Rural Education, Nelson Mandela Institute for (NMiRED)

Portens, K. A., BA *Dartmouth*, MSc *Witw.* Dir.;
    Head*

CONTACT OFFICERS

Accommodation. Housing Co-ordinator:
    Mabeqa, S. M.
Alumni. Director, Alumni Affairs: Mntambo,
    N.
Computing services. IT Director: Moodley, M.
Examinations. Senior Examinations Officer:
    Mogiba, A.
Finance. Chief Financial Officer: Ramoo, C.
Library (chief librarian). University Librarian:
    Soul, Yolisa K.
Marketing. Director, Marketing and
    Communication: Bara, Luthando
Personnel/human resources. Chief Human
    Resources Officer: Dweba, Z., BAdmin *S.Af.*
Quality assurance and accreditation. Director,
    Quality Management and Assurance:
    Marala, K.
Research. Executive Dean, Research and
    Development: Gilbert, Prof. A.
Sport and recreation. Director, Sport: Tison,
    T.
Strategic planning. Institutional Planner: Bally,
    Prof. Rod
Student welfare/counselling. Executive Dean
    of Students: Ngalo-Morrison, L.

[*Information supplied by the institution as at 3 September
2007, and edited by the ACU*]

UNIVERSITY OF THE FREE STATE

Founded 1904

Member of the Association of Commonwealth Universities

Postal Address: PO Box 339, Bloemfontein, 9300 South Africa
Telephone: (051) 401 9111 **Fax:** (051) 401 2117 **E-mail:** info@stig.uovs.ac.za
URL: http://www.uovs.ac.za

RECTOR AND VICE-CHANCELLOR*—Fourie, Prof. Frederick C. v. N., BA OFS, MA OFS, MA Harv., PhD Harv.
VICE-RECTOR: ACADEMIC‡—(vacant)
VICE-RECTOR: ACADEMIC SUPPORT—Khotseng, Prof. B. M., DPhil
CHIEF DIRECTOR: COMMUNITY SERVICE—Jaftha, Rev. Kiepie
CHIEF DIRECTOR: BUSINESS—Viljoen, Prof. Niel

UNIVERSITY OF JOHANNESBURG

Founded 1966

Member of the Association of Commonwealth Universities

Postal Address: PO Box 524, Auckland Park, Johannesburg, 2006 South Africa
Telephone: (011) 489 2911 **Fax:** (011) 489 2191
URL: http://www.uj.ac.za/

VICE-CHANCELLOR AND PRINCIPAL*—Rensburg, Prof. Ihron, BPharm Rhodes, MA Stan., PhD Stan.
PRO-VICE-CHANCELLOR—Mokadi, Prof. Connie
DEPUTY VICE-CHANCELLOR (HUMAN RESOURCES, OPERATIONS AND COMMERCIALISATION)—Higgo, Alf
DEPUTY VICE-CHANCELLOR (STRATEGIC AND INSTITUTIONAL PLANNING AND IMPLEMENTATION)—Redlinghuis, Prof. Aubrey C., BA W.Cape, MA W.Cape, DPhil W.Cape
DEPUTY VICE-CHANCELLOR (ACADEMIC ADMINISTRATION AND EXTERNAL RELATIONS)—Tyobeka, Prof. Errol
DEPUTY VICE-CHANCELLOR (ACADEMIC ADMINISTRATION AND RESEARCH)‡—van der Merwe, Prof. Derek, BA Pret., LLB Pret., LLD Pret.
DEPUTY VICE-CHANCELLOR (FINANCE AND INFORMATION SYSTEMS)—Vorster, Prof. Desiré D., BCom Rand Afrikaans, MCom Rand Afrikaans

GENERAL INFORMATION

History. Originally established in 1966 as Rand Afrikaans University, the university became part of the newly formed University of Johannesburg in 2005.

Admission to first degree courses (see also South African Introduction). South African Matriculation Certificate with full exemption. Special requirements: vary between faculties. International students need a permit required by law; undergraduate students are admitted subject to a matriculation exemption and academic screening.

First Degrees (see also South African Directory to Subjects of Study) (* = with honours). BA*, BA, BA(SocSc), BCom*, BCom, BCur, BInf*, BInf, BIng, BOptom, BSc*, BSc, LLB.
First degree courses normally last 3 years, with an additional 1–2 years for honours.

Higher Degrees (see also South African Directory to Subjects of Study).
Master's. BEd, LLM, MA, MA(SocSc), MCom, MCur, MEd, MIng, MPhil, MSc.
Admission. Applicants for admission to a master's degree must hold a first degree and an honours degree.
Master's courses normally last 2–3 years.
Doctoral. DCom, DCur, DEd, DIng, DLitt&Phil, DPhil, LLD, PhD.
Admission. Applicants must normally hold a master's degree.

Language of Instruction. Afrikaans and English.

Libraries. Volumes: 626,126. Periodicals subscribed to: 2343.

FACULTIES/SCHOOLS

Arts
Tel: (011) 489 2782 Fax: (011) 489 2797
E-mail: jan@lw.rau.ac.za
Dean: Ryan, Prof. Rory
Deputy Director: Reynders, P. J.

Economic and Management Sciences
Tel: (011) 489 3144 Fax: (011) 489 2036
E-mail: ce@eb.rau.ac.za
Dean: Raubenheimer, Prof. I. V. W. (Naas), MCom Potchef., PhD Purdue
Deputy Director: Steyn, L. C.

Education and Nursing
Tel: (011) 489 2678 Fax: (011) 489 2781
Dean: Muller, Prof. M. E., BACur S.Af., MACur S.Af., DCur Rand Afrikaans
Deputy Director: Vermeulen, J. A.

Engineering
Tel: (011) 489 2116 Fax: (011) 489 2054
E-mail: lvdn@ing1.rau.ac.za
Dean: van der Merwe, Prof. P., MSc Pret., PhD Missouri
Deputy Director: Oelofse, T.

Law
Tel: (011) 489 2135 Fax: (011) 489 2049
E-mail: dvdm@regte.rau.ac.za
Dean: Barrie, Prof. G. N., BA Pret., LLB Pret., LLD S.Af.
Deputy Director: Meyer, I. J.

Science
Tel: (011) 489 2418 Fax: (011) 489 3207
E-mail: ddvr@na.rau.ac.za

Dean: Burger, I. C., PhD Rand Afrikaans
Deputy Director: Albertyn, E.

ACADEMIC UNITS

Accounting
De Beer, Johan Sr. Lectr.
Rhodes, Nadia Head*
Other Staff: 7 Lectrs.

Accounting and Taxation
Cilliers, Herda Sr. Lectr.
Coetsee, D., BCom Rand Afrikaans, MCom Rand Afrikaans Prof.
De Jongh, Tessa, BCom Rand Afrikaans Sr. Lectr.
de Villiers, Daniel A. Sr. Lectr.
Dempsey, Amanda, MCom Rand Afrikaans Prof.
du Toit, M. J., BCom Rand Afrikaans Sr. Lectr.
Erasmus, Simone Sr. Lectr.
Griffioen, Samuel Sr. Lectr.
Grosskopf, Liezl Sr. Lectr.
Heathcote, Krysta Sr. Lectr.
Human, E. Sr. Lectr.
Kruges, Michele Sr. Lectr.
Olivier, J., BCom Rand Afrikaans Sr. Lectr.
Pieters, H. N. Prof.
Pietersen, Marita E., MCom Rand Afrikaans Assoc. Prof.
Stegmann, Nerine, BCom Rand Afrikaans, MCom Rand Afrikaans, DCom Rand Afrikaans Assoc. Prof.
Van der Watt, H. Sr. Lectr.
Van Heerden, M. Sr. Lectr.
Van Wyk, A. Sr. Lectr.
Voogt, T. L., BCom Rand Afrikaans Prof.
Wasserman, M. Sr. Lectr.
Other Staff: 3 Lectrs.

Accounting, Cost and Management
Badenhorst, Jacobus Sr. Lectr.
Kocks, Elmare, BCom Stell. Sr. Lectr.
Qua-Enoo, George Sr. Lectr.
Swartz, Marco Prof.
Vermaak, Minnette Head*

African Languages
Groenewald, H. C., BA Rand Afrikaans, MA Rand
   Afrikaans, DLitt&Phil Rand Afrikaans Sr. Lectr.
Kock, J. H. M., MA Rand Afrikaans, DLitt&Phil
   Rand Afrikaans Sr. Lectr.
Posthumus, Lionel C., MA OFS, DLitt OFS
   Prof.
Other Staff: 2 Lectrs.

Afrikaans
Beukes, M. P., MA Potchef., DLitt Bophut., BA
   BPhil Sr. Lectr.
Botha, W. J., BA S.Af., MA S.Af., DLitt&Phil S.Af.
   Prof.
Burger, W. D., BA Potchef., MA Potchef., PhD
   Potchef. Prof.
Coetzee, A. E., DLitt&Phil Rand Afrikaans, BA MA
   Prof.
Conradie, Prof. C. J., BA Stell., MA Stell., DrsLitt
   Utrecht, PhD Witw. Prof.
Van Staden, E., BA Pret., BA Rand Afrikaans, MA
   Rand Afrikaans, DLitt&Phil Rand Afrikaans Sr.
   Lectr.
Other Staff: 1 Lectr.

Anatomy and Physiology
Eagleton, Saramarie Head*
Lakmeeharan, Myriam Sr. Lectr.
Other Staff: 6 Lectrs.

Anthropology and Development Studies
Tel: (011) 489 2859 Fax: (011) 489 2797
   E-mail: jli@lw.rau.ac.za
De Wet, Dorothea, MA OFS, DPhil Flor. Prof.
Ubomba-Jaswa, Peter Assoc. Prof.

Architecture
Bitzer, Martha Sr. Lectr.
Grace, Suzette Sr. Lectr.
Landzaad, Edwin Head*
Van der Merwe, Daniel Sr. Lectr.
Wagener, Annemarie Sr. Lectr.
Other Staff: 3 Lectrs.

Auditing
De Beer, Karin Sr. Lectr.
Labuschagne, Johanna Sr. Lectr.
Marx, Benjamin, BCom OFS, MCom OFS Prof.
Pete, Marco Sr. Lectr.
Schonfeldt, N. Sr. Lectr.
Van der Watt, Alexander, BCom Rand Afrikaans
   Assoc. Prof.
Van Zyl, Mine Sr. Lectr.
Other Staff: 1 Lectr.

Banking and Financial Information
de Villiers, Daniel A. Sr. Lectr.
Pampalis, Andrew Sr. Lectr.
Peer, Abdool Head*
Other Staff: 3 Lectrs.

Biblical and Religious Studies
Tel: (011) 489 2337 Fax: (011) 489 2797
   E-mail: aj@lw.rau.ac.za
Coetzee, J. H., MA S.Af., BD Pret., DD Pret.
   Prof.
du Rand, J. A., MA OFS, DD Pret. Prof.
Nortjé-Meyer, S. J., BEd Rand Afrikaans, MA Rand
   Afrikaans, DLitt&Phil Rand Afrikaans Sr. Lectr.
Viviers, H., BD Pret., DD Pret. Assoc. Prof.

Biomedical Technology
De Villiers, Neil Sr. Lectr.
Hind, Jennifer Sr. Lectr.
Van der Westhuyzen, Ingrid Head*
Other Staff: 1 Lectr.

Biotechnology
Alagiozoglou, Pandeli Sr. Lectr.
Maclean, Kevin Sr. Lectr.
Van Zyl, Frederick Head*
Other Staff: 1 Lectr.

Botany
Tel: (011) 489 2436 Fax: (011) 489 2411
   E-mail: csw@na.rau.ac.za
Tilney, P. M., BSc Witw., PhD Pret. Sr. Lectr.
van der Bank, M., PhD Rand Afrikaans Sr. Lectr.
van Wyk, B.-E., MSc Stell., PhD Cape Town
   Prof.
Venter, Eduard Sr. Lectr.
Whitehead, C. S., BSc Potchef., PhD Rand Afrikaans
   Prof.
Other Staff: 2 Tech. Lectrs.
Research: anatomy of southern African plants;
   molecular systematics of southern African
   plants; post-harvest physiology and
   technology of perishable commodities;
   taxonomy and medicinal uses of southern
   African plants

Built Environment
Thwala, Wellington Sr. Lectr.
Willemse, Barend Head*
Other Staff: 1 Lectr.

Business Communication
Dreyer, Maria Sr. Lectr.
Gila, Bruella Head*
Other Staff: 2 Lectrs.

Business Information Systems
Antrobus, Rosemary Sr. Lectr.
Augustyn, Dave Sr. Lectr.
Barnard, Maria Sr. Lectr.
Grobler, Cornelia Head*
Quevauvilliers, Nola Sr. Lectr.
Other Staff: 4 Lectrs.

Business Management
Boessenkool, Aart L., BCom Rand Afrikaans,
   MCom Potchef. Prof.
Conradie, W. M., BA Pret., MBA S.Af., DBA
   Potchef. Prof.
de Bruyn, Hermanus E. C., MCom Potchef.,
   DCom Potchef. Prof.
Groenewald, D. Sr. Lectr.
Jacobs, H. Sr. Lectr.
Kruger, Stephanus, MCom Potchef., DCom
   Potchef. Prof.
Lessing, Nic, MCom Potchef., DCom Potchef.
   Prof.
Oosthuizen, T. F. J. Sr. Lectr.
Roberts, Ridwaan Sr. Lectr.
Theron, Danie Sr. Lectr.
Other Staff: 1 Principal Lectr.; 4 Lectrs.

Chemical Engineering Technology
Huberts, Robert Sr. Lectr.
Levin, Lance Head*
Mazana, Naison Sr. Lectr.
Mollagee, Mohamed Sr. Lectr.
Peters, Frederich Sr. Lectr.
Ram Reddi, Manogaran Sr. Lectr.
Other Staff: 1 Lectr.

Chemistry, Analytical
De Kock, Lueta-Ann Sr. Lectr.
Du Plessis-Fischer, Hanneli Sr. Lectr.
Mbianda, Xavier Sr. Lectr.
Oosthuizen, Henda Head*
Other Staff: 3 Lectrs.

Chemistry and Biochemistry
Bornman, L., BSc(Agric) Pret., MSc Witw., PhD
   Pret. Assoc. Prof.
Coetzee, P. P., PhD Stell. Prof.
Den Drijver, Laetitia Sr. Lectr.
Dubery, I. A., PhD Rand Afrikaans Prof.
Fischer, J. L., PhD Pret. Sr. Lectr.
Kruger, G. J., DSc Potchef. Prof.
Malan, R. E., MSc Rand Afrikaans Sr. Lectr.
Meyer, D. Sr. Lectr.

Nxumalo, Lawrence Prof.
Van Zyl, W. E., PhD Texas A.& M. Sr. Lectr.
Williams, D. B. G., PhD Rand Afrikaans Assoc.
   Prof.
Other Staff: 6 Lectrs.; 1 Tech. Lectr.
Research: AIDS vaccine development;
   applications of atomic spectroscopy in
   speciation analysis and water quality;
   catalyst systems; chemistry and medicinal
   plants; plant-pathogen interactions

Chemistry, General
Cele, Leskey Sr. Lectr.
Durbach, Shane Sr. Lectr.
Mamba, Bhekie Sr. Lectr.
Shumane, Manelisi Head*
Van Zyl, Adriaan Sr. Lectr.
Other Staff: 7 Lectrs.

Chiropractic
Yelverton, Christopher Head*
Other Staff: 4 Lectrs.

Civil Engineering Technology
Conway, Peter Sr. Lectr.
Elgie, Keith Sr. Lectr.
Fanourakis, George Sr. Lectr.
Lange, Desmond Head*
Shirley, Louius Sr. Lectr.
Other Staff: 4 Lectrs.

Communication Skills
McCormick, Tracey Sr. Lectr.
Other Staff: 4 Lectrs.

Communication Studies
de Wet, G. F. D. Prof.
Tager, Michele Sr. Lectr.
Other Staff: 5 Lectrs.

Computer Science and Information
4 Lectrs.

Construction Management
Fester, Ferdinand Head*
Other Staff: 1 Lectr.

Curriculum Studies
Ankiewicz, P. J., MSc Potchef., DEd Potchef.
   Prof.
de Swardt, A. E., BA Rand Afrikaans, DEd Rand
   Afrikaans Assoc. Prof.
Janse van Rensburg, W. A. Sr. Lectr.
Smit, Brigitte Assoc. Prof.
Strauss, J., BSc OFS, BEd Potchef., DEd Rand
   Afrikaans Prof.
Trümpelmann, M. H., BEd Pret., DPhil Pret.,
   DEd Rand Afrikaans Prof.
Van der Westhuizen, D. Assoc. Prof.
van Rooyen, H. G., BSc Rand Afrikaans, DEd Rand
   Afrikaans Prof.
Other Staff: 6 Lectrs.; 1 Sr. Tech. Assoc.

Economics
Chetty, S., MCom Rand Afrikaans, DCom Rand
   Afrikaans Assoc. Prof.
Greyling, Lorraine, DCom Rand Afrikaans Prof.
Mears, Ronald Prof.
Schaling, E., PhD Tilburg Prof.
Schoeman, C. H., MA Rand Afrikaans, DLitt&Phil
   Rand Afrikaans Sr. Lectr.
van Zyl, G. (Hardus), DCom Rand Afrikaans
   Prof.
Other Staff: 9 Lectrs.

Education
Debeila, James Assoc. Prof.
Pather, Ethel Sr. Lectr.
Steenekamp, Karen Head*
Other Staff: 4 Lectrs.

Educational Sciences
Beekman, Aletha Sr. Lectr.
Bisschoff, T. C., DEd S.Af. Prof.
Conley, Lloyd Sr. Lectr.
Fritz, Elzette Sr. Lectr.

Gravett, S. J., BA Potchef., BEd Rand Afrikaans,
    MEd Rand Afrikaans, DEd Rand Afrikaans   Prof.
Grobler, B. R., BSc Witw., DEd Rand Afrikaans
    Prof.
Grobler, R. C.   Sr. Lectr.
Loock, Coert   Assoc. Prof.
Mestry, R.   Assoc. Prof.
Moloi, K. C.   Assoc. Prof.
Myburgh, C. P. H., BSc Pret., MCom Rand
    Afrikaans, DEd Rand Afrikaans   Prof.
Pillay, J.   Assoc. Prof.
Postma, Dirk   Sr. Lectr.
van der Merwe, M. P., BA(Ed) Rand Afrikaans,
    DEd Rand Afrikaans   Sr. Lectr.
Van der Westhuizen, Gert   Assoc. Prof.
Other Staff: 6 Lectrs.

Emergency Medical Care
4 Lectrs.

Engineering, Civil and Urban
Haarhoff, J., MIng Stell., PhD Iowa State   Prof.
Kruger, D., BSc Pret., BIng Pret., MIng Rand
    Afrikaans   Sr. Lectr.
Legge, T. F. H., BSc(Eng) Witw., MSc Lond.
    Assoc. Prof.
Van Zyl, J.   Assoc. Prof.
Other Staff: 2 Lectrs.; 1 Tech. Lectr.

Engineering, Computer Systems
Buisson-Street, Jane-Anne   Head*

Engineering, Digital and Communication
Ellis, Patrick   Sr. Lectr.
Grobler, Michael   Sr. Lectr.
Nieuwoudt, Johannes   Head*
Other Staff: 8 Lectrs.

Engineering, Electrical and Electronic
Booysen, Andre   Prof.
Boshoff, Hendrick   Assoc. Prof.
Chinnappen, Suvendi   Sr. Lectr.
Clarke, W. A., MIng Rand Afrikaans   Sr. Lectr.
du Plessis, Jan   Sr. Lectr.
Ferreira, H. C., MSc Pret., DSc Pret.   Prof.
Hofsajer, I. W., MIng Rand Afrikaans, DIng Rand
    Afrikaans   Assoc. Prof.
Holm, Stanley   Sr. Lectr.
Meyer, Johan   Assoc. Prof.
Pretorius, J. H. C., MSc St And., DIng Rand
    Afrikaans   Prof.
Swart, P. L., MSc Pret., PhD McM.   Prof.
Other Staff: 2 Lectrs.

Engineering, Mechanical and Manufacturing
Ionescu, Dorina   Head*
Laubscher, R. F., MIng Rand Afrikaans, DIng Rand
    Afrikaans   Assoc. Prof.
Mennad, Abed   Sr. Lectr.
Nel, A. L.   Prof.
Ngongo Kitenge, Emery   Sr. Lectr.
Pretorius, J., MIng Rand Afrikaans   Sr. Lectr.
Stachelhaus, Peter   Sr. Lectr.
Storm, Christoffel   Prof.
Zietsman, Johan   Sr. Lectr.
Other Staff: 12 Lectrs.; 1 Tech. Lectr.

Engineering, Metallurgy
Hattingh, Christian   Sr. Lectr.
Malone, Derek   Sr. Lectr.
Nyembe, Kasongo   Head*
Other Staff: 2 Lectrs.

Engineering, Power
Lazanas, Panagiotis   Head*
Other Staff: 7 Lectrs.

English
Lwanga-Lumu, Joy   Sr. Lectr.
MacKenzie, C. H., MA Durban-W., PhD Rhodes
    Prof.
Mkhize, Jabulani   Sr. Lectr.
Starfield, Jane   Sr. Lectr.
Other Staff: 3 Lectrs.; 1 Sr. Translator

Environmental Health
16 Lectrs.

Extraction Metallurgy
Bell, Desmond   Head*
Dubber, Alexander   Sr. Lectr.
Mulaba, Antoine   Sr. Lectr.
Other Staff: 1 Lectr.

Fashion Design
Cachalia, Fahmida   Sr. Lectr.
Hutchinson, Glenda   Sr. Lectr.
Other Staff: 5 Lectrs.

Finance
Barnard, Etienne   Sr. Lectr.
De Jongh, Tessa, BCom Rand Afrikaans   Sr.
    Lectr.
De Wet, Jacques   Sr. Lectr.
Els, Gideon   Assoc. Prof.
Hattingh, Johann   Sr. Lectr.
Joubert, Dewald   Sr. Lectr.
Van Schalkwyk, Cornelius   Assoc. Prof.
Other Staff: 2 Lectrs.

Fine Art
Berman, Kim   Sr. Lectr.
Farber-Blackbeard, Leora   Sr. Lectr.
Marais, Marialda   Sr. Lectr.
Paton, David   Sr. Lectr.
Von Veh, Karen   Sr. Lectr.
Other Staff: 1 Lectr.

Food Technology
De Kock, Suretha   Sr. Lectr.
Metcalfe, Denise   Head*
Other Staff: 1 Lectr.

French
Snyman, A. E., DLitt&Phil Rand Afrikaans   Sr.
    Lectr.
Other Staff: 2 Lectrs.
Research: autobiography; French novel of the
    twentieth century; seventeenth-century
    French literature; the oeuvre of Marguerite
    Yourcenar; theory of literature

Geographical Sciences
1 Lectr.

Geography, Environmental Management and Energy Studies
Annegarn, Harold   Prof.
Cooper, Christopher   Sr. Lectr.
Harmse, Jacobus   Assoc. Prof.
Meeuwis, June   Sr. Lectr.
Scheepers, Lukas   Sr. Lectr.
Other Staff: 2 Lectrs.

Geology
Barton, J. M., PhD McG.   Prof.
Beukes, N. J., MSc OFS, PhD Rand Afrikaans
    Prof.
Brown, Harry   Head*
Cairncross, B., MSc Natal, PhD Witw.   Prof.
Genis, Jacob   Sr. Lectr.
Gutzmer, J., PhD Rand Afrikaans   Prof.
Huizenga, J. M., PhD Amst.   Sr. Lectr.
Smit, C. A., PhD OFS   Assoc. Prof.
Van Reenen, Dirk   Prof./Researcher
Other Staff: 2 Lectrs.; 1 Researcher/
    Instrumental Scientist
Research: evolution of early life on earth;
    palaeoproterozoic mineral deposits;
    provenance studies; southern African coal
    deposits

German
Knobloch, H.-J., DrPhil Heidel.   Prof.
Other Staff: 1 Lectr.

Graphic Design
Blake, Garth   Sr. Lectr.
Calvani, Ennio   Sr. Lectr.
Groenewald, Marlize   Sr. Lectr.

Hyson, Inge-Lore   Sr. Lectr.
Pretorius, Jacqueline   Head*

Greek and Latin Studies
Wolmarans, J. L. P., BD Pret., MA Pret., DD Pret.
    Prof.
Other Staff: 2 Lectrs.

History
Erlank, M. N.   Sr. Lectr.
Grundlingh, L. W. F, MA OFS, DLitt&Phil Rand
    Afrikaans   Prof.
Verhoef, G., MA Rand Afrikaans, DLitt&Phil Rand
    Afrikaans   Prof.
Other Staff: 4 Lectrs.

Homeopathy
Moiloa, Motlhabane   Head*
Razlog, Radmila   Sr. Lectr.
Solomon, Elizabeth   Sr. Lectr.
Other Staff: 3 Lectrs.

Hospitality Management
Cockeran, Hester   Sr. Lectr.
Nicolaides, Angelo   Sr. Lectr.
Reddy, Sivapalan   Head*
Taylor, Anne-Marie   Sr. Lectr.
Other Staff: 10 Lectrs.

Hospitality Operations
Brian, Arthur   Head*
Muellers, Manfred   Sr. Lectr.
Other Staff: 4 Instrs.

Human Resource Management and Resources Development
Coetsee, Wilhelm J., BCom Potchef., MCom
    Potchef.   Sr. Lectr.
Segalwe, Sello   Head*
Smith, David   Prof.
Van Tonder, C. L., BA Rand Afrikaans, BA S.Af.,
    MA Rand Afrikaans   Sr. Lectr.
Venter, A.   Sr. Lectr.
Other Staff: 5 Lectrs.

Industrial Engineering Technology
Blignaut, Vincent   Sr. Lectr.
De Clercq, Gerhardus   Sr. Lectr.
Nel, Hannelie   Sr. Lectr.
Njapha, Delani   Sr. Lectr.
Peters, Meinhard   Head*

Information Studies
du Toit, A. S. A., MBibl Pret.   Prof.
Rensleigh, C.   Assoc. Prof.
van Brakel, P. A., MBibl OFS, DPhil Pret.   Prof.
Other Staff: 1 Lectr.

Information Technology, Standard Bank Academy of
Ehlers, E. M., PhD Rand Afrikaans   Prof.
Labuschagne, L., MCom Rand Afrikaans   Sr.
    Lectr.
Marais, E., MSc Rand Afrikaans   Sr. Lectr.
Smith, T. H. C., MSc Rand Afrikaans, MS Carnegie-
    Mellon, PhD Carnegie-Mellon   Prof.
von Solms, S. H., PhD Rand Afrikaans   Prof.
Other Staff: 4 Lectrs.
Research: artificial intelligence; information
    security; information technology program
    management; intelligent software agents;
    optimisation

Instrumentation and Control
Lock, Cornelius   Head*
Pentze, David   Sr. Lectr.
Other Staff: 2 Lectrs.

Interior Design
Breytenbach, Amanda   Head*
Gill, Andrew   Sr. Lectr.
Johnston, Ian   Sr. Lectr.
Other Staff: 3 Lectrs.

Labour Relations
Slabbert, Jacobus   Prof.

Law

Boshoff, A., BA Rand Afrikaans, LLB Rand Afrikaans, LLM Rand Afrikaans, LLD Rand Afrikaans Assoc. Prof., Private Law
Burger, Hendrick Sr. Lectr., Public Law
Calitz, Juanitta Sr. Lectr., Mercantile Law
Cornelius, S. J., LLB S.Af., BIur S.Af., LLD Pret. Assoc. Prof., Private Law
De Koker, L., BIur OFS, LLB OFS, LLM OFS, LLM Camb., LLD OFS Prof., Mercantile Law
De Villiers, D. S., BA Pret., LLB Pret., LLD Pret. Prof., Criminal Law and Procedure
Du Preez, Monique Sr. Lectr., Public Law
Du Toit, S. F., BA Rand Afrikaans, LLB Rand Afrikaans, LLD Rand Afrikaans Assoc. Prof., Mercantile Law
Fourie, Elmarie Co-ordinator, Law (Ex. Cur)
Labuschagne, E., BA Pret., LLB Rand Afrikaans, LLM Rand Afrikaans Sr. Lectr., Criminal Law and Procedure
Malherbe, E. F. J., BA Stell., LLB Stell., LLD Rand Afrikaans Prof., Public Law
Neels, J. L., BCom Rand Afrikaans, LLB Rand Afrikaans, LLM Rand Afrikaans, LLD Ley. Prof., Private Law
O'Brien, P. H., BCom Rand Afrikaans, LLB Rand Afrikaans, LLM Rand Afrikaans, LLD Rand Afrikaans Prof., Mercantile Law
Olivier, M. P., BA Pret., LLB Pret., LLD S.Af. Prof., Mercantile Law
Qashani, Nongcaca Sr. Lectr., Private Law
Raffee, Nasima Sr. Lectr., Public Law
Rautenbach, I. M., BA Pret., LLB Pret., LLD S.Af. Prof., Public Law
Smit, N., BLC Pret., LLB Pret., LLD Rand Afrikaans Assoc. Prof., Mercantile Law
Sonnekus, J. C., BA Rand Afrikaans, LLB Rand Afrikaans, LLD Ley. Prof., Private Law
Strydom, H. A., BIur OFS, LLB OFS, LLM OFS, LLD S.Af. Prof., Public Law
Thobejane, Leruma Head, Law and Credit Management
van der Walt, J. W. G., BLC Pret., BA Pret., LLB Pret., MA Pret., LLD Rand Afrikaans Prof., Private Law
Van Heerden, C., BProc Pret., LLB Pret., LLM S.Af. Sr. Lectr., Criminal Law and Procedure
Venter, Anna Sr. Lectr., Mercantile Law
()Watney, Melvina Prof., Criminal Law and Procedure
Other Staff: 8 Lectrs.; 1 Researcher

Leadership Performance

Stanz, Karel Sr. Lectr.

Linguistic and Literary Theory

Beukes, Susanna Sr. Lectr.
Johl, C. S., BA OFS, MA OFS, DLitt&Phil Rand Afrikaans Assoc. Prof.
Pienaar, M. Sr. Lectr.

Management and Entrepreneurship

Clark, Martha Sr. Lectr.
Goldman, Geoffrey Sr. Lectr.
Urban, Boris Sr. Lectr.
Other Staff: 5 Lectrs.

Marketing Management and Retail Management

Berndt, Adele Assoc. Prof.
Dos Santos, Maria Head*
Grove, Tania Assoc. Prof.
Herbst, Frederick Assoc. Prof.
Jooste, Christian Prof.
Klopper, Hendrik Sr. Lectr.
McLaren, Linda
Other Staff: 7 Lectrs.

Mathematics and Statistics

Baard, Charles Sr. Lectr.
Frangos, C. Prof.
Goranko, V. F., PhD Sofia Assoc. Prof.
Jonck, E. Sr. Lectr.
Kirchner, Elmarie Sr. Lectr.
Kotze, Johanna Sr. Lectr.
Liitho, Ndegwa Sr. Lectr.

Lombard, F., MSc Pret., PhD Rand Afrikaans Prof.
Momberg, Josephus Sr. Lectr.
Raubenheimes, H. Prof.
Tlakula, Stanley Sr. Lectr.
Van Wyk, J. L. Sr. Lectr.
Other Staff: 13 Lectrs.

Mathematics, Applied

Prentice, Justin Sr. Lectr.
Steeb, W.-H., DrHabil Kiel Prof.
Villet, C. M., MSc Stell., PhD Rand Afrikaans Prof.
Other Staff: 2 Lectrs.

Statistics

Botha, Elsabe Sr. Lectr.
Periasamy, Jeevasundarie Head*
Theron, Johan Sr. Lectr.
Other Staff: 3 Lectrs.

Mines, School of

Dougall, Andre Sr. Lectr., Mining
Giannakopoulos, Apostolos Sr. Lectr., Mine Surveying
Greyvenstein, Hendrik Sr. Lectr., Mine Surveying
Wilson, David Head, Mine Surveying*
Other Staff: 6 Lectrs.

Multimedia

Edwards, Marc Sr. Lectr.

Nursing

Arries, Ebin Sr. Lectr.
Chabeli, Mahletse Assoc. Prof.
du Plessis, D. W. Sr. Lectr.
Jooste, Karien Assoc. Prof.
Muller, Ann Assoc. Prof.
Nel, Wanda E., BSocSc OFS, DCur Rand Afrikaans Sr. Lectr.
Nolte, Anna G. W., MSocSc OFS, DLitt&Phil S.Af. Prof.
Poggenpoel, Marie, BArt&Sc Potchef., MSocSc OFS, DPhil Potchef. Prof.
Other Staff: 9 Lectrs.

Office Management and Technology

Coetzee, Marijke Sr. Lectr.
Nortje, Helena Head*
Pretorius, Johannes Sr. Lectr.
Other Staff: 5 Lectrs.

Optometry

Ferreira, J. T., BOptom Rand Afrikaans, PhD Rand Afrikaans Prof.
Gillan, W. D. H. Sr. Lectr.
Harris, W. F., BSc(Eng) Witw., BOptom Rand Afrikaans, PhD Minn. Prof.
Richter, Susarah Sr. Lectr.
Rubin, A., MPhil Rand Afrikaans Assoc. Prof.
Von Poser, Patricia Head*
Other Staff: 7 Lectrs.; 1 Tech. Lectr.

Philosophy

Lötter, H. P. P., BTh Stell., LicTheol Stell., DLitt&Phil Rand Afrikaans Prof.
Ruttkamp, Emma Prof.
Snyman, J. J., MA Rand Afrikaans, DLitt&Phil Rand Afrikaans Prof.
Other Staff: 1 Lectr.

Physics

Alberts, H. L., MSc OFS, PhD Rand Afrikaans Prof.
Alberts, V., PhD P.Elizabeth Prof.
Engelbrecht, C. A. Sr. Lectr.
Kotze, Andre Sr. Lectr.
Nair, Periyappurathu Head*
Oelofse, Jan Sr. Lectr.
Prinsloo, A. R. E., DPhil Rand Afrikaans Sr. Lectr.
Reddy, Leelakrishna Sr. Lectr.
Strydom, Andre Assoc. Prof.
Winkles, Hartmut Prof.
Other Staff: 6 Lectrs.

Podiatry

Zipfel, Bernard Head*
Other Staff: 3 Lectrs.

Politics and Governance

Geldenhuys, D. J., MA Pret., PhD Camb. Prof.
Sadie, A. Y., MA Stell., PhD Cape Town Prof.
Venter, A. J., MA S.Af., DLitt&Phil S.Af. Prof.
Other Staff: 5 Lectrs.

Product Design

Du Plessis, Phillip Sr. Lectr., Industrial Design
Nizetich, Andro Sr. Lectr., Jewellery Design
Oosthuizen, Phillip Head*
Other Staff: 5 Lectrs.

Psychology

Beuster, Johannes Principal Lectr.
Burke, A., MA Rand Afrikaans, DLitt&Phil Rand Afrikaans Sr. Lectr.
De Bruin, Karina Sr. Lectr.
Jooste, M. J. L., MA S.Af., DLitt&Phil S.Af. Sr. Lectr.
Novello, A., MA Rand Afrikaans, DLitt&Phil Rand Afrikaans Sr. Lectr.
Oosthuizen, C. J., MA Stell., DLitt&Phil S.Af. Sr. Lectr.
Pretorius, H. G., MA Rand Afrikaans, DLitt&Phil Rand Afrikaans Prof.
Schoeman, W. J., MA OFS, DPhil OFS Prof.
Stuart, A. D., MA Rand Afrikaans, DLitt&Phil Rand Afrikaans Prof.
Other Staff: 14 Lectrs.

Psychology, Industrial

Crafford, Anne Sr. Lectr.
Crous, Frederik Assoc. Prof.
De Bruin, Gideon Prof.
Schmidt, Conrad Sr. Lectr.
Uys, Conradus Prof.
van Vuuren, Leon Assoc. Prof.
Other Staff: 2 Lectrs.

Public Administration

3 Lectrs.

Public Relations Management

Benecke, Dalien Head*
Other Staff: 3 Lectrs.

Quality and Operations Management

Agwa-Ejon, John Sr. Lectr.
Hewitt, Lia Head, Operations Management
Other Staff: 3 Lectrs.

Radiography

Chipeya, Nyamutowa Sr. Lectr.
Motto, Jennifer Head*
Olsson, Jean Sr. Lectr.
Other Staff: 6 Lectrs.

Real Estate

Smith, Nicolaas Sr. Lectr.
Van Niekerk, Willem Head*

Semitic Languages

Janse van Rensburg, Johannes F. J., BD Pret., MA Pret., DLitt Pret. Prof.
Other Staff: 1 Lectr.

Social Work

Nel, J. B. S., MA Rand Afrikaans, DLitt&Phil Rand Afrikaans Assoc. Prof.
Oliphant, E. Sr. Lectr.
Patel, L. Prof.
Roestenburg, W. J. H. Sr. Lectr.
Other Staff: 1 Lectr.; 1 Sr. Researcher

Sociology

Alexander, P., PhD Lond. Assoc. Prof.; Dir., Centre for Sociol. Res.
Moeno, Sylvia Sr. Lectr.
Senekal, A., MA Rand Afrikaans, DLitt&Phil Rand Afrikaans Assoc. Prof.
Smit, R. Sr. Lectr.

Uys, J. M., MA *Rand Afrikaans*, DLitt&Phil *Rand Afrikaans* Prof.

Van Zyl-Schalekamp, Cecilia Assoc. Prof.

Other Staff: 2 Lectrs.; 2 Researchers

Research: comparative labour relations; globalisation and new social identities; HIV/AIDS; race; youth movements

Somatology

5 Lectrs.

Sotho Languages

Khoali, Hellen Sr. Lectr.

Manyaka, Johannes Principal Lectr.

Other Staff: 1 Lectr.

Sport and Movement Studies

Burnett-Louw, Cora, BA *Pret.*, BA *Stell.*, MA *Stell.*, PhD *Stell.* Assoc. Prof.

Lombard, A. J. J. (Rian), BSc *Stell.* Sr. Lectr.

Singh, C. Assoc. Prof.

Other Staff: 2 Lectrs.

Research: gender in sports; indigenous games; sport development; sport didactics; violence in sport

Sport Management

Sierra, Gertrude Sr. Lectr.

Other Staff: 1 Lectr.

Tourism Management

Sumbana, Fhatuwani Sr. Lectr.

Other Staff: 3 Lectrs.

Town and Regional Planning

Brink, Basil Sr. Lectr.

Other Staff: 2 Lectrs.

Transport and Logistics Management

Kilbourn, P. J., MCom *Rand Afrikaans* Sr. Lectr.

Kujawa, Beverley Sr. Lectr.

Mostert, C. W. V., MCom *Rand Afrikaans*, DCom *Rand Afrikaans* Sr. Lectr.

Prinsloo, G. C., MCom *Rand Afrikaans*, DCom *Rand Afrikaans* Prof.

Voortman, Terence Head*

Walters, J., MCom *Rand Afrikaans*, DCom *Rand Afrikaans* Prof.

Other Staff: 1 Lectr.

Research: logistics management; supply chain management; transport economics; transport policy

Zoology

Janse van Vuren, J. H., PhD *Rand Afrikaans* Prof.

Oldewage, A., PhD *Rand Afrikaans* Assoc. Prof.

Pieterse, Gesina Sr. Lectr.

van der Bank, F. H., PhD *Rand Afrikaans* Prof.

Wepener, V. Assoc. Prof.

Other Staff: 4 Lectrs.

Research: aquatic health; aquatic parasitology; biomarkers; ecotoxicology; population genetics

SPECIAL CENTRES, ETC

Banking Law, Centre for

Du Toit, S. F., BA *Rand Afrikaans*, LLB *Rand Afrikaans*, LLD *Rand Afrikaans* Dir.*

Child and Adult Guidance, Institute for

Elie, Fredelene Sr. Psychologist

Comparative Tax Law Studies, Centre for

Olivier, L., BA *Stell.*, LLB *Stell.*, LLM *Rand Afrikaans*, LLD *Rand Afrikaans* Dir.*

Distance Education, Centre for

Tel: (011) 489 2213 Fax: (011) 489 2292

Broere, I., BSc *Pret.*, PhD *Rand Afrikaans* Chief Dir.*

De Wet, E. Dir.

Ramusi, Frans M., BA *S.Af.*, BEd *Witw.*, MEd *Rand Afrikaans*, DEd *Rand Afrikaans* Dir.

Economic Crime, Centre for the Study of

De Koker, L., BIur *OFS*, LLB *OFS*, LLM *OFS*, LLM *Camb.*, LLD *OFS* Dir.*

European Studies, Centre for

Tel: (011) 489 2896 Fax: (011) 489 3038

Olivier, G. C., MA *Pret.*, DPhil *Pret.* Prof.; Dir.*

International and Comparative Labour and Social Security Law, Centre for

Olivier, M. P., BA *Pret.*, LLB *Pret.*, LLD *S.Af.* Dir.*

International Law in Africa, Centre for the Study of

Strydom, H. A., BIur *OFS*, LLB *OFS*, LLM *OFS*, LLD *S.Af.* Dir.*

Islamic Studies, Centre for

Fax: (011) 489 2787

No staff at present

Metropolitan and Regional Administration, Centre for

Tel: (011) 489 2896 Fax: (011) 489 3038

Zybrands, W. J., BA *Pret.*, LLB *S.Af.* Prof.; Head*

Sport Law, Centre for

Cornelius, S. J., LLB *S.Af.*, BIur *S.Af.*, LLD *Pret.* Dir.*

Sports Science and Biokinetics, Centre for

Nowak, Irena Head*

Work Performance, HRM Centre for

Roodt, Gerhard Prof.

CONTACT OFFICERS

Academic affairs. Vice-Rector (Academic): van der Merwe, Prof. Derek, BA *Pret.*, LLB *Pret.*, LLD *Pret.* (E-mail: dvdm@bestuur.rau.ac.za)

Accommodation. Registrar (Operations): Labuschagne, Carl D., BCom *S.Af.* (E-mail: cdl@bestuur.rau.ac.za)

Alumni. Head (Alumni): Van Wyk, Gert J., BEd *Rand Afrikaans*, BA *Rand Afrikaans*, MEd *Rand Afrikaans* (E-mail: gjvw@adfin.rau.ac.za)

Careers. Director (Careers): Botha, Prof. Paul P., BA *S.Af.*, MA *Rand Afrikaans*, MEd *Rand Afrikaans*, DPhil *Potchef.* (E-mail: ppb@adfin.rau.ac.za)

Computing services. Deputy Vice-Chancellor (Finance and Information Systems): Vorster, Prof. Desiré D., BCom *Rand Afrikaans*, MCom *Rand Afrikaans* (E-mail: ddv@bestuur.rau.ac.za)

Equal opportunities. Chief Director (Equal Opportunities): de Wet, Willie M. (E-mail: mala@adfin.rau.ac.za)

Estates and buildings/works and services. Registrar (Operations): Labuschagne, Carl D., BCom *S.Af.* (E-mail: cdl@bestuur.rau.ac.za)

Examinations. Vice-Rector (Academic): van der Merwe, Prof. Derek, BA *Pret.*, LLB *Pret.*, LLD *Pret.* (E-mail: dvdm@bestuur.rau.ac.za)

Finance. Deputy Vice-Chancellor (Finance and Information Systems): Vorster, Prof. Desiré D., BCom *Rand Afrikaans*, MCom *Rand Afrikaans*

Health services. Registrar (Operations): Labuschagne, Carl D., BCom *S.Af.* (E-mail: cdl@bestuur.rau.ac.za)

Industrial liaison. Chief Director (Industrial Liaison): de Wet, Willie M. (E-mail: mala@adfin.rau.ac.za)

Library (enquiries). Chief Director (Library): Sander, J., BSc *Potchef.*, BBibl *Potchef.*, MBibl *Rand Afrikaans* (E-mail: js@bib.rau.ac.za)

Marketing. Head (Marketing): Verwey, Prof. S. (E-mail: sve@lw.rau.ac.za)

Minorities/disadvantaged groups. Chief Director (Minorities/Disadvantaged groups): de Wet, Willie M.

Personnel/human resources. Chief Director (Personnel/Human Resources): de Wet, Willie M.

Purchasing. Director (Purchasing): Pienaar, M. (E-mail: mp@bedryf.rau.ac.za)

Research. Vice-Rector (Academic): van der Merwe, Prof. Derek, BA *Pret.*, LLB *Pret.*, LLD *Pret.* (E-mail: dvdm@bestuur.rau.ac.za)

Safety. Registrar (Operations): Labuschagne, Carl D., BCom *S.Af.* (E-mail: cdl@bestuur.rau.ac.za)

Scholarships, awards, loans. Chief Director (Scholarships, Awards, Loans): Van Schoor, J. (E-mail: jvsc@rau.ac.za)

Schools liaison. Director (Schools Liaison): Botha, Prof. Paul P., BA *S.Af.*, MA *Rand Afrikaans*, MEd *Rand Afrikaans*, DPhil *Potchef.* (E-mail: ppb@adfin.rau.ac.za)

Security. Registrar (Operations): Labuschagne, Carl D., BCom *S.Af.* (E-mail: cdl@bestuur.rau.ac.za)

Sport and recreation. Chief Director (Sport and recreation): Hollander, Prof. Wim J., BSc *Rand Afrikaans*, DEd *Rand Afrikaans* (E-mail: wjho@eb.rau.ac.za)

Staff development and training. Chief Director (Staff Development and Training): de Wet, Willie M.

Student union. Dean of Students: de Jager, Prof. Frederick J., BA *Stell.*, LLB *Stell.*, LLM *S.Af.*, LLD *Rand Afrikaans* (E-mail: fjdj@adfin.rau.ac.za)

Student welfare/counselling. Dean of Students: de Jager, Prof. Frederick J., BA *Stell.*, LLB *Stell.*, LLM *S.Af.*, LLD *Rand Afrikaans* (E-mail: fjdj@adfin.rau.ac.za)

Students from other countries. Dean of Students: de Jager, Prof. Frederick J., BA *Stell.*, LLB *Stell.*, LLM *S.Af.*, LLD *Rand Afrikaans* (E-mail: fjdj@adfin.rau.ac.za)

Students with disabilities. Dean of Students: de Jager, Prof. Frederick J., BA *Stell.*, LLB *Stell.*, LLM *S.Af.*, LLD *Rand Afrikaans* (E-mail: fjdj@adfin.rau.ac.za)

University press. Registrar (Operations): Labuschagne, Carl D., BCom *S.Af.* (E-mail: cdl@bestuur.rau.ac.za)

[*Information supplied by the institution as at 4 July 2005, and edited by the ACU*]

UNIVERSITY OF KWAZULU-NATAL

Founded 1949

Member of the Association of Commonwealth Universities

Postal Address: Private Bag X54001, Durban, KwaZulu-Natal, 4000 South Africa
Telephone: (031) 260 7111 **Fax:** (031) 260 2204 **E-mail:** registrar@ukzn.ac.za
URL: http://www.ukzn.ac.za

VICE-CHANCELLOR AND PRINCIPAL*—Makgoba, Prof. Malegapuru W., AMP, MB ChB Natal, DPhil Oxf., FRCP,
   FRSSAf
DEPUTY VICE-CHANCELLOR (ADMINISTRATION AND CORPORATE GOVERNANCE)—Staniland, Prof. Hilton, BA Natal,
   LLB Natal, LLM S'ton., PhD S'ton.
DEPUTY VICE-CHANCELLOR (RESEARCH, KNOWLEDGE PRODUCTION AND PARTNERSHIPS)—Bawa, Prof. A. C., BSc S.Af.,
   BSc Natal, MSc Durban-W., PhD Durh.
DEPUTY VICE-CHANCELLOR AND HEAD OF COLLEGE (AGRICULTURE, ENGINEERING AND SCIENCE)—Zacharias, Peter J.
   K., BScAgric Natal, MScAgric Natal, DSc Fort Hare
DEPUTY VICE-CHANCELLOR AND HEAD OF COLLEGE (HEALTH SCIENCES)—Uys, Prof. Leana R., BCur Pret., MSocSc
   OFS, DSocSc(Nursing) OFS
ACTING DEPUTY VICE-CHANCELLOR (RESEARCH, KNOWLEDGE PRODUCTION AND PARTNERSHIPS)—Abdool Karim,
   Prof. Salim, MB ChB Natal, MS Col., MMEd Natal, PhD Natal
DEPUTY VICE-CHANCELLOR AND HEAD OF COLLEGE (HUMANITIES)—Mazibuko, Prof. Ntombfikile, BASocWk Zululand,
   BA S.Af., MSocSc Natal, PhD
ACTING DEPUTY VICE-CHANCELLOR AND HEAD OF COLLEGE (LAW AND MANAGEMENT STUDIES)—Msweli-Mbanga,
   Prof. Pumela, BSc Witw., MBA Exe., PhD Exe.
REGISTRAR‡—Mneney, Edith, LLB Dar., LLM Dar., LLD Durban-W.

GENERAL INFORMATION

History. The university was established in
2004 as a result of the merger of the
University of Natal (founded 1949) with the
University of Durban-Westville (founded
1961).
   The university has five campuses, located in
Durban, Pinetown and Pietermaritzburg.

Admission to first degree courses (see also
South African Introduction). Matriculation
exemption or equivalent. International students
require certificates with equivalent
qualifications.

First Degrees (see also South African
Directory to Subjects of Study). BA, BAgric,
BAgricMgt, BAS, BBA, BBusSc, BCom,
BCommunDev, BDevStud, BEd, BMedSc, BMus,
BN, BPsych, BSc, BScAgric, BSc(ConsMgt),
BScDiet, BSc(Eng), BScLS, BScPropDev, BScQS,
BScSur, BSecEd, BSocSc, BSocWork, BTh, LLB,
MB ChB.
   Length of course. Full-time: BA, BAgric,
BAgricMgt, BAS, BBA, BBusSc, BCom,
BCommunDev, BDevStud, BEd, BSc,
BSc(ConsMgt), BScDiet, BScLS, BScPropDev,
BScQS, BScSur, BSecEd, BSocSc, BTh: 3 years;
BMus, BN, BPsych, BSc(Eng), BScAgric,
BSocWork, LLB: 4 years; MB ChB: 5 years.
Part-time: BA, BCom: 5 years; BN: 7 years.

Higher Degrees (see also South African
Directory to Subjects of Study) (* = with
honours).
   Master's. BArch, BBibl*, LLM, MA,
MClinPharm, MCom, MCommunDev, MEd,
MFamMed, MMed, MMedSc, MMus, MN,
MPsych, MRTP, MSc, MScAgric,
MSc(ConsMgt), MScDiet, MScEng, MScQS,
MScSur, MScURP, MSocSc, MSocWork, MTh,
MTRP.
   Admission. Candidates for admission to a
master's degree must hold a 4-year bachelor's
degree or post-bachelor's degree of at least 1
year or equivalent.
   Length of course. Full-time: BBibl*, LLM, MA,
MCom, MCommunDev, MMedSc, MMus, MN,
MPsych, MRTP, MSc, MSc(ConsMgt),
MScAgric, MScDiet, MScEng, MScQS, MScSur,
MScURP, MSocSc, MSocWork, MTh, MTRP: 1
year; BArch: 2 years. Part-time: MClinPharm,
MEd, MFamMed: 2 years; MMed: 4 years.
   Doctoral. MD, PhD.
   Length of course. Full-time: MD, PhD: 2 years.
Part-time: MD, PhD: 4 years.

Libraries. Volumes: 1,335,000. Periodicals
subscribed to: 7660. Special collections:
Campbell (Africana).

FACULTIES/SCHOOLS

Education
Tel: (031) 260 3531 Fax: (031) 260 3600
   E-mail: education@nu.ac.za
Dean: Vithal, Prof. Renuka, BA Durban-W.,
   MPhil Camb., Dr Aalborg
Faculty Manager: Mzizi, H. D. L., BA S.Af.

Engineering
Tel: (031) 260 3179 Fax: (031) 260 1233
   E-mail: thakurpersada@ukzn.ac.za
Dean: Ijumba, Prof. Nelson M., BSc Dar., MSc
   Salf., PhD Strath.
Principal Faculty Officer: Thakurpersad, A. R.
   (Ronal), BCom S.Af., BEd Durban-W., MEd
   Durban-W.

Health Sciences
Tel: (031) 260 7933 Fax: (031) 260 7872
   E-mail: singhvr@ukzn.ac.za
Dean: Essack, Prof. Sabhiya Y., BPharm Durban-
   W., MPharm Durban-W., PhD Durban-W.
Admissions Officer: Singh, V.

Humanities, Development and Social
Sciences
Tel: (031) 260 7933 Fax: (031) 260 7872
   E-mail: bevis@ukzn.ac.za
Dean: McCracken, Prof. Donal P., BA Ulster,
   DPhil Ulster, FRHistS
Faculty Manager: Bevis, A. P., BA Cape Town,
   MA Camb.

Law
Tel: (031) 260 8118 Fax: (031) 260 8119
Dean: Cowling, Prof. Michael G., BA Rhodes,
   LLB Natal, LLM Camb., MPhil Camb.
Faculty Officer: Govender, L. S. (Westville
   Campus)
Faculty Officer: Govender, V. (Pietermaritzburg
   Campus)

Management Studies
Tel: (031) 260 2089 Fax: (031) 260 1312
   E-mail: lancaste@ukzn.ac.za
Dean: Msweli-Mbanga, Prof. Pumela, BSc
   Witw., MBA Exe., PhD Exe.
Faculty Officer: Lancaster, M. L.

Medicine, Nelson R. Mandela School of
Tel: (031) 260 4509 Fax: (031) 260 4410
   E-mail: sibotos@ukzn.ac.za

Dean: Sturm, Prof. A. Willem, MB BS Amst.,
   MD Amst., PhD Amst.
Principal Faculty Officer: Siboto, S. T., BA S.Af.

Science and Agriculture
Tel: (033) 260 5667 Fax: (033) 260 5969
   E-mail: mackrory@ukzn.ac.za
Dean: Cooke, Prof. J. A., BSc Newcastle(UK), PhD
   Newcastle(UK)
Faculty Manager: Mackrory, V. A.

ACADEMIC UNITS

HOWARD COLLEGE
Tel: (031) 260 1111 Fax: (031) 260 2214

Accounting, School of
Tel: (031) 260 2650 Fax: (031) 260 3292
   E-mail: trollip@nu.ac.za
Dawood, M. A. I., BCom Natal, BCompt S.Af.
   Sr. Lectr.
De Waal, F., MCom   Assoc. Prof.
Deodat, L., BAcc Durban-W., MCom Durban-W.
   Sr. Lectr.
Garach, D. I., BCom MCom   Prof.
Haiden, Malcolm A., BCom Natal   Sr. Lectr.
Hemming, N., BCom Natal, BCompt S.Af., MBA
   Natal   Sr. Lectr.
Hopkins, A., BCom Natal, MBA Natal   Sr. Lectr.
Kalideen, S., BCompt S.Af., MCom   Sr. Lectr.
Latiff, Omar A., BCom Durban-W., BCompt S.Af.
   Assoc. Prof.
Maharaj, J. A., BCom S.Af.   Sr. Lectr.
Maitland, C. A., BCom Natal   Sr. Lectr.
Meyer, A., BCom S.Af.   Hon. Prof.
Mitchell, C. G., BSc Cape Town, MM S.Af.
   Assoc. Prof.
Mitchell, Lindsay D., BCom Natal, MAcc Natal,
   DEcon Natal   Prof.; Head*
Montocchio, Jeanine, BCom Natal   Sr. Lectr.
Oakes, David W.   Sr. Lectr.
Razak, M. H. Y., BAcc S.Af.   Sr. Lectr.
Service, Catherine L., BCompt S.Af.   Sr. Lectr.
Skae, F. Owen, MCom Rhodes, MBA Durh.
   Assoc. Prof.
Smith, C., BCom Natal, BCompt S.Af.   Sr. Lectr.
Stainbank, Lesley J., BA Natal, MCom Natal,
   DCom S.Af.   Prof.
Stegen, Philip K., BCom Natal   Assoc. Prof.
Stobie, Bruce S., BCom Natal, MAcc Natal
   Prof.
Sullivan, P. L., BCom LLB LLM   Assoc. Prof.
Vally, Imtiaz A. S., BAcc S.Af., MAcc S.Af.
   Prof.
Vigario, Frisco A. A., BCom Natal   Prof.
Wallach, T. H., BCom S.Af., MCom S.Af.   Sr.
   Lectr.

Willis, S. C., BCom *Cape Town*   Sr. Lectr.
Wood, Nicholas A., BCom *Natal*, MBL *S.Af.*
    Assoc. Prof.
Other Staff: 2 Lectrs.
Research: accountancy students' marks in team-
    based projects; corporate governance and
    executive compensation; effect of culture
    on user interface design; mobile commerce
    platforms in the banking industry; value-
    added statements in South Africa

Adult and Higher Education, School of

Aitchison, John J. W., BA *Natal*, MA *Natal*   Sr.
    Prof.; Head*
Baatjies, I. G., BSc(Ed) *W.Cape*, MA(Ed) *Dal.*
    Sr. Lectr.
John, V. M., BA *Natal*, MA *Natal*   Sr. Lectr.
Lyster, E. S., BA *Natal*, BA *S.Af.*, PhD *Natal*   Sr.
    Lectr.
Mackie, Robin D. A., BCom *Natal*, LLB *Natal*,
    MEd *Cape Town*   Sr. Lectr.
Mbali, V. C., MA *Oxf.*, MPhil *Oxf.*, PhD *Lond.*
    Sr. Lectr.
O'Brien, F., BSocSc *Natal*, MSocSc *Natal*   Sr.
    Lectr.
Rule, P. N., BA *Witw.*, MA *Lond.*   Sr. Lectr.
Searle, Ruth L., BA *Z'bwe.*, MA *Z'bwe.*, MSc *Sur.*
    Sr. Lectr.
Other Staff: 8 Lectrs.

Anthropology, Gender and Historical Studies, School of

Tel: (031) 260 2915 Fax: (031) 260 1519
    E-mail: magwazat@nu.ac.za
Breckenridge, Keith, BA *Witw.*, PhD *Northwestern*
    Assoc. Prof.
Burns, Catherine, BA *Witw.*, PhD *Northwestern*
    Assoc. Prof.
du Toit, M., BA *Stell.*, PhD *Cape Town*   Sr. Lectr.
Goedhals, M., BA *Rhodes*, MA *Rhodes*, PhD *Rhodes*
    Prof.; Head*
Hiralal, K., BPaed *Durban-W.*, BA *Durban-W.*, MA
    Durban-W., DPhil *Natal*   Sr. Lectr.
Leclerc-Madlala, Suzanne, BA *Rhode I.*, MA *George
    Washington*, PhD *Natal*   Assoc. Prof.
Magwaza, Thenji, BA *Zululand*, BA *Natal*, MA
    Natal, PhD *Natal*   Sr. Lectr.
Marschall, S., MA *Tübingen*, PhD *Tübingen*
    Assoc. Prof.
Reddy, Vasu, BA *Natal*, MA *Witw.*, PhD *KwaZulu-
    Natal*   Sr. Lectr.
Singh, A., BA *Durban-W.*, MA *Cape Town*, MSc
    Lond., PhD *Durban-W.*   Assoc. Prof.
Vahed, G., BA *Durban-W.*, MA *Indiana*, PhD
    Indiana   Assoc. Prof.
Vawda, S., MA *Qu.*, PhD *Durban-W.*   Sr. Lectr.
Other Staff: 7 Lectrs.
Research: Afrikaans drama and poetry;
    comparative literature; representations of
    'gaydom'; traditional literature

Architecture, Planning and Housing

Tel: (031) 260 2699 Fax: (031) 260 1252
    E-mail: soobramoneyk1@nu.ac.za
Adebayo, Ambrose A., MArch *Vienna*, DrTechn
    Vienna   Prof.; Head*
Adebayo, Pauline W., BA *Nair.*, MA *Nair.*   Sr.
    Lectr.
Duncan-Brown, Althea S., BBdgA *P.Elizabeth*,
    BArch *P.Elizabeth*, MArch *P.Elizabeth*   Sr. Lectr.
Frescura, Franco, BArch *Witw.*, MArch *Witw.*,
    PhD *Witw.*   Prof.
Kahn, Michael, MSc(TRP) *Witw.*, PhD *Natal*
    Prof.
Odendaal, Nancy, BA *S.Af.*, MRTP *Natal*   Sr.
    Lectr.
Peters, Walter H., BArch *Natal*, MSc *H-W*,
    DrIng *Hanover*   Prof.
Robinson, Peter S., MA *Natal*, MSc *Reading*, PhD
    Natal   Prof.
Wang, Derek T., BSc *Natal*, PhD *Natal*   Assoc.
    Prof.
Other Staff: 5 Lectrs.
Research: alternative technology in tropical
    housing; history of architecture and the
    built environment; land tenure and housing
    development; new forms of land use

management; restructuring migration and
regional planning

Biological and Conservation Sciences, School of

Appleton, Chris C., BSc *Potchef.*, MSc *Rhodes*, PhD
    Murd.   Sr. Prof.
Bate, G., BScAgric *Natal*, MSc *Natal*, PhD *Natal*
    Hon. Prof.
Brothers, Denis J., BSc *Rhodes*, PhD *Kansas*
    Prof.; Head*
Contrafatto, G. C., Dr *Turin*, PhD *Natal*   Sr.
    Lectr.
Cooke, J. A., BSc *Newcastle(UK)*, PhD
    Newcastle(UK)   Sr. Prof.
Goodman, S. M., BS *Mich.*, PhD *Hamburg*   Hon.
    Prof.
Huckett, Barbara I., BSc *Nott.*, MSc *McM.*, PhD
    Natal   Hon. Prof.
Lamb, Jennifer M., MSc *Natal*, PhD *Iowa*   Sr.
    Lectr.
Naidoo, Y., BSc *Durban-W.*, PhD *Durban-W.*   Sr.
    Lectr.
Nicholas, A., BSc *Natal*, MSc *Natal*, PhD *Durban-
    W.*   Assoc. Prof.
Perissonotto, Renzo, Laur *Padua*, PhD *Dal.*
    Assoc. Prof.
Schleyer, M., BSc *Witw.*, MSc *Natal*, PhD *Natal*
    Hon. Prof.
Slotow, R., BSc *Rhodes*, MSc *Natal*, PhD *Calif.*
    Assoc. Prof.
Smith, Alan N., MB BCh *Witw.*, MSc *Sur.*,
    MMed *Witw.*   Hon. Prof.
Smith, Michael T., MSc *Natal*, PhD *Natal*
    Assoc. Prof.
van der Elst, R., MSc *Natal*   Hon. Prof.
Watt, M. Paula, BSc *Witw.*, PhD *Witw.*   Assoc.
    Prof.
Other Staff: 2 Lectrs.; 1 Sr. Res. Fellow; 2
    Hon. Assoc. Profs.; 1 Hon. Sr. Lectr.; 3
    Hon. Lectrs.; 2 Hon. Res. Fellows; 1 Hon.
    Sr. Res. Officer

Business, Graduate School of

Tel: (031) 260 1105 Fax: (031) 260 3157
    E-mail: kingj@nu.ac.za
Challenor, M., BSocSc MBA   Sr. Lectr.
Frank, A. G., CandPolit *Copenhagen*, MBA
    Buckingham, MCom *S.Af.*, DCom *S.Af.*   Assoc.
    Prof.
Kambuwa, M. M., BA *Malawi*, MPA *Manc.*, MA
    Lanc.   Prof.
Singh, A., BA *Durban-W.*, MBA *Durban-W.*, DBA
    Durban-W.   Head*
Other Staff: 1 Lectr.

Chemistry, School of

Tel: (031) 260 3090 Fax: (031) 260 3091
    E-mail: sivild@nu.ac.za
Coombes, P. H., BSc *Rhodes*, BSc *P.Elizabeth*, MSc
    P.Elizabeth, PhD *Natal*   Sr. Lectr.
Crouch, N., BSc *Natal*, MSc *Natal*, PhD *Natal*
    Hon. Prof.
Ford, T. Anthony, BSc *Wales*, MSc *Wales*, PhD
    Dal., FRSChem, FRSSAf   Sr. Prof.
Friedrich, Holge B., BSc *Cape Town*, PhD *Cape
    Town*   Assoc. Prof.
Kindness, Andy, BSc *Aberd.*, MSc *Aberd.*, PhD
    Aberd.   Assoc. Prof.; Head*
Koorbanally, N. A., BSc *Natal*, MSc *Natal*, PhD
    Natal   Sr. Lectr.
Kruger, H. Gert, BSc *Potchef.*, MSc *Potchef.*, PhD
    Potchef.   Sr. Lectr.
Laing, M. J., BSc *Natal*, MSc *Natal*, PhD *Calif.*
    Emer. Prof.
Letcher, Trevor M., BSc *Natal*, BEd *Natal*, MSc
    Natal, PhD *Natal*, FRSChem, FRSSAf   Emer.
    Prof.
Marsh, Jeremy J., BSc *Pret.*, MSc *Pret.*, PhD *Rand
    Afrikaans*   Assoc. Prof.
Martincigh, Bice S., BSc *Natal*, PhD *Natal*
    Assoc. Prof.
Ngila, C., PhD *NSW*, BEdSc MSc   Sr. Lectr.
Taylor, D. A. H., MA *Oxf.*, DPhil *Oxf.*, DSc *Oxf.*
    Emer. Prof.
Williams-Wynn, D. E. A., BSc *Rhodes*, MSc
    Rhodes, PhD *Rhodes*, FRSChem   Emer. Prof.

Other Staff: 4 Lectrs; 1 Hon. Assoc. Prof.; 1
    Hon. Res. Assoc.; 3 Hon. Res. Fellows
Research: co-ordination chemistry;
    environmental analysis; molecular
    spectroscopy; natural product chemistry;
    thermodynamics and photochemistry of
    solutions

Development Studies, School of

Tel: (031) 260 2361 Fax: (031) 260 2359
    E-mail: andersol@nu.ac.za
Bond, P., BA *Swarthmore*, PhD *Johns H.*   Prof.
Lund, Francie J., BSocSc *Cape Town*, MSocSc
    Natal   Assoc. Prof.
May, Julian D., MSocSc *Natal*   Assoc. Prof.;
    Head*
Morris, Michael L., BA *Cape Town*, DPhil *Sus.*
    Sr. Prof.
Mturi, A., MPhil *Cairo*, PhD *S'ton.*, BSc   Assoc.
    Prof.
Padayachee, Vishnu, MCom *Durban-W.*, PhD
    Natal   Sr. Prof.
Other Staff: 1 Sr. Res. Fellow/Lectr.; 9 Res.
    Fellows/Lectrs.
Research: formal-informal economy labour
    dynamics; industrial restructuring in South
    Africa; population and demography;
    poverty and inequality in Kwa-Zulu/Natal;
    the informal economy

Economics and Finance, School of

Tel: (031) 260 2588 Fax: (031) 260 2535
    E-mail: holden@nu.ac.za
Contogiannis, E., BSc *Athens*, MA(Econ) *Manc.*,
    PhD *Kent*   Prof.
Edkins, B. I. M., BCom *Natal*, MCom *Natal*   Sr.
    Lectr.
Fairburn, J. A., BA *Oxf.*, MSc *S'ton.*, PhD *S'ton.*
    Assoc. Prof.
Harris, G. T., BCom *Melb.*, MEc *La Trobe*, PhD
    NE   Prof.
Hart, John S., BA *Rhodes*, MA *S.Af.*, DLitt&Phil
    S.Af.   Assoc. Prof.
Holden, Merle G., BCom *Natal*, MA *Duke*, PhD
    Duke   Prof.
Jones, Trevor B., MA *Natal*   Assoc. Prof.
Kohler, M., BCom *Natal*, MCom *Natal*   Sr.
    Lectr.
Kongolo, M., BSc *Zaire*, PhD *Potchef.*, MSc   Sr.
    Lectr.
Lumby, Anthony B., BCom *Witw.*, PhD *Natal*
    Prof.
Mahadea, D., BA *Lanc.*, MBA *Brad.*, PhD *Durban-
    W.*   Assoc. Prof.
Nichola, Tennassie, MSc *Addis Ababa*, PhD *Purdue*
    Assoc. Prof.
Posel, Dori R., MSocSc *Natal*, PhD *Mass.*   Assoc.
    Prof.
Rhodes, Bruce D., BA *CNAA*, MSc *Lond.*, PhD
    E.Anglia   Sr. Lectr.
Schroenn, J., MCom *Natal*   Sr. Lectr.
Simson, R., MCom *Natal*, PhD *S.Fraser*   Sr.
    Lectr.
Stefanski, Bogdan, MSc *Warsaw*, MPhil *Warsaw*,
    PhD *Warsaw*, DSc *Warsaw*   Sr. Lectr.
Strydom, B., BCom *Natal*   Sr. Lectr.
Tenza, T. B., BCom *S.Af.*, MA *Mich.*   Sr. Lectr.
Viegi, N., MSc *Glas.*, PhD *Strath.*   Sr. Lectr.
Other Staff: 12 Lectrs.
Vacant Posts: Head*
Research: affirmative action; competencies of
    future South African managers; discounting;
    fighting corruption; joint forest
    management programmes

Education Studies, School of

Tel: (031) 260 3531 Fax: (031) 260 3600
    E-mail: education@nu.ac.za
Bhana, D., BPaed *Durban-W.*, MEd *Natal*, PhD
    Natal   Sr. Lectr.
Bojuwoye, O., BSc *Melb.*, PhD *Sask.*   Sr. Prof.
de Lange, N., BAEd *P.Elizabeth*, BEd *P.Elizabeth*,
    MEd *S.Af.*, DEd *P.Elizabeth*   Assoc. Prof.
Jarvis, Brian J., BA *Natal*, BEd *Natal*, MSocSc
    Natal   Sr. Lectr.
Londal, Paul E., BA *Natal*, BEd *Natal*, MEd *Natal*
    Sr. Lectr.

Moletsane, Relebohile T., BA Fort Hare, BEd Fort Hare, MS Indiana, PhD Indiana   Sr. Lectr.

Morrell, Robert G., BJourn Rhodes, BA Rhodes, MA Witw., PhD Natal   Sr. Prof.

Mwamwenda, T. S., MA Ott., MScEd N.Y.State, PhD Alta., BA   Sr. Prof.

Naidoo, Z., BA Durban-W., MSc Kansas, DEd Durban-W.   Sr. Lectr.

Ramrathan, P., BSc S.Af., BEd Durban-W., MEd Durban-W., DEd Durban-W.   Sr. Lectr.; Head*

Shumba, A., BScEd S.Leone, MEd Z'bwe., PhD W.Cape   Sr. Lectr.

Sookrajh, R., BPaed Durban-W., BEd Durban-W., MEd Durban-W., DEd S.Af.   Assoc. Prof.

Other Staff: 12 Lectrs.

Research: adult education in reconstruction and development; children with disabilities in ordinary schools; education and development for out-of-school youth; literacy and language; professional development in adult basic education

Engineering, Chemical, School of

Tel: (031) 260 3115 Fax: (031) 260 1118
   E-mail: arnold@nu.ac.za

Arnold, David R., BSc Aston, PhD Aston   Assoc. Prof.

Buckley, Christopher A., BScEng Natal, MScEng Natal   Prof.

Carsky, Milan, PhD Prague   Prof.

Mulholland, Michael, BScEng Natal, PhD Natal   Prof.

Pocock, Jon, BEng Birm., MPhil Birm., PhD Birm.   Sr. Lectr.

Ramjugernath, Deresh, BScEng Natal, PhD Natal   Prof.; Head*

Starzak, Maciej, BSc Lodz, MSc Lodz, PhD Lodz   Assoc. Prof.

Other Staff: 7 Lectrs.

Research: atmospheric dispersion; cleaner production; mineral processing; process control; water and effluent management

Engineering, Civil, Surveying and Construction, School of

Tel: (031) 260 3055 Fax: (031) 260 1411
   E-mail: kings@nu.ac.za

Botha, Lee G., BScQS Natal   Sr. Lectr.

Crompton, David W., BScQS Natal, MSc Natal   Sr. Lectr.

Everitt, Philip R., BScEng Natal, MScEng Natal   Assoc. Prof.

Forbes, Angus M., BScSur Natal, MScSur Natal   Sr. Lectr.

Jackson, Jonathan, BSc(Eng) Witw., MScSur Cape Town   Sr. Lectr.

Ndege, M., MSc T.U.Cracow, PhD Trondheim   Sr. Lectr.

Pearl, Robert G., MScQS Cape Town   Programme Dir., Property Devel.; Prof., Quantity Surveying

Schreiner, H. Deneys, BScEng Natal, MScEng Natal, PhD Lond.   Prof.

Stretch, Derek D., BScEng Natal, MScEng Natal, PhD Camb.   Assoc. Prof.; Head*

Trois, C.   Sr. Lectr.

Other Staff: 6 Lectrs.

Research: engineering hydrology; environmental fluid dynamics; geotechnical engineering; pavements and materials; traffic and transportation

Engineering, Electrical, Electronic and Computer, School of

Tel: (031) 260 2728 Fax: (031) 260 1300
   E-mail: abroad@nu.ac.za

Afullo, T. J. O., BSc(Eng) Nair., MSEE W.Virginia, PhD Brussels   Assoc. Prof.

Boje, Edward S., BSc(Eng) Witw., MScEng Natal, PhD Natal   AECI Prof., Control

Broadhurst, Anthony D., BScEng Cape Town, MScEng Natal, PhD Cape Town   Prof., Communications

Burton, Bruce, BScEng Natal, MScEng Natal   Sr. Lectr.

Chol, A. M., BSc(Eng) Khart., MSc(Eng) Brad., PhD Brad.   Assoc. Prof.

Davidson, Innocent E., BSc(Eng) Ilorin, MSc(Eng) Ilorin, PhD Cape Town   Sr. Lectr.

Dawoud, David S., BSc Cairo, MSc Cairo, PhD Leningrad   Prof., Computer Engineering

Diana, Gregory G. S., BScEng Natal   Sr. Lectr.

Eitelburg, Eduard, LLM Durban-W., DrIng Karlsruhe, DrIngHabil Karlsruhe, LLD KwaZulu-Natal   Prof.

Hippner, Meciej, MScEng Poznan, PhD Wroclaw   Assoc. Prof.

Hoch, Derek A., BScEng Witw., PhD Witw.   Sr. Lectr.

Ijumba, Nelson M., BSc Dar., MSc Salf., PhD Strath.   Prof.

McDonald, Steven A., BScEng Natal, MScEng Natal   Sr. Lectr.

Mneney, Stanley H., BSc Ghana, MASc Tor., PhD Dar.   Assoc. Prof.

Naidoo, B., BScEng Natal, MScEng Natal   Sr. Lectr.

Nleya, B., PhD St.Petersburg   Assoc. Prof.

Odendal, Eugene J., BScEng Pret., MScEng Natal   Assoc. Prof.

Peplow, Roger C. S., BScEng Natal, MScEng Natal   Assoc. Prof.

Rigby, Bruce, BScEng Natal, MScEng Natal, PhD Natal   Sr. Lectr.

Sewsunker, R., BScEng Natal, MScEng Natal, MSEE Wash.State   Sr. Lectr.

Takawira, Fambirai, BSc Manc., PhD Camb.   Telkom Prof., Digital Communications; Head*

Other Staff: 3 Lectrs.

Research: control systems; electrical machines; high voltage; motion control; power systems

Engineering, Mechanical, School of

Tel: (031) 260 3202 Fax: (031) 260 3217
   E-mail: adali@nu.ac.za

Adali, Sarp, BScEng Cornell, METech Cornell, PhD Cornell, FASME   Sugar Millers' Prof., Mechanical Design

Bright, Glen, BScEng Natal, MScEng Natal, PhD Natal   Prof.

Govender, Saneshan, BSc Durban-W., MSc(Eng) Durban-W., PhD Durban-W.   Prof.

Inambao, F. L., MSc Volgograd, PhD Volgograd   Sr. Lectr.

Kaunda, M. A. E., BSc CNAA, PhD Cape Town, MSc   Sr. Lectr.

Morozov, Evgeny, MSc Moscow, PhD Moscow, DSc Moscow   Prof., Manufacturing Systems

Roy-Aikins, Joseph E. A., BSc Manc., MEng Car., PhD Cran.   Assoc. Prof.

Verijenko, B., BScEng Natal, PhD Natal   Sr. Lectr.

Verijenko, Viktor E., MScEng Kiev, PhD Kiev, DSc Kiev   Prof., Solid Mechanics; Head*

von Klemperer, C. J., BScEng Natal, MScEng Natal, PhD Natal   Sr. Lectr.

Other Staff: 3 Lectrs.

Research: applied mechanics; composite materials and structures; dynamics and vibration of machines; manufacturing systems

Environmental Sciences, School of

Tel: (031) 260 3192 Fax: (031) 260 2029
   E-mail: crawleym@nu.ac.za

Diab, Roseanne D., MSc Natal, PhD Virginia   Sr. Prof.

Ellery, William N., MSc Witw., PhD Witw.   Assoc. Prof.

Garland, Gerald G., MSc I.T.C.Enschede, PhD Natal   Assoc. Prof.

Scott, Di, MA Natal, PhD Natal   Assoc. Prof.

Thompson, A., MA Prin., PhD Bryn Mawr   Hon. Prof.

Watson, Helen K., MSc Natal, PhD Durban-W.   Sr. Lectr.

Other Staff: 4 Lectrs.; 2 Hon. Res. Fellows; 1 Hon. Res. Assoc.

Vacant Posts: Head*

Research: cell and molecular biology; cytogenical aspects of speciation; ecotoxicology; plant physiology; terrestrial, marine and estuarine ecology

Geological Sciences, School of

Tel: (031) 260 2516 Fax: (031) 260 2280
   E-mail: mackroryd@nu.ac.za

Dunlevey, J. N., BSc Durh., MSc Stell., PhD Stell., FGS   Assoc. Prof.

Jermy, Colin A., BSc Wales, MSc Newcastle(UK), FGS   Assoc. Prof.

Liu, K. W., BSc MSc PhD   Assoc. Prof.

Marsh, Carol A., BSc Belf., PhD Belf.   Sr. Lectr.

Maud, Rodney R., BSc Natal, PhD Natal   Hon. Prof.

McCourt, S., BSc Exe., PhD Exe., FGS   Sr. Prof.

Reinhardt, Jurgen, PhD James Cook   Sr. Lectr.

Watkeys, Michael K., BSc Wales, PhD Witw.   Prof.

Wilson, Allan H., BSc Lond., BSc Rhodesia, PhD Rhodesia   Prof.; Head*

Other Staff: 3 Lectrs.

Research: computational learning; engineering geology; environmental geology; geochemistry; geodynamics

Information Systems and Technology, School of

Blewett, Craig, MCom Natal   Sr. Lectr.

Ford, G., BCompt S.Af., BCom Natal, MSc S.Af.   Sr. Lectr.

Gibson, L., BCom S.Af., LLB Natal   Sr. Lectr.

Gokal, Hemraj, BSc Durban-W.   Sr. Lectr.

Lubbe, S., BCom Free State, MCom Cape Town, PhD Witw.   Assoc. Prof.

Maharaj, M. S., BSc Durban-W., MSc Witw., PhD Natal   Assoc. Prof.; Head*

McArthur, Brian, BSc S.Af., MBL S.Af., MA Natal   Assoc. Prof.

Naidoo, K., BSc S.Af., BSc Durban-W.   Sr. Lectr.

Padayachee, Indira, BA Durban-W., BEd Durban-W., BSc Durban-W., BSc S.Af., MSc S.Af.   Sr. Lectr.

Quilling, Rosemary, BSc Natal   Sr. Lectr.

Other Staff: 5 Lectrs.

Isizulu Studies, School of

Tel: (031) 260 2510 Fax: (031) 260 2816
   E-mail: mathonsi@nu.ac.za

Mathonsi, Nhlanhla, BPaed Zululand, BA Natal, MA Natal, PhD Natal   Sr. Lectr.

Muller, Beverley K. B., BA Natal, MA Natal, BSocSc   Sr. Lectr.

Ndimande, N. P., BA Durban-W., MA Durban-W., DLitt Durban-W.   Sr. Lectr.; Head*

Turner, N., BA Durban-W., MA Natal, DLitt Durban-W.   Sr. Lectr.

Zungu, P., BA Zululand, MA Natal, DLitt Durban-W., BEd   Prof.

Other Staff: 6 Lectrs.

Research: linguistics; literature and traditional literature; onomastics; teaching Isizulu as a second language

Language, Literacy and Media Education

Balfour, Robert J., BA Rhodes, MA Natal, PhD Camb.   Assoc. Prof.; Head*

Buthelezi, T., BPaed Zululand, BEd Zululand, MPhil Stell., PhD Zululand   Sr. Lectr.

Soane, Bev A., BA Natal, MA Natal, PhD Zululand   Sr. Lectr.

Other Staff: 9 Lectrs.

Language, Literature and Linguistics, School of

Tel: (031) 260 2617 Fax: (031) 260 1253
   E-mail: kamwanga@nu.ac.za

Balladon, Francesca, LicLett Nice, BA Natal, MA Natal, PhD KwaZulu-Natal   Sr. Lectr.

Desai, U., MA Durban-W., DLitt Durban-W., BA   Assoc. Prof.

Govender, S., BA Durban-W., LLB Durban-W., MA Durban-W.   Assoc. Prof.

Jackson, L., BA Free State, MA P.Elizabeth, DLitt P.Elizabeth   Sr. Lectr.

Jadwat, A., BA Garyounis, PhD St And.   Sr. Lectr.

Lutchman, V., BPaed Durban-W., BA Durban-W., DLitt Durban-W., MA   Sr. Lectr.

Machabeis, Jacqueline M.-A., Lic Paris IV, LicLett Paris X, Maîtrise Paris IV, Drd'État Paris, PhD Paris IV   Assoc. Prof.

Shukla, U., BA Durban-W., MA Durban-W., DLitt Durban-W. Prof.

Tappe, H., MA Hamburg, PhD Hamburg Assoc. Prof.

Tudge, R., BA Durban-W., MA Stell., PhD Durban-W. Sr. Lectr.

Visagie, Andries, BA Stell., MA Stell., DrsLitt Utrecht, DLitt Stell. Sr. Lectr.

Wildsmith-Cromarty, Rosemary, BA Witw., MA Essex, PhD Lond. Prof.; Head*

Zeller, J., PhD Fran. Sr. Lectr.

Other Staff: 2 Lectrs.

Research: bilingualism; code-switching across cultures; English as an international and intranational language; language variation; multilingualism and language planning

Law, School of

Tel: (031) 260 2222 Fax: (031) 260 2522
E-mail: ponquett@nu.ac.za

Bellengere, Adrian H., BA Natal, LLB Natal, LLM Aberd. Sr. Lectr.

Bosch, S., BA Natal, LLM Camb. Sr. Lectr.

Cohen, Tammy J., BA Natal, LLB Natal, LLM Natal Sr. Lectr.

Couzens, Edwin W. F., BA Witw., LLB Witw., LLM Nott. Sr. Lectr.

Cowling, Michael G., BA Rhodes, LLB Natal, LLM Camb., MPhil Camb. Prof.; Head*

du Plessis, Max, BJuris S.Af., LLB Natal, LLM Camb. Assoc. Prof.

Govender, Karthigasen, LLB Lond., LLB Natal, LLM Mich. Prof.

Greenbaum, Lesley A., BA Natal, LLB Natal, MEd Natal Assoc. Prof.

Hulme, D. H., BA Natal, LLB Natal, LLM Natal Sr. Lectr.

Jivan, Usha, BA Durban-W., LLB Durban-W., LLM S.Af. Sr. Lectr.

Konyn, Isobel E., BA Natal, LLB Natal Assoc. Prof.

Leslie, A. B., BA Cape Town, LLB Cape Town, LLM Rhodes Sr. Lectr.

Lumina, C., LLB Zambia, LLM Essex, PhD Griff. Sr. Lectr.

McQuoid-Mason, David J., BCom Natal, LLB Natal, LLM Lond., PhD Natal Prof.

Mowatt, J. G., BA Natal, LLB Natal, LLM Durban-W. Assoc. Prof.

O'Shea, A. G., LLB Coventry, PhD Witw. Assoc. Prof.

Palmer, Robin W., BA Witw., LLB Witw., LLM Natal Assoc. Prof.

Parker, J., BA Natal, LLB Natal Sr. Lectr.

Perumal, Devina, BA Natal, LLB Natal, MA Durban-W. Sr. Lectr.

Pete, Stephen A., BA Natal, LLB Natal, LLM Cape Town, MPhil Camb. Assoc. Prof.

Reddi, M., BA Durban-W., LLB Durban-W., LLM Natal, LLD Durban-W. Assoc. Prof.

Rycroft, Alan J., BA Rhodes, LLB Natal, LLM Lond., PhD S'ton. Prof.

Schembri, Christopher C., BA Natal, LLB Natal, LLM Natal Sr. Lectr.

Steyn, Leienne, BA Natal, LLB Natal, LLM S.Af. Assoc. Prof.

Vahed, M. A., BProc Durban-W. Sr. Lectr.

Woker, Tanya A., BA Natal, LLB Natal, LLM Natal Prof.

Wood-Bodley, Michael C., BCom Natal, LLB Natal, LLM Natal Sr. Lectr.

Yawda, Y. A., BA Durban-W., BProc S.Af., LLM Durban-W. Assoc. Prof.

Zaal, F. N., BA Natal, LLB Natal, LLM Durban-W., LLM Col. Prof.

Other Staff: 15 Lectrs.; 3 Assoc. Lectrs.

Research: advertising; company law; detection and treatment of child abuse; insurance; international insolvency issues

Literary Studies, Media and Creative Arts

Chapman, Michael J. F., BA Lond., MA Natal, DLitt&Phil S.Af. Sr. Prof.; Res. Fellow; Head*

Coullie, J. L., BA Natal, MA Syr., PhD Natal Prof.

Dimitriu, Ileana, MA Timisoara, MA Natal, PhD Natal Assoc. Prof.

Garside, D., BA Cape Town, MA Manc., PhD Cape Town Sr. Lectr.

Green, Michael M., BA Natal, MA Stan., DPhil York(UK) Prof.

Hilton, John L., BA Cape Town, BA S.Af., MA Reading, PhD Natal Assoc. Prof.

Hurst, C., MA Natal Sr. Lectr.

Jacobs, Johan U., BA Pret., BA S.Af., MPhil Col., PhD Col. Prof.; Res. Fellow

Keyan, Tomaselli, BA Witw., MA Witw., PhD Witw. Prof.; Res. Fellow

McMurtry, Mervyn E., BA Natal, MA Natal, PhD Natal Assoc. Prof.

Moran, S., BA Warw., DPhil Sus. Sr. Lectr.

Murray, Sally-Ann, BA Natal, MA Natal, PhD Natal Assoc. Prof.

Narismulu, P., BA Durban-W., MA Durban-W., PhD Durban-W. Assoc. Prof.

Sharland, S., MA Cape Town, PhD Cape Town Sr. Lectr.

Stiebel, L., MA Natal, PhD Natal Prof.

Teer-Tomaselli, Ruth E., BA Witw., MA Witw., PhD Natal Prof.

Wade, Jean-Philippe, BA Natal, MA Essex, PhD Essex Assoc. Prof.

Other Staff: 13 Lectrs.

Management, School of

Bhowan, Kanti, BCom S.Af., MBA Witw. Assoc. Prof.

Brijball Parumasur, S., BAdmin Durban-W., MAdmin Durban-W., DAdmin Durban-W. Assoc. Prof.

Cassim, Shahida, BCom S.Af., MCom Natal Assoc. Prof.

Coldwell, David A. L., BSc Lond., BA(Econ) S.Af., MA S.Af., DLitt&Phil S.Af. Prof.; Head*

Dancaster, Lisa, BCom Natal, LLM Natal Sr. Lectr.

Latiff, Yunus, BCom Durban-W., BProc S.Af., LLB S.Af., MBA Cape Town Sr. Lectr.

Naidoo, J. M., BCom Durban-W., MCom Durban-W. Sr. Lectr.

O'Neill, R. C., BA Stell., BBusAdm Potchef., MBA Potchef., PhD Rhodes Assoc. Prof.

Perumal, S., BCom S.Af., MCom S.Af., DCom Durban-W. Assoc. Prof.

Poovalingam, K., BCom Durban-W., MCom Durban-W., DCom Durban-W. Assoc. Prof.

Poulter, Michael P., BCom Natal, BSc Natal, MSc Natal Sr. Lectr.

Ramdial, S., BAdmin Durban-W., MAdmin Durban-W., DAdmin Durban-W. Sr. Lectr.

Raubenheimer, W. H., BA S.Af., MBL S.Af., DBL S.Af. Assoc. Prof.

Vajeth, T. A. A., BCom Durban-W., MCom Durban-W. Sr. Lectr.

van Uytrecht, Paul M., BIur S.Af., MBA Witw., LLM Natal Prof.

Vigar-Ellis, D. A., BBusSc Cape Town, MBusSc Cape Town Assoc. Prof.

Other Staff: 13 Lectrs.; 2 Assoc. Lectrs.

Mathematical Sciences, School of

Tel: (031) 260 3000 Fax: (031) 260 2632
E-mail: naslop@nu.ac.za

Banasiak, Jacek, MScEng Lodz, PhD Strath., DSc Warsaw Prof.; Head*

Dadhich, Naresh K., MSc SP, PhD Poona Hon. Prof.

Dankelmann, Peter A., DrRerNat T.H.Aachen Assoc. Prof.

Govender, M., BSc Natal, MSc Natal, PhD Natal Sr. Lectr.

Govinder, Kesh S., MSc Natal, PhD Natal Sr. Lectr.

Gutev, Valentin, MSc Sofia, PhD Sofia Assoc. Prof.

Hansraj, S., BSc S.Af., MSc Natal, PhD Natal Sr. Lectr.

Leach, Peter G. L., BSc Melb., MSc La Trobe, PhD La Trobe, DSc Natal, FRSSAf Prof.

Maartens, Roy, BSc Cape Town, PhD Cape Town Hon. Prof.

Maharaj, Sunil D., BSc Durban-W., MSc Witw., PhD Witw., FRAS Sr. Prof.

Meijer, Alko R., BSc Pret., PhD S.Af. Hon. Prof.

Raftery, James G., PhD Natal Prof.

Scribani, L., Laur Genoa, PhD Wat. Sr. Lectr.

Swart, Henda R., MSc Stell., DSc Stell., FRSSAf Emer. Prof.

Swart, John H., MSc Stell., PhD S.Af. Emer. Prof.

Winter, Paul A., BEd Natal, MEd(EdPsych) Natal, MSc Natal, PhD Natal Sr. Lectr.

Other Staff: 7 Lectrs.; 1 Hon. Assoc. Prof.; 1 Hon. Sr. Lectr.; 1 Hon. Res. Fellow; 1 Hon. Res. Assoc.

Research: cosmology and relativity; financial statistics; generalised linear models; graph theory; probability theory

Music Programme

Tel: (031) 260 2377 Fax: (031) 260 1048
E-mail: hodges@nu.ac.za

Ballantine, Christopher J., BMus Witw., MLitt Camb., DMus Cape Town Sr. Prof.; Res. Fellow

Brauninger, Jurgen, MA Calif.State(San Jose), DMus Natal Assoc. Prof.

Brubeck, Darius D., BA Wesleyan Assoc. Prof.; Dir., Music Performance Programme

Franke, Veronica M., MMus Cape Town, DPhil Oxf. Sr. Lectr.

Naidoo, M., BMus Natal, MMus Natal, MM S.Calif. Sr. Lectr.

Opondo, Patricia, BSMusEd Duquesne, MA Pitt., PhD Pitt. Sr. Lectr.

Parker, Beverly L., BMus Boston, MA Mich., PhD Mich. Prof.; Head*

Philp, C.

Smith, David I., BMus Cape Town, PhD Cape Town Prof.

Other Staff: 6 Lectrs.

Research: African music and dance; ethnomusicology; music education; popular music; sociology of music

Nursing, School of

Tel: (031) 260 3316 Fax: (031) 260 1543
E-mail: uys@nu.ac.za

Adejumo, Oluyinka, BSc(Nursing) Ib., MSc Ib., DLitt&Phil S.Af. Assoc. Prof.; Head*

Bhengu, B., BCur S.Af., MCur Rand Afrikaans, PhD Natal Sr. Lectr.

Lee, M. B., BSN St.Louis, PhD Wayne State, MN Assoc. Prof.

Mahlungulu, S., MSc Andrews, PhD Natal Sr. Lectr.

McInerney, Patricia, PhD Witw. Assoc. Prof.

Mtshali, N. G., MCur Natal, PhD Natal Sr. Lectr.

Other Staff: 8 Lectrs.

Research: child abuse; comprehensive psychiatric care in the primary health system; health education in schools; psychosocial rehabilitation; vocational rehabilitation

Philosophy and Ethics, School of

Tel: (031) 260 2292 Fax: (031) 260 3031
E-mail: spurrett@nu.ac.za

Beck, S., MA Rhodes, PhD Cape Town Head*

Collier, J., SB M.I.T., MA Calif., PhD W.Ont. Assoc. Prof.

Giddy, J. P., MA Stell., PhD Cape Town Sr. Lectr.

Gouws, Andries S., BA S.Af., DrsPhil Utrecht Sr. Lectr.

More, M. P., MA Indiana, BA Assoc. Prof.

Spurrett, David, BA Natal, MA Natal, PhD Natal Assoc. Prof.

Other Staff: 4 Lectrs.; 1 Assoc. Lectr.

Research: aspects of liberalism with reference to contemporary South Africa; ethics and their political implications, especially in multicultural societies; Freud's theory of sexuality; Nietzsche; philosophy of the mind

Physics, School of

Tel: (031) 260 2775 Fax: (031) 261 6550
E-mail: lessing@nu.ac.za

Alport, Michael J., MSc Natal, PhD Iowa Assoc. Prof.

Doyle, Terry B., BSc Durh., PhD Witw.   Prof.
Hey, John D., BSc Stell., BSc Cape Town, MSc
   Cape Town, PhD Maryland   Prof.
Mace, R., BSc Natal, PhD Natal   Sr. Lectr.
Matthews, Alan P., BSc Natal, PhD Camb.   Sr.
   Lectr.
Moyo, Thomas, BSc Zambia, PhD Leeds   Sr.
   Lectr.
Petruccione, F., DrRerNat Freib.   Prof.
Pillay, S. R., BPaed Durban-W., BSc Durban-W.,
   MSc Durban-W., PhD Durban-W.   Prof.;
   Head*
Rash, Jonathan P. S., MSc Cape Town, PhD Rhodes
   Assoc. Prof.
Other Staff: 1 Lectr.; 3 Hon. Res. Assocs.; 4
   Hon. Res. Fellows
Research: applied physics; computational physics;
   inter-metallic alloy and magnetic materials;
   plasma spectroscopy; space and plasma
   physics

Politics, School of

Tel: (031) 260 2627 Fax: (031) 260 1061
   E-mail: dekadtr@nu.ac.za
de Kadt, Raphael H. J., BA Witw.   Assoc. Prof.;
   Head*
Freund, W., BA Chic., MPhil Yale, PhD Yale   Sr.
   Prof.; Res. Fellow
Grest, C. Jeremy, BA Rhodes, MA Lond.   Sr.
   Lectr.
Hamilton, L., MA Camb., MPhil Camb., PhD
   Camb.   Sr. Lectr.
Moore, D., BA Guelph, MA York(Can.), PhD
   York(Can.)   Sr. Lectr.
Other Staff: 9 Lectrs.
Research: cities and urban management;
   comparative government and politics;
   modernisation studies; political economy of
   growth and development in South Africa;
   political theory

Psychology, School of

Tel: (031) 260 2401 Fax: (031) 260 2618
   E-mail: ramana@nu.ac.za
Akintola, O., BSc Ilorin, MBA Ilorin, MPh Ib.,
   PhD KwaZulu-Natal   Sr. Lectr.
Bhagwanjee, A., BA Durban-W., MA Durban-W.
   Sr. Lectr.
Bradbury, J., BA Natal, PhD Natal   Assoc. Prof.
Collings, Steven J., MSocSc Natal, PhD Natal
   Assoc. Prof.
Hayes, G., MA Natal   Sr. Lectr.
Le Roux, R., BSocSc Natal, BSocSc S.Af., DCom
   Durban-W.   Assoc. Prof.
Meyer-Weitz, A., BA S.Af., MA S.Af., PhD
   Prof.
Moola, A., BCom Durban-W., MCom Durban-W.,
   DCom Durban-W.   Sr. Lectr.
Parekh, A. G., BA Durban-W., MA Durban-W.,
   DPhil Durban-W., MA   Prof.
Petersen, I., BSc Natal, MSc Natal, PhD Cape Town
   Assoc. Prof.; Head*
Sliep, Y., MCur Rand Afrikaans, PhD Rand
   Afrikaans, EdD Rand Afrikaans   Assoc. Prof.
Wilbraham, L., BA Cape Town, MA Cape Town
   Sr. Lectr.
Other Staff: 10 Lectrs.

Public Administration and Development Management, School of

Moodley, S., BA Durban-W., MA Durban-W.,
   DPhil Durban-W.   Prof.
Penceliah, Y., BA Durban-W., MPA Durban-W.,
   DAdmin Durban-W.   Sr. Lectr.
Pillay, P., BAdmin Durban-W., MAdmin Durban-
   W., DAdmin Durban-W.   Sr. Lectr.
Reddy, P. S., BAdmin Durban-W., MAdmin
   Durban-W., DAdmin Durban-W.   Sr. Prof.
Sing, D., BAdmin Durban-W., MAdmin Durban-
   W., DAdmin Durban-W.   Sr. Prof.
Other Staff: 2 Lectrs.
Vacant Posts: Head*

Religion and Theology, School of

Dangor, S., BA Durban-W., MA Durban-W., DPhil
   Durban-W.   Prof.
Ebrahim, M., BA Al-Azhar, MA Temple, PhD
   Temple   Prof.

Kumar, P. P., PhD Calif.   Prof.
Mekoa, I., BTh Nigeria, MA Natal, PhD
   North(S.Af.)   Sr. Lectr.
Phiri, Isabel A., BEd Malawi, MA Lanc., PhD Cape
   Town   Head*
Smit, J., BA Stell., BTh Stell., MTh Stell., DLitt
   Durban-W.   Assoc. Prof.
Other Staff: 3 Lectrs.

Science, Mathematics and Technology Education, School of

Atagana, H. I.   Sr. Lectr.
de Villiers, M. D., BSc Stell., BEd Free State, MEd
   Stell., DEd Stell.   Assoc. Prof.
Govender, Desmond W., BCom S.Af., BSc
   Durban-W., MA Natal   Sr. Lectr.
Govender, N., BPaed BSc Durban-W., BEd
   Durban-W., MSc Durban-W., PhD W.Cape   Sr.
   Lectr.
Hobden, Paul A., BSc Natal, BEd S.Af., MEd
   Natal, PhD Natal   Assoc. Prof.
Mkhwanazi, W. T., BSc Natal, MSc Natal   Sr.
   Lectr.
Vithal, Renuka, BA Durban-W., MPhil Camb., Dr
   Aalborg   Prof.
Other Staff: 18 Lectrs.
Vacant Posts: Head*

Social Science Education, School of

Forbes, Mary J., BA Stell., BEd Natal, MEd
   Durban-W., DEd Durban-W.   Sr. Lectr.
Moodie, C. A. E., BSc Natal, BA S.Af., MEd
   Natal, DTh S.Af.   Sr. Lectr.
Other Staff: 12 Lectrs.
Vacant Posts: Head*

Social Work and Community Development, School of

Tel: (031) 260 3086 Fax: (031) 260 1168
   E-mail: doorasam@nu.ac.za
Gathiram, N., BA(SocWk) Durban-W.,
   MA(SocWk) Durban-W., DPhil Durban-W.
   Assoc. Prof.
Kasiram, M., BA(SocWk) Durban-W., BA Durban-
   W., DPhil Durban-W., MA   Prof.
Matthias, C., BA(SocialWork) Durban-W.,
   MA(SocialWork) Durban-W., DSW Col.
   Assoc. Prof.
Sewpaul, Vishanti, BA(SocWk) Durban-W.,
   MMedSc Durban-W., PhD Natal   Prof.;
   Head*
Simpson, B., BSocSc(SocWork) Natal,
   BA(SocWk) S.Af., MSocSc Natal, PhD Natal
   Sr. Lectr.
von Kotze, Astrid E., BA Witw., PhD Witw.
   Prof.
Xaba, Thokozani, BA Dartmouth, MA Calif., PhD
   Calif.   Sr. Lectr.
Other Staff: 8 Lectrs.

Sociology and Social Studies, School of

Tel: (031) 260 2302 Fax: (031) 260 2347
   E-mail: mare@nu.ac.za
Bonnin, D., BSocSc Natal, MSocSc Natal   Sr.
   Lectr.
Cebekhulu, E., BAdmin Durban-W., MA Durban-
   W., PhD Durban-W.   Sr. Lectr.
Chetty, V. R., BA S.Af., MA Durban-W., DPhil
   Durban-W.   Sr. Lectr.
Khan, S., BA Durban-W., MA Durban-W., DPhil
   Durban-W.   Sr. Lectr.
Mantzaris, E., MA(SocSc) Cape Town, PhD Cape
   Town   Prof.
Maré, P. Gerhard, BA Natal, BA Witw., MA
   Witw., PhD Natal   Prof.
Marks, Monique, BSocSc Witw., MSocSc Witw.,
   PhD Natal   Sr. Lectr.
Pattman, R., BA Glas., MA Middx., MPhil Sheff.,
   PhD Birm.   Sr. Lectr.
Sitas, A., BA Witw., PhD Witw.   Prof.; Head*
Sooryamoorthy, Radhamany, BSc Kerala, MA
   Kerala, PhD Kerala   Assoc. Prof.
Stears, Louw-Haardt, BA Stell., BEd Stell., DPhil
   Well.   Sr. Lectr.
Other Staff: 10 Lectrs.
Research: police transformation; race thinking
   and thinking about race; social identity

formation; sociology of education;
   sociology of language

MEDICINE, NELSON R. MANDELA SCHOOL OF

Tel: (031) 260 4509 Fax: (031) 260 4410
   E-mail: sibotos@ukzn.ac.za

Anaesthetics

Tel: (031) 260 4326 Fax: (031) 260 4433
   E-mail: kynochs@nu.ac.za
Burrows, Richard C., BA Trinity(Dub.), MB BCh
   BAO Trinity(Dub.)   Sr. Lectr.
Daniel, Clive, MB ChB Cape Town, MMed Stell.
   Sr. Lectr.; Deputy Head
Rout, Chris C., MB BS Lond., FFARCS   Res.
   Prof.
Williamson, Ronald, BSc Brist., MB ChB Brist.,
   FFARCS   Sr. Lectr.; Deputy Head
Other Staff: 11 Lectrs.
Vacant Posts: 1 Prof.
Research: epidural analgesia; HIV+ children and
   intensive care units; obstetrics and
   anaesthesia; paediatric anaesthesia

Behavioural Medicine

Tel: (031) 260 4324 Fax: (031) 260 4357
   E-mail: schlebuschl@nu.ac.za
Pillay, Anthony L., BA Durban-W., MA Durban-
   W., MSc Harv., PhD Natal   Assoc. Prof.
Pillay, Basil J., BA Durban-W., MA Durban-W.,
   PhD Natal   Assoc. Prof.
Schlebusch, Lourens, BA S.Af., MA Natal,
   MMedSc Natal, PhD Natal   Prof.
Other Staff: 14 Lectrs.
Research: cross-cultural health beliefs and
   primary health care; multiple personality
   disorder; psychological aspects of cancer;
   stress management; suicidal behaviour

Cardiothoracic Surgery

Tel: (031) 460 5113 Fax: (031) 461 1724
   E-mail: welman@nu.ac.za
Blyth, F., MB ChB Cape Town, FRCSEd   Sr.
   Lectr.
Other Staff: 5 Lectrs.
Vacant Posts: 1 Prof.
Research: clinical analyses; molecular biology of
   oesophageal carcinoma

Chemical Pathology

Tel: (031) 260 4309 Fax: (031) 260 4517
   E-mail: robertsone@nu.ac.za
Joubert, Septi M., MSc Stell., MB ChB Edin.,
   FRCPath   Emer. Prof
Pegoraro, Rosemary J., BScAgric Natal, PhD
   Natal   Assoc. Prof.
Other Staff: 2 Lectrs.; 3 Hon. Lectrs.
Vacant Posts: 1 Prof.
Research: genetic risk factors for pre-eclampsia
   and coronary heart disease; genetics of
   familial disorders

Dentistry, School of

Laher, M. H. E., BSc Reading, BDS Lond., MSc
   Lond.   Sr. Lectr.
Naiker, V., BDS   Lectr.; Head*
Other Staff: 3 Lectrs.

Family Medicine

Tel: (031) 260 4485 Fax: (031) 260 4465
   E-mail: naidoos79@nu.ac.za
Govender, R. D., BSc Durban-W., MB ChB Natal,
   MFamMed Natal   Sr. Lectr.; Principal
   Specialist*
Naidoo, Soornarain S., MB ChB Natal,
   MFamMed Natal   Prof.
Ross, A. J., MB ChB Cape Town, MFamMed Natal
   Sr. Lectr.; Principal Specialist*
Other Staff: 1 Hon. Assoc. Prof.; 18 Hon.
   Lectrs.
Research: generic prescribing

Forensic Medicine

Tel: (031) 260 4265 Fax: (031) 260 4384
   E-mail: aiyers@nu.ac.za
Naidoo, S. R., MB ChB Natal, MMEd Natal
   Assoc. Prof.

Other Staff: 2 Lectrs.; 2 Hon. Lectrs.
Research: forensic anthropology; human rights
and torture medicine; mortality survey;
pathology of diffuse brain injury

General Surgery

Tel: (031) 260 4219 Fax: (031) 260 4389
  E-mail: ramlal@nu.ac.za
Baker, Lin W., MB BCh Witw., MSc McG.,
  FRCSEd, FRCSGlas Emer. Prof.
Haffejee, Arif A., MB ChB Natal, FRCSEd Prof.
Madiba, T. Enos, MB ChB Natal, MMed Natal,
  FCS(SA) Prof.
Moodley, J., MB ChB Natal, MMedSc Natal,
  FCS(SA) Sr. Lectr.
Muckart, David J. J., MB ChB Dund., MMedSc
  Natal, FRCSGlas Assoc. Prof.
Robbs, John V., MB ChB Cape Town, ChM Cape
  Town, FRCSEd, FCS(SA), FRCPGlas Prof.
Singh, Bhugwan, MB ChB Natal, MD Natal,
  FCS(SA) Assoc. Prof.
Thomson, Sandie R., MB ChB Aberd., ChM
  Aberd., FRCS Prof.
Other Staff: 14 Lectrs.
Research: AIDS-related vasculopathies; biliary
  anatomy variations in Africans; oesophageal
  cancer; surgical nutrition; wound healing

Haematology

Tel: (031) 260 4375 Fax: (031) 260 4289
  E-mail: sarawan@nu.ac.za
Jogessar, Vinod B., MB ChB Natal, MMed Natal,
  FRCPath Assoc. Prof.
Naicker, Vincent L., MB ChB Natal, MMed Natal
  Sr. Lectr.
Other Staff: 3 Lectrs.; 2 Hon. Lectrs.
Research: adaptive immune reponse in neonates;
  HIV; inflammatory central nervous system
  disease; oncology; sickle cell anaemia

Human Physiology

Tel: (031) 260 7976 Fax: (031) 260 7132
  E-mail: perumaln@ukza.ac.za
Channa, M. L., BSc Durban-W., MSc Durban-W.,
  PhD Durban-W. Assoc. Prof.
Higgins-Opitz, Susan B., BSc Cape Town, PhD
  Natal Sr. Lectr.
Mackraj, I., BSc Durban-W., MSc Durban-W., PhD
  Durban-W. Sr. Lectr.
Mclean, M., BSc Natal, MSc Natal, PhD Natal
  Prof.
Musabayane, C. T., BSc Herts., PhD Prof.;
  Acting Head*
Nadar, A., BSc Durban-W., MSc Durban-W., PhD
  Durban-W. Sr. Lectr.
Naidu, Strini G., MSc Witw., PhD Witw. Sr.
  Lectr.
Peters-Futre, Edith M., BA Stell., MSc(Med) Cape
  Town, PhD Pret. Assoc. Prof.
Other Staff: 5 Lectrs.
Research: exercise immunology; exercise
  physiology; medical education

Clinical Anatomy

Tel: (031) 260 4270 Fax: (031) 260 4252
  E-mail: vawda@nu.ac.za
Haffajee, M. R., MB ChB Natal, FRCSEd Prof.
Partab, P., MB ChB S.Af., DA S.Af. Assoc. Prof.
Satyapal, K. S., MD, FRCP Prof.
Vawda, G. Hoosen M., BSc Durban-W., MB ChB
  Natal, PhD Witw. Assoc. Prof.; Acting
  Head*
Other Staff: 5 Lectrs.
Research: cervical nerve root anatomy;
  community accident response; medical
  education and rural community
  empowerment; pharmacokinetic population
  analysis; vascular and neural anatomy in
  reconstructive surgery

Medical Biochemistry

Tel: (031) 260 4364 Fax: (031) 260 4455
  E-mail: hurley@nu.ac.za
Chuturgoon, Anil A., BSc Natal, MSc Natal
  Assoc. Prof.; Acting Head*
Other Staff: 2 Lectrs.

Research: aflatoxins; carcinoma of oesophagus;
  maize storage and health implications;
  mycotoxins

Maternal, Child Health, Obstetrics and Gynaecology

Tel: (031) 260 4250 Fax: (031) 260 4427
  E-mail: gynae@nu.ac.za
Bagratee, Jayntilal S. (Jay), MB ChB Natal,
  MMEd Natal Assoc. Prof.
Green-Thompson, R. W., MB ChB Natal,
  FRCOG Hon. Prof.
Mhlanga, R. E., MD Natal, FRCOG Prof.
Moodley, Jodasa (Jack), MD Natal, FRCOG
  Emer. Prof.
Moodley, M., MB ChB Natal, MMEd Sr. Lectr.
Ncayiyana, D. J., MB ChB Jakarta Hon. Prof.
Pitsoe, Samuel B., MB ChB Natal Sr. Lectr.
Ross, S. M., MB BS Lond., FRCOG Emer. Prof.
Other Staff: 10 Lectrs.; 2 Hon. Lectrs.
Research: hypertensive disorders in pregnancy;
  perinatal HIV infections

Medical Microbiology

Tel: (031) 260 4395 Fax: (031) 260 4431
  E-mail: sturm@nu.ac.za
Bhamjee, Ahmed, FRCPath Sr. Lectr.
Coovadia, Yacoob M., MB ChB Cape Town
  Assoc. Prof.
Kharsany, A. B. M., MMedSc Natal, PhD Natal
  Sr. Lectr.
Moodley, P., MB ChB Natal, MMEd Assoc.
  Prof.
Sturm, A. Willem, MB BS Amst., MD Amst., PhD
  Amst. Prof.
Other Staff: 5 Lectrs.; 1 Hon. Lectr.
Research: antimicrobial resistance; HIV-associated
  infections; sexually transmitted infections

Medicine

Tel: (031) 260 4216 Fax: (031) 260 4420
  E-mail: moodleyu4@nu.ac.za
Adams, E. B., BSc S.Af., BSc Oxf., MD Witw.,
  Hon. MD Natal, FRCP Emer. Prof.
Cassim, Bilkish, MB ChB Natal, MD Natal,
  FCP(SA) Assoc. Prof.
Friedland, G. H., BA Col., MD N.Y. Hon. Prof.
Mody, Girish M., MB ChB Natal, MD Cape Town,
  FCP(SA), FRCP Aaron Beare Family Prof.,
  Rheumatology
Moodley, Y. P., MB ChB Natal, FCP(SA) Sr.
  Lectr.
Motala, A. A., MB ChB Natal, MD Natal, FRCP
  Deputy Head
Omar, M. A. K., MB ChB Natal, MD Natal,
  FCP(SA), FRCP Prof.
Pirie, F. J., MB ChB Cape Town, MD Natal,
  FCP(SA) Sr. Lectr.
Pudifin, Dennis J., MB ChB Cape Town, FRCP,
  FCP(SA) Emer. Prof.
Seedat, Yacoob K., MD N.U.I., Hon. PhD
  Durban-W., FRCP, FRCPI, FACP, FCP(SA)
  Emer. Prof.
Simjee, Ahmed E., MB ChB Natal, FRCP
  Assoc. Prof.
Walker, B. D., BS Colorado, MD Case W.Reserve
  Hon. Prof.
Other Staff: 11 Lectrs.; 1 Hon. Assoc. Prof.; 1
  Hon. Lectr.
Research: diagnostic criteria for psoriatic
  arthritis; genetics of rheumatic arthritis;
  HIV-associated nephropathy;
  microalbuminuria in HIV-infected patients;
  polycystic kidney disease in Kwa-Zulu/
  Natal

Cardiology

Tel: (031) 460 5105 Fax: (031) 468 8734
  E-mail: naidood@nu.ac.za
Mitha, A. S., FCP(SA), FRCP Emer. Prof.
Naidoo, Datshana P., MB ChB Natal, MD Natal,
  FRCP, FCP(SA) Prof.
Other Staff: 2 Lectrs.; 1 Hon. Sr. Lectr.
Research: atrial fibrillation; congestive heart
  failure; hyponatremia; ventricular
  arrhythmias

Dermatology

Tel: (031) 260 4531 Fax: (031) 360 3548
  E-mail: naidooj30@nu.ac.za
Aboobaker, Jamila, MB ChB Natal, FRCP
  Assoc. Prof.
Other Staff: 2 Lectrs.; 1 Hon. Lectr.
Research: common skin diseases in Kwa-Zulu/
  Natal; erythroderma; HTLV-1 in skin
  manifestations; kinins in psoriasis

Gastroenterology

Newton, A. Prof.

Geriatrics

Cassim, Bilkish, MB ChB Natal, MD Natal,
  FCP(SA) Prof.

Nephrology

Assounga, A. G. H., MD Congo(Official), MSc
  PhD Prof.

Neurology

Tel: (031) 460 5038 Fax: (031) 468 6139
  E-mail: seeramaloos@nu.ac.za
Bhigjee, Ahmed I., MB ChB Natal, MMed Cape
  Town, MD Natal, FCP(SA), FRCP Prof.
Bill, Pierre L. A., MB BCh Witw., FRCP,
  FCP(SA) Emer. Prof.
Other Staff: 1 Hon. Lectr.
Research: central nervous system and tuberculous
  meningitis; gene deletions in Duchenne
  muscular dystrophy; HTLV-1 myelopathy

Pulmonology

Lalloo, U. G., MB ChB Natal, FCP(SA), FRCP
  Prof.
Other Staff: 1 Lectr.

Rheumatology

Mody, Girish M., MB ChB Natal, MD Cape Town,
  FCP(SA), FRCP Prof.

Molecular Microbiology

Chetty, R., MB BCh BAO N.U.I., DPhil Oxf.,
  FRCPA, FRCPath Hon. Prof.
Kiepiela, P., BScAgric Natal, MSc Natal, PhD
  Natal Sr. Lectr.
Naidoo, R., BSc Durban-W., MMedSc Natal, PhD
  Natal Sr. Lectr.

Neurosurgery

Tel: (031) 460 5103 Fax: (031) 461 2897
  E-mail: govendesa@nu.ac.za
van Dellen, J. R., MB ChB Witw., PhD Witw.,
  FRCSEd Emer. Prof.
Other Staff: 1 Lectr.
Research: kinin study

Ophthalmology

Tel: (031) 260 4341 Fax: (031) 260 4221
  E-mail: petersa@nu.ac.za
2 Lectrs.; 3 Hon. Lectrs.
Vacant Posts: 1 Prof.
Research: cytomegalovirus (CMV) retinitis in
  AIDS; fungal ulcers; intraocular
  hyaluronidase for vitreous haemorrhage

Optometry

Hansraj, R., BOptom Durban-W., MOptom
  Durban-W., PhD KwaZulu-Natal Sr. Lectr.
Mehta, M., BSc BOptom MOptom Sr. Lectr.
Moodley, V. R., BOptom Durban-W., MOptom
  Durban-W. Sr. Lectr.
Naidoo, K. S., BSc Durban-W., BOptom Durban-
  W., MPH Temple Assoc. Prof.
Seethal, C. H., BOptom Durban-W., PhD Durban-
  W. Sr. Lectr.
Other Staff: 2 Lectrs,

Orthopaedic Surgery

Tel: (031) 260 4297 Fax: (031) 260 4518
  E-mail: katia@nu.ac.za
Goga, Ismail E., LLM, FRCS, FCS(SA) Sr.
  Lectr.
Govender, S. (Teddy), MB BS Bom., FRCSGlas
  Prof.
Rasool, Mahomed N., BSc Durban-W., MB ChB
  Natal, FCS(SA) Sr. Lectr.

Other Staff: 6 Lectrs.; 3 Hon. Lectrs.
Research: adolescent idiopathic scoliosis;
fractures of the thoracolumbar spine; hand
surgery

Otorhinolaryngology

Tel: (031) 260 4292 Fax: (031) 260 4480
E-mail: pillays@nu.ac.za
2 Lectrs.
Vacant Posts: 1 Prof.; 1 Sr. Lectr.
Research: lateral sinus thrombosis; management
of epistaxis; post-operative antibiotics in
children

Paediatric Surgery

Tel: (031) 240 1579 Fax: (031) 240 1667
E-mail: conner@nu.ac.za
Hadley, G. P. (Larry), MB ChB St And., FRCSEd
Prof.
Mickel, Robert E., MB BCh Witw., FRCSEd
Emer. Prof.
Wiersma, Rinus, BSc Natal, MB ChB Rhodesia,
MMedSci Natal, FRCSGlas, FCS(SA)   Sr.
Lectr.
Other Staff: 1 Lectr.
Research: intersex; Wilm's tumour; wound
healing

Paediatrics

Tel: (031) 260 4345 Fax: (031) 260 4388
E-mail: mkhwanazid3@nu.ac.za
Adhikari, Miriam, MB ChB Cape Town, MD Natal
Prof.
Bhimma, Rajendran, MB ChB Natal, FCP(SA)
Assoc. Prof.
Bobat, Razia A., MB ChB Natal, FCP(SA)   Sr.
Lectr.
Coovadia, H. M., MB BS Bom., MSc Birm., MD
Natal, DSc, FCP(SA)   Emer. Prof.
Coutsoudis, Anna, PhD Natal, BSc   Assoc. Prof.
Jeena, Prakash, MB ChB Natal, FCP(SA)   Assoc.
Prof.
Loening, W. E. K., MB ChB Cape Town, FCP(SA)
Emer. Prof.
Rollins, N. C., MB ChB BAO MD, FRCPCH
Assoc. Prof.
Thejpal, Rajendra, MB ChB Natal, FCP(SA)   Sr.
Lectr.
Other Staff: 8 Lectrs.; 2 Hon. Assoc. Profs.; 18
Hon. Lectrs.
Research: breastfeeding and HIV transmission;
childhood cancers; immunologic responses
to HIV; nephrotic syndrome; tubercular
meningitis and encephalopathy

Pathology

see also Chem. Pathol.
Tel: (031) 260 4228 Fax: (031) 205 2711
E-mail: moodleym@nu.ac.za
Chrystal, Vivien, BA S.Af., MB BCh Witw.,
FRCPath   Assoc. Prof.
Ramdial, P. K., MB ChB Natal, MMed Natal
Prof.
Other Staff: 2 Hon. Lectrs.
Research: nephroblastomas; paediatric oncology;
skin cancer

Pharmacy and Pharmacology

E-mail: bagwandeena@ukzn.ac.za
Govender, T., BPharm Durban-W., MPharm
Durban-W., PhD Nott.   Assoc. Prof.; Head*
Ojewole, J. A. O., BPharm Ife, MSc Lond., PhD
Strath.   Sr. Prof.
Rambiritch, V., BSc Durban-W., MMedSc
KwaZulu-Natal, PhD KwaZulu-Natal   Assoc.
Prof.
Other Staff: 5 Lectrs.
Research: antibiotic use and resistance;
antiretroviral therapy in resource-
constrained settings; cardiovascular and
renal drugs; clinical pharmacokinetics;
quality cultures in district-based
pharmaceutical services

Plastic and Reconstructive Surgery

Tel: (031) 460 5202 Fax: (031) 461 3049
E-mail: possolo@nu.ac.za
Madaree, Anil, MB ChB Natal, MMed Natal,
FCS(SA)   Prof.

Other Staff: 1 Lectr.
Research: basal cell carcinomas; cleft lip nose
deformities; cranio-facial surgery;
transcranical Doppler studies in
craniosynostosis; wound healing

Psychiatry

Tel: (031) 260 4321 Fax: (031) 260 4322
E-mail: kuilder@nu.ac.za
Dunn, John A., MSc Witw., MB BCh Witw.,
MMed(Path) Witw., MMed(Psych) Natal   Sr.
Lectr.
Gangat, A. E., MEd Natal   Sr. Lectr.
Mkize, Dan L., MB ChB Natal,
MMed(Psychiatry) Natal   Prof.
Nair, M. G., MB ChB Natal, MD Natal   Prof.
Wessels, Wessel H. C., MB ChB Pret., DM OFS
Emer. Prof.
Other Staff: 13 Lectrs.; 1 Hon. Assoc. Prof.; 1
Hon. Sr. Lectr.; 3 Hon. Lectrs
Vacant Posts: 1 Prof.
Research: African health care systems; cannabis
psychosis; Durban health risk behaviour;
post-traumatic stress disorder; schizophrenia
and schizo-affective disorder

Public Health Medicine

Tel: (031) 260 4383 Fax: (031) 260 4211
E-mail: pillaym@nu.ac.za
Abdool Karim, Salim, MB ChB Natal, MS Col.,
MMEd Natal, PhD Natal   Hon. Prof.
Jinabhai, Champaklal C., BSc Durban-W., MB
ChB Cape Town, MMed Natal, MD Natal
Prof.
Naidoo, Kala, MB ChB Natal, MMed Natal   Sr.
Lectr.
Voce, A. S., BSc Witw.   Sr. Lectr.
Yach, D., MB ChB Cape Town, BSc Stell., MPH
Johns H.   Hon. Prof.
Other Staff: 1 Lectr.; 4 Hon. Assoc. Profs.; 2
Hon. Sr. Lectrs.; 7 Hon. Lectrs.; 1 Adjunct
Prof.
Research: control of parasitic diseases and
sexually transmitted diseases (STDs);
environmental pollutants (especially lead);
HIV/AIDS; policy and planning for health
management

Radiology

Tel: (031) 260 4301 Fax: (031) 260 4621
E-mail: singhm@nu.ac.za
Maharajh, J., MB ChB Natal, MMEd Natal   Sr.
Lectr.
Other Staff: 11 Lectrs.
Vacant Posts: 1 Prof.
Research: magnetic resonance imaging (MRI);
neuro-interventional radiology; ultrasound

Radiotherapy and Oncology

Tel: (031) 327 2182 Fax: (031) 332 4864
E-mail: rikirich@iafrica.com
Jordaan, Johann P., MB ChB Stell., MMed Stell.
Prof.
Other Staff: 1 Lectr.
Research: head and neck cancer; hepato-cellular
cancer; non-small-cell lung cancer; prostate
cancer; supportive care

Sport Science

2 Lectrs.; 4 Lectrs.†

Tele-Health

Tel: (031) 260 4541 Fax: (031) 260 4455
E-mail: medinformatics@nu.ac.za
Mars, Maurice, MB ChB Cape Town, MD Natal
Prof.
Other Staff: 5 Hon. Lectrs.
Research: low-tech telemedicine; tele-health
education

Therapeutics and Medicines Management

Botha, Julia H., BPharm Rhodes, PhD Rhodes
Prof.
Gray, Andy L., BPharm Rhodes, MSc(Pharm)
Rhodes   Sr. Lectr.
Maharaj, Breminand, MB ChB Natal, MD Natal,
PhD Natal, FCP(SA), FRCP   Prof.

Other Staff: 2 Lectrs.; 1 Hon. Assoc. Prof.; 2
Hon. Lectrs.

Urology

Tel: (031) 260 4312 Fax: (031) 260 4340
E-mail: mphangap@nu.ac.za
Bereczky, Zoltan B., MB ChB Bud., MMed(Surg)
Cologne, MMed(Urol) Cologne   Prof.
Fourie, Tjaardt, MB ChB OFS, MMed(Urol) OFS
Sr. Lectr.
Marszalek, Wlodzimierz W., MB ChB Wroclaw,
MD Wroclaw   Emer. Prof.
Other Staff: 3 Hon. Lectrs.
Research: bladder cancer in various population
groups; calculi; cancer of the prostate;
reconstructive urological surgery

Virology

Tel: (031) 260 4403 Fax: (031) 260 4441
E-mail: naidoor35@nu.ac.za
York, Denis F., BSc Natal, MSc Natal, PhD Natal
Sr. Lectr.
Other Staff: 1 Hon. Lectr.
Vacant Posts: 1 Prof.
Research: HIV and AIDS surveillance,
phylogenetic analysis; viral load testing;
influenza surveillance; jaagsiekte sheep
retrovirus; respiratory viruses

SPECIAL CENTRES, ETC

Economic Research Unit

Tel: (031) 260 2588 Fax: (031) 260 2535
E-mail: eru@und.ac.za
Holden, Merle G., BCom Natal, MA Duke, PhD
Duke   Prof.; Dir.*
Research: small business development; South
Africa-European Union (EU) free trade
agreement

Forestry and Forest Products Research Centre

Tel: (031) 260 3275 Fax: (031) 261 1216
E-mail: palan@nu.ac.za
Whiteside, A. W., MA E.Anglia, DEcon Natal
Dir.*
Other Staff: 1 Res. Dir.; 5 Researchers; 1
Project Dir.
Research: forestry; wood science

Health Economics and HIV/AIDS Research Division (HEARD)

Tel: (031) 260 2592 Fax: (031) 260 2587
E-mail: freeman@nu.ac.za
Whiteside, Alan W., MA E.Anglia   Assoc. Res.
Prof.; Dir.*
Research: impact of HIV/AIDS on developing
countries

Jazz and Popular Music, Centre for

Tel: (031) 260 3385 Fax: (031) 260 2085
E-mail: brubeck@nu.ac.za
Brubeck, Darius D., BA Wesleyan   Prof.; Assoc.
Dir.*

Leadership, Centre for

Bodhanya, S. A., BSc Natal, MBA   Sr. Lectr.
Hardman, S. G., MEd Natal   Sr. Lectr.
Taylor, R. G., BSc Natal, MSc Natal   Dir.*

Management Studies Education Unit

Bargate, K., BCom Natal, BCom S.Af., MCom
Cape Town   Sr. Lectr.
Goodier, C., BA Rhodes, MPhil Reading   Sr. Lectr.
Hesketh, J., BA Natal, PhD Sur.   Dir.*
Zikhali, J., BCom Wittenberg   Sr. Lectr.
Other Staff: 1 Lectr./Researcher

Occupational and Environmental Health, Centre for

Gqaleni, N., BSc Natal, MSc Natal, PhD Strath.
Dir.*
Other Staff: 1 Lectr.; 1 Deputy Dir.; 1 Lectr.†

Optics and Imaging Centre

Naicker, T., BSc Durban-W., MMedSc Natal, PhD
Natal   Sr. Lectr.; Manager*

Science Access, Centre for

Parkinson, Jean, BSc Witw., BA Witw., BA S.Af., MA Natal, PhD Natal   Sr. Lectr.
Other Staff: 1 Lectr.
Vacant Posts: Dir.*

PIETERMARITZBURG CAMPUS

Tel: (033) 260 5111 Fax: (033) 260 5788
E-mail: bolton@nu.ac.za

Agricultural Sciences and Agribusiness, School of

Tel: (033) 260 5493 Fax: (033) 260 5970
E-mail: ortmann@nu.ac.za
Adjetey, J. A., BScAgric Ghana, MAgricSc Qld., PhD Syd.   Sr. Lectr.
Bower, J. P., BScAgric Natal, MScAgric Natal, PhD Natal   Prof.
Darroch, Mark A. G., BScAgric Natal, MScAgric Natal   Sr. Lectr.
Dyer, Colin, BSc Witw., MSc Witw., PhD Witw.   Hon. Prof.
Gous, Robert M., BScAgric Natal, MScAgric Natal, PhD Natal   Prof.
Green, J. Maryann, BScHomeEc Stell., BScHomeEcon Natal, PhD Oklahoma State   Prof.
Greenfield, Peter L., BScAgric Natal, MS Wis., PhD Wis.   Prof.
Hendriks, L., BScHomeEcon Natal, MScHomeEcon Natal   Assoc. Prof.
Klug, John R., BScAgric Natal, MScAgric Natal   Sr. Lectr.
Lyne, Michael C., BScAgric Natal, MScAgric Natal, PhD Natal   Prof.
Maunder, Eleni M. W., BSc Lond., PhD Lond.   Prof.; Head*
Modi, Albert T., BScAgric Natal, MScAgric Natal, PhD Oyo State UT   Sr. Lectr.
Nsahlai, Ignatius, BSc Yaounde I, Maîtrise Yaounde I, PhD Reading   Assoc. Prof.
Ortmann, Gerald F., BScAgric Natal, MScAgric Natal, PhD Natal   Prof.
Roberts, Peter J. T., MSc Rhodes, PhD Rhodes   Hon. Prof.
Shanahan, Paul E., BScAgric Natal, PhD Natal   Sr. Lectr.
Zwolinski, Janusz, MSc Cracow Agric., PhD Stell.   Assoc. Prof.
Other Staff: 14 Lectrs.; 1 Hon. Lectr.; 2 Hon. Res. Assocs.; 4 Hon. Res. Fellows
Vacant Posts: 1 Prof.; 1 Lectr.
Research: commercial farming and rural development; determinants of stunting; effect of diet and temperature on broiler chickens; food intake and laying performance in poultry; training courses for women from low-income families

Biochemistry, Genetics, Microbiology and Plant Pathology, School of

Tel: (033) 260 5435 Fax: (033) 260 6127
E-mail: lerouxc@nu.ac.za
Anderson, Trevor R., BScAgric Natal, MScAgric Natal, PhD Natal   Assoc. Prof.
Coetzer, Theresa H. T., BSc Stell., MSc Stell., PhD Natal   Assoc. Prof.
Elliot, Edith, BSc Natal, MSc Natal, PhD Natal   Sr. Lectr.
Fossey, Annabel, BSc Pret., MSc Pret., DSc Pret.   Assoc. Prof.
Goldring, J. P. Dean, BSc Dund., DPhil Z'bwe.Open   Assoc. Prof.
Gubba, A., BSc Z'bwe., MSc Lond., PhD Cornell   Sr. Lectr.
Kormuth, E., BSc Prague, DrRerNat Prague   Prof.; Head*
Laing, M. D., BSc Natal, PhD Natal   Prof.
Quicke, S. G., MScAgric Pret., PhD Wis.   Emer. Prof.
Rijkenberg, F. H. J., BScAgric Natal, MScAgric Natal, PhD Natal   Emer. Prof.
Rogan, J. M., BSc Witw., BA S.Af., MA Col., PhD Calif.   Hon. Prof.
Tivchev, G., MSc Sofia, PhD Sofia   Sr. Lectr.
Tongoona, P., BSc Z'bwe., MPhil Z'bwe., PhD Z'bwe.   Prof.

Wallis, F. M., BScAgric Natal, MScAgric Natal, PhD Natal   Emer. Prof.
Other Staff: 8 Lectrs.; 3 Hon. Lectrs.; 1 Hon. Res. Assoc.
Research: immunoglobulins; infectious bursal disease virus; poultry pathogens; proteinases and cancer; trypanosomal proteinases

Biological and Conservation Sciences, School of

Tel: (033) 260 5104 Fax: (033) 260 5105
E-mail: sec@nu.ac.za
Beckett, Richard P., BSc St And., PhD Brist.   Assoc. Prof.
Brothers, Denis J., BSc Rhodes, PhD Kansas   Sr. Prof.; Head*
Downs, Colleen T., BSc Natal, PhD Natal   Assoc. Prof.
Edwards, Trevor T., BSc Natal, MSc Natal, PhD Natal   Assoc. Prof.
Everson, T. M., BScAgric Natal, MSc Natal, PhD Natal   Sr. Lectr.
Finnie, Jeff F., BSc Natal, PhD Natal   Sr. Lectr.
Granger, J. Edward, BSc Natal, PhD Natal   Sr. Lectr.
Hamer, Michelle L., BSc Natal, MSc Natal, PhD Natal   Sr. Lectr.
Hart, Robert C., BSc Natal, PhD Rhodes, DSc Natal   Prof.
Johnson, Steven D., BSc Cape Town, PhD Cape Town   Sr. Lectr.
Kirkman, Kevin P., BScAgric Natal, MScAgric Natal, PhD Natal   Prof.
Lawes, Michael J., BSc Natal, PhD Natal   Assoc. Prof.
Lovegrove, Barry G., BSc Cape Town, PhD Cape Town   Assoc. Prof.
Olckers, T., BSc Rhodes, PhD Rhodes   Sr. Lectr.
Perrin, Michael R., BSc Lond., PhD Exe., FLS   Prof.
van Staden, Hannes, BSc Stell., MSc Stell., PhD Natal, FRSSAf   Emer. Prof.
Ward, D. M., BSc Natal, PhD Natal   Prof.
Other Staff: 3 Lectrs.; 1 Hon. Assoc. Prof.; 4 Hon. Sr. Lectrs.; 8 Hon. Res. Fellows
Vacant Posts: 1 Sr. Lectr.
Research: African parrot conservation; indigenous plants in small-scale farming; medicinal plants; plant molecular biology; science management

Bioresources Engineering and Environmental Hydrology, School of

Tel: (033) 260 5483 Fax: (033) 260 5818
E-mail: currins@nu.ac.za
Ciolkosz, D. E., BAE Penn.State, BSc Penn.State, PhD Cornell   Sr. Lectr.
Jewitt, Graham P. W., BSc Natal, MSc Natal, PhD Stell.   Assoc. Prof.
Lagrange, L. F., BEng Pret., MEng Pret.   Sr. Lectr.
Lorentz, S. A., BScEng Witw., MS Colorado, PhD Colorado   Assoc. Prof.
Schulze, Roland E., MSc Natal, PhD Natal, FRSSAf   Prof., Hydrology
Smithers, Jeffrey C., MScEng Natal, PhD Natal   Prof., Agricultural Engineering; Head*
Other Staff: 1 Lectr.
Research: groundwater recession; haulage vehicle simulation; hydrological impacts of sugarcane; multimedia-based tools for engineering; optimisation of environment of intensive animal housing

Chemistry, School of

Tel: (033) 260 5326 Fax: (033) 260 5009
E-mail: fieldj@nu.ac.za
Drewes, S. E., BSc Natal, MSc Natal, PhD Rhodes, DSc Natal, FRSChem, FRSSAf   Emer. Prof.
Field, John S., BSc Natal, MSc Natal, PhD Camb.   Sr. Prof.
Jaganyi, Deo, BSc Nair., MSc Nair., PhD Lond.   Assoc. Prof.
Low, Murray R., BSc Natal, PhD Edin.   Sr. Lectr.
Munro, Orde Q., BSc Witw., PhD Witw.   Assoc. Prof.

Nikolaenko, Igor V., BSc Kiev, MSc Kiev, PhD Kiev   Assoc. Prof.
Robinson, R. S., BSc Rhodes, PhD Rhodes   Sr. Lectr.
Southway, Colin, BSc Salf., PhD Salf.   Sr. Lectr.
van Heerden, F. R., BSc Free State, MSc Free State, PhD Free State   Prof.
Other Staff: 3 Lectrs.; 1 Hon. Sr. Lectr.
Research: carbamates and the chelating silicon atom; chemical properties of tea; co-ordination compounds; 'muti' plants extraction; synthetic organic chemistry

Computer Science, School of

Dempster, Robert, BSc Natal, BSc S.Af., MSc Natal   Sr. Lectr.
Murrell, Hugh C., BSc Natal, MSc Rhodes, PhD Natal   Prof.; Head*
Pillay, N., BSc Natal, MSc Natal, PhD KwaZulu-Natal   Sr. Lectr.
Other Staff: 1 Lectr.

Education and Development, School of

Tel: (033) 260 5752 Fax: (033) 260 5080
E-mail: parkerb@nu.ac.za
Christiansen, M., Cand Roskilde, PhD Aalborg   Sr. Lectr.
Cornelius, Lambertus F. B., BSc Pret., BEd Natal   Sr. Lectr.
Dempster, Edith R., BSc Natal, MSc Natal, PhD Natal   Sr. Lectr.
Hart, Mike T., BA Natal, MA Natal   Sr. Lectr.
Hemson, Crispin M. C., BA Natal, BEd Natal, MEd Natal   Sr. Lectr.
Muthukrishna, Anbanithi, BAEd S.Af., BEd S.Af., MEd Birm., MSc Oregon, PhD Notre Dame Sem.   Prof.
Ngwenya, T. H., BA Natal, MA Natal, MEd S.Af., DLitt&Phil S.Af.   Assoc. Prof.
Samuel, M. A., BA Natal, BEd Durban-W., MA Durh., DEd Durban-W.   Assoc. Prof.
Wedekind, Volker R., BA Natal, BEd Natal, MEd Natal, PhD Manc.   Sr. Lectr.; Head*
Zambodla-Barlow, A., BScAgric Mak., PhD S.Af.   Sr. Lectr.
Other Staff: 28 Lectrs.
Research: distance education; leadership and gender: the experience of women principals; models of whole school development; school management; social relations and identity in secondary schools

Environmental Sciences, School of

Tel: (033) 260 5525 Fax: (033) 260 5919
E-mail: bartera@nu.ac.za
Beckedahl, Heinz R., BSc Witw., MSc Witw., PhD Natal   Assoc. Prof.
Breen, C. M., BSc Rhodes, MSc Rhodes, PhD Natal   Emer. Prof.
Fincham, R. J., BA Natal, MA W.Mich., PhD Rhodes   Prof.
Haynes, Richard J., BHortSc Cant., PhD Cant., DSc Lincoln(NZ)   Prof.
Hill, Trevor R., BSc Rhodes, PhD Rhodes   Sr. Lectr.
Hughes, Jeffrey C., BSc Reading, MSc Qu., PhD Reading   Prof.
Maharaj, Brij, BPaed Natal, BA Natal, MA Natal, PhD Natal   Prof.
Mutanga, O., BA Z'bwe., MSc Wageningen, PhD Wageningen   Sr. Lectr.
Rugege, D., BSc NUL, MSc Wageningen, PhD Wageningen   Sr. Lectr.
Savage, Michael J., BSc Natal, PhD Natal   Sr. Prof.
Worth, S. H., BScAgrBus Fresno State, MAgriMgt Natal   Sr. Lectr.
Other Staff: 3 Lectrs.; 1 Adjunct Sr. Lectr.; 2 Hon. Res. Fellows
Research: air pollution; community-based nutrition surveillance; debris deposits in the high Drakensberg; geographical information systems; waterfront developments

Isizulu Studies, School of

Koopman, Adrian, MA Natal, PhD Natal   Prof.; Head*

Maphumulo, Abednego M., BA S.Af., MA S.Af., DLitt&Phil S.Af., BEd   Assoc. Prof.
Other Staff: 3 Lectrs.

Language, Literature and Linguistics, School of

De Meyer, B., MA Antwerp, PhD Cape Town   Assoc. Prof.
Fourie, R., MA Natal, MEd Natal, PhD Witw.   Sr. Lectr.
van der Berg, Dietloff Z., BA Stell., MA Rhodes, PhD Natal   Assoc. Prof.
Wildsmith-Cromarty, Rosemary, BA Witw., MA Essex, PhD Lond.   Prof.
Other Staff: 5 Lectrs.

Law, School of

Tel: (033) 260 5014 Fax: (033) 260 5015
    E-mail: govenderv@nu.ac.za
Carnelley, M., BA Stell., LLB Stell., LLM S.Af., PhD Amst.   Assoc. Prof.
Cowling, Michael G., BA Rhodes, LLB Natal, LLM Camb., MPhil Camb.   Prof.
Farisani, D. M., BProc S.Af., LLB S.Af., LLM S.Af.   Sr. Lectr.
Freedman, W., BCom Witw., LLB Witw., LLM Natal   Prof.
Grant, Brenda, BA Natal, LLB Natal, LLM Natal   Assoc. Prof.
Hoctor, Shannon V., BA Cape Town, LLB Cape Town, LLM Cape Town, DIur Ley.   Prof.
Kidd, Michael A., BCom Natal, LLB Natal, LLM Natal, PhD Natal   Prof.
Mamashela, Motokoa, LLB NUL, LLM Ley., LLM Sheff.   Sr. Lectr.
Pennefather, Rob C., BA Rhodes, BCom Rhodes, LLB Natal   Sr. Lectr.
Sharrock, Robert D., BA Natal, LLB Natal   Prof.
Strode, Ann, BA Natal, LLB Natal, LLM Natal   Sr. Lectr.
Whitear-Nel, Nicci J., BA Natal, LLB Natal   Sr. Lectr.
Williams, Robert C., BA Cape Town, LLB Cape Town, LLM Lond., PhD Macq.   Prof.
Other Staff: 3 Lectrs.
Research: business law; contract law; criminal law and criminal justice; environmental law; gender law

Literary Studies, Media and Creative Arts, School of

Tel: (033) 260 5297 Fax: (033) 260 6213
    E-mail: bowend@nu.ac.za
Armstrong, Juliet, BAFA Natal, MAFA Natal   Assoc. Prof.
Arnott, Jill M., MA Natal, PhD Natal   Sr. Lectr.
Barnes, Hazel S., BA Natal, MA Lanc.   Assoc. Prof.
Baxter, Veronica, BA Natal, MA Natal   Sr. Lectr.
Brown, D., BA Natal, MA Natal, PhD Natal   Prof.
Calder, Ian M. S., BAFA Natal, MAFA Natal   Assoc. Prof.
Clarence-Fincham, Jennifer A., BA Natal, PhD Natal   Assoc. Prof.
Du Toit, J. L., BA Pret., MA Natal, PhD Natal   Sr. Lectr.
King, Terence H., BAFA Witw., MAFA Witw.   Sr. Prof.
Lambert, Michael, BA Natal, MA Natal   Sr. Lectr.
Tennant, Peter M. W., BA Natal, MA Natal, PhD Natal   Assoc. Prof.
van der Hoven, Anton, BA Natal, BA Cape Town, PhD Northwestern   Assoc. Prof.
Woeber, Catherine A., BA Witw., BA Rhodes, MA Cape Town, PhD Witw.   Sr. Lectr.
Other Staff: 8 Lectrs.
Research: coherent writing at tertiary level; early Roman religion; effective communication for teaching and learning; folk culture and ceremony as drama; foundation legends of the Roman state

Mathematical Sciences, School of

Tel: (033) 260 5704 Fax: (033) 260 5648
    E-mail: wraym@nu.ac.za
Ewer, J. P. G., BSc Cape Town, MSc Cape Town, MSc Sus., PhD Z'bwe.   Sr. Lectr.

Henning, Michael A., BSc Natal, MSc Natal, PhD Natal   Prof.
Moori, Jamshid, BSc Meshed, MSc Birm., PhD Birm.   Sr. Prof.
Ng, Siu-Ah, BA Wis., MA Wis., PhD Wis.   Sr. Lectr.
Sibanda, P., BSc Z'bwe., MSc Manc., PhD Manc.   Sr. Lectr.
Swart, Johan, BSc Witw., MSc Witw., PhD S.Af.   Prof.
van den Berg, John E., BSc Natal, MSc Natal, PhD Natal   Assoc. Prof.
Other Staff: 3 Lectrs.; 1 Hon. Sr. Lectr.
Research: combinatorics and graph theory; ecological and financial modelling; finite groups and finite geometrics; ring theory; statistical modelling and optimal design

Philosophy and Ethics, School of

Tel: (033) 260 5180 Fax: (033) 260 5230
    E-mail: lawrencer@nu.ac.za
Beck, Simon M., BA Rhodes, MA Rhodes, PhD Cape Town   Prof.
Prozesky, Martin H., BA Rhodes, MA Oxf., DPhil Rhodesia   Sr. Prof.
Other Staff: 6 Lectrs.

Politics, School of

Piper, L., BA Natal, MPhil Camb., PhD Camb.   Sr. Lectr.
Uzodiki, Nwabufo I., BA Wake Forest, MA S.Carolina, PhD N.Carolina   Sr. Lectr.
Other Staff: 1 Lectr.

Psychology, School of

Tel: (033) 260 5853 Fax: (033) 260 5809
    E-mail: grantham@nu.ac.za
Durrheim, Kevin L., BSc S.Af., BSocSc Cape Town, PhD Cape Town   Prof.
Killian, Beverly J., BSc Cape Town, MSc Cape Town, PhD KwaZulu-Natal   Sr. Lectr.
Lachenicht, Lance G., BA Cape Town, BSc Cape Town, BSc Witw., PhD Witw.   Assoc. Prof.
Lindegger, Graham C., BA S.Af., MA Natal, PhD Natal   Prof.
Mkhize, N. J., BA Natal, MA Iowa, PhD Natal   Sr. Lectr.
O'Neill, Clare M., MSc Cape Town   Sr. Lectr.
van der Riet, M., MA Rhodes   Sr. Lectr.
Wassenaar, Douglas R., BA Natal, MA Natal, PhD Natal   Sr. Lectr.
Other Staff: 6 Lectrs.
Research: adult children of alcoholics; attitudes of nurses towards AIDS and patient care; child molestation; coping mechanisms among trauma counsellors; family support systems and AIDS

Religion and Theology, School of

Tel: (033) 260 5540 Fax: (033) 260 5858
    E-mail: mhladl@nu.ac.za
Balcomb, T., BA S.Af., BSc Natal, BTh S.Af., MA Natal, PhD Natal   Assoc. Prof.
Biyela, M. D., BTh S.Af., MTh Luth.Theol.Sem., Minn., ThD Luth.Theol.Sem., Minn.   Sr. Lectr.
de Gruchy, S. M., MA Cape Town, STM U.T.S.(N.Y.), DTh W.Cape   Assoc. Prof.
Denis, P., Lic Liège, Doctorat Liège   Prof.
Draper, Jonathan A., BA Durh., BD Rhodes, LTh St.Paul's(D.C.), PhD Camb.   Prof.
Farisani, E. B., MTh Natal, PhD Natal   Sr. Lectr.
Haddad, B. G., BASocWk Witw., MA W.Cape, PhD Natal   Sr. Lectr.
Phiri, Isabel A., BEd Malawi, MA Lanc., PhD Cape Town   Prof.; Head*
Ward, Edwina D., MA Calif., PhD Natal   Sr. Lectr.
West, Gerald O., BA Sheff., MA Sheff., PhD Sheff.   Prof.
Other Staff: 8 Lectrs.
Research: contextual theology; gender and theology; growth of the indigenous church in southern Africa; oral historiography; orality, literacy and colonialism

Sociology and Social Studies, School of

Burton, Simon I. R., BSocSc Cape Town, BA Cape Town, MSocSc Natal, PhD Natal   Sr. Lectr.

Lawrence, Ralph, BA Natal, MA Cape Town, MPhil Lond.   Prof.
Manicom, D., BSocSc Natal, MSocSc Natal   Sr. Lectr.
Maxwell, Patrick S., BA Natal, MA Oxf.   Sr. Lectr.
Ngulube, P., MSc Addis Ababa, PhD Natal   Sr. Lectr.
Stilwell, Christine, BA Natal, MIS Natal, PhD Natal   Prof.
Other Staff: 9 Lectrs.

Statistics and Actuarial Science, School of

Mwambi, H. G., BSc Nair., MSc Nair., PhD Nair.   Sr. Lectr.
Njuho, Peter M., BSc Nair., MSc N.Carolina, PhD Kansas   Sr. Lectr.
North, Delia E., MSc Natal, PhD Natal   Head*
Zewotir, T., BSc Asmara, MSc Addis Ababa, PhD Witw.   Sr. Lectr.
Other Staff: 1 Lectr.

SPECIAL CENTRES, ETC

Environment, Agriculture and Development, Centre for

Tel: (033) 260 6223 Fax: (033) 260 6118
    E-mail: robertsk@nu.ac.za
Breen, C. M., BSc Rhodes, MSc Rhodes, PhD Natal   Emer. Prof.
Fincham, R. J., BA Natal, MA W.Mich., PhD Rhodes   Prof.; Dir.*
Rugege, D., BSc NUL, MSc Wageningen, PhD Wageningen   Sr. Lectr.
Other Staff: 1 Lectr.; 1 Adjunct Sr. Lectr.; 2 Hon. Res. Fellows

Science Access, Centre for

3 Lectrs.

WESTVILLE CAMPUS

Audiology, Occupational Therapy and Speech Language Pathology, School of

Van Der Reyden, Dain, BA S.Af.   Head*

Audiology

Govender, C. D., BA Witw., MAudiology Durban-W., MA S.Af.Med.   Sr. Lectr.
Other Staff: 2 Lectrs.

Occupational Therapy

Tel: (031) 260 7310 Fax: (031) 260 2227
Holland, K. E., BOccTher Pret., BOccTher S.Af., MEd   Sr. Lectr.
Joubert, Robin W. E., BA S.Af.   Sr. Lectr.
Linga, T., BOccTher Durban-W., MBA Wales   Sr. Lectr.
Ramlaul, A., BOccTher Durban-W., MMedSc   Sr. Lectr.
Van Der Reyden, Dain, BA S.Af.   Sr. Lectr.

Speech Language Pathology

Pahl, J. A. H., BSc Cape Town, MA Stell.   Sr. Lectr.
Other Staff: 4 Lectrs.

Biochemistry, Genetics, Microbiology and Plant Pathology, School of

Ariatti, M., BSc Lond., DPhil Rhodesia   Sr. Prof.
Gupthar, A., BSc Durban-W., MSc Witw., PhD Witw.   Prof.
Lin, J., BSc Natnl.Tsing Hua, PhD N.Y.State   Assoc. Prof.
Masola, B., PhD Lond.   Sr. Lectr.
Pillay, B., BSc Durban-W., MSc Durban-W., DrRerNat Würzburg   Sr. Prof.
Other Staff: 2 Lectrs.

Chemistry

Tel: (031) 204 4324 Fax: (031) 204 4780
Jonnalagadda, Sreekantha B., BSc And., MSc Vikram, PhD Vikram   Sr. Prof.

Naidoo, S., BSc Durban-W., MSc Durban-W. Sr. Lectr.

Nevines, J. A., BSc Keele, MSc Brist., PhD Natal Sr. Lectr.

Sankar, M., BSc Rhodes, BSc Natal, MSc Natal, PhD Natal Emer. Prof.

Shode, Francis O., MSc Sheff., PhD Sheff., BSc Assoc. Prof.

Other Staff: 2 Lectrs.

Computer Science, School of

Baboolal, S., BSc Durban-W., MSc Durban-W., MSc Dund., PhD Natal Prof.

Goddard, Wayne, BSc Natal, PhD Natal, PhD M.I.T. Hon. Prof.

Meyerowitz, Jane J., MSc Natal Assoc. Prof.

Moodley, D., BSc Durban-W., BSc Natal, MSc Natal Sr. Lectr.

Sartori-Angus, Alan G., BSc Kent, PhD Kent Prof.

Tapamo, J. R., BSc Yaounde, MSc Yaounde, PhD Rouen Assoc. Prof.

Other Staff: 9 Lectrs.

Environmental Sciences, School of

Bob, U., BPaed Durban-W., BA S.Af., MA W.Virginia, PhD W.Virginia Assoc. Prof.

Moodley, V., BA Durban-W., MA Durban-W., PhD Durban-W. Sr. Lectr.

Other Staff: 4 Lectrs.

Mathematical Sciences, School of

Baboolal, D., BSc Durban-W., MSc Oxf., DPhil Oxf. Sr. Prof.

Pillay, P., BSc Durban-W., MSc Durban-W., PhD Durban-W. Sr. Lectr.

Pillay, P., BSc Durban-W., MSc Chic., PhD Witw. Prof.

Singh, P., BSc Durban-W., MSc Durban-W., PhD Natal Sr. Lectr.

Xu, H. K., BSc Zhejiang, MSc Zhejiang, PhD Xi'an Jiaotong Sr. Prof.

Other Staff: 5 Lectrs.

Physics

Tel: (031) 204 4663 Fax: (031) 204 4780

Govender, K., BEng Durban-W., MSc(Eng) Natal, PhD Natal Sr. Lectr.

Naidoo, Krishna, BSc S.Af., MSc S.Af., PhD S.Af. Sr. Lectr.

Ogulu, A., BSc Sund., MSc Sur., PhD Rivers SUST Prof.

Oyoko, H. O., BSc Nair., MSc F.Dickinson, PhD Maine(USA) Sr. Lectr.

Pillay, S. R., BPaed Durban-W., BSc Durban-W., MSc Durban-W., PhD Durban-W. Assoc. Prof.

Other Staff: 3 Lectrs.

Physiotherapy

Tel: (031) 360 3241

Gounden, Poobalan, MPhysiotherapy Durban-W., PhD S.Af.Med. Prof.

Puckree, Thayananthee, BSc(Physio) Durban-W., MEd S.Af., PhD N.Y.State Assoc. Prof.; Head*

Other Staff: 8 Lectrs.

Statistics and Actuarial Sciences, School of

Dale, Andrew I., MSc Cape Town, PhD Virginia Polytech. Prof.

Jordens, Olav, BSc Natal, PhD Natal Sr. Lectr.

Matthews, Glenda B., MSc Pret., PhD Pret. Sr. Lectr.

Moolman, W. Henri, BCom Stell., MCom Natal, DCom Durban-W. Sr. Lectr.

Murray, Michael, MSc Natal, PhD Natal Assoc. Prof.

North, Delia E., MSc Natal, PhD Natal Sr. Lectr.

O'Hara, John G., BSc Ulster, MSc Belf., PhD Witw. Sr. Lectr.

Other Staff: 3 Lectrs.

SPECIAL CENTRES, ETC

Science Access, Centre for

2 Lectrs.
Vacant Posts: Dir.*

[Information supplied by the institution as at 11 October 2006, and edited by the ACU]

UNIVERSITY OF LIMPOPO

Founded 1959

Member of the Association of Commonwealth Universities

Postal Address: Turfloop Campus, Private Bag X1106, Sovenga, 0727 South Africa
Telephone: (015) 268 2121 **Fax:** (015) 267 0154
URL: http://www.unorth.ac.za/

VICE-CHANCELLOR AND PRINCIPAL*—Mokgalong, Prof. Mahlo, PhD
INTERIM DEPUTY VICE-CHANCELLOR AND PRINCIPAL, MEDUNSA CAMPUS—Dyasi, Andile
INTERIM DEPUTY VICE-CHANCELLOR AND PRINCIPAL, TURFLOOP CAMPUS—Franks, Prof. Peter

NELSON MANDELA METROPOLITAN UNIVERSITY

Founded 2005

Member of the Association of Commonwealth Universities

Postal Address: PO Box 77000, Port Elizabeth, 6031 South Africa
Telephone: (041) 504 1111 **Fax:** (041) 504 2574 **E-mail:** info@nmmu.ac.za
URL: http://www.nmmu.ac.za

VICE-CHANCELLOR AND CHIEF EXECUTIVE*—Swartz, Prof. Derrick, BA *W.Cape*, MA *Essex*, PhD *Essex*
DEPUTY VICE-CHANCELLOR (ACADEMIC)—Van Loggerenberg, Prof. Christo, BJuris *P.Elizabeth*, LLB *P.Elizabeth*, DJuris *Ley.*
DEPUTY VICE-CHANCELLOR (RESEARCH, TECHNOLOGY AND PLANNING)—Jeenah, Prof. Mohammed, BSc *Lond.*, MPhil *CNAA*, MBA *S.Af.*, PhD *Natal*
EXECUTIVE DIRECTOR, STUDENT AFFAIRS—Soga, Thoft
EXECUTIVE DIRECTOR, FINANCE—Scheepers, Marius
REGISTRAR‡—Grimbeek, Hugo, MA *S.Af.*, BA

GENERAL INFORMATION

History. The university was founded on 1 January 2005 as a result of the merger between Port Elizabeth Technikon, the University of Port Elizabeth and the Port Elizabeth Campus of Vista University.

The main campus is located in the city of Port Elizabeth, Eastern Cape province, on the southeastern coast of South Africa. Two campuses are located in George in the Southern Cape.

Admission to first degree courses (see also South African Introduction). The standard requirement for admission to a degree programme is the certificate issued by the Matriculation Board of Higher Education South Africa, or an exemption certificate issued by the board.

First Degrees (see also South African Directory to Subjects of Study) (* = with honours). BA, BA*, BAdmin, BA(HumanMovementScience), BA(HumanMovementScience)*, BA(SW), BA(YouthWork), BBdgA(Arch), BCom, BCom*, BCom(Ed), BCom(MercatusMinoris), BCom(Rationum), BCur, BCur(IetA), BEd, BHMS, BMus, BMus(Ed), BPharm, BPsych, BSc, BSc*, BSc(ConstrEcons), BSc(ConstrStudies), BSocSc, LLB.

Honours degree courses extend over at least two semesters.

Length of course. Full-time: BA, BA(HumanMovementScience), BA(YouthWork), BAdmin, BBdgA(Arch), BCom, BCur(IetA), BHMS, BPsych, BSc, BSc(ConstrEcons), BSc(ConstrStudies), BSocSc: 3 years; BA(HumanMovementScience)*, BA(SW), BA*, BCom(Ed), BCom(MercatusMinoris), BCom(Rationum), BCom*, BCur, BEd, BMus, BMus(Ed), BPharm, BSc*, LLB: 4 years.

Higher Degrees (see also South African Directory to Subjects of Study) (* = with honours).

Master's. BArch, BSc(ConstrMan), BSc(ConstrMan)*, LLM, LLM(LabourLaw), LLM(Tax), LLM(TourismLaw), MA, MA(ClinPsych), MA(CounsPsych), MA(Health&WelfareManagement), MArch, MA(SW), MCom, MCom(Tax), MCur, MEd, MEd(EdPsych), MMus, MPA, MPharm, MPhil, MSc, MSc(ConstrMan), MSc(QS), MTech.

Admission. Applicants for admission to BArch and BSc(ConstrMan) must normally hold and appropriate first degree; master's: appropriate first degree with honours.

Minimum 1 year, or 2 years for coursework programmes.

Length of course. Full-time: BSc(ConstrMan), LLM, LLM(LabourLaw), LLM(Tax), LLM(TourismLaw), MA, MA(Health&WelfareManagement), MA(SW),

MArch, MCom, MCom(Tax), MCur, MEd, MPharm, MPhil, MSc, MSc(ConstrMan), MSc(QS): 1 year; BArch, BSc(ConstrMan)*, MA(ClinPsych), MA(CounsPsych), MMus: 2 years; MPA: 3 years.

Doctoral. DArch, DCom, DCur, DEd, DLitt, DMus, DPhil, DSc, DTech, LLD, PhD.

Length of course. Full-time: DSc: 1 year; DArch, DCom, DCur, DEd, DLitt, DMus, DPhil, LLD, PhD: 2 years.

Statistics. Staff (2007): 1424 (524 academic, 900 non-academic). Students (2005–2006): total 21,800.

FACULTIES/SCHOOLS

Arts
Tel: (041) 504 2187 *Fax:* (041) 504 2827
E-mail: gail.ehbel@nmmu.ac.za
Dean: Mayekiso, Prof. Thokozile, BA *Fort Hare*, MA *Fort Hare*, DPhil *F.U.Berlin*

Business and Economic Sciences
Tel: (041) 504 3892 *Fax:* (041) 504 9741
E-mail: reinette.strydom@nmmu.ac.za
Dean: Dorfling, Prof. Niekie J., BCom *P.Elizabeth*, BEd *P.Elizabeth*, MBL *S.Af.*, PhD *Stell.*

Education
Tel: (041) 504 2953 *Fax:* (041) 504 2822
E-mail: ridaa.salie@nmmu.ac.za
Dean: Naidoo, Prof. Ana, BPaed *Durban-W.*, BEd *S.Af.*, MEd *Rhodes*, PhD *Aalborg*

Engineering, the Built Environment and Information Technology
Tel: (041) 504 3238 *Fax:* (041) 504 9447
E-mail: rene.vosloo@nmmu.ac.za
Dean: de Jager, Prof. Henk, DTech *S.Af.*, BA
Faculty Officer (North Campus): Jappie, Rushda
Faculty Officer (South Campus): Szczerbinski, Jackie

Health Sciences
Tel: (041) 504 2815 *Fax:* (041) 504 2854
E-mail: nouwaal.ahmed@nmmu.ac.za
Dean: Naidoo, Prof. Raj, BSc(Pharm) *Rhodes*, BSc *Rhodes*, MSc *Rhodes*, PhD *Rhodes*
Faculty Officer: Ahmed, Nouwaal

Law
Tel: (041) 504 2190 *Fax:* (041) 504 2818
E-mail: marieta.fourie@nmmu.ac.za
Dean: Delport, Prof. Henk, BA *Pret.*, LLD *Pret.*
Faculty Officer: Fourie, Marieta

Science
Tel: (041) 504 2873 *Fax:* (041) 504 2369
E-mail: olivia.barclay@nmmu.ac.za
Dean: Leitch, Prof. Andrew, PhD *P.Elizabeth*
Faculty Officer: Barclay, Olivia

ACADEMIC UNITS

Accounting
Tel: (041) 504 2656 *Fax:* (041) 504 2755
E-mail: frans.prinsloo@nmmu.ac.za
Barnard, Jaco, BCom *P.Elizabeth*   Sr. Lectr.
Diedericks, Suné, BCom *P.Elizabeth*   Sr. Lectr.
Forsyth, Derek, BCom *Natal*   Prof.
Houzet, Neil, BCom *Rhodes*, BCompt *S.Af.*, MCom(Tax) *Pret.*   Sr. Lectr.
Matthee, Peirre, BAcc *Stell.*, BCompt *S.Af.*   Sr. Lectr.
Prinsloo, Frans, MCom *P.Elizabeth*   Assoc. Prof.; Dir.*
Rowlands, Jeff, BCom *Natal*, BEd *Rhodes*, MCom *Rhodes*   Prof.
Shaw, Ronelle, BCom *P.Elizabeth*, BJuris *S.Af.*   Sr. Lectr.
Other Staff: 6 Lectrs.

Agriculture and Game Management
Tel: (041) 504 3527
E-mail: pieter.vanniekerk@nmmu.az.ca
Celliers, Retief, MSc(Agric) *OFS*   Sr. Lectr.
van Niekerk, Pieter du P., BSc(Agric) *Stell.*, DTech *P.Elizabeth Tech.*   Prof.; Head*
Other Staff: 3 Lectrs.

Architectural Technology and Interior Design
Tel: (041) 504 3926
E-mail: johan.pansegrouw@nmmu.ac.za
Pansegrouw, Johan B., BBuild *P.Elizabeth*, BArch *P.Elizabeth*   Sr. Lectr.; Acting Head*
Vosloo, Christo, BArch *Pret.*, MArch *Cape Town*, MBA *Nelson Mandela Met.*   Prof.
Other Staff: 7 Lectrs.

Architecture
Tel: (041) 504 2244
E-mail: stephen.lear@nmmu.ac.za
Flint, J. D., BBuild *P.Elizabeth*, BArch *P.Elizabeth*   Sr. Lectr.
Hardman, C. M., BBuild *P.Elizabeth*, BArch *P.Elizabeth*   Sr. Lectr.
Hardman, T. J., BBuild *P.Elizabeth*, BArch *P.Elizabeth*, MArch *P.Elizabeth*   Sr. Lectr.
Herholdt, A. D., BArch *OFS*, MArch *P.Elizabeth*   Assoc. Prof.
Lear, Stephen C., BBuild *P.Elizabeth*, BArch *P.Elizabeth*   Sr. Lectr.; Head*
McLachlan, G., BBuild *P.Elizabeth*, BArch *P.Elizabeth*, MSc(TRP)   Assoc. Prof.
Palframan, A. G., BBuild *P.Elizabeth*, BArch *P.Elizabeth*, MArch *Gothenburg*   Sr. Lectr.
Rushmere, J. W., BArch *Cape Town*   Assoc. Prof.
Varghese, B. P., BArch *Kerala*, MIndDes   Sr. Lectr.
Other Staff: 7 Lectrs.

Art and Design

Introductory Studies

Tel: (041) 504 3255 Fax: mary.duker@nmmu.ac.za
Duker, G. Mary A., MTech P.Elizabeth   Acting Head*
Hansford, Jonty   Principal Lectr.
Other Staff: 3 Lectrs.

Biochemistry and Microbiology

Tel: (041) 504 2441
    E-mail: ryno.naude@nmmu.ac.za
Naudé, Ryno, PhD P.Elizabeth   Prof.; Head*
Oosthuizen, Vaughan, PhD P.Elizabeth   Sr. Lectr.
Roux, Saartjie, MSc Potchef., DMedSci Pret.   Sr. Lectr.
Somai, Benesh, MSc Durban-W., PhD S.Carolina   Sr. Lectr.
Other Staff: 2 Lectrs.

Biomedical Technology and Radiography

Tel: (041) 504 3354
    E-mail: nanette.smith@nmmu.ac.za
Smith, Nanette, PhD P.Elizabeth   Sr. Lectr.; Head*

Botany

Tel: (041) 504 2397
    E-mail: eileen.campbell@nmmu.ac.za
Adams, J. B., PhD P.Elizabeth   Prof.
Campbell, Eileen E., BSc Stell., PhD P.Elizabeth   Prof.; Head*
Cowling, R. M., PhD Cape Town   Res. Prof.
du Preez, D. R., BSc Witw., PhD P.Elizabeth   Sr. Lectr.; Dir., Sch. of Environmental Scis.
Other Staff: 1 Lectr.

Building and Quantity Surveying

Tel: (041) 504 3201
    E-mail: fanie.buys@nmmu.ac.za
Bekker, J. P., MSc P.Elizabeth   Sr. Lectr.
Buys, Fanie, BBdgA P.Elizabeth, MSc(QS) P.Elizabeth, PhD P.Elizabeth   Prof.; Head*
Vosloo, D., BSc(QS) P.Elizabeth, MSc P.Elizabeth   Dir., Sch. of Built Environment
Other Staff: 2 Lectrs.

Business and Social Sciences, School of

Tel: (044) 801 5561
Doubell, Marianne, BA(Ed) P.Elizabeth, BA P.Elizabeth, MA Natal, MA Durban-W.   Dir.*

Business Management

Tel: (041) 504 2201
    E-mail: johan.bosch@nmmu.ac.za
Arnolds, Cecil, BEcon W.Cape, MCom Vista, DCom P.Elizabeth   Assoc. Prof.
Bosch, Johan, BCom Stell., DBA Stell.   Prof.; Head*
Gray, B., BCom P.Elizabeth   Sr. Lectr.
Mazibuko, Noxolo, BA Vista, MCom Vista, PhD Vista   Assoc. Prof.
Smith, E. E., MCom Vista, PhD Vista   Principal Lectr.
Struwig, F. W., MCom PhD   Prof.
Tait, Madele, DCom P.Elizabeth   Assoc. Prof.
Venter, Elmarie, BCom Free State, MCom Stell., MBA Ghent, DCom P.Elizabeth   Sr. Lectr.
Other Staff: 2 Lectrs.

Chemistry

Tel: (041) 504 3281
    E-mail: cedric.mccleland@nmmu.ac.za
Du Preez, Jan, DSc Stell.   Extraordinary Prof., Inorganic Chemistry
Ferg, E., MSc Witw., DTech P.Elizabeth Tech.   Sr. Lectr., Physical Chemistry
Gerber, S., MSc Stell.   Sr. Lectr.
Gerber, Thomas, BSc P.Elizabeth, MSc OFS, PhD S.Af.   Prof., Inorganic Chemistry
Imrie, Christopher, BSc Leeds, PhD Strath.   Sr. Lectr., Organic Chemistry
Loyson, Peter, BSc S.Af., PhD P.Elizabeth   Prof., Physical Chemistry

McCleland, Cedric, PhD P.Elizabeth   Prof., Organic Chemistry; Head*
Rohwer, Hans, MSc Stell., PhD P.Elizabeth   Prof., Analytical Chemistry
Van Brecht, B., PhD P.Elizabeth   Sr. Lectr., Analytical Chemistry
Venter, R. D., BSc Rhodes   Sr. Lectr., Organic Chemistry
Woolard, C. D., PhD Cape Town   Sr. Lectr., Physical and Polymer Chemistry
Zeelie, Ben, PhD P.Elizabeth   Prof.; Dir., Sch. of Biomolecular and Chemical Scis.
Other Staff: 9 Lectrs.

Computer Science and Information Systems

Tel: (041) 504 2247
    E-mail: janet.wesson@nmmu.ac.za
Barnard, L., BCom P.Elizabeth   Sr. Lectr.
Calitz, A. P., BCom P.Elizabeth, PhD P.Elizabeth   Prof.
Cilliers, C., MSc P.Elizabeth   Sr. Lectr.
Wesson, Janet L., MCom P.Elizabeth, PhD P.Elizabeth   Prof.; Head*
Other Staff: 13 Lectrs.; 2 Asst. Lectrs.; 3 Jr. Lectrs.; 1 Res. Assoc.

Construction Management

Tel: (041) 504 2790
    E-mail: john.smallwood@nmmu.ac.za
Botha, Brink, BTech P.Elizabeth Tech., MSc P.Elizabeth   Sr. Lectr.
Malherbe, A. C., BSc(Eng) Witw.   Sr. Lectr.
Smallwood, John, PhD P.Elizabeth   Prof.; Head*
Steenkamp, Ivan, BSc Stell., BCom P.Elizabeth   Assoc. Prof., Environment and Services

Design, Applied

Tel: (041) 504 3254
    E-mail: bruce.cable@nmmu.ac.za
Cadle, Bruce   Head*
Esterhuizen, Gina, BA(FA) Stell.   Head, Fashion Design
Other Staff: 10 Lectrs.

Development Studies

Tel: (041) 504 2729
    E-mail: richard.haines@nmmu.ac.za
Haines, Richard, MA Natal, PhD Lond.   Prof.; Head*

Economics

Tel: (041) 504 2638
    E-mail: stephen.hosking@nmmu.ac.za
Du Preez, Mario, DCom P.Elizabeth   Sr. Lectr.
Hosking, Stephen, MCom Rhodes, PhD Rhodes   Prof.; Head*
Le Roux, P., DCom OFS   Prof.
Parsons, Raymond, BCom Cape Town, BA Cape Town, Hon. DCom P.Elizabeth   Hon. Prof.
Wait, Charles, DCom Stell.   Hon. Prof.
Woolard, Ingrid, BCom S.Af., PhD Cape Town   Sr. Lectr.
Other Staff: 5 Lectrs.

Education

Tel: (041) 504 2371
    E-mail: ana.naidoo@nmmu.ac.za
Bean, Patrick, BCom(Ed) P.Elizabeth, BEd P.Elizabeth, MEd Rhodes   Prof.; Head, School for Professnl. Teacher Educn.
Blignaut, Sylvan, BA W.Cape, DEd Nelson Mandela Met.   Sr. Lectr.
Botha, Nonnie, BA Pret., DEd   Prof.; Dir., Sch. of Specialised Studies in Educn.
Delport, Alette, BMus(Ed) Stell., BMus Pret., MMus Pret., DEd P.Elizabeth   Sr. Lectr.; Head, Advanced Studies in Educn.
Griesel, Issa   Head, Dept. of Further Educn. and Training
Holdermann, William, BA Rhodes, BEd Rhodes, MA(Ed) Lond., PhD Lond.   Prof.
Illsley, Jeff, BEd Rhodes, BSc Rhodes, MEd Rhodes, PhD Rhodes   Head, Dept. of Sci., Maths. and Technol. Educn.
Mcfarlane, Johann, BEd Stell., MA Stell., PhD Rhodes   Sr. Lectr.

Meiring, Leslie, BSc Rhodes, MEd Rhodes   Head, Dept. of Intermediate Phase Studies
Olivier, M. A. J., BA P.Elizabeth, DEd P.Elizabeth   Prof.
Toni, Noluthando, BPrimEd P.Elizabeth, BEd P.Elizabeth, MEd P.Elizabeth   Head, Dept. of Foundation Phase Studies
Van Rensburg, Susan, BA P.Elizabeth, DEd P.Elizabeth, STD P.Elizabeth   Assoc. Prof.
Other Staff: 1 Lectr.

Engineering, Civil

Tel: (041) 504 3309
    E-mail: debbie.hogan@nmmu.ac.za
Butlion, P. H.   Principal Lectr.
Danoher, Vincent, BSc(Eng) Cape Town, MPA P.Elizabeth
Hogan-Illenberger, Debbie, BSc(Eng) Natal   Head*
Nagel, A.   Sr. Lectr.
Pansegrouw, Pieter, BSc Stell., BEng Stell., MEng Stell., DSc(Agric) Pret.   Principal Lectr.
Other Staff: 2 Lectrs.

Engineering, Electrical

Tel: (041) 504 3208
    E-mail: alistair.scott@nmmu.ac.za
Adlam, Frank, MTech P.Elizabeth Tech.   Sr. Lectr.
Clark, Ian, BSc MSc   Sr. Lectr.
Grebe, S.   Principal Lectr.
Harris, R. T., MTech P.Elizabeth Tech.   Sr. Lectr.
Millroy, P.   Sr. Lectr.
Roberts, A. G.   Principal Lectr.
Schoombie, Sarel
Scott, Alistair G., BCom S.Af., BEd P.Elizabeth   Head*
Other Staff: 6 Lectrs.

Engineering, Industrial

Tel: (041) 504 9124
    E-mail: ann.lourens@nmmu.ac.za
Lourens, Ann S., MBA P.Elizabeth Tech.   Head*
Other Staff: 4 Lectrs.

Engineering, Mechanical

Tel: (041) 504 3644
    E-mail: karl.dupreez@nmmu.ac.za
Du Preez, Karl H.   Head*
Maczek, J.   Principal Lectr.
Phillips, R. L.   Sr. Lectr.
Other Staff: 8 Lectrs.

Environmental Health and Social Development Professions

Tel: (041) 504 3348
    E-mail: charles.qoto@nmmu.ac.za
Maarschalk, Henri, MA P.Elizabeth, PhD P.Elizabeth
Mashologu-Kuse, T. T., BA(SocialWork) Fort Hare, MSW Denver, PhD Witw.   Assoc. Prof.
Pretorius, Blanche, MA(SW) P.Elizabeth, DPhil P.Elizabeth, BSocSc
Qoto, Charles, BCom Vista, BTech P.Elizabeth Tech., MPH S.Af.Med.   Sr. Lectr.; Head*
Van der Westhuizen, H. W. J., MSc   Sr. Lectr.

Financial Accounting

Tel: (041) 504 2351 Fax: (041) 504 2755
    E-mail: amanda.singleton@nmmu.ac.za
Brettenny, Alex, BCom Cape Town, MAcc Natal   Prof.
Joubert, David, BCom Stell., MCom P.Elizabeth   Sr. Lectr.
Singleton, Amanda, BCom P.Elizabeth, MCom P.Elizabeth   Assoc. Prof.; Head*

Geoscience

Tel: (041) 504 2325 Fax: (041) 504 2355
    E-mail: vincent.kakembo@nmmu.ac.za
Booth, Peter, MSc Rhodes, PhD Cape Town   Sr. Lectr.
De Wit, A., MA Free State, DPhil P.Elizabeth   Principal Lectr.
Kakembo, Vincent, MSc Rhodes   Prof.; Head*
Shone, Russel, BSc Rhodes, PhD P.Elizabeth   Assoc. Prof.
Siyongwana, Pakama, PhD P.Elizabeth   Sr. Lectr.

Webb, N. L., BEd *P.Elizabeth*, MA *Rhodes*, MPhil *Stell.*, PhD *P.Elizabeth* Principal Lectr.
Other Staff: 2 Lectrs.

Human Movement Science and Sport Management

Tel: (041) 504 2497
E-mail: rosa.durandt@nmmu.ac.za
Du Randt, Rosa, BSc(PE) *Stell.*, MPhysEd *Stell.*, PhD *Stell.* Prof.; Head*
Du Toit, D. E., MA *P.Elizabeth*, DPhil *P.Elizabeth* Sr. Lectr.
Oosthuizen, V., BAEd *P.Elizabeth*, BA *P.Elizabeth* Sr. Lectr.
Other Staff: 4 Lectrs.

Human Resource Management

Tel: (041) 504 3750
E-mail: paul.poisat@nmmu.ac.za
Poisat, Paul, BCom *P.Elizabeth*, MTech *P.Elizabeth Tech.* Principal Lectr.; Head*

Industrial and Organisational Psychology

Tel: (041) 504 2364
E-mail: robin.snelgar@nmmu.ac.za
Rousseau, G. G. Prof.
Snelgar, Robin J., MA *Rhodes*, PhD *Rhodes* Sr. Lectr.; Head*
Other Staff: 3 Lectrs.

Industrial Psychology and Human Resources

Tel: (041) 504 3831
E-mail: dave.berry@nmmu.ac.za
Berry, Dave M., BA *P.Elizabeth*, MA *Stell.*, DTech *P.Elizabeth Tech.* Prof.; Dir.*
Mey, M. R., BCom *P.Elizabeth*, BCom *S.Af.*, DTech *P.Elizabeth Tech.* Sr. Lectr.
Ngalo, O. T., BTech *P.Elizabeth*, MPhil *P.Elizabeth*, BTech Sr. Lectr.
Poisat, Paul, BCom *P.Elizabeth*, MTech *P.Elizabeth Tech.* Principal Lectr.
Werner, A., BA(Comm) *Potchef.*, MA *Potchef.*, DTech *P.Elizabeth Tech.* Sr. Lectr.

Informatics, Applied

Tel: (041) 504 9100
E-mail: mark.thomson@nmmu.ac.za
Evlambiou, A. Sr. Lectr.
Pottas, Dalenca, BSc *Potchef.*, PhD *Rand Afrikaans*
Thomson, Mark E., MTech *P.Elizabeth Tech.* Sr. Lectr.; Head*
Other Staff: 6 Lectrs.

Information Technology

Tel: (041) 504 3604
E-mail: karen.church@nmmu.ac.za
Botha, R., BSc *P.Elizabeth*, PhD *Rand Afrikaans* Prof.
Church, Karen A., MSc *P.Elizabeth* Principal Lectr.; Head*
Harmse, R. G., BCom *P.Elizabeth*, MTech *P.Elizabeth Tech.* Sr. Lectr.
Schröder, C. H., BSc *P.Elizabeth*, MTech *P.Elizabeth Tech.* Sr. Lectr.
Van de Haar, H., BSc *P.Elizabeth* Sr. Lectr.
Von Solms, R., BSc *P.Elizabeth*, BSc *S.Af.*, PhD *Rand Afrikaans* Prof.
Other Staff: 12 Lectrs.

Journalism and Public Relations

Tel: (041) 504 3330
E-mail: bianca.wright@nmmu.ac.za
Jordaan, D. J., BA(Ed) *P.Elizabeth*, BA *P.Elizabeth*, MA *P.Elizabeth*, DLitt *P.Elizabeth* Prof.
Olivier, G., MA *DPhil STD* Prof.
Wright, Bianca M., BA *P.Elizabeth*, BA *P.Elizabeth*, MPhil *Stell.* Lectr.; Head*
Other Staff: 9 Lectrs.

Language and Literature

Tel: (041) 504 2223
E-mail: helize.vanvuuren@nmmu.ac.za
Goddard, K., MA *Rhodes*, PhD *Rhodes* Sr. Lectr.; Acting Head, English

Jooste, G., BA *OFS*, BA *S.Af.*, MA *Natal*, DLitt *OFS* Prof.
Kwatsha, L. L., BA *Fort Hare*, BA *Fort Hare*, BCom *P.Elizabeth*, MA *Vista*, PhD *Vista* Sr. Lectr.
Maqagi, S., BA *Fort Hare*, MA *Wis.* Sr. Lectr.
Mkonto, B., BA *Fort Hare*, BTh *S.Af.*, BA *Fort Hare*, MA *Fort Hare*, DLitt&Phil *S.Af.* Prof.
Otto, A., BA BA MA *DLitt* Assoc. Prof.
Smith, N., MA *Natal*, PhD *Natal* Sr. Lectr.
Somniso, M., MA *P.Elizabeth*, DLitt *P.Elizabeth* Sr. Lectr.
Thomas, H., BA *S.Af.*, MA *P.Elizabeth*, DLitt *P.Elizabeth* Sr. Lectr.
van Vuuren, Helize E., BA *Stell.*, BA *Stell.*, MA *Stell.*, MA *Natal*, Drs *Utrecht*, DLitt *Stell.* Prof.; Head*
Wozniak, J., BA *Pret.*, BA *P.Elizabeth*, MA *Cape Town*, PhD *Cape Town* Sr. Lectr., German
Other Staff: 10 Lectrs.

Language Studies, Applied

Tel: (041) 504 3266
E-mail: ernst.kotze@nmmu.ac.za
Ayliff, Diana, BA *Rhodes*, BA *P.Elizabeth*, MA *Stell.*, DLitt *P.Elizabeth* Sr. Lectr.
Israel, H. F., BA *Durban-W.*, BEd *S.Af.*, MSEd *Baylor*, EdD *Baylor*
Kotzé, Ernst, BA *Cape Town*, PhD *Witw.* Prof.; Head*
Potgieter, S., BA *Cape Town*, BA *Rhodes*, MEd *Rhodes* Sr. Lectr.
Other Staff: 12 Lectrs.

Law

Tel: (041) 504 2309 Fax: (041) 504 2818
E-mail: marieta.fourie@nmmu.ac.za
Badenhorst, P., BLC *Pret.*, LLM *Witw.*, LLM *Yale*, LLD *Pret.* Prof.
Bohler-Muller, N., BJuris *P.Elizabeth*, LLM *P.Elizabeth* Prof.
Delport, Henk, BA *Pret.*, LLD *Pret.* Prof.; Head, Dept. of Mercantile Law; Head*
Fouché, M., BJuris *Free State*, LLB *Free State* Prof.
Govindjee, A., BA *Rhodes*, LLB *Rhodes*, LLM *P.Elizabeth*, LLD *Nelson Mandela Met.* Sr. Lectr.
Knoetze, E., BJuris *P.Elizabeth*, LLM *P.Elizabeth*, LLD *W.Cape* Assoc. Prof.
Le Roux, L., BJuris *P.Elizabeth*, LLB *P.Elizabeth*, LLM *S.Af.* Sr. Lectr.
Marx, Frans, BCom *Stell.*, BJuris *P.Elizabeth*, LLD *P.Elizabeth* Prof.; Head, Dept. of Private Law
Mukheibir, A., BA *S.Af.*, BMus *P.Elizabeth*, BJuris *P.Elizabeth*, LLB *P.Elizabeth* Sr. Lectr.
Müller, Karen, BA *Rhodes*, LLB *Rhodes*, PhD *Rhodes* Prof.; Head, Dept. of Criminal and Procedural Law
Newton, D. A., BA *W.Cape*, LLB *W.Cape*, LLM *Georgetown* Sr. Lectr.
Olivier, M., BJuris *P.Elizabeth*, LLM *P.Elizabeth* Sr. Lectr.
Price, T., BA *Rhodes*, LLB *Rhodes*, LLM *Stell.* Sr. Lectr.
Tait, A. M., BJuris *P.Elizabeth*, LLB *Stell.*, MBL *S.Af.*, LLM *P.Elizabeth* Assoc. Prof.
Van Der Berg, E., BJuris *P.Elizabeth*, LLB *P.Elizabeth* Sr. Lectr.
Van Der Walt, G., BJuris *P.Elizabeth*, LLB *P.Elizabeth*, LLM *S.Af.*
Van Der Walt, J. A., BJuris *P.Elizabeth*, BA *P.Elizabeth*, LLB *S.Af.* Assoc. Prof.
van Loggerenberg, Christo, BJuris *P.Elizabeth*, LLB *P.Elizabeth*, DJuris *Ley.* Prof.
Vrancken, Patrick, LenDroit *Brussels*, LLD *Cape Town* Prof.; Head, Dept. of Internat., Constitutional and Human Rights Law
Other Staff: 7 Lectrs.

Logistics

Tel: (041) 504 3817
E-mail: gideon.horn@nmmu.ac.za
Horn, Gideon, BCom *P.Elizabeth*, DCom *P.Elizabeth* Prof.; Head*

Management Accounting

Tel: (041) 504 3833 Fax: (041) 504 2755
E-mail: pieter.pelle@nmmu.ac.za
Pelle, Pieter, BCompt *S.Af.*, MCom *P.Elizabeth* Prof.; Head*
Rosenberg, David, BCom *Rhodes* Assoc. Prof.
Other Staff: 2 Lectrs.

Management and Entrepreneurship

Tel: (041) 504 3832
E-mail: norman.kemp@nmmu.ac.za
Kemp, Norman, BSocSc *Rhodes*, BSocSc *S.Af.*, MA *S.Af.*, PhD *Vista* Prof.; Head*

Marketing Management

Tel: (041) 504 3816
E-mail: john.burger@nmmu.ac.za
Burger, John, DTech Head*

Mathematics and Applied Mathematics

Tel: (041) 504 2310
E-mail: werner.olivier@nmmu.ac.za
Ackermann, M., MSc *P.Elizabeth* Sr. Lectr.
Booth, G. L., BSc *Cape Town*, MSc *Rhodes*, PhD *Stell.* Prof.
Boshoff, H. H., BSc *Stell.*, BSc *P.Elizabeth*, BEd *P.Elizabeth*, MSc *P.Elizabeth*, DEd *P.Elizabeth* Sr. Lectr.
Coetzee, J. J., MSc *P.Elizabeth* Sr. Lectr.
France-Jackson, H., MSc *Warsaw*, PhD *Warsaw* Prof.
Gonsalves, J. W., PhD *P.Elizabeth* Assoc. Prof.
Groenewald, N. J., MSc *P.Elizabeth*, PhD *Rhodes* Prof.
Olivier, W. A., PhD *P.Elizabeth* Prof.; Head*
Other Staff: 12 Lectrs.

MBA Unit

Tel: (041) 504 3737
E-mail: kobus.jonker@nmmu.ac.za
Jonker, Kobus, BCom *S.Af.*, MBL *S.Af.*, DCom *Pret.* Prof.; Head*

Mechatronics

Tel: (041) 504 3289
E-mail: igor.gorlach@nmmu.ac.za
Gordon, Mark, BScMechEng *Natal*, MScMechEng *Durban-W.* Sr. Lectr.
Gorlach, Igor A., BSc(MechEng) *Witw.*, MSc(IndEng) *Witw.*, PhD *Potchef.* Prof.; Head*
Other Staff: 1 Lectr.

Music

Tel: (041) 504 2250
E-mail: erik.albertyn@nmmu.ac.za
Albertyn, Erik, MMus *P.Elizabeth*, PhD *Witw.* Assoc. Prof.; Head*
Du Plooy, D., BMus *Witw.*, MMus *Pret.* Sr. Lectr., Piano
Hanken, K. Hon. Prof.
Potgieter, Zelda, BMus *Stell.*, DPhil *P.Elizabeth* Sr. Lectr., Musicology
Van Zyl, Lionel Sr. Lectr., Voice
Other Staff: 11 Lectrs.

Natural Resource Management, School of

Tel: (044) 801 5019
E-mail: jos.louw@nmmu.ac.za
Louw, Jos, PhD *Witw.* Dir.*

Nursing Science

Tel: (041) 504 2112
E-mail: dalena.vanrooyen@nmmu.ac.za
Carlson, Sheree, BCur(IetA) *P.Elizabeth*, MCur *P.Elizabeth*, DCur *P.Elizabeth* Sr. Lectr.
Strümpher, J., BCur *Pret.*, BCur(IetA) *Pret.*, BCur *P.Elizabeth*, MCur(CN) *P.Elizabeth*, DCur *P.Elizabeth* Prof.
Van Rooyen, Dalena, BCur *P.Elizabeth*, BACur *P.Elizabeth*, MCur *P.Elizabeth*, DCur *P.Elizabeth* Prof.; Head*
Wannenburg, Iona, MCur *Pret.*, DCur *P.Elizabeth* Prof.
Other Staff: 8 Lectrs.

Pharmacy

Tel: (041) 504 2128
    E-mail: pieter.milne@nmmu.ac.za
Boschmans, S.-A., MSc P.Elizabeth   Sr. Lectr.
Milne, Pieter J., BPharm Potchef., MSc Potchef.,
    DSc Potchef.   Prof.; Head*
Potgieter, Ben, MSc(Pharm) Potchef., DSc Potchef.
    Prof.
Truter, Ilse, BPharm P.Elizabeth, MSc P.Elizabeth,
    DSc Potchef., DCom P.Elizabeth   Assoc. Prof.
Other Staff: 6 Lectrs.

Physics

Tel: (041) 504 2579
    E-mail: japie.engelbrecht@nmmu.ac.za
Botha, J. R., PhD P.Elizabeth   Assoc. Prof.
Engelbrecht, Japie A. A., PhD P.Elizabeth   Prof.;
    Head*
Leitch, Andrew, PhD P.Elizabeth   Prof.
Mulder, R., BSc Pret., MSc P.Elizabeth   Sr. Lectr.
Neethling, Jan, PhD P.Elizabeth   Prof.
Raubenheimer, Deon, MSc P.Elizabeth, PhD
    P.Elizabeth   Prof.
Van Dyk, E. E., PhD P.Elizabeth   Sr. Lectr.
Venter, A., MSc P.Elizabeth, PhD P.Elizabeth
    Assoc. Prof.
Other Staff: 4 Lectrs.

Political and Governmental Studies

Tel: (041) 504 1139
Masango, R. S., DPhil   Sr. Lectr.
Raga, K., BA P.Elizabeth, MTech P.Elizabeth Tech.,
    DPhil Durban-W.   Head*
Siwisa, B., MA Oxf., DPhil Oxf.   Sr. Lectr.
Snodgrass, Lynn, MA P.Elizabeth, DPhil Nelson
    Mandela Met.   Sr. Lectr.
Taylor, J. D., BSocSc Cape Town, MTech
    P.Elizabeth Tech., DPhil Durban-W.   Sr. Lectr.
Wissink, Henry, PhD Stell.   Prof.
Other Staff: 9 Lectrs.

Psychology

Tel: (041) 504 2354
    E-mail: mark.watson@nmmu.ac.za
Fouché, J. P., MSocSc OFS, DPhil P.Elizabeth   Sr.
    Lectr.
Hoelsen, C. N., MA P.Elizabeth, DPhil P.Elizabeth
    Prof.
Howcroft, J. C., MA P.Elizabeth, PhD Vista   Prof.
Nqweni, Zinzi   Sr. Lectr.
Watson, Mark B., DPhil P.Elizabeth   Prof.;
    Head*
Other Staff: 4 Lectrs.

Public Relations and Communications Studies

Tel: (041) 504 3330
    E-mail: hercules.fourie@nmmu.ac.za
Ferreira, Elizabeth, BA OFS, MA Rand Afrikaans,
    DLitt Rand Afrikaans   Principal Lectr.
Fourie, Hercules S., BBibl S.Af., MBL S.Af., MA
    OFS   Head*
Mak'Ochieng, Murej, CandMag Bergen,
    CandPolit Bergen, PhD Natal   Sr. Lectr.
Other Staff: 3 Lectrs.

Sociology and Anthropology

Tel: (041) 504 2175 Fax:
    peter.cunningham@nmmu.ac.za
Bezuidenhout, Frans, BA P.Elizabeth, BA Pret.,
    DPhil P.Elizabeth   Assoc. Prof.
Cunningham, Peter, MA P.Elizabeth, DPhil
    P.Elizabeth   Prof.; Head*
Herbst, R. O., MA Stell., DPhil Stell.   Sr. Lectr.
Pauw, Henk, BA Pret., MA P.Elizabeth, DPhil
    P.Elizabeth   Assoc. Prof.
Petrus, Theodore, BA P.Elizabeth, MA Lond.
Pretorius, D., BA S.Af., MA P.Elizabeth, PhD
    Warw.   Prof.
Terblanche, Otto, BA Stell., MA P.Elizabeth, PhD
    P.Elizabeth   Assoc. Prof.
Other Staff: 3 Lectrs.

Statistics

Tel: (041) 504 2730
    E-mail: igor.litvine@nmmu.ac.za
Barnard, J. J., MCom P.Elizabeth, MBL S.Af.   Sr.
    Lectr.
Hugo, J., MSc OFS   Sr. Lectr.
Litvine, Igor, MSc Kiev, PhD Kiev   Prof.; Head*
Pietersen, J. J., PhD Pret.   Sr. Lectr.
Venter, Danie, BSc P.Elizabeth   Sr. Lectr.
Other Staff: 6 Lectrs.

Studio Arts

Tel: (041) 504 3494
    E-mail: david.jones@nmmu.ac.za
Cull, Cleone, MFA Rhodes   Prof.
Frankenfeld, E.   Sr. Lectr., Printmaking
Jones, David A., MTech(FA) P.Elizabeth Tech.
    Sr. Lectr.; Head*
Other Staff: 3 Lectrs.

Textile Science

E-mail: lhunter@nmmu.ac.za
Hunter, Lawrence, BSc Cape Town, MSc
    P.Elizabeth, PhD P.Elizabeth   Prof.; Head*
Other Staff: 2 Lectrs.

Tourism

Tel: (041) 504 3766
    E-mail: hugh.bartis@nmmu.ac.za
Bartis, Hugh, BA Fort Hare, BSc Fort Hare, MA
    Ohio   Head*

Zoology

Tel: (041) 504 2690
    E-mail: tris.wooldridge@nmmu.ac.za
Baird, Dan, BSc Pret., PhD Stell.   Prof.
Kerley, Graham, MSc Pret., PhD P.Elizabeth
    Prof.
Rossouw, Gideon, MSc Stell., PhD P.Elizabeth
    Sr. Lectr.
Winter, Paul, PhD P.Elizabeth   Sr. Lectr.
Wooldridge, Tris, BSc Rhodes, PhD P.Elizabeth
    Prof.; Head*
Other Staff: 1 Lectr.

SPECIAL CENTRES, ETC

Automotive Components, Technology Station in

Els-Botes, Annelise, MTech P.Elizabeth Tech.
    Research Manager
Hattingh, Danie, PhD Plym.   Prof.; Technology
    Manager*

Cisco Academy Training Centre (CATC)

Rheeder, R., BTech P.Elizabeth Tech.   Head*

Dragon Technologies Unit

Wessels, J., BTech Nelson Mandela Met.   Head*

Education Research, Technology and Innovation Unit in

Tel: (041) 504 4206
    E-mail: paul.webb@nmmu.ac.za
Webb, Paul, BSc Rhodes, BEd Rhodes, BSc
    P.Elizabeth, MEd Rhodes, MSc P.Elizabeth, STD
    Cape Town, PhD Curtin   Prof.; Dir.*

Information and Communication Technology Advancement, Institute for (IICTA)

Von Solms, R., BSc P.Elizabeth, BSc S.Af., PhD
    Rand Afrikaans   Prof.; Head*

Spatial Technologies Unit

Olivier, A.   Head*

[Information supplied by the institution as at 9 October 2007, and edited by the ACU]

NORTH-WEST UNIVERSITY

Founded 2004

Member of the Association of Commonwealth Universities

Postal Address: Private Bag X6001, Potchefstroom, 2520 South Africa
Telephone: (018) 299 4901 **Fax:** (018) 299 4910 **E-mail:** enquiries@nwu.ac.za
URL: http://www.nwu.ac.za

VICE-CHANCELLOR*—Eloff, Theuns, BJur *Potchef.*, ThB *Potchef.*, ThM *Potchef.*, ThD *Potchef.*
VICE-PRINCIPAL—Takalo, Ngoato M., BA *North(S.Af.)*, BEd *North(S.Af.)*, MA *Boston*, EdM *Col.*, EdD *Col.*
REGISTRAR‡—Van der Walt, Prof. Chris F. C., BJur&Art *Potchef.*, LLB *Rand Afrikaans*, LLD *S.Af.*
CAMPUS RECTOR (MAFIKENG)—Kgwadi, Prof. Ntate D., BSc *Bophut.*, MSc *Ball*, MPhil *North(S.Af.)*, PhD *Potchef.*
CAMPUS RECTOR (POTCHEFSTROOM)—Combrink, Prof. Annette L., BA *Potchef.*, MA *Potchef.*, DLitt *Potchef.*
CAMPUS RECTOR (VAAL TRIANGLE)—Prinsloo, Prof. Piet J. J., DLitt *Potchef.*
EXECUTIVE DIRECTOR, FINANCE AND FACILITIES—Rost, Prof. I. J., MComm *Potchef.*
EXECUTIVE DIRECTOR, RESEARCH AND INNOVATION—Van Niekerk, Prof. F., BSc *Potchef.*, MSc *Potchef.*, DSc *Potchef.*
EXECUTIVE DIRECTOR, CORPORATE AFFAIRS AND RELATIONS—Mmope, P., BA *S.Af.*
EXECUTIVE DIRECTOR, HUMAN CAPITAL DEVELOPMENT—Mothobi, V. L., BA *Rand Afrikaans*

GENERAL INFORMATION

History. The university was originally founded in 1869 as a theological seminary for Christian teaching. In 1919 it became a university college and in 1951 achieved independent university status under the name of Potchefstroom University for Christian Higher Education. In 1966 a satellite campus in the Vaal Triangle was established. On 1 January 2004, the university merged with University of North-West to form the newly reconstituted North-West University.

The university has three campuses: Potchefstroom; at Hoffman Street, Potchefstroom; Vaal Triangle at Vanderbijlpark on the Vaal River; and Mafikeng at Mmabatho, 300km south of Johannesburg.

Admission to first degree courses (see also South African Introduction). Applicants must have full matriculation exemption and also comply with the specific requirements set out by individual faculties.

First Degrees (see also South African Directory to Subjects of Study) (* = with honours). BA*, BA, BA(Comm)*, BA(CommStuds), BA(CTSD), BAdmin*, BA(Ed), BAetSc(Planning), BA(GraphicDesign), BAgric(Ed), BA(IDS), BA(IKS), BA(IndComms), BA(LangTech), BA(LRD), BA(PEC), BA(SocialWork)*, BA(SocialWork), BA(SW), BBA, BComm, BComm*, BComm(BusinessCommunication), BComm(Ed), BCrim*, BCur(Education), BEd, BEd*, BIng, BJur*, BLegum, BMus, BN, BNSc, BPharm, BPrimEd, BProc, BPsych, BSc*, BSc(Agric)*, BSc(ConsumerSc), BSc(Dietetics), BSc(Ed), BSc(IndustSc), BSc(InfoTech), BSocSc, BSocSc*, BTh*, LLB, ThB.
Length of course. Full-time: BA, BA(Comm)*, BA(CTSD), BA(IDS), BA(SocialWork)*, BA*, BAdmin*, BBA, BComm, BComm*, BCrim*, BCur(Education), BJur*, BN, BSc(IndustSc), BSc(InfoTech), BSc*, BSocSc, BTh*, ThB: 3 years; BA(CommStuds), BA(Ed), BA(GraphicDesign), BA(IKS), BA(IndComms), BA(LangTech), BA(LRD), BA(PEC), BA(SocialWork), BA(SW), BAetSc(Planning), BAgric(Ed), BComm(BusinessCommunication), BComm(Ed), BEd, BEd*, BIng, BLegum, BMus, BNSc, BPharm, BPrimEd, BProc, BPsych, BSc(Agric)*, BSc(ConsumerSc), BSc(Dietetics), BSc(Ed), BSocSc*, LLB: 4 years. *Part-time:* BBA, ThB: 3 years; BA, BA(Comm)*, BA(CTSD), BA(IDS), BA(SocialWork)*, BA*, BAdmin*, BComm, BComm*, BCrim*, BCur(Education), BJur*, BN, BSc(IndustSc), BSc(InfoTech), BSc*, BSocSc, BTh*: 4 years; BA(CommStuds), BA(Ed), BA(GraphicDesign), BA(IKS), BA(IndComms), BA(LangTech), BA(LRD), BA(PEC), BA(SocialWork), BA(SW), BAetSc(Planning), BAgric(Ed),

BComm(BusinessCommunication), BComm(Ed), BEd, BEd*, BIng, BLegum, BMus, BNSc, BPharm, BPrimEd, BProc, BPsych, BSc(Agric)*, BSc(ConsumerSc), BSc(Dietetics), BSc(Ed), BSocSc*, LLB: 5 years. *By distance learning:* BA(Comm)*, BA(CTSD), BA(IDS), BAdmin*, BBA, BComm*, BCrim*, BN, BSocSc, ThB: 3 years; BSc*: 3–5 years; BA, BA(SocialWork)*, BA*, BComm, BCur(Education), BJur*, BSc(IndustSc), BSc(InfoTech), BTh*: 5 years; BA(CommStuds), BA(Ed), BA(GraphicDesign), BA(IKS), BA(IndComms), BA(LangTech), BA(LRD), BA(PEC), BA(SocialWork), BA(SW), BAetSc(Planning), BAgric(Ed), BComm(BusinessCommunication), BComm(Ed), BEd, BEd*, BIng, BLegum, BMus, BNSc, BPharm, BPrimEd, BProc, BPsych, BSc(Agric)*, BSc(ConsumerSc), BSc(Dietetics), BSc(Ed), BSocSc*, LLB: 6 years.

Higher Degrees (see also South African Directory to Subjects of Study).
Master's. LLM, MA, MA(Comm), MAdmin, MArt&Sc, MA(SocialWork), MBA, MBibl, MCom, MComm, MConsumerScience, MCuratonis, MDevMan, MDiv, MEd, MIng, MLegum, MMus, MPA, MPharm, MPhil, MSc, MSc(ARST), MSocSc, MSocSc(CP), MSocSc(SW), ThM.
Admission. Applicants must hold a first degree.
Length of course. Full-time: LLM, MA(Comm), MA(SocialWork), MAdmin, MArt&Sc, MBibl, MCom, MComm, MConsumerScience, MCuratonis, MDevMan, MDiv, MEd, MIng, MLegum, MMus, MPharm, MPhil, MSc, MSocSc, ThM: 1 year; MA: 1–2 years; MBA, MPA, MSc(ARST), MSocSc(CP), MSocSc(SW): 2 years. *Part-time:* LLM, MA, MA(Comm), MA(SocialWork), MAdmin, MArt&Sc, MBibl, MCom, MComm, MConsumerScience, MCuratonis, MDevMan, MDiv, MEd, MIng, MLegum, MMus, MPharm, MPhil, MSc, MSocSc, ThM: 1–3 years; MPA, MSc(ARST), MSocSc(CP), MSocSc(SW): 2–3 years; MBA: 2–4 years. *By distance learning:* LLM, MA, MA(Comm), MA(SocialWork), MAdmin, MArt&Sc, MBibl, MCom, MComm, MConsumerScience, MCuratonis, MDevMan, MDiv, MEd, MIng, MLegum, MMus, MPharm, MPhil, MSc, MSocSc, ThM: 1–3 years; MPA, MSc(ARST), MSocSc(CP), MSocSc(SW): 2–3 years; MBA: 2–4 years.
Doctoral. DEd, DLegum, DLit, DMus, DSc, PhD, ThD.
Admission. Applicants must hold a master's degree.
Length of course. Full-time: DEd, DLegum, DLit, DMus, DSc, PhD, ThD: 2 years. *Part-time:* DLegum, DMus, ThD: 2–5 years; DEd, DLit, DSc, PhD: 2–6 years. *By distance learning:* DLegum, DMus, ThD: 2–5 years; DEd, DLit, DSc, PhD: 2–6 years.

Language of Instruction. Mafeking: English only. Potchefstroom: Afrikaans and English; tests/exams may be submitted in either language. Vanderbijpark: Afrikaans and English.

Libraries. Volumes: 643,685. Periodicals subscribed to: 5855. Other holdings: 17,281 other materials. Special collections: Carney Africana; Postma.

Academic Awards (2006–2007). 9572 awards ranging in value from R500 to R45,000.

Income (2006–2007). Total, R1,272,204,155.

Statistics. Staff (2006–2007): 4359 (1165 academic, 3194 non-academic). Students (2006–2007): full-time 20,052 (8538 men, 11,514 women); part-time 32,226 (10,795 men, 21,431 women); international 6832 (2990 men, 3842 women); distance education/external 12,147 (8479 men, 3668 women); undergraduate 48,662 (17,435 men, 31,227 women); master's 2582 (1320 men, 1262 women); doctoral 790 (448 men, 342 women).

FACULTIES/SCHOOLS

Agriculture, Science and Technology (Mafikeng)
Tel: (018) 389 2050 Fax: (018) 389 2052
E-mail: 20561873@nwu.ac.za
Dean: McPherson, Prof. M., BSc *NUL*, MSc *Lanc.*, DSc *Lanc.*
Secretary: Gaebee, N.

Arts (Potchefstroom)
Tel: (018) 299 1481 Fax: (018) 299 4085
E-mail: 10184309@mwu.ac.za
Dean: Swanepoel, Prof. J., BA *Potchef.*, BPhil *Potchef.*, MA *Potchef.*, DLitt *Potchef.*
Secretary: Pretorius, N.

Commerce and Administration (Mafikeng)
Tel: (018) 389 2066 Fax: (018) 389 2090
E-mail: 21108188@nwu.ac.za
Dean: Khumalo, Prof. R., BSc *CNAA*, MA *S.Af.*, PhD *S.Af.*
Secretary: Mokaila, J.

Economics and Management Science (Potchefstroom)
Tel: (018) 299 1340 Fax: (018) 299 1339
E-mail: 10056459@nwu.ac.za
Dean: Eloff, Prof. T., BComm *Potchef.*, BPhil *Potchef.*, MComm *Potchef.*, DComm *Potchef.*
Secretary: Kotze, N.

Education (Mafikeng)

Tel: (018) 389 2364 Fax: (018) 389 2038
E-mail: 20914156@nwu.ac.za
Dean: Gericke, D. H., BA OFS, BEd OFS, MEd
OFS, DEd OFS
Secretary: Mothibi, M. E.

Educational Sciences (Potchefstroom)

Tel: (018) 299 1610 Fax: (018) 299 1755
E-mail: 20918135@nwu.ac.za
Dean: Engelbrecht, Prof. P., BEd Pret., MEd
Pret., PhD Pret.
Secretary: Labuschagne, F. J. C.

Engineering (Potchefstroom)

Tel: (018) 299 1533 Fax: (018) 299 1529
E-mail: 10183906@nwu.ac.za
Dean: Fick, Prof. J. I. J., MScEng Pret., PhD
Cran.
Secretary: Steenkamp, W.

Health Sciences (Potchefstroom)

Tel: (018) 299 2224 Fax: (018) 299 4014
E-mail: 21014639@nwu.ac.za
Dean: Viljoen, Prof. M., BA Pret., MCur Pret.,
DSocSc Free State
Secretary: Du Toit, A.

Human and Social Sciences (Mafikeng)

Tel: (018) 389 2505 Fax: (018) 389 2504
E-mail: 16423445@nwu.ac.za
Dean: Thiba, T., BEd S.Af., MA Durh., PhD
Mich.State
Secretary: Dimpe, P.

Law (Mafikeng)

Tel: (018) 389 2060 Fax: (018) 389 2028
E-mail: 17139066@nwu.ac.za
Dean: Mahao, N. L., BA NUL, LLB NUL, LLM
Edin., LLD W.Cape
Secretary: Tow, A.

Law (Potchefstroom)

Tel: (018) 299 1340 Fax: (018) 299 1339
E-mail: 10057358@nwu.ac.za
Dean: Venter, Prof. F., BJur&Comm Potchef.,
LLB Potchef., LLD Potchef.
Secretary: Du Plooy, E.

Natural Sciences (Potchefstroom)

Tel: (018) 299 2301 Fax: (018) 299 2421
E-mail: 10062092@nwu.ac.za
Dean: Pienaar, Prof. J. J., BSc Potchef., MSc
Potchef., DSc Potchef.
Secretary: Venter, H.

Theology (Potchefstroom)

Tel: (018) 299 1844 Fax: (018) 294 8952
E-mail: 10055878@nwu.ac.za
Dean: Du Plooy, Prof. A. le R., BA Potchef., ThB
Potchef., ThM Potchef., ThD Potchef.
Secretary: Brazer, E.

Vaal Triangle

Tel: (016) 910 3111 Fax: (016) 910 3116
E-mail: 10184546@nwu.ac.za
Dean: Theron, Prof. A. M. C., BA OFS, BEd
OFS, MEd OFS, DEd S.Af.
Secretary: Ward, R.

ACADEMIC UNITS

MAFIKENG CAMPUS

Tel: (018) 389 2111 Fax: (018) 392 5775
E-mail: 10829547@nwu.ac.za

Accounting

Tel: (018) 389 2111 Fax: (018) 392 5575
E-mail: 16119509@nwu.ac.za
Bootha, A. A. I., BCom S.Af. Prof.
Meko, K. M., BCom Bophut., MBA Col. Sr.
Lectr.; Head*
Vacant Posts: 1 Prof.; 1 Lectr.

Adult Education

Tel: (018) 389 2111 Fax: (018) 392 5575
E-mail: 16184262@nwu.ac.za
Sefotlhelo, S. M., BEd Wales, BA(Ed) Potchef.,
MEd Potchef. Head*
Other Staff: 1 Lectr.
Vacant Posts: 2 Sr. Lectrs.; 1 Lectr.

Afrikaans

Tel: (018) 389 2111 Fax: (018) 392 5575
E-mail: 20560737@nwu.ac.za
Buscop, J., BA S.Af., BA Pret., MA Pret., DLitt
Bophut. Assoc. Prof.; Head*

Agricultural Economics and Extension

Tel: (018) 389 2111 Fax: (018) 392 5575
E-mail: 16495306@nwu.ac.za
Antwi, M. A., MScAgric Pret., MBA Potchef.
Lectr.; Head*
Vacant Posts: 1 Prof.; 1 Sr. Lectr.

Animal Health

Tel: (018) 389 2111 Fax: (018) 392 5575
E-mail: 16450442@nwu.ac.za
Bakunzi, R. F., BVMCh S.Af.Med., MSc Guelph,
DSc S.Af.Med. Assoc. Prof.
Mbewe, M., BSc Texas, PhD Camb. Prof.
Mlilo, T., BVMCh Z'bwe. Sr. Lectr.
Molefe, M. S. M., BVMCh S.Af.Med. Sr. Lectr.;
Head*
Ndou, R. V., BVMCh S.Af.Med. Sr. Lectr.
Vester, R. S., BVMCh Pret. Sr. Lectr.
Vacant Posts: 1 Sr. Lectr.

Animal Sciences

Tel: (018) 389 2111 Fax: (018) 392 5575
E-mail: 20561768@nwu.ac.za
Mulugeta, S. D., PhD Free State, BSc MSc Sr.
Lectr.; Head*
Other Staff: 2 Lectrs.
Vacant Posts: 2 Profs.; 1 Sr. Lectr.; 2 Lectrs.

Biological Sciences

Tel: (018) 389 2111 Fax: (018) 392 5575
E-mail: 16284283@nwu.ac.za
Gopane, R. E., BSc North(S.Af.), BSc Potchef., MSc
Bophut. Sr. Lectr.; Head*
Malan, P. W., BScEd Free State, MSc Free State,
PhD Free State Sr. Lectr.
Phalatse, S. D., BSc North(S.Af.), MSc North(S.Af.)
Sr. Lectr.
Other Staff: 1 Lectr.
Vacant Posts: 1 Lectr.

Chemistry

Tel: (018) 389 2111 Fax: (018) 392 5575
E-mail: 20560389@nwu.ac.za
Drummond, H. P., BSc Cape Town, MEd Witw.,
PhD North(S.Af.) Sr. Lectr.
Isabirye, D. A., BSc Mak., PhD HK Sr. Lectr.;
Head*
Marvey, B., BSc North(S.Af.), MSc Howard, PhD
Potchef. Sr. Lectr.
Other Staff: 3 Lectrs.
Vacant Posts: 1 Prof.

Communication

Tel: (018) 389 2111 Fax: (018) 392 5575
E-mail: 17156505@nwu.ac.za
Garside, D. Prof.; Head*
Other Staff: 4 Lectrs.
Vacant Posts: 1 Sr. Lectr.; 1 Lectr.

Crop Science

Tel: (018) 389 2111 Fax: (018) 392 5575
E-mail: 16009800@nwu.ac.za
Funnah, S. M., BScAgric S.Leone, MSc Flor., PhD
Malaya Prof.; Head*
Kasirivu, J. B. K., BScAgric Mak., MScAgric Ib.
Sr. Lectr.
Materechera, S. A., BScAgric Malawi, MSc McG.,
PhD Adel. Prof.
Other Staff: 1 Lectr.

Development Studies

Tel: (018) 389 2111 Fax: (018) 392 5575
E-mail: 16227298@nwu.ac.za
Chikulo, B. C., BA Zambia, MA(Econ) Manc.,
PhD Manc. Prof.
Mpolokeng, P. G., BAEd Bophut., BSocSc Bophut.,
MA Rand Afrikaans Lectr.; Head*

Economics

Tel: (018) 389 2111 Fax: (018) 392 5575
E-mail: 16230868@nwu.ac.za
Daw, O. D., BPA Bophut., MSc Witw. Lectr.;
Head*
Lembede, F. P., BCom Zululand, BCom S.Af., MA
Sr. Lectr.
Louw, S. J. H., BCom Free State, BCom Pret., MA
Penn. Sr. Lectr.
Other Staff: 1 Lectr.
Vacant Posts: 2 Lectrs.

Educational Planning and Administration

Tel: (018) 389 2111 Fax: (018) 392 5575
E-mail: 11211172@nwu.ac.za
Legotlo, M. W., BA S.Af., BEd Bophut., MEd
Bophut., PhD Potchef. Assoc. Prof.; Head*
Other Staff: 1 Lectr.
Vacant Posts: 1 Sr. Lectr.; 2 Lectrs.

English

Tel: (018) 389 2111 Fax: (018) 392 5575
E-mail: 1614782@nwu.ac.za
Hlatswayo, A., BA Swazi., BA S.Af., MEd Manc.
Sr. Lectr.
Moletsane, J. R., BA(Ed) North(S.Af.), BA S.Af.,
MA Potchef. Lectr.; Head*
Ngwenya, T., PhD Potchef. Sr. Lectr.
Segatlhe, D., BA S.Af., BA North(S.Af.), BA Rhodes,
MA Mich.State Sr. Lectr.
Other Staff: 2 Lectrs.
Vacant Posts: 1 Prof.; 2 Sr. Lectrs.; 3 Lectrs.

Foundations of Education

Tel: (018) 389 2111 Fax: (018) 392 5575
E-mail: 16223926@nwu.ac.za
Assan, T. E. B., BCom Cape Coast, BEd S.Af., MA
Lond., MEd N-W(S.Af.) Sr. Lectr.
Loate, I. M., BAPaed North(S.Af.), BEd
North(S.Af.), MEd Witw., PhD Potchef. Sr.
Lectr.
Sebego, G. M., BA North(S.Af.), BEd Cape Town,
MEd Witw. Sr. Lectr.
Other Staff: 2 Lectrs.

Geography and Environmental Science

Tel: (018) 389 2111 Fax: (018) 392 5575
E-mail: 21229198@nwu.ac.za
Drummond, J. H., MA Glas., MA Witw. Sr.
Lectr.; Head*
Hamandawana, H., PhD Botswana Sr. Lectr.
Other Staff: 3 Lectrs.

History

Tel: (018) 389 2111 Fax: (018) 392 5575
E-mail: 16424522@nwu.ac.za
Boemah, D. L., BPaed Zululand, BA Fort Hare, MA
Ohio Sr. Lectr.
Bottomley, J., BA Natal, MA Natal, PhD Qld.
Assoc. Prof.; Head*
Manyane, Prof. R. M., BEd S.Af., MAEd Lond.,
DEd S.Af. Sr. Lectr.
Mbenga, B. K., BA(Educn) Zambia, MA
York(UK), PhD S.Af. Sr. Lectr.

Information Systems

Tel: (018) 389 2111 Fax: (018) 392 5575
E-mail: 20561830@nwu.ac.za
Mavetera, N., BSc S.Af. Sr. Lectr.
Ncube, P. Z., MSc NUST Bulawayo Sr. Lectr.
Nyakwende, E., MSc T.U.Varna, PhD Nott.
Prof.; Head*
Other Staff: 2 Lectrs.
Vacant Posts: 1 Prof.; 1 Sr. Lectr.; 1 Lectr.

Law (Postgraduate Studies)

Tel: (018) 389 2111 Fax: (018) 392 5575
E-mail: 12294608@nwu.ac.za
Khunou, S. F., BJuris N-W(S.Af.), LLB N-
W(S.Af.), LLM N-W(S.Af.)   Sr. Lectr.
Mbao, M. L. M., LLB Zambia, MPhil Camb., PhD
Camb.   Prof.; Head*
Morei, N. L., BJuris N-W(S.Af.), LLM N-W(S.Af.)
Sr. Lectr.
Ndima, D. D., BJuris Fort Hare, LLB S.Af., LLM
S.Af.   Sr. Lectr.
Other Staff: 1 Lectr.
Vacant Posts: 1 Sr. Lectr.

Law (Undergraduate Studies)

Tel: (018) 389 2111 Fax: (018) 392 5575
E-mail: 16448383@nwu.ac.za
Iya, P. F., BA Yale, LLB Mak., PhD Warw.   Prof.
Rossouw, G. L., BA Cape Town, LLB Cape Town,
LLM Cape Town   Sr. Lectr.; Head*
Other Staff: 8 Lectrs.
Vacant Posts: 1 Prof.

Management

Tel: (018) 389 2111 Fax: (018) 392 5575
E-mail: 16432681@nwu.ac.za
Godji, L. J. K., BA Cape Coast, MBA Ghana   Sr.
Lectr.; Head*
Kadama, K. F. R., BSc N-W(S.Af.), MBA N-
W(S.Af.)   Assoc. Prof.
Pelser, A. S., BCom Potchef., MCom Venda   Sr.
Lectr.
Other Staff: 4 Lectrs.

Mathematical Sciences

Tel: (018) 389 2111 Fax: (018) 392 5575
E-mail: 16448588@nwu.ac.za
Kambule, M. T., BSc S.Af., BSc North(S.Af.), MSc
S.Af., PhD Mass.   Assoc. Prof.
Khalique, C. M., BSc Punjab, MSc Islam., MSc
Dund., MPhil Islam., PhD Dund.   Assoc. Prof.
Seretlo, T. T., BSc Fort Hare, MSc Fort Hare   Sr.
Lectr.; Head*
Other Staff: 1 Lectr.
Vacant Posts: 1 Assoc. Prof.; 1 Sr. Lectr.; 2
Lectrs.

Nursing Science

Tel: (018) 389 2111 Fax: (018) 392 5575
E-mail: 16453565@nwu.ac.za
Mokwena, B. A., BACur S.Af.Med., MA Potchef.
Sr. Lectr.
Rakhudu, M. A., BA S.Af., MCur Potchef.
Lectr.; Head*
Other Staff: 7 Lectrs.
Vacant Posts: 1 Assoc. Prof.

Physics

Tel: (018) 389 2111 Fax: (018) 392 5575
E-mail: 20559895@nwu.ac.za
Makgamathe, S., BSc North(S.Af.), BSc Potchef.,
MSc Potchef.   Sr. Lectr.
Perera, A. K., BSc Ceyl., PhD Birm.   Sr. Lectr.;
Head*
Taole, S. H., MSc Wales, PhD Ott.   Prof.
Other Staff: 3 Lectrs.
Vacant Posts: 1 Assoc. Prof.

Political Studies and International Relations

Tel: (018) 389 2111 Fax: (018) 392 5575
E-mail: 16321138@nwu.ac.za
Leepile, B. W., BA North(S.Af.)   Lectr.; Head*
Other Staff: 1 Lectr.
Vacant Posts: 1 Lectr.

Population Training and Research Unit

Tel: (018) 389 2111 Fax: (018) 392 5575
E-mail: 16450418@nwu.ac.za
Kalule-Sabiti, I., BA Mak.   Prof.; Head*
Kibet, M. K., BSc Nair., MSc Nair., PhD Z'bwe.
Sr. Lectr.
Other Staff: 2 Lectrs.
Vacant Posts: 1 Assoc. Prof.

Professional Studies and Internship

Tel: (018) 389 2111 Fax: (018) 392 5575
E-mail: 16518802@nwu.ac.za
Kwayisi, F. N., BSc Ghana, BEd Fort Hare, MEd
Rhodes, PhD North(S.Af.)   Sr. Lectr.; Head*
Mwenesongole, E., BA N.Y., MA Col.   Sr. Lectr.
Vacant Posts: 1 Prof.; 1 Sr. Lectr.; 1 Lectr.

Psychology

Tel: (018) 389 2111 Fax: (018) 392 5575
E-mail: 20560877@nwu.ac.za
Direko, L. P., BA N-W(S.Af.), BA Zululand,
MSocSc N-W(S.Af.)   Sr. Lectr.
Niemand, S. W., BA Stell.   Sr. Lectr.; Head*
Other Staff: 3 Lectrs.
Vacant Posts: 1 Lectr.

Psychology, Industrial

Tel: (018) 389 2111 Fax: (018) 392 5575
E-mail: 16453603@nwu.ac.za
Louw, E. J., BCom S.Af., MCom Free State, DPhil
Free State   Assoc. Prof.; Head*
Mokgele, K. R. F., BA Fort Hare, MBA N-
W(S.Af.)   Sr. Lectr.
Other Staff: 4 Lectrs.

Public Administration

Tel: (018) 389 2111 Fax: (018) 392 5575
E-mail: 16182804@nwu.ac.za
Masilo, L. M., BPA Bophut., BAdmin S.Af., MPA
N.Arizona   Sr. Lectr.; Head*
Tabane, I. A., BA S.Af., MA Pret.   Sr. Lectr.
Other Staff: 2 Lectrs.

Science Foundation

Tel: (018) 389 2111 Fax: (018) 392 5575
E-mail: 16189868@nwu.ac.za
Tsatsimpe, K. W., BCom North(S.Af.), MCom
North(S.Af.)   Lectr.; Head*
Other Staff: 2 Lectrs.
Vacant Posts: 3 Lectrs.

Setswana

Tel: (018) 389 2111 Fax: (018) 392 5575
E-mail: 11191473@nwu.ac.za
Motsilanyane, V. K., BA North(S.Af.)   Lectr.;
Head*
Pooe, E. E., BA(Ed) Bophut., BA Bophut., BA
Witw., MA Potchef.   Sr. Lectr.
Rakgokong, M. P., BA North(S.Af.), MA Potchef.
Sr. Lectr.
Other Staff: 3 Lectrs.

Social Work

Tel: (018) 389 2111 Fax: (018) 392 5575
E-mail: 20560540@nwu.ac.za
Moloto, G. M., BA North(S.Af.), MA Calif.   Sr.
Lectr.
Phetlho-Thekisho, N. G., BA S.Af., BA Fort Hare,
MA Rhodes   Sr. Lectr.
Qalinge, L. I., BA Fort Hare, MA Nebraska, PhD
N-W(S.Af.)   Assoc. Prof.
Ratefane, T. A., BASocWk Bophut., MSocSc Cape
Town   Sr. Lectr.
Setlalentoa, B. M. P., BA North(S.Af.), MASocSc
Rand Afrikaans   Sr. Lectr.; Head*
Other Staff: 2 Lectrs.

Sociology

Tel: (018) 389 2111 Fax: (018) 392 5575
E-mail: 16479726@nwu.ac.za
Kaya, H. O., BA Dar., MA Dar., PhD F.U.Berlin
Assoc. Prof.
Monyatsi, G. A., BA Fort Hare, MA Fort Hare
Lectr.; Head*
Ncala, N., BA Pret., MA Dal., PhD S.Af.   Sr.
Lectr.
Odhav, K. P., MA Essex   Sr. Lectr.
Other Staff: 1 Lectr.

Statistics

Tel: (018) 389 2111 Fax: (018) 392 5575
E-mail: daniel.metsileng@nwu.ac.za
Maruma, N. N., BSc N-W(S.Af.)   Sr. Lectr.

Metsileng, N. N., BCom N-W(S.Af.), MCom N-
W(S.Af.)   Lectr.; Head*
Mosweu, R. N., BCom N-W(S.Af.)   Sr. Lectr.
Sedupane, M. S., BSc Cape Town, MCom N-
W(S.Af.)   Sr. Lectr.
Serumaga Zake, P. A. E., BSc Mak., MSc Rhodes,
PhD Potchef.   Assoc. Prof.
Other Staff: 1 Lectr.

Teaching and Curriculum

Tel: (018) 389 2111 Fax: (018) 392 5575
E-mail: 16954726@nwu.ac.za
Lumadi, M. W., BA S.Af., BEd Witw., MEd Rand
Afrikaans, DEd S.Af.   Sr. Lectr.; Head*
Monobe, R. J., BA North(S.Af.), BEd North(S.Af.),
MEd Rand Afrikaans, DEd Rand Afrikaans   Sr.
Lectr.
Mwenesongole, M. W. A., MA Col., DEd Zambia
Prof.
Other Staff: 1 Lectr.
Vacant Posts: 1 Prof.

SPECIAL CENTRES, ETC

Applied Radiation Science and Technology, Centre for

Tel: (018) 389 2111 Fax: (018) 392 5575
E-mail: 16954181@nwu.ac.za
Van der Linde, H. J., BSc Free State, MSc Free
State, PhD S.Af.   Manager*

Community Law Centre

Tel: (018) 389 2111 Fax: (018) 392 5575
E-mail: 16419987@nwu.ac.za
Bodenstein, J. W., BA Stell., LLB Natal, LLM
Natal   Head*

POTCHEFSTROOM CAMPUS

Tel: (018) 299 1111 Fax: (018) 299 2799
E-mail: 1005597@nwu.ac.za

Accounting Sciences

E-mail: 10056459@nwu.ac.za
Aslett, D., LLB S.Af., LLM S.Af.   Sr. Lectr.
Barnard, R. J. J., BComm Potchef.   Sr. Lectr.
Bibbey, F. J., BComm Potchef., MComm Potchef.
Sr. Lectr.
Buys, P. W., MBA Potchef., PhD Potchef.   Prof.
Coetzee, K., BComm Potchef., BR Potchef.,
MComm Potchef., DCompt S.Af.   Prof.
Eloff, T., BComm Potchef., BPhil Potchef.,
MComm Potchef., DComm Potchef.   Prof.;
Dir.*
Fouche, J. P., BComm Potchef., MComm Potchef.
Assoc. Prof.
Gericke, J. S., BComm Potchef., BR Potchef.,
MCom Rand Afrikaans   Prof.
Jordaan, K., MCom Rand Afrikaans   Prof.
Kilian, P., BComm Potchef., LLB Potchef.   Sr.
Lectr.
Lourens, P. A., BComm Potchef., MComm
Potchef., DComm Potchef.   Sr. Lectr.
Meiring, C. E., BA Rand Afrikaans, BCom Potchef.,
MA North(S.Af.)   Sr. Lectr.
Nel, A. L., BComm Potchef.   Assoc. Prof.
Rademeyer, A., BCom Rand Afrikaans   Prof.
Schutte, D. P., BComm S.Af.   Sr. Lectr.
Stoop, A. A., BComm Potchef., BRek Potchef.,
MComm Potchef.   Assoc. Prof.
Van der Merwe, D. C., MComm Potchef.   Sr.
Lectr.
Van Niekerk, R. J., BComm Potchef., BRek
Potchef.   Assoc. Prof.
Van Romburgh, J. D., BComm Free State   Sr.
Lectr.
Van Rooyen, S., BComm Potchef.   Assoc. Prof.
Van Zyl, A. P., BCom Free State, LLB Free State
Sr. Lectr.
Visser, S. S., BComm Potchef., MComm Potchef.,
DComm Potchef.   Prof.
Weyers, M. M., BCom Potchef.   Sr. Lectr.
Other Staff: 3 Lectrs.
Vacant Posts: 1 Prof.

Art History

E-mail: 10058451@nwu.ac.za
Botha, J. R., BA *Potchef.*, BEd *Potchef.*, MA
Potchef., DEd *Potchef.* Assoc. Prof.; Head*
Other Staff: 2 Lectrs.

Bible Studies and Bible Languages

E-mail: 10059296@nwu.ac.za
Dircksen, M. R., BA *Pret.*, MA *Rand Afrikaans*,
PhD *Rand Afrikaans* Assoc. Prof.
Fick, P. H., BTh *Potchef.* Sr. Lectr.
Janse van Rensburg, J. J., BA *Potchef.*, ThB
Potchef., MA *Potchef.*, ThM *Potchef.*, ThD *Potchef.*
Prof.; Dir.*
Jordaan, G. J. C., BA *Potchef.*, BTh *Potchef.*, ThD
Potchef. Prof.
Jordaan, P. J., DLitt *Rand Afrikaans* Sr. Lectr.
Kruger, P. P., BA *Potchef.*, ThB *Potchef.*, MA
Potchef., ThM *Potchef.*, ThD *Potchef.* Assoc.
Prof.
Lamprecht, A., BA *Free State*, BTh *Free State*, MA
Free State Sr. Lectr.
Viljoen, F. P., BA *Potchef.*, ThB *Potchef.*, MA
Potchef., ThD *Potchef.* Assoc. Prof.
Other Staff: 3 Lectrs.

Biochemistry

E-mail: 11359250@nwu.ac.za
Erasmus, E., BSc *Potchef.*, MSc *Potchef.* Sr. Lectr.
Kotze, H. F., DSc *Free State* Prof.
Mienie, L. J., BSc *Potchef.*, MSc *Potchef.*, DPhil
Potchef. Assoc. Prof.
Pretorius, P. J., BSc *Potchef.*, MSc *Potchef.*, DSc
Potchef. Assoc. Prof.
Van der Westhuizen, F. H., BSc *Potchef.*, MSc
Potchef., PhD *Potchef.* Sr. Lectr.
Van Dijk, A. A., DSc *Potchef.* Assoc. Prof.
Vacant Posts: 1 Assoc. Prof.

Biokinetics, Recreation and Sports Science

E-mail: 10060057@nwu.ac.za
De Ridder, J. H., BA *Potchef.*, MA *Potchef.*, DPhil
Potchef. Prof.
Malan, D. D. J., DSc *Potchef.* Prof.; Dir.*
Vacant Posts: 1 Assoc. Prof.

Adventure and Experience Studies

E-mail: 10057633@nwu.ac.za
Meyer, C. D. P., BA *Free State*, BA *Stell.*, MA
Potchef., PhD *Potchef.* Sr. Lectr.

Biokinetics, Institute for

E-mail: 10068198@nwu.ac.za
Moss, S. J., BSc *Potchef.*, MSc *Potchef.*, PhD *Potchef.*
Sr. Lectr.
Wilders, C. J., BA *Potchef.*, MA *Potchef.*, PhD
Potchef. Assoc. Prof.; Head*

Children Kinetics

E-mail: 10063153@nwu.ac.za
Peens, A., BA *Potchef.*, MA *Potchef.* Sr. Lectr.
Pienaar, A. E., BA *Potchef.*, MA *Potchef.*, PhD
Potchef. Assoc. Prof.; Head*

Botany

E-mail: 10175458@nwu.ac.za
Cilliers, S. S., BSc *Potchef.*, MSc *Potchef.*, PhD
Potchef. Sr. Lectr.
Du Plessis, S., PhD *Free State* Sr. Lectr.
Janse van Vuuren, M. S., PhD *Potchef.* Sr.
Lectr.
Jordaan, A., BSc *North(S.Af.)*, MSc *North(S.Af.)*
Sr. Lectr.
Kellner, K., BSc *Pret.*, MSc *Potchef.*, PhD *Potchef.*
Assoc. Prof.
Maboeta, M. S., DSc *Stell.* Sr. Lectr.
Pieterse, A. J. H., BSc *Potchef.*, MSc *Potchef.*, PhD
Wash. Prof.; Head*
Vacant Posts: 1 Prof.; 1 Sr. Lectr.; 1 Lectr.

Business Mathematics and Informatics

Focus area
E-mail: 10173501@nwu.ac.za
Grobler, J. J., BSc *Potchef.*, MSc *Potchef.*, DMath
Ley. Prof.; Dir.*

Research: computer science/operations research
(decision support systems and mathematical
programming, systems methodologies
(Gabek)); mathematics/statistics (bootstrap
resampling methods and non-parametric
curve, control theory, functional analysis);
risk management and analysis (credit risk,
investment risk, market risk, operational
risk)

Business Mathematics and Informatics Centre

E-mail: 11749318@nwu.ac.za
De Jongh, D. C. J., PhD *Witw.* Prof.
De Jongh, P. J., BComm *Stell.*, MSc *S.Af.*, PhD
Cape Town Prof.; Dir.*
De Waal, D. A., BSc *Potchef.*, MSc *Potchef.*, PhD
Brist. Assoc. Prof.
Other Staff: 2 Lectrs.; 1 Chief Subject Specialist
Vacant Posts: 2 Profs.

Chemistry

E-mail: 10179402@nwu.ac.za
Breedt, E. L. J., BSc *Potchef.*, MSc *Potchef.*, DSc
Potchef. Prof.; Head*
Du Toit, C. J., BSc *Stell.*, BSc *Potchef.*, BEd
Potchef., MSc *Potchef.*, DSc *Potchef.* Assoc.
Prof.
Krieg, H. M., BSc *Stell.*, BSc *Pret.*, MSc *Rutgers*,
PhD *Potchef.* Sr. Lectr.
Kriek, R. J., DSc *Stell.* Sr. Lectr.
Lachman, G., DSc *Potchef.* Sr. Lectr.
Read, C. E., BSc *Potchef.*, MSc *Potchef.*, PhD
Potchef. Sr. Lectr.
Van Sittert, C. G. D. E., PhD *Potchef.* Sr. Lectr.
Viljoen, A. M., BSc *Potchef.*, MSc *Potchef.*, DSc
Potchef. Sr. Lectr.
Vosloo, H. C. M., BSc *Free State*, MSc *Potchef.*,
DPhil *Potchef.* Prof.
Other Staff: 1 Lectr.; 2 Subj. Specialists
Vacant Posts: 1 Assoc. Prof.; 1 Chief Res.
Scientist

Communication Studies

E-mail: 10058192@nwu.ac.za
Fourie, L. M., MA *Potchef.* Sr. Lectr.
Froneman, J. D., BA *Stell.*, MA *Stell.*, PhD *Potchef.*
Assoc. Prof.
Gerber, A. M., BA *Potchef.*, MA *Potchef.*, PhD
Potchef. Assoc. Prof.
Schutte, P. J., BA *Potchef.*, MA *Potchef.*, DLitt
Potchef. Prof.; Dir.*
Swanepoel, T., BA *Potchef.* Sr. Lectr.
Other Staff: 7 Lectrs.; 1 Sr. Subject Specialist

Community Law and Development Centre

E-mail: 10058419@nwu.ac.za
Meyer, S. W. J., BJur *Potchef.* Dir.*

Computer Sciences

E-mail: 10067132@nwu.ac.za
Drevin, G. R., BSc *Potchef.*, MSc *Potchef.*, PhD
Witw. Assoc. Prof.; Head*
Goede, R., BSc *Potchef.*, MSc *Potchef.*, PhD *Potchef.*
Sr. Lectr.
Huisman, H. M., PhD *Potchef.* Sr. Lectr.
Kruger, H. A., BSc *Potchef.*, BSc *Free State*, BCom
Free State, MCom *Free State*, MSc *Free State*, PhD
Potchef. Assoc. Prof.
Oberholzer, J. A., DSc *Potchef.* Sr. Lectr.
Steyn, T., BSc *Potchef.*, MSc *Potchef.*, DSc *Potchef.*
Prof.
Other Staff: 4 Lectrs.
Vacant Posts: 1 Subj. Specialist

Creative Writing

E-mail: 10175288@nwu.ac.za
Du Plessis, H. G. W., BA *Pret.*, BA *S.Af.*, BA
Potchef., MA *S.Af.*, DLitt *S.Af.*, DPhil *Potchef.*
Prof.; Dir.*

Development in the South African Constitutional State

Focus area
E-mail: 10063994@nwu.ac.za
Du Plessis, W., BJur *Potchef.*, LLB *Potchef.*, LLD
Potchef. Prof.; Dir.*

Research: modern-day impact of religious family
systems in South Africa; new thinking in
law; poverty, social exclusion and social
rights; rural and urban land development;
trade and development

Drug Research and Development

Focus area
E-mail: 10065318@nwu.ac.za
Du Plessis, J., BPharm *Potchef.*, MSc *Potchef.*, PhD
Potchef. Prof.; Dir.*
Du Preez, J. L., BPharm *Potchef.*, MSc *Potchef.*,
PhD *Potchef.* Prof.
Liebenberg, W., BPharm *Potchef.*, MSc *Potchef.*,
DSc *Potchef.* Prof.
Other Staff: 2 Subj. Specialists; 1 Scientific
Officer
Research: drug delivery; drug design and
mechanisms in neuropsychiatry

Ecclesiastical Studies

E-mail: 10177582@nwu.ac.za
Coetzee, C. F. C., ThD *Potchef.* Prof.
De Klerk, B. J., BA *Potchef.*, ThB *Potchef.*, ThM
Potchef., ThD *Potchef.* Prof.
De Lange, M. C., BSc *Potchef.*, MA *Potchef.* Sr.
Lectr.
De Wet, F. W., ThD *Potchef.* Assoc. Prof.
Letsosa, R. S., BA *Potchef.*, MA *Potchef.*, PhD N-
W(S.Af.) Sr. Lectr.
Lotter, G. A., BA *Potchef.*, ThB *Potchef.*, DMin
Westminster Theol.Sem., ThD *Potchef.* Prof.
Mashua, T. D., MA *Potchef.* Sr. Lectr.
Vorster, J. M., BA *Potchef.*, ThB *Potchef.*, MA
Potchef., ThM *Potchef.*, DPhil *Potchef.*, ThD
Potchef. Prof.; Dir.*

Economics, Risk Management and International Trade

E-mail: 10064230@nwu.ac.za
Kleynhans, E. P. J., PhD *Potchef.* Sr. Lectr.
Krugell, W. F., BCom *Potchef.*, MCom *Potchef.*,
PhD *N-W(S.Af.)* Assoc. Prof.
Saayman, A., PhD *Potchef.* Assoc. Prof.
Styger, P., BCom *Free State*, MCom *Free State*,
DCom *Potchef.* Prof.
Van Heerden, J. H. P., BSc(Econ) *Potchef.*, BSc
Potchef., MSc *Potchef.*, MComm *Potchef.*,
DComm *Potchef.* Prof.
Viviers, W., BComm *Potchef.*, BEd *Potchef.*,
MComm *Potchef.*, DComm *Potchef.* Prof.;
Dir.*
Other Staff: 5 Lectrs.
Vacant Posts: 1 Lectr.

Education and Training

E-mail: 10064818@nwu.ac.za
Abdool, A. D., BA *Potchef.*, BEd *Potchef.*, MEd
Potchef. Sr. Lectr.
Karstens, A., MEd *Potchef.* Sr. Lectr.
Kirsten, G. J. C., BA *Potchef.*, MEd *Pret.* Sr.
Lectr.
Kok, A., PhD *Potchef.* Sr. Lectr.
Kruger, L. L., MEd *Pret.* Sr. Lectr.
Maarman, R. F. A., BA *W.Cape*, BEd *S.Af.*, MEd
Rand Afrikaans Sr. Lectr.
Mentz, P. J., BA *Pret.*, BEd *Pret.*, MEd *Rand
Afrikaans*, DEd *Potchef.* Prof.; Dir.*
Mosoge, M. J., PhD *Potchef.* Assoc. Prof.
Nel, C., BA *Potchef.*, MA *Potchef.*, PhD *Potchef.*
Prof.
Potgieter, F. J., BA *Pret.*, BA(Ed) *S.Af.*, MEd *S.Af.*
Assoc. Prof.
Rossouw, J. P., DEd *S.Af.* Assoc. Prof.
Steyn, H. J., BEd *Potchef.*, BA *Potchef.*, MEd
Potchef., DEd *Potchef.* Prof.
Viljoen, C. T., DPhil *Potchef.* Sr. Lectr.
Wolhuter, C. C., DEd *Stell.* Assoc. Prof.
Other Staff: 6 Lectrs.
Vacant Posts: 1 Prof.; 1 Lectr.

Education, Postgraduate School of

E-mail: 10179178@nwu.ac.za
Du Toit, P., BA *Pret.*, BEd *Pret.*, MEd *Pret.*, PhD
Pret. Assoc. Prof.
Meyer, L. W., DEd *P.Elizabeth* Assoc. Prof.
Monteith, J. L. de K., BA *Potchef.*, BPhil *Potchef.*,
BEd *Potchef.*, MEd *Potchef.*, DEd *Potchef.* Prof.

Nieuwoudt, H. D., BSc Potchef., BEd Potchef., MSc Potchef., PhD Potchef.   Assoc. Prof.

Van der Westhuizen, P. C., BA Potchef., BEd Potchef., MEd Potchef., DEd S.Af., DEd Potchef. Prof.; Dir.*

Van Vuuren, H. J., MEd Free State   Sr. Lectr.

Engineering, Chemical and Mineral

E-mail: 10059571@nwu.ac.za

Bruinsma, O. S. L., BEng V.U.Amst., PhD V.U.Amst.   Prof.

Campbell, Q. P., BSc Witw.   Sr. Lectr.

Le Roux, M., BEng Potchef., MEng Potchef.   Sr. Lectr.

Marx, S., BEng Stell.   Sr. Lectr.

Neomagus, H. W. J. P., PhD T.H.Twente   Assoc. Prof.

Van der Gryp, P., BEng Potchef., MEng Potchef.   Sr. Lectr.

Van der Merwe, A. F., BEng Potchef., MBA Potchef.   Sr. Lectr.

Waanders, F. B., BSc Potchef., MSc Potchef., DSc Potchef.   Prof.; Dir.*

Engineering, Electrical and Electronics

E-mail: 12363626@nwu.ac.za

Bodenstein, C. P., BEng Pret., BSc Potchef., MSc Potchef., DEng Potchef.   Assoc. Prof.

De Kock, J. A., BEng Stell., MEng Stell., PhD Stell. Prof.

Helberg, A. S. J., BIng Rand Afrikaans, MIng Rand Afrikaans, DIng Rand Afrikaans   Prof.; Dir.*

Hoffman, A. J., PhD Pret.   Prof.

Holm, J. E. W., DEng Pret.   Assoc. Prof.

Holm, S. R., BEng Rand Afrikaans, MEng Rand Afrikaans, DEng Rand Afrikaans   Assoc. Prof.

Rens, A. P. J., BEng Potchef., MEng Potchef.   Sr. Lectr.

Venter, W. C., BSc Potchef., BEng Potchef., MEng Potchef., PhD Iowa   Assoc. Prof.

Other Staff: 3 Lectrs.; 1 Sr. Subject Specialist
Vacant Posts: 1 Prof.; 1 Sr. Lectr.

Engineering, Mechanical and Materials

E-mail: 10199365@nwu.ac.za

Botha, B. W., BEng Pret., MEng Pret.   Sr. Lectr.

Du Toit, C. G. D. K., BEng Stell., MEng Stell., PhD Stell.   Prof.; Dir.*

Grobler, L. J., BEng Pret., MEng Pret., PhD Pret.   Assoc. Prof.

Jonker, A. S., BSc Potchef., BEng Potchef.   Sr. Lectr.

Jordaan, P. W., BSc Stell., BEng Stell.   Sr. Lectr.

Markgraaff, J., BSc Potchef., MSc Potchef., PhD Rand Afrikaans   Assoc. Prof.

Roberts, J. G., BEng Pret., MEng Rand Afrikaans   Sr. Lectr.

Rousseau, P. G., BEng Pret., MEng Pret., PhD Pret.   Prof.; Dir.*

Van Eldik, M., BEng Potchef., MEng Potchef., PhD Potchef.   Sr. Lectr.

Van Niekerk, W. M. K., BEng Pret., MEng Pret.   Sr. Lectr.

Van Schalkwyk, P., BScEng Pret., BEd Potchef., BSc Potchef., MSc Pret., PhD Potchef.   Assoc. Prof.

Vacant Posts: 1 Prof.; 1 Sr. Subject Specialist

Entrepreneurship

E-mail: 10201424@nwu.ac.za

Kroon, J., BComm Potchef., MComm Potchef., DComm Potchef.   Prof.

Mostert, P. G., BCom Pret., DCom Pret.   Assoc. Prof.

Saayman, M., BA(Ed) Pret., BA Pret., MA Pret., DPhil Pret.   Assoc. Prof.; Head*

Other Staff: 3 Lectrs.

Environmental Sciences and Management

Focus area

E-mail: udsgjdt@nwu.ac.za

Du Toit, G. J., BSc Potchef., BScEng Pret., MBL S.Af., PhD Pret.   Dir.*

Van Rensburg, L., BSc Potchef., MSc Potchef., PhD Potchef.   Head*

Research: air quality and atmopheric pollution; aquatic ecology and management; environmental management; remediation and sustainable management of ecosystems; sustainable development and spatial planning

Geography

E-mail: 10066497@nwu.ac.za

Retief, F. P., BA Free State, MSc Free State   Sr. Lectr.

Sandham, L. A., BSc(Ed) Rand Afrikaans, BSc Rand Afrikaans, MSc Rand Afrikaans, PhD Rand Afrikaans   Sr. Lectr.

Van der Walt, I. J., BSc Potchef., MSc Potchef., PhD Potchef.   Assoc. Prof.; Head*

Winde, F., DSc Potchef.   Assoc. Prof.

Other Staff: 1 Lectr.

Geology

E-mail: 10062203@nwu.ac.za

Coetzee, M. S., PhD Free State   Sr. Lectr.

Other Staff: 3 Lectrs.; 1 Subj. Specialist

Graphic Design

De la Harpe, H. E., BA S.Af., BA Potchef., MA Potchef., PhD N-W(S.Af.)   Sr. Lectr.

Marley, I. R.   Sr. Lectr.

Other Staff: 2 Lectrs.

History

E-mail: 20734131@nwu.ac.za

Du Pisani, J. A., BA Free State, MA Free State, PhD Free State   Prof.; Head*

Oosthuizen, G. J., BA Potchef., MA Potchef.   Assoc. Prof.

Other Staff: 1 Lectr.

Labour Relations

E-mail: 10058818@nwu.ac.za

Linde, H. M., BA Free State, MA Potchef., PhD Potchef.   Sr. Lectr.

Visagie, J. C., BCom Potchef., MCom Potchef., DCom Potchef.   Assoc. Prof.; Head*

Other Staff: 1 Lectr.

Languages

E-mail: 10185429@nwu.ac.za

Carstens, W. A. M., BA Stell., MA Stell., DLitt Stell.   Prof.; Dir.*

Du Plooy, H. J. G., BA Potchef., BA Pret., MA Pret., DLitt Potchef.   Prof.

Greyling, S. F., PhD Potchef.   Sr. Lectr.

Hentschel, C. E., BA Potchef., MA Potchef., DLitt Potchef.   Assoc. Prof.

Pretorius, R. S., BA Potchef., MA Potchef., PhD Potchef.   Sr. Lectr.

Terblanche, J. E., PhD Potchef.   Sr. Lectr.

Van der Walt, J. L., BA Potchef., BEd Potchef., MA Potchef., DEd Potchef.   Prof.

Van der Westhuizen, E. S., BA Potchef., MA Potchef., PhD Potchef.   Assoc. Prof.

Van Rooy, A. J., BA Potchef., MA Potchef., PhD Potchef.   Assoc. Prof.

Van Wyk, H. G., BA Potchef., MA Potchef., PhD Potchef.   Sr. Lectr.

Viljoen, H. M., BA Potchef., MA Pret., DLitt Potchef., DrsLitt Gron.   Prof.

Other Staff: 11 Lectrs.
Vacant Posts: 1 Assoc. Prof.; 1 Sr. Lectr.

Languages and Literature in the South African Context

Focus area

E-mail: 10064354@nwu.ac.za

De Lange, A. M., BA Potchef., MA Potchef., PhD Rhodes   Prof.; Dir.*

Van Huyssteen, G., BA Pret.   Assoc. Prof.

Research: applied language studies (language teaching and assessment, sociolinguistics); children's literature; language technology (computational linguistics, computer-assisted language learning (CALL), corpus linguistics, interpreting and subtitling); liminality and hybridity; space and identity in contemporary South African and metropolitan literature

Law

E-mail: 10058176@nwu.ac.za

Crous, A. J., BJur Potchef., LLB Pret., BA Pret.   Assoc. Prof.

De la Harpe, S. P. L. R., LLM Pret.   Assoc. Prof.

Du Plessis, A. A., BA Potchef., LLB Potchef., LLM Potchef.   Sr. Lectr.

Ferreira, G. M., BJur Potchef., LLB Potchef., LLM Rand Afrikaans, LLD Potchef.   Prof.

Horsten, D. A., BCom Potchef., LLB Potchef.   Sr. Lectr.

Jansen van Rensburg, L., BComm Potchef., LLB Potchef., LLD Potchef.   Assoc. Prof.

Kotze, L. J., LLM Potchef.   Sr. Lectr.

Monchusi, P. J., BJur Vista   Sr. Lectr.

Pienaar, G. J., BJur&Comm Potchef., LLB Potchef., LLD Potchef.   Prof.; Head*

Rautenbach, C., BJur Potchef., LLB Potchef.   Prof.

Scholtz, W., LLB Potchef.   Assoc. Prof.

Schutte, P. J. W., BJur Potchef., BA Potchef., LLB Potchef.   Sr. Lectr.

Stander, A. L., BJur Potchef., LLB Potchef., LLM S.Af., PhD Potchef.   Prof.

Swanepoel, J., BA Potchef., BPhil Potchef., MA Potchef., DLitt Potchef.   Prof.; Joint Dir.*

Van der Merwe, A. P. S., BSc Stell., BSc Rand Afrikaans, LLB S.Af., DPhil Witw.   Assoc. Prof.

Van der Schyff, E., LLM Potchef.   Sr. Lectr.

Other Staff: 4 Lectrs.
Vacant Posts: 1 Sr. Lectr.

Mathematics and Applied Mathematics

E-mail: 100556491@nwu.ac.za

Benade, J. G., BSc Rand Afrikaans, DSc Rand Afrikaans   Sr. Lectr.

Burger, I., DSc Potchef.   Sr. Lectr.

De Klerk, J. H., BSc Potchef., MSc Potchef., DSc Potchef.   Prof.; Head*

Groenewald, G. J., BSc W.Cape, MSc Ill., MSc Cape Town, Drs V.U.Amst., PhD V.U.Amst.   Assoc. Prof.

Hitge, M., BSc Free State, BSc Potchef., MSc Potchef., PhD Potchef.

Petersen, M. A., BSc Cape Town, BSc W.Cape, MSc W.Cape, PhD W.Cape   Prof.

Spoelstra, J., BSc Potchef., MSc Potchef., DSc Potchef.   Assoc. Prof.

Other Staff: 4 Lectrs.

Microbiology

Bezuidenhout, C. C., BSc Rhodes, PhD Rhodes   Assoc. Prof.

Esterhuysen, H. A., BSc Potchef., MSc Potchef., DSc Potchef.   Sr. Lectr.

Other Staff: 3 Lectrs.; 1 Sr. Subj. Specialist
Vacant Posts: 1 Assoc. Prof.

Music

E-mail: 10078576@nwu.ac.za

Coetzee, M. G. H., BMus Stell., MMus Potchef.   Sr. Lectr.

Koornhof, H. P., BMus Potchef.   Sr. Lectr.

Kruger, D., BMus Potchef., MMus Potchef., DMus Pret.   Sr. Lectr.

Kruger, J. H., BMus Cape Town, MMus Cape Town, PhD Rhodes   Sr. Lectr.

Oliver, G. J., BMus Potchef., MMus Potchef.   Sr. Lectr.

Petersen, A. B., BMus Cape Town, BEd S.Af., MMus Cape Town, DMus Fort Hare   Sr. Lectr.

Potgieter, H. M., BMus Pret., MMus Pret., DMus Pret.   Assoc. Prof.

Swart, B., MMus Pret.   Sr. Lectr.

Taljaard, D. J., MMus Pret.   Sr. Lectr.

Van der Merwe, P. J., BMus Potchef., MMus Youngstown   Sr. Lectr.; Dir.*

Van Rensburg, H., BMus Potchef., MMus Potchef.   Sr. Lectr.

Watt, M. C., DMus Pret.   Sr. Lectr.

Weyer, W. W., BMus Potchef.   Sr. Lectr.

Other Staff: 4 Lectrs.

Nuclear Science and Engineering, Postgraduate School of

E-mail: 10184945@nwu.ac.za

Greyvenstein, G. P., DIng Pret.   Prof.

Sibiya, G. S., BSc S.Af., BSc Fort Hare   Assoc. Prof.

Nursing

E-mail: 11089016@nwu.ac.za
Bornman, E., BCur S.Af.   Sr. Lectr.
Du Plessis, E. M., MA Potchef.   Sr. Lectr.
Du Plessis, E., MCur Potchef.   Sr. Lectr.
Du Preez, A., MCur Potchef.   Sr. Lectr.
Greeff, M., BA S.Af., MCur Rand Afrikaans, DCur Rand Afrikaans   Prof.
Klopper, H. C., BCur S.Af., MCur Rand Afrikaans, PhD Rand Afrikaans   Prof.; Dir.*
Lekalakala-Mokgele, E., PhD Free State   Assoc. Prof.
Marx, A., MCur Potchef.   Sr. Lectr.
Minnie, C. S.   Sr. Lectr.
Mulaudzi, F. M., BA S.Af., MA S.Af., PhD S.Af.   Assoc. Prof.
Pretorius, R., BCur S.Af., MCur Pret.   Sr. Lectr.
Scrooby, B., MCur Rand Afrikaans   Sr. Lectr.
Van der Walt, E., BCur S.Af., BA Free State   Sr. Lectr.
Van Graan, A. C., BA S.Af., MCur Rand Afrikaans   Sr. Lectr.
Watson, M. J., MCur Potchef.   Sr. Lectr.
Williams, M. J. S., MCur Rand Afrikaans   Sr. Lectr.
Other Staff: 2 Lectrs.

Pharmaceutical Chemistry

E-mail: 10057072@nwu.ac.za
Bergh, J. J., BSc Stell., BSc(Pharm) Potchef., BSc Potchef., MSc Potchef., DSc Potchef.   Prof.; Head*
Breytenbach, J. C., BSc Free State, MSc Free State, PhD Free State   Prof.
Malan, S. F., BPharm Potchef., MSc Potchef., PhD Potchef.   Assoc. Prof.
Terreblanche, G., BPharm Potchef., MSc Potchef., PhD Potchef.   Sr. Lectr.
Van Dyk, S., PhD Potchef.   Sr. Lectr.
Vacant Posts: 1 Subj. Specialist

Pharmaceutics

Tel: 10200142@nwu.ac.za
Kotze, A. F., BPharm Potchef., MSc Potchef., DPharm Potchef.   Assoc. Prof.; Head*
Malan, M. M., BPharm Potchef., MPharm Potchef., DPharm Potchef.   Sr. Lectr.
Marais, A. F., BPharm Potchef., MSc Potchef., DPharm Potchef.   Sr. Lectr.
Steenkamp, J. H., MPharm Potchef.   Sr. Lectr.
Other Staff: 2 Lectrs.; 1 Sr. Subj. Specialist
Vacant Posts: 1 Lectr.

Pharmacology

E-mail: fkldwo@nwu.ac.za
Brand, L., BPharm Potchef., MSc Potchef., DSc Potchef.   Assoc. Prof.
Brink, C. B., BPharm Potchef., MSc(Pharm) Potchef., PhD Potchef.   Assoc. Prof.
Harvey, B. H., BPharm Rhodes, BSc Potchef., MSc Stell., PhD Stell.   Prof.
Meyer, C. L., BSc Potchef., MSc Potchef.   Sr. Lectr.
Viljoen, M., MSc Potchef.   Sr. Lectr.
Other Staff: 1 Lectr.
Vacant Posts: 1 Assoc. Prof.

Pharmacy, Clinical

E-mail: 10056696@nwu.ac.za
Du Plessis, J. M., BMC Pret.   Sr. Lectr.
Gerber, J. J., BSc Potchef., MSc Potchef., DSc Potchef.   Assoc. Prof.; Head*
Lamprecht, J. C., BPharm North(S.Af.), MPharm North(S.Af.), DPhil North(S.Af.)   Sr. Lectr.
Rakumakoe, D. M., DPharm Xavier(La.)   Sr. Lectr.

Pharmacy Practice

E-mail: 10069712@nwu.ac.za
Basson, M. J., BSc Potchef.   Sr. Lectr.
Basson, W. D., BSc Potchef.   Sr. Lectr.
Burger, J. R., MPharm Potchef.   Sr. Lectr.
John, G. K., BPharm S.Af.Med.

Lubbe, M. S., BPharm Potchef., MPharm Potchef., DPharm Potchef.   Assoc. Prof.
Vacant Posts: 1 Assoc. Prof.

Pharmacy, School of

E-mail: 10060855@nwu.ac.za
Oliver, D. W., BPharm Potchef., BSc Potchef., MPharm Potchef., DSc Potchef.   Prof.; Dir.*
Vacant Posts: 1 Assoc. Prof.

Philosophy, School of

E-mail: 10056076@nwu.ac.za
Heyns, M. F., MA Potchef.   Sr. Lectr.
Venter, J. J., BA Potchef., MA Potchef., DrsPhil V.U.Amst., DPhil Potchef.   Prof.; Dir.*
Other Staff: 3 Lectrs.

Physics, School of

E-mail: 10060014@nwu.ac.za
De Jager, O. C., BSc Potchef., MSc Potchef., DSc Potchef.   Prof.
Ferreira, S. E. S., PhD Potchef.   Sr. Lectr.
Moraal, H., BSc Potchef., MSc Potchef., DSc Potchef.   Prof.
Potgieter, M. S., BSc Potchef., MSc Potchef., DSc Potchef.   Prof.; Dir.*
Raubenheimer, B. C., BSc Potchef., MSc Potchef., DSc Potchef.   Prof.
Van der Walt, D. J., BSc Stell., MSc Potchef., DSc Potchef.   Prof.
Other Staff: 1 Lectr.; 2 Subj. Specialists

Physiology, Nutrition and Consumer Sciences, School of

E-mail: 10056173@nwu.ac.za
Malan, N. T., BSc Free State, MSc Free State, DSc Potchef.   Prof.; Dir.*

Consumer Sciences

E-mail: 21070342@nwu.ac.za
De Beer, H., PhD Free State   Sr. Lectr.; Head*
Van der Merwe, M., BSc Free State, MSc Free State, PhD Free State   Sr. Lectr.
Venter, M. D., BSc Potchef., MSc Potchef.   Sr. Lectr.
Other Staff: 2 Lectrs.
Vacant Posts: 1 Sr. Lectr.

Nutrition

Hanekom, S. M., PhD Potchef.   Sr. Lectr.
Huisman, H. W., BSc Potchef., MSc Potchef.   Sr. Lectr.
Jerling, J. C., BSc Stell., BSc Potchef., MSc Potchef.   Prof.; Head*
Kempen, E. L., MA Potchef.   Sr. Lectr.
Kruger, H. S., BSc Potchef., BPharm Potchef., MSc Potchef., DSc Potchef.   Assoc. Prof.
Loots, D., BSc Potchef., MSc Potchef., PhD Potchef.   Sr. Lectr.
Smuts, C. M., BSc Stell., MSc Stell., DSc Stell.   Assoc. Prof.
Wright, H. H., PhD Potchef.   Sr. Lectr.
Other Staff: 3 Lectrs.; 1 Subj. Specialist
Vacant Posts: 1 Sr. Lectr.

Physiology

E-mail: 10059539@nwu.ac.za
Eloff, F. C., BSc Potchef., MSc Potchef., DSc Potchef.   Assoc. Prof.
Huisman, H. W., BSc Potchef., MSc Potchef.   Sr. Lectr.
Malan, L., BSc Potchef., MSc Potchef., PhD N-W(S.Af.)   Sr. Lectr.
Schutte, A. E., PhD Potchef.   Sr. Lectr.
Van Rooyen, J. M., BSc Potchef., MSc Potchef., DSc Potchef.   Assoc. Prof.; Head*
Other Staff: 2 Lectrs.; 2 Subject Specialists

Political Sciences

E-mail: 10187448@nwu.ac.za
Kirsten, J. F., BA Potchef., MA Potchef., DPhil Potchef.   Dir.*
Other Staff: 1 Lectr.

Potchefstroom Business School

E-mail: 10059377@nwu.ac.za
Bisschoff, C. A., BCom S.Af., MCom S.Af., DCom S.Af.   Prof.
Coetsee, L. D., BA Potchef., MA S.Af., DPhil Potchef.   Prof.
Du Plessis, J. L., PhD P.Elizabeth   Prof.
Du Plessis, T. E., MBA Potchef.   Assoc. Prof.; Dir.*
Kotze, J. G., BCom Free State, BCompt S.Af., BCom S.Af., MCom S.Af., DCom S.Af.   Prof.
Lotriet, R. A., BComm Potchef., MComm Potchef., PhD Potchef.   Assoc. Prof.
Nel, I., BCom S.Af., MBA Pret., PhD Free State   Assoc. Prof.
Smit, A. M., BComm Potchef., PhD Potchef.   Sr. Lectr.
Van der Merwe, S. P., BAgric Free State, BSc Free State, MSc Free State, MBA Potchef., PhD Potchef.   Sr. Lectr.
Van der Walt, J. L., DCom Potchef.   Assoc. Prof.
Other Staff: 2 Lectrs.
Vacant Posts: 2 Profs.; 1 Assoc. Prof.; 1 Lectr.

Professional Services

Engineering
E-mail: 10183906@nwu.ac.za
Fick, J. I. J., MScEng Pret., PhD Cran.   Prof.; Dir.*
Kleingeld, M., PhD Pret.   Assoc. Prof.
Mathews, E. H., DEng Potchef.   Prof.
Stoker, P. W., DEng Potchef.   Prof.
Van Rensburg, J. F., BEng Potchef., MEng Potchef.   Sr. Lectr.
Wichers, J. H., DEng Potchef.   Assoc. Prof.
Vacant Posts: 1 Sr. Lectr.

Psychology

E-mail: psgmpw@nwu.ac.za
Botha, K. F. H., BA Potchef., MA Potchef., PhD Potchef.   Prof.
Du Toit, M. M., BSc Potchef., MSc Potchef., PhD Potchef.   Sr. Lectr.
Nienaber, A. W., BSc Potchef., MSc Potchef., PhD Potchef.   Sr. Lectr.
Potgieter, J. C., MSc Free State   Sr. Lectr.
Rankin, P., BA(SW) P.Elizabeth, BA Stell., BA P.Elizabeth, MA P.Elizabeth, PhD Rhodes   Sr. Lectr.
Roos, V., DPhil Pret.   Assoc. Prof.
Temane, Q. M., BA N-W(S.Af.), MA N-W(S.Af.), PhD N-W(S.Af.)   Sr. Lectr.
Van Rensburg, E., BA Potchef., MA Potchef.   Assoc. Prof.
Venter, C. A., BA Potchef., MA Potchef., DPhil Potchef.   Prof.

Psychology, Industrial

E-mail: 10064699@nwu.ac.za
Jonker, C. S., PhD Potchef.   Sr. Lectr.
Mostert, C. S., BCom Potchef., MCom Potchef., PhD Potchef.   Assoc. Prof.
Rabie, G. H., BA S.Af., MA N-W(S.Af.)   Sr. Lectr.
Rothmann, S., BComm Potchef., MComm Potchef., PhD Potchef.   Prof.
Scholtz, P. E., BA Pret., BA S.Af., MA Potchef., DPhil Potchef.   Prof.; Dir.*
Sieberhagen, G. V. D. M., BComm Stell., MComm Stell., DComm Rand Afrikaans   Assoc. Prof.

Psychosocial Behavioural Sciences, School of

Wissing, M. P., BA Potchef., MA Potchef., PhD Potchef.   Prof.; Dir.*

Psychotherapy and Counselling, Institute for

E-mail: 10056971@nwu.ac.za
Du Plessis, W. F., BA Potchef., MA Potchef., PhD Potchef.   Assoc. Prof.; Head*
Kirsten, D. K., BA Potchef., BEd Rand Afrikaans, MEd Rand Afrikaans   Sr. Lectr.

Public Management and Administration

E-mail: 12330841@nwu.ac.za

Van der Waldt, G., BA Stell., MA Stell., PhD Stell.
Assoc. Prof.

Vermeulen, L., BA Pret. Sr. Lectr.

Other Staff: 1 Lectr.

Reformed Theology and the Development of South African Society

Focus area

E-mail: 10058052@nwu.ac.za

Van Rooy, H. F., BA Potchef., ThB Potchef., MA
Potchef., DLitt Potchef. Prof.; Dir.*

Research: equipping people for the development
of society; ethical perspectives on human
rights; socio-historic context of the Bible
and its implications for the reconstruction
and development of South African society

Science, Mathematics and Technology Education, School of

E-mail: fskjjas@nwu.ac.za

Froneman, S., DSc Stell. Sr. Lectr.; Dir.*

Lemmer, M., MSc Potchef. Sr. Lectr.

Other Staff: 5 Lectrs.

Vacant Posts: 1 Prof.; 1 Lectr.

Separation Science and Technology

Focus area

Tel: (018) 299 1111 Fax: (018) 299 2703
E-mail: chioslb@nwu.ac.za

Bruinsma, O. S. L., BEng V.U.Amst., PhD
V.U.Amst. Prof.; Dir.*

Research: catalysis and synthesis; crystallisation
and leaching; membrane technology;
process intensification; supercritical
technology

Social and Government Studies

E-mail: 13250612@nwu.ac.za

Rothmann, J., BA Rand Afrikaans Prof.

Zaaiman, S. J., BA Stell., MA Stell., PhD Stell.
Assoc. Prof.; Head*

Other Staff: 5 Lectrs.

Social Work

E-mail: 10180761@nwu.ac.za

Herbst, A. G., BA Pret., MA Pret., PhD Potchef.
Sr. Lectr.

Rankin, P., BA P.Elizabeth, MA P.Elizabeth, PhD
Rhodes Assoc. Prof.

Roux, A. A., BSc Free State, MA Potchef., PhD
Potchef. Sr. Lectr.

Ryke, E. H., BA Rand Afrikaans, MA Stell. Sr.
Lectr.

Steyn, M. M., BA Potchef., MA Potchef. Sr. Lectr.

Strydom, H., BA P.Elizabeth, MA Pret., PhD Pret.
Prof.

Wessels, C. C., BA Potchef., MA Potchef., PhD
Potchef. Sr. Lectr.

Weyers, M. L., BA Stell., MA Potchef., PhD Pret.
Assoc. Prof.

Sociology

E-mail: 10067248@nwu.ac.za

Cronjé, J. F., BA Potchef., MA Potchef., PhD
Potchef. Sr. Lectr.; Head*

Other Staff: 1 Lectr.

Vacant Posts: 1 Sr. Lectr.

Space Physics, Unit for

Focus area

E-mail: 10188738@nwu.ac.za

Burger, R. A., BSc Potchef., MSc Potchef., DSc
Potchef. Prof.; Dir.*

Other Staff: 1 Sr. Subj. Specialist; 1 Subj.
Specialist

Research: cosmic ray observations in South
Africa and Antarctica; gamma-ray
astrophysics; heliospheric physics; innovative
astro-technology; star formation

Statistics and Operational Research

E-mail: 10177507@nwu.ac.za

Swanepoel, C. J., BSc Potchef., MSc Potchef., DSc
Witw. Assoc. Prof.

Swanepoel, J. W. H., BSc Potchef., MSc Potchef.,
DSc Potchef. Prof.; Head*

Van Graan, F. C., BCom Potchef., MCom Potchef.,
PhD Potchef. Assoc. Prof.

Other Staff: 3 Lectrs.

Vacant Posts: 1 Lectr.

Sustainable Social Development

Focus area

E-mail: 10197125@nwu.ac.za

Duvenhage, A., BA Potchef., MA Potchef., PhD Free
State Dir.*

Van Niekerk, D., BA Rand Afrikaans, PhD N-
W(S.Af.) Sr. Lectr.

Vacant Posts: 1 Assoc. Prof.

Research: AIDS and communication;
desertification (impact on physical and
social environment); land claims and
resettlement

Teachers' Training Human-oriented School Subjects

E-mail: 10088253@nwu.ac.za

Du Toit, BA Potchef., MA Potchef., PhD Potchef.
Sr. Lectr.; Dir.*

Golightly, A., BEd Potchef., BA Potchef., MA
Potchef. Sr. Lectr.

Meyer, S., BA Free State, BA Pret., MA Pret., PhD
S.Af. Sr. Lectr.

Uys, C. C., BA S.Af. Sr. Lectr.

Van den Berg, M., PhD Potchef. Sr. Lectr.

Zerwick, L. J., MA Potchef. Sr. Lectr.

Other Staff: 17 Lectrs.

Vacant Posts: 1 Assoc. Prof.; 1 Sr. Lectr.; 2
Lectrs.

Teachers' Training Nature-oriented School Subjects

E-mail: 10064915@nwu.ac.za

Els, P. L., BA Potchef., BEd Potchef., MEd Potchef.
Sr. Lectr.

Mentz, E., PhD Potchef. Assoc. Prof.; Dir.*

Nieuwoudt, S. M., PhD Potchef. Sr. Lectr.

Reitsma, G. M., BSc Potchef., MSc Potchef., DEd
N-W(S.Af.) Sr. Lectr.

Other Staff: 18 Lectrs.

Vacant Posts: 1 Lectr.

Tourism and Leisure Studies

E-mail: 10219382@nwu.ac.za

Van der Merwe, P., BA Potchef., MA Potchef.,
PhD Potchef. Sr. Lectr.; Head*

Other Staff: 1 Lectr.

Town and Regional Planning

Drewes, J. E., BArt&Sc Potchef., MArt&Sc Potchef.
Sr. Lectr.

Geyer, H. S., BArt&Sc Potchef., MArt&Sc Potchef.,
DPhil Potchef. Prof.

Schoeman, C. B., DSc Calif., DPhil Potchef.
Assoc. Prof.

Other Staff: 1 Lectr.

Transdisciplinary Health Research, Africa Unit for

E-mail: 10062416@nwu.ac.za

Kruger, A., PhD Potchef. Subject Specialist;
Dir.*

Other Staff: 1 Subject Specialist

Research: community-based interventions to
improve quality of life of Africans in
transition in the North-West province of
South Africa; functional foods
(development, sensory testing and
evaluation of physiological and biochemical
effects of new products); indigenous
knowledge (gender issues in the Tswana
culture); nutrition and social work
interventions in HIV/AIDS patients;
psychosocial well-being and quality of life

WorkWell Research Unit for People, Policy and Performance

Focus area

E-mail: 10074988@nwu.ac.za

Naude, W. A., BComm Potchef., MSc Warw.,
MComm Potchef., PhD Potchef. Prof.; Dir.*

Pienaar, J., BA Potchef., MA Potchef., PhD Potchef.
Sr. Lectr.

Zoology

E-mail: 10175709@nwu.ac.za

Bouwman, H., BSc Potchef., MSc Potchef., DSc
Potchef. Prof.

Du Preez, L. H., BSc Free State, MSc Free State,
PhD Free State Assoc. Prof.

Geyer, H. S., BArt&Sc Potchef., MArt&Sc Potchef.,
DPhil Potchef. Prof.

Theron, P. D., BSc Potchef., MSc Potchef., DSc
Potchef. Prof.; Head*

Van den Berg, J., PhD Free State Assoc. Prof.

Weldon, C., DSc N-W(S.Af.) Sr. Lectr.

Wolmarans, C. T., BSc Potchef., MSc Potchef., DSc
Potchef. Sr. Lectr.

Other Staff: 2 Lectrs.

SPECIAL CENTRES, ETC

Education, Potchefstroom College of

E-mail: pokbwr@nwu.ac.za

Janse van Rensburg, J. M., MEd Potchef. Sr.
Lectr.

Kirstein, C. F., PhD Vista Sr. Lectr.

Rens, J. A., BA Potchef., MEd Potchef., DPhil N-
W(S.Af.) Sr. Lectr.

Richter, B. W., PhD Potchef. Assoc. Prof.; Dir.*

Van der Merwe, J., BA S.Af., BEd S.Af., MEd
Rand Afrikaans, DEd Rand Afrikaans Sr. Lectr.

Other Staff: 2 Lectrs.

Teachers' Centre

E-mail: 10187502@nwu.ac.za

Rabe, A. Sr. Lectr.

Spamer, E. J., PhD Stell. Prof.; Dir.*

Other Staff: 7 Lectrs.; 1 Mentor

Vacant Posts: 1 Lectr.; 1 Mentor

VAAL TRIANGLE CAMPUS

Tel: (016) 910 3111 Fax: (016) 910 3116
E-mail: 10057870@@nwu.ac.za

Accountancy and Auditing

E-mail: 10199527@nwu.ac.za

Delport, M., BCompt Free State Sr. Lectr.;
Head*

Janse van Rensburg, P. J., MCom S.Af. Sr.
Lectr.

Marx, M. A., BA S.Af. Sr. Lectr.

Vacant Posts: 1 Sr. Lectr.

African Languages

E-mail: 11806702@nwu.ac.za

Seema, J., BA Vista Sr. Lectr.

Selepe, T. J., BA S.Af., MA S.Af., DPhil S.Af.
Assoc. Prof.; Head*

Afrikaans and Dutch

E-mail: 10119663@nwu.ac.za

Esterhuizen, M., BA Potchef., MA Potchef., PhD
Vista Sr. Lectr.

Nel, A., DLitt Pret. Assoc. Prof.; Head*

Basic Sciences

E-mail: 10186220@nwu.ac.za

Rabali, T. C., BA S.Af., ThB Potchef., ThM
Potchef., DTh S.Af. Assoc. Prof.

Other Staff: 1 Lectr.

Behavioural Sciences

E-mail: bsocdwvw@nwu.ac.za

Van Wyk, C. de W., BComm Potchef., MComm
Potchef., DComm Potchef. Assoc. Prof.; Head*

Business Management

E-mail: 11000732@nwu.ac.za

Pelser, T. G., PhD Potchef. Sr. Lectr.

Van Schalkwyk, P. J., MCom Rand Afrikaans Sr.
Lectr.

Venter, P. F., PhD Vista Assoc. Prof.; Head*

Other Staff: 2 Lectrs.

Business Management and Accountancy
E-mail: 10067450@nwu.ac.za
Janse van Vuuren, H. H., BComm *Potchef.* Sr. Lectr.
Oberholzer, M., BComm *Potchef.*, MSc *Potchef.*, PhD *Potchef.* Assoc. Prof.; Head*
Vacant Posts: 1 Sr. Lectr.

Economic Sciences
E-mail: 10061177@nwu.ac.za
Lucouw, P., BComm *Potchef.*, MComm *Potchef.*, DCom *Pret.* Prof.; Dir.*

Economics
E-mail: 10055851@nwu.ac.za
Slabbert, T. J. C., PhD *Vista* Assoc. Prof.
Van der Westhuizen, G., BCom *Free State*, MCom *Free State*, DPhil *Free State* Prof.; Head*
Other Staff: 4 Lectrs.

Educational Sciences
E-mail: 11704411@nwu.ac.za
De Waal, E. A. S., BA *Potchef.*, BEd *Potchef.*, MEd *W.Cape*, PhD *Potchef.* Sr. Lectr.
De Waal, E., BA *Rand Afrikaans*, BEd *Potchef.*, MEd *Potchef.*, DEd *Potchef.*, PhD *Potchef.* Sr. Lectr.
Fourie, J. E., PhD *Potchef.* Sr. Lectr.
Grosser, M. M., MEd *Vista* Sr. Lectr.
Holtzhausen, H. E., PhD *Vista* Sr. Lectr.
Lombard, B. J. J., DEd *Rand Afrikaans* Assoc. Prof.
Mazibuko, N. J. L., BEd *Zululand*, BPaed *Zululand*, PhD *Free State* Sr. Lectr.
Meyer, L. J., PhD *Vista* Sr. Lectr.
Nel, M., BA *Pret.*, MEd *Potchef.*, PhD *N-W(S.Af.)* Sr. Lectr.
Strydom, E., BA *Potchef.*, BEd *Potchef.*, MEd *Potchef.*, DEd *Potchef.* Sr. Lectr.
Theron, L. C., DEd *S.Af.* Sr. Lectr.
Vermeulen, L. M., BA *Pret.*, BEd *Pret.*, MEd *S.Af.*, DEd *S.Af.* Assoc. Prof.; Head*
Xaba, M. I., PhD *Potchef.* Sr. Lectr.
Other Staff: 4 Lectrs.

English Language and Literature
E-mail: 10868720@nwu.ac.za
Swanpoel, A. C., BA *Potchef.* Lectr.; Head*
Other Staff: 2 Lectrs.

History
E-mail: 10224793@nwu.ac.za
De Klerk, P., BA *Potchef.*, BEd *Potchef.*, MA *Potchef.*, DLitt *Potchef.*, DEd *Potchef.* Prof.
Moller, P. L., BA *Potchef.*, MA *Stell.*, PhD *Potchef.* Sr. Lectr.
Tempelhoff, J. W. N., BA *Pret.*, MA *Pret.*, DLitt *S.Af.* Prof.

Languages
E-mail: 10072578@nwu.ac.za
Kruger, J. L., BA *Potchef.*, MA *Potchef.*, PhD *Potchef.* Sr. Lectr.; Head*
Other Staff: 2 Lectrs.

Law, Commercial
E-mail: 10869964@nwu.ac.za
Pelser-Carstens, V., LLB *Potchef.* Sr. Lectr.; Head*

Modelling Sciences
E-mail: 10187820@nwu.ac.za
Jordaan, D. B., BSc *Potchef.*, MSc *Potchef.*, DSc *Potchef.* Prof.; Head*
Pretorius, P. D., BSc *Potchef.*, MSc *Potchef.*, PhD *Potchef.* Sr. Lectr.
Swanepoel, G., BSc *Potchef.*, MSc *Potchef.*, DSc *Potchef.* Sr. Lectr.
Other Staff: 5 Lectrs.
Vacant Posts: 1 Lectr.

Psychology
E-mail: 10057013@nwu.ac.za
Marais, A., BA *Rand Afrikaans* Sr. Lectr.
Van der Merwe, E. K., BA *Pret.*, BEd *Potchef.*, MEd *Pret.* Sr. Lectr.

Van Eeden, C., BA *Pret.*, BA *Potchef.*, MA *Potchef.*, PhD *Potchef.* Sr. Lectr.; Head*
Williams, H. J., BA *Potchef.*, BA *Rand Afrikaans*, MA *Potchef.* Sr. Lectr.

Psychology, Industrial
E-mail: 10192425@nwu.ac.za
Botha, E., MBA *N-W(S.Af.)* Sr. Lectr.
Deacon, E., BCom *Potchef.*, MA *Potchef.* Sr. Lectr.
Du Toit, D. H., BA *Pret.*, BCom *S.Af.*, MCom *Potchef.* Sr. Lectr.
Stander, M. W., MCom *N-W(S.Af.)* Sr. Lectr.; Head*
Other Staff: 1 Assoc. Prof.

Public Management and Administration
E-mail: 11985631@nwu.ac.za
Ababio, E. P., BA *Ghana*, BA *S.Af.*, MA *S.Af.*, DPhil *S.Af.* Sr. Lectr.
Vyas-Doorgapersad, S., PhD *Potchef.* Sr. Lectr.
Other Staff: 2 Lectrs.
Vacant Posts: 1 Sr. Lectr.; 1 Lectr.

Sociology
E-mail: 10725385@nwu.ac.za
Nell, H. W., BA *Potchef.* Sr. Lectr.; Head*
Other Staff: 1 Lectr.

Sociology, Industrial
E-mail: 10205209@nwu.ac.za
Moolman, L., BCom *Potchef.*, MCom *Potchef.* Sr. Lectr.; Head*
Other Staff: 1 Lectr.

Theology and Philosophy
E-mail: 10139028@nwu.ac.za
Van Deventer, J. H., BA *Potchef.*, BTh *Potchef.*, MTh *Potchef.* Assoc. Prof.; Head*
Other Staff: 1 Lectr.
Vacant Posts: 1 Sr. Lectr.

CONTACT OFFICERS

Academic affairs. (Mafikeng) Manager, Academic Services: Modise, M. R., BA(Comm) *N-W(S.Af.)*, MEd *Arizona* (E-mail: 20559968@nwu.ac.za)
Academic affairs. (Vaal Triangle) Officer-in-Charge: Vermeulen, C. W. (E-mail: 10195726@nwu.ac.za)
Academic affairs. (Potchefstroom) Director (Admissions): Pienaar, W. J., BA *Potchef.* (E-mail: 10000798@nwu.ac.za)
Accommodation. (Mafikeng) Manager (Administration and Facilities): Paadi, R. D., BJuris *Bophut.*, LLB *Bophut.*, LLM *S.Af.*, MDP *Bophut.* (E-mail: 16277465@nwu.ac.za)
Accommodation. (Potchefstroom) Director (Accommodation): De Klerk, W. (E-mail: 1018498@nwu.ac.za)
Admissions (first degree). (Mafikeng) Admissions Officer: Paadi, R. D., BJuris *Bophut.*, LLB *Bophut.*, LLM *S.Af.*, MDP *Bophut.* (E-mail: 16277465@nwu.ac.za)
Admissions (first degree). (Vaal Triangle) Officer-in-Charge: Vermeulen, C. W. (E-mail: 10195726@nwu.ac.za)
Admissions (first degree). (Potchefstroom) Director (Admissions): Pienaar, W. J., BA *Potchef.* (E-mail: 10000798@nwu.ac.za)
Admissions (higher degree). (Mafikeng) Admissions Officer: Paadi, R. D., BJuris *Bophut.*, LLB *Bophut.*, LLM *S.Af.*, MDP *Bophut.* (E-mail: 16277465@nwu.ac.za)
Admissions (higher degree). (Vaal Triangle) Officer-in-Charge: Vermeulen, C. W. (E-mail: 10195726@nwu.ac.za)
Admissions (higher degree). (Potchefstroom) Director (Admissions): Pienaar, W. J., BA *Potchef.* (E-mail: 10000798@nwu.ac.za)
Adult/continuing education. Institutional Director: Zibi, Prof. M. S., BCom *Fort Hare*, MA *Bochum* (E-mail: 11715510@nwu.ac.za)
Alumni. (Potchefstroom) Director, Marketing and Communication: Cloete, T. T., BA *Potchef.* (E-mail: 10187618@nwu.ac.za)

Archives. (Potchefstroom) Archivist: Kellner, A. C., BBibl *Potchef.* (E-mail: 10186069@nwu.ac.za)
Careers. (Potchefstroom) Head (Careers): Kotzé, Prof. H. N., MSc *Potchef.*, DPhil *Potchef.* (E-mail: 10057951@nwu.ac.za)
Computing services. (Mafikeng) Director (Information Services): Pietersen, C. M., BSc *Cape Town*, MBA *N-W(S.Af.)*, MDP *N-W(S.Af.)* (E-mail: 16000102@nwu.ac.za)
Computing services. (Potchefstroom) Director (Computing services): Juyn, A., BJur *Potchef.* (E-mail: 10000437@nwu.ac.za)
Development/fund-raising. (Mafikeng) Manager, Public Relations: Motabogi, S., BA(Comm) *N-W(S.Af.)* (E-mail: 16372603@nwu.ac.za)
Development/fund-raising. (Potchefstroom) Director, Marketing and Communication: Cloete, T. T., BA *Potchef.* (E-mail: 10187618@nwu.ac.za)
Distance education. (Potchefstroom) Director (Admissions): Pienaar, W. J., BA *Potchef.* (E-mail: 10000798@nwu.ac.za)
Estates and buildings/works and services. (Mafikeng) Manager, Maintenance and Operations: Ngakane, B. M., MBA *N-W(S.Af.)*, MBA *S.Af.*, MDP *N-W(S.Af.)* (E-mail: ngakanebm@uniwest.ac.za)
Estates and buildings/works and services. (Potchefstroom) Director (Physical Infrastructure and Planning): Van der Ryst, L. G. (E-mail: 10176608@nwu.ac.za)
Examinations. (Mafikeng) Examinations Officer: Mvana, P. F., BPA *Bophut.*, MDP *Bophut.* (E-mail: 20559402@nwu.ac.za)
Examinations. (Potchefstroom) Director (Examinations): Pienaar, W. J., BA *Potchef.* (E-mail: 10000798@nwu.ac.za)
Finance. (Mafikeng) Manager, General Ledger: Molosiwa, K. C., BCom *N-W(S.Af.)*, BComm *S.Af.* (E-mail: 21158258@nwu.ac.za)
Finance. Executive Director (Finance and Facilities): Rost, Prof. I. J., MComm *Potchef.* (E-mail: 10185380@nwu.ac.za)
General enquiries. (Mafikeng) Manager, Public Relations: Motabogi, S., BA(Comm) *N-W(S.Af.)* (E-mail: 16372603@nwu.ac.za)
General enquiries. (Potchefstroom) Institutional Registrar: Van der Walt, Prof. Chris F. C., BJur&Art *Potchef.*, LLB *Rand Afrikaans*, LLD *S.Af.* (E-mail: 10178384@nwu.ac.za)
Health services. (Mafikeng) Nursing Sister: Motasi, K. M., BN *N-W(S.Af.)* (E-mail: 16460928@nwu.ac.za)
Library (chief librarian). (Mafikeng) University Librarian: Nkosi, N. S., BBibl *Rand Afrikaans* (E-mail: 16808428@nwu.ac.za)
Library (chief librarian). (Potchefstroom) Director, Library Services: Larney, T., BA *Potchef.*, BBibl *Potchef.* (E-mail: 10056378@nwu.ac.za)
Personnel/human resources. (Mafeking) Manager, Human Resources: Motabogi, J. (E-mail: 20560117@nwu.ac.za)
Personnel/human resources. Director, Human Resource Operation: Mothobi, V. L., BA *Rand Afrikaans* (E-mail: 13251767@nwu.ac.za)
Public relations. (Potchefstroom) Director, Marketing and Communication: Cloete, T. T., BA *Potchef.* (E-mail: 10187618@nwu.ac.za)
Publications. (Mafeking) Chairperson (Research): Mosimege, M. (E-mail: 16175166@nwu.ac.za)
Publications. (Potchefstroom) Director, Marketing and Communication: Cloete, T. T., BA *Potchef.* (E-mail: 10187618@nwu.ac.za)
Purchasing. (Mafikeng) Purchasing Officer: Mere, M. I., BCom *Bophut.* (E-mail: 16381424@nwu.ac.za)
Purchasing. (Potchefstroom) Senior Accountant: Earle, E., BCompt *S.Af.* (E-mail: 11360607@nwu.ac.za)

Research. Chairperson (Research): Mosimege, M. (E-mail: 16175166@nwu.ac.za)
Safety. (Potchefstroom) Co-ordinator (Safety): Jackson, F. (E-mail: 20898363@nwu.ac.za)
Scholarships, awards, loans. (Potchefstroom) Director (Scholarships, awards, loans): Hefer, D., MBA N-W(S.Af.) (E-mail: 20283253@nwu.ac.za)
Scholarships, awards, loans. (Mafikeng) Financial Aid and Scholarships Officer: Tlatsana, T. D., BSocSc N-W(S.Af.) (E-mail: 16407040@nwu.ac.za)
Schools liaison. (Potchefstroom) Head, Unit for Educational Services: Gibbs, M. G., BA Potchef. (E-mail: 10055835@nwu.ac.za)
Security. (Mafikeng) Manager, Protection Services: Gaanakgomo, J. (E-mail: 20559518@nwu.ac.za)
Security. (Potchefstroom) Director (Security): Engels, A. S., BA Potchef. (E-mail: dolf.engels@nwu.ac.za)
Sport and recreation. (Mafikeng) Sports Officer: Van Rooyen, F., BA OFS (E-mail: 16415922@nwu.ac.za)
Sport and recreation. (Potchefstroom) Head (Sport and recreation): Stoffberg, J., MBW Potchef. (E-mail: 10183248@nwu.ac.za)

Staff development and training. Director, Organisational Learning and Development: Van der Watt, Prof. C. J., DSc Potchef. (E-mail: 10058516@nwu.ac.za)
Student union. (Vaal Triangle) Chairman (Student Representative Council): Tebakeng, M. (E-mail: 1006015@nwu.ac.za)
Student union. (Mafikeng) Chairman (Student Representative Council): Atau-Rahman, A.
Student union. (Potchefstroom) Chairman (Student Representative Council): Tromp, M. (E-mail: 10173609@nwu.ac.za)
Student welfare/counselling. (Mafikeng) Head, Guidance and Counselling: Mokgoro, T. S., MSocSc N-W(S.Af.) (E-mail: 16169638@nwu.ac.za)
Student welfare/counselling. (Vaal Triangle) Officer-in-Charge: Stavast, H. A. (E-mail: 10060715@nwu.ac.za)
Student welfare/counselling. (Potchefstroom) Students Dean: Reyneke, Prof. H. J., MA Potchef. (E-mail: 10180206@nwu.ac.za)
University press. (Mafikeng) Manager, Public Relations: Motabogi, S., BA(Comm) N-W(S.Af.) (E-mail: 16372603@nwu.ac.za)

CAMPUS/COLLEGE HEADS

Mafikeng Campus, Private Bag X2046, Mmabatho, 2735 South Africa. (Tel: (018) 389 2111; Fax: (018) 392 5775; E-mail: 10829547@nwu.ac.za) Campus Rector: Kgwadi, Prof. Ntate D., BSc Bophut., MSc Ball, MPhil North(S.Af.), PhD Potchef.
Potchefstroom Campus, Private Bag X6001, Potchefstroom, 2520 South Africa. (Tel: (018) 299 1111; Fax: (018) 299 2799; E-mail: 1005597@nwu.ac.za) Campus Rector: Combrink, Prof. Annette L., BA Potchef., MA Potchef., DLitt Potchef.
Vaal Triangle Campus, PO Box 1174, Vanderbijlpark, 1900 South Africa. (Tel: (016) 910 3111; Fax: (016) 910 3116; E-mail: 10057870@@nwu.ac.za) Campus Rector: Prinsloo, Prof. Piet J. J., DLitt Potchef.

[Information supplied by the institution as at 10 October 2007, and edited by the ACU]

UNIVERSITY OF PRETORIA

Founded 1908

Member of the Association of Commonwealth Universities

Postal Address: Pretoria, 0002 South Africa
Telephone: (012) 420 4111 **Fax:** (012) 362 5168
URL: http://www.up.ac.za

VICE-CHANCELLOR AND PRINCIPAL*—Pistorius, Prof. Carl W. I., BSc(Eng) Pret., BEng Pret., MS Ohio State, SM M.I.T., PhD Ohio State, FRSSAf
VICE-PRINCIPAL—De Beer, Prof. C. R., BJur&Art Potchef., LLB Potchef., LLM Rand Afrikaans, DrsJuris Ley., LLD Ley.
VICE-PRINCIPAL—Mogotlane, Prof. R. A., MB ChB Natal, FRCPSGlas, FRCSEd
VICE-PRINCIPAL—Crewe, Prof. Robin M., BScAgric Natal, MScAgric Natal, PhD Georgia
VICE-PRINCIPAL—Ogude, N. A., BSc NUL, MSc Nair., DTE S.Af., PhD Witw.
REGISTRAR‡—Grové, Prof. Nic J., BA Pret., LLB Pret., LLM Pret., LLD Rand Afrikaans
EXECUTIVE DIRECTOR—De Klerk, Prof. A. M., BEng Pret., MEng Pret., MS Stan., PhD Stan.
EXECUTIVE DIRECTOR—Vil-Nkomo, Prof. S., BA Lincoln(Pa.), MA Delaware, PhD Delaware
ADVISOR TO THE VICE-PRINCIPAL AND RECTOR—Melck, Prof. A. P., BComm Stell., BA Camb., MComm Stell., MA Camb., DComm Stell., LLD Stell., DHumL Thomas A. Edison State
EXECUTIVE DIRECTOR—Nel, J. S. J., BCom Pret.
UNIVERSITY LIBRARIAN—Moropa, R., BBibl Fort Hare, BBibl S.Af.

GENERAL INFORMATION

History. Previously established in 1910 as Transvaal University College, the university was founded in 1930.

Admission to first degree courses (see also South African Introduction). Matriculation Exemption Certificate issued by the Matriculation Board. Applicants who do not meet the subject requirements applicable in certain faculties may be admitted through an entrance test.

International candidates: Foreign Conditional Exemption Certificate from Matriculation Board; valid study permit from Department of Home Affairs; Test of English as a Foreign Language (TOEFL) score of (usually) at least 550.

First Degrees (see also South African Directory to Subjects of Study) (* = with honours). BA, BA*, BA(ArtsEducation), BAdmin*, BAdmin, BA(Drama), BA(Drama)*, BA(FineArts), BA(FineArts)*, BA(HumanMovementScience), BA(HumanMovementScience)*, BA(InformationDesign), BA(Languages), BA(Languages)*, BA(Law), BA(Music), BA(Theol), BA(Theol)*, BA(VisualStudies),

BA(VisualStudies)*, BChD, BCom, BCom*, BCommunicationPathology, BConsumerScience, BCur, BCur(IetA), BDietetics, BDietetics*, BEd, BEd*, BEng, BEng*, BHCS, BHCS*, BInstAgrar, BInstAgrar*, BIS, BIS*, BIT, BL*, BMedSci, BMus, BMus*, BOccTher, BPhysT, BPolSci, BPolSci*, BRad, BRad*, BSc, BSc*, BSc(Agric), BSc(Arch), BSc(ConstrMan), BSc(ConstrMan)*, BScInt, BSc(LArch), BSc(QS), BSc(QS)*, BSecEd(Sci), BSocSci, BSocSci*, BSportScience, BTh, BT&RP, BVSc, BVSc*, LLB, MB ChB.

Length of course. Full-time: BL*: 2 years; BA, BA(Drama), BA(HumanMovementScience), BA(Languages), BA(Law), BA(Music), BA(Theol), BA(VisualStudies), BAdmin, BCom, BCur(IetA), BHCS, BIS, BMedSci, BPolSci, BRad, BSc, BSc(Arch), BSc(ConstrMan), BSc(LArch), BSc(QS), BScInt, BSocSci, BSportScience: 3 years; BA(ArtsEducation), BA(Drama)*, BA(FineArts), BA(HumanMovementScience)*, BA(InformationDesign), BA(Languages)*, BA(Theol)*, BA(VisualStudies)*, BA*, BAdmin*, BCom*, BCommunicationPathology, BConsumerScience, BCur, BDietetics, BEd, BEng, BHCS*, BInstAgrar, BIS*, BIT, BMus, BOccTher, BPhysT, BPolSci*, BRad*, BSc(Agric), BSc*, BSecEd(Sci), BSocSci*, BT&RP, BTh, BVSc, LLB: 4 years; BA(FineArts)*, BChD, BDietetics*, BEd*,

BEng*, BInstAgrar*, BMus*, BSc(ConstrMan)*, BSc(QS)*: 5 years; BVSc*, MB ChB: 6 years.

Higher Degrees (see also South African Directory to Subjects of Study).

Master's. LLM, MA, MAdmin, MA(Drama), MA(FineArts), MA(HumanMovementScience), MArch, MA(Theol), MBA, MChD, MCom, MCommPath, MConsumerScience, MCur, MD, MDietetics, MDiplomaticStudies, MDiv, MEd, MEng, MHCS, MInstAgrar, MInt, MIS, MIT, MMEd, MMedVet, MMilMed, MMus, MOccTher, MPA, MPH, MPharmMed, MPhil, MPhysT, MPoliticalPolicyStudies, MRad, MSc, MSc(Agric), MSc(ConstrMan), MSc(Odont), MSc(ProjectManagement), MSc(QS), MSc(RealEstate), MSecurityStudies, MSocialWork, MSocSci, MTh, MT&RP.

Admission. Candidates must normally hold a bachelor's or honours degree as required by the regulations of the relevant faculty.

Length of course. Full-time: MA, MA(Drama), MA(HumanMovementScience), MA(Theol), MAdmin, MArch, MCom, MDiplomaticStudies, MEd, MEng, MHCS, MInstAgrar, MIS, MIT, MMus, MPA, MPhil, MPoliticalPolicyStudies, MSc, MSc(Agric), MSocSci: 1 year; LLM, MA(FineArts), MBA, MCommPath, MConsumerScience, MCur, MD, MDietetics, MDiv, MInt, MMedVet, MOccTher, MPH,

MPhysT, MRad, MSc(ConstrMan),
MSc(Odont), MSc(ProjectManagement),
MSc(QS), MSc(RealEstate), MSecurityStudies,
MSocialWork, MT&RP, MTh: 2 years;
MMilMed, MPharmMed: 3 years; MChD,
MMEd: 4 years.

Doctoral. DAdmin, DBA, DCom, DCur, DD,
DEng, DLitt, DMus, DOccTher, DPhil, DSc,
DSc(Odont), DVSc, LLD, PhD.

Admission. Candidates must normally hold a
master's degree.

Length of course. Full-time: DCur, DD, DEng,
DLitt, DMus, DOccTher, DPhil, DSc,
DSc(Odont), DVSc, LLD, PhD: 2 years; DBA: 3
years; DAdmin, DCom: 4 years.

Language of Instruction. Afrikaans or
English. Afrikaans language courses available.

Libraries. Volumes: 1,763,178. Periodicals
subscribed to: 2785. Other holdings: 32,658
electronic journals; 5334 audio-visual titles.
Special collections: Africana collection; South
African music collection (includes F. Z. van
der Merwe, Mimi Coertse, Marita Napier and
Stefans Grové sheet music collections);
Tukkiana (University of Pretoria publications);
African cultural heritage (Van Warmelo
collection on anthropology); Anglo Boer war;
Birch (waterpaintings, documents, books,
photographs and Old Johannesburg mining
maps); human rights reference; law of Africa;
old authorities (legal books); Netherlands
cultural historical collection; HIV/AIDS
collection.

Academic Awards (2007). 8605 awards
ranging in value from R1000 to R100,000.

Academic Year (2008). Four quarters: 31
January–18 March; 31 March–21 May; 14
July–29 August; 1 September–28 October.

Income (2006). Total, R2,693,000,000.

Statistics. Staff (2006): 4265 (2124
academic, 2141 non-academic). Students
(2007): full-time 34,445 (16,010 men,
18,435 women); part-time 4190 (2141 men,
2049 women); international 2588 (1425 men,
1163 women); distance education/external
14,433 (4746 men, 9687 women);
undergraduate 28,282 (12,556 men, 15,726
women); master's 5143 (2737 men, 2406
women); doctoral 1393 (797 men, 596
women).

FACULTIES/SCHOOLS
Economic and Management Sciences
Tel: (012) 420 2425 Fax: (012) 362 5194
E-mail: irene.vandenberg@up.ac.za
Dean: Koornhof, Prof. Carolina, BCom Pret.,
MCom Witw., DCom Pret.
Secretary: Van den Berg, Irene

Education
Tel: (012) 420 5721 Fax: (012) 420 4215
E-mail: yvonne.munro@up.ac.za
Acting Dean: Eloff, Irma, BA Potchef., BEd Pret.,
MEd Pret., PhD Stell.
Secretary: Munro, Yvonne

Engineering, Built Environment and
Information Technology
Tel: (012) 420 2005 Fax: (012) 420 2208
E-mail: dean@eng.up.ac.za
Dean: Sandenberg, Prof. Roelof F., MEng Pret.,
DEng Pret.
Secretary: Damons, Leola

Health Sciences
Tel: (012) 354 2386 Fax: (012) 329 1351
E-mail: mpume.ngcobo@up.ac.za
Dean: Mariba, Prof. Thanyani J., MB ChB Natal,
FCP(SA), FRCP
Secretary: Ngcobo, Mpume

Humanities
Tel: (012) 420 2318 Fax: (012) 420 4501
E-mail: gwdekaan@up.ac.za
Dean: Muller, Prof. Marie E., MA Pret.,
DLitt&Phil Rand Afrikaans
Secretary: Bicknelle, Hildegard E.

Law
Tel: (012) 420 2412 Fax: (012) 362 5184
Dean: Heyns, Prof. Christoffel H., BA Pret., BLC
Pret., LLB Pret., MA Pret., LLM Yale, PhD
Witw.
Secretary: Botha, Marlene

Natural and Agricultural Sciences
(General)
Tel: (021) 420 2478 Fax: (021) 420 3890
E-mail: dean@bioagric.up.ac.za
Dean: Ströh, Prof. Anton, BSc Pret., MSc Pret.,
PhD Pret.
Secretary: Cronjé, Elmarie

Theology
Tel: (012) 420 2322 Fax: (012) 420 4016
E-mail: teolb@ccnet.up.ac.za
Dean: Vos, Prof. Casparus J. A., BA Pret., DD
Pret.
Secretary: Aucamp, Carla

Veterinary Science
Tel: (012) 529 8201 Fax: (012) 529 8313
E-mail: vetdean@up.ac.za
Dean: Swan, Prof. Gerald E., BVSc Pret.,
MMedVet Pret., PhD Potchef.
Secretary: Prinsloo, Linda

ACADEMIC UNITS
Accounting
Tel: (012) 420 3211 Fax: (012) 362 5142
E-mail: eunice.dutoit@hakuna.up.ac.za
Booysen, Stefaans F., MCompt S.Af., DCom Pret.
Hon. Prof.
Coetzee, Stephen A., BCompt S.Af. Sr. Lectr.
Du Plessis, Daniel E., BCom Pret. Sr. Lectr.
Friedrichs, Juliana, BCom Pret. Sr. Lectr.
Gerber, Thinus C., BA Pret., BD Pret., MDiv Pret.
Sr. Lectr.
Griesel, Sonja, BCompt S.Af., MCom(Acc) Rand
Afrikaans Sr. Lectr.
Haasbroek, Chanette, BCom Pret. Sr. Lectr.
Hattingh, Marteli, BCom Jo'burg. Sr. Lectr.
Janse van Renburg, Cecile E., BCom Pret. Sr.
Lectr.
Leith, Karin B., BCom Natal Sr. Lectr.
Molate, Mosie M. C., BCompt S.Af. Sr. Lectr.
Myburgh, Jean E., DCom Pret. Assoc. Prof.
Oberholster, Johan G. I., MCom Jo'burg.
Assoc. Prof.
Pretorius, Denice, BCompt S.Af., BCom(Accg)
Pret. Sr. Lectr.
Roode, Monika, MCom Pret. Sr. Lectr.
Schumulian, A., BCom Pret. Sr. Lectr.
Smit, Anri, BCom Pret. Sr. Lectr.
Smith, Sonnette E., BCom Cape Town Sr. Lectr.
Terblanche, Andries B., MCom Rand Afrikaans,
DCom Pret. Hon. Prof.
Tomes, Tania, BCom Pret. Sr. Lectr.
Van der Schyf, Daniel B., DCom Potchef. Prof.
Von Well, Rieka, BCom Pret. Sr. Lectr.
Vorster, Quintus, MCom Stell., PhD Stell. Prof.;
Head*
Walters, Stephanie, BCom Pret. Sr. Lectr.
Other Staff: 6 Lectrs.
Research: accounting education; forensic
accounting; global convergence of
accounting standards; sustainable reporting,
including environmental, social and
employee reporting; the financial reporting
process

African Languages
Tel: (012) 420 2320 Fax: (012) 420 3163
E-mail: stienie.venter@up.ac.za
Gauton, Rachélle, MA Pret., DLitt Pret. Assoc.
Prof.
Goslin, Benjamin du P., BA Pret., MEd Pret. Sr.
Lectr.

Mojalefa, Mawatle J., MA Pret., DLitt Pret.
Prof.
Prinsloo, Daniel J., MA Pret., DLitt&Phil S.Af.
Prof.; Head*
Ramagoshi, Refilwe M., BA North(S.Af.), MA
Rand Afrikaans Sr. Lectr.
Skhosana, Philemon B., BA S.Af., BA Pret., MA
Pret. Sr. Lectr.
Taljard, Elizabeth, MA Pret., DLitt Pret. Assoc.
Prof.
Other Staff: 1 Lectr.
Research: African languages (linguistics); African
languages (literature); corpus linguistics;
lexicography; translation

Afrikaans
Tel: (012) 420 4320 Fax: (012) 420 2349
E-mail: celliers@postino.up.ac.za
Bosman, Hendrina J., MA Pret., DLitt Stell. Sr.
Lectr.
Gerwel, Gert J., BA W.Cape, LicGerm Brussels,
DLitt&Phil Brussels Hon. Prof.
Grebe, Heinrich P., MA Stell., DLitt Pret. Sr.
Lectr.
Milton, Viola C., MA Pret., PhD Indiana Sr.
Lectr.
Ohlhoff, Carl H. F., MA Pret., DLitt Pret. Prof.
Willemse, Heinrich S. S., MA W.Cape, MBL
S.Af., DLitt W.Cape Prof.; Head*
Other Staff: 2 Lectrs.
Research: language and culture; language and
development/the politics of language;
language structure; media studies; text and
context

Agricultural Economics, Extension and
Rural Development
Tel: (012) 420 3251 Fax: (012) 420 3247
E-mail: johann.kirsten@up.ac.za
Blignaut, Chris, MSc(Agric) Pret., DScAgric Free
State Prof.
Bostyn, Frank, PhD Ghent Extraordinary Prof.
Coetzee, Gerhardus K., MSc(Agric) Stell., PhD
Pret. Assoc. Prof.
D'Haese, Luc J. G. M. H., PhD Ghent
Extraordinary Prof.
Doyer, Tobias, BSc(Agric) Pret. Sr. Lectr.
Düvel, Gustav H., BSc(Agric) Pret., MInstAgrar
Pret., DInstAgrar Pret. Prof.†
Geyser, Mariëtte, MCom Potchef., DCom Pret.
Sr. Lectr.
Hassan, Rashid M., BSc Khart., MSc Iowa, PhD
Iowa, BSc(Agric) MSc(Agric) Prof.
Kirsten, Johann F., MSc(Agric) Pret., PhD Pret.
Prof.; Head*
Louw, Andre, BSc(Agric) Stell., MSc(Agric)
Pret., DSc(Agric) Pret. Prof.
Machethe, Charles L., BSc(Agric) Fort Hare, MS
Mich.State, PhD Mich.State Prof.
Terblanché, Stephanus E., BSc(Agric) Pret.,
BInstAgrar Pret., MInstAgrar Pret., PhD Pret.
Sr. Lectr.
Thirtle, Colin G., MPhil Col., PhD Col.
Extraordinary Prof.
Van Rooyen, C. Johan, BScAgric Stell.,
MSc(Agric) Pret., DSc(Agric) Pret. ABSA
Prof., Agribusiness Management
Other Staff: 4 Lectrs.; 1 Res. Fellow
Research: agribusiness management; agricultural
and rural finance; agricultural policy;
environmental economics; land reform

Ancient Languages
Tel: (012) 420 3658 Fax: (012) 420 4008
E-mail: henk.potgieter@up.ac.za
Botha, Philippus J., MA Pret., DD Pret. Prof.
Kritzinger, Jacobus P. K., BD Pret., MA Pret.,
DLitt Pret. Sr. Lectr.
Potgieter, Johan H., BA Potchef., MA Pret., DD
Pret. Prof.; Head*
Prinsloo, Gert T. M., DD Pret. Prof.
Stander, Hendrik F., MA Pret., MATheology
Pret., DLitt Pret. Prof.
Swart, Gerhardus J., MA Stell., MA Pret., DLitt
Pret. Assoc. Prof.
Other Staff: 1 Lectr.
Research: Greek language and literature; history
of ancient cultures; Latin language and

literature; patristic studies; Semitic languages and literature

Animal and Wildlife Sciences

Tel: (012) 420 4018 Fax: (012) 420 3290
E-mail: animal&wildlife.sciences@up.ac.za
Bothma, Jacobus du P., MSc Pret., PhD Texas A.& M.   Extraordinary Prof.
Casey, Norman H., MSc(Agric) Natal, DSc(Agric) Pret.   Prof.
Donkin, E. F., BScAgric Natal, MPhil Lond., PhD S.Af.Med.   Assoc. Prof.
Erasmus, Lourens J., MSc(Agric) Pret., PhD Pret.   Assoc. Prof.
Hassen, A., BSc Alemaya, MSc Muslim, Morogoro, PhD Pret.   Sr. Lectr.
Jansen van Ryssen, Jannes B., BSc(Agric) Pret., MSc(Agric) Natal, PhD Natal   Emer. Prof.
Meyer, J. A., MSc(Agric) Pret., PhD Pret.   Sr. Lectr.
Oelofse, A., MSc(Nutrition) Stell., PhD Wageningen   Assoc. Prof.
Schoeman, Stefanus J., DScAgric Free State   Extraordinary Prof.
Strydom, P. E., MSc(Agric) Pret., PhD OFS   Sr. Lectr.
Van Hoven, Wouter, MSc Potchef., DSc Potchef.   Assoc. Prof.
Van Marle-Köster, E., BSc(Agric) Pret., MSc(Agric) Free State, PhD Pret.   Sr. Lectr.
Van Niekerk, Willem A., MSc(Agric) Pret., PhD Pret.   Assoc. Prof.
Webb, Edward C., MSc(Agric) Pret., PhD Pret.   Assoc. Prof.; Head*
Other Staff: 3 Lectrs.; 2 Res. Fellows; 1 Temp. Lectr.
Research: genetics (performance traits and DNA genetic markers); nutrition (wildlife, domesticated ruminants and domesticated monogastrics); physiology (growth, digestion and reproduction); rural development (resource management and production planning); wildlife (resource and wildlife management)

Anthropology and Archaeology

Tel: (012) 420 2595 Fax: (012) 420 4921
E-mail: john.sharp@up.ac.za
Boonzaaier, Carl C., MA Pret., DPhil Pret.   Assoc. Prof.
Cook, Susan E., PhD Yale   Assoc. Prof.
Ebrahim-Vally, Rehana, PhD Paris IV   Assoc. Prof.
Kriel, Johannes D., MA Pret., DPhil Pret.   Assoc. Prof.
Ouzman, Sven, BA Witw., MA Calif., PhD Calif.   Sr. Lectr.
Pikirayi, Innocent, BA Z'bwe., MA Z'bwe., PhD Uppsala   Sr. Lectr.
Sharp, John S., PhD Camb.   Prof.; Head*
Other Staff: 1 Lectr.; 1 Sr. Res. Officer
Research: applied anthropology, community development and tourism; ethnicity and identity politics; ethno-archaeology; power and belief systems; urbanisation and urbanism

Architecture, Landscape Architecture and Interior Architecture

Tel: (012) 420 2550 Fax: (012) 420 2552
E-mail: archi@postino.up.ac.za
Bakker, Karel A., MArch Pret., PhD Pret.   Prof.
De Villiers, Adriaan J., MArch Pret., PhD Pret.   Assoc. Prof.
Fisher, Roger C., MArch Pret., PhD Pret.   Prof.
Jekot, Barbara P., MScArch Gliwice, PhD Warsaw U.T.   Assoc. Prof.
Joubert, Ora, MArch Penn.State, PhD Natal   Prof.; Head*
Le Roux, Schalk W., MArch Pret., PhD Pret.   Prof.
Osman, Amira, BScArch Khart., MScArch Khart., PhD Pret.   Sr. Lectr.
Theron, Gwen, BL Pret., MLA Texas A.& M., PhD Pret.   Assoc. Prof.
Vosloo, Pieter T., BSc Pret., BArch Pret., ML Pret., BSc   Sr. Lectr.

Young, Graham A., BArch Tor., BL Tor.   Sr. Lectr.
Other Staff: 11 Lectrs.; 19 Temp. Lectrs.
Research: appropriate and sustainable technologies; design theory and education; environment and development; heritage and conservation; urbanism and settlement

Arts, Languages, Human Movement Studies Education

Tel: (012) 420 5639 Fax: (012) 420 5637
E-mail: laurel.becker@up.ac.za
Becker, Laurel R., BA Pret., MA Stell.   Sr. Lectr.; Head*
Cloete, Johann L., BA Potchef., MA Pret.   Sr. Lectr.
Van der Westhuizen, Carol N., BA Pret., MA S.Af., DLitt&Phil S.Af.   Sr. Lectr.

Auditing

Tel: (012) 420 4427 Fax: (012) 362 5199
E-mail: tania.laubscher@up.ac.za
Basson, Gideon J., BAdmin S.Af.   Hon. Prof.
Beukes, Bernice, BCom Potchef.   Sr. Lectr.
Coetzee, Georgina P., MCom Pret.   Sr. Lectr.
De Jager, Hermanus, BEd Pret., MEd Potchef., MCom Pret., DCom Pret.   Prof.; Head*
De Kock, Ronel, MCom Rand Afrikaans   Sr. Lectr.
Du Bruyn, Rudrik, MCom Pret.   Sr. Lectr.
Gloeck, Juergen D., MCom Pret., DCom Pret.   Prof.
Joosub, Tasneem, MCom S.Af.   Sr. Lectr.
Koen, Marius, MCom Pret., DCom Pret.   Hon. Prof.
Steyn, Corlia, BCom Pret.   Sr. Lectr.
Sumners, Glenn E., DBA   Hon. Prof.
Van Staden, Johanna M., MCom Free State   Sr. Lectr.
Venter, Anita, MCom S.Af.   Sr. Lectr.
Other Staff: 1 Lectr.
Research: the audit expectation gap

Biblical and Religious Studies

Tel: (012) 420 3155 Fax: (012) 420 2887
E-mail: djhuman@ccnet.up.ac.za
Human, Dirk J., BD Pret., MA Rand Afrikaans, DD Pret.   Prof.; Head*
Other Staff: 1 Lectr.
Research: monotheism; Old Testament theology and exegesis; psalms; scripture and its use in Africa; the historical Jesus

Biochemistry

Tel: (012) 420 3793 Fax: (012) 362 5302
E-mail: albert.neitz@bioagric.up.ac.za
Apostolides, Zeno, MSc(Agric) Pret., DSc(Agric) Pret.   Sr. Lectr.
Beukes, Mervyn, BSc W.Cape, MSc Pret., PhD Pret.   Sr. Lectr.
Birkholtz, Lynn-Marie, MSc Pret., PhD Pret.   Sr. Lectr.
Gaspar, Anabella R. M., MSc Pret., PhD Pret.   Sr. Lectr.
Joubert, Fourie, MSc Pret., PhD Pret.   Assoc. Prof.
Kenyon, Colin, MSc Free State, PhD Rhodes   Extraordinary Prof.
Louw, Abraham I., MSc(Agric) Pret., DSc(Agric) Pret.   Prof.
Morris, Jane E., BSc St And., PhD Aberd.   Extraordinary Prof.
Neitz, Albert W. H., MSc(Agric) Pret., DSc(Agric) Pret.   Prof.
Verschoor, Jan A., MSc(Agric) Pret., DSc(Agric) Pret.   Prof.; Head*
Other Staff: 2 Res. Fellows
Research: biochemical aspects of the quality and health properties of tea; biochemistry, immunology and molecular biology of parasites and bacteria of medical/veterinary significance; bio-informatics; computational biology

Biokinetics, Sport and Leisure Sciences

Tel: (012) 420 6039 Fax: (012) 420 6099
E-mail: tilla.boshoff@up.ac.za
Baechle, Thomas R., EdD S.Dakota   Hon. Prof.

Goslin, Anna E., MA(PhysEd) Pret., MBA Pret., DPhil Pret.   Prof.
Hendriks, Denver J., MA Stell.   Extraordinary Prof.
Jansen van Vuuren, Thomas B. R., MA(PhysEd) PhD   Sr. Lectr.
Kluka, Darlene A., MA Illinois State, PhD   Extraordinary Prof.
Kruger, Pieter E., MA(PhysEd) Pret., DPhil Pret.   Prof.
Steyn, Barend J. M., MEd(PhysEd) Pret., MA Pret., DEd Pret., DPhil Pret.   Prof.
Van Wyk, Gerrit J., BA Free State, MA Pret., DPhil Pret.   Prof.; Head*
Van Wyk, Johannes G. U., MA(PhysEd) Potchef., MEd S.Af., PhD Pret.   Sr. Lectr.
Other Staff: 6 Lectrs.
Research: biokinetics; exercise science; human movement science; recreation science; sport: management

Business Management

Tel: (012) 420 2411 Fax: (012) 362 5198
E-mail: ghnieman@hakuna.up.ac.za
de Villiers, Willem A., BMil Stell., MBA Pret., DBA Pret.   Sr. Lectr.
Janse van Vuuren, Johannes J., MBA Pret., DBA Pret.   Prof.
Le Roux, I., BA Stell., BEd Stell., MPhil Pret., PhD Pret., DCom Pret.   Sr. Lectr.
Maasdorp, Edward F. de V., MBA Pret., DCom Pret.   Prof.
Marx, Andrew E., MCom Pret.   Prof.
Nieman, Gideon H., MBA Pret., PhD Vista   Prof.; Head*
Pretorius, Marius, BSc(Agric) Pret., MSc(Agric) North(S.Af.), MBL S.Af., DTech Tshwane UT   Sr. Lectr.
Raath, Leon, BCom Pret.   Extraordinary Prof.
Segal, N. S., PhD Witw., DPhil Oxf.   Hon. Prof.
Venter, D. J., DCom S.Af.   Extraordinary Prof.
Vögel, A. J., BCom Rand Afrikaans, MCom Pret., DCom Pret.   Sr. Lectr.
Other Staff: 7 Lectrs.
Research: e-commerce; entrepreneurship; international management; logistic management; strategic management

Chemistry

Tel: (012) 420 2512 Fax: (012) 362 5297
E-mail: ignacy.cukrowski@up.ac.za
Bauermeister, Sieglinde, MSc Pret., PhD Pret.   Sr. Lectr.
Cukrowski, Ignacy, MSc Lublin, PhD Lublin, DSc Torún   Prof.; Head*
Landman, Marilé, MSc Pret., PhD Pret.   Sr. Lectr.
Laurens, Johannes B., MSc Pret., PhD Pret.   Sr. Lectr.
Lotz, Simon, MSc Stell., PhD Rand Afrikaans   Prof.
Nkwelo, Mluleki M., MSc Fort Hare, PhD Witw.   Sr. Lectr.
Ozoemena, Kenneth I., MSc Lagos, PhD Rhodes   Sr. Lectr.
Pilcher, Lynne A., MSc Rhodes, PhD Camb.   Sr. Lectr.
Potgieter, Maria, MSc S.Af., PhD Ill.   Sr. Lectr.
Rohwer, Egmont R., MSc Stell., PhD Rand Afrikaans   Prof.
Schoeman, Wentzel J., BCom S.Af., MSc Pret., DSc Pret.   Assoc. Prof.
Schutte, Casper J. H., BSc Potchef., DrMath&Phys Amst., FRSSAf   Hon. Prof.
Van Rooyen, Petrus H., MSc Rand Afrikaans, PhD Rand Afrikaans   Prof.
Venter, Elise M. M., MSc Pret., PhD Rand Afrikaans   Sr. Lectr.
Vleggaar, Robert, MSc Pret., DSc Pret.   Prof.
Other Staff: 3 Lectrs.; 3 Sr. Res. Officers; 1 Res. Fellow
Research: chemical analysis; chemical education; chemical synthesis; industrial chemistry; materials chemistry

Church History and Church Polity

Tel: (012) 420 2889 Fax: (012) 420 4016
E-mail: prakgesk@ccnet.up.ac.za
Duncan, Graham A., BEd *Aberd.*, BD *Aberd.*, MTh
S.Af., DTh *S.Af.*, PhD Pret. Assoc. Prof.;
Acting Head*
Labuschagne, C. J., BA Pret., DD Pret. Sr. Lectr.
Research: contemporary South African church
history; ecumenical church history; history
of the establishment and growth of the
Dutch Reformed Church of Africa;
nineteenth and twentieth century
theological debate; spirituality in the
reformed tradition

Communication Pathology

Tel: (012) 420 2357 Fax: (012) 420 3517
E-mail: brenda.louw@up.ac.za
Kritzinger, Aletta M., MA(Log) Pret., DPhil Pret.
Assoc. Prof.
Louw, Brenda, BA(Log) Pret., MSc *Alabama*,
DPhil Pret. Prof.; Head*
Pottas, Lidia, MCommPath Pret., DPhil Pret. Sr.
Lectr.
Soer, Magdalena E., MA(Log) Pret., DPhil Pret.
Sr. Lectr.
Swanepoel, Daniel C. D., MCommPath Pret.,
DPhil Pret. Sr. Lectr.
Tesner, Hermanus E. C., MA Pret. Sr. Lectr.
Van der Merwe, Anita, MA(Log) Pret., DPhil
Pret. Prof.
Other Staff: 9 Lectrs.
Research: analysis of speech; cochlear implants;
early intervention; hearing disorders in
children; motor-speech disorders

Computer Science

Tel: (012) 420 3120 Fax: (012) 362 5188
E-mail: cgama@cs.up.ac.za
Bishop, Judith M., BSc *Rhodes*, MSc *Natal*, PhD
S'ton. Prof.
Eloff, Jan H. P., BSc *Rand Afrikaans*, MSc *Rand
Afrikaans*, PhD *Rand Afrikaans* Prof.; Head*
Engelbrecht, Andries P., MSc Stell., PhD Stell.
Prof.
Kourie, Derrick G., MSc Pret., MSc *S.Af.*, PhD
Lanc. Prof.
Olivier, Martin S., BSc *Rand Afrikaans*, MSc *Rand
Afrikaans*, PhD *Rand Afrikaans* Prof.
Van den Heever, Roelf J., MSc Pret., MS *Stan.*,
MEng *Calif.*, PhD *Calif.* Extraordinary Prof.
Venter, Hein S., BSc *Rand Afrikaans*, MSc *Rand
Afrikaans*, PhD *Rand Afrikaans* Sr. Lectr.
Watson, Bruce W., PhD *T.U.Eindhoven*
Extraordinary Prof.
Other Staff: 10 Lectrs.
Research: computational intelligence; distributed
components and middleware; information
and computer security architectures;
software engineering, principles and
practice; theoretical and applied computer
science research

Construction Economics

Tel: (012) 420 2576 Fax: (012) 420 3598
E-mail: corrie.pienaar@up.ac.za
Basson, Gert A. J., BSc Pret., BEng Pret. Sr.
Lectr.
Brümmer, Diederick G., MSc(QS) Pret., PhD
Pret. Prof.; Head*
Cloete, Christiaan E., BA Pret., MSc Pret., MBL
S.Af., DSc Pret. Prof.
Maritz, Marthinus J., MSc(QS) Pret., PhD Pret.
Assoc. Prof.
Other Staff: 9 Lectrs.
Research: building technology; construction
procurement; property development;
property management; real estate

Consumer Science

Tel: (012) 420 2531 Fax: (012) 420 2855
E-mail: consumer.science@postino.up.ac.za
De Klerk, Helena M., MHomeEconomics Pret.,
PhD Pret. Assoc. Prof.; Head*
Erasmus, Aletta C., BHomeEconomics Pret., PhD
Pret. Sr. Lectr.
Other Staff: 8 Lectrs.
Research: consumer groups in South Africa;
development, marketing and consumption
of products and services to further small
businesses, retail trade, community
development and tourism; human
behaviour in relation to food, nutrition,
clothing, textiles and interior merchandise

Curriculum Studies

Tel: (012) 420 2207 Fax: (012) 420 3003
E-mail: william.fraser@up.ac.za
Bender, Cornelia J. G., BA Pret., BEd Pret., MA
Pret., DEd Pret. Sr. Lectr.
De Kock, Dorothea M., BA *Stell.*, MA Pret., PhD
Pret. Assoc. Prof.
Du Toit, Pieter H., MEd Pret., PhD Pret. Sr.
Lectr.
Fraser, William J., BSc *Potchef.*, BEd *S.Af.*, MEd
S.Af., DEd *S.Af.* Prof.; Head*
Hartell, Cycil G., BA *S.Af.*, BEd Pret., MEd Pret.,
PhD Pret. Sr. Lectr.
Hattingh, Annemarie, BSc Pret., BEd Pret., MEd
Pret., PhD Pret. Prof.
Howie, Sarah J., BA *Stell.*, MEd *Witw.*, PhD
T.H.Twente Assoc. Prof.
Jita, Loyiso C., BSc *Witw.*, BEd *Zululand*, MA
Mich.State, PhD *Mich.State* Sr. Lectr.
Killen, L. R., BSc *Newcastle(NSW)*, MEd
Newcastle(NSW), PhD *Newcastle(NSW)*
Extraordinary Prof.
Knoetze, Jan G., BSc Pret., BEd Pret., MEd Pret.,
PhD Pret. Assoc. Prof.
Kuhn, Marthinus J., MA Pret., BEd Pret., DLitt
Pret. Assoc. Prof.
Maree, J. G., BA Pret., BEd Pret., MEd Pret., DEd
Pret., PhD Pret., DPhil Pret. Prof.
Pillay, Venitha, BA *W.Cape*, BA *S.Af.*, MA *Natal*,
PhD Pret. Sr. Lectr.
Plomp, Tjeerd, MSc *V.U.Amst.*, PhD *V.U.Amst.*,
PhD *Ghent* Extraordinary Prof.
Slabbert, Johannes A., BSc *Rand Afrikaans*, BEd
Rand Afrikaans, MEd Pret., DEd Pret. Assoc.
Prof.
Van Loggerenberg-Hattingh, Annemarie, BSc
Pret., BEd Pret., MEd Pret., PhD Pret. Sr.
Lectr.
Van Rooyen, Linda, BA *S.Af.*, BEd Pret., MEd
Pret., PhD Pret. Prof.
Vandeyar, Saloshna, BA(Ed) *Witw.*, BA *S.Af.*,
MEd *Witw.*, PhD Pret. Sr. Lectr.
Other Staff: 2 Lectrs.
Research: assessment and quality assurance;
computer-integrated education; learning
facilitation; science and technology; teacher
education

Dogmatics and Christian Ethics

Tel: (012) 420 3397 Fax: (012) 420 4016
E-mail: dogmsend@ccnet.up.ac.za
Buitendag, Johan, BA Pret., MCom *Rand
Afrikaans*, DD Pret. Prof.
De Villiers, D. Etienne, BTh *Stell.*, MA *Stell.*,
ThD *Amst.* Prof.
Veldsman, Daniel P., BA *P.Elizabeth*, DD Pret.
Assoc. Prof.
Wethmar, Conrad J., BA *Stell.*, BTh *Stell.*, MA
Stell., ThD *Amst.* Prof.; Head*
Research: basic issues in ecumenical/reformed
dogmatics; character of Christian morality;
economic justice in South Africa; modern
trends in systematic theology; the nature of
doctrine

Drama

Tel: (012) 420 2558 Fax: (012) 362 5281
E-mail: yrabie@postino.up.ac.za
Coetzee, Marié-Heleen, BA *Natal*, MTech
Pret.Tech., DTech *Pret.Tech.* Sr. Lectr.
Hagemann, Fredrick R., PhD *Natal* Prof.;
Head*
Other Staff: 3 Lectrs.; 1 Sr. Clin. Lectr.
Research: actor training; media studies including
radio, film and television; movement
studies; South African theatre philosophy;
theatre and drama in education and
development

Early Childhood Education

Tel: (012) 420 5641 Fax: (012) 420 5595
E-mail: nkidi@gk.up.ac.za
Phatudi, Nkidi C., BAPaed *North(S.Af.)*, BEd
Rhodes, MPhil Stell., PhD Pret. Lectr.; Head*
Other Staff: 5 Lectrs.; 4 Lectrs.†
Research: development of early childhood
education theories; early childhood
education curriculum development and
teacher training (assessment and evaluation
in early childhood education); early
childhood education policy development;
life skills learning; teaching and learning
strategies in early childhood education
(development of language and
mathematics)

Economics

Tel: (012) 420 2413 Fax: (012) 362 5207
E-mail: graduate@up.ac.za
Abedian, Iraj, MA(Econ) *Cape Town*, PhD *S.Fraser*
Hon. Prof.
Blignaut, James N., MCom Pret., DCom Pret.
Prof.
Breitenbach, Martin, BCom *Vista*, PhD Pret.
Prof.
Du Toit, Charlotte B., MCom Pret., DCom Pret.
Prof.
Fenyes, Tommy I., BSc(Agric) Pret., MSc(Agric)
Pret., DSc(Agric) Pret. Prof.
Franzsen, Riel, LLB Pret., LLD Stell. Prof.
Gupta, Rangan, PhD *Conn.* Assoc. Prof.
Harmse, Chris, MCom *Rand Afrikaans*, DCom
Pret. Hon. Prof.
Jordaan, André C., MCom Pret., DCom Pret.
Assoc. Prof.
Koch, Steven F., MA(Econ) *Penn.*, PhD *Penn.*
Prof.
Mabugu, Margaret R., BSc(Econ) *Z'bwe.*,
MSc(Econ) *Z'bwe.*, PhD *Gothenburg* Assoc.
Prof.
Mboweni Tito, M. A., MA *E.Anglia* Hon. Prof.
Mokate, Renosi, MA *Delaware*, PhD *Delaware*
Hon. Prof.
Parsons, Raymond W. K., BCom *Cape Town*, BA
Cape Town, Hon. DCom *P.Elizabeth* Hon.
Prof.
Schaling, Eric, BSc *Tilburg*, MPhil *Tilburg*, PhD
Tilburg Prof.
Schoeman, Nicolaas J., MA(Econ) Pret., DCom
Pret. Prof.
Scholtz, Frederik J., BCom Pret., LLB Pret. Sr.
Lectr.
Smal, M. M., MCom Pret., DCom Pret. Hon.
Prof.
Van der Merwe, Ernie J., MCom *Potchef.*, DCom
Potchef. Extraordinary Prof.
Van Eyden, Reneé, BSc *Potchef.*, MBA Pret.,
DCom Pret. Assoc. Prof.
Van Heerden, Jan H., BCom Pret., MCom *Rand
Afrikaans*, MA *Rice*, PhD *Rice* Prof.; Head*
Other Staff: 10 Lectrs.
Research: international trade and finance; job
creation (human resources analysis);
macroeconometric modelling; small
business development, local and regional
economic development and growth; tax
policy development

Education Management and Policy Studies

Tel: (012) 420 2902 Fax: (012) 420 3581
E-mail: johan.beckman@up.ac.za
Amsterdam, Christina E. N., BA *S.Af.*, MEd
S.Af., PhD *S.Carolina* Sr. Lectr.
Beckmann, Johannes L., BA *Potchef.*, BEd *Rand
Afrikaans*, MEd *Rand Afrikaans*, DEd Pret. Prof.
Herman, C., BA *Tel-Aviv*, BEd *Witw.*, MEd
Witw., PhD Pret. Sr. Lectr.
Joubert, Rika J., BSc Pret., PhD Pret. Sr. Lectr.
Nieuwenhuis, Jan F. J., BA Pret., BEd Pret., MEd
Pret., MDiac *S.Af.*, DEd *Rand Afrikaans* Sr.
Lectr.
Nkomo, M. N., BA *Penn.*, MEd *Mass.*, EdD *Mass.*
Prof.
Prinsloo, I. J., BA *Potchef.*, MEd *Potchef.*, DEd
S.Af. Sr. Lectr.

Sehoole, M. T., BAEd North(S.Af.), BEd Witw., MEd Witw., PhD Witw.   Sr. Lectr.
Van der Bank, Anita J., BA Pret., BEd Pret., MEd Pret., PhD Pret.   Assoc. Prof.; Head*
Other Staff: 4 Lectrs.
Research: education human resources management; education law and policy; performance indicators; quality assurance; school financial management

Educational Psychology

Tel: (012) 420 3751 Fax: (012) 420 5511
E-mail: adrie.vandyk@up.ac.za
Ebersöhn, Liesel, BPrimEd Pret., MEd Pret., PhD Pret.   Sr. Lectr.
Eloff, Irma, BA Potchef., BEd Pret., MEd Pret., PhD Stell.   Assoc. Prof.; Head*
Prinsloo, Heila M., BA(SocSc) Pret., PhD Pret., DEd Pret.   Sr. Lectr.
Other Staff: 3 Lectrs.
Research: asset-based approaches; HIV/AIDS primary education teaching; positive psychology; transdisciplinary education psychology

Engineering, Academic Development

Tel: (012) 420 4109 Fax: (012) 420 3874
E-mail: iplessis@postino.up.ac.za
Du Plessis, Gloudina, MA Pret., DPhil Pret.   Manager*
Steyn, Tobia M., BA Pret., BEd Pret., MEd Pret.   Sr. Lectr.
Research: counselling psychology; mathematics education

Engineering and Technology Management

Tel: (012) 420 4605 Fax: (012) 362 5307
E-mail: tinus.pretorius@eng.up.ac.za
Amadi-Echendu, Joe E., MS(EE) Wyoming, DPhil Sus., PhD   Prof.
Bekker, Michiel C., BEng Pret., MEng Rand Afrikaans, MBA Stell.   Sr. Lectr.
Brent, Alan C., BEng Stell., MSc Chalmers U.T.   Sr. Lectr.
Buys, André, BEng Cape Town, MEng Cape Town, DEng Pret.   Extraordinary Prof.
De Klerk, A. M., BEng Pret., MEng Pret., MS Stan., PhD Stan.   Prof.
Kachieng'a, Michael O., MSc(ElecEng) Moscow State T.U., PhD Cape Town   Assoc. Prof.
Köster, Manfried J. F., BSc(QS) Pret., MBA Pret., PhD Texas A.& M.   Extraordinary Prof.
Oerlemans, Leon A. G., BSc(Econ) Tilburg, MSc Tilburg, PhD T.U.Eindhoven   Extraordinary Prof.
Paterson, Adrian W., BSc(Chem) Cape Town, PhD Cape Town   Extraordinary Prof.
Pretorius, Marthinus W., BSc Pret., BEng Pret., PhD Pret.   Prof.; Head*
Pretorius, Petrus J., BEng Pret., MBA Pret., PhD Pret.   Sr. Lectr.
Steyn, Hermanus De V., BSc(Eng) Pret., MBA Pret., PhD Pret.   Prof.
Van Waveren, Cornelis C., BEng Pret., MEng Pret.   Sr. Lectr.
Visser, Jacobus K., BSc Stell., BEng Stell., PhD Pret.   Prof.
Other Staff: 1 Lectr.
Research: life cycle engineering; production and operations management; project management; scope and structure of engineering management; technology management

Engineering, Chemical

Tel: (012) 420 2475 Fax: (012) 362 5173
E-mail: philip.devaal@up.ac.za
Chirwa, Evans, PhD   Assoc. Prof.
Christopher, Lew, PhD   Extraordinary Prof.
De Vaal, Philip L., MEng Pret., PhD Pret.   Prof.; Head*
Du Plessis, Barend J. G. W., BEng Pret.   Sr. Lectr.
Du Toit, Elizbé, MEng Pret.   Sr. Lectr.
Focke, Walter W., BEng Pret., MEng Pret., PhD M.I.T.   Prof.

Friend, John F. C., BEng Pret., MScEng Cape Town   Sr. Lectr.
Grimsehl, Uys H. J., BEng Pret., DEng Pret.   Prof.
Heydenrych, Mike D., BSc(Eng) Witw., MScEng Witw., MPD S.Af., PhD T.H.Twente   Assoc. Prof.
Majozi, Thoko, PhD UMIST   Assoc. Prof.
Mandersloot, Willem G. B.   Extraordinary Prof.
Nicol, Willem, BEng Pret., PhD Witw.   Assoc. Prof.
Schoeman, Japie, PhD   Assoc. Prof.
Schutte, Christiaan F., MSc Potchef., MBL S.Af., PhD Cape Town   Prof.
Tolmay, Andries T., MEng Pret.   Sr. Lectr.
Research: air pollution control; polymer engineering; process modelling and control; tribology; water utilisation

Engineering, Civil and Biosystems

Tel: (012) 420 2429 Fax: (012) 362 5218
E-mail: rita.peens@up.ac.za
Burdzik, Walter M. G., MEng Pret., PhD Pret.   Prof.
De Klerk, Anton, MEng Pret.   Sr. Lectr.
Dekker, Nicolaas W., MEng Pret., PhD Witw.   Prof.
Du Plessis, Hendrik L. M., MSc(Eng) Pret., PhD Pret.   Prof.
Heymann, Gerhard, MEng Pret., PhD Sur.   Prof.
Horak, Emile, MEng Pret., MScEng Calif., PhD Pret.   Prof.; Head*
Kearsley, Elizabeth P., MEng Pret., PhD Leeds   Assoc. Prof.
Maree, Leon, MEng Pret., PhD Pret.   Prof.
Michael, Ronnie, MEng Pret.   Sr. Lectr.
Rust, Ebenhaezer, MEng Pret., PhD Sur.   Assoc. Prof.
Smit, Johannes E., BSc(Eng) Stell., MEng Pret.   Sr. Lectr.
Van der Stoep, Isobel, MEng Pret.   Sr. Lectr.
Van der Walt, Adriaan, MSc Potchef., DSc Potchef.   Assoc. Prof.
Van Rensburg, Barend W., MScEng Pret., MSc S'ton., PhD Pret.   Prof.
Van Vuuren, Stefanus J., MEng Pret., MBA Pret., PhD Pret.   Prof.
Venter, Christo J., BEng Stell., MEng Stell., PhD Calif.   Assoc. Prof.
Visser, Alex T., BSc(Eng) Cape Town, BCom S.Af., MSc Witw., PhD Texas   Prof.
Other Staff: 2 Lectrs.
Research: development of materials and design methods; management systems; materials research (fibre-reinforced foamed concrete); mine slime dams; tunnel ageing

Engineering, Electrical, Electronic and Computer

Tel: (012) 420 2164 Fax: (012) 362 5000
E-mail: leuschner@eng.up.ac.za
Barnard, E., BEng Pret., MSc Witw., PhD Carnegie-Mellon   Prof.
Camisani-Calzolari, Ferdinando R., BEng Pret., MEng Pret., PhD Pret.   Sr. Lectr.
Craig, Ian K., BEng Pret., MS M.I.T., MBA Witw., PhD Witw.   Prof.
De Villiers, J. Pieter, BEng Pret., MEng Pret.   Sr. Lectr.
Du Plessis, Monuko, BA S.Af., BCom S.Af., DEng Pret.   Prof.
Geldenhuys, Ronelle, BEng Pret., MEng Pret.   Sr. Lectr.
Gitau, Michael N., BSc(Eng) Nair., PhD Lough.   Assoc. Prof.
Hancke, Gerhardus P., MEng Stell., DEng Pret.   Prof.
Hanekom, Johannes J., MEng Pret., PhD Pret.   Assoc. Prof.
Hanekom, Tania, MEng Pret., PhD Pret.   Sr. Lectr.
Jacobs, Jan P., BEng Pret., BMus S.Af., BMus Pret., MEng Pret., MMus Pret., MMA Yale, DMA Yale   Sr. Lectr.
Joubert, Johan, MEng Pret., PhD Pret.   Prof.
Le Roux, W., BEng Rand Afrikaans, PhD Georgia I.T.   Sr. Lectr.

Leuschner, Friedrich W., MEng Pret., DEng Pret.   Prof.; Head*
Linde, Louis P., BEng Stell., MEng Pret., DEng Pret.   Prof.
Maharaj, Bodhaswar T. J., BScEng Natal, MScEng Natal, MSc Coventry   Sr. Lectr.
Malherbe, J. A. G., BSc Stell., BIng Stell., PhD Stell., DIng Pret., FIEEE   Prof.
Naidoo, Raj M., BSc(Eng) Natal, MSc(Eng) Witw.   Sr. Lectr.
Ngwenya, Dumisa W., BSc MSc   Sr. Lectr.
Odendaal, Johann W., MEng Pret., PhD Pret.   Prof.
Olivier, J. C., BEng Pret., MEng Pret., PhD Pret.   Prof.
Penzhorn, Walter T., BEng Pret., MEng Pret., MSc Lond., PhD Pret.   Assoc. Prof.
Roux, Filippus S., BEng Pret., MEng Pret., PhD Pret., PhD Tor.   Assoc. Prof.
Snyman, Magdaleen, MEng Pret.   Sr. Lectr.
Van Wyk, Jacques H., BEng Pret., MEng Pret.   Sr. Lectr.
Xia, Xiaohua, MEng Beijing Aeron.& Astron., PhD(Eng) Beijing Aeron.& Astron.   Prof.
Yavin, Yaakov, BSc Tel-Aviv, MSc Weizmann, DSc Haifa(Technion)   Extraordinary Prof.

Engineering, Industrial and Systems

Tel: (012) 420 3762 Fax: (012) 362 5103
E-mail: schalk.claasen@up.ac.za
Adendorff, Kris, BSc(Eng) Witw., DBA Pret.   Extraordinary Prof.
Claasen, Schalk J., BScEng Pret., MBA Pret., MScEng Arizona, PhD Pret.   Prof.; Head*
Conradie, Pieter J., BEng Pret., MBA Pret., PhD Pret.   Sr. Lectr.
Jacobs, Pieter J., BScEng Pret., BEng Pret., MScEng Pret., MBA Pret., DBA Pret.   Sr. Lectr.
Janse van Rensburg, Antonie C., BEng Pret., MEng Pret., PhD Pret.   Sr. Lectr.
Kruger, Paul S., MBA Pret., MSc(Eng) Pret., DSc(Eng) Pret.   Prof.
Lubbe, Andries J., BSc Stell., BEng Stell., MBA Pret., DEng Pret.   Assoc. Prof.
Van Dyk, Liezl, BEng Pret., MEng Pret., MSc Warw.   Sr. Lectr.
Van Tonder, Jan A., MA Pret., DPhil Pret.   Extraordinary Prof.
Yadavalli, Venkata V. S., BSc And., MSc Osm., PhD IIT Madras   Prof.
Research: business engineering; decision analysis and resource optimisation; mechatronics; supply chain management

Engineering, Materials Science and Metallurgical

Tel: (012) 420 3182 Fax: (012) 362 5304
E-mail: sarah.havenga@up.ac.za
Bosman, J. B., BEng Pret.   Sr. Lectr.
Davidtz, J. C., PhD Purdue   Prof.
De Villiers, J. P. R., BSc OFS, PhD Ill.   Prof.
Du Toit, Madeleine, BEng Pret., MEng Pret., PhD Pret.   Assoc. Prof.
Garbers-Craig, Andrie M., MSc Pret., SM M.I.T., PhD Pret.   Assoc. Prof.
Groot, Dick R., MSc P.Elizabeth, PhD P.Elizabeth   Sr. Lectr.
Havemann, Paul C. W., BSc(Eng) Pret., MBA Pret.   Sr. Lectr.
Mahlangu, T., DPhil Z'bwe.   Sr. Lectr.
Pistorius, Petrus C., MEng Pret., PhD Camb.   Prof.; Head*
Stumpf, Waldo E., BEng Pret., PhD Sheff.   Prof.
Van Rooyen, G. T., BSc(Eng) Witw., MBA Pret., SM M.I.T., ScD M.I.T.   Prof.
Vermaak, M. K. G., MEng Pret., PhD Pret.   Sr. Lectr.
Von Moltke, Tom v S., BSc Stell., MSc Stell., PhD Pret.   Prof.
Research: minerals processing and hydrometallurgy; physical metallurgy and corrosion; pyrometallurgy

Engineering, Mechanical and Aeronautical

Tel: (012) 420 2590 Fax: (012) 362 5124
E-mail: jmeyer@up.ac.za
Burger, Nicolaas D. L., MEng Pret.   Sr. Lectr.

Craig, Kenneth J., MEng Pret., PhD Stan. Prof.
De Wet, Philippus R., BEng Stell., MEng Stell. Sr. Lectr.
Els, Pieter S., MEng Pret. Sr. Lectr.
Heyns, Philippus S., MEng Pret., PhD Pret. Prof.
Kok, Schalk, MEng Pret., PhD Ill. Sr. Lectr.
Liebenberg, Leon, MEng Rand Afrikaans, MSc Lond., PhD Rand Afrikaans Prof.
Malan, Arnaud G., MEng Wales, PhD Wales(Swansea) Assoc. Prof.
Meyer, Josua P., MEng PhD Prof.; Head*
Snyman, Johannes A., BSc Cape Town, BSc Pret., MSc S.Af., DSc Pret. Prof.
Theron, Nico J., MEng Stell., PhD Rensselaer Assoc. Prof.
Uys, Petronella E., MSc Pret., DSc Pret. Sr. Lectr.
Van Tonder, F., MEng Pret. Sr. Lectr.
Van Wyk, Adriaan J., MEng Pret. Sr. Lectr.
Other Staff: 2 Lectrs.
Research: computational fluid dynamics; experimental heat transfer; machine and product design; multidisciplinary optimisation; structural fatigue

Engineering, Mining

Tel: (012) 420 2443 Fax: (012) 420 4242
E-mail: daleen.gudmanz@up.ac.za
Handley, Matthew F., BSc Natal, MSc(Eng) Witw., PhD Minn. Prof.
Matunhire, Isadore I., BSc(Min) Nott., MSc Nott., PhD Nott. Sr. Lectr.
Thompson, Roger J., MSc CNAA, PhD Pret. Prof.
Van der Merwe, J. Nielen, BSc(Eng) Pret., MSc(Eng) Witw., PhD Witw. Prof.; Head*
Webber-Youngman, Ronald C. W., BEng Pret., MEng Pret. Sr. Lectr.
Other Staff: 2 Lectrs.
Research: coal mining; mine design; mine health and safety; mine ventilation; surface mining

English

Tel: (012) 420 2351 Fax: (012) 420 5191
E-mail: fwelgens@postino.up.ac.za
Brown, Molly A., MA Rhodes, MA Lond. Sr. Lectr.
Chennels, Anthony J., DPhil Z'bwe. Extraordinary Prof.†
Lenahan, Patrick C., BA Rhodes, MEd Rhodes, MPhil Oxf. Sr. Lectr.
Marx, Petronella J. M., BA Pret., MA Stell. Sr. Lectr.
Medalie, David, BA Witw., MPhil Oxf., DPhil Oxf. Prof.
Wessels, Johan A., BA Free State, MPhil Oxf., DLitt&Phil S.Af. Prof.; Head*
Other Staff: 5 Lectrs.
Research: children's literature; English as a second/foreign language; Irish literature; modernism; South African literature

Financial Management

Tel: (012) 420 3795 Fax: (012) 420 3916
E-mail: yvonne.craig@up.ac.za
Antonites, Elbie, BCom Pret. Sr. Lectr.
De Hart, Frediricus J., BCompt OFS, BCompt S.Af. Sr. Lectr.
De Jager, Phillip G., BAcc Stell., BCom S.Af., MCom Jo'burg. Sr. Lectr.
De Kock, Gawie M., BCom(Accg) Pret. Sr. Lectr.
De Wet, Johannes H. v H., BAcc Stell., MBA Stell., DCom Pret. Assoc. Prof.
Erasmus, Yolande, BCom(Accg) Pret., BCom S.Af. Sr. Lectr.
Gouws, Daan G., DCom Potchef. Prof.
Hall, John H., BCom P.Elizabeth, MBA Pret., DBA Pret. Assoc. Prof.
Huyser, Susanna L., BCom(Accg) Pret., MCom(Tax) Pret. Sr. Lectr.
Kruger, Christine J., BCom Pret. Sr. Lectr.
Lambrechts, Hugo A., MCom Stell., MBA Ghent, DBA Pret. Prof.
Lombard, Caren, BCom(Accg) Pret., MCom(Tax) Sr. Lectr.

Maree, Adele, BCom Pret., MCom Pret. Sr. Lectr.
Meyer-Pretorius, Margaret, BPharm Potchef., MBA Pret., DBA Pret. Sr. Lectr.
Oost, Ebo J., BCom Pret., MCom S.Af., DCom S.Af. Prof.; Head*
Plant, Gregory J., BCom(Accg) Pret. Sr. Lectr.
Vermaak, Frans N. S., BCom Potchef., MCom Potchef., DCom Potchef. Assoc. Prof.
Viljoen, Margaret A., BCom Pret., BCom S.Af., MCom Potchef. Sr. Lectr.
Wolmarans, Hendrik P., BCom Pret., BCom S.Af., BSc Pret., MBA Pret., DBA Pret. Assoc. Prof.
Other Staff: 3 Lectrs.
Research: financial, financial risk management and management accounting

Food Science

Tel: (012) 420 3202 Fax: (012) 420 2839
E-mail: food.science@up.ac.za
Buys, Elna M., BSc Stell., BSc Potchef., MSc Pret., PhD Witw. Assoc. Prof.
De Kock, Henrietta L., BH(FoodManagement) Pret., MScAgric Pret., PhD Pret. Sr. Lectr.
Duodu, K. G., BSc Ghana, MInstAgrar Pret., PhD Pret. Sr. Lectr.
Minnaar, Amanda, BSc(Agric) Pret., PhD Pret. Assoc. Prof.; Head*
Taylor, John R. N., BSc CNAA, PhD CNAA, DSc Pret. Prof.
Other Staff: 1 Lectr.
Research: dairy and meat microbiology; grain quality; modern processing technologies for improved quality and safety of foods; natural shelf-life extension of food; sensory test methodologies

Genetics

Tel: (012) 420 3258 Fax: (012) 362 5327
E-mail: ina.goosen@up.ac.za
Bloomer, Paulette, BSc Potchef., PhD Pret. Assoc. Prof.
Fick, Wilma C., BSc(Agric) Pret., MSc Cape Town, PhD Pret. Sr. Lectr.
Greeff, Jacobus M., BSc Pret., BSc Rhodes, PhD Pret. Prof.
Hofmeyr, Jan H., DSc(Agric) Pret. Hon. Prof.
Honey, Engela M., MB ChB Pret., MMed Stell. Sr. Lectr.
Huismans, Hendrik, MSc Stell., DSc Pret. Prof.; Head*
Jansen van Rensburg, Elizabeth, MSc Rand Afrikaans, PhD Stell. Assoc. Prof.
Myburg, Alexander A., MSc Free State, PhD N.Carolina Assoc. Prof.
Oberholster, Anna-Maria, MSc Potchef., PhD Free State Prof.
Roux, Carl Z., MSc Stell., PhD Iowa State Extraordinary Prof.
Van Staden, Vida, BSc Pret., PhD Pret. Sr. Lectr.
Wingfield, Brenda D., BSc Natal, BSc(Med) Cape Town, MSc Minn., PhD Stell. Prof.
Other Staff: 5 Technicians
Research: cereal and forest genomics; molecular ecology and evolution; molecular genetics; molecular virology; plant genetics

Geography, Geo-Information and Meteorology

Tel: (012) 420 2489 Fax: (012) 420 3284
E-mail: reynet.vanniekerk@up.ac.za
Engelbrecht, Francois A., BSc Pret., MSc Pret., PhD Pret. Sr. Lectr.
Horn, André C., MA Pret., DPhil Pret. Assoc. Prof.
Meiklejohn, Keith I., BSc Natal, PhD Natal Assoc. Prof.
Rautenbach, C. J. de W., BSc Pret., PhD Pret. Assoc. Prof.; Head*
Stengel, Ingrid U., DrRerNat Würzburg Assoc. Prof.
Sumner, P. D., BSc Natal, MSc Natal, PhD Pret. Assoc. Prof.
Van der Merwe, Fritz J., BSurveying Pret. Sr. Lectr.

Van Helden, Paul, BA Potchef., MSc(S&S) Pret., PhD Pret. Assoc. Prof.
Other Staff: 10 Lectrs.
Research: environmental sciences; geographical information systems (GIS) and remote sensing; numerical atmospheric modelling; processes and interaction with physical environment; urban, rural, population and decision-making

Geology

Tel: (012) 420 2454 Fax: (012) 362 5219
E-mail: melinda.deswardt@up.ac.za
Altermann, Wlady, DrRerNatHabil Munich Hon. Prof.
Bumby, Adam J., PhD Pret. Sr. Lectr.
Camasani-Calzolari, Ferdi A., DSc Milan Extraordinary Prof.
De Wit, M. C. J., PhD Cape Town Hon. Prof.
Eriksson, Patrick G., PhD Natal, DrRerNatHabil Munich Prof.; Head*
Kijko, A., PhD Polish Acad.Sc. Hon. Prof.
Killick, Andrew M., PhD Rand Afrikaans Hon. Prof.
Merkle, Roland K. W., DrRerNat Mainz Prof.
Nelson, D. R., PhD ANU Hon. Prof.
Stettler, Edgar H., PhD Pret. Hon. Prof.
Theart, Hennie F. J., PhD Stell. Prof.
Van Rooy, J. Louis, PhD Pret. Assoc. Prof.
Witthueser, Kai T., DrRerNat Karlsruhe Sr. Lectr.
Other Staff: 2 Lectrs.; 2 Extraordinary Lectrs.

Health Systems and Public Health, School of

Tel: (012) 354 1472 Fax: (012) 354 2071
E-mail: shsph@up.ac.za
Beke, Andy, MB ChB Ghana, MMed(CommHealth) S.Af.Med. Sr. Lectr.
Bornman, Maria S., MB ChB Pret., DSc Pret. Extraordinary Prof.
Buch, Eric, MB BCh Witw., MSc(Med) Witw. Prof.
De Jager, Christiaan, BSc Free State, MSc Free State, PhD Pret. Assoc. Prof.
Girdler-Brown, Brendan V., BScAgric Natal, MB ChB Rhodesia, MBA Cape Town, MMed Cape Town Extraordinary Prof.
Louwagie, Goedele, MB ChB Leuven, MMed(ComHealth) Free State Sr. Lectr.
Matjila, Maila J., MB ChB Natal, MMed Natal Prof., Community Health; Head*
Mwaka, Mary, MSc Nair. Sr. Lectr.
Njongwe, Patiswa, MB ChB Natal Sr. Lectr.
Rendall-Mkosi, Kirstie, BSc(OT) Witw., MPH W.Cape Sr. Lectr.
Rheeder, Paul, MB ChB Pret., MMed(Int) Pret., MSc Rotterdam, PhD Utrecht Prof.
Terblanche, Petro, BSc Pret., MSc Pret., DSc Pret. Extraordinary Prof.
Van Ginneken, Jeroen, PhD Extraordinary Prof.
Voyi, Kuku, BSc Fort Hare, BSc Cape Town, MSc Cape Town, PhD Cape Town Assoc. Prof.; Chairperson*
Westaway, Margaret S., PhD Witw. Extraordinary Prof.
Other Staff: 3 Lectrs.; 8 Extraordinary Lectrs.
Vacant Posts: 1 Lectr.

Historical and Heritage Studies

Tel: (012) 420 2323 Fax: (012) 420 2656
E-mail: johan.bergh@up.ac.za
Bergh, Johannes S., BA Stell., MA S.Af., DPhil Stell. Prof.; Head*
Ferreira, O. J. O., MA Pret., DPhil Pret., DLitt&Phil S.Af. Hon. Prof.
Grobler, John E. H., MA Pret., DPhil Pret. Sr. Lectr.
Harris, Karen L., MA Stell., DLitt&Phil S.Af. Prof.
Kriel, Lizé, MA Pret., DPhil Pret. Assoc. Prof.
Mlambo, Alois S., MA Lond., MA Wesleyan, PhD Duke Prof.
Phimister, Ian R., BA Nott., DPhil Rhodesia Hon. Prof.
Pretorius, Fransjohan, MA Pret., DrsLitt Ley., DLitt&Phil S.Af. Prof.

Other Staff: 3 Lectrs.
Research: inter-group relations in South African history; minority groups in South African history; political and military resistance in South African history; South Africa in international context, 1945-90; South African cultural historical heritage

Human Resources Management

Tel: (012) 420 3797 Fax: (012) 420 3574
E-mail: lvermeul@hakuna.up.ac.za
Basson, J. S., BSc Potchef., MA Pret., DPhil Pret. Prof.
Brand, H. E., MA Pret., DPhil Pret. Prof.
Buys, M. A., BA Pret., MA S.Af. Sr. Lectr.
De Beer, J. J., MA Pret., DPhil Pret. Assoc. Prof.
Du Plessis, Yvonne, BSc Pret., MDP S.Af., MBA Pret., PhD Pret. Sr. Lectr.
Griesel, Sonja, BCompt S.Af., MCom(Acc) Rand Afrikaans Sr. Lectr.
Schaap, P., BCom Pret., MCom Pret., DCom Pret. Assoc. Prof.
Steyn, G. J., BA Pret., MA Free State Sr. Lectr.
Van der Walt, Ruan v M., MCom Pret., DPhil Pret. Sr. Lectr. (Mamelodi Campus)
Vermeulen, L. P., MA Pret., DPhil Pret. Prof.; Head*
Zinn, S. A., BEd S.Af., MEd W.Cape, EDM Harv., EdD Harv. Extraordinary Prof.
Other Staff: 5 Lectrs.
Research: cultural intelligence; diversity and employment equity; gender issues in aviation; human factors in project management; psychometrics and assessment

Humanities (General)

Tel: (012) 420 2318 Fax: (012) 420 2698
E-mail: gwdekaan@up.ac.za
Muller, Marie E., MA Pret., DLitt&Phil Rand Afrikaans Prof.; Dean*
Potgieter, Johan H., BA Potchef., MA Pret., DD Pret. Prof.; Deputy Dean
Van Onselen, Charles, BSc Rhodes, BA Witw., DPhil Oxf. Prof.
Research: academic development; academic support; curriculum development

Informatics

Tel: (012) 420 3798 Fax: (012) 362 5287
E-mail: carina.devilliers@up.ac.za
Alexander, Patricia M., BSc Cape Town, MSc S.Af., PhD Pret. Sr. Lectr.
Burger, Alewyn P., BSc Rand Afrikaans, PhD Extraordinary Prof.
De Villiers, Carina, BSc Potchef., MEd S.Af., DCom Pret. Prof.; Head*
Du Plooy, Nicolaas F., MSc Potchef., MBA Pret., DCom Pret. Emer. Prof.
Joubert, Pieter, BSc Pret., MCom Pret. Sr. Lectr.
Kroeze, Jan H., BA Potchef., ThB Potchef., MA Potchef., MIT Pret., PhD Potchef. Sr. Lectr.
Krüger, Cornelius J., MBA Pret., MIT Pret. Sr. Lectr.
Leonard, Abraham C., BSc Potchef., MSc S.Af., DCom Pret. Sr. Lectr.
Lotriet, Hugo H., BEng Pret., MEng Stell., PhD Stell. Sr. Lectr.
Matthee, Machdel C., BSc Pret., MSc Pret., DCom Pret. Sr. Lectr.
Phahlamohlaka, Letlibe J., BSc Zululand, MSc Dal., PhD Pret. Sr. Lectr.
Ponelis, Shana, BSc Pret., BA Pret., MIS Pret. Sr. Lectr.
Roode, J. Dewald, BSc Potchef., MSc Potchef., PhD Ley. Extraordinary Prof.
Van Loggerenberg, Johan J., BSc Potchef., MBA Potchef., DCom Pret. Sr. Lectr.
Weilbach, Elizabeth H., MCom Pret. Sr. Lectr.
Other Staff: 5 Lectrs.; 5 Temp. Lectrs.
Vacant Posts: 2 Lectrs.
Research: adoption and use of information technology in organisations; knowledge discovery from data; socio-economic impact of information technology; theoretical aspects of information systems

Information Science

Tel: (012) 420 2921 Fax: (012) 362 5181
E-mail: theo.bothma@up.ac.za
Boon, J. A., MBibl Rand Afrikaans, DLitt&Phil Rand Afrikaans Extraordinary Prof.
Bothma, Theodorus J. D., BA Pret., MA S.Af., DLitt&Phil S.Af. Prof.; Head*
Britz, Johannes J., BA Pret., BD Pret., BBibl Pret., DD Pret. Prof.
Cosijn, Erica, MA Rand Afrikaans, DPhil Pret. Sr. Lectr.
De Beer, C. S., BScAgric Pret., MA Pret., DPhil Pret. Extraordinary Prof.
De Wet, Karen, BA Pret., BLibrarySc Pret., MA Pret., DLitt N-W(S.Af.) Sr. Lectr.
Dick, Archie L., BLibrarySc W.Cape, MLS Wash., PhD Cape Town Prof.
Fourie, Ina, MLibr Free State, DLitt&Phil S.Af. Assoc. Prof.
Galloway, Francina C. J., BA Free State, MA Free State, DLitt Free State Sr. Lectr.
Jacobs, Daisy, BSc Madr., BEd Madr., MSc Bom., MIS Natal, PhD Natal Sr. Lectr.
Lor, Peter J., BA Stell., MBibl Pret., DPhil Pret. Extraordinary Prof.
Snyman, M. M. M., BA Pret., MBibl Rand Afrikaans, DLitt&Phil Rand Afrikaans Assoc. Prof.
Snyman, Maritha E., BA Pret., MA Pret., DLitt Pret. Assoc. Prof.
Other Staff: 6 Lectrs.
Research: hypertext/hypermedia/multimedia; information and knowledge management; information ethics; information for development; information organisation and retrieval

Insurance and Actuarial Science

Tel: (012) 420 3488 Fax: (012) 362 5273
E-mail: johanna.hellberg@up.ac.za
Du Plessis, Hendrick L. M., BSc Witw. Assoc. Prof.
Sauer, Johannes J. C., BCom Pret. Sr. Lectr.
Ströh, Anton, BSc Pret., MSc Pret., PhD Pret. Prof.; Acting Head*
Venter, Marli, BSc Rand Afrikaans, BCom Cape Town Sr. Lectr.
Research: health benefit financing; multidisciplinary studies in mathematics, insurance, actuarial science and risk management

Law, Mercantile and Labour

Tel: (012) 420 2363 Fax: (012) 420 4010
E-mail: hetta.debeer@up.ac.za
Brassey, M. S. M., BA Cape Town, LLB Witw. Hon. Prof.
De Villiers, Willem P., BIur Pret., LLB Pret., LLD Pret. Assoc. Prof.
Delport, Petrus A., BA Pret., LLB Pret., LLD Pret. Prof.
Fourie, Joël D., BIur Pret., LLB S.Af. Extraordinary Prof.
Katz, Michael M., BCom Witw., LLB Witw., LLM Harv. Extraordinary Prof.
Klopper, Hendrik B., LLB Free State, LLD Free State Prof.
Kuper, M. D., BA Witw., LLB Witw. Hon. Prof.
Lombard, Sulette, BLC Pret., LLB Pret., LLM S.Af., LLD Pret. Sr. Lectr.
Lotz, Dirk J., BIur Pret., LLB Pret., LLM Witw., LLD Pret. Prof.
Loubser, R. M., MCom S.Af. Extraordinary Prof.
Louw, Cornelius, BCom Pret., LLB Pret., MCom Pret. Sr. Lectr.
Nagel, Christoffel J., LLB Pret., LLD Pret. Prof.
Roestoff, Melanie, BLC Pret., LLB Pret., LLM Pret., LLD Pret. Prof.
Swart, J. D. M., LLB Pret. Extraordinary Prof.
Van Eck, Bruno P. S., BLC Pret., LLB Pret., LLD Pret. Prof.; Head*
Van Jaarsveld, Stephanus R., BA Pret., LLB Pret., LLD Pret. Prof.
Vettori, S., LLB Witw., LLM S.Af., LLD Pret. Assoc. Prof.
Other Staff: 2 Lectrs.

Law, Private

Tel: (012) 420 2354 Fax: (012) 420 3961
E-mail: trynie.davel@up.ac.za
Buchner-Eveleigh, Mariana, LLB Pret., LLM Pret. Sr. Lectr.
Davel, Catharina J., BA Pret., LLB Pret., LLD Pret. Prof.; Head*
Grové, Nic J., BA Pret., LLB Pret., LLM Pret., LLD Rand Afrikaans Hon. Prof.
Kuschke, Birgit, BLC Pret., LLB Pret. Sr. Lectr.
Maithufi, Ignatius P., LLB North(S.Af.), LLM N-W(S.Af.), LLD Pret. Prof.
Schoeman-Malan, Magdalena C., BA Pret., LLB Pret., LLD Pret. Prof.
Scott, Tobias J., BA Pret., LLB Pret., DrJur Ley. Prof.
Sinclair, June D., BA Witw., LLB Witw., LLD Witw. Hon. Prof.
Van der Linde, Anton, BLC Pret., LLB Pret., LLM Pret., LLD Pret. Assoc. Prof.
Van der Spuy, Pieter de W., BA Pret., LLB Stell. Sr. Lectr.
Van Schalkwyk, Llewelyn N., BA Pret., LLB Pret., LLD Pret. Prof.
Other Staff: 1 Lectr.

Law, Procedural

Tel: (012) 420 3198 Fax: (012) 420 4405
E-mail: hannatjie.louw@up.ac.za
Boraine, André, LLB Pret., LLM Witw., LLD Pret. Prof.; Head*
Church, Jacqueline, BCom Pret., LLB Pret., LLM S.Af. Sr. Lectr.
Cloete, Rian, LLB Pret., LLD S.Af. Prof.
Haupt, Franciscus S., BA Pret., LLB S.Af. Dir., Legal Aid Clinic
Illsley, Ella D., BLC Pret., LLB Pret., LLM McG., LLM S.Af. Sr. Lectr.
Jordaan-Parkin, Ronel, LLB Pret., LLM Pret. Sr. Lectr.
Van der Merwe, Ivy A., BProc Pret., LLB S.Af., LLM Pret., PhD Rhodes Prof.

Law, Public

Tel: (012) 420 2649 Fax: (012) 420 2991
E-mail: cjbotha@up.ac.za
Bekink, Bernard, BLC Pret., LLB Pret., LLM Pret., LLD Pret. Sr. Lectr.
Botha, Christoffel J., BA S.Af., LLB Pret., LLD S.Af. Prof.; Head*
Brand, Jacobus F. D., BLC Pret., LLB Pret., LLM Emory Sr. Lectr.
Carstens, Pieter A., BLC Pret., LLB Pret., LLD Pret. Prof.
Feris, Loretta A., BA Stell., LLB Stell., LLM Georgetown, LLD Stell. Assoc. Prof.
Grobbelaar-Du Plessis, Ilze, BIuris Pret., LLB Pret., LLM Pret. Sr. Lectr.
Le Roux, Jolandi, BIur P.Elizabeth, LLB P.Elizabeth, LLD Pret. Assoc. Prof.
Malan, Jacobus J., BA Pret., BIur S.Af., LLB S.Af., LLD S.Af. Assoc. Prof.
Olivier, Michèle E., BLC Pret., LLB Pret., MA Rand Afrikaans, LLM Pret., LLD S.Af. Prof.
Woolman, Stuart C., BA Wesleyan, MA Col., JD Col., LLD Pret. Sr. Lectr.

Legal History, Comparative Law and Philosophy of Law

Tel: (012) 420 3628 Fax: (012) 420 4524
E-mail: caroline.nicholson@up.ac.za
Kleyn, D. G., BA Pret., LLB Pret., LLD Pret. Prof.
Kok, Johan A., BCom Pret., LLB Pret., LLM Pret. Sr. Lectr.
Madlingozi, Tshepo, LLB Pret., LLM Pret. Sr. Lectr.
Mokgoro, Jennifer Y., BIuris N-W(S.Af.), LLB N-W(S.Af.), LLM N-W(S.Af.), LLM Penn. Hon. Prof.
Nicholson, Caroline M. A., BProc Witw., LLM S.Af., LLD S.Af. Prof.; Head*
Nienaber, Annelize G., BA Pret., BA Witw., LLB Witw., LLB Pret., LLM Pret. Sr. Lectr.
Thomas, Philippus J., MR Rotterdam, LLD S.Af. Prof.
Van der Westhuizen, Johan V., BA Pret., LLB Pret., LLD Pret. Hon. Prof.

Van Marle, Karin, BLC Pret., LLB Pret., LLM
S.Af., LLD S.Af. Prof.
Viljoen, Frans J., BLC Pret., LLB Pret., MA Pret.,
LLM Camb., LLD Pret. Prof.
Other Staff: 2 Lectrs.

Management, Graduate School of

Tel: (012) 420 3355 Fax: (012) 362 5183
E-mail: susan@postino.up.ac.za
Adendorff, Susan A., BEng Pret., MBA Pret., PhD
Pret. Prof.; Deputy Dir.
De Klerk, A. M., BEng Pret., MEng Pret., MS
Stan., PhD Stan. Prof.; Dir.*
De Villiers, Willem A., BMil Stell., MBA Pret.,
DBA Pret. Sr. Lectr.
Roodt, Gert K. A., BMil Stell., MBA Pret., PMD
Harv. Assoc. Prof.
Ward, M. J. D., BScEng Cape Town, MBA Witw.,
PhD Witw. Prof.; Dir.
Other Staff: 1 Res. Officer

Marketing and Communications Management

Tel: (012) 420 3816 Fax: (012) 362 5085
E-mail: ronel.rensburg@up.ac.za
De Wet, Johannes M., BCom Potchef., MComm
Stell., DCom Potchef. Prof.
Du Plessis, Phillipus J., BCom S.Af., MBL S.Af.,
DBL S.Af. Prof.
Ehlers, Lene, MCom Rand Afrikaans, DCom Pret.
Sr. Lectr.
Grobler, Anske F., BA Free State, MA Free State,
PhD Free State Prof.
Jordaan, Yolanda, BCom Pret., MCom Pret.,
DCom Pret. Assoc. Prof.
Kotzé, Theuns G., BCom Pret., MCom Pret. Sr.
Lectr.
North, Ernest J., BCom S.Af., MCom S.Af.,
DCom S.Af. Prof.
Puth, G., DPhil Free State Extraordinary Prof.
Rensburg, Ronél S., BCom P.Elizabeth, MA Rand
Afrikaans, DLitt&Phil S.Af. Prof.; Head*
Schreuder, Andries N., MCom Pret., DCom Rand
Afrikaans Extraordinary Prof.
Van der Waldt, De La Rey, BA Free State, MA
Free State, PhD Potchef. Sr. Lectr.
Van Heerden, Cornelius H., BSc(Agric) Pret.,
BCom Pret., MCom Pret., DCom Pret. Assoc.
Prof.
Other Staff: 9 Lectrs.; 1 Temp. Prof.

Mathematics and Applied Mathematics

Tel: (012) 420 2520 Fax: (012) 420 3893
E-mail: jean.lubuma@up.ac.za
Anguelov, Roumen, MSc Sofia, PhD S.Af.
Assoc. Prof.
Delbaen, Freddy E., PhD V.U.Brussels
Extraordinary Prof.
Diestel, Prof. Joseph, BS Dayton, PhD C.U.A.
Extraordinary Prof.
Duvenhage, Rocco de V., MSc Pret., PhD Pret.
Sr. Lectr.
Engelbrecht, Johannes C., MSc Pret., DSc Potchef.
Prof.
Harding, Anna F., DSc Pret. Assoc. Prof.
Janse van Rensburg, Nicolaas F., BSc Pret., BSc
S.Af., MSc Pret., DSc Pret. Emer. Prof.
Jordaan, Kerstin H., BSc Pret., BSc Witw., MSc
Pret., PhD Witw. Sr. Lectr.
Le Roux, Christiaan, MSc Cape Town, PhD Pret.
Sr. Lectr.
Lubuma, Jean M-S., MSc Louvain, PhD Louvain
Prof.; Head*
Maré, Eben, MSc Witw., PhD Free State Assoc.
Prof.
Möller, Magrieta P., MSc Pret. Sr. Lectr.
Mureithi, Eunice W., MSc Kenyatta, PhD NSW
Sr. Lectr.
Mutangadura, Simba A., BSc Lond., PhD Lond.
Sr. Lectr.
Ntumba, Patrice P., MSc Cape Town, PhD Cape
Town Sr. Lectr.
Penning, Frans D., DSc Pret. Prof.
Pretorius, Lourens M., DSc Pret. Prof.
Rajagopal, Kumbakonam R., PhD Minn.
Extraordinary Prof.

Rosinger, Elemer E., MSc Bucharest, DrSc
Bucharest Emer. Prof.
Sango, Mamadou, MSc Donets, PhD Valenciennes
Prof.
Sauer, Niko, MSc Pret., PhD S.Af.
Extraordinary Prof.
Schoeman, Marius J., MSc Pret., DrSc T.H.Delft
Prof.
Ströh, Anton, BSc Pret., MSc Pret., PhD Pret.
Prof.
Swart, Johan, BSc Potchef., MSc Potchef., DrPhil
Zür. Prof.
Other Staff: 9 Lectrs.
Research: abstract analysis, topology and
applications; discrete mathematics; partial
differential equations, their numerical
analysis and mathematical modelling;
undergraduate mathematics teaching

Microbiology and Plant Pathology

Tel: (012) 420 3265 Fax: (012) 420 3266
E-mail: eugene.cloete@up.ac.za
Ashton, P. J., BSc Rhodes, MSc Rhodes, PhD Rhodes
Extraordinary Prof.
Atlas, R. M., BSc N.Y.State, MSc Rutgers, PhD
Rutgers Extraordinary Prof.
Aveling, Terry A. S., MSC Natal, PhD Natal
Assoc. Prof.
Cloete, Thomas E., MSc Free State, DSc Pret.
Prof.; Head*
Coutinho, Teresa A., MSc Natal, PhD Natal
Assoc. Prof.
Grabow, W. O. K., BSc Pret., MSc Pret., DSc Pret.
Extraordinary Prof.
Kasan, H. C., BSc Witw., MSc Witw., PhD Witw.
Extraordinary Prof.
Korsten, Lise, BSc Stell., MSc Pret., PhD Pret.
Prof.
Labuschagne, Nico, MSc(Agric) Pret.,
DSc(Agric) Pret. Assoc. Prof.
Nel, Louis H., MSc Free State, PhD Pret. Prof.
Pietersen, Gerhard, PhD Extraordinary Prof.
Steenkamp, Emma, PhD Pret. Sr. Lectr.
Theron, Jacques, BSc Pret., MSc Pret., PhD Pret.
Assoc. Prof.
Van der Waals, Jacquie, PhD Pret. Sr. Lectr.
Venter, Stephanus N., MSc Pret., PhD Pret.
Assoc. Prof.
Other Staff: 2 Lectrs.
Research: environmental biotechnology;
integrated disease management; molecular
biology and virology; plantation tree
pathology; protozoon parasites

Modern European Languages

Tel: (012) 420 2352 Fax: (012) 420 3660
E-mail: stephan.muehr@up.ac.za
Mühr, Stephan, PhD Freib. Sr. Lectr.; Acting
Head*
Van Dyk, Jeanne, MA Stras.II, DLitt Pret. Sr.
Lectr.
Other Staff: 3 Lectrs.
Research: anthropological foundations of poetry;
contemporary French poetry; inter-cultural
hermeneutics; language teaching for specific
purposes (architecture, economics, law,
politics, theology); lexicology
(computerised French-Afrikaans dictionary)

Music

Tel: (012) 420 2316 Fax: (012) 420 2248
E-mail: wim.viljoen@up.ac.za
Devroop, Chatradari, MMus Durban-W., DMus
Pret. Assoc. Prof.
Fourie, Ella, BMus Stell., MMus Witw., DPhil
Pret. Prof.
Grové, Stefans, MA Harv., DMus Free State,
Hon. DMus Pret. Extraordinary Prof.
Hinch, John de C., MMus Pret., DMus Pret.
Prof.; Head*
Johnson, Alexander, MMus Pret., DMus Pret.
Sr. Lectr.
Nzewi, Meki E., BA Nigeria, PhD Belf. Prof.
Stanford, Hendrik J., MMus Stell., DPhil W.Cape
Prof.
Van der Mescht, Heinrich H., BA Stell., BMus
Stell., MMus Witw., DMus S.Af. Prof.

Van der Sandt, Johannes T., MMus Pret., DMus
Pret. Assoc. Prof.
Van Niekerk, Caroline, BMus Stell., MMus
Witw., PhD Witw. Prof.
Van Wyk, Wessel, BMus S.Af., MMus Cape Town,
DMus Pret. Sr. Lectr.
Viljoen, Willem D., BMus Pret., MMus Cape
Town, DPhil Pret. Prof.
Walton, Christopher R., MA Camb., MA Oxf.,
DPhil Oxf. Prof.
Other Staff: 3 Lectrs.
Research: African music; music education; music
technology; music therapy; Western art
music

Natural and Agricultural Sciences (General)

Tel: (012) 420 3201 Fax: (012) 420 3890
E-mail: dean.nas@up.ac.za
Ströh, Anton, BSc Pret., MSc Pret., PhD Pret.
Prof.; Dean*

New Testament Studies

Tel: (012) 420 2384 Fax: (012) 420 4016
E-mail: otnt@postino.up.ac.za
Steyn, Gert J., BA Pret., BD Pret., MA Pret., DD
Pret. Assoc. Prof.
Van der Watt, Jan G., BA P.Elizabeth, BD Pret.,
MA Pret., DLitt Pret., DD Pret. Prof.; Head*
Other Staff: 8 Res. Fellows†; 3 Temp. Lectrs.
Research: hermeneutics; Johannine writings;
literary methods in reading New Testament
texts; Pauline writings; the historical Jesus

Old Testament Studies

Tel: (012) 420 2348 Fax: (012) 420 2887
E-mail: pm.venter@up.ac.za
Groenewald, Alphonso, BD Pret., MA Pret., DTL
Nijmegen Sr. Lectr.
Human, Dirk J., BD Pret., MA Rand Afrikaans, DD
Pret. Prof.
Le Roux, Jurie H., MA Pret., DD S.Af., DTh S.Af.
Prof.
Venter, Pieter M., BA Pret., DD Pret. Prof.;
Head*
Research: apocalyptic literature; hermeneutics;
history of Israel's religion; Samaritan
Pentateuch; wisdom literature

Philosophy

Tel: (012) 420 2326 Fax: (012) 420 2698
E-mail: deon.roussouw@up.ac.za
Antonites, Alexander J., BD S.Af., MA Pret.,
DPhil Pret. Prof.
Nethersole, Reingard, PhD Witw.
Extraordinary Prof.
Painter Morland, M. J., PhD Pret. Assoc. Prof.
Rossouw, Gedeon J., PhD Stell. Prof.; Head*
Schoeman, Marinus J., MA Pret. Assoc. Prof.
Wolff, Ernst, MA Rand Afrikaans, DPhil Paris IV
Sr. Lectr.
Other Staff: 3 Lectrs.
Research: ethics; Greek and patristic philosophy;
philosophy of science; political philosophy
and world views; social philosophy and
philosophy of culture

Physics

Tel: (012) 420 2455 Fax: (012) 362 5288
E-mail: malherbe@scientia.up.ac.za
Adam, R. M., BSc Cape Town, BSc S.Af., MSc
S.Af., PhD S.Af. Hon. Prof.
Alberts, Hendrik W., MSc Potchef., DSc Pret.
Prof.
Auret, Francois D., DSc Pret. Prof.
Bharuth-Ram, K., BSc Natal, MSc Natal, DPhil
Oxf. Hon. Prof.
Boeyens, J. C. A., MSc OFS, DSc Pret., FRSSAf
Extraordinary Prof.
Braun, Max W. H., BSc P.Elizabeth, BSc S.Af.,
MSc P.Elizabeth, MSc Pret., DSc Pret. Prof.
Brink, Daniel J., MSc Potchef., DSc Pret. Prof.
Carr, A., BSc Natal, MSc Pret., PhD Pret. Sr.
Lectr.
Friedland, Erich K. H., MSc Pret., DSc Pret.
Extraordinary Prof.
Gaigher, H. L., MSc Pret., DSc Pret.
Extraordinary Prof.

Grayson, D. J., BSc Natal, MSc Natal, MSc PhD Hon. Prof.

Gries, W., BSc Pret., MSc Pret., PhD Stell. Hon. Prof.

Hayes, Michael, MSc P.Elizabeth, PhD Pret. Assoc. Prof.

Kunert, Herbert W., MSc Poznan, PhD Warsaw Assoc. Prof.

Malaza, E. D., BSc Fort Hare, MSc Brown, PhD Camb. Hon. Prof.

Malherbe, Johan B., MSc Pret., DSc Pret. Prof.; Head*

Miller, Henry G., MA N.Y., PhD Sask., DrHabil Fran. Prof.

Plastino, A. R., PhD Prof.

Scheffler, Theophilus B., MSc Stell., DPhil Oxf. Sr. Lectr.

Van der Berg, Nicolaas G., BSc P.Elizabeth, MSc S.Af., DSc Pret. Sr. Lectr.

Van der Merwe, J. H., BSc Stell., MSc Stell., MSc Pret., PhD Brist. Hon. Prof.

Other Staff: 9 Support Staff

Research: application of many body techniques to various fields; experimental solid state physics (ion/solid interactions, thin film physics); quantum information theory; thermal solar energy and desalination of water

Plant Production and Soil Science

Tel: (012) 420 3809 Fax: (012) 420 4120
E-mail: charlie.reinhardt@up.ac.za

Annandale, John G., MSc(Agric) Pret., PhD Wash.State Prof.

Claassens, Andries S., MSc(Agric) Pret., DSc(Agric) Pret. Assoc. Prof.

Du Toit, Elsie S., MSc(Agric) Pret., PhD Pret. Assoc. Prof.

Reinhardt, Carl F., BSc Free State, MSc(Agric) Pret., PhD Pret. Prof.; Head*

Soundy, Puffy, MScAgric Natal, PhD Flor. Sr. Lectr.

Steyn, Joachim M., MSc(Agric) Free State, PhD Pret. Sr. Lectr.

Other Staff: 5 Lectrs.

Research: effect of environment and management practices on growth and development of crops; management of weeds; physical and physico-chemical soil conditions; plant nutrition and soil fertility; soil-plant-atmosphere-water relations and irrigation scheduling

Plant Science

Tel: (012) 420 3770 Fax: (012) 362 5099
E-mail: marion.meyer@up.ac.za

Berger, Dave K., PhD Cape Town Assoc. Prof.

Bredenkamp, George J., MSc Pret., DSc Pret. Prof.

Kunert, Karl J., PhD Constance Prof.

Lall, Namrita, PhD Pret. Assoc. Prof.

Meyer, Jacobus J. M., MSc Pret., PhD Pret. Assoc. Prof.; Head*

Van Rooyen, Margaretha W., PhD Pret. Assoc. Prof.

Van Wyk, Abraham E., MSc Potchef., DSc Pret. Prof.

Other Staff: 2 Lectrs.

Research: commercial and medicinal plants (molecular research and medically active ingredients); ecology of grasslands; ecophysiological studies on dry areas; molecular plant biotechnology; South African flora (management, reproduction biology, taxonomy, utilisation)

Political Sciences

Tel: (012) 420 2464 Fax: (012) 420 3886
E-mail: maxi.schoeman@up.ac.za

Du Plessis, Anton, MA Pret., DPhil Pret. Prof.

Hough, Michael, BA S.Af., BA Pret., MA Pret., DPhil Pret. Prof.

Miti, Katabaro N., DPhil Tor. Prof.

Olivier, Gert C., MA Pret., DPhil Pret. Extraordinary Prof.

Schoeman, Maria M. E., MA Rand Afrikaans, PhD Wales Prof.; Head*

Solomon, Hussein, BA Durban-W., MA Durban-W., DLitt&Phil S.Af. Assoc. Prof.

Other Staff: 3 Lectrs.

Research: conflict and peace studies; diplomacy; public policy studies; South African foreign policy; South African politics

Practical Theology

Tel: (012) 420 2700 Fax: (012) 420 4016
E-mail: julian@ccnet.up.ac.za

Dreyer, Yolanda, BA Pret., PhD Pret. Prof.

Masango, Maake S. J., BA Fort Hare, PhD Columbia Theol.Sem. Assoc. Prof.

Müller, Julian C., BA Pret., DD Pret. Prof.; Head*

Vos, Casparus J. A., BA Pret., DD Pret. Prof.

Other Staff: 21 Lectrs.†

Research: deaconate; hermeneutics; homiletics; liturgy; pastoral care and counselling

Psychology

Tel: (012) 420 2329 Fax: (012) 420 2404
E-mail: maria.marchetti-mercer@up.ac.za

Aronstam, Maurice, MA Pret., DPhil Pret. Sr. Lectr.

Bakker, Therese M., DLitt&Phil S.Af. Assoc. Prof.

Beyers, Dave, BTh Stell., MA S.Af., DPhil Free State Extraordinary Prof.

Cassimjee, Nafisa, MA Pret., PhD Pret. Sr. Lectr.

De la Rey, Ruben R., MA Pret., DPhil Pret. Extraordinary Prof.

Eskell-Blokland, Linda M., MA(ClinPsych) Pret., PhD Pret. Sr. Lectr.

Gildenhuys, Andries A., MA Pret., DPhil Pret. Sr. Lectr.

Human, Lourens H., MDiv Pret., MA(CounsPsych) Rand Afrikaans, MA Potchef., PhD Pret. Sr. Lectr.

Jordaan, Wilhelm J., BA Free State, BA Stell., MA S.Af. Extraordinary Prof.

Marchetti-Mercer, Maria C., MA Rand Afrikaans, DLitt&Phil Rand Afrikaans Prof.; Head*

Maree, David J. F., DPhil Pret. Prof.

Mauer, Karl F., MA Natal, MA S.Af., DLitt&Phil Rand Afrikaans Extraordinary Prof.

Moleko, Anne-Gloria S., MSc S.Af.Med. Sr. Lectr.

Potgieter, Cheryl A., MA Cape Town, PhD W.Cape Assoc. Prof.

Schoeman, Johannes B., MA Pret., DPhil Pret. Prof.

Strümpher, Deodandus G. W., BSc Potchef., MSc Potchef., PhD Purdue Extraordinary Prof.

Van Vuuren, Daniel P., BA S.Af., MA S.Af., DPhil Pret. Extraordinary Prof.

Visser, Maretha J., MA Rand Afrikaans Assoc. Prof.

Wagner, Claire, MA Pret., PhD Pret. Sr. Lectr.

Other Staff: 16 Lectrs.

Research: Alzheimer's disease; cognitive psychology; family therapy; HIV/AIDS; Rorschach

Public Management and Administration, School for

Tel: (012) 420 3334 Fax: (012) 362 5265
E-mail: kuyej@up.ac.za

Bouare, Oumar, MA Paris I, PhD New Sch.Soc.Res.(N.Y.), PhD Paris Extraordinary Prof.

Brynard, Petrus A., MA Pret., DPhil Pret. Prof.

Fourie, David J., MA Pret., DPhil Pret. Assoc. Prof.

Kuye, Jerry O. A., BA Manit., MPA Winn., PhD Manit. Prof.; Head*

Malan, Lianne, BAdmin Pret., MAdmin Pret., DAdmin Pret. Sr. Lectr.

Roux, Nicolaas L., MAdmin Pret., DAdmin Pret. Assoc. Prof.

Thornhill, Chris, BA Pret., MA Pret., DPhil Pret. Emer. Prof.

Van Dijk, Gerda H., BA Pret., MA Pret., DPhil Pret. Sr. Lectr.

Van Rooyen, Enslin J., MAdmin Pret., DAdmin Pret. Prof.

Other Staff: 4 Lectrs.

Research: environmental management and policy; international administration; leadership, governance and public policy; policy studies and analysis; Web-based public administration training

Radiographic Sciences

Tel: (012) 354 1236 Fax: (012) 354 1218
E-mail: annarie.hugo@up.ac.za

Hugo, Gertina A., BRad Pret. Sr. Lectr.; Head*

Mathurine, G. T., BTech Natal Sr. Lectr.

Other Staff: 4 Lectrs.

Research: AIDS; computer-aided tomography; improvement of training, methods, techniques and community services; mammography; tuberculosis

Religion and Missiology, Science of

Tel: (012) 420 2777 Fax: (012) 420 2887, 420 4016 E-mail: gswa@ccnet.up.ac.za

Niemandt, Cornelius J. P., BA Pret., BD Pret., DD Pret. Sr. Lectr.

Van der Merwe, Pieter J., BA Pret., BD Pret., DD Pret. Prof.; Head*

Other Staff: 2 Res. Fellows

Research: missiological and ecumenical research; the Church and reconciliation

Science, Mathematics and Technology Education

Tel: (012) 420 5572 Fax: (012) 420 5621
E-mail: onwu@gk.up.ac.za

De Villiers, Rian J. J. R., BSc Pret., MSc Pret., PhD Pret. Sr. Lectr.

Onwu, Gilbert O. M., BSc Lond., MSc E.Anglia, PhD E.Anglia Prof.; Head*

Research: cognitive development research in science and mathematics; effective schools; problem-solving in chemistry; science process skills assessment; teaching large under-resourced science and technology classes

Social Studies Education

Tel: (012) 420 5635 Fax: (012) 420 5594
E-mail: liza.vanbaalen@up.ac.za

Beukes, Lukas D., BA Free State, MPhil Rand Afrikaans Sr. Lectr.; Head*

Evans, Rinelle, BA Pret., BAEd Pret., MA Pret., PhD Pret. Sr. Lectr.

Roos, N. D., BA Natal, MA Natal, PhD Natal Assoc. Prof.

Van der Walt, C. A., BA Potchef., MA S.Af. Sr. Lectr.

Social Work and Criminology

Tel: (012) 420 2325 Fax: (012) 420 2093
E-mail: antoinette.lombard@up.ac.za

Bezuidenhout, Christiaan, MA Pret., MSc Oxf., DPhil Pret. Sr. Lectr.

Carbonatto, Charlene L., BA(SW) Pret., MSW Wash., MA(SW) Pret., DPhil Pret. Sr. Lectr.

Delport, Catharina S. L., BA(SW) Pret., BA(SW) S.Af., MA Rand Afrikaans, DLitt&Phil Rand Afrikaans Assoc. Prof.

Lombard, Antoinette, BSocSc(SW) Free State, MA Rand Afrikaans, DPhil Pret. Prof.; Head*

Motepe, Maureen M., MSocSc N-W(S.Af.), DPhil Pret. Sr. Lectr.

Pretorius, Ronelle, MA Pret., DPhil Pret. Prof.

Prinsloo, Christina E., BA(SW) Pret., MA(SW) Pret., DPhil Pret. Sr. Lectr.

Spies, Gloudien M., BA(SW) Pret., MA(SW) Pret., DLitt&Phil S.Af. Assoc. Prof.

Terblanche, Lourens S., BSocSc(SW) Free State, MA(SW) S.Af., DSocSc(SocialWork) Free State Assoc. Prof.

Other Staff: 8 Lectrs.

Research: alcohol and drug abuse; community development; community work; poverty; social policy and development

Sociology

Tel: (012) 420 2330 Fax: (012) 420 2873
E-mail: janis.grobbelaar@up.ac.za

Grobbelaar, Janis I., BSocSc Cape Town, MA Stell., DLitt&Phil S.Af. Prof.; Head*

Naidoo, Kammila, MA Durban-W., PhD Manc.
Assoc. Prof.
Neocosmos, Michael, BSc Lough., MA Lond., PhD
Brad. Prof.
Other Staff: 6 Lectrs.
Research: social development; sociology of
poverty and health; sociology of race, class
and gender; sociology of social change and
human rights; sociology of South Africa

Statistics

Tel: (012) 420 3774 Fax: (012) 420 3440
E-mail: petro.britz@up.ac.za
Bekker, Andriette, MSc Jo'burg., PhD S.Af. Sr.
Lectr.
Crowther, Nicolaas A. S., BSc Free State, MSc
P.Elizabeth, DSc Free State Prof.; Head*
Debusho, Legesse D., PhD KwaZulu-Natal, MSc
Sr. Lectr.
Grimbeek, Richard J., MSc Pret. Sr. Lectr.
Groeneveld, Hendrik T., MScAgric Free State,
DSc Pret. Prof.
Kanfer, Frans H. J., MSc Potchef., PhD Potchef.
Sr. Lectr.
Kasonga, Raphael A., MSc Car., PhD Car. Sr.
Lectr.
Louw, Elizabeth M., MSc Pret., PhD Pret. Sr.
Lectr.
Millard, Salomon M., MCom Pret. Sr. Lectr.
Smit, Christian F., DSc Pret. Prof.
Steyn, Hendrik S., MSc Free State, PhD Edin., DSc
Pret. Extraordinary Prof.
Stoker, D. J., MSc Potchef., MSc Stell.,
Dr(Math&Phys) Amst. Hon. Prof.
Swanepoel, Andre, MSc P.Elizabeth Sr. Lectr.
Van Zyl, Gideon J. J., BComm Stell., PhD
N.Carolina Prof.
Other Staff: 16 Lectrs.
Research: distribution-free methods;
econometrics; multivariate analysis;
sampling; time series

Taxation

Tel: (012) 420 4983 Fax: (012) 420 3725
E-mail: gene@up.ac.za
Coetzee, E. S. M., BCom Pret. Sr. Lectr.
Du Preez, H., BCompt S.Af. Sr. Lectr.
Janse van Rensburg, W., BCom(Law) Stell.,
BCom S.Af. Sr. Lectr.
Nel, P. J., BCom Pret., MCom(Tax) Pret. Sr.
Lectr.
Nienaber, S. G., BCom Pret., MCom(Tax) Pret.
Sr. Lectr.
Oberholzer, R., BCom Pret., MCom(Tax) Pret.
Assoc. Prof.
Oosthuizen, R., BCom Potchef. Sr. Lectr.
Smulders, S. A., BCom S.Af., MCom(Tax) Pret.
Sr. Lectr.
Stark, K., BCom Pret. Sr. Lectr.
Steyn, T., BCom Pret., MCom(Tax) Pret. Sr.
Lectr.
Stiglingh, Madeleine, BCom Potchef.,
MCom(Tax) Potchef. Assoc. Prof.; Head*
Other Staff: 2 Staff Members
Research: accountability and financial decision-
making; interim reporting

Tourism Management

Tel: (012) 420 4374 Fax: (012) 420 3349
E-mail: deptour@orion.up.ac.za
Fairer-Wessels, Felicité A., BBibl Pret., MPhil
Wales, DPhil Pret. Sr. Lectr.
Francis, Cyril V., BCom Vista, BCom Rand
Afrikaans, MCom Rand Afrikaans Sr. Lectr.
Heath, Ernie T., BCom Stell., MCom Fort Hare,
DCom P.Elizabeth Prof.; Head*
Lubbe, Berendien A., BCom Rand Afrikaans,
BCom S.Af., MCom S.Af., DCom Pret. Prof.
Wilson, G. D. H., BA Potchef., BA S.Af., MA
Potchef., MURP Free State, DPhil Pret. Assoc.
Prof.
Research: ecotourism; hospitality management;
sustainable tourism development; tourism
marketing; transportation and distribution
channel management

Town and Regional Planning

Tel: (012) 420 3531 Fax: (012) 420 3537
E-mail: mfletc@postino.up.ac.za
Anyumba, Godfrey, BA Nair., MA Nott., PhD
T.H.Delft Sr. Lectr.
Oranje, Mark C., MS&S Pret., PhD Pret. Prof.;
Head*
Other Staff: 2 Lectrs.
Research: development planning; land-use
management; planning futures; planning
theory; urban regeneration

Visual Arts

Tel: (012) 420 2353 Fax: (012) 420 3686
E-mail: smutsn@postino.up.ac.za
Badenhorst, Philip, BA(FineArts) Potchef.,
MA(FineArts) Potchef. Sr. Lectr.
Dreyer, Elfriede, BA Pret., BA(FineArts) S.Af.,
MA(FineArts) S.Af., DLitt&Phil S.Af. Sr.
Lectr.
Du Preez, Amanda A., BA Pret., MA Free State,
DLitt&Phil S.Af. Sr. Lectr.
Slabbert, Margaret L., BA(FineArts) Pret.
Assoc. Prof.
Van Eeden, Jeanne, BA Pret., MA Pret.,
DLitt&Phil S.Af. Prof.; Head*
Van Zyl, H. M., BA(FineArts) Pret., MA Pret.
Sr. Lectr.
Other Staff: 3 Lectrs.; 1 Sr. Clin. Lectr.
Research: design studies (South African design,
South African designers); national and
international arts; post-modern theory;
South African art (painting, sculpture)

Zoology and Entomology

Tel: (012) 420 3233 Fax: (012) 362 5242
E-mail: swinicolson@zoology.up.ac.za
Bastos, Amanda D., PhD Pret. Assoc. Prof.
Bateman, P. W., PhD Open(UK) Sr. Lectr.
Bennett, Nigel C., BSc Brist., MSc Cape Town,
PhD Cape Town Prof.
Best, Peter B., MA Camb., PhD Camb.
Extraordinary Prof.
Bester, Marthan N., BSc Stell., DSc Pret. Prof.
Cameron, Elissa Z., BSc Cant., PhD Massey
Assoc. Prof.
Chimimba, Christian T., MSc W.Aust., PhD Pret.
Assoc. Prof.
Clutton-Brock, Tim H., MA Camb., PhD Camb.,
ScD Camb. Extraordinary Prof.
Crewe, Robin M., BScAgric Natal, MScAgric
Natal, PhD Georgia Extraordinary Prof.
Dippenaar-Schoeman, Ansie S., PhD Rand
Afrikaans Extraordinary Prof.
Du Toit, J. T., PhD Witw. Extraordinary Prof.
Faulkes, C. G., PhD Lond. Extraordinary Prof.
Ferguson, J. Willem H., BSc P.Elizabeth, MSc
Pret., PhD Witw. Prof.
Getz, Wayne M., PhD Witw. Extraordinary
Prof.
Govender, Prem, BSc Natal, MSc Natal, PhD Pret.
Sr. Lectr.
Janse van Rensburg, B., BSc OFS, MSc Pret. Sr.
Lectr.
Krüger, Kerstin, PhD Pret. Sr. Lectr.
Mansell, Mervyn W., PhD Pret. Extraordinary
Prof.
Mills, M. G. L. (Gus), BSc Cape Town, MSc Pret.,
DSc Pret. Extraordinary Prof.
Moritz, Robin F. A., DSc Fran. Extraordinary
Prof.
Nicolson, Sue W., BSc Auck., PhD Camb. Prof.;
Head*
Pimm, Stuart L., PhD New Mexico State
Extraordinary Prof.
Schoeman, Adriaan At. S., DSc(Agric) Pret. Sr.
Lectr.
Scholtz, Clarke H., MSc Pret., DSc Pret. Prof.
Van Aarde, Rudolph J., DSc Pret. Prof.; Dir.,
Conservation Ecol. Res. Unit
Van der Merwe, Meinhardt (Mac), DSc Pret.
Prof.
Other Staff: 1 Lectr.; 12 Res. Fellows
Research: conservation ecology; environmental
studies; mammalogy; molecular biology

HEALTH SCIENCES

Tel: (012) 354 2386 Fax: (012) 329 1351
E-mail: mpume.ngcobo@up.ac.za

Anaesthesiology

Tel: (012) 354 1510 Fax: (012) 329 8276
E-mail: awedders@postillion.up.ac.za
Alberts, Andries N. J. D., MB ChB Pret.,
MMed(Anaesth) Pret. Sr. Lectr.
De Bruin, Johann C., MB ChB Pret.,
MMed(Anaesth) Pret. Sr. Lectr.
Fourie, Pierre H. J. L., MB ChB Pret., MMed
Pret. Prof.
Ingram, H., MB ChB Free State, MMed(Anaesth)
Free State Sr. Lectr.
Nel, Marius S., MB ChB Pret., MMed S.Af.Med.
Sr. Lectr.
Rantloane, J. L. A., MB ChB S.Af.Med.,
MMed(Anaesth) Prof.; Head*
Van der Vyver, J. D., MB ChB Pret.,
MMed(Anaesth) Pret. Sr. Lectr.
Other Staff: 11 Lectrs.; 3 Adjunct Profs.
Research: anaesthesia in the elderly; cerebral
protection; intra-operative awareness;
malignant hyperthermia; pain management

Anatomical Pathology

Tel: (012) 319 2614 Fax: (012) 324 4886
E-mail: leonora.dreyer@up.ac.za
Bloem, Pieter, BSc Pret., MB ChB Pret.,
MMed(Path) Pret. Sr. Lectr.
Campaini, Cinzia, MB BCh Pisa, MMed S.Af.Med.
Sr. Lectr.
Davel, Gerhardus H., MB ChB Pret., MMed
S.Af.Med. Sr. Lectr.
Dinkel, Jurgen E., MB ChB Pret., MMed(Path)
Pret. Sr. Lectr.
Dreyer, Leonora, MB ChB Pret., MMed(Path)
Pret., MD Pret., FCP(SA) Prof.; Head*
Louw, Melanie, MB ChB Pret., MMed(Path) Pret.
Sr. Lectr.
Other Staff: 1 Lectr.
Research: bone and soft tissue tumours; gastric
carcinoma; renal pathology
(glomerulonephritis, renal trauma)

Anatomy

Tel: (012) 319 2233 Fax: (012) 319 2240
E-mail: jmeiring@medic.up.ac.za
Abrahams, P. H., MB BS Lond. Extraordinary
Prof.
Bester, Megan J., BSc Pret., MSc Pret., PhD Witw.
Sr. Lectr.
Bosman, Marius C., BMedSci Pret., PhD S.Af.Med.
Assoc. Prof.
Carmichael, S. W., AB Ohio, PhD Tulane Hon.
Prof.
L'Abbe, E. N., MA Louisiana State, PhD Pret. Sr.
Lectr.
Maat, G. J. R., MB ChB Ley., MD Ley., PhD Ley.
Exraordinary Prof.
Meiring, Johannes H., MB ChB Pret., MPraxMed
S.Af. Prof.; Head*
Navsa, Nadia, BSc W.Cape, MSc Witw. Sr.
Lectr.
Pretorius, Etheresia, BSc Stell., MSc Stell., PhD
Pret. Prof.
Steyn, Maryna, MB ChB Pret., PhD Witw. Prof.
Thackeray, J. F., MSc Cape Town, MPhil Yale,
PhD Yale Hon. Prof.
Other Staff: 7 Lectrs.; 1 Hon. Lectr.
Research: cell biology; clinical anatomy;
embryology; histology; physical
anthropology

Cardiology

Tel: (012) 354 2277 Fax: (012) 354 4168
E-mail: tshimbi.mathivha@up.ac.za
Mathivha, T. M., MB ChB Natal, FCP(SA)
Prof.; Head*
Vacant Posts: 1 Sr. Lectr.

Cardiothoracic Surgery

Tel: (012) 354 1506 Fax: (012) 354 1507
E-mail: profdirk@med.up.ac.za
Du Plessis, Dirk J., MB ChB Pret., MMed Stell.
Prof.; Head*

Jacobs, Aldrich G., BSc *W.Cape*, MSc *Cape Town*, MB ChB *Cape Town*, FCS(SA)
Roos, Willem L., MB ChB *Free State*   Sr. Lectr.
Vacant Posts: 1 Lectr.

Chemical Pathology

Tel: (012) 319 2114 Fax: (012) 328 3600
   E-mail: wvermaak@medic.up.ac.za
Kiabilua, Olivia, BSc *Kinshasa*, MD *Kinshasa*   Sr. Lectr.
Oosthuizen, Nicolette M., MB ChB *Pret.*   Sr. Lectr.
Swanepoel, Eugene, MB ChB *Pret.*   Sr. Lectr.
Vermaak, William J. H., BSc *Pret.*, MB ChB *Pret.*, MMed *Pret.*   Prof.; Head*
Other Staff: 1 Chief Professl. Officer
Research: familiar hypercholesterolaemia, abnormal homocysteine metabolism and vascular disease; screening methods for inborn errors of metabolism on cord blood; susceptibility of black South Africans to a high-fat Western diet

Dentistry, School of

Tel: (012) 319 2327 Fax: (012) 326 2508
   E-mail: ligthelm@medic.up.ac.za
Ligthelm, A. J., BChD *Pret.*, MChD *Pret.*, PhD *Stell.*   Dean*

Community Dentistry

Tel: (012) 319 2418 Fax: (012) 323 7616
   E-mail: pjvanwyk@medic.up.ac.za
Ayo-Yusuf, Olalekan A., BDS *Benin*, MSc(Odont) *Pret.*, MPH *Pret.*   Sr. Lectr.
Botha, Francina S., MSc *Potchef.*, PhD *Pret.*   Sr. Lectr.
Botha, Stephanus J., BSc *Potchef.*, MSc *Pret.*, PhD *Pret.*   Assoc. Prof.
Postma, Thomas C., MChD *Pret.*, DHSM   Sr. Lectr.
Van Wyk, Phillippus J., MChD *Pret.*, PhD *Pret.*   Prof.; Head*
Other Staff: 3 Lectrs.
Research: oral epidemiology; oral health service research; preventive dentistry; tobacco research

Dental and Management Sciences

Tel: (012) 319 2518 Fax: (012) 319 2146
   E-mail: renata.vanaswegen@up.ac.za
Buch, Brian, BScAgric *Natal*, BDS *Witw.*, MScDent *Witw.*   Prof.
Oosthuizen, Marius P., BChD *Stell.*, MEd *Pret.*   Sr. Lectr.
White, J. George, BChD *Stell.*, MBA *Stell.*, PhD *Pret.*   Assoc. Prof.; Acting Head*
Other Staff: 8 Lectrs.
Research: dental practice management; radiation dosimetry (relative safety of dental radiographic procedures); radiographic features of odontogenic neoplasms; Rontgenology localisation of Frankfort horizontal planes

Maxillo-Facial and Oral Surgery

Tel: (012) 319 2232 Fax: (012) 319 2172
   E-mail: kwbutow@medic.up.ac.za
Bütow, Kurt-W., BSc *Rand Afrikaans*, BChD *Stell.*, MChD *Stell.*, DrMedDent *Erlangen-Nuremberg*, PhD *Pret.*, DSc *Pret.*   Prof.; Head*
Jacobs, Frederick J., BChD *Pret.*, MChD *Pret.*   Prof.
Other Staff: 4 Lectrs.; 10 Lectrs.†
Research: cleft lip and cleft palate; implantology; joint prostheses; oral pathology; trauma plate-biomechanical stability studies and design

Odontology

Tel: (012) 319 2443 Fax: (012) 326 2754
   E-mail: fadewet@medic.up.ac.za
Dannheimer, Manfred F. G., MDent *Pret.*   Assoc. Prof.
De Wet, Franscois, MDent *Pret.*, DSc(Odont) *Pret.*   Prof.; Head*
Other Staff: 5 Lectrs.
Research: aesthetic dentistry; clinical biomaterials development; testing of dental materials

Oral Pathology and Oral Biology

Tel: (012) 319 2320 Fax: (012) 321 2225
   E-mail: wvheerd@medic.up.ac.za
Bernitz, Herman, BChD *Pret.*, MSc *Pret.*, PhD *Pret.*   Hon. Prof.
Boy, Sonja C., BChD *Pret.*, MChD *Pret.*   Assoc. Prof.
Hemmer, Joërg, BSc *Mün.*, PhD *Ulm*, DSc *Mün.*   Hon. Prof.
Nzima, Nonhlanhla, BDS *S.Af.Med.*, MDS *S.Af.Med.*   Sr. Lectr.
Swart, Theunis J. P., BChD *Pret.*, MChD *Pret.*, MSc *Pret.*   Assoc. Prof.
Van Heerden, Willem F. P., BChD *Pret.*, MChD *Pret.*, PhD *S.Af.Med.*, DSc *Pret.*   Prof.; Head*
Other Staff: 1 Lectr.
Research: forensic odontology; oral cancer

Orthodontics

Tel: (012) 319 2223 Fax: (012) 328 6697
   E-mail: antoinette.dutoit@up.ac.za
De Muelenaere, Johan J. G. G., MChD *Pret.*   Extraordinary Prof.
Du Toit, Antoinette, BChD *Pret.*   Acting Head*
Grobler, Marthinus, MChD *Pret.*   Extraordinary Prof.
Nel, Stephanus J. P., MChD *Pret.*, PhD *Pret.*   Extraordinary Prof.
Other Staff: 2 Lectrs.
Research: cephalometric norms (data and analyses in various population groups); forces with removable orthodontic appliances (behaviour of springs); Golden Ratio and the human head (cephalometric and photographic investigation); malocclusion epidemiology (prevalence in various population groups); natural head position (photographic study of its establishment)

Periodontics and Oral Medicine

Tel: (012) 319 2336 Fax: (012) 326 3375
   E-mail: andrevanzyl@up.ac.za
Shangasi, Sindiswe L., MDent *S.Af.Med.*   Sr. Lectr.
Van Zyl, Andre W., BChD *Stell.*, MChD *Stell.*   Prof.; Head*
Other Staff: 1 Lectr.
Research: epidemiology

Prosthodontics

Tel: (012) 319 2446 Fax: (012) 323 0561
   E-mail: hemant.dullabh@up.ac.za
Becker, L. H., MChD *Pret.*   Prof.
Dullabh, Hemant D., MSc(Dent) *Witw.*, MDent *Witw.*   Assoc. Prof.; Head*
Other Staff: 7 Lectrs.; 10 Lectrs.†
Research: implant prostheses; improving the strength of denture base materials

Family Medicine

Tel: (012) 354 2141 Fax: (012) 354 1317
   E-mail: karin.ainslie@up.ac.za
Blitz, Julia J., MB BCh *Witw.*, MPraxMed *S.Af.Med.*   Prof.; Head*
Bondo, C., MB ChB *Congo(Official)*, MMEd(FamilyMed) *Pret.*   Sr. Lectr.
Britz, E. N., MB ChB *Pret.*, MPraxMed *Pret.*   Sr. Lectr.
Cameron, D. A., MB ChB *Cape Town*, MPraxMed *S.Af.Med.*, MPhil *Cape Town*   Assoc. Prof.
Chabikuli, N. O., MB ChB *S.Af.Med.*, MSc *Lond.*   Assoc. Prof.
Chundu, R. C., BSc *Zambia*, MB ChB *Zambia*, MMed(FamilyMed) *Pret.*   Sr. Lectr.
De Villiers-Smit, P., MB ChB *Pret.*, MMed *Pret.*   Sr. Lectr.
Delport, Rhena, BCur *Pret.*, MSc *Pret.*, MEd *Pret.*, PhD *Pret.*   Assoc. Prof.
Duvenage, H., MB ChB *Pret.*, MMed(FamilyMed) *Pret.*   Sr. Lectr.
Engelbrecht, A., MB ChB *Pret.*, MMed(FamilyMed) *Pret.*   Sr. Lectr.
Geyser, M. M., BSc *Pret.*, MB ChB *Pret.*, BSc(Pharm) *Potchef.*, MPraxMed *Pret.*   Sr. Lectr.
Heystek, Marthinus J., MPraxMed *Pret.*   Sr. Lectr.

Hitchcock, Sonja A., MB ChB *Pret.*, MPraxMed *Pret.*   Sr. Lectr.
Hugo, J. F. M., MB ChB *Free State*, MPraxMed *Free State*   Assoc. Prof.
Kenny, P. T., MB ChB *Pret.*, MPraxMed *Pret.*   Sr. Lectr.
Lachowicz, Ryszard, MMed(FamilyMed) *Pret.*, MD   Sr. Lectr.
Matthews, Peter A., MB ChB *Cape Town*, MPraxMed *S.Af.Med.*   Prof.
Meyer, Helgard P., MB ChB *Pret.*, MPraxMed *Pret.*   Prof.
Peters, F., MB ChB *Pret.*, MFamMed *Free State*   Sr. Lectr.
Rossouw, Theresa, MB ChB *Stell.*, MPhil *Stell.*   Sr. Lectr.
Smith, S., MB ChB *OFS*, MPraxMed *Pret.*   Sr. Lectr.
Tiamiyu, M. Y., BSc *Stell.*, MB BS *Lagos*, MMed(FamilyMed) *S.Af.Med.*   Sr. Lectr.
Ukpe, I. S., MB BCh *Nigeria*, MMed(FamilyMed) *Pret.*   Sr. Lectr.
Van Ramesdonk, Carl, MB ChB *Pret.*, MFamMed *Free State*   Sr. Lectr.
Van Rooyen, Marietjie, MB ChB *Pret.*, MMed(FamilyMed) *Pret.*   Sr. Lectr.
Other Staff: 14 Lectrs.
Research: chronic diseases (asthma and hypertension); HIV and sexually transmitted diseases; psycho-social aspects of family medicine; sports medicine

Forensic Medicine

Tel: (012) 323 5298 Fax: (012) 323 0921
   E-mail: gsaayman@medic.up.ac.za
Rossouw, Servaas H., MB ChB *Pret.*, MMed *Pret.*, MA *Pret.*   Sr. Lectr.
Saayman, Gert, MB ChB *Pret.*, MMed *Pret.*   Prof.; Head*
Other Staff: 1 Lectr.; 3 Res. Fellows; 4 Hon. Lectrs.
Research: forensic pathology service dispensations in South Africa; lightning and electro-thermal injury; non-natural mortality surveillance; pathology of trauma; suicide deaths (medico-legal perspectives)

Haematology

Tel: (012) 319 2449 Fax: (012) 319 2265
   E-mail: roger.pool@up.ac.za
Moodley, V., MB ChB *Cape Town*, MMed(Haem) *S.Af.Med.*   Sr. Lectr.
Pool, R., MB ChB *Pret.*, MMed(Haem) *S.Af.Med.*   Head*
Swart, A. M., MB ChB *Pret.*, MPraxMed *Pret.*, MMed(Path) *Pret.*   Sr. Lectr.
Other Staff: 2 Lectrs.
Research: electron microscopic aspects of haematology involving platelets; imatinib resistance in CML treatment of aplastic anaemia with ATG; immunophenotyping of malignant disease S-phase fraction in childhood; platelet function; platelets and electron microscopic morphology

Health Sciences (General)

Tel: (012) 354 1121 Fax: (012) 329 1351
   E-mail: james.ker@up.ac.za
Ker, James A., MB ChB *Pret.*, MMed *Pret.*, MD *Pret.*   Prof.; Deputy Dean
Mariba, Thanyani J., MB ChB *Natal*, FCP(SA), FRCP   Prof.; Dean*
Other Staff: 1 Lectr.

Immunology

Tel: (012) 319 2425 Fax: (012) 323 0732
   E-mail: ronald.anderson@up.ac.za
Anderson, Ronald, BSc *Glas.*, MSc *Witw.*, PhD *Witw.*   Prof.; Head*
Theron, Annette J., BSc *Pret.*, MSc *Pret.*, PhD *Pret.*   Assoc. Prof.
Research: characterisation and regulation of the harmful pro-inflammatory activities of microbial toxins; development of novel anti-malaria chemotherapeutic agents; development of novel anti-tuberculosis chemotherapeutic agents; nutrition, cigarette smoking, occupational and

environmental exposure to toxins as causes of oxidant-mediated pulmonary damage in tuberculosis; pharmacological regulation of phagocyte activation in chronic inflammatory disorders

Internal Medicine

Tel: (012) 354 2287 Fax: (012) 329 4168
E-mail: avg@tocmed.com
Ally, Mahmood M. M. T., MB BCh Witw., FCP(SA) Sr. Lectr., Rheumatology
Ellemdin, Sirajudeen, MMed(Int) Pret. Sr. Lectr.
Ker, James A., MB ChB Pret., MMed Pret., MD Pret. Prof.
Mwantembe, Obedy, MB ChB Zambia, PhD Edin. Prof.
Nagel, Gerhardus J., MMed(Int) Pret. Sr. Lectr.
Potgieter, Cornelius D., MMed Pret. Prof.
Retief, Johannes H., MMed Pret., MSc(ClinE) Pret. Prof.
Ribeiro Da Costa, Maria M., MB ChB Pret., MMed(Int) Witw. Sr. Lectr.
Sommers, Rita, MMed(Int) Pret., MPharmMed Pret. Sr. Lectr.
Steyn, George J. S., MB ChB Pret., MMed(Int) S.Af.Med. Sr. Lectr.
Tintinger, Gregory R., MB BCh Witw., MMed(Int) Pret., PhD Pret. Prof.
Van Gelder, Antoine L., MB ChB Pret., FCP, FRCP Prof.; Head*
Visser, Susanna S., MMed Pret., MD Pret., PhD Pret. Assoc. Prof.
Other Staff: 5 Lectrs.
Research: clinical, physiological and radiographic correlation in alpha-1 P1 deficiency; clinical research in diabetes mellitus management; in-vitro neutrophil and inflammation studies; lung disease

Medical Microbiology

Tel: (012) 319 2256 Fax: (012) 321 9456
E-mail: michael.dove@up.ac.za
Delport, J. A., MB ChB Pret., MMed Pret. Sr. Lectr.
Dove, Michael G., MB ChB Pret., MMed Free State Prof.; Acting Head*
Ehlers-Van der Stel, Marthie M., BSc Pret., MSc Pret., PhD Pret. Sr. Lectr.
Lekalakala, M. Ruth, MB ChB S.Af.Med., MMed S.Af.Med. Sr. Lectr.
Research: antimicrobial resistance; infectious diseases; nosocomial infection

Medical Oncology

Tel: (012) 354 1054 Fax: (012) 329 1100
E-mail: susan.botha@up.ac.za
Biddulph, F. J., BSc Pret., MB ChB Pret., MMed Pret. Sr. Lectr.
Dreosti, Lydia M., BSc Witw., MB BCh Witw., MMed Witw., FCP(SA) Prof.; Head*
Voster, A., MB ChB Pret., MMed Pret. Sr. Lectr.
Other Staff: 8 Lectrs.; 7 Res. Officers

Medical Virology

Tel: (012) 319 2351 Fax: (012) 325 5550
E-mail: maureen.taylor@up.ac.za
Taylor, Maureen B., MSc Rhodes, DSc Pret. Assoc. Prof.; Acting Head*
Venter, Marietjie, PhD Pret. Sr. Lectr.
Other Staff: 4 Registrars; 6 Res. Assts.
Research: detection of JC virus in AIDS patients; enteric viruses and environmental virology; molecular biology and pathogenesis of West Nile virus in South Africa; respiratory viruses associated with acute lower respiratory tract disease

Neurology

Tel: (012) 354 1082 Fax: (012) 354 2045
E-mail: roelien.dejager@up.ac.za
Bartel, Peter R., MA Rhodes, PhD Natal, FCP(SA) Prof.
Kakaza, Mandiza, BSc Rhodes, MB ChB Transkei, MMed Pret. Sr. Lectr.

Mafojane, Ntutu A., MB ChB Natal, FCP(SA) Prof.
Pillay, M., MB ChB Pret., MMed Pret. Sr. Lectr.
Schutte, Clara-Maria, MB ChB Pret., MMed Pret., MD Prof.; Head*
Other Staff: 1 Lectr.
Research: dystonia botulinium therapy; facio-scapulo-humeral muscular dystrophy; hereditary neuromuscular diseases; meningitis; neurological complications of HIV

Neurosurgery

Tel: (012) 521 4259 Fax: (012) 521 3510
E-mail: jlochner@medunsa.ac.za
Mokgokong, S., BSc North(S.Af.), MB ChB Natal, MMed S.Af.Med., FCS(SA) Acting Head*
Shapiro, Henry P., BSc Witw., MB BCh Witw., MMed Pret., FCS(SA) Prof.
Research: efficacy and safety of Nimodipine in treatment of traumatic subarachnoid haemorrhage; intra-cranial pressure monitoring; role of magnetic resonance imaging (MRI) in neurosurgery

Nuclear Medicine

Tel: (012) 354 2374 Fax: (012) 354 1219
E-mail: mike.sathekge@up.ac.za
Maes, Alex, MD Leuven, PhD Leuven Hon. Prof.
Meyer, Bernard J., MB ChB Pret., MSc Stell., MD Pret., DSc Pret., DSc Free State Extraordinary Prof.
Mpikashe, Pilisiwe, MB ChB S.Af.Med., MMed S.Af.Med.
Sathekge, Machaba M., MB ChB S.Af.Med., MMed S.Af.Med. Prof.; Head*
Other Staff: 11 Radiographers; 3 Consultants; 3 Registrars; 3 Nursing Sisters
Vacant Posts: 1 Consultant
Research: evaluation of stress fractures in military recruits of different ethnic backgrounds; FDG PET/CT and infection imaging; influence of BMI on Tc-99m MDP in bone and soft tissue; I-131 phenylacetate and cancer therapy; Tc-99m MIBI and Acute Coronary Syndrome

Nursing Science

Tel: (012) 354 2125 Fax: (012) 354 1490
E-mail: nursing@medic.up.ac.za
Du Rand, Eleonora A., MCur Pret. Sr. Lectr.
Leech, Ronell, PhD Pret. Sr. Lectr.
Meyer, Salome M., BCur Pret., MEd Pret., PhD Pret. Sr. Lectr.
Van Wyk, Neltjie C., MSocSc Free State, PhD Free State Prof.; Head*
Other Staff: 11 Lectrs.
Research: integration of technology in nursing education; perinatal health care; problem-orientated learning in clinical nursing science; traditional healers in primary health care; trans-cultural nursing care

Obstetrics and Gynaecology

Tel: (012) 354 2366 Fax: (012) 329 6258
E-mail: glindequ@medic.up.ac.za
Dreyer, Greta, MB ChB Pret., MMed(O&G) Pret. Prof.
Lindeque, Barend G., MB ChB Pret., MMed(O&G) Stell., MD Stell. Prof.; Head*
Lombaard, Hendrik A. d. T., MB ChB Pret., MMed(O&G) Pret. Sr. Lectr.
MacDonald, Angus P., MB ChB Cape Town, MMed(O&G) Pret., FRCOG Prof.
Mouton, Arnold, BSc Potchef., MB ChB Pret., MMed(O&G) Pret., MPraxMed Pret. Sr. Lectr.
Pattinson, Robert C., BSc Witw., MB BCh Witw., MMed(O&G) Stell., MD Stell. Prof.
Snyman, Leon C., MB ChB Pret., MPraxMed Pret., MMed(O&G) Pret. Sr. Lectr.
Other Staff: 2 Lectrs.; 2 Adjunct Profs.
Research: endoscopic surgery; gynaecological oncology; perinatology; reproductive biology and infertility; urogynaecology

Occupational Therapy

Tel: (012) 329 7800 Fax: (012) 329 3255
E-mail: margot.graham@up.ac.za
Graham, Margot, BOccTher Pret., MOccTher Pret., PhD Sr. Lectr.; Head*
McAdam, J. C., BSc(OccTher) Stell., MOccTher Witw. Sr. Lectr.
Other Staff: 7 Lectrs.
Research: hand therapy; rehabilitation in paediatrics; rehabilitation neurology; rehabilitation psychiatry; vocational therapy

Ophthalmology

Tel: (012) 354 1782 Fax: (012) 319 2643
E-mail: polla.roux@up.ac.za
Roux, Paul, MB ChB Pret., MPraxMed Pret., MMed Pret., FCS(SA) Prof.; Head*
Research: epidemiology of glaucoma; glaucoma laser therapy; glaucoma surgery; grafts for ocular surface disorders; retinopathy of prematurity in premature African babies

Orthopaedics

Tel: (012) 354 6528 Fax: (012) 354 6164
E-mail: sibongile.bopape@up.ac.za
Janse van Rensburg, D. Christa, MB ChB Pret., MMed Pret., MSc Pret. Sr. Lectr.
Motsitsi, N. S., MB ChB S.Af.Med. Sr. Lectr.
Mukenge, Felix M., MMed S.Af.Med., FCS(SA) Sr. Lectr.
Myburgh, J. G., MB ChB Pret., MMed Pret. Sr. Lectr.
Neluheni, Eric V. D., MB ChB Natal, FCS(SA) Sr. Lectr.; Head*
Snyckers, Hans M., MMed Pret. Sr. Lectr.
Visser, Christa C., MB ChB Pret., MMed Pret. Sr. Lectr.
Vlok, A. L., MB ChB Stell., MMed Pret. Sr. Lectr.
Other Staff: 9 Lectrs.; 1 Adjunct Prof.
Research: influence of HIV on treatment of open fractures; outcome of fracture treatment; rotator cuff disease

Otorhinolaryngology

Tel: (012) 354 2724 Fax: (012) 354 3723
E-mail: helene.vandermerwe@up.ac.za
Moolman, G. M., MMed Pret. Sr. Lectr.
Mulder, Andries A. H., MPraxMed Pret., MMed(Orl) Pret. Prof.
Swart, Johannes G., MB ChB Witw., MMed(Orl) Witw., MD Pret. Prof.; Head*
Other Staff: 6 Residents/Registrars; 2 Medical Officers; 4 Specialists†; 4 Temp. Lectrs.
Research: cochlear implantation; endolymphatic hydrops; inverted papillomas; laryngeal carcinoma; sub-glottic stenosis

Paediatrics

Tel: (012) 354 5276 Fax: (012) 354 5275
E-mail: dwittenb@medic.up.ac.za
Avenant, Theunis J., MB ChB Pret., MMed Pret. Sr. Lectr.
Bomela, H. N., MB ChB Natal, MMed Witw. Sr. Lectr.
De Witt-Jordaan, Theunsina W., MB ChB Pret., MMed Pret. Sr. Lectr.
Delport, Suzanne D., MMed Pret., MPharmMed Pret., PhD Pret. Assoc. Prof.
Farhangpour, Sirus, MMed(Paed) Jundi Shapur, MD Jundi Shapur Sr. Lectr.
Green, Robin J., MB BCh Witw., MMed(Paed) Witw., PhD Witw. Assoc. Prof.
Kruger, Mariana, MMed Pret., MPhil Stell., PhD Leuven Prof.
Malek, Aletta E., MB ChB Pret., MMed Pret., FCP(SA) Sr. Lectr.
Mitchell, B. J., MB ChB Pret., MMed(Paed) Pret. Sr. Lectr.
Opperman, Johannes C., MMed(Path) Pret., MMed(Paed) Pret. Sr. Lectr.
Reynders, David T., MB ChB Pret. Sr. Lectr.
Smuts, Izelle, BSc Pret., MMed Pret. Sr. Lectr.
Takawira, Farirai F. N., MB ChB Witw., MMed Witw. Sr. Lectr.
Van Biljon, Gertruida, MMed Pret., FCP(SA) Sr. Lectr.

Van Lobenstein, J. A., MMed(Paed) Gron.   Sr.
Lectr.
Wittenberg, Dankwart F., MB ChB Cape Town,
MD Natal, FCP(SA)   Prof.; Head*
Other Staff: 6 Lectrs.
Research: child health and primary care; HIV;
neonatology; oncology

Pharmacology

Tel: (012) 319 2243 Fax: (012) 319 2411
E-mail: jbekker@medic.up.ac.za
Medlen, Constance E., BSc(Agric) Pret., MSc
Pret., PhD Pret.   Prof.
Meeding, Johanna P., MB ChB Pret.,
MPharmMed Pret.   Sr. Lectr.
Outhoff, K., MB ChB Cape Town   Sr. Lectr.
Snyman, Jacques R., MB ChB Pret.,
MPharmMed Pret., MD Pret.   Prof.; Head*
Research: immunopharmacology; pharmaco-
economics; respiratory pharmacology

Physiology

Tel: (012) 319 2138 Fax: (012) 321 1679
E-mail: dvanpape@medic.up.ac.za
Apatu, Richard S. K., MB ChB Ghana, PhD Camb.
Assoc. Prof.
Dippenaar, Nola G., MSc Stell., MPhil Camb.,
PhD S.Af.Med.   Extraordinary Prof.
Du Toit, Peet J., BSc Pret., MSc Pret., PhD Pret.
Sr. Lectr.
Haag, Marianne, MSc Pret., DSc Pret.   Assoc.
Prof.
Joubert, Anna M., MSc Pret., PhD Pret.   Assoc.
Prof.
Ker, James, MB ChB Pret., MMed Pret., PhD Pret.
Sr. Lectr.
Soma, Prasilla, MB ChB S.Af.Med., MSc Pret.   Sr.
Lectr.
Van Papendorp, Dirk H., MB ChB Pret., BSc
Stell., MSc Stell., PhD(Med) Stell.   Prof.;
Head*
Viljoen, Margaretha, MSc Pret., PhD Witw.,
PhD(Psychology) Pret.   Prof.
Willemse, Naudine, MSc Rand Afrikaans, PhD
Witw.   Sr. Lectr.
Other Staff: 2 Lectrs.
Research: fatty acids; metabolic bone disorders,
osteoporosis, vitamin D and calcium;
occupational hygiene;
psychoneuroimmunology; testicular
physiology

Physiotherapy

Tel: (012) 354 2018 Fax: (012) 354 1226
E-mail: tania.vrooijen@up.ac.za
Eksteen, Carina A., BSc Stell., MEd S.Af., PhD
Pret.   Sr. Lectr.
Van Rooijen, Agatha J., BSc Free State, MSc Free
State, PhD Pret.   Sr. Lectr.; Head*
Other Staff: 5 Lectrs.
Research: exercise in type 2 diabetes mellitus;
physiotherapy in public health, community
health and primary health care; pressure-
relieving properties of a novel wheelchair
cushion; rehabilitation of spinal injuries

Psychiatry

Tel: (012) 319 9741, 354 3818 Fax: (012)
319 9617, 354 5130
E-mail: erna.fourie@up.ac.za
De Wet, Paul H., BChD Pret., MB ChB Pret.,
MMed(Psych) Pret.   Sr. Lectr.
Du Preez, Renata R., MB ChB Pret.,
MMed(Psych) Pret.   Sr. Lectr.
Krüger, Christa, MB BCh Witw., MMed(Psych)
Pret., MD Warw.   Assoc. Prof.
Page, Mark L., MB ChB Pret., MMed(Psych)
Pret.   Sr. Lectr.
Roos, Johannes L., MB ChB Pret., MMed(Psych)
Pret., MD Pret.   Prof.; Head*
Scholtz, Jonathan G., BASocSci Jo'burg.,
BA(Psych) Pret., MA(ClinPsych) Pret., PhD
Jo'burg.   Adjunct Prof.; Section Head, Clin.
Psychol.
Van Staden, C. Werdie, MB ChB Pret.,
MMed(Psych) Pret., MD Warw., FTCL
Assoc. Prof.

Weinkove, John V., MB ChB Cape Town,
MMed(Psych) Witw.   Sr. Lectr.
Other Staff: 7 Lectrs.; 23 Jr. Lectrs.; 2 Adjunct
Profs.
Research: medical education; physiology in
psychiatry; psychiatric symptomatology;
schizophrenia

Radiation Oncology

Tel: (012) 354 2940 Fax: (012) 329 1302
E-mail: steyni@medic.up.ac.za
Van Rensburg, Ado J., MSc Free State, MMedSci
Free State, PhD Pret.   Extraordinary Prof.
Wilson, J. A. G., MB ChB   Prof.; Head*
Other Staff: 1 Lectr.
Vacant Posts: 1 Sr. Lectr.
Research: irradiation with or without
chemotherapy for the treatment of cancer;
medical imaging; radiobiology

Radiology

Tel: (012) 354 2406 Fax: (012) 354 2771
E-mail: frieda.vosloo@up.ac.za
Ahmad, Samia, MB BS S.Af.Med., MMed(Radiol)
S.Af.Med.   Sr. Lectr.
Holl, Julian L., MB ChB Pret.   Prof.
Khan, S., MB ChB Pret., MMed Pret.   Sr. Lectr.
Lockhat, Z. I., MB ChB Natal   Prof.; Head*
Prinsloo, S. F., MB ChB Pret., MMed Pret.   Sr.
Lectr.
Small, Bernardus, MB ChB Pret., MMed(RadT)
Pret.   Sr. Lectr.
Van de Werke, Irma E. A., MB ChB Pret., FRCR
Sr. Lectr.
Van der Walt, E., MB ChB Pret., MMedRad Pret.
Sr. Lectr.
Other Staff: 1 Lectr.

Surgery

Tel: (012) 354 2099 Fax: (012) 354 3713
E-mail: hennie.becker@up.ac.za
Becker, Jan H. R., MB ChB Pret., MMed Pret.,
FCS(SA), FRCSGlas, FRCSEd   Prof.; Head*
Coetzee, Petrus F., MMed Pret.   Assoc. Prof.
Durand, Michiel C., MB BCh Witw., MMed Pret.
Sr. Lectr.
Karusseit, Victor O. L., MB ChB Witw., MMed
Pret.   Assoc. Prof.
Luvhengo, Thifhelimbilu, MB ChB, FCS(SA)
Sr. Lectr.
Mokoena, Taole R., MB ChB Natal, DPhil Oxf.,
FRCSGlas   Prof.
Other Staff: 1 Sr. Res. Officer; 22 Jr. Lectrs.; 2
Adjunct Profs.
Research: clinical and experimental organ
transplantation; surgical bleeding;
thrombophilia; thrombosis and haemostasis;
wound healing

Urology

Tel: (012) 354 1513 Fax: (012) 329 5152
E-mail: sreif@medic.up.ac.za
Kok, Etienne L., BA S.Af., MB ChB Pret.   Sr.
Lectr.
Reif, Simon, MMed Pret., FCS(SA)   Prof.;
Head*
Other Staff: 5 Lectrs.
Research: endocrine disruptors; male
reproductive health; prostate cancer; the
ageing male

VETERINARY SCIENCE

Tel: (012) 529 8201 Fax: (012) 529 8313
E-mail: vetdean@up.ac.za

Anatomy and Physiology (Veterinary)

Tel: (012) 529 8267 Fax: (012) 529 8320
E-mail: herman.groenewald@up.ac.za
Boomker, Elizabeth A., DSc Pret.   Assoc. Prof.
Booth, Kenneth K., MSc Iowa, PhD Iowa   Prof.
Chamunorwa, Joseph P., BSc Z'bwe., BVSc
Z'bwe., PhD Liv.   Sr. Lectr.
Fourie, Sheryl L., BVSc Pret., MMedVet Pret.
Sr. Lectr.
Groenewald, Hermanus B., BVSc Pret., PhD Pret.
Prof.; Head*
Hornsveld, Marius, BVSc Pret.   Sr. Lectr.

Madekurozwa, Mary-Cathrine N., BSc Z'bwe.,
BVSc Z'bwe., PhD Glas.   Assoc. Prof.
Meintjes, Roy A., BVSc Pret., MSc Witw., PhD
Pret.   Assoc. Prof.
Soley, John T., BA S.Af., MSc Witw., PhD Pret.
Prof.
Van der Merwe, Nicolaas J., DVSc Pret.   Assoc.
Prof.
Research: anatomy of wildlife; digestive
physiology; offspring recognition; renal
physiology; reproductive biology

Clinical Services (Onderstepoort Veterinary Academic Hospital) (OVAH)

Tel: (012) 529 8207 Fax: (012) 529 8309
E-mail: paul.bland@op.up.ac.za
Bland-van den Berg, Paul, MMedVet Pret., PhD
Texas A.& M.   Prof.; Dir.*

Companion Animal Clinical Studies

Tel: (012) 529 8260 Fax: (012) 529 8308
E-mail: piet.stadler@up.ac.za
Bester, Lynette, BVSc Pret.   Sr. Lectr.
Cilliers, Ingrid, BSc(Agric) Pret., BVSc Pret.   Sr.
Lectr.
Donnellan, Cynthia M. B., BVSc Pret., MMedVet
Pret.   Sr. Lectr.
Du Plessis, Wencke M., BVSc Pret., MMedVet
Pret.   Sr. Lectr.
Goddard, Amelia, BVSc Pret., MMedVet Pret.
Sr. Lectr.
Goodhead, Anthony D., BVSc Pret., MMedVet
Pret.   Sr. Lectr.
Kirberger, Robert M., BVSc Pret., MMedVet Pret.
Prof.
Marais, Hendrik J., BVSc Pret.   Sr. Lectr.
Olivier, Ann, BVSc Pret., MMedVet Pret.   Assoc.
Prof.
Scheepers, Elrien, BSc Pret., BVSc Pret.   Sr.
Lectr.
Schoeman, Johannes P., BVSc Pret., MMedVet
Pret.   Assoc. Prof.
Stadler, Pieter, BVSc Pret., MMedVet(Med) Pret.,
MBA Pret.   Prof.; Head*
Steenkamp, Gerhard, BSc Pret., BVSc Pret.   Sr.
Lectr.
Stegmann, George F., BVSc Pret., MMedVet Pret.
Assoc. Prof.
Turner, Peter H., BVSc Pret., MMedVet Pret.
Sr. Lectr.
Van der Merwe, Liesel, BVSc Pret., MMedVet
S.Af.Med.   Sr. Lectr.
Van Dyk, Enette, BSc(Agric) Pret.,
MMedVet(Gyn) Pret.   Sr. Lectr.
Van Schoor, Mirinda, BVSc Pret., MMedVet Pret.
Sr. Lectr.
Venter, Isak J., BVSc Pret., MMedVet Pret.   Sr.
Lectr.
Other Staff: 5 Lectrs.

Paraclinical Sciences

Pathology Section (Veterinary)

Tel: (012) 529 8054 Fax: (012) 529 8303
E-mail: leon.prozesky@up.ac.za
Duncan, Neil M., BVSc Pret., MMedVet Pret.
Assoc. Prof.
Lawrence, John A., BVSc Edin., DPhil Rhodesia
Extraordinary Prof.
Prozesky, Leon, BVSc Pret., MMedVet Pret.
Assoc. Prof.
Williams, June H., BVSc Pret.   Sr. Lectr.
Williams, Mark C., BVSc Pret., MMedVet Pret.
Assoc. Prof.
Other Staff: 1 Extraordinary Lectr.

Pharmacology and Toxicology Section (Veterinary)

Tel: (012) 529 8023
E-mail: christo.botha@up.ac.za
Botha, Christoffel J., BVSc Pret., MMedVet Pret.,
PhD Oslo   Prof.; Head*
Fourie, Neil, BVSc Pret., PhD Pret.
Extraordinary Prof.
Guilette, Louis J., BS New Mexico, MA Colorado,
PhD Colorado   Extraordinary Prof.

Kellerman, Theunis S., BScAgric Natal, BVSc Pret. Extraordinary Prof.

Myburgh, Jan G., BVSC S.Af.Med., MMedVet S.Af.Med. Sr. Lectr.

Naidoo, Vinasan, BVMCh S.Af.Med., MSc(VetSc) Pret. Sr. Lectr.

Naudé, Theunis W., BVSc Pret., MSc Pret. Emer. Prof.

Other Staff: 2 Extraordinary Lectrs.

Veterinary Public Health Section

Tel: (012) 529 8075 Fax: (012) 529 8311
E-mail: cheryl.mccrindle@up.ac.za
McCrindle, Cheryl M. E., BVSc Pret., PhD Pret. Prof.

Veary, Courtney M., BVSc Pret., MMedVet Pret. Prof.

Woods, Pamela S., BVSc Z'bwe., MSc Mich., PhD Utrecht Sr. Lectr.

Other Staff: 1 Extraordinary Lectr.

Production Animal Studies

Tel: (012) 529 8013 Fax: (012) 529 8315
E-mail: daleen.anderson@up.ac.za
Bath, Gareth F., BVSc Pret. Assoc. Prof.
Bisschop, Shahn P. R., BVSc Pret., MSc(VetSc) Pret., MSc Sr. Lectr.; Dir., Poultry Ref. Centre

Buss, P. E., BVSc MMedVet(Pharm) Extraordinary Prof.

Carrington, Christopher A. P., BVSc Pret., BComm S.Af., MMedVet Pret. Sr. Lectr.

Els, Helena C., MSc(Agric) Pret. Sr. Lectr.
Gummow, Bruce, BVSc Pret., MMedVet Pret., PhD Utrecht Prof.

Harmse, Johan G., BVSc Pret. Sr. Lectr.
Irons, Peter C., BVSc Pret., MMedVet Pret. Assoc. Prof.

Lourens, Dirk C., BVSc Pret., MMedVet Pret. Prof.

Nöthling, Johan O., MMedVet Pret., MBA Pret., PhD Utrecht Prof.

Pettey, Kenneth P., BSc Witw., BVSc Pret. Assoc. Prof.

Petzer, Inge-Marie, BVSc Pret., MScVetSc Pret., MSc Sr. Lectr.

Rautenbach, Gert H., BVSc Pret., MMedVet Pret.; Head*

Schulman, Martin L., BVSc Pret., MMedVet Pret. Assoc. Prof.

Shakespeare, Anthony S., BSc Pret., BVSc Pret., MMedVet Pret. Assoc. Prof.

Skinner, J. D., BSc(Agric) Natal, MSc(Agric) Pret., PhD Camb., FRSSAf Extraordinary Prof.

Spencer, Brian T., BVSc Pret., BComm S.Af., MMedVet Pret. Sr. Lectr.

Stout, T. A. E., VetMB MA PhD Extraordinary Prof.

Thompson, Peter N., BVSc Pret., MMedVet Pret. Assoc. Prof.

Other Staff: 4 Lectrs.; 1 Extraordinary Lectr.; 4 Clin. Assts.

Research: equine and companion animal health and welfare; veterinary aspects of food safety and food security; wildlife and environmental health

Veterinary Tropical Diseases

Tel: (012) 529 8269 Fax: (012) 529 8312
E-mail: koos.coetzer@up.ac.za
Allsopp, Basil A., BSc Lond., PhD Lond. Prof.
Boomker, Joop D. F., BVSc Pret., MMedVet Pret., MSc(Zoology) Rand Afrikaans, DVSc S.Af.Med. Prof.

Bryson, Nigel R., BSc Rhodes, BVSc Pret., MMedVet Pret. Sr. Lectr.

Coetzer, Jacobus A. W., BVSc Pret., MMedVet Pret. Prof.; Head*

Crafford, Jannie, BVSc Pret., MSc(VetSci) Pret. Sr. Lectr.

Godfroid, J., DVM Liège, MSc Brussels, PhD Namur Prof.

Horak, Ivan G., BVSc Pret., DVSc Pret., PhD Natal Extraordinary Prof.

Jonngejan, Frans, BSc(Biol) Amst., MSc Utrecht, PhD Utrecht Extraordinary Prof.

Latif, Abdalla A. I., BVSc Khart., MVSc Khart. Extraordinary Prof.

Majiwa, Phelix A. O., BS Jarvis Christian, MS Texas, PhD Brussels Extraordinary Prof.

Musoke, Anthony J., BVSc Nair., MSc Mich., PhD Mich. Extraordinary Prof.

Penrith, Mary-Lou, BVSc Pret., DSc Pret., PhD Cape Town Extraordinary Prof.

Penzhorn, Barend L., BSc Pret., BVSc Pret., MAgric Texas A.& M., DSc Pret. Prof.

Perry, Brian, OBE, BVM&S MSc DVM&S, FRCVS Extraordinary Prof.

Picard, Jacqueline A., BVSc Pret., MSc(VetSci) Pret. Sr. Lectr.

Rutten, Victor, BSc Utrecht, MSc Utrecht, PhD Utrecht Extraordinary Prof.

Schwan, E. Volker, MVSc Liv., DVM Hanover, DrMedVet Hanover Sr. Lectr.

Stoltsz, W. Hein, BVSc Pret. Sr. Lectr.
Van den Bossche, Peter, DVM Ghent, PhD Pret. Extraordinary Prof.

Van Vuuren, Moritz, BVSc Pret., MMedVet Pret. Prof.

Venter, Estelle H., MSc OFS, PhD Pret. Assoc. Prof.

Vosloo, Wilna, BSc Pret., MSc Pret., PhD Cape Town Extraordinary Prof.

Other Staff: 1 Lectr.; 10 Extraordinary Lectrs.; 1 Sr. Researcher

SPECIAL CENTRES, ETC

Academic Development, Centre for

Tel: (012) 420 2635 Fax: (012) 420 2698
E-mail: ann-louise.deboer@up.ac.za
De Boer, Ann L., BA S.Af., BEd Pret., MEd Pret., DPhil Pret. Assoc. Prof.; Dir.*

Academic Literacy, Unit for

Tel: (012) 420 2334 Fax: (012) 420 3682
E-mail: christelle.alberts@up.ac.za
Carstens, Adelia, MA Pret., DLitt&Phil S.Af. Prof.

Marais, Renee, BA(Mus) Free State, MA Pret. Sr. Lectr.

Weideman, Albertus J., MA Free State, MA Essex, DLitt Free State Prof.; Dir.*

Other Staff: 6 Lectrs.
Research: language course design; language for academic purposes/academic literacy; language testing

Agricultural Extension, South African Institute for

Tel: (012) 420 3246 Fax: (012) 420 3247
E-mail: gustav.duvel@up.ac.za
Düvel, Gustav H., BSc(Agric) Pret., MInstAgrar Pret., DInstAgrar Pret. Prof.; Dir.*

Terblanche, Stephanus E., BSc(Agric) Pret., BInstAgrar Pret., MInstAgrar Pret., PhD Pret. Sr. Lectr.

Other Staff: 1 Lectr.

Applied Materials, Institute of

Tel: (012) 420 2588 Fax: (012) 420 2516
E-mail: walter.focke@up.ac.za
Focke, Walter W., BEng Pret., MEng Pret., PhD M.I.T. Prof.; Dir.*

Morgan, David L., MSc Natal, PhD Cape Town Extraordinary Prof.

Other Staff: 6 Researchers
Research: carbon technology; chemical production process improvements; polymer additives; polymer applications

Augmentative and Alternative Communication, Centre for

Tel: (012) 420 2001 Fax: (012) 420 4389
E-mail: erna.alant@up.ac.za
Alant, Erna, MA(Log) Pret., DPhil Pret. Prof.; Dir.*

Bornman, Juanita, MCP Pret., PhD Pret. Assoc. Prof.

Uys, Catharina J. E., BOccTher S.Af.Med., PhD Pret. Sr. Lectr.

Other Staff: 1 Lectr.
Research: augmentative and alternative communication; communication and life-

skills of people with severe disabilities (complex communications needs); multi-professional and community training; policy making impacting on the lives of people with severe disabilities; severe disabilities (early intervention)

Business and Professional Ethics, Centre for

Tel: (012) 420 2546 Fax: (012) 420 2890
E-mail: mpainter@postino.up.ac.za
Painter Morland, M. J., PhD Pret. Assoc. Prof.
Rossouw, Gedeon J., PhD Stell. Prof.; Dir.*
Research: corruption prevention; narrative ethics

Capacity Building in Africa, UNESCO International Institute for (UNESCO-IICBA)

Tel: (012) 420 5582 Fax: (012) 420 5584
E-mail: tphendla@unesco.iicba.org
Phendla, Thidziambi S., BA Witw., MEd Rand Afrikaans, PhD Mich.State Sr. Lectr.; Dir.*

Child Law, Centre for

Tel: (012) 420 2354 Fax: (012) 420 4499
E-mail: cjdavel@up.ac.za
Davel, Catharina J., BA Pret., LLB Pret., LLD Pret. Prof.; Dir.*

Maithufi, Ignatius P., LLB North(S.Af.), LLM N-W(S.Af.), LLD Pret. Prof.

Clinical Pharmacology, Glaxo Laboratory for

Tel: (012) 319 2243 Fax: (012) 319 2411
E-mail: jbekker@medic.up.ac.za
Meeding, Ronel J. P., MB ChB Pret., MPharmMed Pret. Sr. Lectr.

Snyman, Jacques R., MB ChB Pret., MPharmMed Pret., MD Pret. Prof.; Dir.*

Vacant Posts: 2 Sr. Lectrs.
Research: clinical pharmacodynamics and kinetics of allopathic and natural medicines and herbs; immunopharmacology; pharmaco-economics; respiratory pharmacology

Continuing Theological Education, Centre for

Tel: (012) 420 2015 Fax: (012) 420 4016
E-mail: sevto@ccnet.up.ac.za
Le Roux, Jurie H., MA Pret., DD S.Af., DTh S.Af. Prof.†; Co-Dir.*

Meiring, Pieter G. J., BA Pret., DrsTheol V.U.Amst., DD Pret. Prof.; Co-Dir.*

Corrosion Engineering, Centre for

Tel: (012) 420 3182 Fax: (012) 362 5304
E-mail: chris.pistorius@up.ac.za
Pistorius, Petrus C., MEng Pret., PhD Camb. Prof.; Dir.*

Sandenberg, Roelof F., MEng Pret., DEng Pret. Prof.

Other Staff: 1 Lectr.
Research: coated steel; corrosion of weldments; electrochemical fundamentals; steel corrosion cracking

Creative Writing, Unit for

Tel: (012) 420 4862 Fax: (012) 420 4008
E-mail: henning.pieterse@up.ac.za
Pieterse, Henning J., MA Pret., DLitt&Phil S.Af. Prof.; Dir.*

Other Staff: 2 Lectrs.
Research: creative writing as therapy; narrative therapy; poetry therapy

Early Intervention in Communication Pathology, Centre for

Tel: (012) 420 2303 Fax: (012) 362 2349
E-mail: brenda.louw@up.ac.za
Louw, Brenda, BA(Log) Pret., MSc Alabama, DPhil Pret. Prof.; Dir.*

Economic Policy and Analysis, Bureau for

Tel: (012) 420 3455 Fax: (012) 362 5207
E-mail: njschoem@hakuna.up.ac.za
Schoeman, Nicolaas J., MA(Econ) Pret., DCom Pret. Prof.; Dir.*

Research: international trade and finance; job creation; macroeconometric modelling; small business development; tax policy development

Education Law and Education Policy, Inter-University Centre for

Tel: (012) 420 3484 Fax: (012) 420 3723
E-mail: celp@hakuna.up.ac.za
Joubert, Hendrika J., BSc Pret., BEd Pret., MEd Pret., PhD Pret.   Sr. Lectr.
Research: access to human rights; discipline; labour law; perception of HIV/AIDS; school governance

Electromagnetism, Centre for

Tel: (012) 420 2680 Fax: (012) 362 5000
E-mail: johan.joubert@eng.up.ac.za
Joubert, Johan, MEng Pret., PhD Pret.   Prof.†; Dir.*
Research: antenna design and analysis in the microwave and mm-wave frequency ranges

Environmental Studies, Centre for

Tel: (012) 420 4048 Fax: (012) 420 3210
E-mail: mcilliers@zoology.up.ac.za
Ferguson, J. Willem H., BSc P.Elizabeth, MSc Pret., PhD Witw.   Prof.; Dir.*
Research: conservation planning; integrated environmental management; sustainable development

Equine Research Centre

Tel: (012) 529 8068 Fax: (012) 529 8301
E-mail: aguthrie@op.up.ac.za
Guthrie, Alan J., BVSc Pret., MMedVet(Phys) Pret., PhD Louisiana State   Prof.†; Dir.*

Financial Analysis, Bureau for

Tel: (012) 420 3371 Fax: (012) 362 5299
E-mail: rina.vancoller@up.ac.za
3 Res. Officers
Vacant Posts: Dir.*

Forestry and Agricultural Biotechnology Institute (FABI)

Tel: (012) 420 3938 Fax: (012) 420 3960
E-mail: rose.visser@up.ac.za
Aveling, Terry A. S., PhD Natal   Assoc. Prof.
Berger, Dave K., PhD Cape Town   Assoc. Prof.
Coutinho, Teresa A., MSc Natal, PhD Natal   Assoc. Prof.
Korsten, Lise, BSc Stell., MSc Pret., PhD Pret.   Prof.
Kunert, Karl J., PhD Constance   Prof.
Labuschagne, Nico, MSc(Agric) Pret., DSc(Agric) Pret.   Assoc. Prof.
Marasas, Walter F. O., PhD Witw., DSc(Agric) Pret.   Extraordinary Prof.
Oberholster, Anna-Maria, MSc Potchef., PhD Free State   Prof.
Viljoen, Altus, BSc Free State, PhD Free State   Sr. Lectr.
Wingfield, Brenda D., BSc Natal, BSc(Med) Cape Town, MSc Minn., PhD Stell.   Prof.
Wingfield, Michael J., BSc Natal, MSc Stell., PhD Minn.   Prof.; Dir.*
Other Staff: 1 Lectr.; 2 Sr. Res. Officers
Research: forest pathology; fungal diagnostics; molecular mycology; plant biotechnology; plant-pathogen interactions

Heritage and History, Centre for

Tel: (012) 420 2323 Fax: (012) 420 2656
E-mail: karen.harris@up.ac.za
Bergh, Johannes S., BA Stell., MA S.Af., DPhil Stell.   Prof.
Harris, Karen L., MA Stell., DLitt&Phil S.Af.   Prof.; Head*

Human Nutrition, Division of

Tel: (012) 354 1408 Fax: (012) 354 1232
E-mail: gerda.gericke@up.ac.za
Gericke, Gertruida J., BScDiet Pret., MDietetics Pret.   Sr. Lectr.; Head*
Wenhold, Friedeburg A. M., BScDiet Pret., MDietetics Pret., PhD Pret.   Sr. Lectr.

Other Staff: 3 Lectrs.

Human Rights, Centre for

Tel: (012) 420 3810 Fax: (012) 362 5125
E-mail: chr@up.ac.za
Dugard, C. J. R., BA Stell., LLB Stell., LLB Camb., LLD Camb., Hon. LLD Stell.   Hon. Prof.
Hansungule, M. K., LLB Zambia, LLM Zambia, LLM Lond., PhD Graz   Prof.
Kriegler, J., BA Pret., LLB S.Af.   Hon. Prof.
Kwakwa, E. K., LLB Ghana, LLM Qu., JSB Yale   Assoc. Prof.
Robinson, Mary, LLM Harv., LLD Oxf., LLB MA   Extraordinary Prof.
Research: gender issues; human rights law in Africa

Industrial Metals and Minerals Research, Institute for

Tel: (012) 420 3183 Fax: (012) 362 5304
E-mail: tom.vonmoltke@up.ac.za
Von Moltke, Tom v S., BSc Stell., MSc Stell., PhD Pret.   Prof.; Dir.*
Other Staff: 7 Researchers
Research: corrosion of steel coated with tin, zinc and organic coatings; hot deformation of steels (grain size development, recrystallisation, hot ductility); inclusions in steel

International Political Studies, Centre for

Tel: (020) 420 2696 Fax: (020) 420 3886
E-mail: cips@postino.up.ac.za
Solomon, Hussein, BA Durban-W., MA Durban-W., DLitt&Phil S.Af.   Assoc. Prof.; Dir.*

Leisure Studies, Centre for

Tel: (012) 420 6028 Fax: (012) 420 6099
E-mail: anneliese.goslin@up.ac.za
Goslin, Anna E., MA(PhysEd) Pret., MBA Pret., DPhil Pret.   Prof.†; Dir.*
Research: ethics in sport; leisure management and marketing; sport management; sport psychology; sport tourism

Mammal Research Institute

Tel: (012) 420 3776 Fax: (012) 420 2534
E-mail: ezcameron@zoology.up.ac.za
Cameron, Elissa Z., BSc Cant., MSc Cant., PhD Massey   Assoc. Prof.; Dir.*
Other Staff: 1 Sr. Res. Officer
Research: community ecology; ecology; game; plant-animal interactions

Micro-Electronics, Carl and Emily Fuchs Institute for

Tel: (012) 420 2952 Fax: (012) 362 5115
E-mail: monuko.duplessis@up.ac.za
Du Plessis, Monuko, BA S.Af., BCom S.Af., DEng Pret.   Prof.; Dir.*
Research: complementary metal oxide semiconductor design; component design and electronic circuit techniques; optoelectronics; semiconductor physics

Microscopy and Microanalysis, Laboratory for

Tel: (012) 420 2075 Fax: (012) 362 5150
E-mail: ajbotha@scientia.up.ac.za
Malherbe, Johan B., MSc Pret., DSc Pret.   Prof.; Head*
Other Staff: 3 Operators
Research: materials characterisation; plant morphology and ultrastructure; quality management in microscopy; specimen preparation in biological electron microscopy

Missiological and Ecumenical Research, Institute for

Tel: (012) 420 2891 Fax: (012) 420 4016
E-mail: attie.vanniekerk@up.ac.za
Van Niekerk, Adriaan S., BA Pret., BD Pret., DD Pret.   Sr. Lectr.; Dir.*
Other Staff: 2 Researchers†
Research: functional integration of the household in the African context

New Electricity Studies, Centre for

Tel: (012) 420 2587 Fax: (012) 263 5000
E-mail: werner.badenhorst@up.ac.za
Badenhorst, Werner, BEng Pret.   Lectr.†; Acting Dir.*
Research: demand side management

Public Theology, Centre for

Tel: (020) 420 2885 Fax: (020) 420 4016
E-mail: etienne.devilliers@up.ac.za
De Villiers, D. Etienne, BTh Stell., MA Stell., ThD Amst.   Prof.; Dir.*

Radio and Digital Communication, Centre for

Tel: (012) 420 2168 Fax: (012) 362 5000
E-mail: louis.linde@up.ac.za
Linde, Louis P., BEng Stell., MEng Pret., DEng Pret.   Prof.; Dir.*
Research: channel estimation and modelling; coding mechanisms; wireless communications

Science, Mathematics and Technology Education, Joint Centre for

Tel: (012) 420 2771 Fax: (012) 420 3003
E-mail: annemarie.hattingh@up.ac.za
Hattingh, Annemarie, BSc Pret., BEd Pret., MEd Pret., PhD Pret.   Prof.; Dir.*
Ndlalane, Thembe C., BA Zululand, BEd Natal, MEd Leeds   Sr. Lectr.
Other Staff: 1 Project Co-ordinator
Research: computer-based education; instructional leadership for science and mathematics; mathematics and technology education; school and cluster-based professional development in science; teacher development and change in science and mathematics

Sports Research, Institute for

Tel: (012) 420 6032 Fax: (012) 420 6099
E-mail: ernst.kruger@up.ac.za
Kruger, Pieter E., MA(PhysEd) Pret., DPhil Pret.   Prof.†; Dir.*
Other Staff: 12 Biokineticists
Research: biokinetics; exercise physiology

Statistical and Survey Methodology, Bureau for

Tel: (012) 420 3445 Fax: (012) 420 3440
E-mail: deon.vanzyl@up.ac.za
Van Zyl, Gideon J. J., BComm Stell., PhD N.Carolina   Acting Dir.*
Research: advanced statistical analysis; market research; questionnaire design; sampling methodology; surveys

Strategic Studies, Institute for

Tel: (012) 420 2034 Fax: (012) 420 2693
E-mail: wilma.martin@up.ac.za
Hough, Michael, BA S.Af., BA Pret., MA Pret., DPhil Pret.   Prof.†; Dir.*
Research: migration trends; national security; strategic scenario constructions

Technological Innovation, Institute for

Tel: (012) 420 3843 Fax: (012) 362 5092
E-mail: anthea.vanzyl@up.ac.za
Mugabe, John O., BSc Nair., PhD Amst.   Extraordinary Prof.; Co-Dir.*
Pistorius, Carl W. I., BSc(Eng) Pret., BEng Pret., MS Ohio State, SM M.I.T., PhD Ohio State, FRSSAf   Prof.; Co-Dir.*
Pouris, Anastassios, MScEng Grad.Sch.Indust.St., Salonika, MSc Sur., PhD Cape Town   Prof.
Research: managing the dynamics of technological change; technology policy issues; technology transfer and diffusion

Teletraffic Engineering for the Information Society, Centre for

Tel: (012) 420 2953 Fax: (012) 362 5000
E-mail: walter.penzhorn@up.ac.za
Penzhorn, Walter T., BEng Pret., MEng Pret., MSc Lond., PhD Pret.   Assoc. Prof.; Dir.*
Research: telecommunications

Transport Development, Centre for

Tel: (012) 420 3168 Fax: (012) 362 5218
E-mail: alex.visser@up.ac.za
Venter, Christo J., BEng Stell., MEng Stell., PhD Calif. Assoc. Prof.
Visser, Alex T., BSc(Eng) Cape Town, BCom S.Af., MSc Witw., PhD Texas Prof.; Dir.*

Veterinary Wildlife Studies, Centre of

Tel: (012) 529 8558 Fax: (012) 529 8312
E-mail: nick.kriek@up.ac.za
No staff at present

Vacant Posts: Head*

Welding Engineering, Centre for

Tel: (012) 420 3182 Fax: (012) 362 5304
E-mail: madeleine.dutoit@up.ac.za
Du Toit, Madeleine, BEng Pret., MEng Pret., PhD Pret. Assoc. Prof.; Dir.*
Research: nitrogen and hydrogen behaviour during welding; precipitation behaviour in weldments; weld flux development

Wildlife Management, Centre for

Tel: (012) 420 2627 Fax: (012) 420 6096
E-mail: wildlife.management@up.ac.za
Van Hoven, Wouter, MSc Potchef., DSc Potchef. Assoc. Prof.; Dir.*
Research: carnivore ecology; habitat management; wildlife ecology and management; wildlife nutrition; wildlife ranching

Women's and Gender Studies, Institute for

Tel: (012) 420 3898 Fax: (012) 420 2873
E-mail: marinda.mare@up.ac.za
Fairhurst, Unitia J., MA S.Af., DPhil Pret. Dir.*

CONTACT OFFICERS

Academic affairs. Director (Academic affairs): Marais, D. D., MA Pret., DPhil Pret.
(E-mail: ddmarais@ccnet.up.ac.za)
Accommodation. Director (Residence Affairs and Accommodation): Visser, Prof. R. N., MSc(QS) Pret.
(E-mail: rnvisser@postino.up.ac.za)
Admissions (first degree). Director (Admissions): Marais, D. D., MA Pret., DPhil Pret. (E-mail: ddmarais@ccnet.up.ac.za)
Admissions (higher degree). Director (Admissions): Marais, D. D., MA Pret., DPhil Pret. (E-mail: ddmarais@ccnet.up.ac.za)

Adult/continuing education. Director (Adult/continuing education): Marais, D. D., MA Pret., DPhil Pret.
(E-mail: ddmarais@ccnet.up.ac.za)
Alumni. Head (Alumni): Liebenberg, E. J., DLitt&Phil S.Af.
(E-mail: elmarie.liebenberg@up.ac.za)
Archives. Head (Archives): Harris, Prof. Karen L., MA Stell., DLitt&Phil S.Af.
(E-mail: kharris@postino.up.ac.za)
Careers. Head (Careers): Isaacs, W. J., MA Stell.
(E-mail: wallace.isaacs@up.ac.za)
Computing services. Head/Director (Computing services): Pretorius, J. A., MEng Pret., PhD Tor.
(E-mail: jakkie.pretorius@it.up.ac.za)
Distance education. Head (Distance education): Jorissen, H. W., PhD Pret.
(E-mail: hjorisse@postino.up.ac.za)
Equal opportunities. Vice-Principal: De Beer, Prof. C. R., BJur&Art Potchef., LLB Potchef., LLM Rand Afrikaans, DrsJuris Ley., LLD Ley.
(E-mail: crdebeer@up.ac.za)
Estates and buildings/works and services. Director (Estates and buildings/works and services: (vacant)
Examinations. Director (Examinations): Marais, D. D., MA Pret., DPhil Pret.
(E-mail: ddmarais@ccnet.up.ac.za)
Finance. Director (Finance): Kruger, T. G., BCom Pret., MBA Pret.
(E-mail: tom.kruger@up.ac.za)
General enquiries. Director (General enquiries): Marais, D. D., MA Pret., DPhil Pret. (E-mail: ddmarais@ccnet.up.ac.za)
Health services. Dean, Student Affairs: Speckman, M. T., PhD S.Af.
(E-mail: m.speckman@up.ac.za)
International office. International Co-ordinator: Crewe, Prof. Robin M., BScAgric Natal, MScAgric Natal, PhD Georgia
(E-mail: robin.crewe@up.ac.za)
Library (chief librarian). University Librarian: Moropa, R., BBibl Fort Hare, BBibl S.Af.
(E-mail: robert.moropa@up.ac.za)
Library (enquiries). Director (Library): Moropa, R., BBibl Fort Hare, BBibl S.Af.
(E-mail: robert.moropa@up.ac.za)
Marketing. Director, Marketing and Corporate Communication: Pretorius, I. E., BA
(E-mail: elizabeth.pretorius@up.ac.za)
Minorities/disadvantaged groups. Vice-Principal: De Beer, Prof. C. R., BJur&Art Potchef., LLB Potchef., LLM Rand Afrikaans, DrsJuris Ley., LLD Ley.
(E-mail: crdebeer@up.ac.za)

Personnel/human resources. Director: Van Aswegen, Prof. A., BA(Law) Pret., LLB Pret., LLD S.Af. (E-mail: avanweg@up.ac.za)
Public relations. Director, Marketing and Corporate Communication: Pretorius, I. E., BA (E-mail: elizabeth.pretorius@up.ac.za)
Publications. Director, Marketing and Corporate Communication: Pretorius, I. E., BA (E-mail: elizabeth.pretorius@up.ac.za)
Purchasing. Director (Purchasing): Addendorff, Prof. S. A., BEng MBA PhD (E-mail: susan.adendorff@up.ac.za)
Research. Director (Research): Naidoo, D. P., MSc(Medicine)
(E-mail: deshigen.naidoo@up.ac.za)
Safety. Head (Safety): Lübbe, W. J., BSc Stell., BScEng Stell.
Scholarships, awards, loans. Head (Scholarship, awards, loans): Van der Walt, A. J., BA Pret.
(E-mail: andrevdw@ccnet.up.ac.za)
Schools liaison. Head (Schools liaison): Isaacs, W. J., MA Stell.
(E-mail: wallace.isaacs@up.ac.za)
Security. Head (Security): Fouche, C. C., BA S.Af., BTech Pret.Tech., BA(Pol) S.Af.
(E-mail: colin.fouche@up.ac.za)
Sport and recreation. Registrar: Grové, Prof. Nic J., BA Pret., LLB Pret., LLM Pret., LLD Rand Afrikaans (E-mail: niek.grove@up.ac.za)
Student union. Dean, Student Affairs: Speckman, M. T., PhD S.Af.
(E-mail: m.speckman@up.ac.za)
Student welfare/counselling. Dean, Student Affairs: Speckman, M. T., PhD S.Af.
(E-mail: m.speckman@up.ac.za)
Students from other countries. Dean, Student Affairs: Speckman, M. T., PhD S.Af.
(E-mail: m.speckman@up.ac.za)
Students with disabilities. Dean, Student Affairs: Speckman, M. T., PhD S.Af.
(E-mail: m.speckman@up.ac.za)
University press. Director (University press): Pretorius, J. A., MEng Pret., PhD Tor.
(E-mail: jakkie.pretorius@it.up.ac.za)
Women. Vice-Principal: De Beer, Prof. C. R., BJur&Art Potchef., LLB Potchef., LLM Rand Afrikaans, DrsJuris Ley., LLD Ley.
(E-mail: crdebeer@up.ac.za)

[Information supplied by the institution as at 11 January 2008, and edited by the ACU]

RHODES UNIVERSITY

Founded 1951

Member of the Association of Commonwealth Universities

Postal Address: PO Box 94, Grahamstown, 6140 South Africa
Telephone: (046) 603 8111 **Fax:** (046) 622 5049
URL: http://www.ru.ac.za

VICE-CHANCELLOR*—Badat, M. Saleem, BSc Natal, DPhil York(UK), Hon. PhD Free State
DEPUTY VICE-CHANCELLOR, ACADEMIC AND STUDENT AFFAIRS—(vacant)
DEPUTY VICE-CHANCELLOR, RESEARCH AND DEVELOPMENT—(vacant)
CHAIRMAN OF COUNCIL—Jones, Hon. Mr. Justice R. J. W., BA Rhodes, LLB Rhodes
REGISTRAR‡—Fourie, Stephen, BTh Rhodes, BD Rhodes, DTh S.Af.
PUBLIC ORATOR—Maylam, Prof. P. R., BA Rhodes, MA Qu., PhD Qu.

GENERAL INFORMATION

History. The university was originally established as Rhodes University College in 1904. The decision to create an independent university was taken at the end of the Second

World War and the university was inaugurated in 1951.
It is located at Grahamstown, Eastern Cape Province.

Admission to first degree courses (see also South African Introduction). South African

applicants: matriculation exemption issued by the Matriculation Board. International applicants: General Certificate of Education (GCE) O and A levels or equivalent; exemption certificates from the Matriculation Board are also required.

First Degrees (see also South African Directory to Subjects of Study). BA, BAcc, BBusSc, BCom, BEcon, BEd, BFineArt, BJourn, BMus, BPharm, BSc, BSc(InfSys), BSocSc, LLB.

Length of course. Full-time: BA, BCom, BEcon, BSc, BSc(InfSys), BSocSc: 3 years; BAcc, BBusSc, BEd, BFineArt, BJourn, BMus, BPharm, LLB: 4 years.

Higher Degrees (see also South African Directory to Subjects of Study).

Master's. LLM, MA, MCom, MEcon, MEd, MFineArt, MMus, MPharm, MSc, MSc(Pharm), MSocSc.

Admission. Applicants for admission to master's degrees must normally hold an appropriate first degree with honours (first degree without honours is often acceptable); applicants without formal tertiary qualifications who have extensive work experience may also be accepted.

Length of course. Full-time: MA, MCom, MEcon, MEd, MFineArt, MMus, MSc: 1 year; LLM, MPharm, MSc(Pharm), MSocSc: 2 years.

Doctoral. DEcon, DLitt, DMus, DSc, DSocSc, LLD, PhD.

Admission. PhD: a master's degree.

Length of course. Full-time: PhD: 2 years; DEcon, DLitt, DMus, DSc, DSocSc, LLD: 4 years.

Libraries. Volumes: 400,000. Periodicals subscribed to: 900. Other holdings: electronic journals/periodicals/databases. Special collections: Cory Library for Historical Research (Southern African history).

FACULTIES/SCHOOLS

Commerce

Tel: (046) 603 8305 Fax: (046) 622 5210
E-mail: a.webb@ru.ac.za

Dean: Webb, Prof. A. C. M., PhD *Rhodes*
Secretary: Yule, M.

Education

Tel: (046) 603 8383 Fax: (046) 622 8028
E-mail: g.euvrard@ru.ac.za

Dean: Euvrard, Prof. G. J., BEd *S.Af.*, MA *Rhodes*, DLitt&Phil *S.Af.*
Administrative Assistant: Grunenberg, D.

Humanities

Tel: (046) 603 8362 Fax: (046) 622 5570
E-mail: f.hendricks@ru.ac.za

Dean: Hendricks, Prof. F. T., BA *W.Cape*, MSocSc *Uppsala*, PhD *Uppsala*
Secretary: Kouari, K.

Law

Tel: (046) 603 8432 Fax: (046) 622 8960
E-mail: r.midgley@ru.ac.za

Dean: Midgley, Prof. J. R., BCom *Rhodes*, LLB *Rhodes*, PhD *Cape Town*
Department Administrator: Flanagan, S.

Pharmacy

Tel: (046) 603 8381 Fax: (046) 636 1205
E-mail: r.b.walker@ru.ac.za

Dean: Walker, R. B., BPharm *Rhodes*, PhD *Rhodes*
Secretary: Emslie, L. M.

Science

Tel: (046) 603 8292 Fax: (046) 636 1915
E-mail: p.terry@ru.ac.za

Dean: Terry, Prof. P. D., MSc *Rhodes*, PhD *Camb.*
Secretary: Fischer, C. L.

ACADEMIC UNITS

Accounting

Tel: (046) 603 8201 Fax: (046) 622 8879
E-mail: k.maree@ru.ac.za

Bunting, M., BSc *Rhodes*, BCom *Rhodes* Prof.
Lancaster, J. C. S., MA *Rhodes* Assoc. Prof.
Lester, M., BCom *Rhodes* Assoc. Prof.
Maree, K. W., BCom *Rhodes*, MCom *Rhodes* Assoc. Prof.; Head*
Mokorosi, M., BCom *NUL*, MSc *Stir.* Sr. Lectr.

Pretorius, J. A., BCom *Rhodes* Sr. Lectr.
Stack, E. M., DCompt *S.Af.* Prof.
Stott, A. J. H., LLB *Leeds* Sr. Lectr.
Wagenaar, A., BCom *Rhodes* Sr. Lectr.
Williams, J. H., MCom *Rhodes* Sr. Lectr.
Other Staff: 1 Lectr.
Research: statement and accounting practice; tax; university funding

Anthropology

Tel: (046) 603 8231 Fax: (046) 622 3948
E-mail: d.bekker@ru.ac.za

Boswell, M. J. R., MSocSc *Cape Town*, PhD *V.U.Amst.* Sr. Lectr.
de Wet, C. J., MA *Stell.*, PhD *Rhodes* Prof.
Palmer, R. C. G., BA *Durh.*, DPhil *Sus.* Assoc. Prof.; Head*
Other Staff: 2 Lectrs.
Research: anthropological perspectives on heritage; anthropology of tourism; medical anthropology, including indigenous healing systems; rural development and land reform; social or cultural anthropology

Biochemistry, Microbiology and Biotechnology

Tel: (046) 603 8441 Fax: (046) 622 3984
E-mail: r.dorrington@ru.ac.za

Blatch, G. L., BSc *Natal*, PhD *Cape Town* Prof., Biochemistry
Bradley, G., PhD *P.Elizabeth* Sr. Lectr., Biochemistry
Burgess, J., BSc *Wales*, PhD *Cran.* Sr. Lectr.
Dorrington, R. A., BSc(Agric) *Stell.*, PhD *Cape Town* Assoc. Prof., Biochemistry; Head*
Duncan, J. R., PhD *Natal*, FRSSAf Prof., Biochemistry
Hendry, D. A., MSc *Stell.*, PhD *Cape Town* Assoc. Prof. Emer.
Limson, J., PhD *Rhodes* Sr. Lectr.
Pletschke, B., PhD *P.Elizabeth* Sr. Lectr.
Rose, P. D., BSc *Cape Town*, PhD *Rhodes* Prof., Biotechnology
Whiteley, C. G., PhD *Natal* Assoc. Prof., Biochemistry
Other Staff: 3 Lectrs.; 1 Res. Assoc.
Research: bio-informatics and molecular modelling; bio-organic chemistry and enzymology; environmental and industrial waste management; insect viruses; regulation of gene expression in eukaryotes

Botany

Tel: (046) 603 8592 Fax: (046) 622 5524
E-mail: b.ripley@ru.ac.za

Barker, N. P., MSc *Witw.*, PhD *Cape Town* Assoc. Prof.
Botha, C. E. J., MSc *Natal*, PhD *Natal* Prof.
Dold, A. P., MSc *Rhodes*
Lubke, R. A., BSc *Rhodes*, MSc *Keele*, PhD *W.Ont.* Prof.
Peter, C. I., MSc *Rhodes*
Ripley, B. S., MSc *Natal*, PhD *Rhodes* Assoc. Prof.; Head*
Other Staff: 1 Lectr.
Research: molecular systematics; plant anatomy, stress, cell structure/function; plant ecology (coastal and inland); plant physiology; use of medicinal plants

Business School, Rhodes Investec

Tel: (046) 603 8617 Fax: (046) 603 8613
E-mail: r.parker@ru.ac.za

Pearse, N. J., MSocSci *Cape Town*, PhD *Rhodes* Co-ordinator, Res. and People Management
Staude, G. E., MBA *Cran.*, PhD *Rhodes* Prof.; Dir.*
Whittington-Jones, K., PhD *Rhodes* Sr. Lectr.; Co-ordinator

Chemistry

Tel: (046) 603 8254 Fax: (046) 622 5109
E-mail: m.davies-coleman@ru.ac.za

Brown, M. E., BSc *Witw.*, PhD *Rhodes*, FRSSAf Prof.
Cosser, R. C., PhD *Lond.* Sr. Lectr., Physical Chemistry

Davies-Coleman, M. T., BSc *Rhodes*, PhD *Rhodes* Prof., Organic Chemistry; Head*
Eve, D. J., PhD *Rhodes*, FRSChem Assoc. Prof. Emer.
Galwey, A. K., DSc *Lond.*
Kaye, P. T., BSc *Natal*, BSc *S.Af.*, MSc *Natal*, DPhil *Oxf.*, FRSSAf Prof., Organic Chemistry
Klein, R., BSc *Cape Town*, MSc *Rhodes*, PhD *Miami(Fla.)*
Lamprecht, E., BA *Rhodes*
Lobb, K. A., BSc *Rhodes*
Nyokong, T., BSc *NUL*, MSc *McM.*, PhD *W.Ont.*, FRSSAf Prof., Physical Chemistry
Rivett, D. E. A., MSc *Rhodes*, PhD *Camb.* Prof.
Rosseinsky, D. R., MSc *Rhodes*, PhD *Manc.*, DSc *Manc.*, FRSChem
Sewry, J. D., MSc *Rhodes*
Tshentu, Z., PhD *Nelson Mandela Met.*
Watkins, G. M., PhD *Cape Town* Sr. Lectr., Inorganic and Analytical Chemistry
Research: electrocatalytic and photocatalytic reactions (porphyrins/phthalocyanines; marine natural product chemistry; solid surface chemistry; structure and synthetic organic chemistry; vibrational spectroscopy of inorganic compounds

Computer Science

Tel: (046) 603 8296 Fax: (046) 636 1915
E-mail: g.wells@ru.ac.za

Bangay, S. D., MSc *Rhodes*, PhD *Rhodes* Assoc. Prof.
Bradshaw, K. L., MSc *Rhodes*, PhD *Camb.* Course Co-ordinator
Clayton, P. G., MSc *Rhodes*, PhD *Rhodes* Prof.
Ebden, A. J. B., BSc *Lond.*
Foss, R. J., BSc *Natal*, MSc *S.Af.*, PhD *Rhodes* Assoc. Prof.
Foster, G. G., PhD *Rhodes* Sr. Lectr.
Halse, M. L., BSc *Rhodes* Course Co-ordinator
Irwin, B. V. W., MSc *Rhodes* Sr. Lectr.
Terry, P. D., MSc *Rhodes*, PhD *Camb.* Prof.
Wells, G. C., MSc *Rhodes*, PhD *Brist.* Assoc. Prof.; Head*
Wentworth, E. P., PhD *P.Elizabeth* Prof.
Wright, M. K., BSc *Rhodes*, MA *Camb.* Course Co-ordinator
Research: compilers; computer languages; distributed and parallel processing; distributed multimedia; photorealistic graphics

Drama

Tel: (046) 603 8538 Fax: (046) 636 1582
E-mail: g.gordon@ru.ac.za

Buckland, A. F., BA *Rhodes* Assoc. Prof.
Gordon, G. E., BA *Natal*, MA *CNAA* Prof.; Head*
Other Staff: 3 Lectrs.
Research: choreography; dance studies; mime and directing; performance studies; physical theatre

Economics and Economic History

Tel: (046) 603 8301 Fax: (046) 622 5210
E-mail: h.nel@ru.ac.za

Antrobus, G. G., MSc(Agric) *Natal*, PhD *Rhodes* Prof.
Aziakpono, M. J., MScEcon *Ib.* Sr. Lectr.
Black, P., PhD *Rhodes* Visiting Prof.
Cattaneo, N. S., MSc *Rhodes* Sr. Lectr.
Faure, A. P., PhD *Stell.* Prof.
Guma, X. P., PhD *Manc.* Visiting Prof.
Nel, H., BCom *OFS*, DCom *P.Elizabeth* Prof.; Head*
Snowball, J., PhD *Rhodes* Sr. Lectr.
Webb, A. C. M., PhD *Rhodes* Prof.
Other Staff: 3 Lectrs.
Research: agricultural/conservation economics; banking and business history; macroeconomics monetary policy; poverty and job search; theory of exhaustible resources

Education

Tel: (046) 603 8383 Fax: (046) 622 8028
E-mail: m.schafer@ru.ac.za

Duncan, R., BSc *Natal*

Euvrard, G. J., BEd S.Af., MA Rhodes, DLitt&Phil S.Af. Prof.
Irwin, P. R., BA Natal, MEd Natal, DEd S.Af. Prof.
Lotz-Sisitka, H., BPrimEd P.Elizabeth, BEd Stell., DEd Stell. Assoc. Prof., Environmental Education
Murray, S. R., BA Lanc., MA Reading Sr. Lectr.
O'Donaghue, R. B., BEd Z'bwe., MEd Natal, PhD Rhodes Assoc. Prof.
Schafer, M., BSc Witw., BEd Rhodes, MEd Rhodes, PhD Curtin Head*
Smith, C. K. O., BA Stell., BTh S.Af., BEd S.Af., MSc Oregon, PhD Oregon
Southwood, S. L., BEd Brighton, MEd Lond., PhD Rhodes
van der Mescht, H., BA P.Elizabeth, MA Rhodes, PhD Rhodes Prof.
van Harmelen, U. A., BA S.Af., BEd Rhodes, MEd Rhodes Sr. Lectr.
Westaway, L., BPrimEd Rhodes, MEd Rhodes
Zinn, D., BA Cape Town, DEd Harv.
Other Staff: 4 Lectrs.
Research: educational leadership and management; environmental education; language teacher education; mathematical, science and technology education; school guidance and counselling

English

Tel: (046) 603 8400 Fax: (046) 622 2264
E-mail: g.cornwell@ru.ac.za
Beard, M. M., MA Rhodes, PhD Natal Sr. Lectr.
Cornwell, D. G. N., MA Rhodes, PhD Rhodes Assoc. Prof.; Head*
Jacobson, W. S., BA Lond., PhD Birm. Assoc. Prof.
Marais, M. J., BA Cape Town, MA P.Elizabeth, DLitt&Phil Rand Afrikaans Assoc. Prof.
Walters, P. S., BA Rhodes, PhD Rhodes H. A. Molteno Prof.
Wylie, D., PhD Rhodes Sr. Lectr.
Other Staff: 1 Lectr.
Research: American, South African and African literature; Charles Dickens; colonial and British literature (imperial period); modern and Southern African poetry; Victorian to contemporary fiction

English Language and Linguistics

Tel: (046) 603 8105 Fax: (046) 622 8106
E-mail: r.adendorff@ru.ac.za
Adendorff, R. D., BA Rhodes, MA Indiana, PhD Natal Prof.; Head*
Simango, S. R., BA Malawi, MSc Edin., PhD S.Carolina Sr. Lectr.
Other Staff: 3 Lectrs.
Research: language issues in South Africa; onomastics; socio-linguistics

Environmental Science

Tel: (046) 603 7002 Fax: (046) 622 9313
E-mail: c.shackleton@ru.ac.za
Avis, A. M., PhD Rhodes
Hendricks, H., MSc W.Cape
Shackleton, C., PhD Witw. Assoc. Prof.; Head*
Other Staff: 1 Lectr.; 1 Res. Assoc.
Research: changes in energy use; fibre craft materials; human impacts in biodiversity; sustainable use of natural and modified ecosystems; tenure of access to land and natural resources

Fine Art

Tel: (046) 603 8192 Fax: (046) 622 4349
E-mail: b.schmahmann@ru.ac.za
Schmahmann, B. L., BA Witw., BFineArt Witw., MA Witw., PhD Witw. Prof.; Head*
Simbao, R., BFA Stell., MWS Tor., MPhil Tor., AM Harv. Sr. Lectr.
Thorburn, D., BFineArt Rhodes, MFA Rhodes Assoc. Prof.; Tamarind Professnl. Printer (New Mexico)
Other Staff: 4 Lectrs.
Research: contemporary American and South African art; digital imaging and

printmaking; feminist theory in relation to arts

Geography

Tel: (046) 603 8320 Fax: (046) 636 1199
E-mail: k.rowntree@ru.ac.za
Fox, R. C., PhD Strath. Prof.
Rowntree, K. M., MSc Brist., PhD Strath. Prof.; Head*
Other Staff: 1 Lectr.
Research: fluvial geomorphology; geographic information systems (GIS) applications; quaternary studies; settlement geography; urban, rural and economic geography

Geology

Tel: (046) 603 8309 Fax: (046) 622 9715
E-mail: s.prevec@ru.ac.za
Bordy, E. M., PhD Rhodes
Buttner, S. H., PhD Fran.
Eales, H. V., PhD Rhodes Emer. Prof.
Marsh, J. S., PhD Cape Town Prof.; Head*
Moore, J. M., PhD Cape Town Prof., Exploration Geology
Prevec, S. A., PhD Alta. Sr. Lectr.; Head*
Tsikos, H., PhD Rhodes Sr. Lectr.
Research: chemistry of volcanic rocks; economic mineral deposits; geology of Namibia; mineral deposits and exploration; petrology of igneous rocks

History

Tel: (046) 603 8330 Fax: (046) 622 9953
E-mail: p.maylam@ru.ac.za
Baines, G. P., BA Cape Town, BA S.Af., MA Rhodes, PhD Cape Town Assoc. Prof.
Cobbing, J. R. D., BA Lond., PhD Lanc. Assoc. Prof.
Maylam, P. R., BA Rhodes, MA Qu., PhD Qu. Prof.; Head*
Wells, J. C., BA Colorado Coll., MA Yale, PhD Col. Assoc. Prof.
Other Staff: 2 Lectrs.
Research: Eastern Cape township music; history of racism in South Africa; late nineteenth-century British imperialism; South Africa history of Eastern Cape; women's history (South Africa, Zimbabwe, Africa)

Human Kinetics and Ergonomics

Tel: (046) 603 8468 Fax: (046) 622 3803
E-mail: m.gobel@ru.ac.za
Christie, C., BA P.Elizabeth, BSc Cape Town, MSc Rhodes Sr. Lectr.
Gobel, M., PhD T.H.Aachen Prof.; Head*
Zschernak, S. Sr. Lectr.
Other Staff: 1 Lectr.
Research: ergonomics; gait analysis; macro-micro ergonomics in industrial developing countries; psychophysiology of stress; sports psychology

Ichthyology and Fisheries Science

Tel: (046) 603 8415 Fax: (046) 622 4827
E-mail: p.britz@ru.ac.za
Booth, A. J., PhD Rhodes Assoc. Prof.
Britz, P. J., BSc Cape Town, PhD Rhodes Assoc. Prof.; Head*
Hecht, T., BSc Free State, PhD P.Elizabeth Res. Prof., Fisheries Science
Kaiser, H., DrAgr Bonn Assoc. Prof.
Sauer, W. H. H., PhD P.Elizabeth Assoc. Prof.
Weyl, O. L. F., PhD Rhodes Sr. Lectr.
Other Staff: 1 Aquaculture Devel. Officer
Research: aquaculture; coastal conservation; commercial and recreational fisheries management; fish and shellfish culture; squid and marine linefish biology/management

Information Systems

Tel: (046) 603 8244 Fax: (046) 636 1915
E-mail: d.sewry@ru.ac.za
Freeme, D. M., BSc S.Af., MCom Witw. Course Manager
McNeill, J. B., BSc Rhodes Sr. Lectr.
Palmer, L., BCom Rhodes, MBA Rhodes Course Manager

Rafferty, K., BSc Witw. Course Manager
Sainsbury, M., BSc S.Af., MSc Bath Visiting Prof.
Sewry, D. A., MSc Rhodes, PhD Rhodes Prof.; Head*
Upfold, C., MBA Rhodes
Other Staff: 1 Lectr.
Research: computer graphics; database, language designs and implementation; information system theories; IS audit and control

Journalism and Media Studies

School of Journalism

Tel: (046) 603 7107 Fax: (046) 603 7101
E-mail: j.prinsloo@ru.ac.za
Amner, R., BJourn Rhodes SABMiller Prof., Media and Democracy
Banda, F., BA Zambia, MA Leic., PhD S.Af. Prof.; SAB Miller Chair, Media and Democracy
Berger, G. J. E. G., BJourn Rhodes, BA Rhodes, MA S.Af., PhD Rhodes Prof.; Head of Sch.*
Brand, R. C., BA Pret., BJourn Stell., MPhil Stell. Pearson Prof., Economics Journalism
Du Toit, P., BA P.Elizabeth Project Dir.
Fick, A. C., BA Cape Town, MA Cape Town
Garman, A. C., BA Cape Town, MA KwaZulu-Natal Sr. Lectr.
Mavhunga, J., MA Witw.
Mdlongwa, F. Project Dir.
Prinsloo, J., BA Natal, MA Lond., PhD Witw. Assoc. Prof.
Steenveld, L. N., BA CNAA, MA Rhodes, MA N.Carolina Sr. Lectr.
Strelitz, L. N., BA Rhodes, MA Lond., PhD Rhodes Assoc. Prof.; Deputy Head
Other Staff: 10 Lectrs.
Research: censorship and press freedom; cultural studies; film/television theory and politics; information superhighway; media development

Languages, School of

Tel: (046) 603 8304 Fax: (046) 622 9953
E-mail: r.kaschula@ru.ac.za
Kaschula, R., BA Rhodes, LLB Rhodes, PhD Rhodes Prof.; Head*

African Languages

Tel: (046) 603 8224
Kaschula, R., BA Rhodes, LLB Rhodes, PhD Rhodes Prof.; Head*
Nosilela, B., BA Rhodes, MA Stell. Lectr.; Head*
Other Staff: 2 Lectrs.
Research: Xhosa

Afrikaans and Nederlandic Studies

Tel: (046) 603 8226
E-mail: g.meintjes@ru.ac.za
Meintjes, W. G., PhD Rhodes Sr. Lectr.; Head*
Other Staff: 2 Lectrs.
Research: Afrikaans prose; literary theory

Classics

Tel: (046) 603 8274 E-mail: j.jackson@ru.ac.za
Jackson, J. L., BA Natal, MA Rhodes Head*
Snowball, W. D., BSc(MechEng) Cape Town, BA Rhodes, MA Lond. Sr. Lectr.
Other Staff: 1 Lectr.
Research: ancient Greek; classical civilisation; Latin

French Studies

Tel: (046) 603 8299 E-mail: c.cordell@ru.ac.za
Cordell, C. J., MA Rand Afrikaans, PhD Rand Afrikaans Lectr.; In-Charge*
Other Staff: 2 Lectrs.
Research: French eighteenth-century novel of sensibility; twentieth-century French novel and theatre

German Studies

Tel: (046) 603 8328 E-mail: u.weber@ru.ac.za
1 Lectr.
Research: twentieth-century German literature

Law

Tel: (046) 603 8427 Fax: (046) 622 8960
E-mail: r.midgley@ru.ac.za
Barker, G. W., BA Witw., LLB Natal, LLM Bophut.
  Sr. Lectr.
Campbell, J., BA Cape Town, LLB Cape Town
  Assoc. Prof.
Davies, G. E., BA Rhodes, LLB Rhodes   Sr. Lectr.
de Vos, W., BA Rand Afrikaans, LLB Rand Afrikaans,
  LLM Rand Afrikaans, LLD Rand Afrikaans   Prof.
Glover, G. B., BA Rhodes, LLB Rhodes, PhD Rhodes
  Sr. Lectr.
Keep, H. J., BA Rhodes, LLB Rhodes
Kerr, A. J., BA S.Af., LLB Witw., PhD Natal, LLD
  Rhodes   Emer. Prof.; Res. Fellow
Lehloenya, M. P., BA NUL, LLB NUL, LLM Pret.
Midgley, J. R., BCom Rhodes, LLB Rhodes, PhD
  Cape Town   Prof.; Head*
Mqeke, R. B., BJuris Fort Hare, LLB Fort Hare,
  LLM Rhodes, LLD Fort Hare   Prof.
Otto, J., BA Rhodes
Pringle, P., BA Rhodes, LLB Natal, LLM Witw.
  Dir., Legal Aid Clinic
Roberts, L. J., BA Rhodes, LLB Rhodes   Sr. Lectr.
Schafer, I. D., BA Rhodes, LLB Rhodes, LLD Natal
Other Staff: 4 Lectrs.
Research: constitutional and labour law; law of
  delict; professional development in higher
  education; professional negligence;
  women's rights

Management

Tel: (046) 603 8735 Fax: (046) 603 8913
E-mail: l.louw@ru.ac.za
Amos, T. L., BSocSc Rhodes, MSocSc Rhodes   Sr.
  Lectr.
Court, P. W., BSc(Agric) Stell., MBA Witw., PhD
  Rhodes   Assoc. Prof.
Elliott, R. M., BCom Rhodes, LLB Rhodes, MBA
  Cape Town, PhD Rhodes   Sr. Lectr.
Harvey, N. M., BCom Rhodes, BCom S.Af., MBA
  Indiana   Prof.
Louw, L., BCom Rhodes, LLB Rhodes, MBA Cape
  Town, PhD Rhodes   Prof.; Head*
Other Staff: 3 Lectrs.
Research: financial markets and theory of
  investment; strategic management

Mathematics (Pure and Applied)

Tel: (046) 603 8339 Fax: (046) 603 8897
E-mail: s.mabizela@ru.ac.za
Burton, M. H., BSc Natal, MSc Cape Town, PhD
  Rhodes   Assoc. Prof.
Lubczonok, G., MMath Cracow, PhD Silesia   Sr.
  Lectr.
Mabizela, S. G., MSc Fort Hare, PhD Penn.
  Prof.; Head*
Matutu, P., BSc S.Af., MSc Rhodes, PhD Cape Town
  Sr. Lectr.
Murali, V., MSc Madr., MSc Wales, PhD Rhodes
  Prof.
Other Staff: 2 Lectrs.
Research: functional analysis; fuzzy algebra,
  topology and uniform spaces; mathematical
  modelling

Music and Musicology

Tel: (046) 603 8489 Fax: (046) 622 7111
E-mail: t.radloff@ru.ac.za
Foxcroft, C., BMus Cape Town   Sr. Lectr.
Heunis, D., BAMus Stell., MMus Rhodes   Sr.
  Lectr.
Radloff, T. E. K., BA Rhodes, MMus Rhodes,
  UTLM S.Af., PhD Rhodes   Sr. Lectr.; Head*
Thram, D., PhD Indiana   Assoc. Prof.
Other Staff: 3 Lectrs.
Research: ethnomusicology

Pharmacy, Faculty of

Tel: (046) 603 8381 Fax: (046) 636 1205
E-mail: r.b.walker@ru.ac.za
Daya, S., BSc Durban-W., MSc Rhodes, PhD
  S.Af.Med.   Prof., Pharmacology
Dowse, R., BPharm Rhodes, PhD Rhodes   Assoc.
  Prof., Pharmaceutics
Futter, W. T., MCom Rhodes   Assoc. Prof.,
  Pharmacy Administration and Practice

Haigh, J. M., BSc Rhodes, BSc(Pharm) Rhodes,
  PhD Cape Town   Prof., Pharmaceutical
  Chemistry
Jobson, M. R., MB ChB Cape Town, MPraxMed
  S.Af.Med.
Kanfer, I., BSc(Pharm) Rhodes, BSc Rhodes, PhD
  Rhodes   Prof., Pharmaceutics
Karekezi, C. W., BPharm Nair., MSc Lough., PhD
  Lough.   Sr. Lectr., Pharmaceutical Chemistry
Naidoo, M. J., BSc Durban-W., MSc Rhodes, PhD
  S.Af.Med.   Sr. Lectr.
Oltmann, C., BSc Witw., BPharm Rhodes, MEd
  Witw., MSc Rhodes   Head, Pharmacy
  Practice; Deputy Dean
Robertson, S. S. D., BSc Cape Town, PhD Rhodes
  Sr. Lectr., Physiology and Anatomy
Smith, P., BScPharm Rhodes, MBL S.Af.
Srinivas, S. C., BPharm B'lore., MPharm B'lore.
  Assoc. Prof., Pharmacy Administration and
  Practice
Verbeek, R. K., BSc Leuven, PhD Leuven
Walker, R. B., BPharm Rhodes, PhD Rhodes
  Assoc. Prof., Pharmaceutics; Head*
Wisch, M. H., BPharm Rhodes, MSc Rhodes
Other Staff: 3 Lectrs.
Research: drug absorption release and
  dissolution; drug analysis and absorption;
  neurobiochemistry and the heart;
  percutanious absorption of corticosteroids

Philosophy

Tel: (046) 603 8351 Fax: (046) 622 6460
E-mail: m.vermaak@ru.ac.za
Jones, W. E., BA Calif., DPhil Oxf.   Sr. Lectr.
Martin, T. W., BSc Adel., BA Adel., PhD NSW
  Sr. Lectr.
Vermaak, M. D., BA Stell., DrsPhil Ley.   Assoc.
  Prof.; Head*
Other Staff: 3 Lectrs.
Research: applied philosophy; critical reasoning;
  ethics; Greek philosophy

Physics and Electronics

Tel: (046) 603 8450 E-mail: r.grant@ru.ac.za
Baart, E. E., BSc Rhodes, PhD Liv., FRAS   Emer.
  Prof.
Booth, R. S., PhD Manc.
Chithambo, M. L., BSc Malawi, MPhil Sus., PhD
  Edin.
Grant, R. P. J. S., MSc Rhodes   Sr. Lectr.; Head*
Haggard, R., BSc Rhodes, BSc S.Af., PhD Rhodes
Jonas, J. L., PhD Rhodes   Prof.
McKinnell, L.-A., PhD Rhodes
Poole, A. W. V., PhD Rhodes
Poole, L. M. G., MSc Rhodes, PhD Sheff.
Williams, J. A., BSc Rhodes, PhD Camb.
Research: ionosphere; radio astronomy; square
  kilometre array (SKA) telescope; upper
  atmosphere neural networks

Political Studies

Tel: (046) 603 8354 Fax: (046) 622 4345
E-mail: p.bischoff@ru.ac.za
Bischoff, P. H., BA Witw., MA Lanc., PhD Manc.
  Assoc. Prof.; Head*
Du Toit, B. A., MA Stell., PhD Stell., Drs Ley.
Fluxman, A. P., MA Witw., MA Cornell, PhD
  Cornell   Sr. Lectr.
Matthews, S., BA Pret., MA Pret.
Praeg, L., BA Stell., MA Stell., PhD Stell.   Sr.
  Lectr.
Vale, P., BA Witw., MA Leic., PhD Leic.   Nelson
  Mandela Prof.
Vincent, L., BA Rhodes, DPhil Oxf.   Assoc. Prof.
Wamba Dia Wamba, E., BA W.Mich., MBA
  Claremont, PhD Brandeis
Other Staff: 1 Lectr.
Research: African political economy; Kenyan and
  Lesotho politics; peace and conflict in
  Africa; political philosophy; South African
  politics

Psychology

Tel: (046) 603 8500 Fax: (046) 622 4032
E-mail: c.macleod@ru.ac.za@ru.ac.za
Edwards, A. B., BA Rhodes, MSc Cape Town, PhD
  Rhodes   Assoc. Prof.
Edwards, D. J. A., MA Oxf., PhD Rhodes   Prof.

Knight, Z. G., BA Rhodes, MEd Rhodes, PhD Rhodes
  Sr. Lectr.
Macleod, C. T., BSc Natal, MEd Cape Town, PhD
  Natal   Prof.; Head*
Stones, C. R., MSc Rhodes, PhD Rhodes   Prof.
Swingler, D. D., MB ChB Cape Town   Assoc.
  Prof.
Van Niekerk, R., MA P.Elizabeth, PhD P.Elizabeth
  Sr. Lectr.
Van Ommen, C., BSc Witw., BSc Rand Afrikaans,
  MA(ClinPsych) Rand Afrikaans
Visser, C., BScEng Witw., MB BCh Witw.
Other Staff: 4 Lectrs.; 1 Lectr.†
Research: cognitive psychotherapy; gender
  studies; post-apartheid South Africa;
  transpersonal psychology

Sociology and Industrial Sociology

Tel: (046) 603 8361 Fax: (046) 622 5570
E-mail: m.roodt@ru.ac.za
Adesina, J. O., BSc Ib., MILR Ib., PhD Warw.
  Assoc. Prof.
Coetzee, J. K., BD Pret., MA Pret., DPhil Pret.
  Prof.
Drewett, M. D., MSocSc Rhodes, PhD Rhodes   Sr.
  Lectr.
Hendricks, F. T., BA W.Cape, MSocSc Uppsala,
  PhD Uppsala   Prof.
Klerck, G. G., LLB Natal, PhD Rhodes   Sr. Lectr.
Miller, D. R., MA Johns H., PhD Johns H.   Sr.
  Lectr.
Mtyingizana, B., BA Witw., MA Witw.
Roodt, J. J., BA Rhodes, MA Witw., PhD Rhodes
  Sr. Lectr.; Head*
Other Staff: 1 Lectr.
Research: development, human rights,
  contemporary politics; feminism; narrative
  study of lives; social theory

Statistics

Tel: (046) 603 8680 Fax: (046) 622 2723
E-mail: s.radloff@ru.ac.za
Jaeger, G., PhD Karlsruhe   Assoc. Prof.
Radloff, S. E., MSc Rhodes, PhD Rhodes   Prof.;
  Head*
Szyszkowski, I., MSc Lublin, PhD Lublin   Assoc.
  Prof.
Other Staff: 4 Lectrs.
Research: data analysis; linear models; stochastic
  processes

Zoology and Entomology

Tel: (046) 603 8525 Fax: (046) 622 8959
E-mail: a.hodgson@ru.ac.za
Allanson, B. R., DSc Natal, PhD Cape Town, DSc
  Rhodes, FRSSAf
Bernard, R. F. T., PhD Natal   Prof., Zoology
Craig, A. J. F. K., MSc Cape Town, PhD Natal
  Assoc. Prof., Zoology
Froneman, P. W., PhD Rhodes   Assoc. Prof.,
  Zoology
Hepburn, H. R., PhD Kansas   Emer. Prof.
Hill, M. P., PhD Rhodes   Assoc. Prof.,
  Entomology
Hodgson, A. N., BSc Liv., PhD Manc.   Prof.,
  Zoology; Head*
Hulley, P. E., MSc Rhodes, PhD Lond.   Assoc.
  Prof. Emer.
Lutjeharms, J. R. E., PhD Wash., DSc Cape Town,
  FRSSAf
McQuaid, C. D., PhD Cape Town, FRSSAf   Prof.,
  Zoology
Villet, M. H., PhD Witw.   Assoc. Prof.,
  Entomology
Other Staff: 1 Lectr.
Research: apiculture; marine ecology; molluscan
  biology; ornithology and animal behaviour,
  ecology, systematics, evolution;
  reproductive ecology and physiology of
  African small mammals

CONTACT OFFICERS

Accommodation. Senior Administrative Officer
  (Admissions): Wicks, D.
  (E-mail: registrar@ru.ac.za)
Admissions (first degree). Senior
  Administrative Officer: Wicks, D.
  (E-mail: admissions@ru.ac.za)

Admissions (higher degree). Assistant Registrar: (vacant) (E-mail: academicadmin@ru.ac.za)

Alumni. President, Old Rhodian Union: Walker, R. B., BPharm *Rhodes*, PhD *Rhodes* (E-mail: r.b.walker@ru.ac.za)

Archives. Cory Librarian: Kabwato, S. (E-mail: s.kabwato@ru.ac.za)

Careers. Head, Career Centre: Wetmore, M. R. N., BA *Rhodes* (E-mail: m.wetmore@ru.ac.za)

Computing services. Director, Information Technology: Jacot-Guillarmod, F. F., BSc *Rhodes* (E-mail: jacot@ru.ac.za)

Conferences/corporate hospitality. Conference Manager: Stevenson-Milln, C., MBA *Cape Town* (E-mail: c.stevenson-milln@ru.ac.za)

Development/fund-raising. Executive Director, Development: (vacant)

Estates and buildings/works and services. Director, Estates Division: Reynolds, L. M., BCom *S.Af.* (E-mail: l.m.reynolds@ru.ac.za)

Examinations. Assistant Registrar: (vacant)

Finance. Registrar (Finance): Long, H. A. (E-mail: t.long@ru.ac.za)

General enquiries. Registrar: Fourie, Stephen, BTh *Rhodes*, BD *Rhodes*, DTh *S.Af.* (E-mail: registrar@ru.ac.za)

Health services. Sister-in-Charge: Shaw, J., BCur North(*S.Af.*) (E-mail: j.shaw@ru.ac.za)

Industrial liaison. Director: Human Resources: Fischer, S. A. L., MCom *Rhodes* (E-mail: s.fischer@ru.ac.za)

International office. International Studies Officer: Pienaar, H. (E-mail: h.pienaar@ru.ac.za)

Library (chief librarian). University Librarian: Thomas, G. (E-mail: g.thomas@ru.ac.za)

Personnel/human resources. Director: Human Resources: Fischer, S. A. L., MCom *Rhodes* (E-mail: s.fischer@ru.ac.za)

Purchasing. Senior Buyer: (vacant)

Research. Dean of Research: Duncan, Prof. J. R., PhD *Natal*, FRSSAf (E-mail: j.duncan@ru.ac.za)

Safety. Manager, Campus Protection Unit: Charteris, D. M. (E-mail: d.charteris@ru.ac.za)

Scholarships, awards, loans. Financial Aid Administrator: Bheyili, L. (E-mail: l.bheyili@ru.ac.za)

Schools liaison. Student Recruitment Manager: Norval, S. A., BA(PhysEd) *Rhodes*, BEd *Witw.* (E-mail: s.norval@ru.ac.za)

Security. Chief Campus Protection Officer: Charteris, D. M. (E-mail: d.charteris@ru.ac.za)

Sport and recreation. Head, Sports Administration: Rogers, K. J. (E-mail: k.rogers@ru.ac.za)

Staff development and training. Organizational Development Manager: Robertson, S. (E-mail: susan.robertson@ru.ac.za)

Student welfare/counselling. Head, Counselling Centre: Young, C., MA *Natal* (E-mail: c.young@ru.ac.za)

Students from other countries. Senior Administrative Officer (Admissions): Wicks, D. (E-mail: registrar@ru.ac.za)

Students with disabilities. Head, Counselling Centre: Young, C., MA *Natal* (E-mail: c.young@ru.ac.za)

[*Information supplied by the institution as at 9 January 2008, and edited by the ACU*]

UNIVERSITY OF SOUTH AFRICA

Universiteit van Suid-Afrika

Founded 1916

Member of the Association of Commonwealth Universities

Postal Address: PO Box 392, Pretoria, 0003 South Africa
Telephone: (012) 429 3111 **Fax:** (012) 429 3221 **E-mail:** undergrad/student@alpha.unisa.ac.za
URL: http://www.unisa.ac.za

PRINCIPAL AND VICE-CHANCELLOR*—Pityana, Prof. N. Barney, BA(Law) *S.Af.*, BProc *S.Af.*, BD *Lond.*, PhD *Cape Town*
REGISTRAR (FINANCE) (ACTING)—Lenamile, Dikloff O., BCom *S.Af.*, BCompt *S.Af.*, MBA *Witw.*
VICE-PRINCIPAL (RESEARCH AND PLANNING)—Döckel, Prof. J. A., BSc(Agric) *Stell.*, PhD *Iowa*
VICE-PRINCIPAL (TUITION)—Maimela, Prof. S. S., BA *S.Af.*, DPhil *Harv.*, MTh
REGISTRAR (ACADEMIC) (ACTING)‡—Msimang, Prof. Christian T., LLB *S.Af.*, MA *S.Af.*, DLitt&Phil *S.Af.*
REGISTRAR (HUMAN RESOURCES) (ACTING)—Van Aswegen, Prof. Annél, BA *Pret.*, LLB *Pret.*, LLD *S.Af.*
REGISTRAR (OPERATIONS) (ACTING)—Mosoma, David L., BTh *S.Af.*, MTh *Prin.*, PhD *Prin.*

UNIVERSITY OF STELLENBOSCH

Founded 1918

Member of the Association of Commonwealth Universities

Postal Address: Private Bag X1, Matieland, 7602 South Africa
Telephone: (021) 808 4515 **Fax:** (021) 808 4499 **E-mail:** rk@sun.ac.za
URL: http://www.sun.ac.za

RECTOR AND VICE-CHANCELLOR*—Botman, Prof. H. Russel, BA *W.Cape*, BTh *W.Cape*, MTh *W.Cape*, DTh *W.Cape*
ACTING VICE-RECTOR (RESEARCH)—Van Huyssteen, Prof. Leopoldt, MScAgric *Stell.*, PhD(Agric) *Stell.*
VICE-RECTOR (OPERATIONS)—Smith, Julian F., BA *W.Cape*, MA *W.Cape*, DLitt *W.Cape*
VICE-RECTOR (TEACHING)—(vacant)
DEANS' REPRESENTATIVE—Van Huyssteen, Prof. Leopoldt, MScAgric *Stell.*, PhD(Agric) *Stell.*
EXECUTIVE DIRECTOR, FINANCE—Calitz, Prof. Estian, BComm *Stell.*, BCom *Pret.*, MComm *Stell.*, DComm *Stell.*
MANAGER, INNOVATION—Botha, Prof. Liesbeth, MEng *Pret.*, PhD *Carnegie-Mellon*
REGISTRAR‡—Aspeling, Johann A., MComm *Stell.*

GENERAL INFORMATION

History. The university was originally established in 1874 as the arts department of Stellenbosch Gymnasium. It achieved separate status in 1881, when Stellenbosch College was founded. It was renamed Victoria College of

Stellenbosch in 1887 and became a university under its present name in 1918.

The university is situated in Stellenbosch, about 50km east of Cape Town.

Admission to first degree courses (see also South African Introduction). Recognised South

African School Leaving Certificate with matriculation exemption. Certain subjects or combinations of subjects are required for some degree courses. International students may be admitted if a certificate of exemption is issued by the Joint Matriculation Board. International undergraduate students also require a study permit available from the department of home affairs, Pretoria.

First Degrees (see also South African Directory to Subjects of Study) (* = with honours). BA*, BA, BAcc*, BAcc, BAdmin*, BA(FA)*, BA(FA), BA(FA)(Ed), BAgricAdmin*, BAgricAdmin, BAgric(Ed), BA(SW)*, BA(SW), BB&A*, BBibl*, BBibl, BChD, BComm*, BComm, BCur, BD, BDram*, BDram, BEcon*, BEcon, BEng, BFor, BHMS*, BHomeEcon, BHomeEcon*, BHomeEcon(Ed), BJourn*, BMedSc, BMil*, BMus*, BMus, BMus(Ed), BOccTher*, BOccTher, BPA*, BP&R*, BPrimEd, BSc*, BSc, BScAgric*, BScAgric, BScConsEcol, BScDentSc*, BScDiet, BScFoodSc*, BScFoodSc, BScFor*, BScFor, BScForSc*, BScHomeEcon*, BScHomeEcon(Ed), BScHomeEcon(Food), BScMedSc*, BScMedSc, BScPhysio*, BScPhysio, BScWoodSc*, BScWoodSc, BSp&HTher, BTh, LLB, MB ChB.

Most courses normally last a minimum of 4 years, with an additional 1–2 years for honours.

Length of course. Full-time: BAdmin*, BB&A*, BJourn*, BMedSc, BScMedSc*: 1 year; BPA*: 2 years; LLB: 2–4 years; BA, BAcc, BAgricAdmin, BComm, BDram, BEcon, BMil, BMus, BSc: 3 years; BA(FA), BA(FA)(Ed), BA(SW), BA*, BAcc*, BAgricAdmin*, BComm*, BDram*, BEcon*, BEng, BMil*, BMus*, BOccTher, BPrimEd, BSc*, BScAgric, BScConsEcol, BScDiet, BScFoodSc, BScFor, BSp&HTher: 4 years; BTh: 4–5 years; BA(FA)*, BOccTher*, BScAgric*, BScFoodSc*, BScFor*, BScPhysio*: 5 years; MB ChB: 6 years.

Higher Degrees (see also South African Directory to Subjects of Study) (* = with honours).

Master's. BEd*, BPhil, LLM, MA, MAcc, MAdmin, MA(FA), MAgricAdmin, MA(SW), MBA, MBibl, MChD, MComm, MCur, MD, MDram, MEcon, MEd, MEng, MFamMed, MHMS, MHomeEcon, MJourn, MMEd, MMil, MMus, MNutr, MOccTher, MPA, MPhil, MP&R, MSc, MScAgric, MScConsEcol, MScDentSc, MScEngSc, MScFoodSc, MScFor, MScForSc, MScHomeEcon, MScMedSc, MScPhysio, MScWoodSc, MTh.

Most courses normally last a minimum of 1 year.

Length of course. Full-time: BEd*, BPhil, LLM, MA, MA(FA), MA(SW), MAcc, MAdmin, MAgricAdmin, MBA, MComm, MCur, MDram, MEcon, MEd, MEng, MJourn, MMil, MMus, MNutr, MOccTher, MPA, MPhil, MSc, MScAgric, MScConsEcol, MScEngSc, MScFoodSc, MScFor, MScForSc, MScMedSc, MScPhysio, MTh: 1 year; MP&R: 1–2 years; MFamMed: 3 years; MMEd: 4–5 years. Part-time: MBA: 2 years.

Doctoral. DAdmin, DComm, DCur, DEd, DEng, DLitt, DMil, DMus, DPhil, DSc, DScAgric, DScFoodSc, DScFor, DScHomeEcon, DScMedSc, DScNCons, DSc(Odont), DScWoodSc, DTh, LLD, PhD, PhD(Agric), PhD(AgricAdmin), PhD(Eng), PhDEngSc, PhD(FoodSc), PhD(For), PhDForSc, PhD(HMS), PhD(HomeEcon), PhD(Mil), PhD(NCons), PhD(WoodSc).

Length of course. Full-time: DSc, DScAgric, DScFoodSc, DScFor, DScMedSc: 1 year; DCur, DEd, DEng, DLitt, DMil, DMus, DPhil, DTh, LLD, PhD, PhD(Agric), PhD(AgricAdmin), PhD(FoodSc), PhD(For), PhDEngSc: 2 years; DAdmin, DComm: 3 years.

Language of Instruction. Afrikaans. Other languages may be used where deemed necessary for effective instruction, and in several advanced postgraduate courses English is used.

Libraries. Volumes: 650,922. Periodicals subscribed to: 4945. Special collections: Africana; European Document Centre; rare books and manuscripts.

FACULTIES/SCHOOLS

Agricultural and Forestry Sciences
Tel: (021) 808 4737 Fax: (021) 808 2001
E-mail: kit@sun.ac.za
Acting Dean: Theron, Prof. Karen I., MScAgric Stell., PhD(Agric) Stell.
Faculty Administrator: Jordaan, Leon, BA Stell.

Arts
Tel: (021) 808 2137 Fax: (021) 808 2123
E-mail: hjk@sun.ac.za
Dean: Kotze, Prof. Hennie J., MA S.Af., MA(Econ) Manc., DLitt&Phil Rand Afrikaans
Faculty Administrator: Loxton, M. C. (Leana), BA Stell.

Economic and Management Sciences
Tel: (021) 808 2248 Fax: (021) 808 2409
E-mail: judv@sun.ac.za
Dean: De Villiers, Prof. Johann U., BEng Stell., MBA Stell., PhD Witw.
Faculty Administrator: Eygelaar, Leon, BA Stell.

Education
Tel: (021) 808 2258 Fax: (021) 808 2269
E-mail: yw@sun.ac.za
Dean: Waghid, Prof. Yusaf, BA W.Cape, PhD Stell., DEd W.Cape, DPhil Stell.
Faculty Administrator: De Beer, Johan B., BA Stell., BPA Stell.

Engineering
Tel: (021) 808 4204 Fax: (021) 808 4206
E-mail: august@sun.ac.za
Dean: Schoonwinkel, Prof. Arnold, MEng Stell., MBA Cape Town, PhD Stan.
Faculty Administrator: Pienaar, Minnaar O., BA OFS

Health Sciences
Tel: (021) 938 9204 Fax: (021) 938 9060
E-mail: fcla@sun.ac.za
Dean: Van der Merwe, Prof. Wynand L., MB ChB Stell., MMed Stell., MD Stell.
Faculty Administrator: Mouton, Eben, BA Stell., MBL Stell., MIMM Stell.

Law
Tel: (021) 808 4853 Fax: (021) 886 6235
E-mail: gfl@sun.ac.za
Dean: Lubbe, Prof. Gerhard F., BA Stell., LLB Stell., LLM Yale
Faculty Administrator: Le Roux, Andra, BA Stell., LLB Stell.

Military Science
Tel: (022) 702 3003 Fax: (022) 702 3002
E-mail: lizelb@sun.ac.za
Acting Dean: Van Harte, Edna, BA S.Af., MSc C.U.N.Y., EdM Col., EdD Col.
Faculty Administrator: Petersen, Melanie, BA Stell., BEd Stell.

Science
Tel: (021) 808 3072 Fax: (021) 808 3680
E-mail: mvdworm@sun.ac.za
Dean: Rawlings, Prof. Doug E., BSc Rhodes, PhD Rhodes
Faculty Administrator: Abels, Bevin, BCom Stell.

Theology
Tel: (021) 808 3255 Fax: (021) 808 3251
E-mail: emouton@sun.ac.za
Dean: Mouton, A. Elna J., BA Stell., MA P.Elizabeth, DTh W.Cape
Secretary: Cornelissen, Shirle

ACADEMIC UNITS

Accountancy
Tel: (021) 808 3428 Fax: (021) 886 4176
E-mail: adurand@sun.ac.za
Brown, William, BCom Cape Town, MComm Stell., PhD Stell. Prof.
De Jager, J. Willie, BComm Stell., BCompt S.Af., MAcc Stell. Assoc. Prof.
De Wet, Johan J., BComm Stell. Sr. Lectr.

Fourie, W., BCom Rand Afrikaans, MCom Rand Afrikaans Sr. Lectr.
Loxton, Leon, BSc Stell., BAcc Stell., MBA Stell. Assoc. Prof.
Nel, G. F., BComm Stell., MBA Stell. Sr. Lectr.
Olivier, Pierre, BCompt S.Af., MComm Stell., PhD Stell. Prof.; Chair*
Scholtz, H., BCom Rand Afrikaans, MCom Rand Afrikaans Sr. Lectr.
Steyn, B. Wilna, BAcc Stell., BComm Stell., MBA Stell. Sr. Lectr.
Van Dyk, D. P., MAcc Stell. Sr. Lectr.
Van Schalkwyk, C. J. (Cobus), BAcc Stell., BComm Stell., MComm Stell. Prof.
Van Schalkwyk, Linda, BCom Pret., MCom Pret. Assoc. Prof.
Von Wielligh, S. Pieter J., MAcc Stell. Assoc. Prof.
Wessels, Philip L., MComm Stell. Assoc. Prof.
Wesson, Nicolene, BComm Stell., BCom Rand Afrikaans, MComm Stell. Assoc. Prof.
Wiese, Adel, BComm Stell., BCompt S.Af., MComm Stell. Sr. Lectr.
Other Staff: 26 Lectrs.
Research: information value of accounting indicators; prediction of corporate failure

African Languages
Tel: (021) 808 2210 Fax: (021) 808 2171
E-mail: afrika@sun.ac.za
Dlali, Mawande, MA Stell., DLitt Stell. Sr. Lectr.
Satyo, P. Nomsa, BA S.Af., MA Natal, DLitt Stell. Sr. Lectr.
Visser, Marianna W., MA Stell., DLitt Stell. Assoc. Prof.; Chair*
Zulu, Nogwaja S., DLitt Stell. Prof.
Other Staff: 3 Lectrs.
Research: African linguistics; African literature, especially Xhosa, Zulu and Sesotho; phonetics of African languages

Afrikaans and Dutch
Tel: (021) 808 2158 Fax: (021) 808 3815
E-mail: afrsu@maties.sun.ac.za
Britz, Etienne C., MA Stell., LittDrs Amst., DLitt Stell. Sr. Lectr.
De Stadler, Leon G., MA Stell., DLitt Stell. Assoc. Prof.
Feinauer, A. E. (Ilse), MA Stell., DLitt Stell. Assoc. Prof.; Chair*
Foster, P. H. (Ronel), MA Stell., DLitt Stell. Sr. Lectr.
Gouws, Rufus H., MA Stell., DLitt Stell. Prof.
Huigen, Siegfried, DrsLitt Utrecht, DLitt Utrecht Assoc. Prof.
Van Niekerk, Marlene, MA Stell., PhilDr Amst. Assoc. Prof.
Van Zyl, Dorothea P., MA Stell., LittDrs Utrecht, DLitt&Phil S.Af. Sr. Lectr.
Viljoen, Louise, MA Stell., DLitt Stell. Prof.
Other Staff: 6 Lectrs.
Research: Afrikaans communication studies; Afrikaans linguistics; Afrikaans literature; Dutch literature; literary theory

Agricultural Economics
Tel: (021) 808 4758 Fax: (021) 808 4670
E-mail: nv@maties.sun.ac.za
Karaan, Mohammad, MScAgric Stell., PhD(Agric) Stell. Sr. Lectr.
Kleynhans, Theo E., MScAgric Natal, PhD(Agric) Stell. Assoc. Prof.
Lombard, Jan P., MScAgric Stell., PhD(Agric) Stell. Sr. Lectr.
Vink, Nick, MScAgric Stell., PhD(Agric) Stell. Prof.; Chair*
Other Staff: 2 Lectrs.
Research: agricultural development; agricultural marketing and business; agricultural production management; agricultural strategic management; agriculture in the national economy

Agronomy
Tel: (021) 808 4803 Fax: (021) 887 9273
E-mail: gaa@maties.sun.ac.za
Agenbag, G. André, MScAgric Stell., PhD(Agric) Stell. Prof.; Chair*

Pieterse, Petrus J., BSc OFS, MScAgric Stell., PhD Stell. Sr. Lectr.

Other Staff: 4 Lectrs.

Research: crop production; hydroponics; soil tillage; veld invaders; weed research

Ancient Studies

Tel: (021) 808 3203 Fax: (021) 808 3480
E-mail: sakkie@sun.ac.za

Cook, Johann, BTh Stell., MA Stell., DLitt Stell. Assoc. Prof.

Cornelius, Izak, BTh Stell., MA Stell., DLitt Stell. Prof.; Chair*

Kruger, Paul A., BTh Stell., MA Stell., DLitt Stell. Assoc. Prof.

Thom, Johann C., BA Stell., MA Pret., PhD Chic. Prof.

Thom, Sjarlene, MA Stell., DLitt Stell. Sr. Lectr.

Van der Merwe, Christo H. J., MA Stell., MTh Stell., DLitt Stell. Assoc. Prof.

Zietsman, J. Christoff, MA Pret., DLitt Pret. Sr. Lectr.

Other Staff: 3 Lectrs.; 3 Extraordinary Lectrs.

Research: biblical Hebrew (grammar and teaching); Graeco-Roman religion and philosophy; Graeco-Roman satire, comedy, drama, lyric and elegy; Near Eastern culture and comparative literature; Septuagint proverbs

Animal Sciences

Tel: (021) 808 4916 Fax: (021) 808 4750
E-mail: cwc@maties.sun.ac.za

Cruywagen, Christiaan W., MSc(Agric) Pret., DSc(Agric) Pret. Assoc. Prof.; Chair*

Dzama, Kennedy, MAnimSc Texas A.& M., PhD Texas A.& M. Assoc. Prof.

Hoffmann, Louw C., MScAgric Stell., PhD(Agric) North(S.Af.) Prof.

Lambrechts, Helet, MScAgric Stell., PhD(Agric) Stell. Sr. Lectr.

Other Staff: 2 Lectrs.

Research: animal breeding; meat sciences; poultry studies; ruminant nutrition

Biochemistry

Tel: (021) 808 5862 Fax: (021) 808 5863
E-mail: pswart@sun.ac.za

Bellstedt, Dirk U., PhD(Agric) Stell. Assoc. Prof.

Hofmeyr, Jan-Hendrik S., MSc Stell., PhD Stell. Prof.

Louw, Ann, MSc Stell., PhD Stell. Sr. Lectr.

Rautenbach, Marina, MSc Pret., PhD Stell. Sr. Lectr.

Rohwer, Johann M., MSc Stell., PhD Amst. Assoc. Prof.

Snoep, Jackie, PhD Amst. Prof.

Swart, Pieter, PhD Stell. Prof.; Chair*

Other Staff: 4 Lectrs.

Research: antimicrobial peptides; applied agricultural research; molecular cell physiology; natural products from Salsola tuberculatiformis; regulation of gene expression

Botany and Zoology

Tel: (021) 808 3236 Fax: (021) 808 2405
E-mail: lwillems@sun.ac.za

Bowie, Rauri C. K., PhD Cape Town Sr. Lectr.

Cherry, Michael, BSc Cape Town, DPhil Oxf. Prof.

Chown, Steven L., BSc Pret., PhD Pret. Prof.

Daniels, Savel R., BSc W.Cape, PhD Stell. Sr. Lectr.

Dreyer, Leanne, MSc Stell., PhD Pret. Sr. Lectr.

Flemming, Alex F., MSc Stell., PhD Stell. Sr. Lectr.

Jackson, Sue, BSc Natal, PhD Cape Town Sr. Lectr.

Matthee, Conrad A., MSc Pret., PhD Pret. Assoc. Prof.

Mouton, P. le Fras N. M., MSc Stell., PhD Stell. Assoc. Prof.

Mucina, L., MSc Bratislava, PhD Slovak Acad.Sc., DrRerNat T.U.Berlin Prof.

Reinecke, A. J. (Koot), BProc Potchef., MSc Potchef., DSc Potchef. Prof.

Reinecke, Sophie A., Hon. BSc Potchef., MSc Rand Afrikaans, PhD Rand Afrikaans Assoc. Prof.; Dir.*

Richardson, Dave M., BSc Stell., MSc Cape Town, PhD Cape Town Prof.

Robinson, Terry J., MSc Pret., DSc Pret., FRSSAf Prof.

Smith, Valdon R., BSc Witw., PhD OFS Prof.

Van Jaarsveld, Albert S., BSc Pret., PhD Pret. Prof.

Van Wyk, J. H. (Hannes), MSc Stell., PhD Cape Town Assoc. Prof.

Wossler, Theresa C., PhD Witw. Sr. Lectr.

Other Staff: 6 Lectrs.; 1 Sr. Researcher; 2 Researchers; 2 Emer. Profs.; 2 Temp. Sr. Lectrs.

Research: behavioural ecology, animal-plant interactions, community ecology, conservation planning and biocomplexity; ecology; genomics; invasion biology; plant physiology

Business, Graduate School of

Tel: (021) 918 4111 Fax: (021) 918 4112
E-mail: usbcom@usb.sun.ac.za

Biekpe, Nicholas B., BSc Ghana, MSc Lond., PhD Belf. Assoc. Prof.

Butler, Martin J., MSc Pret., MBA Stell. Sr. Lectr.

Gevers, Wim R., MSc(Eng) Cape Town, MBA Stell., PhD Stell. Prof.

Harris, A. Tony, MA Brown, MBA Babson Sr. Lectr.

Herbst, Frikkie J., DComm Pret. Assoc. Prof.

Krige, J. D. (Niel), MComm Stell., FIA Assoc. Prof.

Mathur-Helm, Babita, MA Gujar., PhD Gujar. Sr. Lectr.

Oosthuizen, Hein, MCom S.Af., DComm Rand Afrikaans Prof.

Smit, Eon v. d. M., DComm Stell. Prof.; Chair*

Smith, Johan d. P., BSc(Eng) Cape Town, BCom S.Af., MBA Stell., PhD Stell. Sr. Lectr.

Other Staff: 12 Lectrs.; 4 Researchers

Research: futures research; investment analysis in Africa; leadership studies

Business Management

Tel: (021) 808 2026 Fax: (021) 808 2226
E-mail: ablather@sun.ac.za

Bloom, Jonathan Z., MComm Stell., PhD Stell. Assoc. Prof.

Boshoff, C., MComm Pret., DComm Pret. Prof.; Chair*

De Villiers, Johann U., BEng Stell., MBA Stell., PhD Witw.

Hough, Johan, BScAgric OFS, MScAgric Pret., DComm S.Af. Prof.

Krige, J. D. (Niel), MComm Stell., FIA Assoc. Prof.

Mostert, F. J. (Erik), MComm Stell., DComm Stell. Prof.

Terblanche, Nic S., BCom S.Af., BEcon Stell., MTRP Stell., DPhil Stell. Prof.

Van Rooyen, Johan H., MCom Rand Afrikaans, DCom Rand Afrikaans Assoc. Prof.

Other Staff: 4 Lectrs.

Research: entrepreneurship and innovation management; financial management; investment management; marketing management in business management

Chemistry and Polymer Science

Tel: (021) 808 3331 Fax: (021) 808 3360
E-mail: hgr@sun.ac.za

Barbour, Len J., PhD Cape Town Assoc. Prof.

Bredenkamp, Martin W., MSc Stell., DSc Pret. Sr. Lectr.

Burger, Ben V., MSc Stell., DSc Stell. Prof.

Crouch, Andrew M., BSc W.Cape, PhD C'dia. Prof.

Dillen, Jan L. M., DSc Antwerp Prof.

Esterhuysen, Catharine E., PhD Rand Afrikaans Sr. Lectr.

Jacobs, Ed P., PhD Stell. Assoc. Prof.

Jardien, M. A., PhD Cape Town Sr. Lectr.

Le Roux, Maritha, PhD Stell. Sr. Lectr.

Mallon, Peter E., PhD P.Elizabeth Sr. Lectr.

Meyer, Connie J., MSc Stell., PhD Stell. Sr. Lectr.

Raubenheimer, Helgard G., MSc Stell., PhD Stell. Prof.; Chair*

Sanderson, Ron D., BSc Cape Town, PhD Akron Prof.

Sandra, Pat J. F., PhD Ghent Prof.

Strauss, Erick, BSc Pret., PhD Cornell Sr. Lectr.

Van Reenen, Albert J., MSc Stell., PhD Stell. Sr. Lectr.

Other Staff: 6 Lectrs.; 2 Researchers

Computer Science

Tel: (021) 808 4232 Fax: (021) 808 4416
E-mail: info@cs.sun.ac.za

Krzesinski, A. E. (Tony), MSc Cape Town, PhD Camb. Prof.

Van der Merwe, A. Brink, BSc Stell., DPhil Texas A.& M. Assoc. Prof.; Chair*

Van Zijl, Lynette, PhD Stell. Sr. Lectr.

Other Staff: 4 Lectrs.

Research: asynchronous transfer mode (ATM) and broadband networks; descriptional complexity; systems software verification

Conservation Ecology

Tel: (021) 808 3304 Fax: (021) 808 3304
E-mail: consecol@sun.ac.za

Esler, Karen J., BSc Cape Town, PhD Cape Town Assoc. Prof.

Leslie, Alison J., BSc Stell., MSc Drexel, PhD Drexel Sr. Lectr.; Acting Chair*

McGeoch, Melodie A., PhD Pret. Assoc. Prof.

Milton, Sue, PhD Cape Town Prof.

Other Staff: 4 Lectrs.

Research: conservation planning and evaluation; environmental effects of forestry and agriculture; quantitative methods in conservation; recreation and ecotourism planning; wildlife management and utilisation

Curriculum Studies

Tel: (0210 808 2300 Fax: (021) 808 2295
E-mail: mlr1@sun.ac.za

Bitzer, Eli M., BA OFS, DEd OFS Prof.; Chair*

Carl, Arend E., BA Stell., DEd Stell. Prof.

Kapp, Chris A., BA P.Elizabeth, BA S.Af., DEd Stell. Prof.

Le Grange, Leslie L. L., BSc W.Cape, BA Cape Town, MEd Cape Town, PhD Stell. Prof.

Menkveld, Hannie, MA Stell., PhD Stell. Sr. Lectr.

Olivier, Alwyn I., BSc Stell., MEd Stell. Sr. Lectr.

Roux, Cornelia D., BA Potchef., DPhil Stell. Assoc. Prof.

Schreuder, Danie R., BSc Stell., BSc S.Af., MEd S.Af., DEd Stell. Prof.

Van der Walt, Christa, MA Potchef., DLitt Pret. Sr. Lectr.

Other Staff: 13 Lectrs.

Research: computer-based education; educational leadership; educational technology; environmental education; general curriculum studies

Drama

Tel: (021) 808 3089 Fax: (021) 808 4336
E-mail: satj@maties.sun.ac.za

Hauptfleisch, Temple, BA OFS, DLitt&Phil S.Af. Prof.; Chair*

Hees, Edwin P. H., BA Witw., DLitt&Phil S.Af. Assoc. Prof.

Kruger, Marie S., DPhil Stell. Sr. Lectr.

Other Staff: 5 Lectrs.

Research: community theatre; film theory analysis; theatre science; youth theatre

Economics

Tel: (021) 808 2247 Fax: (021) 808 4637
E-mail: econ@sun.ac.za

Black, Philip A., PhD Rhodes Prof.†

Calitz, Estian, BComm Stell., BCom Pret., MComm Stell., DComm Stell. Prof.

De Villiers, A. Pierre, MComm Stell., PhD Stell. Sr. Lectr.

Du Plessis, Stan A., BComm *Stell.*, MPhil *Camb.*, PhD *Stell.*   Prof.
Jafta, Rachel C. C., BEcon *W.Cape*, MEcon *Stell.*, PhD *Stell.*   Assoc. Prof.
Keswell, Malcolm M., MSocSci *Natal*, MA *Mass.*, PhD *Mass.*   Assoc. Prof.
McCarthy, Colin L., MA *Stell.*, DPhil *Stell.*   Emer. Prof.
Moore, Basil J., PhD *Johns H.*   Prof.†
Schoombee, G. Andries, BCom *Pret.*, MComm *Stell.*, PhD *Stell.*   Prof.; Chair*
Smit, Ben W., MComm *Stell.*, DComm *Stell.*   Prof.
Terreblanche, Sampie J., MA *Stell.*, DPhil *Stell.*   Emer. Prof.
Van der Berg, Servaas, BCom *Natal*, MCom *Pret.*, PhD *Stell.*   Prof.
Other Staff: 12 Lectrs.; 2 Lectrs.†
Research: business cycles; experimental economics; history of South Africa; macroeconomic policy; social policy (education and social security)

Education Policy Studies

Tel: (021) 808 2419 Fax: (021) 808 2283
   E-mail: yw@sun.ac.za
Berkhout, Sarie J., BCom *Pret.*, BEd *Pret.*   Prof.
De Klerk, J., BA *Stell.*, BEd *S.Af.*, MEd *S.Af.*, DEd *S.Af.*   Sr. Lectr.
Waghid, Yusaf, BA *W.Cape*, PhD *Stell.*, DEd *W.Cape*, DPhil *Stell.*   Prof.; Chair*
Other Staff: 4 Lectrs.
Vacant Posts: 1 Sr. Lectr.
Research: comparative education; culture and community; human interaction in educational organisations; policy analysis and development; theory and ideology (ideological paradigms in education)

Educational Psychology

Tel: (021) 808 2306 Fax: (021) 808 2021
   E-mail: peng@maties.sun.ac.za
Daniels, Doria, BA *W.Cape*, MA *Iowa*, PhD *S.Calif.*   Assoc. Prof.
Newmark, Rona, BA *S.Af.*, MEd *Pret.*, PhD *Stell.*   Assoc. Prof.; Chair*
Swart, R. Estelle, MEd *Rand Afrikaans*, DEd *Rand Afrikaans*   Prof.
Other Staff: 5 Lectrs.
Research: adult basic education; guidance and counselling of at-risk learners; inclusive education; thinking skills

Engineering, Civil

Tel: (021) 808 4369 Fax: (021) 808 4440
   E-mail: icm@sun.ac.za
Basson, Gerrit R., BEng *Pret.*, MEng *Stell.*, PhD(Eng) *Stell.*   Prof.
Bester, Christo J., BSc *Stell.*, MEng *Stell.*, DEng *Pret.*   Prof.; Chair*
Bosman, D. Eddie, BSc *Stell.*, BEng *Stell.*   Sr. Lectr.
De Wet, Marius, BSc(Eng) *Pret.*, MEng *Pret.*, PhD *Stell.*   Sr. Lectr.
Dunaiski, Peter E., MEng *Stell.*, PhD(Eng) *Stell.*   Prof.
Jenkins, K. J., BScEng *Natal*, MScEng *Natal*, PhD(Eng) *Stell.*   Assoc. Prof.
Retief, Johan V., BSc(Eng) *Pret.*, MPhil *Lond.*, DSc(Eng) *Pret.*   Emer. Prof.
Rooseboom, Albert, BSc *Stell.*, BEng *Stell.*, DSc(Eng) *Pret.*   Emer. Prof.
Strasheim, J. A. v. Breda, BSc *S.Af.*, BSc(Eng) *Pret.*, MEng *Stell.*, MBA *Stell.*   Sr. Lectr.
Van Rooyen, Gert C., BSc *OFS*, BSc(Eng) *Pret.*, MEng *Stell.*, PhD *Stell.*   Sr. Lectr.
Van Zijl, Gideon P. A. G., MEng *Stell.*, PhD *T.H.Delft*   Prof.
Wium, Jan A., MEng *Pret.*, PhD *Lausanne*   Sr. Lectr.
Other Staff: 2 Lectrs.
Research: construction and maintenance, flexible pavements, basic and applied soil mechanics; experimental structural mechanics, structural reliability, concrete structures; liquefaction potential; low-cost housing, computer applicatinos, facility management, information technology

applications; traffic engineering, road safety, pavement design

Engineering, Electrical and Electronic

Tel: (021) 808 4368 Fax: (021) 808 4981
   E-mail: wjperold@sun.ac.za
Bakkes, Pieter J., BSc *Stell.*, BEng *Stell.*, MEng *Stell.*, PhD *Stell.*   Assoc. Prof.
Blanckenberg, Mike M., BSc *Stell.*, BEng *Stell.*, BEng *Pret.*, PhD *Stell.*   Sr. Lectr.
Cloete, John H., BSc *Stell.*, BEng *Stell.*, MSc(Eng) *Calif.*, PhD(Eng) *Stell.*   Prof.
Davidson, David B., BEng *Pret.*, MEng *Pret.*, PhD(Eng) *Stell.*   Prof.
De Swardt, Johan B., BEng *Stell.*, MEng *Stell.*, PhD(Eng) *Stell.*   Assoc. Prof.
Du Preez, Johan A., BEng *Stell.*, MEng *Stell.*   Assoc. Prof.
Jones, Thomas, MScEng *Stell.*, PhD *M.I.T.*   Sr. Lectr.
Kamper, Martin J., BEng *Stell.*, MEng *Stell.*, PhD(Eng) *Stell.*   Prof.
Lourens, Johan G., BEng *Stell.*, MEng *Stell.*, PhD(Eng) *Stell.*   Prof.
Meyer, Petrie, BEng *Stell.*, MEng *Stell.*, PhD(Eng) *Stell.*   Assoc. Prof.
Milne, Garth W., BScEng *Natal*, MEng *Stell.*, PhD *Stan.*   Prof.
Mostert, Sias, MEng *Stell.*, PhD *Stell.*   Sr. Lectr.
Mouton, H. du Toit, BEng *Stell.*, MSc *OFS*, PhD *OFS*, PhD *Stell.*   Assoc. Prof.
Niesler, Thomas R., MEng *Stell.*, PhD *Camb.*   Sr. Lectr.
Palmer, Keith D., BEng *Stell.*, MEng *Stell.*, PhD(Eng) *Stell.*   Assoc. Prof.
Perold, Willem J., BEng *Stell.*, MEng *Stell.*, PhD(Eng) *Stell.*   Prof.; Chair*
Randewijk, P. J., MEng *Stell.*   Sr. Lectr.
Reader, Howard C., PhD *Camb.*, BScEng   Prof.
Steyn, Wilhelm H., MEng *Stell.*, MSc *Sur.*, PhD(Eng) *Stell.*   Prof.
Treurnicht, J., BEng *Stell.*, MSc *Cran.*   Sr. Lectr.
Van Niekerk, Cornell, MEng *Stell.*, PhD *Stell.*   Sr. Lectr.
Vermeulen, H. Johan, BEng *Stell.*, MEng *Stell.*, PhD(Eng) *Stell.*   Assoc. Prof.
Other Staff: 10 Lectrs.; 3 Extraordinary Lectrs.
Research: biomedical electronics; computer systems; control systems; converters of photovoltaic and wind energy systems; direct current traction substation technology with active filtering

Engineering, Industrial

Tel: (021) 808 4234 Fax: (021) 808 4245
   E-mail: nddp@sun.ac.za
Bekker, James F. B., MEng *Stell.*   Sr. Lectr.
Dimitrov, D., DrEng *T.U.Dresden*   Assoc. Prof.
Du Preez, Nick D., PhD(Eng) *Stell.*   Prof.
Fourie, C. J. (Neels), BEng *Pret.*, MEng *Stell.*, PhD(Eng) *Stell.*   Prof.; Chair*
Page, Daan C., MEng *Stell.*, MBA *Pret.*, PhD(Eng) *Stell.*   Sr. Lectr.
Von Leipzig, Konrad H., BCom *S.Af.*, MEng *Stell.*   Sr. Lectr.
Other Staff: 5 Lectrs.; 5 Extraordinary Lectrs.; 6 Lectrs.†
Research: facility design; fleet management; industrial ergonomics; information era developments; megatronics

Engineering, Mechanical

Tel: (021) 808 4376 Fax: (021) 808 4958
   E-mail: meganies@sun.ac.za
Basson, Anton H., MEng *Stell.*, PhD *Penn.State*   Prof.
Els, Danie N. J., BEng *Pret.*, MEng *Stell.*   Sr. Lectr.
Harms, Thomas M., BSc(Eng) *Cape Town*, MSc(Eng) *Birm.*, PhD(Eng) *Stell.*   Assoc. Prof.
Reuter, H. C. R., MEng *Stell.*   Sr. Lectr.
Scheffer, Cornie, MEng *Stell.*, PhD *Stell.*   Sr. Lectr.
Schreve, K., MEng *Stell.*, PhD *Stell.*   Sr. Lectr.
Van der Westhuizen, K., MEng *Stell.*   Sr. Lectr.
Van Niekerk, J. L. (Wikus), BEng *Stell.*, MSc(Eng) *Pret.*, PhD(Eng) *Calif.*   Prof.

Von Backstroem, Theo W., MScEng *Pret.*, PhD(Eng) *Stell.*   Prof.
Other Staff: 10 Lectrs.; 1 Extraordinary Lectr.
Research: biaxial yield; design procedure development; emissions and lubricants; fuels; internal combustion engines

Engineering, Process

Tel: (021) 808 4485 Fax: (021) 808 2059
   E-mail: cheming@ing.sun.ac.za
Aldrich, Chris, BEng *Stell.*, MEng *Stell.*, PhD(Eng) *Stell.*   Prof.
Bradshaw, Steven M., MSc *Natal*, PhD *Witw.*   Prof.
Burger, André J., MEng *Stell.*, PhD(Eng) *Stell.*   Prof.; Chair*
Callanan, Linda H., BScChemEng *Cape Town*, PhD *Cape Town*   Sr. Lectr.
Eksteen, Jacques J., BEng *Stell.*, MEng *Stell.*   Sr. Lectr.
Els, E. Raymond, BSc *Pret.*, MBL *S.Af.*, MEng *Potchef.*, PhD(Eng) *Stell.*   Sr. Lectr.
Knoetze, J. H. (Hansie), BEng *Stell.*, PhD(Eng) *Stell.*   Prof.
Lorenzen, Leon, BEng *Stell.*, MEng *Stell.*, PhD(Eng) *Stell.*   Prof.
Other Staff: 2 Lectrs.; 11 Researchers; 5 Extraordinary Lectrs.
Research: artificial intelligence in process engineering; microwave processing; process modelling; pyrometallurgy; safety and environmental protection

English

Tel: (021) 808 2045 Fax: (021) 808 3827
   E-mail: eew@sun.ac.za
Gagiano, Annie H., MA *Stell.*, PhD *Stell.*   Prof.
Jamal, A. A., MA *New Br.*, PhD *Natal*   Sr. Lectr.
Klopper, Dirk C., MA *S.Af.*, DLitt&Phil *S.Af.*   Prof.; Chair*
Other Staff: 8 Lectrs.
Research: cultural studies; gender studies; nineteenth-century British fiction; twentieth-century African/South African fiction and poetry

Entomology and Nematology

Tel: (021) 808 4775 Fax: (021) 808 4336
   E-mail: hge@sun.ac.za
Addison, Pia, BSc *Stell.*, PhD *Natal*   Sr. Lectr.
Pringle, Ken L., MScAgric *Stell.*, PhD(Agric) *Stell.*   Sr. Lectr.
Samways, Mike J., BSc *Nott.*, PhD *Lond.*   Prof.; Chair*
Other Staff: 2 Lectrs.; 3 Researchers
Research: ecology (insects and agricultural ecosystems); nematology (host-parasite relationships, pathogenicity, taxonomy); pest management; systematics (emphasis on lepidoptera associated with fynbos)

Fine Arts

Tel: (021) 808 3052 Fax: (021) 808 4336
   E-mail: sandra@sun.ac.za
Alborough, Alan G., BA *Witw.*, MA *Lond.*   Assoc. Prof.
Brundrit, Jean, MA(FA) *Stell.*   Sr. Lectr.
Cassar, E., BAFA *Stell.*   Sr. Lectr.
Dietrich, Keith, BAFA *Stell.*, MA(FA) *S.Af.*, DLitt&Phil *S.Af.*   Assoc. Prof.
Kannemeyer, Anton, MA(FA) *Stell.*   Sr. Lectr.
Klopper, Sandra, BA *Witw.*, MA *E.Anglia*, PhD *Witw.*   Prof.; Chair*
Von Robbroeck, Lize, MA *Witw.*   Sr. Lectr.
Other Staff: 5 Lectrs.

Food Science

Tel: (021) 808 3578 Fax: (021) 808 3510
   E-mail: voedselw@sun.ac.za
Britz, Trevor J., MSc(Agric) *Pret.*, DSc(Agric) *Pret.*   Prof.
Manley, Marena, BScFoodSci *Stell.*, MSc *Pret.*, PhD *Plym.*   Sr. Lectr.
Witthuhn, R. Corli, PhD *Free State*   Assoc. Prof.; Chair*
Other Staff: 2 Lectrs.
Research: environmental management (liquid and solid waste management in the food

industry); fermented foods; food microbiology; near infrared spectroscopy (NIR); sensory science

Forest and Wood Science

Tel: (021) 808 3318 Fax: (021) 808 3603
E-mail: emg@sun.ac.za
Ackerman, Pierre, BSc Stell., MSc Stell.   Chair*
Bredenkamp, Brian V., MScFor Stell., PhD Virginia Polytech.   Prof.
Chirwa, Paxie, MSc Flor., PhD Nott.   Assoc. Prof.
Du Toit, Ben, MScFor Natal, PhD(For) Witw.   Sr. Lectr.
Meincken, Martina, MSc Constance, PhD Stell.   Sr. Lectr.
Rypstra, Tim, MSc Stell., PhD Stell.   Assoc. Prof.
Theron, J. M. (Kobus), MScFor Stell., PhD(For) Stell.   Sr. Lectr.
Wessels, C. Brand, BEng Stell., MSc Stell.   Sr. Lectr.
Other Staff: 5 Lectrs.; 2 Emer. Lectrs.
Research: dryland forestry; nursery practice; soil-related yield problems; special trials; weed control

Genetics

Tel: (021) 808 5888 Fax: (021) 808 5833
E-mail: lw@sun.ac.za
Brink, Danie D., MScAgric Stell., PhD(Agric) Stell.   Assoc. Prof.
Burger, Johan T., BScAgric Stell., PhD Cape Town   Assoc. Prof.
Hillermann-Rebello, R., PhD Lond.   Sr. Lectr.
Kossman, Jens M., DrRerNatHabil T.U.Berlin, DrScAgr T.U.Berlin   Prof.
Marais, G. Frans, MScAgric Stell., PhD N.Dakota, PhD(Agric) Stell.   Prof.
Warnich, Louise, MSc(MedSc) Stell., PhD Stell.   Prof.; Chair*
Zaahl, Monique, MSc(MedSc) Stell., PhD Stell.   Sr. Lectr.
Other Staff: 5 Lectrs.; 1 Sr. Researcher
Research: cereal breeding and genetic manipulation of wheat; fish breeding; molecular and cytogenetics; quantitative genetics; statistical inference

Geography and Environmental Studies

Tel: (021) 808 3218 Fax: (021) 808 2405
E-mail: geog@sun.ac.za
Barnard, Barnie W. S., BA Stell., MA Stell., DPhil Stell.   Sr. Lectr.; Chair*
Ferreira, Sanet L., BA Rand Afrikaans, MA Rand Afrikaans, DLitt&Phil S.Af.   Sr. Lectr.
Van der Merwe, J. H. (Hannes), DPhil Stell.   Assoc. Prof.
Other Staff: 3 Lectrs.

Geology

Tel: (021) 808 3219 Fax: (021) 808 3129
E-mail: ar@maties.sun.ac.za
De Villiers, Stephanie, BSc Stell., BSc Cape Town, PhD Wash.   Sr. Lectr.
Kisters, Alex F. M., PhD Witw.   Assoc. Prof.
Rozendaal, Abraham, MSc Stell., PhD Stell.   Prof.; Chair*
Stevens, Gary, MSc Rand Afrikaans, PhD UMIST   Prof.
Wickens, H. De Ville, MSc P.Elizabeth, PhD P.Elizabeth   Sr. Lectr.
Other Staff: 2 Lectrs.
Research: geotectonic evolution of the Western Cape; Karoo sediments as a sedimentary model for petroleum reservoir and source rocks; metamorphosed massive sulphide deposits; tanzanite and emerald gemstone deposits; west coast heavy mineral deposits

History

Tel: (021) 808 2177 Fax: (021) 808 2389
E-mail: ch@maties.sun.ac.za
Burden, Mathilda M., MA Stell., DPhil Stell.   Sr. Lectr.
Grundlingh, Albert M., BA OFS, MA S.Af., DLitt&Phil S.Af.   Prof.; Chair*
Visser, Wessel P., MA Stell., DPhil Stell.   Sr. Lectr.

Other Staff: 3 Lectrs.
Research: Afrikaans cultural history and folklore; gender, intellectual history, society and environment; history and society; history of the Anglo-Boer War; labour history and the history of trade unionism

Horticultural Science

Tel: (021) 808 4900 Fax: (021) 808 2121
E-mail: mcp@sun.ac.za
Jacobs, Gerhard, MScAgric Natal, PhD(Agric) Natal   Emer. Prof.
Steyn, Willem J., MScAgric Stell., PhD(Agric) Stell.   Sr. Lectr.; Acting Chair*
Theron, Karen I., MScAgric Stell., PhD(Agric) Stell.   Prof.
Wand, Stephanie J. E., MScAgric Stell., PhD Cape Town   Sr. Lectr.
Other Staff: 6 Lectrs.
Research: ecophysiology (deciduous crops); growth and development (of deciduous, citrus and indigenous floricultural crops); post-harvest physiology (deciduous, citrus and indigenous floricultural crops)

Industrial Psychology

Tel: (021) 808 3008 Fax: (021) 808 3007
E-mail: hhv@sun.ac.za
Boonzaier, William, MComm W.Cape, DTech Cape Peninsula UT
Dannhauser, Zani, MComm Rand Afrikaans, PhD Stell.   Sr. Lectr.
Du Preez, Ronel, MEcon Stell., PhD Stell.   Sr. Lectr.
Engelbrecht, Amos S., MComm Stell., PhD Stell.   Assoc. Prof.
Malan, D. Johan, MA Stell., DPhil Stell.   Prof.; Chair*
Theron, Callie C., MA Stell., PhD Stell.   Assoc. Prof.
Other Staff: 3 Lectrs.
Vacant Posts: 1 Lectr.
Research: consumer behaviour; human resources management; occupational psychology; organisational behaviour; psychometrics

Information Science

Tel: (021) 808 2423 Fax: (021) 808 2117
E-mail: informa@sun.ac.za
Kinghorn, Johann, BA Pret., DTh Stell.   Prof.; Chair*
Müller, Hans P., BTh Stell., MA Stell., DPhil Stell.   Sr. Lectr.
Van der Walt, Martin S., BBibl Stell., MA Stell., DPhil Stell.   Sr. Lectr.
Other Staff: 8 Lectrs.; 1 Researcher
Research: agricultural information systems; information society development; knowledge management; knowledge networks

Journalism

Tel: (021) 808 3488 Fax: (021) 808 3487
E-mail: leona@sun.ac.za
Rabe, Lizette, MJourn Stell., DPhil Stell.   Prof.; Chair*
Wasserman, Herman J., MA Stell., DLitt Stell.   Assoc. Prof.
Other Staff: 2 Lectrs.; 3 Extraordinary Lectrs.
Research: broadcast journalism; media-ethics; print journalism; science journalism

Law, Mercantile

Butler, David W., BComm Stell., LLD Stell.   Prof.
Coetzee, Juana, BA Stell., LLM Stell.   Sr. Lectr.
Da Gama, Mustaqeem M., BProc Pret., LLB Pret., LLM Leuven   Prof.
De Villiers, Roux, LLB Stell., MEng Stell., LLM Lond.   Sr. Lectr.
Du Plessis, Izelle, BComm Stell., LLB Stell., LLM Cape Town   Sr. Lectr.
Dupper, Ockie C., BA Stell., LLB Cape Town, LLM Harv., SJD Harv.   Prof.
Garbers, Christoph J., LLB Pret., LLM Stell.   Sr. Lectr.
Oosthuizen, Pieter G., BA S.Af., BIur S.Af., LLB Pret., LLM Pret.   Sr. Lectr.; Acting Chair*

Stevens, Richard A., BA Stell., LLB Stell., LLM Tübingen   Sr. Lectr.
Sutherland, Philip J., BComm Stell., LLB Stell., PhD Edin.   Prof.
Van der Bijl-Dam, Charnelle, LLB Pret., LLD Pret.   Sr. Lectr.
Other Staff: 1 Lectr.
Research: banking law; company law; international trade law; labour law; law of arbitration

Law, Private and Roman

Tel: (021) 808 3184 Fax: (021) 886 6235
E-mail: evdm@sun.ac.za
De Waal, Marius J., BComm Stell., LLM Stell., LLD Stell.   Prof.
Du Plessis, Jacques E., BComm Stell., LLM Stell., PhD Aberd.   Prof.
Human, C. Sonia, BMil Stell., LLB Stell., LLM S.Af., LLD Stell.   Prof.
Loubser, Max M., BA Stell., LLB Stell., DPhil Oxf.   Prof.
Lubbe, Gerhard F., BA Stell., LLB Stell., LLM Yale   Prof.
Mostert, Hanri, BA Stell., LLM Stell., LLD Stell.   Prof.
Naude, Tjakie, LLB Stell., LLD Stell.   Assoc. Prof.
Pienaar, Juanita M., BJuris Potchef., LLM Potchef., LLD Potchef.   Prof.; Chair*
Other Staff: 2 Lectrs.
Research: children's rights; indigenous law; land reform; law of delict

Law, Public

Tel: (021) 808 3195 Fax: (021) 883 9656
E-mail: ak1@sun.ac.za
Botha, Henk, BLC Pret., LLB Pret., LLM Col., LLD Pret.   Prof.
Du Plessis, Lourens M., BA Stell., BJur&Comm N-W(S.Af.), LLB N-W(S.Af.), BPhil N-W(S.Af.), LLD N-W(S.Af.)   Prof.
Forsyth, Christopher, BSc Natal, LLB Natal, LLB Camb., PhD Camb.   Prof.
Kemp, Gerhard, BA Stell., LLM Stell.   Sr. Lectr.; Acting Chair*
Liebenberg, Sandra, LLB Cape Town, LLM Essex   Prof.
Nel, Mary, BA Stell., LLB Stell., LLM Stell., MPhil Camb.   Sr. Lectr.
Quinot, Geo, BA Stell., LLB Stell., LLM Virginia   Sr. Lectr.
Van der Merwe, Steph E., LLB S.Af., LLD Cape Town, BJuris   Prof.
Van der Walt, A. J., BJur N-W(S.Af.), BA N-W(S.Af.), LLB N-W(S.Af.), LLM Witw., LLD N-W(S.Af.)   Prof.
Research: administrative law; constitutional law; constitutional property law; criminal law; human rights

Linguistics, General

Tel: (021) 808 2010 Fax: (021) 808 2009
E-mail: linguis@sun.ac.za
Anthonissen, Christine, MA Stell., PhD Vienna   Sr. Lectr.; Chair*
Oosthuisen, Johan, MA Stell.   Sr. Lectr.
Southwood, Frenette, MA Stell.   Sr. Lectr.
Van Gass, Kate, MA Stell.   Sr. Lectr.
Research: conceptual issues in evolutionary linguistics; second language acquisition; structure of sign language; syntactic structure of aphasic language

Logistics

Tel: (021) 808 2249 Fax: (021) 808 2409
E-mail: mmt@sun.ac.za
De Kock, Hennie C., MSc Stell., PhD Stell.   Assoc. Prof.
Krygsman, S. C., BEcon Stell., MSS Stell., PhD Utrecht   Sr. Lectr.
Louw, Nicol H., MComm Stell., PhD Stell.   Sr. Lectr.
Nel, J. Hannelie, MBA Stell., DSc Potchef.   Sr. Lectr.
Pienaar, Wessel J., MEcon Stell., MS(Eng) Calif., PhD(Eng) Stell., DCom S.Af.   Prof.; Chair*
Visagie, S. E., MSc Stell., MPhil Stell.   Sr. Lectr.

Other Staff: 5 Lectrs.

Research: benefit-cost analysis; business logistics management; transport costs; transport policy; urban, air, maritime, road, rail and pipeline transport

Mathematics

see also Stats. and Actuarial Sci.

Tel: (021) 808 3282 Fax: (021) 808 3828
E-mail: omarais@sun.ac.za
Breuer, Florian, PhD Paris   Sr. Lectr.
De Villiers, Johan M., BSc Stell., PhD Camb.   G. B. B. Rubbi Prof.
Fransman, A., MSc Stell., PhD Amst.   Sr. Lectr.
Green, Barry W., MSc Cape Town, PhD Cape Town   Prof.; Chair*
Holgate, David B., MSc Cape Town, PhD Cape Town   Assoc. Prof.
Keet, Arnie P., MSc Cape Town, PhD Cape Town   Sr. Lectr.
Laurie, Dirk P., PhD Dund.   Prof.
Mouton, S., MSc Free State, PhD Free State   Sr. Lectr.
Muller, M. Arnold, MSc Stell., PhD Edin.   Sr. Lectr.
Prodinger, H., PhD Vienna   Prof.
Rewitzky, I. M., MSc Cape Town, PhD Cape Town   Assoc. Prof.
Rohwer, Carl H., MSc Stell., DSc Potchef.   Sr. Lectr.
Van Wyk, Leon, MSc Stell., PhD Stell.   Prof.
Wild, Marcel, PhD Zür.   Assoc. Prof.
Other Staff: 3 Lectrs.

Research: arithmetic of curves and applications to coding theory; bi-ideals and quasi-reflective rings; decomposition of LULU operators for analysis and computational efficiency; perfect maps in uniform spaces; spline-wavelet analysis

Mathematics, Applied

Tel: (021) 808 4215 Fax: (021) 808 3778
E-mail: mvann@sun.ac.za
Du Plessis, J. Prieur, MSc Stell., PhD Stell.   Prof.
Grobler, Paul J. P., PhD S.Af.   Sr. Lectr.
Herbst, Ben M., PhD OFS   Prof.
Maritz, Milton F., PhD OFS   Sr. Lectr.
Smit, G. J. Francois, PhD Stell.   Sr. Lectr.; Chair*
Van Vuuren, Jan H., MSc Stell., DPhil Oxf.   Assoc. Prof.
Weideman, Jacob A. C., PhD OFS   Prof.
Other Staff: 3 Lectrs.

Research: computation; numerical analysis; operation research; porous media

Microbiology

see also Health Sciences (Basic and Appl. Health Scis.; Med. Microbiol.), below

Tel: (021) 808 5845 Fax: (021) 808 5846
E-mail: dvdm@sun.ac.za
Bloom, Marinda, MSc Stell., PhD Stell.   Sr. Lectr.
Botha, Alf, BScAgric Stell., MSc Pret., PhD OFS   Assoc. Prof.
Dicks, Leon M. T., BSc OFS, MSc Stell., PhD Stell.   Prof.
Prior, Bernard A., BScAgric Natal, MSc Wis., PhD Wis.   Prof.
Rawlings, Doug E., BSc Rhodes, PhD Rhodes   Prof.; Chair*
Van Zyl, W. H. (Emile), MSc OFS, PhD Prin.   Prof.
Other Staff: 2 Lectrs.

Research: biology of the mucorales; genetic manipulation of yeasts; lignocellulose bioconversion; microbiology of bio-mining; taxonomy of lactic acid bacteria

Military Science

Tel: (022) 702 3093 Fax: (022) 702 3002
E-mail: lizelb@sun.ac.za

Defence Organisation and Resource Management, School of

De Wet, Major H. Francois, MCom Pret., DEcon Vista   Sr. Lectr.

Jansen van Rensburg, Lt.-Col. J. L. (Wikus), BA S.Af., MPA Stell., PhD Stell.   Sr. Lectr.
Theletsane, Lt. K. I., BMil Stell.   Sr. Lectr.
Walters, Lt.-Col. A. N., BMil Stell., MBA Stell.   Sr. Lectr.
Other Staff: 7 Lectrs.

Geospatial Studies and Information Systems, School of

Ayirebi, G. K., BA Ghana, BSc Fort Hare, MA Stell.   Sr. Lectr.; Chair*
Rabé, Lt.-Col. D. J. (Kobus), BSc OFS, MEd OFS   Sr. Lectr.; Chair*
Other Staff: 5 Lectrs.

Human, Organisational and Law Studies, School of

Brits, Col. F. P., LLB Potchef.   Sr. Lectr.
Khashane, K. E., BComm Venda
Kotze, M. Elize, MSc Potchef., PhD Stell.   Assoc. Prof.
Nel, Lt.-Col. M., LLB Pret.
Van Dyk, Lt.-Col. Gielie A. J., BA Stell., BTh Stell., MA Potchef., PhD Potchef.   Chair*
Van Huyssteen, C. E., BA OFS, BEd Stell.
Other Staff: 2 Lectrs.

Science and Technology, School of

Botolo, E. W. L., BSc(Ed) Northwestern, BSc Northwestern, MSc Northwestern
Erasmus, Lt.-Col. J. H., BMil Stell.
Geldenhuys, Lt.-Col. H. J., BMil Stell., BIng Stell.
Neetling, A., PhD Witw.
Thiart, G. P., BSc Stell., MSc Lond., PhD Stell.   Sr. Lectr.
Van Der Merwe, J. P., BSc Potchef., MSc Rand Afrikaans
Other Staff: 6 Lectrs.

Security and Africa Studies, School of

Du Plessis, Major M. J. (Inus), BA OFS, MA Stell.   Sr. Lectr.
Van der Waag, Lt.-Col. Ian, BA P.Elizabeth, MA Pret.   Sr. Lectr.
Visser, Lt.-Col. G. E. (Deon), BA Stell., MA S.Af., DPhil Stell.   Assoc. Prof.; Chair*
Vreÿ, Lt.-Col. Francois, MMil Stell., PhD Stell.   Sr. Lectr.
Other Staff: 5 Lectrs.

Modern Foreign Languages

Tel: (021) 808 2133 Fax: (021) 808 2035
E-mail: ddreyer@sun.ac.za
Annas, Rolf, MA Stell., DLitt Stell.   Sr. Lectr.
Du Toit, Catherine, BA Pret.   Sr. Lectr.
Levéel, Eric C. G., BA Paris IV, MA Paris IV, PhD Natal   Sr. Lectr.
Von Maltzan, Carlotta H., MA Witw., PhD Witw.   Prof.; Chair*
Other Staff: 3 Lectrs.; 8 Lectrs.†
Research: computer-assisted language learning; eighteenth-century studies; travel literature

Music

Tel: (021) 808 2345 Fax: (021) 808 2340
E-mail: mkade@sun.ac.za
Grové, Izak J., MMus OFS, DPhil OFS   Prof.
Herbst, Theo, BMus Stell., MMus Natal   Sr. Lectr.
Lüdemann, Winfried A., MMus OFS, DPhil Stell.   Assoc. Prof.
Matei, Corvin, MMus Bucharest, PhD Cape Town   Sr. Lectr.
Oosthuizen, Magdalena J., MMus Stell.   Sr. Lectr.
Pauw, Niel E., MMus Stell., MMus P.Elizabeth   Sr. Lectr.
Roosenschoon, Hans, MMus Stell., DMus Cape Town   Prof.; Chair*
Roux, Magdalena, BMus Pret.   Sr. Lectr.
Schumann, Nina V., BMus Cape Town, MM Calif.   Assoc. Prof.
Smit, M. (Ria), BA Stell., BMus Stell., BA S.Af., MA Stell., DLitt Stell.   Assoc. Prof.
Wagner, Dietrich N., BMus Witw., MMus Witw.   Sr. Lectr.
Other Staff: 1 Lectr.

Research: composition; historic musicology; music education; music technology; systematic musicology

Old and New Testament

Tel: (021) 808 3267 Fax: (021) 808 3251
E-mail: hlb1@sun.ac.za
Bosman, Hendrik L., BA Pret., DD Pret.   Prof.; Chair*
Jonker, Louis C., MA Stell., DTh Stell.   Assoc. Prof.
Mouton, A. Elna J., BA Stell., MA P.Elizabeth, DTh W.Cape   Assoc. Prof.
Punt, Jeremy, MA Stell., MTh Stell., DTh Stell.   Sr. Lectr.
Research: contextual hermeneutics (interpretation of Old and New Testament in Africa); hermeneutics (reading strategies of Bible study groups); socio-rhetorical interpretation of Matthew; theology and ethics of Old Testament (Exodus); theology of the New Testament (reconciliation in Paul and Matthew)

Philosophy

Tel: (021) 808 2418 Fax: (021) 808 3556
E-mail: lb3@sun.ac.za
Cilliers, F. Paul, BEng Stell., MA Stell., DPhil Stell.   Prof.
Hattingh, Johann P., MA Stell., DPhil Stell.   Prof.; Chair*
Roodt, Vasti, MA Stell., DPhil Stell.   Sr. Lectr.
Van der Merwe, Willie L., BTh Stell., MA Stell., DPhil Stell.   Prof.
Van Niekerk, Anton A., BTh Stell., MA Stell., DPhil Stell.   Prof.
Other Staff: 2 Lectrs.
Research: applied ethics (biomedical and environmental); complexity; philosophy of language, religion and culture

Physics

Tel: (021) 808 3383 Fax: (021) 808 3385
E-mail: fgs@sun.ac.za
Arendse, Gillian J., MSc Stell., PhD Stell.   Sr. Lectr.
Burger, Johan P., MEng Rand Afrikaans, PhD S.Calif.   Sr. Lectr.
Cowley, Anthony A., MSc Pret., DSc Pret.   Prof.
Eggers, Hans, MSc Pret., PhD Arizona   Prof.
Geyer, Hendrik B., MSc Rand Afrikaans, PhD Stell.   Prof.
Heiss, W. Dieter, DrRerNat F.U.Berlin   Prof.
Hillhouse, Greg C., MSc Stell.   Assoc. Prof.
Müller-Nedebock, Kristian K., BSc Stell., PhD Camb.   Sr. Lectr.
Rohwer, Erich G., MSc Zululand, PhD Stell.   Lectr.
Scholtz, Frederik G., MSc Stell., PhD Stell.   Prof.; Chair*
Stander, J. Anton, MSc Stell., PhD Stell.   Sr. Lectr.
Van der Westhuizen, Pieter, MSc Stell., PhD Stell.   Sr. Lectr.
Visser, Kobus, MSc Stell., PhD Stell.   Assoc. Prof.
Von Bergmann, Hubertus M., PhD Natal   Prof.
Other Staff: 7 Lectrs.
Research: laser and spectrophysics (development of atomic reference database, diode laser spectroscopy); nuclear physics (medium energy light ion nuclear physics, nuclear reaction mechanism studies); theoretical physics (complex systems, condensed matter physics, quantum field theory)

Physiological Sciences

Tel: (021) 808 3146 Fax: (021) 808 3145
E-mail: alb@sun.ac.za
Engelbrecht, Anna-Mart, BSc Stell., MMedSc OFS, PhD Stell.   Sr. Lectr.
Essop, Faadiel, BA W.Cape, BSc Cape Town, BSc(Med) Cape Town, PhD Cape Town   Assoc. Prof.
Myburgh, Kathy H., BSc(Med) Cape Town, PhD Cape Town   Prof.; Chair*
Smith, Rob, BSc Sund., PhD Bath   Sr. Lectr.
Other Staff: 3 Lectrs.

Research: exercise physiology and muscle biochemistry; factors affecting the ischaemic heart

Plant Pathology

Tel: (021) 808 4797 Fax: (021) 808 4956
E-mail: altus@sun.ac.za
McLeod, Adele, MScAgric Stell., PhD Cornell Sr. Lectr.
Viljoen, Albertus, BSc Free State, PhD Free State Prof.; Chair*
Research: host-parasite interactions; integrated disease control; mycology; post-harvest pathology (stone and pome fruit and table grapes); small-grain diseases

Political Science

Tel: (021) 808 2414 Fax: (021) 808 2110
E-mail: polsci@sun.ac.za
Breytenbach, Willie J., MA Pret., DLitt&Phil S.Af. Prof.
Cornelissen, Scarlett, BSocSc Cape Town, MA Stell., PhD Glas. Sr. Lectr.
Du Toit, Pierre van der P., MA Stell., DPhil Stell. Prof.; Chair*
Gouws, Amanda, MA Rand Afrikaans, PhD Ill. Prof.
Leysens, Anthony J., MA Stell., DPhil Stell. Sr. Lectr.
Van der Westhuizen, Janis, MA Stell., PhD Dal. Sr. Lectr.
Other Staff: 3 Lectrs.
Research: African studies; comparative political behaviour; democratisation and state-building in Africa; international political economy; South African politics

Practical Theology and Missiology

Tel: (021) 808 3577 Fax: (021) 808 3251
E-mail: hjh@sun.ac.za
August, Karel T., MPA Stell., DTh Stell. Sr. Lectr.
Botman, H. Russel, BA W.Cape, BTh W.Cape, MTh W.Cape, DTh W.Cape Prof.
Cilliers, Johann H., BA Stell., MTh Stell., DTh Stell. Sr. Lectr.
Hendriks, H. Jurgens, BTh Stell., MA Stell., DLitt Stell. Prof.; Chair*
Louw, Daniël J., BTh Stell., MA Stell., DPhil Stell., DTh Stell. Prof.
Other Staff: 3 Lectrs.
Research: church growth and congregational studies (moral leadership for social transformation); homiletics (preaching and social transformation); missiology; pastoral care and counselling (cross-cultural counselling within an African context); youth ministry in context of post-modernity

Psychology

see also Educnl. Psychol., and Indust. Psychol.
Tel: (021) 808 3466 Fax: (021) 808 3584
E-mail: mclr@sun.ac.za
De Vos, Hennie, MA Stell., DPhil OFS, BA Sr. Lectr.
Greeff, Awie P., BEd Stell., MSc Stell., PhD Stell. Assoc. Prof.
Kagee, S. Araf, BA W.Cape, MA Portland, PhD Ball Prof.
Kruger, Lou-Marie, BA Stell., MSocSc Cape Town, MA Boston, PhD Boston Assoc. Prof.
Lesch, Elmien, BA Stell., MA OFS, DPhil Stell. Sr. Lectr.
Meyer, Johan C., MA Stell., DPhil Stell. Assoc. Prof.
Möller, André T., MA Stell., DPhil Stell. Prof.; Chair*
Naidoo, A. V. (Tony), BA W.Cape, MA Ball, PhD Ball Prof.
Smith, Mario R., MA W.Cape, MPhil Col., PhD Col. Sr. Lectr.
Swartz, Leslie P., MSc Cape Town, PhD Cape Town Prof.
Wait, Johnny W. van S., MA Stell., DPhil Stell. Sr. Lectr.
Other Staff: 7 Lectrs.

Research: child psychology; cognitive behaviour therapy; family psychology; social psychology; vocational psychology

Public Management and Planning, School for

Tel: (021) 918 4122 Fax: (021) 918 4123
E-mail: enquiry@sopmp.sun.ac.za
Burger, A. P. J. (Johan), BArch OFS, MPA Stell., PhD Stell. Assoc. Prof.
Cloete, G. S. (Fanie), BJur Potchef., LLB Rand Afrikaans, MA Stell., PhD Stell. Prof.
Fakir, S. (Saliem), BSc Witw., MEnvSc ICL Sr. Lectr.; Assoc. Dir., Centre for Renewable and Sustainable Energy Resources
Ketel, Belinda, MA Stell., PhD Stell. Sr. Lectr.
Müller, J. I. (Anneke), BJuris S.Af., MTRP Stell. Sr. Lectr.
Müller, J. J. (Kobus), BSc(Agric) Stell., MPA Stell., PhD Stell. Assoc. Prof.
Schwella, Erwin, BA Stell., MPA Stell., PhD Stell. Prof.
Swilling, Mark, PhD Warw. Prof.
Theron, Francois, MA Stell. Sr. Lectr.
Uys, Frederik M., BA Stell., MA Pret., PhD Stell. Sr. Lectr.
Other Staff: 2 Lectrs.
Research: development management; planning and environmental law; policy analysis; public management; sustainable development

Social Work

Tel: (021) 808 2069 Fax: (021) 808 3765
E-mail: jic@sun.ac.za
Engelbrecht, Lambert K., MA Stell., DPhil Stell. Sr. Lectr.
Green, Sulina, MASocWork Stell., DPhil Stell. Prof.; Chair*
Other Staff: 3 Lectrs.
Research: child abuse; evaluating effectiveness of social work practice; field practice supervision of students; use of volunteers; welfare policy formulation at national level

Sociology

Tel: (021) 808 2420 Fax: (021) 808 2143
E-mail: hjdw@sun.ac.za
Begg, Rashid M., PhD Tor. Sr. Lectr.
Ewert, Joachim W., MA Stell., DPhil Stell. Sr. Lectr.
Heinecken, Lindy P. T., MSocSc Cape Town, PhD Lond. Assoc. Prof.
Mouton, Johann, BA Rand Afrikaans, DLitt&Phil Rand Afrikaans Prof.
Robins, Steven L., PhD Col. Assoc. Prof.
Van der Waal, C. S. (Kees), MA Pret., DLitt&Phil Rand Afrikaans Prof.
Walker, Cherryl, DLitt Natal Prof.; Chair*
Other Staff: 15 Lectrs.
Research: computer-assisted analysis and presentation of social data; labour and industrial relations; race relations; social control and deviance; the household, family and gender

Soil Science

Tel: (021) 808 4794 Fax: (021) 808 4791
E-mail: waters@sun.ac.za
Ellis, Freddie, MScAgric Stell., PhD(Agric) Stell. Sr. Lectr.
Fey, Martin, BScAgric Natal, PhD Natal Prof.; Chair*
Hoffman, J. Eduard, MScAgric OFS, PhD OFS Sr. Lectr.
Rozanov, Andre, PhD Sr. Lectr.
Other Staff: 2 Researchers
Research: land suitability and soil amelioration (forestry soils, fruit and wine grapes); plant nutrition and environmental effects (of the grapevine); soil classification and genesis; soil physics and irrigation science

Sport Science

Tel: (021) 808 4915 Fax: (021) 808 4817
E-mail: jrp@sun.ac.za
Barnard, J. G. (Sthinus), MA Stell., DPhil OFS Assoc. Prof.

Bressan, Elizabeth S., MSPhysEd N.Carolina, PhD Calif. Assoc. Prof.
Rossouw, Corné M., MPhysEd Stell. Sr. Lectr.
Terblanche, Elmarie, BSc Stell., MSc Stell., PhD Stell. Assoc. Prof.; Chair*
Van der Merwe, Floris J. G., MA Stell., MPhysEd Stell., DPhil Potchef. Assoc. Prof.
Van Deventer, Kallie J., PhD Free State Sr. Lectr.
Venter, Ranel, MPhysEd Stell. Sr. Lectr.
Other Staff: 3 Lectrs.
Research: exercise physiology; kinanthropometry; perceptual motor aspects; sport history; sport psychology

Statistics and Actuarial Science

Tel: (021) 808 3244 Fax: (021) 808 3830
E-mail: brigott@sun.ac.za
Cilliers, H. M., MComm Stell. Sr. Lectr.
Clover, Rob J., BBusSc Cape Town, FIA Sr. Lectr.
Conradie, Willie J., MComm Stell., PhD Cape Town Assoc. Prof.
De Wet, Tertius, MSc Potchef., DSc Potchef. Prof.; Chair*
Le Roux, Niel J., MSc Stell., MSc Camb., MSc S.Af., PhD S.Af. Prof.
Louw, N., BSc Stell., BSc Pret., MSc Potchef., PhD Stell. Assoc. Prof.
Mostert, Paul J., BSc Potchef., MSc Pret., PhD S.Af. Assoc. Prof.
Nel, Daan G., MSc Free State, DSc Free State Prof.
Slattery, P. G., PhD Witw. Prof.
Steel, Sarel J., MSc Stell., PhD Stell. Prof.
Uys, Danie W., MSc Free State, PhD Stell. Sr. Lectr.
Van Deventer, Pieta J. U., BComm Stell., MSc Cape Town, PhD Cape Town Sr. Lectr.
Van Vuuren, Johan O., MSc P.Elizabeth, PhD Stell. Sr. Lectr.
Van Zyl, Natalie, BBusSc Cape Town Sr. Lectr.
Viljoen, Lienki, MMedSc Free State, PhD Potchef. Sr. Lectr.
Other Staff: 6 Lectrs.
Research: classification; extreme value theory; non-linear smoothing; regression; visualisation of multivariate data

Systematic Theology and Church History and Church Polity

Tel: (021) 808 3258 Fax: (021) 808 3251
E-mail: pc@sun.ac.za
Koopman, Nico N., BA W.Cape, DTh W.Cape Assoc. Prof.; Chair*
Smit, Dirk J., MA Stell., DTh Stell. Prof.
Vosloo, R. R., BA Stell., BTh Stell., MTh Stell., DTh W.Cape Sr. Lectr.
Research: church government (study of principles and systems); church history (ecumenical study of church history); ethics (anthropology and ethics); reformed theology in the (post)modern period; systematic theology (Christian doctrine and culture)

Viticulture and Oenology

Tel: (021) 808 4545 Fax: (021) 808 4781
E-mail: dww@sun.ac.za
Bauer, Florian F., MSc Bordeaux, PhD Bordeaux Prof.
Du Toit, Maret, MSc Stell., PhD Stell. Sr. Lectr.
Du Toit, Wessel J., MSc Stell., PhD(Agric) Stell. Sr. Lectr.
Vivier, Melane A., MSc Stell., PhD Stell. Prof.; Chair*
Other Staff: 6 Lectrs.; 3 Adjunct Profs.; 2 Adjunct Assoc. Profs.; 1 Temp. Prof.
Vacant Posts: 1 Sr. Lectr./Assoc. Prof.
Research: characterisation and identification of terrain (terroir); cultivar science (grapevine improvement, propagation, abnormalities and cultivation); grapevine cultivation; grapevine water relations, stress physiology and irrigation; table grape production

HEALTH SCIENCES

Tel: (021) 938 9204 Fax: (021) 938 9060
    E-mail: fcla@sun.ac.za

Anaesthesiology and Critical Care

Tel: (021) 938 9226 Fax: (021) 938 9144
    E-mail: ph1@sun.ac.za
Coetzee, André R., MB ChB Stell., MMed Stell.,
    MD Stell., PhD Stell., FFARCS   Prof.; Chair*
Coetzee, Johan F., BSc Stell., MB ChB Stell.,
    MMed Stell., PhD Stell.   Assoc. Prof.
Other Staff: 13 Consultants
Research: cardiac function, anaesthesia; cerebral
    blood flow, metabolism and function;
    hypotensive anaesthesia; pulmonary surgery
    and right ventricular function; total
    intravenous anaesthesia, pharmacokinetics

Biomedical Sciences

Anatomy and Histology

Tel: (021) 938 9397 Fax: (021) 931 7810
    E-mail: bjp@sun.ac.za
Chase, Carol C., MSc Stell., PhD Stell.   Sr. Lectr.
Du Toit, Don F., MB ChB Stell., PhD Stell., DPhil
    Oxf., FRCSEd   Prof.; Chair*
Labuschagne, Barend C. J., MB ChB Pret., BSc
    Potchef., MSc Pret., DSc Potchef.   Sr. Lectr.
Page, Ben J., MSc Stell., PhD Stell.   Sr. Lectr.
Vorster, Willie, MSc Stell., PhD Stell.   Sr. Lectr.
Other Staff: 1 Lectr.
Research: generation of reactive oxygen species
    (free hydroxil radicals) during infection
    and treatment of tuberculosis-infected
    patients; immune suppression of allogeneic
    transplanted foetal pancreas tissue beneath
    the renal subcapsular space; medical
    education; milky spots in the pleura of
    laboratory animals; return to
    normoglycaemia/euglycaemia in chemically
    induced diabetic laboratory animals

Medical Physiology

Tel: (021) 938 9389 Fax: (021) 938 9476
    E-mail: sa@sun.ac.za
Daniels, Willie M. U., BSc W.Cape, MSc Stell.,
    MBA Stell., PhD Stell.   Assoc. Prof.; Chair*
Du Plessis, Stephan S., MSc Stell., MBA Stell.,
    PhD Stell.   Sr. Lectr.
Du Toit, E. F. (Joss), MSc Stell., PhD Cape Town
    Sr. Lectr.
Koeslag, Johan H., MB ChB Cape Town, PhD
    Cape Town   Prof.
Moolman, Johan A., MB ChB Pret., MMed Stell.
    Assoc. Prof.
Other Staff: 1 Lectr.; 20 Med. Researchers
Research: cardiac ischaemia and reperfusion
    injury, and preconditioning; immunological
    aspects of tuberculosis pericarditis; the heart
    in non-insulin-dependent diabetes;
    tuberculosis

Molecular Biology and Human Genetics

Tel: (021) 938 9401 Fax: (021) 938 9476
    E-mail: serasmus@sun.ac.za
Bardien, Soraya, PhD Stell.   Sr. Lectr.
Van Helden, Paul D., PhD Cape Town   Prof.;
    Chair*
Van Pitius, Nico C. G., MSc Potchef., PhD Stell.
    Sr. Lectr.
Victor, Tommie C., BSc S.Af., PhD S.Af.   Assoc.
    Prof.
Walzl, Gerhard, MB ChB Pret., MMed Stell.,
    FCP(SA)   Assoc. Prof.
Other Staff: 59 Lectrs. and Scientists
Research: inherited genetic disorders;
    tuberculosis

Interdisciplinary Health Sciences

Community Health

Tel: (021) 938 9375 Fax: (021) 938 9166
    E-mail: fla@sun.ac.za
Cameron, Niel A., MB BCh Witw., BSc Stell.
    Sr. Lectr.
Carstens, Sydney E., MB ChB Stell., MMed Stell.
    Sr. Lectr.; Acting Chair*
Mehtar, S., MD Lond.   Assoc. Prof.

Other Staff: 1 Lectr.
Research: epidemiology and biostatistics; health
    administration and management;
    occupational and environmental health

Family Medicine and Primary Care

Tel: (021) 938 9440 Fax: (021) 938 9153
    E-mail: rvdwe@sun.ac.za
Bawoodien, Aziza, MB ChB Natal, MFamMed
    Stell.   Sr. Lectr.
De Villiers, Marietjie R., MB ChB Stell.,
    MFamMed Stell.   Prof.
De Villiers, Pierre J. T., BSc Stell., MB ChB Stell.,
    MFamMed Stell., PhD Stell.   Prof.; Chair*
Hill, P. V., MB ChB Cape Town   Sr. Lectr.
Mash, R. J. (Bob), MB ChB Edin., PhD Stell.
    Assoc. Prof.
Moodley, Keymenthri, MB ChB Natal, MPhil
    Stell.   Sr. Lectr.
Pather, Michael K., MB ChB Cape Town,
    MFamMed Stell.   Sr. Lectr.
Van Velden, David P., MB ChB Stell.,
    MPraxMed Pret.   Sr. Lectr.
Other Staff: 2 Lectrs.
Research: family medicine (clinical medicine as
    appropriate on the primary care level
    health-seeking behaviour of patients,
    preventive medicine, provider/patient
    relationship); practice management/
    community medicine (cost-effective
    medicine, epidemiology in primary care/
    family practice, health care to the indigent
    population, provision of primary health
    care services, surveillance in family
    practice)

Human Nutrition

Tel: (021) 933 1408 Fax: (021) 933 1405
    E-mail: nicus@sun.ac.za
Labadarios, Demetre, BSc Sur., MB ChB Stell.,
    PhD Sur.   Prof.; Chair*
Other Staff: 3 Lectrs.
Research: acute phase response; hospital and
    community malnutrition; micro-nutrient
    status; nutrition in renal disease

Nursing Science

Tel: (021) 938 9095 Fax: (021) 938 9723
    E-mail: umec@sun.ac.za
Chikte, Usef M. E., BChD W.Cape, MDent
    Witw., MSc Lond., PhD Stell.   Prof.; Acting
    Chair*
Stellenberg, Ethelwynn L., BCur W.Cape, MCur
    Stell.   Sr. Lectr.
Other Staff: 4 Lectrs.
Research: community health; critical care;
    maternal and child health

Occupational Therapy

Tel: (021) 938 9307 Fax: (021) 931 9308
    E-mail: nes@sun.ac.za
Beukes, Susan, BOccThy Stell., BScMedSci Stell.
    Sr. Lectr.; Chair*
Smit, M. E., BOccTher Pret., BOccThy Stell.,
    MBA Stell.   Sr. Lectr.
Other Staff: 6 Lectrs.
Research: work rehabilitation and work
    assessment

Physiotherapy

Tel: (021) 938 9300 Fax: (021) 931 7810
    E-mail: erein@sun.ac.za
Bester, M. M. (Ria), MSc W.Cape   Sr. Lectr.
Crous, Linette C., MSc Stell.   Sr. Lectr.; Chair*
Faure, M. R., BA S.Af., MPhil W.Cape   Sr. Lectr.
Frieg, Annette, MPhil Stell.   Sr. Lectr.
Other Staff: 7 Lectrs.
Research: cardiopulmonary research; community
    and primary care; orthopaedics;
    physiotherapy education

Speech-Language and Hearing Therapy

Tel: (021) 938 9586 Fax: (021) 931 7810
    E-mail: susannah@sun.ac.za
Swart, S. M., MSc Cape Town   Sr. Lectr.; Chair*
Other Staff: 6 Lectrs.

Research: communication disorders; disorders of
    fluency and voice; swallowing and feeding
    disorders

Medical Imaging and Clinical Oncology

Nuclear Medicine

Tel: (021) 938 4352 Fax: (021) 938 4694
    E-mail: pjoerdens@sun.ac.za
Ellmann, Annare, MB ChB Stell., MSc Stell.,
    MMed Stell.   Assoc. Prof.; Chair*
Korowlay, Nisaar, MB ChB Natal, MMed Cape
    Town   Sr. Lectr.
Rubow, Sietske M., BPharm Potchef., MSc Stell.,
    PhD Stell.   Sr. Lectr.
Warwick, James, MB ChB Cape Town, MMed
    Stell.   Sr. Lectr.
Other Staff: 3 Lectrs.
Research: functional brain single photon
    emission computer tomography (SPECT);
    infection imaging; management of
    hyperthyroidism; myocardial perfusion
    scintigraphy; oncological scintigraphy

Radiation Oncology

Tel: (021) 938 5992 Fax: (021) 931 0804
    E-mail: jdtoit@sun.ac.za
Vernimmen, Fred J. A. I., MD Ghent, MMed
    Natal   Prof.; Chair*
Other Staff: 3 Specialists; 5 Registrars
Research: electroporation of cells; photodynamic
    theory; prostate carcinoma

Radiodiagnosis

Tel: (021) 938 9320 Fax: (021) 931 7810
    E-mail: aj@sun.ac.za
Scher, Alan T., MB ChB Cape Town, FRCS
    Prof.; Chair*
Other Staff: 17 Registrars
Research: forensic radiology; neurological and
    neurosurgical imaging; rugby injuries to
    the cervical spine and spinal cord

Medicine

Dermatology

Tel: (021) 938 9139 Fax: (021) 932 9071
    E-mail: cdeb@sun.ac.za
Jordaan, H. Francois, MB ChB Stell., MMed Stell.
    Assoc. Prof.; Chair*
Other Staff: 1 Lectr.
Research: atopic dermatitis; macro/micro aspects
    of acne keloidalis nuchea; skin barrier
    function; skin tumours, histopathology;
    tuberculosis/HIV disease and skin

Internal Medicine

Tel: (021) 938 9044 Fax: (021) 931 7442
    E-mail: fsh@sun.ac.za
Ascott-Evans, B. H., MB ChB Cape Town,
    FCP(SA)   Assoc. Prof.
Bolliger, C. T., BSc Stell., MB ChB MMed MD
    Prof.
Bouwens, C. S. H., BSc Stell., MSc Stell., MEd
    Rotterdam, FCP(SA)   Sr. Lectr.
Brice, Edmund A., MB ChB Cape Town, PhD Cape
    Town   Sr. Lectr.
Brink, Paul A., MB ChB Stell., BSc Stell., MMed
    Stell., PhD Stell.   Prof.
Butler, J. T., MB ChB Cape Town, FCP(SA)   Sr.
    Lectr.
Carr, J., MB ChB Cape Town, FCP(SA)   Sr.
    Lectr.
Davids, M. R., MB ChB Stell., MMed Stell.,
    FCP(SA)   Sr. Lectr.
De Kock, A., MB ChB Stell., BSc Stell., MMed
    Stell.   Sr. Lectr.
Doubell, Anton F., BSc Stell., MB ChB Stell.,
    MMed Stell., PhD Stell., FCP(SA)   Prof.
Hough, F. Stephan, BSc Stell., MB ChB Stell.,
    MMed Stell., MD Stell., FCP(SA)   Prof.;
    Chair*
Irusen, E. M., MB ChB Natal, FCP(SA)   Assoc.
    Prof.
Jacobs, P., MB ChB Stell., MD Witw., PhD Witw.
    Extraordinary Prof.
Joubert, James R., BSc Stell., MB ChB Stell.,
    MMed Stell., MD Stell., FCP(SA)   Emer. Prof.

Manie, M., MB ChB *Cape Town*, MMed *Stell.*, FCP(SA) Sr. Lectr.

Moosa, M. R., MB ChB *Cape Town*, FCP(SA) Assoc. Prof.

Prozesky, H. W., MB ChB *Stell.*, MMed *Stell.* Sr. Lectr.

Schmidt, Adrian, MB ChB *Pret.*, MMed *Stell.* Sr. Lectr.

Van de Wal, Bernard W., MB ChB *Pret.*, MMed *Pret.* Assoc. Prof.

Van Rensburg, C. J., MB ChB *Stell.*, MMed *Stell.* Sr. Lectr.

Whitelaw, D. A., MB ChB *Cape Town*, BSc *Witw.*, PhD *Lond.*, FCP(SA) Sr. Lectr.

Wilken, E., MB ChB *Stell.*, MMed *Stell.* Sr. Lectr.

Other Staff: 20 Lectrs.; 3 Med. Researchers
Research: cardiology; endocrinology; gastroenterology; nephrology; neurology

Pharmacology

Tel: (021) 938 9331 Fax: (021) 932 6958
E-mail: pvdb@sun.ac.za

Lamprecht, J. H., MB ChB *Stell.*, BSc *Stell.* Sr. Lectr.

Müller, Gerbus J., BSc *Stell.*, MB ChB *Stell.*, MMed *Stell.*, PhD *Stell.* Sr. Lectr.

Van der Bijl, Pieter, BSc *Cape Town*, BChD *Stell.*, BScMedSci *Stell.*, PhD *Cape Town*, DSc *Stell.* Prof.; Chair*

Other Staff: 1 Lectr.; 15 Med. Researchers
Vacant Posts: 1 Lectr.
Research: biological toxicology; gene delivery to cells; medicinal applications of phytosterols; permeability studies; tuberculosis

Obstetrics and Gynaecology

Tel: (021) 938 9209 Fax: (021) 931 7810
E-mail: hkr@sun.ac.za

De Jong, Grietjie, BSc *Stell.*, MB ChB *Stell.*, MMed *Stell.*, MD *Stell.* Sr. Lectr.

Franken, Danie R., BSc *OFS*, MMedSc *OFS*, PhD *OFS* Assoc. Prof.

Geerts, Lut T. G. M., MD *Leuven* Sr. Lectr.

Hall, D. R., MB ChB *Stell.*, MMed *Stell.*, MD *Stell.* Assoc. Prof.

Kruger, Thinus F., MB ChB *Pret.*, MMed *Pret.*, MMed *Stell.*, MD *Stell.*, FRCOG Prof.; Chair*

Menkveld, R., BScAgric *Stell.*, BSc *Stell.*, MScMedSc *Stell.*, PhD *Stell.* Sr. Lectr.

Reinhardt, G. W., MB ChB *Stell.*, MMed *Stell.* Sr. Lectr.

Steyn, D. W., MB ChB *Stell.*, MMed *Stell.*, MD *Stell.* Assoc. Prof.

Steyn, P. S., MB ChB *Stell.*, MMed *Stell.*, MPhil *Stell.* Sr. Lectr.

Theron, Gerhard B., BSc *Stell.*, MB ChB *Stell.*, MMed *Stell.*, MD *Stell.* Prof.

Van der Merwe, J. P., MB ChB *Stell.*, MMed *Stell.* Sr. Lectr.

Other Staff: 10 Lectrs.
Research: gynaecological oncology; human genetics; maternal foetal medicine; perinatal mortality; reproductive health

Paediatrics and Child Health

Tel: (021) 938 9506 Fax: (021) 938 9138
E-mail: aec1@sun.ac.za

Beyers, Nulda, MB ChB *Stell.*, MSc(Med) *Cape Town*, PhD *Stell.*, FCP(SA) Prof.

Cotton, Mark F., MB ChB *Stell.*, MMed *Stell.*, FCP(SA) Sr. Lectr.

Donald, Peter R., MB ChB *Stell.*, MD *Stell.*, FCP(SA) Emer. Prof.

Gie, Robert P., MB ChB *Stell.*, MMed *Stell.*, FCP(SA) Prof.

Henning, Philip A., MB ChB *Stell.*, MMed *Stell.* Sr. Lectr.

Hesseling, Pieter B., MB ChB *Stell.*, MMed *Stell.*, MD *Stell.* Emer. Prof.

Kirsten, Gert F., MB ChB *Pret.*, MMed *Pret.*, MD *Stell.*, FCP(SA) Prof.

Kling, Sharon, MB ChB *Cape Town*, FCP(SA) Sr. Lectr.

Lawrenson, J., MB ChB *Witw.*, MMed *Cape Town* Sr. Lectr.

Nel, Etienne D., BSc *Stell.*, MB ChB *Stell.*, MMed *Stell.* Sr. Lectr.

Pieper, Clarissa H., MB ChB *OFS*, MMed *Stell.* Sr. Lectr.

Schaaf, H. Simon, MB ChB *Stell.*, MMed *Stell.* Assoc. Prof.

Schoeman, Johan F., MB ChB *Stell.*, MMed *Stell.*, MD *Stell.*, FCP(SA) Assoc. Prof.

Smith, Johan, MB ChB *Stell.*, MMed *Stell.* Assoc. Prof.

Van Buuren, A. J. (Tony), BSc *Stell.*, MB ChB *Stell.*, MMed *Stell.* Sr. Lectr.

Van der Merwe, Peter L., MB ChB *Stell.*, MMed *Stell.*, MD *Stell.*, FCP(SA) Prof.; Chair*

Wessels, Glynn, MB ChB *Stell.*, MMed *Stell.*, MD *Stell.* Assoc. Prof.

Other Staff: 16 Lectrs.
Research: cardiology (congenital anomalies); childhood cancer (epidemiology, Burkitt's lymphoma); HIV/AIDS (apoptosis/family clinic); neonatology (infection, nutrition, ventilation); tuberculosis (epidemiology, meningitis, pharmacology, drugs)

Pathology

Forensic Medicine

Tel: (021) 938 8043 Fax: (021) 933 3367
E-mail: saw@sun.ac.za

Schwar, T. G., MB ChB *Pret.*, MD *Heidel.*, FRCPath Emer. Prof.

Wadee, S. A., BSc *Wat.*, MB ChB *Natal*, MMed *Natal* Prof.; Chief Specialist; Chair*

Other Staff: 3 Lectrs.
Vacant Posts: 1 Specialist Lectr.
Research: gunshot injuries; paraquat poisoning; sudden cardiac death in adults; sudden infant death syndrome

Medical Microbiology

Tel: (021) 938 4032 Fax: (021) 938 4005
E-mail: medmicro@sun.ac.za

Forder, A. A., MB ChB *Cape Town*, MMed *Cape Town* Emer. Prof.

Liebowitz, Lynne D., BSc *Rhodes*, MB BCh *Witw.*, PhD *Witw.*, FRCPath Prof.; Chair*

Wasserman, E., MB ChB *OFS*, MMed *Stell.*, DPhil *Stell.* Prof.

Other Staff: 4 Lectrs.
Research: cross-reactivity between phospholipid antibodies and brain antigens in systemic lupus erythematosus (SLE) patients with cerebral lupus; health and environmental quality studies; immune response of patients in receipt of intra-vesicular Bacille Calmette Guerin (BCG); intestinal parasites; taxonomy and physiology of heparin-degrading bacteria

Medical Virology

Tel: (021) 938 9354 Fax: (021) 938 9361
E-mail: sal@sun.ac.za

Korsman, Stephan, MB ChB *Pret.*, MMed *Stell.* Sr. Lectr.

Preiser, Wolfgang, DrMed *F.H.Frankfurt*, DrMedHabil *F.H.Frankfurt*, DTM *Lond.* Prof.; Chair*

Van Zyl, Gert U., MB ChB *Pret.*, MMed *Stell.* Prof.

Other Staff: 3 Registrars
Research: analysis of host genetic susceptibility to HIV/AIDS; characterisation of human herpes virus 8 (HHV-8) strains circulating in South Africa; construction of a chimeric simian/human immunodeficiency virus (SHIV) using a South African HIV-1 subtype C envelope gene; HIV-1 sub-type C vaccine development for South Africa

Pathology, Anatomical

Tel: (021) 938 4041 Fax: (021) 938 6559
E-mail: jws2@sun.ac.za

Schneider, Johann W., MB ChB *Stell.*, MMed *Stell.* Prof.

Wranz, Peter A. B., MB ChB *Witw.*, MMed *Pret.*, MMed *Stell.*, FRCOG Emer. Prof.

Wright, C. A., MB BCh *Witw.*, FRCPath Assoc. Prof.; Chair*

Other Staff: 8 Lectrs.
Research: dermatopathology, including tuberculosis; gynaecological pathology and cytopathology; paediatric pathology; pulmonary pathology, including tuberculosis; renal pathology

Pathology, Chemical

Tel: (021) 938 4107 Fax: (021) 938 4640
E-mail: rte@sun.ac.za

Erasmus, R. T., MB BS *Ib.* Prof.; Chair*

Meyer, Carel, MB ChB *Stell.*, MMed *Stell.* Sr. Lectr.

Other Staff: 4 Lectrs.; 2 Med. Researchers
Research: endocrinology; HIV; hypoxia and obesity; lipidology; neurodegenerative diseases (Alzheimer's)

Pathology, Haematological

Tel: (021) 938 4610 Fax: (021) 938 4609
E-mail: wk@sun.ac.za

Mansvelt, Erna P. G., MB ChB *Stell.*, MMed *Stell.*, MD *Stell.* Assoc. Prof.; Chair*

Other Staff: 2 Lectrs.
Research: chronic lymphocytic leukaemia; hereditary thrombophilia; myeloma; platelet flow cytometry; platelet function

Psychiatry

Tel: (021) 938 9227 Fax: (021) 938 9116
E-mail: bas@sun.ac.za

Emsley, Robin A., MB ChB *Cape Town*, MMed *Stell.*, MD *Stell.* Prof.; Chair*

Gerber, Mickey F., MA *Stell.*, DPhil *Stell.* Sr. Lectr.

Oosthuizen, Piet P., MB ChB *Free State*, MMed *Stell.* Assoc. Prof.

Pienaar, Willie P., MB ChB *Stell.*, MMed *Stell.*, MD *Stell.*, MPhil *Stell.* Assoc. Prof.

Seedat, S., MB ChB *Natal*, MMed *Stell.* Assoc. Prof.

Other Staff: 22 Lectrs.; 6 Researchers
Research: anxiety and stress disorders; genetics of psychiatric disorders; neuropsychiatry, including Alzheimer's, Tourette's and head injury; psychopharmacology; schizophrenia and first-episode psychosis

Surgical Sciences

Cardiothoracic Surgery

Tel: (021) 938 9432 Fax: (021) 931 7810
E-mail: swvz@sun.ac.za

Rossouw, Gawie J., MB ChB *Stell.*, MMed *Stell.* Assoc. Prof.; Chair*

Other Staff: 4 Specialists
Research: anxiety disorder in rheumatic heart disease; environmental, societal and genetic markers for the development of oesophageal cancer in different population groups in the Western Cape; evaluation of platelet function after cardio-pulmonary bypass; subtle neurologic dysfunction after cardiopulmonary bypass

Neurosurgery

Tel: (021) 938 9265 Fax: (021) 931 7810
E-mail: hbh@sun.ac.za

Hartzenberg, H. Bennie, MB ChB *Cape Town*, MMed *Stell.* Assoc. Prof.; Chair*

Other Staff: 4 Lectrs.; 3 Consultants
Research: craniofacial surgery; intracranial pathology including tumour, vascular and endocrinological surgery; spinal surgery

Ophthalmology

Tel: (021) 938 9380 Fax: (021) 931 8437
E-mail: mms@sun.ac.za

Meyer, David, BSc *Potchef.*, MB ChB *Stell.*, MMed *Stell.* Prof.; Chair*

Other Staff: 7 Lectrs.; 3 Consultants
Research: medical and surgical retina; oculoplastic and orbital surgery; paediatric ophthalmology

Orthopaedic Surgery

Tel: (021) 938 9266 Fax: (021) 931 7810
  E-mail: gjv@sun.ac.za
Vlok, Gert J., MB ChB Stell., MMed Stell.   Prof.;
  Chair*
Other Staff: 6 Specialists; 2 Consultants
Research: foot surgery; paediatric orthopaedics;
  patient care; spinal problems; trauma

Otorhinolaryngology

Tel: (021) 938 9318 Fax: (021) 938 9470
  E-mail: ah@sun.ac.za
Lehmann, Karen, MB ChB Stell., MMed Stell.
  Sr. Lectr.
Loock, J. W., MB ChB Cape Town, FCS(SA)
  Prof.; Chair*
Other Staff: 2 Lectrs.
Research: head and neck surgery; otology and
  paediatric airways; rhinology; voice
  rehabilitation

Plastic and Reconstructive Surgery

Tel: (021) 938 9432 Fax: (021) 931 7810
  E-mail: swvz@gerga.sun.ac.za
Bruce-Chwatt, Andrew J., MD Malta, FRCS   Sr.
  Lectr.
Graewe, Frank R., MB ChB Pret., MMed Stell.,
  DrMed T.U.Munich   Assoc. Prof.; Chair*
Other Staff: 4 Registrars
Research: aesthetic surgery; cranio-facial surgery;
  lower leg reconstruction; microvascular
  surgery; surgery of cleft lip and palate

Surgery (General)

Tel: (021) 938 9273 Fax: (021) 933 7999
  E-mail: me@sun.ac.za
Apffelstaedt, Justus P., MMed Stell., DrMed
  Würzburg, FCS(SA)   Assoc. Prof.
Moore, Sam W., MB ChB Cape Town, MD Cape
  Town, FRCSEd   Prof.
Warren, Brian L., MB ChB Cape Town, MMed
  Stell., FCS(SA), FRCSEd   Prof.; Chair*
Other Staff: 9 Lectrs.
Research: epidemiology and management of
  trauma; gastro-enterology; head, neck and
  breast surgery; laparoscopic surgical
  techniques; paediatric surgery

Urology

Tel: (021) 938 9282 Fax: (021) 933 8010
  E-mail: nsmuts@sun.ac.za
Heyns, Chris F., MB ChB Stell., MMed Stell.,
  PhD Stell., FCS(SA)   Prof.; Chair*
Other Staff: 2 Lectrs.
Research: erectile dysfunction; laparoscopic
  surgery in urology; male urethral strictures;
  molecular genetics and clinical
  epidemiology of prostatic carcinoma

SPECIAL CENTRES, ETC

Advanced Production, Unit for (SENROB)

Tel: (021) 808 4327 Fax: (021) 808 4245
  E-mail: august@sun.ac.za
Fourie, C. J. (Neels), BEng Pret., MEng Stell.,
  PhD(Eng) Stell.   Dir.*

Advanced Study, Stellenbosch Institute for

Tel: (021) 808 2185 Fax: (021) 808 2184
  E-mail: bcl@sun.ac.za
Lategan, Bernard, PhD Stell.   Prof.; Dir.*
Research: complexity theory; good governance
  and poverty relief; HIV strain dynamics;
  renewable bio-energy; the quality of young
  democracies

Anxiety and Stress Disorder Research Unit

Tel: (021) 938 9161 Fax: (021) 933 5790
  E-mail: djs2@sun.ac.za
Steyn, Dan J., PhD Stell.   Dir.*
Other Staff: 1 Researcher
Research: counselling; trauma

Applied Ethics, Centre for

Tel: (021) 808 2418 Fax: (021) 886 3556
  E-mail: aavn@sun.ac.za
Hattingh, Johann P., MA Stell., DPhil Stell.
  Head, Unit for Environmental Ethics
Van Niekerk, Anton A., BTh Stell., MA Stell.,
  DPhil Stell.   Head, Unit for Bioethics; Dir.*

Bible Translation in Africa, Centre for

Tel: (021) 808 3655 Fax: (021) 808 3480
  E-mail: cvdm@sun.ac.za
Van der Merwe, Christo H. J., MA Stell., MTh
  Stell., DLitt Stell.   Dir.*
Other Staff: 2 Co-ordinators; 1 Res. Partner

Care and Rehabilitation of the Disabled, Centre for

Tel: (021) 938 9090 Fax: (021) 931 9835
  E-mail: annettec@sun.ac.za
Mji, G., BSc S.Af.Med., MScPhysio Cape Town
  Head*
Other Staff: 1 Sr. Lectr.
Research: community-based rehabilitation
  (Zambia); criteria for prosthetic prescription
  (lower limb); profiles of disability grant
  recipients; rehabilitation programme
  evaluation

Continuing Theological Training and Research, Bureau for (BUVTON)

Tel: (021) 808 3381 Fax: (021) 886 5701
  E-mail: cwbu@sun.ac.za
Burger, Coenie W., BA Stell., DTh Stell.   Dir.*
Other Staff: 1 Sr. Researcher; 5 Project
  Managers
Research: congregation and community (to
  guide congregations in community
  development); faith formation and value
  formation (principles and guidelines);
  liturgy and worship (programmes and
  lectionaries for congregations); practical
  ecclesiology (bridging the division between
  ideal and reality); responsible citizenship
  (challenging faith communities and their
  value systems)

DNA Sequencer, Unit of

Tel: (021) 808 2836 Fax: (021) 808 2837
  E-mail: hdw@sun.ac.za
Burger, Johan T., BScAgric Stell., PhD Cape Town
  Assoc. Prof.; Dir.*
Other Staff: 1 Analyst
Research: capillary electrophresis; plasmid DNA
  extraction

Economic Research, Bureau for (BER)

Tel: (021) 887 2810 Fax: (021) 883 9225
  E-mail: hhman@sun.ac.za
Kershoff, George, MA Stell.   Deputy Dir.
Smit, Ben W., MComm Stell., DComm Stell.
  Dir.*
Other Staff: 8 Researchers; 4 Consultants

Educational Psychology, Unit for

Tel: (021) 808 2315 Fax: (021) 808 2021
  E-mail: pjn@sun.ac.za
Louw, C., MA Stell.   Head*
Research: behaviour management; development;
  learning

Fluorescence Live Cell Imaging Microscopy Unit

Tel: (021) 808 2836 Fax: (021) 808 2837
  E-mail: hdw@sun.ac.za
Smith, Rob, BSc Sund., PhD Bath   Dir.*
Other Staff: 1 Researcher
Research: Foerster Resonance Energy Transfer
  (FRET); multi-colour and generic frame
  procedure (GFP) imaging; time-lapse
  imaging

Futures Research, Institute for (IFR)

Tel: (021) 918 4144 Fax: (021) 918 4146
  E-mail: future@fir.sun.ac.za
Roux, André, PhD Stell.   Dir.*
Other Staff: 1 Sr. Researcher

Research: future prospects; scenario planning and
  strategic support services for management;
  systems thinking

Geographical Analysis, Centre for

Tel: (021) 808 3103 Fax: (021) 808 2405
  E-mail: geom@sun.ac.za
Van der Merwe, J. H. (Hannes), DPhil Stell.
  Dir.*
Research: resource studies; urban studies

Higher and Adult Education, Centre for

Tel: (021) 808 2277 Fax: (021) 808 2270
  E-mail: dkruger@sun.ac.za
Bitzer, Eli M., BA OFS, DEd OFS   Prof.; Dir.*
Kapp, Chris A., BA P.Elizabeth, BA S.Af., DEd Stell.
  Prof.; Dir.*
Other Staff: 1 Programme Co-ordinator
Research: consultation, mentoring and facilitation
  of processes (transformation, strategic
  planning); instructional and course design;
  instructional and training methods for
  effective learning; leadership development
  and training; staff development

HIV/AIDS Management, Africa Centre for

Tel: (021) 808 3002 E-mail: pdm@sun.ac.za
Du Toit, Jan B., MA Stell., DPhil Stell.   Assoc.
  Prof.; Dir.*
Research: HIV/AIDS awareness; HIV/AIDS
  management

Industrial Engineering, Institute for

Tel: (021) 808 4244 Fax: (021) 808 4245
  E-mail: jb2@sun.ac.za
Von Leipzig, Konrad H., BCom S.Af., MEng
  Stell.   Dir.*

Industrial Mathematics, Bureau for (BIMUS)

Tel: (021) 808 4219 Fax: (021) 808 3778
  E-mail: fsmit@sun.ac.za
Smit, G. J. Francois, PhD Stell.   Dir.*
Other Staff: 12 Experts
Research: coastal hydrodynamics; cryptology;
  graph theory; morphology; non-linear
  waves, signal and image processing

Invasion Biology, Centre for (CIB)

Tel: (021) 808 2832 Fax: (021) 808 2995
  E-mail: rambau@sun.ac.za
Chown, Steven L., BSc Pret., PhD Pret.   Prof.;
  Dir.*
Richardson, Dave M., BSc Stell., MSc Cape Town,
  PhD Cape Town   Deputy Dir.
Other Staff: 15 Researchers

Knowledge Dynamics and Decision-making, Centre for

Tel: (021) 808 2423 Fax: (021) 808 2117
  E-mail: nodysa@sun.ac.za
Kinghorn, Johann, BA Pret., DTh Stell.   Dir.*
Other Staff: 10 Lectrs.; 1 Sr. Researcher

Language and Speech Technology, Centre for (SU-CLaST)

Tel: (021) 808 2017 Fax: (021) 808 3975
  E-mail: jcr@sun.ac.za
Roux, Justus C., DLitt Stell.   Prof.; Dir.*
Other Staff: 9 Researchers; 3 Assocs.

Language Centre

Tel: (021) 808 2167 Fax: (021) 808 3676
  E-mail: mjoyce@sun.ac.za
De Stadler, Leon G., MA Stell., DLitt Stell.
  Assoc. Prof.; Dir.*
Other Staff: 16 Researchers
Research: document design; official South
  African languages

Laser Research Institute (LRI)

Tel: (021) 808 3658 Fax: (021) 808 3358
  E-mail: hmvb@sun.ac.za
Von Bergmann, Hubertus M., PhD Natal
  Prof.; Dir.*
Other Staff: 3 Lectrs.

Research: confocal microscope; femtosecond laser; gas lasers; laser spectroscopy; solid-state lasers

Mass Spectrometry Unit (MSU)

Tel: (021) 808 2836 Fax: (021) 808 2837
   E-mail: hdw@sun.ac.za
Swart, Pieter, PhD *Stell.*   Chair*
Research: amino acid analysis; polar non-volatile molecules

Mathematics and Science Teaching, Institute for (IMSTUS)

Tel: (021) 808 3483 Fax: (021) 808 3000
   E-mail: jhs@sun.ac.za
Smit, J. H. (Kosie), MSc *Stell.*, DrWisNat *Ley.*
   Dir.*
Other Staff: 9 Lectrs.
Research: mathematics material for curriculum 2005; strategies to empower second language learners

Mathematics Education, Research Unit for (RUMEUS)

Tel: (021) 808 2299 Fax: (021) 808 2295
   E-mail: aio@sun.ac.za
Olivier, Alwyn I., BSc *Stell.*, MEd *Stell.*   Sr.
   Lectr.; Dir.*
Other Staff: 1 Sr. Researcher; 6 Res. Fellows
Research: learners' computational and algebraic learning

Mental Health Information, Centre for

Tel: (021) 938 9229 Fax: (021) 931 4172
   E-mail: mhic@sun.ac.za
De Roover, Winnie, MA *Cape Town*, MA *Ghent*
   Dir.*
Other Staff: 1 Manager
Research: mental health consumer research; obsessive compulsive disorder; specific phobia; traumatic stress disorder

Military Studies, Centre for (CEMIS)

Tel: (022) 702 3093 Fax: (022) 702 3060
   E-mail: lindy@ma2.sun.ac.za
Heinecken, Lindy P. T., MSocSc *Cape Town*, PhD
   Lond.   Assoc. Prof.; Deputy Dir.*
Other Staff: 3 Researchers
Research: security studies

Nuclear Magnetic Resonance Laboratory (NMR)

Tel: (021) 808 2836 Fax: (021) 808 2837
   E-mail: hdw@sun.ac.za
Koch, Klaus R., PhD *Cape Town*   Prof.; Dir.*
Other Staff: 1 Researcher; 1 Analyst

Plant Biotechnology, Institute for (IPB)

Tel: (021) 808 3834 Fax: (021) 808 3835
   E-mail: ipb@sun.ac.za
Kossman, Jens M., DrRerNatHabil *T.U.Berlin*,
   DrScAgr *T.U.Berlin*   Prof.; Dir.*
Other Staff: 2 Sr. Researchers; 2 Researchers
Research: genetic manipulation of plant tissue; isolation of plant growth promoters; regulation of carbohydrate and organic acid metabolism

Polymer Science, Institute for

Includes UNESCO Associated Centre for Macromolecules and Materials

Tel: (021) 808 3172 Fax: (021) 808 4967
   E-mail: rds@sun.ac.za
Sanderson, Ron D., BSc *Cape Town*, PhD *Akron*
   Dir.*
Other Staff: 3 Lectrs.; 2 Researchers; 7 Indust.
   Consultants

Process Engineering, Centre for

Tel: (021) 808 4485 Fax: (021) 808 2059
   E-mail: ajburger@sun.ac.za
Burger, André J., MEng *Stell.*, PhD(Eng) *Stell.*
   Prof.; Dir.*
Other Staff: 11 Researchers
Research: high-temperature material processing; intelligent process systems; mineral processing; reactive systems and

environmental technology; thermal separation technology

Religion and Development Research, Unit for (URDR)

Tel: (021) 808 3577 Fax: (021) 808 3251
   E-mail: egdn@sun.ac.za
Hendriks, H. Jurgens, BTh *Stell.*, MA *Stell.*, DLitt
   Stell.   Prof.; Dir.*
Other Staff: 3 Researchers
Research: religious demographic research

Science and Technology, Centre for Research on (CREST)

Tel: (021) 808 2393 Fax: (021) 808 2023
   E-mail: jm6@sun.ac.za
Mouton, Johann, BA *Rand Afrikaans*, DLitt&Phil
   Rand Afrikaans   Prof.; Dir.*
Other Staff: 4 Researchers
Research: dynamics of knowledge production; higher education; science policy studies in South Africa

Single Crystal X-Ray Diffraction Unit

Tel: (021) 808 2836 Fax: (021) 808 2837
   E-mail: hdw@sun.ac.za
Barbour, Len J., PhD *Cape Town*   Assoc. Prof.;
   Dir.*
Esterhuysen, Catharine E., PhD *Rand Afrikaans*
   Sr. Lectr.

Sport Science, Institute for

Tel: (021) 808 4724 Fax: (021) 808 4817
   E-mail: fjgvdm@sun.ac.za
Van der Merwe, Floris J. G., MA *Stell.*,
   MPhysEd *Stell.*, DPhil *Potchef.*   Assoc. Prof.;
   Dir.*
Research: attitudes toward sport; needs of the physically disabled

Statistical Consultation, Centre for

Tel: (021) 808 3240 Fax: (021) 808 3830
   E-mail: dgnel@sun.ac.za
Kidd, M., PhD *Stell.*   Sr. Lectr.
Nel, Daan G., MSc *Free State*, DSc *Free State*
   Prof.; Dir.*
Research: statistical interpretation and analysis

Teaching and Learning, Centre for (SOL)

Tel: (021) 808 3717 Fax: (021) 886 4142
   E-mail: bleibowitz@sun.ac.za
Leibowitz, Brenda, PhD *Stell.*   Sr. Lectr.; Dir.*
Other Staff: 5 Sr. Advisors

Theatre Research, Centre for

Tel: (021) 808 3216 Fax: (021) 808 3086
   E-mail: satj@sun.ac.za
Hauptfleisch, Temple, BA *OFS*, DLitt&Phil *S.Af.*
   Dir.*
Other Staff: 1 Researcher; 6 Assoc. Researchers

Theoretical Physics, Institute for

Tel: (021) 808 3658 Fax: (021) 808 4336
   E-mail: hbg@sun.ac.za
Geyer, Hendrik B., MSc *Rand Afrikaans*, PhD *Stell.*
   Prof.; Dir.*
Other Staff: 4 Sr. Researchers
Research: complex systems; condensed matter physics; quantum field theory

Thermodynamics and Mechanics, Institute for

Tel: (021) 808 4250 Fax: (021) 808 4958
   E-mail: ahb@sun.ac.za
Basson, Anton H., MEng *Stell.*, PhD *Penn.State*
   Prof.; Dir.*
Other Staff: 15 Researchers
Research: air conditioning; computational fluid dynamics; heat exchangers; thermosyphons; transient response of systems

Wine Biotechnology, Institute for (IWBT)

Tel: (021) 808 3770 Fax: (021) 808 3771
   E-mail: iwbt@sun.ac.za
Bauer, Florian F., MSc *Bordeaux*, PhD *Bordeaux*
   Prof.

Du Toit, Maret, MSc *Stell.*, PhD *Stell.*   Sr. Lectr.
Vivier, Melane A., MSc *Stell.*, PhD *Stell.*   Prof.;
   Dir.*
Other Staff: 2 Researchers
Vacant Posts: 1 Sr. Researcher; 1 Researcher
Research: analytical chemistry; grapevine molecular biology and systems biology; wine biotechnology

X-ray and Electron-Microbeam Unit

Tel: (021) 808 2836 Fax: (021) 808 2837
   E-mail: hdw@sun.ac.za
Stevens, Gary, MSc *Rand Afrikaans*, PhD *UMIST*
   Prof.; Dir.*
Other Staff: 3 Analysts
Research: scanning electron microscopy and microanalysis; x-ray diffraction; x-ray fluorescence spectrometry

CONTACT OFFICERS

Academic affairs. Registrar: Aspeling, Johann A., MComm *Stell.* (E-mail: jaa@sun.ac.za)
Accommodation. Head, Admissions and Accommodation: Blanche, Susan E. (E-mail: seb@sun.ac.za)
Admissions (first degree). Head, Admissions and Accommodation: Blanche, Susan E. (E-mail: seb@sun.ac.za)
Admissions (higher degree). Head, Admissions and Accommodation: Blanche, Susan E. (E-mail: seb@sun.ac.za)
Adult/continuing education. Head, Distance Education: De Klerk, A., BA *Stell.* (E-mail: adklerk@sun.ac.za)
Alumni. Co-ordinator, Alumni: Van Heerden, Sydney G., BA *Stell.* (E-mail: svheerd@sun.ac.za)
Archives. Archivist: Heese, Hans F., BA *Stell.*, MA *Cape Town*, PhD *Cape Town* (E-mail: fheese@sun.ac.za)
Careers. Director, Centre for Student Counselling and Development: Cilliers, Prof. Charl D., BA *Stell.*, DEd *Stell.* (E-mail: cdc@sun.ac.za)
Computing services. Senior Director, Information Technology: Dreijer, Helmi W., MBA *Stell.*, MEng *Stell.* (E-mail: mwd@sun.ac.za)
Conferences/corporate hospitality. Head, Marketing and Communication: Van der Merwe, Susan, BJourn *Stell.* (E-mail: svdmerwe@sun.ac.za)
Credit transfer. Registrar: Aspeling, Johann A., MComm *Stell.* (E-mail: jaa@sun.ac.za)
Development/fund-raising. Director, Stellenbosch Foundation: Uys, D. Sunley, BA *Stell.*, MBA *Stell.* (E-mail: dsu@sun.ac.za)
Estates and buildings/works and services. Director, Physical Infrastructure: Du Plessis, Reenen, BEng *Stell.*, MEng *Pret.* (E-mail: rdp2@sun.ac.za)
Examinations. Head, Examinations: Louw, M. C. L., BComm *Stell.* (E-mail: mcllouw@sun.ac.za)
Finance. Senior Director, Finance: Lombard, H. A. J. (Manie), BAcc *Stell.*, BComm *Stell.*, BCompt *S.Af.* (E-mail: hajl2@sun.ac.za)
General enquiries. Registrar: Aspeling, Johann A., MComm *Stell.* (E-mail: jaa@sun.ac.za)
Health services. Medical Officer, Student Health Service: Kotze, H. E., MB ChB *Stell.* (E-mail: hk@sun.ac.za)
International office. Director, International Office: Kotzé, Robert J., BTh *Stell.*, MA *Stell.* (E-mail: rk@sun.ac.za)
Language training for international students. Head of Unit, English Language Programme for International Students: Ellis, Jeanne, BA *Stell.*, MA *Stell.* (E-mail: jellis@sun.ac.za)
Library (chief librarian). Acting Director, Library Services: Engelbrecht, Johan P. J., BBibl *Pret.*, MBibl *Stell.* (E-mail: jpe@sun.ac.za)
Marketing. Manager, Communication: Shaikh, Mohamed, MJourn *Stell.* (E-mail: shaikh@sun.ac.za)

Personnel/human resources. Assistant Director, Human Resources: Geldenhuys, B. Johan, BComm *Stell.* (E-mail: bjg@sun.ac.za)

Public relations. Head, Liaison Services: Van der Merwe, Susan, BJourn *Stell.* (E-mail: svdmerwe@sun.ac.za)

Publications. Manager, Communication: Shaikh, Mohamed, MJourn *Stell.* (E-mail: shaikh@sun.ac.za)

Purchasing. Head, Purchasing and Provision: Durand, Willie H. (E-mail: whdr@sun.ac.za)

Quality assurance and accreditation. Director, Academic Planning and Quality Assurance: Botha, Prof. Jan, ThB *Potchef.*, MA *Stell.*, DTh *Stell.* (E-mail: jb3@sun.ac.za)

Research. Senior Director, Research: Engelbrecht, Petra, MEd *Pret.*, PhD *Pret.* (E-mail: peng@sun.ac.za)

Safety. Head, Campus Security: Van der Walt, Viljoen, BA *S.Af.*, BMil *Stell.* (E-mail: vvdw@sun.ac.za)

Scholarships, awards, loans. (Postgraduate) Head, Postgraduate Bursaries: Zietsman, Elva M., BA *Pret.* (E-mail: ez@sun.ac.za)

Scholarships, awards, loans. (Undergraduate) Head, Bursaries and Loans: Hanekom, Arrie, BSc *Stell.*, BSc *Potchef.*, BEd *S.Af.* (E-mail: ahan@sun.ac.za)

Schools liaison. Deputy Director, Prospective Students: Van den Heever, P. Leon, BA *Stell.*, BEd *Stell.* (E-mail: lvdh@sun.ac.za)

Security. Head, Campus Security: Van der Walt, Viljoen, BA *S.Af.*, BMil *Stell.* (E-mail: vvdw@sun.ac.za)

Sport and recreation. Director, Sports Bureau: Wiese, J. E., BPhysEd *Stell.* (E-mail: jew@sun.ac.za)

Staff development and training. Training Officer: Knight, Jan A., BEcon *Stell.* (E-mail: jkn@sun.ac.za)

Student union. Dean of Students: Kotzé, Robert J., BTh *Stell.*, MA *Stell.* (E-mail: rk@sun.ac.za)

Student welfare/counselling. Director, Centre for Student Counselling and Development: Cilliers, Prof. Charl D., BA *Stell.*, DEd *Stell.* (E-mail: cdc@sun.ac.za)

Students from other countries. Director, International Office: Kotzé, Robert J., BTh *Stell.*, MA *Stell.* (E-mail: rk@sun.ac.za)

Students with disabilities. Director, Services: Human, Etienne, BA *Stell.* (E-mail: eh1@sun.ac.za)

[Information supplied by the institution as at 10 October 2007, and edited by the ACU]

TSHWANE UNIVERSITY OF TECHNOLOGY

Founded 2004

Member of the Association of Commonwealth Universities

Postal Address: Private Bag X680, Pretoria, 0001 South Africa
Telephone: (012) 382 4112 **Fax:** (012) 382 5422 **E-mail:** tyobekaem@tut.ac.za
URL: http://www.tut.ac.za

VICE-CHANCELLOR AND PRINCIPAL*—Tyobeka, Prof. Errol M., BSc *Fort Hare*, MSc *Fort Hare*, PhD *Witw.*
REGISTRAR‡—Stofberg, N. J. vdM., BSc *Pret.*, MEd *S.Af.*

VAAL UNIVERSITY OF TECHNOLOGY

Founded 1966

Postal Address: Private Bag X021, Vanderbijlpark, 1900 South Africa
Telephone: (016) 950 9275 **Fax:** (016) 950 9800 **E-mail:** moutlana@vut.ac.za
URL: www.vut.ac.za

VICE-CHANCELLOR AND PRINCIPAL*—Moutlana, Prof. Irene, BA *Pitt.*, BEd *S.Af.*, MEdu *Harv.*, DEduc *Harv.*

UNIVERSITY OF VENDA

Founded 1982

Member of the Association of Commonwealth Universities

Postal Address: Private Bag X5050, Thohoyandou, Limpopo Province, 0950 South Africa
Telephone: (015) 962 8000 **Fax:** (015) 962 4749 **E-mail:** prd@caddy.univen.ac.za
URL: http://www.univen.ac.za

VICE-CHANCELLOR AND PRINCIPAL*—Mbati, Prof. Peter A., MSc *Kenyatta*, DPhil *Kenyatta*
VICE-PRINCIPAL (ACADEMIC AFFAIRS AND RESEARCH)—Ramogale, Prof. M. M., BA *North(S.Af.)*, PhD *Nott.*
UNIVERSITY REGISTRAR‡—Nemadzivhanani, K. C., BA *Venda*, BA *S.Af.*, MA *McM.*
EXECUTIVE DIRECTOR, FINANCIAL MANAGEMENT AND PLANNING—Madzhie, R. J., BCom *Venda*, MBA *Buckingham*

GENERAL INFORMATION

History. The university was established in 1982.
It is located in Thohoyandou in the far north-eastern corner of Limpopo Province.

Admission to first degree courses (see also South African Introduction). Matriculation

certificate or certificate of exemption. An entrance test or completion of special courses in certain disciplines may be required. International applicants: certificates or diplomas equivalent to matriculation requirements in candidate's country of origin are generally accepted.

First Degrees (see also South African Directory to Subjects of Study) (* = with honours). BA*, BA, BA(Agric), BA(CrimJus)*, BA(CrimJus), BAdmin*, BAdmin, BA(Ed), BA(Ed)Agric, BA(Law), BA(Mus)*, BA(Mus), BA(SW), BCom*, BCom, BCur, BCur*, BCur(PraxExt), BEcon, BEcon*, BEnvSc, BEnvSc*, BProc, BSc, BSc(Agric)*, BSc(Agric), BSc(EnvM), BTh, BURP.

Length of course. Full-time: BA, BA(Agric), BA(CrimJus), BA(Ed), BA(Ed)Agric, BA(Law), BA(Mus), BA(SW), BAdmin, BCom, BCur, BCur(PraxExt), BEcon, BEnvSc, BProc, BSc, BSc(Agric), BSc(EnvM), BTh, BURP: 3 years; BA(CrimJus)*, BA(Mus)*, BA*, BAdmin*, BCom*, BCur*, BEcon*, BEnvSc*, BSc(Agric)*: 4 years.

Higher Degrees (see also South African Directory to Subjects of Study).
Master's. BEd, LLB, LLM, MA, MA(Admin), MA(CrimJus), MA(Mus), MA(SW), MCom, MCurationis, MEcon, MEd, MSc, MSc(Agric).
Length of course. Full-time: LLM, MA, MA(Admin), MA(CrimJus), MA(Mus), MA(SW), MCom, MCurationis, MEcon, MEd, MSc, MSc(Agric): 1 year; BEd, LLB: 2 years.
Doctoral. DAdmin, DEcon, DEd, LLD, PhD.
Length of course. Full-time: DAdmin, DEcon, DEd, LLD, PhD: 3 years.

Libraries. Volumes: 109,321. Periodicals subscribed to: 1085.

Academic Awards. 12 awards ranging in value from R500 to R1000.

FACULTIES/SCHOOLS

Health, Agriculture and Rural Development
Tel: (015) 962 8114 Fax: (015) 962 8647
E-mail: smahoko@univen.ac.za
Executive Dean: Shai-Mahoko, Prof. N. S., BCur *S.Af.*, MSc(Nursing) *Witw.*, DLitt&Phil *S.Af.*

Humanities, Law and Management Sciences
Tel: (015) 962 8502 Fax: (015) 962 8050
E-mail: rralebipi@univen.ac.za
Executive Dean: Ralebipi-Simela, M. D. R., MLS *Pitt.*, PhD *Minn.*

Natural and Applied Sciences
Tel: (015) 962 8514 Fax: (015) 962 4742
Executive Dean: (vacant)

ACADEMIC UNITS

Accounting and Auditing
Manda, D. C., BA *Malawi*, BBus *Strath.*, MBA *Strath.* Sr. Lectr.; Head*
Mashamba, R. F., BCom *North(S.Af.)*, BEd *North(S.Af.)*, BCom *Venda*, MBA *Georgia State* Sr. Lectr.
Oseifuah, E., MSc Sr. Lectr.
Other Staff: 3 Lectrs.

African Languages, Arts and Culture, M. E. R. Mathivha Centre for
Makgopa, M. A., BA *S.Af.*, MA *Stell.*, DLitt&Phil *S.Af.* Head*
Musehane, N. M., BA *S.Af.*, BA *Venda*, MA *Stell.*, DLitt *Stell.* Sr. Lectr.

Northern Sotho
2 Lectrs.
Vacant Posts: 1 Prof.

Tshivenda
Muloiwa, T. W., BA *S.Af.*, MA *Tor.* Assoc. Prof.
Musehane, N. M., BA *S.Af.*, BA *Venda*, MA *Stell.*, DLitt *Stell.* Sr. Lectr.
Other Staff: 2 Lectrs.
Vacant Posts: 1 Prof.

Xitsonga
1 Lectr.
Vacant Posts: 1 Sr. Lectr.

Agricultural Economics and Extension
Oni, S .A., BSc *Calif.*, MSc *Calif.*, PhD *Ib.* Prof.; Head*
Other Staff: 3 Lectrs.

Agriculture and Rural Engineering
Simalenga, T. E., PhD *R.Vet.& Agric., Denmark*, BSc(MechEng) MSc(AgricEng) Prof.; Head*
Other Staff: 1 Lectr.

Animal Science
Acheompong-Boateng, O., BSc *Ghana*, MSc(Agric) *Pret.*, PhD *Pret.* Sr. Lectr.; Head*
Makinde, M. O., DVM *Ib.*, PhD *Ib.* Prof.
Menne, P. F., MSc(Agric) *Pret.* Sr. Lectr.

Biochemistry
Du Toit, P. J., MSc *Pret.*, PhD *Rand Afrikaans* Prof.; Head*
Other Staff: 2 Lectrs.

Biotechnology, Centre for
No staff at present

Biological Sciences
Crafford, J., BSc *Pret.*, PhD *Pret.*
Van der waal, B. c. W., BSc *Pret.*, PhD *Rand Afrikaans* Prof.; Head*
Other Staff: 10 Lectrs.

Business Information Systems
Kadyamatimba, A., MSc PhD Prof.; Head*
Other Staff: 2 Lectrs.

Business Management
4 Lectrs.

Chemistry
Mammino, L., MSc *Pisa*, PhD *Moscow* Assoc. Prof.
Mebe, P., MSc *Texas*, PhD *New Br.* Sr. Lectr.
Ramaite, I. D. I., BSc *Venda*, MSc *Rhodes*, PhD *Rhodes* Sr. Lectr.
Van Ree, T., DSc *Pret.* Prof.; Head*
Vijayan, R. P., BSc *Kerala*, MSc *Saug.*, PhD *Saug.* Assoc. Prof.
Other Staff: 3 Lectrs.

Communication and Applied Language Studies
Phaswana, E. N., BA *Venda*, BEd *Venda*, MA *Stell.*, MPhil *Cape Town*, PhD *Mich.State* Sr. Lectr.; Head*

Computer Science and Information Systems
Van Ree, T., DSc *Pret.* Prof.; Head*
Other Staff: 1 Lectr.

Criminal Adjectival and Clinical Legal Studies
Mawila, P. R., BProc *S.Af.*, LLB *S.Af.* Sr. Lectr.; Head*
Van der Walt, T., BIur *S.Af.*, LLM *S.Af.* Sr. Lectr.
Other Staff: 1 Lectr.

Criminal Justice
Roloefse, C. J. Sr. Lectr.; Head*
Other Staff: 2 Jr. Lectrs.

Curriculum Studies and Teacher Education
Bayona, E. L. M., BEd *Manit.*, MA(Ed) *S'ton.*, PhD *W.Aust.* Prof.; Head*
Other Staff: 3 Lectrs.

Development Studies
Hofmeyr, H. M., BA *Pret.*, BD *Pret.*, DD *Pret.* Sr. Lectr.
Leeuw, J. D. N., MA *Columbia Coll.(N.Y.)*, DTh *Utrecht* Sr. Lectr.
Lukhaimane, E. K., BA *S.Af.*, BA *North(S.Af.)*, MA *North(S.Af.)* Prof.; Head*
Molapo, R. R., BA *Cape Town*, MA *Cape Town*, PhD *W.Cape* Sr. Lectr.
Van der Westhuizen, J. D. N., BA *Pret.*, BD *Pret.* Other Staff: 2 Lectrs.

Ecology and Resource Management
Chimuka, L., BSc *Zambia*, MSc *Botswana*, PhD *Lund* Sr. Lectr.
Stam, E. M., MSc *Amst.*, PhD *V.U.Amst.* Other Staff: 2 Lectrs.

Economics
Gyekye, A. B., BSc *Ghana*, MA *Virginia*, PhD *Ohio State* Prof.; Head*
Other Staff: 3 Lectrs.

Education, Early Childhood and Primary
Ngobeli, D. T., BA *North(S.Af.)*, BA *S.Af.*, BEd *S.Af.*, MEd *S.Af.*, DEd *S.Af.* Sr. Lectr.; Head*

Education, Mathematics and Science

Educational Foundations
Mulaudzi, M. P., BEd *Venda*, MEd *Bowie State*, DEd *S.Af.* Head*
Ngobeli, D. T., BA *North(S.Af.)*, BA *S.Af.*, BEd *S.Af.*, MEd *S.Af.*, DEd *S.Af.* Sr. Lectr.
Phendla, T. S., BA *Venda*, BEd *Witw.*, MED *Rand Afrikaans*, PhD *Mich.*
Ravhudzulo, M. A., BA *S.Af.*, BEd *S.Af.*, MEd *North(S.Af.)*, DEd *S.Af.* Sr. Lectr.; Head*
Sadiki, N. B., BEd *Venda*, MEd *Vista*, DEd *Rand Afrikaans*
Other Staff: 3 Lectrs.
Vacant Posts: 1 Prof.

English
Rafapa, L. P., DLitt *Stell.*, BA MA Head*
Other Staff: 12 Lectrs.
Vacant Posts: 1 Prof.

Family Ecology and Consumer Sciences
Maliwichi, L. L., BSc(Agric) *Malawi*, MSc *Lond.*, PhD *Cornell* Asst. Prof.; Head*

Food Science and Technology
Olorunda, A. O., BSc(Agric) *Ife*, PhD *Aberd.* Prof.; Head*
Other Staff: 2 Lectrs.

Forestry
Ole-Meiludie, R. E., BSc(For) *Dar.*, MSc(For) *Dar.*, PhD *Dar.* Prof.; Head*
Other Staff: 1 Lectr.

Geography and Geoinformation Sciences
Musyoki, A., BEd *Nair.*, MA *Ohio*, PhD *Howard*
Other Staff: 3 Lectrs.

Horticultural Science
Mchau, G. R. A., BSc *Pomona*, MSc(Agric) *Pomona*, PhD *Calif.* Assoc. Prof.; Head*
Other Staff: 1 Lectr.

Human Resources Management and Labour Relations
1 Lectr.
Vacant Posts: Head*; 1 Prof.

Hydrology and Water Resources
Odiyo, J. O., BSc *Egerton*, MSc *Dar.* Sr. Lectr.; Head*
Other Staff: 1 Lectr.

Jurisprudence, History of Law and Comparative Law
Nengome, N. R., LLB *S.Af.*, LLM *S.Af.* Head*
Other Staff: 2 Lectrs.

Law, Mercantile
Letuka, P. P., BA(Law) *NUL*, LLB *NUL*, LLM *Lond.* Sr. Lectr.; Head*
Nengome, N. R., LLB *S.Af.*, LLM *S.Af.*
Other Staff: 1 Lectr.

Law, Private
Choshi, M. K., LLB *S.Af.*, LLM *S.Af.* Sr. Lectr.; Head*
Mphahlele, M. V., BProc *S.Af.*, LLB *S.Af.*, LLM *S.Af.*

Other Staff: 1 Lectr.

Law, Public and International

Choma, H. J., BIur North(S.Af.), LLM Georgetown,
    LLM Howard   Sr. Lectr.; Head*
Lansink, A., LLM S.Af.   Sr. Lectr.
Mireku, O., LLB Ghana, LLM S.Af., DrJur   Prof.
Other Staff: 1 Lectr.

Mathematics and Applied Mathematics

Kirunda, E. F., PhD Moscow   Prof.
Makasu, C.
Moyo, S., MSc Moscow, PhD Brun.   Sr. Lectr.;
    Head*
Tshifhumulo, A. T., BSc Venda, MSc Penn., PhD
    Witw.   Sr. Lectr.
Other Staff: 5 Lectrs.

Microbiology

Bessong, P. O., BSc Lagos, MSc Lagos, PhD Venda
    Head*
Potgieter, N., BSc Rand Afrikaans, MSc Pret., PhD
    Pret.
Other Staff: 1 Lectr.

Mining and Environmental Geology

Da Costa, F. A., BSc Kumasi, MSc Witw., PhD
    Witw.   Sr. Lectr.; Head*
Korkor, F. O., BSc Ghana, MSc Wales   Sr. Lectr.
Ogola, J. S., MSc Moscow, PhD Moscow   Prof.
Tessema, L. S., BSc Addis Ababa, PhD Witw., MSc
    Sr. Lectr.
Walemba, K. M. A., BSc Kumasi, MSc Witw.,
    PhD Witw.   Sr. Lectr.

Music

Lalendle, L. L. T., BPed Fort Hare, MA(MusEd)
    Iowa, PhD Mich.State   Sr. Lectr.
Mugovhani, N. G., BA S.Af., BMus Cape Town,
    UPLM S.Af., MMus Witw., PhD S.Af.   Lectr.;
    Head*
Other Staff: 3 Lectrs.
Vacant Posts: 1 Assoc. Prof.

Nursing Science

Tel: (015) 962 8393 Fax: (015) 962 8647
    E-mail: bkhoza@univen.ac.za
Khoza, L. B., BA(Cur) S.Af., MCur S.Af.,
    DLitt&Phil S.Af.   Prof.; Head*
Netshandama, V. O., MCur S.Af., DCur Rand
    Afrikaans
Other Staff: 6 Lectrs.

Nutrition

Tel: (015) 962 8647 Fax: (015) 962 8647
Mbhenyane, X. G., BSc S.Af.Med., MMed Ill.,
    PhD Potchef.   Prof.; Head*
Other Staff: 3 Lectrs.

Philosophy

Leeuw, T. M. J., MA Col., DTh Utrecht   Sr.
    Lectr.; Head*
Other Staff: 1 Lectr.

Physics

Gohil, A. M., BSc Gujar., MSc Saur.   Assoc.
    Prof.; Head*
Matamba, I. P., BSc North(S.Af.), BSc S.Af., MSc
    Oregon, PhD S.Af.   Sr. Lectr.
Sankaran, V., MSc Annam., PhD Annam.   Sr.
    Lectr.
Vacant Posts: 1 Prof.

Plant Production

Ogola, J. B. O., BSc Nair., MSc Nair., PhD
    Reading   Sr. Lectr.; Head*
Other Staff: 1 Lectr.

Psychology

see also Educn., Psychol. of; and Indust.
    Psychol.

Tel: (015) 962 8341 Fax: (015) 962 8647
    E-mail: sodi@univen.ac.za
Fourie, A. P., BA Pret., BA Stell.   Sr. Lectr.;
    Head*

Sodi, T., BA North(S.Af.), MA(ClinPsy) Witw.,
    PhD Cape Town   Prof.
Other Staff: 8 Lectrs.

Public and Development Administration

Khwashaba, M. P., BAdmin Venda, MAdmin
    S.Af., PhD S.Af.   Sr. Lectr.; Head*
Other Staff: 6 Lectrs.

Public Health

Tel: (015) 962 8161 Fax: (015) 962 8647
    E-mail: tmaluleke@univen.ac.za
Maluleke, T. X., BCur S.Af., BCur S.Af.Med., MSc
    Edin., DLitt&Phil S.Af.   Sr. Lectr.; Head*
Other Staff: 3 Lectrs.

Social Work

Mogorosi, L. D., BS(SW) Zululand, MS Col.,
    DSW Col., PhD Col., BS(SW)   Sr. Lectr.
Thabede, D. G., BA(SW) Zululand, MSW Ohio
    State, PhD Stell.   Sr. Lectr.; Head*
Other Staff: 3 Lectrs.

Anthropology

Dederen, J. L. F., Lic Leuven, PhD Rand Afrikaans
    Sr. Lectr.
Hanisch, E. O. M., MA Pret.   Sr. Lectr.
Other Staff: 2 Lectrs.
Vacant Posts: 1 Prof.

Sociology

Mokhahlane, P. M., BA Fort Hare, MA Vista, PhD
    Vista   Sr. Lectr.
Other Staff: 2 Lectrs.
Vacant Posts: 1 Prof.

Soil Science

Odhiambo, J. J. O., BSc(Agric) Nair.,
    MSc(Agric) Nair., PhD Br.Col.   Sr. Lectr.;
    Head*

Statistics

Amey, A. K. A., BA Ghana, MA Bowling Green,
    PhD Bowling Green   Assoc. Prof.; Head*
Kyei, K. A., BSc Ghana, MD Louvain, DrDroit
    Louvain, PhD Pret.   Sr. Lectr.
Misi, T. S., BSc Malawi, MSc N.Y., PhD

Tourism and Hospitality Management

Spencer, J. P., BCom Cape Town, MEd S.Af., DEd
    Stell.   Prof.; Head*
Steyn, J. N., MA Stell., DPhil Stell.   Prof.

Urban and Regional Planning

Bikam, P., MPhil Paris IV, PhD Paris IV   Sr.
    Lectr.; Head*
Dayomi, M., PhD Aix-Marseilles   Assoc. Prof.

SPECIAL CENTRES, ETC

African Studies, Es'kia Mphahlele Centre for

Nindi, B. C., BA Dar., MA Dar., PhD Hull
    Prof.; Acting Dir.*
Other Staff: 7 Lectrs. (jt. apptd.)

Biokinetics, Recreation and Sport Science, Centre for

Tel: (015) 962 8067 Fax: (015) 962 8647
    E-mail: amusalbw@yahoo.com
Amusa, L. O., BSc Nigeria, MPE Springfield, EdM
    Col., DPE Springfield   Prof.; Head*

Business Career and Placement Centre

No staff at present

Entrepreneurial Studies, Centre for

No staff at present

Entrepreneurship, Innovations and Poverty Eradication, Institute of

Oloo, G., BSc MBA   Sr. Lectr.; Head*
Other Staff: 2 Lectrs.; 1 Lectr. (jt. apptd.)

G. I. S. Resource Centre

1 Sr. Lab. Tech.

Gender Studies, Centre for

Ayuru, R. N., BA Tor., MSc Lond., PhD Leeds
    Prof.; Dir.*
Leeuw, T. M. J., MA Col., DTh Utrecht   Sr.
    Lectr. (joint appointment)
Miti, L. M., BA Zambia, MA York(UK), PhD Lond.
    Assoc. Prof. (joint appointment)
Musehane, N. M., BA S.Af., BA Venda, MA Stell.,
    DLitt Stell.   Sr. Lectr. (joint appointment)
Siachitema, A. K., BA Zambia, MA Leeds, MPhil
    Lond., PhD Edin.   Sr. Lectr.
Other Staff: 1 Lectr.; 1 Lectr. (jt. apptd.)

Government and Policy Studies, Oliver Tambo Institute of

Khwashaba, M. P., BAdmin Venda, MAdmin
    S.Af., PhD S.Af.   Sr. Lectr.
Other Staff: 1 Asst. Prof.

Human and Peoples' Rights, Ismail Mahomed Centre for

Mireku, O., LLB Ghana, LLM S.Af., DrJur   Prof.;
    Dir.*

Legal Aid Clinic

Funyufunyu, T. B., BProc S.Af.   Acting Head*

Rural Development, Centre for

Aja Okorie, F., BSc Ib., MSc Cornell, PhD Ib.
    Prof.

Semi-Arid Environment and Disaster Management, Institute of

No staff at present

Youth Studies, Centre for

Nindi, B. C., BA NUL, MA PhD   Prof.
Other Staff: 1 Lectr.

CONTACT OFFICERS

Academic affairs. University Registrar:
    Nemadzivhanani, K. C., BA Venda, BA S.Af.,
    MA McM. (E-mail: khuliso@univen.ac.za)
Admissions (first degree). Chief Admissions
    Officer: (vacant)
Admissions (higher degree). Chief
    Admissions Officer: (vacant)
Alumni. Development Officer (Alumni and
    Individuals): Neluheni, T. G., BA Venda
Development/fund-raising. Development
    Officer (Corporate): (vacant)
Estates and buildings/works and services.
    Senior Administration Officer (Building
    Maintenance): (vacant)
Estates and buildings/works and services.
    Senior Administration Officer (Grounds
    Maintenance): Nemuhuyuni, T. E., BAdmin
    Venda
Estates and buildings/works and services.
    Acting Director (Estates and buildings/
    works and services): Masiagwala, N. W.,
    BAdmin North(S.Af.), BCom Venda, MSc Pret.,
    MBA Newport
Examinations. Chief Examinations Officer:
    Sadiki, E. N., BA Venda
Finance. Executive Director, Financial
    Management and Planning: Madzhie, R. J.,
    BCom Venda, MBA Buckingham
Finance. Director (Finance): Malima, D. M.,
    BA North(S.Af.), BCompt S.Af., BCom Venda
    (E-mail: malima@univen.ac.za)
General enquiries. Director, Public Relations
    and Development: Kharidzha, R. N.,
    BA(SW) North(S.Af.)
    (E-mail: kharidzha@univen.ac.za)
International office. Executive Director:
    Mogadime, Y. M., BA Hunter, MA N.Y.
    (E-mail: mogadime@univen.ac.za)
Library (chief librarian). Director, Library
    Services: Mulaudzi, M. T.
    (E-mail: tshif@univen.ac.za)
Library (chief librarian). Director, Library
    Services: (vacant)
Library (enquiries). Executive Secretary:
    Mudalahothe, M. S.
    (E-mail: smudala@univen.ac.za)

Marketing. Executive Director: Mogadime, Y. M., BA Hunter, MA N.Y.
(E-mail: mogadime@univen.ac.za)

Public relations. Director, Public Relations and Development: Kharidzha, R. N., BA(SW) North(S.Af.)
(E-mail: kharidzha@univen.ac.za)

Purchasing. Deputy Director, Procurement and Planning: (vacant)

Research. Director, Research and Development: Fatoki, Prof. O. S., BSc Ib.,

MSc Ib., PhD Salf.
(E-mail: fatoki@univen.ac.za)

Schools liaison. Schools Liaison Officer (Acting): Dzaga, T. V., BAdmin Venda
(E-mail: dzaga@univen.ac.za)

Security. Chief Security Officer: (vacant)

Staff development and training. Deputy Director (Staff development and training): Netshivhera, N. S., BAdmin Venda
(E-mail: sollynet@univen.ac.za)

Strategic planning. Vice-Principal (Planning and Resource Management): (vacant)

Student welfare/counselling. Director, Student Counselling and Guidance Bureau: Selepe-Madima, M. C., BA Venda, MA Rand Afrikaans, PhD Zululand

[Information supplied by the institution as at 10 October 2007, and edited by the ACU]

WALTER SISULU UNIVERSITY OF SCIENCE AND TECHNOLOGY

Postal Address: Private Bag X1, UNITRA, Eastern Cape, South Africa
Telephone: (0471) 302 2111 **Fax:** (0471) 26820 **E-mail:** postmaster@getafix.utr.ac.za
URL: http://www.utr.ac.za

VICE-CHANCELLOR*—Balintulo, Prof. Malusi M.
REGISTRAR‡—Bhana, J.

UNIVERSITY OF THE WESTERN CAPE

Founded 1959

Member of the Association of Commonwealth Universities

Postal Address: Private Bag X17, Bellville, Western Cape, 7535 South Africa
Telephone: (021) 959 2111 **Fax:** (021) 951 3126 **E-mail:** imiller@uwc.ac.za
URL: http://www.uwc.ac.za

RECTOR AND VICE-CHANCELLOR*—O'Connell, Prof. Brian, BA S.Af., MA Col., MEd Col.
VICE-RECTOR (ACADEMIC)—(vacant)
VICE-RECTOR (STUDENT DEVELOPMENT)—Tshiwula, Prof. L. J., BA Fort Hare, MA P.Elizabeth, DPhil P.Elizabeth
EXECUTIVE DIRECTOR (HUMAN RESOURCES AND SERVICES)—Hambrook-Glaeser, Amanda, BA Rand Afrikaans, BA Pret.
EXECUTIVE DIRECTOR (FINANCE)—Regal, Abduraghman
REGISTRAR (ACADEMIC)‡—Miller, Ingrid M., BHMS Stell., MHMS Stell., DPhil W.Cape
EXECUTIVE DIRECTOR (INFORMATION AND COMMUNICATION SERVICE)—Keats, Prof. Derek W., PhD Nfld.

GENERAL INFORMATION

History. The university was founded in 1959 as a constituent college of the University of South Africa. In 1983 it achieved university status and was renamed the University of the Western Cape.

The university is situated in the northern suburb of the Cape Peninsula.

Admission to first degree courses (see also South African Introduction). Matriculation certificate or certificate of exemption issued by Joint Matriculation Board.

First Degrees (see also South African Directory to Subjects of Study) (* = with honours). BA*, BA, BAdmin, BAdmin*, BA(HE)*, BA(HE), BA(Law), BA(PhysEd)*, BBibl, BBibl(Ed), BChD, BCom, BCom*, BCom(Law), BCur, BD, BEd*, BEd, BOH, BPharm, BPSych, BSc*, BSc, BSc(CompHlthScis), BSc(Dietetics), BSc(OccTher), BSc(Physiotherapy), BSW, BTh, LLB.

Length of course. Full-time: BEd*: 1 year; BA, BAdmin, BCom, BCom(Law), BOH, BSc: 3 years; BA(HE), BA(PhysEd)*, BA*, BAdmin*, BBibl, BBibl(Ed), BCom*, BCur, BEd, BPharm, BPSych, BSc(Dietetics), BSc(OccTher), BSc(Physiotherapy), BSc*, BSW, BTh, LLB: 4 years; BA(HE)*, BChD, BSc(CompHlthScis): 5 years. Part-time: BEd*: 2 years; BA, BAdmin,

BCom, BCom(Law): 4 years; BA(PhysEd)*, BBibl, BBibl(Ed), BTh, LLB: 5 years; BA*, BAdmin*, BCom*: 6 years.

Higher Degrees (see also South African Directory to Subjects of Study).

Master's. LLM, MA, MAdmin, MA(HE), MA(SW), MBibl, MChD, MCom, MCom(ICTPolicy&Reg), MCom(InfMan), MCur, MEcon, MEd, MPA, MPH, MPharm, MPhil, MPsych, MSc, MScDent, MSc(NutrMgmnt), MSc(OccTher), MSc(Physio), MTh.

Admission. Applicants for admission to master's degrees must normally hold an appropriate first degree.

Length of course. Full-time: LLM, MA, MA(HE), MA(SW), MBibl, MCom, MEcon, MEd, MPharm, MSc, MSc(NutrMgmnt), MSc(Physio), MScDent, MTh: 1 year; MAdmin, MCom(ICTPolicy&Reg), MCom(InfMan), MCur, MPA, MPH, MPhil, MPsych: 2 years; MChD, MSc(OccTher): 3 years. Part-time: MCom(ICTPolicy&Reg), MCom(InfMan), MSc(Physio): 2 years; LLM, MA, MA(HE), MA(SW), MBibl, MCom, MCur, MEcon, MEd, MPharm, MSc, MSc(NutrMgmnt), MSc(OccTher), MScDent, MTh: 3 years; MAdmin, MPA, MPH, MPhil, MPsych: 4 years; MChD: 5 years.

Doctoral. DCur, DPharm, DSc, DTh, LLD, PhD.

Admission. Applicants for admission to a doctorate must normally hold a master's degree.

Length of course. Full-time: DCur, DPharm, DSc, DTh, LLD, PhD: 2 years. Part-time: DCur, DPharm, DSc, DTh, LLD, PhD: 5 years.

Language of Instruction. English and Afrikaans.

Libraries. Volumes: 286,156. Periodicals subscribed to: 1237.

Income (2006). Total, R639,420,558.

Statistics. Staff (2006): 1245 (632 academic, 613 non-academic). Students (2006): full-time 11,720 (4666 men, 7054 women); part-time 3190 (1359 men, 1831 women); international 1259 (701 men, 558 women); undergraduate 12,099 (4584 men, 7515 women); master's 1122 (582 men, 540 women); doctoral 311 (180 men, 131 women).

FACULTIES/SCHOOLS

Arts

Tel: (021) 959 2235, 959 2667 Fax: (021) 959 3636 E-mail: jflusk@uwc.ac.za
Dean: (vacant)
Secretary: Flusk, Jill

Community and Health Sciences

Tel: (021) 959 2746, 959 2631 Fax: (021)
959 2755 E-mail: labels@uwc.ac.za

Dean: Mpofu, Prof. Ratie M., MSc S'ton., DPhil
W.Cape, MCSP
Secretary: Abels, Leonie

Dentistry

Tel: (021) 370 4400 Fax: (021) 392 3250
E-mail: evoight@uwc.ac.za

Dean: Moola, Prof. Mohamed H., BDS Bom.,
MSc Lond.
Secretary: Voight, Esmeralda Z.

Economic and Management Sciences

Tel: (021) 959 2257 Fax: (021) 959 3620
E-mail: svanderschyff@uwc.ac.za

Dean: Tapscott, Prof. Chris, MSocSc Birm., MPA
Cape Town, PhD Lond.
Secretary: Van der Schyff, Shanaaz

Education

Tel: (021) 959 2276 Fax: (021) 959 2647
E-mail: rwales@uwc.ac.za

Dean: Desai, Prof. Zubaida K., BA Lond., MA
Lond.
Secretary: Wales, Rhona

Law

Tel: (021) 959 2176 Fax: (021) 959 2960
E-mail: fhendricks@uwc.ac.za

Dean: Moosa, Prof. Najma, BA W.Cape, LLB
W.Cape, LLM W.Cape, LLD W.Cape
Secretary: Hendricks, Faeda

Science

Tel: (021) 959 2762, 959 2255 Fax: (021)
959 2266 E-mail: mapolles@uwc.ac.za

Dean: Van Bever Donker, Prof. Jan, Drs Ley.,
PhD Cape Town
Secretary: Apolles, Monya

ACADEMIC UNITS

Accounting

Tel: (021) 959 3256 Fax: (021) 959 2578
E-mail: jesmith@uwc.ac.za

Arnold, Ebrahim, BCompt S.Af.   Assoc. Prof.
Bakkes, C. Johan, MCompt S.Af.   Prof.
Briggs, Keith, BCom P.Elizabeth, MCom Rand
Afrikaans, MCom P.Elizabeth   Sr. Lectr.
Brink, Petrus J., MAcc Stell.   Prof.; Chair*
Mohammed, Yusuf, BCom W.Cape, BCompt
S.Af.   Sr. Lectr.
Mollagee, Osman, BCom W.Cape, BCom Cape
Town   Sr. Lectr.
Siebritz, Jacques, BCom Stell., LLB Stell., BCompt
S.Af.   Sr. Lectr.
Other Staff: 4 Lectrs.
Vacant Posts: 1 Prof.
Research: public financial management; taxation;
university financial reporting

Afrikaans and Nederlands

Tel: (021) 959 2113 Fax: (021) 959 2376
E-mail: jpekeur@uwc.ac.za

Coetzee, Abraham J., MA Witw., PhD Witw.
Extraordinary Prof.
Hendriks, Frank S., MA W.Cape, DLitt W.Cape
Assoc. Prof.
Van Wyk, Stuart, BA W.Cape, MA W.Cape, STD
W.Cape, DLitt W.Cape   Assoc. Prof.
Van Zyl, Wium J., MA Stell., DrsLitt Utrecht,
DLitt Stell.   Assoc. Prof.; Chair*

Anthropology/Sociology

Tel: (021) 959 2336 Fax: (021) 959 3401
E-mail: knadasen@uwc.ac.za

Becker, Heike A., MA Mainz, PhD Bremen
Assoc. Prof.
Boonzaaier, Emile A., MA Cape Town   Sr. Lectr.
Gibson, Dianne, MA S.Af., PhD W.Cape   Assoc.
Prof.
Humphreys, Anthony J., MA Cape Town, PhD
Cape Town   Assoc. Prof.
Nadasen, Krishnavelli, BA S.Af., MA Ley., DPhil
Durban-W.   Sr. Lectr.; Chair*
Other Staff: 2 Lectrs.

Vacant Posts: 1 Prof.; 1 Lectr.
Research: crime and deviance in South Africa;
identity and group relations; land and
development issues; medical/health studies;
urban studies

Biodiversity and Conservation Biology

Tel: (021) 959 2301 Fax: (021) 959 2266
E-mail: ivanheerden@uwc.ac.za

Channing, Allan, PhD Natal   Prof.
Gibbons, Mark, BSc Liv., PhD Cape Town
Assoc. Prof.; Chair*
Hofmeyer, Margaretha D., MSc Stell., PhD Cape
Town   Assoc. Prof.
Holtman, Lorna, BSc W.Cape, BEd S.Af., MPhil
W.Cape, PhD Louisiana State   Sr. Lectr.
Knight, Richard S., PhD Cape Town   Sr. Lectr.
Raitt, Lincoln M., PhD Stell.   Assoc. Prof.
Other Staff: 3 Lectrs.
Research: marine biology

Biotechnology

Tel: (021) 959 2215 Fax: (021) 959 2266
E-mail: pat@mbiol.uwc.ac.za

Arieff, Zainunisha, BSc Cape Town, MSc W.Cape,
PhD W.Cape   Sr. Lectr.
Blackburn, J., PhD Camb.   Extraordinary Prof.
Cowan, Donald, PhD Waik.   Prof.; Chair*
Davison, Sean, PhD Otago   Assoc. Prof.
du Preez, Marlene G., BSc Stell., MSc W.Cape
Sr. Lectr.
Gehring, C., PhD Lond.   Prof.
Gouws, Pieter A., PhD W.Cape   Assoc. Prof.
Pugh, David, DPhil Oxf.   Sr. Lectr.
Rees, D. Jasper, MA Oxf., DPhil Oxf.   Prof.
Sayed, Muhammed, PhD Camb.   Sr. Lectr.
Sewel, T., PhD Lond.   Extraordinary Prof.
Other Staff: 4 Lectrs.
Research: environmental microbiology
(metagenomics, microbial diversity); food
microbiology, pathogen diagnostics;
protein; virology (insect viruses, viral
genomics)

Chemistry

Tel: (021) 959 2262 Fax: (021) 959 3055
E-mail: wparring@uwc.ac.za

Ameer, Farouk, PhD Natal   Sr. Lectr.
Green, Ivan R., PhD Cape Town   Prof.
Iwuoha, Emmanuel, PhD Ib.   Prof.
Key, David L., PhD Lond.   Assoc. Prof.; Chair*
Linkov, Vladimer, PhD Stell.   Prof.
Mabusela, Tozamile W., BSc Fort Hare, MSc
Rhodes, PhD Cape Town   Sr. Lectr.
Mapolie, Selwyn F., PhD Cape Town   Prof.
Other Staff: 2 Lectrs.
Research: nanotechnology (energy generation in
fuel cells, electrolysers for hydrogen fuel
production)

Community Oral Health

Tel: (021) 392 8116 Fax: (021) 392 3250
E-mail: evivier@uwc.ac.za

Barrie, Robert B., BChD Stell., MChD Stell., MPA
Stell.   Sr. Lectr.
Lalloo, Ratilal, BChD W.Cape, BSc(Med) Cape
Town, MChD W.Cape, PhD Lond.   Assoc.
Prof.
Louw, Adriaan, BSc Stell., MChD Pret.   Assoc.
Prof.; Chair*
Moola, Mohamed H., BDS Bom., MSc Lond.
Prof.
Myburgh, Niel G., BChD Rand Afrikaans, MChD
W.Cape, PhD Stell.   Assoc. Prof.
Naidoo, Sudeshni, BDS Lond., MChD W.Cape
Assoc. Prof.
Other Staff: 3 Lectrs.
Research: dental health status of under 5-year-
old children; impact of inequity on oral
health status; oral manifestations of
paediatric HIV; planning an oral health
programme for disabled pre-school
children; prevalence of mutant streptoccoci
among disabled pre-school children

Computer Science

Tel: (021) 959 3010 Fax: (021) 959 3055
E-mail: rabbott@uwc.ac.za

Agbinya, Johnson, BSc Ife, MSc Strath., PhD La
Trobe   Extraordinary Prof.
Blackledge, Jonathan M., PhD Lond.   Prof.
Norman, Michael J., BSc W.Cape, MSc Cape Town
Sr. Lectr.; Chair*
Omlin, Christian W. P., PhD Rensselaer
Extraordinary Prof.
Tucker, William D., BA Trinity(Dub.), MS   Sr.
Lectr.
Venter, Isabella M., BSc Stell., MSc S.Af., PhD
Pret.   Sr. Lectr.
Other Staff: 2 Lectrs.
Vacant Posts: 1 Prof.; 1 Sr. Lectr.; 1 Assoc.
Research: broadband ATM transmission;
computationally complete program
languages; computer science education;
neural networks; software engineering and
persistant programming languages

Dentistry, Restorative

Tel: (021) 392 8116 Fax: (021) 392 3250
E-mail: osman@dentistry.uwc.ac.za

Ackermann, Wilhelm D., BSc Stell., BChD Stell.
Sr. Lectr.
de la Harpe, Charl J., BChD Stell., BSc(Pharm)
Potchef.   Sr. Lectr.; Chair*
Geerts, Greta, MChD Stell.   Assoc. Prof.
Ismail, Sharafit B., BSc Stell., BChD Stell.   Sr.
Lectr.
Osman, Yusuf I., BChD W.Cape, MChD W.Cape,
MBA Stell.   Prof.
Patel, Narandra, BDS M'lore., MChD W.Cape   Sr.
Lectr.
Rahbeeni, Rihaz, BChD W.Cape, MChD W.Cape
Sr. Lectr.
Saayman, Charlene M., BChD W.Cape,
MSc(Dent) W.Cape   Sr. Lectr.
Solomon, C., BChD W.Cape, MScDentSc W.Cape,
MChD W.Cape   Sr. Lectr.
Strydom, Christma, BCur P.Elizabeth, BChD Stell.,
MSc(Dent) Stell.   Sr. Lectr.
Wilson, Viviene, BChD W.Cape, MChD W.Cape
Assoc. Prof.
Other Staff: 8 Lectrs.
Vacant Posts: 1 Sr. Specialist
Research: effectiveness of NRC-TM in enamel
conditioning and bonding in orthodontics;
retention of pre-fabricated posts in root
canal-treated teeth

Diagnostic Sciences

Tel: (021) 392 8116 Fax: (021) 392 5050
E-mail: jbotha@uwc.ac.za

Carstens, Hendrik A., BSc Stell., BChD Stell., BPA
Stell., MPA Stell.   Sr. Lectr.
Dreyer, W. P., BDS Witw., PhD Stell.   Emer.
Prof.
Hille, Jos J., MDent Rand Afrikaans, DDS   Prof.
Janse van Rensburg, L., MB ChB Witw.,
MFamMed Free State, MMEd Stell., DSc W.Cape
Extraordinary Prof.
Nortje, Christoffel J., BChD Pret., PhD Stell.,
DSc(Odont) Pret.   Prof.
Norval, Ernst J., BSc Rand Afrikaans, BSc Pret.,
BChD Pret., MChD Stell.   Sr. Lectr.
Parker, Mohamed E., BChD W.Cape, MSc Lond.
Prof.
Phillips, Vincent M., BDS Witw., MChD Stell.
Prof.
Roberts, Tina, BChD W.Cape, MChD W.Cape
Sr. Lectr.
Rossouw, Roelof, BSc Free State, MMedSc Free
State, PhD Stell.   Sr. Lectr.
Shear, Mervin, BDS Witw., MDS Witw.,
DSc(Dent) Witw., Hon. LLD Witw.,
Hon. DChD Pret., FRCPath, FRSSAf
Extraordinary Prof.
Stephen, Lawrence X. G., BChD W.Cape, PhD
Cape Town   Prof.; Chair*
Van Rensburg, Ben G. J., BDS Witw., BSc
Witw., MSc(Dent) Stell.   Emer. Prof.
Other Staff: 8 Lectrs.
Research: dental materials (biocompatibility of
materials in prosthetic dentistry); HIV/
AIDS; need and demand for prosthetic

treatment; oral manifestations of inherited skeletal dysplasias

Dietetics Division

Tel: (021) 959 2760 Fax: (021) 959 3686
E-mail: lcortereal@uwc.ac.za
Swart, E. C., BScDiet Stell., MPhil W.Cape, PhD W.Cape   Assoc. Prof.; Chair*
Other Staff: 5 Lectrs.
Vacant Posts: 1 Sr. Lectr.

Earth Sciences

Tel: (021) 959 2223 Fax: (021) 959 3422
E-mail: njovanovich@uwc.ac.za
Adams, Shafiek, PhD W.Cape   Sr. Lectr.
Carey, Paul, PhD Belf.   Assoc. Prof.
Jovanovic, Nebo, PhD Pret.   Sr. Lectr.; Chair*
Okujeni, C. D., MSc T.U.Berlin, PhD T.U.Berlin   Extraordinary Prof.
Van Bever Donker, Jan, Drs Ley., PhD Cape Town   Prof.
Xu, Y., MSc Chengdu Sci.& Technol., PhD Free State   Prof.
Other Staff: 3 Lectrs.

Economics

Tel: (021) 959 2579 Fax: (021) 959 2578
E-mail: mlangeveld@uwc.ac.za
Adams, Ismail, BCom S.Af., MA W.Mich., MPA Harv.   Assoc. Prof.; Chair*
Jacobs, P., BEcon W.Cape, MA(Econ) Fordham, PhD Fordham   Sr. Lectr.
Loots, Lieb J., BCom Rand Afrikaans   Prof.
Other Staff: 1 Lectr.
Vacant Posts: 1 Prof.; 1 Sr. Lectr.
Research: applied public and labour economics; economics of substance abuse; poverty and inequality; public economics and finance

Education, Faculty of

Tel: (021) 959 2276 Fax: (021) 959 2647
E-mail: stowfie@uwc.ac.za
Desai, Prof. Zubaida K., BA Lond., MA Lond.   Assoc. Prof.
Fataar, Moegamat A., BA W.Cape, MPhil W.Cape, DPhil W.Cape   Sr. Lectr.
Green, Lena, MSocSc Cape Town, PhD Exe.   Assoc. Prof.
Groener, Z., MSc Edin., PhD Calif.   Assoc. Prof.
Herman, Harold D., BSc S.Af., MEd S.Af., DEd W.Cape   Prof.
Kerfoot, Caroline, BA Witw., MA New Mexico   Sr. Lectr.
Lazarus, Sandy, BA S.Af., MA Cape Town, PhD Cape Town   Prof.
Mbekwa, Monde, BA S.Af., BA W.Cape, MPhil W.Cape, PhD W.Cape   Sr. Lectr.
Smith, Juliana M., BCom W.Cape, BEd W.Cape, MA Lanc.   Assoc. Prof.
Thaver, Beverly, BA Cape Town, MA York(UK), DPhil W.Cape   Sr. Lectr.
Vergani, Tania, BA Stell., BA W.Cape, MA W.Cape, MA Freib., PhD Cape Town   Sr. Lectr.
Williams, Clarence G., BA S.Af., BEd Cape Town, MA W.Cape, MEd Stell., DEd W.Cape   Sr. Lectr.
Other Staff: 5 Lectrs.
Vacant Posts: 1 Prof.; 1 Sr. Lectr.
Research: impact of information technology on higher education in South Africa; investigating postgraduate supervision at University of the Western Cape; policy development in South Africa (1994 to present); policy implementation in South Africa: school governance and management

English

Tel: (021) 959 2964 Fax: (021) 959 2202
E-mail: ssampson@uwc.ac.za
Dyers, Charlyn, BA W.Cape, MSc Edin., DLitt W.Cape   Assoc. Prof.
Flockemann, M. M., MA Stell., PhD Natal   Extraordinary Prof.
Hibbert, Liesel, BA Cape Town, MPhil Cape Town, PhD Cape Town   Sr. Lectr.
Katz, Ed, BA Brooklyn, MA N.Y.   Sr. Lectr.
Martin, Julia P., MA Cape Town   Sr. Lectr.

Merrington, Peter J., BA Cape Town, MA Cape Town, PhD Cape Town   Assoc. Prof.
Nas, Loes, PhD Cape Town, DrsLitt Nijmegen   Assoc. Prof.
Parr, Anthony N., BA York(UK), MPhil York(UK), PhD Tor.   Prof.
Woodward, W. V., BA Rhodes, MA Temple, PhD Cape Town   Assoc. Prof.; Chair*
Other Staff: 3 Lectrs.
Research: applied linguistics; early modern travel writing; feminist theory and criticism and African women's writing; landscape theory; media studies

Foreign Languages

Tel: (021) 959 2368 Fax: (021) 959 1251
E-mail: jberry@uwc.ac.za
Mohamed, Yasien, BA Durban-W., MA Cape Town, DrsSemSt V.U.Amst., PhD Fran.   Chair*

Arabic

Tel: (021) 959 3766
E-mail: ymohamed@uwc.ac.za
Mohamed, Yasien, BA Durban-W., MA Cape Town, DrsSemSt V.U.Amst., PhD Fran.   Sr. Lectr.
Research: Arabic language and African Islam

French

1 Lectr.
Research: French as a foreign language; Marcel Schwob

German

Tel: (021) 959 2404 Fax: (021) 959 2376
E-mail: kchubb@uwc.ac.za
Chubb, Karin, MA Cape Town   Sr. Lectr.
Research: didactic materials relating to the Truth and Reconciliation Commission of South Africa; German youth literature

Latin

Tel: (021) 959 2289 Fax: (021) 959 2376
E-mail: bvanzylsmit@uwc.ac.za
1 Lectr.
Research: Latin-Greek roots of English; media in literature and art

Geography and Environmental Studies

Tel: (021) 959 2259 Fax: (021) 959 3422
E-mail: fdewet@uwc.ac.za
Donaldson, Sybrand E., BA Stell., MA North(S.Af.), PhD Stell.   Assoc. Prof.
McPherson, Elsworth A., MA W.Cape, MSc Edin.   Sr. Lectr.
Pirie, Gordon, PhD Witw.   Assoc. Prof.; Chair*
Other Staff: 3 Lectrs.
Vacant Posts: 1 Prof.
Research: environmental processes and problems; global information systems; mobility and transport; tourism; urban restructuring

Government, School of

Tel: (021) 959 3083 Fax: (021) 959 3826
E-mail: lfesters@uwc.ac.za
Bardill, John, BA Oxf., MA(Econ) Manc.   Prof.; Chair*
de Coning, Christo, DLitt&Phil S.Af.   Prof.
Esau, Michelle, MAdmin W.Cape, PhD W.Cape   Sr. Lectr.
Hohls, Orlando E., BA Stell., MAdmin W.Cape   Sr. Lectr.
Mphaisha, Chiseppo J. J., BA Zambia, MPA Pitt., PhD Pitt.   Prof.
Thompson, Lisa, BA Cape Town, BA Rhodes, MA Rhodes, PhD W.Cape   Prof.
Williams, John, BA W.Cape, MA W.Cape, PhD Ill.   Prof.
Research: public policy management, development management and local government; southern African development management

History

Tel: (021) 959 2225 Fax: (021) 959 3598
E-mail: jsmidt@uwc.ac.za
Bank, A., MA Cape Town, PhD Camb.   Sr. Lectr.

Barnes, Theresa, BA Brown, MA Z'bwe., DPhil Z'bwe.   Assoc. Prof.
Hayes, Patricia, BA Oxf., PhD Camb.   Assoc. Prof.
Lalu, Premesh, BA Natal, MA W.Cape, PhD Minn.   Sr. Lectr.
Mesthrie, U. S., BA Durban-W., MA Durban-W., PhD Natal   Assoc. Prof.; Chair*
Newton-King, Susan-Jane, BA Cape Town, MA Lond., PhD Lond.   Sr. Lectr.
Rasool, C., BA Cape Town, LLB Cape Town, MA Northwestern   Assoc. Prof.
Scher, David M., MA S.Af., DPhil S.Af.   Sr. Lectr.
Witz, L., BA Natal, MA Witw., PhD Cape Town   Assoc. Prof.
Other Staff: 2 Lectrs.
Vacant Posts: 1 Prof.
Research: family, household and slavery in Dutch South Africa; group area removals in Cape Town; local history of the Northern Cape (Upington and Gordonia district); popular memory (identity, space and place); production of history

Human Ecology

Tel: (021) 959 2760 Fax: (021) 959 3686
E-mail: lelliott@uwc.ac.za
Cornelissen, Judith, BA W.Cape, MEd W.Cape   Sr. Lectr.
Daniels, Priscilla S., BA W.Cape, BEd W.Cape, MSc Cornell   Assoc. Prof.; Chair*
Maurtin-Cairncross, Anita, BA W.Cape, MPhil W.Cape, PhD W.Cape   Sr. Lectr.
Other Staff: 2 Lectrs.
Vacant Posts: 1 Prof.
Research: academic development, community development and empowerment

Industrial Psychology

Tel: (021) 959 3184 Fax: (021) 959 3184
E-mail: dferrus@uwc.ac.za
Abrahams, Fatima, BEcon S.Af., MEcon W.Cape, DCom S.Af.   Prof.
Bosman, Leon A., B(B&A) Stell., BEcon Stell., MEcon Stell., DCom P.Elizabeth   Chair*
Heslop, Karl, BA Natal, BAdmin Durban-W., MAdmin Durban-W.   Sr. Lectr.
Jano, Rubina, BCom W.Cape, MCom W.Cape   Sr. Lectr.
Other Staff: 2 Lectrs.
Vacant Posts: 1 Assoc. Prof.
Research: employment relations, job satisfaction and motivation, gender-based violence; learning styles and cognition, psychometrics; organisational development, commitment and change management; organisational learning, behaviour and skills development, employee assistance programmes; strategic human resource management, mentoring and coaching, career barriers

Information Systems

Tel: (021) 959 3248 Fax: (021) 959 3522
E-mail: ksmit@uwc.ac.za
Fourie, Louis, MBA Potchef., DTh Stell.   Prof.
Hackney, R., BSc Staffs., MA Keele, PhD Cran.   Extraordinary Prof.
Lim-Banda, Roderick, BCom W.Cape   Sr. Lectr.
Smit, Jacobus, BA Free State, BEd Free State, MEd Free State, PhD Leeds Met.   Sr. Lectr.; Chair*
Other Staff: 5 Lectrs.
Vacant Posts: 1 Prof.; 1 Lectr.
Research: enterprise and information architecture; information management, e-learning and digital literacy; information systems and readiness; women in IT, computers and disabled people

Law, Mercantile

Subject Group

Tel: (021) 959 3302 Fax: (021) 959 2960
E-mail: shawhaal@uwc.ac.za
Abdullah, N., BA W.Cape, LLB W.Cape, LLM Cape Town   Sr. Lectr.
Bosch, Craig S., BA Stell., LLB Stell., LLM Cape Town   Sr. Lectr.

Du Toit, Darcy, BA Cape Town, LLB Cape Town,
LLD Ley.   Prof.
Hamman, D., BA(Law) Stell., LLB Stell., LLM
Cape Town, LLD Cape Town   Assoc. Prof.
Kotze, Fourie, BA Stell., LLB Stell., LLM Stell.
Sr. Lectr.
Malherbe, Ethel D., BA Stell., LLB Stell.   Sr.
Lectr.
Maxwell, C., BA Cape Town, LLB Cape Town, LLM
Camb.
Wandrag, M. S., BIur OFS, LLB OFS, LLM OFS,
LLM Camb.   Sr. Lectr.
Other Staff: 4 Temp. Lectrs.

Law, Private
Subject Group

Tel: (021) 959 3314 Fax: (021) 959 2960
E-mail: mnelson@uwc.ac.za
De Villiers, Francois A., BComm Potchef., LLB
Potchef., LLD Leuven   Prof.
Du Toit, F., BA Stell., LLB Stell., LLM Stell., LLD
Stell.   Assoc. Prof.
Martin, Bernard S. C., BA Natal, LLB Natal   Sr.
Lectr.
Maxwell, C., BA Cape Town, LLB Cape Town, LLM
Camb.
Sarkin, J. J., BA Natal, LLB Natal, LLM Harv., LLD
W.Cape   Prof.
Sulaiman, Mubarak A., BA W.Cape, LLB W.Cape,
LLM Miami(Fla.), DrsIuris Ley.   Sr. Lectr.
Other Staff: 4 Lectrs.
Research: comparative African customary law;
contract (comparative, constitutional,
enforceability, international, socialisation);
law of family persons and property (current
issues); legal education; unjustified
enrichment

Law, Public and Adjective
Subject Group

Tel: (021) 959 3299 Fax: (021) 959 2960
E-mail: tkerridge@uwc.ac.za
De Ville, Jacobus R., BComm Potchef., LLB
Potchef., LLD Stell.   Prof.
De Vos, Pierre F., BComm Stell., LLB Stell., LLM
Stell., LLM Col., LLD W.Cape   Prof.
Fernandez, Lovell D., BA W.Cape, MCJ N.Y.,
PhD Witw.   Prof.
Fredericks, Izak N. A., BA(PubAdmin) Witw.,
LLB W.Cape, LLM Harv.   Sr. Lectr.
McCreath, H., BA Stell., LLB Stell., LLM Stell.
Philippe, X., Drd'État Aix-Marseilles III   Visiting
Prof.
Rugege, S., LLB Mak., LLM Yale, DPhil Oxf.
Prof.
Van Reenen, T. P., BA Free State, LLB Free State,
LLM S.Af., LLD S.Af.   Prof.

Library and Information Sciences

Tel: (021) 959 2137 Fax: (021) 959 3659
E-mail: sstroud@uwc.ac.za
Fredericks, George H., BA S.Af., MBibl W.Cape,
DBibl W.Cape   Assoc. Prof.; Chair*
Hart, Genevieve C., BA Cape Town, BA Witw.,
MEd Cape Town   Sr. Lectr.
Other Staff: 4 Lectrs.
Vacant Posts: 1 Prof.
Research: information literacy; information
services for disadvantaged communities;
information-seeking behaviour;
librarianship, South African children's
literature teaching; library education

Linguistics

Tel: (021) 959 2978 Fax: (021) 050 2376
E-mail: agrovers@uwc.ac.za
Banda, F., BA(Educn) Zambia, MA Brussels, PhD
Brussels   Assoc. Prof.; Chair*
Other Staff: 3 Lectrs.
Vacant Posts: 1 Prof.; 1 Sr. Lectr.
Research: academic literacy; language and
gender; language in education;
multilingualism; varieties of English

Management

Tel: (021) 959 2595 Fax: (021) 959 2578
E-mail: rscheepers@uwc.ac.za
Blackmur, D., BEcon Qld., MLitt Qld., PhD Qld.
Prof.
De Vries, Linda E. R., BCom W.Cape, MBA Stell.
Assoc. Prof.
Gool, S., BSc Cape Town, BEcon W.Cape, MA
Calif.   Prof.
Grutter, A., BA Cape Town, MBA Cape Town   Sr.
Lectr.
Hirschsohn, P., BBusSc Cape Town, BCom S.Af.,
MSc Oxf., PhD M.I.T.   Prof.
Isaacs, Enslin B. H., MCom W.Cape   Lectr.;
Chair*
Mainga, Wise, BSc Zambia, MBA Wales, PhD
Brad.   Sr. Lectr.
May, Christopher J., BCom W.Cape, MBA Stell.
Sr. Lectr.
Mentoor, Etienne R., MCom W.Cape   Sr. Lectr.
Pillay, Rubin, BSc Stell., MSc Luton, MB ChB Cape
Town, MBA Cape Town, PhD Cape Town   Sr.
Lectr.
Visser, Chris, BCom Rand Afrikaans, MCom Rand
Afrikaans, DCom Rand Afrikaans   Prof.
Visser, Dirk J., BCom Stell., BCom S.Af., MCom
W.Cape, PhD Stell.   Sr. Lectr.
Other Staff: 1 Visiting Prof.; 3 Lectrs.
Research: human resource development and
business strategy; lean manufacturing, work
organisation and supply chain strategy; life
histories of trade unions; organisational
learning and knowledge management;
strategy and competitive institutional
frameworks in auto, clothing and tourism
sectors

Mathematics and Applied Mathematics

Tel: (021) 959 3027 Fax: (021) 959 2577
E-mail: ghendricks@uwc.ac.za
Benyah, Francis, PhD W.Aust.   Assoc. Prof.
Fray, Richard L., MSc W.Cape, MSc Stell., PhD
Stell.   Prof.; Chair*
Marcus, Nizar, BSc S.Af., PhD Cape Town   Sr.
Lectr.
Ndogmo, Jean-Claude, PhD Montr.   Sr. Lectr.
Witbooi, Peter J., MSc W.Cape, PhD Cape Town
Prof.
Other Staff: 5 Lectrs.
Research: Abelian group theory; algebraic
topology; nearrings; operator theory;
topology and category theory

Maxillofacial and Oral Surgery, Anaesthesiology and Sedation

Tel: (021) 328116 Fax: (021) 325050
E-mail: jdewet@uwc.ac.za
Hein, Gregory, BSc W.Cape, BChD W.Cape,
MChD W.Cape   Sr. Lectr.
Kariem, G., BChD W.Cape, MChD W.Cape
Assoc. Prof.
Levendal, Allan, BChD W.Cape, BChD Stell.   Sr.
Lectr.
Louw, L. R., BChD Pret., MSc Stell., PhD Stell.
Sr. Lectr.
Morkel, Jean A., MB ChB Stell., MChD Stell.
Assoc. Prof.; Chair*
Roelofse, James, MB ChB Stell., MMed Stell.,
PhD Stell.   Prof.
van der Westhuizen, Albert J., MChD Stell.   Sr.
Lectr.
Other Staff: 8 Lectrs.; 6 Registrars
Research: unicystic ameloblastomas

Medical Bioscience

Tel: (021) 959 2182 Fax: (021) 959 2338
E-mail: nlouw@uwc.ac.za
Africa, Charlene, PhD Lond.   Assoc. Prof.
de Kock, Maryna, PhD Pret.   Assoc. Prof.
Dietrich, Daneel L. L., BSc W.Cape, PhD
V.U.Amst.   Assoc. Prof.
Fielding, Bertram C., PhD W.Cape   Sr. Lectr.
Fisher, David, MSc Cape Town, PhD W.Cape   Sr.
Lectr.
Henkel, Ralf, PhD Phillips   Prof.; Sr. Lectr.
Johnson, Quinton, BSc W.Cape, MSc W.Cape,
PhD W.Cape   Assoc. Prof.

Maritz, Gert S., BSc Stell., B(B&A) Stell.,
MScMedSci Stell., PhD Stell.   Prof.
Van der Horst, Gerhard, MSc Stell., PhD
P.Elizabeth, PhD Stell.   Prof.
Other Staff: 5 Lectrs.; 7 Technologists

Natural Medicine, School of

Tel: (021) 959 3064 Fax: (021) 959 3686
E-mail: zgeyer@uwc.ac.za
Moiloa, Motlhabane R., MD WI, PhD WI
Prof.; Dir.*
Swart, Rina, BSc Stell., MPhil W.Cape, PhD
W.Cape   Sr. Lectr.
Other Staff: 10 Lectrs.
Research: Chinese medicine and acupuncture;
naturotherapy; phytotherapy; Unani-Tibb
medicine

Nursing

Tel: (021) 959 2271 Fax: (021) 959 3686
E-mail: cfester@uwc.ac.za
Julie, Hester, BCur W.Cape, BA S.Af., MPH
W.Cape   Sr. Lectr.
Khanyile, Thembisile, BA S.Af., MEd S.Af., PhD
Natal   Assoc. Prof.; Chair*
Kortenbout, W., BSocSc Natal, MSocSc Natal,
PhD Natal   Prof.
Mbombo, Nomafrench, BCur Fort Hare, MCur
Natal, PhD W.Cape   Sr. Lectr.
Nikodem, Cheryl, BA(Cur) S.Af., MCur Rand
Afrikaans, DCur Rand Afrikaans   Assoc. Prof.
Other Staff: 8 Lectrs.
Research: advanced (graduate) midwifery
practice; community participation in health
development; human research development
for the health sector

Occupational Therapy

Tel: (021) 959 2544 Fax: (021) 959 3151
E-mail: ldavids@uwc.ac.za
De Jongh, Jo-celene, BOccTher Stell., MPhil
W.Cape   Sr. Lectr.; Chair*
Nicholls, Lindsey, BSc(OccTher) Cape Town, MA
Sr. Lectr.
Wegner, Lisa, BSc(OT) Witw., MSc(OT) Cape
Town   Sr. Lectr.
Other Staff: 5 Lectrs.

Oral Hygiene

Tel: (021) 370 4448 Fax: (021) 392 3250
E-mail: eluckhoff@uwc.ac.za
Gordon, Natalie, BA S.Af., MPH Maastricht   Sr.
Lectr.; Chair*
Potgieter, Elizabeth, BSc Stell.   Sr. Lectr.
Rayner, Chrisleen, BA W.Cape   Sr. Lectr.
Viljoen, Porcha M., BA S.Af.   Sr. Lectr.
Other Staff: 2 Lectrs.

Orthodontics and Paediatric Dentistry

Tel: (021) 392 8116 Fax: (021) 392 5050
E-mail: cmyburgh@uwc.ac.za
Harris, Angela M. P., BScMedSc Stell., MChD
Stell.   Prof.; Chair*
Hudson, Athol P. G., BChD Stell., BSc(Dent)
Stell.   Sr. Lectr.
Shaikh, Amenah, BChD W.Cape, MSc(Dent)
W.Cape, MChD W.Cape   Sr. Lectr.
Theunissen, Evan T. L., BChD W.Cape, MChD
W.Cape   Sr. Lectr.
Yasin-Harnekar, Soraya, BChD W.Cape,
MSc(Dent) W.Cape   Sr. Lectr.
Other Staff: 1 Lectr.
Vacant Posts: 1 Prof.
Research: attitudes and concerns of patients with
cleft lip and palate and their parents;
cranio-facial morphology of cleft lip and
palate patients

Pharmacy, School of

Tel: (021) 959 2190 Fax: (021) 959 3407
E-mail: rsymonds@uwc.ac.za
Amabeoku, George J., BSc Portsmouth, MSc
Wales, PhD Nigeria   Assoc. Prof.
Bapoo, Rafik, BSc W.Cape, BSc Potchef., BPharm
W.Cape, BSc(IndPharm) Potchef.   Sr. Lectr.
Bheekie, Angenie, BSc Trinity(Dub.), BPharm
Durban-W., DPharm W.Cape   Sr. Lectr.

Butler, Nadine C., BScMedSci Stell., MPharm W.Cape, PhD Minn. Prof.

Eagles, Peter F. K., MPharm W.Cape, PhD Cape Town Prof.

Gorter, R., MD Cologne, PhD Cologne Extraordinary Prof.

Leng, Henry, BSc W.Cape, MPharm W.Cape, MScMedSci Stell., PhD Cape Town Assoc. Prof.

Mugabo, P., BSc Rwanda, MB ChB Rwanda, MD Louvain, PhD Ghent Assoc. Prof.

Myburgh, Johannes A., MPharm W.Cape Assoc. Prof.; Chair*

Sewram, V., MPH Cape Town, PhD Natal Extraordinary Prof.

Syce, James A., MPharm W.Cape, PhD Kentucky Prof.

Other Staff: 3 Lectrs.

Philosophy

Tel: (021) 959 2167 Fax: (021) 959 2376
E-mail: kabrahams@uwc.ac.za

Abrahams, Jacobus P., MA W.Cape Lectr.; Chair*

Research: philosophy of technology

Physics

Tel: (021) 959 2327 Fax: (021) 959 3474
E-mail: aadams@uwc.ac.za

Adams, Danny, MSc W.Cape, PhD Arizona State Prof.

Demeijer, Rob J., PhD Utrecht Extraordinary Prof.

Julies, Roderick E., MSc W.Cape, PhD Stell. Sr. Lectr.

Knoesen, Dirk, MSc Stell., PhD Stell. Prof.

Krylov, Igor, MSc Moscow, DSc Moscow Prof.

Linder, Cedric J., BSc Rhodes, EdM Rutgers, EdD Br.Col. Prof.

Lindsay, Robert, BSc Stell., DPhil Oxf. Prof.; Chair*

Madjoe, Reginald, MSc W.Cape, PhD W.Cape Assoc. Prof.

Marshall, Delia, BSc Cape Town, DPhil Oxf. Assoc. Prof.

Richter, Werner A., PhD Stell. Extraordinary Prof.

Swanepoel, R., MSc S.Af., PhD Rand Afrikaans Extraordinary Prof.

Other Staff: 1 Lectr.

Research: nuclear physics; physics education; solid state physics (high temperature superconductors, photovoltaic material, thin film metal silicides)

Physiotherapy

Tel: (021) 959 2542 Fax: (021) 959 2804
E-mail: mcoetzee@uwc.ac.za

Frantz, Jose, BSc(Physiotherapy) W.Cape, MSc W.Cape, PhD W.Cape Sr. Lectr.; Chair*

Marais, Margaret R., MSc(Physiotherapy) W.Cape Sr. Lectr.

Struthers, Patricia, BSc(Physio) Cape Town, MPhil W.Cape Sr. Lectr.

Other Staff: 6 Lectrs.

Political Studies

Tel: (021) 959 3228 Fax: (021) 959 2578
E-mail: mhoskins@uwc.ac.za

Gottschalk, Keith A., BA Cape Town Lectr.; Chair*

Van Vuuren, Willem L. J., MA Stell., DPhil Stell. Prof.

von Lieres und Wilkau Zwarenstein, B., MA Witw., PhD Essex Sr. Lectr.

Other Staff: 1 Lectr.

Research: cultural politics; identity politics and democratic consolidation; South African party politics, African Union and pan-African parliament

Psychology

see also Indust. Psychol.

Tel: (021) 959 2283 Fax: (021) 959 3515
E-mail: rklink@uwc.ac.za

Adam, Mohamed E., MA W.Cape, MPsych W.Cape Sr. Lectr.

Ahmed, Rashid, MA Cape Town Sr. Lectr.

Andipatin, Michelle, MA(Psych) W.Cape Sr. Lectr.

Bawa, Umesh L., BA Durban-W., BA S.Af., MA Witw. Sr. Lectr.

Malcolm, Charles, MA Witw., PhD Rhodes Prof.; Chair*

Mwaba, Kelven, MA Syr., PhD Syr. Prof.

Ratele, Kopano, MA Natal, DPhil W.Cape Prof.

Other Staff: 7 Lectrs.

Vacant Posts: 1 Sr. Lectr.; 1 Assoc. Prof.

Research: community psychology; forensic psychology; gender and identity (constructions of masculinities and male identities); health psychology (behavioural dimensions of HIV/AIDS)

Public Health, School of

Tel: (021) 959 2402 Fax: (021) 959 2872
E-mail: dsanders@uwc.ac.za

Hausler, Harry, BSc Br.Col., MPH Johns H., MPhil Lond. Sr. Lectr.

Jackson, Debra, MPH Boston, ScD Boston Sr. Lectr.

Lehmann, Uta, PhD Hanover Sr. Lectr.

Puoane, Thandi, BCur S.Af., MPH Calif., DrPH Calif. Sr. Lectr.

Reagon, G., MB ChB Cape Town Sr. Lectr.

Sanders, David M., MB ChB Birm. Prof.; Dir.*

Other Staff: 4 Lectrs.; 13 Researchers; 3 Hon. Profs.

Research: health information systems; HIV/AIDS; human resource development; maternal and child health; nutrition

Religion and Theology

Tel: (021) 959 2386 Fax: (021) 959 3355
E-mail: cbergstedt@uwc.ac.za

Cloete, Waldemar T. W., BTh Stell., MA Stell., DLitt Stell. Prof.; Chair*

Conradie, Ernst M., BA Stell., DTh Stell. Assoc. Prof.

Lawrie, Douglas G., BTh Stell., BA Stell., DTh W.Cape Assoc. Prof.

Lombard, Christo, BA Stell., DTh W.Cape Assoc. Prof.

Other Staff: 3 Lectrs.

Research: moral education (the formation of a human rights culture); rhetoric of reconciliation; systematic theology in Africa (mapping the terrain)

Social Work

Tel: (021) 959 2277 Fax: (021) 959 2845
E-mail: gdykes@uwc.ac.za

Beytell, Anna-Marie, BA(SW) Pret., BA(SW) Stell., MA(SocSc) Rand Afrikaans, PhD Rand Afrikaans Sr. Lectr.

Bozalek, Vivienne, BA Witw., MSocSc Cape Town, PhD Utrecht Assoc. Prof.; Chair*

Martin, Andrew, BA W.Cape, MA Ohio, DPhil Ohio Sr. Lectr.

Terblanche, Susan S., BA P.Elizabeth, MA(SW) P.Elizabeth, DPhil Rand Afrikaans Assoc. Prof.

Other Staff: 4 Lectrs.

Vacant Posts: 1 Prof.

Sport, Recreation and Exercise Science

Tel: (021) 959 2350 Fax: (021) 959 3688
E-mail: vkensley@uwc.ac.za

Jones, Denise, BA Stell., BA Cape Town, PhD Utrecht Assoc. Prof.

Travill, Andre, BA(PhysEd) Rhodes, MA(PhysEd) San Diego, PhD Witw. Assoc. Prof.; Chair*

Other Staff: 2 Lectrs.

Vacant Posts: 1 Prof.

Research: morphopological studies of beach volleyball; nutritional status, growth, physical performance and maturation of socially disadvantaged boys and girls aged 8-17 living in the Western Cape

Statistics

Tel: (021) 959 3038 Fax: (021) 959 3055
E-mail: lselbourne@uwc.ac.za

Blignaut, Renette J., BSc Rand Afrikaans, MSc Cape Town, PhD Pret. Assoc. Prof.; Chair*

Koen, Chris, MSc Cape Town, PhD Cape Town, PhD Rand Afrikaans Prof.

Kotze, Danelle, MSc S.Af., MBL S.Af., DComm Stell. Prof.

Shell, Robert, PhD Yale Extraordinary Prof.

Tati, Gabriel, MSc Yaounde II, PhD Brist. Sr. Lectr.

Other Staff: 3 Lectrs.

Research: aspects of biostatistics and collaborative learning; demographic analysis and statistical information systems; discriminant analysis (variable selection); multiple regression (outliers and influential observations); neural networks

Women's and Gender Studies

Tel: (021) 959 3360 Fax: (021) 959 2202
E-mail: tshefer@uwc.ac.za

Shefer, T., BA Cape Town, MA Cape Town, DPhil W.Cape Sr. Lectr.; Dir.*

Other Staff: 1 Lectr.

Research: gender, culture and diversity; women, state and policy

Xhosa

Tel: (021) 959 2358 Fax: (021) 959 2376
E-mail: jberry@uwc.ac.za

Neethling, Siebert J., MA P.Elizabeth, DLitt Stell. Prof.; Chair*

van Huyssteen, Alette, BA Stell., MA Stell. Sr. Lectr.

Other Staff: 5 Lectrs.

SPECIAL CENTRES, ETC

Adult and Continuing Education, Centre for

Tel: (021) 959 2231 Fax: (021) 959 2481
E-mail: zgroener@uwc.ac.za

Groener, Z., MSc Edin., PhD Calif. Assoc. Prof.; Dir.*

Child and Youth Research and Training Programme

Tel: (021) 959 2602 Fax: (021) 959 2606
E-mail: rseptember@uwc.ac.za

Barnes-September, R. L., BA(SW) W.Cape, MA Cornell, DPhil W.Cape Prof.; Dir.*

Other Staff: 2 Researchers

Vacant Posts: 3 Researchers

Community Law Centre

Tel: (021) 959 2950 Fax: (021) 959 2411
E-mail: tfortuin@uwc.ac.za

Steytler, Nicolaas C., BA Stell., LLB Stell., LLM Lond., PhD Natal Prof.; Dir.*

Higher Education, Centre for the Study of

Tel: (021) 959 2580 Fax: (021) 959 3278

Thaver, Beverly, BA Cape Town, MA York(UK), DPhil W.Cape Acting Dir.*

Historical Research/Archives, Institute for

Tel: (021) 959 2616 Fax: (021) 959 3178
E-mail: cloff@uwc.ac.za

Loff, Christiaan J., Drs Theol.Sch.Kampen Acting Dir.*

Vacant Posts: 1 Sr. Lectr.

Legal Aid Clinic

Tel: (021) 959 3421 Fax: (021) 959 2747
E-mail: ssamaai@uwc.ac.za

Samaai, Sehaam, BProc W.Cape Dir.*

Multilingualism and Language Profession, Iilwimi Centre for

Tel: (021) 959 2666 Fax: (021) 959 1320
E-mail: cdyers@uwc.ac.za

Dyers, Charlyn, BA W.Cape, MSc Edin., DLitt W.Cape Assoc. Prof.; Dir.*

Vacant Posts: 1 Prof.; 2 Sr. Lectrs.

Research: language attitudes and intervention programmes; mediating discourse between patient and doctor via trained interpreters;

1410   SOUTH AFRICA/WESTERN CAPE

multilingualism, particularly in the Western Cape

Science and Mathematics Education, School of

Tel: (021) 959 2525 Fax: (021) 959 2602
E-mail: cjulie@uwc.ac.za
Julie, Cyril M., MSc W.Cape, PhD Ill.   Prof.;
Chair*
Research: scientific and technological literacy among grades 7-9 teachers and pupils in Western Cape

South African Herbal Science and Medicine Institute

Tel: (021) 959 3030 Fax: (021) 959 3029
E-mail: ocase@uwc.ac.za
Johnson, Quinton, BSc W.Cape, MSc W.Cape,
PhD W.Cape   Dir.*
Klaasen, Jeremy, PhD Penn.State   Sr. Lectr.
Other Staff: 3 Lectrs.

South African National Bio-Informatics Institute (SANBI)

Tel: (021) 959 3645 Fax: (021) 959 2512
E-mail: jjansen@uwc.ac.za
Bajic, Vlad, PhD Zagreb   Visiting Prof.
Gray, C., PhD Witw.   Visiting Prof.
Hide, Winston, PhD Temple   Prof.; Dir.*
Lehvaslaiho, H., PhD
Seoighe, Cathal, PhD Trinity(Dub.)   Visiting
Prof.

Southern African Studies, Centre for

Tel: (021) 959 3859 Fax: (021) 959 3862
E-mail: lthompson@uwc.ac.za
Thompson, Lisa, BA Cape Town, BA Rhodes, MA
Rhodes, PhD W.Cape   Prof.; Dir.*

Student Counselling, Centre for

Tel: (021) 959 2881 Fax: (021) 959 2882
E-mail: mparker@uwc.ac.za
Parker, Mumtaj, BCur W.Cape, BA W.Cape, MA
Durban-W.   Sr. Lectr.
Other Staff: 3 Lectrs.
Vacant Posts: Dir.*; 1 Sr. Lectr.

CONTACT OFFICERS

Academic affairs. Deputy Registrar (Academic affairs): (vacant)
Accommodation. Director, Residential and Catering Services: Seale, Mark
(E-mail: mseale@uwc.ac.za)
Admissions (first degree). Admissions Officer: Vermeulen, Harlene
(E-mail: hvermeulen@uwc.ac.za)
Admissions (higher degree). Admissions Officer: Christians, Nicoline
(E-mail: nchristians@uwc.ac.za)
Alumni. Alumni Office: (vacant)
Archives. Archivist, Institute for Historical Research: Loff, Christiaan J., Drs
Theol.Sch.Kampen (E-mail: cloff@uwc.ac.za)
Computing services. Executive Director, Computer Centre: Keats, Prof. Derek W.,
PhD Nfld. (E-mail: dkeats@uwc.ac.za)
Development/fund-raising. Head, Development: Schuller, Raymond
(E-mail: rschuller@uwc.ac.za)
Finance. Executive Director (Finance): Regal, Abduraghman (E-mail: mregal@uwc.ac.za)
General enquiries. Registrar (Academic): Miller, Ingrid M., BHMS Stell., MHMS Stell.,
DPhil W.Cape (E-mail: imiller@uwc.ac.za)
Health services. Head (Health services): Bagwandeen, M., MB ChB Natal
(E-mail: mbagwandeen@uwc.ac.za)

International office. Director (International office): Persens, Prof. Jan, MSc S.Af., MA
Cornell, PhD Cornell
(E-mail: jpersens@uwc.ac.za)
Library (chief librarian). Head (Library): Ntshuntshe-Matshaya, P.
(E-mail: pmatshaya@uwc.ac.za)
Personnel/human resources. Head (Personnel/human resources): Hambrook-
Glaeser, Amanda, BA Rand Afrikaans, BA Pret.
(E-mail: ahambrook@uwc.ac.za)
Public relations. Public Relations Officer: Philander, Amanda
(E-mail: aphilander@uwc.ac.za)
Publications. Editor: Jaffer, K., MA W.Cape
(E-mail: kjaffer@uwc.ac.za)
Purchasing. Head (Purchasing): Thandeki, Barbara (E-mail: bthandeki@uwc.ac.za)
Research. Dean (Research): Christie, Prof. Renfrew, BCom S.Af., BA Cape Town, MA
Cape Town, DPhil Oxf.
(E-mail: rchristie@uwc.ac.za)
Safety. Head Safety Officer: Adonis, Jeff
(E-mail: jadonis@uwc.ac.za)
Schools liaison. Head (Schools liaison): Petersen, Douglas
(E-mail: mpetersen@uwc.ac.za)
Security. Head, Campus Protection Services: Sam, Frank (E-mail: fsam@uwc.ac.za)
Sport and recreation. Head, Sports Administration: Groenewald, Ihlaam
(E-mail: igroenewald@uwc.ac.za)
Student welfare/counselling. Director (Student welfare/counselling): (vacant)

[Information supplied by the institution as at 28 September 2007, and edited by the ACU]

UNIVERSITY OF THE WITWATERSRAND, JOHANNESBURG

Founded 1922

Member of the Association of Commonwealth Universities

Postal Address: Private Bag 3, Witwatersrand, 2050 South Africa
Telephone: (011) 717 1000 **Fax:** (011) 339 7620
URL: http://www.wits.ac.za

VICE-CHANCELLOR AND PRINCIPAL*—Nongxa, Prof. Loyiso G., BSc Fort Hare, MSc Fort Hare, DPhil Oxf.
CHAIRMAN OF COUNCIL—Cameron, The Hon. Mr. Justice E., BA Stell., LLB S.Af., BCL Oxf., MA Oxf.
DEPUTY VICE-CHANCELLOR (ACADEMIC: INTERNAL)—Ballim, Prof. Y., BSc(Eng) Witw., MSc(Eng) Witw., PhD Witw.
ACTING EXECUTIVE DIRECTOR (FINANCE)—FitzGerald, Prof. P., BA Witw., MPA Liv.
DEPUTY VICE-CHANCELLOR (ACADEMIC: EXTERNAL)—(vacant)
DEPUTY VICE-CHANCELLOR (RESEARCH)—Bozzoli, Prof. Belinda, BA Witw., MA Sus., DPhil Sus.
REGISTRAR (ACADEMIC)‡—Swemmer, Derek K., BA Pret., MA Pret., DLitt&Phil S.Af.

GENERAL INFORMATION

History. The university achieved full university status in 1922.
It is located in Braamfontein, Johannesburg.

Admission to first degree courses (see also South African Introduction). South African applicants under 23 years: matriculation certificate with university exemption. Some faculties set additional requirements. International applicants must obtain exemption from the Matriculation Board. All students must be proficient in English.

First Degrees (see also South African Directory to Subjects of Study) (* = with honours). BA, BA*, BAcc, BA(DramaticArt), BA(Education), BA(FineArts), BA(FineArts)(Education), BAS, BA(SocialWork), BA(Sp&HTherapy), BCom, BCom*, BDS, BEconSc, BEconSc*, BMus, BMus(Education), BNurs, BPharm, BPhysEd,

BPrimaryEd, BSc, BSc*, BSc(Building), BSc(Eng), BSc(LabMed), BSc(OralBiology), BSc(OT), BSc(Physiotherapy), BSc(QS), BSc(TRP), LLB, MB BCh.
Additional 2 years part-time for honours.
Length of course. Full-time: BEconSc*, BSc(LabMed), BSc*: 1 year; BA, BCom, BEconSc, BSc: 3 years; BA(DramaticArt), BA(FineArts), BA(SocialWork), BA(Sp&HTherapy), BA*, BAcc, BCom*, BMus, BNurs, BPharm, BPhysEd, BPrimaryEd, BSc(Physiotherapy), LLB: 4 years; BDS: 5½ years; MB BCh: 6 years. Part-time: BEconSc*: 2-4 years; BCom: 4 years.

Higher Degrees (see also South African Directory to Subjects of Study).
Master's. BArch, BEd, LLM, MA, MA(Audiology), MA(ClinPsych), MA(DramaticArt), MA(FineArts), MArch, MA(SocialWork), MA(SpeechPathology), MBA, MCom, MDent, MEconSc, MFamMed, MM, MMed, MMus,

MPH, MPharm, MSc, MSc(Building), MSc(Dent), MSc(DP), MSc(Eng), MSc(Med), MSc(Nursing), MSc(OT), MSc(Physiotherapy), MSc(QS), MSc(TRP), MUD.
Length of course. Full-time: BEd, LLM, MA, MA(ClinPsych), MA(DramaticArt), MA(FineArts), MA(SocialWork), MA(SpeechPathology), MArch, MBA, MCom, MEconSc, MSc, MSc(Eng), MSc(Med), MSc(Nursing), MSc(Physiotherapy): 1 year; MUD: 1½ years; BArch, MA(Translation), MFamMed, MPH, MSc(DP): 2 years; MDent, MMed: 3-4 years. Part-time: BEd, LLM, MA, MA(ClinPsych), MA(DramaticArt), MA(FineArts), MA(SocialWork), MA(SpeechPathology), MArch, MCom, MEconSc, MSc, MSc(Eng), MSc(Med): 2 years; MSc(Nursing), MSc(Physiotherapy): 2½ years; MBA, MFamMed, MUD: 3 years; MA(Translation), MPH: 4 years.
Doctoral. DArch, DCom, DEconSc, DEd, DEng, DLitt, DMus, DSc, DSc(Arch), DSc(Building), DSc(BusAd), DSc(Dent), DSc(Eng), DSc(Med),

DSc(QS), DSc(TRP), D(TRP), LLD, PhD, PhD(Med).

Admission. Higher doctorates: awarded on published work.

Length of course. Full-time: DEconSc, DEd, DEng, DSc, DSc(Dent), DSc(Eng), DSc(Med), DSc(QS), LLD, PhD, PhD(Med): 2 years. Part-time: DEconSc, DEd, DEng, DSc, DSc(Dent), DSc(Eng), DSc(Med), DSc(QS), LLD, PhD, PhD(Med): 4 years.

Libraries. Volumes: 5,000,000. Periodicals subscribed to: 12,000.

Academic Year (2008). Four terms: 4 February–20 March; 31 March–16 May; 7 July–15 August; 25 August–20 October.

FACULTIES/SCHOOLS

Commerce, Law and Management
Tel: (011) 717 8000
E-mail: 100rwd@mentor.wits.ac.za
Acting Dean: Munro, K. A., BA *Witw.*
Secretary: Variava, F.

Engineering and the Built Environment
Tel: (011) 717 7600 Fax: (011) 403 4657
Dean: Lacquet, Prof. B. M., BSc *Rand Afrikaans*, MSc *Rand Afrikaans*, PhD *Rand Afrikaans*
Secretary: Billett, R.

Health Sciences
Tel: (011) 717 2000 Fax: (011) 643 3418
E-mail: deanhsc@health.wits.ac.za
Dean: Laburn, Prof. H. P., BSc *Witw.*, PhD *Witw.*
Secretary: Holt, L.

Humanities
Tel: (011) 717 7400 Fax: (011) 339 4524
Dean: Kupe, T., BA *Z'bwe.*, MA *Z'bwe.*, PhD *Oslo*
Secretary: Underhay, A.

Science
Tel: (011) 717 6000 Fax: (011) 339 3959
Dean: Bharuthram, Prof. R., BSc *S.Af.*, BSc *Durban-W.*, MSc *Natal*, PhD *Natal*
Secretary: Holmes, M. C.

ACADEMIC UNITS
Arranged by Schools

Accounting
Tel: (011) 717 8020 Fax: (011) 339 7884
E-mail: dicksonp@spa.wits.ac.za
Aucock, M. C., BEd *Natal*, MA *Natal*   Sr. Lectr.
de Koker, A. P., BCom *Cape Town*, MCom *Witw.*   Prof.
Dickson, P. L., BSc *Witw.*   Visiting Prof.
Firer, S., BCom *Natal*, BASc *S.Af.*, MBA *Prague*   Assoc. Prof.
Fridman, B. I., BCompt *S.Af.*   Sr. Lectr.
Kolitz, D. L., BCom *Natal*, BCom *S.Af.*, MCom *Witw.*   Assoc. Prof.
Lowe, N. J., BA *Natal*, MA *Natal*   Sr. Lectr.
Negash, M. M., BA *Addis Ababa*, MBA *Leuven*, DEconSc *Brussels*   Prof.; Head*
Papageorgiou, E., BCom *Stell.*, BCom *S.Af.*, MCom *Rand Afrikaans*   Sr. Lectr.
Rabin, C. E., MCom *Witw.*   Assoc. Prof.
Sanders, N. J., BA *Natal*, MA *Natal*   Sr. Lectr.
Sartorius, K., MCom *Witw.*   Assoc. Prof.
Swartz, G. E., BAcc *Witw.*   Assoc. Prof.
Other Staff: 17 Lectrs.; 7 Assoc. Lectrs.; 2 Lectrs.†

Animal, Plant and Environmental Sciences
Tel: (011) 717 6400 Fax: (011) 403 1429
E-mail: shirley@gecko.biol.wits.ac.za
Alexander, G. J., BSc *Natal*, MSc *Natal*, PhD *Witw.*   Assoc. Prof.
Balkwill, K., BSc *Witw.*, PhD *Natal*   Prof.; Head*
Byrne, M. J., BSc *Lond.*, MSc *Witw.*, PhD *Witw.*   Assoc. Prof.

Cron, G. V., BSc *Witw.*, MSc *Witw.*, PhD *Witw.*   Sr. Lectr.
Duncan, F. D., BSc *Witw.*, MSc *OFS*, PhD *Witw.*   Sr. Lectr.
Erasmus, B. F., BSc *Pret.*, PhD *Pret.*   Sr. Lectr.
Ledger, J. A., BSc *Natal*, MSc *Natal*, PhD *Witw.*   Visiting Assoc. Prof.
Mckechnie, A. E., BSc *Natal*, MSc *Natal*, PhD *Natal*   Sr. Lectr.
Mycock, D. J., BSc *Natal*, PhD *Natal*   Sr. Lectr.
Owen-Smith, R. N., BSc *Natal*, MSc *Natal*, PhD *Wis.*   Prof.
Pillay, N., BSc *Natal*, MSc *Natal*, PhD *Natal*   Assoc. Prof.
Rogers, K. H., BSc *Natal*, PhD *Natal*   Prof.
Sanders, M. R., BSc *Witw.*, MEd *Witw.*, PhD *Cape Town*   Assoc. Prof.
Scholes, Mary C., BSc *Witw.*, PhD *Witw.*   Prof.
Sym, S. D., BSc *Witw.*, MSc *Witw.*, PhD *Witw.*   Sr. Lectr.
Whiting, M. J., MSc *Austin State*, PhD *Stell.*   Assoc. Prof.
Witkowski, E. T. F., BSc *Witw.*, MSc *Witw.*, PhD *Cape Town*   Prof.
Other Staff: 1 Res. Fellow; 1 Visiting Res. Fellow; 1 Res. Assoc.; 1 Researcher; 4 Visiting Researchers; 5 Sr. Tutors; 2 Tutors; 1 Assoc. Lectr.†; 1 Assoc. Researcher†; 1 Tutor†; 11 Hon. Profs.
Research: African ecology and conservation biology; communication and behaviour; ecophysiological studies; parasitology; restoration and conservation biology

Architecture and Planning
Tel: (011) 717 7620 Fax: (011) 403 2308
E-mail: ramanp@archplan.wits.ac.za
Charlton, S. M., BA *Witw.*, MA *Natal*   Sr. Lectr.
Huchzermeyer, M., BL *Pret.*, PhD *Cape Town*   Assoc. Prof.
Irurah, D. K., BArch *Nair.*, MArch *Oregon*, PhD *Pret.*   Sr. Lectr.
Karam, Aly, BScArch *Alexandria*, MArch *Kansas*, PhD *N.Carolina*   Sr. Lectr.
Klein, G. R., BSc *Witw.*, MUD *Witw.*   Sr. Lectr.
Kotze, C. P., BA *Free State*, PhD *Cape Town*   Sr. Lectr.
Le Roux, H. K., BArch *Witw.*, MArch *Witw.*   Sr. Lectr.
Mabin, A. S., BA *Witw.*, MA *Witw.*, PhD *S.Fraser*   Prof.; Head*
Winkler, T. A., BSc *Witw.*, PhD *Br.Col.*   Sr. Lectr.
Other Staff: 3 Visiting Profs.; 6 Lectrs.; 1 Tutor; 7 Adjunct Profs.; 2 Sr. Lectrs.†; 7 Lectrs.†; 2 Sr. Tutors†; 1 Hon. Prof.; 3 Hon. Sr. Lectrs.

Arts
Nettleton, A. C. E., BA *Witw.*, MA *Witw.*, PhD *Witw.*   Prof.; Head*
Other Staff: 1 Lectr.; 1 Res. Assoc.; 2 Lectrs.†; 1 Sr. Tutor†; 1 Hon. Prof.

Digital Multimedia
Doherty, C. M. W., BA *Cape Town*, MA *Natal*   Head*

Dramatic Art
Ebrahim, H., BA *Durban-W.*, MA *Ill.*   Head*
Nebe, W. A., MA *Cape Town*   Sr. Lectr.
Roberts, S. E., BA *Natal*, MA *CNAA*   Assoc. Prof.
Taylor, C. J., BA *Cape Town*, MA *Cape Town*, PhD *Northwestern*   Prof.†
Other Staff: 3 Lectrs.; 1 Assoc. Lectr.; 1 Principal Tutor; 1 Sr. Tutor; 1 Lectr.†; 1 Sr. Tutor†

Fine Arts
Andrew, D. P., BA *Natal*   Sr. Lectr.
Crump, A., BA *Cape Town*, MFA *Cape Town*, MFA   Prof.
Oltman, W., BA *Natal*, MA *Witw.*   Sr. Lectr.
Richards, C. P., BA *S.Af.*, PhD *Witw.*   Personal Prof.
Wafer, J. S., BA *Natal*, MA *Witw.*   Assoc. Prof.; Head*

Other Staff: 1 Principal Tutor; 1 Visiting Researcher; 2 Assoc. Profs.†

History of Art
Bunn, D. N., BA *Rhodes*, MA *Northwestern*, PhD *Northwestern*   Prof.
Freschi, F., BA *Witw.*, BA *Cape Town*   Prof.; Head*

Music
Allen, L., BMus *Natal*, MMus *Natal*, PhD *Camb.*   Sr. Lectr.
Lucia, C. E., MA *Oxf.*, PhD *Rhodes*   Assoc. Prof.
Rorich, M. E., BMus *Cape Town*, PhD *Witw.*   Assoc. Prof.
Zaidel-Rudolph, J., DMus *Pret.*   Prof.; Head*
Other Staff: 1 Lectr.; 2 Principal Tutors

Television Studies
Heatlie, D. J., BA *Cape Town*, MA *Cape Town*   Prof.; Head*
Mistry, J., BA *Witw.*, MA *N.Y.*, PhD *N.Y.*   Assoc. Prof.
Other Staff: 2 Lectrs.; 2 Tutors; 1 Researcher; 1 Sr. Tutor†

Biology, Molecular and Cell
Tel: (011) 717 6310 Fax: (011) 339 7377
E-mail: chrissie@gecko.biol.wits.ac.za
Dabbs, E. R., BA *Camb.*, MA *Camb.*, PhD *Harv.*   Prof.
Dirr, H. W., BSc *Jo'burg.*, MSc *Jo'burg.*, PhD *Jo'burg.*   Prof.
Gray, V. M., BSc *Witw.*, PhD *Witw.*   Sr. Lectr.
McLellan, T., SB *M.I.T.*, PhD *M.I.T.*   Assoc. Prof.
Ntwasa, M. M., BSc *Cape Town*, MPhil *Camb.*, PhD *Camb.*   Sr. Lectr.
Rey, Christine M. E., BSc *Witw.*, PhD *Witw.*   Prof.; Head*
Straker, C. J., BA *Cape Town*, BSc *Cape Town*, PhD *Cape Town*   Assoc. Prof.
Veale, R. B., BSc *Witw.*, PhD *Witw.*   Assoc. Prof.
Von Holy, A., BSc *Witw.*, MSc *Pret.*, PhD *Pret.*   Prof.†
Other Staff: 4 Lectrs.; 2 Principal Tutors; 1 Tutor; 1 Researcher; 2 Visiting Researchers; 1 Lectr.†; 5 Hon. Profs.
Research: protein structure and function

Business Administration, Graduate School of
Tel: (011) 717 3600 Fax: (011) 643 2336
E-mail: thomas.a@wbs.wits.ac.za
Ahwireng-Obeng, F., BSc *Ghana*, PhD *Leeds*   Prof.
Bick, G. N. C., BSc(Eng) *Cape Town*, BCom *S.Af.*, MBA *Calif.*   Sr. Lectr.
Dickinson, D., BA *Natal*, MBA *Witw.*   Prof.
Durand, F. D., BSc *Natal*, MBA *Witw.*   Sr. Lectr.
Heald, G. R., BA *Cape Town*, BAdmin *Stell.*, MBA *Stell.*   Sr. Lectr.
Luiz, J. M., BCom *Witw.*, MCom *Witw.*, PhD *Stell.*   Prof.
Ncube, M., BSc *Ghana*, PhD *Leeds*   Prof.; Head*
Pycraft, M. T. H., BSc *Manc.*, MBL *S.Af.*   Sr. Lectr.
Rijamampianina, R., MBA *Otaru Comm.*, DBA *Hokkaido*   Assoc. Prof.
Stacey, A. G., BScEng *Witw.*, PhD *Witw.*   Sr. Lectr.
Viedge, C., BA *Witw.*, MA *Witw.*   Sr. Lectr.
Whittaker, L., BCom *Witw.*, MCom *Witw.*   Sr. Lectr.
Other Staff: 6 Visiting Profs.; 10 Lectrs.; 1 Lectr.†; 1 Tutor†

Chemistry
Tel: (011) 717 6700 Fax: (011) 339 7967
E-mail: hmarques@aurum.chem.wits.ac.za
Bapoo, A. H., BSc *S.Af.*, BSc *Witw.*, PhD *Witw.*   Sr. Lectr.
Billing, D. G., BSc *Witw.*, MSc *Witw.*, PhD *Witw.*   Sr. Lectr.
Carlton, L., BSc *Brist.*, BSc *Exe.*, PhD *Exe.*   Reader

Coville, N. J., BSc *Witw.*, MSc *Witw.*, PhD *McG.*
  Prof.
Cukrowski, I., DChemSc *Lublin*, DSc *Torún*
  Assoc. Prof.
de Koning, C., BSc *Cape Town*, PhD *Cape Town*
  Sr. Lectr.
de Sousa, A. S., BSc *Witw.*, MSc *Witw.*, PhD
  Witw.   Sr. Lectr.
Levendis, D. C., BSc *Witw.*, MSc *Witw.*, PhD
  Witw.   Assoc. Prof.
Marques, H. M., BSc *Witw.*, PhD *Witw.*   Prof.;
  Head*
Marsicano, F., BSc *Witw.*, PhD *Witw.*   Assoc.
  Prof.
Michael, J. P., BSc *Witw.*, PhD *Witw.*   Prof.
Potgieter, S. S., BSc *Rand Afrikaans*, MSc *Rand
  Afrikaans*   Sr. Lectr.
Scurrell, M. S., BSc *Nott.*, PhD *Nott.*, DSc *Nott.*
  Prof.
Van Otterlo, W. A. L., BSc *Witw.*, MSc *Witw.*,
  PhD *Witw.*   Sr. Lectr.
Other Staff: 2 Visiting Profs.; 3 Lectrs.; 1
  Visiting Lectr.; 4 Principal Tutors; 2 Sr.
  Tutors; 1 Tutor; 1 Researcher; 7 Visiting
  Researchers; 3 Visiting Res. Assocs.; 1
  Prof.†; 7 Hon. Profs.; 3 Hon. Res. Assocs.
Research: molecular design; molecular science

Computer Science

Tel: (011) 717 6170 Fax: (011) 717 6199
  E-mail: conrad@cs.wits.ac.za
Ewert, S., BSc *Stell.*, PhD *Stell.*   Sr. Lectr.
Hazlehurst, S. E., BSc *Witw.*, MSc *Witw.*, PhD
  Br.Col.   Assoc. Prof.
Mueller, C. S., BSc *Witw.*, MSc *Rand Afrikaans*,
  PhD *Witw.*   Prof.
Rock, S. T., BSc *Witw.*, MSc *Witw.*, PhD *Edin.*
  Sr. Lectr.
Sanders, I. D., BSc *Witw.*, MSc(Eng) *Witw.*, PhD
  Pret.   Assoc. Prof.
Wright, C. J., BSc *Witw.*, MPhil *Lond.*, PhD
  Witw.   Prof.; Head*
Other Staff: 1 Lectr.; 2 Principal Tutors; 1
  Lectr.†
Research: highly dependable systems

Construction Economics and Management

Tel: (011) 717 7652 Fax: (011) 339 8175
Pienaar, E. J. A., BSc *Witw.*, MBA *Pret.*, DBA
  Pret.   Prof.; Head*
Talukhaba, A. A., BA *Nair.*, MA *Nair.*, PhD *Nair.*
  Assoc. Prof.
Other Staff: 1 Visiting Prof.; 1 Res. Assoc.
  Prof.; 4 Lectrs.; 1 Principal Tutor; 1 Sr.
  Tutor; 2 Adjunct Profs.; 3 Visiting Profs.†;
  4 Lectrs.†

Economic and Business Sciences

Tel: (011) 717 8084 Fax: (011) 339 7835
  E-mail: 100dave@mentor.wits.ac.za
Addison, T. M., BSc *Cape Town*, MBL *S.Af.*   Sr.
  Lectr.
Benfield, B. C., BCom *P.Elizabeth*, BCom *Witw.*,
  PhD *Witw.*   Visiting Prof.
Cassim, R. I., BA *Natal*, MA *Cape Town*, PhD *Cape
  Town*   Prof.; Head*
Cohen, J. F., BCom *Witw.*, PhD *Witw.*   Sr.
  Lectr.
Gruen, C. A., MA *Abertay*   Sr. Lectr.
Hoenig, S., BEE *Georgia*, MPhil *Col.*, PhD *Col.*
  Visiting Prof.
Mende, J. W. M., BSc *Witw.*, MBL *S.Af.*   Sr.
  Lectr.
Ojah, K., BSc *Oral Roberts*, MFin *St.-Louis*, PhD
  St.-Louis   Assoc. Prof.
Rwigema, H. B., BCom *Nair.*, MBA *Nair.*, PhD
  Nair.   Assoc. Prof.
Simkins, C. E. W., BSc *Witw.*, MA *Oxf.*, PhD
  Natal   Prof.
Vivian, R. W., BSc(Eng) *Witw.*, BProc *S.Af.*, LLB
  S.Af.   Prof.
Zarenda, H., BA *Rhodes*, MA *Witw.*   Assoc. Prof.
Other Staff: 1 Visiting Prof.; 19 Lectrs.; 5
  Visiting Lectrs.; 4 Assoc. Lectrs.; 1 Principal
  Tutor; 2 Sr. Tutors; 1 Sr. Researcher; 1
  Visiting Adjunct Prof.; 1 Prof.†; 2 Adjunct

Profs.†; 5 Lectrs.†; 5 Assoc. Lectrs.†; 1 Sr.
  Principal Tutor†; 1 Tutor†; 1 Hon. Prof.†

Education

Tel: (011) 717 3004 Fax: (011) 339 3956
  E-mail: pendleburys@educ.wits.ac.za
Metcalfe, M. E., BEd *Rhodesia*   Prof.; Head*
Other Staff: 1 Visiting Prof.; 1 Assoc. Lectr.; 2
  Visiting Researchers; 1 Adjunct Prof.; 1
  Assoc. Prof.†; 1 Sr. Tutor†; 1 Tutor†; 4
  Hon. Profs.
Research: education policy

Applied English Language Studies

Janks, H., BA *Witw.*, MA *Witw.*, PhD *Lanc.*
  Personal Prof.†
McFinney, C. W., BA *Cape Town*, BA *Rhodes*, MA
  Lond., PhD *Lond.*   Sr. Lectr.
Stein, P. H., BA *Witw.*, MA *N.Y.State*   Assoc.
  Prof.; Head*
Other Staff: 3 Lectrs.; 2 Principal Tutors

Curriculum Studies

Brodie, K. M., BSc *Witw.*, MEd *Witw.*, PhD *Stan.*
  Assoc. Prof.
Pendlebury, S. A., BA *Witw.*, BEd *Witw.*, MEd
  Witw., DEd *W.Cape*   Prof.; Head*
Shalem, Y. T., BA *Haifa*, BEd *Witw.*, PhD *Witw.*
  Assoc. Prof.
Other Staff: 1 Assoc. Lectr.; 5 Principal Tutors;
  4 Sr. Tutors; 2 Tutors; 1 Tutor†

Economics Education and Information Sciences

Marchant, G. C., BSc *Witw.*, MEd *Jo'burg.*
  Prof.; Head*
Other Staff: 2 Sr. Lectrs.; 1 Principal Tutor; 4
  Tutors; 1 Sr. Tutor†

Education Leadership and Policy Studies

Basson, R. B., BA *Witw.*, BEd *Rhodes*, MA *Lanc.*
  Assoc. Prof.
Carrim, N. H., BEd *Witw.*, MEd *Witw.*   Sr.
  Lectr.
Cross, M., BA *Lourenço Marques*, MEd *Witw.*, PhD
  Witw.   Prof.; Head*
Fleish, B. D., MA *Col.*, PhD *Col.*   Assoc. Prof.
Modiba, M. M., MEd *Witw.*, MA *Keele*, PhD *Keele*
  Sr. Lectr.
Other Staff: 2 Lectrs.

Languages Education and Literacy Development

Cloete, E. L., BA *Stell.*, MA *S.Af.*, PhD *Witw.*
  Sr. Lectr.
Other Staff: 2 Lectrs.; 1 Principal Tutor; 6 Sr.
  Tutors

Mathematics and Science Education

Adler, J. B., BSc *Witw.*, MEd *Witw.*, PhD *Witw.*
  Prof.; Head*
Rollnick, M., BSc *Witw.*, MSc *E.Anglia*, PhD
  Witw.   Prof.
Setati, R. M., BEd *Witw.*, MEd *Witw.*, PhD *Witw.*
  Assoc. Prof.
Other Staff: 4 Lectrs.; 3 Principal Tutors; 7 Sr.
  Tutors; 1 Sr. Lectr.†; 1 Res. Assoc.†

Physical Education

No staff at present

Social Context and Human Development

Castle, P. J., BA *Car.*, MEd *Witw.*, PhD *Witw.*
  Assoc. Prof.
Horsthemke, K. A., BA *Witw.*, MA *Witw.*, PhD
  Witw.   Sr. Lectr.
Kissack, P. M. R., BA *Witw.*, MEd *Witw.*   Sr.
  Lectr.
Osman, R., BA *Witw.*, BEd *S.Af.*, MEd *Witw.*,
  PhD *Witw.*   Sr. Lectr.; Head*
Other Staff: 4 Lectrs.; 2 Assoc. Lectrs.; 1
  Principal Tutor; 4 Sr. Tutors; 1 Sr. Tutor†

Social Science and the Arts

Ludlow, E. H., BA *Cape Town*, MA *Cape Town*
  Sr. Lectr.; Head*

Storbeck, C., MEd *Rand Afrikaans*, PhD *Rand
  Afrikaans*   Sr. Lectr.
Other Staff: 5 Principal Tutors; 4 Sr. Tutors; 4
  Sr. Tutors†

Engineering, Chemical and Metallurgical

Tel: (011) 717 7500 Fax: (011) 339 7213
Fedotova, T., PhD *Ib.*   Sr. Lectr.
Glasser, D., BSc(Eng) *Cape Town*, PhD *Lond.*
  Prof.
Iyuke, S. E., BSc *Nigeria*, BEng *Nigeria*, MSc
  Nigeria, PhD *Kalamazoo*   Sr. Lectr.
Jewell, L. L., BSc *Witw.*, PhD *Witw.*   Sr. Lectr.
Kauchali, S. A., BSc *Witw.*, PhD *Witw.*   Sr.
  Lectr.
Koursaris, A., BSc *Aston*, PhD *Witw.*   Assoc.
  Prof.
Kucukkaragoz, C. S., BSc *Middle East Tech.*, MSc
  Middle East Tech., PhD *Witw.*   Sr. Lectr.
Moys, M. H., BSc(Eng) *Witw.*, MSc(Eng) *Natal*,
  PhD *Natal*   Prof.
Potgieter, J. H., BSc *OFS*, MSc *OFS*, PhD *Witw.*
  Prof.; Head*
Sigalas, I., BSc *Athens*, PhD *Manc.*   Visiting Prof.
Williams, D. A. F., BSc(Eng) *Witw.*, MSc(Eng)
  Witw.   Assoc. Prof.
Woollacott, L. C., BSc *Witw.*, MSc(Eng) *Witw.*
  Sr. Lectr.
Other Staff: 2 Visiting Profs.; 3 Lectrs.; 1 Sr.
  Researcher; 1 Researcher; 1 Hon. Res.
  Assoc.; 3 Hon. Profs.†
Research: materials and process synthesis;
  materials research and education

Engineering, Civil and Environmental

Tel: (011) 717 7103 Fax: (011) 339 1762
  E-mail: ballim@civil.wits.ac.za
Elvin, A. A., BSc(Eng) *Witw.*, MSc(CivilEng)
  M.I.T., PhD *M.I.T.*   Sr. Lectr.
Gohnert, M., BSc(Civil) *Brigham Young*, MEM
  Brigham Young   Assoc. Prof.; Head*
James, C. S., BSc *Witw.*, MS *Colorado State*, PhD
  Witw.   Assoc. Prof.
Li, K., BEng *Witw.*, PhD *Witw.*   Sr. Lectr.
Luker, I., BSc *Brist.*, PhD *Witw.*   Sr. Lectr.
Marjanovic, P., BSc *Glas.*, MSc *Glas.*, MScEng *Ill.*,
  MSc *Calif.*, PhD *Calif.*   Prof.
Ndiritu, J. G., BScEng *Nair.*, MSc *Nair.*, PhD
  Adel.   Sr. Lectr.
Taigbenu, A. E., BSc *Lagos*, MS *Cornell*, PhD
  Cornell   Prof.
Uzoegbo, H. C., MSc *Lond.*, PhD *Lond.*   Sr.
  Lectr.
Other Staff: 4 Assoc. Profs.; 11 Lectr.; 1 Res.
  Fellow; 1 Lectr.†; 1 Res. Assoc.†
Research: employment creation in the
  construction industry; waste impact
  minimisation; water systems

Engineering, Electrical and Information

Tel: (011) 717 7200 Fax: (011) 403 1929
  E-mail: i.jandrell@ee.wits.ac.za
Chitamu, P. J. J., BSc *Dar.*, MSc *Sur.*, PhD *S'ton.*
  Sr. Lectr.
Clark, A. R., BSc *Witw.*, PhD *Witw.*   Assoc.
  Prof.
Dwolatzky, B., BSc *Witw.*, PhD *Witw.*   Personal
  Prof.
Gibbon, G. J., MSc(Eng) *Witw.*, PhD *Witw.*
  Assoc. Prof.
Jandrell, I. R., BSc(Eng) *Witw.*, PhD *Witw.*
  Prof.; Head*
Lacquet, B. M., BSc *Rand Afrikaans*, MSc *Rand
  Afrikaans*, PhD *Rand Afrikaans*   Prof.
Marwala, T., BSc *Case W.Reserve*, MSc *Pret.*, PhD
  Camb.   Assoc. Prof.
Rubin, D. M., MB ChB *Pret.*, MMed *Witw.*,
  MBiomedE *NSW*   Sr. Lectr.
Van Coller, J. M., BSc(Eng) *Witw.*, MSc(Eng)
  Witw., PhD *Witw.*   Sr. Lectr.
Van Olst, R., BSc *Witw.*, MBL *S.Af.*   Assoc.
  Prof.
Wigdorowitz, B., BSc(Eng) *Witw.*, MSc(Eng)
  Witw., PhD *Witw.*   Assoc. Prof.
Other Staff: 1 Personal Prof.; 1 Res. Fellow; 1
  Hon. Lectr.†
Research: computational electromagnetics;
  electron microscopy; power systems

engineering; software engineering; telecommunications

Engineering, Mechanical, Industrial and Aeronautical

Tel: (011) 717 7300 Fax: (011) 339 7997
E-mail: adickson@mech.wits.ac.za
Bailey-McEwan, M., BSc *Witw.*, MSc *Witw.*, PhD *Witw.* Sr. Lectr.
Campbell, H. M., BSc *WI*, MBA *Flor.* Sr. Lectr.
Chandler, H. D., BSc *Leeds*, MSc *Glas.*, PhD *CNAA* Reader
Cipolat, D., BSc(Eng) *Witw.*, MSc(Eng) *Witw.*, MBA *Witw.*, PhD *Witw.* Sr. Lectr.
Ingram, A. J., BSc *Cape Town*, MEng *Jo'burg.* Sr. Lectr.
Iwankiewicz, R. M., DrHabil *T.U.Wroclaw*, PhD *T.U.Wroclaw* Prof.
Law, C., BSc *Witw.*, PhD *Witw.* Sr. Lectr.
Moss, E. A., BSc(Eng) *Witw.*, MSc(Eng) *Witw.*, PhD *Witw.* Assoc. Prof.; Head*
Paskaramoorthy, R., BSc *Peradeniya*, MEng *Asian I.T.*, Bangkok, PhD *Manit.* Assoc. Prof.
Pedro, J. O., MSc *Warsaw*, PhD *Warsaw* Sr. Lectr.
Sheer, T. J., BSc(Eng) *Witw.*, MSc(Eng) *Witw.*, PhD *Witw.* Prof.
Skews, B. W., BSc(Eng) *Witw.*, MSc(Eng) *Witw.*, PhD *Witw.* Prof.
Snaddon, D. R., BSc(Eng) *Witw.*, MBA *Witw.*, PhD *Witw.* Assoc. Prof.
Other Staff: 4 Lectrs.; 2 Assoc. Lectrs.; 1 Res. Assoc.; 1 Principal Tutor; 1 Assoc. Prof.†; 1 Hon. Prof.†
Research: applied thermodynamics; flow research; reinforced plastics composites

Engineering, Mining

Tel: (011) 716 7400 Fax: (011) 339 8295
E-mail: phillips@egoli.min.wits.ac.za
Beaumont, C. R., BSc *Leeds*, BEd *Durh.*, MSc *Leeds* Sr. Lectr.
Cawood, F. T., MSc(Eng) *Witw.*, PhD *Witw.* Sr. Lectr.
MacFarlane, A. S., MSc(Eng) *Witw.* Sr. Lectr.
Mathshediso, I. B. V. G., BSc *Alta.*, MSc *ICL* Sr. Lectr.
Minnitt, R. C. A., BSc *Witw.*, MSc *Witw.*, PhD *Witw.* Prof.
Phillips, H. R., BSc *Brist.*, MSc *Newcastle(UK)*, PhD *Newcastle(UK)* Prof.; Head*
Rawlins, C. A., BEng *Pret.*, MSc *Witw.*, PhD *Witw.* Sr. Lectr.
Reichardt, C. L., BSc *Lond.*, MSc *Lond.* Sr. Lectr.
Stacey, T. R., BSc(Eng) *Natal*, MSc(Eng) *Natal*, DSc *Pret.* Prof.
Other Staff: 9 Lectrs.; 1 Sr. Tutor; 1 Adjunct Prof.; 1 Assoc. Prof.†; 1 Res. Assoc.†; 1 Hon. Prof.†
Research: mineral resource management; sustainability

Geography, Archaeology and Environmental Studies

Tel: (011) 717 6521
Huffman, T. N., BA *Denver*, MA *Ill.*, PhD *Ill.*
Mather, C. T., BA *Witw.*, MA *Br.Col.*, PhD *Belf.* Prof.; Head*
Sadr, K., BSc *S.Methodist*, MA *S.Methodist*, PhD *S.Methodist* Sr. Lectr.
Other Staff: 2 Lectrs.; 1 Sr. Researcher; 1 Tutor; 2 Hon. Profs.†
Research: acacia; archaeological resource management; climatology

Geography and Environmental Studies

Grab, S. W., BSc *Natal*, PhD *Natal* Assoc. Prof.
Mather, C. T., BA *Witw.*, MA *Br.Col.*, PhD *Belf.* Prof.; Head*
Patel, Z., BSc *Natal*, MSc *Natal*, PhD *Camb.* Sr. Lectr.
Rogerson, C. M., BSc *Lond.*, MSc *Witw.*, PhD *Qu.* Prof.
Vogel, C. H., BA *Witw.*, MA *Witw.*, PhD *Witw.* Prof.
Other Staff: 2 Lectrs.; 1 Sr. Tutor; 1 Sr. Tutor†; 1 Hon. Prof.

Geophysics

Cooper, G. R. J., BSc *Manc.*, MSc *Newcastle(UK)*, PhD *N.U.I.* Sr. Lectr.
Dirks, P. H., BSc *Utrecht*, MSc *Utrecht*, PhD *Melb.* Prof.; Head*
Other Staff: 1 Lectr.; 1 Sr. Researcher; 1 Res. Assoc.; 4 Hon. Profs.; 1 Hon. Lectr.†
Research: atmospheric and energy research; bush veld complex; economic geology; lithosophere; palaeoanthropology

Geosciences

Tel: (011) 717 6558
E-mail: dirksp@geosciences.wits.ac.za
Ashwal, L. D., MS *Mass.*, PhD *Prin.* Prof.
Cawthorn, R. G., BSc *Durh.*, PhD *Edin.* Prof.
Charlesworth, E. G., BSc *Natal*, PhD *Natal* Assoc. Prof.
Dirks, P. H., BSc *Utrecht*, MSc *Utrecht*, PhD *Melb.* Prof.; Head*
Gibson, R. L., BSc *Natal*, PhD *Camb.* Assoc. Prof.
Hein, K. A., BSc *Adel.*, PhD *Tas.* Prof.
McCarthy, T. S., BSc *Witw.*, BSc *Cape Town*, MSc *Cape Town*, PhD *Witw.* Prof.
Wilson, A. H., BSc *Lond.*, BSc *Z'bwe.*, PhD *Z'bwe.* Prof.
Other Staff: 1 Visiting Lectr.; 1 Researcher; 2 Visiting Researchers; 1 Principal Tutor; 1 Sr. Tutor; 1 Lectr.†; 1 Researcher†; 9 Hon. Profs.; 2 Hon. Lectrs.; 2 Hon. Res. Fellows
Research: applied mining and exploration geology; atmospheric sciences; economic geology; energy; sedimentology

History

Tel: (011) 717 4310
E-mail: bonnerp@social.wits.ac.za
Bonner, P. L., BA *Nott.*, MA *Lond.*, PhD *Lond.* Prof.; Head*
Bratchel, M. E., BA *Camb.*, MA *Camb.*, PhD *Camb.* Assoc. Prof.
Delius, P. N. S., BA *Lond.*, PhD *Lond.* Prof.
Glasser, C. L., BA *Witw.*, MA *Witw.*, PhD *Camb.* Sr. Lectr.
Hamilton, C. I., BA *Keele*, MA *Camb.*, PhD *Camb.* Assoc. Prof.
Kros, C. J., BA *Witw.*, PhD *Witw.* Sr. Lectr.
Nieftagodien, M. N., BA *Cape Town*, MA *Witw.*, PhD *Witw.* Sr. Lectr.
Other Staff: 1 Lectr.; 1 Assoc. Researcher; 1 Hon. Prof.

Humanities and Social Sciences, Graduate School for

Tel: (011) 717 4034
E-mail: 518pg@muse.wits.ac.za
Jacobsen, K., BA *Witw.*, MA *Boston*, PhD *Mass.* Prof.
Nethersole, R., BA *Witw.*, PhD *Witw.* Prof.
Rodgers, G. E., BA *Witw.*, MA *Witw.*, PhD *Witw.* Prof.
Sacco, T. M., BA *Natal*, MEd *Witw.* Prof.
Van Zyl, S., BA *Natal*, BA *Witw.*, MA *Witw.*, PhD *Witw.* Prof.; Head*
Research: refugees

Constitution of Public Intellectual Life

Hamilton, C. A., BA *Natal*, MA *Witw.*, MA *Johns H.*, PhD *Johns H.* Prof.; Head*
Other Staff: 2 Researchers; 2 Hon. Res. Assocs.

Forced Migration Studies Programme

Landau, L. B., BA *Wash.*, MA *Calif.*, PhD *Calif.* Prof.; Head*
Other Staff: 1 Sr. Tutor; 1 Researcher

Journalism and Media Studies

Cowling, I. J., BA *Witw.*, MA *Ohio State* Sr. Lectr.
Harber, A. P., BA *Witw.* Prof.; Head*
Other Staff: 1 Assoc. Lectr.; 2 Sr. Lectrs.†; 2 Lectrs.†

International Relations

Tel: (011) 717 4380
Ajulu, R., BA *NUL*, MA *NUL*, DPhil *Sus.* Assoc. Prof.
Alence, R. C., BA *Col.*, MA *Stan.*, PhD *Stan.* Assoc. Prof.
Shelton, G. L., BA *Witw.*, MA *Witw.*, PhD *Witw.* Assoc. Prof.; Head*
Other Staff: 5 Lectrs.; 1 Visiting Lectr.; 1 Principal Tutor; 1 Sr. Tutor; 1 Lectr.†

Law

Tel: (011) 717 8420 Fax: (011) 339 4733
Abraham, G., BCom *Witw.*, LLB *Witw.* Assoc. Prof.
Bonthuys, E., BA *Stell.*, LLB *Stell.*, LLM *Stell.*, PhD *Camb.* Assoc. Prof.
Bronstein, V. L., BA *Witw.*, LLB *Witw.*, LLM *Lond.* Sr. Lectr.
Cassim, F. H. I., LLB *Lond.*, LLM *Lond.* Sr. Lectr.
Chaskalson, A., BCom *Witw.*, LLB *Witw.*, Hon. LLD *Natal*, Hon. LLD *Witw.* Hon. Prof.
Christianson, M. A., BA *Cape Town*, LLB *Natal*, LLM *Natal* Sr. Lectr.
Currie, J. B., BA *Witw.*, LLB *Cape Town*, MA *Cape Town* Assoc. Prof.
Domanski, A., BSc *Witw.*, LLB *Witw.*, LLM *S.Af.*
Fick, G. C., BA *Witw.*, LLB *Witw.* Prof.; Head*
Hoexter, C. E., BA *Natal*, BA *Oxf.*, MA *Oxf.* Prof.
Humby, T., BMus *P.Elizabeth* Sr. Lectr.
Itzikowitz, A. J., BA *Stell.*, LLB *Stell.* Prof.†
Jordi, P. R., BA *Witw.*, LLB *Witw.* Assoc. Prof.
Klaaren, N. J., BA *Harv.*, MA *Cape Town* Assoc. Prof.
Moodaliyar, K., BProc *Natal*, LLB *Natal*, LLM *Natal*, MPhil *Camb.* Sr. Lectr.
Mosikatsana, T., BA *NUL*, LLB *Ott.*, MA *Regina* Prof.
Nmehielle, V. O., LLB *Rivers SUST*, LLM *Notre Dame(Ind.)*, DSc *George Washington* Assoc. Prof.
Nortje, M., LLB *Stell.*, LLM *Stell.* Sr. Lectr.
Pantazis, A., BA *Witw.*, LLB *Witw.* Prof.
Pieterse, M., LLB *Pret.*, LLM *Pret.* Assoc. Prof.
Rudolph, Harold G., BA *Witw.*, LLB *Witw.*, LLM *Witw.* Assoc. Prof.
Stern, P. A., BA *Witw.*, BA *S.Af.*, LLB *S.Af.* Sr. Lectr.
Theophilopoulos, C., BSc *Witw.*, LLB *Witw.*, LLM *S.Af.*, LLD *S.Af.* Sr. Lectr.
Unterhalter, D. N., BA *Camb.*, BCL *Oxf.*, LLB *Witw.* Prof.†
Other Staff: 1 Visiting Sr. Lectr.; 15 Lectrs.; 1 Visiting Lectr.; 2 Assoc. Lectrs.; 2 Principal Tutors; 1 Sr. Tutor; 3 Adjunct Profs.; 1 Assoc. Prof.†; 10 Hon. Profs.
Research: applied legal studies

Literature and Language Studies

Kupe, T., BA *Z'bwe.*, MA *Z'bwe.*, PhD *Oslo* Assoc. Prof.; Head*
Other Staff: 5 Profs.; 2 Res. Assocs.†

African Languages

Mjiiyako, L. K., BA *Witw.*, MA *Witw.* Sr. Lectr.; Head*
Other Staff: 2 Sr. Tutors; 2 Tutors

African Literature

Hofmeyr, C. I., BJourn *Rhodes*, BA *Witw.*, MA *Lond.*, MA *Witw.*, PhD *Witw.* Prof.
Ogude, J. A., BEd *Nair.*, MA *Nair.*, PhD *Witw.* Assoc. Prof.
Ojwang, D. O., BA *Nair.*, MA *Witw.* Prof.; Head*
Peterson, B. K. J., BA *Cape Town*, BA *Witw.*, MA *York(UK)*, PhD *Witw.* Assoc. Prof.

English

E-mail: attwell@languages.wits.ac.za
Attwell, D. I. D., BA *Natal*, MA *Cape Town*, PhD *Austin Coll.* Prof.
Gaylard, G. P., BA *Natal*, MA *Natal*, PhD *Natal* Sr. Lectr.

Harris, A. M., BA Witw., PhD Witw.   Sr. Lectr.
Houliston, V. H., BA Cape Town, MA Cape Town, DPhil Oxf.   Prof.; Head*
Koyana, S. Z., BA Smith, MA Yale, PhD Temple   Sr. Lectr.
Newfield, D. R., BA Witw., MA Lond.   Sr. Lectr.
Titlestad, M. F., BA Witw., BA S.Af., MA S.Af., PhD Witw.   Sr. Lectr.
Trengove-Jones, T., BA Natal, MPhil Oxf.   Sr. Lectr.
Williams, M. A., BA Natal, PhD Sheff.   Prof.
Other Staff: 3 Lectrs.; 1 Principal Tutor; 1 Visiting Researcher; 1 Lectr.†

French

Dednam, J. S., BA Witw., BA Cape Town, PhD Witw.   Sr. Lectr.; Head*
Other Staff: 1 Lectr.

German

Horn, A. C., BA Cape Town, MA Cape Town, PhD Cape Town   Assoc. Prof.
Thorpe, K. E., BA Witw., MA Witw., PhD Witw.   Prof.; Head*

Media Studies

Hyde-Clarke, N., BA Witw., MA Witw., PhD Witw.   Sr. Lectr.
Kariithi, N. K., BA Nair., MA Wales, MA Houston, PhD Houston   Prof.; Head*
Other Staff: 1 Lectr.

Modern Languages and Literature

Dednam, J. S., BA Witw., BA Cape Town, PhD Witw.   Sr. Lectr.
Poeti, A., BA Witw., MA Witw.   Sr. Lectr.
Thorpe, K. E., BA Witw., MA Witw., PhD Witw.   Head*
Other Staff: 2 Lectrs.; 1 Asst. Lectr.; 1 Tutor†

Sign Language

Morgans, H. G., BA Wash., MA Stell.   Sr. Lectr.; Head*
Other Staff: 1 Lectr.

Translators and Interpreters, Graduate School for

E-mail: libbym@languages.wits.ac.za
Inggs, J. A., BA Sheff., MA Witw., PhD Witw.   Sr. Lectr.
Meintjes, E. A., BA Witw., PhD Witw.   Sr. Lectr.; Head*

Mathematics

Tel: (011) 717 6200 Fax: (011) 403 2017
E-mail: kathy@maths.wits.ac.za
Berger, M., BA Cape Town, BSc Cape Town, MSc Witw., PhD Witw.   Sr. Lectr.
Goranko, V. F., BSc Sofia, MSc Sofia, PhD Sofia   Assoc. Prof.
Hockman, M., BSc Witw., MSc Witw., PhD Witw.   Sr. Lectr.
Kara, A. H., BSc Witw., MSc Witw., PhD Witw.   Sr. Lectr.
Knopfmacher, A., BSc Witw., PhD Witw.   Res. Prof.
Labuschagne, C. C., BSc Rand Afrikaans, DSc Potchef.   Sr. Lectr.
Love, A. D., BSc(Ed) P.Elizabeth, BSc Witw., MSc Witw., PhD Witw.   Assoc. Prof.
Moller, M. H., MSc T.U.Braunschweig, DrRerNat Regensburg, DrHab Regensburg   Prof.; Head*
van Alten, C. J., BSc Natal, MSc Natal, PhD Natal   Sr. Lectr.
Watson, B. A., BSc Witw., MSc Witw., PhD Witw.   Sr. Lectr.
Zelenyuk, Y., MSc Kiev, PhD Kiev   Assoc. Prof.
Other Staff: 7 Lectrs.; 2 Assoc. Lectrs.; 5 Principal Tutors; 6 Sr. Tutors; 2 Tutors; 2 Visiting Researchers
Research: applicable analysis and number theory

Mathematics, Computational and Applied

Tel: (011) 717 6100 Fax: (011) 403 9317
E-mail: sherwell@cam.wits.ac.za
Abelman, Shirley, BSc OFS, MSc OFS, PhD Potchef.   Sr. Lectr.

Adam, A. A., BSc S.Af., MA W.Mich., PhD Witw.   Sr. Lectr.
Ali, M., BSc Dhaka, MSc Dhaka, PhD Lough.   Sr. Lectr.
Berger, M., BA Cape Town, BSc Cape Town, MSc Witw., PhD Witw.   Sr. Lectr.
Block, D. L., BSc Witw., MSc S.Af., PhD Cape Town   Assoc. Prof.
Guo, B., BSc Shanxi, MSc Chinese Acad.Sc., PhD HK   Prof.
Hockman, M., BSc Witw., MSc Witw., PhD Witw.   Sr. Lectr.
Kulikov, G. Y., MSc Moscow, DSc Moscow, PhD Moscow   Sr. Lectr.
Mahomed, F. M., BSc Durban-W., BSc Witw., MSc Witw., PhD Witw.   Prof.
Mason, D. P., BSc Glas., DPhil Oxf.   Prof.
Momoniat, E., BSc Witw., MSc Witw., PhD Witw.   Sr. Lectr.
Sherwell, D., BSc Witw., PhD St And.   Prof.; Head*
Taylor, D. R., BSc Witw., PhD Witw.   Sr. Lectr.
Wafo, C., BSc Yaounde, MSc Witw., PhD Witw.   Sr. Lectr.
Wong, K. H., BSc Lond., MMath NSW, PhD NSW   Reader
Other Staff: 4 Lectrs.; 2 Assoc. Lectrs.; 3 Sr. Tutors; 2 Tutors†; 3 Hon. Profs.; 2 Hon. Res. Assocs.; 1 Hon. Sr. Lectr.†
Research: control theory and optimisation; differential equations, continuum mechanics and applications; numerical analysis and computational mathematics

Philosophy

Tel: (011) 717 4340
Leon, M., BA Witw., PhD Lond.   Prof.; Head*
Martens, D. B., BA Alta., MA Alta., PhD Brown   Sr. Lectr.
Metz, T., MA Cornell, PhD Cornell   Assoc. Prof.
Other Staff: 3 Lectrs.; 1 Visiting Researcher

Physics

Tel: (011) 717 6800 Fax: (011) 339 8262
E-mail: coleb@physics.wits.ac.za
Carter, J. M., BSc Lond., PhD Witw.   Assoc. Prof.
Cole, B. J., BSc Liv., PhD Liv.   Assoc. Prof.; Head*
Comins, J. D., BSc Natal, PhD Witw.   Ad Hominem Prof.
Connell, S. H., BSc Witw., PhD Witw.   Sr. Lectr.
de Mello Koch, R. S., BSc(Eng) Witw., BSc Witw., MSc Witw., PhD Witw.   Assoc. Prof.
Derry, T. E., MA Camb., PhD Witw.   Reader
Every, A. G., BSc Witw., MSc Witw., PhD Reading   Res. Prof.
Frescura, F. A. M., BSc Witw., PhD Lond.   Sr. Lectr.
Hearne, G. R., BSc Witw., MSc Witw., PhD Witw.   Sr. Lectr.
Joubert, D. P., BSc Stell., MSc Stell., PhD Camb.   Sr. Lectr.
Keartland, J. M., BSc Witw., PhD Witw.   Sr. Lectr.
Lowther, J. E., BSc Hull, PhD Hull   Prof.
Mujaji, M., BSc Z'bwe., PhD Cant.   Sr. Lectr.
Rodrigues, J. A. P., BSc Witw., MSc Brown, PhD Brown   Prof.
Sideras-Haddad, E., BSc Witw., MSc Witw., PhD Witw.   Sr. Lectr.
Watterson, J. I. W., BSc Witw., PhD Witw.   Assoc. Prof.
Other Staff: 2 Lectrs.; 1 Assoc. Lectr.; 1 Principal Tutor; 5 Sr. Tutors; 2 Tutors; 2 Visiting Researchers; 1 Visiting Res. Assoc.; 8 Hon. Profs.
Research: applied and environmental physics; condensed matter physics; f-electron magnetism and heavy fermion physics; non-linear studies; nuclear sciences

Political Studies

Tel: (011) 717 4360
Frankel, P. H., BA Witw., MA Witw., MA Prin., PhD Prin.   Assoc. Prof.

Glaser, D., BA Witw., MA Witw., PhD Manc.   Assoc. Prof.
Hassim, S. A. A., BA Durban-W., MA Natal, DPhil York(UK)   Assoc. Prof.
Hudson, P. A., BA Natal   Sr. Lectr.
Louw, S. J., BA Witw., MA Witw., PhD Witw.   Sr. Lectr.
Meintjes, S. M., BA Rhodes, MA Sus., PhD Lond.   Assoc. Prof.; Head*
Taylor, R. L., BA Kent, MSc(Econ) Lond., PhD Kent   Assoc. Prof.
Other Staff: 1 Lectr.; 1 Visiting Researcher

Psychology

Broom, Y., BA S.Af., BSc E.Anglia, BA Witw., MA Witw., PhD Witw.   Sr. Lectr.
Cockcroft, K. A., BA Witw., MA Witw., PhD Witw.   Sr. Lectr.
Duncan, N. T. F., BA W.Cape, MA Montpellier, DPhil W.Cape   Prof.; Head*
Eagle, G. T., BA Natal, MA Natal, PhD Witw.   Assoc. Prof.
Finshilescu, G., BSc Cape Town, MSc Cape Town, PhD Oxf.   Prof.
Fisher, J. A., BSc Bolton IHE, MSc Lough., PhD Witw.   Prof.
Ivey, G. W., BA Rhodes, MSocSc Rhodes, PhD Natal   Sr. Lectr.
Kasese-Hara, M. C., BA Zambia, MEd Manc., PhD Durh.   Sr. Lectr.
Milner, K. M., BA Witw., MA Witw.   Sr. Lectr.
Potter, C. S., BA Witw., BEd S.Af., MEd S.Af.   Assoc. Prof.
Strydom, J. F., BA OFS, MA OFS, PhD Oxf.   Sr. Lectr.
Thatcher, A. J., BSc Witw., MSc Witw., PhD Witw.   Sr. Lectr.
Other Staff: 21 Lectrs.; 1 Visiting Lectr.; 1 Visiting Researcher; 1 Principal Tutor; 5 Sr. Tutors; 2 Tutors; 2 Lectrs.†

Public and Development Management, Graduate School of

Tel: (011) 717 3700 Fax: (011) 484 2729
E-mail: fitzgerald.p@pdm.wits.ac.za
Ambursley, F., BA Birm., PhD Warw.   Sr. Lectr.
Antonie, F. J., BA Witw., MA Leic., MCA Exe.   Prof.; Head*
Booysen, S., BA Rand Afrikaans, MA Rand Afrikaans, DLitt&Phil Rand Afrikaans   Prof.
Jahed, M. I., BSocSci Cape Town, BA W.Cape, MEcon W.Cape, PhD Pret.   Assoc. Prof.
McLennan, A. C., BA Witw., MEd Witw.   Sr. Lectr.
Mogale, T. M., MSc Lond., PhD Pitt., BA   Sr. Lectr.
Muller, M. W., BSc Witw., MSc Witw., PhD S.Af.   Sr. Lectr.
Sarakinsky, I. H., BA Witw., MA Witw., PhD Witw.   Sr. Lectr.
Solomon, D., BA Cape Town, MA Cape Town   Sr. Lectr.
Other Staff: 2 Visiting Profs.; 2 Lectrs.; 6 Visiting Res. Fellows; 1 Visiting Res. Assoc.; 2 Assoc. Researchers; 1 Sr. Tutor; 1 Educnl. Devel. Officer; 2 Sr. Lectrs.†; 1 Lectr.†; 1 Assoc. Researcher†; 1 Hon. Res. Fellow; 5 Hon. Profs.†

Social Anthropology

Tel: (011) 717 4405
E-mail: copland@social.wits.ac.za
Coplan, D. B., MA Ghana, MA Indiana, PhD Indiana, BA   Prof.; Head*
Czegledy-Nagy, A. P., BA Tor., MSc Lond., PhD Camb.   Sr. Lectr.
Ebr-Vally, R., BA Durban-W., PhD Paris IV   Sr. Lectr.
Thornton, R. J., BA Stan., MA Chic., PhD Chic.   Assoc. Prof.
Other Staff: 1 Principal Tutor; 1 Lectr.†; 1 Visiting Researcher†

Social Work

Mabe, T. S. K., BA Bophut., BA Rhodes, MA Pret., PhD North(S.Af.)   Sr. Lectr.; Head*

Ross, E., BA Witw., MA Witw., PhD Witw.
Assoc. Prof.
Other Staff: 5 Lectrs.; 1 Sr. Tutor; 1 Lectr.†

Sociology

Buhlungu, BA Cape Town, MA Witw., PhD Witw.
Sr. Lectr.
Cock, J. E., BA Rhodes, BSocSc Rhodes, PhD Rhodes
Prof.
Germond, P. A., BA Rhodes, BA Cape Town, MA
Cape Town, MPhil Col. Sr. Lectr.
Gilbert, L., BA Jerusalem, MPH Jerusalem, PhD
Witw. Assoc. Prof.
Greenstein, R., BA Haifa, MA Haifa, PhD Wis.
Assoc. Prof.
Kariiuki, S., BA Kenyatta, MA Nair., PhD Witw.
Kenny, B. C., BA Chic., MA Wis., PhD Wis. Sr.
Lectr.
Pillay, D., BA S.Af., MA York(UK), PhD Essex Sr.
Lectr.
Webster, E. C., BA Rhodes, BPhil York(UK), MA
Oxf., PhD Witw. Prof.; Head*
Other Staff: 5 Lectrs.; 1 Assoc. Lectr.; 2 Sr.
Tutors
Research: history; sociology of work

Specialised Education

Sch. of Human and Community Development
Laauwen, H. M., BA Pret., BEd Pret., PhD Pret.
Prof.; Head*
Storbeck, C., MEd Rand Afrikaans, PhD Rand
Afrikaans Sr. Lectr.
Other Staff: 3 Lectrs.; 1 Assoc. Lectr.; 2 Sr.
Tutors; 3 Lectrs.†; 1 Tutor†

Speech Pathology and Audiology

Jordaan, H. L., BA Witw., MA Witw. Sr. Lectr.
Penn, M. A. C., BA Witw., PhD Witw. Prof.;
Head*
Other Staff: 6 Lectrs.; 2 Tutors; 15 Lectrs.†; 1
Principal Tutor†; 1 Tutor†; 3 Sr. Clin.
Tutors; 1 Sr. Clin. Tutor†
Research: cognitive enrichment techniques;
language- and hearing-impaired children

Statistics and Actuarial Science

Tel: (011) 717 6260 Fax: (011) 339 6640
Beichelt, F., MSc Jena, PhD Freib., DrScTechn
T.U.Dresden Prof.
Fridjhon, P., BSc Witw., MA Lanc. Sr. Lectr.
Galpin, J. S., BSc Witw., MSc S.Af., DSc Potchef.
Prof.; Head*
Kass, G. V., BSc Witw., MSc(Econ) Lond., PhD
Witw. Assoc. Prof.
Lubinsky, D. J., BSc Witw., MSc Witw., PhD
Rutgers Prof.†
Thomson, R. J., BSc Cape Town Visiting Prof.
Other Staff: 1 Lectr.; 3 Assoc. Lectrs.; 6 Sr.
Tutors; 4 Tutors; 1 Tutor†; 1 Hon. Prof.†

Teaching and Learning Unit

Sch. of Human and Community Development
Dison, L., BA Witw., BEd Witw., MEd Witw.
Sr. Lectr.
Mayekiso, T. V., BA OFS, MA OFS, PhD
F.U.Berlin Prof.; Head*
Other Staff: 1 Researcher; 1 Principal Tutor; 1
Sr. Tutor

Wits Language School

E-mail: hallg@coled.wits.ac.za
Hall, G. N., BSc Witw., MEd Bath Prof.; Head*
Other Staff: 11 Sr. Tutor; 1 Tutor; 6 Tutors†

HEALTH SCIENCES

Tel: (011) 717 2000 Fax: (011) 643 3418
E-mail: deanhsc@health.wits.ac.za

Anatomical Sciences

Tel: (011) 717 2305 Fax: (011) 717 2422
E-mail: kramerb@anatomy.wits.ac.za
Daly, T. J. M., BSc Witw., PhD Witw. Assoc.
Prof.
Hosie, M. J., BSc Syd., PhD Syd. Sr. Lectr.
Kramer, Beverley, BSc Witw., PhD Witw. Prof.

Maina, J. N., BVM Nair., PhD Liv., DVSc Liv.
Prof.; Head*
Manger, P. R., PhD Qld. Sr. Lectr.
Strkallj, G., BA Belgrade, MA Belgrade, PhD Witw.
Sr. Lectr.
Other Staff: 7 Lectrs.; 4 Assoc. Lectrs.; 2 Res.
Assocs.; 2 Sr. Tutors; 1 Lectr.†; 1 Res.
Assoc.†; 2 Hon. Profs.; 1 Hon. Sr. Lectr.
Research: embryonic differentiation and
development

Clinical Medicine

Tel: (011) 717 2020
E-mail: hollande@health.wits.ac.za
Holland, E. A., MB ChB Cape Town, PhD Cape
Town Prof.; Head*

Accident Service

Johannesburg Hospital
Veller, M. G., MB BCh Witw., MMed Witw.
Prof.; Head*

Anaesthesiology

Tel: (011) 489 0462
Bhagwanjee, S., MB BCh Natal Prof.; Head*
(Johannesburg Hospital)
De Bacear Gouvei, N. P., MD Louvain Sr. Lectr.
(Chris Hani Baragwanath Hospital)
Emdon, S., MB BCh Witw. Sr. Lectr. (Chris
Hani Baragwanath Hospital)
Faria, R. S., MB BCh Witw. Sr. Lectr. (Chris
Hani Baragwanath Hospital)
Gabriel, C. M., MD F.U.Berlin Sr. Lectr.
(Coronation Hospital)
Klein, D. C., BSc Witw., MB BCh Witw. Sr.
Lectr. (Johannesburg Hospital)
Kuhn, R., MB ChB Stell. Sr. Lectr. (Chris Hani
Baragwanath Hospital)
Lines, D., MB BCh Witw. Sr. Lectr. (Chris
Hani Baragwanath Hospital)
Lundgren, A. C., MB ChB Cape Town Adjunct
Prof. (Chris Hani Baragwanath Hospital)
Paruk, F., MB ChB Natal Sr. Lectr.
(Johannesburg Hospital)
Peltz, B., MB BCh Witw., DA Witw. Sr. Lectr.
(Chris Hani Baragwanath Hospital)
Shung, J., MB BCh Witw. Sr. Lectr.
(Johannesburg Hospital)
Singh, D., MB ChB S.Af.Med. Sr. Lectr.
(Johannesburg Hospital)
Veliotes, G. D., MB BCh Witw. Sr. Lectr.
(Chris Hani Baragwanath Hospital)
Zeilstra, I. E., MB BCh Witw. Sr. Lectr.
(Coronation Hospital)
Other Staff: 8 Lectrs.; 4 Sr. Lectrs.†; 9 Lectrs.†

Cardiology

Chris Hani Baragwanath and Johannesburg
Hospitals
Essop, M. R., MB BCh Witw. Assoc. Prof.;
Head*
Manga, P., MB BCh Witw., PhD Witw. Prof.;
Head, Cardiol. Res. Unit; Chief Specialist
Research: heart failure

Casualty

Alam, M. S., MB BS Dacca Sr. Lectr. (Hillbrow
Hospital)
Hamid, M. A., BSc Bom., MB BCh Cairo Sr.
Lectr. (Hillbrow Hospital)
Jacobs, S. E. C., MB BCh Pret. Sr. Lectr.
(Helen Joseph Hospital)
Kanjl, R., MB ChB Natal, MSc Lond. Sr. Lectr.
(Hillbrow Hospital)
Kliesiewicz, M., MD Warsaw Sr. Lectr.
(Hillbrow Hospital)
Kramer, S. A., MB ChB Pret. Sr. Lectr.; Head*
(Johannesburg Hospital)
Lala, G., LLM Sr. Lectr. (Chris Hani
Baragwanath Hospital)
Langridge, P. H., MB BCh Witw. Sr. Lectr.
(Helen Joseph Hospital)
Lenssen, T. Sr. Lectr. (Helen Joseph Hospital)
Livemore, P. A., MB BCh Witw., BSc Witw. Sr.
Lectr. (Johannesburg Hospital)
Mahomed, K. D., MB ChB Natal Sr. Lectr.
(Hillbrow Hospital)

Mahomed, M. K. Sr. Lectr. (Coronation
Hospital)
Moti, A., MB ChB Natal Sr. Lectr. (Hillbrow
Hospital)
Mukaddam, K., MB BS Sindh Sr. Lectr. (Chris
Hani Baragwanath Hospital)
Mutamba, B. E., MD Zaire Sr. Lectr. (Helen
Joseph Hospital)
Nedeljkovic, V. Sr. Lectr. (Coronation
Hospital)
Palmer, C. H. P., MB BCh Witw., MA Witw.
Sr. Lectr. (Chris Hani Baragwanath
Hospital)
Philip, T. J., MB BS Karn. Sr. Lectr. (Chris
Hani Baragwanath Hospital)
Rajah, L., MB ChB Natal Sr. Lectr. (Hillbrow
Hospital)
Sadigh-Loghmany, S. M. Sr. Lectr. (Hillbrow
Hospital)
Tupy, D., MUDr Bratislava Sr. Lectr. (Hillbrow
Hospital)
Vankatesh, A., BSc Mys., MB BS Mys. Sr. Lectr.
(Chris Hani Baragwanath Hospital)
Other Staff: 5 Lectrs.; 5 Assoc. Lectrs.; 9 Med.
Officers; 17 Assoc. Lectrs.†; 2 Med.
Officers†

Dermatology

Modi, D., MB BCh Witw., MMed Witw.
Head*

Endocrinology

Tel: (011) 488 3808
Raal, F. J., MB BCh Witw., MMed Witw., PhD
Witw. Assoc. Prof.
Van der Merwe, M., MB ChB Pret. Assoc.
Prof.; Sr. Specialist
Wing, J., MB BCh Witw. Sr. Lectr.; Prof.
Other Staff: 1 Lectr.; 1 Researcher; 2 Lectrs.†
Research: heart failure

Family Medicine

Tel: (011) 717 2041
Lonergan, B. F., MB BS Syd. Sr. Lectr.
Reid, D., MB BCh Witw. Sr. Lectr.
Sparks, B. L. W., MB BCh Witw. Prof.; Head*
Wright, A. E., BA Witw., MA Witw., PhD Witw.
Sr. Lectr.
Other Staff: 8 Lectrs.; 2 Sr. Lectrs.†; 4 Lectrs.†;
41 Hon. Lectrs.†

Intensive Care

Chris Hani Baragwanath Hospital
Mathivha, L. R., MB ChB Natal Principal
Specialist; Head*
Other Staff: 1 Lectr.; 2 Assoc. Lectrs.; 2
Specialists; 1 Med. Officer; 1 Specialist†

Internal Medicine

Ally, R., MB BCh Witw. Ad Hoc Prof.;
Principal Specialist (Chris Hani Baragwanath
Hospital)
Chita, G., MB BCh Witw. Sr. Lectr.; Principal
Specialist (Helen Joseph Hospital)
Goldberg, L., MD Novosibirsk, PhD Moscow Sr.
Lectr.; Specialist (Helen Joseph Hospital)
Holland, V. B., BSc S.Af., MB ChB Natal Sr.
Lectr.; Principal Specialist (Helen Joseph
Hospital)
Huddle, K. R. L., MB BCh Witw. Prof.; Chief
Specialist (Chris Hani Baragwanath
Hospital)
MacPhail, A. P., BSc Witw., MB BCh Witw., PhD
Witw. Prof.; Chief Specialist (Helen Joseph
Hospital)
Patel, M., MB ChB Natal, MMed Witw., PhD
Witw. Personal Prof.; Principal Specialist
(Chris Hani Baragwanath Hospital)
Radzikowska-Wasia, M. Sr. Lectr.
(Johannesburg Hospital)
Song, E., MB BCh Witw. Assoc. Prof.;
Principal Specialist (Johannesburg Hospital)
Veriava, Y., MB BCh Witw. Assoc. Prof.;
Head* (Helen Joseph Hospital)
Other Staff: 3 Assoc. Profs.; 16 Lectrs.; 14
Assoc. Lectrs.; 71 Assoc. Lectrs./Registrars;

6 Specialists; 1 Adjunct Prof.; 1 Sr. Lectr.†;
4 Lectrs.†; 4 Assoc. Lectrs.†
Research: carbohydrate and lipid metabolism;
molecular hepatology; movement disorders

Medical Oncology and Clinical Haematology
Johannesburg Hospital

Tel: (011) 488 3869

Ruff, P., MB BCh *Witw.*, MMed *Witw.* Assoc.
Prof.
Veriava, Y., MB BCh *Witw.* Prof.; Head*
Other Staff: 2 Lectrs.; 3 Assoc. Lectrs.

Nephrology
Johannesburg Hospital

Tel: (011) 488 3672

Naicker, S., MB BCh *Natal*, PhD *Natal* Head*

Neurosciences
Modi, G., MB BCh *Witw.*, MSc *Lond.*, PhD *Lond.*
Prof.; Head, Neurology
Vorster, M., BA *Witw.*, MB BCh *Witw.*, BSc
Lond., MSc *Lond.*, PhD *Lond.* Prof.; Head,
Neurosurgery; Head*
Other Staff: 1 Hon. Lectr.

Nuclear Medicine
Donde, B., MB BCh *Witw.*, MMed *Witw.* Prof.
Other Staff: 1 Adjunct Prof.†

Obstetrics and Gynaecology
Adams, R. S., MB BCh *Witw.* Sr. Lectr.
(Coronation Hospital)
Buchmann, E. J., MB BCh *Witw.*, MSc(Med)
Witw. Sr. Lectr. (Chris Hani Baragwanath
Hospital)
Chrysostomou, A., MD *Jassy* Sr. Lectr.
(Johannesburg Hospital)
Guidozzi, F., MB BCh *Witw.* Prof.; Head*
(Johannesburg Hospital)
Hellman, P. R., MB BCh *Witw.* Sr. Lectr.
(Chris Hani Baragwanath Hospital)
Jerkovic-Andrin, M., MD *Novi Sad* Sr. Lectr.
(Johannesburg Hospital)
Levin, S. L., MB BCh *Witw.* Adjunct Prof.;
Principal Specialist (Coronation Hospital)
McIntyre, J. A., MB ChB *Rhodesia* Sr. Lectr.
(Chris Hani Baragwanath Hospital)
Molingoane, S. J., BSc *Fort Hare*, MB BCh *Witw.*
Sr. Lectr. (Coronation Hospital)
Nicolaou, E., MD *Düsseldorf* Sr. Lectr. (Chris
Hani Baragwanath Hospital)
Pirani, N. E., MD *Córdoba* Sr. Lectr. (Chris
Hani Baragwanath Hospital)
Setzen, R., MB BCh *Witw.* Sr. Lectr. (Chris
Hani Baragwanath Hospital)
Smith, T. H., MB BCh *Witw.* Sr. Lectr.
(Johannesburg Hospital)
Sridaran, N., BSc *Bom.*, MB BS *Madr.* Sr. Lectr.
(Coronation Hospital)
Van Gelderen, C. J., MB ChB *Cape Town* Prof.;
Chief Specialist (Chris Hani Baragwanath
Hospital)
Other Staff: 5 Sr. Lectrs.; 10 Lectrs.; 54 Assoc.
Lectrs.; 4 Specialists; 2 Lectrs.†; 1 Hon.
Lectr.
Research: reproductive health

Ophthalmology
Tel: (011) 717 2049
E-mail: 123trc@chiron.wits.ac.za
Carmichael, T. R., MB BCh *Witw.*, PhD(Med)
Witw., FCS(SA) Prof. (Johannesburg
Hospital)
Vorster, M., BA *Witw.*, MB BCh *Witw.*, BSc
Lond., MSc *Lond.*, PhD *Lond.* Prof.; Head*
Other Staff: 1 Lectr.†

Orthopaedic Surgery
Tel: (011) 717 2552
George, J. A., PhD Prof.
Lukhele, M., MD *S.Af.Med.* Prof.; Head*
Other Staff: 1 Assoc. Lectr.; 1 Prof.†; 1 Assoc.
Prof.†; 3 Lectrs.†; 1 Clin. Consultant†

Otorhinolaryngology
Modi, P. C., MB BCh *Witw.*, MMed *Witw.*
Head*
Other Staff: 1 Adjunct Prof.†; 1 Lectr.†

Paediatric Surgery
Beale, P. G., MB ChB *Pret.*, MMed *Pret.* Sr.
Lectr.; Head* (Johannesburg Hospital)
Research: community paediatrics; mineral
metabolism

Paediatrics and Child Health
Tel: (011) 933 1297 Fax: (011) 938 9074
Ballot, D. E., MB BCh *Witw.*, PhD *Witw.*
Assoc. Prof. (Johannesburg Hospital)
Bolton, K. D., MB BCh *Witw.* Assoc. Prof.;
Chief Specialist (Coronation Hospital)
Cooper, P. A., MB ChB *Cape Town*, PhD *Witw.*
Prof.; Chief Specialist (Johannesburg
Hospital)
Davies, V. A., MB BCh *Witw.* Assoc. Prof.
(Johannesburg Hospital)
Jacklin, L. B., MB BCh *Witw.*, MMed *Pret.* Sr.
Lectr.
Kala, Udai K., MB BCh *Witw.*, FCP(SA) Sr.
Lectr. (Chris Hani Baragwanath Hospital)
Mayet, Z., BSc *S.Af.*, MB BCh *Witw.* Sr. Lectr.
(Coronation Hospital)
Monsengo, I. O., MD *Lubumbashi* Sr. Lectr.
(Johannesburg Hospital)
Parbhoo, K. B., MB BCh *Witw.*, MMed *Witw.*
Sr. Lectr. (Chris Hani Baragwanath
Hospital)
Pettifor, John M., MB BCh *Witw.*, PhD *Witw.*,
FCP(SA) Prof.; Head* (Chris Hani
Baragwanath Hospital)
Poole, J. E., MB BCh *Witw.* Sr. Lectr.
(Johannesburg Hospital)
Poyiadjis, S. D. Sr. Lectr. (Chris Hani
Baragwanath Hospital)
Scher, L G., MB BCh *Witw.* Sr. Lectr.
Schwyzer, R., MB BCh *Witw.* Sr. Lectr.
(Johannesburg Hospital)
Thein, O., MB BS *Yangon* Sr. Lectr.
(Coronation Hospital)
Other Staff: 23 Lectrs.; 19 Lectrs.†

Perinatal HIV
Cooper, P. A., MB ChB *Cape Town*, PhD *Witw.*
Prof.; Head*
Other Staff: 1 Assoc. Prof.; 1 Sr. Researcher; 1
Researcher

Plastic and Restorative Surgery
Veller, M. G., MB BCh *Witw.*, MMed *Witw.*
Prof.; Head*

Psychiatry
Moosa, M. Y. H., MB ChB *Natal* Sr. Lectr.
(Johannesburg Hospital)
Szabo, C. P., MB BCh *Witw.*, MMed *Witw.*
Prof. (Johannesburg Hospital)
Voster, M., BA *Rand Afrikaans*, MB BCh *Witw.*,
MMed *Witw.* Head*
Other Staff: 11 Profs.†; 1 Lectr.†

Pulmonology
Tel: (011) 488 3840
Feldman, C., MB BCh *Witw.*, PhD *Witw.* Prof.;
Head* (Johannesburg Hospital)
Richards, G. A., MB BCh *Witw.*, PhD *Witw.*
Assoc. Prof. (Johannesburg Hospital)
Wong, M. L., MB BCh *Witw.* Sr. Lectr. (Chris
Hani Baragwanath Hospital)
Other Staff: 3 Lectrs.; 5 Assoc. Lectrs.
Research: cardiology; human ciliated epithelium;
rheumatology

Radiation Oncology
Donde, B., MB BCh *Witw.*, MMed *Witw.*
Prof.; Head*
Rabin, B. S., MB BCh *Witw.*, MMed *Witw.* Sr.
Lectr.
Other Staff: 1 Prof.; 2 Lectrs.; 1 Adjunct Prof.;
3 Lectrs.†

Radiation Services
Donde, B., MB BCh *Witw.*, MMed *Witw.* Prof.
Other Staff: 1 Lectr.; 3 Clin. Consultants; 1
Hon. Prof.; 5 Hon. Lectrs.

Radiology, Diagnostic
Tel: (011) 720 1175 Fax: (011) 642 9185
Donde, B., MB BCh *Witw.*, MMed *Witw.*
Prof.; Head*
Other Staff: 1 Hon. Prof.

Rheumatology
Christian, B. F., MB BCh *Witw.* Head*

Surgery
Tel: (011) 717 2580 Fax: (011) 484 2717
Candy, G. P., MSc *Natal*, PhD *Witw.* Sr. Lectr.
Veller, M. G., MB BCh *Witw.*, MMed *Witw.*
Prof.; Head*
Other Staff: 1 Researcher; 3 Hon. Profs.; 1
Hon. Lectr.

Urology
Veller, M. G., MB BCh *Witw.*, MMed *Witw.*
Head*

Oral Health Sciences
Essop, A. R. M., BDS *Witw.*, BSc *Bom.*, MDent
Witw. Prof.; Head*
Other Staff: 2 Lectrs.; 1 Assoc. Researcher†

Community Dentistry
Tel: (011) 717 2593
Rudolph, M. J., BDS *Witw.*, MSc *Witw.*, MPH
Harv. Prof.; Head*
Tsotsi, N. M., DD *Bucharest* Sr. Lectr.; Principal
Dentist
Other Staff: 1 Assoc. Lectr.

Maxillo-Facial and Oral Surgery
Lurie, R., BDS *Witw.*, MDent *Witw.* Prof.†
Veller, M. G., MB BCh *Witw.*, MMed *Witw.*
Prof.; Head*
Other Staff: 2 Adjunct Profs.; 2 Sr. Lectrs.†; 10
Lectrs.†; 1 Hon. Prof.; 1 Hon. Lectr.†

Odontology, Experimental
Tel: (011) 407 4163 Fax: (011) 339 3036
Cleaton-Jones, P. E., BDS *Witw.*, MB BCh *Witw.*,
PhD *Witw.*, DSc(Dent) *Witw.* Head*

Oral Medicine and Periodontology
Petit, J., BSc *Lubumbashi*, LDS *Louvain*, MDent
Witw. Prof.; Head*
Other Staff: 4 Lectrs.; 4 Hon. Lectrs.

Oral Pathology
Altini, M., BDS *Witw.*, MDent *Witw.* Chief
Specialist; Head*
Meer, S., BChD *W.Cape* Sr. Lectr.
Other Staff: 1 Hon. Res. Fellow

Orthodontics
Evans, W. G., BDS *Witw.* Prof.; Head*
Gavronsky, G., BDS *Witw.*, MDent *Witw.* Prof.
Other Staff: 1 Adjunct Prof.†; 1 Sr. Lectr.†; 11
Lectrs.†

Paediatric and Restorative Dentistry
Evans, W. G., BDS *Witw.* Prof.; Head*
Other Staff: 1 Lectr.; 8 Lectrs.†; 1 Hon. Assoc.
Prof.

Prosthodontics
Owen, C. P., BDS *Lond.*, MChD *W.Cape*,
MSc(Dent) *W.Cape* Prof.; Head*
Shackleton, J. L., BDS *Witw.*, MDent *Witw.* Sr.
Lectr.
Other Staff: 3 Lectrs.; 1 Adjunct Prof.; 1
Adjunct Prof.†; 2 Lectrs.†; 1 Hon. Lectr.

Pathology
Wadee, A. A., BSc *Tor.*, MSc(Med) *Witw.*, PhD
Witw. Prof.; Head*

Other Staff: 1 Visiting Researcher†

Anatomical Pathology

Grayson, W., MB ChB Free State Assoc. Prof.
King, P. C., MB BCh Witw., FRCPath Sr. Lectr.
Nayler, S. J., BSc Witw., MB BCh Witw. Prof.
Paterson, A. C., MB BCh Witw., PhD Witw. Prof.; Head*
Perner, Y., MB BCh Witw. Sr. Lectr.
Wadee, A. A., BSc Tor., MSc(Med) Witw., PhD Witw. Prof.
Other Staff: 3 Lectrs.; 2 Med. Officers; 2 Adjunct Profs.; 1 Lectr.†; 1 Hon. Prof.

Chemical Pathology

Tel: (011) 489 9000
Crowther, N. J., BSc Sus., DPhil Sus. Assoc. Prof.
Gray, I. P., MB ChB OFS, MMed OFS Prof.†
Ojwang, P. J., MB ChB Nair. Prof.; Chief Specialist
Paiker, J. E., MB ChB Pret., MMed Witw. Sr. Lectr.
Rowe, P., BSc Birm., MB ChB Birm. Sr. Lectr.
Wadee, A. A., BSc Tor., MSc(Med) Witw., PhD Witw. Prof.; Head*
Other Staff: 1 Assoc. Prof.; 11 Lectrs.; 1 Assoc. Lectr.†; 1 Lectr.†; 1 Sr. Clin. Lectr.; 1 Hon. Prof.

Clinical Microbiology and Infectious Diseases

Tel: (011) 717 2022
E-mail: heathercb@mail.saimr.wits.ac.za
Ballard, R., PhD Witw. Assoc. Prof.
Duse, A. G., MB BCh Witw. Prof.; Head*
Frean, J. A., MB BCh Witw., MMed Witw., MSc Lond. Assoc. Prof.
Grobusch, M. P., MMed Bonn Prof.
Huebner, R. E., BSc Ill., MSc Johns H., PhD Wis. Sr. Lectr.
Koornhof, H. J., MB BCh Lond., DSc Cape Town Prof.
Perovic, O., MD Belgrade Sr. Lectr.
Other Staff: 13 Lectrs.; 1 Assoc. Lectr.; 1 Sr. Researcher; 1 Med. Officer; 1 Assoc. Prof.†; 3 Lectrs.†; 1 Hon. Prof.†
Research: human genomic diversity; respiratory and meningeal pathogens

Human Genetics

Christianson, A. L., MB ChB Birm. Personal Prof.
Lane, A. B., BSc Witw., MSc Witw., PhD Witw. Sr. Lectr.
Viljoen, D. L., MB BS Lond., MD Lond. Prof.†; Head*
Other Staff: 2 Assoc. Profs.; 5 Lectrs.; 1 Adjunct Prof.; 3 Lectrs.†; 1 Researcher†; 1 Hon. Personal Prof.; 2 Hon. Assoc. Profs.

Immunology

Wadee, A. A., BSc Tor., MSc(Med) Witw., PhD Witw. Prof.; Head*
Other Staff: 1 Hon. Prof.

Molecular Medicine and Haematology

Tel: (011) 717 2165
E-mail: 075barry@chiron.wits.ac.za
Arbuthnot, P. B., BSc Witw., PhD Witw. Assoc. Prof.
Chetty, N., BSc Durban-W., MSc Witw., PhD Witw. Assoc. Prof.
Mizrahi, V., BSc Cape Town, PhD Res. Prof.
Papathanasopoulos, M. A., BSc Witw., MSc Witw., PhD Witw. Sr. Lectr.
Stevens, W. S., BSc Witw., MB BCh Witw., MMed Witw. Aspro Prof.; Head*
Weinberg, M. S., BSc Witw., MSc Witw., PhD Witw. Sr. Lectr.
Other Staff: 10 Lectrs.; 1 Assoc. Lectr.; 1 Visiting Res. Fellow; 1 Res. Assoc.; 1 Researcher; 1 Adjunct Prof.; 4 Lectrs.†; 1 Researcher†; 1 Sr. Clin. Lectr.; 4 Hon. Profs.; 3 Hon. Lectrs.
Research: hepatitis B; molecular mycobacteriology

Virology

Blackburn, N., MPhil Rhodesia, DPhil Z'bwe. Sr. Lectr.
Morris, L., BSc Witw., PhD Oxf.Brookes Reader; Assoc. Prof.
Schoub, B. D., MB BCh Witw., MMed Stell., MD Pret., DSc Witw. Prof.; Head*
Swanepoel, R., BVSc Pret., PhD Edin. Reader
Other Staff: 1 Lectr.
Research: cancer epidemiology

Physiology

E-mail: laburnhp@physiology.wits.ac.za
Connor, M. D., MB BCh Witw. Sr. Lectr.
Davidson, B. C., PhD Witw. Sr. Lectr.
Erlwanger, K. H., BVSc Z'bwe., MSc Edin. Sr. Lectr.
Fuller, A., BSc Witw., PhD Witw. Sr. Lectr.
Gray, D., BSc Sund., PhD P.Elizabeth Assoc. Prof.
Kamerman, P. R., BSc Witw., PhD Witw. Sr. Lectr.
Laburn, H. P., BSc Witw., PhD Witw. Ad Hominem Prof.; Head*
Mitchell, G., BSc Witw., BVSc Pret., PhD Witw., DVSc Pret. Hon. Prof.
Norton, G. R., BSc Witw., PhD Witw. Assoc. Prof.
Rogers, G. G., BSc Witw., MSc Pret., PhD Witw. Assoc. Prof.
Woodiwiss, A. J., BSc Witw., MSc(Med) Witw., PhD Witw. Sr. Lectr.
Other Staff: 8 Lectrs.; 5 Assoc. Lectrs.
Research: brain function; cardiovascular pathophysiology and genomics; malignant hyperthermia

Public Health

Fonn, S., MB BCh Witw., PhD Witw. Prof.; Head*
Klipstein-Grobusch, K., MSc Rotterdam Assoc. Prof.
Odimegwu, C., PhD Nigeria Assoc. Prof.
Other Staff: 1 Visiting Prof.; 4 Assoc. Profs.; 2 Lectrs.; 1 Assoc. Lectr.; 1 Res. Fellow; 1 Sr. Researcher; 1 Researcher; 1 Sr. Lectr.†; 1 Hon. Prof.; 4 Hon. Assoc. Profs.; 1 Hon. Adjunct Prof.†; 2 Hon. Sr. Lectrs.†; 24 Hon. Lectrs.†; 1 Hon. Res. Assoc.†; 1 Hon. Sr. Researcher†

Community Health

Tel: (011) 717 2051
E-mail: 081pick@chiron.wits.ac.za
Hlungwani, T. M., BCur S.Af.Med., MSc Witw. Sr. Lectr.
Kahn, K., MB BCh Witw., MPH Harv. Sr. Lectr.
Tollman, S. M., BSc Witw., BA Oxf., MB BCh Witw., MMed Witw. Prof.; Head*
Other Staff: 1 Assoc. Lectr.; 1 Sr. Researcher; 1 Researcher; 1 Adjunct Prof.; 1 Sr. Lectr.†; 1 Lectr.†; 1 Adjunct Prof.; 1 Hon. Prof.; 4 Hon. Assoc. Profs.; 1 Hon. Adjunct Prof.; 1 Hon. Sr. Lectr.; 24 Hon. Lectrs.; 1 Hon. Res. Fellow; 1 Hon. Res. Assoc.; 1 Hon. Sr. Researcher

Therapeutic Sciences

Nicholson, C. M., BA Stell., MA Calif. Sr. Lectr.
Rothberg, A. D., BSc Witw., MB BCh Witw., PhD Witw. Prof.; Head*
Other Staff: 1 Lectr.; 1 Adjunct Prof.

Nursing Education

Bruce, J. C., BACur W.Cape, BA(Cur) S.Af., MSc(Nursing) Witw. Prof.; Head*
Minnaar, A., BA S.Af., MA S.Af., PhD Natal Sr. Lectr.
Other Staff: 1 Sr. Lectr.; 4 Lectrs.; 2 Lectrs.†

Occupational Therapy

Tel: (011) 717 3701
de Witt, P. A., MSc(OT) Witw. Sr. Lectr.; Head*
Other Staff: 8 Lectrs.; 2 Lectrs.†; 10 Hon. Lectrs.

Pharmacology

Tel: (011) 717 2041
Danckwerts, M. P., MPharm W.Cape, MBL S.Af., PhD Witw. Aspro Prof.; Head*
Havlik, I., PhD Prague Assoc. Prof.
Other Staff: 3 Lectrs.; 1 Sr. Lectr.†; 3 Lectrs.†

Pharmacy

Chemaly, S. M., BSc Witw., PhD Witw. Sr. Lectr.
Danckwerts, M. P., MPharm W.Cape, MBL S.Af., PhD Witw. Assoc. Prof.; Head*
Pillay, V., BPharm Durban-W., MPharm Durban-W., PhD Temple Assoc. Prof.
Van Vuuren, S. F., MA Witw. Sr. Lectr.
Other Staff: 5 Lectrs.; 1 Sr. Tutor; 1 Lectr.†; 2 Hon. Lectrs.

Physiotherapy

Tel: (011) 488 3450
Mbambo, N. P., BSc(Physio) S.Af.Med., MPhysT Pret. Sr. Lectr.; Academic Head
Stewart, A. V., BSc Witw., MSc(Med) Witw. Assoc. Prof.
Other Staff: 6 Lectrs.; 1 Res. Fellow; 1 Sr. Tutor; 4 Lectrs.†; 1 Tutor†; 17 Hon. Lectrs.

SPECIAL CENTRES, ETC

Africa's International Relations, Centre for

1 Researcher

Applied and Environmental Physics Research Programme

Watterson, J. I. W., BSc Witw., PhD Witw. Prof.

Applied Legal Studies, Centre for

Tel: (011) 717 8609
E-mail: albertync@law.wits.ac.za
Albertyn, C. H., BA Cape Town, LLB Cape Town, MPhil Camb., PhD Camb. Assoc. Prof.; Head*
Cooper, C., BA Witw., LLB S.Af., MA Sus., MA Lond. Assoc. Prof.
Other Staff: 10 Researchers; 1 Assoc. Researcher; 1 Hon. Res. Assoc.

Brain Function Research Unit

Tel: (011) 647 2359
E-mail: 057dunc@chiron.wits.ac.za
Mitchell, D., BSc Witw., MSc Witw., PhD Witw., FRSSAf Dir.*
Other Staff: 1 Res. Officer; 1 Hon. Res. Assoc.

Climatology Research Group

Tel: (011) 716 3400
Piketh, S. J., BA Witw., MSc Witw., PhD Witw. Prof.; Head*
Other Staff: 1 Sr. Researcher; 1 Researcher; 1 Res. Assoc.†; 3 Hon. Profs.†

Defence and Security Management, Centre for

Cawthra, G., BA Natal, PhD Lond. Prof.; Head*
Fisher, L. M., BA Botswana, MBA Botswana, MPA Missouri Sr. Lectr.
Macaringue, P. J., BA E.Mondlane, MSc Lanc., MA Lanc. Sr. Lectr.
Van Nieuwkerk, A., BA Jo'burg., MA Jo'burg., PhD Witw. Sr. Lectr.

Dental Research Institute

Tel: (011) 407 4163 Fax: (011) 339 3036
Cleaton-Jones, P. E., BDS Witw., MB BCh Witw., PhD Witw., DSc(Dent) Witw. Prof.; Dir.*
Other Staff: 1 Res. Assoc.†

Economic Geology Research, Institute of

Tel: (011) 716 2799
Kinnaird, J. A., BSc Lond., MSc St And., PhD St And. Assoc. Prof.
Robb, L. J., BSc Witw., MSc Witw., PhD Witw. Prof.; Head*

Other Staff: 1 Lectr.; 1 Sr. Researcher; 1
Researcher

Education Policy Research Programme

Motala, S., BA Durban-W., BA Cape Town, MA
Warw.   Prof.; Head*
Other Staff: 1 Sr. Researcher; 1 Researcher; 1
Hon. Prof.

Health Policy, Centre for

Tel: (011) 489 9931
Blaauw, D. A., BSc Witw., MB BCh Witw.
Prof.; Head*
Gilson, L. J., BA Oxf., MA E.Anglia, PhD Lond.
Assoc. Prof.
Other Staff: 1 Sr. Researcher; 6 Researchers; 1
Assoc. Prof.†
Research: women's health

Ion Implantation and Surface Studies Research Programme

Derry, T. E., MA Camb., PhD Witw.   Prof.
Research: ion implantation and surface studies

Learning Information Networking Knowledge Centre

Abrahams, L. A., BSc Cape Town   Prof.†; Head*
Gillwald, A., BJourn Rhodes, MA Natal   Assoc.
Prof.
Other Staff: 1 Lectr.; 1 Researcher; 1 Assoc.
Researcher; 1 Assoc. Researcher†

Material Physics Research Institute

Comins, J. D., BSc Natal, PhD Witw.   Prof.

Mathematics, Science and Technology Education, Programme for Research and Development in (RADMASTE)

Tel: (011) 717 6070 Fax: (011) 339 1054
Bradley, J. D., BSc Leeds, PhD Lond.   Assoc.
Prof.; Dir.*
Other Staff: 10 Researchers; 1 Visiting
Researcher; 4 Assoc. Researchers; 1
Researcher†

Mineral Metabolism, MRC-University Research Unit for

Tel: (011) 933 1530 Fax: (011) 938 9074
Pettifor, John M., MB BCh Witw., PhD Witw.,
FCP(SA)   Dir.*
Other Staff: 1 Res. Officer; 1 Hon. Res. Fellow

Molecular Hepatology Research Unit

Tel: (011) 716 3815
Kew, M. C., MB BCh Witw., MD Witw., PhD
Witw., DSc(Med) Witw., FCP(SA), FRCP,
FRSSAf   Sr. Res. Officer; Dir.*
Other Staff: 3 Res. Officers; 1 Sr. Res. Officer†

MRC Bone Research Laboratory

Tel: (011) 647 2144 Fax: (011) 647 2300
Ripamonti, U., LMC Milan, DMD Milan, MDent
Witw., PhD Witw.   Res. Officer; Leader*

Nuclear Physics Research Programme

Cole, B. J., BSc Liv., PhD Liv.   Prof.
Research: nuclear physics

Palaeontological Research, Bernard Price Institute for

Rubidge, B. S., BSc Stell., MSc Stell., PhD
P.Elizabeth   Head*
Other Staff: 1 Sr. Researcher; 1 Researcher; 1
Visiting Researcher; 1 Hon. Prof.

Part-Time Studies, Centre for

Tel: (011) 717 9501
E-mail: munrok@witsplus.wits.ac.za
Reiner, G.   Acting Head*

Refugee Research Programme

Del Valle, H. C.   Leader*
Other Staff: 1 Researcher

Rock Art Research Institute

Smith, B. W., BA Newcastle(UK), PhD Camb.

Science, General College of

Tel: (011) 717 6033
Cameron, A. K., BSc Witw.   Prof.; Head*
Other Staff: 2 Sr. Tutors
Research: earth science; mathematical sciences;
microstructural studies

Social and Economic Research, Wits Institute for

Hyslop, J. R. O., MA Oxf., MA Birm., PhD Witw.
Head*
Mbembe, A., PhD Paris IV   Res. Prof.
Nuttall, S., BA Natal, MA Cape Town   Assoc.
Prof.
Posel, D. B., BA Witw., DPhil Oxf.   Personal
Prof.
Other Staff: 5 Researchers; 1 Visiting
Researcher; 1 Hon. Res. Assoc.

Sociology of Work Research Unit

Tel: (011) 717 4426 Fax: (011) 339 2781
E-mail: 029edw@muse.wits.ac.za
Webster, E. C., BA Rhodes, BPhil York(UK), MA
Oxf., PhD Witw.   Dir.*
Other Staff: 4 Res. Officers

Theoretical Physics Research Unit

Rodrigues, J. A. P., BSc Witw., MSc Brown, PhD
Brown   Prof.

University Learning and Teaching Development, Centre for

Tel: (011) 717 1481
E-mail: orrm@cltd.wits.ac.za
Brown, A. J. V., BA S.Af., BA Witw., MBA Leic.
Sr. Lectr.
Murray, C. B., BA Stell., MEd Witw.   Deputy
Dir.
Orr, M. H., BA Pret., MA Wash., DLitt S.Af.
Dir.*
Zulu, N. G., BEd Rhodes, BA Zululand, MEd OFS
Sr. Lectr.
Other Staff: 1 Principal Tutor; 1 Res. and
Devel. Officer

Wits Northern Accelerator Research Group

Connell, S. H., BSc Witw., PhD Witw.

Wits Rural Facility

Tel: (015) 793 3991 Fax: (015) 793 3992
No staff at present

Vacant Posts: Head*

Wits Writing Centre

Tel: (011) 717 4136
Nichols, C., BA Sus., PhD N.Y.   Head*

CONTACT OFFICERS

Accommodation. Head, Residence Life:
Sharman, R. V., BA Rhodes
(E-mail: sharmanr@residence.wits.ac.za)
Admissions (first degree). Deputy Registrar,
Student Enrolment Centre: Crosley, C.
(E-mail: crosleyc@senc.wits.ac.za)
Admissions (higher degree). Deputy
Registrar, Student Enrolment Centre:
Crosley, C.
(E-mail: crosleyc@senc.wits.ac.za)
Alumni. Head of Alumni Affairs: (vacant)
Archives. Records Manager: (vacant)
Careers. Head and Educational Psychologist,
Counselling and Career Development Unit:
Richards, Zena, BA Witw.
(E-mail: 040zena@cosmos.wits.ac.za)
Computing services. Director, Computer
Network Services: Miller, M. M., BSc Natal,
MA Curtin
Development/fund-raising. Director,
University Foundation: (vacant)
Equal opportunities. Director, Transformation
and Employment Equity Office: Makhubela,
P. L., BBibl Zululand, MLib Wales, DBibl
W.Cape
Estates and buildings/works and services.
Director, Facilities and Services: Prinsloo, E.
(E-mail: prinslooe@pimd.wits.ac.za)
Finance. Financial Director: (vacant)
(E-mail: 147lee@cosmos.wits.ac.za)
General enquiries. Registrar (Academic):
Swemmer, Derek K., BA Pret., MA Pret.,
DLitt&Phil S.Af.
(E-mail: registrar@registrar.wits.ac.za)
Health services. Head: Denga, E.
Industrial liaison. Industrial Relations Adviser:
Smailes, S. C. M., BSocSc Rhodes, LLB Rhodes,
LLM Witw.
International office. Head: Haniff, F.
Library (enquiries). University Librarian:
Ubogu, Felix
(E-mail: ubogu.f@library.wits.ac.za)
Marketing. Director, Communications:
(vacant)
Personnel/human resources. Head, Human
Resources: Taylor, G.
(E-mail: taylor@hr.wits.ac.za)
Public relations. Director, Communications:
(vacant)
Scholarships, awards, loans. Head: Sithole, B.
P., BAdm North(S.Af.)
Schools liaison. Student Recruitment Officer:
Kekana, Yvonne S.
(E-mail: 515keka@atlas.wits.ac.za)
Security. Head of Security: Kemp, R.
(E-mail: 508kemp@atlas.wits.ac.za)
Sport and recreation. Director, Sports
Administration: Baxter, John S., BA(PhysEd)
Rhodes (E-mail: 048bax@mentor.wits.ac.za)
Strategic planning. Director, Strategic
Planning Division: Moore, R. S.
Student welfare/counselling. Dean of
Students: Coopoo, P., BA Durban-W., BA
Durban-W., MMedSc Durban-W.
(E-mail: dean@sao.wits.ac.za)
Students from other countries. Dean of
Students: Coopoo, P., BA Durban-W., BA
Durban-W., MMedSc Durban-W.
(E-mail: dean@sao.wits.ac.za)
Students with disabilities. Head: Lawton-
Misra, Nita, BA S.Af., BEd S.Af., MEd Witw.
(E-mail: nita.lawton-misra@wits.ac.za)

[Information supplied by the institution as at 11 October
2007, and edited by the ACU]

UNIVERSITY OF ZULULAND

Founded 1960

Postal Address: Private Bag X1001, KwadDlangezwa, Kwazulu, Natal, 3886 South Africa
Telephone: (035) 902 6634 **Fax:** (035) 902 6222 **E-mail:** nplungu@pan.uzulu.ac.za
URL: http://www.uzulu.ac.za

VICE-CHANCELLOR*—Gumbi, Prof. R. V., BCur *S.Af.*, MComH *Liv.*, DLitt&Phil *S.Af.*
REGISTRAR‡—Maphisa, G. S., BA *Zululand*, BA *Durban-W.*, MA *Stell.*

SOUTH PACIFIC

DIRECTORY TO SUBJECTS OF STUDY

The table below shows which subjects are available for study and/or research at the University of the South Pacific. U = may be studied for first degree course; M = may be studied for master's degree course; D = research facilities to doctoral level; X = all three levels (UMD).

Subject	Level	Subject	Level
Accountancy/Accounting	X	Estate Management	U
Administration/Administrative Studies	UM	Fashion/Clothing	U
Agriculture/Agricultural Science	X	Film/Photography/Television/Animation	U
Agronomy/Soil Science	UM	Food Science/Nutrition/Home Science/Dietetics	U
Animal Science/Husbandry/Production	UM	Forestry	U
Applied Chemistry	X	French/French Studies	U
Applied Physics	X	Genetics	X
Aquaculture/Fisheries/Marine Science	X	Geography	X
Area Studies	X	Geology/Earth Sciences/Atmospheric Studies	X
Art, History of	U	Hindi	UM
Asian/Pacific Studies	U	History	X
Banking/Finance	UM	Horticulture	U
Biochemistry	U	Industrial Relations/Personnel/HRM	U
Biology	X	Information Science/Studies/Systems	UM
Biology Molecular	X	Land Management/Rehabilitation	UM
Biotechnology	X	Law/Legal Studies	X
Botany/Plant Science	UM	Library/Information Science	U
Business Administration	MD	Linguistics/Translation	UM
Business/Commerce	UM	Management	X
Chemistry	X	Maritime Studies	U
Communication/Journalism/Media Studies	UM	Marketing	X
Communications/Information Management	UM	Mathematics	X
Computer Science	X	Microbiology/Medical Microbiology	X
Conservation Studies	X	Multimedia	U
Counselling	U	Music	U
Creative Writing	U	Occupational Health/Therapy	U
Crop Science/Production	UM	Palaeography	X
Design	U	Parasitology	X
Development Studies	X	Physical Education/Sports Science	U
Drama/Theatre/Dance/Performing Arts	U	Physics	X
E-Commerce	X	Politics/Political Science/Government	X
Ecology	X	Population Studies/Demography	UM
Economic History	U	Psychology	UM
Economics	X	Public Administration	UM
Education	X	Rural Studies/Development	X
Education Distance	UM	Sociology	X
Education Extension	UM	Surveying/Quantity Surveying	U
Education Primary	X	Teacher Training	UM
Education Secondary	X	Textiles/Fibre Science/Technology	U
Education Special	UM	Tourism/Hospitality/Leisure/Recreation	X
Engineering	X	Veterinary Science	U
English	X	Visual Arts	U
Environmental Science/Studies	X	Zoology	X

UNIVERSITY OF THE SOUTH PACIFIC

Founded 1968

Member of the Association of Commonwealth Universities

Postal Address: Suva, Fiji
Telephone: (679) 323 1000 **Fax:** (679) 323 1502
URL: http://www.usp.ac.fj

ACTING VICE-CHANCELLOR*—Chandra, Prof. Rajesh, PhD Br. Col.
ACTING DEPUTY VICE-CHANCELLOR—Williams, Esther, BA Canberra, MA Well., PhD Qld.
PRO-VICE-CHANCELLOR (ALAFUA CAMPUS)—Ebenebe, Prof. Alfred C., BSc Lond., MSc Giessen, PhD Giessen
ACTING PRO-VICE-CHANCELLOR (EMALUS CAMPUS)—Hughes, Prof. Robert, BA NE, PhD NE
PRO-VICE-CHANCELLOR (LAUCALA CAMPUS)—Lynch, Prof. John D., BA Syd., PhD Hawaii
REGISTRAR‡—Fraser, Walter, BA S.Pac.
BURSAR—Latham, Graeme, BCom Melb.
UNIVERSITY LIBRARIAN—Yee, Sin J., BA S.Pac., MBIT RMIT, MCLIP

GENERAL INFORMATION

History. The university was established in 1968 as a regional institution.

It has three campuses (at Fiji, Vanuatu and Samoa) and 13 centres in its Pacific island member countries (Cook Islands, Fiji Islands, Kiribati, Marshall Islands, Naura, Niue, Samoa, Solomon Islands, Tokelau, Tonga, Tuvalu and Vanuatu), and covers 33,000,000 square km of ocean.

Admission to first degree courses. Fiji Form Seven exam with 250 marks out of 400, and with minimum 50% in English and in specified subjects for particular programmes. Equivalent qualifications, including the university's foundation programme, and New Zealand Bursary, may also be accepted.

First Degrees (see also South Pacific Directory to Subjects of Study). BA, BAgr, BEd, BEng, BSc, LLB.

Combined BA/LLB: 4 years full-time.
Length of course. Full-time: BA, BAgr, BEd, BEng, BSc: 3 years; LLB: 4 years.

Higher Degrees (see also South Pacific Directory to Subjects of Study).
Master's. MA, MBA, MSc.
Length of course. Full-time: MBA: 1 year; MA, MSc: 2–3 years. Part-time: MBA: 2 years; MA, MSc: 2½–5 years.
Doctoral. PhD.
Length of course. Full-time: PhD: 3–5 years. Part-time: PhD: 4–7 years.

Language of Instruction. English. English Resources Unit in Centre for the Enhancement of Learning and Teaching is able to assist those for whom English is not their first language.

Libraries. Volumes: 630,000. Periodicals subscribed to: 700. Special collections: Pacific collection.

FACULTIES/SCHOOLS

Agriculture, School of
Tel: (685) 21671 Fax: (685) 22933
E-mail: seuoti_s@samoa.usp.ac.fj
Head: Ebenebe, Prof. Alfred C., BSc Lond., MSc Giessen, PhD Giessen
Secretary (Alafua Campus): Seuoti, Sia

Humanities, School of
Tel: (679) 323 2370 Fax: (679) 323 1552
E-mail: kausimae_p@usp.ac.fj
Head: Kedrayate, Akanisi, MEd Glas., PhD NE
Administrative Assistant: Kausimae, Paul, BA S.Pac.

Law, School of
Tel: (678) 22748 Fax: (678) 22633
E-mail: ngwele_a@vanuatu.usp.ac.fj
Head: Hughes, Prof. Robert, BA NE, PhD NE

Secretary (Emalus Campus): Ngwele, Ala, BA S.Pac.

Pure and Applied Sciences, School of
Tel: (679) 323 2080 Fax: (679) 323 1514
E-mail: fong_ma@usp.ac.fj
Head: Jokhan, Anjeela, BSc S.Pac., MSc S.Pac., PhD Brist.
Administrative Assistant: Fong, Mary

Social and Economic Development, School of
Tel: (679) 323 2580 Fax: (679) 323 1506
E-mail: tuinaceva_t@usp.ac.fj
Head: Qalo, Ropate, BA S.Pac., MA Birm., PhD ANU
Administrative Assistant: Tuinaceva, Titilia

ACADEMIC UNITS

Accounting and Financial Management
Tel: (679) 323 2571 Fax: (679) 323 1506
E-mail: korodrau_l@usp.ac.fj
Fulcher, Peter, LLB Adel., LLM Qld. Sr. Lectr.
Patel, Arvind, BA S.Pac., MCom NSW, PhD Qld. Assoc. Prof.; Head*
Peterson, Ronald, BCom Qld., MAcc Ill. Prof.
Sharma, M. D., BCom Agra, MCom Agra, PhD Agra Prof., Banking
White, Michael, BSc(Econ) Hull, MSc(Econ) Lond. Prof.
Other Staff: 7 Lectrs.; 3 Asst. Lectrs.; 8 Tutors
Research: accounting education; accounting standards; audit evidence; performance measurement in the public sector; working capital management

Agriculture, School of
Tel: (685) 21671 Fax: (685) 22933
E-mail: seuoti_s@samoa.usp.ac.fj

Agricultural Economics, Extension and Education
Bhati, Jagdish, BSc GBP, MSc GBP, MPhil HP, PhD Hawaii Sr. Lectr.; Head*

Animal Science
Ajuyah, Asifo, BSc Ib., MSc Glas., PhD Alta. Sr. Lectr.; Head*
Aregheore, Martin, BSc Tennessee, MSc Ib., PhD Ib. Sr. Lectr.

Biology
Tel: (679) 323 2415 Fax: (679) 323 1513
E-mail: fong_ma@usp.ac.fj
Jokhan, Anjeela, BSc S.Pac., MSc S.Pac., PhD Brist. Sr. Lectr.
Tyagi, A. P., BSc(Ag) Agra, MSc(Ag) Ban., PhD Haryana Ag. Assoc. Prof.; Head*
Winder, Linton, BSc S'ton., PhD S'ton. Sr. Lectr.
Other Staff: 7 Lectrs.; 2 Tutors
Research: conservation biology, ecology and quantitative biology; marine biology; molecular genetics and biotechnology; plant

cytogenetics and breeding; reproductive biology

Business Administration, Master of
Tel: (679) 323 2588 Fax: (679) 323 1506
E-mail: mba@usp.ac.fj
Cook, Christanna, BS Maine(USA), MS Maine(USA), PhD Tennessee Sr. Lectr.
Frodey, Carol, BSc Simmons, MBA Loyola(La.) Sr. Lectr.
Kolay, Mohit, BEng Burd., MEng Calc., PhD Kharagpur Assoc. Prof.
Nowak, Jan, MMath Warsaw, PhD Warsaw Prof.

Business Studies
Tel: (679) 323 2137 Fax: (679) 323 1506
E-mail: pratt_n@usp.ac.fj
Reddy, Narendra, BA S.Pac., MBA NSW, PhD Auck. Co-ordinator*

Chemistry
Tel: (679) 323 2417 Fax: (679) 323 1521
E-mail: cama_t@usp.ac.fj
Agarwal, Ram, BSc C.Sturt, MSc C.Sturt, DSc C.Sturt, PhD C.Sturt Assoc. Prof.
Ali, Sadaquat, BSc S.Pac., MSc S.Pac., PhD S.Pac. Assoc. Prof.
Bonato, John A., BSc NSW, MPhil S.Pac. Sr. Lectr.
Khurma, Jagjit, BSc Punj.Ag., MSc Punj.Ag., PhD Otago Sr. Lectr.
Maata, Matakite, BSc S.Pac., MSc Cant., PhD S.Pac. Sr. Lectr.; Head*
Sotheeswaran, Subramaniam, BSc Ceyl., PhD Hull, DSc Hull Prof.
Other Staff: 5 Lectrs.; 3 Asst. Lectrs.; 2 Tutors
Research: environmental and marine chemistry; food chemistry; natural products and marine natural products chemistry; polymer chemistry

Crop Science
Tofinga, Mareko, BAgrSc PNG, MAgr PNG, PhD Reading Sr. Lectr.; Head*

Development Studies Programme
E-mail: paulo_k@usp.ac.fj
Mohanty, Manoranjan, BSc Utkal, MA Indian Sch.Int.Stud., MPhil Indian Sch.Int.Stud., PhD Indian Sch.Int.Stud. Sr. Lectr.
Reddy, Mahendra, BAgr S.Pac., MSc Hawaii, PhD Hawaii Sr. Lectr.
Robertson, Robert, BA Cant. Prof.; Dir.*

Economics
Tel: (679) 323 2547 Fax: (679) 323 2522
E-mail: singh_js@usp.ac.fj
Gani, Azmat, BCom Lincoln(NZ), MCom Lincoln(NZ), PhD Massey
Jayaraman, Tiruvalangadu, BA Madr., MA Hawaii, PhD Hawaii Sr. Lectr.
Prasad, Biman, BA S.Pac., MCom NSW, PhD Qld. Sr. Lectr.; Head*
Rao, Bhaskara B., BA Ban., BSc Lond., MA Lond., PhD NSW Prof.

Sharma, K. L., BSc(Ag) Ud., MSc IARI, PhD Raj.
Sr. Lectr.
Other Staff: 7 Lectrs.; 1 Asst. Lectr.; 6 Tutors
Research: development economics; electoral
systems in the South Pacific; environment
and tourism; international trade; monetary
and public economics

Education and Psychology

Tel: (679) 323 2203 Fax: (679) 323 1552
E-mail: ah_kee_j@usp.ac.fj
Hughes, Desma, BA Macq., MLitt NE, PhD NE
Sr. Lectr.
Jannif-Dean, Sofia, MSc Wis.   Sr. Lectr.
Kedrayate, Akanisi, MEd Glas., PhD NE   Sr.
Lectr.
Marsh, Connie, BA Open(UK), MPhil Leeds Met.,
PhD Nott.Trent   Sr. Lectr.
Muralidhar, S., BSc Mys., MSc Karn., MSc Keele,
PhD Monash   Assoc. Prof.
Sharma, A., BA S.Pac., MEd NE, EdD Brist.
Assoc. Prof.; Head*
Solomona, U. M. P., BMus N.Y.State   Sr. Lectr.,
Expressive Arts
Solomona, Ueta, BMus N.Y.State   Sr. Lectr.
Thaman, Konai H., BA Auck., MA Calif., PhD
S.Pac.   Prof.
Velayutham, T., BSc Madr., MA Ceyl., PhD La
Trobe   Assoc. Prof.
Other Staff: 9 Lectrs.; 10 Asst. Lectrs.
Research: community stress and coping; human
development studies; learning difficulties;
linguistics; Pacific notions of learning

Engineering

Tel: (679) 323 2223 Fax: (679) 323 1538
E-mail: volau_m@usp.ac.fj
Ahmed, Rafiuddin, BTech J.Nehru U., ME
BIT(Ranchi), PhD IIT Bombay   Sr. Lectr.
Kan, Kiu, BEng RMIT, PhD RMIT   Sr. Lectr.
Onwubolu, Godfrey, BEng Benin, MSc Aston,
PhD Aston   Prof.; Head*
Other Staff: 5 Lectrs.; 3 Asst. Lectrs.
Research: building aerodynamics; modern
manufacturing; modern optimisation
techniques; robotics and automation;
wireless communication systems

Food and Textiles

Tel: (679) 323 2265 Fax: (679) 323 1537
E-mail: seruvatu_e@usp.ac.fj
Jannif-Dean, Jasmine S., MS Wis.   Sr. Lectr.;
Head*
Research: applied design; applied nutrition;
consumer textiles; development using local
foods; food analysis

Geography

Tel: (679) 323 2542 Fax: (679) 323 1506
E-mail: mcgowan_s@usp.ac.fj
Govorov, Micheal, BEng Novosibirsk, PhD
Novosibirsk   Sr. Lectr.
Nunn, P. D., BSc Lond., PhD Lond.   Prof.
Rollings, Nicholas, BSc Adel., MSc NSW
Terry, James, BSc Wales, PhD Wales   Assoc.
Prof.; Head*
Thaman, R. R., BA Calif., MA Calif., PhD Calif.
Prof., Pacific Islands Biogeography
Weber, Eberhand, MA Freib., PhD Freib.   Sr.
Lectr.
Other Staff: 4 Lectrs.; 2 Asst. Lectrs.; 1 Tutor
Research: biodiversity; climate change; islands;
resource vulnerability

Governance Programme

Tel: (679) 323 2764 Fax: (679) 323 1524
E-mail: joseph_d@usp.ac.fj
Hassall, Graham, BEd NSW, BA Syd., PhD ANU
Prof.; Dir.*
Other Staff: 2 Sr. Fellows; 2 Fellows
Research: conflict resolution and peace building;
global, regional and national security issues;
political and ethnic conflict; political parties
and electoral systems; terrorism and war

History/Politics

Tel: (679) 323 2083 Fax: (679) 323 1506
E-mail: hennings_l@usp.ac.fj
Campbell, Ian, BA NE, PhD Adel.   Prof.; Head*

Nicole, Robert, BA S.Pac., MA S.Pac.   Sr. Lectr.
Tarte, Sandra, BA Melb., PhD ANU   Sr. Lectr.
Tuimaleali'ifano, Morgan, BA S.Pac., MA S.Pac.,
PhD S.Pac.   Sr. Lectr.
Other Staff: 4 Lectrs.; 1 Asst. Lectr.
Research: colonial government; Fijian history;
human rights issues; international politics
of the Pacific area; Pacific history

Land Management and Development

Tel: (679) 323 2469 Fax: (679) 323 2507
E-mail: roundswong_c@usp.ac.fj
Boydell, S., BSc Liv., FRICS   Assoc. Prof.;
Head*
Curley, R., MSc Nott., FRICS, FRAS
Other Staff: 2 Lectrs.; 1 Asst. Lectr.; 1 Tutor
Research: developing Pacific property theory;
equitable access to land; forestry and other
resource-related land tenure systems;
tourism on native land; urbanisation, land
use planning and sustainable urban
development

Law, School of

Tel: (678) 22748 Fax: (678) 27785
E-mail: hughes_r@usp.ac.fj
Ahmadu, Mohammed, LLB Jos, LLM Lagos, LLM
Warw.   Sr. Lectr.
Hill, Ted, BA Guelph, LLB Qu.   Sr. Lectr.
Hughes, Robert, BA NE, PhD NE   Prof.; Head*
Macfarlane, Peter, BA Flin., LLB Macq., LLM Syd.
Sr. Lectr.
Paterson, Donald, BA Well., LLB Well., LLM
Well., LLM Yale, JSD Yale   Prof. Emer.
Other Staff: 3 Lectrs.; 2 Asst. Lectrs.
Research: commercial and contract law; company
law; customary law and common law in
the South Pacific; HIV/AIDS law and policy
in the Pacific; Pacific succession and trust
law

Literature and Language

Tel: (679) 323 2214 Fax: (679) 323 1500
E-mail: carson_v@usp.ac.fj
Early, Robert, BA Well., BD Melb.Div.Coll., MA
Auck., PhD ANU   Sr. Lectr.
Gaskell, Ian, BA Wat., MA Tor., PhD Tor.   Prof.
Geraghty, Paul, BA Camb., MA Camb., PhD
Hawaii   Sr. Lectr.
Mugler, France, MA Toledo(Ohio), PhD Mich.
Assoc. Prof.
Prakash, Som, BA Auck., MA Auck., PhD Flin.
Sr. Lectr.
Subramani, BA Cant., MA New Br., PhD S.Pac.
Prof.
Thomas, Larry, BA Canberra   Sr. Lectr.; Head*
Other Staff: 4 Lectrs.; 5 Asst. Lectrs.
Research: creative writing; Pacific journalism;
Pacific languages; Pacific literature

Management and Public Administration

Tel: (679) 323 2134 Fax: (679) 323 1506
E-mail: nasedra_i@usp.ac.fj
Pathak, Raghuvar, BA HP, MBA HP, MPhil HP,
PhD HP   Prof.; Head*
Rahman, Mohammed, BSocSci Dhaka, MSocSci
Dhaka, MEc Wales, PhD Wales   Sr. Lectr.
Reddy, Narendra, BA S.Pac., MBA NSW, PhD
Auck.   Assoc. Prof.
Reguri, Ram R., BA Osm., MA Kakatiya, MPhil
Kakatiya, PhD Kakatiya   Sr. Lectr.
Shee, Himanshu, BEng MBA MTech PhD   Sr.
Lectr.
Wimalasiri, J., BA S.Lanka, MA S.Lanka, MBA
Mich., PhD Lanc.   Assoc. Prof.
Other Staff: 3 Lectrs.; 4 Asst. Lectrs.; 2 Tutors
Research: corporate culture; customer behaviour;
industrial restructuring and labour market
flexibility; managerial effectiveness;
problems and prospects of small businesses

Marine Studies Programme

Tel: (679) 323 2051 Fax: (679) 323 1526
E-mail: zann_l@usp.ac.fj
Pickering, Tim, BSc Well., PhD Well.   Sr. Lectr.
Veitayaki, Joeli, BA S.Pac., MA S.Pac., PhD ANU
Sr. Lectr.
Zann, Leon, BSc NE, PhD NE   Head*

Other Staff: 5 Lectrs.; 1 Asst. Lectr.
Research: aquaculture and post harvest fisheries;
coastal and resources management; coral
reefs and atolls; fisheries ecology,
conservation and management; traditional
marine tenure

Mathematics and Computing Science

Tel: (679) 323 2364 Fax: (679) 323 1527
E-mail: prasad_s@usp.ac.fj
Hosack, John, BSc Cal.Tech., MSc Calif., PhD
Calif.   Assoc. Prof.
Khan, M. G. M., BSc Calc., MSc Alig., PhD Alig.
Li, Zhenquan (Jan), BSc Hebei, PhD S.Qld.   Sr.
Lectr.
Malinin, Dmitry, MSc Belorussian State, PhD
St.Petersburg   Sr. Lectr.
Mnukhin, Valeriy, PhD Moldovan Acad.Sc.   Sr.
Lectr.
Vanualailai, Jito, BSc S.Pac., ME Ryukyus, PhD
Kobe   Sr. Lectr.; Head*
Other Staff: 12 Lectrs.; 4 Asst. Lectrs.; 13
Tutors
Research: applied mathematics; combinatorics
and group theory; constructive analysis;
human computer interaction; statistics

Pacific Studies Programme

Tel: (679) 323 2017 Fax: (679) 323 1524
Huffer, Elise, BA Calif., MA Toulouse, PhD Aix-
Marseilles
Research: agricultural, resource and
environmental economics; inequalities of
development/social consequences of present
economic policies; politics of development;
poverty, housing and urban development
issues

Physics

Tel: (679) 323 2063 Fax: (679) 323 1511
E-mail: bainivalu_a@usp.ac.fj
Garimella, S., BSc And., MSc And., DrRerNat
Mainz   Assoc. Prof.
Prasad, Surendra, BSc S.Pac., MSc S.Pac., PhD
ANU   Sr. Lectr.; Head*
Other Staff: 5 Lectrs.; 1 Asst. Lectr.; 3 Tutors
Research: applications of nuclear techniques;
electrical communication; energy and the
environment; marine physics

Population Studies Programme

Fax: (679) 323 1509
E-mail: seniloli_k@usp.ac.fj
Seniloli, Kesaia, BA S.Pac., MA ANU, PhD ANU
Co-ordinator*
Other Staff: 1 Lectr.
Research: male and young people's attitudes
towards family planning; teenage
pregnancies

Sociology

Tel: (679) 323 2136 Fax: (679) 323 1506
E-mail: singh_m@usp.ac.fj
Prasad, Satendra, BA S.Pac., MA New Br., PhD
Warsaw   Sr. Lectr. (on leave)
Qalo, Ropate, BA S.Pac., MA Birm., PhD ANU
Sr. Lectr.
Other Staff: 1 Lectr.; 3 Asst. Lectrs.
Research: child sex abuse; commercial sex and
sexual health; ethics and professionalism;
male attitudes towards contraception and
pregnancy in the South Pacific

Soil Science and Agricultural Engineering

Eaqub, Mohammed, BAgr Dacca, MSc(Agric)
B'desh.Ag., PhD   Sr. Lectr.; Head*

Tourism and Hospitality

Tel: (679) 323 2688 Fax: (679) 323 1510
E-mail: talikai_n@usp.ac.fj
Short, David, MBA Massey, PhD Lincoln(NZ)   Sr.
Lectr.; Head*
Other Staff: 2 Lectrs.
Research: backpacker tourism; sustainable
tourism development in the South Pacific;
tourism and indigenous entrepreneurship;

tourism policy and planning; tourism training and education

SPECIAL CENTRES, ETC

Agriculture, Institute for Research, Extension and Training in (IRETA)

Umar, Mohammed, BAgrSc Qld., MSc W.Virginia   Dir.*
Research: animal science; bio-pesticides; high-yielding, drought- and disease- resistant taro varieties; social science and agricultural engineering; stress and coping strategies among university students

Applied Sciences, Institute of

Tel: (679) 323 2965 Fax: (679) 323 1534
   E-mail: aalsbersberg@usp.ac.fj
Aalbersberg, William, BA Cornell, PhD Calif.   Dir.*
Other Staff: 4 Fellows
Research: coastal processes; environmental impact of solid and liquid waste management; impact of development on coastal environments; pollution monitoring; water quality and biodiversity

Arts and Culture, Oceania Centre for

Tel: (679) 321 2832 Fax: (679) 330 8542
   E-mail: barrett_a@usp.ac.fj
Hau'ofa, Epeli, BA NE, MA McG., PhD ANU   Prof.; Dir.*
Other Staff: 1 Choreographer
Research: contemporary Oceanic arts, culture and history

Development and Governance, Pacific Institute of Advanced Studies in (PIAS-DG)

Tel: (679) 323 2297 Fax: (679) 323 1523
   E-mail: namoga_m@usp.ac.fj
Duncan, Ronald, BAgEc NE, MAgEc NE, PhD ANU   Prof.; Exec. Dir.*

Distance and Flexible Learning Support Centre

Tel: (679) 323 2585 Fax: (679) 323 1539
   E-mail: ratumaiyale@usp.ac.fj
Bonato, John A., BSc NSW, MPhil S.Pac.   Acting Dir.*
Moala, Emily, BA S.Pac., MEPA Monash   Co-ordinator, Pre-Degree
Veramu, Joseph, BEd S.Pac., MSc S.Bank, MPhil S.Pac.   Co-ordinator, Continuing Education
Other Staff: 24 Tutors; 5 Instrucnl. Designers
Research: expected listening and speaking skills for distance students; impact of programmes provided through a university extension centre; impact of satellite technology on distance education; problems faced by distance students

Education, Institute of

Tel: (679) 323 2361 Fax: (679) 323 1553
   E-mail: reiher_e@usp.ac.fj
Taufe'ulungaki, Ana, BA Auck., MA Leeds, PhD Birm.   Dir.*
Other Staff: 1 Co-ordinator; 4 Fellows; 1 Editor
Research: assessment/evaluation; basic education literacy; education in the University of the South Pacific region; education policy; quality of education

Environment and Sustainable Development, Pacific Centre for

Tel: (679) 323 2184
   E-mail: startoceania@usp.ac.fj
Koshy, K. C., MSc Kerala, PhD WI   Assoc. Prof.; Head*

Justice and Applied Legal Studies, Institute of

Tel: (679) 323 2801
   E-mail: shekhar_p@usp.ac.fj
Ahmadu, Mohammed, LLB Jos, LLM Lagos, LLM Warw.   Assoc. Prof.; Acting Dir.*
Other Staff: 3 Fellows

Research: HIV/AIDS; human rights; legal literacy; women and environment

Learning and Teaching, Centre for the Enhancement of (CELT)

Tel: (679) 323 2608 Fax: (679) 323 1541
   E-mail: ramere_e@usp.ac.fj
Hogan, Robert, BA N.Y., MS N.Y., EdD Flor.   Sr. Lectr.
Marsh, Connie, BA Open(UK), MPhil Leeds Met., PhD Nott.Trent   Sr. Lectr.
Tuimaleali'ifano, Eileen J., BA S.Pac., MA S.Pac., PhD NE   Dir.*
Other Staff: 2 Lectrs.; 1 Asst. Lectr.; 9 Tutors
Research: application of educational technology in remote teaching and learning; good practice in remote and flexible teaching and learning; impact of social and study environment on student learning processes

Marine Resources, Institute of

Tel: (679) 323 2888 Fax: (679) 323 1526
Pickering, Tim, BSc Well., PhD Well.   Acting Dir.*
Other Staff: 1 Fellow
Research: aquaculture and marine protected areas; biosecurity; ciguatera poisoning; coastal and shore ecology; marine botany and invasive species

South Pacific Regional Herbarium

Tuiwawa, Marika, BSc S.Pac., MSc S.Pac.   Curator*

University Centres

Cook Islands Centre

Tel: (682) 29415 Fax: (682) 21315
   E-mail: dixon_ro@usp.ac.fj
Dixon, Roderick, BA Essex, MA ANU   Dir.*

Fiji (Northern) Centre

Tel: (679) 881 7707 Fax: (679) 881 5570
Bogitini, Samuela, BA S.Pac., MEd Qld., PhD Qld.   Deputy Dir.

Fiji (Western) Centre

Tel: (679) 666 6800 Fax: (679) 666 7133
Singh, Anirudh, BSc S.Pac., MSc Auck., PhD Leic.   Deputy Dir.
Other Staff: 2 Lectrs.; 1 Asst. Lectr.; 3 Tutors

Kiribati Centre

Tel: (686) 21085 Fax: (686) 21419
   E-mail: mackenzie_u@usp.ac.fj
Neemia, Ueantabo, BA S.Pac., MA S.Pac., PhD W'gong.   Dir.*
Other Staff: 1 Lectr.; 1 Asst. Lectr.

Marshall Islands Centre

Tel: (692) 625 7279 Fax: (692) 625 7282
   E-mail: tibon_l@usp.ac.fj
Taafaki, Irene, BEd Reading, MEd Mass., PhD Mass.   Dir.*
Other Staff: 1 Asst. Lectr.

Nauru Centre

Tel: (674) 555 6455 Fax: (674) 444 3774
   E-mail: lauti_a@usp.ac.fj
Lauti, Alamanda, BA S.Pac.   Dir.*

Niue Centre

Tel: (683) 4049 Fax: (683) 4315
   E-mail: talagi_ma@usp.ac.fj
Talagi, Maru, BA Auck., MA Auck.   Dir.*

Samoa Centre

Tel: (685) 20874 Fax: (685) 23424
   E-mail: vaa_r@samoa.usp.ac.fj
Va'a, Ruby, BSc Auck., MPhil S.Pac.   Dir.*
Other Staff: 1 Lectr.

Solomon Islands Centre

Tel: (677) 21307 Fax: (677) 24024
   E-mail: galo_g@usp.ac.fj
Galo, Glyn, BSc S.Pac., MBA Qld., EdD Brist.   Dir.*
Other Staff: 1 Tutor; 1 Librarian

Tokelau Centre

Tel: (690) 2178 Fax: (690) 2178
   E-mail: siml_l@usp.ac.fj
Lua, L., BA S.Pac.   Co-ordinator*

Tonga Centre

Tel: (676) 29240 Fax: (676) 29249
   E-mail: fukofuka_s@usp.ac.fj
Fukofuka, Salote, BA NE, MEd Canberra   Dir.*
Other Staff: 2 Lectrs.

Tuvalu Centre

Tel: (688) 20811 Fax: (688) 20704
   E-mail: manuella_d@usp.ac.fj
No staff at present

Vanuatu Centre

Tel: (678) 24568 Fax: (678) 24371
   E-mail: molisa_p@vanuatu.usp.ac.fj
Nirua, Jean-Pierre, BA S.Pac., MBA S.Pac.   Dir.*
Other Staff: 1 Asst. Lectr.

CONTACT OFFICERS

Academic affairs. Registrar: Fraser, Walter, BA S.Pac. (E-mail: fraser_w@usp.ac.fj)
Accommodation. Provost: Fifita, Filimone, BA Hawaii (E-mail: fifita_f@usp.ac.fj)
Admissions (first degree). Registrar: Fraser, Walter, BA S.Pac.
   (E-mail: fraser_w@usp.ac.fj)
Admissions (higher degree). Registrar: Fraser, Walter, BA S.Pac.
   (E-mail: fraser_w@usp.ac.fj)
Adult/continuing education. Acting Director, Distance and Flexible Learning Support Centre: Bonato, John A., BSc NSW, MPhil S.Pac. (E-mail: bonato_j@usp.ac.fj)
Alumni. Registrar: Fraser, Walter, BA S.Pac.
   (E-mail: fraser_w@usp.ac.fj)
Archives. University Librarian: Williams, Esther, BA Canberra, MA Well., PhD Qld.
   (E-mail: williams_e@usp.ac.fj)
Computing services. Director, Information Technology Services: Finau, Kisione, BSc Hawaii, MASc Qld.UT
   (E-mail: finau_k@usp.ac.fj)
Conferences/corporate hospitality. Registrar: Fraser, Walter, BA S.Pac.
   (E-mail: fraser_w@usp.ac.fj)
Consultancy services. Manager, USP Solutions: Hawke, James, MBA Auck.
   (E-mail: hawke_j@usp.ac.fj)
Development/fund-raising. Director, Development: (vacant)
Distance education. Acting Director, Distance and Flexible Learning Support Centre: Bonato, John A., BSc NSW, MPhil S.Pac.
   (E-mail: bonato_j@usp.ac.fj)
Estates and buildings/works and services. Director, Property and Facilities: Broad, Terence, BA(Arch) Auck.
Examinations. Registrar: Fraser, Walter, BA S.Pac. (E-mail: fraser_w@usp.ac.fj)
Finance. Bursar: Latham, Graeme, BCom Melb.
   (E-mail: latham_g@usp.ac.fj)
General enquiries. Registrar: Fraser, Walter, BA S.Pac. (E-mail: fraser_w@usp.ac.fj)
Health services. Provost: Fifita, Filimone, BA Hawaii (E-mail: fifita_f@usp.ac.fj)
Industrial liaison. Registrar: Fraser, Walter, BA S.Pac. (E-mail: fraser_w@usp.ac.fj)
Language training for international students. Director, Centre for Enhancement of Learning and Teaching: Tuimaleali'ifano, Eileen J., BA S.Pac., MA S.Pac., PhD NE
   (E-mail: tuimale_e@usp.ac.fj)

Library (chief librarian). Acting University Librarian: Fong, Elizabeth, BA *S.Pac.*, MA *N.Lond.* (E-mail: williams_e@usp.ac.fj)

Marketing. Director, Marketing and Communications: (vacant)

Personnel/human resources. Acting Manager, Personnel: Kotoisuva, Agnes
(E-mail: kotoisuva_a@usp.ac.fj)

Public relations. Manager, Media and Public Relations: Hussain, Bernadette
(E-mail: hussain_b@usp.ac.fj)

Publications. Publications Manager: Sidal, Adrienne, BA *Massey*
(E-mail: sidal_a@usp.ac.fj)

Purchasing. Purchasing Manager: Mataitini, Leba, MBA *S.Pac.*
(E-mail: mataitini_l@usp.ac.fj)

Research. Chairperson, University Research Committee: Hosack, John, BSc *Cal.Tech.*, MSc *Calif.*, PhD *Calif.*
(E-mail: hosack_j@usp.ac.fj)

Safety. Registrar: Fraser, Walter, BA *S.Pac.*
(E-mail: fraser_w@usp.ac.fj)

Schools liaison. Registrar: Fraser, Walter, BA *S.Pac.* (E-mail: fraser_w@usp.ac.fj)

Security. Provost: Fifita, Filimone, BA *Hawaii*
(E-mail: fifita_f@usp.ac.fj)

Sport and recreation. Provost: Fifita, Filimone, BA *Hawaii*
(E-mail: fifita_f@usp.ac.fj)

Staff development and training. Registrar: Fraser, Walter, BA *S.Pac.*
(E-mail: fraser_w@usp.ac.fj)

Student union. Student Union Office

Student welfare/counselling. Provost: Fifita, Filimone, BA *Hawaii*
(E-mail: fifita_f@usp.ac.fj)

Students from other countries. International Students Officer: Konusi, Litia, BA *W'gong.*
(E-mail: konusi_l@usp.ac.fj)

[*Information supplied by the institution as at 3 May 2006, and edited by the ACU*]

SRI LANKA

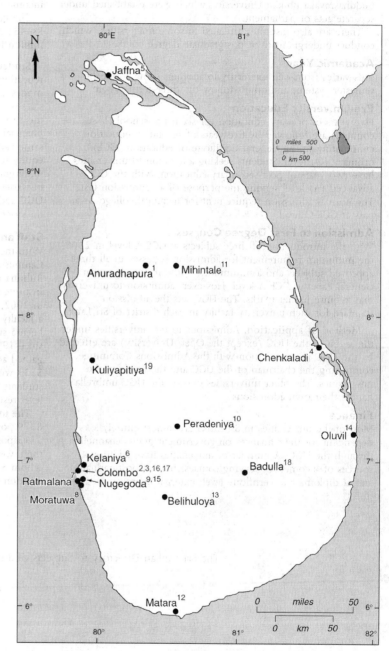

The places named are the seats of the university institutions numbered above

THE UNIVERSITIES OF SRI LANKA

Information compiled by the Committee of Vice-Chancellors and Directors (Sri Lanka) as at 16 May 2005

The University System

The university system in Sri Lanka was established by act of parliament in 1978. There are currently 13 universities functioning under the University Grants Commission (UGC). In addition, two other universities operate outside the ambit of the UGC: Buddhist and Pali University of Sri Lanka and Buddhasravaka Bhikku University, which were established under separate acts of parliament.

There are also institutes affiliated to some universities, which conduct undergraduate or postgraduate degree courses.

Academic Year

This varies from one university to another: some adopt the semester system, and others follow the three-term system.

Pre-University Education

Five years of primary education (or six if pre-school classes are counted) are followed by five years of secondary education culminating in the General Certificate of Education (GCE) ordinary (O) level. Students seeking admission to universities have two years of post-secondary education, with the GCE advanced (A) level serving the purpose of an admission test. The normal admission requirement for technical colleges is a pass at GCE O level.

Admission to First Degree Courses

With the introduction of three subjects at GCE A level in 2000, the minimum requirement for admission is passes in all three approved subjects and a minimum of 30% in the Common General Paper at GCE A level. However, admission to university may require higher marks. The UGC sets the admission standard for each university faculty in each district of Sri Lanka.

Method of application. Admissions to the universities under the ambit of the UGC (except the Open University) are effected by the UGC in consultation with the Admissions Committee, comprising the chairman of the UGC and the heads of the universities. The other universities outside the UGC umbrella handle their own admissions.

Finance

Most of the universities in Sri Lanka are almost entirely dependent for their finances on government grants channelled through the UGC. A number of universities have additional sources of income: fee-levying courses, both at postgraduate and at diploma and certificate level; external degrees; consultations; and charges for hiring playgrounds, gymnasia and halls to outsiders.

In addition fees are levied from undergraduates for examinations, registration, sports, hostels, etc. Universities such as Peradeniya and Colombo also receive fees for accommodation. The Open University obtains most of its income from sources other than the government grant.

The government allocation to the universities for 2004 was Rs4433.85 million for recurrent expenditure and Rs1677 million for capital expenditure.

Student finance. While no tuition fees are charged, students repeating examinations and all external students are charged modest registration and examination fees. There is a scheme of state scholarships, the Mahapola scholarships, awarded partly on the basis of academic merit but mainly to students in need of financial assistance. In addition, the UGC gives bursaries of the same value to needy students who do not receive the Mahapola equity scholarships. At present about two-thirds of the undergraduate population receive these scholarships or bursaries. There are also other scholarships awarded by the UGC and the universities on the basis of criteria stipulated by the donors.

Staff and Student Numbers

With the establishment of the Wayamba University, Tincomalee Campus and the faculty of engineering of the University of Ruhuna in 2000, the Sri Palee Campus in 2001 and the Institute of Technology affiliated to the University of Moratuwa in 2002, in addition to the three new universities in 1997 and a faculty of medical sciences at Sri Jayewardenepura, there has been a substantial increase in the number of students admitted since 1996–97. In 1997–98 the total number of students who gained admission to the universities was 10,755, of whom 5339 were women. In the year 2004, the total number of students admitted to the universities on the basis of the GCE A level results of 2004 was 14,302, of whom 7283 were women.

The universities under the UGC had and approved cadre of 8279 positions for academic and academic support staff, and 1113 positions for non-academic staff. As at October 2003, there were 6257 academic and academic support staff, of whom 3293 were men. The number of non-academic staff in position was 10,056, of whom 8615 were men.

The Sri Lankan Directory to Subjects of Study follows on p. 1428

SRI LANKA: DIRECTORY TO

The table below shows which of the institutions indicated provide facilities for study and/or research in the subjects named. In the case of related subject areas which have been grouped together (eg Botany/Plant Science), it should be borne in mind that one or more of the subjects may be offered by the institution concerned.

	Buddhasravaka Bhiksu	Buddhist & Pali	Colombo	Eastern	Kelaniya	Kotelawala	Open, Sri Lanka	Peradeniya	Ruhuna	South Eastern	Sri Jayewardenepura	Sri Lanka IIT	Wayamba
Accountancy/Accounting			UM	U	UM	U			X	U		U	U
Administration/Administrative Studies										U			U
Advertising							U						
Agricultural Extension and Education													U
Agriculture/Agricultural Science				U				X	X				U
Agronomy/Soil Science				U				X	X				U
Agrotechnology									X				U
American Studies								U					
Anatomical Science/Anatomy			U		X			UM					U
Ancient Indian History and Culture								U					
Animal Nutrition/Animal Physiology								MD					U
Animal Science/Husbandry/Production				U				X	X				U
Animatronics/Computer Arts													U
Anthropology/Folklore			M										
Applied Chemistry			UM										
Applied Physics			UM										
Aquaculture/Fisheries/Marine Science						UM		MD			M		U
Arabic			U	U				X		U			
Archaeology	U	U			X			X	U				
Architectural Design							U						
Architecture							U	U					
Area Studies								U					
Art, Fine				U	X			U					
Art, History of					X			U					
Artificial Intelligence												UM	
Arts, Graphic												U	
Asian/Pacific Studies			U				U						
Aviation							U						
Banking/Finance			UM	U	U	U		U	U	U			U
Behavioural Sciences			U			M							U
Biochemistry			X	U	X			M	U				U
Bioinformatics												U	
Biology			X	U	U			U	U	U			
Biology Molecular			MD		U								
Biomedical Sciences					U								
Biostatistics			U					MD					
Biotechnology			MD		U			MD	U			U	U
Botany/Plant Science			X	U	X		UM	X	UM	U			U
Buddhist Studies	U	X			X			X	X				
Building/Built Environment/Construction						U	UM	U					
Business Administration			UM	U	U			M		X			U

SUBJECTS OF STUDY

For further information about the individual subjects taught at each institution, please refer to the *Index to Subjects of Study* at the end of the Yearbook, but for full details about subjects/courses offered at universities in the Commonwealth each institution's own official publications must be consulted. U = may be studied for first degree course; M = may be studied for master's degree course; D = research facilities to doctoral level; X = all three levels (UMD). **Note**—The table only includes information provided by institutions currently in membership of the Association of Commonwealth Universities.

	Buddhasravaka Bhiksu	Buddhist & Pali	Colombo	Eastern	Kelaniya	Kotelawala	Open, Sri Lanka	Peradeniya	Ruhuna	South Eastern	Sri Jayewardenepura	Sri Lanka IIT	Wayamba
Business Computing			U									U	U
Business Economics													U
Business Information Systems			U									UM	U
Business/Commerce			X	U	UM	U		UM	X	U			U
Catholicism					U								
Chemistry			X	U	X	U	UM	X	X	U			U
Child/Youth Studies				U				U					
Chinese/Chinese Studies					U								
Classics/Greek/Latin/Ancient History					X			UM	U				
Commonwealth Studies								U	U				
Communication Sciences								U				UM	
Communication/Journalism/Media Studies			U		X			U			M		
Communications/Information Management								U	U			U	
Community Health			UM										
Community Medicine								U					
Community Studies					U								
Computer Science	U		X	U	UM	U	U	X	UM	U		UM	U
Conservation Studies					UM								U
Consumer Studies													U
Criminology									U				
Crop Science/Production				U				X	X				U
Cultural Studies				U				U	U				
Dairy Technology								MD					
Defence Studies						M	UM						
Dentistry								X					
Design, Industrial						U		U					
Development Studies								U	U				U
Disability Studies						U							
Drama/Theatre/Dance/Performing Arts			U	U	X				U				
E-Business												UM	
E-Commerce			M									UM	U
Ecology			UM		X				UM				U
Economic History				U			U	M	U	U			
Economics			X	U	X	U	U	X	U	U		U	U
Economics Agricultural/Agribusiness				U				U	X	UM	U		U
Education	U		X				X	MD					
Education Special			U										
Educational Psychology								MD					
Electronics					U	U						U	U
Energy Studies								U					
Engineering							U	X	UM	UM			

	Buddhasravaka Bhiksu	Buddhist & Pali	Colombo	Eastern	Kelaniya	Kotelawala	Open, Sri Lanka	Peradeniya	Ruhuna	South Eastern	Sri Jayewardenepura	Sri Lanka IIT	Wayamba
Engineering Aeronautical/Aerospace						U							
Engineering Agricultural/Fisheries							UD	X					U
Engineering Automobile						U	U						
Engineering Chemical/Petrochemical/Process							U	UM					U
Engineering Civil/Environmental/Structural							U	X	UM	UM			
Engineering Communications/Telecommunications							U	U				U	
Engineering Computer							U	UD	M			U	
Engineering Construction							U						
Engineering Design							U						
Engineering Electrical/Electronic							U	UD	UM	UM		U	
Engineering Geological							U	U	U				
Engineering Industrial							U	UM	U				
Engineering Information Technology							U					U	
Engineering Instrumentation								U					
Engineering Management							U					U	
Engineering Manufacturing								U					
Engineering Marine							U	U					
Engineering Materials/Mineral Resources/Petroleum							U	U					
Engineering Mathematical							U	U	UM				
Engineering Mechanical/Production							U	X	UM	UM			
Engineering Medical								M					
Engineering Metallurgical/Mining						U							
Engineering Software							U					UM	U
English	U	U	X	U	X	U	U	X	U	U			U
English as a Second Language			M									U	
Entomology			U					MD	UM				U
Entrepreneurship												U	
Environmental Health							U						
Environmental Science/Studies			M		X		U	X	X	UM	M		U
Estate Management													U
Ethics							U					U	
Ethnicity/Multiculturalism							U						
Fashion/Clothing							X						
Film/Photography/Television/Animation							U						
Food Science/Nutrition/Home Science/Dietetics					M			X	UM		M		U
Forensic Science			UM		U								
Forestry											M		U
French/French Studies						U		U					
Genetics			M		U								U
Genetics and Plant Breeding								MD					
Geographic Information Systems/Geomatics			U										

	Buddhasravaka Bhiksu	Buddhist & Pali	Colombo	Eastern	Kelaniya	Kotelawala	Open, Sri Lanka	Peradeniya	Ruhuna	South Eastern	Sri Jayewardenepura	Sri Lanka IIT	Wayamba
Geography			X	U	X	U	U	X	U	U			
Geology/Earth Sciences/Atmospheric Studies							U	X		U			
German/Germanic Studies					U								
Health Education					U								
Health Sciences/Studies							U						U
Hindi	U				X								
History	U		X	U	X	U		X	UM	U			
History/Philosophy of Science			U					X					
Horticulture						U		X	UM				U
Human Biology			U										
Human Genetics			U										
Human Movement/Kinesiology/Biomechanics							U						
Human Resource Development													U
Human Rights/Globalisation			UM				U						
Industrial Relations/Personnel/HRM			UM		UM	U				U			U
Information Science/Studies/Systems			UM		UM			M				UM	U
Information Technology					X							UM	U
Insurance													U
International Business						U							U
International Finance						U							
International Finance Economics						U							
International Marketing						M							
International Relations/Studies			X		U	UM				U			
Internet Computing/Technologies												UM	
Islamic/Middle Eastern Studies			U					X		U			
Japanese/Japanese Studies	U		M		U								
Korean/Korean Studies					U								
Labour Studies						M							
Landscape Architecture													U
Language Teaching/Learning			UM										
Language and Communication						UM							
Languages, Modern					U			U					
Law Business/Commercial/Economic/Industrial			U			U						U	U
Law Civil						U							
Law Employment/Labour			U			M							
Law Environmental			U			M							
Law Intellectual Property/Copyright			U			U							
Law International/Comparative/Trade			U			U							
Law Legal Practice			U										
Law Property/Construction/Housing			U										
Law/Legal Studies			X				UM	U					

	Buddhasravaka Bhiksu	Buddhist & Pali	Colombo	Eastern	Kelaniya	Kotelawala	Open, Sri Lanka	Peradeniya	Ruhuna	South Eastern	Sri Jayewardenepura	Sri Lanka IIT	Wayamba
Library/Information Science	U		M		UM								
Linguistics/Translation					X								
Livestock Science								MD					UM
Management			X	U	X	UM	U			U	M	UM	U
Management Information Systems					M							UM	U
Maritime Studies							U						
Marketing			UM	U	UM	U			UM	U		U	U
Materials Science							U						
Mathematics			X	U	X	UM	U	X	UM	U	M	U	U
Medical Ethics			UM										
Medicine, Indian			U										
Medicine, Obstetrics and Gynaecology			UM					UM					
Medicine, Paediatric			UM					X					
Medicine/Surgery			X		X			UM	UM		D		
Meteorology									U				
Microbiology/Medical Microbiology			UM	U	X			UM	U				U
Military Science						M							
Mobile Communications/Telecommunications							U					U	U
Multimedia			U									U	U
Music				U	U								
Natural Resource Studies									U				U
Network Technology/Security												U	U
Neuroscience			U										
Nursing/Midwifery							U						
Occupational Health/Therapy			U										
Operational Research/Operations Management						M							U
Parasitology			UM		X			X	X				
Pathology			UM					X					
Peace/War Studies						M							
Pharmacology			U		X			UM	U				
Pharmacy/Pharmaceutical Science			U										
Philosophy		X			U	X		X			U		
Physical Education/Sports Science				U									U
Physics			X	U	X	U	U	X	UM	U			U
Physiology			UM		U			X	UD				U
Physiotherapy					U								
Planning/Landscape Studies													U
Plant Pathology			U					MD					
Politics/Political Science/Government			X		UM	U	U	X	UD	U			
Population Studies/Demography			UM						UD				
Product Design and Technology							U						

	Buddhasravaka Bhiksu	Buddhist & Pali	Colombo	Eastern	Kelaniya	Kotelawala	Open, Sri Lanka	Peradeniya	Ruhuna	South Eastern	Sri Jayewardenepura	Sri Lanka IIT	Wayamba
Project Management						M						UM	U
Psychiatry			UM					UM					
Psychology	U		M		U		U	X	U				
Public Administration						M	M			U			
Public Health/Population Health													U
Public Relations							U						
Public Sector Management													U
Rehabilitation Medicine/Therapy/Science					U								
Religion/Theology		U					U						
Risk Management							M						U
Robotics												U	
Rural Extension							U						
Rural Studies/Development							U		U				
Russian/Russian Studies					U								
Sanskrit/Pali/Prakrit/Vedic Studies	U	X			X			X					
Sinhala	U	X	X		X	U		X	X	U			
Social Policy							U						
Social Reconstruction							U						
Social Work/Studies	U						U						
Sociology	U		X	U	X	U	UM	X	X	U			
Statistics/Actuarial Science			X		UM	UM		X	UM	U		M	U
Surveying/Quantity Surveying							U		U				
Sustainable Development							U						
Sustainable Economies													U
Tamil	U			U	U	U		X		U			
Taxation							U		U				U
Teacher Training			UM					M					
Textiles/Fibre Science/Technology							X						
Tourism/Hospitality/Leisure/Recreation										U			
Toxicology													U
Transport Studies									X				
United States Studies									U				
Urban Studies							U						
Veterinary Science								M	U				
Visual Arts					U								
Wildlife Management													U
Women's/Gender Studies			UM				U						U
Zoology			X	U	X		UM	X	UM	U			

BUDDHASRAVAKA BHIKSU UNIVERSITY

Founded 1996

Member of the Association of Commonwealth Universities

Postal Address: Nandana Mawatha, Anuradhapura, Sri Lanka
Telephone: (025) 223 5328 **Fax:** (025) 223 5328 **E-mail:** bbuanusl@sltnet.lk

VICE-CHANCELLOR*—Seelakkhandha Thero, Ven. Dr. Thumbulle, BED *Peradeniya*,
   MPhil *Colombo*, PhD *Colombo*
REGISTRAR‡—(vacant)
BURSAR—(vacant)
LIBRARIAN—(vacant)
SENIOR ASSISTANT REGISTRAR—Rathnayaka, K., BA *Peradeniya*
ASSISTANT REGISTRAR—Ekanayake, S. H. P. E. S., BCom *Peradeniya*
ASSISTANT BURSAR—Rathnayaka, G. W., BSc *Rajarata*
ASSISTANT LIBRARIAN—Bandara, Y. K. T., BA *Peradeniya*

GENERAL INFORMATION

History. The university was established in
1996.
   It is located at the sacred city of
Anuradhapura, about 200km from Colombo.

Admission to first degree courses (see also Sri
Lankan Introduction). General School
Certificate (GCE) A level with 4 passes (with
old syllabus) or 3 passes (with new syllabus)
including Pali, Buddhism/Buddhist Studies and
Sanskrit and an aggregate of not less than 180
or 130 marks, or equivalent qualifications.

First Degrees (see also Sri Lankan Directory
to Subjects of Study). BA.
   Length of course. Full-time: BA: 3–4 years.

Language of Instruction. Sinhala and
English.

Libraries. Volumes: 34,000. Periodicals
subscribed to: 400. Special collections:
Thripitaka Sinhalese Character; Burmese
Thripitaka; English Pali text; Sanskrit text.

Academic Awards (2006–2007). 206
awards each with a min. value of Rs1400.

Income (2006–2007). Total, Rs51,285,000.

Statistics. Staff (2007): 64 (26 academic, 38
non-academic). Students (2006–2007): full-
time 206 (206 men.

ACADEMIC UNITS
Buddhist Studies

Dhammapala, Ven. Akmeemana, BA *B&P SLanka*
Dhammapala, Ven. Warakawehera, BA *Buddha
   SK*, MA *Kelaniya*
Gnanissara, Ven. Pathegama, BA *Sri Jay.*, MA
   Kelaniya, MPhil *Kelaniya*
Piyarathana, Ven. Kadawathgama, BA *Kelaniya*,
   MA *Kelaniya*
Saddharatana, Ven. Kanattegoda, BA *Buddha SK*,
   BA *Kelaniya*, MA *Kelaniya*, MPhil *Kelaniya*
Wimalagnana, Ven. Miriswatthe, BA   Head*
Other Staff: 3 Staff Members

Languages Studies

Chandasiri, Ven. Liyanegama, BA *Sri Jay.*, MA
   B&P SLanka, MA *Kelaniya*, MA *Sri Jay.*
Chandrasoma, Ven. Dr. Kanumuldeniye,
   BA(Spe) *S.Lanka*, MA PhD
Rahula, Ven. Kanangamuwe, BA *Peradeniya*,
   MPhil *B&P SLanka*
Rathanasiri, Ven. Kallanchiye, BA(Spe) *Kelaniya*,
   MA *B&P SLanka*
Soratha, Ven. Welivita, BA(Spe) *Kelaniya*, MA
   Kelaniya
Sumanarathana, Ven. Dr. Alahenegama, BA
   Peradeniya, MA *Peradeniya*, PhD *Peradeniya*
   Head*
Sumittha, Ven. Nivithigala, BA *Delhi*, MA *Delhi*
Wimalananda, Ven. Dr. Karagaswewe, BA
   Kelaniya, MA PhD
Other Staff: 2 Staff Members

Practical Buddhist Studies

Chandasiri, Ven. Liyanegama, BA *Sri Jay.*, MA
   B&P SLanka, MA *Kelaniya*, MA *Sri Jay.*   Head*
Dhammadassi, Ven. Anamaduwe, BA(Spe)
   Peradeniya, MA *B&P SLanka*
Other Staff: 2 Staff Members

Social Science and Comparative Studies

Dhammaloka, Ven. Wewala, BA(Spe) *Kelaniya*
   Head*
Dhammananda, Ven. Homagama, BA(Spe)
   Peradeniya, MPhil *Sri Jay.*
Gunananda, Ven. Udugampola, BA *Kelaniya*
Sudhamma, Ven. Wegama, BA(Spe) *Peradeniya*
Wijayasumana, Ven. Waradiwela, BED *Colombo*,
   MPhil *Colombo*
Other Staff: 1 Staff Member

CONTACT OFFICERS

Academic affairs. Head, Department of
Language: Alahenegama Thero, Ven. Dr.
Sumanarathana, BA *Peradeniya*, MA *Peradeniya*,
PhD *Peradeniya*
Admissions (first degree). Assistant Registrar:
Ekanayake, S. H. P. E. S., BCom *Peradeniya*
Library (chief librarian). Librarian: (vacant)

[*Information supplied by the institution as at 3 September
2007, and edited by the ACU*]

BUDDHIST AND PALI UNIVERSITY OF SRI LANKA

Founded 1981

Member of the Association of Commonwealth Universities

Postal Address: Gurulugomi Mawatha, Pitipana North, Homagama 7, Sri Lanka
Telephone: (011) 285 7786 **Fax:** (011) 289 2333 **E-mail:** bplib@sltnet.lk

VICE-CHANCELLOR*—Piyarathana Thero, Ven. Prof. Wegama, BA *B&P SLanka*, BED
   Colombo, MA *B&P SLanka*, MPhil *B&P SLanka*
REGISTRAR (ACTING)‡—Ratnatilake, M. S., BA *Ceyl.*
LIBRARIAN—Amaraweera, J. A., BSc *Vidyod.*, MI
BURSAR (ACTING)—Dharmasena, H. A., BA *Colombo*

GENERAL INFORMATION

History. The university was founded in 1981.
   It is located at Pitipana North, Homagama,
about 20km from Colombo. The external
examinations division is at 214, Bauddhaloka
Mawatha.

Admission to first degree courses (see also Sri
Lankan Introduction). General School

Certificate (GCE) A level with 3 passes
including Pali and Buddhist studies or any
language and an aggregate of not less than
135 marks for the Common General Paper.

First Degrees (see also Sri Lankan Directory
to Subjects of Study). BA, BA(Spe).
   *Length of course. Full-time: BA: 3 years; BA(Spe):
4 years.*

Higher Degrees (see also Sri Lankan
Directory to Subjects of Study).
   Master's. MA, MPhil.
   Admission. Applicants for admission to MA
must normally hold an appropriate first
degree. MPhil: first degree with at least second
class.
   *Length of course. Full-time: MA: 1 year; MPhil: 2
years.*

Doctoral. PhD.
Admission. PhD: appropriate master's degree.
Length of course. Full-time: PhD: 3 years.

Language of Instruction. Sinhala and English.

Libraries. Volumes: 36,300. Periodicals subscribed to: 310. Special collections: Buddha Jayanthi Tripitaka; Burmese Tripitaka; Chinese Tripitaka; Thai Tripitaka.

Income (2007). Total, Rs63,000,000.

Statistics. Staff (2007): 101 (27 academic, 74 non-academic). Students (2007): total 402.

FACULTIES/SCHOOLS

Buddhist Studies
Tel: (011) 285 7782 Fax: (011) 289 2333
  E-mail: bplib@sltnet.lk
Dean: Ekiriyagala Nanda, Ven. Prof., BA
  Peradeniya, MA *Peradeniya,* MPhil *B&P SLanka*

Language Studies
Tel: (01) 285 7783 Fax: (01) 289 2333
Dean: Sumanawansa, Ven. Dr. Neluwe, BA
  Kelaniya, MA *B&P SLanka,* MPhil *Kelaniya,* PhD
  Delhi

ACADEMIC UNITS

Archaeology and Buddhist Art Tradition
Tel: (011) 285 7782 Fax: (011) 289 2333
  E-mail: bplib@sltnet.lk
Amarasekera, K. A. S. N., BA *Kelaniya*   Sr.
  Lectr.
Ekiriyagala Nanda, BA *Peradeniya,* MA *Peradeniya,*
  MPhil *B&P SLanka*   Prof.
Herath, H. M. Y. V. K., BA   Sr. Lectr.

Buddhist Culture
Tel: (011) 285 7782 Fax: (011) 289 2333
  E-mail: bplib@sltnet.lk
Ekiriyagala Nanda, BA *Peradeniya,* MA *Peradeniya,*
  MPhil *B&P SLanka*   Prof.
Other Staff: 2 Lectrs.; 2 Temp. Lectrs.

Buddhist Philosophy
Tel: (011) 285 7782 Fax: (011) 289 2333
  E-mail: bplib@sltnet.lk
Ittademaliye Indasara, Ven. Dr., BA *Kelaniya,* MA
  Delhi, PhD *Delhi*   Sr. Lectr.
Pitigala Vijitha, Ven., BA *Kelaniya,* MA *B&P
  SLanka*   Sr. Lectr.
Wawwe Dhammarakkhitha, Ven., BA *Kelaniya,*
  MA *Kelaniya*   Sr. Lectr.
Other Staff: 2 Temp. Lectrs.

English Language Teaching Unit (ELTU)
Tel: (011) 285 7783
3 Instructors

Pali
Tel: (011) 285 7783 E-mail: bplib@sltnet.lk
Piyarathana Thero, Wegama, BA *B&P SLanka,*
  BED *Colombo,* MA *B&P SLanka,* MPhil *B&P
  SLanka*
Uturawala Dhammaratana, Ven. Dr., BA
  Kelaniya, MA *Kelaniya,* MPhil *Kelaniya,* PhD
  Assoc. Prof.
Other Staff: 2 Lectrs.; 2 Temp. Lectrs.

Religious Studies and Comparative Philosophy
Tel: (011) 285 7782 Fax: (011) 289 2333
  E-mail: bplib@sltnet.lk
Sumanasiri, Gallelle, BA *Kelaniya,* MA *Kelaniya,*
  MPhil *Delhi,* PhD *Delhi*   Prof.
Other Staff: 1 Lectr.

Sanskrit
Tel: (011) 285 7783 E-mail: bplib@sltnet.lk
Sumanawansa, Ven. Dr. Neluwe, BA *Kelaniya,*
  MA *B&P SLanka,* MPhil *Kelaniya,* PhD *Delhi*
  Sr. Lectr.
Other Staff: 1 Temp. Lectr.

Sinhala and Modern Languages
Tel: (011) 285 7783 E-mail: bplib@sltnet.lk
Dunukewatte Gunarathna, Ven., BA *Kelaniya,*
  MPhil *Kelaniya*   Sr. Lectr.
Wickremasinghe, E. A., BA *Kelaniya,* MPhil
  Kelaniya, PhD *Kelaniya*   Assoc. Prof.; Head*

CONTACT OFFICERS
Academic affairs. Vice-Chancellor: Piyarathana
  Thero, Ven. Prof. Wegama, BA *B&P SLanka,*
  BED *Colombo,* MA *B&P SLanka,* MPhil *B&P
  SLanka*
Accommodation. Assistant Registrar:
  Karunaratne, R., BA *Sri Jay.*
Accommodation. Vice-Chancellor: Piyarathana
  Thero, Ven. Prof. Wegama, BA *B&P SLanka,*
  BED *Colombo,* MA *B&P SLanka,* MPhil *B&P
  SLanka*
Admissions (first degree). Assistant Registrar:
  Karunaratne, R., BA *Sri Jay.*
Conferences/corporate hospitality. Vice-
  Chancellor: Piyarathana Thero, Ven. Prof.
  Wegama, BA *B&P SLanka,* BED *Colombo,* MA
  B&P SLanka, MPhil *B&P SLanka*
Consultancy services. Vice-Chancellor:
  Piyarathana Thero, Ven. Prof. Wegama, BA
  B&P SLanka, BED *Colombo,* MA *B&P SLanka,*
  MPhil *B&P SLanka*
Examinations. Senior Assistant Registrar:
  Gunasena, E. A., BA *Sri Jay.*
Finance. Bursar (Acting): Dharmasena, H. A.,
  BA *Colombo*
Library (chief librarian). Librarian:
  Amaraweera, J. A., BSc *Vidyod.,* MI
  (E-mail: bplib@sltnet.lk)
Library (enquiries). Senior Assistant Librarian:
  Karunaratna, C., BA *Ceyl.,* MA *Kelaniya,* MA
  B&P SLanka, MLS *Colombo*
Purchasing. Assistant Registrar: Prabhath, J.,
  BA *Sri Jay.*
Research. Vice-Chancellor: Piyarathana Thero,
  Ven. Prof. Wegama, BA *B&P SLanka,* BED
  Colombo, MA *B&P SLanka,* MPhil *B&P SLanka*
Scholarships, awards, loans. Assistant
  Registrar: Karunaratne, R., BA *Sri Jay.*
Staff development and training. Vice-
  Chancellor: Piyarathana Thero, Ven. Prof.
  Wegama, BA *B&P SLanka,* BED *Colombo,* MA
  B&P SLanka, MPhil *B&P SLanka*
Students from other countries. Assistant
  Registrar: Karunaratne, R., BA *Sri Jay.*

[*Information supplied by the institution as at 3 December 2007, and edited by the ACU*]

UNIVERSITY OF COLOMBO, SRI LANKA

Founded 1978

Member of the Association of Commonwealth Universities

Postal Address: College House, PO Box 1490, No. 94, Cumaratunga Munidasa Mawatha, Colombo 03, Sri Lanka
Telephone: (011) 258 1835 **Fax:** (011) 258 6059
URL: http://www.cmb.ac.lk

VICE-CHANCELLOR*—Hirimburegama, Prof. Kshanika K., BSc *Colombo,* MPhil
  Peradeniya, PhD *Leuven,* FNAS(SL)
REGISTRAR‡—Hussain, W. Husni R., BA *Sri Jay.,* MPA *Sri Jay.*
LIBRARIAN—Jayasuriya, Sumana C., BA *Ceyl.,* MLS *Philippines*
BURSAR—Bandara, Rohini P., BCom *Ceyl.,* MPA *Sri Jay.,* FCA

GENERAL INFORMATION

History. Previously established as Ceylon
University College (1921), University of
Ceylon (1942), University of Ceylon,
Colombo (1968), and Colombo Campus of the
University of Sri Lanka (1972), the university
achieved independent university status under
its present name in 1978.

Admission to first degree courses (see also Sri
Lankan Introduction). General Certificate of
Education (GCE) with passes at A level in three
approved subjects with a minimum mark of

30% for the common general paper and a
minimum aggregate mark of 135.

First Degrees (see also Sri Lankan Directory
to Subjects of Study). BA, BAMS, BBA, BCom,
BCS, BEd, BICT, BIT, BSc, BUMS, LLB, MB BS.
BIT: external.
  Length of course. Full-time: BA, BCS, BICT, BSc:
3–4 years; BBA, BCom, LLB: 4 years; BAMS,
BUMS, MB BS: 5 years. By *distance learning:* BIT:
3 years.

Higher Degrees (see also Sri Lankan
Directory to Subjects of Study).

Master's. LLM, MA, MALS, MBA, MBS,
MCom, MCR, MCS, MD, MEd, MHR, MIT,
MJS, MLS, MMM, MPhil, MS, MSc, MWS.
  Admission. Applicants should normally hold
an appropriate first degree with at least second
class honours.
  Length of course. Full-time: MA, MEd: 1 year;
MBA, MBS, MCom, MD, MLS, MPhil, MS,
MSc: 2 years. Part-time: LLM, MALS, MCR,
MHR, MJS, MMM, MWS: 1 year; MA, MBA,
MCS, MEd, MIT: 2 years; MPhil: 3 years.
  Doctoral. DM, PhD.
  Length of course. Full-time: DM, PhD: 3 years.
Part-time: DM, PhD: 5 years.

Language of Instruction. Sinhala, Tamil and English.

Libraries. Volumes: 451,750. Periodicals subscribed to: 150. Special collections: Sri Lanka collection; IMF depository library.

Academic Awards (2006–2007). 8843 awards ranging in value from Rs1900 to Rs2550.

Academic Year (2007–2008). Three terms/ two semesters:

Income (2006–2007). Total, Rs1,302,918,802.

Statistics. Staff (2006–2007): 1394 (507 academic, 887 non-academic). Students (2006–2007): full-time 814 (444 men, 370 women); part-time 1114 (887 men, 227 women); undergraduate 8658 (3037 men, 5621 women); master's 843 (440 men, 403 women); doctoral 18 (10 men, 8 women).

FACULTIES/SCHOOLS

Arts
Tel: (011) 250 0457 Fax: (011) 250 5758
  E-mail: dean@arts.cmb.ac.lk
Dean: Jayawardane, S. S. R. B. D. A., BA Ceyl., MA Wash., PhD Wash.
Assistant Registrar: Wijekoon, I. K. K., BA Kelaniya

Education
Tel: (011) 258 8812 Fax: (011) 259 6888
  E-mail: postmast@edu.cmb.ac.lk
Dean: Sandrasegaram, Prof. S., BEd Peradeniya, MEd Hiroshima
Assistant Registrar: Nagasinghe, D.

Graduate Studies
Tel: (011) 258 1712 Fax: (011) 259 1395
  E-mail: office@fgs.cmb.ac.lk
Dean: Dissanayake, Prof. D. M. S. S. L., BDevSt Ceyl., MA ANU, PhD ANU
Senior Assistant Registrar: Uyangoda, S., BA Sri Jay., MSc Kelaniya, MPM

Law
Tel: (011) 250 2001 Fax: (011) 250 2001
  E-mail: lawfac@law.cmb.ac.lk
Dean: Selvakkumaran, N., LLB S.Lanka, LLM S.Lanka
Acting Assistant Registrar: Nagasinghe, D.

Management and Finance
Tel: (011) 250 1295 Fax: (011) 259 8324
  E-mail: office@mgmt.cmb.ac.lk
Dean: Gunaratne, P. S. M., BSc Sri Jay., MBA Colombo, PhD Tsukuba
Senior Assistant Registrar: Thambirasah, Sukantheni, BCom Jaffna

Medicine
Tel: (01) 269 8449 Fax: (01) 269 1581
  E-mail: info@medical.cmb.ac.lk
Dean: Fernando, Prof. Dulitha N., MBE, MB BS Ceyl., PhD Lond.
Senior Assistant Registrar: Bandara, P. M. S., BSc Sri Jay.

Science
Tel: (011) 250 3148 Fax: (011) 250 3148
  E-mail: dean@science.cmb.ac.lk
Dean: Wijesundara, Prof. R. L. C., BSc Colombo, PhD Brist.
Senior Assistant Registrar: Gunaratne, R. M., BLE Colombo, MA Colombo

ACADEMIC UNITS

Accounting
Tel: (011) 255 2362 Fax: (011) 255 2362
  E-mail: edba@fmf.cmbmail.cmb.ac.lk
Abeysinghe, A. A. C., BSc Sri Jay., MSc Colombo, MBA Ljubljana, MPhil Colombo   Sr. Lectr.

Rajapakse, R. M. R. B., BCom Colombo, MCom S.Krishna.   Sr. Lectr.
Ranaweerage, G., BCom Sri Jay., MCom S.Krishna.   Sr. Lectr.; Head*
Sabri, H. M. Ali, BBA Jaffna, MBA Colombo   Sr. Lectr.
Other Staff: 4 Lectrs.
Research: accounting; finance

Business Economics
Tel: (011) 255 2363 Fax: (011) 255 2363
  E-mail: edba@fmf.cmbmail.ac.lk
Jayasinghe, H. N. P., BA Colombo, MA Colombo, MPhil Syd., PhD Sing.   Sr. Lectr.; Head*
Karunaratne, H. D., BA S.Lanka, MA Colombo, MA Nagoya, PhD Nagoya   Assoc. Prof.
Padmasiri, H. M. N., BA Colombo, MA Colombo, MCom Kelaniya   Sr. Lectr.
Weeratunga, W. A. S. P., BSc Colombo, MSc Colombo, MA Colombo   Sr. Lectr.
Other Staff: 5 Lectrs.
Research: business and managerial economics; development economics; financial markets; international finance; political economy of development

Chemistry
Tel: (011) 250 3367 Fax: (011) 250 3367
  E-mail: office@chem.cmb.ac.lk
Abeytunga, D. Thusita U., BSc Colombo, PhD Arizona   Sr. Lectr.
Chandrasekharan, N. V., BSc Colombo, PhD Colombo   Sr. Lectr.
Dassanayake, R. S., BSc Peradeniya, PhD HK   Sr. Lectr.
De Costa, M. D. P., BSc Colombo, PhD Dal.   Prof.; Head*
De Silva, E. D., BSc Colombo, PhD Hawaii   Sr. Prof.
De Silva, K. M. N., BSc Colombo, PhD Camb.   Prof.
De Silva, W. Rohini M., BSc Colombo, PhD Camb.   Sr. Lectr.
Deraniyagala, Srianthie A., BSc Ceyl., PhD Dal.   Prof.
Dissanayake, D. P., BSc Peradeniya, MPhil Peradeniya, PhD Texas   Sr. Lectr.
Fernando, S. A., BSc Colombo, MPhil Colombo, PhD Arizona   Sr. Lectr.
Gunaratne, R. D., BSc Colombo, MSc Cornell, PhD Cornell   Sr. Lectr.
Gunawardena, H. D., BSc Ceyl., PhD Salf.   Sr. Prof.
Hettiarachchi, G. H. C. Madhu, BSc Colombo, PhD J.Nehru U.   Sr. Lectr.
Hewage, Sujatha, BSc Ceyl., PhD Newcastle(UK)   Assoc. Prof.
Mahanama, K. R. R., BSc Colombo, MA C.U.N.Y., MPhil C.U.N.Y., PhD C.U.N.Y.   Sr. Lectr.
Perera, R. P., BSc Colombo, MSc Wichita, PhD Wichita   Sr. Lectr.
Sirimanne, Chatu T., BSc Colombo, PhD Wayne   Sr. Lectr.
Wanduragala, C. H. M. S., BSc Peradeniya, PhD Wichita   Sr. Lectr.
Weerasinghe, M. S. S., BSc Colombo, PhD Maine(USA)   Sr. Lectr.
Wijayarathna, C. Dilrukshi, BSc Colombo, MEng Tokyo Agric.& Technol., DrEng Tokyo Agric.& Technol.   Sr. Lectr.
Wijesekera, Ramanee D., BSc Colombo, PhD ANU   Sr. Lectr.
Other Staff: 4 Lectrs.
Research: computational chemistry; environmental chemistry; molecular biology; natural product chemistry

Commerce and Finance
Tel: (011) 250 1294
Azeez, A. A., BCom Peradeniya, MBA Colombo, PhD Yokohama N.   Sr. Lectr.; Head*
Dassanayake, D. M. S., BCom Colombo, MBA Asian I.T., Bangkok   Sr. Lectr.
Fazeel, M. J. M., BA Peradeniya, MA Colombo, PhD Syd.   Sr. Lectr.
Gunaratne, P. S. M., BSc Sri Jay., MBA Colombo, PhD Tsukuba   Sr. Lectr.
Other Staff: 1 Lectr.

Research: asset pricing; banking; corporate governance; financial management; financial markets

Demography
Tel: (011) 258 6111 Fax: (011) 258 1110
  E-mail: info@demo.cmb.ac.lk
Amarabandu, W. P., BSc Ceyl., MSc NSW   Sr. Lectr.
De Silva, W. I., BDevSt Ceyl., MA ANU, PhD ANU   Prof.; Head*
Dissanayake, D. M. S. S. L., BDevSt Ceyl., MA ANU, PhD ANU   Prof.
Siddhisena, K. A. P., BA Ceyl., BPhil Ceyl., MA ANU, MSc Mich., PhD Mich.   Prof.
Ukwatta, S., BDevSt Sri Jay., MA Colombo   Sr. Lectr.
Other Staff: 3 Lectrs.
Vacant Posts: 1 Lectr.
Research: ageing; fertility analysis; mortality; poverty analysis; reproductive health

Economics
Tel: (011) 258 2666 Fax: (011) 250 2722
  E-mail: econ@cmb.ac.lk
Abeyratne, A. D. M. S. A., BA Colombo, MPhil Inst.Soc.Stud.(The Hague), PhD Amst.   Sr. Lectr.
Aluthge, D. C. P., BA Colombo, MA Colombo, PhD Amst.   Sr. Lectr.
Amirthalingam, K., BA Jaffna, MPhil J.Nehru U.   Sr. Lectr.
Aponsu, G. I., BSc Colombo, MA Colombo, MPhil HK   Sr. Lectr.
Attanayake, A. M. G. N. K., BSc Colombo, MA Delhi, PhD Lond.   Prof.
Bandara, R. W. T. B. R., BA Peradeniya, MA Colombo, MSc Norway Ag., PhD Qld.   Sr. Lectr.
Chandrasiri, K. S., BA Ceyl., BPhil S.Lanka, MA S.Lanka, MBA Hartford, PhD La Trobe   Prof.; Head*
De Silva, G. A. Chandani, BA Colombo, MA Colombo, DPhil Sus.   Sr. Lectr.
Ganeshmoorthy, M., BA Peradeniya, MA Colombo, PhD Nijmegen   Sr. Lectr.
Gunaruwan, T. L., BSc Colombo, MSc Asian I.T., Bangkok, PhD Paris I   Sr. Lectr.
Lakshman, R. W. D., BA Colombo, PhD Melb.   Sr. Lectr.
Lakshman, W. D., BA Ceyl., DPhil Oxf.   Sr. Prof.
Liyanarachchi, T. S., BA Colombo, MPhil Colombo   Sr. Lectr.
Mallikahewa, S. N. K., BA Ruhuna, MSc Kelaniya   Sr. Lectr.
Premaratne, S. P., BA Colombo, MA Colombo, PhD T.U.Eindhoven   Sr. Lectr.
Ranasinghe, M. D. A. L., BA Colombo, MA Thammasat, PhD Amst.   Sr. Lectr.
Rodrigo, P. Chandra, BA Ceyl., PhD Camb.   Sr. Prof.
Senanayake, S. M. P., BCom Ceyl., MSc Edin., PhD Brad.   Prof.
Serasinghe, U. P. P., BA Peradeniya, MA Colombo   Sr. Lectr.
Silva, D. A. C., BA Colombo, MA Colombo, MPhil Maastricht, PhD Amst.   Sr. Lectr.
Vidanagama, S. S., BCom Ceyl., MSc Stir.   Sr. Lectr.
Wimalarathana, Rev. W., BA Peradeniya, MA Colombo, PhD Nijmegen   Sr. Lectr.
Other Staff: 4 Lectrs.

Educational Psychology
Tel: (011) 250 4734 Fax: (011) 259 6888
Abeypala, K. R., BEd Ceyl., MPhil Colombo, PhD Colombo   Prof.
Chandradasa, W., BEd Colombo, MPhil Colombo, PhD Colombo   Sr. Lectr.; Head*
Vithanapathirana, M. V., BSc Colombo, MEd Open S.Lanka, PhD Lond.   Sr. Lectr.
Other Staff: 3 Lectrs.
Vacant Posts: 4 Lectrs.
Research: early childhood education; educational measurement and evaluation; educational psychology; school counselling

English

Tel: (011) 250 0438 Fax: (011) 250 0438
De Mel, F. Neloufer S., BA Peradeniya, MA S.Lanka, PhD Kent Prof.
Fernando, M. Siromani, BA Ceyl., PhD Lond. Prof.
Mendis, Dushyanthi, BA Peradeniya, MA Ohio, PhD Mich. Sr. Lectr.
Silva, Neluka M. S., BA Colombo, MSc Oxf., PhD Leeds Sr. Lectr.; Head*
Wijewardene, R. Shermal, BA Delhi, MPhil Oxf. Sr. Lectr.
Other Staff: 2 Lectrs.

English Language Teaching Unit

7 Lectrs.; 1 Sr. Instr.; 22 Instrs.
Vacant Posts: 1 Sr. Lectr.

Geography

Tel: (011) 250 0458 Fax: (011) 250 0458
E-mail: hod@geo.cmb.ac.lk
De Silva, D. H. R. Jayanthi, BA Ceyl., PhD E.Anglia Assoc. Prof.; Head*
Dissanayake, R. M., BA Ceyl. Sr. Lectr.
Gunatilake, R. N., BA Colombo, MPhil Colombo Sr. Lectr.
Karunadasa, D. M., BA Colombo, MPhil Colombo Sr. Lectr.
Karunaratne, H. K. N., BA Peradeniya, MPhil Colombo Sr. Lectr.
Manawadu, L., BA Colombo, MSc Asian I.T., Bangkok Sr. Lectr.
Nobert, S. A., BA Peradeniya, MSc Madr., MPhil Madr. Prof.
Perera, M. O., BA Colombo, MPhil Sr. Lectr.
Piyadasa, R. U. K., BA Moscow, PhD Moscow Sr. Lectr.
Ranasinghe, E. M. S., BA Colombo, MA Brunei Sr. Lectr.
Srikanthan, R., BA Ceyl., BPhil Ceyl., MA Colombo Sr. Lectr.
Wilson, W. N., BA Ceyl., BPhil Ceyl., MA S.Lanka Sr. Lectr.
Other Staff: 3 Lectrs.

History and International Relations

Tel: (011) 250 0433
Ariyaratne, R. A., BA Ceyl., PhD Camb. Assoc. Prof.
Cooray, M. G. A., BA Ceyl., MPhil Colombo Assoc. Prof.
Dewasiri, D. N. N. R., BA Colombo, MPhil Colombo Sr. Lectr.
Jayawardane, S. S. R. B. D. A., BA Ceyl., MA Wash., PhD Wash. Assoc. Prof.
Jayawardena, Janaki, BA Peradeniya, MPhil Peradeniya, PhD Sr. Lectr.
Karunadasa, W. M., BA Ceyl., LLB Ceyl., MA Lond., PhD S.Lanka Prof.
Melegoda, Nayani, BA Colombo, MA Colombo, PhD Leeds Assoc. Prof.; Head*
Wickramasinghe, Nira K., BA Paris, MA Paris, DPhil Oxf. Prof.
Wijegoonawardana, Nirmali, BA Colombo, MA Colombo Sr. Lectr.
Other Staff: 2 Lectrs.

Human Resources Management

Tel: (011) 255 2364 Fax: (011) 255 2364
Dassanayake, M. S., BSc Sri Jay., MBA Otaru Comm., PhD Gakushuin Sr. Lectr.
Kailasapathy, Pavithra, BBA Colombo, MSc N.Y., MSc Mass. Sr. Lectr.
Nawaratne, N. N. J., BSc Sri Jay., MA Keio, PhD Keio Sr. Lectr.; Head*
Tennakoon, T. M. Kamani P., BCom Colombo, MBA Colombo, PhD Sr. Lectr.
Other Staff: 2 Lectrs.
Research: ethics in organisations; gender issues; human decision-making patterns; human resource management

Humanities Education

Tel: (011) 258 6516 Fax: (011) 259 6888
Atukorala, D. R., BEd Ceyl., MA Ceyl. Sr. Lectr.
Perera, Marie E. S., BA Peradeniya, MPhil Colombo, PhD W'gong. Sr. Lectr.; Head*

Other Staff: 4 Lectrs.
Vacant Posts: 1 Prof.
Research: non-formal education; philosophy of education; second language acquisition; second national language

Islamic Civilisation Unit

Tel: (011) 250 0443
2 Lectrs.
Vacant Posts: 1 Sr. Lectr.

Journalism Unit

Tel: (011) 250 0431 Fax: (011) 250 0431
Hapuarachchi, Ajantha, BA Kelaniya, MA Kelaniya, PhD Kelaniya Sr. Lectr.
Herath, H. M. S., BA Colombo, MSc B'lore. Sr. Lectr.
Pathiraja, D., BA Ceyl., MA Peradeniya, PhD Monash Sr. Lectr.
Waleboda, T. D. K., BA Kelaniya, MA Kelaniya Sr. Lectr.; Co-ordinator*
Research: broadcast media; film and television studies; principles of communication; print media, globalisation and contemporary issues; regional development communication

Law

Tel: (011) 250 0942
E-mail: lawfac@law.cmb.ac.lk
Abeyratne, M. D. M., LLB S.Lanka, LLM S.Lanka Sr. Lectr.
Dias, Rev. K. J. F. N., BTh Rome, LLM Lond., MPhil Colombo, PhD Wales Sr. Lectr.
Mahanamahewa, Prathiba, LLB Colombo, LLM Melb., PhD Qld. Sr. Lectr.
Nananayakkara, W. Indira, LLB Colombo, MPhil Colombo Sr. Lectr.
Niriella, Jeeva, LLB Colombo Sr. Lectr.
Perera, Nirmala, LLB S.Lanka, LLM S.Lanka Sr. Lectr.
Sarweswaran, A., LLB Colombo, MPhil Colombo Sr. Lectr.
Scharenguivel, R. Sharya, LLB Ceyl., LLM Harv., MLitt Oxf. Assoc. Prof.
Segarajasingam, Shanthakumari, LLB S.Lanka, MPhil Colombo Sr. Lectr.
Selvakkumaran, N., LLB S.Lanka, LLM S.Lanka Sr. Lectr.
Seneviratne, S. S. M. Wasantha, LLB Colombo, MPhil Colombo Sr. Lectr.
Sivapatham, M., LLB Colombo, MPhil Colombo Sr. Lectr.
Thamilamaran, V. T., LLB Ceyl., MPhil Colombo Sr. Lectr.
Udagama, N. Deepika, LLB S.Lanka, LLM Calif., JSD Calif. Sr. Lectr.; Head*
Wijeyesekera, N. Rose, LLB Colombo, MPhil Colombo Sr. Lectr.
Other Staff: 12 Lectrs.
Vacant Posts: 1 Prof.
Research: constitutional law; environmental law; family law; international humanitarian law

Management and Organisation Studies

Tel: (01) 250 1293 Fax: (01) 259 1293
E-mail: edba@fmf.cmbmail.cmb.ac.lk
De Alwis, W. P. G., BBA Sri Jay., MBA Sri Jay. Assoc. Prof.
Dissanayake, K., BCom Colombo, MBA Colombo, PhD Meiji Sr. Lectr.; Head*
Jayakody, J. A. S. K., BSc Sri Jay., MBA Sri Jay. Sr. Lectr.
Razi, M. J. M., BCom Colombo, MBA Colombo Sr. Lectr.
Senathiraja, R., BCom Jaffna, MSc Sri Jay. Sr. Lectr.
Sridharan, Ushaa, BBA Colombo, MBA Sri Jay. Sr. Lectr.
Other Staff: 5 Lectrs.

Marketing

Tel: (011) 255 2365 Fax: (011) 255 2365
Ahsan, M. J. F. Fazeela, BCom Jaffna, MCom Kerala, PhD Strath. Sr. Lectr.
Dharmadasa, M. P. P., BSc Sri Jay., MBA Colombo Sr. Lectr.

Jayasinghe, J. A. S. C., BCom Peradeniya, MBA Colombo Sr. Lectr.
Kajendra, K., BCom Jaffna, MCom Kelaniya, PhD Delhi Sr. Lectr.
Premarathne, W. G., BSc Sri Jay., MCom Kelaniya Sr. Lectr.; Head*
Randiwela, G. S. P., BCom Peradeniya, MCom Colombo Sr. Lectr.
Wijetunga, D. T., BSc Sri Jay., MBA Sri Jay. Sr. Lectr.
Other Staff: 2 Lectrs.
Research: brand management; consumer behaviour; international business; marketing

Mathematics

Tel: (011) 250 1731
E-mail: office@maths.cmb.ac.lk
Edussuriya, L. C., BSc Colombo, MSc Kaiserslautern Sr. Lectr.
Hameem, M. H. K. M., BSc Colombo, MSc Melb. Sr. Lectr.
Hewage, T. U., BSc Colombo, MA Bowling Green, PhD Bowling Green Sr. Lectr.
Jayawardena, C. J. A., BSc Colombo, MSc Ohio, PhD Memphis State Sr. Lectr.
Jayawardena, D. Romaine, BSc Colombo, PhD Carnegie-Mellon Sr. Lectr.
Karunatilleke, A. D. W., MSc Moscow, PhD Moscow Sr. Lectr.
Premadasa, A. K. K., BSc Colombo, MSc Purdue, PhD Purdue Sr. Lectr.
Samaratunga, R. T., BSc Colombo, MSc S.Fraser, PhD S.Fraser Sr. Lectr.
Wijeratne, C. J., BSc Colombo, MSc Purdue, MSc Ill. Sr. Lectr.; Head*
Wijeratne, J. K., BSc Colombo, MSc Kaiserslautern, PhD Colombo, PhD Kaiserslautern Sr. Lectr.
Other Staff: 8 Lectrs.
Vacant Posts: 2 Profs.; 2 Assoc. Profs.; 2 Lectrs.

Nuclear Science

Tel: (011) 250 2525 Fax: (011) 250 3148
E-mail: office@nuclear.cmb.ac.lk
Hewamanna, Rohini, BSc Colombo, MSc Lond., PhD Lond. Sr. Prof.; Head*
Kulatunga, S., BSc Peradeniya, MSc Cinc., PhD Cinc. Sr. Lectr.
Mahawatte, S. S. B. D. Palee, BSc Colombo, MSc Colombo, MSc Birm. Assoc. Prof.
Vacant Posts: 1 Lectr.
Research: environmental radioactivity; medical physics; nuclear analytical techniques in monitoring pollution

Physics

Tel: (011) 258 4777
E-mail: office@phys.cmb.ac.lk
Ariyaratne, T. R., BSc Ceyl., PhD Durh. Prof.
Coorey, R. V., BSc Colombo, PhD Colombo Sr. Lectr.
Daya, D. D. N. B., BSc Colombo, PhD Colombo Sr. Lectr.
Fernando, I. M. K., BSc Colombo, PhD Colombo Sr. Lectr.
Gamlath, K. A. I. Lanka W., BSc Colombo, PhD NSW Sr. Lectr.
Gomes, G. A. C., BSc Colombo, PhD Colombo Sr. Lectr.
Jayananda, M. K., BSc Colombo, MSc Pitt., PhD Pitt. Sr. Lectr.
Jayanetti, J. K. D. S., BSc Colombo, PhD C.U.N.Y. Prof.; Head*
Jayaratne, K. P. S. C., BSc Colombo, PhD Colombo Sr. Lectr.
Lelwala, R., BSc Colombo, PhD Colombo Sr. Lectr.
Rosa, S. R. D., BSc Colombo, MSc Pitt., PhD Pitt. Sr. Lectr.
Sonnadara, D. U. J., BSc Colombo, MSc Pitt., PhD Pitt. Prof.
Wijayaratne, W. M. K. P., BSc Colombo, PhD Missouri Sr. Lectr.
Other Staff: 2 Lectrs.

Plant Sciences

Tel: (011) 258 5038 Fax: (011) 250 3148
  E-mail: office@pts.cmb.ac.lk
Abeynayake, Kanthi, BSc Ceyl., PhD Lanc.   Sr.
  Prof.
Hirimburegama, Kshanika K., BSc Colombo,
  MPhil Peradeniya, PhD Leuven, FNAS(SL)
  Prof.; Head*
Hirimburegama, W. K., BSc Peradeniya, PhD
  Peradeniya   Sr. Lectr.
Jayasekara, G. A. U., BSc Colombo, MSc Calg.,
  PhD Calg.   Sr. Lectr.
Kathriarachchi, Hashendra S., BSc Peradeniya,
  MPhil Peradeniya, PhD Vienna   Sr. Lectr.
Nanayakkara, Chandrika M., BSc Colombo, MSc
  Kelaniya, PhD Aberd.   Sr. Lectr.
Ranwala, Sudheera M. W., BSc Colombo, PhD
  Aberd.   Sr. Lectr.
Silva, Tara D., BSc Colombo, PhD Reading   Sr.
  Lectr.
Tirimanne, T. L. Shamala, BSc Peradeniya, PhD
  Iowa State   Sr. Lectr.
Wijesundara, R. L. C., BSc Colombo, PhD Brist.
  Sr. Prof.
Other Staff: 3 Lectrs.
Research: cell cultures; comparative genomics
  and phylogeny; micro-propagation;
  production of transgenic plants

Political Science and Public Policy

Tel: (011) 255 4262
Anees, M. S., BA Peradeniya, MA Nagoya, PhD
  Nagoya   Sr. Lectr.
Ariyadasa, K. S. K., BA Peradeniya, MA Colombo
  Sr. Lectr.
Dissanayake, D. M. D., BA S.Lanka, MPhil
  Colombo   Sr. Lectr.
Fernando, L. P., BA Peradeniya, MA New Br., PhD
  Syd.   Prof.
Jayatilleka, A. V. M. D. de S., BA Peradeniya,
  MPhil Colombo   Sr. Lectr.
Keethaponcalan, S. I., BA Jaffna, MA SE(S.Lanka),
  PhD Flor.   Sr. Lectr.
Rambukwella, D. G. N., BA Peradeniya, MA NZ
  Sr. Lectr.
Silva, G. P. V. D. R., BA S.Lanka, MPhil Peradeniya
  Sr. Lectr.
Uyangoda, J., BA Ceyl., PhD Hawaii   Prof.;
  Head*
Other Staff: 1 Lectr.
Research: conflict and peace processes;
  democracy and local governance; political
  institutions

Science and Technology Education

Tel: (011) 250 3147 Fax: (011) 259 6888
  E-mail: destedka@yahoo.com
Karunaratne, W. G., BSc Ceyl., MPhil Ceyl.
  Prof.
Karunasena, N. V., BEd Colombo, MPhil Colombo
  Sr. Lectr.
Pragnadarsana, W. M., BSc Ceyl., MPhil Colombo
  Sr. Lectr.; Head*
Other Staff: 3 Lectrs.
Vacant Posts: 1 Prof.
Research: curriculum development;
  environmental education; informational
  communication; mathematics education;
  science education

Sinhala

Tel: (011) 250 0453
  E-mail: deptofsinhala@yahoo.com
Coperahewa, H. S., BA Colombo, MA Lanc.   Sr.
  Lectr.
Dissanayaka, A. B., BA Ceyl., PhD Amst.   Assoc.
  Prof.
Gurusinghe, Latha, BA Colombo, MPhil Colombo
  Sr. Lectr.
Kumara, L. A. D. A. T., BA Colombo, PhD
  Colombo   Prof.; Head*
Paranavitana, Rohini, BA Ceyl., PhD Ceyl.
  Assoc. Prof.
Premasiri, N. N., BA Colombo, MA Kelaniya,
  MPhil Colombo   Sr. Lectr.
Sirisumana, Rev. A., BA Colombo, MPhil Colombo
  Sr. Lectr.

Wickramasinghe, B. K. A., BA Ceyl., PhD Ceyl.
  Assoc. Prof.
Wijegunasinghe, Piyaseeli D., BA Ceyl., BA
  Leeds, MA Leeds   Assoc. Prof.
Wijesuriya, W. A. D. S., BA Colombo, MPhil
  Colombo   Sr. Lectr.
Other Staff: 2 Lectrs.
Vacant Posts: 1 Prof.

Pali and Buddhist Studies Unit

Ananda, Rev. U., BA Peradeniya, MPhil Peradeniya
  Sr. Lectr.
Dhammajothi, Rev. M., BA Sri Jay., MPhil
  Kelaniya, PhD Nanjing   Sr. Lectr.
Other Staff: 1 Lectr.

Social Science Education

Tel: (011) 259 6887 Fax: (011) 259 6888
Galagamage, S., BA S.Lanka, MEd Ceyl., MPhil
  S.Lanka   Sr. Lectr.
Hettige, Anula M., BEd Colombo, MEd Colombo,
  MPhil Colombo   Sr. Lectr.
Jayawardena, A. A., BEd Colombo, MPhil Colombo,
  PhD Colombo   Sr. Lectr.; Head*
Karunanithy, M., BA Peradeniya, MA Jaffna, PhD
  Colombo   Sr. Lectr.
Karunasekara, R. P., BCom Ceyl., MPhil Colombo
  Sr. Lectr.
Sandarasegaram, S., BEd Ceyl., MEd Hiroshima
  Assoc. Prof.
Other Staff: 3 Lectrs.
Vacant Posts: 3 Sr. Lectrs.
Research: achievement levels and problems in
  multi-grade schools; attitudes towards
  democracy and social cohesion; inter-
  sectoral study of health and education

Sociology

Tel: (011) 250 0452
  E-mail: aishkima@hotmail.com
Abeysinghe, D. N., BA Colombo, MPhil Colombo
  Sr. Lectr.
De Silva, D. A. P., BA Colombo, MA Colombo,
  MSc Edin., PhD Edin.   Sr. Lectr.
De Silva, W. J. S. S., BA Colombo, MA Colombo
  Sr. Lectr.
Edirisinghe, I. V., BA Ceyl., MA Manc.   Sr.
  Lectr.; Head*
Fernando, P. R. N., BA Colombo, MPhil Colombo
  Sr. Lectr.
Gunasekera, Suwineetha S., BA Ceyl., BPhil
  Ceyl., MA Inst.Soc.Stud.(The Hague)   Sr. Lectr.
Haniffa, F. F., BA Colombo, MA Colombo, MPhil
  Colombo, PhD Colombo   Sr. Lectr.
Herath, S. M. K., BA Colombo, MA Colombo, PhD
  Wat.   Sr. Lectr.
Hettiarachchy, Tilak, BA Ceyl., MA McM., PhD
  Lond.   Prof.
Hettige, S. T., BA Ceyl., BPhil Colombo, PhD
  Monash   Sr. Prof.
Hewamanne, Sandya K., BA Colombo, MA Texas,
  MA Kelaniya, PhD Texas   Sr. Lectr.
Jayathilake, S. Ramanie De S., BA Ceyl., BPhil
  Ceyl., MPhil Sus., PhD Delhi   Assoc. Prof.
Karunarathne, I. M., BA Colombo, PhD Melb.   Sr.
  Lectr.
Liyanage, J. H. Chandani, BA Colombo, MA
  Colombo, PhD Delhi   Sr. Lectr.
Niriella, C., BA Colombo, MA Colombo, MPhil Tata
  Inst.Soc.Scis.   Sr. Lectr.
Perera, L. A. S., BA Colombo, MA Calif., PhD
  Calif.   Sr. Lectr.
Samarasinghe, Gameela, BA Paris IV, MA Paris
  IV, PhD Paris IV   Sr. Lectr.
Other Staff: 2 Lectrs.
Vacant Posts: 1 Assoc. Prof.

Statistics

Tel: (011) 259 0111
  E-mail: dst@mail.cmb.ac.lk
Karunaratne, Ariyalatha, BSc Ceyl.   Sr. Lectr.
Sooriyarachchi, M. Roshini, BSc Colombo, MSc
  Reading, PhD Reading   Assoc. Prof.
Weerasekera, D. R., BSc Colombo, MSc Colombo,
  PhD Colombo   Sr. Lectr.; Head*
Wickremasinghe, W. N., BSc Jaffna, MSc Iowa,
  PhD Kansas   Sr. Lectr.

Other Staff: 9 Lectrs.

Zoology

Tel: (011) 250 3399
  E-mail: head@zoology.cmb.ac.lk
Dayawansa, P. N., BSc Colombo, PhD Aberd.   Sr.
  Lectr.
De Silva, Dilrukshi N., BSc Colombo, MSc Rutgers
  Sr. Lectr.; Head*
Ekaratne, S. U. K., BSc Colombo, PhD Wales
  Assoc. Prof.
Jayatunga, Y. N. Amaramali, BSc Peradeniya,
  MPhil Colombo, PhD Lond.   Prof.
Kotagama, S. W., BSc Colombo, PhD Aberd.
  Prof.
Pallewatta, P. K. T. Nirmala S., BSc Colombo,
  PhD Lond.   Sr. Lectr.
Peiris, L. Dinithi C., BSc Colombo, PhD Sheff.
  Sr. Lectr.
Premawansa, W. S., BSc Kelaniya, PhD Colombo
  Sr. Lectr.
Randeniya, Preethi V., BSc Colombo, MSc
  Colombo, PhD Colombo   Sr. Lectr.
Ratnasooriya, W. D., BSc Ceyl., PhD Strath.   Sr.
  Prof.
Weerakoon, H. D. K. G. A., BSc Colombo, MSc
  Ill., PhD Ill.   Sr. Lectr.
Wickremasinghe, Deepthi D., BSc Colombo, MSc
  Colombo, PhD Colombo   Sr. Lectr.
Wijesinghe, Mayuri R., BSc Colombo, PhD Camb.
  Sr. Lectr.
Yapa, W. B., BSc Kelaniya, MPhil Colombo, PhD
  Munich   Sr. Lectr.
Other Staff: 4 Lectrs.

MEDICINE

Tel: (01) 269 8449 Fax: (01) 269 1581
  E-mail: info@medical.cmb.ac.lk

Anatomy

Tel: (01) 269 5300
Anthony, D. J., MB BS Colombo, MS Colombo,
  FRCSEd   Sr. Lectr.; Head*
Dissanayake, M. M., MB BS MD   Sr. Lectr.
Dissanayake, V. H. W., MB BS Colombo, PhD
  Nott.   Sr. Lectr.
Jayasekara, M. M. R. W., MB BS Ceyl., PhD
  Newcastle(UK)   Prof.
Malalasekara, A. P., MB BS MS   Sr. Lectr.
Perera, B. J. J. F., MB BS Ceyl., MS S.Lanka
  Assoc. Prof.
Other Staff: 3 Lectrs.

Biochemistry and Molecular Biology

Tel: (011) 269 7485
Atukorala, T. M. Sunethra, BSc Ceyl., MSc
  Colombo, PhD Sur.   Prof.; Head*
Jayasena, Sharmila M. T., BSc Lond., PhD
  Colombo   Sr. Lectr.
Jeevathayaparan, S., BSc Peradeniya, MSc Colombo,
  PhD Colombo   Sr. Lectr.
Lanerolle, Pulani, BSc S'ton., PhD Colombo   Sr.
  Lectr.
Mathew, C. P. D. W., BSc Kelaniya, MSc Colombo,
  PhD Colombo   Prof.
Siridewa, Kithmini, BSc Colombo, MSc Colombo,
  PhD Colombo   Sr. Lectr.
Sirimanne, S. A. S. R., BSc Peradeniya, PhD Atlanta
  Sr. Lectr.
Soysa, S. S. B. D. Preethi, BSc Sri Jay., MSc
  Colombo, PhD Colombo   Sr. Lectr.
Welihinda, J., BSc Ceyl., PhD Ceyl.   Assoc.
  Prof.; Head*
Wijesundera, W. S. Sulochana, BSc Colombo,
  MSc Brist., PhD Colombo   Sr. Lectr.
Other Staff: 1 Lectr.

Clinical Medicine

Tel: (011) 269 5300 Fax: (011) 268 9188
Constantine, G. R., MB BS Jaffna, MD Colombo
  Sr. Lectr.
Fernando, S. S. D., MB BS Colombo, MD Colombo,
  PhD Lond., FRCP   Prof.; Head*
Gnananthasan, C. Ariaranee, MB BS Peradeniya,
  MD Colombo, MPhil Colombo, FRCP   Sr. Lectr.

Jayasinghe, K. S. A., MB BS Colombo, MD
Colombo, PhD Lond., FRCP Prof.
Lanerolle, R. D., MB BS Colombo, MD Colombo,
MPhil Colombo Sr. Lectr.
Rajapakse, S., MB BS Colombo, MD Colombo Sr.
Lectr.
Sheriff, M. H. Rezvi, MB BS Ceyl., MD Ceyl.,
FRCP, FRCPEd, FACP Hon. Prof.
Other Staff: 3 Lectrs.
Vacant Posts: 1 Lectr.
Research: chronic kidney disease; health
inequalities; non-communicable diseases;
social determinants of health; toxicology

Community Medicine

Tel: (011) 269 5300 Fax: (011) 267 7765
Fernando, Dulitha N., MBE, MB BS Ceyl., PhD
Lond. Sr. Prof.
Gunathunga, M. W., MB BS Colombo, MSc
S.Lanka, MD S.Lanka Sr. Lectr.; Head*
Gunawardana, Nalika S., MB BS Colombo, MSc
S.Lanka, MD Colombo Sr. Lectr.
Lankathilake, M. A. L. Kantha N., BSc Ceyl.,
MSc Chulalongkorn Sr. Lectr.
Rajapaksa, Lalini C., MB BS Ceyl., MSc Colombo,
MD Colombo Prof.
Seneviratne, Rohini S. De A., MB BS Ceyl.,
MMEd Dund., MD S.Lanka Prof.
Other Staff: 5 Lectrs.
Vacant Posts: 1 Prof.
Research: gender issues; health policy transition
in developing countries; maternal and child
health; non-communicable diseases;
primary paradigm of mental health

Forensic Medicine and Toxicology

Tel: (011) 269 4016 Fax: (011) 269 1581
E-mail: formed@yahoo.com
Abeyasinghe, Nilukshi L., MB BS Colombo, MD
S.Lanka Sr. Lectr.; Head*
Fernando, P. R., MB BS Ceyl., MD S.Lanka,
FRCPath, FRCPGlas, FRCPEd Sr. Prof.
Perera, H. Jean M., MB BS Colombo, MD S.Lanka
Sr. Lectr.
Weerasundera, Buddhika J., MB BS Kelaniya, MD
Colombo Sr. Lectr.
Other Staff: 2 Lectrs.
Vacant Posts: 1 Prof.

Microbiology

Tel: (011) 269 7513
E-mail: microcmb@yahoo.com
Corea, Enoka M., MB BS Colombo, MD Colombo
Sr. Lectr.
Perera, Aurelia J., MB BS S.Lanka, MD Colombo
Prof.
Senanayake, C. P., MB BS Colombo, MD Colombo
Sr. Lectr.; Head*
Other Staff: 2 Lectrs.
Vacant Posts: 1 Lectr.
Research: drug resistance patterns; molecular
diagnosis

Obstetrics and Gynaecology

Tel: (011) 534 9567
Colonne, D. J. R., MB BS Colombo, MS Colombo
Sr. Lectr.
Dodampahala, S. H., MB BS Colombo, MS S.Lanka
Sr. Lectr.
Kaluarachchi, A., MB BS Colombo, MS Colombo
Sr. Lectr.
Randeni, C., MB BS Colombo, MS Colombo,
FSLCOG, FRCOG Assoc. Prof.
Senanayaka, H. M., MB BS Colombo, MS S.Lanka,
FRCSEd, FRCOG Prof.
Seneviratne, H. R., MB BS Ceyl., DM, FRCOG,
FSLCOG Sr. Prof.; Head*
Wijeratne, Chandrika N., MB BS Colombo, MD
S.Lanka, FRCP Prof.
Wijeratne, Sumedha, BSc Peradeniya, MSc
Colombo, MPhil Colombo Sr. Lectr.
Other Staff: 1 Lectr.

Paediatrics

Tel: (011) 269 5300
E-mail: paed_colombo@yahoo.com

Ajanthan, R., MB BS Jaffna, MD S.Lanka Sr.
Lectr.
De Silva, K. Shamya H., MB BS Ceyl., MD
S.Lanka, DCH Colombo Sr. Lectr.
Lamabadusuriya, S. P., MBE, MB BS Ceyl., PhD
Lond., FRCPGlas, FRCP, FRCPEd, FRCPCH
Prof.; Head*
Mahamithawa, Udayanthi D., MB BS Colombo,
MD S.Lanka Sr. Lectr.
Rodrigo, G. D. I., MB BS Colombo, MD Colombo,
DCH Colombo, DPhil Oxf. Sr. Lectr.
Senanayake, Manouri P., MB BS Colombo, MD
S.Lanka, FRCP Prof.
Wickramasinghe, V. P., MB BS Colombo, MD
S.Lanka Sr. Lectr.
Other Staff: 2 Lectrs.
Research: childhood and maternal nutrition and
body composition in children; children
with growth hormone deficiency; intersex
disorders in children; outcome of intra-
uterine chikungunya infection

Parasitology

Tel: (011) 269 5300 Fax: (011) 269 9284
E-mail: parasitcmb@yahoo.com
Fernando, Deepika, MB BS Colombo, PhD S.Lanka
Head*
Gunawardena, G. Shamini A., MB BS Colombo,
MPhil Colombo
Karunaweera, Nadira D., MB BS Colombo Prof.
Other Staff: 3 Lectrs.; 1 Res. Officer
Research: filariasis; helminthology; leishmaniasis;
malaria

Pathology

Tel: (01) 269 5300
Angunawela, Preethika, MB BS Ceyl., MD
Colombo, FRCPath Prof.
De Silva, M. V. C., MB BS Colombo, MD S.Lanka
Prof.; Head*
Lokuhetty, M. Dilani S., MB BS S.Lanka, MD
Colombo Assoc. Prof.
Perera, Niranthi R., MB BS Colombo, MD S.Lanka
Sr. Lectr.
Other Staff: 2 Lectrs.
Vacant Posts: 4 Lectrs.
Research: breast and thyroid pathology;
cutaneous lymphomas; perinatal and foetal
pathology; renal pathology

Pharmacology and Pharmacy

Tel: (011) 269 5300 Fax: (011) 269 7483
Abrew, Kusum De W., MB BS Colombo, MD
S.Lanka Prof.
Fernandopulle, B. L. Rohini, MB BS Ceyl., PhD
Colombo Sr. Lectr.
Galappatthy, Priyadarshani, MB BS Colombo, MD
S.Lanka Sr. Lectr.
Jayakody, R. L., MB BS Colombo, PhD Alta.
Prof.; Head*
Kariyawasam, S. Himani, MB BS Colombo, PhD
Aston Sr. Lectr.
Pathirana, W., BPharm Jad., MPharm Jad. Sr.
Lectr.
Sri Ranaganathan, Shalini, MB BS S.Lanka, MD
S.Lanka, PhD Cardiff, DCH S.Lanka Sr. Lectr.
Weeraratne, Chamari L., MB BS Colombo, MD
S.Lanka Sr. Lectr.
Wijayabandara, M. D. J., BSc Sri Jay., PhD Sri
Jay. Sr. Lectr.
Other Staff: 2 Lectrs.
Research: drug information; ethics; paediatrics;
pharmacovigilance

Physiology

Tel: (011) 269 5230
Atapattu, Pushpa M., MB BS Colombo, MD
Colombo Sr. Lectr.
De Silva, P. A., MB BS Sab., BSc Colombo, PhD
Colombo Sr. Lectr.
Dissanayake, S. Angela, MB BS Kelaniya, PhD
S.Lanka Sr. Lectr.
Fernando, A. Dinithi A., MB BS Colombo, MD
Colombo Sr. Lectr.
Gunatilake, Mangala, BVSc Peradeniya, PhD
Colombo Sr. Lectr.
Tennekoon, Kamani H., MB BS Colombo, PhD
Sheff. Sr. Prof.

Wasalathanthri, Sudharshani, MB BS Colombo,
PhD Colombo Sr. Lectr.; Head*
Other Staff: 2 Lectrs.
Research: clinical nutrition; rabies; renal
physiology; reproduction and development;
reproductive endocrinology

Psychological Medicine

Tel: (011) 269 1688
E-mail: psych_med@yahoo.com
De Silva, Varuni, MB BS Colombo, MD Colombo
Sr. Lectr.; Head*
De Zoysa, Piyanjali, MA Delhi, PhD S.Lanka, BA
Sr. Lectr.
Hanwella, D. R. C., MB BS Colombo, MD Colombo
Sr. Lectr.
Mendis, N., MB BS Colombo, FRCPsych Sr.
Prof.
Perera, Hemamali, MB BS Peradeniya, MD
Colombo, FRCPsych Prof.
Samarasinghe, D. S., MB BS Colombo, FRCPsych
Assoc. Prof.
Other Staff: 2 Lectrs.
Research: alcohol and other substance use;
autism; health policy

Surgery

Tel: (01) 269 1111
Abayadeera, Anuja, MB BS Colombo, MD
Colombo, FRCA Sr. Lectr.
Dias, M. N. J. R., MB BS Ceyl., MS Colombo,
FRCSEd Sr. Lectr.
Samarasekara, D. N., MB BS Colombo, MS
Colombo, MD, FRCS, FRCSEd Prof.
Wijeyaratne, S. M., MB BS Colombo, MS Colombo,
MD, FRCS Prof.; Head*
Zoysa, M. I. M., MB BS Colombo, MS Colombo,
FRCS, FRCSEd Sr. Lectr.
Other Staff: 3 Lectrs.

SPECIAL CENTRES, ETC

Biochemistry, Molecular Biology and Biotechnology, Institute of

Tel: (011) 255 2528 Fax: (011) 255 2529
E-mail: director@ibmbb.cmb.ac.lk
Epitawalage, N., BSc Colombo, PhD Colombo Sr.
Lectr.
Handunnetti, S. M., BSc Kelaniya, PhD Colombo
Sr. Lectr.
Karunanayake, U. P. E. H., BSc Ceyl., MSc Lond.,
PhD Lond. Prof.
Tennekoon, Kamani H., MB BS Colombo, PhD
Sheff. Prof.; Dir.*
Weerasena, O. V. D. S. J., BSc Colombo, PhD
Colombo Sr. Lectr.
Research: molecular biology of tropical diseases;
molecular entomology; molecular medicine
(cancer genetics, reproduction and
development, human DNA variations); plant
molecular sciences

Computing, School of

Tel: (011) 248 1245 Fax: (011) 258 7239
E-mail: info@ucsc.cmb.ac.lk
Arunathilake, S. M. K. D., BSc Colombo, MBA Sri
Jay., PhD W.Syd. Sr. Lectr.
Atukorale, D. A. S., BSc Colombo, PhD Qld. Sr.
Lectr.
Dais, G. K. A. D., BSc Colombo, MPhil Cardiff
Sr. Lectr.
De Zoysa, T. N. K., BSc Colombo, PhD Stockholm
Sr. Lectr.
Dharmaratne, A. T., BSc Colombo, MEng
Hiroshima, PhD Hiroshima Sr. Lectr.
Goonathilleke, M. D. J. S., BSc Colombo, MSc
Keele, PhD Cardiff Sr. Lectr.
Hewagamage, K. P., BSc Colombo, PhD Hiroshima
Sr. Lectr.
Karunaratne, D. D., BSc Colombo, MSc Swansea,
PhD Cardiff Sr. Lectr.
Keppitiyagama, C. I., BSc Colombo, MSc Br.Col.,
PhD Br.Col. Sr. Lectr.
Kodikara, N. D., BSc Colombo, MSc Manc., PhD
Manc. Sr. Lectr.; Head, Information Systems
Engin.
Premaratne, H. L., BSc S.Lanka, PhD Sr. Lectr.

Ranasinghe, D. N., BSc Lond., MSc Lond., PhD Cardiff   Sr. Lectr.; Head, Computation and Intelligent Systems
Seneviratne, G. P., BSc Colombo, MSc Cardiff, MPhil Cardiff   Sr. Lectr.
Weerasinghe, A. R., BSc Colombo, MSc Cardiff, PhD Cardiff   Sr. Lectr.; Dir.*
Wikramanayake, G. N., BSc Colombo, MSc Cardiff, PhD Cardiff   Sr. Lectr.; Head, Communication and Media Technologies; Deputy Dir.
Wimalaratne, G. D. S. P., BSc Colombo, PhD Manc.   Sr. Lectr.
Other Staff: 9 Lectrs.
Research: ad hoc sensor networks; data security; distributed systems; multimedia technology; natural language processing

Development Studies Institute

Tel: (011) 534 1296 E-mail: smpsena@sltnet.lk
No staff at present

Human Resource Advancement, Institute of

Tel: (011) 250 3393 Fax: (011) 250 1924
E-mail: ihra@ihra.cmb.ac.lk
Hirimburegama, W. K., BSc Peradeniya, PhD Peradeniya   Sr. Lectr.; Dir.*
Other Staff: 1 Lectr.; 3 Academic Co-ordinators
Research: drug abuse; health promotion; human resource advancement; labour studies; rural development

Indigenous Medicine, Institute of

Tel: (011) 269 4308
Jayawardena, R. S.   Dir.*

Library and Information Science, National Institute of

Tel: (011) 250 7150 Fax: (011) 250 7148
E-mail: diruilis@sltnet.lk
Wijetunge, Pradeepa, BA S.Lanka   Dir.*

Medical Education Development and Research Centre

Karunanayake, I. M., MB BS Colombo, MMEd   Sr. Lectr.
Ponnamperuma, G. G., MB BS Colombo, MMEd   Sr. Lectr.
Other Staff: 2 Lectrs.

Medicine, Postgraduate Institute of

Tel: (011) 268 8649 Fax: (011) 269 7757
E-mail: pgim_dir@sltnet.lk
Sheriff, M. H. Rezvi, MB BS Ceyl., MD Ceyl., FRCP, FRCPEd, FACP   Sr. Prof.; Dir.*

Physiotherapy Unit

2 Lectrs.

CONTACT OFFICERS

Academic affairs. Deputy Registrar: Nanayakkara, D. P. L. J., LLB Open S.Lanka, MBA RMIT (E-mail: acpb@admin.cmb.ac.lk)
Accommodation. Senior Assistant Registrar: Piyaratne, G., BA Peradeniya
Admissions (first degree). Deputy Registrar: Sivalingam, V. S.
Admissions (higher degree). Deputy Registrar (higher degree): Nanayakkara, D. P. L. J., LLB Open S.Lanka, MBA RMIT (E-mail: acpb@admin.cmb.ac.lk)
Adult/continuing education. Deputy Registrar: Nanayakkara, D. P. L. J., LLB Open S.Lanka, MBA RMIT (E-mail: acpb@admin.cmb.ac.lk)
Careers. Senior Assistant Registrar: Silva, T. L. R., BA Open S.Lanka, MBA Colombo
Computing services. Director, School of Computing: Weerasinghe, A. R., BSc Colombo, MSc Cardiff, PhD Cardiff
Consultancy services. Bursar: Bandara, Rohini P., BCom Ceyl., MPA Sri Jay., FCA
Development/fund-raising. Bursar: Bandara, Rohini P., BCom Ceyl., MPA Sri Jay., FCA
Distance education. Director, Staff Development Centre: Ekaratne, S. U. K., BSc Colombo, PhD Wales
Equal opportunities. Registrar: Hussain, W. Husni R., BA Sri Jay., MPA Sri Jay.
Estates and buildings/works and services. Works Engineer: Abeyratna, P. H. M. R. L. B.
Examinations. Deputy Registrar: Sivalingam, S.
Finance. Bursar: Bandara, Rohini P., BCom Ceyl., MPA Sri Jay., FCA
General enquiries. Registrar: Hussain, W. Husni R., BA Sri Jay., MPA Sri Jay.
Health services. Chief Medical Officer: Peiris, R. Grace X., MB BS Ceyl., MD S.Lanka
Industrial liaison. Registrar: Hussain, W. Husni R., BA Sri Jay., MPA Sri Jay.
International office. Vice-Chancellor: Hirimburegama, Prof. Kshanika K., BSc Colombo, MPhil Peradeniya, PhD Leuven, FNAS(SL)
Language training for international students. Senior Assistant Registrar: Uyangoda, S., BA Sri Jay., MSc Kelaniya, MPM
Library (chief librarian). Librarian: Jayasuriya, Sumana C., BA Ceyl., MLS Philippines
Library (enquiries). Assistant Registrar: Dissanayake, D. M. C. U. K., BA Peradeniya

Marketing. Registrar: Hussain, W. Husni R., BA Sri Jay., MPA Sri Jay.
Minorities/disadvantaged groups. Senior Assistant Registrar: Piyaratne, G., BA Peradeniya
Ombudsman. Senior Student Counsellor: Waleboda, T. D. K., BA Kelaniya, MA Kelaniya
Personnel/human resources. Senior Assistant Registrar (Non-Academic): Perera, L. L. W., BA Colombo, LLB S.Lanka
Personnel/human resources. Deputy Registrar (Academic): Ekanayake, A. C. Subalaximi
Public relations. Senior Personal Secretary: Gunawardena, Hiranthi D.
Publications. Deputy Registrar: Nanayakkara, D. P. L. J., LLB Open S.Lanka, MBA RMIT (E-mail: acpb@cmb.ac.lk)
Purchasing. Deputy Bursar: Malalgoda, Damani T., BBM Chaminade, MBA S.Lanka
Research. Deputy Regisar: Nanayakkara, D. P. L. J., LLB Open S.Lanka, MBA RMIT (E-mail: acpb@cmb.ac.lk)
Safety. Senior Assistant Registrar: Piyaratne, G., BA Peradeniya
Scholarships, awards, loans. Deputy Bursar: Jayasuriya, Swarnalatha
Schools liaison. Dean of Education: Sandrasegaram, Prof. S., BEd Peradeniya, MEd Hiroshima
Security. Acting Senior Assistant Registrar: Uyangoda, S., BA Sri Jay., MSc Kelaniya, MPM
Sport and recreation. Acting Director, Physical Education: Hewage, N. W., BDevSt
Staff development and training. Director, Staff Development Centre: Ekaratne, S. U. K., BSc Colombo, PhD Wales
Student union. Senior Assistant Registrar: Piyaratne, G., BA Peradeniya
Student welfare/counselling. Senior Student Counsellor: Waleboda, T. D. K., BA Kelaniya, MA Kelaniya
Student welfare/counselling. Senior Assistant Registrar (Student Welfare): Piyaratne, G., BA Peradeniya
Students with disabilities. Senior Assistant Registrar: Piyaratne, G., BA Peradeniya

CAMPUS/COLLEGE HEADS

Sri Palee Campus, Wewala, Horana, Sri Lanka. (Tel: (034) 226 1371; Fax: (034) 226 1372; E-mail: sripalee@sltnet.lk) Rector: Wilson, W. N., BA Ceyl., BPhil Ceyl., MA S.Lanka

[Information supplied by the institution as at 27 November 2007, and edited by the ACU]

EASTERN UNIVERSITY, SRI LANKA

Founded 1986

Member of the Association of Commonwealth Universities

Postal Address: Vantharumoolai, Chenkalady, Sri Lanka
Telephone: (065) 224 0490, 224 0580 **Fax:** (065) 224 0730 **E-mail:** reception@esn.ac.lk
URL: http://www.esn.ac.lk/

ACTING VICE-CHANCELLOR*—Pathmanathan, N., MSc Moscow, DPhil Sus.
REGISTRAR‡—Harris, A. D., BCom Jaffna, MSc Sri Jay.
BURSAR (ACTING)—Pathmakumar, M. A.
LIBRARIAN—Arulnandhy, T., BA Peradeniya, MLibSc B'lore.

GENERAL INFORMATION

History. The university was established in 1986; it was previously Batticaloa University College, founded 1981.
It is located about 16km north of Batticaloa.

Admission to first degree courses (see also Sri Lankan Introduction). Internal programmes: through University Grants Commission. External programmes: direct to the university.

First Degrees (see also Sri Lankan Directory to Subjects of Study) (* = with honours). BA,

BA*, BBA, BCom, BEcon, BSc, BSc(Acc&FinMgt), BSc(Agric), MB BS.
Length of course. Full-time: BA, BSc: 3 years; BA*, BBA, BCom, BEcon, BSc(Acc&FinMgt), BSc(Agric): 4 years; MB BS: 5 years.

Higher Degrees (see also Sri Lankan Directory to Subjects of Study).

Master's. MA, MPhil.
Length of course. Full-time: MA: 1 year; MPhil: 2 years.
Doctoral. PhD.
Length of course. Full-time: PhD: 3 years.

Language of Instruction. English and Tamil.

Libraries. Volumes: 67,665. Periodicals subscribed to: 1196. Other holdings: 76 Handbook Reports.

FACULTIES/SCHOOLS

Agriculture
Tel: (065) 224 0530 Fax: (065) 224 0740
E-mail: deanagr@sltnet.lk; deanagri@esn.ac.lk
Dean: Premakumar, K., BScAgric *Peradeniya*, MSc *Asian I.T., Bangkok*, PhD *IARI*

Arts and Culture
Tel: (065) 224 0165 Fax: (065) 224 0971
E-mail: deanart@sltnet.lk; deanarts@esn.ac.lk
Dean: Sugumar, B., BA *Peradeniya*, MA *Pondicherry*

Commerce and Management
Tel: (065) 224 0214 Fax: (065) 224 0591
E-mail: deancom@sltnet.lk; deanfcm@esn.ac.lk
Dean: Kanagasingam, V., BBA *Eastern(S.Lanka)*, MSc *Sri Jay.*

Health-Care Science
Tel: (065) 222 7286 Fax: (065) 222 7286
Dean: Karunakaran, K. E., MB BS *Jaffna*, MS *Colombo*

Science
Tel: (065) 224 0528 Fax: (065) 224 0758
E-mail: deansci@sltnet.lk; deansci@esn.ac.lk
Dean: Pathmanathan, N., MSc *Moscow*, DPhil *Sus.*

ACADEMIC UNITS

Agricultural Economics
Tel: (065) 224 0759 E-mail: deanagr@sltnet.lk
Sivarajah, P., BScAgric *Peradeniya*, MSc *Asian I.T., Bangkok* Sr. Lectr.
Thedchanamoorthy, K., BScAgric *Peradeniya*, MSc *TN Ag.* Sr. Lectr.; Acting Head*
Other Staff: 2 Lectrs.

Agronomy
Tel: (065) 224 0760
E-mail: headagron@esn.ac.lk
Arulnandhy, V., BScAgric *Peradeniya*, MSc *Texas*, PhD *Peradeniya* Prof.
Harris, K. D., BScAgric *TN Ag.*, MPhil *Peradeniya* Sr. Lectr.
Jeyakumar, P., BScAgric *Eastern(S.Lanka)*, MPhil *Peradeniya* Sr. Lectr.; Head*
Kajamuhan, A., BScAgric *Eastern(S.Lanka)*, MPhil *Peradeniya* Sr. Lectr.
Mahendran, S., MSc *Peradeniya*, MSc *Jaffna*, PhD *Peradeniya*, BScAgric Sr. Lectr.
Mahendran, T., BScAgric *Peradeniya*, PhD *Reading* Sr. Lectr.
Premakumar, K., BScAgric *Peradeniya*, MSc *Asian I.T., Bangkok*, PhD *IARI* Sr. Lectr.
Premanandarajah, P., BScAgric *SE(S.Lanka)*, MPhil *Peradeniya* Sr. Lectr.
Seran, T. H., BScAgric *Eastern(S.Lanka)*, MSc *Colombo* Sr. Lectr.
Thanaraj, T., BScAgric *Eastern(S.Lanka)*, MPhil *Peradeniya* Sr. Lectr.
Thedchanamoorthy, K., BScAgric *Peradeniya*, MSc *TN Ag.* Sr. Lectr.
Thiruchelvam, T., BScAgric *Eastern(S.Lanka)*, PhD *Brad.* Sr. Lectr.
Other Staff: 6 Lectrs.
Research: association between the onset of rains and the variation of the Maha and Yala seasons in Batticaloa district; effective agricultural decision making through computer special modeling; host range of bruchid beetle; suitability of different

frying oils for the storage of elephant foot yam chips; treatment of prawn farm waste water by common cattail (typha latifilia) under different retention time

Animal Science
Tel: (065) 224 0761 E-mail: headani@esn.ac.lk
Jeyamalar, R., BSc *Peradeniya*, MPhil *Peradeniya* Sr. Lectr.
Mahusoon, M. M., BSc *Peradeniya*, MPhil *Peradeniya*, PhD *Peradeniya* Sr. Lectr.
Pagthinathan, M., BSc *Peradeniya*, MPhil *Peradeniya* Sr. Lectr.; Head*
Other Staff: 1 Lectr.
Research: evaluation of ice cream quality using different treatments, different flavours and fruits; nutritional analysis and yoghurt formulation of hydrogen peroxide treated cow milk; performance analysis of dairy cattle and social economic analysis of dairy cattle farmers in Trincomalee District

Arabic
Tel: (065) 224 0762
E-mail: headarabic@esn.ac.lk
Murugadas, A., BA *Jaffna*, MA *Jaffna*, PhD *Jaffna* Sr. Lectr.; Acting Head*
Other Staff: 2 Lectrs.

Botany
Tel: (065) 224 0757 E-mail: headbot@esn.ac.lk
Jeyasingam, T., BSc *Peradeniya*, PhD *Wales* Sr. Lectr.
Mahendranathan, C., BSc *Eastern(S.Lanka)*, MSc *Peradeniya* Sr. Lectr.
Printhan, M., BSc *Madr.*, MSc *Madr.*, PhD *Durban-W.* Sr. Lectr.; Head*
Sathananthan, S., BSc *Annam.*, MSc *Annam.*, PhD *Eastern(S.Lanka)* Sr. Lectr.
Other Staff: 2 Lectrs.
Research: growth and hydraulic characteristics of two tropical deciduous seedings subjected to different water supply; morphological responses of coastal plant forms in Batticaloa to tidal waves; surveying the post harvesting losses of Brinjal and identifying the causal agents of major post harvest disease

Chemistry
Tel: (065) 224 0755
E-mail: headchem@esn.ac.lk
Vakeesar, K., BSc *Jaffna*, MSc *Peradeniya* Sr. Lectr.; Head*
Other Staff: 4 Lectrs.
Research: heat sensitive gelation of natural rubber latex using polyvinylmethyle ether; spectrophotometric determination of silver using the reaction between bromohenol red and peroxydisulphate

Clinical Sciences
Karunakaran, K. E., MB BS *Jaffna*, MS *Colombo* Sr. Lectr.; Head*

Pathophysiology
1 Lectr.
Vacant Posts: Head*

Commerce
Tel: (065) 224 0736
E-mail: headcomm@esn.ac.lk
Balendran, S., BCom *Eastern(S.Lanka)*, MBA *Sri Jay.* Sr. Lectr.
Logeswaran, N., BCom *Jaffna*, MBA *Sri Jay.* Sr. Lectr.; Head*
Prabakaran, T., BBA *Eastern(S.Lanka)*, MBA *Sri Jay.* Sr. Lectr.
Sritharan, S., BSc *Jaffna*, MSc *Otago* Sr. Lectr.
Uthayakumar, R., BCom *Eastern(S.Lanka)*, MSc *Sri Jay.* Sr. Lectr.

Comparative Religion
Tel: (065) 224 0165 E-mail: deanart@sltnet.lk
Murugadas, A., BA *Jaffna*, MA *Jaffna*, PhD *Jaffna* Sr. Lectr.; Co-ordinator*
Saminathan, Rev. D., PhD *Rome*, BTh LTh Sr. Lectr.

Other Staff: 1 Lectr.

Economics
Tel: (065) 224 0735
E-mail: headecon@esn.ac.lk
Jeyarajah, S., BA *Jaffna*, MPhil *Peradeniya* Sr. Lectr.
Raguragavan, J., BA *Jaffna*, MA *Jaffna* Sr. Lectr. (on leave)
Soundralingam, A., BA *Jaffna*, MPhil *Jaffna* Sr. Lectr.; Head*
Other Staff: 4 Lectrs.

Education
Tel: (065) 224 0165 E-mail: deanart@sltnet.lk
Selvarajah, M., BEd *Peradeniya*, MEd *Colombo*, MPhil *Colombo*, MEd *Leeds* Sr. Lectr.; Co-ordinator*
Other Staff: 1 Lectr.

Fine Arts
Tel: (065) 224 0738
E-mail: headfinearts@esn.ac.lk
Maunaguru, S., BA *Jaffna*, MA *Peradeniya*, PhD *Jaffna* Assoc. Prof.; Head*
Sugumar, B., BA *Peradeniya*, MA *Pondicherry* Sr. Lectr.
Other Staff: 1 Lectr.

Geography
Tel: (065) 224 0165 E-mail: headgeo@esn.ac.lk
Ponniah, S., BA *Peradeniya*, MA *Peradeniya*, MPhil *Peradeniya* Sr. Lectr.; Head*
Thissarajah, A. J., BA *Jaffna*, PhD *Peradeniya* Sr. Lectr.
Other Staff: 2 Lectrs.
Research: displacement and resettlement in Manmunai North Divisional Secretariat in the Batticaloa District in the aftermath of the tsunami; problems and challenges in Karawalai fishing; selection of suitable site for the industrial location in the sand bar of the Batticaloa lagoon by using geographic information system (GIS) as a tool

Human Biology
Tel: (065) 222 7288
Vacant Posts: Head*

Islamic Studies
Tel: (065) 224 0762
E-mail: headislamic@esn.ac.lk
Selvarajah, M., BEd *Peradeniya*, MEd *Colombo*, MPhil *Colombo*, MEd *Leeds* Sr. Lectr.; Acting Head*
Other Staff: 3 Lectrs.

Languages
Tel: (065) 224 0739
E-mail: headlangu@esn.ac.lk
Murugadas, A., BA *Jaffna*, MA *Jaffna*, PhD *Jaffna* Sr. Lectr.
Nadira, K., BA *Jaffna*, MPhil *Jaffna* Sr. Lectr.
Sitralega, M., BA *Jaffna*, MA *Peradeniya*, PhD *Jaffna* Assoc. Prof.; Head*
Yogarajah, S., BA *Colombo*, BPhil *Colombo*, MA *Jaffna*, PhD *Jaffna* Sr. Lectr.
Other Staff: 3 Lectrs.
Research: allowing private institutions to become involved in university education in Sri Lanka (discussions and reality); cultural property affected by tsunami in the east coast of Sri Lanka; re-evaluation on origin and development of Sri Lanka modern Tamil poetry (1940-1960)

Management
Tel: (065) 224 0737 E-mail: headmgt@esn.ac.lk
Andrew, A., BBA *Eastern(S.Lanka)*, MBA *Sri Jay.* Sr. Lectr.; Head*
Kanagasingam, V., BBA *Eastern(S.Lanka)*, MSc *Sri Jay.* Sr. Lectr.
Ragal, V. R., BBA *Eastern(S.Lanka)*, MSc *Sri Jay.* Sr. Lectr.

Raguragavan, G., MBA Sri Jay., PhD Massey, BBA
    Sr. Lectr.
Senthilnathan, S., BSc Jaffna, MSc Sri Jay.   Sr.
    Lectr.
Sriranganathan, S., MBA Colombo, BBA   Sr.
    Lectr.
Other Staff: 2 Lectrs.
Research: a comparative study on impact of
    training on employee's performance of
    bank 'A' and bank 'B' in Batticaloa; effective
    marketing positioning of convenience
    goods in Batticaloa district

Mathematics

Tel: (065) 224 0753
    E-mail: headmaths@esn.ac.lk
Johnpillai, A. G., BSc Eastern(S.Lanka), MSc
    Witw., PhD Witw.   Sr. Lectr.; Head*
Kobindarajah, K., BSc Eastern(S.Lanka), MSc
    Witw., PhD Witw.   Sr. Lectr.
Sritharan, T., BSc Jaffna, DPhil Sus.   Sr. Lectr.
Other Staff: 5 Lectrs.

Medical Education and Research

No staff at present
Vacant Posts: Head*

Physics

Tel: (065) 224 0754 E-mail: headphy@esn.ac.lk
Pathmanathan, N., MSc Moscow, DPhil Sus.   Sr.
    Lectr.
Other Staff: 3 Lectrs.
Research: measurements of terminal conductivity
    and magnetic susceptibility of (Bi.6 Pb0.4)
    Sr2 Ca2 Cu3 Ox superconductor at room
    temperature; preparation and resistance
    measurements of BiPbSrCaCuO
    superconductor

Primary Health Care

No staff at present
Vacant Posts: Head*

Social Science

Tel: (065) 224 0734
    E-mail: headsosci@esn.ac.lk
Gunaratnam, V., BA Jaffna, MPhil Jaffna   Sr.
    Lectr.; Acting Head*
Krishnamohan, S., BA Jaffna, MPhil Peradeniya
    Sr. Lectr.
Thangarajah, C. Y., BA Peradeniya, MA Roch.,
    PhD Roch.   Sr. Lectr.
Other Staff: 7 Lectrs.
Research: ethnic conflict and peace process in Sri
    Lanka

Supplementary Health Sciences

Tel: (065) 222 2059
No staff at present

Vacant Posts: Head*

Zoology

Tel: (065) 224 0756 E-mail: headzoo@esn.ac.lk
Darmaratnam, M., BSc Jaffna, DPhil Sus.   Sr.
    Lectr.
Devadason, C. G., BSc Jaffna, MSc Stir., MPhil
    Aberd.   Sr. Lectr.; Head*
Vinobaba, M., BSc Jaffna, DPhil Sus.   Sr. Lectr.
Vinobaba, P., BSc Jaffna, DPhil Sus.   Sr. Lectr.
Other Staff: 1 Lectr.

SPECIAL CENTRES, ETC

English Language Teaching Unit

Tel: (065) 224 0587 E-mail: headeltu@esn.ac.lk
5 Instrs.
Vacant Posts: Head/Coordinator*

Information and Communication Technology, Centre for

Tel: (065) 224 0166
    E-mail: headcomp@esn.ac.lk
1 Lectr.; 2 Instrs.; 1 Computer Programmer
Vacant Posts: Head/Coordinator*

Svamy Vipulananda Institute of Aesthetic Studies

Tel: (065) 222 2663 Fax: (065) 222 2663
Rajeswaran, B., BA MPhil   Sr. Lectr.; Dir.*
Other Staff: 6 Lectrs.; 4 Instrs.
Research: comparison between yazl and violin

CONTACT OFFICERS

Accommodation. Assistant Registrar, Welfare:
    Selvarasah, V. (E-mail: welfare@esn.ac.lk)
Admissions (higher degree). Senior Assistant
    Registrar, Examinations: Poheenthiran, K.,
    BCom Jaffna (E-mail: examinations@esn.ac.lk)
Adult/continuing education. Senior Assistant
    Registrar, Examinations: Poheenthiran, K.,
    BCom Jaffna (E-mail: examinations@esn.ac.lk)
Alumni. Assistant Registrar, Academic
    Establishments: Kandeepan, V., BScAgric
    Eastern(S.Lanka) (E-mail: estac@esn.ac.lk)
Archives. Librarian: Arulnandhy, T., BA
    Peradeniya, MLibSc B'lore.
    (E-mail: eusllibr@sltnet.lk)
Computing services. Director, Computing
    Services: (vacant)

Development/fund-raising. Bursar (Acting):
    Pathmakumar, M. A.
    (E-mail: bursar@esn.ac.lk)
Estates and buildings/works and services.
    Works Engineer: Sriskandarajah, N.,
    BScEngin Peradeniya
Examinations. (External) Assistant Registrar,
    External Degrees: Pararajasingam, S., BA
    Jaffna (E-mail: externaldegrees@esn.ac.lk)
Examinations. (Internal) Senior Assistant
    Registrar, Examinations: Poheenthiran, K.,
    BCom Jaffna (E-mail: examinations@esn.ac.lk)
Finance. Bursar (Acting): Pathmakumar, M. A.
    (E-mail: bursar@esn.ac.lk)
General enquiries. Registrar: Harris, A. D.,
    BCom Jaffna, MSc Sri Jay.
    (E-mail: registrar@esn.ac.lk)
Health services. Consultant Medical Officer:
    (vacant)
Library (chief librarian). Librarian:
    Arulnandhy, T., BA Peradeniya, MLibSc B'lore.
    (E-mail: eusllibr@sltnet.lk)
Library (enquiries). Librarian: Arulnandhy,
    T., BA Peradeniya, MLibSc B'lore.
    (E-mail: eusllibr@sltnet.lk)
Marketing. Registrar: Harris, A. D., BCom
    Jaffna, MSc Sri Jay.
    (E-mail: registrar@esn.ac.lk)
Personnel/human resources. Registrar:
    Harris, A. D., BCom Jaffna, MSc Sri Jay.
    (E-mail: registrar@esn.ac.lk)
Public relations. Registrar: Harris, A. D.,
    BCom Jaffna, MSc Sri Jay.
    (E-mail: registrar@esn.ac.lk)
Purchasing. Assistant Bursar, Supplies: (vacant)
Safety. Assistant Registrar, Welfare: Selvarasah,
    V.
Security. Chief Security Officer: Sivalingam,
    V., BA Peradeniya
Sport and recreation. Head, Physical
    Education: (vacant)
Student union. President (Student union):
    Nithikumar, K.
Student welfare/counselling. Senior Student
    Counsellor: Saminathan, Rev. D., PhD Rome,
    BTh LTh

CAMPUS/COLLEGE HEADS

Trincomalee Campus, 315 Dockyard Road,
    Trincomalee, Sri Lanka. (Tel: (026) 222
    2769; Fax: (026) 222 2300;
    E-mail: rectotco@slt.lk) Rector: Rajendra, C.
    P., MA PhD

[Information supplied by the institution as at 6 June
2006, and edited by the ACU]

UNIVERSITY OF JAFFNA, SRI LANKA

Founded 1979

Member of the Association of Commonwealth Universities

Postal Address: Thirunelvely, P.O. Box 57, Jaffna, Sri Lanka
Telephone: (021) 222 2294 **Fax:** (021) 222 2294
URL: http://www.jfn.ac.lk/

VICE-CHANCELLOR*—Shanmugalingam, Prof. Nagalingam, BEd Colombo, MA Jaffna,
    PhD Jaffna
ACTING REGISTRAR‡—Kanthasamy, P.
BURSAR—Kanagaratnam, K., BCom S.Lanka, MPhil Jaffna
LIBRARIAN—Pararajasingam, R., BSc Madr., BLIS Madr., MLIS Madr.

UNIVERSITY OF KELANIYA, SRI LANKA

Founded 1978

Member of the Association of Commonwealth Universities

Postal Address: Kelaniya, Sri Lanka
Telephone: (011) 291 1391 **Fax:** (011) 291 3857 **E-mail:** postmast@kln.ac.lk
URL: http://www.kln.ac.lk

VICE-CHANCELLOR*—Wijeyaratne, Prof. M. Jayantha S., BSc S.Lanka, MSc Mich., PhD
Kelaniya, FNAS(SL), FIBiol(SLanka)
DEPUTY VICE-CHANCELLOR—(vacant)
REGISTRAR‡—Karunaratne, W. M., BSc Sri Jay., MSSc Kelaniya
LIBRARIAN—Jayatissa, L. A., BSc Vidyal., MLISc Delhi
ACTING BURSAR—Wanigasekera, A. W. T. S., BSc

GENERAL INFORMATION

History. The university was originally established in 1875 as Vidyalankara Pirivena, a centre of learning for Buddhist monks. It was renamed Vidyalankara University in 1959 and subsequently became the Vidyalankara Campus of the University of Ceylon. In 1978, the university was founded under its present name.
It is located about 10km north of Colombo.

Admission to first degree courses (see also Sri Lankan Introduction). Through University Grants Commission (UGC) and authorised agents. Admission is based on marks obtained at GCE A level. International students with equivalent qualifications are eligible to apply.

First Degrees (see also Sri Lankan Directory to Subjects of Study) (* = with honours). BA, BAMS, BBMgt, BCom, BFA, BNS, BSc, BSc*, MB BS.
Length of course. Full-time: BSc: 3 years; BA: 3–4 years; BBMgt, BCom, BSc*: 4 years; MB BS: 5 years.

Higher Degrees (see also Sri Lanka Directory to Subjects of Study).
Master's. MA, MCom, MDefS, MPhil, MSc, MSSc.
All courses normally last 2 years.
Length of course. Full-time: MPhil, MSc: 2 years.
Doctoral. DM, PhD.
Length of course. Full-time: PhD: 3 years.

Language of Instruction. Sinhalese and English.

Libraries. Volumes: 188,000. Periodicals subscribed to: 132. Special collections: Prof. D. J. Wijayaratne (languages, literature, oriental studies); De Lanerolle Trust (social sciences, humanities); Noel Phoebus; Benedict Dodampegama; Jethawanarama Piriwena.

Statistics. Staff (2006–2007): 1082 (459 academic, 623 non-academic). Students (2006–2007): undergraduate 7986.

FACULTIES/SCHOOLS

Commerce and Management Studies
Tel: (011) 291 7708 Fax: (011) 291 7708
E-mail: sunil@kln.ac.lk
Dean: Sunil Shantha, A. T. H., BSc(BusAdm) Vidyod., MCom Kelaniya
Senior Assistant Registrar: Mallikarachchi, K., BLE Colombo

Graduate Studies
Tel: (011) 290 8165 Fax: (011) 290 8165
E-mail: dangalle1946@yahoo.co.uk
Dean: Dangalle, Prof. N. K., BA Ceyl., MA Flin., PhD Peradeniya
Senior Assistant Registrar: Ranasinghe, G. H., BA Peradeniya

Humanities
Tel: (011) 291 1913 Fax: (011) 290 8787
E-mail: kula@kln.ac.lk
Dean: Kumarasinghe, K., BA S.Lanka, PhD Kelaniya
Assistant Registrar: Yalegama, M. M. N. T. R.

Medicine
Tel: (011) 295 5280 Fax: (011) 295 8337
E-mail: hjdes@sltnet.lk
Dean: Wickremasinghe, Prof. A. R., MB BS Colombo, MPH Tulane, PhD Tulane, PhD
Senior Assistant Registrar: Weerasinghe, R. M. M. L. B.

Science
Tel: (011) 291 1916 Fax: (011) 291 1916
E-mail: kdj@kln.ac.lk
Dean: Jayasuriya, K. A. K. D. D. D., BSc S.Lanka, PhD ANU
Acting Assistant Registrar: Kurugala, G. U. S., BA Sri Jay.

Social Sciences
Tel: (011) 291 1915 Fax: (011) 291 1915
E-mail: maddu@kln.ac.lk
Dean: Maddumabandara, Prof. Y. M. S., BA Vidyal., MA Shiga
Assistant Registrar: Amarathunga, G. S.

ACADEMIC UNITS

Accountancy
Tel: (011) 290 8784 Fax: (011) 290 8784
E-mail: depac@kln.ac.lk
Abeysekara, R., BSc Kelaniya, MBA Colombo Sr. Lectr.
Ariyarathna, J. M. D., BCom Kelaniya, MCom Kelaniya Sr. Lectr.
Gunasekara, U. L. T. P., BSc(BusAdm) Sri Jay., MBA Colombo Sr. Lectr.
Karunaratne, W. V. A. D., BBMgt Kelaniya, MCom Kelaniya, MAAT Sr. Lectr.
Munasinghe, M. A. T. K., BSc(Acct) Sri Jay., MBA Colombo
Ranjani, R. P. C., BCom Kelaniya, MCom Panjab, PhD Panjab Sr. Lectr.; Head*
Thilakerathne, P. M. C., BCom Kelaniya, MCom Panjab, PhD Aegean Sr. Lectr.
Tilakasiri, K. K., BCom Sri Jay., MSc Sri Jay. Sr. Lectr.
Other Staff: 11 Lectrs.; 3 Temp. Lectrs.

Anatomy
Tel: (011) 295 8219 Fax: (011) 295 8337
Hasson, R., MB BS N.C'bo.Med.Coll., PhD Kelaniya Sr. Lectr.
Karunanayake, A. L., MB BS N.C'bo.Med.Coll., DM Kelaniya Sr. Lectr.
Salgado, L. S., MB BS Ceyl., MA Kelaniya, MS Kelaniya Sr. Lectr.
Other Staff: 4 Lectrs.
Research: age changes of the lumber spine; anatomical variations of human body; low backache; placenta in hypertensive disorders of pregnancy; women's health

Archaeology
see also Special Centres, etc

Tel: (011) 290 8779 Fax: (011) 291 1915
Amarasekara, A. A. D., BA Kelaniya, MA Kelaniya Prof.; Sr. Lectr.
Amarasinghe, N. M., BA Kelaniya, MPhil Kelaniya Sr. Lectr.
Gunawardhane, P., BA Kelaniya, MPhil Kelaniya, PhD Kelaniya Sr. Lectr.; Head*
Hettige, U., BA Kelaniya, MPhil Kelaniya Sr. Lectr.
Manathunga, A., BA Kelaniya, MA Poona, MSc Kelaniya Sr. Lectr.
Other Staff: 2 Lectrs.
Research: archaeological heritage of the Kelani valley region; Polonnaruwa city plan; Upper Malwatu Oya archaeological exploration project

Biochemistry and Clinical Chemistry
Tel: (011) 295 3410 Fax: (011) 295 8337
Chakrawarthy, S., BSc Kelaniya, PhD Glas. Sr. Lectr.; Head*
Chandrasena, L. G., BSc Liv., PhD Liv., FIChemC Sr. Prof.
de Silva, L. D. R., BSc Colombo, MSc Colombo, PhD Colombo Sr. Lectr.
Gunasekera, K. A. D. C., MB BS Ruhuna, PhD Nagasaki Sr. Lectr.
Samarawickrama, N. A., BSc ANU, MSc ANU, PhD Qld. Sr. Lectr.; Head*
Thabrew, M. I., BSc Colombo, PhD S'ton., FIChemC, FNAS(SL) Sr. Prof.
Other Staff: 2 Lectrs.
Research: antioxidants; biochemical and pharmacological effects of medicinal plants and traditional Sri Lankan remedies; effect of non-surgical periodontal therapy on protein glycosylation

Botany
Tel: (011) 291 4480 Fax: (011) 291 1916
E-mail: botany@kln.ac.lk
Abeywickrama, K. P., BSc Colombo, MSc Maryland, PhD Maryland Sr. Lectr.
Amarasinghe, M. D., BSc Peradeniya, MPhil Peradeniya, PhD Salf. Sr. Lectr.
Deshapriya, N., BSc Kelaniya, MPhil Kelaniya, PhD Bath Sr. Lectr.
Jayasekera, L. R., BSc Kelaniya, MSc Osnabrück, DrRerNat Osnabrück Prof.
Kannangara, B. T. S. D. P., BSc Kelaniya, PhD Kelaniya Sr. Lectr.
Peiris, B. D., MSc Moscow, MPhil Peradeniya, PhD Hawaii Sr. Lectr.
Ratnayake, R. M. C. S., BSc Peradeniya, MPhil Peradeniya, PhD HK
Senanayake, R. A. S. P., BSc Kelaniya, MPhil Reading Sr. Lectr.
Sirisena, D. M., BSc Kelaniya, MSc Calg., PhD Calg. Assoc. Prof.; Head*
Other Staff: 1 Lectr.
Research: microbial genetics; plant ecology; plant pathology; plant physiology; tissue culture

Chemistry

see also Biochem. and Clin. Chem.

Tel: (011) 291 4486 Fax: (011) 291 1916
    E-mail: chem@kln.ac.lk

De Silva, D. S. M., BSc *Kelaniya*, PhD *Sheff.*   Sr. Lectr.

Deeyamulla, M. P.   Prof.

Gunawardene, N. E., BSc *Peradeniya*, PhD *S'ton.*   Prof.; Head*

Jayasuriya, C. K., BSc *Colombo*, MS *Cinc.*, PhD *Cinc.*   Sr. Lectr.

Jayawardena, B. M., BSc *Colombo*, PhD *Ill.*   Sr. Lectr.

Liyanage, J. A., BSc *Sri Jay.*, PhD *Wales*   Sr. Lectr.

Paranagama, P. A., BSc *Kelaniya*, MPhil *Kelaniya*, PhD *Glas.*   Sr. Lectr.

Pathiratne, K. A. S., BSc *Ceyl.*, MSc *Dal.*, PhD *N.Dakota State*   Sr. Lectr.; Head*

Premaratne, W. A. P. J., BSc *Kelaniya*, PhD *Birm.*   Sr. Lectr.

Ratnatilake, A. A. L., BSc *Kelaniya*, PhD *Zür.*   Sr. Lectr.

Se Silva, R. C. L., BSc *Kelaniya*, PhD *Iowa*

Seneviratne, N. A. K. P. J., BSc *Kelaniya*, PhD *Wayne State*   Sr. Lectr.

Weerasooriya, M. K. B., BSc *Kelaniya*, PhD *Brist.*   Sr. Lectr.

Wickramarachchi, P. A. S. R., BSc *Kelaniya*, PhD *Sheff.*

Wickremesinghe, L. K. G., BSc *Ceyl.*, PhD *S.Fraser*   Sr. Lectr.

Wimalasena, P. S. S., BSc *Ceyl.*, MSc *W.Aust.*   Assoc. Prof.

Other Staff: 3 Lectrs.

Research: analytical chemistry; biochemistry; chemical ecology; environmental chemistry; natural products

Commerce and Financial Management

Tel: (011) 291 4485 Fax: (011) 291 7708
    E-mail: bcom@kln.ac.lk

Amarathunga, S., BA *Sri Jay.*, MA *Colombo*, MSc *Saga*   Sr. Lectr.

Ananda, J. P., BCom *Peradeniya*, MA *Leeds*, PhD *Waik.*   Sr. Lectr.

Edirisinghe, S. D., BA *Sri Jay.*, MSc *Kelaniya*   Sr. Lectr.

Fernando, G. W. J. S., BCom *Kelaniya*, MCom *Kelaniya*   Sr. Lectr.; Head*

Jayasena, M. K., BBAd *Vidyod.*, MCom *Kelaniya*   Sr. Lectr.

Jayathilaka, L. V. K., BCom *Kelaniya*, MPhil *Ruhuna*

Mettananda, G. G., BSc *Vidyod.*, MCom *Kelaniya*   Sr. Lectr.; Head*

Pathirawasam, C., BSc *Sri Jay.*, MBA *Shiga*, PhD *Sri Jay.*   Sr. Lectr.

Ranayake, G. K., BCom *Kelaniya*, MCom *Kelaniya*

Semasinghe, D. M., BCom *Kelaniya*, MCom *Kelaniya*   Sr. Lectr.

Wijerathna, M. M. D., BCom *Kelaniya*, MBA *Colombo*   Sr. Lectr.

Other Staff: 9 Lectrs.; 6 Temp. Lectrs.

Community and Family Medicine

Tel: (011) 295 3411 Fax: (011) 295 8337
    E-mail: commed@mfac.kln.ac.lk

Abeysena, C., BA *Rome*, MB BS *Colombo*, MA *Colombo*, MSc *Colombo*, MD *Colombo*   Sr. Lectr.

De Silva, N., MB BS *Ceyl.*, MD *Colombo*, DCH *Colombo*   Prof., Family Medicine

Jayawardane, P. L., MB BS *Ceyl.*, MSc *Colombo*, MD *Colombo*   Sr. Lectr.

Pathmeswaran, A., MB BS *Colombo*, MSc *Colombo*, MD *Colombo*, MSc   Sr. Lectr.

Wickremasinghe, A. R., MB BS *Colombo*, MPH *Tulane*, PhD *Tulane*, PhD   Prof.; Head*

Other Staff: 1 Lectr.; 3 Probationary Lectrs.

Research: communicable diseases; disability; health information systems; non-communicable diseases; occupational health

Economics

Tel: (011) 291 4488 Fax: (011) 291 1915

Anulawathi, M. H. R., BA *Kelaniya*, MA *Sri Jay.*   Sr. Lectr.

Ariyawansa, D. D. M., BA *Vidyal.*, MA *Kelaniya*   Assoc. Prof.

Bandara, H. M., BEc *S.Lanka*, MA *Sri Jay.*, PhD *Strath.*   Assoc. Prof.

Dissanayaka, A., BA *Kelaniya*, MA *Sri Jay.*   Sr. Lectr.

Gunathilake, M. M., BA *Kelaniya*, MA *Kelaniya*   Sr. Lectr.

Hettiarachchi, U., BA *Peradeniya*, MA *Kelaniya*   Sr. Lectr.

Indrani, G. W., BA *Vidyal.*, MA *Kelaniya*   Sr. Lectr.

Kularatne, M. G., BA *Peradeniya*, MSc   Sr. Lectr.

Maddumabandara, Y. M. S., BA *Vidyal.*, MA *Shiga*   Prof.

Mendis, M. Y. N., BA *Colombo*, MA *Colombo*   Sr. Lectr.

Nawaratne, B. H. M., BA *Kelaniya*, MA *Colombo*, MSc *York(UK)*   Sr. Lectr.

Nayanapriya, T. W. K. O., BA *Colombo*, MA *Colombo*, MSSc *Kelaniya*   Sr. Lectr.

Pathirage, J. M. P., BA *Vidyal.*, MA *Sri Jay.*   Sr. Lectr.

Podimenike, K. M. P., BCom *Peradeniya*, MA *Kelaniya*   Prof.; Head*

Satarasinghe, D. P., BA *Vidyal.*, MA *Tokyo*   Sr. Lectr.

Tennakoon, K. U. A., BA *Vidyal.*, MA *Sri Jay.*, PhD *Auck.*   Sr. Lectr.

Wijekoon, M. K., BA *Vidyod.*, MA *Br.Col.*   Sr. Lectr.

Other Staff: 5 Lectrs.

English

Tel: (011) 290 3740 Fax: (011) 291 1913

Gunasekera, M., BA *S.Lanka*, MA *Mich.*, PhD *Mich.*   Sr. Lectr.

Hewabowala, E. M. J., BA *S.Lanka*, MPhil *Manc.*   Sr. Lectr.; Head*

Wickramasinghe, M. K., BA *S.Lanka*, MA *Lond.*   Sr. Lectr.

Other Staff: 2 Lectrs.

English Language Teaching Unit (ELTU)

Tel: (011) 481 1746 Fax: (011) 291 1913

Rassool, A. R., BA *S.Lanka*, MA *Col.*   Sr. Lectr.

Senaratne, D., BA *Kelaniya*, MA *Kelaniya*, MPhil *Kelaniya*

Other Staff: 4 Lectrs.

Fine Arts

Tel: (011) 290 8785 Fax: (011) 291 1913

Kumarasinghe, K., BA *S.Lanka*, PhD *Kelaniya*   Sr. Lectr.; Acting Head*

Drama and Theatre and Image Arts Unit

Rathnayake, P., BA *Kelaniya*, MA *Sri Jay.*   Sr. Lectr.

Rathnayake, R. M. P. F., BA *Kelaniya*, MA *Nihon*, PhD *Nihon*   Sr. Lectr.; Head*

Other Staff: 1 Lectr.

Performance Arts and Visual Arts Unit

De Silva, T. L. D., BA *Kelaniya*, MSc *Moratuwa*   Sr. Lectr.

Jayatunga, M., BA *Ceyl.*, MA *Kelaniya*   Sr. Lectr.

Nandadeva, B. D., BA *Ceyl.*, MSc *Moratuwa*, PhD *Delaware*   Sr. Lectr.

Narangoda, P., BA *Kelaniya*, MPhil *Kelaniya*   Sr. Lectr.

Other Staff: 2 Lectrs.

Forensic Medicine and Medical Law

Tel: (011) 295 6153 Fax: (011) 295 6153

Edirisinghe, D. A. S., MB BS *N.C'bo.Med.Coll.*, MD *Colombo*   Sr. Lectr.

Perera, B. P. P.   Head*

Other Staff: 2 Lectrs.

Research: child abuse; forensic anthropology

Geography

Tel: (011) 291 4489 Fax: (011) 291 3857
    E-mail: deptofgeography@yahoo.com

Amarasinghe, A. G., BA *Peradeniya*, MPhil *Peradeniya*   Sr. Lectr.

Chandrasena, U. A., BA *Vidyal.*, MSc *Asian I.T.*, *Bangkok*   Sr. Lectr.

Dangalle, N. K., BA *Ceyl.*, MA *Flin.*, PhD *Peradeniya*   Sr. Prof.

Guruge, K. G., BA *Vidyal.*, MA *Kelaniya*, PhD *Kelaniya*   Sr. Lectr.

Harasgama, H. D. A. G., BA *Vidyod.*, MA *Sri Jay.*   Sr. Lectr.

Jayakody, S. K., BA *Ceyl.*, MA *Kelaniya*   Sr. Lectr.

Ratnayake, Ranitha L., BA *Vidyod.*, MA *Kelaniya*, PhD *Nott.*   Sr. Lectr.

Other Staff: 2 Probationary Lectrs.

Hindi

Tel: (011) 481 6510 Fax: (011) 291 1913

Dassanayake, V. I., BA *Lucknow*, MA *Lucknow*, PhD *Lucknow*   Sr. Lectr.

Hewavithanagamage, U. R., BA *Kelaniya*, MPhil *Kelaniya*, PhD *J.Nehru U.*   Sr. Lectr.; Head*

Senevirathna, L., BA *Kelaniya*, MPhil *Kelaniya*   Sr. Lectr.

Other Staff: 1 Lectr.

Research: ancient and modern Hindi literature; Hindi folk drama and folklore; Hindi grammar and lexicography; North Indian culture

History

Tel: (011) 291 4491 Fax: (011) 291 1915

Abayarathne, A. H. M. H., BA *Kelaniya*, PhD *Kelaniya*   Sr. Lectr.

Karunananda, Ukku B., BA *Vidyal.*, PhD *Vidyal.*   Prof.; Head*

Kulasekera, K. M. P., BA *Vidyal.*, PhD *Lond.*   Sr. Lectr.

Sudarmawathi, J. M., BA *Kelaniya*, MSc *Kelaniya*   Sr. Lectr.

Other Staff: 4 Lectrs.

Human Resource Management

Tel: (011) 291 4483 Fax: (011) 291 1483
    E-mail: hrm@kln.ac.lk

Dammika, K. A. S., BBMgt *Kelaniya*, MCom *Kelaniya*   Head*

Dissanayake, D. R., BSc(BusAdm) *Vidyod.*, MCom *Colombo*   Sr. Lectr.

Ganga, P. N., BSc *Sri Jay.*, MSc *Colombo*   Sr. Lectr.

Peiris, M. D. P., BSc *Colombo*, MPhil *Kelaniya*   Sr. Lectr.

Senaratne, P. C., MBA *Sri Jay.*

Sunil, S. A. T. H., BSc(BusAdm) *Vidyod.*, MCom *Kelaniya*   Sr. Lectr.

Welmilla, I., BCom *Sri Jay.*, MCom *Kelaniya*   Sr. Lectr.

Wijesekara, M. P. A. D., BA *Kelaniya*, MBA *Sri Jay.*   Sr. Lectr.

Other Staff: 7 Lectrs.

Industrial Management

Tel: (011) 291 4482 Fax: (011) 291 4482

Abeysinghe, Dhammika P., BSc *Kelaniya*, MBA *Asian I.T.*, *Bangkok*, PhD *Asian I.T.*, *Bangkok*   Sr. Lectr.

Munasinghe, Lalithasewa, BSc(Eng) *Moratuwa*, MSc *Strath.*   Assoc. Prof.; Head*

Nanayakkara, L. D. J. F., BSc(Eng) *S.Lanka*, PhD *Strath.*   Sr. Lectr.

Peter, P. L. S., BSc *Kelaniya*, MSM *Georgia I.T.*   Sr. Lectr.

Pushpakumara, R. L. C. S., BSc *Kelaniya*, PhD *Sheff.Hallam*   Sr. Lectr.

Sunandaraja, Degamboda A. C., BSc(Eng) *Moratuwa*, MEng *Asian I.T.*, *Bangkok*   Assoc. Prof.

Wickramarachchi, A. P. R., BSc *Kelaniya*, MPhil *Camb.*, PhD *Sheff.Hallam*   Sr. Lectr.

Wijayanayake, A. N., BSc *Kelaniya*, MEng *Tokyo I.T.*, DEng *Tokyo I.T.*   Sr. Lectr.

Wijayanayake, W. M. J. I., BSc *Kelaniya*, MEng *Tokyo I.T.*, PhD *Tokyo I.T.*   Sr. Lectr.

Wijayarathna, P. G., BSc *Kelaniya*, DEng   Sr. Lectr.

Other Staff: 5 Probationary Lectrs.

Library and Information Science

Tel: (011) 291 7712 Fax: (011) 291 1915
E-mail: libsci@hotmail.com
Gunathilka, H. M. T. B., BA Kelaniya, MSSc
Kelaniya Sr. Lectr.
Ranasinghe, P., BA S.Lanka, MLib NSW Sr.
Lectr.; Head*
Weerasinghe, W. K. M. M. K., BA Kelaniya,
MLibSc Panjab Sr. Lectr.
Weerasooriya, W. A., BA Kelaniya, MLib Panjab
Sr. Lectr.
Other Staff: 2 Probationary Lectrs.
Research: bibliography; cataloguing;
classification; library administration; user
surveys

Linguistics

Tel: (011) 290 8786 Fax: (011) 291 1913
Disanayake, P., BA Kelaniya, MPhil Kelaniya, PhD
Hitotsubashi Sr. Lectr.
Premaratne, A. C., BA S.Lanka, PhD Lond. Sr.
Lectr.
Rajapaksha, R. M. W., BA S.Lanka, MA Kelaniya,
MA N.Y., PhD Lond.
Wickramasinghe, D. M., BA Ceyl., MA Ceyl.,
PhD Exe. Prof.
Wijeratne, W. M., BA S.Lanka, MA Kelaniya, PhD
Edin. Assoc. Prof.
Wijesekara, G. J. S., BA S.Lanka, MA Delhi, PhD
Kelaniya Sr. Lectr.
Yogarajah, S. J., BA S.Lanka, BTh Rome, MPhil
Kelaniya Sr. Lectr.; Head*
Other Staff: 3 Probationary Lectrs.
Research: applied linguistics and language
acquisition; lexicography; sign language
linguistics; South Asian linguistics; syntax

Marketing Management

Jayaratne, W. A., BCom Sri Jay., MSc
Newcastle(UK)
Mendis, A. P., BCom Kelaniya, MBA Sri Jay. Sr.
Lectr.
Ubayachandra, E. G., BCom Kelaniya, MCom
Kelaniya Sr. Lectr.
Wasanthakumara, D., BCom Kelaniya, MCom
Kelaniya Sr. Lectr.
Weerasiri, R. A. S., BCom Kelaniya, MCom
Kelaniya Head*
Other Staff: 1 Lectr.; 4 Probationary Lectrs.

Mass Communication

Tel: (011) 291 7713 Fax: (011) 291 1915
Athugala, Ariyaratne, BA Kelaniya, MA Kelaniya,
PhD Kelaniya Sr. Lectr.
Gunawardane, H. P. Nihalsiri, BA Kelaniya, MA
Kelaniya Sr. Lectr.
Kulasekera, Ramani A. A. P., BA Kelaniya, MA
Kelaniya Sr. Lectr.
Piyadasa, Rohana L., BA Kelaniya, MA Kelaniya,
PhD Moscow Sr. Lectr.
Rajapaksha, Chandrasiri, BA Kelaniya, MA
Kelaniya, PhD Moscow Sr. Lectr.; Head*
Thilakaratne, M., BA Kelaniya, MA Kelaniya Sr.
Lectr.
Other Staff: 4 Probationary Lectrs.
Research: audience research; folklore and creative
communication; human rights and media;
media and communication; public opinion
and marketing

Mathematics

Tel: (011) 481 1745 Fax: (011) 291 1916
E-mail: math@kln.ac.lk
De Silva, L. N. K., BSc Ceyl., DPhil Sus. Assoc.
Prof.; Head*
Karunatilleke, N. G. A., BSc Kelaniya, MSc
Kaiserslautern Sr. Lectr.
Kulatunga, D. D. Sarath, BSc S.Lanka, MSc
Kyushu, PhD Kyushu Prof.
Mallawarachchi, D. K., BSc Kelaniya, MSc Car.
Sr. Lectr.
Mampitiya, M. A. U., BSc Kelaniya, MSc Ott.,
PhD Ott. Sr. Lectr.
Munasinghe, J., BSc Kelaniya, MSc Kaiserslautern
Sr. Lectr.
Piyadasa, R. A. D., BSc Vidyal., MSc Kyushu, PhD
Kyushu Sr. Lectr.

Senanayake, N. P. W. B. V. K., BSc Kelaniya,
MSc Kyushu, PhD Saga Sr. Lectr.
Tillekeratne, K., BSc Ceyl., MSc Lond., MSc Camb.
Sr. Prof.
Other Staff: 4 Probationary Lectrs.
Research: group theory; mathematical modelling;
mathematical statistics; quantum mechanics;
relativity and cosmology

Medicine

see also Community and Family Med.

Tel: (011) 295 3409 Fax: (011) 295 8337
de Silva, A. P., MSc Oxf., MB BS MD Sr.
Lectr.
de Silva, H. J., DPhil Oxf., MB BS MD, FRCP,
FRCPEd, Hon. FRACP Sr. Prof.
Gunathilake, S. B., MB BS MD, FRCPEd, FRCP,
Hon. FRACP Assoc. Prof.
Premaratne, R., MB BS MD Sr. Lectr.
Premawardhane, A. P., DPhil Oxf., MB BS MD
Sr. Lectr.
Thilakaratne, P. M. Y. I., MB BS MD Sr.
Lectr.; Head*
Research: cerebrovascular disease; inflammatory
bowel disease; liver disease; treatment of
portal hypertension; tropical medicine

Microbiology

Tel: (011) 291 4481 Fax: (011) 291 1916
E-mail: micro@kln.ac.lk
Abeygunawardena, G. A. S. I., BSc Kelaniya,
MPhil Kelaniya, PhD Qld.
Edirisinghe, E. A. A. D., BSc Kelaniya, MSc Sri
Jay.
Gunawardene, M. M., BSc Kelaniya, MPhil Edin.
Sr. Lectr.
Jayaratne, D. L., BSc Colombo, MSc Kelaniya, PhD
Lond. Sr. Lectr.; Head*
Kodikara, C. P., BVSc Peradeniya, PhD Copenhagen
Assoc. Prof.
Ratnayake, I. U., BSc Kelaniya, MSc Sri Jay.
Ratnayake, I. V. N., BSc Kelaniya, MSc Sing.
Widanapathirana, S., BSc Ceyl., MSc H-W, PhD
H-W Sr. Prof.
Other Staff: 3 Lectrs.
Research: agricultural microbiology;
environmental microbiology; food
microbiology; microbial technology;
molecular biology

Microbiology (Medicine)

Tel: (011) 295 8219 Fax: (011) 295 8337
de Silva, N. R., MB BS Colombo, MD Colombo,
DCH Colombo Prof.; Acting Head*
Perera, K. V. H. K. K., MB BS Peradeniya
Perera, R. R. D. P., BVSc Peradeniya, MPhil
Colombo
Sunil-Chandra, N. P., BVSc S.Lanka, MPhil
Peradeniya, PhD Camb. Prof.
Wijesooriya, M. T. W., MB BS Kelaniya
Wijesooriya, W. R.- P. L. I., MB BS Kelaniya
Other Staff: 4 Lectrs.

Modern Languages

Tel: (011) 291 4494 Fax: (011) 291 3857
Amunugama, S., LicLett Paris III, MA Paris III,
PhD Paris III Sr. Lectr.
Chandrasena Premawardhena, K. L. K. N., BA
Kelaniya, MPhil Kelaniya, PhD Siegen Sr.
Lectr.; Head*
De Zoysa, A., MA F.U.Berlin, PhD F.U.Berlin Sr.
Lectr.
Dhammadhina, Ven. Nadalagamuwe, BA MA
Gunananda, Ven. Meemure, MA Moscow
Gunasekara, N. N., BA Kelaniya, LicLett
Montpellier, MA Montpellier
Premawardhena, K. L. K. N. C., BA Kelaniya,
PhD Siegen
Ratnayake, D., BA Kelaniya, MA Kelaniya
Sirisena, H., BA Kelaniya, MA PhD
Other Staff: 5 Lectrs.
Research: Sinhala, German, French, Japanese,
Russian, Chinese (contrastive studies,
foreign language teaching, inter-cultural
communication)

Molecular Medicine Unit

Manamperi, Aresha, BSc Colombo, MSc Colombo,
PhD Colombo Sr. Lectr.
Silva Gunawardena, Nilmini Y. I., BSc Colombo,
MSc Colombo, PhD HK Sr. Lectr.
Research: dengue; filariasis; hepatitis B and C;
malaria; tuberculosis

Obstetrics and Gynaecology

Tel: (011) 295 8219 Fax: (011) 295 8337
E-mail: pswijesinghe@lycos.com
De Silva, B. A., MB BS N.C'bo.Med.Coll., MD
Colombo, FRCA Sr. Lectr.
Dissanayake, D. M. A. B., BSc Sri Jay.
Fernando, W. S., MB BS Ruhuna, MS Colombo
Herath, H. M. R. P., MB BS Colombo
Motha, M. B. C., MB BS Colombo
Padumadasa, G. S., MB BS Colombo, MD Colombo
Palihawadana, T. S., MB BS Colombo
Wijesinghe, P. S., MB BS Peradeniya, MS Colombo,
FRCOG Prof.; Head*
Other Staff: 4 Lectrs.

Paediatrics

Tel: (011) 295 8219 Fax: (011) 295 8337
De Silva, D. G. H., MB BS Ceyl., MSc Birm.,
FRCP Prof.
Fernando, Aswini D., MB BS Colombo, MD
Colombo Sr. Lectr.; Head*
Jayasinghe, C. Y., MB BS Sri Jay., DCH Colombo
Kannangara, M. P., MB BS Peradeniya, MD
Colombo
Karunasekera, K. A. W., MB BS Ruhuna, MMEd
Otago, MD Colombo
Meththananda, D. S. G., MB BS Colombo
Perera, K. P. J., MB BS Colombo, MD Colombo
Rajindrajith, E. G. D. S., MB BS Ruhuna, MD
Colombo
Other Staff: 2 Lectrs.

Pali and Buddhist Studies

see also Special Centres, etc

Tel: (011) 291 4492 Fax: (011) 291 1913
E-mail: pali_bd@hotmail.com
Dammadassi, Ven. D., BA Kelaniya, MA Kelaniya,
MSc
Dammaratana, Ven. T., BA Kelaniya, MA Ban.,
PhD Delhi
Dhammalankara, Ven. N., BA B&P SLanka, MA
B&P SLanka
Dhammananda, Ven. M., BA Kelaniya, MA
Kelaniya, MA B&P SLanka, PhD Delhi ,
Rajakeeya Pandit
Garusinghe, U., MA Otani, PhD Otani
Gnanaratana, Ven. N., BA Kelaniya, MA B&P
SLanka, PhD Delhi
Kariyawasam, T., BA Vidyod., PhD Lanc. Prof.
Mahinda, Ven. K., BA Kelaniya, MA Delhi, PhD
Delhi
Medhananda, Ven. D., BA Kelaniya, MA Kelaniya,
MA B&P SLanka, PhD Delhi Assoc. Prof.;
Head*
Nanda, Ven. K., BA Kelaniya, MA Kelaniya
Pandit, Rajakeeya
Pandita, Prancina
Pannaloka, Ven. D., BA Kelaniya, MA Kelaniya
Sumanapala, G. D., BA Vidyod., MA Kelaniya, PhD
Kelaniya , Pracina Pandita
Upali, Ven. R., BA Peradeniya, MPhil Kelaniya
Wijeratne, A., BA Vidyod., MA Northwestern, PhD
Kelaniya
Wimalagnana, Ven. N., BA Kelaniya, MA Kelaniya
Other Staff: 3 Lectrs.

Parasitology

Tel: (011) 295 8219 Fax: (011) 295 8337
Abeyewickreme, W., BSc S.Lanka, MSc Mahidol,
PhD Liv. Head*
Chandrasena, T. G. A. N., MB BS Colombo, MD
Colombo
De Silva, N. R., MB BS Colombo, MSc Lond., MD
Colombo Prof.
Hapuarachchi, H. A. C., MB BS Kelaniya
Weerasinghe, C. R., MB BS N.C'bo.Med.Coll., MD
Colombo
Other Staff: 2 Lectrs.

Pathology

Tel: (011) 295 3407 Fax: (011) 295 8337
Hewawisenthi, S. J. de S., MB BS Colombo, MD
    S.Lanka   Sr. Lectr.; Head*
Mahendra, B. A. G. G., MB BS Colombo, MD
    Colombo
Rathnayaka, S. A. G. R., MB BS Colombo, MD
    S.Lanka   Sr. Lectr.
Saparamadu, P. A. M., MB BS Colombo, MD
    S.Lanka   Sr. Lectr.
Williams, H. S. A., MB BS Colombo, MD Colombo
Other Staff: 3 Lectrs.

Pharmacology

Tel: (011) 295 8219 Fax: (011) 295 8337
Dassanayaka, A., MB BS Colombo, MD Colombo
    Sr. Lectr.
De Silva, H. A., MB BS N.C'bo.Med.Coll., DPhil
    Oxf.   Sr. Lectr.
Mettananda, K. D. C., MB BS Kelaniya
Ranasinha, C., BSc Lond., MB BS Lond.
Senaviratne, A. N., MB BS Peradeniya
Wijekoon, C. N., MB BS Colombo, MD Colombo
Other Staff: 1 Lectr.
Research: clinical trial methodology;
    epidemiology of dementia; liver cirrhosis;
    respiratory tract infection

Philosophy

Tel: (011) 290 8778 Fax: (011) 291 1915
Daharanitha, K. A. T., BA Kelaniya
Edirisinghe, Daya, BA Vidyod., MA Dongguk   Sr.
    Prof.; Head*
Gamini, K. H. A., BA Kelaniya, MA Kelaniya
Kulasena, V. G., BA Ceyl., MA Kelaniya, PhD
    Ioannina   Assoc. Prof.
Rodrigo, Pushpasiri P. D., BA Vidyod., MA
    Kelaniya, PhD Kelaniya
Seneviratne, Jayanthi H. D. J., BA Kelaniya, MA
    Kelaniya, PhD Kelaniya   Assoc. Prof.
Wimaladhamma, Ven. K., BA Vidyal., MA
    Kelaniya, PhD Ioannina
Other Staff: 1 Lectr.; 4 Probationary Lectrs.

Physics

Tel: (011) 291 4495 Fax: (011) 291 1916
    E-mail: phys@kln.ac.lk
Abeywarna, U. K., BSc Peradeniya, MSc Peradeniya,
    PhD Colombo   Sr. Lectr.
Amarasekera, C. D., BSc Ceyl., MSc Purdue, PhD
    Purdue   Assoc. Prof.
Hewageegana, P. S., BSc Kelaniya
Jayakody, J. R. P., BSc Peradeniya, MA C.U.N.Y.,
    MPhil C.U.N.Y.
Jayasuriya, K. A. K. D. D. D., BSc S.Lanka, PhD
    ANU   Assoc. Prof.
Kalingamudali, S. R. D., BSc Kelaniya, PhD Sheff.
    Sr. Lectr.; Head*
Perera, P. A. A., BSc Colombo, MA Roch., PhD
    Roch.   Sr. Lectr.
Punyasena, M. A., BSc Kelaniya, MSc Alta., PhD
    Alta.   Sr. Lectr.
Samaranayake, W. J. M., BSc Peradeniya, DEng
    Kumamoto   Sr. Lectr.
Siripala, W. P., BSc Ceyl., MSc C.U.N.Y., PhD
    C.U.N.Y.   Prof.
Sumathipala, H. H., BSc Kelaniya, PhD Peradeniya
    Sr. Lectr.
Wijesundara, L. B. D. R. P., BSc Kelaniya, MPhil
    Kelaniya, MIP S.Lanka
Other Staff: 2 Lectrs.
Research: photocatalysis; physics education; solar
    energy research with designing and
    developing new electronic circuits

Physiology

Tel: (011) 295 3410 Fax: (011) 295 8337
Amarasekara, N. D. D. M., MB BS Kelaniya
Amarasiri, W. A. D. L., MB BS Kelaniya
De Silva, D. C., MB BS
Devanarayana, N. M., MB BS Ruhuna
Dewamitta, S. R., MB BS Colombo
Selliah, S., MB BS N.C'bo.Med.Coll., MPhil Colombo
    Head*
Weerasinghe, G. A. K., MB BS Colombo, MD
    Colombo, DCH Colombo, PhD Niigata, FRCPEd
    Prof.

Psychiatry

Tel: (011) 295 8039 Fax: (011) 295 8337
Hapangama, A., MB BS Kelaniya
Kuruppuarachchi, K. A. L. A., MB BS Peradeniya,
    MD Colombo   Prof.
Lawrence, T. S., MB BS Sri Jay.
Peris, M. U. P. K., MB BS Colombo, MD Colombo
    Sr. Lectr.; Head*
Wijeratne, L. T., MB BS Colombo
Williams, S. S., MB BS Jaffna, MD Colombo
Other Staff: 1 Lectr.; 4 Probationary Lectrs.
Research: alcohol-related psychiatric problems;
    culture-bound psychiatric syndromes;
    deliberate self-harm (DSH); liaison
    psychiatry; psychiatric problems in old age

Sanskrit

Tel: (011) 481 6421 Fax: (011) 291 1913
Dhammaratana, Ven. I., BA Kelaniya, MA
    Kelaniya, PhD Pune   Sr. Lectr.
Revata, Ven. N., BA Vidyal., MA Nag.   Sr. Lectr.
Sugatharatana, Ven. K., BA Kelaniya, MA Kelaniya,
    MPhil Kelaniya, PhD Delhi   Sr. Lectr.; Head*
Wijesinghe, S. A. G., BA Vidyal., MA Kelaniya,
    PhD Kelaniya   Sr. Lectr.
Wimalanana, Ven. E., BA Kelaniya
Other Staff: 2 Lectrs.
Research: Buddhist Sanskrit; Mahayanic
    philosophy

Sinhala

Tel: (011) 291 4493 Fax: (011) 291 1913
Abeysekera, W. M. S. P., BA Kelaniya, MA
    Kelaniya   Sr. Lectr.
Balasooriya, Somaratna, BA Vidyal., PhD Paris
    Prof.
Chandrarataane, Ven. M., BA Kelaniya
Danansooriya, J., BA S.Lanka, MA Kelaniya
    Assoc. Prof.
De Silva, A. N., BA Colombo
Dela Bandara, T. R. Gamini, BA S.Lanka, MA
    Kelaniya, PhD Lond.   Assoc. Prof.; Head*
Dias, U. G. H., BA Kelaniya, MA Kelaniya, PhD
    Kelaniya
Goonawardhane, N. D., BA S.Lanka, PhD Kelaniya
    Assoc. Prof.
Ihalagama, H. A. A. S., BA Kelaniya
Kumarasinghe, K., BA S.Lanka, PhD Kelaniya   Sr.
    Prof.
Mallawaarachchi, N. K., BA Kelaniya, MA B&P
    SLanka, MPhil Kelaniya   Sr. Lectr.
Palliyaguruge, C., BA Vidyal., PhD S.Lanka   Sr.
    Prof.
Pannasara, Ven. O., BA Kelaniya, MA B&P SLanka,
    MPhil Kelaniya, PhD Pune   Sr. Lectr.
Ratnayaka, J. K. D. R., BA Kelaniya, MPhil
    Kelaniya   Sr. Lectr.
Other Staff: 3 Asst. Lectrs.
Research: ancient and modern Sinhala literature;
    folk drama and theatre; folklore and folk
    life; palaeography; sociology of literature

Sociology

Tel: (011) 291 4490 Fax: (011) 291 1915
Karunaratne, H. W., BA Peradeniya, MA Sri Jay.,
    PhD Sri Jay.   Sr. Lectr.
Karunathilake, K., BA Sri Jay., MA Sri Jay., PhD
    J.Nehru U.   Sr. Lectr.; Head*
Kumara, G. W. D. N. S., BA Sri Jay., MSSc
    Kelaniya   Sr. Lectr.
Kumari, K. M. G. C., BA Sri Jay., MSSc Kelaniya
    Sr. Lectr.
Subashini, T. M. D., BA Sri Jay., MA Sri Jay.
    Sr. Lectr.
Subasinghe, A. V. K. W., BA Kelaniya, MSSc
    Kelaniya
Ubesekara, D. M., BA Kelaniya, MSSc Kelaniya
Vitharana, L. D. S., BA Kelaniya, MSSc Kelaniya
Other Staff: 2 Probationary Lectrs.

Statistics and Computer Science

Tel: (011) 290 8780 Fax: (011) 291 1916
    E-mail: dscs@kln.ac.lk
De Silva, C. H., BSc Houston, MPhil H-W   Sr.
    Lectr.; Head*
Dias, N. G. J., BSc Colombo, MSc Belf., PhD Wales
    Sr. Lectr.

Hewapathirana, T. K., BSc S.Lanka, MSc Bath
    Sr. Lectr.
Jayasundara, D. D. M., BSc Kelaniya, MSc
    Kaiserslautern, PhD Kaiserslautern   Sr. Lectr.
Perera, D. I., BSc Kelaniya, MSc Tokyo I.T.   Sr.
    Lectr.
Suriyaarachchi, D. J. C., BSc Ceyl., MSc Manc.
    Sr. Lectr.
Weerasinghe, K. G. H. D., BSc Kelaniya
Wickremesinghe, R. I. P., BSc Kelaniya, MSc
    Moratuwa
Wijegunasekara, M. C., BSc Kelaniya, MSc Wales,
    PhD Wales   Sr. Lectr.
Other Staff: 2 Lectrs.
Research: database systems; e-learning; stochastic
    processes; time series analysis

Surgery

Tel: (011) 295 8039 Fax: (011) 295 8337
Ariyarathna, M. H. J., MB BS Colombo, MS
    Colombo, FRCS, FRCSEd   Sr. Lectr.
De Zylva, T. S. U., MB BS NSW, MS Colombo,
    FRCSEd
Deen, K. I., MB BS Peradeniya, MS, FRCS,
    FRCSEd   Assoc. Prof.
Fernando, F. R., MB BS Colombo, MS Colombo,
    FRCSEd   Sr. Lectr.; Head*
Kumarage, S. K., MB BS Colombo, MS Colombo,
    FRSEd
Liyanage, C. A. H., MB BS Colombo
Perera, D. M., MB BS MD, FRCA   Sr. Lectr.
Wijesuriya, S. R. E., MB BS Colombo, MS Colombo

Western Classical and Christian Culture

Tel: (011) 481 6410 Fax: (011) 291 1913
Abeysinghe, Nihal, LLB Open S.Lanka, MA
    Kelaniya, LTh Ans., ThD Ans.   Sr. Lectr.
Gamlath, I., BA Kelaniya, MA Kelaniya   Sr. Lectr.
Jayasekera, I. Kamani, BA Kelaniya, MA Kelaniya
    Sr. Lectr.; Head*
Liyanage, Pulsara N., BA Kelaniya, MA Peradeniya
    Sr. Lectr.
Lowe, N. N. E., BA Kelaniya, MA Sri Jay.   Sr.
    Lectr.
Sumangala, Ven. T., BA Kelaniya, MA Peradeniya
    Sr. Lectr.
Wijesinghe, S. L., BA Rome, PhD Rome   Sr.
    Lectr.

Zoology

Tel: (011) 291 4479 Fax: (011) 291 1916
    E-mail: headzoo@kln.ac.lk
Amarasinghe, L. D., BSc Kelaniya, PhD Lond.   Sr.
    Lectr.
Amarasinghe, U. S., BSc Kelaniya, MSc Wales,
    PhD Ruhuna   Assoc. Prof.
Chandrasekera, W. U., BSc Kelaniya, PhD
    Newcastle(UK)   Sr. Lectr.
Dias, R. K. S., BSc Kelaniya, MSc Asian I.T.,
    Bangkok, PhD Wales   Sr. Lectr.
Epa, U. P. K., BSc Kelaniya, PhD Deakin   Sr.
    Lectr.
Fernando, I. V. S., BSc Ceyl., MSc Lond., PhD
    Manc.   Sr. Lectr.
Ganehiarachchi, G. A. S. M., BSc Kelaniya, MPhil
    Kelaniya   Sr. Lectr.
Hettiarachchi, M., BSc Kelaniya, PhD Nigeria   Sr.
    Lectr.; Head*
Pathiratne, A., BSc Kelaniya, PhD N.Dakota State
    Prof.
Ranawaka, K., BSc Kelaniya
Weerawardhena, S. R., BSc Peradeniya, MPhil
    Kelaniya   Sr. Lectr.
Wijeratne, W. M. D. N., BSc Kelaniya
Wijeyaratne, M. Jayantha S., BSc S.Lanka, MSc
    Mich., PhD Kelaniya, FNAS(SL),
    FIBiol(SLanka)   Sr. Prof.
Research: aquaculture and fish health
    management; aquatic ecology; eco-
    toxicology; fisheries management;
    taxonomy of ants and agricultural pest
    management

SPECIAL CENTRES, ETC

Archaeology, Postgraduate Institute of

Tel: (011) 269 4151 Fax: (011) 269 4151
E-mail: pgiar@pgiar.lanka.net
Adikari, A. M. G., BA Kelaniya, MPhil Kelaniya
Sr. Lectr.
De Silva, T. K. N. P., BSc MSc(Arch) Dir.*
Premathilke, T. R., BSc Sri Jay., MPhil Sri Jay.,
PhD Stockholm Sr. Lectr.
Solangaarachchi, Rose, MPhil Kelaniya Sr.
Lectr.
Somadeva, D. W. R. K., BA Kelaniya, MPhil
Kelaniya, PhD Uppsala Sr. Lectr.
Weerasinghe, J., BFA Kelaniya, MFA
American(D.C.) Sr. Lectr.

Gampaha Wickramarachchi Ayurveda Institute

Tel: (033) 222 2748 Fax: (033) 222 2739
E-mail: ayurgmo@sltnet.lk
Amarasekara, A. A. D., BA Kelaniya, MA Kelaniya
Dir.*
Dhammissara, Ven. M., BA Sri Jay., MA Kelaniya,
MPhil Sri Jay., PhD Jain VB Sr. Lectr.
Peris, K. P. P., MS(Ay) Ban., BAMS Sr. Lectr.
Tissera, M. H. A., MD(Ay) Ban. Assoc. Prof.
Other Staff: 2 Sr. Lectrs.; 21 Lectrs.; 1 Sr. Asst.
Librarian; 1 Asst. Librarian; 2 Temp. Asst.
Lectrs.

Pali and Buddhist Studies, Postgraduate Institute of

Tel: (011) 236 8894 Fax: (011) 533 5369
E-mail: tasanga@sltnet.lk
Tilakaratne, A., BA Peradeniya, MA Hawaii, PhD
Hawaii Prof.; Dir.*
Other Staff: 11 Visiting Lectrs.

Vacant Posts: 2 Profs.

Buddhist Philosophy

Tel: (011) 250 1079 Fax: (011) 533 5369
E-mail: tasanga@sltnet.lk
Tilakaratne, A., BA Peradeniya, MA Hawaii, PhD
Hawaii Prof.; Head*

Pali Studies

Tel: (011) 236 8894 Fax: (011) 533 5369
E-mail: toshiich_endo@hotmail.com
Toshiichi, E., BA Kelaniya, MA Kelaniya, PhD
Kelaniya

CONTACT OFFICERS

Academic affairs. Deputy Registrar/Academic
Establishment: Ranasinghe, A. P., BSc
Admissions (first degree). Senior Assistant
Registrar: Kalansooriya, J., BCom Kelaniya,
MA Colombo
Admissions (higher degree). Dean, Faculty of
Graduate Studies: Dangalle, Prof. N. K., BA
Ceyl., MA Flin., PhD Peradeniya
(E-mail: dangalle1946@yahoo.co.uk)
Computing services. Head, Computer Centre:
Dias, N. G. J., BSc Colombo, MSc Belf., PhD
Wales
Estates and buildings/works and services.
Works Engineer: Gunarathna, K. A. P.
Examinations. Senior Assistant Registrar
(Centre for Open and Distance Learning):
Dharmathilake, K. K. K., BA Colombo, MSSc
Kelaniya
Examinations. Deputy Registrar
(Examinations): Gunaratne, K., BLE Colombo
Examinations. Senior Assistant Registrar
(Centre for Open and Distance Learning):
Kalansooriya, J., BCom Kelaniya, MA Colombo
(E-mail: kala@kln.ac.lk)

Finance. Acting Bursar: Wanigasekera, A. W.
T. S., BSc
General enquiries. Registrar: Karunaratne, W.
M., BSc Sri Jay., MSSc Kelaniya
Health services. Chief Medical Officer:
Jayatissa, J. A. J., MB BS Ceyl., DCH Colombo,
MD Colombo, MSc
Library (chief librarian). Librarian: Jayatissa,
L. A., BSc Vidyal., MLISc Delhi
(E-mail: library@kln.ac.lk)
Publications. Assistant Registrar: Rajeswaran,
R., BA Peradeniya
(E-mail: rajeshwaran1954@yahoo.com)
Purchasing. Deputy Bursar: Wanigasekera, A.
W. T. S., BSc
Research. Assistant Registrar: Rajeswaran, R.,
BA Peradeniya
(E-mail: rajeshwaran1954@yahoo.com)
Sport and recreation. Acting Director: Nihal
Kumara, W. G.
(E-mail: nihalkumara01@yahoo.com)
Student welfare/counselling. Senior Assistant
Registrar (Welfare): Ambegoda, A. C. M. S.
D., BCom Sri Jay.
Student welfare/counselling. Chief Student's
Counsellor: Dodamkumbure Dammadassi
Thero, Rev., BA Kelaniya, MA Kelaniya, MS
Kelaniya
Student welfare/counselling. Deputy
Registrar (Welfare): Gunaratne, K., BLE
Colombo
Student welfare/counselling. Head, Medical
Faculty Counselling Centre: Salgado, L. S.,
MB BS Ceyl., MA Kelaniya, MS Kelaniya
(E-mail: sujee@mfac.kln.ac.lk)

[Information supplied by the institution as at 13 August
2007, and edited by the ACU]

GENERAL SIR JOHN KOTELAWALA DEFENCE UNIVERSITY

Founded 1981

Member of the Association of Commonwealth Universities

Postal Address: Kandawala Estate, Ratmalana, Sri Lanka
Telephone: (011) 263 5268 **Fax:** (011) 260 5160 **E-mail:** kdudefence@sltnet.lk
URL: http://www.kdu.lk

COMMANDANT (VICE-CHANCELLOR)*—Balasuriya, Major General S. R., MSc
ACTING DIRECTOR OF ACADEMIC STUDIES (ACADEMIC AFFAIRS)—Amaradasa, W. M., BA
Sri Jay., LLB Colombo, MA Colombo
REGISTRAR (ADMINISTRATION)‡—Jayasuriya, D. G., BCom Ceyl., MPA Sri Jay., MEd
Manc.
BURSAR (DIRECTOR OF FINANCE)—Galhena, A. P., BSc Sri Jay.
ACTING LIBRARIAN—Ranawella, T. C., BSc Kelaniya, MLS Colombo

GENERAL INFORMATION

History. General Sir John Kotelawala Defence
Academy was founded in 1981 and achieved
university status in 1988. In 2008, it was
renamed General Sir John Kotelawala Defence
University.
It is located in Ratmalana, 15km south of
Colombo City.

Admission to first degree courses (see also Sri
Lankan Introduction). Applicants must have
been pronounced eligible to apply for
university admission by the Commissioner
General of Examinations and have fulfilled the
following requirements: those who offered 3
subjects at GCE A level should have obtained at
least S grades in all three subjects and passed
the common general paper, and have a
minimum of credit pass in English at GCE O
level.

Applicants must be Sri Lankan and aged
between 18 and 22. Physical standards also
apply.

First Degrees (see also Sri Lankan Directory
to Subjects of Study). BA, BCom, BSc(Eng),
BSc(MTS).
Length of course. Full-time: BA, BCom,
BSc(MTS): 3 years; BSc(Eng): 3½ years.

Higher Degrees (see also Sri Lankan
Directory to Subjects of Study).
Master's. MSc.
Length of course. Part-time: MSc: 2 years.

Libraries. Volumes: 18,500. Periodicals
subscribed to: 15. Other holdings: 495 videos;
100 CDs; 592 maps. Special collections: Sri
Lanka collections.

Academic Awards (2007–2008). 17
awards.

Statistics. Staff (2007–2008): 210 (17
academic, 193 non-academic). Students
(2006–2007): full-time 261 (244 men, 17
women); international 5 (5 men); distance
education/external 75 (75 men);
undergraduate 261 (244 men, 17 women).

ACADEMIC UNITS
Cadet Training Wing

Tel: (011) 262 2503
Thilakaratne, Lt-Col. A. L. P. S. Commanding
Officer; Head*
Other Staff: 20 Military Officers

Engineering, Aeronautical

Tel: (011) 263 2028
Pandithasekera, V. N., BSc Kotelawala DA Wing
Commdr.
Other Staff: 24 Visiting Lectrs.

Engineering, Civil

Tel: (011) 263 2028

Fernando, W. C. D. K., BSc Moratuwa   Lectr.;
    Probationary Head* (on leave)
Senerath, D. C. H., BSc Ceyl., MEng Sheff., MSc
    Colombo, PhD Birm., FIE(SL)   Prof.†
Thilakasiri, H. S., BSc Moratuwa, MSc Lond., PhD
    S.Florida   Co-ordinator
Other Staff: 7 Visiting Sr. Lectrs.; 3 Visiting
    Temp. Lectrs.

Engineering, Electrical

Tel: (011) 263 2028

Kuruparan, S. N., BSc Moratuwa, MBA Moratuwa
    Commdr.; Head*
Lucas, J. R., BSc Ceyl., MSc Manc., PhD Manc.,
    FIE(SL), FIEE   Prof.
Perera, H. Y. R., BSc Moratuwa, PhD T.H.Aachen
    Prof.†; Co-ordinator
Other Staff: 2 Visiting Sr. Lectrs.; 6 Visiting
    Temp. Lectrs.

Engineering, Electronic

Tel: (011) 263 2028

Kuruparan, S. N., BSc Moratuwa, MBA Moratuwa
    Commdr.; Head*
Samarasiri, B. S., BSc Moratuwa   Co-ordinator
Other Staff: 1 Visiting Sr. Lectr.; 4 Visiting
    Temp. Lectrs.

Engineering, Mechanical and Marine

Tel: (011) 263 2028

Sirisena, E. J. K. P., BSc Moratuwa, MSc S'ton.,
    MIE PNG   Sr. Lectr.
Thilakasiri, A. M. J., BSc Moratuwa, MSc
    Kotelawala DA   Capt.; Head*

Wimalasiri, W. K., BSc Moratuwa, MSc
    Newcastle(UK), PhD Newcastle(UK)   Co-
    ordinator
Other Staff: 5 Visiting Sr. Lectrs.; 11 Visiting
    Temp. Lectrs.

Humanities

Tel: (011) 263 2028

Amaradasa, W. M., BA Sri Jay., LLB Colombo, MA
    Colombo   Sr. Lectr.; Head*
Other Staff: 1 Visiting Sr. Lectr.; 1 Lectr.
    (Probationary)

Languages

Tel: (011) 263 2028

Amaratunga, W. A. A. K., BA Peradeniya, MA
    Kelaniya   Lectr. (Probationary); Head*
Jayawardena, R. P. T., BA Ceyl., PhD Lond.
    Prof.
Other Staff: 1 Visiting Sr. Lectr.; 3 Instrs.; 1
    Visiting Instructor

Mathematics, Science and Computer Science

Tel: (011) 263 2028

Chandrasiri, L. H. G. S., BSc Tees., MSc Cape
    Town   Sr. Lectr.
Jayasena, V. S. D., BSc Moratuwa, MSc Ill., PhD
    Ill.   Co-ordinator
Karunathilake, T. H. N. M., BSc Peradeniya,
    MPhil Peradeniya   Sr. Lectr.
Rohana, D. A., BSc Colombo, MSc Pune   Sr.
    Lectr.; Head*
Other Staff: 3 Visiting Sr. Lectrs.; 1 Asst. Lectr.;
    1 Instr.

Social Science

Tel: (011) 263 2028

Jayawardena, M. M., BA Ceyl., MA Peradeniya
    Sr. Lectr. (on leave)
Waidyasekera, D. L., BA Sri Jay., MSc Moratuwa
    Sr. Lectr.; Head*
Wattuhewa, I. D., BCom Ruhuna, MBA Sri Jay.
    Sr. Lectr.
Other Staff: 8 Visiting Sr. Lectrs.; 4 Visiting
    Temp. Lectrs.

CONTACT OFFICERS

Academic affairs. Acting Director of Academic
    Studies: Amaradasa, W. M., BA Sri Jay., LLB
    Colombo, MA Colombo
    (E-mail: aweesinghe@hotmail.com)
Examinations. Senior Assistant Registrar
    (Academic): Silva, G. N. R., BSc Sri Jay.,
    MSc Sri Jay.
General enquiries. Registrar: Jayasuriya, D. G.,
    BCom Ceyl., MPA Sri Jay., MEd Manc.
    (E-mail: kda_registrar@yahoo.com)
Library (enquiries). Senior Assistant Librarian:
    Ranawella, T. C., BSc Kelaniya, MLS Colombo
    (E-mail: thanuja_ranawella@yahoo.com)
Personnel/human resources. Acting Senior
    Assistant Registrar (Establishment): Silva, G.
    N. R., BSc Sri Jay., MSc Sri Jay.
    (E-mail: kda_registrar@yahoo.com)
Security. Adjutant (Security): Herath, I. H. M.
    N. N., MSc Kelaniya
    (E-mail: nishantha_herath22@yahoo.com.au)
Students from other countries. Registrar:
    Jayasuriya, D. G., BCom Ceyl., MPA Sri Jay.,
    MEd Manc.
    (E-mail: kds_registrar@yahoo.com)

[Information supplied by the institution as at 18 March
2008, and edited by the ACU]

UNIVERSITY OF MORATUWA, SRI LANKA

Founded 1978

Member of the Association of Commonwealth Universities

Postal Address: Katubedda, Moratuwa, Sri Lanka
Telephone: (011) 265 0301 **Fax:** (011) 265 0622
URL: http://www.mrt.ac.lk

VICE-CHANCELLOR*—Ranasinghe, Prof. Malik, BSc(Eng) Moratuwa, MASc Br.Col., PhD
    Br.Col., FNAS(SL), FIE(SL)
REGISTRAR‡—De Silva, G. H. D. C., BA Ceyl.
BURSAR—Wijesekera, C., BA Ceyl.
LIBRARIAN—Kodikara, R. C., BA Kelaniya, MLS Br.Col.

OPEN UNIVERSITY OF SRI LANKA

Founded 1980

Member of the Association of Commonwealth Universities

Postal Address: PO Box 21, Nawala, Nugegoda, Sri Lanka
Telephone: (01) 285 3615, 285 3777 **Fax:** (01) 243 6858 **E-mail:** postmaster@ou.ac.lk
URL: http://www.ou.ac.lk

VICE-CHANCELLOR*—de Silva, Prof. Nandani, MB BS Ceyl., MD Colombo, DCH Colombo
REGISTRAR‡—Sadique, A. L. J., BSc Jaffna
LIBRARIAN—Seneviratne, R. C. W. M. R. W., BA Kelaniya, MLISc Col.
BURSAR—Premaratne, K. M., BA Sri Jay., MBA Colombo

GENERAL INFORMATION

History. The university was founded in 1980.

Admission to first degree courses (see also Sri Lankan Introduction). Either General Certificate of Education (GCE) A level with at least 3 passes; or completion of levels 1 and 2 of the university's foundation programme.

First Degrees (see also Sri Lankan Directory to Subjects of Study). BA, BAELT, BEd, BI, BMS, BNursing, BSc, BTech(Eng), LLB.
Length of course. By distance learning: BA, BSc, BTech(Eng): 3 years; BAELT, BEd, BI, BMS, BNursing, LLB: 4 years.

Higher Degrees (see also Sri Lankan Directory to Subjects of Study).
Master's. MA, MBA, MEd, MPA, MPhil, MTech.
Admission. Applicants for admission to MTech must hold a relevant first degree and have field or industrial experience. MEd: first degree with at least second class honours and merit pass in postgraduate diploma in education; MPhil: good first degree.
Length of course. By distance learning: MEd: 1½ years; MTech: 1½–2 years; MA, MBA, MPA: 2 years; MPhil: 2–5 years.
Doctoral. PhD.
Admission. PhD: applicants must hold a master's degree by research, or transfer from MPhil.
Length of course. Full-time: PhD: 3–7 years. Part-time: PhD: 5–7 years.

Language of Instruction. English for most programmes with some in Sinhala/Tamil.

Libraries. Volumes: 94,982. Periodicals subscribed to: 74. Other holdings: 231 CD-ROM; 1769 videos.

FACULTIES/SCHOOLS

Education
Tel: (01) 276 8055 Fax: (01) 276 8055
Dean: Lekamge, G. D., BEd Colombo, MPhil Colombo, PhD Open(UK)
Assistant Registrar: (vacant)

Engineering Technology
Tel: (01) 282 2737 Fax: (01) 282 2737
E-mail: deaneng@ou.ac.lk
Dean: Fonseka, H. C. M., BSc(Eng) S.Lanka, MEng Nagoya I.T., MBA Sri Jay.
Assistant Registrar: Kuruppuarachchi, N. D., BSc Open S.Lanka

Humanities and Social Sciences
Tel: (01) 282 0032 Fax: (01) 282 0032
E-mail: deanhss@ou.ac.lk
Dean: Ranasinghe, Prof. R. M. S. W., BPAdm Ceyl., MA(Admin) Sri Jay., PhD Sri Jay.
Assistant Registrar: Jayawardena, S. M. D. B., BSc Sri Jay.

Natural Sciences
Tel: (01) 282 2738 Fax: (01) 282 2738
E-mail: deannsc@ou.ac.lk
Dean: Bandarage, G., BSc Colombo, PhD Alta.
Assistant Registrar: Sanjivanee, K. C., BSc Sri Jay.

ACADEMIC UNITS

Agricultural and Plantation Engineering
Tel: (01) 282 2737 Fax: (01) 282 2737
E-mail: hdagri@ou.ac.lk
De Silva, C. S., BScAgric Peradeniya, MPhil Peradeniya, PhD Cran. Sr. Lectr.
De Silva, R. P., BSc(Eng) Moratuwa, MSc Cran., PhD Cran. Sr. Lectr.
Kulatunga, K. D. G., BSc(Eng) Ceyl., PhD Cran. Sr. Lectr.
Senanayake, S. A. M. A. N. S., BSc(Eng) Moratuwa, MSc Cran., PhD Cran. Sr. Lectr.; Head*
Other Staff: 2 Lectrs.
Research: groundwater flow models; irrigation and management; salinity development due to groundwater use; soil analysis and land use patterns; use of groundwater in hard rock aquifer in Sri Lanka

Botany
Fax: (01) 282 2738
Coomaraswamy, Umarany, BSc Ceyl., PhD Lond., FNAS(SL), FIBiol(SLanka) Sr. Prof.
Daulagala, P. W. H. K. P., BSc Peradeniya, PhD Sr. Lectr.
Jayakody, L. K. R. R., BSc Colombo, PhD Lanc. Sr. Lectr.; Head*
Karunaratne, V. C., BSc Sri Jay., MPhil Open S.Lanka Sr. Lectr.
Pathirana, P. S. K., BSc Colombo, MPhil Open S.Lanka Sr. Lectr.
Samaranayake, A. C. I., BSc Ceyl., PhD Lond. Sr. Lectr.
Senaratne, L. K., BSc Colombo, MPhil Open S.Lanka Sr. Lectr.
Weerakoon, S. R., BSc Colombo, PhD W.Aust. Sr. Lectr.
Weerasinghe, T. K., BSc Kelaniya, PhD Kelaniya Sr. Lectr.
Wickramasinghe, B. K. L., BSc Kelaniya, MPhil Open S.Lanka Sr. Lectr.
Other Staff: 5 Lectrs.
Research: distance education technology; plant breeding; plant ecology; plant taxonomy; soil biology

Chemistry
Fax: (01) 282 2738
Bandarage, G., BSc Colombo, PhD Alta. Sr. Lectr.
Fernando, J. N. O., BSc Ceyl., PhD Lond., FRSChem, FRACI Sr. Prof.
Gunaherath, G. M. K. B., BSc Peradeniya, PhD Peradeniya Prof.
Gunatilleke, M. D. A. D., BSc Sri Jay., PhD Wayne State Sr. Lectr.
Haniffa, M. R. M., BSc Colombo, MSc Hawaii Sr. Lectr.
Hettiarachchi, S. R., BSc Ruhuna, PhD Maine(USA) Sr. Lectr.

Iqbal, S. S., BSc Colombo, PhD Birm. Sr. Lectr.; Head*
Mudalige, A. P., BSc Peradeniya, MPhil Peradeniya, PhD Peradeniya
Perera, K. S. D., BSc Sri Jay., PhD Belf. Prof.
Tantrigoda, R. U., BSc Sri Jay., MPhil Ruhuna Sr. Lectr.
Other Staff: 6 Lectrs.
Research: inorganic, organic and organometallic chemistry; ion-atom collisions; natural products chemistry; synthetic chemistry; water analysis

Early Childhood and Primary Education
Tel: (01) 276 8055 Fax: (01) 276 8055
Talagala, I. M. M., BA Ceyl., MPhil Colombo, PhD Open S.Lanka Sr. Lectr.; Head*
Other Staff: 2 Lectrs.
Research: child development; child psychology; child rights; children in disadvantaged communities

Education, Secondary and Tertiary
Tel: (01) 276 8055 Fax: (01) 276 8055
De Zoysa, T. S. V., BA Ceyl., MPhil Colombo, PhD Open S.Lanka Sr. Lectr.
Ismail, A. G. H., BEd Ceyl., MEd Colombo, PhD Colombo Sr. Lectr.
Jaufer, P. C. P., BSc Jaffna, MPhil Open S.Lanka, PhD S.Fraser Sr. Lectr.
Karunanayake, S. P., BSc Open S.Lanka, MPhil Open S.Lanka, EdD ANU, PhD W'gong. Sr. Lectr.; Head*
Kasthuriarachchi, C., BSc(BusAdmin) Sri Jay., MEd Colombo Sr. Lectr.
Lekamge, G. D., BEd Colombo, MPhil Colombo, PhD Open(UK) Sr. Lectr.
Rajendram, T., BA Ceyl., MEd Colombo, MPhil Jaffna Sr. Lectr.
Other Staff: 13 Lectrs.
Research: child psychology; distance education; gender issues; special education; teacher education

Education, Special Needs
Tel: (01) 276 8055 Fax: (01) 276 8055
Oliver, K. A. D. C., BEd Ceyl., MA Lond., MPhil Open S.Lanka Sr. Lectr.; Acting Head*
Other Staff: 2 Lectrs.
Research: children with special needs

Educational Technology
Tel: (01) 285 3975 Fax: (01) 285 3975
Jayathilake, B. G., BSc Col., MA Lond., PhD Open(UK) Sr. Lectr.
Other Staff: 4 Lectrs.

Engineering, Civil
Fax: (01) 282 2737
Abeysuriya, A. G. K. De S., BSc(Eng) Ceyl., MSc Leeds, PhD Leeds Sr. Lectr.
Aluwihare, P. S. D., BSc(Eng) Peradeniya, MSc Saitama, PhD Saitama Sr. Lectr.
Dolage, D. A. R., BSc(Eng) Moratuwa, MSc Reading, MBA Sri Jay., MA Colombo, FIE(SL) Sr. Lectr.
Liyanagama, J., MSc(Eng) Moscow, PhD Moscow Sr. Lectr.

Liyanage, B. C., BSc(Eng) Moratuwa, PhD Osaka
Sr. Lectr.
Pallewatta, T. M., BSc(Eng) Moratuwa, MEng
Asian I.T., Bangkok, PhD Tokyo, DrEng Tokyo
Sr. Lectr.
Ratnaweera, H. G. P. A., BSc Ceyl., MSc(Mgt)
Lond., DPhil Oxf., FIE(SL)   Sr. Lectr.
Sivaprakasapillai, S., BScEng Ceyl., MSc(Mgt)
Lond., DPhil Oxf., FIE(SL)   Sr. Lectr.
Tantirimudalige, M. N., BSc(Eng) S.Lanka,
MTech Open S.Lanka   Sr. Lectr.; Head*
Udamulla, L. A., BScEng Peradeniya, MPhil HK
Weerasekera, K. S., BSc(Eng) Moratuwa, MEngSc
NSW, PhD NSW   Sr. Lectr.
Wickramayake, P. N., BSc Peradeniya, MSc M.I.T.,
PhD M.I.T.   Sr. Lectr.
Other Staff: 1 Lectr.

Engineering, Electrical/Electronics and Communications/Computer

Fax: (01) 282 2737
de Silva, N. S., MSc Moscow, MPhil Open S.Lanka
Sr. Lectr.
Fonseka, H. C. M., BSc(Eng) S.Lanka, MEng
Nagoya I.T., MBA Sri Jay.   Sr. Lectr.
Perera, C. J. S. A. H., BSc(Eng) Moratuwa, MSc
Munich   Sr. Lectr.; Head*
Ratnayake, K. G. H. U. W., BSc(Eng) Moratuwa,
PhD   Sr. Lectr.
Samaliarachchi, L. A., BSc(Eng) Moratuwa, MEng
Asian I.T., Bangkok   Sr. Lectr.
Sriyananda, H., BSc(Eng) Ceyl., MSc Salf., PhD
Wales   Sr. Prof.
Udayakumar, K. A. C., MSc(Eng) Moratuwa, PhD
Moratuwa   Sr. Lectr.
Udugama, L. S. K., MSc Donetsk T.U., PhD
Donetsk T.U.   Sr. Lectr.
Wickramasinghe, S. N., BScEngin Peradeniya,
MSc Lond.   Sr. Lectr.
Other Staff: 6 Lectrs.

Engineering, Mechanical

Fax: (01) 282 2737 E-mail: hdmech@ou.ac.lk
Arthenayake, N. R., MSc(Eng) Moscow,
MSc(Eng) Strath., FIE(SL), FIE(India)   Sr.
Prof.
De Mel, W. R., BSc Moratuwa, MSc Peradeniya,
MEng NU Singapore   Sr. Lectr.
Dedigamuwa, P. R., BSc(Eng) Moratuwa, MPhil
Open S.Lanka   Sr. Lectr.
Goonetilleke, H. D., BSc(Eng) Ceyl., MASc
Br.Col., PhD Br.Col.   Sr. Lectr.
Jatunarachchi, T. S. S., BSc(Eng) S.Lanka, MPhil
Open S.Lanka   Sr. Lectr.
Liyanage, K. N. H. P., BSc Kelaniya, PhD
Sheff.Hallam   Sr. Lectr.
Medagedara, T. M. D. N., BSc(Eng) Peradeniya,
MPhil Sheff.Hallam   Sr. Lectr.
Sarath Chandra, P. D., BSc(Eng) S.Lanka,
MScEng Moratuwa   Sr. Lectr.; Head*
Wijesundara, W. R. G. A., BSc(Eng) S.Lanka,
MPhil Open S.Lanka   Sr. Lectr.
Other Staff: 5 Lectrs.

Health Sciences

Tel: (01) 282 3921 Fax: (01) 282 3921
Vithanarachchi, S. L. H., BSc Open S.Lanka, MSc
Br.Col.   Sr. Lectr.; Head*
Other Staff: 2 Lectrs.
Research: factors affecting nursing productivity;
impact of spousal emotion; learning
methods experienced and described by
registered nurses; nursing students'
understanding of culture

Language Studies

Fax: (01) 282 0032 E-mail: hglang@ou.ac.lk
Abeysooriya, B. K. P., BA Kelaniya, MA Colombo
Sr. Lectr.; Head*
Devendra, D. E., BA Syd., MA Colombo   Sr.
Lectr.
Madawttegedara, V., BA Kelaniya, MA Ulster   Sr.
Lectr.
Raheem, R., BA Peradeniya, PhD Leeds   Prof.
Ratwatte, H. V. M., BA Peradeniya, MSc Edin.,
PhD Edin.   Sr. Lectr.
Other Staff: 6 Lectrs.

Legal Studies

Fax: (01) 282 0032
Gooneratne, W. D. R. D., LLB Colombo, LLM
Monash   Sr. Lectr.; Attorney-at-Law
Guneratne, C. E., LLB Colombo, LLM Harv.   Sr.
Lectr.; Attorney-at-Law
Hemaratne, T. S. K., LLB Colombo, LLM B'lore.,
PhD Lond.   Sr. Lectr.; Attorney-at-Law
Perera, L. A. A., LLB Colombo, MPhil Lond.   Sr.
Lectr.; Attorney-at-Law
Rajapakshe, N. G. T., LLB Ceyl., LLM Syd.   Sr.
Lectr.; Attorney-at-Law
Ratnayake, R., BA Kelaniya, LLB Open S.Lanka,
MPhil Colombo   Sr. Lectr.; Attorney-at-Law
Silva, K. B. A., LLB Colombo, LLM S'ton., PhD
S'ton.   Sr. Lectr.; Head*
Other Staff: 5 Lectrs.

Management Studies

Edirisinghe, S. S. K., BCom Kelaniya, MCom
Kelaniya   Sr. Lectr.
Gamage, H. R., BSc Colombo, MPA Sri Jay.   Sr.
Lectr.
Gamini, L. P. S., BSc Sri Jay., MCom Kelaniya
Sr. Lectr.
George, R. M. J., BCom Madr., MCom Madr.,
PhD W.Syd.   Sr. Lectr.; Head*
Rajamanthri, S. D., BSc Sri Jay., MCom Colombo,
MAAT   Sr. Lectr.
Rajapaksha Menike, R. M. P. P. L. S., BSc Sri
Jay., MPA Sri Jay.   Sr. Lectr.
Sapukotanage, S., BBA Colombo, MSc Sri Jay.   Sr.
Lectr.
Senanayake, S. A. D., BSc Kelaniya, MBA Delhi
Silva, A. W., MPA Sri Jay.   Sr. Lectr.
Other Staff: 4 Lectrs.

Mathematics and Computer Science

Fax: (01) 282 2738
De Silva, W. P. C. D., BSc Colombo, MSc Asian
I.T., Bangkok
Perera, W. C. W., BSc Colombo, MSc S.Fraser,
PhD S.Fraser   Sr. Lectr.
Ramasinghe, W., BSc Colombo, MS Ohio State,
PhD Ohio State   Sr. Lectr.; Head*
Other Staff: 6 Lectrs.
Research: intelligent learning environment for
statistics and mathematics; knowledge
modelling for expert systems; knowledge-
based systems; natural language processing
for weather reports and Sinhala grammar;
testing parameters of fit models

Mathematics and Philosophy of Engineering

Fax: (01) 282 2737 E-mail: emath@ou.ac.lk
de Zoysa, A. P. K., BSc(Eng) S.Lanka, MSc Lond.,
PhD Colombo   Prof.
Fernando, M. P. W. S., BScEngin Peradeniya,
MPhil Open S.Lanka   Sr. Lectr.; Head*
Other Staff: 4 Lectrs.
Research: energy/environment; philosophy of
science; probabilistic modelling

Physics

Fax: (01) 282 2738
Fernando, G. W. A. R., BSc Peradeniya, MPhil
Peradeniya, PhD Mainz   Sr. Lectr.
Jayasinghe, E. M., BSc Ceyl., PhD Liv.   Sr. Prof.
Liyanage, L. S. G., BSc Ceyl., MSc Baylor, PhD
Baylor   Sr. Lectr.; Head*
Sumathipala, W. L., BSc Ceyl., MSc Hawaii, PhD
Hawaii   Sr. Lectr.
Other Staff: 7 Lectrs.
Research: atmospheric physics; development of
appropriate geophysical method for
groundwater exploration in Sri Lanka;
electronic structure calculations in transition
metal surfaces; petrology

Social Studies

Fax: (01) 282 0032
Abeysinghe, N. S., BA Colombo, MAEcon
Colombo, MA Colombo   Sr. Lectr.
Bulumulla, W. R. W. M. K. S., BA Peradeniya
Sr. Lectr.

Chandrabose, A. S., BA Peradeniya, MA Peradeniya,
MPhil J.Nehru U., PhD J.Nehru U.   Sr. Lectr.
Colombage, S. S., BA Ceyl., MA Manc., PhD
Manc.   Prof.
Dissanayake, S. K., BA Peradeniya, MA Peradeniya
Sr. Lectr.
Mendis, B. M. P., BA Kelaniya, MA Lanc., MPhil
Leic., PhD Sing.   Sr. Lectr.; Head*
Vidanapathirana, U., BA Kelaniya, MSc Asian I.T.,
Bangkok, MBA Sri Jay.   Prof.
Other Staff: 5 Lectrs.

Textile Technology

Fax: (01) 822 2737 E-mail: hdtext@ou.ac.lk
Ariadurai, S. A., BE Osm., PhD UMIST   Sr.
Lectr.; Head*
Delkumurewatta, G. B., MPhil Open S.Lanka   Sr.
Lectr.
Jayananda, G. Y. A. R., MBA Sri Jay., MA
Colombo   Sr. Lectr.
Ovitigala, P., PhD Leeds   Sr. Lectr.
Wimalaweera, W. A., DrIng Stuttgart, FTI   Sr.
Lectr.; Head*
Other Staff: 5 Lectrs.

Zoology

Fax: (01) 282 2738
Chandrananda, W. P. N., BSc Peradeniya, PhD Sri
Jay.   Sr. Lectr.
Dassanayake, V. D., BSc Colombo, MPhil Open
S.Lanka   Sr. Lectr.
Edirisinghe, E. A. D. N. D., BSc Kelaniya, MPhil
Open S.Lanka   Sr. Lectr.
Jayasuriya, H. Thusitha R., BSc Colombo, MSc
Colombo, PhD Lond.   Sr. Lectr.
Jayawardena, K. H., BSc Kelaniya, MPhil Colombo,
PhD Col.   Sr. Lectr.
Nilakarawasam, N., BSc Colombo, PhD Stir.   Sr.
Lectr.
Perera, W. V. J., BSc Sri Jay., MPhil Sri Jay., PhD
Colombo   Sr. Lectr.
Ranawake, G. R. R., BSc Colombo, PhD Lond.
Sr. Lectr.; Head*
Wijesekera, S. K., BSc Peradeniya, PhD Colombo
Sr. Lectr.
Other Staff: 3 Lectrs.
Research: hydrological investigation of water
bodies using macroinvertebrates as
biological indicators; insect molecular
biology and biological control; insecticide
resistance in mosquitoes; wildlife ecology
and conservation biology

Environmental Studies

Padmalal, U. K. G. K., BSc Colombo, MSc
Colombo, PhD Tohoku   Sr. Lectr.; Head*

CONTACT OFFICERS

Academic affairs. Registrar: Sadique, A. L. J.,
BSc Jaffna (E-mail: registrar@ou.ac.lk)
Accommodation. Assistant Registrar, General
Administration: Somanathan, A.
Admissions (first degree). Senior Assistant
Registrar, Student Affairs: Kithsiri, V. D.,
BCom Sri Jay.
Admissions (higher degree). Senior Assistant
Registrar, Student Affairs: Kithsiri, V. D.,
BCom Sri Jay.
Adult/continuing education. (Contact the
Dean of the appropriate faculty)
Alumni. Assistant Registrar, General
Administration: Somanathan, A.
Archives. Registrar: Sadique, A. L. J., BSc Jaffna
(E-mail: registrar@ou.ac.lk)
Computing services. Director, Information
Technology: Prabath, D. D., BSc Colombo,
MSc (E-mail: dirit@ou.ac.lk)
Consultancy services. (Contact the Dean of
the appropriate faculty)
Distance education. (Contact the Dean of the
appropriate faculty)
Estates and buildings/works and services.
Senior Assistant Registrar, Capital Works:
Prabaharan, T., BA Jaffna
Examinations. Senior Assistant Registrar
(Examinations): de Silva, M. W. S., BA
Peradeniya (E-mail: sarexam@ou.ac.lk)

Finance. Bursar: Premaratne, K. M., BA Sri Jay., MBA Colombo
(E-mail: kmpremaratna@yahoo.com)
General enquiries. Registrar: Sadique, A. L. J., BSc Jaffna (E-mail: registrar@ou.ac.lk)
Library (chief librarian). Librarian: Seneviratne, R. C. W. M. R. W., BA Kelaniya, MLISc Col. (E-mail: swene@ou.ac.lk)
Marketing. Director, Marketing: Dharmasiri Thimali, BCom Ceyl.
Personnel/human resources. Acting Senior Assistant Registrar, Establishments (Academic/Non-academic): Suresh, K., BCom Sri Jay. (E-mail: ksure@ou.ac.lk)
Public relations. Director, Public Relations: Wanigasundera, K. H., BA Ceyl.

Publications. Director, Operations: Gamage, H. R., BSc Colombo, MPA Sri Jay.
Purchasing. Senior Assistant Bursar (Purchasing): Pasqual, A. I. N.
Quality assurance and accreditation. Vice-Chancellor: de Silva, Prof. Nandani, MB BS Ceyl., MD Colombo, DCH Colombo
(E-mail: vc@ou.ac.lk)
Research. Deputy Registrar (Academic): Godagama, D., BCom Sri Jay.
Safety. Chief Security Officer: Perera, K. J. M.
Scholarships, awards, loans. Senior Assistant Bursar, Finance: Marcus, B. T.
Schools liaison. Acting Director, Regional Educational Services: De Mel, P. K. J.

Security. Chief Security Officer: Perera, K. J. M.
Staff development and training. Director, Staff Development Centre: Ratnaweera, H. G. P. A., BSc Ceyl., MSc(Mgt) Lond., DPhil Oxf., FIE(SL)
Student welfare/counselling. Senior Assistant Registrar, Student Affairs: Kithsiri, V. D., BCom Sri Jay.
Students from other countries. Director, Public Relations: Wanigasundera, K. H., BA Ceyl.
University press. Printer: Perera, G. A. S. D.

[Information supplied by the institution as at 14 June 2006, and edited by the ACU]

UNIVERSITY OF PERADENIYA, SRI LANKA

Founded 1978

Member of the Association of Commonwealth Universities

Postal Address: Peradeniya, Sri Lanka
Telephone: (081) 238 8301/5 **Fax:** (081) 238 8102 **E-mail:** vc@pdn.ac.lk
URL: http://www.pdn.ac.lk

VICE-CHANCELLOR*—Abeygunawardena, Prof. H., BVSc Ceyl., MSc Ill., PhD Ill.
DEPUTY VICE-CHANCELLOR—Wickremasinghe, Prof. A., BSc Peradeniya, PhD
REGISTRAR‡—De Alwis, Ranjith, BSc Peradeniya, MSc Peradeniya
BURSAR—Ganthune, M. D.

GENERAL INFORMATION

History. The university was founded in 1942 as University of Ceylon, the result of the merger of Ceylon Medical College and Ceylon University College. It subsequently became Peradeniya Campus of the University of Sri Lanka in 1972 and achieved independent university status in 1978.

Admission to first degree courses (see also Sri Lankan Introduction). Application is through University Grants Commission (UGC) and is based on performance at General Certificate of Education (GCE) A level examination.

First Degrees (see also Sri Lankan Directory to Subjects of Study). BA, BDS, BSc, BScAgric, BScEngin, BVSc, MB BS.
Length of course. Full-time: BA, BSc: 3–4 years; BDS, BScAgric, BScEngin, BVSc: 4 years; MB BS: 5 years.

Higher Degrees (see also Sri Lankan Directory to Subjects of Study).
Master's. MA, MBA, MEng, MPhil, MSc, MVSc.
Admission. Applicants should hold an appropriate first degree (with at least second class honours), or (for arts courses) have passed master's preliminary programme.
Length of course. Full-time: MA, MBA, MPhil, MSc: 2 years. Part-time: MA, MEng, MPhil: 3 years.
Doctoral. PhD.

Language of Instruction. Sinhala, Tamil and English.

Libraries. Volumes: 785,642. Periodicals subscribed to: 166.

Income (2006–2007). Total, Rs177,838,050.

Statistics. Staff (2007): 2625 (736 academic, 1889 non-academic).

FACULTIES/SCHOOLS
Agriculture
Tel: (081) 238 8041 Fax: (081) 238 8041
E-mail: bmarambe@pdn.ac.lk
Dean: Marambe, Prof. P. W. M. M. B., BScAgric Peradeniya, MAgr Hiroshima, PhD Hiroshima
Senior Assistant Registrar: Navaratne Banda, K. M., BA Peradeniya

Allied and Health Sciences
Tel: (081) 239 2138 Fax: (081) 238 7394
E-mail: info@ahs.pdn.ac.lk
Acting Dean: Goonasekara, Prof. C. D. A., MB BS Ceyl., MD Ceyl., MPhil Peradeniya, PhD Lond., FFARCSI
Assistant Registrar: Ranawana, C. M. N., BA Open S.Lanka

Arts
Tel: (081) 238 8345 Fax: (081) 238 8933
E-mail: dean@arts.pdn.ac.lk
Dean: Silva, Prof. K. T., BA Ceyl., PhD Monash
Assistant Registrar: Weeraddana, L. S., BA Peradeniya

Dental Sciences
Tel: (081) 238 8045 Fax: (081) 238 8948
E-mail: deandental@pdn.ac.lk
Dean: Amaratunga, E. A. P. D., BDS Peradeniya, MSc Lond., MS Colombo, FDSRCS, FFDRCSI
Assistant Registrar: Wijeyeratne, W. D. V., BA Peradeniya

Engineering
Tel: (081) 238 8322 Fax: (081) 238 8158
E-mail: deaneng@pdn.ac.lk
Dean: Abayakoon, Prof. S. B. S., BSc(Eng) S.Lanka, MASc Br.Col., PhD Br.Col., FIE(SL)
Assistant Registrar: Jayatilake, H. A.

Medicine
Tel: (081) 239 6200 Fax: (081) 238 9106
E-mail: dean@med.pdn.ac.lk
Dean: Amarasinghe, Prof. W. I., MB BS Ceyl., FRCOG, FSLCOG
Assistant Registrar: Weerasinghe, S.

Science
Tel: (081) 238 9126 Fax: (081) 238 8018
E-mail: dean@sci.pdn.ac.lk
Dean: Karunaratne, Prof. S. H. P. P., BSc Peradeniya, PhD Lond.
Assistant Registrar: Herath, P. K.

Veterinary Medicine and Animal Science
Tel: (081) 239 5700 Fax: (081) 238 9136
E-mail: deanvet@pdn.ac.lk
Dean: Abeynayake, Prof. Preeni, BVSc Ceyl., PhD Massey
Assistant Registrar: Madawala Hulugalla, W. M. D. P., BA Peradeniya, MA Peradeniya

ACADEMIC UNITS
Agricultural Biology
Tel: (081) 239 5247 E-mail: abgio@pdn.ac.lk
Ahangama, M. A. D., BScAgric Ceyl., MSc Leip., PhD Texas A.& M.   Sr. Lectr.
Bandara, D. C., BScAgric S.Lanka, MSc Penn.State   Prof.
Bandara, J. M. R. S., BScAgric Ceyl., PhD ANU   Prof.
De Costa, D. M., BSc(Agric) Reading, MSc Reading   Sr. Lectr.
Gunawardena, A. H. L. A. N., BScAgric Peradeniya, MSc Oxf., DPhil Oxf.   Sr. Lectr.
Hemachandra, K. S., BScAgric ICL, MSc ICL   Sr. Lectr.
Karunagoda, R. P., BScAgric Peradeniya, MPhil Wales, PhD Obihiro   Sr. Lectr.
Perera, A. L. T., BScAgric Ceyl., MSc Obihiro, PhD Birm.   Prof.
Sumanasinghe, V. A., BScAgric Ceyl., MSc Penn.State, PhD Penn.State   Sr. Lectr.; Head*
Wickramasinghe, H. A. M. S., BScAgric Peradeniya, MPhil Peradeniya, PhD Obihiro   Sr. Lectr.
Wickramasinghe, I. P., BScAgric Ceyl., MSc Texas A.& M., PhD Peradeniya   Sr. Lectr.
Wijegunasekera, H. N. P., BScAgric Ceyl., MPhil Newcastle(UK)   Sr. Lectr.
Other Staff: 2 Lectrs.
Research: entomology; plant breeding; plant pathology and microbiology; plant physiology; plant systematics

Agricultural Economics

Tel: (081) 239 5500

Ariyawardena, A., BScAgric Peradeniya, MSc Peradeniya   Sr. Lectr.

Bogahawatte, C., BScAgric Ceyl., MSc Philippines, PhD Texas A.& M.   Sr. Prof.

Gunaratne, L. H. P., BScAgric Peradeniya, MSc Hawaii, PhD Hawaii   Sr. Lectr.

Gunatilake, H. M., BScAgric Peradeniya, MSc Norway Ag., PhD Hawaii   Prof.

Kodituwakku, K. A. S. S., BScAgric Peradeniya, MBA Stir., PhD Stir.   Sr. Lectr.; Head*

Thiruchelvam, S., BScAgric Peradeniya, MSc Obihiro, PhD Peradeniya   Assoc. Prof.

Weerahewa, H. L. J., BScAgric Peradeniya, MPhil Peradeniya, PhD Guelph   Sr. Lectr.

Other Staff: 2 Lectrs.

Research: agribusiness; agricultural marketing; consumer behaviour; international trade; production economics and econometrics

Agricultural Extension

Tel: (081) 239 5520

De Silva, J. A. S., BScAgric Peradeniya, MSc Asian I.T., Bangkok, PhD Cran.   Sr. Lectr.

Sivayoganathan, C., BScAgric Ceyl., MAgrSt Qld., PhD Texas A.& M.   Assoc. Prof.; Head*

Wanigasundara, W. A. D. P., BScAgric Ceyl., PhD Reading   Sr. Lectr.

Wickremasuriya, H. V. A., BScAgric Ceyl., MED Penn.State, PhD Penn.State   Sr. Lectr.

Other Staff: 2 Lectrs.

Research: development of computer package for registration and examination procedures; development of computer-based glossary in agricultural extension; impact assessment of micro-credit program of Agrarian Bank; initial development of computer-based information and decision support system for selected crops; social aspects of bulk water allocation in agriculture

Animal Science

Tel: (081) 239 5321

Cyril, H. W., BScAgric Ceyl., MSc Nott., PhD Nott.   Prof.

Dematawewa, C. M. B., BScAgric Peradeniya, PhD Iowa   Sr. Lectr.

Deshappriya, R. C. N., BVSc Peradeniya, MPhil Reading   Sr. Lectr.

Edirisinghe, U. G. de A., BSc Ceyl., MSc Ceyl., PhD Ceyl.   Sr. Lectr.

Ibrahim, M. N. M., BScAgric Ceyl., PhD Melb.   Prof.

Janak Kamil, Y. V. A., BScAgric Peradeniya, MSc Nfld.   Sr. Lectr.

Mahipala, M. P. B., BScAgric Kagawa, MSc Kagawa   Sr. Lectr.

Perera, A. N. F., BScAgric Ceyl., MSc Virginia Polytech., PhD Virginia Polytech.   Prof.

Perera, E. R. K., BScAgric Ceyl., MSc Virginia Polytech., PhD Virginia Polytech.   Prof.

Premaratne, S., BScAgric Ceyl., MSc Virginia Polytech., PhD   Prof.

Samarasinghe, K., BScAgric Ceyl., MSc Ceyl., PhD E.T.H.Zürich   Sr. Lectr.

Silva, G. L. L. P., BScAgric Peradeniya, PhD Syd.   Sr. Lectr.

Silva, K. F. S. T., BVSc Ceyl., MSc Arizona, PhD Calif.   Sr. Lectr.

Wijegunawardena, M. P. B., BVSc Obihiro, MSc Obihiro, PhD Obihiro   Prof.; Head*

Other Staff: 7 Lectrs.

Research: alternate seed additives; evaluation of seed resources for ruminants and non-ruminants; livestock biodiversity and genetic improvement of indigenous animals; meat and milk products; mineral nutrition of ruminants

Arabic and Islamic Culture

Tel: (081) 239 2541

Abdul Barie, M. S., BA Peradeniya, MPhil Peradeniya   Sr. Lectr.; Head*

Asad, M. L. M. K., BA Saudi Arabian Inst., MLitt Edin., PhD Edin.   Sr. Lectr.

Cassim, A., BA Libya, MA IIU Malaysia   Sr. Lectr.

Other Staff: 4 Staff members

Research: Arabic colleges; Holy Quran interpretation; Islamic law; mosques in Sri Lanka; Muslims of Sri Lanka

Archaeology

Tel: (081) 239 2555

Chandraratne, R. M. M., BA Peradeniya, MA Poona, PhD Poona   Sr. Lectr.

Jayaratne, D. K., BA Peradeniya, MSc Kelaniya, PhD Poona   Sr. Lectr.; Head*

Mahinda, Rev. W., BA Peradeniya, MA Peradeniya   Sr. Lectr.

Rambukwella, M. W. N. C. K., BA Peradeniya, MA Peradeniya   Sr. Lectr.

Senanayake, A. M. P., BA Peradeniya, PhD Peradeniya   Sr. Lectr.

Seneviratne, S. D. S., BA Delhi, MA J.Nehru U., MPhil J.Nehru U., PhD J.Nehru U.   Prof.

Other Staff: 1 Staff Member

Research: archaeological information systems; classical archaeology; heritage management; pre- and proto-historic archaeology; pre-industrial technology

Botany

Tel: (081) 239 4521

Abeysekera, C. L., BSc Peradeniya, PhD Peradeniya   Sr. Lectr.

Abeygunasekera, R. M. K., BSc Ceyl., PhD Lond.   Assoc. Prof.

Adikaram, N. K. B., BSc Ceyl., PhD Belf.   Sr. Prof.; Head*

Gunatilake, C. V. S., BSc Ceyl., MSc Aberd., PhD Aberd.   Sr. Prof.

Gunatilake, I. A. U. N., BSc Ceyl., PhD Camb.   Sr. Prof.

Karunaratne, A. M., BSc Ceyl., MSc Nebraska   Sr. Lectr.

Perera, G. A. D., BSc Peradeniya, MSc Oxf., DPhil Oxf.   Sr. Lectr.

Saravanakumar, P., BSc PhD   Sr. Lectr.

Tennakoon, K. U., BSc Peradeniya, PhD W.Aust.   Sr. Lectr.

Weerasinghe, H. M. S. P. M., BSc Peradeniya, MPhil Camb., PhD Camb.   Sr. Lectr.

Yakandawala, D. M. D., BSc Peradeniya, PhD Reading   Sr. Lectr.

Other Staff: 2 Lectrs.

Research: eco-physiology of native plants; forest biology; forestry; plant ecology; Sri Lankan flora

Chemistry

Tel: (081) 239 4422

Bandara, B. M. R., BSc Ceyl., PhD ANU   Prof.

Bandara, H. M. N., BSc Ceyl., MSc Aston, PhD Aston   Prof.

Bandara, W. M. A. T., BSc Peradeniya, PhD Tokyo I.T.   Sr. Lectr.

Ganehenege, M. Y., BSc Peradeniya, PhD   Sr. Lectr.

Gunawardena, R. P., BSc Ceyl., PhD Aberd.   Sr. Prof.

Ileperuma, O. A., BSc Ceyl., PhD Arizona   Sr. Prof.

Karunaratne, N. L. V. V., BSc Colombo, PhD Br.Col.   Prof.; Head*

Kumar, N. S., BSc Ceyl., PhD Lond.   Sr. Prof.

Kumar, V., BSc Ceyl., DPhil Oxf.   Sr. Prof.

Navaratne, M. M. A. N., BSc Peradeniya, MSc Hawaii   Sr. Lectr.

Perera, A. D. L. Chandanie, BSc Peradeniya, MSc Hawaii   Assoc. Prof.

Priyantha, H. M. D. N., BSc Peradeniya, PhD Hawaii   Prof.

Rajapakse, R. M. G., BSc Peradeniya, PhD Lond.   Prof.

Tennekoon, D. T. B., BSc Ceyl., PhD Wales   Sr. Prof.

Wickremasinghe, A., BSc Peradeniya, PhD   Prof.

Other Staff: 6 Lectrs.

Research: bioactive organic molecules (reactive oxygen species); biologically active natural products (isolation, characterisation and synthesis); clay (electronically conducting polymer organic and inorganic heterostructure materials and their applications in optoelectronic devices); solar cell materials, acid rain and air quality monitoring; structural polysaccharide chemistry

Classical Languages

Tel: (081) 239 2524

Weerakkody, D. P. M., BA Ceyl., PhD Hull   Prof., Western Classics; Head*

Wickramasinghe, W. M. M. W. G. C. S. M., BA Peradeniya, PhD Nott.   Sr. Lectr.

Other Staff: 3 Staff Members

Research: Greek philosophy; Sanskrit Buddhist canonical texts; Sanskrit Buddhist philosophical texts; Sanskrit drama; technical literature in Sanskrit

Computer Sciences

see also Stats. and Computer Sci.

Tel: (081) 239 3471

Dewasurendra, S. D., BScEng S.Lanka, MEng Asian I.T., Bangkok, PhD Grenoble   Sr. Lectr.

Sandirigama, M., BScEng Peradeniya, MSc Ehime, PhD Ehime   Sr. Lectr.; Head*

Other Staff: 11 Staff Members

Research: applying design patterns in designing and implementing role based access control; formal description of object-oriented design patterns; public key cryptosystems and their performances

Crop Science

Tel: (081) 239 5111

De Costa, W. A. J. M., BScAgric Peradeniya, PhD Reading   Prof.

Eeswara, J. P., BScAgric Peradeniya, MPhil Aberd., PhD Aberd.   Sr. Lectr.

Hitinayake, H. M. G. S. B., BScAgric Peradeniya, MSc Oxf., MPhil Wales, PhD Wales   Sr. Lectr.

Keerthisinghe, J. P., BScAgric Peradeniya, MSc Birm., MPhil Peradeniya   Sr. Lectr.

Malkanthi Fonseka, R., BScAgric Peradeniya, MSc Ghent, PhD Ehime   Sr. Lectr.

Marambe, P. W. M. M. B., BScAgric Peradeniya, MAgr Hiroshima, PhD Hiroshima   Prof.

Nissanka, N. A. A. S. P., BScAgric Peradeniya, MSc Guelph, PhD Guelph   Sr. Lectr.; Head*

Peiris, B. C. N., BScAgric Peradeniya, MSc Penn.State, PhD Penn.State   Prof.

Peiris, B. L., BSc(Agric) Iowa, MSc Iowa, PhD Iowa   Sr. Lectr.

Peiris, S. E., BScAgric Peradeniya, MSc Penn.State, PhD Lond.   Prof.

Premaratne, K. P., BScAgric Ceyl., MSc Leip., PhD F.U.Berlin   Sr. Lectr.

Pushpakumara, D. K. N. G., BScAgric Peradeniya, MSc Oxf., DPhil Oxf.   Sr. Lectr.

Samitha, S., BScAgric Peradeniya, MPhil Edin., PhD Edin.   Sr. Lectr.

Sangakkara, U. R., BScAgric Ceyl., PhD Massey   Sr. Prof.

Sivanthewerl, T., BScAgric Peradeniya, MSc Norway Ag., PhD Gött.   Sr. Lectr.

Weerakkody, W. A. P., BScAgric Peradeniya, MAgr Peradeniya, PhD Peradeniya   Sr. Lectr.

Weerasinghe, K. W. L. K., BScAgric Peradeniya   Sr. Lectr.

Other Staff: 2 Lectrs.

Research: agronomy; biometry; forestry; horticulture; plantation crops

Economics

Tel: (081) 239 2620

Abayasekera, C. R., BA S.Lanka, PhD Boston   Sr. Lectr.

Abhayaratne, A. S. P., BA Peradeniya, MA Essex, MPhil Peradeniya, PhD Essex   Sr. Lectr.

Ariyadasa, W. G., BA Peradeniya, MPhil Peradeniya   Sr. Lectr.

Dayaratne Banda, O. G., BA Peradeniya, MPhil Peradeniya   Sr. Lectr.

De Mel, S. J. S., BScEng Moratuwa, PhD American(D.C.)   Sr. Lectr.

Gnaneswaran, K., BA Peradeniya, MA Jaffna   Sr. Lectr.

Gunawardena, D. N. B., BA Peradeniya, MA American(D.C.), PhD American(D.C.) Sr. Lectr.

Jayawickrama, J. M. A., BA Peradeniya, MA Thammasat Sr. Lectr.

Kankanamge, A. D. H. K., MSc Peradeniya, PhD Sr. Lectr.

Liyanage, S. G., BA Ceyl., MPhil Colombo Sr. Lectr.; Head*

Madhavie, A. V. K., BA Peradeniya, MPhil Peradeniya Sr. Lectr.

Nigel, J., BA Ceyl., MPhil Peradeniya Sr. Lectr.

Pathberiya, P., BA Peradeniya, MA Thammasat Sr. Lectr.

Perera, W. C. P., BA Peradeniya, MSc Thammasat Sr. Lectr.

Rajeadran, S., BA Peradeniya Sr. Lectr.

Rajeswaram, T., BA Peradeniya, MPhil Peradeniya Sr. Lectr.

Ranjith, J. G., BA Peradeniya, MA Br.Col. Sr. Lectr.

Rantilake, M. B., BA Peradeniya, MPhil Peradeniya Sr. Lectr.

Samarawickrema, N. D., BCom Ceyl., MSc Sur., MA Boston Sr. Lectr.

Sivarajasingham, S., BA Ceyl., MPhil Peradeniya Sr. Lectr.

Vijesandiran, S., BA Peradeniya, MSc Sr. Lectr.

Other Staff: 5 Lectrs.

Research: agricultural policy and marketing; capital market in Sri Lanka; conflict and negotiations; demand analysis; development issues

Education

Tel: (081) 239 2711

Senadeera, S., MA Ceyl., PhD Ceyl. Prof.

Setunga, S. M. P. W. K., BEd Kyoto, MEd Kyoto, PhD Tsukuba Sr. Lectr.; Head*

Sugathapala, R. D., BCom Peradeniya, MEd Colombo Sr. Lectr.

Wijesundara, S. D. K., BSc Sri Jay., MSc Edin. Sr. Lectr.

Research: constructing a general ability test for Sri Lankan students; contribution of the community to curriculum development in Sri Lankan schools; functional literacy of the students in Sri Lankan schools; learning approaches of students; new educational reforms in Sri Lanka (1999 to present)

Engineering, Agricultural

Tel: (081) 239 5454

Alahakoon, A. M. P. M. K., BScEngin Peradeniya, MSc Virginia Polytech., PhD Missouri Sr. Lectr.

Amaratunga, K. S. P., BScAgric Peradeniya, MAgric Kyushu, PhD Kyushu Sr. Lectr.

Ariyaratne, A. R., BScAgric Ceyl., MSc Texas A.& M., PhD Texas A.& M. Sr. Lectr.

Basnayake, B. F. A., BSc Cran., DEng Paris VI Sr. Lectr.

Dayawansa, N. D. K., BSc(Agric) Asian I.T., Bangkok, MSc Asian I.T., Bangkok Sr. Lectr.

De Silva, R. P., BScAgric Peradeniya, MSc Asian I.T., Bangkok, PhD Cran. Sr. Lectr.; Head*

Dharmasena, D. A. N., BScAgric Peradeniya, PhD Cran. Sr. Lectr.

Galagedera, L. W., BScAgric Peradeniya, MSc Guelph, PhD Guelph Sr. Lectr.

Gunawardena, E. R. N., BScAgric S.Lanka, PhD Cran. Prof.

Jayatissa, D. N., BScAgric S.Lanka, MSc Virginia Polytech., PhD Virginia Sr. Lectr.

Mowjood, M. I. M., BSc(Agric) Yamagata, MSc Yamagata, PhD Iwate Sr. Lectr.

Pathmarajah, S., BScAgric Peradeniya, MPhil Peradeniya, PhD Asian I.T., Bangkok Sr. Lectr.

Rambanda, M., BScAgric Peradeniya, MSc Obihiro Sr. Lectr.

Ranjith Premalal, W. P., BScAgric Peradeniya, MSc Asian I.T., Bangkok, PhD Cran. Sr. Lectr.

Other Staff: 4 Lectrs.

Research: crop storage; energy and waste management; farm machinery; food process engineering; instrumentation applications in agriculture and processing systems

Engineering, Chemical

Tel: (081) 239 3690

Chandraratne, M. R., BScEng Peradeniya, MSc Leeds, PhD Sr. Lectr.; Head*

Karunaratne, D. G. G. P., BScEngin Ceyl., PhD Lisbon Sr. Lectr.

Shanthini, R., BScEngin S.Lanka, MSc Alta., PhD Luleå Assoc. Prof.

Other Staff: 1 Lectr.

Research: energy; environmental pollution; industrial process development

Engineering, Civil

Tel: (081) 239 3500

Abayakoon, S. B. S., BSc(Eng) S.Lanka, MASc Br.Col., PhD Br.Col., FIE(SL) Prof.

Abeyruwan, H., BScEngin Ceyl., MPhil HK Sr. Lectr.

Devapriya, D. S., BScEng Peradeniya, MSc Sr. Lectr.

Dissanayake, P. B. R., BScEng Peradeniya, MEng Ehime, PhD Ehime Sr. Lectr.

Dissanayake, U. I., BScEng Peradeniya, PhD Sheff. Sr. Lectr.

Edirisinghe, A. G. H. J., BScEng Peradeniya, MEng Ehime, PhD Ehime Sr. Lectr.

Herath, G. B. B., BScEng Peradeniya, MEng Asian I.T., Bangkok, PhD Tokyo Sr. Lectr.

Herath, K. R. B., BSc(Eng) S.Lanka, MSc Ill., PhD Calif. Sr. Lectr.

Jayawardena, U. de S., BSc S.Lanka, MSc Asian I.T., Bangkok Sr. Lectr.

Keerthisena, H. H. J., BSc(Eng) Ceyl., PhD Ceyl., FIE(SL) Sr. Lectr.

Kurukulasooriya, L. C., BScEng Moratuwa, MEng Saitama, PhD Saitama Sr. Lectr.

Mauroof, A. L. M., BScEng Peradeniya, MEng Asian I.T., Bangkok, DEng Tokyo Sr. Lectr.

Nandalal, K. D. W., BScEng Peradeniya, MEng Asian I.T., Bangkok, PhD Wageningen Sr. Lectr.

Pathirana, K. P. P., BScEng Peradeniya, MEng Leuven, PhD Leuven Sr. Lectr.

Ranaweera, M. P., BSc(Eng) Ceyl., PhD Camb., FIE(SL) Sr. Prof.

Ratnayake, U. R., BScEng Peradeniya, MEng Asian I.T., Bangkok, DEng Asian I.T., Bangkok Sr. Lectr.

Sathyaprasad, I. M. S., BSc S.Lanka, MEng Asian I.T., Bangkok, DEng Yokohama N. Sr. Lectr.

Seneviratne, K. G. H. C. N., BSc(Eng) Ceyl., PhD Camb. Prof.

Somaratne, A. P. N., BSc(Eng) Ceyl., MS Ill., PhD Ill. Sr. Lectr.; Head*

Udayakara, D. de S., BScEng Peradeniya, MEng Asian I.T., Bangkok Sr. Lectr.

Weerakoon, W. M. S. B., BSc(Eng) S.Lanka, MEng Tokyo, DEng Tokyo Sr. Lectr.

Werellagama, D. R. I. B., BScEng Peradeniya, MEng Asian I.T., Bangkok, DEng Nagoya Sr. Lectr.

Wijethunga, J. J., BSc(Eng) Moratuwa, PhD Camb. Sr. Lectr.

Other Staff: 10 Lectrs.

Research: concrete technology; engineering materials; hydraulics; structural engineering; waters resources engineering

Engineering, Electrical and Electronic

Tel: (081) 239 3401

Abeyratne, S. G., BScEng Peradeniya, MScEng Gifu, PhD Gifu Sr. Lectr.

Alahakoon, A. M. U. S. K., BScEng Peradeniya, PhD R.I.T.Stockholm Sr. Lectr.; Head*

Atputharajah, A., BScEng Peradeniya, PhD UMIST Sr. Lectr.

Ekanayake, E. M. N., BScEng Peradeniya, MSc Lond., PhD McM. Prof.

Ekanayake, J. B., BScEng Peradeniya, PhD UMIST Prof.

Fernando, M. A. R. M., BScEng Peradeniya, PhD Chalmers I.T., LicTech R.I.T.Stockholm Sr. Lectr.

Gunawardena, A. U. A. W., BScEng Peradeniya, MSc NSW, PhD Qld.UT Sr. Lectr.

Hoole, S. R. H., BSc(Eng) S.Lanka, MSc(Eng) Lond., PhD Carnegie-Mellon, DSc(Eng) Lond., FIEE Sr. Prof.

Jagathkumara, K. D. R., BScEng Peradeniya, MEngSc NSW, PhD S.Af. Sr. Lectr.

Liyanage, K. M., BScEng Peradeniya, PhD Tokyo Sr. Lectr.

Rathnayake, K. R. M. N., BScEng Peradeniya, MEng Gifu, PhD Gifu Sr. Lectr.

Ratnayake, K. B. N., BScEng Peradeniya, MS Rensselaer, PhD Rensselaer Sr. Lectr.

Samaranayake, B. G. L. T., BScEng Peradeniya, LicTech R.I.T.Stockholm, PhD R.I.T.Stockholm Sr. Lectr.

Wijayakulasooriya, J. V., BScEng Peradeniya, PhD Newcastle(UK) Sr. Lectr.

Other Staff: 11 Lectrs.

Research: communication and information engineering; electronics and instrumentation; information communication technology; power and energy; robotics and motion control

Engineering Mathematics

Tel: (081) 239 3341

E-mail: head@engmath.pdn.ac.lk

Karunasinghe, D. S. K., BScEng Peradeniya, PhD NU Singapore Sr. Lectr.

Perera, K., BSc Sri Jay., MA N.Y.State, PhD N.Y.State Sr. Lectr.

Perera, S. P. C., BScEng Peradeniya, MSc Texas Tech, PhD Texas Tech Sr. Lectr.

Siyambalapitiya, S. B., BSc Ceyl., MSc Newcastle(NSW), PhD Newcastle(NSW) Prof.; Head*

Susantha, K. A. S., BScEng Peradeniya, MEng Asian I.T., Bangkok, DEng Sr. Lectr.

Walgama, K. S., BScEng Moratuwa, MSc Alta., MEng Philips'(Eindhoven), PhD Luleå Prof.

Other Staff: 12 Lectrs.

Research: automatic control systems; mathematical modelling; numerical methods; probability and applied statistics; solar energy and ecology

Engineering, Mechanical

Tel: (081) 239 3600

E-mail: ssivasegaram@pdn.ac.lk

Boyagoda, E. M. P. B., BScEng Peradeniya, MEng Yamaguchi, DEng Yamaguchi Sr. Lectr.; Head*

Rajapakshe, L., BScEng Peradeniya, MEng Asian I.T., Bangkok, PhD Lond. Sr. Lectr.

Ratnaweera, D. A. A. C., BScEng Peradeniya, PhD Melb. Sr. Lectr.

Seneviratne, S. K., BScEngin Ceyl., MSc Leeds Sr. Lectr.

Sivasegaram, S., BScEngin Ceyl., MSc Lond., PhD Lond. Sr. Prof.

Other Staff: 2 Lectrs.; 5 Engin. Teaching Assts.

Research: combustion control energy studies; control engineering; ergonomics

Engineering, Production

Tel: (081) 239 3650

Bandara, G. E. M. D. C., MSc Sofia, PhD Sofia Sr. Lectr.

Pathirana, S. D., BScEngin S.Lanka, MSc Ghent, DEng Tokyo Sr. Lectr.; Head*

Other Staff: 7 Lectrs.

Research: embedded systems; industrial electronics; industrial engineering management; manufacturing engineering; robotics

English

see also Special Centres, etc

Tel: (081) 239 2543

De Silva, C. L., BA Ceyl., MA N.Y.State, PhD N.Texas Sr. Lectr.

Fernando, L. N. A., BA Ceyl., MA Hawaii, PhD Flin. Sr. Lectr.

Herath, R., BA Kelaniya, MA Sr. Lectr.

Jayaweera, N. C., BA Peradeniya, MA Peradeniya Sr. Lectr.

Parakrama, A., BA Peradeniya, MA PhD Prof.; Head*

Perera, S. W., BA Ceyl., MA New Br., PhD New Br. Prof.

Wickramagamage, C. S., BA Ceyl., PhD Hawaii Sr. Lectr.

Other Staff: 1 Lectr.

Research: cultural studies; feminist theory and literary criticism; post colonial theory and literature (Sri Lankan, Indian, American); translation theory and practice

Fine Arts

Tel: (081) 239 2183

Fernando, G. M. D., BA Ceyl., PhD Humboldt Sr. Lectr.

Seneheweera, A. G. L., BFA Kelaniya, MSc Kelaniya Sr. Lectr.; Head*

Other Staff: 2 Lectrs.

Food Science and Technology

Tel: (081) 239 5213

Arampath, P. C., BScAgric Asian I.T., Bangkok, MSc Asian I.T., Bangkok Sr. Lectr.

Ileperuma, D. C. K., BScAgric Peradeniya, MSc(Agric) Peradeniya, PhD Maryland Assoc. Prof.

Jaykodi, J. A. L. P., BScAgric Peradeniya, MSc Nfld. Sr. Lectr.

Prasantha, B. D. R., BScAgric Peradeniya, MScAgric Peradeniya, PhD Sr. Lectr.

Samarajeewa, U., BSc Ceyl., PhD Ceyl., FIBiol, FIChemE Sr. Prof.; Head*

Wijesinghe, D. G. N. G., BScAgric Peradeniya, MSc Philippines, PhD Lond. Sr. Lectr.

Wimalasiri, K. M. S., BSc Peradeniya, PhD Peradeniya Sr. Lectr.

Other Staff: 2 Lectrs.

Research: food and nutrition; microbiology; post-harvest technology; product development

Geography

Tel: (081) 239 2672

Aladuwaka, A. G., BA Peradeniya, MA American(D.C.) Sr. Lectr.

Fernando, W. G., BA Ceyl., MA Ceyl., MSc Asian I.T., Bangkok Sr. Lectr.

Hasbullah, S. H., BA Ceyl., MA Ceyl., MA Br.Col., PhD Br.Col. Sr. Lectr.

Hennayake, H. A. N. M., BA Col., PhD Syr. Sr. Lectr.

Hennayake, H. M. S. K., BA Ceyl., MA Ceyl., PhD Syr. Prof.

Jayakumara, M. A. S., BA Peradeniya, MPhil Norwegian U.S.T. Sr. Lectr.

Mookiah, M. S., BA Ceyl., MA Ceyl., MSc Wales Prof.; Head*

Nanadakumar, V., BA Ceyl., MA Ceyl., MSc Tsukuba Assoc. Prof.

Nawfhal, A. S. M., BA Ceyl., MA Tsukuba Sr. Lectr.

Nelson, M. D., BA Ceyl., MSc Asian I.T., Bangkok, PhD Peradeniya Assoc. Prof.

Razik, M. S. M., BA Peradeniya, MPhil Norwegian U.S.T. Sr. Lectr.

Rekha Nilanthi, G. W. K., BA Peradeniya, MSc Asian I.T., Bangkok Sr. Lectr.

Velmurugu, N., BA Ceyl., MA Ceyl., PhD Ceyl. Sr. Lectr.

Wickramagamage, P., BA Ceyl., MSc Lond., PhD Lond. Assoc. Prof.

Wickremaratne, S. N., BA Ceyl., MS Oregon State, PhD Gifu Sr. Lectr.

Wickremasinghe, A., BA Ceyl., MSc Sheff., PhD Sheff. Sr. Prof.

Other Staff: 2 Lectrs.

Research: coastal zone management; disaster management; gender and development forestry; natural resource management; refugees

Geology

Tel: (081) 239 2011

Amarasinghe, R. M. U. U. B., BSc Peradeniya, MSc Asian I.T., Bangkok Sr. Lectr.

Chandrajith, R. L. R., BSc Peradeniya, MSc Shimane, PhD Erlangen-Nuremberg Sr. Lectr.

Dahanayake, K. G. A., BSc Ceyl., PhD Nancy Sr. Prof.

Dharmagunawardena, H. A., BSc Ceyl., MPhil Peradeniya, PhD Copenhagen Sr. Lectr.

Dissanayake, C. B., BSc Ceyl., DPhil Oxf., DSc Oxf. Sr. Prof.

Gunathilaka, A. A. J. K., BSc Peradeniya, MSc Asian I.T., Bangkok Sr. Lectr.

Jayasena, H. A. H., BSc Ceyl., MSc Colorado State Sr. Lectr.

Nawaratne, S. W., BSc Ceyl. Sr. Lectr.

Perera, L. R. K., BSc Ceyl., MPhil S.Lanka Sr. Lectr.; Head*

Pitawala, H. M. T. G. A., BSc Peradeniya, MPhil S.Lanka, PhD Mainz Sr. Lectr.

Senaratne, A., BSc Ceyl., MSc Lond., PhD Mainz Assoc. Prof.

Research: environmental geochemistry and health (chronic renal failure, fluorosis, goitre); exploration of gold in Sri Lanka; remediation of contaminated land; reservoir induced seismicity in the central highland of Sri Lanka; search for raw material substitutes for ceramic and porcelain industry

History

Tel: (081) 239 2550

Dharamaratne, S. M., BA Peradeniya, MPhil Peradeniya Sr. Lectr.

Dheerananda, Rev. H., BA Peradeniya, MA Peradeniya, PhD J.Nehru U. Prof.

Gajameragedera, B., BA Ceyl., MSc Lond., DPhil Sus. Assoc. Prof.

Hettiarachchi, R., BA Peradeniya, MA Peradeniya Sr. Lectr.

Jayasinghe, R. S., BA Peradeniya, MA Texas Sr. Lectr.

Karunatilake, P. V. B., BA Ceyl., PhD Lond. Prof.

Keerawella, G. B., BA Ceyl., MA Windsor, PhD Br.Col. Prof.; Head*

Meththananada, T. P., BA Ceyl., DPhil Oxf. Assoc. Prof.

Siriweera, W. I., BA Ceyl., PhD Lond. Sr. Prof.

Somathilake, M., BA Peradeniya, MA Peradeniya, PhD J.Nehru U. Assoc. Prof.

Other Staff: 4 Lectrs.

Management Studies

Tel: (081) 239 2624 E-mail: ranasinm@slt.lk

Alfred, M., BCom Peradeniya, MPhil Peradeniya Sr. Lectr.

Kolongahapitiya, K. H. M. A. R., BCom Peradeniya, MA Peradeniya Sr. Lectr.

Nandasena, K. M., BCom Ceyl., MBA Yokohama N. Sr. Lectr.

Ranasinghe, E. P. M., BCom Peradeniya, MSc Osaka, PhD Osaka Sr. Lectr.

Ranasinghe, M., BCom Peradeniya, MSc Peradeniya Sr. Lectr.; Head*

Randeniya, P., BA Ceyl., MA Osaka, PhD Osaka Sr. Lectr.

Subasinghe, S. M. U. T., BCom Peradeniya, MBA Asian I.T., Bangkok Sr. Lectr.

Tharmathasan, V., BCom Peradeniya, MPhil Peradeniya Sr. Lectr.

Other Staff: 2 Lectrs.

Research: business taxation; entrepreneurship development; financial economics; financial management accounting; human resource development (HRD)

Mathematics

see also Engin. Maths.

Tel: (081) 239 4551

Daundasekera, W. B., BSc Peradeniya, MA Alabama, PhD Alabama Sr. Lectr.

Dharmadasa, J. P. D., BSc Ceyl., MPhil Lond. Sr. Lectr.

Dissanayake, U. N. B., BSc Peradeniya, PhD Alta. Sr. Lectr.

Nazeer, H. M., BSc Jaffna Sr. Lectr.

Perera, A. A. I., BSc Peradeniya, MSc Oslo, PhD RMIT Sr. Lectr.; Head*

Perera, A. A. S., BSc Peradeniya, PhD Albany Sr. Lectr.

Seneviratne, H. H. G., BSc Ceyl., PhD Lond. Sr. Prof.

Other Staff: 2 Lectrs.

Research: algebra; analysis; mathematical economics; mathematics education; numerical analysis

Molecular Biology and Biotechnology

Tel: (081) 239 4501

Rajapakshe, R. G. S. C., BSc Peradeniya, MPhil Peradeniya, PhD Hokkaido Sr. Lectr.

Samaraweera, P., BSc Peradeniya, PhD Arizona Sr. Lectr.; Head*

Other Staff: 1 Staff Member

Pali and Buddhist Studies

Tel: (081) 239 2521

Ananada, Rev. D. M., BA Peradeniya, MA Peradeniya, PhD Delhi Sr. Lectr.

Gnananananda, Rev. M., BA Peradeniya, MPhil Peradeniya Sr. Lectr.; Head*

Jayawardena, R. G. D., BA Peradeniya, MA Peradeniya Sr. Lectr.

Rahula, Rev. K., BA Ceyl., MA Peradeniya Sr. Lectr.

Ratnayake, S., BA Peradeniya, MLitt Oxf. Sr. Lectr.

Shanthawimala, Rev. B., BA Peradeniya, MA Peradeniya Sr. Lectr.

Somarathne, G. A., BA Kelaniya, PhD Wayamba Sr. Lectr.

Research: Buddhist philosophy in comparison with Indian and Western philosophical systems; etymology of Pali language; history of Pali literature

Philosophy and Psychology

Tel: (081) 239 2651

Anes, A. S. M., BA Ceyl., MA Ceyl. Sr. Lectr.; Head*

Gnanissara, Rev. A., BA Ceyl., MA Ceyl. Sr. Lectr.

Gunasekera, H. M., BA Ceyl., MA N.Y. Sr. Lectr.

Handagama, H. R. N. P. K., BA Peradeniya, MPhil Peradeniya Sr. Lectr.

Herath, H. M. C., BA Peradeniya, MA Ohio Sr. Lectr.

Jamahir, P. M., BA Peradeniya, MPhil Peradeniya Sr. Lectr.

Karunanayake, D. D. K. S., BA Calg., MS Illinois State, PhD Purdue Sr. Lectr.

Mallikarachchi, D. D., BA Ceyl., MA Ceyl., PhD Lond. Sr. Lectr.

Rajaratnam, M., BA Ceyl., MA Mys. Sr. Lectr.

Other Staff: 4 Lectrs.

Research: Buddhist psychology; comparative religion; eastern and far-eastern thought; German and French philosophy

Physics

Tel: (081) 239 4580

Bandara, L. R. A. K., BSc Peradeniya, PhD Peradeniya Sr. Lectr.

Bandaranayake, P. W. S. K., BSc Peradeniya, PhD Peradeniya Sr. Lectr.; Head*

Careem, M. A., BSc Ceyl., PhD Lond. Prof.

Chandrakanthi, R. L. N., BSc Peradeniya, PhD Peradeniya Sr. Lectr.

Dissanayake, M. A. K. L., BSc Ceyl., MS Indiana, PhD Indiana Sr. Prof.

Ekanayake, P., BSc Peradeniya, MSc Peradeniya, PhD Halle Sr. Lectr.

Hettiarachchi, N. F., BSc Ceyl., PhD Hull Sr. Lectr.

Karunaratne, B. S. B., BSc Ceyl., PhD Warw. Prof.

Karunasiri, R. P. U., BSc Colombo, MS Pitt., MS Calif., PhD Calif. Sr. Lectr.

Leelananda, S. A., BSc Ceyl., MSc Lond., PhD Calg. Sr. Lectr.

Premaratne, K., BSc Ceyl., MS Hawaii, PhD Hawaii Assoc. Prof.

Sivakumar, V., BSc Peradeniya, MSc Georgia, PhD Georgia Sr. Lectr.

Wijewardena, R. L., BSc Peradeniya, MSc Albany Sr. Lectr.

Other Staff: 2 Lectrs.

Research: physics education; physics of materials (ceramics, polymers, semiconductors, solid state ionics)

Political Science

Tel: (081) 239 2625

Amarasinghe, Y. R., BA Ceyl., BPhil York(UK), PhD Lond. Prof.

Ameerdeen, V., BA Ceyl., MA Peradeniya Sr. Lectr.

Cader, M. L. A., BA Ceyl., MA ANU Assoc. Prof.

Liyanage, I. M. K., BA Ceyl., MA Ceyl., PhD Keio Prof.; Head*

Navaratne Bandara, A. M., BA Ceyl., MA Ceyl., DPhil York(UK) Assoc. Prof.

Ranasinghe, R. A. W., BA Ceyl., MA Ceyl. Sr. Lectr.

Saifdeen, N. P. M., BA Ceyl., MA Ceyl. Sr. Lectr.

Samaranayake, S. V. D. G., BA Ceyl., MA Ceyl., PhD St And. Assoc. Prof.

Sivayogalingum, V., BA Ceyl., MA Ceyl. Sr. Lectr.

Witharanawasam, A. G., BA Ceyl., MPhil Peradeniya Sr. Lectr.

Zoysa, de M. O. A., BA Ceyl., MA Tas. Assoc. Prof.

Other Staff: 1 Staff Member

Research: conflict and conflict resolution; devolution of power; gender studies; human rights

Sinhalese

Tel: (081) 239 2549

Attanayake, H. M., BA Ceyl., MA Ceyl. Sr. Lectr.

Gunathilaka, S. K. M. D. D., BA Peradeniya, MPhil Peradeniya Sr. Lectr.

Kularatne, G. G. S., BA Peradeniya, MPhil Peradeniya Sr. Lectr.

Meddegama, U. P., BA Ceyl., PhD Lond. Prof.; Head*

Nugapitiya, E. M. M. R. P. L., BA Peradeniya, MPhil Peradeniya Sr. Lectr.

Other Staff: 6 Lectrs.

Research: language; mass communication and culture; translation techniques

Sociology

Tel: (081) 239 2611

Abeyratne, R. M., BA Bowdoin, MA Wash., MA Mahidol Sr. Lectr.

Amarasekera, D. P. D., BA Ceyl., MA Ceyl., PhD Calc. Sr. Lectr.

Bandaranayake, P. D., BA Ceyl., MA Ceyl., MSc Asian I.T., Bangkok Sr. Lectr.

De Silva, M. W. A., BA Ceyl., MSc Asian I.T., Bangkok, PhD Conn. Prof.

Goonasekara, R. S. A., BA Peradeniya, MA Calif., PhD Calif. Sr. Lectr.

Herath, H. M. D. R., BA Ceyl., MA Delhi, PhD Peradeniya Sr. Lectr.

Karunatissa, S. A., BA Ceyl., MA Ceyl. Sr. Lectr.

Manuratne, M. G., BA Peradeniya, MA Peradeniya Sr. Lectr.

Nanayakkara, V., BA Ceyl., MA Ceyl. Sr. Lectr.; Head*

Pinnawala, M. R. S., BA Ceyl., MA Ceyl. Sr. Lectr.

Pinnawala, S. K., BA Ceyl., MSc Asian I.T., Bangkok, PhD ANU Assoc. Prof.

Rajakaruna, R. M. H. B., BA Vidyod., MA Ceyl. Sr. Lectr.

Razak, M. G. M., BA Peradeniya, MA Colorado Sr. Lectr.

Tudor Silva, K., BA Ceyl., PhD Monash Sr. Prof.

Wanninayake, H. M. S. K., BA Peradeniya, MPhil Peradeniya Sr. Lectr.

Wijesinghe, W. A. S. N., BA Ceyl., MA Mahidol Sr. Lectr.

Other Staff: 1 Lectr.

Soil Science

Tel: (081) 239 5200

Indraratne, S. P., BScAgric Peradeniya, MPhil Peradeniya, PhD Manit. Sr. Lectr.; Head*

Jayakody, A. N., BScAgric Leip., MSc Leip., PhD Giessen Prof.

Kumaragamage, D., BScAgric Peradeniya, MPhil Peradeniya, PhD Manit. Prof.

Mapa, R. B., BScAgric Ceyl., PhD Hawaii Prof.

Nandasena, K. A., BScAgric Peradeniya, MSc Peradeniya, PhD Ghent Sr. Lectr.

Rajapakse, R. M. C. P., BScAgric Peradeniya, MPhil Peradeniya, DPhil Sus. Sr. Lectr.

Ratnayake, J. I. L. B., BScAgric Peradeniya, MSc Syd. Sr. Lectr.

Other Staff: 3 Lectrs.

Research: characterisation and mapping of Sri Lankan soils; isolation of soil micro-organisms; water quality

Statistics and Computer Science

see also Computer Scis.

Tel: (081) 239 4640

Kodituwakku, S. R., BSc Peradeniya, MSc Asian I.T., Bangkok, PhD RMIT Sr. Lectr.; Head*

Thewarapperuma, P. S. S., BSc Peradeniya, MSc Tor., PhD Mich.State Sr. Lectr.

Wijekoon, S. N. M. M. W. W. M. P., BSc Kelaniya, PhD Dortmund Assoc. Prof.

Other Staff: 5 Lectrs.

Research: estimation techniques; linear regression model; Stein rule estimators and their properties; time series analysis

Tamil

Tel: (081) 239 2546

Arunasalam, K., MA Ceyl., PhD Ceyl. Assoc. Prof.

Kanagaratnam, V., BA Ceyl., MA Ceyl. Assoc. Prof.

Maheshwarn, V., BA Peradeniya, MPhil Peradeniya Sr. Lectr.

Manoharan, T., BA Ceyl., MA Ceyl., PhD Ceyl. Sr. Lectr.; Head*

Nuhuman, M. A. M., BA Ceyl., BPhil Ceyl., PhD Annam. Prof.

Thevar, S. R., BA Peradeniya, MPhil Peradeniya Sr. Lectr.

Other Staff: 1 Lectr.

Research: culture and folklore; literary criticism; literary history; literary theory; Tamil linguistics

Zoology

Tel: (081) 239 4471

De Silva, K. H. G. M., BSc Ceyl., PhD Edin. Sr. Prof.

De Silva, P. K., BSc Ceyl., PhD Lanc. Prof.

Edirisinghe, J. P., BSc Ceyl., PhD Adel. Prof.

Karunaratne, S. H. P. P., BSc Peradeniya, PhD Lond. Prof.; Head*

Rajakaruna, R. S., BSc Peradeniya Sr. Lectr.

Ranawana, K. B., BSc Peradeniya, MS N.Y.State, MPhil S.Lanka Sr. Lectr.

Santiapillai, C. V. M., BSc Ceyl., PhD Aberd. Assoc. Prof.

Yatigammana, M. W. S. K., BSc Peradeniya, MSc Peradeniya, PhD Qu. Sr. Lectr.

Other Staff: 3 Lectrs.

DENTAL SCIENCES

Tel: (081) 238 8045 Fax: (081) 238 8948
E-mail: deandental@pdn.ac.lk

Basic Sciences (Dentistry)

Tel: (081) 239 7221

Amarasena, J. K. C., BDS Ceyl., MPhil Ceyl., PhD Tokyo Sr. Lectr.; Head*

Arudechevan, Y., BDS Peradeniya, PhD Sr. Lectr.

Jayawardena, J. A. C. K., BDS Peradeniya, PhD Tokyo Sr. Lectr.

Nanayakkara, C. D., BDS Peradeniya, PhD Ceyl. Prof.

Wimalasiri, W. R., BSc Peradeniya, PhD S.Lanka Sr. Lectr.

Other Staff: 9 Staff Members

Research: ondontogenesis, cholinesterases; ondontometric studies; swallowing, mastication, thermoregulation

Community Dental Health

Tel: (081) 239 7323
E-mail: nandanin@kandyan.net

Amarasena, H. D. N., BDS Peradeniya, MSc MD PhD Sr. Lectr.

Ekanayake, A. N. I., BDS Peradeniya, PhD Lond. Sr. Prof.

Ekanayake, S. L., BDS Peradeniya, PhD Lond. Prof.

Kalyanaratne, K. A., BDS Peradeniya Sr. Lectr.

Nagaratne, S. P. N. P., BDS Peradeniya, MS Prof.

Wijayakumaran, V., BDS MPhil Sr. Lectr.; Head*

Wijeyeweera, R. L., BDS Ceyl., PhD N.Y. Prof.

Other Staff: 3 Lectrs.

Research: low cost dental treatment techniques

Oral and Maxillofacial Surgery

Tel: (081 239 7401

Amaratunga, N. A. de S., BDS Ceyl., PhD Ceyl., DSc, FDSRCSEd Sr. Prof.

Attiyagala, A. M., BDS MS, FDSRCS Sr. Lectr.

Hewapathirana, I. S., BDS MS, FDSRCS Sr. Lectr.

Nandadeva, P. G., MB BS Ceyl., FRCS Sr. Lectr.

Weerasinghe, J. U., BDS Ceyl., MS Colombo Sr. Lectr.

Wijekoon, W. M. P. S. K., BDS Ceyl., MS Head*

Other Staff: 5 Lectrs.

Research: cleft lip and palate; facial abnormalities; oral cancer

Oral Medicine and Periodontology

Tel: (081) 239 7451

Ariyawardena, S. P. A. G., BDS Peradeniya, MS Sr. Lectr.

Chandrasekera, A., BDS Peradeniya, MPhil Peradeniya Sr. Lectr.

Ellepola, A. N. B., BDS Peradeniya, PhD HK Sr. Lectr.

Herath, H. M. T. D. K., MB BS Peradeniya, MD S.Lanka Sr. Lectr.

Panagoda, G. J., BSc Punjab, MSc Kelaniya, PhD HK Sr. Lectr.

Rajapakse, P. S., BDS Peradeniya, MPhil Peradeniya, PhD Sr. Lectr.

Ranasinghe, A. W., BDS Peradeniya, MMedSc Lond., PhD Lond. Sr. Lectr.

Sitheeque, M. A. M., BDS Peradeniya, FDSRCPSGlas Sr. Lectr.

Tilakaratne, A. A., BDS Peradeniya, PhD Peradeniya Sr. Lectr.; Head*

Varathan, V., BDS Peradeniya, PhD Osaka Sr. Lectr.

Other Staff: 3 Lectrs.

Research: congenital abnormalities of head and neck in children in Sri Lanka; development and oral infections (effects of plant extracts on oral microflora); oral-facial pain and oral submucous fibrosis; systemic effects and periodontal disease; ultrasonographic and sialographic findings of salivary gland diseases

Oral Pathology

Tel: (081) 239 7431

Amaratunga, E. A. P. D., BDS Peradeniya, MSc Lond., MS Colombo, FDSRCS, FFDRCSI Sr. Lectr.

Dissanayake, S. B. A., MB BS Ceyl., MPhil Peradeniya, DCh Lond. Sr. Lectr.

Dissanayake, U. B., BDS Peradeniya, MPhil S.Lanka, PhD S.Lanka Sr. Lectr.; Head*

Jayasooriya, P. R., BDS Ceyl., PhD Tokyo Sr. Lectr.

Thilakaratne, W. M., BDS Ceyl., MS Ceyl., FDSRCS Prof.

Other Staff: 2 Lectrs.

Research: candida and fungal infections; oral cancer; osteosarcoma; precancer; salivary gland tumours

Prosthetic Dentistry

Tel: (081) 239 7381
Anandamoorthy, T., BDS, FDSRCPSGlas   Sr. Lectr.; Head*
Other Staff: 3 Lectrs.
Research: speech aid prosthesis

Restorative Dentistry

Tel: (081) 239 7361 E-mail: kaw@pdn.ac.lk
Amarathunga, D. I., BDS Peradeniya, MPhil   Sr. Lectr.
Wettasinghe, K. A., BDS Ceyl., MS Col., FDSRCSEd   Sr. Lectr.
Wijeratne, K. M., BDS Peradeniya, MPhil   Sr. Lectr.; Head*
Other Staff: 1 Lectr.
Research: dental trauma; endodontics bonding techniques; fluorosis

MEDICINE

Tel: (081) 239 6200 Fax: (081) 238 9106
E-mail: dean@med.pdn.ac.lk

Anaesthesiology

Tel: (081) 239 6240
Goonasekara, C. D. A., MB BS Ceyl., MD Ceyl., MPhil Peradeniya, PhD Lond., FFARCSI   Prof.; Head*
Varathan, S., MD Col., PhD Osaka   Sr. Lectr.
Other Staff: 1 Staff Member

Anatomy

Tel: (081) 239 6260
Chandrasekara, M. S., BDS Ceyl., PhD Newcastle(UK)   Prof.
Gunasinghe, N. P. A. D., BDS Ceyl.   Sr. Lectr.
Sabanayagam, M. I., BDS Ceyl., PhD Belf.   Prof.; Head*
Other Staff: 7 Lectrs.

Biochemistry

Tel: (081) 239 6320
Amarasinghe, A. B. C., BSc Ceyl., MS S.Carolina, MSc S.Carolina, PhD Buffalo   Sr. Lectr.
Athauda, S. B. P., BSc Peradeniya, PhD Tokyo   Sr. Lectr.
Fernando, P. H. P., BVSc Ceyl., MAgric Miyazaki, PhD Kagoshima   Sr. Lectr.
Ranasinghe, J. G. S., BVSc S.Lanka, MScAgric Miyazaki   Sr. Lectr.
Sivakanesan, R., BVSc Ceyl., PhD Hull   Assoc. Prof.; Head*
Other Staff: 4 Lectrs.
Research: aspartic proteases; folic acid; lipids in health and diseases; megaloblastic anaemia; oral cancer

Community Medicine

Tel: (081) 239 6490
E-mail: commed@med.pdn.ac.lk
Dharmaratne, S. D., MB BS Col., MSc Col.   Sr. Lectr.
Jayasinghe, A., MB BS Ceyl.   Sr. Lectr.; Head*
Kumarasiri, P. V. R., MB BS Ceyl., MSc Col., MD Col.   Sr. Lectr.
Nugegoda, D. B., MB BS Ceyl., MSc Lond.   Prof.
Pethiyagoda, K., MB BS Peradeniya, MSc Col., PhD   Sr. Lectr.
Other Staff: 4 Lectrs

Forensic Medicine

Tel: (081) 239 6400
Edussuriya, D. H., MB BS N.C'bo.Med.Coll.   Sr. Lectr.; Head*
Other Staff: 3 Lectrs.

Medical Education Unit

Tel: (081) 239 6230
Athuraliya, T. N. C., MB BS, FRCPEd   Dir.*
Other Staff: 1 Lectr.

Medicine

Tel: (081) 239 6470
Hewawitharana, P. B., MB BS Ceyl., MD Ceyl.   Sr. Lectr.

Illangasekera, V. L. U., MB BS Ceyl., MD Ceyl.   Assoc. Prof.
Jayalath, W. A. T. A., MB BS Peradeniya, MD Col.   Sr. Lectr.
Jayasinghe, M. W. C. J., MB BS Ceyl., MD Ceyl.   Sr. Lectr.; Head*
Kularatne, S. A. M., MB BS Ceyl., MD Ceyl.   Prof.
Senanayake, A. M. A. N. K., MD Ceyl., DSc Peradeniya, PhD, FRCP, FRCPEd   Sr. Prof.
Research: epilepsy; poisoning; snake bite

Microbiology

Tel: (081) 239 6531
Thevanesam, V., MB BS Ceyl., DM Peradeniya   Prof.; Head*
Other Staff: 3 Lectrs.
Research: antibiotics; diagnostics in infections; diseases; rhinospordiosis; rickettsial pox

Nuclear Medicine Unit

Tel: (081) 239 6250
Nanayakkara, D. K. K., MB BS Ceyl.   Sr. Lectr.
Udugama, J. M. C., MB BS Ceyl.   Sr. Lectr.; Head*
Watawanna, L., MB BS Ceyl.   Sr. Lectr.
Other Staff: 1 Lectr.

Obstetrics and Gynaecology

Tel: (081) 239 6450
Amarasinghe, W. I., MB BS Ceyl., FRCOG, FSLCOG   Prof.
Karunanada, S. A., MB BS Ceyl., MS Ceyl.   Sr. Lectr.
Samarakoon, E. W., MB BS Ceyl., MS Col.   Sr. Lectr.; Head*
Research: adult health and sexuality; heart diseases and reproductive health

Paediatrics

Tel: (081) 239 6410
Abeygunawardena, A. S., MB BS Peradeniya, MD Col.   Sr. Lectr.
Abeysekara, C. K., MB BS Ceyl.   Sr. Lectr.; Head*
Wickramasinghe, E. M. N., MB BS S.Lanka, MD Colombo   Sr. Lectr.
Wijekoon, A. S. B., MB BS Ceyl., MD S.Lanka   Prof.
Research: nephrology; respiratory diseases

Parasitology

Fax: (081) 239 6510
Edirisinghe, J. S., MB BS Ceyl., MSc Lond., MD Col., PhD Lond.   Prof.
Iddawela, W. M. D. R.
Weilgama, D. J., BVSc Ceyl., MVSc Ceyl., PhD Qld.   Prof.
Wijesundera, M. K. de S., MB BS Ceyl., MSc Lond., MD Col., PhD Ceyl.   Sr. Prof.; Head*
Other Staff: 1 Lectr.
Research: pathogenic free-living amoebae; soil-transmitted helminthiases; toxocariasis and zoonotic diseases

Pathology

Tel: (081) 239 6360
Dissanayake, A. M. S. D. M., MB BS Peradeniya, DPath Col., MD Lond., PhD Lond.   Sr. Lectr.
Gunawardena, R. T. A. W., MB BS Col., MD Col., DPath Col.   Sr. Lectr.
Ratnatunga, N. V. I., MB BS Peradeniya, MD Colombo, PhD Peradeniya, DPath Col.   Prof.; Head*
Other Staff: 1 Lectr.
Research: haemophilia and bleeding disease in Sri Lanka; nutritional anaemia; renal diseases in Sri Lanka; thalassaemia and haemoglobinopathies in Sri Lanka

Pharmacology

Tel: (081) 239 6380
Aturaliya, T. N. C., MB BS Ceyl.   Sr. Lectr.; Head*
Dangahadeniya, U., MB BS Peradeniya, MD Col.   Sr. Lectr.

Other Staff: 2 Lectrs.
Research: drug utilisation studies

Physiology

Tel: (081) 239 6290
Ariyasinghe, A. S., MB BS Peradeniya, PhD   Sr. Lectr.
Kariyawasam, K. P. A., BDS Peradeniya, PhD Tor.   Sr. Lectr.
Nanayakkara, S. D. I., MB BS Peradeniya, MPhil Peradeniya   Sr. Lectr.
Rajaratne, A. A. J., BVSc Ceyl., MPhil Ceyl., PhD Lond.   Sr. Lectr.
Rajaratne, S. A., BVSc Peradeniya, PhD   Sr. Lectr.
Weerasinghe, V. S., BDS S.Lanka, MPhil Peradeniya, PhD S'ton.   Sr. Lectr.; Head*
Other Staff: 1 Lectr.
Research: aspects of human physiology

Psychiatry

Tel: (081) 239 6350
Abeysinghe, D. R. R., MB BS Ceyl., MD Ceyl.   Sr. Lectr.; Head*
Other Staff: 1 Lectr.
Research: alcohol; mental retardation and childhood problems; sex therapy; suicide and childhood problems

Surgery

Tel: (081) 239 6430
Aluwihare, A. P. R., MB BChir Camb., MChir Camb., FRCS, FNAS(SL)   Sr. Prof.
Buthpitiya, A. G., MB BS Ceyl., MS Ceyl.   Sr. Lectr.
Esufali, S. T., MB BS Lond., MS Col., FRCS   Sr. Lectr.
Lamawansa, M. D., MB BS S.Lanka, MS PhD, FRCSEd   Sr. Lectr.
Mathivathaney, M., MB BS MS, FRCS   Sr. Lectr.
Pethiyagoda, A. U. B., MB BS S.Lanka, MS, FRCS, FRCSEd   Sr. Lectr.
Ratnatunga, P. C. A., MB BS Ceyl., FRCS   Sr. Prof.; Head*
Rosairo, S., MB BS S.Lanka, MD Col.   Sr. Lectr.
Other Staff: 2 Lectrs.

VETERINARY MEDICINE AND ANIMAL SCIENCE

Tel: (081) 239 5700 Fax: (081) 238 9136
E-mail: deanvet@pdn.ac.lk

Basic Veterinary Science

Tel: (081) 239 5813
Abeygunawardena, I. S., BVSc Ceyl., MSc Ill.   Sr. Lectr.; Head*
Ariyaratne, H. B. S., BVSc Ceyl., MPhil Ceyl., PhD Tennessee   Sr. Lectr.
Gunawardana, V. K., BVSc Ceyl., PhD Lond.   Sr. Prof.
Jayasekara, N. K., BVSc Ceyl., MSc Ill., PhD Ill.   Sr. Lectr.
Jayasooriya, L. J. P. A. P., BVSc Peradeniya, MAgric Miyazaki, PhD RMIT   Sr. Lectr.
Mohomad, A. R., BVSc S.Lanka, PhD Lond.   Sr. Lectr.
Munasinghe, D. M. S., BVSc Peradeniya, MAgric Miyazaki   Sr. Lectr.
Wanigasekera, W. M. A. P., BSc Peradeniya, MPhil Peradeniya, PhD Kyoto   Sr. Lectr.
Other Staff: 2 Lectrs.
Research: animal endocrinology and reproductive biology; biological chemistry; immunology; livestock farming systems; reproductive biology of Asian elephants

Farm Animal Production and Health

Tel: (081) 239 5926
Abeygunawardena, H., BVSc Ceyl., MSc Ill., PhD Ill.   Prof.
Alexander, P. A. B. D., BVSc Peradeniya, MPhil Peradeniya, PhD Guelph   Sr. Lectr.
de Silva, L. N. A., BVSc S.Lanka, MPhil S.Lanka, MPhil Peradeniya   Sr. Lectr.
Gunaratne, S. P., BVSc S.Lanka, PhD Nott.   Sr. Lectr.
Kalupahana, R. S., BVSc Peradeniya   Sr. Lectr.

Perera, B. M. A. O., BVSc Ceyl., PhD Glas. Prof.

Pushpakumara, P. G. A., BVSc Peradeniya, PhD Lond.   Sr. Lectr.; Head*

Other Staff: 4 Staff Members

Research: farming system research aimed at technology development and dissemination aimed at smallholder dairy production system; repeat breeding in cattle; reproduction in goats

Veterinary Clinical Science

Tel: (081) 239 5869

Dangolla, A., BVSc Ceyl., PhD R.Vet.& Agric., Denmark   Sr. Lectr.

De Silva, D. D. N., BVSc Ceyl., PhD Camb.   Sr. Lectr.

Silva, I. D. D., BVSc Ceyl., PhD Calif.   Prof.; Head*

Other Staff: 2 Lectrs.

Research: canine dermatological conditions; medical problems in elephants; veterinary haematology

Veterinary Pathobiology

Tel: (081) 239 5735

Abeynayake, Preeni, BVSc Ceyl., PhD Massey Prof.

Arulkanthan, A., BVSc Peradeniya, MSc   Sr. Lectr.

Gunawardena, G. S. P. de S., BVSc Peradeniya, PhD Peradeniya   Sr. Lectr.

Hathurusinghe, M. H., BVSc Peradeniya, MPhil Peradeniya   Sr. Lectr.

Rajapakse, R. P. V. J., BVSc Ceyl., PhD Peradeniya Prof.; Head*

Wijewardena, T. G., BVSc S.Lanka, MPhil S.Lanka, PhD Edin.   Prof.

Other Staff: 3 Lectrs.

Research: aetiopathology and clinical manifestation of neurological diseases in domestic animals in Sri Lanka; aetiopathology of plant toxicity in livestock; development of residue monitoring system in food of animal origin; effects of nutrition, water quality, innate immunity and diseases on the productive performance of Tilapia (Oreochromics) species in Sri Lanka; specialised diagnostic techniques for confirming bacterial diseases

SPECIAL CENTRES, ETC

Agribusiness Centre (ABC)

Tel: (081) 239 5161 E-mail: abc@pdn.ac.lk

Kodituwakku, K. A. S. S., BScAgric Peradeniya, MBA Stir., PhD Stir.   Dir.*

Agricultural Biotechnology Centre

Tel: (081) 238 7178 E-mail: agbc@pdn.ac.lk

Basnayake, B. F. A., BSc Cran., DEng Paris VI Dir.*

Research: animal disease diagnosis through molecular techniques; bioinformatics; characterisation of Sri Lankan medicinal plants, aquatic plants by RADP, AFLP technique; genetically modified organism/ foods (GMO/GMF) testing in Sri Lanka; plant genetic transformation

Career Guidance Unit (CGU)

Perera, B. M. K., BA Colombo   Dir.*

Distance and Continuing Education, Centre for

Tel: (081) 239 2209 Fax: (081) 238 9206

Wijeyeweera, R. L., BDS Ceyl., PhD N.Y.   Prof.; Dir.*

Engineering Design Centre

Tel: (081) 239 3667 Fax: (081) 238 8169 E-mail: edc@pdn.ac.lk

Seneviratne, S. K., BScEngin Ceyl., MSc Leeds Dir.*

Other Staff: 3 Staff Members

Engineering Education Unit

Tel: (081) 238 8158 Fax: (081) 238 8029

Nandalal, K. D. W., BScEng Peradeniya, MEng Asian I.T., Bangkok, PhD Wageningen   Dir.*

English Language Teaching Unit

Tel: (081) 239 2544 E-mail: cellawala@yahoo.com

Ellawala, C., BA Peradeniya   Head*

Other Staff: 28 Instrs.

Environmental Studies, Centre for (CES)

Tel: (081) 239 2679

Hennayake, H. M. S. K., BA Ceyl., MA Ceyl., PhD Syr.   Prof.; Co-ordinator*

Other Staff: 2 Staff Members

Information Technology, Centre for

Tel: (081) 239 2070 Fax: (081) 238 4488 E-mail: liya@ee.pdn.ac.lk

Liyanage, K. M., BScEng Peradeniya, PhD Tokyo Dir.*

Maha-Illuppallama Teaching Unit

Tel: (025) 224 9137

Malkanthi Fonseka, R., BScAgric Peradeniya, MSc Ghent, PhD Ehime   Sr. Lectr.

Pathmarajah, S., BScAgric Peradeniya, MPhil Peradeniya, PhD Asian I.T., Bangkok   Sr. Lectr.

Rambanda, M., BScAgric Peradeniya, MSc Obihiro Lectr.-in-Charge*

Somaratne, H. M., BScAgric Peradeniya, MSc Obihiro, PhD Manc.   Sr. Lectr.

Thiruchelvam, S., BScAgric Ceyl., MSc Obihiro, PhD Peradeniya   Sr. Lectr.

Other Staff: 3 Staff Members

Science Education Unit

Tel: (081) 239 4691

Karunaratne, S., BSc Ceyl., MScAgric Peradeniya, MEd Brist., PhD Mich.State   Sr. Lectr.

Other Staff: 1 Staff Member

Staff Development Centre (SDC)

Tel: (081) 239 5265 E-mail: deepthib@pdn.ac.lk

Bandara, D. C., BScAgric S.Lanka, MSc Penn.State Prof.; Dir.*

CONTACT OFFICERS

Academic affairs. Vice-Chancellor: Abeygunawardena, Prof. H., BVSc Ceyl., MSc Ill., PhD Ill. (E-mail: vc@pdn.ac.lk)

Admissions (first degree). Registrar: De Alwis, Ranjith, BSc Peradeniya, MSc Peradeniya (E-mail: registrar@pdn.ac.lk)

Admissions (higher degree). (Contact the Dean of the appropriate faculty)

Computing services. Director, Centre for Information Technology: Liyanage, K. M., BScEng Peradeniya, PhD Tokyo (E-mail: liya@ee.pdn.ac.lk)

Finance. Bursar: Ganthune, M. D. (E-mail: bursar@pdn.ac.lk)

General enquiries. Registrar: De Alwis, Ranjith, BSc Peradeniya, MSc Peradeniya (E-mail: registrar@pdn.ac.lk)

Library (chief librarian). Librarian: Harison Perera, P. E., BA Ceyl., MLS W.Ont. (E-mail: librarian@pdn.ac.lk)

Research. Senior Assistant Registrar (Research): Samarasinghe, P. K. (E-mail: acad@pdn.ac.lk)

Strategic planning. Vice-Chancellor: Abeygunawardena, Prof. H., BVSc Ceyl., MSc Ill., PhD Ill. (E-mail: vc@pdn.ac.lk)

Student union. President: Abeysinghe, D.

[Information supplied by the institution as at 10 October 2007, and edited by the ACU]

RAJARATA UNIVERSITY OF SRI LANKA

Founded 1996

Member of the Association of Commonwealth Universities

Postal Address: Administrative Building, Mihintale, Sri Lanka
Telephone: (025) 66650 **Fax:** (025) 66511
URL: http://www.rjt.ac.lk/

VICE-CHANCELLOR*—Nandasena, Prof. K. A.
REGISTRAR‡—Karunaratne, A. G., BCom Ceyl., MA B&P SLanka
BURSAR—Dassanayake, R. M., BCom Sri Jay. leave
LIBRARIAN—De Silva, W. R. G., BA Ceyl., MLib Monash, FLA

UNIVERSITY OF RUHUNA, SRI LANKA

Founded 1984

Member of the Association of Commonwealth Universities

Postal Address: Matara, Sri Lanka
Telephone: (041) 222 2681-2 **Fax:** (041) 222 2683, 222 2998
URL: http://www.ruh.ac.lk

VICE-CHANCELLOR*—Mendis, Prof. A. L. S., MB BS Ceyl., PhD Ruhuna
REGISTRAR‡—Vineetheratne, A. N. H., BA Peradeniya, MA

GENERAL INFORMATION

History. The university was established as Ruhuna University College in 1979 and achieved full university status in 1984.

Admission to first degree courses (see also Sri Lankan Introduction). General Certificate of Education (GCE) A level in 4 approved subjects with a minimum aggregate mark of 180.

First Degrees (see also Sri Lankan Directory to Subjects of Study). BA(Gen), BA(Spe), BBA, BCom, BSc(Agric), BSc(Eng), BSc(Gen), BSc(Spe), MB BS.

Higher Degrees (see also Sri Lankan Directory to Subjects of Study).
Master's. MA, MBA, MPhil.
Doctoral. DM, PhD.

Language of Instruction. Sinhalese and English.

Libraries. Volumes: 140,000.

FACULTIES/SCHOOLS

Agriculture
Tel: (041) 229 2382 Fax: (041) 229 2384
E-mail: dean@slt.net.lk
Dean: Weerasinghe, Prof. K. D. N., MScAgric P.F.U., Moscow, PhD P.F.U., Moscow

Engineering
Tel: (091) 224 5762
Dean: Liyanage, Kithsiri, BScEng Peradeniya, PhD Tokyo

Humanities and Social Sciences
Tel: (041) 222 7010 Fax: (041) 222 7010
Dean: Wawwage, S., BA Ceyl., MPhil Ruhuna

Management and Finance
Tel: (041) 222 7015 Fax: (041) 222 7015
Dean: Perera, H. S. C., BSc Sri Jay., MCom Ruhuna

Medicine
Tel: (091) 223 4907 Fax: (091) 222 3314
E-mail: dean@sri.lanka.net
Dean: Mendis, Prof. A. L. S., MB BS Ceyl., PhD Ruhuna

Science
Tel: (041) 222 2701 Fax: (041) 222 2701
Dean: Pathirana, Prof. R. N., BSc Colombo, MSc S'ton., PhD S'ton.

ACADEMIC UNITS

Accounting and Finance
Anulawathi, T. M., BCom Ruhuna, MBA Colombo Sr. Lectr.; Head*
Dayananda, A. G., BBA Ruhuna, MMA Sri Jay. Sr. Lectr.
Indrani, M. W., BCom Ruhuna Sr. Lectr.
Other Staff: 8 Lectrs.

Agricultural Biology
Tel: (041) 229 2383 Fax: (041) 229 2384
Nugaliyadda, L., BSc Peradeniya, MSc Philippines, PhD Newcastle(UK)
Punchihewa, R. K. W., BSc(Agr) Peradeniya, MSc Guelph, DPhil Head*
Rajapakse, R. H. S., BScAgric Ceyl., MScAgric Ceyl., PhD Flor. Prof.
Senanyake, S. G. J. N., BScAgric Ceyl., PhD R.Vet.& Agric., Denmark Prof.
Other Staff: 5 Lectrs.

Agricultural Chemistry
Tel: (041) 229 2385
Jayamanna, V. S., BScAgric Ruhuna, MPhil
Wanniarachchi, S. D., BSc(Agric) Ruhuna, MSc Guelph, PhD Guelph Sr. Lectr.; Head*
Wijerathne, Vinitha, BScAgric Ceyl., MSc Ghent, PhD Copenhagen Sr. Lectr.
Other Staff: 5 Lectrs.

Agricultural Economics
Tel: (041) 229 2385
Amarasingha, O., BScAgric Ceyl., MSc Ghent, PhD Ghent Sr. Lectr.
Darmasena, K. H., BScAgric Ceyl., MPhil Peradeniya Sr. Lectr.
De Soyza, M., BScAgric Peradeniya, MSc Wageningen, PhD Tokyo Sr. Lectr.; Head*
Wijerathne, W. M. M. P., BScAgric Ceyl., MSc Ghent, PhD Wageningen Prof.
Other Staff: 4 Lectrs.

Agricultural Engineering
Tel: (041) 229 2386
Alwis, P. L. A. G., BScAgric Peradeniya, DrIng Montpellier, PhD Montpellier Sr. Lectr.; Head*
Navaratne, C. M., BSc Ruhuna, MSc Cardiff Sr. Lectr.
Weerasinghe, K. D. N., MScAgric P.F.U., Moscow, PhD P.F.U., Moscow Prof.
Other Staff: 5 Lectrs.

Animal Science
Tel: (041) 229 2387
Attapaththu, N. S. B. M., BSc(Agric) Ruhuna, MSc NZ Sr. Lectr.
Gunawardane, W. W. D. A., BScAgric Ceyl., PhD Zür. Prof.
Pathirana, K. K., BVSc Ceyl., MSc McG., PhD McG. Prof.
Serasinghe, R. Thakshila, BScAgric Ceyl., PhD Sur. Assoc. Prof.; Head*
Other Staff: 5 Lectrs.

Botany
Tel: (041) 222 7024
Abeysingha, P. D., BSc Ruhuna, MSc V.U.Brussels, PhD V.U.Brussels Sr. Lectr.
De Silva, M. P., BSc Ceyl., PhD T.H.Aachen Prof.
De Silva, P. H. A. Udul, BSc Kelaniya, PhD Reading Sr. Lectr.
Dissanayake, Nanda P., BSc Peradeniya, PhD Reading Sr. Lectr.
Hettiarachchi, S., BSc Kelaniya, MSc Brussels, PhD Brussels Sr. Lectr.
Jayatissa, L. P., BSc Ruhuna, PhD Stir. Sr. Lectr.

Kariyawasam, P. S., BSc Ruhuna, MSc Flor. Sr. Lectr.
Samarakoon, S. P., BSc Ceyl., MSc Qld. Prof.
Sapumohotti, W. P., BSc Kelaniya, MSc Sci.U.Malaysia, PhD Ruhuna Sr. Lectr.
Other Staff: 3 Lectrs.

Chemistry
Tel: (041) 222 7023
De Silva, M. S. W., BSc Peradeniya, PhD Sr. Lectr.
Dissanayaka, A. S., BSc Colombo, PhD Wash.State Sr. Lectr.
Edussuriya, M., MSc Moscow, PhD Moscow Sr. Lectr.
Indurugolla, Deepani, BSc Peradeniya, MSc Kansas, PhD Kansas Sr. Lectr.
Manawadevi, U. G. Y., BSc Peradeniya, MSc PhD Sr. Lectr.
Pathirana, H. M. K. K., BSc Colombo, PhD Aston Assoc. Prof.; Head*
Pathirana, R. N., BSc Colombo, MSc S'ton., PhD S'ton. Prof.
Priyadarshane, B. K. V., BSc Ruhuna, PhD Frib. Sr. Lectr.
Weerasinghe, M. S. S., BSc Colombo, PhD Minn. Sr. Lectr.
Other Staff: 9 Lectrs.

Computer Unit
Tel: (041) 222 7019
No staff at present

Crop Science
Tel: (041) 229 2389
Amarasekara, D. A. B. N., BScAgric Peradeniya, MSc Leuven Sr. Lectr.
Amarasinghe, M. K. T. K., BSc Ruhuna, MPhil Ruhuna Sr. Lectr.
Hettiarichchi, M. P., BSc Peradeniya, PhD Vienna
Liyanage, M. De S., BSc Peradeniya, PhD Colombo, MSc Sr. Lectr.
Subasinghe, S., BSc Ruhuna, MSc Ruhuna, MSc Asian I.T., Bangkok, PhD Ruhuna Assoc. Prof.; Head*
Other Staff: 4 Lectrs.

Economics
Tel: (041) 222 7014
Atapattu, D., BA Ceyl., MA McG., PhD McG. Prof.; Head*
Chandradasa, A. J. M., BA Peradeniya, MA Ruhuna Sr. Lectr.
Dayananda, P. M., BA Vidyal., MPhil Ruhuna Sr. Lectr.
Dervin, S. K., BA Ruhuna, MA Ruhuna Sr. Lectr.
Hemapala, R., BCom Ceyl., MPhil Ruhuna Sr. Lectr.
Nishantha, K. A., BA Sri Jay., MSc Colombo Sr. Lectr.
Rupannada, W., BA Colombo, MSc Asian I.T., Bangkok Sr. Lectr.
Sarath, H. K., BA Ruhuna, MSc Sr. Lectr.
Sumanarathne, B. M., BA Peradeniya, MA Ruhuna Sr. Lectr.
Udayakanthi, K. K. S., BA Sri Jay., MA Ruhuna Sr. Lectr.
Vithanage, P., BA Ceyl., MSc Peradeniya, MPhil Ruhuna Sr. Lectr.

Wijesiri, E. G., BA Peradeniya, MPhil Peradeniya
Sr. Lectr.
Other Staff: 10 Lectrs.

Fish Biology

Tel: (041) 222 7026

Amarasinghe, P. B., BSc Ruhuna, MPhil Ruhuna,
PhD Ruhuna Sr. Lectr.
Cumaranatunga, P. R. T., BSc Vidyal., PhD S'ton.
Sr. Lectr.; Head*
Nissanka, C., BSc Kelaniya, PhD Kelaniya Sr.
Lectr.
Priyadarshana, D. G. T., BSc Ruhuna, MPhil
Ruhuna, PhD Sr. Lectr.
Other Staff: 7 Lectrs.

Geography

Tel: (041) 222 7013

Dayalatha, W. K. V., BA Ruhuna, MA Ruhuna
Sr. Lectr.
Edirisinghe, Gnana, BA Ruhuna, MA Ruhuna Sr.
Lectr.
Fernando, S. L. J., BA Ruhuna, MPhil Ruhuna Sr.
Lectr.
Hewage, P., BA Ceyl., MSc Lond., PhD Ruhuna
Sr. Lectr.
Mohamed Ali, Sitty K., BA Ceyl., PhD Durh.
Sr. Lectr.
Premadasa, L. A., BA Peradeniya, MA Peradeniya,
PhD Peradeniya Assoc. Prof.
Rathnayaka, L. Kanthi, BA Ceyl., PhD Edin.
Prof.
Rathnayaka, M., BA Colombo, MA Colombo Sr.
Lectr.
Razzak, M. A. A., BA Vidyod., MA Colombo Sr.
Lectr.
Senarath, G., BA Colombo, MA Colombo Sr.
Lectr.
Weerakkody, U. C. de S., BA Vidyod., MSc
I.T.C.Enschede, PhD Ruhuna Assoc. Prof.
Wijerathne, S., BA Ruhuna, MA Ruhuna Sr.
Lectr.
Other Staff: 4 Lectrs.

History

Tel: (041) 222 7017

Bohingamuwa, B. H. W., BA Ban., MA Poona
Sr. Lectr.
Kanthi, J. K. A., BA Ruhuna, MA Sri Jay., MPhil
Delhi, PhD Delhi Sr. Lectr.
Piyasena, S. A., BA Peradeniya, MPhil Ruhuna Sr.
Lectr.; Head*
Wawwage, S., BA Ceyl., MPhil Ruhuna Sr.
Lectr.
Other Staff: 4 Lectrs.

Management and Entrepreneurship

Tel: (041) 222 7015

Jinadasa, P. C. V., BSc Sri Jay., MSc Sri Jay. Sr.
Lectr.
Karunanayake, R., BCom Colombo, MA Osaka,
PhD Osaka Sr. Lectr.
Perera, H. S. C., BSc Sri Jay., MCom Ruhuna Sr.
Lectr.; Head*
Rathnayake, R. M., BCom Peradeniya, MCom
Ruhuna Sr. Lectr.
Silva, P. E. D. D., BCom Kelaniya Sr. Lectr.
Sriyani, G. T. M., BCom Ruhuna, MBA Colombo
Sr. Lectr.
Sriyani, K. A. S., BCom Ruhuna, MPhil Ruhuna
Sr. Lectr.
Other Staff: 11 Lectrs.

Mathematics

Tel: (041) 222 7018

Abeyratne, M. K., BSc Kelaniya, MSc Kaiserslautern
Sr. Lectr.; Head*
Geeganage, S. D. L., BSc Colombo, MSc Sri Jay.
Sr. Lectr.
Jayantha, P. A., BSc Kelaniya, MSc Sri Jay. Sr.
Lectr.
Jayasekara, L. A. L. W., BSc Kelaniya, MSc
Kyushu, PhD Kyushu Sr. Lectr.
Shantidevi, K. C. N., BSc Sri Jay., MSc Hiroshima
Sr. Lectr.

Wedagedara, J. R., BSc Kelaniya, PhD Wales Sr.
Lectr.
Wijayasiri, M. P. A., BSc Vidyal., MSc Brad.,
MPhil Kelaniya Sr. Lectr.
Other Staff: 5 Lectrs.

Pali and Buddhist Studies

Tel: (041) 222 7011

Ariyadewa, Rev. V., BA Kelaniya, MA Kelaniya,
PhD Ban. Sr. Lectr.
Dhammajothi, Rev. D., MA Peradeniya, PhD Ban.
Sr. Lectr.
Heenbanda, E. H. M., BA Peradeniya, MPhil
Peradeniya Sr. Lectr.
Mahinda, U., BA Kelaniya, MA Kelaniya, MPhil
Kelaniya Sr. Lectr.
Nandawansa, Rev. M., BA Kelaniya, MA Kelaniya,
PhD J.Nehru U. Sr. Lectr.
Ruhunuhewa, A. J., BA Kelaniya, MA Paris IV,
PhD Paris IV Sr. Lectr.
Siriniwasa, T., BA Kelaniya, MPhil Kelaniya Sr.
Lectr.
Soratha, Rev. M., BA Kelaniya, MA Colombo,
MPhil Ruhuna Prof.; Head*
Other Staff: 5 Lectrs.

Physics

Tel: (041) 222 7022

Dharmarathne, W. G. D., BSc Peradeniya, MSc
Tufts, PhD Tufts Prof.; Head*
Fernando, C. A. N., BSc Colombo, MPhil Ruhuna,
PhD Kanazawa Prof.
Samarasekara, P., BSc Kelaniya, MSc Flor. Sr.
Lectr.
Yapa, K. K. A. S., BSc Kelaniya, MSc Tufts, PhD
Tufts Sr. Lectr.
Other Staff: 3 Lectrs.

Sinhala

Tel: (041) 222 7016

Amarasekare, K. G., BA Kelaniya, MPhil Kelaniya
Sr. Lectr.
Amarasinghe, J., BA Peradeniya, MA Peradeniya
Sr. Lectr.
Ananda, Rev. K., BA Peradeniya, MA Peradeniya
Sr. Lectr.
Dhamminda, Rev. A., BA Vidyal., MA Kelaniya
Sr. Lectr.
Dharmawathie, R. P., BA Kelaniya, MA Ruhuna
Sr. Lectr.
Ekanayake, P. B., MA Vidyal., PhD Peradeniya
Prof.
Kotawalagedara, Angel, BA Peradeniya, MA
Peradeniya Sr. Lectr.
Manawadu, S., BA Vidyal., MA Kelaniya Sr.
Lectr.
Sugathapala, P. D., BA Peradeniya, MPhil Ruhuna
Sr. Lectr.
Wimalasiri, P., BA Peradeniya, MA Peradeniya Sr.
Lectr.
Other Staff: 6 Lectrs.

Sociology

Tel: (041) 222 7012

Amarasinghe, S. W., BA Peradeniya, MSc Asian
I.T., Bangkok, PhD J.Nehru U. Prof.; Head*
Ekanayake, P. R., BA Ruhuna, MA Ruhuna
Perera, M. N. M., BA Colombo, MA Colombo Sr.
Lectr.
Ranaweera Banda, R. M., BA Peradeniya, MA
Colombo, PhD J.Nehru U. Sr. Lectr.
Wijekoon, Banda T. M., BA Peradeniya, MA
Peradeniya Sr. Lectr.
Wijesundara, M. A. C. G., BA Colombo, MSc
Kelaniya
Other Staff: 2 Lectrs.

Zoology

Tel: (041) 222 7025

Amarasinghe, N. J. de S., BSc Ceyl., PhD Namur
Sr. Lectr.
Bogahawatta, Nandanie, BSc Sri Jay., MSc Sri
Jay., PhD Reading Sr. Lectr.
De Silva, M. P. K. S. K., BSc Kelaniya, MSc
V.U.Brussels Sr. Lectr.
Guruge, W. A. H. P., BSc Sr. Lectr.

Wegiriya, H. C. E., BSc Kelaniya, PhD Reading
Sr. Lectr.
Wickramasinghe, M. G. Vinitha, BSc Sri Jay.,
PhD Reading Sr. Lectr.
Other Staff: 4 Lectrs.

ENGINEERING

Tel: (091) 224 5762

Civil and Environmental Engineering

Tel: (091) 224 5765

Alagiyawanna, A. M. N., BSc Asian I.T., Bangkok,
MSc Asian I.T., Bangkok Sr. Lectr.
Silva, G. H. A. C., BSc Peradeniya, MEng Tokyo,
PhD Tokyo Sr. Lectr.
Somasundaraswaran, A. K., BSc Peradeniya, DEng
Asian I.T., Bangkok, PhD Sr. Lectr.; Head*
Wijayaratne, T. M. N., BSc Moratuwa, MEng
Asian I.T., Bangkok, PhD Yokohama N. Sr.
Lectr.
Other Staff: 11 Lectrs.

Electrical and Information Engineering

Tel: (091) 224 5766

Gunawickrama, S. H. K. M. N., MSc PhD Sr.
Lectr.
Wickramaratne, L. S., BSc Moratuwa, DPhil Sus.
Sr. Lectr.
Other Staff: 11 Lectrs.

Interdisciplinary studies

5 Lectrs.

Mechanical and Manufacturing Engineering

Tel: (091) 224 5767

Ambawatta, H. C., MSc Moscow, PhD Moscow
Head*
Baduge, Sumith, BSc Moratuwa, MSc PhD Sr.
Lectr.
Other Staff: 7 Lectrs.

MEDICINE

Tel: (091) 223 4907 Fax: (091) 222 3314
E-mail: dean@sri.lanka.net

Anatomy

Illeperuma, I., BSc Peradeniya, PhD Otago Sr.
Lectr.
Nanayakkara, B. G., BDS S.Lanka, PhD Ruhuna
Sr. Lectr.
Weerasuriya, T. R., MB BS Peradeniya, DMSc
Kyushu Prof.; Head*
Other Staff: 5 Lectrs.

Biochemistry

Jayatilaka, K. A. P. W., MSc Sri Jay., PhD Ruhuna
Sr. Lectr.
Pathirana, C., BSc Peradeniya, PhD S'ton. Prof.;
Head*
Ruwinkumara, N. K. V. M., BSc Kelaniya, MSc
Colombo Sr. Lectr.
Other Staff: 1 Lectr.

Community Medicine

Fonseka, P. H. G., MB BS Colombo, PhD Ruhuna
Prof.; Head*
Liyanage, K. D. C. E., BSc Baroda, MSc Peradeniya
Sr. Lectr.
Wijsiri, W. A. A., MB BS Colombo, MSc Sr.
Lectr.
Wimalasundera, MB BS Peradeniya, PhD Ruhuna
Sr. Lectr.
Other Staff: 7 Lectrs.

Forensic Medicine

Chadrasiri, N., MB BS Ceyl., MD Colombo, DM
Lond., FRCPGlas Prof.; Head*
Widanapathirana, M., MB BS Colombo, MD
Colombo
Other Staff: 2 Lectrs.

Medicine

Ariyananda, P. L., MB BS Ceyl., MD Ceyl., DCH
Ceyl., FRCP Prof.

Mohideen, M. R., MB BS Ceyl., MD Colombo
Prof.

Pathirana, K. D., MB BS Peradeniya, MD Colombo
Sr. Lectr.

Sarath, L. K. L., MB BS Ceyl., MD Colombo   Sr.
Lectr.

Weeraratne, T. P., MB BS Ruhuna, MD Colombo

Other Staff: 1 Lectr.

Microbiology

De Silva, N., MB BS Patna, MD Colombo   Sr.
Lectr.; Head*

Other Staff: 2 Lectrs.

Nuclear Medicine Unit

Liyanage, K. D. C. E., BSc Baroda, MSc Peradeniya
Sr. Lectr.; Head*

Obstetrics and Gynaecology

Gunasekear, A. G. A. de S., MB BS Ceyl.,
FRCOG   Prof.

Gunawardane, I. M. R., MB BS Ceyl., MS
Colombo, FRCOG   Prof.; Head*

Kularatne, M. D. C. S., MB BS Ruhuna, MS
Colombo   Sr. Lectr.

Samarage, L. H., MB BS Peradeniya, MS Colombo
Sr. Lectr.

Other Staff: 2 Lectrs.

Paediatrics

Amarasena, T. S. D., MB BS Ceyl., MD Colombo
Sr. Lectr.; Head*

Devasiri, I. V., MB BS Ruhuna, MD Colombo   Sr.
Lectr.

Gunawardane, T. P. J., MB BS Ruhuna, MD
Colombo   Sr. Lectr.

Jayantha, U. K., MB BS Ruhuna, MD Colombo
Sr. Lectr.

Liyanarachchi, N. D., MB BS Colombo, MD
Colombo

Other Staff: 2 Lectrs.

Parasitology

Mudalige, M. P. S., MB BS Colombo, MD Colombo

Weerasooriya, M. V., MB BS S.Lanka, DMSc
Kyushu   Prof.; Head*

Other Staff: 7 Lectrs.

Pathology

Ajith, L. H., MB BS Colombo, MD Colombo

Mohideen, M. R., MB BS Ceyl., MD Colombo
Sr. Lectr.

Mudduwa, L. K. B., MB BS Colombo, MD Colombo
Head*

Other Staff: 3 Lectrs.

Pharmacology

Fernando, A. I., BA Open(UK), MB BS Ceyl.,
FRCP   Prof.; Head*

Hettiarchchi, L. M., MB BS PhD

Other Staff: 1 Lectr.

Physiology

Gunaweradena, S., MB BS Ruhuna, PhD Ruhuna

Imendra, K. G., MB BS PhD

Mendis, A. L. S., MB BS Ceyl., PhD Ruhuna
Prof.

Somasiri, K. G., MB BS Peradeniya, PhD Ruhuna
Sr. Lectr.; Head*

Other Staff: 4 Lectrs.

Psychiatry

Jayawardene, M. K. G. R. De S., MB BS Ceyl.,
FRCP   Sr. Lectr.; Head*

Other Staff: 2 Lectrs.

Surgery

De Silva, W. A. S. A., MB BS Ceyl., FRCS   Sr.
Lectr.

Kumara, M. M. A. J., MB BS Peradeniya, MS
Colombo, FRCS   Sr. Lectr.

Kumarasinghe, J. P. M., MB BS Ruhuna, MD
Colombo   Sr. Lectr.

Other Staff: 2 Lectrs.

CONTACT OFFICERS

Academic affairs. Academic Establishment:
Renuka, Piyal, BA Sri Jay.

Accommodation. (Senior) Assistant Registrar,
Student Affairs: Kalugama, P. S., BA Sri Jay.,
MA Lond.

Admissions (first degree). Senior Assistant
Registrar, Student Affairs: Kalugama, P. S.,
BA Sri Jay., MA Lond.

Admissions (higher degree). Assistant
Registrar (Examinations): Yapa, Manjula,
BSc Ruhuna

Careers. Director, Careers Guidance Unit:
Hewage, P., BA Ceyl., MSc Lond., PhD Ruhuna

Examinations. Assistant Registrar
(Examinations): Yapa, Manjula, BSc Ruhuna

Finance. Bursar: Gunadasa, Yaddehige, BCom
Sri Jay.

General enquiries. Registrar: Vineetheratne, A.
N. H., BA Peradeniya, MA

Health services. University Medical Officer:
Gunawardena, D. K., MB BS Ceyl.

Library (enquiries). Librarian: Sirisena, K. J.,
BA MALib

Personnel/human resources. Senior Assistant
Registrar, Non-Academic Establishments:
Vineerharatna, M. N. H., BA Peradeniya, MA
Kelaniya

Publications. Assistant Registrar, Academic and
Publication: Yapa, Manjula, BSc Ruhuna

Scholarships, awards, loans. Assistant
Registrar, Student Affairs: Kalugama, P. S.,
BA Sri Jay., MA Lond.

Security. Chief Security Officer: Dias, H. N.

Sport and recreation. Director of Physical
Education: Wijetunge, S.

Staff development and training. Director,
Staff Development Centre: Ariyananda, Prof.
P. L., MB BS Ceyl., MD Ceyl., DCH Ceyl.,
FRCP

Student welfare/counselling. Director,
Student Affairs: Sendanayake, P., BA
Peradeniya, MPhil Ruhuna

Student welfare/counselling. Senior Student
Counsellor: Soratha, Rev. M., BA Kelaniya,
MA Colombo, MPhil Ruhuna

[Information supplied by the institution as at 2 March
2005, and edited by the ACU]

SABARAGAMUWA UNIVERSITY OF SRI LANKA

Founded 1995

Member of the Association of Commonwealth Universities

Postal Address: PO Box 02, Belihuloya 70140, Sri Lanka
Telephone: (045) 80087 **Fax:** (045) 87813 **E-mail:** belihul@mail.ac.lk
URL: http://www.sab.ac.lk/indextt.htm

VICE-CHANCELLOR*—Mahaliyanaarachchi, Prof. Rohana P., MScAgric Plovdiv, PhD
Peradeniya
REGISTRAR‡—Thalagune, T. K. W. T.

SOUTH EASTERN UNIVERSITY OF SRI LANKA

Founded 1995

Member of the Association of Commonwealth Universities

Postal Address: University Park, Oluvil 32360, Sri Lanka
Telephone: (067) 22 55062-4 **Fax:** (067) 22 55217 **E-mail:** seusl@seu.ac.lk
URL: http://www.seu.ac.lk

VICE-CHANCELLOR*—Husain Ismail, A. G., BEd Ceyl., MAEd Colombo, PhD Colombo
ACTING REGISTRAR‡—Hibathul Careem, M. F., BSc Eastern(S.Lanka), MSc Peradeniya
BURSAR—Gulam Rasheed, A.

GENERAL INFORMATION

History. The university was founded in 1995. It is situated in Oluvil on the south-eastern coast of Sri Lanka.

Admission to first degree courses (see also Sri Lankan Introduction). Through University Grants Commission (UGC) on the basis of General Certificate of Education (GCE) A level results.

First Degrees (see also Sri Lankan Directory to Subjects of Study). BA, BBA, BCom, BSc.
Length of course. Full-time: BA, BSc: 3–4 years; BBA, BCom: 4 years.

Higher Degrees (see also Sri Lankan Directory to Subjects of Study).
Master's. MSc.
Length of course. Full-time: MSc: 1 year.

Language of Instruction. English and Tamil.

Libraries. Volumes: 50,000. Periodicals subscribed to: 300. Special collections: Dr. M. M. Uwise (Islamic-Tamil studies); Gate Mudaliyar M. S. Kariapper (local studies).

FACULTIES/SCHOOLS

Applied Science
Tel: (067) 226 0465 Fax: (067) 226 0465
Dean: Ahmed, A. N., BScAgric Peradeniya, MSc Philippines

Arts and Culture
Tel: (067) 225 5068 Fax: (067) 225 5068
Dean: Kaleel, M. I. M., BA Peradeniya, MA Peradeniya

Management and Commerce
Tel: (067) 225 5067 E-mail: deanfmc@seu.ac.lk
Dean: Rauff, F. H. A., BBA Sri Jay., MBA Sri Jay.

ACADEMIC UNITS

Accountancy and Finance
Tel: (067) 225 5069
Amjath, M. B. M., BCom Eastern(S.Lanka), MSc Sr. Lectr.
Ishaq, K., BCom Jaffna, MCom Kerala, PhD S.Af. Sr. Lectr.; Dir., Centre for External Studies

Rauf, A. L. A., BBA Jaffna, MSc(Mgt) Sri Jay. Sr. Lectr.; Head*
Other Staff: 4 Lectrs.

Biological Sciences
Tel: (067) 226 0892
Ahmed, A. N., BScAgric Peradeniya, MSc Philippines Sr. Lectr.
Rizvi, E. M. J. M., BSc Peradeniya, MPhil Peradeniya Sr. Lectr.; Head*
Santhanam, V., BSc Colombo, MPhil Wales Sr. Lectr.
Other Staff: 2 Lectrs.

English Language Teaching Unit
Tel: (067) 225 5179 E-mail: eltu@seu.ac.lk
Navaz, A. M. M., BScAgric Peradeniya, MA Kelaniya Instr.; Head*
Other Staff: 2 Instrs.; 1 Temp. Instr.

Languages
Tel: (067) 225 5180
Jalaldeen, M. S. M., BA Peradeniya, MPhil Peradeniya Sr. Lectr.
Kalideen, K. M. H., BA Ceyl., MA Jaffna Sr. Lectr.; Head*
Rahila Umma, M. L. S., BA Peradeniya, MPhil Peradeniya
Rameez, M. A. M., BA Peradeniya, MPhil Peradeniya Sr. Lectr.
Other Staff: 7 Lectrs.; 1 Temp. Lectr.

Management Studies
Tel: (067) 225 5184
Rauff, F. H. A., BBA Sri Jay., MBA Sri Jay.
Sulaiha Beevi, M. A. C., BBA Jaffna, MSc(Mgt) Sri Jay. Sr. Lectr.
Other Staff: 13 Lectrs.

Mathematical Science
Tel: (067) 226 0467
Faham, M. A. A. M., BSc Peradeniya Co-ordinator*
Other Staff: 5 Lectrs.; 4 Temp. Asst. Lectrs.

Physical Sciences
Ragal, F. C., BSc Eastern(S.Lanka), PhD S.Af. Sr. Lectr.; Head*
Other Staff: 4 Lectrs.; 1 Temp. Asst. Lectr.

Social Sciences
Tel: (067) 225 5182
Aliff, S. M., BA Peradeniya, MPhil Peradeniya Sr. Lectr.
Ameerdeen, S. R., BA Peradeniya, MPhil Peradeniya Sr. Lectr.
Anusiya, S., BA Madr., MA Madr., MPhil Madr., PhD Madr. Sr. Lectr.
Ismail, S. M. M., MSc PhD Sr. Lectr.; Head*
Kaleel, M. I. M., BA Peradeniya, MA Peradeniya Sr. Lectr.
Kanesraja, K., BA Peradeniya, MPhil Peradeniya Sr. Lectr.
Other Staff: 8 Lectrs.; 1 Temp. Asst. Lectr.

CONTACT OFFICERS

Accommodation. (Students) Assistant Registrar (Welfare): Zubair, M. I. M.
Accommodation. (Staff) Acting Registrar: Hibathul Careem, M. F., BSc Eastern(S.Lanka), MSc Peradeniya
Admissions (first degree). Senior Assistant Registrar (Admissions (first degree)): Mansoor, A. C. A. M., BA Jaffna, MEd
Estates and buildings/works and services. Works Engineer: Sideeque, S. M.
Examinations. Senior Assistant Registrar (Admissions (first degree)): Mansoor, A. C. A. M., BA Jaffna, MEd
Finance. Bursar: Gulam Rasheed, A.
General enquiries. Acting Registrar: Hibathul Careem, M. F., BSc Eastern(S.Lanka), MSc Peradeniya
Library (enquiries). Senior Assistant Librarian: Rifaudeen, M. M., BScAgric Eastern(S.Lanka), MLS Colombo
Personnel/human resources. Senior Assistant Registrar (General Administration): Saththar, H. A., BCom Peradeniya
Purchasing. Senior Assistant Bursar (Stores and Supplies): Wickramasinghe, W. A. D. R., BLE Colombo
Security. Acting Registrar: Hibathul Careem, M. F., BSc Eastern(S.Lanka), MSc Peradeniya
Student welfare/counselling. Assistant Registrar (Student welfare/counselling): Zubair, M. I. M.

[Information supplied by the institution as at 23 March 2005, and edited by the ACU]

UNIVERSITY OF SRI JAYEWARDENEPURA, SRI LANKA

Founded 1959

Member of the Association of Commonwealth Universities

Postal Address: Gangodawila, Nugegoda, Sri Lanka
Telephone: (280) 2696 **Fax:** (280) 1604 **E-mail:** unisjay@sjp.ac.lk
URL: http://www.sjp.ac.lk

VICE-CHANCELLOR*—Warnasuriya, Prof. Narada D., MB BS Ceyl., FRCP
REGISTRAR‡—Muttettuwegedara, J., BA *Kelaniya*
LIBRARIAN—Vidanapathirana, P., BA Ceyl., MLS *NSW*, FCLIP
BURSAR—Ranatunga, D. C., BSc *Vidyod.*

GENERAL INFORMATION

History. Originally founded as a traditional seat of learning, Vidyodaya Pirivena, the university was established in 1959.
It is located about 13km from Colombo.

Admission to first degree courses (see also Sri Lankan Introduction). Through University Grants Commission on the basis of General Certificate of Education (GCE) A level results.

First Degrees (see also Sri Lankan Directory to Subjects of Study). BA, BCom, BSc, MB BS.
Length of course. Full-time: BA, BSc: 3–4 years; BCom: 4 years; MB BS: 5 years.

Higher Degrees (see also Sri Lankan Directory to Subjects of Study).
Master's. MA, MPhil, MSc.
Admission. Applicants for admission to master's degree courses should hold a relevant first degree with at least second class honours; other applicants must take a qualifying exam.
Length of course. Full-time: MA, MPhil, MSc: 2 years.
Doctoral. PhD.
Admission. PhD: MPhil in a relevant subject.
Length of course. Full-time: PhD: 2 years.

Language of Instruction. Sinhala and English.

Libraries. Volumes: 180,000. Periodicals subscribed to: 350. Other holdings: 250 databases and accompanying materials; 25 CD-Rom. Special collections: Sri Lanka.

FACULTIES/SCHOOLS

Applied Science
Tel: (280) 2914 Fax: (280) 2914
Dean: Abeysekera, Prof. A. M., BSc Ceyl., PhD Belf.
Secretary: Gunasinghe, U. D. S. S.

Arts
Tel: (280) 3196
Dean: Silva, S. A. C. S., BA Vidyod., MSc Edin.
Secretary: Mendis, A. M. S.

Management Studies and Commerce
Tel: (280) 3343 Fax: (280) 3653
Dean: Silva, W. H. E., BCom Sri Jay., MA Lanc.
Secretary: Rajapaksa, D. V.

Medicine
Tel: (280) 1480 Fax: (280) 1480
Dean: Jayawardana, Prof. M. A. J., MB BS Ceyl., MS Ceyl.
Secretary: Gunarathne, K.

Postgraduate Studies
Tel: (552) 3642 Fax: (552) 3642
Dean: Wijewardena, Prof. K. A. K. K., MB BS Ceyl., MD Ceyl.
Secretary: Rajapaksha, D. V.

ACADEMIC UNITS

Accounting
Tel: (280) 1279
Abayadeera, N., BSc(PubAdm) Sri Jay., MBA Sri Jay.   Sr. Lectr.
Fernando, M. S. J. S. K. D., BCom Sri Jay., MSc Sri Jay.   Sr. Lectr.
Fonseka, K. B. M., BSc Colombo, MBA Colombo   Sr. Lectr.; Head*
Gunawardena, K. D., MBA Colombo, PhD Assum., BSc(BusAdm)   Sr. Lectr.
Kelum, W. G. S., MSc Leningrad Inst.Finance & Econ., PhD Leningrad Inst.Finance & Econ.   Sr. Lectr.
Manawaduge, A. S. P. G., MA Lanc., BSc(PubAdm)   Sr. Lectr.
Ratnasekara, B. Y. G., BSc(PubAdm) Sri Jay., MCom S.Krishna.   Sr. Lectr.
Senarathne, D. S. N. P., BSc(Accty) Sri Jay., MBA Sri Jay.   Sr. Lectr. (on leave)
Silva, W. H. E., BCom Sri Jay., MA Lanc.   Sr. Lectr.
Udayashantha, P. D. C., BSc(Accty) Sri Jay., MBA Sri Jay.   Sr. Lectr.
Wickremarachchi, M. W., BA Vidyod., MA NE, PhD Marath.   Prof.

Botany
Tel: (280) 1414
Dassanayake, P. K. N., BSc Sri Jay., PhD Sri Jay.   Sr. Lectr.
Fernando, K. M. E. P., BSc Vidyod., PhD Lanc.   Sr. Lectr. (on leave)
Hettiarachchi, P. L., BSc Colombo, MSc Brussels, PhD Brussels   Sr. Lectr.
Mahagamasekera, M. G. P., BSc Colombo, MSc NSW, PhD Cant.   Sr. Lectr.
Nandadasa, H. G., BSc Ceyl., PhD Leic.   Sr. Prof.
Saleem, N., BSc Vidyod., PhD Bath   Sr. Lectr.
Senarath, W. T. P. S. K., BSc Peradeniya, PhD Wales   Sr. Lectr.
Wijeratne, S. C., BSc Ceyl., MPhil Kelaniya, PhD Fukuoka   Prof.; Head*
Yapa, P. A. J., BSc Lond., PhD Lond.   Prof.

Business Administration
Tel: (280) 3472
Chandrakumara, P. M. K. A., BSc(BusAdmin) Sri Jay., MBA Sri Jay., PhD Sheff.   Sr. Lectr.; Head*
De Silva, D. V. L. B., BSc(BusAdm) Sri Jay., MBA Colombo   Sr. Lectr. (on leave)
Gunasekera, M. A. M., BSc(BusAdm) Sri Jay., MBA Sri Jay.   Sr. Lectr. (on leave)
Gunathilaka, P. D. H. D., BSc(PubAdm) Sri Jay., MSc Sri Jay.   Sr. Lectr.
Gunatilake, H. W., BSc(BusAdm) Sri Jay., MBA Sri Jay.   Sr. Lectr. (on leave)
Jayawardana, S. D. W., BSc(BusAdm) Sri Jay., MBA Sri Jay.   Sr. Lectr.
Kalyani, M. W., BCom Sri Jay., MSc Sri Jay.   Sr. Lectr.
Karunayake, G. P., BCom Sri Jay., MBA Sri Jay.   Sr. Lectr.
Molligoda, A. G. M. M. N. S. P., BSc(BusAdm) Sri Jay., MBA Leuven   Sr. Lectr.
Pushpakumari, M. D., BSc(PubAdm) Sri Jay., MBA Colombo   Sr. Lectr. (on leave)

Senadeera, G. D. V. R., BSc(BusAdm) Sri Jay., MSc Sri Jay.   Sr. Lectr.
Udayanga, M. V. S. S., BSc(BusAdm) Sri Jay., MSc Sri Jay.   Sr. Lectr.
Wickramasinghe, D. W. A., BSc(BusAdm) Sri Jay., MCom Kelaniya   Sr. Lectr.
Wijesinghe, J. M. R. C., BSc(BusAdm) Sri Jay., MSc Kelaniya   Sr. Lectr.

Business Economics
Tel: (280) 2005
Amaratunga, S. P. P., BA Sri Jay., MA Saga, PhD Kagoshima   Sr. Lectr.; Head*
Anura Kumara, U., BA Sri Jay., MSc Moratuwa   Sr. Lectr. (on leave)
Dodankotuwa, J. B., MEng Kobe, BSc(EstMgt&Valn)   Sr. Lectr.
Lalani, P. P., BCom Sri Jay., MSc Sri Jay.   Sr. Lectr.
Perera, M. S. S., BCom Sri Jay., MBA Sri Jay.   Sr. Lectr.
Thantrigama, G., BA Vidyod., MA Leuven, PhD Delhi   Sr. Lectr. (on leave)
Weerasinghe, E. A., BA Sri Jay., MSc Brad., PhD Osaka   Sr. Lectr. (on leave)

Chemistry
Tel: (280) 4206
Abeysekera, A. M., BSc Ceyl., PhD Belf.   Sr. Prof.
Deraniyagala, S. P., BSc Ceyl., PhD Dal.   Prof.; Head*
Fernando, W. S., BSc Ceyl., PhD Leic.   Sr. Prof. (on leave)
Jayatilleke, W. D. W., BSc Ceyl., MSc Brad.   Assoc. Prof.
Jayaweera, C. D., BSc Sri Jay., PhD Belf.   Sr. Lectr.
Jayaweera, P. P. M., BSc Sri Jay., PhD Belf.   Sr. Lectr.
Karunanayake, L., BSc Sri Jay., PhD N.Lond.   Sr. Lectr.
Liyanayage, S. S. L. W., BSc Sri Jay., PhD Wales   Sr. Lectr.
Mahathanthila, K. C. P., BSc Vidyod., PhD Ott.   Sr. Lectr.
Perera, B. A., BSc Colombo, MS Wichita, PhD Wichita   Sr. Lectr.
Samarasinghe, Shiromi I., BSc Vidyod., MSc Leeds, PhD Leeds   Assoc. Prof. (on leave)
Silva, W. S. J., BSc Sri Jay., PhD Hawaii   Sr. Lectr.

Commerce
Tel: (280) 2513
Dayarathna, E., BCom Peradeniya, MA Thammasat   Sr. Lectr.
Dharmadasa, E. A., BCom Vidyod., MBA Leuven   Sr. Lectr. (on leave)
Hirantha, S. W., BCom Sri Jay., MA Essex, PhD Nagoya   Sr. Lectr.; Head*
Naotunne, S. S., BCom Vidyod., MBA Ott.   Sr. Lectr.
Silva, S. S. M. de, BA Vidyod., MA Sri Jay.   Sr. Lectr.

Economics
Tel: (280) 2014
Atukorala, P., BA Ceyl., MA Peradeniya, PhD Sri Jay.   Sr. Lectr.; Head*

Chandrakumara, D. P. S., BA Sri Jay., MA Kerala
Sr. Lectr.

Herath, H. M. T. N. R., BA Sri Jay., MA Sri Jay.,
PhD Colombo Sr. Lectr. (on leave)

Kodagoda, K. R., BA Ceyl., MSc Lanc. Sr. Lectr.
(on leave)

Nishantha, H. A. A., BA Peradeniya, MPhil
Peradeniya Sr. Lectr.

Purasingha, P. L. T., BA Peradeniya, MA Peradeniya
Sr. Lectr.

Thantrigama, P. M. S., BA Vidyod., MA Leuven
Sr. Lectr.

Wickremasinghe, G. A. U., BA Sri Jay., MA
Thammasat, PhD Hawaii Prof.

Wilson, P., BA Vidyod., MA ANU, PhD Penn.
Assoc. Prof.

English

Tel: (280) 2695

Mawella, I. J., BA Colombo, MA Colombo Sr.
Lectr.; Head*

Estate Management and Valuation

Tel: (280) 2004

Ariyawansa, R. G., BSc(EstMgt&Valn) Sri Jay.,
MSc Sri Jay. Sr. Lectr. (on leave)

Edirisinghe, J., BSc(EstMgt&Valn) Sri Jay., MSc
Asian I.T., Bangkok Sr. Lectr. (on leave)

Hettirachchi, J. N., BSc(EstMgt&Valn) Sri Jay.,
MSc Moratuwa Sr. Lectr.

Premathilake, H. M., BSc(EstMgt&Valn) Sri Jay.,
MPhil Peradeniya Sr. Lectr.; Head*

Weerakoon, K. G. P. K., BSc(EstMgt&Valn) Sri
Jay., MSc Asian I.T., Bangkok Sr. Lectr.

Wickramarachchi, N. C., BSc(EstMgt&Valn) Sri
Jay., MSc Moratuwa Sr. Lectr.

Finance

Tel: (280) 2695

Abeyrathne Bandara, W. M., BSc(BusAdm)
Vidyod., MBA Ott. Sr. Lectr.

Colombage, S. R. N., BSc(BusAdm) Sri Jay.,
MBA Colombo Sr. Lectr. (on leave)

Dissabandara, D. B. P. H., BSc(PubAdm) Sri
Jay., MSc Sri Jay. Sr. Lectr.

Nimal, P. D., BSc(BusAdm) Sri Jay., MBA Sri
Jay., PhD Shiga Sr. Lectr.

Perera, K. L. W., BCom Sri Jay., MB Asian I.T.,
Bangkok Sr. Lectr.

Seelanatha, S. L., BSc(PubAdm) Sri Jay., MSc
Asian I.T., Bangkok Sr. Lectr. (on leave)

Weerakoon Banda, Y. K., BSc(BusAdm) Sri Jay.,
MBA Colombo, PhD Athens Sr. Lectr.; Head*

Food Science and Technology

Tel: (430) 5396

Bamunuarachchi, A. H. De O., BSc Vidyod., MSc
Calif., PhD NSW Prof. (on leave)

Ranaweera, K. K. D. S., MSc P.F.U., Moscow,
PhD Sofia Sr. Lectr.

Forestry and Environmental Science

Tel: (280) 4685

Amarasekera, H. S., BSc Sri Jay., PhD Wales Sr.
Lectr.; Head*

Bandara, N. J. G. J., BSc Punjab, MSc Punjab,
MEDes Calg. Sr. Lectr. (on leave)

Gunawardene, U. A. D. P., BSc Kelaniya, PhD
Edin. Sr. Lectr.

Ranasinghe, D. M. S. H. K., BSc Sri Jay., MSc Sri
Jay., PhD Wales Prof.

Singhekumara, B. M. P., BSc Sri Jay., DPhil Oxf.
Prof.

Subasinghe, S. M. C. U. P., BSc Sri Jay., PhD
Wales Sr. Lectr.

Geography

Tel: (280) 2028

Bandaranayake, G. M., BA Sri Jay., MA Sri Jay.
Sr. Lectr.

Deheragoda, C. K. M., MSc Sofia, PhD Sofia Sr.
Lectr.; Head*

Epitawatta, D. S., BA Vidyod., MSc Moratuwa, PhD
Sheff. Sr. Lectr.

Karunaratna, N. L. A., BA Vidyod., PhD Durh.
Sr. Lectr.

Katupotha, K. N. J., BA Vidyod., MA Hiroshima
Assoc. Prof.

Navaratne Banda, H. M., BA Vidyod., MA Qld.
Sr. Lectr.

Rathnayake, R. M. K., BA Sri Jay., MPhil Sri Jay.,
PhD Sri Jay. Sr. Lectr.

Sangasumana, Rev. P., BA Sri Jay., MA Sri Jay.
Sr. Lectr.

Tennakoon, T. M. S. P. K., BA Sri Jay., PhD Qld.
Sr. Lectr.

Wijesinghe, M. A. S., BA Sri Jay., MPhil Sri Jay.
Sr. Lectr.

Wishwakula, U. H. N., BA Sri Jay., MA Sri Jay.
Sr. Lectr.

History and Archaeology

Tel: (280) 1163

Abayawardhana, D. L., BA Vidyod., PhD Paris
Assoc. Prof.

Alexander, K. M., BA Sri Jay., MSc Kelaniya
Lectr. (on leave)

Karunatillake, G. K. N. D., BA Sri Jay., MA Sri
Jay. Sr. Lectr. (on leave)

Kulatunga, T. G., BA Vidyod., MA Vidyod. Prof.
(on leave)

Mandawala, P. B., BSc Moratuwa, MSc Moratuwa,
MA York(UK) Sr. Lectr.; Acting Head*

Manthriratna, M. A. S. R. S., BA Sri Jay., MA Sri
Jay. Sr. Lectr.

Pathmasiri, K., BA Sri Jay., MA Sri Jay. Sr.
Lectr.

Vajira, Rev. H., BA Sri Jay., MSc Kelaniya Sr.
Lectr. (on leave)

Human Resources Management

Tel: (280) 2010

Aruna Shantha, G. G., BSc(PubAdm) Sri Jay.,
MBA Sri Jay., PhD Meijo Sr. Lectr.

Batagoda, C. K., BSc(PubAdm) Sri Jay., MBA
Colombo Sr. Lectr.

Opatha, H. H. D. N. P., BSc(PubAdm) Sri Jay.,
MSc Sri Jay., PhD Utara Prof.; Head*

Ramanayake, U. B., MA Leningrad, PhD Leningrad
Sr. Lectr.

Tharangani, M. G., BSc(PubAdm) Sri Jay., MBA
Colombo Sr. Lectr.

Information Technology and Decision Sciences

Tel: (280) 2023

Amarasena, T. S. M., BSc(PubAdm) Sri Jay.,
MBA Asian I.T., Bangkok Sr. Lectr.

Gunathunga, R. S., BSc(BusAdm) Sri Jay., MBA
Colombo, MA Hull, PhD E.Cowan Prof.

Hewagamage, Champa, BSc Kelaniya, MA Nagoya,
PhD Hiroshima Sr. Lectr.

Jayasooriya, D. S. P., BSc Sri Jay., MSc Colombo
Sr. Lectr.

Kulathunga, K. M. S. D., BSc Kelaniya, MBA Sri
Jay. Sr. Lectr. (on leave)

Lokuge, A. L., BSc Colombo, MSc Colombo Sr.
Lectr.; Head*

Palawatta, T. M. B., BSc(Math) Sri Jay., MBA
Leuven Sr. Lectr.

Samarasinghe, S. M., BCom Sri Jay., MSc Sri Jay.
Sr. Lectr.

Wedage, D. M., BSc Sri Jay., MSc Colombo Sr.
Lectr.

Wijewickrama, A. K. A., BSc(BusAdm) Sri Jay.,
MBA Colombo Sr. Lectr.

Yapa, S. T. W. S., BSc Kelaniya, MBA Sri Jay.
Sr. Lectr. (on leave)

Languages and Cultural Studies

see also English; Pali and Buddhist Studies; and
Sinhala and Mass Media

Tel: (280) 2695

Chandrasena, R. M. S., BA Sri Jay., MA Sri Jay.
Sr. Lectr.; Head*

Manamperi, A. K. M. S., BFA Kelaniya, MA Sri
Jay. Sr. Lectr.

Ratnayake, D. P., BMus VB, MMus VB Sr.
Lectr.

Wijetunga, B. M., BA Lucknow, MA Lucknow, PhD
Kanpur Sr. Lectr. (on leave)

Marketing Management

Tel: (280) 2009

Ihalanayake, R., BSc(PubAdm) Sri Jay., MA
Victoria UT Sr. Lectr. (on leave)

Samarasinghe, D. S. R., BSc(BusAdm) Sri Jay.,
MBA Sri Jay. Sr. Lectr.; Head*

Warnakulasuriya, B. N. F., BCom Colombo, MBA
Colombo, PhD Pune Sr. Lectr. (on leave)

Mathematics

Tel: (280) 3470

Boralugoda, S. K., BSc Sri Jay., MSc Alta., PhD
Alta. Sr. Lectr.

De Silva, T. P., BSc Ceyl., MSc Monash Sr.
Lectr.; Head*

Kumara, K. K. W. A. S., BSc Colombo, MPhil Sri
Jay. Sr. Lectr.

Liyanage, L. L. M., BSc Sri Jay., MSc Wat., PhD
McM. Sr. Lectr.

Malmini, R. P. K. C., BSc Kelaniya, PhD H-W
Sr. Lectr.

Siriwardane, M. K. N., BSc Ceyl., MSc Flin. Sr.
Lectr.

Weeakoon, Sunethra, BSc Ceyl., MSc Penn., PhD
Penn. Prof. (on leave)

Pali and Buddhist Studies

see also Langs. and Cultural Studies

Tel: (280) 2752

Dhammadassi, Rev. N., BA Sri Jay., PhD Lanc.
Sr. Lectr.

Moratuwagama, H. M., BA Peradeniya, MPhil
Kelaniya Sr. Lectr.

Perera, G. A., BA Vidyod., MA Vidyod., PhD Ban.
Prof.

Perera, W. A. G., BA Kelaniya, MA Kelaniya
Assoc. Prof.

Weerasena, K. A., BA Sri Jay., MA Sri Jay. Sr.
Lectr.; Head*

Wijebandara, W. D. C., BA Peradeniya, PhD Lanc.
Prof. (on leave)

Physics

Tel: (551) 6967

Abeyratne, C. P., BSc Sri Jay., MSc Bowling Green,
PhD Toledo(Ohio) Sr. Lectr.

Geekiyanagage, P., BSc Sri Jay., MSc Sri Jay.,
PhD Sri Jay. Sr. Lectr.

Jayewardene, D. N., BSc Sri Jay., PhD Camb.
Sr. Lectr.

Peiris, M. G. C., BSc Vidyod., MSc Sri Jay. Sr.
Lectr.; Head*

Ranathunga, C. L., BSc Sri Jay., MPhil Sri Jay.
Sr. Lectr. (on leave)

Tantrigoda, D. A., BSc Ceyl., MSc Durh., PhD
Durh. Sr. Prof.

Wijeratne, W. D. A. T., BSc Colombo, PhD Wayne
State Sr. Lectr.

Public Administration

Tel: (280) 2006

Fernando, H. A. C., MA Leuven Sr. Lectr.

Fernando, R. L. S., BSc(PubAdm) Sri Jay., MA
Manc., PhD Natnl.Inst.Devel.Admin., Bangkok Sr.
Lectr.; Head*

Herath, H. M. A., BPAdm Vidyod., MA Car., PhD
Car. Sr. Lectr.

Weeratunge, W. M. N., BA Peradeniya, MA
Peradeniya Sr. Lectr.

Werasinghe, W. N. A. D. C., BSc(PubAdm) Sri
Jay., MA Punjab Sr. Lectr.

Sinhala and Mass Communication

Tel: (280) 2214

Ariyarathne, S., BA Vidyod., PhD Sri Jay. Sr.
Prof.

Dissanayake, W. A. D. G., BA Sri Jay., MA Tokai
Assoc. Prof.; Head*

Harischandra, M. A. S., BA Kelaniya, MCommSt
Pune

Kariyawasam, T., BA Ceyl., MA Ceyl., PhD Lond.
Sr. Prof.

Lankamullage, K., BA Sri Jay., MA Sri Jay. Sr.
Lectr.

Medawatta, K. A. J. P. K., BA Sri Jay., MPhil Sri
Jay. Sr. Lectr.

Narada, Rev. K., BA Sri Jay., MPhil Sri Jay., MA
  B&P SLanka, PhD Pune   Sr. Lectr.
Rathnasiri, A. V. D., BA Sri Jay., MA Sri Jay.
  Sr. Lectr.
Wijeratne, M. W. W., BA Vidyod., PhD Sri Jay.
  Sr. Prof. (on leave)

Social Statistics

see also Stats. and Computer Sci.

Tel: (280) 2751

Dharmasena, K. A., BA Sri Jay., MA Sri Jay.   Sr.
  Lectr.; Head*
Jayatissa, W. A., BSc Vidyod., MA Manc., PhD
  Manc.   Prof. (on leave)
Silva, S. A. C. S., BA Vidyod., MSc Edin.   Sr.
  Lectr.
Silva, S. K. R., BDevS Vidyod., MA Kent   Sr.
  Lectr.
Wijayasiriwardane, A. M. M. J., BSc Vidyod.,
  MEcon NE   Sr. Lectr.

Sociology and Anthropology

Tel: (280) 2207

Abayasundere, A. P. N. de S., BA Sri Jay., MA
  Sri Jay., PhD Ban.   Sr. Lectr.
Abeysekara, D. S. D. J., BA Vidyod., MA Texas,
  PhD Brown   Assoc. Prof.
Buddhadasa, M. P. A. A., BA Sri Jay., MA S.Fraser
  Sr. Lectr.
Danapala, W. M., BA Sri Jay., MPhil Sri Jay.   Sr.
  Lectr.
Ganihigama, E. K., BA Vidyod., MA Sri Jay.   Sr.
  Lectr.
Jayasiri, A. A. Jayantha, BA Sri Jay., MA Sri Jay.,
  PhD Pune   Sr. Lectr.
Jayasundara, W. M., BA Sri Jay., MA S.Fraser
  Sr. Lectr.
Jayathilaka, H. D. Y. Devika, BA Sri Jay., MA Sri
  Jay., PhD J.Nehru U.   Sr. Lectr.
Perera, B. A. T., BA Vidyod., MA Sri Jay.   Prof.
  (on leave)
Perera, Swarnalatha M. C., BA Vidyod., MA Sri
  Jay., PhD   Sr. Lectr.; Head*
Samarakoon, M. T., BA Sri Jay., MA Sri Jay.   Sr.
  Lectr.
Samarasekara, K. M. S., BA Sri Jay., MA Sri Jay.
  Sr. Lectr.
Sunil, R. N., BA Sri Jay., MA Sri Jay.   Sr. Lectr.
Udayakumara, A. R. P. C., BA Sri Jay., MA Sri
  Jay.   Sr. Lectr.
Wijekoon, W. A. S., BA Sri Jay., MA Sri Jay.
  Sr. Lectr.

Statistics and Computer Science

see also Soc. Stats.

Tel: (280) 2695

Ananda Gamini, D. D., BSc Sri Jay., MSc Asian
  I.T., Bangkok   Sr. Lectr.
Banneheka, B. M. S. G., BSc Sri Jay., MSc Lond.,
  PhD S.Fraser   Sr. Lectr.
Dayananda, R. A., BSc Ceyl., PhD Wales   Sr.
  Prof.
Dias, P., BSc Sri Jay., MSc Curtin   Sr. Lectr.
Edirisuriya, E. A. T. A., BSc Sri Jay., MSc
  Shanghai   Sr. Lectr. (on leave)
Kalukottege, C. J. P., BSc Sri Jay., MSc Saga, PhD
  Saga   Sr. Lectr.
Makalanda, G. S., BSc Vidyod., MSc Wales   Sr.
  Lectr.; Head*

Zoology

Tel: (280) 4515

Attygala, Manel V. E., BSc Vidyod., PhD E.Anglia
  Sr. Lectr.
De Alwis, S. M. D. A. U., BSc Kelaniya, MSc
  Bergen, PhD Bergen   Sr. Lectr.
De Silva, B. G. D. N. K., BSc Sri Jay., PhD Sri
  Jay.   Sr. Lectr.
Jinadasa, J., BSc Vidyod., MSc Vidyod., PhD Mass.
  Sr. Prof.
Karunarathne, M. M. S. C., BSc Vidyod., PhD
  S'ton.   Sr. Lectr. (on leave)
Mahaulpotha, W. A. D., BSc Sri Jay., MSc
  Hiroshima, PhD Hiroshima   Sr. Lectr.
Pathmalal, M. M., BSc Sri Jay., PhD Ehime   Sr.
  Lectr.

Piyasiri, S., BSc Peradeniya, PhD Vienna   Prof.;
  Head*
Seneviratne, A. G. D. H., BSc Sri Jay., PhD Cant.
  Sr. Lectr.

MEDICINE

Tel: (280) 1480 Fax: (280) 1480

Anatomy

Tel: (280) 2164

De Silva, K. R. D., MB BS Colombo, MPhil
  Colombo   Sr. Lectr.
Yasawardena, S. G., MB BS Colombo, PhD
  Colombo   Sr. Lectr.; Head*

Biochemistry

Tel: (280) 3578

Chandrika, U. G., BSc Sri Jay., MPhil Massey,
  PhD Sri Jay.   Sr. Lectr.
Ekanayake, S., BSc Peradeniya, MPhil Sri Jay., PhD
  Sri Jay.   Sr. Lectr.
Jansz, E. R., BSc Ceyl., PhD Dal.   Sr. Prof.
Jayawardene, M. I. F. P., BSc Ceyl., MSc Ceyl.,
  PhD Ceyl.   Sr. Lectr.; Head*
Peiris, Hemantha, BVSc Ceyl., MPhil Ceyl., PhD
  Qld.   Prof.

Community Medicine

Gunawardena, C. S. E., MB BS Colombo, MD
  Colombo   Sr. Lectr.
Sivayogan, S., MB BS Ceyl., MD Ceyl.   Prof.;
  Head*
Wijewardena, K. A. K. K., MB BS Ceyl., MD
  Ceyl.   Sr. Prof.

Family Medicine

Tel: (280) 3191

Perera, M. S. A., MB BS Ceyl., MD Ceyl.   Prof.
Seneviratne, A. L. P. de S., MB BS Colombo, MD
  Ceyl.   Sr. Lectr.

Forensic Medicine

Tel: (280) 2182

Gunasekara, I. S., MB BS Colombo, MD Colombo
  Sr. Lectr.; Head*

Medicine

Tel: (280) 2695

Hewage, U. C. L., MB BS Ceyl., MD Ceyl.   Sr.
  Lectr. (on leave)
Indrakumar, J., MB BS N.C'bo.Med.Coll., MD
  Colombo   Sr. Lectr.
Jayaratne, S. D., MB BS Ceyl., MD Ceyl.   Sr.
  Lectr.; Head*
Kamaladasa, S. D., MB BS Ceyl., MD Ceyl.   Sr.
  Lectr.
Wanigasuriya, J. K. P., MB BS Ceyl., MD Ceyl.
  Sr. Lectr.

Microbiology

Tel: (280) 2026

Fernando, S. S. N., MB BS N.C'bo.Med.Coll., PhD
  Lond.   Sr. Lectr.; Head*
Fernando, S., MB BS Ceyl., MSc Lond.   Prof.

Obstetrics and Gynaecology

Tel: (280) 3192

Fernando, T. A. N., MB BS Colombo, MS Colombo
  Sr. Lectr.
Fernandopulle, R. C., MB BS Colombo, MS
  Colombo   Sr. Lectr.
Jayawardena, M. A. J., MB BS Ceyl., MS Ceyl.
  Prof.
Pathiraja, R. P., MB BS Ruhuna, MS Colombo   Sr.
  Lectr.; Head*
Rajapaksa, A. U., MB BS Colombo, MS Colombo
  Sr. Lectr. (on leave)

Paediatrics

Tel: (280) 3191

de Silva, T. G. D. A., MB BS Colombo, MD
  Colombo   Sr. Lectr. (on leave)
Gunasekera, D. P. S., MB BS Ceyl., MD Ceyl.
  Sr. Lectr.
Samarage, D. K., MB BS Ceyl., MD Ceyl.   Sr.
  Lectr.; Head*

Seneviratne, T. R. S., MB BS Kelaniya, MD
  Colombo, DCH Colombo   Sr. Lectr.
Warnasuriya, Narada D., MB BS Ceyl., FRCP
  Prof.

Parasitology

Tel: (280) 1028

Ekanayake, S., BSc Ceyl., MSc Sri Jay., PhD
  Georgia   Assoc. Prof.
Ranasinghe, P. H. K. I. S., MB BS Colombo,
  MPhil S.Calif.   Sr. Lectr.
Wickramasinghe, D. R., BSc Wis., PhD Ceyl.
  Sr. Lectr.; Head*

Pathology

Tel: (280) 1027

Premathilake, I. V., MB BS Manipal AHE, MD
  Colombo   Sr. Lectr.
Samrasinghe, K., MB BS Ruhuna, MD Colombo
  Sr. Lectr.; Head*
Seneviratne, M. B. S., MB BS Kelaniya, MD
  Colombo   Sr. Lectr.
Wijesiriwardena, I. S., MB BS Ceyl., MD Ceyl.
  Sr. Lectr.
Withana, R. J., MB BS Ceyl., MD Ceyl.   Prof.

Pharmacology

Tel: (280) 1491

Fernando, G. H., MB BS Ceyl.   Prof.; Head*
Goonetillaka, A. K. E., MB BS Ceyl., MD Ceyl.
  Sr. Lectr. (on leave)
Gunathunga, W. A. D. K., MB BS Ruhuna, MD
  Colombo   Sr. Lectr.
Wanigathunga, C. A., MB BS Kelaniya, MD
  Colombo   Sr. Lectr.

Physiology

Tel: (280) 2182

Fernando, D. M. S., MB BS Colombo, MPhil
  Colombo   Sr. Lectr.
Hettiarachchi, P., MB BS Colombo, MPhil Sri Jay.
  Sr. Lectr.; Head*
Jiffry, M. T. M., BDS Ceyl., MMedSc Ceyl., MSc
  Lond.   Prof.
Makuloluwa, P. T. R., MB BS Colombo, MD
  Colombo   Sr. Lectr.
Peiris, John R. J., MB BS Kelaniya, MPhil Sri Jay.
  Sr. Lectr.
Ruberu, D. K., MB BS Ceyl.   Sr. Lectr. (on
  leave)
Wimalasekera, S. W., MB BS N.C'bo.Med.Coll.,
  MPhil Colombo   Sr. Lectr.

Psychiatry

Tel: (280) 2497

Dolage, N. S., MB BS Colombo, MD Colombo   Sr.
  Lectr. (on leave)
Kathriarachchi, S. T., MB BS Ceyl., MD Ceyl.
  Assoc. Prof. (on leave)
Weerasundera, R. Y. P., MB BS Kelaniya, MD
  Colombo   Sr. Lectr.; Head*

Surgery

Tel: (280) 2695

De Silva, W. M. M., MB BS Ceyl., MS Ceyl.,
  FRCSEd   Prof.; Head*
Pathirana, A. A., MB BS Colombo, MS Colombo
  Sr. Lectr.
Weerasekera, D. D., MB BS Colombo, MS Colombo
  Sr. Lectr.

SPECIAL CENTRES, ETC

Management, Postgraduate Institute of

Tel: (268) 9639 Fax: (268) 9643
  E-mail: pim@lanka.com.lk
Nanayakkara, G., BSc(PubAdm) Vidyod., MA
  York(Can.), PhD Car.   Prof.; Dir.*

CONTACT OFFICERS

Academic affairs. Deputy Registrar:
  Siriwardena, A. R.
Accommodation. Assistant Registrar
  (Accommodation): Dilrukshika, S. V. C. V.
Admissions (first degree). Deputy Registrar:
  Siriwardena, A. R.

Admissions (higher degree). Deputy Registrar: Siriwardena, A. R.

Adult/continuing education. Assistant Registrar: Krishantha, B. A. N.

Alumni. Deputy Registrar: Siriwardena, A. R.

Computing services. Coordinator: Karunaratne, N. L. A., BA *Vidyod.*, PhD *Durh.*

Credit transfer. Bursar: Ranatunga, D. C., BSc *Vidyod.*

Distance education. Assistant Registrar: Krishantha, B. A. N.

Estates and buildings/works and services. Assistant Registrar: Malkanthi, K. P. Y. T.

Examinations. Senior Assistant Registrar: Perera, K. W. D. D.

Finance. Bursar: Ranatunga, D. C., BSc *Vidyod.*

General enquiries. Registrar: Muttettuwegedara, J., BA *Kelaniya*

Health services. Medical Officer: Welikumbura, R. M. P. K., MB BS *Colombo*

International office. Deputy Registrar: Siriwardena, A. R.

Library (chief librarian). Librarian: Vidanapathirana, P., BA *Ceyl.*, MLS *NSW,* FCLIP

Personnel/human resources. Assistant Registrar (Personnel/Human Resources): Weheragoda, P.

Publications. Deputy Registrar: Siriwardena, A. R.

Purchasing. Senior Assistant Bursar (Purchasing): (vacant)

Research. Deputy Registrar: Siriwardena, A. R.

Scholarships, awards, loans. Assistant Registrar (Scholarships, awards, loans): Dilrukshika, S. V. C. V.

Security. Chief Security Officer: (vacant)

Sport and recreation. Acting Director, Physical Education: Amarasena, T. S. A.

Student welfare/counselling. Director: Liyanage, S. S. L. W., BSc *Sri Jay.*, PhD *Wales*

Students from other countries. Deputy Registrar: Siriwardena, A. R.

[Information supplied by the institution as at 15 May 2006, and edited by the ACU]

SRI LANKA INSTITUTE OF INFORMATION TECHNOLOGY

Founded 1999

Member of the Association of Commonwealth Universities

Postal Address: 16th Floor, BoC Merchant Tower, 28 St Michael's Road, Colombo 03, Sri Lanka
Telephone: (011) 230 1904 **Fax:** (011) 230 1906 **E-mail:** info@sliit.lk
URL: http://www.sliit.lk/

PRESIDENT/CHIEF EXECUTIVE OFFICER*—Gamage, Prof. Lalith D. K. B., BSc *Moratuwa,* MSc *De Mont.*, PhD *Br.Col.*

DEAN (ACADEMIC AFFAIRS)—Kumarawadu, Priyantha, BSc *Moratuwa,* PhD *Saga* leave

DEAN (STUDENT SERVICES)—Kapurubandara, Mahesha, BSc *Colombo,* MSc *Asian I.T., Bangkok*

DEAN (RESEARCH AND DEVELOPMENT)—Pulasinghe, Koliya, BSc *Moratuwa,* PhD *Saga*

DIRECTOR OF ADMINISTRATION‡—Hewawasam, Prof. Lakshman J., BA *Ceyl.*

DIRECTOR OF FINANCE—Wickramasinghe, Suwineetha C.

LIBRARIAN—Perera, Pushpamala, BA *Colombo,* MLS *Colombo*

GENERAL INFORMATION

History. Originally established in 1999, the Institute was granted degree-awarding status by the University Grants Commission in 2000.

The Institute comprises two campuses: Colombo Metropolitan campus, located in the city of Colombo; and Malabe campus, 10km east of Colombo precincts. It also has two centres, Kandy, 120km east, and Matara, 160km south of Colombo.

Admission to first degree courses. Passes in 3 subjects at GCE (Advanced level) examination taken at one sitting, or passes in 3 subjects at GCE (Advanced level) London examination taken at one sitting, plus an aptitude test.

First Degrees (see also Sri Lankan Directory to Subjects of Study). BScIT.
Length of course. Full-time: BScIT: 3–4 years.

Higher Degrees (see also Sri Lankan Directory to Subjects of Study).
Master's. MSc.
Admission. A bachelor's degree in a relevant field or membership of a recognised professional institute, with relevant experience.
Length of course. Full-time: MSc: 2 years.

Language of Instruction. English. Intensive remedial courses are available to students from the beginning of each academic year.

Libraries. Volumes: 11,000. Periodicals subscribed to: 1500. Other holdings: 2000 CD/DVD.

Academic Awards (2007–2008). 40 awards ranging in value from Rs253,000 to Rs506,000.

Academic Year (2008). Two semesters: 1 January–8 June; 16 June–24 October.

Income (2006–2007). Total, Rs260,899,000.

Statistics. Staff (2007): 219 (104 academic, 115 non-academic). Students (2007): full-time 3110; undergraduate 2933; master's 177.

ACADEMIC UNITS

Computer Graphics and Multimedia

Tel: (011) 241 3889 Fax: (011) 241 3916
E-mail: docgm@sliit.lk
Widyasekara, Sirimevan, BSc *Colombo,* PhD *Uppsala* Sr. Lectr.; Head*
Other Staff: 2 Lectrs.; 1 Asst. Lectr.; 4 Instrs.
Vacant Posts: 2 Sr. Lectrs.; 1 Lectr.
Research: WebGIS-based applications; 3D modelling and rendering

Computer Systems and Networking

Tel: (011) 241 3907 Fax: (011) 241 3916
E-mail: docsn@sliit.lk
Jayawardena, Chandimal, BSc *Moratuwa,* MEng *Moratuwa,* PhD *Saga* Sr. Lectr.
Wijesundara, Malitha, BSc *Warw.*, PhD *NU Singapore* Sr. Lectr.; Head*
Other Staff: 2 Lectrs.; 2 Asst. Lectrs.; 5 Instrs.
Vacant Posts: 3 Sr. Lectrs.
Research: autonomous robots; embedded systems; network security; peer-to-peer storage and caching; redundant manipulator controlling

Information Management

Tel: (011) 241 3913 Fax: (011) 241 3916
E-mail: doim@sliit.lk
Robertson, Allan, BA *W.Aust.*, BEd *W.Aust.*, MBus *Curtin* Assoc. Prof.; Head*
Thelijjagoda, Samantha, BA *Sri Jay.*, MEng *Gifu,* PhD *Gifu* Sr. Lectr.
Other Staff: 2 Lectrs.; 2 Asst. Lectrs.; 4 Instrs.
Vacant Posts: 2 Sr. Lectrs.
Research: hypermedia and virtual reality IS; IS performance analysis and estimation

Information Technology

Tel: (011) 241 3911 Fax: (011) 241 3896
E-mail: doit@sliit.lk
Abeysuriya, Dimuth, BSc *Alabama,* MSc *Colombo* Sr. Lectr. (on leave)
Amararachchi, Jayantha, BSc *Sri Jay.*, MSc *Colombo* Sr. Lectr.
Anver, Mohammed, BSc *Moratuwa,* PhD *C.Qld.* Sr. Lectr.
De Silva, Clarence, PhD *M.I.T.*, PhD *Camb.*, FASME, FIEEE Hon. Prof.
Fernando, Chandrika, BSc *Sri Jay.*, MSc *Colombo* Sr. Lectr.
Kapurubandara, Mahesha, BSc *Colombo,* MSc *Asian I.T., Bangkok* Sr. Lectr.
Kodagoda, Nuwan, BSc *Moratuwa,* MPhil *Moratuwa* Sr. Lectr.
Kumarawadu, Priyantha, BSc *Moratuwa,* PhD *Saga* Assoc. Prof. (on leave)
Marikkar, Faiz, BSc *Ruhuna,* MSc *Nanjing,* PhD *Nanjing* Sr. Lectr.
Pulasinghe, Koliya, BSc *Moratuwa,* PhD *Saga* Sr. Lectr.; Head*
Other Staff: 18 Lectrs.; 7 Asst. Lectrs.; 29 Instrs.; 2 Adjunct Profs.
Research: enterprise application development frameworks; lean software development; NL-based programming; semantic web services; XML data integration

CONTACT OFFICERS

Academic affairs. Manager, Academic Affairs: Kulatunga, Jinadasa, BA *Sri Jay.*, MA *Colombo* (E-mail: kulatunga@sliit.lk)

Adult/continuing education. Manager, Professional Development Programmes: Gamage, Uditha, BSc *Moratuwa* (E-mail: uditha.g@sliit.lk)

Computing services. Head, IT Services: Wijesundara, Malitha, BSc *Warw.*, PhD *NU Singapore* (E-mail: docsn@sliit.lk)

Consultancy services. Head, Software
Engineering Services: Mallawarachchi,
Yashas, BA *Moratuwa*, MBA *Moratuwa*
(E-mail: yasas@sliit.lk)
Estates and buildings/works and services.
Director of Engineering: Wijesooriya,
Parakrama, BSc *Peradeniya* (on leave)
Finance. Director of Finance: Wickramasinghe,
Suwineetha C. (E-mail: swineetha.w@sliit.lk)
General enquiries. Director of Administration:
Hewawasam, Prof. Lakshman J., BA *Ceyl.*
(E-mail: hewa@sliit.lk)
Health services. Medical Officer: Jayasuriya,
Shelton, MB BS *Ceyl.*
(E-mail: shelton.e@sliit.lk)

Language training for international students.
Director, English Language Teaching Unit:
Goonatillake, Vineetha
Library (chief librarian). Librarian: Perera,
Pushpamala, BA *Colombo*, MLS *Colombo*
(E-mail: pushpamala@sliit.lk)
Marketing. Manager, Business Development:
Panabokke, Himadri, BCom *W.Syd.*
(E-mail: himadri.p@sliit.lk)
Personnel/human resources. Manager,
Human Resource Development: Jayasooriya,
Savitri, BA *Ceyl.* (E-mail: sjayasuriya@sliit.lk)
Purchasing. Manager, Procurement and
Supplies: Peiris, Harsha, BCom *Sri Jay.*
(E-mail: harsha.p@sliit.lk)

Quality assurance and accreditation. Director,
Curriculum and Academic: Jayawardena,
Chandimal, BSc *Moratuwa*, MEng *Moratuwa*,
PhD *Saga* (E-mail: chandimal.j@sliit.lk)
Research. Director, Centre for Research:
Marikkar, Faiz, BSc *Ruhuna*, MSc *Nanjing*, PhD
Nanjing (E-mail: faiz.m@sliit.lk)
Sport and recreation. Sports Consultant:
Hettiarachchi

[*Information supplied by the institution as at 10
December 2007, and edited by the ACU*]

UVA WELLASSA UNIVERSITY

Founded 2005

Postal Address: Second Mile Post, Passara Road, Badulla 9000, Sri Lanka
Telephone: (055) 222 6400 **Fax:** (055) 222 6370
URL: http://www.uwu.ac.lk

VICE-CHANCELLOR*—Embuldeniya, Chandra

UNIVERSITY OF THE VISUAL AND PERFORMING ARTS

Founded 2005

Postal Address: 2 Albert Crescent, Colombo 07, Sri Lanka
Telephone: (11) 269 6971
URL: http://www.vpa.ac.lk

VICE-CHANCELLOR*—Amunugama, Prof. Sarath

WAYAMBA UNIVERSITY OF SRI LANKA

Founded 1999

Member of the Association of Commonwealth Universities

Postal Address: Kuliyapitiya, Sri Lanka
Telephone: (037) 228 2758 **Fax:** (037) 228 1392 **E-mail:** vc@wyb.ac.lk
URL: http://www.wyb.ac.lk

VICE-CHANCELLOR*—Fonseka, Prof. T. S. G., BSc *Colombo*, MSc *Kelaniya*, PhD *Nott.*
REGISTRAR‡—Muthubanda, R. M. B., AC
BURSAR—Dharmadasa, D. A. Upali, BSc *Kelaniya*

GENERAL INFORMATION

History. The university was previously
established as Wayamba Campus of Rajarata
University in 1995, and was granted university
status in October 1999.
It is located in the North-Western Province
of Sri Lanka, with sites at Kuliyapitiya and
Makandura.

Admission to first degree courses (see also Sri
Lankan Introduction). Selections are made by
the University Grants Commission (UGC) on
the basis of General Certificate of Education
(GCE) A level results.

First Degrees (see also Sri Lankan Directory
to Subjects of Study). BSc, BSc(Agric),
BSc(BusStud), BSc(Food&Nutr).
Length of course. Full-time: BSc: 3–4 years;
BSc(Agric), BSc(BusStud), BSc(Food&Nutr): 4
years.

Higher Degrees (see also Sri Lankan
Directory to Subjects of Study).
Master's. MBA.
Admission. An appropriate first degree and at
least one year work experience.
Length of course. Full-time: MBA: 1 year. Part-
time: MBA: 2 years.

Language of Instruction. English. Intensive
pre-sessional courses are available for all
undergraduate students.

Libraries. Volumes: 45,000. Special
collections: Staff Development; Career
Guidance.

FACULTIES/SCHOOLS
Agriculture and Plantation Management
Tel: (031) 229 9430 Fax: (031) 229 9248
E-mail: deanfapm@wyb.ac.lk
Dean: Attanayake, Prof. D. P. S. T. G., BScAgric
Peradeniya, PhD *Birm.*

Assistant Registrar: Kumari, P. M. D. A. S., BSc *Open S.Lanka*

Applied Sciences

Tel: (037) 228 1749 Fax: (037) 228 1749
E-mail: deanfas@wyb.ac.lk
Dean: Ekanayake, E. M. Piyal, BSc *Kelaniya*, MSc *Kyushu*, DSc *Kyushu*
Assistant Registrar: Siriwardhane, L. M. C., BA *Sri Jay.*, MA *Kelaniya*

Business Studies and Finance

Tel: (037) 228 3621 Fax: (037) 228 3621
E-mail: deanbsf@wyb.ac.lk
Dean: Wickramasinghe, Prof. E. S., BDS *Colombo*, MCom *Kelaniya*
Assistant Registrar: Henegama, H. P., BSc *Peradeniya*

Livestock, Fisheries and Nutrition

Tel: (031) 229 9429 Fax: (031) 229 9870
E-mail: deanflfn@wyb.ac..lk
Dean: Jayasinghe, Prof. J. M. P. K., BSc *Colombo*, MSc *Colombo*, PhD *Sterling*
Assistant Registrar: Christy, A. J., BA *Jaffna*

ACADEMIC UNITS

Accountancy and Business Finance

Tel: (037) 228 4214 E-mail: acc@yahoo.com
Uluwatta, K. H. U. D. N. K., BSc *Sri Jay.*, MSc *Sri Jay.* Sr. Lectr.; Head*
Other Staff: 1 Lectr.

Agribusiness Management

Tel: (031) 229 9246 Fax: (031) 229 9248
E-mail: abm@wyb.ac.lk
Jayasinghe-Mudalige, Udith K., BScAgric *Peradeniya*, MSc(AgricEcon) *Peradeniya*, PhD *Guelph* Head*
Other Staff: 3 Lectrs.

Applied Nutrition

Tel: (031) 229 8120
E-mail: nutrition@wyb.ac.lk
Chandrasekara, G. Anoma P., BSc(Agri) *Peradeniya*, MPhil *Peradeniya*
Silva, Renuka, BSc(Agri) *Peradeniya*, PhD *Reading* Sr. Lectr.; Head*
Other Staff: 6 Lectrs.

Aquaculture and Fisheries

Tel: (031) 229 9874 E-mail: aqua@wyb.ac.lk
Jayasinghe, J. M. P. K., BSc *Colombo*, MSc *Colombo*, PhD *Sterling* Prof.; Head*
Other Staff: 2 Lectrs.

Banking and Finance

Tel: (037) 228 4216
E-mail: banking@wyb.ac.lk
Rathnasiri, R. A., BCom *Sri Jay.*, MA(Econ) *Colombo* Lectr.-in-Charge; Head*
Upananda, W. A., BSc *Peradeniya*, MBA *Peradeniya*, MPS *Cornell*, PhD *Peradeniya* Sr. Lectr.
Other Staff: 3 Lectrs.

Biotechnology

Tel: (031) 229 8119 Fax: (031) 229 9430
E-mail: biotec@wyb.ac.lk
Attanayake, D. P. S. T. G., BScAgric *Peradeniya*, PhD *Birm.* Prof.; Head*
Other Staff: 2 Lectrs.

Business Management

Tel: (037) 228 3618 Fax: (037) 228 4215
E-mail: bm@wyb.ac.lk
Herath, H. M. A., BCom *Ruhuna* Lectr.-in-Charge; Head*
Wickramasinghe, E. S., BDS *Colombo*, MCom *Kelaniya* Sr. Lectr.; Prof.
Other Staff: 3 Lectrs.

Computing and Information Systems

Tel: (037) 228 2759 E-mail: cmis@wyb.ac.lk
Perera, L. D. Rohana D., BSc *Kelaniya*, MPhil *Kelaniya*, PhD *Kyushu* Head*
Other Staff: 4 Lectrs.

Electronics

Tel: (037) 228 3622
E-mail: electronics@wyb.ac.lk
Fernando, C. A. Nandana, BSc *Sri Jay.*, MPhil *Ruhuna*, PhD *Kanazawa* Prof.
Perera, G. A. Kumudu S., BSc *Peradeniya*, PhD *Peradeniya* Head*
Perera, L. D. Rohana D., BSc *Kelaniya*, MPhil *Kelaniya*, PhD *Kyushu* Sr. Lectr.
Vidanapathirana, Kamal P., BSc *Peradeniya*, PhD *Peradeniya* Sr. Lectr.
Other Staff: 3 Lectrs.

Food Sciences and Technology

Tel: (031) 229 9871
E-mail: foodtech@wyb.ac.lk
Fonseka, T. S. G., BSc *Colombo*, MSc *Kelaniya*, PhD *Nott.* Prof.
Jayasinghe, C. V. L., BSc *Sri Jay.*, MPhil *Sri Jay.*, PhD *Tokyo* Head*
Other Staff: 3 Lectrs.

Horticulture and Landscape Gardening

Tel: (031) 229 9249 Fax: (031) 229 9430
E-mail: horticulture@sltnet.lk
Jayasekera, S. J. B. A., BSc(Agric) *Agric.*, *Faisalabad*, PhD *Reading* Prof.
Ranaweera, B., MSc *Moscow*, PhD *Moscow* Sr. Lectr.; Head*
Other Staff: 2 Sr. Lectrs.; 3 Lectrs.

Industrial Management

Tel: (037) 228 3619 E-mail: imgt@wyb.ac.lk
Priyantha, L. D., BSc *Kelaniya*, MPhil *Kelaniya* Head*
Other Staff: 7 Lectrs.

Insurance and Valuation

Tel: (037) 228 4213 Fax: (037) 228 4215
E-mail: ins@wyb.ac.lk
Gamage, S. K., BCom *Kelaniya*, MSSc *Kelaniya* Lectr.; Head*
Other Staff: 1 Lectr.

Livestock and Avian Sciences

Tel: (031) 229 9873
E-mail: livestock@wyb.ac.lk
Ranawana, S. S. E., BVSc *Ceyl.*, PhD *Syd.* Prof.; Head*
Other Staff: 3 Lectrs.

Mathematical Sciences

Tel: (037) 228 3170 E-mail: maths@wyb.ac.lk
Ekanayake, E. M. Piyal, BSc *Kelaniya*, MSc *Kyushu*, DSc *Kyushu* Dean of Fac.
Francisco, Geethamala S., BSc *Kelaniya*, MSc *E.China Normal* Head*
Gunaratne, H. Sunil, BSc *Peradeniya*, PhD *Ill.* Dir.

Priyantha, L. D., BSc *Kelaniya*, MPhil *Kelaniya* Sr. Lectr.
Other Staff: 5 Lectrs.

Plantation Management

Tel: (031) 229 9226 Fax: (031) 229 9870
E-mail: plantation@sltnet.lk
Fernandopulle, M. N. D., BSc *Peradeniya*, MPhil *Colombo*, PhD *Qld.* Sr. Lectr.; Head*
Jayasekera, N. E. M., BSc *Ceyl.*, PhD *Birm.* Prof.
Other Staff: 4 Sr. Lectrs.; 1 Lectr.

SPECIAL CENTRES, ETC

Computer Unit (Kuliyapitiya)

Tel: (037) 228 3622
E-mail: comunitkul@wyb.ac.lk
Gunaratne, H. Sunil, BSc *Peradeniya*, PhD *Ill.* Dir.*
Other Staff: 4 Staff Members
Research: data communication; networking

Computer Unit (Makandura)

Tel: (031) 229 9247
E-mail: comunimk@wyb.ac.lk
Weerakkody, W. J. S. K., BSc *Kelaniya*, PhD *Kelaniya* Dir.*
Other Staff: 5 Staff Members

English Language Teaching Unit (Kuliyapitiya)

Tel: (037) 228 3155 E-mail: eltukul@wyb.ac.lk
Samaranayake, M. K. S. Mohan, BA *Kelaniya*, MA *Kelaniya* Co-ordinator*
Other Staff: 6 Staff Members

English Language Teaching Unit (Makandura)

Tel: (060) 231 4281
E-mail: eltumkd@wyb.ac.lk
Fernando, W. M. Clare, BA *Peradeniya* Co-ordinator*
Other Staff: 2 Instructors

CONTACT OFFICERS

Admissions (first degree). Senior Assistant Registrar (Student Welfare): Banneheke, B. M. N. C., BSc *Sri Jay.*
Careers. Director, Career Guidance Unit: Athauda, A. M. T. P., BSc *Sri Jay.*, MBA *Tsukuba*, PhD *Tokyo*
Examinations. Senior Assistant Registrar: Ekanayake, E. M. G. L., BA *Peradeniya*
Finance. Bursar: Dharmadasa, D. A. Upali, BSc *Kelaniya* (E-mail: bursar@wyb.ac.lk)
Health services. University Medical Officer (Visiting): Dissanayake, D. M. S., MB BS *Peradeniya*
Library (chief librarian). Librarian: Gamlath, W. G. P., BA *Peradeniya*, BLISc *Panjab*, MLISc *Panjab*
Sport and recreation. Instructor in Physical Education: Wellassa, R. J., BSc *Kelaniya*
Staff development and training. Director, Staff Development and Training: Jayasinghe-Mudalige, Udith K., BScAgric *Peradeniya*, MSc(AgricEcon) *Peradeniya*, PhD *Guelph* (E-mail: udith@wyb.ac.lk)

[*Information supplied by the institution as at 4 October 2007, and edited by the ACU*]

SWAZILAND

DIRECTORY TO SUBJECTS OF STUDY

The table below shows which subjects are available for study and/or research at the University of Swaziland. U = may be studied for first degree course; M = may be studied for master's degree course; D = research facilities to doctoral level; X = all three levels (UMD).

Accountancy/Accounting	U		Economics	U
Administration/Administrative Studies	U		Economics Agricultural/Agribusiness	U
Advertising	U		Education	M
African Languages/Studies	U		Education Adult	M
Agricultural Extension and Education	U		Education Extension	M
Agriculture/Agricultural Science	M		Education Primary	M
Agronomy/Soil Science	U		Education Secondary	U
Anatomical Science/Anatomy	U		Education Special	U
Animal Nutrition/Animal Physiology	M		Educational Administration	M
Animal Science/Husbandry/Production	U		Educational Psychology	M
Animatronics/Computer Arts	U		Electronics	U
Applied Chemistry	M		Engineering	U
Aquaculture/Fisheries/Marine Science	M		Engineering Communications/Telecommunications	U
Banking/Finance	U		Engineering Electrical/Electronic	U
Biology	U		English	U
Botany/Plant Science	M		English as a Second Language	U
Business Administration	U		Entomology	M
Business Computing	U		Entrepreneurship	U
Business Economics	U		Environmental Health	U
Business Information Systems	U		Environmental Management	M
Business/Commerce	U		Environmental Science/Studies	U
Chemistry	U		Epidemiology	U
Child Health	U		Ethics	U
Child and Family Psychology	U		Ethics, Law and Governance	U
Communication/Journalism/Media Studies	U		Fashion/Clothing	U
Communications/Information Management	U		Food Science/Nutrition/Home Science/Dietetics	M
Community Education	U		Forestry	M
Community Health	U		French/French Studies	U
Computer Science	U		Genetics	U
Consumer Studies	U		Genetics and Plant Breeding	M
Corporate Governance	U		Geographic Information Systems/Geomatics	U
Counselling	U		Geography	M
Creative Writing	U		Health Education	U
Criminal Justice/Public Policy	U		Health Information	U
Criminology	U		Health Sciences/Studies	U
Crop Science/Production	M		Health and Social Care	U
Curriculum and Assessment Studies	M		Health/Hospital Administration	U
Dairy Technology	U		History	M
Development Studies	U		Horticulture	U
Drama/Theatre/Dance/Performing Arts	U		Human Biology	U
Economic History	U		Human Resource Development	U
Economic Planning and Development	U		Immunology/Infection/Immunity	U

Indigenous Knowledge Systems	U	Music Education	U
Industrial Relations/Personnel/HRM	U	Nursing Education/Administration	U
Information Technology	U	Nursing/Midwifery	U
Insurance	U	Occupational Health/Therapy	U
International Business	U	Parasitology	U
International Finance	U	Physics	U
International Finance Economics	U	Physiology	U
International Marketing	U	Plant Pathology	M
Labour Studies	U	Politics/Political Science/Government	U
Land Management/Rehabilitation	M	Population Studies/Demography	U
Land Resource Science	M	Poultry Science	U
Language Teaching/Learning	U	Project Management	U
Language and Communication	U	Psychology	U
Languages, Modern	U	Public Administration	U
Law Business/Commercial/Economic/Industrial	U	Public Health/Population Health	U
Law Civil	U	Public Relations	U
Law Employment/Labour	U	Public Sector Management	U
Law Environmental	M	Religion/Theology	U
Law Intellectual Property/Copyright	U	Social Work/Studies	U
Law Legal Practice	U	Sociology	U
Law/Legal Studies	U	Sotho	U
Livestock Science	U	Statistics/Actuarial Science	U
Management	U	Sustainable Development	U
Management Information Systems	U	Taxation	U
Marketing	U	Teacher Training	U
Mathematics	U	Textiles/Fibre Science/Technology	U
Microbiology/Medical Microbiology	U	Women's/Gender Studies	M
Multimedia	U	Zoology	U

UNIVERSITY OF SWAZILAND

Founded 1982

Member of the Association of Commonwealth Universities

Postal Address: Private Bag 4, Kwaluseni, Swaziland
Telephone: 518 4011 **Fax:** 518 5276 **E-mail:** postmaster@uniswa.sz
URL: http://www.uniswa.sz

VICE-CHANCELLOR*—Magagula, Prof. Cisco M., BA UBS, BEd Bran., MEd Manit., EdD Tor.
PRO-VICE-CHANCELLOR—Mtetwa, Prof. Victor S. B., BSc UBLS, DPhil Oxf.
REGISTRAR‡—Vilakati, S. S., BA UBLS, MA Ball
LIBRARIAN—Mavuso, Makana R., BA UBLS, MLib Wales
BURSAR—Dlamini, M. E., BCom Swazi., MSc Strath.

GENERAL INFORMATION

History. Founded in 1982, the university was formerly University College of Swaziland, a constituent college of the University of Botswana and Swaziland (founded 1976).

Admission to first degree courses. International General Certificate of Education (IGCE) with at least 6 passes (including English), obtained at no more than two sittings.

First Degrees (see also Swaziland Directory to Subjects of Study). BA, BCom, BEd, BEng, BNSc, BSc, BSc(AgricEd), BSc(Agron), BSc(AnimalSc), BSc(FSNT), BSc(HomeEc), BSc(Hort), BSc(LWM), BSc(TADM), LLB.
  Length of course. Full-time: BA, BEd, BEng, BSc, BSc(AgricEd), BSc(Agron), BSc(AnimalSc), BSc(FSNT), BSc(HomeEc), BSc(Hort), BSc(LWM), BSc(TADM): 4 years; BCom, BNSc, LLB: 5 years. Part-time: BA: 5 years. By distance learning: BCom: 6 years; BA: max. 8 years.

Higher Degrees (see also Swaziland Directory to Subjects of Study).
  Master's. MA, MEd, MSc, MSc(AgAPEC), MSc(AgEd), MSc(AgExt), MSc(CropSc), MSc(ERM).
  Length of course. Full-time: MA, MEd, MSc, MSc(AgAPEC), MSc(AgEd), MSc(AgExt), MSc(CropSc), MSc(ERM): 2 years. Part-time: MA, MEd, MSc, MSc(AgAPEC), MSc(AgEd), MSc(AgExt), MSc(CropSc), MSc(ERM): 3 years.

Libraries. Volumes: 188,350. Periodicals subscribed to: 1500. Special collections: Swaziana.

Academic Awards (2006–2007). 20 awards ranging in value from to E20,000.

Academic Year (2007–2008). Two semesters: 16 August–21 December; 7 January–18 April.

Income (2005–2006). Total, E191,127,986.

Statistics. Staff (2006–2007): 753 (293 academic, 460 non-academic). Students (2006–2007): full-time 3648 (1905 men, 1743 women); international 125; distance education/external 2046 (891 men, 1155 women); undergraduate 5647 (2771 men, 2876 women); master's 47 (25 men, 22 women).

FACULTIES/SCHOOLS

Agriculture
Tel: 527 4021 Fax: 527 4021
  E-mail: bmdlamini@agric.uniswa.sz
Dean: Dlamini, Prof. Barnabas M., BSc UP Ag., MSc W.Virginia, PhD Ohio
Secretary: Ndabandaba, G.

Commerce
E-mail: khan@comm2.uniswa.sz/commerce@uniswa.sz

Dean: Khan, Mohammed A., BCom Alig., MCom Alig., PhD Alig.
Secretary: Mamba, L.

Education
Tel: 518 5811
  E-mail: akusen@uniswacc.uniswa.sz
Dean: Nyakutse, Getrude, BA Lond., MA Georgia, PhD A.Bello
Secretary: Msibi, P.

Health Sciences
Tel: 404 6242 Fax: 404 6241
  E-mail: itzwane@healthsci.uniswa.sz
Dean: Zwane, Isabel T., BSc Howard, MA Maryland, PhD Maryland
Secretary: Dlamini, P.

Humanities
E-mail: hlndlovu@uniswacc.uniswa.sz
Dean: Ndlovu, Hebron L., BA UBS, MA McCormick, MPhil Trinity(Dub.), PhD McM.
Secretary: Kunene, T.

Postgraduate Studies
E-mail: bmdlamini@agric.uniswa.sz
Acting Director: Dlamini, Prof. Barnabas M., BSc UP Ag., MSc W.Virginia, PhD Ohio
Secretary: Shongwe, S.

Science
E-mail: science@uniswa.sz
Dean: Dlamini, M. D., BSc UBS, MSc Lanc., PhD Camb.
Secretary: Simelane, K.

Social Science
E-mail: pqmag@uniswacc.uniswa.sz
Acting Dean: Magagula, P. Q., BA UBS, MA Dar., PhD Durh.
Secretary: Lokothwayo, P.

ACADEMIC UNITS

Accounting
Khan, Mohammed A., BCom Alig., MCom Alig., PhD Alig.   Assoc. Prof.
Ntentesa, M. T., BCom UBS, MSocSc Birm.   Lectr.; Head*
Other Staff: 4 Lectrs.

African Languages and Literature
Sibanda, E. S., BA UBS, MA Ohio   Lectr.; Head*
Other Staff: 1 Lectr.

Agricultural Economics and Management
Tel: 527 4021 Fax: 527 4021
  E-mail: agriculture@uniswa.sz
Dlamini, Phonias M., BSc Ghana, MSc Nair., PhD Manit.   Sr. Lectr.
Masuku, M. B., BScAgric Swazi., MSc Ohio, PhD Pret.   Sr. Lectr.; Head*
Panin, Anthony, BSc Gött., MSc Gött., DrScAgr Gött.   Prof.
Rugambisa, J. I., BA Dar., MSc Wis., PhD Ill.   Sr. Lectr.

Sithole, M. M., BSc Swazi., MSc Curtin, PhD Curtin   Sr. Lectr.
Other Staff: 1 Lectr.

Agricultural Education and Extension
Tel: 527 4021 Fax: 527 4021
  E-mail: agriculture@uniswa.sz
Dlamini, Barnabas M., BSc UP Ag., MSc W.Virginia, PhD Ohio   Prof.
Dlamini, Marrieta P., BScAgEd Luzonian, MSc Ohio State, PhD Ohio State   Assoc. Prof.; Head*
Dube, M. A., BScAgEd W.Virginia, MSc Mich.State, PhD Iowa State   Sr. Lectr.
Mndebele, C. B., BSc W.Virginia, MA W.Virginia, MSc W.Virginia, PhD Virginia Polytech.   Assoc. Prof.
Simelane, M. J., BScAgEd W.Virginia, PhD Ohio, MScAgricEd W.Virginia   Lectr.; Head*
Other Staff: 2 Lectrs.

Animal Production and Health
Tel: 528 3021 Fax: 528 3021
Dlamini, A. M., BSc(AgEd) Swazi., MSc Glas., PhD W.Syd.   Sr. Lectr.
Dlamini, B. J., BSc Oklahoma, MSc New Mexico, PhD Iowa   Head*
Other Staff: 7 Lectrs.

Biological Sciences
E-mail: science@uniswa.sz
Kunene, Innocentia S., BSc S.Leone, MSc Ib., PhD Texas A.& M.   Sr. Lectr.; Head*
Magagula, Cebsile N., BSc Swazi., MSc Dal., PhD Natal   Sr. Lectr.
Mansuetus, A. B., BScAgric Sokoine Ag., MSc Texas A.& M., PhD Texas A.& M.   Sr. Lectr.
Monadjem, A., BSc Witw., MSc Witw., PhD Natal   Assoc. Prof.
Nkosi, B. S., BSc UBS, MSc Lond., PhD Lond.   Sr. Lectr.
Other Staff: 3 Lectrs.

Business Administration
E-mail: commerce@uniswa.sz
Joubert, Patricia N., BCom Swazi., MBA Wales, PhD Wales   Sr. Lectr.; Head*
Other Staff: 7 Lectrs.
Research: behavioural dispositions in organisations; entrepreneurial behaviour in a competitive market (a developing country's perspective); innovation and industrialisation; media advertising in Swaziland; strategies and challenges

Chemistry
Amusan, O. O. G., BSc Ib., MSc Lough., PhD Ib.   Assoc. Prof.
Fadiran, A. O., BSc Ife, MSc A.Bello, PhD Ife   Sr. Lectr.
Lwenje, Salia M., BSc Zambia, MA Brandeis, PhD Brandeis   Sr. Lectr.
Mtetwa, Victor S. B., BSc UBLS, DPhil Oxf.   Prof.
Otieno, D. A., BSc Nair., PhD Nott.   Assoc. Prof.
Thwala, J. M., BSc Swazi., MSc E.Anglia, PhD Brist.   Lectr.; Head*

Other Staff: 2 Lectrs.

Community Health Nursing Science

Tel: 404 0171 Fax: 404 6241

Mabuza, Eunice M., BEdNurs *Wales*, MPH
Jerusalem Lectr.; Head*
Sukati, Nonhlanhla A., BSc *Cuttington*, MA N.Y.,
PhD *Calif.* Sr. Lectr.
Zwane, Isabel T., BSc *Howard*, MA *Maryland*, PhD
Maryland Sr. Lectr.; Head*
Other Staff: 3 Lectrs.

Computer Science

Fax: 518 6903

Ikram, I. M., BSc *Buckingham*, MSc *Brist.*, PhD
Rhodes Sr. Lectr.
Jaju, R. P., BSc *Lucknow*, MSc *Lucknow*, PhD *Agra*
Assoc. Prof.
Mashwama, P. M., BSc *Swazi.*, MSc *Dund.*, PhD
Leeds Lectr.; Head*
Other Staff: 3 Lectrs.

Crop Production

Tel: 527 4021 Fax: 527 4021
E-mail: crop@agric.uniswa.sz

Earnshaw, Diana M., BScAg *Swazi.*, MSc *Guelph*,
PhD *Wales* Lectr.; Head*
Edje, O. T., BSc *Mich.State*, MSc *Mich.State*, PhD
Iowa State Prof.
Masina, G. T., BSc *UBLS*, MSc *Missouri*, PhD *Nair.*
Sr. Lectr.
Ossom, E. M., BSc *Ife*, MSc *Ife*, PhD *Purdue*
Assoc. Prof.
Shongwe, Gideon N., BSc *W.Illinois*, MSc *Guelph*,
PhD *Ohio State* Sr. Lectr.
Other Staff: 4 Lectrs.

Curriculum and Teaching

Gathu, K., BEd *Kenyatta*, MEd *Kenyatta* Sr. Lectr.
Mazibuko, Edmund Z., BEd *Swazi.*, MEd *Wales*,
PhD *E.Cowan* Sr. Lectr.
Mkatshwa, T. Daphne, BA *UBLS*, MA *Ball*, PhD
Penn. Sr. Lectr.
Zwane, Sihle E., BA *UBLS*, MEd *Col.*, MA *Col.*,
EdD *Col.* Lectr.; Head*
Other Staff: 8 Lectrs.

Economics

Mbatha, Thuli M., BA *Swazi.*, MA *Dar.* Lectr.;
Head*
Ojo, F., BA *Bran.*, MA *Alta.*, PhD *Lagos* Prof.
Other Staff: 4 Lectrs.

Education, Adult

Biswalo, P. L., BSc *Indiana State*, MSc *Florida State*
Lectr.; Head*
Mkhwanazi, Almon M., BA *UBLS*, MSEd *Penn.*
Sr. Lectr.
Mutangira, J. P. B., BA(Ed) *Dar.*, MA *Dar.*, PhD
S'ton. Sr. Lectr.
Ngoitiama, Z. M., BA(Ed) *Dar.*, MA *Dar.*, PhD
S'ton. Sr. Lectr.
Other Staff: 3 Lectrs.

Education, In-Service

Tel: 518 4658

Dlamini, F. K., BSc *Swazi.*, MEd *Brist.* Lectr.;
Head*
Magagula, Cisco M., BA *UBS*, BEd *Bran.*, MEd
Manit., EdD *Tor.* Prof.
Other Staff: 3 Lectrs.

Education, Primary

Dlamini, Betty T., BSc *UBS*, BEd *Bran.*, MEd
Manit., PhD *Witw.* Sr. Lectr.; Head*
Other Staff: 5 Lectrs.

Educational Foundations and Management

Famuyide, M. M., BEd *Ib.*, MEd *Ib.*, PhD *Wales*
Sr. Lectr.
Nyakutse, Getrude, BA *Lond.*, MA *Georgia*, PhD
A.Bello Sr. Lectr.
Shongwe, A. B., BA *UBLS*, BEd *UBLS*, MA *Lond.*,
EdD *Col.* Lectr.; Head*

Other Staff: 2 Lectrs.

Electronic Engineering

Egau, P. C., BScEng *Nair.*, MScEng *Nair.*, PhD
Syd. Assoc. Prof.; Head*
Ekemezie, P. N., BEng *Nigeria*, MEng *Nigeria*,
PhD *Nigeria* Sr. Lectr.
Other Staff: 3 Lectrs.

English Language and Literature

Dlamini, Lucy Z., BA *UBS*, MA *Nair.*, DA *Clark
Atlanta* Sr. Lectr.
Tsabedze, Clara, BA *UBLS*, MA *Nair.*, PhD
Penn.State Sr. Lectr.
Zindela, Nomsa C. W., BA *UBS*, MEd *Exe.*
Lectr.; Head*
Other Staff: 1 Lectr.

Environmental Health Science

Tel: 404 6242 Fax: 404 6241
E-mail: jmtshali@healthsci.uniswa.sz

Mtshali, J. S., BSc *Strath.*, MSc *Z'bwe.* Lectr.;
Head*
Other Staff: 6 Lectrs.
Research: community involvement in malaria
control activities in Swaziland; evaluation of
anti-malaria bed net acceptance and use of
insecticide treated bed nets for malaria
control in Swaziland; evaluation of public
participation in the environmental impact
assessment process in Swaziland; types of
medical waste generated by medical
institutions in Swaziland

Geography

Matondo, J. I., BSc *Dar.*, MSc *Dar.*, PhD *Colorado
State* Assoc. Prof.; Head*
Mlipha, M., BA *Swazi.*, MA *Wat.* Sr. Lectr.
Tevera, D. S., BA *S.Leone*, MA *Qu.*, PhD *Cinc.*
Other Staff: 6 Lectrs.

History

Nyeko, B., BA *Mak.*, PhD *Mak.* Assoc. Prof.
Sikhondze, B. A. B., BA *UBLS*, MA *Manit.*, PhD
Lond. Sr. Lectr.; Head*
Simelane, H. S., BA *UBS*, MA *Ohio*, PhD *Tor.*
Assoc. Prof.
Other Staff: 2 Lectrs.

Home Economics

Tel: 527 4021 Fax: 527 4021

Sibiya, Thokozile E., BSc *Tuskegee*, MSc *Tuskegee*,
PhD *Guelph* Lectr.; Head*
Surana, N., BSc *Ud.*, MSc *Baroda*, MPhil *Mumbai*
Sr. Lectr.
Zwane, Pinkie E., BSc *Mich.State*, MSc *Oklahoma
State*, PhD *Florida State* Sr. Lectr.
Other Staff: 5 Lectrs.

Horticulture

Wahome, P. K., MSc *Nair.*, DrRerNat *Humboldt*
Sr. Lectr.; Head*
Other Staff: 2 Lectrs.

Journalism and Mass Communication

Rooney, R. C., BA *Herts.*, MA *Westminster*, PhD
Westminster Prof.; Head*
Other Staff: 3 Lectrs.

Land Use and Mechanisation

Tel: 527 4021 Fax: 527 4021

Manyatsi, A. M., BScAgric *Swazi.*, MSc *Cran.*,
PhD *James Cook* Sr. Lectr.; Head*
Other Staff: 5 Lectrs.

Law

Acheampong, K. A., LLB *Ghana*, LLM *Sask.*
Assoc. Prof.
Mabirizi, D., LLB *Mak.*, LLM *Mak.* Lectr.;
Head*
Other Staff: 2 Visiting Profs.; 5 Lectrs.; 2
Lectrs.†

Mathematics

Motsa, S. S., BSc *Swazi.*, MSc *Z'bwe.*, PhD *Z'bwe.*
Lectr.; Head*
Other Staff: 5 Lectrs.

Midwifery Science

Tel: 404 0171 Fax: 404 6241

Masilela, Bongiwe H., BEdNurs *Botswana*, MMP
Adel. Lectr.; Head*
Other Staff: 4 Lectrs.

Modern Languages: French

Ferreira-Meyers, Karren A. F., BA *Brussels*, MA
Brussels Lectr.; Head*
Other Staff: 2 Lectrs.

Nursing Science

Tel: 404 6242 Fax: 404 6241

Dlamini, Jabulile V., BEd *Wales*, MSc *Manc.*
Lectr.; Head*
Dlamini, Priscilla S., BEd(Nursing) *Botswana*,
MCur *Natal*, PhD *Natal* Sr. Lectr.
Mathunjwa, Mumly D., BSc(Nursing) *New
Orleans*, MSN *Texas*, MPH *Texas*, DLitt&Phil
S.Af. Sr. Lectr.
Mkhabela, Mildred S. P., BSc(Nursing) *Howard*,
MA N.Y. Dir.*
Other Staff: 6 Staff Members
Research: psychological support needs of people
living with HIV/AIDS (families and support
groups); stigma and discrimination of
people living with HIV/AIDS in Swaziland

Physics

Darlington, C. N. W., MA *Camb.*, PhD *Camb.*
Sr. Lectr.
Dlamini, M. D., BSc *UBS*, MSc *Lanc.*, PhD *Camb.*
Assoc. Prof.
Liao, W. H., BSc *Cheng Kung*, MSc *Colorado State*,
PhD *Colorado State* Sr. Lectr.; Head*
Sheth, C. V., BSc *Karn.*, MSc *Karn.*, PhD *Karn.*
Prof.
Varkey, A. J., BSc *Kerala*, MSc *Ravi.*, PhD *Nigeria*
Sr. Lectr.
Other Staff: 3 Lectrs.
Research: development of an indigenous water
filter using anthracite and clay

Political and Administrative Studies

Al-Teraifi, Ahmed A., BSc *Khart.*, MSocSc *Birm.*,
PhD *Pitt.* Prof.
Dlamini, M. P., BA(Admin) *UBLS*, MPA
Union(N.Y.), PhD *Manc.* Assoc. Prof.
Mkhonta, P. B., BA *Swazi.*, MA *St Mary's(Can.)*
Lectr.; Head*
Other Staff: 3 Lectrs.

Sociology

Mathew, R., BSc *Kerala*, MA *Kerala* Sr. Lectr.
Zamberia, A. M., BA *Nair.*, MA *Indiana*, PhD
Indiana Sr. Lectr.; Head*
Other Staff: 3 Lectrs.
Research: HIV/AIDS at the university of
Swaziland (the influence of social-structural
factors)

Statistics and Demography

Dlamini, S. S., BA *Swazi.*, MA *Bowling Green*, PhD
Bowling Green Lectr.; Head*
Other Staff: 4 Lectrs.

Theology and Religious Studies

Ndlovu, Hebron L., BA *UBS*, MA *McCormick*,
MPhil *Trinity(Dub.)*, PhD *McM.* Sr. Lectr.
Omoregbe, J. I., BA *Greg.*, MA *Pontif.Lateran*,
DPhil *Pontif.Lateran*, PhD *Louvain* Prof.
Vilakati, Joyce N., BA *Swazi.*, MA *McCormick*
Lectr.; Head*
Other Staff: 2 Staff Members

SPECIAL CENTRES, ETC

Academic Development Centre

E-mail: adc@uniswa.sz

Mazibuko, Edmund Z., BEd *Swazi.*, MEd *Wales*,
PhD *E.Cowan* Sr. Lectr.; Dir.*

Community Services, Centre for

E-mail: nom@uniswacc.uniswa.sz

Simelane, Nomcebo O., BA UBLS, MA *George Washington*, PhD *Clark*   Lectr.; Dir.*

Consultancy and Training Centre

Masuku, M. B., BScAgric *Swazi.*, MSc *Ohio*, PhD *Pret.*   Sr. Lectr.; Dir.*

Distance Education, Institute of

Tel: 518 7083 Fax: 518 7083
E-mail: ide@uniswa.sz

Sukati, C. Walter S., BSc *UBLS*, BEd *UBLS*, MSc *Harv.*, EdM *Harv.*, DEd *S.Af.*, EdD *Harv.*   Dir.*

Other Staff: 3 Lectrs.

Information and Communication Technology Centre

Tel: 518 6903 Fax: 518 5276

Thwala, Thembela I., BSc *Swazi.*, MSc *Qu.*   Acting Dir.*

Other Staff: 6 Technologists

Swaziland Institute for Research in Traditional Medicine, Medicinal and Indigenous Plants

Tel: 518 6816

Amusan, O. O. G., BSc *Ib.*, MSc *Lough.*, PhD *Ib.*   Assoc. Prof.; Dir.*

Other Staff: 2 Res. Fellows; 1 Pharmacologist

UNISWA Health Information and Counselling Centre

Tel: 527 4021 Fax: 527 4021

Mkhabela, Mildred S. P., BSc(Nursing) *Howard*, MA *N.Y.*   Dir.*

University Planning Centre

E-mail: upc@uniswa.sz

Mndebele, C. B., BSc *W.Virginia*, MA *W.Virginia*, MSc *W.Virginia*, PhD *Virginia Polytech.*   Assoc. Prof.; Dir.*

University Research Centre

Tel: 527 4428 Fax: 527 4418
E-mail: research@iafrica.sz

Dlamini, Marrieta P., BScAgEd *Luzonian*, MSc *Ohio State*, PhD *Ohio State*   Assoc. Prof.; Dir.*

Other Staff: 1 Res. Fellow

CONTACT OFFICERS

Academic affairs. Senior Assistant Registrar (Academic affairs): Masuku, Richard N., BA *Swazi.*, MPM *Carnegie-Mellon* (E-mail: rma@isdu.uniswa.sz)

Accommodation. Dean of Student Affairs: Kunene, M., BEd *Swazi.*, MA *Col.* (E-mail: mkunene@isdu.uniswa.sz)

Admissions (first degree). Senior Assistant Registrar (Admissions (first degree)): Masuku, Richard N., BA *Swazi.*, MPM *Carnegie-Mellon* (E-mail: rma@isdu.uniswa.sz)

Admissions (higher degree). Senior Assistant Registrar (Admissions (higher degree)):

Masuku, Richard N., BA *Swazi.*, MPM *Carnegie-Mellon* (E-mail: rma@isdu.uniswa.sz)

Adult/continuing education. Senior Assistant Registrar (Adult/continuing education): Masuku, Richard N., BA *Swazi.*, MPM *Carnegie-Mellon* (E-mail: rma@isdu.uniswa.sz)

Alumni. Staff Development Fellow: Shongwe, Job M., BEd *Swazi.*, MEd *Bran.* (E-mail: jsh@admin.uniswa.sz)

Careers. Staff Development Fellow: Shongwe, Job M., BEd *Swazi.*, MEd *Bran.* (E-mail: jsh@admin.uniswa.sz)

Consultancy services. Contact Officer (Consultancy Services): Masuku, M. B., BScAgric *Swazi.*, MSc *Ohio*, PhD *Pret.*

Development/fund-raising. Bursar: Dlamini, M. E., BCom *Swazi.*, MSc *Strath.* (E-mail: bursar@admin.uniswa.sz)

Distance education. Director (Distance education): Sukati, C. Walter S., BSc *UBLS*, BEd *UBLS*, MSc *Harv.*, EdM *Harv.*, DEd *S.Af.*, EdD *Harv.* (E-mail: sukati@uniswacc.uniswa.sz)

Examinations. Senior Assistant Registrar (Examinations): Masuku, Richard N., BA *Swazi.*, MPM *Carnegie-Mellon* (E-mail: rma@isdu.uniswa.sz)

Finance. Bursar: Dlamini, M. E., BCom *Swazi.*, MSc *Strath.* (E-mail: bursar@admin.uniswa.sz)

General enquiries. Registrar: Vilakati, S. S., BA *UBLS*, MA *Ball* (E-mail: vilakati@admin.uniswa.sz)

Health services. Deputy Registrar (Corporate Affairs): Gama, Ambrose V., BSc *UBS*, BEd *Bran.*, MEd *Bran.* (E-mail: ambrose@admin.uniswa.sz)

Industrial liaison. Registrar: Vilakati, S. S., BA *UBLS*, MA *Ball* (E-mail: vilakati@admin.uniswa.sz)

International office. Dean of Student Affairs: Kunene, M., BEd *Swazi.*, MA *Col.* (E-mail: mkunene@isdu.uniswa.sz)

Library (chief librarian). Librarian: Mavuso, Makana R., BA *UBLS*, MLib *Wales* (E-mail: mmavuso@uniswacc.uniswa.sz)

Marketing. Deputy Registrar (Corporate Affairs): Gama, Ambrose V., BSc *UBS*, BEd *Bran.*, MEd *Bran.* (E-mail: ambrose@admin.uniswa.sz)

Ombudsman. Registrar: Vilakati, S. S., BA *UBLS*, MA *Ball* (E-mail: vilakati@admin.uniswa.sz)

Personnel/human resources. Registrar: Vilakati, S. S., BA *UBLS*, MA *Ball* (E-mail: vilakati@admin.uniswa.sz)

Public relations. Deputy Registrar (Corporate Affairs): Gama, Ambrose V., BSc *UBS*, BEd *Bran.*, MEd *Bran.* (E-mail: ambrose@admin.uniswa.sz)

Publications. Pro-Vice-Chancellor: Mtetwa, Prof. Victor S. B., BSc *UBLS*, DPhil *Oxf.* (E-mail: mtetwa@admin.uniswa.sz)

Purchasing. Bursar: Dlamini, M. E., BCom *Swazi.*, MSc *Strath.* (E-mail: bursar@admin.uniswa.sz)

Quality assurance and accreditation. Vice-Chancellor: Magagula, Prof. Cisco M., BA

UBS, BEd *Bran.*, MEd *Manit.*, EdD *Tor.* (E-mail: ciscomag@uniswacc.uniswa.sz)

Research. Pro-Vice-Chancellor: Mtetwa, Prof. Victor S. B., BSc *UBLS*, DPhil *Oxf.* (E-mail: mtetwa@admin.uniswa.sz)

Safety. Deputy Registrar (Corporate Affairs): Gama, Ambrose V., BSc *UBS*, BEd *Bran.*, MEd *Bran.* (E-mail: ambrose@admin.uniswa.sz)

Scholarships, awards, loans. Registrar: Vilakati, S. S., BA *UBLS*, MA *Ball* (E-mail: vilakati@admin.uniswa.sz)

Schools liaison. Dean of Student Affairs: Kunene, M., BEd *Swazi.*, MA *Col.* (E-mail: mkunene@isdu.uniswa.sz)

Security. Registrar: Vilakati, S. S., BA *UBLS*, MA *Ball* (E-mail: vilakati@admin.uniswa.sz)

Sport and recreation. Dean of Student Affairs: Kunene, M., BEd *Swazi.*, MA *Col.* (E-mail: mkunene@isdu.uniswa.sz)

Staff development and training. Registrar: Vilakati, S. S., BA *UBLS*, MA *Ball* (E-mail: vilakati@admin.uniswa.sz)

Student welfare/counselling. Assistant Dean of Student Affairs: Mabuza, Theresa P., BA *Swazi.*, MEd *Bran.* (E-mail: tpmabuza@admin.uniswa.sz)

Students from other countries. Dean of Student Affairs: Kunene, M., BEd *Swazi.*, MA *Col.* (E-mail: mkunene@isdu.uniswa.sz)

Students with disabilities. Dean of Student Affairs: Kunene, M., BEd *Swazi.*, MA *Col.* (E-mail: mkunene@isdu.uniswa.sz)

University press. Registrar: Vilakati, S. S., BA *UBLS*, MA *Ball* (E-mail: vilakati@admin.uniswa.sz)

CAMPUS/COLLEGE HEADS

Luyengo Campus, PO Luyengo, Swaziland. (Tel: 527 4021; Fax: 527 4021) Dean: Dlamini, Prof. Barnabas M., BSc *UP Ag.*, MSc *W.Virginia*, PhD *Ohio*

Mbabane Campus, Box 369, Mbabane, Swaziland. (Tel: 404 0171; Fax: 404 6241) Dean: Dlamini, Priscilla S., BEd(Nursing) *Botswana*, MCur *Natal*, PhD *Natal*

Nazarene Nursing College, PO Box 14, Manzini, Swaziland. (Tel: 505 4636; Fax: 505 5077) Principal: Nhlengethwa, W. M., BSc *Boston*, MSc(Nursing) *Howard*

Nazarene Teacher Training College, PO Box 14, Manzini, Swaziland. (Tel: (09268) 505 4129) Principal: Mavuso, Z. M., BSc *Swazi.*

Ngwane Teacher Training College, PO Box 474, Nhlangano, Swaziland. (Tel: 207 8466; Fax: 207 8112) Principal: Dlamini, P., BSc *Bridgewater(Va.)*, MEd *Ohio*

William Pitcher Training College, PO Box 87, Manzini, Swaziland. (Tel: 505 2081; Fax: 505 4690) Principal: Magagula, P., MEd *Ohio*

[*Information supplied by the institution as at 1 November 2007, and edited by the ACU*]

TANZANIA

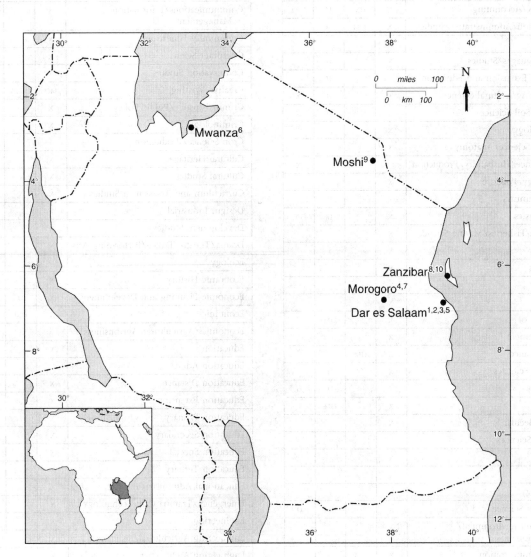

The places named are the seats of the university institutions numbered above

TANZANIA: DIRECTORY TO SUBJECTS OF STUDY

The table below shows which subjects are available for study and/or research at the universities in Tanzania. U = may be studied for first degree course; M = may be studied for master's degree course; D = research facilities to doctoral level; X = all three levels (UMD).

	Dar es Salaam	Mzumbe	Open, Tanzania	Sokoine
Accountancy/Accounting	X	UM	U	
Administration/Administrative Studies	X	UM	U	
Advertising	X			
African Languages/Studies	X		U	
Agricultural Extension and Education			U	
Agriculture/Agricultural Science	X		U	X
Agronomy/Soil Science	X		U	X
Agrotechnology	X			
Anatomical Science/Anatomy	X			
Animal Science/Husbandry/Production				X
Anthropology/Folklore	X			
Applied Chemistry	X		U	
Applied Physics	X		U	
Aquaculture/Fisheries/Marine Science	X			
Archaeology	X			
Area Studies	X			
Art Therapy	X			
Art, Fine	X			
Art, History of	X		UM	
Arts Management	X			
Banking/Finance	X	UM		
Behavioural Sciences	X		U	
Biochemistry	X		U	U
Biology	X		UM	
Biology Molecular	X			
Biomedical Sciences	X			
Biophysics	X			
Biostatistics	X			
Biotechnology	X			
Botany/Plant Science	X		UM	U
Building/Built Environment/ Construction	X			
Business Administration	X	UM	M	
Business Computing		UM		
Business Economics		U		
Business Information Systems	X			
Business/Commerce	X	UM	U	
Chemistry	X		UM	
Communication Sciences	X		U	U
Communication/Journalism/Media Studies	X			

	Dar es Salaam	Mzumbe	Open, Tanzania	Sokoine
Communications/Information Management	X			
Community Education	X			
Computer Science	X			U
Conservation Studies	X			
Creative Writing	MD			
Criminal Justice/Public Policy	X			
Criminology	X			
Crop Science/Production				X
Cultural Heritage	X			
Cultural Studies	X			
Curriculum and Assessment Studies	X			
Design, Industrial	X			
Development Studies	X		U	U
Drama/Theatre/Dance/Performing Arts	X			
Ecology				U
Economic History	X			
Economic Planning and Development	X	U		
Economics	X	UM	UM	
Economics Agricultural/Agribusiness				X
Education	X		UM	
Education Adult	X			
Education Distance	X		M	
Education Extension	X			X
Education Primary	X			
Education Secondary	X			
Education Special	X			
Education Tertiary	X			
Educational Administration	X			
Emergency/Trauma Care Technology	X			
Engineering	X			U
Engineering Agricultural/Fisheries	X			X
Engineering Architectural	X			
Engineering Automobile	X			
Engineering Chemical/Petrochemical/ Process	X			
Engineering Civil/Environmental/ Structural	X			
Engineering Communications/ Telecommunications	X			
Engineering Computer	X			

	Dar es Salaam	Mzumbe	Open, Tanzania	Sokoine
Engineering Construction	X			
Engineering Design	X			
Engineering Electrical/Electronic	X			
Engineering Environmental Geophysics	X			
Engineering Geological	X			
Engineering Industrial	X			
Engineering Instrumentation	X			
Engineering Management	X			
Engineering Manufacturing	X			
Engineering Materials/Mineral Resources/Petroleum	X			
Engineering Mathematical	X			
Engineering Mechanical/Production	X			
Engineering Metallurgical/Mining	X			
English	X	U	UM	
English as a Second Language	X			
Entomology	X			
Entrepreneurship	X			
Environmental Health	X			
Environmental Science/Studies	X		U	X
Ethics, Law and Governance	X			
Ethnomusicology	X			
Film/Photography/Television/ Animation	X			
Food Science/Nutrition/Home Science/ Dietetics			U	X
Forestry				X
French/French Studies	X			
Genetics and Plant Breeding	X			
Geographic Information Systems/ Geomatics	X			
Geography	X		UM	
Geology/Earth Sciences/Atmospheric Studies	X			
Geophysics	X			
Health Information	X			
Health Sciences/Studies	X			
Health/Hospital Administration		UM		
Heritage Studies	UM			
History	X		UM	
History/Philosophy of Science	X			
Horticulture				X
Human Biology	X			

	Dar es Salaam	Mzumbe	Open, Tanzania	Sokoine
Human Movement/Kinesiology/ Biomechanics	X			
Human Resource Development	X			
Human Resource Economics	X			
Human Rights/Globalisation	X			
Indigenous Knowledge Systems	X			
Industrial Relations/Personnel/HRM	X	UM		
Industrial and Organisation Psychology	X			
Information Science/Studies/Systems	X	UM		
Information Technology	UM			
Insurance	X			
International Business	X			
International Finance	X			
International Finance Economics	X			
International Marketing	X			
International Relations/Studies	X			
Internet Computing/Technologies	UM			
Kiswahili/Swahili	X		UM	
Labour Studies	X			
Land Management/Rehabilitation	X			
Land Resource Science	X			
Language Teaching/Learning	X			
Language and Communication	X			
Law Business/Commercial/Economic/ Industrial	X	U		
Law Civil	X			
Law Employment/Labour	X	U		
Law Environmental	X	U		
Law Intellectual Property/Copyright	X			
Law International/Comparative/Trade	X	U		
Law Legal Practice	X	U		
Law Property/Construction/Housing	X			
Law Transport	X			
Law/Legal Studies	X	UM		
Library/Information Science	X			
Linguistics/Translation	X			
Literature, Comparative	X			
Logic/Computation	X			
Management	X	UM		
Management Information Systems	X			
Marketing	X	UM	U	

	Dar es Salaam	Mzumbe	Open, Tanzania	Sokoine
Materials Science	X			
Mathematics	X	UM	UM	
Microbiology/Medical Microbiology	X			
Migration, Refugee and Diaspora Studies	X			
Mobile Communications/ Telecommunications	X			
Multimedia	X			
Music	X			
Music Education	X			
Music Jazz	X			
Natural Resource Studies	X			X
Oceanography/Oceanic Sciences	X			
Operational Research/Operations Management	X	UM		
Pharmacology				X
Philosophy	X			
Physical Education/Sports Science	X			
Physics	X		UM	
Plant Pathology	X			
Politics/Political Science/Government	X			

	Dar es Salaam	Mzumbe	Open, Tanzania	Sokoine
Popular Culture	UM			
Population Studies/Demography	X	UM	U	U
Project Management	X	UM		
Public Administration	X	UM		
Public Health/Population Health	X			
Public Relations	X			
Public Sector Management	X	U		
Publishing	UM			
Rural Studies/Development	X	U		X
Sculpture	X			
Sociology	X			
Statistics/Actuarial Science	X	U		
Sustainable Development	X			
Taxation	X	U		
Teacher Training	X			
Urban Studies	X			
Veterinary Science				X
Wildlife Management	X			
Women's/Gender Studies	X	UM		

UNIVERSITY OF DAR ES SALAAM

Founded 1970

Member of the Association of Commonwealth Universities

Postal Address: PO Box 35091, Dar es Salaam, Tanzania
Telephone: (022) 241 0700 **Fax:** (022) 241 0078 **E-mail:** vc@admin.udsm.ac.tz
URL: http://www.udsm.ac.tz

VICE-CHANCELLOR*—Mukandala, Prof. Rwekaza R. S., BA Dar., MA Dar., PhD Calif.
DEPUTY VICE-CHANCELLOR (ACADEMIC RESEARCH AND CONSULTANCY)—Maboko, Prof. Makenya A. H., BSc Dar., MSc Dar., PhD ANU
DEPUTY VICE-CHANCELLOR (FINANCE, PLANNING AND ADMINISTRATION)‡—Mgaya, Prof. Yunus D., BSc Dar., MSc Br.Col., PhD N.U.I.
PRINCIPAL, DAR ES SALAAM COLLEGE OF EDUCATION—Mosha, Prof. Herme J., BA Dar., MA(Ed) Dar., PhD Alta., Hon. Dr
PRINCIPAL, MKWAWA COLLEGE OF EDUCATION—Mushi, Prof. P. A. K., BAEd Dar., MA(Ed) Dar., PhD S'ton.
PRINCIPAL, COLLEGE OF ENGINEERING AND TECHNOLOGY—Mwamila, Prof. Burton L. M., BSc(Eng) Dar., MSc(Eng) Dar., PhD R.I.T.Stockholm

GENERAL INFORMATION

History. The university was previously founded as a college of the University of London in 1961. In 1963 it became a constituent college of the University of East Africa. Independent university status was gained in 1970.

It is situated 13km from the centre of Dar es Salaam, on the west side of the city.

Admission to first degree courses. Certificate of Secondary Education Examination (CSEE) or equivalent with passes in 5 approved subjects, and Advanced Certificate of Secondary Education Examination (ACSEE) or equivalent.

First Degrees (see also Tanzanian Directory to Subjects of Study) (* = with honours). BA*, BA(Ed)*, BCom*, BEd*, BSc*, BSc(Ed)*, BScEng*, LLB*.

Length of course. Full-time: BA(Ed)*, BA*, BCom*, BSc(Ed)*, BSc*: 3 years; BEd*, BScEng*, LLB*: 4 years.

Higher Degrees (see also Tanzanian Directory to Subjects of Study).

Master's. LLM, MA, MBA, MSc, MScEng.
Length of course. Full-time: LLM, MA, MBA, MSc, MScEng: 2 years. Part-time: MBA: 2 years.
Doctoral. LLD, PhD.
Length of course. Full-time: LLD, PhD: 3 years.

Libraries. Volumes: 600,000. Periodicals subscribed to: 2800. Other holdings: 20,255 volumes (college libraries); 220 periodicals (college libraries). Special collections: Cory Paper (Arabic and Swahili manuscripts); environment and biodiversity databases; regional and civil society databases; economics; education; sociology.

FACULTIES/SCHOOLS

Aquatic Sciences and Technology

Tel: (022) 241 0472 Fax: (022) 241 0472
E-mail: fast@ucc.udsm.ac.tz
Dean: Machiwa, J. F., BSc Dar., MSc Wales, PhD Stockholm

Arts and Social Sciences

Fax: (022) 241 0395 E-mail: fass@udsm.ac.tz
Dean: Mbago, Maurice C. Y., BA Dar., MA Dar., PhD Liv.

Civil Engineering and the Built Environment

Tel: (022) 241 0752 Fax: (022) 241 0029
E-mail: foe@udsm.ac.tz
Dean: Msambichaka, J. J., BSc Mys., MSc Dar., DrIng Dortmund

Commerce and Management

Tel: (022) 241 0510 Fax: (022) 241 0510
E-mail: dean@fcm.udsm.ac.tz
Dean: Chijoriga, Marcellina M., BCom Dar., MBA Leuven, PhD Vienna Bus.Admin.

Education

Tel: (022) 241 0608 Fax: (022) 241 0608
E-mail: dean@ed.udsm.ac.tz
Dean: Bhalalusesa, E. P., BEd Dar., MA Dar., EdD Brist.

Electrical and Computer Systems Engineering

Dean: Nzali, A. H., BSc(Eng) Dar., MSc Aston, PhD Dar.

Informatics and Virtual Education

Tel: (022) 241 0129 Fax: (022) 241 0129
E-mail: dean@five.udsm.ac.tz
Dean: Ikingura, Prof. Justin R., BSc Dar., MSc Car., PhD Car.

Law

Tel: (022) 241 0254 Fax: (022) 241 0254
E-mail: dean@law.udsm.ac.tz
Dean: Mchome, Sifuni E., LLB Dar., LLM Qu., PhD Dar.

Mechanical and Chemical Engineering

Dean: Katima, Jamidu H. Y., BSc(Eng) Dar., MPhil Lough., PhD Leeds

Science

Tel: (022) 241 0129 Fax: (022) 241 0129
E-mail: dean@science.udsm.ac.tz
Dean: Magingo, Francis S. S., BSc Dar., MSc Dar., PhD Dar.

ACADEMIC UNITS

Accounting

Tel: (022) 241 0455 Fax: (022) 241 0455
E-mail: dean@fcm.udsm.ac.tz
Assad, M. J., BCom Dar., MA Dublin City, PhD S'ton.   Sr. Lectr.; Head*
Mushi, R., BA Dar., MBA Dar., PhD Bath   Sr. Lectr.
Nchimbi, M. I., BCom Dar., MA Dublin City, PhD Dar.   Sr. Lectr.
Temu, S., PhD Bremen, MBA T.U.Berlin   Sr. Lectr.
Other Staff: 2 Lectrs.; 8 Asst. Lectrs.
Research: impact of micro-finance services on women's enterprises in Tanzania

Adult Education and Extension

Tel: (022) 241 0608 Fax: (022) 241 0608
E-mail: dean@edu.udsm.ac.tz
Bhalalusesa, E. P., BEd Dar., MA Dar., EdD Brist.   Assoc. Prof.
Mlekwa, V. M., BA(Ed) Dar., MA Dar., PhD Alta.   Assoc. Prof.; Head*
Mutanyatta, J. N. S., BSc Dar., EdD Tor., MA   Sr. Lectr.
Other Staff: 2 Asst. Lectrs.
Research: political democratisation in Tanzania (critical analysis of adult education); sustaining literacy and post-literacy in Tanzania

Botany

Tel: (022) 5141 0764 E-mail: dbot@udsm.ac.tz
Elia, F., MSc Dar., PhD Mich.State   Sr. Lectr.
Friedricks, J. M., MSc Kentucky, PhD Virginia   Sr. Lectr.
Ismail, F. A. R., BSc Dar., MSc Dar., PhD Nijmegen   Sr. Lectr.; Head*
Lyaruu, H. V. M., BSc Dar., MSc Addis Ababa, PhD Uppsala   Sr. Lectr.
Nyomora, A. M., BSc Dar., MSc Dar., PhD Calif.   Sr. Lectr.
Rulangaranga, Z. K., MSc Dar., PhD Essex   Sr. Lectr.
Research: rapid regeneration of endangered Tanzanian tree species; terrestrial vegetation ecology

Chemistry

Tel: (022) 241 0038 Fax: (022) 241 0039
E-mail: science@cc.udsm.ac.tz
Akwilapo, L. D., BSc(Ed) Dar., MSc Dar., PhD Trondheim   Sr. Lectr.
Buchweishaija, J., BSc Dar., MSc Trondheim, PhD Trondheim   Sr. Lectr.
Joseph, C. C., BSc Dar., MSc Dar., PhD Nijmegen   Sr. Lectr.; Head*
Kamwaya, M. E., MSc Kharkov, MSc DrRerNat   Sr. Lectr.
Kishimba, M., MSc Dar., PhD Dar.   Assoc. Prof.
Lugwisha, E., BSc Dar., MSc E.Anglia, PhD E.Anglia   Sr. Lectr.
Mbogo, S. A., MSc Aston, PhD Aston   Sr. Lectr.
Mdachi, S. J. M., BSc(Ed) Dar., MSc Oslo, PhD Oslo   Sr. Lectr.
Mdoe, J. E. G., BSc(Ed) Dar., MSc Dar., DPhil York(UK)   Sr. Lectr.
Mhinzi, G. S., MSc Dar., PhD Salf.   Assoc. Prof.
Mkayula, L. L., MSc Dar., PhD Salf.   Sr. Lectr.
Mosha, D. M. S., BSc Dar., MSc Dar., PhD Liv.   Prof.
Ngassapa, F. N., MSc Moscow, PhD Moscow   Sr. Lectr.
Othman, O. C., MSc Dar., PhD Dar.   Assoc. Prof.
Other Staff: 7 Lectrs.; 6 Asst. Lectrs.
Research: application of semiochemicals in integrated pest management; chemical analysis of salt lakes; chemical studies of Tanzanian medicinal plants; solid state chemistry and catalysis

Computer Science

E-mail: science@cc.udsm.ac.tz
Koda, G. R., MSc Dar., MSc(InfoSys) Car., PhD Dar.   Sr. Lectr.; Head*

Twaakyondo, H. M., BSc Dar., MEng Shinshu, PhD Shinshu Sr. Lectr.
Other Staff: 2 Lectrs.; 7 Asst. Lectrs.

Curriculum and Teaching

Tel: (022) 241 0500
E-mail: dean@edu.udsm.ac.tz
Chonjo, P. N., BSc(Ed) Dar., MA Dar., PhD S'ton. Assoc. Prof.; Head*
Komba, W. L. M., BA(Ed) Dar., MA Dar., PhD Lond. Sr. Lectr.
Mbunda, F. L., BEd Alta., MA Dar., PhD Dar. Prof.
Mushi, P. S. D., BEd Dar., MEd Leeds, PhD Leeds Sr. Lectr.
Njabili, A., BSc(Ed) E.Af., MEd Calif., PhD Hull Prof.
Osaki, K. M., BSc Dar., MA Lond., PhD Alta. Sr. Lectr.
Other Staff: 6 Lectrs.; 3 Asst. Lectrs.
Research: environmental education; evaluation of training programmes; social studies education and curriculum

Economic Research Bureau

Tel: (022) 241 0134 Fax: (022) 241 0212
E-mail: erb@uchumi.udsm.ac.tz
Mabele, R. B. M., BA E.Af., MSc(AgrE) Tennessee, PhD Dar. Assoc. Res. Prof.
Moshi, H. P. B., MA Dar., PhD Mün. Assoc. Res. Prof.
Msambichaka, L. A., BSc(Agric) Leip., MSc Leip., PhD Leip. Res. Prof.
Shitundu, J. L., BA Dar., MA Dar., PhD Dar. Sr. Res. Fellow; Dir.*
Tibaijuka, A. K., BSc Dar., MSc Uppsala, PhD Uppsala Assoc. Res. Prof. (on leave)
Other Staff: 6 Sr. Res. Fellows; 1 Sr. Assoc. Res. Fellow; 5 Res. Fellows; 4 Asst. Res. Fellows
Research: economic, cultural and social development of Tanzania and East Africa

Economics

Tel: (022) 241 0226 Fax: (022) 241 0227
E-mail: econ@uchumi.udsm.ac.tz
Bukuku, E. S. N., MA Dar., PhD Dar. Sr. Lectr. (on leave)
Likwelile, S. B., BA Dar., MA Dar., PhD Dar. Sr. Lectr. (on leave)
Mbelle, A. V. Y., MA Dar., PhD Gothenburg Assoc. Prof.
Mkenda, A. F., BA Dar., MA Dar., PhD Gothenburg
Mtatifikolo, F. P. A., MA Kansas, PhD Kansas Assoc. Prof.
Mwinyimvua, H. H., BA Dar., MA Dar., PhD Dar. Sr. Lectr. (on leave)
Ndanshau, M. O. A., BA Dar., MA Dar., PhD Dar.
Ndanshau, N. O., BA Dar., MA Dar., PhD Dar. Sr. Lectr.
Osoro, E., MA Dar., MSc Ill., PhD Ill. Assoc. Prof.
Rutasitara, L., BA Dar., MA Dar., PhD Dar. Sr. Lectr.; Head*
Rwegasira, D., PhD Harv. Assoc. Prof.
Other Staff: 6 Lectrs.; 7 Asst. Lectrs.
Research: environmental economics; fiscal policy issues; industrial economics; macro- and microeconomic issues; monetary policy

Educational Foundations

Tel: (022) 241 0500
E-mail: dean@edu.udsm.ac.tz
Ishumi, A. G., BA E.Af., EdM Harv., PhD Dar. Prof.
Malekela, George A., BA(Ed) Dar., MA Dar., PhD Chic. Prof.
Masudi, A., BA(Ed) Dar., MA Dar., PhD Leeds Sr. Lectr.
Puja, Grace K., MA Dar. Sr. Lectr.; Head*
Other Staff: 2 Lectrs.; 1 Asst. Lectr.
Research: appraisal of school–community relations; classroom interaction in primary schools; education in Tanzania; gender disparities in education in Tanzania

Educational Planning and Administration

Tel: (022) 241 0500
E-mail: dean@edu.udsm.ac.tz
Alphonce, N. A., BA(Ed) Dar., MA Tor., PhD NZ Sr. Lectr.
Dachi, H., BA(Ed) Dar., MA Dar., PhD Brist. Lectr.; Head*
Galabawa, J. C. J., BSc(Ed) Dar., MA Dar., MDS Inst.Soc.Stud.(The Hague), PhD Alta. Prof.
Mosha, Herme J., BA Dar., MA(Ed) Dar., PhD Alta., Hon. Dr Prof.
Other Staff: 1 Lectr.; 2 Asst. Lectrs.
Research: attitudes to and strategies for education in Tanzania; teacher quality and motivation

Educational Psychology

Tel: (022) 241 0500
E-mail: dean@edu.udsm.ac.tz
Katabaro, J. K., BEd Dar., MA Dar., PhD Camb. Sr. Lectr.; Head*
Lugoe, W. L., BA(Ed) Dar., MA Dar., MSc Bergen, PhD Bergen Sr. Lectr.
Mbise, A. S., BA Dar., MA Col., PhD Alta. Assoc. Prof.
Ndalichako, J., BEd Dar., MA Alta., PhD Alta. Sr. Lectr.
Omari, I. M., BA(Ed) E.Af., MA Col., PhD Col. Prof.
Possi, M. K., BA(Ed) Dar., MA Dar., MA Ball, PhD Ohio State Assoc. Prof.
Other Staff: 4 Lectrs.; 2 Asst. Lectrs.
Research: childhood development milestones in Tanzania; decentralisation of education and the role of education in Tanzania; youth education research and evaluation

Engineering, Chemical and Processing

Tel: (022) 241 0753 E-mail: foe@udsm.ac.tz
Elisante, E., BSc(Eng) Dar., MSc(Eng) Arizona, PhD Tohoku Sr. Lectr.
Halfani, M. R., MSc Tor., PhD Leeds Assoc. Prof.
Katima, Jamidu H. Y., BSc(Eng) Dar., MPhil Lough., PhD Leeds Assoc. Prof.
Kaunde, O., BSc(Eng) Dar., MSc Leeds, PhD Leeds Sr. Lectr.
Kibazohi, O., BSc(Eng) Dar., MSc Wat., PhD Wat. Sr. Lectr.
Manyele, S. V., BSc(Eng) Dar., MSc Dar., PhD W.Ont. Head*
Maronga, S. J. E., BSc(Eng) Dar., MSc Trondheim, PhD Trondheim Sr. Lectr.
Masanja, E., MSc Dar., PhD Edin. Sr. Lectr.
Minja, R. J. A., BSc(Eng) Dar., MSc(Eng) Ott., PhD T.U.Trondheim Sr. Lectr.
Mrema, G. D. E., MSc Dar., PhD Trondheim Assoc. Prof.
Njau, K. N., BSc(Eng) Dar., MSc Trondheim, PhD T.U.Eindhoven Sr. Lectr.
Ntalikwa, J. W., BSc(Eng) Dar., MSc Dar., PhD Wales Sr. Lectr.
Raphael, M. L., MSc Texas A.& M., PhD Sask. Sr. Lectr.
Temu, A. K., BSc(Eng) Dar., MSc Trondheim, PhD Trondheim Sr. Lectr.
Other Staff: 2 Lectrs.; 2 Asst. Lectrs.

Engineering, Computer and Systems

Tel: (022) 241 0753 E-mail: foe@udsm.ac.tz
Bagile, B. R. B., MSc Brad., PhD S'ton. Sr. Lectr.
Mvungi, N. H., MSc Salf., PhD Leeds Sr. Lectr.; Head*
Mwandosya, Mark J., BSc Aston, PhD Birm. Prof. (on leave)
Other Staff: 1 Lectr.; 3 Asst. Lectrs.

Engineering, Construction Technology and Management

Tel: (022) 241 0753
Chamuriho, L. M., BSc(Eng) Dar., MSc Ill., PhD Tokyo Lectr.; Head*
Lema, Prof. N. M., BSc(Eng) Dar., MSc Lough., PhD Lough. Assoc. Prof.
Shirima, L. H. M., BSc(Eng) Dar., MSc(Eng) Dar., DrIng Dortmund Sr. Lectr.
Other Staff: 1 Lectr.; 2 Asst. Lectrs.

Engineering, Design and Production

Tel: (022) 241 0753 E-mail: foe@udsm.ac.tz
Elias, E., BSc(Eng) Dar., MSc(Eng) Newcastle(UK), PhD Strath.
Majaja, B. A. M., BSc Dar., MSc Calif., PhD Calif. Sr. Lectr.
Masuha, John R., DrIng T.U.Berlin Prof.
Mutagahywa, B. M., MSc Dar., PhD Lough. Assoc. Prof.
Nalitolela, N., BSc Dar., MSc Newcastle(UK), PhD Aston Sr. Lectr.
Nshama, W., BSc(Eng) Dar., MSc(Eng) Calif., PhD Calif. Sr. Lectr.; Head*
Nyichomba, B., BSc(Eng) Dar., MSc Birm., PhD Birm. Assoc. Prof.
Opiyo, E. Z., BSc(Eng) Dar., MSc Cran.
Other Staff: 2 Lectrs.; 2 Asst. Lectrs.

Engineering, Electrical Power

Tel: (022) 241 0753 E-mail: foe@udsm.ac.tz
Chambega, D., MSc Moscow, PhD Strath. Assoc. Prof.; Head*
Kundy, B. J., BSc(Eng) Dar., MSc Strath., PhD Stell. Sr. Lectr.
Kyaruzi, A. L., BSc(Eng) Dar., MSc George Washington, DSc George Washington Sr. Lectr.
Lujara, N. K., DIng Rand Afrikaans Sr. Lectr.
Manyahi, M. J., BSc(Eng) Dar., MSc Strath., PhD Uppsala Sr. Lectr.
Mwinyiwiwa, B. M. M., MEng McG., PhD McG. Assoc. Prof.
Nzali, A. H., BSc(Eng) Dar., MSc Aston, PhD Dar. Assoc. Prof.
Other Staff: 2 Asst. Lectrs.

Engineering, Energy

Tel: (022) 241 0753 E-mail: foe@udsm.ac.tz
John, G. R., BSc Dar., MSc Leeds, PhD Leeds Sr. Lectr.
Katalambula, H. H., BSc(Eng) Dar., MSc(Eng) Tech.UNS, PhD Hokkaido Assoc. Prof.
Kawambwa, S. J. M., BSc(Eng) Dar., MSc Reading, PhD Sur. Sr. Lectr.
Kimambo, C. Z. M., BSc(Eng) Dar., MSc Reading, PhD City(UK) Sr. Lectr.
Mhilu, C. F., MSc Leningrad, PhD Leeds Sr. Lectr.
Mkilaha, I. S. N., BSc(Eng) Dar., MEng Toyohashi, DrEng Toyohashi Assoc. Prof.; Head*
Mkumbwa, M. H., BSc(Eng) Dar., MSc(Eng) Strath., PhD Strath. Sr. Lectr.
Mushi, E. M. J., MSc Leeds, PhD Leeds Sr. Lectr.
Rajabu, H. M., BSc(Eng) Dar., MSc Leeds, PhD Dar. Sr. Lectr.
Other Staff: 1 Lectr.

Engineering, Management and Entrepreneurship

Tel: (022) 241 0753
Chungu, BSc(Eng) Dar., MSc(Eng) Asian I.T., Bangkok, PhD Asian I.T., Bangkok Sr. Lectr.
Kundi, B. A. T., MSc Wat., PhD Wat. Assoc. Prof.
Mjema, E. A. M., BSc(Eng) Dar., MSc Alta., DrIng T.H.Aachen Assoc. Prof.; Head*
Victor, M. A. M., BSc(Eng) Dar., MSc(Eng) Arizona State, PhD T.U.Eindhoven Assoc. Prof.
Other Staff: 1 Lectr.; 2 Asst. Lectrs.

Engineering, Materials

Tel: (022) 241 0753 E-mail: foe@udsm.ac.tz
Mshana, John S., BSc Nair., MASc Ott., PhD Ott. Prof.
Mwaikambo, L. Y., MSc(MechEng) Dar., PhD Bath Sr. Lectr.
Nyahumwa, C. W. M., BSc(Eng) Dar., MSc(Eng) Qu., PhD Birm. Sr. Lectr.
Runyoro, J. J., BSc(Eng) Dar., MSc Cran.IT, PhD Birm. Sr. Lectr.
Shine, S. J., BSc E.Af., MSc(Tech) Manc., MBA Botswana, PhD Calif. Assoc. Prof.
Tesha, J. V., BSc Dar., MSc Cran.IT, PhD Cran. Assoc. Prof.; Head*
Other Staff: 2 Lectrs.; 2 Asst. Lectrs.

Engineering, Structural

Tel: (022) 241 0753 E-mail: foe@udsm.ac.tz
Lwambuka, L., DrIng *Kassel*   Sr. Lectr.
Mrema, A. L., BSc Dar., MSc Strath., PhD Colorado
State   Sr. Lectr.
Msambichaka, J. J., BSc Mys., MSc Dar., DrIng
Dortmund   Assoc. Prof.
Mwamila, Burton L. M., BSc(Eng) Dar.,
MSc(Eng) Dar., PhD R.I.T.Stockholm   Prof.
Mwitta, N. G., PhD Leeds   Sr. Lectr.
Ndumbaro, P., MSc UMIST, PhD Lond.   Sr.
Lectr.; Head*
Rubaratuka, I., MSc Dar., DrIng Dortmund   Sr.
Lectr.
Shirima, A. A., BSc(Eng) Dar., DrIng Kassel   Sr.
Lectr.
Other Staff: 2 Lectrs.

Engineering, Technology and Transfer Centre

E-mail: foe@udsm.ac.tz
Katalambula, H. H., BSc(Eng) Dar., MSc(Eng)
Tech.UNS, PhD Hokkaido   Dir.*
Ntalikwa, J. W., BSc(Eng) Dar., MSc Dar., PhD
Wales   Sr. Lectr.
Temu, A. K., BSc(Eng) Dar., MSc Trondheim, PhD
Trondheim   Sr. Lectr.

Engineering, Telecommunications

Tel: (022) 241 0753 E-mail: foe@udsm.ac.tz
Kissaka, M. M., BSc(Eng) Dar., PhD Manc.   Sr.
Lectr.; Head*
Luhanga, M. L., BSc(Eng) Calif.State Polytechnic,
MEng Calif.State Polytechnic, MPhil Col., PhD
Col.   Prof.
Other Staff: 2 Lectrs.; 6 Asst. Lectrs.

Engineering, Transportation and Geotechnical

Tel: (022) 241 0395 Fax: (022) 241 0395
E-mail: foe@udsm.ac.tz
Kyulule, A. L., BSc Nair., MSc Zür., DrScTech
Zür.   Assoc. Prof.
Masaoe, E. N., BSc(Eng) Dar., MSc Strath., PhD
Dar.   Sr. Lectr.; Head*
Mfinanga, D. A., BSc(Eng) Dar., MSc Miyazaki,
PhD Kyushu
Mushule, N. K. M., BSc(Eng) Dar., MSc Calg.,
PhD Dar.
Nyaoro, D. L., BSc(Eng) Dar., MSc Lond., PhD
Lond.
Rwebangira, T., BSc(Eng) Dar., MSc Birm., PhD
Oregon State   Assoc. Prof.
Other Staff: 1 Lectr.; 2 Asst. Lectrs.

Engineering, Water Resources

Tel: (022) 241 0753 E-mail: foe@udsm.ac.tz
Bashar, K. E., MSc Dar., PhD Dar.   Sr. Lectr.
Mashauri, D. A., MSc Tampere, PhD Tampere
Assoc. Prof.
Mayo, A. W., MSc Dar., MSc Tampere, PhD
Tohoku   Assoc. Prof.
Mkhandi, S. H., BSc(Eng) Dar., MSc N.U.I., PhD
Dar.   Sr. Lectr.
Mtalo, F. W., MSc Dar., DrIng Munich   Assoc.
Prof.; Head*
Mwanuzi, F. L. M., MSc Brussels, PhD Brussels
Assoc. Prof.
Other Staff: 4 Lectrs.; 2 Asst. Lectrs.

Finance

Tel: (022) 241 0510 Fax: (022) 241 0510
E-mail: dean@fcm.udsm.ac.tz
Chijoriga, Marcellina M., BCom Dar., MBA
Leuven, PhD Vienna Bus.Admin.   Sr. Lectr.
Kaijage, E. S., BA Dar., MBA Leuven, PhD Sheff.
Assoc. Prof.
Other Staff: 4 Lectrs.; 5 Asst. Lectrs.
Research: microfinancing in Tanzania

Fine and Performing Arts

Tel: (022) 241 0510 Fax: (022) 241 0510
E-mail: fass@udsm.ac.tz
Hatar, A., BA Mak., MA Ohio, PhD Ohio   Sr.
Lectr.

Jengo, Elias, BSc Kent State, MA Sir G.Wms.
Assoc. Prof.
Lihamba, Amandina, BA Minn., MFA Yale, PhD
Leeds   Prof.
Makoye, H. F., BA Dar., MA Dar., PhD Ghana
Sr. Lectr.
Mlama, Penina O. P., BA(Ed) Dar., MA Dar.,
PhD Dar.   Prof. (on leave)
Nyoni, F. P., BA Dar., MA Leeds, PhD Leeds   Sr.
Lectr.; Head*
Strumpf, M., BSc N.Y., MA Ghana, PhD Wash.
Prof.
Other Staff: 2 Lectrs.; 5 Asst. Lectrs.
Research: children's theatre project and festival;
role of traditional media in learning for
change

Foreign Languages and Linguistics

Includes Communication Skills Unit
Fax: (022) 241 0395 E-mail: fass@udsm.ac.tz
Kapoli, I. J., BA(Ed) Dar., MA Dar., PhD Lond.
Sr. Lectr.
Lwaitama, A. F., BA Dar., MSc Aston, PhD Aston
Sr. Lectr.
Maghway, J. B., MA Dar., MLitt Edin., PhD Edin.
Assoc. Prof.
Muzale, H. R. T., BA(Ed) Dar., MA Dar., PhD
Nfld.   Sr. Lectr.
Ndoloi, D. B., BA(Ed) Dar., MA Warw., PhD
Lanc.   Sr. Lectr.; Head*
Qorro, M., BA Dar., MA Wales, PhD Dar.   Sr.
Lectr.
Rubagumya, C. M., BA Dar., MA Lanc., PhD
Lanc.   Assoc. Prof.
Rugemalira, J., BA Dar., MA Lanc., PhD Calif.
Assoc. Prof.
Swilla, I. N., BA Dar., MA Paris IV, PhD Laval
Assoc. Prof.
Yahya-Othman, Saida, BA Dar., MA Dar., MA
York(UK), PhD Dar.   Assoc. Prof.
Other Staff: 4 Lectrs.; 12 Assoc. Lectrs.; 4 Asst.
Lectrs.
Research: languages in contact and in conflict in
Africa; linguistic and cultural atlas of
Tanzania

Geography

Fax: (022) 241 0395 E-mail: fass@udsm.ac.tz
Banyikwa, W. F., BA Dar., MA Dar., MSc Halle,
PhD Halle   Sr. Lectr.
Jambiya, G. K., BA Dar., MA Dar., PhD Halle
Sr. Lectr.
Maro, P. S., BA Dar., MA Minn., PhD Minn.
Assoc. Prof.
Mbonile, M. J., BA(Ed) Dar., MPhil Cairo, PhD
Liv.   Assoc. Prof.
Misana, S. B., MA Dar., PhD Colorado   Assoc.
Prof.
Mwakalila, S., PhD Leuven, BSc(AgricEng) MSc
Sr. Lectr.
Mwamfupe, D., BA Dar., MA Dar., PhD Glas.
Sr. Lectr. (on leave)
Rugumamu, W., MSc Reading, MA Dar., PhD
Dar.   Prof.
Sawio, Fr. C. J., MA N.Y.State, MRP N.Y.State,
PhD Clark   Sr. Lectr.
Sokoni, C. H., BA Dar., MA Dar., PhD Dar.
Lectr.; Head*
Other Staff: 4 Lectrs.; 7 Asst. Lectrs.
Research: fruit and vegetable marketing in Dar es
Salaam; village land management for
resource conservation

Geology

Tel: (022) 241 0013 Fax: (022) 241 0129
E-mail: science@udsm.ac.tz
Ikingura, Justin R., BSc Dar., MSc Car., PhD Car.
Prof.
Kaaya, C. Z., BSc Dar., MSc Dar., DrRerNat
Cologne   Sr. Lectr.
Kinabo, C. P., MSc Lond., DrIng Clausthal   Sr.
Lectr.
Maboko, Makenya A. H., BSc Dar., MSc Dar.,
PhD ANU   Prof.
Malisa, E. J. S., BSc Dar., MSc Ife, PhD Helsinki
Sr. Lectr.
Marobhe, I. M., MSc Lond., PhD Helsinki   Sr.
Lectr.; Head*

Mbede, E. I., BSc Dar., MSc Lond., PhD T.U.Berlin
Assoc. Prof. (on leave)
Mruma, A. H., MSc Dar., PhD Dar.   Assoc.
Prof. (on leave)
Msindai, K. A., BSc Dar., MSc O.Awolowo, MPhil
Turku, PhD Turku   Sr. Lectr.
Mutakyahwa, M. D., MSc Hamburg, DrRerNat
Hamburg   Sr. Lectr.
Mutakyahwa, M. K. D., BSc Dar., MSc Dar.,
DrRerNat Hamburg
Nkotagu, H. H., BSc Dar., MSc Lond., MPhil
T.U.Berlin, DrRerNat T.U.Berlin   Sr. Lectr.
Other Staff: 4 Lectrs.
Research: environmental aspects of mining and
industrialisation in Tanzania

History

including Archaeology
Tel: (022) 241 0397 Fax: (022) 241 0395
E-mail: fass@udsm.ac.tz
Chami, F., MA Brown, PhD Uppsala   Prof.
Kaijage, F. J., BA E.Af., MA Warw., PhD Warw.
Prof.
Kimambo, I. N., BA Pacific Lutheran, MA
Northwestern, PhD Northwestern   Prof.
Lawi, Y. Q., BEd Dar., MA Dar., PhD Boston   Sr.
Lectr.
Luanda, N. N., MA Dar., PhD Camb.   Assoc.
Prof.
Mabula, A., BA Dar., MA Flor., PhD Flor.   Sr.
Lectr.
Mapunda, B., BA Dar., MA Flor., PhD Flor.   Sr.
Lectr.; Head*
Mihanjo, E., BA Dar., MA Dar., PhD Dar.   Sr.
Lectr.
Tambila, K. I., BA Dar., MA Dar., PhD Hamburg
Assoc. Prof.
Other Staff: 3 Lectrs.; 5 Asst. Lectrs.
Research: archaeology; history of the University
of Dar es Salaam

Kiswahili

see also Special Centres, etc
Tel: (022) 241 0396 Fax: (022) 241 0396
E-mail: fass@udsm.ac.tz
Kahigi, K. K., MA Dar., PhD Mich.State   Assoc.
Prof.; Head*
Mkude, D. J., BA Dar., PhD Lond.   Prof.
Mochiwa, Z., MA Dar., PhD Ill.   Assoc. Prof.
Mutembei, A., BA Dar., MA Dar., MA Ley., PhD
Ley.   Sr. Lectr.
Rubanza, Y. I., BA(Ed) Dar., MA Dar., PhD
Mich.State   Assoc. Prof.
Senkoro, F. E. M. K., MA Alta., MA Dar.
Assoc. Prof.
Other Staff: 4 Asst. Lectrs.

Law, Constitutional and Administrative

Tel: (022) 241 0254 E-mail: ghent@ud.co.tz
Mbunda, L. X., LLM Dar., PhD Northeastern
Assoc. Prof.
Mlimuka, A. K. L. J., LLB Dar., LLM Dar., DrIur
Hamburg   Sr. Lectr. (on leave)
Mvungi, S. E. A., LLB Dar., LLM Dar., DrJur
Hamburg   Sr. Lectr.
Mwaikusa, J., LLB Dar., LLM Birm., PhD Lond.
Assoc. Prof.; Head*
Mwakyembe, H. G., LLB Dar., LLM Dar., LLM
Hamburg, DrIur Hamburg   Sr. Lectr. (on
leave)
Shivji, I. G., LLM Lond., PhD Dar.   Prof.
Other Staff: 3 Asst. Lectrs.

Law, Criminal and Civil

Tel: (022) 241 0254 E-mail: ghent@ud.co.tz
Juma, I. H., LLB Dar., LLM Lond., MIL Lund, PhD
Ghent
Mchome, Sifuni E., LLB Dar., LLM Qu., PhD
Dar.   Assoc. Prof.
Migiro, Rose A., LLM Dar., DrJur Constance   Sr.
Lectr. (on leave)
Mtaki, C. K., LLB Dar., LLM Dar., PhD Ghent
Sr. Lectr.; Head*
Rutinwa, B. S., LLB Dar., LLM Qu., BCL Oxf.,
DPhil Oxf.
Shaidi, L. P., LLB Dar., LLM Dar., PhD Dar.
Assoc. Prof.

Wambali, M. K., LLM Dar.   Sr. Lectr.
Other Staff: 1 Lectr.; 4 Asst. Lectrs.

Law, Economic

Tel: (022) 241 0254 E-mail: ghent@ud.co.tz
Kanywanyi, J. L., LLB E.Af., LLM Calif., PhD Dar.
   Assoc. Prof.
Luoga, F. D., LLB Dar., LLM Qu.   Assoc. Prof.
Mapunda, A. M., LLM Dar., PhD Warw.   Sr.
   Lectr.
Mbunda, L. X., LLM Dar., PhD Northeastern
   Assoc. Prof.; Head*
Mgongo-Fimbo, G., LLB Dar., LLM Lond., PhD
   Dar.   Assoc. Prof.
Mtaki, C. K., LLB Dar., LLM Dar., PhD Ghent
   Sr. Lectr.; Head*
Nditi, N. N. N., LLM Dar., PhD Dar.   Assoc.
   Prof.
Other Staff: 8 Asst. Lectrs.

Law, International

Tel: (022) 241 0254 E-mail: ghent@ud.co.tz
Kabudi, P. J., LLM Dar., DrJur Constance   Assoc.
   Prof.; Head*
Kamanga, K., LLM Amst., LLM P.F.U., Moscow,
   PhD P.F.U., Moscow   Sr. Lectr.
Peter, C. M., LLM Dar., DrJur Constance   Prof.
Other Staff: 1 Lectr.; 1 Asst. Lectr.

Law, Legal Theory

Tel: (022) 241 0254 E-mail: ghent@ud.co.tz
Hussain, M. S., MLIS Madr., LLM Osm., MA
   Osm., PhD Osm.   Sr. Lectr.
Majamba, H. I., LLB Dar., LLM Qu., PhD
   Northeastern   Sr. Lectr.
Mapunda, B. T., LLB Dar., PhD Ghent   Lectr.;
   Head*
Tenga, R. W., LLM Cornell, LLM Dar., JSD Cornell
   Sr. Lectr.
Other Staff: 4 Asst. Lectrs.

Literature

Tel: (022) 241 0395 E-mail: fass@udsm.ac.tz
Njozi, H., BA Dar., MA Dar., PhD NU Malaysia
   Assoc. Prof.
Osaki, L. T., BA(Ed) Dar., MA Dar., PhD Flor.
   Sr. Lectr.; Head*
Other Staff: 2 Lectrs.; 4 Asst. Lectrs.

Management, General

Tel: (022) 241 0510 Fax: (022) 241 0510
   E-mail: dean@fcm.udsm.ac.tz
Baradyana, J. S., BA Dar., MBA Arizona, PhD
   Lond.   Sr. Lectr.; Head*
Katunzi, J. M., MBA Arizona, PhD Lond.   Sr.
   Lectr.
Other Staff: 3 Lectrs.; 11 Asst. Lectrs.

Marketing

Tel: (022) 241 0510 Fax: (022) 241 0510
   E-mail: dean@udsm.ac.tz
Lindi, G. M., BCom Dar., MCom Strath., PhD
   Sr. Lectr.
Matambalya, F. A. S. T., BCom Dar., MSc Linz,
   PhD Bochum   Assoc. Prof.
Mboma, L. M., BA Dar., MBA Dar., PhD Strath.
   Sr. Lectr.; Head*
Mwaipopo, L. J., BSc Dar., MBA Dar., PhD
   Nebraska   Sr. Lectr.
Olomi, D. R., BCom Dar., MBA St Mary's(Can.),
   PhD Dar.   Sr. Lectr.
Rutashobya, Lettice H. K., BA Dar., MA Dar.,
   PhD Dar.   Prof.
Other Staff: 1 Lectr.; 8 Asst. Lectrs.
Research: gender role portrayal in advertising in
   Tanzania

Mathematics

Tel: (022) 241 0129 Fax: (022) 241 0129
   E-mail: dean@science.udsm.ac.tz
Alphonce, N. A., BA(Ed) Dar., MA Tor., PhD NZ
   Sr. Lectr.
Klaasen, G., BA Mich., PhD Nebraska   Prof.
Masanja, V. G., MSc Dar., PhD Berl., DrIng
   T.U.Berlin   Assoc. Prof. (on leave)

Massawe, E. S., MSc Trinity(Dub.), PhD
   Trinity(Dub.)   Sr. Lectr. (on leave)
Mshimba, A. S. A., DrRerNat Halle   Prof.
Mushi, A. R., BScEd Dar., MMS N.U.I., PhD
   Dublin City   Head*
Shayo, L. K., MSc Dar., PhD Lond.   Assoc. Prof.
Other Staff: 4 Lectrs.; 1 Asst. Lectr.
Research: dynamical systems; fluid dynamics and
   mathematical modelling

Molecular Biology and Biotechnology

Kivaisi, A. K., BSc Dar., MSc Stockholm, PhD Dar.
   Prof.
Lyimo, T. J., BSc Dar., MSc Dar., PhD Dar.   Sr.
   Lectr.
Magingo, Francis S. S., BSc Dar., MSc Dar., PhD
   Dar.   Assoc. Prof.
Mtui, G. Y. S., BSc Dar., MSc Kanazawa, PhD
   Kanazawa   Sr. Lectr.; Head*
Muruke, M. H. S., BSc Dar., MSc Dar., PhD Dar.
   Sr. Lectr.
Rubindamayugi, M. S. T., BSc Dar., MSc Dar.,
   PhD Dar.   Sr. Lectr.
Other Staff: 3 Lectrs.; 5 Asst. Lectrs.
Research: cultivation of edible mushrooms;
   marine science; minerals and amino acid
   composition of algae

Physical Education, Sport and Culture

Tel: (022) 241 0500
   E-mail: dean@edu.udsm.ac.tz
Ndee, H. S., MSc(Ed) Stockholm, MA Moscow,
   PhD Strath.   Sr. Lectr.; Head*
Other Staff: 1 Lectr.; 5 Asst. Lectrs.

Physics

Tel: (022) 241 0129 Fax: (022) 241 0129
   E-mail: science@cc.udsm.ac.tz
Kainkwa, R. M. R., MSc Dar., PhD Dar.   Sr.
   Lectr.
Kivaisi, R. T., BSc Dar., MSc Dar., PhD Stockholm
   Prof.
Kololeni, Y. I., MSc Dar.   Sr. Lectr.
Makundi, I. N., BSc Dar., MSc Dar., PhD Tokyo
   Sr. Lectr.
Mbise, G. W., BSc Dar., MSc Dar., PhD Dar.
   Sr. Lectr.
Msaki, P. K., BSc Zambia, MSc Reading, PhD
   Stockholm   Assoc. Prof.
Uiso, C. B. S., BSc Dar., PhD Dar.   Sr. Lectr.;
   Head*
Other Staff: 2 Lectrs.; 2 Asst. Lectrs.
Research: environmental pollution; grain storage
   structures

Political Science and Public Administration

Tel: (022) 241 0130 Fax: (022) 241 0395
   E-mail: fass@udsm.ac.tz
Bakari, M. A., BA Dar., MA Dar., PhD Hamburg
   Sr. Lectr.
Baregu, M. L., BA Brock, MA Dar., PhD Stan.
   Prof.
Chaligha, A. E., MA Dar., MPA S.Calif., PhD
   Claremont   Assoc. Prof.
Kente, M. G., MA Villanova, PhD Duquesne   Sr.
   Lectr.
Killian, B., BA Dar., MA Dar., PhD Calif.   Sr.
   Lectr.
Liviga, A. J., MA Dar., PhD Pitt.   Assoc. Prof.
Mallya, E. T., BA Dar., MA Dar., PhD Manc.
   Assoc. Prof.
Mhina, A. K. L., MA Dar., PhD Pau   Assoc.
   Prof.
Mmuya, M., BA(Ed) Dar., MSc Bath, PhD
   Missouri   Assoc. Prof.
Mogella, Fr. C. A., BA Dar., MA Dar., PhD Car.
   Sr. Lectr.
Mukandala, Rwekaza R. S., BA Dar., MA Dar.,
   PhD Calif.   Prof.
Mukangara, D. R., MA Dar., PhD ANU   Assoc.
   Prof.
Munishi, Gasper K. K., BA Dar., MA Dar., PhD
   Wis.   Prof.
Mushi, S. S., BA Lond., MA Calif., PhD Yale
   Prof.
Ndumbaro, L., BA Dar., MA Dar., PhD Flor.   Sr.
   Lectr.; Head*

Nyirabu, M., BA Goshen, MA Kent State, PhD Kent
   State   Assoc. Prof.
Other Staff: 4 Lectrs.; 10 Asst. Lectrs.
Research: education for democracy in Tanzania

Sociology and Anthropology

Tel: (022) 241 0130 Fax: (022) 241 0395
   E-mail: fass@udsm.ac.tz
Lyimo, F. F., BA Dar., MA Dar., PhD Wis.   Sr.
   Lectr.
Maghimbi, S., MA Dar., MSc Lond., PhD Lond.
   Assoc. Prof.
Masanja, P., BA Dar., MA Paris, PhD Hull   Sr.
   Lectr.
Mesaki, B. A., BA Dar., MA Dar., PhD Minn.   Sr.
   Lectr.
Mvungi, A. A. K., BA Dar., MSc Sur., PhD Linz
   Sr. Lectr.; Head*
Mwami, J. A., BA Dar., MA Dar., PhD Linz   Sr.
   Lectr.
Other Staff: 2 Lectrs.; 11 Asst. Lectrs.
Research: baseline study on family profile; health
   knowledge

Statistics

Tel: (022) 241 0395 Fax: (022) 241 0395
   E-mail: fass@udsm.ac.tz
Akarro, R. J., BA Dar., MA Dar., MSc Lond., PhD
   Dar.   Sr. Lectr.
Kamuzora, C. L. A., BA Dar., MA Dar., MA
   Penn., PhD Penn.   Prof.
Mbago, Maurice C. Y., BA Dar., MA Dar., PhD
   Liv.   Assoc. Prof.
Mussa, A. S., BSc Dar., MA Dar., PhD Kent   Sr.
   Lectr.; Head*
Naimani, G. M., MA Dar., PhD Dar.   Sr. Lectr.
Rugaimukamu, D. B. M., MA Dar., MSc S'ton.,
   PhD S'ton.   Sr. Lectr.
Sichona, F. J., MA Dar., PhD N.Carolina State   Sr.
   Lectr.
Other Staff: 5 Asst. Lectrs.

Zoology and Wildlife Conservation

Tel: (022) 241 0129 Fax: (022) 241 0129
   E-mail: science@cc.udsm.ac.tz
Howell, K. M., BSc Cornell, PhD Dar.   Prof.
Kabigumila, J. D. L., BSc Dar., MSc Dar., PhD
   Dar.   Assoc. Prof.
Kasigwa, P. F., MSc Dar., DPhil Sus.   Sr. Lectr.
Kayumbo, H. Y., BSc Lond., PhD Dar.   Prof.
Kyomo, J., BSc Kyushu, PhD Kyushu   Sr. Lectr.
Mturi, F. A., BSc Dar., PhD Dar.   Sr. Lectr.
Nahonyo, C. L., BSc Dar., PhD Kent   Head*
Nikundiwe, A. M., BSc Andrews, MSc Mich., PhD
   Mich.   Assoc. Prof.
Nkwengulila, G., BSc Dar., MSc Liv., PhD Liv.
   Sr. Lectr.
Pratap, H. B., MSc Gujar., PhD Dar.   Sr. Lectr.
Rugumamu, C. P., BSc Dar., MSc Dar., PhD Dar.
   Sr. Lectr.
Senzota, R. B. M., MSc Dar., PhD Texas A.& M.
   Assoc. Prof.
Urasa, F. M., MSc Dar., PhD Dar.   Sr. Lectr.
Wagner, G. M., MSc Dar., PhD Dar.   Sr. Lectr.
Yarro, J. G., MSc Dar., PhD Dar.   Sr. Lectr.
Other Staff: 4 Lectrs.; 6 Asst. Lectrs.
Research: environmental impact assessment of
   various ecosystems; physiological and
   biochemical assessment of health status of
   aquatic organisms in Tanzania; studies in
   local protein feeds for Oreochromis spp

SPECIAL CENTRES, ETC

Computing Centre

Tel: (022) 241 0645 Fax: (022) 241 0380
   E-mail: ucc@udsm.ac.tz
Mutagahywa, B. M., MSc Dar., PhD Lough.
   Dir.*
Research: development of prototype system for
   the retailing supermarket; system
   transformation of Tanzanian society into a
   cashless society

Continuing Education, Centre for

Muruke, M. H. S., BSc Dar., MSc Dar., PhD Dar.
   Dir.*

Development Studies, Institute of

Tel: (022) 241 0755 Fax: (022) 241 0075
E-mail: ids@udsm.ac.tz
Chambua, S. E., BSc Dar., MA Dar., MA Car.,
PhD Car.   Assoc. Prof.
Kamugisha, C. A., BA(Ed) Dar., MA Dar., PhD
Dar.   Sr. Lectr.
Kamuzora, P. C. L., BA Dar., MA Dar., MA Leeds,
PhD Leeds   Sr. Lectr.
Koda, Bertha, MA Dar., PhD Dar.   Assoc. Prof.;
Dir.*
Komba, A. A., MA Dar., PhD George Washington,
BSc(Eng)   Sr. Lectr.
Kopoka, P., BA Dar., MA Dar., PhD Leeds   Sr.
Lectr.
Mlawa, H. M., BA Dar., MA Dar., DPhil Sus.
Prof.
Mongula, B. S., BA Dar., MA Car., MA Dar.,
PhD Dar.   Assoc. Prof.
Mpangala, G., BA Dar., MA Dar., PhD Leip.
Prof.
Mwaigomole, E. A., BA Dar., MA Dar., MA Kobe,
PhD Kobe   Sr. Lectr.
Ngaiza, M. K., BA Dar., MA Dar., MLS Lough.,
PhD Dar.   Sr. Lectr.
Ngware, S. S., BA Dar., MA Dar., MA Minn.,
PhD Minn.   Prof.
Niboye, E. P., BEdSc Dar., DrRerSoc Linz   Sr.
Lectr.
Othman, H. M., LLM Moscow, PhD Dar.   Prof.
Rugumamu, S. M., BA Dar., MA Dar., MA
Maryland, PhD Maryland   Prof.
Shao, I., BA Dar., MA Dar., PhD Dar.   Assoc.
Prof.
Shayo, R., BA Dar., MA Dar., PhD Manc.   Sr.
Lectr.
Other Staff: 3 Lectrs.; 2 Asst. Lectrs.
Research: rural food security policy and
development

Entrepreneurship Centre

Olomi, D. R., BCom Dar., MBA St Mary's(Can.),
PhD Dar.   Dir.*

Journalism and Mass Communication, Institute of

Hatar, A., BA Mak., MA Ohio, PhD Ohio   Sr.
Lectr.
Kapoli, I. J., BA(Ed) Dar., MA Dar., PhD Lond.
Sr. Lectr.
Possi, M. K., BA(Ed) Dar., MA Dar., MA Ball,
PhD Ohio State   Prof.; Dir.*
Other Staff: 1 Lectr.; 3 Asst. Lectrs.

Kiswahili Research, Institute of

Tel: (022) 241 0757 Fax: (022) 241 0328
E-mail: tuki@ikr.udsm.ac.tz
Massamba, D. P. B., BA(Ed) Dar., MA Dar., MA
Indiana, PhD Indiana   Res. Prof.
Mdee, J. S., MA Dar., PhD Leip.   Assoc. Res.
Prof.
Mulokozi, M. M., BA Dar., PhD Dar.   Assoc.
Res. Prof.
Mwansoko, H. J. M., MA Moscow, DPhil
York(UK)   Assoc. Res. Prof.; Dir.*
Other Staff: 6 Sr. Res. Fellows; 5 Res. Fellows
Research: history of poetry; legal dictionary;
Swahili-English dictionary

Marine Sciences, Institute of

Tel: (022) 230741 Fax: (022) 233050
E-mail: ims@zims.udsm.ac.tz
Dubi, A. M., DrIng Trondheim   Dir.*

Other Staff: 8 Sr. Res. Fellows; 8 Res. Fellows;
1 Asst. Res. Fellow
Research: beach erosion; nutrient dynamics in
coral reefs, seagrass beds and mangroves;
seaweed farming and algal physiology
studies

Resource Assessment, Institute of

Tel: (022) 241 0144 Fax: (022) 241 0393
E-mail: ira@udsm.ac.tz
Kangalawe, R. Y. M., MSc Norway Ag., PhD
Stockholm, BSc(Agric)
Mwalyosi, R. B. B., MSc Dar., PhD
Agric.Coll.Norway   Res. Prof.
Ngana, J. O., BSc Dar., MSc N.U.I., PhD
Stockholm   Assoc. Res. Prof.
Shechambo, F. C., BA Dar., MA(Econ) Dar.,
PhD T.U.Berlin
Shishira, E. K., MSc Sheff., PhD Sheff.   Assoc.
Res. Prof.
Yanda, P., BSc Dar., MSc Norway Ag., PhD
Stockholm   Assoc. Prof.; Dir.*
Other Staff: 4 Sr. Res. Fellows; 4 Res. Fellows;
8 Asst. Res. Fellows
Research: human-land interrelations

CONTACT OFFICERS

Alumni. Convocation Liaison Officer: Benedict,
F., BA Dar. (E-mail: caco@admin.usdm.ac.tz)
Careers. Deputy Vice-Chancellor (Finance,
Planning and Administration): Mgaya, Prof.
Yunus D., BSc Dar., MSc Br.Col., PhD N.U.I.
Careers. Deputy Vice-Chancellor (Academic
Research and Consultancy): Maboko, Prof.
Makenya A. H., BSc Dar., MSc Dar., PhD
ANU (E-mail: caco@admin.usdm.ac.tz)
Computing services. Director, Computing
Centre: Mutagahywa, B. M., MSc Dar., PhD
Lough. (E-mail: ucc@udsm.ac.tz)
Consultancy services. Director, University
Consultancy Bureau: Temu, S. S, BCom
Dar., MBA T.U.Berlin, PhD Bremen
(E-mail: ucb@udsm.ac.tz)
Development/fund-raising. Deputy Vice-
Chancellor (Finance, Planning and
Administration): Mgaya, Prof. Yunus D.,
BSc Dar., MSc Br.Col., PhD N.U.I.
Distance education. Deputy Vice-Chancellor
(Academic Research and Consultancy):
Maboko, Prof. Makenya A. H., BSc Dar.,
MSc Dar., PhD ANU
(E-mail: caco@admin.usdm.ac.tz)
Equal opportunities. Deputy Vice-Chancellor
(Academic Research and Consultancy):
Maboko, Prof. Makenya A. H., BSc Dar.,
MSc Dar., PhD ANU
(E-mail: caco@admin.usdm.ac.tz)
Estates and buildings/works and services.
Estates Manager: Mwashihava, M., BSc(Eng)
Dar., MSc(Eng)
Examinations. Principal Administrative Officer:
Mchallo, S. I.
Finance. Bursar: Kaijage, V. R.
(E-mail: bursar@admin.udsm.ac.tz)
General enquiries. Secretary to the Council:
Mtunga, D., MPA Kentucky
(E-mail: stc@admin.udsm.ac.tz)
Health services. Medical Officer-in-Charge:
Mroso, D. M., MD Dar., MMed Dar.
Industrial liaison. Deputy Vice-Chancellor
(Finance, Planning and Administration):
Mgaya, Prof. Yunus D., BSc Dar., MSc
Br.Col., PhD N.U.I.

International office. Senior Administrative
Officer, Links and Projects: Kaaya, M. S.
Library (chief librarian). Director, Library:
Nkhoma-Wamunza, A. G., BA Dar., MA
Lond., PhD N.Carolina
(E-mail: director@libis.udsm.ac.tz)
Minorities/disadvantaged groups. Deputy
Vice-Chancellor (Finance, Planning and
Administration): Mgaya, Prof. Yunus D.,
BSc Dar., MSc Br.Col., PhD N.U.I.
Personnel/human resources. Director: Jambo,
Edward G. M., BA Dar., MSc Manc.
Public relations. Principal Public Relations
Officer: Saule, J. O., BA Nair.
(E-mail: pro@udsm.ac.tz)
Publications. Director of Research and
Publications: Yahya-Othman, Prof. Saida,
BA Dar., MA Dar., MA York(UK), PhD Dar.
(E-mail: research@admin.udsm.ac.tz)
Purchasing. Chief Supplies Officer: Swai, S. H.
N., MSc(Finance) Strath.
Research. Director of Research and
Publications: Yahya-Othman, Prof. Saida,
BA Dar., MA Dar., MA York(UK), PhD Dar.
(E-mail: research@admin.udsm.ac.tz)
Safety. Deputy Vice-Chancellor (Finance,
Planning and Administration: Mgaya, Prof.
Yunus D., BSc Dar., MSc Br.Col., PhD N.U.I.
Scholarships, awards, loans. Dean, Graduate
School: Kivaisi, Prof. R. T., BSc Dar., MSc
Dar., PhD Stockholm
(E-mail: dpgs@admin.udsm.ac.tz)
Security. Deputy Vice-Chancellor (Finance,
Planning, Administration): Mgaya, Prof.
Yunus D., BSc Dar., MSc Br.Col., PhD N.U.I.
Sport and recreation. Acting Principal Games
Coach: Gogomoka, L. H.
(E-mail: dean@edu.udsm.ac.tz)
Staff development and training. Senior
Administrative Officer: Mshigeni, N. G.,
MPA Liv. (E-mail: dpgs@admin.udsm.ac.tz)
Student welfare/counselling. Dean of
Students: Rubagumya, C. M., BA Dar., MA
Lanc., PhD Lanc.
Students from other countries. Senior
Administrative Offier, Co-operation, Links
and Projects Section: Kaaya, M. S.
(E-mail: dpgs@admin.udsm.ac.tz)
Students with disabilities. Dean of Students:
Rubagumya, C. M., BA Dar., MA Lanc., PhD
Lanc.
Women. Deputy Vice-Chancellor: Mgaya, Prof.
Yunus D., BSc Dar., MSc Br.Col., PhD N.U.I.

CAMPUS/COLLEGE HEADS

College of Engineering and Technology, Dar
es Salaam, Tanzania. Principal: Mwamila,
Prof. Burton L. M., BSc(Eng) Dar., MSc(Eng)
Dar., PhD R.I.T.Stockholm
Dar es Salaam College of Education, Dar es
Salaam, Tanzania. Principal: Mosha, Prof.
Herme J., BA Dar., MA(Ed) Dar., PhD Alta.,
Hon. Dr
Mkwawa College of Education, Iringa,
Tanzania. Principal: Mushi, Prof. P. A. K.,
BAEd Dar., MA(Ed) Dar., PhD S'ton.

[Information supplied by the institution as at 25
November 2007, and edited by the ACU]

HUBERT KAIRUKI MEMORIAL UNIVERSITY

Founded 1997

Postal Address: PO Box 65300, Dar es Salaam, Tanzania
Telephone: (022) 270 0021 **Fax:** (022) 277 5591 **E-mail:** info@hkmu.ac.tz
URL: http://www.hkmu.ac.tz

VICE-CHANCELLOR*—Mshigeni, Prof. Keto E., BSc E.Af., PhD Hawaii
DEPUTY VICE-CHANCELLOR FINANCE AND ADMINISTRATION‡—(vacant)

INTERNATIONAL MEDICAL AND TECHNOLOGICAL UNIVERSITY

Postal Address: PO Box 77594, Dar es Salaam, Tanzania
Telephone: (022) 647036 **Fax:** (022) 647038 **E-mail:** imtu@afsat.com
URL: http://www.imtu.edu/imtu.htm

VICE-CHANCELLOR*—Kimati, Prof. Valelian P.

MZUMBE UNIVERSITY

Founded 2001

Member of the Association of Commonwealth Universities

Postal Address: PO Box 1, Mzumbe, Morogoro, Tanzania
Telephone: (023) 260 4380 **Fax:** (023) 260 4382 **E-mail:** idm@raha.com
URL: http://www.mzumbe.ac.tz/

VICE-CHANCELLOR*—Kuzilwa, Prof. Joseph A., BA Dar., MA Lanc., PhD Ill.
DEPUTY VICE-CHANCELLOR (ACADEMIC)—Kuzilwa, Prof. Joseph A., BA Dar., MA Lanc., PhD Ill.

GENERAL INFORMATION

History. Mzumbe University has been established by Act No.21 of 2001 as a product of the transformation of the then Institute of Development Management (IDM).

It is located 22km South-West of Morogoro town and about 220km from Dar es Salaam.

First Degrees (see also Tanzanian Directory to Subjects of Study). BAcc, BBA, BPA, BSc.
Length of course. Full-time: BAcc, BBA, BPA, BSc: 3 years.

Higher Degrees (see also Tanzanian Directory to Subjects of Study).
Master's. MBA, MPA.
Length of course. Full-time: MBA, MPA: 1½ years.
Doctoral. PhD.
Length of course. Full-time: PhD: 3–6 years.

Libraries. Volumes: 24,957. Periodicals subscribed to: 300.

FACULTIES/SCHOOLS

Commerce

Dean: Kasilo, Dominicus M., PhD T.H.Twente, MBA

Law

Dean: Mushi, Eliuter G., LLB Dar., LLM Warw.

Public Administration and Management

Dean: Milanzi, Montanus C., MA Hull, PhD L&H

Science and Technology

Dean: Muna, Prof. Damas, BA Dar., MA Kent, MA Dar.

Social Sciences

Dean: Nagu, Prof. Joseph T., BA E.Af., MSc Tennessee, PhD Tennessee

ACADEMIC UNITS

SPECIAL CENTRES, ETC

Continuing Education, Institute of

Simime, Alto, MSc Aston   Dir.*

Development Studies, Institute of

Shio, Prof. Leonard J., BA Dar., MA Dar., PhD Dir.*

Public Administration, Institute of

Njunwa, Mujwahuzi, BA Dar., MA Dar., PhD Dir.*

CONTACT OFFICERS

Adult/continuing education. Director, Institute of Continuing Education: Simime, Alto, MSc Aston

Computing services. Director, Directorate of Information and Communication Technology: Njovu, Simon, BSc Dar., MSc Hull (E-mail: skmnjovu@yahoo.com)

Library (chief librarian). Director, Directorate of Library and Technical Services: Kuzilwa, Matilda S., MA Lond.

Publications. Director, Directorate of Research, Publications and Postgraduate Studies: Nkya, Prof. Estomihi J., MSc Bucharest, MA Car., PhD Pitt.

Research. Director, Directorate of Research, Publications and Postgraduate Studies: Nkya, Prof. Estomihi J., MSc Bucharest, MA Car., PhD Pitt.

Strategic planning. Director, Directorate of Strategic Business Development: Kiwango, Aristarch

[*Information supplied by the institution as at 17 January 2005, and edited by the ACU*]

OPEN UNIVERSITY OF TANZANIA

Founded 1992

Member of the Association of Commonwealth Universities

Postal Address: PO Box 23409, Dar es Salaam, Tanzania
Telephone: (022) 266 8445 **Fax:** (022) 266 8759 **E-mail:** vc@out.ac.tz
URL: http://www.openuniversity.ac.tz

VICE-CHANCELLOR*—Mbwette, Prof. Tolly S. A., BSc(Eng) Dar., MSc Dar., PhD Lond.
DEPUTY VICE-CHANCELLOR (ACADEMIC)—Shemwetta, Prof. Dunstan T. K., MSc(For) New Br., PhD Oregon, BSc(For)
DEPUTY VICE CHANCELLOR (RESOURCE MANAGEMENT)—Kusiluka, Prof. L. J., MPhil Edin., PhD R.Vet.& Agric., Denmark, BVM
DEPUTY VICE CHANCELLOR (REGIONAL SERVICES)—Bisanda, Prof. E. T., BSc(Eng) Dar., MSc Cran., PhD Bath
DIRECTOR OF PLANNING—Temu, Elisei B., BA(Ed) E.Af., MA(Ed) Dar., PhD Stockholm

GENERAL INFORMATION

History. The university was established in 1992.

It is located on Kawawa Road in Kinondoni Municipality, in the north of Dar es Salaam, and has 25 regional centres throughout Tanzania, including two in Zanzibar.

Admission to first degree courses. Certificate of Secondary Education, or East African Certificate of Education O level or equivalent, with 3 credit passes or passes in 5 approved subjects, and Advanced Certificate of Secondary Education or an equivalent diploma or certificate approved by the university senate.

First Degrees (see also Tanzanian Directory to Subjects of Study). BA, BA(Ed), BBA, BBA(Ed), BCom, BCom(Ed), BEd, BEd(SpecEd), BSc, BSc(Ed), BSc(ICT), LLB.
Length of course. By distance learning: BEd(SpecEd): 3 years; BA, BA(Ed), BBA, BCom, BCom(Ed), BEd, BSc, BSc(Ed), LLB: 3–6 years.

Higher Degrees (see also Tanzanian Directory to Subjects of Study).
Master's. MA, MA(Econ), MA(EGM), MA(Kisw), MA(Ling), MBA, MDistEd, ME, MEd, MEd(Apps), MSc, MSc(Biology), MSc(CED), MSc(Chemistry), MSc(HE), MSc(Maths), MSc(Physics).
Admission. Applicants for admission to master's degrees must normally hold a first degree with at least second class honours or an unclassified/pass degree with grade B or above.
Length of course. By distance learning: MSc(CED): 2 years; MBA: 2–4 years; MA, MA(Econ), MA(EGM), MA(Kisw), MA(Ling), MDistEd, MEd, MEd(Apps), MSc, MSc(Biology), MSc(Chemistry), MSc(HE), MSc(Maths), MSc(Physics): 5 years.
Doctoral. PhD.
Admission. Applicants for admission to PhD must hold a master's degree or equivalent.
Length of course. By distance learning: PhD: 2–6 years.

Libraries. Volumes: 26,000. Periodicals subscribed to: 20. Other holdings: 17 dissertation volumes; 3300 audio cassettes.

FACULTIES/SCHOOLS

Arts and Social Sciences
Tel: (022) 266 8820 E-mail: dfass@out.ac.tz
Dean: Gwalema, Susan, BAEd Dar., MA(Demo) Dar., PhD

Business Management
Tel: (022) 266 8820 E-mail: dfbm@out.ac.tz
Dean: Mhoma, M. A., BA Dar., MA Kyoto, PhD Kyoto

Education
Tel: (022) 266 8820 E-mail: dfed@out.ac.tz
Dean: Bwatwa, Prof. Y. D. M., BA(Soc) MA EdD

Law
Tel: (022) 266 8820 E-mail: dflaw@out.ac.tz
Dean: Kihwelo, Paul F., LLB Dar., LLM Dar.

Science, Technology and Environmental Studies
Tel: (022) 266 8820 E-mail: dfstes@out.ac.tz
Dean: Varisanga, Prof. M. D., MVM Havana Livestock Scis., PhD Yamaguchi, BVM

ACADEMIC UNITS
Arranged by Faculties, etc.

Arts and Social Sciences
Tel: (022) 266 8820 E-mail: dfass@out.ac.tz
Gwalema, Susan, BAEd Dar., MA(Demo) Dar., PhD   Dean*
Other Staff: 3 Profs.; 18 Lectrs.; 20 Asst. Lectrs.

Business Management
Tel: (022) 266 8820 E-mail: dfbm@out.ac.tz
Mhoma, M. A., BA Dar., MA Kyoto, PhD Kyoto   Dean*
Other Staff: 2 Lectrs.; 12 Asst. Lectrs.

Continuing Education, Institute of
Tel: (022) 266 8820 E-mail: dice@out.ac.tz
Muganda, C. K., BA(Ed) Dar., MEd Tor., PhD Massey   Dir.*
Other Staff: 2 Sr. Lectrs.; 4 Lectrs.; 8 Asst. Lectrs.

Education
Tel: (022) 266 8820 E-mail: dfed@out.ac.tz
Bwatwa, Y. D. M., BA(Soc) MA EdD   Prof.; Dean*
Other Staff: 2 Profs.; 6 Sr. Lectrs.; 12 Lectrs.; 17 Asst. Lectrs.

Educational Technology, Institute of
Tel: (022) 266 8820 E-mail: diet@out.ac.tz
Bakari, J. K., BSc MSc PhD   Dir.*
Other Staff: 1 Assoc. Dir., E-learning; 1 Assoc. Dir., Information Resources

Law
Tel: (022) 266 8820 E-mail: dflaw@out.ac.tz
Kihwelo, Paul F., LLB Dar., LLM Dar.   Head*
Other Staff: 1 Prof.; 5 Asst. Lectrs.

Science, Technology and Environmental Studies
Tel: (022) 266 8820 E-mail: dfstes@out.ac.tz
Massenge, Ralph W. P., BSc Würzburg, MSc Oxf., PhD Dar., MA   Prof.
Mhoma, J. R. L., DVM Ukr.Acad.Agric., MSc Ukr.Acad.Agric., MSc James Cook, PhD Murd.   Prof.
Varisanga, M. D., MVM Havana Livestock Scis., PhD Yamaguchi, BVM   Dean*
Other Staff: 9 Profs.; 7 Lectrs.; 16 Asst. Lectrs.

CONTACT OFFICERS

Academic affairs. Deputy Vice-Chancellor (Academic): Shemwetta, Prof. Dunstan T. K., MSc(For) New Br., PhD Oregon, BSc(For) (E-mail: deputyvc@out.ac.tz)

Admissions (first degree). Deputy Vice-Chancellor (Academic): Shemwetta, Prof. Dunstan T. K., MSc(For) New Br., PhD Oregon, BSc(For) (E-mail: deputyvc@out.ac.tz)

Alumni. Deputy Vice Chancellor (Resource Management): Kusiluka, Prof. L. J., MPhil Edin., PhD R.Vet.& Agric., Denmark, BVM (E-mail: dvcrm@out.ac.tz)

Credit transfer. Deputy Vice-Chancellor (Academic): Shemwetta, Prof. Dunstan T. K., MSc(For) New Br., PhD Oregon, BSc(For) (E-mail: deputyvc@out.ac.tz)

Development/fund-raising. Director of Planning and Development: Temu, Elisei B., BA(Ed) E.Af., MA(Ed) Dar., PhD Stockholm (E-mail: dpd@out.ac.tz)

Distance education. Deputy Vice-Chancellor (Academic): Shemwetta, Prof. Dunstan T. K., MSc(For) New Br., PhD Oregon, BSc(For) (E-mail: deputyvc@out.ac.tz)

Estates and buildings/works and services. Deputy Vice Chancellor (Resource Management): Kusiluka, Prof. L. J., MPhil Edin., PhD R.Vet.& Agric., Denmark, BVM (E-mail: dvcrm@out.ac.tz)

Examinations. Deputy Vice-Chancellor (Academic): Shemwetta, Prof. Dunstan T. K., MSc(For) New Br., PhD Oregon, BSc(For) (E-mail: deputyvc@out.ac.tz)

Finance. Deputy Vice Chancellor (Resource Management): Kusiluka, Prof. L. J., MPhil Edin., PhD R.Vet.& Agric., Denmark, BVM (E-mail: dvcrm@out.ac.tz)

General enquiries. Deputy Vice Chancellor (Resource Management): Kusiluka, Prof. L. J., MPhil Edin., PhD R.Vet.& Agric., Denmark, BVM (E-mail: dvcrm@out.ac.tz)

Health services. Deputy Vice Chancellor (Resource Management): Kusiluka, Prof. L. J., MPhil Edin., PhD R.Vet.& Agric., Denmark, BVM (E-mail: dvcrm@out.ac.tz)

Library (enquiries). Deputy Vice-Chancellor (Academic): Shemwetta, Prof. Dunstan T. K., MSc(For) New Br., PhD Oregon, BSc(For) (E-mail: deputyvc@out.ac.tz)

Marketing. Director of Communication and Marketing: Memba, Albert Z., BA Dar., MA (E-mail: dcm@out.ac.tz)

Personnel/human resources. Deputy Vice Chancellor (Resource Management): Kusiluka, Prof. L. J., MPhil Edin., PhD R.Vet.& Agric., Denmark, BVM (E-mail: dvcrm@out.ac.tz)

Public relations. Director of Communication and Marketing: Memba, Albert Z., BA Dar., MA (E-mail: dcm@out.ac.tz)

Publications. Deputy Vice-Chancellor (Academic): Shemwetta, Prof. Dunstan T. K., MSc(For) New Br., PhD Oregon, BSc(For) (E-mail: deputyvc@out.ac.tz)

Purchasing. Deputy Vice Chancellor (Resource Management): Kusiluka, Prof. L. J., MPhil

Edin., PhD R.Vet.& Agric., Denmark, BVM
(E-mail: dvcrm@out.ac.tz)

Quality assurance and accreditation. Deputy
Vice-Chancellor (Academic): Shemwetta,
Prof. Dunstan T. K., MSc(For) New Br., PhD
Oregon, BSc(For)
(E-mail: deputyvc@out.ac.tz)

Research. Deputy Vice-Chancellor (Academic):
Shemwetta, Prof. Dunstan T. K., MSc(For)
New Br., PhD Oregon, BSc(For)
(E-mail: deputyvc@out.ac.tz)

Scholarships, awards, loans. Deputy Vice-
Chancellor (Academic): Shemwetta, Prof.
Dunstan T. K., MSc(For) New Br., PhD
Oregon, BSc(For)
(E-mail: deputyvc@out.ac.tz)

Security. Deputy Vice Chancellor (Resource
Management): Kusiluka, Prof. L. J., MPhil
Edin., PhD R.Vet.& Agric., Denmark, BVM
(E-mail: dvcrm@out.ac.tz)

Staff development and training. Deputy Vice
Chancellor (Resource Management):
Kusiluka, Prof. L. J., MPhil Edin., PhD R.Vet.&
Agric., Denmark, BVM
(E-mail: dvcrm@out.ac.tz)

Student welfare/counselling. Dean of
Students: Libent, Delphine, BA(Ed) Dar., MA
Dar. (E-mail: drmvc@out.ac.tz)

CAMPUS/COLLEGE HEADS

Arusha Regional Centre, PO Box 15244,
Arusha, Tanzania. (Tel: (027) 250 1865;
E-mail: drcarusha@out.ac.tz) Director: Saria,
W. L., MA Dar., BA

Coast Regional Centre, PO Box 30420,
Kibaha, Tanzania. (Tel: (023) 240 2811)
Director: Mori, Joyce, MSc Acad., BSc(Ed)

Dar es Salaam Regional Centre, PO Box
13224, Dar es Salaam, Tanzania. (Tel: (022)
246 0971) Director: Gwalema, Susan, BAEd
Dar., MA(Demo) Dar., PhD

Dodoma Regional Centre, PO Box 1944,
Dodoma, Tanzania. (Tel: (026) 232 2345)
Director: Wawa, A. I., BSc(Ed) Dar., MA
Dar.

Ilala Regional Centre, PO Box 21745, Dar es
Salaam, Tanzania;
E-mail: donafunga@yahoo.com Director:

Fungameza, D., MSc(Forestry) MSc(Agri)
PhD

Iringa Regional Centre, PO Box 1458, Iringa,
Tanzania. (Tel: (026) 270063;
E-mail: drciringa@out.ac.tz) Director:
Makene, V. W., BVM MVM

Kagera Regional Centre, PO Box 1954,
Bukoba, Tanzania. (Tel: (028) 222 0271;
E-mail: drckagera@out.ac.tz) Director:
Mutasingwa, James, BA(Ed) MSc

Kigoma Regional Centre, PO Box 560,
Kigoma, Tanzania. (Tel: (028) 280 2981;
E-mail: drckigoma@out.ac.tz) Director:
Ntabahanyi, S. T. N., BSc(Ed) Durh., MBA
Dar.

Kilimanjaro Regional Centre, PO Box 517,
Kilimanjaro, Tanzania. (Tel: (027) 275
3472; E-mail: drckilimanjaro@out.ac.tz)
Director: Tarimo, Elias C. J., BA(Ed) Dar.,
MA Dar.

Kinondoni Regional Centre, PO Box 13224,
Dar es Salaam, Tanzania. (Tel: (022) 246
0971; E-mail: drcdsm@out.ac.tz) Director:
Mkuchu, S. G. V., BA(Ed) Dar., MA Dar.,
PhD S.Af.

Lindi Regional Centre, PO Box 742, Lindi,
Tanzania. (Tel: (023) 220 2725) Director:
(vacant)

Manyara Regional Centre, PO Box 271,
Babati, Tanzania. (Tel: (027) 253 0319;
E-mail: drcmanyara@out.ac.tz) Director:
Makundi, A. E., BVM MVM PhD

Mara Regional Centre, PO Box 217, Musoma,
Tanzania. (Tel: (028) 262 0401) Director:
Ligembe Nestory, BAEd Dar., MAEd Dar.

Mbeya Regional Centre, PO Box 2803,
Mbeya, Tanzania. (Tel: (025) 250 2607;
E-mail: drcmbeya@out.ac.tz) Director:
Musana, E. Y., BEd Dar., MA Dar.

Morogoro Regional Centre, PO Box 2062,
Morogoro, Tanzania. (Tel: (023) 232 3303;
E-mail: drcmorogoro@out.ac.tz) Director:
Masomo, Said M. A., PhD Leuven, BSc(Agr)
MA

Mtwara Regional Centre, PO Box 322,
Mtwara, Tanzania. (Tel: (023) 233 3977;
E-mail: drcmtwara@out.ac.tz) Director:
Chilumba, J. J., MAEd Dar., BAEd

Mwanza Regional Centre, PO Box 2281,
Mwanza, Tanzania. (Tel: (028) 250 0516;
E-mail: drcmwanza@out.ac.tz) Director:
Ligembe, N. N., MA(Ling) Dar., BA(Ed)

Pemba Regional Centre, PO Box 227,
Chakechake, Tanzania. (Tel: (024) 245
2072; Fax: (024) 245 2223;
E-mail: drepemba@out.ac.tz) Director:
(vacant)

Regional Services, PO Box 23409, Dar es
Salaam, Tanzania. (Tel: (022) 266 8820;
E-mail: dvcrs@out.ac.tz) Deputy Vice
Chancellor (Regional Services): Bisanda,
Prof. E. T., BSc(Eng) Dar., MSc Cran., PhD
Bath

Ruvuma Regional Centre, PO Box 338,
Songea, Tanzania. (Tel: (025) 260 2636;
E-mail: drcruvuma@out.ac.tz) Director:
Chale, B., BA(Ed) Dar., MA Dar.

Shinyanga Regional Centre, PO Box 1203,
Shinyanga, Tanzania. (Tel: (028) 276 3290;
E-mail: drcshinyanga@out.ac.tz) Director:
Mwisomba, S. O., BEd Dar., MA(Ed) Dar.

Singida Regional Centre, PO Box 617,
Singida, Tanzania. (Tel: (026) 250 2451;
E-mail: drcsingida@out.ac.tz) Director:
Msindai, John P. A., MSc P.F.U., Moscow,
PhD Lond.

Tabora Regional Centre, PO Box 1204,
Tabora, Tanzania. (Tel: (026) 266 3227;
E-mail: drctabora@out.ac.tz) Director:
Mbwiliza, Prof. Joseph F., BA(Ed) Dar., MA
Dar., MPhil Col., PhD Col.

Tanga Regional Centre, PO Box 5467, Tanga,
Tanzania. (Tel: (027) 264 4348;
E-mail: drctanga@out.ac.tz) Director:
Msangi, M. A., BSc Dar., MSc Dar., MBA Dar.

Temeke Regional Centre, PO Box 42729, Dar
es Salaam, Tanzania;
E-mail: drcdsm@out.ac.tz Director: Mateka,
H. A., MSc(Env) Dar., BSc(Ed)

Zanzibar Regional Centre, PO Box 2599,
Zanzibar, Tanzania. (Tel: (024) 225 0106;
E-mail: gracekissassi@yahoo.com) Director:
Kissassi, G. R., BA(Ed) Dar., MA(Ed) Dar.

*[Information supplied by the institution as at 4 February
2008, and edited by the ACU]*

ST AUGUSTINE UNIVERSITY OF TANZANIA

Founded 1998

Postal Address: PO Box 307, Mwanza, Tanzania
Telephone: (028) 255 2725 **Fax:** (028) 255 0167 **E-mail:** sautmalimbe@yahoo.com
URL: http://www.saut.ac.tz

VICE-CHANCELLOR*—Kitima, Rev. Fr. Charles H., BA(Theology) JCL JD
DEPUTY VICE-CHANCELLOR FOR ADMINISTRATION AND FINANCE‡—Kachema, Rev. Dr. Herman, PhD(Th)

SOKOINE UNIVERSITY OF AGRICULTURE

Founded 1984

Member of the Association of Commonwealth Universities

Postal Address: PO Box 3000, Chuo Kikuu, Morogoro, Tanzania
Telephone: (232) 604523 **Fax:** (232) 604651 **E-mail:** sua@suanet.ac.tz
URL: http://www.suanet.ac.tz

VICE-CHANCELLOR*—Monela, Prof. G. C., BSc(For) *Sokoine Ag.*, MSc(For) *Sokoine Ag.*, MF *N.Arizona*, PhD *Agric.Coll.Norway*
DEPUTY VICE-CHANCELLOR—Monela, Prof. G. C., BSc(For) *Sokoine Ag.*, MSc(For) *Sokoine Ag.*, MF *N.Arizona*, PhD *Agric.Coll.Norway*
ACTING REGISTRAR‡—Mwageni, E. A., BA(Ed) *Dar.*, MA *Dar.*, PhD *Exe.*
UNIVERSITY BURSAR—Raphael, P., BCom *Dar.*
PRINCIPAL ADMINISTRATIVE OFFICER (PERSONNEL)—Iteba, C. W. A.
CHIEF PLANNING OFFICER—Massawe, R. L., BA(Econ) *Dar.*, MA(Econ) *Nair.*
CHIEF INTERNAL AUDITOR—Mshana, J. J.
CHIEF SUPPLIES OFFICER—Zumo, M. Z.
PRINCIPAL ADMISSIONS OFFICER—Mhagama, G. H. A., MA *GGS Indra.*
DEAN OF STUDENTS—Bisheko, J., BA(Ed) *Dar.*, MA(Ed) *Dar.*

GENERAL INFORMATION

History. The university, formerly the Faculty of Agriculture, Forestry and Veterinary Sciences of the University of Dar es Salaam, was established by act of parliament in 1984.

It is located in the Morogoro region, about 200km from Dar es Salaam.

Admission to first degree courses. Certificate of Secondary Education Examination (CSEE) or East African Certificate of Education ordinary level with passes in five subjects plus two principal level Advanced Certificate of Secondary Education (ACSE) passes. Mature students: equivalent diploma or certificate approved by the Senate with a minimum second class level.

First Degrees (see also Tanzanian Directory to Subjects of Study).
BSc(AgricEcon&Agribusiness),
BSc(AgricEd&Ext), BSc(AgricEng),
BSc(AgricGen), BSc(Agronomy),
BSc(AnimalScience), BSc(Biotechnology),
BSc(EnvironmentalScience),
BSc(FoodSci&Tech), BSc(Forestry),
BSc(HomeEcon&HumanNutrition), BSc(Hort),
BSc(WildlifeMan), BVM.
Length of course. Full-time:
BSc(AgricEcon&Agribusiness),
BSc(AgricEd&Ext), BSc(AgricGen),
BSc(Agronomy), BSc(AnimalScience),
BSc(Biotechnology),
BSc(EnvironmentalScience),
BSc(FoodSci&Tech), BSc(Forestry),
BSc(HomeEcon&HumanNutrition), BSc(Hort),
BSc(WildlifeMan): 3 years; BSc(AgricEng): 4 years; BVM: 5 years.

Higher Degrees (see also Tanzanian Directory to Subjects of Study).
Master's. MA, MBA, MNRSA, MPVM,
MSc(Agric), MSc(AgricEcon), MSc(AgricEng),
MSc(FoodSci), MSc(For),
MSc(SoilScience&LandMangt), MVM.
Length of course. Full-time: MA, MBA, MNRSA,
MSc(Agric), MSc(AgricEcon), MSc(AgricEng),
MSc(FoodSci), MSc(For),
MSc(SoilScience&LandMangt): 2 years; MPVM,
MVM: 3 years.
Doctoral. PhD.
Length of course. Full-time: PhD: 4 years.

Libraries. Volumes: 100,000. Periodicals subscribed to: 200.

Academic Awards (2005–2006). 71 awards ranging in value from Tsh10,000 to Tsh318,000.

Statistics. Staff (2005–2006): 1034 (284 academic, 750 non-academic). Students

(2005–2006): full-time 2654 (1908 men, 746 women); undergraduate 2260 (1626 men, 634 women); master's 337 (231 men, 106 women); doctoral 57 (51 men, 6 women).

FACULTIES/SCHOOLS

Agriculture
Tel: (232) 604649 Fax: (232) 604649
Dean: Mdoe, Prof. N. S. Y. S., BSc(Agric) *Dar.*, MSc *Guelph*, PhD *Reading*

Forestry and Nature Conservation
Tel: (232) 604648 Fax: (232) 604648
Dean: Gillah, P. R., BSc *Sokoine Ag.*, MSc *Wales*, PhD *Brun.*

Science
Tel: (232) 603404 Fax: (232) 603404
Dean: Muzanila, Y. C., BSc(Agric) *Dar.*, MSc *Reading*, PhD *Reading*

Veterinary Medicine
Tel: (232) 604647 Fax: (232) 604647
Dean: Mgasa, M. N., BVM *Nair.*, MVM *Sokoine Ag.*, PhD *R.Vet.& Agric.*, *Denmark*

ACADEMIC UNITS

Agricultural Economics and Agribusiness
Tel: (232) 603415 Fax: (232) 604691, 603080
E-mail: mbiha@suanet.ac.tz
Ashimogo, G. C., BSc(Agric) *Sokoine Ag.*, MSc *Nair.*, PhD *Humboldt* Sr. Lectr.
Kashuliza, A. K., BSc(Agric) *Dar.*, MSc *Guelph*, PhD *Lond.* Sr. Lectr.
Mbiha, R. E., BSc(Agric) *Wis.*, MSc *Wales*, PhD *Lond.* Sr. Lectr.
Mdoe, N. S. Y. S., BSc(Agric) *Dar.*, MSc *Guelph*, PhD *Reading* Prof.
Mlambiti, M. E., BSc(Agric) *E.Af.*, MSc *W.Virginia*, PhD *Dar.* Prof.
Senkondo, E. M., BSc(Agric) *Sokoine Ag.*, MSc *Nair.*, MSc(NRM) *Norway Ag.*, PhD *Wageningen* Assoc. Prof.; Head*
Temu, A. A., BSc *Dar.*, MSc *Guelph*, PhD *Ill.* Sr. Lectr.
Temu, A. E., BSc(Agric) *Dar.*, MSc *Reading*, PhD *Lond.* Assoc. Prof.
Turuka, F. M., BSc(Agric) *Sokoine Ag.*, MSc *Reading*, PhD *Giessen* Sr. Lectr.
Other Staff: 2 Lectrs.; 2 Asst. Lectrs.; 1 Sr. Res. Fellow

Agricultural Education and Extension
Tel: (232) 604795 Fax: (232) 603718
E-mail: daee@suanet.ac.tz
Magayane, F. T., BSc(Agric) *Dar.*, MSc *Ill.*, MSc *Ill.*, PhD *Ill.* Sr. Lectr.
Mattee, A. Z., BA(Agric) *Dar.*, MSc *Wis.*, PhD *Wis.* Assoc. Prof.

Mlozi, M. R. S., MSc(Agric) *W.Virginia*, PhD *Br.Col.* Assoc. Prof.
Mvena, Z. S. K., BSc(Agric) *Dar.*, MSc *Missouri*, PhD *Missouri* Assoc. Prof.; Head*
Mwaseba, D., BSc(Agric) *Sokoine Ag.*, MPhil *O.Awolowo* Sr. Lectr.
Rutatora, D. F., BSc(Agric) *Dar.*, MSc *Guelph*, PhD *Tor.* Prof.
Other Staff: 3 Lectrs.; 4 Asst. Lectrs.

Agricultural Engineering and Land Planning
Tel: (232) 604216 Fax: (232) 603718
Dihenga, Prof. H. O., BSc(Agric) *Dar.*, MSc *Cran.*, PhD *Mich.State* Assoc. Prof.
Hatibu, N., BSc *Cran.IT*, PhD *Newcastle(UK)* Assoc. Prof.
Kihupi, N. I., BSc(Agric) *Dar.*, MSc *Cran.IT*, PhD Assoc. Prof.; Head*
Lazaro, E. L., BSc *Dar.*, MSc *Cran.*, PhD *Newcastle(UK)* Sr. Lectr.
Mahoo, H., BSc *Dar.*, MSc *S'ton.*, PhD *Sokoine Ag.* Assoc. Prof.
Makungu, P. S. J., BSc(Eng) *Dar.*, MSc *Melb.*, PhD *Newcastle(UK)* Assoc. Prof.
Mganilwa, Z. M., BSc *Dar.*, MSc *Miyazaki*, PhD *Kagoshima* Sr. Lectr.
Mpanduji, S. M., BSc *Dar.*, MSc *Newcastle(UK)*, PhD *T.U.Munich* Sr. Lectr.
Mulengera, M. K., BSc *Dar.*, MSc *Newcastle(UK)*, PhD *Newcastle(UK)* Sr. Lectr.
Silayo, V. C. K., BSc *Dar.*, MSc *Reading*, PhD *Newcastle(UK)* Assoc. Prof.
Tarimo, A. K. P. R., BSc *Dar.*, MSc *S'ton.*, PhD *Newcastle(UK)* Assoc. Prof.
Tumbo, S. D., BSc *Sokoine Ag.*, MSc *Dar.*, PhD *Penn.State* Sr. Lectr.
Other Staff: 2 Lectrs.; 1 Asst. Lectr.

Animal Science and Production
Tel: (232) 604617 Fax: (232) 604562
E-mail: dasp@suanet.ac.tz
Aboud, A. A. O., BSc(Agric) *Dar.*, MSc(Agric) *Sokoine Ag.*, PhD *Reading* Sr. Lectr.
Katule, A. M., BSc(Agric) *Dar.*, MSc *Dar.*, PhD *Sokoine Ag.* Assoc. Prof.
Kifaro, G. C., BSc(Agric) *Dar.*, MSc(Agric) *Sokoine Ag.*, PhD *Sokoine Ag.* Assoc. Prof.
Kimambo, A. E., BSc(Agric) *Dar.*, MSc *Adel.*, PhD *Aberd.* Prof.
Kurwijila, R. L. N., BSc(Agric) *Dar.*, MSc *Nair.*, PhD *E.T.H.Zürich* Prof.
Laswai, G. H., BSc(Agric) *Dar.*, MSc(Agric) *Sokoine Ag.*, PhD *Reading* Assoc. Prof.
Lekule, F. P. M., BSc(Agric) *Dar.*, MSc *Sokoine Ag.*, PhD *Sokoine Ag.* Assoc. Prof.; Head*
Mbaga, S. H., BSc(Agric) *Sokoine Ag.*, MSc(Agric) *Sokoine Ag.*, PhD *Edin.* Sr. Lectr.
Mnembuka, B. V., BSc(Agric) *Sokoine Ag.*, MSc(Agric) *Sokoine Ag.*, PhD *Dar.* Sr. Lectr.
Mtenga, L. A., BSc(Agric) *Dar.*, MSc *Reading*, PhD *Reading* Prof.

Mtengeti, E. J., BSc(Agric) Sokoine Ag.,
MSc(Agric) Sokoine Ag., PhD Wales   Sr. Lectr.
Muhikambele, V. R. M., BSc(Agric) Sokoine Ag.,
MSc(Agric) Reading, PhD Reading   Assoc.
Prof.
Mutayoba, S. K., BSc(Agric) Dar., MSc(Agric)
Dar., PhD Aberd.   Assoc. Prof.
Ndemanisho, E., BSc W.Virginia, MSc Wis., PhD
Sokoine Ag.   Sr. Lectr.
Ryoba, R., MSc Reading, PhD Sokoine Ag.   Sr.
Lectr.
Sarwatt, S. V., BSc N.Carolina, MSc Colorado, PhD
Sokoine Ag.   Assoc. Prof.
Shem, M. N., BSc(Agric) Dar., MSc Guelph, PhD
Aberd.   Prof.
Urio, N. A., BSc(Agric) Dar., MSc(Agric) Dar.,
PhD Dar.   Assoc. Prof.
Other Staff: 3 Lectrs.; 1 Asst. Lectr.

Biological Sciences

Muzanila, Y. C., BSc(Agric) Dar., MSc Reading,
PhD Reading   Sr. Lectr.
Mwang'ingo, Patrick, BSc(For) Sokoine Ag., MSc
Sokoine Ag., PhD Wales   Lectr.; Head*
Other Staff: 1 Lectr.; 2 Asst. Lectrs.

Biometry and Mathematics

Karugila, G. K., BSc(Math) Dar., MSc(Math)
Dar., PhD Antwerp   Lectr.; Head*
Other Staff: 3 Asst. Lectrs.

Crop Science and Production

Tel: (232) 603681 Fax: (232) 603718
Lyimo, H. F., BSc Sokoine Ag., MPhil
Newcastle(UK)   Sr. Lectr.
Mabagala, R. B., BSc(Agric) Dar., MSc Mich.,
PhD Mich.   Prof.
Maerere, A. P., BSc(Agric) Sokoine Ag., MSc
Versailles, PhD Nancy I   Sr. Lectr.; Head*
Misangu, R. N., BSc(Agric) Dar., MSc Dar., PhD
Sokoine Ag.   Assoc. Prof.
Nchimbi-Msolla, S., BSc(Agric) Dar., MSc Wis.,
PhD Wis.   Assoc. Prof.
Reuben, S. O. W. M., BSc(Agric) Dar., MSc
Guelph, PhD Wales   Assoc. Prof.
Rweyemamu, C. L., BSc(Agric) Dar., MSc Alta.,
PhD Mich.   Sr. Lectr.
Sibuga, K. P., BSc(Agric) Dar., MSc Guelph, PhD
Nair.   Prof.
Tarimo, A. J. P., BSc(Agric) Dar., MSc Br.Col.,
PhD Qld.   Assoc. Prof.
Other Staff: 6 Lectrs.; 1 Sr. Res. Fellow

Food Science and Technology

Tel: (232) 604402 Fax: (232) 604402
E-mail: foodcil@suanet.ac.tz
Chove, B. E., BSc Dar., MSc Reading, PhD Reading
Assoc. Prof.
Gidamis, A. B., BSc(Agric) Sokoine Ag., MSc
Reading, PhD Kyoto   Prof.
Kinabo, J. L. D., BSc(Agric) Dar., MSc Leeds,
PhD Glas.   Assoc. Prof.
Laswai, H. S., BSc(Agric) Dar., MSc Reading, PhD
Reading   Assoc. Prof.
Lyimo, M. E., BSc Dar., MSc Reading, PhD Reading
Assoc. Prof.
Maeda, E. E., BSc(Agric) Dar., MSc Dar., PhD
Utah   Assoc. Prof.
Mnkeni, A. P., BSc Dar., MSc McG., PhD Sokoine
Ag.   Sr. Lectr.
Mosha, T. C. E., BSc(HomeEcon&HumanNutr)
Sokoine Ag., MSc Tuskegee, PhD Mich.State   Sr.
Lectr.
Msuya, J. M., BSc Dar., MSc Otago, PhD Kiel   Sr.
Lectr.
Mugula, J. K., BSc(Agric) Dar., MSc Reading,
PhD   Assoc. Prof.
Muzanila, Y. C., BSc(Agric) Dar., MSc Reading,
PhD Reading   Sr. Lectr.
Nyaruhucha, C. N.,
BSc(HomeEcon&HumanNutr) Sokoine Ag.,
MSc Lond., PhD Kyoto   Assoc. Prof.
Shayo, N. B., BSc(Agric) Dar., MSc Sask., PhD
Reading   Assoc. Prof.
Tiisekwa, B. P. M., BSc Dar., MSc Reading, PhD
Ghent   Assoc. Prof.; Head*
Other Staff: 6 Lectrs.; 2 Asst. Lectrs.

Forest Biology

Tel: (232) 604944 Fax: (232) 604648
E-mail: dfb@suanet.ac.tz
Chamshama, S. A. O., BSc Dar., MSc(For) Dar.,
PhD Dar.   Prof.
Lulandala, L. L. L., BSc Dar., MSc(For) Dar.,
PhD Sokoine Ag.   Prof.; Acting Head*
Madoffe, S. S., BSc(For) Dar., MSc Sokoine Ag.,
PhD Agric.Coll.Norway, DSc Agric.Coll.Norway,
MSc(For)   Assoc. Prof.
Maliondo, S. M. S., BSc(For) Dar., MSc Wales,
PhD New Br.   Prof.
Munishi, P. K. T., BSc Sokoine Ag., MSc Duke,
PhD N.Carolina   Assoc. Prof.; Head*
Temu, R. P. C., BSc(For) Sokoine Ag., PhD
Uppsala   Assoc. Prof.

Forest Economics

Tel: (232) 604865 Fax: (232) 604648, 603718
E-mail: forest@suanet.ac.tz
Kessy, J. F., BSc Sokoine Ag., MSc
Agric.Coll.Norway, PhD Wageningen   Sr. Lectr.
Monela, G. C., BSc(For) Sokoine Ag., MSc(For)
Sokoine Ag., MF N.Arizona, PhD Agric.Coll.Norway
Prof.
Ngaga, Y. M., BSc(For) Sokoine Ag., MSc(For)
Sokoine Ag., PhD Agric.Coll.Norway   Sr. Lectr.;
Head*
O'Kting'ati, A., BSc(For) Dar., MSc(For) Dar.,
MSc Mich., PhD Sokoine Ag.   Prof.
Other Staff: 3 Asst. Lectrs.

Forest Engineering

Tel: (232) 604387 Fax: (232) 604648
E-mail: fengine@suanet.ac.tz
Abeli, W. S., BSc(For) Dar., MSc(For) Dar., PhD
Sokoine Ag.   Prof.
Migunga, G. A., BSc(For) Dar., MSc(For) Dar.,
PhD Sokoine Ag.   Assoc. Prof.; Head*
Shemwetta, D. T. K., BSc(For) Sokoine Ag., MSc
New Br., PhD Oregon   Assoc. Prof.
Other Staff: 1 Lectr.; 1 Asst. Lectr.

Forest Mensuration and Management

Tel: (232) 604555 Fax: (232) 604648, 603718
E-mail: formens@suanet.ac.tz
Kajembe, G. C., BSc(For) Sokoine Ag., MSc
Agric.Coll.Norway, PhD Wageningen   Prof.;
Head*
Luoga, E. J., BSc(For) Sokoine Ag., MSc Norway
Ag., PhD Witw.   Assoc. Prof.
Malimbwi, R. E., BSc(For) Dar., MSc(For) Dar.,
PhD Aberd.   Prof.
Other Staff: 2 Lectrs.; 2 Asst. Lectrs.

Physical Sciences

Kiangi, P. M. R., BSc Nair., MSc Nair., PhD Nair.
Sr. Lectr.
Mwalilino, J. K., BSc(Agric) Sokoine Ag., MSc
Sokoine Ag., PhD Zhejiang   Head*
Other Staff: 1 Lectr.; 1 Asst. Lectr.

Social Sciences

Mafu, S. T. A., BEd Dar., MSc Aston, PhD Aston
Sr. Lectr.; Head*
Neke, S. M., BA(Ed) Dar., MA Wales, MSc
V.U.Brussels, PhD Ghent   Sr. Lectr.
Other Staff: 1 Lectr.

Soil Science

Tel: (232) 603999 Fax: (232) 603259
E-mail: soil@suanet.ac.tz
Kilasara, M., BSc(Agric) Dar., MSc Reading, PhD
Paris VI   Sr. Lectr.
Mrema, J. P., BSc(Agric) Dar., MSc Reading, PhD
Sokoine Ag.   Sr. Lectr.
Msaky, J. J. T., BSc(Agric) Dar., MSc Calif., PhD
Paris VII   Sr. Lectr.; Head*
Msanya, B. M., BSc(Agric) Dar., MSc Ghent, PhD
Ghent   Prof.
Msumali, G. P., BSc(Agric) Dar., MSc Manit.,
PhD Reading   Assoc. Prof.
Mtakwa, P. W., BSc(Agric) Dar., MSc Sokoine
Ag., PhD Aberd.   Sr. Lectr.
Rwehumbiza, F. B. R., BSc(Agric) Dar., MSc
Sokoine Ag., PhD Aberd.   Assoc. Prof.

Semoka, J. M. R., BSc(Agric) Dar., MSc Calif.,
PhD Calif.   Prof.
Semu, E., BSc(Agric) Dar., MSc Guelph, MSc
Mich., PhD Dar.   Assoc. Prof.
Shayo-Ngowi, A. J., BSc Uppsala, MSc Wash.State,
PhD Newcastle(UK)   Sr. Lectr.
Other Staff: 1 Lectr.; 1 Asst. Lectr.

Wildlife Management

Maganga, S. L. W., BSc(For) Dar., MSc Idaho,
PhD Idaho   Assoc. Prof.; Head*
Songorwa, A., BSc Dar., MSc Guelph, PhD NZ
Sr. Lectr.
Other Staff: 4 Lectrs.; 1 Asst. Lectr.

Wood Utilization

Tel: (232) 603694 Fax: (232) 604648
E-mail: forprod@suanet.ac.tz
Gillah, P. R., BSc Sokoine Ag., MSc Wales, PhD
Brun.   Assoc. Prof.
Hamza, K. F. S., BSc(For) Dar., PhD Freib., MSc
Sokoine Ag.   Prof.
Iddi, S., MSc(For) Dar., PhD Wales   Assoc.
Prof. (on leave)
Ishengoma, R. C., BSc(For) Dar., MSc(For) Dar.,
DSc Agric.Coll.Norway   Prof.
Makonda, F. B. S., BSc(For) Sokoine Ag., MSc
Sokoine Ag., PhD Wales   Sr. Lectr.; Head*
Other Staff: 2 Lectrs.

VETERINARY MEDICINE

Tel: (232) 604647 Fax: (232) 604647

Veterinary Anatomy

Tel: (232) 604979 Fax: (232) 604647
E-mail: anatomy@suanet.ac.tz
Assey, R. J., BVSc Dar., MVM Sokoine Ag., PhD
R.Vet.& Agric., Denmark   Prof.
Mbassa, G. K., BVM Nair., MVM Sokoine Ag.,
PhD Copenhagen Agric.   Prof.; Head*
Other Staff: 2 Asst. Lectrs.

Veterinary Medicine and Public Health

Tel: (232) 604542 Fax: (232) 604647
E-mail: vetmed@suanet.ac.tz
Kambarage, D. M., BVSc Dar., MVM Sokoine Ag.,
PhD Brist.   Prof.
Kazwala, R. R., BVSc Sokoine Ag., MVM N.U.I.,
PhD Edin.   Prof.
Kimera, S. I., BVM Sokoine Ag., MSc Reading, PhD
Reading   Sr. Lectr.
Kusiluka, L. J. M., BVM Sokoine Ag., MPhil Edin.,
PhD R.Vet.& Agric., Denmark   Assoc. Prof.;
Head*
Mellau, L. S. B., BVM Sokoine Ag., MVM Sokoine
Ag., PhD R.Vet.& Agric., Denmark   Sr. Lectr.
Mlangwa, J. E. D., BVM Nair., MSc Lond., PhD
Copenhagen Agric.   Assoc. Prof.
Mtambo, M. M. A., PhD Glas., BVM   Prof.
Muhairwa, A. P., BVM Sokoine Ag., PhD R.Vet.&
Agric., Denmark   Sr. Lectr.
Other Staff: 3 Lectrs.; 3 Asst. Lectrs.

Veterinary Microbiology and Parasitology

Fax: (232) 604647 E-mail: vetbio@suanet.ac.tz
Gwakisa, P. S., MSc Moscow, PhD Moscow   Prof.
Kassuku, A. A., BVM Nair., MSc Edin., PhD
Copenhagen Agric.   Prof.
Kilonzo, B. S., MSc Lond., PhD Dar.   Prof.
Kimbita, E. N., BVSc Sokoine Ag., MVSc Liv., PhD
Sokoine Ag., BVM   Assoc. Prof.
Machang'u, R. S., MSc(Vet) Cluj, DVM Giessen,
PhD Guelph   Prof.
Maeda-Machang'u, A., BVM Nair., PhD Edin.
Prof.
Makundi, R. H., BSc Dar., MSc Newcastle(UK),
PhD Newcastle(UK)   Res. Assoc. Prof.
Silayo, R. S., BVM Nair., MSc Edin., PhD Edin.
Prof.
Wambura, P. N., BVM Sokoine Ag., MVM Sokoine
Ag., PhD Qld.   Sr. Lectr.; Head*
Other Staff: 1 Lectr.

Veterinary Pathology

Tel: (232) 604980 Fax: (232) 604647
    E-mail: vetpath@suanet.ac.tz
Maselle, R. M., DPVM *Copenhagen Agric.*, DVM
    Cluj-Napoca Agric., MVM *Sokoine Ag.*, PhD
    Copenhagen Agric.   Prof.
Matovelo, J. A., BVSc *Dar.*, DSc *Oslo*   Prof.
Mwamengele, G. L., BVSc *Dar.*, MVM *Sokoine
    Ag.*, PhD *R.Vet.& Agric., Denmark*   Assoc.
    Prof.; Head*
Semuguruka, W. D., BVMS *Glas.*, MSc *Ill.*, PhD
    Copenhagen Agric.   Prof.
Other Staff: 1 Lectr.

Veterinary Physiology, Biochemistry, Pharmacology and Toxicology

Tel: (232) 604978 Fax: (232) 604647
    E-mail: vet-phys@suanet.ac.tz
Balthazary, T. S., BVSc *Dar.*, MVM *Sokoine Ag.*,
    DrMedVet *Tier.H., Hannover*   Assoc. Prof.;
    Head*
Kinabo, L. D. B., BVSc *Dar.*, MVM *Sokoine Ag.*,
    PhD *Glas.*   Prof.
Mlay, P. S., BVM *Sokoine Ag.*, MVM *Trinity(Dub.)*,
    PhD *Sokoine Ag.*   Assoc. Prof.
Mosha, R. D., BVM *Nair.*, MVM *Sokoine Ag.*, PhD
    Copenhagen Agric.   Prof.
Mutayoba, B. M., BVSc *Dar.*, MSc *Nair.*, PhD
    Glas.   Prof.
Ngomuo, A. J., BVM *Nair.*, MVM *Glas.*, PhD *Sur.*
    Assoc. Prof.
Pereka, A. E., BVSc *Dar.*, MVM *N.U.I.*, PhD
    Copenhagen Agric.   Prof.
Phiri, E. C. J. H., BVM *Sokoine Ag.*, MVM *Sokoine
    Ag.*, PhD *R.Vet.& Agric., Denmark*   Assoc. Prof.
Other Staff: 1 Lectr.

Veterinary Surgery and Theriogenology

Tel: (232) 603177 Fax: (232) 604647
    E-mail: surgery@suanet.ac.tz
Batamuzi, E. K., BVSc *Dar.*, MVM *Sokoine Ag.*,
    PhD *Copenhagen Agric.*   Prof.; Head*
Bittegeko, S. B. P., BVSc *Sokoine Ag.*, MVM
    Sokoine Ag., PhD *Copenhagen Agric.*   Prof.
Kanuya, N. L., BVM *Sokoine Ag.*, MVM *Sokoine
    Ag.*, PhD *Copenhagen Agric.*   Assoc. Prof.
Kessy, B. M., BVM *Nair.*, PhD *Lond.*   Prof.
Mgasa, M. N., BVM *Nair.*, MVM *Sokoine Ag.*,
    PhD *Copenhagen Agric.*   Prof.
Mgongo, F. O. K., BVM *Nair.*, MSc *Nair.*,
    DrMedVet *Munich*   Prof.
Mpanduji, D. G., BVM *Sokoine Ag.*, MVM *Sokoine
    Ag.*   Sr. Lectr.
Nkya, R., MSc *Moscow*, PhD *Moscow*   Assoc.
    Prof.
Other Staff: 1 Asst. Lectr.

SPECIAL CENTRES, ETC

Computer Centre (CC)

Tel: (232) 604838 Fax: (232) 604562
    E-mail: ccentre@suanet.ac.tz
Kazwala, R. R., BVSc *Sokoine Ag.*, MVM *N.U.I.*,
    PhD *Edin.*   Prof.; Dir.*
Mganilwa, Z. M., BSc *Dar.*, MSc *Miyazaki*, PhD
    Kagoshima   Sr. Lectr.; Assoc. Dir.
Shemwetta, D. T. K., BSc(For) *Sokoine Ag.*, MSc
    New Br., PhD *Oregon*   Assoc. Prof.
Other Staff: 1 Asst. Lectr.

Continuing Education, Institute of (ICE)

Tel: (232) 604559 Fax: (232) 603718
    E-mail: ice@suanet.ac.tz
Isinika, A. C., BSc(Agric) *Dar.*, MSc *Kentucky*,
    PhD *Kentucky*   Assoc. Prof.
Kimbi, G. G., BSc(Agric) *Sokoine Ag.*, MSc *Sokoine
    Ag.*, PhD *Cornell*   Assoc. Prof.; Dir.*
Lyimo-Macha, J. G., BSc(Agric) *Sokoine Ag.*, MSc
    Penn.State, PhD *Penn.State*   Sr. Lectr.; Assoc.
    Dir.
Wambura, R. M., BSc(Agric) *Dar.*, MSc(Agric)
    Sokoine Ag., PhD *N.U.I.*   Assoc. Prof.

Development Studies Institute (DSI)

Tel: (232) 604645
Kapinga, D. S., BA(Ed) *Dar.*, MA *Dar.*, PhD *E.Af.*
    Assoc. Prof.
Kihiyo, V. B. M. S., BSc(For) *Dar.*, PhD *Sokoine
    Ag.*, MSc(For)   Assoc. Prof.
Mwageni, E. A., BA(Ed) *Dar.*, MA *Dar.*, PhD *Exe.*
    Sr. Lectr.; Dir.*
Other Staff: 3 Lectrs.; 4 Asst. Lectrs.

Sustainable Rural Development, Centre for (SCSRD)

Tel: (232) 604279
Mhando, D. G., BSc *Dar.*, MA *Dar.*   Asst. Res.
    Fellow; Head, Soc. Economy
Mtengeti, E. J., BSc(Agric) *Sokoine Ag.*,
    MSc(Agric) *Sokoine Ag.*, PhD *Wales*   Sr. Lectr.;
    Head, Environmental Conservation
Nindi, S. J., BA *Dar.*, MSc *Sokoine Ag.*, PhD *Kyoto*
    Asst. Res. Fellow; Head, Resource
    Management
Rutatora, D. F., BSc(Agric) *Dar.*, MSc *Guelph*,
    PhD *Tor.*   Prof.; Dir.*
Other Staff: 5 Asst. Res. Fellows

CONTACT OFFICERS

Academic affairs. Deputy Vice-Chancellor:
    Monela, Prof. G. C., BSc(For) *Sokoine Ag.*,
    MSc(For) *Sokoine Ag.*, MF *N.Arizona*, PhD
    Agric.Coll.Norway (E-mail: dvc@suanet.ac.tz)
Accommodation. Dean of Students: Bisheko,
    J., BA(Ed) *Dar.*, MA(Ed) *Dar.*
    (E-mail: registrar@suanet.ac.tz)
Admissions (first degree). Principal
    Admissions Officer: Mhagama, G. H. A.,
    MA *GGS Indra.*
    (E-mail: gmhagama92@yahoo.com)
Admissions (higher degree). Director,
    Research and Postgraduate Studies:
    Matovelo, Prof. J. A., BVSc *Dar.*, DSc *Oslo*
    (E-mail: drpgs@suanet.ac.tz)
Adult/continuing education. Director,
    Institute of Continuing Education: Kimbi,
    G. G., BSc(Agric) *Sokoine Ag.*, MSc *Sokoine Ag.*,
    PhD *Cornell* (E-mail: icc@suanet.ac.tz)
Alumni. President, Alumni: Kessy, Prof. B. M.,
    BVM *Nair.*, PhD *Lond.*
    (E-mail: kessy@suanet.ac.tz)
Computing services. Director, Computer
    Centre: Kazwala, Prof. R. R., BVSc *Sokoine
    Ag.*, MVM *N.U.I.*, PhD *Edin.*
    (E-mail: dircc@suanet.ac.tz)
Consultancy services. Co-ordinator, Forestry
    Consultancy (FORCONSULT): Kessy, J. F.,
    BSc *Sokoine Ag.*, MSc *Agric.Coll.Norway*, PhD
    Wageningen (E-mail: jfkessy@yahoo.com)

Consultancy services. Co-ordinator, Bureau
    for Agricultural Consultancy and
    Agricultural Services (BACAS): Semu, E.,
    BSc(Agric) *Dar.*, MSc *Guelph*, MSc *Mich.*, PhD
    Dar. (E-mail: bacas@suanet.ac.tz)
Estates and buildings/works and services.
    Estates Manager: Komba, D. M. T., BSc *Dar.*,
    MSc *Bath* (E-mail: registrar@suanet.ac.tz)
Examinations. Senior Administrative Officer
    (Examinations): Mtapa, J. K., BA *Dar.*
    (E-mail: dvc@suanet.ac.tz)
Finance. University Bursar: Raphael, P., BCom
    Dar. (E-mail: basar@suanet.ac.tz)
General enquiries. Acting Registrar: Mwageni,
    E. A., BA(Ed) *Dar.*, MA *Dar.*, PhD *Exe.*
    (E-mail: registrar@suanet.ac.tz)
Health services. Acting Resident Medical
    Officer: Kapilima, E. H. E.
Library (chief librarian). Director, Sokoine
    National Agricultural Library: Dulle, F. W.,
    BSc *Sokoine Ag.*, MLIS *Botswana*
    (E-mail: library@suanet.ac.tz)
Marketing. Principal Public Relations Officer:
    Msagati, K. A. (E-mail: pro@suanet.ac.tz)
Personnel/human resources. Principal
    Administrative Officer (Personnel): Iteba, C.
    W. A. (E-mail: registrar@suanet.ac.tz)
Public relations. Principal Public Relations
    Officer: Msagati, K. A.
    (E-mail: pro@suanet.ac.tz)
Research. Director, Research and Postgraduate
    Studies: Matovelo, Prof. J. A., BVSc *Dar.*,
    DSc *Oslo* (E-mail: drpgs@suanet.ac.tz)
Safety. Head, Security Department: Rashidi, A.
    (E-mail: registrar@suanet.ac.tz)
Sport and recreation. Senior Games Tutor and
    Head, Sports Department: Madaha, D. A.,
    BA(Ed) *Dar.* (E-mail: registrar@suanet.ac.tz)
Staff development and training.
    Administrative Officer (Staff development
    and training): Kyando-Gellejah, H.
    (E-mail: dvc@suanet.ac.tz)
Staff development and training. (Academic
    staff) Senior Administrative Officer,
    Recruitment and Academic Staff
    Development: Lwiza, W. I.
Strategic planning. Chief Planning Officer:
    Massawe, R. L., BA(Econ) *Dar.*, MA(Econ)
    Nair. (E-mail: plan@suanet.ac.tz)
Student union. President, Sokoine University
    of Agriculture Students' Organisation
    (SUASO) (E-mail: registrar@suanet.ac.tz)
Student welfare/counselling. Dean of
    Students: Bisheko, J., BA(Ed) *Dar.*, MA(Ed)
    Dar. (E-mail: registrar@suanet.ac.tz)

CAMPUS/COLLEGE HEADS

Mazumbai Forest Reserve. Manager: Kiparu,
    S. S., BSc(For) *Sokoine Ag.*, MSc(For) *Sokoine
    Ag.*
Olmotonyi Campus. (Tel: (272) 509348)
    Manager: Mrecha, M. S., BSc(For) *Sokoine
    Ag.*, MSc *Norway Ag.*
Solomon Mahlangu Campus. (Tel: (232)
    604614; Fax: (232) 260 3545) Director:
    Urio, N. A., BSc(Agric) *Dar.*, MSc(Agric)
    Dar., PhD *Dar.*

[Information supplied by the institution as at 6 June
2006, and edited by the ACU]

STATE UNIVERSITY OF ZANZIBAR

Founded 2001

Postal Address: PO Box 146, Zanzibar, Tanzania
Telephone: (024) 223 0724 **Fax:** (024) 223 3337 **E-mail:** takiluki@zanlink.com
URL: http://www.suza.ac.tz/

VICE-CHANCELLOR*—Mshimba, Prof. Ali S.
REGISTRAR‡—Kanduru, Abdullah I., BSc *Dar.*, MSc *Wat.*, MEd *Tor.*, MRD *Wat.*, PhD *Tor.*

TUMAINI UNIVERSITY

Founded 1997

Postal Address: PO Box 2200, Moshi, Tanzania
Telephone: (027) 275 2291 **Fax:** (027) 275 4381 **E-mail:** kcmcadmin@kcmc.ac.tz

VICE-CHANCELLOR*—Shao, Prof. John, MD *Dar.*, MSc *Brun.*

ZANZIBAR UNIVERSITY

Founded 1998

Member of the Association of Commonwealth Universities

Postal Address: PO Box 2440, Zanzibar, Tanzania
Telephone: (024) 223 2642 **Fax:** (024) 223 6388 **E-mail:** zanvarsity@yahoo.com
URL: http://www.zanvarsity.ac.tz

VICE-CHANCELLOR*—Roshash, Prof. Mustafa A. A., LLB *Khart.*, LLM *Khart.*, PhD *Bayero*
ACTING REGISTRAR‡—Omar, Ali A.

UGANDA

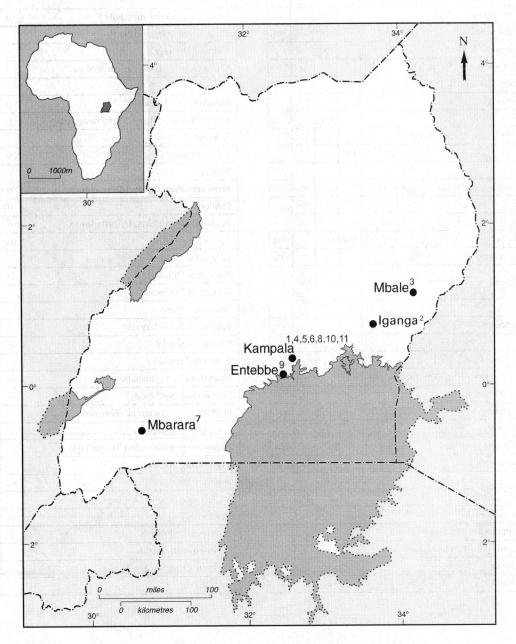

The places named are the seats of the university institutions numbered above

UGANDA: DIRECTORY TO SUBJECTS OF STUDY

The table below shows which subjects are available for study and/or research at the universities in Uganda. U = may be studied for first degree course; M = may be studied for master's degree course; D = research facilities to doctoral level; X = all three levels (UMD).

	Islamic, Uganda	Mbarara	Uganda Christian	Uganda Martyrs
Accountancy/Accounting	UM		U	U
Administration/Administrative Studies	UM		UM	UM
Advertising	U			UM
African Languages/Studies	UM		U	
Agricultural Extension and Education				U
Agriculture/Agricultural Science				U
Agronomy/Soil Science				U
Anatomical Science/Anatomy		X		
Animal Nutrition/Animal Physiology				U
Animal Science/Husbandry/Production				U
Applied Chemistry		UM		
Applied Physics		UM		
Aquaculture/Fisheries/Marine Science				U
Arabic	UM			
Architecture				U
Art, Fine			U	
Arts General			U	
Arts, Graphic			U	
Banking/Finance	UM	U	U	UM
Behavioural Sciences				UM
Biochemistry	U	X		
Bioethics				U
Biology	U	X		
Biomedical Sciences		U		
Biostatistics				M
Botany/Plant Science	UM	X		
Building/Built Environment/Construction				U
Business Administration	UM	U	U	UM
Business Computing	U		U	UM
Business Economics	U		U	UM
Business Information Systems	U		U	UM
Business/Commerce	U		U	UM
Chemistry	U	U		
Classics/Greek/Latin/Ancient History			U	
Communication Sciences			U	
Communication/Journalism/Media Studies	U		U	
Communications/Information Management	U		U	
Community Health		M	M	
Community Medicine		M	M	

	Islamic, Uganda	Mbarara	Uganda Christian	Uganda Martyrs
Community Studies			U	
Computer Science	U	U	U	UM
Corporate Governance				UM
Counselling			M	U
Creative Writing	U			U
Criminal Justice/Public Policy	U			
Crop Science/Production				U
Cultural Heritage				U
Curriculum and Assessment Studies		U	UM	UM
Design				U
Development Studies	U	X	U	UM
Drama/Theatre/Dance/Performing Arts	U			
E-Business				UM
E-Commerce	U		U	UM
Ecology	U	M		
Economic Planning and Development	U			UM
Economics	U		U	UM
Economics Agricultural/Agribusiness	U			U
Education	UM	UM	UM	UM
Education Adult				U
Education Distance	U			UM
Education Extension			UM	
Education Primary	U		U	U
Education Secondary			UM	
Education Special				U
Education Tertiary		UM		
Educational Administration	U	M		
Educational Psychology	U		UM	U
Engineering Agricultural/Fisheries				U
Engineering Computer		U		UM
Engineering Information Technology				U
Engineering Software				UM
English	U		UM	
English as a Second Language				U
Entomology	U	M		
Entrepreneurship	U	U	U	UM
Environmental Health				M
Environmental Science/Studies	U		U	UM
Epidemiology		U		

	Islamic, Uganda	Mbarara	Uganda Christian	Uganda Martyrs
Ethics	M		U	UM
Ethics, Law and Governance			U	X
Film/Photography/Television/Animation			U	
Food Science/Nutrition/Home Science/Dietetics	U			U
French/French Studies	U		U	
Genetics	U	M		
Geography	U		U	
Health Education			U	UM
Health Information				U
Health Sciences/Studies		U	UM	UM
Health/Hospital Administration			M	UM
Hebrew/Semitic Studies			U	
Heritage Studies	U			
History	UM		U	
Horticulture				U
Human Resource Development	UM		M	
Human Resource Economics			U	
Human Rights/Globalisation				UM
Indigenous Knowledge Systems				UM
Industrial Relations/Personnel/HRM	U			UM
Industrial and Organisation Psychology	U			
Information Science/Studies/Systems	U		U	UM
Information Technology	U	U	UM	UM
Insurance	U			U
International Business	U			
International Finance	U			M
International Marketing	U			M
International Relations/Studies	U			U
Internet Computing/Technologies			U	
Islamic/Middle Eastern Studies	X			
Kiswahili/Swahili	X		U	
Laboratory Science Technology		U		
Language Teaching/Learning	U		U	
Language and Communication	U			
Law Business/Commercial/Economic/Industrial	U		U	U
Law Civil	U			
Law Employment/Labour	U		U	U
Law Environmental	U		U	
Law Intellectual Property/Copyright	U		U	

	Islamic, Uganda	Mbarara	Uganda Christian	Uganda Martyrs
Law International/Comparative/Trade	U		U	
Law Legal Practice	U		U	
Law/Legal Studies	U		U	U
Library/Information Science	U			
Linguistics/Translation	U			
Literature, Comparative	U		M	
Management	U		U	U
Management Information Systems	U			
Marketing	UM		U	UM
Mathematics	U	X	U	U
Medical Ethics		U		
Medicine, Obstetrics and Gynaecology		UM		
Medicine, Paediatric		UM		
Medicine, Palliative		U		
Medicine/Surgery		UM		
Microbiology/Medical Microbiology		X		
Nursing/Midwifery		UM	U	
Occupational Health/Therapy		U		M
Operational Research/Operations Management				UM
Ophthalmology		UM		
Parasitology		U		
Pathology		U		
Peace/War Studies		M		UM
Pharmacology		U		
Pharmacy/Pharmaceutical Science		U		
Philosophy			U	
Physics	U	U		
Physiology	U	UM		
Planning/Landscape Studies	U			
Plant Pathology		U		
Politics/Political Science/Government	U		U	
Population Studies/Demography	U		U	
Product Design and Technology				UM
Project Management	U		UM	UM
Psychology	U	U	UM	
Psychology Clinical		UM		
Psychotherapy		M		
Public Administration	UD		U	X
Public Health/Population Health			M	M

	Islamic, Uganda	Mbarara	Uganda Christian	Uganda Martyrs
Public Relations	U		U	
Public Sector Management	UM			U
Radiography/Diagnostic Technology/MRI		U		
Religion/Theology			UM	U
Risk Management	UM			
Rural Extension				U
Rural Studies/Development	U	U	U	X
Sculpture			U	
Social Policy			UM	
Social Work/Studies	U		U	
Sociology	U		U	

	Islamic, Uganda	Mbarara	Uganda Christian	Uganda Martyrs
Statistics/Actuarial Science				U
Sustainable Development			U	UM
Sustainable Economies			U	
Taxation	UM		U	U
Teacher Training	UM	UM	UM	U
Visual Arts			U	
Wildlife Management		M		
Women's/Gender Studies				X
Youth and Community Development				M
Zoology	UM	UM		

BUGEMA UNIVERSITY

Founded 1948

Postal Address: PO Box 6529, Kampala, Uganda
Telephone: (312) 351400 **Fax:** (312) 351460 **E-mail:** registrar@bugemauniv.ac.ug
URL: http://www.bugemauniv.ac.ug

VICE-CHANCELLOR*—Manu, Patrick, MA PhD
ACADEMIC REGISTRAR‡—Cheslim, Paul, BA MA(Ed) MA(Eco)

BUSOGA UNIVERSITY

Postal Address: PO Box 154, Iganga, Uganda
Telephone: (043) 242502 **Fax:** (043) 242345
URL: http://www.busogauniversity.ac.ug/

VICE-CHANCELLOR*—Bakwesegha, Prof. Christopher, PhD
SERCRETARY/REGISTRAR‡—Muyobo, Nathan Ba. K.

ISLAMIC UNIVERSITY IN UGANDA

Founded 1988

Member of the Association of Commonwealth Universities

Postal Address: PO Box 2555, Kumi Road, Mbale, Uganda
Telephone: (035) 251 2100 **Fax:** (045) 443 3502 **E-mail:** info@iuiu.ac.ug
URL: http://www.iuiu.ac.ug

RECTOR*—Sengendo, Kawesa A., BSc Mak., MScEd Kansas, PhD Kansas
VICE-RECTOR (ACADEMIC AFFAIRS)—Mpezamihigo, Mouhamad, BSc Mak., MSc Mak., PhD Glas.
ACTING UNIVERSITY SECRETARY‡—Basalirwa, Asuman, LLB Mak.
ACADEMIC REGISTRAR—Suwed, Saleh A., BA Mak., MEd Mak.
UNIVERSITY BURSAR—Kakande, Siraje, BCom Mak., MBA Mak.
ACTING LIBRARIAN—Ssesanga, Idris, BLIS Mak., MLIS Mak.
UNIVERSITY CO-ORDINATOR (ACCOMMODATION)—Samaali, Abbas, BA Mak., MEd Mak.
UNIVERSITY ENGINEER—Semujju Dauda, Mugejjera, BSc(Eng) Mak.
ACTING UNIVERSITY MEDICAL OFFICER—Nakazibwe, Sauba, MB ChB Mbarara

GENERAL INFORMATION

History. The university was opened in 1988. It is located in Mbale Town, Mbale District, Eastern Uganda.

Admission to first degree courses. At least 5 O level passes and 2 principal passes at A level. International students admitted in accordance with Uganda National Council of Higher Education's equivalence system.

First Degrees (see also Ugandan Directory to Subjects of Study). BA, BAEcon, BAEd, BAIsl/ Arb, BASoc&Da'wah, BBS, BDS, BFSN, BHRM, BHSM, BIT, BLIS, BPA, BPLM, BSAS, BSc, BScCompSci, BScEd, BScEnvSci, BScMassCom, BScPEH, BSS, BStat, BSWSA, LLB.
  Length of course. Full-time: BA, BAEcon, BAEd, BAIsl/Arb, BASoc&Da'wah, BBS, BDS, BFSN, BHRM, BHSM, BIT, BLIS, BPA, BPLM, BSAS, BSc, BScCompSci, BScEd, BScEnvSci, BScMassCom, BScPEH, BSS, BStat, BSWSA: 3 years; LLB: 4 years. Part-time: BHSM: 2 years; BBS, BDS, BHRM, BIT, BPA, BSAS, BScMassCom, BScPEH, BSWSA: 3 years; LLB: 4 years. By distance learning: BEd: 3 years.

Higher Degrees (see also Ugandan Directory to Subjects of Study).

  Master's. MAARB, MAHistory, MAIsl, MARPCR, MASharia, MBA, MEdMgmt&Admn, MScBotany, MScEnvSci, MScZoology.
  Admission. Applicants for admission to master's degrees must normally hold an appropriate first class or good honours first degree or equivalent qualifications.
  Length of course. Full-time: MAARB, MAIsl, MASharia: 2 years. Part-time: MAHistory, MARPCR, MBA, MEdMgmt&Admn, MScBotany, MScEnvSci, MScZoology: 2 years.
  Doctoral. PhD.
  Admission. PhD: appropriate master's degree.
  Length of course. Full-time: PhD: 3 years. Part-time: PhD: 5 years.

Language of Instruction. English, except for Arabic studies and Islamic studies (Arabic) and French and Kiswahili (the relevant language).

Libraries. Volumes: 31,500. Periodicals subscribed to: 50.

Academic Awards (2006–2007). 52 awards ranging in value from to Ush155,000,000.

Income (2007–2008). Total, Ush10,356,529,010.

Statistics. Staff (2007–2008): 299 (133 academic, 166 non-academic). Students (2007–2008): full-time 2029 (1153 men, 876 women); part-time 779 (564 men, 215 women); international 559 (393 men, 166 women); distance education/external 234 (151 men, 83 women); undergraduate 2861 (1735 men, 1126 women); master's 141 (110 men, 31 women).

FACULTIES/SCHOOLS

Arts and Social Sciences
E-mail: fass@iuiu.ac.ug
Dean: Serwanga, Jamil, BAEd Islamic Uganda, MA Mak., PhD Islamic Uganda
Administrative Assistant: Semakula, Hussein, BA Mak.

Education
E-mail: educ@iuiu.ac.ug
Dean: Akbar, Halima W., BAEd Islamic Uganda, MEd Bayero, PhD Birm.
Administrative Assistant: Ozombo, Abdallah, BAEd Islamic Uganda

Islamic Studies and Arabic Language
E-mail: fisal@iuiu.ac.ug
Dean: Bowa, Hussein M., BA Medina, MA Medina, PhD Medina
Administrative Assistant: Mangali, Muhammad, BA Islamic Uganda

Law

E-mail: law@iuiu.ac.ug
Acting Dean: Kamal, Alhaji Da'ud, LLB Maid.,
LLM Jos
Administrative Assistant: Wakhanya, Jawali,
BAEd Islamic Uganda

Management Studies

E-mail: fms@iuiu.ac.ug
Acting Dean: Menya, Muhammad, BAEd Islamic
Uganda, MBA Newport, PhD Newport
Administrative Assistant: Mafabi, Muzamir, BBS
Islamic Uganda

Science

E-mail: science@iuiu.ac.ug
Deputy Dean: Opyene, Eluk P., BSc Mak., MSc
Kent
Administrative Assistant: Walusansa, Yahaya,
BPA Islamic Uganda

ACADEMIC UNITS

Arabic Studies

E-mail: fisal@iuiu.ac.ug
Kabali, Sulait, BA Medina, MA Medina   Lectr.;
Head*
Other Staff: 8 Lectrs.

Biological Science

E-mail: science@iuiu.ac.ug
Makanga, Boniface, BSc Dar., MSc Mak., PhD
Mak.   Assoc. Prof.
Sekimpi, P. S. N. A., BSc Mak., MSc Mak., PhD
Arizona   Sr. Lectr.; Head*
Other Staff: 9 Lectrs.; 1 Asst. Lectr.

Business Studies

E-mail: fms@iuiu.ac.ug
Kitakule, Hussein, BCom Karachi, MBA Flor.
Lectr.; Head*
Kituyi, Zaitun, BAEd Islamic Uganda, MSc Gadjah
Mada, PhD Warw.   Sr. Lectr.
Other Staff: 10 Lectrs.; 3 Asst. Lectrs.

Chemistry and Biochemistry

E-mail: science@iuiu.ac.ug
Opyene, Eluk P., BSc Mak., MSc Kent   Sr.
Lectr.; Head*
Other Staff: 4 Lectrs.

Computer Science

E-mail: science@iuiu.ac.ug
Omujal, George M., BSc E.China U.T., MSc
Shanghai   Lectr.; Head*
Other Staff: 6 Lectrs.; 1 Asst. Lectr.

Curriculum and Instruction

E-mail: educ@iuiu.ac.ug
Muwonge, Victoria M., BScEd Bhopal, MScEd
Bhopal   Lectr.; Head*
Other Staff: 4 Lectrs.

Economics

E-mail: fass@iuiu.ac.ug
Sentongo, Ausi A., BED Mak., MA Mak.   Lectr.;
Head*
Other Staff: 8 Lectrs.
Research: data collection and management as a
basis for local development planning and
evaluation

Educational Foundations

E-mail: educ@iuiu.ac.ug
Hassan, Amina, BAEd Mak., MEd Mak.   Asst.
Lectr.; Head*
Other Staff: 3 Lectrs.; 1 Asst. Lectr.

Educational Management and Administration

E-mail: educ@iuiu.ac.ug
Shalabi, Badrudin, BAEd Islamic Uganda, MEd
Islamic Uganda   Lectr.; Head*
Ssesanga, Abdul K. N., BAEd Mak., MEd Mak.,
PhD Brist.   Lectr.; Dir., Kampala Campus
Other Staff: 4 Lectrs.

Educational Psychology

E-mail: educ@iuiu.ac.ug
Ndagi, M. A., BAEd Sokoto, MEd Lagos   Sr.
Lectr.; Head*
Other Staff: 5 Lectrs.

Geography

E-mail: fass@iuiu.ac.ug
Kiboma, G., BSc Wis., MScEd N.Illinois   Sr.
Lectr.; Head*
Other Staff: 7 Lectrs.

History

E-mail: fass@iuiu.ac.ug
Emudong, Charles P., BA Mak., MA Mak., PhD
Dal.   Sr. Lectr.
Serwanga, Jamil, BAEd Islamic Uganda, MA Mak.,
PhD Islamic Uganda   Lectr.; Head*
Other Staff: 5 Lectrs.; 1 Asst. Lectr.

Islamic Studies

E-mail: fisal@iuiu.ac.ug
Bowa, Hussein M., BA Medina, MA Medina, PhD
Medina   Lectr.; Head*
Other Staff: 7 Lectrs.

Language, Literature and Linguistics

E-mail: fass@iuiu.ac.ug
Nkonge, Ally C., BA Mak., MA Mak.   Lectr.;
Head*
Other Staff: 9 Lectrs.

Law, Common

E-mail: law@iuiu.ac.ug
Kamal, Alhaji Da'ud, LLB Maid., LLM Jos
Lectr.; Head*
Other Staff: 7 Lectrs.; 1 Asst. Lectr.

Law, Islamic

E-mail: law@iuiu.ac.ug
Mayanja, Sowed J., BA(Shariah) Islam.Imam
Mohd.Ibn Saud, MA Islam.Imam Mohd.Ibn Saud,
PhD Islam.Imam Mohd.Ibn Saud   Lectr.; Head*
Other Staff: 2 Lectrs.

Mass Communication

E-mail: fass@iuiu.ac.ug
Adnan, Ali A., BHSc NU Malaysia, MSc NU
Malaysia, MLIS NU Malaysia   Lectr.; Head*
Other Staff: 7 Lectrs.

Mathematics and Statistics

E-mail: science@iuiu.ac.ug
Semogerere, Twaibu, BScEd Islamic Uganda, MSc
Mak.   Lectr.; Head*
Other Staff: 8 Lectrs.

Physics

E-mail: science@iuiu.ac.ug
Taddy, Emmanuel N., BSc Jos, MSc Jos   Lectr.;
Head*
Other Staff: 4 Lectrs.

Political Science

E-mail: fass@iuiu.ac.ug
Kawalya, Isa, BA Islamic Uganda, MSc Gadjah Mada
Lectr.; Head*
Other Staff: 6 Lectrs.; 1 Asst. Lectr.

Public Administration

E-mail: fms@iuiu.ac.ug
Galiwango, Hassan W., BAEd Islamic Uganda,
MPA Islamic Uganda   Lectr.; Head*
Other Staff: 5 Lectrs.

Shariah

E-mail: fisal@iuiu.ac.ug
Lubanga, Ziyad S., BA Islam.Imam Mohd.Ibn Saud,
MA Islam.Imam Mohd.Ibn Saud   Lectr.; Head*
Other Staff: 7 Lectrs.; 1 Asst. Lectr.

Social Work and Social Administration

E-mail: fass@iuiu.ac.ug
Kakaire, Abdul, BA Mak., MSc Gadjah Mada
Asst. Lectr.
Other Staff: 5 Lectrs.; 1 Asst. Lectr.

SPECIAL CENTRES, ETC

English-Arabic Translations Unit

E-mail: fisal@iuiu.ac.ug
Sekitto, Ayoub T., BA Islamic Uganda, MA Khart.,
PhD Khart.   Lectr.; Deputy Dean; Head*
Other Staff: 2 Lectrs.

Information and Communication Technology

E-mail: ict@iuiu.ac.ug
Senyonjo, Ahmed, BCom Mak.   Head*
Other Staff: 3 Staff Members

Postgraduate Studies Programme

E-mail: umarkasule@yahoo.com
Kasule, Umar A., BA Mak., MA Mak., PhD NU
Malaysia   Sr. Lectr.; Dir.*

Vocational Training Centre

E-mail: vtc@iuiu.ac.ug
Kakembo, Moses, BAA Mak.   Head*
Other Staff: 3 Staff Members

CONTACT OFFICERS

Academic affairs. Academic Registrar: Suwed,
Saleh A., BA Mak., MEd Mak.
(E-mail: registrar@iuiu.ac.ug)
Accommodation. University Co-ordinator
(Accommodation): Samaali, Abbas, BA
Mak., MEd Mak.
(E-mail: a.samaali@iuiu.ac.ug)
Admissions (first degree). Academic
Registrar: Suwed, Saleh A., BA Mak., MEd
Mak. (E-mail: registrar@iuiu.ac.ug)
Development/fund-raising. Rector: Sengendo,
Kawesa A., BSc Mak., MScEd Kansas, PhD
Kansas (E-mail: aksengendo@yahoo.com)
Estates and buildings/works and services.
University Engineer: Semujju Dauda,
Mugejjera, BSc(Eng) Mak.
Examinations. Academic Registrar: Suwed,
Saleh A., BA Mak., MEd Mak.
(E-mail: registrar@iuiu.ac.ug)
Finance. University Bursar: Kakande, Siraje,
BCom Mak., MBA Mak.
General enquiries. Acting University
Secretary: Basalirwa, Asuman, LLB Mak.
Health services. Acting University Medical
Officer: Nakazibwe, Sauba, MB ChB Mbarara
International office. Rector: Sengendo,
Kawesa A., BSc Mak., MScEd Kansas, PhD
Kansas (E-mail: aksengendo@yahoo.com)
Library (chief librarian). Acting Librarian:
Ssesanga, Idris, BLIS Mak., MLIS Mak.
(E-mail: library@iuiu.ac.ug)
Marketing. Public Relations Officer: Kaye,
Hussein, BA Al-Azhar
Personnel/human resources. Acting
University Secretary: Basalirwa, Asuman,
LLB Mak.
(E-mail: asumanbasalirwa@yahoo.com)
Public relations. Public Relations Officer:
Kaye, Hussein, BA Al-Azhar
Publications. Chief Editor, Editorial Board:
Akbar, Halima W., BAEd Islamic Uganda, MEd
Bayero, PhD Birm.
Purchasing. University Bursar: Kakande, Siraje,
BCom Mak., MBA Mak.
Quality assurance and accreditation.
Chairman, Quality Assurance Committee:
Mpezamihigo, Mouhamad, BSc Mak., MSc
Mak., PhD Glas.
(E-mail: m.mpeza@iuiu.ac.ug)
Research. Chairman, Research Committee:
Mpezamihigo, Mouhamad, BSc Mak., MSc
Mak., PhD Glas.
(E-mail: m.mpeza@iuiu.ac.ug)

Scholarships, awards, loans. Academic Registrar: Suwed, Saleh A., BA *Mak.*, MEd *Mak.* (E-mail: registrar@iuiu.ac.ug)

Security. Vice-Rector (Academic Affairs): Mpezamihigo, Mouhamad, BSc *Mak.*, MSc *Mak.*, PhD *Glas.* (E-mail: m.mpeza@iuiu.ac.ug)

Sport and recreation. Sports Administrator: Gismallah, Abdallah, BA *Islamic Uganda*

Staff development and training. Academic Registrar: Suwed, Saleh A., BA *Mak.*, MEd *Mak.* (E-mail: registrar@iuiu.ac.ug)

Strategic planning. Chairman, Strategic Planning Committee: Mpezamihigo,

Mouhamad, BSc *Mak.*, MSc *Mak.*, PhD *Glas.* (E-mail: m.mpeza@iuiu.ac.ug)

Student union. University Co-ordinator (Accommodation): Samaali, Abbas, BA *Mak.*, MEd *Mak.* (E-mail: a.samaali@iuiu.ac.ug)

Student welfare/counselling. University Co-ordinator (Accommodation): Samaali, Abbas, BA *Mak.*, MEd *Mak.* (E-mail: a.samaali@iuiu.ac.ug)

Students from other countries. Academic Registrar: Suwed, Saleh A., BA *Mak.*, MEd *Mak.* (E-mail: registrar@iuiu.ac.ug)

CAMPUS/COLLEGE HEADS

Arua Study Centre, PO Box 315, Arua, Uganda. Co-ordinator: Amandu, Yassin I., BBS *Islamic Uganda*, MBA *Mak.*

Kampala Campus, PO Box 7689, Kampala, Uganda. (Tel: (0414) 341561; Fax: (0414) 236400; E-mail: info@iuiukc.ac.ug) Director: Ssesanga, Abdul K. N., BAEd *Mak.*, MEd *Mak.*, PhD *Brist.*

[Information supplied by the institution as at 16 October 2007, and edited by the ACU]

KAMPALA UNIVERSITY

Postal Address: PO Box 25454, Kampala, Uganda
Telephone: (077) 450601 **E-mail:** kuniv@afsat.com

VICE-CHANCELLOR*—Katerega, Prof. Badru

KYAMBOGO UNIVERSITY

Postal Address: PO Box 1, Kyambogo, Uganda
Telephone: (041) 286238 **Fax:** (041) 220464 **E-mail:** itek@starcom.co.ug

VICE-CHANCELLOR*—Lutalo Bosa, Prof. A. J.

MAKERERE UNIVERSITY

Founded 1970

Member of the Association of Commonwealth Universities

Postal Address: PO Box 7062, Kampala, Uganda
Telephone: (041) 532631-4 **Fax:** (041) 533640 **E-mail:** postmaster@muk.ac.ug
URL: http://www.mak.ac.ug/

VICE-CHANCELLOR*—Luboobi, Prof. Livingstone S., BSc *E.Af.*, MASc *Tor.*, PhD *Adel.*, Hon. Dr *Bergen*, FNAS(Uganda)
DEPUTY VICE-CHANCELLOR (ACADEMIC AFFAIRS)—Tibatemwa-Ekirikubinza, L., LLB *Mak.*, LLM *Copenhagen*, PhD *Copenhagen*
DEPUTY VICE-CHANCELLOR (FINANCE AND ADMINISTRATION)—Bakibinga, Prof. D. J., LLB *Mak.*, MA *Lond.*, PhD *Lond.*
UNIVERSITY SECRETARY AND SECRETARY TO COUNCIL‡—Akorimo, Sam S., BA *Mak.*, MA(EdMgt) *Mak.*
ACADEMIC REGISTRAR—Olal-Odur, Amos, BSc *Mak.*, MA *S.Fraser*, PhD *Alta.*
DEAN OF STUDENTS—Ekudu-Adoku, John, BSc *Mak.*
BURSAR—Byambabazi, Ben, BCom *Mak.*, MBA *Mak.*
UNIVERSITY LIBRARIAN—Musoke, Maria G. N., PhD

GENERAL INFORMATION

History. Previously established as Makerere College (founded 1922) and Makerere University College (1949), the university was founded in 1970.

Admission to first degree courses. Uganda Certificate of Education (UCE) or equivalent with at least 6 passes in approved subjects, and 2 passes in approved subjects at the same sitting of the Uganda Advanced Certificate of Education (UACE), or equivalent.

Libraries. Volumes: 550,000.

FACULTIES/SCHOOLS

Agriculture
Tel: (041) 542277
  E-mail: deanagric@agric.mak.ac.ug
Dean: Bekunda-Mateete, Prof. A., BSc *Mak.*, MSc *Wageningen*, PhD *ANU*

Arts
Tel: (041) 542241
  E-mail: deanarts@arts.mak.ac.ug
Dean: Sengendo, H., BA *Mak.*, MA *Leeds*, PhD *Nott.*

Computing and Information Technology
Tel: (041) 540628 E-mail: dean@cit.mak.ac.ug
Dean: Baryamureeba, Prof. V., BSc *Mak.*, MSc *Bergen*, PhD *Bergen*

Education
Tel: (041) 540733
  E-mail: deaneduc@edu.mak.ac.ug
Dean: Masembe-Ssebbunga, C., BA *Mak.*, MEd *Mak.*, PhD *Lond.*

Forestry and Nature Conservation
E-mail: forest@mak.ac.ug
Dean: Kaboggoza, J. R. S., BSc *Mak.*, MSc *Calif.*, PhD *Calif.*

Industrial and Fine Arts, Margaret Trowell School of
Tel: (041) 531423
  E-mail: sifaadimin@sifa.mak.ac.ug
Dean: Kyeyune, George W., BA(FA) MA(FA) PhD

Law

Tel: (041) 542284
E-mail: deanlaw@muklaw.ac.ug
Dean: Tamale, S. R., LLB *Mak.*, LLM *Harv.*, PhD *Minn.*

Medicine

Tel: (041) 541188
E-mail: deanmed@med.mak.ac.ug
Dean: Sewankambo, Prof. N. K., MB ChB *Mak.*, MMed *Mak.*, MSc

Science

Tel: (041) 532401
E-mail: deansci@sci.mak.ac.ug
Dean: Ssembatya, V., BSc MSc PhD

Social Sciences

Tel: (041) 545040 E-mail: deanfss@mak.ac.ug
Dean: Kirumira, Prof. Edward K., BA *Mak.*, MA *Exe.*, PhD *Copenhagen*

Technology

Tel: (041) 545029 E-mail: deantech@mak.ac.ug
Dean: Nawangwe, B., BArch *Mak.*, MSc(Arch) *Mak.*, PhD

Veterinary Medicine

Tel: (041) 554685
E-mail: deanvet@cit.mak.ac.ug
Dean: Kabasa, John D, BVM *Mak.*, MSc *Mak.*, PhD *Gött.*

ACADEMIC UNITS

Agricultural Economics and Agribusiness

Bashaasha, B., BSc *Seoul*, MSc *Seoul*, MA *Ohio*, PhD *Ohio* Sr. Lectr.; Head*
Hyuha, T., BA *S.Fraser*, MSc *Alta.* Sr. Lectr.
Kiiza, B. A., BSc(Agric) *Mak.*, MSc *Minn.*, PhD *Minn.* Sr. Lectr.
Mugisha, J., BSc(Agric) *Mak.*, MSc *Mak.*, PhD *Ohio* Sr. Lectr.
Serunkuma, D., BSc(Agric) *Mak.*, MSc(Agric) *Mak.*, PhD *Minn.* Sr. Lectr.
Tayebwa, B., BA *Mak.*, MSc *Mak.* Sr. Lectr.
Other Staff: 4 Lectrs.; 1 Asst. Lectr.; 1 Visiting Lectr.

Agricultural Extension Education

Biryabaho, F M., BSc(Agric) *Mak.*, MA *Minn.*, PhD *Mak.* Lectr.; Acting Head*
Kibwika, P., BSc(Agric) *Mak.*, MSc *Mak.*, PhD *Wageningen* Sr. Lectr.
Najjingo Mangheni, M., BSc(Agric) *Mak.*, MSc *Ohio*, PhD *Minn.* Sr. Lectr.
Other Staff: 5 Lectrs.; 4 Asst. Lectrs.; 1 Visiting Lectr.; 2 Lectrs.†

Animal Science

Bareeba, F. B., BSc(Agric) *Mak.*, MSc(Agric) *Mak.*, PhD *Manit.* Prof.
Kiwuwa, G. H., BSc(Agric) *Lond.*, MSc *Ill.*, PhD *Cornell* Prof. Emer.
Kyanisima, C., BSc(Agric) *Mak.*, MSc *Syd.*, PhD *Mak.* Sr. Lectr.
Mpairwe, D., BSc(Agric) *Mak.*, MSc(Agric) *Mak.*, PhD *Mak.* Sr. Lectr.
Mutetikka, D. B., BSc(Agric) *Mak.*, MSc *Nair.*, PhD *Ohio* Sr. Lectr.; Head*
Other Staff: 4 Lectrs.; 3 Asst. Lectrs.; 1 Lectr.†

Architecture

Nahdy, Silim, BArch MA Sr. Lectr.; Acting Head*
Nawangwe, B., BArch *Mak.*, MSc(Arch) *Mak.*, PhD Assoc. Prof.
Other Staff: 5 Lectrs.; 6 Asst. Lectrs.; 2 Temp. Asst. Lectrs.

Biochemistry

Enyaru, J. Assoc. Prof.
Kironde, F. S., MASc *N.Y.State*, MSc *N.Y.State*, PhD *N.Y.State* Assoc. Prof.
Kyambadde, J. W., BSc *Mak.*, MSc *Mak.* Sr. Lectr.; Head*
Rutesasira, A., BSc *Mak.*, MSc *Mak.* Sr. Lectr.

Other Staff: 8 Lectrs.; 4 Asst. Lectrs.

Botany

Bukenya-Ziraba, R., BSc *Mak.*, MSc *Ghana*, PhD *Mak.* Prof.
Kakudidi, E. K. Z., BSc *Mak.*, MSc *ANU* Sr. Lectr.
Kalema, J., BSc *Mak.*, MSc *Mak.* Sr. Lectr.
Kasenene, J. M., BSc *Mak.*, MSc *Mak.*, PhD *Mich.* Assoc. Prof.
Kashambuzi, J. T., BSc *Mak.*, MSc *Mak.* Sr. Lectr.
Male, M., BSc *Mak.*, MSc *Mak.* Sr. Lectr.
Mucunguzi, P., BSc *Mak.*, MSc *Mak.*, PhD *Mak.* Sr. Lectr.; Head*
Mutumba, G. M. C., BSc *Dar.*, PhD *Wales* Assoc. Prof.
Nyakaana, S., BSc *Mak.*, MSc *Wales*, PhD Sr. Lectr.
Oryem-Origa, H., BSc *Mak.*, MSc *Mak.*, PhD *Mak.* Prof.
Other Staff: 5 Lectrs.; 2 Asst. Lectrs.

Chemistry

Kiremire, B. T., BSc *Mak.*, MSc *Mak.*, PhD *Windsor* Prof.
Mbabazi, J., BSc *Mak.*, MSc *Mak.*, PhD *Mak.* Sr. Lectr.
Mpango, G. B., BSc *Mak.*, MSc *Mak.*, PhD *Wat.* Sr. Lectr.
Nyakairu, G. W. A., BSc *Mak.*, MSc *Mak.*, DSc *Vienna* Sr. Lectr.
Nyanzi, S. A., BSc *Mak.*, MSc *Nair.*, PhD Sr. Lectr.; Head*
Ssekaalo, H., BSc *Lond.*, MSc *Lond.*, PhD *Nair.* Prof.
Other Staff: 10 Lectrs.; 4 Asst. Lectrs.

Community Forestry and Extension

Buyinza, M., BSc *Islamic Uganda*, MSc *Indonesia*, PhD *Indonesia* Sr. Lectr.
Nabanoga, G., BScFor *Mak.*, PhD *Wageningen*, MSc Sr. Lectr.; Acting Head*
Other Staff: 1 Lectr.; 2 Asst. Lectrs.

Computing and Information Technology

Baryamureeba, V., BSc *Mak.*, MSc *Bergen*, PhD *Bergen* Prof.; Dean*
Wanyama, T., BSc(Eng) *Mak.*, MSc *NSW*, PhD Sr. Lectr.
Other Staff: 2 Lectrs.; 20 Asst. Lectrs.

Construction Economics and Management

Kerali, A. G., BSc(Eng) *Mak.*, PhD *Warw.*, MSc Sr. Lectr.; Head*
Other Staff: 1 Lectr.; 3 Temp. Asst. Lectrs.

Crop Science

Kyamanywa, S., BSc(Agric) *Mak.*, PhD *Mak.* Prof.
Nabasirye, M., BSc(Agric) *Mak.*, MSc *Reading*, PhD *Mak.* Sr. Lectr.
Okon, P., BSc(Agric) *Mak.*, MSc *Mak.*, PhD *Mak.* Sr. Lectr.
Osiru, D. S. O., BSc *E.Anglia*, PhD *Mak.* Prof.
Rubaihayo, P. R., BSc *Lond.*, MSc *Mak.*, PhD *Ill.* Prof. Emer.
Sabiiti, E. N., BSc(Agric) *Mak.*, MSc(Agric) *Mak.*, PhD *New Br.* Prof.
Ssebuliba, J. M., BSc(Agric) *Mak.*, MSc *Nair.*, PhD *Mak.* Sr. Lectr.; Head*
Ssekabembe, C., BSc *Mak.*, MSc *Mak.*, PhD *Ohio* Assoc. Prof.
Tukamuhabwa, BSc(Agric) *Mak.*, MSc *Mak.*, PhD *Mak.* Sr. Lectr.
Other Staff: 6 Lectrs.; 3 Asst. Lectrs.; 1 Visiting Lectr.

Curriculum, Teaching and Media

Nakabugo, M. G., BAEd *Mak.*, MA PhD Sr. Lectr.; Head*
Other Staff: 7 Lectrs.

Economic Policy and Planning

Ddumba-Sentamu, J., BA *Mak.*, MA *Wat.*, PhD *Mak.* Prof.
Mubazi, J. K. E., BA *Mak.*, MA *Kent*, PhD *Vienna* Sr. Lectr.; Head*
Other Staff: 5 Lectrs.; 4 Asst. Lectrs.

Economic Theory and Analysis

Mugume, A., BSc *Mak.*, MAEcon *Botswana*, DPhil *Oxf.* Lectr.; Acting Head*
Other Staff: 4 Lectrs.; 5 Asst. Lectrs.

Economics, Development

Balihuta, A. M., BA *Mak.*, MA PhD Assoc. Prof. (on leave)
Mwebaze, T., BA *Mak.*, MA *Dar.*, PhD *Vienna* Lectr.; Acting Head*
Other Staff: 6 Lectrs.; 4 Asst. Lectrs.

Educational Foundations and Management

Babigumira, D., BAEd MA PhD Lectr.; Acting Head*
Other Staff: 4 Lectrs.; 5 Asst. Lectrs.; 1 Lectr.†

Engineering, Agricultural

Kasisira, BSc *Moscow*, MSc *Moscow*, PhD Sr. Lectr.
Kawongolo, J. B., BSc *Mak.*, MSc *Mak.* Sr. Lectr.
Other Staff: 3 Lectrs.; 2 Asst. Lectrs.

Engineering, Civil

Bagampadde, U., BSc(Eng) *Mak.*, MSc *Dammam* Sr. Lectr.
Mwakali, J. A., BSc(Eng) *Mak.*, MSc *Sur.*, PhD *Sur.* Assoc. Prof.; Head*
Ngirane-Katashaya, G., BSc *Nair.*, PhD *Lond.* Assoc. Prof.
Ziraba, Yasin N. Sr. Lectr.
Other Staff: 3 Lectrs.; 9 Asst. Lectrs.

Engineering, Electrical

Da-Silva, P., MSc *Sao Paulo*, PhD *Sao Paulo* Sr. Lectr.
Kaluuba, L. L., BSc(Eng) *Mak.* Sr. Lectr.
Logujo, E., BSc *Mak.*, MSc(Eng) *Cal.Tech.*, PhD *Cal.Tech.* Assoc. Prof.; Head*
Mugisha, P., BSc(Eng) *Mak.*, MTech *Delhi*, MSc *Oldenburg* Sr. Lectr.
Musaazi, M. K., BSc(Eng) *Mak.*, MSc(Eng) *Lond.*, PhD Sr. Lectr.
Other Staff: 2 Lectrs.; 1 Asst. Lectr.; 1 Temp. Asst. Lectr.

Engineering, Forest Products

Banana, A. Y., BScFor *Mak.*, MSc *Calif.*, PhD *ANU* Assoc. Prof.; Head*
Kaboggoza, J. R. S., BSc *Mak.*, MSc *Calif.*, PhD *Calif.* Sr. Lectr.
Other Staff: 3 Asst. Lectrs.

Engineering, Mechanical

Byaruhanga, J. K., BSc(Eng) *Mak.*, PhD *NSW* Assoc. Prof.
Okure, M. A. E., BSc(Eng) *Mak.*, MSc *Middle East Tech.*, PhD *Northwestern* Sr. Lectr.; Head*
Sebbit, M. A., BSc *T.U.Istanbul*, MSc *T.U.Istanbul* Sr. Lectr.
Other Staff: 5 Lectrs.; 3 Asst. Lectrs.

Engineering Mathematics

Taban-Wani, Gyavira, BSc MSc PhD Sr. Lectr.
Tikodri-Togboa, S. S., MSc(Eng) *Odessa*, PhD *Odessa* Assoc. Prof.
Other Staff: 1 Asst. Lectr.

Finance and Accounts

Nambi Karuhanga, B., BAEd *Mak.*, MBA *Maastricht* Asst. Lectr.; Acting Head*
Other Staff: 1 Lectr.; 1 Asst. Lectr.

Food Science and Technology

Kaaya, A. N., BSc(Agric) *Mak.*, MSc *Flor.*, PhD *Mak.* Sr. Lectr.

Kikafunda, J. K., BSc Mak., MSc Sask., PhD Reading Assoc. Prof.
Kyamuhangire, W., BSc Mak., MSc NSW, PhD ANU Assoc. Prof.
Muyanja, C., BSc Sokoine Ag., MSc ANU, PhD ANU Sr. Lectr.
Muyonga, J. H., BSc Mak., MSc Cornell, PhD Pret. Assoc. Prof.; Head*
Nakimbugwe, D., BSc Mak., MSc Cornell, PhD Leuven Sr. Lectr.
Namutebi, A., BSc Sokoine Ag., MSc ANU, PhD ANU Sr. Lectr.
Other Staff: 6 Lectrs; 2 Asst. Lectrs.

Forest Biology and Ecosystems Management

Bahati, J. B., BSc Mak., MSc Wales Sr. Lectr.
Eilu, Gerald, BScFor Mak., MSc Mak., PhD Mak. Sr. Lectr.
Nyeko, P., BSc Mak., MSc Lond., PhD Wales Sr. Lectr.
Obua, Joseph, BSc Mak., MSc Wales, PhD Wales Prof.; Head*
Okullo, J. B. L., BSc Mak., MSc Mak., PhD Wales Sr. Lectr.
Tweheyo, M., BSc Mak., MSc Mak., DSc Sr. Lectr.
Other Staff: 2 Lectrs.; 2 Asst. Lectrs.

Forest Management

Gombya-Ssembajjwe, W. S., BSc Mak., MSc Edin., PhD Wales Assoc. Prof.; Head*
Muheirwe, C. K., BScFor Mak., MSc Edin., PhD Col. Sr. Lectr.
Other Staff: 3 Lectrs.; 7 Asst. Lectrs.; 2 Lectrs.†

Gender and Women's Studies

Ahikire, J., BA Mak., MA Inst.Soc.Stud.(The Hague), PhD Witw. Sr. Lectr.
Bantebya, K. G., BA Mak., MPhil Camb., PhD Hull Assoc. Prof.; Head*
Kabonesa, C., PhD Ill., BA MA Sr. Lectr.
Kasente, D., BA Mak., MEd Mak., PhD Nair. Sr. Lectr.
Manyire, H., BA Mak., MA Mak., PhD Mak. Sr. Lectr.
Other Staff: 6 Lectrs.; 6 Asst. Lectrs.

Geography

Basalirwa, C. P. K., BSc Dar., MSc Nair., MSc N.U.I., PhD Nair. Assoc. Prof.
Nyakaana, J. B., BA Mak., MA Mak., PhD Amst. Assoc. Prof.; Head*
Sengendo, H., BA Mak., MA Leeds, PhD Nott. Assoc. Prof.
Were, J. W., BA Potsdam, MA N.Y.State Sr. Lectr.
Other Staff: 7 Lectrs.; 6 Asst. Lectrs.; 2 Lectrs.†

Geology

Barifaijo, E., BSc N.Carolina, MSc N.Carolina, PhD Mak. Sr. Lectr.; Head*
Muwanga, A., BSc Mak., MSc Mak., PhD Sr. Lectr.
Teberindwa, J. V., BSc Mak., MSc Mak., PhD Mak. Sr. Lectr.
Other Staff: 7 Lectrs.; 2 Asst. Lectrs.

History

Asiimwe, G. B., BAEd Mak., MA Mak., PhD Inst.Soc.Stud.(The Hague) Lectr.; Head*
Mulira, J., BA E.Af., MA Prin., PhD Prin. Assoc. Prof. (on contract)
Other Staff: 9 Lectrs.

Industrial Art and Design

Kwesiga, P. K., BA(FA) Mak., MA(FA) Mak., PhD Middx. Assoc. Prof.
Other Staff: 6 Lectrs.; 1 Asst. Lectr.

Information Science

Ikoja-Odongo, R. J., BA Delhi, MPhil Stir., PhD Zululand Prof.
Other Staff: 1 Lectr.; 3 Asst. Lectrs.

Information Systems

Dembe, Williams Visiting Sr. Lectr.; Head*
Other Staff: 7 Asst. Lectrs.; 2 Temp. Asst. Lectrs.

Language Education

Masagazi-Masaazi, F., BA Mak., MA Mak. Sr. Lectr.; Acting Head*
Masembe-Ssebbunga, C., BA Mak., MEd Mak., PhD Lond. Assoc. Prof.
Waibi-Walubi, BA Mak., MA Warw. Sr. Lectr.
Other Staff: 5 Lectrs.; 4 Asst. Lectrs.

Languages

Khamalwa, W. W. Sr. Lectr.
Kizza-Mukasa, J. M., BA Mak., MA Mak. Sr. Lectr.
Mukama, R., BA E.Af., MA E.Af., PhD York(Can.) Prof. (on contract)
Muranga, M. J. K., BA Mak., PhD Bayreuth Assoc. Prof.; Dir.*
Natukunda-Togboa, E. R., BA Mak., MA Mak., PhD Aix-Marseilles I Sr. Lectr.
Ndoleriire, O., BA Paris IV, MA Paris IV, PhD Paris IV Prof.
Other Staff: 10 Lectrs.; 8 Asst. Lectrs.

Law and Jurisprudence

Jjuuko, F. W., LLB Mak., LLM Mak. Assoc. Prof.; Head*
Nagitta-Musoke, E. D., LLB Mak., LLM Nott. Sr. Lectr. (on leave)
Tamale, S. R., LLB Mak., LLM Harv., PhD Minn. Assoc. Prof.
Other Staff: 2 Lectrs.; 4 Asst. Lectrs.

Law, Commercial

Kigula, J., LLB Mak., LLM Warw. Sr. Lectr.
Muhwezi, P., LLB Mak., LLM Camb. Asst. Lectr.; Acting Head*
Tumwine-Mukubwa, G. P., LLB Dar., LLM York(Can.), LLD York(Can.) Prof.
Other Staff: 2 Lectrs.; 7 Asst. Lectrs.

Law, Public and Comparative

Barya, J. J., LLB Mak., LLM Warw., PhD Warw. Assoc. Prof.; Head*
Kasimbazi, E. B., LLB Dar., LLM Calg. Sr. Lectr.
Onoria, H., LLB Mak., LLM Camb., PhD Camb. Sr. Lectr.
Twinomugisha, B. K., LLB Mak., LLM Mak., LLD Mak. Sr. Lectr.
Other Staff: 2 Lectrs.; 6 Asst. Lectrs.

Library Science

Kigongo-Bukenya Prof.
Matovu, J., BAEcon Alig., MAEcon Alig., MSc Sr. Lectr.
Other Staff: 1 Asst. Lectr.

Literature

Bukenya, A., BA E.Af., MA Mak. Sr. Lectr.
Dipio, D., BAEd Mak., MA Mak., MA Greg., PhD Greg. Sr. Lectr.; Head*
Gakwandi, Arthur S. Assoc. Prof.
Kiyimba, A., BA Mak., MLitt Strath., PhD Dar. Assoc. Prof.
Okello Ogwang, E., BA Indiana, MA Indiana, PhD Indiana Sr. Lectr.
Other Staff: 6 Lectrs.; 1 Asst. Lectr.

Marketing and Management

Mbidde, H., BBA Mak., MBA Mak. Asst. Lectr.; Acting Head*
Other Staff: 1 Lectr.; 2 Asst. Lectrs.; 1 Temp. Asst. Lectr.

Mass Communication

Chibita, M. B., BAEd Mak., MA Iowa Sr. Lectr.
Mwesige, P. G., BA Mak., MA American(Cairo) Sr. Lectr.; Head*
Nassanga, G. L., BA Mak., MA Wales, PhD Mak. Sr. Lectr.
Other Staff: 3 Lectrs; 4 Asst. Lectrs

Mathematics

Kasozi, J., BSc Mak., MSc Z'bwe., PhD Mak. Lectr.; Acting Head*
Mango, J. M., BSc Mak., MSc Mak., PhD Mak. Sr. Lectr.
Mugisha, J. Y. T., BScEd Mak., MSc Mak., PhD Mak. Assoc. Prof.
Sembayata, V. A., BSc Mak., MSc Mak., PhD Flor. Sr. Lectr.
Tadie, Tadie, PhD Yaounde I Assoc. Prof.
Other Staff: 7 Lectrs.; 5 Asst. Lectrs.

Music, Dance and Drama

Kaahwa, J., BA Benin, MA Mak., PhD Sr. Lectr.; Acting Head*
Mangeni, P., BAEd Mak., MA Leeds Sr. Lectr. (on leave)
Nannyonga Tamusuza, S., BAEd Mak., MA Mak., PhD Pitt. Sr. Lectr.
Ntangaare, M. M., BA Mak., MA Mak., PhD Mak. Sr. Lectr.
Tamusuza, L., BA Mak., MA Belf., PhD Assoc. Prof.
Other Staff: 2 Lectrs.; 3 Asst. Lectrs.

Painting and Art History

Banadda, G. Lectr.; Acting Head*
Ifee, F. X., BA(FA) Mak., MA(FA) Mak. Sr. Lectr.
Kivubbiro, J. M. Sr. Lectr.
Sengendo, P. N., MA(FA) Mak. Prof.
Sserulyo, I., MA(FA) Mak. Sr. Lectr.
Other Staff: 5 Lectrs.; 2 Asst. Lectrs.

Philosophy

Beyaraza, BA Mak., MA Mak., PhD Bayreuth Assoc. Prof.
Byaruhanga, A. R., BA Mak., MA Nair., PhD Mak. Sr. Lectr.
Kaboha, P., BA Lond., MA E.Af. Sr. Lectr.
Kigongo, J. K., BA Mak., MA Mak., PhD Mak. Assoc. Prof.
Mwanahewa, S. A., BA Mak., MA Mak., PhD KwaZulu-Natal Sr. Lectr.
Wamala, E., BA Mak., MA Mak., PhD Mak. Sr. Lectr.; Head*
Other Staff: 3 Lectrs.

Physics

Banda, E. J. B., BSc E.Af., MA Roch., PhD Roch. Prof.
D'ujanga, F. M., BSc Mak., MSc Mak., PhD Mak. Sr. Lectr.
Kaahwa, Y., BSc E.Af., MSc Alta., PhD NSW Prof.
Mugambe, E. K. S., BSc Cal.Tech., DPhil Oxf. Assoc. Prof.
Otiti, Tom, BSc Mak., MSc Reading, PhD Mak. Assoc. Prof.
Twesigomwe, E. M., BSc Mak., MSc Nair., PhD Mak. Sr. Lectr.
Other Staff: 4 Lectrs.; 4 Asst. Lectrs.

Political Science and Public Administration

Bwana, C. N., BA Mak., MA Bordeaux, PhD Bordeaux Sr. Lectr.
Kiiza, J., BA Mak., MPP Syd., PhD Syd. Sr. Lectr.
Muhumuza, W., BA W.Ont., MA W.Ont. Assoc. Prof.
Mukwaya, A. K. K., BA Mak., MA Durh. Sr. Lectr.
Murindwa-Rutunga, BA Mak., MA Mak., PhD Jad. Assoc. Prof.
Nansozi-Muwanga, BA Lond., MA Lond., PhD Tor. Sr. Lectr.
Olum, Y. A. A., BA Mak., MA Manc., PhD Newcastle(UK) Sr. Lectr.; Head*
Sabiti, Makara, BA Mak., MPA Liv. Sr. Lectr.
Tukahebwa, G., BA Mak., MPA Manit. Sr. Lectr.
Other Staff: 10 Lectrs.; 1 Temp. Asst. Lectr.

Psychology, Institute of

Nambi, J. Dir.*

Educational Psychology

Otyala, Robert W.   Teaching Asst.; Head*
Other Staff: 1 Lectr.; 1 Asst. Lectr.

Mental Health and Community Psychology

Nambi, J.   Sr. Lectr.
Other Staff: 2 Lectrs.; 4 Asst. Lectrs.

Organisational and Social Psychology

Baguma, P., BSc Mak., MSc Lond., PhD Lond.
   Assoc. Prof.; Head*
Munene, J. C., BA Mak., MSc Sheff., MSc
   W.Aust., PhD Lond.   Prof.
Other Staff: 3 Lectrs.; 2 Asst. Lectrs.

Records and Archive Management

Magara, E., BLIS Mak., MSc Mak., PhD Zambia
   Assoc. Prof.
Other Staff: 2 Asst. Lectrs.

Religious Studies

Katende, A., BA Mak., MA Mak.   Lectr.; Acting
   Head*
Nkurunziza, Fr. D. R. K., BA Greg., MA CUE Af.,
   PhD Tübingen   Sr. Lectr.
Tinkasimire, T., BAEd Mak., MA Portland, PhD
   Gonzaga   Sr. Lectr.
Other Staff: 10 Lectrs.; 1 Asst. Lectr.

Science and Technical Education

Muhanguzi, H. R., BSc MSc PhD   Sr. Lectr.
Oluka, S. O., BSc Mak., MSc Mak., PhD Alta.
   Sr. Lectr.; Head*
Oonyu, J., BSc Mak., MSc Mak., PhD Mak.   Sr.
   Lectr.
Other Staff: 7 Lectrs.; 2 Asst. Lectrs.

Sculpture

Katende, S., BA(FA) Mak., MA(FA) Mak.   Sr.
   Lectr. (on leave)
Kirumira, R., BA(FA) Mak., MA(FA) Mak.   Sr.
   Lectr.
Kyeyune, George W., BA(FA) MA(FA) PhD
   Sr. Lectr.
Mwesigwa, S., BA(FA) Mak., MA(FA) Mak.
   Lectr.; Acting Head*
Other Staff: 3 Lectrs.; 4 Asst. Lectrs.; 1 Temp.
   Asst. Lectr.

Social Sciences and Arts Education

Kagoda, T. M. A.   Sr. Lectr.
Tamale, B. M., BA Mak., MEd Mak., MA Indiana,
   PhD Mak.   Lectr.; Acting Head*
Other Staff: 8 Lectrs.; 5 Asst. Lectrs.; 1 Temp.
   Asst. Lectr.

Social Work and Social Administration

Asingwire, N., BA Mak., MA McM.   Sr. Lectr.;
   Acting Head*
Lubanga, R., BA Mak., MA Cardiff, MSc Penn.
   Sr. Lectr.
Nuwagaba, A., BA Mak., MSc Lond., PhD Mak.
   Sr. Lectr.
Other Staff: 10 Lectrs.; 3 Asst. Lectrs.

Sociology

Atekyereza, P. R., BA Mak., PhD Mak., MSc   Sr.
   Lectr.; Head*
Kirumira, Edward K., BA Mak., MA Exe., PhD
   Copenhagen   Prof.
Kisamba-Mugerwa, C., BA Mak., MA Nair.   Sr.
   Lectr.
Neema, Stella   Sr. Lectr.
Rwabukwali, C. B., BA Mak., MPA Arizona, MSc
   Case W.Reserve, PhD Case W.Reserve   Assoc.
   Prof.
Other Staff: 11 Lectrs.; 5 Asst. Lectrs.

Soil Science

Bekunda, M. A., BSc Mak., MSc Wageningen, PhD
   ANU   Prof.
Nkwiine, C., BSc(Agric) Mak., MSc(Agric) Mak.
   Sr. Lectr.
Ochwoh, V. O. A., BSc Mak., MSc Mak., PhD
   Pret.   Assoc. Prof.; Head*

Tenywa, J. S., BSc(Agric) Mak., MSc ANU, PhD
   Ohio   Sr. Lectr.
Tenywa-Makooma, M., BSc(Agric) Mak.,
   MSc(Agric) Mak., PhD Ohio   Assoc. Prof.
Tumuhairwe, Joy K., BSc(Agric) Mak., MSc WI
   Sr. Lectr.
Other Staff: 4 Lectrs.; 2 Asst. Lectrs.; 3 Lectrs.†

Sports Science

Kasoma, Sandra S. B.   Asst. Lectr.; Acting
   Head*
Other Staff: 1 Asst. Lectr.

Surveying

Batungi, N. A., BSc Nair., MSc Lagos   Sr. Lectr.
   (on leave)
Mukiibi-Katende, MSc PhD   Sr. Lectr.; Head*
Other Staff: 6 Lectrs.; 3 Asst. Lectrs.

Urban Planning

1 Lectr.

Zoology

Akol Anne, M., BSc Mak., MPhil Camb., PhD
   Sr. Lectr.
Baranga, D. D., BSc Mak., MSc Mak., PhD Mak.
   Assoc. Prof.
Basuta-Isabirye, G., BSc Mak., MSc Mak., PhD
   Mak.   Sr. Lectr.; Head*
Bugenyi, F. W. B., BSc Mak., MSc Mak., PhD
   Mak.   Assoc. Prof.
Kaddu, J. B., BSc E.Af., MSc Liv., PhD Nair.
   Prof.
Muyodi, BSc MSc PhD   Sr. Lectr.
Other Staff: 6 Lectrs.; 3 Asst. Lectrs.

MEDICINE

Tel: (041) 541188
E-mail: deanmed@med.mak.ac.ug

Anaesthesia

Tindimwebwa, J. V. B., MB ChB Mak., MMEd
   Mak.   Sr. Lectr.; Head*
Wabule, A.   Sr. Lectr.

Anatomy

Ibingira, B. R., MB ChB Mak., MMEd Mak.   Sr.
   Lectr.
Ibingira, C., MB ChB Mak., MMEd Mak.
   Head*
Luboga, S., MB ChB Mak., MMed Mak.   Assoc.
   Prof.
Other Staff: 3 Lectrs.; 2 Asst. Lectrs.

Child Health and Development Centre

Katahoire, Anne   Dir.*
Simwogerere, J. J., MB ChB Mak., MMEd Mak.
   Sr. Lectr.
Other Staff: 1 Lectr.; 1 Asst. Lectr.

Community Health and Behavioural Sciences

Atai-Omorot   Acting Head*
Other Staff: 7 Lectrs.; 3 Asst. Lectrs.

Community Practice

Tuunde, S., MB ChB Mak., MMEd Mak.   Hon.
   Lectr.; Acting Head*
Other Staff: 2 Lectrs.; 1 Hon. Lectr.

Dentistry

Muwazi, L. M., BDS Glas.   Sr. Lectr.; Head*
Okullo, I., BDS Mak., MPH Nair., PhD Bergen
   Sr. Lectr.
Other Staff: 7 Lectrs.; 1 Asst. Lectr.; 3 Hon.
   Lectrs.

Disease Control and Environmental Health

Al-Ahamadawy, Bahaa-Eldeen, MB ChB MSc
   PhD   Prof.
Bazeyo, W., MB ChB Mak., MMEd Sing.   Sr.
   Lectr.
Nuwaha, F., MB ChB Mak., MPH Leeds, PhD
   Karolinska   Sr. Lectr.
Oryem-Lalobo, M., BSc Mak., MSPH   Sr. Lectr.

Serwadda, D., MB ChB Mak., MMed Mak., MSc
   Johns H., MPH Johns H., MSc Newcastle(UK)
   Assoc. Prof.
Other Staff: 3 Lectrs.; 3 Asst. Lectrs.

Ear, Nose and Throat

Awubwa, M. D., MB ChB Mak., MMEd Nair.
   Lectr.; Head*
Tumweheire, G. O., MB ChB Mak., MMed Mak.
   Hon. Lectr.; Head*
Tumwikirize, A. W. B., MB ChB Mak., MMed
   Mak., MSc Mak.   Sr. Lectr.
Other Staff: 1 Lectr.; 1 Asst. Lectr.

Epidemiology and Biostatistics

Konde-Lule, J. K., MB ChB Mak., MSc Mak.
   Assoc. Prof.; Head*
Makumbi, F. E., MB ChB Mak., PhD   Sr. Lectr.
Ndungutse, D., MB ChB Mak., MSc Case
   W.Reserve   Sr. Lectr.
Other Staff: 2 Lectrs.; 2 Asst. Lectrs.

Health Policy Planning and Management

Baine, O. S., MB ChB Mak., MPH Leeds, PhD
   Keele   Lectr.; Head*
Pariyo, G. W., MB ChB Mak., PhD Johns H., MSc
   Sr. Lectr.
Wabwire-Manghen, MB ChB Mak., MPH Johns
   H., PhD Johns H.   Assoc. Prof.
Other Staff: 1 Lectr.; 1 Asst. Lectr.

Medical Illustration

3 Asst. Med. Illustrators

Medicine

Freers, O. J., MB ChB Munich, MMed Mak.
   Assoc. Prof.
Kagimu, M., MB ChB Mak., MMed Mak., MSc
   Sr. Lectr.
Kamya, R. M., MB ChB MMEd MPH   Sr.
   Lectr.
Katabira, E. T., MB ChB Mak.   Assoc. Prof.
Mayanja-Kizza, MB ChB Mak., MMed Mak., MSc
   Assoc. Prof.; Head*
Otim, A. M., MB ChB Mak., MMEd Mak., MD
   Mak., FRCP   Prof.
Sewankambo, N. K., MB ChB Mak., MMed
   Mak., MSc   Prof.
Other Staff: 2 Lectrs.; 1 Asst. Lectr.

Microbiology

Abaru, E. D., MB ChB MSc   Sr. Lectr.; Head*
Kaddu-Mulindwa, BVM MSc PhD   Sr. Lectr.
Olobo, J. O., BVM PhD   Assoc. Prof.
Other Staff: 5 Lectrs.; 2 Asst. Lectrs.

Nursing

Rose Nabirye, C.   Lectr.; Acting Head*
Other Staff: 1 Lectr.; 4 Asst. Lectrs.

Obstetrics/Gynaecology

Kaye, Dan, MB ChB MMEd   Sr. Lectr.
Mirembe, F. M., MB ChB Mak., MMed Mak.,
   PhD Mak.   Assoc. Prof.; Head*
Other Staff: 10 Lectrs.

Ophthalmology

Agaba-Ateenyi, C., MB ChB MMEd MSc   Sr.
   Lectr.
Medi Kawuma, A., MB ChB Mak., MD   Assoc.
   Prof.
Mwaka, F. P., MB ChB Mak., MMed   Assoc.
   Prof.
Tibayungwa-Kabuleeta, H., MB ChB Mak.,
   MMEd Nair.   Sr. Lectr.
Other Staff: 1 Lectr.

Orthopaedics

Naddumba, E. K., MB ChB Mak., MMEd Mak.
   Hon Lectr.; Acting Head*
Other Staff: 2 Asst. Lectrs.; 4 Hon. Lectrs.

Paediatrics and Child Health

Karamagi, C. A., MB ChB Mak., MMed Mak.
   Sr. Lectr.

Kiguli, S., MB ChB Mak., MMEd Mak.   Sr. Lectr.

Musoke-Mudido, P., MB ChB Mak., MMEd Mak. Sr. Lectr.

Ndeezi, G., MB ChB Mak., MMEd Mak.   Sr. Lectr.

Serunjogi, L., MSc Mak.   Sr. Lectr.

Tumwine, J., MB ChB Mak., MMed Mak.   Prof.

Other Staff: 2 Asst. Lectrs.

Pathology

Bimenya, G. S., BSc MSc PhD   Assoc. Prof.; Head*

Byarugaba, W., MSc Cologne, PhD Cologne, BSc   Assoc. Prof.

Odida, M., MB ChB MMed   Sr. Lectr.

Wabinga, H. R., MB ChB MMed   Assoc. Prof.

Pharmacology and Therapeutics

Obua, C., MD Dar., MSc Mak.   Sr. Lectr.

Ogwal-Okeng, J. W., MB ChB Mak., MSc Mak., PhD Mak.   Prof.

Waako, P.   Sr. Lectr.; Head*

Other Staff: 6 Asst. Lectrs.

Pharmacy

Odoi, Adome R., BPharm Delhi, MSc Delhi, PhD Mak.   Prof.; Head*

Onegi, B., BPharm Tübingen, PhD Tübingen   Sr. Lectr.

Other Staff: 3 Lectrs.; 6 Asst. Lectrs.

Physiology

Kasolo, J. N., MB ChB Mak., MSc Mak.   Lectr.; Head*

Okullo, J. H., MB ChB Mak., MSc Lond.   Sr. Lectr.

Other Staff: 3 Lectrs.

Psychiatry

Nakasi, G., MB ChB Mak., MMed Mak.   Sr. Lectr.; Head*

Other Staff: 3 Lectrs.; 3 Asst. Lectrs.

Radiology

Ddungu-Matovu, P. F., BSc Mak., MSc Mak.   Sr. Lectr.

Kawooya, M. G., MB ChB Mak., MMed Mak.   Assoc. Prof.

Kiguli Malwadde, MB ChB Mak., MMed Mak.   Assoc. Prof.; Head*

Surgery

Kaggwa, S., MB ChB Mak., MMed Mak.   Sr. Lectr.; Head*

Kato Sebbaale, S., MB ChB Mak., MMEd Mak.   Sr. Lectr.

Kijjambu, S., MB ChB MMed   Sr. Lectr.

Nzarubara, G. R., MB ChB Mak., MMed Mak.   Assoc. Prof.

Other Staff: 2 Lectrs.; 2 Asst. Lectrs.

VETERINARY MEDICINE

Tel: (041) 554685
E-mail: deanvet@cit.mak.ac.ug

Veterinary Anatomy

Bukenya, E. M. F., BSc E.Af., MSc Mak., PhD Cape Town   Sr. Lectr. (on contract)

Epelu Opio, J., BVM Nair., MSc Nair., PhD Nair.   Prof.

Muwazi, R. T., BVM Mak., MSc Mak., PhD Mak.   Assoc. Prof.

Nyatia, E., BVM Mak., MSc Edin., PhD Cape Town   Lectr.; Acting Head*

Other Staff: 3 Lectrs.

Veterinary Medicine

Bizimenyera, E., BVM Mak., MSc Nair.   Sr. Lectr.

Mugisha, A., BVM Mak., MSc Edin.   Sr. Lectr.

Mulaiteyo-Kaahwa, M. S., BVM Mak., MSc Brunei   Sr. Lectr.

Musoke, R. Azuba, BVM Mak., MSc Mak., PhD Mak.   Sr. Lectr.

Waiswa, C., BVM Mak., MSc Mak., PhD Mak.   Sr. Lectr.

Other Staff: 2 Lectrs.; 3 Asst. Lectrs.

Veterinary Parasitology and Microbiology

Lubega, G. W., BVM Mak., MSc McG., PhD McG.   Prof.; Head*

Rubaire-Akiiki, C., BVM Nair., MSc Nair., PhD Mak.   Prof.

Other Staff: 4 Lectrs.; 5 Asst. Lectrs.

Veterinary Pathology

Ojok-Lonzy, BVM Mak., PhD Mak., DrVetMed Giessen   Prof.; Head*

Other Staff: 1 Lectr.; 2 Asst. Lectrs.

Veterinary Physiological Sciences

Kabasa, John D, BVM Mak., MSc Mak., PhD Gött.   Assoc. Prof.

Okello, S., BVM Nair., MSc Mak., PhD   Sr. Lectr.

Olila, D., BVM Mak., MSc Mak., PhD Nair.   Assoc. Prof.

Other Staff: 2 Lectrs.; 3 Asst. Lectrs.

Veterinary Public Health and Preventive Medicine

Ejobi, F., BVM Mak., MVPH Nair., PhD Saar   Assoc. Prof.; Head*

Opuda-Asibo, J., BVM Mak., MPH Minn., PhD Minn.   Prof.

Other Staff: 2 Lectrs.; 6 Asst. Lectrs.

Veterinary Surgery and Reproduction

Acon, J., BVS Mak., MSc Flor., PhD Mak.   Prof.; Head*

Koma, L. M. F. K., BVM Mak., MPhil Edin.   Assoc. Prof.

Ndikuwera, J., BVM Nair., MSc PhD   Sr. Lectr.

Other Staff: 4 Lectrs.

Wildlife and Animal Resources Management

Ocaido, M., BVM Mak., MSc Mak., PhD Mak.   Assoc. Prof.; Head*

Okello, S., BVM Nair., MSc Mak., PhD   Sr. Lectr.

Siefert, L., DrVetMed Hanover   Sr. Lectr.

Other Staff: 2 Lectrs.; 4 Asst. Lectrs.

SPECIAL CENTRES, ETC

Adult and Continuing Education, Institute of

Adult and Communications Studies

Bananuka, T., BAEd MScEd   Asst. Lectr.; Acting Head*

Katahoire, Anne R., BA Hull, MEd Glas.   Assoc. Prof.

Other Staff: 1 Lectr.; 2 Asst. Lectrs.

Community Education and Extra-Mural Studies

Atim, D. K., BA Mak., MEd NE   Sr. Lectr.

Openjuru, G., BA Mak., MEd Mak.   Lectr.; Head* (on leave)

Other Staff: 1 Lectr.; 3 Asst. Lectrs.

Distance Education

Aguti, Jessica N., BA Mak., MEd Mak., PhD   Sr. Lectr.

Siminyu, S. N., BA Mak., MA Mak.   Lectr.; Acting Head*

Other Staff: 3 Lectrs.; 4 Asst. Lectrs.

Environment and Natural Resources, Institute of

Kansenene, J. M., BSc Mak., MSc Mak., PhD Mich.   Acting Dir. (Kibaale)

Kansiime, F., BSc Dar., MScEnv Dar., MSc T.H.Delft, PhD Wageningen   Assoc. Prof.; Dir.*

Kateyo, E., BSc Mak., MSc Mak., PhD Mak.   Sr. Lectr.

Okot-Okum, J., BSc Ghana, MSc T.H.Delft, PhD Mak.   Sr. Lectr.

Pomeroy, D. E., MA Camb., PhD Adel.   Hon. Prof.

Other Staff: 2 Lectrs.; 2 Asst. Lectrs.; 8 Hon. Lectrs.

Higher Education Studies and Development, East African Institute of

Musaazi, J. C. S., BEd E.Anglia, MA Duquesne, PhD Pitt.   Prof.

Nkata, J., BA Mak., MEd Manc., PhD Mak.   Sr. Lectr.

Other Staff: 4 Lectrs.

Human Rights and Peace Centre (HURIPEC)

Oloka-Onyango, J., LLB Mak., LLM Harv., SJD Harv.   Prof.; Dir.*

Tindifa, S. B., LLB Mak., LLM Lund   Sr. Lectr.; Acting Dir.* (on leave)

Other Staff: 3 Lectrs.; 6 Asst. Lectrs.

Library and Information Science, East African School of (EASLIS)

Ikoja-Odongo, R. J., BA Delhi, MPhil Stir., PhD Zululand   Deputy Dir.

Magara, E., BLIS Mak., MSc Mak., PhD Zambia   Dir.*

Makerere University Agricultural Research Institute, Kabanyolo (MUARIK)

Rwakaikara, M. S., BSc(Agric) Mak., MSc(Agric) Mak., PhD Flor.   Acting Dir.*

Social Research, Makerere Institute of

Nakanyike Musisi, BA MA PhD   Dir.*

Other Staff: 2 Res. Fellows; 1 Temp. Sr. Res. Fellow; 2 Temp. Res. Fellows

Statistics and Applied Economics, Institute of

Mugisha, X. R., BA Dar., MSc Manit., PhD Manit.   Dir.*

Odwee, J. J. A. O., BSc Mak., MA Mak., PhD Mak.   Dir.*

Planning and Applied Statistics

Atuhaire, L. K., BStat Mak., MSc S'ton, PhD S'ton.   Sr. Lectr.

Kakuba, C., BStat Mak., MA Mak.   Sr. Lectr.

Kurong, L., BStat Mak., MStat Mak.   Sr. Lectr.

Sekiboobo, A., BStat Mak., MStat Mak.   Sr. Lectr.

Other Staff: 5 Lectrs.; 3 Asst. Lectrs.

Population Studies

Ayiga, 8, BA Mak., MA Mak., PhD Mak.   Sr. Lectr.; Head*

Mulindwa, I. K., BStat Mak., MA Mak., PhD Mak.   Sr. Lectr.

Ntozi, J. P. M., BSc Mak., MSc Mak., PhD Lond.   Prof.

Odwee, J. J. A. O., BSc Mak., MA Mak., PhD Mak.   Sr. Lectr.

Sekatawa, E. K., PhD Penn.   Sr. Lectr.

Ssekamatte, S. J., BA Mak., PhD Brown   Sr. Lectr.

Other Staff: 3 Lectrs.

Statistical Methods

Mwanga, A. Y., BStat Mak., MStat Mak.   Lectr.; Acting Head*

Other Staff: 5 Lectrs.; 5 Asst. Lectrs.

CONTACT OFFICERS

Academic affairs. Academic Registrar: Olal-Odur, Amos, BSc Mak., MA S.Fraser, PhD Alta.

Accommodation. Dean of Students: Ekudu-Adoku, John, BSc Mak.

Admissions (first degree). Deputy Academic Registrar (Admissions): Bazanye-Nkangi, G., BSc Mak., MEd NE

Admissions (higher degree). Deputy Registrar (Admissions (higher degree)): Ngobi, S. M., BA Dar., MSc Nair.

Adult/continuing education. Director, Institute of Adult and Continuing Education: Sentongo, Muua, BA E.Af., MA Indiana

Archives. University Librarian: Musoke, Maria G. N., PhD

Careers. Deputy Academic Registrar (Admissions): Bazanye-Nkangi, G., BSc Mak., MEd NE

Computing services. Acting Director of Computer Science: Mulira, J. N., BA Mak., MSc Lond.

Development/fund-raising. Director (Development/fund raising): Mayanja, M. K., BCom Mak., MA Mak.

Distance education. Director, Institute of Adult and Continuing Education: Sentongo, Muua, BA E.Af., MA Indiana

Estates and buildings/works and services. Senior Assistant Engineer (Estates and buildings/works and services): Kerali, G. A., BSc(Eng) Mak., MSc

Examinations. Deputy Academic Registrar (Examinations): Kiiza, P. N., BA Mak.

Finance. Bursar: Byambabazi, Ben, BCom Mak., MBA Mak.

General enquiries. Academic Registrar: Olal-Odur, Amos, BSc Mak., MA S.Fraser, PhD Alta.

Health services. Acting Director, University Hospital: Bosa, Jane, MB ChB Mak.

Industrial liaison. Lecturer (Industrial liaison): Byaruhanga, J. K., PhD

Library (chief librarian). University Librarian: Musoke, Maria G. N., PhD

Marketing. Acting Public Relations Officer: Kawesa, H., BA Mak.

Ombudsman. Legal Officer: (vacant)

Personnel/human resources. Senior Assistant Secretary, Personnel: Lubwama, F. J. Y., BA Mak., MA Lond.

Public relations. Acting Public Relations Officer: Kawesa, H., BA Mak.

Publications. Senior Assistant Registrar (Publications): Karindiriza, E. S. K., BA(Educn) Mak., MEd Mak.

Purchasing. Senior Assistant Bursar (Purchasing): Mugamba, R., BCom Mak., MBA

Research. Senior Assistant Registrar (Research): Burahure, R. T., BA Mak., MEd Mak.

Scholarships, awards, loans. Academic Registrar: Olal-Odur, Amos, BSc Mak., MA S.Fraser, PhD Alta.

Security. Deputy Vice-Chancellor: Epelu-Opio, Prof. J., BVSc Nair., MSc Nair., PhD Mak.

Sport and recreation. Principal Sports Tutor: Mugisha, E. N. B., BScEd N.Y.State, MScEd N.Y.State

Staff development and training. Acting Deputy Registrar (Staff Development): Basigira, J. G., BAEd Mak., MEd Mak.

Strategic planning. Director (Strategic planning): Mayanja, M. K., BCom Mak., MA Mak.

Student welfare/counselling. Principal Counsellor: Matovu, P. C., BA(Educn) ThM MA PhD

Students from other countries. Deputy Academic Registrar (Admissions): Bazanye-Nkangi, G., BSc Mak., MEd NE

CAMPUS/COLLEGE HEADS

Institute of Teacher Education, Kyambogo. (Tel: (041) 285037; Fax: (041) 220464) Principal: Lutalo-Bosa, A., BSc Lond., MSc McG., PhD McG.

[Information supplied by the institution as at 16 October 2007, and edited by the ACU]

MBARARA UNIVERSITY OF SCIENCE AND TECHNOLOGY

Founded 1989

Member of the Association of Commonwealth Universities

Postal Address: PO Box 1410, Mbarara, Uganda
Liaison Office: PO Box 7062, Kampala; telephone: (041) 533162
Telephone: (0485) 21373 Fax: (0485) 20782 E-mail: vc@must.ac.ug
URL: http://www.must.ac.ug

VICE-CHANCELLOR*—Kayanja, Prof. Frederick I. B., BVetMed Lond., MSc Lond., PhD E.Af., Hon. DSc
DEPUTY VICE-CHANCELLOR—Baranga, Prof. J., BSc(Ed) Mak., PhD Mak.
ACADEMIC REGISTRAR—Bazirake, Stephen B., BA E.Af.
UNIVERSITY SECRETARY‡—Kibirige, Charles K., MB ChB Kalinin
UNIVERSITY BURSAR—Ojambo, D., BCom Mak., MBA Mak.

GENERAL INFORMATION

History. The university was founded in 1989. It is located in Mbarara, 260km southwest of Kampala.

Admission to first degree courses. General Certificate of Education (GCE) O level and passes in at least 2 A levels at the same sitting, or equivalent qualifications. International applicants who do not possess A levels must have completed at least one year of a relevant university course.

First Degrees (see also Ugandan Directory to Subjects of Study) (* = with honours). BBA, BDevSc*, BIT, BMedLabScience, BPharmacy, BScCompt*, BScComptEng, BSc(Ed)*, BSc(Nursing), MB ChB.
Length of course. Full-time: BBA, BDevSc*, BIT, BSc(Ed)*, BScCompt*: 3 years; BMedLabScience, BPharmacy, BSc(Nursing), BScComptEng: 4 years; MB ChB: 5 years.

Higher Degrees (see also Ugandan Directory to Subjects of Study).
Master's. MA(DevSt), MMed, MSc.
Admission. Applicants for admission to master's degree courses should hold a good first degree from a recognised university.
Length of course. Full-time: MA(DevSt), MSc: 2 years; MMed: 3 years.
Doctoral. MD, PhD.
Admission. A relevant master's degree from a recognised university.
Length of course. Full-time: MD, PhD: 3 years.

Libraries. Volumes: 29,248. Periodicals subscribed to: 20. Other holdings: 670 CDs.

Academic Year (2007–2008). August–June.

Income (2006–2007). Total, Ush10,063,000,000.

Statistics. Staff (2006–2007): 350 (184 academic, 166 non-academic). Students (2005–2006): full-time 1606 (1003 men, 603 women); international 19 (12 men, 7 women); undergraduate 1521 (937 men, 584 women); master's 133 (103 men, 30 women); doctoral 28 (21 men, 7 women).

FACULTIES/SCHOOLS

Development Studies
Tel: (0485) 20642
Dean: Mbabazi, Pamela, BA Mak., MA E.Af., MA Leeds, MSc Kumasi, PhD Mbarara
Secretary: Wilfred, Aliguma

Medicine
Tel: (0485) 20642
Dean: Kabakyenga, J., MB ChB Mak., MPH Leeds
Secretary: Night, Natukunda

Science
Tel: (0485) 20851
Dean: Anguma, Simon, BSc Mak., MSc Mak.
Secretary: Kirungi, Harriet, BAS Kyambogo

ACADEMIC UNITS

Anatomy

Kayanja, Frederick I. B., BVetMed Lond., MSc Lond., PhD E.Af., Hon. DSc   Prof.
Muwanga, Grace, BVM Mak., MSc Mak.   Lectr.; Head*
Osinde, S. P., BVM Mak., MSc Mbarara, PhD Mbarara   Sr. Lectr.
Other Staff: 4 Lectrs.
Research: comparative anatomy of pancreatic arterial blood supply; epididymal epithelium in African giant rat

Biochemistry

Tel: (0485) 20720
Isharaza, W. K., MSc Mak., PhD Brussels   Prof.; Head*
Other Staff: 2 Lectrs.; 3 Asst. Lectrs.
Research: extraction and stabilisation of pytolacca docedandra; iron status of pregnant women; molluscicide for field application

Computer Science

Twongyeirwe, Theodora, BEng Leeds, MSc Leeds   Lectr.; Head*
Other Staff: 5 Lectrs.; 3 Asst. Lectrs.

Development Studies

Tel: (0485) 20642
Dornboos, M. R., BA Amst., PhD Calif.   Visiting Prof.
Mbabazi, Pamela, BA Mak., MA E.Af., MA Leeds, MSc Kumasi, PhD Mbarara   Sr. Lectr.

Roberts, Muriisa, BA *Mak.*, MPhil *Bergen*, DrPolSc *Bergen* Head*

Shaw, Timothy, BA *Sus.*, MA *E.Af.*, MA *Prin.*, PhD *Prin.* Visiting Prof.

Other Staff: 6 Lectrs.; 2 Asst. Lectrs.

Research: conflict and peace building; industrial development; milk industry and development of pastoralists; women's empowerment and family stability

Internal Medicine

Tel: (0485) 20007

Pepper, James L., BSc *Mich.State*, MSc *Dayton*, DO *Mich.State* Prof.

Wilson, L. A., MB ChB *Otago*, FRACP, FRCP Prof.; Head*

Other Staff: 4 Lectrs.; 3 Asst. Lectrs.

Research: diabetes; HIV/AIDS; tuberculosis

Mathematics

Tel: (0485) 20851

Kwikiriza, Kenneth Lectr.; Head*

Wanjala, G., BSc(Ed) *Mak.*, MSc *Mak.*, PhD *Gron.* Sr. Lectr.

Other Staff: 4 Lectrs.

Research: Schur functions

Medical Laboratory Science

Apecu, R. O., MSc *Wales* Lectr.; Head*

Other Staff: 3 Lectrs.; 2 Asst. Lectrs.

Microbiology and Parasitology

Byarugaba, Frederick, BVM *Mak.*, MSc *Mbarara*, PhD *Mbarara* Sr. Lectr.; Head*

Labaut Tamara, Tereza, MD *Havana*, MSc *Havana* Assoc. Prof.

Other Staff: 1 Lectr.; 2 Asst. Lectrs.

Research: antibiotic sensitivity of endemic shingella; schistosoma haematobium

Obstetrics/Gynaecology

Sanchez Alarco, C. E., MD Prof.; Head*

Other Staff: 5 Lectrs.; 2 Asst. Lectrs.

Paediatrics and Child Health

Kiwanuka, MB ChB *Mak.*, MTropPaed *Liv.* Sr. Lectr.; Head*

Other Staff: 4 Lectrs.; 3 Asst. Lectrs.

Pathology

Sendikaddiwa, E., MB ChB *Mak.*, MMEd *Mak.* Sr. Lectr.; Head*

Other Staff: 3 Lectrs.

Research: malignant tumours in southwestern Uganda

Pharmacology

Agaba, A., MB ChB *Mak.*, PhD *Morehouse* Sr. Lectr.; Head*

Other Staff: 2 Lectrs.; 1 Asst. Lectr.

Research: herbal medicine

Pharmacy

Reddy, P. R. K., BPharm *Gulb.*, MPharm *BITS*, PhD *Pondicherry* Prof.; Head*

Other Staff: 1 Asst. Lectr.

Physics

Anguma, Simon, BSc *Mak.*, MSc *Mak.* Sr. Lectr.

Luwulira, D., BSc *Mak.*, MSc *Mak.* Lectr.; Head*

Other Staff: 4 Lectrs.

Physiology

Begumya, Y. R., BSc *Mak.*, MB BS *Khart.* Prof.

Kasiisi, B., BVM *Mak.*, MSc *Kansas* Lectr.; Head*

Mukiibi, N., MSc *Moscow*, PhD *Moscow* Assoc. Prof.

Other Staff: 2 Lectrs.; 1 Asst. Lectr.

Psychology/Psychiatry

Maling, S., MB ChB *Mbarara*, MMed *Mak.* Lectr.; Head*

Other Staff: 2 Lectrs.; 2 Asst. Lectrs.

Research: dissociative disorders in southwestern Uganda

Public Health

Kabakyenga, J., MB ChB *Mak.*, MPH *Leeds* Assoc. Prof.

Mulogo, E., BDS *Mak.*, MPH *Mak.*, MSc *Rome* Sr. Lectr.; Head*

Other Staff: 5 Lectrs.; 3 Asst. Lectrs.

Surgery

Bitariho, D., MB ChB *Mak.*, MMed *Mak.* Lectr.; Head*

Kitya, D., MB ChB *Mak.*, MMed *Mak.* Sr. Lectr.

Mutakooha, E. K., MB ChB *Mak.*, MMed *Mak.* Assoc. Prof.

Other Staff: 7 Lectrs.

SPECIAL CENTRES, ETC

Tropical Forest Conservation, Institute of

McNeilage, A., BSc *Edin.*, PhD *Brist.* Dir.*

Research: conservation; forest biology; gorilla census

CONTACT OFFICERS

Academic affairs. Academic Registrar: Bazirake, Stephen B., BA *E.Af.* (E-mail: ar@must.ac.ug)

Accommodation. Dean of Students: Kyagaba, E., BSc(Agric) *Mak.*, MSc *Nair.*

Admissions (first degree). Deputy Registrar: Kibirige, J. L., BA *Mak.*, MA *Mak.* (E-mail: ar@must.ac.ug)

Admissions (higher degree). Academic Registrar: Bazirake, Stephen B., BA *E.Af.* (E-mail: ar@must.ac.ug)

Alumni. Senior Assistant Registrar: Opio, Okello F., BA *Mak.*, MA *Mak.* (E-mail: ar@must.ac.ug)

Estates and buildings/works and services. University Engineer: Nsimbi, T., BScEng *Mak.*

Examinations. Senior Assistant Registrar: Opio, Okello F., BA *Mak.*, MA *Mak.* (E-mail: ar@must.ac.ug)

Finance. University Bursar: Ojambo, D., BCom *Mak.*, MBA *Mak.*

General enquiries. Academic Registrar: Bazirake, Stephen B., BA *E.Af.* (E-mail: ar@must.ac.ug)

Library (chief librarian). Librarian: Gakibayo, Anne, BLIS *Mak.*

Personnel/human resources. University Secretary: Kibirige, Charles K., MB ChB *Kalinin*

Publications. Senior Assistant Registrar: Opio, Okello F., BA *Mak.*, MA *Mak.* (E-mail: ar@must.ac.ug)

Purchasing. Procument Officer: Karuhanga, Stephen, BA(SS) *Mak.*

Research. Academic Registrar: Bazirake, Stephen B., BA *E.Af.* (E-mail: ar@must.ac.ug)

Sport and recreation. Sports Tutor: Tumwesigye, Charles, BScAgric *Mak.*, MEd *Mak.*

Staff development and training. Academic Registrar: Bazirake, Stephen B., BA *E.Af.* (E-mail: ar@must.ac.ug)

[*Information supplied by the institution as at 5 December 2007, and edited by the ACU*]

NDEJJE UNIVERSITY

Postal Address: PO Box 7088, Kampala, Uganda
Telephone: (077) 365927 **Fax:** (041) 610132

VICE-CHANCELLOR*—Senyimba, Bishop Dr. Michael

NKUMBA UNIVERSITY

Founded 1994

Postal Address: PO Box 237, Entebbe, Uganda
Telephone: (042) 320134 **Fax:** (042) 320134 **E-mail:** sbusulwa@hotmail.com
URL: http://www.nkumbauniversity.ac.ug

VICE-CHANCELLOR*—Senteza Kajubi, Prof. William, OM, MSc Chic.
ACADEMIC REGISTRAR‡—Busulwa, S. K., OM, BA E.Af., MA Virginia

UGANDA CHRISTIAN UNIVERSITY

Founded 1997

Member of the Association of Commonwealth Universities

Postal Address: PO Box 4, Mukono, Uganda
Telephone: (041) 429 0828 **Fax:** (041) 429 0800 **E-mail:** ucu@ucu.ac.ug
URL: http://www.ucu.ac.ug

VICE-CHANCELLOR*—Noll, Rev. Prof. Stephen, BA Cornell, MA Grad.Theol.Union, MDiv Church Pacific Div.Sch., PhD Manc.
DEPUTY VICE-CHANCELLOR, FINANCE AND ADMINISTRATION‡—Sajjabi, Florence B., BA Mak., BEd Mak., MEd Melb., PhD Panjab
DEPUTY VICE-CHANCELLOR, ACADEMIC AFFAIRS—Kagume Mugisha, Rev. Dr. Alex, PhD Brist., BD
DEPUTY VICE-CHANCELLOR FOR DEVELOPMENT AND EXTERNAL RELATIONS—Senyonyi, Rev. Canon Dr. John, BSc Nair., MA Trinity Evang.Div.Sch.(Ill.), PhD Melb.

GENERAL INFORMATION

History. Established as a private institution in 1997 by the Church of Uganda, the university was fully accredited in 2004.

It is located in the town of Mukono, 20km outside Kampala on the Kampala-Jinja road.

Admission to first degree courses. Candidates for admission to degree programmes should have a Uganda Certificate of Education (UCE) and Uganda Advanced Certificate of Education (UACE) with at least 2 principal passes, or a diploma from a recognised institution of higher learning, or a pass in Mature Age Examinations.

International students are admitted on a case by case basis depending on their countries' entry requirements. Kenyan applicants require a mean grade of C+ or above.

First Degrees (see also Ugandan Directory to Subjects of Study) (* = with honours). BA, BA(Ed), BBA, BD, BDevS, BEconMan, BEd*, BHA, BSc, BSc(Ed), BSc(Nursing), BSWSA, LLB.

Length of course. Full-time: BEd*: 2 years; BA, BA(Ed), BBA, BD, BDevS, BEconMan, BSc, BSc(Ed), BSc(Nursing), BSWSA: 3 years; LLB: 4 years. Part-time: BEd*: 2 years; BD, BHA: 3 years.

Higher Degrees (see also Ugandan Directory to Subjects of Study).
Master's. MA.
MA in Public Health Leadership/MA in Counselling Psychology; 2 years part-time only. MA in Literature 2 years full-time only.
Length of course. Full-time: MA: 2 years. Part-time: MA: 2 years.

Libraries. Volumes: 80,000. Periodicals subscribed to: 100. Special collections: archives of the Church of Uganda.

Academic Awards (2007–2008). 500 awards ranging in value from US$100 to US$3550.

Income (2006–2007). Total, Ush14,600,000,000.

Statistics. Staff (2006–2007): 430 (200 academic, 230 non-academic). Students (2006–2007): full-time 5306 (2624 men, 2682 women); part-time 439 (259 men, 180 women); international 272; undergraduate 5536 (2741 men, 2795 women); master's 237 (145 men, 92 women).

FACULTIES/SCHOOLS

Business and Administration
Tel: (031) 235 0811
   E-mail: business@ucu.ac.ug
Dean: Owor, Joseph J., BA Dar., MA Marburg

Divinity and Theology
Tel: (031) 235 0810
   E-mail: theology@ucu.ac.ug
Dean: Olwa, Alfred, BD Mak., MTh Brun.

Education and Arts
Tel: (031) 235 0809
   E-mail: education_arts@ucu.ac.ug
Dean: Mwesigwa, Fred S., MEd Leeds, PhD Leeds, BD

Law
Tel: (031) 235 0832 E-mail: law@ucu.ac.ug
Dean: Kasozi, George, BA NUL, LLM Hull

Science and Technology
Tel: (031) 235 0813
   E-mail: technology@ucu.ac.ug
Dean: Nabugoomu, Fabian, BStat Mak., MSc Guelph, PhD Edin.

Social Sciences
Tel: (031) 235 0817 E-mail: swsa@ucu.ac.ug
Dean: Musinguzi, Benon, BSc Mak., MA Mak.

ACADEMIC UNITS

Business and Administration
Tel: (031) 235 0811
   E-mail: business@ucu.ac.ug

Owor, Joseph J., BA Dar., MA Marburg   Lectr.; Head*
Other Staff: 15 Lectrs.

Development Studies
Tel: (031) 235 0835
Kukunda, E. Bacwayo, BA Mak., MA ANU, PhD Massey   Sr. Lectr.; Head*
Other Staff: 5 Lectrs.

Divinity and Theology, Bishop Tucker School of
Tel: (031) 235 0810
   E-mail: theology@ucu.ac.ug
Kalengyo, Edison, BVM Mak., MPhil Nott., PhD Natal, BD   Sr. Lectr.
Mathew, C. V., BA Kerala, BD Benue State, MTh United Theol.Coll.(P.Q.), MA Columbia Internat., PhD Serampore, DTh
Nassaka, Olivia, BD Mak., MA Nott., PhD Edin.   Sr. Lectr.
Obetia, Joel, MA Nott., PhD Leeds, BD   Sr. Lectr.
Olwa, Alfred, BD Mak., MTh Brun.   Lectr.; Head*
Other Staff: 1 Sr. Lectr.; 12 Lectrs.; 1 Sr. Lectr.†

Education
Tel: (031) 235 0809
   E-mail: education_arts@ucu.ac.ug
Byaruhanga, Rev. Canon Christopher, PhD N.Y., BD   Assoc. Prof.
Mwesigwa, Fred S., MEd Leeds, PhD Leeds, BD   Sr. Lectr.; Head*
Opolot, Jethro, MSc Birm., MEd Birm., MA Edin., PhD Edin.   Prof.†
Other Staff: 1 Sr. Lectr.; 13 Lectrs.; 2 Sr. Lectrs.†

General Studies
Tel: (031) 235 0415
Button, Daniel, BA Minn., MDiv Columbia Internat., BA   Lectr.; Head*
Research: integration of faith and learning

Health Sciences

Tel: (013) 235 0414 E-mail: health@ucu.ac.ug
Chamberlain-Froese, Jean, BS Tor., MD Tor.,
MEd McM.   Sr. Lectr.
Fountain, Doug, BS Oregon, MPH N.Carolina
Lectr.; Head*
Mukooza, Edward, MB ChB Mak., MBus S.Af.
Sr. Lectr.
Mutabazi, Jemima, BNS Zambia, MSN Case
W.Reserve   Sr. Lectr.
Other Staff: 6 Asst. Profs.; 6 Sr. Lectrs.; 4
Lectrs.; 1 Sr. Lectr.†
Research: health and wholeness; health
education; maternal and child health;
nursing

Languages and Literature

E-mail: langlit@ucu.ac.ug
Lilford, Grant C., BA Vassar, MA Sus., PhD Cape
Town   Sr. Lectr.; Head*
Other Staff: 5 Lectrs.; 1 Sr. Lectr.†

Law

Tel: (031) 235 0832 E-mail: law@ucu.ac.ug
Mugenyi, Asa, LLB Mak., LLM Mak.   Lectr.;
Head*
Other Staff: 10 Lectrs.; 2 Sr. Lectrs.†

Research: family law; human rights; legal
practice; legislative drafting

Mass Communication

Tel: (031) 235 0824
Ilakut, Ben B., BA Mak., MA Indiana, MA Lond.,
MPhil Lond.   Head*
Other Staff: 8 Lectrs.

Research and Postgraduate Studies

Mangheni, J. Patrick, BSc Mak., MA Oxf., MSc
Oxf., DPhil Oxf.   Assoc. Prof.; Dean*

Science and Technology

Tel: (031) 235 0813
Mangheni, J. Patrick, BSc Mak., MA Oxf., MSc
Oxf., DPhil Oxf.   Assoc. Prof.
Nabugoomu, Fabian, BStat Mak., MSc Guelph,
PhD Edin.   Assoc. Prof.; Head*
Other Staff: 8 Lectrs.; 2 Asst. Lectrs.

Social Work and Social Administration

Tel: (031) 235 0817
Musinguzi, Benon, BSc Mak., MA Mak.   Lectr.;
Head*
Other Staff: 16 Lectrs.

Research: implication of HIV/AIDS on the
development of Uganda

SPECIAL CENTRES, ETC

Mission, Leadership and Public Policy, Global South Institute for

Tel: (031) 235 0827 Fax: (041) 290 800
E-mail: teeuganda@yahoo.com
Tumwine, Rev. Canon John K., BD Uganda
Christian, MA Nairobi Evangelical   Dir.*
Research: African Anglican identity and mission;
leadership development; mission and
evangelism; public policy

Uganda Studies Programme

Tel: (031) 235 0815
E-mail: mbartels@ucu.ac.ug
Bartels, Mark, BA Wheaton(Ill.), MA Wheaton(Ill.)
Dir.*
Smedley, Cynthia T., MS Boston   Co-ordinator

[Information supplied by the institution as at 7 November
2007, and edited by the ACU]

UGANDA MARTYRS UNIVERSITY

Founded 1989

Member of the Association of Commonwealth Universities

Postal Address: PO Box 5498, Kampala, Uganda
Telephone: (038) 410611 Fax: (038) 410100 E-mail: umu@umu.ac.ug
URL: http://www.fiuc.org/umu

VICE-CHANCELLOR*—Olweny, Prof. Charles, MB ChB E.Af., MMEd E.Af., MD, FRACP
DEPUTY VICE-CHANCELLOR (ACADEMIC AFFAIRS)—Kanyandago, Prof. Peter, BTh Louvain, MA Louvain, PhD Louvain
DIRECTOR (HUMAN RESOURCES)—Kikule, Eliza N., BBA Uganda Martyrs, MA(DevSt) Uganda Martyrs
REGISTRAR‡—Byuma, Innocent, BA Mak., MA Hull
FINANCE OFFICER—Mugema, Br. Deogratius, BA Walsh, MBA Akron

GENERAL INFORMATION

History. The university was founded in 1989
and classes began in 1993. It was chartered in
2005. It is a Catholic institution.
It is situated at Nkozi, 82km southwest of
Kampala.

Admission to first degree courses. Uganda
Certificate of Education with at least 2
principal passes at A level. Post-secondary
diplomas are also considered. International
applicants: qualifications required for
university entrance in country of origin are
usually acceptable.

First Degrees (see also Ugandan Directory to
Subjects of Study). BA, BAEd, BArch, BBAM,
BSc, BSc(Agric), BSc(BldgTechn).
Applicants for BArch should hold
BSc(BldgTechn).
Length of course. Full-time: BArch: 2 years; BA,
BBAM, BSc, BSc(BldgTechn): 3 years. By distance
learning: BAEd: 3 years; BSc(Agric): 4 years.

Higher Degrees (see also Ugandan Directory
to Subjects of Study).
Master's. MA, MBA, MSc(HSM), MSc(IS).
Length of course. Full-time: MA, MBA,
MSc(HSM), MSc(IS): 1 year. Part-time: MA,
MBA: 2 years. By distance learning: MA: 3 years.
Doctoral. PhD.
Admission. Applicants should hold a master's
degree.
Length of course. Full-time: PhD: 3–5 years.

Libraries. Volumes: 18,025. Periodicals
subscribed to: 318. Other holdings: 7 online
databases; 2640 book bank volumes; 158 CDs.
Special collections: African Research
Documentation Centre (ARDC).

Academic Awards (2005–2006). 4 awards
ranging in value from US$400 to US$4000.

FACULTIES/SCHOOLS

Agriculture

E-mail: cssekyewa@umu.ac.ug
Dean: Ssekyewa, Charles, BSc Mak., MSc Lond.
Secretary: Omwene Nakyagaba, Sarah, BBA
Uganda Martyrs, MBA Uganda Martyrs

Building Technology and Architecture

E-mail: fbta@umu.ac.ug
Dean: Wadulo, Jackie, BArch Savannah Art & Des.,
MArch Savannah Art & Des.
Secretary: Omwene Nakyagaba, Sarah, BBA
Uganda Martyrs, MBA Uganda Martyrs

Business Administration and Management

Tel: (038) 410615 E-mail: bam@umu.ac.ug
Dean: Ijjo, Alex, BStat Mak., PhD Brad.
Secretary: Nasaka, Justine S., BSE Mak.

Education

Tel: (038) 410643 E-mail: eolupot@umu.ac.ug
Dean: Olupot, Emuron, BA Mak., MA Col., PhD
Alta.

Science

E-mail: mehafflet@umu.ac.ug
Dean: Hafflet, Marie-Esther, BA Detroit, MA
Detroit, MA Notre Dame(Ind.), PhD Notre
Dame(Ind.)
Secretary: Omwene Nakyagaba, Sarah, BBA
Uganda Martyrs, MBA Uganda Martyrs

ACADEMIC UNITS

Ethics and Development Studies, Institute of

E-mail: ides@umu.ac.ug
Kisekka, Joseph, BA Pontif.Urb., MA Pontif.Urb.,
PhD Pontif.Urb.   Dir.*
Other Staff: 1 Sr. Lectr.; 6 Lectrs.; 1 Temp.
Prof.; 2 Temp. Lectrs.

Health Sciences

E-mail: everdmaniple@umu.ac.ug
Everd, Bikaitoha M., MB ChB Mak., MPH Mak.
Head*
Other Staff: 1 Sr. Lectr.; 5 Lectrs.; 2 Temp.
Lectrs.

Information Systems

Tel: (038) 410633 E-mail: victor@umu.ac.ug
van Reijswoud, Victor, MPhil Maastricht, MPhil
Bath, PhD I.M.S., Delft   Prof.; Head*
Other Staff: 3 Lectrs.

Postgraduate Studies, School of

Tel: (038) 410610 E-mail: spgs@umu.ac.ug
Ankunda, Pamela, BA Uganda Martyrs

Carabine, Deirdre, BA Belf., MA Belf., PhD Belf., PhD N.U.I.   Prof.; Dir., Postgrad. Studies

SPECIAL CENTRES, ETC

African Research and Documentation Centre

Tel: (038) 410635 E-mail: ardc@umu.ac.ug
Kanyandago, Peter, BTh Louvain, MA Louvain, PhD Louvain   Prof.; Dir.*
Other Staff: 1 Res. Co-ordinator; 1 Asst. Librarian; 1 Editor†

Extra-Mural Studies, Centre for

No staff at present

Information and Communication Technology

E-mail: ict@umu.ac.ug
Lule, George William, BSc Mak., MSc(IS) Uganda Martyrs   Head*
Other Staff: 5 Staff Members

CONTACT OFFICERS

Academic affairs. Registrar: Byuma, Innocent, BA Mak., MA Hull
    (E-mail: registrar@umu.ac.ug)
Accommodation. Campus Warden: Katusiime, Scholastic (E-mail: warden@umu.ac.ug)
Admissions (first degree). Assistant Registrar (Student Affairs): Nandala, Flora I., BEd Mak., MA Mak. (E-mail: registrar@umu.ac.uk)
Admissions (higher degree). Registrar: Byuma, Innocent, BA Mak., MA Hull
    (E-mail: registrar@umu.ac.ug)
Adult/continuing education. (on hold)
Alumni. Vice-Chancellor: Olweny, Prof. Charles, MB ChB E.Af., MMEd E.Af., MD, FRACP (E-mail: vcumu@umu.ac.ug)
Archives. Acting Librarian: Masereka, John P.
    (E-mail: headlib@umu.ac.ug)
Computing services. Head, Computing Services: Lule, George William, BSc Mak., MSc(IS) Uganda Martyrs
    (E-mail: glule@umu.ac.ug)
Credit transfer. Registrar: Byuma, Innocent, BA Mak., MA Hull
    (E-mail: registrar@umu.ac.ug)

Development/fund-raising. Vice-Chancellor: Olweny, Prof. Charles, MB ChB E.Af., MMEd E.Af., MD, FRACP
    (E-mail: vcumu@umu.ac.ug)
Distance education. (contact relevant faculty/institute)
Equal opportunities. Registrar: Byuma, Innocent, BA Mak., MA Hull
    (E-mail: registrar@umu.ac.ug)
Estates and buildings/works and services. Estates Officer: Ssembatya, Lawrence
    (E-mail: lssembatya@umu.ac.ug)
Examinations. Assistant Registrar (Examinations): Nandala, Flora I., BEd Mak., MA Mak. (E-mail: registrar@umu.ac.uk)
Finance. Finance Officer: Mugema, Br. Deogratius, BA Walsh, MBA Akron
    (E-mail: financeofficer@umu.ac.ug)
General enquiries. Front Desk Officer: Nalumu, Jane (E-mail: umu@umu.ac.ug)
Health services. Nurse: Mugisha Khellen, Evelyn
International office. Vice-Chancellor: Olweny, Prof. Charles, MB ChB E.Af., MMEd E.Af., MD, FRACP (E-mail: vcumu@umu.ac.ug)
Library (enquiries). Acting Librarian: Masereka, John P.
    (E-mail: headlib@umu.ac.ug)
Marketing. Public Relations Officer: Sengooba, Joseph, BA Uganda Martyrs
    (E-mail: pro@umu.ac.ug)
Minorities/disadvantaged groups. Assistant Registrar (Student Affairs): Nandala, Flora I., BEd Mak., MA Mak.
    (E-mail: registrar@umu.ac.ug)
Personnel/human resources. Director (Human Resources): Kikule, Eliza N., BBA Uganda Martyrs, MA(DevSt) Uganda Martyrs
    (E-mail: directorhr@umu.ac.ug)
Public relations. Public Relations Officer: Sengooba, Joseph, BA Uganda Martyrs
    (E-mail: pro@umu.ac.ug)
Publications. UMU Press: Carabine, Prof. Deirdre, BA Belf., MA Belf., PhD Belf., PhD N.U.I. (E-mail: directorspgs@umu.ac.ug)
Purchasing. Purchasing Officer: Tamale, Dominic

Quality assurance and accreditation. Deputy Vice-Chancellor (Academic Affairs): Kanyandago, Prof. Peter, BTh Louvain, MA Louvain, PhD Louvain
    (E-mail: dvcaa@umu.ac.ug)
Research. Deputy Vice-Chancellor (Academic Affairs): Kanyandago, Prof. Peter, BTh Louvain, MA Louvain, PhD Louvain
    (E-mail: dvcaa@umu.ac.ug)
Safety. Security Officer: Mpora, Peter
Scholarships, awards, loans. Deputy Vice-Chancellor (Academic Affairs): Kanyandago, Prof. Peter, BTh Louvain, MA Louvain, PhD Louvain (E-mail: dvcaa@umu.ac.ug)
Schools liaison. Assistant Registrar (Schools liaison): Nandala, Flora I., BEd Mak., MA Mak. (E-mail: registrar@umu.ac.uk)
Security. Security Officer: Mpora, Peter
Sport and recreation. Lecturer (Sport and recreation): Katongole, J. C.
    (E-mail: jckatongole@umu.ac.ug)
Staff development and training. Vice-Chancellor: Olweny, Prof. Charles, MB ChB E.Af., MMEd E.Af., MD, FRACP
    (E-mail: vcumu@umu.ac.ug)
Student union. Assistant Registrar (Student Affairs): Nandala, Flora I., BEd Mak., MA Mak. (E-mail: registrar@umu.ac.ug)
Student welfare/counselling. Assistant Registrar (Student Affairs): Nandala, Flora I., BEd Mak., MA Mak.
    (E-mail: registrar@umu.ac.uk)
Students from other countries. Assistant Registrar (Student Affairs): Nandala, Flora I., BEd Mak., MA Mak.
    (E-mail: registrar@umu.ac.uk)
Students with disabilities. Assistant Registrar (Student Affairs): Nandala, Flora I., BEd Mak., MA Mak. (E-mail: registrar@umu.ac.uk)
University press. Director, School of Postgraduate Studies (SPGS): Carabine, Prof. Deirdre, BA Belf., MA Belf., PhD Belf., PhD N.U.I. (E-mail: directorspgs@umu.ac.ug)

[Information supplied by the institution as at 24 February 2005, and edited by the ACU]

UNITED KINGDOM

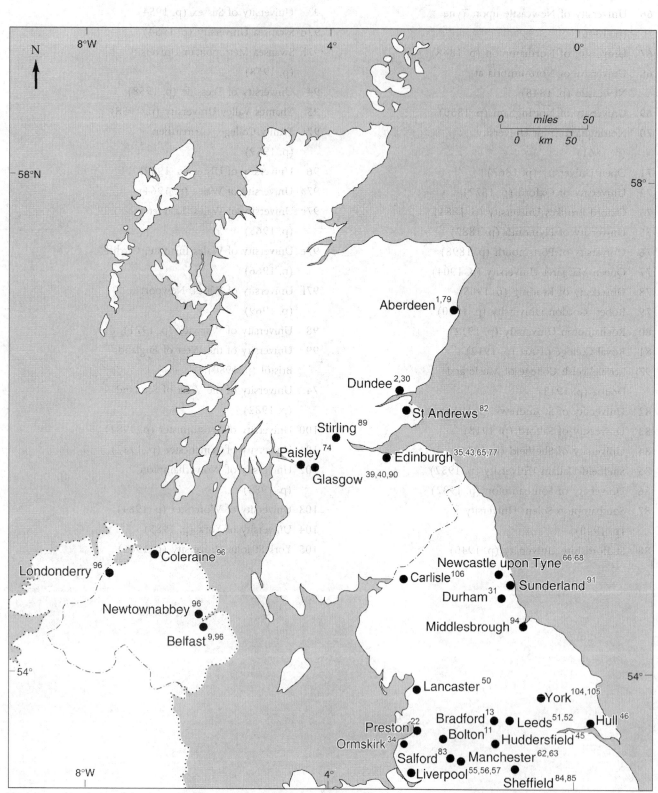

The places named are the seats of the university institutions in Northern England, Northern Ireland and Scotland numbered on p. 1506. For university institutions in the Midlands, Southern England and Wales, see next page

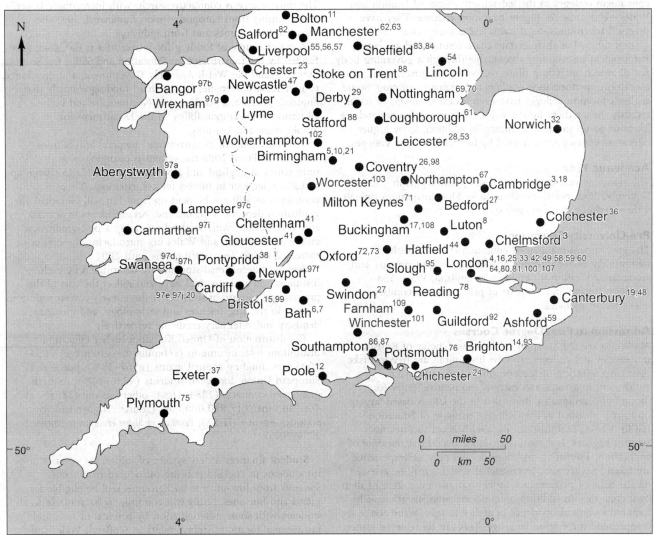

N

Bolton[11]
Salford[82] ● ● Manchester[62,63]
● Liverpool[55,56,57]
● Sheffield[83,84]
Chester[23] ● Stoke on Trent[88] ● Lincoln[54]
Bangor[97b] Newcastle[47]
Wrexham[97g] under ● Derby[29] ● Nottingham[69,70]
Lyme
Stafford[88] ● Loughborough[61] Norwich[32]
Wolverhampton[102] ● Leicester[28,53]
Birmingham[5,10,21]
Coventry[26,98]
Aberystwyth[97a] Worcester[103] ● Northampton[67] Cambridge[3,18]
Milton Keynes[71] ● Bedford[27]
Lampeter[97c] Colchester[36]
Cheltenham[41] Buckingham[17,108] ● Luton[8]
Carmarthen[97i] Gloucester[41] Hatfield[44] Chelmsford[3]
Swansea[97d,97h] Pontypridd[38] Oxford[72,73] ● London[4,16,25,33,42,49,58,59,60,64,80,81,100,107]
Newport[97f] Slough[95]
Cardiff Reading[78]
[97e,97j,20] Swindon[27] Canterbury[19,48]
Bristol[15,99] Farnham[109] Guildford[92] Ashford[59]
Bath[6,7] Winchester[101] Brighton[14,93]
Southampton[86,87] Portsmouth[76]
Exeter[37] Poole[12] Chichester[24]
Plymouth[75]

0 miles 50
0 km 50

50°   50°

4°   0°

The places named are the seats of the university institutions in the Midlands, Southern England and Wales numbered on p. 1506. For university institutions in Northern England, Northern Ireland and Scotland, see previous page

THE UNIVERSITIES OF THE UNITED KINGDOM

Information compiled by Universities UK as at December 2006

The University System

There are currently approximately 168 higher education institutions in the United Kingdom. This encompasses 89 universities, various university institutions—including the constituent colleges of the federal universities of London and Wales—and some 54 higher education colleges. They have diverse backgrounds, legal status and constitutional arrangements, but share certain characteristics and are legally independent institutions, accountable through a governing body for all aspects including funds received from government, monitoring performance, staffing and strategic planning. Some higher education colleges have been awarded university status recently; hence these figures will be subject to changes and are likely to go up in the near future. In addition, some higher education courses are delivered by further education colleges.

Academic Year

The academic year in the United Kingdom begins in September/October and ends in June. Most institutions operate a three-term or two-semester system.

Pre-University Education

The government-maintained education system and the independent sector together provide 13 years of primary and secondary education for children in England, Wales and Northern Ireland and 12 years of primary and secondary education in Scotland.

Admission to First Degree Courses

Applicants are free to apply to their own choice of British universities and colleges, and the institutions are free to make their own selection of students: there is no automatic entitlement to a place and entry is competitive. Entry for 'home' undergraduates, domiciled in the UK, is based largely on results obtained in the General Certificate of Education (GCE) A Level Examination, the Welsh Baccalaureate and Scottish Highers. For 'mature students' over 21 at the time of application, alternative qualifications and previous experience are taken into account. International students may be assessed on the basis of performance in the examination system of their own countries. In addition, international students are usually required to provide evidence of ability to read, write and comprehend the English language. This can be achieved either by passing a British Council Test, or equivalent, or by attending and passing a suitable course at another education provider or the accepting university in the UK.

Method of application. The admissions system for undergraduate programmes is managed by the Universities and Colleges Admissions Service (UCAS), which operates as a central 'clearing house' and provides information and advisory services to the applicants, their advisers, and to the institutions.

Further information on UCAS can be found through: www.ucas.com.

Finance

With the exception of the University of Buckingham, all UK universities receive significant funding, directly or indirectly, from government sources. However, reduced funding from government and its positive policy of encouraging universities to seek more diverse income resources has resulted in an increase in non-government income in recent years.

A large element of income for some universities is external research income. Research income is obtained from three sources. The main source continues to be research studentships and fellowships, and grants, from seven research councils. Research council funds are derived entirely from the government. The second source of research funds is charitable foundations, many of which are related to medical research. The third source is contract research, with increasingly larger sums coming from European Union framework and other research programmes and from industry.

A major source of funding for universities is the block grant, funded by the Department for Education and Skills, the Scottish Executive and the Welsh Assembly Government, and distributed to individual universities by the three funding councils (for England, Wales and Scotland). In Northern Ireland higher education is the responsibility of the Department for Employment and Learning.

The third element in universities' income derives from tuition fees. From 2006 the system is changing with universities in England and Northern Ireland able to charge up to £3000 per year in tuition fee contributions. These contributions will not be paid up front but will be repaid after graduation dependent on income. Arrangements in Scotland and Wales differ, with Scotland operating a post-graduation endowment scheme and Wales not introducing the option of increased tuition fee contributions until 2007.

Fees for international students are determined by each institution on an individual basis and reflect the cost of the programme and are broadly set at three levels corresponding to courses in the arts, sciences and technology, and medicine, dentistry and veterinary medicine respectively.

The distribution of United Kingdom higher education institutions total income in (£cbmillions–percentage) 2004–2005 was: funding council grants (6967–39%); home and European Union domiciled students (4336–24%); research grants and contracts (2884–16%); other income (3806–21%). Total income: £17,990,000,000. (Source: Higher Education Statistics Agency (HESA), *Resources of higher education institutions, 2004–2005*).

Student finance. A new system of tuition fee contributions for students in England is being introduced from 2006. Students from low-income backgrounds will be eligible for grants and bursaries. Loans will continue to be available to all students with some differentiation by parental income and institutional location. Arrangements in Scotland, Wales and Northern Ireland differ and further information can be found through the links below.

British postgraduate students continue to be supported by maintenance grants which together with their fees are paid by the research councils as competitive student awards.

Grants through the Commonwealth Scholarship and Fellowship Plan (CSFP) are available to assist Commonwealth students, while the Overseas Research Awards Scheme (ORS) is available to meet the difference between the home and overseas tuition fees but provides no assistance towards maintenance. Chevening awards are available from the Foreign and Commonwealth Office.

Staff and Student Numbers

In 2004–2005 there were about 2,424,000 students at United Kingdom higher education institutions (HEIs). 1,755,000 students were undergraduates and 533,000 were postgraduate students. Approximately 54,200 undergraduate students came from European Union countries in 2004–2005, and 98,400 from outside the European Union. International students represent a total of approximately 14% of all students. In

2004–2005 there were approximately 161,000 academic members of staff: 9% were professors, 16% senior lecturers, 34% lecturers, 21% researchers and 20% were other members of academic staff.

Further Information

Chevening scholarships. http://www.chevening.com
Commonwealth Scholarship and Fellowship Plan. http://www.csfp-online.org/index.html
Department for Education and Skills (DfES). http://www.dfes.gov.uk/
Department for Employment and Learning Northern Ireland. http://www.delni.gov.uk/studentfinance/

Higher Education and Research Opportunities (HERO). http://www.hero.ac.uk
Higher Education Statistics Agency (HESA). *Resources of higher education institutions, 2004–2005* (http://www.hesa.ac.uk).
Student Awards Agency for Scotland. http://www.student-support-saas.gov.uk
Universities UK. *Higher education in facts and figures, 2006* (http://bookshop.universitiesuk.ac.uk/downloads/Facts 2006.pdf).
—————. *Higher education in facts and figures—international perspectives, 2006*
(http://bookshop.universitiesuk.ac.uk/downloads/Intl_perspectives.pdf).
Welsh Assembly Government. http://www.learning.wales.gov.uk/students/

UNITED KINGDOM : DIRECTORY

The table below shows which of the institutions indicated provide facilities for study and/or research in the subjects named. In the case of related subject areas which have been grouped together (eg Botany/Plant Science), it should be borne in mind that one or more of the subjects may be offered by the institution concerned.

	Aberdeen	Abertay Dundee	Aberystwyth	Aston	Bangor	Bath	Birmingham	Bournemouth	Bristol	Brunel	Cambridge	Cardiff	Coventry	Cranfield	Durham	East Anglia	East London	Edinburgh	Exeter	Glamorgan	Glasgow	Glasgow Caledonian	Greenwich	Heriot-Watt	Hertfordshire	Huddersfield	Hull	Imperial	Keele	Kent	Kingston	Lancaster	Leeds
Accountancy/Accounting	X	X	X	U	X	UM	X	X	X	U		X	U	MD	X	X	U	UD	X	X	X	X	UM	X	X	UD	X		U	X	X	X	X
Administration/Administrative Studies				U	M			M					U					MD					X	UM	U	X	X				U		
Advertising								UD					U					UM					X				U					U	M
African Languages/Studies					X								X					MD															M
Afrikaans/Dutch												X														MD							
Agriculture/Agricultural Science	X		X		X									MD			D	U	X		M		X										
Agronomy/Soil Science	X		X		D									MD			MD	UD															
Agrotechnology														MD				U															
American Studies			X				X			U	MD		D		X			MD		UD	MD						UD		X	X		UM	MD
Anaesthesia/Anaesthesiology																																	MD
Anatomical Science/Anatomy									UD		X	U									X					UM							UM
Ancient Indian History and Culture											X																						
Animal Nutrition/Animal Physiology		X																															
Animal Science/Husbandry/Production	D		X		D		X	U	MD									MD			X												
Animatronics/Computer Arts		X				M	X	M											U						X							M	
Anthropology/Folklore	X						X	MD	X	X	X					X	X	UM	X		U		X		X					X		U	
Applied Chemistry															M			D					UM			UD				UD			
Applied Physics		X																D							X	X							UD
Aquaculture/Fisheries/Marine Science	X	X	X							UD		MD	X					UD	X				X				X					UD	
Arabic											X				X			X	X					MD									X
Archaeology	U		X		X		X		X		X	X			X	X		X	X		X						U			X			
Architectural Design								UM										MD	X	U			U										U
Architecture				X							X	X						X	X	U	X		X				X		M	UM	X		UM
Area Studies			X				X					MD															X						
Art Theory			X																													U	
Art Therapy																									X								
Art, Fine			X	U					X			X			X	X			X	U			X			UD					X	UD	X
Art, History of	X		X				X		X		X	MD	X		UM	X		X	X								UD		D	X	X		X
Artificial Intelligence	UD	X	D	D			X		D						D			X	MD									U					
Arts General																				U			UM										
Arts Management			X																			UM											
Arts and Culture																																	
Arts, Graphic													U				UM						X	U	U		X				X		U
Asian/Pacific Studies			X					MD			MD					MD			X							MD							X
Astronomy/Astrophysics/Space Science							X		X		X	X			MD	X		X	X	UD	X				X			U	D	UD	X	UD	X
Audiology								M	X									U															

TO SUBJECTS OF STUDY

For further information about the individual subjects taught at each institution, please refer to the *Index to Subjects of Study* at the end of the Yearbook, but for full details about subjects/courses offered at universities in the Commonwealth each institution's own official publications must be consulted. U = may be studied for first degree course; M = may be studied for master's degree course; D = research facilities to doctoral level; X = all three levels (UMD). **Note—** The table only includes information provided by institutions currently in membership of the Association of Commonwealth Universities. (*The University of London's subject directory is shown on page 1855.*)

Leeds Metropolitan	Leicester	Lincoln	Liverpool	Liverpool John Moores	London see page 1769	London Metropolitan	London South Bank	Loughborough	Manchester Metropolitan	Middlesex	Napier	Newcastle	Northumbria	Nottingham	Nottingham Trent	Open	Oxford	Oxford Brookes	Plymouth	Portsmouth	Queen Margaret	Queen's, Belfast	Reading	Robert Gordon	Salford	Sheffield	Southampton	St Andrews	Stirling	Strathclyde	Surrey	Swansea	Ulster	Wales: Inst., Cardiff	Wales: Lampeter	Wales: Newport	Warwick	West of England	Wolverhampton	Worcester
X		U	UD	X	X	X	X	X	X	UD	X	X	U	X	X	X		X	X	X		UD	U	UD	UM	X	X		X	X		X	U		U		U	X	X	U
X			MD	U		U			M	U				X	D		UM			U			UM															U		
		U				U				U				U																								U		
			D															MD																						
														X		X	U					UD				UD	X												U	D
														X												X														D
																																								D
UD	U	U	X		U		U	X				U	X		U	X	UM		U	U		UD	D			X		MD	MD			X	X		U		X		U	U
		D															D								D															
		UD														U	MD		U			UD																		
		U	D													U						U																		
UD	X	UD										X		U	X			UD	U			X				X	U										UM	U	U	
		UM																X															UM		U					
		UM												M	X	X				X			MD	U	X		MD			X				X				U		
			UD	X				UM							U			U			U					X								U						
			D														D	U								X														
		X						M	X				X	X	UD				X	X	X		X	X					X					U					
		U											X				UM			X					U															
X		X						X		X	U	X			X	X	X	X		X				X	U				X	X			U						
			X	M		U	U		U	UM				X		UM		D			X				U				U	U									
X		X	X	UM		X	X	MD	X		X	U	X		X	X	X		X	X	UM	X			X	UD				UM										
		UM				MD			X																															
		U						UM																						U										
															MD	M																								
X		X	U	X	X	X	X	X	X		X	X	X	X	X		X	X	U		X				X	UM	U		UM	X	U								
	X	D	UM	UD		X	X	U	X	X	X	X	U	UM	U	X		X				X	X			UD	U			X									
		U	D	MD		U	X	UD	X		U	U	X		X									U		U													
		MD	X		MD	UM	X	X	UM	U	X	U																											
		UM	MD	M		M	X		M																														
		X	MD	UM	MD		X																																
X		U	U	UM	U	X		U				UM	UM	U	X	U									X	UM	UM	U	X	U									
		D	U	U		MD	MD	U	X																														
UD		U	X	UD	UD	MD			UD	U	X	X	X		MD	D																							
					M		X	U																															

	Aberdeen	Abertay Dundee	Aberystwyth	Aston	Bangor	Bath	Birmingham	Bournemouth	Bristol	Brunel	Cambridge	Cardiff	Coventry	Cranfield	Durham	East Anglia	East London	Edinburgh	Exeter	Glamorgan	Glasgow	Glasgow Caledonian	Greenwich	Heriot-Watt	Hertfordshire	Huddersfield	Hull	Imperial	Keele	Kent	Kingston	Lancaster	Leeds
Aviation									UM	U			U	MD											X								U
Banking/Finance	X	X	X	X	X	X	X	X	MD	UM	MD	X		MD	X		UM	MD	X	X	X	X	U	X	X	UD	X	MD	U	X	X	X	X
Behavioural Sciences		UD	D	MD			X	U		U		MD			MD		MD		X	D	M		U	X	UD	U				X	U	X	
Bengali											U																						
Biochemistry	X		X	UD		X	X		X	X	X	UD	X		MD	X	X	U	X	UM		X	X	UM	UD	X	UD		X	UD	X	X	X
Bioengineering	X														MD	D		D										X					
Bioethics							MD				M	D																				D	
Bioinformatics		MD	X				X		X		M			MD				MD	X		MD			D	UM		MD			D			MD
Biology	X	U	X	U	X	X	X	U	X	X	X	UD	X		X	X		X	X	UM	X	U	UM	UD	X	UD	X	X	X	X	X	X	X
Biology Molecular	X		X	UD	U	X	X			U	X	UD	X		D			M	UD		U		UM	D	X		X	X		X		UD	U
Biomedical Sciences	X	U		D	U	D	X	X	M	UM		D	U	MD	UD	U	X	X	X	U	X	X	UM	U	X		X	X	UD	U	X	X	X
Biophysics	X						X								D			MD	X									D				D	
Biostatistics																		MD							MD								
Biotechnology	X	X		MD	X	X	MD				MD	MD	UD	U	MD		X	X	D	U	X		X	X			X	UD		U			UD
Botany/Plant Science	X		X		X	D	X		U			UD			X	X		X			X			D	X			MD		M		X	X
Buddhist Studies									MD			D																					
Building/Built Environment/Construction							X	X	M		UM	X	X	X	MD	MD		UM		X	X	X	X	X	U	UD		X			X		X
Business Administration	MD	X	X	U	UM	X	UM	X		UM	M	X	X	MD	MD	MD	X	MD	MD	X	X	UM	U	X	X		X	MD	X	X	X	X	M
Business Computing	U		X				X	U			M	X						UM	U		UM		U	X	UM		U				U		U
Business Economics			X		U			UM				U			U	UM	U		X	U							U	MD	U			X	
Business Information Systems		U	X					UM							MD		UM	UM	UM		U		X		UM					U			UM
Business/Commerce	X	U	X	X	UM	X	X	X	X			X	X	MD	X	X	UM	X	X	X	X	X	UM	X	X	UD	X	MD	X	X	X	X	X
Canadian Studies							X																										
Caribbean Studies							MD																										
Catholicism	MD														D																		
Celtic/Cornish/Welsh/Irish Studies	X		X		X						X	X						X	X	X	X												
Chemistry	X		U	X	UD	X	X		X		X	X	X		X	X		X	U		X	X	X	X			X	X	X	UD	D	X		X
Child Health								UM	MD							M			D						D								M
Child Welfare								UM								M		UM															
Child and Family Psychology																MD			D													UD	
Child/Youth Studies					U	U	UM		U			U	UM		D		D	UM	X	U	MD		U				U	D					U
Chinese Language and Literature																		X															
Chinese/Chinese Studies					M						X				MD			X			M												X
Civil Care/Security	MD																																
Classics/Greek/Latin/Ancient History									X		X	X	X		X		X		X	X										UD	X	U	X
Cognitive Science				D	MD		MD					D							X								X	D		MD			U

Leeds Metropolitan	Leicester	Lincoln	Liverpool	Liverpool John Moores	London see page 1769	London Metropolitan	London South Bank	Loughborough	Manchester Metropolitan	Middlesex	Napier	Newcastle	Northumbria	Nottingham	Nottingham Trent	Open	Oxford	Oxford Brookes	Plymouth	Portsmouth	Queen Margaret	Queen's, Belfast	Reading	Robert Gordon	Salford	Sheffield	Southampton	St Andrews	Stirling	Strathclyde	Surrey	Swansea	Ulster	Wales: Inst., Cardiff	Wales: Lampeter	Wales: Newport	Warwick	West of England	Wolverhampton	Worcester
					U																				U															
X	X	X	X	X		X	X	X	U	X	X	X	X	UM	X	X	UM		X	U	X		X	X	X	UM	M	X		X	X	M	X	X	X	U		UM	MD	X
X			X	X		D			UM					UD		UD		MD		X						X	X	X	X										D	
	X		X	UD		UD	X					X	UD	U	X	U	X		UD	X	X	UD	UD	UD	X	X	X	X		X	UM	X					X	U	UD	
	D		MD					D						MD											X					X	X	X								MD
			D													U									M															
	M		D					D																															MD	
U	X		X	X			X	U	U	U	X	X	X	X	X	UD	X	X	UD	X	U	X	UD		X	X	X	X	UD	X	X	X	X				X	X	X	U
	D		UD			UD			MD			X		MD	UM		X		X		UD	UD			X					X	M	X					MD	U	UD	
X	U	UD	X	UM		X		D		U	X	X	UM	UD	X			UD		X	UD	U	UD		X	X	X		X	U	UD	X	X				X	X		
															MD														U											
	D																																							
	U	UM										UM	UM	UD	MD			UD		X			X			X					X		X					U	X	
	X		D	X								X	X	UD	X	D	UD	U		D	X				X	D	X	UD										UD	
X		M	UD	X		X	X		D	X	X	X	MD	X			X	U	X		X	X	UD	X	X			MD	X	MD		X	U		UM		X	X		
X	MD	X	MD	U		X	X	M		U	UM	X	X	MD		X	MD	UM	U	X	X	M	U	MD	M	MD	M		X	X	MD	UM	X	UM		UM		X	UM	UM
		X				UD		U				M	UM			UM		X		UM				UD		U			U			U		UM			U	U		U
		X		X		X		X				U	U	U	U		M	MD	X	U	UM		U	X					X	UM	UM					U		U	U	
		X				M	X	UM		UM	UM			M			X			UM			U	U	MD		X			M	X	M	U			UM		U	U	U
X	X	X	X	X		X	X	X	X	X	X	X	UM	X		X	UM	X	X	X	X	X	X	X	X	X	X	X		X	X	X	X	X	U	X	UM	X	X	UM
						U								D																									MD	
						UD																																	MD	
U			X														MD								X			X	UD		X	X		X						
	UD		X	X		UD		X	X			X	X	UD	X	UD	X			UD		X			X	UD	X		X	X	MD					X		MD	
	D		MD								U					U		MD	U						D						UM				M				U
			MD			M	D									U		MD														M							U
			M													UM		MD		M			U									M							U
X		U		U				U	U					UD		U	U		X	U	U										X		UM	X	U		UM	X		U	U
																									D															
		U	U									UM		U		X									X										UD			U		
M																					UM																			
	UD		X									X		X		X	X				X	X			X	X	UM		X			X			X		X		
	U		D			M								U		UM		MD		UM			MD		X															

	Aberdeen	Abertay Dundee	Aberystwyth	Aston	Bangor	Bath	Birmingham	Bournemouth	Bristol	Brunel	Cambridge	Cardiff	Coventry	Cranfield	Durham	East Anglia	East London	Edinburgh	Exeter	Glamorgan	Glasgow	Glasgow Caledonian	Greenwich	Heriot-Watt	Hertfordshire	Huddersfield	Hull	Imperial	Keele	Kent	Kingston	Lancaster	Leeds
Commonwealth Studies																									UM								M
Communication Sciences			X				U		M						M										X				MD		U	UM	X
Communication/Journalism/Media Studies		UM	X		X		U	UM		X			X	X				UM		X	X	UM			X	UD	U	MD	U		U	X	X
Communications/Information Management			X				M	UM		X			X	MD		UM	MD		X				U		U	X			U	X		UM	U
Community Education							X										U	UD		U							U	U					
Community Health		U						UM		UM					D		M				U	MD	UM		UM					MD			
Community Medicine															U							MD			X				D				
Community Studies							X	UM							MD		U		U										D				
Computer Science	X	UD	X	U	X	X	X	X	X	X	X	X	X	X	MD	X	X	UM	X	X	X	X	U	X	X	X	X	X	X	X	X	X	X
Conservation Studies					X	MD	MD		X			X						X		UM			M	MD	X		U	MD		X	M		X
Consumer Studies								X							D								M				U				X		
Corporate Governance								MD							D																		
Counselling	M	UM						MD	X	M	M				U	MD	MD	MD		M	M		X		X				MD	U			M
Creative Writing			X		X			UM		UM			X			X	U	M	MD	X	M						U	U	M		UM	UM	UM
Criminal Justice/Public Policy	M		X		X		MD	UM					UM			UM	MD		X				U		X		UD			M		UM	U
Criminology		U	X		X		MD		MD	MD	X	UM			X		UM	MD		X	D	UM	U		X			X		X	U	U	X
Crop Science/Production	X			MD										MD					D							M							
Cultural Heritage							MD	UM											U	MD													UM
Cultural Studies	X						MD					X						X	MD	X							UM			U		X	X
Curriculum and Assessment Studies																						MD				X							
Dairy Technology																																	
Deaf Studies							MD		X																		U						M
Defence Studies	M		X												MD										UM								
Dentistry							X		X			X						M			X				X								X
Dermatology																																	
Design							X		X			X					UM	M		X	X	UM	U	X	X	UD	U				X		X
Design, Industrial					U	D	X		X			X						M		U			UD	X	X			M			U		
Development Studies					MD		MD	M	M			MD					X	UM				MD	M				X				U	M	X
Diplomacy			X												M		MD															M	
Disability Studies								MD			M	M																		MD			X
Disaster/Emergency							U		M					X	MD				M						MD						U		
Drama/Theatre/Dance/Performing Arts			X		X		X		X	X		M	UM			X	U		X	X	X						U	UD	X	X	U	X	X
E-Business	U			M	U		X				D				M				U			UM	MD		UM		M					UM	
E-Commerce	X				U		X	UM				UM			MD			U			U		UM	MD	U		M			M			U
Eastern European Studies							X													X													
Ecology	X				X		D		X	M	UD	U			U		X		X	D	UM	X			X		U	X			MD	X	U

Leeds Metropolitan	Leicester	Lincoln	Liverpool	Liverpool John Moores	London see page 1769	London Metropolitan	London South Bank	Loughborough	Manchester Metropolitan	Middlesex	Napier	Newcastle	Northumbria	Nottingham	Nottingham Trent	Open	Oxford	Oxford Brookes	Plymouth	Portsmouth	Queen Margaret	Queen's, Belfast	Reading	Robert Gordon	Salford	Sheffield	Southampton	St Andrews	Stirling	Strathclyde	Surrey	Swansea	Ulster	Wales: Inst., Cardiff	Wales: Lampeter	Wales: Newport	Warwick	West of England	Wolverhampton	Worcester
																													UD											
		X				U			X				UM				U			X					X							X								
X	X	X	X	X		X	U	X	X	X	X	X	U		X	UM	U	M	X	X					X	UM	X		X	UM	U	UM	X	U		X	UM		X	U
X		MD	X	U		X		MD	X	M	M	U	UM		UM		X		X						X							M		UM		X	U	UM	UD	U
																									M					UM		U							D	U
			MD			MD								U	MD						M				M											U			UD	U
			MD																		M																		D	
U						U			U																					UM		X				U				X
X	X	X	X	X		X	X	X	X	UD	X	X	X	X	X	X	X	X	X	X			UD	X	UM	UM	X	X	X	X	X	X	X	X	U		X	X	X	X
	X	MD	U							M			UM		X			X	UM	M					M		U		X	X									MD	D
U			U			U			U							U					X				U							UD	U							D
								M				M			M							M	M																	
X	UM		M			MD	M	MD			M	M		M		M									M	U		U		MD	X			X			M		U	
M		U	UM			U	U	UM	U	UM	M		UM				X	U			UM	UM	M	M						UM	M	UD	U	X	U	U	U			U
											U	M	X			UM			U	UM	MD									M						U			UD
	X	X	X	X		U	U	X		X				X		UD	UM	MD	X					X	X	U			X		M	UM	UD						U	UD
											X			X											MD															UD
	M	UM				MD								M	UM	M															U			MD				U		
X			U				UD		MD	X		U	MD	UM		M					X								U	M	U	UD		U	MD		X		UD	
																														UM									D	
																							D																	
									U	U															U															U
																												M												UD
			X									X								U			UD			X							U							
	D																																							
X	X	X				X	UM	X	X	X	X		X	X	UD		X	X						X	X	X		X				X		UM			X		UM	X
		MD	U	X		X	X	X	U				UM				X	U					M	UD	M						X		X				UM			UD
	M		U			M							U	X	MD		U	MD					MD					U			MD	D								MD
														M																										
												M	X				D	U																						U
	M												M										M																	
		X	U			UM	U	X	X		X			D	X		U	X			UM	X	X	U	X					X	X		X	U	U	X	U	X	X	UM
		X	X				M	UD			M	U		U	U	UM	M			U	M				MD					X	M	U	X				U		UM	U
	D	X	X				UM				M	X		M	UM		M	M		U										X	U	X					M	U		U
			D											U											MD														D	
	MD	U					D	M	X				UM		X	UM	X	UD					U	MD		X		X	UD		D	X				MD		UD	U

	Aberdeen	Abertay Dundee	Aberystwyth	Aston	Bangor	Bath	Birmingham	Bournemouth	Bristol	Brunel	Cambridge	Cardiff	Coventry	Cranfield	Durham	East Anglia	East London	Edinburgh	Exeter	Glamorgan	Glasgow	Glasgow Caledonian	Greenwich	Heriot-Watt	Hertfordshire	Huddersfield	Hull	Imperial	Keele	Kent	Kingston	Lancaster	Leeds
Economic History			X				X		U			D			MD	X	X				X						X				U	U	
Economic Planning and Development									M						D						MD												
Economics	X	UD	X		X	X	X		X	X	X	X	UD		X	X	UM	X	X	X	X	U	UM	X	X	UD	X		X	X	X	X	X
Economics Agricultural/Agribusiness			X																D														
Education	X		X		X	X	X		MD	X	X	X	MD		X	MD	X	X	X	X	X		X	X	X		X		UD		X	X	X
Education Adult																		M			MD												
Education Distance								UM										M			D				M		M						
Education Extension																													X				
Education Primary	UM		X		U		M		X			U				M	X	M			X	UM			X		X						
Education Secondary	M		X		U		M		M	UM					MD	M	X	M			MD	UM			X		MD		M				
Education Special									MD		M							UM	MD	MD							X		M				M
Education Tertiary																																	
Educational Administration							D																										
Educational Psychology																		MD			MD	MD								U			
Egyptology							MD		M		X	D									U												
Electronics				UD	X				X	U						U	UD				X	X		X			X					U	X
Emergency/Trauma Care Technology																								UM	M								
Energy Studies	MD									D					M	M	MD			X					MD								X
Engineering	X			UD	X	X	X	X	X	X	X	X	X	X	MD	X	UM	X	X	X	X	X	X	X	X	X	X				X	X	X
Engineering Aeronautical/Aerospace						X	MD		X	X	U	X	D	X	MD	U		U	X		X	D			X						X		U
Engineering Agricultural/Fisheries														MD																			
Engineering Architectural						X						X							X			U											U
Engineering Automobile						X	X		X	UM	U	X	MD								U			X	UD						U		X
Engineering Biomedical				D		UD	U		X	MD		MD			MD			MD							X				U	U	MD	U	
Engineering Business				X					X															UM					X				
Engineering Chemical/Petrochemical/Process	MD			UD		X	X					X			MD	M		X			X	X		D			X						X
Engineering Civil/Environmental/Structural	X	U		UD		X	X		X	X	X	X	X		MD	X		X	X	X	X	X	X	X		UD	X				X		X
Engineering Communications/Telecommunications				X		X	X	X	X	U	X		D	X				X	X	U	X		X		X		X	MD		MD	U	UM	UM
Engineering Computer	X	M	X		X	UD	X	X	X	X	U	X	X	X	MD	X	X	X	X	X	X	X	X	X	X	X	X		U	X			X
Engineering Construction									MD										UM	X			X				X						
Engineering Design						UM	X		U	U		U							X	U	UM	U		X	U							U	
Engineering Electrical/Electronic	X			UD	X	X	X	X	X	X	X	X	X		MD	X	X	X	X	X	X	X	X	X	X	UD	X	X		X	X	UD	X
Engineering Environmental Geophysics																		M								MD							
Engineering Fire																	UD		U		UM												X
Engineering Geological															MD			D								X							MD
Engineering Industrial				U					X							X	U	M			UM			X	X		MD						

Leeds Metropolitan	Leicester	Lincoln	Liverpool	Liverpool John Moores	London see page 1769	London Metropolitan	London South Bank	Loughborough	Manchester Metropolitan	Middlesex	Napier	Newcastle	Northumbria	Nottingham	Nottingham Trent	Open	Oxford	Oxford Brookes	Plymouth	Portsmouth	Queen Margaret	Queen's, Belfast	Reading	Robert Gordon	Salford	Sheffield	Southampton	St Andrews	Stirling	Strathclyde	Surrey	Swansea	Ulster	Wales: Inst., Cardiff	Wales: Lampeter	Wales: Newport	Warwick	West of England	Wolverhampton	Worcester
	X		X						MD					D		MD				X		U									U	D							D	
														M																	M									
X	X		X	X		X	UM	X	X	X	X	X	X	X	X	UD	X	U	X	X		UD	X	UD	X	X	X	X	X	X	X	X	U		U	X	X			
												X									M		MD																U	
X	X	MD	MD	X		X	UM	MD	X	X		MD	X	X	X	X	MD	X	X	X		MD	X		MD	X		X	X	MD	MD	X	U		U	X	X	X	X	UM
							UM							U	M		X													X					U			M	X	UM
									M			M	M	M	U			UM							MD		M			UM								M		UM
	M								X	M			U		UM	M	X	X				X	U							X			U		U		X	U	UM
	M								X	M		U		U	M	X		X				X	UM		MD	MD			M		X	X			UM	U		M		UM
									M			M	M	M	U		UM								MD		UM								M			UD	UM
		M										U					U						MD		X												M	MD		
												M																												
											MD	M	MD	U	M							M		MD			M					U							UM
			X												X														X											
			X			UD			X			X	U	X			U		X		X	X			X	X		X	X	X			U							
																	U																							U
							UM	MD				X	M																	X		MD						D	
X	X		X	X		UM	X	X	M			X	X	X	X	X	X	X	X	X		X	X	X	X	X	X			X	X	X	X	U		X	X	X	X	
			UD				X						UM	U			UD						X	X	X					UM	X					X			
U							U	U						U																X					U	U	UM		U	D
		UM					X										X									X		U								U	UD
		X																						U		X			X	M		X			MD	D
							M			U			M				U							X	U			X	U	X	D
						X	X				X	X	UM	X			X	X	X	X	X
UD			X	X		UM	X			X	X	X	X	U	X	U	UD	X	X	X	X	X	X	X	X	X	UM	X	U	X
X	UD		X	U		U	X	X	UM	UM	X	MD	X	UM	X	MD	UD	X	X	X	X	U	U	U	U	UD
X	X		X	U		X	X	UD	X	UM	UM	MD	X	X	X	U	X	UD	X	X	X	X	X	U	X	U	X	X	U	UD
				UM	MD	UM	UM	U	X	U	U	X
		M	U	X	U	UM	U	M	X	D	X	U	U	UD
X	UD	X	X	X	X	X	X	UM	X	X	X	UD	X	X	X	X	X	X	X	X	X	X	X	X	X	X	U
	MD
U	U	MD	U
	M	M	X	U
X	U	D	UD	X	X

	Aberdeen	Abertay Dundee	Aberystwyth	Aston	Bangor	Bath	Birmingham	Bournemouth	Bristol	Brunel	Cambridge	Cardiff	Coventry	Cranfield	Durham	East Anglia	East London	Edinburgh	Exeter	Glamorgan	Glasgow	Glasgow Caledonian	Greenwich	Heriot-Watt	Hertfordshire	Huddersfield	Hull	Imperial	Keele	Kent	Kingston	Lancaster	Leeds
Engineering Information Technology	U							X										U	U					X									UM
Engineering Instrumentation								X		U												UM		D	X				U				
Engineering Management	U					D		X	MD						U			U	M	U			M		X	MD							
Engineering Manufacturing							X	X	X		X	X	X	X	MD	X		X	MD	M	X		UM	UM	X	X	UD	X	X		X		MD
Engineering Marine											D		MD						X					X		MD							
Engineering Materials/Mineral Resources/Petroleum				D		D						MD						MD	U	MD							U	X					X
Engineering Mathematical						U					UD	U							UD	U													
Engineering Mechanical/Production	X		U			X	X	UD	X	X	X	UD	X	MD	X			X	X	X	X		UM	X	X	X	UD	X	X		X	X	X
Engineering Medical	X			D		U	X	UD				X			MD				D								U	X		D			UM
Engineering Metallurgical/Mining							X					X							X					MD		X							X
Engineering Nuclear																																UM	
Engineering Polymer																																	
Engineering Software	U			D	X	X	MD	X				MD			UD			UM	U	X	X		UM		X	X	UD	X					
English	X		X		X		X		X	X	X	X	U		X	X	UM	X	X	X	X		U		X	UD	X		X	X	X	X	X
English as a Second Language		UM	MD					M							M		U	U	U				M				U		U				M
Entomology																											MD						
Entrepreneurship	UD	M						M					U					U		M	MD	MD			M		MD					UD	
Environmental Geosciences	MD							U										X		X							M			U			
Environmental Health		U	X					MD	X				D										UM			MD						M	
Environmental Management		M	MD		U	M		UM	M			M	MD					U	MD	M	M												X
Environmental Science/Studies	X	D	X	UD	X	MD	X	UM	MD	X	M	X	X	MD	X	X	U	X	D		X		UM	UM	X	X	UD	X	MD	X	X	X	X
Epidemiology																											MD						
Equine Science								U												M			MD										
Ergonomics														MD																			
Estate Management								U				D								U			U	UD							X		
Ethics							MD					D			D					M									U		MD		
Ethics, Law and Governance								X							D									MD							MD		
Ethnicity/Multiculturalism											M																						
Ethnomusicology						M									MD																		
European Studies	X	U	X	X	UM		X	X			M	M	X	X	MD	X	U	X	MD		X		UM	X	X	UD			UD	X	X	X	X
European Union Studies			X									UM																				M	UM
Event Management															U																		
Fashion/Clothing								U					U					U		U			U	X		X						UM	X
Fertility/Embryology																												MD					
Film/Photography/Television/Animation	X				X		M	MD	UM	UM	X		X	UM	X		UM	MD	X	UM	X		M	U	U	D	U				X	M	X
Food Science/Nutrition/Home Science/Dietetics	MD	UM						MD	X	M		UM	MD		MD				M		U	U	UM	U	X		X				X		X

Leeds Metropolitan	Leicester	Lincoln	Liverpool	Liverpool John Moores	London see page 1769	London Metropolitan	London South Bank	Loughborough	Manchester Metropolitan	Middlesex	Napier	Newcastle	Northumbria	Nottingham	Nottingham Trent	Open	Oxford	Oxford Brookes	Plymouth	Portsmouth	Queen Margaret	Queen's, Belfast	Reading	Robert Gordon	Salford	Sheffield	Southampton	St Andrews	Stirling	Strathclyde	Surrey	Swansea	Ulster	Wales: Inst., Cardiff	Wales: Lampeter	Wales: Newport	Warwick	West of England	Wolverhampton	Worcester
									X		UM					UM		UM					U							X		U					M	M		
			U																											X							X			
			M									U	U	MD		UM		U		M										X	M							M		
X			X	X		X	X	MD		UM	X		X			UM	M	X	X			X				UM				X		X	U				X	X	UD	X
			MD	X								X						U										X		X										
			X						X			X		UD		U									MD	X				X	X									
	UD		X	UM		X	X	X			U	X	X	X	X	UD	X	X	X	X		X				X	X	X	UD	X	X	X	X	U			X	X	UM	D
			X							UD		M												MD		X					X	U		MD						D
			X										D											D	MD															
				X							MD	U									UM					MD				X										
X	U		X	X				M			X	X				UM		UM	X		U					X			U	U		U		U	X	U			UM	D
X	X	UD	X	X		X	X	X	X	UD		X	X	X	X	X	X	X	X	X	X	X			X	X	X	X	X	X	X	X	U	X	UM	X	X	X	X	UM
			MD						UM				UM		U	M		UM	X						U												M		U	U
			D																																					
	D		MD			U			MD			U		M		U				U					MD	X	U											MD	M	
			D									M				U	D	U																						
UD									X	UM	MD	U	D			UM											UM				UD	U							UM	
			MD											U	U	M											UM												UM	U
	M		X	X		UM	MD	X	MD	X	MD	X	X	X	X	X	X	X	MD	X	UD	X		M	X	MD	X	X		X	X	X	UM	X	U	U		X	X	U
			X	D												X		U																					UM	U
										X			M																		M									
				U							M	U	UD		UM		U			X		X										X							UM	
			D													UM						U									M		MD							
																M				M																				
																														UM										
			D													UM					UD					MD														
U	UM		U	X		UM	UM	X	X			UM			X	UM				U	X		X		X	X	X		X	UD	UM	UM	UM	UD	U				UD	D
			MD						X							UM														UM										
						UM						M																								U				U
	X		U			U	U	X	X			X		X						U		U		X									UD	U		U		U	U	U
X	U	X	U	U		U	U	U	X		X	M	UM	X	X	UM	U	U	X	U	UM	X			UM	U	X		X			X	X			X	X	X	UM	U
X	X	U		X		X	X	X	UM		U	UM	X	U		X					X	UD	X	UD	UM	MD	M			X	X		X	UM				U		X

	Aberdeen	Abertay Dundee	Aberystwyth	Aston	Bangor	Bath	Birmingham	Bournemouth	Bristol	Brunel	Cambridge	Cardiff	Coventry	Cranfield	Durham	East Anglia	East London	Edinburgh	Exeter	Glamorgan	Glasgow	Glasgow Caledonian	Greenwich	Heriot-Watt	Hertfordshire	Huddersfield	Hull	Imperial	Keele	Kent	Kingston	Lancaster	Leeds
Forensic Science		U							X	U		MD	UM	MD			U	M	U	X	UM		U	UM			UD			U	UM		
Forestry	X				X													X											MD				
French/French Studies	X		X	U	X	X	X		X		X	X	U		X	X	U	X	X		X		X	U	UD	UD				X	X	X	X
Genetics	X		X		X				X		UD	UD			D	X		X	MD		X					X							X
Genetics and Plant Breeding			X		MD														MD														
Geographic Information Systems/ Geomatics	MD										M			MD				U	MD	X			UM		U	D						X	M
Geography	X		X	U		X	U		X		X	UD	X		X	X		X	X	U	X		U	X	UD	X	UD			X		X	X
Geology/Earth Sciences/ Atmospheric Studies	X		X		X	D	X	U	X		X	X			X	X		X	X	U	X		X				UM	D		X	X	X	X
Geophysics							MD				D				MD				X							X						U	UM
German/Germanic Studies	X		X	U	X	X	X		X		X	X	U		X			X	X		X		X	U	UD	UD				X	U	X	X
Gerontology					MD																				U				MD				
Global Studies								MD																									
Greek, Modern/Greek Studies							X				U								X														X
Health Education						D		U											X						X				M				
Health Information			MD		MD																												
Health Sciences/Studies	X	X			X	MD	X	U	MD	X		MD	X		X	MD	UM	U	MD	X	X	X	UM		X	UD	D	MD		MD	UM	X	X
Health and Social Care					X			X	D						D		UM		M												U	M	
Health/Hospital Administration								MD		X							UM		X								MD	MD			X		UM
Hebrew/Semitic Studies											X							U			X												
Heritage Studies					X			MD	X											MD			M							U			
Hindi											X																						
History	X		X		X	X	X	UD	X		X	X	X		X	X	U	X	X	UM	X	X	U	X	X	X			X	X	X	X	X
History/Philosophy of Science						M					X	U			X			D	U					X					MD	X		U	UM
Homeopathy																																	
Horticulture														MD					X	U			U										
Hotel Management								UM																									
Housing/Real Estate	X											MD						U	MD				UM	X									
Human Biology						U									D		U	U	X	U					X					U	U	UD	U
Human Genetics							MD				D				D		MD	M	X						X					X		MD	U
Human Movement/Kinesiology/ Biomechanics								U																									
Human Resource Development		U						MD																	M							X	
Human Resource Economics		U																															
Human Rights/Globalisation	MD		X		M								M				UM				MD									M			MD
Immunology/Infection/Immunity										U								UD			X					MD					D		MD
Indian Languages											X																						
Industrial Chemistry																			D								X						

Leeds Metropolitan	Leicester	Lincoln	Liverpool	Liverpool John Moores	London see page 1769	London Metropolitan	London South Bank	Loughborough	Manchester Metropolitan	Middlesex	Napier	Newcastle	Northumbria	Nottingham	Nottingham Trent	Open	Oxford	Oxford Brookes	Plymouth	Portsmouth	Queen Margaret	Queen's, Belfast	Reading	Robert Gordon	Salford	Sheffield	Southampton	St Andrews	Stirling	Strathclyde	Surrey	Swansea	Ulster	Wales: Inst., Cardiff	Wales: Lampeter	Wales: Newport	Warwick	West of England	Wolverhampton	Worcester
	M	X	D	U		X	UM	U					U							U		U	UD							X	M							UM	U	U
										M					MD																								D	
U	UD		X	X		U			X	UD		X	U	X	UD	U	X	X	U	X		X	X		X	X	X	X	X	U	X	X					X		X	U
	X	UD				M						X		X		U	MD			U	UD					X					M	UD	X						UM	UD
	M		D															UM												U		U								
U	X		X	X				X	X	D		X	UD	X	X	UD	X	UD	UD	X		UD	X		X	X	X	X	U	X		X	X					U	UD	U
	X		X	U								X				UD	X		UD	X			X				U	X	X	UD										UD
	UD		UD							D																X							D							
U	UD		X	X					X	UD		X	U	X	UD	U	X		U	X	UD	UM			X	X	X	UD	X	U	X	X								U
	D		D							D													M					M					D							
										MD	U							X												X										
	X												U			U	X								X				M				X							
MD		MD														U		X		UM		MD								X	M		MD				M		MD	U
						X		MD										X								MD					M				M					
X	M	X	X	X		X	X	D	X	X	UM	MD	UM	D	X	UD	MD	X	X	X	X		MD		X	X	X	MD		X	X	X	X	U			MD	X	X	U
						M							UM		UM				UM						MD												UM	X	UM	
U							M	M					X								M				MD						M	X								
	UD																X									X	U										X			
	X											M	M								M					M						X	M						D	U
															MD																									
X	X	UD	X	X		X				U	X		X	X	X	X	X	X	X	X		X	X		X	X	X	X	X	X		X	X		X	X	X	X	X	UM
	M															U	MD						U										D							
										U																														
															U				D						X								U					U	D	U
																	X		U					U							UM	M		U						
UM		U		U				UM		UM					X	UM		X						M		X		UM												
U	U		U	X					U		U	U	U																									U	U	U
U	X													UD		U				U												U								UD
										MD																				X		D								U
	M												UM					UM								M														
		MD	U										UM		M	U	UM																							
		MD		MD		MD						M	U	D			M													U										
		MD												M																X										
																																								U

	Aberdeen	Abertay Dundee	Aberystwyth	Aston	Bangor	Bath	Birmingham	Bournemouth	Bristol	Brunel	Cambridge	Cardiff	Coventry	Cranfield	Durham	East Anglia	East London	Edinburgh	Exeter	Glamorgan	Glasgow	Glasgow Caledonian	Greenwich	Heriot-Watt	Hertfordshire	Huddersfield	Hull	Imperial	Keele	Kent	Kingston	Lancaster	Leeds
Industrial Hygiene and Safety																																	
Industrial Relations/Personnel/HRM	MD	UM		X		X	X	MD		MD		X	UM	MD	MD			MD		X	D	X	M	X	X	MD	X		X	X	X	X	X
Industrial and Organisation Psychology																																X	
Information Science/Studies/Systems	X	UD	X	U	MD	X	X	UM		X	X	X	X	MD	MD	X	UM	X	X	X	X	UM	UM	X	X	X	X	X	MD		X	X	X
Information Technology	X	MD	X					X			M			M	MD		UM	M	X	M	M			X	U				MD	U		UM	
Insurance										X																							
International Business		U				U		X			M	MD				X			X		U											U	
International Finance		U			M			X		M		MD							X	MD	U											UM	M
International Finance Economics								X				MD								MD	U											UM	
International Marketing								X				MD				X			X	MD	U												M
International Relations/Studies	X				X		X	U		M	X	X	X		MD	X		X		MD		U			MD	UD	X		X	X	U	X	X
Internet Computing/Technologies		UM	X	UM	M		X								MD	X		U	X				UM	U	X		X			U			
Interpreting			MD		M																												D
Islamic/Middle Eastern Studies	MD						X				X				MD	M	X	X			X		D										X
Italian			X		X		X		X		X	X	U		UD		X	X		X							UD			X		X	X
Jainism											D																						
Japanese/Japanese Studies		U			MD		X				X	UD			MD		X																X
Jewish Studies	MD				MD			MD			X																						X
Korean/Korean Studies																																	
Laboratory Science Technology																										X	MD						
Labour Studies																																	
Land Management/Rehabilitation					X										MD		M																
Land Resource Science															MD																		
Landscape Architecture													U								U												
Language Teaching/Learning					M	D															M				MD								M
Language and Communication			X						U														MD			MD							
Languages, Modern	X		X	X	X	X	U	X			X	UD	U		X	X	U	X	X		X			X	U		X			X	U	U	X
Law Business/Commercial/Economic/Industrial	MD	U				M	X	X	M						D				X	MD					M	X					MD	U	M
Law Civil		U	X												D														X			U	
Law Employment/Labour		U						MD	X						D				X	MD					M							U	
Law Enforcement/Security Management																					U												
Law Environmental		X							X											X					M							MD	
Law Intellectual Property/Copyright	MD							MD	X											X	MD												
Law International/Comparative/Trade	MD							MD		M			U		D	M			X	MD					M	MD							M
Law Legal Practice	M		M						X	MD		M						M		MD					M					U			
Law Property/Construction/Housing																				MD													

Leeds Metropolitan	Leicester	Lincoln	Liverpool	Liverpool John Moores	London see page 1769	London Metropolitan	London South Bank	Loughborough	Manchester Metropolitan	Middlesex	Napier	Newcastle	Northumbria	Nottingham	Nottingham Trent	Open	Oxford	Oxford Brookes	Plymouth	Portsmouth	Queen Margaret	Queen's, Belfast	Reading	Robert Gordon	Salford	Sheffield	Southampton	St Andrews	Stirling	Strathclyde	Surrey	Swansea	Ulster	Wales: Inst., Cardiff	Wales: Lampeter	Wales: Newport	Warwick	West of England	Wolverhampton	Worcester
																M															M									
X	MD	UM	MD	MD		UM		X	X	UM	M	UM		MD	M		UM	X	X	M			X	UM	MD		X	X	M		X					UM	MD	MD	X	
X		UM	X	UM		X	X	X	X	X	X	X	X		X	X		X	X	X	MD	UD	X	X	X	X	X	M	X	X	X	MD	D	X	UM	U		X	X	
			X			U		X	X			UM		UM	MD	UM		X			UM		U							X	X						X	UM	UM	U
			U											MD		M																								
						UM		U	X			UM				UM		M	U												U					U	M	U	M	
			X						M	M	MD	M		UM		UM		X	U	U										UM										
			X						MD	MD				UM					U											UM									M	
									MD	M	D			UM		UM														X		U								
MD	UD	MD							X		X	MD		M	UM	MD	X	U	MD	UM	UD	X	U		X	U	X	X	X	U	UM		X	X			MD	X	UM	
	X	D							MD	M	U	UM		U						UM											X	M	U					U	U	
									M			D																												
										U							X									X						X								
UD		U	U			U			X	U				UD	U	X				UM			X		UM	U		X	X									X		
		U				U						U				X	U							X																
																X								U	UM													UD		
						MD										X										X														
																MD											X													
																U																X								
MD																														UM										
																	X					U	UM																U	
X	M		MD							X		M													X												M			
	MD								M					M	UM	M				U								U	X		M								M	
									X			U																												
U	UD		X	X		U	U	X	M	X		X		X	X	X	X	U		X	U		X	X	X	X	X	X	X	U	X	X	X	U			X	U	X	UD
		U				U						M	MD			U		X			UM			UD		D				M								U	UM	MD
														U																										
									M		M	M		D		U			U						MD					UM									M	
M																				UM																				
												M		MD		U																								
									MD						D	U														D										D
		M							MD			M		MD				X		U					MD		M			UM	X								UM	MD
									MD			M													M					M	M								M	U
												M												MD						UM										MD

	Aberdeen	Abertay Dundee	Aberystwyth	Aston	Bangor	Bath	Birmingham	Bournemouth	Bristol	Brunel	Cambridge	Cardiff	Coventry	Cranfield	Durham	East Anglia	East London	Edinburgh	Exeter	Glamorgan	Glasgow	Glasgow Caledonian	Greenwich	Heriot-Watt	Hertfordshire	Huddersfield	Hull	Imperial	Keele	Kent	Kingston	Lancaster	Leeds
Law Transport																																	
Law/Legal Studies	X	UD	X		X		X	X	X	X	X	X	UM		X	X	X	X	X	X	X	UM	UM			X	X	X		X	X	X	X
Library/Information Science			X																							D							
Linguistics/Translation	X		UM	X	M		X		M	U	X	X				MD	U	X			X			X	X		M	MD				X	X
Literature, Comparative	MD																		M		MD						U			X			
Logic/Computation																		D	MD								X			D			
Logistics													U						UM														
Malay Language/Studies																															U		
Management	X	X	X	X	X	X	X	X	X	X	X	X	X	X	MD	X	X	X	MD	X	X	X	X	UM	X	X	UD	X	MD	X	X	X	X
Management Information Systems									X																							U	
Management, Hotel and Catering Technology								UM					U																				
Maritime Studies	MD								M			MD						MD		X			M				UM						
Marketing	MD	X	X	X	UM	MD	MD	X		UM		X	X	MD	MD	MD	X		M	X	MD	UM	UM	X	X	X	X			X	UM	X	X
Materials Science	MD			MD	D	X				X	D				MD	MD		MD						X	X		D		X		D	D	X
Mathematics	X		X	U		X	X		X	X	X	X	X		MD	X	X		X	X	U	X	UM	UM	X	X	UD		X	UD	X	X	X
Mechatronics					M					U									UM	U							U		D			X	U
Mediaeval Studies		MD						MD	X		M	X			X			MD			MD						U			MD		U	MD
Medical Ethics								MD	MD			D									M						MD	M		M		D	M
Medical Physics	MD																	D														U	MD
Medical Transfusion and Transplantation Sciences																											D					D	
Medical/Dental Technology		U																															
Medicine, Alternative																UM																	
Medicine, Chinese																															U		
Medicine, Obstetrics and Gynaecology								MD	MD												D						D						
Medicine, Oncology/Cancer studies									U												D	X					D						
Medicine, Orthopaedic																											D						
Medicine, Otorhinolaryngology/Otolaryngology																																	
Medicine, Paediatric								MD													D						D						
Medicine, Palliative									M																		M	MD		M		D	
Medicine/Surgery	X					D	X		X		X	X			U	U		D	UD		X						UD	X		X	MD	U	X
Mediterranean Studies									X	D								U	D		MD												MD
Meteorology								MD										X															U
Microbiology/Medical Microbiology	X		U	D	D		X		U	M	UD	UD			MD	MD		UM	UD	X		X	UM		UD	X	D	X			X	X	X
Migration, Refugee and Diaspora Studies																			M		D		MD									MD	
Military Science														MD																			
Mobile Communications/Telecommunications					M	M	X					D						MD	UD		X		X	M		UM				X	MD	X	M

Leeds Metropolitan	Leicester	Lincoln	Liverpool	Liverpool John Moores	London see page 1769	London Metropolitan	London South Bank	Loughborough	Manchester Metropolitan	Middlesex	Napier	Newcastle	Northumbria	Nottingham	Nottingham Trent	Open	Oxford	Oxford Brookes	Plymouth	Portsmouth	Queen Margaret	Queen's, Belfast	Reading	Robert Gordon	Salford	Sheffield	Southampton	St Andrews	Stirling	Strathclyde	Surrey	Swansea	Ulster	Wales: Inst., Cardiff	Wales: Lampeter	Wales: Newport	Warwick	West of England	Wolverhampton	Worcester
						MD							M																											
X	X	UM	X	X		X	U		X	X	UM	X	X	X	X	U	X	X	X	X		X	X	X		X	X		UD	X	X	X	X			U	X	X	X	
X				X					X	MD		UM			X						MD			MD			MD			MD									M	D
U	UM		MD	X					X			X		MD	X	UM	MD		X			UD	X		X	X	MD	X	D	X	X	X	X					MD	UM	UD
			U													U			X												M									UD
													UM		M																									
X	X	X	X	M		X	X	X	X	X	X	X	X	X	X	X	X	X	X	X	X	X	UD	X	X	X	X	X	X	X	X	X	X	UD	X	UM	X	UM	X	UM
				M			MD					U			UM		U														UM									
																UM	U													UM										
			MD	U		MD											U	MD								MD					X									
X	MD	X	X	UM		X	X	MD	M	X	UM	U		X	MD	MD	MD	X		X	X	X				X	X		X	X	MD	X	X	U		UM	X	X		UM
	X					M	X	X	M	UM						UD	X	X								X				X	X	X	D					UD		
	UD		X	X		U	X	X	D	X	X	U		UD	UD	X	X	X	X	X	UD		X			UM	X	X	X	UD	X	UD	X	X			X	U	U	U
		U	UM			M	MD			M	UM			U												U					U		X							UD
			MD							MD											M	MD										UD		X						
			MD																								MD										X			
			U																							MD					U						D			
																																								M
								X																																
	U									U																							D							
										U																														
	D		D												MD																						M			
		D													MD	UM																								
		D					M			M					MD																									
		D																																						
	D	D						U						MD			MD			M																				
		D														U		UM		U						D						MD								
	X	X										X		X		X			MD			UD				X	X	U				M	MD						MD	
																U												X	D											
	X	X	U			U	X		MD		U	X	M	UD	UD	UD	MD	D	UD	U		UD	U	D		X	D	X	UD	X	X	D	MD			X	UM	X		
															MD																									
		MD				U		M				U			U						UM					X				X	M	U						M	

	Aberdeen	Abertay Dundee	Aberystwyth	Aston	Bangor	Bath	Birmingham	Bournemouth	Bristol	Brunel	Cambridge	Cardiff	Coventry	Cranfield	Durham	East Anglia	East London	Edinburgh	Exeter	Glamorgan	Glasgow	Glasgow Caledonian	Greenwich	Heriot-Watt	Hertfordshire	Huddersfield	Hull	Imperial	Keele	Kent	Kingston	Lancaster	Leeds
Multimedia		U			X	M	U	X		X			UM				UM		UM		UM			X	X			U			U	UM	
Musculoskeletal Studies									U																				M				
Museum Studies							X					M			M	M							M										UM
Music	X				X		X	MD	X	X	X	X	U		X	X	U	X		X					X	X	X	U	UD		X	X	X
Music Education	U																																
Music Jazz																																	
Music Pop								U																									
Music Technology						M							U				U	UM	U		U			X	X				UD	U		U	X
Nanotechnology					MD		X				MD				MD	D							MD			U		MD					UM
Native Studies																		U															
Natural Resource Studies		UD			X										MD		X	D					M			MD							
Network Technology/Security		UM			M													MD									UD						
Neuroscience	U				MD			MD	U		UD	UD						U			X					MD							U
Nursing Education/Administration																																	
Nursing/Midwifery	MD	U			X			UM	UM			X	U		X		X	UM	X	UM	U			X	UD	X	MD	UD			X		UM
Occupational Health/Therapy	MD							MD	U	UM		X	UM					X	MD		M	UM	UM		M	U			D	D			
Oceanography/Oceanic Sciences					X	D																											
Oenology/Viticulture/Wine Studies																																	
Operational Research/Operations Management		U			M							U						MD							X					D		X	
Ophthalmology									MD																								
Optics/Photonics						D									MD			D						X			MD						
Optometry/Vision Science			UD						UD													X					D						
Palaeography															D			MD															
Palaeontology/Palaeobiology								MD	X						D	D		MD														D	
Parasitology	U	X													D						X					MD	MD					D	
Pastoral Studies	M																																
Pathology									U	X								U			D								D				
Peace/War Studies	MD		X					MD				M						MD							UM					X		X	
Persian											X						X	U	X														
Pharmacology	X		MD		UD	X	X		X			UD	U		MD		M	U		UD	UM	UM			X				UD		X		X
Pharmacy/Pharmaceutical Science			U			X						X	UM					UD						UM	UM		U		MD	UM	X		
Philosophy	X						X		X		X	X			X	X	D	X	X		U	X		U	X		X		X	X		X	X
Physical Education/Sports Science	X	UD	X		X	X	X	U	MD	X			U		U		U	X	X	U		X	U	UD	X	U	UD		U	UD			X
Physics	X		X		UD	X	X		X			UD			X	U		X	X	X	U	U	X	X	D	X	MD	UD	X	D	UD		X
Physiology	X						MD		UD			X	UD		MD	X	UM	UD	D		X	X	U		UM							UD	X
Physiotherapy						M	X			X		X	X				X	UM		X	U		X	U							X	UM	

Leeds Metropolitan	Leicester	Lincoln	Liverpool	Liverpool John Moores	London see page 1769	London Metropolitan	London South Bank	Loughborough	Manchester Metropolitan	Middlesex	Napier	Newcastle	Northumbria	Nottingham	Nottingham Trent	Open	Oxford	Oxford Brookes	Plymouth	Portsmouth	Queen Margaret	Queen's, Belfast	Reading	Robert Gordon	Salford	Sheffield	Southampton	St Andrews	Stirling	Strathclyde	Surrey	Swansea	Ulster	Wales: Inst., Cardiff	Wales: Lampeter	Wales: Newport	Warwick	West of England	Wolverhampton	Worcester
X		U	U	X		X	UM	M	U	UM	X		UM		UM	M		U	U	UM												U	X	U	U	UM			UD	U
			D																																					
	MD	UM										M	M							M							MD													
			X	U								X	X	UM	X	UM	X	UD	X	X	U	M		X	X	X				U	X		X			U				X
						U				M												M								U						U				
			D							U																				U									D	
			X									U	U																											U
						X										U			U			X										X			U	U	UM	U	U	
	D		MD															MD									M					U						D		
	MD																			U										U										D
						M				UM																										U	U			
	UD		MD												U		UM	MD								X														
																	X																							UM
X		U	X	X		UM	X		X	X	UM		UM		X	U		X	U		X	X	UM	X	UM	MD	X		X		X	X	X					X	X	UM
U			UD			MD	UM	M		U				UM	MD		U	UM	UM	X				UD	X		X			M	M		X						U	U
																U		U									X													
			UD																																					
			MD					D																			MD			M							M			
			D															MD						D			D													
																																X								
			UD							U															X							X								
			MD														U			U																				
			MD																																					
																																						D		
	MD		D															MD						D			D													
						U																			U							U	MD						UD	
																								X																
	D		UD			U				MD			X		MD	U	MD			X				D	U	X			X			D							UD	
		X		D									UD		X					X		X	U	X						X	M		D				M	U	UM	
			X			U						X	X	UM		X		X	X	X				X	X			X	X	X	X		MD	X		X	U	X		UD
X		U		X		UM	UM	X	X	U	U			UM	MD		U	UD	X	X				UD	UM	MD	X	MD	X	X		U	X	UM			U	MD	UM	X
	X		X					X				M			X		UD	X		UD				UD	X		X	X	X	X		X	X	X					X	
	X		X					M	MD				X				U	U	X					UD			X	U		X		X	U						U	D
X		U										M	UM	X			UD	U		X					X	U				X		X							U	

	Aberdeen	Abertay Dundee	Aberystwyth	Aston	Bangor	Bath	Birmingham	Bournemouth	Bristol	Brunel	Cambridge	Cardiff	Coventry	Cranfield	Durham	East Anglia	East London	Edinburgh	Exeter	Glamorgan	Glasgow	Glasgow Caledonian	Greenwich	Heriot-Watt	Hertfordshire	Huddersfield	Hull	Imperial	Keele	Kent	Kingston	Lancaster	Leeds
Planning/Landscape Studies	X			U			X	U	MD		X	X					UM		U	MD			UM	X		D						U	MD
Plant Pathology							D											D									MD				X		
Podiatry																		U					X										
Politics/Political Science/Government	X			U	X		X		X	X	X	X	X		X	X	U	X	X	U	X	X	UM			UD	X		X	X	X	X	X
Polymer Science			MD								D							D						MD			D				D		MD
Popular Culture																	UM																
Population Studies/Demography									D											MD	D				D		U	MD					
Portuguese/Portugese Studies							X		X		X							X			X												X
Poultry Science																																	
Product Design and Technology				U			X						U				UM		U	U			UM	U	X	U							
Project Management	M							MD					U				M							M	M							M	
Property	X																			MD													
Psychiatry							MD	MD										M			D												M
Psychology	X	UD	UD	X	X	X	X	U	X	X	X	X	UD	MD	X	X	X	X	X	X	X	X	U	UD	X	UD	X	D	X	X	U	X	X
Psychology Clinical			X		MD		D					D					MD	MD	M		D					D	D				X	D	
Psychotherapy																	M		M												MD		
Public Administration			X		X		M	M		M					D		M	MD	MD	X			UM					X					
Public Health/Population Health	MD				MD		MD		M						D		M	UM	M	MD	M		U			MD							MD
Public Relations		U					X					M									U			UM	U								D
Public Sector Management							UM	UM							D			M						U	U			U					
Publishing								U																	U								
Radiography/Diagnostic Technology/MRI					U							MD		MD					U				UM	X							X		U
Radiology																								X									
Rehabilitation Medicine/Therapy/Science					M		MD	X	M			MD									M												
Religion/Theology	X						X		X		X	X			X			X	X		X		U		X		X			X		X	X
Remote Sensing											M				MD		M	M														UD	
Renewable Energy Studies	MD														MD			MD	UD					MD			MD						
Renewable Resources					D				X											M							MD						
Risk Management	MD																M	M						M				M					
Robotics		X							X			D												X	X	D							
Rural Studies/Development	MD				X	MD	MD	U				D			MD					MD					X								
Russian/Russian Studies			UD		X		X				X							X			X	X	X			UD				D			X
Sanskrit/Pali/Prakrit/Vedic Studies											X							X															
Scandinavian Studies																		X															
Sculpture																																	X
Serbian/Croatian Studies																																	

Leeds Metropolitan	Leicester	Lincoln	Liverpool	Liverpool John Moores	London see page 1769	London Metropolitan	London South Bank	Loughborough	Manchester Metropolitan	Middlesex	Napier	Newcastle	Northumbria	Nottingham	Nottingham Trent	Open	Oxford	Oxford Brookes	Plymouth	Portsmouth	Queen Margaret	Queen's, Belfast	Reading	Robert Gordon	Salford	Sheffield	Southampton	St Andrews	Stirling	Strathclyde	Surrey	Swansea	Ulster	Wales: Inst., Cardiff	Wales: Lampeter	Wales: Newport	Warwick	West of England	Wolverhampton	Worcester
UM			X	X			X					MD	UM		X			X	U			X	UM		U	X							UD						X	D
																														X										
																	U		X					X		U							UD	U						
U	X	X	X	X		X	UM	X	X	UD		X	U	X	X	UD	X	X	X		X	X		X	X		X	X	MD	X	X	X	X	U		U	X	X	X	UM
							X					MD	X		U										MD							D								
										U							M																U							
			MD																						MD	X				UM		D								
			X	U										U			X								U	UD														
			D																																					
		X	MD				U			X		U	U		U	U		U		UM							X		U		U						U	U		
							M	M						X		M				UM				MD					UM			M						M	UD	
														U						UM		UM											UM							
	D		MD											MD		MD																								
U	X	X	X	X		X	UM	X	X	X		UD	X	X	X	X	X	X	X	X	X	X	X	X		X	X	X	X	X	X	X	U		U		X	X	X	UM
	D	UD	MD			MD	UM					D		M							U	D			MD					UM		D								
X	M																								D															D
			MD	U			X	M		X		M	UD	MD	M		M			MD				X			UD		M	M	X					M	D		
	D		MD			D	M						MD		MD	X				UM							UM	MD		M	UM	X								
X	U						UM			X											M					MD			U	X						U				
	D		MD			MD	M					M			M					M							M		M								D	UM	
							X			U	U						X								X			MD			U		U							
	D		UD				UM											X	X				UD	UM					X								UM			
																										D														
			MD							U			X	MD			UM							D	X	M		M		X						U				
										UD			X		UD	X	X	UD	X				X		X	X							X	UM		U				
																				X										X	D								
							X																																	
	UM		M							UM			M																M											
			UD				MD								U			UM					U	UD	D							U				UM				
												X	M			MD	X				M	X																	MD	
			U												UD		X									X		X		X	UM									
																	X																							
			U														M								X														U	
													U																											

	Aberdeen	Abertay Dundee	Aberystwyth	Aston	Bangor	Bath	Birmingham	Bournemouth	Bristol	Brunel	Cambridge	Cardiff	Coventry	Cranfield	Durham	East Anglia	East London	Edinburgh	Exeter	Glamorgan	Glasgow	Glasgow Caledonian	Greenwich	Heriot-Watt	Hertfordshire	Huddersfield	Hull	Imperial	Keele	Kent	Kingston	Lancaster	Leeds
Sign Language									MD																								
Slavonic Languages/Studies							X		U		X										X												D
Social Policy						X	X	X	U		U				MD	UM	X	U	U								X			X		UD	X
Social Reconstruction																																	
Social Work/Studies					U	X	X	X	MD	X		X	UD		MD	X	X	X	MD		X	X	U		X	UD	X		MD	UD	X	X	X
Sociology	X	UD	U	X	X	X			X	X	X	X	UD		X	X	U	X	X	X	X	X	UM				UD	X		X	X	X	X
Sound Recording/Design		U							X										M	UM		U		X			U						
Spanish/Hispanic/Latin American Studies	X		X		X	U	X		X		X	X	U		X			X	X		X			X			UD	UD		X	U	U	X
Speech Science/Pathology/Therapy																		MD															
Statistics/Actuarial Science						UD	X		X	U	M	UD	UD		MD	MD		X	X		X		UM	X	X	D		X		X	X	X	X
Surveying/Quantity Surveying	MD	U										U							UD	MD	U	MD	UM	X	X	U	UD				X		MD
Sustainable Communities																															U		
Sustainable Development	MD			U		U	X				M	MD	D	MD		D	MD	M		MD	U	M	X				U	MD				U	MD
Sustainable Economies																				MD													
Taxation						M			X												M												
Teacher Training	UM				UM	M	M		M	X					X	MD	M	X	X		X		U		X	UD	X				X		MD
Telugu																													M				
Textiles/Fibre Science/Technology								U											U					UD	X								X
Thai/Thai Studies																											U						U
Tourism/Hospitality/Leisure/Recreation		U	X		UM		M	X					UD							MD	U	U	X	UM	X	X	X			U		UM	
Toxicology							MD											M			X						U	D		D			
Transport Studies											X			MD		D				UM				MD	U		MD						X
Turkish/Turkish Studies																																	
United States Studies		X					X											U	MD								UD		X	X			
Urban Studies							X					MD						M			X			X			U			X			
Urdu												U																					
Veterinary Science									X		X							X			X												
Visual Arts		U	X								UM		X		X	UM			UM	X	UM				X		U				U	X	X
Wildlife Management	U					U																		X							X		
Women's/Gender Studies	UD				M	D	M		M			MD			M		U			MD	M						X		D	MD	U	MD	MD
Wood Science																										X							
Youth and Community Development																		U		UM													
Zoology	X		X		UD		X		U		X	UD			UD			X			X						U		X				U

Leeds Metropolitan	Leicester	Lincoln	Liverpool	Liverpool John Moores	London see page 1769	London Metropolitan	London South Bank	Loughborough	Manchester Metropolitan	Middlesex	Napier	Newcastle	Northumbria	Nottingham	Nottingham Trent	Open	Oxford	Oxford Brookes	Plymouth	Portsmouth	Queen Margaret	Queen's, Belfast	Reading	Robert Gordon	Salford	Sheffield	Southampton	St Andrews	Stirling	Strathclyde	Surrey	Swansea	Ulster	Wales: Inst., Cardiff	Wales: Lampeter	Wales: Newport	Warwick	West of England	Wolverhampton	Worcester
																																							U	
														MD			X								M	X													D	
		X	UD			UM	U	UD	MD	M		M	U	X		UM	MD	MD					U			UD			X		M	X					M		UD	
																												X												D
X	MD	X	UD	X		X	UM		X	X			X	MD	U	UD	MD	X	X	UM	U	UD	UM	X	X	X	X		X	X		X	X	U		UM	MD	X	UM	U
U	X		X	X		X	X	UD	X	UD	UD	UD	UM	X	U	X	MD	X	X	X	U	UD			X	X		X	X	X	MD	X	U		U	X	X	UD	U	
				U																											X									U
U	UD		X	X		U		U		X			X	U		X	U	X		U			X			UM			X	X		X	X					UD	UD	
UM										X			UM									UD				X				X		X	U							
										M			UM				MD													UM										
										M		M	UM			U	MD	M				UM							X	M	M								MD	
X	MD		MD	UM		UM	UM	MD	X		MD	UM		X	UM	MD	X	X		M	M		X		MD	X			X	X	D	M	U			UM	UM	X	UM	UM
				U				UD		U		U									UM							X		UM								U		U
X		X		UM		X	U	X	X	UM		X		UD	MD	MD			X	UD	U	X			X		U	MD	X	X		X					X	UM	UM	X
	MD	D										U																			M		U						D	
		U		U				X				X		MD		MD	MD	X	UD	U					D	M						X						X	D	
														X																										
	UD									U		U		U			U				U	U									X									
										M		MD				M	U						X						X			UM							UM	
		X																		U	U								D								MD		U	
X	U		X			UM	U	X		X			X		UM		X			X						X					X	U				UM		X	
		U								M	M			X						U						U				U								UD	D	
		X	U			MD				X				MD					MD					UD		X						U				M	MD		X	D
										X						U	X	U												U										
UD	X	U											U		U		D	X					UD	U					X	U	X	UD					U		U	

UNIVERSITY OF ABERDEEN

Founded 1495

Member of the Association of Commonwealth Universities

Postal Address: Aberdeen, Scotland AB24 3FX
Telephone: (01224) 272000 **Fax:** (01224) 272005
URL: http://www.abdn.ac.uk

PRINCIPAL AND VICE-CHANCELLOR*—Rice, Prof. C. Duncan, MA *Aberd.*, PhD *Edin.*, FRSEd
SENIOR VICE-PRINCIPAL—Logan, Prof. S. D., BSc *St And.*, PhD *St And.*
VICE-PRINCIPAL (TEACHING AND LEARNING)—Macaslan, C., BSc *Aberd.*, MEd *Aberd.*
VICE-PRINCIPAL (RESEARCH AND COMMERCIALISATION)—Houlihan, Prof. D. F., BSc *Brist.*, PhD *Brist.*
VICE-PRINCIPAL (LIBRARY AND INFORMATION SERVICES)—Gane, Prof. C. H. W., LLB *Edin.*
SECRETARY TO THE UNIVERSITY‡—Cannon, Steve, MA *Dund.*
RECTOR—Harper, R., MSP

GENERAL INFORMATION

History. The university was founded by Bishop William Elphinstone in 1495.

It is located in the centre of Aberdeen, north-east Scotland.

Admission to first degree courses (see also United Kingdom Introduction). Through Universities and Colleges Admissions Service (UCAS). Basic requirement is SQA Highers, General Certificate of Education (GCE) A levels, or International Baccalaureate. Other qualifications (eg Scottish Vocational Education Certificate (SCOTVEC), Higher National Certificates and Diplomas (HNCs/HNDs), Scottish Vocational Qualifications (SVQs), General National Vocational Qualifications (GNVQs), and international qualifications) are also recognised.

First Degrees (see also United Kingdom Directory to Subjects of Study). BD, BEd, BEng, BMus, BSc, BScEng, BTh, LLB, MA, MB ChB, MChem, MEng.

Most degrees normally last 4 years, though students with appropriate qualifications may be admitted to second or subsequent years.

Length of course. Full-time: MB ChB, MChem, MEng: 5 years.

Higher Degrees (see also United Kingdom Directory to Subjects of Study).

Master's. ChM, LLM, MBA, MD, MEd, MLE, MLitt, MPhil, MRes, MSc, MScEcon, MTh.

Admission. Applicants for admission to master's degrees must normally hold an appropriate first degree with at least second class honours. ChM: awarded on published work.

Master's degree courses normally last 12 months full-time or 24 months part-time.

Doctoral. DLitt, DMus, DSc, LLD, PhD.

Admission. PhD: candidates for admission must normally hold an appropriate first or master's degree. DLitt, DMus, DSc, LLD, MD: awarded on published work.

PhD: normally 33 months full-time or 60 months part-time.

Language of Instruction. English. Full-time foundation course (October–August), plus summer schools and four-week intensive pre-sessional courses available.

Libraries. Volumes: 1,000,000. Other holdings: 250,000 maps; 6000 journals and periodicals, printed and electronic.

Academic Awards (2007–2008). 40 awards ranging in value from to £2500.

Academic Year (2007–2008). Three terms: 18 September–14 December; 7 January–21 March; 14 April–6 June.

Statistics. Staff (2005–2006): 3166 (1941 academic, 1225 non-academic). Students (2006–2007): full-time 14,200.

FACULTIES/SCHOOLS

Arts and Social Sciences, College of
Tel: (01224) 272084 Fax: (01224) 272082
E-mail: c.h.sim@abdn.ac.uk
Head: MacGregor, Prof. Bryan D., BSc *Edin.*, MSc *H-W*, PhD *Camb.*

Life Sciences and Medicine, College of
Tel: (01224) 551249 Fax: (01224) 550708
E-mail: infoclsm@abdn.ac.uk
Head: Haites, Prof. Neva E., OBE, BSc *Qld.*, PhD *Qld.*, MB ChB

Physical Sciences, College of
Tel: (01224) 272081 Fax: (01224) 272818
E-mail: secy-cops@abdn.ac.uk
Head: Rodger, Prof. A. A., BScEng PhD

ACADEMIC UNITS

Biological Sciences, School of
Tel: (01224) 272861 Fax: (01224) 272396
E-mail: bioscience@abdn.ac.uk

Agriculture and Forestry
Tel: (01224) 274122 Fax: (01224) 273731
E-mail: agf026@abdn.ac.uk
Galbraith, H., BSc *Strath.*, PhD   Sr. Lectr.
Seddon, B., BSc PhD   Hon. Prof.
Woodward, S., BSc *Hull*, PhD *Lond.*   Sr. Lectr.
Other Staff: 7 Lectrs.
Research: animal biology; forestry, rural and environmental economics; organic agriculture; plant pathology

Plant and Soil Science
Tel: (01224) 272257 Fax: (01224) 272703
E-mail: bioscience@abdn.ac.uk
Alexander, Ian J., BSc *Edin.*, PhD *Edin.*, FRSEd   Regius Prof.
Burslem, David F. R. P., BA *Oxf.*, PhD *Camb.*   Sr. Lectr.
Killham, Kenneth S., BSc *Sheff.*, PhD *Sheff.*, FRSEd   Prof.
McDonald, A. James S., BSc *Edin.*, PhD *Edin.*   Sr. Lectr.
Meharg, Andrew A., BSc *Belf.*, PhD *Aberd.*   Prof.
Mullins, Christopher E., BSc *Essex*, MSc *Essex*, PhD *Essex*   Hon. Reader
Paton, Graeme, BSc *Aberd.*, PhD *Aberd.*   Sr. Lectr.
Robinson, David, BSc *Manc.*, PhD *Sheff.*   Prof.; Head*
Smith, Joanna U., BSc *Lond.*, PhD *Reading*   Sr. Lectr.
Smith, Peter, BSc *Lond.*, PhD *Reading*   Reader
Swaine, Michael D., BSc *Wales*, PhD *Wales*   Sr. Lectr.
Wilcock, Christopher C., BSc *Lond.*, MSc *Liv.*, PhD *Lond.*   Sr. Lectr.

Woodin, Sarah J., BSc *Manc.*, PhD *Manc.*   Sr. Lectr.
Other Staff: 4 Lectrs.; 1 Teaching Fellow; 15 Res. Fellows
Research: crop science, including modelling studies; ecology of northern environments; pollution, biosensors and bioremediation; rhizosphere and mycorrhizae; tropical forest ecology, biodiversity and conservation

Biology, Molecular and Cell
Tel: (01224) 555872 Fax: (01224) 555844
E-mail: d.mcb@abdn.ac.uk
Booth, I. R., BSc *Liv.*, PhD *Wales*   Prof.
Booth, Nuala A., BSc *N.U.I.*, PhD *Wales*   Prof.
Brown, A. J. P., BSc PhD   Prof.
Connolly, B., BSc PhD   Sr. Lectr.
Docherty, K., BSc *St And.*, PhD *Edin.*   Macleod-Smith Prof.
Glover, L. Anne, BSc *Edin.*, MPhil *Camb.*, PhD *Camb.*   Prof.
Gow, N. A. R., BSc *Edin.*, PhD   Prof.
Long, W. F., BSc *Lond.*, MSc PhD   Sr. Lectr.
McEwan, I. J., BSc *Strath.*, PhD *Glas.*   Sr. Lectr.
McGlynn, P., BSc *Sheff.*, PhD *Sheff.*   Reader
Mueller, B., PhD *Zür.*   Reader
Porter, A. J. R., BSc *St And.*, PhD *Reading*   Sr. Lectr.
Prosser, J. I., BSc *Lond.*, PhD *Liv.*   Prof.
Shaw, D. J., BSc *St And.*, PhD *St And.*   Prof.
Shennan, K. I. J., BSc *Edin.*, PhD *Birm.*   Sr. Lectr.
Smith, Maggie, BSc *Leeds*, PhD *Brist.*   Prof.
Stansfield, I., BSc *Sheff.*, PhD *Sheff.*   Sr. Lectr.
Other Staff: 9 Lectrs.; 54 Res. Fellows; 4 Teaching Fellows; 1 Hon. Sr. Lectr.; 4 Hon. Lectrs.; 6 Hon. Res. Fellows
Research: biochemistry; genetics; microbiology; molecular and cell pathology; molecular medicine

Biomedical Physics and Bioengineering
Tel: (01224) 681818 Fax: (01224) 685645
E-mail: dept@biomed.abdn.ac.uk
Allen, Alastair R., BSc *Birm.*, DPhil *Sus.*   Sr. Lectr.
Lurie, D. J., BSc *Aberd.*, MSc *Lond.*, PhD *Lond.*   Prof.
Sharp, P. F., BSc *Durh.*, PhD, FIP   Prof.; Head*
Other Staff: 8 Lectrs.; 1 Sr. Res. Fellow; 11 Res. Fellows
Research: free radical imaging; magnetic resonance imaging; radiation protection; radionuclide imaging; retinal imaging

Biomedical Sciences
Tel: (01224) 555717 Fax: (01224) 555719
E-mail: biomedical-sciences@abdn.ac.uk
Bewick, Guy S., BSc *E.Anglia*, PhD *Lond.*   Sr. Lectr.
Bowser-Riley, Frank, BSc *S'ton.*, MSc *Edin.*, PhD *Edin.*   Sr. Lectr.
Cameron, Norman E., BSc *E.Anglia*, DPhil *Sus.*   Prof.
Clegg, E. John, MD *Sheff.*, PhD *Liv.*, FIBiol   Hon. Prof.
Cotter, Mary A., BSc *Birm.*, PhD *Birm.*   Prof.

Davies, Stephen N., BSc Brist., PhD Lond. Sr. Lectr.
Hawksworth, Gabrielle M., BSc Leeds, PhD Lond. Prof.
Hoppler, Stefan P., BSc Zür., MSc Zür., PhD Zür. Sr. Lectr.
MacEwan, David J., BSc Glas., PhD Edin. Sr. Lectr.
McArdle, Harry J., BSc St And., PhD St And. Hon. Prof.
McCaig, Colin D., BSc Edin., PhD Glas. Prof.; Head, Sch. of Med. Scis.
McEwan, Gordon T. A., BSc Glas., PhD Glas. Sr. Lectr.
Micheau, Jacques, BSc Bordeaux, MSc Bordeaux, PhD Bordeaux Hon. Prof.
Nixon, Graeme F., BSc Glas., PhD Glas. Reader
Page, Kenneth R., RD, BSc Aberd., PhD Aberd., FRSChem Sr. Lectr.
Pertwee, Roger G., MA Oxf., DPhil Oxf., DSc Oxf. Prof., Neuropharmacology
Scott, Roderick H., BSc Nott., PhD Nott. Reader
Stewart, Ian J., BSc St And., PhD S'ton. Sr. Lectr.
Wallace, Heather M., BSc Glas., PhD Aberd. Sr. Lectr.
Zhao, Min, MD PhD Prof.
Other Staff: 13 Lectrs.; 7 Res. Fellows; 6 Teaching Fellows; 3 Hon. Readers; 4 Hon. Lectrs.
Vacant Posts: Kosterlitz Chair (Pharmacol.)
Research: Alzheimer's disease; cannabinoid physiology and pharmacology; learning and memory; neural plasticity; neuroscience

Business School

Tel: (01224) 272167 Fax: (01224) 272181
Hughes, Michael D. Prof.; Head*

Accountancy and Finance

Tel: (01224) 272205
    E-mail: t.pascoe@abdn.ac.uk
Arthur, Alex, MA MLitt Sr. Lectr.
Black, Angela, MA Dund., PhD Dund. Prof.
Buckland, Roger, MA Camb., MPhil York(UK) Prof.
Elad, Charles, BA MAcc PhD Sr. Lectr.
Fraser, Patricia, MA PhD Aberdeen Asset Management Prof., Finance and Investment Management
Hoesli, M., MA PhD Prof.
McColgan, P., BA PhD
Molyneaux, D., BA BD PhD, FCA Head*
Roberts, Clare, BSc S'ton., MSc S'ton., PhD Glas. Prof.
Other Staff: 5 Lectrs.
Research: accounting for sustainability; corporate responsibility accountancy; operations and structure of capital markets

Economics

Tel: (01224) 272156
    E-mail: r.naylor@abdn.ac.uk
Barmby, Tim Jaffrey Prof., Political Economy
Battu, Harminder, BA Paisley, MSc Glas., PhD Strath. Sr. Lectr.
Elliot, R. F., BA Oxf., MA Leeds Prof.
Finch, John H., BA Lanc., MTPl Manc., PhD Lanc. Sr. Lectr.
Gazioglu, Saziye, BSc Ankara, MSc Lond., PhD Lond. Sr. Lectr.
Kemp, Alex, MA Schlumberger Prof., Petroleum Economics
McCausland, W. David, BSc Hull, MSc Warw., PhD Keele Sr. Lectr.
McMaster, R., BSc Strath., PhD Strath. Sr. Lectr.
Phimister, E., BSc MA PhD Sr. Lectr.
Skatun, J. D., BSc Leeds, CandMag Bergen, CandPolit Bergen, PhD Essex Sr. Lectr.
Swierzbinski, Joseph E., AB Prin., PhD Harv. Prof.
Theodossiou, I., BSE Piraeus, MPhil Glas., PhD Glas. Prof.
Other Staff: 6 Lectrs.; 6 Res. Fellows
Research: economics of energy and natural resources; labour economics; regional economics

Management Studies

Tel: (01224) 272712
Chia, Robert, MEng MBA PhD, FRSA Prof.
Dawson, Patrick, BSocSci S'ton., PhD S'ton. Prof.
Hyman, Jeff Prof.
Lamb, John
Mauthner, Natasha, BA Camb., PhD Camb. Sr. Lectr.
McKee, Lorna, BSocStud Trinity(Dub.), MA York(UK), DPhil York(UK) Prof.
Other Staff: 8 Lectrs.; 1 Teaching Fellow
Research: change management; family and work; health services management

Property

Tel: (01224) 273555
    E-mail: d.alves@abdn.ac.uk
Hutchison, Norman, BA Prof.
MacGregor, Bryan D., BSc Edin., MSc H-W, PhD Camb. Prof.
Other Staff: 5 Lectrs.
Research: property investment; property market analysis; urban regeneration

Chemistry

Tel: (01224) 272943 Fax: (01224) 272921
    E-mail: chemistry@abdn.ac.uk
Anderson, J., MSc Dund., PhD Dund., FRSChem Prof.
Feldmann, J., PhD Essen Prof.
Glasser, F. P., PhD Penn.State, DSc Aberd., FRSEd Prof.†
Harrison, W. T. A., BA Oxf., DPhil Oxf. Sr. Lectr.
Howe, R. F., BSc Cant., PhD Cant., DSc Cant., FRSChem Prof.
Imrie, C. T., BSc S'ton., PhD S'ton. Prof.; Head, Sch. of Engin. and Phys. Sci.
Jaspars, M., BA Camb., PhD Trinity(Dub.) Prof.
Macphee, D. E., BSc CNAA, PhD CNAA Sr. Lectr.
Plater, M. J., BSc Lough., PhD Lond. Sr. Lectr.
Skakle, J. M. S., MSc Aberd., PhD Aberd. Sr. Lectr.
Storey, J. M. D., BSc Lond., PhD Lond. Sr. Lectr.
Other Staff: 2 Lectrs.; 15 Res. Fellows
Research: environmental chemistry; materials chemistry; medicinal chemistry

Computing Science

Tel: (01224) 272295 Fax: (01224) 273422
    E-mail: ugsec@csd.abdn.ac.uk
Coghill, George M., BSc Aberd., PhD H-W, FRSA Sr. Lectr.
Edwards, Peter, BSc CNAA, PhD Leeds Sr. Lectr.
Hunter, J. R. W., BSc Edin., DPhil Sus. Prof.
Mellish, Chris, BA Oxf., PhD Edin. Prof.
Norman, Tim J. F., BEng Wales, PhD Lond. Sr. Lectr.; Head*
Preece, Alun, BSc Wales, PhD Wales Sr. Lectr.
Reiter, Ehud, BA Harv., MA Harv., PhD Harv. Sr. Lectr.
Sleeman, D. H., BSc Lond., PhD Lond., FRSEd Prof.
Townsend, Steve, BSc CNAA, MSc Oxf., DPhil Oxf. Sr. Lectr.
Van Deemter, Kees, BA Ley., MA Amst., PhD Amst. Reader
Other Staff: 8 Lectrs.; 3 Teaching Fellows; 9 Res. Fellows
Research: information interpretation and communication (including natural image processing; intelligent software agents; knowledge technologies (including semantic web)

Divinity, History and Philosophy, School of

Tel: (01224) 272380 Fax: (01224) 273750

Divinity and Religious Studies

E-mail: divinity@abdn.ac.uk
Clarke, A. D., MA Camb., PhD Camb. Sr. Lectr.
Marshall, I. H., BA Camb., MA Aberd., BD Aberd., PhD Aberd., DD Asbury Prof.
Murphy, F. A., BA Manc., MA Calif., PhD Lond. Reader

Schaper, J., PhD Camb. Reader
Swinton, J., BD Aberd., PhD Aberd. Prof.
Watson, F. B., MA Oxf., DPhil Oxf. Prof.
Webster, J., MA Camb., PhD Camb., DD Aberd. Prof.
Other Staff: 13 Lectrs.; 2 Teaching Fellows
Research: church history; Hebrew and Semitic languages; history of religions; New Testament; practical theology

History

Tel: (01224) 272456 Fax: (01224) 272203
    E-mail: history@abdn.ac.uk
Brotherstone, W. T. C., BA Camb. Sr. Lectr.
Ditchburn, David, MA Edin., PhD Edin. Sr. Lectr.
Dumville, David, BA Camb., MA Camb., PhD Edin., FRHistS Prof.
Frost, Robert, MA St And., PhD Lond. Prof.; Head*
Harper, Marjory, MA Aberd., PhD Aberd. Reader
Macinnes, A. I., MA St And., PhD Glas. Burnett-Fletcher Prof.
Naphy, W. G., BA William & Mary, PhD St And. Sr. Lectr.
Perren, Richard, BA Nott., PhD Nott. Reader, Economic History
Stevenson, Jane, BA Camb., PhD Camb. Prof.
Other Staff: 17 Lectrs.; 6 Teaching Fellows; 4 Res. Fellows; 2 Temp. Lectrs.
Research: early modern European and British history 1500–1800; history of medicine and science in Britain 1800–2000; oral history; Scotland, Ireland and the wider world 1300–2000

History of Art

Tel: (01224) 273733
    E-mail: h.o.art@abdn.ac.uk
Bourdua, Louise, BA McG., MA Lond., PhD Warw. Sr. Lectr.
Gash, John, BA Oxf., MA Oxf. Sr. Lectr.
Geddes, Jane, BA Camb., MA Lond., PhD Lond. Sr. Lectr.
Morrison, John, MA St And., PhD St And. Sr. Lectr.
Other Staff: 1 Lectr.
Research: British art 1700–1900; Italian art 1300–1800; mediaeval art; Scottish architecture

Philosophy

Tel: (01224) 272366
    E-mail: philosophy@abdn.ac.uk
Cameron, J. R., MA St And., BPhil St And. Regius Prof.†, Logic
Other Staff: 4 Lectrs.; 3 Teaching Fellows
Research: aesthetics; epistemology and philosophy of science; ethics and moral philosophy; history of philosophy; logic

Education, School of

Tel: (01224) 274611 Fax: (01224) 274812
    E-mail: education@abdn.ac.uk
Clark, E. M., BEd Sr. Lectr.
Coutts, N. C., MA Aberd. Sr. Lectr.
Duncan, A. G., BSc MEd Sr. Lectr.
Forbes, J. C., BA Strath., MA Open(UK), EdD Stir. Sr. Lectr.
Gray, D., BSc MEd PhD Sr. Lectr.
Hart, N. M., MA Aberd. Sr. Lectr.
Hendry, A. C. Sr. Lectr.
Hurrell, A., MA Sr. Lectr.
Livingston, K. Prof.
McArdle, K. A., MA St And., MEd La Trobe Sr. Lectr.
Pearson, M. Head*
Russell, M. Sr. Lectr.
Stephens, J. P., BA MMus PhD Prof.
Stollery, P., BMus Birm., MA Birm., PhD Birm. Sr. Lectr.
Strang, C. Sr. Lectr.
Williams, R. Sr. Lectr.
Wolfe, A. J., MA Edin., PhD Dund. Sr. Lectr.
Woods, P. Prof.

Other Staff: 55 Lectrs.; 3 Sr. Res. Fellows; 3 Res. Fellows; 13 Teaching Fellows; 3 Hon. Res. Fellows

Engineering

Tel: (01224) 272787 Fax: (01224) 272497
E-mail: s.carnie@eng.abdn.ac.uk
Akisanya, Alfred R., BSc *Camb.*, MSc *Camb.*, PhD *Camb.* Sr. Lectr.
Allen, Alastair R., BSc *Birm.*, DPhil *Sus.* Sr. Lectr.
Baker, Michael J., BSc *Lond.* Prof.; Head, Grad. Sch.
Chandler, Howard W., BSc(Tech) *Sheff.*, PhD *Sheff.* Prof.
Davidson, Paul C., BScEng *Aberd.*, MSc *Lond.*, PhD *Lond.* Sr. Lectr.
Deans, William F., BSc *Strath.*, PhD *Strath.*, FIMMM Sr. Lectr.
Fairhurst, Godred, BSc *Durh.*, PhD *Aberd.* Reader
Grebogi, Celso, BSc *Fed.U.Paraná*, MS *Maryland*, PhD *Maryland*, Hon. Dr Prof.
Guz, Igor A., BEng *Kiev*, PhD *Kiev*, DSc *Kiev* Reader
He, Shiusheng, BSc MSc PhD Sr. Lectr.
Hendry, David C., BSc *Aberd.*, MSc *Aberd.*, PhD *Aberd.* Sr. Lectr.
Imbabi, Mohammed S., BSc *Brun.*, MSc *Brun.*, PhD *Liv.* Sr. Lectr.
Jones, J. Clifford, BSc *Leeds*, PhD *Leeds* Reader
McEwan, Ian, BSc *Aberd.*, PhD *Aberd.* Reader
Neilson, Richard D., MSc *Dund.*, PhD *Dund.* Sr. Lectr.
Nikora, Vladimir, ME *Odessa*, PhD *St.Petersburg* Prof.
O'Donoghue, Thomas, BEng *H-W*, MEngSc *H-W*, PhD *H-W* Sr. Lectr.
Reid, Stephen, BSc PhD Prof.
Spracklen, C. Tim, BSc *Manc.*, PhD *Leic.*, FIP Prof.
Wang, Charles, PhD *Lanc.*, BSc Reader
Watson, John, PhD *St And.*, FIP Prof.
Wiercigroch, Marian, MEng *Silesia*, ScD *Silesia*, FIMA Prof.; Head*
Other Staff: 7 Lectrs.; 8 Res. Assocs.
Research: applied dynamics; communications and optical engineering; environmental hydraulics; materials engineering

Geography and Environment

Tel: (01224) 274365 Fax: (01224) 272331
E-mail: geography@abdn.ac.uk
Edwards, Kevin J., MA *St And.*, PhD *Aberd.* Prof.
Farrington, John H., BSc *Hull*, PhD *Hull* Prof.
Geist, Helmut, BSc PhD Prof.
Gemmell, Alastair M. D., BSc *Aberd.*, PhD *Glas.* Sr. Lectr.
Gibbins, Chris, BSc PhD Sr. Lectr.
Hunter, Colin, BSc *Stir.*, PhD *Leeds* Sr. Lectr.
Macmillan, Douglas C., BSc MS PhD Reader
Mather, Alexander S., BSc *Aberd.*, PhD *Aberd.* Prof.
Mighall, Tim, BSc *Keele*, PhD *Keele* Sr. Lectr.
Scott, Alister, BA *Wales*, PhD *Wales* Sr. Lectr.
Shaw, Jon, BSc PhD, FRGS Sr. Lectr.; Head*
Soulsby, Christopher, BA *Northumbria*, PhD *Wales* Prof.
Spash, Clive, BA MA MSc PhD Prof.
Stockdale, Aileen, BSc *Ulster*, DPhil *Ulster* Sr. Lectr.
Walton, William, BA *Sheff.*, MSc *Wales*, LLM *Aberd.* Sr. Lectr.
Wood, Michael, OBE, BSc *Aberd.*, DSc *Oxf.Brookes* Sr. Lectr.
Wright, Robert, BSc *Glas.*, BSc(PhysEng) *I.T.C.Delft*, MSc *Mich.* Sr. Lectr.
Other Staff: 10 Lectrs.; 3 Res. Fellows
Research: economic and social change in advanced economies; environmental change; environmental management; environmental processes; society and sustainability

Geology and Petroleum Geology

Tel: (01224) 273433 Fax: (01224) 272785
E-mail: geology@abdn.ac.uk
Clift, Peter, BA *Oxf.*, MA *Oxf.*, PhD *Edin.* Prof.

Hartley, A. J., BSc *Manc.*, PhD *Aston* Sr. Lectr.; Head*
Hole, M. J., BSc *Birm.*, MSc *Birm.*, PhD *Lond.* Sr. Lectr.
Hurst, A., PhD *Reading*, BSc, FGS Prof., Petroleum Geoscience
Jolley, David, BSc PhD Sr. Lectr.
Kneller, Ben, BSc *Sheff.*, PhD *Aberd.* Reader
Macdonald, David I., BSc *Glas.*, PhD *Camb.* Prof.; Head, Sch. of Geoscis.
Morton, Andrew, BA *Oxf.*, MA *Oxf.* Sr. Lectr.
North, C. P., BSc *Lond.*, PhD *Brist.* Sr. Lectr.
Parnell, John, BA *Camb.*, MA *Camb.*, PhD *Lond.* Prof.
Rice, C. M., BSc *Sheff.*, PhD *Sheff.* Sr. Lectr.
Schwab, Anne, BSc *Dayton*, MSc *Mich.*, PhD *Aberd.* Sr. Lectr.
Trewin, N. H., BSc *Brist.*, PhD *Keele*, FGS Prof.
Walkden, G. M., BSc *Manc.*, PhD *Manc.* Prof.
Other Staff: 3 Lectrs.; 7 Res. Fellows
Research: geodynamics and petrogenesis; palaeo-environmental studies; petroleum geoscience

Language and Literature, School of

Tel: (01224) 272625, 272163 Fax: (01224) 272624 E-mail: langlit.school@abdn.ac.uk
Fynsk, C., MA *Johns H.*, PhD *Johns H.* Head*

Celtic

Dumville, David, BA *Camb.*, MA *Camb.*, PhD *Edin.*, FRHistS Prof.
Dunbar, R., BA *Tor.*, LLB *York(Can.)*, MA *Tor.*, MBA *York(Can.)*, LLM *Lond.* Head*
Other Staff: 4 Lectrs.
Research: Gaelic language; mediaeval Celtic literature; modern Irish literature; Scottish Gaelic literature

English and Film Studies

Craig, C., OBE, FBA, FRSEd Prof.
Crotty, P. J., BA *N.U.I.*, PhD *Stir.*
Hewitt, D. S., MA *Edin.*, PhD Prof.
Hughes, D. W., BA *Oxf.*, PhD *Liv.* Prof.
Todd, J., MA *Camb.*, PhD *Flor.* Prof.
Other Staff: 7 Sr. Lectrs.; 11 Lectrs.; 4 Teaching Fellows; 2 Hon. Res. Profs.
Research: language and linguistics; Renaissance literature; Romantic and Victorian writing and culture; Scottish and Irish literature; the Enlightenment

French

Dunkley, J., BA *Exe.*, MA *Exe.*, PhD *Exe.* Prof.
Saunders, Alison M., BA *Durh.*, PhD *Durh.* Carnegie Prof.
Syrotinski, Michael, BA *Kent*, MPhil *Yale*, PhD *Yale* Prof.
Other Staff: 2 Sr. Lectrs.; 2 Lectrs.; 1 Teaching Fellow
Research: cultural studies; eighteenth-century theatre; mediaeval and Renaissance studies; sixteenth- and seventeenth-century emblem literature; twentieth-century fiction; literary theory

German

Burgess, G. J. A., BA *Lond.*, MPhil *Lond.*, PhD Prof.
Other Staff: 3 Lectrs.; 2 Lektorin; 2 Teaching Fellows
Research: Austrian studies; exile; German literature 1600–present (especially Baroque, classical and twentieth-century); modernist thought and visual culture

Hispanic Studies

Moreiras, A., MA *Georgia*, PhD *Georgia*
Vilarós, T., MA *Georgia*, PhD *Georgia*
Other Staff: 3 Lectrs.; 1 Teaching Fellow; 1 Hon. Res. Fellow
Research: Basque culture; Hispanic film; Latin-American anthropology (especially Mexico); modern Latin-American narrative; modern Spanish narrative

Law, School of

Tel: (01224) 272440 Fax: (01224) 272442
E-mail: law089@abdn.ac.uk
Anton, A. E., CBE, LLB *Aberd.*, MA *Aberd.*, LLD *Aberd.*, FBA Hon. Prof.
Beaumont, P. R., LLB *Glas.*, LLM *Dal.* Prof.; Head*
Becker, F., LLM *Camb.*, DrJur *Cologne*, DrJurHabil *Bonn* Prof.
Burns, T., LLB *Lond.*, MA *Glas.* Sr. Lectr.
Campbell, A. I. L., LLB *Aberd.*, PhD *Camb.* Sr. Lectr.
Carey Miller, D. L., BA *Natal*, LLB *Natal*, LLM *Edin.*, PhD Prof.
Carty, A., LLB *Belf.*, LLM *Lond.*, PhD *Camb.* Prof.
Dolezalek, G., DrJur *Fran.*, DrJurHabil Prof.
Duff, P. R., LLB *Edin.*, PhD *Aberd.* Prof.; Dir., Res., Coll. of Arts and Soc. Scis.
Dunbar, R., BA *Tor.*, LLB *York(Can.)*, MA *Tor.*, MBA *York(Can.)*, LLM *Lond.* Reader
Evans-Jones, R., PhD *Edin.*, LLB Prof.
Forte, A. D. M., LLB MA Prof.
Gane, C. H. W., LLB *Edin.* Prof., Scots Law
Goldberg, R. S., LLB *Strath.*, LLM *Lond.*, PhD *Lond.* Reader
Hope, Rt. Hon. Lord Hon. Prof.
Lardy, H., LLB *Aberd.*, PhD *Aberd.* Sr. Lectr.
Lessels, D., LLB *Dund.*, BPhil *Hull* Sr. Lectr.
Lyall, F., LLB *Aberd.*, MA *Aberd.*, LLM *McG.*, PhD *Aberd.* Emer. Prof.
MacCormack, G. D., BA *Syd.*, LLB *Syd.*, MA *Oxf.*, DPhil *Oxf.* Emer. Prof
McKenzie Skene, D., LLB *Aberd.* Sr. Lectr.
Meston, M. C., LLB *Aberd.*, MA *Aberd.*, JD *Chic.* Emer. Prof.
Metzger, E. P., AB *Ill.*, JD *Dallas*, DPhil *Oxf.* Prof.
Niglia, L., JD *Milan*, PhD *Florence* Sr. Lectr.
Paisley, R., LLB *Aberd.*, PhD *Aberd.* Prof.
Paterson, J., LLB *Aberd.*, LLM *Edin.*, PhD *European Univ.Inst.* Reader
Radford, M., LLB *Lond.* Reader
Risk, Sheriff Principal D. J., LLB *Glas.*, MA *Camb.* Hon. Prof.
Rodger, Rt. Hon. Lord, QC, LLB *Glas.*, LLB *Aberd.*, MA *Glas.*, DPhil *Oxf.*, FBA Hon. Prof.
Ross, Margaret L., LLB *Aberd.* Sr. Lectr.
Styles, S. C., LLB *Edin.*, MA *Aberd.* Sr. Lectr.
Van der Merwe, C. G., BA *Oxf.*, LLB *Oxf.*, BCL *Oxf.*, LLD *S.Af.* Emer. Prof.
Visser, D. P., BIur *Pret.*, LLB *Pret.*, LLD *Pret.*, DrJur *Ley.* Hon. Prof.
Walker, N., LLB *Strath.*, PhD *Strath.* Prof.
Other Staff: 19 Lectrs.; 4 Teaching Fellows; 1 Basque Government Postdoctoral Fellow
Research: civil law; commercial law; criminal law and criminal justice; European Union law and international law; property law

Mathematical Sciences

Tel: (01224) 272605 Fax: (01224) 272607
E-mail: maths@maths.abdn.ac.uk
Archbold, R. J., MA *Camb.*, PhD *Newcastle(UK)* Prof.
Benson, David, BSc *Camb.*, MA *Camb.*, PhD *Camb.* Prof.
Crabb, M. C., MA *Oxf.*, MSc *Oxf.*, DPhil *Oxf.* Prof.
Geck, Meinolf, MSc PhD Prof.
Hall, G. S., BSc *Newcastle(UK)*, PhD *Newcastle(UK)* Prof.
Hubbuck, J. R., MA *Camb.*, MA *Oxf.*, DPhil *Oxf.*, FIMA Prof.
Kessar, R., BSc MA PhD Sr. Lectr.
Levi, R., BSc *Jerusalem*, MA *Roch.*, PhD *Roch.* Prof.; Head*
Linkelman, Marcus, PhD Prof.
Robinson, Geoffrey, BA *Lanc.*, MA *Oxf.*, DPhil *Oxf.* Prof.
Weiss, M., MSc *Warw.*, PhD *Warw.* Prof.
Wright, John, MA *Aberd.*, MA *Oxf.*, DPhil *Oxf.*, FRSEd Prof.
Other Staff: 6 Lectrs.; 4 Res. Fellows
Research: general relativity; pure mathematics

Psychology, School of

Tel: (01224) 272227 Fax: (01224) 273426
E-mail: psy370@abdn.ac.uk
Crawford, J. R., BSc Stir., PhD   Prof.
Flin, Rhona, MA Aberd., PhD Aberd.   Prof.
Gray, C. D., BSc Belf., PhD Belf.   Sr. Lectr.
Johnston, D., MA Aberd., PhD Hull   Prof.
Johnston, M., BSc Aberd., PhD Hull   Prof.
McGeorge, P., BSc Nott., PhD Nott.   Sr. Lectr.;
Head*
Mearns, K., MA Aberd., PhD Oslo   Sr. Lectr.
Memon, A., BSc E.Lond., PhD Nott.   Prof.
Mon-Williams, M., BSc Aston, PhD G.Caledonian
Sr. Lectr.
Phillips, L., BSc Edin., PhD Manc.   Sr. Lectr.
Sahraie, A., BSc City(UK), PhD City(UK)   Sr.
Lectr.
Other Staff: 11 Lectrs.; 2 Teaching Fellow; 1
Computing Officer
Research: applied psychology(forensic, industrial
and health); cognition and neuroscience;
life span development

Social Science, School of

Tel: (01224) 272725 Fax: (01224) 272552
E-mail: socsci@abdn.ac.uk
Bruce, S., BA Stir., PhD Stir.   Prof.; Head*

Anthropology

Tel: (01224) 273124
E-mail: anthropology@abdn.ac.uk
Anderson, D. G.   Sr. Lectr.
Hallam, Elizabeth, PhD   Sr. Lectr.
Ingold, T., BA Camb., PhD Camb.   Prof., Social
Anthropology; Head*
Other Staff: 4 Lectrs.; 2 Teaching Fellows; 4
Researchers
Research: aboriginal rights in a global context;
anthropology, archaeology, art and
architecture; anthropology of the North;
indigenous media; language in culture and
society

Politics and International Relations

Tel: (01224) 272714
E-mail: pirmail@abdn.ac.uk
Arter, D., BA Manc., MPhil Hull   Prof.
Bennie, L.   Sr. Lectr.
Criddle, B. J., BA Keele, MA Leic.   Reader
Dyer, M.   Sr. Lectr.
Haerpfer, C.   Reader
Jordan, A. Grant, MA Aberd., PhD Strath.   Prof.
Mitchell, N.   Prof.
Pasha, M. K.   Prof.
Rose, R.   Prof.
Salmon, T. C., MA Aberd., MLitt Aberd., PhD St
And.   Dir., Teaching and Learning, Coll. of
Arts and Soc. Sci.; Prof., International
Relations
Wyllie, J. H., BA Stir., MA Lanc.   Reader
Zalewski, M.   Reader
Other Staff: 11 Lectrs.; 1 Sr. Res. Fellow
Research: European integration and regionalism;
interest groups and public policy; political
parties and elections; Scottish politics;
security studies

Sociology

Tel: (01224) 272760
E-mail: sociology@abdn.ac.uk
Blaikie, J. A. D., MA Camb., PhD Lond.   Prof.
Brewer, J.   Prof.
Bruce, S., BA Stir., PhD Stir.   Prof.
Giulianotti, R.   Sr. Lectr.
Glendinning, A.   Sr. Lectr.
Hayes, B.   Prof.
Inglis, D.   Sr. Lectr.
O'Reilly, K.   Reader
Robertson, R., BA Essex   Prof.
Wallace, C.   Prof.
Wright, C.   Sr. Lectr.
Other Staff: 6 Lectrs.; 2 Res. Fellows
Research: global change and historical/
comparative studies; life course, transitions
and bodies; sociology of culture and social
identities; sociology of religion

Zoology

Tel: (01224) 272861 Fax: (01224) 272396
E-mail: nhi915@abdn.ac.uk
Billingsley, P. F., BSc Leeds, PhD Qu.   Sr. Lectr.
Chappell, L. H., BSc Leeds, PhD Leeds, FIBiol
Reader
Gorman, M. L., BSc PhD, FIBiol   Reader
Holliday, Sir Frederick G. T.   Hon. Prof.
Houlihan, D. F., BSc Brist., PhD Brist.   Prof.
Jenkins, D., MA Camb., DPhil Oxf., DSc Oxf.,
FRSEd   Hon. Prof.
Lambin, X., MSc Louvain, DSc Louvain   Prof.,
Population and Wildlife Ecology
McIntyre, A. D., CBE, DSc Glas., FRSEd   Hon.
Prof.
Mordue, Jennifer A., MSc Sheff., PhD Lond.,
FIBiol   Prof.
Noble, L. R., PhD Lond.   Reader
Priede, I. G., BSc Wales, PhD Stir., DSc Aberd.,
FRSEd   Prof.
Racey, P. A., MA Camb., PhD Lond., DSc Aberd.,
FIBiol, FRSEd   Regius Prof.
Secombes, C. J., BSc Leeds, PhD Hull   Prof.;
Head, Sch. of Biol. Scis.
Speakman, J. R., BSc Stir., PhD Stir., DSc Aberd.
Prof.
Steele, J. H., DSc, FRS, FRSEd   Hon. Prof.
Sternberg, J. M., BSc Brist., PhD Edin.   Sr. Lectr.
Thompson, P. M., BSc York(UK), PhD Aberd.
Reader
Usher, M. B., BSc Edin., PhD Edin., FRSEd
Hon. Prof.
Young, M. R., BSc Birm., PhD Birm.   Sr. Lectr.
Other Staff: 9 Lectrs.; 27 Res. Fellows
Research: animal ecology; integration
physiology; marine biology

SPECIAL CENTRES, ETC

Coastal Science and Management, Aberdeen Institute of

Tel: (01224) 274474 Fax: (01224) 272331
E-mail: aicsm@abdn.ac.uk
Ritchie, William, OBE, BSc Glas., BSc Lanc., PhD
Glas., DUniv Stir., FRS, FRICS   Prof.; Dir.*

Cultural History Group

Tel: (01224) 272199 Fax: (01224) 272203
E-mail: history@abdn.ac.uk
Hallam, Elizabeth, PhD   Dir.*

Early Modern Studies, Centre for

Tel: (01224) 272451
E-mail: k.friedrich@abdn.ac.uk
Hughes, D. W., BA Oxf., PhD Liv.   Prof.; Dir.*

Globalisation, Centre for the Study of

Tel: (01224) 273429 E-mail: csg@abdn.ac.uk
Robertson, R., BA Essex   Prof.; Dir.*

History, Languages and Culture of the North of Scotland, Elphinstone Institute for the Study and Promotion of

Tel: (01224) 272996 Fax: (01224) 272728
E-mail: elphinstone@abdn.ac.uk
Russell, I., PhD   Dir.*

Irish and Scottish Studies, Research Institute of

Tel: (01224) 273683 Fax: (01224) 273677
E-mail: riiss@abdn.ac.uk
Craig, C., OBE, FBA, FRSEd   Prof.; Dir.*

Language Centre

Tel: (01224) 272536 Fax: (01224) 276730
E-mail: langcen@abdn.ac.uk
No staff at present

Lifelong Learning, Centre for

Tel: (01224) 273528 Fax: (01224) 272478
E-mail: lifelonglearning@abdn.ac.uk
McAndrews, J., LLB Liv.J.Moores   Dir.*

Linguistic Research, Centre for

Tel: (01224) 272625 Fax: (01224) 272624
E-mail: langlit.school@abdn.ac.uk
No staff at present

Modern Thought, Centre for

Tel: (01224) 272625 Fax: (01224) 272624
E-mail: c.fynsk@abdn.ac.uk
No staff at present

Natural History Centre

Tel: (01224) 493288
E-mail: nat.hist@abdn.ac.uk
No staff at present

Nordic Studies, Centre for

Tel: (01224) 272714 Fax: (01224) 272552
E-mail: d.arter@abdn.ac.uk
Arter, D., BA Manc., MPhil Hull   Prof.; Dir.*

Novel, Centre for the

E-mail: novel@abdn.ac.uk
Todd, J., MA Camb., PhD Flor.   Prof.; Dir.*

Nursing, Centre for Advanced Studies in

Tel: (01224) 553205 Fax: (01224) 550683
E-mail: h.d.robertson@abdn.ac.uk
Kiger, Alice M., BA Towson State, MA Morgan,
MSc Edin., PhD Edin.   Dir.*

Public Policy, Centre for the Study of

E-mail: cspp@abdn.ac.uk
Rose, R.   Prof.; Dir.*

Scottish Studies, Centre for

Tel: (01224) 272195
E-mail: d.n.dumville@abdn.ac.uk
No staff at present

Spirituality, Health and Disability, Centre for

Tel: (01224) 273224 Fax: (01224) 273750
E-mail: j.swinton@abdn.ac.uk
Swinton, J., BD Aberd., PhD Aberd.   Prof.; Dir.*

Walter Scott Research Centre

Tel: (01224) 273777 Fax: (01224) 272624
E-mail: d.s.hewitt@abdn.ac.uk
No staff at present

CONTACT OFFICERS

Academic affairs. Academic Registrar: Webb,
T., BSc CNAA, PhD Hull
(E-mail: t.webb@abdn.ac.uk)
Admissions (first degree). Head of
Admissions: Baverstock, Carol, Hon. BA Hull
(E-mail: sras@abdn.ac.uk)
Admissions (higher degree). Head of Post
Graduate Admissions: Muir, P., BA R.Gordon
(E-mail: pgadmissions@abdn.ac.uk)
Adult/continuing education. Director, Centre
for Lifelong Learning: McAndrews, J., LLB
Liv.J.Moores
(E-mail: lifelonglearning@abdn.ac.uk)
Alumni. Head of Alumni Relations: Moncur,
Laura E-mail: alumni@abdn.ac.uk)
Archives. Senior Curator: Convery, Siobhan
(E-mail: speclib@abdn.ac.uk)
Careers. Head of Careers Service: Madden, J.
L. A., BA Nott., MA York(UK)
(E-mail: careers@abdn.ac.uk)
Consultancy services. Director, Research and
Innovation: Stevenson-Robb, F., MA
Distance education. Director, Centre for
Lifelong Learning: McAndrews, J., LLB
Liv.J.Moores
(E-mail: lifelonglearning@abdn.ac.uk)
Estates and buildings/works and services.
Director of Estates: Donaldson, A. A. M.
(E-mail: estates@abdn.ac.uk)

Finance. Director of Finance: Bews, Irene, BA
R.Gordon
General enquiries. Secretary (General
enquiries): Cannon, Steve, MA Dund.
Health services. Lead GP: Mouat, Walter, MB
Aberd., ChB Aberd.
Industrial liaison. Director, Research and
Innovation: Stevenson-Robb, F., MA
International office. Head of International
Recruitment: Fernandes, Jenny
(E-mail: jenny.fernandes@abdn.ac.uk)
Library (chief librarian). Manager, Library
Services: Pirie, Wendy
Marketing. Head of Marketing: Sandison,
Rachel, MA Aberd.
(E-mail: rachel.sandison@abdn.ac.uk)

Personnel/human resources. Director of
Personnel Services: Inglis, Caroline, MA
Edin. (E-mail: humanresources@abdn.ac.uk)
Publications. Director of External Affairs:
Manders, Lorraine, BA R.Gordon
Purchasing. Purchasing Officer: McKinnon,
Gary (E-mail: purchasing@abdn.ac.uk)
Safety. Safety Officer: Corby, Nigel
(E-mail: n.corby@abdn.ac.uk)
Scholarships, awards, loans. Academic
Registrar: Webb, T., BSc CNAA, PhD Hull
(E-mail: t.webb@abdn.ac.uk)
Schools liaison. Head of Marketing: Sandison,
Rachel, MA Aberd. (E-mail: sras@abdn.ac.uk)
Sport and recreation. Director of Sport and
Recreation: Beattie, David
(E-mail: sportandrec@abdn.ac.uk)

Student welfare/counselling. Head of
Counselling Service: Bolt, Angela
(E-mail: counselling@abdn.ac.uk)
Students from other countries. Head of
International Recruitment: Fernandes, Jenny
(E-mail: jenny.fernandes@abdn.ac.uk)
Students with disabilities. Student Support
Officer: Foley, L., PhD
(E-mail: student.disability@abdn.ac.uk)

[Information supplied by the institution as at 19 October
2007, and edited by the ACU]

UNIVERSITY OF ABERTAY DUNDEE

Founded 1994

Member of the Association of Commonwealth Universities

Postal Address: Bell Street, Dundee, Scotland DD1 1HG
Telephone: (01382) 308000 **Fax:** (01382) 308877 **E-mail:** enquiries@abertay.ac.uk
URL: http://www.abertay.ac.uk

PRINCIPAL AND VICE-CHANCELLOR*—King, Prof. Bernard, CBE, MSc Aston, PhD Aston, FIBiol, FIWSc
VICE-PRINCIPAL (ACADEMIC DEVELOPMENT)—Swanston, Prof. Michael T., MA Camb., PhD Dund.
VICE-PRINCIPAL (PLANNING AND RESOURCES)‡—Terry, Prof. Nicholas, BSc Hull, MSocSc Birm., MPhil Bath
DEPUTE PRINCIPAL (ACADEMIC DEVELOPMENT)—Palfreyman, Prof. John W., BSc Lond., DPhil Sus., FIWSc
DEPUTE PRINCIPAL (PLANNING AND RESOURCES) AND HEAD OF INFORMATION SERVICES—Lloyd, I. G., BA Strath.,
MLib Wales
REGISTRAR—Fraser, Colin, MSc Strath., PhD Strath.

GENERAL INFORMATION

History. Established in 1888 as Dundee
Technical Institute, the university was granted
its charter in 1994.
It is located in the city of Dundee, on the
north bank of the River Tay.

Admission to first degree courses (see also
United Kingdom Introduction). Through
Universities and Colleges Admissions Service
(UCAS). The university welcomes applications
from students with or without traditional
educational qualifications. Minimum Scottish
Qualifications Agency (SQA) requirements: 5
passes, 3 at higher grade and 2 at standard
grade (including English and mathematics).
Mature students (over 21): accredited prior
learning and/or accredited prior experiential
learning. International applicants: qualifications
equivalent to those listed above with evidence
of proficiency in English (eg TOEFL 563 +
TWE 5 or IELTS 6.0 with no individual band
less than 5.0).

First Degrees (see also United Kingdom
Directory to Subjects of Study). BA, BSc.
Most courses may be studied full- or part-
time. Some courses include an additional year's
work placement in business or industry.
Length of course. Full-time: BA, BSc: 3–4 years.

Higher Degrees (see also United Kingdom
Directory to Subjects of Study).
Master's. MBA, MPhil, MSc.
Admission. Applicants for admission to
master's degrees must normally hold an
appropriate first degree and/or have relevant
work experience. International students must
also provide evidence of proficiency in
English, eg. TOEFL 563 +TWE or IELTS 6.0.
Length of course. Full-time: MBA, MSc: 1 year;
MPhil: 2–3 years. Part-time: MSc: 2 years; MBA:
2–3 years; MPhil: 3–4 years.
Doctoral. PhD.

Length of course. Full-time: PhD: 3 years. Part-
time: PhD: 6 years.

Libraries. Volumes: 148,899. Other holdings:
2823 CD-ROM and electronic journal items;
1415 audio-visual items; 30,000 e-books;
10,000 periodicals (print and electronic).
Special collections: Faculty of Procurators and
Solicitors (law); Dundee and Tayside Local
Collection; Computer Games Collection.

Academic Awards (2005–2006). 130
awards ranging in value from £500 to £1125.

Academic Year (2007–2008). Two
semesters: September–December; January–May.

Income (2005–2006). Total, £33,600,000.

Statistics. Staff (2006–2007): 625 (283
academic, 342 non-academic). Students
(2006–2007): full-time 4145 (2103 men,
2042 women); part-time 1324 (676 men, 648
women); international 363 (247 men, 116
women); distance education/external 726
(269 men, 457 women); undergraduate 4386
(2092 men, 2294 women); master's 422 (269
men, 153 women); doctoral 112 (69 men, 43
women).

ACADEMIC UNITS
Arranged by Schools

Computing and Creative Technologies (CCT)
Tel: (01382) 308600 Fax: (01382) 308627
E-mail: computing@abertay.ac.uk
Bradley, D. A., BTech Brad., PhD Brad. Prof.
Crawford, John W., BSc Glas., PhD Lond. Prof.,
Theoretical Biology
Fortuna, H. S., BSc Abertay, PhD Abertay Div.
Leader, Complex Systems
Fullwood, P. Prof., Computer Games
Technology
Harris, P. Prof., Screen Media

Leimich, P., MSc Dund., PhD Dund. Dir.
Academic Programmes
Longair, I. M., BSc CNAA, MPhil CNAA Sr.
Lectr.
Lucas, T. N., BSc Wales, PhD Wales Sr. Lectr.
Lund, G. R., BSc Newcastle(UK), MSc Sheff., PhD
Abertay Sr. Lectr.; Div. Leader, Software
Applications
MacKinnon, Lachlan, BSc H-W, PhD H-W
Prof.*; Head*
Macleod, A. M., BSc Aberd., PhD Abertay
Reader, Software Applications
Miller, C. J., BSc Nott., PhD Nott. Sr. Lectr.
Milne, A. C., MSc St And. Sr. Lectr.
Natanson, L. D., BSc St And., PhD Abertay Sr.
Lectr.; Dir., Academic Programmes
Paris, R. B., BSc Manc., PhD Manc., FIMA Sr.
Lectr.
Sapeluk, A., BSc Abertay Sr. Lectr., Software
Applications
White, G. D. M., BA Aberd., MLitt St And. Div.
Leader, Computer Arts and Media
Other Staff: 45 Staff Members
Research: asymptotic analysis; computer arts;
computer games; computer modelling;
human-computer interaction

Contemporary Sciences
Tel: (01382) 308231 Fax: (01382) 308261
Palfreyman, John W., BSc Lond., DPhil Sus.,
FIWSc Prof.; Head*

Biotechnology and Forensic Sciences
Tel: (01382) 308231 Fax: (01382) 308261
Adya, A., BSc PhD Reader
Bremner, D. H., BSc H-W, MBA Strath., PhD H-
W Prof.; Chair of Appl. Environmental
Sci.
Collier, P. J., MSc Lond., PhD Manc., FRSA, FLS
Dir., Academic Programmes
Spiers, A. J., BSc Auck., MSc Auck., PhD Auck.
Reader
Walker, G. M., BSc H-W, PhD H-W, DSc Abertay
Prof.
White, Nia A., BSc Cardiff, PhD Cardiff Div.
Leader, Biotechnol. and Forensic Sci.

Young, Iain M., BSc *Aberd.*, PhD *Aberd.*   Prof.;
Dir., Res.
Other Staff: 11 Staff Members
Research: environmental science; microbial
physiology; molecular biotechnology; yeast
biotechnology

Built and Natural Environment

Tel: (01382) 308231 *Fax*: (01382) 308261
Akunna, J. C., BEng *Nigeria*, MSc *Lagos*, MSc *Paris
XII*, PhD *Paris XII*   Dir., Postgrad.
Environmental Educn.
Blackwood, D. J., BSc *CNAA*, MSc *Lough.*, PhD
Abertay   Dir., Operations
Jefferies, C., BSc *Leeds*, MSc *Birm.*, PhD *Abertay*
Prof.
Oduyemi, K. O. K., BSc *Birm.*, PhD *Birm.*   Sr.
Lectr.
Preston, R. J., BTech *Brad.*, MSc *Brad.*, PhD *Brad.*
Div. Leader
Other Staff: 7 Staff Members
Research: soil mechanics; sustainable
construction materials; water and
environmental engineering

Health and Food Sciences

Tel: (01382) 308231 *Fax*: (01382) 308261
E-mail: sae@abertay.ac.uk
Bruce, Alan, BSc *CNAA*, PhD *CNAA*   Sr. Lectr.
Colquhoun, A., BA *Open(UK)*   Div. Leader
Zhelev, N., BSc *Sofia*, PhD *Lond.*   Prof., Medical
Biotechnology
Other Staff: 12 Staff Members
Research: bioethics; consumer studies in the
food area; psychology and genetics of
weight control; use of poetry to explain
science

Dundee Business School

Tel: (01382) 308486 *Fax*: (01382) 308400
E-mail: dbs@abertay.ac.uk
Branine, M., BSc *Algiers*, MPhil *Lanc.*, PhD *Lanc.*
Prof., International Human Resource
Management
Hotho, S., MBA *Edin.*, PhD *Gött.*   Sr. Lectr.,
Management and Communication
Malcolm, M., BA *Liv.*, MBA *Durh.*, MPhil *Oxf.*,
PhD *Leeds*   Prof.; Head*
Murphie, J., LLB *Dund.*   Sr. Lectr., Law
Romilly, P., BSc *Lond.*, MA *Leeds*, PhD *Abertay*
Reader, Economics
Seenan, A. J., BEd *Aberd.*, MA *Dund.*   Sr. Lectr.,
Accounting
Siler, P. A., BA *Portland*, MSc *Portland*, PhD *Edin.*
Sr. Lectr., Economics
Staines, H., BSc *Exe.*, MSc *Lond.*, PhD *H-W*
Prof., Applied Statistics
Taylor, A., BA *Paisley*, PhD   Sr. Lectr.,
Information Communications Technology
Willsdon, J. A., BA *H-W*, MSc *Stir.*   Sr. Lectr.,
Accounting
Other Staff: 47 Staff Members
Research: economics; international business;
marketing; small-to-medium enterprise
development and management; tourism

Social and Health Sciences

Tel: (01382) 308700 *Fax*: (01382) 308749
E-mail: shs@abertay.ac.uk
Annetts, J., BA *Reading*, PhD *Reading*   Div.
Leader, Sociol.
Cook, Malcolm J., MA *Aberd.*, PhD *Dund.*   Sr.
Lectr., Psychology
Di Domenico, C., MA *Edin.*, PhD *Ib.*   Prof.
Hardie, S., BSc *Stir.*, PhD *Stir.*   Sr. Lectr.; Div.
Leader, Psychol.
Heeley, D. W., BSc *Sus.*, PhD *Camb.*   Prof.,
Experimental Psychology and Vision Science
Ion, R., BA *Leic.*, MSc *Lond.*   Div. Leader,
Tayside Inst. for Health Studies
Leishman, J. L., MEd *Dund.*   Dir., Academic
Programme, Tayside Inst. for Health Studies
Lindsay, W. R., BA *Strath.*, PhD *Aberd.*   Hon.
Prof.; Chair of Learning Disabilities and
Forensic Psychol.
Lloyd, R., BSc *Manc.*, MSc *Leeds Met.*   Sr. Lectr.
McLeod, J., MA *Edin.*, PhD *Edin.*   Prof.,
Psychology

McPherson, F., MA *Aberd.*, PhD *Edin.*   Hon.
Prof.; Div. Leader, Clinical Psychology
Olivier, Steve, BA *Rhodes*, MA *Rhodes*, PhD *Rhodes*
Prof.; Head*
Wade, N., BSc *Edin.*, PhD *Monash*   Hon. Prof.
Other Staff: 31 Lectrs.; 6 Teaching Fellows
Research: mental health, counselling, well-being;
nurse-led interventions; pain management;
social and environmental issues; sport and
leisure

SPECIAL CENTRES, ETC

AddKnowledge

Tel: (01382) 308909 *Fax*: (01382) 308345
E-mail: p.fullwood@abertay.ac.uk
Fullwood, P.   Prof., Computer Games
Technology; Head*
Research: educational video game development

Computer Games and Virtual Entertainment, International Centre for (IC CAVE)

Tel: (01382) 308909 *Fax*: (01382) 308345
E-mail: info@iccave.org
Fullwood, P.   Prof., Computer Games
Technology; Head*
Other Staff: 4 Staff Members
Research: emerging entertainment technology;
mobile games technology; multi-player
mobile gaming; usability testing and games
quality assurance

Environment, Abertay Centre for the

Tel: (01382) 308543 *Fax*: (01382) 308626
E-mail: m.cowie@abertay.ac.uk
Cowie, M., BSc *Open(UK)*   Dir.*
Other Staff: 8 Staff Members
Research: environmental management; solid
waste management

Golf Solutions

Tel: (01382) 308646 *Fax*: (01382) 308117
E-mail: c.sturrock@abertay.ac.uk
Young, Iain M., BSc *Aberd.*, PhD *Aberd.*   Prof.
Other Staff: 1 Lectr.

Scottish Economic Research

Tel: (01382) 308704 *Fax*: (01382) 308400
E-mail: n.c.mcgregor@abertay.ac.uk
McGregor, N. C., BA *Stir.*, MSc *Stir.*
Research: impact assessment; labour market
analysis; local economic development;
project appraisal and evaluation; regional
economic modelling and forecasting

Scottish Informatics, Mathematics, Biology and Statistics (SIMBIOS)

Tel: (01382) 308640 *Fax*: (01382) 308663
E-mail: j.crawford@abertay.ac.uk
Crawford, John W., BSc *Glas.*, PhD *Lond.*   Prof.
Staines, H., BSc *Exe.*, MSc *Lond.*, PhD *H-W*   Sr.
Lectr.
Young, Iain M., BSc *Aberd.*, PhD *Aberd.*   Prof.
Zhelev, N., BSc *Sofia*, PhD *Lond.*   Prof.
Other Staff: 22 Staff Members
Vacant Posts: 5 Staff Members
Research: cell biology; machine learning; plant
bioscience; soil science; theoretical biology

Teaching and Learning at Abertay

Tel: (01382) 308448 *Fax*: (01382) 308922
E-mail: l.elder@abertay.ac.uk
Elder, L., MA *St And.*, MEd *Dund.*, PhD *Dund.*
Student Experience Co-ordinator
Research: augmentative communications; student
attitudes/retention

Urban Water Technology Centre

Tel: (01382) 308170 *Fax*: (01382) 308117
E-mail: m.golden@abertay.ac.uk
Akunna, J. C., BEng *Nigeria*, MSc *Lagos*, MSc *Paris
XII*, PhD *Paris XII*   Dir., Postgrad. Educn.
Blackwood, D. J., BSc *CNAA*, MSc *Lough.*, PhD
Abertay   Sr. Lectr., Construction and
Environment
Jefferies, C., BSc *Leeds*, MSc *Birm.*, PhD *Abertay*
Prof.; Head*

Other Staff: 1 Lectr.; 1 Res. Fellow
Research: environmental decision-making;
sustainability; sustainable urban drainage
systems; urban water management systems;
waste and wastewater treatment systems

CONTACT OFFICERS

Academic affairs. Vice-Principal (Academic
Development): Swanston, Prof. Michael T.,
MA *Camb.*, PhD *Dund.*
(E-mail: m.swanston@abertay.ac.uk)
Accommodation. Accommodation Officer:
Wassell, Des
(E-mail: d.wassell@abertay.ac.uk)
Admissions (first degree). (Pre-application)
Student Recruitment Office: (vacant)
(E-mail: sro@abertay.ac.uk)
Admissions (higher degree). (Pre-application
(taught)) Student Recruitment Office:
(vacant) (E-mail: sro@abertay.ac.uk)
Alumni. Alumni Development Assistant:
McLemore, Kathy
(E-mail: c.mclemore@abertay.ac.uk)
Archives. Senior Assistant Registrar: Cringle,
Gordon, BSc *Abertay*, MSc *Abertay*
(E-mail: g.cringle@abertay.ac.uk)
Careers. Head of Student Services: Nicholson,
James, BA *Lond.*
(E-mail: j.nicholson@abertay.ac.uk)
Computing services. Depute Principal
(Planning and Resources) and Head of
Information Services: Lloyd, I. G., BA
Strath., MLib *Wales*
(E-mail: i.lloyd@abertay.ac.uk)
Consultancy services. Director of Business
Development: Durrant, Paul, MSc *Brun.*
(E-mail: p.durrant@abertay.ac.uk)
Equal opportunities. Vice-Principal (Planning
and Resources): Terry, Prof. Nicholas, BSc
Hull, MSocSc *Birm.*, MPhil *Bath*
Estates and buildings/works and services.
Head of Estates and Campus Services:
Simpson, Ian
(E-mail: i.simpson@abertay.ac.uk)
Examinations. Registrar: Fraser, Colin, MSc
Strath., PhD *Strath.*
Finance. Head of Finance: Blake, Catriona
(E-mail: c.blake@abertay.ac.uk)
Health services. Student Counsellor:
Richmond, Gail
(E-mail: g.richmond@abertay.ac.uk)
International office. Student Recruitment
Manager: Balfour, Lesley, MSc *Abertay*
(E-mail: sro@abertay.ac.uk)
Library (chief librarian). Depute Principal
(Planning and Resources) and Head of
Information Services: Lloyd, I. G., BA
Strath., MLib *Wales*
(E-mail: i.lloyd@abertay.ac.uk)
Ombudsman. Vice-Principal (Planning and
Resources): Terry, Prof. Nicholas, BSc *Hull*,
MSocSc *Birm.*, MPhil *Bath*
(E-mail: n.terry@abertay.ac.uk)
Personnel/human resources. Vice-Principal
(Planning and Resources): Terry, Prof.
Nicholas, BSc *Hull*, MSocSc *Birm.*, MPhil *Bath*
(E-mail: n.terry@abertay.ac.uk)
Public relations. Director of Communications:
Coe, Kevin, MA *Dund.*
(E-mail: k.coe@abertay.ac.uk)
Publications. Director of Communications:
Coe, Kevin, MA *Dund.*
(E-mail: k.coe@abertay.ac.uk)
Quality assurance and accreditation. Vice-
Principal (Academic Development):
Swanston, Prof. Michael T., MA *Camb.*, PhD
Dund. (E-mail: m.swanston@abertay.ac.uk)
Research. Vice-Principal (Academic
Development): Swanston, Prof. Michael T.,
MA *Camb.*, PhD *Dund.*
(E-mail: m.swanston@abertay.ac.uk)
Safety. Health and Safety Officer: Burke, Ged
(E-mail: g.burke@abertay.ac.uk)
Scholarships, awards, loans. Student
Recruitment Manager: Balfour, Lesley, MSc
Abertay (E-mail: sro@abertay.ac.uk)

Schools liaison. Student Recruitment Manager: Balfour, Lesley, MSc *Abertay* (E-mail: sro@abertay.ac.uk)

Staff development and training. Vice-Principal (Planning and Resources): Terry, Prof. Nicholas, BSc *Hull*, MSocSc *Birm.*, MPhil *Bath* (E-mail: n.terry@abertay.ac.uk)

Student union. President (Student Union): Riddell, Louise

Student welfare/counselling. Head of Student Services: Nicholson, James, BA *Lond.* (E-mail: j.nicholson@abertay.ac.uk)

Students from other countries. International Student Adviser: Parker, Hazel (E-mail: h.parker@abertay.ac.uk)

Students with disabilities. Student Counsellor: Petrie, John (E-mail: j.petrie@abertay.ac.uk)

University press. Vice-Principal (Academic Development): Swanston, Prof. Michael T., MA *Camb.*, PhD *Dund.* (E-mail: m.swanston@abertay.ac.uk)

[Information supplied by the institution as at 30 October 2007, and edited by the ACU]

ABERYSTWYTH UNIVERSITY

Founded 1872

Member of the Association of Commonwealth Universities

Postal Address: PO Box 2, King Street, Aberystwyth, Ceredigion, Wales SY23 2AX
Telephone: (01970) 623111 **Fax:** (01970) 611446
URL: http://www.aber.ac.uk

VICE-CHANCELLOR*—Lloyd, Prof. Noel G., MA *Camb.*, PhD *Camb.*, FTCL
PRO-VICE-CHANCELLOR (RESEARCH AND STAFFING)—Pykett, Prof. Lyn, BA *Lond.*, PhD *Lond.*
PRO-VICE-CHANCELLOR (LEARNING AND TEACHING, WELSH-MEDIUM TEACHING AND STUDENT SUPPORT)—Jones, Prof. Aled G., BA *York(UK)*, MA *Warw.*, PhD *Warw.*, FRHistS
PRO-VICE-CHANCELLOR (NEW INITIATIVES AND SPACE MANAGEMENT)—Harries, John, BSc *Wales*, PhD *Wales*
REGISTRAR AND SECRETARY‡—Hughes, Catrin, BA *Wales*, PhD *Wales*
DIRECTOR OF INFORMATION SERVICES—Hopkins, Mike, BA *Leic.*, PhD *Lough.*

GENERAL INFORMATION

History. Founded in 1872, Aberystwyth was the first university institution to be established in Wales. Formerly a constituent college of the University of Wales, the university achieved full university status in October 2007.

Admission to first degree courses (see also United Kingdom Introduction). Through Universities and Colleges Admissions Service (UCAS).

First Degrees (see also United Kingdom Directory to Subjects of Study). BA, BEng, BSc(Econ), LLB, MEng, MMath, MPhys.
Length of course. Full-time: BA, BSc(Econ), LLB: 3–4 years; BEng, MMath, MPhys: 4 years; MEng: 5 years. *Part-time:* BA, BSc(Econ), LLB: 4–10 years; BEng, MMath, MPhys: 5–10 years; MEng: 6–10 years. *By distance learning:* BSc(Econ): 5 years.

Higher Degrees (see also United Kingdom Directory to Subjects of Study).
Master's. LLM, MA, MPhil, MSc, MSc(Econ). Many courses are also available part-time or through distance learning.
Length of course. Full-time: LLM, MA, MPhil, MSc, MSc(Econ): 1 year. *Part-time:* LLM, MA, MPhil, MSc, MSc(Econ): 2 years. *By distance learning:* LLM, MSc(Econ): 5 years.
Doctoral. PhD.
Length of course. Full-time: PhD: 3 years. *Part-time:* PhD: 5 years.

Language of Instruction. English and Welsh. The university has a language and learning centre where courses are offered to overseas students whose first language may be other than English.

Libraries. Volumes: 730,000. Periodicals subscribed to: 3200. Special collections: George Powell; Celtic; Challinor; John Canmden Hotten; Duff Pamphlet; Johnston; J. B. Willans; Sir John Rhys; Rudler; Dr Ken Robertson; Raymond Durgnat.

Academic Year (2008–2009). Three terms: 22 September–13 December; 12 January–4 April; 27 April–6 June.

Statistics. Staff (2006–2007): 2001 (785 academic, 1216 non-academic). Students (2006–2007): full-time 6677 (3376 men, 3301 women); part-time 3161 (1142 men, 2019 women); international 662 (289 men, 373 women); distance education/external 988 (214 men, 774 women); undergraduate 6362 (3143 men, 3219 women); master's 1620 (610 men, 1010 women); doctoral 313 (173 men, 140 women).

FACULTIES/SCHOOLS

Arts
Fax: (01970) 621872
Dean: (vacant)

Science
Tel: (01970) 622526 Fax: (01970) 621872
E-mail: jdf@aber.ac.uk
Dean: Fish, John D., BSc *Durh.*, PhD *Newcastle(UK)*

Social Sciences
Tel: (01970) 621774 Fax: (01970) 621872
E-mail: gwh@aber.ac.uk
Dean: Huws, Gwilym, BA *Wales*

Welsh Medium Studies, School of
Tel: (01970) 622828 Fax: (01970) 622831
E-mail: imw@aber.ac.uk
Chair: Williams, Prof. Ioan M., BLitt *Oxf.*, MA *Oxf.*, PhD

ACADEMIC UNITS

Art, School of
Tel: (01970) 622460 Fax: (01970) 622461
E-mail: viawww@aber.ac.uk
Crawford, Alistair Res. Prof.
Harvey, John, BA *CNAA*, MA PhD Prof.
Meyrick, Robert K., BA MA Sr. Lectr.; Head*
Vincentelli, Moira, MA Sr. Lectr.
Other Staff: 5 Lectrs.; 1 Curator; 7 Tutors†
Research: art history; ceramics; fine art; material culture; visual religious culture

Biological Sciences, Institute of
Tel: (01970) 622259 Fax: (01970) 622307
E-mail: pew@aber.ac.uk
Barrett, John, MA *Camb.*, MA *Oxf.*, PhD *Camb.*, DSc *Wales* Prof.
Brophy, Peter M., BSc *Stir.*, PhD *Wales* Prof.

Draper, John, BSc *Nott.*, PhD *Nott.* Prof.
Fish, John D., BSc *Durh.*, PhD *Newcastle(UK)* Sr. Lectr.; Dir.*
Gee, John H. R., BSc *Glas.*, DPhil *Oxf.* Sr. Lectr.
Gwynn-Jones, Dylan, BSc *Wales*, PhD *Wales*
Hoffmann, Karl, BSc *Florida I.T.*, PhD *Johns H.* Prof.
Jenkins, Glyn, BA *York(UK)*, PhD *Wales*
Kaderbhai, Mustak A., BSc *Sheff.*, PhD *Kent* Sr. Lectr.
Mur, Luis A. J., BSc *CNAA*, PhD *Brist.* Sr. Lectr.
Scott, Ian M., BA *Camb.*, PhD *E.Anglia* Sr. Lectr.
Scullion, John, BSc *Ulster*, PhD *Wales*
Smith, Aileen R., BSc *Glas.*, MSc *Natal*, PhD *Birm.* Sr. Lectr.
Wilkinson, Michael J., BSc *Leic.*, PhD *Leic.* Prof.
Wootton, Robert J., MA *Camb.*, PhD *Br.Col.* Reader
Young, Michael, BSc *Brist.*, PhD *E.Anglia* Prof.
Other Staff: 11 Lectrs.
Research: cell signalling, genetics and metabolomics; functional and behavioural ecology; molecular microbiology and parasitology

Computer Science
Tel: (01970) 622424 Fax: (01970) 628536
E-mail: rus@aber.ac.uk
Barnes, Dave P., BTech *Brad.*, MSc *Lond.*, PhD *Wales* Sr. Lectr.
King, Ross D., BSc *Aberd.*, PhD *Strath.* Prof.
Lee, Mark H., MSc *Wales*, PhD *Nott.*, FIEE, FRSA Prof.
Long, Fred W., BSc *Lond.*, PhD *Lond.* Sr. Lectr.
Price, Chris J., BSc *Wales*, PhD *Wales*, FBCS Prof.; Head*
Shen, Qiang, BSc *Natnl.U.Defence Technol.*, MSc *Natnl.U.Defence Technol.*, PhD *H-W* Prof.
Tedd, Michael D., MA *Camb.* Hon. Prof.
Zwiggelaar, Reyer, PhD *Lond.* Sr. Lectr.
Other Staff: 15 Lectrs.; 12 Res. Assocs.; 4 Hon. Profs.
Research: advanced reasoning; computational biology; intelligent robotics; vision, graphics and visualisation

Education and Lifelong Learning
Tel: (01970) 622 1580 Fax: (01970) 622258
E-mail: learning@aber.ac.uk
Jones, Bob M., MA *Reading* Reader

Neil, Peter S., MA Edin., MEd Edin., MDiv Belf., PhD Belf. Prof.; Dir.*
Thomas, Malcolm, BSc Wales, PhD Wales Sr. Lectr.
Other Staff: 17 Lectrs.
Research: educational policy (formulation, implementation and evaluation); health education; language, teaching and learning

English Language and Literature

Tel: (01970) 622534 Fax: (01970) 622530
E-mail: jxr@aber.ac.uk
Barry, Peter, BA Lond., MA Lond. Prof.
Davies, Damian W., DPhil Oxf. Sr. Lectr.
Francis, Matthew, BA Camb., MA Camb., PhD S'ton. Reader
Grice, Helena, BA Wales, MA Lanc., PhD Wales Sr. Lectr.
Hutton, Sarah, BA Camb., PhD Lond. Prof.
Marggraf Turley, Richard, BA Leeds, PhD Leeds Sr. Lectr.
Poster, Jeremy P., MA Camb., PhD Nott. Prof.
Prescott, Sarah, BA York(UK), PhD Exe. Sr. Lectr.
Pykett, Lyn, BA Lond., PhD Lond. Prof.
Watt, D., MA Glas., MA Brist., DPhil Oxf. Prof.
Woods, Tim, BA Brist., MA S'ton., PhD S'ton. Prof.; Head*
Other Staff: 13 Lectrs.; 2 Temp. Lectrs.
Research: early modern studies; eighteenth- and nineteenth-century studies; literary theory; mediaeval studies; twentieth-century fiction and poetry

European Languages

Tel: (01970) 622552 Fax: (01970) 622553
E-mail: eurolangs@aber.ac.uk
Trotter, David A., MA Oxf., DPhil Oxf. Prof., French; Head*
Other Staff: 6 Lectrs.; 3 Lectors; 2 Tutors
Research: linguistics and literature

Geography and Earth Sciences, Institute of

Tel: (01970) 622631 Fax: (01970) 622659
Abrahams, Peter W., BSc Manc., PhD Lond. Sr. Lectr.
Dixon, Deborah P., MA Camb., MS Wis., PhD Kentucky Sr. Lectr.
Dodgshon, Robert A., BA Liv., PhD Liv., FBA Prof.†
Duller, Geoffrey A. T., BA Oxf., PhD Wales Prof.
Glasser, Neil F., MA Edin., PhD Edin. Prof.
Grattan, John P., BA Manc., MSc Sheff., PhD Sheff. Reader
Hambrey, Michael J., BSc Manc., MA Camb., PhD Manc. Prof.
Hannah, Matthew G., BS Maryland, MS Penn.State, PhD Penn.State Prof.
Hubbard, Bryn P., BA Oxf., PhD Camb. Reader
Jones, J. Anthony A., BA Lond., MSc McG., PhD Camb. Prof.
Jones, Martin R., BA Manc., PhD Manc., FRSA, AcSS Prof.
Jones, Rhys A., BA Wales, PhD Wales Reader
Kay, David, BSc Leeds, PhD Leeds Prof.
Lamb, Henry F., BA Trinity(Dub.), MSc Minn., PhD Camb. Reader
Lucas, Richard M., BSc Brist., PhD Brist. Reader
Macklin, Mark G., BSc PhD Prof.
Maltman, Alexander J., BSc Liv., MSc Ill., PhD Ill., FGS Prof.†
Pearce, Nicholas J. G., BSc Manc., PhD Durh., FGS Sr. Lectr.
Perkins, William T., BSc CNAA, PhD CNAA, FGS Sr. Lectr.
Tooth, Stephen, BSc S'ton., PhD W'gong. Sr. Lectr.
Whitehead, Mark J., BSc Wales, PhD Wales Sr. Lectr.
Woods, Michael J., BA Wales, PhD Brist. Reader; Acting Dir.*
Other Staff: 11 Lectrs.; 1 Lectr.†; 2 Res. Fellows; 15 Res. Assocs; 5 Temp. Lectrs.; 12 Hon. Profs.

Research: glaciology; historical and cultural geography; new political geographies; quaternary and recent environmental change; river basin dynamics and hydrology

History and Welsh History

Tel: (01970) 622662 Fax: (01970) 622676
E-mail: history-enquiries@aber.ac.uk
Borsay, Peter, BA Lanc., PhD Lanc., FRHistS Prof.
Coopey, Richard G., BA Warw., MA Warw., PhD Warw., FRSA, FRHistS Sr. Lectr.
Davies, Jeffrey L., BA PhD, FSA Sr. Lectr., Archaeology
Jones, Aled G., BA York(UK), MA Warw., PhD Warw., FRHistS Sir John Williams Prof.
Morus, Iwan Rhys, MA Camb., MPhil Camb., PhD Camb. Sr. Lectr.
Nicholas, Sian H., MA Camb., DPhil Oxf., MA, FRHistS Sr. Lectr.
O'Leary, Paul B., BA Wales, PhD Wales, FRHistS Sr. Lectr.
Powell, Martyn J., BA Wales, PhD Wales, FRHistS Sr. Lectr.
Price, Roger D., BA Wales, LittD E.Anglia, FRHistS Prof.
Rubinstein, William D., BA Swarthmore, MA Johns H., PhD Johns H., FRHistS, FAHA, FASSA Prof.
Schofield, Phillipp R., BA Lond., DPhil Oxf., FRHistS Prof., Mediaeval History; Head*
Weiler, Bjorn Ku, MA St And., PhD St And., FRHistS Sr. Lectr.
White, Eryn Mant, BA Wales, PhD Wales Sr. Lectr.
Other Staff: 12 Lectrs.; 1 Sr. Lectr.†
Research: economic and social history; media history; mediaeval and early modern history; modern history and politics; Welsh history

Information Studies

Tel: (01970) 622188 Fax: (01970) 622190
E-mail: dils@aber.ac.uk
Ellis, D., BA MA PhD Prof.
Eyre, G. D., PhD Sheff., BA Head*
Lonsdale, Ray E., BA Wales, MA Open(UK) Reader
Rafferty, Pauline, MA Glas., MSc Strath. Sr. Lectr.
Urquhart, C. J., BSc MSc PhD Sr. Lectr.
Other Staff: 11 Lectrs.
Research: archive administration/records management; electronic sources; information and library studies; knowledge management

International Politics

Tel: (01970) 628563 Fax: (01970) 622709
E-mail: interpol@aber.ac.uk
Abrahamsen, Rita, BSc Wales, PhD Wales Reader
Alexander, Martin, MA Oxf., DPhil Oxf., FRHistS Prof.
Bain, William, BA S.Carolina, MA S.Carolina, PhD Br.Col. Sr. Lectr.
Bird, Graham, MA Oxf. Hon. Prof.
Booth, Kenneth, BA PhD, FBA, AcSS, FRSA E. H. Carr Prof.
Breen-Smyth, Marie, BSc Belf., DPhil Ulster Reader
Clark, Ian, MA Glas., PhD ANU, FBA Prof.
Edkins, Jennifer, BSc(Econ) Open(UK), MSc City(UK), PhD Wales Prof.
Enloe, Cynthia, BA Conn. Hon. Prof.
Falk, Richard, BS Penn., LLB Yale, JSD Harv. Hon. Prof.
Foley, Michael, BA Keele, MA Essex, PhD Essex Prof.
Gaddis, John L., BA Texas, MA Texas, PhD Texas Hon. Prof.
Harvie, Christopher, MA Edin., PhD Edin. Hon. Prof.
Jackson, Peter D., BA Car., MA Calg., PhD Camb., FRHistS Sr. Lectr.
Linklater, Andrew, MA Aberd., MPhil Oxf., PhD Lond., FBA, AcSS Woodrow Wilson Prof.

Mathers, Jennifer G., BA Mt.Holyoke, MPhil Oxf., DPhil Oxf. Sr. Lectr.
MccGwire, Michael, OBE, BSc Wales Hon. Prof.
McInnes, Colin, BScEcon PhD Prof.; Head*
Scott, Len V., BA Nott., MA Lond., DPhil Oxf., FRHistS Prof.
Scully, Roger, BA Lanc., MA Durh., PhD Ohio State Prof.
Suganami, Hidemi, BA Wales, MSc(Econ) Wales, PhD Wales Prof.
Tickner, Ann, BA Lond., MA Yale, PhD Brandeis Hon. Prof.
Wheeler, Nicholas, BA S'ton., MSc S'ton., PhD S'ton. Prof.
Williams, Howard Ll., BSc(Econ) Lond., PhD Durh. Prof.
Williams, Michael, BA Vic.(BC), MA W.Ont., PhD York(Can.) Prof.
Wyn Jones, Richard, BScEcon Wales, MScEcon Wales, PhD Wales Reader
Other Staff: 17 Lectrs.
Research: global rights and responsibilities; international security and intelligence; political philosophy and international relations; regional governance in Wales and Europe; twentieth-century international history

Law

Tel: (01970) 622712 Fax: (01970) 622729
E-mail: law-enquiries@aber.ac.uk
Andrews, John A., JP, MA Oxf., BCL Oxf. Emer. Prof.
Clarke, Alan, BA Middx., BPhil Hull, PhD Nott. Prof.
Davies, Gillian, LèsL Grenoble Hon. Prof.
Drogin, Eric Y., BA New Hampshire, JD Villanova, PhD Hon. Prof.
Harding, Christopher S. P., BA Oxf., LLM Exe. Prof.; Head*
Ireland, Richard W., MA Oxf., LLM Lond. Sr. Lectr.
Jenkins, D., MA Camb., LLM Camb., LittD Camb., FRHistS Emer. Prof.
Jones, Brian, BA Camb., LLB Camb. Hon. Prof.
Kibble, Neil T. E., LLB Warw., LLM Warw. Reader
Kidner, Richard A. W., MA Oxf., BCL Oxf. Emer. Prof.
Piotrowicz, Ryszard, LLB Dund., PhD Glas. Prof.
Rowland, Diane, BSc Kent, LLB Wales, PhD Manc. Prof.
Sherlock, Ann, BCL N.U.I., LLM N.U.I. Sr. Lectr.
Warren, Lynda, LLB Lond., PhD Lond. Emer. Prof.
Williams, John R., LLB Camb., LLB Wales Prof.
Other Staff: 21 Lectrs.; 3 Hon. Lectrs.; 2 Hon. Dept. Fellows
Research: commercial law; criminal law; regional, European and international law; socio-legal and historical law; technology and the law

Management and Business, School of

Tel: (01970) 622202 Fax: (01970) 622409
E-mail: samwww@aber.ac.uk
Akehurst, Gary, BSc Wales, MSc Wales, PhD Nott.Trent Emer. Prof.
Alexander, Nicholas, BA Wales, MPhil Wales, MA York(UK), DPhil Ulster Prof.
Ap Gwilym, Owain, BSc Wales, PhD Wales Prof.; Deputy Dir. and Dir. of Res.
Baker, M. J., BA Durh., BSc(Econ) Lond., DBA Harv. Hon. Prof., Marketing
Cable, John R., BA Nott., MA Manc., PhD Warw. Emer. Prof., Economics
Cowling, K. G., BSc Lond., PhD Ill. Hon. Prof., Economics
Macve, Richard, MA Oxf., MSc Lond., FCA, Hon. FIA Hon. Prof., Accounting
McGuinness, Anthony J., BSc(Econ) Wales, MA Warw. Sr. Lectr., Marketing
Midmore, Peter, BSc(Econ) Wales, PhD Wales Prof., Applied Economics

Perdikis, Nicholas, BSc(Econ) *Wales*, MSc(Econ) *Wales*   Sr. Lectr., Economics and International Business; Acting Dir.*
Thomas, Dennis, BSc(Econ) *Wales*, MSc(Econ) *Wales*   Sr. Lectr., Economics
Other Staff: 15 Lectrs.; 1 Hon. Dept. Fellow
Research: empirical finance and financial markets; marketing; regional and local entrepreneurship

Mathematical and Physical Sciences, Institute of

Tel: (01970) 622802 *Fax*: (01970) 622826
   E-mail: maps@aber.ac.uk
Barnes, Howard A., OBE, BSc *Wales*, PhD *Wales*, FREng   Res. Prof.
Birkinshaw, Keith, BSc *Leeds*, PhD *Leeds*   Prof.
Breen, Andy, BSc *Wales*, PhD *Wales*, FRAS   Sr. Lectr.
Cox, Simon J., BSc *Warw.*, PhD *E.Anglia*   Reader
Evans, Andrew, BSc *Wales*, PhD *Wales*, FIP   Prof.
Gough, John, BSc *N.U.I.*, MSc *N.U.I.*, PhD *N.U.I.*   Prof.
Grande, Manuel, BSc *Warw.*, MA *Leic.*, PhD *Brist.*, FRAS   Prof.
Greaves, G. Neville, BSc *St And.*, PhD *Camb.*, FIP   Prof.; Head*
Jenkins, Tudor E., MA *Oxf.*, DPhil *Oxf.*, FIP   Reader
Kersley, Leonard, BSc *Edin.*, PhD *Edin.*   Emer. Prof.†
Lindley, D. V., MA *Camb.*, FRS   Emer. Prof.
Macdonald, Ian G., MA *Camb.*, FRS   Hon. Prof.
Mavron, Vassili C., MA *Camb.*, MSc *Lond.*, PhD *Lond.*   Prof.
Miszuris, Giennadij, MSc PhD DSc   Prof.
Morris, Alun O., OBE, BSc *Wales*, PhD *Wales*   Emer. Prof.
Oran, E., PhD *Yale*   Hon. Prof.
Pearson, J. R. Anthony, BA *Camb.*, PhD *Camb.*, ScD *Camb.*   Emer. Prof.
Pryse, S. Eleri, BSc *Wales*, PhD *Wales*   Sr. Lectr.
Swinnerton-Dyer, Sir Peter, Bt., KBE, MA *Camb.*, Hon. LLD *Aberd.*, Hon. DSc *Wales*, FRS   Hon. Prof.
Thomas, Kenneth, BSc *Wales*   Hon. Prof.
Thomas, Lance, BSc PhD DSc, FIP, FIEE   Emer. Prof.†
Wade, Richard, BSc *Essex*, PhD *Lond.*, FIEE   Hon. Prof.
Wallard, A., BSc *St And.*, PhD *St And.*, FIP   Hon. Prof.
Walters, Kenneth, BSc *Wales*, PhD *Wales*, DSc *Wales*, FRS   Res. Prof.
Other Staff: 1 Distinguished Res. Prof.; 1 Assoc. Prof.; 13 Lectrs.; 7 Hon. Profs.; 3 Hon. Lectrs.; 7 Hon. Fellows
Research: design theory and permutation groups; glasses; materials physics; non-linear analysis and differential equations; non-Newtonian fluid mechanics

Rural Sciences, Institute of

Tel: (01970) 621986 *Fax*: (01970) 611264
   E-mail: irs-enquiries@aber.ac.uk
Garrod, Brian, BA *CNAA*, MSc *E.Anglia*, PhD *Portsmouth*   Sr. Lectr.
Hannant, Duncan, BSc *Lond.*, MSc *Wales*, PhD *Lond.*   Hon. Prof.
Haresign, William, BSc *Nott.*, PhD *Nott.*   Prof., Agriculture; Dir.*
Harries, John, BSc *Wales*, PhD *Wales*   Sr. Lectr.; Dir., Educn.
Humphreys, Mervyn, BSc *Birm.*, PhD *Birm.*   Hon. Prof.
Lampkin, Nicolas H., BSc *Wales*, PhD *Wales*   Sr. Lectr.
Newbold, Charles J., BSc *Newcastle(UK)*, PhD *Glas.*   Prof.; Dir., Res.
Pollock, Christopher, MA *Camb.*, PhD *Birm.*   Hon. Prof.
Theodorou, Michael, BSc *Lond.*, PhD *Lond.*   Hon. Prof.
Thomas, Christopher, BSc *Wales*, PhD *Glas.*   Prof.

Thomas, Howard, PhD *Wales*, DSc *Wales*   Hon. Prof.
Other Staff: 26 Lectrs.; 8 Res. Assocs.; 1 Farm Manager†
Research: animal science; environmental ecology; sustainable land use; sustainable rural development

Sport and Exercise Science

Tel: (01970) 621545 *Fax*: (01970) 628557
   E-mail: sportexercise@aber.ac.uk
Barrett, John, MA *Camb.*, MA *Oxf.*, PhD *Camb.*, DSc *Wales*   Prof.; Acting Head*
Other Staff: 7 Lectrs.
Research: cardio-respiratory physiology; exercise and sport psychology

Theatre, Film and Television Studies

Tel: (01970) 622828 *Fax*: (01970) 622831
   E-mail: tfts@aber.ac.uk
Barker, Martin, BA *Liv.*, DPhil *W.England*   Prof.
Clos Stephens, E., MA *Oxf.*   Prof.
Creeber, Glen, BA *N.Lond.*, MA *Lanc.*, PhD *E.Anglia*   Sr. Lectr.
Gough, Richard   Sr. Res. Fellow; Prof.; Artistic Dir.
Kear, Adrian K., BA *Manc.*, MSocSc *Birm.*, PhD *Sur.*   Prof.; Head*
O'Malley, Thomas P., BA *Birm.*, PhD *Glam.*   Prof.
Pearson, Michael, BA *Wales*, MA *Wales*   Prof.
Rabey, David I., MA *Calif.*, MA *Birm.*, PhD *Birm.*   Prof.
Williams, Ioan M., BLitt *Oxf.*, MA *Oxf.*, PhD   Prof.
Other Staff: 23 Lectrs.
Research: media and communications studies; theatre, scenographic, performance, film and television studies; Welsh-medium schemes in drama, performance studies, film and television studies and media studies

Welsh Language and Literature

Tel: (01970) 622137 *Fax*: (01970) 622976
   E-mail: gaw@aber.ac.uk
Edwards, Huw M., BA *Wales*, DPhil *Oxf.*   Sr. Lectr.
Haycock, Marged, BA *Camb.*, MA *Camb.*, PhD *Wales*   Prof.
Hincks, Rhisiart J., MA *Wales*, PhD *Wales*   Sr. Lectr.
Hughes, Ian, MA *Wales*, PhD *Wales*   Sr. Lectr.
Huws, Bleddyn O., BA *Wales*, PhD *Wales*   Sr. Lectr.
Sims-Williams, Patrick, MA *Camb.*, PhD *Birm.*, FBA   Prof., Celtic Studies
Williams, Gruffydd A., BA *Wales*, PhD *Wales*   Prof.; Head*
Other Staff: 4 Lectrs.; 1 Res. Fellow; 1 Hon. Dept. Fellow
Research: Celtic languages and literature; Celtic philology

SPECIAL CENTRES, ETC

Farm Business Survey

Tel: (01970) 622253 *Fax*: (01970) 622958
   E-mail: farmsurv@aber.ac.uk
Haresign, William, BSc *Nott.*, PhD *Nott.*   Prof.; Dir.*
Other Staff: 10 Staff Members
Research: economics of farm businesses in Wales

Organic Centre Wales

Tel: (01970) 622248 *Fax*: (01970) 622238
   E-mail: organic@aber.ac.uk
Lampkin, Nicolas H., BSc *Wales*, PhD *Wales*   Sr. Lectr.; Dir.*
Other Staff: 11 Staff Members
Research: organic farming development, education, training and information dissemination

CONTACT OFFICERS

Academic affairs. Academic Registrar: Foster, Brian R., BScEcon *Wales*
   (E-mail: swp@aber.ac.uk)

Accommodation. Director of Residential and Hospitality Services: Wallace, J., BSc *Wales*, MBA *Open(UK)* (E-mail: ehl@aber.ac.uk)
Admissions (first degree). Director of Admissions and Recruitment: Davies, Hywel M., MA *Oxf.*, PhD *Wales* (E-mail: ug-admissions@aber.ac.uk)
Admissions (higher degree). Administrative Assistant (Admissions (higher degree)): Williams, Rhys, BSc *Wales*, PhD *Wales* (E-mail: pg-admissions@aber.ac.uk)
Alumni. Director, Development and External Affairs: Lawrence, Stephen R., MScEcon *Wales* (E-mail: sxl@aber.ac.uk)
Archives. Administrative Assistant (Archives): Salmon, Ian J., MA *Camb.*, MA *Oxf.*, DPhil *Oxf.* (E-mail: ils@aber.ac.uk)
Careers. Director, Careers Advisory Service: Harrison, Emma, BA *Durh.* (E-mail: ohh@aber.ac.uk)
Computing services. Deputy Director of Information Services: Matthews, Roger F., BSc *Lond.* (E-mail: rfm@aber.ac.uk)
Consultancy services. Director, Research, Innovation and Business Services: Craddock, David, BA *Middx.* (E-mail: ccservices@aber.ac.uk)
Credit transfer. Head of Admissions and Recruitment: Davies, Hywel M., MA *Oxf.*, PhD *Wales* (E-mail: ug-admissions@aber.ac.uk)
Development/fund-raising. Director, Development and External Affairs: Lawrence, Stephen R., MScEcon *Wales* (E-mail: sxl@aber.ac.uk)
Distance education. Director, Open Learning Unit: Rogers, Tanya, BSc *Brist.* (E-mail: olu@aber.ac.uk)
Equal opportunities. Equalities Advisor (Equal Opportunities): Petrou, Olympia, MSc *Wales* (E-mail: opp@aber.ac.uk)
Estates and buildings/works and services. Director of Estates: Williams, Jonathan, BSc *Wales*, MA *Lond.Met.* (E-mail: jtw@aber.ac.uk)
Examinations. Academic Secretary: McParlin, David F., BA *Wales* (E-mail: dpm@aber.ac.uk)
Finance. Director of Finance: Lewis, Keith, BA *CNAA* (E-mail: kml@aber.ac.uk)
General enquiries. Registrar and Secretary: Hughes, Catrin, BA *Wales*, PhD *Wales* (E-mail: pjj@aber.ac.uk)
Health services. Director of Student Support: Powell, John Ellis, BD *Wales*, PhD *Wales*, ThM *Harv.*, EdM *Harv.* (E-mail: ejp@aber.ac.uk)
Library (chief librarian). Director of Information Services: Hopkins, Mike, BA *Leic.*, PhD *Lough.* (E-mail: library@aber.ac.uk)
Marketing. Marketing Officer: Davies, D. Russell, BA *Wales*, PhD *Wales* (E-mail: drd@aber.ac.uk)
Minorities/disadvantaged groups. Equalities Advisor (Equal Opportunities): Petrou, Olympia, MSc *Wales* (E-mail: opp@aber.ac.uk)
Personnel/human resources. Director of Human Resources: (vacant)
Public relations. Public Relations Officer: Dafis, Arthur, BA *CNAA* (E-mail: aid@aber.ac.uk)
Publications. Marketing Officer: Davies, D. Russell, BA *Wales*, PhD *Wales* (E-mail: drd@aber.ac.uk)
Purchasing. Director of Finance: Lewis, Keith, BA *CNAA* (E-mail: kml@aber.ac.uk)
Quality assurance and accreditation. Academic Registrar: Foster, Brian R., BScEcon *Wales* (E-mail: brf@aber.ac.uk)
Research. Academic Registrar: Foster, Brian R., BScEcon *Wales* (E-mail: brf@aber.ac.uk)
Safety. Safety and Environmental Adviser: Walker, Andrew G., BA *York(UK)*, DPhil *York(UK)* (E-mail: arw@aber.ac.uk)
Scholarships, awards, loans. Head of Admissions and Recruitment: Davies, Hywel M., MA *Oxf.*, PhD *Wales* (E-mail: ug-admissions@aber.ac.uk)

Schools liaison. Marketing Manager: Richardson, Mary, BEd *Lond.* (E-mail: marketing@aber.ac.uk)

Security. Head of House Services: Stephens, Alan (E-mail: wis@aber.ac.uk)

Sport and recreation. Acting Director, Sports Centre: Rowe, Frank (E-mail: ftr@aber.ac.uk)

Staff development and training. Pro-Vice-Chancellor (Research and Staffing): Pykett, Prof. Lyn, BA *Lond.*, PhD *Lond.* (E-mail: lyp@aber.ac.uk)

Student welfare/counselling. Director of Student Support: Powell, John Ellis, BD *Wales*, PhD *Wales*, ThM *Harv.*, EdM *Harv.* (E-mail: ejp@aber.ac.uk)

Students from other countries. Director, Development and External Affairs: Lawrence, Stephen R., MScEcon *Wales* (E-mail: sxl@aber.ac.uk)

Students with disabilities. Director of Student Support: Powell, John Ellis, BD *Wales*, PhD *Wales*, ThM *Harv.*, EdM *Harv.* (E-mail: ejp@aber.ac.uk)

University press. Public Relations Officer: Dafis, Arthur, BA *CNAA* (E-mail: aid@aber.ac.uk)

Women. Equalities Advisor (Equal Opportunities): Petrou, Olybmia, MSc *Wales* (E-mail: opp@aber.ac.uk)

[Information supplied by the institution as at 30 August 2007, and edited by the ACU]

ANGLIA RUSKIN UNIVERSITY

Founded 1992

Postal Address: Bishop Hall Lane, Chelmsford, Essex, England CM1 1SQ
Telephone: (0845) 196 4858 **Fax:** (01245) 348772 **E-mail:** sandra.hollis@anglia.ac.uk
URL: http://www.anglia.ac.uk

VICE-CHANCELLOR*—Thorne, Prof. Michael P., BSc *Lond.*, PhD *Birm.*, FIMA, FBCS, FRSA
DIRECTOR OF REGISTRY‡—Coward, Joanne, BA *CNAA*

UNIVERSITY OF THE ARTS LONDON

Founded 1989

Member of the Association of Commonwealth Universities

Postal Address: 65 Davies Street, London, England W1K 5DA
Telephone: (020) 7514 6000 **Fax:** (020) 7514 6175
URL: http://www.arts.ac.uk

RECTOR*—Carrington, Nigel
SECRETARY‡—Prince, Martin H., BA *York(UK)*, MA *Reading*

ASTON UNIVERSITY

Founded 1966

Member of the Association of Commonwealth Universities

Postal Address: Aston Triangle, Birmingham, England B4 7ET
Telephone: (0121) 204 3000 **Fax:** (0121) 204 3696 **E-mail:** admissions@aston.ac.uk
URL: http://www.aston.ac.uk

VICE-CHANCELLOR*—King, Prof. Julia, CBE, BA *Camb.*, MA *Camb.*, PhD *Camb.*, FREng, FIMMM, FRAeS, FIMarEST, FCGI, FRSA, FIP
SENIOR PRO-VICE-CHANCELLOR—Hooley, Prof. Graham J., BSc *Warw.*, PhD *Warw.*, FRSA, FCIM, FBAM
PRO-VICE-CHANCELLOR—Reeves, Prof. Nigel B. R., OBE, MA *Oxf.*, DPhil *Oxf.*, FIL, FRSA
PRO-VICE-CHANCELLOR—Saunders, Prof. John A., BSc *Lough.*, MBA *Cran.*, PhD *Brad.*, FBAM, FCIM, FRSA
PRO-VICE-CHANCELLOR—Oakley, M. H., BSc *Newcastle(UK)*, PhD, FCMI
TREASURER—Parnaby, J., CBE
UNIVERSITY SECRETARY-REGISTRAR‡—Packham, R. D. A., BA *Manc.*, FRSA
DIRECTOR OF ESTATES—East, Garry, BEng
DIRECTOR OF FINANCE AND BUSINESS SERVICES—Dhariwal, G. S., BSc *Newcastle(UK)*

GENERAL INFORMATION

History. The university was previously established in 1895 as Birmingham Municipal Technical School and gained its university charter in 1966.

Admission to first degree courses (see also United Kingdom Introduction). Through Universities and Colleges Admissions Service (UCAS).

First Degrees (see also United Kingdom Directory to Subjects of Study). BEng, BSc, MChem, MEng, MPharm.

Length of course. Full-time: BEng, BSc: 3 years; MChem, MEng, MPharm: 4 years.

Higher Degrees (see also United Kingdom Directory to Subjects of Study).
Master's. MBA, MPhil, MSc.
Admission. Applicants for admission to master's degrees must hold a good first degree.

In addition, MBA: at least three years' work experience. MPhil: relevant first degree with first or upper second class honours.
   Doctoral. PhD.
   Admission. PhD: relevant first degree with first or upper second class honours.

Language of Instruction. English. Modern languages courses are partly taught in French and German, as applicable.

ACADEMIC UNITS
Arranged by Schools

Aston Business School
E-mail: business@aston.ac.uk
Ayree, Samuel, BA *Ghana*, MA *McM.*, PhD *McM.* Prof.
Bainbridge, David, BSc *Wales*, LLB *CNAA*, PhD *CNAA* Prof.
Basioudis, Ilias, PhD *Warw.*, MSc Sr. Lectr.
Battisti, Giuliana, BSc *Bologna*, MSc *Lond.*, PhD *Warw.* Sr. Lectr.
Bennett, David J., MSc *Birm.*, PhD *Birm.* Prof.
Binner, Jane, BA *Leeds*, MSc *Leeds*, PhD *Leeds* Reader
Brignall, Stan, BSc *Warw.* Prof.
Brodbeck, Felix, DrHabil *Munich*, PhD *Giessen* Prof.
Broderick, Amanda, BA *Leic.*, PhD *De Mont.* Sr. Lectr.
Budhwar, Pawan, PhD *Manc.*, BA MBA MPhil Prof.
Burcher, Pete, BSc *Birm.*, PhD Sr. Lectr.
Chelley-Steeley, Patricia, BA *Wales*, MA *Manc.*, PhD *Lough.* Reader
Clegg, Stewart, BSc *Aston*, PhD *Brad.* Prof.
Cooper, Stuart, BA *Exe.*, PhD Sr. Lectr.
Davis, Paul, BA *CNAA*, PhD *Greenwich* Sr. Lectr.
Dey, Prasanta, BSc *Calc.*, PhD *Calc.*, MSc Sr. Lectr.
Driffield, Nigel, MA *E.Anglia*, PhD *Reading* Prof.
Edwards, John, MA *Camb.*, PhD *Camb.* Prof.
Fay, Doris, PhD *Amst.* Sr. Lectr.
Gilliland, David, BSc *Tennessee*, MBA *Georgia State*, PhD *Georgia State* Sr. Lectr.
Greenley, Gordon E., BA *Open(UK)*, MSc *Salf.*, PhD *Salf.*, FBAM Prof.
Griffiths, Gareth, BSc *Leic.*, MSc *CNAA*, PhD *Lough.* Sr. Lectr.
Grojean, Michael, BSc *Missouri*, MA *Maryland*, PhD *Maryland* Sr. Lectr.
Harris, Margaret, BSc *Birm.*, MA *Brun.*, PhD *Lond.* Prof.
Higson, Helen, MA *Camb.*, MA *Open(UK)*, PhD *Lond.*, FRSA
Hooley, Graham J., BSc *Warw.*, PhD *Warw.*, FRSA, FCIM, FBAM Prof.
Izushi, Hiro, BEng *Calif.*, MEng *Calif.*, PhD *Calif.* Sr. Lectr.
Jarzabkowski, Paula, PhD *Warw.* Reader
Joseph, Nathan, MBA *Lond.*, PhD *Lond.* Reader
Lee, Nicholas J., BCA *Well.*, PhD Sr. Lectr.
Love, Jim, BA *Strath.*, PhD *Strath.* Prof.
Lowe, Alan, BA *Manc.Met.*, MA *Manc.*, PhD *Waik.* Prof.
Martin, Robin, BA *Plym.*, PhD *Open(UK)* Prof.
Meisel, Frank, LLB *Leeds* Sr. Lectr.
Palmer, Mark, MA *Ulster*, PhD *Ulster* Sr. Lectr.
Pearce, Graham, MSc *Birm.* Sr. Lectr.
Porter, Brian, BA *Car.*, BEd *Tor.*, MEd *McG.*
Roper, Stephen, BA *Durh.*, MPhil *Oxf.*, PhD *Lond.* Prof.
Saunders, John A., BSc *Lough.*, MBA *Cran.*, PhD *Brad.*, FBAM, FCIM, FRSA Prof.
Sena, Vania, MSc *York(UK)*, DPhil *York(UK)* Sr. Lectr.
Shaw, Duncan, BA *Strath.*, PhD *Strath.* Sr. Lectr.
Sillince, John, BA *Manc.*, BSc *Coventry*, MSc *Birm.*, PhD *Lond.* Prof.
Steeley, Jim, BA *Reading*, PhD *Warw.* Prof.
Thannaussoulis, Emmanuel, BSc *Sus.*, MSc *Warw.*, PhD *Warw.* Prof.
Tissington, Patrick, BSc *Westminster*, PhD *Aberd.*
Tricker, Mike, BA *Birm.*, FRGS Sr. Lectr.
Van Dick, Rolf, PhD *Marburg* Prof.

Vasilis, Theoharakis, BEng *N.Y.*, MSc *N.Y.*, MBA *N.Y.*, PhD *Warw.* Sr. Lectr.
West, Michael, BSc *Wales*, PhD *Wales*, FBPsS Prof.; Head*
Wong, Veronica, BSc *Brad.*, MBA *Brad.*, PhD *Manc.* Prof.
Other Staff: 42 Lectrs.; 4 Visiting Profs.; 2 Teaching Fellows; 15 Res. Fellows; 3 Visiting Fellows; 3 Res. Assocs.
Research: management and information systems; marketing and business strategy; organisation studies; public services management; technology and innovation

Engineering and Applied Science
Fax: (0121) 204 3400
Al-Malaika, Sahar, MSc PhD, FRSChem, FIMMM Reader
Amass, Allan J., BSc *Birm.*, PhD *Birm.*, FRSChem Reader
Bennion, Ian, BSc *Glas.*, FIEE, FIP Prof.
Blow, G. Keith, MA *Camb.*, PhD *Camb.*, FIP Prof.
Booth, Richard, MSc *Lond.*, PhD *Warw.*, FIMechE Prof.
Brett, Peter N., BSc *Bath*, PhD *Bath*, FIMechE, FRSA Prof.
Bridgwater, Tony V., BScTech *Manc.*, MSc PhD DSc Prof.
Carpenter, Geof F., BSc *Lond.*, PhD *Lond.* Sr. Lectr.
Clark, Robin, BSc(Eng) *Lond.*, MBA *Lond.*, PhD *Lond.* Sr. Lectr.
Cornford, Dan, BSc *Reading*, MSc *Birm.*, PhD *Birm.*
Elsworth, Edward, MA *Camb.*, PhD *Camb.* Sr. Lectr.
Foot, Nigel I. S., BSc *Leeds*, MEng *Liv.* Sr. Lectr.
Hedges, Peter D., MA *Camb.*, MSc *Birm.*, PhD Sr. Lectr.
Holding, David J., BSc(Eng) *Lond.*, PhD *Lond.*, FIEE Reader
Kettle, Roger J., BSc *Sur.*, MSc *Sur.*, PhD *Sur.*, FRSA Prof.
Kochhar, Ashok, BSc(Eng) *Lond.*, PhD *Brad.*, FREng, FIMechE, FIEE Prof.; Head*
Li, Long-Yuan, BSc *Jiangsu*, PhD *Shanghai*, MSc Sr. Lectr.
Lowe, David, BSc *Warw.*, PhD *Warw.* Prof.
Miller, J. David, MA *Camb.*, PhD *Camb.*, FRSChem Sr. Lectr.
Nabney, Ian, BA *Oxf.*, PhD *Camb.* Prof.
Oliver, Trevor, BSc *CNAA*, PhD
Saad, David, BSc *Haifa(Technion)*, BA *Haifa(Technion)*, MSc *Tel-Aviv*, PhD *Tel-Aviv* Prof.
Short, Neil R., BSc *Sur.*, PhD *Leeds* Sr. Lectr.
Sullivan, John, BSc PhD DSc, FIP, FIEE Prof.
Thornton, Kathryn, BSc *Lond.*, MSc *Oxf.*, MSc *Essex*, DPhil *Strath.* Sr. Lectr.
Tighe, Brian J., BSc PhD, FRSChem Prof.
Traill, Alasdair L., MA *St And.* Sr. Lectr.
Turitsyn, Sergei, BSc *Novosibirsk*, MSc *Novosibirsk*, PhD *Novosibirsk* Prof.
Webb, David, MA *Oxf.*, PhD *Kent* Reader
Williams, John, BSc *Lond.*, PhD *Lond.* Reader
Zhang, Lin, MSc *Sus.*, DPhil *Sus.* Prof.
Other Staff: 42 Lectrs.; 12 Visiting Profs.; 1 Visiting Reader; 32 Res. Fellows; 1 Contract Res. Assoc.; 26 Visiting Fellows

Languages and Social Sciences
Fax: (0121) 204 3700 E-mail: lss@aston.ac.uk
Adab, Beverley, BA *Birm.*, MPhil *Birm.*, PhD Sr. Lectr.
Clark, Urszula Dir. of Studies, English
Coulthard, Malcolm, BA *Birm.*, PhD *Birm.* Dir. of Res.; Prof., English Languages
De Grado, Mercedes, Lic *Madrid*, MA *Durh.*, PhD *Durh.*
Gaffney, John, MA *Sus.*, DPhil *Sus.* Prof., French Government
Grundmann, Reiner, PhD *European Univ.Inst.* Dir. of Studies, Sociol.
Kershaw, Angela, MA *Nott.*, PhD *Nott.* Sr. Lectr.
Kirkbright, Suzanne, BSc *Sur.*, PhD

Larrivée, Pierre, MA *Laval*, PhD *Laval* Sr. Lectr.
Medina, Raquel, MA *S.Calif.*, PhD *S.Calif.* Lectr.; Head, Spanish
Moores, Pamela M., MA *Camb.*, PhD *Leic.* Head*
Reershemius, Gertrud, MA *Hamburg*, DPhil *Hamburg* Prof., German Linguistics
Reeves, Nigel B. R., OBE, MA *Oxf.*, DPhil *Oxf.*, FIL, FRSA Prof., German
Schäffner, Christina Assoc. Dean, Postgrad. Studies; Prof., Translation Studies
Schütte, Uwe Dir., German Studies
Stafford, Hélène Dir., German Studies
Stevens, Anne, MA *Camb.*, MSc(Econ) *Lond.*, PhD *Lond.* Prof., European Studies
Sturge, Kate, MA *Lond.*, PhD *Lond.* Sr. Lectr.; Dir., German
Sutton, Michael Dir., Pol. and Mod. Hist.
Zaborowski, Marcin, MA *Birm.*, PhD *Birm.*, MA
Other Staff: 11 Lectrs.; 2 Lectors; 3 Visiting Staff; 1 Sessnl. Tutor

Life and Health Sciences
Fax: (0121) 204 3000
Anderson, Stephen, BOptom BSc MCOptom PhD Prof.
Bailey, Clifford J., BSc *Sheff.*, PhD, FRCPEd, FRCP Prof.
Barnes, Gareth, PhD
Bill, Roslyn, MA DPhil Reader
Coleman, Mike, BSc *Liv.*, PhD *Liv.* Reader
Furlong, Paul, MPhil PhD Prof.
Georgeson, M. A., MA *Camb.*, DPhil *Sus.* Prof.
Gibson, Jonathon, MB BS *Lond.*, MD *Leic.*, FRCSEd Prof.
Gilmartin, Bernard, BSc *City(UK)*, PhD *City(UK)* Prof.
Griffin, Martin, BSc PhD, FIBiol Prof.; Head*
Griffiths, Helen, BSc *Bath*, PhD *Birm.* Prof.; Dir. of Res.
Hill, Ros, BSc *Warw.*, PhD *Warw.* Sr. Lectr.
Hilton, Anthony, BSc *Birm.*, PhD *Birm.* Sr. Lectr.
Jüttner, Martin, MA *Aston*, PhD *Munich* Sr. Lectr.
Lambert, Peter A., BSc *Lond.*, PhD *Lond.*, DSc *Lough.* Prof.
Marriott, John, BSc PhD Sr. Lectr.; Dir., Postgrad. Programmes
Martin, Ian L., BSc *Birm.*, PhD *Birm.* Prof.
Meese, Tim, BSc *Newcastle(UK)*, PhD *Brist.* Sr. Lectr.
Pattison, Helen, PhD Sr. Lectr.
Perrie, Yvonne, BSc *Strath.*, PhD *Lond.* Prof.
Poyner, David, MA *Camb.*, MPhil *Camb.*, PhD *Camb.* Reader
Rippon, Gina, BSc PhD Sr. Lectr.; Dir., Postgrad. Programmes
Roberts, Brian, PhD Prof.
Romani, Christina, PhD Sr. Lectr.
Schwalbe, Carl H., AM *Harv.*, PhD *Harv.* Prof.
Seri, Stefano, MD Prof.
Stanford, Ian, BSc *S'ton.*, PhD *S'ton.* Reader
Talcott, Joel, PhD Reader
Tisdale, Michael J., BSc *Hull*, PhD *Lond.*, DSc *Lond.* Prof.
Wilson, Keith A., BSc PhD, FRPharmS Prof.
Wolffsohn, James, BSc PhD Prof.
Other Staff: 42 Lectrs.; 1 Visiting Prof.; 8 Res. Fellows; 29 Contract Res. Fellows; 2 Teaching Fellows; 8 Visiting Fellows; 5 Clin. Lectrs./Practitioners

SPECIAL CENTRES, ETC

Voluntary Action Research, Centre for
Cairns, Ben, BA MSc Dir.*

CONTACT OFFICERS
Accommodation. Manager of Residential Services: Reid, Janet, BA *Liv.*
Admissions (first degree). Assistant Registrar (Admissions (first degree)): Hussain, Zahida
Admissions (higher degree). Assistant Registrar (Admissions (higher degree)): Hussain, Zahida

Adult/continuing education. Business Development Manager: Brown, Julia

Alumni. Head, Alumni Relations: Pymm, Sarah E., BA *CNAA*, MSc

Archives. Senior Assistant Registrar (Archives): Walter, John G., BA *CNAA*

Careers. Head, Careers: Tibby, Maureen, BA *Edin.*, MA *C.England*

Computing services. Directo of ICT: Zahini, Fahri, BSc *N.Lond.*, MBA *Birm.*

Conferences/corporate hospitality. Head, Conference Services: Snow, Lynne

Development/fund-raising. Director of Development: (vacant)

Distance education. Business Development Manager: Brown, Julia

Equal opportunities. Equal Opportunities Adviser: Parsons, Kate, BA *Liv.*

Estates and buildings/works and services. Director of Estates: East, Garry, BEng

Examinations. Examinations Officer: Kingston, Gwen

Finance. Director of Finance and Business Services: Dhariwal, G. S., BSc *Newcastle(UK)*

General enquiries. University Secretary-Registrar: Packham, R. D. A., BA *Manc.*, FRSA

Health services. Honorary University Physician: Nye, Matthew N-L., MB ChB *Sheff.*

Industrial liaison. Head, Aston Consulting and Industrial Research: Booth, Michael, MSc *Manc.*, PhD *Manc.*, FIMMM

International office. Head, International Office: Yip, Wendy, BA

Library (chief librarian). Director of Library and Information Services: Smith, Nick R., BSc *S'ton.*, MSc *Sheff.*, PhD *S'ton.*

Marketing. Director of Marketing: Comfort, Stewart, BSc *Lough.*

Personnel/human resources. Director of Human Resources: Thomas, Keith, BA *E.Anglia*

Public relations. Head of University Communications: Harrison, Chris, BA *York(UK)*

Publications. Head of University Communications: Harrison, Chris, BA *York(UK)*

Purchasing. Purchasing Officer: Bloodworth, Sandra

Quality assurance and accreditation. Pro-Vice-Chancellor: Reeves, Prof. Nigel B. R., OBE, MA *Oxf.*, DPhil *Oxf.*, FIL, FRSA

Research. Head, Research Support Unit: Puzey, Sally, BSc *Manc.*, MSc *Open(UK)*

Safety. Safety Advisor: Branston, David S.

Scholarships, awards, loans. Senior Assistant Registrar (Scholarships, awards, loans): Walter, John G., BA *CNAA*

Schools liaison. Head, Schools and Colleges Liaison: Seymour, James, BA *Sheff.*, MSc

Security. Head of Security: Clash, Michael

Sport and recreation. Head of Sport and Recreation: Kirkman, Michael, BSc

Staff development and training. Head of Staff Development: Morton, Ann, BSc *Leic.*, MSc *Leeds*, PhD

Student union. President, Students Guild: Rehal, Dilly

Student welfare/counselling. Manager, Counselling Service: Lawrence, Paul, MEd *Birm.*

Students from other countries. International Student Advisor: Yip, Wendy, BA

Students with disabilities. Disability Co-ordinator: Howarth, Sian, BA *Sheff.*

[*Information supplied by the institution as at 14 September 2007, and edited by the ACU*]

BANGOR UNIVERSITY

Founded 1884

Member of the Association of Commonwealth Universities

Postal Address: Bangor, Gwynedd, Wales LL57 2DG
Telephone: (01248) 351151 **Fax:** (01248) 370451
URL: http://www.bangor.ac.uk

VICE-CHANCELLOR*—Jones, Prof. R. Merfyn, BA *Sus.*, MA *Warw.*, PhD *Warw.*, FRHistS
DEPUTY VICE-CHANCELLOR—Lowe, Prof. C. Fergus, BA Trinity(Dub.), PhD *Wales*, FBPsS
PRO-VICE-CHANCELLOR—Baker, Prof. Colin R., BA *Wales*, PhD *Wales*, FBPsS
PRO-VICE-CHANCELLOR—Farrar, Prof. John F., MA *Oxf.*, DPhil *Oxf.*
PRO-VICE-CHANCELLOR—Hope, Prof. Sian, BSc *CNAA*, MPhil *Wales*
PRO-VICE-CHANCELLOR—Huws, Meri, BScEcon *Wales*, MScEcon *Oxf.*
SECRETARY AND REGISTRAR‡—Roberts, David M., MA *Wales*, PhD *CNAA*
DIRECTOR OF FINANCE—Hughes, Dewi W., BScEcon *Wales*, FRSA

GENERAL INFORMATION

History. Originally founded in 1884 as a constituent of the University of Wales, Bangor University was granted independent university status in 2007.

It is situated on the coast of north Wales.

Admission to first degree courses (see also United Kingdom Introduction). Through Universities and College Admissions Service (UCAS). UK nationals: 2 passes at General Certificate of Education (GCE) A level plus a General Certificate of Secondary Education (GCSE) pass at grade C or above in English language or Welsh language (first language). Vocational and other qualifications are considered. International applicants: qualifications equivalent to those listed above (eg International Baccalaureate), plus a pass in an internationally recognised English language exam such as TOEFL (minimum score of 560) or IELTS (minimum score of 6.0).

First Degrees (see also United Kingdom Directory to Subjects of Study). BA, BD, BEng, BM, BMus, BN, BSc, LLB, MChem, MEng.

Some BA courses may be studied part-time. Four-year science degrees incorporate industrial or European experience; four-year language degrees include a year abroad.

Length of course. Full-time: BD, BEng, BM, BMus, BN, LLB: 3 years; BA, BSc: 3–4 years; MChem, MEng: 4 years.

Higher Degrees (see also United Kingdom Directory to Subjects of Study).

Master's. MA, MBA, MEd, MPhil, MSc, MTh.

Admission. Applicants for admission to master's degree courses must normally hold an appropriate first degree with at least second class honours.

MBA may also be studied by distance learning.

Length of course. Full-time: MA, MBA, MSc: 1 year; MPhil: 1–2 years. Part-time: MA, MPhil, MSc, MTh: 2 years; MEd: 2–5 years.

Doctoral. DClinPsy, PhD.

Admission. PhD, DClinPsy: normally a first class or upper second class degree in an appropriate subject.

Length of course. Full-time: PhD: 2–3 years; DClinPsy: 3 years. Part-time: PhD: 5–7 years.

Language of Instruction. English, except for courses in the School of Welsh, where the language is Welsh. Some degrees may be studied partly or fully in either Welsh or English; students may write exams in either language. International students may attend remedial English classes.

Libraries. Volumes: 750,000. Periodicals subscribed to: 3700. Special collections: Bangor Diocesan Library; Sir Frank Brangwyn (art); department of archives and manuscripts (includes archives of most major estates in north Wales); Owen Pritchard (modern private press); Welsh library (books in Welsh and books in other languages relating to Wales).

Academic Year (2007–2008). Two semesters: 1 October–27 January; 28 January–6 June.

Income (2005–2006). Total, £93,638,000.

FACULTIES/SCHOOLS

Arts and Humanities, College of

Head: Morgan, Prof. D. Densil, BA *Wales*, DD *Wales*, DPhil *Oxf.*

Business, Social Sciences and Law, College of

Head: Gardener, Prof. Edward P. M., MSc *Wales*, PhD *Wales*, Hon. DEcon *Gothenburg*, FCIS

Education and Lifelong Learning, College of

Head: Pritchard, Prof. K. Janet, BSc *Wales*, PhD *Wales*

Health and Behavioural Sciences, College of

Head: Hardy, Prof. J. P. Lew, MA *Wales*, PhD *Wales*

Natural Sciences, College of

Head: Wright, David, BSc *Newcastle(UK)*, PhD *Nott.*

Physical and Applied Sciences, College of

Head: Ashwell, Prof. Geoffrey J., BSc *Nott.*, PhD *Nott.*, PhD *Wroclaw*, DrHabil, FRSChem

ACADEMIC UNITS
Arranged by School

Bangor Business School

Tel: (01248) 383231 E-mail: bbs@bangor.ac.uk
Altunbas, Y., BSc *Ankara*, PhD *Wales*   Sr. Lectr.
Burke, Christopher M., MA *Sheff.*, FCA   Sr. Lectr.
Cain, M., MSc *Sheff.*, PhD *Wales*, FIMA   Prof., Management Science
Chakravarty, Shanti P., BS *George Washington*, MS *Roch.*, PhD *Roch.*   Prof., Economics
Gardener, Edward P. M., MSc *Wales*, PhD *Wales*, Hon. DEcon *Gothenburg*, FCIS   Prof.
Goddard, J., BA *Lanc.*, MSc *Lond.*   Prof., Financial Economics
Hodgkinson, Lynn, BA *CNAA*, PhD *CNAA*   Prof., Accounting
Jones, Stephen J., MSc *Wales*, MBSc *Manc.*   Sr. Lectr.
McLeay, Stuart J., MSc *Brad.*, PhD *Lanc.*, FCA   Prof., Treasury
Molyneux, Philip, MA *Wales*, PhD *Wales*   Prof., Banking and Finance; Head*
Sambrook, Sally, BA *Nott.*, PhD *Wales*, FCIPD   Prof., Human Resource Management
Williams, Jonathan, MA *Wales*, PhD *Wales*   Sr. Lectr.
Other Staff: 12 Lectrs.; 3 Temp. Assoc. Profs.
Research: finance; management studies

Biological Sciences

Tel: (01248) 382527
    E-mail: general.enquiries@sbs.bangor.ac.uk
Braig, Henk R., MSc *Gron.*, PhD *Gron.*   Reader
Carvalho, G. R., BSc *Lond.*, MSc *Wales*, PhD *Wales*, FLS   Prof.
Farrar, John F., MA *Oxf.*, DPhil *Oxf.*   Prof.
Freeman, C., BSc *CNAA*, PhD *Wales*   Prof.
Gadsdon, P. A., PhD *Liv.J.Moores*   Sr. Lectr.
Gliddon, Chris J., BA *Oxf.*, DPhil *Sus.*   Sr. Lectr.
Hughes, Roger N., BSc *Wales*, PhD *Wales*, DSc *Wales*   Prof.
Johnson, D. Barrie, BSc *Wales*, PhD *Wales*   Reader
Lockwood, S. J., BSc *Hull*, PhD *E.Anglia*   Hon. Prof.
Macfarlane, R. J., BSc *Liv.J.Moores*, PhD *Liv.*   Sr. Lectr.
Malhotra, Anita, BA *Oxf.*, PhD *Aberd.*   Sr. Lectr.
Shirsat, A. H., BSc *E.Anglia*, PhD *Durh.*   Sr. Lectr.
Stuart, Nicholas S. A., BM BS *S'ton.*, MD *S'ton.*, FRCP   Prof.
Taylor, Michael, BVMS *Glas.*, PhD *Lond.*   Hon. Prof.
Thorpe, Roger S., BSc *Lond.*, PhD *CNAA*, DSc *Aberd.*   Prof.
Tomos, A. Deri, MA *Camb.*, PhD *Camb.*   Prof.
Turner, George F., BSc *Glas.*, PhD *Wales*   Prof.; Head*
Webster, Simon G., BSc *Liv.*, PhD *Liv.*   Sr. Lectr.
Williams, Dudley D., MSc *W.Ont.*, PhD *W.Ont.*, DSc *Wales*   Hon. Prof.
Other Staff: 5 Lectrs.; 1 Sr. Res. Fellow; 20 Res. Officers; 11 Hon. Lectrs.
Research: bioinformatics and proteomics; cellular and molecular biology; medical and veterinary entomology; molecular and evolutionary ecology; plant biochemistry and physiology

Chemistry

Tel: (01248) 382375
    E-mail: chemistry@bangor.ac.uk
Ashwell, Geoffrey J., BSc *Nott.*, PhD *Nott.*, PhD *Wroclaw*, DrHabil, FRSChem   Prof.
Baird, Mark S., BSc *Lond.*, PhD *Camb.*, DSc *Camb.*, FRSChem   Prof.
Beckett, Michael A., BSc *E.Anglia*, PhD *E.Anglia*, FRSChem   Sr. Lectr.

Holliman, Peter J., BSc *Leic.*, PhD *Leic.*   Sr. Lectr.
Irvine, Stuart J. C., BSc *Lough.*, PhD *Birm.*, DSc *Birm.*   Prof.
Kalaji, Maher, BSc *S'ton.*, PhD *S'ton.*   Prof.; Head*
Murphy, Patrick J., BSc *Manc.*, PhD *Manc.*   Sr. Lectr.
Underhill, A. E., BSc *Hull*, PhD *Hull*, DSc *Wales*, FRSChem   Emer. Prof.
Other Staff: 1 Visiting Prof.; 7 Lectrs.; 1 Res. Assoc.; 1 Lectr.†; 3 Hon. Lectrs.; 4 Hon. Fellows
Research: biological chemistry; computational chemistry and molecular modelling; electrochemistry and sensors; nanomaterials and single molecule chemistry; photovoltaics and optoelectronic materials

Computer Science and Electronics

Tel: (01248) 382686
    E-mail: informatics@informatics.bangor.ac.uk
Bone, Stephen, BSc *Wales*, PhD *Wales*   Sr. Lectr.
Brown, Ronnie, MA *Oxf.*, DPhil *Oxf.*, FIMA   Emer. Prof.
Burt, J. P. H., BSc *Wales*, PhD *Wales*   Sr. Lectr.
Hope, Sian, BSc *CNAA*, MPhil *Wales*   Prof., Computer Science
John, N. W., BSc *Bath*, PhD *Bath*   Prof., Computing; Head, Computer Sci.*
Jones, Dewi I., MSc *Wales*, PhD *Wales*, FIEE   Reader
Kuncheva, L. I., MSc *Sofia*, PhD *Sofia*   Reader
Lambe, L. A., MS *Ill.*, PhD *Ill.*, Hon. Dr *Stockholm*   Hon. Prof.
Last, J. David, BSc *Brist.*, PhD *Sheff.*, DSc *Wales*, FIEE, FRIN   Emer. Prof.
Lewis, T. J., BSc *Lond.*, MSc *Lond.*, PhD *Lond.*, DSc *Lond.*, FIEE, FIP, FIEEE   Emer. Prof.
Pethig, Ron, BSc(Eng) *S'ton.*, PhD *S'ton.*, PhD *Nott.*, DSc *S'ton.*, FIEE   Prof.
Pierce, I., MEng *Wales*, PhD *Wales*, FIP   Sr. Lectr.
Shore, K. Alan, MA *Oxf.*, PhD *Wales*, FIP   Prof.
Spencer, Paul S., BSc *Bath*, PhD *Bath*, FIP   Sr. Lectr.; Head, Electronics*
Taylor, D. Martin, BSc *Wales*, PhD *Wales*, FIP   Prof.
Yates, C. E. Michael, BSc *Manc.*, PhD *Manc.*   Hon. Prof.
Other Staff: 7 Lectrs.; 6 Res. Officers; 8 Hon. Res. Fellows; 4 Hon. Univ. Fellows
Research: crystallographic group theory; homological algebra; information systems; material and sensors; non-Newtonian fluid mechanics

Creative Industries, National Institute for Excellence in the

Tel: (01248) 383215
    E-mail: els609@bangor.ac.uk
Harper, Graeme, BA *Syd.*, MLitt *NE*, DCA *Technol.Syd.*, PhD *E.Anglia*, FRGS, FRSA   Prof.; Dir.*
Lewis, William R., BA *Wales*, PhD *Wales*   Sr. Lectr.
Rumens, Carol, FRSL   Prof.
Other Staff: 7 Lectrs.; 6 Fellows
Research: creative writing practice and critical understanding; drama and performance; film, media and new media; hypertext; writing, book and publishing artefacts

Education

Tel: (01248) 383082
    E-mail: addysg@bangor.ac.uk
Baker, Colin R., BA *Wales*, PhD *Wales*, FBPsS   Prof.
Elliott, John A., BA *Wales*   Sr. Lectr.
Jepson, T., BSc *Leeds*   Sr. Lectr.
Pritchard, K. Janet, BSc *Wales*, PhD *Wales*   Prof.; Head*
Roberts, H. Gareth Ff., MA *Oxf.*, MEd *Wales*, PhD *Nott.*   Emer. Prof.
Roberts, Huw, MEd *Wales*   Sr. Lectr.
Williams, I. W., BSc *Wales*, PhD *Wales*, FRSChem   Emer. Prof.

Williams, P., BSc *Lond.*, MA *Camb.*, PhD *Lond.*, FBPsS   Emer. Prof.
Other Staff: 33 Lectrs.; 8 Lectrs.†; 1 Hon. Sr. Lectr.; 1 Hon. Sr. Res. Fellow; 1 Hon. Res. Fellow
Research: bilingualism; children's literature; information technology; language teaching and learning

English

Tel: (01248) 382102
    E-mail: els029@bangor.ac.uk
Brown, Anthony D., BA *Wales*, MA *Leic.*, PhD *Wales*   Prof.
Corns, Thomas N., MA *Oxf.*, DPhil *Oxf.*, FRHistS   Prof.
Edwards, Justin, MA *Montr.*, PhD *Montr.*   Prof.; Head*
Field, Peter J. C., BLitt *Oxf.*, MA *Oxf.*   Hon. Prof.
Gregson, Ian E., BA *Oxf.*, PhD *Hull*   Reader
Hiscock, Andrew, BA *Lanc.*, MA *Brist.*, PhD *Brist.*   Sr. Lectr.
Humphreys, Emyr, BA *Wales*, Hon. DLitt *Wales*   Hon. Prof.
Sullivan, Ceri, MA *Oxf.*, DPhil *Oxf.*   Reader
Wilcox, Helen, BA *Birm.*, DPhil *Oxf.*   Prof.
Other Staff: 5 Lectrs.
Research: Anglo-Welsh literature; Arthurian literature; contemporary British writing; Romantic literature; seventeenth- to nineteenth-century literature

Environment and Natural Resources

Tel: (01248) 382281 Fax: (01248) 354997
    E-mail: senr@bangor.ac.uk
Cahalan, C. M., BSc *Leic.*, PhD *Wales*   Sr. Lectr.
Edwards-Jones, Gareth, BSc *Manc.*, PhD *Lond.*   Prof.
Godbold, Douglas L., BSc *Sus.*, PhD *Liv.*   Prof., Forest Sciences
Good, John E. G., BSc *Wales*, PhD *Edin.*   Hon. Prof.
Hall, John B., BSc *Lond.*, PhD *Lond.*   Sr. Lectr.
Healey, John R., MA *Oxf.*, PhD *Camb.*   Sr. Lectr.
Jones, David L., BSc *Aberd.*, DPhil *Oxf.*   Prof.
McDonald, Morag A., BSc *Newcastle(UK)*, PhD *Edin.*   Sr. Lectr.
Price, Colin, MA *Oxf.*, DPhil *Oxf.*   Prof.
Reynolds, B., BSc *Nott.*, PhD *Lond.*   Hon. Prof.
Sinclair, Fergus L., BSc *Reading*, PhD *Edin.*   Sr. Lectr.
Wright, David, BSc *Newcastle(UK)*, PhD *Nott.*   Sr. Lectr.; Head*
Wyn-Jones, R. Gareth, BSc *Wales*, MSc *Br.Col.*, DPhil *Oxf.*, DSc *Oxf.*, FIBiol, FRSChem   Hon. Prof.
Other Staff: 13 Lectrs.; 4 Sr. Fellows; 2 Res. Fellows; 7 Res. Officers; 2 Hon. Lectrs.; 1 Hon. Res. Fellow
Research: agroforestry, temperate and tropical; animal science; forestry, temperate and tropical; soil and crop science; wood science

Healthcare Sciences

Tel: (01248) 383189
    E-mail: hss043@bangor.ac.uk
Allsup, David M., BEd *Wales*   Jt. Dir., Pre-Registration Studies
Ashton, Peter R. J., BA *Open(UK)*, MSc *Hudd.*   Sr. Lectr.
Behi, Ruhi H., BSc *Wales*, MSc *Manc.*   Head*
Godwin, J. Malcolm, BEd *Wales*, MA *Keele*, EdD *Manc.Met.*   Dir., Pre-Registration Studies; Deputy Head
Iphofen, R., BA *York(UK)*, BPhil *York(UK)*, MSc *Open(UK)*, PhD *Wales*   Sr. Lectr.
Noyes, Jane, MSc *Manc.*, DPhil *York(UK)*   Noreen Edwards Prof., Nursing Research
Rycroft-Malone, Joanne, BSc *Oxf.Brookes*, MSc *Herts.*, PhD *S'ton.*   Reader
Other Staff: 70 Lectrs.; 1 Sr. Res. Fellow
Research: knowledge, transition and utilisation; language and cultural awareness; longterm conditions; radiography; research methods and ethics

History and Welsh History

Tel: (01248) 382144
E-mail: his203@bangor.ac.uk
Claydon, Anthony M., BA Oxf., PhD Lond.   Sr. Lectr.
Edwards, Nancy, BA Liv., PhD Durh., FSA   Reader
Griffith, William P., BA Wales, PhD Wales, FRHistS   Sr. Lectr.
Karl, R., MPhil Vienna, PhD Vienna   Sr. Lectr.; Head*
Pryce, A. Huw, MA Oxf., DPhil Oxf., FRHistS   Prof.
Tanner, Duncan M., BA Lond., PhD Lond., FRHistS   Prof.
Other Staff: 5 Lectrs.; 2 Hon. Lectrs.; 3 Hon. Res. Fellows
Research: archaeology (particularly north Wales and Ireland); modern British political/educational/social history; relationships between secular and ecclesiastical authority; twentieth-century Europe; Welsh history (mediaeval to modern)

Law

Tel: (01248) 383781
E-mail: sos00c@bangor.ac.uk
Griffiths, Aled W., LLB Wales, MA Wales   Sr. Lectr.
Johnson, Howard A., LLB Birm.   Sr. Lectr.; Acting Head*
Other Staff: 5 Lectrs.; 1 Teaching Fellow; 1 Lectr.†; 1 Teaching Fellow†

Lifelong Learning

Tel: (01248) 382708 E-mail: ll@bangor.ac.uk
Piette, B., BA Wales, PhD CNAA   Head*
Other Staff: 1 Sr. Tutor; 5 Co-ordinating Tutors; 6 Academic Devel. Co-ordinators; 1 Course Promotion Officer

Linguistics and English Language

Tel: (01248) 382264
E-mail: els016@bangor.ac.uk
Crystal, David, OBE, MA Lond., PhD Lond., FBA   Hon. Prof.
Deuchar, Margaret, BA Camb., PhD Stan.   Prof.
Macdonald, Pamela, BA Wales, LLB Wales, PhD Wales   Lectr.; Head*
Thomas, Jennifer A., BA Brad., MA Lanc., PhD Lanc.   Prof.
Williams, E., BA Oxf., MLitt Edin., PhD Reading   Sr. Lectr.
Other Staff: 2 Lectrs.
Research: child language and second language acquisition; computational linguistics; experimental phonetics and pragmatics; psycholinguistics; theoretical and comparative syntax

Modern Languages

Tel: (01248) 382130
E-mail: m.tait@bangor.ac.uk
Bushell, Anthony, BA Ulster, MA Warw., PhD Birm.   Prof., German
Rorato, Laura, BA Bologna, PhD Bologna   Sr. Lectr., Italian
Siefken, Hinrich, DrPhil Tübingen, DLitt Nott.   Hon. Prof.
Tully, Carol, BA Strath., PhD Lond.   Sr. Lectr., German; Head*
Other Staff: 6 Lectrs.
Research: European culture; French, German, Italian and Spanish literature; translation studies

Music

Tel: (01248) 382181
E-mail: music@bangor.ac.uk
Ap Siôn, Pwyll E., BMus Oxf., PhD Wales   Sr. Lectr.
Harper, John M., MA Camb., MA Oxf., PhD Birm., FRCO   RSCM Res. Prof.
Harper, Sally E., MA Birm., DPhil Oxf.   Sr. Lectr.
Lewis, Andrew P., BMus Birm., PhD Birm.   Prof.
Pascall, Robert J., MA Oxf., DLitt Oxf., DPhil Oxf., FRCO   Res. Prof.
Schmidt-Beste, Thomas C., DrHabil Heidel.   Prof.; Head*
Thomas, Wyn, MA Wales   Sr. Lectr.
Wood, Bruce, MusB Camb., MA Camb., PhD Camb., FRCO   Prof.
Other Staff: 5 Lectrs.; 1 Pianoforte Executant; 1 Lectr.†
Research: Celtic traditional music; electro-acoustic composition; historical and editorial musicology; music and the Christian church; popular music culture

Ocean Sciences

Tel: (01248) 382846
E-mail: enquiries@sos.bangor.ac.uk
Beaumont, Andy R., BSc Lond., MSc Wales, DSc Wales   Reader
Bowers, David G., BSc Manc., MSc Wales, PhD Wales   Reader
Davies, Alan G., BSc Lond., MSc Wales, PhD Lond.   Prof., Physical Oceanography
Huthnance, John M., BA Camb., PhD Camb.   Hon. Prof.
Jago, Colin F., BSc Lond., PhD Lond.   Sr. Lectr.; Head*
Jones, Sarah E., MA Camb., PhD Wales   Sr. Lectr.
Kaiser, Michel J., PhD Wales, DSc Liv.   Prof.
Kennedy, Hilary A., BSc Essex, MSc Strath., PhD Leeds   Reader
Le Vay, Lewis, BSc Sus., MSc Wales, PhD Wales   Sr. Lectr.
Naylor, E., OBE, BSc Sheff., PhD Liv., DSc Liv., FIBiol   Emer. Prof.
Richardson, Christopher A., BSc Wales, PhD Wales   Reader
Scourse, James D., MA Oxf., PhD Camb.   Prof.
Seed, Ray, BSc Leeds, PhD Leeds   Prof., Marine Ecology
Simpson, John H., BA Oxf., PhD Liv., DSc Liv.   Prof.
Thomas, David N., BSc Liv., PhD Liv.   Prof.
Thorpe, Stephen A., BSc Lond., PhD Camb., FRS   Hon. Prof.
Turner, John R., BSc Brist., DPhil Oxf.   Sr. Lectr.
Williams, Peter J. leB., BSc Birm., PhD Birm., DSc Birm.   Emer. Prof., Biogeochemistry
Other Staff: 6 Lectrs.; 3 Res. Fellows; 29 Res. Officers; 1 Res. Support Officer; 1 Lectr.†; 1 Res. Fellow†; 1 Hon. Sr. Res. Fellow; 3 Hon. Res. Fellows
Research: geological oceanography (sediment properties and geotechnics); marine biogeochemistry; marine biology (aquaculture, shellfish biology); optical oceanography and remote sensing; physical oceanography (ocean modelling, shelf-edge processes)

Psychology

Tel: (01248) 382211
E-mail: psychology@bangor.ac.uk
Bentall, Richard P., BSc Wales, MA Wales, MClinPsyc Liv., PhD Wales   Prof., Clinical Psychology
Bracewell, Martyn, BM BCh Oxf., MA Oxf., PhD M.I.T.   Sr. Lectr.
Clare, Linda, MA Camb., MSc Lond., PhD Open(UK)   Reader
Cox, W. Miles, BA Georgia S., MA W.Georgia, PhD S.Carolina   Prof., Psychology of Addictive Behaviours
Downing, Paul, BS Calif., MA Prin., PhD Prin.   Reader
Duncan, John, BA Oxf., DPhil Oxf.   Hon. Prof.
Edelman, Shimon, MSc Weizmann, PhD Weizmann   Hon. Prof.
Gathercole, Virginia C., BA St.Louis, MA Kansas, MPhil Kansas, PhD Kansas   Prof.
Giese, Martin, BSc Bochum, MSc Bochum, PhD Bochum   Sr. Lectr.
Hastings, Richard P., BSc S'ton., PhD S'ton., FBPsS   Prof.; Deputy Head
Horne, Pauline J., BA Wales, BSc Sus., MPhil Lond., PhD Wales   Reader
Houghton, George, BA York(UK), MSc Sus., DPhil Sus.   Sr. Lectr.
Ingledew, David K., MA Oxf., MSc Manc., PhD Wales   Sr. Lectr.
Intriligator, J., BA Calif., MA Harv., PhD Harv.   Sr. Lectr.
Jackson, Alan, BSc Manc., MB ChB Manc., PhD Manc., FRCR   Hon. Prof.
Jones, David T., MB ChB Leeds, FRCGP   Hon. Prof.
Klein, Christoph, PhD Constance   Sr. Lectr.
Leek, E. Charles, BSc Keele, MSc Lond., MA Johns H., PhD Johns H.   Sr. Lectr.
Linden, David, BSc Hamburg, PhD Osnabrück, DPhil Oxf., MD   Prof., Biological Psychiatry
Lowe, C. Fergus, BA Trinity(Dub.), PhD Wales, FBPsS   Prof.
Mari-Beffa, Paloma, BA Granada, MSc Granada, PhD Almeria   Sr. Lectr.
Miles, Tim R., MA Oxf., PhD Wales, FBPsS   Emer. Prof.
Morrison, Valerie, MA St And., PhD Edin.   Sr. Lectr.
Pulvermuller, Friedmann, MA Tübingen, PhD Tübingen, PhD Constance, BA   Hon. Prof.
Rafal, Robert D., BA Delaware, MD Penn.   Prof., Clinical Neuroscience and Neuropsychology
Raymond, Jane, BSc Dal., MSc Wash., PhD Dal.   Prof., Experimental Consumer Psychology
Robertson, Ian H., BSc Glas., MPhil Lond., PhD Lond., FBPsS   Hon. Prof.
Schnitzler, Alfons, MD Kiel, PhD Kiel   Prof., Neuroscience and Neurology
Shapiro, Kimron L., BSc N.Carolina, MSc Wash., PhD Dal.   Prof., Cognitive Neuroscience
Tainturier, Marie-Josèphe, MSc Montr., PhD Montr.   Sr. Lectr.
Thierry, Guillaume, MSc Lyons, PhD Toulouse   Sr. Lectr.
Tipper, Steven P., BSc Hudd., MSc Sus., DPhil Oxf.   Prof., Cognitive Science
Turnbull, Oliver, MSc Witw., PhD Camb.   Sr. Lectr.; Head*
Ward, Robert A., BA Austin Coll., MSc Carnegie-Mellon, PhD Carnegie-Mellon   Sr. Lectr.
Williams, J. Mark G., MA Oxf., MSc Oxf., DPhil Oxf., FBPsS   Hon. Prof.
Woods, Robert T., MA Camb., MSc Newcastle(UK), FBPsS   Prof., Clinical Psychology of the Elderly
Other Staff: 10 Lectrs.; 2 Lectr./Practitioners; 2 Teaching Fellows; 1 Sr. Res. Fellow; 23 Res. Officers; 8 Hon. Sr. Lectrs.; 19 Hon. Lectrs.; 7 Hon. Res. Fellows
Research: clinical and health psychology; cognitive psychology and neuroscience; experimental consumer psychology; learning, language and development

Social Sciences

Tel: (01248) 382221
E-mail: sos016@bangor.ac.uk
Davis, Howard H., BA Camb., PhD Edin.   Prof.
Day, Graham A. S., MA Oxf., MPhil Oxf.   Sr. Lectr.; Head*
Hester, Stephen, BA Kent, PhD Kent   Prof.
Hirst, J. David, BSc(Soc) Lond., MA Manc., PhD Wales   Sr. Lectr.
King, Roy D., BA Leic., PhD Lond.   Emer. Prof.
Morris, Delyth, BA Wales, PhD Wales   Sr. Lectr.
Wardhaugh, Julia, BA Stir., PhD Stir.   Sr. Lectr.
Other Staff: 8 Lectrs.; 4 Hon. Res. Fellows
Research: childhood and family; crime and criminal justice; ethnomethodology and conversation analysis; gerontology; rural and community sociology

Sport, Health and Exercise Sciences

Tel: (01248) 382756
E-mail: shes.admissions@bangor.ac.uk
Callow, Nicola, BA Wales, PhD Wales   Lectr.; Deputy Head (Teaching and Learning)
Hardy, J. P. Lew, MA Wales, PhD Wales   Prof.
Khan, A. Michael, BSc Montr., MA W.Ont., PhD Br.Col.   Sr. Lectr.; Head*
Lemmey, A. B., BEd S.Aust., MA Flin., PhD Adel.   Sr. Lectr.

Maddison, P., MB BChir Camb., MA Camb., MD Camb., FRCP Prof.†

Marcora, S., MSc Wis., PhD Wales, BPE Sr. Lectr.

Markland, D., BA Wales, PhD Wales Sr. Lectr.; Deputy Head (Res.)

Walsh, N., MSc Lough., PhD Birm. Sr. Lectr.

Other Staff: 9 Lectrs.; 2 Hon. Res. Fellows

Research: exercise psychology and physiology; health psychology; kinanthropometry and kinesiology; motor control and learning; sport psychology

Theology and Religious Studies

see also Special Centres, etc (Religious Educn., Centre for)

Tel: (01248) 382079
  E-mail: theology@bangor.ac.uk

Allchin, Canon A. M., BLitt Oxf., MA Oxf., Hon. DD Bucharest, Hon. DD Wis., Hon. DD Wales Hon. Prof.

Davies, Eryl W., BA Wales, PhD Camb. Reader; Head*

Kay, William K., MA Oxf., PhD Nott., PhD Reading Reader

Morgan, D. Densil, BA Wales, DD Wales, DPhil Oxf. Prof.

Pope, Robert, BA Wales, PhD Wales Sr. Lectr.

Thomas, J. Heywood, STM N.Y., DD Edin., DD Wales, Hon. DLitt Wales Hon. Prof.

Williams, Catrin H., BA Wales, PhD Camb. Sr. Lectr.

Other Staff: 1 Lectr.; 5 Tutors†; 4 Hon. Academic Fellows

Research: biblical hermeneutics; Hebrew and Greek biblical texts; interaction between Judaism and Christianity; religion in literature; twentieth-century Christianity

Welsh

Tel: (01248) 382240
  E-mail: wes005@bangor.ac.uk

Davies, Jason Walford, BA Wales, PhD Wales Sr. Lectr.

Hunter, T. Gerald, BA Cinc., MPhil Wales, PhD Harv. Sr. Lectr.

Jarvis, Branwen, MA Wales, PhD Wales Prof.

Lynch, Peredur I., BA Wales, PhD Wales Prof.

Rowlands, John, MA Wales, DPhil Oxf. Hon. Prof.

Wiliams, Gerwyn, BA Wales, PhD Wales Prof.; Head*

Other Staff: 2 Lectrs.; 1 Hon. Lectr.

Research: Celtic studies (history, languages, mythology); literature presented on radio, television and film; the bardic tradition; Welsh literature from sixth to twentieth centuries

SPECIAL CENTRES, ETC

Academic Development Unit

Assinder, S. J., BSc Lanc., PhD Lanc. Dir.*

Other Staff: 1 Res. Officer; 1 Skills Devel. Officer

Advanced Software Technology, Centre for

Tel: (01248) 675005 Fax: (01248) 675012
  E-mail: info@techniumcast.com

Hope, Sian, BSc CNAA, MPhil Wales Prof.; Dir.*

Applied Marine Sciences, Centre for

Tel: (01248) 713808
  E-mail: ucs602@bangor.ac.uk

Davies, Alan G., BSc Lond., MSc Wales, PhD Lond. Prof.; Dir.*

Other Staff: 2 Emer. Profs.; 1 Res. Fellow; 15 Res. Assocs.

Research: aquaculture (shellfish, novel species, sustainability); marine chemistry (biofuels, computational chemistry and novel materials); numerical modelling (simulation of coastal currents and winds); oil and chemical spills (predictions of slick movement and fate); remote sensing (analysis and interpretations of satellite data)

Arid Zone Studies Natural Resources, Centre for (CAZS)

Tel: (01248) 382346 E-mail: cazs@bangor.ac.uk

Robinson, W. Ian, BSc Lond., PhD Wales Emer. Dir.

Witcombe, J. R., BSc Wales, PhD Nott. Prof. Res. Fellow; Dir.*

Wyn-Jones, R. Gareth, BSc Wales, MSc Br.Col., DPhil Oxf., DSc Oxf., FIBiol, FRSChem Founding Dir.

Other Staff: 3 Sr. Fellows; 2 Res. Fellows; 1 Res. Co-ordinator; 3 Res. Officers

Research: animal nutrition and husbandry; cereal and legume agronomy; participatory fuel wood and forage use studies; plant breeding for arid areas; soil and water engineering and conservation

BioComposites Centre

Tel: (01248) 370588
  E-mail: biocomposites@bangor.ac.uk

Fowler, Paul, BSc E.Anglia, PhD E.Anglia Dir.*

Other Staff: 16 Res. Staff

Research: natural chemical/material applications in industry; plant fibres in biocomposites; processing non-wood plants; pulp and paper manufacture; wood-based panels

Bioelectronic and Molecular Microsystems, Institute of

Tel: (01248) 382682
  E-mail: martin@informatics.bangor.ac.uk

Burt, J. P. H., BSc Wales, PhD Wales Deputy Dir.

Taylor, D. Martin, BSc Wales, PhD Wales, FIP Prof.; Dir.*

Other Staff: 2 Res. Officers; 1 Commercial Manager

Research: AC electrokinetic properties of cells, micro-organisms and sub-cellular bioparticles; development of novel sensors for application in industry, medicine, biotechnology and the environment; synthesis and evaluation of molecular materials

Business Management Education Ltd

Tel: (01248) 672200 E-mail: a.lock@bme.ac.uk

Banister, Nigel Chief Exec.*

Benson, A. J., BSc Glas., MBA Strath., PhD Newcastle(UK) Academic Dir.

Business Research, Centre for

North West Wales Management Development Centre Ltd

Tel: (01248) 365913
  E-mail: enquiries.cbr@bangor.ac.uk

Pritchard, John, BA Wales, MA Wales Assoc. Dir.

Other Staff: 1 CBR Manager

European Finance, Institute of

Tel: (01248) 382277 E-mail: ief@bangor.ac.uk

Gardener, Edward P. M., MSc Wales, PhD Wales, Hon. DEcon Gothenburg, FCIS Prof.; Jt. Dir.*

Molyneux, Philip, MA Wales, PhD Wales Prof.; Jt. Dir.*

Other Staff: 10 Visiting Res. Fellows

Research: development of financial systems; efficiency of financial services firms; financial services regulation; strategies of banks and financial institutions; structure and performance of financial systems

Industrial and Commercial Optoelectronics (ICON)

Tel: (01248) 382618
  E-mail: alan@sees.bangor.ac.uk

Shore, K. Alan, MA Oxf., PhD Wales, FIP Prof.; Dir.*

Other Staff: 1 Commercial Manager

Industrial Development Bangor Ltd

Tel: (01248) 382749 Fax: (01248) 372105
  E-mail: idb@informatics.bangor.ac.uk

Fielding, Trefor J., PhD Aston Dir.

Hope, Sian, BSc CNAA, MPhil Wales Dir.

Joyner, David J., BSc Wales, PhD Wales Dir.

Roberts, Gwyn, BSc Wales, PhD Wales Dir.

Secker, Philip, BSc Lond., PhD Lond., FIEE, FIP, FCMI Chairman; Dir.*

Spencer, Paul S., BSc Bath, PhD Bath, FIP Dir.

Research: electrostatics instrumentation; global positioning systems, logging and evaluation (transport); instrumentation for hydroelectric power generation industry; instrumentation for nuclear industry; mechatronics and motor control

Medical and Social Care Research, Institute for

Tel: (01248) 388771
  E-mail: imscar@bangor.ac.uk

Rees, Michael R., BSc E.Anglia, MB ChB Sheff., PhD Ioannina, DMRD, FRCR, FRCP Prof., Vascular Studies

Russell, Ian T., MA Camb., MSc Birm., PhD Essex, FRCP, FRCGP Prof., Public Health; Dir.*

Stuart, Nicholas S. A., BM BS S'ton., MD S'ton., FRCP Prof., Cancer Studies

Wenger, G. Clare, MA Calif., PhD Calif., FRAI Emer. Prof.

Woods, Robert T., MA Camb., MSc Newcastle(UK), FBPsS Deputy Dir.; Prof., Clinical Psychology of the Elderly

Other Staff: 4 Sr. Res. Fellows; 8 Res. Fellows; 8 Res. Officers; 1 Clin. Sr. Lectr.; 14 Hon. Sr. Lectrs.; 6 Hon. Lectrs.; 4 Hon. Sr. Res. Fellows; 9 Hon. Res. Fellows

Research: carer support in dementia; health service organisation and delivery; improving partnerships in care; prioritisation of demand for health care; randomised controlled clinical trials/intervention trials

North West Wales Clinical Psychology Programme

Hargreaves, Isabel R., BA Wales, MSc Aberd., PhD Wales Programme and Clin. Dir.*

Hastings, Richard P., BSc S'ton., PhD S'ton., FBPsS Dir., Res.

Jones, Robert S. P., MA Trinity(Dub.), PhD Trinity(Dub.) Dir., Continuing Professional Devel.

Woods, Robert T., MA Camb., MSc Newcastle(UK), FBPsS Academic Dir.

Other Staff: 1 Sr. Lectr./Academic Tutor; 1 Sr. Academic Tutor; 1 Sr. Res. Tutor; 1 Admissions Tutor; 1 Programme Co-ordinator; 1 Clin. Tutor

North West Wales Management Development Centre Ltd

Tel: (01248) 365900
  E-mail: management_centre@bangor.ac.uk

Gardner, C., BA Wales, MSc Wales, PhD Wales, FRSA Chief Executive*

Other Staff: 1 Business and Development Manager; 1 Marketing Manager; 3 Programme Dirs.†

Place Name Research Centre

Tel: (01248) 383214
  E-mail: hywel.w.owen@bangor.ac.uk

Owen, Hywel W., BA Liv., MA Wales, PhD Wales Prof.; Dir.*

Religious Education, Welsh National Centre for

Tel: (01248) 382956
  E-mail: l.j.francis@bangor.ac.uk

Francis, Prof. Leslie J., MA Oxf., MSc Lond., MTh Nott., PhD Camb., DD Oxf., DSc Camb. Dir.*

Other Staff: 5 Res. Staff

Research: church schools; personality in religion; psychology of religion; religious attitudes; theology and education

Social and Cultural Affairs, Welsh Institute for

Tel: (01248) 382133
  E-mail: wisca@bangor.ac.uk

Edwards, A. C., MA Wales, PhD Wales Co-Dir.

Tanner, Duncan M., BA Lond., PhD Lond., FRHistS Prof.; Dir.*
Other Staff: 2 Hon. Fellows

CONTACT OFFICERS

Accommodation. Director of Estates and Facilities: Goodwin, M., BEng Liv.
(E-mail: halls@bangor.ac.uk)
Admissions (first degree). Senior Assistant Registrar (Admissions): Lewis, Ainsley C., BA Wales (E-mail: admissions@bangor.ac.uk)
Admissions (higher degree). Senior Assistant Registrar (Admissions): Lewis, Ainsley C., BA Wales
(E-mail: postgraduate@bangor.ac.uk)
Adult/continuing education. Head of Lifelong Learning: Piette, B., BA Wales, PhD CNAA (E-mail: ll@bangor.ac.uk)
Alumni. Alumni Relations Officer: Davies, Rachel M. L., BA Lanc.
(E-mail: alumni@bangor.ac.uk)
Archives. Archivist: Thomas, Einion W., BA Wales (E-mail: e.w.thomas@bangor.ac.uk)
Careers. Acting Head, Centre for Careers and Opportunities: Preece, Jennie
(E-mail: careersopps@bangor.ac.uk)
Computing services. Director of Information Technology Services: Snelson, Julie, BSc CNAA (E-mail: j.snelson@bangor.ac.uk)
Conferences/corporate hospitality. Director of Estates and Facilities: Goodwin, M., BEng Liv. (E-mail: reservations@bangor.ac.uk)
Consultancy services. Director of University Innovation Bangor: Joyner, David J., BSc Wales, PhD Wales
(E-mail: innovation-enquiries@bangor.ac.uk)
Development/fund-raising. Head of Development and Alumni Relations: Gallagher, Kristen L., BA N.Y.
(E-mail: devtrust@bangor.ac.uk)
Equal opportunities. Senior Human Resources Officer, Pensions and Equal Opportunities: Owen, Siân P., BA Wales
(E-mail: s.p.owen@bangor.ac.uk)
Estates and buildings/works and services. Director of Estates and Facilities: Goodwin,

M., BEng Liv.
(E-mail: estatesoffice@bangor.ac.uk)
Examinations. Senior Assistant Registrar (Examinations): Thomas, Patricia J., BSc Wales, MA Mich., PhD Wales
(E-mail: p.thomas@bangor.ac.uk)
Finance. Director of Finance: Hughes, Dewi W., BScEcon Wales, FRSA
(E-mail: d.w.hughes@bangor.ac.uk)
General enquiries. Secretary and Registrar: Roberts, David M., MA Wales, PhD CNAA
(E-mail: d.m.roberts@bangor.ac.uk)
Health services. Occupational Health Practitioner: Patton, Joe
(E-mail: j.patton@bangor.ac.uk)
Industrial liaison. Director of University Innovation Bangor: Joyner, David J., BSc Wales, PhD Wales
(E-mail: innovation-enquiries@bangor.ac.uk)
International office. Head of International Office: Roberts, Iwan P., BA Wales, MA Essex, MBA Open(UK)
(E-mail: international@bangor.ac.uk)
Language training for international students. Director, English Language Courses for Overseas Students (ELCOS): Pearson, Tony, MA Wales (E-mail: elcos@bangor.ac.uk)
Library (enquiries). Desk Services Manager: Heaton, A. J. (E-mail: library@bangor.ac.uk)
Marketing. Head of Student Recruitment: Roberts, Carys W., BA Wales
(E-mail: c.w.roberts@bangor.ac.uk)
Minorities/disadvantaged groups. Head of Student Services: Tate, Fran, BA Wales
(E-mail: studentservices@bangor.ac.uk)
Personnel/human resources. Director of Human Resources: (vacant)
(E-mail: pos006@bangor.ac.uk)
Public relations. Director of Corporate Communications and Marketing: Parry, Alan, BA Wales
(E-mail: alan.parry@bangor.ac.uk)
Publications. Web and Publications Officer: Wale, Sarah L., BA Wolv.
(E-mail: s.wale@bangor.ac.uk)

Purchasing. Purchasing Officer: Montgomery, Mike, BCom Birm.
(E-mail: m.montgomery@bangor.ac.uk)
Quality assurance and accreditation. Secretary and Registrar: Roberts, David M., MA Wales, PhD CNAA
(E-mail: d.m.roberts@bangor.ac.uk)
Research. Pro-Vice-Chancellor: Farrar, Prof. John F., MA Oxf., DPhil Oxf.
(E-mail: researchoffice@bangor.ac.uk)
Safety. Head of Occupational Health and Safety: Jones, Gareth W.
(E-mail: healthandsafety@bangor.ac.uk)
Schools liaison. Head of Student Recruitment: Roberts, Carys W., BA Wales
(E-mail: c.w.roberts@bangor.ac.uk)
Sport and recreation. Facilities Manager: Roberts, Sharon
(E-mail: sharon.roberts@bangor.ac.uk)
Staff development and training. Training and Development Officer: Ellis Roberts, Mari, BA Wales
(E-mail: mari.ellis-roberts@bangor.ac.uk)
Strategic planning. Senior Assistant Registrar (Planning): Mundy, Kevin, BSc Leeds, PhD Leeds (E-mail: k.mundy@bangor.ac.uk)
Student union. President (Student Union): Burnett, Sam
(E-mail: undeb@undeb.bangor.ac.uk)
Student welfare/counselling. Assistant Registrar (Student welfare/counselling): Barbaresi, Stephanie, BA Wales
(E-mail: aos020@bangor.ac.uk)
Students from other countries. International Student Welfare Adviser: Edwards, Alan
(E-mail: internationalwelfare@bangor.ac.uk)
Students with disabilities. Head of Student Services: Tate, Fran, BA Wales
(E-mail: studentservices@bangor.ac.uk)
University press. Press Officer: Elis-Williams, Elinor, BA Wales
(E-mail: e.elis-williams@bangor.ac.uk)

[Information supplied by the institution as at 3 October 2007, and edited by the ACU]

UNIVERSITY OF BATH

Founded 1966

Member of the Association of Commonwealth Universities

Postal Address: Claverton Down, Bath, England BA2 7AY
Telephone: (01225) 388388 **Fax:** (01225) 462508
URL: http://www.bath.ac.uk

VICE-CHANCELLOR*—Breakwell, Prof. Glynis M., BA Leic., MA Oxf., MSc Strath., PhD Brist., DSc Oxf., Hon. LLD Brist., FBPsS, FRSA, AcSS
DEPUTY VICE-CHANCELLOR—Lunt, Prof. George G., MSc Birm., PhD Birm.
PRO-VICE-CHANCELLOR (RESEARCH)—Edge, Prof. Kevin A., BSc Bath, PhD Bath, DSc Bath, FIMechE, FREng
PRO-VICE-CHANCELLOR (TEACHING AND LEARNING)—Jamieson, Prof. Ian M., BSc Sur., PhD Sur., FRSA
PRO-VICE-CHANCELLOR (STRATEGIC DEVELOPMENTS)—Millar, Prof. Jane, OBE, BA Sus., MA Brun., DPhil York(UK), FRSA
DIRECTOR OF FINANCE—Aderyn, Diane, BA Newcastle(UK), MA(Econ) Manc.
UNIVERSITY SECRETARY‡—Humphriss, Mark, BA Reading

GENERAL INFORMATION

History. The university was originally established as Merchant Venturers Technical College in 1894, receiving university status in 1966.
It is located on Claverton Down, one mile from the centre of Bath.

Admission to first degree courses (see also United Kingdom Introduction). Through Universities and Colleges Admissions Service (UCAS).

First Degrees (see also United Kingdom Directory to Subjects of Study). BA, BEng, BSc, MArch, MBioChem, MBiol, MChem, MEng, MMath, MPharm, MPharmacol, MPhys.
All courses are full-time and normally last 3 years, or 3 years plus 1 year industrial placement. Undergraduate master's degrees: 4 years, or 4 years plus 1 year industrial placement.

Higher Degrees (see also United Kingdom Directory to Subjects of Study).
Master's. MA, MBA, MPhil, MRes, MSc.

Admission. Applicants for admission to postgraduate degrees must normally hold an appropriate first degree with at least second class honours.
Length of course. Full-time: MA, MBA, MRes, MSc: 1 year; MPhil: 1–3 years. Part-time: MA, MSc: 2 years; MPhil: 2–4 years; MBA: 2–8 years. By distance learning: MA, MSc: 2 years.
Doctoral. DBA, DHealth, EdD, EngD, PhD.
Admission. PhD candidates are normally registered in the first instance for MPhil. Application is made direct to the university.
Length of course. Full-time: PhD: 2–4 years; DBA, DHealth, EdD, EngD: 2–5 years. Part-time: PhD:

3–6 years; DBA, DHealth, EdD, EngD: 4–8 years.

Libraries. Volumes: 420,000. Periodicals subscribed to: 2200. Special collections: Pitman (shorthand and orthographic systems, initial teaching alphabet).

Academic Year (2007–2008). Two semesters: 1 September–25 January; 28 January–30 May.

Income (2006–2007). Total, £149,485,000.

Statistics. Staff (2006–2007): 2640 (1480 academic, 1160 non-academic). Students (2006): total 11,965.

FACULTIES/SCHOOLS

Engineering and Design
Tel: (01225) 386389 Fax: (01225) 323255
E-mail: a.k.day@bath.ac.uk
Dean: Day, Prof. Alan K., BArch *Glas.*, PhD *CNAA*
Executive Assistant: Summers, Rachel, BA *Leeds*, MA *Leeds*
Executive Assistant: Pursell, Lucie, BA *N.U.I.*

Humanities and Social Sciences
Tel: (01225) 386013 Fax: (01225) 386113
E-mail: g.d.wood@bath.ac.uk
Dean: Wood, Prof. Geof D., BSc *Sus.*, MPhil *Sus.*, PhD
Executive Assistant: Jacobs, Suzanne E., BA *Sus.*

Lifelong Learning, Division for
Tel: (01225) 326636 Fax: (01225) 386849
E-mail: f.butt@bath.ac.uk
Director: Butt, Faith, BA *Durh.*, MA *Reading*, PhD *Reading*, FRSA
Division Administrator: Birdsall, Margaret, BSc *Wales*, MBA *Open(UK)*, PhD *Newcastle(UK)*

Management, School of
Tel: (01225) 383052 Fax: (01225) 386861
E-mail: a.m.pettigrew@bath.ac.uk
Dean: Pettigrew, Prof. Andrew, BA *Liv.*, PhD *Manc.*, Hon. PhD, FBA, FBAM
School Administrator: Rowe, Catherine A.

Science
Tel: (01225) 383965 Fax: (01225) 383353
E-mail: c.jennison@bath.ac.uk
Dean: Jennison, Prof. Christopher, BA *Camb.*, MA *Camb.*, PhD *Cornell*
Executive Assistant: Bird, Elizabeth, BA *Lond.*

ACADEMIC UNITS

Architecture and Civil Engineering
Tel: (01225) 384495 Fax: (01225) 386691
E-mail: ace@bath.ac.uk
Aish, Robert, MDes *RCA*, PhD *Essex* Visiting Prof.
Barnes, Michael R., BSc *Manc.*, MSc *Manc.*, MA *Manc.*, PhD *City(UK)* Prof.†
Barron, Michael F., BA *Camb.*, MA *Camb.*, PhD *S'ton.* Sr. Lectr.
Caruso, Adam, BSc *Montr.*, BArch *Montr.* Visiting Prof.
Cherry, Martin, BA *Wales*, PhD *Wales* Visiting Prof.
Cooper, Philip, BSc *Leeds*, MA *Camb.* Visiting Prof.
Darby, Antony P., BSc *Bath*, PhD *Camb.* Sr. Lectr.
D'Ayala, Dina F., MSc *Rome*, PhD *Camb.* Sr. Lectr.
Dickson, Michael, BA MS Visiting Prof.
Fordham, Max S., CBE, BA *Camb.*, MA *Camb.*, FREng, Hon. FRIBA Visiting Prof.
Harris, Richard, BSc *Brist.* Prof.†
Hart, Vaughan A., MPhil *Camb.*, PhD *Camb.*, BSc BArch Prof.
Ibell, Timothy J., BSc *Cape Town*, MSc *Cape Town*, PhD *Camb.* Prof.; Head*
McCombie, Paul F., BA *Camb.*, MSc *Lond.* Sr. Lectr.

Richens, Paul N., BA *Camb.*, MA *Camb.* Prof.
Samuel, Flora, BA *Camb.*, PhD *Cardiff* Reader
Walker, Peter, BSc *CNAA*, PhD *Edin.* Prof.
Williams, Christopher J., BA *Camb.*, PhD Sr. Lectr.
Wilson Jones, Mark, BA *Camb.*, PhD Sr. Lectr.
Other Staff: 1 Sr. Lectr.; 13 Lectrs.
Research: advanced studies in architecture; building research establishment (BRE); structural and architectural engineering (lightweight structure, use of fibre-reinforced polymer (FRP) in construction, conservation, natural building materials); window and cladding technology (integrity and construction, physics, the building envelope)

Biology and Biochemistry
Tel: (01225) 386407 Fax: (01225) 386779
E-mail: bio@bath.ac.uk
Acharya, K. Ravindra, BSc *Mys.*, MSc *B'lore.*, PhD *B'lore.* Prof., Structural Biology
Bagby, Stefan, BA *Oxf.*, DPhil *Oxf.* Sr. Lectr.
Beeching, John R., BA *Durh.*, BSc *Wales*, PhD *Warw.* Sr. Lectr.
Brown, D., BSc *Syd.*, MSc *Syd.*, PhD *Syd.* Prof.
Charnley, A. Keith, BSc *Durh.*, PhD *Durh.* Prof.
Cooper, Richard M., MSc *Lond.*, PhD *Lond.* Reader
Danson, Michael J., BSc *Leic.*, PhD *Leic.* Prof., Biochemistry
Furutani-Seiki, Makoto, MD *Yamaguchi*, PhD *Tokyo* Reader; Sr. Res. Fellow
Holman, Geoffrey D., BSc *S'ton.*, PhD *S'ton.* Prof., Cell Biology
Hooley, Richard, BSc *Lond.*, PhD *Lond.* Reader; Head*
Hough, David W., BSc *Manc.*, DPhil *Sus.* Reader
Hurst, Laurence D., BA *Camb.*, DPhil *Oxf.* Prof., Evolutionary Genetics
Karr, Timothy, BA *Calif.*, PhD *Calif.* Reader
Kelsh, Robert N., BA *Camb.*, PhD *Camb.* Reader
Kurtenbach, Klaus, PhD *Bonn* Sr. Lectr.
Mogie, Michael, BSc *Newcastle(UK)*, DPhil *Sus.* Sr. Lectr.
Rayner, Alan D. M., MA *Camb.*, PhD *Camb.* Reader
Reynolds, Stuart E., MA *Camb.*, PhD *Camb.* Prof.
Scott, Rod J., BSc *Nott.*, PhD *Nott.* Prof.
Slack, Jonathan M. W., BA *Oxf.*, PhD *Edin.*, FMedSci Prof., Cell and Molecular Biology
Subramanian, Vasanta, BSc *Gauh.*, MSc *Delhi*, PhD *B'lore.* Sr. Lectr.
Székely, Tamás, PhD Prof.
Tickle, Cheryll, MA *Camb.*, PhD *Glas.* Prof.
Tosh, David, BSc *Belf.*, PhD *Newcastle(UK)* Reader
Ward, Andrew, BSc *Durh.*, PhD *E.Anglia* Reader
Wheals, Alan E., BSc *Leic.*, PhD *Leic.* Sr. Lectr.
Wolstenholme, Adrian J., BSc *Lond.*, PhD *Camb.* Reader
Wonnacott, Susan J., MSc *Lond.*, PhD *Lond.* Prof., Neuroscience
Other Staff: 8 Lectrs.
Research: animal development; biology of micro-organisms; cell cycles; molecular biology; plant development

Chemistry
Tel: (01225) 386444 Fax: (01225) 386231
E-mail: chemistry@bath.ac.uk
Buchanan, Grant Visiting Prof.
Bull, Steven D., BSc *Cardiff*, PhD *Cardiff* Sr. Lectr.
Burrows, Andrew D., BA *Oxf.*, DPhil *Oxf.* Sr. Lectr.
Cox, Jonathan, BSc *Durh.*, PhD *Durh.* Sr. Lectr.
Davidson, Matthew, BSc *Wales*, PhD *Camb.* Prof.
Edler, Karen, BSc *Syd.*, PhD *ANU* Sr. Lectr.
Frost, Christopher G., BSc *Lough.*, PhD *Lough.* Sr. Lectr.
Islam, M. Saiful, BSc *Lond.*, PhD *Lond.* Prof.
James, Tony, BSc *E.Anglia*, PhD *Vic.(BC)* Reader

Kohn, Randolf D., DrRerNat *T.U.Berlin* Sr. Lectr.
Molloy, Kieran C., BSc *Nott.*, PhD *Nott.* Prof.
Parker, Stephen C., BSc *Lond.*, PhD *Lond.* Prof.
Peter, Laurence M., BSc *S'ton.*, PhD *S'ton.* Prof.
Price, Gareth J., BSc *Bath*, PhD *Bath* Sr. Lectr.; Head*
Raithby, Paul, BSc *Lond.*, PhD *Lond.*, MA *Camb.*, ScD *Camb.* Prof.
Roser, Stephen J., BSc *Oxf.*, DPhil *Oxf.* Sr. Lectr.
Whittlesey, Michael, BSc *York(UK)*, DPhil *York(UK)* Sr. Lectr.
Williams, Ian H., BSc *Sheff.*, PhD *Sheff.* Prof.
Williams, Jonathan M. J., BSc *York(UK)*, DPhil *Oxf.* Prof.
Other Staff: 5 Lectrs.
Research: asymmetric catalysis; electrochemistry; organometallic chemistry; polymer chemistry; structural chemistry

Computer Science
E-mail: r.l.clarke@bath.ac.uk
Barry, Alwyn, BSc *Belf.*, PhD *Belf.* Sr. Lectr.
Bradford, Russell, MA *Camb.*, PhD *Bath* Sr. Lectr.
Davenport, James H., MA *Camb.*, PhD *Camb.* Prof.
Edmonds, Ernest, BSc *Leic.*, MSc *Nott.*, FIEE Visiting Prof.
Fitch, John P., MA *Camb.*, PhD *Camb.* Prof.
Hall, Peter M., BSc *Leeds*, PhD *Sheff.* Sr. Lectr.
Johnson, Hilary, BSc *Salf.*, PhD *Birm.* Reader
Johnson, Peter, BSc *Salf.*, PhD *Warw.* Prof., Human Computer Interaction
McCusker, Guy A., BA *Oxf.*, PhD *Lond.* Prof.
O'Neill, Eamonn, BA *Open(UK)*, MSc *Oxf.*, PhD *Lond.* Sr. Lectr.
Padget, Julian A., BSc *Leeds*, PhD Sr. Lectr.
Pym, David J., MA *Camb.*, PhD *Edin.*, FIMA Prof., Logic and Computation
Vorobjov, Nicolai, MSc *Leningrad*, PhD *Leningrad* Prof., Theoretical Computer Science
Willis, Claire, BSc *Lond.*, PhD *Brist.* Sr. Lectr.
Willis, Philip J., BSc *Sus.*, MSc *Essex*, DPhil *Sus.* Prof.; Head*
Other Staff: 8 Lectrs.; 1 Reader†
Research: human-computer interaction; mathematical logic and symbolic computation; media technology

Economics and International Development
Tel: (01225) 383164 Fax: (01225) 383423
E-mail: d.r.ramsey@bath.ac.uk
Abbott, Andrew J., BA *Sund.*, MSc *York(UK)*, PhD *Durh.* Sr. Lectr.
Copestake, James G., BA *Camb.*, MSc *Reading*, PhD *Reading* Sr. Lectr.
Cullis, John G., BA *Nott.*, MA *Leeds*, MPhil *York(UK)* Reader
Heady, C., MA *Yale*, PhD *Yale* Visiting Prof.
Hudson, John R., BSc *Lond.*, MA *Warw.*, PhD *Warw.* Prof.
Jones, Philip R., BA *Wales*, MSc *Leic.*, PhD *Leic.* Prof.
Lawson, Colin W., BSc(Econ) *Lond.*, MSc(Econ) *Lond.*, PhD *Lond.* Reader
Markandya, Anil, BA *York(UK)*, MSc *Lond.*, PhD *Lond.* Prof.†, Quantitative Economics
McGregor, J. Allister, BA *Stir.*, PhD *Bath* Reader
Mishra, A., BA *Utkal*, MA *Delhi*, PhD *Delhi* Sr. Lectr.
Nandeibam, Shasikanta, BA *Madr.*, MA *Delhi*, PhD *Br.Col.* Prof.
Sessions, John, BSc *S'ton.*, MSc *Lond.*, PhD *Lond.* Prof.; Head*
Thomas, Scott M., BA *American(D.C.)*, MSc *Lond.*, PhD *Lond.* Sr. Lectr.
Winnett, Adrian B., BA *Lond.*, MA *E.Anglia*, PhD *E.Anglia* Sr. Lectr.
Other Staff: 18 Lectrs.
Research: economics of taxation; economics of transitional economies; environmental and resource economics; public sector economics

Education

Tel: (01225) 386341 Fax: (01225) 386113
E-mail: education@bath.ac.uk

Bishop, Keith, BSc *Leeds* Sr. Lectr.
Daniels, Harry R. J., BSc *Liv.*, PhD *Lond.Inst.* Prof.
Gough, Stephen R., BSc *Lond.*, PhD *Bath* Sr. Lectr.
Hart, E. Paul, BSc *Sask.*, BEd *Sask.*, MEd *Regina*, PhD *Regina* Visiting Prof.
Hayden, Mary C., BSc *S'ton.*, MPhil *Bath*, PhD *Bath* Sr. Lectr.
James, Chris, BSc *Sheff.*, PhD *Keele* Sr. Lectr.
Lauder, Hugh, BSc *Lond.*, MA *Lond.*, PhD *Camb.* Prof.
Markula-Denison, Pirkko, MSc *Ill.*, PhD *Ill.* Visiting Prof.
Martin, Susan, BSc *Lond.*, PhD *Lond.* Sr. Lectr.
Muschamp, Yolande, BA *Open(UK)*, MEd *Brist.*, PhD *Brist.* Sr. Lectr.; Head*
Porter, Jill, BA *Leic.*, MA *Keele*, PhD *Keele* Sr. Lectr.
Reid, Alan D., BA *Lanc.*, PhD *Bath* Sr. Lectr.
Scott, William A. H., BSc *Leeds*, PhD *Leeds* Prof.
Silk, Michael L., BA *S'ton.*, MA *Alta.*, PhD *Otago* Sr. Lectr.
Stables, Andrew W. G., BA *Lond.*, PhD *Bath* Prof.
Walker, George R., OBE, MA *Oxf.*, MSc *Oxf.* Visiting Prof.
Wikeley, Felicity J., BSc *Sur.*, MPhil *Exe.*, PhD *Exe.* Sr. Lectr.
Young, Michael F. D., BA *Camb.*, BSc *Lond.*, MA *Essex*, Hon. PhD *Joensuu* Prof.†
Other Staff: 15 Lectrs.; 2 Sr. Lectrs.†
Research: culture and environment; curriculum; environmental education; pedagogy; policy management

Engineering, Chemical

Tel: (01225) 386338 Fax: (01225) 385713
E-mail: chem-eng@bath.ac.uk

Arnot, Tom, BSc *Lond.*, PhD *Reading* Sr. Lectr.
Bird, Michael, BSc *Wales*, PhD *Camb.* Sr. Lectr.
Chaudhuri, Julian B., BSc *Lond.*, PhD *Reading*, FIChemE Prof.; Head*
Crittenden, Barry D., BSc *Birm.*, PhD *Birm.*, FREng, FIChemE Prof.
Emery, A., BMet *Sheff.* Visiting Prof.
England, Richard, MSc *Wales*, PhD *Wales* Sr. Lectr.
Greaves, Malcolm, BTech *Lough.*, PhD *Lough.*, FIChemE Emer. Prof.
Howell, John A., MA *Camb.*, PhD *Minn.*, FIChemE Emer. Prof., Biochemical Engineering
Hubble, John, BSc *Bath*, PhD *Bath*, FIChemE Reader
Kolaczkowski, Stanislaw T., BSc PhD, FIChemE Prof.
Lapkin, Alexei, MSc *Novosibirsk*, PhD *Bath* Sr. Lectr.
Lukyanov, Dimitri B., MSc *Moscow*, PhD *Moscow* Sr. Lectr.
Mays, Timothy, BSc *Brist.*, PhD *Bath* Sr. Lectr.
Perera, Semali, BSc *Brun.*, PhD *Brun.* Sr. Lectr.
Plucinski, Pawel, MSc *Warsaw*, PhD *Warsaw*, DrHabil *Munich* Reader
Rigby, Sean, BSc *Open(UK)*, MEng *Camb.*, MA *Camb.*, PhD *Camb.* Sr. Lectr.
Tennison, Stephen, FRSChem Visiting Prof.
Thomas, William J., BSc *Wales*, PhD *Lond.*, DSc *Wales*, FIChemE Emer. Prof.
Other Staff: 1 Lectr.
Research: advanced materials and porous solids; biochemical and biomedical engineering; catalysis and reaction engineering

Engineering, Electronic and Electrical

Tel: (01225) 386063 Fax: (01225) 386305
E-mail: elec-eng@bath.ac.uk

Aggarwal, Raj K., BEng *Liv.*, PhD *Liv.*, FIETE, FRSA Prof.
Allsop, Duncan, BSc *Sheff.*, MSc *Sheff.*, PhD *Sheff.* Sr. Lectr.
Balchin, Martin J., BSc *Lond.*, PhD *Lond.* Sr. Lectr.

Cannon, Paul S., BSc *S'ton.*, PhD *S'ton.*, FREng, FIETE Prof.
Dunn, Roderick W., BSc *Bath*, PhD *Bath* Sr. Lectr.
Eastham, John F., BSc *Manc.*, MSc *Manc.*, PhD *Manc.*, DSc *Manc.*, FREng, FIETE Visiting Prof.
Gosling, William, BSc *Lond.*, DSc, FIETE Emer. Prof.
Johns, Alan T., BSc *Bath*, PhD *Bath*, DSc, FIETE, FRSA Emer. Prof.
Lai, Hong Cheng, BSc *Bath*, PhD *Bath* Sr. Lectr.
Leonard, Paul J., BSc *Aberd.*, PhD *Lond.* Sr. Lectr.
Li, Furong, BEng *Hohai*, PhD *Liv.J.Moores* Sr. Lectr.
Mitchell, Cathryn N., BSc *Wales*, PhD *Wales*, FRAS Reader
Mitchell, Nicolas J., BSc *Sheff.*, PhD *Sheff.*, FRAS Prof.; Head*
Monro, Donald M., MASc *Tor.*, PhD *Lond.*, FIETE Emer. Prof., Electronics
Pennock, Stephen R., BSc *Liv.*, PhD *Liv.* Sr. Lectr.
Phillips, I., BSc *Wales(Swansea)* Visiting Prof.
Redfern, Miles A., BSc *Nott.*, PhD *Camb.* Sr. Lectr.
Rodger, David, BSc(Eng) *Aberd.*, PhD *Aberd.* Prof.
Shepherd, Peter R., BEng *Sheff.*, PhD *CNAA* Sr. Lectr.
Taylor, John T., BSc *Lond.*, PhD *Lond.*, FCA, FIETE Prof.
Wang, Wang N., BSc *Chung Cheng I.T.*, MSc *Iowa State*, MA *Camb.*, PhD *Camb.* Prof.
Watson, Peter, BSc *Durh.*, PhD *Durh.*, FIETE Prof. Emer.
Other Staff: 1 Teaching Fellow; 1 RCUK Fellow (jointly with Dept. of Mech. Eng.)
Vacant Posts: 3 Vacant Posts
Research: advance sensor technology; space, atmospheric and ocean science; sustainable power distribution

Engineering, Mechanical

Includes Aeronautical, Systems and Manufacturing Engineering

Tel: (01225) 383870 Fax: (01225) 386928
E-mail: mech-eng@bath.ac.uk

Almond, Darryl P., BSc *Lond.*, PhD *Lanc.* Prof.; Dir.*
Ansell, Martin P., BSc *Sus.*, PhD *Lond.* Reader
Bowen, Christopher R., BSc *Oxf.*, DPhil *Oxf.* Sr. Lectr.
Bowyer, Adrian, BSc *Lond.*, PhD *Lond.*, FIMA Sr. Lectr.
Brace, Christian J., BEng *Bath*, PhD *Bath* Sr. Lectr.
Bramley, Alan N., BEng *Liv.*, PhD *Liv.*, FIMechE, FIEE Prof.†
Burrows, Clifford R., OBE, BSc *Wales*, PhD *Lond.*, DSc(Eng) *Lond.*, Hon. DrIng *T.H.Aachen*, Hon. DSc *Aston*, FREng, FIMechE, FIEE Prof.†
Butler, Richard, BEng *Wales*, PhD *Wales* Sr. Lectr.
Clift, Sally E., BSc *Birm.*, PhD *Birm.* Sr. Lectr.
Culley, Stephen J., BSc *Brist.* Prof.
Cunningham, James L., BSc *Strath.*, PhD *Brist.*, FIMechE Reader
Darling, Jocelyn, BSc *Bath*, PhD *Bath* Sr. Lectr.
Edge, G. Visiting Prof.
Edge, Kevin A., BSc *Bath*, PhD *Bath*, DSc *Bath*, FIMechE, FREng Prof.
Gursul, Ismet, BSc *T.U.Istanbul*, MScEng *T.U.Istanbul*, PhD *Lehigh*, FRAeS Prof.
Hammond, Geoffrey P., MSc *Cran.IT*, FIMechE Prof.
Hawley, J. Gary, BSc *Sheff.Hallam*, PhD *Exe.* Prof.
Hunt, Giles W., BSc(Eng) *Lond.*, MSc(Eng) *Lond.*, PhD *Lond.*, FIMA Prof.
Johnston, Nigel D., BSc *Bath*, PhD *Bath* Sr. Lectr.
Jupp, J. A. Visiting Prof.
Keogh, Patrick S., BSc *Nott.*, PhD *Manc.* Prof.

Lock, Gary, BSc *Qu.*, MSc *Vic.(Tor.)*, PhD *Tor.* Sr. Lectr.
MacGregor, Stuart A., BSc *Wales*, PhD *Wales* Sr. Lectr.
Maropoulos, Paul, MSc *UMIST*, PhD *UMIST* Prof.
McMahon, Christopher A., BSc *Brist.* Prof.
Medland, Anthony J., PhD *CNAA*, FIMechE, FRSA Prof.†
Meo, Michele, BSc *Naples*, MSc *Cran.*, PhD *Cran.* Sr. Lectr.
Mileham, Anthony R., BSc *CNAA*, PhD *CNAA* Prof.; Head*
Miles, Anthony W., MSc(Eng) *Cape Town* Prof.
Mullineux, Glen, MA *Oxf.*, MSc *Oxf.*, DPhil *Oxf.*, FIMA Reader
Newman, Stephen T., BSc *Aston*, PhD *Lough.* Prof.
Newnes, Linda, BSc *Napier*, PhD *Lough.* Sr. Lectr.
Owen, Geraint, BSc *Bath*, PhD *Bath* Sr. Lectr.
Owen, John M., BSc *Durh.*, DPhil *Sus.* Prof.†
Parker, David A., FREng Visiting Prof.
Plummer, Andrew, BEng *Bath*, PhD *Bath*, FIMechE Prof.
Rees, D. Andrew S., BSc *Lond.*, PhD *Brist.* Reader
Sahinkaya, Mehmet N., BSc *Istanbul*, MSc *Sus.*, DPhil *Sus.* Reader
Stevens, Ronald, BSc *Wales*, PhD *Wales* Prof.
Tilley, Derek G., BSc *Wales*, PhD *Bath* Sr. Lectr.
Turner, Irene G., BSc *Wales*, PhD *Wales* Sr. Lectr.
Vincent, Julian F. V., BA *Camb.*, MA *Camb.*, PhD *Sheff.*, DSc *Sheff.* Prof.
Vogwell, Jeffrey, BSc PhD Sr. Lectr.
Wallace, Frank J. Emer. Prof.
Wilson, Mike, BSc *Bath*, PhD *Bath* Sr. Lectr.
Other Staff: 8 Lectrs.; 11 Res. Fellows; 1 Teaching Fellow
Research: aerothermodynamics; machine systems; manufacturing and materials; sports medicine and materials; structures and bioengineering

European Studies and Modern Languages

Tel: (01225) 383950 Fax: (01225) 386099
E-mail: esml@bath.ac.uk

Andall, Jacqueline M., BA *Cardiff*, MSc *Lond.*, PhD *Cardiff* Sr. Lectr.
Bluhdorn, Ingolfur, MA *Erlangen-Nuremberg*, PhD *Keele* Reader
Brooks, William S., BA *Newcastle(UK)*, PhD Prof., French
Bull, Anna, MA *Reading*, DottLett *Naples*, PhD *Reading* Prof., Italian
Butler, Geoffrey P. G. Emer. Visiting Prof.
Demossier, Marion, Lic *Paris V*, Maîtrise *Paris V*, PhD *E.H.E.S.S., Paris* Sr. Lectr.
Diamond, Hanna E., BA *Sus.*, DPhil *Sus.* Sr. Lectr.
Eatwell, Roger, MA *Oxf.*, DPhil *Oxf.* Prof.; Head*
Everett, Wendy E., BA *Wales*, MA *Lond.* Sr. Lectr.
Gillespie, David C., BA *Leeds*, PhD *Leeds* Prof., Russian
Giorgio, Adalgisa, DottLing *Naples*, PhD *Reading* Sr. Lectr.
Goodbody, Axel H., BA *Trinity(Dub.)*, MA *Kiel*, DrPhil *Kiel* Reader, German
Hyde-Price, Adrian G. V., BSc *Wales*, PhD *Kent* Prof.
Lambert, Peter, BS *Birm.*, PhD *W.England* Sr. Lectr.
Marsh, Rosalind J., MA *Camb.*, DPhil *Oxf.* Prof., Russian
Milner, Susan E., BSc *Aston*, PhD *Aston* Reader, French Studies
Neve, Brian, BA *Reading*, MA *Essex* Sr. Lectr.
Szarka, Joseph P., BA *Liv.*, PhD *Camb.* Reader, French with Management
Tate, George D., BA *Trinity(Dub.)*, MA *McM.*, PhD *Warw.* Prof., German
Wagstaff, Peter J., MA *Exe.*, PhD *Exe.* Sr. Lectr., French

Wharton, Steve, BA Aston, PhD Aston Sr. Lectr.
White, Anne, BA Oxf., PhD Lond. Sr. Lectr.
White, Howard J., BA Camb., MA Camb., MSc
    Lond. Sr. Lectr.
Whitman, Richard G., BA Oxf.Brookes, MA
    E.Anglia, PhD Westminster Prof.
Wiener, Antje, MA F.U.Berlin, PhD Car. Prof.
Other Staff: 12 Lectrs.
Research: conflict and security migration;
    democratic change, social movements and
    political parties; exile and ethnicity;
    integration, governance and territorial
    identities; memory, history and identity

Health, School for

Tel: (01225) 383860 Fax: (01225) 383833
    E-mail: health@bath.ac.uk
Blake, David R., MB ChB, FRCP Prof.
Eccleston, Christopher, BSc Lanc., PhD Reading
    Prof.; Deputy Head
Horrocks, Michael, MB BS Lond., MS Lond., FRCS
    Hon. Consultant Surgeon; Hon. Prof.,
    Surgery
Jones, Roy Hon. Prof.; Dir., Res. Inst. for
    Care of the Elderly (RICE)
Judge, Kenneth, MA Camb., PhD Camb. Prof.;
    Head*
McCabe, Candy, MSc Bath, PhD Bath Sr. Lectr.
Riddoch, Christopher J., PhD Belf. Prof.
Salo, Aki, MSc Jyväskylä, PhD Exe. Sr. Lectr.,
    Sport Biomechanics
Stallard, Paul, BSc Aston, MSc Birm., PhD Bath
    Prof., Child and Family Mental Health
Stevens, Clifford R., BSc Ulster, PhD Lond.
    Reader
Taylor, Gordon, BSc Portsmouth, MSc S'ton.,
    DPhil Ulster Sr. Lectr.
Thompson, Dylan, BA Liv., MSc Lough., PhD
    Lough. Sr. Lectr.
Vince, Russ, BA Sheff.Hallam, PhD Brist. Prof.
Wainwright, David, BA Kent, MSc Lond., PhD
    Kent Sr. Lectr.
Other Staff: 1 Consultant Sr. Lectr.; 9 Lectrs.; 2
    Clin. Dirs.; 2 Clin. Readers; 28 Hon.
    Members
Research: ageing, diabetes, obesity, dementia;
    biomechanics; exercise physiology;
    genomics, healthcare informatics,
    epidemiology, telemedicine; health
    promotion and public health

Management, School of

Tel: (01225) 386742 Fax: (01225) 386473
    E-mail: recep@management.bath.ac.uk
Bayliss, Brian, BSc Lond., PhD Birm. Prof.†
Brammer, Stephen, BA E.Anglia, MA E.Anglia,
    PhD E.Anglia Sr. Lectr.
Brown, Andrew, MSc Sheff., MA Oxf., PhD Sheff.
    Prof.
Butt-Philip, Alan, BA Oxf., DPhil Oxf. Reader
Colville, Ian D., BSc Cardiff, MSc PhD Sr.
    Lectr.
Cooper, Philip, BA Oxf., MBA City(UK), MSc
    Lond., PhD E.Anglia Sr. Lectr.
Elliott, Richard, BSc Lond., PhD Brad. Prof.
Fineman, Stephen, BA Strath., MPhil Strath., PhD
    Lond. Prof.
Ford, Ivan D., MSc Brad., PhD Manc. Prof.,
    Marketing
Goodwin, Paul, BA Liv., MSc Warw., PhD Lanc.
    Prof.
Graves, Andrew, BA Sus., MSc Sus., DPhil Sus.
    Prof. Fellow
Green, Rodney H., BTech Lough., MA Lanc., PhD
    Lanc. Prof.
Harland, Christine, BA CNAA, PhD Warw.
    Prof. Fellow
Howard, Michael B., BA Northumbria, PhD Bath,
    MBA Sr. Lectr.
Huisman, Jeroen, PhD T.H.Twente Prof.
Ioannidis, Christos, BSc MSc MA PhD Prof.
Joinson, Adam, BSc Lond., PhD Herts. Sr. Lectr.
Kinnie, Nicholas J., BSc UMIST, MA Warw., PhD
    Warw. Reader
Lepak, David P., BSc Missouri, MPA Missouri, PhD
    Penn. Prof.
Lewis, Michael, MEng PhD Prof.
Marshall, Judi A., BA Manc., PhD Manc. Prof.

Martin, Brett, MA Auck., PhD Otago Prof.
Mayer, Michael, MA Warw., PhD Warw. Prof.
McGuire, Stephen, BA Calg., MA Tor. Sr. Lectr.
Meeran, Sheik, BEng Cran., MSc Cran., PhD Cran.
    Sr. Lectr.
Meyer, Klaus, BA Gött., MSc Gött., PhD Lond.
    Prof.
Miller, Richard, OBE, BA MA MSc Visiting
    Prof.
Millington, Andrew, BA CNAA, MA Warw., PhD
    Bath Prof.
Morgan, Eleanor J., BSc(Econ) Lond., MA Mass.
    Sr. Lectr.
Naidoo, Rajani, BA Natal, MA Lond., PhD Camb.
    Sr. Lectr.; Dir. of Studies
Panteli, Androniki, PhD Warw. Sr. Lectr.
Pettigrew, Andrew, BA Liv., PhD Manc.,
    Hon. PhD, FBA, FBAM Prof., Strategy and
    Organisation; Head*
Powell, Philip, BSc S'ton., PhD S'ton. Prof.;
    Deputy Dean
Reason, Peter W., BA Camb., PhD Ohio Prof.
Shankar, Avi, BSc Brist., MA W.England, PhD Exe.
    Sr. Lectr.
Strong, Carolyn, BSc Liv.J.Moores, MA W.England,
    MBA Cardiff, PhD Cardiff Sr. Lectr.
Swart, Juani, BCom Bath, PhD Bath Sr. Lectr.
Thompson, Edmund R., BA York(UK), PhD Lond.
    Prof., International Business
Vass, Peter, MSc(Econ) Lond. Sr. Lectr.
Vidgen, Richard, BSc CNAA, MA CNAA, PhD
    Salf. Prof.
Vince, Russ, BA Sheff.Hallam, PhD Brist. Prof.
Zalewska, Ania, MSc Lublin, PhD Lond.Bus.
    Prof.
Other Staff: 23 Lectrs.
Research: accountancy and finance, regulated
    industries and innovative manufacturing;
    decision information systems (IS) for
    strategic and competitive advantage, and e-
    business; international business; operations
    and supply management; strategy
    development, change, performance,
    governance

Mathematical Sciences

Tel: (01225) 386989 Fax: (01225) 386492
    E-mail: enquiries@maths.bath.ac.uk
Besag, Julian, BSc Birm., FRS Prof., Statistics
Britton, Nicholas F., BA Oxf., MSc Oxf., DPhil
    Oxf. Prof., Mathematical Biology; Head*
Budd, Christopher J., MA Camb., DPhil Oxf.
    Prof., Applied Non-Linear Systems and
    PDES, Non-Linear Mechanics
Burstall, Francis E., MA Aberd., MSc Warw., PhD
    Warw. Prof., Geometry
Burton, Geoffrey R., BSc Lond., PhD Lond.
    Prof., Analysis and PDE
Calderbank, David M. J., BA Camb., MSc Warw.,
    PhD Warw. Prof.
Evans, Jonathan, BS Oxf., MA Oxf. Sr. Lectr.,
    Industrial (Applied)
Faraway, Julian, BA Camb., PhD Calif. Prof.,
    Statistics
Fraenkel, Ludwig E., MSc Tor., MA Camb., FRS
    Visiting Prof., Analysis and PDE
Galaktionov, Victor A., MD Moscow Phys.&
    Technol.Inst., PhD Russian Acad.Sc. Prof.,
    Applied Non-Linear Systems and Partial
    Differential Equation
Graham, Ivan G., MA Edin., PhD NSW Prof.,
    Numerical Analysis
Grindrod, Peter, CBE Visiting Prof.
Hill, Adrian, BA Camb., DPhil Oxf. Reader,
    Numerical Analysis
Hurn, Merrilee, BA Oxf., MSc Bath, PhD Bath
    Sr. Lectr.
Jennison, Christopher, BA Camb., MA Camb.,
    PhD Cornell Prof., Statistics
King, Alistair, BA Camb., DPhil Oxf. Prof.,
    Pure Mathematics
Kyprianou, Andreas, BA Oxf., PhD Sheff.
    Reader
Logemann, Hartmut, DrRerNat Bremen Prof.,
    Control Theory
Morters, Peter, PhD Lond. Prof., Probability
    (Statistics)
Movchan, A. B., MSc PhD Visiting Prof.

Penrose, Mathew D., BA Camb., DPhil Edin.
    Prof., Probability
Robinson, Anthony, BSc Newcastle(UK), MSc
    Newcastle(UK), PhD Hull Sr. Lectr.
Ryan, Eugene P., BE N.U.I., PhD Camb. Prof.,
    Mathematics - Control Theory
Sankaran, Gregory K., BA Camb., PhD Camb.
    Reader, Geometry
Shaddick, Gavin, BSc Warw., MSc Lond. Sr.
    Lectr.
Sivaloganathan, Jeyabel, BA Oxf., PhD H-W
    Reader, Continuum Mechanics
Smith, Geoffrey C., MA Oxf., MSc Warw., PhD
    UMIST Sr. Lectr., Group Theory
Smyshlyaev, Valery P., MSc St.Petersburg, PhD
    Russian Acad.Sc. Prof., Continuum Mechanics
    and Non-Linear Mechanics
Spence, Alastair, MSc Edin., DPhil Oxf., FIMA
    Prof., Numerical Analysis, Non-Linear
    Mechanics
Toland, John F., BSc Belf., MSc Sus., DPhil Sus.
    Prof., Mathematics - Analysis and PDE
White, K. A. Jane, BA Oxf., PhD Wash. Sr.
    Lectr.
Willis, John R. Visiting Prof.
Wood, Simon, BSc Manc., PhD Strath. Prof.,
    Statistics
Zhang, Wenyang, PhD Chinese HK Reader,
    Statistics
Other Staff: 13 Lectrs.; 5 Res. Fellows
Research: algebra and geometry; applied
    mathematics; probability; statistics

Pharmacy and Pharmacology

Tel: (01225) 383782 Fax: (01225) 386114
    E-mail: pharmacy-enquiries@bath.ac.uk
Blagbrough, Ian S., BSc Nott., PhD Nott. Sr.
    Lectr.
Bolhuis, Albert, PhD Gron., BSc Sr. Lectr.
De Vries, Corinne, MScPharm PhD Prof.
Dora, Kim, BSc Syd., BSc Tas., PhD Tas. Sr.
    Lectr.
Garland, Christopher J., BSc S'ton., PhD Lond.
    Prof.
Guy, Richard, BA Oxf., MA Oxf., PhD Lond.
    Prof.; Head*
Heal, David J. Visiting Prof.
Husbands, Stephen M., BSc Strath., PhD Strath.
    Sr. Lectr.
Jones, Roland, BSc Brad., MA Oxf., PhD Cardiff
    Reader
Kolios, G. Visiting Prof.
Lewis, John W., BA Oxf., MA Oxf., DPhil Oxf.
    Visiting Prof.
Moss, Stephen H., BPharm Nott., MSc PhD Sr.
    Lectr.
Mrsny, Randall J., BSc Calif., PhD Calif. Prof.†
Penn, C. Visiting Prof.
Potter, Barry V. L., MA Oxf., DPhil Oxf. Prof.,
    Pharmaceutical Chemistry
Price, Robert, BSc Cardiff, PhD Cardiff Reader
Scott, Jenny, BSc PhD Sr. Lectr.
Smirnov, Sergey, BSc PhD Sr. Lectr.
Staniforth, John N. Hon. Prof.
Threadgill, Michael D., MA Camb., PhD Camb.,
    DSc Bath Reader
Tyrrell, Rex M., BPharm Bath, PhD Bath Prof.
Ward, Stephen G., BPharm Lond., PhD Prof.
Watson, Malcolm, BSc Lond., PhD Lond. Sr.
    Lectr.
Welham, Melanie J., BSc Lond., PhD Lond.
    Prof.
Westwick, John, BSc PhD Visiting Prof.
Other Staff: 2 Visiting Readers; 14 Lectrs.; 7
    Teaching Fellows
Research: cardiovascular pharmacology and
    neuropharmacology; clinical pharmacy and
    pharmacy practice (medicine usage,
    pharmaceutical care); immuno-
    pharmacology (inter and intra-cellular
    signalling); pharmaceutical biology
    (mechanisms of and protection from
    infectious diseases and stress);
    pharmaceutical technology (drug delivery,
    pharmaceutical surface science)

Physics

Tel: (01225) 383673 Fax: (01225) 386110
E-mail: physics@bath.ac.uk
Andrews, Steven, BA Oxf., MA Oxf., DPhil Oxf.
Sr. Lectr.
Bending, Simon J., BA Camb., PhD Stan. Prof.
Bird, David M., BA Camb., PhD Camb. Prof.;
Head*
Birks, Timothy T. A., BA Oxf., PhD Limerick
Prof.
Blondel, Phillipe, MPhys Paris, PhD Paris Sr.
Lectr.
Coleman, Paul G., BSc Lond., PhD Lond. Prof.
Crampin, Simon, BSc Lond., PhD Lond. Sr.
Lectr.
Cronin, Nigel J., BSc Lond., PhD Lond. Prof.
Davies, John J., MA Oxf., DPhil Oxf. Prof.
Davies, Steven R., BSc Sheff., MSc Leic., PhD Kent
Sr. Lectr.
Duck, Francis A. Visiting Prof.
Gordeev, Sergey, MSc PhD Sr. Lectr.
James, Richard, BSc PhD Sr. Lectr.
Knight, Jonathan, BSc Cape Town, MSc Cape
Town, PhD Cape Town Prof.
Kovalev, Dmitry, PhD Prof.
Nogaret, Alain, PhD I.N.S.A.Toulouse Sr. Lectr.
Pace, Nicholas G., BSc Durh., PhD Durh. Prof.†
Russell, Philip St. J., BA Oxf., DPhil Oxf.
Prof.†
Salmon, Philip S., BSc Brist., PhD Brist. Prof.
Skryabin, Dmitry, PhD Strath. Sr. Lectr.
Snow, Paul, MA Oxf., DPhil Oxf. Sr. Lectr.
Walker, Alison B., BA Oxf., DPhil Oxf. Reader
Wang, Wang N., BSc Chung Cheng I.T., MSc Iowa
State, MA Camb., PhD Camb. Prof.†
Wilding, Nigel, BSc Edin., PhD Edin. Reader
Wolverson, Daniel, MA Camb., PhD Exe. Sr.
Lectr.
Other Staff: 1 Lectr.; 1 Dir., Teaching and
Resources†
Research: nanoscale physics, nanomagnetism and
superconductivity; photonics, photonic
materials and laser spectroscopy;
semiconductor heterostructures and device
modelling; theoretical condensed matter
physics; underwater acoustics and
astronomic sensors

Psychology

Tel: (01225) 383843 Fax: (01225) 386752
E-mail: psychology-enquiries@bath.ac.uk
Brosnan, Mark, BSc Herts., MSc Manc., PhD Manc.
Sr. Lectr.
Calvert, Gemma, DPhil Oxf. Reader
Gooding, David C., MA Dal., DPhil Oxf. Prof.
Griffin, Christine, BSc Birm., PhD Birm. Prof.;
Head*
Haste, Helen E., BA Lond., MPhil Sus., PhD
Prof.†
Joiner, Richard, BA Sus., MSc Warw., PhD
Open(UK) Sr. Lectr.
Keogh, Edmund, BSc Lond., MSc Lond., PhD Lond.
Sr. Lectr.
Lewis, Alan, BSc Wales, PhD Wales Prof.
Skevington, Suzanne M., BSc Wales, PhD Wales
Prof.
Stanton, Danae, BA Leic., PhD Leic. Reader
Turner-Cobb, Julie, BA Exe., PhD Lond. Sr.
Lectr.
Verplanken, Bas, PhD Ley. Prof.
Weyman, Andrew K., BA Nott.Trent, MSc Lough.,
PhD Nott. Sr. Lectr.
Other Staff: 1 Prof. Fellow; 4 Lectrs.
Research: applied cognition and technology;
health psychology; science, culture and
critical psychology

Social and Policy Sciences

Tel: (01225) 384728 Fax: (01225) 386381
E-mail: socpol-enquiries@bath.ac.uk
Baldwin, Mark J., BSc DPhil Sr. Lectr.
Bauld, Linda, BA Tor., PhD Edin. Reader
Brown, Sarah L., BSc Bath, MSc Bath Sr. Lectr.
Butler, Ian, BA S'ton., MPhil Wales Prof.
Cressey, Peter, BA York(UK), MA York(UK)
Reader
Gough, Ian R., BA Camb., MA Camb., AcSS
Prof., Social Policy

Gould, Nicholas G., BA Sus., MA Sus., MSc Oxf.,
PhD Bath Prof.
Harkness, Susan, BA Camb., MA Sus., PhD Lond.
Sr. Lectr.
Jones, Bryn, BA Lond., PhD Liv. Sr. Lectr.
Kellehear, Allan, BA NSW, PhD NSW Prof.;
Head*
Kuhlmann, Ellen, MA Gött., PhD Bielefeld Sr.
Lectr.
Millar, Jane, OBE, BA Sus., MA Brun., DPhil
York(UK), FRSA Prof.
O'Leary, Patrick, BA S.Aust., PhD Flin. Sr.
Lectr.
Room, Graham J., MA Camb., DPhil Oxf.
Prof., Social Policy
Rose, Michael J., BA Camb., MA Camb., PhD
Camb. Prof.†
Standing, Guy, BA Sus., MA Ill., PhD Camb.
Prof.†, Social and Economic Security
Walter, Julian A., BA Durh., PhD Aberd. Prof.†
Other Staff: 8 Lectrs.; 1 Reader†; 2 Sr. Lectrs.†
Research: social policy (welfare state and welfare
policy in the UK, Europe and globally);
social work (children and families,
community care and professional
education); sociology (criminology and
sociology of law, sociology of employment,
sociology of health and illness)

SPECIAL CENTRES, ETC

Action Research in Professional Practice, Centre for

Tel: (01225) 386792 Fax: (01225) 386473
E-mail: p.w.reason@bath.ac.uk
Marshall, Judi A., BA Manc., PhD Manc. Prof.
Reason, Peter W., BA Camb., PhD Ohio Prof.;
Dir.*
Other Staff: 1 Lectr.
Research: action research in management of
diversity; action research in professional
practice; responsibility and business practice;
sustainability and social justice; theory and
practice of participative inquiry

Advanced Sensor Technologies, Centre for

Allsop, Duncan, BSc Sheff., MSc Sheff., PhD Sheff.
Sr. Lectr.
Sarma, Jayanta, BETelE Jad., MS Ill., PhD Leeds
Reader
Taylor, John T., BSc Lond., PhD Lond., FCA,
FIETE Prof.; Dir.*
Other Staff: 4 Lectrs.

Advertising and Consumption, Centre for Research into

Elliott, Richard, BSc Lond., PhD Brad. Prof.;
Dir.*
Martin, Brett, MA Auck., PhD Otago Prof.;
Deputy Dir.
Shankar, Avi, BSc Brist., MA W.England, PhD Exe.
Sr. Lectr.
Strong, Carolyn, BSc Liv.J.Moores, MA W.England,
MBA Cardiff, PhD Cardiff Sr. Lectr.
Other Staff: 4 Lectrs.

Aerospace Engineering Research Centre

Butler, Richard, BEng Wales, PhD Wales Sr.
Lectr.
Gursul, Ismet, BSc T.U.Istanbul, MScEng
T.U.Istanbul, PhD Lehigh, FRAeS Prof.; Dir.*
Jupp, J. A. Visiting Prof.
Lock, Gary, BSc Qu., MSc Vic.(Tor.), PhD Tor.
Sr. Lectr.
MacGregor, Stuart A., BSc Wales, PhD Wales
Sr. Lectr.
Meo, Michele, BSc Naples, MSc Cran., PhD Cran.
Sr. Lectr.
Rees, D. Andrew S., BSc Lond., PhD Brist.
Reader
Wilson, Mike, BSc Bath, PhD Bath Sr. Lectr.
Research: aerodynamics; aerostructures;
composites; computational fluid dynamics
(CFD); propulsion

Analysis of Social Policy, Centre for the (CASP)

Tel: (01225) 386141 E-mail: casp@bath.ac.uk
Bauld, Linda, BA Tor., PhD Edin. Reader
Brown, Sarah L., BSc Bath, MSc Bath Sr. Lectr.
Cressey, Peter, BA York(UK), MA York(UK)
Reader
Cullis, John G., BA Nott., MA Leeds, MPhil
York(UK) Reader
Gough, Ian R., BA Camb., MA Camb., AcSS
Prof.
Gould, Nicholas G., BA Sus., MA Sus., MSc Oxf.,
PhD Bath Prof.
Harkness, Susan, BA Camb., MA Sus., PhD Lond.
Sr. Lectr.
Hudson, John R., BSc Lond., MA Warw., PhD
Warw. Prof.
Jones, Philip R., BA Wales, MSc Leic., PhD Leic.
Prof.
Kuhlmann, Ellen, MA Gött., PhD Bielefeld Sr.
Lectr.
Millar, Jane, OBE, BA Sus., MA Brun., DPhil
York(UK), FRSA Prof.; Dir.*
Room, Graham J., MA Camb., DPhil Oxf. Prof.
Rose, Michael J., BA Camb., MA Camb., PhD
Camb. Prof.†
Sessions, John, BSc S'ton., MSc Lond., PhD Lond.
Prof.
Standing, Guy, BA Sus., MA Ill., PhD Camb.
Prof.
Research: children and young people;
globalisation, wellbeing and governance;
health and social care; policy analysis and
design; work and welfare

Architecture, Centre for Advanced Studies in (CASA)

Tel: (01225) 386908 Fax: (01225) 386691
E-mail: e.s.j.greeley@bath.ac.uk
Day, Alan K., BArch Glas., PhD CNAA Prof.
Hart, Vaughan A., MPhil Camb., PhD Camb., BSc
BArch Prof.
Richens, Paul N., BA Camb., MA Camb. Prof.;
Dir.*
Samuel, Flora, BA Camb., PhD Cardiff Reader
Wilson Jones, Mark, BA Camb., PhD Sr. Lectr.
Research: computer modelling; history of
architecture; masterplanning; urban design

Biomimetic and Natural Technologies, Centre for

Tel: (01225) 386596 Fax: (01225) 286928
E-mail: j.f.v.vincent@bath.ac.uk
Ansell, Martin P., BSc Sus., PhD Lond. Sr. Lectr.
Bowyer, Adrian, BSc Lond., PhD Lond., FIMA
Sr. Lectr.
Clift, Sally E., BSc Birm., PhD Birm. Sr. Lectr.
Edler, Karen, BSc Syd., PhD ANU Sr. Lectr.
Hubble, John, BSc Bath, PhD Bath, FIChemE
Reader
Reynolds, Stuart E., MA Camb., PhD Camb.
Prof.; Deputy Dir.
Vincent, Julian F. V., BA Camb., MA Camb., PhD
Sheff., DSc Sheff. Prof.; Dir.*
Research: biomimetic locomotion in endoscopy;
fracture mechanics of brittle foods;
functional design of hooks in nature;
integration of biology into engineering;
variable stiffness devices for vibration
control

Business, Organisation and Society, Centre for (CBOS)

Tel: (01225) 383065 Fax: (01225) 386472
E-mail: s.j.a.brammer@bath.ac.uk
Brammer, Stephen, BA E.Anglia, MA E.Anglia,
PhD E.Anglia Sr. Lectr.; Dir.*
Millington, Andrew, BA CNAA, MA Warw., PhD
Bath Reader; Deputy Dir.
Strong, Carolyn, BSc Liv.J.Moores, MA W.England,
MBA Cardiff, PhD Cardiff Sr. Lectr.
Research: corporate social responsibility as a
strategic phenomenon; relationship between
corporations and the societies within which
they operate; the ethical position of modern
corporations in different societal contexts

Death and Society, Centre for (CDAS)

Tel: (01225) 386949 E-mail: cdas@bath.ac.uk
Howarth, Glennys, BA Lond., PhD Lond.
  Reader; Dir.*
Kellehear, Allan, BA NSW, PhD NSW   Prof.;
  Head*
Walter, Julian A., BA Durh., PhD Aberd.   Prof.†
Other Staff: 1 Res. Fellow

Development Studies, Centre for

Tel: (01225) 384514 Fax: (01225) 383423
  E-mail: cds@bath.ac.uk
Copestake, James G., BA Camb., MSc Reading,
  PhD Reading   Sr. Lectr.
Gough, Ian R., BA Camb., MA Camb., AcSS
  Prof., Social Policy
McGregor, J. Allister, BA Stir., PhD Bath
  Reader
White, Sarah, BA Camb., PhD   Dir.*
Winnett, Adrian B., BA Lond., MA E.Anglia, PhD
  E.Anglia   Sr. Lectr.
Wood, Geof D., BSc Sus., MPhil Sus., PhD
  Prof.
Research: globalisation, trade and conflict;
  governance, rights and policy analysis;
  markets and micro-finance; poverty,
  wellbeing and livelihoods; social structures
  and cultural identities

Education and the Environment, Centre for Research in

Tel: (01225) 386648 Fax: (01225) 386113
  E-mail: cree@bath.ac.uk
Gough, Stephen R., BSc Lond., PhD Bath   Sr.
  Lectr.; Deputy Dir.
Reid, Alan D., BA Lanc., PhD Bath   Sr. Lectr.
Scott, William A. H., BSc Leeds, PhD Leeds
  Prof.; Dir.*
Stables, Andrew W. G., BA Lond., PhD Bath
  Prof.
Research: contributions of schools etc. to
  sustainable development; role of learning
  within sustainable development; teacher
  roles and responsibilities

Education in an International Context, Centre for the Study of (CEIC)

Tel: (01225) 386120 Fax: (01225) 386113
  E-mail: ceic@bath.ac.uk
Hayden, Mary C., BSc S'ton., MPhil Bath, PhD
  Bath   Sr. Lectr.; Dir.*
Research: comparative education; development
  education; international curricula and
  assessment; international education,
  nationally and internationally; international
  schools

Engineering and Design of Environments Research Unit

Tel: (01225) 386296 Fax: (01225) 368002
  E-mail: absmn@bath.ac.uk
Barron, Michael F., BA Camb., MA Camb., PhD
  S'ton.   Reader
Fordham, Max S., CBE, BA Camb., MA Camb.,
  FREng, Hon. FRIBA   Visiting Prof.
Gething, William, BA Camb., MA Camb.
  Visiting Prof.
King, Doug, BSc ICL   Visiting Prof.
Ledbetter, Stephen R., BSc Dund., PhD Brist.   Sr.
  Lectr.
Nikolopoulou, Marialena, BEng Cardiff, MPhil
  Camb., PhD Camb.   Dir.*
Other Staff: 6 Lectrs.; 1 Visiting Lectr.; 1 Res.
  Fellow
Research: environmental engineering;
  environmental modelling including
  computational fluid dynamics (CFD)
  technologies; sustainable building design;
  urban microclimate

Environment, International Centre for the

Tel: (01225) 386156 Fax: (01225) 386928
  E-mail: iceoffice@bath.ac.uk
Hammond, Geoffrey P., MSc Cran.IT, FIMechE
  Prof.; Dir.*

Markandya, Anil, BA York(UK), MSc Lond., PhD
  Lond.   Prof.†, Quantitative Economics
Winnett, Adrian B., BA Lond., MA E.Anglia, PhD
  E.Anglia   Deputy Dir.
Research: energy and the environment;
  environmental regulation in the energy and
  water industries; interdisciplinary
  perspectives on environment and
  sustainability; urban sustainability; water
  resources and environmental quality

European Research Institute

Tel: (01225) 386831 Fax: (01225) 386381
  E-mail: eri-enquiries@bath.ac.uk
Bull, Anna, MA Reading, DottLett Naples, PhD
  Reading   Prof., Italian
Butt-Philip, Alan, BA Oxf., DPhil Oxf.   Reader
Cressey, Peter, BA York(UK), MA York(UK)
  Reader
Lawson, Colin W., BSc(Econ) Lond., MSc(Econ)
  Lond., PhD Lond.   Reader
McGuire, Stephen, BA Calg., MA Tor.   Sr. Lectr.
Milner, Susan E., BSc Aston, PhD Aston   Reader
Papadopoulous, Theo, MSc Sur., DPhil York(UK)
  Dir.*
Whitman, Richard G., BA Oxf.Brookes, MA
  E.Anglia, PhD Westminster   Prof.
Other Staff: 2 Lectrs.
Research: contemporary European politics,
  economics, society and culture; European
  governance; European interpretation

Extremophile Research, Centre for

Tel: (01225) 386509 Fax: (01225) 386779
  E-mail: m.j.danson@bath.ac.uk
Bull, Steven D., BSc Cardiff, PhD Cardiff   Sr.
  Lectr.
Danson, Michael J., BSc Leic., PhD Leic.   Prof.;
  Dir.*
Hough, David W., BSc Manc., DPhil Sus.
  Reader
Other Staff: 4 Lectrs.; 4 Postdoctoral Staff; 2
  Technicians
Research: enzymes from extremophiles (stability,
  structure and function); enzymes in
  biotechnology; extremophiles; microbial
  biodiversity and evolution

Higher Education Management, International Centre for (ICHEM)

Tel: (01225) 383304 Fax: (01225) 386543
  E-mail: ichem@management.bath.ac.uk
Abbott, Andrew J., BA Sund., MSc York(UK), PhD
  Durh.   Sr. Lectr.
Brown, Andrew, MSc Sheff., MA Oxf., PhD Sheff.
  Prof.
Colville, Ian D., BSc Cardiff, MSc PhD   Sr.
  Lectr.
Elliott, Richard, BSc Lond., PhD Brad.   Prof.
Fineman, Stephen, BA Strath., MPhil Strath., PhD
  Lond.   Prof.
Huisman, Jeroen, PhD T.H.Twente   Prof.; Dir.*
Lauder, Hugh, BSc Lond., MA Lond., PhD Camb.
  Prof.
Marshall, Judi A., BA Manc., PhD Manc.   Prof.
Mayer, Michael, MA Warw., PhD Warw.   Prof.
Naidoo, Rajani, BA Natal, MA Lond., PhD Camb.
  Sr. Lectr.; Dir. of Studies
Pettigrew, Andrew, BA Liv., PhD Manc.,
  Hon. PhD, FBA, FBAM   Prof., Strategy and
  Organisation; Head*
Powell, Philip, BSc S'ton., PhD S'ton.   Prof.;
  Deputy Dean
Reason, Peter W., BA Camb., PhD Ohio   Prof.
Reid, Alan D., BA Lanc., PhD Bath   Sr. Lectr.
Room, Graham J., MA Camb., DPhil Oxf.
  Prof., Social Policy
Shankar, Avi, BSc Brist., MA W.England, PhD Exe.
  Sr. Lectr.
Other Staff: 1 Lectr.
Research: governance, policy and management;
  international-comparative research;
  internationalisation, Europeanisation and
  globalisation; organisational change;
  programme and institutional diversity

Industrial Marketing and Purchasing Centre (IMP RC)

Tel: (01225) 383699
  E-mail: i.d.ford@bath.ac.uk
Ford, Ivan D., MSc Brad., PhD Manc.   Prof.;
  Dir.*

Information Management, Centre for

Tel: (01225) 383256 Fax: (01225) 386473
  E-mail: mnspp@management.bath.ac.uk
Joinson, Adam, BSc Lond., PhD Herts.   Sr. Lectr.
Kamm, Richard M., BA Camb., MSc W.England,
  PhD Camb.   Sr. Lectr.
Panteli, Androniki, PhD Warw.   Sr. Lectr.;
  Dir.*
Powell, Philip, BSc S'ton., PhD S'ton.   Prof.
Vidgen, Richard, BSc CNAA, MA CNAA, PhD
  Salf.   Prof.
Research: e-business and e-learning; evaluation
  of IT investments; information systems in
  small businesses; information systems
  planning and strategy; virtual teamwork

International Policy Analysis, Institute of

Tel: (01225) 386033 Fax: (01225) 383423
Ramprakash, Deo, MSc Lond.   Visiting Prof.
Wood, Geof D., BSc Sus., MPhil Sus., PhD
  Prof.; Dir.*

Joint Research Unit with the Avon and Wiltshire Mental Health Partnership NHS Trust

Tel: (01225) 384356
  E-mail: hsxwm@bath.ac.uk
Stallard, Paul, BSc Aston, MSc Birm., PhD Bath
  Prof.†
Velleman, Richard D. B., BSc Sus., MSc Exe.,
  PhD Exe.   Prof.†; Dir.*
Research: addictions and substance misuse;
  alcohol, drugs and the family; child and
  adolescent mental health; primary care;
  serious mental illness

Materials Research Centre

Tel: (01225) 386708 Fax: (01225) 386098
  E-mail: d.p.almond@bath.ac.uk
Almond, Darryl P., BSc Lond., PhD Lanc.   Prof.;
  Dir.*

Mathematical Biology, Centre for

Tel: (01225) 386989 Fax: (01225) 386492
  E-mail: n.f.britton@bath.ac.uk
Britton, Nicholas F., BA Oxf., MSc Oxf., DPhil
  Oxf.   Prof.
James, Richard, BSc Bath, PhD Bath   Sr. Lectr.
Mogie, Michael, BSc Newcastle(UK), DPhil Sus.
  Sr. Lectr.; Co-Dir.*
White, K. A. Jane, BA Oxf., PhD Wash.   Sr.
  Lectr.; Co-Dir.*
Research: biological systems (analysis,
  mathematical modelling, simulation);
  dynamics of ecological and epidemiological
  systems; evolution and structure of genetic
  systems; evolution of ecological and
  epidemiological systems; vertebrate
  embryonic development

Media Technology Research Centre

Tel: (01225) 386811 Fax: (01225) 383493
  E-mail: p.j.willis@bath.ac.uk
Fitch, John P., MA Camb., PhD Camb.   Prof.
Hall, Peter M., BSc Leeds, PhD Sheff.   Sr. Lectr.
Willis, Claire, BSc Lond., PhD Brist.   Sr. Lectr.
Willis, Philip J., BSc Sus., MSc Essex, DPhil Sus.
  Prof.; Dir.*
Other Staff: 2 Lectrs.
Research: animation and movies; computer
  graphics; computer vision; music; virtual
  environments

Medical Engineering, Bath Institute of

Tel: (01225) 824103 Fax: (01225) 824111
  E-mail: bime@bath.ac.uk
Orpwood, Roger D., BSc BEng PhD   Hon.
  Prof.; Dir.*
Other Staff: 9 Engineers; 2 Physicists
Research: assistive technology for disabled
  people; clinical infusion systems; healthcare

technology design; robotics for the severely disabled; 'smart' housing for people with dementia

Nonlinear Mechanics, Centre for

Tel: (01225) 386998 Fax: (01225) 386492
E-mail: c.j.budd@bath.ac.uk
Budd, Christopher J., MA Camb., DPhil Oxf. Prof.; Dir.*
Hunt, Giles W., BSc(Eng) Lond., MSc(Eng) Lond., PhD Lond., FIMA Prof.

Orthopaedic Biomechanics, Centre for

Tel: (01225) 385961 Fax: (01225) 386928
E-mail: a.w.miles@bath.ac.uk
Cunningham, James L., BSc Strath., PhD Brist., FIMechE Reader; Deputy Dir.
Miles, Anthony W., MSc(Eng) Cape Town Prof.; Dir.*
Tilley, Derek G., BSc Wales, PhD Bath Sr. Lectr.
Turner, Irene G., BSc Wales, PhD Wales Sr. Lectr.
Research: biomaterials; fracture treatment; orthopaedic biomechanics; pre-clinical test methodologies; total joint replacement

Pain Management Unit

Tel: (01225) 386439 Fax: (01225) 383622
E-mail: pain@bath.ac.uk
Eccleston, Christopher, BSc Lanc., PhD Reading Prof.; Dir.*
Other Staff: 1 Sr. Lectr.†; 2 Consultant Clin. Psychologists; 2 Clin. Psychologists
Research: adolescent and family therapy; chronic pain; contextual cognitive behavioural therapy acceptance; pain management

Photonics and Photonic Materials, Centre for

Fax: (01225) 386110
Bird, David M., BA Camb., PhD Camb. Prof.
Birks, Timothy T. A., BA Oxf., PhD Limerick Prof.
Knight, Jonathan, BSc Cape Town, MSc Cape Town, PhD Cape Town Prof.; Dir.*
Skryabin, Dmitry, PhD Strath. Sr. Lectr.
Snow, Paul, MA Oxf., DPhil Oxf. Sr. Lectr.

Power Transmission and Motion Control, Centre for

Tel: (01225) 386371 Fax: (01225) 386928
E-mail: ptmc@bath.ac.uk
Darling, Jocelyn, BSc Bath, PhD Bath Sr. Lectr.
Edge, Kevin A., BSc Bath, PhD Bath, DSc Bath, FIMechE, FREng Prof.
Johnston, Nigel D., BSc Bath, PhD Bath Sr. Lectr.
Keogh, Patrick S., BSc Nott., PhD Manc. Reader
Plummer, Andrew, BEng Bath, PhD Bath, FIMechE Prof.; Dir.*
Sahinkaya, Mehmet N., BSc Istanbul, MSc Sus., DPhil Sus. Reader
Tilley, Derek G., BSc Wales, PhD Bath Sr. Lectr.
Other Staff: 2 Lectrs.
Research: control of energy transmission systems; electro-hydraulic and hydromechanical power transmission; fluid power systems design and analysis; modelling and computer simulation; pump flowripple and system noise

Powertrain and Vehicle Research, Centre for

Tel: (01225) 386855 Fax: (01225) 386928
E-mail: ensjgh@bath.ac.uk
Brace, Christian J., BEng Bath, PhD Bath Deputy Dir.
Cumming, Brian Visiting Prof.
Hawley, J. Gary, BSc Sheff.Hallam, PhD Exe. Prof.; Dir.*
Kolaczkowski, Stanislaw T., BSc PhD, FIChemE Prof.
Parker, David A., FREng Visiting Prof.
Wallace, Frank J. Emer. Prof.
Other Staff: 1 Lectr.; 1 Advanced Res. Fellow

Research: diesel and gasoline systems; emissions measurement; engine heat transfer; fuel economy; vehicle driveability

Regenerative Medicine, Centre for

E-mail: m.horrocks@bath.ac.uk
Chaudhuri, Julian B., BSc Lond., PhD Reading, FIChemE Prof.
Horrocks, Michael, MB BS Lond., MS Lond., FRCS Hon. Consultant Surgeon; Hon. Prof., Surgery; Head*
Slack, Jonathan M. W., BA Oxf., PhD Edin., FMedSci Prof.
Tickle, Cheryll, MA Camb., PhD Glas. Prof.
Tosh, David, BSc Belf., PhD Newcastle(UK) Reader
Ward, Andrew, BSc Durh., PhD E.Anglia Reader; Co-Dir.*
Welham, Melanie J., BSc Lond., PhD Lond. Prof.; Co-Dir.*
Research: developmental mechanisms; stem cell biology; tissue engineering; tissue regeneration

Regulated Industries, Centre for the Study of (CRI)

Tel: (01225) 383197 Fax: (01225) 383221
E-mail: mnsjsm@management.bath.ac.uk
Vass, Peter, MSc(Econ) Lond. Sr. Lectr.; Dir.*
Other Staff: 1 Res. Officer
Research: consumer representation and regulatory institutions; corporate governance of regulated industries; methodologies for setting price controls; regulatory accounting, environment and corporate social responsibility; the policy framework for effective regulation

Science Studies, Centre for

Tel: (01225) 386335 Fax: (01225) 386752
E-mail: hssdcg@bath.ac.uk
Gooding, David C., MA Dal., DPhil Oxf. Prof.; Dir.*
Gosling, William, BSc Lond., DSc, FIETE Emer. Prof.
Haste, Helen E., BA Lond., MPhil Sus., PhD Prof.†
Joiner, Richard, BA Sus., MSc Warw., PhD Open(UK) Sr. Lectr.
Rayner, Alan D. M., MA Camb., PhD Camb. Reader
Verplanken, Bas, PhD Ley. Prof.
Other Staff: 3 Lectrs.
Research: communication and perception of risk; innovation; public understanding of science; science and culture; science communication

Socio-Cultural and Activity Research, Centre for

Cannon, Paul S., BSc S'ton., PhD S'ton., FREng, FIETE Prof.
Daniels, Harry R. J., BSc Liv., PhD Lond.Inst. Prof.
Other Staff: 3 Lectrs.

Space, Atmospheric and Oceanic Science, Centre for

E-mail: n.j.mitchell@bath.ac.uk
Blondel, Phillipe, MPhys Paris, PhD Paris Sr. Lectr.
Cannon, Paul S., BSc S'ton., PhD S'ton., FREng, FIETE Prof.
Davies, Steven R., BSc Sheff., MSc Leic., PhD Kent Sr. Lectr.
Mitchell, Nicolas J., BSc Sheff., PhD Sheff., FRAS Prof.; Dir.*
Pace, Nicholas G., BSc Durh., PhD Durh. Prof.†

Strategic Purchasing and Supply, Centre for Research into

Tel: (01225) 383492 Fax: (01225) 383223
E-mail: crisps@management.bath.ac.uk
Harland, Christine, BA CNAA, PhD Warw. Prof.; Dir.*
Research: e-business; managing supply networks; public sector supply; supply in health sector; supply strategy

Sustainable Power Distribution, Centre for

Aggarwal, Raj K., BEng Liv., PhD Liv., FIETE, FRSA Prof.; Dir.*
Dunn, Roderick W., BSc Bath, PhD Bath Sr. Lectr.
Redfern, Miles A., BSc Nott., PhD Camb. Sr. Lectr.
Other Staff: 2 Lectrs.; 1 Visiting Fellow

WeD–The Wellbeing in Developing Countries ESRC Research Group

Tel: (01225) 384514 Fax: (01225) 384848
E-mail: wed@bath.ac.uk
Copestake, James G., BA Camb., MSc Reading, PhD Reading Sr. Lectr.
Gough, Ian R., BA Camb., MA Camb., AcSS Prof., Social Policy
McGregor, J. Allister, BA Stir., PhD Bath Reader; Dir.*
Other Staff: 14 Res. Staff
Research: development of conceptual and methodological framework for understanding the social and cultural construction of wellbeing in specific developing societies (framework being developed and tested in Bangladesh, Ethiopia, Peru and Thailand); poverty, inequality and quality of life in developing countries

Window and Cladding Technology, Centre for

Tel: (01225) 386541 Fax: (01225) 386556
E-mail: cwct@bath.ac.uk
Ledbetter, Stephen R., BSc Dund., PhD Brist. Sr. Lectr.; Dir.*
Research: building management (failure mode and effects analysis, supply chain analysis); building materials (durability, finishes, glass, metals); building physics (advanced glazings, condensation, photovoltaics); facade engineering (construction, performance, specification, weathertightness); structural engineering (facade structure interaction, structural use of glass)

WISSP–The Wiltshire Partnership

Tel: (01225) 386949 E-mail: wissp@bath.ac.uk
Cramp, Julia Dir.*

Women's Studies Centre

Tel: (01225) 386876 Fax: (01225) 386099
E-mail: r.j.marsh@bath.ac.uk
Bull, Anna, MA Reading, DottLett Naples, PhD Reading Prof.
Diamond, Hanna E., BA Sus., DPhil Sus. Sr. Lectr.
Giorgio, Adalgisa, DottLing Naples, PhD Reading Sr. Lectr.; Dir.*
Haste, Helen E., BA Lond., MPhil Sus., PhD Prof.†
Marsh, Rosalind J., MA Camb., DPhil Oxf. Prof.
Marshall, Judi A., BA Manc., PhD Manc. Prof.
Millar, Jane, OBE, BA Sus., MA Brun., DPhil York(UK), FRSA Prof.
Tate, George D., BA Trinity(Dub.), MA McM., PhD Warw. Prof.
White, Anne, BA Oxf., PhD Lond. Sr. Lectr.
Other Staff: 7 Lectrs.
Research: feminist methodology, gender and culture; gender and social welfare; women in contemporary Europe: society, culture; women in management; women's psychology and health

Work and Employment Research Centre

Tel: (01225) 386028 Fax: (01225) 386473
E-mail: j.purcell@bath.ac.uk
Colville, Ian, BSc Cardiff, MSc Bath, PhD Bath Sr. Lectr.
Cressey, Peter, BA York(UK), MA York(UK) Reader
Kinnie, Nicholas J., BSc UMIST, MA Warw., PhD Warw. Reader

Purcell, John, MA *Camb.*, MSc *Lond.*, DLitt *Oxf.*
    Prof.; Dir.*
Pye, Annie, BSc PhD   Reader
Other Staff: 3 Lectrs.
Research: corporate governance; change
    management and leadership; employee
    relations of contingent workers; human
    resource management and performance in
    the health sector; knowledge workers in
    professional service firms; strategic human
    resource management and performance

CONTACT OFFICERS

Admissions (first degree). Assistant Registrar:
    Hennessey, Lee, BA *Essex*
    (E-mail: admissions@bath.ac.uk)
Admissions (higher degree). Assistant
    Registrar: Isted, Lisa, BA *Brist.*, PhD *Brist.*
    (E-mail: grad-office@bath.ac.uk)
Adult/continuing education. Director,
    Division for Lifelong Learning: Butt, Faith,
    BA *Durh.*, MA *Reading*, PhD *Reading*, FRSA
    (E-mail: f.butt@bath.ac.uk)
Alumni. Director of Development and Alumni
    Relations: Lutley, Sion, BSc *Bath*
    (E-mail: s.lutley@bath.ac.uk)
Archives. University Archivist: Richmond,
    Elizabeth, MA *St And.*, MA *York(UK)*
    (E-mail: e.richmond@bath.ac.uk)
Careers. Careers Advisor: Hay, Diane, BA *Stir.*
    (E-mail: d.hay@bath.ac.uk)
Computing services. Director of Computing
    Services: Angood, Rod, BA *Open(UK)*, MBA
    Luton (E-mail: ccrsaa@bath.ac.uk)
Consultancy services. Head of KTP and
    Consultancy Services: Cockayne, David,
    BTech *Lough.*
Credit transfer. Academic Registrar: Price,
    Alison, BA *Kent*, MBA *Bourne.*
    (E-mail: adsabjp@bath.ac.uk)

Development/fund-raising. Director of
    Development and Alumni Relations: Lutley,
    Sion, BSc *Bath* (E-mail: s.lutley@bath.ac.uk)
Distance education. Director, Division for
    Lifelong Learning: Butt, Faith, BA *Durh.*, MA
    Reading, PhD *Reading*, FRSA
    (E-mail: f.butt@bath.ac.uk)
Equal opportunities. Human Resources
    Manager: Bertrand, Marlene, BEd *Brist.*, MA
    Warw. (E-mail: m.a.bertrand@bath.ac.uk)
Estates and buildings/works and services.
    Director of Estates: Finch, Patrick, MBA,
    FRICS (E-mail: m.p.finch@bath.ac.uk)
Examinations. Senior Assistant Registrar
    (Examinations): Harris, John, BA *Lond.*, PhD
    Lond. (E-mail: j.harris@bath.ac.uk)
Finance. Director of Finance: Aderyn, Diane,
    BA *Newcastle(UK)*, MA(Econ) *Manc.*
    (E-mail: d.aderyn@bath.ac.uk)
International office. Senior Assistant Registrar
    (International office): Howman, Andrew,
    BA *Nott.*
    (E-mail: international-office@bath.ac.uk)
Library (chief librarian). Librarian:
    Nicholson, Howard, MA *Sus.*
    (E-mail: h.d.nicholson@bath.ac.uk)
Marketing. Director of Communications and
    Development: Reader, Peter, BA *Leeds*
    (E-mail: p.j.reader@bath.ac.uk)
Ombudsman. Postgraduate Ombudsman:
    Threadgill, Michael D., MA *Camb.*, PhD
    Camb., DSc *Bath*
    (E-mail: m.d.threadgill@bath.ac.uk)
Personnel/human resources. Director of
    Human Resources: Williams, Sue, BA
    (E-mail: hr@bath.ac.uk)
Public relations. Director of Communications
    and Development: Reader, Peter, BA *Leeds*
    (E-mail: p.j.reader@bath.ac.uk)
Publications. Director of Communications and
    Development: Reader, Peter, BA *Leeds*
    (E-mail: p.j.reader@bath.ac.uk)

Purchasing. Head of Purchasing Services:
    Andrews, Joanne
    (E-mail: j.m.andrews@bath.ac.uk)
Quality assurance and accreditation. Head of
    Learning and Teaching Enhancement: Van
    der Velden, Gwen
    (E-mail: g.m.vandervelden@bath.ac.uk)
Safety. Head of Safety, Health and
    Environment: Horne, Kevan, BSc *Hudd.*, MA
    Open(UK) (E-mail: safety@bath.ac.uk)
Scholarships, awards, loans. Student Finance
    Officer: Woosey-Griffin, Marica R. S., BSc
    Liv. (E-mail: m.woosey-griffin@bath.ac.uk)
Security. Head of Security: Schofield, Brian
    (E-mail: b.schofield@bath.ac.uk)
Sport and recreation. Director of Sports
    Development and Recreation: Roddy, Ged,
    MBE, BA *Birm.* (E-mail: g.roddy@bath.ac.uk)
Staff development and training. Head of Staff
    Development: Inger, Simon, BSc
    Newcastle(UK), PhD *Open(UK)*
    (E-mail: s.inger@bath.ac.uk)
Student union. General Manager: Robinson,
    Ian W., BA *CNAA*
    (E-mail: i.robinson@bath.ac.uk)
Student welfare/counselling. Student
    Counsellor: Davies, Elizabeth V., MA *Edin.*
    (E-mail: e.v.davies@bath.ac.uk)
Students from other countries. Senior
    Assistant Registrar (Students from other
    countries): Howman, Andrew, BA *Nott.*
    (E-mail: international-office@bath.ac.uk)
Students with disabilities. Head of Student
    Services: Ames, Mark, BA *Birm.*
    (E-mail: m.f.ames@bath.ac.uk)
University press. Librarian: Nicholson,
    Howard, MA *Sus.*
    (E-mail: h.d.nicholson@bath.ac.uk)

[*Information supplied by the institution as at 20
December 2007, and edited by the ACU*]

BATH SPA UNIVERSITY

Founded 2005

Member of the Association of Commonwealth Universities

Postal Address: Newton St Loe, Bath, England BA2 9BN
Telephone: (01225) 875875 **Fax:** (01225) 875444
URL: http://www.bathspa.ac.uk/

VICE-CHANCELLOR*—Morgan, Prof. Frank, BA *Lond.*, MSc *City(UK)*
DEPUTY VICE-CHANCELLOR AND CLERK TO THE BOARD OF GOVERNORS‡—Dewberry, Anthony E.

GENERAL INFORMATION

First Degrees. BA, BSc.
    Length of course. Full-time: BA, BSc: 3 years.
    Part-time: BA, BSc: 5 years.

Higher Degrees.
    Master's. MA, MSc.
    Length of course. Full-time: MA, MSc: 1 year.
    Part-time: MA, MSc: 2 years.
    Doctoral. PhD.
    Length of course. Full-time: PhD: 3 years. *Part-
    time:* PhD: 7 years.

Statistics. Students (2008): international 134;
undergraduate 4564; master's 1766; doctoral
56.

FACULTIES/SCHOOLS

Art and Design, Bath School of

Head: George, Prof. Ron, MA *RCA*

Development and Participation

Head: Hamilton, Derek, BA *CNAA*, MA *Brist.*

Education

Head: Ward, Prof. Stephen, BA *Warw.*, MA
    Leeds, PhD *Bath Spa*

English and Creative Studies

Head: Middleton, Prof. Tim, BA *Kent*, MA
    Warw., PhD *Kent*

Historical and Cultural Studies

Head: Montgomery, Prof. Fiona, MA *Glas.*, PhD
    Glas.

Music and Performing Arts

Head: Smith, Prof. Geoff, BA *Nott.*, MPhil *Oxf.*,
    PhD *Hudd.*

Science and the Environment

Head: Dyson, Allan, MSc *Reading*

Social Sciences

Head: Mears, Prof. Rob, BSc *Leic.*, MSc *Lond.*,
    PhD *Leic.*

UNIVERSITY OF BEDFORDSHIRE

Postal Address: Park Square, Luton, Bedfordshire, England LU1 3JU
Telephone: (01234) 400400 Fax: (01582) 489362
URL: http://www.beds.ac.uk

VICE-CHANCELLOR*—Ebdon, Prof. Les C., BSc ICL, PhD ICL, FRSChem
REGISTRAR‡—Franklin, James, BSc Leeds, PhD Leeds

QUEEN'S UNIVERSITY BELFAST

Founded 1908

Member of the Association of Commonwealth Universities

Postal Address: Belfast, Northern Ireland BT7 1NN
Telephone: (028) 9024 5133 Fax: (028) 9097 5137
URL: http://www.qub.ac.uk

PRESIDENT AND VICE-CHANCELLOR*—Gregson, Prof. Peter J., BSc(Eng) Lond., PhD Lond., FREng, FIMMM, FIE(Ireland)
PRO-VICE-CHANCELLOR—Brown, Prof. Kenneth D., BA Reading, MA McM., PhD Kent, FRHistS
PRO-VICE-CHANCELLOR—Mann, Prof. John, BSc Lond., PhD Lond., DSc Lond., FRSChem
PRO-VICE-CHANCELLOR—McCormac, Prof. Francis G., BSc PhD, FRSA, FSA
REGISTRAR AND CHIEF OPERATING OFFICER‡—O'Kane, James P. J., BA CNAA
HONORARY TREASURER—Prenter, Stephen, BSSc, FCA
DIRECTOR OF FINANCE—Bennett, W. Norman, BSc(Econ)

GENERAL INFORMATION

History. The university, founded in 1908, was previously established as Queen's College, Belfast (1845) and (linked with colleges in Cork and Galway) as Queen's University in Ireland (1850).

The main university site is situated 1 mile from the centre of Belfast.

Admission to first degree courses (see also United Kingdom Introduction). Through Universities and Colleges Admissions Service (UCAS). General requirement: (1) General Certificate of Secondary Education (GCSE), General Certificate of Education (GCE) and Vocational Certificate of Education (VCE) A and AS level, and Scottish Certificate of Education (SCE) ordinary grade and higher grade, with passes in 5 subjects including English language, of which 3 should be at A level (or, for SCE, all 4 at higher grade); (2) Business and Technology Education Council (BTEC) National or Higher National Certificate or Diploma; (3) Advanced General National Vocational Qualification (GNVQ); (4) International Baccalaureate/Diploma; (5) Irish Leaving Certificate, with passes in 5 subjects including English. An approved test in English may be offered in place of English language.

First Degrees (see also United Kingdom Directory to Subjects of Study). BA, BD, BDS, BEd, BEng, BMus, BSc, BTh, LLB, MB BCh BAO, MEng, MPharm, MSci.
Length of course. Full-time: BD, BMus, BTh, LLB: 3 years; BA, BEng, BSc: 3–4 years; BEd, MEng, MPharm, MSci: 4 years; BDS, MB BCh BAO: 5 years. Part-time: BA, BD, BTh: 5 years.

Higher Degrees (see also United Kingdom Directory to Subjects of Study).
Master's. BArch, BSW, LLM, MA, MBA, MD, MEd, MMedSc, MPhil, MSc, MSSc, MTh.
Length of course. Full-time: LLM, MMedSc, MSc, MSSc, MTh: 1 year; MA, MD, MPhil: 1–2 years; BArch: 2 years; BSW: 2–3 years. Part-time: LLM, MBA, MEd, MTh: 2 years; MA, MD, MPhil, MSc, MSSc: 2–3 years.
Doctoral. DLitt, DSc, EdD, LLD, PhD.

Length of course. Full-time: EdD, PhD: 3 years. Part-time: EdD: 4 years; PhD: 6 years.

Academic Awards (2005–2006). 225 awards ranging in value from £690 to £25,300.

Income (2006–2007). Total, £240,989,000.

Statistics. Staff (2006–2007): 3516 (1103 academic, 2413 non-academic). Students (2006–2007): total 19,428.

FACULTIES/SCHOOLS

Arts, Humanities and Social Sciences
Tel: (028) 9097 5347 Fax: (028) 9097 5071
E-mail: deansofficeahss@qub.ac.uk
Dean: Douglas-Cowie, Prof. Ellen E., BA Ulster, PhD Ulster

Engineering and Physical Sciences
Tel: (028) 9097 5443 Fax: (028) 9097 4536
E-mail: deaneps@qub.ac.uk
Dean: Millar, Prof. T. J., BSc Manc., PhD Manc., DSc Manc., FRAS

Medicine, Health and Life Sciences
Tel: (028) 9097 5177 Fax: (028) 9043 4454
E-mail: dean-mhls@qub.ac.uk
Dean: McElnay, Prof. James C., BSc Belf., PhD Belf.

ACADEMIC UNITS
Arranged by Schools

Biological Sciences
Tel: (028) 9097 5786 Fax: (028) 9097 5788
E-mail: sobb.office@qub.ac.uk
Ames, J. M., BSc Reading, PhD Lond.   Prof., Human Nutrition and Health
Dick, J. T. A., BSc Glas., PhD Belf.   Reader
Dring, M. J., BSc Brist., PhD Lond.   Prof., Marine Biology
Elliott, C., MSc Ulster, PhD Belf.   Prof., Food Safety
Elwood, R. W., BSc Reading, PhD Reading   Prof., Animal Behaviour

Fairweather, I., BSc Lond., MSc Liv., PhD Lond.   Reader, Biology
Hutchinson, W. G., BA(Econ) Durh., MBA Belf., PhD Belf.   Prof., Rural and Environmental Economics
Laming, P. R., BSc Reading, PhD Lond.   Reader
Larkin, M. J., BSc CNAA, PhD Wales   Sr. Lectr.
Maggs, C. A., BA Oxf., PhD N.U.I.   Prof., Marine Biology
Marks, N., BSc Belf., PhD Belf.   Reader
Maule, A. G., BSc Belf., PhD Belf.   Prof., Molecular Parasitology
McGrath, J. W., BSc Belf., PhD Belf.
Montgomery, W. I., BSc Manc., PhD Manc.   Prof., Animal Ecology; Head*
Nelson, J., BSc Belf., PhD Belf.   Reader
Paxton, R., BSc Sus., DPhil Sus.   Reader
Prodohl, P., MSc Rio Grande Coll., PhD Belf.   Reader
Quinn, J. P., BSc Wales, DPhil Ulster   Reader
Roberts, D., BSc Liv., PhD Liv., FIBiol   Sr. Lectr.
Savidge, G. J., BSc Wales, PhD Wales   Reader
Other Staff: 27 Lectrs.; 1 Sr. Teaching Fellow; 1 Sr. Res. Officer; 2 Teaching Fellows
Research: bioremediation of pollutants; impact of introduced species and strains; molecular basis of infectious disease; molecular discrimination and affinities of natural populations; sustainable development

Biomedical Sciences
Tel: (028) 9097 5858 Fax: (028) 9097 2124
E-mail: sbs.office@qub.ac.uk
Gardiner, Tom A., PhD Belf.   Reader; Dir., Undergrad. Educn.
Rima, Bertus K., MSc T.H.Delft, PhD McM., FIBiol   Prof., Molecular Biology; Head*

Chemistry and Chemical Engineering
Tel: (028) 9097 5418 Fax: (028) 9097 4687
E-mail: chemistry@qub.ac.uk
Ahmad, Mohammad N., BSc Jordan, MSc Jordan, PhD Belf.   Sr. Lectr.
Allen, S. J., BSc Belf., PhD Belf., FIChemE   Du Pont Prof.
Bell, Steven E. J., BSc PhD   Sr. Lectr.
Burch, Robbie, BSc Belf., PhD Belf., DSc Belf.   Prof., Physical Chemistry; Head*

De Silva, Amilra P., BSc Ceyl., PhD Belf.   Prof.,
Organic Chemistry
Gan, Q., MSc Salf., PhD Wales(Swansea), BEng
Co-ordinator, MSc in Process Engin.; Sr.
Lectr., Process Engineering
Hale, Karl J., BSc Lond., PhD Lond.   Prof.; Chair
of Organic and Medicinal Chem. and
Chem. Biol.
Hardacre, Christopher B. A., PhD Camb.   Sr.
Lectr.
Holland, Clive R., BSc(Tech) Sheff., PhD Sheff.
Sr. Lectr.
Hu, Peijun M. S., PhD Camb.   Reader
James, S., BSc Brist., PhD Brist.   Reader
Magee, T. Ronald A., BSc Belf., PhD Belf.   Prof.
Malone, J. F., BSc N.U.I., PhD Leeds, DSc Belf.
Sr. Lectr.
Mann, John, BSc Lond., PhD Lond., DSc Lond.,
FRSChem   Prof., Organic Chemistry
Migaud, M. E., BSc E.N.S.de Chim., Paris, PhD
Mich.   Sr. Lectr.
Rogers, Robin, BS Alabama, PhD Alabama   Prof.,
Green Chemistry
Rooney, D. R., BSc Belf., PhD Belf.   Co-
ordinator, MSc in Process Engin.; Sr. Lectr.,
Process Engineering
Seddon, Kenneth R., BSc Liv., MA Oxf., PhD Liv.
Prof.
Stevenson, Paul J., BSc Sheff., PhD Belf.   Sr.
Lectr.
Walker, Gavin, BEng Belf., PhD Belf.   Sr. Lectr.
Other Staff: 10 Lectrs.; 1 Res. Fellow; 2
Academic Fellows
Research: catalysis; molecular materials; synthetic
and bio-organic chemistry

Education, School of

Tel: (028) 9097 5941 Fax: (028) 9023 9263
E-mail: education@qub.ac.uk
Connolly, P., BSocSc Birm., MA Warw., MSc
Sheff.Hallam, PhD Leic.   Prof.
Elwood, J., BSc Ulster, MA Lond., PhD Lond.
Prof.
Gallagher, A. M., MSc Belf., PhD Belf.   Prof.;
Head*
Gardner, J. R., MSc Belf., PhD Belf.   Prof.
Hughes, J., BA Belf., PhD Belf.   Prof.
Jay, R., MA Oxf., MPhil Oxf.   Sr. Lectr.
Leitch, M. R., MA Dund., MSc Belf., EdD Brist.
Sr. Lectr.
Lundy, L., LLB Belf., LLM Belf.   Reader
Mark, R. D., BSc Ulster, MEd Glas., MA Hull,
MSc Dublin City, PhD Roskilde   Sr. Lectr.
Mezey, Nicole J. A., BA Sus., MA York(UK)   Sr.
Lectr.
Murphy, C. A., BSc Belf., MSc Belf., MEd Belf.,
PhD Wales   Sr. Lectr.
Other Staff: 17 Lectrs.; 2 Sr. Teaching Fellows;
12 Teaching Fellows
Research: children's rights and participation in
education; contexts of teaching, learning
and assessment; education in divided
societies

Electronics, Electrical Engineering and Computer Science

Tel: (028) 9097 5437 Fax: (028) 9066 7023
Armstrong, B. M., BSc Belf., PhD Belf.   Reader
Armstrong, G. A., BSc Belf., PhD Belf.   Prof.,
Electronic Engineering
Cahill, R., BSc Aston, PhD Kent   Reader
Cowan, C. F. N., BSc Edin., PhD Edin., FIEE
Royal Acad. of Engin./Nortel Telecom
Networks Res. Prof., Telecommunications
Flynn, D., MEng Belf., PhD Belf.   Sr. Lectr.
Fox, B., BSc Belf., PhD Belf.   Reader
Fusco, V. F., BSc Belf., PhD Belf., DSc Belf., FIEE,
FIEEE, FREng   Prof., High Frequency
Engineering
Gamble, H. S., BSc Belf., PhD Belf.   Prof.,
Microelectronic Engineering
Hogg, B. W., BE N.U.I., PhD Liv., DSc N.U.I.,
FIEE, FIAE   Prof. Emer., Electrical
Engineering
Irwin, G. W., BSc Belf., PhD Belf., DSc Belf.,
FREng, FIEEE, FIEE   Dir., Virtual Learning
Centre; Prof., Control Engineering
Linton, D., BSc Belf., PhD Belf.   Reader

Marshall, A. J., BSc Ulster, PhD Aberd.   Prof.,
Telecomms. Engin./Computer Networks/
Digital Comms.
McCanny, J. V., CBE, BSc Manc., DPhil Ulster,
DSc Belf., FRS, FREng, FIEEE, FIAE, FIP,
FRSA   Dir., Inst. of Electronics,
Communications and Information Technol.
(ECIT); Prof., Microelectronics Engineering;
Head*
Mitchell, S. J. N., BSc Belf., PhD Belf.   Sr. Lectr.
Morrow, D. J., BSc Belf., PhD Belf.   Reader
Scanlon, W., BEng Ulster, PhD Ulster   Sr. Lectr.
Schuchinsky, A. G., MSc Rostov State, PhD
Leningrad   Reader
Sellathurai, M., PhD   Reader
Stewart, J. A. C., BSc Belf., PhD Belf., FIEE
Prof. Emer., Electrical Communications
Wang, H. F.
Wilkinson, A. J., BSc Belf., PhD Belf., FIEE   Sr.
Lectr.
Woods, R. F., BSc Belf., PhD Belf., FIEE   Prof.,
Digital Communications
Other Staff: 2 Visiting Profs.; 11 Lectrs.; 14
Res. Fellows
Research: digital communications; electrical
power and energy systems; high-frequency
electronic circuits; intelligent systems and
control microelectronics; semiconductors
and nanotechnology

Computer Science

Tel: (028) 9097 4626 Fax: (028) 9097 5666
E-mail: comp.sci@qub.ac.uk
Bell, D. A., BSc Belf., MPhil Ulster, PhD Ulster,
DSc Ulster   Prof.
Bouridane, A., MEng Algiers, MPhil
Newcastle(UK), PhD Nott.   Reader
Corr, P. H., BSc Belf., PhD Belf.   Sr. Lectr.
Crookes, D., BSc Belf., PhD Belf.   Prof.
Greenwood, L., BSc MSc DPhil   Sr. Lectr.
Hong, J., BSc Jilin, MSc Jilin, PhD Ulster   Sr.
Lectr.
Kilpatrick, P. L., BSc Belf., PhD Belf.   Sr. Lectr.
Liu, W., BSc Jilin, MSc Jilin, PhD Edin.   Reader
McKeag, R. M., BSc Lond., MSc Lond., FBCS   Sr.
Lectr.
Middleton, P., BA Manc., MSc Belf., MBA Ulster,
PhD Lond.   Sr. Lectr.
Milligan, P., BSc Belf., PhD Belf.   Sr. Lectr.
Ming, J., BSc Sichuan, MSc Changsha I.T., PhD
Beijing   Reader
Perrott, R. H., BSc Belf., PhD Belf., FBCS, FRSA,
FIEEE, FACM   Prof., Software Engineering
Scott, N. S., BSc Belf., PhD Belf.   Prof.,
Computational Science
Spence, I. T. A., BSc Belf., PhD Belf.   Sr. Lectr.
Other Staff: 15 Lectrs.; 9 Res. Fellows
Research: high-performance and distributed
computing; knowledge and data
engineering; speech, image and vision
systems; system-on-chip architecture and
programmable systems

Engineering, Mechanical and Aerospace

Tel: (028) 9097 4138 Fax: (028) 9066 1729
E-mail: mech.aero@qub.ac.uk
Armstrong, Cecil G., BSc Belf., PhD Belf.   Prof.
Armstrong, Perry J., BSc Belf., PhD Belf.   Sr.
Lectr.
Artt, David W., BSc Belf., PhD Belf.   Reader
Buchanan, Fraser, BSc(Eng) Lond., PhD Camb.
Sr. Lectr.
Cooper, R. K., BEng Syd., PhD Syd.   Sr. Lectr.
Curran, R. C., BEng Belf., PhD Belf.   Sr. Lectr.
Douglas, Roy, BSc Belf., PhD Belf.   Prof.
Fleck, Robert, BSc Belf., PhD Belf., DSc Belf.
Prof.; Head*
Harkin-Jones, Eileen A., BEng N.U.I., PhD Belf.
Prof.
Hinds, Brendan K., BSc Belf., PhD Belf.   Sr.
Lectr.
Hornsby, Peter, PhD Brun., BSc, FRSChem,
FIMMM   Prof.
Kee, Robert J., BSc Belf., PhD Belf.   Sr. Lectr.
Kenny, Robert G., BSc Belf., PhD Belf.   Sr.
Lectr.
Martin, Peter J., MEng Belf., PhD Belf.   Sr.
Lectr.

McCartney, Jim, BSc Belf., PhD Belf.   Sr. Lectr.
McCullough, Geoffrey, BEng Belf., PhD Belf.
Sr. Lectr.
Orr, John F., BSc Belf., PhD Belf., FIMechE,
FIMMM   Prof.
Price, M. A., BEng Belf., MSc Belf., PhD Belf.
Sr. Lectr.
Raghunathan, S. R., OBE, BE Mys., MTech IIT
Bombay, MSc Belf., PhD IIT Bombay, DSc Belf.,
FRAeS   Prof.
Thompson, Steve, BSc Salf., MSc City(UK), PhD
Reader
Watterson, J. K., MEng Belf., PhD Camb.   Sr.
Lectr.
Other Staff: 15 Lectrs.
Research: aerodynamics; aircraft life cycle costs;
design and manufacture; internal
combustion engine and gas turbines;
polymers

English

Tel: (028) 9097 3320 Fax: (028) 9031 4615
E-mail: english@qub.ac.uk
Brearton, Fran, BA Durh., MA Belf., PhD Durh.
Reader
Burnett, Mark T., BA Exe., MA Calif., DPhil Oxf.
Prof.
Caraher, Brian G., BA Wabash, MA N.Y.State,
PhD N.Y.State   Prof.
Carson, Ciaran, BA Belf.   Prof.; Dir., Seamus
Heaney Centre for Poetry
Haslett, Moyra, BA PhD   Sr. Lectr.
Hughes, Eamonn G. P., BA CNAA, MA Leic.,
PhD Leic.   Sr. Lectr.
Kirk, John M., MA Edin., PhD Sheff.   Sr. Lectr.
Larrissy, Edward, BA Oxf., MA Oxf., DPhil Oxf.
Prof.
Litvack, Leon B., BA Tor., MA Lond., PhD Edin.
Reader
Magennis, Hugh, MA Belf., PhD Belf.   Prof.
McGowan, Philip, BA PhD   Sr. Lectr.
Rahilly, Joan, BA Belf., PhD Belf.   Sr. Lectr.
Roberts, Daniel, BA Madr., MA Hyd., PhD Camb.
Reader
Sheehan, Estelle, BA Belf., PhD Belf.   Prof.
Simpson, Paul W., BA Ulster, DPhil Ulster   Prof.
Thompson, John J., MA Belf., DPhil York(UK),
MA   Prof.; Head*
Other Staff: 14 Lectrs.; 5 Res. Fellows
Research: English language and linguistics;
mediaeval studies (Old and Middle
English); modern literary studies (1700 to
present); poetry and Irish writing,
including creative writing; Renaissance
studies

Geography, Archaeology and Palaeocology

Tel: (028) 9097 5140 Fax: (028) 9097 3212
E-mail: gap@qub.ac.uk

Archaeology and Palaeoecology

Tel: (028) 9097 3186 Fax: (028) 903897
E-mail: arcpal@qub.ac.uk
Baillie, M. G., PhD Belf.   Prof. Emer.
Bennett, K. D., MA Camb., PhD Camb.   Prof.
Gardiner, M., BA Wales, PhD Lond., FSA   Sr.
Lectr.
Hall, V. A., BSc Belf., PhD Belf.   Prof.
Hunt, C. O., MSc Sheff., PhD Wales, FGS
Reader
Mallory, J. P., AB Calif., PhD Calif.   Prof.
Malone, C. A. T., MA Camb., PhD Camb.   Sr.
Lectr.
McCormick, F. M., BA N.U.I., MA N.U.I., PhD
Belf.
McNeill, T. E., MA Oxf., PhD Belf., FSA   Sr.
Lectr.
Murphy, E. M., MSc Sheff., PhD Belf.
Pilcher, J. R., PhD Belf.   Prof. Emer.
Reimer, P. J., PhD Wash.   Sr. Lectr.
Other Staff: 3 Lectrs.; 6 Res. Fellows
Research: archaeological fieldwork; radio-carbon
and isotopes

Geography

Tel: (028) 9097 3350
E-mail: geog.office@qub.ac.uk

Anderson, J., BA Belf., MA Alta.   Prof. Emer.
Betts, N. L., BSc Belf., PhD Belf.   Sr. Lectr.
Boal, F. W., BA Belf., MA Belf., MS Mich., PhD Mich.   Prof. Emer.
Campbell, B. M. S., BA Liv., PhD Camb., FRHistS Prof.
Johnson, N., BA N.U.I., MA N.U.I., PhD Syr.   Reader
Lilley, K. D., BA Birm., PhD Birm.   Sr. Lectr.
Livingstone, D. N., OBE, BA Belf., PhD Belf., FBA, FRSA   Prof.
Orford, J. D., BA Keele, MSc Salf., PhD Reading   Prof., Physical Geography; Head*
Proudfoot, L. J., BA Belf., MA Birm., PhD Belf.   Reader
Royle, S. A., MA Camb., PhD Leic.   Reader
Ruffell, A., BSc Lond., PhD Birm., FGS   Sr. Lectr.
Schwarzacher, W., PhD Innsbruck   Prof. Emer.
Shuttleworth, I. G., BSocSci Leic., MA CNAA, PhD Trinity(Dub.)   Sr. Lectr.
Smith, B. J., BSc Reading, PhD Reading   Prof., Geomorphology
Tomlinson, R. W., BSc Hull, PhD Hull   Sr. Lectr.
Whalley, W. B., BSc Leic., PhD Camb.   Prof., Physical Geography
Other Staff: 8 Lectrs.; 2 Res. Fellows
Research: data digitisation and analysis; environmental change; past cultural change; society, space and culture

History and Anthropology

Tel: (028) 9097 5101 Fax: (028) 9097 3440
E-mail: history@qub.ac.uk
Campbell, J. Brian, BA Belf., DPhil Oxf.   Prof., Roman History
Clinton, Catherine, AB Harv., MA Sus., DPhil Prin.   Prof., American History
Connolly, S. J., BA N.U.I., DPhil Ulster   Prof., Irish History
Curran, J., BA Belf., DPhil Oxf.   Sr. Lectr., Ancient History
Flanagan, Marie T., MA N.U.I., DPhil Oxf., FRHistS   Prof., Mediaeval History
Gray, Peter, BA Camb., PhD Camb., FRHistS   Prof., Modern Irish History
Hayton, D. W., BA Manc., DPhil Oxf.   Reader, Early Modern British and Irish History; Head*
Jeffery, Keith, MA Camb., PhD Camb., FRHistS   Prof., British History
Kelly, Brian, PhD Brandeis   Sr. Lectr., American History
Kennedy, Liam, MSc N.U.I., DPhil York(UK)   Prof., Economic and Social History
Marsh, C. W., BA Camb., PhD Camb.   Reader, Early Modern History
McGarry, Fearghal, BA N.U.I., PhD Trinity(Dub.)   Sr. Lectr., Irish History
O'Connell, Sean, BA Northumbria, PhD Warw.   Sr. Lectr., Modern British History
O'Dowd, Mary, BA N.U.I., PhD N.U.I.   Reader, Irish History
Whitehead, David, MA Camb., PhD Camb.   Prof., Ancient History
Other Staff: 12 Lectrs.; 1 Sr. Teaching Fellow; 1 Res. Fellow
Research: ancient and mediaeval history; modern European and global history; modern Irish and British history

Anthropological Studies

Tel: (028) 9097 3701 Fax: (028) 9097 3700
E-mail: anthropology@qub.ac.uk
Bering, Jesse M., BA Florida Atlantic, MS Louisiana State, PhD Florida Atlantic   Reader
Bowler, P. J., BA Camb., MSc Sus., PhD Tor.   Prof.
Donnan, H. S. C., BA Sus., DPhil Sus., FRAI   Prof.
Josephides, L., BA Lond., PhD Lond.   Reader
Milton, K., BA Durh., PhD Belf.   Prof.
Reily, S. A., BA Salzburg, MA Indiana, PhD Sao Paulo   Reader
Other Staff: 5 Lectrs.; 1 Sr. Teaching Fellow
Research: ethnomusicology; history of science; social anthropology

Languages, Literatures and Performing Arts

Tel: (028) 9097 5363 Fax: (028) 9032 4549
E-mail: modern.languages@qub.ac.uk
Johnston, David W., BA Belf., PhD Belf.   Head*
Research: folklore; language and linguistics; literary studies; theory and practice of film and drama; theory and practice of translation for the stage

Drama Studies

Tel: (028) 9097 5231
E-mail: drama.studies@qub.ac.uk
McMullan, Anna, MA St And., MA Lond., PhD Reading   Prof.; Head*
Other Staff: 5 Lectrs.
Research: actor training; Beckett in performance; gender representation; twentieth-century Irish theatre; Ulster literary theatre

Film Studies

Tel: (028) 9097 5364
E-mail: p.mcmurray@qub.ac.uk
Bell, Desmond L., BA Warw., PhD Warw.   Prof.; Head*
Other Staff: 4 Lectrs.
Research: documentary cinema; French cinema; Irish avant garde cinema; Irish cinema and film theory; Soviet cinema

French Studies

Tel: (028) 9097 5365
E-mail: french@qub.ac.uk
Carruthers, K. Janice, MA Camb., MPhil Camb., PhD Camb.   Sr. Lectr.; Head*
Davies, Simon F., MA Exe., PhD Exe.   Prof.
Lewis, John M., BA Lond., PhD Lond.   Sr. Lectr.
Tame, Peter D., BA Lond., PhD Lond.   Reader
Other Staff: 6 Lectrs.
Research: Caribbean and post-colonial literature and theory; eighteenth-century novel and theatre; French linguistics; French Renaissance, especially Rabelais; literature, politics and society in nineteenth- and twentieth-century France

German Studies

Tel: (028) 9097 5364 Fax: (028) 9032 4547
E-mail: e.childs@qub.ac.uk
Robb, David, MA Edin., PhD Sheff.   Sr. Lectr.; Head*
Other Staff: 2 Lectrs.; 1 DAAD Lector
Research: drama and political song; German music

Irish and Celtic Studies

Tel: (028) 9097 5366 E-mail: celtic@qub.ac.uk
Andrews, Rhian M., BA Wales, MPhil N.U.I., PhD Belf.   Sr. Lectr.
Ò Baoill, Dónall P., BA N.U.I., MA Mich., PhD Mich.   Prof.; Head*
Other Staff: 3 Lectrs.; 2 Res. Fellows
Research: Irish linguistics; Irish place names; Irish-Scottish connections; mediaeval Irish genealogies; mediaeval Welsh poetry

Spanish and Portuguese Studies

Tel: (028) 9097 5362
E-mail: spanish@qub.ac.uk
Johnston, David W., BA Belf., PhD Belf.   Prof., Hispanic Studies
McMullan, T. P. S., BA Belf., PhD Belf.   Sr. Lectr.
Sanchez Espinoza, G., Lic Madrid, PhD Duisburg   Reader
Torres, Isabel M. B., BA Belf., PhD Belf.   Sr. Lectr.; Head*
Other Staff: 4 Lectrs.
Research: Enlightenment studies; Golden Age studies; Latin American studies (Mexico); twentieth-century Portuguese literature and culture; twentieth-century Spanish literature and culture

Law

Tel: (028) 9097 3451 Fax: (028) 9097 3376
E-mail: law-enquiries@qub.ac.uk
Allain, Jean, BA Car., MA Brock, DPA Laur., LLM Geneva, PhD Geneva   Sr. Lectr., Public International Law and Human Rights
Anthony, G., LLB Belf., MSSc Belf., PhD Belf.   Sr. Lectr., Administrative Law
Capper, D. J. S., LLB Belf., LLM Camb.   Reader, Private Law
Conway, H., LLB Belf., PhD Belf.   Sr. Lectr., Comparative Commonwealth Property Law, Land Law
Dawson, N. M., LLB Belf.   Prof., Commercial and Property Law
Doran, S., LLB Belf., MPhil Camb.   Hon. Prof., Public Law
Dowling, J. A., LLB Belf., PhD Belf.   Sr. Lectr., Private Law
Geary, R. V., LLM Glas., Hon. LLB Strath.   Sr. Lectr., Jurisprudence
Grattan, S., LLB Belf.   Sr. Lectr., Private Law
Hadden, Tom B., BA Camb., LLB Camb., PhD Camb.   Hon. Prof., Human Rights
Harvey, Colin, LLB Lanc., PhD Nott.   Prof., Human Rights
•Jackson, J. D., BA Durh., LLM Wales   Prof., Public Law; Head*
Leith, P., BSc Edin., PhD Open(UK)   Prof., Jurisprudence
McEvoy, K., LLB Belf., MSc Edin., PhD Belf.   Prof., Criminology
Morison, J. W. E., LLB Wales, PhD Wales   Prof., Jurisprudence
O'Brien, J., BA Newcastle(UK), MA Belf., PhD Belf.   Sr. Lectr., Corporate Governance
Scraton, Phil, BA Liv., MA Liv., PhD Lanc.   Prof.
Stannard, J. E., MA Oxf., BCL Oxf., PhD Belf.   Sr. Lectr., Public Law
Turner, Sharon, BCL N.U.I., LLM York(Can.)   Prof., Environmental Law
Wheeler, S., MA Oxf., DPhil Oxf.   Prof., Commercial Law and Socio-Legal Studies
Other Staff: 24 Lectrs.

Management and Economics

Tel: (028) 9097 3683 Fax: (028) 9097 5156
E-mail: sme@qub.ac.uk

Accounting

Tel: (028) 9097 3622
Ballantine, J., BA Ulster, MSc Ulster, PhD Warw.   Sr. Lectr.
Demirag, I. S., BSc Aston, MSc Strath., PhD Glas.   Prof.
Forker, J. J., BSc(Econ) Lond., MSc Lond.   Prof.
Hyndman, N. S., BSc CNAA, PhD   Prof.
Other Staff: 4 Lectrs.
Research: accounting education; corporate governance and performance measurement (including non-financial performance measurement); earnings management; governance, performance measurement and accounting in not-for-profit organisations

Economics

Tel: (028) 9097 3287
Black, J. Boyd H., BA Oxf., MBA Col., MIA Col., PhD   Sr. Lectr.
Bradley, Jim F., BComm N.U.I., BA N.U.I., MEconSc N.U.I.   Sr. Lectr.
McVicar, Duncan, BSc(Econ) Lond., MSc S'ton., PhD S'ton.   Reader; Dir., Res.
Prendergast, Catherine C., BE N.U.I., MEconSc N.U.I., PhD   Reader
Other Staff: 4 Lectrs.; 1 Res. Officer
Vacant Posts: 3 Profs.; 1 Lectr.
Research: applied economics and econometrics; development economics; labour economics; macroeconomics; public economics and social choice

Finance

Fax: (028) 9097 5126
Hickson, C., BA Mich., MSc(Econ) Calif., PhD Calif.   Sr. Lectr.

McKillop, D. G., BSc Ulster, MSc(Econ) Ulster Prof.; Dir. of Res.

Moore, M. J., BA Trinity(Dub.), MSc S'ton., PhD N.U.I. Prof.

Turner, J., BA Ulster, MSc Belf., PhD Belf. Sr. Lectr.

Other Staff: 4 Lectrs.

Vacant Posts: 1 Lectr.

Research: economic and financial institutions; financial markets (foreign exchange, bonds, derivatives and equities); not-for-profit financial institutions

Information Systems

Tel: (028) 9097 5010 Fax: (028) 9097 5126

Philip, G., BSc Kerala, MSc Agra, MSc Sheff., PhD Bom., MIInfSc Prof.; Dir. of Res.*

Webb, B. R., BA Belf., MBA Ulster, PhD Lond. Sr. Lectr.

Other Staff: 4 Lectrs.

Research: evaluation of information systems, e-commerce and e-governance; management of technological change and organisational culture; risk management and IT; role of IT and competencies in competitiveness; strategic information systems management

Management

Tel: (028) 9097 5126

Carey, M., BSc Belf., MSocSci Birm., PhD Birm. Prof.

Catterall, M., BSSc Belf., DBA Belf., PhD Ulster Sr. Lectr.

Crone, M., BA Leeds, PhD Sheff. Sr. Lectr.

Harrison, R., BA Belf., PhD Belf. Prof.; Dir., Res.; Head*

Hewitt-Dundas, N., BA Belf., PhD Belf. Sr. Lectr.

Hill, F. M., BA MBA PhD Sr. Lectr.; Dir., MBA Programme

Jeffcutt, P., BSc Lond., MEd Manc., PhD Manc., FRSA Prof.

Leitch, C., BA Stir., MBA Stir., PhD Ulster Sr. Lectr.

Teague, P., BA E.Anglia, MSc Lond., PhD Lond. Martin Naughton Prof.

Other Staff: 6 Lectrs.

Vacant Posts: 1 Prof.; 1 Sr. Lectr.; 1 Lectr.

Research: entrepreneurship; innovation; organisation development and workplace change; supply chain management; transport logistics

Mathematics and Physics

Tel: (028) 9097 3202 Fax: (028) 9097 3997
E-mail: mp@qub.ac.uk

Keenan, Francis P., BSc Belf., PhD Belf., FRAS Head*

Applied Mathematics and Theoretical Physics

Tel: (028) 9097 3189 Fax: (028) 9023 9182
E-mail: applied.maths@qub.ac.uk

Bell, Prof. Kenneth L., BSc Belf., MA Calif., PhD Belf., FRAS, FAPS, FIP Prof., Theoretical Physics

Burke, Philip G., CBE, BSc Lond., PhD Lond., Hon. DSc Exe., Hon. DSc Belf., FIP, FAPS, FRS Prof. Emer.

Crothers, Derrick S. F., MA Oxf., PhD Belf., FIP, FIMA, FIEE, FAPS Prof., Theoretical Physics

Hibbert, Alan, MA Oxf., DPhil Oxf., FIMA, FAPS, FIP Dir., Educn.; Head, Appl. Maths. Teaching Div.; Prof., Applied Mathematics

Hudson, Paul D., BA Camb., PhD Manc. Sr. Lectr.

Kim, Myung, BS Songang, MSc Essex, MBA Warw., PhD Lond. Reader

Kingston, Arthur E., BSc Belf., PhD Belf., FIP Prof. Emer.

Marshall, Adele H., BSc Ulster, DPhil Ulster Sr. Lectr.; Dir., Centre for Statistical Sci. and Operational Res.

McCann, James F., BSc Belf., PhD Belf. Reader

Noble, Clifford J., BSc Auck., MSc Auck., PhD Thomas Jefferson Hon. Prof.

O'Rourke, S. Francesca C., BSc Belf., PhD Belf. Sr. Lectr.

Patterson, Tom N. L., BSc Belf., PhD Belf. Prof. Emer.

Reid, Robert H. G., BSc Belf., PhD Belf. Sr. Lectr.

Scott, M. Penny, BSc Belf., PhD Belf. Sr. Lectr.

Taylor, Kenneth T. A., BSc Belf., PhD Belf. Prof., Physics

Walters, H. R. James, MA Camb., PhD Camb. Dir., Centre for Theoret. and Computational Phys.; Prof., Theoretical Physics

Other Staff: 6 Lectrs. (Appl. Maths.)

Vacant Posts: 1 Prof.; 1 Reader; 3 Lectrs.

Research: intense laser-matter interactions; quantum optics and quantum information; statistics applied to medicine; theoretical atomic and molecular physics

Pure and Applied Physics

Tel: (028) 9097 3941 Fax: (028) 9097 3110
E-mail: physics@qub.ac.uk

Atkinson, Ronald, BSc Salf., PhD Salf., FIP Prof., Physics

Bailey, Mark E., MA Camb., MSc Sus., PhD Edin. Hon. Prof.

Bates, Brian, MSc Nott., PhD Lond. Prof. Emer.

Borghesi, Marco, PhD Lond., Laurea Reader

Bowman, Robert M., BSc Paisley, PhD Strath. Sr. Lectr.; Head, Nanostructured Media Res. Div.

Carolan, Patrick, BSc N.U.I., MSc Belf., PhD Belf. Hon. Prof.

Currell, Fred J., BSc Manc., PhD Manc. Reader; Head, Teaching

Dawson, Paul, BSc Ulster, DPhil Ulster Reader

Dufton, Philip L., MA Camb., PhD Camb. Dir., Astrophys. Res. Centre; Prof., Physics

Fitzsimmons, Alan, BSc Sus., PhD Leic., FRAS Prof., Physics

Gilbody, H. Brian, BSc Lond., PhD Lond., FIP, FAPS Prof. Emer.

Graham, William G., BSc Belf., PhD Belf., FIP, FAPS Dir., Internat. Res. Centre for Exper. Phys.; Prof., Physics

Greenwood, Jason B., BA Oxf., PhD Belf. Sr. Lectr.

Gregg, J. Marty, MA Camb., PhD Camb. Reader

Keenan, Francis P., BSc Belf., PhD Belf., FRAS Prof., Physics

Kohanoff, Jorge J., LicCienFis MagPhil PhD Reader

Lamb, Martin J., BSc Belf., PhD Belf. Sr. Lectr.

Latimer, Colin J., BSc Belf., PhD Belf., FIP Prof., Physics

Lewis, Ciaran L. S., BSc Belf., PhD Belf. Prof., Physics

Lynden-Bell, Ruth M., MA Camb., PhD Camb., ScD Camb., FIP, FRSChem Prof. Emer., Condensed Matter Simulation

Mathoudiakis, Mihalis, PhD Belf. Reader

McCullough, Robert W., BSc Belf., PhD Belf. Prof.

Morrow, Thomas, BSc Belf., PhD Belf. Reader

Paxton, Anthony T., BMet Sheff., DPhil Oxf. Dir., Atomistic Simulation Centre; Prof., Physics

Pollacco, Don L., BSc St And., PhD St And. Reader

Riley, David, BSc Durh., PhD Lond. Sr. Lectr.

Smartt, Stephen J., BSc Belf., PhD Belf. Prof., Physics

Todorov, Tchavdar N., BA Oxf., MA Oxf., DPhil Oxf. Reader

Walmsley, D. George, BSc Belf., MSc McM., PhD McM., DSc Belf., FIP, FAPS Prof. Emer., Physics

Whitaker, M. Andrew B., MA Oxf., PhD Nott., FIP, FIMA Prof., Physics

Williams, Ian D., BSc Belf., PhD Belf., FIP Prof., Physics

Zayats, Anatoly V., MSc Moscow, PhD Moscow Prof., Physics

Other Staff: 5 Lectrs.

Vacant Posts: 1 Reader; 2 Lectrs.

Research: astrophysics and planetary science; atomic and molecular physics; condensed matter physics and materials science;

plasma and laser interactions physics; theory and computer simulation of liquids and solids

Pure Mathematics

Tel: (028) 9097 3661 Fax: (028) 9097 5076
E-mail: pure.maths@qub.ac.uk

Armitage, David H., BSc Liv., PhD Liv. Prof.

Mathieu, Martin, DrRerNatHabil Tübingen Reader

McMaster, T. Brian M., BSc Belf., MSc Belf., PhD Belf. Sr. Lectr.; Head, Undergrad. Teaching

Wickstead, Anthony W., MA Camb., PhD Lond. Prof.; Dir., Pure Maths. Res. Centre

Other Staff: 3 Lectrs.

Vacant Posts: 1 Reader; 2 Lectrs.

Research: banach lattices and their operators; classical potential theory and approximation theory; noncommutative ring theory and algebraic k-theory; operator algebras and noncommutative functional analysis; set theory and order structures in topology

Music and Sonic Arts

Tel: (028) 9097 5534 Fax: (028) 9097 4828
E-mail: somasa@qub.ac.uk

Alcorn, M. P., BA Ulster, MMus Durh., PhD Durh. Prof.; Head*

Carver, A. F., BMus Birm., PhD Birm. Sr. Lectr.

Hellawell, P. R. D., MA Oxf. Prof.

Knapp, R. B., BSc N.Carolina State, MSc Stan., PhD Stan. Sr. Lectr.

Rebelo, P., BMus Edin., MA E.Anglia, PhD Edin. Sr. Lectr.

Smaczny, J. A., MA Oxf., DPhil Oxf. Prof.

Tomita, Y., BMus MMus PhD Prof.

Woodfield, I. D., BMus Nott., MMus Lond., PhD Lond. Prof.

Other Staff: 8 Lectrs.; 2 Res. Fellows

Research: composition; emotion and music; human-computer interaction; musicology; sonic arts

Pharmacy

Tel: (028) 9097 2007 Fax: (028) 9024 7794
E-mail: pharmacyinfo@qub.ac.uk

Collier, P. S., BPharm Lond., PhD Belf. Sr. Lectr.

Gorman, S. P., BSc Belf., PhD Belf. Prof.; Head*

Hirst, D. G., BSc St And., PhD St And. Prof.

Hughes, C. M., BSc Belf., PhD Belf. Prof.

Jones, D. S., BSc Belf., PhD Belf. Prof.

Malcolm, R. K., BSc Belf., PhD Belf. Sr. Lectr.

McCarron, P. A., BSc Belf., PhD Belf. Sr. Lectr.

McCoy, C. P., BSc Belf., PhD Belf. Sr. Lectr.

McElnay, James C., BSc Belf., PhD Belf. Prof.

Millership, J. S., BSc Salf., PhD Salf., FRSChem Sr. Lectr.

Robson, T., PhD Lond. Reader

Shaw, C., BSc Ulster, PhD Belf. Prof.

Walker, Brian, BSc Belf., PhD Belf. Prof.

Woolfson, A. D., BSc Belf., PhD Belf., FRSChem Prof.

Other Staff: 14 Lectrs.; 6 Pharm. Practice Teaching Fellows; 29 Res. Fellows; 1 Hon. Prof.; 1 Hon. Reader; 1 Hon. Sr. Lectr.; 7 Hon. Lectrs.

Vacant Posts: 3 Lectrs.

Research: biomolecular sciences; clinical and professional practice; drug delivery and biomaterials; experimental therapeutics

Planning, Architecture and Civil Engineering

Tel: (028) 9097 4006 Fax: (028) 9066 3754
E-mail: space@qub.ac.uk

Architecture

Gilfillan, J. R., BSc Belf., PhD Belf. Sr. Lectr.

Johnston, L. J. G., MSc Belf. Sr. Lectr.

Larmour, P. F., MSc Belf., PhD Belf. Reader

Ò Cathain, C. S., BArch N.U.I., MSc Trinity(Dub.) Sr. Lectr.

Other Staff: 4 Lectrs.; 1 Sr. Teaching Fellow; 3 Hon. Lectrs.

Research: construction and the built environment

Civil Engineering

Basheer, P. A. Mohammed, BSc(Eng) Kerala, MSc(Eng) Calicut, PhD, FICE   Prof., Structural Materials
Cleland, D. J., BSc Belf., PhD Belf., FICE, FIStructE   Prof.; Head*
Elliot, T., BSc Newcastle(UK), PhD Bath   Sr. Lectr.
Ferguson, J. D., BSc Belf., MSc Leeds, FICE   Sr. Lectr.
Gilbert, S. G., BSc Belf., PhD Belf.   Sr. Lectr.
Hamill, G. A., BSc Belf., PhD Belf.   Sr. Lectr.
Hughes, D. A., BSc Belf., PhD Nott.   Sr. Lectr.
Johnston, H. T., BSc Belf., PhD Belf.   Sr. Lectr.
Long, A. E., PhD Belf., DSc Belf., FREng, FICE, FIStructE   Prof.
Mackinnon, P. A., BSc Belf., PhD Belf.   Sr. Lectr.
Meier-Augenstein, W., MChem Heidel., PhD Heidel.   Sr. Lectr.
Robinson, D. J., BSc Belf., PhD Edin.   Sr. Lectr.
Sen Gupta, B., BChE Calc., MEng B'lore., MBA Calc., PhD Calc.   Sr. Lectr.
Sha, W., BEng Tsinghua, DPhil Oxf.   Reader
Sivakumar, Vinayagamoorthy, BSc S.Lanka, MSc Sheff., PhD Sheff.   Sr. Lectr.
Taylor, S. E., BSc Bath, PhD Belf.   Sr. Lectr.
Whittaker, T. J. T., BSc Belf., PhD Belf., FREng, FICE   Prof.
Other Staff: 10 Lectrs.; 6 Res. Officers; 4 Hon. Lectrs.
Research: construction and the built environment; environmental engineering

Planning

Ellis, Geraint, BSc Birm., MPhil Reading, PhD Cardiff   Sr. Lectr.
Gaffikin, Frank J., BSSc Belf., MSSc Belf.   Prof.
McEldowney, J. Malachy, BSc Belf., MCD Liv.   Prof.
McKay, Stephen, BSc Ulster, MSc Belf., DPhil Ulster   Sr. Lectr.
Murray, Michael R., BA Belf., MSc Belf., PhD Belf.   Reader
Murtagh, Brendan J., BA Belf., MSc Belf., DPhil Ulster   Reader
Sterret, Kenneth W., BA CNAA, MSc Belf., PhD Belf.   Sr. Lectr.
Stockdale, Aileen, BSc Ulster, MPhil Ulster   Reader
Other Staff: 6 Lectrs.
Research: spatial and environmental planning

Politics, International Studies and Philosophy

Tel: (028) 9097 5028 Fax: (028) 9023 5373
E-mail: pisp@qub.ac.uk
Baker, A., DPhil Ulster   Sr. Lectr.
Barry, J., BA N.U.I., MA N.U.I., PhD Glas.   Reader
Bew, P. A. E., MA Camb., PhD Camb.   Prof.
Cullen, Bernard A., BA Belf., BSc(Econ) Belf., MA Mich., PhD Mich., FRSA   Prof.
Dixon, S., MA St And., PhD Camb.   Sr. Lectr.
Elliott, Sydney, BA Belf., PhD Belf.   Sr. Lectr.
English, R. L., BA Oxf., PhD Keele, FRHistS   Prof.; Course Dir., MA in Irish Pol.
Evans, A., MA Camb., LLM Camb., PhD Hull   Reader
Evans, J. D. G., MA Camb., PhD Camb.   Prof., Logic and Metaphysics
Galligan, Y., MA N.U.I., PhD Trinity(Dub.)   Reader; Dir., Centre for Advancement of Women in Pol.
Geoghegan, V., BA Newcastle(UK), PhD Newcastle(UK), FRHistS   Prof., Politics
Gorman, J. L., MA Edin., PhD Camb.   Prof., Moral Philosophy
Guelke, Adrian B., MA Cape Town, PhD Lond.   Prof.
Harmsen, R., BA Alta., PhD Kent   Sr. Lectr.
Lisle, D., PhD Keele   Sr. Lectr.
Macdonald, C., DPhil Oxf.   Prof.
McEvoy, James J., BA Belf., BD Maynooth, MA Belf., PhD Louvain, Hon. DLitt Leic.   Prof.
McGowan, L., BA Ulster, MA Reading, PhD Reading   Sr. Lectr.
Milton-Edwards, B., BA Portsmouth, MA Exe., PhD Exe.   Prof.

Nimni, E., PhD Hull   Reader
O'Neill, S., MA N.U.I., PhD Glas.   Prof.; Head*
Phinnemore, D., BA Kent, PhD Kent   Sr. Lectr.
Walker, B., BA PhD   Prof.
Walker, G. S. W., MA Glas., MA McM., PhD Manc.   Reader
Wiener, Antje, MA F.U.Berlin, PhD Car.   Jean Monnet Prof.
Wilford, R. A., BSc Lond., MSc Bath, PhD Wales   Prof.
Other Staff: 17 Lectrs.

Psychology

Tel: (028) 9097 5445 Fax: (028) 9066 4144
E-mail: psychology@qub.ac.uk
Bell, W. R., BSc Belf., PhD Belf.   Sr. Lectr.
Brown, K., MA Aberd., FPsSI, FBPsS   Emer. Prof.
Carson, R. G., BSc Brist., MSc S.Fraser, PhD S.Fraser   Prof.
Chmiel, N. R. J., BSc Dund., BSc Lond., DPhil Oxf.
Cooper, C., BSc Exe., PhD Exe.   Sr. Lectr.
Cowie, R. I. D., BA Stir., DPhil Sus.   Prof.
Craig, C., MA Edin., PhD Edin.   Sr. Lectr.
Hepper, P. G., BSc Exe., PhD Durh., FBPsS   Prof.; Head*
Kremer, J. M. D., BSc Lough., PhD Lough.   Reader
Lyons, E., BSc Lond., MSc Lond., PhD Lond.   Prof.
McCormack, T., BA Camb., PhD Camb.   Sr. Lectr.
McCusker, C., BA Belf., MSc Lond., PhD Belf.   Dir., Doctorate in Clin. Psychol.
McGuinness, Carol M., MA N.U.I., PhD Belf.   Prof.
Mulhern, G. A., BSc Liv., PhD Belf.   Sr. Lectr.
Rafferty, H., BA Belf., MSc Belf., PhD Belf.   Dir., Educnl. Psychol.
Sneddon, I. A., BSc St And., PhD St And.   Sr. Lectr.
Trew, K. J., BA Belf., PhD Belf.   Reader
Wells, D. L., BA Belf., PhD Belf.   Sr. Lectr.
Other Staff: 18 Lectrs.; 9 Res. Fellows; 1 Temp. Lectr.
Research: behavioural development and welfare; cognition development and education; emotion, perception and individual characteristics (EPIC); health and social issues

Sociology, Social Policy and Social Work

Tel: (028) 9097 5117 Fax: (028) 9097 3943
E-mail: ssp@qub.ac.uk
Campbell, J., BA Belf., PhD Belf.   Sr. Lectr.
Daly, M., BSSc N.U.I., MSSc N.U.I., PhD European Univ.Inst.   Prof., Sociology
Dillenburger, K., BSc Freib., PhD Ulster   Reader
Hill, M., BA Belf., PhD Belf.   Sr. Lectr.
Hillyard, P., BSS Trinity(Dub.), BA Trinity(Dub.), MA Keele, PhD Brist.   Prof., Sociology
Houston, S., BSc Ulster, MSc Leic., PhD Belf.   Sr. Lectr.
Kelly, G. M., MSSc Belf., Hon. BSc(Econ) Belf.   Sr. Lectr.
Leonard, M., BA Belf., PhD Belf.   Prof., Sociology
Macdonald, G., BA Oxf., MA Oxf.   Prof.
McElrath, K., BSc Louisville, MSc Louisville, PhD Florida State   Reader
Miller, R. L., BA Duke, MA Flor., PhD Belf.   Deputy Dir., ARK (Soc. and Pol. Archive for Northern Ireland; Prof., Sociology
O'Dowd, L. G., MA N.U.I., PhD Ill.   Prof., Sociology
O'Hearn, D. A., MA Mich., PhD Mich.   Prof., Sociology
Pinkerton, J. R., BSSc Belf., MSc Lond., MSSc Belf., PhD Belf.   Prof.
Prior, L., BSc(Soc) Lond., BSc Open(UK), MA Reading, PhD Aberd.   Prof., Sociology
Prior, P. M., BSocSc N.U.I., MSc(Econ) Lond., DPhil York(UK)   Sr. Lectr.
Shildrick, M., BA Warw., MSc Warw., PhD Warw.   Reader
Shortall, Sally, BSS N.U.I., MSS N.U.I., PhD N.U.I.   Reader

Skehill, C., BSS Trinity(Dub.), PhD Trinity(Dub.)   Sr. Lectr.
Spratt, T., BSc Ulster, MSc Oxf., PhD Belf.   Sr. Lectr.
Tomlinson, M. W., BA Nott., MPhil Nott.   Head*
Other Staff: 18 Lectrs.; 4 Teaching Fellows
Research: global process and change; social divisions and social conflict; social welfare and social control; social work with children, adults and families

MEDICINE, HEALTH AND LIFE SCIENCES

Tel: (028) 9097 5177 Fax: (028) 9043 4454
E-mail: dean-mhls@qub.ac.uk

Dentistry, School of

Tel: (028) 9063 2734 Fax: (028) 9043 8861
E-mail: dentistry@qub.ac.uk
Burden, D. J., BDS Belf., MSc Manc., PhD Belf., FDSRCPSGlas, FFDRCSI   Prof.
Irwin, C. R., BSc Belf., BDS Belf., PhD Manc., FDSRCPSGlas   Reader/Consultant
Johnston, C. D., BDS Belf., BSc Edin., PhD Belf.   Sr. Lectr.

Microbiology

Tel: (028) 9063 2539
E-mail: w.coulter@qub.ac.uk
Coulter, W. A., BDS Belf., BSc Belf., MSc Belf., PhD Belf.   Sr. Lectr./Consultant

Oral Surgery, Oral Medicine, Oral Pathology and Radiology

Tel: (028) 9063 3106
E-mail: g.cowan@qub.ac.uk
Cowan, G. C., BDS Belf., FDSRCS, FFDRCSI   Sr. Lectr./Consultant
Lamey, P. J., BSc Edin., BDS Edin., MB ChB Glas., DDS Edin., FDSRCPSGlas, FFDRCSI   Prof., Oral Medicine
Marley, J. J., BSc Belf., BDS Belf., PhD Leeds, FDSRCS   Sr. Lectr./Consultant
Other Staff: 1 Lectr.
Vacant Posts: 1 Sr. Lectr./Consultant; 1 Clin. Lectr.

Orthodontics

Tel: (028) 9063 4037
E-mail: c.d.johnson@qub.ac.uk
Burden, D. J., BDS Belf., MSc Manc., PhD Belf., FDSRCPSGlas, FFDRCSI   Prof.
Johnston, C. D., BDS Belf., BSc Edin., PhD Belf.   Sr. Lectr.; Head*
Other Staff: 1 Lectr.

Paediatric and Preventive Dentistry and Dental Public Health

Tel: (028) 9063 2306
No staff at present

Vacant Posts: 2 Profs.

Restorative Dentistry

Tel: (028) 9063 3744
E-mail: g.linden@qub.ac.uk
Clifford, T. J., BDS, FDSRCPSGlas   Sr. Lectr./Consultant
Hussey, D. L., BDS, FDSRCPSGlas   Sr. Lectr./Consultant
Irwin, C. R., BSc Belf., BDS Belf., PhD Manc., FDSRCPSGlas   Reader/Consultant
Kennedy, J. G., BSc Belf., MDS Belf., PhD Belf., FDSRCPSGlas   Sr. Lectr./Consultant
Linden, G. J., BSc Belf., BDS N.U.I., FDSRCS   Prof.; Head*
Lynch, E., BA N.U.I., BDentSc N.U.I., MA N.U.I., PhD Lond., FDSRCS   Prof./Consultant
Mitchell, C. A., BDS Belf., PhD Belf., FDSRCPSGlas   Sr. Lectr./Consultant
Other Staff: 1 Clin. Lectr.
Vacant Posts: 1 Sr. Lectr./Consultant; 1 Clin. Lectr.

Medicine

Tel: (028) 9097 5778 Fax: (028) 9030 2809
E-mail: s.clinmed@qub.ac.uk
Johnston, Patrick G., MD N.U.I., PhD N.U.I.,
FRCPI, FRCP   Prof., Oncology; Head*

Anatomy

Tel: (028) 9097 2131 Fax: (028) 9023 5483
E-mail: anatomy@qub.ac.uk
Wilson, David J., BSc Wales, PhD Wales   Sr.
Lectr.; Head*
Other Staff: 4 Lectrs.; 6 Teaching Fellows

Child Health

Tel: (028) 9063 2703 Fax: (028) 9023 6455
E-mail: f.herbert@qub.ac.uk
Carson, Dennis J., MB Belf., FRCP   Sr. Lectr.
Halliday, H. L., MD Belf., FRCP, FRCPEd   Hon.
Prof.
Jenkins, John G., MD Belf., FRCPCH   Sr. Lectr.
Savage, J. Maurice, MB Belf., FRCP   Prof.,
Paediatrics
Shields, Mike D., MB Brist., MD Brist.   Sr.
Lectr.
Stewart, Moira C., MD Belf., FRCP, FRCPCH
Sr. Lectr.
Research: community child health; neonatology,
nephrology, endocrinology and diabetes;
respiratory disease

Clinical Biochemistry and Metabolic Medicine

Tel: (028) 9063 2470 Fax: (028) 9023 6143
Ennis, Madeleine, BSc Lond., PhD Lond.   Prof.,
Clinical Biochemistry; Head*
Trimble, Elisabeth R., CBE, MD Belf., FRCP,
FRCPath   Prof.
Other Staff: 3 Lectrs.
Research: clinical and basic molecular,
laboratory-based research programmes;
clinical and basic research on the areas of
asthma, bronchiectasis, chronic obstructive
pulmonary disease and cystic fibrosis; major
focus on vascular complication of disease

Epidemiology and Public Health

Tel: (028) 9063 2746 Fax: (028) 9023 1907
E-mail: h.porter@qub.ac.uk
Bradbury, I.   Sr. Lectr.
Craig, David   Sr. Lectr.
Cran, Gordon W., BSc Aberd., PhD Belf.   Sr.
Lectr., Statistics
Crawford, Vivienne L. S., BSc Belf., MSc Belf.,
PhD Belf.   Sr. Lectr.
Donnelly, Michael, BSc Ulster, DPhil Ulster
Reader
Evans, Alun E., MD Belf., FRCP, FFPHM   Prof.,
Epidemiology; Head*
Gavin, Anna T., MSc Belf., MB Belf.   Sr. Lectr.
Kee, Frank, BSc Belf., MSc Edin., MD Belf.
Prof., Public Health Medicine
McCarron, P. G.   Sr. Lectr.
Murray, Liam J., MD   Sr. Lectr.
O'Reilly, Dermott P. J., MB   Sr. Lectr.
Patterson, Chris C., BSc Belf., MSc Lond., PhD
Belf.   Reader
Yarnell, John W. G., MD Manc.   Sr. Lectr.
Other Staff: 1 Lectr.; 2 Hon. Lectrs.
Research: clinical decision-making and genetic
analysis; genetic epidemiology of cancer;
genetic epidemiology of cardiovascular
disease

General Practice

Tel: (028) 9020 4252 Fax: (028) 9031 0202
E-mail: genpractice@qub.ac.uk
Cupples, Margaret E., BSc Belf., MD Belf.,
FRCGP   Sr. Lectr.
Gilliland, A. E. W. (Drew), MD Belf., FRCGP
Sr. Lectr.
McGlade, Kieran J., MD Belf.   Sr. Lectr.
Reilly, Philip M., MD Belf., FRCGP   Prof.;
Head, Div. of Public Health Med. and
Primary Care
Steele, W. Keith, MD Belf., FRCGP   Sr. Lectr.
Other Staff: 1 Lectr.; 3 Res. Fellows; 1
Teaching Fellow; 1 Principal Res. Nurse; 2
Res. Assocs.; 4 Res. Registrars

Medical Education

Tel: (028) 9027 2180 Fax: (028) 9033 0571
Boohan, Mairead I.   Lectr.; Head*
Collins, K. M.   Dir., Clin. Skills
Other Staff: 1 Clin. Sr. Lectr.; 2 Clin. Teaching
Fellows

Medicine and Therapeutics

Tel: (028) 9063 2707 Fax: (028) 9032 9899
Bell, Aubrey L., MD Belf., FRCP   Sr. Lectr./
Consultant, Rheumatology
Bell, David   Sr. Lectr., Pharmacology
Elborn, Stuart, MD, FRCP   Prof., Respiratory
Medicine
Ennis, Madeleine, BSc Lond., PhD Lond.   Prof.,
Immunopharmacology
Fogarty, Damian, BSc MD   Sr. Lectr.,
Nephrology
Hawkins, Stanley A., BSc Belf., MB Belf., FRCP
Reader, Neurology
Heaney, Liam, MD   Sr. Lectr., Respiratory
Medicine
Johnston, G. Dennis, MD PhD, FRCPEd, FRCP
Head, Therapeutics and Pharmacology;
Prof., Therapeutics and Pharmacology
Maxwell, A. Peter, MD Belf., PhD Belf.   Prof.,
Nephrology
McAleer, J. J. A., MD Belf., FRCPEd, FRCR   Sr.
Lectr.
McCluskey, David R., MD Belf., FRCPEd, FRCPI
Sr. Lectr.; Head*
McDermott, Barbara J., BSc PhD   Prof.,
Cardiovascular Pharmacology
McGarvey, Lorcan, MD, FRCP   Sr. Lectr.,
Respiratory Medicine
McGeown, Mollie   Prof. Fellow
McKeown, Pascal P., MD, FRCPEd   Sr. Lectr.,
Cardiology
McMullin, Mary F., MD Belf., FRCPath, FRCPI,
FRCPEd   Reader
McVeigh, Gary E., MD Belf., PhD Belf., FRCP,
FRCPI   Sr. Lectr., Therapeutics and
Pharmacology
Rooney, Madeline, MD, FRCP   Sr. Lectr.,
Rheumatology
van den Berg, Hendrik, BSc Leeds, PhD Leeds
Reader, Oncology
Watson, R. G. Peter, BSc Belf., MD Belf., FRCP
Sr. Lectr./Consultant, Gastroenterology
Young, Ian, BSc MD, FRCP, FRCPath, FRCPI
Prof., Nutrition and Metabolism
Other Staff: 7 Lectrs.; 1 Res. Officer

Obstetrics and Gynaecology

Tel: (028) 9063 2506 Fax: (028) 9032 8247
E-mail: a.mcguinness@qub.ac.uk
Cooke, Inez   Sr. Lectr.
Glenn, David
Hunter, Alyson   Sr. Lectr./Consultant
Lewis, Sheena E. M., PhD Belf.   Prof.; Dir.,
Reproductive Med. Res. Group
McClure, Neil, MD Belf., FRCOG   Prof.; Head*
Other Staff: 1 Lectr.; 2 Res. Fellows; 1
Specialist Consultant
Research: apoptosis in the testis and sperm;
effects of THC on sperm function;
phytoestrogens -: effect on male fertility;
sperm nuclear and mitochondrial DNA
assessment; the effect of Sildenafil on sperm
motility

Pathology

Tel: (028) 9063 2270 Fax: (028) 9031 2265
E-mail: p.clark@qub.ac.uk
Armstrong, Marilyn A., BSc PhD   Sr. Lectr.
Hall, P. A., MD PhD, FRCPath   Musgrave
Prof.; Head*
Hughes, Anne E., BSc Belf., PhD Belf.   Prof.
Patrick, Sheila, BSc Edin., PhD Edin.   Sr. Lectr.
Other Staff: 2 Lectrs.; 3 Res. Fellows; 1 Res.
Officer

Physiology

Tel: (028) 9097 5795 Fax: (028) 9097 1838
E-mail: m.mcgrath@qub.ac.uk
Allen, J. Desmond, MD Belf.   Reader
Allen, Judith A., BSc Belf., MD Belf.   Sr. Lectr.

Hollywood, M., BSc Belf., PhD Belf.   Sr. Lectr.
McGeown, J. G., BSc Belf., MB Belf., PhD Belf.
Sr. Lectr.
McHale, Noel G., BSc Belf., PhD Belf.   Dunville
Prof.
Scholfield, C. Norman, BSc Lond., PhD Lond.
Sr. Lectr.
Thornbury, Keith D., BSc Belf., MB Belf., PhD
Belf.   Reader
Wallace, William F. M., BSc Belf., MD Belf.,
FRCA, FRCP, FRCSEd   Prof. Emer., Applied
Physiology
Other Staff: 3 Lectrs.; 2 Teaching Fellows
Research: blood vessel regulation (human,
disease); calcium transients and control;
cardiac arrhythmias and electrophysiology;
respiratory function; smooth muscle
physiology (lymphatic, vascular, bladder,
urethra, stomach)

Psychiatry and Neurosciences

Tel: (028) 9097 5790 Fax: (028) 9097 5870
E-mail: m.brooks@qub.ac.uk
Cooper, Stephen J., MD Belf., FRCPsych, FRCPI
Sr. Lectr.; Head*
Mulholland, Ciaran C., MB Belf.   Sr. Lectr.
O'Neill, Francis A., MD Belf.   Sr. Lectr.
Reynolds, Gavin P., BA York(UK), PhD Lond.
Prof., Neuroscience
Other Staff: 3 Lectrs.; 1 Res. Fellow; 1 Res.
Officer
Research: functional brain imaging; genetics of
schizophrenia; psychopharmacology of
psychosis

Surgery and Perioperative Care

Tel: (028) 9024 0503 Fax: (028) 9032 1811
Campbell, Charles, MD Glas., FRCS   Prof.;
Head*
Fee, J. P. Howard, MD Belf., PhD Belf., FFARCSI
Prof.
Harkin, Denis   Sr. Lectr.
Khosraviani, Kourosh   Sr. Lectr.
Mirakhur, Rajinder, MD Delhi, PhD, FFARCS,
FFARCSI   Prof.
Murray, James M., MD Belf., FRCA   Sr. Lectr.
Research: gastrointestinal stem cell biology;
incidence and behavioural phenotype of
sporadic colorectal adenomas; minor
germline APC variants; vitamin D3 receptor
(VDR) regulation of neoplastic
transformation

Trauma and Orthopaedic Surgery

Tel: (028) 9090 2848 Fax: (028) 9066 1112
E-mail: orthopaedics@qub.ac.uk
Bell, Aubrey L., MD Belf., FRCP   Sr. Lectr.,
Rheumatology
Dickson, Glenn R., MSc PhD   Sr. Lectr.
Li, Gang, MB Oxf., DPhil Oxf.   Sr. Lectr.
Nixon, J. R., MChOrth, FRCS, FRCSI   Prof.,
Orthopaedic Surgery
Rooney, Madeline, MD, FRCP   Sr. Lectr.
Other Staff: 2 Lectrs.; 7 Researchers; 1
Pathologist

Nursing and Midwifery, School of

Tel: (028) 9097 2233 Fax: (028) 9097 5717
E-mail: nursing@qub.ac.uk
Alderdice, Fiona, BSSc Belf., PhD Belf.   Dir.,
Res.; Sr. Lectr., Nursing Res.
McMurray, Frances, MSc Edin.   Assoc. Head,
Grad. and Continuing Educn.; Sr. Lectr.,
Graduate and Continuing Education/
Midwifery
Moutray, Marianne, MEd Belf.   Sr. Lectr.;
Assoc. Head, Undergrad. Nursing Sci.
Orr, Jean A., BA CNAA, MSc Manc.   Prof.;
Head*
Parkes, Jacqueline, BN Manc., PhD Belf.   Sr.
Lectr.
Porter, Sam, BSSc Belf., PhD Belf.   Prof.,
Nursing Research

SPECIAL CENTRES, ETC

Byzantine Studies, Institute of

Tel: (028) 9097 3817 Fax: (028) 9097 5274
E-mail: byz.studies@qub.ac.uk
Mullett, Margaret E., BA Birm., PhD Birm., FSA
Prof.; Dir., AHRB Centre for Byzantine
Cultural Hist.; Dir.*
Other Staff: 4 Visiting Profs.; 1 Sr. Lectr.; 1
Lectr.; 1 Visiting Sr. Res. Fellow; 6 Res.
Fellows; 1 Teaching Fellow

Canadian Studies, Centre of

Tel: (028) 9097 3927 Fax: (028) 9032 1280
E-mail: canada@qub.ac.uk
Hodgett, S., BSSc Belf., MSSc Belf.   Co-Dir.*
Royle, S. A., MA Camb., PhD Leic.   Co-Dir.*
Research: community development in Canadian
maritime provinces

Cancer Research and Cell Biology, Centre for

Tel: (028) 9026 3911 Fax: (028) 9026 3744
E-mail: oncology@qub.ac.uk
Allen, Ingrid, DBE, CBE, MB BCh BAO Belf.,
MD Belf., DSc Belf., FRCPath, FMedSci   Prof.
Emer.
Campbell, F. Charles, MB ChB Glas., MD Glas.,
FRCS   Prof., Surgery
Cosby, S. L., BSc Belf., PhD Belf., FRCPath
Prof.
Dib, Karim, PhD Paris   Sr. Lectr.
Duprex, W. Paul, BSc Belf., PhD Belf.   Sr. Lectr.
Fennell, Dean A., BSc Lond., MB BS Lond., PhD
Lond.   Sr. Lectr.
Gadina, Massimo, PhD Milan   Sr. Lectr.
Hamilton, Peter W., BSc Ulster, PhD Belf.
Prof., Bioimaging and Informatics
Harkin, D. Paul, BSc N.U.I., PhD Belf.   Prof.,
Molecular Oncology
James, Jacqueline, BSc Belf., BDS Belf., PhD Belf.,
FDSRCS   Sr. Lectr.
Johnston, James A., BSc Ulster, PhD Manc.
Prof., Immunology
Johnston, Patrick G., MD N.U.I., PhD N.U.I.,
FRCPI, FRCP   Prof., Oncology
Lappin, Terence R., MSc Belf., PhD Belf.,
FRCPath, FRSChem   Prof., Haematology
Li, Gang, MB Oxf., DPhil Oxf.   Reader
McCance, Dennis J., BSc Belf., PhD Birm.   Prof.;
Acting Dir.*
McMullin, Mary F., MD Belf., FRCPath, FRCPI,
FRCPEd   Prof.
Mills, Ken, BSc Portsmouth, PhD S'ton., FRCPath
Prof., Experimental Haematology
Morris, Prof. T. Carson M., MB BCh BAO Belf.,
MD Belf., FRCPath   Hon. Prof.
O'Sullivan, Joe M., MD Lond., MB BCh BAO
Belf.   Reader
Power, Ultan F., BSc N.U.I., PhD N.U.I.   Sr.
Lectr.
Prise, Kevin M., BSc Aberd., PhD Aberd.   Prof.,
Radiation Biology
Spence, Roy A. J., OBE, JP, MB BCh BAO Belf.,
MA Belf., MD Belf., FRCS   Hon. Prof.
Van Schaeybroeck, Sandra, MD Leuven, PhD
Leuven
Waugh, David J., BSc Belf., PhD Creighton
Reader
Williamson, Kathleen, MMedSci Belf., PhD Belf.
Sr. Lectr.
Wilson, Richard, MD Belf., FRCS, FRCR   Sr.
Lectr.
Ziebuhr, John K., DMed Jena, PhD Würzburg
Prof., Molecular Microbiology
Ziebuhr, Wilma, DMed Jena, MD Würzburg,
DrHabil Würzburg   Reader, Bacteriology
Other Staff: 8 Lectrs.; 1 Temp. Lectr.
Research: immunology; molecular biology;
molecular virology; prevention, diagnosis
and treatment of cancer

Child Care Research, Institute of

Tel: (028) 9097 5922 Fax: (028) 9097 5900
E-mail: iccr@qub.ac.uk
Macdonald, G., BA Oxf., MA Oxf.   Prof.; Dir.*
Other Staff: 15 Res. Staff

Research: children in the care of public
authoriteis and adopted children; mental
health and disability in children and young
people; parenting and the early years; youth
development, lifestyle and social behaviour

Cognition and Culture, Institute of

Tel: (028) 9097 1333 Fax: (028) 9097 1332
E-mail: icc@qub.ac.uk
Bering, Jesse M., BA Florida Atlantic, MS Louisiana
State, PhD Florida Atlantic   Dir.*
Sousa, Paulo, PhD Mich.   Asst. Dir.
Other Staff: 3 Distinguished Internat. Fellows;
1 Hon. Prof.

Criminology and Criminal Justice, Institute of

Tel: (028) 9097 3472 Fax: (028) 9097 3376
E-mail: iccj@qub.ac.uk
Geary, R. V., LLM Glas., Hon. LLB Strath.   Sr.
Lectr.
Jackson, J. D., BA Durh., LLM Wales   Prof.;
Dir.*
Maruna, S., BA Illinois State, MA Northwestern, PhD
Northwestern   Reader
McEvoy, K., LLB Belf., MSc Edin., PhD Belf.
Prof.
Morison, J. W. E., LLB Wales, PhD Wales   Prof.
Scraton, Phil, BA Liv., MA Liv., PhD Lanc.   Prof.
Stannard, J. E., MA Oxf., BCL Oxf., PhD Belf.
Sr. Lectr.
Other Staff: 5 Lectrs.; 1 Hon. Sr. Lectr.

Human Rights, Centre for

Tel: (028) 9097 3451 Fax: (028) 9097 3376
E-mail: law-enquiries@qub.ac.uk
Allain, Jean, BA Car., MA Brock, DPA Laur., LLM
Geneva, PhD Geneva   Sr. Lectr.
Dickson, S. Brice, BA Oxf., BCL Oxf., MPhil
Ulster   Prof.
Guelke, Adrian B., MA Cape Town, PhD Lond.
Prof.
Hadden, Tom B., BA Camb., LLB Camb., PhD
Camb.   Prof.
Harvey, Colin, LLB Lanc., PhD Nott.   Prof.;
Dir.*
McEvoy, K., LLB Belf., MSc Edin., PhD Belf.
Prof.
Morison, J. W. E., LLB Wales, PhD Wales   Prof.
Scraton, Phil, BA Liv., MA Liv., PhD Lanc.   Prof.
Turner, Sharon, BCL N.U.I., LLM York(Can.)
Prof.
Other Staff: 10 Lectrs.
Research: bills of rights and judges; conflict
resolution, cultural separation and
integration; equality and discrimination;
human rights commissions; international
criminal law

Irish Studies, Institute of

Tel: (028) 9097 3386 Fax: (028) 9097 3388
E-mail: irish.studies@qub.ac.uk
Bryan, Dominic, MPhil Camb., DPhil Ulster
Dir.*
Hughes, Eamonn G. P., BA CNAA, MA Leic.,
PhD Leic.   Asst. Dir.
Other Staff: 1 Lectr.; 3 Res. Fellows
Research: Irish and British identity; physical and
political environment of Ireland

Knowledge Transfer Centre (KTP)

Tel: (028) 9097 5444 Fax: (028) 9097 4011
E-mail: m.flynn@qub.ac.uk
Flynn, Mary, BSc Belf., PhD Belf.   Head*

Marine Resources and Mariculture, Centre for

Tel: (028) 4272 9648 Fax: (028) 4272 9672
E-mail: niall.mcdonough@qub.ac.uk
McDonough, N., BA Trinity(Dub.), PhD Belf.
Manager, Aquaculture and Marine Resources
Roberts, D., BSc Liv., PhD Liv., FIBiol   Co-
ordinator*
Other Staff: 4 Postdoctoral Res. Fellows
Research: marine environment and resource
survey; marine shellfish hatchery and
cultivation technology; re-circulated

seawater cultivation systems; shellfish
fisheries; shellfish handling and purification

Medical Polymers Research Institute

Tel: (028) 9097 4563 Fax: (028) 9066 0631
E-mail: mpri@qub.ac.uk
Hornsby, Peter, PhD Brun., BSc, FRSChem,
FIMMM   Prof.; Dir.*
Price, Denise, BEng Belf.   Project Manager

Northern Ireland Cancer Registry

Tel: (028) 9063 2573 Fax: (028) 9024 8017
E-mail: nicr@qub.ac.uk
Gavin, A. T., MSc Lond., MB Belf.   Dir.*
Murray, L., MD   Sr. Lectr., Epidemiology
Other Staff: 2 Biostatisticians; 1 Data Manager

Northern Ireland Semi-Conductor Research Centre

Tel: (028) 9027 5439 Fax: (028) 9066 4265
Armstrong, B. M., BSc Belf., PhD Belf.   Asst.
Dir., Silicon On Insulator Device Electronics
Armstrong, G. A., BSc Belf., PhD Belf.   Prof.,
Device Modelling
Gamble, H. S., BSc Belf., PhD Belf.   Prof.,
Microelectronic Engineering; Dir.*
Mitchell, S. J. N., BSc Belf., PhD Belf.   Sr.
Lectr., Micro Electro-mechanical Systems
(MEMS), Microfluidics
Other Staff: 1 Lectr.
Research: atomic layer deposition of hafnium
doixide; bonding of silicon wafers for
silicon on insulator substrates; chemical
vapour deposition (CVD) of silicon and
silicon-germanium for production of silicon
on insulator (SOI) substrates; germanium
and silicon for infrared imaging; radio
frequency micro-electromechanical systems
(RF MEMS) employing micromachining of
silicon

Northern Ireland Technology Centre

Tel: (028) 9097 5433 Fax: (028) 9097 4332
E-mail: nitc@qub.ac.uk
Edgar, T., BSc Belf.   Dir.*

Pharmaceutical Education and Training, Northern Ireland Centre for

Tel: (028) 9097 2005 Fax: (028) 9097 2368
E-mail: nicppet@qub.ac.uk
Adair, Colin G., BSc Belf., PhD Belf.   Dir.*
Bell, Heather, BSc PhD   Asst. Dir., Live Educn.
and Training
Lloyd, Fran, BSc   Asst. Dir., Distance Learning
Other Staff: 4 Staff Members
Research: continuing professional development;
pharmacy prescribing; professionalism

Polymer Processing Research Centre

Tel: (028) 9097 4700 Fax: (028) 9066 0631
E-mail: pprc@qub.ac.uk
Clarke, Alan   Extrusion Manager
Kearns, Mark P.   Moulding Res. Manager
McNally, Gerard M. P., MSc Belf., FIMMM   Sr.
Lectr.; Dir.*
Price, Denise, BEng Belf.   Project Manager

Professional Legal Studies, Institute of

Tel: (028) 9097 5567 Fax: (028) 9066 1192
E-mail: iplsenquiries@qub.ac.uk
Fenton, I. Anne, LLB Belf.   Sr. Lectr.; Dir.*
Other Staff: 1 Sr. Lectr.; 3 Lectrs.; 3 Sr.
Teaching Fellows; 1 Teaching Fellow

Queen's University Environmental Science and Technology Research Centre (QUESTOR)

Tel: (028) 9097 5567 Fax: (028) 9066 1462
E-mail: questor@qub.ac.uk
Larkin, M. J., BSc CNAA, PhD Wales   Res.
Cttee. Chairman
McGarel, Wilson, BSc Belf., PhD Belf.   TDP and
IFI Dir.*

Queen's University Ionic Liquid Laboratories (QUILL)

Tel: (028) 9097 5420 Fax: (028) 9066 5297
E-mail: quill@qub.ac.uk
Seddon, Kenneth R., BSc Liv., MA Oxf., PhD Liv.
Prof.; Co-Dir.*
Swindall, Jim W., OBE, MSc Belf., FRSChem
Prof.; Co-Dir.*
Other Staff: 7 Lectrs.; 16 Res. Fellows; 3 Asst.
Dirs.
Research: green chemistry; ionic liquids

Sport and Recreation Services

Tel: (028) 9068 1126 Fax: (028) 9068 1129
E-mail: pec@qub.ac.uk
Cusdin, M., MSc Leic.   Dir.*

Theology, Institute of

Tel: (028) 9097 4170 Fax: (028) 9024 9864
E-mail: theology@qub.ac.uk
Magennis, H., BA MA PhD   Prof.; Dir.*

Vision Sciences, Centre for

Tel: (028) 9063 2729 Fax: (028) 9063 2699
E-mail: cvsvb@qub.ac.uk
Archer, Desmond B., OBE, MB Belf., FRCS
Prof. Emer.
Chakravarthy, Usha, PhD Belf., FRCS, FRCSEd
Prof.
Curry, W. James, BSc Belf., PhD Belf.   Sr. Lectr.
Jackson, A. Jonathan, BSc Glas., PhD Belf.
Hon. Prof.
McVeigh, Gary E., MD Belf., PhD Belf., FRCP,
FRCPI   Prof., Cardiovascular Medicine
Silvestri, Giuliana, MB BCh BAO Belf., MD Belf.,
FRCPEd, FRCS   Sr. Lectr.
Stitt, Alan W., BSc Belf., PhD Belf.   McCauley
Prof., Experimental Ophthalmology; Dir.*
Willoughby, Colin E., BSc Liv., MB ChB Liv.,
MD Liv.   Sr. Lectr.
Other Staff: 4 Lectrs.
Research: retinal microvascular and degenerative
disease

IRISH BAPTIST COLLEGE

Tel: (028) 9261 9267
E-mail: ibc@thebaptistcentre.org
Dowling, M. J., BA Camb., BD Lond., MTh Belf.,
PhD Belf.   Sr. Lectr., Church History and
Theology

ST MARY'S UNIVERSITY COLLEGE

Tel: (028) 9032 7678 Fax: (028) 9033 3719
E-mail: webmaster@stmarys-belfast.ac.uk

Art and Design

Cassidy, Fiona, BEd Belf.   Sr. Lectr.
Flanagan, Mary, BA Ulster, MA(Ed) Open(UK)
Sr. Lectr.
Robson, Deirdre M., BA Ulster, MEd Belf.
Principal Lectr.; Head*

Business Studies

Devlin, Rose O., BA Ulster, MBA Ulster   Sr.
Lectr.
Hennessey, Francis G., BSc(Econ) Belf., MBA
Belf., MA(Ed) Open(UK)   Principal Lectr.;
Head*
Stevenson, Peter, MSc Ulster, MEd Ulster, MBA
Ulster, BSc   Sr. Lectr.

Education

E-mail: m.reynolds@stmarys-belfast.ac.uk
Colohan, Gerald A., BSc Belf., MEd Belf., MBA
Ulster   Sr. Lectr.
Gilliland, Catherine A., BEd Belf., MEd Ulster
Sr. Lectr.
Greenwood, Mary, MEd Ulster   Sr. Lectr.
Hagan, Martin, BEd Belf., MEd Belf.   Principal
Lectr.; Educn. Co-ordinator
Long, Marie Louise, BSSc Belf., MSc Belf.   Sr.
Lectr.
Loughran, Deirdre, BEd Belf., MEd Belf.   Sr.
Lectr.
Magennis, Geraldine, BEd Belf., PhD Belf.   Sr.
Lectr.

McCartan, Dermot, BA Belf., MEd Ulster   Sr.
Lectr.
McKee, Denise, BEd Belf., MEd Belf.   Sr. Lectr.,
Living with Diversity
Murray, Donna, BEd Ulster, MEd Ulster   Sr.
Lectr.
O'Doherty, Siobhan, BEd Belf., MEd Ulster   Sr.
Lectr.
Quinn, Francis, BEd Belf., MEd Belf.   Principal
Lectr.; Numeracy Co-ordinator; Professl.
Studies Co-ordinator; Fac. Co-ordinator
Reynolds, Margaret, BEd Belf., MEd Belf., PhD
Belf.   Dir.*

English/English with Dramatic Art

Cummings, Raymond, BA Belf., MA Belf., PhD
Belf.   Sr. Lectr.
D'Agostino, Olympio G., BA Belf., MA Ulster
Principal Lectr.; Head*
Hanratty, Brian, BA Belf., MA Leeds, DPhil Ulster
Sr. Lectr.
Lombard, Madeleine, BA Open(UK), MA Belf.,
EdD   Sr. Lectr.
Martin, Matthew, BA Indiana, MA Mich., PhD
Mich.   Sr. Lectr.

Geography

Keane, Margaret C., BA Belf., PhD Belf.
Principal Lectr.; Head*
McEntee, Michael, BA Belf., MSc Trinity(Dub.),
PhD Belf.   Principal Lectr.; Adviser of
Studies; Exams Officer
McKay, Tracey, BA Belf., PhD Belf.   Sr. Lectr.

History

Cash, Teresa, BEd Belf., MSc Ulster   Sr. Lectr.
Collins, Peter, BEd Belf., PhD Ulster   Sr. Lectr.
Feeney, Brian J., BA Belf., MA Belf., PhD Reading
Principal Lectr.; Head*
Research: Irish historical commemorations; pre-
reformation Irish ecclesiastical heritage;
twentieth century Irish republicanism

Irish Medium Unit

Garland, Jill, BA Ulster   Sr. Lectr.
Mhic Aoidh, Eibhlín, BA Belf.   Sr. Lectr.
Nig Uidhir, Gabrielle, BA Belf., PhD Belf.
Principal Lectr.

Irish Studies

de Bléine, Pádraig, MA Belf., BEd   Sr. Lectr.
MacLabhrai, Sean, BA Ulster, MA N.U.I.   Sr.
Lectr.
Martin, Micheál J., BA Belf., MEd Belf.   Sr.
Tutor, Student Affairs; Head of Dept./Sr.
Mgmt. Team

Mathematics/Computer and Information Technology

Anthony, Paul G., BA Belf., MEd Belf., MA(Ed)
Belf.   Principal Lectr.; Internat. Officer
McPolin, Peter, BSc Belf., MSc Belf., PhD Belf.
Sr. Lectr.
Rafferty, John, BSc Belf., MSc Belf.   Sr. Lectr.
Trainor, Gerard A., BSc Belf., MSc Belf.
Principal Lectr.; Staff Devel. Officer

Music

Connolly, Claire M., BA Belf., MEd Belf.
Principal Lectr.
Downey, Peter, BSc Belf., MTD Ulster, PhD Belf.
Principal Lectr.; Head*
Nugent, Orla, BMus Ulster, MEd Belf.   Principal
Lectr.

Physical Education

McLaughlin, Elaine, BEd Belf., DPhil Ulster   Sr.
Lectr.; Adviser of Studies
Tally, Patrick J., BEd Belf., MSc Ulster   Sr. Lectr.
Walsh, Ciaran, BA Ulster, MEd Belf.   Sr. Lectr.

Religious Studies

Coll, Rev. Niall, BA N.U.I., BD Maynooth, STL
Greg., STD Greg.   Sr. Lectr.
Curran, Marian P., BEd Belf., MEd Ulster   Sr.
Lectr.; Adviser of Studies
Fleming, Rev. Paul G., BA Belf., BD Maynooth,
STL Greg., PhD Belf.   Principal Lectr.; Fac.
Co-ordinator; Head*

Haughey, Sharon, BEd Belf., MEd Belf.   Sr.
Lectr.
Magennis, Rev. Feidhlimidh, BA Oxf., BD
Maynooth, LSS Pontif.Bibl.Inst.   Sr. Lectr.
Other Staff: 1 Asst. Lectr.

Science

Beggs, James, BSc Belf., PhD Belf.   Principal
Lectr.; Head*
Hickey, Ivor G., BSc Belf., PhD Glas.   Principal
Lectr.
Quinn, Catherine, PhD Belf., Hon. BSc Belf.   Sr.
Lectr.; Adviser of Studies
Sweeney, John J., BSc Belf., MEd Belf., PhD Belf.
Sr. Tutor

Technology and Design

Bradley, Patrick C., MA Ulster, MSc Ulster
Principal Lectr.
McGeown, Kieran, BEd Belf.   Sr. Lectr.
Rice, Arthur, BA Open(UK), MSc Belf.   Principal
Lectr.; In-Service Co-ordinator

SPECIAL CENTRES, ETC

Liberal Arts Faculty

Tel: (028) 9032 7678
E-mail: p.oneill@smucb.ac.uk
Campbell, Joan M., BEd Belf., MBA Ulster
Principal Lectr.; Co-ordinator, Work-Based
Learning
Finn, Peter B., BA Belf., MSSc Belf.   Acting
Principal; Dir. of Fac.*
McCann, Gerard, BA Belf., MA Belf., MEd Ulster,
PhD Belf.   Sr. Lectr.
Schippers, Birgit, MA F.U.Berlin   Sr. Lectr.
Vaulpel, Angela, MA Bochum, PhD Ulster   Sr.
Lectr.
Worley, Jonathan, BA New Hampshire, MA New
Hampshire, MA Rutgers   Sr. Lectr.

STRANMILLIS UNIVERSITY COLLEGE

Independent University College

Tel: (028) 9038 1271 Fax: (028) 9066 4423
E-mail: principal@stran.ac.uk

Early Childhood Education

Carlin, Paula, BA Belf.   Sr. Lectr.
Carville, Sheelagh M., BEd Belf., MEd Ulster
Head*
Gray, Colette, BSSc Belf., PhD Belf.   Sr. Lectr.
Hanna, Karen, BSc Ulster   Sr. Lectr.
Hutchinson, Beverley, BEd Belf., MEd Belf.   Sr.
Lectr.
McConnell, Barbara A., BEd Belf., MA Lond.,
PhD Belf.   Sr. Lectr.
McKee, Bronagh, BA Belf., MA Belf.   Sr. Lectr.
McMillan, Dorothy J., BEd Belf., MEd Belf.   Sr.
Lectr.
Quinn, Louise N., BSc Ulster   Sr. Lectr.
Walsh, Glenda, BEd Belf., PhD Belf.   Sr. Lectr.

Health and Leisure Education

Campbell, Rachel-Ann, BSc Leeds, MPhil Ulster
Sr. Lectr.
Delaney, Brian J., MEd Ulster, MSc Ulster   Sr.
Lectr.
Kelly, Frank R., MSc Ulster   Head*
McKee, David P., BEd Belf., MSc Lough.   Sr.
Lectr.
McLaughlin, Judith A., BEd Belf., PhD Ulster
Sr. Lectr.
Wallace, Stephen, BSc Belf.   Sr. Lectr.

School Partnerships

Eason, E. Gail, BA Open(UK), MSc Ulster, MPhil
Ulster   Head*

Teacher Education (Post-Primary)

Armstrong, David S., BA Ulster, MBA Ulster   Sr.
Lectr.
Blease, Maurice C., MBE, BA Open(UK), MEd
Manc.   Sr. Lectr.
Cummins, Brian J., BEd Belf., MEd Ulster, EdD
Ulster   Sr. Lectr.
Curry, Audrey A. M., BA Ulster, MBA Ulster
Head*

Eaton, Patricia T., BSc Belf., PhD Belf. Sr. Lectr.

Gibson, Kenneth S., BA Open(UK), BEd Belf., MSc Ulster, EdD Belf. Sr. Lectr.

Ievers, Michael A., MEng Belf., PhD Ulster Sr. Lectr.

Mason, Madeline S., BEd Belf., MEd Belf. Sr. Lectr.

McKenzie, Lisa R., BEd Belf., MSc Ulster Sr. Lectr.

Nelson, James H., BEd Belf., MA Lanc. Sr. Lectr.

Purdy, Noel, MA Camb., MEd Belf., MA Open(UK), PhD Belf. Sr. Lectr.

Teacher Education (Primary)

Beale, George M., BEd Belf., MA Belf., PhD Belf., MTh Sr. Lectr.

Bell, Irene T., BSc Belf., MA Belf., EdD Exe. Sr. Lectr.

Burgess, Frances A., BMus Belf., MA Ulster Sr. Lectr.

Donaghy, Colm, BEd Belf., MA Ulster Sr. Lectr.

Dunbar, Carol A., BEd Belf., BA Open(UK), MSc Belf., PhD Belf. Sr. Lectr.

Dunn, Jill E., BSc Belf., MSc Belf., MEd Belf. Sr. Lectr.

Elliott, Denise F., BEd Belf. Sr. Lectr.

Ennis, Harriet G. Sr. Lectr.

Ferguson, James B., BA Trinity(Dub.), PhD Edin. Sr. Lectr.

Gardiner, Joanne, BEd Belf., MEd Belf. Sr. Lectr.

Greenwood, Julian G., BSc Belf., PhD CNAA Sr. Lectr.

Greenwood, Richard O., BSc S'ton., MEd Belf., MPhil Belf. Sr. Lectr.

Kearns, Hugh D., BA Belf., MEd Belf., MSc Belf. Sr. Lectr.

McAlister, Mary G., BEd Belf., MEd Belf. Sr. Lectr.

McClintock, Laura R., BEd Belf., MEd Belf. Sr. Lectr.

McCullagh, John F., BSc Belf., MSc Belf., MEd Belf., PhD Belf. Sr. Lectr.

McCurley, Michael A., BEd Belf., MA Belf. Sr. Lectr.

McMurray, Sharon, BEd Belf., BSc Open(UK), PhD Belf. Sr. Lectr.

Mitchell, Denise R., BA Belf., MA Belf., PhD Belf. Sr. Lectr.

Moffett, Pamela V., BSc Warw., PhD Belf. Sr. Lectr.

Moore, Jayne M., BEd Belf., MA Open(UK) Sr. Lectr.

Phoenix, Eamon G., BA Belf., MA Belf., PhD Belf. Sr. Lectr.

Reid, Christopher I., BEd Belf., MEd Belf., PhD Belf. Sr. Lectr.

Richardson, Norman L., MBE, BEd Belf., MA Belf. Sr. Lectr.

Siberry, Laurence F. G., LèsL Rouen, MA Ulster, MA Open(UK) Sr. Lectr.

Thatcher, Maureen, BA Belf., MEd Belf., EdD Belf. Head*

Wylie, Kenneth W., BA Belf., MA Belf. Sr. Lectr.

CONTACT OFFICERS

Academic affairs. Head of Quality Assurance and Partnerships: Ferguson, R.
(E-mail: qap@qub.ac.uk)

Accommodation. Head of Hospitality Services: Young, Caroline
(E-mail: accommodation@qub.ac.uk)

Admissions (first degree). Head of Admissions: Dwyer, Jennifer
(E-mail: admissions@qub.ac.uk)

Admissions (higher degree). Head of Admissions: Dwyer, Jennifer
(E-mail: postgrad.admissions@qub.ac.uk)

Alumni. Director of Development and Alumni Relations: Sinte, N.
(E-mail: alumni@qub.ac.uk)

Careers. Head of Careers Service: Stirrup, M. Jean, BA Belf., MBA Ulster
(E-mail: careers@qub.ac.uk)

Estates and buildings/works and services. Director of Estates: Jebb, Gary A., BSc, FRICS (E-mail: estates@qub.ac.uk)

Examinations. Head of Student Administrative Services and Systems: Skehin, Joanne
(E-mail: s.records@qub.ac.uk)

Finance. Director of Finance: Bennett, W. Norman, BSc(Econ)
(E-mail: finance.dept@qub.ac.uk)

General enquiries. Communications Office
(E-mail: comms.office@qub.ac.uk)

Health services. Senior GP Partner (University Health Centre): Fair, Barbara E.
(E-mail: reception.157@uhcq.gp.n-i.nhs.uk)

Industrial liaison. Chief Executive of QUBIS Ltd (Queen's University Business and Industrial Services): Lioulias, Panos
(E-mail: info@qubis.co.uk)

International office. Head of Marketing and Recruitment: Anton, Stephen
(E-mail: international@qub.ac.uk)

Library (chief librarian). Director of Information Services: Gormley, John
(E-mail: j.gormley@qub.ac.uk)

Personnel/human resources. Director of Human Resources: McGuickin, Sean, BA
(E-mail: personnel@qub.ac.uk)

Public relations. Director of Communications: Collins, Tom B., BA, FRSA
(E-mail: comms.office@qub.ac.uk)

Publications. Publications Manager: McKinney, T., BA (E-mail: publications@qub.ac.uk)

Purchasing. Head of Purchasing: Massey, Tricia (E-mail: purchasing@qub.ac.uk)

Safety. Head of Safety: Butler, Robin, BSc Belf.
(E-mail: safety@qub.ac.uk)

Scholarships, awards, loans. Administrative Officer: Bennett, M.
(E-mail: qap@qub.ac.uk)

Schools liaison. Head of Admissions: Dwyer, Jennifer (E-mail: admissions@qub.ac.uk)

Security. Security Manager: Chapman, I.
(E-mail: estates@qub.ac.uk)

Sport and recreation. Director of Queen's Sport and Recreation: Cusdin, M., MSc Leic.
(E-mail: sport@qub.ac.uk)

Staff development and training. Training and Development Manager: Guinane, F.
(E-mail: training@qub.ac.uk)

Student welfare/counselling. Head of Counselling Services: McMinn, Jean, BA MSc (E-mail: counsellor@qub.ac.uk)

Students from other countries. Head of Admissions: Dwyer, Jennifer
(E-mail: admissions@qub.ac.uk)

Students with disabilities. Disability Services Co-ordinator: Maguire, Linda
(E-mail: disability.office@qub.ac.uk)

CAMPUS/COLLEGE HEADS

Belfast Bible College, Glenburn House, Glenburn Road South, Dunmurry, Belfast, Northern Ireland BT17 9JP. (Tel: (028) 9030 1551; Fax: (028) 9043 1758; E-mail: reception@belfastbiblecollege.com) Principal: Shepherd, D.

Edgehill Theological College, 9 Lennoxvale, Belfast, Northern Ireland BT9 5BY. (Tel: (028) 9066 5870; Fax: (028) 9068 7204; E-mail: office@edgehillcollege.org) Principal: Clutterbuck, Rev. Richard N., BA Birm., MA Hull, PhD Birm.

Irish Baptist College, 19 Hillsborough Road, Moira, Northern Ireland BT67 0HG. (Tel: (028) 9261 9267; E-mail: ibc@thebaptistcentre.org) Principal: Moore, Rev. H., BD Belf., MTh Belf., PhD Belf.

Loughry Campus, College of Agriculture, Food and Rural Enterprise, Cookstown, County Tyrone, Northern Ireland BT80 9AA. (Tel: (028) 8676 8101; Fax: (028) 8676 1043; E-mail: enquiries@cafre.ac.uk) Deputy Director: Titterington, Ian, BAgri Belf.

St Mary's University College, 191 Falls Road, Belfast, Northern Ireland BT12 6FE. (Tel: (028) 9032 7678; Fax: (028) 9033 3719; E-mail: webmaster@stmarys-belfast.ac.uk) Principal: O'Callaghan, Very Rev. Prof. Martin, BA Belf., BD N.U.I., LSS Pontif.Bibl.Inst.

St Mary's University College, 191 Falls Road, Belfast, Northern Ireland BT12 6FE. (Tel: (028) 9032 7678; Fax: (028) 9033 3719; E-mail: webmaster@stmarys-belfast.ac.uk) Acting Principal: Finn, Peter B., BA Belf., MSSc Belf.

Stranmillis University College, Stranmillis Road, Belfast, Northern Ireland BT9 5DY. (Tel: (028) 9038 1271; Fax: (028) 9066 4423; E-mail: principal@stran.ac.uk) Principal: Heaslett, Anne, BA Ulster, MA Ulster, DPhil Ulster, FRSA

Union Theological College, 108 Botanic Avenue, Belfast, Northern Ireland BT7 1JT. (Tel: (028) 9020 5080; Fax: (028) 9020 5099; E-mail: admin@union.ac.uk) Principal: Taylor, Rev. Prof. J. Patton, TD, MA MTh

[Information supplied by the institution as at 19 December 2007, and edited by the ACU]

UNIVERSITY OF BIRMINGHAM

Founded 1900

Member of the Association of Commonwealth Universities

Postal Address: Edgbaston, Birmingham, England B15 2TT
Telephone: (0121) 414 3344 **Fax:** (0121) 414 3971
URL: http://www.bham.ac.uk

VICE-CHANCELLOR AND PRINCIPAL*—Sterling, Prof. Michael J. H., BEng Sheff., PhD Sheff., DEng Sheff., Hon. DEng Sheff., FREng, FRSA, FIMC, FIET
VICE-PRINCIPAL—Clarke, Prof. M. G., CBE, MA Sus.
PRO-VICE-CHANCELLOR—Cruise, Prof. A. M., BSc Lond., PhD Lond., FIP, FRAS
PRO-VICE-CHANCELLOR—(vacant)
PRO-VICE-CHANCELLOR—Clark, Prof. Les A., OBE, BEng Sheff., PhD Sheff., FIStructE, FICE, FREng
PRO-VICE-CHANCELLOR—Hughes, Prof. Alex, BA Lond., PhD Lond.
REGISTRAR AND SECRETARY AND DIRECTOR OF FINANCE‡—Sanders, Lee, BA Manc.
ACADEMIC REGISTRAR—Hall, David E., BA Reading
LIBRARIAN AND DIRECTOR OF INFORMATION SERVICES—Shoebridge, Michele I., BA Birm., MA Wolv.

GENERAL INFORMATION

History. Established as Mason Science College in 1880, and incorporated as Mason University College in 1898, the university was founded under its present name in 1900.

It is located about 4km from the centre of Birmingham.

Admission to first degree courses (see also United Kingdom Introduction). Through Universities and Colleges Admissions Service (UCAS). General Certificate of Education (GCE) A levels or equivalent qualifications, and English language proficiency (eg General Certificate of Secondary Education (GCSE) grade C). Certain subjects have specific subject requirements.

First Degrees (see also United Kingdom Directory to Subjects of Study). BA, BCom, BD, BDS, BEd, BEng, BLitt, BMedSc, BMus, BNurs, BPhil, BSc, BTheol, LLB, MB ChB, MEng, MNatSc, MSci.

BA/BCom/BSc/LLB with languages: 4 years. LLB honours (graduate entry): 2 years.

Length of course. Full-time: BPhil: 1 year; BD: 2 years; BA, BCom, BEd, BEng, BLitt, BMedSc, BMus, BSc, BTheol, LLB: 3 years; BNurs, MEng, MNatSc, MSci: 4 years; BDS, MB ChB: 5 years. Part-time: BPhil: 2 years. By distance learning: BPhil: 2–3 years.

Higher Degrees (see also United Kingdom Directory to Subjects of Study).

Master's. LLM, MA, MBA, MEd, MJur, MLitt, MMus, MPH, MPhil, MRes, MSc.

Admission. Applicants for admission to postgraduate courses should normally hold a good first degree from a recognised institution.

Length of course. Full-time: LLM, MA, MEd, MJur, MMus, MPH, MRes, MSc: 1 year; MBA, MPhil: 1–2 years; MLitt: 2 years. Part-time: LLM, MA, MEd, MJur, MMus, MPH, MRes, MSc: 2 years; MBA, MPhil: 2–4 years; MLitt: 4 years. By distance learning: MEd: 2–5 years.

Doctoral. ClinPsyD, DDS, DEng, DLitt, DMus, DSc, EdD, EdPsychD, MD, PhD, SocSciD, ThD.

Doctorates normally last 3 years full-time or 6 years part-time.

Length of course. Full-time: ClinPsyD, EdD, EdPsychD, SocSciD, ThD: 3 years; DEng, MD, PhD: 4 years. Part-time: DDS: 4 years; ClinPsyD, EdD, EdPsychD, SocSciD, ThD: 6 years; DEng, PhD: 8 years.

Libraries. Volumes: 2,702,763. Periodicals subscribed to: 13,184. Other holdings: 3,000,000 manuscript and archival items. Special collections: Lord Avon papers (Anthony Eden); Church Missionary Society archives; Harriet Martineau papers; Sir Oswald Mosley papers; Mingana collection (Arabic and Islamic studies); Noel Coward papers; Francis Brett Young papers; YMCA archives; Student

Christian Movement archives; New Shakespeare Company archives; W. H. Dawson papers; Austen, Joseph and Neville Chamberlain papers; Library of St Mary's Church, Warwick; James Rendell Harris.

Statistics. Staff (2005–2006): 5671 (3130 academic, 2541 non-academic). Students (2005–2006): full-time 21,016 (9450 men, 11,566 women); part-time 3751 (1516 men, 2235 women); international 4566 (2327 men, 2239 women); distance education/external 1924 (861 men, 1063 women); undergraduate 19,084 (8513 men, 10,571 women); master's 5249 (2085 men, 3164 women); doctoral 2358 (1229 men, 1129 women).

FACULTIES/SCHOOLS

Arts and Social Sciences

Tel: (0121) 414 7452 Fax: (0121) 414 3149
E-mail: a.j.randall@bham.ac.uk
Dean: Randall, Prof. Adrian J., BA Birm., MA Sheff., PhD Birm.
Secretary: Jenkins, Sarah

Life and Health Sciences

Tel: (0121) 414 7452 Fax: (0121) 414 3149
E-mail: p.m.marquis@bham.ac.uk
Dean: Marquis, Prof. Peter M., BSc Sur., PhD Birm., FIMMM
Secretary: Jenkins, Sarah

Physical Sciences and Engineering

Tel: (0121) 414 7452 Fax: (0121) 414 3149
E-mail: p.w.daniels@bham.ac.uk
Dean: Daniels, Prof. Peter W., BSc Lond., PhD Lond.
Secretary: Jenkins, Sarah

ACADEMIC UNITS

Arranged by Schools

Biosciences

Tel: (0121) 414 5400 Fax: (0121) 414 5925
Bale, J. S., BSc Newcastle(UK), PhD Newcastle(UK) Prof., Environmental Biology
Besra, G., BSc Newcastle(UK), PhD Newcastle(UK) Prof., Microbial Physiology and Chemistry
Blackburn, Tim M., BSc Manc., DPhil Oxf. Prof., Macroecology
Brandstaetter, Roland, MagRerNat Salzburg, DrRerNat Sr. Lectr.
Brown, N. L., BSc Leeds, PhD Leeds, FIBiol, FRSChem, FRSA Prof., Molecular Genetics and Microbiology
Bunce, C. M., BSc Birm., PhD Birm. Sr. Lectr.
Busby, S. J. W., MA Camb., DPhil Oxf., FRS Prof.
Butler, P. J., BSc S'ton., PhD E.Anglia, FIBiol Mason Prof., Comparative Physiology
Callow, J. A., BSc Sheff., PhD Sheff., FIBiol Mason Prof., Botany

Chipman, J. K., BSc Leic., PhD Reading, FIBiol, FRCPath Prof., Cell Toxicology
Cole, J. A., MA Oxf., DPhil Oxf. Head, Academic Programmes; Prof., Microbial Physiology and Biochemistry
Croxall, J. P., BA Oxf., PhD Auck. Hon. Prof.
Dennis, C., BSc Sheff., PhD Sheff. Hon. Prof.
Falciani, F., PhD Florence Sr. Lectr.
Ford-Lloyd, B. V., BSc Birm., PhD Birm. Reader
Franklin, F. C. H., BSc Wales, PhD Wales Prof., Plant Molecular Biology
Franklin-Tong, V. E., BSc Birm., PhD Birm. Prof., Plant Cell Biology
Green, J. R., BA Camb., PhD Camb. Sr. Lectr.
Greenwood, J., CBE, BA Oxf., PhD Manc. Hon. Prof.
Heath, J. K., BSc Glas., MA Oxf., DPhil Oxf. Prof., Biochemistry; Head*
Hidalgo, A., BSc Madrid, DPhil Oxf. Sr. Lectr.
Hotchin, N. A., BSc York(UK), PhD Lond. Sr. Lectr.
Hyde, E. I., BA Oxf., PhD CNAA Sr. Lectr.
Insall, R. H., BA Camb., MA Camb., PhD Camb. Prof., Cell Biology
Jackson, J. B., BSc Brist., PhD Brist. Prof., Bioenergetics
Jones, G. H., BSc Wales, PhD Wales Reader, Cytogenetics
Kearsey, M. J., BSc Wales, PhD Birm. Prof., Biometrical Genetics
Kimber, I., BSc Manc., PhD Manc. Hon. Prof.
Kirk, C. J., BSc Lond., PhD Lond., FIBiol Assoc. Prof.; Reader, Biochemistry
Leadbeater, B. S. C., BSc Lond., PhD Lond., DSc Lond. Reader, Protistology
Levine, B. A., BA Oxf., MPhil Oxf., DPhil Oxf. Reader, Biophysics
Lund, P. A., BA Camb., DPhil Sus. Sr. Lectr.
Luo, Z., BSc Chongqing, MSc Chongqing, PhD Birm. Reader
Macaskie, L. E., BSc Lond., PhD Lond. Prof., Applied Microbiology
Machesky, L. M., BSc Alma, PhD Johns H. Prof., Cell Biology
Martin, Graham R., BSc Sur., PhD Exe., DSc Birm. Prof., Avian Sensory Science
Maxted, N., BSc CNAA, MPhil S'ton., PhD S'ton. Sr. Lectr.
Michelangeli, F., BSc Lanc., PhD S'ton. Sr. Lectr.
Michell, R. H., PhD Birm., DSc Birm., FRS, FMedSci Royal Soc. Res. Prof.
Minchin, S. D., BSc Birm., DPhil Sus. Sr. Lectr.
Minnikin, D. E., MA Oxf., DPhil Oxf. Emer. Prof., Microbial Chemistry
Newbury, H. J., BSc Leeds, PhD Leeds Deputy Head; Reader, Plant Molecular Biology
Page, M. G., BSc Brist., PhD Newcastle(UK) Hon. Prof.
Penn, C. W., BSc Liv., PhD CNAA Prof., Molecular Microbiology
Pooni, H. S., MSc Punjab, PhD Birm. Sr. Lectr.
Pritchard, J., BSc Sus., PhD Wales Sr. Lectr.

Publicover, S. J., BSc Liv., PhD Liv.   Sr. Lectr.

Pullin, A. S., BSc Warw., MSc Durh., PhD CNAA   Reader

Ride, J. P., BSc Birm., PhD Birm.   Sr. Lectr.

Strain, A. J., BSc St And., PhD Lond.   Prof., Biochemistry

Sweet, C., BSc Wales, PhD Wales, DSc Birm., FIBiol   Sr. Lectr.

Taylor, E. W., BSc S'ton., PhD S'ton., FIBiol, FLS   Prof., Animal Physiology

Thomas, C. M., MA Oxf., DPhil Oxf., FIBiol   Dir., Bioscis. Grad. Res. Sch.; Prof., Molecular Genetics

Trayer, I. P., PhD Birm., DSc Birm.   Emer. Prof.

Wang, T., PhD Aarhus, MSc   Hon. Prof.

Waring, R. H., MA Camb., PhD Birm., DSc Birm., FRCPath   Reader, Human Toxicology

Wharton, C. W., BSc Lond., PhD Lond.   Prof., Biochemistry

Wheatley, M., BSc Lond., PhD Nott.   Reader

White, S. A., BSc Edin., PhD Edin.   Reader, Structural Biology

Other Staff: 13 Lectrs.; 4 Sr. Res. Fellows; 82 Res. Fellows; 8 Res. Assocs.; 11 Hon. Sr. Lectrs.; 10 Hon. Lectrs.; 4 Hon. Sr. Res. Fellows; 11 Hon. Res. Fellows

Research: molecular cell and pathology; molecular microbiology; organismal and environmental biology; plant genetics and cell biology; structural biology

Birmingham Business School

Tel: (0121) 414 6225 Fax: (0121) 414 7380

Michie, J., BA Oxf., MSc Lond., DPhil Oxf.   Prof., Management; Dir.*

Research: accounting and finance; business strategy and procurement; industrial relations and labour economics; international management and organisation; marketing

Accounting and Finance

Tel: (0121) 414 6530 Fax: (0121) 414 6678

Adedeji, T. A., BSc Ib., MBA Lagos, PhD Manc.   Sr. Lectr.

Alexander, D. J., BSc Brist., FCA   Prof., International Accounting

Coad, A. F., MBA Aston   Sr. Lectr.

Craner, J. M., MSocSc Birm., FCA, FRSA   Sr. Lectr.

Georgiou, George   Sr. Lectr.

Jelic, R., BSc Belgrade, MSc Belgrade, MSc Lond., PhD Hull   Reader, Finance

Jones, R. H., MA Lanc., PhD Lanc.   Prof., Public Sector Accounting

Lymer, A. M., BSc Wales, MPhil Wales   Sr. Lectr.

Mallin, Christine A., BSc Aston, PhD Nott., FCA, FRSA   Prof., Corporate Governance and Finance

Mullineux, A. W., BA Liv., MSc Lond., PhD CNAA   Prof., Global Finance

Murinde, V., BA Mak., MSc Wales, PhD Wales   Prof., Development Finance

Samuels, J. M., BCom Birm.   Prof., Business Finance

Schroeder, M. A. S., BA Exe., MSc Lond.   Sr. Lectr.

Theobald, M. F., BSc Lond., MA Manc., PhD Manc., FCA   Prof., Finance and Investment; Head*

Other Staff: 7 Lectrs.

Research: corporate finance; emerging financial markets; international accounting; investments; public sector accounting

Business Strategy and Procurement, Centre for

Cox, A. W., BA Lanc., MA Mich., PhD Essex   Prof.; Dir.*

Research: business strategy and procurement

Economic Development Policy, Institute for

Bailey, D. G., BSocSc Birm., MSocSc Birm., PhD Birm.   Sr. Lectr.; Head, Indust. and Labour Econ.

Hanlon, J. P., BSc(Econ) Hull, MA(Econ) Manc., PhD Birm.   Sr. Lectr.

Siebert, W. S., BA Cape Town, MSc Lond., PhD Lond.   Prof., Labour Economics

Slater, J. R., BSc Birm., BCom Birm.   Sr. Lectr.

Sugden, R., BA(Law) Sheff., MA Warw., PhD Warw.   Prof.; Dir.*

Research: industrial and labour economics

International Management and Organisation, Institute for

Child, J., MA Camb., PhD Camb., ScD Camb., Hon. DEcon Helsinki   Prof., International Management and Organisation; Head*

Forrester, P. L., BSc Aston, PhD Aston   Sr. Lectr.

Tann, J., BA Manc., PhD Leic.   Prof., Innovation Studies

Research: international management and organisation

Marketing

Carrigan, Marylyn   Sr. Lectr.

de Chernatony, Leslie, BSc Kent, PhD City(UK), FCIM   Prof., Brand Marketing

Hyde, Peter   Dir., Grad. Diploma Bus. Admin.

Marinova, S. T., MSc Warw., MBA Warw., PhD   Sr. Lectr.

Michie, J., BA Oxf., MSc Lond., DPhil Oxf.   Prof., Management

Szmigin, I. T., BA Reading, MBA City(UK), PhD Birm.   Prof.

Turnbull, P. W., BSc UMIST   Prof.

West, Douglas   Prof.

White, J.   Prof.

Other Staff: 11 Lectrs.; 1 Res. Fellow; 1 Res. Assoc.; 1 Hon. Sr. Visiting Fellow

Research: marketing

Chemistry

Tel: (0121) 414 4361 Fax: (0121) 414 4403
E-mail: chem-sci@bham.ac.uk

Allemann, R. K., BSc Zür., PhD Zür.   Prof., Chemical Biology

Byers, P. K., BSc Tas., PhD Tas.   Assoc. Prof.; Head*

Gameson, I., BSc Wales, PhD Camb.   Sr. Lectr., Inorganic Chemistry

Greaves, C., MA Oxf., DPhil Oxf., FIP, FRSChem   Prof., Solid State Chemistry

Hannon, M. J.   Prof., Chemical Biology

Hriljac, J. A., BSc Ill., PhD Northwestern   Sr. Lectr., Inorganic Chemistry

Johnston, Roy L., MA Oxf., DPhil Oxf.   Reader; Deputy Head

Parsons, I. W.   Sr. Lectr., Physical Chemistry

Pikramenou, Z.   Reader, Supramolecular Chemistry

Preece, J. A., BSc Lough., PhD Birm.   Prof., Nanoscale Chemistry

Rayment, T.   Prof., Physical Chemistry

Smith, Ian W. M., FRS   Emer. Prof., Physical Chemistry

Tucker, J.   Reader, Supramolecular Chemistry

Tuckett, Richard P., BA Camb., PhD Camb., FRSChem   Prof., Chemical Physics

Other Staff: 10 Lectrs.; 1 Royal Society Res. Fellow; 1 EPSRC Res. Fellow; 1 Univ. Res. Fellow; 1 Res. Fellow; 3 Res. Assocs.; 1 Hon. Reader; 2 Hon. Lectrs.

Research: materials chemistry; molecular processes and theory; molecular synthesis and chemical biology

Computer Science

Tel: (0121) 414 3744 Fax: (0121) 414 4281

Barnden, John   Prof.

Bullinaria, John   Sr. Lectr.

Claridge, E., MSc Gdansk, PhD Birm.   Reader, Medical Image Analysis

Coxhead, P., MA Camb., MSc Birm., PhD Camb.   Sr. Lectr.

Dearden, Richard   Sr. Lectr.

Edmondson, W. H., BSc Sur., MA Essex, PhD Lond.   Sr. Lectr.

Hancox, P. J., BA Lough., PhD Lough.   Sr. Lectr.

Jung, A., PhD T.H.Darmstadt   Prof.

Kwiatkowska, M. Z., MSc Cracow, PhD Leic.   Prof.

Reddy, U., MSc BITS, MS N.Carolina, PhD Utah   Prof.; Head*

Rowe, John   Sr. Lectr.

Ryan, M. D., MA Camb., PhD Lond.   Reader

Sloman, Prof. Aaron   Prof.

Theodoropoulos, Georgios   Sr. Lectr.

Vickers, S. J., MA Camb., PhD Leeds   Sr. Lectr.

Wyatt, Jeremy   Sr. Lectr.

Yao, Xin, BSc China U.S.T., MSc China U.S.T., PhD China U.S.T.   Prof.

Other Staff: 18 Lectrs.; 1 Sr. Tutor; 24 Res. Fellows; 8 Res. Assocs.; 2 Hon. Sr. Lectrs.; 4 Hon. Lectrs.; 8 Hon. Res. Fellows

Research: distributed systems, principles of programming; foundations of computer science; modelling and analysis of systems; natural computation, image interpretation and robotics; reasoning and cognition, language and interaction

Dentistry

Tel: (0121) 237 2763 Fax: (0121) 625 8815

Attrill, D. C., BDS Manc., PhD Manc., FDSRCS   Sr. Lectr.

Burke, F. J. T., BDS Belf., MDS Belf., MSc Manc., DDS Manc., FDSRCPSGlas, FDSRCS   Prof., Primary Dental Care

Chapple, I. L. C., BDS Newcastle(UK), PhD, FDSRCPSGlas   Prof., Periodontology

Cooper, P.   Sr. Lectr.

Hamburger, J., BDS MSc, FFDRCSI   Sr. Lectr.

Landini, G., DOdont Republic(Montevideo), PhD Kagoshima   Reader, Oral Pathology

Lumley, P. J., BDS Dund., MDentSc Birm., PhD Glas., FDSRCPSGlas, FDSRCS   Prof., Endodontology; Dir. and Head*

Marquis, Peter M., BSc Sur., PhD Birm., FIMMM   Prof., Biomaterials

Matthews, J. B., BSc Leeds, MSc PhD   Reader, Oral Immunology

Rock, W. P., MBE, JP, BDS DDS, FDSRCS   Reader, Orthodontics

Sammons, R. L.   Sr. Lectr.

Shelton, R. M., BDS PhD   Sr. Lectr.

Shortall, A. C. C., BDS Belf., DDS, FDSRCPSGlas, FFDRCSI   Reader, Restorative Dentistry

Smith, A. J., BSc Liv., PhD Liv.   Prof., Oral Biology

Walmsley, A. D., BDS Manc., MSc Manc., PhD Manc., FDSRCPSGlas   Prof., Restorative Dentistry

White, D. A., BDS Manc., PhD   Sr. Lectr.; Dir., Teaching and Learning

Other Staff: 17 Lectrs.; 5 Res. Fellows; 2 Res. Assocs.; 44 Lectrs.†; 13 Postgrad. Clin. Tutors; 4 Hon. Sr. Lectrs.; 1 Hon. Res. Fellow; 1 Hon. Res. Assoc.; 26 Hon. Sr. Clin. Lectrs.; 47 Hon. Clin. Lectrs.

Research: biomaterial development, mechanistic behaviour, performance and tissue engineering; primary dental care (translational, epidemiology, access/ provision, healthcare); tissue injury and repair (molecular/cellular behaviour, regenerative medicine, diagnosis)

Education

Tel: (0121) 414 4866 Fax: (0121) 414 4865
E-mail: education@bham.ac.uk

Benn, T., BEd Nott., MSc Leic., MEd Exe., PhD Lough.   Assoc. Prof.

Blackledge, A., BA Lond., MEd Birm., PhD Birm.   Sr. Lectr.

Bullock, Alison   Reader

Butt, G. W., MA Lond., MA Oxf., PhD Birm.   Sr. Lectr.

Creese, A., BA Leeds, MSc Penn., PhD Penn.   Reader

Davies, M. L., BA Exe., MEd PhD   Prof., International Education

Gorman, Tom   Strand Leader, Drama

Gray, C., BA Birm., PhD Birm.   Sr. Lectr.

Grosvenor, I. D., BA Hull, PhD Birm.   Prof.; Dir., Learning and Teaching*

Harber, Clive N., BA Reading, MA Leic., PhD Birm.   Prof., International Education; Head*

Hartley, Prof. David   Prof.

Hewitt, D. P., BA Warw., PhD Open(UK)   Sr. Lectr.

Holmes, J. G., BA Liv., MA Manit.   Sr. Lectr.

Jordan, R. R., OBE, BSc Lond., MSc Lond., MA CNAA, PhD Birm.   Prof.
Lacey, P. J., BA Kent, BEd Warw., MEd Birm., PhD Birm.   Sr. Lectr.
Lance, A., BEd Birm., MSocSc Birm.   Sr. Lectr.
Lewis, A., BEd Birm., BPhil C.England, MEd Birm., PhD Warw.   Prof., Special Education and Education Psychology
Lock, R. J., BSc Aberd., PhD Leeds, FIBiol   Sr. Lectr.
Martin, D. M., MSc Birm., PhD Birm.   Sr. Lectr.
Martin-Jones, Marilyn   Prof.
McLinden, Mike   Sr. Lectr.
Mills, J., BA Warw., BPhil Warw., MA Guelph   Sr. Lectr.
Pilkington, R. M., BSc York(UK), PhD Leeds   Sr. Lectr.
Powers, S. G., BA Camb., MA Lond.   Sr. Lectr.
Prestage, S. A., BA Lond., MA Lond.   Sr. Lectr.
Rayner, S. G., BA Nott., MEd Nott., PhD Birm.   Sr. Lectr.; Dir., Res. Studies*
Rhodes, Christopher   Sr. Lectr.
Rutherford, R. J. D., BSc Durh., PhD Durh.   Sr. Lectr.
Schweisfurth, M., MSc Oxf., Hon. BA W.Ont.   Sr. Lectr.
Selwood, Ian   Sr. Lectr.
Sondhi, R., BSc Birm., FRSA   Sr. Lectr.
Thomas, Gary   Prof.
Thomas, H. R., BA Manc., MEd Manc., PhD Birm.   Prof., Economics of Education
Visser, J. G., BA Open(UK), MEd Wales, PhD Birm.   Sr. Lectr.
Watson, Linda   Sr. Lectr.
Watts, R. E., BA Lond., MA Leic., PhD Leic.   Prof.; Co-Dir., DOMUS Res. Centre for Interdisciplinary Res. into the Histories of Educn. and Childhood
Other Staff: 31 Lectrs.; 1 Sr. Res. Fellow; 13 Res. Fellows; 1 Sr. Tutor; 1 Res. Assoc.
Research: culture and heritage; language and education; management and policy; special education and social inclusion; teaching and learning

Engineering

Tel: (0121) 414 4272 Fax: (0121) 414 4269
E-mail: s.m.mcdonald@bham.ac.uk
Acres, G. J. K., OBE, MSc PhD, FIChemE   Royal Academy of Engin. Visiting Prof., Sustainable Development
Blackburn, S., BSc CNAA, MSc Birm., PhD Birm.   Prof.; Head, Interdisciplinary Res. Centre in Materials Processing
Davies, G. J., BSc Wales, PhD Wales, DSc Wales, FREng   Chance Prof.; Head*
Irwin, F. G. E., BA Trinity(Dub.), BAI Trinity(Dub.), MSc Iowa State, FICE, FIStructE   Royal Academy of Engin. Visiting Prof., Principles of Industrial Design
Oates, G., BSc PhD, FREng, FIMMM   Royal Academy of Engin. Visiting Prof., Principles of Industrial Design
Seville, J. P. K., MA Camb., MEng Camb., PhD Sur., FIChemE, FREng   Prof.; Dir., Res. Centres

Biomedical Engineering Research Centre

Arvanitis, Theodoros N., DPhil Sus.   Sr. Lectr.
Hukins, David W. L., BSc Lond., PhD Lond., DSc Manc., FIP, FIPEM, FRSEd   Prof.; Head*
Other Staff: 1 Lectr.; 1 Res. Fellow

Chemical Engineering

Tel: (0121) 414 5355 Fax: (0121) 414 5324
Adams, M. J., PhD, FIChemE, FREng, FIP   Unilever Prof., Product Engineering and Manufacturing
Al-Duri, B., BSc Jordan, PhD Belf.   Sr. Lectr.
Arrowsmith, A., BSc Sheff., PhD Sheff.   Sr. Lectr.
Barigou, M., BEng Brad., PhD Bath   Prof.
Biddlestone, A. J., BSc PhD, FIChemE, FRSA   Emer. Prof.
Blackburn, S., BSc CNAA, MSc Birm., PhD Birm.   Prof., Solids Processing
Fryer, P. J., MA Camb., MEng Camb., PhD Camb., FIChemE, FREng   Prof.

Hewitt, C. J.   Sr. Lectr.
Kendall, K., BSc Lond., PhD Camb., FRS   Prof., Formulation Engineering
Kent, C. A., BSc Birm., PhD Birm.   Sr. Lectr.
Nienow, A. W., PhD Lond., DSc Lond., FREng, FIChemE   Emer. Prof., Biochemical Engineering
Pacek, A. W., MSc T.U.Warsaw, PhD T.U.Warsaw   Reader, Multiphase Processing
Rowson, N. A., BSc CNAA, PhD Leeds   Reader, Minerals Engineering
Seville, J. P. K., MA Camb., MEng Camb., PhD Sur., FIChemE, FREng   Prof.; Head*
Simmons, M. J.   Sr. Lectr.
Thomas, C. R., BA Camb., MA Camb., PhD Lond., FIChemE   Prof., Biochemical Engineering
Thomas, O. R., BSc PhD   Prof., Biochemical Engineering
Winterbottom, J. M., BSc Hull, PhD Hull   Prof., Chemical Reaction Engineering
Zhang, Z., BSc Hefei Technol., MSc Shanghai, PhD Shanghai   Prof.
Other Staff: 2 Lectrs.; 1 Sr. Res. Fellow; 2 Birm. Res. Fellows; 12 Res. Fellows
Research: food and pharmaceutical engineering; formulated products; formulation engineering; multiphase engineering; reaction engineering and supercritical fluid processing

Civil Engineering

Tel: (0121) 414 5049 Fax: (0121) 414 3675
Baker, C. J., BA Camb., MA Camb., PhD Camb., FIHT   Head, Railway Res. Centre; Prof., Environmental Fluid Mechanics; Head*
Bridgeman, J.   Sr. Lectr.
Chan, A. H. C., BSc HK, MPhil HK, PhD Wales   Prof., Computational Engineering
Chapman, D. N., BSc Lough., PhD Lough.   Sr. Lectr.
Clark, Les A., OBE, BEng Sheff., PhD Sheff., FIStructE, FICE, FREng   Prof., Structural Engineering
Coates, L. E., BSc City(UK), PhD City(UK)   Sr. Lectr.; Head, Teaching Devel., Sch. of Engin.
Dawe, Prof. D. J.   Emer. Prof.
Gaterell, M.   Sr. Lectr.; Dir., Res. for Sustainable Engin.
Hamlin, M. J., CBE, BSc Brist., LLD St And.   Emer. Prof.
Jefferson, I.   Sr. Lectr.
Knight, D. W., BSc(Eng) Lond., MSc Aberd., PhD Aberd.   Prof., Water Engineering
Perry, J. G., BEng Liv., MEng Liv., PhD Manc., FICE   Emer. Prof.
Rogers, C. D. F., BSc Leeds, PhD Nott.   Prof., Geotechnical Engineering
Snaith, M. S., MA Trinity(Dub.), BAI Trinity(Dub.), MSc Trinity(Dub.), ScD Trinity(Dub.), PhD Nott., FICE, FREng, FIHT   Emer. Prof., Highway Engineering
Other Staff: 8 Lectrs.; 8 Res. Fellows; 1 Roberts Res. Fellow; 4 Res. Assocs.
Research: computational civil engineering; infrastructure engineering and management; road/railway operations and asset management; water engineering and environmental management; wind engineering and wind loading

Electronic, Electrical and Computer Engineering

Tel: (0121) 414 4285 Fax: (0121) 414 4291
Arvanitis, Theodoros N., DPhil Sus.   Sr. Lectr.
Atkins, P. R., BSc Birm., MPhil(Eng) Birm.   Sr. Lectr.
Baber, C., BA Keele, PhD Aston   Reader, Interactive Systems
Brdys, M. A., MSc Warsaw, PhD Warsaw, DSc Warsaw, FIMA   Sr. Lectr.; Head, Decision Support and Control Sys. Network Res. Centre*
Cherniakov, M., BEng Moscow, PhD Moscow, DSc Moscow   Sr. Lectr.
Constantinou, C. C., BEng Birm., PhD Birm.   Sr. Lectr.

Gardner, P., BA Oxf., MSc Manc., PhD Manc.   Sr. Lectr.
Ghafouri-Shiraz, H., BSc Shiraz, MSc Shiraz, DEng Tokyo   Sr. Lectr.
Goodman, C. J., MA Camb., PhD Camb.   Reader, Traction Systems
Hall, P. S., BSc Sheff., MSc Sheff., PhD Sheff., FIEE, FIEEE   Dir., Wave Solutions; Prof., Communications Engineering
Lancaster, M. J., BSc Bath, PhD Bath   Head, Emerging Device Technol. Res. Centre; Prof., Microwave Engineering; Head*
Megaw, E. D., BA Camb., MSc PhD, FErgS   Sr. Lectr.
Russell, M. J., BSc Hull, PhD Hull, FIMA   Head, Interactive Electronic and Communication Systems Res. Centre; Deputy Head; Prof., Information Engineering
Spann, M., BSc Manc., MSc Manc., PhD Aston   Sr. Lectr.
Stone, R. J., BSc Lond., MSc Lond., FErgS   Chair, Interactive Multimedia Sys.; Dir., Human Interface Technologies Team; Prof., Interactive Multimedia Systems
Other Staff: 14 Lectrs.
Research: communications engineering, radar, antennas and networks; digital systems, vision, speech and acoustics; educational and human interface technologies; electronic materials and devices, and microwave circuits; power electronics, traction systems and control

Mechanical and Manufacturing Engineering

Tel: (0121) 414 4161 Fax: (0121) 414 3958
Aspinwall, D. K., MSc Birm.   Reader, Advanced Manufacturing Technology
Aspinwall, E., BSc CNAA, MSc   Sr. Lectr.
Bakhtar, F., BSc MSc PhD DSc, FIMechE   Hon. Prof.
Ball, A. A., BSc Lond., PhD E.Anglia   Prof., Engineering Design
Dean, T. A., BSc(Eng) Lond., MSc(Eng) Lond., PhD Birm.   Emer. Prof.
Hartley, P., BSc Aston, PhD Birm., FIMechE   Reader, Plasticity
Hodgson, D. C.   Sr. Lectr.
Hukins, David W. L., BSc Lond., PhD Lond., DSc Manc., FIP, FIPEM, FRSEd   Prof., Biomedical Engineering; Head*
Jolly, M.   Sr. Lectr.
Lin, J., BEng Xinjiang Ag., MSc Taiyuan U.T., PhD Sheff.   Sr. Lectr.
Loftus, M., BSc H-W, MSc PhD PhD   Sr. Lectr.
Neal-Sturgess, C. E., BSc CNAA, PhD Birm., FIMechE, FIMMM, FRSA   Dir., Accident Res. Centre; Jaguar Prof., Automotive Engineering
Prewett, P. D., BSc Wales, DPhil Oxf., FIP   Head, Microengin. and Nanotechnol. Res. Centre; Lucas Prof., Microsystems Manufacture and Nanotechnology
Tobias, A. M., BSc Nott., PhD Nott.   Sr. Lectr.
Walton, D., BTech Lough., PhD Brist., FIMechE   Prof., Mechanical Engineering
Ward, M. C. L., BSc Lond., PhD Warw.   Sr. Lectr.
Wyszynski, M. L., MEng Warsaw, PhD Warsaw   Prof.
Xu, H. M.   Reader; Reader, Future Power Sys. Res. Group
Other Staff: 7 Lectrs.; 1 Industrial Tutor; 1 Project Officer; 1 Hon. Reader
Research: biomedical engineering; machining, metalforming and quality; microengineering and nanotechnology; vehicle technology (engines, safety)

Metallurgy and Materials

Tel: (0121) 414 5221 Fax: (0121) 414 5232
Abell, J. S., BSc Reading, PhD Sur., DSc Birm., FIP   Prof., Functional Materials
Bell, T.   Hanson Prof., Metallurgy
Bowen, P., MA Camb., PhD Camb., FIMMM, FIMechE, FREng   Prof., Mechanical Metallurgy; Head*

Campbell, J., OBE, MA Sheff., MMet Sheff., PhD Birm., DEng Birm., FREng, FIMMM Prof., Casting Technology

Chang, I. T. H., BSc Lond., DPhil Oxf. Sr. Lectr.

Davenport, A. J., BA Camb., MA Camb., PhD Camb. Reader, Corrosion Science

Davis, C. L., BA Camb., PhD Camb. Sr. Lectr.

Evans, H. E., BSc Wales, PhD Wales, FIMMM Prof.†, High Temperature Materials

Fernando, G. Prof.

Green, Nick Prof.

Hall, M. G., BMet Sheff., PhD Sheff. Sr. Lectr.

Harris, I. R., BSc Birm., PhD Birm., DSc Birm., FIMMM, FREng Prof., Materials Science

Hay, J. N., BSc Glas., PhD Glas., DSc Birm., FRSChem Reader; Hon. Prof.

Jones, Ian P., MA Camb., PhD, FIP Prof., Physical Metallurgy

Knott, J. F., BMet Sheff., ScD Camb., FRS, FREng, FIMMM, FIMechE Feeney Prof.

Kukureka, S. N., BSc Brist., PhD Camb., FIMMM Sr. Lectr.

Mills, N. J., MA Camb., MSc Cran., PhD Birm., DEng Reader, Polymer Engineering

Ponton, C. B., BSc(Eng) Lond., PhD Lond. Sr. Lectr.

Strangwood, M., MA Camb., PhD Camb. Sr. Lectr.

Other Staff: 2 Lectrs.; 1 Univ. Res. Fellow; 1 Univ. Res. Fellow/Lectr.; 16 Res. Fellows; 1 Visiting Lectr./Hon. Fellow

Research: advanced processing (ceramics, metals, polymers); functional materials (superconductors, magnets, microwave devices); microstructural characterisation, including chemical nano-analysis; sports and biomedical materials; structural materials (fatigue, fracture toughness, failure)

Geography, Earth and Environmental Sciences

Tel: (0121) 414 5544 Fax: (0121) 414 5528

Petts, Judith I., BA Exe., PhD Lough. Prof.; Head*

Research: business, enterprise and local development in developed, developing and transitional economies; climate and atmosphere; earth system sciences; environment, health and risk management; hydroecology and hydrogeology

Earth Sciences

Tel: (0121) 414 6751 Fax: (0121) 414 4942

Chambers, A. D., BSc Durh., PhD Durh. Sr. Lectr.

Mackay, R., BSc Lond., PhD Newcastle(UK) Prof., Hydrogeology

Reston, Tim Prof., Geology

Smith, M. P., BSc Leic., PhD Nott. Prof., Palaeobiology; Dir.*

Tellam, J. H., BSc S'ton., MSc Birm., PhD Birm. Prof., Hydrogeology

Thomas, A. T., BSc Keele, PhD Camb. Sr. Lectr., Palaeobiology; Dir., Learning and Teaching

Turner, J. Sr. Lectr.

Turner, P., PhD Leic., DSc Wales, FGS Reader, Sedimentology

Westbrook, G. K., BSc Lond., PhD Durh., FRAS, FGS Prof., Geophysics

Other Staff: 5 Lectrs.; 6 Res. Fellows; 2 Res. Assocs.; 1 Hon. Reader; 1 Hon. Res. Fellow

Research: earth systems sciences

Environmental Health and Risk Management, Division of

Tel: (0121) 414 3494 Fax: (0121) 414 3709

Brennan, Maurice Head, Teaching

Harrad, S. J., BSc De Mont., MSc E.Anglia, PhD E.Anglia Sr. Lectr.

Harrison, R. M., OBE, BSc Birm., PhD Birm., DSc Birm., FRSChem Queen Elizabeth II Birmingham Centenary Prof.

Lead, J. R., BSc Sus., PhD Lanc. Sr. Lectr.

Other Staff: 3 Lectrs.; 2 Teaching Fellows; 7 Res. Fellows; 3 Res. Assocs.; 2 Hon. Sr.

Lectrs.; 16 Hon. Lectrs.; 8 Hon. Res. Fellows; 7 Hon. Res. Assocs.

Geography and Environmental Sciences

Baker, A., BSc Birm., PhD Birm. Reader, Physical Geography

Bryson, J. R., BA Trinity(Dub.), PhD Leic. Prof., Enterprise and Economic Geography

Cai, X., MSc Fudan, PhD Br.Col. Sr. Lectr.

Cook, Ian Sr. Lectr.

Daniels, Peter W., BSc Lond., PhD Lond. Prof.

Fairchild, I. J., BSc Nott., PhD Nott. Prof., Earth Science Processes

Gwynne, R. N., MA Oxf., BPhil Liv., PhD Liv. Reader, Latin American Development

Hannah, David Sr. Lectr.

Kidd, C., BSc Nott., PhD Brist. Sr. Lectr.

Lawler, D. M., BA Wales, PhD Wales Sr. Lectr.

Milner, A., BSc Aston, MSc Lond., PhD Lond. Reader, Stream Ecology

Petts, Judith I., BA Exe., PhD Lough. Prof., Environmental Risk Management

Sadler, J. P., BSc Sheff., PhD Sheff. Sr. Lectr.

Shaw, Denis J. B., BA Lond., PhD Lond. Reader, Russian Geography

Slater, Terry R., BA Hull, PhD Birm. Reader, Historical Geography

Taylor, M. J., PhD Lond. Prof., Human Geography

Thornes, J. E., BSc Manc.Met., MSc Lond., PhD Lond. Reader, Applied Meteorology

Other Staff: 18 Lectrs.; 6 Res. Fellows; 7 Res. Assocs.; 5 Hon. Sr. Res. Fellows; 16 Hon. Res. Fellows; 4 Hon. Res. Assocs.

Research: business, enterprise and local development in developed, developing and transitional economies; environment, health and risk management

Health Sciences

Tel: (0121) 414 6893 Fax: (0121) 414 3158 E-mail: healthsciences@bham.ac.uk

Clifford, C. M., MSc Manc., PhD Birm. Jenny Jones Prof.; Dir., Res.

Hicks, C. M., BA Exe., MA Exe., PhD Aston Prof., Health Care Psychology

Sackley, C. M., MSc S'ton., PhD Nott. Prof., Physiotherapy

Wrightson, P. A., BA Open(UK), MSocSc Birm. Prof., Physiotherapy; Head of Sch.*

Research: health maintenance and rehabilitation (stroke, musculoskeletal); practice enhancement (genetics, health, practice development)

Nursing

Clifford, C. M. Prof.

Daly, W. N., BSc C.England, PhD Wolv. Sr. Lectr.; Dir., Teaching and Learning

Hewison, A., BSc C.England, MA Warw., PhD Coventry Sr. Lectr.; Dir., Postgrad. Studies

Other Staff: 24 Lectrs.; 2 Clin. Tutors

Physiotherapy

Tel: (0121) 627 2020 Fax: (0121) 627 2021

Broadfield, J. E., BA Open(UK), MSc Sr. Lectr.; Dir.. Undergrad. Studies

Kelly, S. M., MSc Lough., PhD Birm. Sr. Lectr.

Other Staff: 21 Lectrs.; 6 Clin. Tutors

Historical Studies

Tel: (0121) 414 6627 Fax: (0121) 414 7685 E-mail: historical@bham.ac.uk

West, S. C., BA Virginia, PhD St And. Prof.; Head*

Research: ancient, mediaeval and modern history; archaeology, material culture and visual representation; globalisation and global cultures; Mediterranean studies; religion and society

American and Canadian Studies

Tel: (0121) 414 5740 Fax: (0121) 414 6866

Beckford, Robert Lectr.; Diasporan Studies Co-ord.; Chair, Journal of Black Theol.

Ellis, Dick Res. Co-ord.; Head*

Fuller, Danielle Lectr.; Dir., Regional Centre for Canadian Studies

Gair, Chris Sr. Lectr.; Dir., Res.

Other Staff: 4 Lectrs.

Research: history, film, television and television production; post-national studies; trans-Atlantic and global American studies; US and Canadian literature and film; US foreign policy, intelligence and propaganda

Archaeology and Antiquity, Institute of

Tel: (0121) 414 5497 Fax: (0121) 414 3595

Barker, A. D., MA Camb. Prof., Classics

Brickley, M. B., MSc Lond., BA PhD Sr. Lectr.

Brubaker, L., BA Penn., MA Penn., PhD Johns H. Asst. Dir., Res.; Prof., Byzantine Art

Bryer, A. A. M., MA Oxf., DPhil Oxf., FSA Emer. Prof, Byzantine Studies

Costa, C. D. N., BPhil Oxf., MA Oxf. Emer. Prof.

Dowden, K., MA Oxf. Prof., Classics; Dir.*

Esmonde Cleary, A. S., BA Lond., DPhil Oxf., FSA Sr. Lectr.

Fox, M. A., MA Oxf., DPhil Oxf. Sr. Lectr.

Gaffney, V. L., BA Reading, PhD Reading Prof., Landscape Archaeology and Geomatics

Harlow, M. E., BA Leic., PhD Leic. Sr. Lectr., Roman History

Hunter, John R., BA Durh., PhD Durh., FSA Prof., Ancient History and Archaeology

Leahy, M. A., MA Camb., PhD Camb. Sr. Lectr., Egyptology

Limbrey, S. P., BSc Lond., PhD Lond. Emer. Prof., Environmental Archaeology

Livingstone, A., MA Camb., PhD Birm., DrHabil Heidel. Reader, Assyriology

Macrides, Ruth Sr. Lectr., Byzantine Studies

Murphey, W. R., MA Chic., PhD Chic. Reader, Ottoman Studies

Tziovas, D. P., BA Ioannina, PhD Birm. Prof., Modern Greek Studies

Wardle, K. A., MA Camb., FSA Sr. Lectr.

White, R. H., BA Liv., PhD Liv. Sr. Lectr.; Asst. Dir., Devel.

Other Staff: 12 Lectrs.; 4 B'ham Res. Fellows; 3 IARH Fellows; 1 AHRB Res. Fellow; 8 Res. Fellows; 2 Res. Assocs.; 1 Teaching Fellow; 1 Instr.; 1 Hon. Sr. Lectr.; 8 Hon. Lectrs.; 9 Hon. Sr. Res. Fellows; 18 Hon. Res. Fellows

Research: environmental and landscape history and archaeology; Greek, Roman and Byzantine history and archaeology; heritage management; history and archaeology of the Mediterranean; Ottoman and modern Greek studies

First World War Studies, Centre for

Bourne, J. M., BA Leic., PhD Leic., FRHistS Dir.*

Other Staff: 4 Assoc. Members; 1 Hon. Sr. Res. Fellow; 14 Hon. Res. Fellows; 13 Hon. Res. Assocs.

History of Art

Tel: (0121) 414 2218 Fax: (0121) 414 2727

Hemsoll, David E., BA E.Anglia, BSc Lond., MA Lond. Sr. Lectr.; Head*

Verdi, R., OBE, BA Mich., MA Chic., PhD Lond., FRSA Dir., Barber Inst. of Fine Arts; Prof., Fine Art

West, S. C., BA Virginia, PhD St And. Prof.

Other Staff: 3 Lectrs.; 1 Sr. Curator

Research: British and European visual culture; European painting (1500-2000); history of collecting; Italian and German modernism; Italian Renaissance architecture

Medieval History

Tel: (0121) 414 5736 Fax: (0121) 414 3656

Bassett, S. R., BA Birm., PhD Birm., FSA Sr. Lectr.; Head*

Swanson, Robert N., MA Camb., PhD Camb., FRHistS, FSA Prof., Medieval Ecclesiastical History

Wickham, C. J., MA Oxf., DPhil Oxf., FRHistS, FBA Prof., Early Medieval History

Other Staff: 6 Lectrs.; 1 Res. Fellow; 2 Teaching Fellows

Research: early medieval western Europe, including England; late medieval church and society; late medieval social and economic history; medieval landscape history and archaeology; the Anglo-Saxon church

Modern History

Tel: (0121) 414 5736 Fax: (0121) 414 3656

Bourne, J. M., BA *Leic.*, PhD *Leic.*, FRHistS   Sr. Lectr.

Chinn, C. S. A., MBE, BA *Birm.*, PhD *Birm.*   Prof., Birmingham Community History

Crowson, N. J., BA *S'ton.*, PhD *S'ton.*, FRHistS   Sr. Lectr.

Cust, Richard P., BA *Lond.*, PhD *Lond.*, FRHistS   Reader; Head*

Hilton, M. J., BA *Lanc.*, MA *Lanc.*, PhD *Lanc.*   Reader

Jones, Peter M., BA *Leeds*, DPhil *Oxf.*   Dir., Undergrad. Studies; Prof., French History

Lukowski, J. T., BA *Camb.*, PhD *Camb.*   Reader, Polish History

Murdock, Graeme N. J., MA *Oxf.*, DPhil *Oxf.*   Sr. Lectr.

Randall, Adrian J., BA *Birm.*, MA *Sheff.*, PhD *Birm.*   Prof., English Social History

Ross, C. D., BA *E.Mennonite*, MA *Maryland*, PhD *Lond.*   Sr. Lectr.

Ryrie, Alec   Sr. Lectr.

Schwarz, L. D., BA *Oxf.*, DPhil *Oxf.*   Sr. Lectr.

Other Staff: 9 Lectrs.; 1 AHRC Res. Fellow; 5 Teaching Fellows; 4 Assoc. Members; 1 Hon. Reader; 2 Hon. Sr. Res. Fellows; 1 Hon. Res. Fellow; 1 Hon. Res. Assoc.

Research: British social and economic history 1800-1970; European social and political history 1500-present; reformations in Britain and Europe 1500-1700; twentieth-century cultural and political history; twentieth-century military history

Theology and Religion

Tel: (0121) 414 5666 Fax: (0121) 414 4381

Anderson, A. H., BTh *Pret.*, MTh *Pret.*, DTh *Pret.*   Prof., Global Pentecostal Studies

Bhattacharyya, G. S., BA *Oxf.*, PhD *Lond.*   Sr. Lectr.

Felderhof, M. C., BA *Dal.*, MA *St And.*, BD *Dal.*, PhD *Wales*   Sr. Lectr.

Goodacre, M. S., BA *Oxf.*, MPhil *Oxf.*, DPhil *Oxf.*   Sr. Lectr.

Jawad, H. A., BA *Exe.*, MA *Exe.*, PhD *Exe.*   Sr. Lectr.

Khir, B. M., LLB *Khart.*, MSc *Riyadh*, PhD *Edin.*   Sr. Lectr., Islamic Studies

Lynch, Gordon   Sr. Lectr.

McLeod, D. H., BA *Camb.*, PhD *Camb.*   Prof., Church History

Nielsen, Jorgen S., BA *Lond.*, MA *Lond.*, PhD *Beirut*   Deputy Head; Prof., Islamic Studies

Parker, Rev. D. C., MTheol *St And.*, ThD *Ley.*   Prof., New Testament Textual Criticism and Palaeography

Singh, G., BSc *Lond.*, MA *Lond.*, PhD *Lond.*   Nadir Dinshaw Prof., Inter-Religious Relations

Stringer, M. D., BA(Econ) *Manc.*, PhD *Manc.*   Sr. Lectr.; Head*

Sugirtharajah, R. S., BD *B'lore.*, MTh *B'lore.*, PhD *B'lore.*, PhD *Birm.*   Prof., Biblical Hermeneutics

Thomas, D. R., BA *Camb.*, MA *Oxf.*, PhD *Lanc.*   Sr. Lectr.

Ustorf, W., DrTheol *Hamburg*, DrTheolHabil *Heidel.*   Prof., Mission

Vinzent, M., DrTheol *Munich*   H. G. Wood Prof.

Webber, J., BA *Lond.*, DPhil *Oxf.*   UNESCO Prof., Jewish and Interfaith Studies

Wollaston, I. L., BA *Durh.*, PhD *Durh.*   Sr. Lectr.

Other Staff: 11 Lectrs.; 1 Sr. Res. Fellow; 2 Res. Fellows

Research: anthropology, ritual, mission, Pentecostal studies; Asian and western theologies, patristics, church history; biblical and religious texts, languages and manuscripts/versions; Christianity, Judaism, Sikhism, Islam and inter-faith studies; Holocaust studies, black theology, religion and culture

West African Studies, Centre of

Tel: (0121) 414 5128 Fax: (0121) 414 3228
E-mail: cwas@bham.ac.uk

Barber, K. J., BA *Camb.*, PhD *Ife*   Prof., African Cultural Anthropology

Brown, S., BA *CNAA*, MA *Sus.*, PhD *Wales*   Reader, African Literature; Dir.*

Brydon, L., MA *Camb.*, PhD *Camb.*   Sr. Lectr.

Cline-Cole, R. E. A., BA *S.Leone*, Dr3rdCy *Bordeaux*   Sr. Lectr.

McCaskie, T. C., MA *Aberd.*, MA *Ghana*, PhD *Camb.*   Prof., Asante History

Other Staff: 2 Lectrs.; 1 Sr. Res. Fellow; 1 Res. Fellow; 5 Res. Assocs.

Research: African/Caribbean literature and Yoruba studies; gender and development in Ghana; history of Asante (Ghana), Borgu (Benin) and Islam in Mali; natural resources management in Nigeria and Sierra Leone; policing and the state in South Africa

Humanities

Tel: (0121) 414 5994 Fax: (0121) 414 7250
E-mail: humanities@bham.ac.uk

Hughes, Alex, BA *Lond.*, PhD *Lond.*   Prof., Twentieth-Century French Literature; Head*

Kaplan, J. H., BA *Penn.*, MA *Tor.*, PhD *Tor.*   Hon. Prof.

Drama and Theatre Arts

Tel: (0121) 414 5998 Fax: (0121) 414 5998
E-mail: drama@bham.ac.uk

Crow, B., MA *St And.*, PhD *Brist.*   Sr. Lectr.

Jackson, Russell, MA *Oxf.*, MA *Birm.*, PhD *Birm.*, FRSA   Allardyce Nicoll Prof.

Newey, Kate, BA *Syd.*, PhD *Syd.*   Prof.; Head*

Shephard-Barr, Kirsten, BA *Yale*, DPhil *Oxf.*   Sr. Lectr.

Other Staff: 3 Lectrs.

Research: acting processes; dance; gender and theatre; modern and contemporary British and Irish theatre; play-writing studies

English

Tel: (0121) 414 5670 Fax: (0121) 414 5668
E-mail: english@bham.ac.uk

Barnbrook, Geoff, BA MPhil PhD   Sr. Lectr.

Bell, Maureen, BA *Camb.*, MA *Camb.*, MLS *Lough.*, PhD *Lough.*   Reader, English Literature

Caldas-Coulthard, Carmen R., MA *Santa Catarina*, PhD *Birm.*   Sr. Lectr.

Campbell, J., BA *Sus.*, MA *Sus.*, DPhil *Sus.*   Sr. Lectr.

Coulthard, Malcolm, BA *Sheff.*, PhD *Birm.*   Emer. Prof., English Language and Linguistics

Edwards, Corony, BA *Keele*, MA   Sr. Lectr.

Ellis, S. P., BA *Lond.*, PhD *Lond.*   Prof., English Literature

Gasiorek, A. B. P., BA *Sus.*, PhD *McG.*   Reader

Hewings, Martin, BA *S'ton.*, MA *Birm.*, PhD *Birm.*   Sr. Lectr.

Hunston, Susan, BA *Birm.*, MA *Birm.*, PhD *Birm.*   Prof., English Language; Head*

Jowett, John, BA *Newcastle(UK)*, MA *Newcastle(UK)*, PhD *Liv.*   Reader, Shakespeare Studies

Kennedy, Chris, BA *Lond.*, MA *Lanc.*   Assoc. Prof.

Kitson, Simon, BA *Ulster*, DPhil *Sus.*   Sr. Lectr.

Knowles, G. M., MA *Lond.*, MA *Lond.*, PhD *Birm.*   Dir., Centre for Advanced Res. in English (CARE)

Littlemore, Jeannette, BA *Brad.*, MA *E.Anglia*, PhD *Thames V.*   Sr. Lectr.

McDermott, A. C., BA *Birm.*, PhD *Manc.*   Sr. Lectr.

McLuskie, Kate, MA *Glas.*, PhD *Glas.*   Prof.; Dir., Shakespeare Inst.

Moon, R., BA *Exe.*, MA *Exe.*, PhD *Birm.*   Dir., Dictionary Res. Centre

Owen, C. R., BA *Camb.*, MA *Reading*   Sr. Lectr.

Parsons, D. L., BA *Reading*, MA *Reading*, PhD *N.Lond.*   Sr. Lectr.

Rumbold, V., MA *Oxf.*, PhD *Camb.*   Reader

Scase, W. L., BA *Kent*, MPhil *Oxf.*, DPhil *Oxf.*   Geoffrey Shepherd Prof., Medieval English Literature

Sealey, Alison, BA *Kent*, MEd *Birm.*, PhD *Warw.*   Sr. Lectr.

Sinclair, John, MA *Edin.*   Emer. Prof., English Language and Linguistics

Small, I. C., BA *Reading*, PhD *Reading*   Prof., English Literature

Teubert, W., MA *Heidel.*, PhD *Heidel.*   Prof., Corpus Linguistics

Thain, Marion, BA *Birm.*, MPhil *Birm.*, PhD *Birm.*   Sr. Lectr.

Toolan, M., MA *Edin.*, DPhil *Oxf.*   Prof., Applied English Linguistics

Wiggins, Martin, MA *Oxf.*, DPhil *Oxf.*   Sr. Lectr.

Wilcher, Robert, BA *Oxf.*, MA *Birm.*, PhD *Birm.*   Reader, English Studies

Other Staff: 23 Lectrs.; 3 Res. Fellows; 1 Teaching Fellow; 8 Tutors; 1 Hon. Res. Fellow

Research: Chaucer, Shakespeare, Swift, Pope, Wilde and Woolf; corpus linguistics (exploiting computerised language resources); literature, language and culture of medieval Britain; modernisms (culture, literature, modernity 1870-1920); textual editing and history of the book

English Language Studies, Centre for

Tel: (0121) 414 5695 Fax: (0121) 414 3298

Caldas-Couthard, C. R., MA *Brazil*, PhD *Birm.*   Sr. Lectr.

Kennedy, C. J., BA *Lond.*, MA *Lanc.*   Assoc. Prof., English; Dir.*

Other Staff: 4 Lectrs.

European Languages and Cultures, Centre for

Tel: (0121) 414 5965

Hill, D. D., BA *Trinity(Dub.)*, BA *Oxf.*, DPhil *Oxf.*   Prof., German Studies; Dir.*

Research: French literature, thought, cinema, history, politics; German language, linguistics, literature and culture; Hispanic literature, culture and film; Italian literature (mediaeval and modern) and film

French Studies

Tel: (0121) 414 5965 Fax: (0121) 414 5966

Barnwell, Harry, MA *Birm.*, Dr *Montpellier*   Hon. Prof.

Birkett, J., MA *Oxf.*, DPhil *Oxf.*, FRSA   Prof.

Cornick, M., BA *Warw.*, MA *Warw.*, PhD *Warw.*   Reader, Contemporary French Studies

Crossley, E. C. D., BA *Wales*, PhD *Wales*   Prof., Nineteenth Century French Studies

Damamme-Gilbert, B. L. Y., LèsL *Nancy II*, MèsL *Nancy II*, PhD *Birm.*   Sr. Lectr.

Hughes, Alex, BA *Lond.*, PhD *Lond.*   Prof., Twentieth-Century French Literature

Ince, K. L., MA *Oxf.*, MA *Sus.*, DPhil *Sus.*   Sr. Lectr.

Kitson, Simon, BA *Ulster*, DPhil *Sus.*   Sr. Lectr.

Perkins, Wendy, BA *Lond.*, PhD *Lond.*   Sr. Lectr.

Ricketts, P. T., OBE, BA *Birm.*, PhD *Birm.*   Hon. Prof.

Wood, D. M., BA *Lond.*, PhD *Camb.*   Prof., French Literature; Acting Head*

Other Staff: 3 Lectrs.; 1 Lang. Co-ord.; 2 Lang. Tutors; 4 Lecteurs/Lectrices; 1 Hon. Sr. Lectr.; 1 Hon. Sr. Res. Fellow; 5 Tutors†

Research: computerised concordance of mediaeval Occitan; film and media studies; literary, historical and cultural studies; women's studies and gender studies; works of Voltaire, Montesquieu, Constant and Michelet

German Studies

Tel: (0121) 414 5930 Fax: (0121) 414 3834

Butler, M. G., MA *Camb.*, PhD *CNAA*, LittD *Camb.*   Prof., Modern German Literature

Dodd, W. J., BA *Leeds*, MA *Manc.*, PhD *Leeds*
Prof., Modern German Studies
Harris, Nigel W., BA *Oxf.*, DPhil *Oxf.* Sr.
Lectr.
Hill, D. D., BA *Trinity(Dub.)*, BA *Oxf.*, DPhil *Oxf.*
Prof.; Head*
Klapper, John Prof., Foreign Language
Pedagogy
Martin, Nicholas Sr. Lectr.
Speirs, R. C., MA *Aberd.*, PhD *Stir.* Prof.
van der Will, Wilfred Hon. Prof., Modern
German Studies
Other Staff: 4 Lectrs.; 2 Lang. Teachers
Research: contemporary German/Swiss literature
and twentieth-century German literature
(Nietzsche, Kafka, Mann, Brecht); German
corpus linguistics; German culture
(eighteenth-century to the present);
German mediaeval literature; German
unification and re-unification

Hispanic Studies

Tel: (0121) 414 7622 Fax: (0121) 414 3834
E-mail: hispanic@bham.ac.uk
Flitter, D. W., MA *Oxf.*, DPhil *Oxf.* Reader;
Dir., Galician Studies Centre; Head*
Griffiths, N. E. G., MA *Camb.*, PhD *Camb.* Sr.
Lectr.
Lough, Frank Prof.
Odber de Baubeta, P. A., MA *Glas.*, PhD *Glas.*
Sr. Lectr.; Dir., Portuguese Studies
Ward, A. M. M., BA *N.U.I.*, MA *N.U.I.*, PhD
Birm. Sr. Lectr.
Other Staff: 4 Lectrs.; 4 Lang. Instrs.; 3
Teaching Fellows; 1 Visiting Lectr.; 2 Sr.
Hon. Res. Fellows; 2 Hon. Res. Fellows
Research: Golden Age poetry, drama, cultural
history, textual editing; Latin American
fiction, gender and Cuban studies; Luso-
Brazilian, Catalan and Galician
sociolinguistics and translation studies;
mediaeval textual editing and chronicles;
Romanticism and modern historiography,
poetry and fiction

Italian Studies

Tel: (0121) 414 5930 Fax: (0121) 414 5834
E-mail: italian@bham.ac.uk
Caesar, M. P., MA *Camb.* Serena Prof.; Head*
Slowey, Gerry W., MA *Birm.*, PhD *Rome* Sr.
Lectr.
Other Staff: 6 Lectrs.; 1 Lang. Instr.; 1 Hon.
Lectr.; 1 Hon. Res. Fellow
Research: Italian film and cinema; Leopardi,
Romanticism and nineteenth-century
studies; linguistics; modern and
contemporary writing (all genres);
women's history

Music

Tel: (0121) 414 5782 Fax: (0121) 414 5668
E-mail: music@bham.ac.uk
Hamilton, K. L., BMus *Glas.*, MA *Glas.*, DPhil
Oxf. Sr. Lectr.
Harrison, D. J. T., BA *York(UK)*, DPhil *York(UK)*
Prof., Composition and Electroacoustic
Music
Hoyland, D. V., BA *Hull*, DPhil *York(UK)* Prof.,
Composition
Timms, C. R., BA *Camb.*, MMus *Lond.*, PhD *Lond.*
Peyton and Barber Prof.
Vick, G. Hon. Prof.
Whenham, E. J., BMus *Nott.*, MA *Nott.*, DPhil
Oxf. Prof., Music History; Head*
Other Staff: 4 Lectrs.; 1 Dir. of Performance/
Lectr.; 9 Visiting Lectrs.; 4 Hon. Sr. Res.
Fellows; 3 Hon. Res. Fellows
Research: British music (nineteenth- and
twentieth-century); composition; early
music, including performance practice;
eighteenth-century music and aesthetics;
European music (nineteenth- and
twentieth-century)

Shakespeare Institute

Tel: (01789) 293138 Fax: (01789) 414992
Jowett, John D., MA *Newcastle(UK)*, PhD *Liv.*
Reader/Fellow; Deputy Dir.

McLuskie, Kate, MA *Glas.*, PhD *Glas.* Dir.*
Wiggins, Martin J., MA *Oxf.*, DPhil *Oxf.* Sr.
Lectr./Fellow
Other Staff: 1 Lectr./Fellow; 1 Fellow; 2
Assocs.
Research: early modern playwrights and theatre;
reception of Shakespeare; material culture
in the early-modern period; Shakespeare
and the commercialisation of culture;
textual study and editing with reference to
Shakespeare and early modern drama; the
history of Shakespeare performance

Law

Tel: (0121) 414 3637 Fax: (0121) 414 3585
Arnull, Anthony M., BA *Sus.*, PhD *Leic.* Prof.,
European Law
Baldwin, J., BSocSc *Birm.*, PhD *Sheff.* Prof.,
Judicial Administration; Head*
Boyron, S. N. Y., Maîtrise *Paris I* Sr. Lectr.
Brown, Neville Prof.
Cain, Maureen E. Reader
Ellis, E. D., MA *Camb.*, LLM *Birm.*, PhD *Birm.*
Prof., Public Law
Enonchong, N. E., LLB *Yaounde*, LLM *Camb.*, PhD
Camb. Barber Prof.
Girvin, Stephen Assoc. Prof.
Harris, J., BCL *Oxf.*, MA *Oxf.* Prof.,
International Commercial Law
Harvey, Brian W. Prof.
Hodgin, Ray W. Sr. Lectr.
Le Sueur, A. P., LLB *Lond.* Barber Prof.,
Jurisprudence
Lloyd-Bostock, S. M. A., BA *Reading*, MA *Oxf.*,
DPhil *Oxf.* Dir., Inst. of Judicial Admin.;
Prof., Law and Psychology
Lonbay, J. L., LLB *Dund.*, PhD *Florence* Sr. Lectr.
Manchester, C. D., LLB *Lond.*, PhD *Birm.* Prof.,
Licensing Law
McBride, J., LLB *Camb.*, LLM *Birm.* Reader,
International Human Rights Law
Miller, C. John Emer. Prof.
Moodie, Peter C. E. Sr. Lectr.
Morse, G., LLB *Newcastle(UK)* Prof.,
Commercial and Tax Law
Perrins, Bryn Sr. Lectr.
Scott, I. R., LLB *Melb.*, PhD *Lond.* Prof.
Shute, S. C., LLB *CNAA*, BCL *Oxf.*, MA *Oxf.*, PhD
Birm. Prof., Criminal Law and Criminal
Justice
Stevens, A. W. J., BA *Camb.*, BCL *Oxf.* Sr.
Lectr.
Woodman, G. R., BA *Camb.*, LLM *Camb.*, PhD
Camb. Prof., Comparative Law
Other Staff: 19 Lectrs.; 1 Visiting Lectr.
Research: commercial law; criminal justice and
legal theory; European law (European
Community (EC) and European Court of
Human Rights (EHCR)); medical law;
public law and judicial administration

Mathematics

Tel: (0121) 414 6587 Fax: (0121) 414 3389
Blake, J. R., BSc *Adel.*, PhD *Camb.*, FIMA Prof.,
Applied Mathematics; Head*
Butkovic, P., MSc *Prague*, PhD *Prague* Sr. Lectr.;
Head, Management Mathematics Group
Clarke, A. Hon. Prof., Applied Mathematics
Cuninghame-Green, R. A. Emer. Prof.,
Industrial Mathematics
Curtis, R. T., MA *Camb.*, PhD *Camb.* Prof.,
Combinatorial Algebra
Decant, S. P. Head, Applied Mathematics
Group; Reader, Computational Mechanics
Everitt, W. N. Emer. Prof.
Flavell, P. J., MA *Camb.*, DPhil *Oxf.* Sr. Lectr.
Fliege, J. Sr. Lectr.
Gardiner, A. D., BSc *S'ton.*, MSc *Warw.*, PhD
Warw. Reader, Mathematics and
Mathematics Education
Good, C., BA *Oxf.*, DPhil *Oxf.* Sr. Lectr.
Kaye, R. W., BA *Camb.*, PhD *Manc.* Sr. Lectr.
Kyle, J., BSc *Glas.*, PhD *Newcastle(UK)* Sr. Lectr.
MacKerrell, S. O., BSc *Lond.*, PhD *Exe.* Sr.
Lectr.
Parker, C. W., BSc *Manc.*, MSc *Manc.*, PhD *Manc.*
Head, Pure Mathematics Group; Prof.,
Group Theory

Pearson, J. R. A., BA *Camb.*, PhD *Camb.* Hon.
Prof.
Shikhmurzaev, Y. D., MSc *Moscow*, PhD *Moscow*
Reader, Fluid Dynamics
Shpectorov, S. Prof., Group Theory and
Geometry
Sobolev, A. Mason Prof.
Thorpe, B., BSc *Birm.*, PhD *Birm.* Sr. Lectr.
Wilson, R. A., MA *Camb.*, PhD *Camb.* Emer.
Prof.
Other Staff: 14 Lectrs.; 3 Res. Fellows
Research: algebraic and combinatorial
optimisation; wavelets; algebraic groups, lie
groups, model theory; combustion; finite
groups, their geometries, graph theory; free
surface flows and bubble dynamics

Physics and Astronomy

Tel: (0121) 414 4564 Fax: (0121) 414 4577
Bayliss, C. R., BSc *Nott.*, PhD *Cran.* Hon. Prof.
Beddoe, A., BSc *Cant.*, MSc *Cant.*, PhD *Leeds*,
FIPEM Hon. Prof.
Canham, L. T., BSc *Lond.*, PhD *Lond.* Hon.
Prof.
Chaplin, W. J., BSc *Birm.*, PhD *Birm.*, FRAS Sr.
Lectr.
Charles, M. W., PhD *Leic.*, DSc *Leic.*, FIP, FIBiol
Reader, Radiation Physics
Charlton, D. G., BA *Oxf.*, PhD *Birm.* Reader,
Particle Physics
Church, M. J., BSc *Birm.*, PhD *Birm.* Sr. Lectr.
Clarke, N. M., BSc *Lond.*, PhD *Lond.*, DSc *Lond.*,
FIP Sr. Lectr.
Close, F. E., BSc *St And.*, DPhil *Oxf.* Hon. Prof.
Cruise, A. M., BSc *Lond.*, PhD *Lond.*, FIP, FRAS
Prof., Astrophysics and Space Research
Elsworth, Y. P., BSc *Manc.*, PhD *Manc.*, FIP,
FRAS Prof., Helioseismology
Eyles, C. J., BSc *Lond.*, PhD *Lond.* Sr. Lectr.
Forgan, E. M., MA *Camb.*, PhD Prof.,
Condensed Matter Physics
Freer, M., BSc *Aston*, PhD *Birm.* Reader,
Structure and Reactions in Light Nuclei
Gunn, J. M. F., BSc *Edin.*, PhD *Camb.*, FIP
Prof., Theoretical Physics
Guo, Q., BSc *Beijing*, PhD *Lanc.* Sr. Lectr.
Hopewell, J. W., BSc *Hull*, MA *Oxf.*, PhD *Lond.*
Hon. Prof.
Humphreys, R., MA *Camb.*, PhD *Bath* Hon.
Prof.
Jones, R. C., BSc *Manc.*, PhD *Manc.* Sr. Lectr.
Lerner, I. V., PhD *Moscow* Prof., Theoretical
Physics
Long, M. W., BA *Camb.*, PhD *Lond.* Sr. Lectr.
Mayhew, C., BSc *Lond.*, PhD *Lond.*, FIP Sr.
Lectr.
Muirhead, C. M., BSc *CNAA*, PhD *Birm.* Sr.
Lectr.
Palmer, Richard E., MA *Camb.*, PhD *Camb.*, FIP
Prof., Experimental Physics
Parker, D. J., MA *Camb.*, DPhil *Oxf.*, FIP
Reader, Radio-Isotope Techniques
Ponman, T. J., BSc *Warw.*, PhD *Birm.*, FRAS
Prof., Astrophysics
Quinn, T. J., BSc *S'ton.*, DPhil *Oxf.*, FIP Hon.
Prof.
Schofield, A. J., BA *Camb.*, MA *Camb.*, PhD
Camb., FIP Prof., Theoretical Physics
Simnett, G. M., BSc *Lond.*, PhD *Lond.*, FRAS, FIP
Prof., High Energy Astrophysics
Smith, R. A., BA *Camb.*, MSc *Camb.*, MS *Cornell*,
PhD *Cornell* Sr. Lectr.
Speake, C. C., BA *Camb.*, PhD *Camb.* Reader,
Gravitational Physics
Tungate, G., BSc *Birm.*, PhD *Birm.* Sr. Lectr.
Vecchio, A., Laur *Pavia*, PhD *Milan* Sr. Lectr.
Watkins, P. M., BSc *Birm.*, PhD *Birm.* Prof.,
Particle Physics
Watson, A. T., BA *Oxf.*, PhD *Lond.* Sr. Lectr.
Weaver, D. R., MA *Camb.*, PhD *Camb.*, FIP Sr.
Lectr.
Wilcoxon, J. P., BS *Wash.*, PhD *Wash.* Hon.
Prof.
Wilson, J. A., BSc *Aberd.*, PhD *Lond.* Reader,
Experimental Particle Physics
Other Staff: 13 Lectrs.; 5 Sr. Res. Fellows; 43
Res. Fellows; 3 Res. Assocs.; 7 Hon. Sr.

Lectrs.; 9 Hon. Lectrs.; 18 Hon. Sr. Res.
Fellows; 23 Hon. Res. Fellows
Research: astrophysics, solar physics and space
research; condensed matter physics;
nanoscale physics; nuclear physics and
particle physics; theoretical physics

Psychology

Tel: (0121) 414 4932 Fax: (0121) 414 4897
E-mail: psychology@bham.ac.uk
Apperly, Ian   Sr. Lectr.
Beech, Anthony R., BSc CNAA, DPhil Oxf.
Prof., Criminal Psychology
Birchwood, M. J., BSc Hull, MSc PhD   Prof.
Booth, D. A., BSc Oxf., BA Lond., MA Oxf., PhD
Lond., DSc, FBPsS   Prof.
Browne, Kevin D., BSc Lond., PhD CNAA   Prof.,
Forensic and Family Psychology
Copello, Alex   Sr. Lectr.
Crisp, R. J., MA Oxf., PhD Wales   Reader,
Social Psychology
Derbyshire, Stuart   Sr. Lectr.
Greville-Harris, G., BA Open(UK), MSc Open(UK),
PhD Open(UK)   Sr. Lectr.
Hamilton-Giachritsis, Cath   Sr. Lectr.
Harris, M. W., BSc Sus., PhD Brist.   Sr. Lectr.
Higgs, Suzanne   Sr. Lectr.
Humphreys, G. W., BSc Brist., PhD Brist., FBPsS
Prof., Cognitive Psychology; Head*
Kourtzi, Zoe   Prof.
Kroese, Biza   Sr. Lectr.
Meyer, A. S., AM Bochum, PhD Nijmegen   Prof.,
Psycholinguistics
Miall, R. C., BSc Lond., PhD Lond.   Prof., Motor
Neuroscience
Mitchell, I. J., BSc Sheff., DPhil Sus.   Sr. Lectr.
Nouwen, A., BA V.U.Amst., PhD V.U.Amst.   Sr.
Lectr.
Oliver, C., BSc Lough., MPhil Edin., PhD Lond.
Prof., Clinical Psychology
Olson, Andrew   Sr. Lectr.
Orford, J. F., MA Camb., PhD Lond., FBPsS
Prof., Clinical and Community Psychology
Oyebode, J. R., MA Liv., MPsychol Liv., PhD
Newcastle(UK)   Sr. Lectr.
Praamstra, P., MA Nijmegen, MD Nijmegen, PhD
Nijmegen   Reader, Cognitive Neuroscience
Riddoch, M. J., BSc Lond., PhD Lond.   Prof.,
Cognitive Neuropsychology
Terry, P., BSc Lond., PhD Lond.   Reader
Wheeldon, L. R., MA Edin., PhD Camb.   Sr.
Lectr.
Wing, A. M., BSc Edin., PhD McM.   Prof.,
Human Movement
Other Staff: 19 Lectrs.; 29 Res. Fellows; 15
Res. Assocs.; 4 Instrs.; 3 Clin. Tutors
Research: applied social and health psychology;
behavioural neuroscience; cognition and
language, and perceptual systems

Public Policy

Tel: (0121) 414 4986 Fax: (0121) 414 4989
E-mail: spp@bham.ac.uk
Murie, A. S., BA S'ton., MSc Lond.   Prof.; Head*
Other Staff: 1 Hon. Sr. Res. Fellow
Research: global ethics; governance in
developing countries; health policy and
management; housing, urban change and
regeneration; UK public management,
leadership and governance

Global Ethics, Centre for the Study of

Tel: (0121) 693 4687 Fax: (0121) 693 4686
E-mail: globalethics@bham.ac.uk
Hellsten, S., BA Helsinki, PhD Helsinki   Reader
(on leave)
Widdows, Heather   Sr. Lectr.; Acting Dir.*
Other Staff: 1 Lectr.; 6 Assoc. Members
Research: bioethics, medical and genetic
research, and reproductive ethics; ethics,
philosophy and political science; fair trade
development ethics; human rights, women's
rights and combating racism; world poverty

Health Services Management, Centre for

Tel: (0121) 414 7050 Fax: (0121) 414 7051
Bryan, S., BSc Salf., MSc York(UK), PhD Brun.
Prof., Health Economics

Coast, Jo   Prof., Health Economics
Glasby, J., BA Birm., MA Birm., PhD Birm.   Sr.
Lectr.
Ham, C. J., BA Kent, MPhil Kent, PhD Brist.
Prof., Health Policy and Management
Hudson, B., BA Manc.   Hon. Prof., Partnership
Studies
Mullen, P. M., MSc(Eng) Lond.   Sr. Lectr.
Peck, E., MSc Nott., PhD Newcastle(UK)   Prof.,
Healthcare Partnerships; Dir.*
Roberts, T. E., BSc Lond., MPhil Oxf.   Sr. Lectr.
Smith, J. A., BA Birm., MBA Open(UK), MHM
Sr. Lectr.
Spurgeon, P. C., BSc S'ton., PhD Lond.   Prof.
Other Staff: 4 Lectrs.; 8 Sr. Fellows; 2 Visiting
Sr. Fellows; 7 Res. Fellows; 7 Res. Assocs.
Research: health economics, rationing and
priorities; health policy and management;
organisational and leadership development
in healthcare; primary care, social care and
partnership; public participation and patient
involvement

International Development

Tel: (0121) 414 5038 Fax: (0121) 414 7995
Amis, P. H., BSc Brist., PhD Kent   Sr. Lectr.;
Programme Dir.
Batley, R. A., BSocSc Durh., MA Durh., DPhil Sus.
Prof., Development Administration
Campbell, A., BA Brist., PhD Brun.   Sr. Lectr./
Organisational Analyst
Devas, C. N., BA Warw., MCD Liv.   Dir.*
Hubbard, M. E. V., BA Cape Town, MA Sus.,
DPhil Sus.   Reader, Development
Economics
Jackson, Paul B., BA York(UK), MA E.Anglia, PhD
Birm.   Sr. Lectr.
Larbi, George A., BA Ghana, MSocSc Helsinki,
PhD Birm.   Sr. Lectr./Consultant
Rakodi, C. I., BA Manc., PhD Wales   Prof.,
International Urban Development
Other Staff: 2 Lectrs.; 4 Lectrs./Consultants; 2
Res. Fellows; 1 Res. Assoc.
Research: aid effectiveness and donor
harmonisation; decentralisation and local
governance; governance and public
management reform; poverty reduction,
and social and economic development; state
failure, reconstruction and political identity

Local Government Studies, Institute of

Tel: (0121) 414 5008 Fax: (0121) 414 4954
Clarke, M. G., CBE, MA Sus.   Prof., Public
Policy
Coulson, A. C., MA Camb., PhD Camb.   Sr.
Lectr.
Hughes, M. P., BSc Bath, MA Manc.   Assoc.
Prof.; Dir.*
Lyons, Sir Michael, BA Middx., MSc Lond.
Prof., Public Policy
Puffitt, R. G., MA Kent   Sr. Lectr.
Raine, J. W., BA Wales, PhD Wales   Dir.,
Postgrad. Teaching Centre; Prof.,
Management in Criminal Justice
Richards, S., BA Liv., MA Essex   Prof., Public
Management
Rogers, S. A., BA Hull, MSocSc Hull   Sr. Lectr.
Skelcher, C. K., BSc UMIST, MSocSc Birm., PhD
Birm.   Prof.
Spencer, K. M., MA Liv., FRGS   Prof., Local
Policy
Stewart, J. D., MA Oxf., DPhil Oxf.   Emer. Prof.
Watt, P. A., BA Leeds, DPhil York(UK)   Sr.
Lectr.; Assoc. Dir.
Willis, M. H., BA Camb., MSc Aston, MSW Sus.
Sr. Lectr.; Deputy Dir.
Other Staff: 7 Lectrs.; 5 Res. Fellows; 1 Res.
Assoc./Lectr.; 1 Hon. Sr. Lectr.; 2 Hon.
Lectrs.
Research: community governance and local
leadership; management of public services;
modernisation of local governance; policy
and political management in local
government; social care management

Urban and Regional Studies, Centre for

Tel: (0121) 414 5025 Fax: (0121) 414 3279
Beazley, Michael   Sr. Lectr.; Dir., Learning and
Teaching; Dir., Undergrad. Studies

Collinge, C. J., BA Durh., MSc Lond., MPhil
Cran.IT   Sr. Lectr.
Groves, R., MTech Brun.   Sr. Lectr.
Lee, P. W., BSc Brist., MSc York(UK)   Sr. Lectr.
Mullins, D., BA Oxf., MA Brist.   Prof., Housing
Studies
Murie, A. S., BA S'ton., MSc Lond.   Prof.
Niner, P. M., BA Brist., BPhil Glas.   Sr. Lectr.
Walker, J. B., BA E.Anglia   Reader, Housing
Economics
Watson, Chris   Sr. Lectr.; Dir., Graduate Res.
Studies
Other Staff: 11 Lectrs.; 1 Sr. Res. Fellow; 3
Res. Fellows; 3 Res. Assocs.
Research: housing studies and housing policy;
local economic development; urban and
regional planning; urban regeneration and
social exclusion

Social Sciences

Tel: (0121) 414 6630 Fax: (0121) 414 6630
Alcock, P. C., BA Oxf., MPhil CNAA   Prof.,
Social Policy and Administration; Head*
Lee, D., BA Manc., MA Essex, PhD Conn.   Sr.
Lectr.; Deputy Head

Applied Social Studies, Institute of

Tel: (0121) 414 5708 Fax: (0121) 414 5726
Alcock, P. C., BA Oxf., MPhil CNAA   Prof.,
Social Policy and Administration
Barnes, M., BA Sus., MA Sheff., PhD Sheff.
Prof.; Dir., Soc. Res.
Becker, Saul   Dir., Res.; Prof., Social Care and
Health
Bowl, Ric   Dir., Community Mental Health
Programmes
Davis, A., BA York(UK), MSc Lond.   Prof., Social
Work
Doling, J. F., BA Lond., MSc Birm., PhD Birm.
Prof., Housing Studies
Maltby, A. T., BA CNAA, PhD Sheff.   Sr. Lectr.
Nixon, S., BA(Econ) Sheff., MPhil Sheff.   Sr.
Lectr.
Page, R. M., BA Kent, PhD Kent   Reader,
Democratic Socialism and Social Work
Stephenson, D. O., BA Hull, MSocSc Birm.
Assoc. Prof.; Head*
Thomas, Ralph   Dir., Soc. Work Educn.
Other Staff: 1 Lectr./Undergrad. Programme
Dir.; 16 Lectrs.; 2 Sr. Res. Fellows; 4 Res.
Fellows; 3 Teaching Fellows; 1 Lectr.†; 1
Hon. Res. Fellow
Research: children and families; crime and
communities; global social policy; social
care and health, including mental health;
user, citizen participation including
voluntary and community sector

Economics

Tel: (0121) 414 6640 Fax: (0121) 414 7377
Backhouse, R. E., BSc Brist., PhD Birm.   Prof.,
History and Philosophy of Economics
Bailey, Ralph W.   Sr. Lectr.
Cole, M. A., BA De Mont., MA De Mont., PhD
Nott.   Reader
Dickinson, D. G., BA Manc., PhD Sheff.   Assoc.
Prof.; Head*
Dutta, J., MA Delhi, PhD Delhi   Prof.
Elliott, R. J., BA Leic., MA Essex, PhD Nott.   Sr.
Lectr.
Fender, J., MA Oxf., DPhil Oxf.   Prof.,
Macroeconomics
Fielding, A., BSc(Econ) Lond., MSc Lond.
Reader, Social and Educational Statistics
Ford, Jim   Emer. Prof.
Green, Richard   Prof.; Dir., Inst. for Energy
Res. Policy
Maddison, David, MSc Glas., PhD Strath.
Reader
Ray, I., BStat I.Stat.I., MStat I.Stat.I., MA(Econ)
Louvain, PhD Louvain   Reader
Ryan, Cillian, PhD W.Ont., MA   Assoc. Prof.
Sen, S., MA Calc., MSocSc Calc., PhD Warw.
Prof., Development Economics
Sinclair, P. J. N., MA Oxf., DPhil Oxf.   Prof.
Other Staff: 11 Lectrs.; 3 Res. Fellows; 1
Visiting Lectr.†; 1 Hon. Sr. Res. Fellow

Research: econometrics; economic theory; macroeconomics and financial economics; public economics and political economy; trade, energy and environmental economics

German Studies, Institute for

Tel: (0121) 414 7182 Fax: (0121) 414 7329
Grenville, J.   Prof. Fellow
Grix, J., BA Lond., MA Sus., PhD Birm.   Sr. Lectr.
Kaser, M. C.   Hon. Prof.
Longhurst, Kerry A., BA Thames V., MA Wales, PhD Birm.   Sr. Lectr.; Asst. Dir., European Res. Inst.
Paterson, W. E., OBE, MA St And., MSc Lond., PhD Lond., FRSEd, FRSA   Prof.
Poguntke, Thomas   Prof.; Dir.*
Roper, Lord   Hon. Prof.
Van der Will, W., DPhil Cologne   Hon. Prof.
Watson, Lord, CBE   Hon. Prof.
Other Staff: 1 Lectr.; 1 DAAD Sr. Res. Fellow; 11 Visiting Fellows; 1 Assoc. Staff
Research: economic governance and policy in Germany; Germany's relations with East Central Europe; politics and government of unified Germany; role of Germany within the European Union; twentieth-century German history

Philosophy

Fax: (0121) 414 4216
Beebee, Helen   Prof.; Head*
Kölbel, Max   Sr. Lectr.
Miller, Alex   Prof.
Other Staff: 7 Lectrs.
Research: ethics, meta-ethics and applied ethics; metaphysics and epistemology; philosophy of language, mind and action

Political Science and International Studies

Tel: (0121) 414 6526 Fax: (0121) 414 3496
Buckler, N. E., BA S'ton., PhD S'ton.   Sr. Lectr.
Caney, S. L. R., BA Oxf., DPhil Oxf.   Prof.
Caramani, Daniele, BA MA PhD   Reader
Croft, S. J., MSc S'ton., PhD S'ton.   Prof., International Relations
Diez, T., MA Mannheim, DPhil Mannheim, PhD Mannheim   Prof.; Head*
Dunn, D. H., BA Liv., MSc S'ton., PhD Lond.   Sr. Lectr.
Gilson, J. A., BA Leeds, MA Sheff., PhD Sheff.   Sr. Lectr.
Hay, C. S., MA Camb., PhD Lanc.   Prof., Political Analysis
Lassman, P., BA Leic.   Sr. Lectr.
Lee, D., BA Manc., MA Essex, PhD Conn.   Sr. Lectr.
Marsh, D., BA Wales, PhD Exe.   Prof.
Preston, P. W., BA Leeds, PhD Leeds   Prof., Political Sociology (on leave)
Redmond, John, MSc Wales, PhD Warw.   Prof., European Studies
Ryner, Magnus, BA Trent, MA York(Can.), PhD York(Can.)   Sr. Lectr.
Steans, J., PhD Keele, MA   Sr. Lectr.
Terriff, T. R., MA Calg., PhD Lond.   Sr. Lectr.
van Biezen, I., PhD Ley.   Sr. Lectr.
Watson, M., BA Wales, MA Strath., PhD Birm.   Sr. Lectr.
Williams, Paul, BSc MSc PhD   Sr. Lectr.
Wincott, Dan E., BA Manc., MA Manc., PhD Lond.   Sr. Lectr.
Other Staff: 6 Lectrs.; 1 ESRC Res. Fellow; 3 Res. Fellows; 1 Roberts Res. Fellow; 4 Teaching Fellows; 1 Res. Assoc.; 2 Visiting Lectrs.; 1 Visiting Sr. Fellow
Research: international security theory; UK, USA and the 'war on terror'; US evangelicals and foreign policy

Russian and East European Studies

Tel: (0121) 414 6346 Fax: (0121) 414 3423
Ammann, Ronald   Prof., Comparative Politics
Batt, Judy R., BSocSc Birm., PhD Birm.   Prof., Central and South-East European Politics (on leave)
Braithwaite, R., GCMG, MA Camb., LLD Camb.   Hon. Prof.

Cooper, J. M., BSc(Econ) Bath, PhD Birm.   Deputy Dir.; Prof., Russian Economic Studies
Davies, R. W., BA Lond., PhD   Sr. Fellow; Emer. Prof.
Hanson, P., MA Camb., PhD Birm.   Emer. Prof.
Rees, E. A., BA York(UK), PhD Birm.   Reader, Soviet and Russian History (on leave)
Wolczuk, Kataryna, MLaw Gdansk, MSocSc Birm., PhD Birm.   Sr. Lectr.; Dir.*
Other Staff: 7 Lectrs.; 1 Sr. Res. Fellow; 3 Res. Fellows; 1 Lang. Tutor (Russian); 1 Res. Fellow†; 1 Visiting Lectr.†; 2 Hon. Sr. Lectrs.; 1 Hon. Lectr.; 12 Hon. Sr. Res. Fellows; 11 Hon. Res. Fellows; 1 Hon. Res. Fellow/Lectr.†
Research: Russian and East European defence and security; Russian economic transformation and regions; Russian society and culture; Russian, Ukrainian, Central and East European politics; Soviet and Russian history

Security and Diplomacy, Centre for Studies in

Tel: (0121) 414 6950 Fax: (0121) 414 2693
Carter, David, CVO, PhD Durh.   Deputy Dir.
Croft, S. J., MSc S'ton., PhD S'ton.   Prof.; Deputy Dir.
Logan, Sir David, KCMG   Dir.*
Messervy-Whiting, Maj. Gen. G. G., CBE   Deputy Dir.
Other Staff: 7 Fellows; 1 Centre Manager

Sociology

Tel: (0121) 414 6060 Fax: (0121) 414 6061
Abbinnett, R., BA Warw., MA Sus., PhD Warw.   Sr. Lectr.
Brown, Louise   Sr. Lectr.
Budgeon, Shelley, BA Calg., MA Br.Col., PhD Leeds   Sr. Lectr.
Holmwood, John, BA Camb., MA Camb., PhD Camb.   Prof.; Head*
Li, Yaojun, BA Oxf., MA Oxf., MPhil Oxf., DPhil Oxf.   Reader
Mac an Ghaill, Mairtin   Prof.
Marsh, D., BA Wales, PhD Exe.   Prof.; Head*
Toke, David, BA Birm., MSocSci Birm., PhD Birm.   Sr. Lectr.
Other Staff: 8 Lectrs.; 2 Res. Fellows; 2 Teaching Fellows
Research: ethnicity and multiculturalism; gender and sexuality; media; political sociology; sociological theory

Sport and Exercise Sciences

Tel: (0121) 414 4115 Fax: (0121) 414 4121
Brown, M. D., BSc Birm., PhD Birm.   Reader, Cardiovascular Physiology
Carroll, D., BSc Edin., PhD ANU   Prof., Applied Psychology; Head*
Duda, J. L., BA Rutgers, MS Purdue, PhD Ill.   Prof., Sports Psychology
Jeukendrup, A. E., MSc Maastricht, PhD Maastricht   Prof., Exercise Metabolism
Jones, D. A., BSc Lond., PhD Lond.   Prof.
Kaupinnen, Risto   Prof.
Lakie, M. D., BSc Edin., PhD Edin.   Sr. Lectr.
McDonagh, M. J. N., BA Calif., MA Calif., MSc Lond., PhD Brist.   Sr. Lectr.
Moir, I. R., BA Newcastle(UK), MA Leic., MSc Leic.   Sr. Lectr.
Ring, C. M., BSc Hull, MA N.Y., PhD N.Y.   Reader, Psychophysiology
Tipton, Kevin   Sr. Lectr.
Wagenmakers, A., BSc Nijmegen, MSc Nijmegen, PhD Nijmegen   Prof., Exercise Biochemistry
White, M. J., BSc Leeds, PhD Nott.   Reader, Exercise Physiology
Other Staff: 14 Lectrs.; 4 Res. Fellows; 1 Birm. Res. Fellow; 1 Hon. Assoc. Lectr.
Research: cardio-respiratory physiology; exercise biochemistry; health and exercise psychology; motor control; sports psychology

MEDICINE

Tel: (0121) 414 3481 Fax: (0121) 414 6933
Doe, William F., MB BS Syd., MSc Lond., FRCP, FRACP, FMedSci   Prof.; Head and Dean*

Cancer Studies, Division of

Tel: (0121) 414 4491 Fax: (0121) 414 4486
Young, Lawrence S., BSc Birm., PhD Birm., DSc Birm., FRCPath   Prof.; Head*

Cancer Studies

Tel: (0121) 414 4471
Craddock, C. F.   Prof., Haemato-Oncology
Gallimore, P. H., PhD Birm., FIBiol, FRCPath, FMedSci   Prof., Experimental Oncology
Grand, R. J. A., BSc Sheff., PhD Leeds, DSc Leeds   Reader, Experimental Cancer Studies
Hill, F., MB ChB, FRCPath, FRCPCH   Hon. Prof.
James, Nick D., BSc Lond., MB BS Lond., PhD Lond., FRCR, FRCP   Prof., Clinical Oncology
Johnson, Philip J., MB ChB Manc., MD Manc., FRCP, FHKAM   Prof., Oncology
Moss, Paul, BM BCh Oxf., MA Camb.   Prof., Haematology
Overduin, Michael, BSc W.Laur., PhD N.Y.   Prof., Structural Biology
Rickinson, Alan B., MA Camb., PhD Camb., FRS, FMedSci   Prof.
Roberts, Sally, BSc Warw., DPhil Oxf.   Sr. Lectr.
Searle, Peter F., BA Camb., PhD Lond.   Sr. Lectr.
Stankovic, Tanja, MD Belgrade, PhD Birm.   Sr. Lectr.
Taylor, A. Michael R., BSc Lond., PhD Lond.   Prof., Cancer Genetics
Wakelam, Michael J. O., BSc Birm., PhD Birm.   Prof., Molecular Pharmacology
Young, Lawrence S., BSc Birm., PhD Birm., DSc Birm., FRCPath   Prof., Cancer Biology; Head*
Other Staff: 1 Lectr.; 9 Sr. Res. Fellows; 38 Res. Fellows; 6 Res. Assocs.; 5 Sr. Clin. Lectrs.; 1 Sr. Clin. Res. Fellow; 11 Clin. Res. Fellows; 1 Hon. Reader; 3 Hon. Sr. Lectrs.; 1 Hon. Lectr.; 1 Hon. Sr. Res. Fellow; 7 Hon. Res. Fellows; 10 Hon. Res. Assocs.; 15 Hon. Sr. Clin. Lectrs.; 1 Hon. Clin. Lectr.; 1 Hon. Clin. Res. Fellow
Research: DNA viruses linked to human cancer; gene therapy and immunotherapy for cancer; phospholipases and signal transduction; structural biology; the role of DNA repair genes in cancer

Pathology

Tel: (0121) 414 4017 Fax: (0121) 414 4019
Barber, P. C., MA DPhil   Sr. Lectr., Neuropathology
Howie, A. J., MB BChir Camb., MD Camb., MA Camb.   Reader, Renal Pathology
Hubscher, S. G., MB ChB, FRCPath   Reader, Liver Pathology
Jones, E. L., MB ChB Birm., MD Birm., FRCPath   Leith Prof., Lymphoreticular Pathology; Head*
Sanders, D. S. A.   Sr. Lectr., Gastrointestinal and Dermatologic Pathology
Young, J. A.   Sr. Lectr., Cytopathology
Other Staff: 4 Clin. Lectrs.; 1 Hon. Sr. Lectr.
Research: EBV associated tumours; gastrointestinal cancer; liver allograft rejection grading and diagnosis; transplantation pathology

History of Medicine, Centre for the

Tel: (0121) 415 8174 Fax: (0121) 414 6036
Arnott, Robert G., BA Lond., MA Warw., FRHistS   Apothecaries Lectr.; Reader, History and Archaeology of Medicine; Dir.*
Spurgeon, Anne, BSc S'ton., PhD Birm.   Sr. Lectr.
Other Staff: 1 Welcome Trust Res. Fellow and Lectr.; 1 Teaching Asst.; 9 Assoc. Members; 1 Hon. Lectr.; 2 Hon. Sr. Res. Fellows; 1 Hon. Res. Fellow; 1 Hon. Res. Assoc.
Research: ancient medicine, health and palaeodisease; history of medicine and

healthcare in Birmingham and the Black Country; medical education in provincial England, 1800-1948

Immunity and Infection, Division of

Tel: (0121) 414 4068

Anderson, Graham, BSc Birm., PhD Birm. Reader, T-Lymphocyte Biology

Bacon, Paul A., MA Camb., MB BChir Camb., FRCP   Emer. Prof.

Brown, Geoff, BSc Lond., PhD Lond.   Reader, Cellular Immunology

Buchan, Sandy, BSc Aberd., PhD Aberd.   Sr. Lectr.

Buckley, Christopher D., MB BS Lond., MA Oxf., DPhil Oxf.   Campaign Prof., Rheumatology, Arthritis and Rheumatism

Caamaño, Jorge, PhD Buenos Aires   Sr. Lectr.

Freeman, Sylvie

Gordon, John, BSc S'ton., PhD S'ton.   Prof., Cellular Immunology

Hawkey, Peter M., BSc E.Anglia, MS BS Lond., PhD Brist., FRCPath   Prof., Clinical and Public Health Bacteriology

Jenkinson, Eric J., BSc Brist., PhD Wales, FMedSci   Prof., Experimental Immunology; Head*

Lammas, Tony, MSc Wales, PhD Wales   Sr. Lectr.

Lane, Peter J., MB ChB Edin., PhD Birm., FRCPEd, FRCPath   Reader, Immunology

Lord, Janet M., BSc CNAA, PhD Aston   Reader, Molecular Immunology

Maclennan, Ian   Prof., Immunology

Murray, Philip I., MB BS Lond., PhD Amst., FRCS   Prof., Ophthalmology

Pallen, Mark, MA Camb., MB BS Lond., MD Lond., PhD Lond.   Prof., Bacterial Genetics

Piddock, Laura J. V., BSc Birm., PhD Birm.   Prof., Microbiology

Salmon, Mike, BSc Birm., PhD Birm.   Prof., Experimental Rheumatology

Sansom, David   Sr. Lectr.

Savage, Caroline   Prof., Nephrology

Shuttleworth, John, BSc Warw., PhD Warw.   Sr. Lectr.

Turner, Bryan M., BSc Lond., PhD Lond., FMedSci   Prof., Experimental Genetics

Wallace, Graham, BSc PhD   Sr. Lectr., Ophthalmology

Wilton, Joanne C., BSc Newcastle(UK), PhD Reading   Sr. Lectr., Anatomy

Young, Steve P., BSc Lond., PhD Lond.   Sr. Lectr., Rheumatology

Other Staff: 4 Lectrs.; 1 Welcome Trust Sr. Res. Fellow/Hon. Reader; 1 Royal Soc. Res. Fellow; 1 RCUK Roberts Fellow; 1 MRC Career Develop. Fellow; 1 ARC Career Develop. Fellow; 2 Clin. Sr. Lectrs.

Research: cellular and molecular pathways in haemopoiesis; development/selection of the T-cell repertoire; gene suppression, chromatin structure, histone acetylation; molecular signalling in lymphocytes; regulation of immune responses

Medical Sciences, Division of

Tel: (0121) 627 2380 Fax: (0121) 627 2384
E-mail: n.j.roden@bham.ac.uk

Marshall, Janice M., BSc Birm., PhD Birm., DSc Birm., FIBiol, FMedSci   Prof., Cardiovascular Medicine; Head*

Research: cardiovascular science; clinical trials and epidemiology; endocrinology and metabolism; immunity and infection; neurodegradation and repair

Anaesthesia and Intensive Care

Tel: (0121) 627 2060 Fax: (0121) 627 2062

Bion, Julian F., MB BS Lond., MD Lond., FRCA   Reader, Intensive Care Medicine

Clutton-Brock, Tom H., MB ChB Brist., FRCA   Sr. Lectr., Clinical Measurement; Head*

Cooper, Griselda M., MB ChB Birm., FRCA   Sr. Lectr., Day Case and Obstetric Anaesthesia

Hutton, Peter, BSc Birm., MB ChB Birm., PhD Birm., FRCA, FMedSci   Hickman Prof., Cardiac Anaesthesia

Stokes, Monica   , Paediatric Anaesthesia

Other Staff: 6 Hon. Lectrs.; 62 Hon. Sr. Clin. Lectrs.

Research: adult intensive care; cardiac anaesthesia; clinical measurement; obstetric and day case anaesthesia

Applied Gerontology, Centre for

E-mail: gerontology@bham.ac.uk

Nayak, Laxman   Dir.*

Other Staff: 1 Lectr.; 1 Res. Assoc.; 1 Hon. Res. Assoc.; 9 Hon. Sr. Clin. Lectrs.

Cardiovascular Medicine

Tel: (0121) 831 8952 Fax: (0121) 414 3713

Frenneaux, Michael P., MB BS MD, FRCP, FRACP, FACC, FESC   British Heart Foundation Prof., Cardiology; Head*

Gammage, Michael D., MD Birm., FRCP   Reader, Cardiovascular Science

Watson, Steve P., BSc Leeds, PhD Camb., FMedSci   British Heart Foundation Prof., Cardiovascular Sciences and Cellular Pharmacology

Other Staff: 1 Lectr.; 7 Res. Fellows; 2 Res. Assocs.; 1 Hon. Sr. Lectr.; 16 Hon. Sr. Clin. Lectrs.; 4 Hon. Res. Fellows; 1 Hon. Res. Assoc.

Research: alternative pacing sites to optimise cardiac function; cardiovascular control in heart failure; cardiovascular morbidity and mortality in thyrotoxicosis; central mechanisms of cardiovascular control; platelets, receptors and cell signalling

Medicine

Tel: (0121) 627 3360
E-mail: e.a.toney@bham.ac.uk

Adams, David H., MB ChB Birm., MD   Prof., Hepatology

Arlt, Wiebke   Sr. Lectr.; MRC Sr. Clin. Fellow

Barnett, A. H., BSc Lond., MB BS Lond., MD Lond., FRCP   Prof., Diabetes and Obesity

Franklyn, Jayne A., MB ChB Birm., MD Birm., PhD Birm., FRCP, FMedSci   Prof., Endocrinology

Gittoes, Neil J. L., BSc Birm., MB ChB Birm., PhD Birm.   Sr. Lectr.

Gough, Steve C. L., MB ChB Leeds, MD Leeds, FRCP   Prof.

Kendall, Martin J., OBE, MD Birm., FRCP   Prof., Clinical Pharmacology

Langman, M. J. S., BSc Lond., MD Lond., FRCP, FRCPA   Hon. Prof.

Lip, Gregory Y., MD   Hon. Prof., Cardiovascular Medicine

Logan, Ann, BSc Lond., PhD Birm.   Prof., Molecular Neuroscience

Martin, Una, MB BCh Edin., BSc Edin., PhD Edin.   Sr. Lectr., Clinical Pharmacology

Narendran, Parth   Sr. Lectr.

Sheppard, Michael C., MB ChB Cape Town, PhD Cape Town, FRCP, FMedSci   William Withering Prof.; Head*

Stewart, Paul M., MB ChB Edin., MD Birm., FRCP, FMedSci   Prof.

Stockley, R. A., MD DSc, FRCP   Prof.

Other Staff: 4 Lectrs.; 4 Sr. Res. Fellows; 25 Res. Fellows; 6 Res. Assocs.; 14 Clin. Res. Fellows; 1 Hon. Reader; 2 Hon. Sr. Lectrs.; 4 Hon. Lectrs.; 4 Hon. Sr. Res. Fellows; 49 Hon. Res. Fellows; 8 Hon. Res. Assocs.; 100 Hon. Sr. Clin. Lectrs.; 1 Hon. Clin. Lectr.

Research: clinical trials and epidemiology; endocrinology, and hormone action; liver disease and gastroenterology; neurodegeneration and repair; respiratory disease

Physiology

Tel: (0121) 414 6914 Fax: (0121) 414 6919
E-mail: t.l.hayward@bham.ac.uk

Cummins, Peter, BSc Reading, PhD Birm.   Sr. Lectr.

Egginton, Stuart, BSc St And., PhD St And.   Reader

Kumar, Prem, BSc Manc., DPhil Oxf.   Reader, Cardiorespiratory Physiology

Lote, Chris J., BSc Manc., PhD Manc.   Prof., Experimental Nephrology

Lovick, Thelma A., BSc Manc., PhD Birm.   Reader, Neuroscience

Marshall, Janice M., BSc Birm., PhD Birm., DSc Birm., FIBiol, FMedSci   Prof., Cardiovascular Science

Nash, Gerard B., BSc Manc., PhD Lond.   Prof., Cardiovascular Rheology

Rainger, G. Edward, BSc Newcastle(UK)   British Heart Foundation Sr. Lectr.

Ross, H. F., BSc Aberd., FRSS   Sr. Lectr.

Smith, Margaret E., BSc Birm., PhD Birm., DSc Birm.   Prof., Experimental Neurology

Other Staff: 3 Lectrs.; 11 Res. Fellows; 1 Res. Assoc.; 1 Hon. Sr. Lectr.; 1 Hon. Lectr.; 6 Hon. Sr. Res. Fellows; 12 Hon. Res. Fellows; 1 Hon. Res. Assoc.

Research: cardiorespiratory control during hypoxia; leukocyte recruitment in vascular disease; nervous control of heart and circulation; neural degeneration and ageing; regulation of angiogenesis

Surgery

Tel: (0121) 831 2276 Fax: (0121) 472 1230

Bradbury, Andrew W., BSc Edin., MB ChB Edin., MD Edin., FRCSEd   Prof., Vascular Surgery; Head*

Morton, Dion G., MD Birm., FRCS   Reader

Other Staff: 2 Lectrs.; 1 Res. Fellow; 1 Clin. Res. Fellow; 1 Hon. Sr. Lectr.; 1 Hon. Sr. Res. Fellow; 7 Hon. Res. Fellows; 83 Hon. Sr. Clin. Lectrs.

Research: arterial and venous disease and atherosclerosis; colorectal cancer screening and inflammatory bowel disease; epithelial cell adhesion and signalling; haemostasis, thrombosis and fibrinolysis; large bowel adenome prevention

Neuroscience, Division of

Tel: (0121) 414 4508 Fax: (0121) 414 4509

Barnes, Nicholas M., BSc Brad., PhD Wales   Reader, Neuropharmacology

Best, David   Sr. Lectr., Addictions

Bowery, Norman G., Laur Florence, PhD Lond., DSc Lond.   Emer. Prof.

Brockington, Ian, MB ChB Manc., MA Manc., MPhil Lond., MD Camb., FRCPsych, FRCP   Emer. Prof.

Coote, John   Emer. Prof.

Cruikshank, Garth S., BSc MB BS PhD, FRCS, FRCSEd   Prof., Neurosurgery

Cumella, Stuart J., BSc(Econ) Lond., MSc Strath., PhD Lond.   Sr. Lectr., Psychiatry; Head*

Deb, Shoumitro, MB BS Leic., MD Leic., FRCPsych   Program Leader, MSc in Epilepsy; Prof., Neuropsychiatry and Intellectual Disability

Heun, Richard, MD Würzburg, PhD Mainz   Prof., Old Age Psychiatry

Jefferys, J. G. R., BSc Lond., PhD Lond., FMedSci   Prof.; Head, Dept of Neurophysiology

Jones, Lisa   Sr. Lectr., Pharmacology

Keen, Mary, BSc Lond., PhD CNAA   Sr. Lectr., Pharmacology

Lacey, Michael G., BSc Sus., PhD Brist.   Sr. Lectr., Pharmacology

Lendon, Corinne, BSc Lond., PhD Lond.   Sr. Lectr., Molecular Psychiatry

Morrison, Karen, BM BCh Oxf., MA Camb., PhD Oxf.   Head, Dept. of Clin. Neuroscis.; Prof., Neurology

Oyebode, Femi, MB BS Ib., MD Newcastle(UK), PhD Wales, FRCPsych   Hon. Prof.

Spruce, Austen E., MB ChB Leic., PhD Leic.   Sr. Lectr., Pharmacology

Other Staff: 9 Lectrs.; 8 Res. Fellows; 11 Res. Assocs.; 1 Clin. Lectr.

Primary Care, Public and Occupational Health, Division of

Tel: (0121) 414 6022
E-mail: a.e.evans@bham.ac.uk

Parle, Jim V., MB ChB Birm., MD Birm., FRCGP Deputy Head; Prof., Primary Care
Stevens, Andrew J., BA Camb., MB BS Lond., MA Nott., MSc Lond., FFPHM Head*
Research: occupational health; primary care and general practice; public health and epidemiology

Occupational and Environmental Medicine, Institute of

Tel: (0121) 414 6030 Fax: (0121) 414 6217
E-mail: j.b.grainger@bham.ac.uk
Jaakkola, Jouni, MD Helsinki, DMedSci Helsinki, PhD McG. Prof., Environmental Health and Occupational Medicine; Dir.*
Sadhra, Steven, BSc Birm., PhD Birm. Sr. Lectr., Occupational Exposure and Risk Management
Sorahan, Tom M., BSc Birm., PhD Birm., DSc Birm. Prof., Occupational Epidemiology
Other Staff: 1 Lectr.; 2 Res. Assocs.; 1 Res. Statistician; 1 Sr. Clin. Lectr.
Research: environmental health and epidemiology; exposure assessment; occupational health and epidemiology; risk assessment; systematic reviews

Primary Care and General Practice

Tel: (0121) 414 3766 Fax: (0121) 414 6571
E-mail: general-practice@bham.ac.uk
Aveyard, Paul, MB BS Lond., PhD Sr. Lectr.
Delaney, Brendan C., BA Camb., BM BCh Oxf., MA Camb., MD Birm. Prof., Primary Care
Draper, Heather J. A., BA Manc., MA Manc., PhD Birm. Sr. Lectr.
Fitzmaurice, David A., MB ChB Birm. Prof., Primary Care
Freemantle, Nick, BSc Leeds, MA Leeds, PhD Leeds Prof., Clinical Epidemiology and Biostatistics
Greenfield, Sheila M., BSc Aston, MA Aston, PhD Aston Sr. Lectr.
Hobbs, F. D. Richard, MB ChB Brist., FRCGP, FRCP, FMedSci Prof.; Head*
Holder, Roger L., BSc Lond. Head, Statistics
Lester, Helen E., MB ChB Birm., MA Warw., MD Birm. Reader
Mant, Jonathan W. F., MA Camb., MB BS Lond., MSc Lond. Sr. Lectr.
McManus, Richard J., BSc Lond., MB BS Lond., MSc Birm. Sr. Lectr.
Parle, Jim V., MB ChB Birm., MD Birm., FRCGP Prof.
Skelton, John, BA Liv., MA Leeds Prof., Medical Communication
Thomas, Kate P., MB ChB Birm., FRCGP Sr. Lectr.
Other Staff: 12 Lectrs.; 12 Res. Fellows; 5 Teaching Fellows; 1 National Primary Care Postdoctoral Fellow; 7 Res. Assocs.; 2 Res. Nurses; 2 Sr. Project Officers; 1 Statistician; 1 Clin. Sr. Lectr.; 1 Clin. Lectr.; 5 Clin. Res. Fellows; 1 Clin. Tutor
Research: cardiovascular medicine; diagnostic technologies and computer decision support; gastrointestinal medicine; mental health and inequalities in health; screening and cancer

Public Health and Epidemiology

Tel: (0121) 414 3244 Fax: (0121) 414 7878
E-mail: s.t.murphy@bham.ac.uk
Cheng, K. K., BSc HK, MB BS HK, PhD Camb., FFPHM Prof., Epidemiology
Griffiths, Rod, CBE, BSc MB ChB, FRCP Regional Dir. of Public Health; Prof., Public Health Practice
Hawkins, Mike, BSc Wales, MSc Sus., DPhil Oxf. Reader, Epidemiology
Hyde, Chris Sr. Lectr., Public Health
Jolly, Kate Sr. Lectr.
Lilford, Richard J., PhD Lond., MB BCh, FRCOG, FRCP Prof., Clinical Epidemiology
MacArthur, Christine, BSc Salf., BSc Manc., PhD Manc. Prof., Maternal and Child Epidemiology

Marshall, Tim, MBE, BSc Lond., MSc Lond. Sr. Lectr.
Marshall, Tom Sr. Lectr.
Powell, J. E., VetMB Camb., MA Camb., PhD Brist. Sr. Lectr.
Stevens, Andrew J., BA Camb., MB BS Lond., MA Nott., MSc Lond., FFPHM Prof., Public Health; Head*
Taylor, Rod S., BSc Glas., MSc Lond., PhD Glas. Sr. Lectr.
Winter, Heather Sr. Lectr., Maternal and Child Health
Zeegers, Maurice, PhD Reader, Genetic Epidemiology
Other Staff: 1 Lectr.; 1 Sr. Res. Fellow; 6 Res. Fellows; 1 Public Health Fellow; 1 Cancer Res. UK Training Fellow; 12 Res. Assocs.; 1 Res. Asst.; 3 Res. Officers; 1 Sr. Res. Reviewer; 1 Statistician; 1 Biostatistician; 2 Project Officers; 3 Res. Nurses; 1 Academic Manager; 1 Sr. Scientist; 1 Environmental Scientist; 1 Researcher; 1 Programme Manager; 1 Sr. Clin. Lectr.; 1 Hon. Lectr.; 1 Hon. Res. Assoc.; 1 Hon. Clin. Sr. Lectr.
Research: cancer epidemiology; health impact assessment; health services, particularly health care evaluation and health technology assessment; health services research methodology and clinical trials; maternal and child health epidemiology

Reproductive and Child Health, Division of

Tel: (0121) 627 2775 Fax: (0121) 415 4837
Southwood, Taunton R., BM BS Flin., FRACP, FRCPA, FRCPCH, FRCP Prof.; Head*
Research: angiogenesis and vascular biology; clinical trials in paediatrics, obstetrics and gynaecology; fetal and maternal medicine; molecular genetics; systematic review

Medical and Molecular Genetics

Farndon, Peter A., BSc MD, FRCP Hon. Prof., Clinical Genetics
Latif, Farida, BSc Liv., PhD Lond. Reader
Maher, Eamonn, BSc Manc., MB ChB Manc., MD Manc., FRCP Prof., Medical Genetics; Head*
Webb, Tessa P., BSc Birm., PhD Birm. Sr. Lectr.
Other Staff: 2 Lectrs.
Research: autozygosity mapping of rare recessive disorders; genomic imprinting; molecular cytogenetics; molecular pathology of single gene disorders

Obstetrics and Gynaecology

Tel: (0121) 627 2695 Fax: (0121) 414 1576
Gupta, Janesh K., MB ChB Leeds, MSc Leeds, MD Leeds Sr. Lectr.
Khan, Khalid S., MB BS MSc MMed Prof., Obstetrics-Gynaecology and Clinical Epidemiology
Kilby, Mark D., MB BS Lond., MD Nott. Prof., Maternal and Foetal Medicine
Luesley, David M., MA Camb., MD Birm., FRCOG Prof., Gynaecological Oncology
Mann, Chris H., BSc Lough., MB ChB Leic., MD Birm. Sr. Lectr., Gynaecological Oncology and Laparoscopic Surgery
Whittle, Martin J., MD Manc., FRCPGlas, FRCOG Dame Hilda Lloyd Prof., Foetal Medicine; Head*
Other Staff: 4 Lectrs.; 2 Res. Fellows; 1 Res. Assoc.; 1 Clin. Res. Fellow; 1 Hon. Reader; 7 Hon. Sr. Lectrs.; 3 Hon. Sr. Res. Fellows; 3 Hon. Res. Fellows; 2 Hon. Res. Assocs.; 30 Hon. Sr. Clin. Lectrs.; 1 Hon. Clin. Lectr.; 1 Hon. Clin. Res. Fellow
Research: angiogenesis and vascular biology; cervical and ovarian cancer; clinical trials; fetal and maternal medicine; systematic reviews

Paediatrics and Child Health

Tel: (0121) 333 8717 Fax: (0121) 333 8701
Barrett, Timothy G., MB BS Lond. Sr. Lectr., Paediatric Endocrinology

Booth, Ian W., BSc Lond., MB BS Lond., MSc Lond., MD Lond., FRCP, FRCPCH Dir., Inst. of Child Health; Leonard Parsons Prof., Paediatric Gastroenterology
Cummins, Carole L., BA Oxf., MSc Oxf., PhD Birm. Sr. Lectr.
Green, Stuart H., MA Camb., MB BChir Camb., FRCP Sr. Lectr., Paediatric Neurology
Grundy, R. G., BSc Lond., PhD Lond., MB ChB, FRCP Sr. Lectr., Paediatric Oncology
Knutton, Stuart, BSc Birm., PhD Birm. Reader, Cellular Microbiology
Lander, Anthony T. Sr. Lectr., Paediatric Surgery
McConville, Carmel M., BSc Belf., PhD Belf. Sr. Lectr., Paediatric Cancer Genetics
McDonagh, Janet E., MB BS Newcastle(UK) Sr. Lectr., Paediatric Rheumatology
Moy, Robert J., BA Camb., MB BChir Camb., MD Camb. Sr. Lectr., Community Child Health
Murphy, M. Stephen, BSc N.U.I., MB BCh BAO N.U.I., MD N.U.I. Sr. Lectr., Paediatric Gastroenterology
Southwood, Taunton R., BM BS Flin., FRACP, FRCPA, FRCPCH, FRCP Prof., Paediatric Rheumatology; Head*
Other Staff: 1 Lectr.; 16 Res. Fellows; 3 Res. Assocs.; 1 Sr. Clin. Res. Fellow; 4 Clin. Res. Fellows; 1 Hon. Reader; 4 Hon. Sr. Lectrs.; 1 Hon. Sr. Res. Fellow; 3 Hon. Res. Fellows; 1 Hon. Res. Assoc.; 104 Hon. Sr. Clin. Lectrs.; 8 Hon. Clin. Lectrs.; 1 Hon. Clin. Tutor
Research: adolescent and transitional research; clinical trials in paediatrics; disease registries and epidemiology; molecular genetics; paediatric oncology

SPECIAL CENTRES, ETC

Brand Marketing, Centre for Research in

de Chernatony, Leslie, BSc Kent, PhD City(UK), FCIM Prof.; Dir.*

Chemical Physics, Centre for

Johnston, Roy L., MA Oxf., DPhil Oxf. Reader
Palmer, Richard E., MA Camb., PhD Camb., FIP Prof.
Smith, Ian W. M., FRS Emer. Prof.
Tuckett, Richard P., BA Camb., PhD Camb., FRSChem Prof.
Other Staff: 1 Lectr.

Computational Intelligence and Applications, Centre for Research in (CERCIA)

Yao, Xin, BSc China U.S.T., MSc China U.S.T., PhD China U.S.T. Dir.*
Other Staff: 2 Deputy Dirs.; 7 Res. Staff

Corporate Governance Research, Centre for

Mallin, Christine A., BSc Aston, PhD Nott., FCA, FRSA Prof.; Dir.*

Educational Technology and Distance Learning, Centre for (CETADL)

Arvanitis, Theodoros N., DPhil Sus. Dir.*
Other Staff: 1 Deputy Dir.; 1 Res. Assoc.

Electron Microscopy, Centre for

Jones, Ian P., MA Camb., PhD, FIP Prof.; Dir.*

English for International Students Unit

Tel: (0121) 414 5697 Fax: (0121) 414 3600
Hewings, M. J., BA S'ton., MA Birm., PhD Birm. Sr. Lectr.
Littlemore, Jeannette, BA Brad., MA E.Anglia, PhD Thames V. Sr. Lectr.; Acting Dir.*
Overall, C. S., BA Hull, MBA Hull, MA Leeds Dir., Bus. Engl. Programmes
Other Staff: 6 Lectrs.; 6 Tutors

Environmental Research and Training, Centre for

Petts, Judith I., BA Exe., PhD Lough. Prof.; Deputy Dir.

Other Staff: 5 Assoc. Dirs.

Ethnicity and Culture, Centre for the Study of (CSEC)

Abbas, Tahir Sr. Lectr.; Dir.*
Other Staff: 7 Staff Members; 2 Visiting Fellows

European Law, Institute of

Arnull, Anthony M., BA Sus., PhD Leic. Prof.; Dir.*

European Research Institute

Tel: (0121) 414 6928 Fax: (0121) 414 8221
E-mail: eriadmin@bham.ac.uk
Batt, Judy R., BSocSc Birm., PhD Birm. Prof., Central and South-East European Politics (on leave)
Braithwaite, R., GCMG, MA Camb., LLD Camb. Hon. Prof.
Cooper, J. M., BSc(Econ) Bath, PhD Birm. Prof., Russian Economic Studies
Davies, R. W., BA Lond., PhD Sr. Fellow; Emer. Prof.
Grix, J., BA Lond., MA Sus., PhD Birm. Sr. Lectr.
Hanson, P., MA Camb., PhD Birm. Emer. Prof.
Kaser, M. C. Hon. Prof.
Longhurst, Kerry A., BA Thames V., MA Wales, PhD Birm. Sr. Lectr.
Menon, Anand, MA Oxf., MPhil Oxf., DPhil Oxf. Dir., Res. and External Relations; Prof., West European Politics
Paterson, W. E., OBE, MA St And., MSc Lond., PhD Lond., FRSEd, FRSA Prof.
Perrie, M. P., MA Edin., MA Emer. Prof.
Rees, E. A., BA York(UK), PhD Birm. Reader, Soviet and Russian History (on leave)
Roper, Lord Hon. Prof.
Ryan, Cillian, PhD W.Ont., MA Prof.; Dir.*
Van der Will, W., DPhil Cologne Hon. Prof.
Wolczuk, Kataryna, MLaw Gdansk, MSocSc Birm., PhD Birm. Sr. Lectr.
Other Staff: 6 Lectrs.; 2 Sr. Res. Fellows; 1 Res. Fellow; 1 Lang. Tutor; 2 Hon. Sr. Lectrs.
Research: citizenship and identity in Europe; European economic issues; European enlargement; European security; politics and institutions of the EU

Forensic and Family Psychology, Centre for

Beech, Anthony R., BSc CNAA, DPhil Oxf. Course Tutor; Prof., Forensic Psychology
Browne, Kevin D., BSc Lond., PhD CNAA Prof.; Dir.*
Hamilton-Giachritsis, Catherine Course Tutor; Sr. Lectr., Applied Psychology
Harris, Gillian Sr. Lectr., Developmental Psychology
Laws, Richard, PhD Ill., BA MA Hon. Prof.
Ostapiuk, Eugene B., BA Trinity(Dub.), MSc Hon. Prof.
Prins, Herschel, MPhil Hon. Prof.
Thomas-Peter, Brian A., BSc MSc PhD Hon. Prof.
Towl, Graham, BA Durh., MSc Lond., MBA Birm. Hon. Prof.
Other Staff: 2 Lectrs.; 1 Res. Fellow; 1 Instr.; 2 Hon. Sr. Lectrs.; 23 Hon. Lectrs.; 4 Hon. Sr. Res. Fellows

Immune Regulation, Medical Research Council Centre for

Adams, David H., MB ChB Birm., MD Prof., Liver Res. Unit
Anderson, Graham, BSc Birm., PhD Birm. Reader
Buckley, Christopher D., MB BS Lond., MA Oxf., DPhil Oxf. Prof.
Caamaño, Jorge, PhD Buenos Aires Sr. Lectr.
Gordon, John, BSc S'ton., PhD S'ton. MRes Course Tutor; MRC Prof., Cellular Immunology
Jefferis, Royston, BSc PhD DSc, FRSChem, FRCPath Prof., Molecular Immunology
Jenkinson, Eric J., BSc Brist., PhD Wales, FMedSci Prof.; Co-Dir.

Lammas, Tony, MSc Wales, PhD Wales Sr. Lectr.
Lane, Peter J., MB ChB Edin., PhD Birm., FRCPEd, FRCPath Reader
Lord, Janet M., BSc CNAA, PhD Aston Reader; MSc Course Co-ordinator
Maclennan, Ian Prof.; Dir.*
Moss, Paul, BM BCh Oxf., MA Camb. Prof.
Nash, Gerard B., BSc Manc., PhD Lond. Prof.
Rickinson, Alan B., MA Camb., PhD Camb., FRS, FMedSci Prof.; Co-Dir.
Salmon, Mike, BSc Birm., PhD Birm. Prof.
Savage, Caroline Prof.
Wakelam, Michael J. O., BSc Birm., PhD Birm. Prof.
Young, Lawrence S., BSc Birm., PhD Birm., DSc Birm., FRCPath Prof.
Other Staff: 6 Staff Members

International Education and Research, Centre for

Davies, M. L., BA Exe., MEd PhD Prof.; Dir., CIERSE
Harber, Clive R., BA Reading, MA Leic., PhD Birm. Prof.
Other Staff: 2 Lectrs.; 1 Res. Assoc.

Ironbridge Institute

Tel: (01952) 432751 Fax: (01952) 435937
de Haan, David, MSc Programme Dir.
Hunter, John R., BA Durh., PhD Durh., FSA Prof.
White, R. H., BA Liv., PhD Liv. Academic Dir.*
Other Staff: 2 Lectrs.; 47 Visiting Lectrs.

Jean Monnet Centre

Birmingham Jean Monnet European Centre of Excellence

Arnull, Anthony M., BA Sus., PhD Leic. Prof.
Batt, Judy R., BSocSc Birm., PhD Birm. Jean Monnet Prof. (on leave)
Menon, Anand, MA Oxf., MPhil Oxf., DPhil Oxf. Prof., West European Politics
Redmond, John, MSc Wales, PhD Warw. Jean Monnet Prof.
Ryan, Cillian, PhD W.Ont., MA Jean Monnet Prof., European Economics; Dir.*
Other Staff: 15 Affiliated Staff Members

Modern Languages, Centre for

Tel: (0121) 414 7978 Fax: (0121) 414 5919
E-mail: b.a.picariello@bham.ac.uk
Klapper, John M., BA Birm., MLitt Oxf., PhD Birm. Prof., Foreign Language Pedagogy; Dir.*
Wozniak, D., MA Essen Co-ordinator; Deputy Dir.
Other Staff: 3 Lang. Co-ordinators; 9 Lang. Tutors

Ornithology, Centre for

Blackburn, Tim M., BSc Manc., DPhil Oxf. Prof., Macroecology
Brandstaetter, Roland, MagRerNat Salzburg, DrRerNat Sr. Lectr., Animal Biology
Butler, P. J., BSc S'ton., PhD E.Anglia, FIBiol Mason Prof., Comparative Physiology
Martin, Graham R., BSc Sur., PhD Exe., DSc Birm. Prof., Avian Sensory Science; Dir.*
Woakes, A. J. (Tony), BSc Brist., PhD Birm. Sr. Lectr., Animal Physiology
Other Staff: 2 Lectrs.; 1 Roberts Fellow

Reformation and Early Modern Studies, Centre for

Bell, Maureen, BA Camb., MA Camb., MLS Lough., PhD Lough. Reader
Cust, Richard P., BA Lond., PhD Lond., FRHistS Reader
Harris, Nigel W., BA Oxf., DPhil Oxf. Sr. Lectr.
Hemsoll, David E., BA E.Anglia, BSc Lond., MA Lond. Sr. Lectr.
Jones, Peter M., BA Leeds, DPhil Oxf. Prof.

Jowett, John D., MA Newcastle(UK), PhD Liv. Reader/Fellow
Macrides, Ruth Sr. Lectr.
Murdock, Graeme N. J., MA Oxf., DPhil Oxf. Sr. Lectr.
Perkins, Wendy, BA Lond., PhD Lond. Sr. Lectr.
Ryrie, Alec Sr. Lectr.
Shaw, Denis J. B., BA Lond., PhD Lond. Reader
Slater, Terry R., BA Hull, PhD Birm. Reader
Slowey, Gerry W., MA Birm., PhD Rome Sr. Lectr.; Head*
Swanson, Robert N., MA Camb., PhD Camb., FRHistS, FSA Prof.
Wiggins, Martin J., MA Oxf., DPhil Oxf. Sr. Lectr./Fellow
Wilcher, Robert, BA Oxf., MA Birm., PhD Birm. Reader
Other Staff: 5 Lectrs.; 2 Res. Fellows

Research, Medical and Dental Education, Centre for

Frame, J. W., BDS Glas., MSc Manc., PhD Manc., FDSRCS, FDSRCSEd Co-Dir.*
Thomas, H. R., BA Manc., MEd Manc., PhD Birm. Dir.*
Wall, D. W., MB ChB MMed Co-Dir.*

Sociocultural and Activity Theory Research, Centre for

Daniels, H. R. J., BSc Liv., PhD Lond. Co-Dir.*
Edwards, Anne Prof.; Co-Dir.*

Visual Impairment Centre for Teaching and Research

Douglas, G. G. A., BSc Aston, PhD Res. Fellow; Co-ordinator of Res.*
Other Staff: 2 Lectrs.; 2 Res. Fellows

CONTACT OFFICERS

Academic affairs. Academic Registrar: Hall, David E., BA Reading
(E-mail: d.e.hall@bham.ac.uk)
Admissions (first degree). Director of Admissions: Smith, Roderick M., BSc St And.
(E-mail: admissions@bham.ac.uk)
Admissions (higher degree). Director of Admissions: Smith, Roderick M., BSc St And.
(E-mail: admissions@bham.ac.uk)
Adult/continuing education. Head, School of Education: Harber, Prof. Clive R., BA Reading, MA Leic., PhD Birm.
(E-mail: c.r.harber@bham.ac.uk)
Alumni. Director of Development and Alumni Relations: Blinco, Nick
(E-mail: alumnioffice@bham.ac.uk)
Archives. University Archivist: Bassett, Philippa
(E-mail: special-collections@bham.ac.uk)
Careers. Director of Careers Centre: Russell, S.
(E-mail: careers-centre@bham.ac.uk)
Computing services. Librarian and Director of Information Services: Shoebridge, Michele I., BA Birm., MA Wolv.
Conferences/corporate hospitality. Director of Hospitality and Accommodation Services: Pringle, Geoff
(E-mail: r.g.pringle@bham.ac.uk)
Consultancy services. Director of Research and Commercial Services: Wilkie, James
Credit transfer. Academic Registrar: Hall, David E., BA Reading
Distance education. Director of Centre for Distance Education and Learning: Sharples, Prof. M., BSc St And., PhD Edin., FRSA
Equal opportunities. Director of Personnel Services: Paver, Heather
(E-mail: h.paver@bham.ac.uk)
Estates and buildings/works and services. Director of Estate Management: Barker, Ian
(E-mail: i.barker@bham.ac.uk)
Examinations. Academic Registrar: Hall, David E., BA Reading
Finance. Director of Finance: Ball, Gill
(E-mail: g.ball@bham.ac.uk)
General enquiries. Registrar and Secretary: Ball, Gill (E-mail: g.ball@bham.ac.uk)
Health services. University Medical Officer: Raichura, Vijay, MB BS Lond.
(E-mail: vijay.raichura@

pc.birminghamha.wmids.nhs.uk)

Industrial liaison. Director of Research and Commercial Services: Wilkie, James

International office. Director of International Office (Acting): Edwards, Andrea
(*E-mail:* international@bham.ac.uk)

Language training for international students. Director of English for International Students Unit: Lamie, J. M., BA *Warw.*, MA *Warw.*, PhD *Birm.*

Library (chief librarian). Librarian and Director of Information Services: Shoebridge, Michele I., BA *Birm.*, MA *Wolv.*

Marketing. Director of Marketing Services: Lancaster, T.

Personnel/human resources. Director of Personnel Services: Paver, Heather
(*E-mail:* h.paver@bham.ac.uk)

Public relations. Director of Communications: Primmer, Sue J., BA *Camb.*, MA *Camb.*, MLitt *Durh.* (*E-mail:* s.j.primmer@bham.ac.uk)

Publications. Director of Design and Publications: Harris, D.
(*E-mail:* d.e.harris@bham.ac.uk)

Purchasing. Assistant Director of Finance (Procurement): Higgins, B. J.

Quality assurance and accreditation. Director of the Academic Quality Unit: Ruston, Anne, BA *Camb.*
(*E-mail:* a.c.ruston@bham.ac.uk)

Research. Director of Research and Commercial Services: Wilkie, James
(*E-mail:* res.ent@bham.ac.uk)

Safety. Director of Health and Safety Unit: Harrison, David I., BSc *St And.*, MSc *Strath.*
(*E-mail:* healthandsafety@ contacts.bham.ac.uk)

Scholarships, awards, loans. Academic Registrar: Hall, David E., BA *Reading*
(*E-mail:* scholarships@bham.ac.uk)

Schools liaison. Director of Admissions: Murphy, Liz
(*E-mail:* e.murphy@bham.ac.uk)

Security. Security Manager: Allt, Gordon
(*E-mail:* g.g.allt@bham.ac.uk)

Sport and recreation. Director of Sport: Wooldridge, Z.
(*E-mail:* z.j.wooldridge@bham.ac.uk)

Staff development and training. Assistant Director of Personnel (Health, Safety and Staff Development): Harrison, David I., BSc *St And.*, MSc *Strath.*
(*E-mail:* d.i.harrison@bham.ac.uk)

Strategic planning. Director of Planning: Abbott, Christine
(*E-mail:* c.m.abbott@bham.ac.uk)

Student union. General Manager, Guild of Students: Poole, Julia, BSc
(*E-mail:* j.poole@guild.bham.ac.uk)

Student welfare/counselling. Director of Student Support and Counselling Service: Evans, Richard J.
(*E-mail:* r.j.evans@bham.ac.uk)

Students from other countries. International Student Adviser: O'Leary, Claire
(*E-mail:* c.p.oleary@bham.ac.uk)

Students with disabilities. Disability Co-ordinator: Green, Sue
(*E-mail:* s.m.green@bham.ac.uk)

University press. Managing Editor, University Press: McAulay, Alec
(*E-mail:* a.mcaulay@bham.ac.uk)

Women. Women's Officer: Poole, Julia, BSc
(*E-mail:* j.poole@guild.bham.ac.uk)

CAMPUS/COLLEGE HEADS

Birmingham College of Food, Tourism and Creative Studies, Summer Row, Birmingham, England B3 1JB. (Tel: (0121) 604 1000; Fax: (0121) 608 7100; E-mail: marketing@bcftcs.ac.uk) Principal: McIntyre, Eddie F., CBE

[*Information supplied by the institution as at 14 March 2006, and edited by the ACU*]

BIRMINGHAM CITY UNIVERSITY

Founded 1991

Postal Address: Perry Barr, Birmingham, England B42 2SU
Telephone: (0121) 331 5000 **Fax:** (0121) 331 7994 **E-mail:** choices@bcu.ac.uk
URL: http://www.bcu.ac.uk

VICE-CHANCELLOR*—Tidmarsh, Prof. David H., BSc *CNAA*, PhD *CNAA*, FIMechE, FCMI
SECRETARY AND REGISTRAR‡—Penlington, Maxine, BA

UNIVERSITY OF BOLTON

Founded 1989

Postal Address: Deane Road, Bolton, England BL3 5AB
Telephone: (01204) 900600 **Fax:** (01204) 399074 **E-mail:** enquiries@bolton.ac.uk
URL: http://www.bolton.ac.uk

VICE-CHANCELLOR*—Holmes, George, BSc *Leeds*, MBA *Brad.*, PhD *Brist.*

BOURNEMOUTH UNIVERSITY

Founded 1992

Member of the Association of Commonwealth Universities

Postal Address: Talbot Campus, Fern Barrow, Poole, Dorset, England BH12 5BB
Telephone: (01202) 961916 **Fax:** (01202) 962736 **E-mail:** askbuenquiries@bournemouth.ac.uk
URL: http://www.bournemouth.ac.uk

VICE-CHANCELLOR*—Curran, Prof. Paul J., BSc Sheff., MBA S'ton., PhD Brist., DSc Brist., FRGS, FCIM, FRSPSoc
DEPUTY VICE-CHANCELLOR—Willey, David, BSc Lond., MSc Glas., MBA Cran.
PRO-VICE-CHANCELLOR (EDUCATION)—Astin, Brian, BSc Bath, PhD Brist.
PRO-VICE-CHANCELLOR (RESEARCH AND ENTERPRISE)—Petford, Prof. Nick, BSc Lond., MA Camb., PhD Liv.
PRO-VICE-CHANCELLOR (RESOURCES)—Vinney, Prof. John, BEng W.England, PhD W.England
DIRECTOR OF FINANCE—Everett, Karen, BSc Exe., FCA
DIRECTOR OF HUMAN RESOURCES—Riordan, Michael G., BA N.U.I., BD Maynooth
REGISTRAR AND SECRETARY‡—Richardson, Noel D. G., BA Trinity(Dub.)

GENERAL INFORMATION

History. Bournemouth University can trace its origins to the early twentieth century with the foundation of the former Bournemouth College of Technology. The university's modern history began in the mid 1970s with the creation of the Dorset Institute of Higher Education. In 1990 the Institute was redesignated Bournemouth Polytechnic and, two years later, became Bournemouth University.

The university has two campuses: Lansdowne Campus, very near Bournemouth town centre; and Talbot Campus, approximately 3km from the town centre, and within the town of Poole.

Admission to first degree courses (see also United Kingdom Introduction). Through Universities and Colleges Admissions Service (UCAS). UK nationals: entry qualifications are a minimum of 2 General Certificate of Education (GCE) A level passes or equivalent. Candidates will normally be expected to present GCSEs at grade C or above in English and Mathematics or relevant key skills. Other qualifications also accepted include: Access courses, BTEC/EDEXCEL and SCOTVEC National Certificates/Diplomas, Irish Leaving Certificate, International/European Baccalaureate. Specific entry requirements are available from the university registrar. International applicants: a range of qualifications is acceptable for entry. Applicants whose first language is not English must pass an English language test.

First Degrees (see also United Kingdom Directory to Subjects of Study). BA, BEng, BSc, LLB.
Sandwich courses: 4 years.
Length of course. Full-time: BA, BEng, BSc, LLB: 3 years. Part-time: BA, BEng, BSc, LLB: 3–5 years.

Higher Degrees (see also United Kingdom Directory to Subjects of Study).
Master's. LLM, MA, MBA, MPhil, MSc.
Admission. Applicants for admission to master's degree courses must normally hold an appropriate first degree. Relevant professional experience is also considered for entry to some programmes.
MPhil: of varying duration.
Length of course. Full-time: LLM, MA, MBA, MSc: 1 year. Part-time: LLM, MA, MBA, MSc: 2 years.
Doctoral. DBA, PhD.
Admission. Applicants for admission to doctoral degrees must normally hold an appropriate first degree.
DBA, PhD: of varying duration.
Length of course. Full-time: DBA, PhD: 3–4 years. Part-time: DBA, PhD: 6–7 years.

Language of Instruction. English. Pre-sessional courses are available for international students.

Libraries. Volumes: 244,321. Periodicals subscribed to: 7152. Other holdings: 48,000 e-books; 35,000 e-journals; 144 electronic information services. Special collections: Arthur Brown (riots and civil disobedience); Dorset Natural History and Archaeological Society; media history; Segrue (journalism); Wedlake and Greening (archaeology).

Academic Awards (2006–2007). 220 awards each with a min. value of £1000.

Academic Year (2008–2009). Three terms: 29 September–19 December; 12 January–3 April; 27 April–26 June.

Income (2006–2007). Total, £88,830,000.

Statistics. Staff (2007–2008): 1384 (620 academic, 764 non-academic). Students (2007–2008): full-time 11,783; part-time 4359; international 1609; undergraduate 14,560.

FACULTIES/SCHOOLS

Business School
Tel: (01202) 965428 *Fax:* (01202) 965261
E-mail: business@bournemouth.ac.uk
Dean: Brady, Prof. Chris, BEd Lond., MSc S'ton., PhD S'ton.
Secretary: Cutler, Judith

Conservation Sciences, School of
Tel: (01202) 965178 *Fax:* (01202) 965255
E-mail: consci@bournemouth.ac.uk
Dean: Astin, Brian, BSc Bath, PhD Brist.
Secretary: Freeman, Maureen

Design, Engineering and Computing, School of
Tel: (01202) 965339 *Fax:* (01202) 965314
E-mail: dec@bournemouth.ac.uk
Dean: Vinney, Prof. John, BEng W.England, PhD W.England
Secretary: Cooper, Dorothy

Health and Social Care, School of
Tel: (01202) 962115 *Fax:* (01202) 962131
E-mail: hsc@bournemouth.ac.uk
Dean: Thomas, Gail, MSc Brun., PhD Thames V.
Secretary: Joy, Jenny

Media School
Tel: (01202) 965360 *Fax:* (01202) 965530
E-mail: media@bournemouth.ac.uk
Head: Jukes, Stephen, BA Oxf., MA Oxf.
Secretary: Rose, Sandie

Services Management, School of
Tel: (01202) 966966 *Fax:* (01202) 515707
E-mail: sm@bournemouth.ac.uk

Head: Hemmington, Prof. Nigel, BSc Sur., PhD Sur.
Secretary: Lyttle, Sharon

ACADEMIC UNITS

Accounting and Finance
Tel: (01202) 965428 *Fax:* (01202) 965261
E-mail: business@bournemouth.ac.uk
Allerston, Anne, BA Bourne., MSc S'ton. Sr. Lectr.; Assoc. Dean, Undergrad. Studies
Ball, Frazer, BA Bourne. Sr. Lectr.
Day, Robert G., BSc Lond., MSc Lond., MPhil Lond. Sr. Lectr.
Fearnley, Stella, BA Leeds Prof.
Hansford, Ann, BA Liv., PhD W.England Assoc. Prof.
Hardwick, Phillip, BA York(UK), BSc Open(UK), MA Qu., PhD S'ton. Prof., Economics
Hosking, Malcolm, BA Portsmouth Assoc. Dean, Postgrad. Students
Marshall, David, MBA S'ton. Sr. Lectr.
McElroy, Trefor J., BA Manc., MSc Lond. Assoc. Dean; Head*
Stonelake, Bernadette, BA C.Lancs., FACCA Sr. Lectr.
Tauringana, Venancio, MA Glas., PhD Edin. Sr. Lectr.
Webster, Allan, BA E.Anglia, MSc Lond. Reader
Willcocks, Geoff, BA Essex, MBA Bourne., PhD Bourne. Sr. Academic
Other Staff: 4 Visiting Profs.; 3 Visiting Fellows/Res. Fellows; 7 Visiting Lectrs.
Research: finance and risk

Archaeology, Anthropology and Heritage
Tel: (01202) 965178 *Fax:* (01202) 965525
E-mail: consci@bournemouth.ac.uk
Brisbane, Mark, BA S'ton., FSA Prof., Mediaeval Archaeology
Buckland, Paul, BSc Birm., PhD Birm., FSA, FGS, FRES Prof., Environmental Archaeology
Chartrand, Jeffrey, BA Calg., BEd Calg., MA Manit. Sr. Lectr.; Programmes Manager; Programme Leader
Darvill, Timothy, BA S'ton., PhD S'ton., DSc S'ton., FSA Prof.; Dir.*
Gale, John, BA Nott. Sr. Lectr.
Hambleton, Ellen, BSc Sheff., PhD Durh.
Maltby, Mark, BA Sheff., MA Exe., FSA Reader
Parham, David, BA Wales, MSc S'ton. Sr. Lectr., Maritime Archaeology
Russell, Miles, BA Lond., PhD Bourne., FSA Sr. Lectr.
Smith, Helen, BSc Sheff., PhD Sheff. Sr. Lectr.
Staelens, Yvette, BA Exe., FMAS, FSA Programme Leader
Welham, Kate, BSc Portsmouth, MSc Sheff., PhD Sheff. Sr. Lectr.; Assoc. Dean, Postgrad. Studies
Wood, Chris, BSc Lond., PhD Leic. Sr. Lectr.
Other Staff: 3 Visiting Profs.; 4 Lectrs.; 10 Res. Fellows; 3 Visiting Res. Fellows

Computer Animation

Tel: (01202) 965371 Fax: (01202) 965530
E-mail: ncca@bournemouth.ac.uk
Allen, Phillip, BA Bourne., MA Bourne.   Sr. Lectr.
Bell, Stephen, BA CNAA, PhD Lough.   Sr. Lectr.
Callus, Paula, BA Malta, MA Bourne., MA Lond.
Sr. Lectr.
Childs, Lucy, BA E.Lond., MA RCA   Sr. Lectr.
Comninos, Peter, BSc Tees., PhD Tees.   Prof.
Hubbard, Steven, BA Bourne., MA Bourne.
Assoc. Dean; Head*
Macey, Jonathan, BEng Leeds Met., MSc Bourne.
Sr. Lectr.
Nait-Charif, Hammadi, PhD Chiba, BA MSc
Sr. Lectr.
Pasko, Alexander, MSc Moscow, PhD   Prof.
Sarafopoulos, Anargyros, BA Salonika, MA Bourne.
Sr. Lectr.
Vince, John, MTech Brun., PhD Brun.   Prof.;
Head, Academic Group
Zhang, Jian J., BSc Chongqing, MSc Chongqing,
PhD Chongqing   Prof.
Other Staff: 2 Sr. Res. Fellows; 2 Res. Fellows;
2 Programme Leaders

Conservation Ecology and Environmental Change

Tel: (01202) 965352 Fax: (01202) 965255
E-mail: consci@bournemouth.ac.uk
Bennett, Matthew R., BSc Lond., PhD Edin.
Prof.; Deputy Dean, Res. and Enterprise
Britton, John R., BSc Hull, PhD Hull   Sr. Lectr.
Clarke, Ralph, BSc Reading, MSc S'ton.   Prof.
Curran, Paul J., BSc Sheff., MBA S'ton., PhD
Brist., DSc Brist., FRGS, FCIM, FRSPSoc
Prof.
Diaz, Anita, BSc Oxf.Brookes, PhD Exe.   Sr. Lectr.
Fletcher, Stephen, BSc Wales, MSc Bourne.   Sr.
Lectr., Coastal and Marine Affairs
Gozlan, Rodolphe, BA Paris VIII, MSc Aix-
Marseilles, MPhil Aix-Marseilles, PhD Herts.
Reader
Hill, Ross, BA Oxf., MA Oxf., PhD Wales
Reader
Hodder, Kathryn, BSc Wales, PhD S'ton.   Sr.
Lectr.
James, Brian, BSc Bourne.   Sr. Lectr.
Newton, Adrian, BA Camb., PhD Camb.   Prof.;
Dir.*
Petford, Prof. Nick, BSc Lond., MA Camb., PhD
Liv.   Prof.
Stillman, Richard, BSc E.Anglia, PhD E.Anglia
Reader
Other Staff: 1 Visiting Prof.; 3 Lectrs.; 5
Visiting Res. Fellows; 3 Res. Fellows

Corporate and Marketing Communications

Tel: (01202) 965371 Fax: (01202) 965530
E-mail: media@bournemouth.ac.uk
Brissenden, John, BA Westminster   Sr. Lectr.
Caswell, Elsbeth, BA Montr., MA Portsmouth, EdD
S'ton.   Sr. Lectr.
Denegri-Knott, Janice, BA Catholic(Boliviana), MA
Bourne.   Sr. Lectr.
Eccles, Sue, BSc Lanc., PhD Lanc.   Assoc. Dean;
Joint Head*
Haywood, Helen, BA E.Anglia, MSc Leic.   Sr.
Lectr.
Lilleker, Darren, BA Sheff., PhD Sheff.   Sr. Lectr.
Merrett, Colin, BA Exe., MA Exe.   Sr. Lectr.;
Assoc. Dean; Joint Head*
Oliver, John, BA Bourne., MBA Bourne., DBA
Bourne.   Sr. Lectr.
Platt, Carole, BSc Lanc., MBA Bourne.   Sr. Lectr.
Richards, Barry, BA Reading, PhD CNAA   Prof.;
Deputy Dean, Res. and Enterprise
Scullion, Richard, BA Lanc., MA Portsmouth   Sr.
Lectr.
Sekhon, Yasmin, BA S'ton.Solent, MA S'ton.Solent
Sr. Lectr.
VanWyk, Cliff, BCom S.Af., MSc Leic.   Sr.
Lectr.
Watson, Tom, BA NSW, PhD Nott.Trent
Deputy Dean, Educn.

Forensic Sciences

Tel: (01202) 965178 Fax: (01202) 965255
E-mail: consci@bournemouth.ac.uk
Cheetham, Paul, BSc Brad.   Sr. Lectr.
Ginige, Tilak K., LLB N.Lond., LLM Wales   Sr.
Lectr.
Kneller, Paul, MPhil Bourne.   Sr. Lectr.
Korstejns, Amanda, BA Utrecht, MPhil Utrecht,
PhD Utrecht   Sr. Lectr.
Liang, Wei-Jun, BSc Shanxi, MPhil Camb., PhD
Camb.   Sr. Lectr.
Schofield, David, MSc Sur.   Sr. Lectr.
Symonds, Catherine R., BSc Lond., MPhil Lond.
Assoc. Dean, Undergrad. Students
Other Staff: 2 Lectrs.

Law

Tel: (01202) 965428 Fax: (01202) 965261
E-mail: business@bournemouth.ac.uk
Astbury, Nigel S., BA Durh.   Sr. Lectr.
Copp, Stephen E., LLB Exe., PhD Bourne.   Sr.
Lectr.
Davis, Howard, BA S'ton., LLB Lond., PhD Reading
Reader
Grief, Nick, BA Kent, PhD Kent   Prof.; Assoc.
Dean; Head*
Hough, Barry, LLB Exe., LLM Exe.   Prof.
Kretschmer, Martin, LLM Lond., PhD Lond.
Prof.
Martell, Tim, LLB Liv.   Sr. Lectr.
Mytton, Elizabeth A., BA CNAA, LLM S'ton., EdD
S'ton.   Sr. Lectr.; Deputy Dean, Educn.
Pick, Julie K., LLB Reading   Sr. Lectr.
Pond, Ann, BA Bourne.   Sr. Lectr.
Riley, John, MA Camb., MSc Camb.   Sr. Lectr.
Teather, Richard, BA Oxf.   Sr. Lectr.
Towse, Ruth, BA Reading, MSc Lond., PhD
Rotterdam   Prof.
Weston, Sally, BA Kingston(UK)   Sr. Lectr.
Wootton, Danielle, LLB W.England, MA
W.England   Sr. Lectr.
Other Staff: 3 Visiting Profs.; 1 Lectr.; 2
Visiting Fellows/Res. Fellows; 1 Lectr./Res.
Fellow; 9 Visiting Lectrs.

Management

Tel: (01202) 965428 Fax: (01202) 967305
E-mail: business@bournemouth.ac.uk
Armistead, Colin, BSc UMIST, PhD Manc.
Prof.; Head of Res.
Atkinson, Roger, MPhil PhD   Sr. Lectr.
Benmore, Anne, BPharm Bath, MA Bourne.   Sr.
Lectr.
Bobeva, Milena, MSc Sofia, MSc Leeds Met., PhD
Bourne.   Sr. Lectr.
Brady, Chris, BEd Lond., MSc S'ton., PhD S'ton.
Prof.
Burr, Caroline, BA Bourne., MBA Bourne., MA
Bourne.   Sr. Lectr.
Eng, Teck, BEd Sur., MSc UMIST, PhD UMIST
Prof., Marketing
Erdélyi, Peter, MA N.Y.State, MBA Navarra, Mgr
Sr. Lectr.
Freedman, Paul, BSc S'ton., MPhil S'ton., EdD
S'ton.   Sr. Lectr.
Ghosh, Sid, BEng Punjab, MEng Pune, MSc Warw.
Sr. Lectr.
Johnsen, Rhona E., BA Strath., PhD Bath   Sr.
Lectr.
Preget, Louise, BA Bourne., PhD CNAA   Sr.
Lectr.
Ridolfo, Mark, BSc Aston, DMS Bourne.   Sr.
Lectr.
Robson, Julie, BA Staffs., PhD Plym.   Assoc.
Dean; Head*
Roushan, Gelareh, MBA Strath., PhD Bourne.   Sr.
Academic; Assoc. Dean, E-Learning
Wengler, Beate, MA Lanc.   Sr. Lectr.
White, Jennie, BSc Reading   Sr. Lectr.
Wilkinson, Charles, BSc Lough., MA Lanc., PhD
Lanc.   Head, Exec. Educn.
Other Staff: 2 Sr. Academics; 3 Programme
Leaders; 1 Assoc. Sr. Lectr.; 6 Visitng
Fellows/Res. Fellows; 16 Visiting Lectrs.

Media Production, Journalism and Communication

Tel: (01202) 965371 Fax: (01202) 965530
E-mail: media@bournemouth.ac.uk
Allan, Stuart, BA Ryerson, MA Car., PhD Car.
Prof., Journalism
Auckland, Jonathan, BA Cardiff, MSc Cardiff   Sr.
Lectr.
Berger, Richard, BSc E.Lond., MA S'ton., PhD
Bourne.   Sr. Lectr.
Bloore, Peter, BA Brist., MVA Lond.S.Bank
Chignell, Hugh, BA Warw., MA Lond., PhD
Bourne.   Reader
Cownie, Fiona, BA Reading, MA Portsmouth
Assoc. Dean; Head, Media Productn.*
Crawford, E., BA Bourne., MPhil Bourne.   Sr.
Lectr.
Deutsch, Prof. Stephen F., BMus S.Methodist, MA
Calif.   Principal Lectr.
Dungar, Rachel, BA Frib., MPhil Frib.   Sr. Lectr.
Flintham, Joe, BA Lond., MA Lond.   Sr. Lectr.
Foster, John   Principal Lectr.
Fowler-Watt, Karen, BA Camb., MA Camb.   Sr.
Lectr.; Assoc. Dean; Head, Journalism and
Communicn.
Hanson, David M., BA S'ton.   Sr. Lectr.
Hearing, Trevor, BA Sund.   Sr. Lectr.
Helmers, Maike   Sr. Lectr.
Jordan, James, BSc Derby   Sr. Lectr.
MacGregor, Phil, BA Nott.   Sr. Lectr.
Marques Vieira, Claudia G., BA Cardiff
Moon, Jenny, BSc S'ton., MPhil Sur., MEd Glas.,
MSc Cardiff, PhD Glam.   Sr. Lectr.
Parsons, Mik, BSc Leic., MPhil Leic.   Sr. Lectr.
Pullen, Christopher, BA Open(UK), MA Brist.,
PhD Bourne.   Sr. Lectr.
Scattergood, Emma, BA S'ton.   Sr. Lectr.
Street, Sean, PhD Bourne.   Prof.; Dir., Centre
for Broadcasting History
Sykes, Lizzie, BA Lond.Met.   Sr. Lectr.
Thomas, Bronwen, BA Birm., MA E.Anglia, PhD
Manc.   Sr. Lectr.
Wallace, Sue, BA Cardiff   Sr. Lectr.
White, Neal, BA Wales, MA Middx.   Assoc. Sr.
Lectr.
Other Staff: 3 Lectrs.

Nursing and Midwifery

Tel: (01202) 962114 Fax: (01202) 962131
E-mail: hsc@bournemouth.ac.uk
Board, Michelle, BA S'ton., MSc Lond.   Sr. Lectr.
Cheesman, Sarah E., BSc Bourne., MSc Portsmouth
Sr. Lectr., Primary Care
Christensen, Martin, BSc Bourne., MSc Lond., MA
Portsmouth   Sr. Lectr., Adult Nursing
Davis, Elizabeth, BEd Lond.S.Bank, MSc Sur.   Sr.
Lectr.
Davis, Janine A., BSc Bourne., MA Bourne.   Sr.
Lectr.
Donaldson, Ian, BEd Lond.S.Bank, MA Lond.   Sr.
Lectr.
Farasat, Helen, BSc Manc.   Sr. Lectr., Child
Health Care Nursing
Gagan, Mark, MSc
Gale, Debbie, BSc
Glendenning, Nikki, BSc S'ton.   Sr. Lectr.,
Adult Nursing
Halliwell, Diana, BSc Bourne., MSc Manc.
Assoc. Dean; Head, Nursing
Harmsworth, Mark, BSc Chichester, MA Bourne.
Sr. Lectr., Emergency Care Nursing
Hartwell, Matthew, BSc Bourne., MA Wales   Sr.
Lectr., Adult Nursing
Heaslip, Vanessa, BSc S'ton.   Sr. Lectr., Adult
Nursing
Hunt, Jane A., PhD Sur.   Sr. Lectr., Child
Health Nursing
Jordan, Gill, BSc Bourne., MA Bourne.   Sr. Lectr.
Leamon, Jen, BEd Hudd., EdD E.Anglia   Sr.
Lectr.
Lewis, Paul, BSc Lond., MSc Lond.S.Bank   Prof.;
Assoc. Dean; Head, Allied Health
Professions
Little, Christine, BSc Bourne., MPhil S'ton., PhD
S'ton.   Sr. Lectr., Preceptorship
Lockyer-Stevens, Vanessa A., BSc Bourne., MEd
W.Aust.   Sr. Lectr., Child Health
McDonald, Sarah J., BSc Bourne., MA Bourne.

Mills, Anne, MSc S'ton. Sr. Lectr.

Milne, Lesley, BSc Wolv., MSc Edin. Sr. Lectr.

Norton, Liz, BSc Lough., MPhil S'ton. Sr. Lectr.

Phillips, Jill, BSc Bourne., MA Bourne. Sr. Lectr.

Philpott, Andrew J., MSc S'ton. Head, Practice Educn.

Rees, Karen, BSc Lond., MEd Portsmouth, PhD Bourne. Sr. Lectr., Public Health and Health Visiting

Scammell, Janet, BA Open(UK), MSc Lond. Head, Learning and Teaching

Viccars, Anne, BSc W.England, MA Wolv. Sr. Lectr.

Other Staff: 26 Lectr. Practitioners; 5 Acad. Midwife Teachers; 3 Midwife Teachers; 2 Practice Educators

Psychology

Tel: (01202) 965078 Fax: (01202) 965314
E-mail: dec@bournemouth.ac.uk

Burns, Ron, BSc Edin., MSc Cardiff Principal Lectr.

Hallam, John, BSc Brad., MSc Aston, PhD Aston Principal Lectr.

Heathcote, David, BSc C.Lancs., PhD C.Lancs. Sr. Lectr.

House, Becky, BSc Bourne. Sr. Lectr.

McDougall, Sine, MA Glas., PhD Glas. Prof.; Chair*

Stevens, Paul, BSc Lond., PhD Edin. Sr. Lectr.

Taylor, Jacqui, BSc Lond., MSc Portsmouth, PhD Portsmouth Sr. Lectr.

Rehabilitation and Health Science

Tel: (01202) 962115 Fax: (01202) 962131
E-mail: hsc@bournemouth.ac.uk

Fazakarley, Louise, MSc New Br. Sr. Lectr.

Merefield, Sue, MSc S'ton. Sr. Lectr., Physiotherapy

Quincey, Dave, MSc Birm., FIBS

Ryan, Kathleen, BPharm Otago, PhD Otago Reader, Maternal and Perinatal Research

Tarrant, John, BSc Leeds Sr. Lectr., Operating Department Practice

Other Staff: 18 Lectr. Practitioners; 10 Lectrs.; 1 Assoc. Sr. Lectr./Lab. Manager

Social and Community Work

Tel: (01202) 962115 Fax: (01202) 962131
E-mail: hsc@bournemouth.ac.uk

Ashencaen, Sara C., BA Herts., MA Middx., PhD Herts.

Barker, Sue, BSc Open(UK), MSc S'ton. Sr. Lectr., Nursing

Bond, Carol, BA Bourne., MSc Brist., EdD Brist. Sr. Lectr., Informatics

Brown, Keith, BSc Lond., MSc S'ton., MSc Lond.Guild. Head, Post Qualification Practice Based Learning

Fenge, Lee A., BA Exe., MSc Lond. Head, Widening Participation

Galpin, Diane, MA S'ton. Sr. Lectr., Practice Development (PQSW)

Gray, Ivan L., BA Durh., MA Nott., MBA Portsmouth, PhD S'ton. Sr. Lectr., Practice Development

Howe, Kate, BA E.Lond., MA S'ton. Sr. Lectr./ Practice Development Fellow, Social Care

Parker, Jo, BSc Cardiff, MA Cardiff Sr. Lectr., Practice Development

Parker, Jonathan, BA Hull, MA Hull Prof.; Assoc. Dean; Head*

Quinney, Anne, BA Lanc., MA Bourne. Sr. Lectr., Practice Development

Read, Rosie, BA Newcastle(UK), MA Manc., PhD Manc. Sr. Lectr., Community Work and Engagement

Ryden, Julie, BSc S.Bank, MSc Sur. Sr. Lectr., Community Work and Health Studies

Williams, Richard, BA Middx., MA Brun. Sr. Lectr., Social Work

Williams, Sarah, BSc Brist., MA Bourne. Sr. Lectr., Practice Development (PQSW)

Other Staff: 25 Lectr. Practitioners; 5 Lectrs.; 1 Sr. Teaching Fellow; 1 Assoc. Sr. Lectr.; 1 Acad. Midwife Teacher

Software Systems

Tel: (01202) 965078 Fax: (01202) 965314
E-mail: dec@bournemouth.ac.uk

Coles, Melanie, BSc E.Lond., MSc E.Lond. Sr. Lectr.

Gabrys, Bogdan, MSc Gliwice, PhD Nott.Trent Prof.

Gibson, Darrell, BEng Westminster Sr. Lectr.

Jeary, Sheridan P., BSc Bourne. Sr. Lectr.

Jones, Michael, BSc CNAA, MSc Warw. Principal Lectr.

Main, Andrew, BSc Lond., MSc Leic., PhD Leic. Head, Computing

Ncube, Cornelius, BSc Brun., MSc City(UK), PhD City(UK)

Newell, Andrew, BSc Manc., MSc Bourne. Sr. Lectr.

Phalp, Keith T., BSc Kent, MSc Bourne., PhD Bourne. Assoc. Dean; Head, Software Systems and Psychology

Pitman, Ruth J., BSc S'ton. Sr. Lectr.

Sahandi, Reza, BSc Isfahan, MSc Brad., PhD Brad. Assoc. Dean, Acad. Devel. and Resouces

Sheppard, Terry, BSc Wales, MSc Wales, PhD Lond., DSc Wales, FIMechE, FIMMM Prof.

Teal, Martin K., BSc Aston, MSc Lond., PhD City(UK) Sr. Lectr.; Programme Leader, Electronics Postgrad. Framework

Tratt, Laurence, BSc Lond., PhD Lond.

Vincent, Jonathan, BEng Portsmouth, MSc Nott.Trent, PhD Nott.Trent Reader; Assoc. Dean

Other Staff: 1 Visiting Res. Fellow

Sport and Leisure

Tel: (01202) 965146 Fax: (01202) 515707
E-mail: smu@bournemouth.ac.uk

Goodwin, Kelly, BSc Portsmouth, MSc Lond. Sr. Lectr.

Ryland, Philip F., MEd Brist. Sr. Academic; Assoc. Dean, Undergrad. Studies

Shipway, Richard, BA Lough., MSc Lough. Sr. Lectr., Applied Sports Management

Other Staff: 5 Lectrs.

Technology and Design

Tel: (01202) 965078 Fax: (01202) 965314
E-mail: dec@bournemouth.ac.uk

Benjamin, Christopher, BSc City(UK), MSc Bourne. Sr. Lectr.

Cobb, Jon E., MSc S'ton., PhD Bourne. Sr. Lectr.

Dubey, Venky N., BEng Alld., MEng Alld., PhD S'ton. Sr. Lectr.

Dyer, Bryce T. J., BA Bourne., MSc Bourne. Sr. Lectr.

Eves, Bob, BEd Sheff., MSc Sheff., PhD Bourne. Sr. Lectr.

Garland, Nigel, BSc Bourne., PhD Bourne. Sr. Lectr.

Glasspool, Christopher, BA Coventry Sr. Lectr.

Hadfield, Mark, BEng Brun., PhD Brun. Deputy Dean, Res. and Enterprise

Humphries-Smith, Tania M. B., BSc Lond.S.Bank, MPhil Kingston(UK), EdD S'ton. Sr. Academic; Head, Quality and Undergrad. Programmes

Hunt, Clive, BSc Portsmouth, MBA Brist., DMS Brist. Programme Leader

Khan, Zulfiqar, BEng Pesh., MEng Shanghai, PhD Bourne. Sr. Lectr.

Koohgilani, Mehran, BEng S.Bank, MSc Lond., PhD Bourne. Sr. Lectr.

Noroozi, Siamak, BSc Salf., MEng Sheff., PhD Sheff. Prof.

Orman, Timothy G., BEng Bourne. Sr. Lectr.

Palmer, Sarah, BA MA Sr. Lectr.

Randell, Malcolm, MA Bourne. Sr. Lectr.

Reynolds, Tim, BA Bourne. Sr. Lectr.

Roach, Jim, BSc Wales, MSc Wales Deputy Dean, Educn.; Prof.; Knowledge Transfer

Roe, Theodore M., BA Kingston(UK), MDes RCA Sr. Lectr.

Sewell, Phillip, BEng W.England, PhD W.England Sr. Lectr.

Staples, Stephen, BA Brighton, MSc Bourne. Sr. Lectr.

Tobe, Shogo, BA Tokai, PhD Tokyo Metropolitan Reader

Velay, Xavier, BEng Coventry, MSc Coventry, PhD Bourne. Assoc. Dean; Head of Acad. Group, Technol. and Des.

Vinney, Prof. John, BEng W.England, PhD W.England Prof.

Watson, Andrew, BSc Sr. Lectr.

Other Staff: 3 Lectrs.

Tourism and Hospitality

Tel: (01202) 965146 Fax: (01202) 515707
E-mail: smu@bournemouth.ac.uk

Allen, Clive G., BSc Bath, MBA S'ton. Sr. Lectr.

Beer, Sean C., BSc Reading Sr. Lectr.; Winston Churchill Fellow

Blake, Adam, BA Nott., MA Nott., PhD Nott. Prof., Tourism Economics

Boer, Andrew, BA Hudd., MBA Brun. Assoc. Dean, Internat. Devel.

Buhalis, Dimitrios, BBA Aegean, MSc Sur., PhD Sur. Prof., Tourism

Cang, S., BSc Heilongjiang, MSc Lond., PhD Dund.

Curtin, Susanna, BSc Plym., MA Exe. Sr. Lectr.

Dickinson, Janet, BA Manc.Met., MPhil Sheff., PhD Bourne. Sr. Lectr.

Edwards, John, BSc Sur., MSc Sur., PhD Sur. Prof.

Edwards, Jonathan R., BSc Aston, MSc Birm., PhD CNAA Reader

Fairbrother, Crispin, BSc Leeds Met., MSc Strath. Sr. Lectr.

Fletcher, John, BA Wales, MA Wales, PhD Wales Prof.; Head, Grad. Sch.

Fyall, Alan, BA Wolv., MPhil Wolv. Reader; Deputy Dean, Res. and Enterprise

Grant-Braham, Bruce Sr. Lectr.

Hall, Chris, MA Sus., MA Open(UK) Assoc. Dean, Postgrad. Studies

Hartwell, Heather J., BSc Lond., PhD Bourne. Sr. Lectr.

Hayman, Keith, BA Leeds, MSc Cran. Sr. Lectr.

Hemmington, Nigel, BSc Sur., PhD Sur. Prof.

Jackson, Caroline, BA Keele, MSc Lough. Sr. Lectr.; Assoc. Dean, Retail and Events

Johns, Nicholas, BSc Lough., PhD Lough. Prof.

Jones, Ian, BSc MSc PhD Assoc. Dean; Head, Sport and Leisure

Kilburn, David, BA Sheff., MBA Bourne. Assoc. Dean, Enterprise

Ladkin, Adelle, BA Leic., MSc Sur., PhD Sur. Assoc. Dean; Prof., Tourism Employment; Head*

Morgan, Michael, BA Liv., BPhil Liv. Sr. Lectr.

Robbins, Derek K., BSc CNAA, MSc CNAA Sr. Lectr.

Schafheitle, Joachim, MPhil CNAA Sr. Lectr.

Thomas, Simon P., MBA Oxf.Brookes Sr. Lectr.

Tosun, Cevat, MPhil Strath., PhD Strath., MSc Prof.

Vaughan, Prof. David R., BSc Hull, MSc Bath, PhD Edin. Principal Lectr.

Other Staff: 4 Lectrs.; 2 Course Leaders

SPECIAL CENTRES, ETC

Archaeology, Anthropology and Heritage, Centre for

Tel: (01202) 965178 Fax: (01202) 965535
E-mail: consci@bournemouth.ac.uk

Brisbane, Mark, BA S'ton., FSA Prof.

Darvill, Timothy, BA S'ton., PhD S'ton., DSc S'ton., FSA Prof.

Other Staff: 1 Reader; 8 Sr. Lectrs.; 10 Res. Fellows; 3 Visiting Profs.; 3 Visiting Res. Fellows

Computer Animation, National Centre for

Tel: (01202) 965371 Fax: (01202) 965099
E-mail: ncca@bournemouth.ac.uk

Hubbard, Steven, BA Bourne., MA Bourne. Assoc. Dean; Head*

Zhang, Jian J., BSc Chongqing, MSc Chongqing, PhD Chongqing Prof.

Conservation Ecology and Environmental Change, Centre for

Tel: (01202) 965178 Fax: (01202) 965530
E-mail: consci@bournemouth.ac.uk
Bennett, Matthew R., BSc Lond., PhD Edin. Prof.
Clarke, Ralph, BSc Reading, MSc S'ton. Prof.
Curran, Paul J., BSc Sheff., MBA S'ton., PhD Brist., DSc Brist., FRGS, FCIM, FRSPSoc Prof.
Newton, Adrian, BA Camb., PhD Camb. Prof.
Petford, Prof. Nick, BSc Lond., MA Camb., PhD Liv. Prof.
Other Staff: 1 Visiting Prof.; 3 Readers; 6 Sr. Lectrs.

Design Simulation Research Centre

Tel: (01202) 9656446 Fax: (01202) 965530
E-mail: info@cemp.ac.uk
Noroozi, Siamak, BSc Salf., MEng Sheff., PhD Sheff. Prof.; Dir.*
Sheppard, Terry, BSc Wales, MSc Wales, PhD Lond., DSc Wales, FIMechE, FIMMM Prof.
Vinney, Prof. John, BEng W.England, PhD W.England Prof.
Other Staff: 9 Sr. Lectrs.; 1 Bus. Fellow

Event and Sport Research, Centre for

Tel: (01202) 965164 Fax: (01202) 965530
E-mail: smu@bournemouth.ac.uk
Jones, Ian, BSc MSc PhD Assoc. Dean; Head, Sport and Leisure*
Other Staff: 2 Sr. Lectrs.

Excellence in Media Practice, Centre for

Tel: (01202) 965646 Fax: (01202) 965530
E-mail: info@cemp.ac.uk
Heppell, Steven Prof.; Dir.*

Finance and Risk, Centre for

Tel: (01202) 965428 Fax: (01202) 965261
E-mail: business@bournemouth.ac.uk
Fearnley, Stella, BA Leeds Prof.; Dir.*
Other Staff: 1 Prof.; 2 Assoc. Profs.; 1 Reader; 3 Sr. Lectrs.

Food Service and Applied Nutrition Research Group

Tel: (01202) 965127 Fax: (01202) 515707
E-mail: edwardsj@bournemouth.ac.uk
Edwards, J. S., PhD Sur., BSc Prof.; Head*
Other Staff: 4 Visiting Profs./Fellows; 3 Res. Staff†; 6 Temp. Res. Staff
Research: food; food health and safety; food perception and preparation; food service (catering); nutrition

Forensic Science, Centre for

Tel: (01202) 965178 Fax: (01202) 965530
E-mail: consci@bournemouth.ac.uk
Osselton, David, BSc Lond., PhD Lond. Prof.; Head*
Other Staff: 7 Sr. Lectrs.

Legal Studies, Centre for

Tel: (01202) 965428 Fax: (01202) 965261
E-mail: business@bournemouth.ac.uk
Chambers, Claire, LLB Wales, PhD Bourne. Dir.*
Other Staff: 2 Profs.; 2 Readers; 1 Sr. Lectr.

Management, Centre for Research in

Tel: (01202) 965428 Fax: (01202) 967305
E-mail: business@bournemouth.ac.uk
Johnsen, Rhona E., BA Strath., PhD Bath Dir.*
Other Staff: 1 Prof.; 4 Sr. Lectrs.

Market Research Group

Tel: (01202) 963871 Fax: (01202) 963900
E-mail: info@themarketresearchgroup.co.uk
Calver, Stephen J., BSc Sur., MBA City(UK) Head*
Research: data collection, analysis and reporting; market research in tourism, the heritage market, local government and retailing; questionnaire design; survey methodology

Media and Communications Research, Institute for

Tel: (01202) 965360 Fax: (01202) 965530
E-mail: jmccain@bournemouth.ac.uk
Allan, Stuart, BA Ryerson, MA Car., PhD Car. Prof.
Deutsch, Prof. Stephen F., BMus S.Methodist, MA Calif. Prof.
Richards, Barry, BA Reading, PhD CNAA Prof.; Deputy Dean, Res. and Enterprise; Dir., Centre for Public Communication Res.
Street, Sean, PhD Bourne. Prof.; Dir., Centre for Broadcasting History

Midwifery, Maternal and Perinatal Health, Centre for

Tel: (01202) 962114 Fax: (01202) 962131
E-mail: hsc@bournemouth.ac.uk
Lewis, Paul, BSc Lond., MSc Lond.S.Bank Prof.
Ryan, Kathleen, BPharm Otago, PhD Otago Reader
Thomas, Gail, MSc Brun., PhD Thames V.

Postgraduate Medical Research and Education, Centre for

Tel: (01202) 962782 Fax: (01202) 962218
E-mail: copmre@bournemouth.ac.uk
Khattab, A., PhD
Thomas, Peter W., BSc Brist., PhD Brist. Prof.

Practice Development, Centre for

Tel: (01202) 962210
E-mail: practicedevelopment@bournemouth.ac.uk
Andrewes, Clive, BSc Lond. Head*
Hean, Sarah, BSc MSc PhD Sr. Lectr.
Hind, Martin, BSc Bourne., MSc Lond., PhD Lond. Sr. Lectr.
Warr, Jerry, MNurs Wales, PhD S'ton. Reader
Other Staff: 3 Practice Development Fellows; 1 Co-ordinator

Qualitative Research, Centre for

Tel: (01202) 962763 Fax: (01202) 962194
E-mail: cqr@bournemouth.ac.uk
Biley, F., BA MSc MA PhD
Galvin, Kathleen, BSc Ulster, PhD Manc. Prof.; Deputy Dean, Res. and Enterprise
Holloway, Irmgard M., BEd Lond., MA Lond., PhD Lond. Prof.; Co-Dir.*
Jones, Kip, MSc PhD Reader
Matthews, Clive, MSc S'ton. Deputy Dean, Educn.
Todres, Prof. Les, BSocSc Rhodes, MSocSc Rhodes, PhD Sr. Lectr.; Co-Dir.*

Skillset Screen and Media Academy

Tel: (01202) 853681 Fax: (01202) 853601
E-mail: info@bournemouth.ac.uk
Hanson, David M., BA S'ton. Head*

Smart Technology Research Centre

Tel: (01202) 965298 Fax: (01202) 965314
E-mail: bgabrys@bournemouth.ac.uk
Gabrys, Bogdan, MSc Gliwice, PhD Nott.Trent Prof.; Dir.*
Roach, Jim, BSc Wales, MSc Wales Prof.; Deputy Dean, Res. and Enterprise
Other Staff: 10 Sr. Lectrs.

Social Work and Social Policy, Centre for

Tel: (01202) 962114 Fax: (01202) 962131
E-mail: hsc@bournemouth.ac.uk
Keen, Steven, BA Lond., MA Leeds, PhD Leeds Sr. Lectr.
Lewis, Carol, PhD S'ton. Sr. Lectr.
Parker, Jonathan, BA Hull, MA Hull Prof.
Pritchard, Colin, MA Brad., PhD S'ton. Prof.

Software Systems Research Centre

Tel: (01202) 965298 Fax: (01202) 965314
E-mail: bgabrys@bournemouth.ac.uk
Phalp, Keith T., BSc Kent, MSc Bourne., PhD Bourne. Assoc. Dean
Other Staff: 8 Sr. Lectrs.

Sustainable Design Research Centre

Tel: (01202) 965980
E-mail: mhadfield@bournemouth.ac.uk
Hadfield, Mark, BEng Brun., PhD Brun. Prof.; Co-Dir.*
Khan, Zulfiqar, BEng Pesh., MEng Shanghai, PhD Bourne. Sr. Lectr.; Co-Dir.*
Other Staff: 8 Sr. Lectrs.

Tourism and Hospitality Research, International Centre for

Tel: (01202) 595163
E-mail: jfletcher@bournemouth.ac.uk
Blake, Adam, BA Nott., MA Nott., PhD Nott. Prof., Tourism Economics
Buhalis, Dimitrios, BBA Aegean, MSc Sur., PhD Sur. Deputy Dir.; Prof., Tourism
Fletcher, John, BA Wales, MA Wales, PhD Wales Prof.; Dir.*
Other Staff: 4 Readers; 4 Sr. Lectrs.

Wellbeing and Quality of Life, Centre for

Tel: (01202) 962763 Fax: (01202) 962194
E-mail: smitchell@bournemouth.ac.uk
Carr, Eloise, BSc Sur., MSc Lond., PhD Lond. Assoc. Dean; Deputy Dir.
Ersser, Steven, BSc S.Bank, PhD Lond. Prof., Nursing Development (Skin Care); Dir.*
Reid, Jane, BSc Bourne., MSc Lond.S.Bank Assoc. Dean
Other Staff: 9 Sr. Lectrs.

CONTACT OFFICERS

Academic affairs. Head of Academic Services: Hanson, Janet, BA Lanc., PhD Bourne. (E-mail: jhanson@bournemouth.ac.uk)
Accommodation. Head of Accommodation Office: Search, Richard (E-mail: accommodation@bournemouth.ac.uk)
Admissions (first degree). Deputy Registrar (Admissions (first degree)): Gutierrez, Ana (E-mail: agutierr@bournemouth.ac.uk)
Admissions (higher degree). Deputy Registrar (Admissions (higher degree)): Gutierrez, Ana (E-mail: agutierr@bournemouth.ac.uk)
Adult/continuing education. Deputy Registrar (Admissions): Gutierrez, Ana (E-mail: agutierr@bournemouth.ac.uk)
Alumni. Alumni Association Manager: McCabe, Alison, BA Brist. (E-mail: amccabe@bournemouth.ac.uk)
Archives. Assistant Registrar (Student Policy and Support): Barron, Mandi
Careers. Head of Graduate Employment Service: Gush, Jacqui, BA Manc., MBA Bourne. (E-mail: careers@bournemouth.ac.uk)
Computing services. Director of IT Services: Kraftner, Dieter (E-mail: dkraftner@bournemouth.ac.uk)
Consultancy services. Acting Head, Centre for Research and Knowledge Transfer: Francis, Fiona, MBA Bourne. (E-mail: s2b@bournemouth.ac.uk)
Development/fund-raising. Development Officer: McMullan, Iain, BSc Durh. (E-mail: alumni@bournemouth.ac.uk)
Equal opportunities. Diversity and Equality Advisor: Stephens, Emma, BA W.England (E-mail: estephens@bournemouth.ac.uk)
Estates and buildings/works and services. Head of Estates Group: Tierney, Peter, MSc Strath. (E-mail: ptierney@bournemouth.ac.uk)
Examinations. Assistant Registrar (Assessments and Conferments): Young, Andrea, BA Winc., MBA Bourne. (E-mail: ayoung@bournemouth.ac.uk)
Finance. Finance Director: Everett, Karen, BSc Exe., FCA (E-mail: keverett@bournemouth.ac.uk)
General enquiries. (vacant) (E-mail: askbuenquiries@bournemouth.ac.uk)
International office. Head of International Relations: Elster, Dannielle, BA Leic., LLM Lond. (E-mail: inta@bournemouth.ac.uk)

Library (chief librarian). University Librarian: Ball, David, BA *Oxf.*, MLitt *Strath.*
(E-mail: dball@bournemouth.ac.uk)

Marketing. Head of Marketing: Fernandez, Ann
(E-mail: marketing@bournemouth.ac.uk)

Minorities/disadvantaged groups. Manager, Additional Learning Needs Service: Palfreman-Kay, James, BA *Leic.*, MA *Leic.*, PhD *De Mont.*
(E-mail: jmpkay@bournemouth.ac.uk)

Personnel/human resources. Director of Human Resources: Riordan, Michael G., BA *N.U.I.*, BD *Maynooth*
(E-mail: personnel@bournemouth.ac.uk)

Public relations. Press and Public Relations Manager: Elder, Charles
(E-mail: press@bournemouth.ac.uk)

Publications. Publications Manager: O'Sullivan, Mike
(E-mail: mosullivan@bournemouth.ac.uk)

Purchasing. Purchasing Manager: Lifford, David (E-mail: dlifford@bournemouth.ac.uk)

Quality assurance and accreditation. Head of Academic Development and Quality: Biscoe, Adam M., BA *Kent*, PhD *Brist.*
(E-mail: abiscoe@bournemouth.ac.uk)

Research. Head of Research Unit: Johnston, Pamela
(E-mail: pjohnston@bournemouth.ac.uk)

Safety. Head of Estates Group: Tierney, Peter, MSc *Strath.*
(E-mail: ptierney@bournemouth.ac.uk)

Scholarships, awards, loans. Deputy Registrar (Scholarships, awards, loans): Gutierrez, Ana (E-mail: agutierr@bournemouth.ac.uk)

Schools liaison. Education Liaison Manager: Murray-Fagan, Nicola, BA *Oxf.Brookes*

Security. Head of Estates Group: Tierney, Peter, MSc *Strath.*
(E-mail: ptierney@bournemouth.ac.uk)

Sport and recreation. Head of Sport and Recreation: Jenkins, Mark
(E-mail: sports@bournemouth.ac.uk)

Staff development and training. Staff Development Officer: Harding, Colleen
(E-mail: hardingc@bournemouth.ac.uk)

Student union. General Manager, Student Union: James, Alan
(E-mail: subu@bournemouth.ac.uk)

Student welfare/counselling. Head of Student Counselling Service: Morrow, Brian
(E-mail: scounsel@bournemouth.ac.uk)

Students from other countries. Head of International Relations: Elster, Dannielle, BA *Leic.*, LLM *Lond.*
(E-mail: inta@bournemouth.ac.uk)

Students with disabilities. Manager, Additional Learning Needs Service: Palfreman-Kay, James, BA *Leic.*, MA *Leic.*, PhD *De Mont.*
(E-mail: jmpkay@bournemouth.ac.uk)

[*Information supplied by the institution as at 3 June 2008, and edited by the ACU*]

UNIVERSITY OF BRADFORD

Founded 1966

Member of the Association of Commonwealth Universities

Postal Address: Richmond Road, Bradford, West Yorkshire, England BD7 1DP
Telephone: (01274) 233081
URL: http://www.bradford.ac.uk

VICE-CHANCELLOR AND PRINCIPAL*—Cleary, Prof. Mark C., BA *Camb.*, PhD *Camb.*
PRO-VICE-CHANCELLOR (LEARNING AND TEACHING)—Lucas, Prof. Jeff, BSc *Lond.*, MPhil *Lond.*, PhD *Lond.*
PRO-VICE-CHANCELLOR (RESOURCES)—Alderson, Prof. Grace, PhD *Newcastle(UK)*
PRO-VICE-CHANCELLOR (RESEARCH AND INNOVATION)—Pollard, Prof. A. Mark, BA *York(UK)*, DPhil *York(UK)*
REGISTRAR AND SECRETARY‡—Andrew, Nick J., BA *Camb.*
DIRECTOR OF FINANCE—Kershaw, Sue, BA *Newcastle(UK)*, FCA

UNIVERSITY OF BRIGHTON

Founded 1992

Postal Address: Mithras House, Lewes Road, Brighton, England BN2 4AT
Telephone: (01273) 600900 **Fax:** (01273) 642010 **E-mail:** admissions@brighton.ac.uk
URL: http://www.brighton.ac.uk

VICE-CHANCELLOR*—Crampton, Prof. Julian M., BSc *Sus.*, PhD *Warw.*
DEPUTY VICE-CHANCELLOR‡—House, David E., BA *E.Anglia*

UNIVERSITY OF BRISTOL

Founded 1909

Member of the Association of Commonwealth Universities

Postal Address: Senate House, Tyndall Avenue, Bristol, England BS8 1TH
Telephone: (0117) 928 9000
URL: http://www.bris.ac.uk

VICE-CHANCELLOR*—Thomas, Prof. Eric J., MB BS Newcastle(UK), MD Newcastle(UK), Hon. LLD Brist., FRCOG, FRSA, FMedSci, FRCP

PRO-VICE-CHANCELLOR (RESEARCH AND ENTERPRISE)—Anderson, Prof. Malcolm G., BSc Nott., PhD Camb., DSc Brist., FICE

PRO-VICE-CHANCELLOR (RESOURCES)—Knox, Prof. Selby A. R., BSc Brist., PhD Brist., DSc Brist., FRSChem

PRO-VICE-CHANCELLOR (PERSONNEL AND STAFF DEVELOPMENT, LOCAL PARTNERSHIPS)—Clarke, Prof. David N., MA Camb., LLM Camb.

PRO-VICE-CHANCELLOR (EDUCATION)—Waterman-Pearson, Prof. Avril E., BVSc Brist., PhD Brist., FRCVS

REGISTRAR‡—Pretty, Derek W. M., BSc S'ton., MBA Wash.

GENERAL INFORMATION

History. The university was created by the merger in 1893 of University College, Bristol (established 1876) and Bristol Medical School (1833). During negotiations for a university charter these institutions were joined by Merchant Venturers' Technical College (1885; previously Bristol Trade and Mining School), which later became the university's faculty of engineering. Generous gifts from the Wills and Fry families in 1908 were followed by the granting of the charter in 1909, creating the University of Bristol.

The university is situated in Clifton.

Admission to first degree courses (see also United Kingdom Introduction). Through Universities and Colleges Admissions Service (UCAS). Candidates must satisfy university admission tutors that their academic qualifications are sufficient for the course of study. UK applicants: level 3 qualifications accepted include: GCE A levels; BTEC National Diplomas; Irish Highers; Scottish Highers and Advanced Highers; International Baccalaureate, Welsh Baccalaureate, kitemarked Access courses, Open University credits. International applicants: most European and Commonwealth matriculation exams and sufficient command of English (eg satisfactory IELTS test score).

First Degrees (see also United Kingdom Directory to Subjects of Study) (* = with honours). BA*, BDS*, BEng*, BSc*, BVSc*, LLB*, MB ChB*, MEng*, MSci*.

Courses involving study abroad or industrial placements last 4 years. BDS, MB ChB: 6 years if preliminary course is necessary. MB ChB: 4 years fast-track course for suitably qualified graduate entrants. BSc in Chemistry, Physics or Geology: 4 years if preliminary course is necessary.

Length of course. Full-time: BA*, BEng*, BSc*, LLB*: 3 years; MEng*, MSci*: 4 years; BDS*, BVSc*, MB ChB*: 5 years.

Higher Degrees (see also United Kingdom Directory to Subjects of Study).

Master's. ChM, LLM, MA, MClinDent, MEd, MLitt, MMus, MPhil, MRes, MSc, MSocSci, MSW.

Admission. Applicants for admission to higher degrees must normally hold a first degree from a UK university or, subject to senate's approval, an appropriate qualification from any other university.

Length of course. Full-time: ChM, LLM, MA, MEd, MPhil, MRes, MSc: 1 year; MClinDent, MLitt, MMus, MSW: 2 years. Part-time: LLM, MA, MPhil, MRes, MSc: 2 years; MClinDent, MLitt, MMus: 4 years; ChM, MEd: max. 5 years.

Doctoral. DDS, DEdPsy, DSocSci, EdD, EngD, MD, PhD.

Length of course. Full-time: MD: 2 years; DDS, DEdPsy, DSocSci, EdD, EngD, PhD: 3 years. Part-time: MD: 5 years; DEdPsy, DSocSci, EdD, EngD, PhD, DDS: 6 years.

Libraries. Volumes: 1,400,000. Periodicals subscribed to: 9000. Special collections: Brunel (civil engineering); business history; election addresses (British parliamentary history); Eyles (earth sciences); medical history; Penguin Books and Hamish Hamilton Archives (publishers' archives); Wiglesworth (ornithology); architectural history; Bristol university archives; early novels; John Addington Symonds (literary papers); Liberal Party history; Moravian Church history; Pinney papers (West Indies estates).

Academic Awards (2006). 1200 awards ranging in value from £500 to £90,000.

Income (2005–2006). Total, £286,078,000.

Statistics. Staff (2005–2006): 5511 (2214 academic, 3297 non-academic). Students (2006–2007): full-time 14,699; part-time 2433; international 2108; undergraduate 12,169.

FACULTIES/SCHOOLS

Arts
Tel: (0117) 928 7426 Fax: (0117) 925 1129
E-mail: chris.hall@bristol.ac.uk
Dean: Fowler, Prof. Robert L. H., MA Tor., DPhil Oxf.
Assistant Registrar: Hall, Christine

Engineering
Tel: (0117) 928 8108 Fax: (0117) 925 1154
E-mail: engf-office@bristol.ac.uk
Dean: Lieven, Prof. Nicholas A. J., BSc S'ton., DPhil Oxf.
Faculty Administrator: Bevan, Melissa, BA E.Anglia

Medical and Veterinary Sciences
Tel: (0117) 331 1538 Fax: (0117) 331 1889
E-mail: stephen.brooke@bristol.ac.uk
Dean: Hall, Prof. L., BSc Leeds, PhD Leic.
Assistant Registrar: Brooke, Stephen M., BA Wales

Medicine and Dentistry
Tel: (0117) 331 1686 Fax: (0117) 331 1687
E-mail: sylvia.elliott@bristol.ac.uk
Dean: Williams, Prof. Gareth, MA Camb., MD Camb., ScD, FRCPEd
Assistant Registrar: Elliot, Sylvia, BA Qld.

Science
Tel: (0117) 928 9958 Fax: (0117) 925 1129
E-mail: mora.mccallum@bristol.ac.uk
Dean: Orpen, Prof. A. G., BSc Cape Town, PhD Camb.

Head of Academic Administration: McCallum, Mora

Social Sciences and Law
Tel: (0117) 928 8899 Fax: (0117) 925 1129
E-mail: t.r.kinane@bristol.ac.uk
Dean: Evans, Prof. Malcolm D., OBE, MA Oxf., MPhil Oxf.
Assistant Registrar: Kinane, Tania R., BA Leeds

ACADEMIC UNITS

Accounting and Finance
Tel: (0117) 928 8415 Fax: (0117) 928 8577
E-mail: efim-info@bristol.ac.uk
Acker, D. E., MA Camb., PhD Brist. Prof., Accounting
Ashton, David J., BA Open(UK), MA Oxf., MA Lanc., PhD Warw. Prof.; Head*
Dugdale, D., BSc Hull, MSc Hull, PhD Hull Prof., Management Accounting
Ellwood, S. M., BSc Wales, MSc Aston, PhD Aston Prof., Financial Reporting
Lyne, S. R., BSc Brist., PhD Brist. Sr. Lectr., Accounting Management
Ozkan, N., BSc Istanbul, MA Boston, PhD Boston Sr. Lectr., Finance
Payne, R., BSc Brist., MSc Lond., PhD Lond. Prof., Finance
Other Staff: 3 Lectrs.; 2 Teaching Fellows; 2 Teaching Assocs.†
Research: management accounting; theoretical and applied finance

Archaeology and Anthropology
Tel: (0117) 954 6060 Fax: (0117) 954 6001
E-mail: arch-anth@bristol.ac.uk
Bowie, F., BA Durh., DPhil Oxf. Sr. Lectr., Anthropology
Gardiner, P. J., BA Brist., PhD Brist.
Harrison, Richard J., MA Camb., PhD Harv., FSA Prof., European Prehistory
Hodos, T., BA Bryn Mawr, MA Lond., DPhil Oxf. Sr. Lectr.
Horton, Mark C., MA Camb., PhD Camb., FSA Reader, Archaeology
Momigliano, N., Laur Pisa, PhD Lond. Sr. Lectr.
Mowl, T. W., BEd Brist., MA Birm., DPhil Oxf., FSA Prof., History of Architecture and Designed Landscapes
Pike, A. W. G., BSc Brad., DPhil Oxf. Sr. Lectr.
Pollard, C. Joshua, BA Wales, PhD Wales Sr. Lectr.; Head*
Robson Brown, K. A., BA Camb., PhD Camb. Sr. Lectr., Archaeology
Shankland, D. P., MA Edin., PhD Camb. Reader, Anthropology
Theodossopoulos, D., BA Lond., MSc Lond., PhD Lond. Sr. Lectr., Anthropology
Zilhao, J. C., PhD Lisbon Prof., Palaeolithic Archaeology
Other Staff: 2 Lectrs.; 1 Res. Assoc.; 1 Reader†
Research: African and Caribbean archaeology; human origins; materiality and historical

anthropology; Mediterranean worlds; social anthropology

Biological Sciences, School of

Tel: (0117) 928 7475 Fax: (0117) 331 7985
E-mail: biology.dept@bristol.ac.uk
Bailey, A. M., BSc Brist., PhD Sheff. Sr. Lectr.
Bennett, A. T. D., BSc Adel., DPhil Oxf., BSc
  Reader, Sensory and Behavioural Ecology
Cuthill, Innes C., MA Camb., DPhil Oxf. Prof.,
  Behavioural Ecology
Edwards, K. J., BSc Salf., PhD Leic. Prof.,
  Cereal Functional Genomics
Foster, Gary, BSc Belf., PhD Belf. Prof.,
  Molecular Plant Pathology
Franks, N. R., BSc Leeds, PhD Leeds Prof.,
  Animal Behaviour and Ecology
Gibson, Wendy C., BSc Lond., PhD Lond., DSc
  Lond. Prof., Protozoology
Goldsmith, A. R., BSc Wales, PhD Leic. Reader,
  Zoology
Grierson, C. S., BSc Warw., PhD Camb. Reader
Harris, S., PhD Lond., DSc Brist. 2nd Lord
  Dulverton Memorial Prof., Environmental
  Sciences
Hayes, P. K., BSc Wales, PhD Wales Prof.;
  Head*
Hetherington, A. M., BSc St And., PhD St And.
  Melville Wills Prof., Botany
Hiscock, S. J., MA Oxf., DPhil Oxf. Reader
Houston, A. I., MA Oxf., DPhil Oxf. Prof.,
  Theoretical Biology
Jones, G., BSc Lond., PhD Stir. Prof.
Lazarus, C. M., BSc E.Anglia, PhD Brist. Sr.
  Lectr., Molecular Genetics
Memmott, J., BSc Leeds, PhD Leeds Prof.,
  Ecology
Morgan, E. R., MA Camb., VetMB Camb., PhD
  Warw.
Morris, Stephen, BSc Lond., PhD Glas. Prof.
Partridge, Julian C., BSc Brist., PhD Brist.
  Reader, Zoology
Robert, D., PhD Basle Prof., Bionanoscience
Roberts, A., BA Camb., PhD Calif. Prof.,
  Zoology
Soffe, S. R., BSc Aberd., DPhil Sus. Sr. Lectr.
Tinsley, R. C., BSc Leeds, PhD Leeds Prof.,
  Zoology
Viney, M. E., BSc Lond., PhD Liv. Prof.
Wall, R. L., BSc Durh., MBA Open(UK), PhD Liv.
  Prof., Zoology
Other Staff: 3 Lectrs.; 4 Res. Fellows; 1
  Teaching Fellow; 12 Res. Assocs.
Research: behaviour, sensory and neurobiology;
  cell and molecular biology; ecophysiology
  and population biology

Chemistry, School of

Tel: (0117) 928 7645 Fax: (0117) 925 1295
E-mail: c.l.hazell@bristol.ac.uk
Aggarwal, V. K., BA Camb., PhD Camb. Prof.,
  Synthetic Organic Chemistry
Allan, N. L., MA Oxf., DPhil Oxf. Prof.,
  Physical Chemistry
Ashfold, M. N. R., BSc Birm., PhD Birm.,
  FRSChem Prof., Physical Chemistry
Balint-Kurti, G. G., MA Camb., MSc Col., PhD
  Col. Prof., Theoretical Chemistry
Bartlett, Paul, BA Oxf., MA Oxf., DPhil Oxf.
  Reader, Physical Chemistry
Bedford, R. B., BSc Sus., DPhil Sus. Reader,
  Catalysis
Booker-Milburn, Kevin I., BSc CNAA, PhD
  Strath. Prof., Organic Chemistry
Brereton, R. G., MA Camb., PhD Camb. Prof.,
  Chemometrics
Charmant, J. P. H., BSc Brist., PhD Brist. Sr.
  Lectr., X-Ray Crystallography
Connelly, N. G., BSc Sheff., PhD Sheff., DSc Brist.,
  FRSChem Prof., Inorganic Chemistry
Cosgrove, Terence, MSc Manc., PhD Manc., DSc
  Brist. Prof., Physical Chemistry
Cox, R. J., BSc Durh., PhD Durh. Reader
Crosby, J., BSc Hull, PhD Edin. Sr. Lectr.
Crump, M. P., BSc Brist., PhD Brist. Sr. Lectr.,
  Biological NMR Spectroscopy
Davis, A. P., MA Oxf., DPhil Oxf. Prof.,
  Supramolecular Chemistry

Davis, S. A., BSc Bath, PhD Bath Sr. Lectr.
Eastoe, Julian G., BSc E.Anglia, PhD E.Anglia
  Prof.
Evershed, R. P., BSc CNAA, PhD Keele Prof.,
  Biogeochemistry
Faul, C. F. J., BSc Stell., MSc Stell., PhD Stell.
  Sr. Lectr., Inorganic and Materials
  Chemistry
Gallagher, T. C., BSc Wales, PhD Liv., FRSChem
  Prof., Organic Chemistry; Head*
Harvey, J. N., LicSc Louvain, LicPhil Louvain, DrSc
  Louvain Reader
Jeffery, J. C., BSc Warw., PhD Warw. Reader,
  Inorganic Chemistry
Legon, A. C., BSc Lond., PhD Lond., DSc Lond.,
  FRSChem, FRS Prof., Physical Chemistry
Lloyd-Jones, G. C., BSc CNAA, DPhil Oxf.,
  FRSChem Prof.
Manby, F. R., BSc York(UK), DPhil York(UK) Sr.
  Lectr.
Mann, Stephen, BSc UMIST, MSc Manc., DPhil
  Oxf., FRS Prof.
Manners, I., BSc Brist., PhD Brist. Prof.,
  Inorganic and Materials Chemistry
May, P. W., BSc Brist., PhD Brist. Reader,
  Physical Chemistry
Meldrum, F. C., MA Camb., PhD Bath Reader,
  Nanomaterials Chemistry
Mulholland, A. J., BSc Brist., DPhil Brist.
  Reader
Norman, Nicholas C., BSc Brist., PhD Brist.
  Prof., Inorganic Chemistry
O'Doherty, S. J., BSc CNAA, MSc E.Anglia, PhD
  Brist. Reader
Orr-Ewing, A. J., MA Oxf., DPhil Oxf. Prof.
Pancost, R. D., BSc Case W.Reserve, PhD Penn.State
  Reader, Biogeochemistry
Pringle, Paul G., BSc Leic., PhD Leeds Prof.,
  Inorganic Chemistry
Reid, J. P., BA Oxf., DPhil Oxf. Reader
Russell, C. A., BSc Brist., PhD Camb. Sr. Lectr.
Shallcross, D. E., BSc S'ton., DPhil Oxf. Prof.
  Teaching Fellow, Physical Chemistry
Simpson, T. J., BSc Edin., PhD Brist., DSc Edin.,
  FRS, FRSChem Alfred Capper Pass Prof.
Van Duijneveldt, J. S., MSc Utrecht, PhD Utrecht
  Sr. Lectr., Physical Chemistry
Vincent, B., MSc Brist., PhD Brist., DSc Brist.
  Leverhulme Prof., Physical Chemistry
Wass, D. F., BSc Durh., PhD Lond. Sr. Lectr.
Western, C. M., MA Oxf., DPhil Oxf. Reader
Willis, C. L., BSc Lond., DPhil Sus. Prof.,
  Organic Chemistry
Woolfson, D. N., BA Oxf., PhD Camb. Prof.,
  Chemistry and Biochemistry
Wyatt, P. J., MA Camb., PhD Camb. Reader,
  Teaching and Learning
Other Staff: 2 Sr. Res. Fellows; 14 Res.
  Fellows; 1 Teaching Fellow; 1 Jr. Fellow;
  33 Res. Assocs.; 1 Temp. Lectr.
Research: inorganic and materials chemistry;
  organic and biological chemistry; physical
  and theoretical chemistry

Classics and Ancient History

Tel: (0117) 331 7932 Fax: (0117) 331 7933
E-mail: hums-schooloffice@bristol.ac.uk
Buxton, R. G. A., MA Camb., PhD Camb. Prof.,
  Greek Language and Literature
Clark, E. G., MA Oxf., DPhil Oxf. Prof.,
  Ancient History
Hales, S. J., BA Camb., MA Lond., PhD Lond. Sr.
  Lectr.
Kennedy, Duncan F., MA Trinity(Dub.), PhD
  Camb. Prof., Latin Literature and the
  Theory of Criticism; Head*
Leonard, M. A., BA Camb., MPhil Camb., PhD
  Camb. Sr. Lectr., Classics
Michelakis, P., MA Lond., PhD Camb. Sr. Lectr.,
  Classics
Morley, N. D. G., MA Camb., PhD Camb.
  Reader, Ancient History
O'Gorman, E., MA Brist., PhD Brist., BA Sr.
  Lectr., Classics
Zajko, V. D., BA Exe., PhD Exe. Sr. Lectr.,
  Greek Literature and Language
Other Staff: 2 Lectrs.; 1 Res. Assoc.; 1
  Teaching Fellow

Research: archaeology; Greco-Roman culture to
  date; Greece, Rome and classical tradition;
  links between ancient and modern history;
  literary studies

Computer Science

Tel: (0117) 954 5264 Fax: (0117) 954 5208
E-mail: info@cs.bris.ac.uk
Bogacz, R., MEng Wroclaw, PhD Brist. Sr.
  Lectr.
Calway, A. D., BSc Aston, PhD Warw. Sr. Lectr.
Campbell, N. W., BEng Brist., PhD Brist.
  Reader
Cliff, T. D., BSc Leeds, MA Sus., DPhil Sus., FBCS
  Prof.
Eder, K. I., PhD Brist. Sr. Lectr.
Flach, P. A., MSc T.H.Twente, PhD Tilburg Prof.,
  Artificial Intelligence
Fraser, M. C., BSc Nott., PhD Nott. Sr. Lectr.
Gough, J. J. T., MSc Brist., PhD Camb. Reader
Gregory, S., BSc(Eng) PhD Sr. Lectr.
Holyer, I. J., MA Camb., PhD Camb. Sr. Lectr.
Jozsa, Richard O., BSc Monash, MSc Oxf., DPhil
  Oxf. Prof.
Kovacs, T. M. D., BA Car., MSc Birm., PhD Birm.
  Sr. Lectr.
May, M. D., MA Camb., DSc S'ton., FRS Prof.;
  Head*
Melhuish, C. R., BSc Durh., MSc Brist., PhD
  W.England, FBCS Prof.†, Robotics and
  Autonomous Systems
Mirmehdi, M., BSc City(UK), PhD City(UK)
  Reader, Image Analysis
Muller, Henk L., PhD Amst. Reader
Pradhan, D. K., MS Brown, PhD Iowa Prof.
Reinhard, E., PhD Brist. Sr. Lectr.
Smart, Nigel P., BSc Reading, PhD Kent Prof.,
  Cryptology
Other Staff: 9 Lectrs.; 5 Res. Fellows; 5 Res.
  Assocs.
Research: computer languages and architecture;
  cryptography and information security;
  digital media; machine learning; mobile
  and wearable computing

Drama

Theatre, Film, Television

Tel: (0117) 954 5481 Fax: (0117) 331 5082
E-mail: drama-uga@bristol.ac.uk
Adams, John R. J., BA Exe. Sr. Lectr.
Bailes, S. J., MA PhD Sr. Lectr.
Davis, Glyn P., MA Newcastle(UK), PhD Sus. Sr.
  Lectr., Screen Studies
Dovey, J. P., BA Oxf. Reader
Jones, S. J., BA Brist., MLitt Brist., PhD Brist.
  Reader, Performance; Head*
Maningard, J. M., BSocSci Natal, MA Witw.,
  PhD Witw. Sr. Lectr.
Street, Sarah C. J., BA Warw., DPhil Oxf. Prof.,
  Film
White, Martin E., BA Newcastle(UK), MA Birm.
  Prof., Theatre
Other Staff: 1 Lectr.; 1 Sr. Teaching Fellow; 1
  Res. Fellow; 4 Teaching Fellows; 1 Res.
  Assoc.; 2 Teaching Assocs.
Research: contemporary live art performance;
  dramatic theory and practice; film and
  theatre history; film theory and criticism;
  television studies

Earth Sciences

Tel: (0117) 954 5400 Fax: (0117) 925 3385
E-mail: earth-enquiries@bristol.ac.uk
Benton, M. J., BSc Aberd., PhD Newcastle(UK)
  Prof., Vertebrate Palaeontology; Head*
Blundy, J. D., BA Oxf., PhD Camb. Prof.,
  Petrology
Catling, D. C., BSc Birm., DPhil Oxf. Reader
Donoghue, P. C. J., BSc Leic., MSc Sheff., PhD
  Leic. Sr. Lectr.
Elliot, T. R., BA Camb., PhD Open(UK) Reader
Hawkesworth, Chris J., BA Trinity(Dub.), DPhil
  Oxf., FRS Prof.
Helffrich, G. R., BSc Mich., MSc Northwestern,
  PhD Northwestern Prof., Seismology
Kearns, S. L., BSc Dund., PhD CNAA Sr. Lectr.
Kendall, J. M., BSc Qu., PhD Qu. Prof.

Kohn, S. C., BA Oxf., PhD Manc. Reader, Geology

Mader, H. M., BSc York(UK), PhD Brist. Reader

Phillips, J. C., BSc Birm., MPhil Birm., PhD Brist. Sr. Lectr.

Prentice, I. C., BA Camb., PhD Camb. Prof., Earth System Science

Ragnarsdottir, K. Vala, BSc Iceland, MS Northwestern, PhD Northwestern, PhD Prof., Environmental Geochemistry

Robinson, Douglas, BSc Lond., PhD Durh. Sr. Lectr.

Schumacher, J. C., BS Akron, BA Akron, MS Akron, PhD Mass. Sr. Lectr.

Sherman, David M., BS Calif., PhD M.I.T., PhD Calif. Prof., Geochemistry

Sparks, R. S. J., BSc Lond., PhD Lond., DSc Clermont-Ferrand, FRS Chaning Wills Prof., Geology

Talling, P. J., BA Camb., MSc S.Calif., PhD Leeds Sr. Lectr.

Vance, D., BA Trinity(Dub.), PhD Camb. Reader

Walter, M. J., BSc Nebraska, PhD Dallas Reader

Whitaker, F. F., BSc Brist., PhD Brist. Sr. Lectr.

Other Staff: 5 Lectrs.; 1 Sr. Res. Fellow; 11 Res. Fellows; 8 Res. Assocs.; 1 Sr. Tutor†

Research: biogeochemistry and environmental geochemistry; deep earth processes; isotope geochemistry; sedimentology; volcanology and fluid dynamics

Economics

Tel: (0117) 928 8415 Fax: (0117) 928 8577
E-mail: efim-info@bristol.ac.uk

Bhalotra, S. R., BA Delhi, DPhil Oxf. Reader

Brewer, A. A., MA Camb. Prof., History of Economics

Burgess, S. M., MA Camb., DPhil Oxf. Prof.

Demery, David, BScEcon Wales Reader

Duck, N. W., MA Manc., PhD Manc. Reader

Giovannoni, F., MA Stan., PhD Stan. Reader

Gregg, P. A., BSc Kent, MSc Lond. Prof.

Grout, P. A., BA(Econ) Newcastle(UK), MSc(Econ) Lond., PhD Essex Prof., Political Economy; Head*

Halonen-Akatwijuka, M.-L. K., MSc Helsinki, PhD Lond. Sr. Lectr.

Park, I.-U., BA Seoul, MA Cornell, PhD Minn. Leverhulme Prof., Industrial Organisation

Postel-Vinay, F. Y. B., PhD Paris Prof.

Propper, Carol, BSc Brist., MSc Oxf., DPhil York(UK) Prof.

Temple, J. R. W., BA Camb., MPhil Camb., DPhil Oxf. Prof.

Turon, H., MSc Brist., PhD Brist., BSc Sr. Lectr.

Windmeijer, A. L., PhD Amst. Prof., Econometrics

Other Staff: 3 Lectrs.; 2 Teaching Fellows; 6 Teaching Assocs.; 1 Sr. Res. Fellow†; 1 Sr. Teaching Fellow†

Research: macroeconomics, growth and development; theoretical and applied microeconomics

Education, Graduate School of

Tel: (0117) 928 7016 Fax: (0117) 925 5145
E-mail: dominic.freda@bristol.ac.uk

Barnes, S. B., MPhil Open(UK), PhD Brist. Sr. Lectr.

Bond, Tim N., BA Durh., PhD Durh. Prof. Teaching Fellow, Counselling

Brawn, J. R., BSc Salf., MEd Brist. Sr. Lectr., Physics Education

Brown, L. C., MA Oxf., MEd Brist. Sr. Lectr., Mathematics Education

Claxton, G. L., MA Camb., DPhil Oxf. Visiting Prof.

Crossley, M. W., BEd Keele, MA Lond., PhD La Trobe, FRSA Prof., Comparative and International Education

Dale, I. R., BA Leeds, PhD Brist. Visiting Prof.

Deem, R., BA Leic., MPhil Leic., PhD Open(UK) Prof.

Erduran, S., BA Northwestern, MSc Cornell, PhD Vanderbilt Sr. Lectr., Education (Science)

Etherington, R. K., MSc Brist., PhD Brist. Prof.

Feiler, A. C., BA Liv., MSc Lond., PhD Brist. Sr. Lectr., Special Educational Needs

Gall, M. R. Y., MusB Manc. Sr. Lectr.

Garrett, R. M., MA Keele, PhD Keele Sr. Lectr.

Goldstein, H., BSc Manc., FBA Prof., Social Statistics

Howard-Jones, P. A., BSc Manc., PhD Exe. Sr. Lectr.

Hughes, R. Martin, BA Oxf., PhD Edin. ESRC Prof. Res. Fellow

Kiely, R. N., BA N.U.I., MA Essex, PhD Warw. Sr. Lectr., Education (TESOL/Applied Linguistics)

Lazarus, M. E., BA E.Anglia, MA Brist. Sr. Lectr., Education (Modern Foreign Languages)

Lucas, L., MA York(UK), PhD Warw. Sr. Lectr., Education (Research Methods)

Matthewman, S. R. E., MA Brist. Sr. Lectr., Education (English)

McFarlane, A. E., BSc Brist., PhD Brist. Prof.; Head*

McNess, E. M., BEd CNAA, MEd Brist., PhD Brist. Sr. Lectr.

Meadows, Sara A. C., BSc Lond., PhD Lond. Sr. Lectr.

Morgan, J. W., BSc Wales, PhD Lond. Sr. Lectr., Geography Education

Osborn, M. J., BSc Lond., MPhil Lond., PhD Brist. Prof.

Pickering, S. J., BA Sheff., PhD Sheff. Sr. Lectr.

Polat, F., BS Ankara, MS Ankara, MEd Manc., PhD Manc. Sr. Lectr.

Rasbash, J. R., BSc York(UK) Prof. Res. Fellow

Rea-Dickins, Pauline M., MA Lanc., PhD Lanc. Prof., Applied Linguistics in Education

Reed, M. J., BA York(UK), MA Lond., PhD Brist. Sr. Lectr., Education (English)

Robertson, Susan L., BAppSc W.Aust., BEd W.Aust., BSc Curtin, PhD Calg. Prof., Sociology of Education

Speedy, J., BA York(UK), MSc Brist., PhD Brist. Sr. Lectr., Education (Counselling)

Steele, F. A. Reader

Sutherland, Rosamund J., BSc Brist., PhD Lond. Prof.

Thomas, S. M., BSc CNAA, PhD CNAA Reader

Tikly, L. P., BEd CNAA, MPhil Glas., PhD Glas. Prof.

Trahar, S. M., BA CNAA, PhD Brist., MSc Sr. Lectr., Education (Counselling)

Winter, J. C., BSc Warw., MEd Bath Sr. Lectr., Mathematics Education

Wishart, J. M., BSc Reading, PhD Sur. Sr. Lectr., Education (Science)

Other Staff: 5 Lectrs.; 3 Res. Fellows; 7 Res. Assocs.; 5 Teaching Fellows†; 2 Teaching Assocs.†

Research: globalisation, education and societies; international and comparative studies; learning, knowing and interactive technologies; narratives and transformative learnings; psychology and learning in context

Engineering, Aerospace

Tel: (0117) 928 7704 Fax: (0117) 927 2771
E-mail: aero-office@bristol.ac.uk

Allen, C. B., MSc Brist., PhD Brist. Reader, Computational Aerodynamics

Bond, I. P., BSc Bath, PhD Bath Reader

Bunniss, P. C., MSc Cran.IT Sr. Lectr.

Ewins, D., PhD Camb., DSc Lond. Prof.†, Vibration Engineering

Farrow, I. R., BSc S'ton., PhD Cran.IT Sr. Lectr., Aerospace Structural Design

Friswell, M. I., MA Oxf., MSc Open(UK), PhD Aston, DSc Wales Sir George White Prof.

Guha, A., BEng Jad., MEng IISc., PhD Camb. Sr. Lectr.

Hallett, S. R., BSc Cape Town, DPhil Oxf. Sr. Lectr., Aerospace Structures

Hempsell, C. M., BSc Lond., MSc CNAA Sr. Lectr., Space Technology

Isikveren, A. T., BEng NSW, PhD R.I.T.Stockholm Sr. Lectr., Engineering Design

Lieven, Nicholas A. J., BSc S'ton., DPhil Oxf. Prof., Aerospace Dynamics

Lowenberg, M. H., MSc(Eng) Witw., PhD Brist. Sr. Lectr.; Head*

Peng, H.-X., BSc MSc PhD Sr. Lectr.

Potter, K. D., BSc Lond., PhD Reader

Weaver, P. M., BSc Newcastle(UK), PhD Newcastle(UK) Reader, Lightweight Structures

Wisnom, M. R., BSc Lond., PhD Brist. Prof., Aerospace Structures

Other Staff: 7 Lectrs.; 1 Sr. Teaching Fellow; 1 Res. Fellow; 13 Res. Assocs.

Research: dynamics and control systems; fluid flow and aerodynamics; structures and materials

Engineering, Civil

Tel: (0117) 928 7707 Fax: (0117) 928 7783
E-mail: j.dunton@bristol.ac.uk

Agarwal, J., MTech IIT Delhi, PhD Brist. Sr. Lectr., Structural Engineering

Alexander, N. A., BSc(Eng) Lond., PhD Lond. Sr. Lectr., Structural Engineering

Cluckie, Ian D., BSc Sur., MSc Birm., PhD Birm., FREng, FICE Prof., Hydrology and Water Management

Crewe, A. J., BEng Brist., PhD Brist. Sr. Lectr.

Davis, John P., BEng S'ton., PhD Brist. Reader, Engineering Systems

Godfrey, P. S., BSc Lond., FREng, FICE Prof.†, Systems Engineering

Gundry, S. W., BSc Nott., MSc Leic., PhD Edin., FCA Sr. Lectr., Enterprise and Entrepreneurship

Han, D., BEng Hubei, MSc Hubei, PhD Salf. Sr. Lectr.

Ibraim, E., PhD I.N.S.A.Lyons Sr. Lectr.

Lings, M. L., MA Oxf., MSc Lond. Sr. Lectr., Geotechnical Engineering

Loveless, J. H., MSc Lond., PhD Lond. Sr. Lectr.

Macdonald, J. H. G., MA Camb., PhD Brist. Sr. Lectr.

Muir Wood, David, MA Camb., PhD Camb., FICE, FREng Prof.

Nash, David F. T., MA Camb., MSc Lond. Sr. Lectr.

Sebastian, W. M., MA Camb., PhD Camb. Sr. Lectr.

Strachan, P. J., BSc Leeds, MBA Witw., PhD Leeds, MSc Sr. Lectr., Enterprise and Entrepreneurship

Taylor, C. A., BSc Leeds, PhD Brist. Prof., Earthquake Engineering; Head*

Wanous, M., BSc Liv., PhD Liv. Sr. Lectr., Engineering Management

Other Staff: 1 Lectr.; 2 Sr. Teaching Fellows; 1 Res. Fellow; 4 Res. Assocs.

Research: civil engineering systems; earthquake engineering; soil mechanics; structural engineering; water and environmental management

Engineering, Electrical and Electronic

Tel: (0117) 954 5391 Fax: (0117) 925 5206
E-mail: elec-eng@bristol.ac.uk

Armour, S. M. D., BEng Bath, PhD Brist. Sr. Lectr., Software Radio

Barton, M. H., BSc Kent, PhD Wales Sr. Lectr., Microelectronics

Beach, M. A., BSc York(UK), PhD Brist. Prof., Radio Systems Engineering; Head*

Bull, D. R., BSc Exe., MSc Manc., PhD Wales Prof., Signal Processing

Canagarajah, C. N., BA Camb., PhD Camb. Prof., Multimedia Signal Processing

Craddock, I. J., BEng Brist., PhD Brist. Reader

Cryan, M. J., BEng Leeds, PhD Bath Sr. Lectr.

Dagless, E. L., BSc Sur., PhD Sur., FIEE Imperial Group Prof., Microelectronics

Grant, D. A., BSc Manc., PhD Brist. Reader, Industrial Electronics

Hilton, G. S., BSc Leeds, PhD Brist. Sr. Lectr.

Holliday, D. M. J., PhD H-W, BEng Sr. Lectr.

Kaleshi, D., PhD Brist. Sr. Lectr., Communications Networks

Kocak, T., BSc Bosphorus, PhD N.Carolina, MSc Sr. Lectr.

McGeehan, J. P., CBE, BEng Liv., PhD Liv., FREng, FRSA Prof., Communications Engineering

Mellor, P. H., BEng Liv., PhD Liv.   Prof.,
Electrical Engineering
Morris, K. A., BEng Brist., PhD Brist.   Sr. Lectr.,
Radio Frequency Engineering
Munro, A. T. D., BSc Lond., PhD Manc.
Toshiba Prof., Communication Networks
Nix, Andrew R., BEng Brist., PhD Brist.   Prof.,
Wireless Communication Systems
Nunez-Yanez, J. L., BSc Lough., MSc Lough., PhD
Lough.   Sr. Lectr., Electronic Circuit Design
O'Brian, J. L., BSc NSW, PhD NSW   Reader
Railton, C. J., BSc Lond., PhD Bath   Prof.
Rarity, J. G., BSc Sheff., MSc Lond., PhD CNAA
Prof., Optical Communication Systems
Rorison, J. M., BSc McG., DPhil Oxf.   Reader
Warr, P. A., BEng Brist., MSc Brist., PhD Brist.
Sr. Lectr.
Yu, S., BEng Tsinghua, MEng Wuhan, PhD Glas.
Sr. Lectr.
Other Staff: 5 Lectrs.; 3 Sr. Res. Fellows; 10
Res. Fellows; 7 Res. Assocs.
Research: computational electromagnetics;
electrical energy management; optical
communications systems; signal processing
networks and protocols; wireless
communications

Engineering Mathematics

Tel: (0117) 928 9734 Fax: (0117) 954 6833
E-mail: enm-admissions@bristol.ac.uk
Barry, M. D. J., BSc Edin., PhD Edin.   Sr. Lectr.
Campbell, I. C. G., BSc Lond., PhD Lond.
Reader, Mathematics for Information
Technology
Champneys, Alan R., BSc Birm., DPhil Oxf.
Prof., Applied Nonlinear Mathematics;
Head*
Clements, R. R., MBE, MA Camb., PhD Camb.,
FIMA   Prof. Teaching Fellow
Cristianini, N., BSc Trieste, MSc Lond., PhD Brist.
Prof., Artificial Intelligence
Di Bernardo, M., Laurea Naples, PhD Brist.
Reader, Nonlinear Systems and Control
Hogan, S. J., MA Camb., PhD Camb., FIMA
Prof., Mathematics
Homer, M. E., BA Brist., MSc Brist., PhD Brist.
Sr. Lectr.
Krauskopf, B., PhD Gron.   Prof., Applied
Nonlinear Mathematics
Lawry, J., BSc CNAA, PhD Manc.   Reader,
Artificial Intelligence
Martin, T. P., BSc Manc., PhD Brist.   Prof.,
Artifical Intelligent
Osinga, H. M., MSc Gron., PhD Gron.   Reader,
Mathematics
Rossiter, J. M., BEng Brist., MSc Brist., PhD Brist.
Sr. Lectr.
Sims Williams, J. H., MA Camb., MEng Sheff.
Sr. Lectr.
Terry, J. R., BSc Reading, PhD Sur.   Sr. Lectr.
Wilson, R. E., MA Oxf., DPhil Oxf.   Reader
Other Staff: 2 Lectrs.; 3 Res. Assocs.
Research: applied non-linear materials; artificial
intelligence (AI)

Engineering, Mechanical

Tel: (0117) 928 8284 Fax: (0117) 929 4423
E-mail: meng-enquiries@bristol.ac.uk
Alemzadeh, K., BSc CNAA, PhD Brad.   Sr. Lectr.
Booker, J. D., BEng Hull, PhD Hull   Sr. Lectr.,
Design and Manufacture
Burgess, S. C., BSc Brun., PhD Brun.   Prof.,
Design and Nature; Head*
Drinkwater, B. W., BEng Lond., PhD Lond.
Prof., Ultrasonics
Gilbertson, M. A., BEng Liv., DPhil Oxf.   Sr.
Lectr.
Harrison, A. J. L., BEng Brist., PhD Brist.   Sr.
Lectr.
King, A. M., BEng City(UK), MSc Cran., PhD
E.Lond.   Sr. Lectr.
Morgan, J. E., BSc Exe., PhD Exe.   Sr. Lectr.
Pavier, Martyn J., MA Camb., PhD Camb.
Reader, Mechanics of Materials
Poulter, R., BSc Newcastle(UK), PhD Newcastle(UK)
Sr. Lectr.
Quarini, G. L., BSc Lond., PhD Lond.   Prof.,
Process Engineering

Smith, D. J., BSc Newcastle(UK), PhD Lond.
Prof., Engineering Materials
Stoten, D. P., BSc Salf., PhD Camb., DEng Brist.,
FIMechE   Prof., Dynamics and Control
Tierney, M. J., BSc UMIST, PhD Birm.   Sr.
Lectr.
Truman, C. E., BSc Manc., PhD Nott.Trent
Reader
Wagg, D. J., BEng Lond., PhD Lond.   Reader,
Dynamics and Control
Wilcox, P. D., MEng Oxf., PhD Lond.   Sr.
Lectr., Dynamics
Other Staff: 5 Lectrs.; 2 Sr. Teaching Fellows;
8 Res. Assocs.
Research: design and manufacture; dynamics and
control; process engineering; solid
mechanics

English

Tel: (0117) 331 7932 Fax: (0117) 331 7933
E-mail: hums-schooloffice@bristol.ac.uk
Archibald, E. F., PhD Yale   Reader, Medieval
Studies
Bennett, Andrew J., BA Hull, PhD E.Anglia
Prof.; Head*
Cheeke, S. H., BA Camb., PhD Brist.   Sr. Lectr.
Dawson, L. D., BA Lond., MPhil Oxf.   Sr. Lectr.
Hopkins, D. W., MA Camb., PhD Leic.   Prof.,
English Literature
James, S., MA Camb., PhD Lond.   Sr. Lectr.
Lee, J., BA Camb., PhD Brist.   Sr. Lectr.
Lyon, J. M., MA St And., PhD Camb.   Sr. Lectr.
Mason, T. A., BA Oxf., PhD Camb.   Sr. Lectr.
Punter, David G., MA Camb., PhD Camb., DLitt
Stir.   Prof.
Putter, A., Drs Amst., MPhil Camb., PhD Camb.
Reader
Stokes, Myra F. K., MA Brist., PhD Brist.   Sr.
Lectr.
Webb, E. T., BA Trinity(Dub.), MA Trinity(Dub.),
DPhil Oxf.   Prof.
Other Staff: 2 Lectrs.
Research: mediaeval studies; nineteenth- and
twentieth-century fiction; poetry and
poetics 1660–1790; Romantic studies;
Shakespeare and the Renaissance

Exercise, Nutrition and Health Sciences

Tel: (0117) 331 1147 Fax: (0117) 331 1148
E-mail: margaret.thompson@bristol.ac.uk
Cooper, A. R., BSc Brist., PhD Lond., MSc   Sr.
Lectr.; Head*
Fox, Ken R., BSc Lond., MSc Kansas, PhD Arizona
Prof.
Haase, A. M., BA Auck., MSc Auck., PhD Auck.
Sr. Lectr.
Hillsdon, M., PhD Lond.   Sr. Lectr.
Jago, R. P., BSc C&GCHE, PhD Reading   Sr.
Lectr.
Page, A. S., BSc CNAA, PhD Exe.   Sr. Lectr.
Thompson, J. L., BS Calif., MS Calif., PhD Arizona
Prof.
Other Staff: 1 Lectr.; 1 Teaching Fellow; 2 Res.
Assocs.
Research: features of neighbourhoods on activity
patterns and food intake; impact of physical
activity and nutrition on public health;
nutrition in relation to mental health,
metabolic disease and public policy;
physical activity

Experimental Psychology

Tel: (0117) 928 8450 Fax: (0117) 928 8588
E-mail: lesley.barry@bristol.ac.uk
Baddeley, R. J., BA Sus., PhD Stir.   Reader
Benton, C. P., BSc Manc., PhD Lond.   Sr. Lectr.
Bowers, J. S., BSc Tor., PhD Arizona   Prof.
Brunstrom, J. M., BSc Sus., MSc Essex, PhD Birm.
Sr. Lectr.
Damian, M. F. E., MA Rice, PhD Rice   Reader
Farrell, S. A., BSc W.Aust., PhD W.Aust.   Sr.
Lectr.
Frankish, Clive R., BA Liv., MA Camb., PhD
Camb.   Sr. Lectr.
Freeman, N. H., MA Camb., PhD Camb., FBPsS
Prof., Cognitive Development
Gilchrist, I. D., BSc Durh., PhD Birm.   Prof.,
Neuropsychology; Head*

Hood, Bruce M., MA Dund., MPhil Dund., PhD
Camb.   Prof., Developmental Psychology
Jarrold, C. R., MA Camb., PhD Sheff.   Reader,
Cognitive Development
Leonards, U. B., PhD Mainz   Sr. Lectr.
Mattys, S., BA Bruxelles, PhD N.Y.State   Reader
Munafo, M. R., MA Oxf., MSc S'ton., PhD S'ton.
Reader, Biological Psychology
Noyes, J. M., BSc Lough., PhD Lough.   Prof.,
Human Factors of Psychology
Oberauer, K.   Prof., Psychology
Pearce, C. W., BSc Manc., PhD Camb.   Sr. Lectr.
Penton-Voak, I. S., BA Manc., MSc Manc., PhD St
And.   Sr. Lectr., Psychology
Rogers, Peter J., BSc Sus., MSc Sus., PhD Leeds,
FBPsS   Prof., Biological Psychology
Scott-Samuel, N. E., BA Brist., BSc Birm., PhD
Birm.   Sr. Lectr.
Stollery, B. T., BSc Manc., PhD Manc.   Sr. Lectr.
Troscianko, T. S., BSc Manc., PhD City(UK)
Prof., Psychology
Other Staff: 4 Lectrs.; 2 Sr. Res. Fellows; 4 Res.
Fellows; 12 Res. Assocs.
Research: cognitive and biological psychology;
computational neuroscience and
neuropsychology

French

Tel: (0117) 331 8011 Fax: (0117) 331 8010
E-mail: sml-office@bristol.ac.uk
Calder, M. L., BEng Leeds, BA Nott., MA Nott.,
PhD Nott.   Sr. Lectr.
Forman, E. R. B., DPhil Oxf., DPhil   Sr. Lectr.
Freeman, Michael J., BA Leeds, PhD Leeds
Ashley Watkins Prof., French Language and
Literature
Hawkins, Peter G., MA Lond.   Sr. Lectr.
Hobbs, Richard J., BA S'ton., BLitt Oxf.   Sr.
Lectr.
Hurcombe, M. J., BA Brist., PhD Brist.   Sr.
Lectr.
Parkin, J., BA Oxf., PhD Glas.   Prof., French
Literary Studies
Raymond, Gino G., BA Brist., PhD Camb.
Reader
Sampson, R. B. K., MA Camb., MA Manc.
Prof., Romance Philology
Unwin, T. A., MA Camb., MA Exe., PhD Exe.
Prof.; Head*
Other Staff: 2 Lectrs.; 1 Teaching Fellow
Research: critical theory; early modern period;
French culture in developing countries;
nineteenth- and twentieth-century
literature; visual arts and music

Geographical Sciences, School of

Tel: (0117) 928 9954 Fax: (0117) 928 7878
E-mail: geog-office@bristol.ac.uk
Bamber, Jonathan L., BSc Brist., PhD Camb.
Prof.
Bassett, K. A., BA Birm., PhD Brist.   Sr. Lectr.
Bates, P. D., BSc S'ton., PhD Brist.   Prof.,
Hydrology
Dewsbury, J.-D. C., BSc Brist., PhD Brist.   Sr.
Lectr., Human Geography
Flecker, R. M., BA Oxf., PhD Edin.   Sr. Lectr.
Glennie, P. D., MA Camb., PhD Camb.   Sr.
Lectr.
Harris, R. J., BSc Brist., MSc Brist., PhD Brist.
Sr. Lectr.
Harrison, S. P., BA Camb., MSc   Prof., Climate
Dynamics
Hoare, A. G., MA Camb., PhD Camb.   Sr. Lectr.
Johnston, R. J., MA Manc., PhD Monash, LLD
Monash, DU Essex, FBA   Prof.
Jones, K., BSc S'ton., PhD S'ton.   Prof., Human
Quantitative Geography; Head*
Kempson, H. E., CBE, BSc Sus.   Prof., Personal
Finance and Social Policy Research
Larner, W. J., MA Cant., PhD Car.   Prof.,
Human Geography and Sociology
Mayhew, R. J., BA Oxf., DPhil Oxf., PhD Camb.
Reader
Payne, A. J., BSc Stir., PhD Edin.   Prof.,
Glaciology
Plummer, P. S., BA Portsmouth, MA Minn., PhD
Minn.   Reader, Spatial Modelling
Richards, D. A., BSc Brist., PhD Brist.   Sr. Lectr.

Smart, P. L., BSc Brist., MSc *Alta.*, PhD Brist. Prof.

Tranter, M., BSc *E.Anglia*, PhD *E.Anglia* Prof.

Valdes, P. J., BSc Lond., DPhil Oxf. Prof., Physical Geography

Whelan, Y. F., BA PhD Sr. Lectr.

Other Staff: 6 Lectrs.; 3 Sr. Res. Fellows; 1 Sr. Teaching Fellow; 2 Res. Fellows; 11 Res. Assocs.

Research: environmental change and paleoclimate; glaciology; hydrology

German

Tel: (0117) 331 8011 Fax: (0117) 331 8010
E-mail: sml-office@bristol.ac.uk

Allinson, M. A., BA *Salf.*, PhD Lond. Sr. Lectr.; Head*

Carrdus, A. M. R., BA Lond., PhD Lond. Sr. Lectr.

Kosenina, A., MA *F.U.Berlin*, PhD *F.U.Berlin* Prof.

Langer, N., BA *Newcastle(UK)*, MA *Newcastle(UK)*, PhD *Newcastle(UK)* Sr. Lectr.

Simon, K. A., MA Edin., MA *Br.Col.*, PhD Lond. Sr. Lectr.

Other Staff: 1 Lectr.; 1 Teaching Fellow; 2 Teaching Assocs.

Research: German and Austrian history and politics since 1800; German socio- and historical linguistics; literature from the mediaeval period until the present; text and image studies; writing by and for women

Hispanic, Portuguese and Latin American Studies

Tel: (0117) 331 8011 Fax: (0117) 331 8010
E-mail: sml-office@bristol.ac.uk

Brookshaw, D. R., BA Lond., PhD Lond. Prof., Luso-Brazilian Studies

Hook, D., MA Oxf., DPhil Oxf. Prof., Hispanic Studies; Head*

Kitts, S.-A., BA *Sheff.*, PhD *Sheff.* Sr. Lectr., Hispanic Studies

Leu, L. M., BA Lond., MA *Lond.Inst.*, PhD Lond. Sr. Lectr., Portuguese and Brazilian Studies

Lewis-Smith, P., MA Camb., PhD Camb. Sr. Lectr., Hispanic Studies

Romero Salvado, F. J., BA Lond., PhD Lond. Sr. Lectr., Hispanic Studies

Wells, C., BA Lond., MA *Exe.*, PhD *Exe.* Sr. Lectr., Hispanic Studies

Williams, C. A., BA *Warw.*, PhD *Warw.* Sr. Lectr., Latin American Studies

Other Staff: 1 Lectr.; 1 Sr. Teaching Fellow; 4 Teaching Fellows

Research: colonialism; Latin American studies; mediaeval studies; Portuguese, Brazilian and Afro-Portuguese studies; Spanish literature, history and cultural studies

Historical Studies

Tel: (0117) 331 7932 Fax: (0117) 331 7933
E-mail: hums-schooloffice@bristol.ac.uk

Bickers, R. A., BA Lond., PhD Lond. Prof.

Bull, Marcus G., BA Lond., PhD Lond. Sr. Lectr., Mediaeval History

Cervantes, F., MA Oxf., PhD Camb. Sr. Lectr.

Clark, J. G., BA Brist., MA Oxf., DPhil Oxf. Sr. Lectr., Early Modern and Northern European History

Coates, P. A., MA *St And.*, PhD Camb. Prof., American and Environmental History

Cole, T. J., MA Camb., PhD Camb. Sr. Lectr., Social History

Doyle, W., MA Oxf., DPhil Oxf., DU Bordeaux, FRHistS, FBA Prof.

Hutton, R. E., MA Camb., DPhil Oxf., FRHistS, FSA Prof.

Jones, E. T., MA Edin., MA *York(UK)*, PhD Edin. Sr. Lectr., Economic and Social History

Lowe, R., BA Brist., PhD Lond., FRHistS Prof., Contemporary History

MacLeod, Christine, BA Oxf., PhD Camb. Sr. Lectr., Economic and Social History

McLellan, J., BA *Sus.*, MSt Oxf., DPhil Oxf. Sr. Lectr., Modern European History

Middleton, Roger, BA Manc., PhD Camb., FRHistS Prof., History of Political Economy

Pemberton, H. R., BA *Open(UK)*, MA Brist., PhD Brist. Sr. Lectr., Modern British History

Reid, K. M., MA Edin., PhD Edin. Sr. Lectr.

Smith, B. G. C., MA *Trinity(Dub.)*, PhD *Trinity(Dub.)* Reader, Mediaeval History; Head*

Wei, Ian P., BA Manc. Sr. Lectr., Mediaeval European History

Other Staff: 4 Lectrs.

Research: colonialism; mediaeval cultures; reception

History of Art

Tel: (0117) 954 6050 Fax: (0117) 954 6001
E-mail: art-history@bristol.ac.uk

Bann, S., CBE, BA Camb., MA Camb., PhD Camb., FBA Prof.

Liversidge, Michael J. H., BA Lond., FSA Emer. Dean; Head*

O'Mahony, M. J., BA Lond., PhD Lond. Sr. Lectr.

Prettejohn, E. F., BA Harv., MA Lond., PhD Lond. Prof.

Rowe, D. C., BA *Leic.*, PhD *Essex* Sr. Lectr.

Williamson, B. A., BA Oxf., MA Lond., PhD Lond. Sr. Lectr.

Other Staff: 1 Lectr.; 1 Sr. Teaching Fellow; 1 Teaching Fellow

Research: British art; mediaeval studies; nineteenth-century French art and criticism; Renaissance art; twentieth-century Russian art

Italian

Tel: (0117) 331 8011 Fax: (0117) 331 8010
E-mail: sml-office@bristol.ac.uk

Bryce, Judith H., MA *Aberd.*, PhD *Aberd.* Prof.; Head*

Burdett, C. F., MA Oxf., DPhil Oxf. Sr. Lectr.

Duncan, D. E., MA *Aberd.*, PhD Edin. Prof.

Glynn, R. S., BA N.U.I., MA N.U.I., PhD Birm. Sr. Lectr.

Parry, M. M., BA *Wales*, MA Oxf., PhD *Wales* Prof., Italian Linguistics

Other Staff: 1 Lectr.; 2 Teaching Fellows; 1 Teaching Assoc.

Research: mediaeval and Renaissance cultural history; post-unification Italian cultural history

Law, School of

Tel: (0117) 954 5356 Fax: (0117) 925 1870
E-mail: law-ug-admissions@bristol.ac.uk

Bibbings, L. S., LLB *Wales*, MPhil *Wales* Sr. Lectr.

Capps, P. M., BA *Sheff.*, MA *Sheff.*, PhD Brist. Sr. Lectr.

Cowan, D. S., LLB *S'ton.* Prof., Law and Policy

Evans, Malcolm D., OBE, MA Oxf., MPhil Oxf. Prof., Public International Law

Greer, S. C., BA Oxf., MSc Lond., PhD *Belf.* Prof., Human Rights

Griffiths-Baker, J. E., LLB *Wales*, LLM Brist., PhD Brist. Sr. Lectr.

Hill, J. D., LLB Birm., LLM Camb. Prof.

Hitchings, E., LLB *Wales*, PhD *Wales* Sr. Lectr.

Jones, S. P., BA *Durh.* Sr. Lectr.

Kerridge, J. R., LLB Camb., MA Camb. Prof.

Koutrakos, P., LLM Lond., PhD Birm. Prof., European Union Law

Masson, J. M., BA Camb., PhD *Leic.* Prof., Socio-Legal Studies

McDermont, M. A., BA Oxf., LLM Brist., PhD *W.England* Sr. Lectr.

McMeel, G. P., BCL Oxf., MA Oxf. Prof.

McVea, H., LLB *Belf.*, PhD *H-W* Sr. Lectr.

Morgan, M. M., LLB *Belf.*, PhD *H-W* Prof., Socio-Legal Studies

Murray, R. H., LLB *Leic.*, LLM Brist., PhD *W.England* Prof., International Human Rights

Norman, H. E., LLM Birm. Sr. Lectr.

Novitz, T. A., LLB Camb., BCL Oxf., DPhil Oxf. Reader

Prosser, J. A. W., LLB *Liv.* Prof., Public Law

Quick, O. L., LLB *Wales*, PhD *Wales* Sr. Lectr.

Rivers, A. J., BA Camb., MA Camb., LLM Camb., PhD Prof., Jurisprudence

Rose, Francis, MA Oxf., BCL Oxf., MA Camb., PhD Lond. Prof., Commercial Law

Seabourne, G. C., BA Camb., BCL Oxf., PhD Brist. Sr. Lectr.

Skordas, P.-A., LLB *Athens*, PhD *Fran.* Reader

Stanton, K. M., BA Oxf., BCL Oxf. Prof.; Head*

Sufrin, Brenda E., LLB Birm. Prof.

Syrett, K. J., MA Lond., PhD Lond. Sr. Lectr.

Syrpis, P. A. J., MA Camb., BCL Oxf., DPhil Oxf. Sr. Lectr.

Tsagourias, N., LLB Brist., LLM Brist., PhD Nott. Sr. Lectr.

Villiers, C. L., LLM Lond. Prof., Company Law

Watterson, S. W., BA Oxf., DPhil Oxf. Sr. Lectr.

Willmore, C. J., LLB Brist. Sr. Lectr.

Young, R. P., LLB Birm., PhD Birm. Prof., Law and Policy Research

Other Staff: 4 Lectrs.; 2 Sr. Res. Fellows; 2 Res. Fellows; 2 Res. Assocs.; 3 Teaching Assocs.

Research: family law and practice; governance and regulation; housing; human rights; legal profession

Management

Tel: (0117) 928 8415 Fax: (0117) 928 8577
E-mail: efim-info@bristol.ac.uk

Bourne, R. H. L., MBA *City(UK)*, PhD Cran. Sr. Lectr.

Friedman, A. L., BA *Manit.*, MA *Tor.* Prof., Management and Economics

Phillips, M. E., BA Bath, MA *Reading*, PhD *Reading* Sr. Lectr.

Rippin, A. J., BA *Wales*, MSc Brist., PhD *Wales* Sr. Lectr.

White, L. A., BSc Birm., MSc Birm. Sr. Lectr.; Head*

Other Staff: 3 Lectrs.; 2 Teaching Assocs.

Research: management domain; management theory and research practice

Mathematics

Tel: (0117) 928 7978 Fax: (0117) 928 7999
E-mail: helen.craven@bristol.ac.uk

Andrieu, C., MA *I.N.S.A.Lyons*, MA Paris, PhD Paris Reader, Statistics

Boyd, W. G. C., BSc Dund., PhD Dund. Sr. Lectr.

Chatters, A. W., BSc Birm., PhD Leeds Reader

Chuang, J., BA Harv., MSc *Chic.*, PhD *Chic.* Reader, Pure Mathematics

Collins, E. J., BSc Leeds, MSc Manc., PhD Manc. Sr. Lectr., Statistics

Conrey, J. B., BSc Mich., PhD Mich. Prof., Number Theory

Dettmann, C. P., BSc *Melb.*, PhD *Melb.* Reader, Applied Mathematics

Eggers, J. G., MSc T.H.*Aachen*, PhD Marburg Prof., Applied Mathematics

Evans, David V., BSc Manc., PhD Manc. Prof., Applied Mathematics

Green, B. J., PhD Camb. Prof., Pure Mathematics

Green, P. J., BA Oxf., MSc *Sheff.*, PhD *Sheff.*, FRS Henry Overton Wills Prof.

Hogg, A. J., MA Camb., PhD Camb. Sr. Lectr., Applied Mathematics

Keating, Jonathan P., BA Oxf., PhD Brist. Prof., Mathematical Physics

Kerswell, R. R., MA Camb., MA *Calif.*, PhD M.I.T. Prof., Applied Mathematics

Linden, Noah, BA Camb., PhD Lond. Prof., Theoretical Physics

Liskevich, Vitali, MS Kiev, PhD *Ukr.Acad.Sc.* Prof.

Marklof, J., PhD Ulm Reader, Mathematical Physics

McNamara, J. M., MA Oxf., MSc *Sus.*, DPhil Oxf. Prof., Mathematics and Biology

Mezzadri, F., Laurea Parma, PhD Brist. Sr. Lectr., Applied Mathematics

Moroz, V. B., MSc *Belarus State*, PhD *Belarus State* Sr. Lectr., Pure Mathematics

Nason, G. P., BSc Bath, PhD Bath Prof., Statistics

Netrusov, Y., PhD Leningrad Sr. Lectr., Pure Mathematics

Pila, J., BSc Melb., PhD Stan.   Sr. Lectr., Discrete Mathematics
Rickard, J. C., MA Camb., PhD Lond.   Prof.
Robbins, Jonathan M., BS Yale, PhD Calif.   Reader, Applied Mathematics
Rudnev, M., MSc Moscow Phys.& Technol.Inst., PhD Cal.Tech.   Sr. Lectr., Applied Mathematics
Schofield, A. H., BA Camb., PhD Lond.   Prof., Pure Mathematics
Tourigny, Y. J. M., BSc Montr., MSc Wat., PhD Dund.   Sr. Lectr., Numerical Analysis
van den Berg, Michiel, MSc T.H.Delft   Prof., Pure Mathematics
Volkov, S., MSc Moscow, MSc Wis., MA Moscow, PhD Moscow   Reader, Statistics
Welch, P. D., BSc Lond., MSc Oxf., DPhil Oxf.   Prof.
Wiggins, S. R., PhD Cornell   Prof., Applied Mathematics; Head*
Winter, A. J., PhD Bielefeld   Prof., Physics of Information
Wooley, T. D., MA Camb., PhD Lond.   Prof., Pure Mathematics
Other Staff: 16 Lectrs.; 17 Res. Fellows; 8 Res. Assocs.
Research: applied mathematics; pure mathematics; statistics and applied probability

Music

Tel: (0117) 954 5028 Fax: (0117) 954 5027
E-mail: music-info@bristol.ac.uk
Banfield, S. D., MA Camb., DPhil Oxf., FRCO   Stanley Hugh Badock Prof.; Res. Fellow
Irving, John A., BMus Sheff., PhD Sheff.   Reader, Historical Musicology; Head*
Pickard, J., BMus Wales, PhD Wales   Sr. Lectr.
Poole, G. R., BA E.Anglia, BMus S'ton., DMus S'ton.   Prof., Composition
Other Staff: 4 Lectrs.; 1 Sr. Teaching Fellow
Research: British music; film music; history of music in Britain; music in the Soviet Union; music of Mozart

Philosophy

Tel: (0117) 928 7825 Fax: (0117) 928 8626
E-mail: susan.frost@bris.ac.uk
Bird, Alexander J., BA Oxf., MPhil Camb., PhD Camb.   Prof.; Head*
Doyle, J. A., MA Camb., PhD Virginia   Sr. Lectr.
Ladyman, J. A. C., BA York(UK), MSc Lond., PhD Leeds   Sr. Lectr.
Leitgeb, H., MSc Salzburg, PhD Salzburg   Reader, Mathematical Logic and Philosophy of Maths
Morgan, D. S., PhD Leeds   Sr. Lectr.
Okasha, S., MA Oxf., BPhil Oxf., DPhil Oxf.   Reader, Philosophy of Science
Pyle, A. J., BA Brist., PhD Brist.   Reader, Early Modern Philosophy
Woodfield, A. R., MA Oxf., MLitt Edin., DPhil Oxf.   Reader
Other Staff: 3 Lectrs.; 1 Teaching Assoc.
Research: knowledge; philosophy of science; reality

Physics

Tel: (0117) 928 8731 Fax: (0117) 925 5624
E-mail: victoria.johnson@bristol.ac.uk
Alam, M. A., MSc Halle, PhD E.Anglia, FIP   Prof.
Annett, James F., MA Camb., MS Oregon, PhD Camb.   Prof.
Barham, P. J., BSc Warw., MSc Brist., PhD Brist.   Reader
Barnes, A. C., BSc Brist., PhD Brist.   Reader
Berry, Sir Michael, BSc Exe., PhD St And., DSc Exe., ScD Trinity(Dub.), FRS   Royal Soc. Res. Prof.
Birkinshaw, Mark, MA Camb., PhD Camb., FRAS   William P. Coldrick Prof., Cosmology and Astrophysics
Bremer, M. N., BSc Lond., PhD Camb.   Reader, Astrophysics
Brook, N. H., BSc Manc., PhD Manc.   Prof. Res. Fellow
Carrington, A., BSc Warw., PhD Camb.   Reader

Cherns, D., MA Camb., MA Oxf., PhD Camb.   Prof.
Dugdale, S. B., BSc Brist., PhD Brist.   Sr. Lectr.
Evans, R., BSc Birm., PhD Brist., FIP   Prof.; Head*
Goldstein, J., BA Camb., PhD Boston   Sr. Lectr.
Hanna, S., MA Camb., PhD Camb.   Reader
Hannay, J. H., BA Camb., PhD Camb.   Prof.
Hayden, S. M., MA Camb., PhD Camb.   Prof.
Heath, Gregory P., BSc Sus., PhD Lond.   Prof.
Heath, H. F., BA Oxf., MA Oxf., PhD Brist.   Sr. Lectr.
Henshaw, D. L., BSc Lond., PhD Nott.   Prof.
Hill, C. S., BA Dartmouth, MSc Calif., PhD Calif.   Sr. Lectr.
Hoerber, J. K. H., MA Munich, PhD Munich   Prof., Nanobiophysics
Hussey, N. E., DPhil Sus.   Reader
Kuball, M. H. H., PhD Stuttgart   Reader
McMaster, T. J., BSc Brist., PhD Brist.   Reader
Miles, M. J., MSc Birm., PhD Birm., BSc   Prof.
Newbold, D. M., BSc Manc., PhD Brist.   Reader
Odell, J. A., MSc Brist., PhD Brist.   Reader
Phillipps, S., MSc Sus., PhD Durh., FRAS   Prof.
Popescu, Sandu, PhD Tel-Aviv   Prof.
Richardson, Robert M., BSc Brist., PhD Brist., DSc Brist.   Prof.
Schmidt, C. M.   Sr. Lectr.
Schwarzacher, W., MA Camb., PhD Camb.   Prof.
Smith, V. J., MBE, MA Oxf., PhD Brist.   Reader
Steeds, J. W., BSc Lond., PhD Camb., FIP, FRS   H. O. Wills Prof.
Tapper, R. J., MA Camb., PhD Camb.   Reader
Worrall, D. M., BSc Durh., PhD Durh., FRAS   Prof.
Other Staff: 2 Lectrs.; 1 Sr. Res. Fellow; 1 Sr. Teaching Fellow; 7 Res. Fellows; 18 Res. Assocs.
Research: condensed matter physics; interaction between theoretical and experimental physics

Policy Studies, School for

Tel: (0117) 954 6755 Fax: (0117) 954 6756
E-mail: sps-enquiries@bristol.ac.uk
Ayres, S. A., BSc Aston, PhD Aston   Sr. Lectr.
Bartlett, William J., BA Camb., MSc Lond., PhD Liv.   Reader, Social Economics
Berridge, D., BSc Brun., PhD Brist., DLitt Luton   Prof., Child and Family Welfare
Bridge, G. H., MA Oxf., MA Calif., DPhil Oxf.   Prof., Urban Studies
Burgess, H. C., MA Oxf.   Sr. Lectr.
Cameron, A. M., BA Exe., MSc Lond.   Sr. Lectr.
Carpenter, J. S. W., BSc Brist.   Prof., Social Work and Applied Social Sciences
Cemlyn, S. J., BA Oxf., MA Brun.   Sr. Lectr.
Doogan, K. J., BA Trinity(Dub.)   Sr. Lectr.
Doyal, Lesley, BA Lond., MSc Lond.   Prof.
Farmer, E. R. G., BA Nott.   Prof., Child and Family Studies
Forrest, R. S., MSocSc Birm., PhD Brist.   Prof., Urban Studies
Gordon, D., BSc Sus., PhD Brist.   Prof. Res. Fellow, Social Justice
Hague, G. M., BSc S'ton., PhD Brist.   Prof. Res. Fellow
Hester, M., BA Oxf., MA Leeds, PhD Leeds   Prof., Gender, Violence and International Policy
Kennett, P. A., BSc Brist., PhD Brist.   Sr. Lectr.
Lart, R. A., BA Lond., PhD Lond.   Sr. Lectr.
Lloyd, E. H. R. R., BA Amst., BSc E.Lond.   Sr. Lectr., Early Childhood Studies
Lloyd, R. E., BSc Brun., PhD Brist.   Sr. Lectr., Social Work
Marinelli, M., BA Bologna   Sr. Lectr., East Asian Studies
Marsh, A. D., BSc Warw., MSocSc Birm.   Prof., Public Policy; Head*
Murphy, R. A., BA Murd., PhD Camb.   Sr. Lectr., East Asian Studies
Pantazis, C., MA S'ton.   Sr. Lectr.
Payne, S., BA CNAA, PhD Brist.   Reader
Platt, W. D. G., MA Dund., PhD E.Anglia   Sr. Lectr., Social Work (Child Care)
Rivett, M. J., BA Lanc., MSc Wales   Sr. Lectr.
Selwyn, J. T., MSc(Econ) Wales   Sr. Lectr., Social Work

Watson, D. L., BSc Exe., PhD Exe.   Sr. Lectr., Childhood Studies
Other Staff: 10 Lectrs.; 3 Sr. Res. Fellows; 2 Res. Fellows; 2 Teaching Fellows; 6 Res. Assocs.
Research: family policy and child welfare; gender and violence; health and social care; poverty and social justice; urban studies

Politics

Tel: (0117) 928 7898 Fax: (0117) 331 7500
E-mail: politics@bristol.ac.uk
Acharya, A., BA Utkal, MA J.Nehru U., PhD Murd.   Prof., Global Governance
Carver, Terrell F., BA Col., BPhil Oxf., DPhil Oxf.   Prof., Political Theory
Childs, S. L., BA Sus., MA York(UK), PhD Kingston(UK)   Sr. Lectr.
Cini, M. M. C., BA Kent, MSc Lond., PhD Exe.   Reader, European Politics
Colomer, J., BA Barcelona, PhD Barcelona   Prof., Comparative European Politics
Duffield, M. R., BA Sheff., PhD Birm.   Prof., Development Politics
Edmunds, T. P., BA Brad., PhD Sheff.   Sr. Lectr.
Herring, E., MA Aberd., MScEcon Wales, PhD Wales   Sr. Lectr., International Politics
Hewitt, V. M., BA E.Anglia, DPhil Oxf.   Sr. Lectr.
Higate, P. R., MA Glas., DPhil York(UK)   Sr. Lectr.
Krahmann, E., BA Marburg, MA F.U.Berlin, PhD Lond.   Sr. Lectr.
Little, Richard, BSc Lond., MA Lehigh, PhD Lanc.   Prof., International Politics
Pridham, Geoffrey F. M., MA Camb., PhD Lond.   Prof., European Politics
Ross, F. A., BA Strath., MA Pitt., PhD Pitt.   Sr. Lectr.
Sanford, George, BA Brist., MPhil Lond., PhD Lond.   Reader
Shell, D. R., BSc(Econ) Lond., MA Essex   Sr. Lectr.
Squires, J. A., MA Edin., PhD Lond.   Prof., Political Theory; Head*
Weldes, J. E., BA Penn.State, PhD Minn.   Reader, International Relations
Wickham-Jones, Mark, MA Edin., PhD Manc.   Sr. Lectr.
Wyatt, A. K. J., BA Lanc., MA Brist., PhD Brist.   Sr. Lectr.
Other Staff: 1 Lectr.; 1 Sr. Res. Fellow; 3 Teaching Assocs.
Research: comparative politics; international politics; political development; political theory

Russian

Tel: (0117) 331 8011 Fax: (0117) 331 8010
E-mail: sml-office@bristol.ac.uk
Basker, M. G., BA Oxf.   Prof., Russian Literature
Beumers, B., BA CNAA, DPhil Oxf.   Reader
Chitnis, R. A., BA Sheff., MA Lond., PhD Lond.   Sr. Lectr.
Coates, R. A., BA Brist., DPhil Oxf.   Sr. Lectr.
Cornwell, Neil J., BA Lond., PhD Belf.   Prof., Russian and Comparative Literature
Offord, D. C., BA Camb., PhD Lond.   Prof., Russian Intellectual History; Head*
Other Staff: 2 Teaching Fellows; 1 Teaching Assoc.
Research: Russian intellectual history; Russian literature, culture, theatre and cinema; twentieth-century Czech and Slovak culture; twentieth-century Czech and Slovak literature

Sociology

Tel: (0117) 928 8216 Fax: (0117) 954 6609
E-mail: tim.maughan@bristol.ac.uk
Bradley, Harriet K., BA Brist., BA Leic., PhD Durh.   Prof.
Dermott, E. M., BA Camb., MSc Edin., PhD Essex   Sr. Lectr.
Fenton, C. S., BA Hull, MA McM., PhD Duke   Prof.

Flanagan, Kieran D. P., BSocSc N.U.I., MA Minn., DPhil Sus. Reader

Levitas, Ruth A., BA Sheff., PhD Sheff. Prof.; Head*

Marshall, L. K. R., BA Warw., MA Warw., PhD Warw. Sr. Lectr.

McLennan, Gregor, BA Brist., MA Birm., PhD Birm. Prof.

Modood, T., MBE, MA Durh., PhD Wales Prof., Sociology, Politics and Public Policy

Osborne, T. S. D., BA Oxf., MSc Lond., PhD Brun. Reader; Res. Fellow, Social Theory

Skultans, V., BA Lond., PhD Wales Prof., Social Anthropology

Statham, P. D., BA Sus., PhD Prof., Political Sociology

Surridge, P., BSc Warw. Sr. Lectr.

West, Jacqueline A., MA Exe. Sr. Lectr.; Head*

Other Staff: 5 Lectrs.; 3 Res. Assocs.; 1 Teaching Assoc.

Research: ethnicity, multiculturalism and citizenship; gender relations; inequality and social exclusion; social and cultural theory

Theology and Religious Studies

Tel: (0117) 331 7932 Fax: (0117) 331 7933
E-mail: hums-schooloffice@bristol.ac.uk

Campbell, J. G., BD Aberd., DPhil Oxf. Sr. Lectr., Biblical Studies and Judaism

D'Costa, Gavin G., BA Birm., PhD Camb. Reader, Christian Theology

Gethin, Rupert M. L., MA Manc., PhD Manc. Reader, Buddhist Studies

Kieschnik, J. H., BA Calif., MA Stan., PhD Stan. Reader, Buddhist Studies

Lyons, W. J., MA Sheff., PhD Sheff. Sr. Lectr., New Testament Studies

Muessig, C. A., BA N.Y.State, MA Tor., MSL Pontif.Inst.Tor., PhD Montr. Sr. Lectr., Mediaeval Theology; Head*

Williams, Paul M., BA Sus., DPhil Oxf. Prof., Indian and Tibetan Philosophy

Other Staff: 2 Lectrs.; 1 Res. Fellow

Research: Buddhist studies; Christian culture; mediaeval studies; religion and contemporary society

MEDICAL AND VETERINARY SCIENCES

Tel: (0117) 331 1538 Fax: (0117) 331 1889
E-mail: stephen.brooke@bristol.ac.uk

Anatomy

Tel: (0117) 928 7400 Fax: (0117) 929 1687
E-mail: elaine.sparey@bristol.ac.uk

Bashir, Z. I., BSc Newcastle(UK), PhD Glas. Prof., Cellular Neuroscience

Bortolotto, Z. A., PhD Sao Paulo Sr. Lectr.

Brown, M. W., MA Camb., PhD Camb., FRS Prof., Anatomy and Cognitive Neuroscience

Clarke, G., BPharm Lond., PhD Lond. Sr. Lectr., Anatomy

Colborne, G. R., BSc Guelph, MHK Windsor, PhD Qu. Sr. Lectr., Comparative Anatomy

Collingridge, Graham L., BSc Brist., PhD Lond., FRS Prof., Neuroscience in Anatomy

Dolan, P., BSc CNAA, PhD CNAA Reader, Biomechanics

Fuller, C. J., BVSc Liv., PhD Brist. Sr. Lectr.

Greene, J. R.T., BSc Lond., MB BS Lond., PhD Lond. Sr. Lectr.

Henley, Jeremy M., BSc Aston, PhD Lond. Prof., Molecular Neuroscience; Head*

Molnar, E., MD Albert Szent-Györgyi Med., PhD Hungarian Acad.Sc. Prof.

Randall, A. D. Prof., Applied Neurophysiology

Sharif, M., BSc Ulster, PhD Lond. Sr. Lectr.

Tortonese, D. J., DVM La Plata, DrVet La Plata, PhD W.Virginia Sr. Lectr.

Wakerley, J. B., BSc Nott., PhD Brist. Reader

Wakley, G. K., MSc Sheff., PhD Brist., BSc Sr. Lectr.

Warburton, E. C., BSc Reading, PhD Lond. Sr. Lectr.

Other Staff: 4 Lectrs.; 1 Sr. Res. Fellow; 3 Res. Fellows; 2 Teaching Fellows; 18 Res. Assocs.

Research: equine science; musculoskeletal science; neuroscience

Biochemistry

Tel: (0117) 331 2167 Fax: (0117) 331 2168
E-mail: bioc-office@bristol.ac.uk

Banting, G. S., BSc Salf., PhD CNAA Prof., Molecular Cell Biology; Head*

Booth, Paula J., MA Oxf., PhD Lond. Prof., Physical Biochemistry

Brady, Robert L., BSc Macq., DPhil York(UK) Prof.

Clarke, Anthony R., BSc Sheff., PhD Brist. Prof.

Collinson, I. R., BSc Warw., PhD Camb. Sr. Lectr.

Cullen, P. J., BSc E.Anglia, PhD E.Anglia Prof.

Dempsey, C. E., BSc St And., PhD Lond. Sr. Lectr.

Denton, R. M., MA Camb., PhD Camb., DSc Brist., FRS, FMedSci Prof.

Frayne, J., BSc Nott., PhD Brist. Sr. Lectr.

Gaston, K. L., BSc Leic., PhD Birm. Reader

Hadfield, A. T., MA Oxf., DPhil Oxf. Sr. Lectr.

Halestrap, A. P., MA Camb., PhD Brist., DSc Brist. Prof.

Halford, S. E., BSc Brist., PhD Brist., FRS Prof.

Hall, L., BSc Leeds, PhD Leic. Prof., Molecular Genetics

Jones, M. R., BSc Wales, PhD Wales Reader

Kuwabara, P. E., BA Johns H., PhD Penn. William P. Coldrick Prof., Genomics

Mellor, A. H., BSc Edin., PhD Brist. Reader

Rivett, A. J., BSc Birm., PhD Camb. Prof.

Savery, N. J., BSc Birm., PhD Birm. Sr. Lectr.

Stephens, D. J., BSc Lond., PhD Lond. Reader

Szczelkun, M. D., BSc Liv., PhD S'ton. Reader

Tavaré, J. M., BSc Brist., PhD Brist. Prof.

Wood, P. M., MA Camb., PhD Camb., DSc Brist. Sr. Lectr.

Other Staff: 2 Lectrs.; 1 Wellcome Advanced Fellow; 6 Sr. Res. Fellows; 1 Sr. Teaching Fellow; 14 Res. Fellows; 25 Res. Assocs.

Research: cell biology; cell shape and movement; control of cell death and proliferation; intracellular trafficking; structural biology and biophysics

Cellular and Molecular Medicine

Tel: (0117) 331 2050 Fax: (0117) 331 2091
E-mail: enquiries-cellmolmed@bristol.ac.uk

Avison, M. B., BSc Brist., PhD Brist. Sr. Lectr., Microbiology

Bidwell, Jeffrey L., PhD CNAA, FIBiol, FRCPath Reader, Molecular Immunogenetics

Blocker, A. J., BSc Lond., PhD Paris XI Sr. Lectr., Microbiology

Braun, G. J., PhD Tübingen Sr. Lectr., Parasite Immunology

Brown, K. W., MA Camb., MSc Birm., PhD Birm. Reader, Molecular Pathology

Collins, C. M. P., BA Camb., MB BChir Camb. Consultant Sr. Lectr., Pathology

Davidson, A. D., BSc Qld., PhD Qld. Sr. Lectr., Virology

Dick, Andrew D., BSc Lond., MB BS Lond., MD Aberd., FRCS, FRCSEd, FRCPEd Prof.

Finn, A. H. R., MA BCh Oxf., MA Camb., PhD Lond., FRCP, FRCPCH Prof.†, Paediatrics

Heyderman, Robert S., BSc Lond., MB BS Lond., PhD Lond., FRCP Prof., Infectious Diseases and International Health

Hollander, A. P., BSc Bath, PhD Brist. ARC Prof., Rheumatology and Tissue Engineering

Jones, R. H., BSc Lond., MB BCh Oxf., PhD Lond. Consultant Sr. Lectr., Medical Oncology

Kearns, P. R., BSc Newcastle(UK), MB ChB Newcastle(UK), PhD Newcastle(UK) Consultant Sr. Lectr.

MacGowan, A. P., MB ChB Aberd., BMedBiol Aberd., MD Brist. Prof., Clinical Microbiology and Antimicrobial Therapeutics

Malik, K. T. A., BSc Sur., PhD Camb. Sr. Lectr.

Morgan, Andrew J., BSc Bath, PhD Camb. Prof., Molecular Virology

Morgan, D. J., BSc Brist., PhD Warw. Sr. Lectr., Immunology

Paraskeva, C., BSc Manc., DPhil Oxf. Prof., Experimental Oncology

Pignatelli, Massimo, MD Bologna, PhD Lond. Prof., Histopathology

Siddell, S. G., BSc Liv., PhD Warw. Prof., Virology

Sohail, M., MB BS Karachi, MPhil Karachi Consultant Sr. Lectr., Histopathology

Standen, G. R., BPharm Nott., BMedSci Nott., BM BS Nott., PhD Lond. Consultant Sr. Lectr., Pathology (Haematology)

Steward, C. G., BM BCh Oxf., MA Camb., PhD Brist. Reader, Stem Cell Transplantation

Virji, M., BSc Leeds, PhD Leeds Prof., Molecular Microbiology

Williams, A. C., BSc Brist., PhD Brist. Reader, Experimental Oncology

Williams, Neil A., BSc Birm., PhD Brist. Prof., Immunology; Head*

Wraith, David C., BSc Newcastle(UK), PhD Lond. Prof., Pathological Science

Other Staff: 1 Wellcome Lectr.; 7 Lectrs.; 1 Sr. Res. Fellow; 6 Res. Fellows; 1 Teaching Assoc.

Research: cancer biology; immunology; microbiology; virology

Clinical Veterinary Science

Tel: (0117) 928 9236 Fax: (01934) 853400
E-mail: vetsci-info@bristol.ac.uk

Bailey, Allen, BSc Lond., MA Camb., PhD Birm., ScD Camb., FRSChem Emer. Prof.; Sr. Res. Fellow, Biochemistry, Muscle and Collagen

Bailey, M., BVSc Brist., PhD Camb. Prof., Comparative Immunology

Barr, A. R. S., MA Camb., VetMB Camb., PhD Brist. Prof., Veterinary Surgery

Barr, F. J., MA Camb., VetMB Camb., PhD Brist. Sr. Lectr., Veterinary Imaging Techniques

Batt, R. M., BVSc Brist., MSc Lond., PhD Lond., FRCVS Visiting Prof.

Bland, P. W., BSc Belf., BAgr Belf., PhD Glas. Sr. Lectr., Mucosal Immunology

Bostock, Christopher, BSc Edin., PhD Edin. Hon. Visiting Prof.

Bradley, A. J., VetMB Camb., MA Camb., PhD Sr. Lectr.

Bradshaw, J. W. S., BA Oxf., PhD S'ton. Reader, Companion Animal Behaviour

Browne, W. J., MSc Bath, PhD Bath Prof., Biostatistics

Corry, J. E. L., BSc Reading, MSc Brist., PhD Sur., FIFST Reader, Food Microbiology

Day, Michael J., BSc Murd., BVMS Murd., PhD Murd., FRCVS, FASM Prof., Veterinary Pathology

Duffus, W. P. H., BVSc Liv., MA Camb., PhD Liv. Prof., Veterinary Medicine

Grogono-Thomas, R., BSc Lond., BVetMed Lond., MSc Edin., PhD Lond. Sr. Lectr., Farm Animal Science

Gruffydd-Jones, T. J., BVetMed Lond., PhD Brist. Prof., Feline Medicine

Hall, Edward J., MA Camb., VetMB Camb., PhD Liv. Prof.

Hill, P. B., BVSc Liv., PhD Edin. Sr. Lectr., Veterinary Imaging Techniques

Holt, P. E., BVMS Glas., PhD Brist., FRCVS, FIBiol Prof., Veterinary Surgery

Humphrey, T. J., BSc E.Anglia, PhD E.Anglia, FRCPath Prof., Veterinary Zoonotic Bacteriology

Knowles, T. G., BSc CNAA, PhD Camb., MSc Reader, Farm and Food Science

Lane, J. G., BVetMed Lond., FRCVS Sr. Lectr., Veterinary Surgery

Long, Susan E., BVMS Glas., PhD Glas. Sr. Lectr., Animal Reproduction

Main, D. C. J., BVetMed Lond., PhD Brist. Sr. Lectr., Animal Welfare

Mendl, M. T., MA Camb., PhD Camb. Reader, Animal Behaviour and Welfare

Miller, Bevis G., BSc S'ton., PhD S'ton. Sr. Lectr., Animal Husbandry

Morris, J. A. Visiting Prof.

Morrison, William, BVMS Glas., PhD Glas., FRCPath, FRSEd Visiting Prof.

Murison, P. J., BVMS Glas. Sr. Lectr., Veterinary Anaesthesia

Newell, D. G.   Visiting Prof.

Nicol, C. J., BA Oxf., DPhil Oxf.   Prof., Animal Welfare

Owen, M. R., BSc Liv., BVSc Liv., PhD Liv.   Sr. Lectr., Small Animal Orthopaedics

Papasouliotis, K., DVM Salonika, PhD Brist.   Sr. Lectr., Veterinary Clinical Pathology

Pearson, G. R., BVMS Glas., PhD Belf., FRCPath   Prof., Veterinary Pathology

Preston, A., BA Oxf., DPhil Oxf.   Sr. Lectr.

Ricketts, S. W.   Visiting Prof.

Roe, J. M., BVSc Brist., PhD Brist.   Sr. Lectr., Veterinary Medicine

Shaw, S. E., BVSc Syd., MSc Kansas, FACVSc   Sr. Lectr., Dermatology/Applied Immunology

Stokes, C. R., BSc S'ton., PhD Lond.   Prof., Mucosal Immunology

Tasker, S., BSc BVSc PhD   Sr. Lectr., Small Animal Medicine

Taylor, Frank G. R., BVSc Liv., PhD Brist.   Sr. Lectr., Equine Medicine; Head*

Thorns, C. J.   Visiting Prof.

Tremaine, W. H., BVetMed Lond., MPhil Edin.   Sr. Lectr., Equine Surgery

Vazquez-Boland, J. A.   Prof., Veterinary Molecular Microbiology

Wood, Jeff D., BSc Newcastle(UK), PhD Cornell   Prof., Food Animal Science

Other Staff: 10 Lectrs.; 11 Sr. Res. Fellows; 4 Sr. Teaching Fellows; 14 Res. Fellows; 10 Teaching Fellows; 21 Res. Assocs.; 11 Teaching Assocs.

Research: animal behaviour and welfare; food science and food safety; veterinary infection and immunity; veterinary matrix biology

Physiology and Pharmacology

Tel: (0117) 331 1465 Fax: (0117) 331 2288
E-mail: phph-deptoffice@bristol.ac.uk

Apps, R., BSc Brist., PhD Brist.   Prof., Neuroscience

Bates, D. O., BSc Newcastle(UK), PhD Lond.   Prof. Res. Fellow

Brennan, P. A., MA Camb., PhD Camb.   Reader

Donaldson, L. F., BSc Edin., BDS Edin., PhD Edin.   Sr. Lectr.

Hancox, J. C., BSc Leeds, PhD St And.   Prof., Cardiac Electrophysiology

Harris, J. R., BSc Lond., PhD Lond.   Prof., Medical Sciences Education

Headley, P. M., BVSc Brist., BSc Brist., PhD Brist.   Prof., Physiology

Henderson, Graeme, BSc Glas., MA Aberd., PhD Aberd.   Prof.

James, A. F., BSc E.Anglia, DPhil York(UK)   Sr. Lectr.

Jane, D. E., BA Camb., PhD Salf.   Reader, Clinical Pharmacology

Kasparov, S., MD Moscow, PhD Moscow   Reader, Molecular Physiology

Kelly, Eamonn P., BSc Sheff., PhD Lond.   Reader, Molecular Pharmacology

Kennedy, H. J., BSc Brist., PhD Brist.   Sr. Lectr., Physiology

Kozlowski, Roland Z., BSc Bath, MPhil Camb., PhD Camb.   Reader

Langton, P. D., BSc Lanc., PhD Lanc.   Sr. Lectr.

Lawson, S. N., BSc Brist., PhD Brist.   Prof.

Lisney, S. J. W., JP, BSc Brist., BDS Brist., PhD Brist.   Prof.

Lumb, B. M., BSc Birm., PhD Birm.   Reader

Marrion, N. V., BSc Lond., PhD Lond.   Prof., Neuroscience

Martin, P. M., BSc Sus., PhD Lond.   Prof., Cell Biology

Meech, R. W., BSc S'ton., PhD S'ton., DSc S'ton.   Reader

Orchard, C. H., BSc Lond., PhD Lond.   Prof.; Head*

Paton, J. F. R., BSc Birm., PhD Lond.   Prof. Res. Fellow

Poole, A. W., VetMB Camb., MA Camb., PhD Camb.   Prof., Pharmacology and Cell Biology

Ranatunga, K. W., BSc S.Lanka, PhD Brist.   Reader

Roberts, P. J., PhD Brist., DSc Dund.   Prof., Neurochemical Pharmacology; Head*

Sheppard, D. N., BSc Brad., PhD Camb.   Sr. Lectr.

Sitsapesan, R. M. A., BSc Aberd., MSc Leeds, PhD Strath.   Reader

Usowicz, Maria M., BSc Lond., PhD Lond.   Sr. Lectr.

Woolley, D. M., BVSc Liv., PhD Edin.   Sr. Lectr.

Other Staff: 4 Lectrs.; 11 Res. Fellows; 1 Teaching Fellow; 27 Res. Assocs.; 2 Teaching Assocs.

Research: biochemistry; cardivascular pharmacology and physiology; cell signalling; neuropharmacology; synthetic organic chemistry

MEDICINE AND DENTISTRY

Tel: (0117) 331 1686 Fax: (0117) 331 1687
E-mail: sylvia.elliott@bristol.ac.uk

Clinical Science at North Bristol

Tel: (0117) 959 6236 Fax: (0117) 959 5342
E-mail: julia.bingham@bristol.ac.uk

Betmouni, S., BSc Lond., MB BS Lond., DPhil Oxf.   Consultant Sr. Lectr.

Bingley, Polly J., MB BS Lond., MD Lond., FRCP   Prof., Diabetes

Byron, M. A., BSc Leeds, MB ChB Leeds, MD Leeds, FRCP   Consultant Sr. Lectr.; Sr. Teaching Assoc.

Case, C. Patrick, MB ChB Brist., MSc Oxf., DPhil Oxf.   Consultant Sr. Lectr., Orthopaedic Surgery and Pathology

Gale, Edwin A. M., MB BChir Camb., FRCP   Prof., Diabetic Medicine; Head*

Hamilton-Shield, J. P., MB ChB Brist., MD Brist., FRCPCH   Reader, Diabetes and Metabolic Endocrinology

Hollander, A. P., BSc Bath, PhD Brist.   ARC Prof., Rheumatology and Tissue Engineering

Holly, Jeffrey M. P., BSc Lond., PhD Lond.   Prof.

Jackson, M., MB BS Lond., FRCSEd, FRCS   Consultant Sr. Lectr., Surgery

Learmonth, Ian D., MB ChB Stell., FRCS, FRCSEd, FCS(SA)   Prof., Orthopaedic Surgery

Love, S., MB BCh Witw., PhD Lond., FRCP, FRCPath   Prof., Neuropathology

Mathieson, Peter W., MB BS Lond., PhD Camb., FRCP, FMedSci   Prof., Renal Medicine

Millar, Ann B., MB ChB Liv., MD Liv., FRCP   Consultant Sr. Lectr., Respiratory Medicine

Saleem, Moin, MB BS Lond., PhD Lond., FRCP   Consultant Sr. Lectr.

Satchell, S. C., MB BS Lond., PhD Brist.   Consultant Sr. Lectr.

Scolding, Neil, PhD Wales, FRCP   Burden Prof., Clinical Neurosciences

Smith, R. M., BM BCh Oxf., MA Camb., PhD Camb.   Consultant Sr. Lectr.

Whitelaw, Andrew G. L., MB BChir Camb., MD Camb., FRCPCH   Prof., Neonatal Medicine

Other Staff: 4 Lectrs.; 2 Sr. Res. Fellows; 2 Res. Fellows; 10 Res. Assocs.

Research: clinical neurosciences; dementia; diabetes and metabolism; human renal cell biology; rheumatology

Clinical Science at South Bristol

incorporating the Bristol Heart Institute

Tel: (0117) 342 0484 Fax: (0117) 342 0178
E-mail: jackie.phelon@bristol.ac.uk

Angelini, G. D., MD Siena, MCh Wales, FRCSGlas   British Heart Foundation Prof., Cardiac Surgery; Dir.*

Armitage, W. J., BSc Lond., PhD CNAA   Prof. Res. Fellow; Dir., Tissue Banking

Ascione, R., MD Naples, ChM Brist., MSc Brist., FRCS   Reader, Cardiac Surgery Sciences

Blazeby, J. M., BSc Brist., MB ChB Brist., MD Brist., FRCS   Prof., Surgery

Cahill, David J., MB BCh BAO N.U.I., MD Brist., FRCOG   Consultant Sr. Lectr.

Caputo, M., MD Naples, ChM Brist.   Reader

Churchill, A. J., BSc Leeds, MB ChB Leeds, PhD Leeds   Consultant Sr. Lectr.

Dick, Andrew D., BSc Lond., MB BS Lond., MD Aberd., FRCS, FRCSEd, FRCPEd   Prof., Ophthalmology

Emanueli, C., PhD Catania   Sr. Lectr.

Finn, A. H. R., BM BCh Oxf., MA Camb., PhD Lond., FRCP, FRCPCH   Prof., Paediatrics

Fleming, Peter J., CBE, MB ChB Brist., PhD Brist., FRCPCan, FRCP, FRCPCH   Prof., Infant Health and Developmental Physiology

George, S. J., BSc Wales, PhD Wales   Reader

Glew, Susan S., BSc Manc., MB ChB Manc., MD Manc.   Consultant Sr. Lectr.

Gordon, Uma D., MB BS S.Venkat., MD   Consultant Sr. Lectr., Reproductive Medicine

Hamilton-Shield, J. P., MB ChB Brist., MD Brist., FRCPCH   Consultant Sr. Lectr., Child Health

Hanks, Geoffrey W. C., BSc Lond., MB BS Lond., DSc, FRCP, FRCPEd, FFPHM   Prof.

Henderson, Alexander J. W., MB ChB Manc., MD Manc., FRCP   Consultant Sr. Lectr.

Holmes, C. H., BSc E.Anglia, PhD Nott.   Sr. Lectr., Obstetrics and Gynaecology

Hunt, L. P., BSc Brist., MSc Manc., PhD Manc.   Sr. Lectr., Medical Statistics

Karsch, Karl R., MD Düsseldorf, FRCP, FACC, FAHA, FESC   Prof., Cardiology

Kearns, P. R., BSc Newcastle(UK), MB ChB Newcastle(UK), PhD Newcastle(UK)   Consultant Sr. Lectr., Paediatric Oncology

Kirwan, J. R., BSc Lond., MB BS Lond., MD Lond., FRCP   Prof., Rheumatic Diseases

Lopez Bernal, A., LMC Murcia, DPhil Oxf.   Prof., Human Reproductive Biology

Lovell, A. T., BSc Lond., MB BS Lond., FRCA   Consultant Sr. Lectr.

Madeddu, P. R.   Prof., Experimental Cardiology

Mayer, E. J., BM BCh Oxf., PhD Camb.   Consultant Sr. Lectr.

Newby, Andrew C., MA Camb., PhD Wales   British Heart Foundation Prof., Vascular Cell Biology

Oberhoff, M. A., MBCh Düsseldorf, MD Tübingen, PhD   Consultant Sr. Lectr.

Pickering, A. E., BSc Birm., MB ChB Birm., PhD Birm., FRCA   Consultant Sr. Lectr.

Pignatelli, Massimo, MD Bologna, PhD Lond.   Prof., Histopathology; Head, Clinical Science at South Bristol*

Probert, C. S. J., MB ChB Birm., MD Leic.   Prof., Gastroenterology

Schindler, M., MB BS NSW   Consultant Sr. Lectr., Paediatric Intensive Care Medicine

Soothill, Peter W., BSc Lond., MB BS Lond., MD Lond., FRCOG   Prof., Maternal and Fetal Medicine

Stevens, M. C. G., MB BS Lond., MD Lond., FRCP, FRCPCH, FRCR   Cancer and Leukaemia in Childhood Prof., Paediatric Oncology

Suleiman, M.-S., BSc Beirut, PhD Essex, DSc   Prof., Cardiac Cellular Physiology

Thoresen, Marianne, MD Oslo, PhD Oslo   Prof., Neonatal Neuroscience

Tobias, Jonathan H., BA Camb., MB BS Lond., MD Lond., PhD Lond., FRCP   Reader, Rheumatology

Winters, Zoe E., MB ChB Witw., DPhil Oxf., FRCS, FCS(SA)   Consultant Sr. Lectr.

Zacharowski, K. D., MD Mainz, PhD Lond.   Prof., Cardiovascular Anaesthesia and Critical Care

Other Staff: 4 Lectrs.; 13 Sr. Res. Fellows; 22 Res. Fellows; 31 Res. Assocs.

Research: child health; gastroenterology; obstetrics and gynaecology; ophthalmology; rheumatology

Community-Based Medicine

Tel: (0117) 331 3839 Fax: (0117) 331 3828
E-mail: sharon.ritchie@bristol.ac.uk

Amos, H. T., MB BS Lond., MA Oxf., MSc Manc.   Consultant Sr. Lectr., Forensic Psychiatry

Araya, R.   Prof., Psychiatry

Emond, A. M., MB BChir Camb., MA Camb., MD Camb., FRCP, FRCPCH   Prof., Community Child Health

Evans, J., MB ChB Birm., MD   Consultant Sr. Lectr.

Harrison, Glynn L., MB ChB Dund., MD Dund., FRCPsych   Norah Cooke Hurle Prof., Mental Health

Hay, A. D., MB ChB Sheff., MD   Consultant Sr. Lectr.

Lewis, G. H., MB BS Lond., MSc Lond., PhD Lond. Prof., Psychiatric Epidemiology

Lingford-Hughes, A. R., BM BCh Oxf., MA Oxf., PhD Camb.   Reader

Malizia, A. L., BA Open(UK), MD Brist., MB BS   Consultant Sr. Lectr.

Montgomery, A. A., BSc Glas., MSc Lond., MSc Lond., PhD St And.   Sr. Lectr.

Nutt, D. J., BA Camb., MB BChir Camb., DM Oxf., FRCP, FRCPsych, FMedSci   Prof., Psychopharmacology; Head*

Peters, T. J., BSc Exe., MSc Oxf., PhD Exe. Prof., Primary Care Health Services Research

Potokar, J. P., MB ChB Birm., MD   Consultant Sr. Lectr.

Salisbury, C. J., MB ChB Brist., MSc Lond., MD, FRCGP   Prof.

Sayal, K. S., BM S'ton., PhD Lond.   Sr. Clin. Lectr., Child and Adolescent Psychiatry

Sharp, Deborah J., BM BCh Oxf., MA Oxf., PhD Lond., FRCGP   Prof.

Other Staff: 11 Lectrs.; 1 Sr. Res. Fellow; 6 Res. Fellows; 1 Teaching Fellow; 23 Res. Assocs.

Research: addictions; epidemiological and health services; forensic mental health; primary health care; psychopharmacology

Medical Education

Mumford, D. B., MA Camb., MB ChB Brist., MPhil Edin., MD Brist.   Prof., Cross-Cultural Psychiatry; Head*

Other Staff: 1 Teaching Fellow; 2 Teaching Assocs.

Oral and Dental Science

Tel: (0117) 928 4307 Fax: (0117) 928 4150
  E-mail: geraldine.vines@bristol.ac.uk

Addy, M., BDS Wales, MSc Wales, PhD Wales, FDSRCS   Prof., Periodontology

Cowpe, Jonathan G., BDS Manc., PhD Dund., FDSRCSEd, FDSRCS   Prof., Oral Surgery; Head*

Crawford, P. J. M., BDS Sheff., MScD Wales, FDSRCSEd   Consultant Sr. Lectr., Child Dental Health

Dymock, D., BSc Dund., PhD Cran.   Sr. Lectr., Oral Microbiology

Eveson, J. W., BSc Brist., BDS Brist., PhD Glas., FDSRCPSGlas, FRCPath, FDSRCS   Prof., Head and Neck Pathology

Gray, G. B., BDS MSc DDS   Sr. Lectr., Restorative (Conservative) Dentistry

Hague, A., BSc York(UK), PhD Wales   Sr. Lectr., Cancer Biology

Hooper, S. M., BDS Lond., MSc Brist., FDSRCS Sr. Lectr.

Jagger, D. C., BDS Wales, MSc Brist., PhD Brist., FDSRCS   Prof., Restorative Dentistry

Jagger, R. G., MScD Wales, FDSRCS   Consultant Sr. Lectr.

Jenkinson, H. F., BSc Warw., PhD Nott.   Prof., Oral Microbiology

Moran, J. M., BDS Wales, MScD Wales, PhD Wales, FDSRCS   Consultant Sr. Lectr., Periodontology

O'Sullivan, D. J., BDS Brist., PhD Brist., FDSRCS Consultant Sr. Lectr.

Paterson, I. C., BSc Lond., PhD Bath   Sr. Lectr., Cancer Studies

Prime, S. S., BDS Birm., PhD Melb., FDSRCPSGlas, FRCPath   Prof., Experimental Pathology

Sandy, J. R., BDS Lond., MSc Lond., PhD Lond., FDSRCS, FDSRCSEd, FMedSci, FFDRCSI Prof., Orthodontics

Su, B., MSc Birm., PhD Birm.   Sr. Lectr., Dental Materials Science

Thomas, Steven J., BDS Lond., MB BCh Wales, PhD Qld., FDSRCS   Consultant Sr. Lectr.

West, N. X., BDS Wales, PhD Wales, FDSRCS Consultant Sr. Lectr., Restorative Dentistry

Other Staff: 6 Lectrs.; 1 Res. Fellow; 4 Teaching Fellows; 1 Res. Assoc.

Research: biomaterials and dental materials science; experimental pathology; oral bioscience

Social Medicine

Tel: (0117) 928 7279 Fax: (0117) 928 7325
  E-mail: socmed@bristol.ac.uk

Ben-Shlomo, Yoav, MB BS Lond., MSc Lond. Consultant Sr. Lectr.

Brookes, S. T., BSc Exe., MSc S'ton.   Sr. Lectr., Medical Statistics

Campbell, R. M., BSc CNAA, MSc Lond., PhD Lond.   Sr. Lectr.

Davey Smith, George, MB BChir Camb., MA Oxf., MSc Lond., MD Camb.   Prof., Clinical Epidemiology

Donovan, Jenny L., BA Liv., PhD Lond.   Prof.; Head*

Gunnell, David J., MB ChB Brist., PhD Brist. Prof., Epidemiology

Hickman, M., BSc Lanc., MSc Aberd., PhD Lond. Reader

Lambert, H. S., BA Oxf., MA Oxf., DPhil Oxf. Sr. Lectr., Medical Anthropology

Lawlor, D. A., MB ChB Brist., MSc Lond., MPH Leeds, PhD Brist.   Consultant Sr. Lectr.

Martin, R. M., BMedSci Nott., BM BS Nott., MSc Lond.   Reader, Clinical Epidemiology

Sterne, Jonathan A. C., BA Oxf., MSc Lond., PhD Lond.   Prof., Medical Statistics and Epidemiology

Tilling, K., BSc Warw., MSc Oxf., PhD Lond.   Sr. Lectr., Medical Statistics

Yao, Y., BA Nebraska, MA Nebraska, PhD Col. Reader, Genetic Epidemiology

Other Staff: 5 Lectrs.; 1 Sr. Res. Fellow; 5 Res. Fellows; 24 Res. Assocs.

Research: epidemiology; genetic epidemiology; health services

SPECIAL CENTRES, ETC

Advanced Computing Research Centre

Tel: (0117) 331 5044
  E-mail: caroline.gardiner@bristol.ac.uk

Stewart, I. B., BSc H-W, MSc Dund., PhD Dund. Dir.*

Research: high performance computing

Advanced Studies, Institute for

Tel: (0117) 928 9172 Fax: (0117) 928 9173
  E-mail: karine.taylor@bristol.ac.uk

Sykes, K. E., BSc Brist., PhD Brist.   Collier Prof., Public Engagement in Science and Engineering

White, Martin E., BA Newcastle(UK), MA Birm. Prof.†; Provost*

Other Staff: 4 Visiting Fellows

Research: interdisciplinary research; research in developing countries; water research opportunities

Bristol Colloid Centre

Tel: (0117) 929 8398 E-mail: bcc@bristol.ac.uk

Vincent, B., MSc Brist., PhD Brist., DSc Brist. Leverhulme Prof., Physical Chemistry; Dir.*

Other Staff: 1 Sr. Res. Fellow; 2 Res. Fellows; 1 Res. Assoc.; 2 Res. Fellows†

Research: colloid science

Bristol Glaciology Centre

Tel: (0117) 928 9954 Fax: (0117) 928 7878
  E-mail: geog-office@bristol.ac.uk

Payne, A. J., BSc Stir., PhD Edin.   Prof.; Head*

Research: cryospheric biogeochemical research; cryospheric evolution of Central Antarctic plate; polar observation and modelling

Colonial and Post-Colonial Societies, Centre for the Study of

Tel: (0117) 928 8117
  E-mail: kirsty.reid@bristol.ac.uk

Howe, S. J., BA Oxf., MA Oxf., DPhil Oxf. Prof., History and Cultures of Colonialism; Co-Dir.*

Reid, K. M., MA Edin., PhD Edin.   Sr. Lectr., History; Co-Dir.*

Research: colonialism and post-colonialism

Communications Research, Centre for

Tel: (0117) 954 5171 Fax: (0117) 954 5207
  E-mail: j.p.mcgeehan@bristol.ac.uk

McGeehan, J. P., CBE, BEng Liv., PhD Liv., FREng, FRSA   Prof., Communications Engineering; Dir.*

Other Staff: 10 Res. Assocs.

Research: electromagnetics; networks and protocols; optics; signal processing; wireless communications

Deaf Studies, Centre for

Tel: (0117) 954 6900 Fax: (0117) 954 6921
  E-mail: enquiries-cds@bristol.ac.uk

Kyle, J. G., MA Glas., MSc Stir., PhD Lond., FBPsS   Harry Crook Prof.

Ladd, N. P., BA Reading, MSc Reading, MA Lond., PhD Brist.   Sr. Lectr.

Sutton-Spence, R. L., BA Oxf., PhD Brist.   Sr. Lectr.

Other Staff: 1 Lectr.; 1 Teaching Fellow; 1 Sr. Lectr.†

Research: deaf community and culture; education, cognition and psychological wellbeing; sign language; sign language acquisition; technological applications

East Asian Studies, Centre for

Tel: (0117) 331 8007 Fax: (0117) 954 6604
  E-mail: ceas-admin@bristol.ac.uk

Mok, K. J., BA HK, PhD Lond.   Prof.; Dir.*

Research: East Asian society; housing and housing reforms in East Asia; school and university governance in East Asia

Ethics in Medicine, Centre for

Tel: (0117) 331 0720 Fax: (0117) 331 0732
  E-mail: anne.lavender@bristol.ac.uk

Huxtable, R., LLB Nott., MA Sheff., PhD Brist. Sr. Lectr.; Deputy Dir.

ter Meulen, R. H. J., MSc Nijmegen, PhD Nijmegen Prof.; Dir.*

Other Staff: 1 Lectr.; 1 Res. Fellow; 3 Res. Assocs.

Research: biotechnology ethics; ethics, regulations and European policy; young people and research ethics

Food Refrigeration and Process Engineering Research Centre

Tel: (0117) 928 9239 Fax: (0117) 928 9314
  E-mail: wendy.larder@bristol.ac.uk

James, S. J., BA Open(UK)   Dir.*

Other Staff: 1 Sr. Res. Fellow; 5 Res. Fellows; 1 Res. Fellow†

Research: food decontamination; food refrigeration; modelling of thermal processes; robotics and low-cost automation

Governance Research Centre

Tel: (0117) 331 6793 Fax: (0117) 331 7500
  E-mail: governance-research@bristol.ac.uk

Acharya, A., BA Utkal, MA J.Nehru U., PhD Murd. Prof., Global Governance; Dir.*

Research: European governance; gender and governance; international development and governance; security and governance

Hearing and Balance Studies, Centre for

Tel: (0117) 331 7503 Fax: (0117) 954 6809
  E-mail: office-chbs@bristol.ac.uk

Hoyle, M., BSc Hull   Head*

Other Staff: 4 Lectrs.†; 1 Res. Fellow†; 1 Sr. Teaching Fellow†

Research: balance; hearing; rehabilitation

Humanities and Arts, Bristol Institute for

Tel: (0117) 928 8892
  E-mail: sam.barlow@bristol.ac.uk

Unwin, T. A., MA Camb., MA Exe., PhD Exe. Prof.; Head*

Research: colonialism; mediaeval culture; performativity, place and space; reception; science, knowledge and reality

Integrative Neuroscience and Endocrinology, Henry Wellcome Laboratories for

Tel: (0117) 331 3161 Fax: (0117) 331 3162
E-mail: jill.locke-edmunds@bristol.ac.uk
Andrews, R. C., MB ChB PhD   Consultant Sr. Lectr.
Dawbarn, D., BSc Bath, PhD Brist.   Reader, Medicine (Care of the Elderly)
Dayan, C. M., MB BS Lond., MA Oxf., PhD Lond.   Head, Clin. Res.
Levy, A., BMedSci Nott., BM BS Nott., PhD Lond., FRCP   Prof., Medicine
Lightman, S. L., MB BChir Camb., MA Camb., PhD Camb., FRCP, FMedSci   Prof., Medicine; Dir.*
Linthorst, A. C. E., PhD Utrecht   Sr. Lectr.
McArdle, C. A., BSc CNAA, PhD CNAA   Prof., Medicine
Murphy, David, BSc Edin., PhD Lond.   Prof., Experimental Medicine
Norman, Michael R., BSc Lond., PhD Lond., FRCPath   Sr. Lectr., Medicine
Reul, J. M. H. M., PhD Utrecht   Reader
Uney, James B., BSc Sur., MSc Lond., PhD Lond.   Prof., Molecular Neuroscience
Wynick, David, BSc Lond., MB BS Lond., MD Lond., PhD Open(UK), FRCP   Prof., Molecular Medicine
Other Staff: 2 Lectrs.; 5 Sr. Res. Fellows; 7 Res. Fellows; 16 Res. Assocs.; 2 Res. Fellows†; 2 Res. Assocs.†; 1 Clin. Res. Fellow
Research: clinical endocrinology; neuroendocrinology; rheumatoid arthritis; signal transduction mechanisms

Interface Analysis Centre

Tel: (0117) 331 1171 Fax: (0117) 925 5646
E-mail: julie.gray@bristol.ac.uk
Allen, G. C., BSc S'ton., PhD Brist., DSc Brist., FRSChem   Prof., Materials Science; Dir.*
Other Staff: 3 Res. Fellows; 2 Res. Assocs.
Research: analysis of interfaces between dissimilar materials; development of equipment for interface analysis; relationship between interfaces and macroscopic properties

Language Centre

Tel: (0117) 331 0909 Fax: (0117) 331 0870
E-mail: language-centre@bristol.ac.uk
Collard, R., BA Sheff., MA Portsmouth   Sr. Lectr.
Satchell, Ray, BA CNAA, FRSA   Dir.*
Other Staff: 1 Sr. Teaching Fellow; 8 Teaching Fellows; 1 Teaching Assoc.

Learning and Research Technology, Institute for

Tel: (0117) 928 7193 Fax: (0117) 928 7112
E-mail: ilrt-reception@bristol.ac.uk
Hooper, T. A.   Inst. Manager; Asst. Dir.
Huxley, L., BA Wales, EdD Brist.   Res. Dir.; Dir.*
Other Staff: 1 Res. Fellow

Market and Public Organisation, Centre for

Tel: (0117) 331 0799 Fax: (0117) 331 0705
E-mail: cmpo-office@bristol.ac.uk
Burgess, S. M., MA Camb., DPhil Oxf.   Prof.; Dir.*
Gregg, P. A., BSc Kent, MSc Lond.   Prof.
Grout, P. A., BA(Econ) Newcastle(UK), MSc(Econ) Lond., PhD Essex   Prof., Political Economy
Propper, Carol, BSc Brist., MSc Oxf., DPhil York(UK)   Prof., Economics
Other Staff: 2 Sr. Res. Fellows; 2 Res. Assocs.

Research: competition, benchmarking and incentives; families, welfare and children; markets and regulations; neighbourhoods and peer groups; organisation and culture

Norah Fry Research Centre

Tel: (0117) 331 0987 Fax: (0117) 331 0978
Johnson, K., BA Melb., MA Melb., PhD Melb.   Dir.*
Ward, L. M., OBE, BSc Lond., PhD Brist.   Prof., Disability and Social Policy
Other Staff: 5 Sr. Res. Fellows; 2 Res. Fellows; 2 Res. Assocs.
Research: adults with intellectual disabilities; disabled children

Parents and Children, Avon Longitudinal Study of (ALSPAC)

Tel: (0117) 331 1711 Fax: (0117) 331 1704
E-mail: b.j.stowe@bristol.ac.uk
Davey Smith, George, MB BChir Camb., MA Oxf., MSc Lond., MD Camb.   Prof., Clinical Epidemiology; Dir.*
Golding, M. J., MA Oxf., PhD Lond., DSc Brist., FFPHM, FMedSci   Hon. Emer. Prof., Paediatric and Perinatal Epidemiology
Other Staff: 2 Res. Fellows; 5 Res. Assocs.; 1 Res. Statistician; 1 Sr. Res. Fellow†; 2 Res. Fellows†; 2 Res. Assocs.†; 1 Soc. Scientist†
Research: health and development of children

Reproductive Medicine, In-Vitro Centre for

Tel: (0117) 902 1100 Fax: (0117) 902 1101
E-mail: admin@repromed.co.uk
Gordon, Uma D., MB BS S.Venkat., MD   Dir.*

Safety Systems Research Centre

Tel: (0117) 928 7707 Fax: (0117) 928 7783
E-mail: j.may@bristol.ac.uk
May, J. H. R., BSc Brist., PhD Brist.   Dir.*
Other Staff: 1 Res. Fellow†
Research: hierarchical systems modelling for wicked systems; holistic systems analysis; human tolerant systems; software fault tolerance; uncertainty tolerant systems

CONTACT OFFICERS

Academic affairs. Academic Registrar: Robinson, Lynn, BSc Sheff.
(E-mail: l.robinson@bristol.ac.uk)
Accommodation. Accommodation Officer: Lawrence-Archer, Pru, BA Brist.
(E-mail: accom-office@bristol.ac.uk)
Admissions (first degree). Admissions Officer: Walker, Catherine D., BA Open(UK)
(E-mail: admissions@bristol.ac.uk)
Alumni. Director of Campaigns and Alumni Relations: Rawlinson, Tania J., BA Dartmouth, MLitt
(E-mail: development-alumni@bristol.ac.uk)
Careers. Director of Careers Advisory Service: Goodman, Jeffrey A., BA Lond.
(E-mail: careers-gen@bristol.ac.uk)
Computing services. Director, Information Systems: Phillips, Tim, BSocSc Birm., MSc Open(UK) (E-mail: cc-enquiries@bristol.ac.uk)
Development/fund-raising. Director of Campaigns and Alumni Relations: Rawlinson, Tania J., BA Dartmouth, MLitt
(E-mail: development-alumni@bristol.ac.uk)
Equal opportunities. Equality and Diversity Manager: Brunnock-Cook, Tracy, MBA
(E-mail: tracy.brunnock-cook@bristol.ac.uk)
Estates and buildings/works and services. Bursar: Phipps, Michael, BSc Manc.
(E-mail: mike.phipps@bristol.ac.uk)
Examinations. Examinations Officer: Gadd, Lynzie, LLB Nott.Trent
(E-mail: exams-office@bristol.ac.uk)
Finance. Finance Director: Crawford, Ian
(E-mail: ian.crawford@bristol.ac.uk)

General enquiries. Registrar: Pretty, Derek W. M., BSc S'ton., MBA Wash.
(E-mail: registrar@bristol.ac.uk)
Health services. Director, Students' Health Service: Butler, Anthony V. J., MB ChB Brist.
(E-mail: tony.butler@bristol.ac.uk)
International office. Head of International Office: Axel-Berg, Claire, MEd Brist.
(E-mail: axel-berg@bristol.ac.uk)
Library (chief librarian). Deputy Registrar and Director of Information Services: Allden, Alison, BA Brist., MSc Lond.
(E-mail: library-enquiries@bristol.ac.uk)
Marketing. Director of Communications and Marketing: Taylor, Barry, BA Sus., MA Exe.
(E-mail: barry.taylor@bristol.ac.uk)
Personnel/human resources. Personnel Services and Staff Development Director: Gregory, Guy, BA CNAA
(E-mail: guy.gregory@bristol.ac.uk)
Public relations. Assistant Director of Communications and Marketing Services: Cartwright, Jill, BSSc Belf., MBA Belf.
(E-mail: public-relations@bristol.ac.uk)
Publications. Publications Officer: Brown, Hilary, BA Lond.
(E-mail: public-relations@bristol.ac.uk)
Purchasing. Purchasing Manager: How, Mandy
(E-mail: mandy.how@bristol.ac.uk)
Quality assurance and accreditation. Director of Teaching Support Unit: Clarke, Gill, MSc City(UK) (E-mail: gill.clarke@bristol.ac.uk)
Research. Director of Research and Enterprise Development: Langley, David, BSc Lond., PhD Lond. (E-mail: red-office@bristol.ac.uk)
Safety. Director of Health and Safety: Adams, Peter, BEng Bath
(E-mail: bristol-safety@bristol.ac.uk)
Scholarships, awards, loans. Student Funding Manager: Fitzwalter, Jane, BA Westminster
(E-mail: student-funding@bristol.ac.uk)
Security. Security Services Manager: Woods, Jerry, BSc W.England, MA Lough.
(E-mail: security-office@bristol.ac.uk)
Sport and recreation. Director of Sport: Reeves, Robert A., MEd Brist.
(E-mail: bob.reeves@bristol.ac.uk)
Staff development and training. Head of Staff Development: England, Kim, FCIPD
(E-mail: kim.england@bristol.ac.uk)
Student union. General Manager (Student Union): Brackstone, Keith, LLB Brist.
(E-mail: info@ubu.org.uk)
Student welfare/counselling. Director, Student Counselling Service: Booth, Rosemary P. E., BA Lond.
(E-mail: r.booth@bristol.ac.uk)
Students from other countries. Senior International Adviser: Stueber, Ri'Anna, BA Brist., LLM Brist. (E-mail: os-as@bristol.ac.uk)

CAMPUS/COLLEGE HEADS

Bristol Baptist College, The Promenade, Clifton Down, Clifton, Bristol BS8 3NJ. (Tel: (0117) 946 7050; Fax: (0117) 946 7787; E-mail: admin@bristol-baptist.ac.uk; Principal: Finamore, Rev. Stephen, LLB MA DPhil

Trinity College, Stoke Hill, Bristol BS9 1JP. (Tel: (0117) 968 2803; Fax: (0117) 968 7470; E-mail: admissions@trinity-bris.ac.uk; Principal: Kovoor, Rev. Canon George, BA BD

Wesley College, Bristol, College Park Drive, Henbury Road, Bristol BS10 7QD. (Tel: (0117) 959 1200; Fax: (0117) 950 1277; E-mail: admin@wesley-college-bristol.ac.uk; Principal: Pye, Rev. Jonathan, BA Durh., MA Durh., PhD Leeds

[Information supplied by the institution as at 19 October 2007, and edited by the ACU]

BRUNEL UNIVERSITY

Founded 1966

Member of the Association of Commonwealth Universities

Postal Address: Uxbridge, Middlesex, England UB8 3PH
Telephone: (01895) 274000 **Fax:** (01895) 232806
URL: http://www.brunel.ac.uk

VICE-CHANCELLOR*—Jenks, Prof. Christopher, BSc Sur., MSc Lond., PhD Norwegian U.S.T., AcSS
VICE PRINCIPAL—Sarhadi, Prof. Mansoor, BSc Reading, MSc Sur., PhD Lond.
PRO-VICE-CHANCELLOR (EXTERNAL RELATIONS)—Thomas, Prof. Linda, BSc Wales, MEd Wales, PhD Lond.
PRO-VICE-CHANCELLOR (STUDENT EXPERIENCE)—Macredie, Prof. Robert, BSc Hull, PhD Hull
MANAGING DIRECTOR (RESOURCES AND OPERATIONS)—Thomas, Paul, CBE, BSc City(UK)
DIRECTOR OF BRUNEL INTERNATIONAL—Chang, Christopher, LLB
DIRECTOR OF FINANCE—Eastwood, Rob

GENERAL INFORMATION

History. Named after Isambard Kingdom Brunel, the university was established in 1966 as one of ten new universities created from colleges of advanced technology in the mid-1960s.

Admission to first degree courses (see also United Kingdom Introduction). Through Universities and Colleges Admissions Service (UCAS). General Certificate of Secondary Education (GCSE) in English, or equivalent, and 2 or 3 General Certificate of Education (GCE) A levels, or equivalent (such as Business and Technology Education Council (BTEC), International Baccalaureate or other recognised overseas qualifications). Mature students (21 years old or over) may offer alternative qualifications, and, where appropriate, relevant work experience.

First Degrees (see also United Kingdom Directory to Subjects of Study). BA, BEng, BSc, LLB.
Length of course. Full-time: BA, BEng, BSc, LLB: 3 years. Part-time: BA, BSc: 4–6 years. By distance learning: BSc: 4 years.

Higher Degrees (see also United Kingdom Directory to Subjects of Study).
Master's. LLM, MA, MBA, MEng, MPhil, MSc.
Admission. Applicants for admission to master's degrees should hold an appropriate first degree, or equivalent qualification.
Length of course. Full-time: LLM, MA, MBA, MEng, MPhil, MSc: 1 year. Part-time: LLM, MA, MBA, MEng, MSc: 2 years; MPhil: 3 years. By distance learning: MA, MBA, MSc: 5 years.
Doctoral. DBA, EdD, EngD, PhD.
Admission. Doctorates: good first degree or master's degree.
Length of course. Full-time: DBA, EdD, EngD, PhD: 3 years. Part-time: DBA, EdD, EngD, PhD: 4 years.

Language of Instruction. English. Pre-entry EFL courses available.

Libraries. Volumes: 430,000. Periodicals subscribed to: 12,000. Special collections: transport history; working class autobiographical archive; Murray (early children's books); British and Foreign School Society archive; Runnymede campus.

Academic Awards (2006). 2161 awards.

Academic Year (2008–2009). Three terms: 29 September–19 December; 12 January–3 April; 27 April–29 August.

Income (2005–2006). Total, £118,257,000.

Statistics. Staff (2005–2006): 2819 (1380 academic, 1439 non-academic). Students (2006–2007): full-time 11,499 (5876 men, 5623 women); part-time 1983 (1004 men, 979 women); international 2052; distance education/external 374; undergraduate 10,138 (5045 men, 5093 women); master's 2584 (1340 men, 1244 women); doctoral 760 (495 men, 265 women).

FACULTIES/SCHOOLS

Arts
Fax: (01895) 266059
E-mail: diane.woodhead@brunel.ac.uk
Head: Dixon, Prof. Steve, BA Manc., MA Middx.
School Manager: Woodhead, Diane

Brunel Business School
Tel: (01895) 265278 Fax: (01895) 269865
E-mail: joinbbs@brunel.ac.uk
Head: Irani, Prof. Zahir, BEng Salf., MPhil Salf., PhD Brun.
School Manager: Snowden, Dave

Brunel Law School
Tel: (01895) 266728 Fax: (01895) 269724
E-mail: tracey.alexis@brunel.ac.uk
Head: Olowofoyeku, Prof. Abimbola, LLB Lagos, LLM Lond., PhD Lond.
School Administrator: Alexis, Tracey

Engineering and Design
Tel: (01895) 265732 Fax: (01895) 203205
E-mail: paul.worthington@brunel.ac.uk
Head: Tassou, Prof. Savvas A., BSc CNAA, MBA Westminster, PhD Westminster
School Manager: Worthington, P.

Graduate School
Fax: (01895) 265931
E-mail: pat.holloway@brunel.ac.uk
Head: Rodgers, Prof. Geoff J., BSc Lond., PhD Manc.

Health Sciences and Social Care
Tel: (01895) 203338 Fax: (01895) 274348
E-mail: gelvinder.nothey@brunel.ac.uk
Head: De Souza, Prof. Lorraine, BSc Brist., MSc Brist., PhD Lond.
School Manager: Nothey, Gelvinder

Information Systems, Computing and Mathematics
Tel: (01895) 266031 Fax: (01895) 251686
E-mail: john.park@brunel.ac.uk
Head: Darby-Dowman, Prof. Kenneth, BSc Brad., MSc Brun., PhD Brun.
School Manager: Park, John

Social Sciences
Tel: (01895) 266561 Fax: (01895) 203105
E-mail: elizabeth.jones@brunel.ac.uk
Head: Nobus, Prof. Dany, BSc Ghent, MSc Ghent, MA Ghent, PhD Ghent
School Manager: Jones, Elizabeth

Sport and Education
Tel: (01895) 255490 Fax: (01895) 269769
E-mail: jac.aldous@brunel.ac.uk
Head: Capel, Prof. Susan, BEd Wales, MBA Open(UK), MSc Lough., DPhil Oregon
School Manager: Aldous, Jac

ACADEMIC UNITS

Anthropology
Tel: (01895) 265951 Fax: (01895) 269723
E-mail: veronica.johnson@brunel.ac.uk
Beatty, Andrew, BA York(UK), MSt Oxf., DPhil Oxf. Sr. Lectr.
Helman, Cecil, MB ChB Cape Town Prof.
Hirsch, Eric, BSc Missouri, MSc Lond., PhD Lond. Reader
Kuper, Adam, BA Witw., PhD Camb. Prof.
Other Staff: 5 Res. Lectrs.
Research: anthropology of education; child-focused anthropology; medical anthropology; psychological and psychiatric anthropology

Biosciences
Tel: (01895) 266301 Fax: (01895) 274348
E-mail: biosciences@brunel.ac.uk
Arlett, Colin, BSc Wales, PhD Birm. Reader; Prof.
Bridger, Joanna, BSc Lond., PhD Dund. Sr. Lectr.
Evans, Robert, BA Oxf., PhD Brist. Prof.
Kill, Ian R., BSc Portsmouth, DPhil Sus. Sr. Lectr.
Li, Su-Ling, MD Suzhou, PhD Karolinska Reader
Newbold, Robert, BSc Aston, PhD Lond., DSc Lond., FIBiol Prof.
Parris, Christopher N., BSc Nott., PhD Lond. Sr. Lectr.
Pook, Mark, BSc Leeds, PhD Manc. Sr. Lectr.
Rand-Weaver, Mariann, BSc Lond., PhD Lond. Sr. Lectr.; Dir.*
Slijepcevic, Predrag, MSc Sarajevo Sr. Lectr.
Other Staff: 9 Lectrs.; 2 Res. Fellows; 3 Postdoctoral Staff

Brunel Business School
Fax: (01895) 203175
E-mail: zahir.irani@brunel.ac.uk
Abdel-Kader, Magdy, BCom Cairo, MPhil Cairo, PhD W.England Sr. Lectr.
Aston, John, MBA Brun. Sr. Lectr.
Athreye, Suma, BA Delhi, MA J.Nehru U., DPhil Sus. Reader
Balmer, John Prof.
Blundel, Richard, BSc Lond., MBA Brad., PhD Birm. Sr. Lectr.
Bourlakis, Michael, BSc Athens, MBA Edin., PhD Edin. Sr. Lectr.
Cohen, Geraldine, PhD Brun. Sr. Lectr.
Cornelius, Nelarine, PhD Sr. Lectr.
Dickson, Keith, BE NZ, MSc Birm. Prof.
Eames, Michael, DPhil Sus. Prof.
Eldabi, Tillal Sr. Lectr.
Evans, Chris, BSc Sus., MSc Sus., PhD Lond. Sr. Lectr.
Fan, Ying, BSc Peking, MBA Peking, PhD Ulster Sr. Lectr.
Gallear, David, BEng Nott., MEng Nott., PhD Middx. Sr. Lectr.

Hackney, Ray   Prof.

Irani, Zahir, BEng Salf., MPhil Salf., PhD Brun. Head*

Koufopoulos, Dimitrios, BSc Athens, MBA Wales, PhD Wales   Sr. Lectr.

Melewar, T. C., BSc Indiana, MBA Cleveland, PhD Lough.   Prof.

Pitt, Martyn, PhD   Sr. Lectr.

Sharif, Amir, BEng City(UK), PhD Brun.   Prof.

Simpson, Ruth, BA Cardiff, MSc PhD   Sr. Lectr.

Smith, Stephen, BA Brun., MSc Brun., PhD Brun. Sr. Lectr.

Spence, Laura, BA Bath, MSc PhD   Sr. Lectr.

Tollington, Tony, PhD Lond.   Sr. Lectr.

Woods, Adrian G. W., BA Lanc., BA CNAA, MA Lanc., PhD Brun., FRSA   Foundation Prof.

Other Staff: 22 Lectrs.; 2 Res. Fellows; 1 Res. Officer; 6 Lectrs.†

Research: business computing; consumer and social marketing; enterprise, innovation, sustainability and ethics; international business and strategy; organisation and systems design

Design and Advanced Manufacturing and Enterprise Engineering

Tel: (01895) 265874 Fax: (01895) 269861

Balachandran, Wamedeva, BSc Ceyl., MSc Brad., PhD Brad.   Prof.

Cheng, Kai, BSc Harbin, MSc Harbin, PhD Liv.J.Moores   Prof.; Head of Design*

Giacomin, Joseph A., BME C.U.A., MME C.U.A., PhD Sheff.   Prof.; Head of Advanced Manufacturing and Enterprise Engin.*

Grieve, Robert J., BSc Salf., MSc Manc., PhD Manc.   Reader

Harrison, David J., BSc Exe., PhD Portsmouth Prof.

Holland, Raymond, MSc City(UK), PhD   Sr. Lectr.

Qin, Shengfeng, BEng Anhui, MSc S.W.China Jiaotong, PhD Wales   Sr. Lectr.

Rakowski, Richard, BSc Lond., MSc Lond., PhD Lond.   Sr. Lectr.

Rees, David, MA MSc PhD   Sr. Lectr.

Sivaloganathan, Sangarappillai, MSc Birm., PhD Lond.   Sr. Lectr.

Stanton, Neville A., BSc Hull, MPhil Aston, PhD Aston   Prof.

Turnock, Paul, BA Lond., MDes RCA   Sr. Lectr.

Wright, David K., BSc Lond., PhD Warw.   Prof.

Other Staff: 16 Lectrs.; 3 Teaching Assocs.; 1 Sr. Lectr.†; 17 Lectrs.†

Research: engineering systems and mechanics; environmentally sensitive design; manufacturing systems; measurement systems; polymedia design

Economics and Finance

Tel: (01895) 203169 Fax: (01895) 203384
E-mail: margaret.hunt@brunel.ac.uk

Bennett, John S., BA Camb., MA Camb., DPhil Sus.   Prof.

Bennett, Paul B., MA Trinity(Dub.), MA Calif. Sr. Lectr.

Bhaumik, Sumon, BSc Calc., MA S.Calif., PhD S.Calif.   Sr. Lectr.

Campos, Nanso, MSc S.Calif., PhD S.Calif.   Prof.

Caporale, Guglielmo, MSc Lond., PhD Lond. Prof.

Davis, Philip, MA Oxf., MPhil Oxf.   Prof.; Head*

Fidrmuc, Jan, Ing T.U.Bratislava, MA Missouri, PhD Tilburg   Sr. Lectr.

Georgellis, Yannis, BA Athens, MA Athens, PhD W.Virginia   Sr. Lectr.

Ghosh, Sugata, MSc Calc., MPhil Camb., PhD Camb.   Reader

Gregoriou, Andros, BSc Brun., MSc Brun., PhD Brun.   Sr. Lectr.

Iossa, Elisabeta, BA Naples, MSc York(UK), PhD Naples, FRS   Prof.

Karanasos, Menelaos, BSc Athens, MSc Lond., PhD Lond.   Prof.

Liu, Guy, BSc Shanghai, MPhil Liv., DPhil Oxf. Sr. Lectr.

Martin, Chris, BSc Brist., MSc Lond., PhD Durh. Prof.

Pal, Sarmistha, MSc Calc., MPhil Camb., PhD Lond.   Reader

Roy, Jaideep, BSc Calc., MA Delhi, PhD Madrid Sr. Lectr.

Skerrat, Len, BSc Lond.   Assoc. Prof.

Spagnolo, Fabio, Laurea Naples, PhD Lond. Reader

Spagnolo, Nicola, BSc Naples, PhD Lond.   Sr. Lectr.

Other Staff: 10 Lectrs.

Research: financial markets; health economics; labour economics; macroeconomics and econometrics; microeconomic theory and industrial organisation

Engineering, Electronic and Computing

Tel: (01895) 265140 Fax: (01895) 269695

Aggoun, Amar, Ing Algiers, PhD Nott.   Reader

Al-Raweshidy, Hamid, BEng Baghdad, MSc Baghdad, PhD Strath.   Prof.

Amira, Abbes, BEng Algiers, PhD Belf.   Sr. Lectr.

Cosmas, John P., BEng Liv., PhD Lond.   Prof.

Darwish, Mohamed, BSc Helwan, PhD Brun.   Sr. Lectr.

Hadjinicolaou, Marios, BSc Lond., MSc Brun., PhD Brun.   Sr. Lectr.

Hobson, Peter R., BSc Edin., PhD Lond.   Prof.

Holland, Andrew D., BSc Durh., PhD Leic. Prof.

Irving, Malcolm, PhD Sheff.   Prof.

Khan, Akram, BSc Lond., PhD   Reader

Owens, Thomas J., BSc Warw., MScTech Sheff., PhD Strath.   Sr. Lectr.

Powell, Roger, BEng Sheff., PhD Durh.   Sr. Lectr.

Sadka, Abdul-Hamid, BSc Beirut, MSc Middle East Tech., PhD Sur.   Prof.

Sheng-Uei Guan, Steven, BS Tsinghua, MEng Tamkang, PhD N.Carolina   Prof.

Stonham, T. John, BSc Kent, MSc Kent, PhD Kent Prof.

Vaseghi, Saeed, BSc Newcastle(UK), PhD Camb. Prof.

Other Staff: 18 Lectrs.

Research: bio-inspired intelligent systems; communication and signal processing; multimedia systems and parallel computing technology; networks and power systems control; sensors, instrumentation and radiation effects

Engineering, Mechanical

Tel: (01895) 267120 Fax: (01895) 256392

Brown, Chris, BSc Leeds   Reader

Esat, Ibrahim, BSc Lond., PhD Lond.   Prof.

Fan, Zhongyn, PhD Sur., BSc   Prof.

Jiang, Xi, BEng Nanjing Sci. & Tech., MSc Nanjing, PhD China U.S.T.   Sr. Lectr.

Kamineni, Srinath, MB BCh BSc, FRCSEd, FRCS Prof.

Karayiannis, Tassos, BSc City(UK), PhD W.Ont., FIMechE   Prof.

Kirby, Ray, BEng Hull, PhD Hull   Sr. Lectr.

Kolokotroni, Maria, MSc Lond., PhD Lond. Reader

Megaritis, Thanos, BSc ICL, PhD ICL   Sr. Lectr.

Mokhtarzadeh-Dehghan, Mohammad-Reza, BSc Arya-Mehr, MSc Lond., PhD Lond.   Sr. Lectr.

Silver, Jack, BSc Lond., PhD Lond., DSc Lond. Prof.

Song, Jim, BEng MSc PhD, FIMechE   Sr. Lectr.

Stolarski, Tadeusz A., MSc Gdansk, PhD Gdansk, DSc Cracow   Prof.

Tassou, Savvas A., BSc CNAA, MBA Westminster, PhD Westminster   Prof.; Head*

Withnall, Robert, BA Camb., MA Camb., MSc E.Anglia, PhD E.Anglia   Prof.

Wrobel, Luiz, MSc Brazil, PhD S'ton.   Prof.

Zhao, Hua, BEng Tianjin, PhD Leeds   Prof.

Other Staff: 17 Lectrs.; 1 Teaching Assoc.; 6 Lectrs.†

Research: biomedical engineering; energy and environmental engineering; fluid mechanics; mechanical systems

English

Tel: (01895) 266248 Fax: (01895) 269768
E-mail: suzanne.wills@brunel.ac.uk

Brayfield, Celia   Reader

Leahy, William, BA Herts., MA Essex, PhD Brun. Head*

Mondal, Anshuman, MA Edin., PhD Leeds   Sr. Lectr.

Moran, Maureen, BA Calg., MA Calg., PhD Lond. Prof.

Taunton, Nina, BA MA PhD   Sr. Lectr.

Tew, Philip, BA Leic., MPhil Leic., PhD Westminster   Prof.

Watkin, William, BA Manc., MA Sus., PhD Belf. Sr. Lectr.

Weldon, Fay, MA St And., PhD St And.   Prof.

Other Staff: 7 Lectrs.; 1 Sr. Tutor

Research: contemporary literature; creative writing; post-colonial literature; Renaissance studies; Victorian literature and culture

Film and Television Studies, Modern Drama and Music

Tel: (01895) 266248 Fax: (01895) 816224
E-mail: suzanne.wills@brunel.ac.uk

Barrett, Richard, BSc Lond.   Prof.

Birringer, Johannes, BA Trier, MA Trier, PhD Trier, PhD Yale   Prof.

Broadhurst, Susan, BA Murd., PhD Murd. Reader; Subject Head, Drama

Croft, John, PhD   Subject Head, Music

Dixon, Steve, BA Manc., MA Middx.   Prof.; Head*

Edwards, Barry, BA Sus., MA Essex   Reader

Fox, Christopher, BA Liv., BMus S'ton., DPhil York(UK)   Prof.

Freeman, John, BA Manc.Met., MA Lanc., PhD Brun.   Sr. Lectr.

Hunt, Leon, BEd CNAA, MA E.Anglia   Sr. Lectr.

King, Geoff, BA Roeh., MA Sus., DPhil Sus. Prof.; Subject Head, Film Studies

Krzywinska, Tanya, BA Reading, MA CNAA, PhD CNAA   Prof.

Niblock, Sarah, BA Coventry, MA Middx., PhD Middx.   Reader

Petley, Julian, BA Exe., MA Exe., PhD Exe.   Prof.

Wayne, Michael, BA N.Lond., MA Westminster, PhD Middx.   Sr. Lectr.

Wiegold, Peter, BMus Wales, MMus Wales, PhD Durh.   Prof.

Other Staff: 16 Lectrs.

Research: drama (aesthetic potentials of digitised technology for performance, interdisciplinary performance, live capture (sound, film) plus performance, solo performance and new performance writing, somatic practice and performance composition); film and television studies (cult media and transgression, dominant and alternative cinemas, spectacle, documentary and the real, the politics of representative and cultural identity, video games and digital media); music (composition, digital arts, electronic music and live electronic transformation, improvisation, meeting points between popular, world and 'classical' cultures)

Health and Social Care

Tel: (020) 8891 0121 Fax: (020) 8847 2030

Allotey, Pascale, BA Ghana, MMedSci W.Aust., PhD W.Aust.   Prof.

Anderson-Ford, David, LLB Liv.   Sr. Lectr.

Andrews, Brian, BSc Reading, MSc Sheff., PhD Strath.   Prof.

Aymer, Cathy, BSc Sus., MSc Aberd.   Sr. Lectr.

Banning, Maggi, BSc Lond.Guild., MSc Lond., EdD Brun.   Sr. Lectr.

Barrett, Geraldine, BA Lond., MSc Lond., PhD Lond.   Sr. Lectr.

Beresford, Peter, OBE, BA Oxf., PhD Middx. Prof.

Craik, Christine J., MPhil R.Gordon   Sr. Lectr.

De Souza, Lorraine, BSc Brist., MSc Brist., PhD Lond.   Prof.; Head*

Farrow, Alexandra, BSc Lond., MSc Wales, PhD Brist.   Sr. Lectr.

Gilhooly, Mary L. M., BS Oregon, MPhil Glas., PhD Aberd.   Prof.

Harwin, Judith E., BA Oxf.   Prof.

Madge, Nicola, BA Sus., MSc Lond., PhD Lond. Reader

Marsland, David, BA Camb., MA Camb., PhD Brun.   Prof.
McDonald, Marilynn, BA Ohio, MSW Maryland, PhD Calif.   Reader
Naylor, Sandra, MEd Brun.   Sr. Lectr.
Nowicky, Alexander, BA Ill., PhD Ohio   Sr. Lectr.
Parkin, Paul, BSc Sur., MSc Lond.   Sr. Lectr.
Peacock, Janet, BSc Reading, MSc Lond., PhD Lond.   Prof.
Reidpath, Daniel, BA Swinburne I.T., PhD W.Aust.   Prof.
Reynolds, Frances, BSc Nott., PhD Lond.   Sr. Lectr.
Scriven, Angela, BA Open(UK), MEd Bath   Sr. Lectr.
Wilson, Lesley, BSc Newcastle(UK)   Sr. Lectr.
Other Staff: 70 Lectrs.; 19 Lectrs.†
Research: community health studies; health promotion; healthcare evaluation; healthcare policy; nursing research

Information Systems and Computing

Tel: (01895) 203374 Fax: (01895) 251686
Angelides, Marios C., BSc Lond., PhD Lond.   Prof.
Avison, David, BA Leic., MSc N.Lond., PhD Aston   Prof.
Chen, Sherry, MLS Maryland, PhD Sheff., BA   Reader
Clarke, Malcolm, BSc Lond., PhD Lond.   Sr. Lectr.
Counsell, Steve, BSc Brighton, MSc City(UK), PhD Lond.   Sr. Lectr.
Elliman, Anthony D., BTech Brun., PhD   Sr. Lectr.
Fitzgerald, Guy, BA Essex, MSc Lond.   Prof.
Ghinea, George, BSc Witw., MSc Witw., PhD Reading   Reader
Hall, Tracy, BA Tees., MSc Tees., PhD City(UK)   Reader
Hierons, Robert, BA Camb., MA Camb., PhD Brun.   Prof.
Hone, Kate, BA Oxf., MS Birm., PhD Birm.   Sr. Lectr.
Kuljis, Jasna, MS Pitt., PhD Lond.   Prof.
Liu, Xiaohui, BEng Hohai, PhD H-W   Prof.
Lycett, Mark, BSc Oxf.Brookes, MSc Brun., PhD Brun.   Reader
Macredie, Robert, BSc Hull, PhD Hull   Prof.; Head*
McGrath, Kathy, BSc Kent, MSc Lond., PhD Lond.   Sr. Lectr.
Perry, Mark, BA Wales, MSc Wales, PhD Brun.   Sr. Lectr.
Shepperd, Martin, BSc Exe., MSc Aston, PhD   Prof.
Stergioulas, Lampros, MSc Liv., PhD Liv.   Sr. Lectr.
Taylor, Simon, BSc Sheff.Hallam, MSc Sheff.Hallam, PhD Leeds Met.   Sr. Lectr.
Wang, Zidong, BSc Suzhou, MSc E.China Inst.Technol., PhD Nanjing I.T.   Prof.
Williams, David S., BSc Lond., MSc Lond.   Sr. Lectr.
Yongmin, Li, BSc Tsinghua, MSc Tsinghua, PhD Lond.   Sr. Lectr.
Young, Terry, BSc Birm., PhD Birm.   Prof.
Other Staff: 23 Lectrs.; 8 Res. Fellows
Research: applied simulation modelling; information systems development; modelling interfaces; neural and evolutionary systems; strategic information systems

Law

Tel: (01895) 266229 Fax: (01895) 810476
E-mail: adrienne.obrien@brunel.ac.uk
Abass, Ademola, LLB Lagos, LLM Camb., PhD Nott.
Beresford-Hartwell, Geoffrey   Assoc. Prof.
Chigara, Ben, BA Keele, LLM Hull, PhD Nott.   Prof.
Corbett, Claire, BSc Lond., MPhil Camb., PhD Lond.   Sr. Lectr.

Easton, Susan, BSc Wales, MA Lond., PhD S'ton.   Reader
Jaffey, Peter, MA Camb., LLM Lond.   Prof.
Kaganas, Felicity, BA Lond., LLB Lond., LLM Lond.   Sr. Lectr.
Kaikobad, Kaiyan H., BA Punjab, LLB Punjab, LLM Lond., PhD Lond.   Prof.
Mushkat, Roda, LLM Well., LLD S.Af., LLB   Prof.
Olins, Andrew   Assoc. Prof.
Olowofoyeku, Abimbola, LLB Lagos, LLM Lond., PhD Lond.   Prof.; Head*
Piper, Christine, BA Brist., MA Brun., PhD Brun.   Reader
Polden, Patrick, BA Reading, PhD Reading   Prof.
Rehman, Javaid, BA Punjab, LLB Reading, LLM Hull, PhD Hull   Prof.
Weston, Robert   Assoc. Prof.
Other Staff: 14 Lectrs.; 4 Lectrs.†
Research: international and public law

Mathematical Sciences

Tel: (01895) 265733 Fax: (01895) 269732
E-mail: kay.lawrence@brunel.ac.uk
Akemann, Gernot, PhD Hanover   Prof.
Beasley, John, BA Camb., MSc ICL, PhD ICL, DSc Lond.   Prof.
Darby-Dowman, Kenneth, BSc Brad., MSc Brun., PhD Brun.   Prof.
Date, Paresh, BE Pune, MTech Mumbai, PhD Camb.   Sr. Lectr.
Furter, Jacques E., PhD Lausanne   Sr. Lectr.
Greenhow, Martin J., BSc Exe., PhD Exe., DrTechn Trondheim   Sr. Lectr.
Heuer, Norbert, DrRerNat Hanover   Prof.
Kaplunov, Julius, MA Moscow, PhD Moscow, DSc Moscow, FIMA   Prof.; Head*
Krasikov, Ilia, MSc Moscow, PhD Tel-Aviv   Sr. Lectr.
Lawrie, Jane B., BSc Leeds, PhD Lond.   Sr. Lectr.
Lucas, Cormac, BSc Brun., PhD Brun.   Sr. Lectr.
Maischak, Matthias, DerRerNat Hanover   Sr. Lectr.
Mitra, Gautam, BEE Jad., MSc Lond., PhD Lond.   Prof.
Mladenovic, Nenad, BSc Belgrade, PhD Belgrade   Reader
Rawlins, Anthony D., BSc Aston, MSc Sur., PhD Sur.   Reader
Rodgers, Geoff J., BSc Lond., PhD Manc.   Prof.
Shaw, Simon, BEng Portsmouth, MSc ICL, PhD Brun.   Sr. Lectr.
Whiteman, John R., BSc St And., PhD Lond., FIMA   Prof.
Winter, Matthias, PhD Stuttgart   Sr. Lectr.
Yu, Keming, MSc E.China Normal, PhD Open(UK), BSc   Reader
Other Staff: 10 Lectrs.; 7 Res. Staff; 4 Lectrs.†
Research: applied mathematics; computational optimisation and modelling; mathematical physics; numerical analysis and computation

Politics and History

Tel: (01895) 812595
Dale, Gareth, BA Manc., PhD Manc.   Sr. Lectr.
Davies, Philip, PhD   Sr. Lectr.
Fisher, Justin T., BA Lond.Guild., PhD Brun.   Prof.; Head*
Folly, Martin, BA Camb., MA Camb., PhD Lond.   Sr. Lectr.
Glees, P. Anthony, MA Oxf., BPhil Oxf., MPhil Oxf., DPhil Oxf.   Prof.
Hughes, Matthew, BA Lond., MSc(Econ) Lond., PhD Lond.   Sr. Lectr.
Kleinberg, Jay, BA Pitt., MA Pitt., PhD Pitt.   Prof.
MacMillan, John, BA Keele, DPhil Oxf.   Sr. Lectr.
Morgan, Kenneth, BA Leic., DPhil Oxf.   Prof.
Neocleous, Mark, BSc City(UK), MSc Lond., PhD Middx.   Sr. Lectr.
Spencer, Tom   Hon. Prof.
Thatcher, Ian, BA Tees., MSc Tees., MLitt Glas., PhD Glas.   Sr. Lectr.

Warleigh-Lack, Alex, BA Brist., PhD Nott.   Prof.
Other Staff: 7 Lectrs.; 2 Res. Fellows
Research: democratic evaluation; government; intelligence and security; international relations; war and conflict

Psychology

Tel: (01895) 265951 Fax: (01895) 269723
E-mail: veronica.johnson@brunel.ac.uk
Bunce, David, BA Kent, PhD Sheff.   Prof.
Cheeta, Survjit, BSc Lond.Met., PhD Wales   Sr. Lectr.
Gaines, Stanley, BSc Texas, PhD Texas   Sr. Lectr.
Gobet, Fernand, MSc Frib., PhD Frib.   Prof.
Goodwin, Robin, BSc Kent, PhD Kent   Prof.
Nobus, Dany, BSc Ghent, MSc Ghent, MA Ghent, PhD Ghent   Prof.
Wright, Michael, BSc Camb., PhD Camb.   Prof.
Wydell, Taeko, BSc Lond.   Prof.
Other Staff: 15 Lectrs.; 4 Lectrs.†; 1 Temp. Lectr.
Research: cognition and neuro-imaging; expertise; health and illness; infant behaviour

Sociology/Communications

Tel: (01895) 265951 Fax: (01895) 269723
E-mail: veronica.johnson@brunel.ac.uk
Gane, Nicholas, BA Warw., MA Warw., PhD Lond.   Sr. Lectr.
Hutchby, Ian, BA Middx., DPhil York(UK)   Prof.
Lunt, Peter, BSc Lond., DPhil Oxf.   Prof.
Robinson, Ian C., MA Nott.   Prof.
Seale, Clive, BEd S'ton., MSc Lond., PhD CNAA   Res. Prof.
Tulloch, John, BA Camb., MA Camb., DPhil Sus.   Prof.
Wilkin, Peter, BSc S'ton., PhD S'ton.   Reader
Other Staff: 4 Lectrs.; 1 Res. Lectr.; 2 Lectrs.†
Research: media globalisation and risk

Sport Sciences and Education

Tel: (01895) 266494 Fax: (01895) 269769
E-mail: sse.ugcourses@brunel.ac.uk
Alldred, Pam, PhD E.Lond.   Sr. Lectr.
Ansell, Nicola   Sr. Lectr.
Armstrong, Gary, PhD Lond.   Reader
Barlex, David, BSc Leic., PhD Leic.   Sr. Lectr.
Blazevich, Anthony, PhD S.Cross   Reader
Brackenridge, Celia, PhD Sheff.Hallam   Prof.
Bradford, Simon, MPhil Brun., PhD Brun.   Sr. Lectr.
Breckon, Peter, MEd Brun.   Sr. Lectr.
Buckingham, Susan, BA CNAA, MSc Lond.   Sr. Lectr.
Campbell, Ian, PhD Lough.   Prof.
Capel, Susan, BEd Wales, MBA Open(UK), MSc Lough., DPhil Oregon   Prof.; Head*
Evans, Roy, BSc Wales, MA Wales, PhD Wales   Prof.
Fisher, Robert, BA Lond., PhD Brun.   Prof.
Gervis, Misia, MSc Flor.   Sr. Lectr.
Girginov, Vassil, PhD Lough.   Reader
Godfrey, Richard, PhD Cran.   Sr. Lectr.
Gonzalez-Alonzo, Jose, PhD Texas   Prof.
Green, Andrew, EdD Brun.   Sr. Lectr.
Jones, Deborah, EdD Brun.   Sr. Lectr.
Karageorghis, Costas, PhD Brun.   Reader
Korff, Thomas, PhD Texas   Sr. Lectr.
Koshy, Valsa, BSc Kerala, MA Keele, MPhil Lond., PhD Lond.   Reader
Linthorne, Nick, PhD W.Aust.   Sr. Lectr.
McConnell, Alison, PhD Lond.   Prof.
Murray, Jean, PhD Lond.   Sr. Lectr.
Romer, Lee, PhD Birm.   Sr. Lectr.
Sharp, Norman, PhD Glas.   Emer. Prof.
Shave, Rob, PhD Wolv.   Reader
Smith, Fiona, BA Reading, PhD Reading   Sr. Lectr.
Watts, Mike, PhD Sur.   Prof.
Other Staff: 28 Lectrs.; 1 Res. Fellow†
Research: education (gifted and talented, pedagogies for inclusive practice, public professionals and their communities, youth work studies); sport science (biomechanical analysis, exercise physiology, physical education/youth sport, sport philosophy, sport psychology, sport sociology)

SPECIAL CENTRES, ETC

Advanced Powertrain and Fuels Research, Centre for

Tel: (01895) 266698
    E-mail: hua.zhao@brunel.ac.uk
Jiang, Xi, BEng Nanjing Sci. & Tech., MSc Nanjing, PhD China U.S.T.   Sr. Lectr.
Ma, T.   Assoc. Prof.
Megaritis, Thanos, BSc ICL, PhD ICL   Sr. Lectr.
Zhao, Hua, BEng Tianjin, PhD Leeds   Prof.; Dir.*
Other Staff: 3 Lectrs.; 3 Res. Fellows
Research: advanced automotive powertrain; alternative and bio fuels (impact on environment)

Advanced Solidification Technology, Brunel Centre for (BCAST)

Tel: (01895) 816391 Fax: (01895) 816393
    E-mail: bcast@brunel.ac.uk
Evans, Roy   Assoc. Prof.
Granasy, Laszlo, PhD Bud.   Prof.
Hunt, John, FRS   Assoc. Prof.
Ralph, Brian, FRS   Emer. Prof.
Scamans, Geoff, BSc ICL, PhD ICL   Prof.
Zhongyun, Fan, BSc Beijing, MSc Beijing, PhD Sur.   Prof.; Dir.*
Other Staff: 11 Res. Fellows
Research: rheo-casting; rheo-diecasting; rheo-extrusion; rheo-mixing; rheo-moulding

American, Trans-Atlantic and Caribbean History, Centre for

Tel: (01895) 267238 Fax: (01895) 269775
    E-mail: tony.tollington@brunel.ac.uk
Tollington, Tony, PhD Lond.   Dir.*
Research: intangible assets

Analysis of Risk and Optimisation Modelling Application, Centre for the (CARISMA)

Tel: (01895) 265187 Fax: (01895) 269732
    E-mail: ann.wilkes@brunel.ac.uk
Mitra, Gautam, BEE Jad., MSc Lond., PhD Lond.   Prof.; Dir.*
Other Staff: 6 Staff Members; 8 Res. Leaders; 3 Res. Assocs.
Research: modelling and solution algorithms of linear programming and discrete optimisation problems; models and solution methods for optimisation under uncertainty; risk measures and optimum risk decisions; robust estimation, systems identification and semi definite programming; time series and stochastic volatility models

Bio-Engineering, Brunel Institute for

Tel: (01895) 271206 Fax: (01895) 274608
    E-mail: bioengineering@brunel.ac.uk
Sutherland, Ian, PhD Brist.   Prof.; Dir.*
Other Staff: 1 Prof. Assoc.; 2 Res. Fellows; 3 Academic Staff; 7 Staff Members
Research: bioengineering; medical engineering; rehabilitation; space science and engineering

Brunel Able Children's Centre

Tel: (01895) 267152 Fax: (01895) 269805
    E-mail: catherina.emery@brunel.ac.uk
Casey, Ron   Co-Dir.*
Koshy, Valsa, BSc Kerala, MA Keele, MPhil Lond., PhD Lond.   Co-Dir.*
Research: educational provision for gifted and talented children

Brunel Information Technology (BITLab)

Tel: (01895) 265541 Fax: (01895) 203357
    E-mail: bitlab@brunel.ac.uk
Stanton, Neville A., BSc Hull, MPhil Aston, PhD Aston   Prof.; Dir.*

Brunel Macroeconomics Research Centre

Tel: (01895) 266644
    E-mail: christopher.martin@brunel.ac.uk
Davis, Philip, MA Oxf., MPhil Oxf.   Prof.
Ghosh, Sugata, MSc Calc., MPhil Camb., PhD Camb.   Reader
Gregoriou, Andros, BSc Brun., MSc Brun., PhD Brun.   Sr. Lectr.
Karanasos, Menelaos, BSc Athens, MSc Lond., PhD Lond.   Prof.
Martin, Chris, BSc Brist., MSc Lond., PhD Durh.   Prof.; Dir.*
Yannis, Georgellis, BA Athens, MA Athens, PhD W.Virginia   Sr. Lectr.
Research: factors underlying economy growth rate and differences in growth rates between countries (analysis of productivity, impact of demographic structures); monetary policy; unemployment and the labour market

Brunel University Random Systems Research Centre (BURST)

Tel: (01895) 265733 Fax: (01895) 269732
    E-mail: kay.lawrence@brunel.ac.uk
Rodgers, Geoff J., BSc Lond., PhD Manc.   Prof.; Dir.*
Other Staff: 10 Staff Members

Cancer Genetics and Pharmacogenomics, Brunel Institute of

Tel: (01895) 266290 Fax: (01895) 274348
    E-mail: robert.newbold@brunel.ac.uk
Newbold, Robert, BSc Aston, PhD Lond., DSc Lond., FIBiol   Prof.; Dir.*
Research: genetic mechanisms involving ultraviolet light in the development of cutaneous malignant melanoma; identification and isolation of susceptability genes involved in radiation-induced cancer in humans; the role of telomerase in human cancer development and evaluation of its potential as a therapeutic target

Cell-Chromosome Biology Group

Fax: (01895) 274348
    E-mail: ian.kill@brunel.ac.uk
Kill, Ian R., BSc Portsmouth, DPhil Sus.   Dir.*
Other Staff: 3 Academic Staff
Research: ageing; biomaterials; nuclear biology

Child-Focused Anthropological Research, Centre for (C-FAR)

Tel: (01895) 265956 Fax: (01895) 269724
    E-mail: admin@c-far.co.uk
Toren, Christina, BSc Lond., MPhil Lond., PhD Lond.   Head*
Other Staff: 1 Fellow; 1 Postdoctoral Fellow; 2 Res. Staff

Citizen Participation, Centre for

Tel: (01818) 918308 Fax: (01818) 918266
    E-mail: hilary.everitt@brunel.ac.uk
Beresford, Peter, OBE, BA Oxf., PhD Middx.   Prof.; Dir.*
Research: community involvement and regeneration; political participation and representation; social exclusion; the democratisation of public policy, agencies and services

Cognition and Neuroimaging, Centre for

Tel: (01895) 265957 Fax: (01895) 269724
    E-mail: michael.wright@brunel.ac.uk
Wright, Michael, BSc Camb., PhD Camb.   Prof.; Co-Dir.*
Wydell, Taeko, BSc Lond.   Prof.; Co-Dir.*
Other Staff: 13 Academic Staff
Research: consciousness; event-related potentials (ERP); functional magnetic resonance imaging (fMRI); perceptual skills in sport; visual attention, blindness, emotion and facial expressions

Computational Mathematics, Brunel Institute of (BICOM)

Tel: (01895) 265745 Fax: (01895) 269732
    E-mail: maths@brunel.ac.uk
Whiteman, John R., BSc St And., PhD Lond., FIMA   Dir.*
Research: mathematical theory, application and computational implementation of the finite element method

Contemporary Music Practice, Centre for

Tel: (01895) 266583 Fax: (01895) 269768
    E-mail: peter.wiegold@brunel.ac.uk
Wiegold, Peter, BMus Wales, MMus Wales, PhD Durh.   Dir.*
Other Staff: 9 Lectrs.
Research: composition; musicology; performance; philosophy of music

Contemporary Writing, Brunel Centre for

E-mail: philip.tew@brunel.ac.uk
Brayfield, Celia   Reader
Gaston, Sean, PhD Melb.   Sr. Lectr.
Mondal, Anshuman, MA Edin., PhD Leeds   Deputy Dir.; Sr. Lectr., D
Morrison, Jago, PhD Nott.   Sr. Lectr.
Tew, Philip, BA Leic., MPhil Leic., PhD Westminster   Prof.; Dir.*
Watkin, William, BA Manc., MA Sus., PhD Belf.   Reader
Weldon, Fay, MA St And., PhD St And.   Prof.
Other Staff: 7 Lectrs.; 2 Hon. Res. Fellows
Research: contemporary prose; creative writing and practice-based research; poetry and poetics; postcolonial literatures and theory

Electronic Imaging, Centre for

Tel: (01895) 268000 Fax: (01895) 269773
    E-mail: andrew.holland@brunel.ac.uk
Holland, Andrew D., BSc Durh., PhD Leic.   Prof.; Dir.*
Other Staff: 3 Staff Members
Research: imaging for space and terrestrial applications; imaging sensor development instrumentation

Emotion Work, Centre for Research into (CREW)

Tel: (01895) 265298 Fax: (01895) 203191
    E-mail: nelarine.cornelius@brunel.ac.uk
8 Academic Staff

Enterprise, Sustainability and Riches, Brunel Research into (BRESE)

Fax: (01895) 203191
    E-mail: alice.lam@brunel.ac.uk
Lam, Alice, PhD Lond.   Prof.; Dir.*
Other Staff: 2 Assoc. Dirs.; 3 Academic Staff; 1 Res. Fellow
Research: enterprise, ethics and accountability; innovation, risk and environmental sustainability; knowledge, innovation and organisational change

Environment, Institute for the

Tel: (01895) 266104 Fax: (01895) 269765
    E-mail: ife@brunel.ac.uk
Kershaw, Stephen, BSc Manc., PhD Wales, FGS   Sr. Lectr.
Leroy, Suzanne, DSc Louvain   Prof.
Scrimshaw, Mark, BSc PhD   Sr. Lectr.
Skelly, Chris, BA W.Ont., MSc W.Ont., PhD Macq., DPH Otago   Reader
Sumpter, John, BA Wales, PhD Wales, DSc Wales   Prof.; Dir.*
Other Staff: 5 Academic Staff; 6 Res. Fellows; 2 Hon. Lectrs.
Research: clean process technology; ecosystems and disease environments; ecotoxicology; environmental change/climate change/ geological and hydrological hazards; waste and wastewater treatment

Epidemiology and Health Services, Centre for (CEHSR)

Tel: (01895) 268818
E-mail: janet.peacock@brunel.ac.uk
Barrett, Geraldine, BA Lond., MSc Lond., PhD Lond.   Sr. Lectr.
Peacock, Janet, BSc Reading, MSc Lond., PhD Lond. Prof.
Other Staff: 6 Academic Staff; 6 Res. Fellows
Research: maternal and child health; occupational and environmental health; respiratory health methodology

Health Economics Research Group (HERG)

Tel: (01895) 203331 Fax: (01895) 203330
E-mail: nicky.dunne@brunel.ac.uk
Buxton, Martin, BA Leic.   Prof.; Dir.*
Other Staff: 2 Sr. Res. Fellows; 3 Res. Assocs.; 8 Res. Fellows
Research: assessment of the 'payback' on health research; development of economic evaluation methods; economic evaluation of health care technologies

Human Centred Design Institute (HCDI)

Tel: (01895) 265340 Fax: (01895) 269763
E-mail: linda.edgecock@brunel.ac.uk
Giacomin, Joseph A., BME C.U.A., MME C.U.A., PhD Sheff.   Prof.; Co-Dir.**
Stanton, Neville A., BSc Hull, MPhil Aston, PhD Aston   Prof.; Co-Dir.**
Turnock, Paul, BA Lond., MDes RCA   Sr. Lectr.
Other Staff: 5 Lectrs.
Research: augmented cognition systems; perception enhancement systems

Information and Knowledge Management, Centre for (CIKM)

Tel: (01895) 266002 Fax: (01895) 251686
E-mail: robert.hierons@brunel.ac.uk
Counsell, Steve, BSc Brighton, MSc City(UK), PhD Lond.   Sr. Lectr.
Hall, Tracy, BA Tees., MSc Tees., PhD City(UK)   Reader
Hierons, Robert, BA Camb., MA Camb., PhD Brun.   Prof.; Dir.*
Liu, Xiaohui, BEng Hohai, PhD H-W   Prof.
Shepherd, Martin, BA Exe., MSC Aston, PhD Open(UK)
Stergioulas, Lampros, MSc Liv., PhD Liv.   Reader
Taylor, Simon, BSc Sheff.Hallam, MSc Sheff.Hallam, PhD Leeds Met.   Sr. Lectr.
Wang, Zidong, BSc Suzhou, MSc E.China Inst.Technol., PhD Nanjing I.T.   Prof.
Other Staff: 6 Lectrs.; 6 Res. Fellows
Research: evolutionary algorithms; image analysis and signal processing; modelling temporal glaucomatous visual field data; multivariate time series; robotics navigation

Intelligence and Security Studies, Brunel Centre for (BCISS)

E-mail: katie.bridge@brunel.ac.uk
Glees, P. Anthony, MA Oxf., BPhil Oxf., MPhil Oxf., DPhil Oxf.   Prof.; Dir.*
Other Staff: 2 Lectrs.; 2 Res. Fellows
Research: clandestine intelligence operations in Latin America; defence and military intelligence; intelligence and security politics; radicalisation and extremism; security and counter-terrorism policy in the UK and the EU

Intelligent Data Analysis, Centre for

Tel: (01895) 265989 Fax: (01895) 251686
E-mail: xiahui@brunel.ac.uk
Liu, Xiaohui, BEng Hohai, PhD H-W   Prof.; Dir.*

Wang, Zidong, BSc Suzhou, MSc E.China Inst.Technol., PhD Nanjing I.T.   Prof.
Other Staff: 8 Lectrs.; 6 Res. Fellows
Research: biomedical informative, genomics and systems biology; data mining and intelligent systems; dynamics, signals and time series; visual computing

International and Public Law, Centre for (CIPL)

Tel: (01895) 266107
E-mail: roda.mushkat@brunel.ac.uk
Abass, Ademola, LLB Lagos, LLM Camb., PhD Nott.
Chigara, Ben, BA Keele, LLM Hull, PhD Nott. Prof.
Jaffey, Peter, MA Camb., LLM Lond.   Prof.
Kaikobad, Kaiyan H., BA Punjab, LLB Punjab, LLM Lond., PhD Lond.   Prof.
Mushkat, Roda, LLM Well., LLD S.Af., LLB   Prof.
Olowofoyeku, Abimbola, LLB Lagos, LLM Lond., PhD Lond.   Prof.; Head*
Rehman, Javaid, BA Punjab, LLB Reading, LLM Hull, PhD Hull   Prof.
Xanthaki, Alexandra, LLB Athens, LLM Belf., PhD Keele   Sr. Lectr.
Other Staff: 9 Lectrs.
Research: international criminal law; international human rights; public international law; public law

Materials Processing, Wolfson Centre for

Tel: (01895) 266166
E-mail: wolfson@brunel.ac.uk
Allan, Peter A., BSc Liv., PhD Liv.   Tech. Dir.
Silver, Jack, BSc Lond., PhD Lond., DSc Lond.   Prof.; Exec. Dir.*
Tarverdi, K., BSc PhD   Dir., Extrusion Technol.
Other Staff: 4 Res. Staff Members; 3 Res. Assocs.
Research: biomedicine; ceramics processing; polymer processing; waste management

Media and Communications Research, Centre for (CMCR)

Tel: (01895) 265459 Fax: (01895) 269724
E-mail: cmcr@brunel.ac.uk
Henderson, Lesley, BA CNAA, PhD Glas.   Acting Dir.*
Other Staff: 8 Academic Staff
Research: conversation analysis and broadcast talk; ethnographies of reception and consumption; journalistic practice and pressure group advocacy; media regulation, policy and governance; media representations and interactions

Media, Globalisation and Risk, Centre for

E-mail: john.tulloch@brunel.ac.uk
Allotey, Pascale, BA Ghana, MMedSci W.Aust., PhD W.Aust.   Prof.
Chigara, Ben, BA Keele, LLM Hull, PhD Nott. Prof.
Reidpath, Daniel, BA Swinburne I.T., PhD W.Aust. Prof.
Tulloch, John, BA Camb., MA Camb., DPhil Sus.   Prof.; Dir.*
Wilkin, Peter, BSc S'ton., PhD S'ton.   Reader
Research: civil society, space and place; diaspora, representation and identity; risk, uncertainty and insecurity

People and Interactivity Research Centre (PANDI)

E-mail: disc-pandi@brunel.ac.uk
Angelides, Marios C., BSc Lond., PhD Lond. Prof.
Chen, Sherry, MLS Maryland, PhD Sheff., BA   Reader
Ghinea, George, BSc Witw., MSc Witw., PhD Reading   Reader
Hone, Kate, BA Oxf., MS Birm., PhD Birm.   Reader

Kuljis, Jasna, MS Pitt., PhD Lond.   Prof.; Dir.*
Love, Steve, BA Glas., MSc Strath., PhD Edin.   Sr. Lectr.
Macredie, Robert, BSc Hull, PhD Hull   Prof.
Perry, Mark, BA Wales, MSc Wales, PhD Brun.   Sr. Lectr.
Other Staff: 1 Visiting Prof.; 8 Lectrs.; 2 Res. Fellows
Research: design for diver user groups; human factors; information visualisation; mobile technology designing for novel input/ output devices; multimedia

Rehabilitation, Centre for Research in

Tel: (01895) 26755
De Souza, Lorraine, BSc Brist., MSc Brist., PhD Lond.   Dir.*
Other Staff: 4 Academic Staff
Research: low back pain; multiple sclerosis

Screen Media Research Centre

Tel: (01895) 265826 Fax: (01895) 269768
E-mail: geoff.king@brunel.ac.uk
King, Geoff, BA Roeh., MA Sus., DPhil Sus.   Dir.*
Other Staff: 10 Academic Staff
Research: cult media and transgression; dominant and alternative cinemas; politics of representation and cultural identity; spectacle, documentary and the real; video games and digital media

Youth Work Studies, Centre for

Tel: (020) 8891 0121 Fax: (020) 8744 2960
Bradford, Simon, MPhil Brun., PhD Brun.   Dir.*

CONTACT OFFICERS

Accommodation. Accommodation Officer: Lockhart, Barbara
(E-mail: barbara.lockhart@brunel.ac.uk)
Admissions (first degree). Assistant Registrar: Gemmill, Sue
(E-mail: admissions@brunel.ac.uk)
Admissions (higher degree). Academic Registrar: Lapworth, Susan
(E-mail: susan.lapworth@brunel.ac.uk)
Alumni. Alumni Officer: Curley, Sue
(E-mail: sue.curley@brunel.ac.uk)
Careers. Head of Careers Services: Standley, Jane (E-mail: careers@brunel.ac.uk)
Computing services. Director (Computing Services): Bonney, Norman
(E-mail: colette.belza@brunel.ac.uk)
Conferences/corporate hospitality. Head, Conference Management: Killen, Sheila
(E-mail: conference@brunel.ac.uk)
Credit transfer. Assistant Registrar (Quality and Standards): (vacant)
Distance education. (Contact the appropriate Course Director)
Estates and buildings/works and services. Head, Operations: Berresford, Peter
(E-mail: peter.berresford@brunel.ac.uk)
Examinations. Head of Registry: Lapworth, Susan (E-mail: susan.lapworth@brunel.ac.uk)
Finance. Director of Finance: Eastwood, Rob
(E-mail: christine.smith@brunel.ac.uk)
International office. Director, Brunel International: Chang, Christopher, LLB
(E-mail: international-office@brunel.ac.uk)
Library (chief librarian). Head of Library Services: Bevan, Nick
(E-mail: library@brunel.ac.uk)
Personnel/human resources. Director of Human Resources: Doyle, Paul
(E-mail: tina.miller@brunel.ac.uk)
Publications. Head, Publications: Bevis, Marianne E., BA Lond.
(E-mail: publications@brunel.ac.uk)
Purchasing. Procurement Officer: Lloyd, David, MSc UMIST, PhD Manc., FIChemE
(E-mail: david.lloyd@brunel.ac.uk)
Quality assurance and accreditation. Assistant Registrar (Quality and Standards): (vacant)
Safety. Safety Officer: Covell, Mike
(E-mail: mike.covell@brunel.ac.uk)

Scholarships, awards, loans. Head of Student Services: Bufton, Denise
(E-mail: denise.bufton@brunel.ac.uk)

Schools liaison. Schools and Colleges Liaison Officer: Bennett, Amanda
(E-mail: amanda.bennett@brunel.ac.uk)

Security. Head, Operations: Berresford, Peter
(E-mail: peter.berresford@brunel.ac.uk)

Sport and recreation. Director, Sport and Recreation: Dimmock, Paul

Strategic planning. Acting Head of Planning: Dearn, Frances
(E-mail: planning@brunel.ac.uk)

Student welfare/counselling. Head of Counselling: Caleb, Ruth
(E-mail: brunel-counselling@brunel.ac.uk)

Students from other countries. Director, Brunel International: Chang, Christopher, LLB
(E-mail: international-office@brunel.ac.uk)

Students with disabilities. Policy and Planning Manager: Smith, Martin
(E-mail: martin.smith@brunel.ac.uk)

University press. Manager (University press): Leach, Gary
(E-mail: print-room@brunel.ac.uk)

[Information supplied by the institution as at 12 October 2007, and edited by the ACU]

UNIVERSITY OF BUCKINGHAM

Founded 1973

Postal Address: Hunter Street, Buckingham, England MK18 1EG
Telephone: (01280) 814080 **Fax:** (01280) 822245 **E-mail:** marketing@buckingham.ac.uk
URL: http://www.buckingham.ac.uk

VICE-CHANCELLOR*—Kealey, Terence, MB BS Lond., BSc Lond., MA Camb., DPhil Oxf.
REGISTRAR‡—Evans, Prof. Len, MSc Wales, PhD Wales, DSc Wales

BUCKINGHAMSHIRE NEW UNIVERSITY

Founded 1893

Postal Address: High Wycombe Campus, Queen Alexandra Road, High Wycombe, Buckinghamshire, England
HP11 2JZ
Telephone: (01494) 522141 **Fax:** (01494) 524392
URL: http://www.bucks.ac.uk/

VICE CHANCELLOR AND CHIEF EXECUTIVE*—Farwell, Ruth, BSc Kent, PhD Kent

UNIVERSITY OF CAMBRIDGE

Member of the Association of Commonwealth Universities

Postal Address: The Old Schools, Trinity Lane, Cambridge, England CB2 1TN
Telephone: (01223) 337733 **Fax:** (01223) 332332
URL: http://www.cam.ac.uk

VICE-CHANCELLOR*—Richard, Prof. Alison F., BA Camb., MA Camb., PhD Lond.
PRO-VICE-CHANCELLOR (PLANNING AND RESOURCES)—Minson, Prof. Anthony C., BSc Birm., PhD ANU, MA
PRO-VICE-CHANCELLOR (EDUCATION)—McKendrick, Prof. Melveena C., BA Lond., MA Camb., PhD Camb.
PRO-VICE-CHANCELLOR (HUMAN RESOURCES)—Cliff, Prof. Andrew D., BA Lond., MA Northwestern, MA Camb., PhD
  Brist., DSc Brist., FBA
PRO-VICE-CHANCELLOR (RESEARCH)—Leslie, Prof. Ian M., MASc Tor., PhD Camb.
PRO-VICE-CHANCELLOR (INTERNATIONAL STRATEGY)—Pretty, Katherine B., MA Camb., PhD Camb., FSA
HIGH STEWARD—Ogilvie, Dame Bridget, DBE, ScD Camb.
COMMISSARY—Mackay of Clashfern, Lord, KT, LLB Edin., MA Edin.
REGISTRARY‡—Nicholls, Jonathan W., BA Brist.
ACADEMIC SECRETARY—Allen, Graham P., MA Oxf., MA Camb.
DIRECTOR OF FINANCE—Reid, Andrew, MA Oxf., MBA Cran., FCA

GENERAL INFORMATION

History. The university was founded in the thirteenth century. Statutes granted to the university by Elizabeth I remained in force for 300 years, and were replaced twice in the nineteenth century and again in 1926. The university has 31 constituent colleges, each of which is a separate foundation with its own statutes. The fellows of the colleges provide the majority of the teaching staff of the university.

Admission to first degree courses (see also United Kingdom Introduction). Through

Universities and Colleges Admissions Service (UCAS) and the university's individual colleges. United Kingdom students: General Certificate of Education (GCE) A level with several high passes. International students: normally a degree from a university in the student's home country.

First Degrees (see also United Kingdom Directory to Subjects of Study). BA, BTh, BVetMed, MB BChir, MusB.
  Length of course. Full-time: BTh, MusB: 3 years; BA: 3–4 years; BVetMed, MB BChir: 6 years.

Higher Degrees (see also United Kingdom Directory to Subjects of Study).
  Master's. BD, LLM, MA, MBA, MChir, MEd, MEng, MLitt, MPhil, MSc, MSci, MStud.
  Admission. Applicants for admission to master's degrees must normally hold a first degree with first class honours. MA: awarded without examination to members of the university of a certain standing. MEng, MSci: awarded after 4-year honours courses in various triposes.
  Length of course. Full-time: LLM: 1 year; MBA, MPhil: 1–2 years; MEd, MLitt, MSc, MStud: 2

years; BD, MChir: 5 years. *Part-time:* MLitt, MSc: 5 years.

Doctoral. DD, EngD, LittD, LLD, MD, MusD, PhD, ScD, VetMD.

Admission. PhD: also awarded on published work. Higher doctorates: only awarded to senior members of the university for distinguished work.

Length of course. Full-time: EngD, PhD: 3 years. *Part-time:* PhD: 5 years.

Language of Instruction. English. Pre-sessional courses available for international students.

Libraries. Volumes: 5,811,231. Other holdings: 1,303,833 serial volumes (62590 serial titles); 157,186 manuscripts; 1,151,087 maps; 1,800,824 microforms; other central, faculty and departmental libraries: several million items, including historic collections; college libraries: historical collections, manuscripts and current literature.

Academic Year (2007–2008). Three terms: 2 October–30 November; 15 January–14 March; 22 April–13 June.

Income (2005–2006). Total, £563,600,000.

Statistics. Staff (2006–2007): 7933 (4003 academic, 3930 non-academic). Students (2005–2006): full-time 18,126 (9438 men, 8688 women); part-time 2832; international 3144; undergraduate 11,903 (6001 men, 5902 women).

ACADEMIC UNITS

Anglo-Saxon, Norse and Celtic

Tel: (01223) 335070 Fax: (01223) 335079
E-mail: asnc@hermes.cam.ac.uk
Blackburn, Mark A. S., MA *Oxf.*, PhD *Camb.*, FSA   Reader; Keeper of Coins and Medals, Fitzwilliam Museum (Cai.)
Dance, Richard, MA *Oxf.*, DPhil *Oxf.*   Sr. Lectr. (S.Cat.)
Keynes, Simon D., MA *Camb.*, PhD *Camb.*, LittD *Camb.*, FBA, FSA   Elrington and Bosworth Prof., Anglo-Saxon (Trin.)
Love, Rosalind, BA *Camb.*, PhD *Camb.*   Sr. Lectr. (Rob.)
Ní Mhaonaigh, Maire, MA *N.U.I.*, PhD *N.U.I.*   Sr. Lectr. (S.Joh.)
Quinn, Judy E., BA *Melb.*, PhD *Syd.*   Sr. Lectr.; Head* (Newn.)
Russell, Paul, MA *Oxf.*, MPhil *Oxf.*, DPhil *Oxf.*   Reader, Celtic (Pem.)
Other Staff: 1 Lectr.; 1 Teaching Assoc.†

Anthropology, Biological

Tel: (01223) 764700 Fax: (01223) 764710
E-mail: jb574@cam.ac.uk
Foley, Robert A., MA PhD   Prof., Human Evolution; Head* (King's)

Lahr, Marta M., MA PhD ScD   Reader, Human Evolutionary Biology (Cla.)
Mascie-Taylor, C. G. Nicholas, MA PhD ScD   Prof., Human Population Biology and Health (Chur.)
Petraglia, M. D., MA PhD   Sr. Lectr., Evolution of Human Behaviour and Palaeolithic Archaeology (Qu.)
Other Staff: 5 Lectrs.

Anthropology, Social

Tel: (01223) 334599 Fax: (01223) 335993
E-mail: socanth-admin@lists.cam.ac.uk
Howe, Leo E. A., PhD *Edin.*   Sr. Lectr.; Head* (Darw.)
Humphrey, Caroline, MA PhD   Sigrid Rausing Prof., Collaborative Anthropology (King's)
Macfarlane, Alan, MA *Oxf.*, MA *Camb.*, DPhil *Oxf.*, PhD *Lond.*   Prof., Anthropological Science (King's)
Strathern, Dame Marilyn, DBE, MA *Camb.*, PhD *Camb.*, FBA   William Wyse Prof. (Gir.)
Other Staff: 9 Lectrs.; 4 Affiliated Lectrs.; 1 Sr. Asst. in Res.

Archaeology

see also Classics

Tel: (01223) 333520 Fax: (01223) 333503
E-mail: archanth-enquiries@lists.cam.ac.uk
Barker, Graeme W. W.   Disney Prof.; Dir., McDonald Inst. for Archaeol. Res.; Head* (S.Joh.)
Chakrabarti, Dilip K.   Prof., South Asian Archaeology (Gir.)
French, Charles A. I., BA *Wales*, MA *Lond.*, PhD *Lond.*   Reader, Geoarchaeology (Gir.)
Hills, Catherine M., BA *Durh.*, MA *Camb.*, PhD *Lond.*   Sr. Lectr. (Newn.)
Jones, Martin K., MA PhD   George Pitt-Rivers Prof., Archaeology Science (Darw.)
Mellars, Paul A., MA PhD ScD, FBA, FSA   Prof., Prehistory and Human Evolution (Corp.)
Postgate, J. Nicholas, MA *Camb.*, FBA   Prof., Assyriology (Trin.)
Ray, John D., MA *Camb.*, FBA, FSA   Herbert Thompson Prof., Egyptology (Selw.)
Robb, John E., PhD   Sr. Lectr.
Sørensen, Marie L. S., BA *Aarhus*, CandPhil *Aarhus*, PhD *Camb.*   Sr. Lectr. (Jes.)
Stoddart, Simon K. F., MA *Camb.*, PhD *Camb.*   Sr. Lectr. (Magd.)
Other Staff: 6 Lectrs.; 1 Asst. Dir. of Res.; 1 Sr. Asst. in Res.

Archaeology and Anthropology, Museum of

Tel: (01223) 333516
Boast, Robin B., BA MA PhD   Sr. Curator, World Archaeology (Hug.)
Chippindale, Christopher R., MA PhD, FSA   Reader, Archaeology; Sr. Curator, British Archaeology (Gir.)

Herle, Anita C., BA MPhil   Sr. Curator, Anthropology (Qu.)
Salmond, Amiria J. M., BDesign BA MPhil PhD   Sr. Curator, Anthropology (Cai.)
Thomas, Nicholas J., PhD, FAHA, FBA   Prof., Historical Anthropology; Dir.* (Trin.)

Architecture

Tel: (01223) 332950 Fax: (01223) 332960
E-mail: arct-info@lists.cam.ac.uk
Bullock, Nicholas O. A., MA PhD   Reader (King's)
Carl, Peter W., MArch *Prin.*, MA   Sr. Lectr. (Cai.)
Echenique, Marcial H., DrArch *Barcelona*, MA   Prof., Land Use and Transport Studies; Head* (Chur.)
Penz, François A.   Reader, Architecture and the Moving Image
Pullan, Wendy A.   Sr. Lectr. (Cla.)
Short, Charles A., MA   Prof. (Cla.H.)
Spence, Robin J. S., MSc *Cornell*, MA PhD   Prof., Architectural Engineering (Magd.)
Steemers, Koen A., BSc *Bath*, MPhil *Camb.*, PhD *Camb.*   Prof., Sustainable Design (Wolfs.)
Other Staff: 5 Lectrs.; 1 Sr. Tech. Officer

Asian and Middle Eastern Studies

Tel: (01223) 335106 Fax: (01223) 335110
E-mail: webmaster@oriental.cam.ac.uk
Bennison, Amira K., MA PhD   Sr. Lectr., Middle Eastern and Islamic Studies
Bowring, Richard J., MA *Camb.*, PhD *Camb.*, LittD *Camb.*   Prof., Japanese Studies (Selw.)
Gordon, Robert P., MA *Camb.*, PhD *Camb.*   Regius Prof., Hebrew (S.Cat.)
Kahrs, Eivind G., MA *Oslo*, PhD *Oslo*   Reader, Sanskrit (Qu.)
Kemp, Barry J., BA *Liv.*, MA *Camb.*, FBA   Prof., Egyptology (Wolfs.)
Khan, Geoffrey A., BA *Lond.*, PhD *Lond.*, FBA   Prof., Semitic Philology (Wolfs.)
Kornicki, Peter F., MA *Oxf.*, MSc *Oxf.*, DPhil *Oxf.*, FBA   Prof., East Asian Studies (Rob.)
Melville, Charles P., MA PhD   Reader, Persian History (Pemb.)
Montgomery, James E., PhD   Prof., Classical Arabic (Trin.H.)
Sterckx, Roel, PhD   Prof., Chinese
Suleiman, Yasir, BA PhD, FRSEd   His Majesty Sultan Qaboos Bin Said Prof., Modern Arabic Studies
van de Ven, Hans J., BA PhD   Prof., Modern Chinese History (S.Cat.)
Yuan, Boping, BA MA MSc PhD   Sr. Lectr. (Chur.)
Other Staff: 14 Lectrs.; 2 Lectors; 3 Sr. Lang. Teaching Officers; 2 Lang. Teaching Officers; 1 Asst. Dir of Res.; 4 Res. Staff

Astronomy, Institute of

see also Phys.

Tel: (01223) 337548 Fax: (01223) 337523
E-mail: ioa@ast.cam.ac.uk
Carswell, Robert F., BSc *Otago*, MSc *Br.Col.*, DPhil *Sus.*   Prof. (S.Joh.)
Chapman, Scott C., BSc *Br.Col.*, MSc *Br.Col.*, PhD *Br.Col.*   Reader
Clarke, Catherine J., MA *Camb.*, DPhil *Oxf.*   Reader (Cla.)
Efstathiou, George P., MA *Oxf.*, MA *Camb.*, PhD *Durh.*, FRS, FIP, FRAS   Head of Dept.; Prof., Astrophysics; Dir.* (King's)
Evans, N. Wyn, BSc *Camb.*, PhD *Camb.*   Reader (King's)
Fabian, Andrew C., BSc *Lond.*, PhD *Lond.*, FRS   Prof. (Darw.)
Gilmore, Gerard F., BSc *Cant.*, PhD *Cant.*   Prof. (King's)
Gough, Douglas O., MA PhD, FRS   Prof., Theoretical Astrophysics (Chur.)
Haehnelt, Martin, BSc *Düsseldorf*, PhD *Camb.*   Reader (S.Joh.)
Hewett, Paul C., BSc *Edin.*, MA *Camb.*, PhD *Edin.*   Prof., Observational Cosmology and Astrophysics (Corp.)

The abbreviation in round brackets after a teacher's name denotes the college of which the teacher is a present fellow. The names of the colleges are indicated by abbreviations as follows:

Chr.	Christ's College	Magd.	Magdalene College
Chur.	Churchill College	New H.	New Hall
Cla.	Clare College	Newn.	Newnham College
Cla.H.	Clare Hall	Pemb.	Pembroke College
Corp.	Corpus Christi College	Pet.	Peterhouse
Darw.	Darwin College	Qu.	Queens' College
Down.	Downing College	Rob.	Robinson College
Emm.	Emmanuel College	Selw.	Selwyn College
Fitz.	Fitzwilliam College	Sid.	Sidney Sussex College
Gir.	Girton College	S.Cat.	St Catharine's College
Cai.	Gonville and Caius College	S.Edm.	St Edmund's College
Hom.	Homerton College	S.Joh.	St John's College
Hug.	Hughes Hall	Trin.	Trinity College
Jes.	Jesus College	Trin.H.	Trinity Hall
King's	King's College	Wolfs.	Wolfson College
L.Cav.	Lucy Cavendish College		

Note—For fellows of colleges the usual postal address is the college, and for other staff the university department, laboratory, museum, etc.

Irwin, Michael J., BA York(UK), PhD Camb. Reader, Astrophysics

Kennicutt, Robert, BS Rensselaer, MS Wash., PhD Wash. Plumian Prof., Astronomy and Experimental Philosophy

Mackay, Craig D., MA PhD   Reader (Corp.)

McMahon, Richard G., BSc Belf., PhD Camb. Reader (Cla.H.)

Parry, Ian R., BSc St And., MSc Sus., PhD Durh. Sr. Lectr.

Pettini, Max, BSc Lond., PhD Lond.   Prof.

Pringle, James E., MA PhD   Prof., Theoretical Astronomy (Emm.)

Rees of Ludlow, Lord Martin, MA PhD DSc Sus., DSc Leic., DSc Copenhagen, DSc Keele, DSc Uppsala, DSc Newcastle(UK), DSc Tor., DSc Durh., DSc Oxf., PRS   Royal Society Prof., Cosmology and Astrophysics (Trin.)

Tout, Christopher A., MA Camb., PhD Camb. Reader (Chur.)

Biochemistry

Tel: (01223) 333600 Fax: (01223) 333345
E-mail: examtchg@mole.bio.cam.ac.uk

Blundell, Sir Thomas, BA Oxf., DPhil Oxf., FRS Sir William Dunn Prof.; Head* (Sid.)

Brindle, Kevin M., BA Oxf., DPhil Oxf.   Prof., Biomedical Magnetic Biochemistry (Fitz.)

Carrington, David M., BA Camb., PhD Camb. Reader, Molecular Biology (S.Joh.)

Dupree, Paul, MA Camb., PhD Camb.   Reader, Plant Cell Biology (Magd.)

Farndale, R. W., BA Camb., PhD CNAA Reader, Receptor Biochemistry (Fitz.)

Gay, N. J., BSc Leeds, PhD Camb.   Reader, Cell Signalling and Development (Chr.)

Hesketh, T. R., BSc Lond., PhD Lond., MA   Sr. Lectr. (Selw.)

Howe, Christopher J., MA Camb., PhD Camb., FLS   Prof., Plant and Microbial Biochemistry

Jackson, A. J., BA Oxf., PhD Camb.   Sr. Lectr.

Laue, E. D., MA Camb., MA CNAA, PhD CNAA Prof., Structural Biology (S.Joh.)

Leadlay, Peter F., MA Oxf., DPhil Oxf., PhD Prof., Molecular Enzymology (Cla.)

Oliver, S. G., BSc Brist., PhD CNAA   Prof., Systems Biology and Biochemistry

Rubery, P. H., MA Camb., PhD Camb., ScD   Sr. Lectr. (Down.)

Salmond, George P. C., BSc Strath., PhD Warw. Prof., Molecular Microbiology (Wolfs.)

Smith, C. W. J., BSc Brist., PhD Lond.   Prof., RNA Molecular Biology

Standart, Nancy M., MA Camb., PhD Wales   Sr. Lectr. (Gir.)

Thomas, Dame Jean, CBE, DBE, MA Wales, MA Camb., PhD Wales, ScD, FRS   Prof., Macromolecular Biochemistry (S.Cat.)

Other Staff: 5 Lectrs.; 7 Asst. Dirs. of Res.; 1 Sr. Tech. Officer; 2 Computer Officers

Biotechnology, Institute of

Tel: (01223) 334160 Fax: (01223) 334162
E-mail: admin@biotech.cam.ac.uk

Hall, Elizabeth A. H., BSc Lond., PhD Lond., MA Prof., Analytical Biotechnology (Qu.)

Lowe, Christopher R., BSc Birm., PhD Birm. Prof.; Head; Dir.* (Trin.)

Murray, James A. H., BA Camb., PhD CNAA Prof., Molecular Biotechnology (King's)

Tunnacliffe, Alan H., BA Lond., PhD Lond. Reader (Pemb.)

Other Staff: 1 Clin. Lectr.

Business and Management

Judge Business School

Tel: (01223) 337051 Fax: (01223) 339701
E-mail: enquiries@jbs.cam.ac.uk

Barker, Richard G., BA Oxf., MPhil Camb.   Sr. Lectr.; Dir., MBA Course (Wolfs.)

Barrett, Michael I., BSc WI, MSc Ott., MBA McM., PhD Camb.   Reader, Information Technology and Innovation (Chur.)

Bell, Simon, PhD Melb.   Sr. Lectr. (Hug.)

Dawson, Dame Sandra J. N., BA Keele, MA Camb., Hon. DSc Keele, FCGI   KPMG Prof.; Head; Dir.* (Sid.)

de Meyer, Arnoud C. L.   Head; Prof., Management Studies; Dir.* (Jes.)

de Rond, Mark E. J., DPhil Oxf.   Reader, Strategy and Organisation (Darw.)

Deakin, Simon F., MA Camb., PhD Camb., FBA Robert Monks Prof., Corporate Governance (Pet.)

Dissanaike, Gishan R., BA Peradeniya, MPhil Camb., PhD Camb.   Reader, Finance (Trin.)

Eatwell, Lord, AM Harv., MA Camb., PhD Harv. Dir., Cambridge Endowment for Res. in Finance; Prof., Financial Policy (Qu.)

Fleming, Peter   Sr. Lectr. (Wolfs.)

Holweg, Matthias, MSc Buckingham, PhD Cardiff Sr. Lectr.

Hope, Christopher W., MA Oxf., PhD   Reader, Policy Modelling (Cla.H.)

Hughes, Alan, MA Camb.   Margaret Thatcher Prof., Enterprise Studies (Sid.)

Jiang, Houyuan   Sr. Lectr.

Kattuman, Paul, BA Calicut, MA Calicut, MPhil Camb., PhD Camb.   Sr. Lectr. (Corp.)

Meeks, Geoff, BA Camb., PhD Edin.   Prof., Accounting (Darw.)

Munir, Kamal A., PhD McG.   Sr. Lectr.

Nolan, Peter H., MA Camb., MSc Lond., PhD Lond.   Sinyi Prof., Chinese Management (Jes.)

Pitelis, Christos N., BA Panteios, MA Warw., PhD Warw.   Barclay's Bank Reader; Reader, International Business and Competitiveness

Pollitt, Michael G., DPhil   Reader, Business Economics (Sid.)

Ralph, Daniel, BSc Melb., MS Wis., PhD Wis. Prof., Operations Research (Chur.)

Roberts, John D., BSc Manc., PhD Manc. Reader, Organisational Analysis (S.Cat.)

Runde, Jochen H., MPhil Camb., PhD Camb. Reader, Economics (Gir.)

Scholtes, Stefan, PhD Karlsruhe   Prof.

Steinberg, Richard, BA Reed, MMath Wat., MBA Chic., PhD Wat.   Reader, Operations Management

Stiles, Philip, BA Kent, MPhil Lond., PhD Lond. Sr. Lectr.

Walsham, Geoffrey, BA Oxf., MA Warw., MSc Warw.   Prof.

Other Staff: 10 Lectrs.

Chemistry

Tel: (01223) 336454 Fax: (01223) 336362
E-mail: reception@ch.cam.ac.uk

Abell, Christopher, MA PhD   Prof., Biological Chemistry (Chr.)

Alavi, Ali, BA Camb., PhD Camb.   Reader, Theoretical Chemistry (Trin.)

Althorpe, Stuart, BA Camb., PhD Camb. Reader, Theoretical Chemistry (King's)

Balasubramanian, Shankar, MA PhD   Reader, Chemical Biology (Trin.)

Clarke, Jane, BA York(UK), MSc Camb., PhD Camb.   Reader, Molecular Biophysics (Jes.)

Clarke, Stuart M., BA Oxf., DPhil Oxf.   Sr. Lectr. (Jes.)

Davies, Paul B., BSc Liv., MA PhD   Reader, Spectroscopy (Corp.)

Dobson, Christopher M., BSc Oxf., MA Oxf., DPhil Oxf., Hon. DSc, FRS, FMedSci   John Humphrey Plummer Prof., Chemical and Structural Biology (S.Joh.)

Duer, Melinda J., MA PhD   Sr. Lectr. (Rob.)

Elliott, Stephen R., MA PhD   Prof., Chemical Physics (Trin.)

Fersht, Sir Alan R., MA PhD, FRS   Herchel Smith Prof., Organic Chemistry (Cai.)

Frenkel, Daniel, PhD   Prof.

Glen, Robert C., BSc Paisley, PhD Stir.   Unilever Prof., Molecular Sciences Informatics (Cla.)

Goodman, Jonathan M., MA PhD   Sr. Lectr. (Cla.)

Hansen, Jean-Pierre, LèsSPhys Liège, PhD Paris XI, FRS   Prof. (Cla.)

Huck, Wilhelm T. S., MSc Ley., PhD T.H.Twente Prof., Macromolecular Chemistry (Cai.)

Jackson, Sophie E., MA Oxf., PhD Camb.   Sr. Lectr. (Pet.)

Jefferson, David A., MA PhD   Reader, Crystallography (Cai.)

Jones, Rod L., MA Oxf., DPhil Oxf.   Prof., Atmospheric Science (Qu.)

Jones, William, BSc Wales, PhD Wales   Prof., Materials Chemistry; Head* (Sid.)

Keeler, James H., MA Oxf., DPhil Oxf., PhD Camb.   Sr. Lectr. (Selw.)

Klenerman, David, PhD Camb.   Prof., Biophysical Chemistry (Chr.)

Klinowski, Jacek, MSc Cracow, PhD Cracow, PhD Lond., MA   Prof., Chemical Physics (Pet.)

Lambert, Richard M., BA Oxf., DPhil Oxf., MA Prof., Surface Chemistry (King's)

Leeper, Finian J. J., MA PhD   Sr. Lectr. (Emm.)

Ley, Steven V., CBE, BSc Lough., MA Camb., PhD Lough., DSc Lond., FRS, FRSChem   BP Prof., Organic Chemistry (Trin.)

Murray-Rust, Peter   Reader, Molecular Informatics (Chur.)

Paterson, Ian, BSc St And., PhD   Prof., Organic Chemistry (Jes.)

Pyle, John A., BSc Durh., DPhil Oxf., PhD Prof., Atmospheric Science (S.Cat.)

Rawson, Jeremy M., MA Camb., PhD Durh.   Sr. Lectr. (Magd.)

Robinson, Carol V., MSc Wales, PhD Camb. Royal Soc. Res. Prof., Chemical Biology (Chur.)

Sanders, Jeremy K. M., BSc Lond., MA PhD ScD, FRSChem, FRS   Prof., Inorganic Chemistry (Selw.)

Spencer, Jonathan B., BA S'ton., MA Camb. Reader, Biological Chemistry ((S.Joh.))

Sprik, Michiel, MSc Amst., PhD Amst.   Prof., Theoretical Chemistry (Cla.)

Wales, David J.   Reader, Chemical Physics (Down.)

Wright, Dominic S., PhD   Reader, Inorganic Chemistry (Cai.)

Other Staff: 7 Lectrs.; 1 Asst. Dir. of Res.; 4 Sr. Tech. Officers; 2 Tech. Officers; 7 Computer Officers

Classics

Tel: (01223) 335152
E-mail: pu10000@cam.ac.uk

Austin, Colin F. L., MA Oxf., MA Camb., DPhil Oxf., FBA   Prof., Greek (Trin.H.)

Beard, W. Mary, MA Camb., PhD Camb.   Prof., Roman History (Newn.)

Cartledge, Paul A., MA Oxf., DPhil Oxf., PhD, FSA   Prof., Greek History (Cla.)

Clackson, James P. T., MA PhD   Sr. Lectr. (Jes.)

Denyer, Nicholas C., MA   Sr. Lectr. (Trin.)

Diggle, J., MA Camb., PhD Camb., LittD Camb., FBA   Prof., Greek and Latin (Qu.)

Goldhill, Simon D., MA Camb., PhD Camb. Prof., Greek Literature (King's)

Henderson, John G. W., BA Oxf., MA Camb., DPhil Oxf., PhD Camb.   Prof. (King's)

Horrocks, Geoffrey C., MA Camb., PhD Camb. Prof., Comparative Philology (S.Joh.)

Hunter, Richard L., BA Syd., MA Camb., PhD Camb.   Regius Prof., Greek (Trin.)

Hurst, Henry R., MA Camb.   Curator, Museum of Classical Archaeol.; Reader, Classical Archaeology (Chur.)

Kelly, Christopher M., BA PhD   Sr. Lectr. (Corp.)

Meissner, Torsten, DPhil PhD   Sr. Lectr. (Pemb.)

Millett, Martin J.   Laurence Prof., Classical Archaeology (Fitz.)

Millett, Paul C., MA PhD   Sr. Lectr. (Down.)

Morales, Helen L., MA PhD   Sr. Lectr. (Newn.)

Oakley, Stephen P., MA PhD   Kennedy Prof., Latin (Emm.)

Osborne, Robin G., MA PhD, FBA   Prof., Ancient History (King's)

Patterson, James R., MA PhD   Sr. Lectr. (Magd.)

Reeve, Michael D., MA Oxf., MA Camb., FBA Prof., Latin (Pemb.)

Schofield, Malcolm, MA Camb., PhD Camb., DPhil Oxf., FBA   Prof., Ancient Philosophy (S.Joh.)

Sedley, David N., MA *Oxf.*, MA *Camb.*, PhD *Lond.*, FBA Laurence Prof., Ancient Philosophy (Chr.)

Wardy, Robert B. B., MA *Camb.*, PhD *Camb.* Reader, Ancient Philosophy (S.Cat.)

Warren, James I., MA *Camb.*, MPhil *Camb.*, PhD *Camb.* Sr. Lectr. (Corp.)

Other Staff: 9 Lectrs.; 3 Lang. Teaching Officers; 1 Computer Officer

Research: Greco-Roman philosophy in the first century BC; Greek colonization and European development; Greek lexicon

Computer Laboratory

Tel: (01223) 763500 *Fax:* (01223) 334678
E-mail: reception@cl.cam.ac.uk

Anderson, Ross J., MA *Camb.*, PhD *Camb.* Prof., Security Engineering (Trin.)

Bacon, Jean M., BSc *Lond.*, MSc *CNAA*, MA *Camb.*, PhD *CNAA* Prof., Distributed Systems (Jes.)

Blackwell, Alan F., BEng *Auck.*, MSc *Well.*, PhD *Camb.* Reader, Interdisciplinary Design (Darw.)

Briscoe, Edward J., BA *Lanc.*, PhD Prof. (Gir.)

Copestake, Ann A., MA *Camb.*, DPhil *Sus.* Reader (Wolfs.)

Crowcroft, Jon A., BA *Camb.*, MSc *Lond.*, PhD *Lond.*, FREng Marconi Prof., Communication Systems (Wolfs.)

Daugman, John G., AB *Harv.*, PhD *Harv.* Reader

Dawar, Anuj, BTech *Delhi*, MS *Delaware*, PhD *Penn.* Reader, Logic and Algorithms (Rob.)

Dodgson, Neil A., BSc *Massey*, PhD *Camb.* Reader, Graphics and Imaging (Emm.)

Fiore, Marcelo P. Reader, Mathematical Foundations of Computer Science (Chr.)

Gibbens, Richard J., MA *Camb.*, PhD *Camb.* Sr. Lectr. (Cai.)

Gordon, Michael J. C., BA *Camb.*, PhD *Edin.*, FRS Prof., Computer-Assisted Reasoning

Greaves, David J., MA *Camb.*, PhD *Camb.* Sr. Lectr. (Corp.)

Hand, Steven M., BSc *N.U.I.*, MSc *N.U.I.*, PhD *Camb.* Sr. Lectr. (Wolfs.)

Holden, Sean B., BSc *E.Anglia*, PhD *Camb.* Sr. Lectr. (Trin.)

Hopper, Andrew, CBE, BSc *Wales*, MA *Camb.*, PhD *Camb.*, FRS Prof., Computer Technology; Head* (Corp.)

King, Frank H., MA *Camb.*, PhD *Camb.* Sr. Lectr. (Chur.)

Leslie, Ian M., MASc *Tor.*, PhD *Camb.* Prof., Computer Science (Chr.)

Lio, Pietro Sr. Lectr. (Fitz.)

Moore, Simon W. Sr. Lectr. (Trin.H.)

Mycroft, Alan, MA *Camb.*, PhD *Edin.*, ScD *Camb.* Prof. (Rob.)

Paulson, Lawrence C., BSc *Pasadena*, PhD *Stan.*, MA Prof., Computational Logic (Cla.)

Pitts, Andrew M., MA *Camb.*, PhD *Camb.* Prof., Theoretical Computer Science (Darw.)

Pratt, Ian A., MA *Camb.*, PhD *Camb.* Sr. Lectr. (King's)

Robinson, Peter, MA *Camb.*, PhD *Camb.* Prof. (Cai.)

Sewell, Peter M. Sr. Lectr. (Wolfs.)

Stajano, Francesco M. Sr. Lectr.

Teufel, Simone H. Sr. Lectr.

Wassell, Ian J., BSc *Lough.*, BEng *Lough.*, PhD *S'ton.* Sr. Lectr. (Chur.)

Winskel, Glynn, MSc *Oxf.*, MA *Camb.*, PhD *Edin.*, ScD *Camb.* Robert Sansom Prof., Computer Science (Emm.)

Other Staff: 5 Lectrs.; 1 Sr. Computer Officer; 6 Computer Officers

Criminology, Institute of

Tel: (01223) 335360 *Fax:* (01223) 335356
E-mail: enquiries@crim.cam.ac.uk

Eisner, M. P. Reader

Farrington, D. P., MA PhD Prof., Psychological Criminology (Darw.)

Gelsthorpe, Loraine R. R., BA *Sus.*, MPhil *Camb.*, PhD *Camb.* Reader (Pemb.)

Grounds, Adrian T., DM *Nott.*, FRCPsych Sr. Lectr. (Darw.)

Liebling, Alison, BA *York(UK)*, MA *Hull*, PhD *Camb.* Prof., Criminology and Criminal Justice (Trin.H.)

Lösel, Friedrich A. Prof.; Dir.* (Wolfs.)

Sherman, Lawrence W., MA *Chic.*, PhD *Yale*, Hon. MA *Penn.*, FRSA Wolfson Prof.

Wikstrom, Per-Olof H., BA *Stockholm*, PhD *Stockholm* Prof., Ecological and Developmental Criminology (Gir.)

Other Staff: 4 Lectrs.

Divinity

see also Hist.

Tel: (01223) 332590 *Fax:* (01223) 332582
E-mail: divinity-office@lists.cam.ac.uk

Carlton Paget, James N. B., MA *Camb.*, PhD *Camb.* Sr. Lectr. (Pet.)

Coakley, Sarah, BA *Camb.*, ThM *Harv.*, PhD *Camb.* Norris-Hulse Prof.

Davies, Graham I., MA *Oxf.*, PhD *Camb.*, DD *Oxf.*, FBA, FSA Prof., Old Testament Studies (Fitz.)

de Lange, Nicholas R. M., MA *Oxf.*, DPhil *Oxf.*, PhD *Camb.*, DD *Camb.* Prof., Hebrew and Jewish Studies (Wolfs.)

Dell, Katharine J., MA *Oxf.*, DPhil *Oxf.* Sr. Lectr. (S.Cat.)

Duffy, Eamon, BA *Hull*, PhD *Camb.*, DD *Camb.* Prof., History of Christianity (Magd.)

Ford, David F., BA *Trinity(Dub.)*, MA *Camb.*, STM *Yale*, PhD *Camb.* Regius Prof. (Selw.)

Graumann, Thomas, DTh *Mün.* Sr. Lectr.

Hedley, D., BA *Oxf.*, MSt *Oxf.*, PhD *Munich* Sr. Lectr. (Cla.)

Horbury, William, MA *Oxf.*, MA *Camb.*, PhD *Camb.*, DD *Camb.* Prof., Jewish and Early Christian Studies (Corp.)

Lieu, Judith M., BA *Durh.*, MA *Durh.*, PhD *Birm.* Lady Margaret's Prof.

Lipner, Julius J., BA *Pune*, MA *Camb.*, MA *Calc.*, PhD *Lond.* Prof., Hinduism and the Comparative Study of Religion (Cla.H.)

Pickstock, Catherine J. C., MA *Camb.*, PhD *Camb.* Reader, Philosophy and Theology (Emm.)

Rex, R. A. W., MA *Camb.*, PhD *Camb.* Reader, Reformation History (Qu.)

Soskice, Janet M., BA *Cornell*, MA *Sheff.*, DPhil *Oxf.* Reader, Philosophical Theology (Jes.)

Stanton, Graham N., BD *Otago*, BA *Otago*, MA *Otago*, PhD *Camb.* Prof. (Fitz.)

Thompson, David M., BD *Camb.*, MA *Camb.*, PhD *Camb.*, FRHistS Dir., Centre for Advanced Religious and Theol. Studies; Prof., Modern Church History (Fitz.)

Watts, Rev. Fraser N., BA *Oxf.*, MSc *Lond.*, MA *Camb.*, PhD *Camb.* Reader, Theology and Science (Qu.)

Other Staff: 4 Lectrs.; 2 Asst. Dirs. of Res.; 2 Teaching Assocs.

Earth Sciences

Tel: (01223) 333400 *Fax:* (01223) 333450
E-mail: mij10@esc.cam.ac.uk

Artacho, Emilio, PhD Prof., Theoretical Mineral Physics (Cla.H.)

Bickle, M. J., DPhil *Oxf.*, FRS Prof., Tectonics (Qu.)

Butterfield, Nicholas J., BSc *Alta.*, MA *Camb.*, PhD *Harv.* Sr. Lectr. (Selw.)

Carpenter, Michael A., MA PhD Curator, Museums of Mineral. and Petrol.; Prof., Mineralogy and Mineral Physics (Magd.)

Conway Morris, Simon, BSc *Brist.*, MA PhD, FRS Prof., Evolutionary Palaeobiology (S.Joh.)

Dove, Martin T., BSc *Birm.*, PhD *Birm.* Prof., Computational Mineral Physics (Trin.)

Elderfield, Henry, BSc *Liv.*, MA *Camb.*, PhD *Liv.*, ScD *Camb.* Prof., Geochemistry (S.Cat)

Farnan, Ian, BSc *E.Anglia*, PhD *E.Anglia* Sr. Lectr. (Cla.H.)

Galy, Albert J. B., PhD *Nancy* Sr. Lectr. (S.Joh.)

Gibson, Sally A. Sr. Lectr.

Haines, A. John, MSc *Well.*, PhD *Camb.* Reader, Geodesy and Geophysics (S.Edm.)

Holland, T. J. B. Reader, Petrology (Fitz.)

Holness, Marian B. Reader, Petrogenesis (Trin.)

Jackson, James A., MA PhD Prof., Active Tectonics (Qu.)

McCave, I. N., MA *Oxf.*, DSc *Oxf.*, PhD *Brown*, ScD, FGS Woodwardian Prof., Geology (S.Joh.)

McKenzie, Dan P., MA PhD, FRS Royal Society Res. Prof. (King's)

Norman, David B., BSc *Leeds*, PhD *Lond.* Reader; Curator, Sedgwick Museum of Earth. Scis. (Chr.)

Priestly, Keith F. Reader, Seismology (Qu.)

Redfern, Simon A. T., MA *Camb.*, PhD *Camb.* Prof., Mineral Physics (Jes.)

Salje, Ekhard K. H., PhD *Hanover*, MA, FRS Prof., Mineralogy Petrology; Head* (Cla.H.)

Scott, James F. Symetrix Prof., Ferroics

White, Nicholas J. Reader, Basin Analysis (Emm.)

White, Robert S., MA PhD, FRS Prof., Geophysics (S.Edm.)

Woodcock, Nigel H., BSc *Manc.*, MSc *Lond.*, PhD *Lond.*, MA Sr. Lectr. (Cla.)

Woods, Andrew W., MA *Camb.*, PhD *Camb.* BP Prof., Petroleum Science (S.Joh.)

Other Staff: 9 Lectrs.; 1 Academic Fellow; 2 Sr. Tech. Officers; 2 Tech. Officers; 3 Computer Officers

Economics

see also Hist., and Land Economy

Tel: (01223) 335200 *Fax:* (01223) 335475
E-mail: faculty@econ.cam.ac.uk

Aidt, Toke S., MA *Aarhus*, PhD Sr. Lectr. (Jes.)

Brown, William A., CBE, BA *Oxf.*, MA *Camb.* Montagu Burton Prof., Industrial Relations (Darw.)

Chang, Ha-Joon, BA *Seoul*, MPhil *Camb.*, PhD *Camb.* Reader, Political Economy of Development (Wolfs.)

Dasgupta, Sir Partha, BSc *Delhi*, BA *Camb.*, PhD *Camb.*, FBA Frank Ramsey Prof. (S.Joh.)

Edwards, Jeremy S. S., BA *Camb.*, BPhil *Oxf.*, DPhil *Oxf.* Reader (S.Joh.)

Evans, Robert A., BA *Oxf.*, MSc *Lond.* Reader, S.Joh.

Goyal, Sanjeev, BA *Delhi*, MA *Cornell*, PhD *Cornell*, MBA Prof.

Harris, Christopher J., BA *Oxf.*, MPhil *Oxf.*, DPhil *Oxf.* Prof. (King's)

Harvey, Andrew C., BA *York(UK)*, MSc *Lond.*, FBA Prof., Econometrics (Corp.)

Holly, M. J. Sean, BA *Reading*, PhD *CNAA* Reader; Exec. Dir., Res.

Honkapohja, Seppo M. S., MSocSc *Helsinki*, DSocSc *Helsinki* Prof., International Macroeconomics (Cla.)

Horrell, Sara H., BSc *Bath*, MPhil *Camb.*, PhD *Camb.* Sr. Lectr. (New H.)

Krishnan, Pramila, BStat *I.Stat.I.*, MStat *I.Stat.I.*, PhD *Flor.* Sr. Lectr. (Jes.)

Lawson, Tony, BSc *Lond.*, MSc *Lond.*, PhD *Camb.* Reader (King's)

Low, Hamish W., BA *Oxf.*, MPhil *Oxf.*, PhD *Lond.* Sr. Lectr. (Trin.)

Newbery, David M. G., MA *Camb.*, PhD *Camb.*, ScD *Camb.*, FBA Prof., Applied Economics (Chur.)

Ogilvie, Sheilagh C., MA *St And.*, MA *Chic.*, PhD *Camb.* Prof., Economic History (Trin.)

Palma, J. Gabriel, BSc *Chile*, DPhil *Oxf.*, DPhil *Sus.* Sr. Lectr. (Sid.)

Pesaran, M. Hashem, BSc *Salf.*, PhD *Camb.*, FBA Prof. (Trin.)

Robertson, Donald, MA *Camb.*, MSc *Lond.*, PhD *Lond.* Sr. Lectr. (Pem.)

Rustichini, Aldo, BA *Florence*, MA *Manc.*, PhD *Minn.* Prof., Political Economy

Sabourian, Hamid, BA *Camb.*, MSc *Lond.*, PhD *Camb.* Prof., Economics and Game Theory (King's)

Satchell, Stephen E., BA *NSW*, MCom *NSW*, MA *Syd.*, MA *Camb.*, PhD *Camb.*, PhD *Lond.* Reader, Financial Econometrics (Trin.)

Singh, Ajit, BA *Punjab*, MA *Howard*, MA *Camb.*, PhD *Calif.*   Prof. (Qu.)

Smith, Richard J., BA *Camb.*, MA *Camb.*, MA *Essex*, PhD *Camb.*   Prof., Econometric Theory and Economic Statistics (Cai.)

Solomou, Solomos N., BSc *Lond.*, MSc *Lond.*, PhD *Camb.*   Sr. Lectr. (Pet.)

Weeks, Melvyn J., BA *Reading*, MA *Ill.*, PhD *Penn.*   Sr. Lectr. (Cla.)

Other Staff: 10 Lectrs.; 1 Asst. Dir. of Res.; 1 Librarian; 2 Computer Officers

Education

Tel: (01223) 767600 Fax: (01223) 767602

Andrews, Paul R., BSc *Nott.*, MEd *Wolv.*, MA *Camb.*, PhD *Manc.Met.*   Sr. Lectr.

Anghileri, Julia, BSc MSc PhD   Sr. Lectr.

Arnot, Madeleine M., MA *Edin.*, PhD *Open(UK)*   Prof., Sociology of Education (Jes.)

Brindley, Susan, BA MA   Sr. Lectr.

Burnard, Pamela A., BMus *Melb.*, MMus *Indiana*, MEd *Qld.*, PhD *Reading*   Sr. Lectr.

Chaplain, Roland P., BEd *Lanc.*, MA *Lanc.*   Sr. Lectr. (Hom.)

Cliff-Hodges, Gabrielle, BA *Newcastle(UK)*, MA *Lond.*   Sr. Lectr. (Hom.)

Colclough, Christopher L., BA *Brist.*, PhD *Camb.*   Prof., Economics of Education

Counsell, Christine, MA MEd   Sr. Lectr.

Cunningham, Peter J., MA *Camb.*, MA *E.Anglia*, PhD *Leeds*   Sr. Lectr. (Hom.)

Dillabough, Jo-Anne, BA *W.Ont.*, MA *Br.Col.*, PhD *McG.*   Reader

Doddington, Christine, BEd *Leic.*, MA *Lond.*, MA *Camb.*   Sr. Lectr. (Hom.)

Evans, Michael J., BA *E.Anglia*, PhD *Warw.*   Sr. Lectr. (Cla.H.)

Frost, David C., BEd *Lond.*, MA *Kent*, PhD *E.Anglia*   Sr. Lectr. (Wolfs.)

Gardner, Philip W., BA *E.Anglia*, MA *E.Anglia*, DPhil *Sus.*, MA   Sr. Lectr. (S.Edm.)

Goalen, Paul S. P., MA *Camb.*, MEd *Sheff.*   Sr. Lectr.

Goswami, Usha C., BA *Oxf.*, DPhil *Oxf.*   Prof. (S.Joh.)

Gray, John M., MA *Oxf.*, EdM *Harv.*, DPhil *Sus.*, FBA   Prof. (Hom.)

Hargreaves, Linda, BSc *Durh.*, MA(Ed) *Leic.*, PhD *Leic.*   Sr. Lectr. (Hom.)

Hickman, Richard D., BA *Nott.Trent*, MA *De Mont.*, MA *Camb.*, PhD *Reading*   Sr. Lectr. (Hom.)

Howe, Christine, BA *Sus.*, PhD *Camb.*   Prof.

MacBeath, John E. C., OBE, MA *Glas.*, MEd *Glas.*   Prof., Educational Leadership (Hug.)

McLaughlin, Colleen, BEd *Camb.*, MEd *Wales*, MA *Camb.*   Sr. Lectr. (Cla.H.)

Mercer, Neil M., BSc *Manc.*, PhD *Leic.*   Prof.

Moore, Robert, BSc *Lond.*, MA *Lond.*, PhD *Lond.*   Sr. Lectr. (Hom.)

Opfer, V. Darleen, BA *Stetson*, MEd *Virginia*, PhD *Virginia*   Sr. Lectr.

Reay, Diane, BA *Newcastle(UK)*, MA *Lond.*, PhD *S.Bank*   Prof.

Rowland, Timothy, BSc *S'ton.*, MSc *S'ton.*, MA *Camb.*, PhD *Open(UK)*   Sr. Lectr. (Hom.)

Ruthven, Kenneth B. H., MA *Oxf.*, MA *Camb.*, PhD *Stir.*   Prof. (Hug.)

Sinkinson, Anne J., BEd *Camb.*, MPhil *Camb.*, PhD *E.Anglia*   Sr. Lectr. (Hom.)

Stephenson, Philip, BSc *Manc.*, MA *Camb.*   Sr. Lectr. (Hom.)

Styles, Morag, BSc   Reader, Children's Literature and Education (Hom.)

Sugrue, Ciaran, PhD *Tor.*, BA MA MEd   Reader

Taber, Keith S., BSc *Nott.*, MSc *Sur.*, PhD *Sur.*   Sr. Lectr.

Whitebread, David G., BA *Keele*, MEd *Nott.*, PhD *Nott.*   Sr. Lectr. (Hom.)

Wyse, Dominic, MPhil *Leeds Met.*, PhD *Liv.J.Moores*   Sr. Lectr. (Chur.)

Younger, Michael R., BA *Leic.*, MA *Lond.*   Sr. Lectr.; Head* (Hom.)

Other Staff: 28 Lectrs.; 1 Sr. Tech. Officer; 1 Computer Officer; 1 Librarian

Engineering

Tel: (01223) 332600 Fax: (01223) 332662
E-mail: reception@eng.cam.ac.uk

Allwood, Julian M., MA *Camb.*, MBA *Lond.*, PhD *Lond.*   Sr. Lectr. (Cai.)

Al-Tabbaa, Abir, MPhil *Camb.*, PhD *Camb.*   Reader, Geotechnical Engineering (Sid.)

Amaratunga, Gehan A. J., PhD *Camb.*   Prof. (Chur.)

Babinsky, Holger, PhD *Cran.*   Reader (Magd.)

Barlow, Claire   Sr. Lectr. (Newn.)

Beaumont, Peter W. R.   Reader (Wolfs.)

Bolton, Malcolm D., MSc *Manc.*, MA PhD   Prof., Soil Mechanics (Chur.)

Britter, Rex E., BE *Monash*, PhD *Monash*, MA   Prof., Environmental Fluid Dynamics (Pemb.)

Burgoyne, Christopher J., MSc *Lond.*, PhD *Lond.*, MA   Reader (Emm.)

Campbell, Archibald M., MA PhD   Prof., Electromagnetism (Chr.)

Cant, R. Stewart, BSc *St And.*, PhD *Cran.*   Reader (Selw.)

Cardwell, David A., MA *Camb.*, PhD *Warw.*   Prof., Superconducting Engineering (Fitz.)

Cebon, David, BE *Melb.*, PhD   Prof., Mechanical Engineering (Qu.)

Cipolla, Roberto, MA *Camb.*, MSE *Penn.*, MEng *Tokyo*, DPhil *Oxf.*, PhD *Camb.*   Prof., Information Engineering (Jes.)

Clarkson, Peter J., MA PhD   Prof., Engineering Design (Trin.H.)

Coles, Harry J.   Prof., Photonics of Molecular Materials

Collings, Nicholas, BSc *Brist.*, PhD   Prof., Applied Thermodynamics (Rob.)

Coombs, Tim A., MA *Camb.*, PhD *Camb.*   Sr. Lectr. (Magd.)

Crossland, William A., BSc *Lond.*   Prof., Photonics (Hug.)

Davidson, Peter A., BSc *Aberd.*, PhD *Camb.*   Prof., Fluid Mechanics (Chur.)

Dawes, William (Bill) N., MA PhD   Francis Mond Prof., Aeronautical Engineering (Chur.)

Deshpande, Vikram S., BTech *IIT Bombay*, MPhil *Camb.*, PhD *Camb.*   Sr. Lectr. (Pemb.)

Dowling, Dame Ann P., DBE, MA *Camb.*, PhD *Camb.*, FREng   Prof., Mechanical Engineering (Sid.)

Drummond, Thomas W.   Sr. Lectr. (S.Cat.)

Fitzgerald, William J., MSc *Birm.*, PhD *Birm.*   Prof., Applied Statistics and Signal Processing (Chr.)

Fleck, Norman A., MA PhD, FRS   Prof., Mechanics of Materials (Pemb.)

Flewitt, Andrew, BSc *Birm.*, PhD *Camb.*   Sr. Lectr. (Sid.)

Gales, Mark J. F., PhD   Reader (Emm.)

Garnsey, Elisabeth W., BA *Oxf.*, PhD *Calif.*, MA   Reader, Innovation Systems (Cla.H.)

Gee, Andrew H., PhD   Reader (Qu.)

Ghahramani, Zoubin, BEng *Penn.*, BA *Penn.*, PhD *M.I.T.*   Prof., Information Engineering

Glover, Keith, BSc *Lond.*, SM *M.I.T.*, PhD *M.I.T.*, MA, FRS   Prof.; Head* (Sid.)

Godsill, Simon J., MA PhD   Reader (Corp.)

Graham, Will   Sr. Lectr. (Trin.)

Gregory, Michael J., BSc *S'ton.*, MA *Camb.*   Prof., Manufacturing Engineering (Chur.)

Guest, Simon D., MA *Camb.*, PhD *Camb.*   Reader, Structural Mechanics (Trin.H.)

Guthrie, Peter M., FCGI, FREng, FICE   Prof., Sustainable Development (S.Edm.)

Hochgreb, Simone   Prof., Experimental Combustion

Hodson, Howard P., MA PhD   Prof., Aerothermal Technology (Gir.)

Holburn, David   Sr. Lectr. (Cai.)

Hunt, Hugh E. M., BE *Melb.*, PhD   Sr. Lectr. (Trin.)

Hutchings, Ian M., MA PhD   Prof., Manufacturing Engineering (S.Joh.)

Hynes, Tom P., BA *Camb.*, PhD *Camb.*   Sr. Lectr. (S.Joh.)

Johnson, Aylmer L.   Sr. Lectr. (Cla.)

Kelly, Michael J., FREng, Hon. FRS   Prince Philip Prof., Technology (Trin.H.)

Kingsbury, Nicholas G., MA PhD   Prof., Signal Processing (Trin.)

Langley, Robin S., BSc *Leic.*, MSc *Cran.*, PhD *Cran.*   Prof., Mechanical Engineering (Fitz.)

Lees, Janet M., BEng *McG.*, MSc *Lond.*, PhD *Camb.*   Sr. Lectr. (S.Joh.)

Maciejowski, Jan M., BSc *Sus.*, MA PhD   Prof., Control Engineering (Pemb.)

Madabhushi, Gopal   Reader, Geotechnical Engineering (Chur.)

Mair, Robert J., MA *Camb.*, PhD *Camb.*, FREng, FICE   Prof. (Jes.)

Mastorakos, Epaminondas, BEng *Lond.*, MS *Cornell*, PhD *Lond.*   Reader (Fitz.)

McFarlane, Duncan C., BE *Melb.*, PhD *Camb.*   Reader, Automation Systems (Qu.)

McMahon, Richard A., MA PhD   Sr. Lectr. (Corp.)

McRobie, F. Allan, BSc *Brist.*, MSc *S'ton.*   Reader (S.Edm.)

Middleton, Campbell R., BE *Tas.*, MSc *Lond.*, PhD *Camb.*   Sr. Lectr. (King's)

Migliorato, Piero, DottFis *Rome*   Prof., Physical Electronics (Trin.)

Milne, William I., BSc *St And.*, PhD *Lond.*, MA   Prof., Electrical Engineering (Chur.)

Morley, Christopher T., BA PhD   Sr. Lectr. (Trin.)

Nickels, Timothy B., BEng(Mech) *Melb.*, PhD *Melb.*   Reader, Experimental Fluid Mechanics (Emm.)

O'Neill, William   Reader, Laser Engineering

Palmer, Patrick R., MA PhD   Reader, Electrical Engineering (S.Cat.)

Parks, Geoffrey T., BA *Camb.*, MA *Camb.*, PhD *Camb.*   Sr. Lectr. (Jes.)

Peake, Nigel, MA *Camb.*, PhD *Camb.*   Prof., Applied Mathematics (Emm.)

Pellegrino, Sergio, LaurCivIng *Naples*, MA PhD   Prof., Structural Engineering (Corp.)

Penty, Richard V., MA PhD   Prof., Photonics (Pem.)

Platts, Kenneth W., MA *Camb.*, PhD *Camb.*   Reader (Fitz.)

Prager, Richard W., MA PhD   Reader (Qu.)

Probert, David R., MA *Camb.*   Reader, Technology Management (S.Cat.)

Robertson, John, BA *Camb.*, PhD *Camb.*   Prof., Electronics (Chur.)

Scholtes, Stephan   Prof., Management Science

Seffen, Keith A., BA *Camb.*, MA *Camb.*, PhD *Camb.*   Sr. Lectr. (Corp.)

Shercliff, Hugh R., MA *Camb.*, PhD *Camb.*   Sr. Lectr. (Gir.)

Smith, Malcolm C., MA MPhil PhD   Prof., Control Engineering (Cai.)

Soga, Kenichi, BSc *Kyoto*, MEng *Kyoto*, PhD *Calif.*   Prof., Civil Engineering (Chur.)

Sutcliffe, Michael P. F., MA PhD   Reader, Mechanics of Materials (S.Cat.)

Wallace, Kenneth M., BSc *Manc.*, MA   Prof., Engineering Design (Selw.)

Welland, Mark E., BSc *Leeds*, MSc *Brist.*, PhD *Brist.*, MA   Prof., Nanotechnology (S.Joh.)

White, Alexander J.   Sr. Lectr. (Pet.)

White, David J., BA *Camb.*, PhD *Camb.*   Sr. Lectr. (Down.)

White, Ian H., MA PhD   Van Eyck Prof. (Jes.)

Wilkinson, Timothy D., BE *Cant.*, PhD *Camb.*   Sr. Lectr. (Jes.)

Williams, John A., MA PhD   Prof., Engineering Tribology (Rob.)

Wolpert, Daniel M., BA *Camb.*, BM BCh *Oxf.*, DPhil *Oxf.*   Prof. (Trin.)

Woodhouse, James, MA PhD   Prof., Structural Dynamics (Cla.)

Woodland, Philip C., MA MPhil   Prof., Information Engineering (Pet.)

Young, John B., MSc *Birm.*, PhD *Birm.*, MA   Hopkinson and Imperial Chemical Industries Prof., Applied Thermodynamics (King's)

Young, Stephen J., MA *Camb.*, PhD *Camb.*   Prof., Information Engineering (Emm.)

Other Staff: 41 Lectrs.; 1 Asst. Dir. of Res.; 3 Sr. Des. Engineers; 1 Des. Engineer; 3 Sr. Tech. Officers; 1 Tech. Officer; 1 Sr. Lang.

Teacher; 1 Sr. Computer Officer; 10 Computer Officers

Engineering, Chemical

Tel: (01223) 334777 Fax: (01223) 334796
E-mail: research@cheng.cam.ac.uk,
tripos@cheng.cam.ac.uk

Cardoso, Silvana S. S., BA *Oporto*, PhD *Camb.* Reader, Fluid Mechanics and the Environment (Pemb.)

Chase, Howard A., MA *Camb.*, PhD *Camb.*, ScD *Camb.*, FREng Prof., Biochemical Engineering (Magd.)

Dennis, John S., MA *Camb.*, PhD *Camb.* Sr. Lectr. (Selw.)

Fisher, Adrian C., BSc *E.Anglia*, DPhil *Oxf.* Reader, Electrochemistry

Gladden, Lynn F., CBE, BSc *Brist.*, PhD *Camb.*, FRS, FREng Shell Prof., Chemical Engineering Science; Head* (Trin.)

Johns, Mike L., BSc *Natal*, PhD *Camb.* Sr. Lectr. (S.Cat.)

Kaminski, Clemens, BSc *Reading*, DPhil *Oxf.* Reader (Rob.)

Kraft, Markus, DrRerNat *Kaiserslautern* Reader (Chur.)

Mackley, Malcolm R., BSc *Leic.*, MSc *Brist.*, PhD *Brist.*, MA, FREng Prof., Process Innovation (Rob.)

Moggridge, Geoff D., MA *Camb.*, PhD *Camb.* Sr. Lectr. (King's)

Paterson, William R., BSc *Edin.*, MA *Camb.*, PhD *Edin.* Sr. Lectr. (Wolfs.)

Scott, David M., MA *Camb.*, PhD *Camb.* Sr. Lectr. (Fitz.)

Slater, Nigel K. H., MA *Camb.*, PhD *Camb.*, FREng, FIChemE Prof. (Sid.)

Vassiliadis, Vassili S., PhD *Camb.* Sr. Lectr.

Wilson, D. Ian, MA *Camb.*, MEng *Camb.*, PhD *Br.Col.* Reader (Jes.)

Other Staff: 2 Lectrs.; 3 Asst. Dirs. of Res.; 4 Sr. Tech. Officers; 3 Computer Officers

English

see also Anglo-Saxon, Norse and Celtic

Tel: (01223) 335070 Fax: (01223) 335075
E-mail: english-faculty@lists.cam.ac.uk

Beadle, H. Richard L., DPhil *York(UK)*, MA Reader, English History and Historical Bibliography (S.Joh.)

Cannon, Christopher D., MA *Harv.*, PhD *Harv.* Sr. Lectr. (Gir.)

Chothia, Jean K., BA *Durh.*, PhD Reader, Drama and Theatre (Selw.)

Collini, Stefan A., MA *Yale*, MA *Camb.*, PhD Prof., Intellectual History and English Literature (Cla.H.)

Cooper, E. Helen, MA *Camb.*, PhD *Camb.*, DLitt *Oxf.* Prof., Medieval and Renaissance English

de Bolla, P. L., MA *Camb.*, PhD *Camb.* Reader, Cultural History and Aesthetics (King's)

Glen, Heather J., BA *Syd.*, MA *Camb.*, PhD *Camb.* Prof., English Literature (New H.)

Gopal, Priyamvada, MA *J.Nehru U.*, MA *Purdue*, PhD *Cornell* Sr. Lectr. (Chur.)

Harvey, John R., MA *Camb.*, PhD *Camb.* Reader, Literature and Visual Culture (Emm.)

Hawkins, John A., MA *Camb.*, PhD *Camb.* Prof., English and Applied Linguistics (Trin.H.)

Heath, Stephen C., MA *Camb.*, PhD *Camb.* Reader, Cultural Studies (Jes.)

Jacobus, Mary L., MA *Oxf.*, DPhil *Oxf.* Prof. (Chur.)

Jarvis, Simon J., MA *Camb.*, PhD *Camb.* Gorley Putt Reader, Poetry and Poetics (Rob.)

Kerrigan, John F., MA *Oxf.* Prof., English Literature (S.Joh.)

Lyne, Raphael T. R., MPhil *Camb.*, PhD *Camb.* Sr. Lectr. (New H.)

Meer, Sarah, BA *Camb.*, PhD *Camb.* Sr. Lectr. (Selw.)

Mengham, Rod, MA *Camb.*, PhD *Edin.* Reader, Modern English Literature (Jes.)

Page, Christopher H., BA *Oxf.*, DPhil *York(UK)* Reader, Mediaeval Literature and Music (Sid.)

Parker, G. Fred, MA *Camb.*, PhD *Camb.* Sr. Lectr. (Cla.)

Poole, Adrian D. B., MA *Camb.*, PhD *Camb.* Prof., English Literature (Trin.)

Trotter, Wilfred D., MA *Camb.*, PhD *Camb.* King Edward VII Prof., English Literature (Cai.)

Wheeler, Kathleen M., PhD *Camb.* Reader, English Literature (Darw.)

Windeatt, Barry A., MA *Camb.*, PhD *Camb.*, LittD *Camb.* Prof. (Emm.)

Wright, Laura C. Sr. Lectr. (L.Cav.)

Other Staff: 18 Lectrs.

French

Tel: (01223) 335009 Fax: (01223) 335062
E-mail: french-department@lists.cam.ac.uk

Bayley, Peter J., MA *Camb.*, PhD *Camb.* Drapers Prof. (Cai.)

Bennett, Wendy M. A., MA *Oxf.*, MA *Camb.*, DPhil *Oxf.*, PhD *Camb.* Prof., French Philology and Linguistics (New H.)

Burgwinkle, Bill E., BA *Amherst*, MA *Boston Coll.*, PhD *Stan.* Reader, Mediaeval French and Occitan Literature (King's)

Collier, Peter J., BA *Lond.*, PhD *Lond.*, MA Sr. Lectr. (Sid.)

Crowley, Martin P. V., MA *Oxf.*, MA *Nott.*, DPhil *Oxf.* Sr. Lectr. (Qu.)

Darlow, Mark R., MA *Kent*, PhD *Kent* Sr. Lectr. (Chr.)

Ford, Philip J., MA *Camb.*, PhD *Camb.* Prof., French and Neo-Latin Literature (Cla.)

Hammond, Nicholas G., MA *Rhodes*, DPhil *Oxf.* Reader, Early Modern French Theatre and Thought (Cai.)

Huot, Sylvia, BA *Calif.*, PhD *Prin.* Prof., Medieval French Literature (Pemb.)

Jones, Mari C., BA *Aberd.*, MPhil *Camb.*, PhD *Camb.* Sr. Lectr. (Pet.)

Kenny, Neil F., MA *Camb.*, DPhil *Oxf.* Reader, Early Modern French Literature and Thought (Chur.)

Mander, Jenny S., MA *Camb.*, PhD *Camb.* Sr. Lectr. (Newn.)

White, Nicholas J., MA *Camb.*, PhD *Camb.* Sr. Lectr. (Emm.)

Wilson, Emma F., MA *Camb.*, PhD *Camb.* Reader, Contemporary French Literature and Film; Head* (Corp.)

Other Staff: 5 Lectrs.; 2 Lang. Teaching Officers

Genetics

Tel: (01223) 333999 Fax: (01223) 333992
E-mail: info@gen.cam.ac.uk

Ashburner, Michael, MA *Camb.*, PhD *Camb.*, ScD *Camb.*, FRS Prof., Biology (Chur.)

Glover, David M., BA *Camb.*, PhD *Lond.*, FRSEd Arthur Balfour Prof. (Fitz.)

MacDonald, Donald W. B., BSc *Aberd.*, MA *Camb.*, PhD *E.Anglia* Sr. Lectr. (Wolfs.)

Majerus, Michael E. N., MA *Camb.*, PhD *Lond.* Prof., Evolution (Cla.)

Martinez Arias, Alfonso, Lic *Madrid*, PhD *Chic.* Prof.

O'Kane, Cahir J., MA *Camb.*, PhD *Trinity(Dub.)* Reader (Chur.)

Summers, D. K., MA *Camb.*, DPhil *Oxf.* Sr. Lectr.; Head* (Cai.)

Other Staff: 6 Lectrs.

Geography

Tel: (01223) 333399 Fax: (01223) 333392
E-mail: enquiries@geog.cam.ac.uk

Adams, Bill M., MSc *Lond.*, MA *Camb.*, PhD *Camb.* Moran Prof., Conservation and Development (Down.)

Bayliss-Smith, Tim P., MA *Camb.*, PhD *Camb.* Reader, Pacific Geography (S.Joh.)

Bennett, Robert J., MA *Camb.*, PhD *Camb.*, FBA Prof. (S.Cat.)

Cliff, Andrew D., BA *Lond.*, MA *Northwestern*, MA *Camb.*, PhD *Brist.*, DSc *Brist.*, FBA Prof., Theoretical Geography (Chr.)

Dowdeswell, Julian A., BA *Camb.*, PhD *Camb.* Prof., Physical Geography (Jes.)

Duncan, James S., BA *Dartmouth*, MA *Syr.*, PhD *Syr.* Reader, Cultural Geography (Emm.)

Friend, Andrew D., BSc *Lond.*, PhD *Camb.* Sr. Lectr.

Gibbard, Philip L., BSc *Sheff.*, PhD *Camb.* Prof., Quaternary Palaeoenvironments (Darw.)

Graf, Hans-F. Prof., Environmental Systems Analysis

Haining, Robert P., MSc *Northwestern*, MA *Camb.*, PhD *Northwestern* Prof., Human Geography (Fitz.)

Howell, P. M. R. Sr. Lectr. (Emm.)

Kearns, Gerry P., BA *Camb.*, PhD *Camb.* Sr. Lectr. (Jes.)

Martin, Ron L., MA *Camb.*, PhD *Camb.* Prof., Economic Geography (S.Cat.)

Oppenheimer, Clive M. M., BA *Camb.*, PhD *Open(UK)* Reader, Volcanology and Remote Sensing (Sid.)

Owens, Susan E., OBE, MA *Camb.*, PhD *E.Anglia* Prof., Environment and Policy (Newn.)

Radcliffe, Sarah A., BSc *Lond.*, MA *Camb.*, PhD *Liv.* Sr. Lectr. (New H.)

Rees, William G., MA *Camb.*, PhD *Camb.* Sr. Lectr. (Chr.)

Richards, Keith S., MA *Camb.*, PhD *Camb.* Prof. (Emm.)

Smith, Richard M., BA *Lond.*, MA *Oxf.*, PhD *Camb.* Prof., Historical Geography and Demography; Head* (Down.)

Spencer, Tom, MA PhD Sr. Lectr. (Magd.)

Trudgill, Stephen T., BSc *Brist.*, PhD *Brist.* Sr. Lectr. (Rob.)

Vira, Bhaskar, MA *Camb.*, PhD *Camb.* Sr. Lectr. (Fitz.)

Warrington, Molly, MA *Camb.*, PhD *Camb.* Sr. Lectr. (Hom.)

Willis, Ian C., BSc *Camb.*, PhD *Camb.* Sr. Lectr. (S.Cat.)

Other Staff: 11 Lectrs.; 2 Asst. Dirs. of Res.; 1 Sr. Tech. Officer; 2 Tech. Officers; 3 Computer Officers

German and Dutch

Tel: (01223) 335037 Fax: (01223) 335062
E-mail: mml-german-managers@lists.cam.ac.uk

Boyle, Nicholas, MA *Camb.*, LittD *Camb.*, FBA Schröder Prof. (Magd.)

Chinca, Mark, MA PhD Sr. Lectr. (Trin.)

Hutchinson, Peter, MA *Camb.*, PhD *Lond.*, LittD *Camb.* Reader (Trin.H.)

Midgley, David R., BA *Oxf.*, DPhil *Oxf.*, PhD *Camb.* Reader (S.Joh.)

Minden, Michael R., MA *Camb.*, PhD *Camb.* Sr. Lectr. (Jes.)

Nisbet, Hugh B., MA *Edin.*, MA *Camb.*, PhD *Edin.* Prof., Modern Languages (Sid.)

Stewart, Mary E., MA *Oxf.*, DPhil *Oxf.* Sr. Lectr. (Rob.)

Strietman, Elsa G. C., CandLitt *Gron.*, MA Sr. Lectr. (New H.)

Webber, Andrew J., MA *Camb.*, PhD *Camb.* Reader, Modern German and Comparative Culture (Chur.)

Whaley, Joachim, MA *Camb.*, PhD *Camb.*, FRHistS Sr. Lectr. (Cai.)

Young, Christopher J., MA *Camb.*, PhD *Camb.* Sr. Lectr.; Head* (Pemb.)

Other Staff: 2 Lectrs.; 2 Sr. Lang. Teaching Officers

Research: fifteenth- and sixteenth-century drama of the Low Countries

History

see also Classics, and Asian and Middle Eastern Studies

Tel: (01223) 335340 Fax: (01223) 335968
E-mail: gen.enq@hist.cam.ac.uk

Abulafia, D. S. H., MA *Camb.*, PhD *Camb.*, LittD *Camb.* Prof., Mediterranean History (Cai.)

Andrew, Christopher M., MA *Camb.*, PhD *Camb.* Prof., Modern and Contemporary History (Corp.)

Badger, Anthony J., MA *Camb.*, PhD *Hull*, Hon. DLitt *Hull* Paul Mellon Prof., American History (Cla.)

Bayly, Prof. Sir Christopher A., KBE, MA *Oxf.*, DPhil *Oxf.*, PhD, FBA Vere Harmsworth Prof., Imperial and Naval History (S.Cat.)

Berend, N., MA *Paris*, PhD Sr. Lectr. (S.Cat.)

Biagini, Eugenio F., PhD *Pisa* Reader, Modern British and European History (Rob.)

Blanning, Timothy C. W., MA *Camb.*, PhD *Camb.* Prof., Modern European History (Sid.)

Brett, Annabel S., MA *Camb.*, PhD *Camb.* Sr. Lectr. (Cai.)

Carpenter, M. Christine, MA *Camb.*, PhD *Camb.* Prof., Medieval English History (New H.)

Clark, Christopher, PhD *Camb.* Reader, Modern European History (S.Cat.)

Daunton, Martin J., MA *Camb.*, PhD *Camb.*, LittD *Camb.*, FBA, FRHistS Prof., Economic History (Trin.H.)

Drayton, Richard, AB *Harv.*, MA *Oxf.*, MPhil *Yale*, PhD *Yale*, FRHistS Sr. Lectr. (Corp.)

Evans, Richard J., MA *Oxf.*, DPhil *Oxf.*, LittD *E.Anglia*, FBA Prof., Modern History (Cai.)

Goldie, Mark A., MA *Camb.*, PhD *Camb.* Sr. Lectr. (Chur.)

Harper, Timothy N., MA *Camb.*, PhD *Camb.* Reader, Southeast Asian and Imperial History (Magd.)

Hatcher, M. J., BSc(Econ) *Lond.*, MA *Camb.*, PhD *Lond.*, LittD *Camb.* Prof., Economics and Social History (Corp.)

Hilton, A. J. Boyd, MA *Oxf.*, MA *Camb.*, DPhil *Oxf.*, PhD, FRHistS Prof., Modern British History (Trin.)

Jahn, Hubertus, MA *Munich*, PhD *Georgetown*, DrPhilHabil *Erlangen* Sr. Lectr. (Cla.)

Klein, Lawrence E., MA *Johns H.*, PhD *Johns H.* Sr. Lectr. (Emm.)

Lane, M. S., PhD *Camb.* Sr. Lectr. (King's)

Laven, Mary R., PhD *Leic.* Sr. Lectr. (Jes.)

Lawrence, Jon M., PhD *Camb.* Sr. Lectr. (Emm.)

Mandler, Peter, MA *Harv.*, PhD *Harv.* Reader, Modern British History (Cai.)

McKitterick, Rosamond D., BA *W.Aust.*, MA *Camb.*, PhD *Camb.*, LittD *Camb.*, FRHistS Prof., Medieval History (Sid.)

Morrill, John S., MA *Oxf.*, DPhil *Oxf.*, LittD *E.Anglia*, FRHistS, FBA Prof., British and Irish History (Selw.)

Muldrew, J. Craig, BA *Alta.*, MA *Alta.*, PhD *Camb.* Sr. Lectr. (Qu.)

O'Brien, Michael, MA *Camb.*, PhD *Camb.* Prof., American Intellectual History (Jes.)

Parry, Jonathan P., MA *Camb.*, PhD *Camb.* Reader, Modern British History (Pemb.)

Peterson, Derek R., BA *Roch.*, PhD *Minn.* Sr. Lectr. (Selw.)

Reynolds, David J., MA *Camb.*, PhD *Camb.* Prof., International History (Chr.)

Rublack, U., MA *Camb.*, PhD *Camb.* Sr. Lectr. (S.Joh.)

Skinner, Quentin R. D., MA *Camb.*, LittD *E.Anglia*, FBA Regius Prof., Modern History (Chr.)

Stedman Jones, Gareth, MA *Oxf.*, MA *Camb.*, DPhil *Oxf.* Prof., Political Science (King's)

Szreter, Simon R. S., MA *Camb.*, PhD *Camb.* Reader, History and Public Policy (S.Joh.)

Thornton, Jonathan M., MPhil *Yale*, PhD *Yale* Pitt Prof., American History and Institutions (Jes.)

Tombs, Robert P., MA *Camb.*, PhD *Camb.* Prof., French History (S.Joh.)

Tooze, J. Adam, BA *Lond.*, PhD *Lond.* Reader, Twentieth-Century History (Jes.)

Vaughan, Megan A., BA *Kent*, PhD *Lond.* Smuts Prof., Commonwealth History (King's)

Webber, M. Tessa J., MA *Oxf.*, MA *Oxf.*, DPhil *Oxf.* Sr. Lectr. (Trin.)

Wood, Betty C., BA *Keele*, MA *Lond.*, MA *Camb.*, PhD *Penn.* Reader, American History (Gir.)

Other Staff: 13 Lectrs.; 1 Sr. Lang. Teaching Officer; 2 Computer Officers

History and Philosophy of Science

Tel: (01223) 334500 Fax: (01223) 334554
E-mail: hps-admin@lists.cam.ac.uk

Forrester, John P., MA PhD Prof. (King's)

Jardine, Nicholas, MA PhD Prof. (Darw.)

Kusch, Martin P. H., MA *Oulu*, PhD *Oulu* Prof. (King's)

Lipton, Peter, BA *Wesleyan*, BPhil *Oxf.*, DPhil *Oxf.* Prof.; Head* (King's)

Schaffer, Simon J., MA *Harv.*, MA *Camb.*, PhD Prof. (Darw.)

Secord, James A., BA *Pomona*, PhD *Prin.* Prof. (Chur.)

Taub, Liba, BA *Tulane*, MA *Chic.*, PhD *Oklahoma* Reader; Dir. and Curator, Whipple Museum of the Hist. of Sci.

Other Staff: 4 Lectrs.

History of Art

Tel: (01223) 332975 Fax: (01223) 332976
E-mail: mj10007@cam.ac.uk

Binski, Paul, MA PhD Reader, History of Mediaeval Art (Cai.)

Howard, Deborah J., MA PhD Prof., Architectural History (S.Joh.)

Joannides, Paul E. A., MA PhD Prof. (Cla.H.)

Mahon, Alyce, MA PhD Sr. Lectr. (Trin.)

Massing, Jean Michel, MHistArt *Stras.*, Dr *Stras.*, MA Prof. (King's)

Watkin, David J., MA PhD LittD, FSA Prof., History of Architecture; Head* (Pet.)

Other Staff: 6 Lectrs.

Italian

Tel: (01223) 335038 Fax: (01223) 335062
E-mail: nt272@cam.ac.uk

Antonello, Pierpaolo, Laurea *Bologna*, MA *Stan.*, PhD *Stan.* Sr. Lectr. (S.Joh.)

Baranski, Zygmunt G., BA Serena Prof. (New H.)

Gordon, Robert S. C., MA *Oxf.*, PhD *Camb.* Reader, Modern Italian Culture (Cai.)

Kirkpatrick, Robin, BA *Oxf.*, MA *Oxf.*, PhD *Camb.* Prof. (Rob.)

Ledgeway, Adam N., BA *Salf.*, MA *Manc.*, PhD *Manc.* Sr. Lectr.; Head* (Down.)

Other Staff: 2 Lectrs.; 2 Affiliate Lectrs.; 1 Sr. Lang. Teaching Officer; 1 Postdoctoral Res. Fellow; 2 Hon. Res. Fellows

Research: cultural studies; film; linguistics; literature (Middle Ages, Renaissance, post-Unification to the present); women's studies

Land Economy

Tel: (01223) 337147 Fax: (01223) 337130

Bond, Shaun A., BEcon *Qld.*, MPhil *Camb.*, PhD *Camb.* Sr. Lectr. (Hug.)

Dixon, Martin J., MA *Oxf.*, PhD *Camb.* Reader, Law of Real Property (Qu.)

Fingleton, Bernard, BA *Wales*, MPhil *Camb.*, PhD *Wales*, PhD *Camb.* Reader (Darw.)

Glascock, John, BSBA *Tennessee*, MBA *Stetson*, MA *Virginia Polytech.*, PhD *N.Texas*, FRICS Grosvenor Prof., Real Estate Finance (Pemb.)

Hodge, Ian D., BSc *Reading*, PhD *Lond.*, FRICS Prof., Rural Economy; Head* (Hug.)

McCombie, John S. L., MA *McM.*, MA PhD Reader, Applied Economics (Down.)

McHugh, Paul G., LLB *Well.*, LLM *Sask.*, PhD *Camb.* Reader, Comparative Common Law (Sid.)

Tyler, Peter, MSc MA PhD Prof., Urban and Regional Economics (S.Cat.)

Whitehead, Christine M. E., BSc *Lond.*, PhD *Lond.* Dir., Cambridge Centre for Housing and Planning Res.

Other Staff: 8 Lectrs.; 1 Dir. of Res.; 1 Asst. Dir. of Res.

Law

see also Criminol., Inst. of

Tel: (01223) 330033 Fax: (01223) 330055
E-mail: admin@law.cam.ac.uk

Albors-Llorens, Albertina, LicDr *Valencia*, LLM *Lond.*, PhD *Camb.* Sr. Lectr. (Gir.)

Allan, Trevor R. S., BCL *Oxf.*, MA *Oxf.*, MA *Camb.* Prof., Public Law and Jurisprudence (Pemb.)

Allison, John W. F., BA *Stell.*, LLB *Stell.*, LLM *Camb.*, MPhil *Camb.*, PhD *Camb.* Sr. Lectr. (Qu.)

Andrews, Neil H., BCL *Oxf.*, MA *Oxf.* Reader, Civil Justice (Cla.)

Bainham, Andrew W. E., LLM *Camb.*, PhD *Camb.* Reader, Family Law and Policy (Chr.)

Baker, Sir John, KCB, QC, LLB *Lond.*, MA *Camb.*, PhD *Lond.*, LLD *Camb.*, Hon. LLD *Chic.*, FBA Downing Prof., Laws of England (S.Cat.)

Barnard, Catherine S., MA *Camb.*, LLM *European Univ.Inst.*, PhD *Camb.* Reader, European Union Law (Trin.)

Bell, John S., MA *Camb.*, DPhil *Oxf.* Prof. (Pemb.)

Bently, Lionel, MA *Camb.* Herchel Smith Prof., Intellectual Property Law (Emm.)

Cheffins, Brian R., LLB *Vic.(BC)*, LLM *Camb.* S. J. Berwin Prof., Corporate Law (Trin.H.)

Clarke, Malcolm A., LLB *Camb.*, MA *Camb.*, PhD *Camb.* Prof., Commercial Contract Law (S.Joh.)

Crawford, James R., BA *Adel.*, LLB *Adel.*, DPhil *Oxf.*, LLD *Camb.* Whewell Prof., International Law (Jes.)

Dashwood, Alan A., CBE, BA *Rhodes*, MA *Oxf.* Prof., European Law (Sid.)

Deakin, Simon F., MA *Camb.*, PhD *Camb.*, FBA Prof., Labour Law (Pet.)

Elliott, Mark C., MA *Camb.*, PhD *Camb.* Sr. Lectr. (S.Cat.)

Feldman, David J., BCL *Oxf.*, MA *Oxf.* Rouse Ball Prof., English Law (Down.)

Fentiman, Richard G., BCL *Oxf.*, MA *Oxf.*, MA *Camb.* Reader, Private International Law (Qu.)

Ferran, Eilis V., MA *Camb.*, PhD *Camb.* Prof., Company and Securities Law (S.Cat.)

Forsyth, Christopher F., BSc *Natal*, LLB *Natal*, LLB *Camb.*, PhD *Camb.* Prof., Public Law and Private International Law (Rob.)

Fox, David M., BA *Otago*, LLB *Otago*, PhD *Camb.* Sr. Lectr. (S.Joh.)

Gray, Christine D., MA *Camb.*, PhD *Camb.* Prof., International Law (S.Joh.)

Gray, Kevin J., MA *Camb.*, PhD *Camb.*, LLD *Camb.*, DCL *Oxf.* Prof. (Trin.)

Harris, Peter, LLB *Camb.*, LLM *Camb.*, PhD *Camb.* Sr. Lectr. (Chur.)

Ibbetson, David J., MA *Camb.*, PhD *Camb.*, FBA Regius Prof., Civil Law (Corp.)

Jones, Neil G., MA *Camb.*, LLM *Camb.*, PhD *Camb.* Sr. Lectr. (Magd.)

Kramer, Matthew H., BA *Cornell*, PhD *Camb.*, JD *Harv.*, LLD *Camb.* Prof., Legal and Political Philosophy (Chur.)

Munday, Roderick J., MA *Camb.*, PhD *Camb.* Reader (Pet.)

Nolan, Richard C., MA *Camb.* Reader, Corporate and Trust Law (S.Joh.)

O'Sullivan, Janet A., MA *Camb.* Sr. Lectr. (Selw.)

Padfield, Nicola M., MA *Oxf.* Sr. Lectr. (Fitz.)

Palmer, Stephanie M., LLB *Adel.*, LLM SJD Sr. Lectr. (Gir.)

Rogerson, Philippa J., MA *Camb.*, PhD *Camb.* Sr. Lectr. (Cai.)

Simmonds, Nigel E., MA *Camb.*, LLM *Camb.*, PhD *Camb.* Reader, Jurisprudence (Corp.)

Spencer, John R., QC, LLB *Camb.*, MA *Camb.* Prof. (Selw.)

Tiley, John, CBE, BCL *Oxf.*, MA *Camb.*, LLD *Camb.* Prof., Law of Taxation (Qu.)

Virgo, Graham J., BCL *Oxf.*, MA *Camb.* Prof., English Private Law (Down.)

Other Staff: 17 Lectrs.; 1 Computer Officer

Linguistics

Tel: (01223) 335010 Fax: (01223) 335053
    E-mail: ling-admin@lists.cam.ac.uk
Hawkins, Sarah, BSc S'ton., PhD Camb.   Prof.,
    Phonetic Sciences (Cla.H.)
Jaszczolt, Katarzyna M., MA Lodz, MPhil Lodz,
    DPhil Oxf., PhD Camb.   Reader, Linguistics
    and Philosophy of Language (Newn.)
Nolan, Francis J. D., MA Camb., PhD Camb.
    Prof., Phonetics; Head* (Fitz.)
Roberts, Ian G., BA Wales, PhD S.Calif.   Prof.
    (Down.)
Willis, David W. E., MA Oxf., MPhil Oxf., DPhil
    Oxf.   Sr. Lectr. (Selw.)
Other Staff: 1 Lectr.

Materials Science and Metallurgy

Tel: (01223) 334300 Fax: (01223) 334567
    E-mail: web-replies@msm.cam.ac.uk
Barber, Zoe H., BA Camb., PhD Camb.   Sr.
    Lectr. (Down.)
Best, Serena M., BSc Sur., PhD Lond.   Reader,
    Ceramics and Medical Materials (S.Joh.)
Bhadeshia, Harshad K. D. H., BSc CNAA, PhD,
    FRS, FREng   Prof., Physical Metallurgy
    (Darw.)
Blamire, Mark G., MA Camb., PhD Camb.
    Prof., Device Materials (Hug.)
Bristowe, Paul D., BSc E.Anglia, PhD Sur.
    Reader, Computational Material Science
    (Cla.)
Burstein, Gordon T., MA Auck., MSc Auck., PhD
    Auck.   Prof., Materials Chemistry and
    Corrosion
Cameron, Ruth E., BA Camb., PhD Camb.
    Reader, Polymers and Medical Materials
Cheetham, Anthony K., BA Oxf., DPhil Oxf.
    Prof.
Clegg, William J., BSc Manc., DPhil Oxf.
    Reader, Ceramics (Selw.)
Clyne, Trevor W., MA PhD   Prof., Mechanics
    of Materials (Down.)
Driscoll, Judith L., BScEng ICL, PhD Camb.
    Reader, Materials Science (Trin.)
Fray, Derek J., BSc Lond., MA Camb., PhD Lond.
    Prof., Materials Chemistry (Fitz.)
Glowacki, Bartlomiej A., MA Camb., MSc
    Wroclaw, PhD Polish Acad.Sc.   Reader, Applied
    Superconductivity (Darw.)
Greer, Alan L., MA Camb., PhD Camb.   Prof.,
    Materials Science; Head* (Sid.)
Humphreys, C. J., BSc Lond., MA Oxf., PhD
    Goldsmiths' Prof., Materials Science (Selw.)
Knowles, Kevin M., DPhil Oxf., MA   Sr. Lectr.
    (Chur.)
Kumar, Ramachandran V., BTech Bom., PhD
    McM.   Sr. Lectr. (Trin.H.)
Little, John A., MA PhD   Sr. Lectr. (S.Cat.)
Midgley, Paul A., BSc Brist., MSc Brist., PhD
    Brist.   Prof. (Pet.)
Wallach, Eric R., MSc Qu., MA PhD   Sr. Lectr.
    (King's)
Windle, Alan H., BSc(Eng) Lond., PhD   Prof.
    (Trin.)
Other Staff: 3 Lectrs.; 1 Asst. Dir. of Res.; 3 Sr.
    Tech. Officers; 1 Tech. Officer; 1 Computer
    Officer

Mathematics, Applied, and Theoretical Physics

Tel: (01223) 765000 Fax: (01223) 765900
    E-mail: enquiries@damtp.cam.ac.uk
Allanach, Benjamin C., PhD S'ton.   ,
    Theoretical Physics
Barrow, John D., DPhil Oxf., FRAS, FRSA
    Prof., Mathematical Sciences (Cla.H.)
Berloff, Natalia G., PhD Flor.   Sr. Lectr. (Jes.)
Cowley, Stephen J., PhD   Sr. Lectr.
Dalziel, Stuart B., PhD   Sr. Lectr. (Sid.)
Davis, Anne C., BSc Lond., PhD Brist.   Prof.,
    Theoretical Physics (King's)
Dorey, Nicholas, PhD Edin.   Reader,
    Theoretical Physics
Eglen, Stephen J., BSc Nott., PhD Sus.   Sr. Lectr.
Fokas, Thanasis S., BSc Lond., PhD Cal.Tech., MD
    Miami(Fla.)   Prof., Nonlinear Mathematical
    Science (Cla. H.)

Gibbons, Gary W., MA PhD, FRS   Prof.,
    Theoretical Physics (Trin.)
Goldstein, Raymond E., PhD Cornell
    Schlumberger Prof., Complex Physical
    Systems (Chur.)
Green, Michael B., MA PhD, FRS   John
    Humphrey Plummer Prof., Theoretical
    Physics (Cla.H.)
Hawking, Stephen W., CBE, CH, BA Oxf., MA
    PhD Hon. ScD, FRS   Lucasian Prof.,
    Mathematics (Cai.)
Haynes, Peter H., MA PhD   Prof., Applied
    Mathematics; Head* (Qu.)
Hinch, E. John, MA PhD, FRS   Prof., Fluid
    Mechanics (Trin.)
Horgan, Ronald R., BSc Reading, DPhil Oxf., PhD
    Camb.   Prof., Theoretical and Mathematical
    Physics (Sid.)
Huppert, Herbert E., BSc Syd., MSc ANU, MSc
    Calif., PhD Calif., MA ScD, FRS   Prof.,
    Theoretical Geophysics (King's)
Iserles, Arieh, MA   Prof., Numerical Analysis
    of Differential Equations (King's)
Kent, Adrian P. A., PhD Camb.   Reader,
    Quantum Physics (Wolfs.)
Lister, John R., MA Camb., PhD Camb.   Reader,
    Fluid Dynamics (Trin.)
Manton, Nicholas S., MA PhD, FRS   Prof.,
    Mathematical Physics (S.Joh.)
McIntyre, Michael E., BSc Otago, PhD, FRS
    Prof., Atmospheric Dynamics (S.Joh.)
Osborn, Hugh, BSc Lond., PhD Lond., MA, FRS
    Prof., Quantum Field Theory (Trin.)
Papaloizou, John C. B., BSc Lond., DPhil Sus.,
    FRS   Prof., Mathematical Physics
Peake, Nigel, MA Camb., PhD Camb.   Prof.,
    Applied Mathematics (Emm.)
Pedley, Timothy J., MA Camb., PhD Camb., ScD
    Camb., FRS   GI Taylor Prof., Fluid
    Mechanics (Cai.)
Perry, Malcolm J., ScD   Prof., Theoretical
    Physics (Trin.)
Proctor, Michael R. E., MA Camb., PhD Camb.,
    ScD Camb.   Prof., Astrophysical Fluid
    Dynamics (Trin.)
Quevedo, Fernando, BSc PhD   Prof.,
    Theoretical Physics (Cai.)
Rallison, John M., MA PhD   Reader, Fluid
    Mechanics (Trin.)
Shellard, E. Paul S.   Sr. Lectr. (Trin.)
Stewart, John M., MA PhD   Reader,
    Gravitational Physics (King's)
Stuart, David M. A., MA Camb., MSc Prin., PhD
    Prin.   Reader, Non-linear Partial Differential
    Equations (S.Joh.)
Townsend, Paul K., PhD Brandeis, MA, FRS
    Prof., Theoretical Physics (Qu.)
Turok, Neil, MA Camb., PhD Lond.   Prof.,
    Mathematical Physics (Down.)
Wadhams, Peter, MA Camb., PhD Camb., ScD
    Camb.   Prof., Ocean Physics (Chur.)
Williams, Ruth M., MA PhD   Reader,
    Mathematical Physics (Gir.)
Willis, John R., BSc Lond., PhD Lond., FRS
    Prof., Theoretical Solid Mechanics (Fitz.)
Worster, M. Grae, MA PhD   Prof., Fluid
    Dynamics (Trin.)
Other Staff: 8 Lectrs.; 2 Asst. Dirs. of Res.; 1
    Sr. Computer Officer; 2 Computer Officers

Mathematics, Pure, and Mathematical Statistics

Tel: (01223) 337999 Fax: (01223) 337920
    E-mail: office@dpmms.cam.ac.uk
Brooks, Stephen P., PhD   Prof. (Wolfs.)
Carne, T. Keith, MA PhD   Sr. Lectr. (King's)
Coates, John H., BSc ANU, PhD, FRS
    Sadleirian Prof., Pure Mathematics (Emm.)
Dafermos, Michail   Reader, Mathematical
    Physics
Fritz, Peter K.   , Stohastic Analysis and
    Quantitative Finance (King's)
Gowers, W. Timothy, BA Camb., PhD Camb.
    Rouse Ball Prof., Mathematics (Trin.)
Grimmett, Geoffrey R., MA Oxf., MSc Oxf.,
    DPhil Oxf.   Prof., Mathematical Statistics;
    Head* (Chur.)
Grojnowski, Ian   Prof., Representation Theory

Hyland, J. Martin E., MA Oxf., MA Camb., DPhil
    Oxf., PhD   Prof. (King's)
Johnstone, Peter T., MA PhD ScD   Prof.,
    Foundations of Mathematics (S.Joh.)
Kelly, Frank P., BSc Durh., MA Camb., PhD
    Camb., FRS   Prof., Mathematics of Systems
    (Chr.)
Körner, Thomas W., MA PhD ScD   Prof.,
    Analysis (Trin.H.)
Leader, Imre B., MA PhD   Prof. (Trin.)
Norris, James R., MA Oxf., DPhil Oxf.   Prof.,
    Stochastic Analysis (Chur.)
Paternain, Gabriel P.   Reader (Trin.)
Pitts, Susan M., MA MSc PhD   Sr. Lectr.
    (Newn.)
Rogers, L. Chris G.   Prof., Statistical Science
    (S.Joh.)
Saxl, Jan, BSc Brist., MA Camb., MSc Oxf., DPhil
    Oxf., PhD Camb.   Prof. (Cai.)
Scholl, Anthony J.   Kuwait Prof., Number
    Theory and Algebra
Shepherd-Barron, Nicholas I., PhD Warw., BA
    Prof., Algebraic Geometry (Trin.)
Smith, Ivan   Reader, Pure Mathematics (Cai.)
Suhov, Yuri M., MA Moscow, MA Camb., PhD
    Moscow   Prof., Probability (S.Joh.)
Thomason, Andrew G., MA PhD   Prof.,
    Combinatorial Mathematics (Cla.)
Totaro, Burt J., AB Prin., PhD Calif.   Lowndean
    Prof., Astronomy and Geometry
Weber, Richard R., MA Camb., PhD Camb.
    Churchill Prof., Mathematics for
    Operational Research (Qu.)
Wilson, Pelham M. H., MA PhD ScD   Prof.
    (Trin.)
Other Staff: 8 Lectrs.; 2 Computer Officers

Music

Tel: (01223) 763481 Fax: (01223) 335067
    E-mail: tkw23@cam.ac.uk
Cross, Ian R. M., PhD   Reader, Music and
    Science (Wolfs.)
Davis, Ruth F., BMus PhD   Sr. Lectr. (Corp.)
Ennis, Martin W., MA PhD   Sr. Lectr. (Gir.)
Fenlon, Iain A., BMus Reading, MA Birm., PhD
    Birm.   Prof., Historical Musicology (King's)
Frolova-Walker, Marina, MA Moscow State Cons.,
    PhD Moscow State Cons.   Sr. Lectr. (Cla.)
Holloway, Robin G., MA PhD MusD   Prof.,
    Musical Composition (Cai.)
Jones, Andrew V., MA Oxf., MA Camb., DPhil
    Oxf., PhD   Sr. Lectr. (Selw.)
Marston, Nicholas J., MA PhD   Reader, Music
    Theory and Analysis (King's)
Parker, Roger, MMus Lond., PhD Lond.   Prof.
    (S.Joh.)
Rankin, Susan K., MMus Lond., MA PhD   Prof.,
    Mediaeval Music (Emm.)
Other Staff: 4 Lectrs.

Other Languages (Modern Greek Section)

Tel: (01223) 335038 Fax: (01223) 335062
    E-mail: nt272@cam.ac.uk
Holton, David W., MA Oxf., DPhil Oxf., PhD
    Prof., Modern Greek; Head* (Selw.)
Other Staff: 2 Res. Assocs.
Research: mediaeval, Renaissance and modern
    Greek literature

Pathology

Tel: (01223) 333695 Fax: (01223) 333346
    E-mail: admin@path.cam.ac.uk
Affara, Nabeel A., BSc Edin., MA Camb., PhD
    Glas.   Prof., Molecular Genetics and
    Genomics (Hug.)
Ajioka, James W.   Sr. Lectr. (Jes.)
Arends, Mark J., MA Camb., PhD Edin., MB ChB,
    FRCPath   Reader, Histopathology (Fitz.)
Brierley, Ian, BSc Leeds, DPhil York(UK)   Reader,
    Molecular Virology
Brown, Thomas D. K., BA Oxf., PhD Leic.   Sr.
    Lectr.
Clark, Michael R.   Reader, Therapeutic and
    Molecular Immunology (Darw.)
Collins, V. Peter, MB BCh BAO N.U.I., MD
    Stockholm, FRCPI   Prof., Histopathology

Cooke, Anne, BSc *Glas.*, DPhil *Sus.* Prof., Immunobiology (King's)

Digard, P. Sr. Lectr. (S.Joh.)

Du, Ming-Qing Prof., Oncological Pathology

Dunne, David W., BSc *Brist.*, PhD *Lond.* Prof., Parasitology

Edwards, Paul A. W., MA PhD Sr. Lectr. (Cla.)

Efstathiou, Stathi, BA *Leeds*, PhD Reader, Virology (Chur.)

Field, M. C. Reader, Cell Biology

Hughes, Colin, BSc *Kent*, PhD *Kent*, ScD *Camb.* Prof., Microbiology (Trin.)

Koronakis, Vassilis Prof., Molecular Biology

Minson, Anthony C., BSc *Birm.*, PhD *ANU*, MA Prof., Virology (Wolfs.)

Moffett, Ashley Reader, Reproductive Immunology

Trowsdale, John, BSc *Birm.*, PhD *Birm.* Prof., Immunology

Watson, Christine J., BSc *Glas.*, PhD *Lond.* Reader, Cell Signalling (Newn.)

Wyllie, Andrew H., BSc *Aberd.*, MB ChB *Aberd.*, PhD *Aberd.*, FRCPath, FRS Prof.; Head* (S.Joh.)

Xuereb, John H., MA MD Sr. Lectr. (S.Cat.)

Other Staff: 6 Lectrs.; 11 Assoc. Lectrs.; 1 Clin. Lectr.

Pharmacology

Tel: (01223) 334000 Fax: (01223) 334100
E-mail: drj23@cam.ac.uk

Barrand, Margery A., BSc *Lond.*, PhD *Lond.* Sr. Lectr. (Down.)

Cooper, Dermot M. F., BSc *N.U.I.*, MSc *N.U.I.*, PhD *Wales* Prof.

Edwardson, J. Michael, MA *Camb.*, PhD *Camb.* Reader (Fitz.)

Fan, Tai-Ping D., BSc *Lond.*, PhD *Lond.* Sr. Lectr. (Emm.)

Henderson, Robert M., BSc *Lond.*, MA *Camb.*, PhD *Lond.* Reader (Emm.)

Hiley, C. Robin, MA *Camb.*, PhD *Camb.* Reader (New H.)

Hladky, Stephen B., BA *Dartmouth*, MA PhD Reader (Jes.)

Irvine, Robin F., BA *Oxf.*, PhD, FRS Prof., Molecular Pharmacology (Corp.)

McNaughton, Peter A., BSc *Auck.*, DPhil *Oxf.* Prof.; Head* (Chr.)

Morton, A. Jennifer, BSc *Otago*, PhD *Otago* Reader (Newn.)

Murrell-Lagnado, Ruth D., BSc PhD Sr. Lectr. (Newn.)

Taylor, Colin W., MA *Camb.*, PhD *Camb.* Prof., Cellular Pharmacology (Down.)

Van Veen, Hendrik W., MSc *Wageningen*, PhD *Wageningen* Sr. Lectr. (Cla.)

Other Staff: 3 Lectrs.; 1 Computer Officer

Philosophy

see also Classics, and Hist. and Philos. of Sci.

Tel: (01223) 335090 Fax: (01223) 335091
E-mail: phil-admin@lists.cam.ac.uk

Blackburn, Simon W., MA *Camb.*, PhD *Camb.*, Hon. LLD *Sund.* Prof. (Trin.)

Cassam, Quassim, BA *Oxf.*, BPhil *Oxf.*, DPhil *Oxf.* Knightbridge Prof. (King's)

Geuss, Raymond, BA *Col.*, PhD *Col.* Prof.

Heal, Barbara J., MA PhD Prof. (S.Joh.)

Lillehammer, Hallvard, BA *Camb.*, MPhil *Camb.*, PhD *Camb.* Sr. Lectr. (King's)

Oliver, Alexander D., MA *Camb.*, MA *Yale*, MPhil *Yale*, PhD *Camb.* Reader (Cai.)

Olsaretti, Serena M., MA *Oxf.*, MPhil *Oxf.*, DPhil *Oxf.* Sr. Lectr. (S.Joh.)

Potter, Michael D., MA *Camb.*, DPhil *Oxf.* Reader, Philosophy of Mathematics (Fitz.)

Other Staff: 3 Lectrs.; 2 Temp. Lectrs.; 2 Res. Fellows

Physics

see also Maths., Appl., and Theoret. Phys.

Tel: (01223) 337200 Fax: (01223) 363263
E-mail: administration@phy.cam.ac.uk

Alexander, Paul, BA *Camb.*, PhD *Camb.* Sr. Lectr. (Jes.)

Allison, William, MA *Camb.*, PhD *Lond.* Reader, Experimental Physics (Fitz.)

Ansorge, Richard E., MA *Camb.*, PhD *Camb.* Sr. Lectr., Fitz.

Batley, John R., BA *Camb.*, DPhil *Oxf.* Sr. Lectr. (Chr.)

Bland, James A. C., MA *Camb.*, PhD *Camb.* Prof., Experimental Physics (Selw.)

Carter, Janet R., MA *Camb.*, PhD *Camb.* Prof., Experimental Particle Physics

Chaudhri, Mohammad M., PhD *Camb.* Reader (Darw.)

Cooper, John R., BSc *Lond.*, PhD *Lond.* Reader, Physics of High Temperature Superconductors (Darw.)

Cooper, Nigel R., BA *Camb.*, DPhil *Oxf.* Prof., Theoretical Physics (Pemb.)

Donald, Athene M., MA *Camb.*, PhD *Camb.* Prof., Experimental Physics (Rob.)

Duffett-Smith, Peter J., MA *Camb.*, PhD *Camb.* Reader, Experimental Radio Physics (Down.)

Ford, Christopher J. B., BA *Camb.*, PhD *Camb.* Reader, Quantum Electrics (Girt.)

Friend, Sir Richard, MA *Camb.*, PhD *Camb.*, FRS Cavendish Prof. (S.Joh.)

Gibson, Valerie Reader, High Energy Physics (Trin.)

Green, David A. Sr. Lectr. (Chur.)

Greenham, Neil C., BA *Camb.*, PhD *Camb.* Reader (Cla.)

Gull, Stephen F., MA *Camb.*, PhD *Camb.* Prof. (S.Joh.)

Haniff, Christopher A., MA *Camb.*, PhD *Camb.* Prof. (Down.)

Hills, Richard E., PhD *Calif.*, BA Prof., Radio Astronomy (S.Edm.)

Hobson, Michael P., BA *Camb.*, PhD *Camb.* Reader, Astrophysics and Cosmology (Trin.H.)

Hughes, Howard P., BSc *Lond.*, MA *Camb.*, PhD *Camb.*, ScD *Camb.* Reader (S.Joh.)

Jones, Geraint A. C., BSc *Wales*, PhD *Wales*, MA Reader, Nanoelectronics (Rob.)

Josephson, Brian D., MA *Camb.*, PhD *Camb.*, DSc *Exe.*, Hon. DSc *Wales*, FRS Prof. (Trin.)

Lasenby, Anthony N., MSc *Lond.*, MA *Camb.*, PhD *Manc.* Prof., Astrophysics and Cosmology (Qu.)

Liang, Wei Yao, BSc *Lond.*, PhD *Camb.* Prof., Superconductivity (Cai.)

Littlewood, Peter B., BA *Camb.*, PhD *Camb.* Prof.; Head* (Trin.)

Longair, Malcolm S., BSc *St And.*, MA *Camb.*, PhD *Camb.*, LLD *Dund.*, FRS, FRAS, FRSEd Jacksonian Prof., Natural Philosophy (Cla.H.)

Lonzarich, Gilbert G., BA *Calif.*, MS *Minn.*, PhD *Br.Col.*, MA, FRS Prof., Condensed Matter Physics (Trin.)

MacKay, David J. C., BA *Camb.*, PhD *Calif.* Prof., Natural Philosophy (Darw.)

Needs, Richard J., BSc *Brist.*, PhD *Camb.* Prof., Theoretical and Computational Physics (Rob.)

Parker, Michael A., MA *Camb.*, PhD *Lond.* Prof., High Energy Physics (Pet.)

Payne, Michael C., MA *Lond.*, PhD *Lond.* Prof., Computational Physics (Pemb.)

Pepper, Sir Michael, BSc *Reading*, PhD *Reading*, MA ScD, FRS Prof. (Trin.)

Phillips, Richard T., MA *Camb.*, PhD *Camb.* Prof., Quantum Physics (Cla.)

Richer, John S. Reader, Astrophysics (Chur.)

Ritchie, David A., MA *Oxf.*, DPhil *Sus.* Prof., Experimental Physics (Rob.)

Simons, Benjamin D., MA *Camb.*, PhD *Camb.* Prof., Theoretical Physics (S.Joh.)

Sirringhaus, Henning, PhD *E.T.H.Zürich* Hitachi Prof., Electron Device Physics (Chur.)

Smith, Charles G., MA *Camb.*, PhD *Camb.* Prof., Experimental Quantum Physics (Cla.H.)

Steiner, Ullrich, PhD *Weizmann* John Humphrey Plummer Prof., Polymer Physics

Terentjev, Eugene M., MsD *Moscow*, PhD *Russian Acad.Sc.* Prof., Polymer Physics (Qu.)

Thomson, Mark A., BA *Oxf.*, DPhil *Oxf.* Reader, Experimental Partide Physics (Emm.)

Ward, David R., MA *Camb.*, PhD *Camb.* Prof., Particle Physics (Qu.)

Warner, Mark, MA *Camb.*, PhD *Lond.* Prof., Theoretical Physics (Corp.)

Webber, Bryan R., MA *Oxf.*, MA *Camb.*, PhD *Calif.* Prof., Theoretical Physics (Emm.)

Withington, Stafford, BTech *Brad.*, PhD *Manc.* Prof., Analytical Physics (Down.)

Other Staff: 7 Lectrs.; 1 Asst. Dir. of Res.; 1 Sr. Asst. in Res.; 8 Sr. Tech. Officers; 4 Tech. Officers; 5 Computer Officers

Physiology, Development and Neuroscience

Tel: (01223) 333750, 333899 Fax: (01223) 333840 E-mail: reception@pdn.cam.ac.uk

Barnes, Richard J., MB BChir MA PhD Sr. Lectr. (Emm.)

Brand, Andrea H., BA *Oxf.*, PhD *Camb.*, FMedSci Prof., Developmental Neurobiology (King's)

Bray, Sarah J., BA *Camb.*, MPhil *Camb.*, PhD *Camb.* Reader, Developmental Biology (Down.)

Brown, Nick H., PhD *Harv.* Reader, Cell Biology

Burton, Graham J., MB BChir MA MD Prof., Reproductive Biology (S.Joh.)

Carpenter, Roger H. S., MA PhD Reader, Oculomotor Physiology (Cai.)

Chivers, David J., MA PhD Reader, Primate Biology and Conservation (Selw.)

Colledge, William H., BSc *Lond.*, PhD *Lond.* Reader, Molecular Physiology (Chur.)

Crawford, Andrew C., MA PhD, FRS Prof., Neurophysiology (Trin.)

Dyball, Richard E. J., MA *Camb.*, VetMB *Camb.*, PhD *Brist.*, ScD *Camb.* Reader (Cla.)

Edgley, Stephen A., BSc *Brist.*, MA *Brist.*, PhD *Brist.* Reader, Sensorimotor Neuroscience (S.Joh.)

Ferguson-Smith, Anne C., BSc *Glas.*, MS *Yale*, PhD *Yale* Reader, Developmental Genetics (Darw.)

Fettiplace, Robert, PhD *Camb.*, FRS Prof.

Fowden, Abigail L., MA *Camb.*, PhD *Camb.* Prof., Perinatal Physiology (Gir.)

Guissani, Dino A., BSc *Lond.*, PhD *Lond.* Reader, Developmental Cardiovascular Physiology and Medicine (Cai.)

Hardie, Roger C., BA *Camb.*, PhD *ANU* Prof., Cellular Neuroscience (Emm.)

Harris, William A., BA *Calif.*, PhD *Cal.Tech.*, FRS, FMedSci Prof., Anatomy; Head* (Cla.)

Holt, Christine E., BSc *Sus.*, PhD *Lond.*, FMedSci Prof., Developmental Neuroscience (Cai.)

Huang, Christopher L.-H., BM BCh *Oxf.*, MA *Oxf.*, MA *Camb.*, DM *Oxf.*, DSc *Oxf.*, MD *Camb.*, PhD *Camb.*, ScD *Camb.* Prof., Cell Physiology (New H.)

Johnson, Martin H., MA PhD Prof., Reproductive Sciences (Chr.)

Keynes, Roger J., MA MB BChir, FMedSci Prof., Neuroscience (Trin.)

Matthews, Hugh R., MA PhD Reader, Sensory Physiology (S.Joh.)

Roberts, Angela C. Reader, Behavioural Neuroscience (Gir.)

Robinson, Hugh P. C. Sr. Lectr. (Corp.)

Sage, Stewart O., MA PhD Reader, Cell Physiology (Selw.)

Schofield, Paul N., MA PhD Sr. Lectr. (Corp.)

Schultz, Wolfram, BA *Heidel.*, DrMed *Heidel.* Prof., Neuroscience (Chur.)

Surani, M. Azim H., CBE, BSc *Lond.*, MSc *Strath.*, PhD, FRS Mary Marshall and Arthur Walton Prof., Physiology of Reproduction (King's)

Tolhurst, David J., MA PhD Sr. Lectr. (Emm.)

White, Robert A. H., BA *Oxf.*, DPhil *Oxf.* Reader, Developmental Biology (Selw.)

Winter, Ian M. Sr. Lectr. (S.Joh.)

Other Staff: 7 Lectrs.; 2 Assoc. Lectrs.; 3 Sr. Tech. Officers; 2 Computer Officers; 1

Univ. Clin. Anatomist; 1 Univ. Clin. Vet. Anatomist; 1 Univ. Physiologist

Plant Sciences

Tel: (01223) 333900 Fax: (01223) 333953
E-mail: reception@plantsci.cam.ac.uk
Baulcomb, David C., BSc Leeds, PhD Edin. Prof., Botany
Carr, John P., BSc Liv., PhD Liv. Sr. Lectr.
Davies, Julia M., BSc Wales, PhD Liv. Sr. Lectr. (Rob.)
Gilligan, Chris A., BA Oxf., MA Prof., Mathematical Biology (King's)
Glover, Beverley, BSc St And., PhD Norwich Sr. Lectr. (Qu.)
Gray, John C., BSc Birm., PhD Birm., MA Prof., Plant Molecular Biology; Head* (Rob.)
Griffiths, Howard, BSc Dund., PhD Dund. Prof., Plant Ecology (Cla.)
Hanke, David E., BA Oxf., PhD Sr. Lectr. (Jes.)
Hibberd, Julian, BSc Wales, PhD Wales
Johnstone, Keith, PhD Sr. Lectr. (Qu.)
Parker, John S., MA Oxf., DPhil Oxf. Dir., Botanic Garden; Curator, Herbarium; Prof., Plant Cytogenetics (S.Cat)
Smith, Alison G., PhD Prof., Plant Biochemistry (Corp.)
Tanner, Edmund V. J., MA PhD Sr. Lectr. (Cai.)
Webb, Alex A. R., BSc Stir., PhD Lanc. Sr. Lectr.
Other Staff: 2 Lectrs.; 1 Sr. Tech. Officer; 1 Asst. Curator, Herbarium

Polar Research

Scott Polar Research Institute

Tel: (01223) 336540 Fax: (01223) 336549
E-mail: enquiries@spri.cam.ac.uk
Dowdeswell, Julian A., BA Camb., PhD Camb. Prof., Physical Geography; Dir.* (Jes.)
Other Staff: 1 Librarian

Psychology, Experimental

Tel: (01223) 333552 Fax: (01223) 333564
E-mail: reception@psychol.cam.ac.uk
Bussey, Timothy J., BSc (Chem) Vic.(BC), BSc(Psych) Br.Col., PhD Camb. Sr. Lectr. (Pemb.)
Clayton, Nicola S., MA PhD Prof., Comparative Cognition (Cla.)
Dickinson, Anthony, BSc Manc., DPhil Sus. Prof., Comparative Psychology (Hug.)
Everitt, Barry J., BSc Hull, PhD Birm., ScD Camb., FRS Prof., Behavioural Neuroscience (Down.)
Mollon, John D., BA Oxf., DPhil Oxf., MA Prof., Visual Neuroscience (Corp.)
Moore, Brian C. J., MA PhD Prof., Auditory Perception (Wolfs.)
Robbins, Trevor W., MA PhD Prof., Cognitive Neuroscience; Head* (Down.)
Russell, James, MA Oxf., PhD Lond. Reader, Cognitive Development
Saksida, Lisa M., MA Br.Col., MSc Edin., PhD Carnegie-Mellon Sr. Lectr. (Newn.)
Tyler, Lorraine K., PhD Prof. (Cla.)
Other Staff: 9 Lectrs.

Slavonic Studies

Tel: (01223) 335007 Fax: (01223) 335062
E-mail: slavon@hermes.cam.ac.uk
Etkind, Alexander M., PhD Leningrad Reader, Russian Literature and Cultural History (King's)
Franklin, Simon C., DPhil Oxf., MA PhD Prof.; Head* (Cla.)
Kelly, Aileen M., MA PhD Reader, Intellectual History and Russian Culture (King's)
Ward, C. E., BEd Lond., MA Lanc., PhD E.Anglia Sr. Lectr. (Rob.)
Widdis, E. K., MA PhD Sr. Lectr. (Trin.)
Other Staff: 2 Lectrs.; 1 Sr. Lang. Teaching Officer

Social and Political Sciences

Tel: (01223) 334520 Fax: (01223) 334550
E-mail: sps-enquiries@lists.cam.ac.uk
Baert, Patrick J. N., DPhil Oxf. Sr. Lectr. (Selw.)
Born, Georgina E. M., BSc Lond., PhD Lond. Prof., Sociology Anthropology and Music (Emm.)
Brown, William A., CBE, BA Oxf., MA Camb. Montagu Burton Prof., Industrial Relations; Chairman* (Darw.)
Burchell, Brendan J., BSc Warw., PhD Warw. Sr. Lectr. (Magd.)
Dunn, John M., MA Camb. Prof., Political Theory (King's)
Duveen, Gerard M., BSc Sur., MSc Strath., DPhil Sus. Reader, Genetic Social Psychology (Corp.)
Gamble, Andrew M., BA Camb., MA Durh., PhD Camb. Prof., Politics (Qu.)
Golombok, Susan E., BSc Glas., MSc Lond., PhD Lond. Prof., Family Research
Hines, Melissa, BA Prin., MA Calif., PhD Calif. Prof., Psychology
Hughes, Claire H., PhD Camb. Reader, Developmental Psychology (Newn.)
Ingham, Geoffrey K., PhD Camb. Reader, Political Economy and Sociology (Chr.)
Lamb, Michael E., MPhil Yale, PhD Yale Prof., Psychology in the Social Sciences
Lane, Christel O., BA Essex, MA Camb., PhD Lond. Prof., Economic Sociology (S.Joh.)
Lehmann, A. David, DPhil Oxf. Reader (Wolfs.)
Mitchell, Juliet C. W., MA Oxf. Prof., Psychoanalysis and Gender Studies (Jes.)
Runciman, David, BA Camb., PhD Camb. Sr. Lectr. (Trin.H.)
Scott, Jacqueline L., BA Sus., MA Mich., PhD Mich. Prof., Empirical Sociology (Qu.)
Therborn, Göran, FilKand Lund, FilLic Lund, FilDr Lund Prof., Sociology
Thompson, Helen E. Sr. Lectr. (Cla.)
Thompson, John B., BA Keele, PhD Camb. Prof., Sociology (Jes.)
Other Staff: 7 Lectrs.; 1 Computer Officer

Spanish and Portuguese

Tel: (01223) 335005 Fax: (01223) 335062
E-mail: spanport@hermes.cam.ac.uk
Boldy, Steven R., MA Camb., PhD Camb. Sr. Lectr., Latin-American Studies; Head* (Emm.)
Haywood, Louise M., BA Lond., MA Lond., PhD Lond. Sr. Lectr. (Trin.H.)
Kantaris, E. Geoffrey, MA Camb., PhD Camb. Sr. Lectr. (S.Cat.)
Keown, Dominic, PhD Sheff. Reader, Catalan (Fitz.)
Lisboa, Maria Manuel G., BSc MA PhD Reader, Portuguese (S.Joh.)
McKendrick, Melveena C., BA Lond., MA Camb., PhD Camb. Prof., Spanish Golden Age Literature, Culture and Society (Gir.)
Sinclair, Alison S., MA Camb., PhD Camb. Prof., Modern Spanish Literature and Intellectual History (Cla.)
Smith, Paul J., MA Camb., PhD Camb. Prof., Spanish (Trin.H.)
Other Staff: 3 Lectrs.; 1 Sr. Lang. Teaching Officer

Veterinary Medicine

Tel: (01223) 339900 Fax: (01223) 339903
E-mail: ubss@mole.bio.cam.ac.uk
Allen, William R., BVSc Syd., PhD Camb. Jim Joel Prof., Equine Reproduction (Rob.)
Archer, F. Joy, VMD MS PhD Sr. Lectr.
Blacklaw, Barbara A. Sr. Lectr. (Newn.)
Blakemore, William F., BVS Brist., PhD Lond., MA ScD Prof., Neuropathology (Wolfs.)
Brearley, Jacqueline C., VetMB MA Sr. Lectr. (L.Cav.)
Broom, Donald M., MA Camb., PhD Camb. Colleen Macleod Prof., Animal Welfare (S.Cat)

Bryant, Clare E., BSc S'ton., BVetMed Lond., PhD Lond. Sr. Lectr. (Qu.)
Dobson, Jane M., BVetMed Lond., MA Camb., DVetMed Lond. Sr. Lectr. (Darw.)
Field, Hugh J., BSc Lond., PhD Brist., MA Reader, Comparative Virology (Qu.)
Franklin, Robin J. M., BSc Lond., BVetMed Lond., PhD Camb. Prof., Neuroscience (Pemb.)
Gibson, John S., MA Camb., VetMB Camb., PhD Camb. Reader, Pathophysiology (Cla.)
Herrtage, Michael E., BVSc Liv., MA Liv., DVSc Liv. Reader, Small Animal Medicine (S.Edm.)
Holmes, Mark A., MA PhD VetMB Sr. Lectr. (Fitz.)
Jefferies, Andrew R., MA VetMB Univ. Pathologist (Gir.)
Jeffery, Nicholas D., BVSc Brist., PhD Camb. Prof., Veterinary Clinical Studies
Langley-Hobbs, Sorrel J., BVetMed MA Univ. Surgeon (S.Edm.)
Lloyd, Sheelagh S., MVB Trinity(Dub.), PhD Penn. Sr. Lectr. (Wolfs.)
Maskell, Duncan J., MA Camb., PhD Camb. Marks and Spencer Prof., Farm Animal Health, Food Science and Food Safety; Head* (Wolfs.)
McConnell, Ian, BVMS Glas., MA PhD Prof., Veterinary Science
Mueller, Karin, MVSc Giessen Univ. Physician
Sargan, David R., PhD Lond., MA Sr. Lectr. (S.Joh.)
Scase, Timothy J., BSc Edin., BVM&S Edin., PhD Camb. Sr. Lectr.
Tucker, Alexander W. Sr. Lectr. (Pemb.)
Watson, Penelope J., VetMB MA Sr. Lectr.
Other Staff: 5 Lectrs.; 7 Assoc. Lectrs.; 2 Sr. Tech. Officers; 17 Residents; 1 Sr. Asst. in Res.
Research: genetics; infection and immunity; neurology

Zoology

Tel: (01223) 336600 E-mail: jj280@cam.ac.uk
Akam, Michael E., BA Camb., DPhil Oxf. Prof.; Dir., Museum of Zool. (King's)
Amos, William Reader, Evolutionary Genetics (Gir.)
Balmford, Andrew P., MA Camb., PhD Camb. Prof., Conservation Science (Cla.)
Barnes, Richard S. K., BSc Lond., PhD Qld. Sr. Lectr. (S.Cat.)
Bate, C. M., BA Oxf., PhD Camb. Royal Society Prof., Developmental Neurobiology (King's)
Burrows, Malcolm, MA Camb., MA Oxf., PhD St And., ScD Camb., FRS Prof.; Head* (Wolfs.)
Clack, Jennifer A. C., BSc Newcastle(UK), MA Camb., PhD Newcastle(UK) Curator, Vertebrate Palaeontol. (Museum of Zool.); Prof., Vertebrate Palaeontology (Darw.)
Clutton-Brock, Timothy H., MA PhD ScD, FRS Prince Philip Prof., Ecology and Evolutionary Biology (Magd.)
Davies, Nicholas B., MA Oxf., MA Camb., DPhil Oxf., FRS Prof., Behavioural Ecology (Pemb.)
Ellington, Charles P., BA Duke, MA PhD, FRS Prof., Animal Mechanics (Down.)
Foster, William A., MA PhD Sr. Lectr.; Curator (Insects), Museum of Zool. (Cla.)
Hedwig, Berthold G. Reader, Neurobiology (Wolfs.)
Jackson, Stephen P., BSc Leeds, PhD Edin. Quick Prof., Biology (S.Joh.)
Johnstone, Rufus A., DPhil Oxf. Reader, Evolution and Animal Behaviour (Trin.)
Keverne, E. Barry, BSc Lond., PhD Lond., MA, FRS Prof., Behavioural Neuroscience (King's)
Laskey, Ronald A., MA Oxf., DPhil Oxf., PhD, FRS Charles Darwin Prof., Animal Embryology (Darw.)
Laughlin, Simon B., PhD ANU, MA, FRS Prof., Neurobiology (Chur.)
Simpson, Patricia A., BSc S'ton., PhD Paris, FRS Prof., Comparative Embryology (Newn.)
Skaer, Helen L. B. Reader, Developmental Biology (Jes.)

Smith, Derek J., PhD *New Mexico*   Prof.,
    Infectious Disease Informatics
Smith, James C., MA *Camb.*, PhD *Lond.*, FRS
    John Humphrey Plummer Prof., Cell
    Biology (Chr.)
Sutherland, William J., PhD *CNAA*   Miriam
    Rothschild Prof., Conservation Biology
Other Staff: 9 Lectrs.; 76 Res. Staff; 1
    Computer Officer

MEDICINE

Faculty of Clinical Medicine—for Anatomy,
Pathology, Pharmacology, Physiology, see
above

Tel: (01223) 336700 Fax: (01223) 336709
Silverman, Jonathan D.   Assoc. Dean
Wood, Diana F., MD *Birm.*, FRCP   Dir., Med.
    Educn./Clin. Dean

Biochemistry, Clinical

Tel: (01223) 336792 Fax: (01223) 330598
    E-mail: lacp1@cam.ac.uk
Luzio, J. Paul, MA PhD, FMedSci   Prof.,
    Molecular Membrane Biology (S.Edm.)
O'Rahilly, Stephen, MB BCh BAO *N.U.I.*, MD
    N.U.I., FRS   Prof., Clinical Biochemistry
    and Medicine; Head* (Chur.)
Owen, David, BA DPhil   Reader, Structural
    and Molecular Biology
Robinson, Margaret, PhD   Prof., Molecular
    Cell Biology
Siddle, Ken, MA PhD   Serono Prof., Molecular
    Endocrinology (Chur.)
Vidal-Puig, Antonio, MD PhD   Reader,
    Human Metabolism
Other Staff: 2 Lectrs.

Genetics, Medical

Tel: (01223) 331154 Fax: (01223) 331206
    E-mail: lms28@cam.ac.uk
Clayton, David G.   Prof., Biostatistics (non-
    clinical)
Ffrench-Constant, Charles K., MA *Camb.*, MB
    BChir *Camb.*   Prof., Neurological Genetics
    (Pemb.)
Karet, Fiona E., BSc MB BS PhD, FRCP,
    FMedSci   Prof., Nephrology
Raymond, F. L., MA DPhil, FRCP   Sr. Lectr.
    (S.Joh.)
Rubinzstein, David C., BSc(Med) MB ChB PhD,
    FMedSci, FRCPath   Prof., Molecular
    Neurogenetics
Sandford, R. N., BSc(Med) MB PhD, FRCP
    Reader, Renal Genetics
Todd, John A., BSc *Edin.*, PhD *Camb.*   Prof.
    (Cai.)
Wicker, Linda S.   Prof., Immunogenetics
    (non-clinical)
Woods, C. G., MB MD, FRCP   Reader,
    Human Genetics
Yates, John R. W., MA *Oxf.*, MA *Camb.*, MB BS
    Lond.   Prof.; Acting Head* (S.Cat.)
Other Staff: 2 Clin. Lectrs.
Research: genes contributing to X-linked disease,
    particularly intellectual disability; genetic
    components of neurological disease,
    including cellular mechanisms of
    neurodegeneration and developmental
    biology of neural cell development and
    repair; genetics of eye diseases (age-related
    macular degeneration and retinoschisis);
    genetics of inflammatory disorders and
    juvenile diabetes

Haematology

Tel: (01223) 336820 Fax: (01223) 762670
Allain, J.-P., MD *Paris*, PhD *Paris*   Prof.,
    Transfusion Medicine (Corp.)
Gottgens, Berthold   Reader, Molecular
    Haematology
Green, Anthony R., MB BS *Lond.*, MA *Camb.*,
    PhD *Lond.*, FRCP, FRCPath   Prof., Haemato-
    Oncology; Head* (Qu.)
Huntington, James A.   Reader, Molecular
    Haemostasis
Lee, Helen H., BSc *N.Y.*, MSc *Oxf.*, PhD *N.Y.*
    Reader, Biomedical Technology (L.Cav.)

Ouwehand, Willem H., MD PhD, FRCPath
    Reader, Platelet Biology and Genetics
    (Trin.)
Read, R. J., PhD *Alta.*   Prof., Protein
    Crystallography
Warren, A. J., MB ChB *Glas.*, PhD *Camb.*, FRCP,
    FRCPath, FMedSci   Prof. (Cai.)
Williamson, L. M., BSc *Edin.*, MB ChB *Edin.*,
    MD *Edin.*, FRCP, FRCPath   Reader,
    Transfusion Medicine (L.Cav.)
Other Staff: 1 Asst. Dir. of Res.

Medicine

Tel: (01223) 336844 Fax: (01223) 336846
    E-mail: nf258@medschl.cam.ac.uk
Bennett, Martin R., MB BCh *Wales*, MA *Camb.*,
    PhD *Wales*, FRCP, FMedSci   British Heart
    Foundation Prof., Cardiovascular Sciences
Blackwell, Jenefer M., BSc *W.Aust.*, PhD *W.Aust.*,
    FMedSci   Glaxo Prof., Molecular
    Parasitology (Newn.)
Brown, Morris J., MSc *Lond.*, MD, FRCP, FAHA,
    FMedSci   Prof., Clinical Pharmacology
    (Cai.)
Chatterjee, Vengali K. K., BM BCh *Oxf.*, MA
    Camb., FRCP, FMedSci   Prof.,
    Endocrinology (Chur.)
Chilvers, Edwin R., BMedSci *Nott.*, BM BS *Nott.*,
    PhD *Lond.*, MA, FRCPEd, FRCP, FMedSci
    Prof., Respiratory Medicine (S. Edm.)
Compston, Juliet E., BSc *Lond.*, MD *Lond.*, FRCP,
    FRCPath, FMedSci   Prof., Bone Medicine
    (Jes.)
Cox, Timothy M., BS *Lond.*, MSc *Lond.*, MD
    Lond., MD *Camb.*, MA, FRCP, FMedSci   Prof.
    (Sid.)
Davenport, Anthony P., BSc MA PhD   Reader,
    Cardiovascular Pharmacology (S.Cat.)
Fearon, Doug T., FRS   Sheila Joan Smith Prof.,
    Immunology (Trin.)
Gaston, John S. H., BM BCh *Oxf.*, MA *Oxf.*, PhD
    Brist., FRCP   Prof., Rheumatology (S. Edm.)
Lehner, Paul J., PhD, FRCP, FMedSci   Prof.,
    Immunology and Medicine
Lever, Andrew M. L., BSc *Wales*, MD *Wales*,
    FRCP, FRCPEd, FRCPath, FRSCan, FMedSci
    Prof., Infectious Diseases (Pet.)
Lomas, David A., PhD *Camb.*, ScD *Camb.*, FRCP,
    FMedSci   Prof., Respiratory Biology (Trin.)
Menon, David K., MD *Madr.*, PhD *Lond.*,
    FFARCS, FMedSci   Prof., Anaesthesia
    (Qu.)
Morrell, Nicholas W., BSc *Lond.*, MD, FRCP
    Prof., Cardio-Pulmonary Medicine
O'Shaughnessey, Kevin M., BM BCh *Oxf.*, DPhil
    Oxf., FRCP   Sr. Lectr. (Cai.)
Sinclair, John H., BSc *Essex*, PhD *Essex*   Prof.,
    Molecular Virology (Wolfs.)
Sissons, J. G. Patrick, MA *Camb.*, MD *Lond.*,
    FRCP   Regius Prof., Physic; Head* (Darw.)
Smith, Kenneth G. C., BMedSci *Melb.*, MB BS
    Melb., MA *Camb.*, PhD *Melb.*, FRCP   Prof.,
    Experimental Medicine (Pemb.)
Sterling, Jane C., MA PhD, FRCP   Sr. Lectr.
    (Newn.)
Other Staff: 4 Lectrs.; 1 Assoc. Lectr.; 4 Clin.
    Lectrs.

Neurosciences, Clinical

E-mail: vas33@cam.ac.uk
Barker, Roger A.   Reader (Sid.)
Baron, Jean-Claude   Prof., Stroke Medicine
    (Cla.H.)
Carpenter, Thomas A., MA PhD   Reader,
    Imaging Sciences (Cla.H.)
Compston, David A. S., MB BS *Lond.*, PhD *Lond.*,
    FRCP   Prof., Neurology; Head* (Jes.)
Czosnyka, M.   Reader, Brain Physics
Fawcett, James W.   Merck Company
    Foundation Prof., Experimental
    Neurobiology (King's)
Hodges, John R.   Prof., Behavioural Neurology
    (King's)
Pickard, John D., MA MB MChir, FRCS,
    FRCSEd   Prof., Neurosurgery (S.Cat)
Spillantini, Maria-Grazia   Prof., Molecular
    Neurology (Cla.H.)

Other Staff: 2 Lectrs.; 2 Sr. Tech. Officers

Obstetrics and Gynaecology

Tel: (01223) 336881 Fax: (01223) 215327
    E-mail: obgyn-headofdept@lists.cam.ac.uk
Charnock-Jones, D. Stephen, BSc *Lond.*, PhD
    Camb.   Reader, Reproductive Biology
    (Corp.)
Prentice, Andrew, BSc *Glas.*, MB ChB *Glas.*, MA
    Camb., MD *Newcastle(UK)*, FRCOG   Sr. Lectr.;
    Hon. Consultant
Smith, Gordon C. S., BSc *Glas.*, MB ChB *Glas.*,
    MD *Glas.*, PhD *Glas.*   Prof.; Head*
Other Staff: 1 Lectr.

Oncology

Tel: (01223) 404124 Fax: (01223) 404128
    E-mail: bruce.ponder@cancer.org.uk
Burnet, N. G., MD *Camb.*, FRCS, FRCR
    Reader, Radiation Oncology (Cla.)
Caldas, Carlos, MD *Lisbon*, FACP, FRCP   Prof.,
    Clinical Oncology
Earl, H. M., MB BS *Lond.*, PhD *Lond.*, FRCP
    Reader, Clinical Cancer Medicine
Murphy, Gillian, BSc *Birm.*, PhD *Birm.*   Prof.,
    Cell Biology
Neal, David E., BSc *Lond.*, MB BS *Lond.*, MS
    Lond., FRCS, Hon. FRCSEd, FMedSci   Prof.,
    Surgical Oncology
Ponder, Bruce A. J., KB, MA *Camb.*, MB BChir
    Camb., PhD *Lond.*, FRCP, FRCPath, FMedSci,
    FRS   Li Ka Shing Prof.; Head* (Jes.)
Tavare, Simon, BSc *Sheff.*, MSc *Sheff.*, PhD *Sheff.*
    Prof., Cancer Research (Bioinformatics and
    Computational Biology) (Cai.)
Venkitaraman, Ashok R., MB BS *Madr.*, MA
    Camb., PhD *Lond.*, FMedSci   Ursula Zoëllner
    Prof., Cancer Research (New H.)
Other Staff: 1 Lectr.; 1 Clin. Lectr.
Research: cellular and molecular biology of
    cancer, imaging, genomics, genetics;
    clinical cancer research; epidemiology;
    genetics

Paediatrics

Tel: (01223) 336885
    E-mail: medschl-paediatrics@lists.cam.ac.uk
Acerini, Carlo L., MA *Camb.*, MD *Dund.*   Sr.
    Lectr.
Dunger, David B., MA *Oxf.*, MD *Lond.*, FRCP,
    FRCPCH   Prof.
Hughes, Ieuan A., MA *Camb.*, MD *Wales*, FRCP
    Prof.; Head* (Fitz.)
Tasker, Robert C., MB BS *Lond.*, MA *Camb.*,
    FRCP   Sr. Lectr. (Selw.)
Other Staff: 2 Clin. Lectrs.

Psychiatry

Tel: (01223) 336965 Fax: (01223) 336968
Baron-Cohen, Simon, BA *Oxf.*, MPhil *Lond.*, PhD
    Lond.   Prof., Developmental
    Psychopathology (Trin.)
Bullmore, Edward T., BA *Oxf.*, MB BS *Lond.*,
    PhD *Lond.*   Prof. (Wolfs.)
Croudace, Tim J., PhD   Sr. Lectr.
Fletcher, Paul, MB BS *Lond.*, PhD *Lond.*   Reader
Goodyer, Ian M., MD *Lond.*   Prof., Child and
    Adolescent Psychiatry (Wolfs.)
Holland, Tony J.   Prof., Learning Disability
    Psychiatry
Huppert, Felicia A., PhD   Prof., Psychology
    (Darw.)
Jones, Peter B., PhD *Lond.*, FRCP, FMedSci
    Prof.; Head* (Wolfs.)
Sahakian, Barbara J., BA *Mt.Holyoke*, PhD *Camb.*
    Prof., Neuropsychology (Cla.H.)
Other Staff: 4 Lectrs.; 4 Clin. Lectrs.
Research: affective disorder; cognitive function;
    epidemiology; neuropsychiatry; psychosis

Public Health and Primary Care

Tel: (01223) 330300 Fax: (01223) 330330
    E-mail: smt14@medschl.cam.ac.uk
Benson, John A., MB ChB *Birm.*, MSc MD,
    FRCGP   Sr. Lectr.
Brayne, Carol E. G., MB BS *Lond.*   Prof., Public
    Health Medicine (Darw.)

Danesh, John Prof., Epidemiology and
Medicine; Head*
Easton, Douglas F. Prof., Genetic
Epidemiology (Trin.H.)
Khaw, Kay-Tee, MSc Lond., MA MB BChir
Prof., Clinical Gerontology (Cai.)
Kinmonth, Ann-Louise, MA Camb., MB BChir
Camb., MSc Lond., MD Camb., FRCGP, FRCP
Prof., General Practice (S.Joh.)
Powles, J. W. Sr. Lectr., Public Health
Medicine
Sutton, Stephen R. Prof., Behavioural Science
Zimmern, Ronald H. Dir., Inst. of Public
Health (Hug.)
Other Staff: 3 Lectrs.; 1 Consultant Occupnl.
Physician; 1 Asst. Dir. of Res.

Radiology

Tel: (01223) 336890 Fax: (01223) 330915
Dixon, Adrian K., MD, FRCR, FRCP, FRCS,
FMedSci Prof.; Head* (Pet.)
Gillard, Jonathan H., MD, FRCR Reader,
Neuroradiology (Chr.)
Lomas, David J., MB BChir MA, FRCR
Amersham Prof., Clinical Magnetic
Resonance Imaging (Emm.)
Other Staff: 3 Lectrs.; 1 Clin. Lectr.
Research: aspects of imaging (computer-aided
tomography (CT), magnetic resonance
imaging (MRI), ultrasonography (US))

Surgery

Tel: (01223) 336978 Fax: (01223) 410772
Bradley, J. Andrew, MB ChB Leeds, PhD Glas.,
FMedSci Prof.; Head* (Wolfs.)
Neal, David E., BSc Lond., MB BS Lond., MS
Lond., FRCS, Hon. FRCSEd, FMedSci Prof.,
Cancer Research (Cell Biology)
Pedersen, R. A. L., PhD Prof. (Chur.)
Rosengard, B. R. British Heart Foundation
Prof., Cardiac Surgery
Rushton, Neil, MB BS Lond., MA Camb., MD
Camb., FRCS Prof., Orthopaedics (Magd.)
Watson, Christopher J. E., MA MD, FRCS
Reader (Hug.)
Other Staff: 3 Lectrs.; 1 Asst. Dir. of Res.; 1
Assoc. Lectr.; 1 Clin. Lectr.

SPECIAL CENTRES, ETC

African Studies, Centre of

Tel: (01223) 334396 Fax: (01223) 334396
E-mail: african-studies@lists.cam.ac.uk
Peterson, Derek R., BA Roch., PhD Minn. Dir.*
(Selw.)

Arts, Social Sciences and Humanities, Centre for Research in (CRASSH)

Tel: (01223) 766886 Fax: (01223) 765276
E-mail: crassh-admin@lists.cam.ac.uk
Jacobus, Mary L., MA Oxf., DPhil Oxf. Prof.,
English; Dir.* (Chur.)

Business Research, Centre for

Tel: (01223) 335244 Fax: (01223) 335768
E-mail: enquiries@cbr.cam.ac.uk
Cosh, Andrew D., MA Camb., PhD Camb. Asst.
Dir.; Reader, Management Economics and
Accounting (Qu.)
Deakin, Simon F., MA Camb., PhD Camb., FBA
Robert Monks Prof., Corporate Governance
(Pet.)
Hughes, Alan, MA Camb. Margaret Thatcher
Prof., Enterprise Studies; Dir.* (Sid.)

Continuing Education, Institute of

Tel: (01954) 280280 Fax: (01954) 280200
E-mail: registration@cont-ed.cam.ac.uk
Kalnins, Mara I., MA Edin., PhD Edin. Reader,
Modern English Literature
Rawlings, Susan, MA Camb. Dep. Dir. (L.Cav.)
Taylor, Richard K. S., MA Oxf., PhD Leeds
Prof.; Dir.* (Wolfs.)
Other Staff: 12 Staff Tutors

Educational Technologies, Centre for Applied Research in

Tel: (01223) 765040 Fax: (01223) 765505
Norman, John R., BSc Birm., MA Calif. Dir.*
Other Staff: 1 Chief Technol. Officer; 2
Computer Officers
Vacant Posts: 1 Asst. Dir.

English and Applied Linguistics, Research Centre for

Tel: (01223) 767397 Fax: (01223) 767398
E-mail: bej12@cam.ac.uk
Hawkins, John A., MA Camb., PhD Camb.
Prof.; Dir.*
Other Staff: 4 Asst. Dirs. of Res.; 3 Sr. Res.
Assocs.

International Studies, Centre of

Tel: (01223) 767235 Fax: (01223) 767236
E-mail: intstudies@lists.cam.ac.uk
Barkawi, Tarak K., MSc Lond., PhD Minn., BA
Sr. Lectr.
Edwards, Geoffrey R., BA Wales, PhD Lond.
Reader, European Studies (Pemb.)
Haslam, Jonathan G., BSc(Econ) Lond., MLitt
Camb., PhD Birm. Prof., History of
International Relations (Corp.)
Hill, Christopher J., BA Oxf., DPhil Oxf. Sir
Patrick Sheehy Prof., International Relations;
Dir.*
Jones, Charles A., BA Camb., MA Warw., PhD
Camb. Reader, International Relations
(Wolfs.)
Simms, Brendan P., BA Trinity(Dub.), PhD Camb.
Reader, History of International Relations
(Pet.)
Smith, Julie E., MA Camb., DPhil Oxf. Sr.
Lectr.; Deputy Dir.
Towle, Philip A., MA Camb., MA Lond., PhD
Lond. Reader, International Relations (Qu.)
Weller, Marc, MALD Tufts, MA Camb., PhD
Camb. Reader, International Law and
International Relations
Other Staff: 3 Lectrs.

Language Centre

Tel: (01223) 335040 Fax: (01223) 335040
E-mail: enquiries@langcen.cam.ac.uk
King, Anny N., MA Dir.* (Chur.)
Other Staff: 2 Sr. Lang. Advisers; 2 Lang.
Advisers; 4 Computer Officers; 1 Librarian;
1 Deputy Dir.

Latin-American Studies, Centre of

Tel: (01223) 335390 Fax: (01223) 335397
E-mail: general@latin-american.cam.ac.uk
Jones, Charles A., BA Camb., MA Warw., PhD
Camb. Dir.* (Wolfs.)

Mathematical Sciences, Isaac Newton Institute for

Tel: (01223) 335999 Fax: (01223) 330508
E-mail: info@newton.cam.ac.uk
Hunt, Robert E., PhD Camb. Dep. Dir. (Chr.)
Wallace, Sir David, CBE, BSc Edin., PhD Edin.,
Hon. DEng H-W, Hon. DSc Edin., FRS,
FRSEd, FIP, FREng N. M. Rothschild &
Sons Prof.; Dir.* (Chur.)

Medical Genetics and Policy, Centre for

Tel: (01223) 331154 Fax: (01223) 331206

Vacant Posts: Dir.*

Middle Eastern and Islamic Studies, Centre of

Tel: (01223) 335103 Fax: (01223) 335110
E-mail: secretary@cmeis.cam.ac.uk
Suleiman, Yasir, BA PhD, FRSEd His Majesty
Sultan Qaboos Bin Said Prof., Modern
Arabic Studies; Dir.*

South Asian Studies, Centre of

Tel: (01223) 338094 Fax: (01223) 767094
E-mail: webmaster@s-asian.cam.ac.uk

Vacant Posts: Dir.*

University Biomedical Support Services

Veterinary Studies
Tel: (01223) 336767
Coetzee, M. Asst. Dir./Named Vet. Surgeon
Gentry, Charles B. Dir.*
Keeley, J. R. Asst. Dir./Named Vet. Surgeon
(Newn.)
Shortland, A. Asst. Dir./Named Vet. Surgeon
Other Staff: 1 Trg. Sch. Manager; 1 Sr. Tech.
Officer

Wellcome Trust Cancer Research UK Gurdon Institute

Tel: (01223) 334088 Fax: (01223) 334089
E-mail: info@gurdon.cam.ac.uk
Smith, James C., MA Camb., PhD Lond., FRS
Chairman* (Chr.)

CHRIST'S COLLEGE

Tel: (01223) 334900 Fax: (01223) 334967
Bowkett, Kelvin M., BSc Wales, MA Camb., PhD
Camb. Sr. Tutor
Halstead, Michael P., MA Camb., PhD Camb.
Bursar
Kelly, Frank P., BSc Durh., MA Camb., PhD
Camb., FRS Master*
Payne, Geoffrey S., BA Sheff., MA Camb.
Domestic Bursar

CHURCHILL COLLEGE

Tel: (01223) 336000 Fax: (01223) 336180
E-mail: info@chu.cam.ac.uk
Halson, Paula, BA Open(UK) Registrar
Kingston, I. Barry, PhD Brist. Tutor for
Advanced Students
Packwood, Allen, MPhil Camb. Dir. of the
Archives Centre
Partington, Richard J., MA Camb. Sr.
Admissions Tutor; Sr. Tutor
Rigby, Jennifer M., MA Oxf., MBA Cran.
Bursar
Tristram, Andrew G., MA St And., PhD Camb.
Vice-Master
Wallace, Sir David, CBE, BSc Edin., PhD Edin.,
Hon. DEng H-W, Hon. DSc Edin., FRS,
FRSEd, FIP, FREng Master*

CLARE COLLEGE

Tel: (01223) 333200 Fax: (01223) 333219
Badger, Anthony J., MA Camb., PhD Hull,
Hon. DLitt Hull Master*
Fara, Patricia, MSc PhD Sr. Tutor
Foster, William A., MA PhD Admissions
Tutor, Scis.
Hearn, Donald, MA Bursar
Knighton, Tess, MA PhD Admissions Tutor,
Arts
Tasioulas, Jackie Financial Tutor

CLARE HALL

Tel: (01223) 332360 Fax: (01223) 332333
Barrow, John D., DPhil Oxf., FRAS, FRSA
Vice-President
Blake, Andrew, PhD Edin., FREng, FRS Tutor
Harris, Sir Martin, CBE, MA PhD LCD
President*
Hawthorn, Geoffrey P., BA Oxf., MA Vice-
President
Luff, Rosemary M., PhD Camb. Tutor
Rhodes, Daniela, PhD Camb. Assistant
Praelector
Stewart, Murray J., BSc Syd., MA Camb., PhD
Syd. Praelector
Tate, Trudi, PhD Camb. Tutor
Wells, Roberta S., MA Brad., PhD Camb. Sr.
Tutor

Womack, Joanna, MA Camb. Bursar and Steward

CORPUS CHRISTI COLLEGE

Tel: (01223) 338000 Fax: (01223) 338061
  E-mail: info@corpus.cam.ac.uk
Andrew, Christopher M., MA Camb., PhD Camb. President
Brookes, Christopher J. B., MA PhD Tutor for Advanced Studies
Dawson, Diane, MA Calif. Tutor
Drayton, Richard, AB Harv., MA Oxf., MPhil Yale, PhD Yale, FRHistS Tutor
Duveen, Gerard M., BSc Sur., MSc Strath., DPhil Sus. Vice-Master
Foster, Juliet L. H., MA Lond., MSc Lond., PhD Tutor
Frasca-Spada, Marina, MA Rome, PhD Sr. Tutor
Godsill, Simon J., MA PhD Tutor
Ibbetson, David J., MA Camb., PhD Camb., FBA Warden of Leckhampton
Mellars, Paul A., MA PhD ScD, FBA, FSA Acting Master*
Taylor, Melanie A., MA Lond., DPhil York(UK) Tutor
Warren, James L., MA MPhil PhD Tutor

DARWIN COLLEGE

Tel: (01223) 335600 Fax: (01223) 335667
Branson, Nicholas J. B. A., MA Camb., PhD Camb. Coll. Secretary
Brindle, Peter J., MPhil Camb. Bursar
Brown, William A., CBE, BA Oxf., MA Camb. Master*
Cone, Margaret, MPhil Oxf., PhD Oxf. Assoc. Dean
Fabian, Andrew C., BSc Lond., PhD Lond., FRS Vice-Master
Howe, Leo E. A., PhD Edin. Dean
Jones, Matthew R., BSc Newcastle(UK), PhD Reading Deputy Dean
Leedham-Green, Elisabeth S., BLitt Oxf., MA Oxf., MA Camb., DPhil Oxf., PhD, FSA Archivist

DOWNING COLLEGE

Tel: (01223) 334800 Fax: (01223) 467934
Barrand, Margery A., BSc Lond., PhD Lond. Tutor for Grads.
Evans, Peter D., ScD Tutor
Everitt, Prof. Barry J., BSc Hull, MA Birm., PhD Birm., ScD Camb. Master*
James, Ian R., MA Warw., PhD Warw. Tutor for Grads.; Fellow Librarian
Lintott, Susan E., MA Kent, PhD Kent Bursar
McCombie, John S. L., MA McM., MA PhD Tutor
Millett, Paul C., MA PhD Tutor for Admissions
Phillips, Cathy L., BA Qu., MA Tor., PhD Tutor
Rubery, Philip H., MA ScD Tutor; Asst. Admissions Tutor
Smith, Richard M., BA Lond., MA Oxf., PhD Camb. Vice-Master
Stibbs, Richard J., MA Praelector; Fellows' Steward and Sec. to the Governing Body
Stock, Jay T., BA Trent, MSc Guelph, PhD Tor. Tutor
Virgo, Graham J., BCL Oxf., MA Camb. Sr. Tutor
White, David J., BA Camb., PhD Camb. Tutor

EMMANUEL COLLEGE

Tel: (01223) 334200 Fax: (01223) 334426
Barnes, Richard J., MB BChir MA PhD Sr. Tutor
Caddick, Jeremy L., MA Camb. Dean
Gross, Mike J., MA PhD Bursar
Wilson of Dinton, Lord, GCB, MA LLM Master*

FITZWILLIAM COLLEGE

Tel: (01223) 332000 Fax: (01223) 477976
Abayasekara, D. Robert E., PhD Lond. Dir. of Studies in Med. and Vet. Med.
Alcántara, José I., MA Camb., PhD Melb. Tutor; Dir. of Studies in Nat. Sci. (Biol.); Disability Officer
Allison, William, MA Camb., PhD Lond. Tutor for Grad. Students
Ansorge, Richard E., MA Camb., PhD Camb. Tutor; Asst. Dir. of Studies in Maths. for Nat. Sci.
Bukhari, Natasha, MSt Oxf., DPhil Oxf. Dir. of Studies in Engl.
Camina, Rachel D., MSc Lond., PhD Lond. Dir. of Studies in Maths; Outreach Officer
Cardwell, David A., MA Camb., PhD Warw. Tutor, Financial, and Admissions Tutor (Scis.)
Chirico, Paul A., PhD Camb. Sr. Tutor
Clark, Alan, MA Camb., PhD Camb. Admin. Sec., Registrary
Cleaver, John R. A., MA Camb., PhD Camb. Fellow Librarian
Cole, David J., MA Camb., PhD Camb. Data Protection Officer
Coomes, David A., MA Camb., PhD Camb. Tutor; Asst. Dir. of Studies in Nat. Sci. (Biol.)
Davies, Graham I., MA Oxf., PhD Camb., DD Oxf., FBA, FSA Dir. of Studies in Theol.
Elliott, James A., MA Camb., PhD Brist. Asst. Dir. of Studies in Nat. Sci. (Phy.)
Holly, M. J. Sean, BA Reading, PhD CNAA Dean of College
Hooley, Prof. Richard J. A., MA Camb. Dir. of Studies in LLM; Steward and SCR Steward
Horrox, Rosemary E., MA Camb., PhD Camb., FRHistS Admissions Tutor (Arts); Dir. of Studies in Hist.
Keown, Dominic, PhD Sheff. Dir. of Studies in Mod. and Med. Lang.
Leigh, John D., MA Camb., PhD Camb. Tutor; Dir. of Studies in Mod. and Mediaeval Lang.
Lethbridge, Robert D., BA Kent, MA McM., MA Camb., PhD Camb. Master*
Liò, Pietro, PhD Florence Dir. of Studies in Comp. Sci.
Möller, Iris, MPhil Wales, PhD Camb. Asst. Dir. of Studies in Geog.
Mukherji, Subha, MPhil Camb., PhD Camb. Dir. of Studies in Engl.
Newby, Elisa M. S., MA Helsinki Dir. of Studies in Econ.
Owen, Sara S., MPhil Camb., PhD Camb. Tutor; Dir. of Studies in Classics
Padfield, Nicola M., MA Oxf. Tutor; Dir. of Studies in Law
Platts, Kenneth W., MA Camb. Dir. of Studies in Engin. and Management Studies
Pooley, G. G., MA Camb., PhD Camb. Dir. of Studies in Nat. Sci. (Phys.)
Potter, Michael D., MA Camb., DPhil Oxf. Dir. of Studies in Philos.; President
Pratt, Christopher L., MA Camb. Bursar
Rentfrow, P. Jason, PhD Texas Dir. of Studies in Soc. and Pol. Sci.
Saeb-Parsy, Kourosh, MA Camb., MB BChir Camb., PhD Camb. Dir. of Studies in Clin. Med.
Scott, David M., MA Camb., PhD Camb. Dir. of Studies in Chem. Engin.
Seabrooke, William, PhD Reading, FRICS Dir. of Studies in Land Econ.
Slater, Nigel K. H., MA Camb., PhD Camb., FREng, FIChemE Fellow Safety Officer
Tavernor, Angie S., PhD Camb. Tutor
Thompson, David M., BD Camb., MA Camb., PhD Camb., FRHistS Archivist
Vira, Bhaskar, MA Camb., PhD Camb. Dir. of Studies in Geog.; Tutor for Grad. Students
Wheatley, Andrew E. H., PhD Camb. Asst. Dir. of Studies in Chem.; Tutor for Grad. Students

GIRTON COLLEGE

Tel: (01223) 338999 Fax: (01223) 338896
  E-mail: info@girton.cam.ac.uk
Barden, Dennis, MA Camb., PhD Camb. Grad. Tutor
Barnes, Crispin H. W., BSc Lond., PhD Lond. Tutor
Duke, Alison, MA Camb. Registrar Emer. of the Roll
Gandy, Frances, BA Open(UK), MA Camb. Librarian; Tutor
Hackett, Maureen J., BA S'ton., MA S'ton.
Hopkins, Charity A., OBE, MA Camb., LLB Sec. to Council
Lowther, Deborah, MA Camb. Bursar
Pugh, Emma, BSc Keele, PhD Camb. Tutor
Randall, Roland E., MSc McG., MA Camb., PhD Camb. Tutor
Riley, Julia M., MA Camb., PhD Camb. Admissions Tutor
Rubery, Eileen D., CB, MB ChB Sheff., PhD, FRCR, FRCPath Registrar of the Roll
Strathern, Dame Marilyn, DBE, MA Camb., PhD Camb., FBA Mistress*

GONVILLE AND CAIUS COLLEGE

Tel: (01223) 332400 Fax: (01223) 332456
Herd, Ian R. Domestic Bursar
Hum, Sir Christopher, KCMG, MA Camb. Master*

HOMERTON COLLEGE

Tel: (01223) 507111 Fax: (01223) 507120
Bryan, Richard G. Bursar
Pretty, Katherine B., MA Camb., PhD Camb., FSA Principal*
Warner, Peter M., PhD Leic. Sr. Tutor
Watts, Steve, BA Camb., MA Camb., PhD Camb. Admissions Tutor

HUGHES HALL

Tel: (01223) 334898 Fax: (01223) 311179
  E-mail: enquiries@hughes.cam.ac.uk
Affara, Nabeel A., BSc Edin., MA Camb., PhD Glas. Tutor; Vice-President
Carr, Gillian C., MA MPhil PhD Tutor
Devereux, Bernard J., BA Nott.Trent, MA Nott., PhD Nott. Graduate Admissions Tutor
Franklin, Michael J., MA Camb., PhD Camb., FSA, FRHistS Praelector; Undergrad. Admissions Tutor; Tutor and Registrary
Lambert, Jean F., BA Lond., BA Open(UK), MA Camb., MA Anglia Ruskin Tutor
Lemons, Tony D., BA Open(UK), MA Camb. Dir. of Phys. Educn.
Malone, Caroline A. T., MA PhD, FSA, FSA Sr. Tutor
McVeigh, Keith J. A., MA Oxf., MA Camb. Dir. of Studies in Law; Under-Librarian
Meggitt, Justin J., BA PhD Tutor
Moseley, Charles W. R. D., MA Camb., PhD E.Anglia, FSA Tutor
Raffan, John G., MA Tutor; Vice-President
Raymont, Rev. P. R., BA Qld., BEdStud Qld., MEd Melb., PhD Camb.
Richards, Peter M., MA Camb., PhD Camb. Tutor
Sargent, Carole A., BA Oxf., MA Oxf., DPhil Oxf., PhD Camb. Tutor; Admissions Tutor for Graduate Course in Medicine
Sinclair Brown, Nicholas, LLB Leic. Vice-President
Singal, N., BA Delhi, MA Delhi, MPhil Camb., PhD Camb. Tutor
Squire, Sarah, MA Camb. President*

JESUS COLLEGE

Tel: (01223) 339339 Fax: (01223) 339313
Arnot, Madeleine M., MA Edin., PhD Open(UK) Tutor for Grads.
Crouch, Anthony T., BA Keele, MA Penn. Sr. Bursar
Dennis, Richard J. P. Devel. Dir.

Ingram, David M., BA Camb., PhD Camb. Admissions Tutor (Scis.)

Jenkins, Timothy D., MA Oxf., MLitt Oxf., PhD Camb., BA Dean of Chapel

Mair, Robert J., MA Camb., PhD Camb., FREng, FICE Master*

Parks, Geoffrey T., BA Camb., MA Camb., PhD Camb. Admissions Tutor (Arts)

Siklos, Stephen T. C., MA Camb., PhD Camb. Sr. Tutor

Wilkinson, Timothy D., BE Cant., PhD Camb. Deputy Tutor for Grads.

KING'S COLLEGE

Tel: (01223) 331100 Fax: (01223) 331315
E-mail: info@kings.cam.ac.uk

Adkins, Tess, MA Camb., PhD Camb. Vice Provost

Burgwinkle, Bill E., BA Amherst, MA Boston Coll., PhD Stan. Grad. Tutor

Cleobury, Stephen J., MA MusB Dir. of Music

Fenlon, Iain A., BMus Reading, MA Birm., PhD Birm. Sr. Tutor

Harrison, Prof. Ross T., MA Camb., PhD Camb. Provost*

Jones, Peter M., MA Oxf. Librarian

Laidlaw, James A., BA Camb., MA Camb., PhD Camb. Sr. Tutor

Moggridge, Geoff D., MA Camb., PhD Camb. Sr. Tutor

Reavley, Martin, MA Camb. First Bursar

Thompson, Rev. Ian M., BTh Aberd., MA Camb. Dean of Chapel

Zeeman, Nicky, MA Camb., PhD Camb. Admissions Tutor for Undergrads.

LUCY CAVENDISH COLLEGE

Tel: (01223) 332190 Fax: (01223) 332178
E-mail: lcc-admin@lists.cam.ac.uk

Brindley, Susan, BA MA Tutor

Carter, David Bursar

Curry, Allison J. Asst. Grad. Tutor; Admissions Tutor (Medical Scis.)

Dashwood, Julie D. Sr. Tutor

Ellington, Stephanie K. L. Tutor

Greatorex, Jane Tutor

Houghton, M. Christine, BA Ulster, MA Camb. Domestic Bursar

McLarty, Jane Admissions Tutor

Sapir Abulafia, Anna B., Drs Amst., PhD Amst., MA Vice-President

Spivack, Orsola, PhD Grad. Tutor

Sutherland, Dame Veronica E., DBE, CMG, BA S'ton., MA S'ton., Hon. LLD Trinity(Dub.) President*

Vinnicombe, Alison A., BA Leeds, MA Camb. Registrar

MAGDALENE COLLEGE

Tel: (01223) 332100 Fax: (01223) 462589
E-mail: admissions@magd.cam.ac.uk

Burchell, Brendan J., BSc Warw., PhD Warw. Admissions Tutor (Recruitment); Dir. of Studies in Social and Political Science

Daybell, Peter J., MBE, MA Lond. Asst. Bursar; Rooms Tutor

Dupree, Paul, MA Camb., PhD Camb. Tutor for Grad. Students; Dir. of Studies in Natural Scis.

Martin, Stuart, MA Glas., MA Oxf., DPhil Oxf., PhD Camb. Sr. Tutor; Dir. of Studies in Maths.

Morris, Steven, MA Sr. Bursar

Rawson, Jeremy M., MA Camb., PhD Durh. Admissions Tutor (Undergrads.); Dir. of Studies in Natural Scis.

Rigney, Rev. James T., MA Camb., DPhil Oxf. Chaplain; Dir. of Studies in Theol.

Robinson, D. Duncan, MA Camb., MA Yale, FRSA Dir. of Sudies in Hist. of Art; Master*

Spencer, Tom, MA PhD Admissions Tutor (Grads.); Dir. of Studies in Geog.

NEW HALL

Tel: (01223) 762100 Fax: (01223) 763110
E-mail: enquiries@newhall.cam.ac.uk

Acton, Elizabeth, MA PhD Dir. of Studies, Engineering

Ahmed, Seema, PhD Tutor

Ardavan, Houshang, BSc M.I.T., PhD Dir. of Studies, Maths.

Ball, Stephen, DPhil Oxf. Grad. Tutor

Barnes, Jennifer President*

Basso, Franco G. G. Dir. of Studies, Classics; Arts Admissions Tutor

Bennett, Wendy M. A., MA Oxf., MA Camb., DPhil Oxf., PhD Camb. Dir. of Studies, Mod. and Mediaeval Langs and Linguistics

Benson, Susan N., MA PhD Dir. of Studies, Soc. and Pol. Scis. and Archaeol. and Anthropol.; Tutor

Burt, Caroline, MPhil Dir. of Studies, History Part I

Dawson, James R., PhD Cardiff Tutor

Drayson, Elizabeth A., MA Camb., PhD Camb. Tutor

Durrani, Zahid A., MPhil PhD Tutor

Filippucci, Paola, BA Sheff., MPhil Camb., PhD Camb. Tutor

Forster, Peter, PhD Hamburg, MA Praelector

Glen, Heather J., BA Syd., MA Camb., PhD Camb. Dir. of Studies, English Part II

Harris, Harriet E., MA Lond., PhD Lond. Admissions Tutor; Dir. of Studies, Nat. Scis. (Biol.)

Henson, Frances M. D., MA Camb., VetMB Camb., PhD Camb. Dir. of Studies, Vet. Med.

Hiley, C. Robin, MA Camb., PhD Camb. Dir. of Studies, Pharmacology

Horrell, Sara H., BSc Bath, MPhil Camb., PhD Camb. Dir. of Studies, Economics

Huang, Christopher L.-H., BM BCh Oxf., MA Oxf., MA Camb., DM Oxf., DSc Oxf., MD Camb., PhD Camb., ScD Camb. Dir. of Studies, Med.

Lyne, Raphael T. R., MPhil Camb., PhD Camb. Dir. of Studies, Engl. Part 1

Radcliffe, Sarah A., BSc Lond., MA Camb., PhD Liv. Dir. of Studies, Geog.

Roberts, Mark, MA PhD Dir. of Studies, Land Economy

Saxton, W. Owen, MA PhD Sr. Tutor; Dir. of Studies, Nat. Scis. (Phys.)

Sinnatamby, Ruchi, MB BChir MA MA, FRCR Dir. of Studies, Clin. Med.

Steane, Mary Ann, MPhil Dir. of Studies, Archit.

Strietman, Elsa G. C., CandLitt Gron., MA Grad. Tutor

Thomas, Dame Jean, CBE, DBE, MA Wales, MA Camb., PhD Wales, ScD, FRS Dir. of Studies, Biochem.

Turenne, Sophie Dir. of Studies, Law

Wilson, Alison M., BA Brist., MSc Lond., MLitt Camb. Coll. Librarian

Wilson, Penelope B., MA Edin., MA Camb., DPhil Oxf. Secretary, Seniors' Committee

Wright, Nicholas R. M., BA Sheff. Bursar

NEWNHAM COLLEGE

Tel: (01223) 335700 Fax: (01223) 357898
E-mail: enquiries@newn.cam.ac.uk

Apter, Terri, MA Camb., PhD Camb. Sr. Tutor

Baker, Harry, BA Open(UK), MSc CNAA, DSc Open(UK) Asst. Grad. Tutor

De Waal, Clarissa, MA Edin., MPhil Camb., PhD Camb. Tutor

Du Quesnay, Ian M. Le M., BA Birm. Bursar

Edgcombe, Katherine, MA Camb. Financial Tutor; Tutor

Evans, Wendy Domestic Bursar

Fleet, Kate, BA Lond., PhD Lond. Dir., Skilliter Centre for Ottoman Studies; Tutor

Forhead, Alison, BSc Camb., PhD Camb. Asst. Tutor

Golombok, Susan E., BSc Glas., MSc Lond., PhD Lond. Asst. Tutor

Hazlehurst, Frances A., BA Open(UK) Coll. Sec.

Hills, Catherine M., BA Durh., MA Camb., PhD Lond. Secretary of the Governing Body

Hirsch, Pam, MA Camb., PhD Camb. Grad. Tutor

Hodder, Deborah K., MA Lond., MA Camb. Librarian

Hodgson, Dame Patricia A., DBE, MA Camb., Hon. ScD City(UK), Hon. DPhil Essex Principal*

Hubbard, Penny D., MA Camb. Dir. of Devel.; Registrar of the Roll

Ridley, Rosalind M., PhD Lond., MA ScD Tutor

Seville, Catherine, BMus Lond., MA Camb., LLM Camb., PhD Camb. Vice-Principal; Asst. Grad. Tutor

Stock, Ute B. C., MA Camb., MPhil Camb., PhD Camb. Admissions Tutor; Asst. Tutor

Taub, Liba, BA Tulane, MA Chic., PhD Oklahoma Asst. Tutor

Watson, Christine J., BSc Glas., PhD Lond. Asst. Tutor

PEMBROKE COLLEGE

Tel: (01223) 338100 Fax: (01223) 338163
E-mail: enquiries@pem.cam.ac.uk

Baskey, Nicholas S., BA Yale, MA Camb., MBA Ohio State Treasurer and Bursar

Edwards, Geoffrey R., BA Wales, PhD Lond. Jean Monnet Dir. of European Studies

Raingold, Howard P., MA Devel. Dir.

Stobbs, Susan H., MA Camb. Admissions Tutor

Wormald, M. R., BA Oxf. Tutor

PETERHOUSE

Tel: (01223) 338200 Fax: (01223) 337578
E-mail: info@pet.cam.ac.uk

Golding, Martin S., MA Ward Librarian

Mandelbrote, Scott H., MA Tutor for Admissions (Undergrads.); Perne Librarian

Pattenden, Philip, MA Camb., MA Oxf., DPhil Oxf., PhD Sr. Tutor; Graduate Admissions Tutor, Praelector

Plevy, Neil R., MA Camb. Devel. Dir.

Quash, J. Ben, MA Camb., PhD Camb. Chaplain; Dean

Turner, D. Mike, MA PhD Jr. Bursar

Wilson of Tillyorn, Lord, KT, GCMG, PhD, FRSEd Master*

Woodman, Veronica E. Domestic Bursar

QUEENS' COLLEGE

Tel: (01223) 335511 Fax: (01223) 335522

Bollom, Lee A., MA Camb. Steward

Cosh, Andrew D., MA Camb., PhD Camb. Sr. Bursar

Eatwell, Lord, AM Harv., MA Camb., PhD Harv. President*

Holmes, Rev. J. M., MA VetMB PhD Chaplain; Dean

Milgate, Murray J., MEc Syd., MA Essex, PhD Camb. Sr. Tutor

ROBINSON COLLEGE

Tel: (01223) 339100 Fax: (01223) 351794

Guild, Elizabeth M., MA St And., MA Camb., PhD Sr. Tutor

Jones, Geraint A. C., BSc Wales, PhD Wales, MA Grad. Tutor

Milloy, Peter D. G., BSc Manc., MEng Wales Domestic Bursar

Murk Jansen, Saskia M., MA Camb., PhD Camb. Praelector

Reason, Ross G., MA Camb. Finance Bursar

Smith, Julie E., MA Camb., DPhil Oxf. Grad. Tutor

Warner, Christopher D., MA Camb., PhD Manc. Admissions Tutor

Yates, Anthony D., MA Camb., MA Oxf. Warden*

SELWYN COLLEGE

Tel: (01223) 335846 Fax: (01223) 335837
E-mail: master@sel.cam.ac.uk
Bowring, Richard J., MA Camb., PhD Camb.,
LittD Camb.   Master*
Butterfield, Nicholas J., BSc Alta., MA Camb.,
PhD Harv.   Tutor for Advanced Students
Downer, Nicholas J. A., MA Camb.   Bursar
Fox, Peter K., BA Lond., MA Sheff., MA Camb.
Univ. Librarian
Keeler, James H., MA Oxf., DPhil Oxf., PhD
Camb.   Tutor for Admissions (Science)
Kennedy, Joseph, BSc Edin., BD Edin., MSt Oxf.,
DPhil Oxf.   Dean of Chapel
Sewell, Michael J., MA Camb., PhD Camb.
Tutor for Admissions (Arts)
Smith, David L., MA Camb., PhD Camb., FRHistS
Tutor for Advanced Students
Tilby, Michael J., MA Camb., PhD Camb.   Sr.
Tutor

SIDNEY SUSSEX COLLEGE

Tel: (01223) 338800 Fax: (01223) 338884
Britton, Colin, BA Open(UK)   Domestic Bursar
and Steward
Dawson, Dame Sandra J. N., BA Keele, MA
Camb., Hon. DSc Keele, FCGI   Master*
Larkum, Charles P., MA Oxf.   Bursar
Partington, Richard J., BA Camb., MA Camb.
Admissions Dir.
Preston, Claire E., MPhil Yale, DPhil Oxf., PhD
Camb.   Grad. Tutor
Straughan, Keith, BA Camb., MA Camb., PhD
Lond.   Sr. Tutor

ST CATHARINE'S COLLEGE

Tel: (01223) 338300 Fax: (01223) 338340
Bainbridge, David, PhD   Tutor
Borzym, Irena, BA   Tutor
Clark, Christopher, PhD Camb.   Tutor
Crawford, Charles M. C., MA Camb.   Sr. Bursar
Dell, Katharine J., MA Oxf., DPhil Oxf.   Tutor
Hartle, Paul N., MA PhD   Sr. Tutor
Johns, Michael, PhD   Tutor
Oliver, Philip, BSc MA PhD   Admissions Tutor
Richmond, Rev. Patrick, DPhil   Tutor;
Chaplain
Summers, Simon, MA   Sr. Bursar
Thomas, Prof. Dame Jean, FRS, FMedSci
Master*
Wardle, Fiona, BA PhD   Tutor
Wardy, Robert B. B., MA Camb., PhD Camb.
Tutor

ST EDMUND'S COLLEGE

Tel: (01223) 336250 Fax: (01223) 762822
Bunbury, Judith, BSc Durh., PhD Durh.
Undergrad. Admissions Tutor; Tutor
Dunstan, P., MA PhD   Tutor
Gannon, A., MA PhD, FSA   Asst. Undergrad.
Admissions Tutor; Tutor
Gardiner, M. B., MA   Bursar
Harter, A., MA PhD, FIETE, FBCS   Tutor
Herrtage, Michael E., BVSc Liv., MA Liv., DVSc
Liv.   Vice-Master
Jenkins, S., PhD   Rooms Tutor
Jongkind, Dirk, MA Camb., MPhil Camb., PhD
Camb.   Tutor
Kaminski, Ann, BSc Glas., PhD   Grad.
Admissions Tutor; Tutor
Langley-Hobbs, Sorrel J., BVetMed MA   Tutor
Luzio, J. Paul, MA PhD, FMedSci   Master*
Mason, Helen, BSc Lond., PhD Lond., MA   Sr.
Tutor; Tutor
McRobie, A., BSc Brist., MSc S'ton., FIMA
Tutor
Mitton, S. A., MA Oxf., MA PhD   Treasurer
Robson, Rev. Dr. M., BA Kent, PhD Camb.,
FRHistS   Dean; Praelector and Tutor

ST JOHN'S COLLEGE

Tel: (01223) 338600 Fax: (01223) 337720
E-mail: enquiries@joh.cam.ac.uk
Colwell, Susan M., MA PhD   Tutor for Grad.
Affairs
Dobson, Christopher M., BSc Oxf., MA Oxf.,
DPhil Oxf., Hon. DSc, FRS, FMedSci
Master*
Dormor, Duncan J., BA MSc   Dean of Chapel
and Tutor
Dörrzapf, Matthias, MA Camb., PhD Camb.   Sr.
Tutor
Ewbank, Christopher F., MA Camb.   Sr. Bursar
Harris, Commodore John W. R.   Domestic
Bursar
Hughes, Howard P., BSc Lond., MA Camb., PhD
Camb., ScD Camb.   Tutor
Linehan, Peter A., MA Camb., PhD Camb.   Dean
of College
McConnel, Richard E., BE NZ, DPhil Oxf.
Tutor
Metaxas, Andrew C., BSc Lond., PhD Lond., MA
Tutor
Nethsingha, Andrew M., BA Camb.   Dir. of
Music
Ní Mhaonaigh, Maire, MA N.U.I., PhD N.U.I.
Tutor
Nicholls, A. Mark, MA Camb., PhD Camb.
Librarian
Plaisted, Kate C., BSc Lond., PhD Camb.   Tutor
Schofield, Malcolm, MA Camb., PhD Camb.,
DPhil Oxf., FBA   Praelector
Spencer, Jonathan B., BA S'ton., MA Camb.
Tutor
Watson, Helen E., BA Belf., PhD Camb.
Admissions Tutor

TRINITY COLLEGE

Tel: (01223) 338400 Fax: (01223) 338564
Landman, Rory B., MA Camb.   Sr. Bursar
McKitterick, David J., MA Camb., LittD Camb.,
FBA   Librarian
Pullen, Roderick A., BA Oxf., DPhil Sus.   Jr.
Bursar
Rallison, John M., MA PhD   Sr. Tutor
Rees of Ludlow, Lord Martin, MA PhD DSc
Sus., DSc Leic., DSc Copenhagen, DSc Keele, DSc
Uppsala, DSc Newcastle(UK), DSc Tor., DSc Durh.,
DSc Oxf., PRS   Master*
Wingfield, Paul, BA MPhil PhD   Tutor for
Admissions

TRINITY HALL

Tel: (01223) 332500 Fax: (01223) 332537
Bampos, Nick, BSc MA PhD   Sr. Tutor
Daunton, Martin J., MA Camb., PhD Camb.,
LittD Camb., FBA, FRHistS   Master*
Ffolkes David, Paul, MA, FSA   Bursar; Steward
Miles, Richard, MA PhD   Tutor for
Undergrad. Admissions
Morris, Jeremy N., MA DPhil   Dean; Chaplain

WOLFSON COLLEGE

Tel: (01223) 335900 Fax: (01223) 335908
Jarvis, David, BA Camb., MA Lanc., PhD Lanc.
Sr. Tutor; Dean
Johnson, Gordon, MA Camb., PhD Camb.
President*
Seagrave, J. R., BA Durh., MA Camb., MA Oxf.,
PhD Birm.   Bursar

CONTACT OFFICERS

Academic affairs. Academic Secretary: Allen,
Graham P., MA Oxf., MA Camb.
(E-mail: academic.secretary@
admin.cam.ac.uk)
Accommodation. Secretary, Accommodation
Syndicate: Blanning, Nicky, BA Sus.
(E-mail: accommodation_service@
admin.cam.ac.uk)
Admissions (first degree). Admissions Officer:
(vacant) (E-mail: admissions@cam.ac.uk)
Admissions (higher degree). Acting Secretary,
Board of Graduate Studies: Maxwell,

Catherine, BSc Newcastle(UK), PhD
Newcastle(UK)
(E-mail: admissions@gradstudies.cam.ac.uk)
Adult/continuing education. Director,
Continuing Education: Taylor, Prof. Richard
K. S., MA Oxf., PhD Leeds
(E-mail: intenq@cont-ed.cam.ac.uk)
Alumni. Alumni Relations Manager: Zinovieff,
Jenny
(E-mail: alumni@foundation.cam.ac.uk)
Careers. Secretary, Careers Service:
Chesterman, Gordon, MA Camb.
(E-mail: enquiries@careers.cam.ac.uk)
Computing services. Director, Computing
Service: Lewis, Ian J., BSc Lond., PhD Camb.
(E-mail: reception@ucs.ca.ac.uk)
Credit transfer. Administrative Secretary:
Clark, Alan, MA Camb., PhD Camb.
Development/fund-raising. Director,
Development Office: Agar, Peter, BA Camb.,
MBA Lond.
(E-mail: alumni@foundation.cam.ac.uk)
Distance education. Director, Continuing
Education: Taylor, Prof. Richard K. S., MA
Oxf., PhD Leeds
(E-mail: intenq@cont-ed.cam.ac.uk)
Equal opportunities. Interim Head of Equality
and Diversity: Showunmi, Victoria
(E-mail: equality@admin.cam.ac.uk)
Estates and buildings/works and services.
Director, Estate Management and Building
Service: Bienias, Michael R., MA Camb.
Examinations. Head of Examinations:
Rainsbury, Diane, BSc Reading
Finance. Director of Finance: Reid, Andrew,
MA Oxf., MBA Cran., FCA
General enquiries. Head, Communications
Office: Hayman, Gregory, MA Sus.
(E-mail: communications@admin.cam.ac.uk)
Health services. Director of Health and Safety
Division: Cooper, Sara, BA Oxf., MPhil Sur.
International office. International Education
Officer (International Office): Chang, Tao-
Tao
Library (chief librarian). Librarian: Fox, Peter
K., BA Lond., MA Sheff., MA Camb.
(E-mail: library@ula.cam.ac.uk)
Library (enquiries). Head of Reader Services:
Harper, Anthony C., BSc Newcastle(UK)
(E-mail: library@ula.cam.ac.uk)
Marketing. Head of Communications Services:
(vacant) (E-mail: communicationsservices@
admin.cam.ac.uk)
Personnel/human resources. Director of
Personnel: Deer, Peter J., BA Lond.
Public relations. Head of External Affairs and
Communications: Jolly, Stephen, MA Camb.,
MA Sus. (E-mail: communicationsservices@
admin.cam.ac.uk)
Publications. Head of Communications
Services: (vacant)
(E-mail: communicationsservices@
admin.cam.ac.uk)
Quality assurance and accreditation. Deputy
Academic Secretary: McCallum, Duncan P.
F., MA Camb., MA Sus.
Research. Director of Research Services
Division: (vacant)
(E-mail: rcoenquiries@rsd.cam.ac.uk)
Schools liaison. Schools Liaison Officer:
(vacant)
Sport and recreation. Director of Physical
Education: Lemons, Tony D., BA Open(UK),
MA Camb.
(E-mail: enquiries@sport.cam.ac.uk)
Student union. President, Graduate Union:
(vacant)
(E-mail: enquiries@gradunion.cam.ac.uk)
Student union. President, Cambridge
University Students' Union: Fletcher, Mark
(E-mail: info@cusu.cam.ac.uk)
Student welfare/counselling. Head (Student
welfare/counselling): Phippen, Charles M.,
BSc Kent
(E-mail: reception@counselling.cam.ac.uk)
Students with disabilities. Disability Adviser:
Jesky, Judith M., BA Sus.
(E-mail: ucam-disability@lists.cam.ac.uk)

University press. Chief Executive and University Printer: Bourne, Stephen (E-mail: information@cup.cam.ac.uk)
Women. Interim Head of Equality and Diversity: Showunmi, Victoria

CAMPUS/COLLEGE HEADS

Christ's College, Cambridge, England CB2 3BU. (Tel: (01223) 334900; Fax: (01223) 334967) Master: Kelly, Prof. Frank P., BSc Durh., MA Camb., PhD Camb., FRS

Churchill College, Cambridge, England CB3 0DS. (Tel: (01223) 336000; Fax: (01223) 336180; E-mail: info@chu.cam.ac.uk) Master: Wallace, Sir David, CBE, BSc Edin., PhD Edin., Hon. DEng H-W, Hon. DSc Edin., FRS, FRSEd, FIP, FREng

Clare College, Cambridge, England CB2 1TL. (Tel: (01223) 333200; Fax: (01223) 333219) Master: Badger, Prof. Anthony J., MA Camb., PhD Hull, Hon. DLitt Hull

Clare Hall, Cambridge, England CB3 9AL. (Tel: (01223) 332360; Fax: (01223) 332333) President: Harris, Sir Martin, CBE, MA PhD LLD

Corpus Christi College, Cambridge, England CB2 1RH. (Tel: (01223) 338000; Fax: (01223) 338061; E-mail: info@corpus.cam.ac.uk) Acting Master: Mellars, Prof. Paul A., MA PhD ScD, FBA, FSA

Darwin College, Cambridge, England CB3 9EU. (Tel: (01223) 335600; Fax: (01223) 335667) Master: Brown, Prof. William A., CBE, BA Oxf., MA Camb.

Downing College, Cambridge, England CB2 1DQ. (Tel: (01223) 334800; Fax: (01223) 467934) Master: Everitt, Prof. Barry J., BSc Hull, MA Birm., PhD Birm., ScD Camb.

Emmanuel College, Cambridge, England CB2 3AP. (Tel: (01223) 334200; Fax: (01223) 334426) Master: Wilson of Dinton, Lord, GCB, MA LLM

Fitzwilliam College, Cambridge, England CB3 0DG. (Tel: (01223) 332000; Fax: (01223) 477976) Master: Lethbridge, Robert D., BA Kent, MA McM., MA Camb., PhD Camb.

Girton College, Cambridge, England CB3 0JG. (Tel: (01223) 338999; Fax: (01223) 338896; E-mail: info@girton.cam.ac.uk) Mistress: Strathern, Dame Marilyn, DBE, MA Camb., PhD Camb., FBA

Gonville and Caius College, Cambridge, England CB2 1TA. (Tel: (01223) 332400; Fax: (01223) 332456) Master: Hum, Sir Christopher, KCMG, MA Camb.

Homerton College, Cambridge, England CB2 2PH. (Tel: (01223) 507111; Fax: (01223) 507120) Principal: Pretty, Katherine B., MA Camb., PhD Camb., FSA

Hughes Hall, Cambridge, England CB1 2EW. (Tel: (01223) 334898; Fax: (01223) 311179; E-mail: enquiries@hughes.cam.ac.uk) President: Squire, Sarah, MA Camb.

Jesus College, Cambridge, England CB5 8BL. (Tel: (01223) 339339; Fax: (01223) 339313) Master: Mair, Prof. Robert J., MA Camb., PhD Camb., FREng, FICE

King's College, Cambridge, England CB2 1ST. (Tel: (01223) 331100; Fax: (01223) 331315; E-mail: info@kings.cam.ac.uk) Provost: Harrison, Prof. Ross T., MA Camb., PhD Camb.

Lucy Cavendish College, Lady Margaret Road, Cambridge, England CB3 0BU. (Tel: (01223) 332190; Fax: (01223) 332178; E-mail: lcc-admin@lists.cam.ac.uk) President: Sutherland, Dame Veronica E., DBE, CMG, BA S'ton., MA S'ton., Hon. LLD Trinity(Dub.)

Magdalene College, Cambridge, England CB3 0AG. (Tel: (01223) 332100; Fax: (01223) 462589; E-mail: admissions@magd.cam.ac.uk) Master: Robinson, D. Duncan, MA Camb., MA Yale, FRSA

New Hall, Cambridge, England CB3 0DF. (Tel: (01223) 762100; Fax: (01223) 763110; E-mail: enquiries@newhall.cam.ac.uk) President: Barnes, Jennifer

Newnham College, Cambridge, England CB3 9DF. (Tel: (01223) 335700; Fax: (01223) 357898; E-mail: enquiries@newn.cam.ac.uk) Principal: Hodgson, Dame Patricia A., DBE, MA Camb., Hon. ScD City(UK), Hon. DPhil Essex

Pembroke College, Cambridge, England CB2 1RF. (Tel: (01223) 338100; Fax: (01223) 338163; E-mail: enquiries@pem.cam.ac.uk) Master: Dearlove, Sir Richard, OBE, KCMG, MA Camb.

Peterhouse, Cambridge, England CB2 1RD. (Tel: (01223) 338200; Fax: (01223) 337578; E-mail: info@pet.cam.ac.uk) Master: Wilson of Tillyorn, Lord, KT, GCMG, PhD, FRSEd

Queens' College, Cambridge, England CB3 9ET. (Tel: (01223) 335511; Fax: (01223) 335522) President: Eatwell, Lord, AM Harv., MA Camb., PhD Harv.

Robinson College, Cambridge, England CB3 9AN. (Tel: (01223) 339100; Fax: (01223) 351794) Warden: Yates, Anthony D., MA Camb., MA Oxf.

Selwyn College, Cambridge, England CB3 9DQ. (Tel: (01223) 335846; Fax: (01223) 335837; E-mail: master@sel.cam.ac.uk) Master: Bowring, Prof. Richard J., MA Camb., PhD Camb., LittD Camb.

Sidney Sussex College, Cambridge, England CB2 3HU. (Tel: (01223) 338800; Fax: (01223) 338884) Master: Dawson, Dame Sandra J. N., BA Keele, MA Camb., Hon. DSc Keele, FCGI

St Catharine's College, Cambridge, England CB2 1RL. (Tel: (01223) 338300; Fax: (01223) 338340) Master: Thomas, Prof. Dame Jean, FRS, FMedSci

St Edmund's College, Cambridge, England CB3 0BN. (Tel: (01223) 336250; Fax: (01223) 762822) Master: Luzio, Prof. J. Paul, MA PhD, FMedSci

St John's College, Cambridge, England CB2 1TP. (Tel: (01223) 338600; Fax: (01223) 337720; E-mail: enquiries@joh.cam.ac.uk) Master: Dobson, Prof. Christopher M., BSc Oxf., MA Oxf., DPhil Oxf., Hon. DSc, FRS, FMedSci

Trinity College, Cambridge, England CB2 1TQ. (Tel: (01223) 338400; Fax: (01223) 338564) Master: Rees of Ludlow, Lord Martin, MA PhD DSc Sus., DSc Leic., DSc Copenhagen, DSc Keele, DSc Uppsala, DSc Newcastle(UK), DSc Tor., DSc Durh., DSc Oxf., PRS

Trinity Hall, Cambridge, England CB2 1TJ. (Tel: (01223) 332500; Fax: (01223) 332537) Master: Daunton, Prof. Martin J., MA Camb., PhD Camb., LittD Camb., FBA, FRHistS

Wolfson College, Cambridge, England CB3 9BB. (Tel: (01223) 335900; Fax: (01223) 335908) President: Johnson, Gordon, MA Camb., PhD Camb.

[Information supplied by the institution as at 17 October 2007, and edited by the ACU]

CANTERBURY CHRIST CHURCH UNIVERSITY

Founded 1962

Postal Address: Canterbury, Kent, England CT1 1QU
Telephone: (01227) 767700 **Fax:** (01227) 470442
URL: http://www.canterbury.ac.uk

VICE-CHANCELLOR*—Wright, Prof. Michael, LLM Hon. DL, FRSA

CARDIFF UNIVERSITY

Founded 1988

Member of the Association of Commonwealth Universities

Postal Address: Cardiff, Wales CF10 3XQ
Telephone: (029) 2087 4000
URL: http://www.cardiff.ac.uk

VICE-CHANCELLOR*—Grant, David, CBE, PhD Durh., FREng, FIEE
DEPUTY VICE-CHANCELLOR—Blood, Prof. Peter, BSc Leeds, PhD Leeds, FIP
PRO VICE-CHANCELLOR, LEARNING AND TEACHING AND STUDENTS—Osmond, Prof. Jonathon P., MA Oxf., DPhil Oxf.
PRO VICE-CHANCELLOR, RESEARCH—Rees, Prof. Teresa, CBE, BA Exe., PhD Wales
PRO VICE-CHANCELLOR, STAFF—Threadgold, Prof. Terry R., MA Syd.
PRO VICE-CHANCELLOR EXTERNAL AFFAIRS—Woodhouse, Prof. Ken W., BM S'ton., MD Newcastle(UK), FRCP
PRO VICE-CHANCELLOR, HEALTH AND ESTATES—Jones, Prof. M. L., BDS Wales, MSc Lond., PhD Wales, FDSRCSEd
DIRECTOR OF CORPORATE SERVICES AND HUMAN RESOURCES AND UNIVERSITY SECRETARY—Turner, Christopher B., BA Wales, PhD Wales
DIRECTOR OF INFORMATION SERVICES—Harrow, Martyn, BSc Bath
DIRECTOR OF FINANCIAL AND PHYSICAL RESOURCES—Davies, Mike D., BScEcon Wales
DIRECTOR OF REGISTRY AND STUDENT SUPPORT—Cryer, Anthony, BSc Sheff., PhD Sheff.
DIRECTOR OF STRATEGIC DEVELOPMENT—Casella, Louise C., BScEcon Wales

GENERAL INFORMATION

History. Originally founded in 1883, Cardiff University was established in 1988, following the merger of University College, Cardiff and the University of Wales Institute of Science and Technology and, like its predecessors, was a constituent institution of the federal University of Wales. On 1 August 2004, the university merged with the University of Wales College of Medicine, which was originally established in 1931 as the Welsh National School of Medicine. In 2005, Cardiff University achieved the status and title of a university in its own right and at that point ceased to be a constituent institution of the University of Wales, though it retains affiliated status.

The main campus is located in Cardiff's civic centre in the heart of the city, and the Heath site campus shares a 53-acre site with the University Hospital of Wales Healthcare NHS Trust at Heath Park, some 5km north of the centre of Cardiff.

Admission to first degree courses (see also United Kingdom Introduction). Through Universities and Colleges Admissions Service (UCAS).

First Degrees (see also United Kingdom Directory to Subjects of Study). BA, BArch, BDS, BEng, BMus, BN, BSc, BScEcon, BTh, LLB, MB BCh, MChem, MEng, MESci, MPharm, MPhys.
Length of course. Full-time: BA, BEng, BMus, BSc, BScEcon, BTh, LLB: 3 years; MChem, MEng, MESci, MPharm, MPhys: 4 years; BArch: 5 years.

Higher Degrees (see also United Kingdom Directory to Subjects of Study).
Master's. LLM, MA, MBA, MCh, MMus, MPH, MPhil, MSc, MScD, MScEcon, MTh.
Length of course. Full-time: LLM, MA, MBA, MCh, MMus, MPH, MScEcon, MTh: 1 year; MPhil, MSc: 1–2 years. Part-time: LLM, MA, MBA, MCh, MPH, MScEcon, MTh: 2 years; MPhil, MSc: 2–3 years; MScD: 3 years.
Doctoral. DClinPsy, EdD, EngD, MD, PhD.
Length of course. Full-time: MD: 1 year; PhD: 2–3 years; DClinPsy, EngD: 3 years. Part-time: PhD: 3–5 years; EdD: 5 years.

Language of Instruction. English. The university offers facilities for international students to improve their English.

Libraries. Volumes: 1,300,000. Periodicals subscribed to: 16,000. Special collections: European Documentation Centre and United Nations documentation; Salisbury Library (Welsh language, history and culture); Sir Archie Cochrane archive; Edward Thomas archive.

Academic Year (2007–2008). Two semesters: 26 September–27 January; 28 January–13 June.

Income (2005–2006). Total, £3,344,437,000.

Statistics. Staff (2006–2007): 5487 (2669 academic, 2818 non-academic). Students (2005–2006): undergraduate 19,673; master's 5139.

ACADEMIC UNITS
Arranged by Schools

Architecture, Welsh School of

Tel: (029) 2087 4430 Fax: (029) 2087 4926
E-mail: archi@cardiff.ac.uk
Forster, Wayne P., BSc Wales, BArch Wales, PhD Wales   Sr. Lectr.; Deputy Head
Hardy, Adam   Sr. Lectr.
Jones, Phillip J., BSc Wales, PhD Wales   Prof.; Head*
Knight, Ian P., BSc Leeds, PhD Wales   Sr. Lectr.
Lupton, Sarah A., MA Edin.   Sr. Lectr.
Powell, Christopher G., BArch Brun., MTech Brun.   Sr. Lectr.
Other Staff: 6 Lectrs.; 1 Sr. Teaching Fellow; 1 Sr. Res. Fellow; 3 Sr. Res. Assocs.; 4 Professl. Tutors†
Research: architectural practice and research-led design; environmental design and sustainable development in the built environment; historical understanding and theory of architecture

Biosciences

Tel: (029) 2087 4829 Fax: (029) 2087 4116
Allen, Nicholas D., BSc Lond., PhD Camb.   Reader
Archer, Charles W., BSc Wales, PhD Wales   Prof.
Benjamin, M., BSc Wales, PhD Wales   Prof.
Berry, Colin, BSc S'ton., PhD Brist.   Sr. Lectr.
Boddy, L., BSc Lond., PhD Lond., DSc Exe., FRSA   Prof.
Borri, P., Laurea Florence, PhD Florence, DrHabil Dortmund   Reader
Bowen, I. D., BSc Wales, PhD Wales, DSc Wales, FIBiol   Prof.
Brambilla, R., PhD Milan   Reader
Bruford, Michael W., BSc Portsmouth, PhD Leic.   Prof.
Buchanan, K. L., BSc Glas., PhD Lond.   Sr. Lectr.
Buchman, V. L., MD Moscow, PhD Moscow   Prof.

Cable, J., BSc Lond., PhD Lond.   Sr. Lectr.
Carter, David A., BSc Bath, PhD Lond.   Reader
Caterson, Bruce, BSc Monash, PhD Monash   Prof.
Clarke, Alan R., BSc Brist., PhD Camb.   Prof.; Joint Head of Res.
Crunelli, V., Laur Catania   Prof.
Dale, Trevor C., BSc Lond., PhD Lond.   Prof.
Dancer, B. N., BSc Sheff., DPhil Oxf.   Sr. Lectr.
Davies, A., MB ChB Liv., BSc Liv., PhD Lond.   Prof.
Davies, M. S., BSc Wales, PhD Reading   Sr. Lectr.
Day, M. J., BSc CNAA, PhD Lond.   Reader
Dickinson, J. R., BSc Warw., PhD Warw.   Reader
Duance, Victor C., BSc Bath, PhD Brist.   Prof.
Dunnett, Stephen B., BSc Lond., MA Camb., PhD Camb., DSc Camb.   Prof.
Ehrmann, Michael, PhD Constance   Prof.
Evans, Martin J., MA Camb., MA Lond., PhD Lond., ScD Camb.   Prof.
Ferns, P. N., BSc Manc., PhD Exe.   Sr. Lectr.
Foster, George A., BA Camb., MA Camb., PhD S'ton.   Reader
Fox, Kevin D., BSc Bath, PhD Lond.   Prof.; Joint Head of Res.
Francis, Dennis, BSc Newcastle(UK), PhD Newcastle(UK), DSc Newcastle(UK)   Reader
Fry, John C., BSc Wales, PhD Wales   Prof.
Griffiths, S., BSc Wales, MSc Oxf., PhD St And.   Sr. Lectr.
Harwood, A., BA Oxf., PhD Edin.   Prof.
Harwood, John L., PhD Birm., DSc Birm.   Prof.; Head*
Huber, R., DrRerNat T.H.Munich, DrHabil T.H.Munich   Prof.
Hughes, C., BSc Lond., PhD Lond.   Sr. Lectr.
Jacob, Timothy J. C., BSc Sus., PhD E.Anglia   Prof.
Jervis, M. A., BSc Lond., PhD Wales   Sr. Lectr.
John, R. A., BSc Wales, PhD Wales   Prof.
John, R. M., PhD Lond.   Sr. Lectr.
Jones, T. H., BSc Lond., PhD Lond.   Sr. Lectr.
Kay, John, BSc Edin., PhD Edin.   Prof.
Kemp, P., BSc Oxf., DPhil Oxf.   Prof.
Kidd, N. A. C., BSc Glas., PhD Glas.   Reader
Kille, Peter, BSc Wales, PhD Wales   Sr. Lectr.; Dir., Bio-Initiatives
Lloyd, D., PhD Wales, DSc Sheff.   Prof.
Mahenthiralingam, Eshwar, BSc Wales, PhD CNAA   Reader
Major, G., BA Oxf., BA Camb., MA Oxf., MA Camb., DPhil Oxf.   Sr. Lectr.
Morgan, A. J., BSc Wales, PhD Wales, DSc Wales   Reader
Moxham, Bernard J., BSc Brist., BDS Brist., PhD Brist.   Prof.; Head of Teaching
Ormerod, Stephen J., BSc CNAA, MSc Wales, PhD Wales   Prof.
Pascoe, David, BSc Wales, PhD Wales   Reader

Ralphs, James R., BSc Lond., PhD CNAA Sr. Lectr.

Ramji, Dipak P., BSc Leeds, PhD Leeds Reader

Riccardi, D., BS Milan, MRes Milan, PhD Milan Reader

Rogers, H., BSc Lond., PhD Lond. Sr. Lectr.

Santer, Robert M., BSc St And., PhD St And. Sr. Lectr.

Sengpiel, F., MA Oxf., DPhil Oxf., DrHabil Munich Prof.

Stickler, D. J., BSc Wales, MA Trinity(Dub.), DPhil Oxf. Reader

Symondson, William O. C., BA Keele, PhD Wales Reader

Taylor, Michael V., MA Camb., PhD Camb. Sr. Lectr.

Thomas, K. L., BSc Swansea, PhD Lond. Sr. Lectr.

Venables, W. A., BSc Wales, PhD Wales Sr. Lectr.

Watson, Alan H. D., BSc Edin., PhD St And. Sr. Lectr.

Weightman, A. J., BSc Kent, PhD Warw. Prof.

Wells, T., BSc Leeds, PhD Lond. Sr. Lectr.

White, Graham F., BSc Lond., PhD Lond., DSc Lond. Reader

Wilson, D. J., BSc Wales, PhD Wales Prof.

Wyatt, S., BSc S'ton., PhD Lond. Sr. Lectr.

Other Staff: 15 Lectrs.; 6 Sr. Professnl. Tutors; 13 Sr. Res. Assocs.; 14 Professnl. Tutors; 16 Res. Fellows; 5 Hon. Profs.; 6 Hon. Lectrs.; 4 Hon. Res. Fellows

Research: biodiversity and ecological processes; connective tissue biology; genetics and neuroscience; microbiology; molecular cell biology

Business

Tel: (029) 2087 6013 Fax: (029) 2087 4419

Ashworth, Rachel, BA Glam., PhD Cardiff Sr. Lectr.

Beresford, Anthony, BA Manc., PhD E.Anglia Sr. Lectr.

Beynon, Malcolm J., BSc Wales, PhD Wales Reader

Blyton, Paul R., BA Leic., PhD Sheff. Prof.

Boyne, George A., MA Aberd., MLitt Aberd., PhD Bath Prof.

Boyns, Trevor, BSc Warw., PhD Wales Prof.

Bridge, John, BScEcon Wales, MA Sheff., PhD Wales Sr. Lectr.

Byers, John D., BA Durh., MSc Lond., PhD Wales Sr. Lectr.

Chandler, Roy A., BScEcon Wales Prof., Accounting

Clarke, Roger, BSc Wales, MA Essex, PhD Leic. Prof., Industrial Economics

Clatworthy, Mark, BSc Wales, PhD Wales Sr. Lectr.

Collie, David R., BSc Birm., BCom Birm., MSc(Econ) Lond., PhD Lond. Prof.

Copeland, Laurence S., BA Oxf., MA(Econ) Manc., PhD Manc. Prof.

Curry, Bruce, BA(Econ) Manc., MSc Sus. Prof.

Davies, Annette, BSc Wales, PhD Brun. Sr. Lectr.

Davies, Anthony J., BA Open(UK), MSc Wales, PhD Wales Prof., Electronic Commerce

Delbridge, Richard I., BScEcon Wales, PhD Wales Prof.

Disney, Stephen, BEng Wales, MSc Wales, PhD Wales Sr. Lectr.

Dixon, Huw D., MA Oxf., MPhil Oxf., PhD Oxf. Prof.

Doyle, John, BSc Newcastle(UK), MA Lanc., DPhil Sus. Prof.

Edwards, J. Richard, MScEcon Wales, FCA Prof.

Ezzamel, Mahmoud A., BCom Alexandria, PhD S'ton. Prof. Fellow

Foreman-Peck, James S., BA Essex, MSc(Econ) Lond., PhD Lond. Prof., Welsh Economic Research

Foster, Deborah J. Sr. Lectr.

Foxall, Gordon R., MSc Salf., PhD Strath., PhD Birm., DSocSc Birm. Prof.

Gillman, Max, BA Mich., MA Chic., PhD Chic. Prof.

Gould-Williams, Julian, BSc Wales, PhD Wales Sr. Lectr.

Heery, Edmund J., BA Camb., MA Essex Prof.

Heravi, Saeed, BSc Mashhad, MSc Manc., PhD Manc. Reader

Hines, Peter A., MA Camb. Prof.

Hodges, Susan L., LLB Sing., LLM Lond., PhD Wales Sr. Lectr.

Holtham, Gerald, BA Oxf., MPhil Oxf. Visiting Prof.

Hood, Christopher P., BA Sheff., PhD Sheff. Sr. Lectr.

Jamal, Ahmad, PhD Brad. Sr. Lectr.

Jones, Michael J., BA Oxf., FCA Prof., Financial Reporting

Kaleka, Anna, PhD Cardiff Reader

Karbari, Yusuf, BA CNAA, MBA Wales, PhD Wales Reader

Kitchener, Martin J., BSc Wales, MBA Wales, PhD Cardiff Prof.

Luintel, Kul, BA Kathmandu, BL Kathmandu, MA Kathmandu, MPhil Glas., PhD Glas. Prof.

Makepeace, Gerald H., BA Durh., MSocSc Birm. Prof., Labour Economics

Marginson, David, BA Lond., MA Lanc., PhD Lanc. Prof.

Marlow, Peter B., MScEcon Wales, PhD Wales Prof.; Head, Logs. and Ops.

Martin, Stephen J., BA Oxf., PhD Aston Prof.; Dir., Local Govt. Management

Matthews, Derek R., BSc(Econ) Hull, MA Leeds, PhD Hull Prof.

Matthews, Kent G. P., MSc(Econ) Lond., PhD Liv. Sir Julian Hodge Prof., Banking and Finance

McNabb, Robert, BSc Brist., MA Qu., PhD Wales Prof.; Dean*

Mellett, Howard J., MScEcon Wales, FCA Prof.; Head, Accounting

Minford, A. Patrick L., CBE, BA Oxf., MSc Lond., PhD Lond. Prof.; Head, Econ.

Morgan, Claire Louise, BSc MSc Assoc. Dean

Morgan, Peter H., BSc(Tech) Wales, PhD Wales Sr. Lectr.

Morgan, Robert, BScEcon Wales, PhD Wales, FCIM Prof.

Morris, Jonathan L., BA Oxf., MPhil Lond. Prof.; Head, Human Res. Management

Munday, Maxim C. R., BA CNAA, PhD Wales Reader

Naim, Mohamed M., BEng(Tech) Wales, MSc Wales, PhD Wales Reader

Ogbonna, Emmanuel O., MBA Wales, PhD Wales Prof.

Peel, Michael J., LLB Leeds, MBA Brad. Prof.

Pendlebury, Maurice W., MA Lanc., PhD Wales Prof., Accounting

Poole, Michael J. F., BA(Econ) Sheff., PhD Sheff. Prof., Human Resource Management

Powell, John H. Prof.

Reed, Robert I., BScEcon Wales, PhD Wales Prof.

Roberts, Annette, BSc(Econ) PhD Sr. Lectr.

Robson, Keith, BA(Econ) Manc., MA(Econ) Manc., PhD Manc. Prof.

Sadler, P., MSc(Econ) Lond. Hon. Prof.

Shorey, John C., BA(Econ) Manc., MSc(Econ) Lond., PhD Lond. Sr. Lectr.

Smith, Ian G., MScEcon Wales, PhD Wales Sr. Lectr.

Solomon, Jill, MSc Durh., PhD Manc., BA Sr. Lectr.

Thomas, Robyn, BScEcon Wales, PhD Glam. Prof.

Turnbull, Peter J., BA Leeds, MA Warw. Prof.

Walker, Stephen P., BA Kent, PhD Edin. Prof.

Wallace, Allan M., BA Camb., MA Camb., PhD E.Anglia Prof.

Wass, Victoria, BSc Wales, MSc Lond., PhD Wales Sr. Lectr.

Wells, Peter, BA Leeds, MSc Wales, PhD Wales Reader

Whitfield, Keith L., MA Camb., DPhil Oxf. Prof.

Williams, David Sr. Lectr.

Willmott, Hugh, BSc Manc., PhD Manc. Prof.

Xiao, Jason Z., MEcon Beijing, MSc CNAA, PhD Napier Prof.

Other Staff: 54 Lectrs.; 2 Sr. Professnl. Tutors; 5 Distinguished Sr. Res. Fellows; 1 Sr. Res. Fellow; 14 Sr. Res. Assocs.; 4 Res. Fellows; 7 Professnl. Tutors; 1 Lectr.†; 1 Distinguished Sr. Res. Fellow†; 1 Sr. Res. Fellow†; 4 Sr. Res. Assocs.†

Research: accounting and finance; employment and related organisational research; macro- and microeconomics relevant to business and the national economy; marketing; supply chain and operations management

Chemistry

Tel: (029) 2087 4023 Fax: (029) 2087 4030

Aldridge, Simon, BA Oxf., DPhil Oxf. Sr. Lectr.

Allemann, Rudolf K., DrScNat E.T.H.Zürich, PhD E.T.H.Zürich, FRSChem Prof.

Attard, Gary A., BSc Liv., PhD Liv. Prof.

Bagley, Mark C., BA Oxf., DPhil Oxf. Reader

Bochtler, Matthias, PhD T.U.Munich, DrHabil Polish Acad.Sc. Dir., Structural Biol.

Bowker, Michael, BSc E.Anglia, PhD Liv., FRSChem Prof.

Carpenter, Barry K., BSc Warw., PhD Lond. Prof.

Cavell, Kingsley J., MSc La Trobe, PhD La Trobe, FRSChem Prof.; Head*

Coogan, Michael P., BSc Leic., PhD Leic. Sr. Lectr.

Davies, Philip R., BSc S'ton., PhD Wales Sr. Lectr.

Edwards, Peter G., BSc Lond., PhD Lond. Prof.

Fallis, Ian A., BSc Glas., PhD Glas. Sr. Lectr.

Griffiths, Peter C., BSc Wales, PhD Brist. Reader

Harris, Kenneth D. M., BSc St And., PhD Camb., FRSChem Prof.

Hutchings, Graham J., BSc Lond., PhD Lond., FRSChem Prof.

Jones, Cameron, BSc W.Aust., PhD Griff. Prof.

Knight, David W., BSc Nott., PhD Nott., FRSChem Prof.

Knowles, Peter J., MA Camb., PhD Camb. Prof.

McKeown, Neil B., BSc E.Anglia, PhD E.Anglia Prof.

Mella, Massimo, PhD Milan Reader

Murphy, Damien M., PhD Dublin I.T. Sr. Lectr.

Platts, James A., BSc Glas., PhD Cardiff Sr. Lectr.

Richter, Gerald, PhD Munich Prof.

Roberts, M. Wyn, PhD Wales, DSc Wales, FRSChem Res. Prof.

Smith, Keith, BSc Manc., MSc Manc., PhD Manc., FRSChem Prof.

Spencer, Michael S., MA Camb., PhD Camb., FRSChem Hon. Prof.

Taylor, Stuart H., BSc Brun., PhD Liv. Sr. Lectr.

Wells, Peter B., BSc Hull, PhD Hull, FRSChem Prof.

Williams, David R., OBE, BSc Wales, PhD Wales, DSc St And., FRSChem, FRSA Res. Prof.

Willock, David J., BSc Salf., PhD Lond. Sr. Lectr.

Wirth, Thomas, PhD T.U.Berlin Prof.

Other Staff: 11 Lectrs.; 2 Res. Fellows; 1 Dir., External Liaison; 1 Dir., Undergrad. Studies

Research: chemical biology; heterogeneous catalysis and surface science; solid state materials chemistry; synthesis (metals in synthesis, organic synthesis); theoretical and computational chemistry

City and Regional Planning

Tel: (029) 2087 4022 Fax: (029) 2087 4845

Biddulph, Mike J., BSc Oxf.Brookes, MA Oxf.Brookes Sr. Lectr.

Bristow, Gillian I., BA(Econ) Cardiff, PhD Cardiff Sr. Lectr.

Brown, Alison M, BSc Nott., MCD Liv. Sr. Lectr.

Clapham, David F., BA CNAA, MSc Lond., PhD Lond. Prof.

Cooke, Philip N., BA Liv., FRSA Prof.

Cowell, Richard W., BA Camb., PhD Camb. Sr. Lectr.

Crow, H. Stephen, CB, MA Camb., FRTPI, FRICS Hon. Prof.

Feindt, Peter H., PhD Hamburg Sr. Lectr.

Flynn, Andrew C., BA *Essex*, PhD *Lond.* Sr. Lectr.
Guy, Clifford M., BA *Camb.*, MPhil *Lond.*, PhD *Reading* Prof.
Hooper, Alan J., BSc(Econ) *Lond.*, MSc *Wales* Prof.
Jones-Evans, Dylan, BSc *Cardiff*, MSc *Manc.*, PhD, FRSA Prof.
Kunzmann, Klaus R., DrTech *T.U.Vienna* Hon. Prof.
Lovering, John, BA *Wales* Prof.
Marsden, Terry K., BA *Hull*, PhD *Hull* Prof.; Head*
Meadows, Graham, MA *Edin.* Hon. Prof.
Milbourne, Paul, BA *Wales*, PhD *Wales* Reader
Morgan, Kevin J., BA *Leic.*, MA *McM.*, DPhil *Sus.* Prof.
Punter, John V., BA *Newcastle(UK)*, MA *Tor.*, PhD *Tor.* Prof.
Senior, Martyn L., BA *Leeds*, PhD *Leeds* Sr. Lectr.
Smith, Robert S. G., BA *Sheff.*, PhD *Sheff.* Sr. Lectr.
Tayler, Kevin, BSc *Birm.*, MSc *Manc.* Hon. Prof.
Thomas, A. Huw, BA *Oxf.*, MPhil *Lond.* Reader
Walker, Richard M., BA *CNAA*, PhD *Reading* Sr. Lectr.
Webster, Christopher J., MSc *Wales*, PhD *Hull* Prof.
Wu, Fulong, BSc *Nanjing*, MSc *Nanjing*, PhD *HK* Prof.
Other Staff: 13 Lectrs.; 5 Res. Fellows; 1 Hon. Res. Fellow
Research: environmental planning and sustainability; housing management and development; spatial analysis; urban design; urban planning and transport

Computer Science

Tel: (029) 2087 4812 *Fax:* (029) 2087 4598
E-mail: office@cs.cardiff.ac.uk
Allen, Stuart M., BSc *Nott.*, PhD *Reading* Sr. Lectr.
Avis, Nicholas J., BSc *Reading*, PhD *Sheff.* Prof.
Brown, Brian M., BSc *Wales*, PhD *Wales* Prof.
Craig, K. H., BSc *Glas.*, DPhil *Oxf.*, FIEE Hon. Prof.
Eastham, Michael S. P., MA *Oxf.*, DPhil *Oxf.*, DSc *Oxf.*, FIMA Hon. Prof.
Fiddian, Nicholas J., MSc *Lond.*, PhD *S'ton.* Prof.; Head*
Gray, W. Alex, MA *Edin.*, MSc *Newcastle(UK)* Prof.
Hu, Shi-Min, BSc *Jilin*, PhD *Zhejiang* Hon. Prof.
Hurley, Stephen, BSc *CNAA*, MSc *Reading* Prof.
Jeffrey, Keith G., BSc *Exe.*, PhD *Exe.*, FGS Hon. Prof.
Jones, Andrew C., BSc *Wales*, PhD *Wales* Sr. Lectr.
Jones, C. B., BSc *Brist.*, PhD *Newcastle(UK)* Prof.
Marshall, A. David, BSc *Wales*, PhD *Wales* Reader
Martin, Ralph R., MA *Camb.*, PhD *Camb.* Prof.
McIntosh, Stephen B., BA *Open(UK)*, MSc *Cran.* Dir.
Pollington, A. D., BA *Lond.*, MSc *Lond.*, PhD *Lond.* Hon. Prof.
Rana, Omer F., BEng *Lond.*, MSc *S'ton.*, PhD *Lond.* Prof.
Rosin, Paul, BSc *Strath.*, PhD *City(UK)* Reader
Shao, Jianhua, BSc *Shanghai*, MPhil *CNAA*, PhD *Ulster* Sr. Lectr.
Taylor, Ian J., BSc *Wales*, PhD *Wales* Sr. Lectr.
Walker, David W., MA *Camb.*, PhD *Lond.* Prof.
Whitaker, Roger M., BSc *Keele*, PhD *Keele* Sr. Lectr.
Wilson, Brian, BSc *Nott.*, PhD *Nott.* Hon. Prof.

Dentistry

Tel: (029) 2074 2468 *Fax:* (029) 2074 6343

Adult Dental Health

Tel: (029) 2074 4356 *Fax:* (029) 2074 3120
E-mail: krip@cardiff.ac.uk
Dummer, P. M. H., BDS *Wales*, MScD *Wales*, PhD *Wales*, DDSc *Wales*, FDSRCSEd Prof., Restorative Dentistry; Head*
Gilmour, A. S. M., BDS *Edin.*, PhD *Edin.*, FDSRCSEd Sr. Lectr.
Jacobsen, P. H., BDS *Lond.*, MDS *Lond.*, FDSRCS Reader
Jenkins, S. M., BDS *Wales*, MSc *Wales*, PhD *Wales*, FDSRCSEd Sr. Lectr.
Lynch, C., BDS *N.U.I.* Sr. Lectr.
McAndrew, R., BDS *Dund.*, MScD *Edin.*, MRD *Edin.* Sr. Lectr.
Rees, J., BDS *Wales*, MScD *Wales*, PhD *Wales* Prof., Restorative Dentistry
Sweet, J., BDS *Wales*, MSc *Lond.* Sr. Lectr.
Thompson, S. A., BDS *Wales*, MPhil *Wales*, PhD *Wales* Sr. Lectr.
Wilson, J., BDS *Lond.*, MSc *Lond.*, FDSRCS Sr. Lectr.
Other Staff: 16 Lectrs.
Research: biomaterials and biomechanics; endodontology; epithelial cell biology; inflammation and host responses

Dental Health and Biological Sciences

Tel: (029) 2074 2447 *Fax:* (029) 2074 2447
E-mail: denhealth@cardiff.ac.uk
Aeschlimann, D. P., MSc *Basle*, PhD *Basle* Prof.; Head, Biol. Scis. Unit
Chadwick, Barbara L., BDS *Lond.*, MScD *Wales* Sr. Lectr.
Hunter, L., BDS *Wales*, MScD PhD, FDSRCS Sr. Lectr.
Jones, M. L., BDS *Wales*, MSc *Lond.*, PhD *Wales*, FDSRCSEd Prof.
Knauper, V. Sr. Lectr.
Middleton, J., BSc *Wales*, MSc *Wales*, FRSA Prof., Biol. Scis. Unit
Oliver, R. G., BDS *Wales*, MScD *Wales*, PhD *Wales*, FDSRCSEd Prof.
Richmond, S., BDS *Sheff.*, MScD *Wales*, PhD *Manc.*, FDSRCS Prof.; Head, Dent. Health; Head*
Treasurer, E. T., BDS *Birm.*, PhD *Birm.*, FRACDS Prof.
Waddington, R. J., BSc *Birm.*, PhD *Liv.* Sr. Lectr.
Other Staff: 11 Lectrs.; 3 Lectrs.†; 2 Hon. Sr. Lectrs.
Research: adult dental health survey; biomaterials and biomechanics; oral connective tissue biology; orthodontics

Oral Surgery, Medicine and Pathology

Tel: (029) 2074 4215 *Fax:* (029) 2074 2442
E-mail: oralsm-p@cardiff.ac.uk
Hill, C. M., BDS *Brist.*, MSc *Glam.*, MDSc *Leeds*, FDSRCSEd Sr. Lectr., Oral Surgery
Lewis, M. A. O., BDS *Dund.*, PhD *Glas.*, FDSRCPSGlas, FDSRCSEd Reader; Prof., Oral Medicine
Moore, S., BSc PhD Sr. Lectr.
Potts, A. J. C., BSc *Manc.*, BDS *Manc.* Sr. Lectr., Oral Pathology
Shepherd, J. P., CBE, BDS *Lond.*, MSc *Oxf.*, PhD *Brist.*, DDSc *Wales*, FDSRCSEd, Hon. FDSRCSEd Prof., Oral and Maxillofacial Surgery; Head*
Sivarajasingam, V., BDS *Dund.*, BMSc *Dund.* Sr. Lectr.
Sloan, A., BSc *Wales*, PhD *Birm.* Sr. Lectr., Bone Biology and Tissue Engineering
Stephens, P., BSc *Leeds*, PhD *Leeds* Sr. Lectr., Oral Molecular Biology
Stringer, B., BSc *Sus.*, MSc *Wales*, PhD *Wales* Prof., Dental Science
Thomas, D. W., BDS *Wales*, MScD *Wales*, PhD *Brist.*, FDSRCSEd Prof., Oral and Maxillofacial Surgery
Williams, D., BSc *Wales*, PhD *Wales* Reader, Oral Microbiology
Wilson, M., BDS *Belf.* Sr. Lectr., Oral Microbiology
Other Staff: 4 Lectrs.; 1 Instr.; 6 Clin. Teachers; 1 Hon. Sr. Registrar
Research: clinical decisions; oral microbiology; violence; wound healing

Earth and Ocean Sciences

Tel: (029) 2087 4830 *Fax:* (029) 2087 4326
E-mail: earth-ug@cf.ac.uk
Bassett, Michael G., BSc *Wales*, PhD *Wales*, DSc *Wales*, FGS Hon. Prof.
Cartwright, Joseph, MA *Camb.*, DPhil *Camb.*, FGS Prof. Fellow
Cherns, Lesley, BA *Keele*, PhD *Glas.* Sr. Lectr.
Cope, John C. W., BSc *Brist.*, PhD *Brist.*, DSc *Brist.*, FGS Hon. Prof.
Davies, John H., BSc *Camb.*, MA *Camb.*, MS *Cal.Tech.*, PhD *Cal.Tech.* Sr. Lectr.
Edwards, Dianne, CBE, BA *Camb.*, MA *Camb.*, PhD *Camb.*, ScD *Camb.*, FGS, FLS, FRS Prof.; Head*
Hall, Ian R., BSc *Wales*, PhD *S'ton.* Reader
Harris, Anthony Hon. Visiting Prof.; Distinguished Res. Fellow
Harris, Charles, BSc *Durh.*, PhD *Reading*, FGS Prof.
Hemsley, Alan R., BSc *Lond.*, PhD *Lond.* Sr. Lectr.
James, David, MA *Oxf.*, PhD *Wales*, FGS Prof.; Hon. Res. Fellow
Jones, Timothy P., PhD *Lond.*, BSc Sr. Lectr.
Kerr, Andrew C., BSc *St And.*, PhD *Durh.* Sr. Lectr.
Leake, Bernard, BSc *Liv.*, PhD *Liv.*, DSc *Brist.*, DSc *Glas.* Hon. Prof.
Lisle, Richard J., BSc *Birm.*, MSc *Lond.*, ScD *Birm.*, PhD *Lond.* Prof.
Luther, George W., BA *La Salle(Penn.)*, PhD *Pitt.* Hon. Prof.; Distinguished Visiting Fellow
MacLeod, Christopher J., BSc *Durh.*, PhD *Open(UK)*, FGS Sr. Lectr.
Parkes, R. John, BEd *Birm.*, PhD *Aberd.* Dist. Prof. Fellow
Pearce, Julian A., BA *Camb.*, PhD *E.Anglia* Prof. Fellow
Pearson, Paul N., BA *Oxf.*, PhD *Camb.* Prof.; Deputy Head; Dir., Res.
Pike, Jennifer, BSc *Birm.*, PhD *S'ton.* Sr. Lectr.
Prichard, Hazel M., BSc *Hull*, PhD *Newcastle(UK)* Sr. Lectr.
Ramsay, Anthony T. S., BSc *Wales*, PhD *Wales* Sr. Lectr.; Hon. Res. Fellow
Ramsay, John G., CBE, PhD *Lond.*, DSc *Lond.*, Hon. Doctorat *Rennes*, FRS, Hon. FGS Hon. Prof.
Rickard, David T., BSc *Lond.*, PhD *Lond.*, FGS Prof.
Riding, Robert E., BSc *Sheff.*, PhD *Sheff.* Reader
Smith, Hance D., BSc *Aberd.*, PhD *Aberd.*, FRICS Reader
Wakefield, Simon J., PhD *Leeds* Sr. Lectr.; Deputy Head; Dir., Teaching
Wooldridge, Christopher F., BSc *Wales*, PhD *Wales*, FRICS, FRGS Sr. Lectr.
Wright, Victor P., BSc *Wales*, PhD *Wales*, DSc *Wales* Prof.
Yang, Yuesuo, PhD *Jilin* Sr. Lectr.
Other Staff: 15 Lectrs.; 1 Sr. Tutor; 1 Res. Fellow; 8 Hon. Lectrs.; 1 Hon. Res. Fellow
Research: basin dynamics, magmatic processes and computational geodynamics; geomicrobiology, palaeobiology, palaeoclimate; marine and coastal environment, geo-environment, carbonates

Engineering

Tel: (029) 2087 4070 *Fax:* (029) 2087 4716
Barrow, David A., BSc *Wales*, PhD *Wales* Prof. Fellow
Belcher, Allan, BSc *Wales*, PhD *Sur.* Prof.
Bowen, Philip J., BSc *Wales*, PhD *Wales* Prof.
Evans, Henry P., BSc *Exe.*, PhD *Exe.* Prof.
Evans, Sam L., BEng *S'ton.*, PhD *S'ton.* Sr. Lectr.
Falconer, Roger A., BSc *Lond.*, MSCE *Wash.*, PhD *Lond.*, DSc *Lond.*, DEng *Birm.*, FICE Prof.
Featherston, Carol A., BEng *Birm.*, PhD *Oxf.* Sr. Lectr.
Griffiths, Anthony J., BEng *Wales*, PhD *Wales* Prof.
Griffiths, Huw, BSc *Wales* Sr. Lectr.
Grosvenor, Roger I., BEng(Tech) *Wales*, MEng *Wales*, PhD *Wales* Reader

Haddad, Abderrahmane, Ing Éc.Nat.Polytech., Algiers, PhD Wales Prof.
Holford, Karen M., BEng(Tech) Wales, PhD Wales, FIMechE Prof.
Holt, Catherine, BEng Wales, PhD Wales, FIMechE Sr. Lectr.
Howson, W. Paul, BEng Liv., PhD Birm. Sr. Lectr.
Hughes, Tim G., MSc Wales, PhD Wales, FICE Prof.; Deputy Head, Teaching
Jefferson, Anthony D., BSc CNAA, MSc Wales, PhD Wales Sr. Lectr.
Jiles, David C., BSc Wales, PhD Wales, FIP, FIEEE, FIEE, FAPS, FIMMM, FIMA Prof.
Karihaloo, B. L., BSc(Eng) Ranchi, MTech Bom., PhD Moscow, DEng Syd., FIEAust, FASCE Prof.
Kennedy, David, MA Camb., PhD Wales Reader
Lark, Robert J., BSc PhD Sr. Lectr.
Lever, Kenneth V., BSc Liv., MSc Essex Prof.
Lin, BinLiang, BSc(Eng) Tsinghua, MSc(Eng) Tianjin, PhD Beijing, PhD Brad. Reader
Loxham, Michael, BSc Leic., Doctorat T.H.Delft Prof.
McWhirter, J. G., BSc Belf., PhD Belf., FREng, FIEE, FIMA Distinguished Res. Prof.
Meydan, Turgut, BSc Birm., MSc Wales, PhD Wales Reader
Miles, John C., BSc Manc., MSc Birm., PhD Birm. Prof.
Morgan, D. Vernon, BSc Wales, PhD Camb., DSc Leeds, FIEE, FREng, FIP, FCGI, FRSA Prof.
Moses, Anthony J., BEng(Tech) Wales, PhD Wales, DSc Wales, FIEE, FIP Prof.
Nokes, Leonard D. M., BEng Wales, MB BCh Wales, MSc Wales, PhD Wales, FIMechE Prof.
Nussey, I., OBE, MA Camb., PhD Lond., FREng, FIMechE Hon. Prof.
O'Doherty, D., BEng Wales, PhD Brist. Sr. Lectr.
O'Doherty, T., BEng Wales, PhD Wales, FIMechE Reader
Porch, Adrian, MA Camb., PhD Camb. Prof.
Prickett, Paul W., BEng(Tech) Wales Sr. Lectr.
Roberts, Terry M., BSc Wales, PhD Wales Prof.
Rowe, David M., OBE, BSc Wales, MSc Brist., PhD Wales, DSc Wales, FIEE Prof.
Sanei, Saeid, BSc Lond., PhD Lond. Sr. Lectr.
Setchi, Rossitza, PhD Wales Sr. Lectr.
Snidle, Raymond W., BSc Leic., PhD Leic., DSc Leic., FIMechE Prof.
Snyder, John E., BS MS PhD Sr. Lectr.
Syred, Nicholas, BEng Sheff., PhD Sheff., FIMechE Prof.
Tasker, Paul J., BSc Leeds, PhD Leeds Prof.; Deputy Head, Res.
Thomas, Hywel R., BSc Wales, MSc Lond., PhD Wales, DSc Wales, FICE, FGS, FREng Prof.; Head*
Watton, John, BSc Wales, PhD Wales, DSc Wales, FIMechE Prof.
Williams, Fred W., MA Camb., ScD Camb., PhD Brist., FICE, FIStructE, FRAeS, FREng Prof.
Williams, Keith P., MSc Wales, PhD Wales Prof.
Wilson, Catherine A. M. E., BEng Sheff., PhD Brist. Sr. Lectr.
Woodcock, J. P., OBE, BSc Durh., MPhil Lond., PhD Lond., DSc Durh., FIP Prof.
Other Staff: 29 Lectrs.; 6 Sr. Res. Assocs.; 1 Res. Fellow; 4 Professnl. Tutors; 10 Hon. Lectrs.; 1 Hon. Res. Fellow
Research: advanced materials and energy systems; information systems and integration technology; machines and structures (theoretical, applied and computational mechanics); medical engineering and medical physics; sustainability, energy and environmental management

English, Communication and Philosophy
Tel: (029) 2087 6049 Fax: (029) 2087 4502
Aldridge-Waddon, Michelle, BA Wales, PhD Wales Sr. Lectr.
Attfield, Robin, MA Oxf., PhD Prof.

Badmington, Neil, BA Exe., PhD Wales Sr. Lectr.
Buchanan, Ian, BA Murd., PhD Murd. Prof.
Connolly, Claire, BA N.U.I., PhD Wales Reader
Cotterill, Janet, BSc Aston, PhD Birm. Reader
Coupland, Justine, BA Wales, PhD Wales Reader
Coupland, Nikolas J., BA Oxf., BLing Manc., MA Reading, PhD Wales Prof.
Coyle, Martin J., BA Nott., PhD Nott. Prof.
Edgar, Andrew R., BA Lanc., MA Sus., DPhil Sus. Sr. Lectr.
Garrett, Peter D., BScEcon Lond. Sr. Lectr.
Gramich, Katie, BA Wales, PhD Alta. Sr. Lectr.
Hammill, Faye, BA Birm., PhD Birm. Sr. Lectr.
Jaworski, Adam, MA Poznan, PhD Poznan Prof.
Kayman, Martin A., BA York(UK), DPhil York(UK) Prof. Fellow; Head*
Knight, Stephen T., BLitt Oxf., MA Oxf., PhD Syd. Prof.
Milesi, Laurent, BA Dijon, DPhil Oxf. Sr. Lectr.
Mohanram, Radhika, MA Madr., PhD Arizona Reader
Moore, Jane, BA Wales, PhD Wales Sr. Lectr.
Norris, Christopher C., BA Lond., PhD Lond. Distinguished Res. Prof.
Phelpstead, Carl L., BA Sheff., MPhil Oxf., DPhil Oxf. Sr. Lectr.
Phillips, Helen, BA Oxf., PhD Nott. Prof.
Plasa, Carl A., BA Oxf., MA S'ton., PhD S'ton. Reader
Sarangi, S. K., MA Utkal, MLitt Lanc., PhD Lanc. Prof.
Sedgwick, Peter R., BA CNAA, PhD Wales Sr. Lectr.
Skilton, David J., MA Camb., MLitt Camb. Prof.
Tanesini, Alessandra, PhD Hull, Laurea Bologna Reader
Thomas, Julia, BA Wales, PhD Wales Sr. Lectr.
Thornborrow, Joanna S., BA Hull, MLitt Strath., PhD Strath. Reader
Weedon, Christine M., BA S'ton., PhD Birm. Prof.
Williams, Angela M., BSc Brist., PhD Calif. Sr. Lectr.
Wilson, Richard, BA York(UK), DPhil York(UK) Prof.
Wray, Alison M., BA York(UK), DPhil York(UK) Prof.
Other Staff: 20 Lectrs.; 3 Hon. Profs.
Research: applied ethics; critical and cultural theory; editorial and intertextual research; English literature; language and communication

European Studies
Tel: (029) 2087 4889 Fax: (029) 2087 4946
Berendse, Gerrit-Jan, MA Utrecht, DPhil Utrecht Prof.
Bettinson, Christopher D., BA Reading, PhD Reading Sr. Lectr.
Boucher, David, BA Wales, MSc Lond., PhD Liv., FRHistS Prof. Fellow
Broughton, David J., BA Sus., MSc Strath., PhD Essex Sr. Lectr.
Cole, Alistair M., BSc(Econ) Lond., DPhil Oxf. Prof. Fellow
Compston, H. W., BA ANU, BLitt ANU, PhD ANU Reader
Cumming, Gordon, MA Glas., PhD Sr. Lectr.
Donovan, Mark P., BA CNAA, BA Open(UK), MSc Lond., PhD Lond. Sr. Lectr.
Dorey, Peter, BA Sus., MA Leeds, PhD Hull Reader
Dyson, Kenneth H. F., BSc Lond., MSc Lond., PhD Liv., FRHistS, FRSA, FBA Prof.
Furlong, Paul, PhL Greg., MA Oxf., PhD Reading Prof.; Head*
Garrard, Graeme, BA Trin.Coll.(Tor.), MA Tor., DPhil Oxf. Sr. Lectr.
Gorrara, C. J., BA Leeds, MSt Oxf., DPhil Oxf. Reader
Haddock, B. A., BA Leic., DPhil Oxf., FRHistS Prof.
Hanley, David L., MA Oxf., PhD Warw. Prof.
Jackson, David A., MA Oxf., DPhil Oxf. Prof.
Kelley, Charles, MA PhD Sr. Lectr.

Langford, Rachael, BA Oxf., MA Camb., PhD Camb. Sr. Lectr.
Loughlin, John P., BA CNAA, PhD Florence Prof.
Lunati, Montserrat, BA Cardiff, PhD Cardiff Sr. Lectr.
Marsh, Stephen I., BA Swansea, PhD Cardiff Sr. Lectr.
Nuselovici, Alexis, MPhil PhD Prof.
Parsons, Nicholas, BA CNAA, MA Reading, PhD Lond. Reader
Pateman, Carole, DLitt ANU, FASSA Hon. Prof.
Sutch, Peter, BA Swansea, MA Swansea, PhD Swansea, FRHistS Sr. Lectr.
Topping, Margaret, MA Oxf., MSt Oxf., DPhil Oxf. Sr. Lectr.
Vighi, Fabio, BA Reading, PhD Reading Sr. Lectr.
Other Staff: 13 Lectrs.; 1 Prof. Tutor
Research: European histories, memories and fictions; European ideologies and intellectuals; political parties, social movements and institutions; regionalism, nationalism and federalism

Healthcare Studies
Tel: (029) 2074 4185 Fax: (029) 2074 7763
E-mail: martind@cardiff.ac.uk
Mansfield, Roger, MA Camb., PhD Camb. Sir Julian Hodge Prof., Management; Head*

Occupational Therapy
Tel: (029) 2074 2257
E-mail: occupational-therapy@cardiff.ac.uk
Boniface, G., MSc PhD Sr. Lectr.
Clouston, T. J., MBA Sr. Lectr.
Hearle, D., MSc Sr. Lectr.
Roberts, G. W., MA Sr. Lectr.; Hon. Fellow
Other Staff: 18 Lectrs.; 4 Hon. Clin. Teachers

Operating Department Practice
Tel: (029) 2074 5067 Fax: (029) 2074 4552
E-mail: seawardde@cardiff.ac.uk
Morgan, A., BSc Wales, PhD Wales Sr. Lectr.; Dir.*
Other Staff: 6 Lectrs.

Physiotherapy
Tel: (029) 2074 2267 Fax: (029) 2074 2267
E-mail: physiotherapy@cardiff.ac.uk
Evans, E., BSc Wales, MSc Wales Sr. Lectr.
Everett, A., BA Open(UK), MEd Wales Sr. Lectr.; Deputy Dir.
Lipscombe, H. F., BA Open(UK), MEd Wales Sr. Lectr.
Palastanga, Nigel P., BA Open(UK), MA Lond. Prof.
Phillips, N., MSc Wales, PhD Wales Sr. Lectr.
Richardson, S., BA MSc Sr. Lectr.
van Deursen, R., BSc Utrecht, MSc Amst., PhD Penn. Sr. Lectr.; Dir.*
Other Staff: 16 Lectrs.

Radiography
Tel: (029) 2074 4169 Fax: (029) 2074 3836
E-mail: radiography-l@cardiff.ac.uk
Brown, P. N., MScEcon Wales, PhD Wales Asst. Dir.
Gambling, Tina S., BSc BSc PhD Sr. Lectr.
Newton, J., BEd Wales, MEd Wales, MSc Wales Dir.*
West, M. K., MPhil Glam. Deputy Dir.
Other Staff: 15 Lectrs.; 11 Clin. Lectrs.

History and Archaeology
Tel: (029) 2087 4259 Fax: (029) 2087 4929
Bailey, Douglass W., AB Dartmouth, PhD Camb. Sr. Lectr.
Benton, Gregor, MA Camb., PhD Leeds Prof. Fellow
Bivins, Roberta E., BA Col., PhD Sr. Lectr.
Coss, Peter R., BA Wales, PhD Birm., FSA Prof.
Edbury, Peter W., MA St And., PhD St And. Prof.
Fisher, Nicholas R. E., MA Oxf., DPhil Oxf. Prof.
Freestone, Ian C. Prof. Fellow

Hines, John A., MA Oxf., DPhil Oxf.   Prof.

Hudson, Patricia, BSc(Econ) Lond., DPhil York(UK)   Prof.

Jones, William D., BA Wales, PhD Wales   Reader

Lambert, Stephen D., MA Oxf., DPhil Oxf.   Sr. Lectr.

Lane, Alan M., MA Glas., PhD Lond., FSA   Sr. Lectr.

Mulville, Jacqueline   Sr. Lectr.

Newton, Christopher C. S., MA Camb., PhD Birm.   Sr. Lectr.

Nicholson, Helen J., MA Oxf., PhD Leic.   Sr. Lectr.

Nicholson, Paul T., BA Sheff., PhD Sheff.   Sr. Lectr.

Osmond, Jonathon P., MA Oxf., DPhil Oxf.   Prof.; Head*

Passmore, Kevin, BA Warw., PhD Warw.   Reader

Pringle, Reginald D., BA S'ton., DPhil Oxf.   Prof. Fellow

Sharples, N. M., MA Glas.   Sr. Lectr.

Tougher, Sean F., BA Belf., PhD St And.   Sr. Lectr.

Waddington, Keir, BA E.Anglia, PhD Lond.   Sr. Lectr.

Walker, Garthine, BA Liv., PhD Liv.   Sr. Lectr.

Watkinson, David E., MSc Wales   Sr. Lectr.

Whitley, A. J. M., MA Camb., PhD Camb.   Sr. Lectr.

Whittle, Alasdair W. R., MA Oxf., DPhil Oxf., FSA   Distinguished Res. Prof.

Wiliam, E., BA Wales, MA Manc., PhD Manc., FSA   Hon. Prof.

Other Staff: 22 Lectrs.; 1 Professnl. Tutor; 5 Hon. Lectrs.; 2 Hon. Res. Fellows

Research: ancient history and archaeology (Egypt, Greece and Rome); archaeological science and conservation; mediaeval history and archaeology (British Isles and Europe); modern history (British Isles, Europe and the Middle East); prehistory (British Isles and Europe)

Journalism, Media and Cultural Studies

Tel: (029) 2087 4041 Fax: (029) 2023 8832

Barrell, Howard, DPhil Oxf.   Sr. Lectr.

Branston, Gillian A., MA Leeds, MA Lond.   Sr. Lectr.

Cater, Cynthia, PhD Wales   Sr. Lectr.

Cottle, Simon, BA Sus., MSc Birm., PhD Leic.   Prof.

Franklin, Robert, MA Hull, PhD Hull   Prof.

Hargreaves, Ian R., MA Camb.   Prof.

Hills, Matt, MA Lond., PhD Sus.   Sr. Lectr.

Kitzinger, Jenny, BA Camb., PhD Glas.   Prof.

Lewis, J. W., BA Sus., PhD Sheff.   Prof.; Head*

Mason, Paul J., LLB S'ton., PhD Brist.   Sr. Lectr.

Tait, Richard G., BA Oxf., MA Oxf., DPhil Oxf.   Prof.

Threadgold, Terry R., MA Syd.   Prof.

Wahl-Jorgensen, Karin, PhD Stan.   Sr. Lectr.

Other Staff: 16 Lectrs.; 1 Sr. Professnl. Tutor; 8 Professnl. Tutors; 2 Professnl. Tutors†; 1 Sr. Res. Fellow†; 1 Res. Fellow†; 4 Hon. Res. Fellows

Research: broadcast news and communicating science; communication and 'risk society' (health and environmental risk); television and its effects on children); cultural citizenship and policy; digital story-telling and alternative media practices and formations; fandom, media reception and cultural mobility in theatre, cinema and museum audiences

Law

Tel: (029) 2087 6705 Fax: (029) 2087 4097   E-mail: law@cardiff.ac.uk

Chadwick, Ruth, BA Oxf., BPhil Oxf., LLB Lond., DPhil Oxf.   Prof.

Clements, Luke J., BSc Newcastle(UK), MSc Leeds   Prof.

Cobley, Catherine M., LLB Wales, LLM Wales   Sr. Lectr.

Doe, C. Norman, LLM Wales, MTh Wales, PhD Camb.   Prof.

Douglas, Gillian F., LLB Manc., LLM Lond.   Prof.; Head*

Fennell, Philip W. H., BA Kent, MPhil Kent, PhD Wales   Prof.

Field, S. A., BA Oxf., MPhil Camb., DPhil Oxf.   Sr. Lectr.

Fogelman, Valerie M., LLM Ill., MSc Texas   Prof.

Gunningham, Neil, LLM Sheff., MA Sheff., PhD ANU   Distinguished Res. Prof.

Harpwood, Vivienne, LLM Birm.   Prof.

Holm, Søren, BA Copenhagen, MA Manc., MD Copenhagen, PhD Copenhagen   Prof.

Kariyawasan, Rohan, BSc Kent, PhD Lond.   Sr. Lectr.

Khaliq, Urfan, LLB Lond., LLM Nott., PhD Lond.   Sr. Lectr.

Lee, Robert G., LLB Brun.   Prof.

Lewis, Richard K., MA Oxf., LLD Cardiff   Prof.

Lowe, Nigel V., LLB Sheff.   Prof.

Luxton, Peter, LLB Leic., LLM Lond., PhD Lond.   Prof.

Miers, David R., LLM Leeds, DJur Tor.   Prof.

Moorhead, Richard L., LLB Warw.   Prof.

Nelken, David, MA Camb., PhD Camb.   Distinguished Res. Prof.

Priaulx, Nicolette, LLB Kent, PhD Kent   Sr. Lectr.

Pribán, Jirí, JUD Prague   Prof.

Smismans, Stijn, LicLaw Leuven, PhD Florence, MA   Reader

Smith, Keith J. M., LLM Lond., DPhil Oxf.   Prof.

Wylie, John C. W., LLD Belf., LLM Harv.   Prof.

Wylie, O. Philip, LLB Belf., FCA   Sr. Lectr.

Other Staff: 16 Lectrs.; 2 Res. Fellows; 6 Professnl. Tutors; 1 Sr. Res. Assoc.†; 3 Hon. Res. Fellows

Vacant Posts: 1 Prof.; 3 Lectrs.

Research: bio-medicine, ethics and society; governance and constitutionalism; procedural justice; regulation of commercial activity

Lifelong Learning, Cardiff Centre for

Tel: (029) 2087 0000 Fax: (029) 2066 8935   E-mail: learn@cardiff.ac.uk

Evans, Richard G., BA Lond., MA Camb., PhD Lond.   Dean*

Sobiesierski, Z., BSc Exe., MSc Glam., PhD Exe.   Sr. Lectr.

Webster, P. V., BA Manc., MPhil Lond., DLitt Wales, FSA   Sr. Lectr.

Other Staff: 11 Lectrs.

Mathematics

Tel: (029) 2087 4811 Fax: (029) 2087 4199   E-mail: mathematics@cardiff.ac.uk

Balinsky, Alexander, MSc Moscow, PhD Moscow   Prof.

Burenkov, Victor, MSc Moscow, PhD Moscow, DSc Moscow   Prof.

Davies, A. Russell, MSc Oxf., DPhil Oxf.   Prof.; Head*

Davies, Christopher, MSc Warw., PhD Warw.   Sr. Lectr.

Edmunds, David E., PhD Wales   Distinguished Res. Prof.

Elliott, George A., MSc Qu., PhD Tor.   Hon. Prof.

Evans, David E., BA Oxf., MSc Oxf., DPhil Oxf.   Prof.

Evans, W. Desmond, BSc Wales, DPhil Oxf.   Prof.

Everitt, William N., BSc Birm., MA Oxf., DPhil Oxf., FIMA   Hon. Prof.

Greaves, George R. H., MA Edin., BA Camb., PhD Brist.   Reader

Griffiths, Jeffrey D., BSc Wales, PhD Wales, FIMA   Prof.

Harper, Paul R., BSc Bath, MSc S'ton., PhD S'ton.   Prof.

Hollands, Levitin, PhD Moscow   Prof.

Hollands, Stefan, PhD York(UK)   Reader

Hooley, Christopher, MA Camb., PhD Camb., ScD Camb., FRS   Distinguished Res. Prof.

Huxley, Martin N., MA Camb., PhD Camb.   Prof.

Jones, J. Edward, MSc Manc., PhD Manc.   Reader

Jones, Vaughan F. R., MSc Auck., DSc Geneva, Hon. DSc Auck., Hon. DSc Wales, FRS   Hon. Prof.

Khukhro, E. I., PhD Novosibirsk   Res. Prof.

Leonenko, Mykola N., PhD Moscow Technol.Inst., DSc   Prof.

Marletta, Marco, BSc Edin., MSc Oxf., PhD Cran.   Prof.

Phillips, Tim N., MA Oxf., MSc Oxf., DPhil Oxf., DSc Oxf.   Prof.

Schmidt, Karl M., DrRerNat Munich   Sr. Lectr.

Williams, Janet E., BSc Wales, PhD Wales   Sr. Lectr.

Zhigljavsky, Anatoly A., MS St.Petersburg, PhD St.Petersburg   Prof.

Other Staff: 8 Lectrs.; 9 Res. Assocs.; 1 Hon. Res. Fellow

Research: applied mathematics (fluid mechanics, numerical analysis, electrical discharge in gases, statistical mechanics and conformal field theory); pure mathematics (analytic number theory, differential equations and analysis, operator algebras); statistics/operational research

Medicine

Tel: (029) 2074 2020 Fax: (029) 2074 3199

Wynford-Thomas, D., MB BCh Wales, PhD Wales, DSc, FRCPath, FMedSci   Prof.; Dean*

Research: Epstein-Barr virus biology; immune evasion by viruses; immunity and development of vaccines; influenza immunobiology; progression of renal disease

Anaesthetics and Intensive Care Medicine

Tel: (029) 2074 3110 Fax: (029) 2074 7203

Hall, J. E., BA Newcastle(UK), MB ChB Liv., FRCA   Reader

Hodzovic, I., MD Belgrade, FRCA   Sr. Lectr.

Jenkins, B. J., MB BS Lond., FRCA   Sr. Lectr.

Taylor, A. M., BN Wales, MSc Wales   Sr. Lectr., Pain Management

Other Staff: 2 Lectrs.

Research: anaesthetic equipment; cerebral protection during cardiac surgery; inhaled volatile anaesthetics; perioperative pain management

Cardiology

Tel: (029) 2074 2338 Fax: (029) 2074 3500   E-mail: scaccia@cardiff.ac.uk

Blayney, L. M., BSc Cardiff, PhD Cardiff   Sr. Lectr.

Cockcroft, J. R., BSc Lond., MB ChB Leic., FRCP   Prof.

Fraser, A. G., BSc Edin., MB ChB Edin., FRCP   Reader

James, P. E., BSc Cardiff, PhD Cardiff   Reader

Lai, F. A., BSc Lond., PhD Lond.   Prof.; Head*

Williams, A. J., BSc Lanc., PhD Lanc.   Prof.

Other Staff: 1 Lectr.; 2 Hon. Lectrs.

Research: cardiac excitation-contraction coupling; cardiac ultrasound; endothelial function; large artery physiology and ventriculovascular coupling; ryanodine receptor calcium release channel

Child Health

Tel: (029) 2074 4187 Fax: (029) 2074 4283   E-mail: bullenmj@cardiff.ac.uk

Cartlidge, P. H. T., MB ChB Sheff., DM Nott., FRCP, FRCPCH   Sr. Lectr.

Evans, Bronwen   Sr. Lectr.

Gregory, John W., MD Dund., MB ChB, FRCPCH, FRCP   Prof., Paediatric Endocrinology

Hain, R. D., MSc Tor., MD Lond., FRCPCH   Sr. Lectr.

Kemp, A. M., MB BCh Wales   Reader

Kotecha, Sailesh   Clin. Prof.

Payne, Elizabeth H., MB BS Lond.   Sr. Lectr.

Spiller, O. Bradley   Sr. Lectr.

Webb, E. V. J., BSc Lond., MB BS Lond., MSc, FRCPCH, FRCP   Sr. Lectr.

Other Staff: 3 Lectrs.; 2 Clin. Sr. Lectrs.

Research: community and population (making the environment safer for children); neonatal/paediatric respiratory medicine; paediatric endocrinology

Dermatology

Tel: (029) 2074 2247 Fax: (029) 2074 4312
E-mail: finlayay@cardiff.ac.uk
Bowden, P. E., BSc *Newcastle(UK)*, PhD *Newcastle(UK)*   Sr. Lectr.
Finlay, A. Y., MB BS, FRCP, FRCPGlas   Prof.; Head*
Gonzalez, Maria, MB BS *Cardiff*, MSc *Cardiff*, DDSc *Cardiff*   Reader
Other Staff: 1 Lectr. (Cell Biology); 3 Lectrs. (Teaching)
Research: cosmetic dermatology; development of dermatology clinical outcome measures and quality; medical education with an emphasis on E-learning; photodermatology, porphyria; skin biology (epidermal differentiation, hair differentiation, sebaceous gland differentiation, keratinocyte cell biology, investigation of keratin G genodermatoses)

Emergency Medicine

Tel: (029) 2074 8090 Fax: (029) 2074 8062
E-mail: roger.evans@cardiffandvale.wales.nhs.uk
2 Consultants; 1 Hon. Clin. Teacher

Endocrinology and Diabetes

Alcolado, J., BM *S'ton.*, DM *S'ton.*   Reader, Diabetes
Ludgate, M., BSc *Wales*, PhD *Wales*   Reader
Luzio, S., BSc *Wales*, MSc *Camb.*, PhD *Wales*   Sr. Lectr., Diabetes
Owens, D. R., CBE, MD, FRCP, FIBiol   Prof., Clinical Diabetes
Rees, D. A., MB BCh *Wales*, PhD *Wales*
Scanlon, M. F., BSc *Newcastle(UK)*, MB BS *Newcastle(UK)*, MD *Newcastle(UK)*, FRCP   Head, Centre for Endocrine and Diabetes Sciences; Prof., Endocrinology
Other Staff: 3 Lectrs.; 1 Hon. Sr. Lectr.
Research: aetiology and medical therapy of pituitary tumours; endocrine regulation of vascular function; hormonal control of adipocyte differentiation; role of thyroid stimulating hormone receptor in bone function; thyroid function and pregnancy

Forensic Medicine

Tel: (029) 2074 2911 Fax: (029) 2048 4358
E-mail: chilcotta@cardiff.ac.uk
Davison, Andrew M., BSc MB ChB   Sr. Lectr.
James, D. S., MB ChB *Sheff.*   Sr. Lectr.
Leadbeatter, S., MB ChB *Brist.*   Sr. Lectr.
Vacant Posts: 1 Prof.

Genito-Urinary Medicine

Tel: (029) 2073 5207 Fax: (029) 2048 7096
2 Staff Members

Geriatric Medicine

Tel: (029) 2071 6986 Fax: (029) 2071 1267
E-mail: greens3@cardiff.ac.uk
Bayer, A. J., MB BCh *Wales*   Sr. Lectr.; Dir., Memory Team; Acting Head*
Hasan, M., MB BS *Patna*, MD *Patna*   Sr. Lectr.
Meara, R. J., MA *Camb.*, MB BChir *Camb.*, MD *Camb.*   Sr. Lectr.
O'Mahony, Sinead, BSc *N.U.I.*, MB *N.U.I.*   Sr. Lectr.
Woodhouse, Ken W., BM *S'ton.*, MD *Newcastle(UK)*, FRCP   Prof.
Other Staff: 1 Lectr.; 2 Postgrad. Res. Fellows
Research: biomedical gerontology and biology of ageing; community care; dementia; geriatric pharmacology; movement disorders

Haematology

Tel: (029) 2074 2375 Fax: (029) 2074 4655
E-mail: edwardssa1@cardiff.ac.uk
Bowen, D. J., BSc *Wales*, PhD *Wales*   Sr. Lectr.

Burnett, A. K., MD *Glas.*, FRCPGlas, FRCPEd, FRCPath, FRCP, FMedSci   Prof.; Head*
Collins, Peter, BA *Camb.*, MA MD, FRCP, FRCPath   Sr. Lectr.
Darley, Richard L., BSc PhD   Sr. Lectr.
Hills, Robert K., MA *Oxf.*, MSc DPhil   Sr. Lectr.
Pepper, Christopher J., PhD   Sr. Lectr.
Wilson, K., MB BS   Sr. Lectr.
Worwood, M., BSc *Exe.*, PhD *Lond.*, FRCPath, FMedSci   Prof.
Other Staff: 1 Lectr.; 2 Fellows; 3 Clin. Sr. Lectrs.
Research: molecular and cellular biology of haemopoiesis and its disorders, particularly leukaemia and preleukaemia; molecular basis and treatment of disorders of coagulation

Medical Biochemistry and Immunology

Tel: (029) 2074 2799 Fax: (029) 2074 4905
E-mail: thomasdj3@cardiff.ac.uk
Ager, E. Ann   Reader
Badminton, M. N., BSc *Cape Town*, MB ChB *Cape Town*, PhD *Wales*   Sr. Lectr.
Brennan, Paul   Sr. Lectr.
Campbell, A. K., MA *Camb.*, PhD *Camb.*   Prof.
Dormer, R. L., BSc *Leeds*, PhD *Brist.*   Reader
Errington, Rachel J.   Sr. Lectr.
Evans, W. H., PhD *Lond.*, DSc *Liv.*, FIBiol   Prof.
Gallimore, A. M., BSc *Bath*, DPhil *Oxf.*   Sr. Lectr.
Harris, C. L., BSc *Wales*, PhD *Wales*   Sr. Lectr.
Jones, Simon A.   Reader
Labeta, Mario O.   Sr. Lectr.
Man, Stephen T.   Sr. Lectr.
Matthews, Reginald J., BA *Oxf.*, PhD *Wales*   Sr. Lectr.
McDowell, I. F. W., BM BCh *Oxf.*, BA MSc   Sr. Lectr.
Morgan, B. P., BSc *Wales*, MB BCh *Wales*, PhD *Wales*, FRCPath, FMedSci   Prof.; Wellcome Trust Sr. Clin. Fellow; Head*
Moser, Bernhard, PhD   Prof.
O'Donnell, V. B., PhD *Brist.*, BSc   Sr. Lectr.; Wellcome Trust Res. Career Devel. Fellow
Sewell, Andrew   Res. Prof.
Wang, Edward C., BA *Camb.*, PhD *Camb.*   Sr. Lectr.
Other Staff: 2 Lectrs.; 2 Hon. Sr. Lectrs.; 1 Hon. Sr. Res. Fellow
Research: biochemical immunology; cell signalling and communication

Medical Education Unit

Allen, A. K., BA *Nott.*, MA *Lond.*, MEd *Open(UK)*   Sr. Lectr.
Houston, Prof. Helen L. A., MB BCh *Wales*, MD *Wales*, FRCGP   Prof.; Head*
Knight, Lynn V.   Sr. Lectr.
Other Staff: 1 Clin. Teaching Fellow

Medical Genetics

Tel: (029) 2074 4672 Fax: (029) 2074 7603
E-mail: harperps@cardiff.ac.uk
Cheadle, J. P., BSc *UMIST*, PhD *Wales*   Sr. Lectr.
Clarke, A. J., DM *Oxf.*, BMedSci   Reader
Cooper, D. N., BSc *Edin.*, PhD *Edin.*   Prof., Human Molecular Genetics
Harper, P. S., CBE, MA *Oxf.*, DM *Oxf.*, FRCP   Prof.
Jones, A. L., BSc *Wales*, PhD *Wales*   Sr. Lectr.
Sampson, J. R., DM *Nott.*, FRCP   Prof.; Head/Clinical Prof.*
Other Staff: 4 Lectrs.; 5 Hon. Sr. Lectrs.; 1 Hon. Lectr.
Research: causative mechanisms underlying gene mutation and their consequences; thrombosis and vascular biology

Medical Microbiology

Tel: (029) 2074 2168 Fax: (029) 2074 2161
E-mail: angoveml@cardiff.ac.uk
Barnes, Rosemary A., MA *Camb.*, MB BS *Lond.*, MD *Lond.*   Sr. Lectr.; Hon. Consultant; Acting Head*

Bugert, Jozchim J., MD *Heidel.*, PhD *Heidel.*   Sr. Lectr.
Duerden, B. I., MD *Edin.*, BSc, FRCPath   Prof.; Med. Dir., Public Health Lab. Service
Walsh, Timothy R.   Prof.
Wilkinson, Gavin W. G.   Prof.
Other Staff: 2 Lectrs.
Research: microbial pathogenesis (bacterial, fungal and viral infections)

Medical Physics and Bioengineering

Tel: (029) 2074 2008 Fax: (029) 2074 2012
E-mail: jon.woodcock@cardiffandvale.wales.nhs.uk
Woodcock, J. P., OBE, BSc *Durh.*, MPhil *Lond.*, PhD *Lond.*, DSc *Durh.*, FIP   Prof.
Other Staff: 1 Res. Fellow; 3 Hon. Lectrs.; 2 Hon. Sr. Res. Fellows
Research: basic vascular studies; electrical impedance tomography; hand-arm vibration syndrome; image processing; resonance imaging

Medicine

Freedman, A. R., MA *Camb.*, MB BChir *Camb.*, MD *Camb.*   Sr. Lectr., Infectious Diseases
Shale, Dennis J., BSc *Newcastle(UK)*, MB BS *Newcastle(UK)*, MD *Newcastle(UK)*, FRCP   Prof., Respiratory and Communicable Disease
Stephens, S. D. G., MB BS *Lond.*, BSc MPhil   Hon. Prof., Audiological Medicine
Topley, N., BSc *Wales*, PhD *Wales*   Prof.; Sub-Dean of Research Operations
Williams, J. D., BSc *Wales*, MB BCh *Wales*, MD *Wales*, FRCP   Prof.; Dir. of Med.

Nephrology

Phillips, A. O., BSc *Wales*, MD *Wales*   Prof.; Dir.*
Steadman, R., BSc *Wales*, PhD *Wales*   Sr. Lectr., Nephrology

Neurology

Tel: (029) 2074 3798 Fax: (029) 2074 4166
E-mail: johnslm@cardiff.ac.uk
Morgan, J. E., BA *Camb.*, BM BCh *Oxf.*, DPhil *Oxf.*   Sr. Lectr.
Robertson, N. P., MD   Sr. Lectr.
Rosser, E. A., MB BChir *Camb.*, PhD *Camb.*   Sr. Lectr.; Prof., Neuroscience and Neurology
Wiles, C. M., BSc *Lond.*, MB BS *Lond.*, PhD *Lond.*, FRCP   Prof., Neurology; Head*
Other Staff: 5 Staff Members
Research: mobility in neurological disease; multiple sclerosis; neurogenic dysphagia

Obstetrics and Gynaecology

Tel: (029) 2074 3235 Fax: (029) 2074 4399
E-mail: rileym@cf.ac.uk
2 Clin. Lectrs.
Research: human papillomavirus (HPV); reproductive medicine and infertility

Oncology

Tel: (029) 2031 6964 Fax: (029) 2052 9625
E-mail: masonmd@cardiff.ac.uk
Mason, M., MB BS *Lond.*, MD *Lond.*, FRCR, FRCP   Prof.; Head*
Tabi, Zsuzsanna, BSc MSc PhD   Sr. Lectr.
Other Staff: 3 Clin. Sr. Lectrs.; 13 Staff Members
Research: cell adhesion and cancer; clinical trials; Cochrane cancer network; tumour immunology

Oto-Rhino-Laryngology

Tel: (029) 2074 2583 Fax: (029) 2074 2783
E-mail: deborah.hayharris@uhw-tr.wales.nhs.uk
Mills, R. G. S., BA *Camb.*, MB BChir *Camb.*, FRCS   Sr. Lectr.

Pathology

Tel: (029) 2074 2700 Fax: (029) 2074 4276
E-mail: kingt2@cardiff.ac.uk
Baird, Duncan M.   Sr. Lectr.

Douglas-Jones, A. G., MA Camb., MB BChir Camb., PhD Auck., FRCPA   Sr. Lectr.

Griffiths, D. F. R., BA Camb., MB BCh Wales, FRCPath   Sr. Lectr.

Jasani, B., BSc Glas., MB ChB Birm., PhD Birm., FRCPath   Sr. Lectr.

Jones, C. J., BSc Wales, PhD Wales   Sr. Lectr.

Kipling, D. G., BA Camb., DPhil Oxf.   Sr. Lectr.

Lammie, A., MB BChir Camb., MA Camb., PhD Lond.   Sr. Lectr.

Lazda, E. J., MB BS Lond., MA Lond.   Sr. Lectr., Paediatric Pathology

Leadbeatter, S., MB ChB Brist.   Dir.*

Neal, J. W., BSc Brist., MB ChB Brist., DPhil Oxf., FRCPath, FRCS   Sr. Lectr., Neuropathology

Pooley, Frederick D., MSc Wales, PhD Wales   Prof.

Reed, Simon HH.   Sr. Lectr.

Smith, P. J., BSc Brist., PhD Manc.   Prof., Cancer Biology

Vujanic, G. M., DM Belgrade, DS Belgrade, PhD Belgrade, FRCPath   Sr. Lectr.

Waters, Raymond   Prof.

Williams, G. T., BSc Wales, MB BCh Wales, MD Wales, FRCP, FRCPath   Prof.

Wynford-Thomas, D., MB BCh Wales, PhD Wales, DSc, FRCPath, FMedSci   Prof.; Head*

Other Staff: 1 Lectr.; 2 Clin. Sr. Lectrs.

Research: control of proliferative lifespan by tumour suppressor genes; DNA damage and genomic stability; oncogenes and tumour initiation

Pharmacology, Therapeutics and Toxicology

Tel: (029) 2074 2062 Fax: (029) 2074 8316
    E-mail: longem@cardiff.ac.uk

Lang, Derek   Sr. Lectr.

Lewis, M. J., MB BCh Wales, PhD Wales, DSc Wales   Prof., Cardiovascular Pharmacology

Marshall, R. W., BSc Glas.   Sr. Lectr.

Routledge, P. A., OBE, MB BS Newcastle(UK), MD Newcastle(UK), FRCP   Prof., Clinical Pharmacology; Head*

Thompson, J. P., BMedSci Sheff., MB ChB Sheff.   Sr. Lectr.

Van Den Berg, C. W., PhD Utrecht, BSc MSc   Sr. Lectr.

Wilson, J. F., BSc Leeds, PhD Wales   Sr. Lectr.

Other Staff: 2 Lectrs.; 1 Clin. Sr. Lectr.

Research: drug metabolism; mechanisms of homocysteine-induced endothelial function; pharmaco-epidemiology and toxico-epidemiology; post-angioplasty neointimal hyperplasia; role of endothelial function in cardiovascular disease

Primary Care and Public Health

Tel: (029) 2074 2321 Fax: (029) 2074 3500
    E-mail: atkinsonse@cardiff.ac.uk

Allen, A. K., BA Nott., MA Lond., MEd Open(UK)   Sr. Lectr.

Butler, C., BA Rhodes, MB ChB Cape Town, MD Wales   Prof.

Chamberlain, D. A., CBE, MA Camb., MD Camb., BSc Hon. DSc, FRCP, FRCA   Hon. Prof.

Colquhoun, M. C., BSc Lond., MB BS Lond., FRCP   Sr. Lectr.

Dunstan, F. D., MA Camb., MSc Oxf., DPhil Oxf.   Prof.

Edwards, Adrian G., MB BS Newcastle(UK), MPhil Wales, PhD Wales   Prof.

Elwood, P. C., MD Belf., FRCP   Hon. Prof.

Elwyn, Glyn   Clin. Prof.

Evans, M. R., MB BCh Wales, BA Open(UK), FRCP, FFPHM   Sr. Lectr.

Fone, D., MB BS Lond.   Sr. Lectr.

Gallacher, J., BSc Wales, PhD Wales

Grant, A. J., MB BS Maastricht, MHPE Maastricht   Sr. Lectr.

Hawthorne, K., BM BCh Oxf., MA MD, FRCGP   Sr. Lectr.

Hood, K., BSc PhD   Sr. Lectr.

Houston, Prof. Helen L. A., MB BCh Wales, MD Wales, FRCGP   Prof.; Sr. Lectr.; Head*

Kinnersley, P., MB ChB Brist., MD Brist.   Reader

Matthews, I. P., BSc Liv., MSc Sur., PhD Sur.   Prof.

Newcombe, R., BA Camb., MA Camb., PhD Wales   Reader

Nix, B., BSc Wales, PhD Wales   Sr. Lectr.

Palmer, S. R., MB BChir Camb., MA Camb., FRCP, FFPHM   Mansel Talbot Prof., Epidemiology and Public Health; Head*

Potter, C. C., BSc Lond., PhD Bath   Sr. Lectr.

Robbé, I. J., BSc Lond., MB BS Lond., MSc   Sr. Lectr.

Rollnick, S., BSocSci Cape Town, MSc Strath., PhD Wales   Prof.

Tapper-Jones, Lorna, BDS Wales, MD Wales, FRCGP   Reader

Vetter, N. J., MB ChB Edin., MD Edin.   Reader

Watkins, J., BSc Wales, MD Wales, BCh Wales   Sr. Lectr.

Wilkinson, Clare E.   Clin. Prof.

Other Staff: 2 Clin. Sr. Lectrs.

Psychological Medicine

Tel: (029) 2074 4534 Fax: (029) 2074 7839
    E-mail: enquiries@psychmed.cardiff.ac.uk

Beyer, S. J., BSc Warw., PhD Brist.   Sr. Lectr.

Buckland, P. R., BSc Leeds, PhD Leeds   Reader

Craddock, N. J., MA Camb., MB ChB Birm., MMedSci Birm., PhD Wales   Prof.

Felce, D., BSc S'ton., MSc Oxf., PhD S'ton.   Prof.; Dir., Welsh Centre for Learning Disabilities Appl. Res. Unit

Healy, D. T., MD N.U.I., FRCPsych   Reader

Holmans, P. A., BA Camb., MSc Sheff., MA Camb., PhD Camb.   Prof., Biostatistics and Genetic Epidemiology

Isles, Anthony R.   Sr. Lectr.

Jones, A. L., BSc Wales, PhD Wales   Sr. Lectr.

Kerr, M. P., MB ChB Brist.   Prof., Mental Handicap

Kirov, G., MD Sofia   Sr. Lectr.

Menkes, D. B., BA Calif., MD Yale, PhD Yale, FRANZCP   Prof.

O'Donovan, M. C., BSc Glas., MB ChB Glas., PhD Wales, FRCPsych   Prof.

Owen, M. J., BSc Birm., MB ChB Birm., PhD Birm., FRCPsych, FMedSci   Prof.; Head*

Taylor, Pamela J., MB BS Lond., FRCPsych, FMedSci   Prof.

Thapar, A., MB BCh Wales, PhD Wales   Prof., Child and Adolescent Psychiatry

Thomas, H. V., BSc E.Anglia, DPhil Oxf.   Sr. Lectr.

Van den Bree, Marianne B., BSc MSc PhD   Sr. Lectr.

Williams, J., BSc Wales, PhD Wales   Prof., Psychological Genetics

Williams, Nigel M.   Sr. Lectr.

Other Staff: 4 Lectrs.; 50 Res. Staff; 3 Clin. Sr. Lectrs.; 3 Hon. Sr. Lectrs.; 9 Hon. Lectrs.

Research: Alzheimer's disease; bipolar disorder; Huntington's disease; psychiatric genetics; schizophrenia

Radiology, Diagnostic

Tel: (029) 2074 3070 Fax: (029) 2074 4726
    E-mail: birchallc@cardiff.ac.uk

Edwards, D. H., MPhil Wales, PhD Wales   Sr. Lectr.

Griffith, T. M., MB BCh Wales, MA Camb., PhD Wales, FRCR   Prof.; Head*

Hourihan, Margaret D., MB BCh Wales, FRCR   Sr. Lectr.

Other Staff: 2 Lectrs.; 1 Hon. Lectr.

Research: magnetic resonance imaging; vascular physiology and pathophysiology

Radiotherapy

Tel: (029) 2061 5888 Fax: (029) 2052 2694
    E-mail: jean.roper@velindre-tr.wales.nhs.uk
No staff at present

Renal Medicine

Tel: (029) 2073 5651 Fax: (029) 2045 3643

Fraser, Donald J.   Sr. Lectr.

Other Staff: 2 Lectrs.; 1 Clin. Sr. Lectr.; 1 Hon. Lectr.

Research: peritoneal host defence; progression of renal disease

Respiratory Medicine

Tel: (029) 2071 6936 Fax: (029) 2070 8973

Freedman, A. R., MA Camb., MB BChir Camb., MD Camb.   Sr. Lectr., Infectious Diseases; Head*

Shale, Dennis J., BSc Newcastle(UK), MB BS Newcastle(UK), MD Newcastle(UK), FRCP   Clin. Prof.

Other Staff: 1 Clin. Reader; 4 Staff Members

Research: cystic fibrosis; metabolic impact of chronic pulmonary infection/inflammation

Rheumatology

Tel: (029) 2074 3575 Fax: (029) 2074 4388
    E-mail: matthewsaj@cardiff.ac.uk

Williams, Anwen S.   Sr. Lectr.

Other Staff: 2 Clin. Sr. Lectrs.; 2 Staff Members

Research: complement inhibition and its effects on experimental arthritis; minocycline-induced Lupus syndrome; targeted drug delivery

Surgery

Tel: (029) 2074 2896 Fax: (029) 2076 1623
    E-mail: surgery@cf.ac.uk

Dent, Colin M., MB BS Lond., FRCS   Clin. Prof.

Hallett, M., BSc Lond., PhD Lond.   Sr. Lectr., Surgical Immunology

Harding, K. G., MB ChB Birm., FRCS   Head*

Jiang, Wen Guo, MB Beijing, MD Wales   Sr. Lectr., Tumour Biology

Mansel, R. E., CBE, MB BS Lond., MS Lond., FRCS   Prof.

Puntis, M. C. A., PhD Camb., MB BCh, FRCSEd, FRCS   Sr. Lectr.

Sweetland, Helen M., MB ChB Sheff., MD Sheff., FRCS   Reader

Other Staff: 2 Lectrs.; 7 Res. Fellows; 2 Clin. Sr. Lectrs.

Research: breast cancer; cell signalling; hepatobiliary and pancreatic cancer; metastasis; oncology

Surgery, Cardiothoracic

Tel: (029) 2074 3578
2 Staff Members

Surgery, Neurological

Tel: (029) 2074 5014
2 Staff Members

Surgery, Paediatric

Tel: (029) 2074 5342
4 Staff Members

Surgery, Traumatic and Orthopaedic

Tel: (029) 2074 3219 Fax: (029) 2049 4855

Dent, Colin M., MB BS Lond., FRCS   Sr. Lectr.

Evans, R.   Sr. Lectr.

Other Staff: 5 Staff Members

Surgery, Urological

Tel: (01633) 234989
4 Staff Members; 1 Hon. Sr. Lectr.

Surgery, Vascular

Tel: (029) 2074 7747
2 Res. Fellows; 8 Staff Members

Surgery: Wound Healing Research Unit

Tel: (029) 2074 4505 Fax: (029) 2075 6334
    E-mail: admin@whru.co.uk

Harding, K. G., MB ChB Birm., FRCS   Prof.; Clin. Dir.

Price, P., BA Wales, PhD Wales   Dir., Academic Res. and Educn.

Other Staff: 1 Sr. Res. Fellow; 20 Staff Members

Research: clinical trials; non-invasive measurement; tissue repair; wound healing; wound models

Music

Tel: (029) 2087 4816 Fax: (029) 2087 4379
E-mail: music-eng@cardiff.ac.uk
Gloag, Kenneth, BMus Sur., MMus Lond., PhD Exe. Sr. Lectr.
Jones, David W., BMus Wales, MA Wales, PhD Wales Prof.
Jones, Richard E., BA Wales, MMus Wales, PhD Wales, FRCO Sr. Lectr.
O'Connell, John, MA Oxf., PhD Calif. Sr. Lectr.
Powers, Anthony J. W., BA York(UK), DPhil York(UK) Prof.
Stowell, Robin, MA Camb., PhD Camb. Prof.; Head*
Thomas, Adrian T., BMus Nott., MA Wales Prof.
Tyrell, John, BMus Cape Town, DPhil Oxf. Prof.
Walsh, M. Stephen, MA Camb. Prof.
Weir, Judith, CBE, MA Camb. Prof.
Other Staff: 6 Lectrs.; 1 Sr. Prof. Tutor; 1 Hon. Lectr.
Research: aesthetics (music and politics); composition; ethnomusicology; historical musicology (eighteenth-century, twentieth-century); performance practice

Nursing and Midwifery Studies

Tel: (029) 2074 4160 Fax: (029) 2074 2259
Alabaster, Erica, MSc Manc., PhD Wales Sr. Lectr.
Allen, Davina, BA Nott., PhD Nott. Dir., Res. Centre
Beer, Elaine, BEd Wales, MBA Leic. Dir., Adult Nursing; Deputy Head
Bennett, Paul, BA Plym., MSc Plym., PhD Birm. Prof.
Burnard, P., MSc Sur., PhD Wales Dir., Postgrad. Res.
Cooper, Linda, BEd Wales, MSc Dir., Mental Health and Learning Disabilities
Davies, Jane, BSc Open(UK), LLM Cardiff Acting Dir., Children and Young People's Directorate
Featherstone, Katie, BSc Lond., PhD Brist. Sr. Lectr.
Hannigan, Ben, BA Sheff., MA Lond., PhD Wales Sr. Lectr.
Harden, Jane Sr. Lectr.
Hunt, Sheila, MSc(Econ) Wales, MBA Nott., PhD Warw. Head*
Lankshear, Annette Reader
Lowes, Lesley, MSc Wales, PhD Wales Sr. Lectr.
Parsons, Evelyn P., BSc Lond., PhD Wales Res. Prof.
Rowlands, Nicola Sr. Lectr.
Smith, Christine, MN Wales, PhD Wales Dir., Primary Care/Community Nursing
Watkins, Dianne, MSc Wales Dir., Educnl. Devels.
Williams, Anne Prof.
Williams, Gail, BSc(Econ) Lond., MSc Wales Dir., Midwifery
Other Staff: 100 Lectrs.
Research: clinical effectiveness in nursing; managing interfaces in healthcare; planning; practice and education

Optometry and Vision Sciences

Tel: (029) 2087 4374 Fax: (029) 2087 4859
Drexler, Wolfgang, MSc Vienna, PhD Vienna Prof.
Erichsen, Jonathon T., BA Harv., DPhil Oxf. Sr. Lectr.
Guggenheim, Jeremy A., BSc Wales, PhD Wales Sr. Lectr.
Margrain, T., BSc Aston, PhD City(UK) Sr. Lectr.
Meek, Keith M. A., BSc Manc., PhD Manc. Prof.
Murphy, Paul J., BSc Wales, PhD G.Caledonian Sr. Lectr.; Dir. of Teaching
North, Rachel V., MSc Aston, PhD Wales Sr. Lectr.
Quantock, A. J., BSc E.Anglia, PhD Open(UK) Sr. Lectr.
Votruba, M., BA Oxf., BM BCh Oxf., MA Oxf., PhD Lond. Clin. Prof.

Wess, Timothy J., BSc Newcastle(UK), PhD Edin. Prof.; Head*
Wild, John, BSc City(UK), MSc Aston, PhD Aston Prof. Fellow
Woodhouse, J. Margaret, BSc Aston, PhD Camb. Sr. Lectr.
Other Staff: 11 Lectrs.; 1 Sr. Res. Assoc.; 1 Sr. Prof. Tutor; 1 Distinguished Res. Fellow†; 1 Sr. Res. Assoc.†; 1 Hon. Res. Fellow
Research: biophysics (cornea, ion transport, tears, transparency, connective tissue); cell and molecular biology (wound healing, angiogenesis, light damage, ageing, age-related macular degeneration, myopia, neural control of accommodation, molecular genetics); clinical investigation and visual function (visual development, vision and visual defects in infancy and children with disabilities, perimetry, retinal imaging in glaucoma and diabetes, electrophysiology, psychophysics, peripheral spatial vision)

Pharmacy, Welsh School of

Tel: (029) 2087 4151 Fax: (029) 9087 4149
Baxter, Gary F., BPharm Nott., MSc Lond., PhD De Mont., FIBiol, FESC, FAHA Prof.
Brain, Keith R., BPharm Nott., PhD Bath Sr. Lectr.
Broadley, Kenneth J., BPharm Lond., PhD Lond., DSc Lond., FRPharmS Prof.
Daniels, Stephen, MA Oxf., DPhil Oxf. Sr. Lectr.
Denyer, Stephen P., BPharm Nott., PhD Nott. Prof.; Head*
Duncan, Ruth, BSc Liv., PhD Keele Prof. Fellow
Gumbleton, Mark, BPharm Wales, MSc Aberd., PhD Wales Sr. Lectr.
John, David N., BPharm Wales, LLM Wales, PhD Wales Sr. Lectr.
Jones, Arwyn T., BSc Coventry, MSc Leeds, PhD Lond. Sr. Lectr.
Luscombe, David K., BPharm Lond., PhD Lond., FIBiol, FRPharmS Prof.
Maillard, Jean-Yves, BSc Wales, PhD Wales Sr. Lectr.
McGuigan, Christopher, BSc Birm., PhD Birm. Prof.
Moncada, Salvador, MD El Salvador, PhD Lond., DSc Lond., FRCP, FRS Hon. Prof.
Mrsny, Randall J., BS Calif., PhD Calif. Prof.
Nicholson, Robert I., BSc Reading, PhD Wales Prof.
Sewell, Robert D. E., BPharm Brad., PhD Wales Sr. Lectr.
Shayegan-Salek, Mir-Saeed, BSc Oklahoma, PhD Wales Prof.
Simons, Claire, BSc PhD Sr. Lectr.
Taylor, Glyn, BSc Aston, PhD Manc. Sr. Lectr.
Walker, Roger D., BPharm Brad., PhD Aston Prof.
Walker, S. R., BSc Lond., PhD Lond., FRSChem, FIBiol Hon. Prof.
Wann, K. T., BSc Aberd., PhD Aberd. Sr. Lectr.
Other Staff: 13 Lectrs.; 1 Sr. Res. Fellow; 8 Sr. Res. Assocs.; 2 Sr. Prof. Tutors; 2 Sr. Teaching Fellows; 3 Res. Fellows; 7 Hon. Lectrs.
Research: design and synthesis of drugs; drug delivery; health and medicines; molecular and cellular basis of drug action

Physics and Astronomy

Tel: (029) 2087 4458 Fax: (029) 2087 4056
Ade, P. A. R., BSc Lond., PhD Lond. Prof.
Blood, Peter, BSc Leeds, PhD Leeds, FIP Prof.
Chow, W. W., BS Colorado, MS Arizona, PhD Arizona Hon. Prof.
Coles, Peter, MA Camb., DPhil Sus. Prof.
Davies, Jonathan I., BA Open(UK), BSc Brist., PhD Wales, FRAS Sr. Lectr.
Eales, Stephen A., MA Camb., PhD Camb. Prof.
Edmunds, Michael G., MA Camb., PhD Camb., FRAS Prof. Emer.
Elliott, Martin, BSc Sus., DPhil Sus. Sr. Lectr.
Ellison, B. N., BSc Lond. Hon. Prof.
Fiarhurst, Stephen Sr. Lectr.

Gear, Walter K., BSc Lond., PhD Lond. Prof.; Head*
Greenaway, Alan, BSc Brun., PhD Lond. Hon. Prof.
Griffin, M. J., BE Dublin City, MSc Lond., PhD Lond. Prof.; Deputy Head
Griffiths, Huw, BSc Brist., PhD Brist. Hon. Prof.
Grishchuk, Leonid P., PhD Moscow, DSc Moscow, FRAS Prof.
Ivanov, Alexei L., PhD Moscow, DSc Moscow Prof.
Langbein, Wolfgang W., PhD Karlsruhe Prof.
Macdonald, J. Emyr, BSc Wales, DPhil Oxf. Reader
Matthai, Clarence C., BSc Lond., DPhil Oxf. Reader
Mauskopf, Phillip D., BA Harv., MA Calif., PhD Calif. Prof.
Richardson, Bernard E., BSc Salf., PhD Wales Reader
Romano, Joseph D., BS Cornell, MS Syr., PhD Syr. Sr. Lectr.
Sathyaprakash, Bangalore S., BSc B'lore., MSc IIT Madras, PhD IISc. Prof.
Schutz, Bernard F., BSc Clarkson, PhD Cal.Tech., FRAS Prof.†
Scott, M. D., MSc Wales, PhD Wales Hon. Prof.
Smowton, Peter M., BSc(Tech) Wales, PhD Wales Reader
Summers, Huw D., BSc Cardiff, PhD Cardiff Sr. Lectr.
Sutton, Patrick J., BSc St FX, PhD Alta. Sr. Lectr.
Ward-Thompson, Derek, MA Oxf., MSc Durh., PhD Durh. Prof.
Whitworth, Anthony P., MA Oxf., PhD Manc., FRAS Prof.
Other Staff: 5 Lectrs.; 3 Sr. Res. Assocs.; 4 Res. Fellows; 1 Sr. Res. Fellow†; 1 Lectr.†; 1 Res. Fellow†; 3 Hon. Lectrs.
Research: astrophysics (galaxies, star formation, gravitational waves, CBR); biological and mesoscopic physics; instrumentation for sub-millimetre astronomy; musical acoustics; optoelectronics (theoretical and experimental studies of quantum well and quantum dot laser diodes and vertical cavity devices)

Postgraduate Medical and Dental Education

Tel: (029) 2074 2144 Fax: (029) 2075 4966
E-mail: powelljf@cardiff.ac.uk
Allery, Lynne A., BA Warw., MA Sheff. Sr. Lectr., Medical Education
Brigley, S. J., BA Wales, MPhil Exe., PhD Exe. Sr. Lectr.
Davies, S., MB BChir MA MSc, FRCP Deputy Dir., Hosp. Practice
Donnelly, Peter, BA Open(UK), FRCPsych Assoc. Dean, E-Learning
Gallen, Derek, MMEd, FRCGP Dean*
Jones, Melanie J. T., MB BCh Wales Assoc. Dean
Lewis, M. Sian, MB BCh, FRCP, FRCPath Assoc. Dean
Lewis, M., MB BS LLM Dir., Gen. Practice
Matthews, P., MB BS MSc Deputy Dir., Gen. Practice
Midha, A., BSc(Econ) MBA PhD Assoc. Dir., Business and Planning
Nash, E. S., BDS Wales, MSc Wales, FDSRCS Dir., Postgrad. Dent. Educn.
Pugsley, L., BSc MSc PhD Sr. Lectr.
Rockey, A., BDS Deputy Dir., Postgrad. Dent. Educn.
Straczewski, Anthony R., BSc MB ChB Assoc. Dean
Williams, S., BA Wash., MA Leeds Sr. Lectr.
Yapp, Thomas R., MB BCh Wales, FRCP Assoc. Dean
Young, H. L., ChM Dund., MBA, FRCS Vice Dean
Other Staff: 5 Lectrs.; 3 Hon. Sr. Lectrs.; 2 Hon. Lectrs.

Psychology

Tel: (029) 2087 6707 Fax: (029) 2087 4858

Aggleton, John P., MA Camb., DPhil Oxf.   Prof.
Aylward, Mansel, CB, BSc Lond., MB BS Lond., FRCP   Hon. Prof.
Boivin, Jacky L., MA C'dia., PhD C'dia.   Sr. Lectr.
Buehner, Marc J., MA Calif., PhD Sheff.   Sr. Lectr.
Culling, John F., BSc Sus., DPhil Sus.   Reader
Dwyer, Dominic M., BSc Syd., PhD Camb.   Sr. Lectr.
Farmer, Eric W., BSc Glas., PhD Glas.   Hon. Prof.
Freeman, Thomas C. A., BSc Birm., PhD Birm.   Sr. Lectr.
Gattis, Meredith, PhD Calif.   Sr. Lectr.
Good, Mark A., BSc Lond., DPhil York(UK)   Sr. Lectr.
Graham, Kim, BSc Edin., PhD Camb.   Prof.
Gray, Nicola S., MSc Lond., PhD Lond., FBPsS   Reader
Griffiths, Robert D. P., BA Manc., MA Lond., PhD Lond., FRCS, FBPsS   Hon. Prof.
Haddock, Geoffrey, BSc Tor., MA Wat., PhD Wat.   Reader
Hahn, Ulrike, MSc Edin., DPhil Oxf.   Sr. Lectr.
Halligan, Peter W., MA N.U.I., DSc N.U.I., PhD Oxf.Brookes, FBPsS, FPsSI   Prof. Fellow
Hare, R. D., MA Alta., PhD W.Ont.   Hon. Prof.
Harold, Gordon T., MS Iowa, PhD Wales   Reader
Hay, Dale F., BA Allegheny, PhD N.Carolina   Prof.
Honey, Robert C., BSc Sus., DPhil York(UK)   Reader
Jones, Derek, BSc MSc PhD   Prof.
Jones, Dylan M., BSc(Tech) Wales, PhD Wales, DSc Wales, FBPsS   Prof.; Head*
Killcross, A. Simon, BA Camb., PhD Camb.   Reader
Lewis, Michael, BSc Birm., PhD Wales   Sr. Lectr.
Macken, William J. M., MA N.U.I., PhD Wales   Sr. Lectr.
Maio, Gregory R., BSc York(Can.), MA W.Ont., PhD W.Ont.   Prof.
Manstead, Antony, BSc Brist., DPhil Sus.   Prof.
Miles, Christopher, BSc Wales, PhD Wales   Sr. Lectr.
Oakley, David, BSc Lond., PhD Lond., FBPsS, FAPA   Hon. Prof.
Patrick, John, BA Hull, PhD Hull, FBPsS   Sr. Lectr.
Pearce, John M., BSc Leeds, DPhil Sus.   Prof.
Pigdeon, Nick, BA Keele, PhD Brist.   Prof.
Singh, Krish, BSc Durh., PhD Open(UK)   Prof.
Smith, Andrew P., BSc Lond., PhD Lond., FBPsS   Prof.
Snowden, Robert J., BSc York(UK), PhD Camb.   Prof.
Spears, Russell, BSc Brist., PhD Exe.   Prof.
van Goozen, Stephanie, MSc Amst., PhD Amst.   Reader
Waddell, Gordon, CBE, BSc Glas., MB ChB Glas., MD Glas., DSc Glas., FRCS   Hon. Prof.
White, Peter A., BA Nott., DPhil Oxf.   Prof.
Wilding, Edward, BSc Sheff., MSc Edin.   Sr. Lectr.
Wilkinson, Lawrence, BSc Sheff., PhD Wales   Prof.
Wright, Patricia, BSc Lond., MA Camb., PhD Lond., FBPsS   Prof.
Other Staff: 11 Lectrs.; 1 Sr. Res. Assoc.; 1 Sr. Res. Fellow; 7 Res. Fellows; 1 Lectr.†; 3 Professnl. Tutors†; 7 Hon. Lectrs.; 8 Hon. Res. Fellows; 6 Hon. Assoc. Professnl. Tutors
Research: behavioural neuroscience; developmental psychology; perception and cognitive neuropsychology; pure and applied cognition; social and health psychology

Religious and Theological Studies

Tel: (029) 2087 4240 Fax: (029) 2087 4500

Deeg, Max, MA Würzburg, PhD Würzburg   Sr. Lectr.
Gilliat-Ray, Sophie, BA Wales, MA Wales, PhD Wales   Sr. Lectr.
Johnson, William J., BA Sus., DPhil Oxf.   Sr. Lectr.
King, John, BSc MSc PhD, FRINA   Prof.; Acting Head*
Lossl, Josef, PhD Regensburg, DrHabil Mün.   Reader
Samuel, Geoffrey B., MA Oxf., PhD Camb.   Prof. Fellow
Trevett, Christine, MA Sheff., PhD Sheff.   Prof.
Trombley, Frank R., BA San Diego, MA Calif., PhD Calif.   Reader
Watt, John W., MA Camb., PhD St And.   Reader
Other Staff: 3 Lectrs.; 4 Res. Fellows; 1 Res. Fellow†; 1 Hon. Lectr.; 3 Hon. Res. Fellows
Research: Indian/Asian religion, especially Jainism and Buddhism; inter-faith issues (chaplaincy, health care, management, theology and practice); practical theology, especially Church, mission and society; religion in late antiquity (Syriac, Patristics, Byzantium, the Christianisation of Europe)

Social Sciences

Tel: (029) 2087 5179 Fax: (029) 2087 4175

Adam, Barbara E., BScEcon Wales, PhD Wales, DScEcon Cardiff   Prof.
Ashton, David N., BA Leic.   Hon. Prof.
Atkinson, Paul A., MA Camb., PhD Edin., FRAI   Res. Prof.; Dir., Centre for Economic and Social Aspects of Genomics (CESAGen)
Baker, Susan C., MA N.U.I., PhD Florence   Prof.
Bellin, Wynford, MA Oxf., DPhil Sus.   Sr. Lectr.
Beynon, Huw, BA Wales, DSc Manc.   Prof.; Head*
Brown, Phillip, BEd CNAA, PhD Wales   Prof.
Chaney, Paul, BA Wales, PhD Leic.   Sr. Lectr.
Coffey, Amanda J., BA Exe., MSc Brist., PhD Wales   Prof.
Collins, Harold M., BSc(Econ) Lond., MA Essex, PhD Bath   Distinguished Res. Prof.
Davies, W. Brian, BSc(Econ) Lond., MA Lond.   Prof.
Delamont, K. Sara, MA Camb., PhD Edin., DScEcon Cardiff   Reader
Dicks, Bella, BA Reading, MA CNAA, PhD Wales   Reader
Drakeford, Mark, BA Kent, BPhil Exe., PhD Wales   Prof.
Epstein, Deborah A., BA Sus., PhD Birm.   Prof.
Evans, Robert, BSc Bath, MSc Bath, PhD Bath   Sr. Lectr.
Fairbrother, Peter, BA Monash, DPhil Oxf.   Prof. Fellow
Felstead, Alan, BA Camb., MA Warw., PhD Lond.   Prof.
Fevre, R. W., BA Durh., PhD Aberd.   Prof.
Fitz, John, BA Tas., MA Lond., PhD Open(UK)   Prof.
Glasner, Peter E., BSc Lond., PhD Lond.   Prof. Res. Fellow
Gorard, Stephen A. C., BSc Lond., MEd Wales, PhD Wales   Prof.
Hall, Tom, BA Camb., MA Camb., PhD Camb.   Sr. Lectr.
Henwood, Karen, BSc Brist., PhD Brist.   Sr. Lectr.
Holland, Sally, MA Aberd., MSc Oxf., PhD Wales   Sr. Lectr.
Housley, William, BA Wales, PhD Wales   Sr. Lectr.
Hughes, Gordon, BSc Leic., MPhil Leic., MSoc Birm., PhD Open(UK)   Prof.
Innes, Martin, BA Lond., MSc Lond., PhD Lond.   Prof.; Dir., Universities Police Sci. Inst. (UPSI)
Jephcote, Martin, BEd Brist., PhD Wales   Sr. Lectr.
Jones, Trevor D. B., BSc Oxf., MSc Oxf.   Reader
Keep, Ewart, BA Lond., PhD Warw.   Dir., ESRC Centre on Skills, Knowledge and Organisational Perfomance (SKOPE)
Latimer, Joanna, BA Lond., PhD Edin.   Reader
Levi, Michael, BA Oxf., PhD S'ton., DScEcon Cardiff   Prof.
Maguire, E. Michael W., BA Oxf., BLitt Oxf.   Prof.

Moore, Laurence A. R., BSc Brist., MSc Lond., PhD Brist.   Dir., Cardiff Inst. of Society, Health and Ethics (IHSE)
Nichols, William A. T., MA Hull, DSc Brist.   Distinguished Res. Prof.
Pithouse, Andrew J., BScEcon Wales, PhD Wales   Prof.
Power, Sally, BEd CNAA, PhD CNAA   Prof. Res. Fellow; Prof.
Rees, Gareth M., BA Oxf., MPhil Oxf.   Prof.
Rees, Terry L., BA Exe., PhD Wales   Prof.
Renold, Emma, BA Wales, PhD Wales   Sr. Lectr.
Richardson, John, BA Strath.   Sr. Lectr.
Robinson, Amanda, BSc Alabama, MSc Alabama, PhD Mich.   Sr. Lectr.
Salisbury, Jane, BEd Wales, MEd Wales, PhD Wales   Sr. Lectr.
Sampson, Helen, BA Durh., PhD Salf.   Prof.; Dir., Seafarers International Res. Centre
Scourfield, Jonathan, BA Camb., MA Wales, PhD Wales   Sr. Lectr.
Taylor, Chris, BA Leic., PhD Leic.   Sr. Lectr.
Walkerdine, Valerie, MA Lond., PhD Brist.   Prof.
Walters, David, BSc Lond., MMedSci Nott., PhD S.Bank   Prof.
Welsh, Ian, BA CNAA, PhD Lanc.   Reader
Williams, Gareth H., BA CNAA, MSc Lond., PhD Manc.   Prof. Fellow
Other Staff: 24 Lectrs.; 1 Sr. Res. Fellow; 3 Res. Fellows; 5 Sr. Res. Assocs.; 2 Professnl. Tutors; 1 Distinguished Visiting Fellow; 4 Lectrs.†; 2 Sr. Res. Fellows†; 2 Sr. Res. Assocs.†; 10 Professnl. Tutors†; 1 Hon. Lectr.; 9 Hon. Res. Fellows
Research: crime and criminal justice; economic and social transformation (comparative analysis); education and lifelong learning; knowledge, expertise and science; sociology of health and human services

Welsh

see also Special Centres, etc

Tel: (029) 2087 4843 Fax: (029) 2087 4604

Davies, Sioned M., BA Wales, DPhil Oxf.   Prof.; Head*
James, E. Wyn, BA Wales, PhD Wales   Sr. Lectr.
Mac Giolla Chriost, Diarmait, BA Belf., PhD Wales   Sr. Lectr.
Owen, T. M., MA Wales, FSA   Hon. Prof.
Roberts, B., MA Wales, PhD Wales   Hon. Prof.
Williams, Colin H., BScEcon Wales, PhD Wales   Prof.
Other Staff: 3 Lectrs.; 2 Tutors; 1 Postdoc. Fellow; 4 Res. Assts.; 2 Hon. Lectrs.; 1 Hon. Res. Fellow
Research: applied Welsh (education, language planning and policy); Welsh American studies (the language, literary history and culture of the Welsh in the United States, Canada and Patagonia); Welsh linguistic studies (historical and contemporary linguistics of Welsh; dialectology, geolinguistics, and sociolinguistics); Welsh literary studies (textual transmission: oral and written; identity and cultural interpretation; literary theory and translation)

SPECIAL CENTRES, ETC

Astrobiology, Cardiff Centre for

Tel: (029) 2087 4201 Fax: (029) 2087 6425

Napier, W. M., BSc Glas., PhD Glas.   Hon. Prof.
Wickramasinghe, Nalin C., BSc Ceyl., MA Camb., PhD Camb., ScD Camb., FRAS   Prof.; Dir.*
Other Staff: 2 Hon. Res. Fellows

Business Relationships, Accountability, Sustainability and Society, Research Centre for

Tel: (029) 2087 6562 Fax: (029) 2087 6061
E-mail: mullinsp@cardiff.ac.uk
Peattie, Kenneth J., BA Leeds   Prof.; Dir.*
Other Staff: 3 Sr. Res. Assocs.

Cardiff and the Vale of Glamorgan Welsh for Adults Centre

Heath-Davies, Rachel, BA *Wales*, PhD *Wales* Dir.*

Price, Adrian, BA *Wales*, PhD *Glam.* Dir., Teaching

Other Staff: 2 Principal Tutors; 4 Sr. Tutors; 8 Tutors

Common Cold and Nasal Research Centre

Tel: (029) 2087 4099 Fax: (029) 2087 4093
Eccles, Ronald, BSc *Liv.*, DSc *Liv.* Prof.
Jawad, Moutaz S. M., MB ChB *Baghdad*, FRCPEd Dir.*

Diabetes Research Unit

Tel: (029) 2071 5299 Fax: (029) 2035 0147
E-mail: owensdr@cardiff.ac.uk
Owens, D. R., CBE, MD, FRCP, FIBiol Prof.; Consultant Diabetologist
Other Staff: 15 NHS Res. Staff
Research: insulin secretion and resistance; nephropathy; pathophysiology of Type 2 diabetes; retinopathy; tele-medicine

Japanese Studies Centre

Tel: (029) 2087 4959 Fax: (029) 9087 4419
E-mail: cjsc@cardiff.ac.uk
Hood, Christopher P., BA *Sheff.*, PhD *Sheff.* Dir.*
Other Staff: 2 Lectrs.

Manufacturing Engineering Centre

Tel: (029) 2087 4429 Fax: (029) 2087 4003
E-mail: mec@cf.ac.uk
Dimov, Stefan S., PhD *Moscow* Prof., Advanced Manufacturing Technology
Pham, Duc T., OBE, BE *Cant.*, PhD *Cant.*, DEng, FREng, FIMechE Prof., Computer Controlled Manufacture; Head*
Other Staff: 1 Lectr.; 2 RCUK Fellows; 23 Sr. Res. Fellows; 15 Res. Fellows; 1 Sr. Res. Fellow†
Research: industrial engineering; intelligent systems; manufacturing engineering; systems engineering

Professional Legal Studies, Centre for

Tel: (029) 2087 4964 Fax: (029) 9087 4984
E-mail: webbj@cardiff.ac.uk
Brookfield, Ian C., LLB *Wales* Dir.*
Devereux, Angela, BA *York(UK)* Sr. Prof. Tutor
Dixon, David, BA *Tor.*, LLB *Wales* Sr. Prof. Tutor
Hughes, Ceri, LLB *Manc.* Sr. Prof. Tutor
Jerram, Andrew, BSc *Edin.* Sr. Prof. Tutor
Jones, Byron, LLB *Lond.* LPC Course Leader
Lebasci, Jetsun, LLB *Cardiff* BVC Course Leader
Other Staff: 19 Lectrs.; 7 Sr. Prof. Tutors

Social Sciences, Centre for Advanced Studies in the

Tel: (029) 2087 4945 Fax: (029) 2087 4994
Cooke, Philip N., BA *Liv.*, FRSA Prof.; Dir.*
Other Staff: 3 Sr. Res. Assocs.

CONTACT OFFICERS

Academic affairs. Director of Registry: Cryer, Anthony, BSc *Sheff.*, PhD *Sheff.*
(E-mail: registry@cardiff.ac.uk)

Accommodation. Residences Administration Manager: Pycroft, Tracey D.
(E-mail: residences@cardiff.ac.uk)

Admissions (first degree). Director of Registry: Cryer, Anthony, BSc *Sheff.*, PhD *Sheff.* (E-mail: admissions@cardiff.ac.uk)

Admissions (higher degree). Director of Registry: Cryer, Anthony, BSc *Sheff.*, PhD *Sheff.* (E-mail: pgadmissions@cardiff.ac.uk)

Adult/continuing education. Dean of Cardiff University Centre for Lifelong Learning: Evans, Richard G., BA *Lond.*, MA *Camb.*, PhD *Lond.* (E-mail: learn@cardiff.ac.uk)

Alumni. Head of Alumni Relations: Price, Sarah J., BA *Leic.*
(E-mail: alumni@cardiff.ac.uk)

Archives. University Records Manager: Burrow, Lucy M., BSc *Wales*, MScEcon *Wales* (E-mail: burrowl@cardiff.ac.uk)

Careers. Director of Careers Service: Thomas, Nigel R., BA *Lanc.*
(E-mail: careers@cardiff.ac.uk)

Computing services. Director of Information Services: Harrow, Martyn, BSc *Bath*
(E-mail: insrvconnect@cardiff.ac.uk)

Conferences/corporate hospitality. Conference Manager: Emmott, Samantha E., BSc *Wales* (E-mail: conference@cardiff.ac.uk)

Consultancy services. Deputy Director and Head of Research Policy and Management: Pittard Davies, Kathy J., BSc *Wales*, PhD *Wales* (E-mail: davieskp2@cardiff.ac.uk)

Development/fund-raising. Director of Development and Alumni Relations: Berezny, Alan
(E-mail: streeters@cardiff.ac.uk)

Distance education. Senior Assistant Registrar (Distance education): Evans, Rhodri P., BEng *Wales*, MBA *Wales*
(E-mail: admissions@cardiff.ac.uk)

Estates and buildings/works and services. Director of Estate Development: Lomer, Ian
(E-mail: lomer@cardiff.ac.uk)

Examinations. Senior Assistant Registrar (Examinations): Evans, Rhodri P., BEng *Wales*, MBA *Wales*
(E-mail: exams@cardiff.ac.uk)

Finance. Director of Financial and Physical Resources: Davies, Mike D., BScEcon *Wales*
(E-mail: daviesmd@cardiff.ac.uk)

Health services. Director of Occupational Safety, Health and Environment: Salmon, M. L., MSc *Sur.*
(E-mail: health@cardiff.ac.uk)

Industrial liaison. Director of Research and Commercial Division: Jones, Geraint W., BSc *Wales* (E-mail: jonesgw@cardiff.ac.uk)

International office. Director of International Development: Elliott, Sandra, MA *Edin.*
(E-mail: international@cardiff.ac.uk)

Language training for international students. Deputy Director of International Development: Evans, Helen, BA *Leeds*
(E-mail: elt@cardiff.ac.uk)

Library (chief librarian). Senior Assistant Deputy Director of Information Services and University Librarian: Peters, J.
(E-mail: petersjm@cardiff.ac.uk)

Library (enquiries). Deputy University Librarian: Mellowes, Richard, BA *Brist.*, MA *Lond.* (E-mail: library@cardiff.ac.uk)

Marketing. Director of Public Relations and Communications: Richardson, Brian J., BA *Liv.*, MBA *Wales*
(E-mail: williamsm14@cardiff.ac.uk)

Personnel/human resources. Director of Human Resources: Dowden, Jayne
(E-mail: jardineur@cardiff.ac.uk)

Public relations. Director of Public Relations and Communications: Richardson, Brian J., BA *Liv.*, MBA *Wales*
(E-mail: williamsm14@cardiff.ac.uk)

Publications. Publications Officer: Roberts, Laura (E-mail: robertsl9@cardiff.ac.uk)

Purchasing. Assistant Purchasing Director: Coulbeck, Norman B.
(E-mail: buyline@cardiff.ac.uk)

Quality assurance and accreditation. Quality Assurance Officer: Moore, K. T.
(E-mail: moorekt@cardiff.ac.uk)

Research. Director of Research and Commercial Division: Jones, Geraint W., BSc *Wales* (E-mail: jonesgw@cardiff.ac.uk)

Safety. Director of Occupational Safety, Health and Environment: Salmon, M. L., MSc *Sur.*
(E-mail: safety@cardiff.ac.uk)

Scholarships, awards, loans. Head of Student Advisory Service: Lewis, Ben, MSc *Wales*
(E-mail: studentadvisory@cardiff.ac.uk)

Schools liaison. Schools and Colleges Liaison Officer: Thomas, Ruth, BA *Wales*
(E-mail: enquiries@cardiff.ac.uk)

Security. Head of Security Services: Oliver, Anthony W. (E-mail: olivera1@cardiff.ac.uk)

Sport and recreation. Head of Sports and Exercise: Stephens, Gary C., BSc *Wales*
(E-mail: sport@cardiff.ac.uk)

Staff development and training. Deputy Director Training and Development: Midha, Susan M., BA *Wales*
(E-mail: midha@cardiff.ac.uk)

Strategic planning. Director of Planning: Hybart, Sue, BSc *Nott.*, PhD *Nott.*
(E-mail: planning@cardiff.ac.uk)

Student union. Student President: Cox, Jonny
(E-mail: studentsunion@cardiff.ac.uk)

Student welfare/counselling. Head of Counselling: Cowley, John, MA *Durh.*
(E-mail: counsellling@cardiff.ac.uk)

Students from other countries. Director of International Development: Elliott, Sandra, MA *Edin.*
(E-mail: international@cardiff.ac.uk)

Students with disabilities. Senior Student Advisor (Disability and Dyslexia Service): Werrell, C. (E-mail: disability@cardiff.ac.uk)

[Information supplied by the institution as at 13 November 2007, and edited by the ACU]

UNIVERSITY OF CENTRAL LANCASHIRE

Founded 1992

Postal Address: Preston, Lancashire, England PR1 2HE
Telephone: (01772) 201201 **Fax:** (01772) 892911 **E-mail:** reception@uclan.ac.uk
URL: http://www.uclan.ac.uk

VICE-CHANCELLOR*—McVicar, Malcolm T., MA Exe., PhD Lond.

UNIVERSITY OF CHESTER

Founded 2005

Postal Address: Parkgate Road, Chester, England CH1 4BJ
Telephone: (01244) 511000 **Fax:** (01244) 511300 **E-mail:** d.stevens@chester.ac.uk
URL: http://www.chester.ac.uk/

VICE-CHANCELLOR*—Wheeler, Prof. Timothy, DL, BA PhD DL, FRSA

UNIVERSITY OF CHICHESTER

Founded 2005

Postal Address: College Lane, Chichester, England PO19 6PE
Telephone: (01243) 816000 **Fax:** (01243) 816080
URL: http://www.chiuni.ac.uk

VICE-CHANCELLOR*—Baker, Robin, CMG, BA Lond., PhD E.Anglia
CHIEF FINANCIAL OFFICER‡—Child, Ian, BA S'ton.

CITY UNIVERSITY

Founded 1966

Postal Address: Northampton Square, London, England EC1V 0HB
Telephone: (020) 7040 5060 **Fax:** (020) 7040 5070
URL: http://www.city.ac.uk

VICE-CHANCELLOR AND PRESIDENT*—Gillies, Prof. Malcolm, BA ANU, MA Camb., MMus Lond., PhD Lond., LMusA, FAHA
DIRECTOR OF RESOURCES‡—Toop, Frank, BA N.U.I.

COVENTRY UNIVERSITY

Founded 1992

Member of the Association of Commonwealth Universities

Postal Address: Priory Street, Coventry, England CV1 5FB
Telephone: (024) 7688 7688 **Fax:** (024) 7688 8638
URL: http://www.coventry.ac.uk

VICE-CHANCELLOR*—Atkins, Prof. Madeleine J., BA *Camb.*, PhD *Nott.*
SECRETARY AND REGISTRAR‡—Quantrell, Kate
PRO-VICE-CHANCELLOR (LEARNING AND STUDENT EXPERIENCE)—Pennington, Prof. Donald, BA *Warw.*, PhD *Warw.*
PRO-VICE-CHANCELLOR (RESOURCES)—Soutter, David, BA *Oxf.*, MA *Oxf.*, FCA
PRO-VICE-CHANCELLOR (INTERNATIONAL AFFAIRS)—Jawaid, Prof. Ashraf, BSc *Lahore UET*, MSc *Birm.*, PhD *Birm.*
PRO-VICE-CHANCELLOR (BUSINESS DEVELOPMENT)—Latham, John, MBA *Coventry*
ASSOCIATE PRO-VICE-CHANCELLOR (RESEARCH)—Marshall, Prof. Ian M., BA BSc PhD
LIBRARIAN—Noon, Patrick, BA *CNAA*, MBA *Leic.*

GENERAL INFORMATION

History. The university was originally founded as the School of Design, a predecessor to the School of Art and Design, in 1843. It was later established as Lanchester Polytechnic (1970), Coventry (Lanchester) Polytechnic (1980) and Coventry Polytechnic (1987), and became a university following the 1992 Further and Higher Education Act.

The university is situated in Coventry city centre.

First Degrees (see also United Kingdom Directory to Subjects of Study). BA, BEng, BSc, LLB, MEng, MSci.

Courses normally last 3 years full-time or equivalent part-time. Sandwich courses: 4 years.

Higher Degrees (see also United Kingdom Directory to Subjects of Study).

Master's. MA, MPhil, MSc.

Taught master's courses last 12 months full-time. Part-time and research courses vary.

Doctoral. DSc, PhD.

Libraries. Volumes: 350,000. Periodicals subscribed to: 2000. Other holdings: 3000 electronic periodicals subscribed to. Special collections: Frederick Lanchester Collection; Anthony Hobson papers; Gulf Support Group papers.

FACULTIES/SCHOOLS

Art and Design, Coventry School of
Tel: (024) 7688 8248 Fax: (024) 7688 8667
E-mail: afuture.ad@coventry.ac.uk
Dean: Tovey, Prof. Michael, MDes *RCA*
Secretary: McAllister, Jane

Business, Environment and Society, Faculty of
Tel: (024) 7688 8410 Fax: (024) 7688 8400
E-mail: info.cbs@coventry.ac.uk
Co-Dean: Gillingham, Prof. David, BSc *Hull*, PhD *Brad.*
Co-Dean: Noon, D. M.
Secretary: MacDonald, Ingrid

Engineering and Computing, Faculty of
Tel: (024) 7688 8365 Fax: (024) 7655 3007
E-mail: genenq.eng@coventry.ac.uk
Dean: Marshall, Prof. Ian M., BA BSc PhD
Secretary: Sleath, Jill

Health and Life Sciences, Faculty of
Tel: (024) 7688 8357 Fax: (024) 7688 8784
E-mail: genenq.hls@coventry.ac.uk
Dean: Merriman, Linda, MPhil *Cran.IT*, PhD *Leic.*
Secretary: Crisp, Julia

Lifelong Learning, School of
Tel: (024) 7679 5059 Fax: (024) 7679 5082
E-mail: lifelonglearning.soll@coventry.ac.uk
Dean: Bibby, D.

ACADEMIC UNITS
Arranged by Faculties/Schools

Art and Design, Coventry School of
Tel: (024) 7688 8248 Fax: (024) 7688 8667
Atkinson, P., BA *CNAA*, MSc *CNAA*   Sr. Lectr.
Aust, I.   Sr. Lectr.
Ball, T. G., BA *CNAA*, MA *CNAA*   Sr. Lectr.
Barker, P., BSc *CNAA*, MDes *RCA*   Principal Lectr.
Barton, W., BA *Warw.*, BSc *Warw.*, MA *Coventry*   Sr. Lectr.
Barzey, A.   Sr. Lectr.
Beck, A. D., BA *Kent*, MA *Hudd.*, FRSA   Principal Lectr.
Bell, S., BA *Reading*   Sr. Lectr.
Birch, A., BA *CNAA*, MA *CNAA*   Sr. Lectr.
Birtley, N.   Sr. Lectr.
Bleetman, J., BA *Jerusalem*, MSc *Glas.*   Sr. Lectr.
Browne, D., BA *Leeds*   Principal Lectr.
Bull, K., BA *Brist.*, MA *C.England*, PhD *C.England*   Sr. Lectr.
Clough, B. A., BA *CNAA*   Sr. Lectr.
Davies, S., MSc *Lough.*   Sr. Lectr.
Dawkins, S. L., BA *CNAA*, MA *Leeds*   Sr. Lectr.
Devane, J., BA *CNAA*, MA *RCA*   Sr. Lectr.; Head of Subj. Group (Visual Arts)
Draycott, P. A.   Head, Dept. of Media and Communicn.
Evans, M., BA *York(UK)*   Principal Lectr.
Fitzpatrick, D., DA *Edin.*   Sr. Lectr.
Fry, M., BA *Birm.*, PhD *Lond.*   Sr. Lectr.
Garrett, N.   Sr. Lectr.
Gehlhaar, R., BA *Yale*   Sr. Lectr.
Georgiou, D., BA *W.England*, MA *C.England*   Sr. Lectr.
Hall, L., BSc *Coventry*   Sr. Lectr.
Hides, D. S., BA *Leic.*   Sr. Lectr.
Hull, N.   Sr. Lectr.
Johnson, C.   Sr. Lectr.; Head of Subj. Group (Indust. Des.)
Journeaux, J., BA *Humb.*   Prof.; Assoc. Dean
Kim, J.   Sr. Lectr.
Knyspel, M. R., BA *Coventry*, PhD *Coventry*   Sr. Lectr.
Lee, M. J., BA *CNAA*   Sr. Lectr.
Mackie, E., BSc *Aston*, MA *De Mont.*   Sr. Lectr.
Moody, C. L.   Sr. Lectr.
Muirhead, A.   Principal Lectr.
Noble, J., BA *RCA*, MA *RCA*   Sr. Lectr.
Owen, J., BA *CNAA*, MA *RCA*   Co-ordinator, Overseas Devel.
Palka, A., BA *Kent*, MA *Warw.*   Sr. Lectr.
Pullen, A. M.   Sr. Lectr.
Ramskill, R., BMus *Wales*, MMus *Wales*   Sr. Lectr.
Richards, C., MPhil *CNAA*, PhD *RCA*   Prof.; Assoc. Dean
Ross, K., BA *CNAA*, PhD *Warw.*   Prof., Mass Communication

Shaw, J., BA *W.England*, MA *C.England*   Sr. Lectr.
Sherriffs, R.   Sr. Lectr.
Super, K., BA *CNAA*, MA *C.England*   Principal Lectr.
Thorley, M.   Principal Lectr.
Tovey, Michael, MDes *RCA*   Prof.; Dean*
Webb, L., BA *CNAA*, MA *CNAA*   Sr. Lectr.
Whatley, Sarah, PhD *Sur.*   Head of Subj. Group (Performing Arts)
Willcocks, G., BA *De Mont.*   Sr. Lectr.
Other Staff: 16 Assoc. Sr. Lectrs.; 20 Lectrs.; 4 Assoc. Lectrs.; 1 Res. Fellow

Business, Environment and Society
Tel: (024) 7688 8410 Fax: (024) 7688 8400
E-mail: info.cbs@coventry.ac.uk
Astley, Sonja, BA *Trier*   Sr. Lectr.
Bagge-Gillingham, C.   Sr. Lectr.
Barrett, Hazel, BA *Sus.*, MA *Birm.*, PhD *Birm.*   Reader; Head of Subj. Group, Geog. and Environmental Bioscis.
Bass, T.   Subj. Convenor
Bateman, Mark, PhD   Sr. Lectr.
Bayley, Vida, BA *Northwestern*, MA *Lond.*, MSc *Coventry*   Sr. Lectr.
Beech, J., MA *Camb.*, MBA *Camb.*   Sr. Lectr.; Head of Subj. Group (Leisure, Sport and Tourism)
Bird, L., BSc *Lond.*, MBA *W.England*   Sr. Lectr.
Blair, A., MA *Aberd.*, PhD *Leic.*   Prof.
Blight, D., BA *CNAA*, MSc *Lond.*   Principal Lectr.
Brathwaite, T., BA *York(Can.)*, MA *Leic.*   Sr. Lectr.
Brick, A. W., MSc   Sr. Lectr.
Broadbent, D., BSc *Lond.*, MSc *Brad.*, FICE   Sr. Lectr.
Brooke, W. C., BA *Warw.*, MA *Coventry*   Sr. Lectr.
Brown, R., BA *Exe.*, MA *Coventry*   Sr. Lectr.
Browne, Angela, BA *Sheff.*, MA *Newcastle(UK)*, PhD *CNAA*   Principal Lectr.
Buckle, P. D.   Sr. Lectr.
Butler, C.   Sr. Lectr.
Byers, T.   Principal Lectr.
Bywaters, P. W., MA *Oxf.*   Prof.; Dir., Centre for Soc. Justice
Campbell, Lesley, BSc *Wales*, MSc *Aston*   Dir., Engl. Academy
Cashian, P., BA *Keele*, MA *Essex*   Assoc. Dean (Undergrad. Study)
Charlesworth, S. M., BA *Open(UK)*, PhD *Coventry*   Sr. Lectr.
Chubarov, A., PhD *Moscow*   Sr. Lectr.
Clements, N., BA *Coventry*   Sr. Lectr.
Clowes, J., BEd *Leeds*, MSc *Mass.*   Head, Marketing and Recruitment; Assoc. Dean
Cole, P., BSc *CNAA*, PhD *CNAA*   Sr. Lectr.
Coles, E.   Sr. Lectr.
Coluccello, S.   Sr. Lectr.
Donnelly, T., BA *Strath.*, PhD *Aberd.*   Prof.
Doster, L.   Sr. Lectr.
Duckers, L., BSc *E.Anglia*, PhD *E.Anglia*   Principal Lectr.
Dunham, P. J., BSc *CNAA*, PhD *Coventry*   Sr. Lectr.

Dunn, C., BA Coventry, MA Coventry   Principal Lectr.

Evans, R., MSc Lond.   Sr. Lectr.

Farnell, R., BA Manc., MPhil CNAA   Prof.

Finlay, D. C., BCom Birm., MBA Nott., PhD Nott.   Assoc. Dean, Postgrad.

Forbes, N., BA Hull, MA Lond., PhD Kent   Head of Subj. Group (Hist., Internat. Relations and Pol.)

Foster, S., BA CNAA, LLM Lond.   Principal Lectr.

Fox, A.   Sr. Lectr.

Gallacher, P. J.   Sr. Lectr.

Gillingham, Prof. David, BSc Hull, PhD Brad.   Prof.; Co-Dean*

Gilmour, E.   Sr. Lectr.

Gingell, R., LLB Warw., MSocSc Birm.   Sr. Lectr.

Gomes, E.   Sr. Lectr.

Goodall, G., BA Durh., MSc Birm., MSocSc Birm.   Sr. Lectr.

Graham, W. R.   Sr. Lectr.

Gray, K. E., BA CNAA, MPhil CNAA   Sr. Lectr.

Guest, J., BA CNAA, MA E.Anglia   Sr. Lectr.

Gurden, H.   Principal Lectr.

Halborg, A., BSc Lond., MBA City(UK)   Principal Lectr.

Hammersley, Geraldine, BA CNAA, MA Leic.   Sr. Lectr.

Harris, P., BSc Bath, PhD Glas.   Internat. Devel. Officer; Prof., Plant Science

Harrop, W.   Sr. Lectr.

Holt, S. A., BA Nene, MA Warw.   Sr. Lectr.

Horsman, S., BA CNAA, MBA Warw., FCA   Sr. Lectr.

Hughes, S., BA Wales, MA Manc.   Sr. Lectr.

Hunt, C. J.   Sr. Lectr.

Hunter, A.   Sr. Lectr.

Idriss, M.   Sr. Lectr.

Ilbery, Brian, BA Wales, PhD Wales, FRGS   Assoc. Dean; Prof., Human Geography

Jackson, Roselyn, BSc Durh., MSc Sheff., PhD S'ton.   Sr. Lectr.

Jackson, T. P., MBA Stir.   Sr. Lectr.

Jeffree, Debra, LLB CNAA   Principal Lectr.

Johnson, J. A., LLB Coventry, LLM Leic.   Sr. Lectr.

Jones, D., BA Wales, MA Lond., MA Birm.   Principal Lectr.

Kane-Iturrioz, R.   Sr. Lectr.

Kazamias, A., BA CNAA, MA Birm., PhD Lond.   Sr. Lectr.

Kellet, M.   Sr. Lectr.

Kinross, R.   Sr. Lectr.

Knyspel, M. R., BA Coventry, PhD Coventry   Sr. Lectr.

Kohler-Ridley, Monika, BA Warw.   Sr. Lectr.

Krauth, K.   Sr. Lectr.

Lewis, J., BA CNAA, MSocSci Birm.   Head of Subj. Group (Langs.)

Magee, F., BA Leeds, PhD Leeds   Sr. Lectr.

Majeed, A.   Sr. Lectr.

Manak, S. K.   Sr. Lectr.

Marlow, J., BA Essex, MA Essex, PhD Essex   Sr. Lectr.

Marsh, G. L. J.   Sr. Lectr.

Marshall, A.   Sr. Lectr.

Massey, S.   Sr. Lectr.

Maynard, J. A.   Undergrad. Programme Manager, Business

McGuire, S.   Sr. Lectr.

McKay, N., LLB CNAA, LLM Warw.   Programme Manager, Law

Mitchell, B., LLB Birm.   Prof.

Montague, T., BA Warw.   Dir., Policy and Programmes

Moore, T.   Sr. Lectr.

Morris, D.   Prof.; Dir., E-Learning

Moseley, Leslie A.   Head of Subj. Group, Disaster Management

Mountain, R.   Sr. Lectr.

Noon, D. M.   Co-Dean*

Old, J., BSc Lond., MA Warw.   Principal Lectr.

Orsini-Jones, Marina, DottLett Bologna, MA Warw.   Sr. Lectr.

O'Sullivan, Marion   Sr. Lectr.; Head of Subj. Group, Human Resource Management

Page, Caroline, BA Reading, PhD Reading   Sr. Lectr.

Panesar, S., LLB Coventry, LLM Warw.   Sr. Lectr.

Panther, J., MA Oxf., MSc Warw.   Principal Lectr.

Parker, E., BSc Wales, MSc Durh., PhD Liv.   Sr. Lectr.

Parra-Ramirez, G., BA Warw., MA Warw.   Sr. Lectr.

Perkin, C., BA CNAA, LLM Birm.   Principal Lectr.

Pritchard, A. R., BA C.Lancs., MSc Salf.   Sr. Lectr.

Proctor, R., BA Lond., MBA Warw.   Sr. Lectr.

Redhead, K., BSc Brad., MA Leeds, MSc Lond., MPhil Warw.   Principal Lectr.

Reeves, T. J.   Sr. Lectr.

Richards-Bray, J. E.   Sr. Lectr.

Rickers, W., BA   Sr. Lectr.

Rigby, A., BSocSc Birm., MA Essex, PhD Birm.   Dir., Centre for the Study of Forgiveness and Reconciliation

Roberts, A., BA Lond., MPhil Warw.   Sr. Lectr.

Robertson, M. J.   Prof.

Rodgers, T., BA Stir., MSc York(UK)   Sr. Lectr.

Rogers, P., BA Wolv., MA Keele   Sr. Lectr.

Rogers, R., BA CNAA, MBA CNAA   Sr. Lectr.

Rosser, M., BA Essex, MA Warw.   Principal Lectr.; Head, Quality Assurance

Ryan, M.   Sr. Lectr.

Sandhu, R., BA CNAA   Sr. Lectr.

Sara, G., BSc Lond., MSocSc Birm.   Head, Internat./EU Devel.

Saunders, R. J.   Sr. Lectr.

Sekhon, H., BA Kingston(UK), MBA Sur., PhD Nott.   Sr. Lectr.; Head of Subj. Group (Marketing)

Shaw, G., MA S'ton.   Sr. Lectr.

Shirole, R.   Sr. Lectr.

Skinner, D.   Prof.

Skipper, A. C., BA E.Anglia, MA Warw.   Sr. Lectr.

Smith, S. J., BSc Exe., PhD Open(UK)   Principal Lectr.

Squires, N., LLM Warw.   Sr. Lectr.

Steventon, B., BSc Bath   Head of Subj. Group

Syson, A. J., BSc Lanc., PhD Lanc.   Deputy Dir., E-Learning

Tanna, S., BSc Lond., MSc Lond., PhD CNAA   Sr. Lectr.

Tasker, R., BSc Manc.   Sr. Lectr.; Assoc. Head, Disaster Management

Teoh, L. K.   Sr. Lectr.

Thandi, S., BSc Hull, MSc Lond.   Sr. Lectr.; Head, Econ., Finance and Acctg.

Thompson, R. H.   Sr. Lectr.

Thomson, A., MA York(UK), PhD Lanc., BA   Principal Lectr.

Trodd, N. M.   Principal Lectr.

Tyrrell, Julia, BSc Lough., MBA Coventry   Sr. Lectr.

Urwin, G., BA CNAA, MBA Aston   Sr. Lectr.

Velo, V.   Sr. Lectr.

Vickery, Susan, LLB CNAA   Principal Lectr.

Vollans, T., LLB Leeds   Sr. Lectr.

Walsh, M., BA CNAA, MA Birm.   Sr. Lectr.

Webster, I. A.   Sr. Lectr.

Wilkinson, R., BA E.Anglia, MSc Aston   Sr. Lectr.

Williams, M. T., LLB Sheff.   Sr. Lectr.

Wood, A. M., BSc Lond., PhD Wales   Sr. Lectr.

Wood, J.   Sr. Lectr.

Yavash, Perihan, BA CNAA, MSc Lond.   Sr. Lectr.

Other Staff: 5 Assoc. Sr. Lectrs.; 4 Lectrs.; 2 Assoc. Lectrs.

Engineering and Computing

Tel: (024) 7688 8888 Fax: (024) 7688 7661

Abdel-Gayed, R.   Sr. Lectr.

Amin, S. A., MPhil Brun., PhD Lough.   Sr. Lectr.

Anane, R., BSc Manc., MSc Birm.   Sr. Lectr.

Anderson, R. D.   Principal Lectr.

Arochena, H. E.   Sr. Lectr.

Aslam, F., BSc Lond., MSc Wolv.   Sr. Lectr.

Aslam, T.   Sr. Lectr.

Bali, R., MSc Sund., PhD Sheff.Hallam   Sr. Lectr.

Basini, M. J.   Sr. Lectr.

Bate, S., BSc Sheff., PhD   Principal Lectr.

Baxter, J., MSc CNAA   Principal Lectr.

Beck, M. S., BSc CNAA, PhD Birm.   Principal Lectr.

Bell, A. R.   Sr. Lectr.

Benjamin, S., BSc Lond., PhD Lond.   Reader

Blake, M., BSc CNAA   Sr. Lectr.

Bland, C., MEng Wales   Principal Lectr.

Blundell, M., BSc CNAA, MSc Lond.   Sr. Lectr.

Booth, G. P.   Sr. Lectr.

Briscoe, G., BCom Birm.   Sr. Lectr.

Burnham, K., PhD CNAA   Prof.; Dir., Centre for Control Theory and Applications

Byrne, P. J.   Internat. Programme Manager

Carson, R., BA Salf., PhD Brist.   Sr. Lectr.

Chao, K. M., PhD Sund.   Sr. Lectr.

Chapman, M., BSc Warw., PhD Warw.   Sr. Lectr.

Claisse, P., BA Oxf., PhD Leeds   Reader, Construction Materials

Cook, R., BSc Liv., MSc CNAA   Programme Manager, Postgrad. Courses

Cooke, G.   Sr. Lectr.

Cross-Rudkin, P., MBA Strath., MA Camb.   Sr. Lectr.

Davies, John W., BSc Wales, MSc Wales, PhD CNAA   Sr. Lectr.; Head of Subj. Group, Civil Engin. and Bldg.

Davis, T. J., MEng Sheff.   Sr. Lectr.

Dunn, I. K., BEng CNAA   Assoc. Dean

Dunn, W., BSc Glas., BA Open(UK)   Sr. Lectr.

Evatt, M., BA Open(UK)   Sr. Lectr.

Every, P., BA Coventry, MS Coventry   Sr. Lectr.

Farmer, R., BSc Warw.   Assoc. Dean

Ganijan, M.   Sr. Lectr.

Garner, Wendy, BEng Manc.   Principal Lectr.

Gatward, R., BA Open(UK), MSc CNAA   Principal Lectr.

Gaura, E., PhD Coventry   Sr. Lectr.

Giannasi, F. J., BA Open(UK), BSc Newcastle(UK), MSc Birm.   Progamme Manager, Computer Sci.

Gleeson, J., BSc Aston, MSc   Sr. Lectr.

Glendinning, Irene, BSc CNAA   Internat. Programme Manager

Goodall, D., BSc CNAA, MSc Dund., PhD Bath   Sr. Lectr.

Goodyer, J., BEng CNAA   Sr. Lectr.

Green, P.   Sr. Lectr.

Griffiths, P., BSc Birm.   Principal Lectr.

Guo, H., MEng S'ton., PhD S'ton., BSc   Sr. Lectr.

Haas, O. C.   Sr. Lectr.

Halloran, J.   Sr. Lectr.

Hargrave, S.   Sr. Lectr.

Hooper, M.   Sr. Lectr.

Hough, D., BSc Manc., MSc Brun., PhD Brun.   Sr. Lectr.

Hulse, Ray, BSc MSc, FICE   Assoc. Dean

Hunt, D., BSc Nott., PhD Nott.   Principal Lectr.

James, Anne E., BSc Aston, PhD Aston   Res. Group Leader

Jarvis, R., BA MSc   Sr. Lectr.

Jinks, R., BEng CNAA   Sr. Lectr.

Jones, R. M., BSc CNAA, PhD CNAA   Sr. Lectr.

Karadelis, J. N., BSc Brun., MPhil   Sr. Lectr.

Kenna, R.   Sr. Lectr.

Kenning, G., BA Lond., BA Open(UK), MA Essex, MSc Open(UK), MEd Open(UK)   Sr. Lectr.

Khan, Z.   Sr. Lectr.

Kinross, R.   Sr. Lectr.

Kondrat, M. W., BSc CNAA, PhD CNAA   Sr. Lectr.

Kotecha, S.   Sr. Lectr.

Kruntcheva, M., PhD R.Gordon, MPhil   Sr. Lectr.

Lawson, D., BA Oxf., DPhil Oxf.   Assoc. Dean

Lehaney, B., BSc S.Bank, BSc Sheff.Hallam, MSc S.Bank, PhD Brun., PhD Hull   Head, Knowledge and Information Management

Lewis, M., BEng CNAA   Sr. Lectr.

Lovett, Philip J.   Sr. Lectr.

Low, R., MA Aberd., DPhil Oxf.   Reader

Mahtani, P., BEng Liv., MSc Warw.   Sr. Lectr.

Mansfield, R., BA Open(UK)   Sr. Lectr.

March, C., BSc UMIST   Sr. Lectr.

Marshall, Ian M., BA BSc PhD   Prof.; Dean*

Martin, S. H.   Principal Lectr.

Mashhoudy, H., MSc Lond., PhD Warw.   Sr. Lectr.
Molokov, S., PhD Latvia   Reader, Applied Mathematics
Naguib, R. N., BSc Cairo, MSc Lond., PhD Lond.   Prof., Biomedical Computing
Newman, R., BSc Birm., PhD Coventry   Head of Subj. Group, Digital Entertainment and Creativity
Ngami, S. C.   Sr. Lectr.
Odetayo, M. O., MSc Lond., PhD Glas.   Principal Lectr.
Oliver, M.   Sr. Lectr.
Owen, S. E., BSc Aston, BA Open(UK)   Sr. Lectr.
Page, C., BSc Nott., PhD Nott.   Reader, Manufacturing Systems
Payne, Lisa, BSc E.Anglia, MSc CNAA   Principal Lectr.
Petrovic, D., PhD Warw.   Reader
Poole, N., BSc Leeds   Principal Lectr.
Popplewell, K., BA Coventry   Prof.; Head of Subj. Group (Manufacturing Engin. and Management)
Porter, B., BSc   Sr. Lectr.
Pye, T., BA CNAA   Assoc. Head
Railton, A., BSc Lond.   Principal Lectr.
Reeves, C., BSc CNAA, MPhil CNAA   Prof.
Richards, O., BSc Wales, PhD Wales   Sr. Lectr.
Rider, R. J., BSc CNAA, PhD CNAA   Principal Lectr.
Rizzuto, J., BSc CNAA, MSc Kingston(UK)   Sr. Lectr.
Saidani, M., BEng Algiers, PhD Nott.   Sr. Lectr.
Samra, P. K.   Sr. Lectr.
Sassman, R., BSc Leeds, MSc Lond.   Sr. Lectr.
Sherwin, G.   Sr. Lectr.
Simons, M., BSc CNAA, MSc Brist.   Principal Lectr.
Singh, G., BSc Lond.   Principal Lectr.
Slaich, A., BSc Nott., MSc Nott.Trent   Sr. Lectr.
Smalov, L., MSc PhD   Sr. Lectr.
Smith, E. G., BSc Manc., MSc Brist., PhD Brist.   Sr. Lectr.
Smith, K.   Sr. Lectr.
Southey, P., BSc CNAA   Sr. Lectr.
Stavrinides, A., BSc Lond., PhD Birm.   Principal Lectr.
Tabor, J., BSc Lond., PhD Lond.   Head, Mathl. Scis.
Todman, A.   Sr. Lectr.
Trepess, D. H., BSc CNAA, PhD S'ton.   Sr. Lectr.
Tyrell, S. E.   Sr. Lectr.
Vella, C., BSc Birm., MSc CNAA   Principal Lectr.
Vershinin, Y.   Sr. Lectr.
Wall, B., BSc Aston, MSc Coventry   Sr. Lectr.
White, P., BSc Nott., PhD Nott.   Head of Subj. Group, Mech. Engin.; Reader, Thermofluid Dynamics
Williamson, J.   Sr. Lectr.
Wood, R., MSc CNAA   Sr. Lectr.
Wright, J. A., BTech Brad., MSc H-W   Sr. Lectr.
Wright, N.   Sr. Lectr.
Wu, H.   Sr. Lectr.
Yaacob, N., PhD Exe.   Sr. Lectr.
Yan, S. Y.   Principal Lectr.
Yates, P.   Sr. Lectr.
Young, M. A.   Sr. Lectr.
Zhang, B.   Prof., Applied Mathematics
Zhou, Q., BSc S.China U.T., MSc S.China U.T., PhD Chinese HK   Sr. Lectr.
Other Staff: 1 Assoc. Sr. Lectr.; 1 Internat./ Marketing Manager

Health and Life Sciences

Tel: (024) 7679 5959 Fax: (024) 7679 5950
E-mail: hlsgen@coventry.ac.uk
Al-Daffaee, H., BSc Baghdad, PhD Aston   Principal Lectr.
Archer, K.   Sr. Lectr.
Astley-Cooper, Jean, BSc Edin.   Principal Lectr.
Awang, D., MA C.England   Sr. Lectr.
Ballard, H.   Sr. Lectr.
Ballard, V. J.   Sr. Lectr.
Banyard, I., BA Coventry   Sr. Lectr.
Barker, H., BSc Dund.   Programme Manager, Dietetics

Barlow, J. H., BA CNAA, PhD Coventry   Prof.
Barnes, K. V., BSc Coventry, MSc Coventry, PhD Leic.   Sr. Lectr.
Barry, S.   Co-ordinator, Physiotherapy
Bearne, C. A.   Sr. Lectr.
Bell, R.   Sr. Lectr.
Bluteau, P. A., BA Warw.   Sr. Lectr.
Blydon, S.   Sr. Lectr.
Bollard, M. R.   Sr. Lectr.
Booth, J.   Sr. Lectr.
Brooks, S., BSc Lond.   Principal Lectr.
Brown, Maureen, BSc CNAA, MSc Warw.   Sr. Lectr.
Brown, S., BSc Wales, MSc Wales, PhD Manc.   Sr. Lectr.
Brown, Y.   Sr. Lectr.
Bywaters, P. W., MA Oxf.   Prof.; Dir., Centre for Soc. Justice
Canning, B., LLB   Sr. Lectr.
Carpenter, C. M.   Sr. Lectr.
Carson, R., BA Leeds   Sr. Lectr.
Chamley, C., BA Lond.   Sr. Lectr.
Clampin, A.   Sr. Lectr.
Clarke, E.   Sr. Lectr.
Clay, C., BSc Coventry   Sr. Lectr.
Clouder, Lynne, BSc Birm., MA Warw., PhD Warw.   Sr. Lectr.
Cole, K., BSc Leic., MSc Coventry   Programme Manager, Pre-Registration Nursing
Colombo, A., BA Leic., MPhil Camb., PhD Camb.   Sr. Lectr.
Conneeley, A. L., MSc Exe.   Sr. Lectr.
Cook, S.   Sr. Lectr.
Coolican, A. H.   Principal Lectr.
Cooper, C.   Head, Healthcare
Corbett, S., BSc Hudd.   Sr. Lectr.
Court, D.   Sr. Lectr.
Coveney, J., BSc Lond., PhD Warw.   Sr. Lectr.
Cowden, S., BA Coventry   Sr. Lectr.
Cox, M. J., BSc Lond.   Sr. Lectr.
Cox, V., BSc Liv., PhD Liv.   Sr. Lectr.; Head, Physiol./Sports Sci.
Craig, K.   Sr. Lectr.
Cross, Dawn, MA Coventry   Programme Manager, Occupnl. Therapy
Cullen, S. M., BSc Wolv.   Sr. Lectr.
Cushway, D., BA Reading, PhD Birm.   Prof.; Programme Dir., Clin. Psychol.
Dalley, J., MSc Coventry   Sr. Lectr.
Daly, G. B. J.   Assoc. Dean
Davies, B. M., BSc Coventry   Sr. Lectr.
Davies, K. L.   Sr. Lectr.
Dignon, A. M., BA Brighton, BSc Leic.   Sr. Lectr.
Drake, A. P.   Sr. Lectr.
Drake, M. F.   Sr. Lectr.
Dring, P. L.   Sr. Lectr.
Dunn, O., BSc Brun., PhD Warw.   Sr. Lectr.
Eames, C., BSc Lond., DPhil York(UK)   Sr. Lectr.
Farr, C.   Sr. Lectr.
Ford, H., BSc C.England   Sr. Lectr.
Gilbert, F. M., BA Open(UK)   Sr. Lectr.
Gilchrist, M.   Principal Lectr.
Godfrey, S., BSc Coventry, MSc Coventry   Assoc. Head, Nursing
Godson, N.   Sr. Lectr.
Goodman, M.   Sr. Lectr.
Gopee, L. N., BA Open(UK), MEd Warw.   Sr. Lectr.
Gordon, I. P.   Sr. Lectr.
Goy, S.   Principal Lectr.
Gray, A. D.   Sr. Lectr.
Greaney, B. G.   Sr. Lectr.
Green, Ann, MSc Liv.   Assoc. Head, Physiotherapy and Dietetics
Green, C.   Sr. Lectr.
Green, E. F., BSc Leic., MPhil Camb., PhD Camb.   Sr. Lectr.
Greene, G.   Sr. Lectr.
Gregory, P.   Sr. Lectr.
Gurden, Helen, BA Sus., MPhil Warw.   Sr. Lectr.
Guy, J. S.   Principal Lectr.
Hargreaves, J. P., BSc CNAA   Sr. Lectr.
Harrison, Karen, BEd CNAA, MSc Aston   Prof.; Head of Subj. Group, Physiother. and Dietetics
Harrower, J. A.   Head of Subj. Group (Psychol.)

Hastings, J., BA Manc.   Sr. Lectr.
Hawcroft, E. M.   Sr. Lectr.
Haycock, C. G.   Sr. Lectr.
Heames, Ruth, MA Leic.   Head of Subj. Group (Occupnl. Therapy)
Heeney, S. L., MSc Wolv.   Sr. Lectr.
Henderson, Janey, BSc Aberd., MSc Manc., PhD Durh.   Sr. Lectr.; Head of Subj. Group (Biological and Molecular Scis.)
Heptinstall, J., BSc Sheff., PhD Sheff.   Sr. Lectr.
Horner, L., BA CNAA, MSc Aston   Sr. Lectr.
Howat, D. J.   Principal Lectr.
Hume, I.   Sr. Lectr.
Igo, S., MSc Greenwich   Sr. Lectr.
James, L. G.   Sr. Lectr.
James, R. S., BSc Leeds, PhD Leeds   Sr. Lectr.
Javed, T., BSc Salf., PhD Salf.   Sr. Lectr.
Keay, T. J.   Sr. Lectr.
Khanna, R., BA C.Lancs.   Sr. Lectr.
King, A.   Sr. Lectr.
Knight, E.   Academic Dir., Clin. Psychol.
La Fontaine, J. H.   Principal Lectr.
Lahiff, J. F.   Sr. Lectr.
Lambon, Nicola, MA Keele   Programme Manager, Physiother.
Langton, H.   Assoc. Dean
Law, S. M., BSc Wales   Sr. Lectr.
Lawrence, A.   Sr. Lectr.
Lees, S., BSc Wolv.   Sr. Lectr.
Lister, S., BSc CNAA, MA Lond.   Sr. Lectr.
Lund, P., BSc Witw., DPhil Oxf.   Sr. Lectr.
Lynch, D., BA Qld., MA Qld., PhD Qld.   Sr. Lectr.
Maddock, H.   Sr. Lectr.
Mainwaring, J. E.   Sr. Lectr.
Marr, M.   Sr. Lectr.
Mason, T., BSc S'ton., PhD S'ton.   Prof., Chemistry
McCarrick, D.   Head, Soc. and Community Care
McClement, A.   Sr. Lectr., Operating Department Practice
McGhee, A., MSc Nott.   Sr. Lectr.
Merriman, Linda, MPhil Cran.IT, PhD Leic.   Dean*
Mian, R., BSc Liv., PhD Birm.   Sr. Lectr.
Middleton, A.   Sr. Lectr.
Mills, Natalie, BSc Warw., BEd Warw., MEd Warw.   Assoc. Head, Nursing
Mitchell, A.   Sr. Lectr.
Morgan, M., BSc CNAA, MSc Greenwich   Sr. Lectr.
Morrow, R. J., BSc Ulster, MSc E.Anglia, PhD E.Anglia   Sr. Lectr.
Morse, T., BSc Coventry, MSc Coventry   Sr. Lectr.
Navarro, D. C., MA Warw.   Sr. Lectr.
Norman, B.   Sr. Lectr.
Norrish, M., BSc Wales   Sr. Lectr.
Odedra, S., BA CNAA   Principal Lectr.
Paniwnyk, L.   Sr. Lectr.
Parker, N. D.   Principal Lectr.
Parkes, J.   Sr. Lectr.
Patel, A.   Sr. Lectr.
Percy, C.   Sr. Lectr.
Perry, J.   Sr. Lectr.
Pettifer, A. R.   Sr. Lectr.
Phimister, D., BSc C.England, MA Coventry   Sr. Lectr.
Phull, S. S., BSc Manc., PhD Warw.   Sr. Lectr.
Pinchess, C.   Sr. Lectr.
Plester, B. A., BA Brigham Young   Sr. Lectr.
Poole, H.   Sr. Lectr.
Price, M.   Sr. Lectr.
Ramsay, J., BA Warw., MSc Birm.   Sr. Lectr.
Rodney, C., MA Coventry   Sr. Lectr.
Roebuck, A.   Sr. Lectr.
Ross, L., BSc C.England   Sr. Lectr.
Russell, K.   Sr. Lectr.
Saranga, J.   Sr. Lectr.
Sausman, J.   Sr. Lectr.
Savin-Baden, M., MA Lond., PhD Lond.   Prof.
Scullion, P. A., BSc C.England, MA Warw.   Sr. Lectr.
Sellars, J.   Sr. Lectr.
Shannon, J. T., BA Open(UK)   Sr. Lectr.
Simons, K.   Sr. Lectr.
Singh, Gurnam, MSc Brad., PhD   Sr. Lectr.
Smith, M., BA Newcastle(UK)   Sr. Lectr.

Srivastava, A., BSc N.Lond. Sr. Lectr.
Steed, Anita, MA Coventry Sr. Lectr.
Steptoe-Warren, G. L. Sr. Lectr.
Steventon, G., BA Sheff., MA Oxf.Brookes, PhD Warw. Sr. Lectr.
Taylor, L., BSc Birm., PhD Birm. Sr. Lectr.
Thake, C. D. Sr. Lectr.
Thunhurst, C. Principal Lectr.
Tighe, B., BSc CNAA Sr. Lectr.
Toms, J., MA Coventry Sr. Lectr.
Turner, T. Sr. Lectr.
Twining, F. Sr. Lectr.
Webb, A. K., BSc Wolv., MEd Warw. Sr. Lectr.
Welyczko, A. L. Sr. Lectr.
Wilcock, E. J., BSc Sund., MSc Brist. Sr. Lectr.
Williams, B. E. Sr. Lectr.
Williams, J. Sr. Lectr.
Williams, N. A., BSc CNAA, MSc Lough. Sr. Lectr.
Wilson, A., BSc Coventry, MSc Birm. Sr. Lectr.
Wilson, N. Sr. Lectr.
Wilson, R. Sr. Lectr.
Wimpenny, K., MSc Birm. Sr. Lectr.
Wood, C. P. Sr. Lectr.
Woodhouse, C. E., BSc Birm., MSc Birm. Sr. Lectr.
Yorke, A. Sr. Lectr.
Other Staff: 27 Assoc. Sr. Lectrs.; 3 Assoc. Lectrs.; 3 Inter-Prof. Practice Facilitators; 1 Clin. Tutor/Lectr.; 1 Clin. Health Skills Instructor

Lifelong Learning

Tel: (024) 7679 5059 Fax: (024) 7679 5082
E-mail: lifelonglearning.soll@coventry.ac.uk
Bhanot, R. C. Subj. Convenor, Health, Org. Learning
Bibby, D. Dir.*
Harris, S. Subj. Convenor
Rumbelow, J. Asst. Dir.
Other Staff: 1 Learner Service Support Manager

SPECIAL CENTRES, ETC

Study of Higher Education, Centre for (CSHE)

Tel: (024) 7688 7599 Fax: (024) 7688 7599
E-mail: info.ched@coventry.ac.uk
Blackmore, Paul, BA E.Anglia, MEd Bath, PhD Warw. Dir.*

Clouder, Lynne, BSc Birm., MA Warw., PhD Warw. Pedagogical Res. Fellow
Courtney, K., BA Sus., MPhil Warw. Sr. Lectr.
Deepwell, F., BA Manc., MA Kent Sr. Lectr.
Dickinson, A., BSc PhD Sr. Lectr.
Ganobcsik-Williams, L., BA Bowling Green, MA Maine(USA), PhD Miami(Ohio) Co-ordinator, Centre for Academic Writing
King, Virginia, BA Lanc. Pedagogical Res. Fellow
Orsini-Jones, Marina, DottLett Bologna, MA Warw. Sr. Lectr.
Savin-Baden, M., MA Lond., PhD Lond. Prof., Higher Education Research
Singh, Gurnam, MSc Brad., PhD Sr. Lectr.
Turner, A. P., BSc CNAA, PhD CNAA Sr. Lectr.
Other Staff: 1 Res. Fellow; 1 Res. Asst.

Sustainable Regeneration, Applied Research Centre in

Tel: (024) 7679 5757
E-mail: surge.bes@coventry.ac.uk
Berkeley, N. P., BSc MA Dir., Centre for Local Econ. Devel.
Donnelly, T., BA Strath., PhD Aberd. Prof.
Farnell, R., BA Manc., MPhil CNAA Prof.
Other Staff: 1 Lectr.; 1 Sr. Res. Fellow; 3 Res. Fellows; 2 Sr. Res. Assts.; 1 Res. Asst.; 2 Res. Administrators

CONTACT OFFICERS

Accommodation. Halls Manager: Morgan, Christine
(E-mail: accomm.ss@coventry.ac.uk)
Admissions (first degree). Head, Recruitment and Admissions Office: Bamforth, Claire
(E-mail: info.rao@coventry.ac.uk)
Admissions (higher degree). Graduate and CPD Centre Manager: Mann, Inderjit
(E-mail: grad.uni@coventry.ac.uk)
Alumni. Head of Alumni and Fundraising: Moore, Ian
(E-mail: i.moore@coventry.ac.uk)
Careers. Assistant Director of Student Services (Careers and Counselling): Derby, Joanna
(E-mail: careers.ss@coventry.ac.uk)

Computing services. Director of Computing Services: Dimmer, Paul, BSc Lond., PhD Leic.
(E-mail: help.csv@coventry.ac.uk)
Consultancy services. Pro-Vice-Chancellor (Business Development): Latham, John, MBA Coventry
(E-mail: genenq.cad@coventry.ac.uk)
Estates and buildings/works and services. Director of Estates: Woolhead, William
(E-mail: genenq.est@coventry.ac.uk)
Finance. Group Director of Finance: Soutter, David, BA Oxf., MA Oxf., FCA
(E-mail: genenq.fin@coventry.ac.uk)
General enquiries. Secretary and Registrar: Quantrell, Kate
(E-mail: genenq.sec@coventry.ac.uk)
International office. Assistant Director (International Affairs): Hunt, Timothy
(E-mail: interlink@coventry.ac.uk)
Library (chief librarian). Librarian: Noon, Patrick, BA CNAA, MBA Leic.
(E-mail: lbxaal@coventry.ac.uk)
Marketing. Director of Marketing and Communications: Stokes, Nick
(E-mail: m.dyer@coventry.ac.uk)
Personnel/human resources. Director of Personnel: Kendall, Donna, MA
(E-mail: genenq.per@coventry.ac.uk)
Public relations. Press and Publicity Officer: Beales, Katie
(E-mail: k.beales@coventry.ac.uk)
Quality assurance and accreditation. Pro-Vice-Chancellor (Learning and Student Experience): Pennington, Prof. Donald, BA Warw., PhD Warw.
(E-mail: d.pennington@coventry.ac.uk)
Research. Associate Pro-Vice-Chancellor (Research): Marshall, Prof. Ian M., BA BSc PhD (E-mail: i.marshall@coventry.ac.uk)
Students with disabilities. Disabilities Officer: Bogusz, Helen
(E-mail: h.bogusz@coventry.ac.uk)

[Information supplied by the institution as at 14 June 2006, and edited by the ACU]

CRANFIELD UNIVERSITY

Founded 1969

Member of the Association of Commonwealth Universities

Postal Address: Cranfield, Bedfordshire, England MK43 0AL
Telephone: (01234) 750111 **Fax:** (01234) 750972
URL: http://www.cranfield.ac.uk

VICE-CHANCELLOR*—O'Reilly, Prof. Sir John J., BTech Brun., PhD Essex, DSc Brun., FREng, FIET, FIP, FBCS, FRAeS, CCMI, Hon. FIChemE
PRO-VICE-CHANCELLOR—Nellis, Prof. Joe G., BSc(Econ) Ulster, MA Warw., PhD Cran.
DEPUTY VICE-CHANCELLOR—Friend, Prof. Clifford M., BSc Sur., PhD Sur., FIMMM
DIRECTOR OF FINANCE—Aspinall, Philip J., BA Sheff.
ACTING ACADEMIC REGISTRAR‡—Truesdale, Susan, MBA Dund.
DIRECTOR OF HUMAN RESOURCES AND DEVELOPMENT AND ACTING SECRETARY—Altman, Ruth
UNIVERSITY LIBRARIAN—Woodward, Hazel M., BA CNAA, PhD Lough.
CHANGE PROGRAMME DIRECTOR—Stephens, Prof. William, BSc Edin., MSc Cran., PhD Cran., FIAE
DIRECTOR OF IT—Lusignani, Gio

GENERAL INFORMATION

History. The university has its origins in the College of Aeronautics established in 1946. It was incorporated by royal charter as Cranfield Institute of Technology in 1969, and the present name was adopted in 1993.

The university has campuses at Cranfield and Silsoe in Bedfordshire; it is also responsible for the academic work at the Defence College of Management and

Technology, part of the Defence Academy of the United Kingdom at Shrivenham in Oxfordshire.

Higher Degrees (see also United Kingdom Directory to Subjects of Study).

Master's. MA, MBA, MDA, MPhil, MRes, MSc, MTech.

Admission. Applicants must normally hold an appropriate first degree with at least second class honours, or equivalent.

Length of course. Full-time: MA, MBA, MDA, MRes, MSc: 1 year; MPhil, MTech: 2 years.

Part-time: MA, MBA, MDA, MSc: 2 years; MPhil: 4 years.

Doctoral. DBA, DM, EngD, PhD.

Admission. Admission: Applicants must normally hold an appropriate first degree with at least second class honours or equivalent, or an appropriate master's degree.

Length of course. Full-time: DBA, DM, PhD: 3 years; EngD: 4 years. Part-time: DBA: 4 years; DM, PhD: 6 years.

Libraries. Volumes: 439,009. Periodicals subscribed to: 10,045. Special collections: Conservation Trust (at Silsoe); disaster management (at Shrivenham).

Academic Year (2007–2008). October–September (Cranfield and Silsoe) or September–August (Shrivenham):

Income (2005–2006). Total, £140,000,000.

Statistics. Staff (2006): 1355 (384 academic, 971 non-academic). Students (2006): full-time 2856; part-time 1202; international 541; undergraduate 87; master's 1923; doctoral 716.

FACULTIES/SCHOOLS

Defence and Security
Tel: (01793) 785434 Fax: (01793) 785768
E-mail: academicreg@cranfield.ac.uk
Dean: Neal, Prof. Derrick J., BE Kent, MBA Cran., PhD Kent
Faculty Board Secretary: Truesdale, Susan, MBA Dund.

Engineering and Aerospace
Tel: (01234) 754008 Fax: (01234) 752462
E-mail: registry@cranfield.ac.uk
Dean: Muir, Prof. Helen C., OBE, MA St And., PhD Lond., FRAeS
Faculty Board Secretary: Bailey, Phil

Environment, Science and Manufacturing
Tel: (01234) 754008 Fax: (01234) 752462
E-mail: registry@cranfield.ac.uk
Dean: Kay, Prof. John M., BSc Nott., PhD Nott., FIEE
Faculty Board Secretary: Marshall, Kate

Management
Tel: (01234) 754008 Fax: (01234) 752462
E-mail: registry@cranfield.ac.uk
Dean: Bowman, Prof. Cliff, BA Liv., MBA Liv., PhD Cran.
Faculty Board Secretary: Marshall, Kate

Medicine and Biosciences
Tel: (01234) 754008 Fax: (01234) 752462
E-mail: registry@cranfield.ac.uk
Dean: Barr, Prof. Hugh, MB ChB Liv., MD Liv., ChM Liv.
Academic Dean: Higson, Prof. Seamus P., PhD S'ton.
Faculty Board Secretary: Marshall, Kate

ACADEMIC UNITS

Applied Sciences, School of
Tel: (01234) 754086 Fax: (01234) 754109
E-mail: sims.enquiries@cranfield.ac.uk
Alcock, Jeffrey R., BSc Leeds, PhD Leeds Sr. Lectr.; Course Dir., Motorsport Engin.
Allen, David M., BSc Wales, PhD Wales Prof., Microengineering
Allwood, Robert L., BSc Reading, PhD H-W Sr. Lectr., Underwater Technology
Baines, Timothy S., MSc Cran., PhD Cran., FIEE, FIMechE Prof., Strategic Manufacturing
Ball, Peter D., BEng Aston, PhD Aston Sr. Lectr.
Carter, Richard C., MA Camb., MSc S'ton., PhD Cran., FGS Prof.
Evans, Stephen, BSc Bath, PhD Bath Prof., Life Cycle Engineering
Fan, I., BSc HK, PhD Cran. Sr. Lectr.
Farris, Ian, BA Arts(Lond.) Sr. Lectr.
Franceys, Richard, PhD Lough. Sr. Lectr.
Fuller, Graham D., MPhil Cran. Sr. Lectr.; Course Dir., Integrated Pharmaceut. and Med. Engin.
Gao, Xiaoyu, BSc Dalian I.T., MSc UMIST, PhD UMIST Sr. Lectr.

Goatman, Michael C., BA Arts(Lond.), MA Herts. Sr. Lectr.
Godwin, Richard J., BSc CNAA, MS Ill., PhD Reading, FREng, FIAE Prof., Agricultural Engineering
Greenough, Richard M., BA Oxf., MSc Lond., PhD Cran. Sr. Lectr., Manufacturing Systems
Harris, James A., BSc CNAA, PhD CNAA, FLS, FGS, FIAE, FIBiol Prof., Environmental Technology
Harrison, Paul T. C., BSc Lond., PhD Lond., FIBiol, FRSA Dir., Inst. of Environment and Health
Hess, Tim M., BSc Wales, MSc Cran., PhD Cran. Sr. Lectr.
Holman, Ian P., BSc E.Anglia, PhD E.Anglia Sr. Lectr., Groundwater Hydrology
Irving, Philip, BSc Birm., PhD Birm., FIMMM Prof., Damage Tolerance
Judd, Simon J., BSc Bath, MSc S'ton., PhD Cran. Prof., Membrane Technology
Julien, Denyse M., BSc WI, PhD Nott., MBA Sr. Lectr.
Kay, John M., BSc Nott., PhD Nott., FIEE Prof., Manufacturing Systems Engineering
Kibblewhite, Mark G., BA York(UK), MBA Cran., PhD Aberd., FRSChem, FIAE Prof., Applied Soil Science
Kirby, Paul B., BSc Lanc., PhD Camb. Sr. Lectr.
Kirk, Guy J. D., BSc Newcastle(UK), DPhil Oxf. Prof., Soil Systems
Leeds-Harrison, Peter B., BSc CNAA, PhD Reading Prof., Soil and Water Management
Lester, J., BSc Brad., MSc Lond., PhD Lond., DSc Lond. Prof., Water Technology
Levy, Len, BSc Manc., MSc Manc., PhD Lond. Prof., Environmental Health
Longhurst, Philip J., BEd Sheff.Hallam, PhD Cran. Sr. Lectr., Waste Strategy
Mehnen, Jorn, MSc Dortmund, PhD Dortmund Sr. Lectr.
Morris, Joe, BSc Reading, MSc Lond., PhD Prof., Resource Economics and Management
Neame, Charles, BA Liv., MSc Lond. Sr. Lectr.
Nicholls, John R., BSc(Eng) Lond., PhD Lond., FIMMM Prof., Coatings Technology
Parsons, Simon, BSc Leic., PhD Leic. Prof., Water Sciences
Partridge, Ivana K., BA Camb., MA Camb., PhD Cran., FIMMM Prof., Polymer Composites
Pollard, Simon, BSc Lond., PhD Lond., FRSChem Prof., Waste and Environment Risk Management
Ramsden, Jeremy J., BA Camb., MA Camb. Prof., Nanotechnology
Rickson, R. Jane, BSc Lond., MSc Cran., PhD Cran. Prof., Soil Erosion and Conservation
Ritz, Karl, BSc Reading, PhD Brist. Prof., Soil Biology
Roy, Raj, MSc Plym., PhD Plym. Prof., Decision Engineering
Sackett, Peter, MSc Manc., PhD Manc. Prof., Integrated Systems
Sansom, Christopher L., BSc Liv., DPhil Sus. Sr. Lectr.
Shaw, Trevor W., BSc Wales, PhD Wales Sr. Lectr.
Shore, Paul, MSc Cran., PhD Cran. Prof., Ultra Precision Engineering
Smart, Palminder K., BSc Plym., MSc Cran., PhD Cran. Sr. Lectr.
Soltan-mohammadi, H., BSc Aston, MSc Sr. Lectr.
Stephenson, David J., BSc Brun., PhD Brun., FIMechE, FIMMM Prof., Materials Processing
Stephenson, Tom, BSc York(UK), PhD Lond., FIChemE Lorch Prof., Water Sciences; Head*
Taylor, John C., MS Iowa, PhD Iowa Prof., Land Resources Monitoring and Remote Sensing
Tyrrel, Sean F., BSc Leeds, MPhil Cran., PhD Cran. Sr. Lectr.
Wainwright, Charles, BEng CNAA, PhD UMIST Sr. Lectr., Enterprise Simulation

Weatherhead, E. Keith, BA Oxf., MA Oxf., PhD Cran. Sr. Lectr.
Whelan, Michael J., BSc Leeds, PhD Leeds Sr. Lectr.
White, Susan M., BEng Liv., MSc Birm., PhD Exe. Prof., Integrated Catchment Management
Williams, Stewart W. Prof., Welding Science and Technology
Yapp, David, BSc Sheff., MMet Sheff. Sr. Lectr.

Cranfield Health
Tel: (01525) 863005 Fax: (01525) 863360
E-mail: c.wright@cranfield.ac.uk
Bessant, Conrad, BSc Nott., PhD Cran. Sr. Lectr.
Cullen, David C., BSc E.Anglia, PhD Camb. Reader
Higson, Seamus P., PhD S'ton. Prof., Bio and Electroanalysis
Houghton, Joan Sr. Lectr.
Lunec, Joe, BSc Lond., PhD Lond., DSc Lond. Prof.; Head*
Magan, Naresh, BSc Exe., MSc Exe., PhD Reading, FIBiol Prof., Applied Mycology
Piletsky, Sergey, PhD Moscow Prof., Bio-Organic Polymer Chemistry
Turner, Tony P. F., BSc E.Lond., MSc Kent, PhD Portsmouth, DSc Kent, FIBiol, FRSChem Distinguished Prof., Biotechnology
Warner, Philip J., BSc Lond., PhD Kent Prof., Industrial Molecular Biology
Woodman, Anthony C., BSc Sund., MSc Lond., PhD Lond. Reader

Engineering, School of
Tel: (01234) 755561 Fax: (01234) 750728
E-mail: soe@cranfield.ac.uk
Anker, Ralph W. J., MSc Warw. Sr. Lectr.
Badr, Ossama M. H., BSc Cairo, PhD Cran. Sr. Lectr.; Course Dir.
Batty, William J., MSc Cran., PhD Cran. Sr. Lectr.
Braithwaite, Graham R., BSc Lough., PhD Lough., FRAeS Dir., Safety and Accident Investigation Centre; Prof., Safety and Accident Investigation
Brennan, F., MSc Lond., PhD Lond. Prof., Offshore Engineering
Cook, Michael V., BSc S'ton., MSc Cran., FRAeS, FIMA Sr. Lectr.
Cooke, Alastair, BTechnol Lough., BEng Lough., MSc Cran., PhD Cran. Sr. Lectr.
Dorn, Lisa Sr. Lectr.
Drikakis, Dimitris, PhD T.U.Athens Head, Aerospace Scis.; Prof., Fluid Mechanics and Computational Science
Fielding, John P., MSc Cran., PhD Cran., FRAeS Prof., Aircraft Design
Garry, Kevin P., BSc S'ton., MSc Cran., PhD Cran. Prof., Experimental Aerodynamics
Gelman, Leonid Prof., Vibro-Acoustic Monitoring
Greenhalgh, Douglas A., BSc Newcastle(UK), PhD Newcastle(UK), FIP Head, Automotive Mech. and Structures Engin.; Prof., Non-Intrusive Measurement of Combustion and Flow
Guenov, Marin D., MEng T.U.Sofia, PhD Napier, FIMechE Prof., Engineering Design
Guo, Shijun, MSc Northwest(Xi'an), PhD Herts. Sr. Lectr.
Hammond, David W., BSc Lond., PhD Cran. Sr. Lectr.
Harrison, Matthew F., BEng S'ton., PhD S'ton. Sr. Lectr.
Haslam, Anthony S., BSc Edin., MSc Cran. Sr. Lectr.; Course Dir.
Hobbs, Stephen E., BA Camb., PhD Cran. Sr. Lectr.; Dir., Cranfield Space Res. Centre
James, Stephen W. Sr. Lectr.
John, Philip, BSc Lond., PhD Lond. Academic Tech. Dir.; Prof., Systems Engineering
Lawson, Nicholas J., BSc Lough., PhD Lough. Sr. Lectr.
Mason, Keith J., BA Leic., PhD Plym. Sr. Lectr.; Dir., Bus. Travel Res. Centre
Mba, David U., BEng Herts., PhD Cran. Sr. Lectr.; Course Dir.

Moss, J. Barrie, BSc *Leeds*, MSc *Cran.*, PhD *Cran.*, FIMechE Prof., Thermofluids and Combustion

Muir, Helen C., OBE, MA *St And.*, PhD *Lond.*, FRAeS Dir., Cranfield Inst. for Safety Risk and Reliability; Prof., Aerospace Psychology

Patel, Minoo, BSc *Lond.*, PhD *Lond.*, FREng, FIMechE Prof.; Head*

Pilidis, Pericles, BSc *Glas.*, MBA *Glas.*, PhD *Glas.* Prof., Gas Turbine Performance Engineering

Poll, D. Ian A., OBE, BSc(Eng) *Lond.*, PhD *Cran.*, FRAeS, FREng, FCGI Prof., Aerospace Engineering

Savill, Mark, BA *Camb.*, MA *Camb.*, PhD *Camb.* Prof., Computational Aerodynamics Design

Singh, Riti, BSc *Delhi* Prof., Gas Turbine Engineering

Smith, Howard, BSc *City(UK)*, MSc *Cran.*, DPhil *Cran.* Sr. Lectr.

Snow, John E., BSc *S'ton.*, MSc *Cran.* Sr. Lectr.

Stocking, Phil J., MSc *Cran.* Sr. Lectr.; Course Dir.

Tatam, Ralph P., BSc *Exe.*, PhD *CNAA*, DSc *Exe.*, FIP Prof., Engineering Photonics

Thompson, Christopher P., BA *Oxf.*, MSc *Oxf.*, DPhil *Bergen* Prof., Applied Computation

Tirovic, Marco, MSc *Belgrade*, PhD *Belgrade*, FIMechE Sr. Lectr.

Tomlinson, Michael A., BSc *CNAA*, MPhil *CNAA* Sr. Lectr.

Vaughan, Nicholas D., BSc *Lond.*, PhD *Brist.*, FIMechE Prof., Automotive Engineering

Vignjevic, Rade, MSc *Sarajevo*, PhD *Cran.* Prof., Structural Mechanics

Wang, Frank Z., MSc *Plym.* Prof., e-Science and Grid Computing

Whidborne, James F., BA *Camb.*, MSc *UMIST*, PhD *UMIST* Sr. Lectr.

Williams, George, BSc *City(UK)*, MA *Leeds*, PhD *Cran.* Sr. Lectr.

Yeung, H. C., BSc(Eng) *HK*, PhD *Newcastle(UK)* Sr. Lectr.

Zhang, Xiang, PhD *Lond.*, MSc, FRAeS Sr. Lectr.; Course Dir.

Other Staff: 70 Staff Members

Management, School of

Tel: (01234) 751122 Fax: (01234) 751806

Allen, Peter M., BSc *Hull*, PhD *Hull* Prof., Evolutionary Complex Systems

Ambrosini, Veronique L. Sr. Lectr.

Baines, P. R. Sr. Lectr.

Bender, Ruth, BA *Liv.J.Moores*, MBA *Cran.*, PhD *Warw.*, FCA Sr. Lectr.

Bernon, Michael P., BA *Brighton*, MSc *Cran.* Sr. Lectr.

Bourne, Michael C. S., BSc *Birm.*, BCom *Birm.*, MBA *Aston*, PhD *Camb.* Prof., Business Performance

Bowman, Cliff, BA *Liv.*, MBA *Liv.*, PhD *Cran.* Prof., Strategic Management

Braganza, Ashley, MBA *Strath.*, PhD *Cran.* Sr. Lectr.

Buchanan, David A., BA *H-W*, PhD *Edin.*, FRSA, FCIPD Prof., Organisational Behaviour

Burke, Andrew Prof., Entrepreneurship

Butcher, David J., BA *Leeds*, MA *Leeds*, PhD *Brad.* Sr. Lectr.

Christopher, Martin G., BA *Lanc.*, MSc *Brad.*, PhD *Cran.*, FCILT, FCIM Prof., Marketing and Logistics

Clark, Graham R., BSc *Leeds*, MSc *Lond.* Sr. Lectr.

Edwards, Chris, MA *Sheff.*, PhD *Strath.* Prof., Management Information Systems

Glen, John, BSc *Wales*, MSc *Salf.* Sr. Lectr.

Goffin, Keith R. H., BSc *Durh.*, MSc *Aberd.*, PhD *Cran.* Prof., Innovation Management

Grayson, David Dir., Doughty Centre; Prof., Corporate Responsibility

Grundy, Tony N., MA *Camb.*, MBA *City(UK)*, MSc *Lond.*, PhD *Cran.* Sr. Lectr.

Harrison, Alan, MA *Oxf.*, MSc *Oxf.*, PhD *Cran.*, FIEE Dir., Res.; Prof., Operations and Logistics

James, Kim, BSc *Lond.*, PhD *Aston* Dir., DBA; Prof., Executive Learning

Jenkins, Mark Prof., Business Strategy

Kakabadse, Andrew, BSc *Salf.*, MA *Brun.*, PhD *Manc.*, FBPsS, FCMI Prof., International Management Development

Kelliher, Clare, BSc *Sur.*, MA *Warw.*, PhD *Lond.Bus.* Sr. Lectr.

Knox, Simon D., BSc *Sheff.*, PhD *Sheff.* Prof., Brand Marketing

Kwiatkowski, Richard, BSc *Lond.*, MSc *CNAA* Sr. Lectr.

Lambert, Robert D., MSc *Bath* Sr. Lectr.

Levene, Ralph J., BSc *Lond.*, PhD *Lond.* Sr. Lectr.

Maylor, Harvey R., BEng *Brun.*, MPhil *Brun.*, PhD *Cardiff* Sr. Lectr.

Neely, Andrew D., BEng *Nott.*, MA *Camb.*, PhD *Nott.* Prof., Operations Strategy and Performance

Nellis, Joe G., BSc(Econ) *Ulster*, MA *Warw.*, PhD *Cran.* Prof., International Management Economics

Osbaldeston, Michael D., BSc *Liv.*, MBA *Liv.*, FRSA Prof.; Dir.*

Palmer, Roger A., MBA *Cran.*, PhD *Cran.*, FCIM Sr. Lectr.

Parker, David, BSc *Hull*, MSc *Salf.*, PhD *Cran.* Prof., Privatisation and Regulation

Partington, David L., BSc *Manc.*, MSc *Cran.*, PhD *Cran.* Sr. Lectr., Project Management

Peppard, Joseph Prof., Information Systems

Peters, Melvyn J., BTech *Brun.*, MSc *Cran.* Sr. Lectr.

Poshakwale, Sunil Prof., International Finance

Regan, Stephen J., BA *Warw.*, MBA *Warw.* Sr. Lectr.

Rickard, Sean M., BSc *Lond.*, MSc *Lond.*, MBA *Cran.* Sr. Lectr.

Ryals, Lynette J., BA *Oxf.*, MA *Oxf.*, PhD *Cran.*, MBA Prof., Strategic Sales and Account Management

Saw, Richard J., MA *Camb.*, MA *Lanc.* Sr. Lectr.

Schoenberg, Richard J., BSc *E.Anglia*, MBA *Warw.*, PhD *Lond.* Sr. Lectr.

Srikanthan, Sri., MBA Sr. Lectr.

Steele, W. Murray B., BSc *Glas.*, MSc *Glas.*, MBA *Cran.* Sr. Lectr.

Sudarsanam, P. Sudi., BSc *Madr.*, MSc *Madr.*, MSc *City(UK)*, PhD *City(UK)* Prof., Finance and Corporate Control

Sweeney, Mike T., MSc *Bath* Prof., Operations Management

Towriss, John G., BSc *Portsmouth*, MSc *Cran.*, PhD *Cran.* Sr. Lectr.

Tranfield, David R., BA *CNAA*, MA *Leeds*, PhD *CNAA* Prof.

Tyson, Shaun J. J., BA *Lond.*, PhD *Lond.*, FCIPD, FRSA Prof., Human Resource Management

Vinnicombe, Susan M., OBE, MA *Lanc.*, PhD *Manc.*, FRSA Prof., Organisational Behaviour and Diversity Management

Ward, John M., BA *Camb.*, MA *Camb.* Prof., Strategic Information Systems

Wilding, Richard D., BSc *Sheff.*, PhD *Warw.* Prof., Supply Chain Risk Management

Wilson, H., MA *Oxf.*, PhD *Cran.* Prof., Strategic Marketing

Other Staff: 118 Staff Members

SHRIVENHAM SITE

Tel: (01793) 782551 Fax: (01793) 783878

Management and Technology, Defence College of

Tel: (01793) 785434 Fax: (01793) 785768
E-mail: academicreg@cranfield.ac.uk

Akhavan, Jacqueline, BSc *S'ton.*, MPhil *S'ton.*, PhD *S'ton.* Sr. Lectr.

Allsop, Derek F., MSc *City(UK)*, PhD *CNAA* Sr. Lectr.

Barton, Peter C., BSc *Manc.* Sr. Lectr.

Bathe, Mike R., BSc *Reading*, MSc *Sus.* Sr. Lectr.; Head, Operational Analysis, Modelling and Simulation Group

Bellamy, Christopher D., BA *Oxf.*, MA *Lond.*, PhD *Edin.* Prof., Military Science and Doctrine

Bellerby, John M., BSc *York(UK)*, PhD *Camb.* Sr. Lectr.

Blacknell, D., BA *Camb.*, MSc *Lond.*, PhD *Sheff.* Prof., Radar Systems

Braithwaite, Prof. Martin, BSc(Eng) *Lond.*, PhD *Camb.*, FRSChem, FIChemE William Penney Prof., Chemical Physics

Bray, Derek, BEng *Wales*, PhD *Cran.* Sr. Lectr.

Brown, Robert D. Sr. Lectr.

Carr, Karen, MA *Edin.*, MSc *Birm.*, PhD *Birm.* Prof.; Head, Centre for Human Systems

Chivers, H. Prof., Information Systems

Cleary, Laura J., BA *Indiana*, PhD *Glas.* Sr. Lectr.; Dir., Res.

Collins, Brian S., MA *Oxf.*, DPhil *Oxf.*, FBCS, FIEE Prof., Informatics and Simulation

Crowley, Anna B., MA *Oxf.*, MSc *Oxf.*, DPhil *Oxf.* Prof., Ballistics

Davies, N., BSc *Sheff.*, PhD *Sheff.* Sr. Lectr.

Dunbar, David, BA *Open(UK)* Sr. Lectr.

Durodie, William J. L. Sr. Lectr.

Edwards, Mike R., BSc(Eng) *Lond.*, PhD *Lond.*, FIMMM Sr. Lectr.

Fitz-Gerald, Ann M., PhD *Cran.*, MA Reader

Goyder, Hugh G. D., BSc *S'ton.*, PhD *S'ton.* Sr. Lectr.

Griffiths, Hugh, BA *Oxf.*, PhD *Lond.*, DSc *Lond.* Prof.; Principal*

Grint, Keith, BA *Open(UK)*, BA *York(UK)*, PhD *Oxf.* Prof., Defence Leadership

Hameed, Amer Sr. Lectr.

Harrison, A., BA *Open(UK)*, MSc *City(UK)*, PhD *Open(UK)* Sr. Lectr.

Hazell, Paul J., BEng *Leeds*, EngD *Cran.* Sr. Lectr.

Hetherington, Janice I., BSc *Kent*, PhD *Strath.* Sr. Lectr.

Hetherington, John G., MA *Camb.*, PhD *Cran.* Prof., Engineering Design

Holmes, E. Richard, BA *Camb.*, MA *Camb.*, PhD *Reading* Prof., Military and Security Studies

Horsfall, Ian, BSc *Sur.*, PhD *Cran.* Sr. Lectr.

Hughes, Evan J., BEng *Brad.*, MEng *Brad.*, PhD *Cran.* Sr. Lectr.

Hutchinson, Philip, BSc *Durh.*, PhD *Newcastle(UK)*, FREng, FIP Prof., Statistical Fluid Mechanics

Iremonger, Michael J., BSc(Eng) *Lond.*, PhD *Lond.*, FIMechE Sr. Lectr.

Jackson, Sylvia, MBA *Staffs.*, PhD *Cran.* Sr. Lectr.

James, D., BSc *Cardiff*, PhD *Cran.* Sr. Lectr.

Jolly, Colin K., BSc *S'ton.*, MSc *S'ton.*, PhD *S'ton.*, FIStructE Sr. Lectr.

Kirby, Marc L., BA *Warw.*, MSc *Cran.* Sr. Lectr.

Knowles, Kevin, BSc *Exe.*, PhD *Exe.*, FRAeS Prof., Aeromechanical Systems

Lane, David W., BSc *Lough.*, PhD *Cran.* Sr. Lectr.

Lee, Martin P., BA *Lond.*, MSc *Keele*, FBCS Sr. Lectr.

Luk, Patrick C., MPhil *Sheff.*, PhD *Glam.* Sr. Lectr.

Matthews, Ron G., BSc *Aston*, MSc *Wales*, MBA *Warw.*, PhD *Glas.* Academic Leader; Prof., Defence Economics

Mays, Geoff C., BSc *Brist.*, PhD *Dund.*, FICE Prof., Civil Engineering

Moore, David, MBA *Wales* Sr. Lectr.

Morrison, Keith, BSc *Leic.*, PhD *St And.* Sr. Lectr.

Moss, Peter J., BSc *Lond.*, PhD *Cran.* Sr. Lectr.

Neal, Derrick J., BE *Kent*, MBA *Cran.*, PhD *Kent* Prof., Defence Strategic Change

Ormondroyd, Richard F., BEng *Sheff.*, PhD *Sheff.* Prof., Communications and Wireless Networks

Peck, Helen L., PhD *Cran.* Sr. Lectr., Corporate and Supply Chain Risk

Picton, R. S., BSc *Lond.*, MSc *Leeds* Sr. Lectr.

Purdy, David J., BSc *Leeds*, PhD *Cran.* Sr. Lectr.

Reid, Stuart C., BSc *S'ton.*, MSc *Cardiff*, PhD *Glam.* Sr. Lectr.

Richardson, Mark A. Sr. Lectr.

Rogers, Keith D., BSc *Wales*, PhD *Wales* Reader

Sammes, Tony J., BSc *Lond.*, MPhil *Lond.*, PhD *Lond.* Prof., Computer Science

Sastry, Venkat V. S., BSc *Madr.*, MSc *Madr.*, PhD *B'lore.* Sr. Lectr.
Sayle, Dean C. Sr. Lectr.
Scott, Bernard C., MSc *Lond.* Sr. Lectr.
Simpson-Horn, G., MSc *Cran.* Sr. Lectr.
Smith, Jeremy D., BSc *Oxf.* Sr. Lectr.
Stacey, Barry, MSc *Birm.*, PhD *Birm.* Sr. Lectr.
Szmelter, Joanne M., PhD *Wales* Sr. Lectr.
Taylor, Trevor, BSc *Lond.*, MA *Lehigh*, PhD *Lond.* Prof.
Tsourdos, Antonios Sr. Lectr.
Wallace, Ian G., BSc *H-W*, PhD *H-W*, FRSChem Prof.
Walters, Bob, BSc *Leeds*, PhD *Cran.* Sr. Lectr.
White, Brian A., BSc *Leic.*, MSc *UMIST*, PhD *UMIST* Prof., Control and Guidance
Whitford, Ray, BSc *CNAA* Sr. Lectr.
Whitworth, Ian R., MA *Camb.* Sr. Lectr.
Witty, Robert W., BTech *Brun.*, PhD *Brun.*, FREng, FIEE, FBCS Prof., Information Systems Engineering
Yuen, Peter, PhD *Lond.* Sr. Lectr.
Zioupos, Peter, BSc *Ioannina*, PhD *Strath.* Sr. Lectr.

Other Staff: 297 Staff Members

CONTACT OFFICERS

Accommodation. Facilities Director: Oxenham, Andrew J., BSc *W.England* (E-mail: c.major@cranfield.ac.uk)
Archives. Archivist: Harrington, John, MA *Lond.* (E-mail: j.harrington@cranfield.ac.uk)
Computing services. Director, IT Department: Lusignani, Gio (E-mail: g.lusignani@cranfield.ac.uk)
Computing services. Acting Director, Computer Centre: Jeffrey, Howard (E-mail: h.jeffrey@cranfield.ac.uk)
Estates and buildings/works and services. Facilities Director: Oxenham, Andrew J., BSc *W.England* (E-mail: c.major@cranfield.ac.uk)
Finance. Director of Finance: Aspinall, Philip J., BA *Sheff.* (E-mail: p.aspinall@cranfield.ac.uk)
Library (chief librarian). University Librarian: Woodward, Hazel M., BA *CNAA*, PhD *Lough.* (E-mail: h.woodward@cranfield.ac.uk)

Personnel/human resources. Director of Human Resources and Development and Acting Secretary: Altman, Ruth (E-mail: r.altman@cranfield.ac.uk)
Purchasing. Facilities Director: Oxenham, Andrew J., BSc *W.England* (E-mail: c.major@cranfield.ac.uk)
Security. Facilities Director: Oxenham, Andrew J., BSc *W.England* (E-mail: c.major@cranfield.ac.uk)

CAMPUS/COLLEGE HEADS

Shrivenham Site, Cranfield University, Defence College of Management and Technology, Shrivenham, Swindon, Wiltshire, England SN6 8LA. (Tel: (01793) 782551; Fax: (01793) 783878) Principal: Griffiths, Prof. Hugh, BA *Oxf.*, PhD *Lond.*, DSc *Lond.*

[*Information supplied by the institution as at 24 October 2007, and edited by the ACU*]

UNIVERSITY FOR THE CREATIVE ARTS

Postal Address: Falkner Road, Farnham, Surrey, England GU9 7DS
Telephone: (01252) 722441 **Fax:** (01252) 892616
URL: http://www.ucreative.ac.uk

RECTOR*—Thomas, Prof. Elaine

UNIVERSITY OF CUMBRIA

Postal Address: Fusehill Street, Carlisle, England CA1 2HH
Telephone: (01228) 616234 **Fax:** (01228) 616235
URL: http://www.cumbria.ac.uk/

VICE-CHANCELLOR*—Carr, Prof. Chris, BCL MA

DE MONTFORT UNIVERSITY

Founded 1992

Postal Address: The Gateway, Leicester, England LE1 9BH
Telephone: (0116) 255 1551 **Fax:** (0116) 257 7515 **E-mail:** enquiry@dmu.ac.uk
URL: http://www.dmu.ac.uk

VICE-CHANCELLOR*—Tasker, Prof. Philip W., BSc *Birm.*, PhD *Birm.*, FIP, FRSChem
ACADEMIC REGISTRAR‡—Critchlow, Eugene, BA *Leic.*, MA *Sheff.*

UNIVERSITY OF DERBY

Founded 1993

Postal Address: Kedleston Road, Derby, England DE22 1GB
Telephone: (01332) 590500 **Fax:** (01332) 597731 **E-mail:** postmaster@derby.ac.uk
URL: http://www.derby.ac.uk

VICE-CHANCELLOR*—Coyne, Prof. John, BA *Nott.*
DIRECTOR OF STUDENT SUPPORT AND INFORMATION SERVICES‡—Hughes, June

UNIVERSITY OF DUNDEE

Founded 1967

Postal Address: Dundee, Scotland DD1 4HN
Telephone: (01382) 384000 **Fax:** (01382) 201604
URL: http://www.dundee.ac.uk

PRINCIPAL AND VICE-CHANCELLOR*—Langlands, Sir Alan, KT, BSc *Glas.*, DUniv *Glas.*, FRCSEd, FRSEd, FRCPEd,
FRCPGlas, FRCGP, FIA, FFPHM, FRCP, FCGI
SECRETARY OF THE UNIVERSITY‡—Duncan, David, MA *Aberd.*, MA *Qu.*, PhD *Qu.*

DURHAM UNIVERSITY

Founded 1832

Member of the Association of Commonwealth Universities

Postal Address: University Office, Old Elvet, Durham, England DH1 3HP
Telephone: (0191) 334 2000 **Fax:** (0191) 334 6250
URL: http://www.dur.ac.uk

VICE-CHANCELLOR AND WARDEN*—Higgins, Prof. Christopher F., BSc *Durh.*, PhD *Durh.*, FRSA, FMedSci, FRSEd, FAE
PRO-VICE-CHANCELLOR (REGIONAL STRATEGY AND QUEEN'S CAMPUS)—Hudson, Prof. Raymond, BA *Brist.*, PhD *Brist.*, DSc *Brist.*, FBA
PRO-VICE-CHANCELLOR (RESEARCH)—Stirling, Prof. W. James, CBE, MA *Camb.*, PhD *Camb.*, FIP, FRS
PRO-VICE-CHANCELLOR (LEARNING AND TEACHING)—(vacant)
EXECUTIVE DEAN (FACULTY OF ARTS AND HUMANITIES)—Kunin, Prof. Seth D., BA *Col.*, MA *Jewish Theol.Sem.*, PhD *Camb.*
EXECUTIVE DEAN (FACULTY OF SCIENCE)—Orford, Keith J., TD, BSc *Durh.*, PhD *Durh.*, FIP, FRAS
EXECUTIVE DEAN (FACULTY OF SOCIAL SCIENCES AND HEALTH)—Forster, Prof. Anthony, BA *Hull*, MPhil *Oxf.*, DPhil *Oxf.*
REGISTRAR AND SECRETARY‡—(vacant)
TREASURER—Lubacz, Paulina, BA *CNAA*

GENERAL INFORMATION

History. The university was founded in Durham in 1832. From 1852, until Newcastle became a separate university in 1963, there were also students in Newcastle upon Tyne.

Situated in Durham City with a campus at Stockton on Tees (University of Durham Queen's Campus). All colleges are situated in Durham apart from George Stephenson College and John Snow College which are situated in Stockton.

Admission to first degree courses (see also United Kingdom Introduction). Through Universities and Colleges Admissions Service (UCAS). UK nationals: normally a minimum of 3 passes at General Certificate of Education (GCE) A level and 2 at General Certificate of Secondary Education (GCSE). Equivalent qualifications, eg Vocational Certificate of Education (VCE) or BTEC National Diploma, are acceptable subject to specific prerequisites for individual programmes. Mature applicants (aged over 21) are considered individually. International students: high levels in International Baccalaureate or European Baccalaureate or, in many cases, qualifications acceptable for university entrance in applicant's own country. Minimum English language qualifications also apply.

First Degrees (see also United Kingdom Directory to Subjects of Study). BA, BEng, BSc, LLB, MChem, MEng, MMath, MPhys, MSci.

Courses including a foreign language or European studies normally last 3 years plus 1 year abroad.

Length of course. Full-time: BA, BEng, BSc, LLB: 3 years; MChem, MEng, MMath, MPhys, MSci: 4 years. Part-time: BA, BSc: 6–9 years.

Higher Degrees (see also United Kingdom Directory to Subjects of Study).

Master's. LLM, MA, MBA, MEd, MJur, MLitt, MMus, MPhil, MProf, MSc, MTh.

Admission. Applicants for admission must normally hold a good honours degree in an appropriate subject.

All degrees except LLM may be taken by combinations of full-time and part-time study.

Length of course. Full-time: LLM, MA, MBA, MJur, MProf, MSc, MTh: 1 year; MEd, MLitt, MMus, MPhil: 2 years. Part-time: MTh: 1–2 years; MA, MBA, MJur, MProf, MSc: 2 years; MEd, MLitt, MMus, MPhil: 4 years. By *distance learning*: MBA: 2–8 years.

Doctoral. DBA, DD, DLitt, DMin, DMus, DSc, EdD, PhD, PhD(DCE).

Admission. DD, DLitt, DMus, DSc: awarded on published work.

All degrees except DD, DLitt, DMus and DSc may be taken by combinations of full-time and part-time study.

Length of course. Full-time: DBA, DMin, EdD, PhD, PhD(DCE): 3 years. Part-time: DBA, DMin, EdD, PhD, PhD(DCE): 6 years.

Libraries. Volumes: 1,498,000. Periodicals subscribed to: 6000. Special collections: archives of Durham Cathedral (monastic to 1539) and Diocese; Earl Grey (political); mediaeval manuscripts; north-east local collection (including family papers); Sudan archive (political).

Academic Awards (2005–2006). 750 awards ranging in value from £300 to £25,050.

Academic Year (2007–2008). Three terms: 3 October–12 December; 14 January–14 March; 21 April–20 June.

Income (2006–2007). Total, £193,704,000.

Statistics. Staff (2006–2007): 3516 (1732 academic, 1784 non-academic). Students (2006–2007): full-time 13,422 (6499 men, 6923 women); part-time 1632 (952 men, 680 women); international 1964 (1065 men, 899 women); distance education/external 494 (356 men, 138 women); undergraduate 11,497 (5535 men, 5962 women); master's 1479 (705 men, 774 women); doctoral 1027 (629 men, 398 women).

FACULTIES/SCHOOLS

Arts and Humanities
Tel: (0191) 334 2904 Fax: (0191) 334 2905
Dean: Kunin, Prof. Seth D., BA *Col.*, MA *Jewish Theol.Sem.*, PhD *Camb.*
Faculty Administrator: Child, Victoria

Postgraduate Studies
Tel: (0191) 334 4668 Fax: (0191) 334 4578
Dean of the Graduate School: Halliday, Douglas P., BSc *Edin.*, PhD *Nott.*
Personal Assistant: McAlhone, Carolyn

Science
Tel: (0191) 334 1017 Fax: (0191) 334 1018
Dean: Orford, Keith J., TD, BSc *Durh.*, PhD *Durh.*, FIP, FRAS
Faculty Administrator: Cutmore, Janet

Social Sciences and Health
Tel: (0191) 334 2904 Fax: (0191) 334 2905
Dean: Forster, Prof. Anthony, BA *Hull*, MPhil *Oxf.*, DPhil *Oxf.*
Executive Assistant: Allison, Margaret E.

ACADEMIC UNITS

Anthropology

Tel: (0191) 334 6100 Fax: (0191) 334 6101
E-mail: anthropology@durham.ac.uk

Ball, Helen L., BSc CNAA, MA Mass., PhD Mass. Prof.

Barton, Robert A., BSc Brist., MSc Lond., PhD St And. Prof.; Head*

Bell, Sandra, BA Newcastle(UK), PhD Durh. Sr. Lectr.

Bentley, Gillian, BA Lond., MA Chic., PhD Chic. Prof.

Bilsborough, Alan, MA Camb., DPhil Oxf. Prof.

Carrithers, Michael B., MA Conn., DPhil Oxf. Prof.

Collins, Peter J., BSc Wales, PhD Manc. Sr. Lectr.

Edgar, Iain R., BA York(UK), MPhil Durh., PhD Keele Sr. Lectr.

Hampshire, Katherine R., BA Oxf., MSc Lond., PhD Lond. Sr. Lectr.

Hill, Russell A., BSc Brist., MPhil Camb., PhD Liv. Reader

Layton, Robert H., BSc Lond., MPhil Lond., DPhil Sus. Prof.

Lyon, Stephen M., BSc Lond., PhD Kent Sr. Lectr.

Panter-Brick, Catherine, MA Oxf., MSc Oxf., DPhil Oxf. Prof.

Russell, Andrew J., BA Oxf., MS Penn., DPhil Oxf. Sr. Lectr.

Sant Cassia, Paul, BA Malta, PhD Camb. Reader

Sillitoe, Paul, MA Durh., MSc Lond., MSc Newcastle(UK), PhD Camb., ScD Camb. Prof.

Simpson, Robert, BA Durh., PhD Durh. Reader

Smith, Malcolm T., BSc Nott., MSc Liv., PhD Durh. Sr. Lectr.

Other Staff: 10 Lectrs.; 1 Sr. Res. Fellow

Research: development (participation, indigenous knowledge, local rights); environmental anthropology (ethnoscience, human ecology, conservation); evolutionary anthropology (primates, genetics, behavioural biology); medical anthropology (infant-child, international health); public culture (nationalism, ethnicity, migration, globalisation)

Applied Social Sciences, School of

Tel: (0191) 334 6820 Fax: (0191) 334 6821

Bailey, Diane, BSc Warw., MSc Oxf. Reader

Banks, Sarah J., MA Edin., PhD Reading Prof., Community and Youth Work

Blackman, Timothy J., BA Durh., PhD Durh. Prof.

Boyne, Roy D., BSocSc Birm., PhD Leeds Prof.

Byrne, David S., BA Newcastle(UK), MSc(Econ) Lond., PhD Durh. Prof.

Dominelli, Lena, BA S.Fraser, MA Sus., DPhil Sus. Prof.

Giulianotti, Richard, MA Aberd., MLitt Aberd., PhD Aberd. Prof.

Hackett, Simon J., BA Hull, MA Manc. Reader; Head*

Jack, Gordon, BSc Sheff., MSc Oxf. Reader

McKay, Jim, BA McM., BPE McM., MSc Wat., PhD ANU Prof.

Palmer, Catherine, PhD Adel. Reader

Phoenix, Joanna B., BSc Brist., MSc Brist., PhD Bath Reader

Williams, Robin, BSc(Soc) Lond. Prof.

Other Staff: 14 Lectrs.; 3 Res. Fellows

Research: crime, policing and interpersonal violence; identity, technologies, professional ethics and society; innovative research methodologies; international social, youth and community work; sport, health, social policy

Archaeology

Tel: (0191) 334 1100 Fax: (0191) 334 1101
E-mail: enquiries.arch@durham.ac.uk

Bailiff, Ian K., BSc Sus., MSc Oxf. Prof.

Caple, Christopher, BSc Wales, PhD Brad. Sr. Lectr.

Chapman, John C., BA Lond., PhD Lond. Reader

Coningham, Robin, BA Camb., PhD Camb. Prof.; Head*

Diaz-Andreu, A. Margarita, MA Madrid, PhD Madrid Sr. Lectr.

Gerrard, Christopher M., BA Brist., PhD Brist., FSA Reader

Graves, C. Pamela, MA Glas., PhD Glas. Sr. Lectr.

Hingley, Richard, BA Durh., PhD S'ton. Reader

Millard, Andrew R., BA Oxf., DPhil Oxf. Sr. Lectr.

Philip, Graham, MA Edin., PhD Edin. Prof.

Richards, Michael, BA S.Fraser, MA S.Fraser, DPhil Oxf. Prof.†

Roberts, Charlotte A., BA Leic., MA Sheff., PhD Brad. Prof.

Rowley-Conwy, Peter A., MA Camb., PhD Camb. Prof.

Scarre, Christopher, BA Camb., PhD Camb. Prof.

Skeates, Robin G., BA Lond., DPhil Oxf. Sr. Lectr.

White, Mark J., BA Lond., PhD Camb. Sr. Lectr.

Wilkinson, Tony, BSc Lond., MSc W.Ont. Prof.

Other Staff: 9 Lectrs.; 2 Res. Fellows

Research: archaeology from late antiquity to capitalism; bioarchaeology; emergence of complex societies in prehistory; Graeco-Roman world and its neighbours; science-based conservation and archaeology

Biological and Biomedical Sciences

Tel: (0191) 334 1200 Fax: (0191) 334 1201
E-mail: biosci.office@durham.ac.uk

Baxter, Robert, BSc Manc., PhD Manc. Sr. Lectr.

Benham, Adam, BA Oxf., MSc Oxf., PhD Lond. Sr. Lectr.

Croy, Ronald R. D., BSc Edin., PhD Aberd. Reader

Edwards, Robert, BSc Bath, PhD Lond. Prof.

Gatehouse, John A., BA Oxf., DPhil Oxf. Reader

Gates, Phillip J., BA Oxf., PhD Durh. Sr. Lectr.

Hoelzel, A. Rus, BA Portland, MSc Sus., PhD Camb. Prof.

Hole, Nicholas, BSc Durh., PhD Liv. Sr. Lectr.

Huntley, Brian, MA Camb., PhD Camb. Prof.

Hussey, Patrick J., BSc Liv., PhD Kent Prof., Plant Molecular Cell Biology

Hutchison, Christopher J., BSc Sus., PhD Lond. Prof., Animal Cell Biology; Head*

Jahoda, Colin A. B., BSc Dund., PhD Dund. Prof.

Knight, Marc R., BSc Durh., PhD Glas. Prof.

Lindsay, Steven W., BSc Wales, PhD Lond. Prof.

Lindsey, Keith, BA Oxf., PhD Edin. Prof., Plant Molecular Biology

Lucas, Martyn C., BSc Lond., PhD Aberd. Sr. Lectr.

Pohl, Ehmke, PhD Gött. Reader, Biology and Chemistry

Przyborski, Stefan A., BSc Sheff., PhD Sheff. Reader

Quinlan, Roy A., BSc Kent, PhD Kent Prof., Biomedical Sciences

Sharples, Gary J., BSc Glas., PhD Nott. Sr. Lectr.

Slabas, Antoni R., BSc Lond., DPhil Oxf. Prof., Plant Sciences

Walmsley, Adrian R., BSc Lanc., PhD Manc. Prof., Infectious Diseases

Watson, Martin D., BSc S'ton., PhD S'ton. Sr. Lectr.

Other Staff: 16 Lectrs.; 1 Res. Fellow

Research: cytoskeleton and cell architecture; ecology and evolutionary biology; molecular biology of infectious diseases; plant development and metabolic engineering; stem cell biology

Chemistry

Tel: (0191) 334 2076 Fax: (0191) 384 4737
E-mail: chemistry.office@durham.ac.uk

Badyal, Jas-Pal S., BA Camb., PhD Camb. Prof.

Bain, Colin D., BA Camb., PhD Harv., FRSChem Prof.

Beeby, Andrew, BSc E.Anglia, PhD E.Anglia Reader

Bryce, Martin R., BSc CNAA, DPhil York(UK) Prof.

Cameron, Neil R., BSc Strath., PhD Strath. Reader

Clarke, Nigel, BSc Sheff., PhD Sheff. Sr. Lectr.

Cooper, Sharon J., BSc Brist., PhD Brist. Sr. Lectr.

Dillon, Keith B., MA Oxf., DPhil Oxf. Reader

Dyer, Philip W., BSc Durh., PhD Durh. Sr. Lectr.

Evans, John S. O., MA Oxf., DPhil Oxf. Prof.

Howard, Judith A. K., CBE, DSc Brist., DPhil Oxf., FRS, FRSChem Prof.; Head*

Hughes, Andrew K., MA Oxf., DPhil Oxf. Sr. Lectr.

Hutson, Jeremy M., MA Oxf., DPhil Oxf. Prof.

Kataky, Ritu, BEd NE Hill, BSc Gauh., MSc IIT Delhi, PhD Newcastle(UK), FRSChem Reader

Khosravi, Ezat, BSc Sus., BSc Reader

Low, Paul J., BSc Adel., PhD Adel. Reader

Marder, Todd B., BSc M.I.T., PhD Calif. Prof.

Parker, David, MA Oxf., DPhil Oxf., FRS, FRSChem Prof.

Pohl, Ehmke, PhD Gött. Reader, Chemistry and Biology

Prassides, Kosmas, MA Oxf., DPhil Oxf. Prof.

Sandford, Graham, BSc Durh., PhD Durh. Sr. Lectr.

Steed, Jonathan W., BSc Lond., PhD Lond., FRSChem Prof.

Steel, Patrick G., MA Oxf., DPhil Oxf. Sr. Lectr.

Tozer, David J., BA Camb., PhD Camb. Reader

Whiting, Andrew, BSc Newcastle(UK), PhD Newcastle(UK) Reader

Williams, J. A. Gareth, MA Oxf., PhD Durh. Sr. Lectr.

Wilson, Mark R., BSc Sheff., PhD Sheff. Reader

Other Staff: 11 Lectrs.; 4 Res. Fellows

Research: biological chemistry; inorganic materials, polymers, supramolecular chemistry; organic and inorganic synthesis and reactivity; spectroscopy and dynamics (gases, solutions, interfaces); theoretical and computational chemistry

Classics and Ancient History

Tel: (0191) 334 1670 Fax: (0191) 334 1671
E-mail: classics.dept@durham.ac.uk

Boys-Stones, George R., MA Camb., DPhil Oxf. Sr. Lectr.

Ceccarelli, Paola Reader

Gildenhard, Ingo, PhD Prin. Reader

Graziosi, Barbara, BA Oxf., MSt Oxf., PhD Camb. Sr. Lectr.

Harris, Edward M., BA Oxf., MA Harv., PhD Harv. Prof.; Head*

Haubold, Johannes H., MPhil Camb., PhD Camb. Sr. Lectr.

Hunt, E. David, MA Oxf., DPhil Oxf. Sr. Lectr.

Rowe, Christopher J., MA Camb., PhD Camb. Prof., Greek

Other Staff: 10 Lectrs.

Research: ancient philosophy; epic traditions; Greek social and cultural history; the ancient Near East; the classical tradition and reception

Computer Science

Tel: (0191) 334 1700 Fax: (0191) 334 1701
E-mail: computer.science@durham.ac.uk

Broersma, Hajo J., MSc T.H.Twente, PhD T.H.Twente Prof.

Budgen, David, BSc Durh., PhD Durh. Prof.; Head*

Burd, Elizabeth L., BEd CNAA, MSc York(UK), DPhil York(UK), PhD Durh. Reader

Gallagher, Keith B., BA Penn., MSc Mich., PhD Maryland Sr. Lectr.

Holliman, Nicolas S., BSc Durh., PhD Leeds Sr. Lectr.

Krokhin, Andrei, MSc Ural State, PhD Ural State Prof.

Lau, Rynson W. H., BSc Kent, PhD Camb. Prof.

Munro, Malcolm, BSc Leic., MSc Liv. Prof.

Stewart, Iain A., MA Oxf., PhD Lond. Prof.

Other Staff: 14 Lectrs.

Research: algorithms and complexity; computer graphics and visualisation; software engineering; technology-enhanced learning; web intelligence, services and agents

Durham Business School

Tel: (0191) 334 5200 Fax: (0191) 334 5201
E-mail: dbs.reception@durham.ac.uk
Andriani, Pierpaolo, MSc *Bari*, MBA *Durh.*   Sr. Lectr.
Antoniou, Antonios, BA *CNAA*, MSc *Lond.*, DPhil *York(UK)*   Prof., Economics and Finance
Ashworth, John S., BA(Econ) *Manc.*, MA(Econ) *Manc.*   Prof.†, Economics and Finance
Bannerjee, Anurag, BS *Calc.*, MS *Delhi*, PhD *Tilburg*   Reader
Barr, David G., BSc *Lond.*, MSc *Lond.*, PhD *Lond.*   Prof.†
Basu, Parantap, MPhil *Calc.*, PhD *Calif.*   Prof., Economics
Bozionelos, Nikos, MA *Liv.*, MPhil *Cran.*, PhD *Strath.*   Prof.
Carroll, Glen R., BA *Indiana*, MA *Stan.*, PhD *Stan.*   Prof.†
Clark, Timothy, BA *Leic.*, PhD *De Mont.*   Prof., Organisational Behaviour
Darnell, Adrian C., BA *Durh.*, MA *Warw.*   Prof.†, Economics and Finance
Dixon, Robert, MA *Leic.*   Prof., Managerial Accounting
Galariotis, Emilios, MA *Middx.*   Sr. Lectr.
Greatbatch, David, BA *Warw.*, PhD *Warw.*   Prof.†
Hadri, Kaddour, MSc *Birm.*, MA *Manc.*, PhD *Exe.*   Prof.
Hamilton, Peter M., MA *Glas.*, MSc *UMIST*, PhD *Lond.*   Sr. Lectr.
Hannon, Michael T., AB *Worcester State*, MA *N.Carolina*, PhD *N.Carolina*   Prof.†
Harrison, Glenn, BEcon *Monash*, MEcon *Monash*, MA *Calif.*, PhD *Calif.*   Prof.
Holmes, Philip R., BA *CNAA*, MA *Newcastle(UK)*, PhD *Brun.*   Prof., Economics and Finance
Jessop, Alan T., BSc *Leeds*, MSc *Lond.*, PhD *H-W*   Sr. Lectr.
Laffin, Martin, BA *Sus.*, PhD *Brad.*   Prof., Public Policy and Management
Lau, Morten I., BSc *Copenhagen*, MSc *Tilburg*, PhD *Copenhagen*   Reader
McKendrick, David G., AB *Calif.*, MA *Calif.*, PhD *Calif.*   Prof., Strategy
Moore, Geoffrey A., BA *Camb.*, MSc *Durh.*, MA *Camb.*   Prof.
Negro, Giacomo, BA *Bocconi*, PhD *Bocconi*   Sr. Lectr.
Parker, Simon C., BSc(Econ) *Wales*, PhD *Durh.*   Prof., Entrepreneurship
Paudyal, Krishna, MBAC *Tribhuvan*, MSc *Strath.*, PhD *Strath.*   Prof.
Pescetto, Gioia M. R., Dott *Turin*, MA *Maryland*, PhD *Durh.*   Sr. Lectr.
Polos, Laszlo, PhD *Bud.*   Prof.
Read, Daniel, BA *Ott.*, MA *Br.Col.*, PhD *Tor.*   Prof., Psychology
Redman, Tom, BSc *UMIST*, MSc *Salf.*   Prof.
Robson, Martin T., BA *Newcastle(UK)*, MA *Warw.*, PhD *Sheff.*   Sr. Lectr.
Robson, Paul J. A., BA *Sund.*, MSc *York(UK)*, MPhil *Camb.*, PhD *Camb.*   Reader
Swaninathan, Anand, PhD *Calif.*   Prof.†
van Witteloostuijn, Arjen, BSc *Gron.*, PhD *Maastricht*   Prof., Strategy
Wade, James B., MBA *Texas*, PhD *Calif.*   Prof.†
Watson, Robert, BA *Hull*, PhD *Manc.*   Prof., Financial Management
Westhead, Paul, BA *Wales*, PhD *Wales*   Prof.
Wright, George, BSc *Lond.*, MPhil *Brun.*, PhD *Brun.*   Prof., Management
Other Staff: 23 Lectrs.
Research: accounting, applied economics and applied econometrics; financial economics, corporate finance, international finance, behavioural finance; organisation theory, organisational behaviour, organisational ecology; small business, entrepreneurship and enterprise development; strategy, decision-making, public policy and management

Earth Sciences

Tel: (0191) 334 2300 Fax: (0191) 334 2301
E-mail: durham.geolsci@durham.ac.uk
Allen, Mark, BSc *Durh.*, PhD *Leic.*   Reader
Armstrong, Howard A., MSc *Sheff.*, PhD *Nott.*   Sr. Lectr.
Davidson, Jon P., BSc *Durh.*, PhD *Leeds*   Prof., Earth Sciences
Davies, Richard J., BSc *Reading*, PhD *Edin.*   Prof.
Foulger, Gillian R., MA *Camb.*, MSc *Durh.*, PhD *Durh.*   Prof.
Goulty, Neil R., MA *Oxf.*, PhD *Camb.*   Prof.
Holdsworth, Robert E., BSc *Liv.*, PhD *Leeds*, FGS   Prof.; Head*
Macpherson, Colin G., BSc *Edin.*, PhD *Lond.*   Sr. Lectr.
McCaffrey, Kenneth J. W., BSc *Belf.*, PhD *Durh.*   Sr. Lectr.
Milne, Glenn A., BSc *Edin.*, MSc *Tor.*, PhD *Tor.*   Reader
Niu, Yaoling, BSc *Lanzhou*, MS *Alabama*, PhD *Hawaii*   Prof.
Pearson, D. Graham, BSc *Lond.*, PhD *Leeds*   Prof.
Peirce, Christine, BSc *Wales*, PhD *Camb.*   Reader
Searle, Roger C., MA *Camb.*, PhD *Newcastle(UK)*   Prof., Geophysics
Tucker, Maurice E., BSc *Durh.*, PhD *Reading*, FGS   Prof.
Worrall, Fred, BA *Camb.*, PhD *Reading*   Reader
Other Staff: 11 Lectrs.; 1 Res. Fellow
Research: earth systems; geochemistry, geophysics, structural and petroleum geology; life cycle of the lithosphere; structures and geofluids; the convecting mantle

Education, School of

Tel: (0191) 334 8310 Fax: (0191) 334 8311
Bagley, Carl A., BSc *Brad.*, PhD *Open(UK)*   Prof.
Beverton, Susan L., BA *Hull*, MA *Reading*, PhD *CNAA*   Sr. Lectr.
Byram, Michael S., MA *Camb.*, PhD *Camb.*   Prof.
Coe, Robert, BA *Oxf.*, MPhil *Camb.*, PhD *Durh.*   Reader
Cooper, Barry, BA *Camb.*, MA *Sus.*, DPhil *Sus.*   Prof.
Elliot, Julian, BEd *Durh.*, MA *Durh.*, PhD *Durh.*   Prof.
Fleming, Michael P., BA *Durh.*, PhD *Durh.*   Sr. Lectr.
Gott, Richard, BSc *Leeds*, MA *Leeds*, PhD *Leic.*   Prof.
Harries, Anthony V., BSc *Brist.*, MEd *Brist.*, PhD *Brist.*   Sr. Lectr.
Higgins, Steven E., BA *Oxf.*, PhD *Newcastle(UK)*   Prof.
Hillyard, S.   Sr. Lectr.
Johnson, Philip M., BSc *Lond.*, PhD *Durh.*   Sr. Lectr.
Meyer, Jan H. F., BSc *Witw.*, MSc *Witw.*, PhD *Witw.*   Prof.; Dir., Centre for Learning, Teaching and Res. in Higher Educn.
Newton, Lynn D., BEd *Durh.*, MA *Durh.*, PhD *Newcastle(UK)*   Prof.; Head*
Palmer-Cooper, Joy A., BEd *Birm.*, MEd *Birm.*, PhD *Durh.*, MA *Stan.*   Prof.
Riddick, Barbara, BSc *Exe.*, MA *Nott.*   Sr. Lectr.
Ridgway, James E., BSc *Sheff.*, MSc *Stir.*, PhD *Lanc.*   Prof.
Roberts, Rosalyn, BSc *Brist.*, MEd *Brist.*   Sr. Lectr.
Simpson, Adrian, BSc   Reader
Smith, Richard D., BA *Oxf.*, MEd *Birm.*   Prof.
Stevens, David J., BA *Middx.*, MPhil *Open(UK)*, MEd *Camb.*   Sr. Lectr.
Tymms, Peter B., MA *Camb.*, MEd *Newcastle(UK)*, PhD *Camb.*   Prof.
Other Staff: 12 Lectrs.
Research: assessment and value-added in schools; curriculum analysis; intercultural studies in education; maths and science education; policy studies in education

Engineering, School of

Tel: (0191) 334 2400 Fax: (0191) 334 2408
Augarde, Charles E., BSc *Lanc.*, MSc *H-W*, PhD *Oxf.*   Sr. Lectr.
Bennett, Keith H., BSc *Manc.*, MSc *Manc.*, PhD *Manc.*, FIEE   Prof.
Bumby, James R., BSc *Durh.*, PhD *Durh.*   Reader
Crouch, Roger, BSc *CNAA*, MSc *Lond.*, PhD *Manc.*   Prof.
Dominy, Robert G., BSc *CNAA*, PhD *Lond.*   Reader
Green, Sarah M., BEng *Sheff.*, PhD *Nott.*   Sr. Lectr.
He, Li, MSc *Beijing*, PhD *Camb.*   Prof.
Petty, Michael C., PhD *Lond.*, DSc *Sus.*, FIEE   Prof.
Purvis, Alan, BSc *Leeds*, PhD *Camb.*   Prof.
Salous, Sana, BSc *Beirut*, MSc *Birm.*, DPhil *Birm.*   Prof., Communications Engineering
Scott, Richard H., MSc *Lond.*, PhD *Durh.*, FIStructE   Reader
Swift, James S., BSc *Leeds*   Sr. Lectr.
Tavner, Peter, MA *Camb.*, PhD *S'ton.*   Prof., New and Renewable Energy; Head*
Taylor, Philip C., BEng *Liv.*, MSc *Manc.*, EngD *Manc.*   Sr. Lectr.
Toll, David G., BSc *Wales*, PhD *Lond.*   Sr. Lectr.
Trevelyan, Jonathan, BSc *Brist.*, PhD *Brist.*   Reader
Unsworth, Anthony, BSc *Salf.*, MSc *Leeds*, PhD *Leeds*, DEng *Leeds*, FIMechE   Prof.
Vitanov, Valentin, MEng MSc PhD   Prof.
Wood, David, BSc *Hull*, PhD *Hull*   Prof.
Other Staff: 16 Lectrs.
Research: biomedical engineering; communications networks and renewable energy; computational fluid and solid mechanics; industrial automation and robotics; molecular and nanoscale electronics

English Studies

Tel: (0191) 334 2500 Fax: (0191) 334 2501
Clark, Timothy J. A., BA *Oxf.*, DPhil *Oxf.*   Prof.
Clemit, Pamela A., MPhil *Oxf.*, DPhil *Oxf.*   Prof.
James, Simon J., BA *Camb.*, PhD *Camb.*   Sr. Lectr.
Knights, Pamela E., BA *Durh.*, MA *Keele*, PhD *Keele*   Sr. Lectr.
McKinnell, John S., MA *Oxf.*   Prof.
O'Neill, Michael S. C., MA *Oxf.*, DPhil *Oxf.*   Prof.
Reeves, Gareth E., BA *Oxf.*, MA *Stan.*, PhD *Stan.*   Reader
Regan, Stephen, BA *Hull*, PhD *Tor.*   Prof.
Sandy, Mark R., BA *Wales*, MA *Durh.*, PhD *Durh.*   Sr. Lectr.
Saunders, Corrine J., MA *Tor.*, DPhil *Oxf.*   Prof.
Shell, Alison E. M., BA *Oxf.*, DPhil *Oxf.*   Reader
Waugh, Patricia, BA *Birm.*, PhD *Birm.*   Prof.; Head*
Wilson, Penelope B., MA *Edin.*, DPhil *Oxf.*   Reader†
Other Staff: 14 Lectrs.; 1 Reader†
Research: editing (all periods from mediaeval to modern); literary theory, literature, science and medicine; mediaeval literatures (Chaucer, Old Norse, romance, mediaeval texts); romantic and Victorian poetry and prose; twentieth-century and contemporary poetry and prose

Geography

Tel: (0191) 334 1800 Fax: (0191) 334 1801
E-mail: geog.dept@durham.ac.uk
Amin, Ash, BA *Reading*, PhD *Reading*, FBA   Prof.
Atkins, Peter J., MA *Camb.*, PhD *Camb.*   Prof.
Atkinson, Sarah, BA *Durh.*, MSc *Lond.*, PhD *Durh.*   Reader
Bentley, Michael J., BSc *Edin.*, PhD *Edin.*   Reader
Bracken, Louise J., BSc *Leeds*, PhD *Birm.*   Sr. Lectr.
Bridgland, David R., BSc *CNAA*, PhD *CNAA*   Sr. Lectr.

Burt, Timothy P., MA Camb., MA Car., PhD Brist., DSc Brist., FRGS   Prof.†
Campbell, David, BA Melb., PhD ANU   Prof., Cultural and Political Geography
Crang, Michael A., BA Camb., PhD Brist.   Reader
Curtis, Sarah, BA Oxf., DPhil Kent   Prof.
Densmore, Alexander, BS Cal.Tech., PhD Calif.   Reader
Donoghue, Daniel N. M., BSc Aberd., PhD Durh.   Reader
Dunn, Christine E., BSc Wales, PhD Hull   Sr. Lectr.
Elden, Stuart R., BSc Brun., PhD Brun.   Prof.
Evans, David, BA Wales, MSc Nfld.   Reader
Evans, Ian S., MA Camb., MS Yale, PhD Camb.   Reader
Ferguson, Robert I., PhD Camb.   Prof., Physical Geography
Graham, Stephen, MPhil Newcastle(UK), PhD Manc.   Prof.
Hudson, Raymond, BA Brist., PhD Brist., DSc Brist., FBA   Prof.†
Lane, Stuart, PhD Camb., PhD Lond.   Prof.
Long, Antony J., BA Durh., PhD Durh.   Prof.; Head*
MacLeod, Donald G., BA Paisley, MA Lanc., PhD Lanc.   Reader
Macnaghten, Philip, BA S'ton., PhD Exe.   Prof.
McEwan, Cheryl, BSc Lough., PhD Lough.   Sr. Lectr.
O'Cofaigh, Colm, BA Trinity(Dub.), MSc Trinity(Dub.), PhD Alta.   Reader
Pain, Rachel H., BA Lanc., PhD Edin.   Reader
Painter, Joseph M., BA Camb., PhD Open(UK)   Prof.
Petley, David N., BSc Lond., PhD Lond.   Prof.
Rigg, Jonathan D., BA Lond., PhD Lond.   Prof.
Shennan, Ian, BSc Durh., PhD Durh.   Prof.
Smith, Susan J., MA Oxf., DPhil Oxf.   Prof., Human Geography
Stokes, Christopher, BSc Sheff., PhD Sheff.   Reader
Warburton, Jeff, BSc Wales, MA Colorado, PhD S'ton.   Reader
Zong, Yongqiang, PhD Durh.   Sr. Lectr.
Other Staff: 19 Lectrs.
Research: catchment, river and hillslope science, links to ecology and tectonics; living and material cultures (national identity, ethnicity, belonging, socio-economics); politics, state, space (popular geopolitics, boundaries, citizenship, urban governance); quaternary (environmental change, human impact, palaeoceanography, sea-level change, stratigraphy); social well-being and spatial justice (risks and knowledge, social polarisation, human welfare)

Government and International Affairs, School of

Ehteshami, Anoushiravan, BA CNAA, PhD Exe.   Prof.; Head*

Middle Eastern and Islamic Studies, Institute for

Tel: (0191) 334 5660 Fax: (0191) 334 5661
E-mail: sgia.pgadmissions@durham.ac.uk
Ehteshami, Anoushiravan, BA CNAA, PhD Exe.   Prof.
Murphy, Emma C., BSocSc Birm., MA Exe., PhD Exe.   Prof.
Wilson, Rodney J. A., BSc(Econ) Belf., PhD Belf.   Prof.
Other Staff: 4 Lectrs.

Politics

Tel: (0191) 334 5680 Fax: (0191) 334 5661
E-mail: politics.department@durham.ac.uk
Chan, Gerald C. W., MA Kent, PhD Griff.   Prof.
Dumbrell, John, BA Camb., MA Keele, PhD   Prof.
Stapleton, Julia, BA Wales, MA Sus., DPhil Sus., FRHistS   Reader
Stirk, Peter M. R., BA CNAA, PhD Exe.   Sr. Lectr.
Williams, John C., BA Hull, MA Hull, PhD Warw.   Sr. Lectr.
Other Staff: 8 Lectrs.

Research: British and European politics (ideas and history); contemporary China (politics and foreign policy); international relations and strategic studies (theory and foreign policy); political theory (history of political thought); the contemporary Middle East (politics and political economy)

Health, School for

Tel: (0191) 334 0320 Fax: (0191) 334 0374
Cornford, Charles S., MD Newcastle(UK), EdD Newcastle(UK)   Sr. Lectr.
Evans, H. Martyn, BA Wales, PhD Wales   Prof.†, Humanities in Medicine
Hungin, A. Pali S., OBE, MB BS Newcastle(UK), FRCGP   Prof.; Dean of Med.*
Macnaughton, R. Jane, MB ChB Glas., MA Glas., PhD Glas.   Sr. Lectr.
Mason, James, BSc S'ton., MSc York(UK), PhD S'ton.   Prof.
McLachlan, John C., BSc Glas., PhD Lond.   Prof.
Other Staff: 5 Lectrs.
Research: arts and humanities in health and medicine (evaluating the health impact of architecture and design); clinical and economic evaluation and implementation research; clinical management development (systematising clinical work, ethical and cultural change); history of medicine and disease (ethics, sexuality, infectious diseases, pharmacology); public health and policy (evaluating public policy, influencing health investment)

History

Tel: (0191) 334 1040 Fax: (0191) 334 1041
Brooks, Christopher W., BA Prin., DPhil Oxf., FRHistS   Prof.
Davies, Sarah R., MA St And., MA Lond., DPhil Oxf.   Sr. Lectr.
Fox, Joanne C., BA Kent, PhD Kent   Sr. Lectr.
Gameson, Richard, BA Oxf., DPhil Oxf.   Prof.
Harris, Howell J., MA Oxf., DPhil Oxf.   Prof.
Michie, Ranald C., MA Aberd., PhD Aberd.   Prof.
Moon, David, BA Newcastle(UK), PhD Birm.   Prof.
Osborne, Toby, MA Oxf., DPhil Oxf.   Sr. Lectr.
Prestwich, Michael C., MA Oxf., DPhil Oxf., FRHistS, FSA   Prof.
Rollason, David W., MA Oxf., PhD Birm., FSA, FRHistS   Prof.
Stephenson, Paul, MSc Oxf., MA Camb., PhD Camb., FRHistS   Reader
Williamson, Philip A., MA Camb., PhD Camb., FRHistS   Prof.; Head*
Willis, Justin, BA Lond., PhD Lond.   Reader
Other Staff: 16 Lectrs.
Research: American history; Imperial and African history; mediaeval British and European history; modern British and European history

Law

Tel: (0191) 334 2800 Fax: (0191) 334 2801
E-mail: law-dept@durham.ac.uk
Allen, Thomas, BA Qu., LLB Dal., LLM Lond.   Prof.
Baker, Aaron C., BA St.Louis, JD St.Louis, BCL Oxf.   Sr. Lectr.
Beever, Allan, BA Auck., MA Auck., LLM Tor., PhD Auck.   Reader
Beyleveld, Deryck, BA Camb., PhD E.Anglia   Prof.
Bohlander, Michael, DrJur Saar   Prof.
Campbell, David I., BSc Wales, LLM Mich., PhD Edin.   Prof.
Cullen, Holly A., BCL McG., LLB McG., LLM Essex   Reader
Fenwick, Helen M., BA Newcastle(UK), LLB CNAA   Prof.
Fox, Lorna, LLB Belf., PhD Belf.   Sr. Lectr.
Leigh, Ian D., LLB Wales, LLM Wales   Prof.; Head*
McGlynn, Clare M. S., BA Durh., MJur Durh.   Prof.
O'Mahony, David, BSocSci Ott., MA Ott., MPhil Camb.   Reader

Pattinson, Shaun, LLB Hull, LLM Sheff., PhD Sheff.   Reader
Phillipson, Gavin, BA Durh., LLM Camb.   Prof.
Riley, Christopher A., LLB Hull   Reader
Spaventa, Eleanor, LLM Camb., DPhil Oxf.   Reader
Ulph, Janet S., LLB Nott., LLM Camb., LLM Harv.   Sr. Lectr.
Wells, Celia K., LLB Warw., LLM Lond.   Prof.
Other Staff: 12 Lectrs.
Research: commercial and corporate law; European Community law; gender and the law; human rights; international criminal justice

Mathematical Sciences

Tel: (0191) 334 3050 Fax: (0191) 334 3051
E-mail: maths.office@durham.ac.uk
Abel, Steven A., BSc Brist., PhD Brist.   Reader
Abrashkin, Victor A., PhD Moscow, DSc Moscow   Prof.
Blowey, James F., BSc Sus., DPhil Sus.   Reader
Bolton, John, BSc Liv., PhD Liv.   Reader
Chu, Chong-Sun, BSc HK, PhD Calif.   Reader
Coolen, Franciscus P. A., MSc T.U.Eindhoven, PhD T.U.Eindhoven   Prof.
Coolen-Schrijner, Pauline, MSc Tilburg, PhD T.H.Twente   Reader
Dorey, Patrick E., BA Oxf., PhD Durh.   Prof.
Farber, Michael S., MSc Azerbaijan, PhD Azerbaijan, DSc Georgia State   Prof., Pure Mathematics
Goldstein, Michael, BA Oxf., MSc Oxf., DPhil Oxf.   Prof., Statistics; Head*
Gregory, Ruth A. W., MA Camb., PhD Camb.   Prof., Mathematical Sciences and Physics
Kanti, Panagiota, PhD Ioannina   Reader
Kearton, Cherry, MA Camb., PhD Camb., ScD Camb.   Reader, Pure Mathematics
Mansfield, Paul, BA Oxf., PhD Camb.   Prof.
Martin, Nigel, MA Camb., PhD Camb.   Sr. Lectr.†
Menshikov, Mikhail V., PhD Moscow, DSc Moscow   Prof., Statistics
Parker, John R., BSc Durh., PhD Camb.   Reader
Pennington, Michael R., BSc Edin., PhD Lond., FIP   Prof., Mathematical Sciences and Physics
Ross, Simon F., BSc Wat., PhD Camb.   Reader
Seheult, Allan H., BSc Lond., PhD N.Carolina   Sr. Lectr.
Smith, Douglas J., BSc Glas., PhD Glas.   Sr. Lectr.
Stirling, W. James, CBE, MA Camb., PhD Camb., FIP, FRS   Prof., Mathematical Sciences and Physics
Straughan, Brian, BSc Newcastle(UK), MSc Newcastle(UK), PhD H-W   Prof., Numerical Analysis
Sutcliffe, Paul M., BSc Durh., PhD Durh.   Prof.
Taormina, Anne, PhD Mons   Prof.
Ward, Richard S., MSc Rhodes, DPhil Oxf., FRS   Prof.
Zakrzewski, Wojciech J. M., MSc Warsaw, PhD Camb.   Prof.
Other Staff: 18 Lectrs.; 2 Sr. Lectrs.
Research: applied mathematics and mathematical physics; numerical analysis and computational mathematics; pure mathematics; statistics, applied probability and operational research

Modern Languages and Cultures, School of

Tel: (0191) 334 3420 Fax: (0191) 334 3421
E-mail: modern.languages@durham.ac.uk
Saul, Nicholas D. B., BA Camb., PhD Camb.   Prof.; Head*

Arabic

Newman, Daniel, BA Ghent, MA Lond., PhD Lond.   Sr. Lectr.
Starkey, Paul G., MA Oxf., DPhil Oxf.   Prof.
Other Staff: 1 Lang. Instr.
Research: Arabic language and linguistics; Arabic literature; middle eastern cultures

French

Barnet, Marie-Claire, PhD Calif.   Sr. Lectr.
Cairns, Lucille, BA Lond., PhD Lond.   Prof.

Clarke, Janet L., BA Warw., MA Warw., PhD Warw. Prof.
Cowling, David J., MA Oxf., DPhil Oxf. Prof.
Dousteyssier-Khoze, Catherine, LèsL Clermont-Ferrand, MA Durh., PhD Durh. Sr. Lectr.
Lloyd, Christopher D., MA Oxf., PhD Warw. Prof.
Maber, Richard G., MA Oxf., DPhil Oxf. Prof.
Taylor, Jane H. M., MA Oxf., DPhil Oxf. Prof.†
Welch, Edward J., MA Oxf., MSt Oxf., DPhil Oxf. Sr. Lectr.
Wiseman, Boris N. D., BA Lond., PhD Lond. Sr. Lectr.
Other Staff: 3 Lectrs.; 1 Sr. Lang. Instr.
Research: early modern French culture; French culture; gender studies; modern and contemporary French culture

German

Long, Jonathan J., BA Oxf., MA Nott., PhD Nott. Prof.
Musolff, Andreas, MA Düsseldorf, DrPhil Düsseldorf Prof.
Saul, Nicholas D. B., BA Camb., PhD Camb. Prof.
Thomas, Neil E., BA Wales, PhD Wales Reader
Other Staff: 2 Lectrs.; 1 Sr. Lang. Instr.
Research: fifteenth- and sixteenth-century German literature; literary theory; neo-Latin; Orientalism and post-colonialism; twentieth-century German literature

Italian

Caruso, Carlo, DrPhil Zür., PhD Turin Prof.
Cracolici, Stefano, MA Tor., MD Freib., PhD Tor. Sr. Lectr.
Other Staff: 2 Lectrs.; 1 Lang. Instr.
Research: classic tradition and book history; comparative literature (French/German/Italian/Latin); Italian cinema and visual culture; mediaeval and renaissance culture; medicine and the arts

Russian

Harrington, Alexandra K., BA Nott., MA Nott., PhD Nott. Sr. Lectr.
O'Meara, Patrick, BA Keele, MA Trinity(Dub.), DPhil Oxf. Prof.†
Renfrew, Alastair, BA Strath., PhD Sheff. Reader
Other Staff: 1 Lectr.; 1 Sr. Lang. Instr.; 1 Lang. Instr.
Research: history of Imperial Russia; literary and critical theory; modern Russian fiction; Russian and Soviet cinema; twentieth-century Russian poetry

Spanish

Beresford, Andrew M., BA Lond., MA Lond., PhD Lond. Sr. Lectr.
Noble, Andrea, BA Camb., PhD Birm. Prof.
Thompson, Michael P., BA Durh., PhD Brist. Sr. Lectr.
Other Staff: 3 Lectrs.; 2 Sr. Lang. Instrs.; 1 Lang. Instr.
Research: gender studies; mediaeval Spanish hagiography and chronicles; modern Spanish theatre and censorship; Spanish and Latin-American film and photography; Spanish and Latin-American literature

Music

Tel: (0191) 334 3140 Fax: (0191) 334 3141
Dibble, Jeremy C., BA Camb., PhD S'ton. Prof.
Fitch, Fabrice J., MMus McG., PhD Manc. Sr. Lectr.
Harry, Martyn, MA Camb., PhD City(UK) Sr. Lectr.
Kanno, Mieko, PhD York(UK) Sr. Lectr.
Manning, Peter D., BA Durh., PhD Durh. Prof.
Paddison, Max H., MA Exe., PhD Exe. Prof.
Spitzer, Michael, BA Oxf., PhD S'ton. Reader
Zon, Bennett M., BMus Mich., MMus Edin., DPhil Oxf. Reader; Head*
Other Staff: 2 Lectrs.
Research: composition and music technology; ethnomusicology; music theory and analysis; musicology; performance

Philosophy

Tel: (0191) 334 6550 Fax: (0191) 334 6551
E-mail: philosophy.department@durham.ac.uk
Cooper, David E., MA Oxf., BPhil Oxf. Prof.
Hamilton, Andrew J., MA St And., MPhil St And., PhD St And. Sr. Lectr.
Hendry, Robin F., BSc Lond., PhD Lond. Reader
Hinzen, Wolfram, MA Lond., DPhil Berne Prof.; Head*
Lowe, E. Jonathan, MA Camb., DPhil Oxf. Prof.
Maehle, A.-Holger, DrMed Bonn, DrMedHabil Gött. Prof., History of Medicine and Medical Ethics
Ratcliffe, Matthew J., BA Durh., MPhil Camb., PhD Camb. Reader
Reader, Soran, MA Camb., PhD Camb. Reader
Scarre, Geoffrey F., MA Camb., MLitt Camb., PhD Open(UK) Prof.
Zangwill, Nick, PhD Lond. Prof.
Other Staff: 8 Lectrs.
Research: aesthetics, moral philosophy and applied ethics; history and philosophy of science and medicine; metaphysics and philosophy of mind; phenomenology and continental philosophy; philosophy of language and linguistics

Physics

Tel: (0191) 334 3520 Fax: (0191) 334 5823
E-mail: physics.office@durham.ac.uk
Abram, Richard A., BSc Manc., PhD Manc., FIP Prof.; Head*
Adams, Charles S., BA Oxf., MEng McM., PhD Strath. Prof.
Ball, Patricia, DrRerNat Heidel. Prof.
Bower, Richard G., BA Oxf., PhD Durh. Prof.
Brand, Stuart, BSc Newcastle(UK), PhD Newcastle(UK) Sr. Lectr.
Brinkman, Andrew W., BSc Nott., PhD Nott. Reader
Chadwick, Paula M., BSc Lond., PhD Durh., FRAS Reader
Chamberlain, J. Martyn, MA Oxf., DPhil Oxf., FIP Prof.†, Applied Physics
Clark, Stewart J., BSc Aberd., PhD Edin. Reader
Cole, Shaun M., BA Oxf., PhD Camb. Prof.
Cross, Graham H., BSc CNAA, PhD CNAA Sr. Lectr.
Done, Christine, BSc St And., PhD Camb. Prof.
Durose, Kenneth, BSc Durh., PhD Durh. Prof.
Edge, Alistair, BSc York(UK), PhD Leic. Reader
Flower, David R., BSc Lond., PhD Lond. Prof.
Frenk, Carlos S., BSc Mexico Natnl., PhD Camb., FRAS, FRS Ogden Prof., Fundamental Physics
Glover, E. W. Nigel, MA Camb., PhD Durh., FIP Prof.
Gregory, Ruth A. W., MA Camb., PhD Camb. Prof.
Halliday, Douglas P., BSc Edin., PhD Nott. Sr. Lectr.
Hampshire, Damian P., MA Oxf., DPhil Oxf. Prof.
Hatton, Peter D., BSc Leic., PhD Leic. Prof.
Hughes, Ifan G., BSc Lond., DPhil Oxf. Sr. Lectr.
Khoze, Valentin, MSc St.Petersburg, PhD Lund Prof.
Love, Gordon D., BSc Durh., PhD Durh. Reader
Lucey, John R., BSc Leic., DPhil Sus. Sr. Lectr.
Maxwell, Christopher J., BSc Lond., PhD Lond. Sr. Lectr.
Monkman, Andrew P., BSc Lond., PhD Lond. Prof.
Morris, Simon L., BSc Durh., PhD Camb. Prof.
Osborne, John L., BSc Durh., PhD Durh., FRAS Sr. Lectr.
Pennington, Michael R., BSc Edin., PhD Lond., FIP Prof., Mathematical Sciences and Physics
Potvliege, Robert M., LicSci Brussels, DocSci Brussels Reader
Shanks, Thomas, MSc Lond., PhD Durh. Prof.
Sharples, Raymond M., BSc St And., PhD Edin. Prof.

Stirling, W. James, CBE, MA Camb., PhD Camb., FIP, FRS Prof.†, Mathematical Sciences and Physics
Tanner, Brian K., MA Oxf., DPhil Oxf., FIP, FRSA Prof.
Ward, Martin J., BSc Lond., MA Camb., MSc Sus., DPhil Sus. Prof.
Weiglein, Georg, PhD Würzburg Prof.
Other Staff: 11 Lectrs.
Research: advanced instrumentation; astronomy; atomic and molecular physics; condensed matter physics; high energy particle theory

Psychology

Tel: (0191) 334 3240 Fax: (0191) 334 3241
Campbell, Anne C., BA Reading, DPhil Oxf. Prof.
Drewett, Robert F., BA Hull, DPhil Oxf. Reader
Eacott, Madeline J., BSc Reading, DPhil Oxf. Prof.
Easton, Alexander, MA Oxf., DPhil Oxf. Sr. Lectr.
Feeney, Aidan, BA Trinity(Dub.), PhD Plym. Sr. Lectr.
Fernyhough, Charles P., BA Camb., PhD Camb. Sr. Lectr.
Findlay, John M., MA Camb., PhD Camb. Prof.
Hausmann, Markus Sr. Lectr.
Heywood, Charles A., BSc St And., DPhil Oxf. Prof.; Head*
Kentridge, Robert W., BSc Leeds, PhD Durh. Reader
Leekam, Susan R., BA Open(UK), DPhil Sus. Reader
Meins, Elizabeth, MA Camb., PhD Camb. Sr. Lectr.
Milner, A. David, MA Oxf., PhD Lond. Prof., Cognitive Neuroscience
Muncer, Steven J., BA Oxf., PhD Lond. Sr. Lectr.
Reissland, Nadja N., BSc Lond., MA Sus., DPhil Oxf. Sr. Lectr.
Schenk, Thomas, MS Constance, PhD Munich Sr. Lectr.
Other Staff: 14 Lectrs.
Research: cognition and cognitive science; developmental and child health psychology; social and evolutionary psychology; vision and visual cognition

Theology and Religion

Tel: (0191) 334 3940 Fax: (0191) 334 3941
Barclay, John M. G., MA Camb., PhD Camb. Lightfoot Prof., Divinity; Head*
Barton, Rev. Stephen C., BA Macq., MA Lanc., PhD Lond. Reader
Davies, Douglas J., BA Durh., MLitt Oxf., PhD Nott., DLitt Oxf. Prof., Study of Religion
Hardman, Charlotte E., BA Sus., BLitt Oxf., PhD Lond. Sr. Lectr.
Harrison, Carol, BA Oxf., DPhil Oxf. Reader
Hayward, C. T. Robert, MA Durh., DPhil Oxf. Prof., Hebrew
Loughlin, Gerard P., BA Wales, MA Wales, PhD Camb. Prof.
Louth, Andrew, MA Camb., MA Oxf., MTh Edin., DD Oxf. Prof., Patristic and Byzantine Studies
Moberly, Rev. R. Walter L., MA Oxf., MA Camb., PhD Camb. Prof.
Murray, Paul D., BA Durh., MA Durh., PhD Camb. Sr. Lectr.
Ryrie, Alec, MA Oxf., DPhil Oxf. Reader
Song, Robert J., BA Oxf., DPhil Oxf. Sr. Lectr.
Stuckenbruck, Loren T., BA Milligan, MD Princeton Theol.Sem., PhD Princeton Theol.Sem. Brooke Fosse Wescott Prof., Biblical Studies
Telford, R. William, BD Glas., MA Glas., STM U.T.S.(N.Y.), PhD Camb. Sr. Lectr.
Watson, Francis, PhD Oxf. Prof., New Testament Studies
Weeks, Stuart D. E., MA Oxf., MPhil Oxf., DPhil Oxf. Sr. Lectr.
Other Staff: 3 Lectrs.
Research: contemporary theology (systematics, ethics, philosophy of religion, gender); historical theology (patristics, Byzantine/

orthodox theology, Northumbrian, reformation); New Testament (criticism, theology, hermeneutics, Second Temple Judaism); Old Testament, biblical theology, Israelite history, early Judaism; religion (anthropology/sociology of religion, film studies)

COLLEGE OF ST HILD AND ST BEDE

Tel: (0191) 334 8300 Fax: (0191) 334 8301
Carr, Carol A.   Sr. Tutor
Pearson, J. Alan, BSc *Wales*, PhD *Wales*   U. Lectr.†, Biological Sciences; Principal*

COLLINGWOOD COLLEGE

Tel: (0191) 334 5000 Fax: (0191) 334 5035
Corrigan, F. Edward, MA *Camb.*, PhD *Camb.*, FRS   Principal*
Rayner, Stephen M., BA *Oxf.*, PhD *Durh.*   Vice-Principal and Sr. Tutor
Taylor, Jane H. M., MA *Oxf.*, DPhil *Oxf.*   Univ. Prof.†, French

GEORGE STEPHENSON COLLEGE

Tel: (0191) 334 0114 Fax: (0191) 334 0054
Darnell, Adrian C., BA *Durh.*, MA *Warw.*   Univ. Prof.†, Economics and Finance; Principal*
Marlow, Mandy, BA *Camb.*, MA *Camb.*, MPhil *Camb.*   Vice-Principal; Sr. Tutor

GREY COLLEGE

Tel: (0191) 334 5900 Fax: (0191) 334 5901
Chamberlain, J. Martyn, MA *Oxf.*, DPhil *Oxf.*, FIP   Univ. Prof.†, Physics; Master*
Cleaver, Antony E., BSc *Wales*, MSc *Lond.*   Vice-Master and Sr. Tutor

HATFIELD COLLEGE

Tel: (0191) 334 2633 Fax: (0191) 334 3101
Burt, Timothy P., MA *Camb.*, MA *Car.*, PhD *Brist.*, DSc *Brist.*, FRGS   Univ. Prof.†, Geography; Master*
Widdison, P. E., BA BSc MSc PhD   Sr. Tutor

JOHN SNOW COLLEGE

Tel: (0191) 334 0034 Fax: (0191) 334 0029
Evans, H. Martyn, BA *Wales*, PhD *Wales*   Univ. Prof.†, Health; Principal*
Wesson, Karen L., BSc *Camb.*, PhD *Camb.*   Sr. Tutor
Wilson, Laura, BSc   Sr. Tutor

JOSEPHINE BUTLER COLLEGE

Tel: (0191) 334 7270 Fax: (0191) 334 7259
Simpson, Adrian, BSc   Univ. Reader†, Education; Principal*
Tidmarsh, Jill, BA PhD   Sr. Tutor

ST AIDAN'S COLLEGE

Tel: (0191) 334 5769 Fax: (0191) 334 5770
Frenk, Susan F., BA MPhil PhD   Sr. Tutor; Acting Principal*

ST CHAD'S COLLEGE

Tel: (0191) 334 3358 Fax: (0191) 334 3371
E-mail: st-chads@durham.ac.uk
Cassidy, Rev. Canon Joseph P. M., BA *C'dia.*, STB *Tor.*, MA *Detroit*, MDiv *Tor.*, PhD *Ott.*, ThD *St Paul(Ott.)*   Principal*
Masson, Margaret J., PhD *Durh.*   Sr. Tutor

ST CUTHBERT'S SOCIETY

Tel: (0191) 334 3400 Fax: (0191) 334 3401
Boyne, Roy D., BSocSc *Birm.*, PhD *Leeds*   Univ. Prof., Applied Social Sciences; Principal*
Richardson, Sharon, BA MA   Sr. Tutor

ST JOHN'S COLLEGE

Tel: (0191) 334 3500 Fax: (0191) 334 3501
Ogden, Mark, PhD   Sr. Tutor
Wilkinson, Rev. David, BSc MA PhD   Principal*

ST MARY'S COLLEGE

Tel: (0191) 334 5719 Fax: (0191) 334 5720
E-mail: st.marys.college@durham.ac.uk
Boughton, Gillian E., BA *Durh.*, PhD *Durh.*   Sr. Tutor; Vice-Principal
Gilmartin, Philip, BSc PhD   Principal*

TREVELYAN COLLEGE

Tel: (0191) 334 7000 Fax: (0191) 334 5371
E-mail: enquiries@trevcoll.ac.uk
Latham, Ian, MPhys PhD   Sr. Tutor
Martin, Nigel, MA *Camb.*, PhD *Camb.*   U. Sr. Lectr.†, Mathematical Sciences; Principal*

UNIVERSITY COLLEGE

Tel: (0191) 334 4099 Fax: (0191) 334 3801
Stirling, Paula H., LLB *Warw.*   Sr. Tutor
Tucker, Maurice E., BSc *Durh.*, PhD *Reading*, FGS   U. Prof., Earth Sciences; Master*

USTINOV COLLEGE

Tel: (0191) 334 5470 Fax: (0191) 334 7231
McKinven, Theresa, MA *Glas.*, MSc *Aston*   Vice-Principal and Sr. Tutor
Wilson, Penelope B., MA *Edin.*, DPhil *Oxf.*   Principal*

VAN MILDERT COLLEGE

Tel: (0191) 334 7100 Fax: (0191) 334 7130
O'Meara, Patrick, BA *Keele*, MA *Trinity(Dub.)*, DPhil *Oxf.*   Univ. Prof.†, Russian; Master*
Points, Petra, BA *Liv.*, MA *Newcastle(UK)*   Sr. Tutor

CONTACT OFFICERS

Academic affairs. Academic Registrar: Fowler, Carolyn B., BA *Durh.*
Accommodation. Commercial Director: Strangward, Helen
Admissions (first degree). Senior Assistant Registrar (Admissions (first degree)): Emborg, Richard, BA *Durh.*, MA *Nott.*
Admissions (higher degree). Postgraduate Admissions Officer: Houghton, Nicola, BA *Newcastle(UK)*
Adult/continuing education. Academic Registrar: Fowler, Carolyn B., BA *Durh.*
Alumni. Alumni Relations Officer: Wallace, Emily, MA *Glas.*
Archives. Records Manager: Philipson, Sophie, BA *Northumbria*
Careers. Head of Careers Advisory Service: Richardson, Catherine L., BA *CNAA*
Computing services. Director of Information Technology Service: Beddie, Lesley, BSc *Edin.*
Conferences/corporate hospitality. Commercial Director: Strangward, Helen
Consultancy services. Knowledge Exploitation Manager: White, John R., BA *Durh.*
Credit transfer. Academic Registrar: Fowler, Carolyn B., BA *Durh.*

Development/fund-raising. Director of Development and Communications: Elder, Liesl A., BA *Minn.*
Distance education. Academic Registrar: Fowler, Carolyn B., BA *Durh.*
Equal opportunities. Director of Human Resources: Boyd, Jack, MA *Glas.*
Estates and buildings/works and services. Director of Estates and Buildings: Robinson, Peter S., FRICS
Examinations. Assistant Registrar: Parks, Michael A., MBA *Tees.*
Finance. Treasurer: Lubacz, Paulina, BA *CNAA*
General enquiries. Registrar and Secretary: Sanders, Lee, BA *Manc.*
Industrial liaison. Director of Research and Economic Development Support Service: Statham, Robin T., MA *Camb.*, MA *Sheff.*
International office. Director of International Office: Baker, David, BA *CNAA* (E-mail: international.office@durham.ac.uk)
Language training for international students. Acting Academic Director of Language Centre: Davenport, Michael J. S., MA *Edin.*
Library (chief librarian). University Librarian: Hall, John T. D., BA *Manc.*, MA *Camb.*, PhD *Manc.*
Marketing. Director of Development and Communications: Elder, Liesl A., BA *Minn.*
Minorities/disadvantaged groups. Deputy Academic Registrar: Dale, Sam, BA *York(UK)*, MBA *Lond.*
Ombudsman. Registrar and Secretary: Sanders, Lee, BA *Manc.*
Personnel/human resources. Director of Human Resources: Boyd, Jack, MA *Glas.*
Public relations. Senior Marketing and Communications Manager: Lavery, Michael, BA *Sund.*
Publications. Public Relations Officer: Hamil, Dionne, BA *Inst.Soc.Stud.(The Hague)*
Purchasing. Director of Procurement: Holmes, Alison
Quality assurance and accreditation. Senior Assistant Registrar: Harrison, Richard D., BA *Lanc.*, PhD *Lanc.*
Research. Head of Research Grant Applications: Harle, Wendy, BA *Newcastle(UK)*, MA *Durh.*
Safety. University Health and Safety Adviser: Watson, Allan, BSc *Lond.*
Scholarships, awards, loans. Academic Registrar: Fowler, Carolyn B., BA *Durh.*
Schools liaison. Assistant Registrar: Worden, Lee, BA *Durh.*, MA *Durh.*
Security. Assistant Director (Facilities) of Estates and Buildings: Sharp, Stuart A.
Sport and recreation. Director of Sport: Warburton, Peter A., BA *Durh.*, PhD *Hull*
Staff development and training. Director of Human Resources: Boyd, Jack, MA *Glas.*
Strategic planning. Director of Strategic Planning and Change Unit: Chadwick, Stephen A., BA *Exe.*, MA *Northumbria*
Student union. Academic Registrar: Fowler, Carolyn B., BA *Durh.*
Student welfare/counselling. Director and Senior Counsellor, University Counselling Service: Fraser, M. Ruth, MA *Edin.*
Students from other countries. Director of International Office: Baker, David, BA *CNAA*
Students with disabilities. Acting Director, Service for Students with Disabilities: Osborne, Hilary A., BEd *Sund.*
Women. Deputy Director of Human Resources: Race, Joanne E.

[Information supplied by the institution as at 6 February 2008, and edited by the ACU]

UNIVERSITY OF EAST ANGLIA

Founded 1964

Member of the Association of Commonwealth Universities

Postal Address: Norwich, England NR4 7TJ
Telephone: (01603) 456161 **Fax:** (01603) 458553
URL: http://www.uea.ac.uk

VICE-CHANCELLOR*—Macmillan, Prof. William D., BSc Brist., MA Oxf., PhD Brist.
CHAIRMAN OF COUNCIL—Holmes, Stuart
TREASURER—Sisson, Jonathan, FCA
PRO-VICE-CHANCELLOR—Acton, Prof. E. D. J., BA York(UK), PhD Camb.
PRO-VICE-CHANCELLOR—Davies, Prof. T. D., BSc Sheff., PhD Sheff.
REGISTRAR AND SECRETARY‡—Summers, Brian, BSc
LIBRARY DIRECTOR—Lewis, Nicholas

GENERAL INFORMATION

History. The university was established in 1964.

It is located on the outskirts of Norwich.

Admission to first degree courses (see also United Kingdom Introduction). Applicants must fulfil the general entrance requirement and any special requirement for the course. International students: qualifications accepted for admission to universities in student's own country together with an approved English language qualification. European qualifications, including International or European Baccalaureate, must include an English language element.

First Degrees (see also United Kingdom Directory to Subjects of Study). BA, BEd, BEng, BSc, LLB, MChem, MMath.

Most full-time courses last 3 years. Many programmes may also be taken by part-time study.

Higher Degrees (see also United Kingdom Directory to Subjects of Study).
Master's. LLM, MA, MBA, MEd, MMus, MPhil, MSc.
Admission. Applicants for admission to master's level degrees must normally hold an appropriate first degree with at least second clas honours.
Length of course. Full-time: LLM, MA, MBA, MEd, MMus, MSc: 1 year; MPhil: 2 years. *Part-time:* LLM, MA, MBA, MEd, MMus, MSc: 2 years; MPhil: 4 years.
Doctoral. ClinPsyD, DLitt, DSc, DSW, EdD, LLD, MD, PhD.
Admission. MPhil and doctorates: an appropriate first degree with at least second class honours or, in some cases, an appropriate master's degree and/or professional experience. MD and PhD: also awarded on published work; DLitt, DSc and LLD: awarded on published work.
Length of course. Full-time: ClinPsyD, DSW, EdD, MD, PhD: 3 years. *Part-time:* ClinPsyD, DSW, EdD, MD, PhD: 6 years.

Libraries. Volumes: 750,000. Periodicals subscribed to: 2000.

Academic Year (2007–2008). Two semesters: September–December; January–June.

Income (2005–2006). Total, £138,000,000.

Statistics. Students (2006–2007): full-time 10,950; part-time 4031; international 1416; undergraduate 11,629; master's 2102; doctoral 1250.

FACULTIES/SCHOOLS

Arts and Humanities

Dean: Cook, Prof. Jon, BA Camb., MA E.Anglia

Health

Dean: Kopelman, Prof. P., MB BS MD, FRCP, FFPH

Science

Dean: Richardson, Prof. D. J., BSc Keele, PhD Birm.

Social Sciences

Dean: Hargreaves-Heap, Prof. S. P., BA Oxf., PhD Calif.

ACADEMIC UNITS

Arranged by Schools

Allied Health Professions

Tel: (01603) 593891 Fax: (01603) 593166
E-mail: jayne.rogers@uea.ac.uk
Bunning, K., MA E.Anglia, PhD City(UK)   Sr. Lectr.
Cross, J. L., MSc E.Anglia, EdD E.Anglia   Sr. Lectr.
Drachler, M. L., MD Rio Grande do Sul, MPhil Rio Grande do Sul, PhD Lond.   Sr. Lectr.
Hartley, S. D., MEd Ib., PhD Lond.   Prof.
Jerosch-Herold, C., MSc S'ton., PhD E.Anglia   Reader
Mcalistar, J., MA PhD   Sr. Lectr.
Poland, F., BA Manc., MA Manc., PhD Manc.   Sr. Lectr.; Dir., Res.
Pomeroy, V. M., BA Open(UK), PhD S'ton.   Prof.
Richardson, B., MSc Lond., PhD E.Anglia   Reader, Physiotherapy
Song, F., BA Tongji, MA Tongji, PhD Lond.   Reader
Spalding, N., BSc Anglia PU, BEd E.Anglia, MA E.Anglia   Sr. Lectr.
Stephenson, R. C., BA Brad., MSc Leeds, PhD E.Anglia   Reader; Head*
Watson, M. J., MSc S'ton.   Sr. Lectr.
Wells, C. A., BEd E.Anglia

American Studies

Tel: (01603) 592280 Fax: (01603) 507728
Bigsby, C. W. E., MA Sheff., PhD Nott., BA, FRSL   Prof.
Churchwell, S., BA Vassar, PhD Prin.   Sr. Lectr.
Crockatt, R. D. G., MA Edin., DPhil Sus.   Prof.; Head*
Fear-Segal, J., BA E.Anglia, PhD Lond.   Sr. Lectr.
Lloyd-Smith, A. G., BA Sus., MA Sus., PhD Indiana   Sr. Lectr.
Selby, N., BA Exe., DPhil York(UK)   Sr. Lectr.

Biological Sciences

Staff based at the John Innes Centre are individually indicated

Tel: (01603) 592269 Fax: (01603) 592250
E-mail: enqoff.bio@uea.ac.uk
Baulcombe, D., BSc Leeds, PhD Edin., FRS   Prof.
Bell, D., BSc Wales, PhD Wales   Sr. Lectr.
Bourke, A. F. G., BA Camb., PhD Bath   Prof.
Bowater, R. P., BSc Sheff., PhD Lond.   Sr. Lectr.
Butt, J. N., BA Oxf., PhD Calif.   Reader
Chantry, A., BSc Birm., PhD Lond.   Sr. Lectr.
Chapman, T., BSc Bath, PhD Edin.   Reader

Clark, I. M., BSc Brist., PhD CNAA   Reader
Coen, E. S., BA Camb., PhD Camb., FRS   Prof. (John Innes Centre)
Dalmay, T., BSc Bud., PhD   Sr. Lectr.
Davy, A. J., BSc Lond., PhD Lond.   Reader
Edwards, D., MA Camb., PhD Lond.   Prof., Cancer Studies
Ellis, V., BSc Liv., PhD Liv.   Prof.
Emerson, B. C., BSc Otago, PhD Otago   Reader
Gage, M., BSc Manc., MSc Manc.   Reader
Gale, M. D., BSc Birm., PhD Wales, FRS   Prof.
Gavrilovic, J., BSc Lond., PhD CNAA   Sr. Lectr.
Gill, J. A., BSc Edin., PhD E.Anglia   Reader
Hayward, S. J., BSc Brist., PhD Edin.   Sr. Lectr.
Hemmings, A. M., BSc Lond., PhD Lond.   Reader
Johnston, A. W. B., BSc Edin., PhD Edin.   Prof., Biology
Jones, J. D. G., BSc Camb., PhD Camb.   Prof.
Lamb, C. J., BA Camb., PhD Camb.   Prof.
Mayer, U., PhD Munich   Sr. Lectr.
Munsterberg, A. E., MSc Heidel., PhD   Reader
Poschl, E., PhD Munich   Sr. Lectr.
Richardson, D. J., BSc Keele, PhD Birm.   Prof.
Turner, J. G., BSc Leeds, MSc Missouri, PhD Missouri   Prof., Plant Science; Head*
Watkinson, A. R., BA York(UK), PhD Wales   Prof.
Watmough, N. J., BSc Lond., PhD Newcastle(UK)   Reader
Williams, M. R., BSc E.Anglia, PhD E.Anglia   Sr. Lectr.
Research: arthritis, cancer, cardiovascular disease, cataract development, gastroenterology, biomedicine; molecular biology (micro-organisms, protein structure, plant molecular biology); molecular evolution, sexual conflict, social insects; population and conservation biology

Chemical Sciences and Pharmacy

Tel: (01603) 593145 Fax: (01603) 592003
E-mail: r.g.smith@uea.ac.uk
Andrews, D. L., BSc Lond., PhD Lond.   Prof.
Barker, S.   Sr. Lectr., Pharmacy
Belton, P., BSc Lond., PhD Lond.   Prof.
Bochmann, M., BSc Lond., PhD Lond.   Prof.; Head*
Butt, J., PhD Calif.   Reader
Cammidge, A., BSc E.Anglia, PhD E.Anglia   Reader
Clayden, N. J., BA Oxf., DPhil Oxf.   Sr. Lectr.
Cook, M. J., BSc Birm., PhD Birm.   Prof., Chemistry
Craig, D. Q. M., BPharm Bath, PhD Lond.   Prof.; Head, Pharmacy
Field, R. A., BSc E.Anglia, PhD E.Anglia   Prof.
Hemmings, A. M., BSc Lond., PhD Lond.   Reader
Hoogeweff, J., BSc MSc PhD   Sr. Lectr.
Jayasooriya, U. A., BSc Ceyl., MSc E.Anglia, PhD E.Anglia   Reader
LeBrun, N., PhD E.Anglia   Sr. Lectr.
MacEwan, D.   Prof., Pharmacy
MacMillan, F. J., BSc Sheff., PhD   Reader
Mayes, A., BSc Bath, PhD Bath   Sr. Lectr.

Meech, S. R., BSc E.Anglia, PhD S'ton. Prof., Chemistry

Moore, G. R., BSc CNAA, MSc Lond., DPhil Oxf. Prof., Chemistry

Nann, T., DrHabil Freib. Prof.

O'Connall, M., BSc PhD Sr. Lectr.

Pickett, C., BSc S'ton., PhD S'ton. Prof., Chemistry

Redshaw, C., BSc Newcastle(UK), PhD Newcastle(UK) Sr. Lectr.

Richards, C. J., BSc Bath, PhD Warw. Reader

Russell, D. A., BSc PhD Prof., Chemistry

Sach, T., BA Kent, BSc York(UK), PhD Nott. Sr. Lectr.

Searcy, M., BSc Lough., PhD Herts. Reader

Stephenson, G. R., MA Camb., PhD Camb. Reader, Chemistry

Steytler, D. C., BSc Exe., PhD Kent Sr. Lectr.

Stockman, R. A., BSc Bath, PhD Brist. Sr. Lectr.

Wright, D. Sr. Lectr., Pharmacy

Other Staff: 20 Lectrs.; 4 Sr. Fellows

Research: biological chemistry; drug formulation and delivery; medicinal chemistry; physical and analytical chemistry; synthesis chemistry

Computing Sciences

Tel: (01603) 592847 Fax: (01603) 593345

Bagnall, A. J., BSc Herts., MSc E.Anglia, PhD E.Anglia Sr. Lectr.

Bangham, J. A., BSc Lond., PhD Lond. Prof.

Cawley, G. C., BEng Essex, PhD Essex Sr. Lectr.

Chardaire, P., PhD E.Anglia Reader

Cox, S. J., BSc Reading, MPhil Reading, PhD E.Anglia Prof.

Day, A. M., BSc E.Anglia, PhD E.Anglia Prof.

Finlayson, G. D., BSc Strath., PhD S.Fraser Prof.

Fisher, M. H., BSc Aston, MSc UMIST Sr. Lectr.

Glauert, J. R. W., BA Camb., MSc Manc., PhD Camb. Prof.

Harvey, R. W. H., BSc E.Anglia, PhD E.Anglia Sr. Lectr.

Hayward, S. J., BSc Brist., PhD Edin. Sr. Lectr.

Janacek, G. J., BSc UMIST, PhD Nott. Sr. Lectr.

Mayhew, Pamela J., BSc E.Anglia, PhD E.Anglia Sr. Lectr.

McKeown, G. P., MSc Manc., PhD Manc. Sr. Lectr.

Milner, B., BEng E.Anglia, PhD E.Anglia Sr. Lectr.

Moulton, V., BSc Warw., PhD Duke, MSc Prof.

Rayward-Smith, V. J., MA Oxf., PhD Lond. Prof.

Smith, G. D., BSc H-W, MSc E.Anglia, PhD E.Anglia Sr. Lectr.

Wang, W. J., BSc Northeastern(Shenyang), PhD Manc. Sr. Lectr.

Other Staff: 1 Prof. Fellow; 3 Sr. Fellows

Research: databases, distributed information systems (data mining); graphics and computational geometry; image processing algorithms and architectures (2D and 3D constrained non-linear methods); speech, music and pattern processing (speech recognition and synthesis)

Development Studies

Tel: (01603) 592807 Fax: (01603) 451999
E-mail: dev.general@uea.ac.uk

Brown, K., BSc Newcastle(UK), MSc Reading, PhD Nott. Prof.

Cameron, J., BA Essex, MA Essex, PhD E.Anglia Reader

Conway, D., BSc Wales, MSc Leic., PhD E.Anglia Sr. Lectr.

Ellis, F. T., BSc Reading, MSc Lond., DPhil Sus. Prof.

Jackson, Cecile, BSc Lond., PhD Lond. Prof.

Jenkins, R. O., BA Camb., DPhil Sus. Prof.

Lankford, B. A., BSc Reading, MSc Newcastle(UK), PhD Newcastle(UK) Sr. Lectr.; Head*

Lloyd-Sherlock, P. G., BA Oxf., MA Lond., PhD Lond. Reader

Locke, C. H., BA Camb., MA E.Anglia, PhD Wales Sr. Lectr.

Martin, A. C. R., BA Greenwich, MSc Salf., PhD Cran.

McDonagh, J. F., BSc Brist., MSc Kent, PhD Lond. Sr. Lectr.

Palmer-Jones, R., BA Camb., PhD Reading Sr. Lectr.

Pereira, A. W., BA Sus., MA Harv., PhD Harv. Sr. Lectr.

Rao, N., BA Delhi, MA E.Anglia, PhD E.Anglia Sr. Lectr.

Russell, S. J., BA Camb., MA E.Anglia, PhD Lond. Sr. Lectr.

Seeley, J. A., BA Durh., MPhil Camb., PhD Camb. Sr. Lectr.

Research: education; gender analysis; international development, including development economics; politics; social and rural development

Economics

Tel: (01603) 592065 Fax: (01603) 456259
E-mail: g.neff@uea.ac.uk

Connolly, S. J., BA Liv., MPhil Oxf., DPhil Oxf. Sr. Lectr.

Davies, S. W., BA Warw., MA Warw., PhD Warw. Prof., Economics; Head*

Hargreaves-Heap, S. P., BA Oxf., PhD Calif. Prof., Economics

Loomes, G., BA Essex, MSc Lond. Prof.

Lyons, B. R., BSc Wales, MSc(Econ) Lond., MA Camb., PhD Sheff. Prof., Economics; Head*

Moffatt, P. G., BA Warw., MSc S'ton., PhD Brist. Reader

Saha, B., PhD S.Calif. Sr. Lectr.

Sugden, R., BA York(UK), MSc Wales Prof., Economics

Zizzo, D. J., Laurea Parma, MA Oxf., MPhil Oxf. Sr. Lectr.

Research: economics (experimental economics, game theory, industrial economics)

Education and Lifelong Learning

Cockburn, A. D., BSc St And., MSc Strath., PhD E.Anglia Reader

Martin, L. C., BSc Lough., PhD Oxf. Reader

Norris, N. F. J., BA E.Anglia, PhD E.Anglia Prof.; Head*

Towner, E. G., BSc Wales Sr. Lectr.

Walker, R., BSc(Soc) Lond., MPhil Lond., PhD Lond. Prof.

Environmental Sciences

Tel: (01603) 592542 Fax: (01603) 591327
E-mail: sarah.reynolds@uea.ac.uk

Adger, W. N., MA Edin., MSc Lond., PhD E.Anglia Prof.

Andrews, J., BSc E.Anglia, PhD Leic. Prof.

Barclay, J., BSc Edin., PhD Brist. Sr. Lectr.

Bateman, I. J., BSc Birm., MA Manc., PhD Nott. Prof.

Bentham, C. G., BA Camb., MA Camb. Prof.

Boar, R. R., BSc E.Anglia, PhD E.Anglia Sr. Lectr.

Bond, A. J., BSc Lanc., PhD Lanc. Sr. Lectr.

Brimblecombe, P., BSc Auck., MSc Auck., PhD Auck. Prof.

Burgess, J. A., BA Hull, PhD Hull Prof.; Head*

Burton, P. W., MA Camb., PhD Durh. Reader

Chroston, P. N., BSc Wales, PhD Wales Sr. Lectr.

Clegg, S., BSc E.Anglia, PhD E.Anglia Prof.

Davies, T. D., BSc Sheff., PhD Sheff. Prof.

Day, B. H., BA Camb., MSc Lond. Sr. Lectr.

Dolman, P. M., BSc E.Anglia, PhD E.Anglia Sr. Lectr.

Dorling, S. R., BSc E.Anglia, PhD E.Anglia Sr. Lectr.

Grant, A., BSc Wales, PhD Wales Reader

Hassall, M., BSc Leeds, PhD Leeds Reader

Haynes, R. M., BA Brist., PhD Penn. Reader

Heywood, K. J., BSc Brist., PhD S'ton. Prof.

Hiscock, K. M., BSc E.Anglia, PhD Birm. Sr. Lectr.

Hulme, M., BSc Durh., PhD Wales Prof.

Jickells, T. D., BSc Reading, MSc S'ton., PhD S'ton. Prof.

Jones, A. P., BSc E.Anglia, PhD E.Anglia Sr. Lectr.

Jordan, A. J., BSc E.Anglia, PhD E.Anglia Prof.

Kendall, A. C., BSc Lond., PhD Lond. Sr. Lectr.

Le Quéré, C., BSc Montr., MSc McG., PhD Paris VI Reader

Leeder, M. R., BSc Durh., PhD Reading Prof.

Lenton, T. M., BA Camb., PhD E.Anglia Prof.

Liss, P. S., BSc Durh., PhD Wales Prof.

Lovett, A., BA Wales, PhD Wales Prof.

Matthews, A. J., BA Camb., MSc E.Anglia, PhD Reading Sr. Lectr.

Peres, C. A., BSc Brazil, MSc Flor., PhD Camb. Reader

Reid, B. J., BSc Edin., PhD Lanc. Sr. Lectr.

Renfrew, I. A., BSc Edin., PhD Reading Reader

Robinson, C., BSc Newcastle(UK), PhD Newcastle(UK) Reader

Sturges, W. T., BSc Lanc., PhD Lanc. Reader

Tovey, N. K., MA Camb., PhD Camb. Reader

Turner, R. K., BA Wales, MA Leic. Prof.

Van Glasow, R., PhD Reader

Vincent, C. E., BSc Lond., PhD S'ton. Prof.

Watson, A. J., BSc Lond., PhD Reading Prof.

Watson, R. T., BSc Lond., PhD Lond. Prof.

Other Staff: 12 Lectrs.; 1 Tutor; 107 Res. Assocs./Sr. Res. Assocs.; 80 Visiting Fellows; 5 Hon. Profs.; 2 Hon. Lectrs.; 1 Hon. Res. Fellow

Film and Television Studies

Tel: (01603) 592743 Fax: (01603) 507728
E-mail: m.waters@uea.ac.uk

Higson, A. D., BEd Brist., MA Leic., PhD Kent Prof.

Holmes, S., BA Sus., MA S'ton., PhD S'ton. Prof.

Jancovich, Mark, BA Keele, PhD Kent Prof.; Head*

Kramer, P., MA E.Anglia Sr. Lectr.

Negra, D., BA Guilford, PhD Texas Prof.

Tasker, Y. M., BA Warw., MPhil Birm., PhD Warw. Prof.

Other Staff: 3 Lectrs.

History

Tel: (01603) 592070 Fax: (01603) 250434
E-mail: k.brandish@uea.ac.uk

Acton, E. D. J., BA York(UK), PhD Camb. Prof.

Butler, L. J., BA N.Lond., PhD Lond. Sr. Lectr.

Carmichael, C. D., BA Brad., PhD Brad. Sr. Lectr.

Casey, J. G., BA Belf., PhD Camb., FRHistS Reader

Charmley, J. D., BA Oxf., DPhil Oxf., FRHistS Prof.; Head*

Cherry, S., BA E.Anglia, MA E.Anglia, PhD E.Anglia Reader

Church, S. D., BA CNAA, PhD Lond. Sr. Lectr.

Farr, I., BA Durh. Sr. Lectr.

Gaskill, M. J., BA Camb., PhD Camb. Reader

Harper-Bill, C., BA Lond., PhD Lond. Prof.

Howe, A. C., BA Oxf., DPhil Oxf. Prof.

Morgan, V. F. G., BA E.Anglia, PhD E.Anglia, FRHistS Sr. Lectr.

Rawcliffe, C., BA Sheff., PhD Sheff. Prof.

Vincent, N. C., BA Camb., MA Camb., MPhil Camb., PhD Camb., DPhil Prof.

Waldron, P. R., BA Lond., PhD Lond. Prof.

Warde, P. S., BA Camb., PhD Camb. Reader

Williamson, T., BA Camb., PhD Camb. Prof.

Wood, A., BA York(UK), PhD Camb. Prof.

Other Staff: 10 Lectrs.; 1 Res. Fellow; 1 Postdoctoral Fellow; 1 Res. Assoc.

Research: history (economic and social, English, European, medical)

Language, Linguistics and Translation Studies

Tel: (01603) 592749 Fax: (01603) 250599
E-mail: k.baxter@uea.ac.uk

Garton, Janet, MBE, MA Camb., PhD Prof.

Kenning, M.-M., PhD E.Anglia, LèsL Sr. Lectr.

Lodge, K. R., BA Manc., PhD Reader; Head*

Other Staff: 1 Lectr.

Law

Tel: (01603) 592520 Fax: (01603) 250245
E-mail: law@uea.ac.uk

Banakas, Stathis, LLB Athens, PhD Camb. Sr. Lectr.

Hviid, Morten, CandOceon *Aarhus*, MA *Warw.*, PhD *Warw.*   Prof., Competition Law

Mead, D. J., LLB *Camb.*, LLM *Lond.*   Sr. Lectr.; Solicitor

Mullis, Alastair C., LLB *Lond.*, LLM *Camb.*   Prof.

Naldi, Gino, LLB *Birm.*, LLM *Birm.*, PhD *Birm.*   Sr. Lectr.

Pattenden, Rosemary D., BCom *NSW*, LLB *NSW*, DPhil *Oxf.*   Prof.

Sheehan, D. K., BCL *Oxf.*, MA *Oxf.*, DPhil *Oxf.*   Sr. Lectr.

Smith, Ian, MA *Camb.*, LLB *Camb.*   Clifford Chance Prof., Employment Law

Thomas, Gareth, LLB *Wales*, BCL *Oxf.*   Sr. Lectr.; Head*

Wadlow, Chris, MA *Camb.*   Reader

Literature and Creative Writing

Tel: (01603) 592743 Fax: (01603) 507728
  E-mail: m.waters@uea.ac.uk

Benson, S., BA *Newcastle(UK)*, MA *Lond.*, PhD *Lond.*   Sr. Lectr.

Boase-Beier, Jean, MA *Regensburg*, PhD *Regensburg*   Sr. Lectr.

Chaudhuri, A., BA *Oxf.*, MA *E.Anglia*, PhD *Keele*   Prof.

Clark, Robert, BA *Essex*, MA *Essex*, PhD *Essex*, FRSA   Reader

Cook, Jon, BA *Camb.*, MA *E.Anglia*   Prof.

Cowan, Andrew, BA MA   Sr. Lectr.

Currie, Mark, BA PhD   Prof.; Head*

Foden, G., BA *Camb.*   Prof.

Garton, Janet, MBE, MA *Camb.*, PhD   Prof.

Greenlaw, L., BA *Kingston(UK)*, MA *Lond.*   Prof.

Holmes, R., OBE, BA *Camb.*, Hon. LittD *E.Anglia*, FBA, FRSL   Prof.

Hughes, K., BA *Oxf.*, MA *E.Anglia*, PhD *Keele*   Prof.

Marshall, Tim A., BA *Kent*, MA *Sus.*, PhD   Sr. Lectr.

Potter, R., BA *Camb.*, MA *Sus.*, PhD *Camb.*   Sr. Lectr.

Raymond, Joad, BA *E.Anglia*, DPhil *Oxf.*   Prof.

Riley, D., BA *Camb.*, MA *Sus.*, DPhil *Sus.*   Prof.

Roberts, M. B., MA *Oxf.*   Prof.

Sage, V. R. L., BA *Durh.*, MA *Birm.*, PhD *E.Anglia*   Prof.

Scott, C., MA *Oxf.*, MPhil *Oxf.*, DPhil *Oxf.*, FBA   Prof.

Stonebridge, Lyndsay, BA *CNAA*, MA *Sus.*, PhD *Lond.*   Sr. Lectr.; Prof.

Stott, R., BA *York(UK)*, MA *York(UK)*, DPhil *York(UK)*   Prof.

Szirtes, G., BA *Leeds*, PhD *Anglia Ruskin*   Reader

Womack, Peter, BA *Oxf.*, PhD *Edin.*   Sr. Lectr.

Woodcock, M. R., BA *Exe.*, MSt *Oxf.*, DPhil *Oxf.*   Sr. Lectr.

Yarrow, R., BA *Reading*, MA *Manc.*, PhD *Manc.*   Prof.

Management

Tel: (01603) 592263 Fax: (01603) 593343
  E-mail: l.snell@uea.ac.uk

Ashton, J., BSc *Swansea*, MSc *Portsmouth*, PhD *Bourne.*   Sr. Lectr.

Barnes, S., BSc *Lond.*, PhD *Manc.*   Prof.

Baruch, Y., BSc *Ben Gurion*, MSc *Haifa(Technion)*, DSc *Haifa(Technion)*   Prof.

Dewing, I. P., BA *Kent*, MAEd *Open(UK)*, FCA   Sr. Lectr.

Fletcher, K. P., MA *Lanc.*, PhD *Strath.*, FRSA, FCIM   Prof.

Granleese, J., BSc *Ulster*, MEd *Ulster*, DPhil *Ulster*   Sr. Lectr.

Kaye, R., BA *Manc.*, MSc *Sheff.Hallam*   Prof.

Lettice, F., BSc *Brad.*, BA *Open(UK)*, MSc *Cran.*, PhD *Cran.*, FRSA   Sr. Lectr.

Lowson, R. H., BA *W.England*, MBA *Open(UK)*, PhD *Cardiff*   Prof.

McLarty, R. W., MBA *Strath.*, PhD *E.Anglia*   Sr. Lectr.

Ozbilgin, M., BA *Bosphorus*, MA *Marmara*, PhD *Brist.*   Prof.

Pandit, N. R., BA(Econ) *Manc.*, MSc *Manc.*, PhD *Manc.*   Prof.

Peters, L. D., BA *Lond.*, MBA *Strath.*, PhD *E.Anglia*   Sr. Lectr.

Pressey, A., BA *Luton*, PhD *Luton*   Sr. Lectr.

Russell, P. O., BSocSc *Birm.*, MA(Econ) *Manc.*, FCA   Sr. Lectr.

Tzokas, N., BSc *Athens*, MBA *Athens*, PhD *Bath*   Prof.; Head*

Waddams, C. M., BSc *Nott.*, PhD *Nott.*   Prof.

Williams, B. C., BSc *Lond.*, PhD *E.Anglia*, FCA   Sr. Lectr.

Witcher, B. J., BA *Leic.*, PhD *Stir.*   Sr. Lectr.

Other Staff: 6 Lectrs.

Research: implementation of strategy and innovation; management of market-based relationships; regulation and the management of change

Mathematics

Tel: (01603) 592844 Fax: (01603) 593868
  E-mail: a.holdom@uea.ac.uk

Cooker, M. J., BSc *Oxf.*, MSc *Oxf.*, PhD *Brist.*   Sr. Lectr.

Dzamonja, M., BS *Sarajevo*, MA *Wis.*, PhD *Wis.*   Reader

Evans, D., BA DPhil   Reader; Head*

Everest, G. R., BSc *Lond.*, PhD *Lond.*   Prof.

Korobkin, A. A., MSc *Novosibirsk*, PhD *Novosibirsk*, DSc *Novosibirsk*   Prof.

Matthews, A. J., BA *Camb.*, MSc *E.Anglia*, PhD *Reading*   Sr. Lectr.

Scott, N. H., BA *Camb.*, MSc PhD   Reader

Siemons, I. J., PhD *Lond.*   Reader

Stevens, D. P., BSc *E.Anglia*, MSc *E.Anglia*, PhD *E.Anglia*   Reader

Stevens, S. A. R., BA *Camb.*, PhD *Lond.*   Reader

Ward, T. B., BSc *Warw.*, MSc *Warw.*, PhD *Warw.*   Prof.

Other Staff: 5 Lectrs.

Research: fluid dynamics (sonic booms, stability of boundary-layer flows); geophysical fluid dynamics (ocean circulation); logic, model theory and set theory; mechanics of solids (composite materials, fabric in polar ice sheets); representation theory and algebraic combinatorics

Medicine, Health Policy and Practice

Tel: (01603) 593061 Fax: (01603) 593752
  E-mail: janet.higgs@uea.ac.uk

Abubakar, I., MB BS *Nigeria*, MSc *Lond.*   Sr. Lectr.

Bachmann, Max, MB ChB *S.Af.*, MSc *Lond.*, PhD *Brist.*   Prof., Healthcare Interfaces

Barrett, Ann, MB BS *Lond.*, MD *Lond.*, FRCP, FRCR   Prof., Clinical Oncology

Beales, I. L. P., BSc *Lond.*, MB BS *Lond.*, MD *Lond.*   Sr. Lectr.

Cassidy, Aedin, BSc *Ulster*, MSc *Aberd.*, PhD *Camb.*   Prof., Nutrition

Fairweather-Trait, S., BSc *Lond.*, MSc *Lond.*, PhD *Lond.*   Prof.

Fordham, Richard, BA *York(UK)*, MA *Leeds*, PhD *W.Aust.*   Sr. Lectr., Social Psychiatry

Fowler, David, BSc *Leeds*, MSc *Leeds*   Prof., Social Psychology

Harvey, Ian, BA *Camb.*, MB BCh *Wales*, PhD *Wales*   Prof., Epidemiology and Public Health

Heylings, David, BSc *Belf.*, MB BCh BAO *Belf.*   Sr. Lectr., Anatomy

Holland, R. C., BA *Camb.*, BM BCh *Oxf.*, PhD *E.Anglia*   Sr. Lectr.

Howe, Amanda, BA *Camb.*, MB BS *Lond.*, MD *Sheff.*, MMedEd *Sheff.*, FRCGP   Prof., Primary Care

Hunter, Paul, MBA *Open(UK)*, MB ChB *Manc.*, MD *Manc.*, FIBiol, FRCPath   Prof., Health Protection

Jennings, Barbara, BSc *E.Anglia*, PhD *E.Anglia*   Sr. Lectr., Molecular Medicine

Leinster, Prof. Samuel J., BSc *Liv.*, MB ChB *Liv.*, MD *Liv.*, FRCS, FRCSEd   Prof., Medical Education; Head*

Loke, Y. K., MB BS *Lond.*   Sr. Lectr.

MacGregor, Alexander, MB BS *Lond.*, MA *Camb.*, MSc *Manc.*, MD *Lond.*, FRCP   Prof., Chronic Illness

Mackintosh, B., BSc *Sus.*, DPhil *Sus.*   Sr. Lectr.

Mugford, Miranda, BA *Stir.*, DPhil *Oxf.*   Prof., Health Economics

Potter, J. F., BMedSci *Nott.*, BM *Nott.*, FRCP   Prof.

Price, D., BA *Camb.*, MB BChir *Camb.*   Prof.

Reynolds, Shirley A., BSc *Wales*, MSc *Leic.*, PhD *York(UK)*   Prof. and Academic Course Organiser, Clinical Psychology

Robinson, Angela, BA *Northumbria*, MSc *York(UK)*   Sr. Lectr., Health Economics

Shepstone, Lee, BSc *CNAA*, MSc *Leic.*, PhD *Brist.*   Reader, Medical Statistics

Smith, Richard, MA *York(UK)*, MSc *York(UK)*   Reader, Health Economics

Song, Fujian, PhD *Leeds*, BM MMEd   Reader, Research Synthesis

Steele, N., MB ChB *Brist.*, MSc *E.Anglia*   Sr. Lectr.

Waynforth, D. C., BSc *Lond.*, PhD *New Mexico*   Sr. Lectr.

Wileman, T. E., BPharm *Lond.*, PhD *Liv.*   Prof.

Wilson, A. M., MB ChB *Edin.*, MD *Edin.*   Sr. Lectr.

Other Staff: 17 Lectrs.; 6 Clin. Sr. Lectrs.

Research: chronic illness (asthma, diabetes, musculoskeletal disease); health economics and health policy; infection and immunity (water-borne disease, health protection, trypanosomes); psychological health; public health medicine and health sciences

Music

Tel: (01603) 592452 Fax: (01603) 250454

Impett, J. F., BMus *Lond.*, MMus *Lond.*, MSc *City(UK)*, PhD *Camb.*   Head*

Waters, S. J., BA *Nott.*, MMus *E.Anglia*, PhD *E.Anglia*   Sr. Lectr.

Other Staff: 5 Lectrs.

Nursing and Midwifery

Tel: (01603) 597001/2 Fax: (01603) 597019
  E-mail: l.dack@uea.ac.uk

Elsegood, J., BEd *E.Anglia*   Sr. Lectr.

Guyon, K., MA *E.Anglia*   Head*

Lindsay, B., BA *CNAA*   Sr. Lectr.

Pfeil, Michael, BSc MSc PhD   Sr. Lectr.

Robinson, J. E., BSc *Lond.*, PhD *E.Anglia*   Dir., Learning and Teaching

Philosophy

Tel: (01603) 592070 Fax: (01603) 250434
  E-mail: k.brandish@uea.ac.uk

Hagberg, G. L., BA *Oregon*, MA *Oregon*, PhD *Oregon*   Prof.

O'Hagan, T. D. B., BA *Oxf.*, MA *Oxf.*, DPhil *Oxf.*   Prof.

Osborne, C. J., BA *Camb.*, MA *Camb.*, PhD *Camb.*   Head*

Read, R. J., BA *Oxf.*, PhD *Rutgers*   Reader

Other Staff: 1 Lectr.; 1 Hon. Lectr./Tutor

Political, Social and International Studies

Tel: (01603) 592070 Fax: (01603) 250434

Bowker, Mike, BA *CNAA*, MA *Essex*   Sr. Lectr.

Goodwin, Barbara L., BA *Oxf.*, MA *Oxf.*, DPhil *Oxf.*   Prof., Politics

Greenaway, J. R., MA *Camb.*, PhD *Leeds*   Sr. Lectr.

Kassim, H., BA *Oxf.*, MPhil *Oxf.*, DPhil *Oxf.*   Prof.

Kemp-Welch, Tony, BSc *Lond.*, PhD *Lond.*   Sr. Lectr.

Street, J. R., BA *Warw.*, DPhil *Oxf.*   Prof.; Head*

Social Work and Psychosocial Sciences

Tel: (01603) 592068 Fax: (01603) 593552
  E-mail: swk.info@uea.ac.uk

Brandon, M. J., BA *E.Anglia*, MA *E.Anglia*   Sr. Lectr.

Crozier, R., BA *Belf.*, MSc *Stir.*, PhD *Keele*   Prof.

Dickens, J. E., BA *Camb.*, MSc *Sur.*, MA *Nott.*, PhD *E.Anglia*   Sr. Lectr.

Howe, D. K., BSc *Durh.*, MA *Nott.*, PhD *E.Anglia*   Prof.

McDonald, E. A., LLB *Hull*, MA *E.Anglia*   Sr. Lectr.; Head*

Neil, E. C., BSc *Leic.*, MA *E.Anglia*, PhD *E.Anglia*   Sr. Lectr.

Nobes, G., MA Oxf., PhD Bath Sr. Lectr.
O'Brien, M., BSc Lond., PhD Lond. Prof.
Schofield, G. L., BA Birm., MA Calif., MSW E.Anglia, PhD E.Anglia Prof.
Sellick, C., MSW E.Anglia Sr. Lectr.
Stone, N. A., LLB Exe., LLB Camb., LLM Col., MA Nott. Sr. Lectr.
Other Staff: 8 Lectrs.; 1 Tutor
Research: child and family; community care; international child welfare; policy and practice; psychosocial sciences

World Art Studies and Museology

Tel: (01603) 592817 Fax: (01603) 593642
E-mail: b.youngman@uea.ac.uk
Dell, S., BA Lond., PhD Lond. Lectr.; Head*
Heslop, T. A., BA Lond., FSA Sr. Lectr.; Head*
Hodges, R. A., OBE, BA S'ton., PhD S'ton., FSA Prof.
Mack, John, MA DPhil, FSA Prof.
Mitchell, J. B., BA Penn., FSA Reader
Thofner, M., MA Lond., MA Lond., DPhil Sus. Sr. Lectr.
Research: arts of Africa, Oceania and the Americas; Asian art; European art and archaeology; Japanese arts and culture

SPECIAL CENTRES, ETC

Arts of Africa, Oceania and the Americas, Sainsbury Research Unit for the

Tel: (01603) 592498 Fax: (01603) 259401
Hooper, S. J. P., BSc Brad., PhD Camb. Dir.*

Audio Visual Services

Tel: (01603) 592833 Fax: (01603) 593859
Browne, C. Manager*

Climatic Research Unit

Tel: (01603) 592722 Fax: (01603) 507784
E-mail: j.burgess@uea.ac.uk
Briffa, K. R., BSc E.Anglia, PhD E.Anglia Prof.; Deputy Dir.
Jones, P., BA Lanc., MSc Newcastle(UK), PhD Newcastle(UK) Prof.; Dir.*
Research: climate change; global warming

Counselling Studies, Centre for

Tel: (01603) 592651 Fax: (01603) 592668
E-mail: csr@uea.ac.uk
Moore, J., BA Reading, PhD Liv. Dir.*

East Anglian Studies, Centre of

Tel: (01603) 592667 Fax: (01603) 592660
E-mail: j.tanimoto@uea.ac.uk
Rawcliffe, C., BA Sheff., PhD Sheff. Dir.*

Research: nature and development in the regions of Britain

Overseas Development Group

Tel: (01603) 592813 Fax: (01603) 505262
E-mail: odg.gen@uea.ac.uk
McDonagh, J. F., BSc Brist., MSc Kent, PhD Lond. Sr. Lectr.; Chief Exec.*

Public Choice Studies, Centre for

Tel: (01603) 592067 Fax: (01603) 250434
Street, J. R., BA Warw., DPhil Oxf. Dir.*

Religious Education, Keswick Hall Centre for Research and Development in

Tel: (01603) 593179 Fax: (01603) 507728
Rudge, L., BA E.Anglia, MA E.Anglia Dir.*

Visual Arts Education, Applied Research in

Tel: (01603) 592465 Fax: (01603) 259401
Sekules, V., BA Lond., PhD Lond. Dir.*

Visual Arts, Sainsbury Centre for

Tel: (01603) 592466 Fax: (01603) 259401
E-mail: scva@uea.ac.uk
Johnson, J. N., BA Essex, MA Essex Dir.*

CONTACT OFFICERS

Academic affairs. Academic Registrar (Acting): Evans, Robin, BA E.Anglia, BPhil E.Anglia, MA E.Anglia (E-mail: r.evans@uea.ac.uk)
Accommodation. Accommodation Manager: Richards, M. A. (E-mail: accom@uea.ac.uk)
Admissions (first degree). Head of Admissions and Outreach: Beard, J., BA E.Anglia (E-mail: jon.beard@uea.ac.uk)
Admissions (higher degree). Head of Recruitment and Admissions Office: Beard, J., BA E.Anglia (E-mail: jon.beard@uea.ac.uk)
Adult/continuing education. Director, Continuing Education: Towner, E. G., BSc Wales (E-mail: cont.ed@uea.ac.uk)
Alumni. Alumni and Development Officer: Street, David (E-mail: david.street@uea.ac.uk)
Careers. Director, Careers Centre: Benson, Anne H., BA Essex, MA E.Anglia (E-mail: careers.centre@uea.ac.uk)
Computing services. Director, Information Services (Acting): Colam, Jonathan (E-mail: itcs.reception@uea.ac.uk)
Credit transfer. Academic Registrar (Acting): Evans, Robin, BA E.Anglia, BPhil E.Anglia, MA E.Anglia (E-mail: r.evans@uea.ac.uk)

Estates and buildings/works and services. Director of Estates and Buildings: Bond, Roger, MBA
Examinations. Examinations Officer: Ward, L. (E-mail: l.ward@uea.ac.uk)
Finance. Director of Finance: Donaldson, S. (E-mail: y.johnson@uea.ac.uk)
Health services. Senior Partner (Health services): Coathup, P. A. (E-mail: ums@uea.ac.uk)
Library (chief librarian). Library Director: Lewis, Nicholas (E-mail: nicholas.lewis@uea.ac.uk)
Personnel/human resources. Director of Personnel: Piper, C. (E-mail: d.whalen@uea.ac.uk)
Public relations. Director of Marketing and Communications: Preece, Alan, BA Open(UK) (E-mail: c.burford@uea.ac.uk)
Purchasing. Purchasing Officer: Boardman, S. (E-mail: s.c.boardman@uea.ac.uk)
Quality assurance and accreditation. Head of Learning, Teaching and Quality Office/ Assistant Registrar: Rhodes, A. (E-mail: w.forsdich@uea.ac.uk)
Research. Director, Research and Business Services (Acting): McCormick, Ian
Safety. Director, Safety Services: Donson, P. (E-mail: p.donson@uea.ac.uk)
Security. Superintendent, Security Services: McCormack, M. (E-mail: security@uea.ac.uk)
Sport and recreation. Director, Physical Recreation: Nicholls, K., BEd Lond., MA Leeds (E-mail: j.rumball@uea.ac.uk)
Staff development and training. Head of Centre for Staff and Educational Development: Levy, P. (E-mail: d.slaughter@uea.ac.uk)
Student union. Communications Officer: Boddington, Rowena (E-mail: su.comm@uea.ac.uk)
Student welfare/counselling. Dean of Students: Grant, A. E., BA Camb., MA Camb., PhD Camb. (E-mail: dos@uea.ac.uk)
Students from other countries. Dean of Students: Grant, A. E., BA Camb., MA Camb., PhD Camb. (E-mail: dos@uea.ac.uk)
Students with disabilities. Disability Co-ordinator: (vacant)
University press. Press Officer: Ogden, Anne, BA Liv. (E-mail: a.ogden@uea.ac.uk)

[Information supplied by the institution as at 6 December 2007, and edited by the ACU]

UNIVERSITY OF EAST LONDON

Founded 1992

Member of the Association of Commonwealth Universities

Postal Address: University Way, London, England E16 2RD
Telephone: (020) 8223 3000 **Fax:** (020) 8223 2900
URL: http://www.uel.ac.uk

ACTING VICE-CHANCELLOR*—Price, Prof. Susan, BSc MBA PhD
DEPUTY VICE-CHANCELLOR—Price, Prof. Susan, BSc MBA PhD
SECRETARY AND REGISTRAR‡—Ingle, Alan, BA MBA
DIRECTOR OF FINANCE—Borkhataria, Nirmal
DIRECTOR OF LEARNING SUPPORT SERVICES AND LIFELONG LEARNING—McDonald, Andrew
DIRECTOR OF INNOVATION AND STRATEGIC DEVELOPMENT—Snee, Carole, BA MA

GENERAL INFORMATION

History. The university was founded as North East London Polytechnic in 1970, incorporated as the Polytechnic of East London in 1989, and gained its current title in 1992.

The university's campuses are located at Docklands and Stratford.

Admission to first degree courses (see also United Kingdom Introduction). Through Universities and Colleges Admissions Service (UCAS).

First Degrees (see also United Kingdom Directory to Subjects of Study). BA, BEng, BSc, LLB, MEng.

Part-time study options and sandwich courses are widely available, as is the option to study a combination of 2 or 3 subjects.

Length of course. Full-time: BA, BEng, BSc, LLB: 3–4 years; MEng: 4 years. *Part-time:* BA, BEng, BSc, LLB: 5–6 years.

Higher Degrees (see also United Kingdom Directory to Subjects of Study).

Master's. LLM, MA, MBA, MPhil, MSc.

Admission. Applicants for admission to master's degrees must normally hold a first degree, a postgraduate diploma or equivalent, or have had substantial experience or employment in a relevant field.

Length of course. Full-time: LLM, MA, MBA, MPhil, MSc: 1 year. *Part-time:* LLM, MA, MBA, MPhil, MSc: 2 years.

Doctoral. PhD.

Academic Year (2007–2008). Three semesters: 24 September–14 December; 7 January–14 March; 31 March–20 June.

ACADEMIC UNITS

Arranged by schools

Architecture and the Visual Arts

Tel: (020) 8223 3405
      E-mail: s.g.harris@uel.ac.uk
Abdu'Allah, Faisal   Sr. Lectr.
Aleman, C.   Sr. Lectr.
Barrett, Martin   Sr. Lectr.
Bass, David   Sr. Lectr.
Beardsall, P.   Sr. Lectr.
Blackhall, Tessa   Sr. Lectr.
Buck, David   Sr. Lectr.
Callaghan, Carl   Sr. Lectr.
Carpenter, B.   Sr. Lectr.
Carter, Helen   Sr. Lectr.
Chandler, Alan   Sr. Lectr.
Charif, R.   Sr. Lectr.
Christiansen, Marianne   Sr. Lectr.
Ciurlo-Walker, S.   Sr. Lectr.
Coates, Paul   Sr. Lectr.
Coker, M.   Sr. Lectr.
Cook, J.   Sr. Lectr.
Court, Caryl   Sr. Lectr.
Craft, P.   Sr. Lectr.
Danicic, Amanda   Sr. Lectr.
Davey, Granville   Sr. Lectr.
Davey, K.   Sr. Lectr.
Derix, Christian   Sr. Lectr.
Foster, Tim   Principal Lectr.
Georgeson, M.   Sr. Lectr.
Gonzalez-Cebrian, Hildegard   Sr. Lectr.
Grasby, C.   Sr. Lectr.
Great-Rex, Eric J.   Sr. Lectr.
Groothuizen, C.   Sr. Lectr.
Hadrys, C.   Sr. Lectr.
Hall, R.   Sr. Lectr.
Harding, Emma   Sr. Lectr.
Hauck, Eva   Sr. Lectr.
Hay, I.   Sr. Lectr.
Hayduk, M.   Sr. Lectr.
Hertel, Kristina   Sr. Lectr.
Higgott, Andrew N.   Principal Lectr.
Hoshino, T.   Sr. Lectr.
Insull, J.   Sr. Lectr.
Kajita, Masashi   Sr. Lectr.
Kantonen, M.   Sr. Lectr.
Keller, T.   Sr. Lectr.
Kohn, Michael   Sr. Lectr.
Kraft, Clara   Sr. Lectr.
Liang, H.   Sr. Lectr.
Liebe, Jan   Sr. Lectr.
Logue, L.   Sr. Lectr.
Loh, Paul   Sr. Lectr.
Mann, Dave   Sr. Lectr.
McGuire, E.   Sr. Lectr.
Modeen, T.   Sr. Lectr.
Mooney, S.   Sr. Lectr.
Morris, Gareth   Sr. Lectr.
Mueller, M.   Sr. Lectr.
Nevin, Pete   Principal Lectr.
Nicholls, Cliff   Head*
Nigianni, P.   Sr. Lectr.
O'Pray, Mike   Prof.
O'Sullivan, Julie   Sr. Lectr.
Pegg, J.   Sr. Lectr.
Pelsmaker, S.   Sr. Lectr.

Phillips, David   Sr. Lectr.
Piesse, J.   Sr. Lectr.
Pinsky, M.   Sr. Lectr.
Poletto, M.   Sr. Lectr.
Raney, K.   Sr. Lectr.
Riches, Jane   Principal Lectr.
Robertson, L.   Sr. Lectr.
Rodic, S.   Sr. Lectr.
Roelofsma, Michele   Sr. Lectr.
Sapsford, S.   Sr. Lectr.
Senatore, A.   Sr. Lectr.
Sheng, G.   Sr. Lectr.
Sirch, D.   Sr. Lectr.
Smith, John   Prof.
Steven, U.   Sr. Lectr.
Stockwell, S.   Sr. Lectr.
Svenningsen, H.   Sr. Lectr.
Thum, Robert   Sr. Lectr.
Turko, J.   Sr. Lectr.
Vanden-Berghe, V.   Sr. Lectr.
Vasilschenko, G.   Sr. Lectr.
Ward, I.   Sr. Lectr.
Winckle, Alison   Principal Lectr.
Other Staff: 1 Reader; 24 Sr. Lectrs.; 13 Lectrs.;
      4 Subject Dirs.; 1 Technical Support

Business School

Tel: (020) 8223 6277 E-mail: r.patel@uel.ac.uk
Barry, Jim   Prof.
Bashir, Tariq   Sr. Lectr.
Bathgate, Ian   Course Dir.*
Binns, David   Sr. Lectr.
Burgess, Peter   Sr. Lectr.
Chaharbarghi, Kazem   Prof.
Chandler, John   Principal Lectr.
Clews, Emma   Sr. Lectr.
Clingan, John   Programme Dir.
Cocking, John   Principal Lectr.
Cooper, John   Sr. Lectr.
Crawshaw, Jonathan   Sr. Lectr.
Cripps, Sandy   Principal Lectr.
D'Cruz, Brendan   Principal Lectr.
Eglin, Greg   Principal Lectr.
Everitt, Mary   Sr. Lectr.
Heath, Margaret   Sr. Lectr.
Little, Robin   Sr. Lectr.
Malinowski, Carolyn   Sr. Lectr.
Marney, John   Sr. Lectr.
Marshall, Mike   Sr. Lectr.
Mottershead, Peter   Sr. Lectr.
Nwankwo, Sonny   Prof.
O'Connor, William   Sr. Lectr.
Piranfar, Hosein   Sr. Lectr.
Pontier, Maarten   Sr. Lectr.
Sandland, Stephanie   Sr. Lectr.
Sheldrake, John   Sr. Lectr.
Sparrowhawk, John   Principal Lectr.
Stirk, Christina   Sr. Lectr.
Symon, Graham   Sr. Lectr.
Taylor, Peter   Sr. Lectr.
Wright, Graham   Sr. Lectr.
Yu, Pei   Sr. Lectr.
Other Staff: 19 Lectrs.

Computing and Technology

Tel: (020) 8223 6700 E-mail: l.james@uel.ac.uk
Arunachalam, Subramaniam   Sr. Lectr.
Aybet, Jahid   Sr. Lectr.
Bailey, Wilton   Sr. Lectr.
Bayliss, Roy   Sr. Lectr.
Beaver, Rae   Principal Lectr.
Bolissian, Jacqueline   Sr. Lectr.
Brown, Sharon   Sr. Lectr.
Burr, John   Principal Lectr.
Cazan, Adrian   Sr. Lectr.
Chanerley, Andrew   Sr. Lectr.
Ciupala, Mihaela   Sr. Lectr.
Cox, Julian   Sr. Lectr.
Dixon-Gough, Robert   Sr. Lectr.
Dodds, Stephen   Prof.
Everitt, Michael   Principal Lectr.
Ford, Graham   Principal Lectr.
Freeman, Richard   Sr. Lectr.
Griffiths, Michael   Sr. Lectr.
Hakimazari, Hamid   Sr. Lectr.
Harston, Jill   Principal Lectr.
Hosny, Wada   Principal Lectr.
Hyslop, Ian   Sr. Lectr.

Imafidon, Chris   Sr. Lectr.
Ioannou, Constantinos   Principal Lectr.
Jahankhani, Hamid   Sr. Lectr.
Jahankhani, Hossein   Sr. Lectr.
Kans, Aaron   Sr. Lectr.
Kretsis, Michael   Sr. Lectr.
Latham, Richard   Principal Lectr.
Marriott, Martin   Principal Lectr.
Martin, Stephen   Principal Lectr.
Moorehead, Francis   Sr. Lectr.
Noor, Faiz   Principal Lectr.
Perryman, Roy, BSc PhD   Prof.
Pimenidis, Elias   Sr. Lectr.
Prendiville, Alison   Sr. Lectr.
Preston, David   Principal Lectr.
Ruocco, Ray   Principal Lectr.
Safieddine, Fadi   Sr. Lectr.
Saidpour, Seyed   Principal Lectr.
Slawson, Alan   Principal Lectr.
Smith, Paul   Head*
Snailum, Nic   Sr. Lectr.
Webb, Patricia   Sr. Lectr.
Whiting, Brian   Principal Lectr.
Wijeyesekera, Prof. Chitral   Principal Lectr.
Williams, Godfried   Sr. Lectr.
Xiao, Di-Chen   Sr. Lectr.
Other Staff: 11 Lectrs.; 48 Staff Members

Education

Adams, Paul   Sr. Lectr.
Ang, Lynn, BA MA PhD   Sr. Lectr.
Ashby, Penny   Sr. Lectr.
Blows, Genevieve   Sr. Lectr.
Bosanquet, Paula   Sr. Lectr.
Brennan, Caroline   Sr. Lectr.
Chakrabarty, Namita   Sr. Lectr.
Czerniawski, Gerry   Sr. Lectr.
Dalladay, Chris   Sr. Lectr.
Dean, Jim   Sr. Lectr.
Dixon, Sue, BSc MA   Principal Lectr.
Dreese, Alison   Sr. Lectr.
Garlick, Su   Sr. Lectr.
Golabek, Charles   Sr. Lectr.
Gray, John, BA MA   Sr. Lectr.
Griffiths, Alison   Sr. Lectr.
Hafez, Rania   Sr. Lectr.
Herrington, Neil   Sr. Lectr.
Kenworthy, Joanne N., BA MA   Sr. Lectr.
Kilshaw, Ian   Sr. Lectr.
Lambrou, Marina, BA MA   Sr. Lectr.
Macklin, John   Sr. Lectr.
Masterson, Helen   Sr. Lectr.
Mitchell, Helen, BA MA   Principal Lectr.
Monger, David   Sr. Lectr.
Morris, David   Sr. Lectr.
Neeves, Ramona   Sr. Lectr.
Nehusi, Kimani, BA MA PhD   Sr. Lectr.
Ogunsola, Abiola   Sr. Lectr.
Penn, Helen, BA PhD   Prof.
Preston, John   Sr. Lectr.
Quarshie, Richard   Sr. Lectr.
Serdar, Heather   Sr. Lectr.
Silberfeld, Carolyn, BSc MEd   Sr. Lectr.
Simpson, Robert   Principal Lectr.
Slater, Ann, BA BSc   Head*
Todd, Barbara   Sr. Lectr.
Trushell, J. M., BEd PhD   Sr. Lectr.
Weiss, Nina   Sr. Lectr.
Weston, Carrie   Sr. Lectr.
Woodage, Simon   Sr. Lectr.
Other Staff: 13 Lectrs.; 32 Staff Members

Health and Bioscience

Tel: (020) 8223 4066
      E-mail: r.d.worgan@uel.ac.uk
Aceijas, Carmen   Sr. Lectr.
Adigwe, Gloria   Sr. Lectr.
Armstrong, Paul   Sr. Lectr.
Atkinson, Karen   Sr. Lectr.
Baldry-Currens, Julie   Principal Lectr.
Beale, James   Sr. Lectr.
Bone, Anthony   Principal Lectr.
Brook, Josephine   Sr. Lectr.
Carpenter, Roger   Sr. Lectr.
Catwell, Barbara   Principal Lectr.
Copnell, Graham   Sr. Lectr.
Corcoran, Nova   Sr. Lectr.
Corcoran, Olivia   Sr. Lectr.

Cramp, Mary Sr. Lectr.
Culpan, Jane Sr. Lectr.
Cutler, Ron Principal Lectr.
Cutler, Sally Sr. Lectr.
Dourida, Maria Sr. Lectr.
Doyle, Gary Sr. Lectr.
Gaimster, Cindy Sr. Lectr.
Garlick, John Principal Lectr.
George, John Sr. Lectr.
Goodfellow, Barbara Sr. Lectr.
Hill, Tom Sr. Lectr.
Holt, Sandra Sr. Lectr.
Howes, Shan Sr. Lectr.
Hughes, Mike Sr. Lectr.
Hunt, Richard Principal Lectr.
Izod, Alexander Sr. Lectr.
Johnstone, James Sr. Lectr.
Lam, Ray Sr. Lectr.
Lindsay, Richard Principal Lectr.
Meah, Mohammed Sr. Lectr.
Moffett, Bruce Sr. Lectr.
Morgan, Winston Principal Lectr.
Morrissey, Ilana Sr. Lectr.
Needham, Joy Sr. Lectr.
Nicholls, Elizabeth Sr. Lectr.
Parslow, Charlotte Sr. Lectr.
Pendry, Barbara Sr. Lectr.
Petterson, Stephanie Sr. Lectr.
Potter, Jacqui Principal Lectr.
Punchard, Neville Prof.; Head*
Ranasinghe, Rane Sr. Lectr.
Rees, Sharon Sr. Lectr.
Resteghini, Carol Sr. Lectr.
Rostron, John Sr. Lectr.
Rowley, Dave Principal Lectr.
Salmon, Mike Sr. Lectr.
Savage, Patsy Sr. Lectr.
Shaw, Phil Sr. Lectr.
Simmonite, Neil Sr. Lectr.
Smith, Patricia Sr. Lectr.
Smith, Roland Sr. Lectr.
Steele, Wilson Sr. Lectr.
Steer, Jonathan Sr. Lectr.
Terrazzini, Nadia Sr. Lectr.
Tkatchenko, Elena Sr. Lectr.
Tocher, Joanne Principal Lectr.
Watkinson, Dave Sr. Lectr.
Webb, Geoff Sr. Lectr.
Westhead, Elizabeth Sr. Lectr.
Williamson, Andy Sr. Lectr.
Wright, John Principal Lectr.
Wylde, Charmain Sr. Lectr.
Other Staff: 8 Lectrs.; 53 Staff Members

Law

Tel: (020) 8223 2113
E-mail: p.berwick@uel.ac.uk
Fairweather, Fiona, LLB Sr. Lectr.; Head*
Griffiths, Anne Sr. Lectr.
Gunter, Anthony Sr. Lectr.
Levy, Sharon I., LLB Sr. Lectr.
Lim, H., LLB MA Principal Lectr.
Silke, Andrew Principal Lectr.
Stirk, Ian Sr. Lectr.
Strawson, John Sr. Lectr.
Torgbor, Shan Sr. Lectr.
Wilson, A. P. Sr. Lectr.
Other Staff: 10 Lectrs.; 1 Assoc. Lectr.; 1
Temp. Lectr.; 1 Lectr.†

Psychology

Tel: (020) 8223 4480
E-mail: i.linton@uel.ac.uk
Ahmed, Bipasha Sr. Lectr.
Anderson, Irina Principal Lectr.
Attree, Elizabeth Principal Lectr.
Baker, Martyn Sr. Lectr.
Bayne, Rowan Prof.
Boniwell, Ilona Sr. Lectr.
Boyle, Mary Prof.
Burton, Andy Principal Lectr.
Cahill, Sharon Sr. Lectr.
Clifford, Brian Prof.
Collard, Patrizia Sr. Lectr.
Dancey, Christine Prof.
Dawkins, Lynne Sr. Lectr.
Dell, Pippa Principal Lectr.
Dickins, Tom Principal Lectr.

Edmonds, Caroline Sr. Lectr.
Gersch, Irvine Prof.
Harper, David Sr. Lectr.
Holloway, Mark Principal Lectr.
Jansari, Ashok Principal Lectr.
Java, Ros Sr. Lectr.
Jinks, Gordon Principal Lectr.
Jones-Chesters, Matthew Sr. Lectr.
Lasite, Claudia Sr. Lectr.
Lawrence, Jane Sr. Lectr.
Macdonald, Alison Sr. Lectr.
Moore, Derek Prof.
Mulvey, Rachel Principal Lectr.
Passmore, Jonathan Sr. Lectr.
Patel, Nimisha Sr. Lectr.
Pawson, Chris Sr. Lectr.
Popovic, Nebojsa Sr. Lectr.
Rahman, Qazi Principal Lectr.
Ridley, Donald Principal Lectr.
Roberts, Amanda Sr. Lectr.
Rose, David, BSc PhD, FBPsS Prof.; Head*
Spragg, Melanie Sr. Lectr.
Summers, Lucia Sr. Lectr.
Thoma, Volker Sr. Lectr.
Thompson, Kate Sr. Lectr.
Thomson, Rob Sr. Lectr.
Tribe, Rachel Sr. Lectr.
Turner, John Principal Lectr.
Vitkovitch, Melanie Principal Lectr.
Walsh, James Sr. Lectr.
Wolfendale, Sheila Prof.
Other Staff: 10 Lectrs.; 1 Assoc. Lectr.; 46 Staff
Members

Social Science, Media and Cultural Studies

Tel: (020) 8223 4216
E-mail: j.c.sherman@uel.ac.uk
Andrews, Molly Sr. Lectr.
Bandyopadhyay, Mamata Sr. Lectr.
Blake, Andrew Assoc. Head*
Breed, Ananda Sr. Lectr.
Burnett, Judith Principal Lectr.
Cannon, Robert Sr. Lectr.
Carson, Fiona Assoc. Subject Area Co-
ordinator
Cassidy, Jules Sr. Lectr.
Craig, Linda Sr. Lectr.
Dave, Paul Sr. Lectr.
De Miranda, Alvaro Sr. Lectr.
Diamond, Nicola Sr. Lectr.
Dona, Giorgia Sr. Lectr.
Dorrington, David Sr. Lectr.
Eastwood, Steven Sr. Lectr.
Edwards, Judith Sr. Lectr.
Garrett, Roberta Sr. Lectr.
Hobden, Stephen Sr. Lectr.
Hodgkin, Kate Sr. Lectr.
Jeffers, Sydney Sr. Lectr.
Jeffery, Graham Sr. Lectr.
Johns, Robert Principal Lectr.
Jones, David Sr. Lectr.
Joseph, Marie Sr. Lectr.
Kempadoo, Roshini Sr. Lectr.
Luddick, Dawn Sr. Lectr.
Lynn, Simon Sr. Lectr.
Marriott, John Sr. Lectr.
McWatt, Tessa Sr. Lectr.
Mellor, Noha Sr. Lectr.
Mitchell, Grethe Sr. Lectr.
Mutter, Robin Sr. Lectr.
Myles, John Sr. Lectr.
Nava, Mica Subject Area Co-ordinator
Newman, Mary Sr. Lectr.
Parfitt, Trevor Sr. Lectr.
Parkinson, Clare Sr. Lectr.
Pogoda, Stacey Sr. Lectr.
Poynter, Gavin Prof.
Reddington, Helen Sr. Lectr.
Richardson, Malcolm Sr. Lectr.
Robbins, Derek Sr. Lectr.
Sharma, Ashwani Principal Lectr.
Sims, Lionel Sr. Lectr.
Sims, Martin Sr. Lectr.
Squire, Corinne Sr. Lectr.
Stepulage, Linda Sr. Lectr.
Stokes, Jane Sr. Lectr.
Storr, Merl Sr. Lectr.

Taylor, Barbara Sr. Lectr.
Thomas, Graham Sr. Lectr.
Tiwari, Meera Sr. Lectr.
Turner, Eva Principal Lectr.
Valentine, Paul Sr. Lectr.
Vitali, Valentina Sr. Lectr.
Von Schelling, Vivian Sr. Lectr.
Ward, Adrian Sr. Lectr.
Other Staff: 53 Lectrs.; 1 Assoc. Lectr.; 2
Visiting Lectrs.; 2 Lectrs.†

CONTACT OFFICERS

Academic affairs. Secretary and Registrar:
Ingle, Alan, BA MBA
(E-mail: a.ingle@uel.ac.uk)
Accommodation. Residential Services
Manager: Smith, Tracy
(E-mail: t.smith@uel.ac.uk)
Adult/continuing education. Director, Centre
for Widening Participation: (vacant)
(E-mail: continuum@uel.ac.uk)
Alumni. Development and Alumni Manager:
Salehi-Kellaway, Fariba
(E-mail: f.salehi-kellaway@uel.ac.uk)
Careers. Head of Employability: Bola, Femi
(E-mail: employability@uel.ac.uk)
Computing services. Director of Information
Technology Services: Wright, Tony
(E-mail: t.wright@uel.ac.uk)
Equal opportunities. Equality and Diversity
Manager: Wahab, Abdul
(E-mail: a.wahab@uel.ac.uk)
Estates and buildings/works and services.
Secretary to Director of Facilities: Hines,
Theresa (E-mail: t.hines@uel.ac.uk)
Examinations. Secretary and Registrar: Ingle,
Alan, BA MBA (E-mail: a.ingle@uel.ac.uk)
Finance. Director of Finance: Borkhataria,
Nirmal (E-mail: n.k.borkhataria@uel.ac.uk)
General enquiries. Applicant Enquiries Co-
ordinator: Morley, Emma
(E-mail: e.l.morley@uel.ac.uk)
International office. Head, International
Office: Clarke, Adrienne
(E-mail: international@uel.ac.uk)
Library (chief librarian). Director of Learning
Support Services and Lifelong Learning:
McDonald, Andrew
(E-mail: a.mcdonald@uel.ac.uk)
Marketing. Director of Corporate Marketing
and International Office: Hollis, Sandra, BA
MA (E-mail: s.hollis@uel.ac.uk)
Public relations. Public Relations Manager:
Wilson, Patrick (E-mail: p.wilson@uel.ac.uk)
Publications. Assistant Head of Student
Recruitment Marketing: Cole, Neil
(E-mail: n.cole@uel.ac.uk)
Quality assurance and accreditation. Quality
Assurance Manager: Carter, Ruth
(E-mail: r.carter@uel.ac.uk)
Research. Director, Research: Loughrey, Bryan
(E-mail: b.loughrey@uel.ac.uk)
Safety. Health and Safety Officer: Basi, Del
(E-mail: d.s.basi@uel.ac.uk)
Scholarships, awards, loans. Marketing
Support Officer: Moreton, Vicki
(E-mail: v.moreton@uel.ac.uk)
Schools liaison. Schools Partnership Co-
ordinator: Mclinden, Maggie
(E-mail: m.mclinden@uel.ac.uk)
Security. Director of Security: Hickling, Marcia
(E-mail: m.hickling@uel.ac.uk)
Student union. General Secretary (Student
union): Matewu, Caston
(E-mail: c.matewu@uel.ac.uk)
Student welfare/counselling. Secretary and
Registrar: Ingle, Alan, BA MBA
(E-mail: a.ingle@uel.ac.uk)
Students with disabilities. Disability/Dyslexia
Advisor: Asad, Fozya
(E-mail: f.asad@uel.ac.uk)
University press. Assistant Head of Student
Recruitment Marketing: Cole, Neil
(E-mail: n.cole@uel.ac.uk)

[Information supplied by the institution as at 16 January
2008, and edited by the ACU]

EDGE HILL UNIVERSITY

Founded 1885

Member of the Association of Commonwealth Universities

Postal Address: St Helens Road, Ormskirk, Lancashire L39 4QP
Telephone: (01695) 575171 **Fax:** (01695) 579997
URL: http://www.edgehill.ac.uk

VICE-CHANCELLOR*—Cater, John, BA PhD
UNIVERSITY SECRETARY‡—Munro, Lesley

UNIVERSITY OF EDINBURGH

Founded 1583

Member of the Association of Commonwealth Universities

Postal Address: Old College, South Bridge, Edinburgh, Scotland EH8 9YL
Telephone: (0131) 650 1000 **Fax:** (0131) 650 2147 **E-mail:** communications.office@ed.ac.uk
URL: http://www.ed.ac.uk

PRINCIPAL AND VICE-CHANCELLOR*—O'Shea, Prof. Sir Timothy M. M., KB, BSc Sus., PhD Leeds
VICE-PRINCIPAL—Boulton, Prof. Geoffrey S., OBE, BSc Birm., PhD Birm., DSc Birm., FRS, FRSEd
VICE-PRINCIPAL—Bownes, Prof. Mary, BSc Sus., DPhil Sus., FIBiol, FRES, FRSEd
VICE-PRINCIPAL—Chapman, Prof. Stephen K., BSc Newcastle(UK), PhD Newcastle(UK), FRSEd
VICE-PRINCIPAL, DEVELOPMENT—Dawkins III, Young P., BA Dartmouth
VICE-PRINCIPAL—Haywood, Prof. J., BSc Edin., PhD Open(UK)
VICE-PRINCIPAL—Kenway, Prof. Richard D., BSc Exe., DPhil Oxf., FRSEd
VICE-PRINCIPAL—van Heyningen, Simon, MA Camb., PhD Camb., FRSChem, FIBiol
VICE-PRINCIPAL—Bruce, Prof. Vicki, OBE, MA PhD, FBA, FRSEd
VICE-PRINCIPAL—Savill, Prof. Sir. J. S., KB, BA PhD, FRCP
VICE-PRINCIPAL—Bulfield, Prof. G. J., BSc Leeds, PhD, FRSEd
VICE-PRINCIPAL—Waterhouse, Prof. Lorraine, BA W.Ont., MSW
UNIVERSITY SECRETARY‡—Cornish, Melvyn, BSc Leic.
RECTOR—Ballard, Mark, MA
ACADEMIC REGISTRAR AND DEPUTY SECRETARY—Nelson, D. Bruce, BSc Glas., PhD Glas., MBA
DIRECTOR OF FINANCE—Gorringe, Jon

GENERAL INFORMATION

History. The university was originally founded in 1583 as the College of Edinburgh, or Tounis College, by the town council of Edinburgh under the charter of King James VI.

Admission to first degree courses (see also United Kingdom Introduction). Through Universities and Colleges Admissions Service (UCAS).

First Degrees (see also United Kingdom Directory to Subjects of Study). BA, BD, BEd, BEng, BMus, BSc, BScMedSci, BScSocSci, BScVetSc, BVM&S, LLB, MA, MB ChB, MChem, MChemPhys, MEng, MPhys.

Honours degrees normally last 4 years full-time or 6-10 years part-time. General/Ordinary degrees normally last 3 years full time or 5-8 years part-time.

Length of course. Full-time: BScSocSci, MA: 3 years; BScMedSci, BScVetSc: 3–4 years; BVM&S, MB ChB, MChem, MChemPhys, MEng, MPhys: 5 years.

Higher Degrees (see also United Kingdom Directory to Subjects of Study).

Master's. LLM, MBA, MEd, MLitt, MMus, MPhil, MRes, MSc, MSW, MTh.

Admission. Applicants for admission to master's degrees must normally hold an appropriate first degree with at least good second class honours, or have appropriate equivalent professional experience.

Taught modular master's: 1 year full-time or 2–6 years part-time. MBA in international business: 15 months full-time. MSW: 21 months full-time.

Length of course. Full-time: LLM, MBA, MEd, MMus, MRes, MSc, MTh: 1 year; MLitt, MPhil: 2 years. Part-time: LLM, MEd, MMus, MSc, MTh: 2–3 years; MBA: 2½ years; MLitt, MPhil: 3–5 years.

Doctoral. DClinPsychol, DD, DDS, DLitt, DMus, DPsychol, DSc, DVM&S, EdD, EngD, LLD, MD, PhD.

Admission. PhD: at least upper second class honours; DDS, MD, DPsychol, DVM&S: awarded on submission of a thesis; DD, DLitt, DSc, LLD, DMus: awarded on published work.

Length of course. Full-time: DPsychol, DVM&S: 1½ years; DDS, MD: 1½–5 years; DClinPsychol, PhD: 3 years; EngD: 4–5 years. Part-time: DPsychol, DVM&S: 1½ years; DDS, MD: 1½–5 years; EdD, PhD: 4–6 years.

Libraries. Volumes: 3,817,500. Periodicals subscribed to: 9400. Special collections: A. S. Cumming (Italian studies); Adam Smith (literature, classics, political economy, science); Alexander Cameron and Donald Mackinnon (Celtic studies and theology); Arthur Berriedale Keith (Indian literature, history and politics, constitutional history of British Commonwealth); Arthur Koestler (literature); Barry Bloomfield (W. H. Auden and associated 1930s writers); Clement Littill (theology); David Laing (Scottish charters, mediaeval and modern manuscripts on Scottish history and literature, early Scottish music texts, letters of artists); Donald Tovey (music scores); Dugland Stewart (political economy, moral philosophy, mathematics); Halliwell-Phillipps (Shakespeare, seventeenth- and eighteenth-century English drama); Hugh Cleghorn (Indian forestry, land use and botany); James Corson (Sir Walter Scott); James Geikie (geology); James Nairn

(theology, philosophy, history and literature); James Thin (hymnology); James V. Compton (American history); John Stuart Blackie (Greek); Lord Abercromby (archaeology, ethnology, linguistics); Marjorie Kennedy-Fraser (Scottish music, dance, history and literature); Penguin Books; Robert Bertram Serjeant (Middle Eastern studies); Sigfoes Bl[154]ndal (Icelandic studies); Sir John Murray (zoology, geography, geology); Sophie Weiss (Beethoven); W. B. Hodgson (economics); William Drummond of Hawthornden (English, Latin, Italian, French and Spanish literature); William Montgomery Watt (Islamic studies); William Speirs Bruce (oceanography and Polar studies); also libraries of Dumfries Presbytery, Edinburgh Mathematical Society, Royal Physical Society, Royal Scottish Forestry Society.

Academic Year (2007–2008). Two semesters: 17 September–14 December; 7 January–23 May.

Income (2005–2006). Total, £435,015,000.

Statistics. Staff (2006–2007): 7691 (4241 academic, 3450 non-academic). Students (2006–2007): full-time 21,737 (9514 men, 12,223 women); part-time 3854 (1691 men, 2163 women); international 6078 (2743 men, 3335 women); undergraduate 18,440 (7851 men, 10,589 women); master's 3481 (1385 men, 2096 women); doctoral 3670 (1969 men, 1701 women).

FACULTIES/SCHOOLS

Humanities and Social Science, College of

Tel: (0131) 650 4646 Fax: 0131) 650 6512
E-mail: chss@ed.ac.uk
Head of College: Bruce, Prof. Vicki, OBE, MA PhD, FBA, FRSEd
College Registrar: Gribben, Frank, BA Stir., MPhil Stir.

Medicine and Veterinary Medicine, College of

Tel: (0131) 242 6531 E-mail: mvm@ed.ac.uk
Head of College: Savill, Prof. Sir. J. S., KB, BA PhD, FRCP
College Registrar: Golightley, Louis, BSc(Econ) Lond., MBA

Science and Engineering, College of

Tel: (0131) 650 5759 Fax: (0131) 650 5738
E-mail: sciengmail@ed.ac.uk
Head of College: Bulfield, Prof. G. J., BSc Leeds, PhD, FRSEd
College Registrar: Welch, D. A., BSc Camb., PhD Camb.

ACADEMIC UNITS

Arts, Culture and Environment, School of

Tel: (0131) 650 6329 Fax: (0131) 651 4229
E-mail: ace@ed.ac.uk
Brennan, John, MA   Sr. Lectr.
Bury, Michael, MA Camb., MA Lond.   Sr. Lectr.
Cairns, Stephen, BA BArch PhD   Sr. Lectr.
Cowling, Elizabeth G., BA Oxf., MA Lond.   Prof., 20th Century European Art
Coyne, Richard D., BArch PhD   Prof., Architectural Computing; Head*
Dorrian, M. W., BArch PhD   Sr. Lectr.
Edwards, Michael, BA Brist., MMus Brist., MA Stan.   Sr. Lectr.
Frith, Simon, BArch PhD   Prof.; Tovey Chair of Music
Hammer, Martin A., BA Lond.   Reader
Hillenbrand, Robert, MA Camb., DPhil Oxf., FRSEd   Prof., Islamic Art
Howarth, David, MA Camb., PhD Camb.   Reader
Kitchen, John P., BMus Glas., MA Glas., PhD Camb., FRCO   Sr. Lectr.
Lawson, Jim, MA PhD   Sr. Lectr.
Lee, John R., MA PhD   Sr. Lectr.
Lewis, D.   Hon. Prof.
Lowrey, J. P., MA St And.   Sr. Lectr.
MacDonald, A. J., BSc PhD   Prof., Architectural Studies
McLachlan, Fiona, MA   Sr. Lectr.
Myers, Arnold, BSc St And., PhD   Prof., Organology
Nelson, Peter W., BMus Glas., MA Glas., MMus   Prof., Music and Technology
O'Regan, Noel, BMus N.U.I., MSc N.U.I., DPhil Oxf.   Sr. Lectr.
Osborne, N., BA Oxf., BMus Oxf.   Reid Prof.
Pedreschi, Remo, BSc Strath., PhD   Prof., Architectural Technology
Russell, Terence M., BArch Sheff., PhD Sheff., FRIAS   Reader
Thomson, Richard, BA MA PhD, FRSEd   Watson Gordon Prof.
Tolley, Thomas S., BA E.Anglia, PhD E.Anglia   Sr. Lectr.
Turnbull, Michael, MA Oxf., DPhil Oxf.   Sr. Lectr.
Whyte, Iain B., BA Nott., MPhil Nott., MA Leeds, PhD Camb., FRSEd   Prof., Architectural History
Wiszniewski, Dorian, BArch   Sr. Lectr.
Other Staff: 17 Lectrs.; 1 Sr. Res. Fellow; 8 Res. Assocs.; 2 Res. Fellows; 23 Hon. Fellows
Vacant Posts: 1 Forbes Prof.

Biological Sciences, School of

Tel: (0131) 650 5525 Fax: (0131) 650 6556
E-mail: hossbs@ed.ac.uk
Aitken, Alastair, BSc H-W, MSc Newcastle(UK), PhD   Prof., Protein Biochemistry
Allan, James, BSc Edin., PhD Edin.   Reader
Allen, J. E., BS PhD   Prof., Immunobiology
Allshire, Robin, BA Edin., PhD Edin.   Prof., Chromosome Biology
Anderton, Steve, BSc CNAA, PhD Newcastle(UK)   Prof., Therapeutic Immunology
Barlow, Paul N., BSc PhD   Prof., Structural Biology
Barton, N. H., BA Camb., PhD E.Anglia, FRS, FRSEd   Prof., Evolutionary Genetics
Beggs, Jean D., BSc Glas., PhD Glas., FRS, FRSEd   Prof., Molecular Biology
Bird, Adrian P., CBE, BSc Sus., PhD, FRS, FRSEd   Buchanan Prof., Genetics
Blackmore, Stephen, BSc PhD, FIBiol, FRSEd   Hon. Prof.
Blaxter, M. L., BSc PhD   Prof., Evolutionary Genomics
Bond, D. J., BSc Wales, PhD Camb.   Sr. Lectr.; Dir., Biol. Teaching Orgn.
Bownes, Mary, BSc Sus., DPhil Sus., FIBiol, FRES, FRSEd   Prof., Developmental Biology
Braithwaite, V. A., BA DPhil   Sr. Lectr.
Carter, R., BSc PhD   Prof. Fellow
Charlesworth, Brian, BA Camb., PhD Camb., FRS, FRSEd   Prof. Fellow
Charlesworth, Deborah, BA PhD, FRSEd, FRS   Prof. Fellow
Corbet, P. S., BSc Reading, DSc Reading, PhD Camb., ScD Camb., FRSEd, FIBiol, FESC   Hon. Prof.
Coulson, Andrew, MA Oxf., DPhil Oxf.   Sr. Lectr.
Davis, Ilan, BSc PhD   Prof., Cell Biology
Deacon, J. W., BSc PhD   Sr. Lectr.
Deag, J. M., BSc Leic., PhD Brist.   Sr. Lectr.
Doerner, Peter, DrRerNat   Sr. Lectr.
Earnshaw, W. C., BA Colby, PhD M.I.T., FRSEd   Prof. Fellow
Ennos, Richard, MA Camb., PhD Liv.   Reader
Fantes, Peter A., MA Camb., PhD Leic.   Reader
Finnegan, David J., BSc Adel., PhD, FRSEd   Prof., Molecular Genetics
French, Vernon, BSc Sus., DPhil Sus.   Sr. Lectr.
Fry, Stephen C., BSc Leic., PhD Leic., FRSEd   Prof., Plant Biochemistry
Gallagher, M. P., BSc Strath., PhD Strath.   Sr. Lectr.
Gray, David, BSc Wales, MSc Birm., PhD Birm.   Prof., Immunology
Haley, Chris, BSc Birm., PhD Birm., FRSEd   Hon. Prof.
Halliday, Karen J., BSc PhD   Sr. Lectr.
Harrington, Lea A., BSc McM., MSc Tor., PhD N.Y.   Reader
Healy, Sue, BSc Otago, DPhil Oxf.   Sr. Lectr.
Hudson, A. D., BA Oxf., PhD E.Anglia   Prof., Developmental Genetics
Hughes, Gareth, BA York(UK), DPhil York(UK), FIMA   Reader
Illius, Andrew, PhD Nott., BSc   Prof., Animal Ecology; Head*
Keightley, Peter D., BSc Edin., PhD Edin.   Prof., Evolutionary Genetics
Lancaster, J., BSc Br.Col., MSc Br.Col., PhD Lond.   Sr. Lectr.
Leach, David R. F., BSc Sus., DPhil Sus.   Prof., Molecular Genetics
Leigh-Brown, Andrew J., BSc Lond., PhD Leic.   Prof., Evolutionary Genetics
Loake, Gary J., BSc W.England, PhD Durh.   Prof., Molecular Plant Sciences
Maizels, R. M., BSc PhD, FRSEd   Prof., Zoology
Matthews, Keith, BSc Brun., PhD Glas.   Prof., Parasite Biology
McBride, J. S., MSc Prague, PhD   Sr. Lectr.
Medvinsky, A., BSc Moscow, PhD   Prof., Haematopoietic Stem Cell Biology
Millar, Andrew J., BA PhD   Prof., Systems Biology
Nee, S., BA MA DPhil   Prof., Social Evolution

Oparka, K. J., BSc PhD, FRSEd   Regius Prof., Plant Science
Pemberton, J. M., BA Oxf., PhD Reading   Prof., Evolutionary Ecology
Preston, Patricia M., BSc Lond., PhD Lond.   Sr. Lectr.
Read, Andrew, BSc Otago, DPhil Oxf., FRSEd   Prof., Natural History
Read, N. D., BSc Brist., PhD Brist.   Prof., Fungal Cell Biology
Reid, Graeme A., PhD Dund., BSc   Prof., Molecular Microbiology
Sawyer, Lindsay, BSc PhD, FRSChem   Prof., Biomolecular Structure
Stone, G. N., BA DPhil   Sr. Lectr.
Telfer, Evelyn, BSc CNAA, PhD Edin.   Sr. Lectr.
Tollervey, David, BSc PhD, FRS, FRSEd   Prof. Fellow
Tyers, Michael D., BSc PhD, FRSChem   Prof., Systems Biology
Visscher, Peter, MSc Edin., PhD Edin., BSc   Reader
Walkinshaw, M. D., BSc PhD, FRSEd   Prof., Structural Biochemistry
Walliker, David, BA Oxf., PhD Lond.   Hon. Prof.
Ward, Bruce, MA Oxf., MSc Newcastle(UK), PhD Birm.   Sr. Lectr.
West, Stuart A., BA Camb., PhD Camb.   Prof., Evolutionary Ecology
Woolliams, John, MA DSc   Hon. Prof.
Other Staff: 12 Lectrs.; 6 Sr. Res. Fellows; 106 Res. Fellows; 25 Res. Assocs.; 1 Hon. Lectr.; 25 Hon. Fellows
Vacant Posts: 1 Regius Prof., Molecular Biology

Chemistry, School of

Tel: (0131) 650 7546 Fax: (0131) 650 6453
E-mail: chemistry@ed.ac.uk
Arnold, Polly L., MA DPhil   Reader
Attfield, J. Paul, BA Oxf., MA Oxf., DPhil Oxf.   Prof., Materials Science at Extreme Conditions
Bailey, Philip J., BSc Lough., PhD Camb.   Sr. Lectr.
Barlow, Paul N., BSc PhD   Prof., Structural Biology
Baxter, R. L., BSc Glas., PhD Glas.   Prof., Chemical Biology
Bradley, Mark, BA Oxf., DPhil Oxf.   Prof., Chemical Biology
Cape, J. Neil, BSc St And., PhD Camb., DSc St And., FRSChem   Hon. Prof.
Chapman, Stephen K., BSc Newcastle(UK), PhD Newcastle(UK), FRSEd   Prof., Biological Inorganic Chemistry
Donovan, Robert J., OBE, BSc Wales, PhD Camb., FRSChem, FRSEd   Prof., Physical Chemistry
Dryden, David T. F., BSc Glas., PhD Glas.   Reader
Harrison, Andrew, MA Oxf., DPhil Oxf., FRSEd   Prof., Solid State Chemistry
Heal, Matthew R., MA Camb., DPhil Oxf.   Sr. Lectr.
Hulme, Alison N., BA Camb., PhD Camb.   Sr. Lectr.
Jones, Anita C., BSc Wales, PhD Wales   Reader
Langridge-Smith, Pat, BSc Brist., PhD Brist.   Reader
Leigh, David A., BSc PhD, FRSChem, FRSEd   Forbes Prof., Organic Chemistry
Love, Jason B., BSc Salf., PhD Salf.   Sr. Lectr.
Madden, Paul, BSc MA DPhil, FRS, FIP   Prof., Physical Chemistry
McDougall, Gordon, BSc E.Anglia, PhD Glas.   Sr. Lectr.
McNab, Hamish, BSc St And., PhD St And.   Prof., Heterocyclic Chemistry
Mount, Andrew R., BSc Lond., MA Camb., PhD Lond.   Reader
Parsons, Simon H., BSc Durh., PhD New Br.   Prof., Crystallography
Paton, R. Michael, BSc St And., PhD St And.   Reader
Pulham, Colin R., BA Oxf., DPhil Oxf.   Sr. Lectr.

Rankin, David W. H., MA *Camb.*, PhD *Camb.*, FRSEd   Prof., Structural Chemistry
Robertson, Neil, BSc *Edin.*, PhD *Edin.*   Sr. Lectr.
Tasker, Peter A., BA *Oxf.*, MA *Oxf.*, DPhil *York(UK)*, FRSChem   Prof., Industrial Chemistry
Yellowlees, Lesley J., MBE, BSc PhD   Prof., Inorganic Electrochemistry; Head*
Other Staff: 7 Lectrs.; 1 Sr. Res. Fellow; 28 Res. Fellows; 2 Res. Assocs.; 14 Hon. Fellows
Vacant Posts: 1 Crum Brown Prof.

Divinity, School of

Tel: (0131) 650 8900 Fax: (0131) 650 7952
   E-mail: divinity@ed.ac.uk
Adams, Nicholas S., BA MA PhD   Sr. Lectr.
Althaus-Reid, Marcella M., PhD *St And.*   Prof., Contextual Theology
Barstad, Hans, DrTheol *Oslo*   Prof., Hebrew and Old Testament Studies
Bond, Helen K., PhD *Durh.*   Sr. Lectr.
Brown, Stewart J., BA *Ill.*, MA *Chic.*, PhD *Chic.*, FRHistS   Prof., Ecclesiastical History
Cox, James L., BA *Wichita*, PhD *Aberd.*   Prof., Religious Studies
Dawson, Jane, BA *Durh.*, PhD *Durh.*, FRHistS   Prof., Reformation History
Fergusson, David, MA *Glas.*, BD *Edin.*, DPhil *Oxf.*, FRSEd   Prof.
Foster, Paul, BSc *W.Aust.*, BEd *W.Aust.*, BD *Murd.*, MSt *Oxf.*, DPhil *Oxf.*   Sr. Lectr.
Hurtado, L. W., MA PhD   Prof., New Testament Language, Literature and Theology; Head*
Lim, Timothy H., BA MPhil DPhil   Prof., Hebrew Bible and Second Temple Judaism
McDowell, J. C., BD PhD   Sr. Lectr.
Mitchell, J. P., MA *Camb.*, MA *Durh.*, PhD *Edin.*   Sr. Lectr.
Northcott, Michael S., BA *Durh.*, MA *Durh.*, PhD *CNAA*   Prof., Ethics
O'Donovan, Oliver, MA DPhil   Prof., Christian Ethics
Openshaw, Jeanne, BA PhD   Sr. Lectr.
Purcell, Michael, MA PhD   Sr. Lectr.
Reimer, David J., BA MA DPhil   Sr. Lectr.
Thompson, Jack, BA *Belf.*, PhD   Sr. Lectr.
Walls, Andrew F., OBE, MA *Oxf.*, BLitt *Oxf.*, DD *Aberd.*   Hon. Prof.
Other Staff: 9 Lectrs.; 1 Res. Assoc.; 8 Hon. Fellows

Education, Moray House School of

Tel: (0131) 651 6138 Fax: (0131) 651 6052
   E-mail: education@ed.ac.uk
Anderson, C. D. B., MA *St And.*, MEd PhD   Sr. Lectr.
Arshad, Rowena, OBE, MEd *H-W*   Sr. Lectr.
Carr, David, BA *Leeds*, MA *Lond.*   Prof., Philosophy of Education
Clough, Sharon, BEd *Lond.*, BA *Open(UK)*, MA *Leeds*   Sr. Lectr.
Coleman, S., BA PhD   Sr. Lectr.
Conlon, Tom, MSc *Glas.*, BSc PhD   Sr. Lectr.
Cosford, Brian D., BSc(SocialSciences) *S'ton.*, MPhil *Sur.*   Sr. Lectr.
Crowther, J., BSc *Newcastle(UK)*, MA *York(UK)*   Sr. Lectr.
Cunningham, Elizabeth, BA *Open(UK)*, LLB *Strath.*, MEd *Glas.*   Sr. Lectr.
Currie, Candace, BSc *St And.*, PhD *Edin.*   Prof., Child and Adolescent Health
Cutting, Joan, MSc PhD   Sr. Lectr.
Day, Katherine J., BA *S'ton.*, PhD *Edin.*   Sr. Lectr.
Entwistle, Noel, BSc *Sheff.*, PhD *Aberd.*, FSRHE, FBPsS   Hon. Prof.
Frame, John, BA *Stir.*, MSc   Sr. Lectr.
Griffiths, Morwenna, BSc *Brist.*, MEd *Brist.*, PhD *Brist.*   Prof., Classroom Learning
Haywood, J., BSc *Edin.*, PhD *Open(UK)*   Dir., Media and Learning Technol. Service; Prof., e-Learning
Higgins, Peter, BSc *Kent*, MSc *Lond.*, PhD *Aberd.*   Prof., Outdoor and Environmental Education
Hill, Peter, BEd MEd   Sr. Lectr.

Horne, John D., BA *CNAA*, MA *Essex*, PhD *Edin.*   Sr. Lectr.
Hounsell, Dai, BA *Lond.*, PhD *Lanc.*   Prof., Higher Education
Jess, Mike, BEd *Glas.*, MEd *Glas.*   Sr. Lectr.
Kreber, Carolin, BA *Freib.*, MEd *St.Catherine(Minn.)*, PhD *Tor.*   Prof., Teaching and Learning in Higher Education
Lawn, Martin   Hon. Prof.
Lingard, Robert   Bell Prof.
Lloyd, Gwynedd, BA MA   Sr. Lectr.
Macintyre, Tom, BSc *Edin.*, MSc *Edin.*   Sr. Lectr.
Macleod, Hamish, BSc PhD   Sr. Lectr.
Maile, Andrew J., BA *Birm.*, MA *Leeds*   Sr. Lectr.
Martin, Brian, BA *Essex*, MEd *Edin.*   Sr. Lectr.
Martin, Ian S., BA MSc   Reader
McCulloch, Ken, MEd *H-W*, PhD *Edin.*   Sr. Lectr.
Munn, Pamela, OBE, MA *Aberd.*, MLitt *Aberd.*   Prof., Curriculum Research
O'Brien, Jim, MA MEd PhD, FRSA   Sr. Lectr.; Head*
Ozga, Jenny, MA *Aberd.*, MEd *Aberd.*, PhD *Open(UK)*   Prof., Educational Research
Parton, N. T., BA *Stir.*, MEd *Stir.*   Sr. Lectr.
Paterson, Lindsay, MA *Aberd.*, PhD *Edin.*   Prof., Educational Policy
Quickfall, Mike, BSc *Manc.*, BA *Open(UK)*, BA *Edin.*, MBA   Sr. Lectr.
Raffe, David, BA *Oxf.*, BPhil *Oxf.*   Prof., Sociology of Education
Reid, Gavin, BEd *Aberd.*, MEd *Aberd.*, MA *Open(UK)*, MAppSci *Glas.*, PhD *Glas.*   Sr. Lectr.
Riddell, Sheila, BA PhD   Prof., Inclusion and Diversity
Sanders, Ross, PhD *Qld.*   Prof., Sport Science
Sharp, Stephen, BA *Sheff.*, MSc *Stir.*, PhD *Liv.*   Sr. Lectr.
Skinner, Don, BSc *Edin.*, MEd *Edin.*   Sr. Lectr.
Sproule, John S., BEd MSc PhD   Sr. Lectr.
Squire, Patrick J., MA *Birm.*   Sr. Lectr.
Tett, Lyn, BA *Open(UK)*, MEd *H-W*   Prof., Community Education and Lifelong Learning
Thomson, David K., MSc *Edin.*   Sr. Lectr.
van der Kuyl, Anthony, MA *Dund.*, BEd   Sr. Lectr.
Wishart, Jennifer G., MA *Edin.*, PhD *Edin.*   Prof., Special Education
Other Staff: 66 Lectrs.; 5 Sr. Res. Fellows; 9 Res. Fellows; 7 Res. Assocs.; 1 Hon. Fellow

Engineering and Electronics, School of

Tel: (0131) 650 5567 Fax: (0131) 650 6554
   E-mail: see@ed.ac.uk
Arslan, T., BEng PhD   Prof., Integrated Electronic Systems
Barthelmie, Rebecca J., BSc PhD   Prof.; Ewart Farvis Chair of Renewable Energy
Bialek, Janusz W., MEng *Warsaw U.T.*, PhD *Warsaw U.T.*   Bert Whittington Prof. of Electrical Engin.
Biggs, Mark J., BEng *NSW*, PhD *Adel.*   Sr. Lectr.
Blackford, Jane, BEng *Sheff.*, PhD *Sheff.*   Sr. Lectr.
Brandani, Stefano, PhD   Prof., Chemical Engineering
Bryden, I. G., BSc PhD, FIP, FIMechE   Prof., Renewable Energy
Chen, J. F., BEng *Zhejiang*, MSc *Zhejiang*, PhD *Edin.*   Reader
Cheung, Rebecca, BSc *Glas.*, PhD *Glas.*   Prof., Nanoelectronics
Christy, John R. E., MA *Camb.*, PhD, FIChemE   Sr. Lectr.
Cooper, Jonathan M.   Prof., Micro and Nano Systems
Davies, Mike, MA PhD   Jeffrey Collins Chair of Signal Processing
Denyer, Peter, BSc *Lough.*, PhD, FIEE, FREng, FRSEd   Hon. Prof.
Easson, William J., BSc PhD   Prof., Fluid Mechanics
Eccles, Harry, MPhil PhD   Visiting Prof.
Ewen, Peter J. S., BSc PhD   Sr. Lectr.

Flynn, Brian W., BSc PhD   Sr. Lectr.
Forde, Michael C., BEng *Birm.*, MSc *Birm.*, PhD *Birm.*, FICE, FIEE   Carillion Prof., Civil Engineering Construction
Glass, D. H., BSc *Manc.*, PhD *Camb.*, FIChemE   Sr. Lectr.
Grant, Peter M., BSc *H-W*, PhD, FIEE, FIEEE, FREng, FRSEd   Prof., Electronic Signal Processing; Head*
Hall, Christopher, MA *Oxf.*, DPhil *Oxf.*, DSc *Oxf.*, FRSChem, FIMMM   Prof., Materials
Hamilton, Alister, BSc *Napier*, MSc *H-W*, PhD   Sr. Lectr.
Hannah, J. M., BSc *Strath.*, PhD   Sr. Lectr.
Haworth, L. I., BSc *Salf.*, PhD *Salf.*   Sr. Lectr.
Ingram, David, BSc *Greenwich*, PhD *Manc.Met.*   Reader
Jack, M. A., BSc *H-W*, MSc *H-W*, MBA *Open(UK)*, PhD, FIEE, FRSEd   Prof., Electronic Systems
Koutsos, Vasileios, BSc PhD   Sr. Lectr.
Laurenson, D. I., BEng *Edin.*, PhD *Edin.*   Sr. Lectr.
Lu, Yong, BEng *Tongji*, MSc *Southeast(Nanjing)*, PhD *T.U.Athens*   Prof., Structural Mechanics
Macpherson, Ewen, BSc *Edin.*, PhD *Edin.*, FIEE   Sr. Lectr.
McLaughlin, Steve, BSc *Glas.*, PhD *Edin.*, FRSEd   Prof., Electronic Communications Systems
Mill, Frank G., BSc *Napier*, PhD *Edin.*, FIMechE   Sr. Lectr.
Milne, A. D., OBE, MSc PhD, FREng, FRSEd, FIEE   Hon. Prof.
Mueller, Markus, BSc *ICL*, PhD *Camb.*   Sr. Lectr.
Mulgrew, Bernie, BSc *Belf.*, PhD, FIEE   Prof., Signals and Systems
Murray, Alan, BSc *Edin.*, PhD *Edin.*, FIEE, FRSEd   Prof., Neural Electronics
Ooi, Jin Y., BEng *Auck.*, PhD *Syd.*   Prof., Particulate Solid Mechanics
Pankaj, Pankaj, PhD *Wales*   Sr. Lectr.
Ponton, J. W., BSc PhD, FIChemE, FREng   Prof., Chemical and Process Systems Engineering
Reekie, Martin, BSc *Edin.*, PhD *Edin.*   Sr. Lectr.
Renshaw, D., BSc MSc PhD   Sr. Lectr.
Rotter, J. Michael, MA *Camb.*, PhD *Syd.*, FREng, FRSEd, FICE, FIEAust   Prof., Civil Engineering
Roulston, J. F., OBE, BSc *Belf.*, MSc, FRSEd, FIEE   Visiting Prof.
Schaefer, A. I., PhD *Syd.*   Prof., Environmental Engineering
Scholz, Miklas, BEng MSc PhD   Sr. Lectr.
Seaton, Nigel A., BSc PhD   Prof., Interfacial Engineering
Sefiane, Khellil, PhD   Reader
Sheikholeslami, Roya, BSc PhD, FIEAust   Prof., Chemical Process Engineering
Smith, Simon D., BEng *Lough.*, PhD *Edin.*   Sr. Lectr.
Snell, Anthony J., BSc *Nott.*, PhD *Nott.*   Sr. Lectr.
Thompson, John, BEng PhD   Reader
Torero, Jose, BS *Calif.*, MSc *Calif.*, PhD *Calif.*   Prof., Fire Safety Engineering
Underwood, Ian, BSc *Glas.*, MSc *Strath.*, PhD, FRSEd   Prof., Electronic Displays
Usmani, Asif S., PhD *Wales*   Prof., Structural Engineering and Computational Mechanics
Wallace, Robin, BSc PhD   Prof., Renewable Energy Systems
Walton, Anthony J., MSc *Newcastle(UK)*, PhD *CNAA*, FRSEd   Prof., Microelectronic Manufacturing
Wardlaw, Robin B., BSc *Strath.*, PhD *Strath.*, FICE   Sr. Lectr.
Zaiser, Michael, DrRerNatHabil   Reader
Other Staff: 29 Lectrs.; 3 Sr. Res. Fellows; 43 Res. Fellows; 20 Res. Assocs.; 1 Univ. Fellow; 1 Lectr.†; 19 Hon. Fellows
Vacant Posts: 1 Regius Prof.; 1 Prof., Electrical Engineering

GeoSciences, School of

Tel: (0131) 650 4845 Fax: (0131) 668 3184
E-mail: info@geos.ed.ac.uk
Aitken, Ian D., OBE, BVMS PhD Hon. DVM&S, FRSA   Hon. Prof.
Atkinson, David, BSc PhD, FIBiol, FRSA   Hon. Prof.
Bondi, Liz, PhD Manc., MA   Prof., Social Geography
Boulton, Geoffrey S., OBE, BSc Birm., PhD Birm., DSc Birm., FRS, FRSEd   Regius James Hutton Prof., Geology
Cannell, Melvin G. R., OBE, DSc Reading, PhD Reading, FRSEd   Hon. Prof.
Christie, Mike   Hon. Prof.
Collins, Lyn, BA Hull, MA Tor., PhD Tor.   Sr. Lectr.
Corbett, Patrick   Hon. Prof.
Cowie, Gregory L., BS MS PhD   Sr. Lectr.
Cowie, Patience A., BSc MA MPhil PhD   Reader
Crampin, S., BSc Lond., PhD Camb., FRSEd   Hon. Prof.
Crowley, Thomas, MS PhD   Prof., Earth Systems Science
Curtis, Andrew, BSc Edin., DPhil Oxf.   Reader
Danesh, Ali   Hon. Prof.
Dixon, J. E., BA Camb., PhD Camb.   Sr. Lectr.
Dugmore, Andrew J., BSc Birm., PhD Aberd.   Prof.
Dunai, T. J., PhD   Sr. Lectr.
Essery, Richard, BSc PhD   Reader
Fallick, A. E., BSc PhD   Hon. Prof.
Farmer, John G., BSc Glas., PhD Glas., FRSChem, FGS   Prof., Environmental Geochemistry
Finnigan, John, BSc PhD   Hon. Prof.
Fitton, J. Godfrey, BSc Durh., PhD Durh., FGS, FRSEd   Prof., Igneous Petrology
Gill, Maggie, BA BSc PhD   Hon. Prof.
Grace, J., BSc Sheff., PhD Sheff., FRSEd, FIBiol   Prof., Environmental Biology
Graham, Colin M., BSc PhD, FGS, FRSEd   Prof., Experimental Geochemistry
Graham, Margaret C., BSc PhD   Sr. Lectr.
Harley, Simon L., BSc NSW, MA Tas., DPhil Oxf., FRSEd   Prof., Lower Crustal Processes
Harte, Ben, MA Camb., PhD Camb., FRSEd   Prof., Metamorphism
Haszeldine, Stuart, BSc Edin., PhD Strath., FRSEd   Prof., Sedimentary Geology
Heal, Kate, MA Oxf., PhD Leeds   Sr. Lectr.
Heal, O. W., BSc Durh., PhD Durh., FIBiol   Hon. Prof.
Hegerl, Gabriele, BA MS PhD   Reader
Hillman, J. R., BSc Wales, PhD Wales, FLS, FIBiol, FRSEd   Hon. Prof.
Hipkin, Roger G., BSc Lond., PhD Newcastle(UK), FRSEd   Sr. Lectr.
Hobbs, B. A., BSc Exe., PhD Exe., FRAS   Sr. Lectr.
Hughes, C. George, BA MA   Sr. Lectr.
Hulton, Nicholas R. J., BSc PhD   Sr. Lectr.
Jacobs, Jane M., BA Adel., MA Adel., PhD Lond.   Prof., Cultural Geography
Last, Fred, OBE, PhD Lond., DSc Lond., FRSEd   Hon. Prof.
Legg, Colin, BSc Wales, PhD Aberd.   Sr. Lectr.
Li, X. Y., BSc MSc PhD   Hon. Prof.
MacBeth, C., BA Oxf., MA PhD   Hon. Prof.
Mackaness, William A., BSc PhD   Sr. Lectr.
Main, Ian G., BSc St And., MSc Durh., PhD   Prof., Seismology and Rock Physics
Malthus, Tim J., BSc Otago, PhD Otago   Sr. Lectr.
McDermott, Christopher I., BSc PhD   Sr. Lectr.
McLeod, Andy, BSc Exe., MSc Wales, PhD Exe., FIBiol   Sr. Lectr.
Meir, Patrick W., BA PhD   Sr. Lectr.
Mencuccini, Maurizio, BSc PhD   Reader
Merchant, Chris, BA MSc PhD   Sr. Lectr.
Metcalfe, S. E., BA Camb., MA Camb., DPhil Oxf.   Prof., Environmental Change
Moncrieff, John B., BSc Nott., PhD Nott.   Prof., Micrometeorology
Monteith, J. L., BSc PhD Hon. DSc, FRS, FRSEd   Hon. Prof.

Ngwenya, Bryne, BSc Reading, PhD Reading   Sr. Lectr.
Nienow, Peter W., BA PhD   Sr. Lectr.
Penrose, J. M., BA McG., MA McG., PhD Tor.   Sr. Lectr.
Pumphrey, Hugh C., BA Camb., MA Camb., PhD Mississippi   Reader
Rigby, Sue, MA Oxf., PhD Camb.   Sr. Lectr.
Robertson, Alastair, MA Camb., PhD Leic., BSc, FRSEd   Prof., Geology
Rounsevell, Mark, BSc Newcastle(UK), PhD Cran.   Prof., Rural Economy and Environmental Sustainability
Russell, Graham, BSc Nott., PhD Nott.   Sr. Lectr.
Scrutton, Roger A., BSc Durh., PhD Camb., FRSEd, FGS   Reader
Shepherd, Andrew, BSc Leic., PhD Leic.   Reader
Siegert, Martin J., BSc PhD, FRSEd   Prof.; Head*
Sinclair, Hugh D., BSc DPhil   Reader
Staeheli, Lynn, BA MS PhD   Ogilvie Prof., Geography
Sugden, D. E., BA Oxf., DPhil Oxf.   Prof., Geography
Summerfield, M. A., MA Oxf., DPhil Oxf.   Prof., Geomorphology
Tett, Simon F. B., BSc PhD   Prof., Earth System Dynamics
Thompson, R., BSc Reading, PhD Newcastle(UK)   Prof., Environmental Geophysics
Tudhope, Sandy, BSc PhD   Prof., Climate Studies
Underhill, John R., BSc Brist., PhD Wales, FGS, FRSEd   Prof., Stratigraphy
Usher, M. B., OBE, BSc PhD   Hon. Prof.
van Gardingen, Paul, BSc Cant., PhD Cant.   Sr. Lectr.
Whaler, Kathy, BSc PhD, FRSEd   Prof., Geophysics
Whittemore, Colin T., BSc Newcastle(UK), PhD Newcastle(UK), DSc, FIBiol, FRSEd   Prof., Agriculture and Rural Economics
Williams, Mat, BA Oxf., PhD E.Anglia   Sr. Lectr.
Williams, W., BSc Lond., PhD Camb.   Prof., Mineral Physics
Wilson, Ronald M., BSc Glas., MSc Aberd., PhD Aberd.   Sr. Lectr.
Withers, Charles W. J., BSc St And., PhD Camb., FRGS, FRSA   Prof., Geography
Woodhouse, I., BSc MSc PhD   Sr. Lectr.
Ziolkowski, Anton M., MA Camb., MSc Lond., PhD Camb., FRSEd   PTSI Prof., Petroleum Geoscience
Other Staff: 30 Lectrs.; 6 Sr. Res. Fellows; 21 Res. Fellows; 16 Res. Assocs.; 3 Hon. Lectrs.; 28 Hon. Fellows
Vacant Posts: 1 Prof., Agricultural Resource Management; 1 Prof., Forestry and Natural Resources; 1 Prof., Mineralogy

Health in Social Sciences, School of

Tel: (0131) 650 3890 Fax: (0131) 650 3891
E-mail: health@ed.ac.uk
Fawcett, Tonks, BSc City(UK), MSc   Sr. Lectr.
Laidlaw, Kenneth, MA MPhil   Sr. Lectr.
Mander, Rosemary, MSc PhD   Prof., Midwifery
McQueen, Anne, BA Open(UK), MSc Edin., MPhil Edin.   Sr. Lectr.
Melia, Kathleen M., BNurs Manc., PhD   Prof., Nursing Studies; Head*
Pollock, Allyson   Prof., Health Policy
Power, Mick, BSc MSc DPhil   Prof., Clinical Psychology
Price, David, BSc Lond.   Sr. Lectr.
Smith, Graeme D., BA PhD   Sr. Lectr.
Tilley, S. C., BA PhD   Sr. Lectr.
Other Staff: 10 Lectrs.; 14 Lectrs.†; 9 Hon. Fellows
Research: cancer nursing and palliative care; community care and primary-secondary care interface; nursing and health care of elderly people; women's health

History, Classics and Archaeology, School of

Tel: (0131) 650 6693 Fax: (0131) 651 3070
Ahonen, Pertti T., BA MA MPhil PhD   Sr. Lectr.
Anderson, Robert D., MA Oxf., DPhil Oxf., FRHistS   Prof., Modern History
Bailey, Paul, BA Leeds, MA Lond., PhD Br.Col., FRHistS   Prof., Modern Chinese History
Barringer, Judith M.   Prof., Greek Art and Archaeology
Bates, Crispin, MA Camb., PhD Camb., FRAS   Reader
Berry, Dominic H., BA MA DPhil   Sr. Lectr.
Bloxham, D., BA PhD, FRHistS   Prof., Modern History
Boardman, S. I., MA PhD, FRHistS   Reader
Bonsall, J. Clive, BA Sheff., FSA   Reader
Breeze, D. J., BA PhD, FSA, FRSEd, FRSA   Hon. Prof.
Brown, Andrew D., MA DPhil, FRHistS   Sr. Lectr.
Brown, T. S., PhD Nott., MA   Reader
Cairns, D. L., MA Glas., PhD Glas.   Prof., Classics; Head*
Cameron, Ewen, MA Aberd., PhD Glas., FRHistS   Sr. Lectr.
Chick, Martin, MA Camb., PhD Lond.   Sr. Lectr.
Cogliano, Francis D., BA Tufts, MA Boston, PhD Boston, FRHistS   Prof., American History
Crang, Jeremy A., BA Stir., PhD, FRHistS, FRSA   Sr. Lectr.
Davidson, Roger, MA Camb., PhD, FRHistS   Prof., Social History
Davies, Glenys M., BA Lond., PhD Lond.   Sr. Lectr.
Day, Alan F., BA S'ton., MA Johns H., MA McM., PhD Johns H., FRHistS   Sr. Lectr.
Devine, T. M., OBE, BA PhD   Sir William Fraser Prof., Scottish History and Palaeography
Erskine, Andrew, MA Oxf., DPhil Oxf.   Prof., Ancient History
Fox, A. P., MA Camb., PhD Camb., FRHistS   Reader
Goodare, Julian, MA Edin., PhD Edin., FRHistS   Reader
Greasley, David G., BA Liv., BPhil Liv., PhD Liv.   Reader
Green, Judith, BA DPhil, FRHistS   Prof., Medieval History
Griffiths, Trevor, BA Oxf., MA Oxf., DPhil Oxf.   Sr. Lectr.
Harding, D. W., MA DPhil, FRSEd   Abercromby Prof., Archaeology
Jackson, Alvin   Richard Lodge Prof., History
Jackson, L. A., BA MA PhD   Sr. Lectr.
Jeffreys-Jones, Rhodri, BA Wales, PhD Camb., FRHistS   Prof., American History
Mason, Robert, BA Oxf., DPhil Oxf.   Sr. Lectr.
McMillan, James F., MA DPhil, FRHistS, FRSEd   Richard Pares Prof.
Mercer, Roger, MA, FRSEd, FSA   Hon. Prof.
Midgley, Magdalena S., MA PhD   Sr. Lectr.
Morris, R. J., BA Oxf., DPhil Oxf., FRHistS   Prof., Economic and Social History
Murdoch, Alexander J., BA PhD, FRHistS   Sr. Lectr.
Nenadic, Stana, BA Strath., PhD Glas.   Sr. Lectr.
Newman, Mark, BA Leic., MA Wales, PhD Mississippi   Reader
Nugent, Paul, BA Cape Town, MA Lond., PhD Lond., FRHistS   Prof., Comparative African History
Peltenburg, Edgar, BA Birm., PhD Birm., FSA   Prof., Archaeology
Ralston, Ian, MA PhD, FSA   Prof., Prehistoric European Archaeology
Rodger, R., MA PhD   Prof., Economic and Social History
Rothwell, V. H., BA Nott., PhD Leeds, FRHistS   Reader
Sauer, Eberhard W., MSc Oxf., DPhil Oxf., FSA   Reader
Stephenson, A. Jill R., MA PhD, FRHistS   Prof., Modern German History
Other Staff: 24 Lectrs.; 6 Res. Fellows; 1 Lectr.†; 35 Hon. Fellows

Vacant Posts: 1 Prof., Modern British History

Informatics, School of

Tel: (0131) 650 2690 Fax: (0131) 651 1426
E-mail: informatics@ed.ac.uk
Anderson, Stuart, BSc H-W   Sr. Lectr.
Arvind, D. K., BSc Lond.   Reader
Atkinson, Malcolm, BA MA PhD, FBCS, FRSEd
Prof., e-Science
Bishop, Christopher M., BA Oxf., PhD   Prof.,
Computer Science
Bradfield, J. C., MA Camb., PhD   Reader
Brebner, Gordon, BSc PhD   Hon. Prof.
Bundy, Alan R., BSc Leic., PhD Leic., FRSEd
Prof., Automated Reasoning
Buneman, Peter, MA PhD, FRSEd   Prof.,
Database Systems
Cole, Murray I., BSc PhD   Sr. Lectr.
Etessami, Kousha, MSc Mass., PhD Mass.
Reader
Fan, Wen Fei, BS MS PhD   Prof., Web Data
Management
Fisher, Robert B., BS Cal.Tech., MS Stan., PhD
Prof., Computer Vision
Fourman, M. P., BSc Brist., MSc Oxf., DPhil Oxf.
Prof., Computer Systems; Head*
Gilmore, Stephen, BSc Belf., PhD Belf.   Reader
Goddard, Nigel H., BA PhD   Reader
Goryanin, Igor   Hon. Prof., Systems Biology
Gray, J. P., BSc PhD   Hon. Prof.
Hayes, G. M., BA Oxf., MSc Edin., PhD Birm.
Sr. Lectr.
Hillston, Jane, BA York(UK), MSc Lehigh, PhD,
FRSEd   Prof., Quantitative Modelling
Jerrum, M. R., MA Camb., PhD   Hon. Prof.
Kalorkoti, K. A., BSc Nott., MSc Lond., PhD Lond.
Sr. Lectr.
Klein, Ewan, BA Camb., MA Reading, PhD Camb.
Prof., Cognitive Systems
Lascarides, Alex, BSc Durh., MSc Edin., PhD Edin.
Reader
Lee, John R., MA PhD   Sr. Lectr.
Libkin, Leonid, BSc MSc PhD   Prof.,
Foundations of Data Management
McKenzie, Eric, MSc H-W   Sr. Lectr.
Moore, Johanna D., PhD Calif., FRSEd   Prof.,
Artificial Intelligence
Oberlander, Jon, MA Camb., PhD Edin.   Prof.,
Epistemics
O'Boyle, Michael, BSc Aston, MSc UMIST, PhD
UMIST   Prof., Computer Science
Pain, H. G., BA Wales, PhD   Sr. Lectr.
Plotkin, G. D., BSc Glas., PhD, FRS, FRSEd
Prof., Computation Theory
Renals, Steve, BSc Sheff., MSc Edin., PhD Edin.
Prof., Speech Technology
Robertson, D. S., BSc PhD   Sr. Lectr.
Sannella, D. T., BSc Yale, MSc Calif., PhD
Prof., Computer Science
Schweizer, P., BA Calif., PhD Calif.   Sr. Lectr.
Shillcock, Richard, BSc Sus., DPhil Sus.   Reader
Simpson, Alex, BA MSc PhD   Reader
Steedman, Mark, BSc Sus., PhD   Prof.,
Cognitive Science
Stenning, Keith, MA Oxf., PhD Rockefeller   Prof.,
Human Communications
Stevens, Perdita, BA Camb., MA Camb., MSc
Warw., PhD Warw.   Reader
Stirling, C., MA Oxf., DPhil Oxf.   Prof.,
Computation Theory
Tate, Austin, BA Lanc., PhD   Prof., Knowledge-
Based Systems
Thompson, Henry S., MA Calif., MS Calif., PhD
Calif.   Reader
Topham, N. P., BSc Manc., PhD Manc.   Prof.,
Computer Systems
Vijayakumar, Sethu, BTech Tokyo I.T., MEngg
Tokyo I.T., PhD Tokyo I.T.   Reader
Wadler, Philip, BSc MSc PhD   Prof.,
Theoretical Computer Science
Webb, Barbara, BSc PhD   Reader
Webber, B., PhD, FRSEd   Prof., Intelligent
Systems
Williams, Christopher K. I., MA Camb., MSc
Tor., MSc Newcastle(UK), PhD Tor.   Prof.,
Machine Learning
Willshaw, David, MA Camb., MSc Lond., PhD
Prof., Computational Neurobiology

Other Staff: 26 Lectrs.; 5 Sr. Res. Fellows; 35
Res. Fellows; 1 Univ. Fellow; 18 Res.
Assocs.; 21 Hon. Fellows

Law, School of

Tel: (0131) 650 2006 Fax: (0131) 650 6317
E-mail: law@ed.ac.uk
Bankowski, Zenon, LLB Dund.   Prof., Legal
Theory
Barr, Alan R., MA LLB   Sr. Lectr.; Dir., Legal
Practice Unit
Bertram, R. D., LLB MA   Visiting Prof.
Boyle, A. E., BA BCL   Prof., Public
International Law
Brodie, Douglas, LLB PhD   Prof., Employment
Law; Head*
Cairns, John W., LLB Edin., PhD Edin.   Prof.,
Legal History
Carter, C. A., BA Cardiff, PhD   Sr. Lectr.
Chalmers, James, LLB LLM   Sr. Lectr.
Clive, Eric, CBE, LLB LLM MA, FRSEd
Visiting Prof.
Craufurd Smith, R., BA LLM PhD   Sr. Lectr.
Eden, Sandra M., BA Kent, LLB   Sr. Lectr.
Edward, D. A. O., CMG, QC, MA Oxf., LLB,
FRSEd   Hon. Prof.
Finnie, Wilson, LLB Aberd.   Sr. Lectr.
Gilmore, William C., LLM Lond., LLM Edin., MA
Car., PhD Lond.   Prof., International
Criminal Law
Gordon, Sir Gerald, FRSEd   Visiting Prof.
Gretton, George L., BA Durh., LLB   Lord
President Reid Prof.
Griffiths, Anne M. O., LLB PhD   Prof.,
Anthropology of Law
Himsworth, C. M. G., BA Camb., LLB Camb.
Prof., Administrative Law
Hogg, Martin, LLB LLM, FRSA   Sr. Lectr.
Johnston, D. E. L., MA PhD LLD   Hon. Prof.
Lane, R. C., MA Car., DPhil Oxf.   Sr. Lectr.
Laurie, Graeme T., LLB PhD   Prof., Medical
Jurisprudence
MacCormick, D. Neil, MA Glas., MA Oxf.,
Hon. LLD Uppsala, Hon. LLD, FRSEd, FBA
Regius Prof., Public Law and the Law of
Nature and Nations
Macgregor, Laura J., LLB LLM   Sr. Lectr.
MacQueen, Hector L., LLB PhD, FRSEd   Prof.,
Private Law
Maher, Gerry, LLB Glas., BLitt Oxf.   Prof.,
Criminal Law
McAra, Lesley, MA PhD   Sr. Lectr.
Munro, Colin R., BA Open(UK), LLB Aberd.
Prof., Constitutional Law
Neff, Stephen C., AB Harv., LLM Virginia, JD
Virginia   Reader
Nic Shuibhne, Niamh, LLM N.U.I., PhD Edin.
Reader
Reid, Elspeth C., MA LLB   Sr. Lectr.
Reid, K. G. C., LLB Edin., MA Camb., FRSEd
Prof., Property Law
Schafer, Burkhard, MA Munich, LLM Lanc.   Sr.
Lectr.
Scott, Drew, MA H-W   Prof., European Union
Studies
Shaw, Jo, BA, FRSA   Prof.; Salvesen Chair of
European Insts.
Siems, Mathias M., LLM PhD   Reader
Smith, David J., MA   Hon. Prof.
Sparks, Richard, BA MPhil PhD   Prof.,
Criminology
Sutton, Alistair, LLB LLM   Hon. Prof.
Tierney, Stephen, LLB Glas., LLM Liv., LLM Tor.
Reader
Waelde, C., LLB PhD   Sr. Lectr.
Watson, Alan, LLB MA DPhil LLD   Visiting
Prof.
Whitty, Niall R., MA St And., LLB   Visiting
Prof.
Zimmerman, Reinhard, PhD, FRSEd   Visiting
Prof.
Other Staff: 15 Lectrs.; 1 Sr. Res. Fellow; 4
Res. Fellows; 2 Res. Assocs.; 16 Hon.
Fellows

Literatures, Languages and Cultures, School of

Tel: (0131) 650 3638 Fax: (0131) 651 1311
E-mail: llc@ed.ac.uk
Astley, Ian, BA DPhil   Sr. Lectr.
Barker, Andrew W., MA PhD   Prof., Austrian
Studies
Bell, Bill R., BSc MA PhD   Sr. Lectr.
Bennett, Philip E., BA Exe., MA Exe.   Reader
Beugnet, Martine, BA Lille, MA Lille, PhD Edin.
Reader
Campbell, Ian, MA Aberd., PhD Edin.   Prof.,
Scottish and Victorian Literature
Carpenter, Sarah M., MA Oxf., DPhil Oxf.   Sr.
Lectr.
Christianson, Aileen, MA Aberd.   Sr. Lectr.
Colebrook, Claire M., BA Melb., BLitt ANU, PhD
Edin.   Prof., Literary Theory
Colvin, Sarah, BA MA DPhil   Prof., German
Davies, P. J., MA Manc., DPhil   Sr. Lectr.
Dayan, Peter T., MA Oxf., DPhil Oxf.   Prof.,
French
Duffy, Jean H., MA Glas., DPhil Oxf.   Prof.,
French
Dundas, Paul, MA Edin.   Reader
Fielding, Penny, MA Oxf., DPhil Oxf.   Sr. Lectr.
Frow, John, BA ANU, PhD Cornell, MA, FAHA
Regius Prof., Rhetoric and English Literature
Gentz, Natascha, MA PhD   Prof., Chinese
Gillies, William, BA Oxf., MA, FRSEd, FRHistS
Prof., Celtic Languages, Literature, History
and Antiquities
Graves, Peter A., MA Aberd.   Sr. Lectr.; Head*
Hillenbrand, Carole, BA Oxf., MA Camb., PhD,
FRSEd   Prof., Islamic History
Kruse, Arne   Sr. Lectr.
Lewis, Huw A., BA Oxf., MA Oxf., DPhil   Sr.
Lectr.
Loxley, James, BA Lond., PhD Lond.   Sr. Lectr.
Mackay, Margaret A., BA Tor., PhD   Sr. Lectr.
Manning, Susan, MA Camb., PhD Camb., FRSEd
Dir., Inst. for Advanced Studies in the
Humanities; Grierson Prof., English
Literature
McClellan, Tommy, MA Edin., PhD Edin.   Sr.
Lectr.
McLeod, Wilson, BA Haverford, MSc PhD   Sr.
Lectr.
Meek, Donald E., MA Camb., MA Glas., PhD
Glas., FRHistS, FRSEd   Prof., Scottish and
Gaelic Studies
Millard, K., DPhil   Sr. Lectr.
Newman, Andrew J., BA Dartmouth, MA Calif.,
PhD Calif.   Sr. Lectr.
Nicholson, C. E., BA Leeds   Prof., Eighteenth
Century and Modern Literature
Nocentini, Claudia, PhD Lond.   Sr. Lectr.
Pedriali, Federica G., DottLett Genoa   Reader
Revie, Ian, MA PhD   Sr. Lectr.
Robbins, J. M. W., MA Oxf., DPhil Oxf.   Prof.,
Hispanic Studies
Rogers, G. V., BA   Sr. Lectr.
Ryazanova-Clarke, Lara I., MA St.Petersburg, PhD
Strath.   Sr. Lectr.
Saval, Jose V., MA C.U.A., PhD Virginia   Reader
Schmid, Marion, PhD Camb.   Reader
Shaw, John W., BA Harv., MA Harv., PhD Harv.
Sr. Lectr.
Spinks, Lee, BA Leeds, PhD Edin.   Sr. Lectr.
Stevenson, Randall, MA Oxf., MLitt Oxf.   Prof.,
Twentieth Century Literature
Taxidou, Olga, BA MSc PhD   Reader
Thomsen, Bjarne T.   Sr. Lectr.
Trill, Suzanne, BA S'ton., PhD Liv.   Sr. Lectr.
Usher, Jon, BA Reading   Prof., Italian
Webster, William T., MA PhD   Sr. Lectr.
West, Gary J., MA Edin., PhD Edin.   Sr. Lectr.
Other Staff: 41 Lectrs.; 2 Res. Fellows; 3 Res.
Assocs.; 25 Hon. Fellows
Vacant Posts: 1 Regius Prof. of English
Literature; 1 John Orr Prof. of French; 1
Prof. of Scottish Ethnology; 1 Saintsbury
Chair of English Literature

Management School and Economics

Tel: (0131) 650 8362 Fax: (0131) 668 3053
E-mail: school.of.management@ed.ac.uk
Abhyankar, A.   Baillie Gifford Prof., Financial
Markets

Adams, Andrew T., BSc Newcastle(UK), MSc Newcastle(UK), PhD   Sr. Lectr.

Andre, Paul, PhD   Sr. Lectr.

Ansell, J. I., MSc PhD   Prof., Risk Management

Archibald, T. W., BSc PhD   Prof., Business Modelling

Banasik, John L., BA McG., MA Tor., PhD Edin.   Sr. Lectr.

Carr, Chris, MA DPhil   Prof., Corporate Strategy

Clark, Simon, BSc Lond., MSc Lond., PhD   Sr. Lectr.

Crook, Jonathan N., BA Lanc., MSc Wales   Prof., Business Economics

Duncan, Colin, BCom MPhil   Sr. Lectr.

Findlay, Patricia, BA Strath., LLB Strath., DPhil Oxf.   Sr. Lectr.

Fleck, James, MSc Manc., BSc MA   Visiting Prof.

Fransman, M. J., MA Witw., DPhil Sus.   Prof., Economics

George, Donald A. R., BSc Sus., BPhil Oxf.   Sr. Lectr.

Glen, J. J., BSc Glas., MSc Strath., PhD   Reader

Graham, I. R., BSc   Sr. Lectr.

Hardman Moore, John H., MA Camb., MSc Lond., PhD Lond., FBA, FRSEd   Prof., George Watson's and Daniel Stewart's Political Economy

Harris, Simon, BA Nott., MBA Strath., PhD Leeds   Sr. Lectr.

Harrison, Tina S., BA Hudd., PhD   Sr. Lectr.

Henley, John S., BSc Lond., PhD Lond., FRSA   Prof., International Management

Hine, James A. H. S., BA PhD   Sr. Lectr.

Hopkins, Ed H. K., BA MSc PhD   Prof., Economics

Hughes, G. A., BA Camb., PhD Camb.   Visiting Prof.

Ibrahim, Essam, BCom MSc PhD   Sr. Lectr.

Jeacle, Ingrid, MA PhD   Sr. Lectr.

Kanbur, Ravi, MA MPhil DPhil   Visiting Prof.

Kinder, Tony, BSc MA MBA PhD   Sr. Lectr.

Koop, Gari, PhD Tor.   Visiting Prof.

Lapsley, I. McL., BCom PhD   Prof., Accountancy

Lloyd, Ashley D., BSc Stir., MBA H-W, PhD H-W   Sr. Lectr.

Loretto, Wendy A., BCom PhD   Sr. Lectr.

Main, Brian, BSc St And., MA Calif., MBA Calif., PhD Calif., FRSEd   Prof., Business Economics

Marrian, I., MA   Visiting Prof.

Marshall, D. W., BSc Newcastle(UK), PhD Newcastle(UK)   Prof., Marketing and Consumer Behaviour

McCrone, Gavin, CB, MA Camb., MSc Wales, PhD Glas., Hon. LLD Glas., FRSEd   Visiting Prof.

Mitchell, F., BCom   Prof., Management Accounting

Moles, Peter, MA Camb., MBA City(UK), PhD City(UK)   Sr. Lectr.

Molina, A. H., MPhil Brad., PhD   Prof., Technology Strategy

Nutley, Sandra, BA BPhil PhD   Prof., Public Management

O'Donohoe, S., BSc Trinity(Dub.), PhD   Sr. Lectr.

Oliver, Nick, MA PhD   Prof., Management; Head*

Osborne, Stephen, BA MSc MSocSci PhD   Prof., International Public Management

Pong, C. K. M., MSc PhD   Sr. Lectr.

Pudelko, Markus, PhD Cologne   Sr. Lectr.

Rosa, Peter, BA PhD   Prof., Entrepreneurship and Family Business

Sakovics, Jozsef, MSc Stan., PhD Stan.   Prof., Economic Theory

Sayer, Stuart, BA Oxf., BPhil Oxf.   Sr. Lectr.

Schofield, Jill   Somers Chair of Healthcare Management

Shen, Xiaobai, BSc Edin., Hon. MPhil PhD   Sr. Lectr.

Snell, Andrew J., BSc Hull, MA Warw., PhD Warw.   Prof., Economics and Econometrics

Taffler, Richard   Martin Currie Chair of Finance and Investment

Thomas, Jonathan P., MA MPhil DPhil   Prof., Economics

Tregear, Angela E. J., BA MPhil PhD   Sr. Lectr.

Yoshikawa, T., BE MB MS   Visiting Prof.

Other Staff: 31 Lectrs.; 4 Res. Fellows; 2 Hon. Fellows

Vacant Posts: 1 Morrison Prof. of Internat. Bus.; 1 Prof. of Management Sci.; Dixons Chair of Entrepreneurship and Innovation; 4 Profs. of Accounting; 1 Prof. of Management and Organisation; 1 Prof. of Organisation of Industry and Commerce

Mathematics, School of

Tel: (0131) 650 5060 Fax: (0131) 650 6553
E-mail: queries@maths.ed.ac.uk

Aitken, C. G. G., PhD Glas., BSc   Prof., Forensic Statistics

Atiyah, Michael, MA Camb., PhD Camb., FRS, FRSEd   Hon. Prof.

Bailey, Toby, MA Camb., DPhil Oxf.   Reader

Braden, H. W., BSc Syd., PhD Camb.   Prof., Integrable Systems

Byatt-Smith, J. G., BSc Brist., PhD Brist.   Sr. Lectr.

Carbery, A., BA Oxf., PhD Calif.   Colin MacLaurin Prof.

Davie, A. M., BA Camb., PhD Dund.   Prof., Mathematical Analysis

Eggar, Mike, BSc Syd., DPhil Oxf.   Sr. Lectr.

Figueroa-O'Farrill, Jose, BSc M.I.T., PhD N.Y.State   Prof., Geometric Physics

Fletcher, R., MA Camb., PhD Leeds, FRS, FRSEd   Hon. Prof.

Gilbert, A. D., MA Camb., PhD Camb.   Sr. Lectr.

Gillespie, T. Alastair, BA Camb., PhD, FRSEd   Prof., Mathematical Analysis

Gondzio, Jacek, PhD Warsaw   Prof., Optimisation

Gordon, Iain, BSc PhD   Prof.

Gould, N. I. M., BA DPhil   Visiting Prof.

Gy[154]ngy, I. J., PhD Moscow, FRSEd   Prof., Probability

Heggie, Douglas C., MA Camb., PhD Camb., FRSEd   Prof., Mathematical Astronomy

Leimkuhler, Ben, BS MS PhD   Prof., Applied Mathematics

Lenagan, T. H., BSc Lond., PhD Leeds   Prof., Noncommutative Algebra

Maciocia, Antony, MA Camb., DPhil Oxf.   Sr. Lectr.

Martin, John, MA Camb., PhD Manc.   Sr. Lectr.

McKinnon, Ken, BSc Glas., PhD Camb., FRSEd   Prof., Operational Research

O'Carroll, Liam, MSc Belf., PhD Belf.   Reader

Olde Daalhuis, Ardi B., PhD Amst.   Sr. Lectr.

Prentice, Michael J., BSc Manc.   Sr. Lectr.

Radcliffe, Nicholas J., BSc Sus., PhD   Visiting Prof.

Ranicki, A. A., MA Camb., PhD Camb., FRSEd   Prof., Algebraic Surgery

Richardson, S., MA Camb., PhD Camb.   Reader

Ruffert, Maximilian, DrRerNat   Reader

Singer, Michael, BA DPhil   Prof., Geometry; Head*

Smyth, Chris J., BA ANU, MA Adel., PhD Camb.   Reader

Smyth, Noel, BSc Qld., PhD Cal.Tech.   Reader

Teleman, Constantin, BA MA MSc PhD   Prof.

Toland, J. F., BSc MSc DPhil, FRS, FRSEd   Hon. Prof.

Vanneste, Jacques, PhD   Reader

Volberg, Alex, PhD DSc   Sir Edward Whittaker Prof.

Wright, James, BA Chic., MSc Wis., PhD Wis.   Prof., Mathematical Analysis

Other Staff: 20 Lectrs.; 3 Res. Fellows; 2 Res. Assocs.

Philosophy, Psychology and Language Sciences, School of

Tel: (0131) 651 3083 Fax: (0131) 651 3190
E-mail: ppls@ed.ac.uk

Abrahams, Sharon, BSc PhD   Sr. Lectr.

Austin, E. J., MA Oxf., DPhil Oxf.   Reader

Bard, E. G., BA Smith, MA Harv., MLitt Harv., PhD Harv.   Reader

Bates, Tim, BA Auck., MA Auck., PhD Auck.   Reader

Cann, Ronnie, BA Lond., DPhil Sus.   Reader

Caryl, P. G., MA Camb., PhD Camb.   Sr. Lectr.

Clark, Andy, BA DPhil   Prof., Logic and Metaphysics

Deary, Ian J., BSc MB ChB PhD, FRCPEd, FRSEd, FBA   Prof., Differential Psychology

Della Sala, Sergio, MSc MD PhD, FBPsS, FRSA, FRSEd   Prof., Human Cognitive Neuroscience

Donaldson, Morag L., MA PhD   Sr. Lectr.

Ferreira, Fernanda, BA MS MA PhD   Prof., Language and Cognition

Gafaranga, J., MA PhD   Sr. Lectr.

Giegerich, H. J., MA Mainz, PhD, FRSEd   Prof., English Linguistics

Gisborne, Nikolas, BA MA PhD   Sr. Lectr.

Henderson, John, BSc MSc PhD   Prof., Visual Cognition and Cognitive Neuroscience

Heycock, Caroline, BA Camb., MA Camb., PhD Penn.   Prof., Syntax

Hurford, James R., BA Camb., PhD Lond.   Prof., General Linguistics

Hurley, S. L., BA BPhil DPhil   Visiting Prof.

Joseph, John E., MA Mich., PhD Mich., FRSA   Prof., Applied Linguistics

Ketland, Jeffrey, BA MA PhD   Sr. Lectr.

Kirby, Simon, MA Edin., PhD Edin.   Reader

Ladd, D. R., MA Cornell, PhD Cornell   Prof., Linguistics

Lewis, Peter, BA Wales   Sr. Lectr.

Logie, Robert H., BSc Aberd., PhD Lond., FRSEd, FBPsS, FRSA   Prof., Human Cognitive Neuroscience

McCarthy, David   Reader

McGonigle, M., MA PhD   Sr. Lectr.

McKinlay, Andy, BA MA PhD   Sr. Lectr.

McMahon, April, MA Edin., PhD Edin., FRSEd   Forbes Prof., English Language; Head*

Meyerhoff, Miriam, BA Well., MA Well., PhD Penn.   Prof., Sociolinguistics

Pickering, Martin, BA Durh., PhD   Prof., Psychology of Language and Communication

Pritchard, Duncan, BA Hull, MLitt St And., PhD St And.   Prof., Philosophy

Pullum, Geoffrey, BA PhD   Prof., General Linguistics

Ridge, Michael R., BA MA PhD   Prof., Moral Philosophy

Scaltsas, Theodore, BS Duke, MA Brandeis, DPhil Oxf.   Prof., Ancient Philosophy

Sorace, Antonella, PhD Edin., MA, FRSA   Prof., Developmental Linguistics

Sturt, Patrick, BA MA PhD   Reader

Trousdale, Graeme M., BA Manc., MSc PhD   Sr. Lectr.

Turk, Alice, PhD Cornell   Reader

Watt, Caroline, MA St And., PhD Edin.   Sr. Lectr.

Whiteman, Martha C., BA Colby, MSc PhD   Sr. Lectr.

Wright, Peter, MA Oxf., DPhil Oxf.   Sr. Lectr.

Other Staff: 35 Lectrs.; 18 Res. Fellows; 5 Res. Assocs.; 2 Lectrs.†; 14 Hon. Fellows

Vacant Posts: 1 Koestler Prof., Parapsychol.

Physics, School of

Tel: (0131) 650 5249 Fax: (0131) 650 5902
E-mail: physics@ed.ac.uk

Ackland, Graeme J., BA DPhil   Prof., Computer Simulation

Ball, Richard D., BA Camb., PhD Camb.   Prof., Mathematical Physics

Bates, Simon P., MA Camb., PhD Manc.   Sr. Lectr.

Branford, D., BSc Hull, PhD Manc., FIP   Prof., Photonuclear Physics

Campbell, Murray, BSc PhD   Prof., Musical Acoustics

Cates, Michael, MA PhD   Prof., Natural Philosophy

Clarke, Peter, BSc S'ton., DPhil Oxf.   Prof., E-Science

Cole, Jamie, BSc Liv., PhD Liv.   Sr. Lectr.

Crain, Jason, BSc PhD   Prof., Applied Physics
Dunlop, James S., BSc PhD   Prof.,
  Extragalactic Astronomy
Ellis, K. Visiting Prof.
Evans, Martin R., BSc PhD   Reader
Halliday, Ian, MA Edin., MSc Edin., PhD Camb.,
  Hon. DSc Edin. Prof.
Heavens, Alan F., MA Camb., PhD Camb. Prof.,
  Theoretical Astrophysics
Hossack, William J., BSc Lond., MSc Lond., PhD
  Lond. Sr. Lectr.
Huxley, Andrew, MA Camb., MS Penn., PhD
  Camb. Prof., Quantum Ordering at
  Extreme Conditions
Kennedy, A. D., BA Oxf., DPhil Sus. Prof.,
  Computational Science
Kenway, Richard D., BSc Exe., DPhil Oxf.,
  FRSEd   Tait Prof., Mathematical Physics
Lawrence, Andrew, BSc PhD, FRSEd   Regius
  Prof., Astronomy; Head*
Loveday, John, BSc Brist., PhD Brist.   Reader
MacPhee, Cait Reader
McMahon, Malcolm, BSc PhD   Prof., High
  Pressure Physics
Meiksin, Avery, MA PhD   Reader
Muheim, Franz, PhD Zür. Prof., Particle
  Physics
Nelmes, R. J., OBE, MA Camb., ScD Camb., PhD,
  FIP, FRSEd, FRS Prof., Physical
  Crystallography
Peacock, J. A., MA Camb., PhD Camb. Prof.,
  Cosmology
Playfer, Stephen M., BA PhD   Prof.,
  Experimental Particle Physics
Poon, Wilson C. K., MA Camb., PhD Camb., FIP,
  FRSEd   Prof., Condensed Matter Physics
Pusey, P. N., MA Camb., PhD Pitt., FIP, FRS,
  FRSEd   Prof.
Shotter, Alan C., BSc Lond., DPhil Oxf., FIP,
  FRSEd   Prof., Experimental Physics
Trew, A. S., BSc PhD   Prof., Computational
  Science
Walker, Alan, BSc Lond.   Sr. Lectr.
Woods, P. J., BSc Manc., PhD Manc.   Prof.,
  Nuclear Physics
Other Staff: 18 Lectrs.; 5 Sr. Res. Fellows; 23
  Res. Fellows; 22 Res. Assocs.; 6 Hon.
  Fellows

Social and Political Studies, School of

Tel: (0131) 650 3925 Fax: (0131) 650 3945
  E-mail: ssps@ed.ac.uk
Adler, Michael E., BA Oxf., AM Harv., PhD
  Prof., Socio-Legal Studies
Aspinwall, Mark, BA Middlebury, MA Rhode I.,
  MSc Lond., PhD Lond. Sr. Lectr.
Banner, Michael C., BA MA DPhil Prof.,
  Ethics and Public Policy in Life Sciences
Barnard, Alan J., BA Wash., MA McM., PhD Lond.
  Prof., Anthropology of Southern Africa
Bloor, David, BA Keele, MA Camb., PhD Prof.,
  Sociology of Science
Bomberg, Elizabeth, PhD Santa Barbara, BA MA
  Sr. Lectr.
Boswell, Elizabeth, BA PhD   Sr. Lectr.
Bray, Francesca, BA Camb., MA Camb., PhD
  Camb. Prof., Social Anthropology
Brown, Alice, MA PhD   Hon. Prof.
Cannizzo, J. E., BA MA PhD   Sr. Lectr.
Carsten, J. F., BSc Lond., PhD Lond. Prof.,
  Social and Cultural Anthropology
Castles, Francis G., BA DLitt, FASSA Prof.,
  Social and Public Policy
Clark, Chris, BSc Birm., PhD Edin. Prof., Social
  Work Ethics
Cohen, A. P., BA S'ton., MSc S'ton., PhD S'ton.,
  FRSEd Hon. Prof.
Cree, Viviene E., BA Open(UK), MA St And., PhD
  Prof., Social Work Education
Dannreuther, Roland, BA Oxf., MSc Lond., DPhil
  Oxf. Sr. Lectr.
Fabre, Cécile, BA DPhil Prof., Political Theory
Faulkner, Wendy, BSc Sus., MSc Sus., DPhil Sus.
  Reader
Fraser, Neil M., BA Oxf., BPhil Oxf. Sr. Lectr.
Freeman, Richard, BA PhD Sr. Lectr.
Good, Anthony, BSc Edin., PhD Durh. Prof.,
  Social Anthropology in Practice; Head*

Hayward, Tim, BA Warw., MA Warw., DPhil
  Warw. Prof., Environmental Political
  Theory
Hearn, Jonathan S., BA Bard, MA C.U.N.Y., PhD
  C.U.N.Y. Sr. Lectr.
Henry, John, BA Leeds, MPhil Leeds, PhD
  Open(UK) Reader
Howarth, David, BA Oxf., MPhil Oxf., DPhil Oxf.
  Sr. Lectr.
Jamieson, Lynn H. A., MA PhD   Prof.,
  Sociology of Families and Relationships
Jean-Klein, Iris, BA S.Fraser, MA Nfld., PhD
  Manc.Met. Sr. Lectr.
Jeffery, Charles, BA Lough., PhD Prof., Politics
Jeffery, P. M., MA Camb., MA Nott., PhD Brist.
  Prof., Sociology
Jeffery, Roger, MA Camb., MSc Brist., PhD
  Prof., Sociology of South Asia
MacInnes, John, MA PhD   Prof., Sociology
Mackay, F. S., BA Manc., PhD Edin. Sr. Lectr.
MacKenzie, Donald A., BSc PhD, FRSEd, FBA
  Prof., Sociology
March, Luke, MA Camb., MSocSc Birm., PhD
  Birm. Sr. Lectr.
McCrone, David, MA MSc, FRSEd Prof.,
  Sociology
McEwen, Nicola, BA Strath., MA W.Ont., PhD
  Sheff. Sr. Lectr.
McGhee, J., BSc Stir., LLB Sr. Lectr.
Parry, Richard H., MA Strath., MSc Strath.
  Reader
Perry, Richard W., BA Open(UK), MA Warw.
  Sr. Lectr.
Peterson, John, BSc Ithaca, MA Ithaca, PhD Lond.
  Prof., International Politics
Preda, Alexandru, DrRerSoc Sr. Lectr.
Prior, Nick, BA York(UK), MA York(UK), PhD
  Edin. Sr. Lectr.
Raab, Charles D., BA Col., MA Yale, FRSA
  Prof., Government
Raffel, Stanley H., AB Col., PhD Reader
Robertson, Sandy, MA PhD Hon. Prof.
Russell, Stewart, BA MSc PhD Sr. Lectr.
Smith, James, MA Dund., MSc Witw., PhD Sr.
  Lectr.
Spencer, Jonathan, AM Chic., DPhil Oxf., MA
  Prof., Anthropology of South Asia
Stanley, Liz, BSc MSc PhD Prof., Sociology
Tait, Joyce, CBE, BSc Glas., PhD Camb. Prof.
  Fellow
Thin, Neil, BA PhD Sr. Lectr.
Thompson, Andrew G. H., BSc Manc., PhD
  Manc. Sr. Lectr.
Timpson, Annis May, BSc Brist., MSc Oxf., PhD
  Tor. Sr. Lectr.; Dir., Centre of Canadian
  Studies
Tisdall, E. Kay, PhD Reader
Wasoff, Fran, MA Penn., PhD Penn. Prof.,
  Family Politics
Waterhouse, Lorraine, BA W.Ont., MSW
  Prof., Social Work
Webb, J., BSc Hull, PhD Nott. Prof., Sociology
  of Organisations
Whyte, W. T., MA Prof., Social Work
Williams, Robin A., MA Camb., MSc Aston, PhD
  Aston Dir., Research Centre for Social
  Sciences; Prof., Social Research on
  Technology
Yearley, Steven, MA DPhil Prof., Sociology of
  Scientific Knowledge
Other Staff: 49 Lectrs.; 1 Sr. Res. Fellow; 9
  Res. Fellows; 1 Res. Assoc.; 32 Hon.
  Fellows

MEDICINE AND VETERINARY MEDICINE, COLLEGE OF

Tel: (0131) 242 6531 E-mail: mvm@ed.ac.uk

Biomedical Sciences, School of

Tel: (0131) 650 3114 Fax: (0131) 651 1835
  E-mail: bcls@ed.ac.uk
Harmar, Tony, MA Camb., PhD Camb., FRSEd
  Prof., Molecular Pharmacology; Head*
Other Staff: 8 Sr. Res. Fellows; 24 Res.
  Fellows; 19 Res. Assocs.

Biomedical Sciences Teaching Organisation

Ellis, David, BSc Leic., PhD Leic. Sr. Lectr.
Findlater, Gordon S., BSc PhD   Sr. Lectr.

Kristmundsdottir, F., BSc Lough., PhD Nott. Sr.
  Lectr.
Poyser, Norman L., BPharm Lond., PhD DSc
  Sr. Lectr.
Stewart, John, BSc PhD   Sr. Lectr.
Wilson, Norrie, BSc PhD, FRSChem Sr. Lectr.

Cognitive and Neural Systems, Centre for

Morris, Richard G. M., CBE, MA Oxf., DPhil
  Oxf., FMedSci, FRS, FRSEd Prof.,
  Neuroscience
Wood, Emma R., BSc St And., PhD Br.Col. Sr.
  Lectr.

Infectious Diseases, Centre for

Amyes, S. G. B., BSc Lond., MSc Reading, PhD
  Lond., DSc Lond., FIBiol, FRCPath Prof.,
  Microbial Chemotherapy
Crawford, Dorothy, OBE, MD PhD DSc, FRCP,
  FRSEd   Robert Irvine Prof.
Cubie, Heather A., BSc MSc PhD   Hon. Prof.
Govan, J. R. W., BSc PhD DSc Prof.,
  Microbial Pathogenicity
Poxton, Ian R., BSc PhD DSc Prof., Microbial
  Infection and Immunity
Simmonds, P., BM S'ton., PhD Prof., Virology
Talbot, Simon J., BSc PhD Sr. Lectr.
Woolhouse, Mark E. J., OBE, BA MSc PhD,
  FRSEd Prof., Veterinary Public Health and
  Quantitative Epidemiology
Other Staff: 1 Lectr.; 6 Hon. Fellows; 10 Hon.
  Teaching Staff; 2 Clin. Teaching Staff

Integrative Physiology, Centre for

Ashley, Richard H., MB BS Lond., MSc PhD Sr.
  Lectr.
Bard, Jonathan, MA Camb., PhD Manc. Prof.,
  Bioinformatics and Development
Cousin, Mike A., BSc Edin., PhD Dund. Sr.
  Lectr.
Davies, Jamie, MA Camb., PhD Camb. Prof.,
  Experimental Anatomy
Douglas, Alison J., BSc PhD Sr. Lectr.
Dutia, Manyank B., BSc Lond., PhD Glas.
  Reader
Flatman, Peter W., MA Camb., PhD Camb. Sr.
  Lectr.
Hall, A. C., BSc PhD Sr. Lectr.
Jarman, Andrew P., BA Oxf., DPhil Oxf. Prof.,
  Developmental Cell Biology
Kaufman, M. H., MA Camb., PhD Camb., MB
  ChB DSc, FRCPEd, FRCSEd Prof., Anatomy
Kind, P. C., BSc Dal., DPhil Oxf. Sr. Lectr.
Leng, Gareth, BSc Warw., MSc Birm., PhD Birm.
  Prof., Experimental Physiology
Ludwig, Mike, BSc Leip., MSc Leip., PhD Leip.
  Prof., Neurophysiology
Maciver, S. K., BSc PhD Sr. Lectr.
MacLeod, Nikki, BSc Lond., MSc Lond., PhD St
  And. Sr. Lectr.
Mason, John O., BSc PhD Sr. Lectr.
Parson, Simon, BSc PhD Sr. Lectr.
Price, D. J., DPhil Oxf., BSc MB ChB Prof.,
  Developmental Neurobiology
Russell, John A., BSc MB ChB PhD Prof.,
  Neuroendocrinology
Shipston, Michael J., BSc PhD Prof.,
  Physiology
Spears, Norah, BSc Edin., DPhil Oxf. Reader
van Heyningen, Veronica, MA MS DPhil,
  FRSEd Hon. Prof.
Other Staff: 2 Lectrs.; 7 Hon. Fellows; 2 Hon.
  Teaching Staff

Neuroscience Research, Centre for

Grant, S. G. N., BSc Syd., MB BS Syd. Prof.,
  Molecular Neuroscience
Harmar, Tony, MA Camb., PhD Camb., FRSEd
  Prof., Molecular Pharmacology; Head*
McCulloch, James, BSc PhD Prof.,
  Neuropharmacology
McQueen, Daniel S., BPharm Lond., PhD Lond.,
  DSc, FIBiol Prof., Sensory Pharmacology
Nimmo, W. S., BSc MD, FRCP, FRCA Hon.
  Prof.
Overman, Henry J., BSc Glas., PhD Camb. Sr.
  Lectr.

Ribchester, Richard R., BSc Durh., PhD
Newcastle(UK) Prof., Cellular Neuroscience
Skehel, P. A., BSc Lond., PhD ICL Sr. Lectr.
Wyllie, David J. A., BSc Glas., PhD Lond. Sr.
Lectr.
Other Staff: 12 Hon. Fellows

Pathway Medicine, Division of

Ghazal, Peter, BSc Wales, PhD Prof.,
Molecular Genetics and Biomedicine
Haas, Juergen, MD Munich, PhD Munich Reader
Other Staff: 1 Hon. Fellow

Clinical Sciences and Community Health, School of

Tel: (0131) 242 6357 Fax: (0131) 242 6483
E-mail: csch@ed.ac.uk
Garden, James, BSc MD, FRCSEd, FRCSGlas
Regius Prof., Clinical Surgery; Head*
Henderson, Kirsty J., MB ChB Sr. Lectr.
Hoare, P., MA Oxf., BM BCh Oxf., DM Oxf.,
FRCPsych Sr. Lectr.
Huby, G. O., PhD Reader
Lamb, J. R., BA Oxf., PhD Lond., BDS MA,
FRCPath, FMedSci, FRSEd Hon. Prof.
MacKinlay, Marna E., BSc Aberd., MB ChB Aberd.
Sr. Lectr.
McIntosh, Neil, BSc Lond., MB BS Lond., FRCP,
FRCPEd, FRCPCH Edward Clark Prof.,
Child Life and Health
McKenzie, R. C., MBA BSc PhD Sr. Lectr.
Ridgen, Jessica, MB ChB Sr. Lectr.
Sinclair, Alison, MB ChB Sr. Lectr.
Warren, Patricia M., BSc Sheff., PhD Sheff. Sr.
Lectr.
Other Staff: 3 Sr. Res. Fellows; 56 Res.
Fellows; 15 Res. Assocs.

Clinical and Surgical Sciences, Division of

Brash, Harry M., BSc PhD Sr. Lectr.
Clegg, Gareth, BSc MB ChB Sr. Lectr.
Court-Brown, C. M., BSc MD, FRSEd Hon.
Prof.
Cumming, Allan D., BSc MB ChB MD, FRCP
Prof., Medical Education
Currie, Colin T., BSc MB ChB, FRCPEd Sr.
Lectr.
Dhillon, Baljean, BMedSci Nott., BM Nott., BS
Nott., FRCS, FRCPath Hon. Prof.
Drummond, Gordon B., MA Camb., MB ChB,
FRCA, FRCP Sr. Lectr.
Fearon, K. C. H., MD Glas., FRCSGlas Prof.,
Surgical Oncology
Forbes, Stuart J., BSc MB ChB PhD Prof.,
Transplantation and Regenerative Medicine
Forsythe, J. L. R., MD Newcastle(UK), FRCS
Hon. Prof.
Frier, Brian M., BSc MD, FRCPEd, FRCPGlas
Hon. Prof.
Garden, James, BSc MD, FRCSEd, FRCSGlas
Regius Prof., Clinical Surgery; Head*
Gregory, Chris, BSc Sheff., PhD Sheff. Prof.,
Inflammatory Cell Biology
Hayes, Peter C., BMSc Dund., MB ChB Dund.,
PhD, FRCPEd Prof., Hepatology
Hirani, N. A., BMedSci BM BS Sr. Lectr.
Hughes, Jeremy, MA Camb., MB BS Lond., PhD
Lond. Reader
Iredale, John, DM S'ton., FRCP, FMedSci Prof.,
Medicine
Kluth, David, BSc MB BS Sr. Lectr.
MacLullich, Alasdair M. J., BSc MB ChB Sr.
Lectr.
Mead, Gillian, MA Camb., MB BChir Camb., MD
Camb. Sr. Lectr.
Noble, Brendon S., BSc PhD Sr. Lectr.
Parks, R. W., MD, FRCS Reader
Phelps, Richard G., MA Camb., PhD Lond. Sr.
Lectr.
Porter, D. E., BSc MB ChB MD, FRCSEd,
FRCSGlas Sr. Lectr.
Powell, James John, BSc Glas., MB ChB Glas.,
MD Edin. Sr. Lectr.
Power, Ian, BSc Glas., MB ChB Glas., MD Glas.,
FRCA Prof., Anaesthesia, Critical Care and
Pain Management
Robertson, Colin, BA MB ChB, FRCSEd,
FRCPEd Hon. Prof.

Ross, J. A., BSc Strath., PhD Strath. Reader
Savill, J. S., KB, BA PhD, FRCP Prof.,
Medicine
Simpson, A. H. R. W., BM BCh Oxf., MA
Camb., FRCSEd George Harrison Law Prof.
Simpson, Ken, MSc MD PhD, FRCPEd Sr.
Lectr.
Turner, A. Neil, BM BCh Oxf., MA Camb., PhD
Lond., FRCP, FRCPEd Prof., Nephrology
Young, Archie, BSc MD, FRCPGlas, FRCP,
FRCPEd Prof., Geriatric Medicine
Other Staff: 14 Lectrs.; 21 Sr. Lectrs.†; 88
Hon. Teaching Staff; 24 Hon. Fellows; 98
Clin. Teaching Staff
Vacant Posts: 1 Prof., Rehabilitation Sci.; 1
Forbes Prof., Ophthalmol.

Community Health Sciences, Division of

Amos, Amanda, BA Camb., PhD Camb., MSc
Prof., Health Promotion
Backett-Milburn, K. C., MA PhD Prof.,
Sociology of Families and Health
Bhopal, Raj, BSc Glas., MD Glas., FRCPEd
Bruce and John Usher Prof., Public Health;
Head*
Campbell, H., BSc MSc MD, FRCPEd, FFPHM
Prof., Genetic Epidemiology and Public
Health
Cunningham-Burley, S., BSc Birm., PhD Aberd.
Prof., Medical and Family Sociology
Donnelly, P. D., MD, FRCP, FFPHM Hon.
Prof.
Fairhurst, K., MB BS Sr. Lectr.
Forbes, John F., BA Calif., MSc York(UK), PhD
Glas. Reader
Fowkes, F. G. R., MSc Lond., MSc Edin., MB ChB
Wales, PhD Wales, FRCPEd, FFPHM Prof.,
Epidemiology
Hallowell, N., BSc MA DPhil Reader
Murray, Gordon D., MA Camb., PhD Glas.,
FRCPEd Prof., Medical Statistics
Murray, Scott A., MB ChB Aberd., FRCGP,
FRCPEd St Columba's Hospice Prof.,
Primary Palliative Care
Pagliari, Claudia, BSc Ulster, PhD Edin. Sr.
Lectr.
Platt, Stephen, BA MSc PhD Prof.
Porter, Mike, BA Durh., MPhil Durh. Sr. Lectr.
Prescott, Robin J., BSc Reading, MSc S'ton., PhD
Liv., FRCPEd Prof., Health Technology
Assessment
Price, Jackie, BSc MB ChB Sr. Lectr.
Robertson, J. Roy, MBE, BSc, FRCP, FRCGP
Reader
Sheikh, A., BSc MB BS MSc, FRCGP Prof.,
Primary Care Research and Development
Thomson, Donald M., BSc MB ChB, FRCPEd,
FRCGP Sr. Lectr.
Warner, Pamela, BSc Natal Sr. Lectr.
Weller, D., MB BS PhD, FRACGP, FAFPHM
James Mackenzie Prof.
Wild, Sarah, BSc MSc MB BChir PhD Sr.
Lectr.
Other Staff: 3 Lectrs.; 37 Hon. Teaching Staff;
41 Hon. Fellows; 41 Clin. Teaching Staff

Medical and Radiological Sciences, Division of

Andrew, Ruth, BSc PhD Sr. Lectr.
Baldock, R. A., BSc PhD Hon. Prof.
Bastin, M. E., BSc York(UK), MSc Edin., DPhil
Oxf. Reader
Best, Jonathan, MSc Lond., MB ChB MSc,
FRCPEd, FRCR Forbes Prof., Medical
Radiology
Boon, N. A., MD Camb., FRCPEd Hon. Prof.
Brown, Roger, BA Camb., BM BCh Oxf., PhD
Sr. Lectr.
Chapman, Karen E., BSc Newcastle(UK), PhD
Newcastle(UK) Reader
Denvir, M. A., BSc MB ChB PhD, FRCP Sr.
Lectr.
Donaldson, Ken, BSc Stir., PhD DSc, FIBiol,
FRCPath Prof., Respiratory Toxicology
Douglas, Neil J., MB ChB MD, FRCPEd, FRCP
Prof., Respiratory and Sleep Medicine
Dransfield, I., BSc York(UK), PhD Sheff. Prof.,
Leukocyte and Lung Cell Biology
Forbes, Shareen Sr. Lectr.

Ford, M. J., MD, FRCPEd Hon. Prof.
Fox, Keith A. A., BSc MB ChB, FRCP, FMedSci
Prof.; Duke of Edinburgh Chair of
Cardiology; Head*
Gray, Gillian A., BSc Aberd., PhD Strath. Sr.
Lectr.
Greening, Andrew P., BSc MB ChB, FRCPEd
Prof., Pulmonary Disease
Hart, Simon P., BSc Edin., MB ChB Edin., PhD
Edin. Sr. Lectr.
Haslett, Chris, BSc MB ChB, FRCP, FRCPEd
Prof., Respiratory Medicine
Holmes, Megan C., BSc Lond., PhD Lond.
Reader
Hoskins, P. R., BA MSc PhD Reader
Ludlam, Christopher, BSc PhD, FRCP, FRCPath
Hon. Prof.
MacNee, William, MD Glas., FRCPEd, FRCPGlas
Prof., Respiratory and Environmental
Medicine
Marshall, Ian, MA Oxf., PhD Prof., Magnetic
Resonance Physics
Maxwell, Simon, BSc MB ChB MD PhD, FRCP,
FRCPEd Sr. Lectr.
McDicken, W. N., BSc Glas., PhD Glas. Prof.,
Medical Physics and Medical Engineering
Mullins, John, BSc PhD Prof. Fellow
Newby, Dave, BA Open(UK), BSc S'ton., BM
S'ton., DM S'ton., PhD Edin., FRCP Prof.,
Cardiology
Nyirenda, Moffat, BSc MB BS PhD Sr. Lectr.
Rees, Jonathan L., BSc, FRCP, FMedSci Grant
Prof., Dermatology
Reynolds, Rebecca M., MA Oxf., PhD Edin. Sr.
Lectr.
Riemersma, Rudolph A., MSc Ley., PhD,
FRCPEd Sr. Lectr.
Rossi, Adriano, BSc Glas., PhD Glas. Prof.,
Respiratory and Inflammation
Pharmacology
Seckl, Jonathan R., BSc Lond., MB BS Lond., PhD
Lond., FRCPEd, FMedSci, FRSEd Moncrieff
Arnott Prof.
Sethi, Tariq J., BA Lond., BSc Camb., MB BS
Edin., PhD Edin. Prof., Respiratory and
Lung Cancer Biology
Simpson, John, BMedBiol MB ChB, FRCPEd
Sr. Lectr.
Walker, Brian R., BSc MB ChB MD, FRCPEd
Prof., Endocrinology
Webb, David J., MB BS Lond., MD, FRCP,
FRCPEd, FMedSci, FFPM, FRSEd Christison
Prof., Therapeutics and Clinical
Pharmacology
Weller, R., MD Lond., MB BS Sr. Lectr.
Other Staff: 8 Lectrs.; 11 Sr. Lectrs.†; 1 Hon.
Reader; 58 Hon. Teaching Staff; 22 Hon.
Fellows; 33 Clin. Teaching Staff
Vacant Posts: 1 Prof., Medical Physics and
Medical Engineering

Postgraduate Dental Institute

Tel: (0131) 536 4970 Fax: (0131) 536 4971
Ibbetson, Richard J., BDS MSc, FDSRCS Sr.
Lectr., Primary Dental Care; Head*
Ross, Margaret K., BA Sheff. Sr. Lectr.
Other Staff: 2 Lectrs.; 1 Sr. Lectr.†; 17 Hon.
Teaching Staff; 12 Hon. Fellows

Reproductive and Developmental Sciences

Anderson, Richard, BSc MB ChB PhD MD
Prof., Clinical Reproductive Science
Beckett, Geoff, BSc UMIST, PhD, FRCPath
Reader
Bramley, T. A., BSc Birm., PhD Birm. Sr. Lectr.
Calder, Andrew, MD Glas., FRCPGlas, FRCPEd,
FRCSEd, FRCOG Prof., Obstetrics and
Gynaecology; Head*
Critchley, Hilary, BSc MB ChB MD, FRCOG,
FRACOG Prof., Reproductive Medicine
Duncan, Colin, BSc Edin., MB ChB Edin., MD
Edin. Sr. Lectr.
Fraser, Hamish M., BSc Dund., MSc Dund., PhD
Dund., DSc Dund. Hon. Prof.
Glasier, A. F., BSc Brist., MD Brist., FRCOG
Hon. Prof.

Hillier, Stephen G., MSc *Leeds*, PhD *Wales*, DSc, FRCPath   Prof., Reproductive Endocrinology
Kelly, R. W., BSc PhD   Hon. Prof.
Kelnar, Chris, MA *Camb.*, MD *Camb.*, FRCP, FRCPCH   Hon. Prof.
MacKinlay, Gordon A., MB BS *Lond.*, FRCS, FRCSEd   Sr. Lectr.
Mason, J. Ian, BSc PhD, FRCPath   Prof., Clinical Biochemistry
McNeilly, Alan S., BSc *Nott.*, PhD *Reading*, DSc, FRSEd   Hon. Prof.
Midgley, P., MB ChB *Aberd.*, FRCPCH, FRCPEd   Sr. Lectr.
Millar, R. P., BSc MSc PhD   Hon. Prof.
Minns, Robert A., JP, MB BS *Qld.*, PhD, FRCPEd, FRCPCH   Prof., Paediatric Neurology
O'Hare, Anne E., MB BS   Hon. Prof.
Penney, Gillian, MB ChB *Edin.*, MD *Edin.*, FRCOG   Sr. Lectr.
Riley, Simon C., BSc PhD   Sr. Lectr.
Saunders, Philippa, BSc *Brist.*, PhD *Camb.*   Hon. Prof.
Sharpe, Richard, BSc MSc PhD   Hon. Prof.
Walker, Simon W., MA *Oxf.*, MB BS *Lond.*, DM   Sr. Lectr.
West, John D., BSc *E.Anglia*, PhD   Reader
Wilmut, I., OBE, BSc PhD, FRS, FRSEd   Hon. Prof., Reproductive Science
Wilson, D. C., MD, FRCP, FRCPCH   Sr. Lectr.
Other Staff: 4 Lectrs.; 9 Sr. Lectrs.†; 46 Hon. Teaching Staff; 19 Hon. Fellows; 33 Clin. Teaching Staff
Vacant Posts: 1 Prof., Edward Clark Chair of Life and Child Health

Lister Postgraduate Institute

Tel: (0131) 650 2609 Fax: (0131) 662 0580
MacPherson, Stuart G., MB ChB, FRCS   Prof., Postgraduate Medical Education; Head*
Other Staff: 1 Clin. Teaching Staff; 2 Hon. Clin. Sr. Lectrs.

Molecular and Clinical Medicine, School of

Tel: (0131) 537 2506 Fax: (0131) 537 2506
E-mail: mcm@ed.ac.uk
Andrew, Ruth, BSc PhD   Sr. Lectr.
Baldock, R. A., BSc PhD   Hon. Prof.
Best, Jonathan, MSc *Lond.*, MB ChB MSc, FRCPEd, FRCR   Forbes Prof., Medical Radiology
Brown, Roger, BA *Camb.*, BM BCh *Oxf.*, PhD   Sr. Lectr.
Busuttil, Anthony, OBE, MD *Malta*, FRCPath, FRCPEd, FRCPGlas, FRCSEd   Prof., Forensic Medicine
Cameron, David, MB BS MA MSc MD   Sr. Lectr.
Chapman, Karen E., BSc *Newcastle(UK)*, PhD *Newcastle(UK)*   Reader
Denvir, M. A., BSc MB ChB PhD, FRCP   Sr. Lectr.
Ford, M. J., MD, FRCPEd   Hon. Prof.
Greening, Andrew P., BSc MB ChB, FRCPEd   Prof., Pulmonary Disease
Hayward, Richard L., BSc MB ChB PhD   Sr. Lectr.
Holmes, Megan C., BSc *Lond.*, PhD *Lond.*   Reader
Maxwell, Simon, BSc MB ChB MD PhD, FRCP, FRCPEd   Sr. Lectr.
McLaren, Kathryn M., BSc MB ChB, FRCPath, FRCSEd, FRCPEd   Sr. Lectr.
Porteous, Mary, MSc *Glas.*, MD *Glas.*, FRCP   Reader
Ralston, Stuart H., MB ChB MD, FRCP   Prof.; Arthritis Res. Council Chair of Rheumatol.; Head*
Reynolds, Rebecca M., MA *Oxf.*, PhD *Edin.*   Sr. Lectr.
Seckl, Jonathan R., BSc *Lond.*, MB BS *Lond.*, PhD *Lond.*, FRCPEd, FMedSci, FRSEd   Moncrieff Arnott Prof.
Walker, Brian R., BSc MB ChB MD, FRCPEd   Prof., Endocrinology

Webb, David J., MB BS *Lond.*, MD, FRCP, FRCPEd, FMedSci, FFPM, FRSEd   Christison Prof., Therapeutics and Clinical Pharmacology
Other Staff: 5 Sr. Res. Fellows; 44 Res. Fellows; 48 Res. Assocs.

Clinical Neuroscience, Division of

Dennis, Martin S., MB BS *Lond.*, MD *Lond.*, FRCPEd   Prof., Stroke Medicine
Ffrench-Constant, Charles, MA MB MChir PhD   MS Society Prof., Multiple Sclerosis
Kelly, P. A. T., PhD *Glas.*, BSc   Reader
Knight, Richard S. G., BA BM BCh, FRCPEd   Reader
Sandercock, Peter, MA *Oxf.*, DM *Oxf.*, FRCPEd, FMedSci   Prof., Medical Neurology
Sudlow, Catherine L. M., BM BCh MSc DPhil, FRCPEd   Sr. Lectr.
Wardlaw, Joanna M., BSc MB ChB, FRCR   Prof., Applied Neuro-imaging
Warlow, Charles, BA *Camb.*, MD *Camb.*, FRCP, FRCPEd, FRCPGlas   Prof., Medical Neurology
Whittle, Ian R., MD *Adel.*, PhD, FRACS, FRCSEd   Forbes Prof., Surgical Neurology
Will, R. G., CBE, MA MD, FRCP, FRCPEd   Prof., Clinical Neurology
Zeman, Adam, BM BCh MA   Hon. Prof.
Other Staff: 3 Lectrs.; 4 Sr. Lectrs.†; 5 Hon. Fellows; 10 Hon. Clin. Sr. Lectrs.

Edinburgh Cancer Centre

Ball, Kathryn, BSc PhD   Prof., Biochemistry and Cell Signalling
Dunlop, M. G., MB ChB MD, FRCS   Prof., Coloproctology
Erridge, Sara C., MB BS *Lond.*, FRCR   Sr. Lectr.
Fallon, Marie T., MB ChB, FRCP   St Columba's Hospice Prof., Palliative Medicine
Forrester, Lesley M., BSc PhD   Reader
Gourlay, Charles, BSc MB ChB PhD   Sr. Lectr.
Habib, Fouad K., BA *Utah*, PhD *Leeds*, DSc, FRSChem   Reader
Harrison, D. J., BSc MB ChB, FRCPath, FRCPEd   Prof., Pathology; Head*
Hooper, Martin, MA *Camb.*, PhD *Camb.*, FRCPEd, FRSEd   Prof., Molecular Pathology
Hupp, Ted, BSc PhD   Prof., Cancer Research
Jodrell, Duncan D. M., MSc *S'ton.*, MSc *Lond.*, FRCPEd   Prof., Cancer Therapeutics
Kunkler, Ian, MB BChir MA, FRCPEd, FRCR, FRSA   Hon. Prof.
Melton, David W., MA *Camb.*, PhD *Camb.*   Prof., Somatic Cell Genetics
Price, Allan, MB BCh *Wales*, PhD *Lond.*, FRCR   Hon. Prof.
Smyth, J. F., MA *Camb.*, MD *Camb.*, MSc *Lond.*, FRCP, FRCPEd, FRSEd, FRCR   Prof., Medical Oncology
Turner, Marc, MB ChB *Manc.*, PhD *Edin.*, FRCPEd   Prof., Cellular Therapy
Other Staff: 2 Lectrs.; 4 Sr. Lectrs.†; 2 Hon. Fellows; 1 Clin. Teaching Staff; 29 Hon. Clin. Sr. Lectrs.

Molecular Medicine, Centre for

Abbott, Cathy, BSc *Reading*, PhD *Reading*   Reader
Bickmore, Wendy, BA *Oxf.*, PhD *Edin.*, FRSEd   Hon. Prof.
Cooke, Howard, BA *Oxf.*, PhD   Hon. Prof.
Gray, Mohini   Sr. Lectr.
Hill, Robert, BSc PhD   Hon. Prof.
Jackson, Ian J., MA *Oxf.*, PhD *Lond.*   Hon. Prof.
Porteous, David J., BSc PhD, FRSEd, FMedSci, FIBiol   Prof., Human Molecular Genetics and Medicine; Head*
Ralston, Stuart H., MB ChB MD, FRCP   Prof.; Arthritis Res. Council Chair of Rheumatol.; Head, Rheumatic Diseases Unit
Satsangi, Jack, DPhil *Oxf.*, BSc MB BS   Prof., Gastroenterology
van Heyningen, Veronica, MA MS DPhil, FRSEd   Hon. Prof.
Wright, Alan F., MB ChB *St And.*, PhD   Hon. Prof.
Other Staff: 3 Lectrs.; 2 Hon. Readers; 2 Hon. Teaching Staff; 2 Hon. Fellows

Pathology, Division of

Al-Nafussi, Awatif I., DPhil *Oxf.*, MB ChB, FRCPath   Sr. Lectr.
Bartlett, John M. S., BSc PhD   Reader
Bell, Jeanne E., CBE, BSc *Newcastle(UK)*, MD *Newcastle(UK)*, FRCPath, FRSEd, FMedSci   Prof., Neuropathology
Bellamy, Christopher, BSc *Lond.*, MB BS *Lond.*, PhD *Lond.*   Sr. Lectr.
Brownstein, David G., BSc DVM   Sr. Lectr.
Duvall, Edward, MA *Oxf.*, DPhil *Oxf.*, MB ChB, FRCPath   Sr. Lectr.
Gilmour, Hugh M., MB ChB, FRCPath, FRCSEd   Sr. Lectr.
Grigor, Ken, BSc *Glas.*, MD, FRCPath, FRSEd   Sr. Lectr.
Harrison, D. J., BSc MB ChB, FRCPath, FRCPEd   Prof.; Head*
Howie, Sarah E. M., BSc *St And.*, PhD *Lond.*   Prof., Immunopathology
Ironside, James W., MB ChB *Dund.*, FRCPath, FRCPEd, FMedSci   Prof., Clinical Neuropathology
Manson, Jean C., BSc MSc PhD   Hon. Prof.
Reid, W. A., BSc MD, FRCPath   Sr. Lectr.
Salter, Donald M., BSc MB ChB, FRCPath   Prof., Osteoarticular Pathology
Smith, Colin, MB ChB *Glas.*, BS   Sr. Lectr.
Williams, Alistair R. W., BSc MD, FRCPath   Reader
Other Staff: 2 Lectrs.; 1 Hon. Reader; 8 Hon. Fellows; 4 Clin. Teaching Staff; 16 Hon. Clin. Sr. Lectrs.
Vacant Posts: 1 Regius Prof.

Psychiatry, Division of

Blackwood, Douglas, MB ChB PhD, FRCP, FRCPsych   Prof., Psychiatric Genetics
Ebmeier, Klaus P., MD *Aberd.*   Hon. Prof.
Hoare, P., MA *Oxf.*, BM BCh *Oxf.*, DM *Oxf.*, FRCPsych   Sr. Lectr.
Johnstone, Eve C., CBE, MD *Glas.*, FRCPEd, FRCPGlas, FRCPsych   Prof.; Head*
Lawrie, Stephen M., MB ChB *Aberd.*, MPhil   Prof., Psychiatric Imaging
MacIntyre, D. J., BSc MB ChB   Sr. Lectr.
McIntosh, Andrew, BSc MB ChB MSc MPhil MD   Sr. Lectr.
Muir, Walter J., BSc MB ChB, FRCPsych   Reader
Owens, D. G. Cunningham, MB ChB MD, FRCPGlas, FRCPsych   Prof., Clinical Psychiatry
Sharpe, Michael, MA *Oxf.*, MB BChir *Camb.*, MD *Camb.*   Prof., Psychological Medicine and Symptoms Research
Thomson, Lindsay D. G., MB ChB MPhil   Sr. Lectr.
Other Staff: 7 Lectrs.; 2 Sr. Lectrs.†; 4 Hon. Fellows; 21 Clin. Teaching Staff; 11 Hon. Clin. Sr. Lectrs.

Undergraduate Learning and Teaching, Directorate of

Cumming, Allan D., BSc MB ChB MD, FRCP   Prof., Medical Education; Head*

Learning Technology Section

Tel: (0131) 651 1564 Fax: (0131) 651 3011
E-mail: learning.technology.section@ed.ac.uk
Dewhurst, D. E.   Dir., Med. Illustration; Prof., Student Learning (e-Learning); Head*

Medical Teaching Organisation

Boyd, Kenneth M., BD MA PhD, FRCPEd   Prof., Medical Ethics
Cameron, Helen S., BSc MB ChB   Sr. Lectr.; Head*
Carlson, Robert, BSc *Cant.*, MB ChB *Otago*, FAFPHM   Sr. Lectr.
Cumming, Allan D., BSc MB ChB MD, FRCP   Prof., Medical Education
Warren, Patricia M., BSc *Sheff.*, PhD *Sheff.*   Sr. Lectr.
Other Staff: 1 Lectr.; 4 Teaching Fellows; 5 Hon. Fellows; 1 Hon. Clin. Sr. Lectr.

Veterinary Studies, Royal (Dick) School of

Tel: (0131) 650 6130 Fax: (0131) 650 6585
E-mail: dick.vet@ed.ac.uk
25 Lectrs.; 7 Sr. Res. Fellows; 31 Res. Fellows;
7 Res. Assocs.; 1 Sr. Lectr.†; 2 Lectrs.†; 33
Hon. Fellows

Easter Bush Veterinary Centre

Hume, David   Head*

Veterinary Biomedical Sciences

Archibald, A., BSc PhD   Hon. Prof.
Becker, Catherina G., PhD   Sr. Lectr.
Bradshaw, Jeremy P., MA Oxf., DPhil Oxf.,
FIBiol   Reader
Brophy, Peter J., BSc Lond., PhD Lond., FIBiol
Mary Dick Prof., Veterinary Anatomy and
Cell Biology
Bruce, M., BSc PhD   Hon. Prof.
Cottrell, David F., BVSc Liv., MSc PhD   Sr.
Lectr.
Dalziel, R. G., BSc Glas., PhD Glas.   Sr. Lectr.
Fazakerley, John K., BSc MBA PhD, FRCPath
Prof., Virology
Fleetwood-Walker, S. M., BSc Birm., MSc Birm.,
PhD Birm.   Prof., Pain Biology
Gally, D. L., BSc PhD   Prof., Microbial
Genetics
Harkiss, G. D., BSc Edin., PhD Camb.   Prof.,
Veterinary Immunopathology
Hopkins, John, BSc Liv., PhD Lond., DSc Edin.
Prof., Veterinary Immunology
Ingham, Cali A., BSc Brist., MSc ANU, DPhil
Oxf.   Sr. Lectr.
Kempson, Susan A., BSc Leeds, PhD Liv.   Sr.
Lectr.
Lawrence, A., BSc PhD   Hon. Prof.
Macdonald, Alastair A., BSc Glas., MBA PhD
Sr. Lectr.
Molony, V., BVSc Liv., MSc Cornell, PhD Liv.
Hon. Prof.
Nash, A. A., BSc MSc PhD, FMedSci   Prof.,
Veterinary Pathology
Pearson, G. T., BSc Dund., PhD Dund.   Sr. Lectr.
Pettigrew, Graham W., BSc PhD   Prof.,
Bioenergetics
Other Staff: 8 Lectrs.; 9 Hon. Fellows

Veterinary Clinical Sciences

Argyle, David, BVMS PhD   William Dick
Prof., Veterinary Clinical Studies
Barakzai, S. Z., BVSc   Sr. Lectr.
Blissitt, Karen J., BVSc PhD   Sr. Lectr.
Chandler, Marjorie, DVM Colorado, MS   Sr.
Lectr.
Cleaveland, Sarah, BA BSc PhD   Sr. Lectr.
Clutton, R. E., BVSc Liv.   Prof., Veterinary
Anaesthesiology
Cockram, Michael, BVetMed Lond., PhD Liv.
Sr. Lectr.
Collie, David, BVM&S MPhil PhD   Sr. Lectr.
Corcoran, Brendan M., PhD   Dir., Hospital for
Small Animals; Prof., Veterinary
Cardiopulmonary Medicine
Cuddeford, D., BSc Lond., MSc Aberd., PhD   Sr.
Lectr.
Dixon, Padraic, MVB N.U.I., PhD   Prof.,
Equine Surgery
Eisler, Mark C., BA MSc PhD   Sr. Lectr.
Else, R. W., BVSc Brist., PhD Brist., FRCPath
Prof., Diagnostic Veterinary Pathology
French, Anne, MVB   Sr. Lectr.
Griffin, Harry, BSc MBA PhD   Hon. Prof.
Gunn-Moore, Danielle, BSc BVM&S PhD
Prof., Feline Medicine
Hahn, C. N., BS MSc PhD   Sr. Lectr.
Lamb, J. R., BA Oxf., PhD Lond., BDS MA,
FRCPath, FMedSci, FRSEd   Prof., Veterinary
Clinical Immunology
Maudlin, I., BSc MSc PhD   Prof. Fellow
McGorum, Bruce, BSc PhD   Prof., Equine
Medicine
McKeever, Declan, PhD   Moredun Prof.
Milne, Elspeth, BVSc PhD, FRCVS   Sr. Lectr.
Morrison, Ivan, BVMS Glas., PhD Glas.,
FRCPath, FRSEd   Prof. Fellow
Mosley, John R., BVM&S PhD   Sr. Lectr.

Penny, C. D., BVM&S   Sr. Lectr.; Dir., Large
Animal Practice
Pirie, R. S., BVM&S   Sr. Lectr.
Rhind, S. M., BVMS Glas., PhD   Prof.,
Veterinary Medical Education
Ridyard, A., BVSc   Sr. Lectr.
Sargison, N., BA, FRCVS   Sr. Lectr.
Scott, Philip R., BVM&S MPhil, FRCVS   Reader
Simpson, James W., BVM&S MPhil   Prof.,
Canine Medicine
Smith, Sionagh, BVMS Glas., PhD   Sr. Lectr.
Stead, A. C., BVMS Glas., FRCVS   Sr. Lectr.
Taylor, David W., BSc S'ton., PhD Camb.   Prof.,
Tropical Animal Health
Thoday, K. L., BVetMed Lond., PhD   Prof.,
Veterinary Dermatology
Thrusfield, M. V., BVMS Glas., MSc Birm., FIBiol
Sr. Lectr.
Van den Broek, A. H. M., BVSc Liv., FRCVS
Sr. Lectr.
Watson, E. D., BVMS Glas., MVM Glas., PhD
Brist., FRCVS   Prof., Veterinary
Reproduction; Head*
Welburn, Susan, BSc PhD   Prof., Medical and
Veterinary Molecular Epidemiology
Yool, D., BVMS PhD   Sr. Lectr.
Other Staff: 24 Lectrs.; 7 Sr. Res. Fellows; 31
Res. Fellows; 7 Res. Assocs.; 1 Sr. Lectr.†; 1
Lectr.†; 23 Hon. Fellows

SPECIAL CENTRES, ETC

Language Studies, Applied, Institute for

Tel: (0131) 650 6200 Fax: (0131) 667 5927
E-mail: ials.enquiries@ed.ac.uk
Glendinning, Eric H., MA   Sr. Lectr.; Dir.*
Lynch, Tony, MA Camb., MSc PhD   Sr. Lectr.
Trappes-Lomax, Hugh R. N., MA Oxf., PhD
Sr. Lectr.
Other Staff: 2 Lectrs.; 2 Res. Assocs.
Research: analysing language needs of business
and industry; teaching and learning English
as a foreign language; teaching and learning
for special purposes; teaching and learning
modern languages

Lifelong Learning, Office of

Tel: (0131) 650 4400 Fax: (0131) 667 6097
E-mail: cce@ed.ac.uk
Gillen, C., BSc Glas., BA Open(UK), MEd Aberd.,
PhD Glas., FGS   Sr. Lectr.; Dir.*
Other Staff: 4 Lectrs.

Stem Cell Research, Institute for

Tel: (0131) 650 5828 Fax: (0131) 650 7773
E-mail: cgrinfo@ed.ac.uk
Smith, A. G., BA Oxf., PhD, FRSEd   Dir.*
Other Staff: 1 Sr. Res. Fellow; 15 Res. Fellows

Teaching, Learning and Assessment, Centre for

Tel: (0131) 651 6661 Fax: (0131) 651 6664
E-mail: tla.centre@ed.ac.uk
Day, Katherine J., BA S'ton., PhD Edin.   Sr.
Lectr.; Co-Dir.*
Macleod, Hamish, BSc PhD   Sr. Lectr.; Co-
Dir.*

CONTACT OFFICERS

Academic affairs. Academic Registrar and
Deputy Secretary (Academic Affairs):
Nelson, D. Bruce, BSc Glas., PhD Glas., MBA
Accommodation. Director of Accommodation
Services: Kington, Richard
(E-mail: accommodation@ed.ac.uk)
Admissions (first degree). Director of Student
Recruitment and Admissions: Lister,
Elizabeth, BSc
(E-mail: sra.enquiries@ed.ac.uk)
Admissions (higher degree). (Admissions are
distributed to College Postgraduate Offices)
Academic Policy Manager: Honeyman, Gail
(E-mail: postgrad@ed.ac.uk)
Adult/continuing education. Director, Centre
for Lifelong Learning: Gillen, C., BSc Glas.,
BA Open(UK), MEd Aberd., PhD Glas., FGS
(E-mail: cce@ed.ac.uk)

Alumni. Director, Development and Alumni
Services: Fleming, Robert
(E-mail: development@ed.ac.uk)
Archives. Sub-Librarian: Wilson, Arnott T.,
MA
Careers. Director, Careers Service: Ali, Lynda,
BSc (E-mail: careersbp@ed.ac.uk)
Computing services. Vice-Principal,
Knowledge Management, CIO and Librarian
to the University: Haywood, Prof. J., BSc
Edin., PhD Open(UK)
(E-mail: eucs.reception@ed.ac.uk)
Conferences/corporate hospitality. Director,
Corporate Services: Paul, Nigel, BA
Conferences/corporate hospitality. Director
of Accommodation Services: Kington,
Richard (E-mail: edinburgh.first@ed.ac.uk)
Consultancy services. Director of Research
Services: Waddell, Derek, BA
(E-mail: research.innovation@ed.ac.uk)
Credit transfer. Director of Student
Recruitment and Admissions: Lister,
Elizabeth, BSc
Development/fund-raising. Director,
Development and Alumni Services:
Fleming, Robert
(E-mail: development@ed.ac.uk)
Equal opportunities. Equality and Diversity
Manager: Bettison, Ian, BA Sund.
(E-mail: equal.opportunities@ed.ac.uk)
Estates and buildings/works and services.
Director of Estates and Buildings: Currie,
A., FRICS
Examinations. Senior Administrative Officer:
(vacant) (E-mail: registry@ed.ac.uk)
Finance. Director of Finance: Gorringe, Jon
(E-mail: deptsec.finance@ed.ac.uk)
General enquiries. University Secretary:
Cornish, Melvyn, BSc Leic.
(E-mail: communications.office@ed.ac.uk)
Health services. Physician-in-Charge: Brown,
Tim S., BSc MB ChB
(E-mail: health.service@ed.ac.uk)
Industrial liaison. Director of Research
Services: Waddell, Derek, BA
(E-mail: research.innovation@ed.ac.uk)
International office. Director, International
Office: Mackay, Alan, BA
(E-mail: enquiries.international@ed.ac.uk)
Language training for international students.
Director, Institute for Applied Language
Studies: Glendinning, Eric H., MA
(E-mail: ials.enquiries@ed.ac.uk)
Library (chief librarian). Librarian/University
Librarian: Hayes, Helen, BA
(E-mail: library@ed.ac.uk)
Marketing. Communications and Marketing:
Cavani, John, BA
(E-mail: communications.office@ed.ac.uk)
Personnel/human resources. Director of
Human Resources: Gupta, Sheila, MBE, MA
Keele (E-mail: human.resources@ed.ac.uk)
Public relations. Communications and
Marketing: Conn, Ian, BA MBA
(E-mail: communications.office@ed.ac.uk)
Publications. Communications and Marketing:
Conn, Ian, BA MBA
(E-mail: communications.office@ed.ac.uk)
Purchasing. Director of Procurement:
Bowman, Karen, MA
(E-mail: procurement.office@ed.ac.uk)
Quality assurance and accreditation. Director
of Quality Assurance: van Heyningen,
Simon, MA Camb., PhD Camb., FRSChem,
FIBiol
Research. Director of Research Services:
Waddell, Derek, BA
(E-mail: research.innovation@ed.ac.uk)
Safety. Director, Health and Safety: Reid,
Alistair, BSc (E-mail: health.safety@ed.ac.uk)
Scholarships, awards, loans. Assistant
Secretary: Lawrie, Robert, BD Glas., MSc
Strath.
Schools liaison. Director of Student
Recruitment and Admissions: Lister,
Elizabeth, BSc
(E-mail: enquiries.slcs@ed.ac.uk)

Security. Chief Security Officer: Conn, Adam
(E-mail: security@ed.ac.uk)
Sport and recreation. Director, Centre for
Sport and Exercise: Aitken, Jim, BEd
Staff development and training. Director of
Staff Development: MacArthur, Elspeth C.,
MA *Aberd.*
(E-mail: staff.development@ed.ac.uk)
Strategic planning. Director of Planning:
Easson, Alexis R., MA PhD
Student union. President, EUSA: MacAlister,
John (E-mail: eusa.enquiry@ed.ac.uk)
Student welfare/counselling. (Counselling)
Head, Student Counselling Service: Jackson,

Susie, MA *Edin.*
(E-mail: student.counselling@ed.ac.uk)
Student welfare/counselling. Director,
Careers Service: Ali, Lynda, BSc
(E-mail: careersbp@ed.ac.uk)
Students from other countries. Director of
Student Recruitment and Admissions: Lister,
Elizabeth, BSc
Students with disabilities. Special Needs
Officer: Roadburg, Marnie, BEd
(E-mail: disability.office@ed.ac.uk)
University press. Chief Executive, Edinburgh
University Press: Wright, Timothy E., BA
Sund. (E-mail: editorial@eup.ed.ac.uk)

CAMPUS/COLLEGE HEADS

New College, The Mound, Edinburgh,
Scotland EH1 2LU. Principal: Lyall, Rev.
David, STM *Yale,* BSc BD PhD
Scottish Agricultural College: Edinburgh,
The King's Buildings, West Mains Road,
Edinburgh, Scotland EH9 3JG. Acting
Principal: Linklater, Prof. K. A., BVM&S
PhD, FRCVS

[Information supplied by the institution as at 22 October 2007, and edited by the ACU]

UNIVERSITY OF ESSEX

Founded 1965

Postal Address: Wivenhoe Park, Colchester, England CO4 3SQ
Telephone: (01206) 873333 **Fax:** (01206) 873598 **E-mail:** registrar@essex.ac.uk
URL: http://www.essex.ac.uk

VICE-CHANCELLOR*—Riordan, Prof. Colin, BA *Manc.,* PhD *Manc.*
REGISTRAR AND SECRETARY‡—Rich, Tony, BA *Manc.,* PhD *Manc.,* FRSA

UNIVERSITY OF EXETER

Founded 1955

Member of the Association of Commonwealth Universities

Postal Address: Northcote House, The Queen's Drive, Exeter, Devon, England EX4 4QJ
Telephone: (01392) 661000 **Fax:** (01392) 263108
URL: http://www.exeter.ac.uk

VICE-CHANCELLOR*—Smith, Prof. Steve, BSc *S'ton.,* MSc *S'ton.,* PhD *S'ton.,* DSc *S'ton.*
DEPUTY VICE-CHANCELLOR—Armstrong, Prof. Neil, BEd *Lough.,* MSc *Lough.,* PhD *Exe.,* DSc *Exe.,* FIBiol, FRSA
DEPUTY VICE-CHANCELLOR—Kain, Prof. Roger J. P., CBE, BA *Lond.,* PhD *Lond.,* DLit *Lond.,* FBA, FSA
DEPUTY VICE-CHANCELLOR—Kay, Prof. Janice M., BA *Newcastle*(UK), PhD *Camb.*
DEPUTY VICE-CHANCELLOR—Overton, Prof. Mark, BA *Exe.,* MA *Camb.,* PhD *Camb.,* FRHistS
TREASURER—Sturtridge, Gerald, BSc(Eng) *Brist.*
REGISTRAR AND SECRETARY‡—Allen, David J., BA *Wales,* MEd *Wales,* FRSA
LIBRARIAN—Paterson, Alasdair T., MA *Edin.,* MA *Sheff.*

GENERAL INFORMATION

History. Established as University College of
the South West of England in 1922, the
university was founded under its present name
in 1955.
   The main site overlooks the city of Exeter.
The school of education shares a second site in
Exeter with departments from the school of
sport and health sciences. The Cornwall
campus is based at Penryn near Falmouth and
incorporates the Camborne School of Mines.

Admission to first degree courses (see also
United Kingdom Introduction). Through
Universities and Colleges Admissions Service
(UCAS). Part-time students apply direct to the
university. General entrance requirement: at
least 2 passes at General Certificate of
Education (GCE) A level (or equivalent
qualifications), together with acceptable levels
of literacy and numeracy.

First Degrees (see also United Kingdom
Directory to Subjects of Study). BA, BA(Ed),
BEd, BEng, BM BS, BMus, BSc, BSc(Ed), LLB,
LLB(Eur), MChem, MEng, MMath, MPhys,
MStat.

   Full-time degrees normally last 3 years.
Modern language degrees and degrees with
European study: 3 years plus 1 year abroad.
All undergraduate degrees may be taken on a
part-time basis by arrangement with the school
concerned.
   Length of course. Full-time: BA, BEng, BSc, LLB:
3 years; LLB(Eur), MEng, MMath, MPhys: 4
years; BM BS: 5 years. Part-time: BA: 6 years. By
distance learning: BA: 6 years.

Higher Degrees (see also United Kingdom
Directory to Subjects of Study).
   Master's. LLM, MA, MBA, MD, MEd, MMus,
MPhil, MSc.
   Admission. Applicants must normally hold an
appropriate first degree with at least second
class honours.
   Most courses last 1 year full-time or 2 years
part-time.
   Doctoral. DClinPsych, DD, DEng, DLitt, DMus,
DSc, EdD, LLD, PhD.
   Admission. EdD: master's degree in education
or a related discipline; DD, DEng, DLitt, DMus,
DSc, LLD: awarded on published work of
distinction.
   Length of course. Full-time: PhD: 3 years. Part-
time: PhD: max. 6 years.

Language of Instruction. English. Pre-
sessional and and in-sessional courses are
available for students whose first language is
not English.

Libraries. Volumes: 1,000,000. Periodicals
subscribed to: 3250. Special collections:
personal library of Sir John Betjeman.

Statistics. Students (2005–2006):
undergraduate 9951 (9951 men; master's
2553 (2553 men); doctoral 907 (907 men).

FACULTIES/SCHOOLS
Postgraduate Studies
Tel: (01392) 263074 Fax: (01392) 263108
Dean: Lappin-Scott, Prof. Hilary M., BSc *Warw.,*
PhD *Warw.*

Undergraduate Studies
Tel: (01392) 263328 Fax: (01392) 263108
E-mail: ugfaculty@ex.ac.uk
Dean: Macnair, Prof. Mark R., BA *Camb.,* MA
Camb., PhD *Liv.*

ACADEMIC UNITS

Arranged by Schools

Arabic and Islamic Studies, Institute of

Tel: (01392) 264036 Fax: (01392) 264035
E-mail: iais-info@ex.ac.uk
Al-Qasimi, H.H. Shaikh Sultan bin Mohammed
Visiting Prof.
El-Enany, Rasheed, BA Cairo, PhD Prof.,
Modern Arabic Literature; Dir.*
Gleave, Robert, BA York(UK), MA Manc., PhD
Manc. Prof., Arabic Studies
Niblock, Timothy C., BA Oxf., DPhil Sus.
Prof., Arab Gulf Studies
Stansfield, Gareth R. V., BA Durh., MA Durh.,
PhD Durh. Reader
Other Staff: 3 Visiting Profs.; 1 Sr. Lectr.; 7
Lectrs.; 2 Teaching Fellows; 1 Lectr.†; 10
Hon. Univ. Fellows
Vacant Posts: 1 Prof.
Research: anthropology and sociology of the
Middle East; Arabic language, literature and
culture; history of the Middle East; Islamic
studies; Middle East politics and political
economy

Biosciences

Tel: (01392) 264674 Fax: (01392) 263700
E-mail: a.c.r.trick@exeter.ac.uk
Aves, Stephen J., BA York(UK), PhD Brist. Sr.
Lectr.
Bryant, David M., BSc Lond., PhD Lond., FRSEd
Prof., Environmental Biology
Bryant, John A., MA Camb., PhD Camb., FIBiol
Prof.†
Cresswell, James E., BSc S'ton., PhD Mich. Sr.
Lectr.
Evans, Matthew R., BSc Brist., PhD Camb.
Prof., Environmental/Conservation Biology
Grant, Murray, PhD Prof.
Harper, J. L., CBE, MA Oxf., DPhil Oxf., FRS
Visiting Prof.
Hoskin, David, BSc W.Aust., PhD W.Aust.
Reader, Ecology
Hunt, Roderic, BSc Sheff., PhD Sheff. Visiting
Prof.
Lappin-Scott, Hilary M., BSc Warw., PhD Warw.
Prof., Environmental Microbiology
Littlechild, Jennifer A., PhD Lond. Prof.,
Biological Chemistry
Macgregor, Herbert, BSc St And., PhD St And.
Visiting Prof.
Macnair, Mark R., BA Camb., MA Camb., PhD
Liv. Prof., Evolutionary Genetics
Moore, Allen, BSc Arizona, PhD Colorado Prof.,
Evolutionary Genetics
Moore, Patricia J., BA St.Louis, PhD Colorado Sr.
Lectr.
Shaw, Andrew M., MA Camb., PhD S'ton. Sr.
Lectr.
Smirnoff, Nicholas, BSc Brist., PhD St And.
Reader, Physiology and Metabolism
Stevens, James, BSc CNAA, PhD Brist. Reader,
Molecular Systematics
Talbot, Nicholas J., BSc Wales, PhD E.Anglia
Prof., Molecular Genetics; Head*
Tyler, Charles R., BSc Lanc., MSc Plym., PhD
Aston Prof., Environmental Biology
Wilson, Roderic W., BSc Birm., PhD Birm. Sr.
Lectr.
Other Staff: 4 Emer. Profs.; 8 Lectrs.; 5
Teaching Fellows; 31 Res. Fellows; 2 Exper.
Officers; 3 Hon. Res. Fellows
Research: chemical biology and biocatalysis;
conservation and ecology; environmental
biology; plant and microbial sciences

Business and Economics

Tel: (01392) 263200 Fax: (01392) 263242
E-mail: sobe@exeter.ac.uk
Research: accounting; business and management;

economics and econometrics; finance

Accounting and Finance

including the XFi Centre for Finance and
Investment

Tel: (01392) 263201/263463 Fax: (01392)
263210/262475
E-mail: c.i.down/r.phillips@exeter.ac.uk
Bulkley, I. George, MA Essex, PhD Calif. Prof.
Collier, Paul A., BSc Aston, PhD Exe., FCA Jt.
Head, Acctg.; Sr. Lectr., Accounting
Cooke, Terry E., BSc(Econ) Lond., PhD Exe., FCA
Prof., Accounting
Draper, Paul R., BA Exe., MA Reading, PhD Stir.
Prof., Finance; Head of Sch.*
Gregory, Alan, MSc Lond. Prof., Business and
Finance
Gwilliam, David R., MA Camb., FCA Prof.,
Accounting
Harris, Richard D. F., BSc(Econ) Lond., MSc
Lond., PhD Exe. Prof., Finance
Jackson, Richard H. G., BSc Exe., MBA Cran.,
FCA Sr. Lectr.; Jt. Head, Acctg.
Rhys, Huw P., MA Oxf., MSc Leeds, MSc CNAA
Sr. Lectr.
Other Staff: 7 Lectrs.
Vacant Posts: 1 Sr. Lectr./Reader
Research: accounting history; auditing and
corporate governance; capital markets;
management accounting; risk management
and financial econometrics

Economics

Balkenborg, D. G., BA Duisburg, MSc Lond., MA
Bonn, PhD Bonn Reader
Davidson, James, BSocSc Birm., MSc Lond.
Prof., Econometrics
Kaplan, Todd R., BS Cal.Tech., MA Minn., PhD
Minn. Reader
Kelsey, David, MA Oxf., MPhil Oxf., DPhil Oxf.
Prof.
Kotsogiannis, Christos, BA Essex, MA Essex, PhD
Essex Sr. Lectr.
MacMillen, Malcolm J. J., BA Keele, MA Sus.
Sr. Lectr.
Maloney, John, BA Camb., PhD Nott. Reader,
Political Economy
McCorriston, Steven, BA Strath., MSc Reading
Prof., Agricultural Economics; Head*
Myles, Gareth D., BA Warw., MSc(Econ) Lond.,
DPhil Oxf. Prof., Economics
Wren-Lewis, Simon, MA Camb., MSc Lond.
Dir., Res.; Bertie Black Prof., Business
Economics
Other Staff: 9 Lectrs.
Research: agricultural economics; applied
statistics and econometrics; economic
theory, decision theory, theory of the firm;
environmental economics; evolutionary
game theory and experimental economics

Management

Brown, Steve, BA MBA DPhil Prof.; Head*
James, Simon R., BSc(Econ) Lond., MSc Lond.,
MA Open(UK), MBA Open(UK), LLM Leic., PhD
Leeds Met. Reader, Economics
Maull, Roger S., BAEcon CNAA, MSc CNAA,
PhD CNAA Prof.
Murray, Gordon C., BSc Nott., PhD E.Anglia,
MBA Prof.
Newton, Tim, BSc Brun., MA Sheff., PhD H-W
Prof., Organisation and Society
Schroeder, Jonathan E., BA Mich., MA Calif.,
PhD Calif. Prof., Marketing
Shaw, Gareth, BSc Hull, PhD Hull Prof.,
Tourism Studies
Smart, Andrew P., BSc Plym., PhD Plym. Sr.
Lectr.
Other Staff: 10 Lectrs.
Research: business process analysis; consumer
behaviour, advertising and branding;
operations management; organisational
behaviour and organisation theory;
technology management

Classics, Ancient History and Theology

Tel: (01392) 264200 Fax: (01392) 264377
E-mail: classics@exeter.ac.uk
Research: Greek literature of the archaic and
classical period; Hellenistic culture; ideas of
personality in the ancient world; Latin
literature and science; relations of Greece
and north-eastern Europe

Classics and Ancient History

Borg, Barbara E., PhD Gött. Prof., Classical
Archaeology
Braund, David C., MA Camb., PhD Camb., FSA
Prof., Mediterranean and Black Sea History
Gill, Christopher J., MA Camb., PhD Yale Prof.,
Ancient Thought
Mitchell, Lynette G., BA NE, PhD Durh. Sr.
Lectr.
Mitchell, Stephen, BA Oxf., DPhil Oxf.
Leverhulme Prof., Hellenistic Culture
Ogden, Daniel, BA Oxf., DPhil Oxf. Prof.
Seaford, Richard A. S., MA Oxf., DPhil Oxf.
Prof., Greek Literature
Whitmarsh, Timothy J. G., MA Camb., MPhil
Camb., PhD Camb. Reader
Wilkins, John M., MA Camb., PhD Camb.
Prof., Greek Culture
Other Staff: 6 Lectrs.; 12 Hon. Univ. Fellows
Research: Greek literature of the archaic and
classical period; Hellenistic culture; ideas of
personality in the ancient world; Latin
literature and science; relations of Greece
and north-eastern Europe

Theology

Tel: (01392) 264241 Fax: (01392) 264195
E-mail: theology@exeter.ac.uk
Gorringe, Tim, BA Oxf., MPhil Leeds St. Luke's
Foundation Prof., Theological Studies
Higton, Mike A., MA Camb., PhD Camb. Sr.
Lectr.; Head*
Horrell, David G., MA Camb., PhD Camb.
Reader, New Testament Studies
Logan, Rev. Alistair H. B., MA Edin., BD Edin.,
ThM Harv., PhD St And. Sr. Lectr.
Wynn, Mark, BA Oxf., DPhil Oxf. Sr. Lectr.
Other Staff: 3 Lectrs.; 4 Teaching Fellows; 1
Prof. Res. Fellow†; 1 Lectr.†; 10 Hon.
Univ. Fellows
Research: biblical studies; historical and
systematic theology; philosophy of religion;
theological ethics and politics; theology and
culture

Drama

Tel: (01392) 264580 Fax: (01392) 264594
E-mail: drama@exeter.ac.uk
Balfour, Michael, BA Ulster, PhD Lanc. Sr.
Lectr.
Giannachi, Gabriella, BA Turin, DPhil Oxf. Sr.
Lectr.
Kaye, Nick, BA Birm., PhD Manc. Prof.,
Performance Studies
Ley, Graham K. H., BA Oxf., MPhil Lond.
Reader, Drama and Theory
Mangan, Michael, BA Camb., PhD Camb. Prof.
McCullough, Christopher J., BA CNAA, MA Leeds
Prof., Theatre; Head of Sch.*
Wade, Lesley A., MA Br.Col., PhD Exe. Sr.
Lectr.
Zarrilli, Phillip, BA Ohio, MDiv McCormick, MA
Minn., PhD Minn. Prof., Performance
Practice
Other Staff: 13 Lectrs.; 2 Res. Fellows; 4
Teaching Fellows; 1 Tech. Manager; 1 Sr.
Lectr.†; 5 Hon. Univ. Fellows
Research: actor and character in performance;
ancient Greek theatre performance and
stages; Brecht, Meyerhold and political
theatre; gender and performance;
Shakespeare's stage then and now

Education

Tel: (01392) 264892 Fax: (01392) 264922
E-mail: ed.ipso@exeter.ac.uk
Bayliss, Philip D., BA York(UK), PhD Brist. Sr.
Lectr.

Biesta, Gerardus J. J., BPhil Amst., BPhil Ley., MPhil Rotterdam, MPhil Ley., PhD Ley.   Prof.

Blewitt, John D., BSc Wales, MA Hudd., MEd Hudd., PhD Wales   Sr. Lectr.

Burden, Robert L., BA Hull, PhD Exe., FBPsS Prof., Applied Educational Psychology

Chedzoy, Susan M., BEd Lond., MEd Hull   Sr. Lectr.

Copley, Terence D., BA Nott.   Prof., Religious Education

Cunliffe, Leslie   Reader

Ernest, Paul, BSc Sus., MSc Lond., PhD Lond., FIMA   Prof., Philosophy of Mathematics Education

Fisher, Rosalind J., BA Manc., MEd Manc., PhD Plym.   Sr. Lectr.

Holden, Cathie, BA Wales, MPhil CNAA   Reader

Hunt, Cheryl M., BA Sheff., MEd Sheff., PhD Sheff.   Sr. Lectr.

MacLeod, Flora J., BA Open(UK), PhD Exe.   Sr. Lectr.

Mitchell, Christine H., BEd Lond., MA Lond.   Sr. Lectr.

Myhill, Deborah A., BA Exe., MPhil Exe., PhD Exe.   Prof.

Norwich, Brahm, MA Camb., MSc Lond., PhD Lond.   Prof., Educational Psychology

Postlethwaite, Keith C., BA Camb., DPhil Oxf.   Sr. Lectr.

Richardson, William, BA Brist., DPhil Oxf.   Prof.; Head of Sch.*

Skinner, Nigel C., BSc Lond., PhD CNAA   Sr. Lectr.

Trend, Roger D., BA Sheff., MSc Keele, PhD Exe.   Sr. Lectr.

Wegerif, Rupert B., BA Kent, MSc Lond., PhD Open(UK)   Prof.

Wood, Elizabeth A., BA CNAA, MEd Leeds   Reader

Research: cultures of learning beyond school; language; learning and educational needs; science education; teaching and teacher education

Engineering, Computer Science and Mathematics

Tel: (01392) 263628 Fax: (01392) 217965
E-mail: s.j.randle@exeter.ac.uk

Computer Science

Tel: (01392) 263655 Fax: (01392) 264067
E-mail: s.l.addo@ex.ac.uk

Djordjevic, S.   Sr. Lectr.

Everson, Richard M.   Sr. Lectr.

Galton, Anthony P., BA Camb., PhD Leeds   Reader, Knowledge Representation

Kapelan, Z.   Sr. Lectr.

Partridge, Derek, BSc Lond., PhD Lond.   Prof.

Yang, Zheng R.   Sr. Lectr.

Zunic, Jovisa   Sr. Lectr.

Research: artificial intelligence and cognitive science; media computing; neural computing; parallel systems; visualisation and visual programming

Engineering

Tel: (01392) 263651 Fax: (01392) 217965
E-mail: s.a.costello@exeter.ac.uk

Belmont, Michael R., BSc Wales, PhD Wales   Sr. Lectr.

Butler, David   Prof.

Chapman, Robin J.   Sr. Lectr.

Childe, Stephen J.   Sr. Lectr.

Davies, Thomas W., BScTech Sheff., PhD Sheff., FIChemE   Prof., Thermofluids Engineering

Evans, Kenneth E., BSc Lond., PhD Camb.   Prof., Materials Engineering; Head of Sch.*

Khu, Soon T.   Sr. Lectr.

Newman, David M.   Reader

Savic, Dragan A., MSc Belgrade, PhD Manit.   Prof., Hydroinformatics

Wadee, Khurram M., BSc Nott., MSc CNAA, PhD CNAA   Sr. Lectr.

Wright, David C., PhD CNAA   Prof., Electronics Engineering

Young, Phillipe G., BSc W.Ont., PhD W.Ont.   Sr. Lectr.

Zhang, David, BSc Gansu U.T., MSc Gansu U.T., PhD Brun.   Prof., Manufacturing Systems

Research: control and computational engineering; electronic and systems engineering; materials and process engineering; structure and infrastructure

Mathematical Sciences

Tel: (01392) 263994 Fax: (01392) 263997
E-mail: h.crispin@maths.exeter.ac.uk

Ashwin, Peter B., BA Camb., PhD Warw.   Reader, Applied Mathematics

Bailey, Trevor C., MSc Lond., PhD Exe.   Sr. Lectr.

Byott, Nigel P.   Sr. Lectr.

Gilbert, Andrew D., MA Camb., PhD Camb.   Reader

Hill, Roger M., MA Camb., MSc Warw., PhD Exe.   Sr. Lectr.

Krzanowski, Wojtek J., BSc Leeds, PhD Reading   Prof., Statistics

Langer, A.   Prof.

Saidi, Mohamid   Reader

Smith, David K., MA Camb., PhD Lanc., FIMA   Sr. Lectr.

Soward, Andrew M., PhD Camb., ScD Camb., FRS   Prof., Applied Mathematics

Thuburn, John   Prof.

Townley, Stuart B., BSc Warw., PhD Warw.   Prof., Applied Mathematics

Vámos, Peter, PhD Sheff., DSc Sheff.   Prof., Pure Mathematics

Zhang, Keke, BSc Nanjing, MSc Calif., PhD Calif.   Prof., Fluid Dynamics

Research: computational number theory; control theory; fluid dynamics; multivariate statistics; stochastic modelling

English

Tel: (01392) 264265 Fax: (01392) 264361
E-mail: english@ex.ac.uk

Brown, Andy, BSc Leeds   Sr. Lectr.

Edwards, Karen, MA Yale, MPhil Yale, PhD Yale   Sr. Lectr.

Gagnier, Regenia, BA Calif., PhD Calif.   Prof., English Literature

Jolly, Margaretta, BA Camb., MA York(UK), DPhil Sus.   Sr. Lectr.

Lawson-Peebles, Robert, MA Sus., DPhil Oxf.   Sr. Lectr.

McCabe, Colin, BA Camb., PhD Camb.   Prof.

McDowell, Nicholas, BA Camb., MPhil Oxf., DPhil Oxf.   Sr. Lectr.

McRae, Andrew D., BA Monash, MPhil Camb., PhD Camb.   Prof.

Neale, Stephen B. M., BA Exe.   Prof.

Richardson, Angelique, BA Oxf., MA Lond., PhD Lond.   Sr. Lectr.

Rylance, Richard, BA Leic., PhD Leic.   Prof.; Head*

Spencer, Jane, BA Hull, DPhil Oxf.   Prof.

Tauchert, Ashley, BA Camb., PhD Lond.   Sr. Lectr.

Taylor, Helen R., BA Lond., MA Louisiana State, DPhil Sus.   Prof.

Other Staff: 21 Lectrs.; 2 Lectrs.†; 13 Hon. Univ. Fellows

Research: creative writing; critical theory; film studies; modern and mediaeval English literature

Geography, Archaeology and Earth Resources

Tel: (01392) 263310 Fax: (01392) 263342
E-mail: sogaer-schooloffice@exeter.ac.uk

Van de Noort, R., BA Utrecht, Drs Amst.   Head*

Archaeology

Tel: (01392) 264350 Fax: (01392) 264358
E-mail: archaeology@exeter.ac.uk

Bradley, Bruce A., BA Arizona, PhD Camb.   Sr. Lectr.

Coles, Bryony J., BA Brist., MPhil Lond., FSA   Prof., Prehistoric Archaeology

Harding, Anthony F., MA Camb., PhD Camb., FBA, FSA   Anniversary Prof.

Hurcombe, Linda M., BA S'ton., PhD Sheff., FSA   Sr. Lectr.; Head*

Maxfield, Valerie A., BA Leic., PhD Durh., FSA   Prof., Roman Archaeology

Outram, Alan K., BA Durh., MSc Sheff., PhD Durh., FSA   Sr. Lectr.

Rippon, Stephen J., BA Reading, PhD Reading   Reader, Landscape Archaeology

Van de Noort, R., BA Utrecht, Drs Amst.   Sr. Lectr.

Other Staff: 5 Lectrs.; 5 Res. Fellows; 2 Teaching Fellows; 13 Hon. Univ. Fellows

Research: cultural landscapes, landscape archaeology, military landscapes; material culture; resource exploitation; wetland archaeology

Geography

based at Exeter and Cornwall campuses

Tel: (01392) 263341
E-mail: geography@exeter.ac.uk

Brace, Catherine, BA CNAA, MA Tor., PhD Brist.   Sr. Lectr.; Head, Cornwall Dept.* (Cornwall Campus)

Brown, Antony G., BSc Lond., PhD S'ton.   Prof., Physical Geography and Palaeoenvironmental Analysis

Buller, Henry, BA Lond., PhD Lond.   Prof., Rural Geography

Caseldine, Christopher J., MA St And., PhD St And.   Prof., Quaternary Environmental Change (Cornwall Campus)

Cloke, Paul, BA S'ton., PhD Lond., DSc Brist.   Prof., Human Geography

Goodwin, Mark, BA Sus., PhD Lond.   Prof., Human Geography

Harrison, Stephan, BSc Leic., PhD CNAA   Sr. Lectr., Physical Geography (Cornwall Campus)

Harvey, David C., BA Exe., PhD Exe.   Sr. Lectr.

Kain, Roger J. P., CBE, BA Lond., PhD Lond., DLit Lond., FBA, FSA   Montefiore Prof.

Little, Jo K., BA Wales, PhD Reading   Prof., Gender and Social Geography

Nicholas, Andrew P., BSc Leeds, PhD Exe.   Sr. Lectr.

Quine, Timothy A., BSc Lond., PhD Strath.   Reader, Earth Surface Processes; Head, Exeter Dept.*

Walling, Desmond E., BA Exe., PhD Exe.   Reardon Smith Prof.

Webb, Bruce W., BSc Exe., PhD Exe.   Prof., Physical Geography

Winter, D. Michael, OBE, BSc Lond., PhD Open(UK)   Prof., Rural Policy

Other Staff: 8 Lectrs.; 3 Teaching Fellows; 15 Res. Fellows; 2 Sr. Lectrs.†; 6 Hon. Univ. Fellows

Research: environmental change and environmental modelling; historical-cultural geography; nature, society, rurality; river basin science; space, power and political economy

Mines, Camborne School of

Tel: (01326) 371800 Fax: (01326) 371859
E-mail: cornwall@exeter.ac.uk

Barley, Robert W., BSc Lond., MSc Lond., PhD Lond.   Sr. Lectr.

Coggan, John S., MSc Newcastle(UK), PhD Newcastle(UK)   Sr. Lectr.

Glass, Hylke J., MSc T.H.Delft, PhD T.U.Eindhoven   Rio Tinto Prof., Mining and Minerals Engineering

Pine, Robert, BSc Lond., MSc Lond., PhD CNAA, FREng, FIMMM   Prof., Geotechnical Engineering

Pirrie, Duncan, BSc CNAA, PhD CNAA   Reader

Scott, Peter W., BSc Newcastle(UK), PhD Lond., FGS   Prof., Industrial Geology

Other Staff: 4 Sr. Lectrs.; 18 Lectrs.; 4 Res. Fellows

Research: environmental and minerals engineering; fundamental and applied geology; geomechanics and mining engineering; renewable energy

Historical, Political and Sociological Studies

Tel: (01392) 264631 Fax: (01392) 263305
E-mail: j.e.ashby@exeter.ac.uk

History

Tel: (01392) 264297
Barry, Jonathan, BA Camb., MA Oxf., DPhil Oxf., FRHistS Sr. Lectr.; Head of Sch.*
Barton, Simon F., BA Wales, MA York(UK), DPhil York(UK), FRHistS Prof., Spanish History
Black, Jeremy M., MBE, MA Camb., PhD Durh., FRHistS Prof.
Booth, Alan E., BA Kent, PhD Kent Reader
Crick, Julia C., BA Camb., PhD Camb., FRHistS Sr. Lectr.
Duffy, Michael D., MA Oxf., DPhil Oxf., FRHistS Reader, British History
Hamilton, Sarah, BA Camb., MA Lond., PhD Lond., FRHistS Sr. Lectr.
Jackson, Mark A., BSc Lond., MB BS Lond., PhD Leeds Prof., History of Medicine
Melling, Joseph L., BSc Brad., PhD Glas., FRHistS Reader, Social Welfare and Industrial Health
Orme, Nicholas I., MA Oxf., DPhil Oxf., DLitt Oxf., FSA, FRHistS Prof.
Overton, Mark, BA Exe., MA Camb., PhD Camb., FRHistS Prof., Economic and Social History
Overy, Richard, MA Camb., PhD Camb., FBA Prof., Modern History
Rees, Tim, MA Lond., DPhil Oxf. Sr. Lectr.
Rodger, Nicholas A. M., MA Oxf., DPhil Oxf. Prof., Naval History
Smith, Joseph, BA Durh., PhD Lond., FRHistS Reader, American Diplomatic History
Thomas, Martin, MD Oxf., DPhil Oxf. Reader
Thorpe, Andrew J., BA Birm., PhD Sheff., FRHistS Prof., British History
Walsham, Alexandra M., MA Melb., PhD Camb., FRHistS Prof., Reformation History
Whittle, Jane C., MA Manc., DPhil Oxf. Sr. Lectr.
Other Staff: 8 Lectrs.; 2 Res. Fellows; 2 Sr. Lectrs.†; 5 Hon. Res. Fellows
Research: Africa; Asia; mediaeval and modern Britain and Europe; the Americas

Politics

Tel: (01392) 263164
Armstrong, James D., BSc Lond., MSc Lond., PhD ANU Prof., International Relations
Banducci, Susan, BSc Santa Barbara, MA Santa Barbara, PhD Santa Barbara Sr. Lectr., Political Science
Castiglione, Dario, DottFil Palermo, MA Sus., DPhil Sus. Sr. Lectr.
Doern, G. Bruce, BComm Manit., MA Car., PhD Qu. Prof., Public Policy
Dumper, Michael, BA Lanc., MPhil Lanc., PhD Exe. Reader, Middle East Politics
Dunne, Tim, BA E.Anglia, MPhil Oxf., DPhil Oxf. Reader, International Relations; Head*
Hampsher-Monk, Iain W., BA Keele, FSA Prof., Political Theory
Ismail, Salwa, BA American(Cairo), MA Manc., PhD McG. Sr. Lectr., Middle East Politics
James, Oliver, BA Oxf., MSc Lond., PhD Lond. Reader, Public Policy
Karp, Jeff, BA Calif., MA Calif., PhD Calif. Sr. Lectr., Political Science
Radaelli, Claudio, PhD Florence Prof., Political Science
Sadiki, Larbi, MA Syd., PhD ANU Sr. Lectr., Middle East Politics
Smith, Steve, BSc S'ton., MSc S'ton., PhD S'ton., DSc Prof., International Relations
Wilks, Stephen R. M., BA Lanc., PhD Manc., FCA Prof., Public Policy
Other Staff: 6 Lectrs.; 7 Res. Fellows; 5 Hon. Res. Fellows
Research: electoral politics; international politics; Middle East politics; political theory; public policy and administration

Sociology and Philosophy

Tel: (01392) 263276
E-mail: r.w.webber@ex.ac.uk

Barnes, S. Barry, BA Camb., MSc Leic., MA Essex Prof.
Davie, Grace R. C., BA Exe., PhD Lond. Prof., Sociology of Religion
DeNora, Tia, BA Westchester, MA Calif., PhD Calif. Prof., Sociology of Music
Dupre, John A., BA Oxf., MA Oxf., DPhil Oxf., PhD Camb. Prof., Philosophy of Science
Guala, Francesco, BA Milan, MA Lond., PhD Lond. Sr. Lectr.
King, Anthony C., BA Camb., MA Mich., PhD Salf. Reader
Moss, Lenny, PhD Calif., PhD Northwestern Reader
Pleasants, Nigel, BA Brist., MPhil Camb., PhD Camb. Sr. Lectr.
Rappert, Brian, BA Mich., MA Rensselaer, PhD Anglia Ruskin Reader
Vincent, John A., BA Sus., DPhil Sus. Sr. Lectr.
Other Staff: 5 Lectrs.; 1 Sr. Res. Fellow; 13 Res. Fellows
Research: philosophy and sociology of science; sociology of culture

Law

Tel: (01392) 263365 Fax: (01392) 263196
E-mail: s.hammond@exeter.ac.uk
Addo, Michael K., LLB Ghana, LLM Essex, PhD Essex Sr. Lectr.
Betlem, Gerrit, PhD Utrecht, LLM Gron. Reader, European Private Law
Drury, Robert R., LLB Newcastle(UK) Sr. Lectr.
Economides, Kim M., BA CNAA, LLM Lond. Prof., Legal Studies; Head*
Honeyball, Simon E., LLB Birm., PhD Birm. Sr. Lectr.
McEwan, Jenny A., LLB Exe., BCL Oxf. Prof., Criminal Law
Musson, Anthony Sr. Lectr.
Stebbings, Chantal, LLB Exe., PhD Exe. Prof., Modern Legal History
Tettenborn, Andrew M., MA Camb., LLB Camb. Bracton Prof.
Other Staff: 11 Lectrs.; 2 Hon. Univ. Fellows; 4 Teaching Fellows
Research: commercial law; European law; legal ethics; professional legal studies

Modern Languages

Tel: (01392) 264391 Fax: (01392) 264391
E-mail: e.a.stewart@exeter.ac.uk

French

Tel: (01392) 264216 Fax: (01392) 264222
E-mail: j.curry@exeter.ac.uk
Cook, Malcolm C., BA Warw., PhD Warw. Prof., French Eighteenth-Century Studies
Coveney, Aidan B., BA York(UK), PhD Newcastle(UK) Sr. Lectr.
Davison, Ray, BA Leeds, MPhil Leeds Sr. Lectr.
Hayward, Susan, MA Exe., PhD Exe. Prof.
Kearns, James, MA Warw., PhD Warw. Sr. Lectr.
Orr, Mary M., MA St And., PhD Camb. Prof., Modern French Studies
Sorrell, Prof. Martin R. M., BA Oxf., MA Kent Prof., French Poetry and Translation Studies
Other Staff: 7 Lectrs.; 4 Lectors; 6 Hon. Res. Fellows
Research: French cinema; French literature and culture from earliest times to present day; French thought from the Renaissance to the present day; literary translation; sociolinguistics of French

German

Tel: (01392) 264335 Fax: (01392) 264339
E-mail: german@exeter.ac.uk
Lauster, Martina, BA Marburg, PhD Marburg Prof.
Paver, Chloe E. M., BA Oxf., DPhil Oxf. Sr. Lectr.
Robertshaw, Alan T., BA Durh., PhD Durh. Prof.
Sharpe, Lesley, MA Oxf., DPhil Oxf. Prof.
Smart, Sara C., BA Reading, PhD Reading Sr. Lectr.

Zitzlsperger, Ulrike, MA F.U.Berlin, PhD F.U.Berlin Sr. Lectr.
Other Staff: 2 Lectrs.; 2 Lectors.; 1 Tutor; 1 Lectr.†; 2 Hon. Univ. Fellows
Research: Austrian literature of the nineteenth and twentieth centuries; literature of the classical period (particularly mediaeval lyric poetry, Schiller, and Oswald von Wolkenstein); literature of the Reformation and Baroque era; post-war fiction

Hispanic Studies

Tel: (01392) 264245 Fax: (01392) 264390
E-mail: spanish@exeter.ac.uk
Barton, Simon F., BA Wales, MA York(UK), DPhil York(UK), FRHistS Reader, Mediaeval Spanish History
Canaparo, Claudio, MA F.L.A.C.S.O., PhD Lond. Reader, Latin American Studies
Walters, Gareth, BA Wales, PhD Wales Prof.
Other Staff: 7 Lectrs.; 2 Lectors; 1 Tutor; 2 Lang. Co-ordinators
Research: contemporary Spanish society; Golden Age Spanish literature; Latin American literature; mediaeval Spain; modern Spanish literature

Italian

Tel: (01392) 264214 Fax: (01392) 264214
E-mail: n.i.welsh@exeter.ac.uk
Bruni, Roberto L., DottLett Pisa Sr. Lectr.
Davie, R. Mark, MA Camb., PhD Reading Sr. Lectr.; Head of Sch.*
Diffley, Paul B., MA Oxf., DPhil Oxf. Prof.
Other Staff: 3 Lectrs.; 1 Lector; 1 Sr. Lectr.†; 1 Hon. Univ. Fellow
Research: contemporary Italian literature and society; Dante's writings; Italian book publishing; late Renaissance literature and humanism; vernacular literature of the fourteenth and fifteenth centuries

Russian

Tel: (01392) 264310 Fax: (01392) 264300
E-mail: w.oldfield@exeter.ac.uk
Hodgson, Katharine M., MA Camb., PhD Camb. Sr. Lectr.
Other Staff: 3 Lectrs.; 1 Lector; 2 Sr. Lectrs.†; 1 Hon. Univ. Fellow
Research: Gothic literature; nineteenth-century Russian literature; post-revolutionary Russian literature; Russian women writers; 1920s Russian literature

Peninsula Medical School

Tel: (01752) 437444 Fax: (01752) 517842
Bligh, Prof. John, BSc MMEd MD, FRCGP Assoc. Dean (Educn.); Dir., Inst. of Clin. Educn.
Logan, Stuart, MB ChB MSc, FRCPCH Prof.; Dir., Health and Social Care Res.
MacLeod, Kenneth, MB ChB MD, FRCPEd, FRCP Dir., Clin. Studies
Pinching, Anthony, BM BCh Oxf., MA Oxf., DPhil Oxf., FRCP Prof.; Assoc. Dean (Cornwall)
Shore, Angela, BSc PhD Prof.; Dir., Biomed. and Clin. Res.
Sneyd, J. Robert, MB BChir MD MA, FRCA Assoc. Dean; Prof., Anaesthesia
Strobel, Prof. Stephan, MD PhD, FRCP Prof.; Dir., Postgrad. Clin. Educn.; Chair, Peninsula Postgrad. Health Inst.
Tooke, Prof. John, BM BCh Oxf., MA Oxf., MSc Oxf., DM Oxf., DSc Oxf., FRCP, FMedSci Dean*

Physics

Tel: (01392) 264171 Fax: (01392) 264111
E-mail: physics@exeter.ac.uk
Barnes, William L., BSc Exe., PhD Exe. Prof., Photonics
Bate, Matthew R., BSc Massey, PhD Camb. Prof., Theoretical Astrophysics
Hicken, Robert J., BA Oxf., MA Johns H., PhD Johns H. Sr. Lectr.

Inkson, John C., BSc Manc., MA Camb., PhD Camb., ScD Camb.   Prof., Theoretical Physics; Head*
Jones, Bob, BSc Manc., MSc Wales, PhD Wales, Hon. FD Umeå   Prof., Computational Physics
Matcher, Stephen J., BSc Lond., PhD Lond.   Sr. Lectr.
McCaughrean, Mark J., BSc Edin., PhD Edin.   Prof., Astrophysics
Naylor, Tim, MA Oxf., DPhil Oxf., FRAS   Norman Lockyer Prof., Astrophysics
Sambles, J. Roy, BSc Lond., PhD Lond., FRS   Prof., Experimental Physics
Savchenko, Alexander K., MSc Moscow Physico-Tech., PhD Russian Acad.Sc., DSc Russian Acad.Sc.   Prof., Condensed Matter Physics
Srivastava, Gyaneshwar P., PhD Ban., DSc Ban.   Prof., Theoretical Semiconductor Physics
Summers, Ian R., MA Oxf., PhD Lond.   Sr. Lectr.
Usher, Alan, MA Oxf., DPhil Oxf.   Reader
Williams, Charles D. H., BSc Durh., PhD Durh.   Sr. Lectr.
Winlove, C. Peter, BSc Lond., MSc Oxf., DPhil Oxf.   Prof., Biophysics
Wyatt, Adrian F. G., BSc Brist., DPhil Oxf.   Prof.†
Other Staff: 14 Lectrs.; 14 Res. Fellows; 4 Exper. Officers; 7 Hon. Res. Fellows
Research: astrophysics; biomedical physics; electromagnetic materials; medical imaging (diagnostic radiography); quantum interacting systems

Psychology

Tel: (01392) 264625 Fax: (01392) 264623
E-mail: psyadmin@exeter.ac.uk
Burgoyne, Carole B., BSc Brist., PhD Bath   Sr. Lectr.
Haslam, Alexander, MA St And., PhD Macq.   Prof., Social Psychology
Haslam, Catherine, BSc NSW, MSc Macq., PhD ANU   Sr. Lectr.
Hodgson, Tim, BSc Cardiff, PhD Lond.   Sr. Lectr.
Jetten, Jolanda, PhD Amst.   Prof.
Kay, Janice M., BA Newcastle(UK), PhD Camb.   Prof.
Kuyken, Willem, BSc Lond., PhD Lond.   Reader
Lea, Stephen E. G., MA Camb., PhD Camb., FBPsS   Prof.; Head*
Mitchell, Don C., BSc Manc., PhD Lond.   Prof., Experimental Psycholinguistics
Monsell, Stephen, MA Oxf., DPhil Oxf.   Prof., Cognitive Psychology
Pendry, Louise F., BA Kent, PhD Wales   Sr. Lectr.
Postmes, Thomas T., MSc Amst., PhD Amst.   Prof.
Slater, Alan M., BSc Wales, PhD Durh.   Reader, Child Development
Watkins, Edward R., BA Oxf., MSc Lond., PhD Lond.   Reader
Williams, W. Huw, BA Wales, DClinPsy Wales, PhD Wales   Sr. Lectr.
Wills, Andrew, BSc S'ton., PhD Camb.   Sr. Lectr.
Other Staff: 11 Lectrs.
Vacant Posts: 1 Prof. (Animal Behaviour); 1 Prof. (Cognition); 3 Lectrs.
Research: animal behaviour; clinical psychology; cognitive psychology and cognitive neuroscience; social, economic and organisational psychology

Sport and Health Sciences

Tel: (01392) 262896 Fax: (01392) 264726
E-mail: sshs-school-office@exeter.ac.uk
Armstrong, Neil, BEd Lough., MSc Lough., PhD Exe., DSc Exe., FIBiol, FRSA   Prof., Health and Exercise Science
Dixon, Sharon, BSc Lough., PhD Lough.   Sr. Lectr.
Eston, Roger, BEd Birm., MEd Springfield, PhD Springfield   Prof., Human Physiology
Jones, Andrew, BSc Brighton, PhD Brighton   Prof., Applied Physiology

Parfitt, Gaynor, BA Wales, PhD Wales   Sr. Lectr.
Sparkes, Andrew C., BEd Lough., MA Durh., PhD Lough.   Prof., Social Theory
Taylor, Adrian H., MSc Ithaca, PhD Tor.   Reader, Exercise and Sport Psychology
Welsman, Joanne, BSc Sur., PhD Exe.   Sr. Res. Fellow; Deputy Dir.
Williams, Craig A., BEd Exe., MSc Alta., PhD Exe.   Sr. Lectr.
Other Staff: 8 Lectrs.; 7 Res. Fellows; 2 Teaching Fellows
Research: children's health and exercise; sport and exercise physiology; sport, exercise and health psychology; sports biomechanics

SPECIAL CENTRES, ETC

Children's Health and Exercise Research Centre

Tel: (01392) 264812 Fax: (01392) 264706
E-mail: a.e.husband@exeter.ac.uk
Armstrong, Neil, BEd Lough., MSc Lough., PhD Exe., DSc Exe., FIBiol, FRSA   Prof., Health and Exercise Science; Dir.*
Eston, Roger, BEd Birm., MEd Springfield, PhD Springfield   Prof., Human Physiology
Parfitt, Gaynor, BA Wales, PhD Wales   Sr. Lectr.
Welsman, Joanne, BSc Sur., PhD Exe.   Sr. Res. Fellow; Deputy Dir.
Williams, Craig A., BEd Exe., MSc Alta., PhD Exe.   Sr. Lectr.
Other Staff: 4 Lectrs.; 4 Res. Fellows
Research: children's physical activity patterns; children's responses to exercise training; coronary prevention in children; paediatric exercise science including children's physiological responses to exercise; sex differences in children's exercise responses

Cornish Studies, Institute of

Tel: (01872) 263457 Fax: (01872) 223449
E-mail: p.j.payton@exeter.ac.uk
Payton, Philip J., BSc Brist., PhD Adel., PhD CNAA, FRHistS   Reader; Dir.*
Other Staff: 1 Lectr.; 1 Res. Fellow; 4 Hon. Res. Fellows
Research: Celtic studies; culture; education; history; territorial politics

Educational Development and Co-operation, Centre for

Tel: (01392) 264865 Fax: (01392) 411274
Delve, Ronald A., MEd   Co-Dir.*
Olek, Hilary, BA Brist., MA Exe.   Co-Dir.*
Other Staff: 2 Res. Fellows
Research: curriculum development; education in Central and Eastern Europe; European education policy; evaluation; professional development

Energy and the Environment, Centre for

Tel: (01392) 264144 Fax: (01392) 264143
E-mail: cee@exeter.ac.uk
Preist, Trevor W., BSc Brist., PhD Brist.   Dir.*
Other Staff: 6 Res. Fellows
Research: building acoustics; computational methods; energy in building; environmental campaigns; waste strategies

English Language, Centre for

Tel: (01392) 264282 Fax: (01392) 264277
E-mail: elc@exeter.ac.uk
Lewis, Derek R., BA Lond., MPhil Lond.   Sr. Lectr.; Dir.*
Other Staff: 2 Lectrs.

European Legal Studies, Centre for

Tel: (01392) 263380 Fax: (01392) 263381
No staff at present

Research: effects of European Community law in the UK and other member states

European Studies, Centre for

Tel: (01392) 264490 Fax: (01392) 263305
E-mail: europe@exeter.ac.uk
Banducci, Susan, BSc Santa Barbara, MA Santa Barbara, PhD Santa Barbara   Dir.*

Davie, Grace R. C., BA Exe., PhD Lond.   Prof.
Longman, Chris, MA Exe., PhD Reading   Deputy Dir.
Research: European electoral politics; European history; European identity; gender and European politics; modern European society

Evidence-based Social Services, Centre for

Tel: (01392) 263323 Fax: (01392) 263324
E-mail: s.e.bosley@exeter.ac.uk
Jones, Ray, BSc Bath, MPhil Bath, PhD Bath   Visiting Prof.
Little, Michael, BA Birm., PhD Lanc.   Visiting Prof.
Macdonald, Geraldine, BA Oxf., MSc Oxf.   Visiting Prof.
Sheldon, Brian, MPhil Birm., PhD Leic.   Prof.; Dir.*
Shepperd, Michael, BSc Warw., MA Warw., PhD Warw.   Visiting Prof.
Other Staff: 3 Hon. Univ. Fellows
Research: evaluations of critical appraisal skill training for social care staff; matching needs and services for children; rehabilitation work with frail, elderly people; training of foster carers in the management of challenging behaviours; translation of results of existing research into service and practice development

Finance and Investment, Centre for (XFI)

Tel: (01392) 263420
E-mail: s.hudson@ex.ac.uk
Tonks, Ian, BA Leic., MA Warw., PhD Warw.   Prof., Finance; Dir.*
Other Staff: 2 Lectrs.
Research: asset pricing; corporate finance; financial management; performance of financial markets; portfolio performance measurement

Foreign Language, Centre for

Tel: (01392) 264293 Fax: (01392) 264377
E-mail: avril.smith@exeter.ac.uk
Lewis, Derek R., BA Lond., MPhil Lond.   Dir.*
Other Staff: 2 Lectrs.†

Genomics in Society, ESRC Centre for (EGENIS)

Tel: (01392) 262053 Fax: (01392) 264676
E-mail: egenis@ex.ac.uk
Barnes, S. Barry, BA Camb., MSc Leic., MA Essex   Prof.; Co-Dir.
Dupre, John A., BA Oxf., MA Oxf., DPhil Oxf., PhD Camb.   Prof.; Dir.*
Hughes, Stephen G., MS Edin., PhD Edin.   Prof.; Co-Dir.
Other Staff: 9 Res. Fellows; 3 Hon. Univ. Fellows
Research: application of genomics, from genetically modified crops to human cloning; genopragmatics; genosemantics

History of Cinema and Popular Culture, Bill Douglas Centre for the

Tel: (01392) 264352 Fax: (01392) 264361
1 Res. Fellow; 1 Hon. Res. Fellow
Research: cinema history; relationship between cinema and pre-cinema; social impact of cinema

Leadership Studies, Centre for

Tel: (01392) 262555 Fax: (01392) 262559
E-mail: leadership@exeter.ac.uk
Alvesson, Mats, BA Lund, PhD Lund   Visiting Prof.
Bennis, Warren, PhD M.I.T.   Visiting Prof.
Gosling, Jonathan, BA E.Anglia, MBA City(UK)   Prof.; Dir.*
Rajan, Amin, BA MA   Visiting Prof.
Other Staff: 2 Lectrs.; 2 Res. Fellows; 1 Res. Asst.; 3 Project Dirs.; 15 Hon. Univ. Fellows
Research: improving leadership development; new ways of thinking about leadership; personal challenges of leadership;

relationship between leadership and
organisational performance

Learning Society, Research Centre for the

Tel: (01392) 264917
  E-mail: j.s.moncur@ex.ac.uk
Biesta, Gerardus J. J., BPhil Amst., BPhil Ley.,
  MPhil Rotterdam, MPhil Ley., PhD Ley.   Prof.;
  Co-Dir.*
Richardson, William, BA Brist., DPhil Oxf.
  Prof.; Co-Dir.*
Other Staff: 1 Sr. Lectr.; 1 Res. Fellow
Research: adult life transformations; assessment
  of performance and mastery; learning in the
  life-course; learning, inclusion and
  democracy; skills development for policy-
  makers

Maritime Historical Studies, Centre for

Tel: (01392) 264324 Fax: (01392) 263305
  E-mail: m.duffy@exeter.ac.uk
Duffy, Michael D., MA Oxf., DPhil Oxf., FRHistS
  Dir.*
Rodger, Nicholas A. M., MA Oxf., DPhil Oxf.
  Prof., Naval History
Other Staff: 1 Lectr.; 3 Hon. Res. Fellows
Research: British maritime history; maritime
  archives; naval history

Medical History and Related Social Studies, Centre for

Tel: (01392) 263297 Fax: (01392) 263297
  E-mail: j.l.melling@exeter.ac.uk
Barry, Jonathan, BA Camb., MA Oxf., DPhil Oxf.,
  FRHistS   Sr. Lectr.
Jackson, Mark A., BSc Lond., MB BS Lond., PhD
  Leeds   Prof., History of Medicine; Dir.*
Melling, Joseph L., BSc Brad., PhD Glas., FRHistS
  Asst. Dir.; Reader, Social Welfare and
  Industrial Health
Other Staff: 2 Lectrs.; 4 Res. Fellows; 4 Hon.
  Univ. Fellows
Research: gender and health; history of
  environmental health; history of insanity;
  history of medical statistics and patient
  records; history of occupation health

Mediterranean Studies, Centre for

Tel: (01392) 264038 Fax: (01392) 264035
  E-mail: m.s.omri@exeter.ac.uk
Omri, Mohamed-Salah, MA Wash., Maîtrise
  Tunis   Dir.*
Other Staff: 5 Hon. Univ. Fellows
Research: archaeology; cultural studies; history
  and ancient history; identity; Romance
  languages

Rural Research, Centre for

Tel: (01392) 263836 Fax: (01392) 263852
  E-mail: crr@exeter.ac.uk
Winter, D. Michael, OBE, BSc Lond., PhD
  Open(UK)   Prof., Rural Policy; Dir.*
Other Staff: 2 Sr. Res. Fellows; 4 Res. Fellows;
  7 Investigational Officers; 2 Hon. Univ.
  Fellows
Research: animal health and welfare economics;
  farm economics; rural development; rural
  development and policy appraisal; transition
  in Central and Eastern Europe

Wetland Research, Centre for

Tel: (01392) 264351 Fax: (01392) 263377
  E-mail: b.j.coles@exeter.ac.uk
Coles, Bryony J., BA Brist., MPhil Lond., FSA
  Prof.; Dir.*
Research: conservation and excavation of wetland
  archaeology; wetland archaeology; wetland
  conservation and management; wetland
  palaeoecology; wetlands and environmental
  change

CONTACT OFFICERS

Accommodation. Accommodation Office
  (E-mail: accommodation@ex.ac.uk)
Admissions (first degree). Undergraduate
  Admissions Officer: Hoad, Pamela A.
  (E-mail: admissions@ex.ac.uk)
Alumni. Director, Development and Alumni
  Relations Office: Smith, Elizabeth
  (E-mail: alumni@ex.ac.uk)
Archives. Modern Records Clerk: Cross, Suzie
Careers. Director: Hodges, Ian
  (E-mail: careers@exeter.ac.uk)
Computing services. Director: Brooks, Sue
Consultancy services. Head of Enterprise
  Development: Tiltman, Paul
  (E-mail: res@exeter.ac.uk)
Development/fund-raising. Director,
  Development and Alumni Relations: Smith,
  Elizabeth (E-mail: alumni@ex.ac.uk)
Distance education. Distance Learning Office
  (E-mail: dll@ex.ac.uk)
Equal opportunities. Equality and Diversity
  Manager: Devlin, Kate
  (E-mail: k.m.devlin@ex.ac.uk)
Estates and buildings/works and services.
  Director of Buildings and Estate: Alcock,
  Robert J., BA Brist.
  (E-mail: r.j.alcock@exeter.ac.uk)
Examinations. Assistant Registrar
  (Examinations): Able, Neil
  (E-mail: exams@ex.ac.uk)
Finance. Director of Finance: Lindley, Jeremy
  (E-mail: s.e.harrington@exeter.ac.uk)
General enquiries. Registrar and Secretary:
  Allen, David J., BA Wales, MEd Wales, FRSA

Health services. Principal Medical Officer:
  Thomas, Kate, MB BS Lond.
  (E-mail: studenthealth@exeter.ac.uk)
International office. International Officer:
  Withrington, John K. B., BA Camb., MA
  Leic., DPhil York(UK)
  (E-mail: intoff@exeter.ac.uk)
Library (chief librarian). Librarian: Paterson,
  Alasdair T., MA Edin., MA Sheff.
  (E-mail: library@exeter.ac.uk)
Marketing. Director of Marketing: Brook,
  Amanda F., BA Brist., MBA Warw.
  (E-mail: a.f.brook@exeter.ac.uk)
Personnel/human resources. Director of
  Personnel and Staff Development: Cooper,
  Stephen J. C., BA Kent
  (E-mail: personnel@ex.ac.uk)
Public relations. Public Relations Manager:
  Franklin, Stuart D., BA S'ton.
  (E-mail: s.d.franklin@exeter.ac.uk)
Publications. Publications Manager: Pollard,
  Ann, BSc Brist.
  (E-mail: a.m.j.pollard@exeter.ac.uk)
Purchasing. Purchasing Co-ordinator: Hill,
  Kathy (E-mail: k.a.hill@ex.ac.uk)
Quality assurance and accreditation. Deputy
  Vice-Chancellor: Kay, Prof. Janice M., BA
  Newcastle(UK), PhD Camb.
Research. (Funding) Assistant Registrar
  (Research): Loughlin, Helen, BA CNAA
  (E-mail: research@exeter.ac.uk)
Safety. Safety Officer: Adams, Paul H., BSc
  Reading, PhD Reading
  (E-mail: hse.office@exeter.ac.uk)
Scholarships, awards, loans. Scholarship
  Office (E-mail: money@ex.ac.uk)
Schools liaison. Education Liaison Officer:
  Hogbin, Saskia
  (E-mail: schools-liaison@exeter.ac.uk)
Security. Security Officer: Paddon, Mike
Sport and recreation. Director of Sport:
  Attwell, Philip, BA Sus., MSc Sheff.
  (E-mail: p.j.attwell@exeter.ac.uk)
Student union. Permanent Secretary to the
  Students' Guild: Fishwick, Simon
  (E-mail: s.n.fishwick@ex.ac.uk)
Student welfare/counselling. Head of Service:
  Halpern, Lisa (E-mail: counselling@ex.ac.uk)
Students from other countries. Secretary,
  International Office: Adkins, Carol
  (E-mail: intoff@ex.ac.uk)
Students with disabilities. Disability Co-
  ordinator: (vacant)
  (E-mail: disability@ex.ac.uk)
University press. Publisher for the University
  Press: Baker, Simon C., BA Camb.
  (E-mail: uep@exeter.ac.uk)

[Information supplied by the institution as at 10 May
2006, and edited by the ACU]

UNIVERSITY OF GLAMORGAN

Founded 1992

Member of the Association of Commonwealth Universities

Postal Address: Pontypridd, Wales CF37 IDL
Telephone: (01443) 480480 **Fax:** (01443) 480558 **E-mail:** enquiries@glam.ac.uk
URL: http://www.glam.ac.uk

VICE-CHANCELLOR*—Halton, Prof. David J., BA *Greenwich*, MSc *Aston*, EdD *Leic.*, FRSA
UNIVERSITY SECRETARY‡—Bracegirdle, J. Leigh, BA BPhil MEd
PRO VICE CHANCELLOR (ACADEMIC)—Lydon, Julie E., BA *Wolv.*, MBA *Wolv.*
PRO VICE CHANCELLOR (LEARNING AND STUDENT SUPPORT)—Mulholland, Prof. Clive
PRO-VICE-CHANCELLOR (RESEARCH AND REGENERATION)—Hobbs, Prof. Brian
PRO VICE CHANCELLOR (RESOURCES)—Williams, Huw R., LLB
DEAN OF QUALITY AND ACADEMIC REGISTRAR—O'Shea, John, BA

GENERAL INFORMATION

History. The university was founded in 1992. It was previously established as South Wales and Monmouthshire School of Mines (1913), Glamorgan College of Technology (1958), and the Polytechnic of Wales (1970).

It is located about 15km north-west of Cardiff.

Admission to first degree courses (see also United Kingdom Introduction). Through Universities and Colleges Admissions Service (UCAS). International applicants are considered on an individual basis.

First Degrees (see also United Kingdom Directory to Subjects of Study). BA, BEng, BSc, LLB, MEng, MMath.
Length of course. Full-time: BA, BEng, BSc, LLB, MEng, MMath: 3 years. *Part-time:* BA: 4 years; BEng: 5 years.

Higher Degrees (see also United Kingdom Directory to Subjects of Study).
Master's. LLM, MA, MBA, MSc.
Admission. Applicants for admission to master's degrees should normally hold a first degree with honours and/or appropriate work experience.
Length of course. Full-time: LLM, MA, MBA, MSc: 1 year. *Part-time:* LLM, MA, MBA, MSc: 3–4 years.
Doctoral. PhD.
Length of course. Full-time: PhD: 3–5 years. *Part-time:* PhD: 4–6 years.

Language of Instruction. English. Pre-sessional English language course available.

Libraries. Volumes: 250,000. Periodicals subscribed to: 2727.

Academic Year (2007–2008). Three terms: 22 September–12 December; 5 January–27 March; 20 April–5 June.

Income (2006–2007). Total, £88,838,000.

Statistics. Staff (2006–2007): 2009 (980 academic, 1029 non-academic). Students (2006–2007): full-time 10,823; part-time 10,593; international 2500.

ACADEMIC UNITS

Advanced Technology, Faculty of

Tel: (01443) 482957 Fax: (01443) 482169
Djialli, Demetri A., BSc   Head, Knowledge Transfer
Hodson, Peter J., BSc MSc EdD, FIEE, FBCS   Prof.; Dean*
Story, Dawn L., BSc PhD   Head, Learning, Teaching and Collaboration
Watkins, Mike, BSc   Assoc. Dean
Wiltshire, Ronald J., BSc PhD, FIMA, FIP   Head, Res.

Research: built environment; civil engineering; hypermedia and information security; mechanical and manufacturing engineering

Computing and Mathematical Sciences

Al-Begain, Khalid, MSc PhD   Prof.
Hammoudeh, Akram M.   Head, Telecommunications
Otung, Ifiok E.   Principal Lectr.
Ware, Andrew, BSc MSc PhD   Head*
Other Staff: 30 Staff Members
Research: applied mathematics and statistics; artifical intelligence technologies modelling; computer-based teaching and learning; data and software integrity; geographical information systems

Engineering

Garwood, Roy, MSc PhD   Head*

Engineering, Electronics and Computer Systems

Jones, Lee   Head*
Price, Michael H., BSc PhD   Head, Microelectronics and Embedded Systems

Environmental Technology, Construction and Management

Evans, Peter, BSc(MechEng) MSc   Head, Quality, Environment and Safety Management
Lloyd, Stephen, BEng(Tech) PhD   Head*
Price, Trevor, MSc PhD   Leader, Environmental Management Scheme
Williams, Trefor, BSc MPhil   Head, Construcn. and Real Estate

Business Faculty

Tel: (01443) 654364 Fax: (01443) 483396
Lovell, Alan, MSocSc PhD, FRSA   Dean*
Research: competitive advantage; consumption, markets and culture; enterprise; governance and leadership

Accounting, Finance and Information Management

Coombs, Hugh, BSc MPhil PhD   Prof., Accounting and Finance
Davies, Marlene, BSc(Econ) MSc   Leader, Division of Corporate Systems
Marriott, Pru, BA   Leader, Division of Financial Reporting
Other Staff: 21 Staff Members

Learning and Professional Development

Colebourne, David, BA MSc   Leader*
Other Staff: 7 Staff Members

Management

Jones, Paul, BA MSc   Leader, Enterprise Scheme; Sr. Lectr., Small Business Management
Packham, Gary, BA PhD   Leader, Division of Enterprise and Econ. Devel.

Marketing, Division of

Stephens, Paula, BSc MA   Leader*
Other Staff: 7 Staff Members

Organisational Behaviour and Human Resource Management

Daunton, Lyn, MSc   Leader*
Other Staff: 9 Staff Members

Supply Chain and Strategic Management, Division of

Lee, Chris, MBA   Sr. Lectr.
Mason-Jones, Rachel, BEng PhD   Leader*
Other Staff: 12 Staff Members

Creative and Cultural Industries, Cardiff School of

Tel: (01443) 654067 Fax: (01443) 654178
Blandford, Steve J., BA MA   Assoc. Dean
Carklin, Mike, BJourn *Rhodes*, BA *Rhodes*, MA *Rhodes*, MA *Lond.*   Head, Drama and Music
Mitchell, Philip   Head, Media and Communicn.
Robertson, Peter, BSc PhD   Dean*
Sharma, Pradeep   Head, Art and Design
Traynor, Mary J., BA   Head, Teaching and Learning
Wilson, Mike, BA PhD   Head, Res.
Other Staff: 45 Staff Members

Health, Sport and Science, Faculty of

Tel: (01443) 482451 Fax: (01443) 482285
Brown, Rhobert G. (Bob), BSc PhD, FRSChem   Prof.; Assoc. Dean
Davies, Ruth, BN MPhil   Head, Dept. of Care Scis.
Evans, Linda   Assoc. Head (Service Provision), Professnl. Educn. and Service Delivery
Kell, Terry, BSc PhD   Jt. Head, Teaching and Learning Quality
Kirk, Maggie, BSc PhD   Head, Res.; Prof., Genetics Education
Lee, Christopher, BSc MSc PhD   Head, Dept. of Sci. and Sport
Lewis, Rhobert H., BSc PhD   Head, Sci. and Sport; Dir., Centre for Police Scis.
Mead, Donna M., MSc PhD   Prof.; Head*
Rogers, Andrew, BEd MSc   Head, Dept. of Professl. Educn. and Service Delivery
Woolley, Norman, MSc MN   Head, Teaching and Learning Quality
Other Staff: 150 Staff Members
Research: care sciences; genomics; health and social care; health economics and policy; intellectual disability

Humanities and Social Sciences, Faculty of

including Law Sch.

Tel: (01443) 482662 Fax: (01443) 482138
Dubrow-Marshall, Rod, PhD   Prof.
John, Tim G., LLB *Staffs.*, MSc *Wales*   Head, Learning and Teaching (Postgrad.)
Jones, Cath   Head, Learning and Teaching (Undergrad.)

McNorton, Maggy, BEd Brist. Assoc. Dean
Stuart-Hamilton, Ian, MA Oxf., PhD Head,
Res. and External Activity
Research: border studies; education; history;
lifespan research; modern and
contemporary Wales

Humanities and Languages

England, Anne Head, Langs. Div.
Evans, Chris, BA PhD Head, Hist. Div.
Wallace, Diana, BA PhD Head, Engl. Div.
Wallace, Jeff, BA MA PhD Prof.; Head*
Other Staff: 40 Staff Members

Law School

Power, Helen, BA LLM Assoc. Head
Stuckey, Michael, BA LLB LLM PhD Prof.;
Head*
Other Staff: 25 Staff Members

Psychology, Education and Careers

Dunning, Gerald, BMus MEd PhD Head,
Educn. and Careers Div.
Mayer, Peter, BSc PhD Head*
Taylor, Rachel, BA PhD Head, Psychol. Div.
Other Staff: 30 Staff Members

Social Sciences

Brookman, Fiona, BSc MSc PhD Head,
Criminol. Div.
Farrell, Catherine, BA PhD Head, Policy,
Politics and Philos. Div.
Jones, Alan, BSc Lond., LLB Lond., MSc *Wales*
Head*
Oerton, Sarah, MA MSc PhD Head, Sociol.
Div.
Other Staff: 30 Staff Members

SPECIAL CENTRES, ETC

Learning and Corporate Support Services (LCSS)

Tel: (01443) 482401 Fax: (01443) 482424
Cobley, Ronald S., MEd DBA, FBCS Head*

Learning Resources Centre

Tel: (01443) 483593 Fax: (01443) 482629
E-mail: lrcenq@glam.ac.uk
Atkinson, P. Jeremy, BSc MPhil Head*

Life-Long Learning, Centre for

Tel: (01443) 482567 Fax: (01443) 482931
Saunders, Daniel M., BA MSc PhD Prof.;
Head*

CONTACT OFFICERS

Academic affairs. Pro-Vice-Chancellor
(Academic): Carter, Prof. Joy, BSc PhD
Accommodation. Manager, Accommodation
and Hospitality Services: Matthews, Robert
Admissions (first degree). Head, Student
Registry: Williams, Denise
Admissions (higher degree). Head, Student
Registry: Williams, Denise
Adult/continuing education. Head, Centre
for Lifelong Learning: Saunders, Prof.
Daniel M., BA MSc PhD
Archives. Senior Administrative Officer
(Quality): Williams, Stephanie
Careers. Manager, Careers Centre: Evans, Euros
J., BA
Computing services. Head, Information
Systems and E-Learning Services: Cobley,
Ronald S., MEd DBA, FBCS
Consultancy services. Manager, University of
Glamorgan Commercial Services Office:
Hughes, Alun, BSc MPhil PhD
Distance education. Head, Centre for Lifelong
Learning: Saunders, Prof. Daniel M., BA
MSc PhD
Equal opportunities. University Secretary:
Bracegirdle, J. Leigh, BA BPhil MEd
Estates and buildings/works and services.
Head, Estates and Facilities: Woodruff, Alun
J., BA MSc
Finance. Director of Finance: Williams, Huw
R., LLB
General enquiries. University Secretary:
Bracegirdle, J. Leigh, BA BPhil MEd
Health services. Nurse Manager: Sharp,
Althea, BA
Industrial liaison. Manager, University of
Glamorgan Commercial Services Office:
Hughes, Alun, BSc MPhil PhD
Library (chief librarian). Librarian/Head of
Learning Resources Centre: Atkinson, P.
Jeremy, BSc MPhil
Personnel/human resources. Head of Human
Resources: Emanuel, Bethan, MSc
Purchasing. Purchasing Manager: Thomas, D.
Alun
Quality assurance and accreditation.
Manager, Quality and Policy Office: Ryall,
Paul, PhD
Research. Manager, Research Office: Bright,
Louise, PhD
Safety. Health and Safety Officer: Curtis, John
Scholarships, awards, loans. Head, Student
Finance Centre: Smith, David
Security. Head, Estates and Facilities:
Woodruff, Alun J., BA MSc

Sport and recreation. Deputy Head, Campus
Services: Williams, W. Tudor, BA MA PhD
Staff development and training. Assistant
Head, Personnel Services (Training): Baker,
Robert, MSc
Strategic planning. Manager, Strategy Office:
Richards, Leanne, BA
Student union. President: Rees, Philip
Student welfare/counselling. Head, Student
Services: Jack, Gillian, BSc LLB
Students from other countries. International
Officer, Student Services: Davies, Julie, BSc
Students with disabilities. Student Adviser
(Special Needs): Bond, Sharon

CAMPUS/COLLEGE HEADS

Bridgend College, Cowbridge Road, Bridgend,
Wales CF31 3DF. (Tel: (01656) 766588;
Fax: (01656) 663912;
E-mail: enquiries@bridgend.ac.uk) Principal:
Hampton, Roger, BA BSc MSc
Coleg Gwent, Headquarters, The Rhadyr, Usk,
Monmouthshire, Wales NP23 6GT,. (Tel:
(01495) 333333; Fax: (01495) 333526;
E-mail: info@coleggwent.ac.uk) Principal:
(vacant)
Coleg Llandrillo, Llandudno Road, Rhos-on-
Sea, Colwyn Bay, Conwy, Wales LL28
4HZ,. (Tel: (01492) 546666; Fax: (01492)
543052;
E-mail: admissions@llandrillo.ac.uk)
Principal: Evans, Huw, OBE, BSc MPhil
Coleg Morgannwg, Ynys Terrace, Rhydyfelin,
Pontypridd, Wales CF37 5RN,. (Tel:
(01443) 662800; Fax: (01443) 663028;
E-mail: college@pontypridd.ac.uk) Principal:
Knight, Jan, MA
Coleg Sir Gâr, Sandy Road, Llanelli,
Carmarthenshire, Wales SA15 4DN,. (Tel:
(01554) 748000; Fax: (01554) 756088;
E-mail: admissions@colegsirgar.ac.uk)
Principal: Robinson, Brian, BSc MSc
Pembrokeshire College, Haverfordwest,
Pembrokeshire, Haverfordwest, Wales SA61
1SZ,. (Tel: (01437) 765247; Fax: (01437)
767279;
E-mail: admissions@pembrokeshire.ac.uk)
Principal: Jones, Glyn

[*Information supplied by the institution as at 9 January
2008, and edited by the ACU*]

UNIVERSITY OF GLASGOW

Founded 1451

Member of the Association of Commonwealth Universities

Postal Address: Glasgow, Scotland G12 8QQ
Telephone: (0141) 330 2000 **Fax:** (0141) 330 4808 **E-mail:** publicityservices@gla.ac.uk
URL: http://www.gla.ac.uk

PRINCIPAL AND VICE-CHANCELLOR*—Russell, Sir Muir, KCB, BSc *Glas.*, DUniv *Glas.*, Hon. LLD *Strath.*, FRSEd, FIP, Hon. FRCPSGlas

CLERK OF SENATE—Nash, Prof. Andrew, BVMS *Glas.*, PhD *Glas.*, FIBiol

VICE-PRINCIPAL (LEARNING, TEACHING AND INTERNATIONALISATION)—Nolan, Prof. Andrea M., MVB *Trinity(Dub.)*, PhD *Brist.*

VICE-PRINCIPAL (RESEARCH AND ENTERPRISE)—Beaumont, Prof. Steve, OBE, MA PhD, FRSEd

VICE-PRINCIPAL (LIFE SCIENCES AND MEDICINE)—Coggins, Prof. John R., MA *Oxf.*, PhD *Ott.*, FRSEd

VICE-PRINCIPAL (STRATEGY AND RESOURCES)—Juster, Prof. Neil, BSc PhD

PRO VICE-PRINCIPAL—Holmes, Prof. Peter H., OBE, BVMS *Glas.*, PhD *Glas.*, FRSEd

PRO-VICE-PRINCIPAL—Leake, Prof. Robin E., MA *Oxf.*, DPhil *Oxf.*

DEAN OF FACULTIES—McDonald, Prof. Jan, MA, FRSEd, FRSA

SECRETARY OF THE UNIVERSITY COURT‡—Newall, David, BA

DIRECTOR OF FINANCE—Fraser, Robert, BSc MBA

GENERAL INFORMATION

History. The university was founded in 1451. The university moved to its current campus on Gilmorehill, in the west end of the city of Glasgow, in 1870.

Admission to first degree courses (see also United Kingdom Introduction). Through Universities and Colleges Admissions Service (UCAS).

First Degrees (see also United Kingdom Directory to Subjects of Study) (* = with honours). BA, BA*, BAcc, BAcc*, BAL, BAL*, BArch, BArch*, BCLD, BD, BD*, BDS, BEd*, BEng*, BES, BMus, BMus*, BN*, BSc, BSc*, BSc(DentSci)*, BSc(MedSci)*, BSc(VetSci)*, BTechEd, BTechEd*, BTheol, BVMS, LLB, LLB*, MA, MA*, MA(SocSci), MA(SocSci)*, MB ChB, MEng*, MSci*.

Most courses are full-time and normally last 4 years.

Length of course. Full-time: BA, BAcc, BAL, BArch, BCLD, BD, BES, BMus, BN, BSc, BTechEd, BTheol, LLB, MA, MA(SocSci): 3 years; BA*, BAcc*, BAL*, BArch*, BD*, BEd*, BEng*, BMus*, BN*, BSc(DentSci)*, BSc(MedSci)*, BSc(VetSci)*, BSc*, BTechEd*, LLB*, MA(SocSci)*: 4 years; MA*: 4–5 years; BDS, BVMS, MB ChB, MEng*, MSci*: 5 years. Part-time: BArch: 4 years; BSc, MA, MA(SocSci): 5 years; BA, BA*: 6 years.

Higher Degrees (see also United Kingdom Directory to Subjects of Study).

Master's. LLM, MAcc, MArch, MBA, MCC, MDes, MEd, MFA, MFin, MLitt, MMus, MPH, MPhil, MRes, MSc.

Admission. Applicants for admission to master's degrees must normally hold an appropriate first degree with at least second class honours.

MLitt (research) lasts 2–3 years; MLitt (taught) lasts 1–2 years.

Length of course. Full-time: LLM, MAcc, MBA, MDes, MEd, MFin, MLitt, MMus, MPH, MRes, MSc: 1 year; MArch, MFA, MPhil: 2 years. Part-time: LLM, MAcc, MBA, MCC, MEd, MFin, MMus, MPH, MSc: 2 years; MArch, MLitt, MPhil: 3 years.

Doctoral. DBA, DClinPsy, DDS, DLitt, DMus, DSc, DVM, DVS, EdD, LLD, MD, PhD.

Admission. PhD: candidates for admission must normally hold an appropriate master's degree or equivalent; DLitt, DMus, DSc, DVM, DVS, LLD: awarded on published work.

Length of course. Full-time: DDS, MD: 2 years; DClinPsy, PhD: 3 years. Part-time: DDS, MD: 4 years; EdD, PhD: 5 years.

Libraries. Volumes: 2,000,000. Periodicals subscribed to: 14,410. Other holdings: 14,800 microfilms; 3880 sound recordings; 200,000 manuscripts; 1000 incunabula. Special collections: European Documentation Centre for the European Union; Council of Europe publications.

Academic Awards (2005–2006). 624 awards ranging in value from £16 to £25,000.

Academic Year (2007–2008). Two semesters: 25 September–18 January; 21 January–30 May.

Income (2005–2006). Total, £312,300,000.

Statistics. Staff (2005–2006): 5581 (1294 academic, 4287 non-academic). Students (2005–2006): full-time 17,855 (7608 men, 10,247 women); part-time 5707 (2104 men, 3603 women); international 1978 (869 men, 1109 women); distance education/external 837 (271 men, 566 women); undergraduate 19,076 (7862 men, 11,214 women); master's 1618 (745 men, 873 women); doctoral 1322 (666 men, 656 women).

FACULTIES/SCHOOLS

Arts

Tel: (0141) 330 6319 Fax: (0141) 330 4537
E-mail: dean@arts.gla.ac.uk
Dean: Moignard, Prof. Elizabeth A., MA *Oxf.*, DPhil *Oxf.*
Faculty Secretary: Goldie, Debbie, MA *Glas.*

Biomedical and Life Sciences

Tel: (0141) 330 3524 Fax: (0141) 330 4758
E-mail: dean@bio.gla.ac.uk
Dean: Hagan, Prof. Paul, BSc PhD, FRSEd
Faculty Secretary: Donald, Nancy, MA

Dental School

Tel: (0141) 211 9600
Head: Bagg, Prof. Jeremy, BDS *Edin.*, PhD *Edin.*, FDSRCSEd, FRCPath, FDSRCPSGlas
Administrator: Millard, M., MA *Glas.*

Education

Tel: (0141) 330 3202 Fax: (0141) 330 3499
E-mail: dean@educ.gla.ac.uk
Dean: Conroy, Prof. James C., BEd *Lond.*, MA *Lanc.*, PhD *V.U.Amst.*
Faculty Secretary: Boyle, Linda, BSc *Glas.*

Engineering

Tel: (0141) 330 5858 Fax: (0141) 330 4885
E-mail: engineering@gla.ac.uk
Dean: Coton, Prof. Frank N., BSc *Glas.*, PhD *Glas.*, FRAeS
Faculty Secretary: Duncan, Patricia, MA *Glas.*

Information and Mathematical Sciences

Tel: (0141) 330 4269 Fax: (0141) 330 2359
E-mail: gs@fims.gla.ac.uk
Dean: Fearn, Prof. David R., BSc *St And.*, PhD *Newcastle(UK)*, FIMA
Faculty Secretary: Alexander, Lynne A., BA *Open(UK)*, MBA *Glas.*

Law, Business and Social Sciences

Tel: (0141) 330 2514 Fax: (0141) 330 3547
E-mail: enquiries@lbss.gla.ac.uk
Dean: Burrows, Prof. Noreen, LLB *Edin.*, PhD *Edin.*, FRSA
Faculty Secretary: Young, Helen, LLB *Glas.*

Medicine

Tel: (0141) 330 5921 Fax: (0141) 330 5440
E-mail: execdean@clinmed.gla.ac.uk
Executive Dean: Barlow, Prof. D. H., BSc MA MD, FRCOG, FMedSci, FRCPGlas
Faculty Secretary: Clugston, Carol, BSc *Glas.*, PhD *Glas.*

Physical Sciences

Tel: (0141) 330 4374 Fax: (0141) 330 4371
E-mail: physci@gla.ac.uk
Dean: Saxon, Prof. David H., OBE, MA *Oxf.*, DPhil *Oxf.*, DSc *Oxf.*, FRSEd
Faculty Secretary: McNeil, Iain C., MBA

Veterinary Medicine

Tel: (0141) 330 5706 Fax: (0141) 942 7215
E-mail: reception@vet.gla.ac.uk
Dean: Reid, Prof. Stuart W. J., BVMS *Glas.*, PhD DVM, FRSA, FRSEd
Faculty Secretary: Chiodetto, Sarah, BSc *Edin.*, MBA *G.Caledonian*

ACADEMIC UNITS

Accounting and Finance

Tel: (0141) 330 4138 Fax: (0141) 330 4442
Beattie, Vivien A., MA *St And.*, PhD   Prof., Accounting
Danbolt, Jo, BA *H-W*, PhD *H-W*   Prof., Finance
Emmanuel, Clive R., BSc *Wales*, MA *Lanc.*, PhD *Lanc.*   Prof., Accountancy
Holland, John B., BSc *Aston*, MBA *Liv.*, PhD   Prof., Finance
Kinnon, David H., MA *Glas.*, MAcc *Glas.*   Johnstone Smith Prof.†
McKernan, John F., MBA PhD   Sr. Lectr.
McPhail, Kenneth J., BA *Dund.*, PhD *Dund.*   Prof.
Opong, Kwaku, BCom MSc PhD   Prof.; Head*
Weetman, Pauline, BA BSc PhD   Prof.

Other Staff: 8 Lectrs.; 4 Univ. Teachers

Research: auditing; capital markets; disclosure issues in financial reporting (accounting narratives, graphical reporting, intellectual capital); managerial accounting and control; social, ethical and environmental accounting

Adult and Continuing Education

Tel: (0141) 330 1835 Fax: (0141) 330 1821
E-mail: dace-query@educ.ac.uk

Barr, Prof. Jean L., MA(Ed) MA PhD   Prof.

Findsen, Brian, BSocSci Waik., MA Waik., EdD N.Carolina State   Sr. Lectr.; Head*

Hamilton, Robert, MA Glas., MPhil Glas., PhD H-W   Sr. Lectr.

Kane, William F., MA   Sr. Lectr.

MacKinnon, Alexander L., BSc PhD, FRAS   Sr. Lectr.

MacLachlan, Kathleen E., BA MEd MPhil   Sr. Lectr.

Preece, Julia, BA BPhil MEd PhD   Chair, Adult and Lifelong Educn.; Dir., CRADALL

Other Staff: 9 Lectrs.; 2 Res. Fellows; 4 Univ. Teachers

Research: adult participation and widening access; community and popular adult education; gender and education; historical, philosophical and policy studies in adult and higher education; policy studies in adult and higher education

Archaeology

Tel: (0141) 330 5690 Fax: (0141) 330 3544
E-mail: enquiries@archaeology.gla.ac.uk

Campbell, Ewan, BSc Glas., PhD Cardiff, FSA   Sr. Lectr.

Driscoll, Stephen T., BA Penn., MSc Penn., PhD Glas.   Prof.; Res. Dir., GUARD

Hall, Allan, BSc Edin., PhD Durh.   Sr. Lectr.; Convener, Hons.

Hanson, William S., BA Manc., PhD Manc., FSA   Prof.

Huggett, Jeremy W., BA Leeds, PhD CNAA   Sr. Lectr.; Head*

Jones, Richard E., CBE, BSc Kent, MSc Warw., PhD Wales, FSA   Sr. Lectr.; Convener, Exams

Knapp, A. Bernard, BA Akron, MA Calif., PhD Calif.   Prof.; Convener, Postgrad. Res.

van Dommelen, Peter, MA Ley., PhD Ley.   Sr. Lectr.; Convener, Postgrad. Teaching

Other Staff: 6 Lectrs.; 1 Tutor; 1 Sr. Lectr.†; 1 Lectr.†

Research: archaeological theory (ethnohistory, phenomenology, insularity, agency and identity); historical archaeology (early mediaeval, Roman, Viking); landscape archaeology and regional studies (Mediterranean, Scotland, North Atlantic); material culture studies (technological, typological, contextual and social interpretations); science-based archaeology and information technology

Biomedical and Life Sciences, Institute of

Tel: (0141) 330 3524 Fax: (0141) 330 4758
E-mail: dean@bio.gla.ac.uk

Research: biochemistry and molecular biology (cancer, cell signalling and membrane biology, molecular medicine, proteins, enzymes and X-ray crystallography, transcriptional and cell cycle control); environmental and evolutionary biology (ecophysiology, fish behaviour and ecology, ornithology, taxonomy and biodiversity); infection and immunity (microbiological pathogenesis, pathogen immunity); molecular genetics (animal models of human disease, human genetics); neuroscience and biomedical systems (cardiovascular studies/heart failure, neuroscience, sports and exercise science)

Biochemistry and Molecular Biology

Tel: (0141) 330 5902

Amtmann, Anna D., PhD   Sr. Lectr.

Blatt, Michael R., BSc PhD   Regius Prof., Botany

Bryant, Nia, BSc PhD   Sr. Lectr.

Campbell, Ailsa M., BSc Edin., PhD, FRSEd   Prof., Biochemical Immunology

Cogdell, Richard J., BSc Brist., PhD Brist., FRSEd   Hooker Prof., Botany

Cushley, William, BSc PhD   Prof., Molecular Immunology

Dominy, Peter J., BSc PhD   Sr. Lectr.

Dow, Jocelyn W., BSc NZ, PhD N.Y.   Sr. Lectr.

Gillespie, David A., BSc PhD   Prof., Transcription and Cell Cycle Control

Gould, Gwyn W., BSc S'ton., PhD S'ton.   Prof., Membrane Biology

Herzyk, Pawel, MSc PhD   Head, Bioinformatics

Houslay, Miles D., BSc Manc., PhD Camb.   Gardiner Prof., Biochemistry

Jenkins, Gareth I., BSc Liv., PhD Leeds   Prof., Plant Cell and Molecular Biology

Kolch, Walter, MD   Prof., Molecular and Cellular Biology

Lindsay, Gordon, BSc PhD   Prof., Medical Biochemistry

McInergy, Christopher J., BSc MSc PhD   Reader

Milligan, Graeme, BSc Birm., PhD Nott.   Dir., Res.; Prof., Molecular Pharmacology

Milner, Joel J., BA DPhil   Reader

Milner-White, E. J., BSc Aberd., PhD Lond.   Prof., Structural Bioinformatics

Nimmo, Hugh G., MA Camb., PhD Camb., FRSEd   Prof., Plant Biochemistry; Head*

Palmer, Timothy M., BSc PhD   Sr. Lectr.

Pitt, Andrew   Sr. Lectr., Proteomics

Price, Nicholas C., MA Oxf., DPhil Oxf.   Prof., Protein Science

Strang, Robin H., BSc St And., PhD Edin.   Sr. Lectr.

Waugh, Robert, PhD   Hon. Prof.†

White, Robert J., BSc Oxf., PhD   Prof., Gene Transcription

Zaccolo, M., PhD   Reader

Other Staff: 7 Lectrs.; 3 Res. Fellows; 6 Hon. Lectrs.

Research: cancer; cell signalling and membrane biology; molecular medicine, proteins, enzymes and x-ray crystallography; transcriptional and cell cycle control

Environmental and Evolutionary Biology

Tel: (0141) 330 5975

Adams, Colin E., BSc PhD   Sr. Lectr.

Crozier, Alan, BSc Durh., PhD Lond.   Prof., Plant Biochemistry and Human Nutrition

Downie, J. Roger, BSc Glas., PhD Glas.   Prof., Zoological Education

Furness, Robert W., BSc Durh., PhD Durh.   Prof., Seabird and Fishing Interactions

Haydon, Daniel   Prof., Population Ecology and Epidemiology

Houston, David C., BSc Brist., DPhil Oxf.   Prof., Zoology

Huntingford, Felicity A., BA Oxf., DPhil Oxf., FRSEd   Prof., Functional Ecology

Kennedy, Malcolm W., BSc Glas., PhD Glas.   Prof., Infection Biology

Lindstrom, Jan E., MSc PhD   Sr. Lectr.

Metcalfe, Neil B., BSc Durh., PhD Glas.   Prof., Behavioural Ecology; Head*

Monaghan, Patricia, BSc Durh., PhD Durh., FRSEd   Dir., Res.; Prof., Animal Ecology

Murphy, Kevin J., BSc Liv., PhD Liv.   Sr. Lectr.

Nager, Rudolf, MA PhD   Sr. Lectr.

Neil, Douglas M., MA Camb., PhD Camb.   Prof., Animal Physiology

Page, Roderic D. M., BSc Auck., MSc Auck., PhD Auck.   Prof., Taxonomy

Ruxton, Graeme D., BSc PhD   Prof., Theoretical Ecology

Taylor, Alan C., BSc Liv., PhD Liv.   Prof., Physiological Ecology

Wanless, S., PhD   Hon. Prof.†

Other Staff: 2 Lectrs.; 1 Sr. Res. Fellow; 11 Hon. Lectrs.; 5 Hon. Sr. Res. Fellows; 8 Hon. Res. Fellows

Research: biodiversity; cophysiology; fish behaviour and ecology; ornithology; taxonomy

Infection and Immunity

Tel: (0141) 330 4642

Aitken, Robert, BSc DPhil   Sr. Lectr.

Barrett, Michael P., BSc PhD   Reader

Byron, Olwyn, BSc MSc PhD   Sr. Lectr.

Coote, John G., BSc Leeds, PhD Leeds   Reader

Douce, Gillian, BSc PhD   Sr. Lectr.

Douglas, L. Julia, BSc Newcastle(UK), PhD Newcastle(UK)   Sr. Lectr.

Everett, Roger D., PhD   Hon. Prof.†

Graham, Sheila V., BSc PhD   Sr. Lectr.

McCulloch, Richard, BSc PhD   Sr. Lectr.

McGeoch, Duncan J.   Hon. Prof.†

Mitchell, Timothy J., BSc PhD   Prof., Microbiology

Muller, Sylke, PhD   Prof., Molecular and Biochemical Parasitology

Parton, Roger, BSc Birm., PhD Birm.   Sr. Lectr.

Phillips, R. Stephen, BSc Lond., PhD Camb., FIBiol   Prof., Parasitology

Preston, Christopher M., PhD   Hon. Prof.†

Ranford-Cartwright, Lisa C., BA PhD   Sr. Lectr.

Riehle, Mathis, DLitt   Reader

Thompson, Russell, BSc Brist., PhD Edin.   Sr. Lectr.

Turner, Charles M. R., BSc Lond., PhD Lond.   Prof., Parasitology; Head*

Other Staff: 2 Lectrs.; 1 Sr. Res. Fellow; 4 Res. Fellows; 1 Clin. Sr. Lectr.; 1 Clin. Res. Training Fellow; 13 Hon. Lectrs.; 7 Hon. Sr. Res. Fellows; 7 Hon. Res. Fellows

Research: microbiological pathogenesis; pathogen immunity

Molecular Genetics

Tel: (0141) 330 6219

Davies, Roger W., BA Camb., MA Camb., PhD Camb., FRSEd   Robertson Prof., Biotechnology

Davies, Shireen A., BSc PhD   Reader

Dow, Julian A., BA Camb., PhD Camb.   Prof., Molecular and Interactive Physiology

Goodwin, Stephen, BSc PhD   Sr. Lectr.

Johnstone, Iain L., BSc PhD   Sr. Lectr.

Monckton, Darren G., BSc PhD   Prof., Human Genetics

O'Dell, Kevin M., BSc PhD   Sr. Lectr.

Stark, William M., BSc Glas., PhD Glas.   Prof.; Head*

Sutcliffe, Roger G., BSc Manc., PhD Edin.   Sr. Lectr.

Wilson, Joanna B., BSc Sus., PhD Lond.   Reader

Wilson, Richard H., MA PhD   Sr. Lectr.

Other Staff: 2 Lectrs.; 1 Hon. Res. Fellow

Research: animal models of human disease; human genetics

Neuroscience and Biomedical Systems

Tel: (0141) 330 4483

Baxendale, Ronald H., BSc PhD   Reader

Cobb, Stuart, BSc DPhil   Sr. Lectr.

Ferrell, William R., MB ChB Glas., PhD Glas.   Prof., Clinical Physiology

Gill, Jason, BSc MSc PhD   Sr. Lectr.

Gilmore, Desmond P., BSc NZ, PhD Lond.   Sr. Lectr.

Kennedy, Simon, PhD   Sr. Lectr.

MacFarlane, Niall G., BSc PhD   Sr. Lectr.

MacKay, Sarah, BSc Birm., PhD Birm.   Sr. Lectr.

MacLean, Margaret, BSc Edin., PhD Edin.   Prof., Pulmonary Pharmacology

Martin, William, BSc PhD   Prof., Cardiovascular Pharmacology; Head*

Maxwell, David, BSc Edin., PhD Edin.   Prof., Neuroanatomy

Maxwell, William L., BSc Brist., PhD Brist.   Sr. Lectr.

McDonald, Stuart W., BSc MB ChB PhD   Sr. Lectr.

McGrath, John C., BSc PhD   Regius Prof., Physiology

Morris, Brian J., MA Camb., PhD Brist.   Prof., Molecular Neurobiology

Payne, Anthony P., BSc *Reading*, PhD *Birm.*
Prof., Anatomy
Riddell, John S., BSc PhD Sr. Lectr.
Shaw-Dunn, John, BSc MB ChB PhD Sr.
Lectr.
Skett, Paul, BSc *Liv.*, PhD Reader
Smith, Godfrey L., BSc PhD Prof.,
Cardiovascular Physiology
Smith, Robert A., MA *Oxf.*, PhD *S'ton.* Prof.,
Cellular Anatomy
Stone, Trevor W., BPharm *Lond.*, PhD *Aberd.*,
DSc *Lond.* Prof., Pharmacology
Todd, Andrew J., BSc *Lond.*, MB BS *Lond.*, PhD
Lond. Prof., Neuroscience
Vida, Imre, PhD Sr. Lectr.
Other Staff: 4 Lectrs.; 1 Univ. Teacher; 2 Res.
Fellows; 1 Clin. Res. Fellow; 1 Hon. Lectr.;
3 Hon. Sr. Res. Fellows; 6 Hon. Res.
Fellows
Research: cardiovascular studies/heart failure;
neuroscience; sports and exercise science

Celtic

Tel: (0141) 330 4222 Fax: (0141) 330 4222
E-mail: celtic@arts.gla.ac.uk
Clancy, Thomas O., BA *N.Y.*, PhD *Edin.* Prof.
O'Maolalaigh, Roibeard, BA *N.U.I.*, MA *N.U.I.*,
PhD *Edin.* Prof.; Head*
Other Staff: 4 Lectrs.
Research: Irish and Scottish Gaelic language;
mediaeval Gaelic and Welsh literatures;
mediaeval Irish and Scottish history and
culture; mediaeval Irish and Welsh law;
Scottish Gaelic literature

Central and East European Studies

Tel: (0141) 330 5585 Fax: (0141) 330 5594
Berry, Richard R., BA MPhil Sr. Lectr.
Cox, Terence M. Prof.
Flynn, Moya B., BA MSc PhD Sr. Lectr.
Kay, Rebecca L. Prof., Russian and Gender
Studies; Head*
Oldfield, Jonathan Sr. Lectr.
Smith, David J., BA MA PhD Reader
Swain, Geoffrey R. Chair, Alex Nove Centre
for East European Studies
White, James D., MA *Glas.*, PhD *Glas.* Hon.
Prof.†
Other Staff: 5 Lectrs.; 1 Czech Lektor; 1 Polish
Lektor
Research: Central and East European economics;
history and historiography; politics and
transition

Chemistry

Tel: (0141) 330 4708 Fax: (0141) 330 4888
E-mail: hod@chem.gla.ac.uk
Barron, Laurence D., BSc *Lond.*, DPhil *Oxf.*,
FRSEd Gardiner Prof.
Clark, J. Stephen, BSc *Edin.*, PhD *Camb.* Prof.
Cooke, Graeme Sr. Lectr.
Cooper, A., BSc *Manc.*, PhD *Manc.*, FRSChem,
FIP Prof., Biophysical Chemistry
Cronin, Leroy, BSc *York(UK)*, DPhil *York(UK)*
Prof.; Head, Res.
Farrugia, Louis J., BA *Oxf.*, PhD *Brist.* Sr.
Lectr.
Freer, Andrew A., BSc *Paisley*, PhD *Glas.* Sr.
Lectr.
Gilmore, Chris J., BSc *Brist.*, PhD *Brist.*, DSc
Glas., FRSChem Prof.
Gregory, Duncan Prof.
Hargreaves, Justin, BSc *Brist.*, PhD Sr. Lectr.
Hartley, Richard C., BA *Camb.*, MA *Camb.*, PhD
Camb. Reader
Hecht, Lutz, BSc *Essen*, PhD *Essen* Reader
Hill, Robert A., MA PhD, FRSChem Prof.;
Head, Teaching
Isaacs, Neil W., BSc *Qld.*, PhD *Qld.*, FRSEd
Prof.
Jackson, Samuel D., BSc *Glas.*, PhD *Glas.* Prof.;
Head*
Jarvis, Michael C., BSc *Glas.*, PhD *Glas.* Reader
Kadodwala, Michael Sr. Lectr.
Kocovsky, Pavel, MSc *Prague*, PhD *Prague*, DSc
Leic. Prof.
Lapthorn, Adrian J. Sr. Lectr.

Lennon, David, BSc *E.Anglia*, PhD *E.Anglia* Sr.
Lectr.
Malkov, Andrei Reader
McGrady, John E. Prof., Theoretical
Chemistry
Pulford, Ian D., BSc PhD Sr. Lectr.
Wilson, Charles, BSc *Glas.*, PhD *Dund.* Regius
Prof.
Wimperis, Stephen, BA *Oxf.*, PhD *Lausanne*
Prof.
Other Staff: 7 Lectrs.; 1 Res. Fellow; 1 Univ.
Teacher†
Research: biological chemistry; catalysis, solid
state and surface science; environmental,
agricultural and analytical chemistry;
synthesis; theory, structure and
spectroscopy

Classics

Tel: (0141) 330 5695 Fax: (0141) 330 4459
E-mail: enquiries@classics.arts.gla.ac.uk
Fox, Matthew A., BA *Oxf.*, MA *Oxf.*, DPhil *Oxf.*
Prof.
Green, Roger P. H., BLitt *Oxf.*, MA *Oxf.* Prof.
Knox, Ronald A., MA *Edin.*, DPhil *Oxf.* Sr.
Univ. Teacher
Panayotakis, Costas, BA *Crete*, PhD *Glas.* Sr.
Lectr.
Steel, Catherine E. W., BA *Oxf.*, MA *Oxf.*, DPhil
Oxf. Prof.; Head*
Other Staff: 3 Lectrs.
Research: Greek literature (comedy, epigram, the
novel, literatures of the Roman period);
Greek visual and material culture; Latin
literature (comedy, mime, oratory, epic,
the novel); post-classical Latin literature and
Christian thought; Roman history

Computing Science

Tel: (0141) 330 4256 Fax: (0141) 330 4913
E-mail: enquiries@dcs.gla.ac.uk
Brewster, Stephen, BSc *Herts.*, DPhil *York(UK)*
Prof.
Calder, Muffy, BSc *Stir.*, PhD *St And.*, FIEE,
FRSEd Prof.
Chalmers, Matthew J., BSc *Edin.*, PhD *E.Anglia*
Reader
Cockshott, William P., BA *Manc.*, MSc *H-W*,
PhD *Edin.* Reader
Cooper, Richard L., BSc *Lond.*, MSc *Lond.*, PhD
Glas. Sr. Lectr.
Cutts, Quintin, BSc *St And.*, MSc *St And.* Sr.
Lectr.
Dickman, Peter, MA *Camb.*, PhD *Camb.* Sr.
Lectr.
Gay, Simon J., MA *Camb.*, PhD *Lond.* Sr. Lectr.
Gilbert, David R., BSc *Lond.*, MSc *Lond.*, PhD
Lond. Prof.
Girolami, Mark, BEng *Glas.*, PhD *Paisley* Prof.
Gray, Philip, BA *Wittenberg*, MSc *Glas.* Sr. Lectr.
Irving, Robert W., BSc *Glas.*, PhD *Glas.* Sr.
Lectr.
Johnson, Christopher W., BA *Camb.*, MA *Camb.*,
MSc *York(UK)*, DPhil *York(UK)* Prof.
Jose, Joeman M., BSc *Calc.*, MSc *Cochin*, PhD
R.Gordon Sr. Lectr.
Mackenzie, Lewis M., BSc *Glas.*, PhD *Glas.* Sr.
Lectr.
Murray-Smith, Roderick W., BEng *Strath.*, PhD
Strath. Prof.
Ould-Khaoua, Mohamed, BSc *Algiers*, MAppSci
Glas., PhD *Glas.* Reader
Ounis, Iadh, MEng *ENSI Tunis*, MSc
Inst.Nat.Poly.Grenoble, PhD *Grenoble I* Reader
Prosser, Patrick, BSc *Strath.*, PhD *Strath.* Sr.
Lectr.
Purchase, Helen C., BSc *Rhodes*, MPhil *Camb.*,
PhD *Camb.* Sr. Lectr.
Renaud, Karen V., BSc *Pret.*, MSc *S.Af.*, PhD
Glas. Sr. Lectr.
Sventek, Joseph S., BA *Roch.*, PhD *Calif.*, FRSEd
Prof.
van Rijsbergen, Cornelis J., BSc *W.Aust.*, PhD
Camb., FIEE, FBCS, FRSEd Prof.
Watt, David A., BSc *Glas.*, PhD *Glas.* Prof.
Welland, Raymond C., BSc *Reading*, MSc *Lond.*
Prof.; Head*

Other Staff: 5 Lectrs.; 1 Sr. Res. Fellow; 5 Res.
Fellows
Vacant Posts: 1 Royal Acad. of Engin./
Microsoft Res. Prof., Information Retrieval
Research: bioinformatics; embedded, networked
and distributed systems; formal analysis,
theory and algorithms; human-computer
interaction; information retrieval

Crichton Campus of the University of Glasgow

Tel: (01387) 702001 Fax: (01387) 702005
E-mail: admissions@crichton.gla.ac.uk
Bold, Valentina, MA *Edin.*, PhD *Glas.* Sr. Lectr.
Cowan, Edward J., MA Prof., Scottish History
and Literature; Dir.*
Hill, Carol M., BA PhD Sr. Lectr.
Jessop, Ralph, MA *Glas.*, PhD *Camb.* Sr. Lectr.
Johnston, Sean F., BSc *S.Fraser*, MSc *S.Fraser*, PhD
Leeds Reader
Macleod, Donald, BA DPhil Sr. Lectr.
Pow, Thomas, MA *St And.* Sr. Lectr.
Other Staff: 4 Lectrs.; 4 Univ. Teachers; 3
Univ. Teachers†
Research: environmental studies/carbon
management; history, folklore, philosophy
and literature; history of science and
technology; Scottish heritage and culture;
tourism

Curriculum Studies

Tel: (0141) 330 3054 Fax: (0141) 330 3012
E-mail: m.mcwilliams@educ.gla.ac.uk
Aitkenhead, Elizabeth Sr. Univ. Teacher
Baumfield, Vivienne, BA PhD Prof.
Blee, Henry Sr. Lectr.; Head*
Campbell, Theresa, BEd *Edin.* Sr. Univ.
Teacher
Dickson, Beth Sr. Lectr.
Donnelly, Philip, BEd *Glas.* Sr. Lectr.
Farrell, Maureen A., MA MPhil Sr. Lectr.
Lally, Victor Sr. Univ. Lectr.
Livingston, Kay, BEd MEd PhD Prof.
McGonigal, James, MA *Glas.*, MPhil PhD
Prof.; Subj. Leader, Lang. and Lit.
Menter, Ian J. Prof.
Neilson, Marion B. Sr. Univ. Teacher
Pitcathley, John, BMus *Glas.* Sr. Lectr.
Templeton, Brian C., MA *Glas.*, MEd *Glas.*
Reader
Other Staff: 5 Univ. Lectrs.; 20 Univ. Teachers
Research: curriculum, policy innovation in
statutory and pre-statutory education; global
citizenship; professional knowledge in
teacher education (PKITE)

Economics

Tel: (0141) 330 4618 Fax: (0141) 330 4940
E-mail: n.birkin@lbss.gla.ac.uk
Cozzi, Guido Bonar McFie Prof.
Findlay, Jeanette, BA *Strath.*, MSc *Brist.* Sr.
Lectr.
Harris, Richard I., BA *Kent*, MA *Lanc.*, PhD *Belf.*
Cairncross Prof.
Huff, William G., MSc *Penn.*, PhD *Penn.* Prof.
Kovalenkov, Alexander Reader
Leith, Campbell B., BA *Strath.*, MSc *Glas.*, PhD
Exe. Prof., Macroeconomics
Malley, James, BA MPhil PhD Prof.
McDonald, Ronald Adam Smith Prof.,
Political Economy
McGillivray, Mark A. Hon. Prof.†
McLaughlin, Andrew Hon. Prof.†
Milne, Robin G., MA *Edin.*, MPhil *Lond.* Sr.
Lectr.
Noorbakhsh, Farhad, PhD *Birm.*, BSocSci
Natnl.Iran Prof., Development Economics;
Head*
Paloni, Alberto, MSc *Lond.*, PhD *Lond.* Sr. Lectr.
Quinn, Brian Hon. Prof.†
Talmain, Gabriel Jack Daniel Prof.
Other Staff: 1 Sr. Univ. Teacher; 9 Lectrs.
Vacant Posts: 1 Prof./Reader; 2 Lectrs.
Research: economic development and growth;
international finance and business cycles;
modelling macroeconomic performance;
monetary economics and financial markets;
regional economics

Education, Religious

Tel: (0141) 330 3434 Fax: (0141) 330 3470
E-mail: re@educ.gla.ac.uk
Davis, Robert A., BA Strath., MLitt Stir., PhD Stir.
Sr. Lectr.; Head*
Other Staff: 3 Lectrs.; 5 Univ. Teachers
Research: childhood; faith education; global
citizenship; ideals in education; religion
and culture

Educational Studies

Tel: (0141) 330 4407 Fax: (0141) 330 5451
Clancy, Kevin, MA MLitt MEd Sr. Lectr.;
Head*
Forde, Christine M., MA Glas., MEd Glas., MLitt
Strath., PhD Strath. Sr. Lectr.
Kane, Jean, MA MEd Sr. Lectr.
McPhee, Alastair D., MA MEd PhD, FRSA Sr.
Lectr.
Reid, Norman, BSc MA PhD, FRSA, FRSChem
Dir., Centre for Sci. Educn.
Whitehead, Rex R., BSc Melb., MSc Melb., PhD
Melb., DSc Glas., FRSEd Deputy Dir., Centre
for Sci. Educn.; Prof., Theoretical Physics
Wilkinson, John E., BSc St And., MEd Dund.,
PhD, FRSA Prof.
Other Staff: 12 Lectrs.; 5 Univ. Teachers; 12
Assoc. Tutors
Research: access, social capital, additional
support needs, inclusion; citizenship and
values education; leadership and
management, policy studies in education;
professional education; science and
technology education

Engineering, Aerospace

Tel: (0141) 330 3575 Fax: (0141) 330 5560
Benard, Emmanuel P. Sr. Lectr., Aero/Fluid
Dyamics
Brown, Richard Mechan Prof., Engineering
Cameron, Dugald Hon. Prof.†
Galbraith, Roderick A. McD., BSc CNAA, PhD
Camb. Shoda Prof., Aerospace Systems
Gillies, Augustine, PhD Sr. Lectr.
Goodchild, Colin, BSc Essex, MSc Cran.IT, PhD
Sr. Lectr.
Green, Richard B., BSc PhD Sr. Lectr.
Houston, Stewart S., BSc Glas., PhD Glas. Sr.
Lectr.
McGookin, Euan W., MEng PhD Sr. Lectr.
Radice, Gianmarco, PhD Sr. Lectr.
Smrcek, Ladislav, PhD Glas. Sr. Lectr.
Thomson, Douglas G., BSc Glas., PhD Glas. Sr.
Lectr.
Vezza, Marco, BSc Strath., PhD Glas. Sr. Lectr.;
Head*
York, Christopher B., BEng Wales, PhD Wales
Sr. Lectr.
Other Staff: 4 Lectrs.; 1 Res. Fellow; 1 Sr.
Project Manager; 1 Hon. Sr. Res. Fellow
Vacant Posts: 1 Lectr.
Research: air traffic management systems;
computational fluid dynamics (CFD);
control (including helicopter flight
dynamics and space systems); design and
structures; low speed aerodynamics

Engineering, Civil

Tel: (0141) 330 4077 Fax: (0141) 330 4557
E-mail: grant@civil.gla.ac.uk
Bicanic, Nenad J., PhD Wales(Swansea) Regius
Prof.
Davies, Trevor G., BSc Wales, PhD Wales Sr.
Lectr.
Ervine, D. Alan, BSc Belf., PhD Belf. Prof.,
Water Engineering
Gallipoli, Domenico Sr. Lectr.
Pearce, Christopher J., BSc Wales(Swansea), MSc
Wales(Swansea), PhD Wales(Swansea) Sr. Lectr.
Sloan, William T., BSc H-W, MSc Wales, PhD
Newcastle(UK) Prof., Environmental
Engineering
Stewart, William, BSc PhD Sr. Lectr.
Tanner, Kathleen E. Prof., Mechanics of
Material and Structures
Wheeler, Simon J., MA Camb., DPhil Oxf.
Cormack Prof.; Head*

Other Staff: 4 Lectrs.; 3 Univ. Teachers; 1 Res.
Fellow; 2 Res. Assocs.; 3 Hon. Sr. Res.
Fellows
Research: geotechnical (boundary element
method, constitutive modelling, numerical
modelling, soft clays, unsaturated soils);
structural (complex structures, concrete
failure, finite elements, modelling
discontinua, modelling extreme events);
water (biotechnology, catchment
hydrology, developing countries, estuary
behaviour, hydraulic structures)

Engineering, Electronics and Electrical

Tel: (0141) 330 5218 Fax: (0141) 330 4907
Acha, Enrique, BSc Mexico, PhD NZ Prof.,
Electrical Power Systems
Arnold, John M., BEng Sheff., PhD Sheff. Prof.,
Applied Electromagnetics; Head*
Asenov, Asen M., BSc Sofia, PhD Bulgarian Acad.Sc.
Prof., Device Modelling
Bailey, Nicholas J., BSc PhD Sr. Lectr.
Barker, John R., BSc Edin., MSc Durh., PhD
Warw. Prof.
Barretino, Diego R. Sr. Lectr.
Bryce, Ann C., BSc MSc PhD Prof. Res.
Fellow
Cooper, Jonathan M., BSc S'ton., MSc Cran.IT,
PhD Cran.IT Prof., Bioelectronics and
Bioengineering
Cumming, David, BEng Glas., PhD Camb.
Prof., Microelectronics
Davies, John H., MA Camb., PhD Camb. Prof.,
Physical Electronics
De La Rue, Richard M., BSc Lond., PhD Lond.,
MASc Tor. Prof., Optoelectronics
Dorrell, David G., PhD Sr. Lectr.
Hersh, Marion, MA MSc PhD Sr. Lectr.
Hutchings, David C., BSc PhD Prof., Optical
and Quantum Electronics
Ironside, Charles N., BSc H-W, PhD H-W
Prof., Quantum Electronics
Kelly, Anthony E. Sr. Lectr.
Li, Yun, BA Warw., BSc Warw., MPhil Oxf. Sr.
Lectr.
Macauley, Martin W. S., BSc Glas., PhD Glas.
Sr. Lectr.
Marsh, John H., BA Camb., MEng Liv., PhD
Sheff. Prof., Optoelectronic Systems
Miller, Timothy J. E., BSc Leeds, PhD Leeds
Prof.
O'Reilly, John, PhD Belf., DSc Belf., FIMA
Prof., Control Engineering
Paul, Douglas J. Prof.
Roy, Scott A., BSc PhD Reader
Stanley, Colin R., BEng Sheff., PhD S'ton. Prof.,
Semi-conductor Materials
Thayne, Iain G., BSc Glas., PhD Glas. Prof.,
Ultrafast Systems
Weaver, Jonathan M. R., MA DPhil Prof.,
Applied Nanofabrication
Williamson, John G., BSc Edin., PhD Sheff. Sr.
Lectr.
Other Staff: 9 Lectrs.; 3 Res. Fellows; 1 Res.
Assoc.; 4 Res. Technologists; 1 Speed Lab.
Manager; 3 Hon. Lectrs.; 1 Hon. Sr. Res.
Fellow; 2 Hon. Res. Fellows
Vacant Posts: 1 Researcher
Research: bioelectronics (cellular engineering,
molecular electronics, sensing); control
aerospace and electromechanical systems;
nanoelectronic device design (simulation
and assessment); optoelectronics; robotics

Engineering, Mechanical

Tel: (0141) 330 5914 Fax: (0141) 330 4343
E-mail: hod-sec@mech.gla.ac.uk
Ballance, Donald, BA Oxf., DPhil Oxf. Sr.
Lectr.; Head*
Cartmell, Matthew P., BSc Edin., PhD Edin.
James Watt Prof.
Green, Graham, BSc Napier, MTech Lough., PhD
Glas. Sr. Lectr.
Hancock, John W., BSc Birm., PhD Birm. Prof.
Hashim, Safa A., BSc MSc PhD Sr. Lectr.
Howell, John, BEng Sheff., PhD Glas. Reader
Hunt, Kenneth J., BSc Strath., PhD Strath.
Wylie Prof.

Lucas, Margaret, BSc Aberd., PhD Lough. Prof.,
Ultrasonics
Thomson, Ronald D., BSc Glas., PhD Glas. Sr.
Lectr.
Watson, Ian A., BSc S.Bank, PhD Glas. Sr.
Lectr.
Whittaker, Arthur R., MSc Birm., PhD Birm.
Sr. Lectr.
Other Staff: 7 Lectrs.; 1 Univ. Teacher; 1 Hon.
Sr. Lectr.; 2 Hon. Sr. Res. Fellows; 2 Hon.
Res. Fellows
Research: control; design; dynamics; laser and
optical systems engineering; marine
technology materials (including fracture
mechanics and corrosion)

English Language

Tel: (0141) 330 6340 Fax: (0141) 330 3531
E-mail: enquiries@englang.arts.gla.ac.uk
Caie, Graham D., MA Aberd., MA McM., PhD
McM., FRSA, FRSEd Prof.
Corbett, John B., MA Glas., MA New Br., PhD
Prof.
Emmott, Catherine, BA Birm., MA Birm., PhD
Birm. Sr. Lectr.
Hough, Carole A., BA Brist., MA Lond., PhD
Nott., FSA, FRHistS Reader
Lowe, Kathryn A., BA Nott., PhD Camb. Sr.
Lectr.
MacMahon, Michael K. C., BA Durh., PhD,
FRSA Prof.
Smith, Jennifer, MA Durh., DPhil York(UK) Sr.
Lectr.
Smith, Jeremy J., BA Lond., MPhil Oxf., PhD
Prof.; Head*
Stuart-Smith, Jane, BA MPhil DPhil Reader
Other Staff: 1 Lectr.; 1 Univ. Teacher; 1 RCUK
Fellow
Research: historical English language (Old and
Middle English, codicology, dialectology,
onomastics, historical linguistics and
philology); interdisciplinary mediaeval
studies; literary and linguistic computing;
modern English language (discourse
analysis, grammar, lexicography, phonetics,
phonology semantics, sociolinguistics,
stylistics); Scots

English Literature

see also Scottish Lit.

Tel: (0141) 330 5296 Fax: (0141) 330 4601
E-mail: enquiries@englit.arts.gla.ac.uk
Coyle, John G., MA PhD Head*
Cronin, Richard, BA Oxf., BLitt Oxf. Prof.
Cummings, Robert M., BLitt Oxf., MA Sr.
Lectr.
Gair, Chris, BA MA PhD Sr. Lectr.
Gillespie, Stuart F., MA Camb., PhD Camb.
Reader
Goldman, Jane, MA PhD Reader
Grant, Robert A., MA Camb., PhD Camb. Prof.
Jenkins, Alice, MA PhD Sr. Lectr.
Kolocotroni, Vassiliki, BA MSc PhD Sr. Lectr.
Leask, Nigel J., MA PhD Regius Prof.
Leonard, Tom Prof.
Lyons, Patrick G., MA Trinity(Dub.) Sr. Lectr.
Maley, William, BA Strath., PhD Camb. Prof.
Maslen, Robert W., MA DPhil Sr. Lectr.
McMillan, Dorothy A., MA Sr. Lectr.
Newell, David J., BPhil MA Sr. Univ. Teacher
Pascoe, David A., MA Oxf., DPhil Oxf. Reader
Pittock, Murray, MA DPhil, FRSEd Bradley
Prof.
Schmidt, Michael, MA Oxf. Prof.
Other Staff: 9 Lectrs.; 3 Tutors; 1 Univ.
Teacher
Research: European modernism (especially
France, England); Irish and intercultural
studies; literature and translation;
Romanticism; the early modern period/
Renaissance

Geographical and Earth Sciences

Tel: (0141) 330 4782 Fax: (0141) 330 4894
E-mail: ges-secretaries@ges.gla.ac.uk
Bishop, Paul, BA Syd., PhD Syd. Prof.; Chair,
Phys. Geog.
Briggs, John A., BA Lond., PhD Wales Prof.

Brown, Roderick, BSc PhD   Prof.
Cumbers, Andrew D.   Sr. Lectr.
Curry, Gordon B., BA Trinity(Dub.), PhD Lond.
   Reader
Cusack, Maggie, BSc Glas., PhD Liv.   Prof.
Dempster, Timothy J., BSc Lond., PhD Edin.   Sr.
   Lectr.
Dickinson, Gordon J., BSc PhD   Sr. Lectr.
Drummond, Jane E., BSc Newcastle(UK), MEng
   New Br., PhD I.T.C.Enschede   Sr. Lectr.
Forrest, David, BSc Glas., MA Qu., PhD Glas.
   Sr. Lectr.
Hansom, James D., MA Aberd., PhD Aberd.
   Reader
Hoey, Trevor, BA Camb., PhD NZ   Prof.,
   Numerical Geoscience; Head*
Lee, Martin, BSc PhD   Sr. Lectr.
Lorimer, Hayden, BA Lough., MA Aberd., PhD
   Lough.   Sr. Lectr.
Lowder, Stella M., BA Nott., PhD Liv.   Sr. Lectr.
Owen, Alan W., BSc Durh., PhD Glas.   Reader
Paddison, Ronan, BA Durh., PhD Aberd.   Prof.,
   Geography
Philo, Christopher, BA Camb., PhD Camb.   Prof.
Routledge, Paul, BA Kingston(UK), MSc Lond.,
   PhD Syr.   Reader
Sharp, Joanne P., BA Camb., PhD Syr.   Sr.
   Lectr.
Waldron, Susan, BSc PhD   Sr. Lectr.
Other Staff: 5 Lectrs.; 9 Res. Fellows
Research: earth surface dynamics (evolution of
   the earth's surface and near-surface
   environment, geodynamic and tectonic
   processes, physical and biological processes
   of surface modification); human geography
   (environment and development, impacts of
   globalisation, restructuring in Britain
   (especially Scotland), space/power and the
   environment)

History

Tel: (0141) 330 4509 Fax: (0141) 330 5000
   E-mail: enquiries@history.arts.gla.ac.uk
Abrams, Lynn, BA E.Anglia, PhD E.Anglia   Prof.,
   Gender History
Airlie, Stuart R., MA DPhil, FRHistS, FSA   Sr.
   Lectr.
Ball, Simon J., BA Oxf., PhD   Reader
Black, Christopher F., MA Oxf., BLitt   Hon.
   Prof.
Broadie, Alexander, MA Edin., BLitt PhD, FRSEd
   Prof.
Brown, Dauvit, BA PhD   Sr. Lectr.
Cohn, Samuel, BA MA PhD   Prof., Mediaeval
   History
Dunn, Marilyn, MA Edin., PhD Edin.   Sr. Lectr.
Glassey, Lionel K. J., MA Oxf., DPhil Oxf.,
   FRHistS   Sr. Lectr.
Kidd, Colin C., MA DPhil   Prof., Modern
   History
Maver, Irene E., MA DPhil   Sr. Lectr.
Mawdsley, Evan, MA Chic., PhD Lond.   Prof.,
   International History
Moskowitz, Marina, BA MA MPhil PhD
   Reader
Munck, Thomas, MA St And., PhD E.Anglia
   Reader
Newman, Simon P., BA Nott., MA Wis., PhD
   Prin.   Sir Denis Brogan Prof., American
   History
O'Brien, Phillips P., MA DPhil   Sr. Lectr.
Roach, Andrew P., MA DPhil   Sr. Lectr.
Small, Graeme P., MA PhD, FRHistS   Sr. Lectr.
Smith, Julia   Edwards Prof., Medieval History
Spaeth, Donald A., BA MA PhD   Sr. Lectr.;
   Head*
Strickland, Matthew J., MA Camb., PhD Camb.
   Prof., Medieval History
Other Staff: 6 Lectrs.
Research: American history and culture;
   mediaeval history (politics, society,
   religion, culture); Scottish history (medieval
   to modern); social and gender history; war
   studies and international relations

History, Economic and Social

Tel: (0141) 330 5992 Fax: (0141) 330 4889
   E-mail: a.mulholland@arts.gla.ac.uk
Dupree, Marguerite W., BA Mass., MA Prin.,
   DPhil Oxf., PhD Camb.   Prof.
French, Michael J., BA E.Anglia, MSc Lond., PhD
   Lond.   Prof.
Gordon, Eleanor J., MA Edin., PhD   Prof.,
   Gender and Social History
Nicolson, Malcolm A., BSc Aberd., PhD Edin.
   Reader
Phillips, Keith J., MA PhD   Sr. Lectr.
Rollings, Neil, BSc Brist., PhD Brist.   Sr. Lectr.;
   Head*
Ross, Duncan M., MA Glas., PhD Lond.   Sr.
   Lectr.
Schenk, Catherine, BA Tor., MA Lond., PhD Lond.
   Prof., International Economic History
Stokes, Raymond G., BA S.Florida, MA Ohio State,
   PhD Ohio State   Prof., International
   Industrial History
Other Staff: 2 Lectrs.
Research: British economic policy since 1945;
   business history (financial institutions,
   business and state, industrial relations,
   history of technology, China, Europe, USA,
   Britain); social history (crime, gender,
   history, medical, culture)

History of Art

Tel: (0141) 330 5677 Fax: (0141) 330 3513
   E-mail: enquiries@arthist.arts.gla.ac.uk
Gibbs, Robert J., BA Lond.   Prof.
Hopkins, David, BA CNAA, MA Essex, PhD Essex
   Prof.
Kinchin, Juliet L. C., MA Cant., MA Lond.   Sr.
   Lectr.
MacDonald, Margaret, BA Leeds, DLitt Glas.
   Prof.
Pearce, Nicholas J., BA Hudd., MA Lond.   Prof.
Richards, John, MA Glas., PhD Glas.   Sr. Lectr.
Stirton, Paul A. W., MA Edin., MA Lond.   Sr.
   Lectr.
Warwick, Genevieve, BA Oxf., PhD Johns H.
   Sr. Lectr.
Willsdon, Clare A. P., MA Cant., PhD Cant.   Sr.
   Lectr.
Yarrington, Alison W., BA Reading, PhD Camb.,
   FSA   Prof.; Head*
Other Staff: 3 Lectrs.
Research: Chinese and related areas of art and
   decorative arts; Eastern European art; Italian
   Renaissance; nineteenth-century art,
   including Whistler; seventeenth-century art
   (Dutch, Flemish)

Humanities Advanced Technology and Information Institute (HATII)

Tel: (0141) 330 5512 Fax: (0141) 330 2793
   E-mail: director@hatii.arts.gla.ac.uk
Ross, Prof. Seamus, AB Vassar, MA Penn., DPhil
   Oxf.   Prof.; Dir.*
Stuart, Susan, BA PhD   Sr. Lectr.
Other Staff: 1 Lectr.; 1 Hon. Sr. Res. Fellow; 2
   Hon. Res. Fellows; 1 Hon. Prof. Res.
   Fellow†
Research: computing for libraries, archives and
   museums; digital preservation; digitisation
   (image and audio); humanities computing
   and informatics; virtual reality and virtual
   environments

Law, School of

Tel: (0141) 330 6075 Fax: (0141) 330 5140
Anderson, Gavin W., LLB LLM   Sr. Lectr.
Brown, John L., MA   Sr. Univ. Teacher
Carruthers, Janeen M., LLB PhD   Reader
Christodoulidis, Emilios, LLB LLM PhD   Prof.
Connelly, Clare, LLB Glas., MA Glas.   Sr. Lectr.
Crawford, Elizabeth A., LLB PhD   Prof.,
   International Private Law
Crerar, Lorne D., LLB Glas.   Prof., Banking
   Law
Farmer, Lindsay, LLB Edin., MPhil Camb., PhD
   European Univ.Inst.   Prof.
Finlay, John, LLB PhD   Sr. Lectr.
Furse, Mark, BA LLM PhD   Prof., Competition
   Law and Policy

Greaves, Rosa   Prof.
Guthrie, Thomas G., LLB Glas.   Sr. Lectr.
Hiram, Hilary, LLB   Sr. Lectr.
Leverick, Fiona   Sr. Lectr.
MacNeil, Iain G., LLB PhD   Reader
Mair, Jane   Sr. Lectr.
Martin, Robert R.   Hon. Prof.†
McHarg, Aileen T., LLB Edin., PhD Edin.   Sr.
   Lectr.
McLean, Sheila A. M., LLB Glas., MLitt Glas.,
   PhD Glas., FRSEd   International Bar Prof.,
   Law and Ethics in Medicine
Metzger, E., DPhil   Prof., Public Law
Mullen, Thomas J., LLB Glas., LLM Harv.   Prof.;
   Head*
Murdoch, James L., LLB Glas., LLM Calif., MA
   Open(UK)   Prof., Public Law
Reid, George   Hon. Prof.†
Rennie, Robert, LLB Glas., PhD Glas., FRSA
   Prof.†, Conveyancing
Tomkins, Adam, LLB LLM   John Millar Prof.,
   Public Law
Van der Walt, Johan W.   Prof.
Veitch, Thomas S., LLB Edin., PhD Edin.
   Reader
Woolfson, Charles A., BA PhD, FRSA   Prof.,
   Labour Studies
Other Staff: 16 Lectrs.; 2 Res. Fellows; 1
   Researcher
Research: European and public international law;
   legal and political theory; medical law and
   ethics; private law (private international
   law, Scots private law); public law
   (administrative law and theory,
   constitutional law and theory, human rights
   law)

Management

Tel: (0141) 330 4131 Fax: (0141) 330 5669
Beaumont, Philip B., BEcon Glas., MEcon Glas.,
   PhD Glas.   Prof., Employee Relations
Beirne, Martin J., BA CNAA, MSc Strath., PhD
   Strath.   Prof., Management and
   Organisational Behaviour
Bell, Sheena H.   Sr. Univ. Teacher
Castledine, Pamela, BSc CNAA, MPhil CNAA,
   MBA Strath.   Sr. Lectr.; Programme Dir.,
   MBA
Docherty, Iain W., BSc PhD   Sr. Lectr.
Fischbacher, Moira, BA PhD   Sr. Lectr.
Furlong, Andy, BSc Leic., PhD Leic.   Prof.,
   Sociology
Huczynski, Andrzej A., BSc(Soc) Lond., PhD
   Sr. Lectr.
Hudson, James R.   Prof. Sr. Res. Fellow†
Jones, Marian V., MSc PhD   Prof.,
   International Business and Entrepreneurs
Laing, Angus W.   Prof., Business and
   Management; Head*
Logan, David W., BSc MBA   Sr. Univ. Teacher
Macbeth, Douglas K., MSc Strath., BSc   Hon.
   Prof.†
MacLean, Donald, BSc MBA PhD   Prof. Res.
   Fellow
McGregor, Alan, BAcc Glas., MA Glas.   Prof.,
   Economics Development
McIntosh, Robert   Prof., Supply Chain
   Management
McMaster, Robert   Sr. Lectr.
Moutinho, Luiz A., BA Sheff., MA Sheff., PhD
   Sheff.   Prof., Marketing
Pate, Judith M., MA MSc PhD   Sr. Lectr.
Paton, Robert A., MSc Strath.   Prof.
Shaw, Deirdre   Sr. Lectr.
Smith, Denis, BSc BEd MSc MBA PhD   Prof.
Southern, Geoffrey, MSc Birm., PhD   Sr. Lectr.
Veloutsou, Cleopatra, BA PhD   Sr. Lectr.
Wilson, Fiona M., BA Leeds, MA Manc., PhD
   Manc.   Prof., Organisational Behaviour
Wilson, James M., BScTech Houston, BSc Houston,
   MA Houston, MBA Houston, PhD Houston   Sr.
   Lectr.
Young, Stephen   Prof. Res. Fellow†
Other Staff: 3 Lectrs.; 2 Univ. Teachers; 1 Sr.
   Res. Fellow; 2 Res. Fellows; 1 Res. Assoc.;
   1 KTP Assoc.; 1 Principal Res. Fellow†; 1
   Sr. Res. Fellow†; 6 Hon. Res. Fellows

Research: enterprise, change and internationalisation; marketing and consumers; organisation and employees

Mathematics

Tel: (0141) 330 5176 Fax: (0141) 330 4111
E-mail: hod@maths.gla.ac.uk
Athorne, Christopher, MA Kent, PhD Durh. Sr. Lectr.
Baker, Andrew J., BSc Manc., PhD Manc. Reader
Bees, Martin A., BA MA PhD Reader
Brown, Kenneth A., MSc Warw., PhD Warw., BSc Prof.
Cohen, Stephen D., BSc PhD Prof., Number Theory
Dickson, Neil K. Sr. Univ. Teacher
Gilson, Claire R., MA PhD Sr. Lectr.
Goldman, Frances H. Sr. Teaching Fellow
Haughton, David M., BSc Bath, PhD Bath Sr. Lectr.
Hill, Nicholas A., MSc E.Anglia, PhD Lond. Simson Prof.
Kropholler, Peter Prof., Pure Mathematics; Head*
Leinster, Thomas S., BA MSc PhD Reader
Lindsay, Kenneth A., BSc Oxf., MSc Oxf., DPhil Oxf. Prof.
Luo, Xiaoyu Reader
Moore, David J. Sr. Univ. Teacher
Nair, Mohan K. N., BA Oxf., PhD Nott. Sr. Lectr.
Nimmo, Jonathan J. C., BSc Leeds, PhD Leeds Reader
Ogden, Raymond W., MA Camb., PhD Camb., FRSEd George Sinclair Prof.
Pott, Sandra Sr. Lectr.
Pride, Stephen J., BSc Monash, PhD ANU Prof.
Smith, Patrick F., MA Aberd., MSc Aberd., PhD Leeds Prof.†
Steiner, Richard J., MA Camb., PhD Camb. Sr. Lectr.
Stothers, Wilson W., PhD Camb., BSc Sr. Lectr.
Strachan, Ian, BA MA PhD Reader
Stroppel, Catharina Reader
Wassermann, A. Simon, MA Camb., PhD Camb. Reader
Webb, Jeffrey R. L., BSc Sus., DPhil Sus. Prof.
Other Staff: 1 Sr. Univ. Teacher; 2 Sr. Teaching Fellows; 8 Lectrs.; 3 Res. Fellows; 1 Advanced Fellow; 1 Royal Society Res. Fellow; 4 Hon. Res. Fellows
Research: algebra, analysis, discrete mathematics; elasticity, mathematical biology; fluid mechanics and magnetohydrodynamics; geometry and topology, number theory; non-linear evolution equations and systems

Modern Languages and Cultures, School of

Tel: (0141) 330 5521 Fax: (0141) 330 3381
E-mail: enquiries@smlc.arts.gla.ac.uk
Donnelly, Paul J., BA Oxf., MA Oxf., DPhil Oxf. Sr. Lectr.; Head*
Martin, Laura, BA Eckerd, MA Emory, PhD Emory Sr. Lectr.

French Section

Tel: (0141) 330 4583 Fax: (0141) 330 4234
E-mail: enquiries@french.arts.gla.ac.uk
Adams, Alison R., BA Brist., PhD Brist. Prof., Emblem Studies
Campbell, John, BA Belf., PhD Prof.
Dickson, William J., MA Aberd. Sr. Lectr.
Grove, Laurence F., BA Durh., MA Pitt., PhD Pitt. Sr. Lectr.
Lloyd, Heather, BA Belf., PhD Glas. Sr. Lectr.
Marshall, Bill J., BA Lond., MA Lond., MèsL Paris, DPhil Oxf. Prof., Modern French Studies
Peacock, Noel A., BA Wales, MA Wales Marshall Prof., French Language and Literature
Reader, Keith A., BA Camb., BPhil Oxf., DPhil Oxf. Prof., Modern French Studies
Salazar-Ferrer, Ramona D., BA MA DPhil Sr. Lectr.

Simpson, James R., MA Camb., PhD Camb. Sr. Lectr.; Head*
Wygant, Amy, BMus AM MA PhD
Other Staff: 1 Lectr.; 1 Univ. Teacher; 5 Univ. Native Lang. Teachers†
Research: Atlantic studies; French culture, language, cinema and politics; mediaeval and Renaissance French literature (including emblems); Quebec; seventeenth- to twentieth-century literature and thought

German Section

Tel: (0141) 330 5377 Fax: (0141) 330 3512
E-mail: enquiries@german.arts.gla.ac.uk
Bishop, Paul C., BA Oxf., MA Oxf., DPhil Oxf. Prof.
Burns, Barbara Sr. Lectr.
Dickson, Sheila Sr. Lectr.
Stephenson, Roger H., BA Lond., PhD Lond. Prof.
Ward, Mark Prof.; Head*
Other Staff: 1 Univ. Teacher; 1 Teaching Assoc.; 2 Univ. Native Lang. Teachers†
Research: aesthetics, history of ideas, modern German thought; age of enlightenment (classicism, romanticism); ethnography (comparative literature, cultural studies, feminism); mediaeval culture and literature; twentieth-century literature and culture

Hispanic Studies Section

Tel: (0141) 330 4135 Fax: (0141) 339 3381
E-mail: enquiries@hispanic.arts.gla.ac.uk
Donnelly, Paul J., BA Oxf., MA Oxf., DPhil Oxf. Sr. Lectr.
Gonzalez, Mike A., BA Leeds Prof.; Head*
Pastor, Brigida M., LicFil&Lett Alicante, PhD Brist. Sr. Lectr.
Other Staff: 1 Lectr.; 1 Univ. Teacher; 1 Teaching Assoc.; 2 Univ. Native Lang. Teachers†
Vacant Posts: 1 Stevenson Prof.
Research: Latin American studies (culture, film, music, poetry, prose); Lusophone, particularly Brazilian, literature (film, prose, poetry); Spanish golden age literature (drama, ideas, prose)

Italian Section

Tel: (0141) 330 4135
E-mail: enquiries@italian.arts.gla.ac.uk
Morris, Penelope, BA DPhil Sr. Lectr.
O'Ceallachain, Eanna, MA N.U.I., PhD Camb. Sr. Lectr.; Head*
Other Staff: 1 Lectr.; 1 Univ. Teacher†
Research: Italian resistance to fascism; modern Italian history and literature; modern Italian poetry

Slavonic Studies Section

see also Central and E. European Studies
Tel: (0141) 330 5418 Fax: (0141) 330 2297
E-mail: enquiries@slavonic.arts.gla.ac.uk
Bates, John M., BA MPhil DPhil Lectr.; Head*
Rogatchevski, Andrei, BA Moscow, MA Moscow, PhD Glas. Sr. Lectr.
Other Staff: 4 Lectrs.; 1 Univ. Native Lang. Teacher; 2 Lectrs.†
Research: Czech literature and cultural history; mass media in Central and Eastern Europe; Polish literature and cultural history; Russian literature and cultural history

Music

Tel: (0141) 330 4093 Fax: (0141) 330 3518
E-mail: enquiries@music.gla.ac.uk
Butt, John A., BA Camb., MPhil Camb., PhD Camb., FRSEd, FBA Gardiner Prof.
Cloonan, Martin, BA York(UK), MA York(UK), PhD Liv. Sr. Lectr.; Convener, Postgrad. Studies
Edwards, Warwick A., MA Camb., MusB Camb., PhD Camb. Reader
Fells, Nick, BA York(UK), PhD York(UK) Sr. Lectr.
Hair, Graham B., MMus Melb., PhD Sheff. Dir., Music†

Rycroft, Marjorie E., MA Aberd., PhD Aberd. Prof.
Sweeney, William Sr. Lectr.; Head*
Other Staff: 3 Lectrs.
Research: composition, electro-acoustic composition and twentieth-century composers; computer applications including artificial intelligence; early music and performance practice; musicology (aesthetics, criticism, historical, philosophy of music); Scottish music and musicians

Naval Architecture and Marine Engineering

Tel: (0141) 330 4322 Fax: (0141) 330 5917
Barltrop, Nigel, BSc S'ton. Prof.†
Das, Purnendu K., PhD Prof.†, Marine Structures
Vassalos, Dracos Prof.†
Other Staff: 2 Sr. Lectrs.
Research: computational fluid dynamics (manoeuvring and model testing, slamming and deck wetness); dynamics of fixed and offshore structures (ro-ro survivability, structural adhesives reliability and fatigue analysis, wind engineering); optimisation in design (marine vehicle performance at design stage, resistance and propulsion)

Philosophy

Tel: (0141) 330 5692 Fax: (0141) 330 4112
E-mail: philosophy@arts.gla.ac.uk
Carter, Alan B., MA Kent, MPhil Sus. Prof., Moral Philosophy
Kemp, Gary, PhD Calif. Sr. Lectr.
Knowles, Dudley R., BA Oxf., MLitt Glas. Prof.
Stalley, Richard F., BPhil Oxf., MA Oxf. Prof., Ancient Philosophy
Weir, Alan J., MA Edin., BPhil Oxf., DPhil Oxf. Prof.; Head*
Other Staff: 9 Lectrs.
Research: epistemology and metaphysics; history of philosophy (ancient); meta-, normative and applied (especially environmental) ethics; philosophies of logic, language, mathematics, religion, science; philosophy of mind/psychology

Physics and Astronomy

Tel: (0141) 330 4709 Fax: (0141) 330 5299
E-mail: enquiries@physics.gla.ac.uk
Brown, John C., PhD Glas., DSc Glas., FRSEd Regius Prof., Astronomy
Bussey, Peter J., MA Camb., PhD Camb. Reader
Buttar, Craig M., BSc PhD Reader
Chapman, John N., MA Camb., PhD Camb., FRSEd Prof.
Craven, Alan J., MA Camb., PhD Camb. Prof.
Davies, Christine T. H., OBE, MA Camb., PhD Camb., FRSEd Prof.
Diver, Declan, BSc Glas., PhD Glas. Reader
Doyle, Anthony T., BSc Manc., PhD Manc. Prof.
Hendry, Martin A., BSc Glas., PhD Glas. Sr. Lectr.
Hough, James, BSc Glas., PhD Glas., FRAS, FRSEd, FRS Prof.
Ireland, David G. Sr. Lectr.
Kaiser, Ralf Prof.
Land, David V., BSc PhD Sr. Lectr.
Long, Andrew R., MA Camb., PhD Camb. Prof.; Head*
MacGregor, Ian J. D., BSc Glas., PhD Glas., FIP Reader
McVitie, Stephen, BSc Glas., PhD Glas. Sr. Lectr.
O'Shea, Valentine, PhD Reader
Padgett, Miles, BSc York(UK), MSc St And., PhD Camb., FRSEd Prof.
Rosner, Guenther, BSc Munich, MSc Heidel., DrRerNat Mainz Cargill Prof.
Rowan, Sheila, BSc Glas., PhD Glas. Prof.
Saxon, David H., OBE, MA Oxf., DPhil Oxf., DSc Oxf., FRSEd Kelvin Prof.
Soler, Paul, MSc Syd., PhD Syd. Reader
St Denis, Richard, BS Ill., MS Harv., PhD Harv. Sr. Lectr.
Strain, Kenneth A., BSc Glas., PhD Glas. Prof.

Ward, Henry, BSc PhD   Sr. Lectr.
Woan, Graham, MA Camb., PhD Camb.   Reader
Other Staff: 4 Lectrs.; 3 Sr. Res. Fellows; 12
Res. Fellows; 7 Res. Assocs.; 3 Univ.
Teachers; 2 Programmers; 1 Electron
Microscopist
Research: astronomy/astrophysics; gravitation
and optics; nuclear physics; particle physics
experiment, particle physics theory; solid
state physics, microwave thermography

Politics

Tel: (0141) 330 5130 Fax: (0141) 330 5071
Berry, Christopher J., BA Nott., PhD Lond.
Prof., Political Theory
Clements, Alan   Hon. Prof.†
Duckett, Jane, BA Leeds, MSc Lond., PhD Lond.
Reader
Girvin, Brian, BA N.U.I., MA N.U.I., PhD N.U.I.
Prof.
Graham, Paul, BA MSc PhD   Sr. Lectr.
Lockyer, Andrew A., BA Leic., MA Sheff.   Prof.,
Citizenship and Social Theory
Miller, William L., MA Edin., PhD Newcastle(UK),
FBA, FRSA, FRSEd   Edward Caird Prof.
Mills, Kurt   Sr. Lectr.
Oates, Sarah, BA MA PhD   Sr. Lectr.
O'Toole, Barry J., BA Durh., MSc Strath., PhD
Strath.   Prof., Government; Head*
Thornhill, Christopher J.   Prof.
White, Stephen L., MA Trinity(Dub.), MA Oxf.,
DPhil Oxf., PhD Glas.   Prof., Government
Young, Alasdair, BA DPhil   Sr. Lectr.
Other Staff: 7 Lectrs.; 1 Res. Fellow; 1 Univ.
Teacher; 1 Hon. Res. Fellow
Research: British and Scottish politics;
comparative politics (especially Eastern
Europe, EU, Latin America, West Africa);
political theory (conceptual and historical);
public opinion (surveys and methodology)

Psychology

Tel: (0141) 330 5485 Fax: (0141) 330 4606
E-mail: info@psy.gla.ac.uk
Belin, Pascal, MSc Paris, PhD Paris, DrHabil Paris
V   Prof.
Biello, Stephany M., AB Smith, PhD Tor.
Reader
Burton, A. Michael, BSc Nott., PhD Nott.   Prof.
Bushnell, Ian W., BA Strath., PhD Camb.   Sr.
Lectr.
Dafters, Richard I., BSc S'ton., MSc Sus., DPhil
Sus.   Sr. Lectr.
Draper, Stephen W., BSc Sus., MSc Manc., DPhil
Sus.   Sr. Univ. Teacher
Garrod, Simon C., BA Oxf., MA Prin., PhD Prin.
Prof., Cognitive Psychology
Gross, Joachim, BSc Angelo State, PhD Leip.
Prof.
Harvey, Monika, BSc Bielefeld, MSc Bielefeld, PhD
St And.   Sr. Lectr.
Jones, Barry T., BSc Durh., PhD Edin.   Prof.
Kilborn, Kerry W., BA Oregon, PhD Calif.   Sr.
Lectr.
Leuthold, Hartmut, BSc Constance, MSc Constance,
PhD   Reader
Martin, Margaret, MA PhD   Sr. Univ. Teacher
Mayes, Gillian M., MA Glas., PhD Glas.   Sr.
Lectr.
Moxey, Linda M., MA Glas., MSc Glas., PhD
Glas.   Sr. Lectr.
Muckli, Lars F., PhD Maastricht   Sr. Lectr.
O'Donnell, Patrick J., MA Glas.   Prof.,
Teaching, Learning and Assessment
Pollick, Frank E., BSc M.I.T., MSc Case W.Reserve,
PhD Calif.   Reader
Sanford, Anthony J., BSc Leeds, PhD Camb.
Prof.
Schyns, Philippe, BSc Rhode I., PhD Rhode I.
Prof.; Head*
Sereno, Sara C., BS N.Illinois, MS Mass., PhD
Mass.   Sr. Lectr.
Other Staff: 9 Lectrs.; 3 Univ. Teachers; 4 Res.
Fellows; 1 Researcher; 1 Hon. Sr. Res.
Fellow
Research: cognitive and behavioural
neuroscience; language and

communication; perception and cognition;
physiology and health

Scottish Literature

Tel: (0141) 330 5093 Fax: (0141) 330 2431
E-mail: enquiries@scotlit.arts.gla.ac.uk
Carruthers, Gerard C., BA Strath., MPhil Glas.,
PhD Glas.   Reader; Head*
Riach, Alan S., MA Camb., PhD Glas.   Prof.
Other Staff: 4 Lectrs.; 1 Writer-in-Residence
Research: eighteenth-century Scottish literature;
fiction, poetry and drama in twentieth-
century Scotland and Ireland; literature of
the Renaissance and Reformation; mediaeval
Scottish literature; nineteenth-century
Scottish literature

Social Work

Tel: (0141) 330 5029 Fax: (0141) 330 8035
Barr, A., BSocSc Birm., PhD Glas.   Sr. Lectr.
Green Lister, Pamela, BA PhD   Sr. Lectr.
Kendrick, Andrew J.   Head*†
McNeill, Fergus E., MA MSc   Sr. Lectr.
Nellis, Mike   Prof.†, Community and Criminal
Justice
Orme, Joan E., BA Sheff.   Prof.
Other Staff: 1 Visiting Lectr.
Research: children and society; community
development; criminal justice; social work
education and practice

Sociology, Anthropology and Applied Social Sciences

Tel: (0141) 330 5981 Fax: (0141) 330 8022
Bourque, Lisa N., BA New Br., PhD Camb.   Sr.
Lectr.
Burman, Michele J., BA Cape Town, MSc Edin.,
PhD Edin.   Prof., Criminology
Cartmel, Fred, BSc   Sr. Lectr.
Evans, David T., BA(Econ) Sheff., PhD Glas.   Sr.
Lectr.
Ferguson, Harvie, MA Edin., PhD Glas., DSc Edin.
Prof.
Fowler, Bridget, BA Leeds, PhD Glas.   Prof.
Moorhouse, Herbert F., BA Leic., MSc(Econ)
Lond.   Sr. Lectr.
Philo, Gregory, BSc Brad., PhD Glas.   Prof.,
Communications and Social Change
Reith, Gerda, PhD   Sr. Lectr.
Torres, Rodolfo D.   Hon. Prof.†
Virdee, Satnam, MA Brun., PhD Warw.   Prof.
Watson, Nicholas, BSc Liv., MSc Dund., PhD
Edin.   Prof., Disability Studies; Head*
Other Staff: 8 Lectrs.; 2 Sr. Res. Fellows; 3 Res.
Fellows; 3 Hon. Res. Fellows
Research: criminology and socio-legal studies;
modernity, leisure, sport and consumption;
social anthropology (caste and religion);
sociologies of media, racism and migration;
youth education and employment

Statistics

Tel: (0141) 330 5024 Fax: (0141) 330 4814
E-mail: secretary@stats.gla.ac.uk
Bowman, Adrian W., BSc PhD, FRSEd   Prof.
Gilmour, W. Harper, BSc Glas., MSc Glas.   Sr.
Lectr.
MacAulay, Vincent, MA Oxf., DPhil Oxf.   Sr.
Lectr.
McColl, John H., MA Glas., MSc Glas.   Prof.
Scott, E. Marian, BSc PhD, FRSEd   Prof.;
Head*
Senn, Stephen J., BA Exe., MSc Exe., PhD Dund.
Prof.
Titterington, D. Michael, BSc Edin., PhD Camb.,
FRSEd   Prof.
Torsney, Bernard, BSc Strath., MSc Lond., PhD
Sr. Lectr.
Other Staff: 5 Lectrs.; 2 Res. Fellows; 1 Lectr.†;
1 Hon. Prof.; 3 Hon. Sr. Res. Fellows
Research: biostatistics and bio-informatics;
environmetrics; Markov chains Monte Carlo
(MCMC) and Bayesian methodology; neural
networks, analysis of images and spatial
patterns; non-parametric modelling

Theatre, Film and Television Studies

Tel: (0141) 330 3809 Fax: (0141) 330 4142
E-mail: tftsoffice@arts.gla.ac.uk
Boyle, Raymond, BA Ulster, MA Dublin City, PhD
Stir.   Sr. Lectr.
Caughie, John, MA Glas.   Prof.
Craven, Ian P., BA Exe., PhD Exe.   Sr. Lectr.
Doyle, Gillian, BA Trinity(Dub.), PhD Stir.   Sr.
Lectr.
Eleftheriotis, Dimitris, BA Warw., PhD Glas.   Sr.
Lectr.
Geraghty, Christine, BA Hull, MA Keele   Prof.;
Head*
Heddon, Dee, MA Glas., PhD Glas.   Sr. Lectr.
Lury, Karen E., BA Exe., MPhil Liv., PhD Liv.
Sr. Lectr.
Schlesinger, Philip, BA Oxf., PhD Lond.   Prof.
Scullion, Adrienne C., MA Glas., PhD Glas.
Prof.
Other Staff: 7 Lectrs.; 1 Teaching Fellow; 1
Creative Fellow; 1 Res. Fellow
Research: cultural policy; film and television
aesthetics; history and theory of theatre,
cinema and broadcasting; performance
theory and analysis; world cinema

Theology and Religious Studies

Tel: (0141) 330 6256 Fax: (0141) 330 4943
Hazlett, Rev. William I., BA Belf., BD St And.,
DrTheol Mün.   Reader; Head*
Hunter, Rev. Alastair G., BD Glas., MSc Glas.,
PhD Glas.   Sr. Lectr.
Jasper, David, BA Camb., BD Oxf., MA Oxf., PhD
Durh.   Prof.
Newlands, George M., MA Edin., BD Edin., PhD
Edin.   Prof.
Schmidt-Leukel, Perry H., DrTh Munich,
DrHabil Munich   Prof.
Sherwood, Yvonne, BA Sheff., PhD Sheff.   Sr.
Lectr.
Siddiqui, Mona, BA Leeds, MA Manc., PhD Manc.,
Hon. DLitt Wolv.   Prof.
Other Staff: 6 Lectrs.; 2 Univ. Teachers†
Research: biblical studies and hermeneutics; early
church history and Reformation studies;
Islam and interfaith studies; literature,
theology and the arts; modern theology,
systematic and practical

Urban Studies

Tel: (0141) 330 5993 Fax: (0141) 330 4668
Adams, David, MA Camb., MCD Liv., PhD Camb.
Ian MacTaggart Prof., Property and Urban
Studies
Bailey, Nick, BA   Sr. Lectr.
Bannister, Jonathan, BSc Lond.   Sr. Lectr.
Gibb, Kenneth D. G., MA Glas., MPhil Glas.
Prof., Housing Economics; Head*
Hastings, Annette L., BA Camb., MPhil Glas.
Sr. Lectr.
Kearns, Ade J., BA Camb.   Prof.
Kintrea, Keith J., BA Sus., MPhil Edin.   Sr.
Lectr.
Lennon, Michael   Hon. Prof.†
MacKenzie, Mhairi F., BA   Sr. Lectr.
Munro, Moira A., BA Durh., MSc York(UK)
Prof.
Murray, Kevin   Hon. Prof.†
Parr, John B., BSc(Econ) Lond., PhD Wash., MA
Prof., Applied Economics
Pryce, Gwilym B. J., BA Leeds, MSc Warw., PhD
Glas.   Prof.
Tiesdell, Steven A., BA Nott., MA Nott., PhD
Nott.   Sr. Lectr.
Turok, Ivan, BSc Brist., MSc Wales, PhD Reading
Prof., Urban Economic Development
Other Staff: 4 Lectrs.; 7 Res. Fellows; 1 Univ.
Teacher; 1 Res. Assoc.; 1 Health Care
Researcher; 1 Hon. Sr. Res. Fellow
Research: housing policy; public policy; real
estate economics and finance; real estate,
planning and regeneration; social justice

Veterinary School and Hospital

Tel: (0141) 330 5706 Fax: (0141) 942 7215
E-mail: reception@vet.gla.ac.uk
Research: animal production and public health
(epidemiology, zoonoses, genetic

resistance, food quality/safety); clinical and translational science (diagnostics, acute phase, non-invasive assay, pain); oncology and virology (papillomavirus, transgenics, leukaemia, FIV, animal models); parasitic diseases (molecular parasitology, population biology, host-parasite interactions); reproductive and developmental diseases (testis, ovary, hypothalmus, pituitary, infertility, hormone)

Veterinary Animal Production and Public Health Division

Tel: (0141) 330 5739 Fax: (0141) 330 5729
Barrett, David C., BSc BVSc   Sr. Lectr.
Chang, Kin C., BVSc Brist., MSc Lond., PhD Lond. Reader
Eckersall, Peter D., BSc Liv., PhD Edin., MBA, FRCPath   Prof., Veterinary Biochemistry
Kao, Rowland R.   Sr. Lectr.
Logue, David N., BVM&S PhD, FRCVS   Prof., Food Animal Disease
Mellor, Dominic J., BVMS PhD   Sr. Lectr.
Parkins, James J., BSc Glas., PhD Glas., FIBiol   Prof., Animal Health
Stear, Michael J., BSc Aberd., PhD Edin.   Prof., Immunogenetics
Steele, William B., BVMS   Sr. Lectr.
Taylor, David J., MA Camb., VetMB Camb., PhD Camb.   Prof., Veterinary Bacteriology and Public Health; Head*
Other Staff: 1 Registrar; 2 Lectrs.; 1 AWF Lectr.; 1 Postdoctoral Lectr.; 5 Res. Fellows

Veterinary Cell Sciences Division

Tel: (0141) 330 5771 Fax: (0141) 330 4874
Bain, Maureen M., BSc PhD   Sr. Lectr.
Evans, Neil P., BSc PhD   Prof., Integrative Physiology; Head*
Griffiths, Ian, BVMS PhD, FRCVS   Prof., Comparative Neurology
Jeffcoate, Ian A., BSc PhD   Sr. Lectr.
Mihm, Monika, PhD   Sr. Lectr.
O'Shaughnessy, Peter J., PhD Brist., BSc   Prof., Reproductive Biology
Purton, Michael D., BSc PhD   Sr. Univ. Teacher
Robinson, Jane E., PhD   Sr. Lectr.
Other Staff: 2 Lectrs.; 3 Res. Fellows

Veterinary Companion Animal Sciences Division

Tel: (0141) 330 5739 Fax: (0141) 330 5279
Anderson, Thomas J., BVMS Edin., MVM Glas., PhD Glas.   Sr. Lectr.
Bennett, David, BSc BVetMed PhD   Prof., Small Animal Clinical Studies
Carmichael, Stuart, BVMS Glas., MVM Glas.   Prof., Veterinary Clinical Studies
Flaherty, Derek, BVMS DVA   Sr. Univ. Teacher
Jackson, Mark, BS DVM PhD   Sr. Lectr.
King, Alison M., BVMS   Sr. Lectr.
Knottenbelt, Clare   Lectr.; Head*
Lischer, Cristoph, DrMedVet   Prof., Equine Clinical Studies
Love, Sandy, BVMS PhD   Prof., Equine Clinical Studies
Penderis, Jacques, BVSc MVM PhD   Sr. Lectr.
Ramsey, Ian, BVSc PhD   Sr. Lectr.
Sullivan, Martin, BVMS Glas., PhD Glas.   Prof., Veterinary Surgery and Diagnostic Imaging
Wotton, Paul R.   Sr. Lectr.
Yam, Phillipa, BVMS BSc PhD   Sr. Lectr.
Other Staff: 1 Sr. Registrar; 4 Lectrs.; 2 Univ. Teachers; 1 Res. Fellow; 1 Sr. Univ. Clinician; 1 Sr. Clin. Fellow
Vacant Posts: 4 Sr. Lectrs.

Veterinary Infection and Immunity Division

Tel: (0141) 330 3040
Britton, Collette, BSc PhD   Sr. Lectr.
Devaney, Eileen, BSc Glas., PhD Liv.   Prof., Parasite Immunobiology; Head*
Everest, Paul H., MSc PhD   Sr. Lectr.
Gilleard, John S., BVSc PhD   Prof., Veterinary and Molecular Parasitology

Nicolson, Lesley, BSc Aberd., PhD Glas.   Sr. Lectr.
Onions, David E.   Hon. Prof.†
Page, Antony P., BSc PhD   Prof. Res. Fellow
Roberts, Mark, BSc E.Anglia, PhD Leic.   Prof., Molecular Bacteriology
Shiels, Brian R., BSc Glas., PhD Camb.   Prof., Parasite Cell Biology
Smith, David G., BSc PhD   Prof.
Tait, Andrew, BSc Edin., PhD Edin., FRSEd   Prof., Veterinary Parasitology
Willett, Brian J., BSc PhD   Reader
Other Staff: 1 Lectr.; 1 Sr. Res. Fellow; 1 Res. Fellow; 1 Researcher; 1 Res. Technician

Veterinary Pathological Sciences Division

Tel: (0141) 330 5773 Fax: (0141) 330 5602
Cameron, Ewan R., BVMS PhD   Prof., Molecular and Cellular Oncology
Campo, Saveria, PhD Edin., BSc   Prof., Viral Oncology
Jarrett, Ruth F., MB ChB Glas., FRCPath   Prof., Molecular Pathology
Johnston, Pamela   Sr. Lectr.
Melendy, Thomas   Sr. Lectr.
Morgan, Iain M., BSc PhD   Prof., Molecular Oncology
Morris, Joanna S., BVSc Brist., BVSc BSc, FRCVS   Sr. Lectr.
Nasir, Lubna, BSc MSc PhD   Sr. Lectr.
Neil, James C., BSc PhD, FRSEd   Prof., Virology and Molecular Oncology
Palmarini, Massimo, DVM PhD   Prof., Molecular Pathogenesis; Head*
Philbey, Adrian W., BVSc PhD   Sr. Lectr.
Thompson, Harold, BVMS PhD   Sr. Lectr.
Other Staff: 2 Lectrs.; 5 Res. Fellows; 1 RCUK Fellowship; 2 Postdoctoral Res. Scientists; 1 Postdoctoral Scientist; 1 Wellcome Intermediate Clin. Fellow
Vacant Posts: 1 Prof.

MEDICINE

Tel: (0141) 330 5921 Fax: (0141) 330 5440
E-mail: execdean@clinmed.gla.ac.uk

Cancer Sciences and Molecular Pathology, Division of

Tel: (0141) 211 2233 Fax: (0141) 337 2494

Forensic Medicine and Science Section

Tel: (0141) 330 4574 Fax: (0141) 330 4602
E-mail: pathology@formed.gla.ac.uk
Anderson, Robert A., BSc Glas., PhD Glas., FRSChem   Sr. Lectr.
Cooper, Gail A. A., BSc PhD   Sr. Lectr.
Scott, Karen S., BSc PhD   Sr. Lectr.
Other Staff: 5 Consultant Pathologists; 2 Consultant Toxicologists
Research: advanced methodologies in forensic toxicology; alcohol and drugs in the community; deaths due to alcohol and drug abuse; sudden unexpected deaths in epilepsy; use of alternative matrices in forensic toxicology

Haemato Oncology Section

Fitzsimons, Edward, BSc Glas., MB ChB Glas., MD Glas., FRCPath, FRCPGlas   Sr. Lectr.
Franklin, Ian M., PhD, FRCP, FRCPath   Prof., Transfusion Medicine
Holyoake, Tessa, MB ChB PhD, FRCPGlas, FRCPath   Prof., Experimental Haematology
Other Staff: 1 Sr. Lectr.; 1 Lectr.; 1 Scientific Officer
Research: cancer stem cells in CML; molecular lymphopoiesis; stem cell biology; stem cell technology

Medical Oncology Section

Tel: (0141) 330 4161 Fax: (0141) 330 4127
Cassidy, J., MB ChB MSc MD   Prof.
Evans, T. R. J., MB BS Lond., MD Lond., FRCP   Prof.
Jones, Robert J., BA Glas., MB ChB Glas., MA Glas., PhD Glas.   Sr. Lectr.
Keith, William, BSc Edin., PhD Glas.   Prof.

Welsh, John, BSc MB ChB, FRCP   Dr Olav Kerr Prof., Palliative Medicine
Other Staff: 1 Clin. Sr. Lectr.
Research: pharmacology and new drug development; telemerase-directed molecular therapeutics

Pathology Section

Tel: (0141) 221 2233 Fax: (0141) 337 2494
Gusterson, Barry A., BSc Lond., BDS Lond., MB BS Lond., PhD Lond., FRCPath   Prof.; Head*
Iwata, Tomoko   Sr. Lectr.
Jamieson, Susan, BSc PhD   Sr. Univ. Teacher
Vetrie, David   Sr. Lectr.
West, Adam   Sr. Lectr.
Other Staff: 6 Lectrs.; 1 Clin. Reader; 2 Clin. Sr. Lectrs.
Research: fibroblast growth factors (FGF) receptor signalling; mechanisms involved in cellular migration and branching morphogenesis during breast development; pathogenesis of biological tumours; RNA interference (function and technology); role of chromatin insulator elements in gene expression

Radiation Oncology Section

Tel: (0141) 330 4161 Fax: (0141) 330 4127
Mairs, Robert J., BSc PhD DSc   Reader
Rampling, Roy, BSc Lond., MB BS Lond., MSc Lond., PhD Lond., FRCR   Prof., Neuro-oncology
Research: targeted radionuclide therapy

Squamous Cell Biology and Dermatology Section

Tel: (0141) 330 4012 Fax: (0141) 330 4008
Edward, Michael, BSc H-W, PhD H-W   Reader; Section Head*
Greenhalgh, David A., BSc Salf., PhD Manc.   Sr. Lectr.
Other Staff: 1 Clin. Sr. Lectr.
Research: genetic basis of skin disease; mechanisms of fibrosis; psoriasis; skin cancer (non-melanoma/melanoma; wound healing and extracellular matrix

Surgery Section

Tel: (0141) 211 2166 Fax: (0141) 211 1972
E-mail: r.o'hara@clinmed.gla.ac.uk
Angerson, Wilso J., BA Oxf., DPhil Sus.   Reader
Bartlett, John, BSc Bath, PhD Edin.   Sr. Lectr.
Cooke, Timothy G., MD Liv., FRCS, FRCSGlas   St. Mungo Prof.; Head, Royal Infirmary
George, W. D., MB BS Lond., MS Lond., FRCS, FRCSGlas   Prof.; Head, Western Infirmary; Head*
Horgan, P., MB ChB PhD, FRCS   Clin. Sr. Lectr.; Dir., Clin. Skills
McKay, Colin, MB ChB Glas., FRCSGlas   Sr. Lectr.
O'Dwyer, Patrick J., BAO MB ChB MCh, FRCSI   Prof., Gastrointestinal Surgery
Shiels, Paul, BA Trinity(Dub.), PhD Glas.   Sr. Lectr.
Stuart, Robert C., MB BCh BAO MCH, FRCSI   Sr. Lectr.
Other Staff: 1 Clin. Sr. Lectr.
Research: breast cancer; gastroenterology; hernia; transplantation

Cardiovascular and Medical Sciences, Division of

Tel: (0141) 211 2320 Fax: (0141) 211 2895
E-mail: j.l.reid@clinmed.gla.ac.uk
Caslake, Muriel   Prof.
Hillis, William S., MB ChB, FRCPGlas   Prof., Cardiovascular and Exercise Medicine
Langhorne, Peter, BSc MB ChB PhD, FRCP   Prof., Stroke Care
Lees, Kennedy R., BA MB ChB MD, FRCP   Prof., Cerebrovascular Medicine
Lowe, Gordon D., MB ChB MD, FRCP   Prof., Vascular Medicine
Macfarlane, Peter W., BSc Glas., PhD Glas., DSc Glas., FRSEd, FBCS   Prof., Electrocardiology
McColl, Kenneth E. L., MB ChB MD, FRCP   Prof., Gastroenterology

McInnes, Gordon T., BSc *Glas.*, MB ChB *Glas.*, MD *Glas.*, FRCP   Prof., Clinical Pharmacology

McKillop, James H., BSc MB ChB PhD, FRCP, FRCR, FMedSci, FRCPEd, FRCPGlas   Muirhead Prof.

Reid, John L., MA *Oxf.*, BM BCh *Oxf.*, DM *Oxf.*, FRCPGlas, FRCP, FRSEd, FMedSci   Regius Prof., Medicine and Therapeutics

Stott, David J., MB ChB MD, FRCP   David Cargill Prof., Geriatric Medicine

Other Staff: 1 Univ. Teacher; 1 Res. Dietician; 4 Clin. Sr. Lectrs.; 1 Clin. Lectr.; 3 Clin. Res. Fellows; 1 Hon. Reader; 1 Hon. Lectr.; 11 Hon. Consultants; 2 Hon. Sr. Res. Fellows; 2 Hon. Res. Fellows; 70 Hon. Clin. Sr. Lectrs.; 2 Hon. Clin. Lectrs.; 5 Hon. Clin. Teachers

British Heart Foundation Glasgow Cardiovascular Research Centre

Tel: (0141) 330 2045 Fax: (0141) 330 6997

Baker, Andrew H., BSc   Prof., Molecular Medicine

Cobbe, Stuart M., MB MA MD   Walton Prof.

Connell, John, MD   Prof., Endocrinology

Dominiczak, Anna F., MD   Prof., Cardiovascular Medicine; Head*

Hamilton, Carlene A., BSc PhD   Sr. Lectr.

Jardine, Alan G., BSc MB ChB MD   Clin. Prof.

McMurray, John J., MD   Prof., Cardiology

Pell, Jill   Prof., Epidemiology

Rankin, Andrew C., BSc MB ChB MD   Prof., Medical Cardiology

Sattar, Naveed A., MB ChB   Prof., Metabolic Medicine

Other Staff: 6 Lectrs.; 1 Res. Fellow; 3 Clin. Sr. Lectrs.; 6 Clin. Lectrs.; 10 Clin. Res. Fellows; 8 Hon. Consultants

Community Based Sciences, Division of

Tel: (0141) 211 0692
E-mail: divadmin-cbs@clinmed.gla.ac.uk

General Practice and Primary Care Section

Tel: (0141) 330 8330

Mair, Frances   Prof.†, Primary Care Research

Morrison, Jillian M., MB ChB *Glas.*, MSc *Glas.*, PhD *Glas.*, FRCGP, FRCPEd, FRCPGlas   Prof.

O'Donnell, Catherine, BSc PhD   Sr. Lectr.

Watt, Graham C. M., BMedBiol *Aberd.*, MB ChB *Aberd.*, MD, FRCP, FRCGP   Norie-Miller Prof.; Clin. Academic Consultant

Other Staff: 2 Sr. Univ. Teachers; 1 Lectr.; 6 Res. Fellows; 1 Clin. Sr. Lectr.; 1 Clin. Lectr.

Psychological Medicine Section

Tel: (0141) 211 3927

Campbell, Elizabeth A., MA MPhil DPhil   Sr. Lectr.

Cavanagh, Jonathan, MB ChB *Glas.*, MPhil *Edin.*, MD *Edin.*   Sr. Lectr.

Cooper, Sally-Ann, BSc *Lond.*, MB BS *Lond.*, MD *Lond.*, FRCPsych   Prof., Learning Disabilities

Espie, Colin A., BSc *Glas.*, MSc *Glas.*, PhD *Glas.*, FBPsS   Prof., Clinical Psychology

Evans, Jonathan J.   Prof., Applied Neuropsychology

Gumley, Andrew I.   Sr. Lectr.

McKenna, Peter J., BA MB   Chair, Psychiatry

McMillan, Thomas M., BSc *Aberd.*, MSc *Glas.*, PhD *Lond.*   Prof., Clinical Neurospsychology

Millar, Keith, BA *Stir.*, PhD *Dund.*, FBPsS   Prof., Medical Psychology

Wilson, Sarah L., BSc *Wales*, PhD *Lond.*   Sr. Lectr.

Other Staff: 1 Univ. Teacher; 2 Res. Fellows; 1 Clin. Sr. Reader; 1 Clin. Reader; 1 Clin. Sr. Lectr.; 1 Clin. Res. Fellow

Public Health and Health Policy Section

Tel: (0141) 211 4039

Atkinson, Jacqueline M., BA *Hull*, PhD *Hull*   Prof., Mental Health Policy

Briggs, Andrew H., BA MSc DPhil   Chair, Health Policy and Econ. Evaluation

Hanlon, Philip W., BSc *Glas.*, MB ChB *Glas.*, MD *Glas.*, FRCP   Prof., Public Health

Reid, Margaret E., MA *Aberd.*, PhD   Prof., Women's Health

Other Staff: 3 Lectrs.; 3 Univ. Teachers; 3 Res. Fellows; 1 Clin. Lectr.

Dental School

Tel: (0141) 211 9701 Fax: (0141) 331 2798

Ayoub, Ashraf F., BDS *Cairo*, PhD *Glas.*, MDS, FRCS, FDSRCS   Prof.

Bagg, Jeremy, BDS *Edin.*, PhD *Edin.*, FDSRCSEd, FRCPath, FDSRCPSGlas   Prof., Clinical Microbiology; Head*

Macpherson, Lorna M., BDS PhD, FRCDCan   Prof., Dental Public Health

McCord, James F., BDS   Prof., Restorative Dentistry

Orchardson, Richard, BSc BDS PhD   Sr. Lectr.

Ramage, Gordon, BSc PhD   Sr. Lectr.

Riggio, Marcello P., BSc PhD   Sr. Lectr.

Welbury, Robert R., MB BS BDS PhD, FDSRCS, FRCPCH   Prof., Paediatric Dentistry

Wray, David, BDS MB ChB MD, FMedSci, FDSRCPSGlas, FDSRCSEd   Prof., Oral Medicine

Other Staff: 3 Univ. Teachers; 1 Res. Fellow; 1 Locum Consultant; 1 Dental Instr.; 1 Clin. Reader; 7 Clin. Sr. Lectrs.; 10 Clin. Lectrs.; 4 Clin. Sr. Univ. Teachers; 5 Clin. Univ. Teachers; 1 Clin. Res. Fellow; 2 Hon. Lectrs.; 4 Hon. Sr. Res. Fellows; 2 Hon. Res. Fellows; 15 Hon. Consultants; 8 Hon. Clin. Sr. Lectrs.; 5 Hon. Clin. Lectrs.; 25 Hon. Clin. Teachers

Developmental Medicine, Division of

Asbury, Adrian J., MB ChB *Birm.*, MD *Sheff.*, PhD *Sheff.*, FRCA   Reader

Carachi, Robert, MD PhD   Prof., Surgical Paediatrics

Connor, J. M., BSc *Liv.*, MD *Liv.*, MB ChB, FRCP   Burton Prof.; Head*

Edwards, Christine, BSc *Sheff.*, PhD *Sheff.*   Prof., Nutritional Physiology

Freeman, Dilys, BSc PhD   Sr. Lectr.

Hankey, Catherine R., BSc MSc PhD   Sr. Lectr.

Hepburn, Mary, BSc *Edin.*, MD *Edin.*, FRCOG   Sr. Lectr.

Lean, M. E. J., BA *Camb.*, MB BChir *Camb.*, MA *Camb.*, MD *Camb.*, FRCP   Prof., Human Nutrition

Lumsden, Mary Ann, BSc *Lond.*, MB BS *Lond.*, MD *Lond.*, FRCOG   Prof.

Lyall, Fiona, BSc PhD   Prof., Maternal and Fetal Health

Malkova, Dalia, BSc PhD   Sr. Lectr.

Norman, Jane E., MB ChB *Edin.*, MD *Edin.*   Prof., Obstetrics and Gynaecology

Reilly, John J., BSc *Glas.*, PhD *Wales*   Prof., Paediatric Energy Metabolism

Stone, David H., BSc MB ChB MD, FRCP, FRCPCH   Prof., Paediatric Epidemiology

Weaver, Lawrence T., BA *Camb.*, BChir *Camb.*, MA *Camb.*, MD *Camb.*, FRCP, FRCPCH   Samson Gemmell Prof.

Wright, Charlotte M., MSc MD   Prof., Community Child Health

Other Staff: 2 Lectrs.; 1 Res. Fellow; 1 Res. Assoc.; 2 Gen. Teaching Facilitators; 2 Clin. Readers; 4 Clin. Sr. Lectrs.; 3 Clin. Lectrs.; 6 Clin. Res. Fellows

Education and Administration, Division of

Tel: (0141) 330 8040

Barton, Peter J., MB ChB, FRCGP   Dir., Clin. Skills*

Brown, Ian, BSc *Glas.*, MB ChB *Glas.*, FRCPath   Sr. Lectr.; Convenor, Undergrad. Medicine Admissions Committee

Burke, Joanne M., BSc MEd PhD   Sr. Univ. Teacher

Clark, Barry, BSc *St And.*, PhD *Glas.*   Dir., Vale

Jamieson, Susan, BSc PhD   Sr. Univ. Teacher

Lumsden, Mary Ann, BSc *Lond.*, MB BS *Lond.*, MD *Lond.*, FRCOG   Prof.

McKillop, James H., BSc MB ChB PhD, FRCP, FRCR, FMedSci, FRCPEd, FRCPGlas   Prof.

Morrison, Jillian M., MB ChB *Glas.*, MSc *Glas.*, PhD *Glas.*, FRCGP, FRCPEd, FRCPGlas   Prof.; Head, Undergrad. Med. Sch.

Murray, T. Stuart, MD PhD, FRCPEd, FRCPGlas, FRCGP   Prof., General Practice (Postgraduate Medicine)

Reid, John L., MA *Oxf.*, BM BCh *Oxf.*, DM *Oxf.*, FRCPGlas, FRCP, FRSEd, FMedSci   Regius Prof., Medicine and Therapeutics

Sturrock, Roger D., MB BS MD, FRCP, FRCPGlas   Prof.

Other Staff: 8 Univ. Teachers

Immunology, Infection and Inflammation, Division of

Tel: (0141) 211 2251 Fax: (0141) 337 3217

Research: adjuvants and virulence factors in bacteria; autoimmunity and Ig V-gene repertoire; cytokine network and immune regulations; mucosal immunity and oral tolerance; signalling in the immune system

Immunology and Bacteriology Section

Evans, Thomas J., MA PhD   Prof., Molecular Microbiology

Gemmell, Curtis G., BSc *Glas.*, PhD *Glas.*, FRCPath   Prof.

Gracie, J. Alastair, BSc PhD   Sr. Lectr.

Graham, Gerard   Prof., Molecular and Structural Immunology

Harnett, Margaret, BSc *Glas.*, PhD *Glas.*   Prof., Immune Signalling

Liew, Foo Y., BSc *Monash*, PhD *ANU*, DSc *ANU*, FRCPath, FRSEd   Prof.; Head*

Mowat, Allan M., MB ChB PhD, FRCPath   Prof., Mucosal Immunology

Nibbs, Robert, BA PhD   Sr. Lectr.

Stott, David I., BSc *Manc.*, PhD *Camb.*   Reader

Other Staff: 3 Res. Fellows; 2 Clin. Sr. Lectrs.; 5 Clin. Res. Fellows; 7 Hon. Clin. Sr. Lectrs.

Respiratory Medicine Section

Tel: (0141) 211 3241 Fax: (0141) 211 3464

Thomson, Neil C., MB ChB MD, FRCP   Prof.

Other Staff: 1 Clin. Res. Fellow

Rheumatology Section

Tel: (0141) 211 4687 Fax: (0141) 211 4878

Field, Max, BSc MD   Reader

McInnes, Iain, PhD   Prof., Experimental Medicine

Sturrock, Roger D., MB BS MD, FRCP, FRCPGlas   Macleod ARC Prof.

Other Staff: 2 Clin. Res. Fellows

Neurosciences, Clinical, Division of

Tel: (0141) 201 2474 Fax: (0141) 201 2993
E-mail: m.a.mccoll@clinmed.gla.ac.uk

Hillan, Edith M., MSc *Strath.*, MPhil PhD   Prof.†, Midwifery

Neuroinflammation and Neurobiology Section

Barnett, Susan C., BSc PhD   Prof., Cellular Neuroscience

Kennedy, Peter G. E., MLitt MPhil MD PhD DSc, FRCP, FRCPGlas, FRCPath, FRSEd, FMedSci   Head*

Willison, Hugh J., MB BS *Lond.*, PhD, FRCP   Prof., Neurology

Other Staff: 1 Lectr.; 1 Clin. Sr. Lectr.; 1 Clin. Res. Fellow; 3 Hon. Consultants

Research: fundamental mechanisms in inflammatory demyelinating neuropathy and ganglioside biology; glial cell biology; neurovirology; virus/gene therapy

Wellcome Surgical Institute

Tel: (0141) 330 5826 Fax: (0141) 943 0215
E-mail: gpne02@udcf.gla.ac.uk

Dewar, Deborah, PhD   Sr. Lectr.

Macrae, Iseabail M., BSc *Glas.*, PhD *Glas.*   Prof., Neuroscience

Other Staff: 5 Lectrs.; 1 Univ. Teacher; 1 Res. Fellow

Research: experimental stroke research; models of brain injury; neurochemical pathology; oestrogen and brain injury; receptor imaging

Nursing and Health Care, School of

Tel: (0141) 330 4051 Fax: (0141) 330 3539
  E-mail: s.hendry@clinmed.gla.ac.uk
Comerasamy, Claudette, BA MSc PhD
McDowell, Joan R., MN   Sr. Lectr.
O'Neill, Anna, BN *Glas.*, MN *Glas.*, PhD   Sr. Univ. Teacher
Paul, Lorna, BSc *Glas.*, MPhil *Glas.*, PhD *Glas.*
Smith, Lorraine N., BScN *Ott.*, MEd *Manc.*, PhD *Manc.*   Prof., Nursing
Sneddon, Margaret C., MSc *Glas.*   Sr. Univ. Teacher; Head*
Other Staff: 5 Lectrs.; 1 Univ. Teacher; 1 Res. Fellow
Research: acute and chronic health challenges; cardiac care; contracture management in multiple sclerosis, effect of vibration therapy in multiple sclerosis; lyphoedema; stroke

SPECIAL CENTRES, ETC

Biostatistics, Robertson Centre for

Tel: (0141) 330 4744 Fax: (0141) 330 5094
Ford, Ian, BSc PhD   Prof.; Head*
Other Staff: 1 Res. Fellow; 1 Health Economist; 1 Sr. Statistician; 1 Biostatistician; 3 Consultant Statisticians; 1 Data Manager/Statistician

Drugs Misuse Research, Centre for

Tel: (0141) 330 3616 Fax: (0141) 330 2820
McKeganey, Neil, BA *Sus.*, MSc *Lond.*, PhD *Aberd.*   Prof.; Head*
Thom, Elizabeth   Hon. Prof.†
Other Staff: 1 Prof. Res. Fellow; 1 Sr. Res. Fellow; 2 Res. Fellows; 2 Tutors
Research: drugs misuse

History of Medicine, Centre for

Tel: (0141) 330 6071 Fax: (0141) 330 3511
Dupree, Marguerite W., BA *Mass.*, MA *Prin.*, DPhil *Oxf.*, PhD *Camb.*   Sr. Lectr.
Nicolson, Malcolm A., BSc *Aberd.*, PhD *Edin.*   Sr. Lectr.
Research: history of child health; history of clinical medicine in modern Britain; Scottish medical history

Molecular Parasitology, Wellcome Centre for

Glasgow Biomedical Research Centre
Tel: (0141) 330 4875 Fax: (0141) 330 5422
  E-mail: j.barry@vet.gla.ac.uk
Barry, J. David, BSc   Prof.; Dir.*
Mottram, Jeremy C., BSc PhD   Prof., Molecular and Cellular Parasitology
Other Staff: 2 Res. Fellows; 2 Postdoctoral Researchers

Scottish Universities Environmental Research Centre

Consortium of two universities (Edinburgh and Glasgow)
Tel: (01355) 223332 Fax: (01355) 229898
  E-mail: director@suerc.gla.ac.uk
Cook, Gordon T., BSc *Glas.*, PhD *Glas.*   Reader
Ellam, Robert M., BSc *Lond.*, PhD *Open(UK)*   Prof., Isotope Geochemistry
Fallick, Anthony E., BSc *Glas.*, PhD *Glas.*, FRSA, FRSEd   Prof., Isotope Geosciences; Dir.*

Freeman, Stewart P.   Prof.
Mackenzie, Angus B., BSc *Glas.*, PhD *Glas.*   Prof., Environmental Geochemistry
Preston, Thomas, BSc *St And.*, PhD *Dund.*   Prof.
Sanderson, David C. W., BSc *Durh.*, MPhil *Brad.*, PhD *Paisley*   Reader
Stuart, Finlay M.   Sr. Lectr.
Other Staff: 1 Lectr.; 1 Marie Curie Fellow; 1 AMS Scientist; 1 Hon. Sr. Res. Fellow
Research: biomedical and ecological processes (stable isotope approaches); environmental geochemistry and environmental radioactivity; isotope geology and geochronology; quaternary dating; waste disposal, pollution and health

CONTACT OFFICERS

Academic affairs. Clerk of Senate: Nash, Prof. Andrew S., BVMS *Glas.*, PhD *Glas.*, FIBiol
Accommodation. Director (Residential Service): Campbell, Neil, BSc *Edin.*
  (E-mail: accom@gla.ac.uk)
Admissions (first degree). Director, Central Admissions Service: Brown, James
  (E-mail: admissions@gla.ac.uk)
Admissions (higher degree). Assistant Director (Graduate): Wilber, Ann
  (E-mail: pgadmissions@gla.ac.uk)
Adult/continuing education. Head, Adult and Continuing Education: Findsen, Prof. Brian, BSocSci *Waik.*, MA *Waik.*, EdD *N.Carolina State*
  (E-mail: enquiry@educ.gla.ac.uk)
Alumni. Head, Development and Alumni Office: Bell, Catherine, MA
  (E-mail: campaign@gla.ac.uk)
Archives. Head, University Archives: Richmond, Lesley M., MA
Careers. Director, Careers Service: Weir, Jane, MA (E-mail: careers@admin.gla.ac.uk)
Computing services. Director, Computing Services: Gilmour, Rowland A.
  (E-mail: admin@compserv.gla.ac.uk)
Conferences/corporate hospitality. Director, Hospitality Services: McInnes, Aileen G.
Consultancy services. Director, Research and Enterprise: Cullen, Kevin, PhD *Edin.*
  (E-mail: r-e@gla.ac.uk)
Credit transfer. Director, Student Recruitment: Andrews, Fiona
Development/fund-raising. Director, Development and Alumni Office: Bell, Catherine, MA (E-mail: campaign@gla.ac.uk)
Equal opportunities. Deputy Director, Staff Development Services: Chandler, Jean F.
  (E-mail: sds@admin.gla.ac.uk)
Estates and buildings/works and services. Director, Estates and Buildings: McConnel, Jim
Examinations. Head of Registry: Lowther, Christine R., BA
  (E-mail: reg.enq@admin.gla.ac.uk)
Finance. Director of Finance: Fraser, Robert M., BSc MBA
General enquiries. Head of Registry: Lowther, Christine R., BA
  (E-mail: reg.enq@admin.gla.ac.uk)
Health services. Medical Officer: Hamilton, Gordon M., MB ChB *Glas.*, MPhil
Industrial liaison. Director, Research and Enterprise: Cullen, Kevin, PhD *Edin.*
  (E-mail: r-e@gla.ac.uk)
International office. Director, International and Postgraduate Service: Procter, Sharne, BEd
Language training for international students. Director of EFL Unit: Daborn, Esther, MA PhD (E-mail: efl@gla.ac.uk)

Library (chief librarian). Director of Library Services: Durndell, Helen A.
  (E-mail: library@lib.gla.ac.uk)
Marketing. Director, Corporate Communications: Stewart, Susan
  (E-mail: communications@gla.ac.uk)
Personnel/human resources. Director, Human Resources: Black, Ian
  (E-mail: humanresources@gla.ac.uk)
Public relations. Director, Corporate Communications: Stewart, Susan
  (E-mail: communications@gla.ac.uk)
Publications. Director, Corporate Communications: Stewart, Susan
  (E-mail: communications@gla.ac.uk)
Purchasing. Head of Procurement: McAra, Tom
Research. Director, Research and Enterprise: Cullen, Kevin, PhD *Edin.*
  (E-mail: r-e@gla.ac.uk)
Safety. Safety Officer: Rankine, Andrew D., BSc *Glas.*, PhD *Glas.*, FRSChem
  (E-mail: safety@gla.ac.uk)
Scholarships, awards, loans. Scholarships Officer
Schools liaison. UK Recruitment Officer, Recruitment, Admissions and Participation Service: Campbell, Kelly
  (E-mail: k.campbell@admin.gla.ac.uk)
Security. Central Services Manager: Edgar, Laurence W.
Sport and recreation. Acting Director (Sport and recreation): Ommer, Julie
  (E-mail: c.stuart@admin.gla.ac.uk)
Staff development and training. Deputy Director of Personnel Services: Chandler, Jean F. (E-mail: sds@admin.gla.ac.uk)
Strategic planning. Head, Planning Office: Sim, Alastair
  (E-mail: planningoffice@gla.ac.uk)
Student union. Acting President, Students' Representative Council: Tomlinson, Sarah
  (E-mail: enquiries@src.gla.ac.uk)
Student welfare/counselling. Head, Student Counselling and Advisory Service: McManus, Davina
Students from other countries. Head, International and Postgraduate Service: Procter, Sharne, BEd
Students with disabilities. Senior Disability Adviser: Robertson, Shona
  (E-mail: studentdisability@gla.ac.uk)

CAMPUS/COLLEGE HEADS

Crichton Campus, Crichton University Campus, Bankend Road, Dumfries, Scotland DG1 4ZL. (Tel: (01387) 702131; Fax: (01387) 702005;
  E-mail: information@crichton.gla.ac.uk)
  Director: Cowan, Prof. Edward J., MA
Glasgow School of Art, 67 Renfrew Street, Glasgow, Scotland G3 6RQ. (Tel: (0141) 353 4500; E-mail: info@gsa.ac.uk) Director: Reid, Prof. Seona, CBE, BA *Strath.*, DLitt, FRSA
Scottish Agricultural College, Donald Hendrie Building, Auchincruive, Ayr, Scotland KA6 5HW. (Tel: (0800) 269453;
  E-mail: recruitment@sac.ac.uk) Chief Executive and Principal: McKelvey, Prof. Bill

[*Information supplied by the institution as at 19 November 2007, and edited by the ACU*]

GLASGOW CALEDONIAN UNIVERSITY

Founded 1993

Member of the Association of Commonwealth Universities

Postal Address: City Campus, Cowcaddens Road, Glasgow, Scotland G4 0BA
Telephone: (0141) 331 3000 **Fax:** (0141) 331 3005
URL: http://www.caledonian.ac.uk

PRINCIPAL AND VICE-CHANCELLOR*—Gillies, Prof. Pamela A., BSc *Aberd.*, MMedSci *Nott.*, MEd *Aberd.*, PhD *Nott.*, AcSS, FFPH, FRCP, Hon. FRCPSGlas
VICE-PRINCIPAL—Dickson, Prof. G. C. A.
EXECUTIVE DIRECTOR (UNIVERSITY SECRETARY)—Rooney, A.
PRO-VICE-CHANCELLOR—Watson, L.
HEAD OF ACADEMIC ADMINISTRATION‡—Ferguson, E. Brendan, BSc
DEPUTY HEAD OF ACADEMIC ADMINISTRATION—Struthers, A. Ian

GENERAL INFORMATION

History. The university was founded in 1993 by the merger of The Queen's College, Glasgow (1875) and Glasgow Polytechnic (1971).

The university's sole campus is located in the centre of Glasgow.

Admission to first degree courses (see also United Kingdom Introduction). Through Universities and Colleges Admissions Service (UCAS).

First Degrees (see also United Kingdom Directory to Subjects of Study) (* = with honours). BA, BA*, BEng, BEng*, BSc, BSc*.
Length of course. Full-time: BA, BEng, BSc: 3 years; BA*, BEng*, BSc*: 4 years.

Higher Degrees (see also United Kingdom Directory to Subjects of Study).
Master's. LLM, MBA, MPhil, MSc.
Admission. Admission to master's degree courses is made directly to the university.
Length of course. Full-time: MBA, MSc: 1 year; LLM: 3 years. *Part-time:* MSc: 2 years; MBA: 3 years.
Doctoral. PhD.

Libraries. Volumes: 342,501. Periodicals subscribed to: 6243. Special collections: Norman and Janey Buchan, Scottish and Northern Book Distribution Centre, Norrie McIntosh, and Mike Scott (all left-wing politics and labour movement); Queen's College (cookery and home economics); RSSPCC Archive (child welfare and abuse); Anti-Apartheid Movement in Scotland Archive; Heatherbank Museum of Social Work (book library, photo library, ephemera and resources library, journals and periodicals library); custodianship of Gallagher Memorial Library (left-wing politics).

Academic Year (2007–2008). Two semesters: September–January; February–May.

FACULTIES/SCHOOLS

Built and Natural Environment, School of the
Tel: (0141) 331 3170 Fax: (0141) 331 3370
E-mail: schoolbne@gcal.ac.uk
Dean: Hardcastle, Prof. Cliff, BSc MSc PhD
Personal Assistant: Graham, Liz

Caledonian Business School
Tel: (0141) 331 3117 Fax: (0141) 331 3172
E-mail: cbs@gcal.ac.uk
Dean: Robson, Prof. Ian
Personal Assistant: Connolly, Patricia

Computing and Mathematical Sciences, School of
Tel: (0141) 331 3277 Fax: (0141) 331 8445
E-mail: schoolcms@gcal.ac.uk

Dean: Mannion, Prof. Mike, BSc *Brun.*, PhD *Brist.*
Personal Assistant: Hill, Christine

Engineering, Science and Design, School of
Tel: (0141) 331 3530 Fax: (0141) 331 3690
E-mail: schoolesd@gcal.ac.uk
Acting Dean: Harrison, Prof. David, BSc *CNAA*, MSc *Manc.*, PhD *Manc.*
Personal Assistant: (vacant)

Health and Social Care, School of
Tel: (0141) 331 8151 Fax: (0141) 331 8112
E-mail: shsc@gcal.ac.uk
Dean: Durward, Brian, MSc PhD
Personal Assistant: MacAskill, Moira

Law and Social Sciences, School of
Tel: (0141) 331 8657 Fax: (0141) 331 3439
E-mail: lss@gcal.ac.uk
Dean: Huntley, Prof. John
Personal Assistant: Lawley, Nicola

Life Sciences, School of
Tel: (0141) 331 3600 Fax: (0141) 331 3500
E-mail: lifesciences@gcal.ac.uk
Dean: Gartland, Prof. Kevin, BSc *Leeds*, PhD *Nott.*
Personal Assistant: Clark, Yvonne

Nursing, Midwifery and Community Health, School of
Tel: (0141) 331 8311 Fax: (0141) 331 8312
E-mail: nmch@gcal.ac.uk
Dean: Parfitt, Prof. Barbara, CBE, MSc MCommH PhD
Personal Assistant: McKinlay, Ann

ACADEMIC UNITS

Accounting and Finance, Division of
Tel: (0141) 331 3360 Fax: (0141) 331 3171
Crawford, Margaret, MSc *Glas.*   Sr. Lectr.
Devlin, Patrick, BSc MAcc   Acting Head*
Forbes, David J., BA *Strath.*, PhD *Osm.*   Sr. Lectr.
Henry, William N., MPhil *Edin.*   Sr. Lectr.
Hill, Wan Ying, BSc PhD   Sr. Lectr.
Hillier, Joseph D., BSc   Sr. Lectr.
McArthur, Archie, MA *Edin.*   Sr. Lectr.
McChlery, Stuart, BA *Strath.*   Sr. Lectr.
McKendrick, James E., MA *Glas.*, MPhil *Glas.*   Sr. Lectr.
Merrouche, Cherif N., BA *Algiers*, MSc *Wales*   Sr. Lectr.
Rolfe, Thomas F., MAcc *Glas.*   Sr. Lectr.
Tarbert, Heather, BA *Paisley*, MSc *Glas.*   Sr. Lectr.
Webb, Robert, PhD *Anglia PU*   Sr. Lectr.
White, Siobhan, BAcc *Glas.*   Sr. Lectr.
Other Staff: 15 Lectrs.

Biological and Biomedical Sciences
Tel: (0141) 331 3209 Fax: (0141) 331 3208
E-mail: bio@gcal.ac.uk
Aidoo, Kofi E., BSc MSc PhD   Reader

Bartholomew, C., BSc *Leic.*, PhD *Leic.*   Reader
Blackstock, Jim, BSc PhD   Sr. Lectr.
Craft, John, BSc PhD   Prof.
Finbow, M. E., BSc PhD   Prof.
Graham, Ann, PhD   Reader
Grant, Alison   Sr. Lectr.
Hillier, Christopher, BSc PhD   Prof.
Logan, Niall, BSc PhD   Prof.
MacDonald, Allan, BSc PhD   Reader
Tester, Richard, BSc MSc PhD   Sr. Lectr.
Wilkie, Iain, BSc PhD   Sr. Lectr.; Head*
Wood, Les, BSc PhD   Sr. Lectr.
Other Staff: 26 Lectrs.; 5 Res. Fellows

Built and Natural Environment, School of
Tel: (0141) 331 3629 Fax: (0141) 331 3370
Akintoye, Akintola, BSc MSc PhD   Prof.; Dean, Res. and Knowledge
Baird, James, BSc PhD   Prof.; Manager, Caledonian Shanks Centre
Crowther, John, BA *Oxf.*, DPhil *Oxf.*   Sr. Lectr.
Cullen, Martin, BSc *Paisley*, MBA *Newcastle(UK)*   Sr. Lectr.
Hardcastle, Cliff, BSc MSc PhD   Prof.
Hytiris, Nicholas, BSc *Tees.*, MSc *Strath.*, PhD *Strath.*, FGS   Sr. Lectr.
Kennedy, Peter, MSc   Sr. Lectr.; Dean, Marketing and Income
Madden, Harry   Sr. Lectr.
Sommerville, James, MSc PhD   Sr. Lectr.
Taylor, Gavin, BSc *Strath.*, PhD *Strath.*, FIMechE   Sr. Lectr.

Business Information Management, Division of
Tel: (0141) 331 3179 Fax: (0141) 331 3193
Barr, Stephen, MSc *Glas.*   Sr. Lectr.
Edgar, David, BA PhD   Head*
Grant, Kevin, BA *Napier*, MSc *Lanc.*   Sr. Lectr.
Jordan, Michael, MSc *Brad.*   Sr. Lectr.
McCready, Ann, MBA *Strath.*, PhD *G.Caledonian*   Sr. Lectr.
Reid, Vivien, MBA *Strath.*   Sr. Lectr.
Williamson, Elizabeth   Sr. Lectr.
Other Staff: 14 Lectrs.

Computing, Division of
Tel: (0141) 331 3279 Fax: (0141) 331 8445
E-mail: s.cranston@gcal.ac.uk
Buggy, Tom   Head
Foley, Richard   Sr. Lectr.
Gray, Eddie   Sr. Lectr.
Lambie, Iain   Sr. Lectr.
Larijani, Hadi   Sr. Lectr.
Mair, Quentin   Sr. Lectr.
Mannion, Mike, BSc *Brun.*, PhD *Brist.*   Prof.; Head*
Murray, Grace   Sr. Lectr.
Newman, Julian, BA *Oxf.*, BA *Lond.*   Reader
Parker, Caroline   Assoc. Dean
Riley, Jackie   Assoc. Dean
Tianfield, Huaglory   Prof.
Other Staff: 20 Lectrs.

Economics and Enterprise, Division of

Tel: (0141) 331 3309 Fax: (0141) 331 3292
E-mail: acdo@gcal.ac.uk
Bailey, Stephen, MA Dund., MLitt Dund., PhD Strath. Prof.
Cooper, John, BA Strath., PhD Strath. Sr. Lectr.
Dow, Alistair, MA St And., MA S.Fraser, PhD Manit. Prof.
Doyle, Carole Sr. Lectr.
Hutton, Alan, BCom Leeds, MA Leeds Sr. Lectr.
Leahy, James, BA Strath. Sr. Lectr.
Radford, Alan, BSc MPhil Sr. Lectr.
Riddington, Geoffrey, BA Sus., PhD Wales, MPhil Reader
Whigham, David, MA Glas., MPhil Glas. Sr. Lectr.
Other Staff: 14 Lectrs.

Engineering, Science and Design, School of

Tel: (0141) 331 3530 Fax: (0141) 331 3974
E-mail: schoolesd@gcal.ac.uk
Allan, Malcolm, BSc Strath., PhD G.Caledonian Sr. Lectr.
Ansell, Raymond O., BSc Lond., PhD Newcastle(UK) Reader
Campbell, Michael, BSc Paisley, PhD Glas. Reader
Champaneri, Ramesh, BSc Aston, MPhil Northumbria Sr. Lectr.
El-Sharif, Mahmoud R., MSc Glas. Prof.
Fortune, J. D., BSc Glas., MSc Aberd., PhD Glas. Sr. Lectr.
Gordon, David R., BSc Strath., PhD Strath. Sr. Lectr.
Knight, Elizabeth, BSc Glas. Sr. Lectr.
MacLachlan, John, BSc Glas., PhD Glas. Sr. Lectr.
McKee, Willie, BA Open(UK), MSc Glas. Sr. Lectr.
Pugh, John R., BSc Glas., PhD Glas. Prof.; Head, Div. of Measurement and Control
Temple, Bryan K., BTech Brad., PhD Leeds Sr. Lectr.
Westwood, Tom, BSc Glas., MSc Strath. Sr. Lectr.; Head, Div. of Electronic and Electr. Engin.
Other Staff: 42 Lectrs.; 2 Res. Fellows
Research: electric plant condition monitoring; insulating materials (degradation and breakdown); intelligent manufacturing technologies; multimedia learning; processing materials for manufacture

Human Resource Management and Development, Division of

Fax: (0141) 331 3003
E-mail: j.boyd@gcal.ac.uk
Barclay, Jean, MA Glas., PhD Strath. Sr. Lectr.
Beattie, Rona, MA PhD Sr. Lectr.; Head, Subject Group*
Cousins, John, MSc Bath, MLitt H-W Sr. Lectr.
Kellock-Hay, Gillian, MA Sr. Lectr.
Maxwell, Gillian, BA Strath., MPhil Strath. Prof.
McLean, Morag, BA Strath., MSc Strath. Sr. Lectr.
Other Staff: 6 Lectrs.

Law, Division of

Tel: (0141) 331 8429 Fax: (0141) 331 3798
Chisholm, Marcella, LLM Sr. Lectr.
O'Donnell, Aidan, BA LLM Head*
Research: business regulation; international economic law; Islamic law; law of the sea; public international law

Management, Division of

Tel: (0141) 331 3410 Fax: (0141) 331 3269
Falconer, Peter, BA MA PhD Sr. Lectr.
Lennon, John J., BSc Oxf.Brookes, MPhil Strath. Prof.
Leslie, David, BA Strath., MPhil Ulster Reader
Levy, Roger, BA MPhil PhD Sr. Lectr.
Litteljohn, David, BA Strath., MSc Manc. Prof.; Section Head, Travel, Tourism and Hospitality
Livingstone, Ron, BSc MSc MBA Assoc. Dean

Mackie, Robert, BA Strath., MSc Strath. Sr. Lectr.
McTavish, Duncan, BA MBA PhD Sr. Lectr.
Moxen, John, BA Sr. Lectr.
Ogden, Susan Sr. Lectr.
Penlington, John, BSc Newcastle(UK), MA Manc. Sr. Lectr.
Pyper, Robert, MA Glas., PhD Glas. Prof.
Scott, Bernadette, BA Strath., MSc Strath. Programme Leader/Lectr.
Younis, Tal, BSc Birm., MEd Birm., PhD Birm. Reader
Other Staff: 15 Lectrs.

Marketing, Division of

Tel: (0141) 582 0431 Fax: (0141) 582 0359
Birtwistle, Grete, PhD Stir. Sr. Lectr.
Connell, John, MSc PhD Sr. Lectr.
Doyle, Stephen Sr. Lectr.
Lochhead, Malcolm Sr. Lectr.
MacArthur, Sheena, BA Open(UK), MSc Glas. Sr. Lectr.
Moore, Christopher, MA Glas., MBA Stir., PhD Stir. Prof.
Roberts, Gillian, MSc PhD Sr. Lectr.
Vaughan, Elizabeth, BA Strath., MSc Strath. Sr. Lectr.
Other Staff: 14 Lectrs.

Mathematics, Division of

Tel: (0141) 331 3609 Fax: (0141) 331 3608
E-mail: maths@gcal.ac.uk
Bradley, Roy, BSc Durh., MSc Newcastle(UK), PhD Glas., FIMA Prof.
Gardiner, William P., BSc Strath., PhD Strath. Head*
Gomatam, Jagannathan, BSc Madr., MSc Madr., PhD Syr. Prof.
Macaulay, Alexander B., BSc Strath., MSc Strath. Sr. Lectr.
McFadyen, Angus K., BSc Paisley, MSc Strath. Sr. Lectr.
Speller, Martin Assoc. Dean
Williamson, Geoffrey H., BSc Lough. Sr. Lectr.
Other Staff: 11 Lectrs.; 1 Res. Fellow

Media, Culture and Leisure Management, Division of

Tel: (0141) 331 3259 Fax: (0141) 331 3264
Cook, John, MA Edin., PhD Glas. Sr. Lectr.
Foley, M. T., MSc Edin. Prof. Sr. Lectr.
Garner, Ken, BA Lond. Sr. Lectr.
McPherson, C. G., BA H-W Sr. Lectr.
O'Donnell, H., MA Glas., PhD Glas. Prof.
Other Staff: 10 Lectrs.

Nursing, Midwifery and Community Health, School of

Tel: (0141) 331 8311 Fax: (0141) 331 8312
E-mail: nmch@gcal.ac.uk
Crossan, Frank, BA MN Assoc. Dean, Planning and Operations
Currie, Kay, BSc MN Head of Div., Post-Registration Nursing and Health
Ferguson, Dorothy, BSc MPH EdD Head of Div., Community Health
Fleming, Valerie, PhD Prof.; Head of Div., Midwifery
Parfitt, Barbara, CBE, MSc MCommH PhD Prof.; Dean*
Reid, Gerald W., BA MSc Assoc. Dean, Quality
Strachan, Kathy, BA MEd EdD Head of Div., Pre-Registration Nursing
Tolson, Debbie, BSc MSc PhD Prof.; Assoc. Dean, Res.
Other Staff: 20 Staff Members

Occupational Therapy, Division of

Tel: (0141) 331 8381 Fax: (0141) 331 8382
E-mail: otadmissions@gcal.ac.uk
McKay, Vincent Head*
Pratt, J., PhD G.Caledonian Sr. Lectr.
Other Staff: 8 Staff Members

Physiotherapy, Division of

Tel: (0141) 331 8129 Fax: (0141) 331 8130
E-mail: physio.admissions@gcal.ac.uk
Brown, Helen, MSc Sr. Lectr.
Curr, Margaret C. H., MEd Edin. Head*
Grant, Margaret, MSc Liv. Sr. Lectr.
Gray, H., MSc Sr. Lectr.
Keir, K., MSc Sr. Lectr.
Stachura, S., MSc Sr. Lectr.
Webster, V., PhD G.Caledonian Sr. Lectr.
Other Staff: 17 Lectrs.

Podiatric Medicine and Surgery, Division of

Tel: (0141) 331 8128 Fax: (0141) 331 8130
E-mail: podadmissions@gcal.ac.uk
Baird, Stuart A., BSc Brighton Head*
Burrow, Gordon, BA MPhil Sr. Lectr.
Campbell, Robert, MSc G.Caledonian Sr. Lectr.
O'Donnell, Maureen, BSc Sund. Sr. Lectr.
Other Staff: 6 Lectrs.

Psychology, Division of

Tel: (0141) 331 3119 Fax: (0141) 331 3636
E-mail: psy@gcal.ac.uk
Brodie, Eric, BA Stir., PhD Stir. Reader
Cooke, David, BSc St And., MSc Newcastle(UK), PhD Glas., FBPsS Prof.†
Durndell, A., BSc Lond., PhD Aberd. Head*
Egan, Vincent, BSc Lond., PhD Edin., DClinPsy Leic. Prof.
Forbes, Douglas, MA Aberd., PhD Aberd. Sr. Lectr.
Hammersley, Richard, PhD Prof.
Hetherington, Marion, PhD Prof.
McGee, A., BA Birm., PhD Birm. Sr. Lectr.
Shewan, D., MA Glas. Reader
Tuohy, Alan, BSc Lond., PhD Strath. Sr. Lectr.
Wrennall, Mike, BSc Lond., MPhil Lond. Sr. Lectr.
Yule, Fred, MA Aberd. Sr. Lectr.
Other Staff: 26 Lectrs.; 7 Res. Staff

Radiography, Division of

Tel: (0141) 331 8128 Fax: (0141) 331 8130
E-mail: radadmissions@gcal.ac.uk
Cuthbertson, Lynn, MSc G.Caledonian Sr. Lectr.
Ellis, Brian, PhD Head*
Gallagher, Helen, PhD Sr. Lectr.
Lee, Rosemary, MSc Sr. Lectr.
Meredith, Cathy, BA Open(UK), MPH Glas. Sr. Lectr.
Other Staff: 7 Lectrs.; 1 Clin. Tutor

Risk, Division of

Tel: (0141) 331 3159 Fax: (0141) 331 3229
E-mail: m.louden@gcal.ac.uk
Adams, Jennifer, MPhil Glas., BA Sr. Lectr.
Drennan, Lynn, BA Strath., PhD Glas. Sr. Lectr.; Head*
Ring, Patrick, LLB MSc Sr. Lectr.
Stein, William, PhD G.Caledonian, BA Sr. Lectr.
Thomson, Mary, PhD G.Caledonian Reader
Watson, Alan B., MPhil G.Caledonian, PhD Sr. Lectr.
Webb, Robert, PhD Anglia PU Sr. Lectr.
Other Staff: 11 Lectrs.; 1 Res. Fellow

Social Sciences, Division of

Tel: (0141) 331 3437 Fax: (0141) 331 3439
Charlton, Roger, BSc Sheff., MA Sheff. Reader
Culbert, John, BSc Strath. Sr. Lectr.
Hughes, William G., BA Aberd., PhD Aberd. Sr. Lectr.
Liddell, Peter, BSc Lond., MSc Strath. Sr. Lectr.
McFarland, Elaine, MA Glas., PhD Glas. Reader; Acting Head*
Nottingham, Chris, BA Sheff., MA Sheff., PhD Sheff., DPhil Amst. Sr. Lectr.
Other Staff: 6 Lectrs.

Social Work, Division of

Tel: (0141) 331 3104 Fax: (0141) 331 8130
E-mail: swadmissions@gcal.ac.uk
Brodie, Ian J., BA MPhil Sr. Lectr.
Hooton, Lynne Sr. Lectr.

Kelly, Timothy, PhD Head*
Watson, David, PhD G.Caledonian Sr. Lectr.
Other Staff: 7 Lectrs.

Vision Sciences, Division of

Tel: (0141) 331 3379 Fax: (0141) 331 3387
E-mail: vis@gcal.ac.uk
Button, Norman, BSc G.Caledonian, PhD
G.Caledonian Sr. Lectr.
Doughty, Michael, BSc Lond., MSc Warw., PhD
Lond. Res. Prof.
Dutton, Gordon Res. Prof.
Gray, Lyle, BSc PhD Sr. Lectr.
Heron, Gordon, MSc UMIST, PhD UMIST Sr.
Lectr.
Logvinenko, Alexander Res. Prof.
Manahilov, Velitchko, BSc PhD Reader
McCulloch, Daphne L., OD Wat., PhD Indiana
Reader
Orbach, Harry, PhD Reader
Strang, Niall, BSc PhD Sr. Lectr.
Tomlinson, Alan, BSc Manc., MSc Brad., PhD
Manc., DSc UMIST Prof.; Head*
Walsh, Glyn, BSc UMIST, MSc UMIST, PhD
UMIST Sr. Lectr.
Watson, Lesley, BEd Sr. Lectr.
Other Staff: 9 Lectrs.; 1 Res. Fellow

SPECIAL CENTRES, ETC

Academic Practice Unit

Tel: (0141) 273 1316 Fax: (0141) 273 1318
E-mail: m.warburton@gcal.ac.uk
Drysdale, Jan, BSc Dund., MSc Strath., MBA
Strath. Sr. Lectr.
Other Staff: 1 Lectr.; 1 Learning Technol.
Adviser

Family Enterprise, Centre for

No staff at present

Lifelong Learning, Centre for Research in

Tel: (0141) 273 1347 Fax: (0141) 273 1318
E-mail: crll@gcal.ac.uk
Gallacher, Prof. Jim, MA Glas., MSc Lond.
Head*

Other Staff: 1 Sr. Res. Fellow; 4 Res. Fellows

Open Campus Learning

Tel: (0141) 331 8841 Fax: (0141) 332 8535
E-mail: j.black@gcal.ac.uk
Bissell, Bob, MA Glas. Dir.*
Research: adult guidance; adult literacy and
numeracy; dyslexia; lifelong learning;
student retention

CONTACT OFFICERS

Academic affairs. Head of Academic
Administration: (vacant)
Accommodation. Accommodation Manager:
Lamberton, Angelina, MA G.Caledonian
(E-mail: accommodation@gcal.ac.uk)
Adult/continuing education. Adult Education
Officer: (vacant)
Alumni. Alumni Officer: Martin, Debbie, MA
(E-mail: deborah.martin@gcal.ac.uk)
Archives. Archivist: McCallum, Carole, BA Stir.
(E-mail: c.mccallum@gcal.ac.uk)
Careers. Deputy Head of Student Services
Department: Houston, Deborah
(E-mail: d.houston@gcal.ac.uk)
Computing services. Director of Learning
Resources: Garden, Louise
(E-mail: ithelp@gcal.ac.uk)
Conferences/corporate hospitality.
Conference and Events Manager: James,
Jane (E-mail: jane.james@gcal.ac.uk)
Consultancy services. Dean, Faculty of Science
and Technology: (vacant)
Credit transfer. Academic Co-ordinator: Davis,
Margaret (E-mail: m.davis@gcal.ac.uk)
Development/fund-raising. Development
Officer: (vacant)
Distance education. Workbased Learning and
Research/Development: Nimmo, Alison
Equal opportunities. Executive Director of
Human Resources: Sinclair, Mark
(E-mail: mark.sinclair@gcal.ac.uk)
Estates and buildings/works and services.
Head of Facilities Management: Fraser,
Therese (E-mail: t.fraser@gcal.ac.uk)
Examinations. Registry Manager (Assessment):
Blaber, Jane

Finance. Head of Finance Office: Boyle, John
General enquiries. Schools and Colleges
Liaison Assistant: Meikle, Lisa
(E-mail: lisa.meikle@gcal.ac.uk)
Health services. University Doctor:
MacPherson, Fergus
International office. Head of International
Office: McQuire, Lynn
(E-mail: international@gcal.ac.uk)
Library (chief librarian). Senior Librarian:
(vacant)
Personnel/human resources. Executive
Director of Human Resources: Sinclair,
Mark (E-mail: mark.sinclair@gcal.ac.uk)
Publications. Marketing Communications
Officer: Bell, Marylin
(E-mail: marylin.bell@gcal.ac.uk)
Purchasing. Purchasing Adviser: (vacant)
Quality assurance and accreditation. Director
of Quality: Eadie, Andrew
(E-mail: a.s.eadie@gcal.ac.uk)
Safety. Head of Facilities Management: Fraser,
Therese
Scholarships, awards, loans. Student Funding
Adviser: (vacant)
(E-mail: funding@gcal.ac.uk)
Schools liaison. Schools and Colleges Liaison
Assistant: Meikle, Lisa
(E-mail: l.meikle@gcal.ac.uk)
Sport and recreation. Recreation Manager:
Menzies, Corinne, BA Strath.
(E-mail: c.menzies@gcal.ac.uk)
Staff development and training. Training and
Development Manager: Armstrong, Melanie
Student welfare/counselling. Head of Student
Services: Finnegan, Tom
(E-mail: counselling@gcal.ac.uk)
Students from other countries. Head of
International Office: McQuire, Lynn
(E-mail: international@gcal.ac.uk)
Students with disabilities. Student Adviser:
(vacant) (E-mail: disability@gcal.ac.uk)

[Information supplied by the institution as at 27 July
2006, and edited by the ACU]

UNIVERSITY OF GLOUCESTERSHIRE

Founded 1847

Postal Address: The Park, Cheltenham, Gloucestershire, England GL50 2RH
Telephone: (08707) 210210 **Fax:** (01242) 714433 **E-mail:** admissions@glos.ac.uk
URL: http://www.glos.ac.uk

VICE-CHANCELLOR*—Broadfoot, Prof. Patricia M., CBE, BA Leeds, MEd Edin., PhD Open(UK), DSc Brist.
UNIVERSITY REGISTRAR AND SECRETARY‡—van Rossum, Paul, BScTech Sheff., MA Open(UK), FCIPD

GLYNDWR UNIVERSITY

Postal Address: Plas Coch Campus, Mold Road, Wrexham, Wales LL11 2AW
Telephone: (01978) 290666 **Fax:** (01978) 290008
URL: http://www.glyndwr.ac.uk

CHIEF EXECUTIVE AND PRINCIPAL OF COLLEGE*—Scott, Prof. Michael, BA MA PhD, FRSA

UNIVERSITY OF GREENWICH

Founded 1992

Member of the Association of Commonwealth Universities

Postal Address: Old Royal Naval College, Park Row, Greenwich, London, England SE10 9LS
Telephone: (020) 8331 8000 **Fax:** (020) 8331 8876
URL: http://www.gre.ac.uk

VICE-CHANCELLOR*—Blackstone, Baroness Tessa, BSc(Soc) Lond., PhD Lond.
DEPUTY VICE-CHANCELLOR (RESOURCES)—Wills, Prof. David J., MPhil HK, FRICS
PRO-VICE-CHANCELLOR (LEARNING AND QUALITY)—Noble, Margaret, BA Wales, PhD Hull
PRO-VICE-CHANCELLOR (RESEARCH AND ENTERPRISE)—Humphreys, Prof. John, BSc MSc MEd PhD, FIBiol
SECRETARY AND REGISTRAR TO THE UNIVERSITY‡—Cording, Linda, MA Glas.
DIRECTOR OF STUDENT AFFAIRS—Rose, Christine H., MSc Lond., FRSA, FCMI
DIRECTOR OF FINANCE—Daly, Reginald V.
DIRECTOR OF INFORMATION AND LIBRARY SERVICES—Castens, Maureen E., BSc MA
DIRECTOR OF PERSONNEL—Brockett, R. J., BA Kent, MA Kent

GENERAL INFORMATION

History. The university was founded in 1992.
It was previously established as Thames
Polytechnic (originally founded in 1890 as
Woolwich Polytechnic Young Men's Christian
Institution).

The university has three campuses in
London and Kent.

Admission to first degree courses (see also
United Kingdom Introduction). Through
Universities and Colleges Admissions Service
(UCAS). General Certificate of Secondary
Education (GCSE), or equivalent qualification,
with passes in 3 approved subjects and passes
in 2 subjects at A level. International
applicants: equivalent qualifications. Students
whose first language is not English must
normally pass either English language at GCSE
or an approved test in English (eg IELTS).

First Degrees (see also United Kingdom
Directory to Subjects of Study). BA, BEng, BSc,
LLB, MChem, MEng, MSci.
    Length of course. Full-time: BA: 2–4 years; BSc: 3
years; BEng, LLB: 3–4 years; MChem, MEng,
MSci: 4 years. Part-time: BA, BEng, BSc, LLB,
MChem, MEng, MSci: 5–7 years. By distance
learning: BA, BEng, BSc, LLB, MChem, MEng,
MSci: 5–7 years.

Higher Degrees (see also United Kingdom
Directory to Subjects of Study).
    Master's. LLM, MA, MBA, MEd, MPA, MPhil,
MSc.
    MA, LLM: available as taught and research
degrees.
    Length of course. Full-time: LLM, MA, MBA,
MEd, MPA, MPhil, MSc: 1 year. Part-time: LLM,
MA, MBA, MEd, MPA, MPhil, MSc: 2–3 years.
    Doctoral. EdD, PhD.
    Length of course. Full-time: EdD, PhD: 3 years.
Part-time: EdD, PhD: 5 years.

Libraries. Volumes: 412,757. Periodicals
subscribed to: 5524.

Academic Year (2007–2008). Three terms:
1 October–14 December; 7 January–14 March;
7 April–27 June.

Income (2005–2006). Total, £131,408,000.

Statistics. Staff (2006–2007): 1671 (749
academic, 922 non-academic). Students
(2005–2006): full-time 14,389 (6901 men,
7488 women); part-time 10,453 (4855 men,
5598 women); international 3956 (2631 men,
1325 women); distance education/external
5863 (3292 men, 2571 women);
undergraduate 17,294 (7760 men, 9534
women); master's 7136 (3776 men, 3360
women); doctoral 441 (249 men, 192
women).

ACADEMIC UNITS
Arranged by Schools unless otherwise indicated

Architecture and Construction

Tel: (020) 8331 9100 Fax: (020) 8331 9105
Adeline, Julie A., BSc MSc   Sr. Lectr.
Allan, S., BSc MSc   Principal Lectr.
Berntsen, D.   Sr. Lectr.
Brown, H.   Sr. Lectr.
Bull, G., BA MA DPhil   Sr. Lectr.
Clelford, A. J., BA MSc   Sr. Lectr.
Coffey, M., BSc MSc PhD, FRICS   Sr. Lectr.
Cooper, R. A., BA   Sr. Lectr.
Cummings, M., BA   Sr. Lectr.
Daley, M. V. J., BA   Sr. Lectr.
Dalton, P. M., BSc MSc, FCIOB   Principal
    Lectr.; Dir., Resources
Daniell, Gillian, BA BEng MA   Sr. Lectr.
Delage, Corine C. F., MLA Harv.   Dir.,
    Learning and Quality
Falconer, R. E., BSc MSc   Principal Lectr.
Fantie, Shirley, BSc   Sr. Lectr.
Frith, E. J., BA   Sr. Lectr.
Gilby, H., BA   Sr. Lectr.
Goode, P., MA DPhil   Sr. Lectr.
Graef, A., MSc   Sr. Lectr.
Harrison, Charlotte, BA   Sr. Lectr.
Hayward, R., BArch BA PhD   Head*
Heil, Sybille   Sr. Lectr.
Hirst, Nicola   Sr. Lectr.
Holden, R., BA   Sr. Lectr.
Holder, Ann T., BSc MBA PhD   Principal
    Lectr.
Isaac, D. W. L., BSc(Econ) MSc PhD, FRICS
    Prof.; Dir., Res.
Jobst, Marco, MArch MSc PhD   Principal
    Lectr.
Jones, K. G., BSc PhD   Reader
Kelly, A., BSc MSc   Sr. Lectr.
Kotzen, Benz, BA MA   Sr. Lectr.
Liversedge, J., BA   Sr. Lectr.
McDonald, T., BSc   Principal Lectr.
Pillans, G. N., BSc PhD   Sr. Lectr.
Powers, A.   Reader
Rhoden, Maureen D., MA   Sr. Lectr.
Rosling, Robert, BA   Sr. Lectr.
Scott, Fred   Sr. Lectr.
Seijo, R. E.   Sr. Lectr.
Shokoohy, M., BArch MArch MSc PhD DSc
    Prof.
Stoppani, T., DrArch DrRic   Sr. Lectr.
Titman, Mark, BA   Sr. Lectr.
Tuckey, Jonathan, BA   Sr. Lectr.
Turner, T. H. D., MA   Principal Lectr.
Wagner, Franziska   Principal Lectr.
Watson, D.   Sr. Lectr.
Watson, J., BSc MA   Sr. Lectr.
Weisser, Cordula, MSc
Other Staff: 2 Res. Fellows

Business

Fax: (020) 8331 9003
Allen, C. J., MSc MBA   Sr. Lectr.
Andrescu, A. F., CM, BSc MSc   Sr. Lectr.

Atkinson, M., MA   Sr. Lectr.
Ayres, R. I., BA(Econ) MSc PhD   Prof.; Head
    of Economics
Barry, T., BSc MBA   Sr. Lectr.
Baynes, P. T., BA MA   Dir., Resources; Deputy
    Head
Booth, E., MA   Sr. Lectr.
Brady, N., BA MA MBA   Sr. Lectr.
Cagliesi, M. G., BSc MSc PhD   Principal Lectr.
Catchpowle, Leslie J., BA MSc PhD   Principal
    Lectr.
Chen, J., BSc MBA   Sr. Lectr.
Corby, Susan R., BA MA   Reader
Cronin, B., MA PhD   Sr. Lectr.; Dir., Postgrad.
    Programmes
Cullinane, J., BMS MMS PhD   Sr. Lectr.
De Domenici, M. C., BA MA   Sr. Lectr.
De Mel, Sandy, MA   Sr. Lectr.
Dennison, P. H., BSc MBA   Principal Lectr.
Edmunds, M. D., BSc MA PhD   Principal
    Lectr.; Dir., Learning and Quality
Evans, A., BA MSc   Sr. Lectr.; Head,
    Marketing
Farinas Almeida, M., BA MSc   Sr. Lectr.
Ghanei, M., BSc MSc   Sr. Lectr.
Gould, J. J., BA MA MBA   Principal Lectr.
Halicioglu, R. F., BSc MSc PhD   Sr. Lectr.,
    Economics
Hall, D. J., BA BPhil MA
Hallam, G., BA MSc
Hand, N. G., BComm MSc   Principal Lectr.
Hearne, W., BSc MSc   Prof./Principal Lectr.
Hickman, S. P., MBA   Sr. Lectr.
Holden, P. R., BSc MA   Sr. Lectr.
Holtom, K., BA MA   Sr. Lectr.
Hopwood, J. M., BA MA   Sr. Lectr.
Housden, M. J., BA   Sr. Lectr.
Huang, Jing   Sr. Lectr.
Hughes, D. A., BEd MSc   Principal Lectr.
Hugill, C. W., BSc   Sr. Lectr.
Jarrar, R., BSc MSc PhD   Sr. Lectr.
Johnson, L., BA PhD   Prof.; Head*
Jones, C. A., MA   Principal Lectr.
Kandler, A. C., BA MA   Sr. Lectr.
Kelly, C., BA PhD   Sr. Lectr.
Khoe, M., MSc   Sr. Lectr.
Kirkby, M. E. P., BA MA MBA   Sr. Lectr.
Kitromilides, Y., BSc MA PhD   Principal Lectr.
Kuenzel, S., BA MA PhD   Sr. Lectr.
Laycock, M., MBA   Sr. Lectr.
Lewis, B. K., BSc   Sr. Lectr.
Lin, X., BA MA   Sr. Lectr.
Macleod, N., MA   Sr. Lectr.
Madonia, G., PhD
Mambu Ma Khenzu, E., MSc PhD   Sr. Lectr.
Mateus, C.   Sr. Lectr.
Mayne, Daphne M., MA   Sr. Lectr.
Mayor, R. J., BSc MBA   Principal Lectr.;
    Head, Management Dept.
Mundy, J., BSc MBA PhD   Sr. Lectr.
Murayama, M.   Sr. Lectr.
Owen, G. N., BA   Sr. Lectr.
Qi, Hantang, BSc PhD   Sr. Lectr.
Rajah, K. K., BSc MSc PhD   Sr. Lectr.
Riley, J., BSc MSc   Sr. Lectr.

Rock, C., BSc MBA   Sr. Lectr.
Ryan, Bernadette A. B., BA MBA   Sr. Lectr.
Saidi, L.   Sr. Lectr.
Saint Hilaire, Antoinette, BSc MBA PhD   Sr. Lectr.
Sevic, Z., LLB LLM MSc PhD   Prof.; Dir. of Res.
Shaw, R. I., BA   Sr. Lectr.
Slater, Alix C. J., BA   Sr. Lectr.
Smith, Melanie K., BA MSc   Sr. Lectr.
Smullen, J., BSc MSc MA MBA   Sr. Lectr.
Spencer-Wood, J. E., MSc   Sr. Lectr.
Stanworth, Celia, BSc MA PhD   Reader
Strojanovic, A., BSc MSc MBA PhD   Sr. Lectr.
Stubbs, J.   Sr. Lectr.
Tilley, I., BComm MSc PhD   Reader
Tsahuridu, E. E., BA MBA PhD   Sr. Lectr.
Ugur, M., BSc MSc PhD   Reader; Principal Lectr.
Veersma, U., MA PhD   Sr. Lectr.
Vellam, Iwona, BA   Principal Lectr.
White, G. K., BA MA   Prof. (on leave)
Wild, N., BSc MA   Sr. Lectr.
Wilde, N. P., BA MA   Sr. Lectr.
Williams, D. E., BA MA   Sr. Lectr.
Williams, N., BA MA   Sr. Lectr.
Williamson, P.   Sr. Lectr.
Yeshin, A. D., BScComm BSc(Econ)   Sr. Lectr.
Zhou, L.   Sr. Lectr.
Other Staff: 19 Lectrs.; 2 Teachers; 4 Sr. Res. Fellows; 1 Res. Fellow; 4 Sr. Lectrs.†

Computing and Mathematical Sciences

Tel: (020) 8331 8503 Fax: (020) 8331 8665
E-mail: cmsinfo@greenwich.ac.uk
Ackroyd, A., MA MSc   Principal Lectr.
Ades, Y., BSc MSc   Sr. Lectr.
Al-Zobaidie, A., BSc MSc PhD   Principal Lectr.
Anthony, R. J., BSc DPhil   Sr. Lectr.
Bacon, Elizabeth A., BSc PhD   Head*
Bainbridge, Brian, BA BSc DPhil   Sr. Lectr.
Brass, C. B., BEd MSc   Sr. Lectr.
Butler, A. R., BSc MSc   Sr. Lectr.
Chadwick, D. R., BSc   Sr. Lectr.
Chen, A., MSc PhD   Principal Lectr.
Clipsham, P. S., BSc   Principal Lectr.
Cowell, D. F., BSc PhD   Sr. Lectr.
Cumpson, I., BSc   Sr. Lectr.
Dastbaz, M., BSc PhD   Principal Lectr.; Head, Information Systems
Dench, P., BSc   Sr. Lectr.
Dolden, B., BSc MA   Sr. Lectr.; Dir., Learning and Quality
Edwards, D., BSc PhD, FRAS   Sr. Lectr.
Fedorec, A. M., BSc, FIMA, FBCS   Sr. Lectr.
Finney, Kate, BSc MSc PhD   Principal Lectr.
Flynn, Ryan, BSc   Sr. Lectr.
Galea, E., BSc PhD, FIMA, FRAS   Prof.; Dir., Res.
Gan, Diane E., BSc DPhil   Sr. Lectr.
Ibrahim, M., BSc MSc   Principal Lectr.
Ierotheou, C. S., BSc PhD, FIMA   Reader
Jones, R. A. C., BA MA   Principal Lectr.
Kiernan, Mary, BSc MSc   Sr. Lectr.
Knight, Joan, BEd MSc   Sr. Lectr.
Koulopoulos, C., BSc MSc PhD   Sr. Lectr.
Lai, C.-H., BSc PhD, FIMA   Prof.
Ma, Chaoying, BEng PhD   Sr. Lectr.
Ma, Jixin, BSc MA MSc PhD   Reader
Major, Elaine, BSc   Principal Lectr.
Malcolm, Jan M., BSc   Sr. Lectr.
Mann, A. J. S., MA   Sr. Lectr.; Head, Mathl. Scis.
McKenzie, Sati, BSc MSc PhD   Principal Lectr.
McManus, K.   Sr. Lectr.
Morris, P. N., BSc MSc   Principal Lectr.
Newbutt, Nigel, BSc   Sr. Lectr.
Njovu, C., BSc MSc PhD   Sr. Lectr.
Parrott, A. K., MA PhD   Prof.; Dir., Resources
Patel, M. K., BSc MSc PhD, FIMA   Reader
Pericleous, K., BSc PhD   Prof.
Peter, Sophie, BSc MSc   Sr. Lectr.
Petridis, M., MSc PhD   Reader; Head, Computer Sci.
Ramesh, N. I., BSc DPhil   Sr. Lectr.
Rennolls, K., BSc MSc   Prof.
Smith, P. A., BEng MSc   Principal Lectr.
Soper, A. J., BA MSc PhD   Sr. Lectr.

Stanley, A. J., BA MSc   Sr. Lectr.
Stoneham, R., BSc PhD   Principal Lectr.
Strusevich, V., PhD   Prof.
Sue, R. E., BSc MSc PhD   Principal Lectr.
Tambyrajah, A., BSc MSc PhD   Principal Lectr.
Valsamidis, A. P. B., BA MSc   Sr. Lectr.
Windall, G., BSc MSc   Sr. Lectr.
Woollard, C. C., BSc PhD   Principal Lectr.
Other Staff: 18 Sr. Res. Fellows; 1 Teacher; 14 Res. Fellows

Education and Training

Tel: (020) 8331 9500 Fax: (020) 8331 9504
Ade-Ojo, G., BA MA   Sr. Lectr.
Ainley, P. J. D., BA PhD   Prof.
Aldridge, H.   Sr. Lectr.
Bailey, S., BEd   Sr. Lectr.
Barnard, J., BSc MSc PhD   Sr. Lectr.
Bath, D.   Sr. Lectr.
Bland, R., BA MA   Sr. Lectr.
Bloor, M., BSc MSc   Sr. Lectr.
Bourne, D.   Sr. Lectr.
Bradley, S., BEd   Sr. Lectr.
Brunskell-Evans, Heather, BA MA   Sr. Lectr.
Carpenter, A., BA MA   Sr. Lectr.
Choak, C., BA   Sr. Lectr.
Colquhorn, Susan, BA MA   Sr. Lectr.
Cox, Anne, BSc MA   Principal Lectr.
Cranwell, K., BSc MA   Sr. Lectr.
Crisp, M., BA MA   Sr. Lectr.
Davies, R., BA MA   Sr. Lectr.
Dixon, Lynne, BA MA   Sr. Lectr.
Durrell, J., BEd   Sr. Lectr.
Evans, K., BA   Sr. Lectr.
Farmer, G. T., BA MSc MBA   Principal Lectr.; Head, Educn. and Community Studies
Farr, Jackie, BEd MA   Sr. Lectr.
Field, Jennifer, BEd   Sr. Lectr.
Flynn, A., BEd   Sr. Lectr.
Freedman, Elizabeth, BA   Sr. Lectr.
Freeman, A., BEd MSc   Sr. Lectr.
Garner, L., BA PhD   Sr. Lectr.
Gibson, A. J., MEd   Sr. Lectr.
Goddard, W. D., BEd MEd MPhil   Principal Lectr.; Head, Educn. Leadership and Devel.
Golden, J. W., BHum MA   Principal Lectr.
Good, K. W., BEd   Sr. Lectr.
Grant, Pat, BEd MSc   Principal Lectr.
Gravelle, Margaret R., BA MA   Sr. Lectr.
Gregory, P., MA   Sr. Lectr.
Hall, N., MEd PhD   Principal Lectr.
Hallmond, S., BSc   Sr. Lectr.
Headington, Rita, BEd MA   Sr. Lectr.
Hilditch, Felicity, MA   Principal Lectr.; Head, Dept. of Primary Educn.
Hornsby, Rosamund M., BSc   Sr. Lectr.
Huish, Barbara, MA   Principal Lectr.
Jameson, Jill, BA MA PhD   Principal Lectr.
Kazim, R., BSc MSc   Sr. Lectr.
Kilderry, A., BA MEd   Sr. Lectr.
Kinchington, Francia, BEd MA EdPsychD   Principal Lectr., Postgraduate Professional Development
Kitchener, I.   Sr. Lectr.
Kotecha, K., MBA MA   Sr. Lectr.
Leahong, T., BSc   Sr. Lectr.
Leggatt, S., BA   Sr. Lectr.
Martin, Mary-Clare, PhD   Sr. Lectr.
McKelvey, C., MA   Sr. Lectr.
McNay, Iain, BA   Prof.
Meers, Tricia, BSc MA PhD   Head*
Mindel, Carla, BA MA   Sr. Lectr.
Morgan, R., BA MA   Sr. Lectr.
Morrison, E., BSc PhD   Sr. Lectr.
Orpin, H., BA   Sr. Lectr.
Page, D., BA   Sr. Lectr.
Parsons, J., BEd MA   Sr. Lectr.
Partridge, T., BA   Sr. Lectr.
Patterson, J., BA PhD   Sr. Lectr.
Philpott, C., BEd MA   Principal Lectr.; Head, Dept. of Secondary Educn.
Randall, C., BEng   Sr. Lectr.
Rawlinson, Christine, BEd MA   Sr. Lectr.
Reeves, C. G., BHum MEd PhD   Principal Lectr.
Reynolds, D.   Sr. Lectr.
Ross, H., BSc   Sr. Lectr.
Rowlands, D., MA MSc   Sr. Lectr.

Ryan, M., MEd   Principal Lectr.
Saridogan, Alison, BHumS MA   Sr. Lectr.
Sidorenko, E., BA PhD   Sr. Lectr.
Smith, J., BA MA PhD   Sr. Lectr.
Smith, Penny A., BEd   Sr. Lectr.
Smith, S., BA   Sr. Lectr.
Speare, Jane, BA MA   Sr. Lectr.
Steele, Susanna, MA   Sr. Lectr.
Tanish, Y., BSc   Sr. Lectr.
Taylor, Janet, BA MA   Sr. Lectr.
Tharia, S., BEd   Sr. Lectr.
Thomas, S. D., BSc MSc   Sr. Lectr.
Walker, S. H., BA MA   Principal Lectr.
Watmore, J., BA MA   Sr. Lectr.
Webb, M., BEd   Sr. Lectr.

Engineering

Tel: (01634) 883495 Fax: (01634) 883153
E-mail: eng-courseinfo@greenwich.ac.uk
Archer, S. J., BA MBA   Sr. Lectr.
Armour-Chelu, D. I., BEng PhD   Principal Lectr.
Ashenden, S. J., BSc PhD   Principal Lectr.; Dir., Resources and Recruitment
Bakalis, P., BSc MSc PhD   Sr. Lectr.
Baker, G., MA MEng   Sr. Lectr.
Beams, R., BA Open(UK)   Sr. Lectr.
Benterkia, Z., MSc PhD   Sr. Lectr.
Bhatti, R. S., BSc MSc PhD   Principal Lectr.
Bingley, M. S., BSc PhD   Sr. Lectr.
Butler, M. D., BSc MSc PhD   Principal Lectr.
Clements, M. M., BSc   Sr. Lectr.
Coutroubis, A. D., BSc MSc MBA DBA PhD, FIMarEST   Principal Lectr.; Visiting Prof.
Doncheva, Radi, MSc   Sr. Lectr.
Ekere, N., BEng MSc PhD, FIEE   Prof.; Head*
Essop, I., BSc MSc   Sr. Lectr.
Frankland, J. W., MSc   Sr. Lectr.
Gao, J. X., PhD   Prof.
Grant, A., BSc Glas.   Principal Lectr.; Dir., Learning and Quality
Harireche, O., BEng MSc PhD   Sr. Lectr.
Hettiaratchi, K., BEng PhD   Sr. Lectr.
Ho, Tan K., BScEng MSc   Sr. Lectr.
Huang, K.-C., BSc MEng PhD   Sr. Lectr.
Israel, D. J., BEng   Sr. Lectr.
Jenner, R., BEng PhD   Sr. Lectr.
Kang, I., BEng MSc   Sr. Lectr.
Li, Chun-Qing, BEng MSc PhD   Prof.; Head, Dept. of Civil Engin.
Mandlik, J., BScEng   Sr. Lectr.
McKillop, D., BSc MSc MBA DMS   Sr. Lectr.
Rapajic, P., BE ME PhD   Prof.
Reed, A. R., BSc PhD, FIMechE   Prof.
Seals, R. C., BSc PhD   Principal Lectr.
Sharp, M. W., BEd   Principal Lectr.
Smith, M. J., BSc MSc   Principal Lectr.
Snelling, P. D., BEng MPhil   Sr. Lectr.
Wetherall, J., BEng   Sr. Lectr.
Whapshott, Grazyna F., MSc   Sr. Lectr.
Woodhead, S. R., BSc PhD   Dir., Res. and Enterprise; Reader, Computer Systems and Networks
Wu, R., BEng MEng PhD   Sr. Lectr.
Zhou, X., BEng MEng PhD   Sr. Lectr.
Other Staff: 3 Lectrs.; 1 Sr. Res. Fellow; 3 Res. Fellows

Greenwich Maritime Institute

Tel: (020) 8331 7688 Fax: (020) 8331 7690
E-mail: gmi@gre.ac.uk
Palmer, Sarah, BA Durh., MA Indiana, PhD Lond., FRSA, FRHistS   Prof., Maritime History; Dir.*

Health and Social Care

Tel: (020) 8331 9151 Fax: (020) 8331 8060
Alexander, Victoria, MSc Greenwich   Sr. Lectr.
Allen, Carol, BA Open(UK)   Sr. Lectr.
Allen, Patricia J., MSc S.Bank   Sr. Lectr.
Baxter, Lynn C., MA Lond.   Sr. Lectr.
Beeby, Jayne, BSc MSc   Sr. Lectr.
Billington, Mary, BA York(UK), MSc Manc.   Principal Lectr.; Lead Midwife for Educn.
Blaber, Amanda Y., BSc Oxf.Brookes, MSc Greenwich   Sr. Lectr.
Bowden, Julie, BSc Greenwich, MSc Sur.   Sr. Lectr.

Bruneau, Ben, BA Open(UK), MSc Greenwich Sr. Lectr.
Brunswic, Myriam, MSc Lond. Sr. Lectr.
Chandler, Karen, MSc Cant. Sr. Lectr.
Chojnacka, Irena, BSc Greenwich Principal Lectr.
Chummun, N. Harry, BSc Greenwich, PhD Greenwich Sr. Lectr.
Cleaver, Karen P., BEd S.Bank, MSc S.Bank Principal Lectr.; Head, Family Care and Mental Health
Cork, Alison D., BSc Greenwich, MSc Greenwich, MA Greenwich Sr. Lectr.
Corney, Rosalyn H., BSc Manc., MSc Lond., MSc Lond., PhD Lond. Prof.
Cornish, Yvonne, BA Sus., MSc Brist., PhD City(UK) Principal Lectr.
Crapnell, Denis, BEd CNAA, MSc Lond.Guild. Principal Lectr.; Dir., Resources and Health Services Liaison
Crowley, Colm, MA Antioch, MSc Lond. Sr. Lectr.
Crowley, John J., BA E.Lond., BSc Greenwich, MSc Lond. Sr. Lectr.
Dale, Zoe, MA E.Lond. Sr. Lectr.
Dalton-O'Connor, Ann M., BSc Manc. Sr. Lectr.
Delaney, Ros, BSc Manc. Sr. Lectr.
Demetre, James D., BA Sheff., PhD Strath. Sr. Lectr.
Dike, Priscilla, BSc City(UK), MSc Lond. Sr. Lectr., Midwifery
Ferns, Terry, BSc Manc., MA Greenwich Sr. Lectr.
Fowler, Nicki, MSc Kent Principal Lectr.
French, Carolyn, MSc Sur., PhD Sur. Sr. Lectr.
Fuller, Elizabeth, BA Greenwich Sr. Lectr.
Gale, Elizabeth A., BSc Greenwich Sr. Lectr.
George, Mildred E. R., BSc Greenwich Sr. Lectr.
Gill, Anne, BSc S.Bank, MSc Northumbria Sr. Lectr.
Goble, Colin, BA Portsmouth, MSc Portsmouth Sr. Lectr.
Gousy, Mamood H., BEd Greenwich, MSc S.Bank Principal Lectr.
Grainger, Claire, BSc Manc. Sr. Lectr.
Habgood, Veronica A., BSc Salf. Principal Lectr.; Dir., Learning and Quality
Hardath, Geeta, BSc Greenwich, MA Greenwich Sr. Lectr.
Heptinstall, Tina, BSc S'ton., MSc S.Bank Sr. Lectr.
Hocking, Avril, BSc Greenwich Sr. Lectr.
Hunter, Lis, BSc Lond. Sr. Lectr.
Ibe, Jude C. W., BA Lond., MSc Lond. Principal Lectr.
Jackson, Patricia A., BA Leeds Sr. Lectr.
Jump, Lynne, BSc E.Lond., MA Open(UK) Sr. Lectr.
Jump, Richard, MSc Greenwich Sr. Lectr.
Knight, Anneyce E., BA Greenwich, MSc Kent Sr. Lectr.
Lees, John, BA Camb., MA Camb., PhD Greenwich Sr. Lectr.
Lewis, Tina, BSc Anglia PU Sr. Lectr.
Longstaff, Mitchell G., BSc Newcastle(NSW), PhD Newcastle(NSW) Sr. Lectr.
Lutchman, S. Anita Sr. Lectr.
Maharajh, Asha, MSc Sur. Sr. Lectr.
Maras, Pamela F., BA Kent, PhD Kent Principal Lectr./Reader; Head, Psychol. and Counselling
Marriott, Mike, BA Camb., MA Lond. Sr. Lectr.
McArdle, Simon, BA Sheff.Hallam Sr. Lectr.
McKeown, M. M. Olive, MSc S.Bank, PhD Kent Sr. Lectr.
McMahon, Teresa, BSc Greenwich Sr. Lectr.
McNaught, Allan G., BSc CNAA, MPhil CNAA, PhD Keele Sr. Lectr.
Meek, Rhona, BA Manc., MA Keele Sr. Lectr.
Meerabeau, Elizabeth, BSc Sur., MBA Lond., PhD Lond. Prof.; Head*
Mehmet, Nevin, BSc Greenwich Sr. Lectr.
Mitchelmore, Mandy, BA Thames V., MSc City(UK), MSc Greenwich Sr. Lectr.
Monks, Claire, BSc Lond., MSc Reading, PhD Reading Sr. Lectr.

Montgomery, Anthony M. J., BSc Lond., MSc Exe., DPhil Sus. Principal Lectr./Reader
Morgan, Mary, BSc Lond., BSc Greenwich, MA Greenwich Sr. Lectr.
Mounty, Maureen, BSc Greenwich, MSc Kent Principal Lectr.; Head, Health Devel.
Narramore, Naomi P., MA Cant.CCC Sr. Lectr.
O'Gorman, Josephine, BA Newcastle(UK), MSc Lond. Sr. Lectr.
O'Reilly, Nuala, BA Middx., MSc Sr. Lectr.
Pass, Pat, BSc Lond. Principal Lectr.
Patchay, Sandhi, BSc Aix-Marseilles, MSc Aix-Marseilles, PhD Aix-Marseilles Sr. Lectr.
Patel, Swatee, MSc S'ton. Principal Lectr.
Payne, Julie A., MSc Westminster Sr. Lectr.
Perez-Navarro, Jose M., BSc Valencia, PhD Coventry Sr. Lectr.
Ramnawaz, Sheila, BA Middx. Sr. Lectr.
Rankin, Sandra, MSc G.Caledonian Sr. Lectr.
Redfern, Morag, BSc Sur., MA Greenwich Principal Lectr.
Reeves, Jane E., BA Lanc., MPhil Kent, PhD Open(UK) Sr. Lectr.
Rich, Ann B., BSc Manc. Sr. Lectr.
Robinson, Oliver, MPhil Lond., MSc Nott., MA Edin. Sr. Lectr.
Scott, Janet M., BA Otago, MSc Edin., MA Kent, PhD Kent Sr. Lectr.
Shepherd, Jean M., MSc City(UK) Sr. Lectr.
Sims, David, BA Kingston(UK), MA Lond. Principal Lectr.
Spender, Linda, BSc Open(UK), MSc Lond. Sr. Lectr.
Spittles, Heather A., BSc Greenwich Principal Lectr.; Head, Acute and Continuing Care
Stacey, Christine G., BSc Greenwich Sr. Lectr.
Stevenson, Mandy J., BSc Lond., MSc S.Bank, MA Brighton Sr. Lectr.
Stewart, Jill L., BSc Greenwich, MSc Brist., PhD Greenwich Sr. Lectr.
Stimpson, Quentin, MSc Sus. Principal Lectr.
Stokes, Jane, BA Camb., MPhil City(UK) Sr. Lectr.
Street, Paul A., BSc Lond., MSc Greenwich, EdD Greenwich Principal Lectr.
Sumoreeah, Lyn, MSc Greenwich Principal Lectr.
Thatcher, Janet L., BA Manc. Sr. Lectr.
Thomas, Raja K., BA E.Lond., MSc Lond. Principal Lectr.
Thorne, Linda, MA Sus. Principal Lectr.
Townsend, J. Phillip, BSc Lond.Met. Sr. Lectr.
Veeramah, R. Ven., BSc Lond., MSc Lond., MSc Open(UK), PhD Greenwich Principal Lectr.
Walia, Surinder, MA Greenwich, BSc Sr. Lectr.
Wallman, Jill L., BA Keele, MBA Greenwich Sr. Lectr.
Webb, Janet S., BEd Sus., MSc Greenwich Sr. Lectr.
West, Liz, BSc Edin., MSc Calif., MA Cornell, PhD Cornell Prof.; Dir., Res.
Whitnell, Jacqueline, BSc E.Lond., MA Greenwich Sr. Lectr.
Willson, Rob, BSc Dal., MA Br.Col., PhD Br.Col. Sr. Lectr.
Winter, Claire, BEd Greenwich Sr. Lectr.
Woodward, Lynn, MA Greenwich Sr. Lectr.
Woodward, Peter, MSc Lond. Sr. Lectr.
Wright, Kerri, BSc Lond., MA Greenwich Sr. Lectr.
Yare, Brinley Sr. Lectr.
Yaskey, Jackie, BA Hull Sr. Lectr.
Other Staff: 3 Lectrs.; 4 Sr. Res. Fellows; 6 Clin. Lectrs.; 12 Hon. Lectrs.
Vacant Posts: 5 Sr. Lectrs.

Humanities

Tel: (020) 8331 8800 Fax: (020) 8331 8805
E-mail: humanities@gre.ac.uk
Acton, Thomas A., MA DPhil Prof.
Adil, Alev, BSc MA Principal Lectr.; Head, Creative, Critical and Communicn. Studies
Alsford, Mike, BA PhD
Alsford, Sally, BA PhD
Baillie, Justine, BA MA PhD
Balshaw, June, BA MA PhD Principal Lectr.
Bavidge, Jenny, BA MA PhD
Bell, Louise

Benati, Alessandro, PhD DottLett Principal Lectr.; Head, Lang. and Internat. Studies
Bowles, Michael J., BA MA PhD Sr. Lectr.
Brown, Carolyn M. H., BA MA PhD Sr. Lectr.
Campbell, Noel, BA MA PhD Sr. Lectr.
Cannon, Margaret J., LLB Sr. Lectr.
Cannon, Terence G., BA MSc MPhil Reader
Clarke, Sandra Sr. Lectr.
Cormack, Anne, PhD
Dasgupta, Nandini, BA MA MPhil PhD Reader; Dir., Res.
Davies, Rosamund
Dawson, Andrew, BScEcon PhD Principal Lectr.
Derbyshire, Harry, BA PhD
Devlin, Fiona M. E., BD Sr. Lectr.
Dunne, John, BA MA PhD
Dye, Simon, MA
Everett, Kim, LLB Principal Lectr.
Gaborak, Margaret J., LLB LLM Sr. Lectr.
Golding, Sue, BA MA PhD Prof.
Goulbourne, Selina, LLB LLM Head, Law
Greer, Sarah J., BA MA Sr. Lectr.
Guard, Pippa, BA
Hanmore, Lynne Sr. Lectr.
Harrison, Rebecca J., BA MA DPhil Sr. Lectr.
Healey, Suzanne M., LèsL MA Sr. Lectr.
Howe, Leonie, PhD Sr. Lectr.
Humble, Kristian
Humm, Peter, BA MPhil Sr. Lectr.; Head, Engl. and Performance Studies
Jackson, Martin, BSc Sr. Lectr.
Jones, Kathleen R., BA MA PhD Sr. Lectr.
Jones, Peter, BA PhD Principal Lectr.; Dir., Learning and Quality
Kaspersson, Maria Sr. Lectr.
Kennedy, Stephen, BA PhD Sr. Lectr.
Langan, Michael, BA MA PhD
Laval, Cecile Sr. Lectr.
Laycock, Angela, BA LLB LLM Sr. Lectr.
Leach, Bridget, BA MEd Sr. Lectr.
Lund, Sian
Manz, Stefan, BA MA PhD Sr. Lectr.
McClean, Mairead, BA Reader
McLean, John
Moodley, Devadas D. S., BA Sr. Lectr.
Morris, Craig
Ottley, Mike, LLB LLM Sr. Lectr.
Pawlowska, Chrisoulla, LLB Sr. Lectr.
Pawlowski, Mark, LLB Prof.
Pettit, Zoe Sr. Lectr.
Phillips, Edward P., LLB Principal Lectr.
Rowland, Susan A., MA PhD Reader
Ryan, M. C., BA MA Prof.
Sigthorsson, Gauti, MA PhD
Sinaniotis, Dimitrios, PhD
Smith, Caroline
Smyth, Cherry Sr. Lectr.
Stanton, Sylvia, MA Sr. Lectr.
Stuart, Doug I., BA MA PhD Head, Sociol., Criminology and Cultural Studies
Thompson, I.
Tsukada Bright, Bob
Urpeth, Jim R., BA PhD Sr. Lectr.
Wild, Richard, BA PhD Sr. Lectr.
Williams, John R., BA DPhil Prof.
Yeatman, Lucy, BA LLM Sr. Lectr.
Zell, M. L., BA MA PhD Reader
Other Staff: 6 Sr. Lectrs.; 21 Lectrs.
Research: British, European and world history since 1500; English literature and theory; languages and international studies; media and performing arts; modern European philosophy

Natural Resources Institute (NRI)

Tel: (020) 8331 9800 Fax: (020) 8331 9805
E-mail: nri@greenwich.ac.uk
Belmain, S. R., BA MSc PhD Sr. Scientist
Bennett, C. J., BA MSocSc Principal Economist
Bostock, T. W., BSc MSc Principal Scientist
Burt, P. A., BSc PhD Principal Scientist
Chancellor, T. C. B., BA MSc PhD Principal Scientist
Cheke, R. A., BSc PhD Prof.; Principal Scientist
Cherry, A., BSc MSc PhD Principal Scientist

Colvin, J., BA MSc MA PhD   Principal
  Scientist
Conroy, M. A., BA MSc   Reader; Principal
  Scientist
Cooper, J. F., BSc MSc   Principal Scientist
Coote, Hilary C., BA BSc MSc   Principal
  Scientist
Cork, A., BSc MSc PhD   Reader; Principal
  Scientist
Coulter, J. P., MBA   Principal Economist
Dobson, Hans, BSc MSc   Principal Scientist
Downham, M. C. A., BSc MSc PhD   Sr.
  Scientist
Farman, D. I.   Sr. Scientist
Gibson, R. W., BSc PhD   Principal Scientist
Graffham, A. J., BSc PhD   Sr. Scientist
Grzywacz, D., BSc   Principal Scientist
Hall, D., BA PhD   Prof.; Principal Scientist
Hillocks, R. J., BSc MSc PhD   Principal
  Scientist
Hodges, R. J., BSc PhD   Reader; Principal
  Scientist
Holt, J. G., BSc PhD   Sr. Scientist
Kleih, U. K., MSc   Principal Scientist
Lamboll, R. I., BSc MSc   Principal Scientist
Legg, J. P., MA PhD   Sr. Scientist
Linton, J.   Dir., Commercial
Martin, Adrienne M., BA   Principal Scientist
Morton, J. F., BA PhD   Principal Scientist
Nelson, Valerie J., BA MSc   Sr. Scientist
Nicolaides, Linda, MPhil   Principal Scientist
Onumah, G. E., BSc MSc PhD   Sr. Scientist
Orchard, J. E., BSc PhD   Principal Scientist
Orr, A. W., MA MSc PhD   Principal Scientist
Parnell, M., MSc   Sr. Scientist
Poulter, R. G., BSc PhD   Principal Scientist;
  Dir.*
Quan, J. F., BA MSc   Principal Scientist
Rees, Deborah, BA DPhil   Principal Scientist
Riches, Charlie, BSc MSc PhD   Principal
  Scientist
Ridgway, R. B., BSc PhD   Principal Scientist
Russell, D. A., BSc MA PhD   Principal Scientist
Stathers, Tanya E., BSc MSc   Sr. Scientist
Sutherland, A. J., MPhil PhD   Principal
  Scientist
Tomlins, K. I., BSc MPhil   Principal Scientist
Torr, S., BSc MSc PhD   Principal Scientist
Westby, A., BSc PhD   Principal Scientist; Dir.,
  Res.; Prof., Food Technology

Pharmacy, Medway School of

Tel: (01634) 883150 Fax: (01634) 883413
Calzolai, Luigi, PhD   Sr. Lectr.
Cumming, K. Iain, MRPharmS PhD   Prof.;
  Head*
Dodds, Linda, BPharm MPharmSc   Sr. Lectr.
Gibbs, Bernard, PhD   Sr. Lectr.
Keating, Min, MPharmSc DMS   Sr. Lectr.
Mathie, Alistair, PhD   Dir., Res.; Prof.,
  Pharmacology/Electrophysiology
Nokhodchi, A., PhD   Sr. Lectr.
Paget, T., PhD   Reader
Other Staff: 10 Lectrs.; 4 Teaching
  Practitioners; 11 Clin. Lectrs.
Research: medicines management and
  pharmaceutical technology

Science

Tel: (020) 8331 9800 Fax: (020) 8331 9805
  E-mail: sciencequeries@gre.ac.uk
Acott, T. G., BSc PhD   Principal Lectr.
Amuna, P., MD   Sr. Lectr.
Benee, L., BSc PhD   Sr. Lectr.
Bishop, A. H., BSc PhD   Sr. Lectr.
Blackburn, R., BSc MSc PhD   Head, Life and
  Sports Sciences
Burt, P. A., BSc PhD   Principal Scientist
Carey, Paula J., BSc PhD, FGS   Principal Lectr.
Chowdhry, B. Z., BSc MSc PhD   Prof.
Dyer, P., BSc MSc   Sr. Lectr.
Edwards, M., BSc MSc PhD   Sr. Lectr.
El Daher, S., BSc PhD   Sr. Lectr.

Evans, I. H., BSc MSc PhD   Reader
Goss-Sampson, M. A., MA PhD   Principal
  Lectr.
Habtemariam, S., BSc MSc PhD   Sr. Lectr.
Haggart, B. A., MS PhD   Sr. Lectr.
Harbige, L. S., BSc PhD   Reader
Harvey, Patricia J., BSc PhD   Prof.; Dir.,
  Resources
Hills, C. D., BSc PhD, FGS   Reader
Karsten, Bettina, BSc   Sr. Lectr.
Knight, S., BSc MSc PhD   Sr. Lectr.
Leach, M. J., PhD   Reader
Leharne, S. A., BSc PhD   Prof.
McGibbon, M. J., BA MA PhD   Principal
  Lectr.
Mitchell, J., BSc MSc PhD   Prof.; Head,
  Medway Scis.
Newbery, J. E., BSc MA PhD, FRSChem
  Principal Lectr.; Head*
Nicholson, J., BSc MSc PhD   Prof.
Pecorino, Lauren, BSc PhD   Sr. Lectr.
Pollard, Lucie, BSc PhD   Sr. Lectr.; Dir.,
  Learning and Quality
Rahman, M. A., BSc MSc PhD   Sr. Lectr.
Richardson, S., BSc MSc PhD   Sr. Lectr.
Simon, Richie, BSc MSc PhD   Principal Lectr.
Snowden, M. J., BSc MSc PhD   Prof.; Dir.,
  Res.
Spencer, J., PhD   Reader
Strickland, Jenny, BSc   Sr. Lectr.
Swan-Wallis, J., BSc PhD   Sr. Lectr.
Thomas, M. J. K., BSc PhD, FRSChem   Head,
  Chem. Pharm. Sci. and Environmental Sci.
Todd, M., BSc PhD   Sr. Lectr.
Vidgeon, E. A., PhD   Principal Lectr.
Wray, D. S., BSc PhD, FGS   Reader
Other Staff: 8 Lectrs.; 1 Sr. Res. Fellow; 7 Res.
  Fellows

CONTACT OFFICERS

Academic affairs. Director of Student Affairs:
  Rose, Christine H., MSc *Lond.*, FRSA, FCMI
  (*E-mail:* c.h.rose@greenwich.ac.uk)
Accommodation. Head of Accommodation
  Services: Chandler, Jonathan, BA *York(UK)*
  (*E-mail:* j.e.s.chandler@greenwich.ac.uk)
Admissions (first degree). Director,
  Recruitment and Admissions: Wallis, Steve
  E., BSc, FBCS
  (*E-mail:* s.e.wallis@greenwich.ac.uk)
Admissions (higher degree). Director,
  Recruitment and Admissions: Wallis, Steve
  E., BSc, FBCS
  (*E-mail:* s.e.wallis@greenwich.ac.uk)
Alumni. Alumni Officer: Stephenson, Martyn,
  BA *Birm.*
  (*E-mail:* m.h.stephenson@greenwich.ac.uk)
Archives. Head of Student Progression and
  Conferment: Hill, Henry
  (*E-mail:* h.hill@greenwich.ac.uk)
Careers. Head of Guidance and Employability:
  Kehoe, Eleanor (*E-mail:* e.kehoe@gre.ac.uk)
Computing services. Head of Information and
  Communications Technology: Broadaway,
  Alan (*E-mail:* a.broadaway@gre.ac.uk)
Consultancy services. Director of Research,
  Enterprise and Regional Affairs: Hume, M.
  (*E-mail:* m.s.hume@greenwich.ac.uk)
Credit transfer. Quality Assurance Manager:
  Harper, Chris, MA *Greenwich*
  (*E-mail:* c.h.harper@greenwich.ac.uk)
Equal opportunities. Director of Personnel:
  Brockett, R. J., BA *Kent*, MA *Kent*
  (*E-mail:* r.j.brockett@greenwich.ac.uk)
Estates and buildings/works and services.
  Head of Estates and Building Services:
  Fotheringham, Peter
  (*E-mail:* p.fotheringham@gre.ac.uk)
Examinations. Head of Exams and Standards:
  Glennon, Dionne, BA
  (*E-mail:* d.m.glennon@greenwich.ac.uk)

Finance. Director of Finance: Daly, Reginald V.
  (*E-mail:* r.v.daly@greenwich.ac.uk)
General enquiries. Secretary and Registrar to
  the University: Cording, Linda, MA *Glas.*
  (*E-mail:* l.cording@greenwich.ac.uk)
Health services. Director of Student Affairs:
  Rose, Christine H., MSc *Lond.*, FRSA, FCMI
  (*E-mail:* c.h.rose@greenwich.ac.uk)
International office. Head of International
  Office: Davis, Maxine E.
  (*E-mail:* m.e.davis@gre.ac.uk)
Library (chief librarian). Head of Learning
  Services: Murphy, Ann
  (*E-mail:* a.e.murphy@gre.ac.uk)
Marketing. Head of Marketing: Woods,
  Alison, BA *S'ton.*, MA *S'ton.*
  (*E-mail:* a.l.woods@greenwich.ac.uk)
Minorities/disadvantaged groups. Director of
  Student Affairs: Rose, Christine H., MSc
  Lond., FRSA, FCMI
  (*E-mail:* c.h.rose@greenwich.ac.uk)
Ombudsman. Director of Student Affairs:
  Rose, Christine H., MSc *Lond.*, FRSA, FCMI
  (*E-mail:* c.h.rose@greenwich.ac.uk)
Personnel/human resources. Director of
  Personnel: Brockett, R. J., BA *Kent*, MA *Kent*
  (*E-mail:* r.j.brockett@greenwich.ac.uk)
Public relations. Head of Public Relations
  Unit: Jones, Caron, BSc *Brist.*
  (*E-mail:* caron.jones@greenwich.ac.uk)
Publications. Head of Marketing: Woods,
  Alison, BA *S'ton.*, MA *S'ton.*
  (*E-mail:* a.l.woods@greenwich.ac.uk)
Purchasing. Director of Procurement and
  Business Services: John, Vincent, BA *CNAA*,
  MA *CNAA*, MBA *E.Lond.*
  (*E-mail:* v.m.john@greenwich.ac.uk)
Quality assurance and accreditation. Head of
  Learning and Quality: Cealey-Harrison,
  Wendy P. A., PhD
  (*E-mail:* w.p.a.cealeyharrison@
  greenwich.ac.uk)
Research. Pro-Vice-Chancellor (Research and
  Enterprise): Humphreys, Prof. John, BSc
  MSc MEd PhD, FIBiol
  (*E-mail:* j.humphreys@greenwich.ac.uk)
Safety. Safety Advisor: Ellis, Kevin
  (*E-mail:* r.k.ellis@greenwich.ac.uk)
Scholarships, awards, loans. Head of Student
  Finance, Financial Support and Records:
  Currie, Lorri, MBA *Greenwich*
  (*E-mail:* l.d.currie@greenwich.ac.uk)
Schools liaison. School and College Liaison
  Officer: Solomon, Ami
  (*E-mail:* a.k.solomon@greenwich.ac.uk)
Security. Head of Campus Services: Ellis,
  Helen D.
Sport and recreation. Head of Estates and
  Building Services: Fotheringham, Peter
  (*E-mail:* p.fotheringham@gre.ac.uk)
Staff development and training. Staff
  Development Manager: Behn, Kevin, BSc
  CNAA (*E-mail:* k.r.behn@greenwich.ac.uk)
Student welfare/counselling. Head of Pastoral
  Support and Student Access: Stein, Suzanna,
  BA *Lond.*, MA
  (*E-mail:* s.s.i.stein@greenwich.ac.uk)
Students from other countries. International
  Officer: Ifinnwa, Isaac
  (*E-mail:* i.ifinnwa@greenwich.ac.uk)
Students from other countries. Director of
  Student Affairs: Rose, Christine H., MSc
  Lond., FRSA, FCMI
  (*E-mail:* c.h.rose@gre.ac.uk)
Students with disabilities. Director of Student
  Affairs: Rose, Christine H., MSc *Lond.*, FRSA,
  FCMI (*E-mail:* c.h.rose@greenwich.ac.uk)

[*Information supplied by the institution as at 2 October
  2007, and edited by the ACU*]

HERIOT-WATT UNIVERSITY

Founded 1966

Member of the Association of Commonwealth Universities

Postal Address: Edinburgh, Scotland EH14 4AS
Telephone: (0131) 449 5111 **Fax:** (0131) 449 5153
URL: http://www.hw.ac.uk

PRINCIPAL AND VICE-CHANCELLOR*—Muscatelli, Prof. Anton, MA Glas., PhD Glas., FRSA
VICE-PRINCIPAL—Walker, Prof. A. C., BA Essex, MSc Essex, PhD Essex, FIP, FRSEd
DEPUTY PRINCIPAL (RESEARCH AND KNOWLEDGE TRANSFER)—Gibson, Prof. G. J., BSc PhD, FRSEd
DEPUTY PRINCIPAL (INTERNATIONAL, ACADEMIC AND BUSINESS DEVELOPMENT)—Smart, Prof. B. G. D., BSc Strath.,
    PhD Strath., FREng
DEPUTY PRINCIPAL (LEARNING AND TEACHING)—Craik, Prof. R. J. M., BSc H-W, MSc H-W, PhD H-W
DEPUTY PRINCIPAL (STRATEGY AND RESOURCES)—Jones, Prof. J. D. C., OBE, BSc Wales, PhD Wales, FRSEd, FIP
SECRETARY OF THE UNIVERSITY AND DIRECTOR OF ADMINISTRATION‡—Wilson, Peter L., BSc Glas., MA Lond.
DIRECTOR OF FINANCE AND INFORMATION SERVICES/INFORMATION TECHNOLOGY—McNaull, Philip G., BA Strath.,
    MBA Edin.

GENERAL INFORMATION

History. The university was founded in 1966; it traces its origins back to the Edinburgh School of Arts established in 1821.

Admission to first degree courses (see also United Kingdom Introduction). Through Universities and Colleges Admissions Service (UCAS). Normally Scottish Certificate of Education (SCE) Highers, General Certificate of Education (GCE) A levels or Irish Leaving Certificate. Further education qualifications also accepted; applications from mature students encouraged.
    International students: contact the university's international office, recruitment and admissions office.

First Degrees (see also United Kingdom Directory to Subjects of Study) (* = with honours). BA, BA*, BEng, BEng*, BSc, BSc*, MA, MChem, MEng, MPhys.
    Part-time students are expected to complete a course within 10 years. The university's management programme is also available through supported distance learning.
    Length of course. Full-time: BA, BEng, BSc: 3 years; BA*, BEng*, BSc*, MA: 4 years; MPhys: 4–5 years; MChem, MEng: 5 years.

Higher Degrees (see also United Kingdom Directory to Subjects of Study).
    Master's. MBA, MPhil, MSc, MTM, MURP.
    Admission. Applicants for admission to master's degrees must normally hold an appropriate first degree with at least second class honours. Professional experience is recognised for entry purposes to some courses.
    Courses are available part-time, and some are offered as mixed-mode and distance learning.
    Length of course. Full-time: MBA, MSc: 1 year; MPhil: 1–2 years; MTM, MURP: 2 years.
    Doctoral. DBA, EngD, PhD.
    Length of course. Full-time: PhD: 3 years; DBA: 3–5 years; EngD: 4 years. Part-time: DBA: 3–7 years. By distance learning: DBA: 3–10 years.

Language of Instruction. English. Short courses in English as a foreign language available.

Libraries. Volumes: 200,000. Periodicals subscribed to: 3500.

Academic Year (2007–2008). Three terms: 1 October–7 December; 7 January–14 March; 14 April–20 June.

Income (2005–2006). Total, £99,500,000.

Statistics. Staff (2006–2007): 1750 (430 academic, 1320 non-academic). Students (2006–2007): full-time 6242 (3831 men, 2411 women); part-time 416 (229 men, 187 women).

FACULTIES/SCHOOLS

Art, Humanities and Social Sciences

E-mail: a.prior@hw.ac.uk
Dean: Prior, Prof. A. A., BSc H-W, MLitt Glas.

Science and Engineering

E-mail: j.sawkins@hw.ac.uk
Dean: Sawkins, Prof. J. W., MA Edin., MSc Glas., PhD Edin.

ACADEMIC UNITS

Built Environment

Tel: (0131) 451 4644 Fax: (0131) 451 4617
    E-mail: a.j.ormston@hw.ac.uk
Adeloye, A. J., MSc Newcastle(UK), PhD
    Newcastle(UK)   Sr. Lectr.
Aspinall, P. A., BSc Edin., MSc Edin., PhD Edin.
    Prof.
Baird, D.   Hon. Prof.
Baker, G. J.   Hon. Prof.
Banfill, Phillip F. G., BSc S'ton., PhD Liv.,
    FRSChem   Prof.
Beard, A. N., BSc Leic., PhD Durh.   Reader
Binnie, R. B.   Hon. Prof.
Bowles, G., BSc Dund., PhD Abertay   Sr. Lectr.
Bramley, G., BSc Brist., PhD Brist.   Prof.; Dir.,
    Centre for Res. into Socially Inclusive
    Services (CRSIS)
Cairns, J. J., BSc Glas., PhD Glas.   Sr. Lectr.
Campbell, D. P., BA Open(UK), PhD H-W   Sr.
    Lectr.
Cantley, W. R. D.   Hon. Prof.
Carley, M., BSc Mich.State, MSc Lond., PhD Br.Col.
    Prof.
Cheesman, P. G., MSc H-W   Sr. Lectr.
Chrisp, T. M., BSc Newcastle(UK), MSc Brist., PhD
    H-W   Sr. Lectr.
Craik, R. J. M., BSc H-W, MSc H-W, PhD H-W
    Prof.
Dhillon, B., BMedSci Nott., BM BS Nott.,
    FRCPSGlas   Prof.
Dunse, N. A., BLandEc Aberd., PhD Paisley   Sr.
    Lectr.
Finch, E. F., BSc Kingston(UK), PhD Reading
    Reader
Floyd, J. D.   Hon. Prof.
Grant, I., BSc Edin., PhD Edin., FIP   Prof.
Haldane, D., BSc H-W   Sr. Lectr.
Higgins, M. G., BA Rhode I., MPhil Edin.   Sr.
    Lectr.
Hull, A. D., BA Newcastle(UK), BPhil
    Newcastle(UK), MA Newcastle(UK), PhD
    Newcastle(UK)   Prof.
Jack, L. B., BEng Napier, PhD H-W   Sr. Lectr.
Jenkins, P., MA Edin., PhD H-W   Reader; Dir.,
    Centre for Environmental and Human
    Settlements
Jones, C. A., BA York(UK), MA Manc.   Prof.

Jowitt, Paul W., BSc(Eng) Lond., PhD Lond.,
    FICE, FRSA, FRSEd, FCGI   Prof., Civil
    Engineering Systems
Kaka, A. P., BSc Lough., PhD Salf.   Prof.; Dir.,
    Teaching and Learning
Linfoot, B. T., BEng Liv.   Sr. Lectr.
MacLeary, A. R.   Hon. Prof.
May, I. M., BEng Brad., MSc Warw., PhD Warw.
    Prof.
McBeth, D.   Hon. Prof.
McCarter, W. J., BSc Edin., PhD Edin., DSc H-W
    Prof.
McCarthy, J. P., BA Manc., BPlanning Manc.
    Reader
Meikle, J. L.   Hon. Prof.
Netto, G., PhD   Dir., Scottish Ethnic
    Minorities Res. Unit
Pawson, H., BSc S'ton., MPublPol Brist.   Prof.
Paxton, R. A., MBE, MSc PhD Hon. DEng,
    FICE, FRSEd   Hon. Prof.
Pender, G., BSc Strath., PhD Strath., FICE   Prof.;
    Dir., Res.
Prior, A. A., BSc H-W, MLitt Glas.   Prof.
Raemaekers, J. J., MA Camb., MPhil Edin., PhD
    Camb.   Sr. Lectr.
Robertson, B. S., BSc Strath.   Sr. Lectr.
Schvidchenko, A. B., MSc Leningrad, PhD Glas.
    Prof.
Swaffield, J. A., BSc Brist., MPhil City(UK), PhD
    City(UK)   Prof.; Head*
Val, D., MSc Moscow, DSc Haifa(Technion)
    Reader
Wallis, S. G., BSc Birm.   Sr. Lectr.
Wang, Y. P., BSc Shanxi Teachers, PhD H-W
    Reader
Webb, R. S., BEng Liv., MSc Lond.   Sr. Lectr.
White, M. J., BSc Belf., MA Manc., PhD Aberd.
    Reader
Wilson, D.   Hon. Prof.
Other Staff: 32 Lectrs.; 1 Academic Fellow; 3
    Teaching Fellows
Research: construction and property economics
    and management; construction materials,
    structures and geomechanics; flood
    management, urban and building drainage;
    planning, housing, urban regeneration and
    governance; systems engineering, safety and
    sustainability

Edinburgh Business School

Tel: (0131) 451 3090 Fax: (0131) 451 3002
    E-mail: enquiries@ebs.hw.ac.uk
Henderson, I. S., BSc H-W, MBA Dund., PhD H-
    W   Sr. Teaching Fellow
Jamieson, B. M., BA H-W, MBA H-W   Sr.
    Teaching Fellow
Kennedy, G., BA Strath., PhD Brun.   Prof. Emer.
Lothian, N., BA H-W   Prof.
Lumsden, K. G., MA Edin., PhD Stan.   Prof.
    Fellow; Dir.*
Peacock, Sir Alan, DSC, MA St And.,
    Hon. DUniv Stir., Hon. DEcon Zür.,
    Hon. DSc Buckingham, Hon. DSc(SocSci)
    Edin., Hon. LLD St And., Hon. LLD Dund.,

FRSEd, FBA Hon. Res. Prof., Public Finance

Roberts, A., MBA Lond., PhD Lond., FCIS, FACCA Prof. Fellow

Scott, A., MA Edin., MSc Edin., PhD Prof. Fellow

Wallace, W. A., BSc Leeds, MSc Lough., PhD H-W Sr. Teaching Fellow

Other Staff: 1 Lectr.; 1 Teaching Fellow

Engineering and Physical Sciences, School of

Tel: (0131) 451 3082 Fax: (0131) 451 3136
E-mail: l.bruce@hw.ac.uk

Abraham, E., BSc Buenos Aires, PhD Manc. Sr. Lectr.

Adams, D. R., BSc PhD Reader

Baker, H. J., BSc Manc., PhD Manc. Prof.

Barton, J. S., MA Camb., PhD Liv. Reader

Bell, J. M., MEng H-W, PhD H-W Sr. Lectr.

Belyaev, A., MS Moscow, PhD Moscow Reader

Brown, K. E., BSc Edin., PhD Edin. Sr. Lectr.

Buller, G. S., BSc H-W, PhD H-W Reader

Cameron, J. H., BSc PhD, FRSChem Sr. Lectr.

Cowie, J. M. G., BSc PhD DSc, FRSChem, FRSEd Prof. Emer.

Davidson, J. L., BSc PhD Reader

Desmulliez, M. P. Y., MSc Lond., PhD H-W Prof.

Dhariwal, R. S., BSc Coventry, MSc Aston Sr. Lectr.

Dunnigan, M. W., BSc Glas., PhD H-W Sr. Lectr.

Fischer, I., PhD Marburg Prof.

Fruh, W. G., BSc Freib., DPhil Oxf. Sr. Lectr.

Galbraith, I., BSc H-W, PhD H-W Prof.

Greenaway, A. H., BSc Brun., PhD Lond. Prof.

Greenhalgh, D. Prof.; Head*

Gutowski, M., PhD Warsaw Prof.

Hall, Dennis R., BSc Manc., MBA H-W, MPhil Lond., PhD Case W.Reserve, FIP, FIEE, FRSEd Prof.

Hand, D. P., BSc St And., PhD S'ton. Prof.

Harrison, R. G., BSc Lond., PhD Lond., FRSEd Prof. Emer.

Harvey, A. R., BSc Durh., MSc Leic., PhD St And. Sr. Lectr.

John, P., BSc PhD DSc Prof., Physical Chemistry

Jones, J. D. C., OBE, BSc Wales, PhD Wales, FRSEd, FIP Prof., Optics

Jonson, M. Prof.

Kar, A. K., MSc Delhi, MSc Essex, PhD Essex Reader

Keane, M. A., BSc N.U.I., PhD N.U.I. Prof.

Kew, P. A., MA Camb., PhD H-W Sr. Lectr.

Lane, D. M., BSc H-W, PhD H-W Prof.

MacGregor, S. A., BSc Edin., PhD Edin. Reader

Markx, G., PhD Prof.

McCoustra, M. R. S., BSc H-W, PhD H-W, DSc H-W, FRSChem Prof.

McCullough, K. J., BSc PhD, FRSChem Sr. Lectr.

McKendrick, K., BSc DPhil Prof., Physical Chemistry

McNeil, D. A., BSc Strath., PhD Strath. Sr. Lectr.

Murray, J. L., BSc MSc, FIMechE Prof. Emer., Computer-Aided Engineering

Newborough, M., MSc Cran., PhD Cran. Prof.

Ni, X.-W., BSc Chongqing, PhD Leeds Prof., Chemical Engineering

Ocone, R., Laur Naples, MA Prin., PhD Prin. Prof., Chemical Engineering

Parker, J. E., BSc PhD, FRSChem Sr. Lectr.

Pidgeon, C. R., BSc Reading, PhD Reading, FIP, FRSEd Prof. Emer.

Powell, A. V., MA DPhil Reader

Prior, K. A., MA Camb., PhD Camb. Reader

Reay, D. A., MSc Brist., BSc(Eng) Visiting Prof.

Reid, D. T., MA Camb., PhD St And. Prof.

Reuben, R. L., BSc Strath., PhD Open(UK) Prof., Materials Engineering

Ritchie, J. M., BSc MSc Sr. Lectr.

Sangster, A. J., BSc(Eng) Aberd., MSc Aberd., PhD Aberd., FIEE Prof., Microwave Engineering

Snowdon, J. F., BSc H-W, PhD H-W Sr. Lectr.

Taghizadeh, M. R., BSc Meshed, MSc Meshed, MSc Essex, PhD Reader

Tao, S., MSc China U.S.T., PhD China U.S.T. Reader

Vorobyov, S., MSc PhD Reader

Waldie, B., BSc Durh., PhD Newcastle(UK), FIChemE Prof. Emer., Chemical and Offshore Process Engineering

Walker, A. C., BA Essex, MSc Essex, PhD Essex, FIP, FRSEd OCLI Prof., Modern Optics

Wallace, A. M. F., BSc Edin., PhD Edin. Prof.

Wang, X., MEng China U.Electronic S.T., PhD Chinese HK Sr. Lectr.

Warburton, R. J., MA Oxf., DPhil Oxf. Prof.

Welch, Alan J., BSc PhD, FRSChem Prof., Inorganic Chemistry

Wherrett, B. S., BSc Reading, PhD Reading, FRSEd Prof., Theoretical Physics

White, G. Sr. Lectr.

Wightman, R. H., MA PhD, FRSChem Sr. Lectr.

Wilkinson, D., BSc Brist., PhD H-W Sr. Lectr.

Wilson, J. I. B., BSc Durh., PhD Durh. Prof., Materials Processing

Other Staff: 5 Emer. Profs.; 121 Lectrs.; 70 Res. Assocs.; 1 RCUK Academic Fellow

Research: design and manufacture, mechanical engineering; microengineering, image processing, intelligent systems; molecular, particle and process engineering; physical, inorganic and organic chemistry; physics, photonics, laser devices and applications

Engineering, Petroleum, Institute of

Tel: (0131) 451 3567 Fax: (0131) 451 3127
E-mail: jane.wells@pet.hw.ac.uk

Bagci, S. A., BSc Middle East Tech., MSc Middle East Tech., PhD Middle East Tech. Sr. Lectr.

Christie, M., BSc Lond., PhD Lond. Prof.

Corbett, Patrick W. M., BSc Exe., MSc Lond., PhD H-W Prof.; Head*

Couples, G. D., BS Texas A.& M., MA Rice, PhD Texas A.& M. Sr. Lectr.

Danesh, A., BSc Abadan, PhD Manc. Prof.

Davies, D., BSc Exe., PhD Exe. Sr. Lectr.

Ford, J. T., BSc Newcastle(UK), MEng H-W, PhD H-W Prof.

MacBeth, C., BA Oxf., MA Oxf., PhD Edin. Prof.

McDougall, S., BSc St And., PhD H-W Prof.

Potter, D., BSc Leeds, MSc Newcastle(UK), PhD Newcastle(UK) Sr. Lectr.

Side, J. C., BSc H-W, PhD H-W, FRICS Prof., Sustainable Development

Smart, B. G. D., BSc Strath., PhD Strath., FREng Prof.

Sorbie, K. S., BSc Strath., DPhil Sus. Prof.

Tehrani, A. D. H., BSc Teheran Hon. Prof.†

Todd, A. C., BTech Lough., PhD Lough., FIChemE Prof.

Tohidi, B., BSc Abadan, PhD H-W Reader

Other Staff: 5 Lectrs.; 3 Res. Fellows

Research: drilling and production; flow in porous media; geomechanics; production chemistry; reservoir description and simulation

Life Sciences

Tel: (0131) 451 3619 Fax: (0131) 451 3735
E-mail: j.e.j.lodder@hw.ac.uk

Austin, B., BSc Newcastle(UK), PhD Newcastle(UK), DSc H-W Prof.; Head*

Brotherton, C. J., BA Hull, PhD Hull Prof.

Bryce, J. H., BSc St And., PhD Camb. Sr. Lectr.

Green, P. R., BA Oxf., PhD Camb. Sr. Lectr.

Hughes, P. S., BSc Lond., PhD Lond. Prof.

Jamieson, D. J., BSc Dund., PhD Dund. Reader

Kingston, P. F., BSc Lond. Sr. Lectr.

Lyndon, A. R., BSc Aberd., PhD Aberd. Sr. Lectr.

Mair, J. M. D. (Hamish), BSc Glas., PhD Liv. Sr. Lectr.

Meaden, P. G., BSc Lond., PhD Lond. Sr. Lectr.

Mitchell, W. J., BSc Aberd., PhD Aberd. Reader

Moore, C. G., BSc Liv., PhD Liv. Sr. Lectr.

Morris, P. C., BSc Leeds, PhD Nott. Sr. Lectr.

North, A., BSc Manc., PhD Leic. Prof.

Paul, M. A., BA Open(UK), BSc E.Anglia, PhD E.Anglia, FGS Prof., Engineering and Environmental Geology

Schweizer, H. M., BSc Würzburg, PhD Erlangen-Nuremberg, DSc Prof.

Sewell, D. A., BA Birm., PhD CNAA Sr. Lectr.

Stewart, G. G., BSc Wales, PhD Bath, DSc Bath Prof., Brewing and Distilling

Timmons, J., BSc Glas., PhD Nott. Prof.

Wilkinson, M., BSc Liv., PhD Liv. Prof.

Other Staff: 13 Hon. Profs.; 20 Lectrs.; 2 Sr. Res. Fellows; 2 Sr. Res. Officers; 1 Res. Fellow; 5 Res. Assocs.; 1 Teaching Fellow; 1 Experimental Officer (Diving)

Vacant Posts: 1 Prof.; 2 Lectrs.

Research: aquaculture; cereals, fermentation, food science and nutrition; environmental and marine sciences; psychology; sports and exercise science

Management and Languages

Tel: (0131) 451 8143 Fax: (0131) 451 3498
E-mail: enquiries@sml.hw.ac.uk

Bhattacharya, P. C., BA Gauh., MA Alld., MSc Lond., PhD Lond. Sr. Lectr.

Böser, U., PhD Edin. Prof.; Dir., Learning and Teaching

Brown, J. D., BA Iowa, PhD Penn. Sr. Lectr.

Christie, A. J. M., BAcc Glas. Hon. Prof.

Cobham, D., BA Manc., PhD Manc. Prof.

Collins, P., BA S'ton., BA Lond., MSc Cran., PhD Cran. Sr. Lectr.

Craig, V., LLB Edin. Prof.

Cullinane, S., BA Stir., PhD Plym. Sr. Lectr.

Davies, M. A. P., BA Strath., MSc Strath. Sr. Lectr.

Earle, J., MA Stan., PhD Stan. Prof.

Fernie, J., MA Dund., MBA Brad., PhD Edin. Prof.

Gardiner, P. D., MA Lond., PhD Durh. Sr. Lectr.

Gordon, P. D., BA Kent, MA Lanc., FCA Sr. Lectr.

Halliday, J., MA St And. Sr. Lectr., Russian

Hare, P. G., BA Camb., DPhil Oxf. Prof., Economics

Hogg, G., MA Dund., PhD Stir., FRSA Prof.; Head*

Kahn, H., MA Glas., MSc UMIST, PhD UMIST Sr. Lectr.

Keogh, W., BSc Stir. Prof.

Leslie, J., BA H-W, MLitt H-W Sr. Lectr.

Marks, A., BSc Newcastle(UK), MSc Sheff., PhD Strath. Sr. Lectr.

Marston, C. L., MA F.U.Berlin, MA San Jose State Coll., MA Calif., MSc Calif., PhD Prof., Accounting

Mason, I., BA Lond., PhD Lond. Prof., Interpreting and Translating

McKinnon, A. C., MA Aberd., MA Br.Col., PhD Lond. Prof.

Melitz, J., BA Calif., PhD Prin. Visiting Prof.

Mochrie, R. I., BSc St And., MScEcon Warw., PhD(Econ) Warw. Sr. Lectr.

Moore, C., MA Glas., MBA Stir., PhD Stir. Prof.

Paisey, N., BA Leeds, MEd Aberd. Sr. Lectr.

Roslender, R., BA Leeds, PhD Leeds Prof.

Sawkins, J. W., MA Edin., MSc Glas., PhD Edin. Reader

Schaffer, M. E., AB Harv., MA Stan., MSc Lond., PhD Lond. Prof., Economics

Sharwood-Smith, M. A., MA St And., PhD Poznan Prof., Languages

Shaw, W. N., BSc Strath., MBA Strath., PhD Strath. Sr. Lectr.

Song, D.-W., MSc Plym., PhD Plym., BA Reader

Tinker, C. G., BA Birm., MPhil Birm., PhD Birm. Sr. Lectr.

Torrance, T. S., MA St And., PhD Edin. Sr. Lectr.

Towers, N., BSc Oxf.Brookes, MBA Staffs., PhD UMIST, FCMI Sr. Lectr.

Turner, G. H., BA York(UK), MA Durh. Prof.

Wyatt, G. J., BA Keele, DPhil York(UK) Reader

Other Staff: 53 Lectrs.; 1 Sr. Teaching Fellow; 7 Teaching Fellows; 5 Res. Assocs.; 3 Foreign Lang. Assts.

Research: acquisition of second or other languages; business law, entrepreneurship and international business; corporate accounting and finance; financial markets, analysis and reporting; retail marketing (green logistics, international fashion marketing, logistics)

Mathematical and Computer Sciences

Tel: (0131) 451 3420 Fax: (0131) 451 3327
E-mail: enquiries@macs.hw.ac.uk
Aylett, R. S., BSc Lond. Prof.
Beevers, C. E., OBE, BSc Manc., PhD Manc. Prof. Emer.
Brown, K. J., BSc Aberd., PhD Dund., FRSEd Prof.
Burger, A., BSc Augsburg, MSc Missouri, PhD Edin. Sr. Lectr.
Cairns, A. J. G., MA Camb., PhD H-W, FFA Prof.
Carr, J., BSc Bath, MSc Oxf., DPhil Oxf., FRSEd Prof.
Cawsey, A. J., MA Camb., PhD Edin. Sr. Lectr.
Chantler, M. J., BSc Glas., PhD H-W Prof.
Corne, D. W., MSc Edin., PhD Edin. Prof.
Currie, I. D., BSc St And., PhD H-W Reader
Davis, R. H., BSc Belf., PhD Belf. Sr. Lectr.
De Wilde, P., MSc Ghent, PhD Ghent Prof.; Head*
Eilbeck, J. C., BA Oxf., PhD Lanc., FIMA, FRSEd Prof.
Foss, S., MSc Russian Acad.Sc., PhD Russian Acad.Sc. Prof.
Gibson, G. J., BSc PhD, FRSEd Prof., Statistics
Gilbert, N. D., BSc Lond., PhD Lond. Sr. Lectr.
Gray, R., BSc St And. Sr. Lectr.
Hansen, J., BA Carleton(Minn.), MSc Warw., PhD Minn. Sr. Lectr.
Howie, J., BSc St And., PhD Lond., FRSEd Prof.
Ireland, A., BSc Stir., PhD Stir. Sr. Lectr.
Johnston, D. A., BA Camb., PhD Lond. Prof.
Kamareddine, F., BSc Beirut, MSc Essex, PhD Edin., FIMA, FBCS Prof.
Knops, R. J., BSc Nott., PhD Nott., FRSEd Prof. Emer.
Konstantopolous, P. T., MSc Calif., PhD Calif. Reader
Korabinski, A. A., BSc H-W, MSc Lond. Sr. Lectr.
Kuskin, S., MSc Moscow, PhD Moscow Prof.
Lacey, A. A., MA Oxf., MSc Oxf., DPhil Oxf., FRSEd Prof.
Lord, G. J., BSc Sus., PhD Bath Reader
Macdonald, A. S., BSc Glas., PhD H-W, FFA Prof.; Head, Actuarial Maths. and Stats.
Marwick, D. H., MSc Trinity(Dub.) Sr. Lectr.
McNeil, A. J., BSc Lond., PhD Camb., ScD Camb. Prof.; Maxwell Chair
Michaelson, G. J., BA Essex, MSc St And., PhD H-W Prof.; Head, Computer Sci.
Mollison, D., MA Camb., PhD Camb., ScD Camb. Prof. Emer.
Mueller, A., PhD Karlsruhe Sr. Lectr.
Penrose, O., BSc Lond., PhD Camb., FRS, FRSEd Prof. Emer.
Pooley, R. J., BSc Brist., MSc Brad., PhD Edin. Prof.
Prince, A. R., MA Oxf., DPhil Oxf., MSc Col. Sr. Lectr.
Rynne, B. P., BSc Manc., PhD Dund. Reader
Schroers, J. A., BA Camb., DPhil Oxf. Prof.
Sherratt, J. A., BA Camb., DPhil Oxf. Prof.
Szabo, R. J., BSc McG., MSc Br.Col., PhD Br.Col. Prof.
Taylor, N. K., BSc Wales, MSc Lond., PhD Nott. Sr. Lectr.
Trinder, P. W., BSc Rhodes, DPhil Oxf. Sr. Lectr.
Waters, H. R., MA Oxf., DPhil Oxf., FIA, FFA Prof.
White, A. R., BSc Liv., MSc Bath, PhD Liv. Sr. Lectr.
Wilkie, A. D., MA Camb., FFA, FIA Hon. Prof.
Williams, M. H., BSc Rhodes, PhD Rhodes, DSc Rhodes Prof.
Zachary, S., MA Camb., PhD Durh. Reader
Other Staff: 3 Sr. Lectrs.; 29 Lectrs.; 3 Sr. Res. Fellows; 21 Res. Assocs.; 7 Teaching Fellows; 8 Computing Officers
Research: actuarial and financial mathematics, genetic testing, life assurance solvency, life office modelling, risk theory mortality

studies and permanent health insurance; applied analysis; database, information and knowledge based systems, biomedical informatics systems, engineering vision, interactive and graphical environments, image and texture analysis; intelligent systems; probability and stochastic models

Textiles and Design

Tel: (01896) 892130 Fax: (01896) 758965
E-mail: l.a.lindsay@hw.ac.uk
Christie, R. M., BSc St And., PhD St And. Reader
McInnes, I. C., BA CNAA Sr. Lectr.
Stylios, G. K., MSc Leeds, PhD Leeds Prof.
Taylor, S., BA MPhil Reader
Walker, R.
Wardman, Prof. R. H., BTech Brad., PhD Brad. Head*
Other Staff: 22 Lectrs.; 7 Res. Assocs.
Research: fashion; materials and colour chemistry; textile and clothing technology; textile design

SPECIAL CENTRES, ETC

Biomedical Textiles Research, Centre for

Tel: (01896) 892168 Fax: (01896) 758965
E-mail: b.t.r.c@hw.ac.uk
Fotheringham, A. Dir.*
Research: biomedical structures and scaffolds fabricated from textiles; conducting and medical polymers; medical applications of gas plasma treatments; processing biopolymers as fibres for knitted/woven structures; synthetic fibre processing for biomedical applications

Brewing and Distilling, International Centre for

Tel: (0131) 451 3184 Fax: (0131) 449 7459
E-mail: p.s.hughes@hw.ac.uk
Hughes, P. S., BSc Lond., PhD Lond. Prof.; Dir.*
Other Staff: 2 Profs.; 2 Reader; 2 Sr. Lectrs.; 1 Lectr.; 1 Sr. Teaching Fellow
Research: beer quality and stability; innovative management; product safety and integrity; raw materials, particularly hops

Economic Reform and Transformation, Centre for

Tel: (0131) 451 3485 Fax: (0131) 451 3498
E-mail: ecocert@hw.ac.uk
Schaffer, M. E., AB Harv., MA Stan., MSc Lond., PhD Lond. Prof.; Dir.*
Other Staff: 3 Profs.; 2 Readers; 5 Lectrs.; 6 Res. Assocs.
Research: development economics; economics of the European Union; economics of transition: Eastern and Central Europe, former Soviet Union and China

Flexible Materials, Research Institute for

Tel: (01896) 892133 Fax: (01896) 758965
Stylios, G. K., MSc Leeds, PhD Leeds Prof.; Dir.*
Other Staff: 4 Res. Assocs.
Research: drapability of fabrics; plasma treatment of wool fabrics; shape memory alloys and polymers for apparel and interior textiles; smart garments incorporating electronic devices; technology for producing traditional Ikat Limar fabrics

Genetics and Insurance Research, Centre for

Tel: (0131) 451 3209
E-mail: a.s.macdonald@hw.ac.uk
Macdonald, A. S., BSc Glas., PhD H-W, FFA Prof.; Dir.*
Other Staff: 2 Res. Assocs.
Research: insurance and financial implications of genetics; mathematical modelling of genetics disorders

Integrated Systems, Institute for

Tel: (0131) 451 8216
E-mail: p.j.thompson@hw.ac.uk
Cunningham, C. R. Board of Directors, UK Astronomy Technol. Centre
Greenaway, A. H., BSc Brun., PhD Lond. Deputy Dir.; Dir., Postgrad. Studies
Walton, A. Dir., Univ. of Edinburgh
Research: biomedical imaging and instrumentation; electromagnetic detector technologies; micro- and nano-systems; micro electrical machine system (MEMS), micro-opto-electromechanical systems (MOEMS); optics and photonics systems

Island Technology, International Centre for

Renewable Energy
Tel: (01856) 850605 Fax: (01856) 851349
E-mail: icit@hw.ac.uk
Side, J. C., BSc H-W, PhD H-W, FRICS Prof.; Dir.*
Other Staff: 1 Prof.; 2 Lectrs.; 3 Res. Assocs.
Research: fisheries and bio-resource development and management; marine resource and coastal management; renewable energy and energy planning

Logistics Research Centre

Tel: (0131) 451 3850 Fax: (0131) 451 3498
E-mail: a.c.mckinnon@hw.ac.uk
McKinnon, A. C., MA Aberd., MA Br.Col., PhD Lond. Prof.; Dir.*
Other Staff: 1 Prof.; 2 Sr. Lectrs.; 1 Lectr.; 1 Res. Assoc.
Research: assessing the environmental impact of logistical activity; container shipping and port development; development of freight transport strategy; effects of e-commerce on logistics and supply chain management; management of retail logistics

Marine Biodiversity and Biotechnology, Centre for

Tel: (0131) 451 3303 Fax: (0131) 451 3009
E-mail: p.f.kingston@hw.ac.uk
Kingston, P. F., BSc Lond. Sr. Lectr.
Other Staff: 2 Profs.; 1 Reader; 2 Sr. Lectrs.; 2 Lectrs.; 1 Res. Assoc.
Research: biodiversity of marine vertebrates; biotechnological products from marine organisms; effects of pollution on marine ecosystems

Mathematical Sciences, International Centre for

Tel: (0131) 220 1777 Fax: (0131) 220 1053
E-mail: enquiries@icms.org.uk
Dart, Tracey, MA Camb. Exec. Dir.*
Toland, J. F., BSc Belf., MSc Sus., DPhil Sus., Hon. DSc Belf., FRS, FRSEd Prof.; Sci. Dir.

Microsystems Engineering Centre (MISEC)

Tel: (0131) 451 3340 Fax: (0131) 451 4155
E-mail: m.desmulliez@hw.ac.uk
Desmulliez, M. P. Y., MSc Lond., PhD H-W Prof.; Dir.*
Other Staff: 6 Lectrs.; 24 Res. Assocs.; 1 Experimental Officer
Research: advanced packaging of micro electro-mechanical systems (MEMS); high level design language using analogue mixed signal; manufacturing of microsystems and micro electro-mechanical systems using UV-LIGA process; microactuator design and testing; radio frequency micro electro-mechanical systems

Ocean Systems Laboratory

Tel: (0131) 451 3350 Fax: (0131) 451 3180
E-mail: d.m.lane@hw.ac.uk
Lane, D. M., BSc H-W, PhD H-W Prof.; Dir.*
Other Staff: 1 Reader; 2 Sr. Lectrs.; 3 Lectrs.
Research: acoustics, sonar design and communications; autonomous vehicles; sonar video, navigation processing,

classification and data fusion; subsea robotics

Photonics, Centre for

Tel: (0131) 451 3031 Fax: (0131) 451 3180
E-mail: j.jones@hw.ac.uk
Baker, H. J., BSc Manc., PhD Manc.   Prof.
Greenaway, A. H., BSc Brun., PhD Lond.   Dir., Postgrad. Studies
Hall, Dennis R., BSc Manc., MBA H-W, MPhil Lond., PhD Case W.Reserve, FIP, FIEE, FRSEd Prof.
Harrison, R. G., BSc Lond., PhD Lond., FRSEd Prof.
Jones, J. D. C., OBE, BSc Wales, PhD Wales, FRSEd, FIP   Prof.; Dir.*
Walker, A. C., BA Essex, MSc Essex, PhD Essex, FIP, FRSEd   Prof.
Other Staff: 8 Readers; 1 Sr. Lectr.; 2 Lectrs.; 30 Postdoctoral Res. Assocs.
Research: adaptive optics; fibre sensors; laser device physics; laser microprocessing applications; ultra-fast laser applications

Scottish Manufacturing Institute

Tel: (0131) 451 3001 Fax: (0131) 451 3744
E-mail: d.j.nisbet@hw.ac.uk
Jones, J. D. C., OBE, BSc Wales, PhD Wales, FRSEd, FIP   Prof., Optics; Dir.*
Other Staff: 4 Profs.; 2 Readers; 2 Sr. Lectrs.; 2 Lectrs.; 15 Res. Assocs.
Research: computer-aided design for manufacture, process and assembly; digital tools for manufacturing; geometric reasoning about manufactured artefacts and surfaces; optical technology and manufacturing processes; photonics for manufacturing

Social Enterprise Institute

Tel: (0131) 451 3855 Fax: (0131) 451 3008
E-mail: r.d.donnelly@hw.ac.uk
Donnelly, R., BA Strath., MEd Glas., MBA H-W, PhD Strath.   Consultant
Jones, D., BA Strath.   Dir.*
Kahn, H., MA Glas., MSc UMIST, PhD UMIST Dir., Res.
Research: financial exclusion in central Scotland; lottery funding for social enterprises; provision of financial services in rural Scotland

Sustainable Technology, Scottish Institute of

Tel: (0131) 451 8162 Fax: (0131) 451 8150
E-mail: joanne.pope@sistech.co.uk
Jowitt, Paul W., BSc(Eng) Lond., PhD Lond., FICE, FRSA, FRSEd, FCGI   Dir.*
Other Staff: 7 Staff Members
Research: construction and the built environment; energy; transport; waste; water resources

Technology and Research Services

Tel: (0131) 451 3192 Fax: (0131) 451 3193
E-mail: trs@hw.ac.uk
McFadzean, Gillian E., MA Aberd.   Dir.*
Other Staff: 16 Staff Members

Theoretical Modelling in Medicine, Centre for

Tel: (0131) 451 3740 Fax: (0131) 451 3249
E-mail: jas@ma.hw.ac.uk
Sherratt, J. A., BA Camb., DPhil Oxf.   Prof.; Dir.*
Other Staff: 1 Lectr.
Research: cancer, psoriasis and wound healing

Translation and Interpreting Studies in Scotland, Centre for

Tel: (0131) 451 4218 Fax: (0131) 451 3079
E-mail: i.mason@hw.ac.uk
Turner, G. H., BA York(UK), MA Durh.   Prof.
Other Staff: 5 Lectrs.
Research: contrastive textology; interactional aspects of dialogue interpreting; linguistic and pragmatic approaches to the study of translation and interpreting; provision, quality and standards of public service interpreting; theory of communication

CONTACT OFFICERS

Accommodation. Director, Student Welfare Services: Johnston, Christine
(E-mail: c.johnston@hw.ac.uk)
Admissions (first degree). Director, Recruitment and Admissions: Bates, Michael, MA Aberd.
(E-mail: m.bates@hw.ac.uk)
Admissions (first degree). Admissions Officer: McLean, Patricia S., BSc CNAA
(E-mail: p.s.mclean@hw.ac.uk)
Admissions (higher degree). Admissions Officer: McLean, Patricia S., BSc CNAA
(E-mail: p.s.mclean@hw.ac.uk)
Adult/continuing education. Director, Continuing Professional Development: Inglis, Tom A., BSc Strath., MEng H-W
(E-mail: t.a.inglis@hw.ac.uk)
Alumni. Acting Head, Development and Alumni: Travers, Bronwyn
(E-mail: b.travers@hw.ac.uk)
Archives. Archivist: Jones, Ann, BA York(UK), MArAd Liv. (E-mail: a.e.jones@hw.ac.uk)
Careers. Director, Careers Advisory Service: Thow, Nick W., MA
(E-mail: n.w.thow@hw.ac.uk)
Computing services. Director, University Information and Computing Services: Rundell, David R., BSc St And., MSc H-W, FBCS (E-mail: d.r.rundell@hw.ac.uk)
Conferences/corporate hospitality. General Manager, Edinburgh Conference Centre: Day, Thomas K., BSc CNAA
(E-mail: t.k.day@hw.ac.uk)
Consultancy services. Manager, Technology Transfer: Cox, Michael, BSc Manc., MSc Manc., PhD Manc. (E-mail: trs@hw.ac.uk)
Credit transfer. Assistant Registrar (Learning Strategies): King, Margaret, MA Glas., PhD Edin., FSA (E-mail: m.king@hw.ac.uk)
Development/fund-raising. Head, Development and Alumni: Travers, Bronwyn (E-mail: b.travers@hw.ac.uk)
Estates and buildings/works and services. Director, Estate and Building Services: Kerr, Peter G. (E-mail: p.g.kerr@hw.ac.uk)
Examinations. Registry Office Manager: MacArthur, Karen, BA R.Gordon
(E-mail: k.macarthur@hw.ac.uk)
Finance. Director of Finance and Information Services/Information Technology: McNaull, Philip G., BA Strath., MBA Edin.
(E-mail: p.mcnaull@hw.ac.uk)
General enquiries. Management Services Assistant: O'Brien, Lynsey
(E-mail: enquiries@hw.ac.uk)
Health services. Physician-in-Charge, University Health Service: de Lima, Victor, MB ChB Edin.
(E-mail: v.r.f.de_lima@hw.ac.uk)
Industrial liaison. Director of Technology and Research Services: McFadzean, Gillian E., MA Aberd. (E-mail: trs@hw.ac.uk)
International office. Senior International Officer: Bates, Michael, MA Aberd.
(E-mail: m.bates@hw.ac.uk)

Library (chief librarian). Librarian: Breaks, Michael L., BA Leeds
(E-mail: m.l.breaks@hw.ac.uk)
Marketing. Director, Corporate Affairs: (vacant)
Ombudsman. Secretary of the University: Wilson, Peter L., BSc Glas., MA Lond.
(E-mail: p.l.wilson@hw.ac.uk)
Personnel/human resources. Director, Human Resources: Cook, Margaret C., BA Strath. (E-mail: m.c.cook@hw.ac.uk)
Public relations. Press Officer: Dempster, Caroline, BSc(SocSci) Edin.
(E-mail: c.m.l.dempster@hw.ac.uk)
Public relations. Public Relations Manager: Wilson, Kirsty (E-mail: pr@hw.ac.uk)
Publications. Publications Officer: Larter, Karen, MA Dund. (E-mail: k.larter@hw.ac.uk)
Purchasing. Director of Procurement, Procurement Services: Newjem, Anthony E.
(E-mail: a.e.newjem@hw.ac.uk)
Quality assurance and accreditation. Director of Quality Development: Craik, Prof. R. J. M., BSc H-W, MSc H-W, PhD H-W
(E-mail: r.j.m.craik@hw.ac.uk)
Research. Head, Research and Legal Services: Weir, Anthony, BSc Edin., MSc Stir., PhD Wales (E-mail: trs@hw.ac.uk)
Safety. Manager, Health and Safety: Pender, Craig G. (E-mail: c.g.pender@hw.ac.uk)
Scholarships, awards, loans. Student Welfare Services: West, Lesley P.
(E-mail: l.p.west@hw.ac.uk)
Schools liaison. Director, Recruitment and Admissions: Bates, Michael, MA Aberd.
(E-mail: m.bates@hw.ac.uk)
Security. Manager, Security and Operations: Taylor, William J.
(E-mail: w.j.taylor@hw.ac.uk)
Sport and recreation. Director, Sport and Exercise: Fitchett, Michael, BEd Keele, MPhil H-W (E-mail: m.a.fitchett@hw.ac.uk)
Staff development and training. Director, Educational Development Unit: Bamber, Veronica (E-mail: v.bamber@hw.ac.uk)
Strategic planning. Director, Planning: McGookin, W. R., BA Oxf., MA Oxf.
(E-mail: r.w.r.mcgookin@hw.ac.uk)
Student welfare/counselling. Director, Student Welfare Services: Johnston, Christine (E-mail: c.johnston@hw.ac.uk)
Students from other countries. International Students Advisor: Blackwood, Eileen
(E-mail: e.e.blackwood@hw.ac.uk)
Students with disabilities. Disability Adviser: Sabiston, Sandra, BEd Edin., BSc QM Edin.
(E-mail: s.sabiston@hw.ac.uk)

CAMPUS/COLLEGE HEADS

Dubai Campus, Dubai Academic City, Dubai PO Box 294345, United Arab Emirates.
(Tel: +971 (0)4 361 6999; Fax: +971 (0)4 360 4800;
E-mail: dubaienquiries@hw.ac.uk) Head: Cornwell, Prof. Keith J., BSc City(UK), PhD Lond., DEng H-W, FIMechE
Scottish Borders Campus, Netherdale, Galashiels, Selkirkshire, Scotland TD1 3HF.
(Tel: (01896) 753351; Fax: (01896) 758965; E-mail: l.a.lindsay@hw.ac.uk) Head, School of Textiles and Design: Wardman, Prof. R. H., BTech Brad., PhD Brad.

[Information supplied by the institution as at 1 October 2007, and edited by the ACU]

UNIVERSITY OF HERTFORDSHIRE

Founded 1992

Member of the Association of Commonwealth Universities

Postal Address: College Lane, Hatfield, Hertfordshire, England AL10 9AB
Telephone: (01707) 284000 **Fax:** (01707) 284115
URL: http://www.herts.ac.uk

VICE-CHANCELLOR*—Wilson, Prof. R. J. Tim, BSc *Reading*, MA *Lanc.*, PhD, FRSA, CCMI
DEPUTY VICE-CHANCELLOR—(vacant)
DEPUTY VICE-CHANCELLOR—Leinonen, Prof. Eeva K., BSc *Aston*, MPhil *Exe.*, PhD *CNAA*
DEPUTY VICE-CHANCELLOR AND DIRECTOR OF FINANCE—Neville, Terry M.
SECRETARY AND REGISTRAR‡—Waters, Philip E., BSc(SocialSciences) *S'ton.*, FRSA
PRO VICE-CHANCELLOR (REGIONAL AFFAIRS)—Boffey, Stephen A., MA *Camb.*, PhD *Camb.*, FIBiol
PRO VICE-CHANCELLOR (RESEARCH)—Senior, Prof. John M., BSc *Birm.*, MSc *UMIST*, DSc *Manc.Met.*, FIEE, FRSA
DIRECTOR OF LEARNING AND INFORMATION SERVICES—Wingate-Martin, Prof. Diana E., BA *Lond.*, MA *Middx.*

GENERAL INFORMATION

History. The institution was established in 1952 and became successively a technical college, a college of technology and a polytechnic, before receiving its university status in 1992.

The main campus is at Hatfield, 16km north of London, with a further campus housing the School of Law at St Albans.

Admission to first degree courses (see also United Kingdom Introduction). Applications for full-time or sandwich first degree courses should be made through the Universities and Colleges Admissions Service (UCAS). Applicants from outside the UK, if their first language is not English, must provide evidence of English competence equivalent to British Council IELTS 6.0.

First Degrees (see also United Kingdom Directory to Subjects of Study). BA, BEd, BEng, BSc, LLB, MChem, MEng, MPhys.

BEng and BSc may also be taken as sandwich courses lasting 4 years. MChem, MEng and MPhys may also be taken as sandwich courses lasting 5 years.

Length of course. Full-time: BA, BEd, BEng, BSc, LLB: 3 years; MChem, MEng, MPhys: 4 years. Part-time: BA, BEng, BSc, LLB: 5 years.

Higher Degrees (see also United Kingdom Directory to Subjects of Study).

Master's. LLM, MA, MBA, MEd, MPhil, MRes, MSc.

Admission. Applicants for admission to master's degrees must normally hold an appropriate first degree with at least second class honours. MPhil: good honours or master's degree.

Length of course. Full-time: LLM, MA, MBA, MRes, MSc: 1 year; MPhil: 2 years. Part-time: LLM, MA, MBA, MEd, MPhil, MSc: 3 years. By distance learning: MSc: 3 years.

Doctoral. DLitt, DSc, LLD, PhD.

Admission. Candidates for admission should normally hold a good honours or master's degree. All doctoral degrees are awarded on published work.

Length of course. Full-time: PhD: 3–4 years. Part-time: PhD: 5–6 years.

Libraries. Volumes: 500,000. Special collections: Fransella Personal Construct Psychology Collection.

Academic Year (2007–2008). Two semesters: 24 September–18 January; 21 January–30 May.

Income (2005–2006). Total, £160,171,000.

Statistics. Staff (2006–2007): 2441 (1132 academic, 1309 non-academic). Students (2006–2007): full-time 19,165 (9475 men, 9690 women); part-time 4330 (1110 men,

3220 women); international 5430 (2950 men, 2480 women); distance education/external 235 (190 men, 45 women); undergraduate 20,245 (8855 men, 11,390 women); master's 2800 (1140 men, 1660 women); doctoral 455 (265 men, 190 women).

FACULTIES/SCHOOLS

Business
Tel: (01707) 285401 Fax: (01707) 285409
E-mail: s.harrison-barker@herts.ac.uk
Dean (Acting): Newlan, Julie A., MBA *Lond.Guild.*
Secretary: Tetsell, Margot M.

Creative and Cultural Industries
Tel: (01707) 285301 Fax: (01707) 285312
E-mail: l.uttley@herts.ac.uk
Dean: McIntyre, C., BA *CNAA*
Secretary: Kaye, Joni

Engineering and Information Sciences
Tel: (01707) 284300 Fax: (01707) 284781
E-mail: n.m.thomas@herts.ac.uk
Dean: Senior, Prof. John M., BSc *Birm.*, MSc *UMIST*, DSc *Manc.Met.*, FIEE, FRSA
Secretary: Hollinshead, Jill

Health and Human Sciences
Tel: (01707) 284428 Fax: (01707) 284415
E-mail: r.m.jones@herts.ac.uk
Dean: Hunt, W. Barry, BPharm *Nott.*, PhD *Nott.*
Secretary: Blay, Janet

Humanities, Law and Education
Tel: (01707) 285633 Fax: (01707) 285611
E-mail: e.a.1.clark@herts.ac.uk
Dean: Clutterbuck, Andrew H., BEd *Camb.*, MSc *Sus.*, PhD *Lond.*
Secretary: Hubbard, Hilary J.

Interdisciplinary Studies
Tel: (01707) 285200 Fax: (01707) 285202
E-mail: k.wakely@herts.ac.uk
Dean: Boffey, Stephen A., MA *Camb.*, PhD *Camb.*, FIBiol
Secretary: Allen, Mary

ACADEMIC UNITS

Accounting, Finance and Economics
Tel: (01707) 285490 Fax: (01707) 285410
E-mail: m.broadbent@herts.ac.uk
Andersson, Tord, BSc MSc Sr. Lectr.
Awadallah, Emad, PhD *Essex* Sr. Lectr.
Beaumont, Sarah, MAEd *Middx.* Sr. Lectr.
Broadbent, Mick, MA *Sheff.*, MSc *Bath*, FRSA Prof.; Head*
Byass, Edwina, MBA *Brun.* Sr. Lectr.
Bywaters, D., BA *Essex*, MA *Middx.* Sr. Lectr.
Cobb, R. J. Sr. Lectr.
Currie, Frank, BSc *Strath.*, PhD *Strath.* Sr. Lectr.
Dagdeviren, Hulya, BA *Marmara*, MSc *Lond.*, PhD *Lond.* Sr. Lectr.
Easter, J. P., BA *Durh.* Sr. Lectr.

Gayfer, David, MA *Herts.* Assoc. Dean (Academic)
Hardy, Jane A., BSc *Bath*, MA *Lond.Guild.*, PhD *Durh.* Reader
Haslam, C. J., BSc *Wales*, PhD *Wales* Prof.
Hodgson, G. M., BSc *Manc.*, MA *Manc.*, MA *Camb.*, DLitt *Camb.* Res. Prof.
Kerr, E., MBA *Cran.* Sr. Lectr.
Kraithman, D. A., BSc *Hull*, MA *Sus.*, MSc *Herts.* Principal Lectr.
Lee, Edward, PhD *Lond.Inst.* Sr. Lectr.
Malik, Muhammed, PhD *Middx.* Sr. Lectr.
Marambos, P., BCom *Witw.*, BAcc *Witw.* Sr. Lectr.
Modi, Monica, BSc *Herts.* Sr. Lectr.
Newman, Peter, BSc *Lond.*, MBA *Strath.* Principal Lectr.
Paananen, Mari, PhD Principal Lectr.
Riordan, Joseph, BA *Lanc.*, MA *Staffs.* Sr. Lectr.
Roarty, Michael, BA *Essex*, MSc *Reading* Sr. Lectr.
Salmon, Keith G., BA *Sheff.*, MA *Sheff.*, PhD *Luton* Sr. Lectr.
Shah, Syed, MA MBA Sr. Lectr.
Simpson, Mary, BA *Middx.*, MSc *Lond.* Sr. Lectr.
Taylor, M. E., MSc *UMIST* Assoc. Head
Thomas, D. G., BA *CNAA*, MSc *Lond.*, PhD *Herts.* Sr. Lectr.
Tsitsianis, Nicholas, BSc MSc DPhil Sr. Lectr.
Waksman, J., BSc *Lond.*, MSc *Lond.* Sr. Lectr.
Ye, Zhen, LLM *Newcastle(UK)*, DPhil *Herts.* Sr. Lectr.
Yin, Shuxing, PhD *Manc.* Sr. Lectr.
Yin, Y. P., BSc *Beijing*, PhD *Strath.* Sr. Lectr.
Other Staff: 2 Visiting Profs.; 4 Lectrs.; 3 Res. Staff; 3 Lectrs.†

Art and Design
Tel: (01707) 285313 Fax: (01707) 285350
E-mail: j.glasman@herts.ac.uk
Adams, Richard, BSc *Salf.*, MSc *Salf.* Principal Lectr.
Adams, Steven R., BA *Lond.Inst.*, MA *RCA*, PhD *Leeds* Assoc. Head
Anderson, Benedict, MA DPhil Principal Lectr.
Biggs, Michael A. R., BA *CNAA*, MA *CNAA*, PhD *Reading* Prof.; Assoc. Dean (Res.)
Bloxam, L., BA *C.England*, MA *C.England* Sr. Lectr.
Borstrock, Stephen, MA *Lond.* Assoc. Head
Brown, Philippa K. S., BA *Bath* Sr. Lectr.
Carter, M. R. Sr. Lectr.
Cheung, Sophie, MA *RCA* Sr. Lectr.
Cooke, Felicity M., BA *CNAA*, MA *RCA* Principal Lectr.
Dalwood, A., BA *Newcastle(UK)*, MFA *Reading* Sr. Lectr.
Dorey, Roger W., MA *Herts.* Sr. Lectr.
Felstead, Cathie, MA *RCA* Sr. Lectr.
Freshwater, Sally, BA *Lond.*, MA *RCA* Principal Lectr.
Glasman, Judy, BA *Lond.*, MSc *Lond.*, MBA *Leic.* Head*
Graff, Adam Sr. Lectr.

Harris, Jessica, BA C.Lancs.   Sr. Lectr.

Illner, Antje, BA RCA, MA RCA   Sr. Lectr.

Jury, Samantha, MFA Cornell   Sr. Lectr.

Lees-Maffei, Grace, BA Wales, MA RCA, PhD Portsmouth   Sr. Lectr.

Lewis, Tessa C., BA CNAA, MA RCA   Sr. Lectr.

Lindley, Julian K., BA CNAA   Sr. Lectr.

Lockhart-Nelson, S. D., BA(VisArt) Syd.   Sr. Lectr.

Marsh, Huren, MA   Sr. Lectr.

Marsh, J. Lynne M., BA C'dia., MA Lond.   Sr. Lectr.

Marshall-Tierney, Andrew, MA Essex   Sr. Lectr.

McGonigal, Stephen, BA Tees., MA De Mont.   Sr. Lectr.

McGravie, Dave, BA CNAA, MA Herts.   Principal Lectr.

McIntosh, Roderick, BA Sheff.Hallam   Sr. Lectr.

Palmer, Pauline, MPhil Camb.   Sr. Lectr.

Rosella, Tony, BA Nott.Trent   Principal Lectr.

Rothwell, K. E., BA CNAA   Sr. Lectr.

Schooley, M., MA RCA   Sr. Lectr.

Shellard, Annie, BA Belf.   Sr. Lectr.

Shortt, Linda J., BA CNAA   Assoc. Head

Simpson, P. A., BA Essex, PhD Essex   Sr. Lectr.

St James, M., BA Wales   Prof.

Sykes, J. A., BA CNAA, MA E.Lond.   Sr. Lectr.

Wright, Michael J., BAFA Liv., MA Herts.   Sr. Lectr.

Other Staff: 5 Lectrs.; 2 Res. Fellows; 2 Res. Staff; 1 Des. Tutor; 2 Sr. Lectrs.†

Research: art history (design, nineteenth-century French painting, twentieth-century Soviet art); art therapies (art therapy and autism, efficacy studies in arts therapies for people with learning difficulties, story-telling and therapy, theoretical developments in drama therapy); fine art (fine art and new technologies, fine art/craft interface, site-specific art)

Combined Studies

Tel: (01707) 285203 Fax: (01707) 285202
E-mail: p.lockett@herts.ac.uk

Bygate, Dominic, BSc Birm., MSc Herts.   Sr. Lectr.

Duplain, Nicole G. M., LèsL St.-Etienne   Sr. Lectr.

Foster, I. V. J., BA CNAA, LLM Camb.   Sr. Lectr.

Fowler, M. A., BSc CNAA, MAEd Herts.   Sr. Lectr.

Gillett, Andrew, BSc Durh., MA Kent   Principal Lectr.

Hammond, Angela C., BA Leeds, MA Herts.   Sr. Lectr.

Korgaonkar, Gill, LLM Lond.   Sr. Lectr.

Kynnersley, J. Dave, BSc Leeds, MSc CNAA, MPhil Leeds   Principal Lectr.

Leonard, Jenifer A., BA Camb.   Sr. Lectr.

Lockett, Philip E., MA Camb.   Assoc. Dean; Head*

Martala-Locket, Mary   Sr. Lectr.

Omer, Karry   Sr. Lectr.

Rapley, Eve   Sr. Lectr.

Roberts, Paul B., BA Liv.   Principal Lectr.

St John, Judy   Principal Lectr.

Winder, Julia S., MSc Lond., MBA Herts., PhD CNAA   Principal Lectr.

Wray, Elizabeth   Sr. Lectr.

Other Staff: 1 Lectr.

Computer Science

Tel: (01707) 284327 Fax: (01707) 284781
E-mail: j.a.hewitt@herts.ac.uk

Adams, Roderick G., BSc Leic., MSc Leic., MSc CNAA, PhD CNAA   Principal Lectr.

Albrecht, Andreas A., MSc Moscow, DrRerNat Humboldt, DrScNat Humboldt   Sr. Lectr.

Baddoo, Nathan, BSc Northumbria, PhD Herts.   Sr. Lectr.

Baillie, E. Jean, BSc Wales, MSc CNAA, PhD Herts.   Principal Lectr.

Barker, Trevor, BA Open(UK), MSc CNAA, PhD Herts.   Principal Lectr.

Bennett, Steven J., BA Birm., MA Middx., MPhil Oxf.   Sr. Lectr.

Berkhout, Mariette E., BA Gron., MSc Herts.   Sr. Lectr.

Bhinder, F. S., BSc Punjab, PhD Lond.   Visiting Prof.

Bowes, David H., BSc Lond., MSc Herts.   Sr. Lectr.

Calcraft, Lee G. A., BA Essex, PhD Leeds   Sr. Lectr.

Canamero, Lola M., BA Madrid, MSc Madrid, PhD Paris XI   Sr. Lectr.

Christianson, D. Bruce, MSc Well., DPhil Oxf.   Res. Prof.

Crouch, Rosalind M., BA Reading, BSc Open(UK), MA CNAA   Principal Lectr.

Dai, Haihong, BSc Wuhan, PhD Ulster   Sr. Lectr.

Dautenhahn, Kerstin, DrRerNat Bielefeld   Res. Prof.

Davey, Neil, BSc Manc., MSc Lond., MSc Brun.   Principal Lectr.

Dawkins, K. Tony, BSc CNAA, MBA Herts.   Sr. Lectr.

Dickerson, Robert G., BA E.Anglia, MSc Lond.   Principal Lectr.

Doolan, Martina A., BSc Herts., MSc Herts.   Principal Lectr.

Egan, Colin   Sr. Lectr.

Folgate, Sandra, BA Herts., PhD Herts.   Sr. Lectr.

Frank, Raymond J., BSc Lond., MSc Lond., MSc City(UK)   Principal Lectr.

Hall, Tracy, BA CNAA, MSc CNAA, PhD City(UK)   Principal Lectr.

Hewitt, Jill A., BA E.Anglia, MSc CNAA   Prof.; Head*

Hunt, Stephen P., BSc Lond., MSc CNAA   Sr. Lectr.

Jefferies, Amanda L. J., BA Lond., MSc CNAA   Principal Lectr.

Jenkin, J. Mark, BSc Birm., MSc Birm.   Principal Lectr.

Ji, W., PhD Coventry, BEng MEng   Sr. Lectr.

Lane, Peter, BA Oxf., MSc Exe., DPhil Exe.   Sr. Lectr.

Lilley, Marian, MSc Herts.   Sr. Lectr.

Malcolm, James A., MA Camb.   Principal Lectr.

Marczyk, Alexandra A., BA Keele, MEd Lond., MSc Herts.   Sr. Lectr.

Nehaniv, Christopher L., BSc Mich., PhD Calif.   Res. Prof.

Oliver, Roger G., BA Open(UK), BSc Hull, MTech Brun., PhD Hull   Assoc. Head

Polani, Daniel, DrRerNat Mainz   Principal Lectr.

Pye, Lynette J., BA Stir., MSc Cran.IT   Sr. Lectr.

Quick, Patrick C., MA Camb.   Sr. Lectr.

Rainer, Austen W., BSc Bourne., PhD Bourne.   Sr. Lectr.

Sapsford, John, BSc CNAA, MSc CNAA   Principal Lectr.

Saward, Guy R. E., BSc Warw., PhD Warw.   Sr. Lectr.

Scholz, S.-B., DerRerNat Kiel, DrHabil Kiel   Sr. Lectr.

Shafarenko, Alex, MSc Novosibirsk, PhD Novosibirsk   Res. Prof.

Spring, William, MSc Lond.   Sr. Lectr.

Tiwari, Ashok, MSc Cran.IT, MBA Lond., FRSA   Sr. Lectr.

Trainis, Simon A., BEd Leeds, MSc CNAA, PhD Herts.   Principal Lectr.

Wernick, Paul D., BSc Lond., MSc Lond., PhD Lond.   Sr. Lectr.

Werry, Iain, BSc Westminster   Sr. Lectr.

Wood, Michael F., BSc Lond., MSc Herts.   Sr. Lectr.

Xiao, Hannan, BEng MEng DPhil   Sr. Lectr.

Yip, Pik-Yee, MSc Herts.   Sr. Lectr.

Other Staff: 7 Lectrs.; 3 Res. Fellows; 3 Visiting Res. Fellows; 6 Res. Staff; 2 Sr. Lectrs.†

Continuing Education and Partnerships

Tel: (01707) 284668 Fax: (01707) 284284
E-mail: s.culliford@herts.ac.uk

Cochrane, Jill   Sr. Lectr.

Culliford, Steve, BSc Lond., MSc CNAA   Head*

Flynn, S. J., BSc N.Lond., MA Open(UK)   Sr. Lectr.

Hartley, J., BSc Portsmouth, MSc Portsmouth   Sr. Lectr.

Jones, C. F., BA CNAA, MSc Brun.   Principal Lectr.

Messenger, Hazel   Sr. Lectr.

Pinn, Keith, BSc Lond., MA CNAA, MA Herts.   Principal Lectr.

Other Staff: 5 Lectrs.

Education

Tel: (01707) 285675 Fax: (01707) 285409
E-mail: m.read@herts.ac.uk

Akinbode, Adenike, BSc Leic.   Sr. Lectr.

Allen, Rosemary K., MA Herts.   Principal Lectr.

Berry, Jonathan H., BA CNAA   Sr. Lectr.

Bloomfield, Peter A., BSc E.Anglia, MA Lond.   Sr. Lectr.

Bowtell, Julie M., MA Herts.   Sr. Lectr.

Brundrett, M., BA CNAA, MA Keele, MEd Keele, EdD Leic., PhD Herts., FRSA, FCT   Visiting Prof.

Bulman, Una K., BEd S'ton., MA S'ton.   Sr. Lectr.

Burchell, Helen, BSc Lond., MSc Lond., PhD Herts.   Assoc. Head

Dall, Hazell, BEd Kent   Sr. Lectr.

Dell, Eric R., MA Brun.   Sr. Lectr.

Gould, C., BSc Leeds, MEd Nott., PhD Sheff., FIBiol   Visiting Prof.

Graham, Sally F., BA CNAA, MA Lond.   Sr. Lectr.

Hume, Caroline, BEd Leic.   Sr. Lectr.

Jarvis, Joy, BEd Exe., MA Herts., PhD Herts.   Principal Lectr.

Jones, E. Trevor, BA Lond., MA McM., MA(Ed) Keele   Sr. Lectr.

Lenten, P. E., BEd Exe., MA Lond.   Sr. Lectr.

Levy, Roger R., BA Manc., MA Lond., PhD Greenwich   Sr. Lectr.

Mansey, P. Anne, BA Reading, MA De Mont.   Sr. Lectr.

McLauchlin, Alison K., BEd Kent, MA De Mont.   Sr. Lectr.

Mercer, Alex W. B., BA Open(UK), MEd Sheff.   Sr. Lectr.

Phillips, Mandy A., BEd CNAA   Sr. Lectr.

Platt, A. Mike, BSc Warw.   Sr. Lectr.

Powell, Stuart D., BEd CNAA, PhD Birm.   Res. Prof.

Punter, Anne L., BA Wales, MEd Herts., PhD Luton   Sr. Lectr.

Quinn, David, BA Open(UK), BSc Durh.   Sr. Lectr.

Rawlings, Bernice M., BA Manc.   Sr. Lectr.

Read, Mary E., MA Open(UK)   Head*

Rees, Mary E., BPhil(Ed) Exe., MEd Herts.   Principal Lectr.

Ruback, Prue E., BA Leeds, MA Lond.   Sr. Lectr.

Seliet, H., BSc Cairo, MEd Hudd.   Sr. Lectr.

Short, Geoff A., BA Leeds, BSc Lond., MEdPsych Sus., PhD Newcastle(UK)   Reader

Silcock, P. J., MEd Birm., PhD Birm.   Visiting Prof.

Thomas, Kit R., BA Liv., PhD Herts.   Assoc. Head

Thomas, N., CBE, Hon. DLitt Herts., Hon. FCP   Visiting Prof.

Timson, Carol J., BEd Bath, MA Lond.   Sr. Lectr.

Trodd, Lyn F., BA York(UK), MEd Open(UK)   Sr. Lectr.

Warren, Val N., BSc Lond., MA Herts.   Principal Lectr.

White, S., BA Kingston(UK)   Sr. Lectr.

Woolhouse, Marian, BEd Newcastle(UK), MA Lond.   Sr. Lectr.

Other Staff: 1 Res. Staff; 8 Sr. Lectrs.†

Research: autism; equal opportunities; literacy; teaching and learning

Engineering, Aerospace, Automotive and Design

Tel: (01707) 284250 Fax: (01707) 285086
E-mail: a.starr@herts.ac.uk

Ali, Rashid, BSc Punjab, BTech Lough., PhD Lough.   Sr. Lectr.

Angel, Geoff, BSc Herts.   Sr. Lectr.

Ash, Howard, MEng Leeds, PhD Leeds

Ashall, David, PhD Herts.   Sr. Lectr.

Badi, Mohammed N. M., BSc(Eng) Lond., MSc Lond., PhD Lond. Sr. Lectr.

Bevis, K. I., BSc(Eng) Lond., MSc City(UK) Academic Manager

Byrne, C. Liz I., BSc Brist., MPhil CNAA, PhD Herts. Sr. Lectr.

Calay, R. K., BSc(Eng) Punjab, MSc Cran., PhD Cran. Sr. Lectr.

Chen, Yong K., BSc Taiyuan U.T., MSc Taiyuan U.T., PhD Birm. Sr. Lectr.

Chrysanthou, Andreas, BSc(Eng) Lond., PhD Lond. Sr. Lectr.

Combes, Alan J., BSc Keele Jt. Head*

Day, Rodney A., BEng CNAA, MBA Herts., PhD Herts. Sr. Lectr.

Dell, D. J., BSc Exe. Sr. Lectr.

Folkson, R., BSc Lond., FIMechE Visiting Prof.

Fowler, M. A., BSc CNAA, MAEd Herts. Sr. Lectr.

Germany, David A., BSc Lough., MSc Cran. Principal Lectr.

Haritos, George, BSc CNAA, MSc Aston, PhD Staffs. Sr. Lectr.

Harrington, Matthew J., BSc Lond., BEng Herts. Sr. Lectr.

Hart, Ken J., BSc Sus., DPhil Sus. Principal Lectr.

Jawad, Saad A., BSc Newcastle(UK), PhD Brun. Sr. Lectr.

Khoudian, Petros, BSc CNAA, MBA City(UK) Assoc. Head

King, J. A., BSc CNAA, Hon. DSc Herts., FIMechE Visiting Prof.

Knight, Jason J., BEng Herts., PhD Warw. Sr. Lectr.

Lewis, Andrew P., MA Oxf., MSc Cran.IT, PhD Lond. Assoc. Head

Loke, Siew K., BSc Aston, PhD Aston Sr. Lectr.

Mays, I. D., BSc Reading, PhD Reading Visiting Prof.

McAndrew, Ian R., BA Open(UK), MSc Open(UK), MA Luton, PhD Herts. Sr. Lectr.

Mitchell, Les, MBA Newcastle(UK), PhD Herts., FIEE, FIMechE Sr. Lectr.

Mughal, H. G., BSc Open(UK), BSc Birm., MSc Birm., Hon. DSc Herts. Visiting Prof.

Murray, Susan, BSc CNAA Sr. Lectr.

Nasser, Sami H., BSc(Eng) Baghdad, MSc Leeds, PhD Leeds Sr. Lectr.

Pearce, Dave M., BSc CNAA Principal Lectr.

Peters, Jeff, BSc CNAA Principal Lectr.

Russell, Mark B., BEng Herts. Principal Lectr.

Sayigh, A. A. M., BSc Lond., PhD Lond., FIEE Visiting Prof.

Starr, Andrew, BEng Leeds, PhD Manc. Head*

Tiu, William P., BSc Lond., PhD City(UK) Sr. Lectr.

Wibberley, Brian L., MSc CNAA Sr. Lectr.

Wilkinson, Ray, BTech Lough. Sr. Lectr.

Xu, Y., BEng Zhejiang, MEng Zhejiang, PhD S'ton. Sr. Lectr.

Other Staff: 4 Res. Fellows; 5 Visiting Res. Fellows

Research: engineering, aeronautical; engineering, automotive

Engineering, Electronic, Communication and Electrical

Tel: (01707) 284151 Fax: (01707) 284199
E-mail: r.sotudeh@herts.ac.uk

Alinier, Nandini D., BEng Leeds, PhD Leeds Sr. Lectr.

Alukaidey, Talib, BSc Baghdad, MSc Brun., PhD Brun. Academic Manager

Ariyaeeinia, Aladdin M., BEng Tehran, MSc Keele, PhD CNAA Reader

Chakaveh, Sepideh, PhD Kent Sr. Lectr.

Cloutman, Richard W. G., BSc Lond., MSc Lond. Assoc. Head

Hayes, John, BEng Sheff., MSc Sheff.Hallam Sr. Lectr.

Hou, Baochun, BSc Harbin, MSc Harbin, PhD Harbin Sr. Lectr.

Kadhim, Naj J., BSc Salf., MSc Salf., PhD CNAA Sr. Lectr.

Kourtessis, Pandelis, BEng City(UK), MSc Essex, PhD Essex Sr. Lectr.

Lambert, Alan, BA Lond., LLB Lond., MA Lond. Sr. Lectr.

Lauder, David M., BSc Essex Sr. Lectr.

Lee, David C., BSc Nott., PhD Lond. Assoc. Head

Meads, David J. N., BSc Leeds Sr. Lectr.

Ramalingam, Soodamani, PhD Melb., BEng Sr. Lectr.

Siau, Johann, BEng Herts. Sr. Lectr.

Sotudeh, Reza, BSc CNAA, PhD CNAA, FRSA Prof.; Head*

Sun, Yichuang, BSc Dalian Maritime, MSc Dalian Maritime Prof.; Academic Manager*

Williams, Kate E., MEng Wales, MSc Herts. Sr. Lectr.

Xiao, Scarlet A., MSc Portsmouth, BEng Sr. Lectr.

Zhu, Q. Felix, MSc Portsmouth Sr. Lectr.

Other Staff: 5 Lectrs.; 2 Res. Fellows; 1 Sr. Lectr.†

Research: engineering (communications, electrical, electronic)

Film, Music and Media

Tel: (01707) 285304 Fax: (01707) 285350
E-mail: a.marden@herts.ac.uk

Arnold, Peter, MA Herts. Assoc. Head

Bahanovich, David, MMus Music Leader

Beaufoy, John Sr. Lectr.

Blinko, Timothy J., BMus Lond., MMus Lond. Assoc. Head

Bowman, Martin, BA CNAA Sr. Lectr.

Carboni, Marius, MA Lond. Sr. Lectr.

Collopy, Dennis, BA E.Anglia, MA Westminster Sr. Lectr.

Dearden, I., BA Leeds, MMus E.Anglia Sr. Lectr.

Ferris, Malcolm, MA RCA Res. Leader

Filoseta, Roberto, BSc Herts. Sr. Lectr.

Godman, Robert, BMus Lond. Reader

Goodbrey, Daniel, BSc Herts., MA Herts. Sr. Lectr.

Horrox, Alan Prof.

Hunt, Stephen D., BA CNAA, MA Bath Spa UC Sr. Lectr.

Jayalakshmi, Garrabost, PhD Open(UK) Programme Tutor

Larkum, Adam, MA Edin. Sr. Lectr.

Marden, Adrian, BA CNAA Assoc. Dean; Head*

Mitchell, Ian, BA CNAA, MA Herts. Principal Lectr.

Morgan, Nicholas Sr. Lectr.

Morgan, Simon Sr. Lectr.

Paley-Menzies, Lucille, MA Middx. Sr. Lectr.

Peacock, Alan D., BEd Camb. Principal Lectr.

Phillips, Ivan J., BA Manc., MA Nott., PhD Wales Sr. Lectr.

Pinn, Ashley J., BA CNAA, FRSA Principal Lectr.

Rayburn, Nicholas, BA Programme Leader

Rogers, Soloman, MA Herts. Sr. Lectr.

Smith, David, MA Camb. Sr. Lectr.

Squires, Richard, MFA Lond. Sr. Lectr.

Thomas, Rebecca, PhD E.Lond. Sr. Lectr.

Walden, Kim, BA Nott., MA Lond. Sr. Lectr.

Waring, Sarah, MFA RCA Sr. Lectr.

Wright, Rob, BEd Leeds Met., BSc Herts., MSc Herts. Sr. Lectr.

Other Staff: 6 Lectrs.; 1 Res. Staff; 7 Sr. Lectrs.†

Research: design, philosophy and the diagrammatical; new and electronic media; product design and information technology user interface; rapid prototyping

Health and Emergency Professions

Tel: (01707) 284962 Fax: (01707) 284977
E-mail: r.c.price@herts.ac.uk

Adeyemi, S. S., MA Sus. Sr. Lectr.

Alinier, Gullaume, MPhys Portsmouth Principal Lectr.

Anders, Anna M., MSc Herts. Sr. Lectr.

Arnold, N. D., BSc Open(UK) Sr. Lectr.

Baber, N., MB Clin. Dir.

Balston, C., BSc Witw., MSc Lond. Sr. Lectr.

Beeton, Karen, BSc E.Lond., MPhtySt Qld., PhD Herts. Assoc. Head

Brice, Tristan, BSc Trinity(Dub.) Sr. Lectr.

Brown, David, MSc E.Anglia Sr. Lectr.

Brown, Naomi Sr. Lectr.

Browning, Paul, MSc Salf. Sr. Lectr.

Cairns, Melinda, PhD Coventry Sr. Lectr.

Canning, Ian, BSc Herts. Sr. Lectr.

Catterall, Mathew, BSc Herts. Sr. Lectr.

Chisnall, Demelza, BSc City(UK) Sr. Lectr.

Clark, Louisa, BSc Derby Sr. Lectr.

Cook, Nicola J., BSc Lond. Sr. Lectr.

Cuffaro, Gill, BSc Herts. Sr. Lectr.

Davenport, H. Sally, MSc Lond. Sr. Lectr.

Davis, Diane H., MA Herts. Sr. Lectr.

Doel, Louise, MA Brun. Sr. Lectr.

Donaghy, John, BSc Herts. Sr. Lectr.

Dowries, Heidi Sr. Lectr.

Edwards, Hazel, MA Herts. Sr. Lectr.

Exelby, Linda Sr. Lectr.

Fairey, Gail, MSc Lond.S.Bank Sr. Lectr.

Fitzpatrick, Louise, BSc Cape Town, BSc Stell., MSc Stell. Sr. Lectr.

Gannon, Eliane, MSc Lond.S.Bank Assoc. Head

Glendinning, Samantha, BSc Herts. Sr. Lectr.

Gordon, L., MSc Herts. Principal Lectr.

Gregory, H., BSc Derby Sr. Lectr.

Harwood, Colin, BA Open(UK) Academic Manager

Harwood, Patricia, MSc City(UK) Sr. Lectr.

Heasman, Fraser, MSc Lond.Inst. Sr. Lectr.

Henderson, Julia E., MSc Sur. Assoc. Head

Higgs, Tony, MA Herts. Sr. Lectr.

Hilliard, Alan P., MSc Herts. Sr. Lectr.

Hoggard, Victoria, BSc Tees. Sr. Lectr.

Jardine, Sarah, BSc Coventry Sr. Lectr.

Jones, Carolyn Sr. Lectr.

Knowles, Linda, BSc Sur. Sr. Lectr.

Lewis-Brindley, Debbie J., MSc Brun. Sr. Lectr.

Lorimer, Jane E. M. Sr. Lectr.

MacGregor, Jayne, BSc E.Lond. Sr. Lectr.

Madden, Angela, PhD Lond. Principal Lectr.

Mann, T. Sr. Lectr.

McCarthy, Zoe, BSc Herts. Sr. Lectr.

McClinchy, Jane, MSc Herts. Sr. Lectr.

Meyer, Toni C., BSc Herts. Sr. Lectr.

Moulson, A., MSc Herts. Sr. Lectr.

Murray, Susan, MSc Herts. Sr. Lectr.

Newman, Sharon, MSc Lond. Sr. Lectr.

Nicholls, Tracey, BSc Anglia PU Sr. Lectr.

Owens, Andrew, BSc Open(UK) Sr. Lectr.

Papadopoulos, Solomon, MSc Brun. Sr. Lectr.

Parry-Jones, Elaine, BSc Anglia PU Sr. Lectr.

Payne, L. C., LLB Brist., MSc Leic. Sr. Lectr.

Pearson, Joanne, MSc Nott. Sr. Lectr.

Pine, Thomas, BSc Lond. Sr. Lectr.

Power, Paul, BSc Middx. Sr. Lectr.

Price, Richard C., MSc Lanc. Head*

Pulling, Jenny M. Sr. Lectr.

Ramlaul, Aarthi, BSc Sr. Lectr.

Richards, Ann, BA Open(UK), MSc Herts. Sr. Lectr.

Rickard, Scott, BSc Cape Town Sr. Lectr.

Roscoe, Susan Sr. Lectr.

Ryder, Dionne, MSc Coventry Sr. Lectr.

Sayliss, Lesley, MSc E.Lond. Sr. Lectr.

Schreuder, Fiona M., BAppSc Syd., MSc Wales Sr. Lectr.

Sexton, Mary, MA Principal Lectr.

Sharma, Meera, MA Sr. Lectr.

Simmonds, Jane, MA Lond. Sr. Lectr.

Smith, Jane, MA Lond. Sr. Lectr.

Smith, L. M., MA Reading Sr. Lectr.

Terrett, J. Sr. Lectr.

Thayre, Karen W., MSc Herts. Sr. Lectr.

Thornton, Heather, MBA Open(UK) Principal Lectr.

Venstone, G., BSc Herts. Sr. Lectr.

Vickers, Margaret, DPhil Lond.Inst. Res. Dir.

Vosper, Martin R., BSc Hull, MSc Herts. Sr. Lectr.

Watson, Tim, BSc CNAA, PhD Sur. Prof.; Academic Manager

Webber, Janet R. Sr. Lectr.

Wiehahn, Austin, MA ANU Sr. Lectr.

Williams, Julia, BSc Sur. Principal Lectr.

Williams, Laurie E., MSc City(UK) Sr. Lectr.

Wyer, S., MSc Sr. Lectr.

York, Helen Principal Lectr.

Other Staff: 2 Lectrs.; 1 Res. Fellow; 1 Res. Staff; 23 Sr. Lectrs.†

Research: clinical decision-making in radiography; curriculum design, competence and the extended role of radiographers; management issues in radiography; occupational standards in radiography

Humanities

Tel: (01707) 285722 Fax: (01707) 285409
E-mail: s.grainger@herts.ac.uk
Avery, S. J., BA Anglia PU, MA Nott., PhD Anglia PU   Sr. Lectr.
Boak, Helen L., BA Manc., PhD Manc.   Assoc. Dean
Bradley, Janette E., BA Reading, MA Lond.   Sr. Lectr.
Clutterbuck, Andrew H., BEd Camb., MSc Sus., PhD Lond.
Cragoe, Matthew F., BA Lond., MA Wales, DPhil Oxf.   Res. Prof.
Davies, O., BA Wales, PhD Lanc.   Reader
Goose, Nigel R., BA Kent, MA Lond., PhD Camb.   Res. Prof.
Grainger, Stephanie, BA Open(UK), MA Middx.   Head*
Groefsema, Marjolein, MA Lond., PhD Lond., BEd   Sr. Lectr.
Hitchcock, Tim, BA Calif., DPhil Oxf., FRHistS   Prof.; Assoc. Dean
Holderness, Graham, MA Oxf., BPhil Oxf., MPhil Open(UK), PhD Sur., DLitt Herts.   Res. Prof.
Hutto, Dan D., BA Marist, MPhil St And., DPhil York(UK)   Res. Prof.
Larvor, Brendon P., MA Oxf., MA Qu., DPhil Oxf.   Sr. Lectr.
Lippitt, John A., BSc Manc., MLitt Durh., PhD Essex   Reader
Loughrey, B., BA Sus., MA Sus., PhD Sur.   Visiting Prof.
MacKinnon, K. M., BSc(Econ) Lond., MA(Ed) Lond., PhD Lond.   Visiting Prof.
Maunder, Andrew C., BA Leic., MA Lond., MSc Tees., PhD Nott.   Principal Lectr.
Morris, Jonathan, BA Camb., PhD Camb., FRHistS   Res. Prof.
O'Sullivan, Mary M., BA Lond.   Sr. Lectr.
Parke, Tim H., BA Reading, MA Lond., PhD Reading   Principal Lectr.
Rowlands, Mark, BA Manc., DPhil Oxf.   Res. Prof.
Schelletter, Christina, MLing Manc., PhD Reading   Sr. Lectr.
Shaw, Tony, BA Leeds, DPhil Oxf.   Reader
Singleton, Jane, BA Exe., DPhil Sus.   Principal Lectr.
Stafford-Clark, Max R. G., BA Trinity(Dub.), Hon. DLitt Herts., Hon. DLitt Oxf.Brookes   Visiting Prof.
Styles, John, BA Camb., MA Camb.   Res. Prof.
Thomson, Alan, MA Camb., PhD Lond.   Academic Manager
Tripp, Anna F., BA Essex, MA Wales, PhD Wales   Sr. Lectr.
Wheeler, Pat A., BA Herts., MA Herts.   Sr. Lectr.
Zakrzewski, V. M., BSc Salf.   Sr. Lectr.
Other Staff: 1 Principal Lectr.; 5 Lectrs.; 1 Res. Fellow; 1 Visiting Fellow; 5 Sr. Lectrs.†
Research: history (countryside, demography, film, masculinities, regional and local, Wales, women); linguistics (bilingual/ disordered/first/second language acquisition, lexical semantics, pragmatics); literature (early modern, modernism, postmodernism (colonial, post-colonial), Victorian); philosophy (epistemology, ethics, Kierkegaard, metaphysics, mind, philosophy of language, religion and science, Wittgenstein)

Law

Tel: (01707) 283231 Fax: (01707) 283205
E-mail: c.wild@herts.ac.uk
Barnett, Ian S., LLB Hudd.   Sr. Lectr.
Bell, C. D., LLB Birm., LLM Birm., PhD Birm.   Visiting Prof.
Camp, Ralph D., LLB Brist.   Sr. Lectr.
Carey, Penny J., LLB CNAA, LLM Lond.   Principal Lectr.; Assoc. Dean, European and Internat. Affairs

Clark, Karen K., LLB Herts., MA Oxf.
Cotterell, Curtiz A., LLB CNAA, LLM Lond.   Sr. Lectr.
Crook, Heather J., BA Wales, LLM Herts.
D'Alton-Harrison, Rita, LLB E.Anglia   Sr. Lectr.
Farquhar, Sharon, LLB Birm.
Hamilton, Marina, LLB Hudd., LLM Herts.   Sr. Lectr.
Johnson, Maureen C., LLB Herts.
Korek, Sharon L., BSc Hull, LLB Herts., LLM Herts.   Sr. Lectr.
Kyriakides, Klearchos A., LLB Birm., MPhil Camb., PhD Camb.   Sr. Lectr.
O'Brien, John, LLB Camb., MA Camb., LLM Lond.   Principal Lectr.
Rendell, Catherine A., BA Durh., BCL Durh.   Assoc. Dean
Roy, James G., BA City(UK)   Principal Lectr.
Ruben, Eira A., MA Brandeis, MA Edin., LLM Lond.   Sr. Lectr.
Slee, David, BA Kent, LLM Lond.   Sr. Lectr.
Stockdale, E., LLB Lond., BSc(Econ) Lond., LLM Lond., MSc Cran., PhD Lond., Hon. LLD Herts.   Visiting Prof.
Tarassenko, Sophie, BA Oxf.   Sr. Lectr.
Watkins, Los, BA Leeds, LLB Staffs., LLM Staffs.   Sr. Lectr.
Weinstein, Stuart, BA Williams(Mass.), JD Col.   Principal Lectr.; Assoc. Head, Professl.
White, Richard J., BA Kent, LLM Lond.   Sr. Lectr.
Wiggins, Penny J., BA CNAA, LLM Lond.   Assoc. Head, Academic
Wild, Charles R., BSc(Econ) Lond., LLM Sheff., PhD Sheff.   Head*
Other Staff: 10 Lectrs.; 3 Sr. Lectrs.†
Research: corporate and commercial law; data protection and telecommunications law; e-commerce (e-contracts, e-crime, e-finance); international commercial law; public and private international law

Life Sciences

Tel: (01707) 284546 Fax: (01707) 285046
E-mail: r.j.slater@herts.ac.uk
Aldsworth, Timothy, PhD Glas.   Sr. Lectr.
Argent, Elesa, PhD Lough.   Sr. Lectr.
Barefoot, Helen C., BSc Herts., PhD Camb.   Sr. Lectr.
Baydoun, Anwar R., BSc Sund., PhD Sund.   Res. Prof.
Benham, Christopher, PhD Lond.   Sr. Lectr.
Blumhof, Jennifer, MA Middx.   Principal Lectr.
Brodie, M., BSc Edin., PhD Otago   Sr. Lectr.
Bryson, E., MA Lodz, MSc York(UK), PhD Open(UK)   Sr. Lectr.
Bugeja, Virginia, BSc Lond., PhD Lond.   Principal Lectr.
Burton, M. Agneta S., BSc Aberd., PhD Lond.   Sr. Lectr.
Corness, Jacqueline, DPhil   Sr. Lectr.
Crook, Darren S., BSc Hudd., MSc Hudd., PhD Hudd.   Sr. Lectr.
Edmonds-Brown, Veronica, PhD Lond.   Sr. Lectr.
Fletcher, Ian, BSc Brun., MSS U.S.Sports Acad.   Sr. Lectr.
Fox, Rachel, PhD Sund.   Sr. Lectr.
Garrett, Andrew, PhD   Sr. Lectr.
Goyal, Madhu, BSc Panjab, MSc Panjab, PhD Pg.IMER   Sr. Lectr.
Graeme-Cook, Kate, BA Trinity(Dub.), PhD Trinity(Dub.)   Sr. Lectr.
Hall, Avice M., BSc Leic., MSc Exe., PhD Exe.   Principal Lectr.
Hall, Steve J., BSc Wales, MSc Birm., PhD CNAA   Sr. Lectr.
Hoffman, Richard, BSc Lond., PhD E.Anglia   Sr. Lectr.
Huang, Jeffrey, PhD Manc.   Sr. Lectr.
Hughes, Stephen, PhD   Sr. Lectr.
Jones, David H., BSc N.Lond.   Sr. Lectr.
Jones, Heddwyn, BSc Wales, PhD Wales   Sr. Lectr.
Jones, Peter, BSc Liv.J.Moores   Sr. Lectr.
Kukol, Andreas, MSc Bielefeld   Sr. Lectr.
Lou, Fang, BSc China U.S.T., PhD Lund   Sr. Lectr.

McMullan, Niall M., BSc Salf., PhD N.U.I.   Sr. Lectr.
Mitchell, Andrew, MSc Tennessee   Sr. Lectr.
Molleman, Areles, BSc Ley., MSc Ley., PhD Gron.   Sr. Lectr.
Naseby, David C., BSc Wales, PhD Sur.   Sr. Lectr.
Naseby, Judith V., BSc Aberd., MSc Lough., PhD Liv.J.Moores   Sr. Lectr.
Pack, Stephen, DPhil   Sr. Lectr.
Pearlman-Houghie, Deborah   Sr. Lectr.
Pearson, J., MA Oxf., MA Camb., PhD Camb.   Visiting Prof.
Peterson, Dale W., BA Augsburg, PhD Minn.   Principal Lectr.
Piccaver, Howard, BSc N.Lond.   Sr. Lectr.
Porter, Philip, PhD Leeds   Sr. Lectr.
Price, Karen, DPhil   Sr. Lectr.
Rapley, Ralph, BSc CNAA, PhD Birm.
Roberts, Michael G., BSc Lond., PhD Lond.   Principal Lectr.
Rubiu, Monica, MSc Westminster   Sr. Lectr.
Sands, Tim B., BSc CNAA, PhD Herts., FRGS   Sr. Lectr.
Sewell-Hobbs, Bruce, BSc N.Lond.   Sr. Lectr.
Slater, Robert J., BSc Leeds, PhD Nott., FIBiol   Head*
Southern, Richard, MA Dund., PhD St And., FRGS   Sr. Lectr.
Stanbury, Peter F., BSc Wales, MSc Lond.   Assoc. Head
Thakur, Shori, BSc N.Lond.   Sr. Lectr.
Turner, David, MSc Luton   Sr. Lectr.
Webley, Sherael, PhD Lond.   Sr. Lectr.
Whelan, Clifford, PhD De Mont.   Sr. Lectr.
Willis, Jackie, PhD Birm.   Sr. Lectr.
Zukowskyj, Paul, MSc Greenwich   Sr. Lectr.
Other Staff: 7 Lectrs.; 4 Res. Fellows; 6 Visiting Res. Fellows; 1 Principal Lectr.†; 13 Sr. Lectrs.†
Research: medicinal chemistry; molecular biology and biotechnology; physiology and pharmacology

Management, Leadership and Organisation

Tel: (01707) 285463 Fax: (01707) 285455
E-mail: a.e.a.boussofiane@herts.ac.uk
Allsop, David, BA CNAA, MA Middx.   Principal Lectr.
Ashwin, S. M. A., BA CNAA, MSc Lond., MSc City(UK), PhD Lond.   Sr. Lectr.
Baker, Sue, BA St And.   Sr. Lectr.
Balawender, Richard, BSc Lond.S.Bank   Sr. Lectr.
Bond, Angela, MBA Henley   Sr. Lectr.
Choudrie, Jyoti, MSc Brun., DPhil Brun.   Reader
Cubric, M., BSc Belgrade, PhD C'dia.   Sr. Lectr.
Currie, Frank, BSc Strath., PhD Strath.   Assoc. Head
Debenham, Susan, MA Thames V.   Sr. Lectr.
Delliston, A., MA Herts.   Sr. Lectr.
Filosof, Jana, BA Herts., MBA Herts.   Sr. Lectr.
Fletcher, Jane, BSc   Assoc. Head
Forrester, Jerry W., BA CNAA, MPhil CNAA   Head*
Forson, Cynthia, LLM Penn., MBA Herts.   Sr. Lectr.
Gall, Gregor, MA Aberd., PhD UMIST   Prof.
Gee, Christine A., BA Lough.   Sr. Lectr.
Grey, Susan, BA N.U.I., MA N.U.I., MSc Birm., PhD Nott.   Assoc. Dean
Herman, Mike J., MSc Herts.   Sr. Lectr.
Hobson, John B., BSc(Econ) Hull, MSc City(UK)   Principal Lectr.
Hogan, John, BA Essex, MA Leeds   Sr. Lectr.
Holder, Carol A., BA Open(UK), MBA Durh.   Sr. Lectr.
Hollinshead, Graham, MSc Lond.   Principal Lectr.
Imani, Y., BA Teheran, MSc Lond.   Sr. Lectr.
Jacobs, E., MA Manc.   Sr. Lectr.
Kirkham, Janet D., BA Sheff., PhD Sheff.   Academic Manager
Moody, Kim, MA   Sr. Lectr.
Noble, Dorothea, BA Manc., MBA Brad., PhD Brad.   Principal Lectr.
Pye, Michael, BSocSc Waik., MSc Wales   Sr. Lectr.

Randle, Keith R., BSc Bath, BPhil Liv., PhD Herts., FCIPD   Academic Manager
Rosier, Mike J., BSc(Econ) Lond., MSc City(UK), MSc CNAA   Assoc. Dean
Seed, Keith, BA Manc., MA N.Lond.   Sr. Lectr.
Shelley, Steve M., BSc S'ton., MA Herts., PhD Herts.   Principal Lectr.
Smith, Paul, MA Warw., MSc Lond.   Assoc. Head
Spurr, Ian G., BA CNAA, MA Lond., MPhil City(UK)   Principal Lectr.
Stacey, Ralph D., BCom Witw., MSc(Econ) Lond., PhD Lond.   Academic Manager
Stead, Bob, BSc Herts., MSc Herts.   Sr. Lectr.
Wells, Hany, BSc S.Bank, MSc Herts.   Sr. Lectr.
Other Staff: 2 Visiting Profs.; 1 Lectr.; 1 Principal Res. Fellow; 2 Res. Fellows; 3 Sr. Lectrs.†

Marketing and Enterprise

Tel: (01707) 285494 Fax: (01707) 285455
E-mail: a.f.francis@herts.ac.uk
Banks, Judith, BA Manc.Met.   Sr. Lectr.
Beck, Siegrid, BA Greifswald   Sr. Lectr.
Brown, Christopher, BSc Lond.S.Bank, MA Middx.   Sr. Lectr.
Bunce, Sally A., MA Lond.   Principal Lectr.
Catulli, Maurizio, MA Kingston(UK)   Sr. Lectr.
Cooray, Muditha, MBA Keele   Sr. Lectr.
Cottee, Michaela J., BSc Lond., MSc Lond., PhD Open(UK)   Principal Lectr.
Crimes, Branden A., BA CNAA   Sr. Lectr.
Culkin, Nigel, BA CNAA, MA Herts.   Assoc. Dean
De Villez, Julian, MA Brun.   Sr. Lectr.
Deuchar, M., BA Open(UK), MBA Durh.   Sr. Lectr.
Ewen, Mark, BEd MA   Sr. Lectr.
Francis, A. F., BA De Mont., MA Warw.   Head*
Fraser, Peter J., MA Edin., MSc Lond., PhD Herts.   Sr. Lectr.
Glass, Lesley, MSc   Sr. Lectr.
Goodsall, Adrian E., MBA CNAA   Sr. Lectr.
Hall, Eric, MSc Strath.   Principal Lectr.
Herman, Ruth, BA Herts., MA Herts., PhD Open(UK)   Sr. Lectr.
Jones, Martyn H., BSc CNAA, FIEE   Sr. Lectr.
Kelvin, Alex, MA Ott., PhD Wales   Sr. Lectr.
Large, Caroline F., BA Lanc., MA Lanc., MBA Lanc.   Assoc. Head
Leboir, M. R., BEng Algiers, MSc Lond., PhD Lond.   Sr. Lectr.
Martin, Susan, BA York(UK), MSocSci Birm., MBA Lond., PhD Birm.   Sr. Lectr.
Mulholland, A. Gary, BSc Manc., MBA Herts.   Sr. Lectr.
Omar, Ogenyi, MSc Sheff.   Prof.
Paleologos, Issidora, MA Greenwich   Sr. Lectr.
Paterson, Dave J., BSc Reading, MSc Herts.   Sr. Lectr.
Proudlove, Diane, MBA Herts.   Sr. Lectr.
Relph, Amanda, BSc Open(UK), MAEd Open(UK)   Sr. Lectr.
Robins, Fiona M., BSc Herts., MSc Herts.   Sr. Lectr.
Robins, Karen E., BSc Lough., MSc Sus., MSc Herts.   Assoc. Head
Seamark, Christine, BSc Sus.   Sr. Lectr.
Sellars, Aletha D., BA Tees., MSc Birm.   Sr. Lectr.
Shah, B., BSc Kent, MBA Exe.   Sr. Lectr.
Shevlane, Nicola, BA Salf., MBA Brun.   Sr. Lectr.
Slater, Anne M., LèsL Lyons, Maîtrise Lyons   Sr. Lectr.
Spencer, Neil H., BSc Reading, MSc(SocialSciences) S'ton., PhD Lanc.   Principal Lectr.
Taylor, Paul C., BSc Bath, PhD Bath   Sr. Lectr.
Thompson, Nicholas, PhD Oxf.Brookes   Sr. Lectr.
Tofallis, Chris, BSc Lond., MSc Lond., PhD Lond.   Sr. Lectr.
Willard, James, BSc Brist., MSc Lond.   Sr. Lectr.
Other Staff: 4 Visiting Profs.; 1 Principal Lectr.; 5 Lectrs.; 3 Res. Staff; 5 Sr. Lectrs.†
Research: marketing and small to medium enterprises; niche tourism

Nursing and Midwifery

Tel: (01707) 285296 Fax: (01707) 285299
E-mail: l.karstadt@herts.ac.uk
Anderson, M. Irene, BSc Herts.   Sr. Lectr.
Atkins, Ann-Marie, BSc Herts.   Sr. Lectr.
Beary, Thomas, BSc Middx.   Sr. Lectr.
Birtles, A. Pat, BSc Manc.   Sr. Lectr.
Boyle, Sally A., BSc Open(UK), MBA Herts.   Assoc. Head
Brennan, Maureen P., BA Open(UK), MSc Manc.   Sr. Lectr.
Briggs, David, BA Lond., MSc Manc.   Sr. Lectr.
Byrne, Geraldine S. M., BA Sus., PhD Northumbria   Sr. Lectr.
Cahill, M. Jo, BSc Herts., MSc Lond.   Deputy Assoc. Dean
Campbell, Denise   Sr. Lectr.
Campbell, Garry, MA Exe.   Sr. Lectr.
Carr, Susan   Sr. Lectr.
Charles, Michele B., MSc City(UK)   Assoc. Head
Chelvanayagam, Sonya, MSc Lond.   Sr. Lectr.
Clapham, Jane, BSc Lond., MSc Lond.   Sr. Lectr.
Clare, Carl, MSc   Sr. Lectr.
Cloudsdale, Steve J., BA Open(UK)   Sr. Lectr.
Cook, Janet, MSc Sur.   Sr. Lectr.
Darby, Victoria, BSc City(UK)   Sr. Lectr.
Davidson, Maggie H., BA Manc.   Sr. Lectr.
Davies, Debbie S., BSc Open(UK), MSc Brun.   Sr. Lectr.
Dawson-Goodey, Emma, MA Herts.   Sr. Lectr.
Deane-Gray, Tandy   Sr. Lectr.
Dolby, Evelyn   Sr. Lectr.
Donnelly, Mary, BSc Herts.   Sr. Lectr.
Duncombe, Caroline, MSc Herts.   Sr. Lectr.
Entwistle, Francesca   Sr. Lectr.
Fearns, Debra, BA CNAA, MA N.Lond.   Sr. Lectr.
Flanagan, Madeleine, MSc Sheff.   Principal Lectr.
Fletcher, Jacqui, BSc Hudd.   Principal Lectr.
Flynn, Sheila   Sr. Lectr.
Freeman, Pauline, MSc Manc.   Sr. Lectr.
Gault, Christine A., MSc Sur.   Principal Lectr.
Goode, Rev. K. P., BSc CNAA, MSc Brun.   Sr. Lectr.
Gormley-Fleming, E. A., BSc Manc., MA Keele   Sr. Lectr.
Goulden, Barbara A., BSc Manc., MSc Middx.   Sr. Lectr.
Hamilton, Cathy J., BSc City(UK), MSc S.Bank   Sr. Lectr.
Harris, Denise, MA Herts.   Sr. Lectr.
Hemming, Laureen J., BA Open(UK), BPhil Exe.   Sr. Lectr.
Heyes, Mary J., MA Herts.   Sr. Lectr.
Hill, Carolyn, BSc Herts.   Sr. Lectr.
Houston, Melsa L., BA CNAA, MSc Lond.   Sr. Lectr.
Hulse, Jackie L., BA Durh., MSc Brun.   Sr. Lectr.
Janda-Schwab, Salamah, MBA Herts.   Sr. Lectr.
Jay, Annabel M., BA Leic., MA Herts.   Sr. Lectr.
Jenner, Liz A., BSc Sur., MEd Herts.   Principal Lectr.
Karstadt, Lyn, BA Open(UK), MA Open(UK)   Head*
Kell, B., BSc De Mont.   Sr. Lectr.
Kelly, Jackie A., MA E.Lond.   Sr. Lectr.
Kempson, Audrey, MSc Leic.   Sr. Lectr.
Knight, Denise A., BSc CNAA, MSc Lond., MSc Middx.   Principal Lectr.
Knopp, Noel, BSc Herts., MSc S.Bank   Sr. Lectr.
Korgaonkar, Gill, LLM Lond.   Sr. Lectr.
Laird-Pratt, Lorraine, BA Luton   Sr. Lectr.
Lancaster, Jerry C., BSc Reading   Sr. Lectr.
Lawrence, Chris, BSc Lond., MSc Herts.   Principal Lectr.
Lawson, Louise G., BSc Manc.   Sr. Lectr.
Lewinson, Lesline, MSc Brun.   Sr. Lectr.
Loughran, Tony, MSc Lond.   Sr. Lectr.
Maher, David, MSN Lond.S.Bank   Sr. Lectr.
Mallon, Sean, MSc   Sr. Lectr.
Maloret, Paul, BA Luton   Sr. Lectr.
McErlean, Louise, BSc Herts.   Sr. Lectr.
McIver, Malcolm, DPhil   Sr. Lectr.
McLaren, Paula, BSc Herts.   Principal Lectr.
McMorran, Pat, BEd CNAA, MSc Brun.   Sr. Lectr.

Mead, Marianne M. P., BA Open(UK), PhD Herts.   Principal Lectr.
Mehta, Lilla, BEd Hudd.   Sr. Lectr.
Migliozzi, Janet G., BSc Herts., MSc Lond.   Sr. Lectr.
Miller, Sue M., BSc Manc., MSc Manc.   Sr. Lectr.
Mitchell, Yvonne, BEd Sus.   Sr. Lectr.
Montague, Sue E., BSc Sur.   Assoc. Head
Murray, Lorraine, MSc Sur.   Sr. Lectr.
Nair, M., BSc Sur., MSc Sur.   Sr. Lectr.
Nash, C., MBA Herts.   Sr. Lectr.
Offredy, V. Maxine, BA Lond., MPhil Lond., PhD Herts.   Reader
Owen, Diane, BA Luton   Sr. Lectr.
Peate, Ian G., BEd Sus., MA Lond., LLM Wales   Assoc. Head
Ponapalam, Bala, BSc Herts.   Sr. Lectr.
Pratt, Laura, MA Herts.   Sr. Lectr.
Price, Jacqueline, BSc Middx.   Sr. Lectr.
Quinlivan, Lynn, BSc Open(UK)   Sr. Lectr.
Ragoo, Jay G., BSc Lond., MSc Lond.   Sr. Lectr.
Rajoo-Naidu, Vijaya   Sr. Lectr.
Randle, Alan, MA Hull   Professl. Leader
Rooney, Greg, MSc City(UK)   Professl. Leader
Rosenfeld, Virginia, MA Herts.   Sr. Lectr.
Say, Jane, MSc Sur.   Sr. Lectr.
Shaw, Mary A., MSc Herts.   Sr. Lectr.
Simmons, Kingsley L., BSc CNAA, MSc City(UK), PhD Lond.   Principal Lectr.
Sooben, Roja D., MA Lond.   Sr. Lectr.
Stephenson, Carol N., MSc Manc.   Sr. Lectr.
Surfraz, Mohammed N., BA Westminster, MSc Lond.   Sr. Lectr.
Thompson, Brian, MA Anglia PU   Sr. Lectr.
Titchener, Theresa M.   Sr. Lectr.
Todd, Margaret, BA Manc., MBA Oxf.Brookes   Sr. Lectr.
Tomlin, Margaret, MA Leic.   Sr. Lectr.
Tunbridge, Susan, BSc Herts.   Sr. Lectr.
Turner, Jan A., BSc Open(UK)   Assoc. Dean
Turney, Christiane, BA Luton   Sr. Lectr.
Vickers, Peter S., BA Open(UK), PhD Northumbria   Sr. Lectr.
Walter, Kim, BNur Herts.   Sr. Lectr.
Walton, Alan, MSc Herts.   Assoc. Dean
Weinrabe, David P., BEd CNAA   Principal Lectr.
Welch, Rachel, MA Westminster   Sr. Lectr.
Whatton, Susan S.   Sr. Lectr.
Wheeldon, Anthony, MSc Lond.   Sr. Lectr.
Whiting, Lisa S., BA Manc., MSc Manc.   Sr. Lectr.
Wilderman, T. F. Celia, BEd Lond.   Sr. Lectr.
Wilson, Patricia, BEd Lond.S.Bank   Sr. Lectr.
Wood, Pat L., MA Open(UK)   Sr. Lectr.
Yagambrun, Saga, MA E.Anglia   Sr. Lectr.
Yearley, Carol, MSc Brun.   Sr. Lectr.
Young, Kathryn, DPhil E.Anglia   Sr. Lectr.
Other Staff: 12 Lectrs.; 33 Sr. Lectrs.†
Research: assessment of newborn; bullying and child health; midwife decision-making

Pharmacy

Tel: (01707) 284570 Fax: (01707) 284506
E-mail: s.dhillon@herts.ac.uk
Bassin, J., PhD Herts.   Sr. Lectr.
Brown, Marc, PhD Lough.   Sr. Lectr.
Curtiss, S. J., BPharm Nott., MSc Lond.   Sr. Lectr.
Dhillon, Soraya, BPharm Lond., PhD Lond.   Prof.; Head*
Evans, B.   Principal Lectr.
Evans, Sara, PhD Kingston(UK)   Sr. Lectr.
Fergus, Suzanne, DPhil   Sr. Lectr.
Foulsham, Russell M., BSc Leic., MSc Liv.J.Moores, PhD Lond.   Principal Lectr.
Gallagher, Cathal, PhD Nott.   Sr. Lectr.
Garnier, Tracy, BSc Strath., PhD Lond.   Sr. Lectr.
Griffiths, David G., BSc S'ton., PhD Kent   Sr. Lectr.
Hopkins, Kelly   Principal Lectr.
Kravits, Laura, BSc Manc.   Sr. Lectr.
Moss, Gary, PhD Belf.   Principal Lectr.
O'Neill, Richard C., BPharm Lond., LLB Herts., LLM Herts., PhD Lond.   Assoc. Head
Peterson, Dale W., BA Augsburg, PhD Minn.   Sr. Lectr.
Rossiter, Sharon, DPhil   Sr. Lectr.

Schifano, Fabrizio, MD   Chair
Traynor, Mathew, DPhil   Sr. Lectr.
Other Staff: 5 Lectrs.; 3 Practitioners; 7
   Visiting Fellows; 2 Sr. Lectrs.†

Physics, Astronomy and Mathematics

Tel: (01707) 283068 Fax: (01707) 284256
   E-mail: s.g.ryan@herts.ac.uk
Axon, David J., BSc Durh., PhD Durh.   Visiting
   Prof.
Bartholomew-Biggs, M. C., BSc Exe., PhD Lond.
   Reader
Beddiaf, Salah, MSc Dund.   Sr. Lectr.
Brinks, E., BSc Ley., MSc Ley., PhD Ley.   Res.
   Prof.
Busolini, Don T., BSc Manc., MSc Lond., MPhil
   Reading   Assoc. Head
Chrysostomou, Antonio, BSc Lond., PhD Edin.
   Sr. Lectr.
Cioni, Maria-Rosa, BSc Bologna   Sr. Lectr.
Collett, Jim L., MA Camb., PhD Camb.
   Principal Lectr.
Davies, Alan J., BSc S'ton., MSc(Eng) Lond., PhD
   Lond., FIMA   Prof.
Drew, Janet, PhD Lond.   Prof.
Fitzharris, Andrew M., MA CNAA, MSc CNAA
   Principal Lectr.
Fritze, U., BSc Gött., MSc Gött., PhD Gött.,
   DrHabil Gött.   Reader
Granot, Jonathan, BSc MSc PhD   Principal
   Lectr.
Huelga, Susanna, Lic Salamanca, PhD Oviedo   Sr.
   Lectr.
Jones, Hugh, DPhil   Prof.
Kane, Steve J., BSc S'ton., PhD S'ton.   Sr. Lectr.
Lucas, Philip, BA Oxf., DPhil Oxf.   Sr. Lectr.
McCall, Alan, BSc Bath, BSc Open(UK), PhD Herts.
   Sr. Lectr.
Napiwotzki, R., PhD Kiel   Reader
Plenio, M. B., DrRerNat Gron.   Visiting Prof.
Ryan, Sean, BSc ANU, MBA ANU, PhD ANU
   Head*
Shlosman, I., BSc Haifa(Technion), MSc Tel-Aviv,
   PhD Tel-Aviv   Visiting Prof.
Singh, Kuldeep, BSc Lond., MSc Lond.   Sr. Lectr.
Stansfield, Gillian, BSc Brist., MA Oxf.   Sr.
   Lectr.
Steuernagel, Ole, MSc Munich, PhD Humboldt
   Sr. Lectr.
Tanvir, Nial, BSc Durh., PhD Durh.   Reader
Thompson, Mark, BSc Newcastle(UK), MSc
   Newcastle(UK), PhD Kent   Sr. Lectr.
Other Staff: 2 Lectrs.; 2 Fellows; 7 Res.
   Fellows; 2 Sr. Lectrs.†

Postgraduate Medicine

Tel: (01707) 286438
   E-mail: d.w.empey@herts.ac.uk
Dean, Guy, BNur Herts.   Principal Lectr.
Empey, Duncan W., FRCP   Prof.; Head*
Hunter, Cheri L., BA Lond., MSc Luton   Assoc.
   Dean; Assoc. Head
McLaughlin, Philomena, MSN S.Bank   Principal
   Lectr.
O'Connell, Rachel, BA Open(UK)   Sr. Lectr.
Parker, Andrea   Principal Lectr.
Richardson, Marion, BD Lond.Inst.   Programme
   Leader
Other Staff: 1 Sr. Lectr.†

Psychology

Tel: (01707) 284622 Fax: (01707) 285073
   E-mail: b.fletcher@herts.ac.uk
Annett, Lucy E., BA Oxf., MA Oxf., PhD Lond.
   Sr. Lectr.
Anthony, Sue H., BSc Herts., MA Herts.   Assoc.
   Head
Cowley, Stephen J., BA Camb., MA Camb., MA
   Leeds, PhD Camb.   Sr. Lectr.
Dittrich, Winand, DrRerNat Marburg   Reader
Done, D. John, BA Leic., PhD Wales   Academic
   Manager
Fletcher, Ben, BA Keele, DPhil Oxf.   Prof.;
   Head*
George, Christeen, BA Sheff., MSc Aston, PhD
   Brun.   Principal Lectr.

Gilhooly, Kenneth, MA Edin., MSc Stir., PhD
   Stir.   Res. Prof.
Hasenöhrl, Rudiger U., DerRerNat Düsseldorf,
   DrHabil Düsseldorf   Reader
Holland, Angela E., BSc CNAA, MSc Herts.
   Assoc. Head
Keville, Saskia, BSc Hull, DClinPsy Hull
   Principal Lectr.
Kvavilashvili, Lia, PhD Tbilisi   Reader
Laws, K. R., BSc CNAA, PhD Camb.   Res. Prof.
Lovatt, Peter, BSc Sus., MSc Stir., PhD Essex
   Reader
Marcell, A. T., BA Reading, PhD Reading   Res.
   Prof.
Page, Mike P. A., BA Oxf., PhD Wales   Reader
Pine, K. J., BSc Herts., PhD Herts.   Reader
Schmeer, Stefanie, DPhil T.U.Darmstadt   Sr.
   Lectr.
Schulz, Joerg, PhD Herts.   Sr. Lectr.
Slaski, A. Mark, BSc Lough., MSc UMIST, PhD
   UMIST   Sr. Lectr.
Solomons, Wendy, MSc Lond.   Academic
   Manager
Sullman, Mark, DPhil   Sr. Lectr.
Troop, Nicholas, PhD   Sr. Lectr.
Wiseman, Richard J., BSc Lond., PhD Edin.   Res.
   Prof.
Other Staff: 6 Lectrs.; 3 Res. Fellows; 1 Res.
   Tutor; 1 Principal Lectr.†; 2 Sr. Lectrs.†; 2
   Clin. Lectrs.
Research: applied social cognition;
   human–computer/technology interaction;
   mental health and clinical psychology;
   neuropsychology and psychopharmacology

Social, Community and Health Studies

Tel: (01707) 284495 Fax: (01707) 285237
   E-mail: b.littlechild@herts.ac.uk
Ansbro, Maria, MSc Oxf.   Sr. Lectr.
Booth, Jean, MSc Herts.   Sr. Lectr.
Brooks, Susan D. M., BA Open(UK), MSc Oxf.,
   MA Lond., MBA Open(UK)   Sr. Lectr.
Buckroyd, Julia M., MA St And., MA McM., PhD
   Camb.   Res. Prof.
Byers, Carmel, BA   Sr. Lectr.
Davies, Keith F., BA Reading, MSc Lond.   Sr.
   Lectr.
de Chenu, L., BA Hull, MSc Manc.   Sr. Lectr.
Dwyer, Alison M., BSc Brist.   Principal Lectr.;
   Head*
Evans, Jeremy, MA Herts.   Sr. Lectr.
Fitzgibbon, D. W. M., BA CNAA, MA Middx.
   Sr. Lectr.
Gaitanidis, Anastasios, PhD Kent   Sr. Lectr.
Green, Roger D., BA CNAA, MA CNAA, PhD
   Herts.   Principal Lectr.
Hahn, Sue, MA Wales   Sr. Lectr.
Hansen, Grethe D., MA Copenhagen, MA Brun.
   Sr. Lectr.
Jaffe, Alyson, MSocSc Cape Town   Sr. Lectr.
Lee, Soo, MSc Lond.   Principal Lectr.
Linton, Andrew J., BSc CNAA, MSc Oxf.,
   MSc(Econ) Lond.   Sr. Lectr.
Littlechild, Brian, MA CNAA, PhD Herts.   Prof.;
   Acting Head*
Massil, Ros, MA   Sr. Lectr.
Meffan, Caroline, MA Middx.   Sr. Lectr.
Middleton, Susan, BA Brad.   Sr. Lectr.
Mills, K., BA Brist.   Sr. Lectr.
Neal, David, BA Sus., MA Lond., MSc S.Bank   Sr.
   Lectr.
Payne, Helen L., MPhil Manc., PhD Lond.
   Reader
Popple, Gillian, PhD Sheff.   Sr. Lectr.
Rostom, Manjit, MSc City(UK)   Assoc. Head
Stowe, N. V., BA Manc.Met., MSc Lond.   Sr.
   Lectr.
Warrener, J., MA Keele   Sr. Lectr.
Wysling, G. Dave, BA CNAA, BSc Open(UK), MSc
   Aston, MPhil Cran.   Sr. Lectr.
Other Staff: 2 Lectrs.; 8 Sr. Lectrs.†
Research: counselling (adolescent emotional
   welfare, eating disorders); criminal justice;
   social work

SPECIAL CENTRES, ETC

Astrophysics Research, Centre for

Tel: (01707) 284500 Fax: (01707) 284514
   E-mail: j.h.hough@herts.ac.uk
Hough, J. J., BSc Leeds, PhD Leeds, FRAS   Dir.*
Research: active galactic nuclei; chemical
   evolution and evolved stars; high-energy
   astrophysics; star formation; structure,
   formation and evolution of galaxies

Atmospheric and Instrumentation Research, Centre for

Tel: (01707) 284173 Fax: (01707) 284185
   E-mail: p.h.kaye@herts.ac.uk
Kaye, Paul H., BSc CNAA, PhD CNAA, FIP
   Prof.; Head*
Research: atmospheric dynamics and air quality;
   light scattering and radioactive processes;
   particle instruments and diagnostics

Biodeterioration Centre

Tel: (01707) 284522 Fax: (01707) 285046
   E-mail: biodet@herts.ac.uk
Smith, Rick N.   Dir.*
Research: biocide testing; biodegradation;
   diagnosis and control of microbial spoilage
   (Legionnaires' disease and risk assessments,
   water microbiology); microbiology of
   middle distillate fuels

Community Research, Centre for

Tel: (01707) 284105 Fax: (01707) 285860
   E-mail: r.d.green@herts.ac.uk
Green, Roger D., BA CNAA, MA CNAA, PhD
   Herts.   Head*
Research: applied community studies; probation
   and criminal justice; social work and social
   care; youth justice and youth studies

Complexity and Management, Centre for Research in

Tel: (01707) 285449 Fax: (01707) 285455
   E-mail: r.d.stacey@herts.ac.uk
Stacey, Ralph D., BCom Witw., MSc(Econ)
   Lond., PhD Lond.   Prof.; Head*
Research: implications of complexity theories for
   consulting, development, management,
   research, writing and other areas within
   organisations

Computer Science and Informatics Research, Centre for

Tel: (01707) 284328 Fax: (01707) 284304
   E-mail: r.g.adams@herts.ac.uk
Adams, Roderick G., BSc Leic., MSc Leic., MSc
   CNAA, PhD CNAA   Prof.; Head*
Research: algorithms; biological and neural
   computation; system engineering

Electronic Art and Communication, Centre for Research in

Tel: (01707) 285383 Fax: (01707) 285350
   E-mail: m.j.ferris@herts.ac.uk
Ferris, Malcolm, MA RCA   Head*
Research: effect of digital technology on studio
   practice in art and design; hyperfictions and
   non-linear narratives; issues in
   contemporary arts practice; practice based
   research; role of the artefact in research

Employment Studies, Centre for Research in

Tel: (01707) 285405 Fax: (01707) 285455
   E-mail: g.gall@herts.ac.uk
Gall, Gregor, MA Aberd., PhD UMIST   Prof.;
   Head*
Research: gender and equality; industrial
   relations; organisation behaviour and work
   organisation/organisational culture; public
   sector employment relations; trade unionism

Engineering and Applied Sciences Research, Centre for

Tel: (01707) 284168 Fax: (01707) 284185
   E-mail: m.c.tracey@herts.ac.uk
Tracey, Mark C., BEng Herts., PhD Herts.
   Head*

Research: agriculture and environment; fluid mechanics; materials and structures; microfluids and microengineering; radio and mobile communication networks

Finance and Accounting, Centre for Research into

Tel: (01707) 285518
E-mail: c.j.haslam@herts.ac.uk
Haslam, C. J., BSc Wales, PhD Wales   Prof.; Head*
Research: business analysis and corporate performance; financial reporting and governance; management control in the private and public sector; markets and intermediation

FIT Corporation Limited, The

Tel: (01707) 284622 Fax: (01707) 285073
E-mail: b.fletcher@herts.ac.uk
Fletcher, Ben, BA Keele, DPhil Oxf.   Head*
Research: company profiling for investment, management and development; FIT science in relation to organisational selection, assessment, classification, growth and development; FIT science in relation to personal development and change; FIT science in relation to personal organisational coaching and FIT Brief Therapy

Health Research and Development Support Unit

Tel: (01707) 284638 Fax: (01707) 285073
E-mail: d.j.done@herts.ac.uk
Done, D. John, BA Leic., PhD Wales   University Health Res. Co-ordinator; Manager*
Research: NHS-based health research (cancer research, forensic dentistry, learning disability, mental health, plastic surgery)

Information Management and Technology, Centre for (CIMTECH Ltd)

Tel: (01707) 281060 Fax: (01707) 281061
E-mail: c.cimtech@herts.ac.uk
Hendley, A. M.   Managing Dir.*

Institutional Economics, Centre for Research in

Tel: (01707) 285525 Fax: (01707) 285409
E-mail: g.m.hodgson@herts.ac.uk
Hodgson, G. M., BSc Manc., MA Manc., MA Camb., DLitt Camb.   Res. Prof.; Head*
Research: theoretical and empirical research in the 'new' and 'old' traditions in institutional economics (analysis of evolution of business, effects of institutional structures on economic performance, nature of business firms)

International Law, Centre for Research in

Tel: (01707) 283231 Fax: (01707) 283205
E-mail: c.wild@herts.ac.uk
Wild, Charles R., BSc(Econ) Lond., LLM Sheff., PhD Sheff.   Head*
Research: corporate and commercial law; data protection and telecommunications law; e-commerce (e-contracts, e-crime, e-finance); international commercial law; public and private law

Lifespan and Chronic Illness Research, Centre for

Tel: (01707) 286291 Fax: (01707) 286388
E-mail: d.m.wellsted@herts.ac.uk
Wellstead, David, BMus Lond., MMus Lond.   Head*
Research: adult mental health disorders; dialysis; rheumatoid arthritis

Makers of Things

Tel: (01707) 285322 Fax: (01707) 285310
E-mail: s.freshwater@herts.ac.uk
Freshwater, Sally, BA Lond., MA RCA   Head*
Research: contemporary crafts, process and manipulation; physical objects and materials

Music Centre

Tel: (01707) 284440 Fax: (01707) 285098
E-mail: t.blinko@herts.ac.uk
Blinko, Timothy J., BMus Lond., MMus Lond.   Prof.; Head*
Research: artistic (composition, performance); critical and aesthetic; technological (human-computer interaction and sound cognition)

Normativity and Narrative, Centre for

Tel: (01707) 285682 Fax: (01707) 285611
E-mail: j.a.lippitt@herts.ac.uk
Lippitt, John A., BSc Manc., MLitt Durh., PhD Essex   Reader; Head*
Research: Aristotle, Kierkegaard, Wittgenstein, Sellars; epistemology; ethics; idealism and realism; metaphysics

Practice, Centre for Research into

Tel: (01707) 285341 Fax: (01707) 285350
E-mail: m.a.biggs@herts.ac.uk
Biggs, Michael A. R., BA CNAA, MA CNAA, PhD Reading   Prof.; Head*
Research: art and design (fundamental principles, philosophies and problems in studio-based research); contribution of research to the development of the discipline; problem of the relationship of image, object, presentation and word

Primary and Community Care, Centre for Research in

Tel: (01707) 283380 Fax: (01707) 285995
E-mail: s.kendall@herts.ac.uk
Kendall, Sally A., BSc CNAA, PhD Lond.   Prof.; Head*
Research: adolescent and child health; health care of older people; patient experience and public involvement; primary health care; public health and health protection

Professional and Work-Related Learning, Centre for Research in

Tel: (01707) 385662 Fax: (02707) 285626
E-mail: h.burchell@herts.ac.uk
Burchell, Helen, BSc Lond., MSc Lond., PhD Herts.   Head*
Research: facilitation of learning through action research; impact of learning on practice; mentoring in school and higher education contexts; professional learning in the initial training of teachers; school governance

Regional and Local History, Centre for

Tel: (01707) 285637 Fax: (01707) 285611
E-mail: n.goose@herts.ac.uk
Goose, Nigel R., BA Kent, MA Lond., PhD Camb.   Prof.; Head*
Research: history (local, demographic, social economic); nineteenth-century aristocracy and rural politics; poverty and charity in eighteenth-century Britain; seventeenth-century local history of Hertfordshire; witchcraft, magic, popular culture and religion

Theorizing the Visual Arts and Design Group

Tel: (01707) 285369 Fax: (01707) 285350
E-mail: g.lees-maffei@herts.ac.uk
Lees-Maffei, Grace, BA Wales, MA RCA, PhD Portsmouth   Prof.; Head*

CONTACT OFFICERS

Academic affairs. Academic Registrar: Grant, Sue C., BSc CNAA
(E-mail: s.c.grant@herts.ac.uk)
Accommodation. Director of Hospitality Services and Contracts: Thorp, Amanda, BA Hull (E-mail: a.l.thorp@herts.ac.uk)
Admissions (first degree). Manager, University Admissions: MacFadyen, Alastair, BA(Econ) Manc., MBA Open(UK)
(E-mail: admissions@herts.ac.uk)
Admissions (higher degree). Manager, University Admissions: MacFadyen, Alastair,

BA(Econ) Manc., MBA Open(UK)
(E-mail: admissions@herts.ac.uk)
Adult/continuing education. Head, Department of Continuing Education and Partnerships: Culliford, Steve, BSc Lond., MSc CNAA (E-mail: s.culliford@herts.ac.uk)
Alumni. Head of Development and Alumni: Coles, Alison, BA Sheff.
(E-mail: alumni@herts.ac.uk)
Archives. Director of Learning and Information Services: Wingate-Martin, Prof. Diana E., BA Lond., MA Middx.
(E-mail: d.martin@herts.ac.uk)
Careers. Director of Graduate Employment: Everson, Anusha, BSc Westminster, BSc Sur.
(E-mail: a.everson@herts.ac.uk)
Computing services. Head of Information and Communication Technology: Coombs, Geoffrey R., BSc(Eng) S'ton., MSc Manc.
(E-mail: g.r.coombs@herts.ac.uk)
Computing services. Head of Information Services: Wroot, Andrew J., BSc Alta., MSc Alta., PhD Lond.
(E-mail: a.j.wroot@herts.ac.uk)
Consultancy services. Director of Marketing and Communications: Longden, Tim
(E-mail: t.longden@herts.ac.uk)
Development/fund-raising. Head of Development and Alumni: Coles, Alison, BA Sheff. (E-mail: a.j.coles@herts.ac.uk)
Equal opportunities. Head of Equality Unit: Wright, K. Marcella, BA Durh., MPubPol ANU (E-mail: m.wright@herts.ac.uk)
Estates and buildings/works and services. Acting Director of Estates: Thorp, Amanda, BA Hull (E-mail: a.l.thorp@herts.ac.uk)
Examinations. Assistant Registrar (Examinations and Conferments): Walmsley, Anne
(E-mail: a.v.walmsley@herts.ac.uk)
Finance. Deputy Vice-Chancellor and Director of Finance: Neville, Terry M.
(E-mail: t.m.neville@herts.ac.uk)
General enquiries. Secretary and Registrar: Waters, Philip E., BSc(SocialSciences) S'ton., FRSA (E-mail: p.e.waters@herts.ac.uk)
Health services. Dean of Students: Ball, David, BSc Lond. (E-mail: d.ball@herts.ac.uk)
Industrial liaison. Director of Marketing and Communications: Longden, Tim
(E-mail: t.longden@herts.ac.uk)
International office. Head of the International Office: Harris, Cath
(E-mail: international@herts.ac.uk)
Library (enquiries). Administrative Manager (Library): Meredith, Elizabeth A., BA Herts.
(E-mail: lisadmin@herts.ac.uk)
Marketing. Director of Marketing and Communications: Longden, Tim
(E-mail: t.longden@herts.ac.uk)
Minorities/disadvantaged groups. Head of Equality Unit: Wright, K. Marcella, BA Durh., MPubPol ANU
(E-mail: m.wright@herts.ac.uk)
Personnel/human resources. Director of Human Resources: Holloway, Naomi
(E-mail: n.holloway@herts.ac.uk)
Public relations. Director of Marketing and Communications: Longden, Tim
(E-mail: t.longden@herts.ac.uk)
Publications. Editorial Manager: Davies, Valerie, BA Keele
(E-mail: v.davies@herts.ac.uk)
Purchasing. Procurement Manager: Wakeling, Jill C. (E-mail: j.wakeling@herts.ac.uk)
Quality assurance and accreditation. Assistant Registrar (Academic Quality): Bennett, Helen, BA Sund.
(E-mail: h.l.bennett@herts.ac.uk)
Research. Director of Research: Senior, Prof. John M., BSc Birm., MSc UMIST, DSc Manc.Met., FIEE, FRSA
(E-mail: j.m.senior@herts.ac.uk)
Safety. Director of Health and Safety: Thomas, Clive, BA Open(UK)
(E-mail: c.l.thomas@herts.ac.uk)
Scholarships, awards, loans. Secretary and Registrar: Waters, Philip E.,

BSc(SocialSciences) S'ton., FRSA
(E-mail: p.e.waters@herts.ac.uk)
Schools liaison. Head of Education Liaison:
Douglas, Ian C., BEng Sheff., MSc CNAA
(E-mail: i.c.douglas@herts.ac.uk)
Sport and recreation. Head of Sport and
Recreation: Brooking, Nicholas J., BEd
CNAA (E-mail: n.brooking@herts.ac.uk)
Staff development and training. Head of
People Development: Bryant, Linda
(E-mail: l.bryant@herts.ac.uk)

Student union. General Manager (Student
Union): Veal, Michael C. A.
(E-mail: uhsu@herts.ac.uk)
Student welfare/counselling. Dean of
Students: Ball, David, BSc Lond.
(E-mail: d.ball@herts.ac.uk)
Students from other countries. Head of the
International Office: Harris, Cath
(E-mail: international@herts.ac.uk)
Students with disabilities. Head of Equality
Unit: Wright, K. Marcella, BA Durh.,

MPubPol ANU
(E-mail: m.wright@herts.ac.uk)
University press. Manager, University of
Hertfordshire Press: Housham, Jane J., MA
Camb. (E-mail: j.j.housham@herts.ac.uk)
Women. Head of Equality Unit: Wright, K.
Marcella, BA Durh., MPubPol ANU
(E-mail: m.wright@herts.ac.uk)

[Information supplied by the institution as at 19
November 2007, and edited by the ACU]

UNIVERSITY OF HUDDERSFIELD

Founded 1992

Member of the Association of Commonwealth Universities

Postal Address: Queensgate, Huddersfield, England HD1 3DH
Telephone: (01484) 422288 **Fax:** (01484) 516151
URL: http://www.hud.ac.uk

VICE-CHANCELLOR*—Cryan, Prof. Bob, BSc PhD DSc
DEPUTY VICE-CHANCELLOR—(vacant)
PRO-VICE-CHANCELLOR (RESOURCES)—Page, Prof. Michael I., PhD Glas., DSc CNAA, FRSChem
PRO-VICE-CHANCELLOR (ACADEMIC AFFAIRS)—Frost, Prof. Susan A., BA Open(UK), MPhil Bath
PRO-VICE-CHANCELLOR (EXTERNAL RELATIONS)—Boatswain, Prof. Timothy, BA Birm.
UNIVERSITY SECRETARY‡—Mears, Anthony, MBA
DIRECTOR OF FINANCE—McConnell, Andrew, BSc Manc., FCA
HEAD OF REGISTRY—Sherlock, Kathy
DIRECTOR OF HUMAN RESOURCES—McClelland, Julie, BSocSc Birm., MA Lond.

GENERAL INFORMATION

History. The university's history dates back to
the formation of the Young Men's Mental
Improvement Society in 1841, later renamed
the Mechanics' Institution (1844),
Huddersfield Technical School and Mechanics'
Institution (1894) and Huddersfield Technical
College (1896). In 1958 the institution
expanded to become Huddersfield College of
Technology, and in 1970 a merger with
Oastler College of Education created
Huddersfield Polytechnic. The polytechnic was
enlarged in 1974 by its absorption of
Huddersfield College of Education. The
institution was established as a university in
1992.
   The university is situated almost entirely in
the centre and immediate suburbs of the town
of Huddersfield.

Admission to first degree courses (see also
United Kingdom Introduction). Through
Universities and Colleges Admissions Service
(UCAS). General Certificate of Education (GCE)
and General Certificate of Secondary Education
(GCSE) with passes in 2 subjects at GCE A
level and in 3 other subjects at GCSE (grade C
or above). Wide range of equivalent
qualifications accepted.
   Mature entrants lacking formal educational
qualifications: either by completion of a
recognised Access course or by satisfying the
university that they will be able to benefit
from the proposed course. International
students: qualifications judged equivalent to
those specified above. Applicants whose first
language is not English will be required to
demonstrate proficiency in English.

First Degrees (see also United Kingdom
Directory to Subjects of Study). BA, BEd, BEng,
BMus, BSc, LLB, MChem, MEng.
   BEd: 2 years full-time with 1 additional
part-time year for honours. BA, BEd, BEng,
BSc and LLB may also be taken part-time.
   Length of course. Full-time: BA, BEng, BMus, BSc,
LLB: 3 years; MChem: 4 years.

Higher Degrees (see also United Kingdom
Directory to Subjects of Study).
   Master's. MA, MBA, MEd, MPhil, MSc.
   Admission. Applicants for admission must
normally hold an appropriate first degree or
equivalent (for MPhil a degree with at least
second class honours).
   MA, MBA, MEd and MSc may also be taken
part-time. MSc in geographical information
systems and in multimedia and education
offered by distance learning.
   Length of course. Full-time: MA, MBA, MEd,
MSc: 1 year; MPhil: 2 years. Part-time: MPhil: 3
years.
   Doctoral. EdD, PhD.
   Admission. PhD: an appropriate master's
degree; EdD: normally a higher degree or
professional qualification.
   EdD: 24 months part-time taught
programme, with additional research element.
   Length of course. Full-time: PhD: 2 years. Part-
time: PhD: 3 years.

Language of Instruction. English. A lecturer
in English as a foreign language assists
international students.

Libraries. Volumes: 379,163. Periodicals
subscribed to: 1800. Special collections:
George Henry Wood (social, political and
economic history); John Yudkin (food and
nutrition); historic journals and newspapers
(many relating to politics); local history (West
Riding of Yorkshire).

FACULTIES/SCHOOLS
Applied Sciences, School of
Tel: (01484) 472169 Fax: (01484) 472182
   E-mail: sasweb@hud.ac.uk
Acting Dean: Bamford, Prof. Colin G., BA Leeds,
FCILT
Secretary: Goodridge, Janet

Art and Design, School of
Tel: (01484) 472289 Fax: (01484) 472940
Dean: Calderbank, Geoffrey, BArch Strath., MSc
Strath.
Secretary: Farnell, Judith S.

Computing and Engineering, School of
Tel: (01484) 472100 Fax: (01484) 421106
   E-mail: scomoff@hud.ac.uk
Dean: Yip, Prof. Yau Jim, BSc PhD, FIMechE,
FBCS
Secretary: Moorhouse, Kay

Education and Professional Development, School of
Tel: (01484) 478249 Fax: (01484) 478120
   E-mail: sepd@hud.ac.uk
Dean: Bridge, Freda A., BA Open(UK), MSc
CNAA, EdD Leeds Met.
Secretary: Bond, Pauline

Huddersfield University Business School
Tel: (01484) 473338 Fax: (01484) 473212
   E-mail: hubs.enquiries@hud.ac.uk
Dean: Smith, Prof. David, BA CNAA, MSc Salf.
Secretary: Monaghan, Doreen

Human and Health Sciences, School of
Tel: (01484) 473338 Fax: (01484) 473212
Dean: Bernhouser, Sue, BSc MBA
Secretary: Ward, Joyce

Music and Humanities, School of
Tel: (01484) 472242 Fax: (01484) 472655
Dean: Thornton, Tim, MA Oxf., DPhil Oxf.,
FRHistS
Secretary: (vacant)

ACADEMIC UNITS
Adult and Children's Nursing Studies
Tel: (01924) 465105 Fax: (01484) 450839
Doggett, Cathy, BEd Leeds Met., MEd Leeds Met.
   Head*

Adult Nursing, Division of
Armstrong, Barry, BEd Leeds Met.   Sr. Lectr.
Belk, Dennis, BA Brad.   Sr. Lectr.
Bland, Andrew   Sr. Lectr.
Cheung, Sui, BEd Leeds Met.   Sr. Lectr.
Cranmer, Pam, BSc CNAA, MA Leeds   Sr. Lectr.
Delbridge, Bronwyn, BEd Leeds   Sr. Lectr.
Finn, Vincent   Sr. Lectr.

Gren, Elizabeth R., BSc *Hudd.* Sr. Lectr.
Hirst, Ian, BA *Open(UK)*, MSc *Hudd.* Principal Lectr.
Hope, Angela Sr. Lectr.
Machin, David, BEd *Leeds* Sr. Lectr.
Nhemachena, Jean, BSc *Brighton*, MSc *Sur.* Sr. Lectr.
Ormrod, Graham Sr. Lectr.
O'Sullivan, Patricia A., BA *Open(UK)*, BEd *Manc.*, MA *Leeds* Sr. Lectr.
Quashie, Charles, MA *Lanc.* Sr. Lectr.
Saville, Joanne
Shuttleworth, Margaret, BEd *CNAA* Sr. Lectr.
Spilsbury, Hilary, BSc *Hull*, MA *Sheff.Hallam* Sr. Lectr.; Head*
Straw, James A. Sr. Lectr.
Sutton, Andrew
Thomas, Paul, BSc *Leeds* Sr. Lectr.
Thurgood, Graham, MSc *Aston* Sr. Lectr.
Ward, Keith, BSc *Hudd.* Sr. Lectr.
Williams, Jane, BSc *Hudd.* Sr. Lectr.

Children's Nursing

Nicholls, Rebecca
Rhodes, Christine
Wilbourn, Veronica, BA *Open(UK)* Sr. Lectr.
Wood, Barbara, BEd *Leeds*, MSc *Leeds* Sr. Lectr.; Head*

Applied Sciences, School of

Chemical and Biological Sciences

Tel: (01484) 473138
E-mail: j.e.goodridge@hud.ac.uk
Ardrey, Robert E., BSc *Sur.*, PhD *Sur.* Sr. Lectr.
Balac, Pauline A., BSc *Sheff.*, PhD *Sheff.* Sr. Lectr.
Barnes, Philip A., BSc *Wales*, PhD *Brist.* Prof.; Head*
Brown, Robert, BSc *Birm.*, PhD *Leic.* Reader
Burns, Shamus P., BSc *Lond.*, PhD *Lond.* Sr. Lectr.
Clarke, Dougie J., BSc *Strath.*, PhD *Dund.* Sr. Lectr.
Clemenson, Peter I., MSc *Salf.*, PhD *Wales* Sr. Lectr.
Dogariou, Catalin, MD *Bucharest*, MSc *Marshall* Sr. Lectr.
Garner, Cathy, BSc *Manc.*, PhD *Manc.* Sr. Lectr.
Golshekan, Hamid R., MEng *Brad.*, PhD *Brad.* Sr. Lectr.
Hall, Carl E., BSc *Leeds*, PhD *CNAA* Sr. Lectr.
Hemming, Karl, BSc *Salf.*, PhD *Salf.* Sr. Lectr.
Jewsbury, Roger A., BSc *Brist.*, PhD *Brist.*, FRSChem Principal Lectr.
Lamont, Christine L. A., BSc *Bath*, PhD *S'ton.* Sr. Lectr.
Laws, Andrew P., BSc *Lanc.*, DPhil *Sus.* Sr. Lectr.
Lawton, Joanna J., BSc *Liv.*, PhD *Liv.* Communicator in Sci.
Leonard, Michael N., BSc *Nott.*, PhD *Nott.* Sr. Lectr.
McDonald, Ruth L., BSc *Leeds*, PhD *Leeds* Sr. Lectr.
Midgley, Gary, BA *York(UK)*, DPhil *York(UK)* Sr. Lectr.
Mortimer, Michael G., BSc *Leeds*, PhD *Leeds* Principal Lectr.
Parkes, Gareth M. B., BSc *E.Anglia*, PhD *Leeds* Sr. Lectr.
Pye, David A., BSc *Manc.*, PhD *Manc.* Sr. Lectr.
Rice, Craig R., BSc *Leic.*, PhD *Kent* Sr. Lectr.
Saul, Michael W., BA *Camb.*, DPhil *Sus.* Sr. Lectr.
Other Staff: 1 Lectr.
Research: analytical chemistry (development of sensors and mass-spectrometer interfaces); biomolecular sciences (design and synthesis of therapeutic agents); catalysis (characterisation, preparation and application, heterogeneous catalysis); thermal analysis

Environmental and Geographical Sciences

Tel: (01484) 472012 Fax: (01484) 472347
E-mail: sasweb@hud.ac.uk
Allan, Robert L., MA *Glas.*, PhD *Glas.* Sr. Lectr.

Couch, Ian R., BA *Nott.*, MA *Manc.*, PhD *Manc.* Principal Lectr.
Dykes, Alan P., BSc *Brist.*, PhD Sr. Lectr.
Gunn, John, BSc *Wales*, PhD *Auck.* Prof.
Humphreys, Paul N., BSc *Manc.Met.*, PhD *S.Bank* Sr. Lectr.
Hunt, Christopher O., BA *Sheff.*, MSc *Sheff.*, PhD *Wales* Reader
Hunt, Clive, BSc *Lond.*, PhD *Hudd.* Sr. Lectr.
Jones, Anne M., BSc *Lond.*, DPhil *Oxf.* Principal Lectr.
Lawson, John M., BSc *Lond.* Sr. Lectr.
Marshall, Valerie M. E., BSc *Aberd.*, PhD *Reading* Prof.; Head*
Vann, Anthony R., BSc *Wales*, PhD *Wales* Sr. Lectr.
West, Ann, BSc *Lond.* Principal Lectr.
Wood, Adrian P., BA *Durh.*, PhD *Liv.* Prof.
Other Staff: 2 Lectrs.
Research: bioremediation of land and water; hydrology and geomorphology; karst (hydrology, geomorphology and ecology); resource management and sustainable development; urban, economic and social geography

Logistics and Hospitality Management

Tel: (01484) 472614 Fax: (01484) 472562
E-mail: sasweb@hud.ac.uk
Bamford, Colin G., BA *Leeds*, FCILT Prof.; Head*
Corns, Christine, BSc *Hudd.* Sr. Lectr.
Crompton, Richard, BSc *Hudd.*, MSc *C.England* Sr. Lectr.
Hubbard, Nicholas J., BSc *Liv.*, MPhil *Brad.*, PhD *Brad.* Sr. Lectr.
Jenkins, Andi, BSc *Oxf.Brookes*, MSc *Strath.* Sr. Lectr.
Mazurkiewicz, Margaret, BA *Strath.* Principal Lectr.
Norcliffe, Zineb, BSc *Hudd.* Sr. Lectr.
Savage, Christopher, MSc *Salf.* Sr. Lectr.
Shaw, Janet, BSc *Hudd.* Sr. Lectr.
Thompson, Elizabeth J., BSc *Sheff.Hallam*, MSc *Salf.* Sr. Lectr.
Tipi, Nicoleta, BEng *Cluj*, MPhil *Sheff.*, PhD *Sheff.* Sr. Lectr.
Turner, Margaret Sr. Lectr.
Waite, J. Andy, BA *Open(UK)* Sr. Lectr.
Research: customer usage of hotels; database analysis of UK hotel groups; managing workplace diversity

Art and Design, School of

Tel: (01484) 472289 Fax: (01484) 472940

Creative Technologies

Tel: (01484) 472281 Fax: (01484) 472440
E-mail: architecture@hud.ac.uk
Adams, Roderick, BA MA Sr. Lectr.
Atkinson, Paul, BA *CNAA*, MA *Middx.* Principal Lectr.; Manager, Professl. Devel.
Bareham, Gerard E. Sr. Lectr.
Bartlett-Rawlings, Jon R. Sr. Lectr.
Benincasa, Caterina A., BA MA Sr. Lectr.
Bush, Jonathon G. Sr. Lectr.
Carling, Denis, BA *CNAA*, MSc *Leeds* Sr. Lectr.
Dale, Julia E. S., BA *Newcastle(UK)*, BArch *Wales*, MA *Nott.* Sr. Lectr.
Edwards, Robert J., BA Principal Lectr.
Fellows, Richard A., MPhil *York(UK)* Head*
Hales, D., BA *Hudd.* Principal Lectr.
Hartley, Stuart A. Sr. Lectr.
Hippisley-Cox, Charles I., BA *Sheff.*, BSc *Sheff.* Sr. Lectr.
Howard, Christopher J., BA *CNAA* Sr. Lectr.
Lannon, Tracy A., BSc *Hudd.* Sr. Lectr.
Lycett, Robert S. Sr. Lectr.
Meddings, Carl, BA *Hudd.* Principal Lectr.
Nicholls, Richard, BSc *CNAA*, MSc *Manc.* Sr. Lectr.
Pettican, Anneke, BA Sr. Lectr.
Sinclair, Barry Sr. Lectr.
Southern, Jennifer A., BA MFA Sr. Lectr.
Swann, David M., MDes *CNAA*, MA *RCA* Sr. Lectr.
Tancock, David J., BSc *City(UK)*, MSc *Cran.IT* Sr. Lectr.

Unver, Ertugrul, BSc MSc PhD Sr. Lectr.
Wood, Susan, MA Sr. Lectr.

Design

Tel: (01484) 472064 Fax: (01484) 472940
E-mail: d.phillips@hud.ac.uk
Allen, Claire, BA MSc Sr. Lectr.
Almond, Kevin, MDes *RCA*, BA Principal Lectr.
Annable, Raymond G., BSc *Leeds*, PhD *Leeds* Sr. Lectr.
Beale, Joanna M., BA *CNAA*, MSc *Salf.* Principal Lectr.
Beck, Marion E., BA Sr. Lectr.
Beever, Christopher J., BSc Sr. Lectr.
Bland, Douglas Sr. Lectr.
Burton, Simon Sr. Lectr.
Clarkson, Garry, BA *Westminster* Sr. Lectr.
Halstead, Graham, BSc *CNAA* Sr. Lectr.
Harris, Joanne M., BA *Manc.Met.* Sr. Lectr.
Hilditch, Julie, BA Sr. Lectr.
Little, Beverley A., BA *Lough.*, MA *RCA* Sr. Lectr.
Macbeth, Penelope A., BA MA Principal Lectr.
Malik, Sophia, BA Sr. Lectr.
Mason, Suzy J., BA Sr. Lectr.
Norris, Peter T. T., BA MSc Sr. Lectr.
Oliver, Michael G. Principal Lectr.
Pearson, John S., BSc *Leeds*, MPhil *Leeds*, PhD *Leeds* Head*
Perren, Nicola, BSc *Hudd.* Sr. Lectr.
Rickwood, A. G. (Rick), BSc *Lond.*, MA *Lanc.* Sr. Lectr.
Ritchie, Jane Sr. Lectr.
Shearer, Allan J. Sr. Lectr.
Short, J. Margot, BA *Leeds* Sr. Lectr.
Spink, Irene Sr. Lectr.
Squires, Paul L., BA *Lond.* Principal Lectr.
Swindells, Stephen M. P., BA MA PhD Principal Lectr.
Other Staff: 1 Lectr.
Research: digital printing on textiles; inter-relationship between education and industry; new finishes for textile products (crease resistance, reduction of UV penetration, flame retardation); production of new materials from textile waste; textile graduate employment

Behavioural Sciences

Tel: (01484) 473354 Fax: (01484) 473760
Research: autobiographical memory; health psychology; nationalism; personal construct psychology; social identity

Criminology/Sociology, Division of

Arevalo, Mavis, BSc *CNAA*, MSc *Brad.* Sr. Lectr.
Gibbs, Graham, BSc *S'ton.*, MSc *Kent*, MA Reader
McAuley, James W., BSc *Ulster*, PhD *Leeds* Reader
Roberts, Brian, BA *CNAA*, LLM *Sheff.*, PhD *Birm.* Principal Lectr.
Skinns, David, BSc *CNAA*, MA *Sheff.*, MPhil *Camb.*, PhD *Hull* Principal Lectr.
Sparks, Geoffrey H., BSc *Lond.*, MSc *Birm.* Principal Lectr.
van Kemenade, Rudyard J. J., BA *Rhodes*, MSc *Lond.*, MA *Brad.* Sr. Lectr.
Whitehead, Antony, BA *S'ton.*, PhD *S'ton.* Sr. Lectr.
Other Staff: 2 Lectrs.

Politics, Division of

Blakeley, Georgina, BA *Liv.*, MA *Liv.*, PhD *Brad.* Principal Lectr.
Bryson, Valerie, BA *Kent*, MA *Manc.*, PhD *Kent* Prof.
Evans, Brendan J., BA *Manc.*, MA *Manc.*, PhD *Manc.* Prof.
Other Staff: 2 Lectrs.

Psychology, Division of

Burr, Vivien, BA *CNAA*, PhD *CNAA* Principal Lectr.

Butt, Trevor W., BSc Leeds; MSc Leeds, PhD Reader

Hearn, Jeff, BA Oxf., MA Oxf., MA Leeds, PhD Brad.   Prof.

Hickling, Keith, BSc Hudd.   Principal Lectr.

Horrocks, Christine, BSc Hudd., PhD Hudd.   Sr. Lectr.

Kelly, Nancy, BSc CNAA, MSc CNAA   Sr. Lectr.

King, Nigel, BA Kent, PhD Sheff.   Reader

McAdie, Tina, PhD   Sr. Lectr.

Palmer, Derrol, MA York(UK), PhD York(UK), BSc Sr. Lectr.

Peebles, David, BSc MSc PhD   Sr. Lectr.

Ward, Robert, BA Hull, MSc Manc., PhD Hull Reader

Other Staff: 5 Lectrs.

Clinical and Health Sciences

Renwick, Penelope A., MA Leeds   Principal Lectr.; Head*

Health and Sports, Division of

Bartholomew, Michelle, BSc MSc   Sr. Lectr.

Cliff, Malcolm S., BSc MSc   Sr. Lectr.

Latham, Nicky, BSc MSc   Head*

Lewis, Kiara, BA Leeds Met., MSc   Sr. Lectr.

Sellers, Chris   Sr. Lectr.

Wray, Sharon, PhD   Sr. Lectr.

Other Staff: 4 Lectrs.

Midwifery, Division of

Deery, Ruth M., BSc Hudd.   Sr. Lectr.

Howarth, Christina, BA   Sr. Lectr.

Jarvis, Yvonne, BEd Leeds Met., MSc Leeds Met. Sr. Lectr.

Jones, Patricia A., BSc Hudd.   Sr. Lectr.

McGuire, Glenys, BSc Manc.   Sr. Lectr.

Parkin, J.   Sr. Lectr.

Phillips, Mari A., BA Open(UK), MEd Hudd. Head*

Rogan, Kathryn, BSc   Sr. Lectr.

Simpson, Marion O., MEd Leeds   Sr. Lectr.

Occupational Therapy, Division of

Stead, J.

Operating Department Practice, Division of

Hauxwell, Jonathan M., BSc Leic.   Principal Lectr.

Smith, Martin E.   Principal Lectr.

Taylor, Brian, BA Lanc., MEd Leeds   Sr. Lectr.

Tyas, Moira   Sr. Lectr.

White, Stephen   Sr. Lectr.

Other Staff: 1 Implementation Manager

Physiotherapy, Division of

Chipperfield, Sarah

Fletcher-Cook, Phyl, MEd Leeds   Sr. Lectr.

Flynn, Jonathan

Green, Joanne

Lyon, Alison

Malone, Jacqueline

Milligan, James

Robinson, Gillian M.   Sr. Lectr.

Thornton, Sandra E., MEd Leeds   Principal Lectr.; Head*

Williams, Pamela

Podiatry, Division of

Barnes, Celia

Davies, Christopher S., BSc Salf., MEd   Sr. Lectr.

McDonald, Veronica   Sr. Lectr.

Pickard, James M., MSc Salf.   Sr. Lectr.

Smith, Wendy   Sr. Lectr.

Other Staff: 4 Lectrs.

Computing and Engineering, School of

Tel: (01484) 472000 Fax: (01484) 421106

Computing and Mathematical Sciences

Tel: (01484) 472929 Fax: (01484) 421106
E-mail: computing@hud.ac.uk

Allen, Gary, BA Hudd., PhD Hudd.   Sr. Lectr.

Baker, Paul C., BSc Sheff., MSc Hull, MSc Sheff., PhD Sheff.   Sr. Lectr.

Booth, Dexter J., BSc Wales, MSc Wales, PhD Vic.(BC), FIMA   Principal Lectr.

Hood, Peter W. L., BSc CNAA, MSc Open(UK) Sr. Lectr.

Jackson, Adrian R., BSc Manc., MSc Aston, DPhil York(UK)   Head*

Lu, Joan, BSc Shaanxi Normal, PhD Birm.   Sr. Lectr.

McCluskey, Thomas L., BSc Newcastle(UK), MSc Warw., PhD City(UK)   Prof.

Osborne, Hugh R., BSc Manc., MSc Nijmegen, PhD Nijmegen   Sr. Lectr.

Turner, John K., BSc Wales, PhD Newcastle(UK) Sr. Lectr.

Other Staff: 1 Sr. Res. Fellow

Research: artificial intelligence and formal methods (artform); numerical and neural computing; software engineering

Engineering and Technology

Tel: (01484) 472150
E-mail: engtech@hud.ac.uk

Baron, John K., MSc Manc.   Sr. Lectr.

Barrans, Simon M., BSc Manc., PhD Hudd.   Sr. Lectr.

Blunt, Liam A., BSc Coventry, PhD Coventry Prof.

Dales, Mark R., BA Open(UK), MSc Aston   Sr. Lectr.

Daykin, Christopher I., MA Camb.   Sr. Lectr.

Fieldhouse, John D., BSc CNAA, PhD Hudd. Principal Lectr.

Hewson, Peter, BEng Salf., MSc Warw.   Sr. Lectr.

Johnson, Anthony D., BSc CNAA   Sr. Lectr.

Kelly, Philip F., BSc CNAA, MSc CNAA, PhD Hudd.   Principal Lectr.

Little, David, BTech Lough.   Prof.

Lockwood, Stephen, BEng Hudd., PhD Hudd. Sr. Lectr.

Lucas, Gary P., BSc Brist., MSc Manc., PhD Manc. Prof.

Lunn, Paul, BSc MSc   Sr. Lectr.

Mather, Peter J., BEng Hudd., PhD Hudd.   Sr. Lectr.

Mavromihales, Michael, BSc CNAA, MPhil CNAA Sr. Lectr.

Mehrdadi, Behrooz, BSc Brad., MSc Brad., PhD Brad.   Principal Lectr.

Mishra, Rakesh, PhD IIT Delhi, BEng   Sr. Lectr.

Myers, Alan, BSc CNAA   Principal Lectr.

Raczkowycz, Julian, BSc Manc., PhD CNAA   Sr. Lectr.

Rao, Vasudeva H., BE And., MTech Kharagpur, PhD Kharagpur   Prof.

Sibley, Martin J. N., BSc CNAA, PhD CNAA Reader

Talbot, Christopher J., BSc Manc., PhD Brad. Sr. Lectr.

Tian, Gui Yun, BEng Derby, MSc Derby, PhD Derby   Reader

Ubbi, Kuldip S., BEng Brad.   Sr. Lectr.

Wakefield, Jonathan P., BSc Manc., MSc Lanc., PhD Hudd.   Sr. Lectr.

Ward, Stephen, BSc CNAA, PhD CNAA   Head*

Research: distributed controllers; embedded systems; intelligent systems; measurement/ control systems; ultra-precision electronics

Multimedia and Information Systems

Tel: (01484) 472450
E-mail: newmedia@hud.ac.uk

Bonner, John V. H., BSc Lough., PhD Lough. Principal Lectr.

Brignell, David, BA Open(UK), MEd Hudd.   Sr. Lectr.

Clayton, Sam J., BSc Durh.   Sr. Lectr.

Eccles, Ruth, MA Sheff.Hallam   Sr. Lectr.

Kelly, John R., BA CNAA   Sr. Lectr.

Lloyd-Owen, Rob, BSc Leeds, MSc Hudd.   Sr. Lectr.

McDowell, James B., BA Wales, MA Lanc., MSc Tees.   Sr. Lectr.

O'Grady, Michael, BSc Newcastle(UK), MSc Hudd., PhD Newcastle(UK)   Sr. Lectr.

Powell, Sandra, BSc Brad., MSc Hudd.   Sr. Lectr.

Prigmore, Martyn S., BSc St And., MSc Brist., PhD Brist.   Sr. Lectr.

Reeve, Derek E., BA Manc., MA Manc., MSc Brad. Principal Lectr.

Stepney, Roy J., LLB Warw., MSc Lanc.   Sr. Lectr.

Taylor, David, BSc CNAA, PhD CNAA   Prof.; Head*

Wade, Stephen J., BSc CNAA, MSc Sheff., PhD Sheff.   Sr. Lectr.

Watts, Graham J., MA Hudd.   Sr. Lectr.

Wilkinson, Julie, BA Leeds, MSc Hudd.   Sr. Lectr.

Wolfson, Shelley, BA Brad.   Sr. Lectr.

Xu, Zhijie, PhD Derby, BEng MPhil   Sr. Lectr.

Other Staff: 1 Lectr.

Education and Professional Development, School of

see also Continuing Professional Development (Health and Community Studies)

Tel: (01484) 478249 Fax: (01484) 478120
E-mail: sepd@hud.ac.uk

Ashmore, Lyn H., BEd Hudd., MA Hudd.   Sr. Lectr.

Ashmore, Melvyn J., BA Leic., MEd Manc.   Sr. Lectr.

Avis, James, BSc Manc., MA Kent, PhD Birm. Prof., Post Compulsory Education and Training

Beaumont, Joanne, BA Liv.   Sr. Lectr.

Bennett, Elizabeth, BSc Sheff.   Sr. Lectr.

Boyd, Lyn M., BA Liv., MEd Liv.   Sr. Lectr.

Breckin, Michael J., BA Lond., PhD Lond. Principal Lectr.

Bridge, Freda A., BA Open(UK), MSc CNAA, EdD Leeds Met.   Head*

Butroyd, Robert, BA Hull, MEd Manc., PhD Hudd. Sr. Lectr.

Crawford, Roger A., BSc Hull, MSc Brad., EdD Leeds   Sr. Lectr.

Cullingford, Cedric I., BA Camb., MA Tor., MA Oxf., MPhil Oxf., MPhil Lanc., PhD Hudd. Prof., Education

Denby, Neil M., BSc Wales, MEd Manc.   Sr. Lectr.

Dixon, Elizabeth, MEd Hudd., MSc Hudd.   Sr. Lectr.

Eastwood, Linda I., BA Open(UK), MEd Sheff. Sr. Lectr.

Findlay, Ian, BA Coventry, MEd Manc.   Sr. Lectr.

Fisher, Roy, BA Wales, MSc Brad., MPhil Leeds, PhD Hudd.   Principal Lectr.

Fulford, Amanda, BA Sheff., MEd Sheff.   Sr. Lectr.

Gibson, F. Anne, BA Sus., MSc Leeds Met.   Sr. Lectr.

Gorf, Alison M. R., BSc Hudd., MSc Hudd.   Sr. Lectr.

Hall, Lyn A., BA Brad., MA Manc.   Sr. Lectr.

Harris, M. Ann, BA Newcastle(UK), MA Newcastle(UK), PhD Nott.   Sr. Lectr.

Hatton, Jean, BSc Birm., MEd Leeds   Sr. Lectr.

Hunter, Christine, BA Sheff.   Sr. Lectr.

Jarvis, Christine A., BA Warw., MA Warw., PhD Leeds   Head, Dept. of Community and Internat. Educn.

Jones, Helen M. F., BA Leeds, MEd Leeds, EdD Leeds   Sr. Lectr.

Karolia, Mohammed, BA Hudd., MA Sheff.Hallam Sr. Lectr.

Kidder, Judith, BA Leeds   Sr. Lectr.

Lord, David, BSc Nott., MSc Manc., PhD Manc. Sr. Lectr.

Marsden, Frances, BA Hudd.   Sr. Lectr.

McComish, John, BTech Brad., PhD Brad.   Sr. Lectr.

McGrath, Thomas, BA Stir., MA Napier   Sr. Lectr.

McMahon, Samantha, BSc CNAA   Sr. Lectr.

McNichol, John, BEd Hudd., MEd Hudd.   Sr. Lectr.

Morley, Graham, MEd Leeds Met.   Sr. Lectr.

Neve, David J., BEd CNAA, MEd Hudd.   Sr. Lectr.

Oliver, Paul, BEd CNAA, MPhil Leeds, PhD CNAA Principal Lectr.

Ollin, Ros E., BA Warw., MEd Sheff.   Principal Lectr.

Ormondroyd, Christopher, BEd Leeds   Sr. Lectr.

Owen, Geraint, BA CNAA Sr. Lectr.
Patterson, Eira W., BSc Leeds, PhD Durh. Sr.
Lectr.
Pearson, Joanne, BA Sheff. Sr. Lectr.
Pearson, Lesley, BMus Hull, MEd Leeds Sr.
Lectr.
Price, Jayne, BEd Leeds, MA Open(UK) Sr. Lectr.
Robertson, Roderick, BEd CNAA, MEd Liv., MA
Open(UK), EdD Hudd. Sr. Lectr.
Robinson, Denise, BSc Lond., MEd Leeds
Deputy Dir., Consortium for Post
Compulsory Educn. and Trg.
Sanderson, Peter J., BA Camb., MPhil York(UK),
PhD Leeds Sr. Lectr.
Schofield, Margaret V., BEd CNAA, MSc
York(UK) Sr. Lectr.
Swift, Helen D., BA CNAA, MA York(UK), EdD
Hudd. Principal Lectr.; Head, Devel.
Continuing Professl. Devel.
Thomas, Paul, BA Sheff. Sr. Lectr.
Thompson, David L., BA Camb., MA Kent Sr.
Lectr.
Thompson, Ronald, BSc Lond. Sr. Lectr.
Trafford, Anthony J., BA Oxf., MA Oxf. Head,
Dept. of Initial Teacher Educn. and
Continuing Professl. Devel.
Trorey, Gillian M., BSc Reading, MBA Leic., PhD
CNAA Principal Lectr.
Turner, Alwyn, BA Open(UK), MEd Hudd. Sr.
Lectr.
Walker, Martyn A., BA Open(UK), MA Nott.
Head, Dept. of Post Compulsory Educn. and
Training
Webb, Keith F. G., BSc Lond., MA Leeds, MA
York(UK) Dir., Consortium for Post
Compulsory Educn. and Training
Woodhouse, Fiona J., BSc CNAA, MBA Hudd.
Sr. Lectr.
Youde, Andrew, BA Manc., MSc Hudd. Sr.
Lectr.
Research: culture and education; information
technology and education; lifelong and
continuing education; school improvement;
vocational and professional education

Health and Community Studies
Firth, Janet E., MEd Hudd. Head*

Community Studies, Division of
Arthurs, Joyce, BEd Brad., MEd Leeds Sr. Lectr.
Hepworth, Sylvia, BA Open(UK), MEd Hudd.
Principal Lectr.
Rae, Rosemary J., BSc CNAA, MSc Lond. Sr.
Lectr.
Riordan, Linda, BA Leeds Principal Lectr.
Smith, Carole, BA Open(UK) Sr. Lectr.
Snowden, Michael, BSc Leeds, MA Manc. Sr.
Lectr.
Wallis, Timothy J., BSc Hudd. Sr. Lectr.
Westwood, Linda, BA CNAA Sr. Lectr.
Other Staff: 1 Lectr.

Continuing Professional Development, Division of
Bradshaw, Peter L., BMus Manc., MA Leeds
Prof.
Chirema, Kathleen, BA Open(UK), MA Leeds Sr.
Lectr.
Durkan, Patricia M., BSc Hudd. Sr. Lectr.
Farrell, Jane S., BSc Hudd. Sr. Lectr.
Farrell, Winifred, BEd Brad., MEd Hudd. Sr.
Lectr.
Heaton, Margaret, BSc Leeds, MA York(UK) Sr.
Lectr.
Leach, Ann, BSc Hudd. Sr. Lectr.
Logue, Anna, BA MA Sr. Lectr. Practitioner
Michell, Frank Head*
Mills, Joe, BA Hudd., MPhil Hudd. Sr. Lectr.
Williams, Jane, BSc MA Sr. Lectr.
Research: cancer care; care in the community;
child care and child protection; evaluation
of human services; infertility and surrogacy

Primary Care, Division of
Bindless, Linda, BA Open(UK), MA Manc.
Principal Lectr.
Brammall, Sandra

Brooke, Shelagh M., BSc Aston, PhD Liv.
Principal Lectr.
Ellis, Rona, BSc Hudd. Sr. Lectr.
Lord, John, MB ChB MMedSc Prof.
Mills, Valerie, BSc Hudd. Sr. Lectr.
Phillips, Stephen Sr. Lectr.
Other Staff: 5 Lectrs.

Health, Social Work and Community Studies

Learning Disability Studies, Division of
Burton, Robert, BSc CNAA, MEd Hudd. Sr.
Lectr.
Dew, Niall, BSc Hudd. Sr. Lectr.
Gething, Linda, BA Leeds Sr. Lectr.
Rodak, Jenny, BSc Hudd., MEd Nott. Sr. Lectr.
Shaw, Sue, BEd Hudd., MA Sheff. Sr. Lectr.

Mental Health, Division of
Addison, S.
Ascroft, Biljiana, BEd Sarajevo, MEd Hudd.
Head*
Foo, Shih Liang, BA Manc.Met., MSc Manc. Sr.
Lectr.
Jones, James Sr. Lectr.
Joyce, Patrick, BSc Hudd., MSc Hudd. Sr. Lectr.
Leckey, Jill, BSc Leeds Met. Sr. Lectr.
Lucock, Mike, BSc Leeds, MSc Leeds, PhD Durh.
Prof.
Lyon, Steven, BEd MSc Sr. Lectr.
Padgett, Katherine, BSc Leeds Sr. Lectr.
Tramposch, Val, BA Sheff.Hallam Sr. Lectr.

Social Work, Division of
Balen, Rachel, BA Leeds, MA Brad. Sr. Lectr.
Ball, Dorothy M., BA CNAA, MA Brad. Sr.
Lectr.
Blyth, Eric D., BA York(UK), MA Brun. Reader
Chillery, Richard
Gorman, Kevin Sr. Lectr.
Hayles, Michelle, BA Sus., MA Brad. Sr. Lectr.
Jordan, William, BA Oxf., MA Oxf. Prof.
Makin, Philip, BA Leeds, MA Nott. Sr. Lectr.
Masson, Helen C., BA Nott. Principal Lectr.
Neville, Ruth Sr. Lectr.
Richardson, Ian
Stogdon, Christine Head*
Warwick, Ian Sr. Lectr.

Huddersfield University Business School
Tel: (01484) 473063 Fax: (01484) 473638
E-mail: hubs@hud.ac.uk

Accountancy
Tel: (01484) 472327 Fax: (01484) 473062
E-mail: accountancy@hud.ac.uk
Cowton, Christopher J., BA Sheff., MA Wales,
MScEcon Wales, PhD, FRSA Prof.
Derwin, Garry A., BSc Nott., MSc Brist., PhD
Brist. Sr. Lectr.
Drake, Julie E., BA CNAA Principal Lectr.
Drury, Colin, BA Open(UK), MBA Brad. Prof.
English, John M., BA Hudd. Sr. Lectr.
Fiddler, Wayne, BA CNAA Sr. Lectr.
Griffin, Keith, BSc MSc PhD Principal Lectr.
Leach, William J., BA CNAA, MBA Hudd. Sr.
Lectr.
Mackenzie, Orysia, BA Nott. Sr. Lectr.
McGrath, Pamela A., BA CNAA Sr. Lectr.
Mehafdi, Messaoud, MSc Manc., PhD CNAA, Lic
Sr. Lectr.
Price, Christine, MSc Leic. Sr. Lectr.
Pryce, Linda, BSc MSc Sr. Lectr.
Teviotdale, Wilma W., BA Strath., FCA
Principal Lectr.; Head*
Webb, Brian J., BA Sheff., MBA Sheff.Hallam, FCA
Principal Lectr.
Research: accounting and financial ethics;
accounting education; management
accounting and control

Business Studies
Tel: (01484) 472206 Fax: (01484) 473062
E-mail: businessstudies@hud.ac.uk
Anchor, John R., BSc Manc., PhD Manc. Head*
Buckley, Martin W., BCom Leeds, MA Sheff. Sr.
Lectr.

Cafferty, Peter, BA Leeds, MA Leeds, MSc Lond.
Sr. Lectr.
Casserley, Damian J., BA Leeds, MSc(Econ) Lond.,
PhD Hudd. Sr. Lectr.
Day, Janine C., BSc Hull, MBA Hudd. Sr. Lectr.
Day, John, BSc Hull, MSc Salf. Sr. Lectr.
Duty, Denis J., BA Liv., MBA Keele Sr. Lectr.
Fitzsimons, Vincent G., BA CNAA, MA(Econ)
Manc. Sr. Lectr.
Goodale, Paula, BSc CNAA, MSc Leeds Met. Sr.
Lectr.
Hardaker, Glenn, BA Kingston(UK), PhD Hudd.
Prof.
Marsh, G., MA Oxf., MA Warw. Visiting Prof.
Rowles, Kevin J., BA Leeds, MA Leeds Sr. Lectr.
Scott, Steve, BA Lanc., MSc Salf., MPhil Hudd.
Sr. Lectr.
Thompson, John L., BA CNAA, MBA Cran.IT
Prof.
Trick, Robert R., BA Lond. Principal Lectr.
Warmington, Robert V., BA Warw., MA McM.
Principal Lectr.
Wraith, Peter C., BSc Aston, MSc Aston Sr.
Lectr.
Other Staff: 2 Lectrs.
Research: entrepreneurship; European business
strategy; international business; strategic
management

Law
Tel: (01484) 472192 Fax: (01484) 472279
E-mail: law@hud.ac.uk
Ascroft, Phillip, BEd Manc., MPhil Hudd. Sr.
Lectr.
Broad, Chris, BA Hull Sr. Lectr.
Clark, Anne, LLB Nott. Sr. Lectr.
Cockerill, Alan, LLB Liv. Sr. Lectr.
Coidan, Nicholas A., LLB S'ton., LLM Lond. Sr.
Lectr.
Cook, Carol A., LLB CNAA Sr. Lectr.
Edwards, Mark, LLB Hudd. Sr. Lectr.
Fellowes, Melanie G., LLB Sheff., LLM Sheff. Sr.
Lectr.
Foxcroft, Lynne C., LLB CNAA Sr. Lectr.
Hatfield, Emma, LLB Staffs. Sr. Lectr.
Hunter, Philip, LLB Hull Sr. Lectr.
Lazer, Susan, LLB Leeds Sr. Lectr.
Manning, Gemma, LLB Reading, MA Leeds Sr.
Lectr.
Murphy, Martin B., BA Camb., MA Camb. Sr.
Lectr.
Ndi, George, LLB Yaounde, LLM Dund., PhD Dund.
Sr. Lectr.
Norris, Terence L., BA Nott., LLM Leic. Sr.
Lectr.
Richards, Paul H., LLB CNAA, PhD CNAA
Head*
Sagar, David P., LLB Leeds, LLM Leeds Principal
Lectr.
Seagreaves, Emma M., LLB Sheff. Principal
Lectr.
Wolstencroft, Timothy G., BA Durh., MA CNAA
Principal Lectr.
Wood, Anne E., LLB CNAA Sr. Lectr.
Research: civil liberties; employment and
discrimination law; European Community
law; international economic and energy
law; medical law and ethics

Management and Marketing
Tel: (01484) 472026 Fax: (01484) 473174
E-mail: management@hud.ac.uk
Carmichael, Janis L., BSc Brad. Sr. Lectr.
Collins, Chris, BA Open(UK), MA Hudd. Sr.
Lectr.
Cook, John A., BSc Brad., MSc Strath., PhD Nott.
Sr. Lectr.
Crowther, Geoffrey, BA Sheff., MSc Brad. Sr.
Lectr.
Du-Lieu, Lisa, BA Hudd., MBA Hudd. Sr. Lectr.
Edwards, David J., BA Open(UK), PhD Cran.IT
Sr. Lectr.
Foot, Margaret D., BA Newcastle(UK), MA Alta.,
MBA York(Can.) Sr. Lectr.
Forbes, Giles R., BSc Wales, MBA Brad. Sr.
Lectr.
Graham, Richard J., BA Keele, MA E.Anglia Sr.
Lectr.

Hall, Roger D., BA *Leeds*, MSc *UMIST*, MSc *Salf.*, MEd *Manc.*, PhD *Salf.*   Principal Lectr.
Handley, Janet, BA *CNAA*, MSc *Hudd.*   Sr. Lectr.
Harvey, David J., BA *CNAA*   Sr. Lectr.
Hook, Caroline M., BA *Leeds*, MEd *CNAA*   Sr. Lectr.
Jackson, Howard E., MBA *Brad.*   Sr. Lectr.
Johnson, Terence, BSc *Wales*   Sr. Lectr.
Jones, Glynis, MA *C.Lancs.*   Sr. Lectr.
Kong, Kai P., BA *C.Lancs.*, MBA *Leeds*   Sr. Lectr.
Leah, Christopher, BA *Manc.Met.*, MBA *Manc.*   Sr. Lectr.
Marr, Norman E., MSc *Cran.IT*, PhD *Cran.IT*   Prof.
Morland, Leigh, BA *Liv.*   Sr. Lectr.
Parsons, M.   Visiting Prof.
Reynolds, Paul L., BA *CNAA*, MSc *Manc.*   Sr. Lectr.
Rollins, Ralph P., BSc *Brad.*, PhD *Hudd.*   Sr. Lectr.
Routledge, Christopher W., BSc *Newcastle(UK)*, MSc *Lough.*, PhD *Lough.*   Principal Lectr.
Rowland, Caroline A., BA *Wolv.*, MBA *Henley*, PhD *Manc.*   Sr. Lectr.
Sheldrick, Kate, BA *Sheff.*   Sr. Lectr.
Varley, Rosemary, BA *CNAA*   Sr. Lectr.
Withey, Frank, BA *CNAA*, MA *Leeds*   Sr. Lectr.
Worsdale, Graham J., BA *Lanc.*, MSc *UMIST*, PhD *Lanc.*   Head*
Yeadon, Annie, BA *Leeds*, MA *Brad.*   Sr. Lectr.
Research: change and human resource management; communications; database marketing; financial services; management strategy

Music

Tel: (01484) 472003 Fax: (01484) 472656
   E-mail: music@hud.ac.uk
Adkins, Mathew, MA *Camb.*, PhD *E.Anglia*   Sr. Lectr.
Bryan, John H., BA *York(UK)*, BPhil *York(UK)*   Principal Lectr.
Clarke, J. Michael, BA *Durh.*, PhD *Durh.*   Prof.
Cummings, Graham H., BMus *Birm.*, MA *Birm.*, PhD *Birm.*   Sr. Lectr.
Fox, Christopher, BA *Liv.*, BMus *S'ton.*, DPhil *York(UK)*   Prof.
Jan, Steven, BA *Leeds*, PhD *Leeds*   Sr. Lectr.
Russ, Michael, BMus *Sheff.*, MA *Belf.*, DPhil *Ulster*   Head*
Webb, Barrie E. R., BA *Camb.*, MA *Camb.*   Principal Lectr.
Research: computer music and computer-assisted learning; contemporary music (composition, electroacoustic music, musicology, performance); gender issues; Handel in London; historically aware performance practice (sixteenth–eighteenth century)

Music and Humanities, School of

English

Burrow, Merrick, BA *Lanc.*, MA *Sus.*, DPhil *Sus.*   Sr. Lectr.; Pathway Leader
Crutchley, Alison, BA *York(UK)*, MA *Lond.*, PhD *Manc.*
Foot, Robert, BA *Wales*, MA *Alta.*, PhD *Alta.*   Sr. Lectr.
Hodgson-Wright, Stephanie, BA *Lanc.*, MA *Liv.*, PhD *Leeds*   Sr. Lectr.
Holden, Catherine J., BA *E.Anglia*, PhD *E.Anglia*   Sr. Lectr.
Jeffries, Lesley, BA *Reading*, PhD *Leeds*   Principal Lectr.; Head*
Pollard, Malcolm C., BA *Sus.*, PhD *Brist.*   Sr. Lectr.; Mod. Langs. Co-ordinator*
Research: cultural theory, popular culture, conversational analysis; feminist linguistic

theory; literature (critical linguistics, Irish, post-colonial theory, stylistics, text analysis)

History

Cullum, Patricia H., BA *Keele*, MA *York(UK)*, DPhil *York(UK)*, FRHistS   Principal Lectr.; Head*
Davies, Peter J., BSc(Econ) *Wales*, PhD *Wales*   Sr. Lectr.
Laybourn, Keith, BSc *Brad.*, MA *Lanc.*, PhD *Lanc.*, FRHistS   Prof.
Lewis, Katherine, BA *Warw.*, MA *York(UK)*, DPhil *York(UK)*   Sr. Lectr.
Stafford, William, MA *Oxf.*, DPhil *Oxf.*, FRHistS   Prof.
Thornton, Tim, MA *Oxf.*, DPhil *Oxf.*, FRHistS
Ward, Paul, BA *Lond.*, PhD *Lond.*   Sr. Lectr.
Woodfine, Philip L., BA *Camb.*, MA *Camb.*, PhD *Hudd.*, FRHistS   Reader
Research: British politics (parties and policy making); crime and policing (nineteenth-to twentieth-century); gender and women's history, particularly mediaeval; labour history, Labour Party, co-operative movement; political history (sixteenth- to eighteenth century)

Media

Billam, Alistair, BA *Lanc.*   Sr. Lectr.
Butterick, Keith, BA   Sr. Lectr.
Cooper, Martin, BA *Camb.*, MA *York(UK)*, FRGS   Sr. Lectr., Radio Journalism
Dorril, Stephen, BSc *Hudd.*   Sr. Lectr.
Easterman, Max, MA *Camb.*   Sr. Lectr.
Ette, Mercy, BA *Calabar*, MA *Wales*, PhD *Leeds*   Sr. Lectr.
Jones, Eileen   Sr. Lectr.
Kelly, Stephen, BSc(Econ) *Lond.*, FRSA   Sr. Lectr., Media and Journalism
Prior, Christopher N., BA *Camb.*, MA *Camb.*   Principal Lectr.; Head*
Small, Robin, BA *Lanc.*, MA *Sheff.Hallam*   Sr. Lectr.
Williams, Granville, BA *Leeds*, MA *Exe.*   Sr. Lectr.

SPECIAL CENTRES, ETC

Applied Childhood Studies, Centre for

Featherstone, Brigid   National Society for the Prevention of Cruelty to Children Reader
Hanson, Sue
Parton, Nigel A., BA *Brad.*, MA *Essex*   Prof.; Dir.*

Evaluation Studies, Centre for

Kazi, Mansoor A. F., BSc *Lond.*, MA *Hull*   Reader; Dir.*

CONTACT OFFICERS

Academic affairs. Pro-Vice-Chancellor (Resources): Page, Prof. Michael I., PhD *Glas.*, DSc *CNAA*, FRSChem (E-mail: m.i.page@hud.ac.uk)
Admissions (first degree). Assistant Registrar (Admissions): McGregor, Linda (E-mail: admissions@hud.ac.uk)
Admissions (higher degree). Assistant Registrar (Admissions): McGregor, Linda (E-mail: admissions@hud.ac.uk)
Adult/continuing education. Chairman of Equal Opportunities Committee: Lee, Prof. Barry S., BA *Camb.*, MA *Camb.*, MEd *Manc.* (E-mail: b.s.lee@hud.ac.uk)
Alumni. Alumni Officer: Rundstrom, Claire, BA *Leic.* (E-mail: c.e.rundstrom@hud.ac.uk)
Careers. Head of Careers Advisory Service: Bristowe, Sharon, BA *Leeds*, MA *Reading* (E-mail: careers@hud.ac.uk)

Conferences/corporate hospitality. Conference Officer: Senior, Liz (E-mail: m.e.senior@hud.ac.uk)
Consultancy services. Head of Regional Development: Downs, Denise, BA *Lanc.*, MA *Open(UK)*, MSc *Manc.* (E-mail: d.downs@hud.ac.uk)
Equal opportunities. Chairman of Equal Opportunities Committee: Lee, Prof. Barry S., BA *Camb.*, MA *Camb.*, MEd *Manc.* (E-mail: b.s.lee@hud.ac.uk)
Estates and buildings/works and services. Director of Estates and Facilities: Blair, Colin, MSc *H-W* (E-mail: c.r.blair@hud.ac.uk)
Finance. Director of Finance: McConnell, Andrew, BSc *Manc.*, FCA (E-mail: a.mcconnell@hud.ac.uk)
Health services. University Medical Officer: Shortt, M., MB ChB (E-mail: health-centre@gp-b85062.nhs.uk)
Industrial liaison. Head of Regional Development: Downs, Denise, BA *Lanc.*, MA *Open(UK)*, MSc *Manc.* (E-mail: d.downs@hud.ac.uk)
International office. Director (International Office): Wood, Graham, BA *Hudd.*, MA *Griff.* (E-mail: international.office@hud.ac.uk)
Language training for international students. EFL Tutor: Hemsley, Michael J., BA *E.Anglia*, MA *Warw.* (E-mail: m.j.hemsley@hud.ac.uk)
Library (chief librarian). Director of Library and Computing Services: Lancaster, John, MPhil *Salf.* (E-mail: j.m.lancaster@hud.ac.uk)
Marketing. Head of Public Relations: Williams, Philip, BA *Leeds*, MA *Leeds* (E-mail: p.williams@hud.ac.uk)
Ombudsman. (Contact the appropriate Dean or Director/Head of Service or the Vice-Chancellor and Principal)
Personnel/human resources. Director, Human Resources: McClelland, Julie, BSocSc *Birm.*, MA *Lond.* (E-mail: j.mcclelland@hud.ac.uk)
Public relations. Head of Public Relations: Williams, Philip, BA *Leeds*, MA *Leeds* (E-mail: p.williams@hud.ac.uk)
Publications. Publications Manager: Hirstle, Ian (E-mail: i.hirstle@hud.ac.uk)
Purchasing. Purchasing Co-ordinator: Thompson, John (E-mail: john.thompson@hud.ac.uk)
Research. Senior Administrative Assistant (Research): Pitchford, Ian (E-mail: i.pitchford@hud.ac.uk)
Safety. Deputy Health and Safety Adviser: Wood, Gary (E-mail: g.r.wood@hud.ac.uk)
Schools liaison. Head, School and College Liaison: Pink, Julie, BA *Leeds* (E-mail: j.pink@hud.ac.uk)
Security. Security Officer: Tain, Graham (E-mail: g.tain@hud.ac.uk)
Sport and recreation. Sports Supervisor: Nettleton, Laurie (E-mail: l.j.nettleton@hud.ac.uk)
Staff development and training. Head of Staff Development Group: Sharp, Belinda (E-mail: b.j.sharp@hud.ac.uk)
Student union. President, University of Huddersfield Student Union: Johnson, Tom (E-mail: su-president@exchange01.ac.uk)
Student welfare/counselling. (Counselling) Counsellor: Forbes, Maggie, BA *Reading*
Student welfare/counselling. (Welfare) Director of Student Services: Wilcock, Rev. Paul T., BA *Brist.*, MA *Leeds* (E-mail: p.t.wilcock@hud.ac.uk)

[Information supplied by the institution as at 25 January 2005, and edited by the ACU]

UNIVERSITY OF HULL

Founded 1954

Member of the Association of Commonwealth Universities

Postal Address: Hull, England HU6 7RX
Telephone: (01482) 346311 **Fax:** (01482) 465936
URL: http://www.hull.ac.uk

VICE-CHANCELLOR*—Drewry, Prof. David J., BSc Lond., PhD Camb., Hon. DSc Humb., Hon. DSc R.Gordon, Hon. DSc Anglia PU, Hon. DSc Lincoln(UK), FRGS, FRSA, CCMI
TREASURER—Parkes, Deputy Lt. J. A., CBE, MA
DEPUTY VICE-CHANCELLOR (PRO-VICE-CHANCELLOR, ACADEMIC AFFAIRS)—Bruce, Prof. J. W., BA Liv., MSc Liv., PhD Liv.
PRO-VICE-CHANCELLOR (ENTERPRISE)—Winn, Prof. Barry, BSc CNAA, MCOptom Lond., PhD CNAA
PRO-VICE-CHANCELLOR (LEARNING AND TEACHING)—Lutzeier, Prof. Peter
QUALITY DIRECTOR/REGISTRAR AND SECRETARY‡—Owen, Frances, BA E.Anglia, MSc CNAA
DIRECTOR OF FINANCE—Stephenson, Keith, MBA Sheff., MA Camb.
LIBRARIAN AND DIRECTOR OF ACADEMIC SERVICES—Heseltine, Richard G., BA Sus., DPhil Sus.

GENERAL INFORMATION

History. The university was established in 1928 as a college of the University of London and achieved its independence in 1954.

Admission to first degree courses (see also United Kingdom Introduction). Through Universities and Colleges Admissions Service (UCAS). Candidates whose first language is not English will normally be expected to possess a recognised qualification in English language or to submit acceptable evidence of proficiency.

First Degrees (see also United Kingdom Directory to Subjects of Study). BA, BEng, BMus, BSc, BScEcon, LLB, MChem, MMath, MPhys, MPhysGeog.
Length of course. Full-time: BMus, BScEcon: 3 years; BA, BEng, BSc, LLB: 3–4 years; MChem, MMath, MPhys, MPhysGeog: 4 years. Part-time: BA, BEng, LLB: 5–6 years.

Higher Degrees (see also United Kingdom Directory to Subjects of Study).
Master's. LLM, MA, MBA, MEd, MMus, MPhil, MRes, MSc, MScEcon.
Length of course. Full-time: LLM, MA, MBA, MEd, MMus, MSc, MScEcon: 1 year; MPhil, MRes: 2 years. Part-time: LLM, MA, MBA, MEd, MMus, MSc, MScEcon: 2 years; MPhil: 3 years. By distance learning: MBA, MEd: 2 years.
Doctoral. ClinPsyD, DD, DLitt, DSc, DSc(Econ), EdD, LLD, MD, PhD, PsyD.
Admission. DD, DLitt, DSc, DSc(Econ), LLD: by submitted work.
Length of course. Full-time: MD: 1 year; ClinPsyD: 2½ years; EdD, PhD: 3 years. Part-time: MD, PsyD: 2 years; EdD, PhD: 4 years.

Language of Instruction. English. Pre-sessional English language courses available.

Libraries. Volumes: 1,018,000. Periodicals subscribed to: 10,000. Other holdings: 50 electronic databases. Special collections: Philip Larkin; Stevie Smith (lecturer); Hull Grammar School; Holy Trinity Hull (local history); Labour history (political history); South East Asia (map collection).

FACULTIES/SCHOOLS

Applied Science and Technology
Tel: (01482) 465377 Fax: (01482) 466660
E-mail: j.l.smith@hull.ac.uk
Dean: Wills, D. P. M., BSc Hull
Secretary: Smith, J. L.

Arts and Social Sciences
Tel: (01482) 465860 Fax: (01482) 465991
E-mail: p.g.escreet@hull.ac.uk
Dean: Talbot, G. R., BA Trinity(Dub.), PhD Trinity(Dub.)
Secretary: Escreet, P.

Hull York Medical School
Tel: (01482) 464701 Fax: (01482) 464705
E-mail: j.saunderson@hull.ac.uk
Dean: Gillespie, W. J., OBE, BSc Edin., MB ChB Edin.
Secretary: Saunderson, J.

Science and the Environment
Tel: (01482) 465377 Fax: (01482) 466660
E-mail: j.l.smith@hull.ac.uk
Dean: Sewell, D. F., BA Sheff., PhD Sheff.
Secretary: Smith, J. L.

ACADEMIC UNITS

Business School
Tel: (01482) 466096 Fax: (01482) 466097
E-mail: d.e.gibbs@hull.ac.uk

Accounting and Finance Subject Group
Maunders, K. T., BA Hull   Prof.
Simon, J., BSc(Econ) Hull, MA Lanc., MBA Wales   Sr. Lectr.
Other Staff: 8 Lectrs.
Research: international accounting and finance

Business and Leisure Management Subject Group
O'Hara, M., BSc Strath., MPhil CNAA, PhD Exe.   Principal Lectr.
Watson, S., BA CNAA, MA York(UK), MPhil York(UK)   Principal Lectr.
Other Staff: 12 Lectrs.
Research: regional business development

Economics Subject Group
Biswas, T. K., MA Roch., PhD Roch.   Sr. Lectr.
Green, R. J., BA Camb., MPhil Camb., PhD Camb.   Prof.; Head*
Hammond, Christopher J., BA Warw., MSc Lond.   Sr. Lectr.
Ryan, M. J., BSc Birm., MCom Birm., PhD Texas   Sr. Lectr.
Other Staff: 8 Lectrs.
Research: economic policy

Management Systems Subject Group
Jackson, M. C., BA Oxf., MA Oxf., MA Lanc.   Prof.; Dir. of School*
Keys, P., BSc St And., PhD Hull   Sr. Lectr.
Murray, P. J., BSc Cape Town, MSc Cape Town, PhD Camb., MBA   Sr. Lectr.
Yusuf, Y., BEng Bayero, MSc A.Bello, PhD Liv.   Sr. Lectr.
Other Staff: 5 Lectrs.; 2 Sr. Res. Fellows
Research: systems studies

Marketing and Business Strategy Subject Group
Johnson, D., BA Oxf., MA Oxf.   Sr. Lectr.
Kitchen, P. J., BA CNAA, MSc UMIST, MBSc Manc., PhD Keele, FRSA, FCIM   Prof.
O'Neill, N. J., BA York(UK), PhD Hull   Sr. Lectr.
Tucker, D., BA Hull, MA Hull   Sr. Lectr.; Head*
Zhu, Z., MSc Hull, PhD Hull   Sr. Lectr.

Other Staff: 9 Lectrs.
Research: international business; marketing and communications

Organisational Behaviour and Human Resource Management (HRM) Subject Group
Allan, B., BSc Birm., MA Hull, MSc City(UK)   Sr. Lectr.
Armstrong, S. J., BSc De Mont., MBA Sheff., PhD Leeds   Sr. Lectr.
Bright, D., BA CNAA, MSc Lond., PhD CNAA   Sr. Lectr.
Brown, M., BA Brist.   Sr. Lectr.
Carter, P., MA Lanc.   Sr. Lectr.
Milson, B., MSc Sheff.Hallam   Deputy Dir.
Other Staff: 5 Lectrs.
Research: management and organisational learning

Chemistry
Tel: (01482) 465461 Fax: (01482) 466418
E-mail: d.e.low@hull.ac.uk
Binks, B. P., BSc Hull, PhD Hull, FRSChem   Prof.
Boyle, R. W., BSc Paisley, PhD Paisley   Reader
Coupland, K., DSc Hull   Hon. Prof.
Fletcher, P. D. I., BSc Lond., PhD Kent, FRSChem   Prof.
Greenway, G. M., BSc CNAA, PhD Manc., FRSChem   Prof.
Haswell, S. J., BSc CNAA, PhD CNAA   Prof.
Hird, M., BSc Hull, PhD Hull, FRSChem   Reader
Kelly, S. M., BSc Sheff., PhD Hull   Prof.; Head*
Lacey, D., BSc CNAA, PhD CNAA   Reader
Mackenzie, G., BTech Brad., PhD Brad., FRSChem   Reader
Mehl, G. R. H., DrRerNat Freib.   Sr. Lectr.
Overton, T. L., PhD CNAA   Prof.
Paunov, V. N., MSc Sofia, PhD Sofia   Sr. Lectr.
Stillings, M. R., BSc Leic., DPhil York(UK)   Hon. Prof.
Townshend, A., BSc Birm., PhD Birm., DSc Birm., FRSChem   Emer. Prof.
Walker, R. W., BSc Hull, PhD Hull, FRSChem   Emer. Prof.
Warrington, B., PhD Lond.   Hon. Prof.
Young, N. A., BSc Lond., PhD S'ton.   Sr. Lectr.
Other Staff: 16 Lectrs.; 2 Lectrs.†; 2 Hon. Sr. Fellows; 1 Hon. Res. Assoc.
Research: analytical chemistry and chemometrics (chemiluminescence, immobilised reagents, microanalytical systems, microwave-enhanced reactors, process analysis, organopholomics); biological chemistry (drug design, heterocyclic chemistry, nucleosides, synthesis); heterogeneous chemistry (asymmetric synthesis, clean-technology, colloid science, surface chemistry, surfactants); inorganic chemistry (bio-inorganic, co-ordination chemistry, crystallography, fullerenes, metallomesogens, matrix-isolation); liquid crystals and advanced organic materials

(electrorheological fluids, ferroelectrics, liquid crystal polymers, non-linear optics, photochromics)

Comparative and Applied Social Sciences

Tel: (01482) 466213 Fax: (01482) 466366
E-mail: s.m.richards@hull.ac.uk
Argyrou, V., BSc MSc PhD   Sr. Lectr.
Bottomley, A. K., MA Camb., PhD Camb.   Prof.
Craig, G., BSc Lond., PhD Brad.   Prof.
Dawson, A., BA Essex, PhD Essex   Sr. Lectr.
Jewkes, Y., BA CNAA, MA Leic., PhD Camb.   Sr. Lectr.
Johnson, J. M., BA Simpson, MA Lond., PhD Lond.   Sr. Lectr.
Mullard, M., BA Portsmouth, MPhil S'ton., PhD Hull   Sr. Lectr.
Okely, J., BA Oxf., MA Oxf., DPhil Oxf.   Prof.
Seymour, J. O., BSc Hull, MA Manc., PhD Manc.   Head*
Young, P., BSc Lond., MA Sheff., PhD Edin.   Prof.
Other Staff: 12 Lectrs.; 7 Res. Fellows; 1 Emer. Fellow
Research: criminal justice and crime control; disability and health; gender/sexuality and the life course; migration and identity; social study of childhood

Computer Science

Tel: (01482) 465951 Fax: (01482) 466666
E-mail: h.m.el-sharkawy@hull.ac.uk
Bottaci, L., BA Essex, PhD Brun.   Sr. Lectr.
Brookes, G. R., MA Camb., MSc Manc., PhD Glas., FBCS   Prof.
Kambhampati, C., BE Nag., PhD Lond.   Reader
Mohsen, A. M. M., PhD Hull, MB BCh, FRCSEd   Hon. Prof.
Papadopoulos, Y. I., BSc Grad.Sch.Indust.St., Salonika, MSc Cran., PhD York(UK)   Sr. Lectr.
Phillips, R., BSc Manc., PhD Manc.   Prof.
Viant, W. J., BSc Hull   Sr. Lectr.; Head*
Wills, D. P. M., BSc Hull   Sr. Lectr.
Wright, H., MA Camb., DPhil York(UK)   Sr. Lectr.
Other Staff: 13 Lectrs.; 1 Clin. Res. Fellow
Research: distributed reliable intelligent systems; distributed systems engineering; simulation and visualisation

Drama and Music

Drama

Tel: (01482) 466210 Fax: (01482) 466727
E-mail: p.j.lambert@hull.ac.uk
Boon, R. P., BA Sheff., PhD Sheff.   Prof.
Meech, A. J., BA Manc., MA Brist.   Sr. Lectr.; Head*
Peacock, D. K., BA Leeds, PhD Exe.   Sr. Lectr.
Roy, D. H., MA Wales, FRSA   Emer. Prof.
Walton, J. M., MA St And., PhD Hull   Emer. Prof.
Other Staff: 7 Lectrs.
Research: British, German, and Japanese theatre; theory and practice (folk theatre, pantomime, set design, translation for performance, the actor, the director, drama in therapy, clowning)

Music

Tel: (01482) 465998 Fax: (01482) 465998
E-mail: p.a.muse@hull.ac.uk
Borthwick, A. B., BSc Lond., MMus Sheff., PhD Lond.   Sr. Lectr.
Sadler, A. G., BMus Nott., PhD Hull   Reader
Other Staff: 5 Lectrs.
Research: Baroque (especially French Baroque); composition; music analysis and twentieth-century music; performance studies; psychology of music

Engineering

Tel: (01482) 465141 Fax: (01482) 466664
E-mail: s.j.batch@hull.ac.uk
Attenborough, Keith, BSc Lond., PhD Leeds, FIA   Prof., Acoustics

Cole, G. H. A., PhD Lond., DSc Lond., FRAS, FIP, FIMechE   Prof.
Cummings, A., BSc Lond., MSc Liv., PhD Liv., DEng Liv., FIMechE, FIEE   Prof.
Fagan, M. J., BSc Exe., PhD Exe.   Sr. Lectr.
Gilbert, J. M., BSc Hull, PhD Hull   Sr. Lectr.
Haywood, Stephanie K., BA Oxf., PhD CNAA   Prof.
James, R. D., BSc S'ton., PhD CNAA, FIMechE, FIEE   Sr. Lectr.
Judah, S. R., BEng Jab., MSc Lond., PhD Lond.   Sr. Lectr.
Matthews, Allan, BSc Salf., PhD Salf., FIMechE, FIEE, FIMMM   3M Prof.
Patton, R. J., BEng Sheff., MEng Sheff., PhD Sheff.   Prof.
Pugh, A., BSc Wales, PhD Nott., FREng, FIEE, FRSA   Emer. Prof.
Pulko, S. H., BSc Lond., PhD Nott.   Sr. Lectr.
Riley, N. G., BEng Sheff., MSc Essex   Sr. Lectr.
Selke, K. K. W., BSc Hull, PhD Hull   Sr. Lectr.
Swift, K. G., BSc Salf., MSc Salf., PhD Lucas   Prof.
Other Staff: 11 Lectrs.
Research: acoustics and communications; design, analysis and manufacture control and intelligent systems; materials and devices; medical engineering

Geography

Tel: (01482) 465385 Fax: (01482) 466340
E-mail: geo@hull.ac.uk
Atkinson, D. A., BSc Brist., PhD Lough.   Sr. Lectr.
Boehmer-Christiansen, S. A., BA Adel., MA Sus., DPhil Sus.   Reader
Bradley, P. N., BSc Lond., MSc Lond., PhD Camb.   Sr. Lectr.
Bunting, M. J., BA Camb., PhD Camb.   Sr. Lectr.
Coulthard, T. J., BSc Leeds, PhD Leeds   Prof.
Eden, S. E., BA Durh., PhD Leeds   Sr. Lectr.
Ellis, S., BSc Reading, PhD Reading   Sr. Lectr.; Head*
Frostick, L. E., BSc Leic., PhD E.Anglia, FGS   Prof.
Gibbs, D. C., BA Manc., PhD Manc.   Prof.
Hardisty, J., BSc Lond., MSc Wales, PhD Hull   Prof.
Haughton, G., BA Hull, PhD Hull   Prof.
Jonas, A. E., BA Durh., MA Ohio, PhD Ohio   Prof.
Pedley, H. M., BSc Leic., PhD Hull, DSc Leic.   Reader
Rumsby, B. T., BSc Wales, PhD Newcastle(UK)   Sr. Lectr.
Other Staff: 9 Lectrs.; 8 Res. Fellows
Research: critical environmental policy and politics; environmental change, palaeoecology and wetland archaeology; environmental monitoring and modelling (fluvial and coastal processes, remote sensing); knowledge, economy and exclusion (economic, cultural and social geography); waste and pollution (physical and biological processing of waste)

Graduate School

Tel: (01482) 466846 Fax: (01482) 466846
E-mail: gri@hull.ac.uk
King, V. T., BA Hull, MA Lond., PhD Hull   Prof.; Dir.*

Health and Social Care, Faculty of

Tel: (01482) 464582 Fax: (01482) 464587
E-mail: catherine.hughes@hull.ac.uk
Beacock, S., MA York(UK)   Head, Nursing Studies and Midwifery
Hall, M. T., BSc MEd   Head, Appl. Health Studies
Holloway, M., BA York(UK), PhD Manc.   Prof., Social Work
Parry, R., BSc C.England, MSc C.England   Dean*
Shields, L., BAppSci MMedSci PhD   Prof., Nursing Practice and Education
Other Staff: 153 Staff Members
Research: death, dying and bereavement; dementia; nurse education; nursing

workforce; social aspects of chronic illness, especially Parkinson's

History

Tel: (01482) 465344 Fax: (01482) 466126
E-mail: f.e.hanson@hull.ac.uk
Ambler, R. W., BA Lond., PhD Hull, FRHistS, FSA   Sr. Lectr.
Ayton, A. C., BA Hull, PhD Hull   Sr. Lectr.
Burgess, G., MA Well., PhD Camb., FRHistS   Prof.; Head*
Crouch, D. B., BA Wales, PhD Wales, FRHistS   Prof.
English, B. A., MA St And., PhD St And., FSA, FRHistS   Emer. Prof.
Flint, V. I. J., BA Oxf., DPhil Oxf., FRHistS   Emer. Prof.
Haseldine, J. P., MA Oxf., PhD Camb.   Sr. Lectr.
Hoppen, K. T., MA N.U.I., PhD Camb., FBA, FRHistS   Emer. Prof.
Lloyd, H. A., BA Wales, DPhil Oxf., FRHistS   Emer. Prof.
Morgan, P. J., MA Camb., PhD Reading   Sr. Lectr.
Omissi, D. E., BA Lanc., MA Lond., PhD Lond.   Sr. Lectr.
Palmer, J. J. N., BA Oxf., BLitt Oxf., PhD Lond., FRHistS   Emer. Prof.
Pearson, R., MA Edin., PhD Leeds   Prof.
Price, J. L., BA Lond., PhD Lond.   Reader
Reid, D. A., BA Birm., PhD Birm.   Sr. Lectr.
Richardson, P. D., BA Manc., MA Manc.   Prof., Economic and Social History
Saville, J., BSc Lond.   Emer. Prof., Economic and Social History
Smith, S. C., BA Lond., MA Lond.   Sr. Lectr.
Starkey, D. J., BA Leeds, MA Exe., PhD Exe.   Sr. Lectr.
Turner, M. E., BSc Lond., PhD Sheff.   Prof., Economic and Social History
Woodward, D. M., BA Manc., MA Manc.   Emer. Prof., Economic and Social History
Other Staff: 8 Lectrs.
Research: British history; European history (especially French, German and Dutch); Indian and Southeast Asian history; maritime and Atlantic history; military history

Humanities

Tel: (01482) 465995 Fax: (01482) 466122
Gilbert, Paul, MA Camb.   Head*

American Studies

Tel: (01482) 465303 Fax: (01482) 466107
E-mail: s.m.tynan@hull.ac.uk
Abramson, E. A., BA N.Y., MA Iowa, PhD Manc.   Sr. Lectr.
Virden, J., BA Wash.State, MA Wash.State, PhD Wash.   Sr. Lectr.
Other Staff: 3 Lectrs.; 1 Emer. Reader
Research: history (history and film, war and society, World War II); literary and cultural studies (Anglo-American literature and historiography, visual art, film, Jewish American fiction, poetry, women's literature, 1930s fiction)

Cultural and Media Studies

Tel: (01482) 466620 Fax: (01482) 466107
E-mail: s.stathers@hull.ac.uk
Griffin, G., BA Leic., MA Lond., PhD Leic.   Prof.
Other Staff: 3 Lectrs.
Research: gender and development; gender and society; gender and young peoples' life choices; gender science and knowledge; gender theory

English

Tel: (01482) 465309 Fax: (01482) 465641
E-mail: g.e.cowper@hull.ac.uk
Arnold, P. M., BA Leeds, MA Leeds, PhD Leeds   Sr. Lectr.
Booth, James, BA Oxf., BLitt Oxf., PhD Hull   Prof.
Chapple, J. A. V.   Emer. Prof.
Cockin, K. M., BA Leic., MA Leic., PhD Leic.   Sr. Lectr.

Heilmann, A., MA PhD Prof.
McAlindon, T. E. Emer. Prof.
O'Mara, V., BA N.U.I., MA N.U.I., PhD Leeds Sr. Lectr.
Rumens, C., FRSL Prof.
Sanders, Valerie R., BA Camb., MA Camb., DPhil Oxf. Prof.; Dir. of Studies
Stoneman, P. M., BA Lond., MA Lond., PhD Hull Emer. Reader
Woodcock, Bruce, BA Leic., PhD Leic. Sr. Lectr.
Other Staff: 8 Lectrs.; 1 Res. Fellow†
Research: contemporary writing, especially poetry and film; creative writing; mediaeval and Renaissance periods; nineteenth and twentieth centuries; women's writing

Film Studies

Tel: (01482) 466496 Fax: (01482) 465641
E-mail: g.e.colins@hull.ac.uk
Sinyard, N. R., BA Hull, MA Manc. Prof.; Dir. of Studies
Other Staff: 2 Lectrs.
Research: adaptation; British television; documentary; post-war British cinema; post-1970s Hollywood cinema

Philosophy

Tel: (01482) 465995 Fax: (01482) 466122
E-mail: c.m.coulson@hull.ac.uk
Gilbert, Paul, MA Camb. Prof.
Lennon, Kathleen, BA Kent, BPhil Oxf., DPhil Oxf. Sr. Lectr.
Uniacke, Suzanne, BA La Trobe, MA La Trobe, PhD Syd. Reader
Other Staff: 3 Lectrs.; 1 Teaching Fellow
Research: ethics, applied philosophy and philosophy of law; gender theory; history of philosophy; philosophy of mind; political philosophy (ethnicity, nationalism, terrorism)

Theology Unit

Tel: (01482) 465995 Fax: (01482) 466122
E-mail: d.v.bagchi@hull.ac.uk
Bagchi, David V. N., MA Oxf., DPhil Oxf., FRHistS Dir.*
Grabbe, Lester, MA Pasadena, PhD Claremont, DD Hull Prof.
Other Staff: 2 Lectrs.
Research: biblical studies; Christian social ethics; church history; Indian religions

Law

Tel: (01482) 465857 Fax: (01482) 466388
E-mail: law@hull.ac.uk
Bevan, H. P., JP, LLM Wales, LLD Wales Emer. Prof.
Birkinshaw, P. J., LLB Hull Prof.
Burchill, R. M., BA Maine(USA), MA Hull, PhD Nott. Sr. Lectr.
Cownie, F., LLB Leic., LLM Lond. Prof.; H. K. Bevan Prof.
Edles, G. J., BA N.Y., LLM George Washington, SJD George Washington, JD N.Y. Visiting Prof.
Feintuck, M. J., LLB Sheff., PhD Sheff. Prof.
Johnstone, J. G., BA N.U.I., MSc Edin., PhD Edin. Prof.; Head*
La Torre, M., PhD Florence Prof.
Mitchell, C. E., LLB Essex, LLM Aberd. Sr. Lectr. (on leave)
Moir, L., LLB Edin., LLM Camb., PhD Camb. Sr. Lectr.
Parry, D. L., MBE, BA(Law) Sheff. Sr. Lectr.
Parry, M. L., LLB Leic. Emer. Reader
Van Der Borght, K., LicIur Brussels Sr. Lectr.
Ward, T., LLB Lond., LLM Lond., PhD De Mont. Reader
Whitehouse, L. A., LLB Hull Sr. Lectr.
Other Staff: 15 Lectrs.
Research: contract law and criminal law; human rights; international law, including law of the sea and armed conflict; legal philosophy and legal theory; public law, including European public law

Learning, Institute for

Tel: (01482) 466871 Fax: (01482) 466135
E-mail: ifl@hull.ac.uk
Stern, J., BA Oxf., BPhil Oxf., PhD Lond. Dean*
Other Staff: 1 Lectr.

Educational Studies, Centre for

Tel: (01482) 465406 Fax: (01482) 466133
E-mail: ces@hull.ac.uk
Bottery, M. P., BA Oxf., MEd Hull, PhD Hull Prof.
Colquhoun, D., BEd Leeds, MSc Lough., PhD Qld. Prof.
English, R. W., BSc Hull, MPhil Hull Sr. Lectr.
Howie, D. R., MA Auck., PhD Auck. Sr. Lectr.
Male, T. D., BEd Reading, MA Lond. Sr. Lectr.
Waugh, D. G., BA York(UK), MA Hull, PhD Hull Sr. Lectr.
Wright, N. G., BA Reading, MA Reading Sr. Lectr.
Other Staff: 1 Emer. Reader; 14 Lectrs.; 9 Tutors
Research: community, work-based and lifelong learning; information and communication technology (ICT) and learning; leadership, policy and management; religion and education; teaching and history of education

Lifelong Learning, Centre for

Tel: (01482) 465666 E-mail: cll@hull.ac.uk
Lewis, D., BEd Leeds, MA Lincoln(UK) Sr. Lectr.; Head*
Shuttleworth, S. J., BA Lanc., PhD Lanc. Sr. Lectr.
Vulliamy, Daniel L., BA Lanc., MA Warw., LLM Leic. Sr. Lectr.
Other Staff: 6 Lectrs.; 200 Sessional Tutors; 3 Hon. Fellows
Research: collaborative related learning; community learning; informal learning; widening participation; work-based learning

Mathematics

Tel: (01482) 466460 Fax: (01482) 466218
E-mail: d.j.hill@hull.ac.uk
Beckett, P. M., MA Oxf., PhD Emer. Prof.
Bingham, M. S., MSc Sheff., PhD Sheff. Sr. Lectr.
Collinson, C. D., BSc Lond., PhD Lond. Emer. Prof.
Cutland, N. J., MA Camb., PhD Brist. Prof.
Killingbeck, J. P., PhD Nott., DSc Nott. Emer. Reader
Kopp, P. E., BSc Stell., DPhil Oxf., Hon. Dr Rostov State Emer. Prof.
Lukaschuk, S., PhD Novosibirsk Reader
Scott, T., BSc Lond., PhD Lond. Sr. Lectr.
Shaw, R., BA Camb., PhD Camb., ScD Camb. Emer. Prof.
Strauss, D., MSc Cape Town, PhD Camb. Emer. Reader
Other Staff: 2 Lectrs.; 1 Sr. Fellow
Research: applied mathematics (continuum mechanics, mathematical physics); statistics

Modern Languages

Tel: (01482) 465043 Fax: (01482) 465020
E-mail: languages@hull.ac.uk

Dutch Studies

King, P. K., MA Lond., MA Camb. Emer. Prof.
Schludermann, B., BA McG., MA Manit., PhD Camb. Emer. Prof.
Other Staff: 1 Lectr.
Research: Dutch detective fiction; Dutch gender studies; mediaeval Dutch culture (German-Dutch language mix)

French

Tel: (01482) 465990 Fax: (01482) 465345
E-mail: french@hull.ac.uk
Hindley, A., BA Hull, PhD Hull Sr. Lectr.
Smith, Pauline M., BA Lond., PhD Lond. Emer. Prof.
Williams, D. A., BA Oxf., BPhil Oxf. Emer. Prof.

Other Staff: 4 Lectrs.; 5 Emer. Fellows
Research: cultural studies (popular culture, the media and cinema); language studies (European multilingual dictionary, Old French-English dictionary, simultaneous interpreting); literature (mediaeval, Renaissance, Enlightenment, nineteenth- and twentieth-century)

German

Tel: (01482) 465356 Fax: (01482) 465015
E-mail: j.r.cogman@hull.ac.uk
2 Lectrs.; 2 Lektorinnen; 1 Emer. Reader
Research: reception of mediaeval German literature in the twentieth century; twentieth-century German literature (narrative fiction)

Hispanic Studies

Tel: (01482) 465990
Beardsell, P. R., MA Manc., PhD Sheff. Emer. Prof.
Powell, B. J., BA Birm., PhD Camb. Sr. Lectr.; Head*
Other Staff: 3 Lectrs.; 2 Lectors
Research: applied linguistics (computer-assisted language learning); Latin American studies (post-colonial studies and education, twentieth-century literature); Spanish film

Italian

Tel: (01482) 465993 Fax: (01482) 465360
E-mail: g.r.talbot@hull.ac.uk
Moloney, B., BA Camb., PhD Camb. Emer. Prof.
Talbot, G. R., BA Trinity(Dub.), PhD Trinity(Dub.) Sr. Lectr.; Head*
Thompson, D., BA Leeds, MA Reading, MPhil Leeds, PhD Hull Emer. Prof.
Williams, Pamela A., BA Wales, PhD Camb. Sr. Lectr.
Other Staff: 3 Lectrs.; 1 Lector
Research: computer applications in language, the arts and humanities; literary, historical and cultural studies (the Middle Ages, the Renaissance and the eighteenth, nineteenth and twentieth centuries); modern Italian history and culture

Scandinavian Studies

Holmes, P. A., BA Hull, PhD Hull Emer. Reader
Other Staff: 1 Lector

Physics

Tel: (01482) 465501 Fax: (01482) 465606
E-mail: physics@hull.ac.uk
Dunning-Davies, J., BSc Liv., PhD Wales, FRAS
Dyer, P. E., BSc Hull, PhD Hull, FIP Prof.
O'Neill, M., BSc N.U.I., PhD Strath. Prof.
Sands, D., BTech Brad., PhD Brad. Sr. Lectr.
Other Staff: 4 Lectrs.
Research: chemical physics (lasers, novel materials, spectroscopy, theoretical underpinning); lasers and applications (ablation, analysis, carbon dioxide/excimer lasers, micromachining); modelling and theory, soft matter physics, semiconductors and devices, plasma and astrophysics; organic optoelectronics (alignment theory, organic semi-conductors, liquid crystals)

Politics and International Studies

Tel: (01482) 466209 Fax: (01482) 466208
E-mail: c.l.hairsine@hull.ac.uk
Dai, X., MA Nankai, DPhil Sus. Sr. Lectr.
Lee, S. D., BA Hull Sr. Lectr.
Magone, J. M., MPhil Vienna, DPhil Vienna Sr. Lectr.
Morris, J. C., LLB CNAA, MA Hull Sr. Lectr.
Norton of Louth, Lord, BA Sheff., MA Penn., PhD Sheff., FRSA AcSS Prof.; Head*
O'Sullivan, N. K., BSc(Econ) Lond., PhD Lond. Prof.
Tyler, C., BA Reading, MA York(UK), DPhil York(UK) Sr. Lectr.
Wurzel, R. K., MA Augsburg, MA Hull, PhD Lond. Reader

Other Staff: 8 Lectrs.; 1 Emer. Sr. Fellow

Research: European Union studies; legislative studies; security studies and international relations

Postgraduate Medical Institute

Tel: (01482) 465348 Fax: (01482) 463421
    E-mail: j.kitson@hull.ac.uk
Stafford, N. D., MB ChB, FRCS   Clin. Prof./ Consultant; Dir.*
Research: cancer; cardiovascular disease; clinical psychology; musculoskeletal ailments; psychoneuroimmunology

Academic Surgical Unit

Tel: (01482) 623225 Fax: (01482) 623274
    E-mail: h.binks@hull.ac.uk
Drew, P. J., BSc MD, FRCSEd, FRCSGlas   Clin. Sr. Lectr./Consultant
Duthie, G. S., MD Edin., BMedBio, FRCSEd   Reader/Consultant
Gunn, J., MB ChB, FRCS   Clin. Sr. Lectr./ Consultant
Hartley, J. E., BSc MD, FRCS   Clin. Sr. Lectr./ Consultant
Monson, J. R. T., MB BCh BAO Trinity(Dub.), MD, FRCSI, FACS, FRCS   Clin. Prof./ Consultant; Head*
Other Staff: 1 Reader; 7 Clin. Lectrs.
Research: anorectal trauma; neorectal dynamics; neural networks (prognosticate in patients with colorectal cancer); wound healing

Cardiology

Tel: (01482) 624084 Fax: (01482) 624085
    E-mail: j.g.cleland@hull.ac.uk
Cleland, J. G. F., MD, FRCPGlas, FRCP   Clin. Prof./Consultant; Head*
Other Staff: 1 Clin. Reader
Research: heart failure

Clinical Psychology

Tel: (01482) 464106 Fax: (01482) 464093
    E-mail: b.j.leak@hull.ac.uk
Clement, S., BSocSc Birm., MSc Leic.   Clin. Sr. Lectr./Consultant
Glover, L. F., BSc York(UK), MSc Lond., PhD Lond.   Sr. Lectr.
Hoghughi, M., BA Hull, PhD Newcastle(UK), FBPsS   Hon. Prof./Consultant
Lam, D. H., BSc Lond., PhD Lond.   Prof.; Dir., ClinPsyd Programme; Head*
Moniz-Cook, E. D., BSc Leeds   Clin. Sr. Lectr./ Consultant
Other Staff: 1 Lectr.; 1 Hon. Sr. Fellow; 18 Hon. Clin. Lectrs.
Research: Alzheimer's disorder, detection management and carer support; developing cognitive therapy for bipolar affective disorder; measures and organisation for people with long-term disabilities; psychological factors contributing to individual illness experiences

Diabetes and Endocrinology

Tel: (01482) 675365 Fax: (01482) 675370
    E-mail: s.l.atkin@hull.ac.uk
Atkin, S. L., BSc Newcastle(UK), MB BS Newcastle(UK), PhD Liv.   Prof./Consultant; Head*
Research: breast cancer; cytokine production by human anterior pituitary adenomas; diabetic neuropathy (collagen sub-types in human sural nerve); tumour radiosensitisation

Magnetic Resonance Investigations, Centre for

Tel: (01482) 674084 Fax: (01482) 320137
    E-mail: s.p.hunter@hull.ac.uk
Turnbull, L. L. W., BSc Edin., MB ChB Edin., MD Edin., FRCR   Clin. Prof.; Dir.*
Other Staff: 2 Res. Fellows; 1 Clin. Lectr.; 1 Hon. Res. Fellow
Vacant Posts: 1 Lectr.; 1 Clin. Sr. Lectr.; 1 Hon. Res. Fellow
Research: magnetic resonance diffusion-weighted/perfusion imaging; magnetic resonance imaging of breast, prostate and ovary; magnetic resonance imaging/ spectroscopy of brain

Medical Physics

Tel: (01482) 464562
    E-mail: c.m.langton@hull.ac.uk
Langton, C. M., BSc Hull, MSc Aberd., PhD Hull, FIP   Reader; Head*
Other Staff: 5 Hon. Fellows
Research: stimulation (ultrasound propagation in cancellous bone, bone pathophysiology); technology development (propensity to fall radiotherapy)

Metabolic Bone Disease, Centre for

Tel: (01482) 675302 Fax: (01482) 675301
    E-mail: c.m.langton@hull.ac.uk
1 Clin. Res. Fellow
Research: accuracy and precision of bone mineral densitometry; natural history of perimenopausal bone loss; osteoporosis and related fractures in the Yorkshire population; primary care prediction of osteoporosis; selective oestrogen receptor modulators (SERMs)

Obstetrics and Gynaecology

Tel: (01482) 382757 Fax: (01482) 382751
    E-mail: s.r.killick@hull.ac.uk
Killick, S. R., BSc Lond., MB BS Lond., MD Lond., FRCOG   Clin. Prof./Consultant; Head*
Lindow, S. W., MB ChB Sheff., MMed Cape Town, FRCOG   Clin. Sr. Lectr./Consultant
Other Staff: 4 Clin. Lectrs/Clin. Res. Fellows
Research: human physiology (explanations of function, novel imaging techniques); obstetrics (epidural analgesia, sphincter imaging, oxytocin physiology, electrical impedance studies)

Oncology

Tel: (01482) 676807
    E-mail: m.j.lind@hull.ac.uk
Lind, M. J., BSc MD, FRCP   Clin. Prof./ Consultant; Head*
Maraveyas, A., PhD   Clin. Sr. Lectr./ Consultant
Other Staff: 1 Lectr.
Research: development and testing of new drugs for the treatment of malignant disease; investigating lung, breast and ovarian carcinoma

Otolaryngology and Head and Neck Surgery

Tel: (01482) 465348 Fax: (01482) 463421
    E-mail: j.kitson@hull.ac.uk
Stafford, N. D., MB ChB, FRCS   Clin. Prof./ Consultant; Head*
Research: counselling of patients with head and neck cancer; molecular aspects of tumours of the larynx and pharynx; prediction of prognosis in head and neck cancer

Psychiatry

Tel: (01482) 464565 Fax: (01482) 464569
    E-mail: j.t.branton@hull.ac.uk
Mortimer, A. M., BSc Leic., MB ChB Leic., MMedSci Leeds, FRCPsych   Prof./ Consultant; Head*
Other Staff: 2 Res. Assocs.; 1 Clin. Sr. Lectr./ Consultant
Research: cognitive neuropsychology; psychosis (atypical neuroleptics); social management of psychiatric genetics

Public Health and Primary Care

Tel: (01482) 463037
    E-mail: p.d.campion@hull.ac.uk
Campion, P. D., MA Oxf., PhD Liv., BM BCh Oxf., FRCGP   Clin. Prof./Consultant; Head*
Research: chronic fatigue syndrome; communication in children's asthma; doctor-patient interaction; problems of couples undergoing fertility treatment; quality of life in diabetes

Rehabilitation and Therapies, Institute of

Tel: (01482) 675046 Fax: (01482) 675636
    E-mail: a.f.adams@hull.ac.uk
Moffett, J., PhD   Prof.
Walker, L. G., MA PhD   Prof.; Dir.*
Other Staff: 5 Researchers; 1 Clin. Sr. Lectr.
Research: back pain; barriers to research in the therapies; chronic fatigue syndrome; musculoskeletal disorders; neck-related pain

Respiratory Medicine

Tel: (01482) 624067 Fax: (01482) 624068
    E-mail: j.l.crawford@hull.ac.uk
Morice, A. H., MA Camb., MD Camb.   Clin. Prof./Consultant; Head*
Research: mechanism of hypocic vasoconstriction in vitro; respiratory disease; the cough reflex

Vascular Surgery

Tel: (01482) 674704
Chetter, I., MB ChB Leeds, MD Leeds, FRCS   Clin. Sr. Lectr./Consultant
McCollum, P. T., BA Trinity(Dub.), MB ChB BAO Trinity(Dub.), MCh Trinity(Dub.)   Clin. Prof./Consultant; Head*

Psychology

Tel: (01482) 466154 Fax: (01482) 465599
    E-mail: l.baldwin@hull.ac.uk
Clough, P. J., BSc Brad., PhD Aberd.   Sr. Lectr.
Crawshaw, C. M., BSc S'ton., PhD S'ton.   Sr. Lectr.
Flowers, K. A., MA Camb., PhD Camb.   Sr. Lectr.
Johnston, R. S., BA Hull, PhD Hull   Prof.
Lavidor, M.   Sr. Lectr.
Sheridan, M. R., BSc Hull, PhD Hull   Head*
Singleton, C. H., BA Nott., PhD Nott., FBPsS   Sr. Lectr.
Venneri, A.   Prof.
Williams, D. I., BSc Hull, PhD Hull, FBPsS   Sr. Lectr.
Other Staff: 13 Lectrs.
Research: application of psychology to medicine (movement disorders, pain, psychogynaecology); cognition and emotion (action, attention, learning, memory, perception); human factors and cognitive ergonomics (human computer systems, performance, work design); psychological health and lifestyle (coping, drugs, sport/exercise, stress, wellbeing); psychological testing and assessment (cognitive/physical difficulties, dyslexia screening, psychometrics)

Scarborough School of Arts and New Media

Tel: (01723) 357341 Fax: (01752) 347340
    E-mail: ssa@hull.ac.uk
Hockley, L.
Holt, D., MA Lond.   Dir., External Validations
Howle, T., BA Keele, PhD Keele
Other Staff: 20 Lectrs.

Creative Music Technology

King, A., MRes Northumbria   Dir. of Studies*
Other Staff: 5 Lectrs.
Research: electro-acoustic composition for tape alone and mixed media (image, instruments, live electronics, movement, theatre); electro-acoustic music, learning technology and educational psychology; jazz post 1960 (free form composition, avant-garde techniques, minimalist music, electronics in live performance); musical development and audiovisual associations in children (applications for music technology and digital art in pre-school and primary education, interactive response, synthesis and signal processing); theory and analysis (analytical issues in early music, nineteenth-century German song, popular song writing, sixteenth-century style study

Dance

3 Lectrs.
Research: aesthetic development, collaborative processes in art-making behaviour; gender and race politics (Phoenix Dance Theatre); politics in choreographic processes (chiropractic as an impact on dance training and education, non-literal/non-narrative performance)

English

E-mail: f.bannon@hull.ac.uk
Bannon, F., PhD Manc. Dir. of Studies*
Other Staff: 3 Lectrs.
Research: contemporary British fiction; literary and political culture of the Renaissance period; nineteenth-century British and Irish fiction; Old Norse-Icelandic language and literature; theories of postmodernity and postmodernism

Language Institute

E-mail: g.f.gibson@hull.ac.uk
Gibson, G., BA York(UK), MSc Aston, FRSA Dir., EFL*
Other Staff: 3 Lectrs.†
Research: academic writing, bilingualism and bilingual education; music and song in the language classroom; training language teaching mentors

Theatre and Performance Studies

E-mail: ssa@hull.ac.uk
Andrews, S., PhD Lanc. Dir. of Studies*
Other Staff: 5 Lectrs.
Research: aesthetics, culture and performance; performance and new media; politics and performing place and past; practice as research; site based performance and institutional practice

Sport, Health and Exercise Science

Tel: (01482) 466404
E-mail: k.m.williams@hull.ac.uk
McNaughton, L. R., BEd Nedlands C.A.E., MSc Oregon, MBA Bath, PhD Oregon Prof.; Head*
Other Staff: 10 Lectrs.; 1 Teaching Fellow
Research: cardiac rehabilitation; falling in elderly and diabetic patients; health and fitness of children; physiological and biomechanical testing of athletes; psychology of elite athletes

SPECIAL CENTRES, ETC

Chemistry in Industry

Tel: (01482) 465455 Fax: (01482) 470225
E-mail: s.c.pace@hull.ac.uk
1 Lectr.

Childhood, Centre for the Social Study of

Tel: (01482) 465713 Fax: (01482) 466366
James, A., BA Durh., PhD Durh. Reader; Dir.*
Other Staff: 6 Lectrs.; 2 Res. Fellows
Research: child health and welfare; childhood and children as social actors; children's time use; education and schooling; family life

City and Regional Studies

Tel: (01482) 465330 Fax: (01482) 466340
E-mail: d.c.gibbs@hull.ac.uk
Gibbs, D. C., BA Manc., PhD Manc. Dir.*
Haughton, G., BA Hull, PhD Hull Prof.
Other Staff: 1 Lectr.; 2 Res. Fellows
Research: best practice and new developments in urban and regional restructuring and regeneration; local regeneration strategies

Economic Policy, Centre for

Tel: (01482) 466217 Fax: (01482) 466216
E-mail: econ@hull.ac.uk
Biswas, T. K., MA Roch., PhD Roch. Sr. Lectr.
Green, R. J., BA Camb., MPhil Camb., PhD Camb. Prof.
Hammond, Christopher J., BA Warw., MSc Lond. Sr. Lectr.

Ryan, M. J., BSc Birm., MCom Birm., PhD Texas Sr. Lectr.; Dir.*

Education, Scarborough School of

Tel: (01723) 357265 Fax: (01723) 370815
Billett, S., MA Durh. Sr. Lectr.
Jackson, S. A., MA Lond. Sr. Lectr.
James, R., BA Open(UK), MSc Hull Lectr.; Head*
Other Staff: 14 Lectrs.
Research: early years in education; information communication technology (ICT) in primary education; partnership working with primary and early years settings

Environmental Technologies Centre for Industrial Collaboration (ETCIC)

Tel: (01482) 466940 Fax: (01482) 466884
E-mail: f.hartnett@hull.ac.uk
Adams, J., BSc Nott., PhD Newcastle(UK)
Calvert, D., BSc Kingston(UK), PhD Lough.
Foulkes, A., BSc De Mont.
Frostick, L. E., BSc Leic., PhD E.Anglia, FGS Prof.; Dir.*
Segrott, A., BSc Brad.
Other Staff: 1 Res. Fellow; 1 Adjunct Reader
Research: composting; flux of pollutants associated with contaminated land; sustainable resource use

Estuarine and Coastal Studies, Institute of

Tel: (01482) 464558 Fax: (01482) 464130
E-mail: iecs@hull.ac.uk
De Jonge, V. N., PhD Hon. Prof.
Elliott, Michael, BSc Lond., PhD Stir., FIBiol Prof.; Dir.*
Research: estuarine and coastal science management; estuarine and marine fish assessment; marine policy; seabed ecology; water quality

European Public Law, Institute of

Tel: (01482) 465917 Fax: (01482) 466388
Birkinshaw, P. J., LLB Hull Prof.; Dir.*
Feintuck, M. J., LLB Sheff., PhD Sheff. Sr. Lectr.

International Accounting and Finance, Institute for

Tel: (01482) 466636 Fax: (01482) 466637
E-mail: d.j.hill@hull.ac.uk
Briston, R. J., BSc(Econ) Lond., FCA Acting Dir.*
Other Staff: 4 Lectrs.

Learning Development, Centre for

Tel: (01482) 466227 Fax: (01482) 341334
E-mail: ifl@hull.ac.uk
Atkinson, S. A., BA CNAA, MA Exe. Head*
White, I. K., BSc Brad., PhD York(UK) Sr. Lectr.

E-Learning

Tel: (01482) 466186 Fax: (01482) 341334
3 Staff Members

Information and Communications Technology (ICT) Training

Tel: (01482) 465477 Fax: (01482) 466135
Saville, L., BA CNAA Head*
Other Staff: 4 Staff Members

Study Advice Services

Tel: (01482) 466344 Fax: (01482) 466135
E-mail: studyadvice@hull.ac.uk
Barnett, K. Head*
Other Staff: 8 Tutors

Legislative Studies, Centre for

Tel: (01482) 465863 Fax: (01482) 466208
E-mail: p.norton@hull.ac.uk
Norton of Louth, Lord, BA Sheff., MA Penn., PhD Sheff., FRSA Dir.*
Other Staff: 1 Dir., Legal Res.; 2 Lectrs.; 3 Visiting Scholars; 1 Assoc. Scholar; 1 Postdoctoral Res. Fellow

Research: comparative legislative studies; parliamentary behaviour

Management and Organisational Learning, Centre for

Tel: (01482) 466639 Fax: (01482) 466637
E-mail: j.arnold@hull.ac.uk
Armstrong, S. J., BSc De Mont., MBA Sheff., PhD Leeds Dir.*
Other Staff: 7 Lectrs.

Marketing and Communications, Centre for

Tel: (01482) 466639 Fax: (01482) 466637
E-mail: j.arnold@hull.ac.uk
Kitchen, P. J., BA CNAA, MSc UMIST, MBSc Manc., PhD Keele, FRSA, FCIM Dir.*
Other Staff: 6 Lectrs.

Regional Business Development, Centre for

Tel: (01482) 466636 Fax: (01482) 466637
E-mail: d.j.hill@hull.ac.uk
O'Neill, N. J., BA York(UK), PhD Hull Dir.*
Other Staff: 10 Lectrs.

Systems Studies, Centre for

Tel: (01482) 466636 Fax: (01482) 466637
E-mail: d.j.hill@hull.ac.uk
Midgley, G. R., BA Lond., MA City(UK), MPhil City(UK), PhD City(UK) Sr. Res. Fellow; Dir.*
Other Staff: 8 Lectrs.

University of Hull International Fisheries Institute

Tel: (01482) 466421 Fax: (01482) 470129
E-mail: hifi@hull.ac.uk
Cowx, I. G., BSc Liv., PhD Exe. Reader; Dir.*
Research: aquaculture; fisheries policy and planning; fisheries stock management; fisheries technology; inland fisheries management

Wetland Archaeology and Environment Research Centre

Tel: (01482) 465325 Fax: (01482) 465362
E-mail: waerc@hull.ac.uk
Lillie, M. C., BA Nott., MSc Sheff., PhD Sheff. Dir.*
Other Staff: 2 Res. Fellows; 1 Adjunct Sr. Lectr.; 2 Adjunct Lectrs.
Research: archaeological and environmental mitigation; environmental analysis; groundwater monitoring

CONTACT OFFICERS

Admissions (first degree). Admissions Officer: Dowling, Sheila C., BSc Bath (E-mail: admissions@hull.ac.uk)
Admissions (higher degree). Admissions Officer: Dowling, Sheila C., BSc Bath (E-mail: admissions@hull.ac.uk)
Alumni. Alumni Officer: Mustard, Bridget E. (E-mail: b.e.mustard@hull.ac.uk)
Archives. Archivist: Burg, Judy, BA York(UK) (E-mail: archives@hull.ac.uk)
Careers. Head of Careers and Appointments Service: Franks, John C., BA Hull (E-mail: car@hull.ac.uk)
Computing services. Librarian and Director of Academic Services: Heseltine, Richard G., BA Sus., DPhil Sus. (E-mail: r.g.heseltine@hull.ac.uk)
Consultancy services. Pro-Vice-Chancellor (Enterprise): Winn, Prof. Barry, BSc CNAA, MCOptom Lond., PhD CNAA (E-mail: b.winn@hull.ac.uk)
Credit transfer. Acting Head, Student Administration Services: Ord, Derek, BSc Hull (E-mail: d.j.ord@hull.ac.uk)
Distance education. International Officer, Off-Campus Programmes: Clarke, Robert, BA Hull, MPhil Hull (E-mail: r.clarke@hull.ac.uk)

Estates and buildings/works and services.
Estates Development Officer: Farr, Richard,
JP, BA *Wales* (E-mail: r.farr@hull.ac.uk)

Finance. Director of Finance: Stephenson,
Keith, MBA *Sheff.*, MA *Camb.*

General enquiries. Quality Director/Registrar
and Secretary: Owen, Frances, BA *E.Anglia*,
MSc *CNAA* (E-mail: d.j.lock@hull.ac.uk)

Industrial liaison. Pro-Vice-Chancellor
(Enterprise): Winn, Prof. Barry, BSc *CNAA*,
MCOptom *Lond.*, PhD *CNAA*
(E-mail: b.winn@hull.ac.uk)

International office. Director of International
Office: Richardson, James
(E-mail: international@hull.ac.uk)

Library (chief librarian). Librarian and
Director of Academic Services: Heseltine,
Richard G., BA *Sus.*, DPhil *Sus.*
(E-mail: r.g.heseltine@hull.ac.uk)

Marketing. Marketing Manager: Shepherd,
Gillian (E-mail: g.shepherd@hull.ac.uk)

Ombudsman. Assistant Registrar
(Ombudsman): Burton, Tim, LLB *CNAA*,
PhD *Hull* (E-mail: t.p.burton@hull.ac.uk)

Personnel/human resources. Director of
Human Resources: Howie, Rory
(E-mail: r.howie@hull.ac.uk)

Public relations. Public Relations Officer:
Fletcher, Tracy, BA *Birm.*, MPhil *Birm.*
(E-mail: t.fletcher@hull.ac.uk)

Purchasing. Purchasing Officer: Gurling, Susan
E. A. (E-mail: s.e.gurling@hull.ac.uk)

Quality assurance and accreditation. Deputy
Academic Registrar: Newham, Derek, BA
Kent (E-mail: d.newham@hull.ac.uk)

Research. Pro-Vice-Chancellor (Enterprise):
Winn, Prof. Barry, BSc *CNAA*, MCOptom
Lond., PhD *CNAA* (E-mail: b.winn@hull.ac.uk)

Safety. Director, Health and Safety Services:
Stephenson, Rachel
(E-mail: d.h.watson@hull.ac.uk)

Schools liaison. Head, Student Recruitment
Service: Jones, Hilary A., BA *Hull*
(E-mail: srs@hull.ac.uk)

Security. Assistant Director (Services and
Administration): Campbell, Sally A.
(E-mail: s.campbell@hull.ac.uk)

Staff development and training. Staff
Development Manager: Kelsey, M.
(E-mail: m.kelsey@hull.ac.uk)

Student welfare/counselling. Head of Student
Support Services: Allison, Simon, BSc *Hudd.*,
MA *Open(UK)*
(E-mail: studentwelfare@hull.ac.uk)

Students from other countries. Director of
International Office: Richardson, James
(E-mail: international@hull.ac.uk)

Students with disabilities. Disabilities Officer:
Harrison, P. L.
(E-mail: disabilityservices@hull.ac.uk)

CAMPUS/COLLEGE HEADS

Bishop Grosseteste College, Newport,
Lincoln, England LN1 3DY. (Tel: (01522)
527347; Fax: (01522) 530243) Principal
(Dean): Baker, Prof. E.

Greenwich School of Management, Meridian
House, Royal Hill, Greenwich, London,
England SE10 8RD. (Tel: (0208) 516 7800;
Fax: (0208) 516 7801;
E-mail: david@greenwich-college.ac.uk)
Principal: Hunt, William, MA

Scarborough Campus, Filey Road,
Scarborough, North Yorkshire YO11 3AZ.
(Tel: (01752) 357203; Fax: (01752)
357337; E-mail: c.gaskell@hull.ac.uk) Dean:
Gaskell, C., BSc *Hull*, PhD *Hull*

*[Information supplied by the institution as at 9 October
2007, and edited by the ACU]*

IMPERIAL COLLEGE LONDON

Founded 1907

Member of the Association of Commonwealth Universities

Postal Address: South Kensington Campus, London, England SW7 2AZ
Telephone: (020) 7589 5111
URL: http://www.imperial.ac.uk

RECTOR*—Anderson, Sir Roy, PhD *Lond.*, FRS, FMedSci
PRO RECTOR (COMMERCIAL AFFAIRS)—Habib, Prof. Nagy A., MB BCh *Ain Shams*, ChB *Brist.*, BMedSci, FRCS
PRO RECTOR (EDUCATIONAL QUALITY)—Buckingham, Prof. Julia C., BSc *Sheff.*, PhD *Lond.*, DSc *Lond.*
PRO RECTOR (POSTGRADUATE AND INTERNATIONAL AFFAIRS)—Ritter, Prof. Mary A., BA *Oxf.*, MA *Oxf.*, DPhil *Oxf.*
DIRECTOR OF FINANCE—Murphy, Andrew C., BEng *Birm.*
DIRECTOR OF STRATEGY AND PLANNING/COLLEGE SECRETARY AND CLERK TO THE COURT AND COUNCIL‡—Eastwood,
    Rodney, BSc *Newcastle(UK)*, PhD *Newcastle(UK)*
CHIEF OPERATING OFFICER—Knight, Martin, BA *Oxf.*, DPhil *Oxf.*

GENERAL INFORMATION

History. The college is made up of the
former Royal College of Science, City and
Guilds College, Royal School of Mines, St
Mary's Hospital Medical School, National Heart
and Lung Institute, Charing Cross and
Westminster Medical School, Royal
Postgraduate Medical School, Kennedy Institute
for Rheumatology, and Wye College.

It has seven campuses in west London, a
rural campus in Kent and a field station in
Berkshire.

Admission to first degree courses (see also
United Kingdom Introduction). Through
Universities and Colleges Admissions Service
(UCAS). International candidates are normally
required to take an English language test.

First Degrees (see also United Kingdom
Directory to Subjects of Study). BEng, BSc, MB
BS, MEng, MSci.

Length of course. Full-time: BEng, BSc: 3–4 years;
MEng: 4 years; MSci: 4–5 years; MB BS: 6
years.

Higher Degrees (see also United Kingdom
Directory to Subjects of Study).

Master's. MBA, MEd, MPH, MPhil, MRes,
MSc.

Admission. Applicants for admission to higher
degree courses must normally possess the

equivalent of a University of London first or
second class honours degree.

Length of course. Full-time: MBA, MEd, MPH,
MRes, MSc: 1 year; MPhil: 2 years. Part-time:
MBA, MEd, MRes, MSc: 2 years; MPH: 2–3
years; MPhil: 3 years.

Doctoral. EngD, MD(Res), PhD.

Length of course. Full-time: MD(Res): 2 years;
PhD: 3 years; EngD: 4 years. Part-time:
MD(Res), PhD: 4 years.

Libraries. Volumes: 500,000. Periodicals
subscribed to: 23,000. Special collections:
Annan (history of metal mining and
metallurgy).

Academic Year (2007–2008). Three terms:
29 September–14 December; 3 January–19
March; 26 April–27 June.

Income (2005–2006). Total, £503,564,000.

Statistics. Staff (2007–2008): 6409 (1511
academic, 4898 non-academic). Students
(2006–2007): full-time 12,129 (7650 men,
4479 women); part-time 895 (560 men, 335
women); international 5649; distance
education/external 918; undergraduate 8346
(5312 men, 3034 women); master's 1759
(1054 men, 705 women); doctoral 2024
(1284 men, 740 women).

FACULTIES/SCHOOLS

Engineering
Tel: (020) 7594 1282 Fax: (020) 7594 8609
    E-mail: eng.web@imperial.ac.uk
Principal: Wood, Prof. John, BSc *Sheff.*, PhD
    Sheff.

Medicine
Tel: (020) 7594 9836
    E-mail: r.a.shaw@imperial.ac.uk
Principal: Smith, Prof. Stephen K., DSc,
    FMedSci

Natural Sciences
Tel: (020) 7594 5477 Fax: (020) 7594 1418-9
    E-mail: julie.talbot@imperial.ac.uk
Principal: Knight, Prof. Sir Peter, BSc *Sus.*,
    DPhil *Sus.*, FRS

Tanaka Business School
Tel: (020) 7589 5111 Fax: (020) 7823 7685
Principal: Begg, Prof. David K. H., BA *Camb.*,
    MPhil *Oxf.*, PhD *M.I.T.*

ACADEMIC UNITS
Aeronautics
Tel: (020) 7594 5100 Fax: (020) 7584 8120
Aliabadi, Mohammad H., BSc *Tees.*, PhD *Tees.*
    Prof., Aerostructures
Doorly, Denis J., DPhil *Oxf.*, MA   Reader

Falzon, Brian G., BSc Syd., BEng Syd., PhD Syd.
Sr. Lectr., Advanced Aerostructures
Galvanetto, Ugo, MSc DPhil   Sr. Lectr.
Graham, J. Michael R., MA Camb., PhD Lond.
Prof., Unsteady Aerodynamics
Greenhalgh, Emile S., PhD Lond., Hon. BSc Lond.
Sr. Lectr.
Hillier, Richard, BA Camb., MA Camb., PhD
Camb.   Prof., Compressible Flow; Head*
Hodgkinson, John M., MSc Manc., PhD
Sheff.Hallam, FIMMM   Sr. Lectr.
Iannucci, Lorenzo, BSc Lond., MSc Lond., PhD
Lond.   Sr. Lectr.
Leschziner, Michael A., MSc Lond., PhD Lond.,
DSc Manc.Met.   Prof., Computational
Aerodynamics
Morrison, Jonathan F., BSc Durh., PhD Durh.
Prof., Experimental Fluid Mechanics
Olsson, Robin, MSc M.I.T., MSc R.I.T.Stockholm,
PhD R.I.T.Stockholm   Sr. Lectr.
Peiro, Joaquim, PhD Wales   Sr. Lectr.
Robinson, Paul, BSc UMIST, MSc UMIST, PhD
UMIST   Sr. Lectr.; Head, Composites Centre
Serghides, Varnavos C., BSc Manc., PhD Cran.,
DPhil   Sr. Lectr.
Sherwin, Spencer J., BSc Lond., MSc Prin., PhD
Prin.   Prof., Computational Fluid Mechanics
Tsinober, Arkady A., PhD   Prof. Res. Fellow;
Marie Curie Chair
Vassilicos, Christos, PhD Camb.   Prof., Fluid
Mechanics
Research: aerodynamics and fluid dynamics;
composite materials; numerical simulation
techniques; structures and materials

Bioengineering

Tel: (020) 7594 5179 Fax: (020) 7594 9817
E-mail: bme-admissions@imperial.ac.uk
Barahona, Mauricio, Lic Madrid, PhD M.I.T.
Reader, Biomathematics
Bharath, Anil A., BEng Lond., PhD Lond.
Reader, Image Analysis
Boutelle, Martyn G., BSc Lond., PhD Lond.
Reader, Biomedical Sensors Engineering
Bull, Anthony M. J., BEng Lond., PhD Lond.
Reader, Musculoskeletal Mechanics
Burdet, Etienne, PhD E.T.H.Zürich, MSc   Sr.
Lectr.
Cashman, Peter M. M., BSc Warw., DPhil Lond.
Sr. Lectr.
Dickinson, Robert J., MA Camb., MBA Lond.,
PhD Lond.   Sr. Lectr.
Drakakis, Emmanuel M., BSc MSc   Sr. Lectr.
Ethier, C. Ross, PhD   Prof.; Head*
Kitney, Richard I., OBE, MSc Sur., PhD Lond.,
DSc Lond., FREng   Prof., Biomedical
Systems Engineering
Krams, Robert, PhD   Prof.
Krapp, Holger G., PhD Tübingen   Sr. Lectr.
O'Hare, Danny, BSc Lond., PhD Lond.   Reader,
Sensor Research
Weinberg, Peter D., BA Lond., BA Camb., MA
Camb., MSc Lond., PhD Lond.   Reader,
Cardiovascular Mechanics
Research: biological and healthcare technologies;
biological mechanics; medical imaging;
physiological fluid mechanics; systems
analysis and design

Biology, Division of

Tel: (020) 7594 5393 Fax: (020) 7584 2056
E-mail: r.butler@imperial.ac.uk
Agnew, David J., BSc PhD   Reader
Archer, Simon A., BSc Lond., PhD Brist.   Sr.
Lectr.
Barraclough, Timothy G., BA Camb., DPhil Oxf.
Sr. Lectr.
Bates, Jeffrey W., BSc Brist., PhD Brist.   Sr.
Lectr.
Beddington, John R., CMG, BSc MSc DPhil,
FRS   Prof.
Bidartondo, Martin I., BSc Alaska, PhD Calif.State
Sr. Lectr.
Bishop, Gerard J., BSc Brist., PhD E.Anglia   Sr.
Lectr., Plant Sciences
Buck, Martin, BSc Lond., PhD Lond.   Prof.
Burt, Austin, BSc PhD   Prof., Evolutionary
Genetics

Coulson, Timothy N., BSc York(UK), PhD Lond.
Reader, Population Biology
Coutts, Robert H. A., BSc Lond., PhD Nott.
Reader
Crawley, Michael J., BSc Edin., PhD Lond., FRS
Prof.
Hardie, Robert J., BSc Brun., PhD Birm., DSc
Lond., FIBiol   Prof., Insect Physiology
Jeger, Michael J., BA Open(UK), MSc York(UK),
PhD Wales   Prof.
Koella, Jacob C., MEng Zür., PhD Basle   Prof.,
Epidemiology
Lande, Russell, BSc PhD   Royal Society Res.
Prof.
Leak, David J., MA Camb., MSc Newcastle(UK),
PhD Warw.   Sr. Lectr.
Leather, Simon R., BSc Leeds, PhD E.Anglia
Reader, Applied Ecology
Leroi, Armand M., PhD   Reader, Evolutionary
Developmental Biology
Lorenzen, Kai, MSc Lond., PhD Lond.   Sr. Lectr.
Mace, Georgina M., BSc Liv., DPhil Sus.   Dir.,
CPB; Prof., Conservation Science
Mansfield, John, PhD Lond.   Prof.
Milner-Gulland, Eleanor J., BA Oxf., MA Oxf.,
PhD Lond.   Reader, Conservation Science
Murphy, Richard J., BSc Lond., PhD Lond.   Sr.
Lectr.
Nixon, Peter J., BA Lond., MA Camb., PhD Lond.
Reader, Biochemistry
Owens, Ian, BSc Liv., PhD Leic.   Prof.,
Evolutionary Ecology
Powell, Glen, BSc Sheff., PhD Lond.   Sr. Lectr.
Power, Sally A., BSc Lond., PhD Lond.   Sr. Lectr.
Purvis, Andrew J., BA Camb., DPhil Oxf.   Prof.,
Biodiversity
Quicke, Donald L. J., BA Oxf., PhD Nott.
Reader, Systematics
Rossiter, John T., BSc Lond., PhD Lond.   Sr.
Lectr.
Savolainen, Vincent, BSc Geneva, MSc Geneva,
PhD Geneva   Reader, Ecology and
Evolutionary Biology
Spanu, Pietro D., PhD Basle   Sr. Lectr.
Tristem, Michael, BSc Newcastle(UK), PhD Camb.
Sr. Lectr.
Turnbull, Colin G. N., BSc Edin., PhD Camb.
Sr. Lectr.
Vogler, Alfried P., PhD   Reader, Molecular
Systematics
Williams, Huw D., PhD Lond., BSc   Reader,
Microbiology
Wright, Denis J., BSc Newcastle(UK), PhD
Newcastle(UK)   Prof., Pest Management
Research: biomolecular structure, function and
bio-informatics; biophysics; cell biology
(immunology, infection); evolution
(microbial sciences, plant sciences);
structural biology

Cell and Molecular Biology, Division of

Brick, Peter, BSc Lond., PhD Lond.   Reader,
Structural Biology
Brickley, Stephen G., BSc Cardiff, PhD Cardiff
Sr. Lectr.
Brown, Katherine A., PhD Lond., BSc BA
Reader, Biochemistry
Caron, Emmanuelle N. M., BSc Paris, MSc Paris,
PhD Montpellier   Sr. Lectr.
Christophides, George K., BSc   Sr. Lectr.
Crisanti, Andrea, MD Basle, PhD Basle   Prof.,
Molecular Parasitology
Curry, Stephen, BSc PhD   Reader, Structural
Biology
Dallman, Margaret J., BSc Brist., MA Oxf., DPhil
Oxf.   Prof.; Head, Immunology and
Infection
Davis, Daniel M., BSc Manc., PhD Strath.   Prof.,
Molecular Immunology
Deonarain, Mahendra P., BSc Lond., PhD Camb.
Sr. Lectr.
Djamgoz, Mustafa B. A., BSc Lond., PhD Lond.
Prof., Cancer Biology
Fairweather, Neil F., BSc Edin., PhD Leic.
Reader, Molecular Microbiology
Filloux, Alain A. M., PhD   Prof., Molecular
Microbiology
Frankel, Gad M., BSc PhD   Prof., Molecular
Pathogenesis

Franks, Nicholas P., BSc Lond., PhD Lond.,
FMedSci   Prof., Biophysics and
Anaesthetics
Gounaris, Kleoniki, PhD Lond.   Sr. Lectr.
Hosie, Alastair, BSc PhD   Sr. Lectr.,
Neuroscience
Kafatos, Fotis C., BSc Cornell, MA Harv., PhD
Harv.   Prof., Insect Immunogenomics
Mann, David, PhD Sheff.   Sr. Lectr.
O'Hare, Kevin, BA Camb., PhD Edin.   Sr. Lectr.
Okuse, Kenji, PhD   Sr. Lectr.
Onesti, Silvia C. E., Lic Pavia, PhD Lond.   Sr.
Lectr.
Selkirk, Murray E., BSc Salf., PhD Lond.   Prof.,
Biochemical Parasitology
Sinden, Robert E., BSc Newcastle(UK), PhD Edin.,
DSc Lond., FMedSci   Prof.
Tippins, John, PhD Lond.   Sr. Lectr.
Ushkaryov, Yuri A., MSc PhD   Reader,
Neurobiology
Weinzierl, Robert O. J., BSc PhD   Sr. Lectr.
Woscholski, Rudiger, DPhil Freib., BSc MSc
Sr. Lectr.

Chemistry

Tel: (020) 7594 5827
E-mail: chemistry.studies@imperial.ac.uk
Armstrong, Alan, BSc Lond., PhD Lond.   Prof.,
Organic Chemistry
Barrett, Anthony G. M., BSc Lond., PhD Lond.,
FRS   Head, Sythesis
Bearpark, Michael J., BSc Lond., PhD Camb.
Reader, Computational Chemistry
Blackmond, Donna G., BSc Penn., MSc Penn.,
PhD Carnegie-Mellon   Prof., Catalysis
Braddock, David C., BA Oxf., DPhil Oxf.   Sr.
Lectr.
Bresme, Fernando, MSc DPhil   Sr. Lectr.
Britovsek, George J. P., BSc PhD   Sr. Lectr.
Craig, Donald, BSc Lond., PhD Lond.   Prof.,
Organic Synthesis
Davies, Robert P., BSc Brist., PhD Camb.   Sr.
Lectr.
de Mello, Andrew J., BSc Lond., PhD Lond.
Prof., Chemical Nanosciences
de Mello, John C., BSc Oxf., PhD Camb.   Sr.
Lectr.
Durrant, James R., BA Camb., MA Camb., PhD
Lond.   Prof., Photochemistry
Gibson, Susan E., BA Camb., DPhil Oxf.   Prof.
Gibson, Vernon C., BSc Sheff., DPhil Oxf., FRS
Sir Edward Frankland BP Prof., Inorganic
Chemistry
Gould, Ian R., BSc Manc., PhD Manc.   Sr. Lectr.,
Biol. and Biophys. Group
Harrison, Nicholas, BSc Birm., PhD Birm.
Prof., Computational Materials Science
Hii, K. K. Mimi, BSc Leeds, PhD Leeds   Sr.
Lectr., Inorganic Chemistry
Holmes, Andrew B., BSc Melb., MA Camb., MSc
Melb., PhD Lond., DSc Camb., FRS   Prof.,
Organic and Polymer Sciences
Klug, David R., BSc Lond., PhD   Prof.
Kornyshev, Alexei A., MSc Russian Acad.Sc., PhD
Russian Acad.Sc., DSc Russian Acad.Sc.   Prof.,
Chemical Physics
Kucernak, Anthony R. J., BSc Auck., MSc Auck.,
PhD S'ton.   Reader, Physical Chemistry
Law, Robert V., BSc Wales, PhD Strath.   Sr.
Lectr.
Leatherbarrow, Robin J., BSc Liv., DPhil Oxf.
Prof.
Lickiss, Paul D., BSc Sus., DPhil Sus.   Reader,
Organometallic Chemistry
Long, Nicholas J., BSc Durh., PhD Exe.   Reader,
Catalysis and Advanced Materials Group
Miller, Andrew D., BSc Brist., PhD Camb.
Prof., Organic Chemistry and Chemical
Biology
Quirke, Nicholas, PhD Leic.   Prof., Physical
Chemistry
Robb, Michael A., BSc Tor., MSc Tor., PhD Tor.,
DSc Lond., FRS   Prof.
Rzepa, Henry S., PhD Lond.   Prof.,
Computational Chemistry
Seddon, John M., BSc Stir., PhD Lond.   Prof.,
Physical Chemistry
Shaffer, Milo S. P., BA Camb., PhD Camb.
Reader

Spivey, Alan C., BSc *Nott.*, DPhil *Oxf.* Reader, Organic Synthesis

Steinke, Joachim H. G., PhD *Strath.* Sr. Lectr.

Templer, Richard, BSc *Brist.*, DPhil *Oxf.* Prof.; Head*

Vilar Compte, Ramon, BSc *Lond.*, PhD *Lond.* Sr. Lectr., Inorganic Chemical Biology

Welton, Thomas, BSc DPhil Prof., Sustainable Chemistry

Wilde, C. Paul, BSc PhD Sr. Lectr.

Williams, Charlotte K., BSc *Lond.*, PhD *Lond.* Sr. Lectr.

Yaliraki, Sophia, PhD Sr. Lectr.

Research: biological and biophysical chemistry; catalysis and advanced materials; nanostructured materials and devices; synthetic chemistry; theoretical and experimental physical chemistry

Computing

Tel: (020) 7594 8298 Fax: (020) 7581 8024

Broda, Krysia B., BSc *Lond.*, BA *Lond.*, MSc *Lond.*, PhD *Lond.* Sr. Lectr.

Clark, Keith L., BA *Durh.*, MA *Camb.*, PhD *Lond.* Prof.

Colton, Simon G., BSc *Durh.*, MA *Liv.*, PhD *Edin.* Sr. Lectr.

Cunningham, Margaret R., BSc *Lond.* Sr. Lectr.

Darlington, John, BSc *Edin.*, PhD *Edin.* Prof.; Dir., London e-Science Centre

Drossopoulou, Sophia, PhD *Karlsruhe* Reader, Programming Languages

Dulay, Naranker, PhD *Lond.* Sr. Lectr.

Edalat, Abbas, BSc *Lond.*, MSc *Lond.*, MSc *Warw.*, PhD *Warw.* Prof., Computer Science and Mathematics

Eisenbach, Susan, BA *Vassar*, MSc *Lond.* Prof.

Field, Anthony J., BSc *Reading*, PhD *Lond.* Reader, Performance Engineering

Gardner, Philippa A., PhD Sr. Lectr.

Gillies, Duncan F., BMus *Lond.*, MA *Camb.*, MSc *Lond.*, PhD *Lond.* Prof., Biomedical Data Analysis

Guo, Yi-Ke, BSc *Tsinghua*, PhD *Lond.* Prof., Computing Science

Harrison, Peter G., BA *Camb.*, MA *Camb.*, MSc *Lond.*, PhD *Lond.* Prof., Computing Science

Hodkinson, Ian, MA *Camb.*, MSc *Lond.*, PhD *Lond.* Prof., Logic and Computation

Hogger, Christopher J., BSc *Lond.*, PhD *Lond.* Sr. Lectr.

Huth, Michael R. A., MSc PhD Sr. Lectr., Computer Science

Kelly, Paul H. J., BSc *Lond.*, PhD *Lond.* Reader

Knottenbelt, William J., BSc *Cape Town*, MSc *Cape Town*, MPhil *Cape Town*, PhD *Lond.* Sr. Lectr.

Kramer, Jeffrey, BSc *Natal*, MSc *Lond.*, PhD *Lond.*, FIEE Prof.

Lomuscio, Alessio R., PhD *Birm.* Sr. Lectr.

Luk, Wayne W.-C., MA *Oxf.*, MSc *Oxf.*, DPhil *Oxf.* Prof., Computer Engineering

Lupu, Emil C., MEng *Grenoble*, PhD *Lond.* Sr. Lectr.

Magee, Jeffrey N., BSc *Belf.*, MSc *Lond.*, PhD *Lond.* Prof.; Head*

Maros, Istvan, MSc *Bud.*, PhD *Bud.* Prof., Computational Methods of Operations Research

McBrien, Peter, BA *Camb.*, PhD *Lond.* Sr. Lectr.

McCann, Julie A., BSc *Ulster*, DPhil *Ulster* Sr. Lectr.

Mencer, Oskar, BSc MSc PhD Sr. Lectr.

Muggleton, Stephen H., BSc *Edin.*, PhD *Edin.* Prof., Bioinformatics

Pantic, Maja, PhD Reader, Multimodal Human Computer Interaction

Phillips, Iain C. C., BA *Oxf.*, MA *Oxf.*, DPhil *Oxf.* Sr. Lectr.

Rueckert, Daniel, PhD Prof., Visual Information Processing

Rustem, Berc, BSc *Istanbul*, MSc *Lond.*, PhD *Lond.*, FIMA Prof.

Sadri, Fariba, BSc *Lond.*, PhD *Lond.* Sr. Lectr.

Sergot, Marek J., BA *Camb.*, MA *Camb.* Prof., Computational Logic

Shanahan, Murray P., BSc *Lond.*, PhD *Camb.* Reader, Computational Intelligence

Sloman, Morris S., BSc *Cape Town*, PhD *Essex* Prof.; Deputy Head; Dir., Res.

Toni, Francesca, BSc *Lond.*, PhD *Lond.* Sr. Lectr.

Ucitel, Sebastian, PhD *Lond.* Reader, Software Engineering

Wiklicky, Herbert, MSc *Vienna*, PhD *Vienna* Sr. Lectr.

Wolf, Alexander L., BA *Camb.*, MA *Mass.*, PhD *Mass.* Prof.

Yang, Guang-Zhong, BSc *Lond.*, PhD *Lond.* Prof.; Dir., Med. Imaging

Yoshida Honda, Nobuko, BSc *Keio*, MSc *Keio*, PhD *Keio* Reader, Computer Science

Research: computational bioinformatics; computer systems; distributed software engineering; high performance informatics; logic and artificial intelligence

Earth Science and Engineering

Tel: (020) 7594 7333 Fax: (020) 7594 7444

Allen, Philip A., BSc *Wales*, MA *Oxf.*, PhD *Camb.* Prof., Earth Science

Allison, Peter A., BSc PhD Sr. Lectr.

Berry, Andrew J., BSc *Syd.*, DPhil *Oxf.* Sr. Lectr., Earth Sciences

Blunt, Martin J., BA *Camb.*, MA *Camb.*, PhD *Camb.* Prof., Petroleum Engineering

Brandon, Nigel P., BSc *Lond.*, PhD *Lond.* Prof., Sustainable Development in Energy

Carter, Jonathan N., BSc *S'ton.*, PhD *Warw.* Sr. Lectr.

Cilliers, Johannes J., BSc *Witw.*, MSc *Witw.*, MBA *Manc.Met.*, PhD *Cape Town*, FIChemE, FIMMM Prof., Mineral Processing

Collier, Jennifer S., BSc *Brist.*, MSc *Durh.*, PhD *Camb.* Sr. Lectr.

Cosgrove, John W., BSc *Aston*, MSc *Lond.*, PhD *Lond.* Reader, Structural Geology

de Oliveira, Cassiano R. E., PhD *Lond.*, BSc MSc Sr. Lectr.

Durucan, Sevket, BSc *Middle East Tech.*, MSc *Middle East Tech.*, PhD *Nott.* Prof., Mining and Environmental Engineering

Gringarten, Alain C., MSc *Calif.*, PhD *Calif.* Prof., Petroleum Engineering

Gupta, Sanjeev, BA PhD Reader, Sedimentology

Hampson, Gary J., BA *Liv.*, PhD *Camb.* Sr. Lectr.

Harrison, John P., BSc *Lond.*, MSc *Lond.*, PhD *Lond.* Sr. Lectr.

Jackson, Matthew D., PhD *Liv.* Sr. Lectr.

Jakubowicz, Helmut, BA MA MSc PhD PGS Prof., Petroleum Geophysics

Johnson, Howard D., BSc *Liv.*, DPhil *Oxf.*, FGS Prof., Petroleum Geology

King, Peter R., BA *Camb.*, MA *Camb.*, PhD *Camb.* Prof., Petroleum Engineering

Korre, Anna, BSc *Lond.*, PhD *Lond.* Sr. Lectr.

Latham, John-Paul, BSc *Brist.*, MSc *Lond.*, PhD *Lond.* Sr. Lectr.

Liu, J. Guo, BSc MSc PhD Sr. Lectr.

Lonergan, Lidia, BA *Oxf.*, DPhil *Oxf.* Reader, Geotectonics

Matthai, Stephen K., PhD *ANU* Sr. Lectr.

Morgan, Joanna V., BSc *S'ton.*, PhD *Camb.* Reader, Geophysics

Muggeridge, Ann H., BSc *Lond.*, DPhil *Oxf.* Sr. Lectr.

Neethling, Stephen, BSc PhD Sr. Lectr.

Plant, Jane A., BSc *Liv.*, PhD *Leic.*, DSc *Exe.*, DSc *Open(UK)*, FIMMM Anglo-American Prof., Applied Geochemistry

Rehkamper, Mark, PhD Sr. Lectr.

Sephton, Mark A., BSc *Durh.*, MSc *Newcastle(UK)*, PhD *Open(UK)* Reader, Organic Geochemistry and Meteoritics

Vesovic, Velisa, BSc *Lond.*, PhD *Lond.* Sr. Lectr.

Wang, Yanghua, BSc *Jilin*, MSc *Monash*, PhD *Lond.* Dir., CRG; Prof., Reservoir Geophysics

Warner, Michael R., BA *York(UK)*, DPhil *York(UK)* Prof.; Head*

Weiss, Dominik J., MSc *Zür.*, PhD Sr. Lectr.

Wilkinson, Jamie J., BA *Camb.*, PhD *S'ton.* Reader, Hydrothermal Geochemistry

Zimmerman, Robert W., PhD *Calif.*, BSc MSc Reader, Rock Mechanics

Research: earth and planets; energy, environment, modelling and minerals; petroleum geoscience and engineering

Engineering, Chemical, and Chemical Technology

Tel: (020) 7594 5575

Adjiman, Claire S. J., MEng *Lond.*, PhD *Prin.* Sr. Lectr.

Bismarck, Alexander, DSc *Hull* Reader, Advanced Materials

Briscoe, Brian J., BSc *Hull*, MA *Camb.*, PhD *Hull*, DSc, FRSChem, FIP, FIMMM Prof.

Chadwick, David, BSc *Lond.*, PhD *Lond.* Prof.

Dugwell, Denis R., BSc *Sheff.*, PhD *Sheff.*, FIChemE Prof., Chemical Engineering

Galindo, Amparo Reader, Physical Chemistry

Hellgardt, Klaus, PhD *Lond.* Sr. Lectr.

Jackson, George, BSc *Lond.*, DPhil *Oxf.*, FRSChem Prof., Chemical Physics

Kalliadasis, Serafim, PhD Reader, Fluid Mechanics

Kandiyoti, Rafael, BSc *Col.*, PhD *Lond.*, FIChemE Prof.

Kazarian, Sergei G., MSc PhD, FRSChem Dir., Postgrad. Studies, Physical Chemistry

Kelsall, Geoffrey H., BSc MSc PhD Prof., Electrochemical Engineering

Kogelbauer, Andreas, MEng *Vienna*, PhD *Vienna* Sr. Lectr.

Lawrence, Christopher J., BA *Camb.*, MA *Camb.*, PhD *N.Y.* Prof., Fluid Mechanics

Li, Kang, MSc *Salf.*, PhD *Salf.* Reader, Chemical Engineering

Livingston, Andrew G., BEng *Cant.*, MSc *Lond.*, PhD *Camb.* Prof.

Luckham, Paul F., BSc *Brist.*, PhD *Brist.* Prof., Particle Technology

Macchietto, Sandro, MS *Conn.*, PhD *Conn.*, BEng Prof., Process Systems Engineering

Maitland, Geoffrey C., BA *Oxf.*, MA *Oxf.*, DPhil *Oxf.*, Energy Engineering

Mantalaris, Athanasios, BSc *W.Ont.*, MSc PhD Reader, Biological Systems Engineering

Matar, Omar K., MEng *Lond.*, PhD *Prin.* Sr. Lectr.

Muller, Erich A., MSc *Simón Bolívar*, PhD *Cornell* Reader, Thermodynamics

Pantelides, Constantinos C., BEng *Lond.*, MS *M.I.T.*, PhD *Lond.* Prof.

Pistikopoulos, Stratos N., DPhil *Carnegie-Mellon* Prof.

Richardson, Stephen M., BSc *Lond.*, PhD *Lond.*, FIChemE, FREng Prof.; Head*

Shah, Nilay, MEng *Lond.*, PhD *Lond.* Prof., Process Systems Engineering

Stepanek, Frantisek, MEng *Prague Chem.Technol.*, PhD *Prague Chem.Technol.* Sr. Lectr.

Stuckey, David C., BE *Melb.*, MEngSc *Melb.*, PhD *Stan.* Prof., Biochemical Engineering

Thornhill, Nina F., BA *Oxf.*, MEng *Melb.*, PhD *Lond.* Prof., Process Automation

Trusler, J. P. Martin, BSc *Lond.*, PhD *Lond.* Prof., Thermophysics

Williams, Daryl R., BSc *Melb.*, MSc DPhil Sr. Lectr.

Xu, Xiao Y., BSc *City(UK)*, MSc *City(UK)*, PhD Reader, Biofluid Mechanics

Research: biomedical engineering; biotechnology and bioprocess engineering; complex materials; energy engineering; environmental engineering

Engineering, Civil and Environmental

Tel: (020) 7594 5929 Fax: (020) 7594 5934
E-mail: cvenquiries@imperial.ac.uk

Bell, Michael G. H., BA *Camb.*, MSc *Leeds*, PhD *Leeds* Prof., Transport Operations

Bommer, Julian J., BSc *Lond.*, MSc *Lond.*, PhD *Lond.* Reader, Earthquake Hazard Assessment

Buenfeld, Nicholas R., BSc MSc PhD Prof., Concrete Structures

Butler, Adrian P., BSc *Lond.*, MSc *Lond.*, PhD *Lond.* Reader, Subsurface Hydrology

Cheeseman, Christopher R., BSc *Warw.*, DPhil *Oxf.* Reader, Waste Management

Coop, Matthew R., BSc Lond., DPhil Oxf.
Reader, Experimental Soil Mechanics
Elgazhouli, Ahmed Y., BSc MSc PhD   Reader,
Engineering Structures
Evans, Andrew W., MA Camb., MSc Lond., PhD
Birm.   Lloyds Register Prof., Transport Risk
Management
Fenton, Clark H., BSc Glas., PhD Glas.   Sr.
Lectr.
Fisk, David J., CB, MA Camb., PhD Manc.Met.,
ScD Camb., FREng   BP/RAEng Prof.,
Sustainable Development
Gardner, Leroy, BEng S'ton., MSc Lond., PhD
Lond.   Sr. Lectr.
Glaister, Stephen, BA Essex, MA Lond., PhD Lond.
Prof., Transport and Infrastructure
Graham, Nigel J. D., BA Camb., MA Camb., MSc
Lond., PhD, FICE   Prof.
Grimes, Susan M., BSc Lond., MBA City(UK),
PhD City(UK)   Prof.
Hunt, Gary R., BSc Plym., PhD Leeds   Sr. Lectr.
Izzuddin, Bassam A., BEng Beirut, MSc Lond.,
PhD Lond.   Reader, Computational
Structural Mechanics
Jardine, Richard J., BSc Lond., MSc Lond., PhD
Lond.   Prof., Geomechanics
Lloyd Smith, David, BEng Sheff., MSc Lond., PhD
Lond., FICE   Prof., Structural Mechanics
Louca, Luke A., BSc Greenwich, MSc Lond., PhD
Sur.   Sr. Lectr.
Mcintyre, Neil R., BEng Edin., MSc Lond.   Sr.
Lectr.
Nethercot, David A., BSc Wales, DSc Wales, PhD
Wales, FIStructE, FICE, FREng   Prof., Civil
Engineering; Head*
Noland, Robert B., BA Penn., MSc Penn., PhD
Penn.   Reader, Transport and Environmental
Policy
Ochieng, Washington Y., BSc(Eng) Nair., MSc
Nott., PhD Nott.   Reader, Geomatics and
Transport Telematics
Onof, Christian J., PhD Lond.   Sr. Lectr.
Pavlovic, Milija N., BE Melb., MEngSc Melb.,
PhD Camb., PhD Lond., DSc Camb.   Prof.
Polak, John W., BSc Lond., MSc Birm., MA Oxf.
Prof., Transport Demand
Potts, David M., BSc Camb., PhD Camb., ScD
Camb., FICE, FREng   Prof.
Smith, Stephen R., BSc Reading, PhD Reading
Reader, Environmental Biochemistry
Sobey, Rodney J., BEng Lond., PhD Lond.   Prof.,
Fluid Mechanics
Standing, James R., BSc Dund., MSc Lond., PhD
Lond.   Sr. Lectr.
Swan, Christopher, BSc Lond., PhD Camb.
Prof., Hydrodynamics
Vollum, Robert, BA Oxf., MSc Lond., PhD Lond.
Sr. Lectr.
Wadee, Md. Ahmer, BEng Lond., MSc Lond.,
PhD Bath   Sr. Lectr.
Wheater, Howard S., MA Camb., PhD Brist.,
FICE, FREng   Prof., Hydrology
Zdravkovic, Lidija, BSc Belgrade, MSc Belgrade,
PhD Lond.   Sr. Lectr.
Research: concrete structures; environmental
water resource engineering; fluid
mechanics; soil mechanics, geotechnics

Engineering, Electrical and Electronic

Tel: (020) 7594 6185
E-mail: c.drysdale@imperial.ac.uk
Allwright, John C., BSc(Eng) Lond., PhD Lond.
Sr. Lectr.
Astolfi, Alessandro, BSc PhD   Prof., Non-
Linear Control Theory
Barria, Javier A., BSc MSc PhD   Reader,
Communication Networks
Brookes, D. Michael, BA Camb., MA Camb.
Reader, Signal Processing
Cheung, Peter Y.-K., BSc Lond.   Prof., Digital
Systems
Constantinides, Anthony G., BSc Lond., MEng
Lond., PhD Lond., FIEE, FREng   Prof.
Demiris, Tiannis, BSc Edin., PhD Edin.   Sr.
Lectr.
Dragotti, Pier L., MSc Naples, PhD E.T.H.Zürich
Sr. Lectr.
Fobelets, Kristel, PhD   Sr. Lectr.

Gelenbe, Erol, BSc Middle East Tech., MSc
N.Y.Polytech., PhD N.Y.Polytech., DSc Paris VI,
FACM, FIEEE, FIEE   Prof., Computer and
Communication Networks
Green, Timothy C., BSc Lond., PhD H-W
Reader, Power Engineering
Gurcan, Mustafa K., BSc Birm., PhD Birm.   Sr.
Lectr.
Haigh, David G., BSc Brist., PhD Lond.   Reader,
Analogue Circuits
Holmes, Andrew S., MA Camb., PhD Lond.
Reader, Micro-electro-mechanical Systems
Jaimoukha, Imad M., BSc S'ton., MSc Lond., PhD
Lond.   Sr. Lectr.
Leung, Kin Kwong, BSc HK, MS Calif., PhD
Calif.   Tanaka Prof., Internet Technology
Limebeer, David J. N., MSc Natal, PhD Natal,
DSc, FREng   Prof., Control Engineering;
Head*
Lucyszyn, Stepan, BSc Lond., MSc Sur., PhD Lond.
Sr. Lectr.
Mandic, Danilo, BSc Banja Luka, MSc Banja Luka,
PhD Lond.   Reader, Signal Processing
Manikas, Athanassios, BEd Athens, BSc Essex, PhD
Lond.   Prof., Communications and Array
Processing
Naylor, Patrick A., BEng Sheff., PhD Lond.   Sr.
Lectr.
Pal, Bikash C., BE Jad., MEng IISc., PhD Lond.
Sr. Lectr.
Papavassiliou, Christos M., BSc MSc PhD   Sr.
Lectr.
Petrou, Maria, BSc Salonika, PhD Camb., FREng
Prof., Signal Processing
Pike, William T., MA Camb., PhD Camb.   Sr.
Lectr.
Pitt, Jeremy V., BSc Manc., PhD Lond.   Reader,
Intelligent Systems
Stathaki, Panagiota T., MEng Lond.   Sr. Lectr.
Strbac, Goran, BSc Novi Sad, MSc Belgrade, PhD
Belgrade   Prof., Electrical Energy Systems
Syms, Richard, MA Oxf., DPhil Oxf., FREng
Prof.
Vinter, Richard B., BA Oxf., PhD Camb., ScD
Camb.   Prof.
Weiss, George, MSc Bucharest, PhD Weizmann
Prof., Systems and Control
Yeatman, Eric M., BSc Dal., MSc Dal., PhD Lond.
Prof., Microengineering
Research: circuits and systems; communications
and signal processing; control and power
engineering; intelligent systems and
networks; optics and semiconductor devices

Engineering, Mechanical

Tel: (020) 7594 7002
E-mail: s.spargo@imperial.ac.uk
Amis, Andrew A., BSc Leeds, PhD Leeds, DSc Lond.
Prof., Orthopaedic Mechanics
Blackman, Bamber R. K., BEng Lond., PhD Lond.
Sr. Lectr.
Bluck, Michael J., BSc Kent, PhD Lond.   Sr.
Lectr.
Cawley, Peter, BSc Brist., PhD Brist.   Prof.
Charalambides, Maria, BEng Lond., PhD Lond.
Sr. Lectr.
Cumpsty, Nicholas A., BSc Lond., MA Camb.,
PhD Camb., FREng   Prof.; Head*
de Oliveira, Cassiano R. E., PhD Lond., BSc MSc
Sr. Lectr.
Dear, John P., MA Camb., PhD Camb.   Reader
Ewins, David J., BEng Lond., PhD Camb., DSc
Lond., FRS, FREng, FCGI   Prof.
Fenner, Roger T., BSc(Eng) Lond., PhD Lond.,
DSc Lond., FIMMM, FIMechE   Prof.
Gibbins, Jonathan R., BSc Lond., PhD Lond.   Sr.
Lectr.
Hardalupas, Ioannis, PhD Lond.   Reader,
Multiphase Flows
Heyes, Andrew L., BEng MSc PhD   Sr. Lectr.
Imregun, Mehmet, BSc(Eng) Istanbul, MSc Lond.,
PhD Lond.   Prof., Computational
Engineering Dynamics
Isherwood, David P., BSc Lond., PhD Lond.
Assoc. Lectr.
Jones, William P., BSc Wales, MSc Lond., PhD
Lond., FIP   Prof., Combustion
Kinloch, Anthony J., BSc Lond., PhD Lond.,
FREng   Prof.

Kronenburg, Andreas, PhD Syd.   Reader,
Combustion
Leevers, Patrick S., BSc MSc PhD   Reader
Lindstedt, R. Peter, MEng Chalmers U.T., PhD
Lond.   Prof.
Lowe, Michael J. S., BSc Edin., MSc Lond., PhD
Lond.   Reader
Marquis, Andrew J., BEng Lond., MSc Lond., PhD
Lond.   Sr. Lectr.
Martinez-Botas, Ricardo F., MEng Lond., PhD
Sr. Lectr.
Nikbin, Kamran Mohmmad-Pour, DPhil PhD
Prof., Structural Integrity
Olver, Andrew V., BSc Exe., PhD Lond.   Reader
Pullen, Keith R., BEng Lond., PhD Lond.   Sr.
Lectr.
Ristic, Mihailo, BSc Lond., MSc Lond., PhD Lond.
Sr. Lectr.
Robb, David A., BTech Lough., MSc Lond.   Sr.
Lectr.
Sayles, Richard S., BSc CNAA, PhD CNAA
Reader
Smith, Roderick A., BA Oxf., MA Oxf., PhD
Camb., ScD Camb., FREng   Prof.; Head*
Spikes, Hugh A., MA Camb., PhD Lond.   Prof.,
Lubrication
Taylor, Alexander M. K. P., MA Lond., PhD Lond.
Prof.
Walker, Simon P., BSc Lond., PhD Lond., FIEE,
FIMechE   Reader
Research: biomechanics; computational
mechanics; dynamics; mechatronics in
medicine; non-destructive testing

Environmental Policy, Centre for

Tel: (020) 7594 9300 Fax: cep@imperial.ac.uk
ApSimon, Helen M., MA Oxf., PhD St And.,
FRAS   Prof., Air Pollution
Bell, J. Nigel B., BSc Manc., MSc Wat., DSc
Wat., PhD Manc.   Prof., Environmental
Pollution
Blaza, Andrew J., BSc MSc   Principal Res.
Fellow
Conway, Gordon R., BSc Wales, PhD Calif., FRS
Prof., International Development
Derwent, Richard G., OBE, MA Camb., PhD
Camb.   Prof., Atmospheric Chemistry
Knight, Jonathan D., BSc Glas., PhD Leeds   Sr.
Lectr.
Makuch, Zen A., BA LLB LLM MSc   Reader,
Law
Mourato, Susana M. de F. B., MSc Lisbon, PhD
Lond.   Sr. Lectr.
Mumford, John D., BSc Purdue, PhD Lond.
Prof., Natural Resources Management;
Head*
Pearson, Peter J. G., BA Keele, MSc Lond., PhD
Sur.   Reader, Energy and Environmental
Studies
Potter, Clive A., BSc Hudd., PhD E.Anglia
Reader
Sheate, William R., BSc Exe., MSc Lond.
Reader, Environmental Assessment
Thirtle, Colin G., BSc Lond., MS Ill., MPhil Col.,
PhD Col.   Prof., Agricultural Economics
Voulvoulis, Nikolaos, BSc Herts., PhD Lond.   Sr.
Lectr.
Research: environmental and mining
engineering; environmental measurement
modelling and assessment; environmental
policy and management; renewable
resources assessment

Humanities

Tel: (020) 7594 8756
E-mail: humanities@imperial.ac.uk
Brinson, Charmian E. J., BA Lond., MA Lond.,
PhD Lond.   Prof., German Studies
Edgerton, David E. H., BA Oxf., PhD Lond.
Hans Rausing Prof.
Iliffe, Robert, BA Leeds, MPhil Camb., PhD Camb.
Reader, History of Science
Mendelsohn, John A., BA Prin., MA Prin., PhD
Prin.   Sr. Lectr.
Russell, Nicholas C., BSc Exe., MSc Lond., PhD
Sur.   Sr. Lectr.; Dir.*
Shuttleworth, B. Mark, BA Oxf., MA Oxf., MA
Birm.   Sr. Lectr.

Warwick, Andrew C., MA Camb., PhD Camb. Prof., History of Science; Head*
Research: Chinese and Japanese studies; German, Russian and Spanish studies; public understanding of science; science communication; translation studies

Materials

Tel: (020) 7594 6767 Fax: (020) 7594 6757
Alford, Neil M., BSc St And., PhD Lond. Prof., Materials Chemistry
Atkinson, Alan, BA Camb., MA Camb., PhD Leeds, FIP, FIMMM Prof., Materials Chemistry
Boccaccini, Aldo R., MSc PhD Reader, Materials Science
Dashwood, Richard J., BEng Lond., PhD Lond. Sr. Lectr.
Finnis, Michael W., BA Camb., MA Camb., PhD Camb. Prof., Materials Theory and Simulation
Grimes, Robin W., BSc Nott., PhD Keele, MSc Prof., Materials Physics
Haynes, Peter D., BA PhD Reader, Materials and Physics
Hill, Robert G., BSc Wales, MSc Wales, PhD Lond. Reader
Kilner, John A., MSc Birm., PhD Birm. Prof.
Lee, Peter D., BSc Tor., MSc Tor., DPhil Oxf. Prof., Materials Science
Lee, William E., BSc Aston, DPhil Oxf. Prof.; Head*
McComb, David W., BSc Glas., PhD Camb. Reader, Materials Characterisation
McPhail, David S., BSc Brist., PhD Lond. Sr. Lectr.
Riley, D. Jason, MA Oxf., DPhil Oxf. Sr. Lectr.
Ryan, Mary P., BSc Manc., MSc UMIST, PhD UMIST Sr. Lectr.
Shollock, Barbara A., BS Lehigh, MS Lehigh, DPhil Oxf. Sr. Lectr.
Skinner, Stephen J., BSc Aberd., PhD Open(UK) Sr. Lectr.
Stevens, Molly M., BPharm Bath, PhD Nott. Reader, Regenerative Medicine and Nanotechnology
Research: advanced metals; biomaterials; ceramics and glasses; materials modelling; nanotechnology

Mathematics

Tel: (020) 7594 8517 Fax: (020) 7594 8483
E-mail: maths.enquiry@imperial.ac.uk
Atkinson, Colin, BSc Leeds, PhD Leeds, FRS Prof., Applied Mathematics
Barnett, Christopher, BSc Hull, PhD Hull Reader
Barrett, John W., BSc S'ton., PhD Reading Prof.; Head, Numerical Analysis Section
Beardmore, Robert E., BSc Edin., MSc Bath, PhD Brun. Sr. Lectr.
Berkshire, Francis H., MA Camb., PhD Lond. Sr. Lectr.
Brody, Dorje C., PhD Lond. Reader
Buzzard, Kevin M., BA Camb., MA Camb., PhD Camb. Prof., Pure Mathematics
Cash, Jeffrey R., BSc Lond., PhD Camb. Prof., Numerical Analysis
Chen, Yang, BSc Sing., MSc Ill., PhD Mass. Prof., Mathematical Physics
Coleman, Rodney, BSc Leeds, PhD Camb. Sr. Lectr.
Corti, Alessio, BSc Pisa, PhD Utah Prof., Pure Mathematics
Craster, Richard V., PhD Lond., BSc Prof., Applied Mathematics
Crisan, Dan O., PhD Edin. Sr. Lectr.
Crowder, Martin J., BSc Manc., PhD Sur. Prof., Stochastic Modelling
Crowdy, Darren G., MA Camb., PhD Calif.State Prof., Applied Mathematics
Davis, Mark H. A., BA Camb., MEng Calif.State, DEng Calif.State, ScD Camb. Prof.; Head, Mathematical Science Section
Donaldson, Simon K., BA Camb., DPhil Oxf., FRS Prof.
Elgin, John N., BSc H-W, PhD Camb. Prof., Applied Mathematics; Head*

Gibbon, John D., BSc Birm., PhD UMIST Prof., Applied Mathematics
Gibbons, John, BA Camb., DPhil Oxf. Sr. Lectr.
Gogolin, Alexander O., PhD Prof., Mathematical Physics
Hall, Philip, DPhil Prof.; Dir., Mathl. Scis. Res. Inst.
Hand, David J., BA MA MSc PhD Prof.
Haskins, Mark, BA Oxf., PhD Texas Reader
Holm, Darryl D., BSc Minn., MSc Mich.State, PhD Mich.State Prof., Applied Mathematics
Howard, Martin J., BA Oxf., DPhil Oxf. Reader, Biological Physics
Ivanov, Alexander A., DSc Moscow Prof., Pure Mathematics
Jensen, Henrik J., MSc Aarhus, PhD Aarhus Prof., Mathematical Physics
Lamb, Jeroen S. W., MSc PhD Reader, Applied Mathematics
Laptev, Ari, MMath Leningrad, PhD Leningrad Prof., Pure Mathematics
Liebeck, Martin W., BA Oxf., DPhil Oxf. Prof.; Head, Pure Mathematics
Luzzatto, Stefano, BSc Warw., MSc PhD Reader, Applied Mathematics
McCoy, Emma J., BSc Bath, MSc Bath, PhD Lond. Sr. Lectr.
Mestel, A. Jonathan, PhD Camb. Reader, Applied Mathematics
Moore, Daniel R., AB Prin., PhD Camb. Reader, Computational Applied Mathematics
Moore, Gerald, BSc Bath, PhD Bath Reader, Numerical Analysis
Nurnberg, Robert, PhD Lond. Sr. Lectr.
Parry, Andrew O., BSc Brist., PhD Brist. Prof.; Acting Head, Mathematical Physics Section
Ruzhansky, Michael, MSc PhD Reader, Pure Mathematics
Skorobogatov, Alexei N., BSc Moscow, PhD Moscow Prof., Pure Mathematics
Stark, Jaroslav, BA Camb., PhD Warw. Prof., Applied Mathematics
Thiffeault, Jean-Luc, BSc McG., MA Texas, PhD Texas Reader, Applied Mathematics
Thomas, Richard P. W., BA Oxf., MA Oxf., DPhil Oxf. Prof., Pure Mathematics
Walden, Andrew T., BSc Wales, MSc S'ton., PhD S'ton. Prof., Statistics
Walton, Andrew G., BSc Lond., PhD Lond. Sr. Lectr.
White, Lynda V., PhD Lond. Sr. Lectr.
Wu, Xuesong, BSc Fudan, MSc Tianjin, PhD Lond. Reader, Applied Mathematics
Young, G. Alastair, BSc Edin., PhD Camb. Prof., Statistics
Zegarlinski, Boguslaw, MASc Gliwice, PhD Wroclaw Prof., Pure Mathematics
Zheng, Harry, BSc Fudan, MSc Fudan, PhD Br.Col. Sr. Lectr.
Research: applied mathematics; mathematical finance; mathematical physics; pure mathematics; statistics

Molecular Biosciences, Division of

Baldwin, Geoffrey S., PhD Sheff., BSc Sr. Lectr.
Barber, James, BSc E.Anglia, MA E.Anglia, PhD E.Anglia, FRSChem, FRS Ernst Chain Prof., Biochemistry
Byrne, Bernadette, BSc Liv., PhD Aberd. Sr. Lectr.
Dell, Anne, BSc W.Aust., PhD Camb., FRS Prof., Carbohydrate Biochemistry
Drickhamer, Kurt, BSc Stan., PhD Harv. Prof., Biochemistry
Endres, Robert G., PhD Calif., MSc Sr. Lectr., Systems Biology
Freemont, Paul S., BSc H-W, PhD Aberd. Prof., Protein Crystallography
Gilardi, Gianfranco, PhD Lond., BSc Reader, Protein Engineering
Iwata, So, BSc Tokyo, MSc Tokyo, PhD Tokyo David Blow Prof., Biophysics
Matthews, Stephen J., PhD Prof., Chemical and Structural Biology
Stark, Jaroslav, BA Camb., PhD Warw. Dir., CISBIC
Sternberg, Michael J. E., BA Camb., MSc Lond., DPhil Oxf. Prof.; Dir., Centre for Bioinformatics

Stumpf, Michael P. H., MSc Gothenburg, DPhil Oxf. Reader
van Heel, Marin Prof., Structural Biology
Zhang, Xiaodong, BSc Beijing, PhD N.Y.State Reader, Molecular Structure and Function

Physics

Tel: (020) 7594 5111
Bradley, Donal D. C., BSc Lond., PhD Camb. Lee-Lucas Prof., Experimental Physics; Head*
Campbell, Alasdair J., BSc Lond., MSc Lond. Sr. Lectr.
Cargill, Peter J., MSc St And., PhD St And. Prof.
Chittenden, Jeremy P., BSc Lond., DSc Lond. Sr. Lectr.
Christensen, Kim, MSc Aarhus, PhD Aarhus Prof., Theoretical Physics
Cohen, Lesley, BSc Lond., PhD Camb. Prof., Solid State Physics
Coppins, M., BSc Lond., PhD Lond. Sr. Lectr.
Cowburn, Russell P., MA Camb., PhD Camb. Prof., Nanotechnology
Cowley, Stephen C., MA PhD Prof., Plasma Physics
Dainty, J. Christopher, MSc Lond., PhD Lond. Prof., Applied Optics
Damzen, Michael J., BSc Lond., PhD Lond. Prof., Experimental Laser Physics
Dauncey, Paul D., BA Oxf., DPhil Oxf. Reader, High Energy Physics
Davies, Gavin J., BSc Lond., PhD Lond. Reader, Experimental Particle Physics
Dornan, Peter J., BA Camb., PhD Camb. Prof.
Dougherty, Michele K., BSc Natal, PhD Natal Prof., Space Physics
Dowker, Helen F., BA Camb., PhD Camb. Reader, Theoretical Physics
Duff, Michael J., BSc Lond., PhD Lond. Abdus Salam Prof., Theoretical Physics
Egede, Ulrik, BSc Copenhagen, PhD Lund Reader
Evans, Roger G., BSc Wales, PhD Wales Prof.
Evans, Timothy S., MA Lond., PhD Lond. Sr. Lectr.
Forsyth, Robert J., BSc Aberd., PhD Aberd. Sr. Lectr.
Foudas, Constantinos, MA Col., MSc Col., PhD Col. Reader, High Energy Physics
Foulkes, W. Matthew C., MA Camb., PhD Camb. Prof.
Frasinski, Leszek J., MSc Cracow, PhD Cracow Prof.
French, Paul M. W., BSc Lond., PhD Lond. Prof.; Head, Photonics Group
Gauntlett, Jerome P., BSc W.Aust., PhD Camb. Prof., Theoretical Physics
Haigh, Joanna D., MA Oxf., MSc Lond., DPhil Oxf. Prof., Atmospheric Physics
Hall, Geoffrey, BSc Lond., PhD Lond. Prof.
Halliwell, Jonathan J., BSc Brist., MSc Camb., PhD Camb. Prof., Theoretical Physics
Hanany, Amihay, PhD Reader, Theoretical Physics
Harries, John E., BSc Birm., PhD Lond. Prof., Earth Observation
Hassard, John F., BSc Manc., PhD Manc.Met. Reader
Hinds, Edward A., BA Oxf., MSc Oxf., DPhil Oxf., FRS Prof.
Horbury, Timothy S., BSc PhD Reader
Hull, Christopher M., BA Camb., PhD Camb. Prof., Theoretical Physics
Isham, Christopher J., BSc Lond., PhD Lond., FIP Prof., Theoretical Physics
Jaffe, Andrew H., BSc MSc PhD Reader, Astrophysics
Lebedev, Sergey V., MSc Novosibirsk, PhD Novosibirsk Reader, Z-pinch Physics
Lee, Derek K. K., BA Camb., PhD Camb. Sr. Lectr.
Long, Kenneth R., BSc Nott., DPhil Oxf. Prof., Experimental Particle Physics
Mackinnon, Angus, BSc H-W, PhD Lond. Prof.
Magueijo, Joao C. R., PhD Reader, Theoretical Physics
Marangos, Jonathan P., BSc Lond., PhD Lond. Prof., Laser Physics

McCall, Martin W., BSc Lond., PhD Lond.
Reader, Photonics
Murray, Raymond, BSc H-W, PhD Reading   Sr.
Lectr.
Najmudin, Zulfikar, BA Oxf., PhD Lond.
Reader
Nandra, Kirpal, MA Camb., PhD Leic.   Prof.,
Astrophysics
Nash, Jordan A., PhD   Reader
Neil, Mark A. A., MA Camb., PhD Camb.
Reader, Photonics
Nelson, Jenny, BA Camb., PhD Brist.   Reader,
Solid State Physics
New, Geoffrey H. C., MA Oxf., DPhil Oxf.
Prof., Nonlinear Optics
Parry, Gareth, BSc Lond., PhD Lond., FIEE, FREng
Prof., Applied Physics
Pendry, John B., MA Camb., PhD Camb., FRS
Prof., Theoretical Solid State Physics
Phillips, Christopher C., BA Camb., PhD Lond.
Prof., Experimental Solid State Physics
Plenio, Martin B., PhD   Prof., Quantum
Physics
Rivers, Raymond J., BA Camb., PhD Lond.
Prof., Theoretical Physics
Rose, Steven J., BA Oxf., DPhil Oxf.   Head,
Plasma Physics Group; Prof., Plasma Physics
Rowan-Robinson, Michael, BA Camb., PhD Lond.
Prof., Astrophysics
Sauer, Benjamin E. (Ben), BA Wesleyan, MA
N.Y.State, PhD N.Y.State   Reader,
Experimental Physics
Schwartz, Steven J., BSc Cornell, PhD Camb.
Prof., Space Physics
Sedgbeer, Julia K., BSc Birm., PhD Lond.   Sr.
Lectr.
Segal, Daniel M., BSc Manc., PhD Lond.   Reader,
Quantum Optics
Smith, Robin W., MA Camb., PhD Lond.   Prof.;
Head*
Smith, Roland A., BSc PhD   Reader, Laser
Physics
Southwood, David J., BA Lond., PhD Lond.
Prof.
Stelle, Kellogg S., BA Harv., PhD Brandeis   Prof.;
Head, Theoretical Physics
Sumner, Timothy J., BSc Sus., DPhil Sus.   Prof.,
Experimental Astrophysics
Sutton, Adrian P., BA Oxf., MSc Oxf., PhD Penn.,
FRS   Prof., Nanotechnology; Head, CMT
Taylor, James R., BSc PhD   Prof., Ultrafast
Physics and Technology
Thompson, Richard C., BA Oxf., MA Oxf., DPhil
Oxf.   Prof., Experimental Physics
Tisch, John W. G., BSc Tas., PhD Lond.
Reader, Laser Science
Torok, Peter, DPhil Oxf., PhD   Reader
Toumi, Ralf, PhD   Reader, Atmospheric
Physics
Tseytlin, Arkady, DPhil Russian Acad.Sc., DSc
Russian Acad.Sc.   Prof., Theoretical Physics
Unruh, Yvonne C., MSc Sus., PhD Sus.   Sr.
Lectr.
Virdee, Tejinder S., BSc Lond., PhD Lond.   Prof.
Vvedensky, Dimitri, SM M.I.T., PhD M.I.T., BSc
Prof.
Waldram, Daniel J., BA Oxf., PhD   Reader,
Theoretical Physics
Wark, David L., BSc Indiana, MSc Cal.Tech., PhD
Cal.Tech.   Prof., High Energy Physics
Warren, Stephen J., BA MA PhD   Reader,
Astrophysics
Websdale, David M., BSc Lond., PhD Lond.
Prof.
Weir, Kenneth, BSc Edin., PhD Reading   Sr.
Lectr.; Assoc. Head
Zhang, Jing, BSc PhD   Reader
Research: astrophysics, condensed matter theory,
theoretical physics; experimental solid state
physics; high energy physics, plasma
physics; photonics, quantum optics and
laser science; space and atmosphere physics,
high energy physics

Tanaka Business School

Tel: (020) 7589 5111 Fax: (020) 7823 7685
Abadir, Karim M., BA American(Cairo), MA
American(Cairo)   Prof., Financial
Econometrics

Atun, Rifat A., MB BS Lond., MBA Lond.   Dir.,
Centre for Health Management
Autio, Erkko T., MSc Helsinki, PhD Helsinki, DSc
Helsinki   Prof., Technology Transfer and
Entrepreneurship
Barlow, James G., BA Lond., PhD Lond.   Prof.,
Technology and Innovation Management
Begg, David K. H., BA Camb., MPhil Oxf., PhD
M.I.T.   Prof., Economics; Principal*
Bessant, John R., BSc Aston, PhD Aston   Prof.,
Innovation Management
Breedon, Francis, BSc Lond., MPhil Camb.   Sr.
Lectr.
Buraschi, Andrea, MA Chic., PhD Chic., BA
Calvet, Laurent, MA Yale, PhD Yale   Prof.,
Finance
Cathcart, Lara, PhD   Sr. Lectr.
Chemla, Gilles H., BSc Paris, MSc Paris, PhD
Lond.   Reader, Finance
Clarysse, Bart, PhD   Prof., Entrepreneurship
Cox, Benita M., MA S.Af., MSc Lond., PhD Lond.
Reader, Operational Research
Davies, Andrew C., BSc MSc PhD   Reader,
Innovation and Enterpreneurship
Ditaso, Walter, BSc Bari, PhD Bari, PhD York(UK)
Sr. Lectr., Financial Econometrics
Dolan, Paul H. R., BSc Wales, MSc York(UK),
DPhil York(UK)   Prof., Economics
Driver, Ciaran, MA Lanc., MSc Camb., PhD
CNAA, FICE   Prof., Economics
El-Jahel, Lina, MSc Lond., PhD Lond.   Sr. Lectr.
Gann, David M., BSc Reading, MSc Sus., DPhil
Sus.   Prof., Technology and Innovation
Management
George, Gerard, MMS BITS, PhD Virginia
Commonwealth   Dir., Rajiv Gandhi Centre
Griffiths, Dorothy S., MSc Bath   Prof., Human
Resource Management
Hadjiconstantinou, Eleni, BSc City(UK), MSc
Lond., PhD Lond.   Sr. Lectr.
Klumpes, Paul J. M., BComm NSWUT, LLB
Open(UK), MComm NSWUT, PhD NSWUT
Prof., Accounting
Lawton, Thomas C., BA N.U.I., MSc Lond., PhD
European Univ.Inst.   Sr. Lectr., Strategic
Management
Leippold, Markus, BSc MSc PhD   Sr. Lectr.,
Quantitative Finance
MacCulloch, Robert J., BSc Auck., MComm
Auck., MPhil Oxf., DPhil Oxf.   Prof.,
Economics
McCarthy, David G., BSc Witw., PhD Penn.   Sr.
Lectr.
Meade, Nigel, BSc Sheff., MSc Sheff., PhD Lond.
Prof., Quantitative Finance
Meddahi, Nour, PhD Toulouse   Reader, Finance
Naramsimhan, Anand, BEng BITS, PhD Vanderbilt
Reader, Organisational Behaviour
Perraudin, William R. M., BA Oxf., MSc Lond.,
MSc Harv., PhD Harv.   Prof., Finance
Phillips, Nelson W., BSc Calg., MBA Calg., PhD
Alta.   Prof., Strategy and Organisational
Behaviour
Prabhu, Jaideep C., BTech IIT Delhi, PhD
Prof., Marketing
Propper, Carol, BAcc Brist., BCom Brist., MRes
Oxf., MSc Oxf., PhD York(UK)   Prof.,
Economics
Salter, Ammon J., BA C'dia., DPhil Sus.   Sr.
Lectr.
Sefton, James A., BA Camb., PhD Camb.   Prof.,
Economics
Stein, Mark, BA Warw., MSc Lond., MPhil Camb.,
PhD Brun.   Sr. Lectr.; Dir., MSc
Management
Szymanski, Stefan A., BA Lond., MSc Lond., PhD
Lond.   Prof., Economics
Tether, Bruce S., BA PhD   Prof., Design and
Innovation
Touzi, Nizar M.   Prof., Mathematical Finance
Valletti, Tommaso, MSc Lond., PhD Lond.
Reader, Economics
Wang, Pengguo, BSc Huazhong U.S.T., PhD Strath.
Sr. Lectr.
Zaffaroni, Paolo, MSc Lond., PhD Lond.   Reader,
Financial Econometrics
Research: accounting; finance; innovation and
entrepreneurship; organisation

MEDICINE

Tel: (020) 7594 9836
E-mail: r.a.shaw@imperial.ac.uk

Clinical Sciences, Division of

Edwards, Anthony D., MA MB BS MA, FRCP,
FRCPCH, FMedSci   Prof.
Hajnal, Joseph V., BSc Brist., PhD Brist.   Prof.,
Imaging Science
Larkman, David J., BSc Liv.J.Moores, PhD Manc.
Sr. Lectr.
Leen, Edward L. S., MD Durban-W., MB BCh
BAO, FRCR   Prof., Radiology (Ultrasound)
Li, Meng, BMedSc Beijing, PhD Edin., MMedSc
Reader, Experimental Medicine
Research: biological and clinical imaging; cell
biology; genomics

Epidemiology, Public Health and Primary Care, Division of

E-mail: r.a.shaw@imperial.ac.uk
Anderson, Roy M., BSc Lond., PhD Lond., FRS,
FMedSci   Prof., Infectious Disease
Epidemiology
Balding, David J., DPhil Oxf.   Prof., Statistical
Genetics
Basanez, Maria-Gloria, BSc Liv., MSc Liv., PhD
Lond.   Sr. Lectr.
Best, Nicola G., BSc MSc PhD   Reader,
Statistics and Epidemiology
Blane, David, MB BS Lond., MSc Lond.   Prof.,
Medical Sociology
Booton, Paul, BSc Lond., MB BS Lond.   Dir.,
Undergrad., Primary Care Educn.
Briggs, David J., BA Sheff., PhD Brist.   Prof.,
Environmental and Health Sciences
Donnelly, Christl A., BA Oberlin, MSc Harv., ScD
Harv.   Prof., Statistical Epidemiology
Elliott, Paul, BA Camb., MA Camb., MSc Lond.,
PhD Lond., FRCP, FMedSci   Prof.; Head*
Enright, Mark C., BSc Stir., MSc Dund., PhD
Aberd.   Reader, Molecular Epidemiology
Fenwick, Alan, OBE, BSc Liv., MSc Liv., PhD Liv.
Prof., Tropical Parasitology
Ferguson, Neil M., BSc Oxf., DPhil Oxf.   Prof.,
Mathematical Biology
Fisher, Matthew, BSc Edin., PhD Edin.   Sr.
Lectr.
Fraser, Christophe, BSc Edin., PhD Wales
Reader, Theoretical Biology
Garnett, Geoffrey P., BSc Sheff., MSc York(UK),
PhD Sheff.   Prof., Microparasite
Epidemiology
Gregson, Simon, MA Oxf., MSc Lond., MPhil
Lond., DPhil Oxf.   Sr. Lectr.
Hansell, Anna L., BA Camb., MB BChir Camb.,
MA Camb., MSc Lond.   Biobank London Co-
ordinator
Jarup, Lars, MSc Lond., MD Stockholm, PhD
Stockholm   Reader, Environmental Medicine
and Public Health
Jarvelin, Marjo-Riitta, MSc Lond., PhD Oulu
Prof., Life Course Epidemiology
Little, Mark P., BA Camb., DPhil Oxf.   Reader,
Statistics
Majeed, F. Azeem, MB BS Wales, MD Wales,
FFPHM   Prof., Primary Care and Social
Medicine
Michael, Edwin, BSc Madr., MSc Madr., PhD
Lond.   Sr. Lectr.
Michaud, Dominique S., ScD Harv., BA
Reader, Cancer Epidemiology
Peeters, Petra H. M., MEdu PhD   , Chronic
Disease Epidemiology
Riboli, Elio, BSc Milan, MSc Harv., MD Milan
Prof., Cancer Epidemiology and Prevention
Richardson, Sylvia, PhD Nott., Drd'État Paris XI
Prof., Biostatistics
Schatzkin, Arthur, PhD Col., BA MD   Prof.,
Nutritional Epidemiology
Spratt, Brian G., CBE, BSc Lond., PhD Lond.,
FMedSci, FRS   Prof., Molecular
Microbiology
Toledano, Mireille B., BA MA   Sr. Lectr.
Vineis, Paolo, MD Turin, PhD Turin   Prof.,
Environmental Epidemiology
Ward, Helen, DPhil Oxf., MB BS MSc   Reader,
Social Epidemiology

Webster, Joanne P., BSc Stir., DPhil Oxf.
Head, Res. Surveillance; Reader, Parasite
Epidemiology

Research: epidemiology and public health;
infectious disease epidemiology; medical
and community genetics; primary health
care and general practice; social science and
medicine

Investigative Science, Division of

E-mail: r.a.shaw@imperial.ac.uk

Allday, Martin J., BSc Lond., MSc Brun., PhD
Lond.   Prof., Virology
Altmann, Daniel M., BSc Lond., PhD Brist.
Prof., Immunology
Apperley, Jane F., MB ChB Birm., MD Birm.,
FRCP, FRCPath   Prof., Haematology
Arst, Herbert N., AB Prin., PhD Camb., ScD
Camb.   Prof.
Aspinall, Richard, BSc Brist., PhD Birm.
Reader, Immunology
Bangham, Charles R. M., MB BChir Camb., MA
Camb., PhD, FRCPath, FMedSci   Prof.,
Immunology
Bishop, Anne E., BSc Lond., PhD Lond.   Reader
Bloom, Stephen R., MA Camb., MB BChir
Camb., MD Lond., DSc Lond., FRCP, FRCPath,
FMedSci   Prof.; Head*
Cook, H. Terence, BA Oxf., MB BS Lond.,
FRCPath   Prof., Renal Pathology
Dilworth, Stephen M., BA Camb., MA Camb.,
PhD Lond.   Reader, Tumour Cell Biology
Farrell, Paul J., MA Camb., PhD Camb., FRCPath,
FMedSci   Prof., Tumour Virology
Franzoso, Guido, MD PhD   Head, Dept. of
Immunology
Friedland, Jonathan S., MA Camb., MB BS Lond.,
PhD Lond., FRCP, FRCPEd   Prof., Infectious
Diseases and Microbiology
Gardiner, James V., BA Birm., PhD Lond.   Sr.
Lectr.
Ghatei, Mohammad A., BSc Pahlavi, MSc Pahlavi,
PhD Lond.   Prof., Peptide Endocrinology
Goldin, Robert D., MEd   Sr. Lectr.
Gordon, Myrtle Y. A., BSc Liv., PhD Lond., DSc
Liv., FRCPath   Prof.
Gotch, Frances M., MSc Oxf., DPhil Oxf.   Prof.
Grimm, Stefan W., MSc Tübingen, PhD Tübingen
Prof., Toxicology
Haynes, Kenneth, BSc Brist., PhD Lond.   Reader,
Molecular Mycology
Holden, David W., BSc Durh., PhD Lond.,
FMedSci, FRS   Prof.
Holmes, Alison H., BA Camb., MA Camb., MB
BS Lond., MD Lond., FRCP   Sr. Lectr.,
Hospital Epidemiology and Infection
Control
Imami, Nesrina, MSc Zagreb, PhD Lond., MD
Reader, Immunology
Jones, Michael D., BSc Birm., PhD Birm.   Sr.
Lectr.
Laffan, Michael A. (Mike), BA Oxf., BM BCh
Oxf., MD Oxf., FRCPath, FRCP   Prof.,
Haemostasis and Thrombosis
Lane, David A., BSc Essex, PhD Lond.   Prof.
Meeran, M. Karim, BSc Lond., MB BS Lond., MD
Lond.   Reader, Endocrinology
Moore, David A. J., MSc Birm., MD Lond.
Reader, Infectious Diseases and Tropical
Medicine
Muller, Ingrid, BSc F.U.Berlin, PhD   Reader,
Immunology
Porter, Andrew C. G., BSc Brist., DPhil Oxf.
Reader, Haematology
Roberts, Irene, MD Glas., FRCP   Prof.,
Paediatric Haematology
Robertson, Brian D., BSc Edin., PhD Lond.   Sr.
Lectr.
Shaunak, Sunil, BSc Lond., MB BS Lond., PhD
Lond., MD, FRCPEd, FRCP   Prof., Infectious
Diseases
Smith, Geoffrey L., BSc Leeds, MA Camb., MA
Oxf., PhD Lond., FMedSci, FIBiol, FRS   Prof.
Sriskandan, Shiranee, MB BChir Camb., PhD
Lond., MA, FRCP   Hon. Consultant; Reader,
Infectious Disease
Stamp, Gordon W., MB ChB Liv., FRCPath
Prof., Clinical Investigative Sciences

Stanley, Sarah A., BSc Camb., MB BS Lond.   Sr.
Lectr.; Hon. Consultant
Tang, Christoph M., MB ChB Liv., PhD Lond.,
FRCP   Reader, Infectious Diseases
Vaz de Melo, Junia V., MD Minas Gerais, PhD
Lond.   Prof., Molecular Haematology
Walker, Marjorie M., BM BS Nott., FRCPath
Reader, Gastrointestinal Pathology
Watson, Roger J., BSc Warw., PhD Glas.
Reader
Wharton, John, BSc Sur., PhD Lond.   Sr. Lectr.,
Experimental Medicine and Toxicology
Wilkins, Martin R., MD Birm.   Clin. Prof.;
Head*
Young, Douglas B., BSc Edin., DPhil Oxf.,
FMedSci   Prof.

Research: haematology; histopathology;
infectious diseases and immunology;
metabolic medicine; virology

Medicine, Division of

Ashcroft, Margaret, BM Brist., PhD Brist.
Reader, Cancer Biology
Ashton-Rickardt, Philip G., BSc Lond., PhD Edin.
Prof., Immunology
Bell, Derek, BSc Edin., MB BS Edin., MD Edin.,
FRCSGlas, FRCPEd, FRCP   Prof., Acute
Medicine
Blair, Mitchel E., BSc Lond., MB BS Lond., MSc
Lond., FRCP, FRCPCH   Reader, Paediatrics
and Child Public Health
Blakemore, Alexandra I. F., PhD Sheff.   Sr.
Lectr.
Boobis, Alan R., BSc Glas., PhD Glas., FIBiol
Prof.
Botto, Marina, MD   Prof., Rheumatology
Bou-Gharios, George E., BSc Lond., MD Lond.
Sr. Lectr.
Brown, Susan C., BSc Reading, PhD Lond.   Sr.
Lectr.
Cherepanov, Peter P.   Sr. Lectr., Virology
Domin, Jan, BSc Lond., PhD Lond.   Sr. Lectr.
Dyson, Peter J., BSc Sus., PhD Lond.   Reader,
Immunology
Festenstein, Richard J., MB BS Lond., PhD
Open(UK)   Clin. Prof., Molecular Medicine
Froguel, Philippe, MB Paris, PhD Paris   Prof.,
Genomic Medicine
George, Andrew J. T., BA Camb., MA Camb.,
PhD S'ton.   Prof., Molecular Immunology
Ghosh, Subrata, MD Edin.   Prof.,
Gastroenterology
Gibson, Fernando, BSc Leic., PhD Leeds   Sr.
Lectr.
Gilks, Charles F., BA Camb., MSc Lond., MA
Camb., DPhil Oxf., FRCP   Prof.,
International Health
Godsland, Ian F., BA Oxf., PhD Lond.   Wynn
Reader, Human Metabolism
Huang, Fang-Ping   Sr. Lectr.
Johnston, Desmond G., MB ChB Edin., PhD
S'ton., MEd   Clin. Prof.
Karayiannis, Peter, BSc Liv., PhD Liv., FRCPath
Reader, Molecular Virology
Khakoo, Salim I., BSc Lond., MB BS Lond., MD
Lond.   Clin. Prof., Hepatology
Korchev, Yuri E., BSc MSc PhD   Prof.,
Biophysics
Kroll, John S., BA Oxf., BM BCh Oxf., MA Oxf.,
FRCPCH, FRCP   Prof.; Dean*
Langford, Paul R., BSc Wales, PhD Aston
Reader, Paediatrics (Molecular Infectious
Diseases)
Levin, Michael, MB BCh Witw., PhD, FRCP,
FMedSci, FRCPCH   Prof., Paediatrics and
International Child Health
Marelli-Berg, Federica M., PhD Lond., MD   Sr.
Lectr.
Maxwell, Patrick H., MB BS Lond., BA Oxf., MA
Oxf., DPhil Oxf.   Prof., Nephrology
MazarakisMazarakis, Nicholas D., PhD Lond.
Head, Dept. of Gene Therapy; Prof., Gene
Therapy
McClure, Myra O., BSc Lond., MSc Lond., PhD
Lond., DSc Lond., MPhil   Prof., Retrovirology
McGarvey, Michael J., BSc Glas., PhD Glas.   Sr.
Lectr.
Modi, Neena, MB ChB Edin., MD Edin., FRCP,
FRCPCH   Prof., Neonatal Medicine

Morgan, Jennifer   Reader, Cell Biology
Morley, Bernard J., BSc Liv., DPhil Oxf.   Prof.,
Molecular Genetics
Muntoni, Francesco, MB BS, FRCPCH   Prof.,
Paediatric Neurology
Pasvol, Geoffrey, MB ChB Cape Town, MA Oxf.,
DPhil Cape Town, FRCPEd, FRCPath   Clin.
Prof.
Purohit, Atul, BSc Lond., MSc Leeds, PhD Leeds
Sr. Lectr.
Pusey, Charles D., BA Camb., MA Camb., MB
BChir Camb., MSc Lond., DSc Lond., FRCPath,
FRCP, FMedSci, FAMS   Prof.
Reed, Michael J., BSc MSc PhD DSc, FRCPath
Prof.
Rogers, Nicola J., BSc Nott., MSc Lond., PhD
Lond.   Sr. Lectr.
Rutter, Guy A., BSc Nott., PhD Brist.   Head,
Dept. of Cell Biol.; Prof., Cell Biology
Scott, Diane M., BSc Lond., DPhil Oxf.   Sr.
Lectr.
Screaton, Gavin R., BA Camb., BM BCh Oxf.,
DPhil Oxf., FMedSci   Prof.
Tam, Frederick, MB BChir Camb., MA Camb.,
PhD Lond.   Sr. Lectr., Renal Medicine
Taylor, Graham P., MB BS Birm.   Sr. Lectr./
Hon. Consultant
Taylor-Robinson, Simon D., MD Lond., MB BS,
FRCP   Reader
Thomas, Howard C., BSc Newcastle(UK), MB BS
Newcastle(UK), PhD Glas., FRCP, FMedSci,
FRCPath, FRCSGlas   Clin. Prof.
Thursz, Mark R., MB BS Lond., MD Lond., MEd
Reader
Tudor-Williams, Gareth, MB BS Lond., PhD
Reader, Paediatric Infectious Diseases
Vyse, Timothy J., BA Camb., MD Lond., PhD
Lond.   Reader, Rheumatology
Walczak, Henning, MSc PhD   Prof., Tumour
Immunology
Warner, Jill A., BSc Lond., PhD Lond.   Reader,
Allergy and Immunology
Warner, John O., MB BS Sheff., MD Sheff.,
FMedSci, FRCPCH, FRCP   Head, Dept. of
Paediatrics; Prof., Paediatrics
Warrens, Anthony N., BSc Glas., BM BCh Oxf.,
MD Oxf., PhD Lond., FRCP   Sr. Lectr.
Weber, Jonathan N., BA Camb., MB BChir
Camb., PhD Camb., FRCP, FRCPath, FMedSci
Clin. Prof.
Wilkinson, Robert J., BM BCh Oxf., MA Camb.,
DPhil Oxf., FRCP   Prof., Infectious Diseases
Williams, Graham R., BSc Lond., MB BS Lond.,
PhD Birm., FRCP   Clin. Prof.,
Endocrinology

Research: dermatology, endocrinology and
metabolic medicine, rheumatology;
experimental genetics, experimental
medicine and toxicology, gastroenterology;
glycoenterology, glycobiology, hepatology,
infectious diseases; medical genetics,
proteomics, renal medicine; medicine,
immunology, care of the elderly

National Heart and Lung Institute

E-mail: r.a.shaw@imperial.ac.uk

Adcock, Ian, BSc Lond., PhD Lond.   Prof.,
Respiratory Cell and Molecular Biology
Alton, Eric W. F. W., BA Camb., MA Camb., MB
BS Lond., MD Lond., FRCP, FMedSci   Prof.,
Gene Therapy
Barnes, Peter J., MA Camb., BM BCh Oxf., DM
Oxf., DSc Oxf.   Prof., Thoracic Medicine
Barton, Paul J. R., BSc Leic., PhD Lond.   Reader
Belvisi, Maria G., BSc Lond., PhD Lond.   Prof.,
Respiratory Pharmacology
Brand, Nigel J., BSc PhD   Sr. Lectr.
Burney, Peter G. J., BA Oxf., MB BS Lond., MA
Oxf., MD Lond., FFPHM, FRCP, FMedSci
Prof., Respiratory Epidemiology and Public
Health
Bush, Andrew, MB BS Lond., MA Camb., MD
Camb., FRCP, FRCPCH   Prof.
Chaturvedi, Nishi, MB BS Lond., MSc Lond., MD
Lond.   Prof., Clinical Epidemiology
Chester, Adrian H., BSc PhD   Sr. Lectr.
Chung, K. Fan, MB BS Lond., MD Lond., DSc
Lond., FRCP   Prof.
Clark, Peter, BSc Strath., PhD Strath.   Sr. Lectr.

Clerk, Angela, BSc PhD   Reader, Biochemistry and Cell Biology

Collins, Peter, MB BChir Camb., MA Camb., MD, FRCPath   Prof., Clinical Cardiology

Cookson, William O. C., MB BS W.Aust., MD W.Aust., MA Oxf., DPhil Oxf., FMedSci   Prof., Respiratory Genetics

Coutelle, Charles, DrMed Jena, DrScMed Humboldt   Prof.

Cowie, Martin R., MB ChB Aberd., MSc Lond., MD Aberd.   Prof., Cardiology (Health Services Research)

Cullinan, Paul, MB BS Lond., MD Lond., MSc McG.   Reader, Respiratory Epidemiology

Curtin, Nancy A., BSc Penn., PhD Penn.   Prof., Muscle Physiology

Davies, Jane C., BSc Lond., MB ChB Dund., MD Dund.   Sr. Lectr., Gene Therapy

Donnelly, Louise E., BSc PhD   Sr. Lectr.

Durham, Stephen R., MA Camb., MB BChir Camb., MD Camb., FRCPath   Clin. Prof.

Evans, Paul, BSc MSc PhD   Sr. Lectr.

Ferenczi, Michael A., BSc Lond., PhD Lond.   Head, Bio-Nanoscience; Prof., Physiological Science

Firmin, David N., BSc Sur., MPhil Brist., PhD Lond.   Prof., Biomedical Imaging

Fry, Christopher H., BA BSc PhD Hon. DSc   Prof., Cardiac Electrophysiology

Griesenbach, Uta, BSc MSc PhD   Sr. Lectr.

Hansel, Trevor, BSc Liv., MB BCh Wales, MSc Birm., PhD Lond., FRCPath   Med. Dir.

Harding, Sian E., BSc Lond., PhD Lond.   Prof., Cardiac Pharmacology

Haskard, Dorian O., BA Oxf., MB BS Lond., MA Oxf., DM Oxf., FRCP, FMedSci   Prof.; Dir., Eric Bywaters Centre

Ho, S. Yen, BSc Malaya, MPhil Lond., PhD Lond.   Reader, Morphology

Hodson, Margaret E., MSc MD, FRCP   Prof., Respiratory Medicine

Hughes, Alun D., BSc Lond., MB BS Lond., PhD Lond.   Prof., Clinical Pharmacology

Ito, Kazuhiro, BSc Hokkaido, MSc Hokkaido, PhD Hokkaido   Reader, Respiratory Molecular Cell Biology

Johnston, Sebastian L., MB BS Lond., PhD S'ton., FRCP   Prof., Respiratory Medicine

Kemp, Paul, BSc S'ton., DPhil Oxf.   Sr. Lectr.

Lalvani, Ajit, BA Oxf., MB BS Lond., MD Oxf., FRCP   Prof., Infectious Diseases

Lindsay, Mark A., PhD Nott.Trent   Reader, Biopharmaceutics

Lloyd, Clare M., BSc Lond., PhD Lond.   Reader, Leukocyte Biology

Macleod, Kenneth T., BSc Aberd., PhD Edin.   Reader, Cardiac Physiology

Magee, Anthony I. (Tony), BSc Sheff., PhD Lond., FIBiol   Prof., Membrane Biology

Marston, Steven B., BA Oxf., MA PhD DSc   Prof.

Mason, Justin C., BSc Lond., MB BS Lond., PhD Lond., FRCP   Sr. Lectr.

Mitchell, Jane A., BSc Lanc., PhD Lond.   Prof., Pharmacology in Critical Care Medicine

Moffat, Miriam F., BSc Reading, DPhil Oxf.   Reader, Respiratory Genetics

Morrell, Mary J., BSc E.Lond., PhD Lond.   Sr. Lectr.

Nihoyannopoulos, Petros, MD Stras., MD Athens   Prof., Cardiology

Openshaw, Peter J. M., BSc Lond., MB BS Lond., PhD Brun.   Prof.

Partridge, Martyn R., MB BS Manc., MD Manc.   Prof., Repiratory Medicine

Pease, James E., BSc Manc., PhD Sheff.   Sr. Lectr.

Pennell, Dudley J., BA Camb., MB BChir Camb., MA MD, FRCP   Prof., Cardiology

Pepper, John, MB BChir Camb., MChir Camb., MA Camb., FRCS   Prof., Cardiothoracic Surgery

Peters, Nicholas S., MD Lond.   Prof., Cardiac Electrophysiology

Poole-Wilson, Philip A., BA Camb., MB BChir Camb., MA Camb., PhD Camb., FRCP, FESC, FACC, FMedSci   Prof.

Poulter, Neil R., MB BS Lond., MSc Lond., FRCP   Prof., Preventive Cardiovascular Medicine

Rankin, Sara M., BSc Lond., PhD Lond.   Sr. Lectr.

Rogers, Duncan F., BSc PhD   Reader

Rose, Marlene L., BSc Hull, MSc Lond., PhD Edin.   Prof., Transplant Immunology

Rosenthal, Nadia A., BHB Harv.   Scientific Dir.; Prof., Cardiovascular Science

Schachter, Michael, BSc Lond., MB BS Lond.   Sr. Lectr.

Schmidt-Weber, Carsten B.   Reader, Allergy and Clinical Immunology

Schneider, Michael D., MD Penn., BA   Head, Cardiovascular Sci.; Prof., Cardiology

Scott, James, MB BS MSc PhD, FRS, FMedSci   Prof.

Seabra, Miguel C., MD Lisbon, PhD Texas   Prof., Molecular Biology

Sever, Peter S., PhD Lond., MChem, FRCP   Prof., Clinical Pharmacology and Therapeutics

Severs, Nicholas J., BSc Lond., PhD Lond., DSc Lond.   Prof.

Shaheen, Seif O.   Sr. Lectr., Epidemiology

Sheridan, Desmond J., MB BCh BAO N.U.I., MD N.U.I., PhD Newcastle(UK), FRCP   Prof., Cardiology

Shovlin, Claire L., BA Camb., MB BChir Camb., MA Camb., PhD Lond., FRCP   Sr. Lectr., Respiratory Medicine

Smith, Susan F., BSc Liv., PhD Lond.   Sr. Lectr.

Sugden, Peter H., BA Oxf., MA Oxf., DPhil Oxf.   Prof.

Sutton, George C., MD Camb., FRCP   Sr. Lectr.

Taylor, Kenneth M., MB ChB Glas., MD Glas., FRCS   Clin. Prof.

Terracciano, Cesare M. N., MD   Sr. Lectr.

Tetley, Teresa D., BSc Wales, PhD Wales   Reader, Lung Cell Biology

Thom, Simon A. McG., MB BS Lond., MD Lond., FRCP   Clin. Prof., Cardiovascular Pharmacology

Underwood, S. Richard, BM BCh Oxf., MA Oxf., BA MD, FRCP, FRCR   Prof.

Williams, Timothy J., PhD Lond.   Prof.

Wood, David A., MB ChB Dund., MSc Lond., FRCP, FRCPEd, FFPHM   Garfield Weston Prof.

Research: allergy and clinical immunology; cardiovascular medicine; heart/lung medicine and surgery; molecular medicine, gene therapy and lung pathology; respiratory and thoracic medicine

Neuroscience and Mental Health, Division of

E-mail: r.a.shaw@imperial.ac.uk

Anand, Praveen, BA Oxf., MD Camb., BM MA, FRCP   Prof.

Bain, Peter G., MB BS Lond., MA Oxf., MD Lond., FRCP   Reader, Clinical Neurological Medicine

Barnes, Thomas R., DSc Lond., MB BS MD, FRCPsych   Prof., Clinical Psychiatry

Beckmann, Christian F.   Sr. Lectr.

Bronstein, Adolfo M., PhD Lond., FRCP   Prof.

Brooks, David J., MD Lond., DSc Lond., MB BS, FRCP, FMedSci   Hartnett Prof.

Crawford, Michael J., MB BS Lond., MSc Lond., MD Lond.   Reader, Mental Health Services Research

Croucher, Martin J., BSc PhD   Sr. Lectr.

de Belleroche, Jacqueline S., BA Trinity(Dub.), MSc Lond., PhD Lond., DSc Lond.   Prof.

Dexter, David T., BSc Brad., PhD Lond.   Sr. Lectr.

Ellaway, Peter H., BSc Lond., PhD Lond.   Prof.

Garralda Hualde, M. Elena, MD Navarra, MPhil Lond., FRCPCH, FRCPsych   Clin. Prof.

Gentleman, Stephen M., BSc Aberd., PhD Lond.   Reader, Experimental Neuropathology

Gillies, Glenda E., BPharm Lond., PhD Lond.   Reader

Grasby, Paul M., BSc Lond., MB BS Lond., MD Lond., FRCPath, FMedSci   Clin.Prof.

Gregory-Evans, Kevin, BSc Lond., MD Lond., MB BS, FRCS   Reader, Molecular Ophthalmology

Hodes, Matthew, BSc Lond., MSc Lond., PhD Lond., FRCPsych   Sr. Lectr.

Jen, Ling S., PhD Wash.State, BSc MSc   Reader, Neurodevelopment and Plasticity

Kennard, Christopher, BSc Lond., MB BS Lond., PhD Lond., FRCP, FMedSci   Prof.

Laruelle, Marc, MD   Prof., Biological Psychiatry

Laycock, John F., BSc Lond., PhD Lond.   Prof., Endocrine Physiology

Lowrie, Margaret B. (Maggie), BSc Birm., PhD Lond.   Sr. Lectr.

Maden, Anthony, BSc Lond., MB BS Lond., MD Lond.   Prof.

Mathias, Christopher J., MB BS B'lore., DPhil Oxf., DSc Lond., FRCP, FMedSci, FRCSGlas   Clin.Prof.

Matthews, Paul McM., BMedSci Oxf., DM Stras., DPhil Oxf.   Prof., Clinical Neuroscience

Middleton, Lefkos, MD Stras.   Head, Neurosci. and Mental Health; Prof., Clinical Neurology

Reynolds, Richard, BSc Lond., PhD Lond.   Prof., Cellular Neurobiology

Sensky, Thomas, BSc Lond., MB BS Lond., PhD Lond., FRCPsych   Prof., Psychological Medicine

Sharma, Pankaj, PhD Cant.CC   Reader, Clinical Neurology

Solito, Egle, PhD   Sr. Lectr.

Turkheimer, Federico E., PhD   Sr. Lectr.

Tyrer, Peter J., BA Camb., MB BChir Camb., MD, FRCPsych, FRCP, FMedSci   Prof., Community Psychiatry

Weaver, Timothy D., MSc Open(UK), BA   Sr. Lectr., Mental Health Services Research

Wells, Dominic J., BA Camb., MA Camb., PhD Wyoming   Prof., Gene Transfer

Wise, Richard J. S., BM Oxf., MA Oxf., DM Oxf., PhD   Prof., Neurology

Research: cognitive neuroscience and neuroendocrinology; neurogenetics and neuroinflammation; neuropathology and neuromuscular diseases; ophthalmology and psychological medicine; sensorimotor systems, integrative and molecular neuroscience

Rheumatology, Kennedy Institute of

E-mail: r.a.shaw@imperial.ac.uk

Brennan, Fionula M., BSc Brist., PhD Wales   Prof.

Clark, Andrew R., BA Camb., PhD Birm.   Sr. Lectr.

Dazzi, Francesco, PhD   Head, Stem Cell Biology; Prof., Stem Cell Biology

Feldmann, Marc, BSc Melb., MB BS Melb., PhD Melb., FRCP, FRCPath, FMedSci   Clin. Prof.; Head*

Foxwell, Brian M., BSc Newcastle(UK), PhD Brist., FRCPath   Prof., Immune Cell Signalling

Hussell, Tracy, BSc Nott.Trent, PhD Lond.   Reader, Immunology

Itoh, Yoshifumi, BSc Tokyo, MSc Tokyo, PhD Tokyo   Sr. Lectr.

Maini, Ravinder N., BA Camb., MB BChir Camb., FRCP, FRCPEd, FMedSci   Prof.

Nagase, Hideaki, BSc MSc PhD   Prof., Matrix Biology

Nanchalal, Jagdeep, BSc Lond., MB BS Lond., PhD Lond., FRCS   Prof., Hand, Plastic and Reconstructive Surgery

Paleolog, Ewa, BSc Lond., PhD   Sr. Lectr.

Saklatvala, Jeremy, PhD, FMedSci   Prof.

Taylor, Peter C., BA Camb., MB BCh Oxf., MA Camb., PhD Lond., FRCP   Reader, Experimental Rheumatology

Venables, Patrick J., BA   Clin. Prof.

Wait, Robin, MA Oxf., PhD Greenwich   Sr. Lectr., Proteomics

Williams, Richard, BSc Wales, MSc Wales, PhD Lond.   Sr. Lectr.

Research: biological and pathological functions of proteases; cell signalling and gene expression; clinical research; imaging and ultrasound; immunity and inflammation, viruses and autoimmunity

Surgery, Oncology, Reproductive Biology and Anaesthetics, Division of

E-mail: r.a.shaw@imperial.ac.uk

Abel, Paul D., MB BS Liv., MS Liv., FRCS, FRCSEd   Prof., Urology

Ali, Simak, BSc Lond., DSc Edin.   Reader, Medical Endocrine Oncology

Allen-Mersh, Timothy G., BSc St And., MB ChB Dund., MD Dund., FRCS   Clin. Prof.

Bello, Fernando, PhD Lond., BSc   Sr. Lectr., Surgical Graphics and Computing

Bennett, Phillip R., BSc Lond., MB BS Lond., MD Lond., PhD Lond.   Clin. Prof.

Bevan, Charlotte L., MA Camb., PhD Camb.   Sr. Lectr.

Brosens, Jan J., BMedSci Leuven, PhD Lond.   Prof., Reproductive Sciences

Brown, Robert, BSc Edin., PhD CNAA   Prof., Translational Oncology

Buluwela, Lakjaya (Laki), BSc Lond., PhD Lond.   Reader, Cancer Medicine

Cobb, Justin P., BA Oxf., BM BCh Oxf., MCh Oxf., FRCS   Prof., Orthopaedic Surgery

Coombes, Raoul C., MB BS Lond., MD Lond., PhD Lond., FRCP, FMedSci   Clin. Prof.

Darzi, Sir Ara, MD Trinity(Dub.), MB BCh, FRCSI, FRCS, FACS, FMedSci   Clin. Prof.; Head*

Dibb, Nicholas J., BSc Sheff., PhD E.Anglia   Sr. Lectr.

Firth, Anthony J., MA Camb., PhD Lond.   Prof.

Fisk, Nicholas M., MB BS Syd., PhD Lond.   Clin. Prof.

Franks, Stephen, MB BS Lond., MD Lond., FRCP   Clin. Prof.

Gabra, Hani, BSc Glas., MB ChB Glas., MSc Edin., PhD Edin.   Prof., Medical Oncology

Glover, Vivette A. S., BA Oxf., PhD Lond., DSc Lond.   Prof., Perinatal Psychobiology

Gooderham, Nigel J., BSc Liv., PhD Lond., FRSChem   Prof., Molecular Toxicology

Habib, Nagy A., MB BCh Ain Shams, ChB Brist., BMedSci, FRCS   Prof., Hepto-biliary Surgery

Hardy, Katharine, MA Camb., PhD Lond.   Reader, Reproductive Biology

Higham, Jennifer M., MB BS MD   Reader, Obstetrics and Gynaecology

Holmes, Elaine, BSc Lond., PhD Lond.   Prof., Chemical Biology

Huhtaniemi, Iipo T., MD Helsinki, PhD Helsinki   Prof., Reproductive Biology

Jass, Jeremy R., MB BS Lond., MD Lond., DSc Lond., BSc Lond., FRCPath   Clin. Prof., Gastrointesntinal Pathology

Kneebone, Roger L., BSc St And., MB BS Manc., FRCSEd   Sr. Lectr.

Lam, Eric W., PhD   Prof., Molecular Oncology

Lin, Chen-Lung S., DPhil Oxf., MD   Prof., Paediatric Surgery

Maze, Mervyn, MB ChB, FRCP, FRCA, FMedSci   Prof.; Deputy Head

McGregor, Alison H., MSc Sur., PhD Lond.   Sr. Lectr.

Nagy, Istvan, DPhil   Sr. Lectr.

Nicholson, Jeremy K., BSc Liv., PhD Lond., FIBiol, FRSChem, FRCPath   Prof., Biological Chemistry

Parker, Malcolm G., BSc UMIST, PhD Leic., FMedSci   Prof.; Head, Obstet. and Gynaecol.

Regan, Lesley, MB BS Lond., MD Lond.   Clin. Prof.

Rice, Andrew S. C., MD Lond., FRCA   Reader, Pain Research

Seckl, Michael, BSc Lond., MB BS Lond., DPhil Lond., FRCP   Prof., Molecular Cancer Medicine

Sullivan, Mark H. F., BA Oxf., PhD Lond.   Sr. Lectr.

Takata, Masao, PhD   Prof., Molecular Physiology and Critical Care

Vincent, Charles A., BA Oxf., MPhil Lond., PhD Lond.   Smith and Nephew Prof., Clinical Safety Research

Waxman, Jonathan, BSc Lond., MB BS Lond., MD Lond., FRCP   Clin. Prof.

Williamson, Catherine, BSc Manc.Met., MB ChB Manc.   Sr. Lectr.

Research: anaesthetics and intensive care; intracellular signalling and gene expression; neuromuscular disease; paediatric infectious diseases; surgery

SPECIAL CENTRES, ETC

Biomedical Engineering, Institute of

Tel: (020) 7594 0701 Fax: (020) 7594 0704
E-mail: biomedeng@imperial.ac.uk

Cass, Anthony E. G., BA PhD   Deputy Dir.; Res. Dir.

Toumazou, Christofer, BSc Oxf.Brookes, PhD Oxf.Brookes   Dir.*

Climate Change, Grantham Institute for

Tel: (020) 7594 5477
E-mail: p.knight@imperial.ac.uk

CONTACT OFFICERS

Academic affairs. Academic Registrar: McClure, F. Vernon, BA Lond.
(E-mail: v.mcclure@imperial.ac.uk)

Accommodation. Head of Residences: Brown, Sharine (E-mail: s.r.brown@imperial.ac.uk)

Admissions (first degree). Director of Access: Thody, Melanie
(E-mail: admissions@imperial.ac.uk)

Admissions (higher degree). Director of Access: Thody, Melanie
(E-mail: admissions@imperial.ac.uk)

Adult/continuing education. Director, Centre for Professional Development: Jones, Mervyn, BSc Lond., MSc Lond., PhD Lond.
(E-mail: m.jones@imperial.ac.uk)

Alumni. Director of Alumni and Development: Kirk, Fiona (E-mail: f.kirk@imperial.ac.uk)

Archives. College Archivist and Corporate Records Manager: Barrett, Anne, BA Middx., MA Lond. (E-mail: a.barrett@imperial.ac.uk)

Careers. Director, Careers Advisory Service: Farrar, Elspeth A., BSc Stir.
(E-mail: e.farrar@imperial.ac.uk)

Computing services. Director of ICT: Allan, Heather, BA Camb., MSc Edin.
(E-mail: h.allan@imperial.ac.uk)

Conferences/corporate hospitality. Head of Catering and Conferences: Neary, Jane
(E-mail: j.neary@imperial.ac.uk)

Consultancy services. Chief Executive, IC Consultants: Docx, Paul, BA Keele, MSc(Econ) Lond.
(E-mail: p.docx@imperial.ac.uk)

Development/fund-raising. Director of Alumni and Development: Kirk, Fiona
(E-mail: f.kirk@imperial.ac.uk)

Equal opportunities. Deputy Director of Human Resources: Everitt, Kim, BA Warw.
(E-mail: k.everitt@imperial.ac.uk)

Estates and buildings/works and services. Chief Operating Officer: Knight, Martin, BA Oxf., DPhil Oxf.
(E-mail: m.knight@imperial.ac.uk)

Examinations. (Medicine) Deputy Academic Registrar (Student Services and Medicine): Richardson, Lorna, BA Lond.
(E-mail: l.richardson@imperial.ac.uk)

Examinations. (Engineering and natural sciences) Deputy Academic Registrar (Engineering and Natural Sciences): Wheatley, Nigel, BA Lond.
(E-mail: n.wheatley@imperial.ac.uk)

Finance. Director of Finance: Murphy, Andrew C., BEng Birm.
(E-mail: a.murphy@imperial.ac.uk)

Health services. Senior Partner: Weinreb, Irene, MB BS Lond., MBA Lond.
(E-mail: healthcentre@imperial.ac.uk)

International office. Director: Baker, Piers
(E-mail: piers.baker@imperial.ac.uk)

Language training for international students. Director, Humanities Programme and Co-ordinator, Language Studies: Brinson, Prof. Charmian E. J., BA Lond., MA Lond., PhD Lond. (E-mail: c.brinson@imperial.ac.uk)

Library (chief librarian). Director of Library Services: Shorley, Deborah C., BA Durh.
(E-mail: d.shorley@imperial.ac.uk)

Minorities/disadvantaged groups. Diversity and Equal Opportunities Consultant: Yates, C. (E-mail: c.yates@imperial.ac.uk)

Personnel/human resources. Director of Human Resources: Gosling, Chris, MA Camb. (E-mail: c.gosling@imperial.ac.uk)

Public relations. Director, Communications: Miller, Tom E., BSc Lond.
(E-mail: t.miller@imperial.ac.uk)

Publications. Managing Editor: Daniel, Saskia K., BA Sus. (E-mail: s.daniel@imperial.ac.uk)

Purchasing. Head of Purchasing: Whitlow, John, BA Lond.
(E-mail: j.whitlow@imperial.ac.uk)

Research. Director, Research Contracts: Cox, Lynne (E-mail: l.cox@imperial.ac.uk)

Safety. Safety Director: Gillett, Ian, BSc Lond.
(E-mail: i.gillett@imperial.ac.uk)

Scholarships, awards, loans. Assistant Registrar (Student Services): Surtees, Dean
(E-mail: d.surtees@imperial.ac.uk)

Schools liaison. Schools Liaison Officer: Lockwood, Paul
(E-mail: schliaison@imperial.ac.uk)

Security. Head of Security, Fire and Postal Services: Davies, Ceri
(E-mail: c.davies@imperial.ac.uk)

Sport and recreation. Head of Sport and Leisure: Mosley, Neil, MSc Keele
(E-mail: n.mosley@imperial.ac.uk)

Strategic planning. Director of Planning: Coupland, Michelle, BA Exe.
(E-mail: m.coupland@imperial.ac.uk)

Student union. General Manager: Haldane, Peter (E-mail: p.haldane@imperial.ac.uk)

Student welfare/counselling. Senior Student Counsellor: Allman, David, BA Liv.
(E-mail: d.allman@imperial.ac.uk)

Students with disabilities. Disabilities Officer: O'Callaghan, Loretto
(E-mail: l.ocallaghan@imperial.ac.uk)

[*Information supplied by the institution as at 8 November 2007, and edited by the ACU*]

UNIVERSITY OF KEELE

Founded 1962

Member of the Association of Commonwealth Universities

Postal Address: Staffordshire, England ST5 5BG
Telephone: (01782) 621111 **Fax:** (01782) 632343 **E-mail:** a.howells@vco.keele.ac.uk
URL: http://www.keele.ac.uk

VICE-CHANCELLOR*—Finch, Prof. Dame Janet, DBE, BA Lond., PhD Brad., Hon. DLitt W.England, Hon. DSc Edin., Hon. DSc S'ton., Hon. DEd Lincoln(UK), DL, AcSS
DEPUTY VICE-CHANCELLOR—Pearson, Margaret, BA Camb., PhD Liv.
PRO VICE-CHANCELLOR (STAFF AND STUDENTS)—Cocks, Prof. Raymond C., BA Camb.
PRO VICE-CHANCELLOR (RESEARCH AND ENTERPRISE)—Jones, Prof. Peter W., BSc Reading, MSc Reading, PhD Wales
PRO VICE-CHANCELLOR (RESEARCH AND ENTERPRISE)—Phillipson, Prof. Christopher R., BA CNAA, PhD Durh.
HONORARY TREASURER—Myatt, C.
SECRETARY AND REGISTRAR‡—Morris, Simon J., BA Durh.
DIRECTOR OF ACADEMIC REGISTRY—Howells, Allan, BSc Wales
DIRECTOR OF FINANCE AND INFORMATION TECHNOLOGY—Clarke, Karen, MA Oxf.
DIRECTOR OF HUMAN RESOURCES AND STUDENT SUPPORT—Doran, Judith M., BA Leeds
DIRECTOR OF COMMERCIAL FACILITIES MANAGEMENT—Tucker, Jennifer A., BSc DBA

GENERAL INFORMATION

History. The university was founded as University College of North Staffordshire in 1949 and became University of Keele in 1962.

It is located in the North Staffordshire countryside, close to the city of Stoke-on-Trent.

Admission to first degree courses (see also United Kingdom Introduction). Through Universities and Colleges Admissions Service (UCAS). General Certificate of Secondary Education (GCSE)/General Certificate of Education (GCE): minimum 5 subjects (including English language and mathematics or a science subject at grade C or above) with 2 at A level. Candidates offering 4 AS levels in place of 2 A levels: minimum 7 subjects, including GCSE qualifications. International Baccalaureate: minimum 26 points; European Baccalaureate: minimum 60%. Other qualifications may be considered provided they satisfy senate.

First Degrees (see also United Kingdom Directory to Subjects of Study). BA, BEd, BMid, BN, BSc, LLB, MPharm, MSci.

Courses normally last 3 years. Sandwich courses: 4 years.

Length of course. Full-time: BA, BMid, BN, BSc: 3 years; MPharm, MSci: 4 years.

Higher Degrees (see also United Kingdom Directory to Subjects of Study).

Master's. LLM, MA, MBA, MCh(Orth), MLitt, MMedSci, MPhil, MS, MSc.

Courses normally last 1 year full-time or 2 years part-time.

Length of course. Full-time: LLM, MA, MBA, MCh(Orth), MMedSci, MSc: 1 year; MLitt, MPhil: 2 years. Part-time: LLM, MA, MBA, MCh(Orth), MMedSci, MSc: 2 years; MLitt, MPhil: 4 years.

Doctoral. MD, PhD.

Length of course. Full-time: PhD: 3 years. Part-time: PhD: 6 years.

Libraries. Volumes: 500,000. Periodicals subscribed to: 1700. Special collections: Air Reconnaissance Archive (TARA) (wartime reconnaissance photographs); Wedgwood and Spode (pottery industry); European Documentation Centre (EU official documents); Arnold Bennett Collection; British Parliamentary Papers Collection; Local Collection (Staffordshire and neighbouring counties); LePlay Collection (sociology); Karl Mannheim Papers (sociology); Warrilow Collection (historical photographs of Staffordshire).

Statistics. Staff (2006): 1098 (552 academic, 546 non-academic). Students (2006): full-time 5312 (2150 men, 3162 women); international 573 (246 men, 327 women).

FACULTIES/SCHOOLS

Health

Tel: (01782) 583902 Fax: (01782 583903
E-mail: a.garner@hfac.keele.ac.uk
Dean: Garner, Prof. Andrew, BSc Leic., PhD Leic.

Humanities and Social Sciences

Tel: (01782) 584385 Fax: (01782) 583195
E-mail: s.j.scott@keele.ac.uk
Dean: Scott, Prof. Susan J., BSc Newcastle(UK), MA Manc.

Natural Sciences

Tel: (01782) 584583 Fax: (01782) 715261
E-mail: j.laybourn-parry@natsci.keele.ac.uk
Dean: Laybourn-Parry, Prof. Joanna, BSc Reading, MSc Wales, PhD Stir., DSc Reading

Postgraduate Medicine

Tel: (01782) 716047 Fax: (01782) 747319
E-mail: p.crome@pmed.keele.ac.uk
Dean: Crome, Prof. Peter, MB BS Lond., MD Lond., PhD Lond., FRCP, FRCPEd, FRCPGlas

ACADEMIC UNITS

Computing and Mathematics, School of

Quinney, Douglas A., BSc Nott., MSc Oxf., DPhil Oxf.   Prof.; Head*

Computer Science

Tel: (01782) 583446 Fax: (01782) 713082
Brereton, O. Pearl, BSc Sheff., PhD Keele   Reader
Hawksley, Christopher, BSc Manc.   Sr. Lectr.
Kitchenham, Barbara A., BSc Leeds, MSc Leeds, PhD Leeds   Prof.
Linkman, Stephen, BSc Leic.   Sr. Lectr.
Rugg, Gordan, BA Reading, PhD Reading   Sr. Lectr.
Other Staff: 8 Lectrs.

Mathematics

Tel: (01782) 583257 Fax: (01782) 584268
Bedford, David, BSc Sur., MA Essex, PhD Sur.   Sr. Lectr.
Chapman, Christopher J., BA Camb., MA Camb., PhD Brist.   Prof.
Fu, Yibin, BSc Changsha Railway Inst., MSc E.Anglia, PhD E.Anglia   Prof.
Grieve, Andrew P., BSc S'ton., MSc S'ton., PhD Nott.   Hon. Prof.
Healey, Johnathan J., BA Oxf., DPhil Oxf.   Reader
Heckl, Maria A., PhD Camb.   Sr. Lectr.
Jones, J. Mary, MSc Lond., PhD Manc.   Sr. Lectr.

Jones, Peter W., BSc Reading, MSc Reading, PhD Wales   Prof.
Osborne, Anthony D., BSc City(UK), PhD City(UK)   Sr. Lectr.
Preater, John, BSc UMIST, MSc Manc., PhD Keele   Sr. Lectr.
Quinney, Douglas A., BSc Nott., MSc Oxf., DPhil Oxf.   Prof.; Head*
Rogerson, Graham A., BSc Leic., MSc E.Anglia, PhD E.Anglia   Prof.
Shrira, Victor I., MSc Gorky State, PhD Moscow   Prof.
Smith, Peter, BSc Nott., PhD Nott.   Emer. Prof.
Wilks, Graham, BSc Manc., PhD Manc., FIMA   Emer. Prof.
Other Staff: 3 Lectrs.

Criminology, Education, Sociology and Social Work, School of

Williams, Charlotte, BA Wales, MA Wales, PhD Wales   Prof.; Head*

Criminology

Tel: (01782) 583084 Fax: (01782) 584269
Carlen, Patricia, BA Leeds, PhD Leeds   Visiting Prof.
Gadd, David, BSc Keele, MPhil Camb., PhD Keele   Sr. Lectr.
Godfrey, Barry, BA Liv., MA Leeds, PhD Leic.   Reader
Hope, Timothy J., BA Leeds, MSc Lond., PhD Lond.   Prof.
Jefferson, Anthony J., BEd Lough., MA Birm.   Prof.
Karstedt, Susanne, MA Hamburg, PhD Bielefeld   Prof.
Lippens, Ronnie, BA Leuven, MA Ghent, PhD Ghent   Reader
Mattinson, Kevin, MA Lanc.   Sr. Lectr.
Melossi, Dario, Laurea Bologna, PhD Calif.   Visiting Prof.
Shearing, Clifford, BSocSci Natal, MA Tor., PhD Tor.   Visiting Prof.
Stenning, Philip, BA Camb., LLM Tor., DJur Tor.   Prof.
Worrall, Ann J., BA Keele, MA Keele, PhD Keele   Prof.; Head*
Yar, Majid, BA York(UK), MA York(UK), PhD Lanc.   Sr. Lectr.
Other Staff: 7 Lectrs.; 1 Visiting Fellow

Education

Tel: (01782) 583114 Fax: (01782) 583555
Alexiadou, Nafsika, BEd Oxf., MEd Oxf., MSc Oxf., DPhil Oxf.   Sr. Lectr.
Bale, John R., BSc(Econ) Lond., MPhil Lond.   Emer. Prof.
David, M. E., BA Leeds, PhD Lond., FRSA   Emer. Prof.
Hunter, Phillip, CBE, BSc PhD   Hon. Prof.

Jones, Kenneth W., BA Oxf., MA Lond., MA
   Essex, PhD Keele   Prof.
Kempa, Richard F., PhD Lond., FRSChem
   Emer. Prof.
King, Christopher J. H., BSc Brist., MSc Reading
   Prof.
Maden, Margaret, BA Leeds   Emer. Prof.
Mattinson, Kevin, MA Lanc.   Sr. Lectr.
Miller, David J., BA Camb.   Sr. Lectr.
Shain, Farzana, BA Liv., PhD Keele   Sr. Lectr.
Whitehead, Stephen, MA Leeds Met., PhD Leeds
   Met.   Sr. Lectr.
Other Staff: 12 Lectrs.

Social Relations, School of

Tel: (01782) 584063 Fax: (01782) 584069
Allan, Graham, BA MA PhD   Prof.
Bernard, Miriam, BA Keele, PhD Keele   Prof.
Brown, Hilary, PhD Kent   Hon. Prof.
Chambers, Patricia, BA Keele, MA Keele   Sr.
   Lectr.
Frankenberg, Ronald J., BA Camb., MA Manc.,
   PhD Manc., DLitt Keele   Emer. Prof.
Jones, G. E., BA Reading, MSc Sur., PhD Sur.
   Emer. Prof.
Leach, Rebecca, BA CNAA, MA Lanc., PhD
   W.England   Sr. Lectr.
Martens, Lydia D., MA Glas., PhD Glas.
Morgan, David H. J., BSc Hull, MA Hull, PhD
   Manc.   Visiting Prof.
Pahl, Ray, BA Camb., MA Camb., PhD Lond.
   Visiting Prof.
Parish, Jane A. E., BA Liv., PhD Liv.   Sr. Lectr.
Phillipson, Christopher R., BA CNAA, PhD Durh.
   Prof.
Pugh, Richard G., BSc Lond., MA Keele, PhD Keele
   Prof.
Scharf, Thomas, BA Newcastle(UK), PhD Aston
   Reader
Werbner, Pnina, BA Jerusalem, MA Manc., PhD
   Manc.   Prof.
Other Staff: 11 Lectrs.

Economic and Management Studies, School of

Lawrence, Peter R., MA Sus., PhD Leeds   Sr.
   Lectr.; Head*

Economics

Tel: (01782) 583091 Fax: (01782) 717577
Bladen-Hovell, Robin C., BSc Wales, MA(Econ)
   Manc.   Prof.
Cornes, Richard C., MSc S'ton., PhD ANU
   Visiting Prof.
Lanot, Gautier, PhD Stras.   Prof.
Milas, Costas, BSc Athens, MSc Warw., PhD
   Warw.   Prof.
Symons, Elizabeth, MSc S'ton., PhD S'ton.   Sr.
   Lectr.
Wenselburger, Jan, PhD   Reader
Worrall, Timothy S., BA Liv., MA Essex, PhD Liv.
   Prof.
Other Staff: 7 Lectrs.

Health Planning and Management

Tel: (01782) 583191 Fax: (01782) 711737
Beech, Roger, BSc Staffs., MSc Warw., PhD
   Warw.   Reader
Birch, Katherine E., BA Reading, PhD Liv.   Sr.
   Lectr.
Cowpe, Jennifer, BA York(UK), MBA Keele   Sr.
   Lectr.
Cropper, Stephen A., BSc Dund., PhD Wales
   Prof.
Edwards, Brian, CBE, Hon. FRCPath   Hon.
   Prof.
Empey, Duncan, MB BS Lond., FRCP   Hon.
   Prof.
James, Marilyn, BA Liv., MSc York(UK), PhD
   Manc.   Sr. Lectr.
Paton, Calum R., MA Oxf., MPP Harv., DPhil
   Oxf.   Prof.
Peskett, Sheila, BM BCh Oxf., BA Oxf., MA
   York(UK)   Sr. Lectr.
Rigby, Michael J., BA Keele   Prof.
Scrivens, Ellie, BA Exe., PhD Lond.   Prof.

Whitney, David J., BA Exe., MA Lond.   Prof.;
   Dir., Clin. Management
Other Staff: 2 Lectrs.

Human Resource Management and Industrial Relations

Tel: (01782) 583254 Fax: (01782) 584271
Ironside, Michael D., BSc Aston, MA Warw.   Sr.
   Lectr.
Lyddon, David, BA Oxf., MSc(Econ) Lond., PhD
   Warw.   Sr. Lectr.
McIlroy, John, LLB Lond., LLM Lond.   Prof.
Roberts, Ivor, BSc Liv., BA Liv., MA Liv., MA
   Cologne   Hon. Prof.
Seifert, Roger V., BA Oxf., MSc(Econ) Lond.,
   PhD Lond.   Prof.
Smith, Paul A., BA Warw., MA Warw., PhD
   Warw.   Sr. Lectr.
Thornley, Carol R., MPhil Camb., PhD Warw.
   Sr. Lectr.
Whitston, Colin, MA Warw.   Sr. Lectr.
Other Staff: 5 Lectrs.

Management

Tel: (01782) 583089 Fax: (01782) 584272
Bridgeman, John S., BSc Wales   Visiting Prof.
Hassard, John, BA Lanc., MSc Aston, PhD Aston
   Visiting Prof.
Kelemen, Mihaela, PhD Bucharest, DPhil Oxf., BA
   Prof.
Klaes, Matthias, PhD Edin.   Prof.
Knights, David, BSc Salf., MSc Manc., PhD Manc.
   Prof.
McCabe, Darren, BA Lanc., MA Warw., PhD
   Wolv.   Reader
McLaran, Pauline E., MA Ulster, PhD Ulster
Munro, Rolland J. B., BA Stir., PhD Edin.   Prof.
Willis, Paul, MA Camb., MSc Lond., PhD Birm.
   Prof.
Other Staff: 16 Lectrs.

Health and Rehabilitation, School of

Tel: (01782) 584190 Fax: (01782) 584255
Andrews, Marilyn, MEd Manc.   Prof.; Head*
Bucher, Catherine, BSc Salf.   Sr. Lectr.
Sim, Julius W., BA Durh., MSc S.Bank, PhD Keele
   Prof.
Waterfield, Jacqueline, MSc Sur.   Sr. Lectr.
Other Staff: 23 Lectrs.; 1 Hon. Lectr.

Humanities, School of

Vaughan, Michael P., BA CNAA, PhD Nott.
   Prof.; Head*

American Studies

Tel: (01782) 583010 Fax: (01782) 583460
Adams, David K., OBE, MA Camb., AM Yale,
   MA Oxf., DPhil Oxf., DLitt Keele   Emer.
   Prof.; Fellow
Bell, Ian F. A., BA Reading, PhD Reading   Prof.,
   American Literature
Bonwick, Colin C., MA Oxf., PhD Maryland,
   FRHistS   Emer. Prof.
Crawford, Martin S., BA Keele, MPhil Oxf., DPhil
   Oxf.   Prof.
Frascina, Francis A., BA CNAA   Emer. Prof.
Harris, Oliver C.G., BA Oxf., DPhil Oxf.   Prof.
Mills, Stephen F., BA Keele, MA Maryland, PhD
   Keele   Sr. Lectr.
Schaefer, Axel R., MA Oregon, PhD Wash.
Other Staff: 2 Lectrs.

English

Tel: (01782) 583138 Fax: (01782) 713468
Amigoni, David, BA Wales, MA Keele, PhD CNAA
   Prof.
Bruce, Susan, BA Camb., MA Cornell, PhD Cornell
   Sr. Lectr.
Knowles, James, BA Lond., DPhil Oxf.   Prof.
McCracken, Maurice, BA Camb., PhD Lond.
   Prof.
McLaverty, James, BLitt Oxf., MA Oxf.   Prof.
McNaughton, David A., BA Newcastle(UK), BPhil
   Oxf.   Emer. Prof.
Ruston, Sharon, BA Liv., MA Liv., PhD Liv.   Sr.
   Lectr.

Tomlinson, A. Charles, MA Camb., MA Lond.,
   DLitt Keele, FRSL   Hon. Prof.
Other Staff: 6 Lectrs.; 1 Hon. Lectr.

History

Tel: (01782) 583195 Fax: (01782) 583195
Atherton, Ian J., BA Camb., PhD Camb., FRHistS
   Sr. Lectr.
Crook, Malcolm H., BA Wales, PhD Lond.   Prof.
Cushing, Kathleen, BA N.Y., LMS Tor., MPhil
   Oxf., DPhil Oxf.   Sr. Lectr.
Galeotti, Mark, MA Camb., PhD Lond.   Sr. Lectr.
Harrison, Christopher J., BA Keele, PhD Keele,
   FRHistS   Sr. Lectr.
Hughes, Ann L., BA Liv., PhD Liv., FRHistS
   Prof.
Hunt, Karen, BA Kent, MA Manc., PhD Kent
   Prof.
Jackson, Peter, MA Camb., PhD Camb., FRHistS
   Prof.
Maxwell, David J., BA Manc., DPhil Oxf.   Sr.
   Lectr.
Morgan, Philip J., BA Lond., PhD Lond.   Sr.
   Lectr.
Richmond, Colin F., BA Leic., DPhil Oxf.
   Emer. Prof.
Townshend, Charles J. N., MA Oxf., DPhil Oxf.,
   FRHistS   Prof.
Tringham, N., BA Wales, PhD Aberd.   Sr. Lectr.
Other Staff: 6 Lectrs.; 5 Fellows; 1 Hon. Lectr.

Languages, Culture and Creative Arts

Tel: (01782) 584075 Fax: (01782) 584238
Andrew, Joseph M., BA Oxf.   Prof.
Baron, Britta, MA Bonn   Hon. Prof.
Dickinson, Peter, MA Camb., FRCO   Hon. Prof.
Fischman Steremberg, Rajmil A., BSc
   Haifa(Technion), DPhil York(UK)   Prof.
Garro, Diego, BSc Padua, MA Keele, PhD Keele
   Sr. Lectr.
Kelly, Barbara L., MM Ill., MA Glas., PhD Liv.
   Sr. Lectr.
Kratz, Annette, BSc Aston, PhD Aston   Head,
   Centre for International Exchange and
   Languages
Levy, Silvano C., BA Reading, PhD Kent   Reader
Reid, Robert E., BA Birm.   Reader
Rock, David, BA Wales   Sr. Lectr.
Uduman, Sohrab M., BMus Sur., MMus Sur.,
   PhD Birm.   Sr. Lectr.
Williams, Alastair, BSc City(UK), DPhil Oxf.   Sr.
   Lectr.
Other Staff: 7 Lectrs.; 7 Teaching Fellows; 1
   Fellow

Law, School of

Tel: (01782) 583218 Fax: (01782) 583228
Bradney, Anthony, BA Open(UK), LLB Hull
   Prof.
Brammer, Alison K., BA Sus.   Sr. Lectr.
Cocks, Raymond C., BA Camb.   Prof.
Cownie, Fiona C., BA Brist., LLB Leic., LLM Lond.
   Prof.
Dawson, Angus J., BA Sus., MSc Liv., PhD Manc.
   Sr. Lectr.
Dugdale, Anthony M., BA Oxf., BCL Oxf.   Prof.
Fletcher, Ruth, LLB Trinity(Dub.), MA N.U.I.,
   LLM York(Can.), DJur York(Can.), PhD
   York(Can.)   Sr. Lectr.
Fox, Marie D., LLB Belf.   Prof.
Garrard, Eve, BA Lanc., MPhil Manc.   Sr. Lectr.
Haley, Michael A., LLB Liv., LLM Leic.   Prof.
Manji, Ambreena, BA York(UK), LLM Warw.
   Reader
Sharpe, Andrew N., LLB Warw., LLM   Prof.
Thomson, Michael A., LLB S'ton., PhD Birm.
   Prof.; Head*
Wasik, Martin, LLB Manc., MA Keele   Prof.
Wilkinson, Stephen, BA Lanc., MA Sus., DPhil
   Sus.   Prof.
Other Staff: 22 Lectrs.; 1 Fellow

Life Sciences, School of

Tel: (01782) 583057 Fax: (01782) 583055
Arme, Christopher, BSc Leeds, PhD Leeds, DSc
   Keele, FIBiol   Prof.

Chevins, Peter F. D., BSc *Leeds*, PhD *Leeds* Sr. Lectr.; Dir. of Studies
Cooper, Nigel, BSc *Keele*, PhD *Keele* Sr. Lectr.
Corfield, Douglas, BSc *Lond.*, PhD *Lond.* Reader
Duncan, Ruth, BSc *Liv.*, PhD *Keele* Visiting Prof.
Eggleston, Paul, BSc *Birm.*, PhD *Birm.* Prof.
Exley, Christopher, BA *Stir.*, PhD *Stir.* Reader
Fettiplace, Robert, BA *Camb.*, PhD *Camb.*, FRS Visiting Prof.
Foster, David H., PhD *Lond.*, DSc *Lond.*, FIP, FIMA Hon. Prof.
Furness, David N., BSc *Manc.*, PhD Reader
Greenhough, Trevor J., BSc *Nott.*, MSc *Sur.*, PhD *Sur.* Prof.
Hamilton, James, BSc *Wales*, MSc *Wales*, PhD *Virginia* Sr. Lectr.
Hoole, David, BSc *Leeds*, PhD *Sund.* Sr. Lectr.
Hurd, Hilary, BSc *Wales*, PhD *Keele* Prof.
Kirk, William, MA *Camb.*, PhD *Camb.*, FRES Sr. Lectr.
Loweth, Anne C., BSc *Keele*, PhD *Keele* Sr. Lectr.
Mills, John, BSc *Birm.*, PhD *Lond.* Sr. Lectr.; Head*
Moreland, Jack D., BSc *Lond.*, PhD *Lond.* Emer. Prof.
Thomas, Peter A., BSc *Exe.*, MSc *Aberd.*, PhD *New Br.* Sr. Lectr.
Ward, Richard D., BSc *Lond.*, MSc *Lond.*, PhD *Lond.* Prof.
Williams, Gwyn T., BSc *Warw.*, DPhil *Sus.* Prof.
Other Staff: 12 Lectrs.

Medicine, School of

Tel: (01782) 583937 Fax: (01782) 584637
Ashton, Brian, BSc DPhil Sr. Lectr.
Atherton, John C., BSc PhD Sr. Lectr.
Bartlam, Andrew S., MB ChB *Manc.*, FRCGP Sr. Lectr.
Bashford, C. Lindsay, BA *Oxf.*, MA *Oxf.*, DPhil *Oxf.* Reader
Clayton, Richard N., BSc *Lond.*, MB BS *Lond.*, MD *Birm.*, FRCP Prof.
Cooper, Vincent, MB ChB *Brist.* Sr. Lectr.
Cox, John L., BM BCh *Oxf.*, MA *Oxf.*, DM *Oxf.*, FRCPsych, FRCP, FRCPEd Emer. Prof.
Crome, Ilana, BA *Camb.*, MA *Camb.*, MB ChB *Birm.*, MD *Birm.*, MPhil *Lond.*, FRCP Prof.
Crome, Peter, MB BS *Lond.*, MD *Lond.*, PhD *Lond.*, FRCP, FRCPEd, FRCPGlas Prof.; Head, Postgrad. Med.
Davies, Simon J., BSc *Lond.*, MB BS *Lond.*, MD, FRCP Prof.
Deakin, Mark, MB ChB *Liv.*, ChM *Liv.*, FRCS Sr. Lectr.
Dziedzic, Krysia S. G., PhD *Keele* Sr. Lectr.
Elder, James B., MB ChB *Glas.*, MD *Glas.*, FRCS Emer. Prof.
Farrell, William, BSc *Liv.*, MSc *Manc.*, PhD *Manc.* Prof.
Ghodse, Abdon-Hamid, CBE, MD *Edin.*, PhD *Edin.*, FRCPEd, FRCPsych Visiting Prof.
Gray, Carol, BSc *Lond.*, MB BS Sr. Lectr.
Hassell, Andrew B., MB ChB *Manc.*, MD *Manc.* Sr. Lectr.
Hawkins, Clive, BM BS *Nott.*, DM *Nott.* Prof.
Hay, Elaine, MB ChB *Sheff.*, MD *Sheff.*, FRCP Prof.
Hays, Richard B., MB BS MD PhD, FRACGP Prof.; Head*
Henshaw, Carol A., MB ChB *Aberd.*, MD *Aberd.* Sr. Lectr.
Hill, Simon, MB BS *Newcastle(UK)*, FRCP Sr. Lectr.
Hoban, Paul R., BSc *Newcastle(UK)*, PhD *Newcastle(UK)*
Hodgson, Richard E., MB ChB *Liv.*, MSc *Liv.* Sr. Lectr.
Ismail, Khaled, MB BCh *Ain Shams*, MSc *Ain Shams*, MD *Ain Shams* Sr. Lectr.
Lefroy, Janet, MA *Camb.*, MB BS Sr. Lectr.
Liu, Isaac, PhD *Lond.*, BSc MSc Sr. Lectr.
Lovatt, Lisetta M., BSc *Lond.* Sr. Lectr.
Maffulli, Nicola, MS MD PhD Prof.
Mahon, Michael, BSc *Sheff.* Sr. Lectr.

Main, Christopher J., MA *Edin.*, MPhil *Edin.*, PhD *Glas.* Prof.
McCall, Ian W., MB ChB *Birm.*, FRCR Prof.
Melville, Colin A. S., MB ChB *Aberd.* Sr. Lectr.
Middleton, James F.S., BSc *Bath*, PhD *Lanc.* Reader
Naish, Patrick F., MB BS *Lond.*, FRCP Sr. Lectr.
Neal, Nicholas C., MB ChB *Birm.*, FRCSEd Sr. Lectr.
O'Brien, P. M. Shaughn, MB BCh *Wales*, MD *Wales*, FRCOG Prof.
O'Mahony, Fidelma, MB ChB Sr. Lectr.
Ong, Pauline B. N., BA *Nijmegen*, BEd *Nijmegen*, MA *Nijmegen*, PhD *Manc.* Prof.
Pantin, Charles F. A., MB BS *Lond.*, MSc *Camb.*, PhD *Camb.* Sr. Lectr.
Peat, George M., BSc *Edin.*, MSc *Edin.*, PhD *Manc.* Sr. Lectr.
Redmond, A. D., OBE, MB ChB MD, FRCP Emer. Prof.
Richardson, James B., MB ChB *Birm.*, MD *Birm.*, FRCSEd Prof.
Roberts, Sally, BSc PhD Reader
Roffe, Christine Sr. Lectr.
Samuels, Martin, BSc *Lond.*, MB BS *Lond.*, MD *Lond.* Sr. Lectr.
Semenov, Serguei, MS *Moscow*, PhD *Moscow*, DSc *Moscow* Prof.
Shammakhi, Nureddin, MB BCh *Libya*, PhD, FRCSEd Prof.
Smith, David, BA PhD DSc Hon. DSc, FIP, FRS Prof.
Smith, Ian, BSc *Lond.*, MB BS *Lond.*, FRCA Sr. Lectr.
Spanel, Patrick, RNDr *Prague*, PhD *Innsbruck* Hon. Prof.
Spencer, S. Andrew, BMedSci *Nott.*, BM BS *Nott.*, DM *Nott.*, FRCPCH Reader
Spiteri, Monica, PhD *Lond.* Prof.
Strange, Richard C., BSc *Lond.*, PhD *Lond.* Prof.
Templeton, John R., MB BCh BAO, FRCS Emer. Prof.
Thomas, Peter B. M., MB BS *Lond.*, FRCS, FRCSEd Sr. Lectr.
Walsh, Aideen K. M., MD *Leic.*, BSc MB BCh Sr. Lectr.
Williams, Val, MB ChB *Manc.*, FRCA Sr. Lectr.
Other Staff: 15 Lectrs.; 3 Sr. Clin. Lectrs.; 2 Clin. Lectrs.; 1 Hon. Reader; 4 Hon. Sr. Lectrs.; 2 Hon. Lectrs.
Research: genetic susceptibility to cancers; lung injury and inflammation; musculoskeletal pain; pituitary tumours; tumour suppressor genes

Medicines Management

Tel: (01782) 584133 Fax: (01782) 713586
Black, Patricia E., BSc *CNAA*, MBA *Aston*, MA *Open(UK)* Sr. Lectr.
Blenkinsopp, Alison, BPharm *Brad.*, PhD *Aston* Prof.; Dir., Educn. and Res.
Brennan, Mark, BSc *Leic.*, MA *Cardiff* Sr. Lectr.
Chapman, Stephen R., BSc *Liv.*, PhD *Lond.* Prof.; Dir., Prescribing Analysis; Head*
Curtis, Anthony D. M., BSc *Manc.*, PhD *Manc.* Sr. Lectr.
Frischer, Martin, BA *Strath.*, PhD *Edin.* Sr. Lectr.
Tan, Chick, MSc MRPharmS PhD Sr. Lectr.
Wells, Nicholas, BA *Leeds* Visiting Prof.
Other Staff: 4 Lectrs.; 2 Hon. Lectrs.; 20 Hon. Assoc. Lectrs.
Research: concordance; drug misuse; evaluation of healthcare developments; implementing evidence-based practice; pharmaco-epidemiology

Nursing and Midwifery, School of

Tel: (01782) 552948 Fax: (01782) 712941
Jester, Rebecca, BSc *Wolv.*, MPhil *Birm.*, PhD *Birm.* Reader
Maslin-Prothero, Sian, MSc *Brist.*, PhD *Nott.* Prof.
Priest, Helena, BA *Open(UK)*, MSc *Lond.*, PhD *Keele* Sr. Lectr.
Read, Susan C., MA *Keele* Sr. Lectr.
Roberts, Paula, MA *Open(UK)*, PhD *Keele* Sr. Lectr.

Traylor, Sarah E. A., BA *Staffs.*, MA *Warw.* Head, Pre-Registration Nursing Studies
Walsh, Pauline N., MA *Keele* Sr. Lectr.
Other Staff: 26 Lectrs.; 1 Hon. Sr. Clin. Lectr.
Research: acute and critical care; cancer and palliative care; educational evaluation; mental health

Physical and Geographical Sciences, School of

Earth Sciences and Geography

Tel: (01782) 583169 Fax: (01782) 715261
Burley, Stuart D., BSc *Hull*, PhD *Hull*, FGS Hon. Prof.
Collinson, John D., BA *Oxf.*, DPhil *Oxf.*, FGS Hon. Prof.
Egan, Stuart, BSc *Keele*, PhD *Keele*, FGS Sr. Lectr.
Fairchild, Ian J., BSc *Nott.*, PhD *Nott.*, FGS Visiting Prof.
Kelling, Gilbert, OBE, BSc *Edin.*, PhD *Edin.*, FGS Emer. Prof.
Knight, Peter G., BA *Oxf.*, PhD *Aberd.* Sr. Lectr.
Park, R. Graham, BSc *Glas.*, PhD *Glas.*, FGS Emer. Prof.
Phillips, Anthony D. M., BA *Lond.*, PhD *Lond.* Reader
Quilley, Stephen A., BA *Camb.*, MA *Manc.*, PhD *Manc.* Sr. Lectr.
Styles, Peter, BA *Oxf.*, PhD *Newcastle(UK)*, FRAS, FGS Prof.
Torrens, Hugh, BA *Oxf.*, PhD *Leic.*, FGS Emer. Prof.
Williams, Graham D., BSc *Leic.*, PhD *Wales*, FGS Prof.
Winchester, John A., MA *Oxf.*, DPhil *Oxf.*, FGS Prof.
Other Staff: 12 Lectrs.

Physics and Chemistry

Adam, Craig D., BSc *Edin.*, DPhil *Oxf.* Sr. Lectr.
Boehm, Fritz W., MD Hon. Prof.
Catlow, Richard, MA *Oxf.*, DPhil *Oxf.* Visiting Prof.
Davis, Nicola J., BSc *Birm.*, PhD *Birm.* Sr. Lectr.
Evans, Aneurin, BSc *Wales*, PhD *Wales*, FRAS Prof.
Fitch, Andrew N., BA *Oxf.*, DPhil *Oxf.* Visiting Prof.
Forsyth, Trevor V., BSc *Keele*, PhD *Keele* Prof.
Fuller, Watson, BSc *Lond.*, PhD *Lond.*, FIP Emer. Prof.
Hellier, Coel, BA *Oxf.*, PhD *Lond.* Reader
Hogarth, Cyril A., BSc *Lond.*, PhD *Lond.*, DSc *Lond.*, FIP, FRSA Visiting Prof.
Howell, James A. S., MSc *Vic.(BC)*, PhD *Camb.*, FRSChem Prof.
Jackson, Robert A., BSc *Lond.*, PhD *Lond.*, DSc *Lond.*, FRSChem Reader
Jeffries, Robin D., BSc *Birm.*, PhD *Birm.* Reader
Jones, Graeme R., BSc *Liv.*, PhD *Camb.* Sr. Lectr.
Jones, Gurnos, BSc *Sheff.*, PhD *Sheff.*, DSc *Keele*, FRSChem Emer. Prof.
Lainé, Derek C., BSc *S'ton.*, PhD *S'ton.*, DSc *S'ton.*, FIP, FIEE Emer. Prof., Molecular Physics
Mahendrasingam, Arumugam, BSc *S.Lanka*, PhD *Keele* Reader
McGarvey, David J., BSc *CNAA*, PhD *CNAA* Sr. Lectr.
Millar, Ian T., BSc *Lond.*, PhD *Camb.*, FRSChem Emer. Prof.
Morgan, E. David, BSc *Dal.*, MA *Oxf.*, DPhil *Oxf.*, FRSChem Emer. Prof.
Mortimer, Colin T., DSc *UMIST*, FRSChem Emer. Prof.
Plesch, Peter H., MA *Camb.*, PhD *Keele*, ScD *Camb.* Emer. Prof.
Ramsden, Christopher A., BSc *Sheff.*, PhD *Sheff.*, DSc *Sheff.*, FRSChem Prof., Organic Chemistry
Stirling, William G., BSc *Edin.*, PhD *Edin.*, FIP Hon. Prof.

Truscott, T. George, BSc Wales, PhD Wales, DSc Wales, FRSChem, FRSEd   Hon. Prof.

Wadhams, Lester J., BA Keele, PhD Keele, DSc Keele   Hon. Prof.

Williams, Edward W., BSc Nott., PhD Nott., FIP   Emer. Prof.

Wilson, Ian D., BSc UMIST, MSc UMIST, PhD Keele   Hon. Prof.

Zholobenko, Vladimir, MSc Moscow, PhD Moscow   Sr. Lectr.

Other Staff: 10 Lectrs.; 3 Fellows; 1 Hon. Lectr.

Politics, International Relations and the Environment, School of

Tel: (01782) 583452 Fax: (01782) 583592

Bailey, Christopher, MA Oxf., DPhil Oxf.   Prof.; Head*

Constantinou, Costas M., BSocSci Keele, MA Lanc., PhD Lanc.   Sr. Lectr.

Dobson, Andrew N. H., BA Reading, DPhil Oxf.   Prof.

Doherty, Brian J. A., BA Durh., MA Kent, PhD Manc.   Sr. Lectr.

D'Oro, Guiseppina, BA Essex, PhD Essex   Sr. Lectr.

Gokay, Bulent, PhD Camb., BA   Sr. Lectr.

Harrison, Martin, BA Manc., DPhil Oxf.   Emer. Prof.

Horton, John, MSc(Econ) Wales   Prof.

James, Alan M., BSc Lond.   Emer. Prof.

Ladrech, Robert, BA Calif., MA Calif., PhD Calif.   Sr. Lectr.

Lloyd, Lorna, BSc(Econ) Lond., PhD Lond.   Sr. Lectr.

Luther, Kurt R., BA CNAA, PhD CNAA   Sr. Lectr.

Newey, Glen, BA York(UK), MA Camb., DPhil York(UK)   Prof.

O'Kane, Rosemary H. T., BA Essex, MA Essex, PhD Lanc.   Prof.

Porritt, Jonathon, MA Oxf.   Hon. Prof.

Proops, John L. R., BA Keele, PhD Keele   Emer. Prof.

Quilley, Stephen A., BA Camb., MA Manc., PhD Manc.   Sr. Lectr.

Rogers, G. A. John, BA Nott., PhD Keele   Emer. Prof.

Thornberry, Patrick, LLB CNAA, LLM Keele, PhD Keele   Prof.

Vogler, John F., BA Reading, MSc Lond., PhD Lond.   Prof.

Walker, Robert B. J., BA Wales(Swansea), MA Qu., PhD Qu.   Prof.

Waller, D. Michael, BA Manc., MA Oxf.   Emer. Prof.

Wyman, Matthew D., BA Oxf., MSocSc Birm., PhD Birm.   Sr. Lectr.

Other Staff: 15 Lectrs.; 2 Fellows

Psychology, School of

Tel: (01782) 583380 Fax: (01782) 583387

Edelstyn, Nicola, BSc Keele, PhD Keele   Sr. Lectr.

Hartley, James, BA Sheff., PhD Sheff.   Hon. Prof.

Hegarty, John R., BA Nott., PhD Keele   Sr. Lectr.

Hunter, Ian M. L., BSc Edin., DPhil Oxf.   Emer. Prof.

Hutt, S. John, BA Manc., MA Oxf.   Emer. Prof.

Lamont, Alexandra M., BA Camb., MA City(UK), PhD Camb.   Sr. Lectr.

Murray, Michael, BSc Ulster, PhD Stir.   Prof.

Robson, Margaret, BA Open(UK), MA Durh., PhD Durh.   Sr. Lectr.

Rotenberg, Kenneth J., MA Guelph, PhD   Prof.

Sloboda, John A., MA Oxf., PhD Lond., FBPsS   Prof.

Trueman, Mark, BA Keele, MA Keele, PhD Keele   Sr. Lectr.; Head*

Wearden, John, BSc Manc., DSc Manc.   Prof.

Other Staff: 11 Lectrs.; 1 Fellow; 2 Teaching Fellows; 1 Hon. Lectr.

SPECIAL CENTRES, ETC

Continuing and Professional Education

Tel: (01782) 583436 Fax: (01782) 583248

Whittaker, Marian, BA Keele, PhD Keele   Programme Manager

Environment, Physical Sciences and Applied Mathematics, Institute of the

Tel: (01782) 584439
E-mail: s.p.courtholds@keele.ac.uk

Styles, Peter, BA Oxf., PhD Newcastle(UK), FRAS, FGS   Prof.; Dir.*

Other Staff: 3 Res. Fellows

Research: astrophysics; environmental and sustainable chemistry; green chemistry; utilisation of biomass and renewable feedstocks; waste management

Humanities, Institute of

Tel: (01782) 583200
E-mail: j.street@his.keele.ac.uk

Amigoni, David, BA Wales, MA Keele, PhD CNAA   Prof.; Dir.*

Other Staff: 2 Res. Fellows

Research: American studies: literature and history; English literature; history; musicology, composition and music technology; Russian literature and culture

Law, Politics and Justice, Institute of

Tel: (01782) 583245
E-mail: ri_office@ilpj.keele.ac.uk

Godfrey, Barry, BA Liv., MA Leeds, PhD Leic.   Dir.*

Research: criminology; law, ethics and society; politics and international studies

Life Course Studies, Institute of

Tel: (01782) 584568
E-mail: s.e.humphries@humss.keele.ac.uk

Bernard, Miriam, BA Keele, PhD Keele   Prof.; Dir.*

Other Staff: 2 Res. Fellows

Research: cognition and cognitive development psychology; gender and ageing; music psychology; social inclusion and exclusion, participation and citizenship; social theory and social policy of ageing

Primary Care and Health Sciences, Institute of

Tel: (01782) 584722
E-mail: c.ashmore@cphc.keele.ac.uk

Croft, Peter, BA Camb., MB ChB Birm., MSc Lond., MD Birm.   Prof.; Dir.*

Other Staff: 4 Res. Fellows

Research: back pain; chronic widespread pain; joint pain in older people; methodological expertise; population and clinical epidemiology

Public Policy and Management, Institute for

Tel: (01782) 584577
E-mail: t.wood@ippm.keele.ac.uk

Cropper, Stephen A., BSc Dund., PhD Wales   Prof.; Dir.*

Research: culture, organisation and markets; economics; education policy and institutional cultures; health planning and management; industrial relations

Science and Technology in Medicine, Institute of

Tel: (01782) 555234
El-Haj, Alicia, BSc Hull, MSc Manc., PhD Aberd.   Prof.; Dir.*

Other Staff: 9 Res. Fellows

Research: applied entomology and parasitology; cell and tissue engineering; human disease and genomics; medical imaging, diagnostics and assessment; neurosciences

CONTACT OFFICERS

Academic affairs. Director, Academic Registry: Howells, Allan, BSc Wales, PhD Wales
(E-mail: a.howells@acad.keele.ac.uk)

Accommodation. Accommodation Services Manager: Bradshaw, Rosemarie
(E-mail: r.bradshaw@kfm.keele.ac.uk)

Admissions (first degree). Academic Registrar: Thorley, Helena A., BA Oxf., MA Oxf. (E-mail: h.a.thorley@acad.keele.ac.uk)

Admissions (higher degree). Head of Graduate School: MacLeod, Marie, BD St And. (E-mail: m.macleod@acad.keele.ac.uk)

Alumni. Alumni Co-ordinator: Wain, Christopher M., MA Oxf., MA Sheff.
(E-mail: c.m.wain@uso.keele.ac.uk)

Archives. Head of Digitisation Services: Williams, Allan R.
(E-mail: a.r.williams@lib.keele.ac.uk)

Careers. Head of Careers Service: Whittaker, Marian, BA Keele, PhD Keele
(E-mail: m.whittaker@cpe.keele.ac.uk)

Computing services. Director of Finance and Information Technology: Clarke, Karen, MA Oxf. (E-mail: k.j.clarke@fin.keele.ac.uk)

Conferences/corporate hospitality. Head of Facilities Management: Tucker, Jennifer A., BSc DBA (E-mail: j.tucker@kfm.keele.ac.uk)

Equal opportunities. Director of Human Resources and Student Support: Doran, Judith M., BA Leeds
(E-mail: j.m.doran@per.keele.ac.uk)

Estates and buildings/works and services. Head of Estates: Leech, Michael G.
(E-mail: m.g.leech@est.keele.ac.uk)

Examinations. Examinations Officer: Bromage, Kathleen L.
(E-mail: k.l.bromage@acad.keele.ac.uk)

Finance. Director of Finance and Information Technology: Clarke, Karen, MA Oxf.
(E-mail: k.clarke@fin.keele.ac.uk)

Health services. Medical Officer: O'Byrne, Evan, MB BCh BAO N.U.I.

Health services. Occupational Health Nurse: Gaskell, Cathy, BA Salf.
(E-mail: c.gaskell@per.keele.ac.uk)

Industrial liaison. Industrial Liaison Manager: Gallagher, Rosalind, MSc
(E-mail: r.gallagher@uso.keele.ac.uk)

International office. Head of Postgraduate Division: Coleman, Gillian, BA Keele
(E-mail: g.coleman@acad.keele.ac.uk)

International office. (Overseas Students) Head of Undergraduate Division: Moulton, Angela J., BA Wales
(E-mail: a.j.moulton@acad.keele.ac.uk)

Library (chief librarian). Director of Information Services: Reynolds, Paul R., BA Lanc., MA Manc.Met.
(E-mail: p.r.reynolds@lib.keele.ac.uk)

Marketing. Head of Marketing: Williams, Phillip, BA Leeds, MA Leeds
(E-mail: p.williams@kfm.keele.ac.uk)

Minorities/disadvantaged groups. Equality and Diversity Manager: Brown, Richard
(E-mail: r.w.brown@per.keele.ac.uk)

Personnel/human resources. Head of Human Resources: Capewell, Jane D.
(E-mail: j.d.capewell@per.keele.ac.uk)

Public relations. Head of External Relations: Gallagher, Rosalind, MSc
(E-mail: r.gallagher@uso.keele.ac.uk)

Publications. (General) Head of External Relations: Gallagher, Rosalind, MSc
(E-mail: r.gallagher@uso.keele.ac.uk)

Publications. (Prospectuses) Head of Undergraduate Division: Thorley, Helena A., BA Oxf., MA Oxf.
(E-mail: h.a.thorley@acad.keele.ac.uk)

Purchasing. Procurement Manager: Sutton, Linda (E-mail: l.sutton@fin.keele.ac.uk)

Quality assurance and accreditation. Director (Quality assurance and accreditation): Pike, Christopher R., MA Edin.
(E-mail: c.r.pike@acad.keele.ac.uk)

Research. Pro Vice-Chancellor (Research): Jones, Prof. Peter W., BSc Reading, MSc Reading, PhD Wales
(E-mail: p.w.jones@vco.keele.ac.uk)

Safety. Safety Advisor: Rosiek, Clive W., BSc Wales (E-mail: c.w.rosiek@uso.keele.ac.uk)

Scholarships, awards, loans. Director, Academic Registry: Howells, Allan, BSc *Wales*, PhD *Wales*
(E-mail: a.howells@acad.keele.ac.uk)
Schools liaison. Head of Widening Participation: Cross, Kylie
(E-mail: k.cross@acad.keele.ac.uk)
Schools liaison. Head of Undergraduate Recruitment: Firth, Amanda L.
(E-mail: a.l.firth@acad.keele.ac.uk)
Security. Security Officer: Brayford, Ray
(E-mail: r.brayford@kfm.keele.ac.uk)

Sport and recreation. Leisure Centre Manager: Dale, Angela J.
(E-mail: a.j.dale@kfm.keele.ac.uk)
Staff development and training. Head, Staff Training and Development: Mountford, Carol, BA *Wales*, MS *Leeds*
(E-mail: c.mountford@per.keele.ac.uk)
Strategic planning. Director, Planning Support Unit: Chilton, Andrea
(E-mail: a.chilton@vco.keele.ac.uk)
Student union. General Manager: McCormack, Martyn, BSc *Brun.*
(E-mail: m.j.mccormack@kusu.keele.ac.uk)

Student welfare/counselling. Student Support Officer: Ronald, Bernadette
(E-mail: i.ronald@acad.keele.ac.uk)
Students with disabilities. Disability Services Manager: Whittaker, Marian, BA *Keele*, PhD *Keele* (E-mail: m.whittaker@acad.keele.ac.uk)
Women. Director of Human Resources and Student Support: Doran, Judith M., BA *Leeds*
(E-mail: j.m.doran@per.keele.ac.uk)

[Information supplied by the institution as at 12 October 2007, and edited by the ACU]

UNIVERSITY OF KENT

Founded 1965

Member of the Association of Commonwealth Universities

Postal Address: Canterbury, Kent, England CT2 7NZ
Telephone: (01227) 764000
URL: http://www.kent.ac.uk

VICE-CHANCELLOR*—Goodfellow, Prof. Julia M., CBE, BSc *Brist.*, PhD *Open(UK)*, FMedSci, FIBiol, FIP, FRSA
PRO-VICE-CHANCELLOR—Davies, Prof. Phillip A., BSc *Kent*, PhD *Kent*
PRO-VICE-CHANCELLOR—Nightingale, David R., MA *Oxf.*
PRO-VICE-CHANCELLOR—Mander, Prof. Keith C., BSc *Nott.*, PhD *Nott.*
PRO-VICE-CHANCELLOR—Baker, Robin, BA *Lond.*, PhD *E.Anglia*
TREASURER—Marshall, Valerie, MA *Camb.*, MSc *Lond.*

GENERAL INFORMATION

History. The university was founded in 1965. The main campus is situated on the outskirts of Canterbury. Other bases are in Chatham, Tonbridge and Brussels.

Admission to first degree courses (see also United Kingdom Introduction). Through Universities and Colleges Admissions Service (UCAS). Normal entry requirements: 3 A levels, or equivalent qualifications.

First Degrees (see also United Kingdom Directory to Subjects of Study). BA, BBA, BEng, BSc, LLB, MChem, MDram, MPharm, MPhys.
Most courses are full-time and last at least 3 years. Sandwich courses, courses with a year abroad or foundation year: 4 years.
Length of course. Full-time: BA, BBA, BEng, BSc, LLB: 3 years; MChem, MDram, MPharm, MPhys: 4 years. Part-time: BA, BBA, BSc, LLB: max. 6 years.

Higher Degrees (see also United Kingdom Directory to Subjects of Study).
Master's. LLM, MA, MBA, MClinSci, MPhil, MRes, MSc, MSurg.
Admission. Applicants should normally hold an appropriate first or second class honours degree.
Length of course. Full-time: LLM, MA, MBA, MRes, MSc, MSurg: 1 year; MPhil: 2 years. Part-time: LLM, MA, MBA, MRes, MSc, MSurg: 2 years; MPhil: 3 years; MClinSci: 3–4 years.
Doctoral. DClinSci, MD, PhD.
Length of course. Full-time: PhD: 3 years. Part-time: MD: 2–5 years; PhD: 4 years; DClinSci: 5–6 years.

Language of Instruction. English, except for language courses (French, German, Italian and Spanish), where classes may be taught in the relevant language.

Libraries. 1,000,000 books, periodicals, pamphlets, slides and microforms. Special collections: Melville, Pettingell, Reading Rayner, playbills (drama); Weatherill papers

(parliamentary practices and procedures); Crow collection (ballad and song, bibliography, English Renaissance, proverbs and language); Maddison (seventeenth- to nineteenth-century science and technology); Farquharson (Greek and Roman classics 1800–1939); Lloyd George (part of his private library); Kent local history; modern first editions; modern poetry.

FACULTIES/SCHOOLS
Humanities
Tel: (01227) 823918 Fax: (01227) 827134
E-mail: humanities-dean@kent.ac.uk
Dean: Turley, Prof. David M., MA *Camb.*, PhD *Camb.*

Science, Technology and Medical Studies
E-mail: u.d.fuller@kent.ac.uk
Dean: Fuller, Ursula, MA *Camb.*, MA *Kent*

Social Sciences
Tel: (01227) 823655 Fax: (01227) 823959
E-mail: ssdean@kent.ac.uk
Dean: Baldock, Prof. John C., BA *Oxf.*, MA *Kent*

ACADEMIC UNITS
Anthropology
Fax: (01227) 827289
E-mail: anthro-office@kent.ac.uk
Bodmer, Richard, PhD   Reader, Conservation Ecology
Corbin, John, BA *Lond.*, PhD *Lond.*   Sr. Lectr.
Ellen, Roy F., BSc *Lond.*, PhD *Lond.*   Prof., Anthropology and Human Ecology
Fischer, Michael D., MA *Texas*, PhD *Texas*   Reader
Griffiths, Richard, BSc *Lond.*, PhD *Lond.*   Reader, Biological Conservation
Harrop, Stuart, LLB *Leeds*   Prof., Wildlife Management Law
Just, Roger   Prof., Social Anthropology; Head*
Leader-Williams, Nigel, BVSc *Liv.*, PhD *Camb.*   Prof., Biodiversity Management
Walkey, Michael, BSc *Durh.*, PhD *Durh.*   Sr. Lectr.
Watson, Bill, BA *Brist.*, MA *Hull*, PhD *Camb.*   Prof.

Zeitlyn, David, BA *Oxf.*, PhD *Camb.*   Reader, Social Anthropology
Other Staff: 9 Lectrs.; 1 Lectr.†
Research: biodiversity management; biological anthropology; environmental anthropology; social anthropology; sustainable development

Durrell Institute of Conservation and Ecology
Bodmer, Richard, PhD   Reader
Griffiths, Richard, BSc *Lond.*, PhD *Lond.*   Reader
Harrop, Stuart, LLB *Leeds*   Prof., Wildlife Management Law
Leader-Williams, Nigel, BVSc *Liv.*, PhD *Camb.*   Prof., Biodiversity Management; Head*
Other Staff: 1 Lectr.

Biosciences
Tel: (01227) 823743 Fax: (01227) 763912
Baines, Anthony J., BSc *Lond.*, PhD *Lond.*   Reader, Molecular Cell Biology
Blomfield, Ian   Sr. Lectr., Molecular Microbiology
Blower, Philip, BA *Camb.*, DPhil *Sus.*   Sr. Lectr., Radiochemistry
Bruce, Ian   Prof., Nanobiotechnology
Geeves, Michael A., BSc *Birm.*, PhD *Brist.*, DSc *Brist.*   Prof., Physical Biochemistry
Griffin, Darren, PhD   Reader, Genetics
Gullick, William   Prof., Cancer Biology
Jeffries, Peter, BSc *Lond.*, PhD *Lond.*   Prof., Microbiology; Head*
Muhlschlegel, Fritz, PhD   Reader, Medical Microbiology
Nicholls, Peter J., BSc *S'ton.*, PhD *Lond.*   Sr. Lectr., Molecular and Cellular Biology
Robinson, Gary, PhD   Sr. Lectr., Microbial Biotechnology
Tuite, Michael F., BSc *Lond.*, DPhil *Oxf.*   Prof., Molecular Biology
Other Staff: 13 Lectrs.; 2 Lectrs.†
Research: cancer; cell biology and development; infectious disease; protein science

Computing Laboratory
Fax: (01227) 762811
Boiten, Eerke, MSc *T.H.Twente*, PhD *Nijmegen*   Sr. Lectr.

Bowman, Howard, BSc Lanc., PhD Lanc.
Reader, Cognition and Logic
Chadwick, David   Prof., Computer Science
Eager, Bob D., BSc Essex, MSc Essex   Sr. Lectr.
Hanna, F. Keith, BSc Brist., PhD Camb.   Reader,
Formal Design Methods
Hopkins, Tim, BSc S'ton., PhD Liv.   Reader,
Numerical Computing
Jones, Richard E., MA Oxf., MSc   Sr. Lectr.
Kemp, Zarine P., BCom Bom., BSc(Econ) Lond.
Sr. Lectr.
King, Andrew M., BSc Bath, PhD S'ton.   Sr.
Lectr.
Kolling, Michael P., PhD   Sr. Lectr.
Linington, Peter F., MA Camb., PhD Camb.
Prof., Computer Communication
Mander, Keith C., BSc Nott., PhD Nott.   Prof.,
Computer Science
Marshall, Ian   Prof., Distributed Systems
Roberts, Jonathan   Sr. Lectr.
Slater, John, MA Oxf., DPhil Oxf., FIMA, FBCS
Emer. Prof., Computing
Spratt, Brian, BSc Nott., PhD Durh., FIMA
Emer. Prof., Computing
Sutton, Roger   Sr. Lectr.
Thompson, Simon J., MA Camb., DPhil Oxf.
Prof., Logic and Computation; Head*
Timmis, Jonathan, PhD   Sr. Lectr.
Utting, Ian, BSc Kent   Sr. Lectr.
Waters, Gill, BSc Brist., PhD Essex   Sr. Lectr.
Welch, Peter H., BSc Warw., PhD Warw.   Prof.,
Parallel Computing
Other Staff: 28 Lectrs.; 7 Res. Assocs.
Research: applied and interdisciplinary
informatics; cognitive systems; information
systems security; pervasive computing;
theoretical computer science

Drama, Film and Visual Arts, School of

Fax: (01227) 827846
Davis, Jill, BA Hull   Prof.; Head*

Art, History and Philosophy of

Tel: (01227) 827228
Clarke, Graham, MA Essex, PhD Essex   Reader
Friday, Jonathan   Sr. Lectr.
Reason, David A., BA Essex   Sr. Lectr.; Head*
Other Staff: 4 Lectrs.
Research: contemporary aesthetics and the
history of art theory; historical interplay of
image, theory and institutions; the
photograph

Drama and Theatre Studies

Tel: (01227) 827567 Fax: (01227) 827464
E-mail: dramasecs@kent.ac.uk
Allain, Paul, PhD   Prof., Theatre Performance
Baugh, Christopher, BA Manc., MA Manc.
Prof., Drama
Davis, Jill, BA Hull   Prof., Drama
Grantley, Darryll, BA Lond., BA Witw., PhD Lond.
Sr. Lectr.
Shaughnessy, Robert   Prof., Theatre
Other Staff: 9 Lectrs.; 1 Res. Fellow
Research: British theatre history; investigations of
performance; place/space of performance;
radio drama and radio acting

Film Studies

Tel: (01227) 823177
Cowie, Elizabeth J., BA S'ton.   Reader
Grant, Katie, PhD   Sr. Lectr.; Head*
Smith, Murray, BA Liv., MA Wis., PhD Wis.
Prof.
Stanfield, Peter   Sr. Lectr.
Other Staff: 6 Lectrs.

Economics

Fax: (01227) 827850
E-mail: econ-enquiries@kent.ac.uk
Carruth, Alan A., BA Stir., MA Warw., MSc
Strath., PhD Warw.   Prof.; Head*
Green, Francis, BA Oxf., MSc Lond., PhD Lond.
Prof.
Krolzig, Hans-Martin   Prof.
Leon-Ledesma, Miguel   Sr. Lectr.
Peirson, John, BA Camb., PhD S'ton.   Sr. Lectr.

Thirlwall, Anthony P., BA Leeds, MA Clark, PhD
Leeds   Prof., Applied Economics
Vickerman, Roger W., MA Camb., DPhil Sus.
Jean Monnet Prof., European Economics
Other Staff: 8 Lectrs.
Research: European economics including
migration; international trade and finance;
labour economics and applied
microeconomics; macroeconomics, money,
finance and development; regional and
transport economics

Electronics

Fax: (01227) 456084
E-mail: electronics@kent.ac.uk
Ashworth, David G., BSc Manc., PhD Manc.,
FRAS   Reader, Solid State Electronics
Davies, Phillip A., BSc Kent, PhD Kent   Prof.,
Optical Communications
Deravi, Farzin, PhD   Reader, Information
Engineering
Fairhurst, Michael C., BSc PhD   Prof.,
Computer Vision; Head*
Gomes, Nathan, BSc Sus., PhD Lond.   Sr. Lectr.
Jastrzebski, A. K., MSc Warsaw   Reader,
Electronic Engineering
Kelly, Stephen, MSc Kent   Sr. Lectr.
Langley, Richard, BSc Kent, PhD Kent   Prof.,
Antenna Systems
Lee, Peter, BSc Sus.   Sr. Lectr.
Pepper, M. G., BSc PhD   Sr. Lectr.
Walczowski, L. T., BSc Lond., PhD   Sr. Lectr.
Waller, W. A. J., BSc Sur., MSc   Sr. Lectr.
Other Staff: 16 Lectrs.; 18 Res. Assocs.
Research: broadband and wireless
communication; embedded systems and
instrumentation; image processing and
vision

English, School of

Tel: (01227) 823054 Fax: (01227) 827001
E-mail: english@kent.ac.uk
Andrews, Malcolm Y., MA Camb., PhD Lond.
Prof., Victorian and Visual Studies
Ayers, David, BA Lond., PhD S'ton.   Sr. Lectr.
Brown, Peter, BA Sus., DPhil York(UK)   Prof.,
Mediaeval English Literature
Claridge, G. Henry, BA Warw., MA Ill.   Sr.
Lectr.
Edmond, Rod S., BA Well., BPhil Oxf.   Prof.,
Modern Literature and Cultural History
Ellis, David G., MA Camb., PhD Camb.   Emer.
Prof.
Gurnah, Abdulrazak, BEd Lond., PhD Kent
Prof., English and Postcolonial Literature;
Head*
Hallet, Nicky A., PhD   Sr. Lectr.
Herd, David, PhD   Sr. Lectr.
Hutchinson, Stuart, MA Leeds   Sr. Lectr.
Irwin, Michael, BA Oxf., BLitt Oxf.   Emer.
Prof., English Literature
Montefiore, Janet, BA Oxf., BPhil Oxf., PhD Kent
Reader, English and American Literature
O'Connor, Marion F., BA Tor., MPhil Lond., PhD
Lond.   Sr. Lectr.
Rooney, Caroline, DPhil Oxf.   Sr. Lectr.
Scofield, Martin P., BA Oxf., BPhil Oxf.   Sr.
Lectr.
Other Staff: 10 Lectrs.; 1 Hon. Sr. Res. Fellow

European Culture and Languages, School of

Tel: (01227) 823638 Fax: (01227) 823641
E-mail: secl-contact@kent.ac.uk

Classical and Archaeological Studies

Anderson, Graham, MA Glas., MPhil N.U.I.,
DPhil Oxf.   Prof., Classics; Head*
Keaveney, Arthur, MA N.U.I., PhD Hull   Sr.
Lectr., Classical Studies
Ward, Anthony, MA Camb., PhD Nott.   Sr.
Lectr., Archaeology
Other Staff: 7 Lectrs.
Research: archaeology of Britain, northwest
Europe and the Aegean; classical history
and literature

French

Tel: (01227) 824099
E-mail: d.peretti@kent.ac.uk
Robinson, Philip E. J., BA Wales, PhD Wales
Prof.; Head of Sch.*
Williams, James S., BA Lond., PhD Lond.   Sr.
Lectr.
Other Staff: 3 Lectrs.
Research: European studies, film studies,
comparative literary studies; language,
literature and culture; seventeenth-century
to present day French

German

Tel: (01227) 823638
E-mail: n.temple@kent.ac.uk
Durrani, Osman, MA Oxf., DPhil Oxf.   Prof.;
Head*
Preece, Julian, BA Oxf., DPhil Oxf.   Sr. Lectr.
Other Staff: 2 Lectrs
Research: eighteenth- and twentieth-century
literature and culture; German syntax,
pragmatics and sociolinguistics

Italian

Tel: (01227) 824099
E-mail: d.peretti@kent.ac.uk
Behan, Tom, BA Reading, PhD Reading   Sr. Lectr.
Schachter, Elizabeth, BA Leeds   Sr. Lectr.
Other Staff: 2 Lectrs.
Research: cultural politics; early nineteenth-
century to present in national and regional
contexts; interrelation between literature
and other cultural forms; organised crime
and labour history

Philosophy

Tel: (01227) 827785
E-mail: a.priest@kent.ac.uk
Harcourt, Edward, PhD   Sr. Lectr.
Sayers, Sean P., MA Camb., PhD Kent   Prof.
Tanney, Julia, BA Calif., MA Mich., PhD Mich.
Sr. Lectr.
Thomas, Alan, PhD   Sr. Lectr.; Head*
Other Staff: 2 Lectrs.

Religious Studies

Tel: (01227) 827785
E-mail: a.priest@kent.ac.uk
Gill, Robin, BD Lond., MSocSc Birm., PhD Lond.
Michael Ramsey Prof., Modern Theology;
Head*
Other Staff: 5 Lectrs.
Research: applied theology; cosmology and
divination; mysticism and religious
experience

Spanish

Tel: (01227) 823638
E-mail: n.temple@kent.ac.uk
4 Lectrs.
Research: Catalan studies; Latin America; the
avant-garde; twentieth-century theatre,
poetry and narrative

History

Fax: (01227) 827258
Connelly, Mark, PhD   Reader, Media History;
Head*
Ditchfield, Grayson M., BA Durh., PhD Camb.,
FRHistS   Reader, Eighteenth-Century
History
Fincham, Kenneth C., BA Oxf., PhD Lond.
Reader, Seventeenth-Century English
History
Gameson, Richard, MA Oxf., DPhil Oxf.
Reader, Mediaeval History
Ormrod, David, BSc(Econ) Lond., PhD Camb.,
FRHistS   Reader, Economic and Social
History
Potter, David L., BA Durh., PhD Camb.   Sr.
Lectr.
Smith, Crosbie, MA Camb., PhD Camb.   Prof.,
History of Science
Turley, David M., MA Camb., PhD Camb.
Prof., Cultural and Social History

Welch, David A., BA *Wales*, PhD *Lond.*   Prof.,
Modern European History
Other Staff: 8 Lectrs.
Research: history of science; mediaeval and
Tudor studies/early modern history;
modern history

Kent Business School

Tel: (01227) 827726 Fax: (01227) 761187

Bevan, John M., MA *Oxf.*   Sr. Lectr., Operation
Research
Crompton, Gerald, MA *Camb.*   Sr. Lectr.,
Economic and Social History
Fuller, Michael F., MA *Camb.*   Sr. Lectr.,
Econometrics and Social Statistics
Gilman, Mark, PhD   Sr. Lectr., Industrial
Relations and Human Resource
Management
Hampton, Mark, PhD   Sr. Lectr., Tourism
Management
Jones, Martyn   Head*
Liu, Wenbin, MSc *Wuhan*, PhD *Leeds*, BSc
Prof., Management Science and
Computational Mathematics
Mar Molinero, Cecilio   Prof., Management
Science
Mingers, John   Prof.
Phillips, Paul   Prof.
Rutherford, Brian A., BA *Exe.*, PhD   Prof.,
Accounting
Scase, Richard, BA *Leic.*, MA *Leic.*, PhD *Kent*
Prof., Organisational Behaviour
Sharp, John A., MA *Camb.*, PhD *Brad.*   Prof.,
Management
Other Staff: 35 Lectrs.; 2 Sr. Teaching Fellows
Research: accounting and finance; human
resource management, industrial relations
and organisational behaviour; management
science; strategy, operations and marketing

Kent Law School

Tel: (01227) 827636 Fax: (01227) 827831
E-mail: kls-office@kent.ac.uk

Arai, Yutaka   Sr. Lectr.
Bottomley, Anne, BA *Sus.*, LLM *Lond.*, MPhil
Camb.   Sr. Lectr.
Carr, Indira, PhD   Reader, International
Commercial Law
Conaghan, Joanne A. F., BA *Oxf.*, BCL *Oxf.*
Prof.
Cooper, Davina   Prof.
Drakopoulou, Maria, LLB *Athens*, MA *Sus.*   Sr.
Lectr.
Fitzpatrick, John F., BA *Oxf.*   Sr. Lectr.
Herman, Didi   Prof.
Howarth, William, BA *Keele*, LLM *Wales*   Prof.,
Environmental Law
Ireland, Paddy W., BA *Kent*   Prof.
Jackson, Nick, LLB *Camb.*, MA *Camb.*   Sr. Lectr.
Mansell, Wade, BA *Well.*, LLM *Well.*   Sr. Lectr.
McGillivray, Donald, LLB *Aberd.*, MA *Sheff.*   Sr.
Lectr.
Millns, Susan   Sr. Lectr.
Muchlinski, Peter   Prof., Law and International
Business
Rubin, Gerry R., LLB *Glas.*, MA *Sus.*, PhD *Warw.*
Prof.
Ryan, Bernard, BCL *N.U.I.*   Sr. Lectr.
Samuel, Geoffrey, MA *Camb.*, LLB *Camb.*, PhD
Camb.   Prof.
Slaughter, Marty, BA *Wis.*, MA *Wis.*, PhD *Wis.*,
JD *Calif.*   Reader
Uglow, Steve P., BA *Oxf.*, BCL *Oxf.*   Prof.,
Criminal Justice
Wightman, John, MA *Camb.*, LLB *Camb.*   Sr.
Lectr.; Head*
Other Staff: 19 Lectrs.; 1 Sr. Visiting Fellow; 2
Teachers†
Research: criminal justice; environmental law;
European Union and European comparative
law; gender, sexuality and law; public
international law, international commercial
and economic law

Mathematics, Statistics and Actuarial Science, Institute of

Tel: (01227) 827181 Fax: (01227) 827932
E-mail: imssecs@kent.ac.uk

Actuarial Science

Brown, Malcolm S.   Prof.
Other Staff: 5 Lectrs.

Mathematics

Chisholm, J. Roy S., BA *Oxf.*, MA *Oxf.*, DPhil
Oxf.   Emer. Prof., Applied Mathematics
Clarkson, Peter A., BA *Oxf.*, MA *Oxf.*, DPhil *Oxf.*
Prof.
Common, Alan K., BSc *Lond.*, PhD *Lond.*, FIP
Emer. Prof., Applied Mathematics
Fleischmann, Peter, PhD *Essen*   Prof., Pure
Mathematics; Head of Inst.*
Mansfield, Elizabeth, BSc *Syd.*, MSc *Syd.*, PhD
Syd.   Reader
Shank, R. James, PhD   Sr. Lectr.
Sutcliffe, Paul M., BSc *Durh.*, PhD *Durh.*   Prof.,
Mathematical Physics
Woodcock, Chris F., MA *Oxf.*, DPhil *Oxf.*   Sr.
Lectr.
Other Staff: 4 Lectrs.
Research: computational and applied algebra;
discrete mathematics; representation theory
and invariant theory of finite groups;
symmetries, solitons and integrable systems

Statistics

Bassett, Eryl E., BA *Oxf.*, MSc *Wales*, PhD *Wales*
Sr. Lectr.
Brown, Philip J., BSc *Leic.*, MSc *Wales*, PhD *Lond.*
Pfizer Prof., Medical Statistics
Morgan, Byron J. T., BSc *Lond.*, PhD *Camb.*
Prof., Applied Statistics
Preece, Donald A., MA *St And.*, PhD, FIMA
Hon. Prof., Combinatorial Mathematics
Ridout, Martin S.   Reader
Walker, Stephen   Prof.
Other Staff: 7 Lectrs.
Research: Bayesian statistics; bioinformatics and
medical statistics; biometry and ecological
statistics; nonparametric statistics

Medicine and Health Sciences, Kent Institute of

Tel: (01227) 827312 Fax: (01227) 824054
E-mail: kimhs-enquiries@kent.ac.uk

Aw, Tar-Ching   Prof., Occupational Medicine
Bonner, Adrian   Sr. Lectr., Addictive
Behaviours
Colchester, Alan, BA BM BCh PhD, FRCP
Prof., Clinical Neuroscience and Medical
Image Computing
Hale, Anthony S., BSc *Lond.*, MB BS *Lond.*, PhD
Lond.   Prof., General Psychiatry
James, Roger   Prof., Oncology
Katona, Cornelius   Prof.; Head*
Other Staff: 9 Lectrs.
Research: addictive behaviours; neurosciences
and medical image computing;
occupational health; oncology;
psychotherapy

Physical Sciences, School of

Tel: (01227) 823759 Fax: (01227) 827558
Burchell, Mark   Head*
Other Staff: 12 Res. Assocs.

Chemistry

Tel: (01227) 462594 Fax: (01227) 827724
Benfield, Prof. Robert, MA *Camb.*, PhD *Camb.*
Sr. Lectr., Inorganic Chemistry
Boyle, Laurence, PhD   Sr. Lectr.
Chadwick, Alan V., BSc *Manc.*, PhD *Manc.*
Prof., Physical Chemistry
Holder, Simon   Sr. Lectr., Organic Chemistry
Jones, Richard G., MSc *NZ*, PhD *Leeds*, FRSChem
Emer. Prof., Polymer Science
Todd, John F. J., BSc *Leeds*, PhD *Leeds*, FRSChem
Emer. Prof., Mass Spectroscopy
Went, Michael J., BSc *Brist.*, PhD *Brist.*   Reader,
Inorganic Chemistry
Other Staff: 3 Lectrs.
Research: materials

Physics

Fax: (01227) 827558
Burchell, Mark   Reader, Space Sciences
Dore, John C., BSc *Birm.*, PhD *Birm.*   Emer.
Prof., Condensed Matter Physics
Newport, Robert J., BSc *Leic.*, PhD *Leic.*   Head,
Functional Materials Group; Prof., Materials
Physics
Podoleanu, Adrian, MEng *T.U.Bucharest*, PhD
T.U.Bucharest   Prof., Biomedical Optics
Solomon, Chris, BSc *Durh.*, PhD *Lond.*   Sr.
Lectr.
Strange, John H., BSc *Lond.*, PhD *Lond.*, FIP
Emer. Prof., Experimental Physics
White, Glenn   Prof., Space Sciences
Other Staff: 5 Lectrs.
Research: applied optics; astrophysics and
planetary science; functional materials

Politics and International Relations

Tel: (01227) 823678 Fax: (01227) 827033
Abbey, Ruth, PhD   Sr. Lectr., Politics
Burgess, Michael   Prof., Federal Studies
Groom, A. J. R., BSc(Econ) *Lond.*, MA *Lehigh*,
DèsScPol *Geneva*   Prof., International
Relations
Saalfeld, Thomas, BA *Munich*, MA *Munich*, PhD
Munich   Sr. Lectr., Politics
Sakwa, Richard, BA *Lond.*, PhD *Birm.*   Prof.,
Russian and European Politics; Head*
Williams, Andrew J., BA *Keele*, DèsScPol *Geneva*
Prof., International Relations
Other Staff: 12 Lectrs.
Research: conflict and peace; European and
comparative governance; federal studies

Psychology

Tel: (01227) 823961 Fax: (01227) 827030
E-mail: psych-gen@kent.ac.uk

Abrams, W. Dominic J., BA *Manc.*, MSc *Lond.*,
PhD   Prof., Social Psychology
Forrester, Mike A., MSc *Strath.*, PhD *Strath.*   Sr.
Lectr.
Houston, Diane, MA *Dund.*, PhD *Kent*   Prof.
Lloyd-Jones, Toby, PhD   Sr. Lectr.
Quine, Lyn, BA PhD   Prof., Health
Psychology; Head*
Rutland, Adam, PhD   Sr. Lectr.
Rutter, Derek R., BA *Nott.*, PhD *Nott.*   Prof.,
Health Psychology
Van Vugt, Mark   Prof., Social Psychology
Wilson, Clare, PhD   Sr. Lectr., Forensic
Psychology
Other Staff: 14 Lectrs.; 2 Res. Fellows; 3 Res.
Assocs.
Research: cognitive psychology and
neuropsychology; developmental
psychology; forensic psychology; group
processes; health behaviour

Social Policy, Sociology and Social Research, School of

Tel: (01227) 823684 Fax: (01227) 824014
E-mail: socio-office@kent.ac.uk

Alaszewski, Andy   Prof., Health Studies
Baldock, John C., BA *Oxf.*, MA *Kent*   Prof.,
Social Policy
Elliott, Anthony   Prof., Sociology
Evans, Mary S., MSc(Econ) *Lond.*, DPhil *Sus.*
Prof., Women's Studies
Furedi, Frank, BA *McG.*, MA *Lond.*, PhD *Lond.*
Prof., Sociology
Hale, Christopher, BA *Keele*, MSc *Kent*, PhD *Kent*
Prof., Criminology
Jenkins, William I., BSc *Lond.*, PhD *Lond.*   Prof.,
Public Policy and Management
Liddiard, Mark, MScEcon *Wales*   Sr. Lectr.,
Social Policy
Netten, Ann, BA *CNAA*, PhD *Kent*   Prof., Social
Welfare
Pack, Chris   Sr. Lectr., Social Work
Pahl, Jan, MA *Camb.*, PhD *Kent*   Emer. Prof.,
Social Policy
Pickvance, Chris G., MA(Econ) *Manc.*   Prof.,
Urban Studies; Head*
Ray, Larry, BA *Lanc.*, MA *Sus.*, DPhil *Sus.*   Prof.,
Sociology

Rootes, Christopher A., BA Qld., BPhil Oxf. Reader, Environmental Politics and Political Sociology

Sayers, Janet V., MA Camb., PhD   Prof., Psychoanalytical Psychology

Song, Miri, BA Harv., PhD Lond.   Sr. Lectr., Sociology

Taylor-Gooby, Peter F., BA Brist., MPhil York(UK), PhD   Prof., Social Policy

Twigg, Julia, BA Durh., MSc Lond., PhD Lond. Prof., Social Policy and Sociology

Vickerstaff, Sarah, BSc Leic., PhD Leeds   Prof., Work and Employment

Other Staff: 21 Lectrs.; 1 Res. Fellow

Research: criminology; social policy; sociology; urban studies; women's studies

Tizard Centre

Fax: (01227) 763674
   E-mail: tizard-gen@kent.ac.uk

Cambridge, Paul, BA CNAA   Sr. Lectr., Learning Disability

Mansell, Jim M., MScEcon Wales   Prof., Applied Psychology of Learning Disability; Head*

McCarthy, Michelle, BA Exe., BPhil Exe., MA Middx.   Sr. Lectr., Learning Disability

McGill, Peter, BSc Glas., MPhil Lond.   Sr. Lectr., Learning Disability

Milne, Alisoun, BA Liv., MA Lond.   Sr. Lectr., Social Gerontology

Watters, Charles, BA CNAA, MA Lanc., DPhil Sus. Sr. Lectr., Mental Health

Other Staff: 12 Lectrs.; 1 Res. Assoc.; 1 Hon. Sr. Lectr.; 1 Hon. Res. Fellow

Research: intellectual and developmental disabilities; migration studies; social inequalities and community care

SPECIAL CENTRES, ETC

American Studies, Centre for

Tel: (01227) 823140 Fax: (01227) 827060

Conyne, George, AB Haverford, JD Tulane, PhD Camb.   Dir.*

Astrophysics and Planetary Science, Centre for

Tel: (01227) 823759 Fax: (01227) 827558

Burchell, Mark   Reader, Space Sciences

White, Glenn   Prof., Space Sciences; Dir.*

Other Staff: 2 Lectrs.

Cartoons and Caricature, Centre for the Study of

Tel: (01227) 823127
   E-mail: cartoon-centre@kent.ac.uk

Hiley, Nicholas, PhD   Head*

Colonial and Postcolonial Research, Centre for

Edmond, Rod S., BA Well., BPhil Oxf.   Prof., Modern Literature and Cultural History

Gurnah, Abdulrazak, BEd Lond., PhD Kent Prof., English and Postcolonial Literature

Innes, Lyn, BA Syd., MA Oregon, PhD Cornell Prof., Postcolonial Literatures

Rooney, Caroline, DPhil Oxf.   Sr. Lectr.; Dir.*

European, Regional and Transport Economics, Centre for

Tel: (01227) 823642 Fax: (01227) 827784

Vickerman, Roger W., MA Camb., DPhil Sus. Prof.; Dir.*

Group Processes, Centre for the Study of

Tel: (01227) 823961 Fax: (01227) 827030

Abrams, Dominic, BA Manc., MSc Lond., PhD Kent   Prof.; Dir.*

Houston, Diane, MA Dund., PhD Kent   Prof., Psychology

Van Vugt, Mark   Prof., Social Psychology

Other Staff: 4 Lectrs.; 1 Res. Fellow; 1 Res. Assoc.

Health Behaviour, Centre for Research in

Tel: (01227) 823082 Fax: (01227) 827032

Quine, Lyn, BA PhD   Prof., Health Psychology

Rutter, Derek R., BA Nott., PhD Nott.   Dir.*

Other Staff: 2 Lectrs.

Health Services Studies, Centre for

Tel: (01227) 823940 Fax: (01227) 827868

Alaszewski, Andy   Prof., Health Studies; Dir.*

Carpenter, I., BSc MD, FRCP, FRCPEd   Reader, Health Care of Older People

Other Staff: 1 Lectr.; 3 Res. Fellows; 3 Res. Assocs.

History and Cultural Studies of Science, Unit for the

Smith, C. W., MA Camb., PhD Camb.   Prof., History of Science; Dir.*

Other Staff: 2 Res. Fellows

Humanities, Kent Institute for Advanced Studies in the

International Studies, Brussels School of

Fax: (0032) 2641 1720

Wiener, Jarrod, BA PEI, MA Kent, PhD Kent Dir.*

Other Staff: 2 Lectrs.

Kent Crime and Justice Centre

Tel: (01227) 823275 Fax: (01227) 827038

Hale, Christopher, BA Keele, MSc Kent, PhD Kent Prof., Criminology; Dir.*

Other Staff: 1 Sr. Res. Officer

Kent Law Clinic

Tel: (01227) 823311

Fitzpatrick, John F., BA Oxf.   Sr. Lectr.; Dir.*

Medieval and Tudor Studies, Canterbury Centre for

Tel: (01227) 823140 Fax: (01227) 827060

Potter, David L., BA Durh., PhD Camb.   Sr. Lectr.; Dir.*

Modern Poetry, Centre for

E-mail: modernpoetry@kent.ac.uk

Ayers, David, BA Lond., PhD S'ton.   Sr. Lectr.; Dir.*

Herd, David, PhD   Sr. Lectr.

Montefiore, Janet, BA Oxf., BPhil Oxf., PhD Kent Reader, English and American Literature

Music Technology, Centre for

Arundell, Clive   Dir.*

Fuller, Ursula, MA Camb., MA Kent   Dir.*

Personal Social Services Research Unit

Fax: (01227) 827038

Davies, Bleddyn P., MA Camb., DPhil Oxf. Prof., Social Policy

Netten, Ann, BA CNAA, PhD Kent   Prof., Health and Social Welfare; Dir.*

Other Staff: 1 Sr. Res. Fellow; 1 Res. Fellow; 6 Res. Officers

Propaganda, Centre for the Study of

Tel: (01227) 823837

Welch, David A., BA Wales, PhD Lond.   Prof.; Dir.*

Social and Political Movements, Centre for the Study of

Rootes, Christopher A., BA Qld., BPhil Oxf. Dir.*

Social Anthropology and Computing, Centre for

Fischer, Michael D., MA Texas, PhD Texas Reader; Dir.*

Zeitlyn, David, BA Oxf., PhD Camb.   Reader, Social Anthropology

Social Services, European Institute of

Fax: (01227) 827246
   E-mail: eiss-group@kent.ac.uk

Pizani Williams, Linda   Dir.*

Sports Studies, Centre for

Tel: (01227) 823670 Fax: (01227) 824025

Uglow, Steve P., BA Oxf., BCL Oxf.   Prof., Criminal Justice; Dir.*

Other Staff: 4 Lectrs.

Urban and Regional Studies Unit

Tel: (01227) 827005
   E-mail: socio-office@kent.ac.uk

Pickvance, Chris G., MA(Econ) Manc.   Prof.; Dir.*

Women's Studies, Centre for

Fax: (01227) 827005
   E-mail: socio-office@kent.ac.uk

Evans, Mary S., MSc(Econ) Lond., DPhil Sus. Prof.; Dir.*

CONTACT OFFICERS

Academic affairs. Director of Academic Administration and Deputy Registrar: Pink, Jon

Accommodation. Accommodation Officer: Goss, Derek (E-mail: accomm@kent.ac.uk)

Admissions (first degree). Assistant Registrar (Admissions): Holdcroft, Steven (E-mail: recruitment@kent.ac.uk)

Admissions (higher degree). Assistant Registrar (Admissions): Holdcroft, Steven (E-mail: recruitment@kent.ac.uk)

Adult/continuing education. Assistant Registrar (Admissions): Holdcroft, Steven (E-mail: part-time@kent.ac.uk)

Alumni. Alumni Relations Manager: Burn, Killara, BA Calif. (E-mail: alumni-office@kent.ac.uk)

Careers. Head of Careers Advisory Service: Greer, John W., MA Trinity(Dub.)

Computing services. Head of Computing Services: Sotillo, John (E-mail: j.sotillo@kent.ac.uk)

Development/fund-raising. Director of Communications and Development Office: Shepherd, Sue

Equal opportunities. Equal Opportunities Officer: Dimond, Judith

Estates and buildings/works and services. Estates and Buildings Officer: Czarnomski, Peter

Examinations. Senior Assistant Registrar: Ovenden, Jeremy, BA Nott., PhD S'ton.

Finance. Director of Finance: Everitt, Denise R., BA Kent

General enquiries. Secretary: Hollands, Janice (E-mail: censec-staff@ukc.ac.uk)

Health services. Head of Student Health Service (Senior Partner): Bowhay, Alyson, BSc Lond., MB BS Lond., MS Lond. (E-mail: medsecs@kent.ac.uk)

International office. Director of International Office: Cross, Pamela A., BA Lanc. (E-mail: international-office@kent.ac.uk)

Library (chief librarian). Librarian: (vacant)

Minorities/disadvantaged groups. Equal Opportunities Officer: Dimond, Judith

Personnel/human resources. Director of Personnel: Mee, David

Publications. Publications Manager: Saunders, Hilary, BA Warw.

Purchasing. Purchasing Officer: Gallop, Clive, BSc Lond. (E-mail: purchasing@kent.ac.uk)

Research. Head, Research and Enterprise
Services: Forsyth, Jacqui
Safety. Director, Safety, Health and
Environment: Salmon, Mike
Schools liaison. Executive Officer, Schools and
Colleges Liaison: Rowe, Michelle
Sport and recreation. Director of Sport and
Recreation: Wilkins, Michael, BA
Student welfare/counselling. Director,
Student Guidance and Welfare: Greer, John
W., MA Trinity(Dub.)
Students from other countries. Director of
International Office: Cross, Pamela A., BA

Lanc.
(E-mail: international-office@kent.ac.uk)
Students with disabilities. Disability Support
Co-ordinator: Velarde, Andy
(E-mail: inclusive_learning@kent.ac.uk)

CAMPUS/COLLEGE HEADS

Darwin College. Fax: (01227) 824060;
E-mail: darwin_reception@kent.ac.uk)
Master: Ward, Anthony, MA Camb., PhD
Nott.
Eliot College.
(E-mail: eliot_reception@kent.ac.uk) Master:
Nicholls, Peter J., BSc S'ton., PhD Lond.

Keynes College. Fax: (01227) 827362;
E-mail: keynes_reception@kent.ac.uk)
Master: Reason, David A., BA Essex
Rutherford College.
(E-mail: rutherford_reception@kent.ac.uk)
Master: Forrester-Jones, Rachel

[Information supplied by the institution as at 28 June
2005, and edited by the ACU]

KINGSTON UNIVERSITY

Founded 1992

Member of the Association of Commonwealth Universities

Postal Address: River House, 53-57 High Street, Kingston upon Thames, Surrey, England KT1 1LQ
Telephone: (020) 8547 2000 **Fax:** (020) 8547 8067
URL: http://www.kingston.ac.uk

VICE-CHANCELLOR*—Scott, Sir Peter, KBE, BA Oxf., Hon. PhD Anglia PU, Hon. LLD Bath, Hon. DLitt CNAA,
Hon. DLitt Grand Valley, FRSA, Hon. FUMIST
DEPUTY VICE-CHANCELLOR—Stuart, Prof. Mary, BA Cape Town, BA Oxf., DPhil Oxf.
PRO VICE-CHANCELLOR (EXTERNAL AFFAIRS AND BUSINESS DEVELOPMENT)—Jones, Prof. Martyn, BSc MA, FRGS
PRO VICE-CHANCELLOR (SCIENCE)—Lister, Prof. Paul, MSc PhD, FIEE
PRO VICE-CHANCELLOR (ARTS)—Sparke, Prof. Penny, BA PhD, FRCA, FRSA
UNIVERSITY SECRETARY‡—Beaton, D. Donald, BA Manc., MBA Dund.
FINANCE DIRECTOR—Butcher, Terence M.
HUMAN RESOURCES DIRECTOR—Rogers, Nick

GENERAL INFORMATION

History. The university's origins date from
the establishment of Kingston Science, Art and
Technical Institute in 1899. Kingston
Polytechnic was created in 1970 by the merger
of Kingston College of Art and Kingston
College of Technology. Gypsy Hill College of
Education joined the polytechnic in 1975. It
attained university status in 1992.
The university has four campuses located in
the outskirts of London.

Admission to first degree courses (see also
United Kingdom Introduction). Through
Universities and Colleges Admissions Service
(UCAS).

First Degrees (see also United Kingdom
Directory to Subjects of Study). BA, BEng,
BMus, BSc, LLB, MChem, MEng, MPharm.
Many courses are offered full- or part-time;
some are sandwich courses.
Length of course. Full-time: BA, BEng, BMus, BSc,
LLB: 3 years; MChem, MEng, MPharm: 4
years.

Higher Degrees (see also United Kingdom
Directory to Subjects of Study).
Master's. LLM, MA, MArch, MBA, MEd,
MPhil, MSc.
Admission. Applicants for admission to
master's degree courses and for MPhil should
normally hold an appropriate first degree.
Length of course. Full-time: LLM, MA, MArch,
MBA, MEd, MSc: 1 year; MPhil: 2 years. Part-
time: LLM, MA, MArch, MBA, MEd, MSc: 2
years; MPhil: 4 years.
Doctoral. DBA, PhD.
Admission. Applicants for PhD should
normally hold an appropriate first degree.
DBA: master's degree.
Length of course. Full-time: PhD: 4 years. Part-
time: DBA: 4 years; PhD: 8 years.

Libraries. Volumes: 430,000. Periodicals
subscribed to: 2200. Special collections: Iris

Murdoch; Mineralogical Society; Vane
Ivanovic.

Academic Year (2007–2008). Three terms:
24 September–14 December; 2 January–14
March; 31 March–4 July.

Income (2005–2006). Total, £132,332,000.

Statistics. Staff (2005–2006): 1783 (938
academic, 845 non-academic). Students
(2005–2006): full-time 15,448; part-time
3413; international 2636; distance education/
external 1903; undergraduate 16,309; master's
2318; doctoral 234.

FACULTIES/SCHOOLS

Art, Design and Architecture
Tel: (020) 8547 8219 Fax: (020) 8547 7069
E-mail: m.scourfield@kingston.ac.uk
Dean: Ofield, Simon
Personal Assistant: Scourfield, Marylin

Arts and Social Sciences
Tel: (020) 8547 7291 Fax: (020) 8547 7292
E-mail: l.corcoran@kingston.ac.uk
Dean: Cunningham, Prof. Gail R., MA DPhil
Faculty Secretary: Corcoran, Linda

Business and Law
Tel: (020) 8547 7228 Fax: (020) 8547 7024
E-mail: b.varney@kingston.ac.uk
Dean: Ezingeard, Prof. Jean-Noel, MSc PhD,
FRSA
Faculty Secretary: Varney, Barbara

Computing, Information Systems and Mathematics
Tel: (020) 5847 8043 Fax: (020) 8547 7971
E-mail: ku34041@kingston.ac.uk
Dean: Ellis, Prof. Tim
Administrator: Denholm-Price, Kerry

Engineering
Tel: (020) 8547 8043 Fax: (020) 8547 7971
E-mail: k.rowan@kingston.ac.uk

Dean: Mason, Peter J., PhD
Personal Assistant: Rowan, Kate

Health and Social Care Sciences
Tel: (020) 8725 2155 Fax: (020) 8725 2159
E-mail: dbunyan@hscs.sgul.ac.uk
Dean: Ross, Prof. Fiona, BSc PhD DN
Personal Assistant: Bunyan, Debs

Science
Tel: (020) 8547 7421 Fax: (020) 8547 7437
E-mail: t.staussi@kingston.ac.uk
Dean: Mackintosh, David, BSc PhD
Personal Assistant: Staussi, Thelma

ACADEMIC UNITS
Arranged by Schools

Accounting and Finance
Tel: (020) 8547 7353 Fax: (020) 8547 7026
Alexandrou, George, BA PhD   Principal Lectr.
Archibold, Stuart, BA MSc PhD   Head*
Cottingham, Juliet, BSc PhD   Principal Lectr.
Dunhill, Andrea J.   Principal Lectr.
Forgan, John, BA(Econ), FCA   Principal Lectr.
Holland, C. J., BSc(Soc) MSc, FCA   Principal
Lectr.
Myers, V. J., MA, FCA   Principal Lectr.
Salami, Ayodele, BA PhD   Principal Lectr.
Turner, Geoffrey, MBA PhD   Principal Lectr.
Woodward, Marie-Therese, BA PhD   Principal
Lectr.
Other Staff: 8 Sr. Lectrs.; 2 Lectrs.

Architecture
Tel: (020) 8547 7193 Fax: (020) 8547 7186
Brown, Patricia J., BSc   Principal Lectr.
Chaplin, Sarah   Head*
Farren Bradley, Judith V.   Principal Lectr.
Lee, Susan A., MA   Principal Lectr.
Other Staff: 2 Sr. Lectrs.; 1 Assoc. Sr. Lectr.; 6
Sr. Lectrs.†
Research: green audit built environment

Art and Design History

Tel: (020) 8547 7112
Lloyd, Frances A., MA   Head*
McDermott, Catherine E., MA   Reader
Other Staff: 4 Sr. Lectrs.†; 1 Lectr.†
Research: collecting and curating in art and
   design – Dorich House

Business Information Management

Tel: (020) 8547 7214 Fax: (020) 8547 7452
Avery, B., BSc MSc   Principal Lectr.
Benson, V., MSc PhD   Principal Lectr.
Ennals, J. R., MA   Prof., Business Information
   Technology
Fitkov-Norris, E., BSc MSc PhD   Principal
   Lectr.
Fitzgerald, S. J., BSc(Econ) MA   Principal
   Lectr.
Lees, Rebecca, BA MSc   Principal Lectr.
List, M. J., BA MSc   Principal Lectr.
Molyneux, S. P., MSc   Principal Lectr.
Panayiotidis, Andreas, BSc MSc   Principal
   Lectr.
Reade, C., BSc MSc PhD   Head*
Russell, D. J., MSc   Principal Lectr.
Skok, W., MSc PhD   Principal Lectr.
van den Berg, R., MA PhD   Principal Lectr.
Yeghiazarian, A., BSc MPhil   Principal Lectr.
Other Staff: 7 Sr. Lectrs.

Business Strategy and Operations

Tel: (020) 8547 7454 Fax: (020) 8547 7026
Annan-Diab, Fatima, BA MSFM   Principal
   Lectr.
Dixon, S., BA MBA   Principal Lectr.
Doran, D., BA MCPS PhD   Principal Lectr.
El Kahal MacLean, S., BA MA PhD   Principal
   Lectr.
Foster, M. John, MSc PhD   Dir., Overseas
   Programmes and Quality Assurance
Logan, John, MSc   Principal Lectr.
Lowe, S., BA MA PhD   Reader
Matthews, R. D. C., BA(Econ) MSc(Econ)
   Prof., International Business Policy
Pinder-Young, Deborah, MA   Principal Lectr.
Robson, David, MSc MBA   Principal Lectr.
Sims, A. J.   Principal Lectr.
Watkins-Mathys, Lorraine, BA MA PhD
   Head*
Wilson, N., MA Camb., MBA   Principal Lectr.
Other Staff: 7 Sr. Lectrs.

Computing, Information Systems and Mathematics

Tel: (020) 8547 8242 Fax: (020) 8547 7972
Atkins, N., BSc PhD   Principal Lectr.
Bali, H. N., MSc PhD   Principal Lectr.
Bidgood, Penelope L., BSc MSc PhD   Principal
   Lectr.
Bloxham, P. A., BSc(Eng) MSc   Principal
   Lectr.
Briggs, J. H., BSc(Eng)   Reader; Prof., New
   Media Design
Ellis, Tim   Prof.; Dean*
Hatton, L.   Prof.
Istepanian, R.   Prof.
Jones, G. A., BSc PhD   Reader
Lindsay, J. M., BA BLS   Reader
Ling, E. N., PhD   Principal Lectr.
Lyle, Svetlana, BSc PhD   Dir., Joint Studies
Malyan, R. R., BA MSc PhD   Principal Lectr.
Marks, S. M., MSc   Principal Lectr.
Mellor, R. B.   Principal Lectr.
Morris, John L. L., BSc PhD, FIMA   Prof.
Novak, M.   Dir., Postgrad. Programmes
Rapley, Anne, MSc   Assoc. Dean
Remagnino, P.   Reader
Riha, Karel, BA MSc PhD   Principal Lectr.
Roberts, R. E.   Principal Lectr.
Robson, M. J., BSc MSc PhD   Principal Lectr.
Shihab, A.   Principal Lectr.
Soan, P. H., MSc PhD   Principal Lectr.
Thomson, M., BA MSc   Principal Lectr.
Tompsett, C. P., MA   Principal Lectr.
Tsaptsinos, D.   Principal Lectr.
Wallin, Paul I., BSc   Principal Lectr.
Wertheim, D.   Reader

Wills, C. C., MA   Principal Lectr.
Other Staff: 38 Sr. Lectrs.
Research: applied research in information
   systems; digital imaging research; granular
   and heterogeneous mechanics; mobile
   information and networking technologies;
   numerical analysis

Earth Sciences and Geography

Tel: (020) 8547 7524 Fax: (020) 8547 7562
Clemens, John D., PhD, FRMIT, FGS   Prof.;
   Assoc. Dean, Res.
Jarvis, Ian, BSc DPhil, FGS   Reader
Jarvis, Kym E., BSc PhD, FGS   Principal Lectr.
Petford, Nick, BSc MA PhD   Reader
Rankin, Andy H., BSc PhD, FGS   Prof.; Head*
Robinson, Guy M., BSc DPhil, FRGS   Prof.
Sutcliffe, Peter J. C., BSc PhD, FGS   Principal
   Lectr.
Swan, Andy, BSc PhD   Principal Lectr.
Taylor, Rosalind M., BSc PhD   Principal Lectr.
Thomas, Neil, BSc PhD   Principal Lectr.
Treloar, Peter J., BSc PhD, FGS   Reader
Walford, Nigel S., BA Sus., PhD Lond., FRGS
   Prof.
Other Staff: 14 Sr. Lectrs.; 1 Lectr.
Research: geodynamics and crustal processes;
   palaeoenvironmental change; remote
   sensing; rural geography and socio-
   economic change

Economics

Tel: (020) 8547 7335 Fax: (020) 8547 7388
Auerbach, Paul R., MA PhD   Reader
Butler, Nick, BA MSc   Principal Lectr.
Daly, Vince D., MSocSc   Head*
Drummond-Thompson, P. H., BA MA PhD
   Principal Lectr.
Humm, A. L., BA MSc PhD   Principal Lectr.
Hyett, A. J., MSc(Econ) PhD   Principal Lectr.
Li, Hong, MA PhD   Sr. Lectr.
Pollock, Catherine M., BA MSc PhD   Principal
   Lectr.
Sanchez-Fung, Jose, MA PhD   Sr. Lectr.
Shamsavari, Ali, MA PhD   Sr. Lectr.
Shaw, Arthur W., MSc(Econ)   Principal Lectr.
Siddiki, Jalal, PhD   Sr. Lectr.
Spanjers, Willy, DrRerPol   Sr. Lectr.; Deputy
   Head
Stibora, Joachim, MPhil PhD   Sr. Lectr.
Tackie, Alex, MSc PhD   Sr. Lectr.
Wells, Julian, MSc   Sr. Lectr.
Other Staff: 4 Lectrs.
Research: economics in transition; financial
   environment of development; growth and
   development; small and medium
   enterprises; trade and factor mobility

Education

Tel: (020) 8547 7635 Fax: (020) 8547 7116
Anderson, Arlene, BEd MA   Sr. Lectr.
Ashfield, Jean E., BA MA   Dir., PGCE Primary
   Programmes
Basini, Urszula, MA   Sr. Lectr.
Bowell, Pamela, BPhil   Principal Lectr.
Briten, Elizabeth, BEd MA   Sr. Lectr.
Broad, Elizabeth, BA MA   Deputy Dir.,
   Primary PGCE
Broughton, Sylvia, BA BPharm   Sr. Lectr.
Colvert, Helen, BEd MA   Sr. Lectr.
Cooper, Ann   Head, Admin.
Coultas, Valerie, BA MA   Sr. Lectr.
Edwards, Jonathan, BSc MSc, FRSA   Principal
   Lectr., Geography and Education
Evans, Jill, BEd BA   Sr. Lectr.
Ford, Michael, BEd MBA   Sr. Lectr.
Goddard, Linda, BEd   Sr. Lectr.
Grieves, Keith R., BEd PhD   Dir., Res.; Reader,
   History
Haig, John, BSc   Sr. Lectr.
Hiley, Sue, BEd MA   Sr. Lectr.
Hodson, Pamela, BEd MA   Sr. Lectr.
Hudson, Andy   Head*
Humble, Mark, BEd MA   Principal Lectr.
Jackson-Stevens, Sarah, BA   Sr. Lectr.
Jefferson, Wayne, MA EdD   Sr. Lectr.
Johnson, Helen   Reader

Jones, Cynthia, BA MPhil, FRSA   Dir.,
   Continuing Professl. Devel. Programmes
Lancaster-Smith, Greg, BSc BA(Ed) MA
   Principal Lectr.
Lloyd, Beth, BA   Sr. Lectr.
Maisey, Daryl, BEd MA   Sr. Lectr.
McCrum, Elizabeth, BA MA(Ed)   Deputy Dir.,
   Secondary PGCE
McMurtary, Jennifer, BA MA   Sr. Lectr.
Owens, Trina, BEd   Sr. Lectr.
Perselli, Victoria, MA PhD   Sr. Lectr.
Phillips, Gordon, BA MA   Sr. Lectr.
Poku, Veronica, BA MA   Sr. Lectr.
Powell, Andrew   Dir., Undergrad. Primary
   Programme
Rawlings, Anne, BEd   Sr. Lectr.
Robson, Ken, BSc   Dir., Secondary PGCE
Wood, Ruth, BEd MA(Ed)   Sr. Lectr.

Engineering

Tel: (020) 8547 7979 Fax: (020) 8547 7992
Aboutorabi, A. A., BSc MSc PhD   Deputy
   Head
Bromhead, E. N., MSc PhD, FGS   Prof.,
   Geotechnical Engineering
Harris, A. H., BSc MSc, FGS   Assoc. Dean
   (courses)
Karwatzki, John M., MPhil PhD, FIMechE
   Principal Lectr.
Lung, A. W. M., BSc PhD   Principal Lectr.
Mason, Peter J., PhD   Dean*
Roome, R. L., MSc   Principal Lectr.
Ryan, E. C., MSc   Principal Lectr.
Shepherd, K. L., BSc PhD   Principal Lectr.
Stephenson, Pauline M., MSc   Principal Lectr.
Vasudevan, M. S., BSc PhD, FRAeS   Principal
   Lectr.
Wagstaff, P. G., BSc(Met) MSc   Principal
   Lectr.
Welch, C. S., MSc PhD   Principal Lectr.
Other Staff: 29 Sr. Lectrs.
Research: aerospace engineering; applied
   engineering; concrete and masonry;
   sustainable technology

Fashion

Tel: (020) 8547 7101 Fax: (020) 8547 7098
Renfrew, Elinor   Head*
Other Staff: 1 Sr. Lectr.; 2 Sr. Lectrs.†
Research: fashion theory (imaging fashion)

Fine Art

Tel: (020) 8547 7128 Fax: (020) 8547 7041
Dellow, Jeffrey, MA   Principal Lectr.
Hodgson, Carole   Principal Lectr.
Russell, B. J., MA Lond.   Prof.; Head*
Yule, A. A.   Reader
Other Staff: 2 Sr. Lectrs.†

Foundation Studies

Tel: (020) 8547 7090
Stafford, Paul, BA   Head of Foundation*
Other Staff: 1 Sr. Lectr.; 2 Sr. Lectrs.†

Graphic Design

Tel: (020) 8547 7135 Fax: (020) 8547 7148
Hudd, Penelope A.   Head*
Kennard, Malcolm, MA   Principal Lectr.
Other Staff: 1 Sr. Lectr.; 3 Sr. Lectrs.†
Research: sustainability in art and design

Human Resource Management

Tel: (020) 8547 7220 Fax: (020) 8547 7026
Daskalaki, M., BA MA PhD   Principal Lectr.
Edwards, Christine Y., BA MSc   Prof.; Head*
Gourlay, S. N., MA PhD   Reader
MacNeil, C., BA MBA, FCIPD   Principal Lectr.
Narendran, Sunitha, MA PhD   Principal Lectr.
Pidduck, Jasmine, BA MA   Principal Lectr.
Rees, C., BSc MA PhD   Reader
Sachdev, Sanjir, BA MA   Principal Lectr.
Smith, Lesley J., BEd   Principal Lectr.
Soane, E., BSc MSc PhD   Reader
Truss, Katie, BA PhD   Prof.
Other Staff: 8 Sr. Lectrs.
Research: industrial performance; quality
   management and employee responses

Humanities

Tel: (020) 8547 7305 Fax: (020) 8547 7292
Annesley, James, DPhil   Sr. Lectr.
Atherton, Barbara, MA   Sr. Lectr.; English
   Lang. Support Co-ordinator
Bahjat-Abbas, Niran, MA PhD   Sr. Lectr.
Barber, Stephen, BA PhD   Prof., Media Arts
Barnes, Hugh, BA   Sr. Lectr.
Baron, Adam, MA   Lectr./Sr. Lectr.
Bastow, Steve, MA PhD   Principal Lectr.; Field
   Leader, Media and Cultural Studies
Brewster, Beth, MA   Field Leader, Journalism
Brick, Noelle M. C., LèsL MA   Principal Lectr.,
   French
Campbell, Siobhan, MA   Reader/Sr. Lectr.
Carey, Brycchan, BA MA PhD   Sr. Lectr.
Carter, Fan, BA DPhil   Sr. Lectr.
Cathcart, Brian, BA   Sr. Lectr.
Clarke, Norma, BA   Sr. Lectr.
Goldsworthy, Vesna, PhD   Sr. Lectr.
Hannaford, Alex, BA   Lectr./Sr. Lectr.
Horner, Avril, BA MA PhD   Prof., English
   Literature
Jensen, Meg, MA PhD   Sr. Lectr.; Field Leader,
   Creative Writing
Kiernan, Anna, BA MA   Sr. Lectr.
Kyratzis, Sakis, PhD   Sr. Lectr.
Lane, Patricia, BA MA   Sr. Lectr.
Longfellow, Erica, DPhil   Sr. Lectr.
McConnell, Sara, MA   Sr. Lectr.
Mencia, Maria, MA PhD   Sr. Lectr.
Nectoux, François, MPhil PhD   Prof.,
   Contemporary European Studies
O'Brien, Catherine, PhD   Sr. Lectr.
Pinnock, Winsome, BA MA   Sr. Lectr.
Powell, George, MA PhD   Lectr./Sr. Lectr.
Pratt, Lande, DPhil   Sr. Lectr.
Rogers, David L., BA Arkansas, MA Arkansas,
   MPhil Rutgers, PhD Rutgers   Head*
Rothwell, Libby, BA   Principal Lectr., Applied
   English Language and Linguistics
Sceats, Sarah, BA MA PhD   Field Leader,
   English Literature
Siegel, Fleeta, BFA MPS   Sr. Lectr.
Teverson, Andrew, BA Durh., MA PhD   Lectr./
   Sr. Lectr., English Literature
Vyas, Devyani, MA   Sr. Lectr.
Wilks, Clarissa F., BA Oxf., MA Lond.   Principal
   Lectr.; Dir., Undergrad. Modular Scheme
Yilmaz, Aybige, MPhil PhD   Lectr./Sr. Lectr.
Research: conversation in modernist texts; early
   Tudor writing; food and fiction; gender
   and sexuality in representation; women's
   writing in the nineteenth and twentieth
   centuries

Law

Tel: (020) 8547 7322 Fax: (020) 8547 7038
Aries, N., LLB MA   Principal Lectr.
Bermingham, V., MA   Principal Lectr.
Darbyshire, Penny, MA PhD   Reader
Follows, T. J.   Principal Lectr.
Holmes, R. J., LLB   Head*
Knight, Sue, LLB LLM   Principal Lectr.
O'Reilly, M., BEng LLB PhD   Prof.
Saunders, M., BA   Principal Lectr.
Thompson, John J., LLB   Principal Lectr.
Tolmie, Fiona, BA LLM   Dir., Undergrad.
   Programmes
Wynn, M., LLB LLM   Principal Lectr.
Other Staff: 19 Sr. Lectrs.
Research: civilist legal systems

Life Sciences

Tel: (020) 8547 7502 Fax: (020) 8547 7562
Augousti, Andy T., BSc Kent, PhD Kent, MBA,
   FIP, FIEE   Prof.
Cook, Richard, BSc MSc PhD   Principal Lectr.
Easmon, Sue, BSc PhD   Principal Lectr.
Flowers, Alan, BSc PhD   Principal Lectr.
Jones, Lucy, BSc PhD   Sr. Lectr.
Manly, Ralph, BSc PhD
Mistry, Calli, BSc PhD   Sr. Lectr.
Naughton, Declan, BSc PhD   Prof.
Opara, Elizabeth, BSc DPhil   Principal Lectr.
Petroczi, Andrea, BSc MSc PhD   Sr. Lectr.
Piper, Ian, BSc PhD   Sr. Lectr.
Russell, Angela J., BSc MSc PhD   Prof.

Seddon, A. M., PhD   Principal Lectr.; Acting
   Head*
Other Staff: 21 Sr. Lectrs.; 3 Lectrs.
Research: biomedical science; environmental
   biology; exercise physiology; forensic
   sciences; parasite biology

Marketing

Tel: (020) 8547 7226 Fax: (020) 8547 7026
Anderson, Deborah, BA MA   Principal Lectr.
Dall'Olmo Riley, Francesca, BA PhD   Reader
East, J. Robert, BA(SocSc) DPhil   Principal
   Lectr.; Prof., Consumer Behaviour
Eldred, J. G., BSc   Principal Lectr.
Harris, Patricia M.   Principal Lectr.
Kalafatis, S. P., BA MPhil PhD   Prof.
Lomax, A. Wendy, BSc PhD   Head*
Masikunas, G. D., MA   Principal Lectr.
McGill, J., MA PhD   Principal Lectr.
Riley, D., MBA PhD   Principal Lectr.
Robinson, Helen R., BA   Principal Lectr.
Other Staff: 5 Sr. Lectrs.
Research: marketing and consumer behaviour;
   relationship marketing

Music

Tel: (020) 8547 7118
Gartrell, Carol A., BMus PhD   Principal Lectr.
Osbon, David   Head*
Pearson, Ingrid, BMus LMusA PhD   Sr. Lectr.;
   Dir., Music Performance
Searby, M. D., MMus, FTCL   Principal Lectr.
Other Staff: 3 Sr. Lectrs.; 1 Sr. Lectr.†
Research: ethnomusicology (gamelan research);
   recursive algorithms for music generation

Nursing and Midwifery

Tel: (020) 8725 2247 Fax: (020) 8725 2248
Acton, Lesley   Principal Lectr.
Cheng, Linda, BA Open(UK), MSc Lond.
   Principal Lectr.
Collington, Val, BSc MSc PhD   Head of
   Midwifery*
Coppard, Susan P., MSc   Principal Lectr.
Fergy, Susan P., BEd PhD   Principal Lectr.
Forte, Denise, MSc   Principal Lectr.
Gale, Julia, BSc PhD   Head, Mental Health and
   Learning Disability Nursing
Gault, Iris, BSc MSc   Principal Lectr.
Heatley, Susan   Principal Lectr.
Jackson, Diane   Principal Lectr.
Lopez, Jane   Principal Lectr.
Mohammed, Nizam I., BEd MBA MSc
   Principal Lectr.
Pedley, Gillian, BSc MSc   Principal Lectr.
Rees Jones, Ian, BA MSc PhD   Prof., Sociology
   of Health and Illness
Rush, Susan C., MSc   Principal Lectr.
Sheridan, Val   Principal Lectr.
Spurway, Maggie, MSc   Head, Primary Care
   Nursing
Start, Kath, BSc MSc   Deputy Dean; Head,
   Nursing*
Strong, Susan E., BSc   Principal Lectr.
Tye, Chris, BSc PhD   Course Dir.; Head, Acute
   Care Nursing
Webb, Patricia A.   Principal Lectr.
Other Staff: 69 Sr. Lectrs.; 10 Sr. Lectrs.†
Research: evidence-based practice; nutrition;
   primary care

Performance and Screen Studies

Archbold, Paul   Sr. Lectr.
Brooker, Will, MA PhD   Lectr./Sr. Lectr., Film
   Studies
Brown, Simon, BA MA   Lectr./Sr. Lectr.
Busen-Smith, Maria   Principal Lectr.
Chambon, Philip   Sr. Lectr.
Elcock, Mary , Audio Technology and Music
   Industry Studies
Ewers, Tim, MMus AMusD   Sr. Lectr.
Fletcher, Abbe, BA MA   Lectr./Sr. Lectr.
Fredrics, Howard   Sr. Lectr.
Gartrell, Carol A., BMus PhD   Deputy Head
Kennedy, Michael, LLB   Sr. Lectr.
O'Brien, Catherine, PhD   Sr. Lectr., Film
Osbon, David   Sr. Lectr.
Parker, Michael   Sr. Lectr.

Potter, Caroline   Sr. Lectr.
Rabalska, Carmen, BA MA   Sr. Lectr.
Rinke, Andrea, PhD   Sr. Lectr.
Searby, M. D., MMus, FTCL   Principal Lectr.
Smith, Ian   Lectr./Sr. Lectr., Television Studies
Toplis, Gloria   Principal Lectr., Music
Whately, Frank, BA   Head*

Pharmacy

Brown, John E., BPharm MSc PhD   Prof.;
   Head*
Other Staff: 2 Sr. Lectrs.
Research: pharmacy

Pharmacy and Chemistry

Tel: (020) 8547 7955 Fax: (020) 8547 7562
Ahmed, Sabbir, BSc Cardiff, PhD Cardiff   Prof.
Brown, John E., BPharm MSc PhD   Prof.;
   Head*
Buckley-Dhoot, Eileen, BSc PhD   Principal
   Lectr.
Cairns, Chris, BSc MSc, FRPharmS   Prof.
Coombes, Alan, BSc PhD   Prof.
Foot, Peter J. S., BSc Brighton, MSc S'ton., PhD
   Brighton   Prof.
Koenders, Curt   Prof.
Sewell, Graham, BPharm PhD   Prof.
Singer, Richard, BSc PhD   Principal Lectr.
Skinner, G. A., BSc Leic., DPhil   Principal
   Lectr.
Tyrrell, Elizabeth, BA PhD   Principal Lectr.
Williams, Neil, BSc PhD   Principal Lectr.
Other Staff: 16 Sr. Lectrs.; 3 Lectrs.
Research: biomedical and pharmaceutical
   sciences; materials

Physiotherapy

Tel: (020) 8725 2274 Fax: (020) 8725 2200
Bithell, Chris, MA(Education) Lond.   Head*
King, Linda, MSc   Principal Lectr.
Other Staff: 13 Sr. Lectrs.

Radiography

Tel: (020) 8547 7399 Fax: (020) 8547 8800
Dennis, Tony   Principal Lectr.
Francis, Geraldine, BSc MSc   Principal Lectr.
Jadva-Patel, Hansa   Principal Lectr.
Lock, Nicholas, MSc   Principal Lectr.
Morgan, Graham, BA MA   Head*
Rogers, Nigel   Principal Lectr.
Other Staff: 6 Sr. Lectrs.

Social Science

Tel: (020) 8547 7319 Fax: (020) 8547 7388
Almog, Orna, BA MA PhD   Lectr./Sr. Lectr.
Bailey, Joe, BA MSc   Prof., Sociology; Head*
Barker, Chris, BSc PhD   Principal Lectr.
Barlow-Brown, Fiona, PhD   Sr. Lectr.
Beck, Peter J., BSc(Econ) PhD   Prof.,
   International History
Bowen, Stephen, MA LLM   Sr. Lectr.
Brivati, Brian L., PhD   Dir., Grad. Studies;
   Prof., Contemporary History
Butler, Georgia, BSc PhD   Sr. Lectr.
Casey, Emma, BA PhD   Sr. Lectr.
Collins-Mayo, Sylvie, PhD   Sr. Lectr.
Davis, John, MA PhD   Dir., Postgrad. Studies;
   Reader, History
Dixon, Paul, PhD   Sr. Lectr.
Eaton, Stephanie, MSc   Sr. Lectr.
Esgate, Anthony, BSc MSc PhD   Lectr./Sr.
   Lectr.
Favretto, Ilaria, PhD   Prof.
French, Chris J., MA PhD   Principal Lectr.
Gordon, Jane, BA LLM   Sr. Lectr.
Hawkins, Mike J., BSc PhD   Reader
Hayman, Stephanie, MSc PhD   Sr. Lectr.
Humphreys, James   Principal Lectr.
Huq, Rupa, MSc PhD   Lectr./Sr. Lectr.
La Rooy, David, MSc PhD   Sr. Lectr.
Linton, Marisa, PhD   Sr. Lectr.
Locke, Simon, BSc PhD   Sr. Lectr.
Mitchell, Amy   Lectr./Sr. Lectr.
Nikcevic, Ana, PhD   Sr. Lectr.
Penson, Mark, BSc MA   Principal Lectr.,
   Sociology
Pond, R. J., MSc(Soc)   Principal Lectr.

Prior, Jessica, PhD   Sr. Lectr.
Roberts, Mike A., MA *Leeds*   Principal Lectr.
Roberts, Ronald, PhD   Sr. Lectr.
Sawyer, Joanna, LLB LLM   Sr. Lectr.
Stuart, John   Sr. Lectr.
Sullivan, Terry J., BSc(Econ) MSc   Principal Lectr., Politics
Tenenbaum, Harriett, PhD   Sr. Lectr.
Towers, Bridget, MA DPhil   Principal Lectr.
Vallee-Tourange, Frederic, PhD   Principal Lectr.
Warwick-Haller, Sally   Sr. Lectr.
Whittingham, Mike   Sr. Lectr.
Research: cognitive, behavioural and social psychology; contemporary nationalism; democratic standards and election observers; international conflict; South European and Mediterranean politics

Social Work

Tel: (020) 8547 7072 Fax: (020) 8547 8657
Bell, Lorna, PhD   Principal Lectr.
Elliot, Nigel   Principal Lectr.
Hodgson, D. R., BA MA   Principal Lectr.
Lindsay, J. F., MA MSc   Principal Lectr.
Tompsett, Hilary M., BPhil MA   Principal Lectr.; Head*
Other Staff: 7 Sr. Lectrs.

Surveying

Tel: (020) 8547 7070 Fax: (020) 8547 7087
Bennett, T. P., BSc   Principal Lectr.
Gillett, Alan H.   Visiting Prof.
Lewis, Amanda   Postgrad. Course Dir.
Sayce, Sarah L., BSc, FRICS   Head*
Other Staff: 6 Sr. Lectrs.; 2 Sr. Lectrs.†

Three-Dimensional Design

Tel: (020) 8547 7165
Warren, M. D., MDes *RCA*   Principal Lectr.
Other Staff: 2 Sr. Lectrs.; 2 Sr. Lectrs.†
Research: sustainability in art and design

SPECIAL CENTRES, ETC

Earth and Environmental Sciences Research, Centre for (CEESR)

E-mail: g.robinson@kingston.ac.uk
Robinson, Guy M., BSc DPhil, FRGS   Dir.*

Economic Research and Intelligence, Centre for (CERI)

Tel: (020) 8547 7505
Garside, Peter, BA PhD   Dir.*

Enterprise Exchange

Tel: (020) 8547 7200 Fax: (020) 8547 8844
E-mail: j.deacon@kingston.ac.uk
Lipscombe, Marguerite, MSc   Dir., Knowledge Transfer*
McEwan, Ann Marie, BA(Econ) PhD   Lead Facilitator
Stokes, David   Dir., Enterprise and Innovation*

European Research Centre

Fax: (020) 8547 7292
E-mail: j.bailey@kinston.ac.uk
Bailey, Joe, BA MSc   Prof., Sociology
Barber, Stephen, BA PhD   Prof., Media Arts
Nectoux, François, MPhil PhD   Prof., Contemporary European Studies; Dir.*

Iris Murdoch Studies, Centre for

E-mail: a.rowe@kingston.ac.uk
Rowe, Anne, BA MA PhD   Sr. Lectr.; Dir.*

Local History Studies, Centre for

Tel: (020) 8547 7359
E-mail: c.french@kingston.ac.uk
French, Chris J., MA PhD   Principal Lectr.; Dir.*
Other Staff: 2 Res. Fellows; 1 Researcher; 1 Project Devel. Consultant

NTI Centre (New Technology Institutes)

Tel: (020) 8547 8321 Fax: (020) 8547 8781
E-mail: j.woods@kingston.ac.uk
Alsop, Graham   Assoc. Dir., Teaching and Learning
Guest, James   Dir.*
Wallin, Paul I., BSc   Assoc. Dir., Teaching and Learning

Simulation and Control Centre

Fax: (020) 8547 7992
Mason, Peter J., PhD   Dir.*

Small Business Research Centre

Tel: (020) 8547 7247 Fax: (020) 8547 7140
Blackburn, R. A., MA PhD   Prof.; Head*
Hart, M., BA PhD   Prof.
Smallbone, Prof. D., BSc MSc   Assoc. Dir.
Other Staff: 6 Researchers

Society and Politics, Centre for the Study of (CUSP)

Fax: (020) 8547 7292
E-mail: b.brivati@kingston.ac.uk
Brivati, Brian L., PhD   Prof.; Dir.*

CONTACT OFFICERS

Academic affairs. Deputy Vice-Chancellor: Stuart, Prof. Mary, BA *Cape Town*, BA *Oxf.*, DPhil *Oxf.* (E-mail: m.stuart@kingston.ac.uk)
Accommodation. Director of Accommodation: Armstrong, Bruce (E-mail: b.armstrong@kingston.ac.uk)
Admissions (first degree). Head of Admissions Office: Bhugeloo, Nick (E-mail: n.bhugeloo@kingston.ac.uk)
Admissions (higher degree). Head of Graduate School: Manly, Ralph, BSc PhD (E-mail: r.manly@kingston.ac.uk)
Admissions (higher degree). (Taught courses) Head of Admissions Office: Bhugeloo, Nick (E-mail: n.bhugeloo@kingston.ac.uk)
Alumni. Head of Development (Alumni, Events and Fundraising): Trott, Helen, BSc PhD (E-mail: h.trott@kingston.ac.uk)
Careers. Head of Careers: Hankins, Katharine
Computing services. Head of Infrastructure: (vacant) (E-mail: r.volo@kingston.ac.uk)
Conferences/corporate hospitality. Head of Commercial Services, Kingston University Service Company: Jewitt, Richard (E-mail: r.jewitt@kingston.ac.uk)
Credit transfer. Director of Academic Development: Roberts, Larry H., BSc PhD (E-mail: l.roberts@kingston.ac.uk)
Development/fund-raising. Head of Development (Alumni, Events and Fundraising): Trott, Helen, BSc PhD (E-mail: h.trott@kingston.ac.uk)
Development/fund-raising. Pro Vice-Chancellor (External Affairs and Business Development): Jones, Prof. Martyn, BSc MA, FRGS (E-mail: m.jones@kingston.ac.uk)
Equal opportunities. Human Resources Director: Rogers, Nick
Finance. Finance Director: Butcher, Terence M. (E-mail: t.butcher@kingston.ac.uk)

General enquiries. University Secretary: Beaton, D. Donald, BA *Manc.*, MBA *Dund.* (E-mail: j.barry@kingston.ac.uk)
Health services. Head of Health and Counselling: Deane, Gillian (E-mail: g.deane@kingston.ac.uk)
International office. (European office) European Office Manager: Carbonell Porro, Joan-Anton (E-mail: ja.carbonell@kingston.ac.uk)
International office. Head of International Development: Forland, Heather (E-mail: h.forland@kingston.ac.uk)
Language training for international students. English Language Support Co-ordinator: Atherton, Barbara, MA (E-mail: b.atherton@kingston.ac.uk)
Library (chief librarian). Director of Library Services: Bulpitt, Graham, MA (E-mail: g.bulpitt@kingston.ac.uk)
Marketing. Head of Marketing and Communications: Cahn, Alison (E-mail: a.cahn@kingston.ac.uk)
Minorities/disadvantaged groups. Dean of Students: Hopkins, Kenneth V. J., BA *Lond.*, BD *Lond.*, PhD *Hull* (E-mail: k.hopkins@kingston.ac.uk)
Ombudsman. Head of Student Affairs: Jones, Glyn (E-mail: g.r.jones@kingston.ac.uk)
Personnel/human resources. Human Resources Director: Rogers, Nick
Public relations. Media and Public Relations Manager: Gupta, Anita (E-mail: a.gupta@kingston.ac.uk)
Publications. Head of Marketing and Communications: Cahn, Alison (E-mail: a.cahn@kingston.ac.uk)
Purchasing. Finance Director: Butcher, Terence M. (E-mail: t.butcher@kingston.ac.uk)
Quality assurance and accreditation. Academic Registrar: Stokes, Allison M. (E-mail: a.stokes@kingston.ac.uk)
Research. Assistant Registrar: Smith, Michelle, BA *Reading* (E-mail: m.smith@kingston.ac.uk)
Safety. Health and Safety Manager: Appleford, Ian (E-mail: i.appleford@kingston.ac.uk)
Scholarships, awards, loans. Director of Student Services: Marshall, Margo, BA (E-mail: m.marshall@kingston.ac.uk)
Schools liaison. UK Marketing Manager: Pollard, Mike (E-mail: m.pollard@kingston.ac.uk)
Security. Head of Security: Pattern, Tony (E-mail: t.bretherick@kingston.ac.uk)
Sport and recreation. Director of Sport: Muschamp, Phil (E-mail: p.muschamp@kingston.ac.uk)
Staff development and training. Head of Staff Development and Training: King, Pat
Student welfare/counselling. Head of Health and Counselling: Deane, Gillian (E-mail: g.deane@kingston.ac.uk)
Students from other countries. Head of Student Affairs and International Student Advisor: Jones, Glyn (E-mail: g.r.jones@kingston.ac.uk)
Students from other countries. Head of International Development: Forland, Heather (E-mail: h.forland@kingston.ac.uk)
Students with disabilities. Diversity Manager: Stow, Jan (E-mail: j.stow@kingston.ac.uk)
Women. Human Resources Director: Rogers, Nick

[*Information supplied by the institution as at 9 November 2007, and edited by the ACU*]

UNIVERSITY OF LANCASTER

Founded 1964

Member of the Association of Commonwealth Universities

Postal Address: University House, Lancaster, England LA1 4YW
Telephone: (01524) 65201 **Fax:** (01524) 63806
URL: http://www.lancaster.ac.uk

VICE-CHANCELLOR*—Wellings, Prof. Paul W., BSc Lond., MSc Durh., PhD E.Anglia
PRO-VICE-CHANCELLOR, COLLEGES AND THE STUDENT EXPERIENCE—Chetwynd, Prof. Amanda G., MSc Nott., PhD
  Open(UK)
PRO-VICE-CHANCELLOR, EXTERNAL RELATIONS—Cooper, Prof. Cary L., CBE, BS Calif., MBA Calif., MSc Manc., PhD
  Leeds, Hon. DLitt H-W, Hon. DBA Wolv., Hon. DSc Aston, Hon. DUniv Middx.
PRO-VICE-CHANCELLOR, ACADEMIC DEVELOPMENT—McKinlay, Prof. Robert D., BSocSc Birm., DPhil York(UK)
PRO-VICE-CHANCELLOR, RESEARCH—McMillan, Prof. Trevor J., BSc Lanc., PhD Lond.
DIRECTOR, REGIONAL OUTREACH—Seward, Prof. Derek W., BSc Salf., MSc Brad., PhD Lanc.
SECRETARY‡—Aiken, Fiona M., BA Sheff.
DIRECTOR, FINANCE AND RESOURCES—Neal, Andrew C., BA York(UK), MA York(UK)

GENERAL INFORMATION

History. The university was founded in 1964. It is located 2km south of the city of Lancaster.

Admission to first degree courses (see also United Kingdom Introduction). Through Universities and Colleges Admissions Service (UCAS). At least 2 passes at General Certificate of Education (GCE) A level and evidence of competence in English language. Additional requirements specified for each scheme of study.

First Degrees (see also United Kingdom Directory to Subjects of Study) (* = with honours). BA*, BBA*, BEng*, BMus*, BSc*, LLB*, MEng*, MMath*, MPhys*, MSci*.

All courses are full-time and normally last 3 years. Some courses (principally languages, management) last 4 years.

Length of course. Full-time: BA*, BEng*, BMus*, BSc*, LLB*: 3 years; BBA*: 3–4 years; MEng*, MMath*, MPhys*, MSci*: 4 years.

Higher Degrees (see also United Kingdom Directory to Subjects of Study).

Master's. MA, MBA, MMus, MPhil, MRes, MSc.

Admission. The normal requirement for admission to a master's degree is either a second class honours degree of a British university (or CNAA), or a relevant professional qualification at an equivalent level.

Length of course. Full-time: MA, MBA, MMus, MPhil, MRes, MSc: 1 year. Part-time: MA, MBA, MMus, MPhil, MRes, MSc: 2 years.

Doctoral. DClinPsychol, PhD.

Admission. The normal requirement for admission to doctoral degrees is a good honours degree of a recognised university or comparable institution, or evidence of equivalent qualifications with exceptional ability.

Length of course. Full-time: PhD: 3 years. Part-time: DClinPsychol: 3 years; PhD: 5 years.

Language of Instruction. English. Pre-sessional remedial courses available from Institute for English Language Education.

Libraries. Volumes: 1,000,000. Periodicals subscribed to: 3200. Special collections: Ruskin library (works of John Ruskin).

FACULTIES/SCHOOLS

Arts and Social Sciences
E-mail: fass@lancaster.ac.uk
Dean: Gatrell, Prof. Anthony C., BSc Brist., MS Penn., PhD Penn.
Administrator: (vacant)

Graduate School
Director: Park, Prof. Christopher C., BSc Ulster, PhD Exe.
Secretary: (vacant)

Management
E-mail: management@lancaster.ac.uk
Dean: Cox, Susan J., BSc Nott., MPhil Nott.
Administrator: Atherton, Susan, BA Sheff.

Science and Technology
E-mail: j.q.quinn@lancaster.ac.uk
Dean: Smyth, Prof. Mary M., BA Trinity(Dub.), MSc Leic., PhD Leic., FBPsS
Administrator: Thorne, Lucy E., BSc Brad., PhD Middx.

ACADEMIC UNITS
Accounting and Finance
E-mail: l.airey@lancaster.ac.uk
Bartram, Söhnke M., BBA Saar, MBA Saar, PhD Sr. Lectr.
Lambrecht, Bart M., BA Antwerp, MA Camb., MPhil Camb., PhD Camb.   Prof.
O'Hanlon, John F., BA Hull, MA Lanc., FCA Prof.
Otley, David T., MA Camb., MTech Brun., PhD Manc.   Prof.
Peasnell, Kenneth V., MSc(Econ) Lond., PhD Lanc., FCA   Prof.
Pope, Peter F., BCom Liv., MA Lanc.   Prof.
Shackleton, Mark B., BA Oxf., MBA Europ.Inst.Bus.Admin.   Prof.
Taylor, Stephen J., BA Camb., MA Lanc., PhD Lanc.   Prof.; Head*
Widdicks, Martin, BSc Manc., PhD Manc.   Sr. Lectr.
Yadav, Pradeep K., BSc Delhi, MSc Delhi, MSc Strath., PhD Strath.   Prof.
Young, Steven E., BA Wales, PhD Lanc.   Sr. Lectr.
Other Staff: 13 Lectrs.; 5 Res. Fellows; 7 Teaching Assocs.
Research: corporate finance; corporate governance; financial markets; financial reporting; mathematical finance

Applied Social Science
E-mail: v.holmes@lancaster.ac.uk
Grover, Christopher G., BA Lanc., PhD Lanc.   Sr. Lectr.
May-Chahal, Corinne, BA Lanc., PhD Lanc.   Prof.
McIvor, Gill C., BA Stir., PhD Stir.   Prof.
Measham, Fiona, BA Camb., MA Warw., PhD Manc.   Sr. Lectr.
Paylor, Ian, BA Lanc., PhD Lanc.   Sr. Lectr.
Penna, Susan E., BA Lanc., PhD Lanc.   Sr. Lectr.
Sapey, Bob J., MA Plym.   Sr. Lectr.; Head*
Smith, David B., MA Oxf., BPhil Exe.   Prof.
Taylor, Carolyn P., BA Warw., PhD Salf.   Sr. Lectr.

White, Susan J., BSc Brad., MA Salf., PhD Salf. Sr. Lectr.
Wise, Susan, MA Manc., PhD Manc.   Prof.
Other Staff: 7 Lectrs.; 3 Tutorial Fellows
Research: child care; community care; criminal justice

Biological Sciences
E-mail: biology@lancaster.ac.uk
Allsop, David, BSc Lond., PhD Lond.   Prof.
Bardgett, Richard D., BSc Newcastle(UK), PhD Lanc.   Prof.
Benson, Fiona, BSc Hull, PhD Nott.   Sr. Lectr.
Brown, Gavin, BSc Lanc., PhD Lanc.   Sr. Lectr.
Davies, William J., BSc Reading, PhD Wis.   Prof.
Forde, Brian, BSc Belf., PhD Belf.   Prof.
Fullwood, Nigel J., BSc Manc., MPhil CNAA, PhD Open(UK)   Sr. Lectr.
Grant, Karen, BSc Strath., PhD Strath.   Sr. Lectr.
Hartley, Ian, BSc Newcastle(UK), PhD Leic.   Sr. Lectr.
Huckerby, Thomas N., BSc Birm., PhD Birm., DSc Lanc.   Reader
Jones, Keith, BSc Nott., PhD Lond.   Sr. Lectr.
Lea, Peter J., PhD Liv., DSc Liv., FIBiol   Prof.†
Martin, Frank, MSc Lond., PhD Lond., BSc   Sr. Lectr.
McAinsh, Martin R., BSc Sus., PhD Lanc.   Reader
McKean, Paul, BSc Nott., PhD Nott.   Sr. Lectr.
McMillan, Trevor J., BSc Lanc., PhD Lond.   Prof.†
Nieduszynski, Ian A., BSc Leeds, PhD Leeds   Prof.
Owen-Lynch, P. Jane, BA Camb., PhD Leic.   Sr. Lectr.
Parry, Jacqueline D., BA Camb., PhD Leic.   Sr. Lectr.
Paul, Nigel D., BSc Reading, PhD Lanc.   Reader; Head*
Piearce, Trevor G., BSc Wales, PhD Wales   Sr. Lectr.
Price, Clive, BSc Aberd., PhD Newcastle(UK)   Sr. Lectr.
Shirras, Alan D., BSc Edin., PhD Camb.   Sr. Lectr.
Taylor, Jane E., BSc Nott., PhD Wales   Sr. Lectr.
Tollrian, Ralph   Reader
Wilson, Kenneth, BSc Nott., PhD Sheff.   Reader
Other Staff: 10 Lectrs.; 1 Res. Fellow; 18 Res. Assocs.
Research: medical, plant and environmental biology

Communications Systems
E-mail: j.wiggins@lancaster.ac.uk
Honary, Bahram, BSc Mashhad, MSc Kent, PhD Kent   Prof.
Honary, Farideh, BSc Tehran, PhD Kent   Prof.; Head*
Xydeas, Costas S., MSc Lough., PhD Lough., DEng Athens   Prof.
Other Staff: 6 Lectrs.; 2 Teaching Fellows; 12 Res. Assocs.

Research: coding and modulation; image, speech and digital signal processing; ionosphere and radio propagation

Computing

E-mail: computing@comp.lancs.ac.uk

Blair, Gordon S., BSc *Strath.,* PhD *Strath.* Prof.; Head*

Blair, Lynne, BSc *Lanc.,* PhD *Lanc.* Sr. Lectr.

Cheverst, Keith, BSc *Lanc.,* PhD *Lanc.* Sr. Lectr.

Coulson, Geoffrey, BSc *Lanc.,* PhD *Lanc.* Prof.

Davies, Nigel A. J., BSc *Lanc.,* PhD *Lanc.* Prof.

Dix, Alan, BA *Camb.,* DPhil *York(UK)* Prof.

Finney, Joe, BSc *Lanc.,* PhD *Lanc.* Sr. Lectr.

Friday, Adrian, BSc *Lond.,* PhD *Lanc.* Sr. Lectr.

Gellersen, Hans W., MSc *Karlsruhe,* PhD *Karlsruhe* Prof.

Hutchison, David, BSc *Edin.,* MTech *Brun.,* PhD *Strath.* Prof.

Kotonya, Gerald, BSc *Nair.,* PhD *Lanc.* Sr. Lectr.

Mariani, John A., BSc *Strath.,* PhD *Strath.* Sr. Lectr.

Marshall, Ian, BSc *Durh.* Prof.

Mathy, Laurent, PhD *Lanc.* Sr. Lectr.

Mauthé, Andreas U., PhD *Lanc.* Sr. Lectr.

Pink, Steve, BA *Minn.,* MA *Cornell,* PhD *Stockholm* Prof.

Rashid, Awais, BSc *Lahore UET,* MSc *Essex,* PhD *Lanc.* Prof.

Salmation, Kave, MBA *Isfahan,* MSc *Isfahan,* PhD *Paris XI* Reader

Sawyer, Peter H., BSc *Lanc.,* PhD *Lanc.* Sr. Lectr.

Scott, Andrew C., BSc *Lanc.,* PhD *Lanc.* Sr. Lectr.

Whittle, Jon, BA *Oxf.,* MSc *Edin.,* PhD *Edin.* Prof.

Other Staff: 12 Lectrs.; 2 Res. Fellows; 36 Res. Assocs.

Research: cooperative and interactive systems; co-operative systems engineering; mobile and ubiquitous computing; networked and distributed systems; software systems engineering

Contemporary Arts, Lancaster Institute for the

Aston, Elaine, BA *E.Anglia,* MA *Warw.,* PhD *Warw.* Prof.

Boynton, Neil A., MA *City(UK),* PhD *Camb.* Sr. Lectr.

Cooper, Rachel, BA *Staffs.,* PhD *Manc.Met.* Prof.; Dir.*

Davies, Gerald, BA *CNAA,* MA *Lond.* Sr. Lectr.

Harris, Geraldine M., BA *Manc.,* MA *Manc.,* PhD *Lanc.* Prof.

Marsden, Alan A., BA *S'ton.,* PhD *Camb.* Sr. Lectr.

Mawer, Deborah H., BMus *Lond.,* PhD *Lond.* Sr. Lectr.

Quick, Andrew J., BA *Newcastle(UK),* MA *Brist.,* PhD *Brist.* Sr. Lectr.

Rai, Takayuki, BMus *Toho Gakuen* Prof.

Rose, Emma, BA *CNAA,* MA *Lond.* Sr. Lectr.

Whiteley, Nigel S., BA *Wales,* PhD *Lanc.* Prof.

Other Staff: 9 Lectrs.; 1 Res. Fellow; 1 Teaching Fellow

Research: cultural criticism; design; graphic art; musical analysis; theatre in practice

Continuing Education

E-mail: conted@lancaster.ac.uk

Percy, Keith A., BSc *Lond.,* MA *Camb.,* MA *Nott.,* PhD *Lanc.* Prof.; Dir.*

Other Staff: 4 Staff Tutors; 4 Staff Tutors†

Research: post-compulsory and adult education

Cultural Research, Institute for

E-mail: icr@lancaster.ac.uk

Gere, Charles E., MA *Middx.,* PhD *Middx.* Reader; Dir.*

Kuhn, Annette F., BA(Econ) *Sheff.,* MA *Sheff.,* PhD *Lond.* Prof.†

Wilson, Scott T., BA *CNAA,* PhD *Wales* Reader

Other Staff: 9 Lectrs.

Research: cultural identity and cultural memory; culture of modern societies

Economics

E-mail: economics@lancaster.ac.uk

Bradley, Steven, BA *Leeds,* MA *Lanc.,* PhD *Lanc.* Prof.

Ingham, Hilary, BSc *Lough.,* MA *Manc.,* PhD *Glas.* Sr. Lectr.

Johnes, Geraint, BSc *Bath,* MSc *Lanc.,* PhD *Lanc.* Prof.; Head*

Johnes, Jill, BA *Lanc.,* PhD *Lanc.* Sr. Lectr.

Kirby, Maurice W., BA *Newcastle(UK),* PhD *Sheff.* Prof.

Paya, Ivan, BSc *Alicante,* BA *Alicante,* PhD *Cardiff* Sr. Lectr.

Peel, David, BA *Warw.* Prof.

Read, Robert A., BA *Essex,* PhD *Reading* Sr. Lectr.

Rothschild, Robert, MA *Cape Town* Prof.

Simmons, R., MA *Manc.,* PhD *Leeds* Sr. Lectr.

Snowden, P. Nicholas, BCom *Liv.,* MA *Leeds,* PhD *Leeds* Sr. Lectr.

Steele, R. Gerald, BA *Sheff.,* MA *Sheff.* Reader

Taylor, James, MA *Liv.,* PhD *Lanc.* Prof.

Other Staff: 7 Lectrs.

Research: economic theory; human resource economics; international business; macroeconomics, international economics, finance and financial markets

Educational Research

E-mail: kathryn.doherty@lancaster.ac.uk

Hamilton, Mary E., BA *Sus.,* PhD *Lond.* Prof.; Head*

Jackson, Carolyn, BSc *Lanc.,* PhD *Lanc.* Sr. Lectr.

McConnell, David, BA *Stir.,* PhD *Sur.* Prof.

Rogers, Colin G., BA *Sheff.,* PhD *Leic.* Prof.

Saunders, Murray S., BA *Essex,* MA *Lanc.,* PhD *Lanc.* Prof.

Solomon, Yvette, BSc *CNAA,* PhD *Lanc.* Reader

Tight, Malcolm, BSc *Lond.,* PhD *Lond.* Prof.

Trowler, Paul, BA *CNAA,* MA *Lanc.,* PhD *Lanc.* Prof.

Warin, Jo, BA *York(UK),* MA *Lanc.,* PhD *Lanc.* Sr. Lectr.

Other Staff: 9 Lectrs.; 1 Sr. Res. Fellow; 1 Res. Fellow; 1 Teaching Fellow; 3 Res. Assocs.

Research: educational policy; gender; learning technology; literacy and evaluation studies; post-compulsory education; psychology of learning

Engineering

E-mail: engineering@lancaster.ac.uk

Aggidis, George A., BEng *Brad.,* MSc *Cran.* Sr. Lectr.

Carter, Richard G., MA *Camb.,* PhD *Wales,* FIEE Prof.

Dexter, Amos, BSc *Liv.,* PhD *Liv.* Sr. Lectr.

Joyce, Malcolm, BSc *Liv.,* PhD *Liv.* Sr. Lectr.

Kemp, Roger J., BSc *Sus.* Prof.

Richardson, Andrew M. D., BA *Manc.,* PhD *Lanc.* Prof.

Seward, Derek W., BSc *Salf.,* MSc *Brad.,* PhD *Lanc.* Prof.†

Taylor, C. James, BSc *Liv.,* PhD *Liv.* Sr. Lectr.

Turvey, Geoffrey J., BSc *Birm.,* MSc *Lond.,* PhD *Birm.* Sr. Lectr.

Widden, Martin B., MA *Camb.* Sr. Lectr.; Head*

Other Staff: 5 Lectrs.; 1 Res. Officer; 8 Res. Assocs.; 2 Teaching Fellows

Research: communications; electronics; mechatronics

English and Creative Writing

see also Linguistics and Mod. Engl. Lang.

E-mail: a.stewart-whalley@lancaster.ac.uk

Appelbaum, Robert, BA *Chic.,* MA *San Francisco,* PhD *Calif.* Sr. Lectr.

Bainbridge, Simon J., BA *Lond.,* MA *York(UK),* DPhil *York(UK)* Prof.; Head*

Bradley, Arthur H., BA *Liv.,* PhD *Liv.* Sr. Lectr.

Bushell, Sally C., BA *Lond.,* MA *York(UK),* PhD *Camb.* Sr. Lectr.

Cosslett, A. Therese, BA *Oxf.,* BLitt *Oxf.,* DPhil *Oxf.* Reader

Elliott, Kamilla L., BA *Colorado,* PhD *Harv.* Sr. Lectr.

Farley, Paul, BA *Lond.* Prof.

Findlay, Alison G., BA *York(UK),* MA *Birm.,* PhD *Birm.* Prof.

Greaney, Michael J., BA *Oxf.,* MA *Newcastle(UK),* PhD *Lanc.* Sr. Lectr.

Green, George, MA *Lanc.,* PhD *Lanc.* Sr. Lectr.

Hanley, Keith A., MA *Oxf.,* BLitt *Oxf.,* PhD *Lanc.* Prof.

Hinds, Hilary, BA *Birm.,* PhD *Birm.* Sr. Lectr.

Horsley, Lee S., BA *Minn.,* MPhil *Reading,* PhD *Birm.* Sr. Lectr.

Mort, Graham, BA *Liv.,* DPhil *Glam.* Sr. Lectr.

Pearce, Lynne, BA *Hull,* MA *Wales,* PhD *Birm.* Prof.

Pinkney, Tony A., BA *Brist.,* MA *Warw.,* MLitt *Oxf.* Sr. Lectr.

Schad, S. John, BA *York(UK),* PhD *Wales* Prof.

Sharpe, Anthony E., MA *Camb.,* PhD *Camb.* Sr. Lectr.

Spooner, Catherine L., BA *Oxf.,* MA *Lond.,* PhD *Lond.* Sr. Lectr.

Other Staff: 7 Lectrs.; 2 Res. Assocs.

Research: creative writing; early modern literature; nineteenth and twentieth centuries and contemporary literature

Environmental Science

E-mail: e.harrison@lancaster.ac.uk

Beven, Keith J., BSc *Brist.,* PhD *E.Anglia* Prof.

Binley, Andrew M., BSc *Aston,* PhD *Aston* Prof.; Head*

Chappell, Nicholas A., BSc *CNAA,* PhD *CNAA* Sr. Lectr.

Chotai, Arunkumar, BSc *Bath,* PhD *Bath* Sr. Lectr.

Davison, William, BSc *Newcastle(UK),* PhD *Newcastle(UK),* FRSChem Prof.

Gilbert, Jennifer S., BSc *Lond.,* PhD *Camb.* Sr. Lectr.

Hamilton-Taylor, John, BSc *Wales,* PhD *Edin.* Reader

Hewitt, C. Nicholas, BA *Lanc.,* PhD *Lanc.* Prof.

Jones, Kevin C., BSc *Lond.,* PhD *Lond.* Prof.

MacKenzie, A. Robert, BSc *Edin.,* PhD *Essex* Reader

Meju, Max, BSc *Nigeria,* PhD *Edin.* Reader

Pinkerton, Harry, BSc *Strath.,* PhD *Lanc.,* FGS Prof.

Quinton, John, BSc *Reading,* PhD *Cran.* Sr. Lectr.

Semple, Kirk T., BSc *Napier,* PhD *Newcastle(UK)* Reader

Wilson, Lionel, BSc *Birm.,* PhD *Lond.,* FRAS, FGS Prof.†

Zhang, Hao, BSc *Qingdao Sci.&Technol.* Sr. Lectr.

Other Staff: 5 Lectrs.; 1 Sr. Res. Fellow; 4 Res. Fellows; 12 Res. Assocs.; 1 Res. Officer; 1 Teaching Asst.

Research: environmental chemistry; hydrology and modelling; volcanology

European Languages and Cultures

E-mail: delc@lancaster.ac.uk

Bartram, Graham, MA *Oxf.,* DPhil *Oxf.* Sr. Lectr., German

Camino, Mercedes, BA *Auck.,* MA *Auck.,* PhD *Auck.* Prof.

Crawshaw, Robert H., BA *Exe.,* MèsA *Paris,* PhD *Lanc.* Sr. Lectr., French

Fiddler, Allyson, BA *S'ton.,* PhD *S'ton.* Prof., German

Kallis, Aristotle, BA *Athens,* PhD *Brist.* Sr. Lectr.

Rossi, Paolo L., MA *Glas.* Sr. Lectr., Italian

Slawinski, Maurice P. P., MA *Camb.* Sr. Lectr., Italian

Waine, Anthony E., BA *Newcastle(UK),* PhD *Lanc.* Sr. Lectr., German

Whitton, David W., BA *Durh.,* PhD *Durh.* Prof., French; Head*

Other Staff: 7 Lectrs. (European Studies 1, French 2, German 1, Italian 1, Spanish 2); 8 Teaching Fellows (European Studies 1, French 2, German 1, Italian 2, Spanish 2)

Research: applied linguistics; contemporary, romantic and Renaissance literature; film and theatre; socio-cultural studies

Geography

E-mail: geography@lancaster.ac.uk
Barker, Philip A., BSc Hull, PhD Lough.   Reader; Head*
Chapman, Graham P., BA Camb., PhD Camb.   Prof.
Clark, Gordon, MA Edin., PhD Edin.   Sr. Lectr.
Maher, Barbara A., BSc Liv., PhD Liv.   Prof.
Pooley, Colin G., BA Liv., PhD Liv.   Prof.
Walker, Gordon, BA Leeds, PhD Leeds   Prof.
Whyte, Ian D., MA Edin., PhD Edin., DSc Edin.   Prof.
Other Staff: 10 Lectrs.; 1 Sr. Res. Fellow; 1 Res. Fellow
Research: catchment and aquatic processes; environment and society; environmental change and pollution; organisms and the environment

Health Research, Institute for

E-mail: ihr@lancaster.ac.uk
Clark, David, BA Newcastle(UK), MA Newcastle(UK), PhD Aberd.   Prof.
Emerson, Eric B., BSc S'ton., MSc Manc., PhD Manc.   Prof.
Gatrell, Anthony C., BSc Brist., MS Penn., PhD Penn.   Prof.†
Grinyer, Anne, BA Lanc., PhD Lanc.   Sr. Lectr.
Hatton, Christopher R., BSc Manc., PhD Manc.   Prof.; Head*
Milligan, Christine, BA Strath., PhD Strath.   Sr. Lectr.
Mort, Maggie, BA Liv., PhD Lanc.   Sr. Lectr.
Murphy, Glynis, BA Oxf., MSc Birm., PhD Lond.   Prof.
Popay, Jennie, BA Massey, MA Essex   Prof.
Thomas, Carol, BA Sheff., PhD Warw.   Reader
Welshman, John, BA York(UK), DPhil Oxf.   Sr. Lectr.
Other Staff: 4 Lectrs.; 2 Sr. Res. Fellows; 3 Res. Fellows; 6 Res. Assocs.
Research: disability and service provision; health inequalities and public health; health service users and their careers

History

E-mail: l.drake@lancaster.ac.uk
Barber, Sarah, BA Trinity(Dub.), PhD Trinity(Dub.)   Sr. Lectr.
Blinkhorn, R. Martin, BA Oxf., AM Stan., DPhil Oxf., FRHistS   Prof.†
Constantine, Stephen, BA Oxf., DPhil Oxf., FRHistS   Sr. Lectr.
Ealham, Christopher M., BA Lond., PhD Lond.   Sr. Lectr.
Grant, Alexander, BA Oxf., DPhil Oxf., FRHistS   Reader
Harman, Peter M., BA Oxf., MA Oxf., MA Camb., PhD Leeds   Prof., History of Science
Jotischky, Andrew, BA Camb., MA Yale, PhD Yale   Prof.
Mullett, Michael A. A., BA Wales, MLitt Camb., PhD Lanc.   Prof.
Palladino, Paolo, AB Col., PhD Minn., PhD Edin.   Sr. Lectr.; Head*
Phillips, Gordon A., MA Oxf., DPhil Oxf.   Sr. Lectr.
Pumfrey, Stephen, BA Camb., PhD Lond.   Sr. Lectr.
Richards, Jeffrey M., MA Camb., FRHistS   Prof.
Rohkramer, Thomas, MA Freib., PhD Freib.   Sr. Lectr.
Sayer, Derek G., BA Essex, PhD Durh.   Prof.
Stringer, Keith J., MA Camb., PhD Camb., FSA, FRHistS   Prof.
Winchester, Angus J. L., BA Durh., PhD Durh.   Sr. Lectr.
Winstanley, Michael J., BA Oxf., MA Lanc., PhD Lanc., FRHistS   Sr. Lectr.
Other Staff: 7 Lectrs.; 1 Teaching Fellow; 1 Teaching Fellow†
Research: history of science; international and imperial history; social and cultural history

Law

E-mail: law@lancaster.ac.uk
Biggs, Hazel, BA Kent, PhD Kent   Prof.
Bryan, Ian, LLB Warw., PhD Warw.   Sr. Lectr.

Howells, Geraint, LLB Brun.   Prof.; Head*
Milman, David, LLB Birm., PhD Birm.   Prof.
Picciotto, Solomon, BA Oxf., JD Chic.   Prof.
Rowe, Peter, LLB Belf., LLM Lond., PhD Liv.   Prof.
Skogly, Sigrun, BA Oslo, LLM Essex, PhD Oslo   Reader
Sugarman, David, LLB Hull, LLM Camb., LLM Harv., SJD Harv., FRHistS   Prof.
Other Staff: 12 Lectrs.; 1 Teaching Fellow
Research: comparative and international law; gender and family; history of law; legal theory

Linguistics and English Language

E-mail: linguistics@lancaster.ac.uk
Alderson, J. Charles, MA Oxf., PhD Edin.   Prof.
Allwright, Richard L., BA Reading, MLitt Edin., PhD Lanc.   Sr. Lectr.
Baker, John Paul, BSc C.Lancs., MSc Lanc., PhD Lanc.   Sr. Lectr.
Barton, David P., BA Sus., MA Essex, PhD Lond.   Prof.
Bygate, Martin, BA Leic., MA Manc., PhD Lond.   Prof.
Culpepper-Williams, Jonathan V., BA Lanc., PhD Lanc.   Sr. Lectr.
Ivaniĉ, Rosalind E., BA Brist., MA Lanc., PhD Lanc.   Prof.
Johnson, Keith, MA Oxf., MA Essex, PhD Essex   Prof.
Katamba, Francis X., BA Mak., PhD Edin.   Prof.
Kerswill, Paul, BA Camb., MPhil Camb., PhD Camb.   Prof.
Knowles, Gerald, MA Camb., PhD Edin.   Sr. Lectr.
Kormos, Judit, MA E.L.Bud., PhD E.L.Bud.   Sr. Lectr.
McEnery, Anthony, BA Lanc., MSc De Mont., PhD Lanc.   Prof.
Myers, Gregory A., BA Claremont, MA Col., PhD Col.   Prof.
Sebba, Mark, BA Witw., MSc Manc., DPhil York(UK)   Reader
Semino, Elena, BA Genoa, MA Lanc., PhD Lanc.   Sr. Lectr.
Short, Michael H., BA Lanc., MA Birm., PhD Lanc.   Prof.
Siewierska, Anna M., MA Melb., PhD Melb.   Prof.; Head*
Sunderland, Jane, BA Liv., MLitt Qld., MA Lanc., PhD Lanc.   Sr. Lectr.
Waters, Alan, MA Lanc., MA Glas., PhD Lanc.   Sr. Lectr.
Wodak, Ruth, PhD Vienna   Prof.
Other Staff: 10 Lectrs.
Research: computer corpus; formal and descriptive linguistics; stylistics

Management Learning and Leadership

E-mail: j.roberts@lancaster.ac.uk
Burgoyne, John G., BSc Lond., MPhil Lond., PhD Manc.   Prof.
Collinson, David, BSc UMIST, MSc UMIST, PhD UMIST   Prof.
Easterby-Smith, Mark P. V., BSc Durh., PhD Durh.   Prof.
Grint, Keith, BA Open(UK), BA York(UK), DPhil Oxf.   Prof.
Hodgson, Vivien, BSc Birm., PhD Sur.   Prof.; Head*
Other Staff: 6 Lectrs.; 3 Res. Assocs.
Research: social learning process

Management Science

E-mail: managementscience@lancaster.ac.uk
Brown, David H., MA Lanc.   Prof.
Busby, Jeremy S., MA Camb., MSc Lond., PhD Lanc.   Sr. Lectr.
Chiasson, Michael, BCom Alta., PhD Br.Col.   Sr. Lectr.
Cox, Susan J., BSc Nott., MPhil Nott.   Prof.
Eglese, Richard W., BA Camb., MA Lanc.   Prof.
Fildes, Robert A., BA Oxf., MA Calif., PhD Calif.   Prof.
Glazebrook, Kevin, BA Camb., DPhil Oxf.   Prof.†
Hendry, Linda C., BSc Lanc., PhD Lanc.   Prof.; Head*

Letchford, Adam N., BSc Nott., MSc Lanc., PhD Lanc.   Prof.
Pidd, Michael, BTech Brun., MSc Birm.   Prof.
Rand, Graham K., BSc Liv.   Sr. Lectr.
Spring, Martin, BTech Lough., PhD Stir.   Sr. Lectr.
Teunter, Ruud, MSc Gron., PhD Gron.   Prof.
Worthington, David J., BSc Birm., MSc Reading, PhD Reading   Sr. Lectr.
Wright, Michael B., BA Oxf., MSc Oxf.   Sr. Lectr.
Other Staff: 7 Lectrs.; 6 Res. Assocs.
Research: operational research and management; systems and information

Marketing

E-mail: b.moss@lancaster.ac.uk
Araujo, Luis M. P. M. D., LMechEng Oporto, MA Lanc., PhD Lanc.   Prof.; Head*
Easton, Geoffrey, BSc Brist., PhD Lond.   Prof.
Hogg, Margaret, MA Edin., MA Lanc., PhD Manc.   Prof.
Hopkinson, Gillian, BA E.Anglia, PhD Brad.   Sr. Lectr.
Mouzas, Stefanos, BSc Athens, LLM Brist., PhD Lanc.   Sr. Lectr.
Other Staff: 7 Lectrs.; 4 Teaching Fellows
Research: business-to-business (B2B) industrial networks; consumer research; quantitative marketing

Mathematics and Statistics

E-mail: maths@lancaster.ac.uk
Blower, Gordon, BSc Glas., DPhil Oxf.   Prof.; Head*
Chetwynd, Amanda G., MSc Nott., PhD Open(UK)   Prof.
Fearnhead, Paul, MA Oxf., DPhil Oxf.   Prof.
Francis, Brian J., BSc Lond., MSc Sheff.   Prof.
Glazebrook, Kevin, BA Camb., DPhil Oxf.   Prof.†
Jameson, Graham J. O., MA Camb., PhD Edin.   Sr. Lectr.
Lancaster, Gillian A., BSc Glam., MSc Leic., PhD Lanc.   Sr. Lectr.
Lindsay, J. Martin, BSc Lond., PhD Nott.   Prof.
Mukherjee, Kanchan, BStat Calc., MStat Calc., PhD Mich.   Sr. Lectr.
Pettitt, Antony N., BSc Nott., MSc Nott., PhD Nott.   Prof.
Power, Stephen C., BSc Lond., PhD Edin., DSc Edin.   Prof.
Tawn, Jonathan A., BSc Lond., PhD Sur.   Prof.
Towers, David A., BSc Newcastle(UK), PhD Leeds   Sr. Lectr.
Tunnicliffe-Wilson, Granville, BA Camb., PhD Lanc.   Reader
Whitehead, John, BA Oxf., MSc Sheff., PhD Sheff.   Prof.
Whittaker, Joseph C., MSc Lond., PhD Lond.   Sr. Lectr.
Other Staff: 13 Lectrs.; 8 Res. Assocs.; 1 Teaching Fellow
Research: analysis and algebra; computational statistics; statistical modelling of complex data

Organisation, Work and Technology

E-mail: owt@lancaster.ac.uk
Ackroyd, Stephen C., BA Newcastle(UK), MSc(Econ) Lond., PhD Lanc.   Prof.
Blackler, Frank H. M., BA Brist., MPhil Lond.   Prof.
Bloomfield, Brian, BSc Lanc., PhD Open(UK)   Prof.
Bolton, Sharon, BA CNAA, PhD Lanc.   Reader
Fleetwood, Stephen, BA Liv.J.Moores, MPhil Camb., PhD Camb.   Sr. Lectr.
Introna, Lucas D., BCom S.Af., BA Pret., MA Pret., PhD Pret., PhD Rotterdam   Prof.; Head*
Vurdubakis, Theodore, BSc Athens, MSc UMIST, PhD UMIST   Prof.
Other Staff: 7 Lectrs.
Research: knowledge, work and competitive advantage

Philosophy

E-mail: (none listed)
Archard, David, BA Oxf., PhD Lond.   Prof.
Cooper, Rachel, BSc Nott., MPhil Camb., PhD Camb.   Sr. Lectr.

Levitt, Mairi, BA Edin., MA Edin., PhD Exe.   Sr. Lectr.; Head*
Manson, Neil, BA Lond., MPhil Lond., DPhil Oxf.   Sr. Lectr.
Stone, Alison, BA Kent, DPhil Sus.   Sr. Lectr.
Other Staff: 5 Lectrs.; 2 Res. Assocs.
Research: cultural perspectives on risk and environment; intersection of policy, science and technology; public engagement with emerging technologies

Physics

Bertram, Iain A., BSc Melb., PhD Melb.   Reader
Bradley, D. Ian, BSc Lanc., PhD Lanc.   Sr. Lectr.
Falko, Vladimir, MSc Moscow, PhD Moscow   Prof.
Fisher, Shaun N., BSc Lanc., PhD Lanc.   Prof.
Jones, Roger W. L., BA Birm., MA Birm., PhD Birm.   Prof.
Krier, Anthony, BSc Hull, PhD Hull   Prof.
Lambert, Colin J., BSc Hull, PhD Hull   Prof.
McClintock, Peter V. E., BSc Belf., DSc Belf., DPhil Oxf., FIP   Prof.
McDonald, John, BSc Sus., DPhil Sus.   Reader
Pickett, George R., BA Oxf., DPhil Oxf., FRS   Prof.
Ratoff, Peter N., BA Lond., PhD Lond.   Prof.; Head*
Schomerus, Henning, MSc Essen, PhD Essen   Reader
Stefanovska, Aneta, MEng Ljubljana, MSc Ljubljana, PhD Ljubljana   Reader
Tucker, Robin W., MA Camb., PhD Camb., FIP   Prof.
Other Staff: 16 Lectrs.; 1 Sr. Res. Fellow; 38 Res. Assocs.; 4 Res. Officers
Research: experimental condensed matter physics; experimental elementary particle physics; theoretical physics

Politics and International Relations

E-mail: m.worthington@lancaster.ac.uk
Bishop, Patrick J., BA NE, PhD Adel.   Sr. Lectr.
Cochrane, Feargal E., BA Belf., PhD Belf.   Sr. Lectr.
Denver, David T., MA Glas., BPhil Dund.   Prof.
Dillon, G. Michael, BA Liv., MA Dal., PhD Lanc.   Prof.
Geyer, Robert R., BA Calif., MA Essex, MA Wis., PhD Wis.   Prof.
Hands, H. T. Gordon, BA Oxf., BPhil Oxf.   Sr. Lectr.
May, Christopher, BA Open(UK), MA Kent, PhD Nott.Trent   Prof.; Head*
Misra, Amalendu, MA Delhi, MPhil Delhi, MA Hull, PhD Hull   Sr. Lectr.
Sum, Ngai-Ling, BSocSci Birm., MA HK, MEd HK, MSocSci HK, PhD Lanc.   Sr. Lectr.
Sylvester, Christine, BA Albertus Magnus, MA Boston, PhD Kentucky   Prof.
Weber, Cynthia L., BA W.Virginia, MA Sus., PhD Arizona State   Prof.
Other Staff: 7 Lectrs.; 1 Teaching Fellow
Research: comparative international politics; defence; electoral studies; political theory

Psychology

E-mail: psychology@lancaster.ac.uk
Ball, Linden, BSc Plym., PhD CNAA   Sr. Lectr.
Bremner, J. Gavin, BSc St And., DPhil Oxf., FBPsS   Prof.
Cain, Kate, BSc Sus., DPhil Sus.   Sr. Lectr.
Collins, Alan, BA Reading, PhD Lanc.   Sr. Lectr.
Condor, Susan G., BA Wales, PhD Brist.   Prof.
Crawford, Thomas J., BSc Warw., PhD Durh.   Sr. Lectr.
Dewhurst, Stephen A., BSc Lanc., PhD Lanc.   Sr. Lectr.
Dixon, John, BA Cape Town, BSocSci Cape Town, MA Cape Town, PhD Exe.   Sr. Lectr.
Hay, Dennis C., BSc Aberd., MSc UMIST, PhD Aberd.   Sr. Lectr.
Howe, Mark L., BA W.Ont., MA W.Ont., PhD W.Ont.   Prof.
Levine, R. Mark, BA Exe., PhD Exe.   Sr. Lectr.
Lewis, Charles N., BA Lanc., MA Nott., PhD Nott.   Prof.
Monaghan, Padraic, BSc Manc., MSc Edin., PhD Edin.   Prof.

Morris, Peter E., BA Exe., PhD Exe., FBPsS   Prof.
Ormerod, Thomas C., BSc Leeds, PhD CNAA   Prof.; Head*
Plack, Chris, MA Camb., PhD Camb.   Prof.
Smyth, Mary M., BA Trinity(Dub.), MSc Leic., PhD Leic., FBPsS   Prof.†
Subbotsky, Eugene V., PhD Moscow, DSc Moscow   Reader
Taylor, Paul J., BSc Essex, MSc Liv., PhD Liv.   Sr. Lectr.
Towse, John, BA Manc., PhD Manc.   Sr. Lectr.
Vogt, Stefan, BSc Mün., PhD Bremen   Sr. Lectr.
Walker, Peter S., BSc Lond., PhD Lond.   Reader
Other Staff: 7 Lectrs.; 20 Res. Assocs.; 1 Res. Fellow
Research: cognition; infancy; infant and child development; memory; social, conceptual and historical psychology

Religious Studies

E-mail: relstud@lancaster.ac.uk
Heelas, Paul L. F., MA Oxf., DPhil Oxf.   Prof.
Partridge, Chris H., BD Aberd., PhD Aberd.   Sr. Lectr.
Ram-Prasad, Chatravarthi, BA SSSIHL, MA SSSIHL, DPhil Oxf.   Prof.; Head*
Sawyer, Deborah F., BA Newcastle(UK), MLitt Newcastle(UK), PhD Edin.   Sr. Lectr.
Smith, David J., BA Oxf., DPhil Oxf.   Reader
Woodhead, Linda J. P., MA Camb.   Prof.
Other Staff: 5 Lectrs.
Research: eastern and western traditions; method and theory

Sociology

E-mail: sociology@lancaster.ac.uk
Cronin, Anne, BA Hull, MA York(UK), PhD Lanc.   Sr. Lectr.
Fortier, Anne-Marie, BA Laval, MSc Montr., PhD Lond.   Sr. Lectr.
Gilloch, Graeme, BA Durh., MA York(UK), PhD Camb.   Reader; Head*
Jessop, Robert D., BA Exe., MA Camb., PhD Camb.   Prof.
Law, John, BSc(Econ) Wales, PhD Edin.   Prof.
Penn, Roger D., BA Camb., MA Brown, PhD Camb.   Prof.
Sayer, R. Andrew, BA Lond., MA Sus., DPhil Sus.   Prof.
Shapiro, Daniel Z., MA Oxf.   Prof.
Shove, Elizabeth, BA York(UK), DPhil York(UK)   Reader
Stacey, Jackie, BA Sus., MA Kent, PhD Birm.   Prof.
Suchman, Lucy A., AB Calif., MA Calif., PhD Calif.   Prof.
Urry, John R., MA Camb., PhD Camb.   Prof.
Walby, Sylvia, BA Reading, MA Essex, PhD Essex   Prof.
Other Staff: 5 Lectrs.
Research: culture; environment; gender; political economy; technology and work

SPECIAL CENTRES, ETC

Accounting, International Centre for Research in

Pope, Peter F., BCom Liv., MA Lanc.   Dir.*
Research: accounting and finance

Advanced Learning Technology, Centre for Studies in

McConnell, David, BA Stir., PhD Sur.   Prof.; Dir.*

Advanced Studies, Institute for

Jessop, Robert D., BA Exe., MA Camb., PhD Camb.   Prof.; Dir.*

Applications of Computers to Music, Centre for Research into the

Marsden, Alan A., BA S'ton., PhD Camb.   Sr. Lectr.; Dir.*

Bioethics and Medical, Centre for

Archard, David, BA Oxf., PhD Lond.   Prof.; Dir.*

Collaborative Intervention in the Public Sector, Centre for

Blackler, Frank H. M., BA Brist., MPhil Lond.   Prof.; Dir.*

Computer Corpus Research on Language, Centre for

Rayson, Paul E., BSc Lanc., PhD Lanc.   Dir.*

Contemporary Performance Practice, Centre for the Advanced Study of

Aston, Elaine, BA E.Anglia, MA Warw., PhD Warw.   Prof.; Dir.*

Economic and Social Aspects of Genomics, Centre for the

Wynne, Brian E., MPhil Edin., MA Camb., PhD Camb.   Prof.; Dir.*

Education and Training, Centre for the Study of

Saunders, Murray S., BA Essex, MA Lanc., PhD Lanc.   Dir.*
Other Staff: 1 Prof.; 5 Res. Officers
Research: policy and practice; upper secondary and post-compulsory education

Entrepreneurship and Enterprise Development, Institute for

Hamilton, Eleanor E., BA CNAA, MA Lanc., PhD Lanc.   Dir.*
Howorth, Carole, BSc Brad., PhD Brad.   Sr. Lectr.
Jack, Sarah, BA Aberd., PhD Aberd.   Sr. Lectr.
Rose, Mary B., BAEcon Liv., PhD Manc.   Prof.
Other Staff: 2 Lectrs.; 1 Teaching Fellow; 2 Res. Fellows
Research: entrepreneurial learning; entrepreneurship; family business; innovation; social networks

Environmental Change, Centre for the Study of

Szerszynski, Bronislaw, BA Lanc., PhD Lanc.   Dir.*

Forecasting, Lancaster Centre for

Fildes, Robert A., BA Oxf., MA Calif., PhD Calif.   Prof.; Dir.*

Gender and Women's Studies, Centre for

Fortier, Anne-Marie, BA Laval, MSc Montr., PhD Lond.   Sr. Lectr.; Dir.*

Human Development, Centre for Research in

Bremner, J. Gavin, BSc St And., DPhil Oxf., FBPsS   Prof.; Dir.*

InfoLab21: Research and Knowledge Transfer Centre

Hutchison, David, BSc Edin., MTech Brun., PhD Strath.   Prof.; Dir.*

Innovation and Enterprise Unit

Dawes, Frank, BSc Lanc., MSc City(UK)   Dir.*
Other Staff: 1 Lectr.

Language in Social Life, Centre for

Sebba, Mark, BA Witw., MSc Manc., DPhil York(UK)   Dir.*

Law and Society, Centre for

Sugarman, David, LLB Hull, LLM Camb., LLM Harv., SJD Harv., FRHistS   Prof.; Dir.*

Literacy Research Centre

Barton, David P., BA Sus., MA Essex, PhD Lond.   Dir.*

Management School: Development Division

Watson, Sally E., BSc Manc., MA CNAA, PhD Lanc.   Sr. Teaching Fellow; Dir.*
Other Staff: 9 Teaching Fellows

Mobilities Research, Centre for

Urry, John R., MA Camb., PhD Camb.   Prof.; Dir.*

Nanoscale Dynamics and Mathematical Physics, Centre for

Lambert, Colin J., BSc Hull, PhD Hull   Prof.; Dir.*

North-West Regional Studies, Centre for

Whiteside, Jacqueline M., MA Oxf.   Dir.*†
Other Staff: 7 Hon. Res. Fellows
Research: political history; social history; tourism

Peace Studies, Richardson Institute for

Cochrane, Feargal E., BA Belf., PhD Belf.   Dir.*
Other Staff: 1 Lectr.; 1 Hon. Lectr.
Research: conflict resolution; peace and conflict

Performing and Learning and Teaching Innovation Network (PALATINE)

Bray, Roger W., MA Oxf., DPhil Oxf.   Dir.*

Practice and Theory: Research into Composition, Centre for

Rai, Takayuki, BMus *Toho Gakuen*   Prof.; Dir.*

Ruskin Centre

Hanley, Keith A., MA Oxf., BLitt Oxf., PhD Lanc.   Dir.*
Other Staff: 13 Hon. Profs.; 1 Res. Assoc.
Research: John Ruskin and his circle

Science Studies, Centre for

Law, John, BSc(Econ) *Wales*, PhD Edin.   Prof.; Dir.*

Technology and Organisation, Centre for the Study of

Bloomfield, Brian, BSc Lanc., PhD Open(UK)   Prof.; Dir.*

Training and Development, Centre for

O'Brien, Jane, MA Oxf.   Dir.*
Other Staff: 2 Devel. Managers

Transcultural Writing and Research, Centre for

Mort, Graham, BA Liv., DPhil *Glam.*   Sr. Lectr.; Dir.*

Wordsworth Centre

Pinkney, Tony A., BA Brist., MA *Warw.*, MLitt Oxf.   Sr. Lectr.; Dir.

CONTACT OFFICERS

Academic affairs. Director of Governance and Planning: Graves, Paul M., BA *Lanc.*, MA *Lanc.*
(E-mail: angela.pearson@lancaster.ac.uk)
Academic affairs. Academic Registrar: Wareing, Lesley M., BA Lanc.
(E-mail: l.wareing@lancaster.ac.uk)
Admissions (first degree). Undergraduate Admissions Officer: Willes, Heather A., BA Lond. (E-mail: h.willes@lancaster.ac.uk)
Admissions (higher degree). Postgraduate Admissions Officer: Pacey, Catherine, BSc Lanc., MA Liv.
(E-mail: c.pacey@lancaster.ac.uk)
Adult/continuing education. Director, Continuing Education: Percy, Prof. Keith A., BSc Lond., MA Camb., MA Nott., PhD Lanc.
(E-mail: k.percy@lancaster.ac.uk)
Alumni. Alumni Officer: (vacant)
Careers. Head of Career Service: Blackmore, Paul, BSc CNAA, MEd Sheff.
(E-mail: p.blackmore@lancaster.ac.uk)
Computing services. Director, Information Services: Gallagher, John J., BSc *Wales*, MA Lanc. (E-mail: j.gallagher@lancaster.ac.uk)
Conferences/corporate hospitality. Director (Conferences/corporate hospitality): Peeks, David (E-mail: d.peeks@lancaster.ac.uk)
Equal opportunities. Director, Human Resources: Walshe, Valerie C., BA *Warw.*
(E-mail: v.walshe@lancaster.ac.uk)
Estates and buildings/works and services. Director (Estates and buildings/works and services): Swindlehurst, Mark, MBA *Sheff.Hallam*
(E-mail: m.swindlehurst@lancaster.ac.uk)
Examinations. Head, Student Registry: Denny, Ian, BA CNAA
(E-mail: i.denny@lancaster.ac.uk)
Finance. Director, Finance and Resources: Neal, Andrew C., BA York(UK), MA York(UK)
(E-mail: a.neal@lancaster.ac.uk)
General enquiries. Secretary: Aiken, Fiona M., BA Sheff. (E-mail: f.aiken@lancaster.ac.uk)
Health services. Medical Officer: (vacant)
International office. International Officer: Thomas, Adrian, BA Leeds, MA Sheff.
(E-mail: intoffice@lancaster.ac.uk)
Library (enquiries). Librarian: Whiteside, Jacqueline M., MA Oxf.
(E-mail: j.whiteside@lancaster.ac.uk)

Marketing. Director (Marketing): McGovern, John J., BA S'ton., MSc Edin.
(E-mail: j.mcgovern@lancaster.ac.uk)
Personnel/human resources. Director, Human Resources: Walshe, Valerie C., BA *Warw.* (E-mail: v.walshe@lancaster.ac.uk)
Public relations. Press Officer: Tyrrell, Victoria L., BA CNAA
(E-mail: v.tyrrell@lancaster.ac.uk)
Purchasing. Head, Strategic Purchasing: Holt, Hilary, MBA Lanc.
(E-mail: h.holt@lancaster.ac.uk)
Quality assurance and accreditation. Academic Registrar: Wareing, Lesley M., BA Lanc. (E-mail: l.wareing@lancaster.ac.uk)
Research. Research Accountant: Fox, Yvonne (E-mail: y.fox@lancaster.ac.uk)
Safety. Safety and Radiation Protection Officer: Madeley, Anthony T., MSc *Aston*
(E-mail: a.madeley@lancaster.ac.uk)
Scholarships, awards, loans. Student Support Officer: Dray, Terry
(E-mail: t.dray@lancaster.ac.uk)
Schools liaison. Admissions Liaison Officer: Gould, Roger S., BA Lanc., MA Open(UK)
(E-mail: r.gould@lancaster.ac.uk)
Security. Head (Security): Evans, Anthony G., BA Open(UK)
(E-mail: a.g.evans@lancaster.ac.uk)
Sport and recreation. Director, Sport and Physical Recreation: Montgomery, Kim, BA Kent (E-mail: k.montgomery@lancaster.ac.uk)
Staff development and training. Training and Development Officer: Rodaway, Paul
(E-mail: p.rodaway@lancaster.ac.uk)
Strategic planning. Strategic Planning Officer: (vacant)
Student union. General Manager (Student Union): Elliott, Peter R., BA Lanc., MBA Strath. (E-mail: peter.elliott@lancaster.ac.uk)
Student welfare/counselling. Counsellor (Student welfare/counselling): Elder, John, BA Oxf., MSc Birm.
(E-mail: j.elder@lancaster.ac.uk)
Students from other countries. Head, Study Abroad and Exchange: Atkinson, Jane, BA Lond. (E-mail: j.atkinson@lancaster.ac.uk)
Students with disabilities. Disabilities Adviser: Quinn, Christine
(E-mail: c.quinn@lancaster.ac.uk)

[*Information supplied by the institution as at 18 October 2007, and edited by the ACU*]

UNIVERSITY OF LEEDS

Founded 1904

Member of the Association of Commonwealth Universities

Postal Address: Leeds, England LS2 9JT
Telephone: (0113) 243 1751 **Fax:** (0113) 244 3923 **E-mail:** office@scf.leeds.ac.uk
URL: http://www.leeds.ac.uk

VICE-CHANCELLOR*—Arthur, Prof. Michael J. P., BM S'ton., DM S'ton., FRCP, FMedSci, FRSA
DEPUTY VICE-CHANCELLOR—Fisher, Prof. John, BSc Birm., PhD Glas., DEng Leeds, FIMechE
PRO-VICE-CHANCELLOR—Atack, Prof. Margaret K., BA Lond., PhD Lond.
PRO-VICE-CHANCELLOR—Jones, Vivien M., MA Oxf., DPhil Oxf.
PRO-VICE-CHANCELLOR—Scott, Prof. Stephen K., BSc Leeds, PhD Leeds
PRO-VICE-CHANCELLOR—Williams, Prof. Richard A., BSc(Eng) Lond., PhD Lond., FREng, FIMMM, FIChemE
FINANCE AND COMMERCIAL DIRECTOR—Smith, Berenice, BA Oxf.Brookes
MARKETING DIRECTOR—Holmes, Martin, BA Sheff.
DIRECTOR OF HUMAN RESOURCES—Knight, Matthew, MA Camb., FCIPD
DIRECTOR OF ESTATES—Sladdin, Robert D., FRICS
SECRETARY TO THE UNIVERSITY‡—Gair, J. Roger, MA Oxf.

GENERAL INFORMATION

History. The antecedents of the university were Leeds School of Medicine, founded in 1831, and Yorkshire College of Science, founded in 1874. These combined in 1884, eventually to form a constituent part of the federal Victoria University (founded 1887). The university received its charter in 1904.

Admission to first degree courses (see also United Kingdom Introduction). Through Universities and Colleges Admissions Service (UCAS). Acceptable levels of literacy are required for all degree programmes, together with specified requirements for individual degree programmes.

First Degrees (see also United Kingdom Directory to Subjects of Study). BA, BChD, BEng, BHSc, BMus, BSc, LLB, MB ChB, MChem, MEng, MGeog, MGeol, MGeophys.

BA, BSc and LLB may also be taken 4 years full-time if taken with a foreign language or time spent in industry.

Length of course. Full-time: BHSc: $1\frac{1}{2}$–3 years; BA, BEng, BSc, LLB: 3 years; BMus, MChem, MEng, MGeog, MGeol, MGeophys: 4 years; BChD, MB ChB: 5 years. Part-time: BHSc: 2–5 years; BA, BSc: 5–6 years; LLB: 6 years.

Higher Degrees (see also United Kingdom Directory to Subjects of Study).

Master's. ChM, LLM, MA, MA, MBA, MCFS, MDentSci, MDS, MEd, MHSc, MMedSc, MMid, MMus, MPH, MPhil, MPsychObs, MPsychother, MRes, MSc, MSc, MSc(Eng).

Length of course. Full-time: LLM, MA, MBA, MEd, MHSc, MMus, MPH, MRes, MSc, MSc(Eng): 1 year; MA: 1–2 years; ChM, MDS, MPhil: 2 years; MDentSci: 2–3 years. Part-time: MBA, MSc: 1–5 years; MHSc: $1\frac{1}{2}$–5 years; ChM, LLM, MA, MCFS, MMus, MRes, MSc: 2 years; MDentSci: 2–3 years; MEd, MMid, MPH, MSc(Eng): 2–5 years; MMedSc: $2\frac{1}{2}$–5 years; MDS, MPsychObs, MA: 3 years; MPhil, MPsychother: 4 years. By *distance learning:* MA: 2–5 years.

Doctoral. DClinPsychol, DDSc, EdD, MD, PhD.

Length of course. Full-time: MD: 2 years; DClinPsychol, DDSc, EdD, PhD: 3 years. Part-time: MD: 2 years; DClinPsychol: 3 years; DDSc, EdD, PhD: 5 years.

Libraries. Volumes: 2,700,000.

FACULTIES/SCHOOLS

Arts

Dean: Thompson, Prof. Andrew S., BA Oxf., DPhil Oxf.

Biological Sciences

Dean: Homans, Prof. Steven W., BA Oxf., DPhil Oxf.

Business

Dean: Lock, Prof. Andrew R., BA Leeds, MSc Lond., PhD Lond., FRSA, FCIM

Education, Social Sciences and Law

Dean: Leach, Prof. John T., BSc Brist., PhD Leeds, FRSChem

Engineering

Dean: Pollard, Prof. Roger D., BSc Leeds, PhD Leeds, FIEE

Environment

Dean: Mackie, Prof. Peter J., BA Nott.

Mathematics and Physical Sciences

Dean: Wilson, Prof. Michael J., MA Camb., PhD Camb.

Medicine and Health

Dean: McWilliam, Prof. Peter N., BSc Dund., PhD Glas.

Performance, Visual Arts and Communications

Dean: Cooper, Prof. David G., BA Leeds, BA Open(UK), DPhil York(UK)

ACADEMIC UNITS

Biological Sciences

temporary combined faculty

Tel: (0113) 343 3112 Fax: (0113) 343 3167
Adams, David G., BSc Liv., PhD Liv.   Sr. Lectr.
Adams, David J., BSc Edin., PhD Aberd.   Sr. Lectr.
Alexander, R. McNeill, CBE, MA Camb., PhD Camb., DSc Wales, Hon. DSc Aberd., FIBiol, FRS   Res. Prof., Zoology
Altringham, John D., BA York(UK), PhD St And.   Prof., Biomechanics
Atkinson, Howard J., BSc Newcastle(UK), PhD Newcastle(UK)   Prof., Nematology
Baker, Alison, MA Camb., PhD Edin.   Reader, Plant Cell and Molecular Biology
Baldwin, Stephen A., MA Camb., PhD Camb.   Prof., Biochemistry
Bateson, Alan N., PhD Lond., BSc   Sr. Lectr.
Beech, David J., BSc Lond., PhD Lond.   Dir., Res. Inst.; Prof., Cellular and Molecular Physiology
Benton, Timothy G., BA Oxf., PhD Camb.   Dir., Res. Inst.; Prof., Population Ecology
Berry, Alan, BSc S'ton., PhD S'ton.   Sr. Lectr.
Billeter-Clark, Rudolph, MSc Zür., PhD Zür.   Sr. Lectr.
Birch, Karen M., BSc Liv., PhD Liv.J.Moores   Sr. Lectr.

Blair, G. Eric, BSc Edin., PhD Warw.   Reader, Biochemistry and Molecular Biology
Booth, Andrew G., BSc Leeds, PhD Leeds   Prof., Online Learning
Bowmer, Christopher J., BSc Liv., PhD Liv.   Sr. Lectr.
Brown, Stanley B., BSc Durh., PhD Newcastle(UK)   Yorkshire Cancer Res. Prof.
Buckley, Noel J., BA Camb., MA Camb., PhD Lond.   Prof., Neuroscience
Butlin, Roger K., MA Camb., PhD Nott.   Visiting Prof.
Carding, Simon R., BSc Coventry, PhD Lond.   Prof., Molecular Immunology
Chopra, Ian, MA Dublin City, PhD Brist., DSc Brist.   Prof., Microbiology
Coates, David, BSc Leeds, PhD E.Anglia, FIBiol   Visiting Prof.
Colyer, John, BSc CNAA, MPhil Lond., PhD S'ton.   Sr. Lectr.
Compton, Stephen G., BSc Hull, PhD Hull   Reader, Behavioural Ecology
Cove, David J., MA Camb., PhD Camb., FIBiol   Visiting Prof.
Cove, Jonathan H., BSc Lond., PhD CNAA   Sr. Lectr.
Cripps, R. E., BA Camb., PhD Warw.   Visiting Prof.
Cuming, Andrew C., BA Oxf., PhD Camb.   Sr. Lectr.
Davies, Brendan H., BSc Lond., PhD CNAA   Reader, Plant Development
Denecke, Jurgen, MSc(Eng) Brussels, PhD Ghent   Reader, Plant Cell Biology and Biotechnology
Deuchars, James, BSc Glas., PhD Lond.   Prof., Systems Neuroscience
Donnelly, Daniel, BSc Lond., PhD Lond.   Sr. Lectr.
Dunn, Alison, BA Oxf., PhD Leeds   Reader, Evolutionary Ecology
Edwards, John P., BSc Brun., PhD S'ton.   Visiting Prof.
Findlay, John B. C., BSc Aberd., PhD Leeds   Prof., Biochemistry
Forbes, J. Michael, BSc Nott., PhD Leeds, DSc Nott.   Res. Prof.
Fromm, Hillel, BSc Jerusalem, PhD Weizmann   Visiting Prof.
Gilmartin, Philip M., BSc Leeds, PhD Warw.   Prof., Plant Molecular Genetics
Grahame, John W., BSc WI, PhD Wales   Sr. Lectr.
Hale, Anthony D., MA Lond., MB BS Lond., MSc Lond., FRCPath   Visiting Sr. Lectr.
Hamer, Keith C., BSc Manc., PhD Glas.   Reader, Animal Ecology
Hames, B. David, BSc Brist., PhD Leic.   Reader, Developmental Biochemistry
Handyside, Alan H., BA Camb., MA Camb., PhD Camb.   Visiting Prof.
Hardy, Anthony J., MA Oxf., PhD Aberd.   Visiting Prof.

Harris, Mark P. G., BSc Plym., PhD Glas. Reader, Molecular Virology

Harrison, Simon M., BSc Leeds, PhD Glas. Sr. Lectr.

Henderson, Peter J. F., BSc Brist., MA Camb., ScD Camb., PhD Brist. Prof., Biochemistry and Molecular Biology

Henderson, Zaineb, BSc Lond., PhD Camb. Reader, Integrative Neuroscience

Heritage, John, BA York(UK), DPhil Sus. Sr. Lectr.

Hiscox, Julian, BSc Lond., PhD Reading Sr. Lectr.

Hobson, Richard P., MB BS Lond., PhD Lond. Sr. Lectr.

Hodgman, T. Charles, BSc Newcastle(UK), PhD Camb. Visiting Prof.

Holden, Arun V., BA Oxf., PhD Alta. Prof., Computational Biology

Holland, Keith T., BSc Leeds, PhD Leeds, FIBiol Prof., Microbiology

Homans, Steven W., BA Oxf., DPhil Oxf. Prof., Structural Biology; Head*

Hooper, Nigel M., BSc Leeds, PhD Leeds Prof., Biochemistry

Hope, Ian A., BA Oxf., PhD Edin. Sr. Lectr.

Hughes, Ian E., BSc Leeds, PhD Leeds Prof., Pharmacology Education

Hunter, Malcolm, BSc Newcastle(UK), PhD Manc. Reader, Epithelial Physiology

Iles, David, BSc Lond. Sr. Lectr.

Ingham, Eileen, BSc Leeds, PhD Leeds Prof., Medical Immunology

Isaac, R. Elwyn, BSc Wales, PhD Wales Prof., Comparative Biochemistry

Kearney, John N., BSc Leeds, PhD Leeds Visiting Prof.

Killington, Richard A., BSc Birm., PhD Birm. Prof., Virology Education

King, Anne E., BSc Aberd., PhD S'ton. Reader, Neuroscience

Klapper, Paul E., BSc Nott., PhD Manc., FRCPath Visiting Sr. Lectr.

Knight, Peter J., BSc Lond., PhD Lond. Reader, Molecular Cell Biology

Knox, J. Paul, BSc Newcastle(UK), PhD Wales Prof., Plant Cell Biology

Krause, Jens, MPhil Camb., PhD Camb. Prof., Behavioural Ecology

Kunin, William E., MA Harv., PhD Wash. Sr. Lectr.

Lewis, David I., BSc Leeds, PhD Birm. Sr. Lectr.

Marsh, Derek, BA Oxf., MA Oxf., DPhil Oxf. Visiting Prof.

McConkey, Glenn A., BSc Mich., PhD N.Y. Sr. Lectr.

McConnell, Patricia, BSc Birm., PhD Birm. Sr. Lectr.

McDowall, Kenneth J., BSc Edin., PhD Glas. Sr. Lectr.

McPherson, Michael J., BSc Leeds, PhD Leeds Dir., Undergrad. Studies; Prof., Biochemistry and Molecular Biology

Meyer, Peter, PhD Cologne Prof., Plant Genetics

Miller, Helen M., BSc Edin., MSc Reading, PhD Alta. Sr. Lectr.

Millner, Paul A., BSc Leeds, PhD Leeds Sr. Lectr.

Morrison, John F. B., MB ChB Edin., BSc Edin., PhD Edin., FRCSEd Visiting Prof.

Newman, Steven M., BSc Oxf.Brookes, PhD Open(UK) Visiting Prof.

Pearson, Hugh, BSc Lond., PhD Lond. Sr. Lectr.

Peckham, Michelle, BA York(UK), PhD Lond. Sr. Lectr.

Phillips, Simon E. V., BSc Lond., PhD Lond., FRSChem Astbury Prof., Biophysics

Phillips-Jones, Mary K., BSc Wales, PhD Wales Sr. Lectr.

Pilbeam, David J., BSc Lond., PhD Lond. Sr. Lectr.

Ponnambalam, Sreenivasan, BSc Birm., PhD Birm. Sr. Lectr.

Quatrano, Ralph, AB Colgate, MS Ohio, PhD Yale Visiting Prof.

Radford, Sheena E., BSc Birm., PhD Camb. Prof., Structural Molecular Biology

Rayner, Jeremy M. V., BA Camb., MA Camb., PhD Camb. Alexander Prof., Zoology

Richards, Martin B., BSc Sheff., PhD UMIST Sr. Lectr.

Roberts, David J. H., PhD Leeds Sr. Lectr.

Robertson, Brian, BSc Aberd., PhD Prof., Neurobiology

Robinson, Anne C., BSc Leeds, PhD Leeds Sr. Lectr.

Rodway, Richard G., BSc Lond., PhD Birm. Sr. Lectr.

Shaw, Marie-Anne, BSc Lond., PhD Sr. Lectr.

Shorrocks, Bryan, BSc Leic., PhD Manc. Sr. Fellow; Prof., Population Biology

Sivaprasadarao, Asipu, BSc Leeds, PhD Leeds Sr. Lectr.

Smith, Judith E., BSc Edin., PhD Camb. Head, Grad. School; Prof., Parasitology

Steele, Derek S., BSc Glas., PhD Glas. Sr. Lectr.

Stockley, Peter G., BSc Lond., PhD Camb. Prof., Biological Chemistry

Thomas, Christian D., BA Camb., MSc Wales, PhD Texas Visiting Prof.

Tompkins, David S., MB ChB Birm., FRCPath Visiting Sr. Lectr.

Trinick, John A., BSc Leic., PhD Leic. Prof., Animal Cell Biology

Turner, Anthony J., MA Camb., PhD Camb. Prof., Biochemistry

Utley, Andrea, BA Leeds Met., PhD Leeds Sr. Lectr.

Walker, John H., BSc Nott., PhD Nott. Sr. Lectr.

Ward, Susan A., BA Oxf., DPhil Oxf. Prof.

Waters, Dean, BSc E.Anglia, PhD Brist. Sr. Lectr.

Westhead, David, BA Camb., DPhil Oxf. Sr. Lectr.

Whitaker, Elaine M., BSc Dund., MSc Leeds, PhD Leeds Sr. Lectr.

White, Edward, BSc Wales, PhD Reading Reader, Neuroscience

White, Stanley J., BSc Manc., PhD Manc. Sr. Lectr.

Whitehouse, Adrian, BSc Sheff., DPhil Oxf. Reader, Molecular Virology

Whiteley, Geoffrey M., BSc Reading, PhD Adel. Sr. Lectr.

Wilcox, Mark H., BMedSci Nott., BM BS Nott., MD Nott. Prof., Medical Microbiology

Withington, Deborah J., BSc Nott., PhD Birm. Prof., Auditory Neuroscience

Wray, Dennis A., BA Camb., MSc Lond., DPhil Oxf. Prof., Pharmacology

Wright, Stephanie C., BA Oxf., PhD Lond. Sr. Lectr.

Yates, Michael S., BSc Liv., PhD Liv. Sr. Lectr.

Other Staff: 42 Lectrs.; 1 EPSRC Lectr.; 10 Visiting Lectrs.; 3 Assoc. Lectrs.; 1 Fac. Devel. Fellow; 1 Leverhulme Fellow; 2 Fac. Acad. Fellows; 1 Leverhulme Emer. Fellow; 6 Univ. Res. Fellows; 5 Marie Curie Res. Fellows; 1 BBSRC Res. Fellow; 1 EPSRC Res. Fellow; 1 Wellcome Trust Res. Fellow; 6 Visiting Res. Fellows; 2 Res. Assocs.; 95 Res. Fellows/Res. Assts.; 1 MRC Clin. Fellow; 3 Hon. Sr. Lectrs.; 1 Hon. Res. Fellow

Chemistry, School of

Tel: (0113) 343 6543 Fax: (0113) 343 6565

Beddard, Godfrey, BSc Lond., PhD Lond. Prof., Chemical Physics

Compton, Bruce, PhD Montr. Visiting Prof.

Fisher, Julie F., BSc Lanc., PhD Liv. Sr. Lectr.

Fishwick, Colin W. G., BSc Liv., PhD Liv. Sr. Lectr.

Gibb, Terence C., BSc Durh., PhD Newcastle(UK) Reader, Inorganic Chemistry

Griffiths, John F., BSc Birm., PhD Birm. Res. Prof.

Grigg, Ronald E., PhD Nott. Res. Prof.

Halcrow, Malcolm A., BA Camb., PhD Edin. Reader

Hamley, Ian W., BSc Reading, PhD S'ton. Prof., Polymer Materials

Hardie, Michaela J., BSc Melb., PhD Melb. Sr. Lectr.

Heard, Dwayne E., MA Oxf., DPhil Oxf. Prof., Atmospheric Chemistry

James, Keith, PhD Camb. Visiting Prof.

Johnson, A. Peter, MSc Manc., PhD Manc. Res. Prof.

Kee, Terence P., BSc Durh., PhD Durh. Sr. Lectr.

Kennedy, John D., BSc Lond., PhD Lond., FRSChem Prof., Inorganic Chemistry

Kocieński, Philip J., PhD Brown Prof., Organic Chemistry; Head*

Marsden, Stephen P., BSc Lond., PhD Lond. Reader, Organic Chemistry

McGowan, Patrick C., BSc Stir., DPhil Oxf. Sr. Lectr.

Nelson, Adam, BA Camb., PhD Camb. Prof., Chemical Biology

Pilling, Michael J., MA Camb., PhD Camb., FRSChem Prof., Physical Chemistry

Rayner, Christopher M., BSc Liv., PhD Liv. Prof., Organic Chemistry

Reid, Gavin D., BSc Manc., PhD Manc. Sr. Lectr.

Roberts, David, PhD Leeds Visiting Prof.

Scott, Stephen K., BSc Leeds, PhD Leeds Prof., Mathematical Chemistry

Seakins, Paul W., BSc Birm., DPhil Oxf. Reader

Warriner, Stuart, BA Camb., PhD Camb. Sr. Lectr.

Whitaker, Ben J., BSc Sus., DPhil Sus. Prof., Chemical Physics

Other Staff: 1 Prof. Fellow; 4 Lectrs.; 3 Sr. Res. Fellows; 31 Res. Fellows; 1 Sr. Fellow; 1 Academic Fellow; 2 Univ. Fellows

Classics, School of

Tel: (0113) 343 3537 Fax: (0113) 343 3554

Berry, Dominic H., MA Oxf., DPhil Oxf. Sr. Lectr.

Brock, Roger W., MA Oxf., DPhil Oxf. Sr. Lectr.; Head*

Clare, Raymond J., PhD Camb., BA Sr. Lectr.

Heath, Malcolm F., MA Oxf., DPhil Oxf. Prof., Greek Language and Literature

Levene, David S., MA Oxf., DPhil Oxf. Prof., Latin Language and Literature

Maltby, Robert, MA Camb., PhD Camb. Prof., Latin Philology

Stafford, Emma J., MA Camb., PhD Lond. Sr. Lectr.

Other Staff: 4 Lectrs.; 1 Hon. Lectr.; 2 Hon. Res. Assocs.

Research: ancient philosophy; Greek and Latin literature; Greek and Roman history and society

Colour Science

Tel: (0113) 343 2930 Fax: (0113) 343 2947

Carbonnel Costa, José, DSc Barcelona Visiting Prof.

Davison, John W., PhD Leeds, FRSChem Visiting Prof.

Griffiths, John F., BSc Birm., PhD Birm. Res. Prof.

Guthrie, James T., PhD Salf., FRSChem Prof., Polymer Surface Coatings and Science and Technology

Hefford, Robert J. W., BSc Leeds, PhD Leeds, FRSChem Visiting Prof.

Heron, B. Mark, PhD C.Lancs. Sr. Lectr.

Hunt, Robert W. G., BSc Lond., PhD Lond., DSc Lond. Visiting Prof.

Lewis, David M., BSc Leeds, PhD Leeds, FRSChem Res. Prof.

Lin, Long, BSc Zhejiang, MSc Zhejiang, PhD Leeds Sr. Lectr.

Luo, Ming R., BSc Prov.Taipei I.T., Taiwan, PhD Brad. Prof., Colour and Imaging Science

MacWilliams, James, BSc Open(UK), PhD Open(UK) Visiting Prof.

Nobbs, James H., BSc Leeds, PhD Leeds Head*

Oakes, John, BSc Leic., PhD Leic. Visiting Prof.

Perrier, Sebastien, PhD Warw. Sr. Lectr.

Pointer, Michael, BSc Lond., PhD Lond. Visiting Prof.

Rigg, Brian, BSc Brad., PhD Brad. Visiting Prof.

Tapley, Kelvin N., BSc Leeds, PhD Leeds Sr. Lectr.

Other Staff: 2 Lectrs.; 3 Sr. Res. Fellows; 7 Res. Fellows; 3 Visiting Res. Fellows; 1 Sr. Teaching Fellow; 1 Teaching Fellow; 4 Hon. Lectrs.

Research: colour physics (metallic paints, surface coatings, textile coloration); cosmetic science (bleaches, hair dyeing, permanent waves); new chromophores (Infrared (IR) absorbing dyes, medical uses of dyes); polymer and surface coatings (polymer structure, printing inks, ultra-violet (UV) curing); textile coloration (new reactive dyes, no salt cotton dyeing)

Communications Studies, Institute of

Tel: (0113) 343 5820 Fax: (0113) 343 5820

Brown, Robin C. M., BA Keele, MSc Wales, PhD Wales   Sr. Lectr., International Communications

Howells, Richard P., BA Harv., MPhil Camb., PhD Camb.   Sr. Lectr., Communications Arts

Morrison, David E., BA Hull, MA Leic., PhD Leic.   Prof., Communications Research

Popple, Simon, BA Salf., MA Leeds   Sr. Lectr., Cinema

Roberts, Graham, BA Kingston(UK), MA Sus., DPhil Sus.   Sr. Lectr., Communications Arts; Dir.*

Statham, Paul, BA Sus., PhD European Univ.Inst.   Reader, European Political Communications

Taylor, Paul A., MA Edin., PhD Edin.   Sr. Lectr., Communications Theory

Taylor, Philip M., BA Leeds, PhD Leeds, FRHistS   Prof., International Communications

Voltmer, Katrin, PhD F.U.Berlin   Sr. Lectr., Political Communication

Other Staff: 7 Lectrs.; 1 Principal Teaching Fellow; 1 Sr. Fellow; 5 Sr. Teaching Fellows; 3 Teaching Fellows

Research: film and television studies; international communications; political communications and communications policy; social impact of communications and audience research

Computing, School of

Tel: (0113) 343 5430 Fax: (0113) 343 5468

Atwell, Eric S., BA Lanc.   Sr. Lectr.

Baines, Michael, BSc Lond., PhD Lond.   Visiting Prof.

Barnett, Jeremy   Visiting Prof.

Berzins, Prof. Martin, BSc Leeds, PhD Leeds, FIMA   Prof., Scientific Computation

Boyle, Roger D., BA York(UK), DPhil York(UK)   Prof.; Head*

Braunstein, Samuel, BSc Melb., MSc Melb., PhD   Visiting Prof.

Brindley, Lynne J., DBE, BA Reading, MA Lond., FRSA   Visiting Prof.

Brodlie, Kenneth W., BSc Edin., MSc Dund., PhD Dund.   Prof., Visualisation

Cliff, David, BSc Leeds, DPhil Sus.   Visiting Prof.

Cohn, Anthony G., BSc Essex, PhD Essex, FIEEE   Prof., Automated Reasoning

Dew, Peter M., BTech Brad., PhD Brad.   Prof., Computer Science

Duke, David J., BSc Qld., PhD Qld.   Reader

Dyer, Martin E., BSc Leeds, MSc Lond., PhD Leeds   Prof., Theoretical Computer Science

Green, Thomas, BA Oxf., PhD Sheff.   Visiting Prof.

Hogg, David C., BSc Warw., MSc W.Ont., DPhil Sus.   Prof., Artificial Intelligence

Jimack, Peter K., BSc Brist., PhD Brist.   Prof., Scientific Computing

Kessel, David, BA Camb., MA Camb., MB BS Lond., FRCR   Visiting Sr. Lectr.

Kwan, Raymond S., BSc Leeds, PhD Leeds   Sr. Lectr.

Muller, Haiko, DrRerNat Jena, DrRerNatHabil Jena   Sr. Lectr.

Ng, Kia C., BSc Leeds, PhD Leeds   Sr. Lectr.

Phillips, Nicholas I., BSc Leeds, MB ChB Edin., PhD Lond., FRCS   Visiting Sr. Lectr.

Proll, Leslie G., BSc Liv., PhD Liv.   Sr. Lectr.

Roberts, Stuart A., BSc Sus., PhD Lond.   Sr. Lectr.

Ruddle, Roy, BSc Lough., PhD Wales   Sr. Lectr.

Smith, Barbara, BSc Lond., MSc Sheff., PhD Lond.   Visiting Prof.

Stell, John G., BSc Manc., MSc Manc., PhD Manc.   Sr. Lectr.

Vŭsković, Kristina, PhD Carnegie-Mellon, BA   Sr. Lectr.

Xu, Jie, BEng Chongqing, MSc Chongqing, PhD Newcastle(UK)   Prof.

Other Staff: 11 Lectrs.; 1 Assoc. Sr. Lectr.; 1 Assoc. Lectr.; 2 Sr. Res. Fellows; 1 Leverhulme Res. Fellow; 8 Res. Fellows; 1 Univ. Res. Fellow; 3 Sr. Teaching Fellows; 1 Teaching Fellow

Research: artificial intelligence; information systems and management; internet computing; scheduling and constraint management; scientific computation

Design, School of

Tel: (0113) 343 3700 Fax: (0113) 343 3704

Anderson, J. Micheal, MA Leeds Met.   Sr. Lectr.

Blackburn, Richard, BSc Leeds, PhD Leeds   Sr. Lectr.

Burkinshaw, Stephen M., BSc Brad., PhD Brad.   Prof., Textile Chemistry

Cassidy, Tom, MA De Mont., PhD CNAA   Prof.

Hann, Michael A., BA Leeds, MPhil Leeds, PhD Leeds, FTI   Prof., Design Theory

Hay, Kenneth G., BA Leeds, MA Wales, PhD Wales, FRSA   Prof., Contemporary Art Practice

Lawrence, Carl A., BSc CNAA, PhD Brad., FRSA   Prof., Textile Engineering

Leaf, Gerald A. V.   Visiting Prof.

Russell, Stephen, PhD Leeds   Sr. Lectr.

Ward, Robert, BA Newcastle(UK), MA Reading   Sr. Lectr.

Westland, Stephen, BSc Leeds, PhD Leeds   Prof., Colour Science and Technology; Head*

Other Staff: 10 Lectrs.; 1 Sr. Res. Fellow; 9 Res. Fellows; 6 Sr. Teaching Fellows; 13 Teaching Fellows; 1 Sr. Tutor

Earth and Environment, School of

Tel: (0113) 343 5222 Fax: (0113) 343 5259

Yardley, Bruce W. D., BSc Exe., PhD Brist., DSc Brist., FGS   Head*

Atmospheric Sciences, Institute for

Blyth, Alan, BSc Edin., PhD UMIST   Reader, Atmospheric Measurement

Carslaw, Kenneth, BSc E.Anglia, MSc E.Anglia, PhD E.Anglia   Prof.

Chipperfield, Martyn, BA Camb., PhD Camb.   Prof., Atmospheric Chemistry

Gadian, Alan, BA Keele, MSc Lond., PhD Lond.   Sr. Lectr.

Mobbs, Stephen D., BSc Leeds, PhD Leeds   Prof., Atmospheric Dynamics

Parker, Douglas, MA Reading, PhD Reading   Sr. Lectr.

Smith, Michael H., BSc UMIST, PhD UMIST   Prof., Atmospheric Physics; Head*

Other Staff: 6 Lectrs.; 16 Res. Fellows; 1 Univ. Res. Fellow; 1 NERC Res. Fellow

Earth Surface Processes and Environment, Institute of

Benning, Liane G., BSc Kiel, MSc E.T.H.Zürich, PhD E.T.H.Zürich   Reader, Geobiology

Best, James L., BSc Leeds, PhD Lond.   Prof., Process Sedimentology

Bottrell, Simon H., BA Oxf., PhD E.Anglia   Prof., Environmental Isotope Geochemistry

Collier, Richard E. L., BSc Lond., PhD Leeds   Sr. Lectr.

Francis, Jane E., BSc S'ton., PhD S'ton.   Prof., Palaeoclimatology; Head*

Hencher, Stephen R., BSc Lond., PhD Lond.   Visiting Prof., Engineering Geology and Rock Mechanics

Hudson, John A., BSc H-W, PhD Minn., DSc   Visiting Prof., Rock Engineering

Krom, Michael D., MA Camb., PhD Edin.   Prof., Marine and Environmental Geochemistry

West, L. Jared, BA Camb., PhD Leeds   Sr. Lectr.

Wignall, Paul B., BA Oxf., PhD Birm.   Prof., Palaeoenvironments

Other Staff: 6 Lectrs.; 5 Visiting Lectrs.; 1 Sr. Res. Fellow; 7 Res. Fellows; 3 Visiting Res. Fellows; 1 Visiting Sr. Fellow; 1 Hon. Res. Fellow

Geochemistry, Institute of

Chapman, Robert J., MSc Birm., PhD Leeds   Sr. Lectr.

Cliff, Robert A., BA Oxf., DPhil Oxf., FGS   Sr. Lectr.

McCaig, Andrew M., BA Camb., MSc W.Ont., PhD Camb.   Sr. Lectr.

Raiswell, Robert W., MSc Liv., PhD Liv.   Prof., Sedimentary Geochemistry

Shepherd, Thomas J., BSc Durh., PhD Durh.   Visiting Prof., Fluid-Rock Geochemistry

Yardley, Bruce W. D., BSc Exe., PhD Brist., DSc Brist., FGS   Prof., Metamorphic Geochemistry; Head*

Other Staff: 2 Sr. Res. Fellows; 1 Marie Curie Res. Fellow; 3 Visiting Res. Fellows; 1 Hon. Res. Fellow

Geophysics and Tectonics, Institute of

Butler, Robert, BSc Leeds, PhD Wales   Reader, Orogenic Geology

Clark, Roger A., BSc Leeds, PhD Leeds   Sr. Lectr.

Fairhead, J. Derek, BSc Durh., MSc Newcastle(UK), PhD Newcastle(UK), FRAS   Prof., Applied Geophysics

Gubbins, David, BA Camb., PhD Camb., FRS   Res. Prof., Earth Sciences

Houseman, Gregory A., BSc Syd., PhD Camb.   Prof., Geophysics; Head*

Jackson, Andrew, BA Camb., PhD Camb.   Prof., Mathematical Geophysics

Knipe, Robert J., BSc Wales, MSc Lond., PhD Lond.   Prof., Structural Geology

Lloyd, Geoffrey E., BSc Nott., MPhil Nott., PhD Birm.   Reader, Microgeodynamics

Neuberg, Jurgen, PhD Karlsruhe   Prof., Physical Volcanology

Smit, Dirk J., BSc Amst., PhD Utrecht   Visiting Prof., Geophysics

Stuart, Graham W., BSc Leic., PhD Reading   Sr. Lectr.

Wilson, B. Marjorie, BA Oxf., MA Calif., PhD Leeds   Prof., Igneous Petrogenesis

Other Staff: 3 Lectrs.; 2 Visiting Lectrs.; 8 Res. Fellows; 2 Visiting Res. Fellows; 1 Univ. Res. Fellow; 1 Sr. Fellow; 1 Teaching and Res. Fellow

Education, School of

Tel: (0113) 343 4545 Fax: (0113) 343 4541

Anning, Angela J. E., BA Leeds, MEd Leic.   Emer. Hon. Prof.

Asoko, Hilary M., BSc Birm., MEd Leeds   Sr. Lectr.

Bates, Inge, BA Birm., PhD Leeds   Prof., Education and Work

Baynham, Michael J., BA Camb., MA Reading, PhD Reading   Prof., TESOL

Beveridge, Sally E., BA Manc., PhD Manc.   Sr. Lectr.

Borg, Simon, BEd Malta, MEd Exe., PhD Exe.   Sr. Lectr.

Burke, Catherine, BA Wales, MEd Sheff., PhD Sheff.Hallam   Sr. Lectr.

Burtonwood, Neil, BSc Lond., MEd Leeds, PhD Leeds   Sr. Lectr.

Cameron, Lynne J., BA Oxf., MA York(UK), PhD Lond.   Prof., Applied Linguistics

Chambers, Gary N., BA Belf., MA Lond., PhD Leeds   Sr. Lectr.

Deignan, Alice, BA Brist., MA Birm., PhD Birm.   Sr. Lectr.

Donnelly, James F., BSc Lond., MEd Leeds, PhD Leeds   Prof., Science Education

Hall, Kenneth W., MA Leeds   Sr. Lectr., Teaching

Hartley, J. Roger, BA Keele, MA Keele   Emer. Hon. Prof.

Higham, Jeremy J. S., BA Leeds, MEd Leeds, EdD Leeds   Sr. Lectr.

Hodkinson, Philip M., BA Hull, MPhil Exe., PhD Exe.   Prof., Lifelong Learning
Jenkins, Edgar W., BSc Leeds, MEd Leeds, FRSA, FRSChem   Emer. Hon. Prof.
Leach, John T., BSc Brist., PhD Leeds, FRSChem   Prof., Science Education
Lewis, Jennifer, BSc E.Anglia, PhD E.Anglia   Sr. Lectr.
Malderez, Angi, MEd Exe.   Sr. Lectr.
Monaghan, John D., BA Lanc., MSc Warw., PhD Bath   Sr. Lectr.
Osler, Audrey H., BA Leeds, MA Leeds, PhD Birm., FRSA   Prof., Science Education
Pike, Mark, BA Leeds, MA(Ed) Open(UK), PhD S'ton.   Sr. Lectr.
Prosser, John D., BA Birm., MA E.Anglia, DPhil York(UK)   Sr. Lectr.
Roper, Thomas, BSc Manc., MSc Leeds   Sr. Lectr.; Head*
Ryder, James, BSc Brist., PhD Brist.   Sr. Lectr.
Scott, Philip H., BSc Sheff., MEd Leeds, PhD Leeds   Prof., Science Education
Sugden, David A., MSc Calif., PhD Calif.   Prof., Special Needs in Education
Threlfall, John, BA Leeds, PhD Leeds   Sr. Lectr.
Wiegand, Patrick A., BSc Lond., MA Lond., EdD Leeds   Reader, Geography Education
Zukas, Miriam, BSc Exe.   Prof., Adult Learning
Other Staff: 11 Lectrs.; 5 Lectrs. (Teaching); 2 Principal Res. Fellows; 4 Res. Fellows; 1 Principal Teaching Fellow; 5 Sr. Teaching Fellows; 2 Teaching Fellows
Research: computer-based learning; post-fourteen education and training; pre-school, primary and teacher education; psychology and special educational needs; science and mathematics education

Engineering, Civil, School of

Tel: (0113) 343 2269 Fax: (0113) 343 2265
Barton, John, BSc Leeds   Sr. Lectr.
Bonsall, Peter W., BA Oxf.   Prof., Transport Planning
Bower, Denise, BEng UMIST, PhD UMIST   Prof.; Deputy Head
Cousens, Terrence W., BSc Leeds, PhD Camb.   Sr. Lectr.
Forth, John P., BEng Sheff., PhD Leeds   Sr. Lectr.
Garash, Fikry   Hon. Visiting Prof.
Horan, Nigel J., BSc Salf., MSc Hull, PhD Hull   Reader, Public Health Engineering
Lam, Dennis, BEng Sheff., MPhil Sheff., PhD Nott.   Sr. Lectr.
Male, Stephen P., BSc H-W, MSc H-W, PhD H-W   Balfour Beatty Prof., Building Engineering and Construction Management
Mara, Duncan D., BSc St And., PhD Dund., DSc(Eng) Leeds, FICE, FIBiol, FRSA   Prof.
Page, Christopher L., MA Camb., PhD Camb., FICE   Prof., Civil Engineering Materials
Richardson, Ian G., BSc CNAA, DPhil Oxf.   Sr. Lectr.
Robery, Peter C., BSc Leeds, PhD Leeds, FIMMM   Hon. Visiting Prof.
Sleigh, P. Andrew, BSc Leeds, PhD Leeds   Sr. Lectr.
Smith, Nigel J., BSc Birm., MSc Manc., PhD Manc., FICE   Prof., Project and Transport Infrastructure Management; Head*
Stentiford, Edward I., MA Camb., MSc Leeds   Biwater Prof., Public Health Engineering
Stewart, Douglas I., BSc Lond., MPhil Camb., PhD Camb.   Sr. Lectr.
Tight, Miles R., BSc Liv., PhD Lond.   Sr. Lectr.
Tinker, John A., BSc Aston, MSc Manc., PhD Salf.   Sr. Lectr.
Uren, John, BSc Leeds, PhD Leeds   Sr. Lectr.
Watson, Alastair S., BTech Brad., PhD Brad.   Sr. Lectr.
Wells, Matthew, BSc BArch   Hon. Visiting Prof.
Ye, Jianqiao, PhD Wales, BEng MEng   Sr. Lectr.
Other Staff: 3 Lectrs.; 8 Assoc. Lectrs.; 7 Res. Fellows; 4 Visiting Res. Fellows; 1 Univ. Res. Fellow; 3 Sr. Teaching Fellows; 1 Teaching Fellow

Research: construction management; fluid mechanics; materials; structures; tropical public health engineering

Engineering, Electronic and Electrical, School of

Tel: (0113) 343 2000 Fax: (0113) 343 2032

Electronic and Electrical Engineering

Corda, Jasmin, MSc Zagreb, PhD Leeds   Sr. Lectr.
Harrison, Paul, BSc Hull, PhD Newcastle(UK)   Prof., Quantum Electronics; Head*
Howes, Michael J., BSc Leeds, PhD Leeds, FIEE   Prof., Electronic Engineering
Hughes, Austin, BSc Brist., PhD Brist.   Sr. Lectr.
Iezekiel, Stavros, BEng Leeds, PhD Leeds   Sr. Lectr.; Dir., Learning and Teaching
Mei, Tian Xang, BSc Shanghai, MSc Shanghai, MSc Manc., PhD Lough.   Sr. Lectr.
Wilson, David A., BSc(Eng) Lond., PhD Camb.   Reader, Control Engineering
Zhang, L. I., BSc Chungking, PhD Brad.   Sr. Lectr.
Other Staff: 1 Lectr.; 1 Visiting Sr. Fellow; 1 Sr. Teaching Fellow; 2 Teaching Fellows

Integrated Information Systems, Institute of
incorporating the CAA Institute of Satellite Navigation

Tel: (0113) 343 2054
Boussakta, Said, MEng Algiers, PhD Newcastle(UK)   Reader, Digital Communications and Signal Processing
Cooper, John A., MEng Leeds, PhD Leeds   Sr. Lectr.
Hoyle, Brian S., BSc CNAA, MPhil CNAA, PhD CNAA   Deputy Head; Prof., Vision and Image Systems
Markarian, Garik, PhD Odessa   Prof., Communication Systems; Dir.*
McLernon, Desmond C., BSc Belf., MSc Belf., PhD Lond.   Sr. Lectr.
O'Farrell, Tim, BSc Birm., MSc Manc., PhD Manc.   Sr. Lectr.
Strangeways, Hal J., BSc Lond., PhD S'ton., FRAS   Deputy Dir.; Reader, Electromagnetic Wave Propagation
Walsh, David, BSc Leeds, MSc Lond., PhD Nott.   Dir., Inst. of Satellite Navigation
Other Staff: 3 Lectrs.; 2 Sr. Res. Fellows; 1 Royal Academy of Engineering Res. Fellow; 1 Principal Res. Engineer; 1 Res. Engineer

Microwaves and Photonics, Institute of

Tel: (0113) 343 2070
Arnone, Donald D., BSE Penn., BS Penn., MPhil Camb., PhD Camb.   Visiting Prof.
Davies, A. Giles, BSc Brist., PhD Camb.   Prof., Electronic and Photonic Engineering; Dir.*
Eisele, Heribert, MS Munich, PhD Munich   Reader, Millimetre and Submillimetre Wave Electronics
Harrison, Paul, BSc Hull, PhD Newcastle(UK)   Prof., Quantum Electronics
Hunter, Ian C., BSc Leeds, PhD Leeds, FIEE   Prof., Microwave Signal Processing
Iezekiel, Stavros, BEng Leeds, PhD Leeds   Sr. Lectr.
Kelsall, Robert W., BSc Durh., PhD Durh.   Sr. Lectr.
Linfield, Edmund, BA Camb., PhD Camb.   Prof., Terahertz Electronics
Lowe, Lawrence, BSc Warw., MSc Warw., PhD Warw.   Visiting Prof.
Miles, Robert E., BSc Lond., PhD Lond.   Prof., Semiconductor Materials and Devices
Pollard, Roger D., BSc Leeds, PhD Leeds, FIEE   Agilent Technologies Prof., High Frequency Measurements
Rhodes, J. David, CBE, OBE, BSc Leeds, PhD Leeds, DSc Leeds, DEng Brad., FIEE, FREng, FRS   Emer. Prof.
Robertson, Ian D., BSc(Eng) Lond., PhD Lond.   Centenary Prof., Microwave and Millimetre Wave Circuits
Steenson, D. Paul, BSc UMIST, PhD Nott.   Sr. Lectr.

Other Staff: 1 Lectr.; 3 Sr. Res. Fellows; 12 Res. Fellows; 2 Visiting Res. Fellows; 1 Royal Academy of Engineering Res. Fellow; 1 Univ. Res. Fellow

Engineering, Mechanical, School of

Tel: (0113) 343 2186 Fax: (0113) 242 4611
Abbott, Steven J., BSc Oxf., PhD Harv.   Visiting Prof.
Barton, David C., BSc Brist., MSc Manc., PhD Manc., FIMechE   Prof., Solid Mechanics; Head*
Bradley, Derek, BSc Leeds, PhD Leeds, FRS, FIMechE   Res. Prof.
Brooks, Peter C., BSc Leeds, PhD Leeds   Sr. Lectr.
Childs, Thomas H. C., BA Camb., MA Camb., PhD Camb., FIMechE   Prof., Manufacturing Engineering
Coy, Richard C., BSc Leic., PhD Aston   Visiting Prof.
De Pennington, Alan, OBE, MSc Manc., PhD Manc.   Emer. Prof., Computer Aided Engineering
Dearnley, Peter A., BSc Birm., PhD Birm.   Sr. Lectr.
Decre, Michel, BSc Brussels, PhD Éc.Normale Sup., Paris   Visiting Prof.
Dixon-Lewis, Graham, MA Oxf., DPhil Oxf., FRS   Hon. Prof.
Dowson, Duncan, CBE, BSc Leeds, PhD Leeds, DSc Leeds, Hon. DTech Chalmers U.T., Hon. DSc I.N.S.A.Lyons, FREng, FRS, FIMechE   Res. Prof.
Fisher, John, BSc Birm., PhD Glas., DEng Leeds, FIMechE   Prof.
Fox, Malcolm, BSc Lond., PhD Lond.   Visiting Prof.
Gaskell, Philip H., BSc Leeds, PhD Leeds   Prof., Fluid Mechanics
Hall, Richard M., BSc Leeds, PhD Lanc.   Sr. Lectr.
Isaac, Graham H., BSc Leeds, MSc Leeds, PhD Leeds   Visiting Prof.
Jin, Zhong Min, PhD Leeds, BSc   Prof., Computational Bioengineering
Jordan, Patrick W., BEng Brad., MSc(Eng) Birm., PhD Glas., FRSA   Prof., Engineering Design
King, Tim, BSc(Eng) Lond., MDes CNAA, PhD CNAA, FIEE, FIMechE, FRSA   Hon. Prof.
Lawes, Malcolm, BSc CNAA, PhD Leeds   Sr. Lectr.
Levesley, Martin C., BSc Brun., PhD S'ton.   Sr. Lectr.
McKay, Alison, BEng Brad., PhD Leeds   Sr. Lectr.
Neville, Anne, BEng Glas., PhD Glas.   Dir., Res.; Prof., Tribology and Surface Engineering
Priest, Martin, BSc Leeds, PhD Leeds   Dir., Learning and Teaching; Jost Prof., Tribology
Querin, Osvaldo M., BE Syd., ME(Res) Syd., PhD Syd.   Sr. Lectr.
Raffo, David, BA Manc.   Visiting Prof.
Sheppard, Christopher G. W., BSc Leeds, PhD Leeds   Prof., Applied Thermodynamics and Combustion Science
Singh, Gurvinder, BSc Manc., PhD Lond., FIEEE, FIMA   Prof., Robotics and Control
Summers, Jonathan L., BSc Leeds, PhD Leeds   Sr. Lectr.
Taylor, Richard S., OBE, BSc Wolv.   Visiting Prof.
Thompson, Harvey M., MA Camb., PhD Leeds   Sr. Lectr.
Vladimirov, Vladimir A., MPhil PhD DrSci   Visiting Prof.
Walker, Peter G., BSc(Eng) Lond., PhD Lond.   Sr. Lectr.
Wroblewski, Michael, MB ChB Leeds, FRCSEd   Visiting Prof.
Other Staff: 6 Lectrs.; 26 Res. Fellows; 4 Teaching and Res. Fellows; 2 EPSRC Adv. Res. Fellows; 1 Royal Academy of Engin. Postdoctoral Sr. Res. Fellow
Research: biomedical engineering; combustion; computer-aided design and manufacture; tribology and thin films; vehicle dynamics and control

Engineering, Process, Environmental and Materials, School of

Tel: (0113) 343 2444 Fax: (0113) 343 2549

Davies, Reginald, BSc Lond., PhD Lough. Visiting Prof.

Denson, Anthony K., BSc Leeds, PhD Leeds Visiting Prof.

Dixon-Lewis, Graham, MA Oxf., DPhil Oxf., FRS Visiting Emer. Prof.

Docherty, Robert, BSc Strath., PhD Strath. Visiting Prof.

Dunn, Robert B., BEng Sheff., FREng   Visiting Prof.

Fan, Liang Shim, BSc Natnl.Taiwan, MSChE W.Virginia, MS Kansas State, PhD W.Virginia Visiting Prof.

Farmer, Ian, BSc Nott., PhD Sheff., DEng Sheff. Visiting Prof.

Ford, Leslie J., BSc Lond., FRSA   Visiting Prof.

Fray, Derek J., BSc(Eng) Lond., MA Camb., PhD Lond., FREng   Visiting Prof.

Geldart, Derek, BSc Durh., MSc Durh., PhD Brad., FIChemE   Visiting Prof.

Harnby, Norman, BEng Lond., PhD Brad., FIChemE   Visiting Prof.

Harrison, James S., BSc, FIChemE   Visiting Prof.

Heggs, Peter J., BSc Leeds, PhD Leeds, FIChemE Visiting Prof.

Higashitani, Ko, BSc Kyoto, MSc Wis., PhD Wis. Visiting Prof.

Kleingeld, Wynard J., PhD E.S.N.des Mines, Paris, BSc   Visiting Prof.

Koopmans, Rudolf, MSc Antwerp, PhD Antwerp Visiting Prof.

Morley, Christopher, MA Camb., PhD Camb. Visiting Prof.

Napier-Munn, Timothy J., BSc Lond., MSc(Eng) Witw., PhD Lond.   Visiting Prof.

Oliver, Raymond, BSc PhD, FREng, FIChemE Visiting Prof.

Oran, Elaine S., AB Bryn Mawr, MPh Yale, PhD Yale   Visiting Prof.

Palmer, Francis H., BSc Lond., FIMechE Visiting Prof.

Phillips, Mark A., BSc Lough., FIChemE Visiting Prof.

Pourkashanian, Mohamed, MSc Leeds, PhD Leeds Prof.; Head*

Pugh, Robert J., BTech Lough., MSc Brist., PhD Lond.   Visiting Prof.

Ramachandran, Ganapathy, MA Madr., PhD Lond., DSc Lond.   Visiting Prof.

Riddles, Gordon P., BSc Aberd., MBA Strath. Visiting Prof.

Roberts, John R., BSc   Visiting Prof.

Ruddick, Simon, BSc CNAA   Visiting Prof.

Slatter, Paul T., BSc Natal, MSc Cape Town, PhD Cape Town   Visiting Prof.

Stoylov, Stoyl, BSc Sofia, PhD Sofia, DSc Sofia Visiting Prof.

Svoboda, Jan, MSc T.U.Prague, PhD Prague, DSc Stell.   Visiting Prof.

Walton, Geoffrey, BSc Brist., PhD Nott. Visiting Prof.

Wedlock, David J., BSc Salf., PhD Salf.   Visiting Prof.

Wilson, Christopher W., BTech Lough., PhD Leeds   Visiting Prof.

York, David W., BSc Leeds, PhD Leeds   Visiting Prof.

Other Staff: 6 Visiting Lectrs.; 2 Visiting Fellows; 7 Hon. Lectrs.

Energy and Resources Research Institute

Tel: (0113) 343 2498 Fax: (0113) 242 7310

Andrews, Gordon E., BSc Leeds, PhD Leeds Prof., Combustion Engineering

Dupont, Valerie A., Ing I.N.S.A.Lyons, PhD Leeds Sr. Lectr.

Fairweather, Michael, BSc Leeds, PhD Leeds Prof., Thermo Fluids and Combustion

Fowell, Robert J., BSc Leic., MEng Sheff., PhD Newcastle(UK)   Reader, Mining Engineering

Gibbs, Bernard M., BScTech Sheff., PhD Sheff. Reader, Applied Combustion and Energy Technology

Hampartsoumian, Edward, BSc Leeds, PhD Leeds Reader, Combustion Technology

Jones, Jenny M., BSc Bath, MSc Brist., PhD Calg. Reader, Sustainable Energy

McIntosh, Andrew C., BSc Wales, PhD CNAA, DSc Wales   Prof., Thermodynamics and Combustion Theory

Phylaktou, Herodotos N., BEng Leeds, PhD Leeds Sr. Lectr.

Pourkashanian, Mohamed, MSc Leeds, PhD Leeds Prof., High-Temperature Combustion Processes

Staggs, John E. J., BSc St And., DPhil Oxf.   Sr. Lectr.

Tomlin, Alison, BSc Leeds, PhD Leeds   Reader, Environmental Modelling

Williams, Alan, CBE, BSc Leeds, PhD Leeds, FRSA, FREng, FRSChem   Emer. Prof.

Williams, Paul T., BSc Lond., MSc Leeds, PhD Leeds, FGS   Prof., Environmental Engineering; Dir.*

Other Staff: 2 Lectrs.; 4 Sr. Res. Fellows; 12 Res. Fellows; 1 Visiting Res. Fellow

Research: atmospheric pollution modelling (dispersion of gases and particulate pollutants); combustion engineering (combustion of coal, gas, oil and biomass); engine research (alternative fuels, diesels, gasolines, gas turbines); fire and explosion engineering (explosion, fire hazards, smoke, smouldering); pollution control (clean coal technology, NOx reduction)

Materials Research, Institute for

Tel: (0113) 343 2348 Fax: (0113) 242 2351

Bell, Andrew J., BSc Birm., PhD Leeds   FIM Prof., Electronic Materials; Dir.*

Brydson, Richard M., BSc Leeds, PhD Camb. Prof., Nanoscale Materials Characterisation

Cochrane, Robert F., MA Camb., PhD Camb. Sr. Lectr.

Edmonds, David V., BSc Birm., MA Camb., MA Oxf., PhD Birm., FIMMM   Prof., Metallurgy

Gee, Robert, MSc Manc., PhD Manc.   Sr. Lectr.

Hammond, Christopher, MA Camb., PhD Leeds Sr. Lectr.

Jha, Animesh, BE Roor., ME B'lore., PhD Lond. Prof., Applied Materials Science

Kale, Girish M., MSc BITS, PhD B'lore.   Sr. Lectr.

Milne, Steven J., BSc Aberd., PhD Aberd. Reader, Ceramic Science

Mullis, Andrew M., BSc Durh., DPhil York(UK) Sr. Lectr.

Rand, Brian, MSc Durh., PhD Newcastle(UK), FIMMM   Prof., Ceramics

Other Staff: 3 Sr. Res. Fellows; 7 Res. Fellows; 1 Academic Res. Fellow; 1 Univ. Res. Fellow; 1 Royal Society China Fellow

Particle Science and Engineering, Institute of

Tel: (0113) 343 2404 Fax: (0113) 343 2405

Biggs, Simon R., BSc Brist., PhD Brist., FRACI Leeds BNFL Res. Alliance and Royal Academy of Engin. Prof., Particle Science and Technology

Ding, Yulong, BSc Beijing U.S.T., MSc Beijing U.S.T., PhD Birm.   Sr. Lectr.

Fairweather, Michael, BSc Leeds, PhD Leeds Prof., Thermo Fluids and Combustion

Ghadiri, Mojtaba, BSc Teheran, MSc Lond., PhD Camb.   Prof., Chemical Engineering; Dir.*

Mahmud, Tariq, MSc(Eng) Dhaka, PhD Newcastle(NSW)   Sr. Lectr.

Papadaki, Maria, PhD Salonika   Sr. Lectr.

Poole, Colin, BSc Leeds, PhD Leeds   Sr. Lectr.

Roberts, Kevin J., BSc CNAA, PhD CNAA, FRSChem   Brotherton Prof., Chemical Engineering

Wang, M. I., BSc UMIST, MSc UMIST, PhD UMIST   Reader, Process Tomography

Wang, Xue Zhong, MSc Beijing, PhD Beijing Reader, Process Monitoring Control and Analytics

Williams, Richard A., BSc(Eng) Lond., PhD Lond., FREng, FIMMM, FIChemE   Prof., Mineral and Process Engineering

Other Staff: 2 Lectrs.; 2 Sr. Res. Fellows; 19 Res. Fellows; 1 Univ. Fellow; 1 Teaching Fellow

Research: geostatistics (geological and environmental modelling and prediction); mineral processing (comminution, flocculation, hydrometallurgy, pyrometallurgy); particle and colloid engineering (colloid hydrodynamics, particle manufactuing systems); rock mechanics (excavation engineering, rock mass characterisation); sensors (novel sensor development)

English, School of

Tel: (0113) 343 4739 Fax: (0113) 343 4774

Batt, Catherine, BA Lond., MA Liv., PhD Liv.   Sr. Lectr.

Becket, Fiona, MA Warw., PhD Warw.   Sr. Lectr.

Bennett, Bridget, BA York(UK), DPhil York(UK) Sr. Lectr.

Brennan, Michael G., MA Oxf., MA Camb., DPhil Oxf.   Reader, Renaissance Studies

Brown, Richard H., BA Lond., PhD Lond. Reader, Modern Literature

Butler, Martin H., MA Camb., PhD Camb. Prof., Renaissance Drama

Fairer, David, MA Oxf., DPhil Oxf.   Prof., Eighteenth-Century English Literature

Flannery, Denis J. M., DPhil Oxf., MA   Sr. Lectr.

Fraser Gupta, Anthea, MA Newcastle(UK), DPhil York(UK)   Sr. Lectr.

Gidley, Mick, BA Manc., MA Chic., DPhil Sus. Prof., American Literature

Hammond, Paul, MA Camb., PhD Camb., LittD Camb.   Prof., Seventeenth-Century English Literature

Hargreaves, Tracy, BA Lond., MA Lond., PhD Lond.   Sr. Lectr.

Hill, Joyce M., BA Lond., DPhil York(UK), FRSA Visiting Prof.

Huggan, Graham, BA Camb., MA Br.Col., PhD Br.Col.   Prof., Commonwealth and Post-Colonial Literatures

Jones, Vivien M., MA Oxf., DPhil Oxf.   Prof., Eighteenth-Century Gender and Culture

Lindley, David, BPhil Oxf., MA Oxf.   Prof., Renaissance Literature

Mapanje, Jack, BA Malawi, MPhil Lond., PhD Lond.   Visiting Prof. Fellow

Marshall, Gail, BA Durh., MA Leeds, PhD Camb. Sr. Lectr.

McLeod, John, BA Leeds, MA Leeds, PhD Leeds Sr. Lectr.

McTurk, Rory W., MA Oxf., BPhilol Iceland, PhD N.U.I.   Reader, Icelandic Studies

Murray, Stuart, BA Exe., MA Exe., PhD Waik. Sr. Lectr.

O'Gorman, Francis, MA Oxf., DPhil Oxf., FRHistS   Reader, Victorian Literature; Head*

Prosser, Jay, BA Lond., MA N.Y., PhD N.Y.   Sr. Lectr.

Salmon, Richard, MA Leeds, PhD Lond.   Sr. Lectr.

Upton, Clive, BA Wales, MA Wales, PhD Leeds Prof., Modern English Language

Wawn, Andrew, BA Birm., PhD Birm.   Prof., Anglo-Icelandic Studies

Whale, John C., BA Leeds, PhD Leeds   Reader, Romantic Literature

Other Staff: 11 Lectrs.; 1 Assoc. Lectr.; 1 Visiting Res. Fellow; 1 Hon. Reader; 2 Hon. Fellows

Research: American literature; Beowulf to the present; Commonwealth and post-colonial literatures; English language and world Englishes; English literature

Fine Art, History of Art and Cultural Studies, School of

Tel: (0113) 343 5260 Fax: (0113) 245 1977

Day, Gail, BA CNAA, MA Leeds, PhD Leeds   Sr. Lectr.

Engh, Barbara, MA Minn., PhD Minn.   Sr. Lectr.

Green, Vanalyne, BFA Calif.   Prof., Fine Art

Hill, David, BA *Leeds*, PhD *Lond.*   Harewood
    Prof., Fine Art
Jackson, David, BA *Wales*, PhD *Edin.*   Prof.;
    Head*
Kelly, Mary   Visiting Prof.
Lichtenberg-Ettinger, Bracha   Visiting Prof.
McQuillan, Martin, MA *Glas.*, PhD *Glas.*   Prof.,
    Cultural Theory and Analysis
Orton, Lionel F., MA *Lond.*   Prof., Art History
    and Cultural Theory
Palmer, Roger   Prof., Fine Art
Pollock, Griselda F. S., BA *Oxf.*, MA *Lond.*, PhD
    Lond.   Prof., Social and Critical Histories of
    Art
Read, Benedict W., BA *Oxf.*, BA *Lond.*, FSA   Sr.
    Lectr.
Taylor, Christopher, BA *Leeds Met.*, MA *Leeds Met.*
    Sr. Lectr.; Deputy Head
Other Staff: 13 Lectrs.; 1 Teaching Fellow; 2
    Postdoctoral Fellows; 3 Hon. Lectrs.; 1
    Hon. Fellow; 1 Henry Moore Scholar

Food Science, Procter Department of

Tel: (0113) 343 2958 Fax: (0113) 343 2982
Dickinson, Eric, BSc *Sheff.*, PhD *Sheff.*, DSc *Leeds*
    Prof., Food Colloids
Ettelaie, Rammile, BSc *Manc.*, PhD *Manc.*   Sr.
    Lectr.
Georgala, Douglas L., CBE, BSc *Stell.*, PhD *Aberd.*
    External Prof.
Gilbert, John, MSc *Leeds*, PhD *Leeds*   Visiting
    Prof.
Gould, Grahame W., BSc *Brist.*, PhD *Aberd.*
    External Prof.
Horne, David, BSc *CNAA*, PhD *Edin.*   Visiting
    Prof.
Khokhar, Santosh, BSc *Haryana Ag.*, MSc *Haryana
    Ag.*, PhD *Haryana Ag.*   Sr. Lectr.
Morgan, Michael R., BSc *Sus.*, MSc *Leeds*, PhD
    Sheff.   Prof., Food Biochemistry; Head*
Murray, Brent S., BSc *Leeds*, PhD *Leeds*   Reader,
    Food Colloids
Povey, Malcolm J. W., BA *Lanc.*, PhD *Lanc.*, FIP
    Prof., Food Physics
Robinson, David S., BSc *Manc.*, PhD *Manc.*
    Hon. Prof.
Wedzicha, Bronislaw L., BSc *Lond.*, PhD *Lond.*
    Prof.
Other Staff: 1 Lectr.; 5 Res. Fellows; 6 Hon.
    Lectrs.

Geography, School of

Tel: (0113) 343 3300 Fax: (0113) 343 3308
Bailey, Adrian J., BSc *Brist.*, MA *Indiana*, PhD
    Indiana   Prof., Migration Studies
Butlin, Robin A., OBE, BA *Liv.*, MA *Liv.*, PhD
    Liv., DLitt *Lough.*   Emer. Prof., Historical
    Geography
Carver, Stephen J., BSc *Hudd.*, PhD *Newcastle(UK)*
    Sr. Lectr.
Chapman, Pippa J., BSc *Reading*, PhD *Lond.*   Sr.
    Lectr.
Clarke, David B., BA *Manc.*, PhD *Manc.*   Sr.
    Lectr.
Clarke, Graham P., BA *Wales*, PhD *Leeds*   Prof.,
    Business Geography
Clarke, Martin C., BA *Leeds*, PhD *Leeds*   Prof.,
    Geographic Modelling
Drake, Frances, BSc *St And.*, MSc *Leic.*, PhD *Liv.*
    Sr. Lectr.
Grainger, Alan, BSc *Birm.*, MSc *CNAA*, MPhil
    CNAA, DPhil *Oxf.*   Sr. Lectr.
Gupta, Avijit, BA *Calc.*, MA *Calc.*, PhD *Johns H.*
    Sr. Lectr.
Kirkby, Michael J., MA *Camb.*, PhD *Camb.*
    Emer. Prof., Physical Geography
Kneale, Pauline E., BSc *Lond.*, PhD *Brist.*   Prof.,
    Applied Hydrology
Leigh, Christine M., BA *Leeds*, PhD *Leeds*   Emer.
    Prof.
Lloyd, Jonathan J., BSc *ANU*, PhD *Adel.*
    Centenary Prof., Earth System Science
McDonald, Adrian T., BSc *Edin.*, PhD *Edin.*
    Yorkshire Water Prof., Environmental
    Management; Head*
Phillips, Deborah A., BA *Lond.*, MA *Br.Col.*, PhD
    Camb.   Sr. Lectr.

Phillips, Oliver, BA *Camb.*, PhD *Wash.*   Reader,
    Tropical Ecology
Purvis, Martin C., MA *Oxf.*, DPhil *Oxf.*   Sr.
    Lectr.
Rees, Philip H., MA *Camb.*, MA *Chic.*, PhD *Chic.*
    Prof., Population Geography
See, Linda, BSc *Tor.*, MSc *McM.*, PhD *Leeds*   Sr.
    Lectr.
Stillwell, John C. H., BA *Leeds*, PhD *Leeds*   Prof.,
    Migration and Regional Development
Tzedakis, Polychronis C., BA *Boston*, ScM *Brown*,
    PhD *Camb.*   Prof., Quaternary Earth System
    History
Valentine, Gill, BA *Durh.*, PhD *Reading*   Prof.,
    Human Geography
Waley, Paul T., BA *Oxf.*, PhD *Lond.*   Sr. Lectr.
Other Staff: 13 Lectrs.; 2 Sr. Res. Fellows; 5
    Res. Fellows; 6 Visiting Res. Fellows; 1
    NERC Fellow; 2 Visiting Res. Assocs.
Research: earth surface processes and
    environmental change (fluvial
    geomorphology, glaciology and
    hydrology); environmental management
    (environmental change, sustainable
    development, resource appraisal);
    geocomputation and business geographics
    (applied geography, artificial intelligence,
    GIS, spatial modelling); population, society
    and space

History, School of

Tel: (0113) 343 3586 Fax: (0113) 234 2759
Gooch, John, BA *Lond.*, PhD *Lond.*   Prof.;
    Chairman of Sch.*
Research: economic and social history;
    international and military history; modern
    British and European history; Russian and
    East Asian history

Ancient History

1 Lectr.

Medieval History

Childs, Wendy R., MA *Camb.*, PhD *Camb.*
    Prof., Later Medieval History
Loud, Graham A., MA *Oxf.*, DPhil *Oxf.*   Prof.,
    Medieval Italian History
Wood, Ian M., MA *Oxf.*, DPhil *Oxf.*   Prof.,
    Early Mediaeval History

Modern History

Bailey, Mark, BA, FRHistS   Visiting Sr. Lectr.
Black, Robert D., BA *Chic.*, PhD *Lond.*   Prof.,
    Renaissance History
Burrows, Simon F., BA *Oxf.*, DPhil *Oxf.*   Sr.
    Lectr.
Chartres, John A., MA *Oxf.*, DPhil *Oxf.*   Prof.,
    Social and Economic History
Chase, Malcolm S., BA *York(UK)*, MA *Sus.*, DPhil
    Sus.   Reader, Labour History
Childs, John C. R., BA *Hull*, PhD *Lond.*   Prof.,
    Military History
Dixon, Simon M., MA *Camb.*, PhD *Lond.*   Prof.
Gooch, John, BA *Lond.*, PhD *Lond.*   Prof.,
    International History
Green, Simon J. D., MA *Oxf.*, DPhil *Oxf.*
    Reader, Modern British History
Harris, James R., BA *Tor.*, MA *Tor.*, PhD *Chic.*
    Sr. Lectr.
Honeyman, Katrina, BA *York(UK)*, PhD *Nott.*
    Reader, Social and Economic History
Spiers, Edward M., MA *Edin.*, PhD *Edin.*   Prof.,
    Strategic Studies
Thompson, Andrew S., BA *Oxf.*, DPhil *Oxf.*
    Prof., Commonwealth and Imperial History
Thornton, Martin, BA *S'ton.*, MA *Kent*, PhD *Lond.*
Tolliday, Stephen W., BA *Camb.*, PhD *Camb.*
    Prof., Economic History
Waddington, Geoffrey T., BA *Leeds*, PhD *Leeds*
    Sr. Lectr.
Whiting, Richard C., MA *Oxf.*, DPhil *Oxf.*
    Reader
Wilson, Keith M., BA *Oxf.*, DPhil *Oxf.*   Reader,
    International History
Wright, Anthony D., MA *Oxf.*, DPhil *Oxf.*
    Reader, Ecclesiastical History

Other Staff: 10 Lectrs.; 1 Principal Teaching
    Fellow; 1 Assoc. Lectr.; 4 Hon. Lectrs.

Law, School of

Tel: (0113) 343 5033 Fax: (0113) 343 5056
Ackers, H. Louise, BSc *Lond.*, MA *Lond.*, LLM
    Brist., PhD *Lond.*   Prof., European Law
Akdeniz, Yaman, LLB *Leeds*, MA *Leeds*, PhD *Leeds*
    Sr. Lectr.
Campbell, Andrew, BA *Wales*, MPhil *Wales*
    Reader
Cardwell, Michael N., MA *Oxf.*   Sr. Lectr.
Cram, Ian G., LLB *Lanc.*, MA *Sheff.*   Sr. Lectr.
Crawford, T. Adam, BA *Warw.*, MPhil *Camb.*,
    PhD *Leeds*   Prof., Criminology and Criminal
    Justice
Ellison, Louise E., LLB *Leeds*, PhD *Leeds*   Sr.
    Lectr.
Gerstenberg, Oliver, DrIur *Fran.*   Reader
Halson, Roger, LLB *Newcastle(UK)*, MLitt *Oxf.*
    Prof.; Head*
Hucklesby, Anthea, BA *CNAA*, MA *Hull*, PhD
    Glam.   Sr. Lectr.
Keay, Andrew, LLB *Adel.*, MDiv *Conservative Baptist
    Theol.Sem.*, MA *Qld.*, PhD *Qld.*   Prof.,
    Corporate and Commercial Law
Lodge, Juliet, BA *CNAA*, MA *Reading*, MPhil
    Reading, PhD *Hull*, DLitt *Reading*   Prof.,
    European Studies
Masselot, Annick, Lic *Nancy II*, Maîtrise *Nancy II*
    Sr. Lectr.
McMullen, John, MA *Camb.*, PhD *Camb.*   Prof.,
    Labour Law
Morrow, Karen L., LLB *Belf.*, LLM *Lond.*   Sr.
    Lectr.
Ormerod, David, LLB *Essex*   Prof.
Subedi, Surya P., LLB *Tribhuvan*, MA *Tribhuvan*,
    LLM *Hull*, DPhil *Oxf.*   Prof., International
    Law
Vincent-Jones, Peter, BA *Camb.*, MA *Sheff.*, PhD
    Sheff.   Prof.; Dir., Res.
Walker, Clive P., LLB *Leeds*, PhD *Manc.*   Prof.,
    Criminal Justice
Wall, David S., BA *CNAA*, MA *York(UK)*, MPhil
    York(UK), PhD *Leeds*   Prof., Criminal Justice
    and Information Technology
Wallbank, Julie A., LLB *Leic.*, PhD *Leic.*   Sr.
    Lectr.
Wheatley, Steven M., LLB *CNAA*, LLM *Nott.*
    Sr. Lectr.
Wincup, Emma L., BA *Camb.*, MPhil *Camb.*, PhD
    Wales   Sr. Lectr.
Other Staff: 15 Lectrs.; 1 Sr. Fellow; 4 Visiting
    Fellows

Leeds University Business School

Tel: (0113) 343 6321 Fax: (0113) 343 4885
Allen, David, BA *Lanc.*, MSc *Stir.*, PhD *Sheff.*   Sr.
    Lectr.
Allinson, Christopher W., BSc *Brad.*, MA *Leeds*,
    PhD *Brad.*   Sr. Lectr.
Arestis, Philip, BA *Athens*, MSc *Lond.*, MBA *Sheff.*,
    PhD *Sur.*   Visiting Prof.
Barnes, Bradley R., BA *Sheff.Hallam*, MSc *Hudd.*,
    PhD *Leeds*   Sr. Lectr.
Buckley, Peter J., BA(Econ) *York(UK)*, MA
    E.Anglia, PhD *Lanc.*   Prof., International
    Business
Burgess, Thomas F., MBA *Brad.*, PhD *Leeds*   Sr.
    Lectr.; Dir., PhD Programme
Chapman, Malcolm, BLitt *Oxf.*, MBA *Brad.*, MA
    Oxf., DPhil *Oxf.*   Sr. Lectr.
Clegg, L. Jeremy, BA *Nott.*, PhD *Reading*   Jean
    Monnet Prof., European Integration and
    International Business Management
Collins, Mae B., BA *Manc.*, MA *Leeds*, PhD *Leeds*
    Sr. Lectr.
Collins, Michael, BSc(Econ) *Lond.*, PhD *Lond.*
    Prof., Financial History
Cornelissen, Joep P., BA *Utrecht*, PhD *Manc.Met.*
    Sr. Lectr.
Cross, Adam R., BSc *CNAA*, MSc *UMIST*   Sr.
    Lectr.
Duxbury, Darren, BA *Leeds*, MA *Leeds*, PhD *Leeds*
    Sr. Lectr.
Fontona, Guiseppe, Laurea *Naples*, MA *Leeds*,
    PhD *Leeds*, PhD *Naples*   Sr. Lectr.

Gardiner, Jean, BA Camb., MSc Lond. Sr. Lectr.

Gerrard, William J., MA Aberd., MPhil Camb., DPhil York(UK) Prof., Sport Management and Finance

Hayes, John, BSc(Econ) Hull, PhD Leeds Prof., Management Studies

Hillier, David, BSc Paisley, PhD Strath. Ziff Prof., Financial Markets

Hodgkinson, Gerard P., BA CNAA, MSc Hull, PhD Sheff., FRSA Prof., Organisational Behaviour and Strategic Management

Hudson, Robert S., BSc Nott., MA Leeds Sr. Lectr.

Katsikeas, Constantine S., BSc Athens, MA Lanc., PhD Wales Arnold Ziff Res. Prof., Marketing and International Management

Keasey, Kevin, BA Durh., MA Newcastle(UK), PhD Newcastle(UK) Leeds Permanent Building Soc. Prof., Financial Services

King, Stephen F., BTech Brad., MPhil Brad., PhD Warw. Sr. Lectr.

Kirkpatrick, Ian, BA York(UK), MSc Lond., PhD Wales Sr. Lectr.

Lewis, Paul, MA Liv., PhD Leeds Sr. Lectr.

Lock, Andrew R., BA Leeds, MSc Lond., PhD Lond., FRSA, FCIM Prof., Marketing and Business Administration; Head*

Mackenzie, Robert F., BA Leeds, MA Leeds, PhD Leeds Sr. Lectr.

Mackie, Peter J., BA Nott. Prof., Transport Studies

Maule, A. John, BA Durh., PhD Dund. Prof., Human Decision Making

McNulty, Terence H., BA Nott.Trent, PhD Nott.Trent Prof., Management and Governance

Michell, Paul C. N., BSc(Econ) Lond., MSBA Boston, PhD Brun. Prof., Marketing and Communications

Moizer, Peter, MA Oxf., MA(Econ) Manc., PhD Manc., FCA Prof., Accounting

Nash, Christopher A., BA Reading, PhD Leeds Prof., Transport Economics

Nolan, Peter, BA E.Anglia, MSc Lond. Dir., Econ. and Soc. Res. Council Future of Work Programme; Montague Burton Prof., Industrial Relations

Oakland, John S., PhD Salf. Prof., Business Excellence and Quality Management

O'Donnell, Kathleen, BA E.Anglia, MSc(Econ) Lond., PhD Lond. Sr. Lectr.

Okada, Adamantios D. M., BA Waseda, MA Doshisha, PhD Kyoto Visiting Prof.

Outram, Quentin, BA Camb., BA Open(UK), MA Camb., PhD Camb. Sr. Lectr.

Pearman, Alan D., BSocSc Birm., MA Leeds, PhD Leeds Prof., Management Decision Analysis

Pérotin, Virginie, MA Cornell, PhD Cornell Prof., Economics

Porter, Leslie J., BSc Lond., MSc Sur., MBA Sheff., PhD Sur. Visiting Prof.

Reilly, Kevin T., BA Dal., MA Tor., PhD Tor. Sr. Lectr.

Robinson, Andrew M., BA Lanc., MSc York(UK), PhD Brad. Sr. Lectr.

Sawyer, Malcolm C., BA Oxf., MSc(Econ) Lond. Prof., Economics

Schenk-Hoppé, Klaus R., MSc Bremen, PhD Bremen Centenary Prof., Financial Mathematics

Shin, Yong Cheol, BA Hankuk Foreign, MA Hankuk Foreign, PhD Mich. Prof., Applied Econometrics

Short, Helen, BA Kent, PhD Leeds Sr. Lectr.

Spencer, David A., BA CNAA, MA Leeds, PhD Leeds Sr. Lectr.

Spender, John-Christopher, BA Oxf., MA Oxf., PhD Manc. Visiting Prof.

Stuart, Mark, BA CNAA, MA Warw., PhD Leeds Prof., Human Resource Management and Employment Relations

Summers, Barbara A., BSc Leeds, MBA Brad., PhD Brad. Sr. Lectr.

Thorpe, Richard, MSc Strath., PhD Lanc., FRSA Prof., Management Development

Thwaites, Desmond, BSc CNAA, MBA Brad., PhD Brad. Sr. Lectr.

Toner, Jeremy P., BSocSc Birm., MA Leeds, PhD Leeds Sr. Lectr.

Wilson, Nicholas, BA Nott., PhD Nott. Inst. of Credit Management Prof.

Wilson, Thomas D., BSc Lond., PhD Sheff. Visiting Prof.

Yu, Byungchul, BA Sung Kyun Kwan, MA Mich., PhD Ohio Visiting Prof.

Zhang, Hao, BA Virginia, PhD Texas Sr. Lectr.

Other Staff: 32 Lectrs.; 1 Visiting Lectr.; 2 Principal Res. Fellows; 1 Sr. Res. Fellow; 7 Res. Fellows; 2 Univ. Res. Fellows; 7 Sr. Teaching Fellows; 3 Teaching Fellows; 5 Visiting Res. Fellows; 2 Visiting Teaching Fellows; 2 Visiting Fellows; 4 Hon. Lectrs.

Mathematics, Applied

Tel: (0113) 343 5101 Fax: (0113) 343 5090

Bloor, Malcolm I. G., BSc Manc., PhD Manc. Prof.

Brindley, John, BSc Lond., PhD Lond. Emer. Res. Prof.

Cole, Eric A. B., BSc Wales, PhD Wales Sr. Lectr.

Elliott, Lionel, BSc Manc., PhD Manc. Sr. Lectr.

Falle, Samuel A. E. G., BA Camb., MSc Sus., DPhil Sus. Prof., Astrophysical Fluid Dynamics

Fordy, Alan P., MSc Lond., PhD Lond. Prof., Nonlinear Mathematics

Harlen, Oliver G., MA Camb., PhD Camb. Sr. Lectr.

Hollerbach, Reiner, BA Chic., PhD Calif. Reader, Astrophysical Fluid Dynamics

Hughes, David W., MA Oxf., PhD Camb. Prof.; Head*

Ingham, Derek B., BSc Leeds, PhD Leeds, DSc Leeds, FIMA Prof.

Jones, Christopher A., BA Camb., PhD Camb., ScD Camb. Prof., Applied NonLinear Dynamics

Kelmanson, Mark A., BSc Leeds, PhD Leeds Prof.

Klein, Richard, BSc Rensselaer, PhD Brandeis Visiting Prof.

Komissarov, Serguei, PhD St.Petersburg Reader

Kuznetsov, Vadim, MSc Leningrad, PhD Leningrad Reader, Applied Analysis

Lesnic, Daniel, MSc Leeds, PhD Leeds Reader

Merkin, John H., MSc Manc., PhD Manc. Prof.

Mikhailov, Alexander V., ScD Russian Acad.Sc. Prof., Mathematical Physics

Pedley, Timothy J., ScD Camb., FIMA, FRS Visiting Prof.

Rucklidge, Alastair M., BASc Tor., SM Mass., PhD Camb. Reader

Sleeman, Brian D., BSc Lond., PhD Lond., DSc Dund., FIMA Res. Prof.

Tobias, Steven M., BA Camb., PhD Camb. Reader

Weiss, Nigel O., ScD Camb., FRS Visiting Prof.

Wilson, Michael J., MA Camb., PhD Camb. Prof.

Other Staff: 4 Lectrs.; 1 Res. Fellow; 1 Univ. Res. Fellow; 1 Marie-Curie Inter-European Fellow; 1 Academic Fellow; 3 Postdoctoral Res. Assocs.

Mathematics, Financial

Schenk-Hoppé, Klaus R., MSc Bremen, PhD Bremen Centenary Prof.

Other Staff: 1 Lectr.

Mathematics, Pure

Tel: (0113) 343 5140 Fax: (0113) 343 5090

Allenby, Reginald B. J. T., MScTech Manc., PhD Wales Sr. Lectr.

Carter, Sheila, MSc Liv., PhD Liv. Sr. Lectr.

Cooper, S. Barry, BA Oxf., PhD Leic. Prof.

Crawley-Boevey, William W., MA Camb., PhD Camb. Prof.

Dales, H. Garth, MA Camb., PhD Newcastle(UK) Prof.

Houston, Kevin, BSc Newcastle(UK), MSc Warw., PhD Warw. Sr. Lectr.

Lance, E. Christopher, MA Camb., PhD Camb. Prof.

MacPherson, H. Dugald, MA Oxf., DPhil Oxf. Prof.

Partington, Jonathan R., MA Camb., PhD Camb. Prof.

Pillay, Anand, BA Oxf., MSc Lond., PhD Lond. Prof.

Rathjen, Michael, PhD Mün. Prof.

Read, Charles J., MA Camb., PhD Camb. Prof.

Robson, J. Christopher, BSc Durh., PhD Leeds Prof.

Rouquier, Raphael, PhD Paris Prof., Representation Theory

Salinger, David L., MA Camb., PhD Camb. Sr. Lectr.; Head*

Truss, John K., BA Camb., PhD Leeds Prof.

Wainer, Stanley S., MSc Leeds, PhD Leeds Prof.

Wood, John C., BA Oxf., MSc Warw., PhD Warw. Prof.

Other Staff: 4 Lectrs.; 4 Res. Fellows; 1 Univ. Res. Fellow; 2 Principal Teaching Fellows; 4 Hon. Visiting Fellows

Research: differential geometry; functional analysis; mathematical logic; non-commutative algebra

Modern Languages and Cultures, School of

Tel: (0113) 343 2698 Fax: (0113) 343 2699

Nagib, Lucia, BA Sao Paulo, MA Sao Paulo, PhD Sao Paulo Dir., Postgrad. Studies and Res.; Centenary Prof., World Cinema

Williams, Mark B., MA Oxf., MA Calif., PhD Calif. Prof.; Head*

Arabic and Middle Eastern Studies

Tel: (0113) 343 3421 Fax: (0113) 343 3426

Abdul-Raof, Hussein, BA Baghdad, MA Lond., PhD Leeds Sr. Lectr.

Agius, Dionisius A., MA Tor., PhD Tor. Prof., Arabic and Islamic Material Culture

Salhi, Zahia S., PhD Exe. Sr. Lectr.; Head*

Sirriyeh, Hussein M., MA Beirut, DPhil Oxf. Sr. Lectr.

Other Staff: 1 Teaching Fellow; 1 Assoc. Fellow; 1 Postdoctoral Res. Fellow

Research: Arabic linguistics; Islamic philosophy; naval vocabulary in the Gulf; North African literature and Kurdish literature; Palestinian-Israeli negotiation

East Asian Studies

Tel: (0113) 343 3460 Fax: (0113) 343 6741

Christiansen, Flemming, MA Aarhus, PhD Ley. Sr. Lectr.

Davin, Delia, BA Leeds, PhD Leeds Emer. Prof., Chinese Studies

Dent, Christopher M., BA Oxf.Brookes, MA Leeds, PhD Hull Sr. Lectr.

Dosch, Joern, MA Mainz, DPhil Mainz Sr. Lectr.

King, Victor T., BA Hull, MA Lond., PhD Hull Prof., South-East Asian Studies

Li, Ruru, MA Shanghai, PhD Leeds Sr. Lectr.

Parnwell, Michael J., BA Hull, PhD Hull Reader, South-East Asian Geography

Rose, Caroline, BA Leeds, PhD Leeds Sr. Lectr.; Head*

Williams, Mark B., MA Oxf., MA Calif., PhD Calif. Prof., Japanese Studies

Other Staff: 10 Lectrs.; 3 Sr. Teaching Fellows; 3 Teaching Fellows

Research: Chinese revolutionary history; contemporary Chinese society and economy; economy of Japan and newly-industrialising Asian countries; Japanese literature; overseas Chinese in Europe and Asia

French

Tel: (0113) 343 3479 Fax: (0113) 343 3477

Armstrong, Nigel R., BA Newcastle(UK), PhD Newcastle(UK) Sr. Lectr.

Atack, Margaret K., BA Lond., PhD Lond. Prof.

Brown-Grant, Rosalind, BA Manc., PhD Manc. Sr. Lectr.

Goulbourne, Russell J., MA Oxf., MSt Oxf., DPhil Oxf. Sr. Lectr.

Holmes, Diana, BA *Sus.*, MèsL *Paris III*, DPhil *Sus.* Prof.

Jenkins, Brian J., BA *Camb.*, MSc *Lond.*, PhD *Lond.* Res. Prof.

Killick, Rachel, BA *Oxf.*, PhD *Leeds* Prof., Quebec Studies and Nineteenth-Century French Studies

Looseley, David L., BA *Exe.*, PhD *Exe.* Prof., Contemporary French Culture

Platten, David P., BA *Liv.*, PhD *Liv.* Sr. Lectr.; Head*

Roe, David, MA *Oxf.*, DPhil *Oxf.* Dir., Undergrad. Studies

Salhi, Kamal, MPhil *Exe.*, PhD *Exe.* Sr. Lectr.

Silverman, Maxim, BA *E.Anglia*, PhD *Kent* Prof., Modern French Studies

Stafford, Andrew J., BA *Nott.*, MA *Nott.*, PhD *Nott.* Sr. Lectr.

Waters, Sarah, MA *N.U.I.*, PhD *N.U.I.*, BA Sr. Lectr.

Other Staff: 4 Lectrs.; 4 Lecteurs; 1 Teaching Fellow; 2 Hon. Res. Assocs.

Research: cultural studies; francophone studies; French literary studies; linguistics; social and cultural studies

German

Tel: (0113) 343 3508 Fax: (0113) 343 3508

Bridgham, Frederick G. T., BA *Belf.*, PhD *Camb.* Sr. Lectr.

Cooke, Paul A., BA *Birm.*, MA *Nott.*, PhD *Birm.* Sr. Lectr.

Cornils, Ingo, MA *Hamburg*, DPhil *Hamburg* Sr. Lectr.; Head*

Donald, Sydney G., MA *St And.*, PhD *St And.* Sr. Lectr.

Sharp, Ingrid, MA *Oxf.* Sr. Lectr.

Taberner, Stuart J., MA *Camb.*, MA *Chic.*, PhD *Camb.* Prof.

Other Staff: 3 Lektorinnen

Italian

Tel: (0113) 343 3630 Fax: (0113) 343 3634

Honess, Claire E., BA *Reading*, PhD *Reading* Sr. Lectr.; Head*

Richardson, Prof. Brian F., MA *Oxf.*, MPhil *Lond.* Prof.

Other Staff: 3 Lectrs.; 2 Teaching Fellows; 1 Hon. Res. Fellow

Research: history of the Italian language; modern Italy; regional identity; Renaissance Italy; theatre history

Linguistics and Phonetics

Tel: (0113) 343 3563 Fax: (0113) 343 3566

Johnson, Sally, BA *Salf.*, PhD *Salf.* Prof., Linguistics; Head*

Other Staff: 3 Lectrs.; 2 Sr. Fellows

Research: historical linguistics; pragmatics; socio-phonetics; suprasegmental phonology; syntactic and morphological theory

Russian and Slavonic Studies

Tel: (0113) 343 3285 Fax: (0113) 343 3287

Sutton, Jonathan F., BA *Durh.*, PhD *Durh.* Sr. Lectr.; Head*

Other Staff: 2 Lectrs.; 2 Teaching Fellows; 1 Assoc. Res. Fellow; 1 Hon. Res. Fellow

Research: rise and fall of the Tsarist and Soviet empires; Russian and East European media; Russian literature; Siberian studies; translation theory and practice

Spanish and Portuguese

Tel: (0113) 343 3516 Fax: (0113) 343 3517

Cleminson, Richard, BA *Salf.*, PhD *W.England* Sr. Lectr.

Dennison, Stephanie, BA *Lond.*, PhD *Liv.* Sr. Lectr.

Frier, David, MA *Glas.*, PhD *Glas.* Sr. Lectr.; Head*

Garner, Paul, BA *Birm.*, PhD *Liv.* Cowdray Prof.

Smith, Angel, BA *Manc.*, PhD *Lond.* Sr. Lectr.

Other Staff: 2 Lectrs.; 1 Leitor; 1 Sr. Lang. Teaching Fellow; 2 Lang. Teaching Fellows; 1 Hon. Res. Fellow

Research: Iberian and Latin-American cultural studies; Iberian and Latin-American history; literature in Iberia and Latin America; Spanish and Latin-American gender issues; Spanish and Latin-American society

Music, School of

Tel: (0113) 343 2583 Fax: (0113) 343 2586

Barber, Graham D., BA *E.Anglia*, MMus *E.Anglia*, FRCO Prof., Performance Studies

Brown, Clive, MA *Kent*, MA *Oxf.*, DPhil *Oxf.* Prof., Applied Musicology; Head*

Chuan Ng, Kia, BSc *Leeds*, PhD *Leeds* Sr. Lectr.

Cooper, David G., BA *Leeds*, BA *Open(UK)*, DPhil *York(UK)* Prof., Music and Technology

Cowgill, Rachel E., BMus *Lond.*, MMus *Lond.*, PhD *Lond.* Sr. Lectr.

Dawe, Kevin N., BA *Plym.*, BSc *Open(UK)*, MSc *Lond.*, PhD *Belf.* Sr. Lectr.

Holman, Peter, BMus *Lond.*, MMus *Lond.*, DMus *Lond.* Reader, Historical Musicology

Rastall, G. Richard, MA *Camb.*, MusB *Camb.*, PhD *Manc.*, FSA Prof., Historical Musicology

Windsor, W. Luke, BSc *City(UK)*, MA *City(UK)*, PhD *City(UK)* Sr. Lectr.

Other Staff: 4 Lectrs.; 1 Visiting Res. Fellow; 1 Sr. Fellow; 4 Sr. Teaching Fellows; 1 Teaching Fellow

Vacant Posts: West Riding Prof. of Music

Research: composition (commercial, electro-acoustic, mixed media, notated); critical musicology (film, jazz, popular, post-modernism, theory); historical musicology (analysis, classical, mediaeval, nineteenth-century, opera, twentieth-century); music and science (artificial intelligence, electro-acoustics, multimedia, psychology, technology); performance (contemporary, historical, theatrical, theory)

Performance and Cultural Industries, School of

Tel: (0113) 343 9109 Fax: (0113) 343 9186

Boon, Richard P., BA *Sheff.*, PhD *Sheff.* Prof., Performance Studies

Collis, Peter E., BEd *Leeds*, MA *Lond.*, FRSA Dir., Learning and Teaching

Daniels, Susan M., BA *Warw.*, MA *Leeds* Head*

Stephenson, Tim J., BMus *Lond.*, MMus *Lond.*, MEd *Durh.*, PhD *Sur.* Sr. Lectr.

Taylor, Calvin F., BSc *City(UK)*, PhD *Glas.* Sr. Lectr.; Dir., Knowledge Transfer

Wallis, Mick, BA *Manc.* Dir., Res.; Prof., Performance and Culture

Other Staff: 16 Lectrs.; 4 Sr. Teaching Fellows

Philosophy, School of

Tel: (0113) 343 3260 Fax: (0113) 343 3265
E-mail: philosophy@leeds.ac.uk

Cantor, Geoffrey N., BSc *Lond.*, PhD *Lond.* Emer. Prof., History of Science

Christie, John R. R., MA *Edin.* Sr. Lectr.

Francks, Richard, MA *Camb.*, PhD *Lond.* Sr. Lectr.

French, Steven R. D., BSc *Newcastle(UK)*, PhD *Lond.* Prof., Philosophy of Science; Head*

Gooday, Graeme J. N., MA *Camb.*, PhD *Kent* Sr. Lectr.

Hodge, M. Jonathan S., BA *Camb.*, MS *Wis.*, PhD *Harv.* Sr. Lectr.

Holdcroft, David, MA *Camb.* Emer. Visiting Prof.

Kieran, Matthew, BA *Brist.*, PhD *St And.* Sr. Lectr.

Le Poidevin, Robin D., MA *Oxf.*, PhD *Camb.*, FRSA Prof., Metaphysics

Macdonald Ross, George, MA *Camb.* Sr. Lectr.

Millican, Peter J. R., MA *Oxf.*, BPhil *Oxf.*, PhD *Leeds* Sr. Lectr.

Parry, S. James, BA *Wales*, MA *Leeds*, MEd *Manc.*, MJur *Manc.*, EdD *Leeds* Sr. Lectr.

Simons, Peter M., BSc *Manc.*, MA *Manc.*, PhD *Manc.* Prof.

Wilson, Adrian F., BMedSc *Adel.*, MA *Camb.*, DPhil *Sus.* Sr. Lectr.

Other Staff: 9 Lectrs.; 2 Teaching Fellows; 1 Hon. Lectr.

Research: history of ancient and modern philosophy; history of science, technology and medicine; meta-ethics and applied ethics; metaphysics; philosophy of logic and language

History and Philosophy of Science Division

Tel: (0113) 343 3262

Cantor, Geoffrey N., BSc *Lond.*, PhD *Lond.* Prof., History of Science

Christie, John R. R., MA *Edin.* Sr. Lectr.

French, Steven R. D., BSc *Newcastle(UK)*, PhD *Lond.* Prof., Philosophy of Science

Gooday, Graeme J. N., MA *Camb.*, PhD *Kent* Sr. Lectr.

Hodge, M. Jonathan S., BA *Camb.*, MS *Wis.*, PhD *Harv.* Sr. Lectr.

Radick, Gregory, BA *Rutgers*, MPhil *Camb.*, PhD *Camb.* Sr. Lectr.; Chair*

Wilson, Adrian F., BMedSc *Adel.*, MA *Camb.*, DPhil *Sus.* Sr. Lectr.

Other Staff: 2 Lectrs.; 3 Hon. Lectrs.

Research: history and philosophy of physics; history and philosophy of technology; history of biology; history of chemistry; history of medicine

Physics and Astronomy, School of

Tel: (0113) 343 3860 Fax: (0113) 343 3900

Adolf, David B., BSc *Minn.*, PhD *Wis.* Sr. Lectr.

Batchelder, David N., BA *Williams(Mass.)*, MSc *Ill.*, PhD *Ill.* Res. Prof.

Blitz, Leo, BSc *Cornell*, PhD *Col.* Visiting Prof.

Christenson, Hugo K., BSc *Stockholm*, MSc *Missouri*, PhD *ANU* Reader, Molecular Physics

Cywinski, Robert, BSc *Manc.*, PhD *Salf.*, FRSA Prof., Experimental Physics

Dyson, John E., BSc *Lond.*, PhD *Manc.*, DSc *Manc.* Prof., Astronomy

Evans, Stephen D., BSc *Lond.*, MSc *Lanc.*, PhD *Lanc.* Prof., Molecular and Nanoscale Physics

Greig, Denis, BSc *St And.*, PhD *Aberd.* Emer. Res. Prof.

Hartquist, Thomas W., BA *Rice*, MA *Harv.*, PhD *Harv.* Prof., Astrophysics

Henderson, James R., BSc *Well.*, PhD *Well.* Reader, Liquid State Physics

Hickey, Bryan J., BA *Leeds*, BSc *Leeds*, PhD *Leeds* Prof.; Head*

Hillas, A. Michael, BSc *Leeds*, PhD *Leeds* Emer. Res. Prof.

Hoare, Melvin G., BSc *Lond.*, PhD *Lond.*, FRAS Sr. Lectr.

Kilcoyne, Susan H., BSc *Liv.*, PhD *Liv.* Sr. Lectr.

Knapp, Johannes, MSc *Karlsruhe*, PhD *Karlsruhe* Sr. Lectr.

Knoll, Wolfgang, PhD *Constance* Visiting Prof.

Lawrie, Ian D., BA *Oxf.*, DPhil *Sus.* Prof., Theoretical Physics

Lloyd-Evans, J., BSc *Leeds*, PhD *Leeds* Sr. Lectr.

Marrows, Christopher H., BSc *Leeds*, PhD *Leeds* Reader, Condensed Matter Physics

McLeish, Thomas C. B., MA *Camb.*, PhD *Camb.* EPSRC Sr. Res. Fellow/Prof., Polymer Physics

Morgan, Gwynne J., BSc *Manc.*, MSc *St And.*, PhD *Lond.*, FIP Cavendish Prof., Theoretical Physics

Myers, Philip C., AB *Col.*, PhD *M.I.T.* Visiting Prof.

Olmstead, Peter D., BA *Cornell*, MS *Ill.*, PhD *Ill.* Prof., Complex Fluids

Oudmaijer, Rene, BSc *Gron.*, MA *Gron.*, PhD *Gron.* Sr. Lectr.

Rose, H. Joachim, MSc *T.H.Aachen*, PhD *T.H.Aachen* Sr. Lectr.

Savage, Michael D., BSc *Manc.*, PhD *Leeds* Prof., Thin Liquid Films and Coatings

Smith, D. Alastair, BSc *Manc.*, PhD *Manc.* Reader, Molecular Biophysics

Vedral, Vlatko, BSc *Lond.*, PhD *Lond.* Centenary Prof., Quantum Information Science

Voice, Alison M., BSc *Exe.*, PhD *Leeds* Sr. Lectr.

Ward, Ian M., MA Oxf., DPhil Oxf., FRS   Emer. Res. Prof.

Watson, Alan A., BSc Edin., PhD Edin., FRAS, FIP   Res. Prof.

Weekes, Trevor C., BSc PhD   Visiting Prof.

Wiser, Nathan, BSc Wayne State, PhD Chic.   Visiting Prof.

Other Staff: 6 Lectrs.; 2 Sr. Res. Fellows; 1 Visiting Sr. Res. Fellow; 18 Res. Fellows; 3 Visiting Res. Fellows; 4 Sr. Fellows; 2 Advanced Fellows; 3 Royal Society Fellows; 2 Hon. Res. Fellows

Research: magnetism and superconductivity; molecular self-assembly, spectroscopy and atomic force microscopy (AFM)/scanning tunneling microscope (STM) imaging; observational astronomy; theoretical and experimental polymer physics; theoretical and high energy astrophysics

Politics and International Studies, School of

Tel: (0113) 343 4382 Fax: (0113) 343 4400

Aydin, Zulkuf, BA Ankara, PhD Durh.   Sr. Lectr.

Beetham, D., BA Oxf., MA(Econ) Manc., PhD Manc.   Emer. Prof.

Bell, David S., MA Aberd., MSc S'ton., DPhil Oxf.   Prof., French Government and Politics

Blaug, Ricardo, BA Mass., MA Mass., PhD Manc.   Sr. Lectr.

Bluth, Christoph, BA Trinity(Dub.), MPhil Trinity(Dub.), PhD Lond.   Prof., International Studies

Bush, Raymond C., BA CNAA, MA Leeds, PhD Leeds   Sr. Lectr.

Cliffe, Lionel R., BA Nott.   Emer. Prof.

Crawford, Gordon, BA Leeds, MA Leeds, PhD Leeds   Sr. Lectr.

Dyer, Caroline, BA Liv., PhD Edin.   Sr. Lectr.

Dyer, Hugh C., BA Vic.(BC), MA Dal., PhD Lond.   Sr. Lectr.

Fry, Geoffrey K., BSc(Econ) Lond., PhD Lond.   Emer. Prof.

Hills, Aice, BA Lanc., PhD Lond.   Sr. Lectr.

Jones, Clive A., BA Tees., MA E.Anglia, PhD Wales   Sr. Lectr.; Head*

McCargo, Duncan J., MA Lond., PhD Lond.   Prof., South-East Asian Politics

Minkin, Lewis, BA Leeds, DPhil York(UK)   Hon. Prof.

Pearson, Ruth, BA Camb., MA Sus., DPhil Sus.   Prof., Development Studies

Radice, Hugo K., BA Camb., MA Warw.   Sr. Lectr.

Ralph, Jason G., BSc(Econ) Wales, MSc(Econ) Wales, PhD Lond.   Sr. Lectr.

Ramsay, Maureen A., BA Manc., PhD Manc.   Sr. Lectr.

Schwarzmantel, John J., BA Oxf., BPhil Oxf., PhD Leeds   Sr. Lectr.

Seawright, David, BA G.Caledonian, PhD Strath.   Sr. Lectr.

Theakston, Kevin, BSc(Econ) Lond., PhD Lond., FRHistS   Prof., British Government

Winn, Neil, BSc Plym., MA Hull, PhD Florence   Sr. Lectr.

Other Staff: 8 Lectrs.; 1 Sr. Fellow; 1 Sr. Teaching Fellow; 1 Teaching Fellow; 1 Academic Fellow; 2 Hon. Sr. Res. Fellows; 1 Hon. Visiting Res. Fellow

Sociology and Social Policy, School of

Tel: (0113) 343 4418 Fax: (0113) 343 4415

Bagguley, Paul, BA E.Anglia, MA Sus., DPhil Sus.   Sr. Lectr.

Barnes, Colin, BA Leeds, PhD Leeds   Prof., Disability Studies

Deacon, Alan J., BSc(Soc) Lond., PhD Lond.   Prof., Social Policy

Dwyer, Peter, BSc Brad., PhD Leeds   Sr. Lectr.

Ellison, Nick   Prof.; Head*

Harrison, Malcolm L., MA Camb., PhD Camb.   Reader

Irwin, Sarah, BA Leeds, PhD Edin.   Sr. Lectr.

Kilminster, Richard C. J., BA Essex, MA Leic., PhD Leeds   Sr. Lectr.

Law, Ian G., BA Liv., PhD Liv.   Reader

Mann, Kirk, BA Leeds, PhD Leeds   Sr. Lectr.

Mercer, Geoffrey, BA Durh., MA S.Fraser, PhD Strath.   Reader

Pawson, R. D., BA Essex, PhD Lanc.   Reader

Priestley, Mark, BA Leeds, MA Leeds, PhD Leeds   Reader

Roseneil, Sasha, BSc(Econ) Lond., PhD Lond.   Prof., Sociology and Gender Studies

Sevenhuijsen, Selma, MA Amst., PhD Amst.   Visiting Prof.

Williams, Fiona, OBE, BSc(Soc) Lond., PhD Open(UK)   Prof., Social Policy

Other Staff: 5 Lectrs.; 1 Assoc. Lectr.; 1 Principal Res. Fellow; 3 Res. Fellows; 2 Visiting Res. Fellows; 1 Principal Teaching Fellow; 1 Sr. Teaching Fellow; 1 Teaching Fellow; 1 Hon. Sr. Res. Fellow

Research: disability; ethnicity; gender; theory and methods; welfare reform

Statistics

Tel: (0113) 343 5102 Fax: (0113) 343 5090

Aykroyd, Robert G., BSc Newcastle(UK), MSc Sheff., PhD Sheff.   Sr. Lectr.

Bogachev, Leonid V., MSc Moscow, PhD Moscow   Reader

Kent, John T., BA Harv., PhD Camb.   Prof.; Head*

Mardia, Kanti V., MSc Bom., MSc Poona, PhD Raj., PhD Newcastle(UK), DSc Newcastle(UK)   Sr. Res. Prof.

Taylor, Charles C., MSc Lond., PhD Lond.   Prof.

Veretennikov, Alexander U., MSc Moscow, PhD Moscow, DSc Moscow   Prof.

Other Staff: 5 Lectrs.; 1 Res. Fellow; 3 Hon. Visiting Fellows

Research: image analysis; pattern recognition, classification and data-mining; shape analysis; spatial statistics, spatial temporal modelling; statistical inference, robustness, Markov Chain Monte Carlo (MCMC)

Theology and Religious Studies, School of

Tel: (0113) 343 3644 Fax: (0113) 343 3654

Elliott, J. Keith, BA Wales, DPhil Oxf., DD Wales   Prof., New Testament Textual Criticism

Knott, Kim, MA Leeds, PhD Leeds   Prof., Religious Studies

McFadyen, Alistair I., BA Birm., PhD Birm.   Sr. Lectr.

McLoughlin, Seán, BA Manc., MA Manc., PhD Manc.   Sr. Lectr.

Mellor, Philip A., MA Sus., PhD Manc.   Reader, Religion and Social Theory; Head*

Sirriyeh, Elizabeth M., MA Edin., PhD Manc.   Sr. Lectr.

Stewart, Jacqueline A., BSc Edin., PhD Edin., PhD Leeds   Sr. Lectr.

Ward, Kevin, MA Edin., PhD Camb.   Sr. Lectr.

Other Staff: 2 Lectrs.; 1 Leverhulme Res. Fellow; 9 Visiting Fellows

Transport Studies, Institute for

Tel: (0113) 343 5325 Fax: (0113) 343 5334

Bell, Margaret, BSc Durh., PhD Durh.   Prof., Traffic and Environmental Pollution

Bonsall, Peter W., BA Oxf.   Prof., Transport Planning

Carr, John, BSc Leeds, MSc Leeds   Visiting Sr. Lectr.

Carsten, Oliver M. J., BA Oxf., MA Mich., PhD Mich.   Prof., Transport Safety

Daly, Andrew, BA Oxf.   Visiting Prof.

de Jong, Gerard, MA Rotterdam, PhD Amst.   Visiting Prof.

Fowkes, Anthony S., BA Leeds, PhD Leeds   Reader, Transport Economics

Grant-Muller, Susan, BSc CNAA, PhD CNAA   Sr. Lectr.; Dir., Res.

Guehnemann, Astrid, PhD Karlsruhe   Sr. Lectr.

Gwilliam, Ken, BA Oxf.   Visiting Prof.

Mackie, Peter J., BA Nott.   Prof.

Marsden, Gregory, MEng Nott., PhD Nott.   Sr. Lectr.

May, Anthony D., OBE, MA Camb., FREng, FICE   Prof., Transport Engineering

Montgomery, Francis O., BSc CNAA, MSc Leeds   Sr. Lectr.; Dir., Teaching and Learning

Nash, Christopher A., BA Reading, PhD Leeds   Prof., Transport Economics

Quinn, Derek, BA Wales, PhD Aston   Visiting Prof.

Smith, Nigel J., BSc Birm., MSc Manc., PhD Manc., FICE   Prof., Project and Transport Infrastructure Management

Tight, Miles R., BSc Liv., PhD Lond.   Sr. Lectr.

Toner, Jeremy P., BSocSc Birm., MA Leeds, PhD Leeds   Sr. Lectr.

Van Vuren, Tom, MSc T.H.Delft, PhD Leeds   Visiting Prof.

Wardman, Mark, BSocSc Birm., MA Leeds, PhD Leeds   Prof., Transport Demand Analysis; Dir.*

Watling, David, BSc Sheff., PhD Sheff.   Centenary Prof., Transport Analysis

Whelan, Gerard, BSc Hull, MSc Leeds   Sr. Lectr., Transport Economics and Transport Policy

Whiteing, Anthony, BSc Hull, MA Leeds, PhD Leeds   Sr. Lectr.

Other Staff: 2 Lectrs.; 2 Principal Res. Fellows; 15 Sr. Res. Fellows; 12 Res. Fellows; 4 Marie Curie Res. Fellows; 5 Visiting Res. Fellows; 1 Univ. Res. Fellow; 1 Sr. Fellow

Research: driver behaviour and safety issues; economic appraisal and public transport systems; network analysis and traffic modelling; policy and environment; traffic demand management and control

MEDICINE AND HEALTH

Genetics, Health and Therapeutics, Leeds Institute of (LIGHT)

Wild, Christopher P., BSc Manc., PhD Manc.   Prof.; Dir.*

Cardiovascular Medicine

Tel: (0113) 243 2799

Ball, Stephen G., MB BChir Camb., MA Camb., PhD Leeds, FRCP   British Heart Foundation Prof., Cardiology; Head*

Batten, Trevor F. C., BSc Sheff., PhD Sheff.   Reader, Autonomic Science

Drinkhill, Mark J., BSc Leeds, PhD Leeds   Sr. Lectr.

Greenwood, John P., MB ChB Leeds, PhD Leeds   Sr. Lectr.

Hall, Alistair S., MB ChB Leeds, PhD Leeds   Prof., Clinical Cardiology

Peers, Christopher S., BSc Lond., PhD Lond.   Prof., Cellular Physiology

Sivananchan, Mohan, MB BS S.Lanka, MD S.Lanka   Hon. Prof., Clinical Cardiac Imaging and Intervention

Other Staff: 5 Sr. Res. Fellows; 1 Principal Res. Fellow; 16 Res. Fellows; 12 Sr. Clin Lectrs.; 1 Hon. Reader; 11 Hon. Sr. Lectrs.; 2 Hon. Lectrs.; 1 Hon. Res. Fellow

Epidemiology and Biostatistics, Centre for

Tel: (0113) 343 6602

Bishop, D. Tim, BSc Brist., MSc Brist., PhD Sheff.   Prof., Genetic Epidemiology

Bishop, Julia N.   Prof., Dermatology

Cade, Janet E., BSc S'ton., PhD S'ton.   Prof., Nutritional Epidemiology and Public Health

Forman, David, BA Keele, PhD S'ton.   Prof., Cancer Epidemiology

Gilthorpe, Mark S., BSc Nott., PhD Aston   Reader, Statistical Epidemiology

Haward, Robert A., MB ChB Brist.   Prof., Cancer Studies

Hay, Alastair, BSc Lond., PhD Lond.   Prof., Environmental Toxicology

McKinney, Patricia A., BSc Birm., PhD Leeds   Prof., Paediatric Epidemiology

West, Robert, BSc Lond., DPhil Oxf.   Sr. Lectr.

Wild, Christopher P., BSc Manc., PhD Manc.   Prof., Molecular Epidemiology; Head*

Other Staff: 7 Lectrs.; 4 Principal Res. Fellows; 3 Sr. Res. Fellows; 11 Res. Fellows; 1 Internat. Fellow; 1 Clin. Res. Fellow

Molecular Vascular Medicine

Tel: (0113) 243 2799

Ariëns, Robert A. S., BSc *Utrecht*, PhD *Maastricht* Reader
Burr, William   Visiting Prof.
Grant, Peter J., MB ChB *Brist.*, MD *Brist.*, FRCP Prof.; Head*
Scott, D. Julian, MB ChB *Leic.*, MD, FRCS Hon. Prof.
Tan, Lip-Bun, BSc *Oxf.*, MB BCh *Oxf.*, DPhil *Oxf.*, FRCP   Reader
Other Staff: 1 Principal Res. Fellow; 1 Sr. Res. Fellow; 7 Res. Fellows; 1 Univ. Res. Fellow; 6 Sr. Clin. Lectrs.; 5 Clin. Res. Fellows; 6 Hon. Sr. Lectrs.; 1 Hon. Sr. Clin. Lectr.

Health Sciences and Public Health Research, Institute of

House, Allan O., BSc *Lond.*, MB BS *Lond.*, DM *Nott.*   Acting Dir.*
Research: development of health planning systems in developing countries; interface between health and community care; management and leadership; public health, in particular the epidemiology and health care of long-term problems; role of non-governmental organisations

Health and Social Care, Centre for

Harding, Nancy, BSc *Wales*, PhD *Wales*   Sr. Lectr.
Hurst, Keith, PhD *CNAA*   Sr. Lectr.
Keen, Justin, BSc *Lond.*, MSc *Lond.*, PhD *City(UK)* Prof., Health Politics and Information Management
Other Staff: 2 Lectrs.; 3 Sr. Res. Fellows; 1 Sr. Fellow; 1 Teaching Fellow

International Health and Development, Nuffield Centre for

Green, Andrew T., BA *Oxf.*, MA *Sus.*, PhD *Leeds* Prof., International Health Planning
Newell, James, BA *Camb.*, MA *Camb.*, MSc *Leeds*, PhD *Leeds*   Sr. Lectr.
Walley, John D., MB BS *Newcastle(UK)*, MSc *Liv.* Sr. Lectr.
Other Staff: 13 Visiting Sr. Lectrs.; 4 Lectrs.; 9 Visiting Lectrs.; 3 Assoc. Lectrs.; 2 Sr. Res. Fellows; 1 Visiting Sr. Res. Fellow; 3 Res. Fellows; 3 Visiting Res. Fellows; 3 Sr. Teaching Fellows; 2 Teaching Fellows; 1 Visiting Teaching Fellow; 2 Visiting Fellows

Primary Care

Tel: (0113) 343 4179 Fax: (0113) 343 4181

Atkin, Karl, BA *Birm.*, DPhil *York(UK)*   Dir., Res.; Sr. Lectr., Ethnicity and Primary Care
Heywood, Philip L., MB ChB, FRCGP   Prof.; Head*
Leese, Brenda, BSc *Lond.*, MB BS *Lond.*, DPhil *York(UK)*   Reader
Other Staff: 1 Lectr.; 4 Sr. Assoc. Lectrs.; 8 Sr. Res. Fellows; 5 Res. Fellows; 4 Visiting Res. Fellows; 2 Sr. Teaching Fellows; 5 Sr. Clin. Lectrs.; 1 Clin. Res. Fellow; 2 Sr. Clin. Teaching Fellows; 9 Hon. Sr. Lectrs.; 62 Hon. Lectrs.

Psychiatry and Behavioural Sciences

Tel: (0113) 343 2701 Fax: (0113) 343 3719

Adams, Clive, MB BCh BAO *Belf.*, MSc *Lond.* Prof., Adult Psychiatry and Mental Health Services Research
Bekker, Hilary, BSc *Leeds*, MSc *Leeds*, PhD *Leeds* Sr. Lectr., Behavioural Sciences
Butler, Alan W. J., BA *Brad.*, MA *Wales*, MA *Leeds*   Sr. Lectr., Mental Health Social Work
Cottrell, David J., BA *Oxf.*, MB BS *Lond.*, MA *Oxf.*, FRCPsych   Prof., Child and Adolescent Psychiatry
Hewison, Jenny, BA *Camb.*, MSc *Lond.*, PhD *Lond.*   Prof., Healthcare Psychology
Hill, Andrew J., BSc *Leeds*, PhD *Leeds*   Sr. Lectr., Behavioural Sciences

Holmes, John D., BM BCh *Oxf.*, MA *Oxf.*, MMedSc *Leeds*   Sr. Lectr., Old Age Liaison Psychiatry
House, Allan O., BSc *Lond.*, MB BS *Lond.*, DM *Nott.*   Prof., Liaison Psychiatry; Head*
Morley, Stephen J., BSc *Lond.*, MPhil *Lond.*, PhD *Lond.*, FBPsS   Prof., Clinical Psychology
Owens, David W., BSc *Leeds*, MB ChB *Leeds*, MD *Leeds*   Sr. Lectr., Psychiatry
Worrall-Davies, Anne, MB ChB *Leeds*, MMedSc *Leeds*, MD *Leeds*   Sr. Lectr., Child and Adolescent Psychiatry
Other Staff: 2 Lectrs.; 16 Sr. Assoc. Lectrs.; 1 Sr. Res. Fellow; 1 Visiting Sr. Res. Fellow; 2 Res. Fellows; 1 Postdoctoral Res. Fellow; 1 Teaching Fellow; 26 Sr. Clin. Lectrs.; 41 Hon. Sr. Lectrs.; 35 Hon. Lectrs.; 6 Hon. Tutors

Public Health

Robinson, Michael, MA *Camb.*, MSc *Lond.*, MD *Lond.*, MB BS   Sr. Lectr.
Shickle, Darren, MB BCh *Wales*, MPH *Wales*, MA *Wales*, MD *Wales*, FFPHM   Prof.
Smith, Iain D., BSc *Edin.*, MB *Edin.*, FRCP   Sr. Lectr.
Other Staff: 2 Lectrs.; 1 Sr. Res. Fellow

Healthcare, School of

Tel: (0113) 343 1202 Fax: (0113) 343 1204

Allison, Jean, BA BSc MBA   Sr. Lectr.
Baldwin, Susan, MSc *Leeds Met.*   Sr. Lectr., Nursing
Bharj, Kuldip K., BSc *Brad.*, MSc *Brad.*   Sr. Lectr.
Brown, Rev. Alan G., BSc *Brad.*, MBA *Leeds*   Sr. Lectr.
Cheater, Francine, MA *St And.*, PhD *Nott.* Prof., Public Health Nursing
Clarke, David J., BSc *Leeds Met.*, MSc *Leeds Met.* Sr. Lectr., Nursing
Closs, José, BSc *Nott.*, MPhil *Nott.*, PhD *Edin.* Prof., Nursing Research
Cortis, Joseph D., BSc *Hudd.*, MSc *Brad.*, PhD *Leeds*   Sr. Lectr., Nursing
Dodsworth, Pauline, BSc *Leeds Met.*, MA *Leeds* Sr. Lectr., Nursing
Easthope, Gary, BA *Leeds*, MA *Leeds*, PhD *Exe.* Visiting Reader
Forster, Anne, BA *Brad.*, PhD *Brad.*   Reader, Elderly Care
Freshwater, Dawn   Prof.; Head*
Grigor, Ian E., MPhil *Leeds*   Sr. Lectr.
Hale, Claire, BA *Strath.*, PhD *Manc.*   Dame Kathleen Raven Prof., Clinical Nursing
Hargreaves, Janet, BA *Open(UK)*, MA *Leeds*   Dir., Practice; Sr. Lectr., Nursing
Harkness, Gail A., BS *Roch.*, MS *Roch.*   Visiting Prof.
Hinds, Marian, BA *Brad.*, MA *Leeds*   Sr. Lectr., Midwifery
Holt, Janet, BA *Leeds*, MPhil *Manc.*   Sr. Lectr.
Howarth, J. Steve   Sr. Lectr., Nursing
Kay, Elizabeth, BPharm *Nott.*, MSc *Manc.* Visiting Prof.
Kelsey, Amanda, MSc *Lond.*, PhD *Lond.*   Sr. Lectr., Primary Care/Public Health
Lascelles, Margaret A., BA *CNAA*, MA *Leeds*   Sr. Lectr., Nursing
Lee, Jacquie M., BEd *Leeds Met.*, MEd *Leeds*   Sr. Lectr., Ultrasound
Long, Andrew, BA *Sheff.Hallam*, MSc *Sheff.Hallam*, MPhil *Leeds*   Prof., Health Systems Research
Maclean, Joan, BSc *Leeds Met.*, PhD *Hudd.*   Sr. Lectr., Nursing
Marshall, Paul, BSc *Leeds*, PhD *Glas.*   Dir., Learning and Teaching; Sr. Lectr., Nursing
McNichol, Elaine, BSc *Leeds Met.*, MA *Hudd.* Co-ordinator, Centre for the Devel. of Healthcare Policy and Practice
McWilliam, Peter N., BSc *Dund.*, PhD *Glas.* Prof., Cardiovascular Physiology
Morrall, Peter A., BA *Greenwich*, MSc *S.Bank*, PhD *Lough.*   Sr. Lectr., Health and Sociology
Mountain, Gary, BA *Sheff.Hallam*, MA *Leeds*   Sr. Lectr., Child Health
Nelson, Andrea, BSc *Lond.*, PhD *Strath.*   Reader, Wound Healing

Quinn, Helen R., BA *Newcastle(UK)*, MSc *CNAA* Sr. Lectr.
Raynor, Theo K., BPharm *Nott.*, PhD *Brad.* Dir., Res.; Prof., Pharmacy Practice, Medicines and their Users
Shaw, Paul, BSc *Leeds*, MSc *Manc.*   Sr. Lectr., Audiology
Sowter, Julie R., BPharm *Nott.*, MEd *Leeds*   Sr. Lectr., Pharmacy
Strickland-Hodge, Barry, BSc *Aston*, MSc *City(UK)*, PhD *Aston*   Sr. Lectr., Pharmacy
Thomas, Kate, BA *Sus.*, MA *Sheff.*   Prof., Complementary and Alternative Medicine
Thyer, Nick, BSc *Reading*, MSc *S'ton.*, PhD *Qld.* Sr. Lectr.
Tovey, Philip, BA *Leeds*, PhD *Hull*   Reader, Health Sociology
Truscott, John, BSc *Salf.*, MSc *Edin.*, PhD *Leeds* Sr. Lectr., Medical Imaging
Wilson, Jean, BEd *Leeds Met.*, MEd *Leeds*   Sr. Lectr., Radiography
Woolridge, Mike W., BSc *Oxf.*, DPhil *Oxf.*   Sr. Lectr.
Other Staff: 102 Lectrs.; 2 Assoc. Lectrs.; 2 Sr. Res. Fellows; 3 Visiting Sr. Res. Fellows; 5 Res. Fellows; 1 Sr. Teaching Fellow; 2 Teaching Fellows; 1 Visiting Fellow; 1 Hon. Res. Fellow; 47 Hon. Tutors; 2 Hon. Res. Assocs.

Leeds Dental Institute

Kellett, Margaret, BDS *Manc.*, MSc *Manc.*, PhD *Manc.*, FDSRCS   Dir.*

Acute Dental Care

Speirs, Alastair F., BDS *Brist.*, MSc *Glas.*, FDSRCS Hon. Clin. Lectr.; Head*
Other Staff: 1 Dental Tutor†

Adult Integrated Care

Nattress, Brian R., BChD *Leeds*, PhD *Leeds*, FDSRCS   Sr. Lectr.; Head*
Other Staff: 1 Clin. Teaching Fellow; 1 Clin. Tutor; 4 Hon. Clin. Lectrs.

Cariology

Manogue, Michael, BDS *Dund.*, MDSc *Leeds*, PhD *Leeds*   Sr. Lectr.; Dir., Learning and Teaching
Martin, D. Muir, BDS *Edin.*, MDSc *Leeds*, FDSRCSEd   Sr. Lectr.; Head*
Other Staff: 1 Lectr.; 1 Sr. Instr.; 1 Clin. Teaching Fellow

Fixed and Removable Prosthodontics

Brunton, Paul A, BChD *Leeds*, MSc *Manc.*, PhD *Manc.*   Prof., Restorative Dentistry; Head*
Clarkson, Brian   Visiting Prof.
Watson, Christopher J., BDS *Wales*, PhD *Wales*, FDSRCS   Sr. Lectr.
Other Staff: 4 Lectrs.; 1 Lectr.†; 1 Dental Tutor†

Oral Biology

Tel: (0113) 343 6159 Fax: (0113) 343 6165

Bonass, William A., PhD *Leeds*   Sr. Lectr.
Brookes, Steven J., BSc *Leeds*, PhD *Leeds*   Sr. Lectr.
Devine, Deirdre A., BSc *Reading*, PhD *Lond.*   Sr. Lectr., Oral Microbiology
Kirkham, Jennifer, BSc *CNAA*, PhD *Leeds*   Prof.; Dir., Res.; Head*
Marsh, Philip D., BSc *Sheff.*, PhD *Lond.*   Prof., Oral Microbiology
Robinson, Colin, BSc *Leeds*, PhD *Leeds*   Prof.
Shore, Roger C., BSc *Leeds*, MPhil *CNAA*, PhD *Brist.*   Sr. Lectr.
Wood, David J., BSc *CNAA*, PhD *Greenwich* Prof., Dental Materials
Other Staff: 1 Lectr.; 2 Sr. Res. Fellows; 2 Univ. Res. Fellows; 1 Fellow

Oral Medicine and Pathology

Chattergee, Rana P., BDS *Dund.*   Sr. Lectr.
High, Alec S., BDS *Newcastle(UK)*, PhD *Leeds*, FDSRCSEd, FRCPath   Sr. Lectr., Oral Pathology

Hume, William J., BDS Edin., PhD Manc., FRCPath   Consultant Prof.

Mighell, Alan J., BSc Leeds, BChD Leeds, MB ChB Leeds, PhD Leeds, FDSRCS   Sr. Lectr., Oral Medicine; Head*

Oral Surgery

Tel: (0113) 343 6121 Fax: (0113) 343 6165

Fisher, Sheila E., MB ChB Birm., BDS Manc., MSc Birm., FDSRCS, FFDRCSI, FRCS   Sr. Lectr., Oral and Maxillofacial Surgery

Pedlar, Jonathan, BDS Lond., MSc Lond., PhD Lond., FDSRCS   Deputy Head; Sr. Lectr., Oral and Maxillofacial Surgery

Russell, John L., BDS Edin., MB ChB, FDSRCSEd, FRCSEd   Sr. Clin. Lectr., Oral and Maxillofacial Surgery; Head*

Other Staff: 2 Lectrs.; 3 Sr. Clin. Lectrs.; 1 Clin. Tutor; 1 Hon. Lectr.; 5 Hon. Tutors

Orthodontics

Luther, Friedy, BDS Brist., PhD Leeds   Sr. Lectr.; Head*

Other Staff: 3 Sr. Clin. Lectrs.; 3 Clin. Lectrs.; 1 Hon. Tutor

Paediatric Dentistry

Tel: (0113) 343 6139 Fax: (0113) 343 6165

Duggal, Monty S., BDS Punjab, MDS Leeds, PhD Leeds   Prof., Child Dental Health; Head*

Kwan, Stella Y. L., OBE, BSc Open(UK), MDentSci Leeds, MPH Leeds   Sr. Lectr.

Toumba, K. Jack, BSc Leeds, BChD Leeds, MSc Leeds, PhD Leeds, FDSRCS   Sr. Lectr.

Williams, Sonia A., MBE, BDS Lond., MDSc Leeds, PhD Lond.   Prof., Oral Health Services Research

Other Staff: 3 Lectrs.; 3 Res. Fellows; 2 Sr. Clin. Lectrs.; 1 Hon. Lectr.

Periodontology

Clerehugh, D. Valerie, BDS Manc., PhD Manc.   Prof.; Postgrad. Res. Tutor

Other Staff: 1 Lectr.; 12 Clin. Res. Fellows; 2 Hon. Sr. Clin. Lectrs.

Radiology

Carmichael, Fiona A., MSc, FDSRCPSGlas   Clin. Lectr., Oral and Maxillofacial Radiology; Head*

Other Staff: 1 Hon. Tutor

Medical Education Unit

Tel: (0113) 343 4212 Fax: (0113) 343 4373

Morris, Penelope A., BA York(UK)   Sr. Lectr., Communication Skills

Murdoch-Eaton, Deborah G., MB BS Lond., MD Lond.   Prof.

Roberts, Trudie E., BSc Manc., MB ChB Manc., PhD Manc., FRCP   Prof.; Dir.*

Sandars, John, MB ChB Sheff., MSc   Sr. Lectr., Community Based Skills

Other Staff: 1 Lectr.; 2 Sr. Teaching Fellows

Medical Physics

Tel: (0113) 343 6871

Berry, Elizabeth, BSc Hull, PhD Lond.   Sr. Lectr.

Cowen, Arnold R., BSc Nott.   Sr. Lectr.

Evans, J. Anthony, BSc Leeds, MSc Aberd., PhD Wales   Sr. Lectr.; Head*

Thwaites, David I., BA Camb., MA Camb., MSc Aberd., PhD Dund.   Hon. Prof., Oncology Physics

Other Staff: 1 Sr. Res. Fellow; 1 Visiting Sr. Res. Fellow; 3 Res. Fellows; 1 Sr. Clin. Lectr.; 3 Hon. Sr. Lectrs.; 10 Hon. Lectrs.

Molecular Medicine, Epidemiology and Cancer Research

General Surgery, Medicine and Anaesthesia

Tel: (0113) 243 3144 Fax: (0113) 242 9722

Axon, Anthony T. R., MD Lond., FRCP   Hon. Prof., Gastroenterology

Bellamy, Mark C., MB BS Lond., MA Lond., FRCA   Hon. Prof., Critical Care Anaesthesia

Brownjohn, Alex, MB BS, FRCP   Sr. Lectr., Medicine

Burke, Dermot, MB ChB Manc., PhD Lond., FRCS   Sr. Lectr., Surgery

Crabtree, Jean E., BSc Leeds, DPhil York(UK)   Reader, Experimental Pathology

Guillou, Pierre J., BSc Leeds, MD Leeds, FRCS, FRCPSGlas, Hon. FMedSci   Prof., Surgery

Heatley, Richard V., MD Wales, FRCP   Sr. Lectr., Medicine

Hopkins, Philip M., MB BS Lond., MD, FRCA   Prof., Anaesthesia

Howdle, Peter D., BSc Leeds, MD Leeds, FRCP   Prof., Clinical Education; Head*

Howell, Simon J., MB BS Lond., MA Camb., MSc Lond., FRCA   Sr. Lectr., Anaesthesia

Hull, Mark A., MB ChB Oxf., MA Camb., PhD Nott., FRCP   Prof., Molecular Gastroenterology

Jayne, David, MB ChB Wales, BSc, FRCS   Sr. Lectr., Surgery

Kay, Simon P. J., BA Oxf., BM BCh Oxf., FRCS   Hon. Prof., Plastic Surgery

Lodge, Peter A., MB ChB Leeds, MD, FRCS   Hon. Prof., Surgery

McMahon, Michael J., MB ChB Sheff., ChM Sheff., PhD Birm., FRCS   Prof., Surgery

Mulley, Graham P., MB ChB Leeds, DM Nott., FRCP   Hon. Prof., Medicine of the Elderly

Robinson, Philip J. A., FRCP, FRCR   Hon. Prof., Radiology

Sandle, Geoffrey I., BSc Leeds, MD Leeds, PhD Manc., FRCP   Prof., Clinical Science

Scott, D. Julian, MB ChB Leic., MD, FRCS   Hon. Prof., Vascular Surgery

Thomas, David F. M., BA Camb., MB BChir Camb., MA, FRCS   Hon. Prof., Paediatric Surgery

Other Staff: 3 Lectrs.; 1 Sr. Res. Fellow; 1 Visiting Res. Fellow; 1 Teaching Fellow; 217 Sr. Clin. Lectrs.; 1 Hon. Reader; 167 Hon. Sr. Lectrs.; 8 Hon. Lectrs.; 2 Hon. Sr. Clin. Lectrs.

Molecular Medicine

Tel: (0113) 243 3144

Anwar, Rashida, BSc UMIST, MSc UMIST, MBA Leeds, PhD Manc.   Sr. Lectr.

Bonifer, Constanze, PhD Heidel., DrHabil Freib.   Prof., Experimental Haematology

Bonthron, David T., BM BCh Oxf., MA Camb., FRCPEd, FRCPath   Centenary Prof.; Head*

Boylston, Arthur W., BA Yale, MD Harv., FRCPath   Prof., Pathology

Cockerill, Peter, BSc Melb., PhD Lond.   Reader

Coletta, P. Louise, BSc Salf., PhD Liv.   Sr. Lectr.

Crabtree, Jean E., BSc Leeds, DPhil York(UK)   Reader

Hull, Mark A., MB ChB Oxf., MA Camb., PhD Nott., FRCP   Prof., Molecular Gastroenterology

Inglehearn, Christopher, BSc Edin., PhD Edin.   Prof., Molecular Ophthalmology

Jones, Pamela, BA Oxf., DPhil Oxf.   Sr. Lectr.

Markham, Alexander F., KB, BSc Birm., MB BS Lond., PhD Birm., DSc Birm., FRCPath, FRCP   Prof., Medicine

McDermott, Michael, MB BCh BA   Prof., Experimental Rheumatology

Meredith, David A., BSc Brist., PhD Leeds   Reader

Mighell, Alan J., BSc Leeds, BChD Leeds, MB ChB Leeds, PhD Leeds, FDSRCS   Sr. Lectr.

Morgan, Ann W., BSc Leeds, MB ChB Leeds   Sr. Lectr.

Robinson, Philip, BSc Birm., PhD Manc.   Reader

Sandle, Geoffrey I., BSc Leeds, MD Leeds, PhD Manc., FRCP   Prof., Clinical Science

Speirs, Valerie, BSc Aberd., PhD Glas.   Sr. Lectr.

Other Staff: 13 Sr. Res. Fellows; 26 Res. Fellows; 2 Univ. Res. Fellows; 1 Royal Soc. Fellow; 3 Sr. Clin. Lectrs.; 6 Clin. Res. Fellows; 6 Hon. Sr. Lectrs.

Musculoskeletal Disease

Tel: (0113) 343 4940 Fax: (0113) 244 6066

Bhakta, Bipinchandra B., BSc Manc., MB ChB Manc., MD, FRCP   Charterhouse Prof., Rehabilitation Medicine

Bird, Howard A., MB BChir Camb., MA Camb., MD Camb., FRCP   Prof., Pharmacological Rheumatology

Conaghan, Philip, MB BS, FRACP   Prof., Musculoskeletal Medicine

Dickson, Robert A., MA Oxf., MD Edin., ChM Edin., DSc Edin., FRCS, FRCSEd   Prof., Orthopaedic Surgery

Emery, Paul, MA Camb., MD Camb., FRCP   ARC Prof., Rheumatology; Head*

Giannoudis, Panagiotis P., MD Leeds, BSc MB   Prof., Orthopaedic Surgery

Helliwell, Philip S., MB BCh Oxf., MA Oxf., MD Oxf., PhD Leeds, FRCP   Sr. Lectr., Rheumatology

Kent, Ruth M., BMedSci MD   Sr. Lectr., Neurological Rehabilitation

Limb, David L., BSc Lond., FRCSEd   Sr. Lectr., Orthopaedic Surgery

McDermott, Michael, MB BCh BA   Prof., Experimental Rheumatology

McGonagle, Dennis, MB BCh BAO PhD   Prof., Investigative Rheumatology

Milner, Peter A., BSc Leeds, MB ChB Leeds, FRCS   Sr. Lectr., Orthopaedic Surgery

Morgan, Ann W., BSc Leeds, MB ChB Leeds   Sr. Lectr., Rheumatology

Neumann, Vera, MD   Sr. Lectr., Rehabilitation Medicine

Seedhom, Bahaa B., BSc Assiut, PhD Leeds   Reader, Bioengineering

Tennant, Alan, BA CNAA, PhD Leeds   Prof., Rehabilitation Studies

Wakefield, Richard, BM   Sr. Lectr., Rheumatology

Other Staff: 5 Lectrs.; 6 Res. Fellows; 3 Visiting Res. Fellows; 9 Sr. Clin. Lectrs.; 7 Hon. Sr. Lectrs.

Oncology and Haematology

Tel: (0113) 243 3144 Fax: (0113) 242 9886

Anthoney, Alan, BSc Glas., MB ChB Glas., PhD Glas.   Sr. Lectr.

Banks, Rosamonde E., BSc St And., MSc Sur., PhD St And.   Reader, Biomedical Proteomics

Bishop, D. Tim, BSc Brist., MSc Brist., PhD Sheff.   Prof., Genetic Epidemiology

Burchill, Sue A., BSc CNAA, PhD Newcastle(UK)   Reader, Adolescent and Paediatric Cancer Research (Children's Cancer Res. Lab.)

Chester, John, BA Oxf., MB BS Lond., PhD Glas.   Sr. Lectr.

Child, J. Anthony, MD Lond., FRCPath   Visiting Prof.

Duffy, Sean G., MD Glas., FRCS   Sr. Lectr., Obstetrics and Gynaecology

Hall, Geoff, BMedSci Sheff., MB ChB Sheff., PhD Leeds   Sr. Lectr.

Hanby, Andrew M., BM S'ton., FRCPath   Prof., Breast Pathology

Hillmen, Peter, PhD Lond.   Sr. Lectr.

Kiltie, Anne, MA Oxf., DM Oxf., FRCR   Sr. Lectr.

Kinsey, Sally   Sr. Lectr.

Knowles, Margaret, BSc Brist., PhD Lond.   Prof., Experimental Cancer Research

MacLennan, Ken A., MB BS Lond., DM   Prof., Tumour Pathology

Marples, Maria, BA Oxf., BM BCh Oxf., MA Oxf., PhD Lond., FRCP   Sr. Lectr.

Melcher, Alan, BA Oxf., BM BCh Oxf., PhD Lond., FRCR   Sr. Lectr.

Newton Bishop, Julia, MB ChB Sheff., MD Sheff., FRCP   Hon. Prof., Dermatology

O'Donnell, Dearbhaile, MB   Sr. Lectr.

Parmar, Mahesh K. B.   Hon. Prof., Clinical Cancer Studies

Selby, Peter J., CBE, MB BChir Camb., MA Camb., MD Camb., FRCP   Prof., Cancer Medicine; Dir.*

Seymour, Matt T., MA Camb., MD Lond.   Prof., Gastrointestinal Medicine

Spurr, Nigel K., PhD *Lond.* Visiting Prof.
Stark, Dan, BA *Camb.*, PhD *Leeds*, MB BChir MA
  Sr. Lectr.
Tooze, Reuben, MB BS *Lond.*, PhD *Lond.* Sr.
  Lectr.
Trejdosiewicz, Ludwik K., BSc *Exe.*, PhD *Birm.*
  Reader, Epithelial Immunology
Twelves, Chris, BMedSci *Sheff.*, MB ChB *Sheff.*,
  MD *Sheff.*, FRCP, FRCPSGlas Prof., Clinical
  Pharmacology and Oncology
Velikova, Galina, BM BS Sr. Lectr.
Vile, Richard, PhD *Lond.* Hon. Prof.,
  Immunotherapy
Workman, Paul, BSc *Leic.*, PhD *Leeds*, FIBiol
  Visiting Prof.
Other Staff: 1 Principal Res. Fellow; 4 Sr. Res.
  Fellows; 24 Res. Fellows; 28 Sr. Clin.
  Lectrs.; 10 Clin. Res. Fellows; 13 Hon. Sr.
  Lectrs.; 6 Hon. Lectrs.; 3 Hon. Tutors

Paediatrics, Obstetrics and Gynaecology

Tel: (0113) 243 2799
Walker, James J., MD *Glas.*, FRCP, FRCOG
  Prof., Obstetrics and Gynaecology

Pathology

Tel: (0113) 343 3387 Fax: (0113) 343 3404
Burns, Philip A., BSc *Edin.*, PhD *Edin.* Sr. Lectr.
Hanby, Andrew M., BM *S'ton.*, FRCPath Prof.,
  Breast Pathology
Ilyas, Mohammad, MB ChB *Brist.*, DPhil *Oxf.*
  Sr. Lectr.
Jones, Richard G., BM BCh *Oxf.*, MA *Oxf.*, DM
  Oxf. Sr. Lectr., Chemical Pathology and
  Immunology
Kerr, Michael A., BSc *Leeds*, PhD *Leeds*, FRCPath
  Hon. Prof., Immunology
MacLennan, Ken A., MB BS *Lond.*, DM Prof.,
  Tumour Pathology
Quirke, Philip, BM *S'ton.*, PhD *Leeds*, FRCPath
  Prof.; Head*
Other Staff: 1 Lectr.; 1 Sr. Assoc. Lectr.; 1 Sr.
  Teaching Fellow; 1 Visiting Res. Fellow; 18
  Sr. Clin. Lectrs.; 16 Hon. Sr. Lectrs.; 5 Hon.
  Lectrs.; 1 Hon. Principal Res. Fellow

Psychological Sciences, Institute of

Tel: (0113) 343 5724 Fax: (0113) 343 5749
Barkham, Michael, BEd *Sus.*, MSc *Sur.*, MA
  Camb., PhD *Brighton* Prof., Clinical and
  Counselling Psychology
Blundell, John E., BSc *Leeds*, PhD *Lond.*, FBPsS
  Prof., Psychobiology
Conner, Mark T., BSc *Lanc.*, PhD *Birm.* Prof.,
  Applied Social Psychology
Conway, Martin A., BSc *Lond.*, PhD *Open(UK)*
  Prof., Cognitive Pscyhology; Dir.*
Cottrell, David J., BA *Oxf.*, MB BS *Lond.*, MA
  Oxf., FRCPsych Assoc. Prof.
Dye, Louise, BSc *Aston*, PhD *Leeds* Sr. Lectr.
Fielding, Dorothy M., MSc *Leeds*, PhD *Leeds*,
  FBPsS Visiting Prof.
Gardner, Peter H., BA *Sheff.*, MSc *CNAA*, PhD
  Sheff. Sr. Lectr.
Gough, Brendan, BSc *Belf.*, PhD *Belf.* Sr. Lectr.
Hendrie, Colin A., BA *CNAA*, PhD *Brad.* Sr.
  Lectr.
Hewison, Jenny, BA *Camb.*, MSc *Lond.*, PhD
  Lond. Assoc. Prof.
Jones, Fiona A., BA *Nott.*, MA *Brun.*, PhD *Herts.*
  Sr. Lectr.
King, Neil A., BSc *Wales*, MSc *Sheff.*, PhD *Leeds*
  Sr. Lectr.
Lawton, Rebecca J., BA *Nott.*, PhD *Nott.* Sr.
  Lectr.
Madill, Anna L., MA *Edin.*, PhD *Sheff.* Sr. Lectr.
McKeown, J. Denis, BSc *Ulster*, DPhil *Sus.* Sr.
  Lectr.
Näsland, Erik B., MD *Stockholm*, PhD *Stockholm*
  Visiting Prof.
O'Connor, Daryl, BA *Liv.*, PhD *Liv.* Sr. Lectr.
Rodgers, R. John, BSc *Belf.*, PhD *Belf.*, DSc *Belf.*,
  FBPsS Prof., Behavioural Pharmacology
Shapiro, David A., BA *Oxf.*, MSc *Lond.*, PhD
  Lond., FBPsS Visiting Prof.
Smith, Lawrence R., BA *Wales*, PhD *Wales* Sr.
  Lectr.

Waterman, Mitchell G., BSc *Lanc.*, PhD *Keele*
  Sr. Lectr.
Westerman, Stephen J., MSc *Wolv.*, PhD *Aston*
  Sr. Lectr.
Other Staff: 14 Lectrs.; 1 Visiting Lectr.; 1 Sr.
  Res. Fellow; 4 Visiting Sr. Res. Fellows; 1
  Res. Fellow; 1 Visiting Res. Fellow; 1 Sr.
  Teaching Fellow; 1 Teaching Fellow; 1
  Assoc. Res. Fellow; 1 Hon. Sr. Lectr.; 1
  Hon. Lectr.
Research: biological psychology (appetite, drugs
  and behaviour, nutrition, performance);
  health care psychology (clinical evaluation,
  patient–hospital interaction, stress); human
  factors (cognitive psychology, IT, transport,
  work performance); qualitative psychology
  (discourse analysis, grounded theory,
  narrative approach); social and
  developmental psychology (alcoholism,
  bullying, family therapy, planned
  behaviour, smoking)

SPECIAL CENTRES, ETC

African Studies, Leeds University Centre for (LUCAS)

Tel: (0113) 343 4722
  E-mail: j.e.plastow@leeds.ac.uk
Plastow, Jane, MA *Manc.*, MPhil *Manc.*, PhD
  Manc. Sr. Lectr.; Dir.*

Animal Sciences, Centre for

Forbes, J. Michael, BSc *Nott.*, PhD *Leeds*, DSc
  Nott. Res. Prof.
Miller, Helen M., BSc *Edin.*, MSc *Reading*, PhD
  Alta. Sr. Lectr.; Dir.*
Rodway, Richard G., BSc *Lond.*, PhD *Birm.* Sr.
  Lectr.

Antimicrobial Research, Centre for

Chopra, Ian, MA *Dublin City*, PhD *Brist.*, DSc
  Brist. Prof.; Dir.*
Henderson, Peter J. F., BSc *Brist.*, MA *Camb.*,
  ScD *Camb.*, PhD *Brist.* Prof.

Architecture and Material Culture, Centre for

Bristol, Kerry, BFA *Manit.*, MA *Tor.*, PhD *Lond.*
  Dir.*

Art, Institute for Advanced Study in

Includes Centre for Studies in Archit. and
  Material Culture; AHRC Centre for Cultural
  Analysis, Theory and History; Centre for
  Cultural Studies; Centre for Jewish Studies
McQuillan, Martin, MA *Glas.*, PhD *Glas.* Prof.;
  Exec. Dir.*

Banking and Financial Services, International Institute of

Keasey, Kevin, BA *Durh.*, MA *Newcastle(UK)*, PhD
  Newcastle(UK) Prof.; Dir.*
Other Staff: 1 Sr. Res. Fellow; 1 Res. Fellow

Bionanoscience, Institute of

Tel: (0113) 343 3092
  E-mail: p.g.stockley@leeds.ac.uk
Phillips, Simon E. V., BSc *Lond.*, PhD *Lond.*,
  FRSChem Astbury Prof.; Deputy Dir.
Stockley, Peter G., BSc *Lond.*, PhD *Camb.* Prof.;
  Dir.*

Bioscience, Centre for

Tel: (0113) 343 3001 Fax: (0113) 343 5894
  E-mail: ltsnbioscience@leeds.ac.uk
Hughes, Ian E., BSc *Leeds*, PhD *Leeds* Prof.; Co-
  Dir.
Wood, Edward J., MA *Oxf.*, DPhil *Oxf.* Prof.;
  Dir.*

British Government, Centre for

Tel: (0113) 343 4384 Fax: (0113) 343 4400
Seawright, David, BA *G.Caledonian*, PhD *Strath.*
  Sr. Lectr.; Deputy Dir.
Theakston, Kevin, BSc(Econ) *Lond.*, PhD *Lond.*,
  FRHistS Prof.; Dir.*

Business and Professional Ethics, Centre for

Tel: (0113) 343 3280
Megone, Christopher B., BPhil *Oxf.*, MA *Oxf.*,
  DPhil *Oxf.* Sr. Lectr.; Dir.*
Other Staff: 1 Hon. Res. Fellow

Business History, Centre for

Tel: (0113) 343 4474
Tolliday, Stephen W., BA *Camb.*, PhD *Camb.*
  Prof.; Dir.*

Business Law and Practice, Centre for

Tel: (0113) 343 5039
Keay, Andrew, LLB *Adel.*, MDiv *Conservative Baptist
  Theol.Sem.*, MA *Qld.*, PhD *Qld.* Prof.; Dir.*

Canadian Studies, Centre for

Tel: (0113) 343 4023
Huggan, Graham, BA *Camb.*, MA *Br.Col.*, PhD
  Br.Col. Prof.; Deputy Dir.
Killick, Rachel, BA *Oxf.*, PhD *Leeds* Prof.; Dir.*

Cardiovascular Research Unit at Leeds (CRISTAL)

Tel: (0113) 343 4174
  E-mail: c.s.peers@leeds.ac.uk
Peers, Christopher S., BSc *Lond.*, PhD *Lond.*
  Prof.; Dir.*

Chinese Business and Development, Centre for

Christiansen, Flemming, MA *Aarhus*, PhD *Ley.*
  Sr. Lectr.; Deputy Dir.
Cross, Adam R., BSc *CNAA*, MSc *UMIST* Dir.*

Cinema, Photography and Television, Louis Le Prince Interdisciplinary Centre for Research in

Tel: (0113) 343 5826
  E-mail: g.roberts@leeds.ac.uk
Morrison, David E., BA *Hull*, MA *Leic.*, PhD *Leic.*
  Prof.; Deputy Dir.
Roberts, Graham, BA *Kingston(UK)*, MA *Sus.*,
  DPhil *Sus.* Dir.*

Combustion and Energy Studies, Centre for

Tel: (0113) 343 2117
Gaskell, Philip H., BSc *Leeds*, PhD *Leeds* Prof.;
  Dir.*
Gray, Peter, FRS Visiting Prof.
Greenhalgh, Douglas Visiting Prof.

Computational Fluid Dynamics, Centre for

Tel: (0113) 343 2512
Pourkashanian, Mohamed, MSc *Leeds*, PhD *Leeds*
  Prof.; Dir.*

Computational Geography, Centre for

Tel: (0113) 343 3392
  E-mail: i.j.turton@leeds.ac.uk
Turton, Ian, BSc *Newcastle(UK)*, PhD *Edin.* Prof.;
  Dir.*

Computer Analysis of Language and Speech, Centre for

Tel: (0113) 343 5761
Atwell, Eric S., BA *Lanc.* Dir.*

Contemporary China, Institute for Research on

Christiansen, Flemming, MA *Aarhus*, PhD *Ley.*
  Sr. Lectr.; Dir.*

Credit Management Research Centre

Wilson, Nicholas, BA *Nott.*, PhD *Nott.* Prof.;
  Dir.*

Criminal Justice Studies, Centre for

Tel: (0113) 343 5033
Crawford, T. Adam, BA *Warw.*, MPhil *Camb.*,
  PhD *Leeds* Prof.; Dir.*

Cultural Analysis, Theory and History, AHRC Centre for

Tel: (0113) 343 1629
Pollock, Griselda F. S., BA Oxf., MA Lond., PhD Lond.   Prof.; Dir.*

Cultural Studies, Centre for

Tel: (0113) 343 5267
Engh, Barbara, MA Minn., PhD Minn.   Sr. Lectr.; Dir.*

Decision Research, Centre for

Tel: (0113) 343 2614
Maule, A. John, BA Durh., PhD Dund.   Prof.; Dir.*

Democratisation Studies, Centre for

Tel: (0113) 343 4481
Schwarzmantel, John J., BA Oxf., BPhil Oxf., PhD Leeds   Sr. Lectr.; Dir.*

Development Studies, Centre for

Tel: (0113) 343 4393 Fax: (0113) 343 6784
Pearson, Ruth, BA Camb., MA Sus., DPhil Sus.   Prof.; Dir.*
Other Staff: 1 Visiting Res. Fellow

Disability Studies, Centre for

Tel: (0113) 343 3927 Fax: (0113) 343 3944
Barnes, Colin, BA Leeds, PhD Leeds   Prof.; Dir.*

Earth and Biosphere Institute

Tel: (0113) 343 5213
    E-mail: m.d.krom@earth.leeds.ac.uk
Krom, Michael D., MA Camb., PhD Edin.   Prof.; Dir.*

Energy, Earth and Environment Institute

Tel: (0113) 343 5208
    E-mail: r.knipe@earth.leeds.ac.uk
Jimack, Peter K., BSc Brist., PhD Brist.   Prof.; Deputy Dir.
Knipe, Robert J., BSc Wales, MSc Lond., PhD Lond.   Dir.*

Ethnicity and Racism Studies, Centre for

Law, Ian G., BA Liv., PhD Liv.   Dir.*

European Political Communications, Centre for

Statham, Paul, BA Sus., PhD European Univ.Inst.   Dir.*

Family, Kinship and Childhood, Centre for Research on

Tel: (0113) 343 4874
Vacant Posts: Dir.*

Faraday Packaging Partnership

Tel: (0113) 343 6028
    E-mail: w.e.lewis@leeds.ac.uk
Lewis, Walter E., BSc Manc., PhD Manc.   Dir.*

Finance, Centre for Advanced Studies in

Keasey, Kevin, BA Durh., MA Newcastle(UK), PhD Newcastle(UK)   Prof.; Dir.*

French and Francophone Cultural Studies, Centre for

Tel: (0113) 343 3486
    E-mail: m.silverman@leeds.ac.uk
Silverman, Maxim, BA E.Anglia, PhD Kent   Prof.; Dir.*

Future Communications, Research Centre for

Morrison, David E., BA Hull, MA Leic., PhD Leic.   Prof.; Dir.*
Svennevig, Michael, BSc Newcastle(UK)   Dir., Res.
Other Staff: 7 Visiting Fellows; 1 Hon. Res. Fellow

Health Informatics, Yorkshire Centre for

Clamp, Susan E., PhD Leeds   Sr. Lectr.

Heritage Research, Centre for

Tel: (0113) 343 3274
    E-mail: g.j.n.gooday@leeds.ac.uk
Gooday, Graeme J. N., MA Camb., PhD Kent   Dir.*

Informatics Institute

Tel: (0113) 343 3312
    E-mail: m.h.birkin@leeds.ac.uk
Birkin, Mark, BA Leeds, PhD Leeds   Dir.*

Interdisciplinary Ethics, Applied

Tel: (0113) 343 3278
    E-mail: c.b.megone@leeds.ac.uk
Megone, Christopher B., BPhil Oxf., MA Oxf., DPhil Oxf.   Sr. Lectr., Philosophy; Dir.*
Other Staff: 3 Res. Fellows

Interdisciplinary Gender Studies, Centre for

Tel: (0113) 343 2532
    E-mail: r.e.cowgill@leeds.ac.uk
Cowgill, Rachel E., BMus Lond., MMus Lond., PhD Lond.   Sr. Lectr.; Deputy Dir.
Gough, Brendan, BSc Belf., PhD Belf.   Lectr.; Deputy Dir.
Harding, Nancy, BSc Wales, PhD Wales   Sr. Lectr.; Deputy Dir.
Holliday, Ruth, BA Keele, PhD Staffs.   Sr. Lectr.; Dir.*

International Business, Centre for

Tel: (0113) 343 4592 Fax: (0113) 343 4465
Buckley, Peter J., BA(Econ) York(UK), MA E.Anglia, PhD Lanc.   Prof.; Dir.*
Chapman, Malcolm, BLitt Oxf., MBA Brad., MA Oxf., DPhil Oxf.   Sr. Lectr.
Cross, Adam R., BSc CNAA, MSc UMIST   Sr. Lectr.
Other Staff: 2 Lectrs.; 1 Univ. Res. Fellow; 1 Res. Fellow
Research: accountancy and finance, including financial services; economics; human resource management and industrial relations; international business; marketing and strategic management

International Studies, Centre for

Tel: (0113) 343 4382 Fax: (0113) 343 4400
Bluth, Christoph, BA Trinity(Dub.), MPhil Trinity(Dub.), PhD Lond.   Prof.; Dir.*

Jean Monnet Centre of Excellence

Tel: (0113) 343 4512
    E-mail: l.j.clegg@lubs.leeds.ac.uk
Clegg, L. Jeremy, BA Nott., PhD Reading   Prof.; Co-Dir.
Lodge, Juliet, BA CNAA, MA Reading, MPhil Reading, PhD Hull, DLitt Reading   Prof.; Co-Dir.*

Jewish Studies, Centre for

Tel: (0113) 343 5197 Fax: (0113) 245 1977
Frojmovic, Eva, BA Freib., MA Munich, PhD Munich   Dir.*

Law and Policy in Europe, Centre for the Study of

Tel: (0113) 343 5065
Ackers, H. Louise, BSc Lond., MA Lond., LLM Brist., PhD Lond.   Prof.; Dir.*

Leeds Humanities Research Centre

Tel: (0113) 343 4741
    E-mail: d.lindley@leeds.ac.uk
Lindley, David, BPhil Oxf., MA Oxf.   Prof.; Dir.*

Leeds Nanomanufacuring Institute

Tel: (0113) 343 2801
    E-mail: r.a.williams@leeds.ac.uk
Evans, Stephen D., BSc Lond., MSc Lanc., PhD Lanc.   Co-Dir.*
Williams, Richard A., BSc(Eng) Lond., PhD Lond., FREng, FIMMM, FIChemE   Prof.; Co-Dir.*

Leeds Social Sciences Institute (LSSI)

Tel: (0113) 343 3204
    E-mail: n.frost@leeds.ac.uk
Frost, Nicholas P., BA Wales, MA Warw.   Deputy Dir.
Valentine, Gill, BA Durh., PhD Reading   Prof.; Dir.*
Other Staff: 4 Res. Fellows

Lifelong Learning Institute

Tel: (0113) 343 3242
    E-mail: m.zukas@leeds.ac.uk
Hodkinson, Philip M., BA Hull, MPhil Exe., PhD Exe.   Prof.
Zukas, Miriam, BSc Exe.   Prof.; Dir.*

Manufacturing and Information Systems Engineering, Keyworth Institute of

Tel: (0113) 343 2147
Childs, Thomas H. C., BA Camb., MA Camb., PhD Camb., FIMechE   Keyworth Prof.
Dalgarno, Kenneth W., BEng Strath., PhD Brad.   Dir.*
De Pennington, Alan, OBE, MSc Manc., PhD Manc.   Keyworth Prof.
Male, Stephen P., BSc H-W, MSc H-W, PhD H-W   Keyworth Prof.
Narayanan, R. S., BE Madr., MSc Lond., FREng, FIStructE   Visiting Prof.
Phillips, Mark A., BSc Lough., FIChemE   Visiting Prof.
Roberts, John R., BSc   Visiting Prof.
Taylor, Richard S., OBE, BSc Wolv.   Visiting Prof.
West, M. R., BSc Leeds, PhD Leeds   Shell Visiting Prof.
Williams, Richard A., BSc(Eng) Lond., PhD Lond., FREng, FIMMM, FIChemE   Keyworth Prof.
Xu, Jie, BEng Chongqing, MSc Chongqing, PhD Newcastle(UK)   Keyworth Prof.

Medical and Biological Engineering, Institute of

Tel: (0113) 343 2128
    E-mail: j.fisher@leeds.ac.uk
Fisher, John, BSc Birm., PhD Glas., DEng Leeds, FIMechE   Prof.; Dir.*

Medical Imaging Research, Centre for

Tel: (0113) 243 2799
Berry, Elizabeth, BSc Hull, PhD Lond.   Co-Dir.
Boyle, Roger D., BA York(UK), DPhil York(UK)   Prof.; Dir.*
Brodlie, Kenneth W., BSc Edin., MSc Dund., PhD Dund.   Prof.; Co-Dir.
Bulpitt, Andrew J., BEng Liv., PhD Liv.   Co-Dir.
Walker, Peter G., BSc(Eng) Lond., PhD Lond.   Co-Dir.
Other Staff: 3 Lectrs.; 5 Res. Fellows

Medieval Studies, Institute for

Tel: (0113) 343 3620
    E-mail: medieval-studies@leeds.ac.uk
Morris, Richard, OBE, BPhil MA, FSA   Head*
Swan, Mary, BA Keele, MA Leeds, PhD Leeds   Sr. Lectr.; Dir. of Studies
Other Staff: 1 Lectr.

Mediterranean Studies, Centre for

Tel: (0113) 343 3569 Fax: (0113) 343 3568
Agius, Dionisius, MA Tor., PhD Tor., FRAS   Prof.; Dir.*

Military History, Centre for

Tel: (0113) 343 3603
Childs, John C. R., BA Hull, PhD Lond.   Prof.; Dir.*
Gooch, John, BA Lond., PhD Lond.   Prof.; Deputy Dir.

Molecular Biophysics, Institute of (IMB)

Tel: (0113) 343 3170
    E-mail: s.e.radford@leeds.ac.uk

Radford, Sheena E., BSc *Birm.*, PhD *Camb.*   Co-Dir.*

Smith, D. Alastair, BSc *Manc.*, PhD *Manc.*   Co-Dir.*

Music, Interdisciplinary Centre for Scientific Research in (ICSRiM)

Tel: (0113) 343 2572
  E-mail: k.c.ng@leeds.ac.uk
Boyle, Roger D., BA *York(UK)*, DPhil *York(UK)*   Prof.; Deputy Dir.
Ng, Kia C., BSc *Leeds*, PhD *Leeds*   Dir.*
Windsor, W. Luke, BSc *City(UK)*, MA *City(UK)*, PhD *City(UK)*   Sr. Lectr.; Deputy Dir.

Non-Linear Studies, Centre for

Tel: (0113) 343 6463
Fordy, Alan P., MSc *Lond.*, PhD *Lond.*   Prof.; Dir.*
Gray, Peter, FRS   Visiting Prof.
Holden, Arun V., BA *Oxf.*, PhD *Alta.*   Prof.; Deputy Dir.
Other Staff: 3 Visiting Res. Fellows

Photobiology and Photodynamic Therapy, Centre for

Tel: (0113) 343 3166
Brown, Stanley B., BSc *Durh.*, PhD *Newcastle(UK)*   Prof.; Dir.*
Griffiths, John F., BSc *Birm.*, PhD *Birm.*   Prof., Chemistry
Roberts, David J. H., PhD *Leeds*   Sr. Lectr.
Other Staff: 1 Sr. Res. Fellow; 4 Res. Fellows; 10 Res. Assocs.; 1 Sr. Clin. Lectr.

Plant Sciences, Centre for

Davies, Brendan H., BSc *Lond.*, PhD *CNAA*   Dir.*

Polar Science, Centre for

Tel: (0113) 343 6761
  E-mail: j.e.francis@earth.leeds.ac.uk
Francis, Jane E., BSc *S'ton.*, PhD *S'ton.*   Prof.; Dir.*

Policy Studies in Education, Centre for

Tel: (0113) 343 4656
Sugden, David A., MSc *Calif.*, PhD *Calif.*   Prof.; Dir.*

Polymer Science and Technology, Interdisciplinary Research Centre in

Universities of Leeds, Bradford, Durham

Tel: (0113) 343 3810 Fax: (0113) 343 3846
Cameron, Neil R., BSc *Strath.*, PhD *Strath.*   Assoc. Dir.
Coates, P. D., BSc *Lond.*, MSc *Leeds*, PhD *Leeds*, FIMechE   Prof., Polymer Engineering (University of Bradford)
Cunningham, Anthony, BSc *Leeds*, PhD *Leeds*   Prof.; Technol. Strategy Dir.
Harlen, Oliver G., MA *Camb.*, PhD *Camb.*   Sr. Lectr.
Jones, Frank R.   Prof. (University of Sheffield)
Jones, Richard A. L., BSc *Camb.*, PhD *Camb.*   Prof. (University of Sheffield)
McLeish, Thomas C. B., MA *Camb.*, PhD *Camb.*   Prof., Polymer Physics; Dir.*
Ryan, Anthony J., BSc *Manc.*, PhD *Manc.*   Prof. (University of Sheffield)
Other Staff: 3 Lectrs.; 1 Sr. Res. Fellow

Psychological Therapies Research Centre

Tel: (0113) 343 1955 Fax: (0113) 343 1956
Barkham, Michael, BEd *Sus.*, MSc *Sur.*, MA *Camb.*, PhD *Brighton*   Prof., Clinical and Counselling Psychology; Dir.*
Hardy, Gillian, BA *Sheff.*, MSc *Sheff.*, MSc *Leeds*, PhD *Leeds*   Reader, Clinical and Occupational Psychology
Parry, Glenys, BA *Manc.*, PhD *Sheff.*, FBPsS   Visiting Prof.
Stiles, William B., BA *Oberlin*, MA *Calif.*, PhD *Calif.*   Visiting Hon. Prof.

Other Staff: 1 Visiting Sr. Res. Fellow; 1 Visiting Res. Fellow

Science and Mathematics Education, Centre for Studies in

Tel: (0113) 343 4540
Donnelly, James F., BSc *Lond.*, MEd *Leeds*, PhD *Leeds*   Dir.*

Self-Organising Molecular Systems, Centre for

Tel: (0113) 343 6453
Aggeli, Amalia   Deputy Dir.
Colyer, John, BSc *CNAA*, MPhil *Lond.*, PhD *S'ton.*   Sr. Lectr.; Deputy Dir.
Evans, Stephen D., BSc *Lond.*, MSc *Lanc.*, PhD *Lanc.*   Prof.; Deputy Dir.
Hamley, Ian W., BSc *Reading*, PhD *S'ton.*   Prof.; Dir.*
Kelsall, Robert W., BSc *Durh.*, PhD *Durh.*   Sr. Lectr.; Deputy Dir.
Other Staff: 3 Res. Fellows

Skin Research, Centre for

Tel: (0113) 343 5647 Fax: (0113) 343 5638

Vacant Posts: Dir*

Structural Molecular Biology, Astbury Centre for

Homans, Steven W., BA *Oxf.*, DPhil *Oxf.*   Prof.; Deputy Dir.
Stockley, Peter G., BSc *Lond.*, PhD *Camb.*   Prof.; Dir.*

Sustainability Research Institute

Dougill, Andrew, BSc *Sheff.*, PhD *Sheff.*   Lectr.; Head*
Other Staff: 5 Lectrs.; 3 Res. Fellows; 5 Teaching Fellows

Translation Studies, Centre for

Tel: (0113) 343 3285 Fax: (0113) 343 3287
Delin, Judy, BA *Nott.*, PhD *Edin.*   Prof.; Deputy Dir.
Hartley, Tony, BSc *Salf.*, MSc *Sus.*   Prof.; Dir.*

University of Leeds Consulting Ltd

Tel: (0113) 343 7478
  E-mail: k.n.mapp@adm.leeds.ac.uk
Mapp, Katherine N., BA *Wales*   Dir.*

CONTACT OFFICERS

Accommodation. Director of Residential and Commercial Services: Hopper, Dennis
Admissions (first degree). Head, Course Enquiries and Admissions: Maller, Simon
Admissions (higher degree). Senior Assistant Registrar (Admissions (higher degree)): Findlay, Jacqueline Y., BA *Warw.*, MA *Birm.*
Alumni. Director of Development: Calvert, Michelle
Archives. University Archivist: Giffen, Liza, MA *Edin.*, MA *Liv.*
Careers. Director of Careers Centre: Gilworth, Robert B., BA *Sheff.Hallam*, MBA *Sheff.*
Computing services. Director, Information Systems Services: Coghill, Colin M., BSc *Durh.*
Conferences/corporate hospitality. Assistant Director (Catering and Conferencing): Kenny, Beverley
Equal opportunities. Head of Equality Service: Pay, Levi, BComm *Edin.*
Estates and buildings/works and services. Director of Estates: Sladdin, Robert D., FRICS
Examinations. Examinations Officer: Winning, Carol
Finance. Finance and Commercial Director: Smith, Berenice, BA *Oxf.Brookes*
General enquiries. Secretary of the University: Gair, J. Roger, MA *Oxf.*
Industrial liaison. Head of Enterprise and Innovations Office: Holt, Gill, BSc *Cardiff*

International office. Head, International Office: Brown, Jacqueline A., LLB *Lond.*
Library (chief librarian). University Librarian and Keeper of the Brotherton Collection: Coutts, Margaret, MA *Glas.*, MA *Sheff.*
Marketing. Director of Marketing: Holmes, Martin, BA *Sheff.*
Personnel/human resources. Director of Human Resources: Knight, Matthew, MA *Camb.*, FCIPD
Public relations. Director of Media Relations: Bridge, Vanessa, BA *Hull*
Purchasing. Head, Procurement: Brannon, Tim, BA *Nott.Trent*
Quality assurance and accreditation. Head, Academic Quality and Standards Team: Barker-Read, Geoff, BSc *Aston*, MSc *Wales*, PhD *Wales*
Safety. Director, Well-being, Safety and Health: Tideswell, Gary, MSc *Manc.*, LLM *Leeds Met.*
Scholarships, awards, loans. Senior Assistant Registrar (Scholarships, awards, loans): Findlay, Jacqueline Y., BA *Warw.*, MA *Birm.*
Schools liaison. Head, Student Recruitment Team: Clapham, Helen
Security. Head, Security and Support Services: Exley, Steven, MSc *Leic.*
Sport and recreation. Director, Physical Education Service: Ross, Stewart M., BA *Reading*
Staff development and training. Director (Staff development and training): Hatton, Penelope M., MA *Leeds*
Student welfare/counselling. Head of Student Counselling Service: Humphrys, Nigel R., BA *CNAA*, MSEd *Maine(USA)*
Students from other countries. Head, International Student Office: Manns, Katy J., BA *Liv.*, MA *Wolv.*
Students with disabilities. Head of Equality Service: Pay, Levi, BComm *Edin.*
University press. Financial Services Manager: Smith, Helena, BSc *Manc.*

CAMPUS/COLLEGE HEADS

Askham Bryan College, Askham Bryan, York, England YO23 3FR. (Tel: (01904) 772211; Fax: (01904) 772288; E-mail: sf@askham-bryan.ac.uk) Principal: Rees, Prof. Gareth
Barnsley College, PO Box 266, Church Street, Barnsley, England S70 2YW. (Tel: (01226) 216216; Fax: (01226) 298514; E-mail: programme.enquiries@barnsley.ac.uk) Principal: West, Joe
College of the Resurrection, Mirfield, West Yorkshire, England WF14 0BW. (Tel: (01924) 494318; Fax: (01924) 490489; E-mail: community@mirfield.org.uk) Principal: Irvine, Fr. Christopher
Leeds College of Art and Design, The Jacob Kramer Building, Blenheim Walk, Leeds, England LS2 9AQ LS2 9AQ. (Tel: (0113) 202 8000; Fax: (0113) 202 8001; E-mail: info@leeds-art.ac.uk) Principal: Wigan, E.
Leeds College of Music, 3 Quarry Hill, Leeds, England LS2 7PD. (Tel: (0113) 222 3400; Fax: (0113) 243 8798; E-mail: enquiries@lcm.ac.uk) Principal: Hoult, D.
Northern School of Contemporary Dance, 98 Chapeltown Road, Leeds, England LS7 4BH. (Tel: (0113) 219 3000; Fax: (0113) 219 3030; E-mail: admissions@nscd.ac.uk) Principal: Hukam, G.
Trinity and All Saints College, Brownberrie Lane, Horsforth, Leeds, England LS18 5HD. (Tel: (0113) 283 7100; Fax: (0113) 283 7200; E-mail: admissions@tasc.ac.uk) Principal: Coughlan, M. L.

[*Information supplied by the institution as at 30 November 2007, and edited by the ACU*]

LEEDS METROPOLITAN UNIVERSITY

Founded 1970

Member of the Association of Commonwealth Universities

Postal Address: Civic Quarter, Leeds, England LS1 3HE
Telephone: (0113) 812 2600 **E-mail:** university-secretary@leedsmet.ac.uk
URL: http://www.leedsmet.ac.uk

VICE-CHANCELLOR*—Lee, Prof. Simon, BA Oxf., LLM Yale
PRO-VICE-CHANCELLOR—Anderson, Vivienne, BA Exe., MSc
PRO-VICE-CHANCELLOR—Brown, Prof. Sally
PRO-VICE-CHANCELLOR—Chapman, Deborah
PRO-VICE-CHANCELLOR—Peachey, Linda
PRO-VICE-CHANCELLOR—Pickford, Ruth, MSc
PRO-VICE-CHANCELLOR—Pioro, Teresa
PRO-VICE-CHANCELLOR—Rotheram, Bob
PRO-VICE-CHANCELLOR—Sinclair, Georgina
PRO-VICE-CHANCELLOR—Thomas-Osborne, Rhiannon
DIRECTOR OF FINANCE—Willis, Stephen

GENERAL INFORMATION

History. The university was originally established as Leeds Polytechnic in 1970 following the merge of four colleges (Leeds College of Technology founded as Leeds Mechanics Institute in 1824; Leeds College of Art founded in 1846; Leeds College of Commerce founded in 1845; and Yorkshire College of Education and Home Economics founded in 1874). In 1976 City of Leeds Training College was joined to the polytechnic. The polytechnic gained university status in 1992.

The university has campuses in the Civic Quarter of Leeds, in Headingley and in Harrogate.

Admission to first degree courses (see also United Kingdom Introduction). Normally through Universities and Colleges Admissions Service (UCAS). Two 6-unit qualifications at GCE/VCE Advanced Level, or one 12-unit VCE Double Award plus three subjects at General Certificate of Secondary Education (GCSE) grade C, or equivalent.

First Degrees (see also United Kingdom Directory to Subjects of Study) (* = with honours). BA*, BEng*, BSc*, LLB*.

Courses may be taken full-time (normally 3 years), part-time (normally 4–6 years) or on a sandwich basis (normally 3 years plus 1 year industrial placement).

Length of course. Full-time: LLB*: 3 years; BA*, BEng*, BSc*: 3–4 years. Part-time: LLB*: 4 years; BA*, BEng*, BSc*: 4–6 years.

Higher Degrees (see also United Kingdom Directory to Subjects of Study).

Master's. LLM, MA, MBA, MPhil, MSc.

Admission. Applicants for admission to postgraduate courses must either hold a relevant honours degree or must have other qualifications and relevant work experience.

Length of course. Full-time: LLM, MA, MBA, MSc: 1 year. Part-time: MBA: 2 years; MA, MSc: 2–3 years; LLM: 3 years. By distance learning: MSc: 2–3 years.

Doctoral. DEng, DLitt, DSc, DTech, EdD, LLD, PhD.

Length of course. Full-time: DEng, EdD, PhD: 5 years. Part-time: DEng, EdD, PhD: 6 years.

Libraries. Volumes: 365,000. Periodicals subscribed to: 11,900.

Academic Year (2007–2008). Two semesters: September–January; February–June. Summer session: June–October 2008.

FACULTIES/SCHOOLS

Arts and Society
Tel: (0113) 812 3035 Fax: (0113) 812 3444
E-mail: v.moore@leedsmet.ac.uk
Dean: Bailey, Prof. Christopher
Personal Assistant: Moore, Viki

Business and Law
Tel: (0113) 812 6127 Fax: (0113) 812 7508
E-mail: admissions.fblug@leedsmet.ac.uk
Dean: Whittington, Brian
Personal Assistant: (vacant)

Health
Tel: (0113) 812 1907 Fax: (0113) 812 1908
E-mail: m.huby@leedsmet.ac.uk
Dean: Hodgson, Richard
Personal Assistant: Huby, Michelle

Innovation North
Tel: (0113) 812 7421 Fax: (0113) 812 7599
E-mail: j.stewart@lmu.ac.uk
Dean: Orange, Cath
Personal Assistant: Stewart, Jillian

Leslie Silver International Faculty
Tel: (0113) 812 3202
E-mail: international@leedsmet.ac.uk
Dean: Jones, Elspeth, BA Reading, MA Lond.
Personal Assistant: Chard, Dianne

Sport and Education, Carnegie Faculty of
Tel: (0113) 812 6167 Fax: (0113) 812 7508
E-mail: l.hepworth@leedsmet.ac.uk
Dean: Kirk, Prof. David
Personal Assistant: Hepworth, Linda

ACADEMIC UNITS
Arranged by Faculties

Arts and Society
Tel: (0113) 812 3035 Fax: (0113) 812 3444
E-mail: t.gray@leedsmet.ac.uk
Baldwin, Alistair, BA   Sr. Lectr.
Bloor, Chris   Sr. Lectr.
Bozeat, Rupert, BA   Sr. Lectr.
Brien, Alyson, BA CNAA, MA Lond.   Sr. Lectr.
Brown, Ron, BA Portsmouth, MA Sus., DPhil Sus.
   Sr. Lectr.
Cain, Judith B.   Sr. Lectr.
Chinneck, James   Sr. Lectr.
Egginton, Clive, BA Sheff.Hallam   Sr. Lectr.
Evans, Adrian, BA   Sr. Lectr.
Felix, Robert, BArch PhD   Principal Lectr.
Gething, Fleure, BA   Sr. Lectr.
Gray, Len, BA Glas., MA Lond.   Sr. Lectr.
Harrison, Marion   Sr. Lectr.
Heycock, Mary, BSc Lond., MA Calg.   Head*
Heywood, Ian, BA Lond., DPhil York(UK)
   Principal Lectr.
Hoffman, A. Steven, BA   Sr. Lectr.

Horton, Derek, MA Leeds, PhD Leeds   Sr. Lectr.
Howes, Jaki, BA   Principal Lectr.
James, Alby   Sr. Lectr.
Julier, Guy, BA MA PhD   Sr. Lectr.
Kappa, Juha, MPhil   Head, Three-dimensional Des.
Knighton, Edwin J., BA   Principal Lectr.
Lowe, Robert J., MA PhD   Principal Lectr.
MacDermott, Julie, BA Leeds   Sr. Lectr.
Macdonald, Ian   Principal Lectr.
Mayfield, Wendy, BSc Lough., MPhil Nott.
   Principal Lectr.
Mayson, William L., BA   Sr. Lectr.
McCallion, Brian   Sr. Lectr.
Millard, Andrew V., BSc PhD   Sr. Lectr.
Millard, Lesley S.   Sr. Lectr.
Morant, Steven A., BA MA   Sr. Lectr.
Morgan, Alice   Principal Lectr.
Morgan, Jill, BA Wales   Head, Visual Studies
Noble, Elizabeth   Sr. Lectr.
Oswin, Pamela   Sr. Lectr.
Peacock, Briton R.   Sr. Lectr.
Rees, Anthony L., BA   Principal Lectr.; Head, Archit.
Royffe, Christopher D., MA   Assoc. Dean
Sandle, C. Douglas, BA Leeds   Reader; Principal Lectr., Visual Studies
Simpkins, Nigel B., BA Leeds   Sr. Lectr.
Simson, Alan J.   Sr. Lectr.
Stirling, Elizabeth, BA MA   Sr. Lectr.
Teasdale, Geoffrey G.   Principal Lectr.
Thomas, Vernon, BEd   Sr. Lectr.
Thwaites, Kevin, BA PhD   Sr. Lectr.
Treen, Colin, BA PhD   Reader
Truelove, Ian, BA MA   Sr. Lectr.
Wakefield, John R., BA MA   Sr. Lectr.
Wilson-Lambeth, Andrew, BA   Sr. Lectr.
York, Denise R., BA Natal, MA Natal   Sr. Lectr.
Research: architecture, landscape and design; built environment; contemporary art and graphic design; cultural studies; film, television and performing arts

Architecture, Landscape and Design
Tel: (0113) 812 4087
E-mail: aadenquiries@leedsmet.ac.uk
Knighton, Edwin J., BA   Principal Lectr.; Head, Landscape Archit.
Royffe, Christopher D., MA   Head*
Research: design practices and strategy; history and theology of design and architecture; landscape architecture; urban environmental design; user-centred design

Built Environment
Fax: (0113) 812 3190
E-mail: beenquiries@leedsmet.ac.uk
Bates, Mike, BSc MSc   Sr. Lectr.
Bell, Malcolm, MSc   Principal Lectr.
Bingel, Pawel R., BSc Leeds, MSc Leeds, PhD Leeds
   Sr. Lectr.
Cook, Andrew E., BSc   Sr. Lectr.
Douglas, Ian, BA MPhil MA   Sr. Lectr.

Edwards, Janice, BSc   Sr. Lectr.
Ellis, Robert C., BSc CNAA, MSc Lough., FRICS
　　Principal Lectr.
Emmitt, Steve, BA PhD   Sr. Lectr.
Garbett, Christopher, BSc MSc   Sr. Lectr.
Garrison, Philip   Sr. Lectr.
Gordon, Peter B., BSc   Sr. Lectr.; Head, Civil
　　Engin.
Gorse, Christopher, BSc PhD   Sr. Lectr.
Green, Martin, BTech Brad., BSc Leeds Met.   Sr.
　　Lectr.
Hargreaves, Robert C., BSc MSc   Head*
Harrington, John R., BSc   Sr. Lectr.
Hart, Trevor J., BA   Sr. Lectr.
Heathcote, John   Sr. Lectr.
Highfield, David, BSc MPhil   Sr. Lectr.
Hirst, Paul, BSc PhD   Sr. Lectr.
Jeffrey, John, BSc CNAA   Sr. Lectr.
Johnston, David, BEng Strath., MSc Strath., PhD
　　Leeds Met.   Sr. Lectr.
Keel, David A., BSc MSc   Head, Surveying
Kettle, Jane, BSc Lond., MA Leeds   Sr. Lectr.
May, Graham, BA MA   Principal Lectr.
Maye-Banbury, Angela, MSc   Sr. Lectr.
Pearce, David G., BSc LLB MSc   Sr. Lectr.
Pritchard, Martin, BEng Bolton Inst., PhD Manc.
　　Sr. Lectr.
Ray, Tony   Sr. Lectr.
Rodgers, David G., BSc LLB   Sr. Lectr.
Seavers, Jennifer   Sr. Lectr.
Smales, Lindsay M., BA PhD   Sr. Lectr.
Strange, Ian, BA MA PhD   Reader
Sturges, John L., MSc   Sr. Lectr.
Thomas, Kevin, BSc MPhil   Sr. Lectr.
Walley, Ed, BA Lond., MEd Leeds, MA York(UK),
　　DPhil York(UK)   Sr. Lectr.
West, Beverley, BSc Salf., PhD UMIST   Sr.
　　Lectr.
Whitehead, Paul G., BSc MSc   Sr. Lectr.
Whitney, David, BA MA MPhil   Head,
　　Planning and Housing
Research: buildings and sustainability;
　　construction and project management;
　　landscape architecture; materials and
　　structures

Contemporary Art and Graphic Design

Tel: (0113) 812 3108 Fax: (0113) 812 3094
　　E-mail: t.gray@leedsmet.ac.uk
Teasdale, Geoffrey G.   Principal Lectr.; Head*

Cultural Studies

Tel: (0113) 812 3474 Fax: (0113) 812 3112
　　E-mail: cspublicity@leedsmet.ac.uk
Abbinnett, Ross, BA Warw., MA Sus., PhD Warw.
　　Sr. Lectr.
Bekker, Pieter C., BA Witw., PhD Leeds
　　Principal Lectr.
Blackledge, Paul R., BA Newcastle(UK), MA
　　Northumbria, MSc York(UK), DPhil York(UK)
　　Sr. Lectr.
Bousfield, Christine B., BSc Brad., MA Brad.   Sr.
　　Lectr.
Caygill, Matthew J., BA Leeds, MA York(UK)   Sr.
　　Lectr.
Cowman, Krista, BA Keele, MA Lond., DPhil
　　York(UK)   Sr. Lectr.
Cox, Nicholas J., BA Hull, PhD Lanc.   Sr. Lectr.
Douglas, Janet, BA Leeds, MA Hull   Sr. Lectr.;
　　Co-ordinator, Undergrad. Studies
Eagleton, Mary, BA Leic., MA Lanc.   Reader,
　　English
Farrar, Max, BA Leeds, PhD Leeds Met.   Sr. Lectr.;
　　Fellow
Gunn, Simon, BA Lanc., MA Lanc., PhD Manc.
　　Reader; Co-ordinator, Postgrad. Studies
Herron, Tom, BA Newcastle(UK), MA Strath., PhD
　　Aberd.   Sr. Lectr.
Jackson, Louise, BA Oxf., MA Exe., PhD Sur.
　　Sr. Lectr.
Jagger, Gill, BA York(UK), MA York(UK), PhD
　　Hull   Sr. Lectr.
Johnston, Gordon, BSc Lond., MA Leeds, PhD
　　Leeds   Head*
Lynch, John J., BA Manc., MA Leeds, PhD Manc.
　　Sr. Lectr.
Merrin, William, BA Leic., MA Nott.   Sr. Lectr.
Morrison, Jago, BA Nott., PhD Nott.   Sr. Lectr.

Pettitt, Lance, BA Kent, MA N.U.I., PhD N.U.I.
　　Principal Lectr.
Rawnsley, Stuart J., BSc Brad., PhD Brad.
　　Principal Lectr.
Stinson, Marie, BA Leeds, PhD Leeds   Principal
　　Lectr.
Watkins, Susan M., BA Liv., PhD Sheff.   Sr.
　　Lectr.
Other Staff: 1 Lectr.; 1 Lectr.†
Research: cultural history and gender; media and
　　popular culture; post-colonial studies;
　　women's writing

Film, Television and Performing Arts

Tel: (0113) 812 8018
　　E-mail: j.balfour@leedsmet.ac.uk
Palmer, Susan P., BA Open(UK)   Principal
　　Lectr.; Head*
Other Staff: 48 Staff Members

Social Sciences

Tel: (0113) 812 5916 Fax: (0113) 812 6757
　　E-mail: sssenquiries@leedsmet.ac.uk
Batson, Brian, MSc   Principal Lectr.
Bray, Monica, BA MPhil   Sr. Lectr.
Brown, Fraser, BA Leeds   Sr. Lectr.
Charlton, Marion   Principal Lectr.
Cheesman, Brian E., BA Leeds, MA Leeds
　　Principal Lectr.
Chiosso, Rosamond, BA MA   Sr. Lectr.
Crookston, R. Ian, BA Hull, PhD Reading   Sr.
　　Lectr.
Fawbert, Jack, BA Anglia PU, MA Essex   Sr.
　　Lectr.
Foster, Sally A., BA Leeds, MA Leeds, MSc Manc.
　　Sr. Lectr.
Hall, Alison, BSc Lough.   Principal Lectr.
Keighley, David A., BSc Wales, MSc Lond., PhD
　　Leeds   Sr. Lectr.
Landells, Jennifer, MA   Sr. Lectr.
Lavery, Gerard, BA CNAA, MA Warw.   Sr.
　　Lectr.
McFarlane, Kay, MSc MSc MA   Sr. Lectr.
Mobbs, Kenneth L., BA Leeds, MA Lanc., MA
　　York(UK)   Sr. Lectr.
Moran, Gerald F., BA Liv., MSc Lond.   Sr. Lectr.
Moran, Terence P., BSc LLB LLM   Principal
　　Lectr.; Head*
Palmer, Susan P., BA Open(UK)   Principal Lectr.
Paul, Stephen, BA Brad., MSc CNAA   Principal
　　Lectr.
Pelham, Geoff, BSc PhD   Sr. Lectr.
Pender, John, BA Belf., MA N.U.I.   Sr. Lectr.
Peters, Michael, BA Leeds   Sr. Lectr.
Rennie, Stephen A., MA Leeds Met.   Sr. Lectr.
Ross, Alison J., MA Leeds, MPhil Sheff.   Head,
　　Speech and Lang. Scis.
Sayers, Stephen F., BA York(UK), DPhil York(UK)
　　Sr. Lectr.
Smalle, Yvette, MA   Sr. Lectr.
Spoor, Christopher, BSc Edin., MSc Sheff.
　　Principal Lectr.
Winter, Barry, BA Leeds, MA Leeds Met.   Sr.
　　Lectr.
Wobbaka, Patrick N., BA Liv.J.Moores, MBA Brad.
　　Sr. Lectr.

Business and Law

Tel: (0113) 812 7503 Fax: (0113) 812 7508
　　E-mail: lbs-enquiries@leedsmet.ac.uk

Accounting and Finance

Tel: (0113) 812 7544 Fax: (0113) 812 7507
　　E-mail: s.s.harrison@leedsmet.ac.uk
Altshul, Ronald, MBA Aston, FCA   Sr. Lectr.
Banfield, Rachel, FCA   Sr. Lectr.
Boateng, Agyenim, MBA H-W, MA Lond.Met.,
　　PhD Leeds   Sr. Lectr.
Booth, Richard, MA, FCA   Principal Lectr.
Bottone, John, BSc MSc PhD   Sr. Lectr.
Britton, Ann E., BA Hull   Head*
Burnup, John T., MSc Brad.   Principal Lectr.
Combs, Alan M., BA Leic., MSc CNAA   Sr.
　　Lectr.
Evans, Jonathan   Sr. Lectr.
Foster, John W.   Principal Lectr.
Hancock, Pandora, BSc Lond.   Principal Lectr.

Henderson, Roger, BA S'ton., MBA Brad.
　　Reader
Jones, Christopher, BSc Lond.   Principal Lectr.
Knight, David L., BA York(UK)   Sr. Lectr.
Lambell, Jill, BSc Lond.   Sr. Lectr.
Manners, John M., FCA   Sr. Lectr.
O'Sullivan, Colin, BA Lond.   Sr. Lectr.
Payn, Elaine, BA Leeds   Principal Lectr.
Shead, Janet, BA Hudd.   Sr. Lectr.
Silberstein, Martin B., BA Leeds, MPhil Leeds   Sr.
　　Lectr.
Smith, Richard J., MBA Brad.   Principal Lectr.
Waterston, Christopher, BA Manc.   Principal
　　Lectr.
Wilson, Derrick, BA   Sr. Lectr.
Wood, Peter M., BEd Leeds, FCA   Sr. Lectr.

Business Strategy

Tel: (0113) 812 7544 Fax: (0113) 812 7507
　　E-mail: a.poffley@leedsmet.ac.uk
Akamavi, Raphael, MBA PhD   Sr. Lectr.
Allis, Ann, BSc Birm., MBA Sheff.   Principal
　　Lectr.
Allison, David, MBA   Sr. Lectr.
Beedham, Ruth, BA Hull, MA Hull   Sr. Lectr.
Bellamy, Lawrence, BEng MSc MBA   Sr. Lectr.
Beresford, Shirley, BA   Sr. Lectr.
Berrow, Terry, BSc MSc   Sr. Lectr.
Carroll, Alan, BA Wat., MA Wat.   Sr. Lectr.
Chippindale, Peter M., BSc Brad.   Sr. Lectr.
Dennis, June, BSc Brad., MBA Hull   Teaching
　　Fellow; Course Leader, BA Business Studies;
　　Principal Lectr., Marketing
Fawkes, Johanna, BA Kent, MA Lanc.   Sr. Lectr.
Gibson-Sweet, Monica   Head*
Gregory, Anne   Res. Prof.
Holgate, Stuart, BA Brad.   Sr. Lectr.
Hughes, Graham, MA Lanc.   Principal Lectr.
Lane, David, BSc PhD   Sr. Lectr.
Lowensberg, Daniel, MA Lond.   Sr. Lectr.
Naylor, Carole, BA   Sr. Lectr.
Powell, Melanie, MA MPhil   Sr. Lectr.
Robertson, Martyn R., FRSA, FACCA, FIBA   Sr.
　　Lectr.
Sheard, Marie-Paul   Sr. Lectr.
Temperley, John, BSc MSc   Sr. Lectr.
Tench, Ralph, BA Sheff.   Principal Lectr.
Toth, John L., MBA Sheff.   Sr. Lectr.
Webster, Philip A., MA Leeds   Sr. Lectr.
Williams, Gareth, BA Warw., MBA Brad.
　　Principal Lectr.
Yeomans, Elizabeth, BA S'ton., MSc Stir.   Sr.
　　Lectr.

Economics and Human Resource Management

Tel: (0113) 812 7549 Fax: (0113) 812 3206
　　E-mail: c.drake@leedsmet.ac.uk
Allen, Martin, BA PhD   Sr. Lectr.
Barnett, Neil, BA Nott., MSc Aston   Sr. Lectr.
Barras, Judith, BA Birm., MA Lanc.   Principal
　　Lectr.
Beachill, Robert, BA Brad., MA Hull   Sr. Lectr.
Burrell, Catherine, BA MBA   Sr. Lectr.
Davies, David, BSc MSc MA   Sr. Lectr.
Divers, Peter, BA MPhil   Sr. Lectr.
Finnigan, Valerie, BA Leeds   Sr. Lectr.
Godfrey, Graham, BSc MSc   Sr. Lectr.
Gold, Jeffrey, BA   Principal Lectr.
Griffiths, Robert O., BA Essex, MSc Lond.   Sr.
　　Lectr.
Hamblett, John W., BA MA   Sr. Lectr.
Hamilton, Leslie, BA MSc   Sr. Lectr.
Holden, Richard J., BA Sheff., PhD Exe.
　　Principal Lectr.
Jones, Stephen W., MBA Brad.   Principal Lectr.
Judge, Eamonn J., BA Leeds, MA Sheff.   Prof.;
　　Reader, Res. Degrees
Landen, Mary, BA Dublin City, MBA Cran.   Sr.
　　Lectr.
Lawson, Jonathan S., BA Sheff.Hallam, MBA
　　Sheff.Hallam   Head*
Leach, Robert F., BA Oxf., BSc Lond.   Principal
　　Lectr.
McCauley, Patrick T., BA Nott., MSc City(UK)
　　Sr. Lectr.
Michaud, Ann, BA Leeds, MBA Brad.   Sr. Lectr.
Otter, Dorron, BA Oxf., MA Leeds   Sr. Lectr.
Petrick, Karl, BSc MA PhD   Sr. Lectr.

Sheehan, Brendan M., BA MPhil Sr. Lectr.
Shutt, John, BSc MPhil Prof., Regional Bus. Devel.
Sinclair, Lynda, BA Principal Lectr.
Spoor, Christopher, BSc Edin., MSc Sheff. Principal Lectr.
Stead, Richard, BSc Lond., MEd Leeds Sr. Lectr.
Stewart, Gerald, BA Brad. Principal Lectr.
Sutherland, John, BA Strath., MSc Manc. Reader
Thackray, John, BA Leeds Principal Lectr.
Thompson, Frank, BA Leeds, MA Leeds Sr. Lectr.
Thursfield, Denise, BA MA PhD Sr. Lectr.
Watson, Colin, BA Leeds, BA Manc. Sr. Lectr.
Watson, Stuart, BA Sr. Lectr.
Wetherly, Paul A., BA Leeds, MA Leeds, PhD Tees. Principal Lectr.
Whittaker, Lesley, BA Brad., MBA Brad. Principal Lectr.

Law

Tel: (0113) 812 7549 Fax: (0113) 812 3206
E-mail: s.bridgwood@leedsmet.ac.uk
Amos, David, BSc Brist. Sr. Lectr.
Askew, Melissa, LLB Newcastle(UK) Sr. Lectr.
Balchin, Daphne, LLB Birm. Sr. Lectr.
Beech, Nicholas, BA MBA Sr. Lectr.
Birtwistle, Timothy, BA Manc. Jean Monnet Prof., Law and Policy of Higher Education
Bradby, Philip Sr. Lectr.
Cousins, Lynn, LLB Lond. Sr. Lectr.
Creasey, Julian, BA Oxf. Principal Lectr.
Gale, Christopher J., LLB Wales Sr. Lectr.
Hawker, John R., BA Oxf. Principal Lectr.
James, Annabelle, LLB Leeds, MA Leeds Sr. Lectr.
Johnson, Sandra, LLB Leeds, MA Sr. Lectr.
Joyce, Pauline, BA Leeds Principal Lectr.
Letza, Steve, MA MSc Prof., Corporate Governance
Lister, Robin, BA Oxf. Sr. Lectr.
Manzoor, Tasnim, LLB Leeds Sr. Lectr.
Martin, Derek H., LLB Belf. Principal Lectr.
Myers, Maxine, LLB Manc. Sr. Lectr.
Price, Robert, LLB Exe., LLM Exe. Sr. Lectr.
Shaw, Darren, LLB Leeds Sr. Lectr.
Silberstein, Sandra J., LLB Leeds Sr. Lectr.
Tighe, Maria, LLB Head*
Turner, John, BA Oxf. Sr. Lectr.
Walker, Bridget, BA Durh. Principal Lectr.
Wolstencroft, Patricia A., LLB Leeds Sr. Lectr.

Policy Research Institute

Fax: (0113) 812 3224
E-mail: a.davis@leedsmet.ac.uk
Burden, Thomas A., BSc MA Principal Lectr.
Hawtin, Murray, MA York(UK) Sr. Lectr.
Sanderson, Ian, BA Newcastle(UK), PhD Prof.; Head of Unit

Health

Tel: (0113) 283 1907 Fax: (0113) 283 1908
E-mail: h.davies@leedsmet.ac.uk

Allied Health Professions

Tel: (0113) 812 3883 Fax: (0113) 812 3416
E-mail: ahpenquiries@leedsmet.ac.uk
Ellis, Ieuan Assoc. Dean; Head*
Research: childhood obesity; nutrition and dietetics; physiotherapy; speech therapy; the spine

Health and Community Care

Tel: (0113) 812 1914 Fax: (0113) 812 1916
E-mail: hccenquiries@leedsmet.ac.uk
Cash, Keith, BA Open(UK), MSc Open(UK), PhD Manc. Prof.
Cattan, Mima, BSc Helsinki, MSc Leeds Met., PhD Newcastle(UK) Sr. Lectr.
Clegg, Philip L., BA Lond., MSc Sur. Sr. Lectr.
Dimmock, Gary W., BA Liv., MA Sheff. Head, Soc. Work
Dixey, Rachael A., BA PhD Head, Health Educn.
Fatchett, Anita B., BA Leeds, MA Leeds Sr. Lectr.
Green, Jacqueline, MB BS Lond., MSc Leeds Met. Prof., Health and Community Care
Green, Mary Sr. Lectr.

Harrison, Fiona Sr. Lectr.
Hinchliffe, Elizabeth, BA Essex Sr. Lectr.
Karban, Kathryn Sr. Lectr.
Kershaw, Sheila Sr. Lectr.
Llewellyn, M. Ann, BA Leeds, PhD Leeds Sr. Lectr.
Lowry, Michael, BEd CNAA, MEd Curtin Sr. Lectr.
Merrick, Susan, BSc Leeds Met., MA Leeds, PhD Leeds Sr. Lectr.
Miller, Ian Sr. Lectr.
Norton, Lavinia, BSc Leeds, MA Leeds, PhD Leeds Principal Lectr.
Nutman, Peter N., BA MA PhD Head*
Patel, Sunita, BSc Leeds Met., MSc Hudd. Sr. Lectr.
Piercy, Jenny, BA Open(UK), MA Leeds Head, Nursing
Shergill, Markan, MA Brad. Sr. Lectr.
Sherwin, Susan A., BA Leeds Sr. Lectr.
Sidhu, Harcharan Sr. Lectr.
Slavin, S. Fiona, BSc Hudd. Sr. Lectr.
Thomas, Terence V., BA Hull, MSc Hudd. Reader
Trenchard, Stephen, BA Manc. Sr. Lectr.
Walker, Bryony Sr. Lectr.
Walker, Diane F., BA Manc., MA Manc. Sr. Lectr.
White, Alan K., BSc Sur., MSc Leeds Met., PhD Manc. Sr. Lectr.
Research: mens' health; prescribing and administering medication; road safety

Health and Human Sciences

Tel: (0113) 812 2600 Fax: (0113) 812 3124
E-mail: hsenquiries@leedsmet.ac.uk
Airey, Bill, BA CNAA, PhD CNAA Sr. Lectr.
Asghar, Mandy, MSc Sr. Lectr.
Aslett-Bentley, Avril D., BSc Sheff., MSc Lond. Sr. Lectr.
Atkinson, Stephen Sr. Lectr.
Auty, P. Linda, BSc Leeds, MPhil Leeds Sr. Lectr.
Caswell, Alison M., BSc PhD Sr. Lectr.
Clough, Angela, MSc Leeds Met., MPhil Leeds Met. Sr. Lectr.
Coates, Catherine, BSc Sr. Lectr.
Conroy, Carole Sr. Lectr.
Cooper, Keith J., BSc Hull, MSc Nott., PhD Nott. Principal Lectr.
Copeman, June P., BSc Lond., MSc Lond., MEd Leeds Met. Sr. Lectr.
Cram, Geoff, BSc Lond., PhD Manc., FRSChem Sr. Lectr.
Daltrey, Diana C., BSc Lond., PhD Manc., FRS Head*
Davies, Derek, BSc MSc PhD Sr. Lectr.
Dyson, Judith, BA Wales, MEd Sheff. Sr. Lectr.
Eastburn, Sara, BSc Sheff., MSc Sheff.Hallam Sr. Lectr.
Edmondson, Alan S., BSc PhD Principal Lectr.
Fitzgerald, Pauline Sr. Lectr.
Freeman, Alan, BSc Lond., MPhil Hudd., MSc Manc. Sr. Lectr.
Garwood, Jeanette, BSc MSc MSc DPhil Sr. Lectr.
Hartford, Trudy, BSc PhD Sr. Lectr.
Hirst, Sarah, BSc Sr. Lectr.
Johnson, Mark I., BSc Leeds, PhD Newcastle(UK) Principal Lectr.
Jones, Steve, BA Liv., PhD Manc. Sr. Lectr.
Kelly, Mike, BSc CNAA, MSc Nott. Reader
Khan, Mumtaz A. Sr. Lectr.
Lewis, Mark, BE BSc Sr. Lectr.
Mackay, Elizabeth, BA CNAA, MSc Nott. Sr. Lectr.
Martin, Steve Sr. Lectr.
Mera, Steven L., BA PhD Sr. Lectr.
Mitchell, Bets, BA Uppsala Sr. Lectr.
Mwanje, Zach Sr. Lectr.
Neal, Debbie, BSc Leeds, MSc Sheff.Hallam Sr. Lectr.
Phillips, Gillian, MSc MCSP Sr. Lectr.
Redshaw, Jane Sr. Lectr.
Rickett, Bridgette Sr. Lectr.
Sahota, Pinky Sr. Lectr.
Sanderson, Catherine, BSc Newcastle(UK), PhD Open(UK) Sr. Lectr.
Sharples, Paul, MSc Leeds Met. Sr. Lectr.

Smalley, Neil Sr. Lectr.
Smith, Susan, MA Warw. Sr. Lectr.
South, Tim, BA Sr. Lectr.
Standing, Marilyn, BTech Sr. Lectr.
Tabasam, Ghazala, BSc PhD Sr. Lectr.
Taylor, Jill, BSc Lond., PhD Leeds Sr. Lectr.
Teal, Brian, BSc Sr. Lectr.
Unsworth, Bridget A., BSc Bath, PhD Brad. Principal Lectr.
Wild, Dianne, BSc Leeds Met. Sr. Lectr.
Wilkinson, Jacqueline, BSc Leeds Sr. Lectr.
Young, Michael, BA Sr. Lectr.
Research: childhood and adult obesity; eating disorders; microbiology; noise and vibration; pain management

Information and Technology

Tel: (0113) 812 3090 Fax: (0113) 812 3110
E-mail: j.stewart@leedsmet.ac.uk

Computing

Tel: (0113) 812 3756 Fax: (0113) 812 3182
E-mail: c.l.smith@leedsmet.ac.uk
Allen, Patricia, BSc Edin., MSc Brad., PhD Brad. Sr. Lectr.
Balls, Timothy, MSc Principal Lectr.
Beard, David J., BSc Aston, MSc Aston Sr. Lectr.
Bowring, Nicholas, MSc Sr. Lectr.
Calvert, Maurice, BSc Leeds, PhD Leeds Sr. Lectr.
Cook, Leonard, MEd Sr. Lectr.
Coxhead, John F., MPhil CNAA Principal Lectr.
Cullen, Eddie, MSc Sr. Lectr.
Dacre, Anthony N., BA Oxf., MSc Lond., MA Oxf. Principal Lectr.
De Boni, Marco, MSc Sr. Lectr.
Dixon, Mark, PhD Sr. Lectr.
Doney, Paul, MA Sr. Lectr.
Dowd, Norman, MSc Sr. Lectr.
Duddell, David, BA Oxf., PhD Brist. Principal Lectr.
Earle, Lesley, MSc Sr. Lectr.
Ellyard, John, BSc Lough. Sr. Lectr.
Fabri, Marc Sr. Lectr.
Fenton, John, MSc Sr. Lectr.
Finlay, Janet, BA York(UK), MSc York(UK), DPhil York(UK) Prof., Interactive Systems
Godfrey, Rob, BSc Sr. Lectr.
Gould, Howard, MSc Sr. Lectr.
Gray, John, BSc Principal Lectr.
Grierson, Alec, BSc Sr. Lectr.
Guest, Elizabeth, BSc Sr. Lectr.
Harland, David M., BA Oxf., BA Open(UK), MSc York(UK) Sr. Lectr.
Harris, Terence, MSc Sr. Lectr.
Harvey, John, BSc Liv. Principal Lectr.
Ingham, Patrick, BA Sus., MSc Salf. Sr. Lectr.
Jennings, Neil, BA Open(UK) Principal Lectr.
Jones, Richard J., BSc Wales Principal Lectr.
Kemp, Douglas J., BA Leeds, MSc Leeds Principal Lectr.
Kennedy, Nairn F., BSc Glas., PhD Glas. Sr. Lectr.
Martin, Ian, BSc CNAA Sr. Lectr.
McGrath, Paul, MSc Head*
Mullier, Duncan, BSc Sr. Lectr.
Old, Julian, BSc Sr. Lectr.
Palmer-Brown, Dominic, BSc MSc PhD Prof., Neurocomputing
Pattinson, Colin, BSc Leeds, PhD Leeds Principal Lectr.
Pickford, Ruth, MSc Sr. Lectr.
Ponciano, Joao, MEng Sr. Lectr.
Ramachandran, Muthu, BSc Madur., MSc Madur., PhD Lanc., MTech Principal Lectr.
Rayner, Bernard, BA Oxf., BA Open(UK), MA Sr. Lectr.
Richards, Louise, BSc Sr. Lectr.
Scorer, Paul, BSc Nott. Sr. Lectr.
Shaghouei, Ebbie, PhD Sr. Lectr.
Sharpe, Simon, MSc Sr. Lectr.
Soosay-Manickam, Meg, BSc Sr. Lectr.
Taylor, Steve, MSc Principal Lectr.
Willoughby, H. Lynette, BSc Sur., MSc Brad. Sr. Lectr.
Research: computational intelligence; computer communications; interactive systems and

learning environments; software practice and methods

Information Management

Tel: (0113) 812 7553 Fax: (0113) 812 3142
E-mail: p.coleman@leedsmet.ac.uk
Ahmed, Fiaz, MSc   Sr. Lectr.
Bailey, Trevor, MA   Sr. Lectr.
Bilby, Linda, BA   Principal Lectr.
Black, Alistair, BA Lond., MA Lond., PhD CNAA   Prof.
Blake, John D., BSc Leic., MSc Newcastle(UK)   Head*
Broughton, Linda M., BSc Leeds   Deputy Head
Brunt, Rodney M., BA Belf.   Sr. Lectr.
Bryant, Anthony, BA Camb., MA Camb., MSc Brad., PhD Lond.   Prof.
Burke, Alan, BSc Sheff., MSc Lanc.   Sr. Lectr.
Cockerill, Steve, MSc   Sr. Lectr.
Cookson, Anne I., BA Nott.   Sr. Lectr.
Crann, Melvyn P., BA Open(UK)   Sr. Lectr.
Douglas, John, BSc   Sr. Lectr.
Durham, Martin, MSc   Principal Lectr.
Gibbs, Sally E., BA Wales, MA CNAA   Principal Lectr.
Gosnay, Cynthia, MSc   Sr. Lectr.
Griffin, David, MSc   Sr. Lectr.
Grogan, John, BSc   Sr. Lectr.
Hall, John, BA Belf.   Sr. Lectr.
Halpin, Edward, MA   Reader
Hamill, John, MA   Sr. Lectr.
Heyworth, H. Lee, BSc Leeds   Principal Lectr.
Hirst, Stuart L., MSc Birm.   Principal Lectr.
Howard, Alan W., BSc Nott., MSc Salf.   Sr. Lectr.
Howell, Barbara, PhD   Sr. Lectr.
Lazarevski, Sanela, BSc Lund, MSc Leeds Met.   Sr. Lectr.
Livesey, J. Brian, BSc Leeds, PhD Leeds   Principal Lectr.
Meikle, Fiona, MSc   Sr. Lectr.
Moon, Joanna, MA Edin., MBA Edin.   Principal Lectr.
Muddiman, David J., BA Leic., MSc Open(UK)   Principal Lectr.
Nicholls, Paul   Sr. Lectr.
Nottingham, Annet, MSc   Sr. Lectr.
O'Donovan, Brian   Sr. Lectr.
Orange, Graham, MA   Principal Lectr.
Procter, Dave, MSc   Sr. Lectr.
Rankin, Carolynn, MA   Sr. Lectr.
Robson, Peter, BA   Sr. Lectr.
Sarwar, Dilshad, MA   Sr. Lectr.
Savage, John P., MSc Reading   Sr. Lectr.
Smith, Paul, BSc   Sr. Lectr.
Steadman, Chris, MSc   Sr. Lectr.
Strickler, Linda, MSc   Sr. Lectr.
Towers, Keith, BSc Wales, MSc Liv.   Principal Lectr.
Trayhurn, Deborah, BEd Camb.   Principal Lectr.
Uttley, Patricia M., BEd Lond., MEd Leeds   Principal Lectr., Change Management
Vilinskis, Karen   Sr. Lectr.
Walker, Steve, MSc   Sr. Lectr.
Weatherlake, Cecil, MSc   Sr. Lectr.
Williams, Leonard T., BSc Aston, MBA Brad.   Principal Lectr.
Willis, Diane, MPhil DPhil   Sr. Lectr.
Young, Jane, MSc   Sr. Lectr.
Research: business information management; information systems; knowledge management; public library studies; sociology and information

Technology

Tel: (0113) 812 6747 Fax: (0113) 812 3110
E-mail: p.wainwright@leedsmet.ac.uk
Briggs, Martin, MA   Sr. Lectr.
Carter, Peter S., BSc Manc., PhD Manc.   Sr. Lectr.
Challis, Ben, MSc   Sr. Lectr.
Cheng, Kai, PhD   Prof.
Conway, Paul A., BEng PhD   Principal Lectr.
Cope, Nicholas, BSc Salf., PhD S'ton   Principal Lectr.
Cowey, Jeffrey E., MSc Manc., PhD Essex, FIEE   Principal Lectr.

Crispin, Alan J., BSc E.Anglia, PhD E.Anglia   Principal Lectr.
Darwish, Mostafa, BSc Cairo, PhD Brun.   Sr. Lectr.
Edmonds, John, MA   Sr. Lectr.
Folley, Duncan A., BSc Salf., MSc Salf.   Sr. Lectr.
Gledhill, David, BSc   Sr. Lectr.
Larkman, Brian, BA   Sr. Lectr.
Meek, Trevor, MSc   Sr. Lectr.
Mercer, Francis, BSc CNAA, MSc Nott.   Sr. Lectr.
O'Toole, Bernard M., MSc   Principal Lectr.
Parker, Stephen, BSc Bath, MSc CNAA   Sr. Lectr.
Ratcliff, Paul, MSc CNAA   Principal Lectr.
Reed, Edward W., BA Camb., MA Camb., PhD   Sr. Lectr.
Rush, Gary E., PhD Leeds   Sr. Lectr.
Singh, Balbir, BEng   Sr. Lectr.
Strudwick, Salam, BA   Principal Lectr.
Sutton, Terence W., BA Hull, BSc Lond., MSc Lond., MSc Hull, PhD Hull   Sr. Lectr.
Tasker, Joy, BA   Sr. Lectr.
Taylor, Peter L., BTech Brad.   Sr. Lectr.
Thomson, Simon, BA   Sr. Lectr.
Ward, Robert L., BSc MPhil PhD   Principal Lectr.
Waterworth, Geoffrey, BEng   Sr. Lectr.
Webb, David C., BSc CNAA, DPhil York(UK), FRAS, FRSA   Prof., Engineering Modelling and Simulation
Whitbread, Martin J., MPhil Open(UK)   Principal Lectr.
Wilkinson, Stephen P., BSc CNAA, PhD   Principal Lectr.
Research: object orientated 3-D games; signal processing for music and media applications (multi-media and animation, music technology, the theremin); synthetic camera image generation; 3-D character animation systems; 360 degree video viewing

Leslie Silver International Faculty

Tel: (0113) 812 7440 Fax: (0113) 812 5966
E-mail: cls@leedsmet.ac.uk

Applied Global Ethics

E-mail: d.otter@leedsmet.ac.uk
Research: business ethics; corporate social responsibility; engineering; ethical theory; ethics and culture

Languages

Tel: (0113) 812 7440 Fax: (0113) 812 5966
E-mail: sol@leedsmet.ac.uk
Barnes, Jayne, BA   Sr. Lectr.
Buchanan, Heather, BA S'ton   Sr. Lectr.
Foster, Bernard, BA Hull, LèsL Lille, MA CNAA, PhD Bath   Principal Lectr.
Jones, Elspeth, BA Reading, MA Lond.   International Dean
Keinhorst, Wolfgang   Sr. Lectr.
Killick, David, BEd Leeds, MEd Leeds   Principal Lectr.
Leconte, Marie-Odile, PhD Amiens   Head*
Leggott, Dawn, BA MEd   Sr. Lectr.
Mallinson, J. Stephen, BA Lond.   Principal Lectr.
Masuhara, Hitomi, BA Aichi, MA Reading, PhD Luton   Sr. Lectr.
Moulds, Gisela   Sr. Lectr.
Roy, James, MA Reading   Principal Lectr.
Shaw, Nigel, MA Camb.   Sr. Lectr.
Timmis, Ivor, MA Newcastle(UK)   Sr. Lectr.
Turnbull, Sarah, MA Lond.   Sr. Lectr.
Von Knorring, Catherine, MA W.Ont., MA Edin.   Sr. Lectr.
Webb, Graham, BA Portsmouth   Principal Lectr.
Yarborough, Claire, MA Leeds   Sr. Lectr.
Zoellner, Ricarda, BA   Principal Lectr.
Research: cross-cultural communications and capability materials development; materials development

Tourism, Hospitality and Events

Tel: (0113) 812 5937 Fax: (0113) 812 3111
E-mail: v.harris@leedsmet.ac.uk
Blackwell, Ruth, BA E.Anglia, MA Warw.   Sr. Lectr.
Bowdin, Glenn A. J., BA MPhil   Principal Lectr.
Brearley, Helen, BA   Sr. Lectr.
Church, Ivor, BSc CNAA, MPhil Leeds Met.   Sr. Lectr.
Clarkson, L. Barry, BSc CNAA, MSc Brad.   Sr. Lectr.
Clifton, Warwick, BA   Principal Lectr.; Head, Hospitality and Retailing
Coll, Patricia   Sr. Lectr.
Cullen, Peter, BSc MA   Sr. Lectr.
Curland, Susan, MBA Leeds   Sr. Lectr.
Eaglen, Andrew, BSc MSc   Sr. Lectr.
Fitzgerald-Moore, Deborah, BSc CNAA, MSc   Sr. Lectr.
Font, Xavier, MSc   Sr. Lectr.
Gaunt, Allan, BSc CNAA, BEd CNAA   Sr. Lectr.
Graham, David, BSc CNAA   Sr. Lectr.
Harris, Vicky, BA Open(UK), MA   Head*
Hayward, Robert, BA MSc   Sr. Lectr.
Headley, Greig, BSc   Sr. Lectr.
Hind, David, BA MBA   Principal Lectr.
Jameson, Stephanie, BA CNAA, MPhil   Sr. Lectr.
Johnson, Janice, BA MA   Sr. Lectr.
Jones, Steven, MSc   Sr. Lectr.
Jordan, N., MA MBA   Sr. Lectr.
Kenyon, Alex, MA   Sr. Lectr.
Lincoln, Guy, BSc CNAA   Sr. Lectr.
Machin, Alan   Sr. Lectr.
Masterman, Guy, MBA   Sr. Lectr.
McKellen, Sue, BSc MSc   Principal Lectr.
Morpeth, Nigel, BA MSc   Sr. Lectr.
Nightingale, John, BA   Sr. Lectr.
Parsons, Anthony, BSc Nott., PhD Nott.   Principal Lectr.
Pearson, Catherine, BEd CNAA, MSc   Principal Lectr.
Piso, Anne-Marie, MA   Sr. Lectr.
Raj, Razaq, BA MSc   Sr. Lectr.
Richardson, Adrian P., BSc DPhil   Principal Lectr.
Rodger, Carole, BA CNAA   Sr. Lectr.
Shacklock, Raisa, BEd MSc   Principal Lectr.
Thomas, Rhodri, BA MA PhD   Principal Lectr.
Tum, Julia, MBA   Sr. Lectr.
Walsh, Stella, BEd Leeds, MEd Leeds   Sr. Lectr.
Ward, David, MBA Brad., MPhil Brad., MSc Leic.   Principal Lectr.
Whitworth, Graham, MSc   Sr. Lectr.
Williamson, Philip, BA   Sr. Lectr.
Wood, Emma, MSc   Sr. Lectr.
Xie, Guozhong, BSc Shanghai, MSc Leeds, PhD Leeds   Sr. Lectr.
Research: consumer behaviour; events management; food science; sustainable tourism

Sport and Education, Carnegie Faculty of

Childhood and Community

Tel: (0113) 812 3169 Fax: (0113) 812 7508
E-mail: j.riley@leedsmet.ac.uk
Cameron, Joy   Head, Initial Teacher Training
Doherty, Jonathan, BA Wales, MEd Manc.Met.   Sr. Lectr.; Head, Early Childhood Educn.
Gilchrist, Denise, BEd CNAA   Principal Lectr.; Head*
Hawkin, Wendy, BEd Reading, MA Lond.   Principal Lectr.
Jones, Phil   Sr. Lectr.
Lindsay, Vivienne, BEd Leeds, MEd Edin.   Sr. Lectr.
Little, David, BA Open(UK), MSc Sheff.Hallam   Sr. Lectr.
McManus, Michael, BA Open(UK), MEd Leeds   Principal Lectr.
Moss, Dorothy   Sr. Lectr.
Olusoga, Vinka   Sr. Lectr.
Richter, Ingrid   Sr. Lectr.
Tomlinson, Pat, MSc Leeds Met.   Principal Lectr.
Walker, Gary   Sr. Lectr.
Waterton, Angela   Sr. Lectr.

Welch, Susan E., BSc Birm., BSc CNAA, MSc CNAA   Principal Lectr.

Education and Professional Development

Tel: (0113) 812 7408 Fax: (0113) 812 3138
E-mail: epdenquiries@leedsmet.ac.uk
Ableson, Marilyn   Assoc. Sr. Lectr.
Adam, Jill, BEd   Principal Lectr.
Allan, Christine, BEd CNAA, MA Tees.
   Principal Lectr.
Anderson, Vivienne, BA Exe., MSc   Principal Lectr.
Barber, Jane, BEd Camb., MEd Leeds Met.   Sr. Lectr.
Barker, David   Sr. Lectr.
Barrett, Francis, BA Open(UK), MA Lond.   Sr. Lectr.
Beasley, Elizabeth, BEd CNAA, MEd   Principal Lectr.
Betts, Janet, BA Manc., BA Liv.   Sr. Lectr.
Botsaris, Nicholas, BEd CNAA   Principal Lectr.
Bowles, Andrew, BEd CNAA   Sr. Lectr.
Cameron, Joy   Head, Initial Teacher Training
Christian, Margaret, BA Lond., MEd Liv.
   Principal Lectr.
Cooper, Brigitte, PhD   Sr. Lectr.
Dean, Jacqueline, BA Natal, MEd Exe.   Sr. Lectr.
D'Sena, Peter, BA S'ton., MPhil Open(UK)
   Principal Lectr., History and Education
Figgess, Hugh   Sr. Lectr.
Flecknoe, Mervyn, BSc Lond., MA York(UK)   Sr. Lectr.
Hamilton, Philippa, BEd CNAA   Sr. Lectr.
Holmes, Gary, BA Lond., MSc Oxf.   Prof.; Head*
Hurst, Paul   Sr. Lectr.
Little, David, BA Open(UK), MSc Sheff.Hallam   Sr. Lectr.
Marshall, Paul, BEd E.Anglia, MSc Leeds   Sr. Lectr.
Martin, Paul, BA Oxf., MA Leeds   Sr. Lectr.
Metcalfe, Christopher, BEd York(UK), MA York(UK), MPhil York(UK)   Principal Lectr.
Poole, Iain, BA Lond., MEd Leeds, MA E.Anglia   Principal Lectr.
Tan, Jon, PhD   Sr. Lectr.
Tanner, Julia, BSc Salf., MEd Keele   Principal Lectr.
Tarbitt, Valerie, BPhil Newcastle(UK), MA   Sr. Lectr.
Valli, Yasmin, MA Lanc.   Sr. Lectr.
Warren, Susan, BA Open(UK), MEd CNAA, PhD Leeds Met.   Principal Lectr.
White, David   Sr. Lectr.
Other Staff: 2 Lectrs.; 1 Assoc. Res. Asst.
Research: curriculum; educational change and leadership; learning and assessment in primary education; teaching and learning in further and higher education

Leisure and Sport Management

Fax: (0113) 812 7575
E-mail: m.rhyne@leedsmet.ac.uk
Abrams, Jeffrey, BSEd N.Y.State, MA Kent   Principal Lectr.
Bramham, Peter, BSc Lond., MA Essex, MA CNAA, PhD Leeds   Reader
Green, Angela, BA Northumbria, MA Leeds Met.   Sr. Lectr.
Hartley, Hazel, BEd Leeds, MEd Leeds, PhD Lanc.   Principal Lectr.
Hylton, Kevin, BA Leeds, MA Leeds Met., PhD Leeds Met.   Sr. Lectr.
Jackson, David, BSc Brad.   Sr. Lectr.
Long, Jonathan, BSc Brist., MA McM., PhD Leeds Met.   Prof.
Robson, Stephen, MSc Northumbria   Sr. Lectr.
Scraton, Sheila, BEd Liv., PhD Open(UK)   Prof.

Spink, John, BA Leeds, MA Manit.   Sr. Lectr.
Totten, Michael, BA Brad., MA Leeds Met.   Sr. Lectr.
Watson, Rebecca, BA Leeds Met., PhD Leeds Met.   Sr. Lectr.
Whitrod-Brown, Helen, BSc Lough., MA Sheff.   Principal Lectr.; Head*
Wolsey, Christopher, BA Staffs., MA Sheff., MEd Nott.   Principal Lectr.
Research: active lifestyle; gender and equality; operations and leisure policy

Sport, Exercise and Physical Education

Fax: (0113) 812 7575
E-mail: m.rhyne@leedsmet.ac.uk
Adams, Gordon, BA CNAA   Sr. Lectr.
Bissas, Anthanassios, BA Athens, MSc Leeds Met.   Sr. Lectr.
Borkoles, Erika, BSc Herts., MSc Exe., PhD Leeds Met.   Sr. Lectr.
Butterly, Ronald, BEd Liv., MA Leeds, PhD Leeds   Principal Lectr.
Cooke, Carlton, BSc Birm., PhD Birm.   Prof.; Head*
Flintoff, Anne, BEd Leeds, MA Leeds, PhD Open(UK)   Reader, Physical Education and Educational Development
Gately, Paul, BA Leeds Met.   Sr. Lectr.
Gilson, Nicholas, BA Leeds Met.   Sr. Lectr.
King, Roderick, BSc Bath, PhD Leeds   Sr. Lectr.
Lloyd, Edward, BSc Wash.State, MEd Leeds   Principal Lectr.
Polman, Remco, Drs Amst., DPhil York(UK)   Sr. Lectr.
Pringle, Andy, BA Staffs., MSc Leeds Met.   Sr. Lectr.
Twinem, Janette, BPhil Exe.   Sr. Lectr.

SPECIAL CENTRES, ETC

Yorkshire First Foundation

Tel: (0113) 812 6158 Fax: (0113) 812 3142
E-mail: j.dishman@leedsmet.ac.uk
Dishman, John   Dean*

CONTACT OFFICERS

Accommodation. Accommodation Officer: Webster, Ann, BA CNAA
   (E-mail: accommodation@leedsmet.ac.uk)
Admissions (first degree). Admissions Officer: Senior, Deborah
   (E-mail: d.senior@leedsmet.ac.uk)
Admissions (higher degree). Admissions Officer: Senior, Deborah
   (E-mail: d.senior@leedsmet.ac.uk)
Alumni. Alumni Development Manager: Roberts, Mark
   (E-mail: alumni@leedsmet.ac.uk)
Archives. Deputy University Secretary: Rushall, Martin, BA Leeds, MA Leeds
   (E-mail: m.rushall@leedsmet.ac.uk)
Careers. Careers Development Manager: Marsland, Phillip, BA CNAA
   (E-mail: p.marsland@leedsmet.ac.uk)
Computing services. Electronic Services Development Manager: Webb, David
   (E-mail: david.webb@leedsmet.ac.uk)
Conferences/corporate hospitality. Conference Co-ordinator: Bradshaw, Jeremy
   (E-mail: j.bradshaw@leedsmet.ac.uk)
Consultancy services. Head of Office for Leeds and Yorkshire: Rodgers, Peter
   (E-mail: p.rodgers@leedsmet.ac.uk)
Equal opportunities. Director of Human Resources: Pashley, Steve
   (E-mail: s.pashley@leedsmet.ac.uk)

Estates and buildings/works and services. Director of Facilities: Holmes, Susan
   (E-mail: s.m.holmes@leedsmet.ac.uk)
Examinations. Principal Officer, Student Administration: Bradley, Sue, BA Leeds Met.
   (E-mail: s.bradley@leedsmet.ac.uk)
Finance. Director of Finance: Willis, Stephen
   (E-mail: s.willis@leedsmet.ac.uk)
General enquiries. Deputy University Secretary: Rushall, Martin, BA Leeds, MA Leeds
   (E-mail: m.rushall@leedsmet.ac.uk)
Health services. Health Centre Manager: Heslop, Joanne, BSc Leeds Met.
   (E-mail: j.heslop@leedsmet.ac.uk)
Industrial liaison. Head of Office for Leeds and Yorkshire: Rodgers, Peter
   (E-mail: p.rodgers@leedsmet.ac.uk)
International office. Head of International Office: Braham, David
   (E-mail: d.braham@leedsmet.ac.uk)
Language training for international students. International Dean: Jones, Elspeth, BA Reading, MA Lond.
   (E-mail: e.jones@leedsmet.ac.uk)
Library (chief librarian). Head of Learning Support Services: Norry, Jo, BA Northumbria
   (E-mail: j.norry@leedsmet.ac.uk)
Marketing. Director of Communications and Marketing: Kelly, Dennis
Ombudsman. University Secretary: Denton, Steve (E-mail: s.denton@leedsmet.ac.uk)
Personnel/human resources. Director of Human Resources: Pashley, Steve
   (E-mail: s.pashley@leedsmet.ac.uk)
Purchasing. Purchasing and Environment Officer: Briggs, Mike
   (E-mail: m.briggs@leedsmet.ac.uk)
Quality assurance and accreditation. Academic Quality Manager: Murphy, Stephen (E-mail: s.murphy@leedsmet.ac.uk)
Research. Director of University Research: Scraton, Sheila
   (E-mail: s.j.scraton@leedsmet.ac.uk)
Safety. Senior Health and Safety Officer: Richold, Chris
   (E-mail: c.richold@leedsmet.ac.uk)
Schools liaison. Education Liaison Officer: Smith, Joyce
   (E-mail: j.c.smith@leedsmet.ac.uk)
Security. Security Manager: Haines, Peter
   (E-mail: j.balmforth@leedsmet.ac.uk)
Sport and recreation. University Head of Sport: Brown, Malcolm, BEd BA MA
   (E-mail: university-sport@leedsmet.ac.uk)
Staff development and training. Staff Development Manager: Penock, Sara
   (E-mail: s.penock@leedsmet.ac.uk)
Student welfare/counselling. Head of Student Services: Arblaster, David, BA Leic., MPhil Leic., MBA Leic.
   (E-mail: d.arblaster@leedsmet.ac.uk)
Students from other countries. International Students' Adviser: Braham, David
   (E-mail: d.braham@leedsmet.ac.uk)
Students with disabilities. Disability Services Officer: Reaney, John, BA Sheff.Hallam, MA Derby (E-mail: j.reaney@leedsmet.ac.uk)

CAMPUS/COLLEGE HEADS

Harrogate College. (Tel: (01423) 879466; Fax: (01423) 879829;
E-mail: j.hudson@leedsmet.ac.uk) Principal: Hudson, Julie, BSc MA

[Information supplied by the institution as at 28 September 2007, and edited by the ACU]

UNIVERSITY OF LEICESTER

Founded 1957

Member of the Association of Commonwealth Universities

Postal Address: University Road, Leicester, England LE1 7RH
Telephone: (0116) 252 2522 **Fax:** (0116) 252 2200
URL: http://www.le.ac.uk

VICE-CHANCELLOR*—Burgess, Prof. Robert G., BA Durh., PhD Warw., AcSS
SENIOR PRO-VICE-CHANCELLOR—Thompson, Prof. Mark P., LLB Leic., LLM Keele
PRO-VICE-CHANCELLOR—Fothergill, Prof. John C., BSc Wales, MSc Wales, PhD Wales, FIEE, FIEEE
PRO-VICE-CHANCELLOR—Fyfe, Christine
PRO-VICE-CHANCELLOR—Postlethwaite, Prof. Ian, BSc Lond., MA Oxf., PhD Camb., FREng, FIEEE, FIMC, FIEE, FIETE
REGISTRAR AND SECRETARY‡—Hall, David, BA
ACADEMIC REGISTRAR—Williams, Katherine E., BA Reading
DIRECTOR OF FINANCE—Hunt, H. James, MA Oxf., MBA Warw.

GENERAL INFORMATION

History. The university was founded in 1921 as Leicester, Leicestershire and Rutland College, received a royal charter in 1950 as University College of Leicester, and became the University of Leicester in 1957.

It is located in the East Midlands, about 160km north of London.

Admission to first degree courses (see also United Kingdom Introduction). Through Universities and Colleges Admissions Service (UCAS). Minimum requirement: three General Certificate of Education (GCE) A levels or vocational A levels; or two A levels and two AS levels; or equivalent qualification. A wide range of international qualifications are accepted.

First Degrees (see also United Kingdom Directory to Subjects of Study). BA, BEng, BSc, LLB, MB ChB, MBiol, MChem, MEng, MGeol, MMath, MPhys.

All courses are full-time and normally last 3 years or 4 years sandwich. Foundation degree: 2–4 years.

Length of course. Full-time: BA, BSc, LLB: 3 years; BEng: 3–4 years; MBiol, MChem, MGeol, MMath: 4 years; MB ChB, MEng, MPhys: 4–5 years. Part-time: BA: 3–5 years.

Higher Degrees (see also United Kingdom Directory to Subjects of Study).

Master's. LLM, MA, MBA, MD, MEd, MPhil, MSc.

Admission. Applicants for admission to postgraduate degrees should normally hold a good first degree or equivalent qualification.

Length of course. Full-time: LLM, MA, MBA, MEd, MSc: 1 year; MPhil: 1–2 years; MD: 2–5 years. Part-time: LLM, MA, MEd, MSc: 2 years; MPhil: 2–5 years. By distance learning: LLM, MA, MSc: 2–4 years; MBA: 2–5 years.

Doctoral. DClinPsy, DLitt, DMus, DSc, DSocSc, EdD, LLD, PhD.

Length of course. Full-time: DSocSc, EdD: 2–3 years; PhD: 2–4 years; DClinPsy: 3 years. Part-time: EdD, PhD: 3–6 years.

Language of Instruction. English. Preparatory English language courses offered during the year.

Libraries. Volumes: 1,200,000. Periodicals subscribed to: 18,000. Special collections: English local history; Orton papers.

Statistics. Students (2005–2006): full-time 9679 (4544 men, 5135 women); part-time 1307; international 1525; distance education/external 7231; undergraduate 9507; master's 7377; doctoral 1373.

FACULTIES/SCHOOLS

Arts
Tel: (0116) 252 2679 Fax: (0116) 252 5213
E-mail: arts@le.ac.uk
Dean: Shattock, Prof. E. Joanne, BA New Br., MA Leeds, PhD Lond., Hon. DLitt New Br.
Secretary: Baddiley, Kathy, BA Lanc.

Biological Sciences, School of
Tel: (0116) 252 3321 Fax: (0116) 252 5659
E-mail: biolsci@le.ac.uk
Head: Roberts, Prof. Gordon C. K., BSc Lond., PhD Lond., FRSChem, FMedSci
Director of Biological Studies: Scott, John J. A., BSc Durh., PhD Durh.

Education, School of
Tel: (0116) 252 3688 Fax: (0116) 252 3653
E-mail: soed@le.ac.uk
Head: Ainley, Prof. Janet, BA York(UK), MEd Warw., PhD Warw.
Secretary: Rouse, Pam

Law
Tel: (0116) 252 2363 Fax: (0116) 252 5023
E-mail: law@le.ac.uk
Dean: Bonner, Prof. David, LLB Leic., LLM W.Ont.
Secretary: Lad, Sangita

Leicester Medical School
Tel: (0116) 252 2966 Fax: (0116) 252 3013
E-mail: med-admis@le.ac.uk
Dean: Lauder, Prof. Ian, MB BS Newcastle(UK), FRCPath, FMedSci
Secretary: Siesage, Nigel P., JP, MA Oxf.

Science
Tel: (0116) 252 5012 Fax: (0116) 252 2770
E-mail: science@le.ac.uk
Dean: Hillman, Prof. A. Robert, BSc Lond., DPhil Oxf.
Secretary: Goddard, C. A.

Social Sciences
Tel: (0116) 252 2842 Fax: (0116) 252 5073
E-mail: socsci@le.ac.uk
Dean: Jackson, Prof. Peter M., BA Strath., PhD Stir., FRSA, FCIM
Secretary: Pabla, Jasbir

ACADEMIC UNITS

Archaeology and Ancient History, School of
Tel: (0116) 252 2611 Fax: (0116) 252 5005
E-mail: archaeology@le.ac.uk
Haselgrove, Colin, BSc Sus., MA Camb., PhD Camb., FSA Prof.; Head of Sch.*

Ancient History
Cowan, Eleanor R., BA Syd., LLB Syd., PhD Exe.
Foxhall, Lin, MBE, BA Bryn Mawr, MA Penn., PhD Liv., FSA Prof.
Katsari, Constantina, BA Athens, PhD Lond.

Shipley, D. Graham J., MA Oxf., DPhil Oxf., FSA Prof.
Other Staff: 1 Visiting Prof.; 2 Univ. Fellows; 1 Res. Fellow; 1 Hon. Lectr.
Research: classical towns, cities and urbanism; gender, material culture and the past; Hellenistic world; Mediterranean landscape and land use; Roman Europe

Archaeology
Allison, Penelope M., BA Cant., MA Syd., PhD Syd., FSA Reader
Christie, Neil J., BA Newcastle(UK), PhD Newcastle(UK), FSA Reader
Gillings, Mark, BSc Brad., PhD Brad. Sr. Lectr.
Horning, Audrey J., BA William & Mary, MA Penn., PhD Penn., FSA Sr. Lectr.
James, S. T., BSc Lond., PhD Lond., FSA Reader
Mattingly, David J., BA Manc., PhD Manc., FSA, FBA Prof., Roman Archaeology
Palmer, Marilyn, MA Oxf., PhD Leic., FSA Prof., Industrial Archaeology
Pluciennik, Mark Z., BA Sheff., PhD Sheff. Sr. Lectr.
Tarlow, Sarah, BA Sheff., MPhil Camb., PhD Camb. Sr. Lectr.
Van der Veen, Marijke, CandDr Gron., MA Sheff., PhD Sheff., FSA Prof., Archaeology
Other Staff: 1 Emer. Prof.; 1 Visiting Prof.; 6 Lectrs.; 2 Univ. Fellows; 1 Wellcome Trust Univ. Fellow; 1 Res. Fellow; 1 Leverhulme Early Career Res. Fellow; 1 British Acad. Postdoctoral Fellow; 1 Hon. Lectr.
Research: colonial archaeology (ancient to modern); environmental archaeology and archaeology of food; historical archaeology (classical to modern); landscape archaeology (prehistoric to industrial); material culture and heritage

Biochemistry
Tel: (0116) 252 3471 Fax: (0116) 252 3369
E-mail: biochemistry@le.ac.uk
Bagshaw, Clive R., BSc Birm., PhD Brist. Prof.
Carr, Mark D., BSc Birm., DPhil Oxf. Reader
Cohen, Gerald M., BSc Leeds, PhD Minn. Hon. Prof., Biochemical Toxicology
Critchley, David R., BSc Brist., PhD Brist. Prof.
Cundliffe, Eric, MA Camb., PhD Camb., ScD Camb. Prof.
Eperon, Ian C., BSc Brist., PhD Camb., FRSChem Prof.
Farmer, Peter B., BA Oxf., MA Oxf., DPhil Oxf. Hon. Prof., Biochemical Toxicology
Fry, Andrew M., BA Oxf., DPhil Oxf. Reader
Gescher, Andreas J., BSc Fran., PhD Würzburg, DSc Aston Hon. Prof., Biochemical Toxicology
Harrison, Timothy M., BSc Wales, PhD Camb. Sr. Lectr.; Head*
Moody, Peter C. E., BA York(UK), PhD Lond. Sr. Lectr.
Pitchard, Catrin A., BA Oxf., PhD Lond. Reader
Roberts, Gordon C. K., BSc Lond., PhD Lond., FRSChem, FMedSci Prof.

Willmott, Christopher J. R., BSc Leic., PhD Leic.
Sr. Lectr.
Other Staff: 8 Lectrs.; 1 Univ. Fellow; 1 Hon.
Reader; 5 Hon. Lectrs.
Research: biochemistry of gene expression; cell
regulation and signalling; structural biology
and molecular enzymology

Biology

Tel: (0116) 252 3344 Fax: (0116) 252 3330
E-mail: biology@le.ac.uk
Cann, Alan J., BSc Sheff., PhD Leic.   Sr. Lectr.
Gornall, Richard J., BSc St And., MSc Birm., PhD
Br.Col.   Sr. Lectr.; Dir., Gardens and
Herbarium
Harper, David M., MA Oxf., PhD Dund., FLS
Sr. Lectr.
Hart, Paul J. B., BSc Liv., BA Open(UK), PhD Liv.
Prof.
Heslop-Harrison, J. S. (Pat), BSc Wales, PhD
Camb.   Prof., Plant Cell Biology/Molecular
Cytogenetics
Jarvis, Robert P., BSc Durh., PhD E.Anglia
Reader
Twell, David, BSc Durh., PhD Lond.   Prof., Plant
Biology
Whitelam, Garry C., BSc Leeds, PhD Reading
Prof., Plant Molecular Physiology; Head*
Other Staff: 5 Lectrs.; 1 Indust. Fellow; 1
Royal Society Rosenheim Res. Fellow/
Lectr.; 1 Royal Society Res. Fellow/Lectr.; 9
Hon. Visiting Fellows
Research: behavioural biology; biodiversity,
evolution and ecology; cell and molecular
biology

Cancer Studies and Molecular Medicine

Tel: (0116) 258 7597 Fax: (0116) 258 7599
E-mail: jm65@le.ac.uk
Al-Alousi, Louay M., PhD Glas., MB ChB,
FRCPGlas, FRCPath   Sr. Lectr.
Barwell, Julian R., BSc Lond., MB BS Lond., PhD
Lond.   Sr. Lectr.
Bell, Stephen C., BSc W.Aust., PhD Liv., FRCPath
Prof., Reproductive Sciences
Brown, Karen, BPharm Brad., PhD Brad.   Sr.
Lectr.
Cooke, Marcus S., BSc Liv., MSc Leic., PhD Leic.
Sr. Lectr.
Dyer, Martin J. S., MB BChir Camb., MA Oxf.,
DPhil Oxf., FRCP, FRCPath   Prof.,
Haemato-Oncology
Farmer, Peter B., BA Oxf., MA Oxf., DPhil Oxf.
Prof., Cancer Biomakers
Gescher, Andreas J., BSc Fran., PhD Würzburg,
DSc Aston   Hon. Prof., Biochemical
Toxicology
Griffiths, Thomas L., BSc Lond., MB BS Lond.,
MD Newcastle(UK), FRCSEd, FRCS   Sr. Lectr.
Habiba, Marwan A., MSc Cairo, PhD Leic., PhD
Wales, FRCOG   Sr. Lectr.
Heney, David, MB ChB Leeds, MD Leeds   Sr.
Lectr.
Jones, George D. D., BSc Leic., MSc Birm., PhD
Leic.   Sr. Lectr.
Konje, Justin C., MB BS Ib., MD Leic.   Prof.
Manson, Margaret M., BSc St And., PhD Edin.
Prof., Cancer Chemoprevention
McParland, Penelope C., MB BS Newcastle(UK),
PhD Leic.   Sr. Lectr.
Mellon, J. Killian, MB BCh BAO Belf., MD
Newcastle(UK), FRCSEd, FRCSI, FRCS   Prof.,
Urology
Morgan, Bruno, BM BCh Oxf., MA Oxf., FRCR
Sr. Lectr.
Nicholson, Stephen, MB BS Lond., PhD Lond.
Sr. Lectr.; Hon. Consultant, Medical
Oncology
Pringle, James H., BSc CNAA, PhD Warw.
Reader
Rutty, Guy, MB BS Lond.   Prof., Forensic
Pathology
Saldanha, Gerald, MB ChB Leic.   Sr. Lectr.
Shaw, Jacqueline A., BSc Leic., PhD Lond.   Sr.
Lectr.
Steward, William P., MB ChB Manc., PhD Manc.,
FRCPCan, FRCPGlas, FRCP   Prof.,
Oncology; Head*

Symonds, Raymond Paul, TD, MB BS
Newcastle(UK), MD Newcastle(UK), FRCP, FRCR
Reader
Taylor, David J., MB BS Newcastle(UK), MD
Newcastle(UK), FRCOG   Prof., Obstetrics and
Gynaecology
Thomas, Anne L., BM S'ton., PhD Nott.   Sr.
Lectr.
Thornton, Steven, BM S'ton., MA Camb., DM
S'ton.   Hon. Prof., Obstetrics and
Gynaecology
Tincello, Douglas, BSc Edin., MB ChB Edin., MD
Edin.   Sr. Lectr.
Walker, Rosemary A., MB ChB Birm., MD Birm.,
FRCPath   Prof., Histopathology
Other Staff: 14 Lectrs.; 1 Hon. Reader; 11
Hon. Sr. Lectrs.; 3 Hon. Lectrs.; 3 Hon.
Visiting Fellows; 12 Hon. Visiting Clin.
Fellows; 1 Hon. Clin. Res. Asst.
Research: cancer biomarkers and prevention;
cellular interaction and cell signalling;
genome instability; reproductive science

Cardiovascular Sciences

Tel: (0116) 256 3021 Fax: (0116) 287 5792
E-mail: jh77@le.ac.uk
Barnett, David B., MD Sheff., FRCP   Prof.,
Clinical Pharmacology
Brindle, Nicholas P., BSc Leeds, PhD Manc.
Reader
Coats, Timothy J., MB BS Lond., MD Lond., FRCS
Prof.
Davies, Melanie J., MB ChB Newcastle(UK), MD
Newcastle(UK), FRCP   Prof.
Evans, David H., BSc Sur., PhD Leic., DSc Sur.,
FIP   Prof., Medical Physics
Fotherby, Martin D., BSc Leic., MB ChB Leic.,
MD Leic., FRCP   Sr. Lectr.
Galiñanes, Manuel, MD Salamanca, PhD Lond.,
FRCS   Prof., Cardiac Surgery
Goodall, Alison H., BSc Lond., PhD Lond.   Prof.,
Thrombosis and Haemostasis
Gottlob, Irene, MD Vienna   Prof.,
Ophthalmology
Herbert, Karl E., BSc Brun., PhD Lond.   Sr.
Lectr.
Hillhouse, Edward W., MB BS Lond., BSc Lond.,
PhD Lond., FRCP   Hon. Prof., Medicine and
Therapeutics
Horsfield, Mark A., BSc Brist., PhD Camb.
Reader
Lambert, David G., BSc Aston, PhD Aston   Prof.
London, Nicholas J. M., MB ChB Birm., MD
Leic., FRCS   Prof., Surgery
Naylor, A. Ross, MD Aberd., FRCS   Hon. Prof.,
Surgery
Ng, Ghulam A., MB ChB Glas., PhD Glas.   Sr.
Lectr.
Ng, Leong L., MA Camb., MD Camb., FRCP
Prof., Medicine and Therapeutics
Norman, Robert I., BSc Leic., PhD Lond.   Sr.
Lectr.
Panerai, Ronney B., BSc Rio Grande do Sul, MSc
Rio de Janeiro, PhD Lond.   Prof., Physiological
Measurement
Potter, John F., BMedSci Nott., DM Nott., FRCP
Prof., Medicine for the Elderly
Robinson, Thompson G., BMedSci Nott., BM BS
Nott., MD Leic.   Sr. Lectr.
Samani, Nilesh J., BSc Leic., MB ChB Leic., MD
Leic., FRCP, FACC, FMedSci   Prof.,
Cardiology; Head*
Sayers, Robert D., MB ChB Birm., MD Leic.,
FRCS   Reader
Squire, Iain B., BSc Strath., MB ChB Glas., MD
Glas.   Sr. Lectr.
Thompson, Jonathan P., BSc Leic., MB ChB Leic.,
MD Leic., FRCA   Sr. Lectr.
Thompson, Matthew M., MA Camb., MB BS
Lond., MD Leic., FRCS   Visiting Prof.,
Surgery
Thurston, Herbert, BSc Manc., MD Manc., FRCP
Prof., Medicine
Toff, William D., BSc Lond., MB BS Lond., MD
Lond.   Sr. Lectr.
Trembath, Richard C., BSc Lond., MB BS Lond.,
FRCP, FMedSci   Hon. Prof., Medical
Genetics

Williams, Bryan, BSc Lond., MB BS Lond., MD
Leic., FRCP   Prof., Medicine
Woods, Kent L., MA Camb., ScM Harv., MD
Camb., FRCP   Prof., Therapeutics
Other Staff: 11 Lectrs.; 1 Hon. Reader; 11
Hon. Sr. Lectrs.; 8 Hon. Lectrs.; 5 Hon.
Visiting Fellows; 1 Hon. Sr. Res. Nurse; 8
Hon. Res. Nurses; 2 Hon. Clin. Res.
Fellows; 7 Hon. Visiting Clin. Fellows
Research: ageing and stroke medicine; cardiac
surgery; cardiology; pharmacology and
therapautics; vascular medicine and surgery

Cell Physiology and Pharmacology

Tel: (0116) 252 3088 Fax: (0116) 252 5045
E-mail: cpp@le.ac.uk
Challiss, R. A. John, BSc Bath, DPhil Oxf.
Prof., Molecular and Cellular Pharmacology
Davies, Noel W., BSc Wales, PhD St And.   Sr.
Lectr.
Evans, Richard J., BSc Bath, DPhil Oxf.   Prof.,
Molecular Physiology and Pharmacology
Fern, Robert E., BSc Lond., PhD Lond.   Reader
Grubb, Blair D., BSc Edin., PhD Newcastle(UK)
Sr. Lectr.; Head*
Hartell, Nicholas, BSc Herts., PhD Brist.   Prof.,
Neuroscience
Mahaut-Smith, Martyn P., BSc Sheff., MA Camb.,
PhD Brist.   Prof., Cellular Molecular
Physiology and Pharmacology
Mitcheson, John S., BSc Lond., PhD Brist.
Reader
Nicotera, Pierluigi, MD Pavia, PhD Karolinska
Hon. Prof., Neuroscience
Standen, Nicholas B., MA Camb., PhD Camb.,
FMedSci   Prof., Physiology
Tobin, Andrew B., BSc Lond., DPhil Oxf.   Prof.,
Cell Biology
Willars, Gary, BSc Aston, PhD Aston   Sr. Lectr.
Other Staff: 7 Lectrs.; 2 Res. Fellows; 1 Hon.
Prof.
Research: cardiovascular physiology (arterial
resistance vessels, vasodilation); cell
signalling (intracellular calcium,
phosphoinositides); electrophysiology
(inwardly rectifying potassium-channels);
neurophysiology (arthritis, auditory
processing, inflammation); receptors
(adrenoceptors, matabotropic glutamate
receptors, muscarinic acetylcholine)

Chemistry

Tel: (0116) 252 2100 Fax: (0116) 252 3789
E-mail: chemistry@le.ac.uk
Abbott, Andrew P., BSc CNAA, PhD S'ton.   Sr.
Lectr.
Cullis, Paul M., BSc Exe., DPhil Oxf., FRSChem
Prof., Organic Chemistry
Davies, David L., BSc Brist., PhD Brist.   Sr.
Lectr.
Ellis, Andrew M., BSc S'ton., PhD S'ton.   Sr.
Lectr.
Hillman, A. Robert, BSc Lond., DPhil Oxf.
Prof., Physical Chemistry
Hope, Eric G., BSc S'ton., PhD S'ton.   Prof.,
Inorganic Chemistry; Head*
Jenkins, Paul R., BSc Wales, PhD Wales   Sr.
Lectr.
Monks, Paul S., BSc Warw., DPhil Oxf.   Reader
Percy, Jonathan M., BSc Lond., PhD Camb.
Prof., Organic Chemistry
Raven, Emma, BSc Leic., PhD Newcastle(UK)
Reader
Other Staff: 8 Lectrs.; 1 Univ. Fellow; 2
Indust. Assocs.; 1 Hon. Lectr.; 2 Hon.
Visiting Fellows
Research: biological chemistry; fluorine
chemistry; green chemistry; molecular
properties

Criminology

Tel: (0116) 252 3946 Fax: (0116) 252 5788
E-mail: criminology@le.ac.uk
Beck, Adrian, BA Leic.   Reader
Hedderman, Carol, BA Staffs., MPhil Camb.,
DPhil Camb.   Prof.; Head*
Jewkes, Yvonne, BA CNAA, MA Leic., PhD Camb.
Other Staff: 8 Lectrs.; 1 Teaching Fellow

Research: community safety and crime reduction partnerships; globalisation, security and policing; penology, interventions and evaluations; social exclusion and community partnerships

Economics

Tel: (0116) 252 2887 Fax: (0116) 252 2908
    E-mail: economics@le.ac.uk
Charemza, Wojciech, DrEcon *Gdansk*, DrHabEcon *Gdansk*   Prof.
De Fraja, Giovanni, BA *Pisa*, PhD *Siena*, DPhil *Oxf.*   Prof.
Demetriades, Panicos, BA *Essex*, MA *Essex*, PhD *Camb.*   Prof.
Fraser, Clive D., BSocSci *Birm.*, PhD *S'ton.*   Prof.; Head*
Hall, Stephen, BSc *Lond.*, MSc *Lond.*, PhD *Lond.*   Prof.
Lee, Kevin C., BA *Sheff.*, MSc *Brist.*, PhD *Lond.*, FRSA   Prof.
McCrorie, James R., BSc *St And.*, MA *Essex*, PhD *Essex*   Reader
Mezzetti, Claudio, BA *Pisa*, PhD *Siena*, DPhil *Oxf.*   Prof.
Strachan, Rodney W., BA *Qld.*, MSc *NE*, PhD *Monash*   Sr. Lectr.
Wheatley Price, Stephan, BSc *Leic.*, MA *Leic.*, PhD *Leic.*   Sr. Lectr.
Other Staff: 1 Visiting Prof.; 1 Sr. Lectr.; 9 Lectrs.; 1 Assoc. Sr. Lectr.; 1 Univ. Fellow
Research: applied macroeconomics; applied microeconomics; business and financial economics; economic and econometric theory

Education, School of

Tel: (0116) 252 3688 Fax: (0116) 252 3653
    E-mail: soed@le.ac.uk
Bell, Leslie A., BSc *Lond.*, MA *Warw.*, PhD *Warw.*, MSc *CNAA*   Prof., Educational Management
Briggs, Ann R. J., BA *Lond.*, MBA *Leic.*, PhD *Leic.*   Sr. Lectr.
Busher, Hugh C., BA *Manc.*, MEd *Birm.*, PhD *Leeds*   Sr. Lectr.
Cajkler, Wasyl, BA *Wales*, MSc *Aston*   Sr. Lectr.
Comber, Christopher J. F., BA *Leic.*, PhD *Leic.*   Sr. Lectr.
Cooper, Paul W., BA *Stir.*, MEd *Dund.*, MA *Camb.*, PhD *Birm.*   Prof.; Dir., Centre for Innovation in Raising Educnl. Achievement; Dir. of Sch.*
Cremin, Hilary, BA *Warw.*, PhD *Leic.*   Sr. Lectr.
Dimmock, Clive A. J., BSc(Econ) *Lond.*, MEd *Reading*, PhD *Lond.*   Dir., Centre for Educnl. Leadership and Management; Prof., Educational Management
Harrison, Jennifer, BSc *Sur.*, MEdStud *Leic.*   Sr. Lectr.
Jarvis, Tina J., BSc *Birm.*, PhD *Leic.*   Sr. Lectr.; Dir., East Midlands Sci. Learning Centre
Lawson, Tony, MA *Camb.*, MEd *Leic.*, PhD *Leic.*   Sr. Lectr.
Merry, Roger, BA *Keele*, MSc *Aston*, PhD *Aston*   Sr. Lectr.
Pole, Christopher J., BA *Warw.*, PhD *Leic.*   Reader
Rogers, Laurence, MSc *Nott.*, PhD *Leic.*   Sr. Lectr.
Sage, Rosemary J. W., BA *Open(UK)*, MPhil *Open(UK)*, PhD *Leic.*   Sr. Lectr.
Wilkins, Christopher, BEd *Brighton*, PhD *Leic.*   Sr. Lectr.
Other Staff: 27 Lectrs.; 1 Sr. Tutor; 2 Teaching Fellows; 2 Visiting Lectrs.; 1 Lectr.†; 5 Teaching Fellows†
Research: citizenship and social inclusion; education management; language, culture and applied linguistics; learning and teaching

Engineering

Tel: (0116) 252 2559 Fax: (0116) 252 2619
    E-mail: engineering@le.ac.uk
Aroussi, A., BSc *CNAA*, PhD *CNAA*   Prof.
Atkinson, Helen, BA *Camb.*, MA *Camb.*, PhD *Lond.*, FIMMM, FREng, FIMechE   Prof.

Bates, Declan, BEng *Dublin City*, PhD *Dublin City*   Sr. Lectr.
Coats, Christopher M., BSc *Leeds*, PhD *Leeds*   Sr. Lectr.
Dissado, Leonard A., BSc *Lond.*, PhD *Lond.*, DSc *Lond.*   Prof.
Dodd, S., BSc *Lond.*, PhD *Lond.*   Sr. Lectr.
Edwards, Christopher, BSc *Warw.*, PhD *Leic.*   Sr. Lectr.
Folkard, Geoffrey K., BSc *Edin.*, MSc *Lond.*, PhD *Lond.*   Sr. Lectr.
Fothergill, John C., BSc *Wales*, MSc *Wales*, PhD *Wales*, FIEE, FIEEE   Prof.
Gill, Simon P. A., BSc *Brist.*, PhD *Strath.*   Sr. Lectr.
Gostelow, J. Paul, BEng *Liv.*, MA *Camb.*, MA *Lond.*, PhD *Liv.*, DEng *Liv.*, FIEAust, FRAeS   Emer. Prof.
Gu, Da Wei, BA *Fudan*, MSc *Shanghai Jiaotong*, PhD *Lond.*   Reader
Hainsworth, Sarah V., BEng *Newcastle(UK)*, PhD *Newcastle(UK)*   Sr. Lectr.
Jones, N. Barrie, BSc *Manc.*, MEng *McM.*, DPhil *Sus.*, FIEE   Emer. Prof.
Manners, William, MA *Camb.*, PhD *Lond.*   Sr. Lectr.
Pan, Jingzhe, BSc *Shenyang Technol.*, MSc *Dalian U.T.*, PhD *Shanghai Jiaotong*   Prof.
Pearce, T. C., BEng *Warw.*, PhD *Warw.*, FIP   Sr. Lectr.
Pollock, Charles, BSc *Lond.*, PhD *H-W*   Prof.
Pont, Michael J., BSc *Glas.*, PhD *S'ton.*, MBCS   Reader
Ponter, Alan R. S., BSc *Lond.*, MA *Camb.*, MS *Brown*, PhD *Lond.*   Emer. Prof.
Postlethwaite, Ian, BSc *Lond.*, MA *Oxf.*, PhD *Camb.*, FREng, FIEEE, FIMC, FIEE, FIETE   Prof.
Quian Quiroga, Rodrigo, BSc *Buenos Aires*, MSc *Buenos Aires*, PhD *Lübeck*   Reader
Schlindwein, Fernando, BEng *Rio Grande do Sul*, MSc *Rio de Janeiro*, PhD *Leic.*, DSc *Rio de Janeiro*   Sr. Lectr.
Spurgeon, Sarah K., BSc *York(UK)*, DPhil *York(UK)*, FIMA, FIMC, FIEE   Prof.; Head*
Stocker, Alan J., BSc *Leic.*, PhD *Leic.*   Sr. Lectr.
Warrington, E. Michael, BSc *Durh.*, PhD *Leic.*, FIETE   Prof.
Other Staff: 4 Royal Academy of Engineering Visiting Profs.; 16 Lectrs.; 1 Hon. Visiting Prof.; 4 Hon. Visiting Fellows
Research: control and instrumentation; electrical and electronic power; mechanics of materials; radio systems; thermo and fluid engineering

English

Tel: (0116) 252 2620 Fax: (0116) 252 2065
    E-mail: english@le.ac.uk
Campbell, Gordon R., MA *Qu.*, DPhil *York(UK)*, DLitt *York(UK)*, DrHC *Bucharest*, FRHistS, FRGS   Prof., Renaissance Literature
Coleman, Julie, BA *Manc.*, MA *Lond.*, PhD *Lond.*   Reader
Dawson, Gowan, BA *E.Anglia*, MA *Nott.*, PhD *Sheff.*   Sr. Lectr.
Foulkes, Richard, BA *Wales*, MA *Birm.*, PhD *Leic.*   Prof., Theatre History; Head*
Halliwell, Martin R., BA *Exe.*, MA *Exe.*, PhD *Nott.*   Prof.
Newey, Vincent A., MA *Oxf.*, BLitt *Oxf.*, PhD *Liv.*, FRSA   Emer. Prof.
Parker, Emma, BA *Birm.*, PhD *Birm.*   Sr. Lectr.
Rawlinson, Mark J., BA *Oxf.*, MPhil *Oxf.*, DPhil *Oxf.*   Sr. Lectr.
Shattock, E. Joanne, BA *New Br.*, MA *Leeds*, PhD *Lond.*, Hon. DLitt *New Br.*   Prof., Victorian Literature
Shaw, Philip J., BA *Liv.*, PhD *Liv.*   Reader
Stannard, Martin J., BA *Warw.*, MA *Sus.*, DPhil *Oxf.*   Prof., Modern English Literature
Treharne, Elaine M., BA *Manc.*, MA *Liv.*, PhD *Manc.*   Prof., Mediaeval Literature
Other Staff: 14 Lectrs.
Research: mediaeval literature; modern literature and cultural theory; nineteenth-century literature, Romantic and Victorian; Renaissance literature (in particular reign of Henry VIII and Shakespeare)

Genetics

Tel: (0116) 252 3374 Fax: (0116) 252 3378
    E-mail: genetics@le.ac.uk
Borts, Rhona, ScB *Brown*, PhD *Wis.*   Prof.
Brookes, Anthony J., BSc *Manc.*, MB ChB *Manc.*, PhD *Lond.*   Prof.
Cashmore, Annette M., BSc *Sus.*, PhD *CNAA*   Sr. Lectr.
Dalgleish, Raymond W. M., BSc *Glas.*, PhD *Lond.*   Sr. Lectr.
Dubrova, Yuri, BSc *Kiev*, PhD *Kiev*, DrSci *Moscow*   Prof.
Jeffreys, Sir Alec J., BA *Oxf.*, MA *Oxf.*, DPhil *Oxf.*, DSc *Open(UK)*, FRS, FLS, FRCPath, FIBiol, Hon. FRCP, FMedSci   Royal Society Wolfson Res. Prof.
Jobling, Mark, BA *Oxf.*, DPhil *Oxf.*   Prof.
Ketley, Julian M., BSc *Birm.*, PhD *Birm.*   Prof.
Kyriacou, Charalamos P., BSc *Birm.*, PhD *Sheff.*, FMedSci   Prof.
Meacock, Peter A., BSc *Newcastle(UK)*, MSc *Newcastle(UK)*, PhD *Leic.*   Reader
Orr, Eli, MSc *Jerusalem*, PhD *Jerusalem*   Sr. Res. Lectr.
Rosato, Ezio, PhD *Ferrara*   Reader
Royle, Nicola, BSc *Manc.*, PhD *Reading*   Sr. Lectr.
Williams, Peter H., BSc *Lond.*, PhD *E.Anglia*   Prof.; Head*
Other Staff: 9 Lectrs.; 1 Hon. Lectr.; 1 Hon. Visiting Fellow
Research: behavioural and developmental genetics; genetic variability, mutation and evolution; human and medical genetics; microbial genetics and pathogenicity

Geography

Tel: (0116) 252 3823 Fax: (0116) 252 3854
    E-mail: geog@le.ac.uk
Balzter, Heiko, DrAgr *Giessen*   Prof., Physical Geography
Bradshaw, Michael J., BSc *Birm.*, MA *Calg.*, PhD *Br.Col.*   Prof., Human Geography; Head*
Brunsdon, Christopher, BSc *Durh.*, MSc *Newcastle(UK)*, PhD *Newcastle(UK)*   Prof.
Fisher, Pete P., BSc *Lanc.*, MSc *Reading*, PhD *CNAA*   Prof.
Jarvis, Claire, BSc *Edin.*, MSc *Edin.*, PhD *Edin.*   Sr. Lectr.
Madge, Clare, BSc *Birm.*, PhD *Birm.*   Sr. Lectr.
McLaren, Sue J., BSc *Lond.*, PhD *Lond.*   Sr. Lectr.
Page, Sue E., BSc *Nott.*, PhD *Nott.*   Sr. Lectr.
Phillips, Martin P., BA *Lond.*, MA *Lond.*, PhD *Exe.*   Reader
Powell, Mark, BSc *Leeds*, PhD *Leeds*   Sr. Lectr.
Smalley, Ian J., PhD *City(UK)*   Hon. Prof., Applied Geomorphology
Tate, Nicholas J., BA *Durh.*, PhD *E.Anglia*   Sr. Lectr.
Turnock, David, MA *Camb.*, PhD *Camb.*   Emer. Prof., Human Geography
Other Staff: 16 Lectrs.
Research: environmental change; geographical information science; governance, postcolonialism and transformation; media, technology and culture; nature, environment and society

Geology

Tel: (0116) 252 3912 Fax: (0116) 252 3918
    E-mail: geology@le.ac.uk
Aldridge, Richard J., BSc *S'ton.*, PhD *S'ton.*, FGS   F. W. Bennett Prof.
Cunningham, William D., AB *Dartmouth*, MSc *Arizona*, PhD *Texas*   Sr. Lectr.
Davies, Sarah J., BSc *Leeds*, PhD *Leic.*   Sr. Lectr.
Hill, Ian A., BSc *Leic.*, MSc *Birm.*, PhD *Birm.*, FGS   Sr. Lectr.
Lovell, Michael A., BSc *Reading*, MSc *Wales*, PhD *Wales*, FGS   Prof., Petrophysics; Head*
Parrish, Randell R., BA *Middlebury*, MSc *Br.Col.*, PhD *Br.Col.*   Prof., Isotope Geology
Saunders, Andrew D., BSc *Sheff.*, MSc *Birm.*, PhD *Birm.*, FGS   Prof., Geochemistry
Siveter, David J., BSc *Leic.*, PhD *Leic.*, DSc *Leic.*, FGS   Prof., Palaeontology

Other Staff: 18 Lectrs.; 4 Univ. Fellows; 2 Indust. Assocs.; 1 Adjunct Lectr.; 20 Hon. Visiting Fellows

Research: crustal processes; geophysics and borehole research; palaeobiology

Health Sciences

Tel: (0116) 252 3205 Fax: (0116) 252 3272
E-mail: pp15@le.ac.uk

Abrams, Keith R., BSc Warw., MSc Leic., PhD Liv.   Prof., Medical Statistics

Baker, Richard H., OBE, MB BS Lond., MD Lond., FRCGP   Prof., Quality in Health Care; Head*

Brugha, Traolach S., MB BCh BAO N.U.I., MD N.U.I., FRCPsych   Deputy Head; Prof., Psychiatry

Burton, Paul, BSc Leic., MB ChB Leic., MSc Lond., MD Leic.   Prof., Genetic Epidemiology

Dennis, Michael S., MB BCh Wales   Sr. Lectr.

Dixon-Woods, Mary M., BA Dublin City, MSc Oxf., DPhil Oxf.   Reader

Dogra, Nisha, BM S'ton., MA Nott.   Clin. Sr. Lectr.

Draper, Elizabeth S., BSc Lough., MPhil Leic.   Reader

Field, David J., MB BS Lond., MD Nott., FRCPCH, FRCPEd   Prof., Neonatal Medicine

Harper, William M., MB ChB Leic., MD Leic., FRCSEd   Prof., Orthopaedic Trauma Surgery

Jagger, Carol, BSc Leeds, MSc Leeds, PhD Leic.   Prof., Epidemiology

Jones, David R., BA Camb., MSc E.Anglia, PhD E.Anglia   Prof., Medical Statistics

Karim, Khalid, MB ChB Leic.   Sr. Lectr.

Khunti, Kamlesh, MB ChB Dund., MD Leic., FRCGP   Sr. Lectr.

Lambert, Paul C., BSc Sheff.Hallam, MSc Leic., PhD Leic.   Sr. Lectr.

Lindesay, James E. B., MA Oxf., DM Oxf., FRCPsych   Prof., Psychiatry for the Elderly

McGrother, Catherine W., MB BS Newcastle(UK), FFPHM   Sr. Lectr.

McKinley, Robert K., BSc Belf., MB BCh BAO Belf., MD Belf., FRCGP   Sr. Lectr.

Meltzer, Howard I., BSc Lond., MSc Lond., PhD Hull   Prof.

Palmer, Emma J., MA Camb., PhD Birm.   Sr. Lectr.

Rowbotham, David J., MB ChB Sheff., MD Sheff., FRCA, FFARCSI   Prof., Anaesthesia and Pain Management

Sheehan, Nuala, BA N.U.I., MA N.U.I., MSc Wash.State, PhD Wash.State   Sr. Lectr., Statistical Genetics

Stokes, Timothy N., MA Oxf., MB ChB Edin., MPhil Camb., MPH Nott., PhD Leic.   Clin. Sr. Lectr.

Sutton, Alexander J., BSc Newcastle(UK), MSc Leic., PhD Leic.   Sr. Lectr.

Thompson, John R., BSc Exe., PhD Open(UK)   Prof., Ophthalmic Epidemiology

Tobin, Martin D., MB ChB Leic.   Sr. Lectr., Genetic Epidemiology

Vostanis, Panos, PtyLat Athens, MD Birm.   Prof., Child and Adolescent Psychiatry

Wailoo, Michael P., MB ChB Manc., MD Manc., FRCP   Sr. Lectr.

Watson, Paul J., BSc Manc., MSc Manc., PhD Manc.   Sr. Lectr.

Wilson, Andrew D., MB BS Newcastle(UK), MD Newcastle(UK), FRCGP   Reader

Other Staff: 12 Visiting Profs.; 3 Lectrs.; 17 Univ. Fellow; 16 Hon. Sr. Lectrs.; 8 Hon. Lectrs.; 20 Hon. Visiting Fellows; 1 Hon. Res. Nurse; 11 Hon. Visiting Clin. Fellows

Research: community paediatrics and neonatology; epidemiology and public health; general practice and primary health care; orthopaedic surgery; psychiatry

Clinical Consultation Research and Development Unit

Tel: (0116) 258 4873 Fax: (0116) 258 4892
E-mail: hmw10@le.ac.uk

McKinley, Robert K., BSc Belf., MB BCh BAO Belf., MD Belf., FRCGP   Sr. Lectr.; Dir.*

Clinical Governance Research and Development Unit

Tel: (0116) 258 4873 Fax: (0116) 258 4982
E-mail: cgrdu@le.ac.uk

Baker, Richard H., OBE, MB BS Lond., MD Lond., FRCGP   Prof., Quality in Health Care; Head*

Stokes, Timothy N., MA Oxf., MB ChB Edin., MPhil Camb., MPH Nott., PhD Leic.   Clijn. Sr. Lectr.

Other Staff: 2 Hon. Sr. Lectrs.; 1 Hon. Lectr.; 1 Hon. Visiting Fellow

Nuffield Community Care Studies Unit

Tel: (0116) 252 5422 Fax: (0116) 252 5423
E-mail: nccsu@le.ac.uk

Jagger, Carol, BSc Leeds, MSc Leeds, PhD Leic.   Prof., Epidemiology

Research: boundaries in health and social care; economics of health and welfare; evaluation of community care policy/practice; inequalities in health and social care; population forecasting for community care needs

Historical Studies, School of

Tel: (0116) 252 2802 Fax: (0116) 252 3986
E-mail: histstud@le.ac.uk

Aston, Nigel R., BA Durh., DPhil Oxf., FRHistS   Reader

Ball, Stuart R., MA St And., PhD St And., FRHistS   Reader

Clapp, Elizabeth, BA Lond., PhD Lond., FRHistS   Sr. Lectr.

Coffey, John D., BA Camb., PhD Camb.   Reader

Colls, Robert M., BA Sus., DPhil York(UK)   Prof., English History

Cottrell, Phillip L., BSc Hull, PhD Hull   Prof., Financial History

Davies, Martin L., MA Oxf.   Reader

Dyer, Christopher C., BA Birm., PhD Birm., FBA, FSA, FRHistS   Prof., Regional and Local History

Gentilcore, David C., BA Tor., MA McM., PhD Camb.   Prof., Early Modern History

Gunn, Simon, BA Lanc., MA Lanc., PhD Manc.   Prof., Urban History

Housley, Norman J., MA Camb., PhD Camb., FRHistS   Prof., History; Head*

Lewis, George D. G., BA Newcastle(UK), MA Newcastle(UK), PhD Newcastle(UK)   Reader

Musgrave, Peter J., MA Camb., PhD Camb.   Sr. Lectr.

Prestel, Claudia, MA Munich, PhD Munich   Reader

Snell, Keith D. M., MA Camb., PhD Camb., FRAI   Prof., Rural and Cultural History

Story, Joanna, BA Durh., PhD Durh.   Sr. Lectr.

Sweet, Rosemary H., BA Oxf., DPhil Oxf., FSA, FRHistS   Prof., Urban History

Szejnmann, Chris C. W., BA Lond., PhD Lond.   Reader

Other Staff: 15 Lectrs.; 1 Hon. Sr. Lectr.; 21 Hon. Visiting Profs.; 1 Hon. Lectr.; 3 Hon. Fellows; 6 Hon. Univ. Fellows; 1 Hon. Univ. Res. Fellow

Research: contemporary history; modern economic history

History of Art and Film

Tel: (0116) 252 2866 Fax: (0116) 252 5128
E-mail: arthistory@le.ac.uk

Chapman, James, BA E.Anglia, MA E.Anglia, PhD Lanc.   Prof.

Ekserdjian, David P. M., BA Camb., MA Lond., PhD Lond.   Prof.; Head*

Lindley, Phillip G., MA Camb., PhD Camb., FSA   Reader

Other Staff: 3 Lectrs.

Research: British art 1700-1900; European art and architecture 1500-1770; European art 1890-1990; Gothic and Renaissance architecture and art; sculpture 1750-1914

Infection, Immunity and Inflammation

Tel: (0116) 252 2951 Fax: (0116) 252 5030
E-mail: sam20@le.ac.uk

Andrew, Peter W., BSc Wales, PhD Wales   Prof., Microbial Pathogenesis; Head*

Barer, Michael R., BSc Lond., MB BS Lond., MSc Lond., PhD Lond., FRCPath   Deputy Head; Prof., Clinical Microbiology

Barratt, Jonathan, BSc Manc., MB ChB Manc., PhD Leic.   Clin. Sr. Lectr.

Beardsmore, Caroline, BSc Lond., PhD Lond.   Sr. Lectr.

Bradding, Peter, DM S'ton.   Prof.

Brightling, Christopher, BSc Lond., MB BS Lond., PhD Leic.   Clin. Sr. Lectr.

Browning, Michael J., BSc Glas., BM BCh Oxf., PhD Glas.   Sr. Lectr.

Brunskill, Nigel J., MB ChB Leic., PhD Leic., FRCP   Sr. Lectr., Renal Medicine

Camp, Richard D. R., MB ChB Cape Town, PhD Lond., FRCP   Prof., Dermatology

Feehally, John, MB BS Lond., MA Oxf., DM Oxf., FRCP   Hon. Prof., Renal Medicine

Furness, Peter N., BA Camb., BM BCh Oxf., PhD Nott.   Hon. Prof., Renal Pathology

Grant, William D., BSc Edin., PhD Edin.   Prof.

Grigg, Jonathan M., BSc Lond., MB BS Lond., MD Lond., FRCPCH   Sr. Lectr.

Harris, Kevin P. G., MB BS Lond., MA Camb., MD Leic., FRCP   Reader

James, Roger F. L., BSc Sus., MSc Lond., PhD McG.   Reader

McCrae, Malcolm, BSc Edin., PhD Glas.   Hon. Prof., Microbiology

Nicholson, Karl G., MB BS Lond., MD Lond., FRCP   Prof., Infectious Diseases

Nicholson, Michael L., BMedSci Nott., BM BS Nott., MD Leic., FRCS   Prof., Transplant Surgery

O'Callaghan, Christopher L. P., BMedSci Nott., BM BS Nott., DM Nott., PhD Leic., FRCP, FRCPCH   Prof., Paediatrics

Ockleford, Colin D., BSc St And., PhD St And., FRCPath   Sr. Lectr.

Rajakumar, Kumar, MB BS Melb., MBiotech Monash, PhD Monash, FRCPA   Sr. Lectr.

Schwaeble, Wilhelm   Prof., Immunology

Topham, Peter, MB ChB Birm.   Sr. Lectr.

Wardlaw, Andrew J., BA Camb., MB BChir Camb., PhD Lond., FRCP   Dir., Inst. of Lung Health; Prof., Respiratory Medicine

Ziegler-Heitbrock, Hans W. L., MD Hamburg   Prof., Immunology

Other Staff: 7 Lectrs.; 2 Hon. Lectrs./Res. Fellows; 3 Hon. Lectrs.

Research: adult and childhood respiratory studies; infection and immunity studies; microbiology; renal studies

Labour Market Studies, Centre for

Tel: (0116) 252 5950 Fax: (0116) 252 5953
E-mail: clms1@le.ac.uk

Ashton, David N., BA Leic.   Emer. Prof.

Goodwin, John D., BSc Lough., PhD Leic.   Sr. Lectr.

Rainnie, Al F., BA York(UK), PhD Newcastle(UK)   Prof.; Chair*

Other Staff: 8 Lectrs.; 1 Sr. Res. Fellow; 2 Tutors; 4 Hon. Visiting Fellows

Research: academic practice and distance learning; employability and locality; skills, performance and development; work and worker organisation; youth transitions to work

Law

Tel: (0116) 252 2363 Fax: (0116) 252 5023
E-mail: law@le.ac.uk

Andenas, Mads, CandJur Oslo, MA Oxf., PhD Camb., DPhil Oxf.   Prof.

Bell, Mark, BA Ulster, PhD European Univ.Inst.   Reader

Bonner, David, LLB Leic., LLM W.Ont.   Prof.

Buck, Trevor G., LLB C.Lancs., LLM Lanc.   Sr. Lectr.

Clarkson, Christopher M. V., BA Cape Town, LLB Cape Town, LLM Lond.   Prof.

Cumper, Peter, LLB Belf., LLM Essex   Sr. Lectr.

Cygan, Adam J., LLB Middx., LLM Lond., PhD Lond.   Sr. Lectr.

Dromgoole, Sarah K., LLB S'ton., PhD S'ton.   Reader

Graham, Cosmo, BA Sus., LLM Lond.   Prof.

Kavanagh, Aileen, MA N.U.I., MLE Hanover, DPhil Oxf.   Reader
McHale, Jean V., LLB Manc., MPhil Manc.   Prof.
Minkkikken, Panu P., LLM Helsinki, LLD Helsinki   Prof.
Parry, Rebecca, LLB Sheff., MA Sheff., LLM Newcastle(UK), PhD Manc.   Sr. Lectr.
Shaw, Malcolm N., QC, LLB Liv., LLM Jerusalem, PhD Keele, FRGS   Sir Robert Jennings Prof., International Law
Snaith, Ian, BA Keele, MA Manc.   Sr. Lectr.; Nelsons Fellow
Szyszczak, Erika M., LLB Hull, LLM Exe., PhD Kent   Prof.
Thompson, Mark P., LLB Leic., LLM Keele   Prof.
White, Robin C. A., MA Oxf., LLM Virginia   Prof.; Head*
Other Staff: 32 Lectrs.; 1 Mahatma Gandhi Visiting Prof.; 18 Tutors†; 1 Hon. Visiting Fellow
Research: criminal law and criminal justice; employment law and labour law; European law, European convention on human rights; family law; health care law and ethics

Lifelong Learning, Leicester Institute of

Tel: (0116) 252 5911 Fax: (0116) 252 5909
E-mail: lifelonglearning@le.ac.uk
Benyon, John T., BA Warw.   Prof.
Dunne, Jackie, BA Liv., MA Warw.   Dir., Lifelong Learning; Head*
Poplawski, Richard P., BEd Derby, MA Wales, PhD Wales   Sr. Lectr.
Wheeler, Sue J., BA Newcastle(UK), MSc Warw., PhD Birm.   Prof.; Dir., Counselling and Psychotherapy
Other Staff: 3 Visiting Profs.; 3 Lectrs.; 1 Dir., Richard Attenborough Centre; 1 Dir. of Studies, Vaughan College; 1 Dir. of Studies, Northampton Centre; 1 Sr. Lectr.†; 1 Hon. Visiting Prof.; 1 Hon. Visiting Fellow
Research: adult and lifelong learning; counselling and psychotherapy; English (D. H. Lawrence); politics, law and order

Management, School of

Tel: (0116) 252 5520 Fax: (0116) 252 3949
E-mail: ulsm@le.ac.uk
Armstrong, Peter, BSc Brist., MSc Bath, PhD Brist.   Prof.
Arnold, Anthony, MSc Brad., PhD Lond., FCA   Prof.
Bátiz-Lazo, Bernardo, BSc(Econ) Mexico Natnl., MSc A.U.Barcelona, PhD Manc.   Sr. Lectr.
Bresnen, Mike J., BA Nott., PhD Nott.   Prof.
Brewis, Joanna, BSc UMIST, PhD UMIST   Reader
Brown, Stephen, BA Reading, PhD Reading   Prof.
Bryman, Alan E., BA Kent, MA Kent   Prof.; Head*
Burrell, W. Gibson, BA Leic., MPhil Leic., PhD Manc.   Prof.
Casey, Catherine, BA Waik., MA Waik., PhD Roch.   Prof.
Conway, Stephen, BSc Aston, MBA Aston, PhD Aston   Sr. Lectr.
Davies, Andrea, BSc Lanc., MA Warw., PhD Open(UK)   Sr. Lectr.
Fitchett, James, BSc Lanc., PhD Sterling   Reader
Fournier, Valerie, Maîtrise Grenoble, MBA Edin., PhD Manc.   Sr. Lectr.
Haven, Emmanuel, BA(Econ) McG., MA(Econ) McG., PhD C'dia.   Reader
Higgins, Matthew, BA W.England, MA W.England, PhD Keele   Sr. Lectr.
Jack, Gavin, BA H-W, PhD H-W   Reader
Jackson, Peter M., BA Strath., PhD Stir., FRSA, FCIM   Prof.
Jones, Campbell A., BA Auck., MCom Otago, PhD Keele   Sr. Lectr.
Keenoy, Thomas W., BA Strath., DPhil Oxf.   Prof.
Lightfoot, Geoffrey, BA Open(UK), MSc(Econ) Lond., PhD Kingston(UK)   Sr. Lectr.
Lilley, Simon D., BSc Lond., PhD Edin.   Reader
Parker, Martin, BA Sus., MA Lond., PhD Staffs.   Prof.
Saren, Michael, BA H-W, PhD Bath   Prof.

Other Staff: 20 Lectrs.; 5 Hon. Visiting Profs.; 2 Hon. Visiting Fellows
Research: accounting, finance and political economy; business ethics; knowledge and innovation; marketing and consumption; organisational theory

Mathematics and Computer Science, School of

Tel: (0116) 252 3884 Fax: (0116) 252 3915
E-mail: secretary@mcs.le.ac.uk

Computer Science

Crole, Roy, MA Camb., PhD Camb.   Sr. Lectr.
Erlebach, Thomas R., PhD Munich   Prof.
Fiaderio, Jose L., BSc Lisbon, PhD T.U.Lisbon   Prof.; Head*
Heckel, Reiko, PhD T.U.Berlin   Prof.
Raman, Rajeev B., BTech IIT Delhi, MSc Roch., PhD Roch.   Prof.
Thomas, Richard M., MA Oxf., MSc Oxf., DPhil Oxf., FBCS   Prof.
Ulidowski, Irek, BSc Lond., MSc Lond., PhD Lond.   Sr. Lectr.
Other Staff: 12 Lectrs.
Research: algebraic and categorical structures and methods; algorithm design, analysis and engineering; computational complexity and algebraic structures; deduction, rewriting and transformation; models of software intensive systems

Mathematics

Davidchack, Ruslan, PhD Kansas   Sr. Lectr.
Gorban, Alexander, MSc PhD   Prof.
Hunton, John R., MA Camb., PhD Camb.   Prof.
Leimkuhler, Ben J., BS Purdue, MS Ill., PhD Ill.   Prof.
Levesley, Jeremy, BSc Manc., PhD Coventry   Prof.; Head*
Marsh, Robert J., BA Oxf., MSc Warw., PhD Warw.   Reader
Snashall, Nicole J., MA Oxf., PhD Leic.   Sr. Lectr.
Tretyakov, Michael, MSc Ural State, PhD Ural State   Prof.
Other Staff: 5 Lectrs.
Research: applied mathematics (mathematical modelling, numerical analysis, scientific computing); pure mathematics (algebra, geometry, representative theory, topology)

Media and Communications

Tel: (0116) 252 3863 Fax: (0116) 252 5276
E-mail: cmcr@le.ac.uk
Dickinson, Roger D., BA CNAA, MA Leic.   Sr. Lectr.
Gibson, Rachel, BA Salf., PhD Texas   Prof.
Gunter, Barrie, BSc Wales, MSc Lond., PhD E.Lond.   Prof.; Head*
Youngs, Gillian, BA Sus., MA Sus., PhD Nott.Trent   Sr. Lectr.
Other Staff: 7 Lectrs.
Research: film; globalisation, new media and information society; media effects and audiences; political communication, international communication; science, health, risk and the environment

Medical and Social Care Education

Tel: (0116) 223 2946 Fax: (0116) 223 1585
E-mail: ns55@le.ac.uk
Anderson, Elizabeth S., BSc Lond., PhD Leic.   Sr. Lectr.
Gulamhusein, Amirali P., BSc Mak., PhD Lond.   Sr. Lectr.; Dir., Human Morphology
Hales, Jonathon M., BSc Birm., PhD Portsmouth   Sr. Lectr.
Hastings, Adrian, MB ChB Birm.   Sr. Lectr.
Heney, David, MB ChB Leeds, MD Leeds   Sr. Lectr.; Deputy Head
Lakhanpaul, Monica, MB BS   Sr. Lectr.
Law, Robert O., BSc Brist., MA Camb., PhD Brist.   Sr. Lectr.
Lennox, Angela I. A., MB BS Lond.   Sr. Lectr.; Head, Professnl. Devel. Unit
Owusu-Bempah, Kwame, BA Leeds, MA Leeds, PhD Lough.   Reader

Petersen, Stewart A., MA Camb., PhD Edin.   Prof., Medical Education; Head*
Smith, Roger S., MA Leic., PhD Leic.   Sr. Lectr.
Other Staff: 1 Assoc. Sr. Lectr.; 13 Lectrs.; 2 Assoc. Lectrs.; 10 Hon. Sr. Lectrs.; 2 Hon. Lectrs.; 16 Hon. Clin. Demonstrators
Research: medical education; social care

Medicine, School of

E-mail: dbb1@le.ac.uk
Lauder, Ian, MB BS Newcastle(UK), FRCPath, FMedSci   Dean of Sch.*
Research: coronary heart disease and hypertension; immunology of skin disease; molecular biology and cell signalling; pathogenesis of renal disease; vascular biology

Modern Languages, School of

Tel: (0116) 252 2662 Fax: (0116) 252 3633
E-mail: modern.lang@le.ac.uk
Kenworthy, H. Martin, BA Leeds, MA Leeds   Dir., Engl. Lang. Teaching Unit
Miller, A., BA Leeds, MA Lond., PhD Newcastle(UK)   Sr. Lectr.; Dir. of Studies, French
Penn, Sheldon, BA Nott., MA Nott., PhD Birm.   Lectr.; Dir. of Studies, Spanish
Spunta, M., DottLing&LettStran Bologna, MPhil Exe., PhD Birm.   Sr. Lectr.; Dir. of Studies, Italian
Wood, Sharon, BA Brist., PhD Brist.   Prof., Italian; Head*
Other Staff: 7 Lectrs.; 7 Lang. Tutors
Research: European cinema, film and popular culture; francophone studies and immigration studies; modern European literature and culture; theoretical and applied linguistics; women's studies

Museum Studies

Tel: (0116) 252 3963 Fax: (0116) 252 3960
E-mail: museum.studies@le.ac.uk
Hooper-Greenhill, Eilean R., BA Reading, MA Lond., PhD Lond., FRSA   Prof.
Knell, Simon J., BSc Leeds, MSc Manc., PhD Keele, FGS   Prof.; Head*
Pearce, Susan M., MA Oxf., PhD S'ton., FSA   Emer. (Assoc.) Prof.
Other Staff: 9 Lectrs.
Research: material culture studies; museum education and communication; museum history and historiography; museums and new technologies; museums as agents of social regeneration

Physics and Astronomy

Tel: (0116) 252 3575 Fax: (0116) 252 2770
E-mail: pmp4@le.ac.uk
Barstow, Martin A., BA York(UK), PhD Leic., FIP   Prof., Astrophysics and Space Science; Head*
Binns, Christopher R., BSc Leic., PhD Leic.   Prof., Nanoscience
Cowley, Stanley W. H., BSc Lond., PhD Lond.   Prof., Solar-Planetary Physics
Dehnen, Walter, PhD Heidel.   Prof.
Fraser, George W., BSc Aberd., PhD Leic.   Prof., Detector Physics
Gurman, Stephen J., BSc S'ton., PhD Camb.   Sr. Lectr.
Jameson, Richard F., MA Oxf., DPhil Oxf.   Sr. Lectr.
King, Andrew R., MA Camb., PhD Camb.   Prof., Astrophysics
Lester, Mark, BSc Sheff., PhD Sheff.   Prof., Solar Terrestrial Physics
Maksym, Piotr A., BA Camb., MSc Leic., PhD Warw.   Prof., Quantum Physics
Norris, Colin, BSc Reading, PhD Reading   Prof., Surface Physics
O'Brien, Paul, BSc Lond., PhD Lond.   Sr. Lectr.
Raine, Derek J., MA Camb., PhD Camb.   Sr. Lectr.
Remedios, John J., MA Oxf., DPhil Oxf.   Sr. Lectr.
Robinson, Terence R., BSc Birm., MSc Leic., PhD Leic.   Prof., Space Plasma Physics

Stewart, Gordon C., BSc St And., PhD St And.
Reader
Turner, Martin J. L., CBE, BSc Durh., PhD Durh.,
DSc Durh.   Hon. Prof.; Principal Res.
Fellow
Warwick, Robert S., BSc Birm., PhD Manc.
Prof., X-Ray Astronomy
Watson, Michael G., MA Oxf., MSc Sus., PhD
Leic.   Prof., High Energy Astrophysics
Willingale, Richard, BSc Camb., MSc Leic., PhD
Leic.   Sr. Lectr.
Wynn, Graham A., BSc Leic., PhD Leic.   Sr.
Lectr.
Yeoman, Timothy K., BSc Brist., DPhil York(UK)
Reader
Other Staff: 11 Lectrs.; 68 Res. Staff
Research: condensed matter physics; radio and
space plasma physics; space research;
theoretical astrophysics; X-ray and
observational astronomy

Politics and Industrial Relations

Tel: (0116) 252 2702 Fax: (0116) 252 5082
E-mail: politics@le.ac.uk
Berridge, Geoffrey, BA Durh., MA Sus., PhD
Durh.   Assoc. Prof., International Politics
Brace, Laura A., BA Manc., PhD Manc.   Sr.
Lectr.
Dumbrell, John, BA Camb., MA Keele, PhD Keele
Prof.
Garner, Robert W., BA Salf., MA Manc., PhD
Manc.   Reader
Henderson, Karen, BA Brad., MA Lond.   Sr.
Lectr.
Hyde-Price, Adrian G. V., BSc Wales, PhD Kent
Prof., Politics and International Relations;
Head*
Lynch, Philip L., BA Leeds, MA York(UK), PhD
Warw.   Sr. Lectr.
Other Staff: 7 Lectrs.
Research: African politics and international
relations; American foreign policy; British
and European politics; European and
international security; political theories of
state sovereignty, democracy and human
rights

Psychology

Tel: (0116) 252 2170 Fax: (0116) 252 2067
E-mail: psychology@le.ac.uk
Young, Andrew M. J., BSc Nott., PhD Birm.
Head*
Research: behavioural neuroscience; language,
perception and cognitive processes; social
and applied psychology

Taught Postgraduate Courses

Tel: (0116) 252 5057 Fax: (0116) 252 1057
E-mail: appliedpsych@le.ac.uk
Bull, Ray, BSc Exe., MSc Exe., DSc Portsmouth,
FBPsS   Prof., Forensic Psychology
Egan, Vincent, BSc Lond., PhD Edin.
Robertson, Noelle, MA Aberd.   Sr. Lectr.,
Clinical Psychology
Stammers, Robert B., BSc Hull, PhD Hull, FBPsS,
FErgS   Prof., Occupational Psychology
Wang, Michael   Prof.; Dir. Clin. Psychol.
Other Staff: 1 Sr. Lectr.; 7 Lectrs.; 3 Sr. Clin.
Tutors; 3 Clin. Tutors; 17 Hon. Lectrs.

Undergraduate Section

Tel: (0116) 229 7198 Fax: (0116) 229 7196
Beech, John R., BSc Lond., MPhil Reading, DPhil
Ulster, FBPsS   Sr. Lectr.
Boon, Julian, MA Aberd., PhD Aberd.   Sr. Lectr.
Colley, Anne M., BA Sheff., PhD Sheff.   Prof.
Colman, Andrew M., MA Cape Town, PhD
Rhodes, FBPsS   Prof.
De Lillo, Carlo, BSc Rome, PhD Edin.
Gillett, Raphael T., MA Glas., MSc Stir., PhD
Stir., FBPsS   Sr. Lectr.
Hollin, Clive R., BSc Lond., PhD Lond., FBPsS
Prof.
Jordan, Timothy R., BA Reading, PhD Reading
Prof.
Other Staff: 10 Lectrs.; 3 Hon. Lectrs.; 1 Hon.
Visiting Prof.; 1 Hon. Visiting Fellow

Sociology

Tel: (0116) 252 2750 Fax: (0116) 252 5259
E-mail: sociology@le.ac.uk
Annandale, Ellen C., BSc Leic., MA Brown, PhD
Brown   Sr. Lectr.
Bartram, David, BA Kenyon, MSc Wis., PhD Wis.
Hutchby, Ian, BA Middx., DPhil York(UK)
Lazaridis, Gabriella, BSc Leeds, MA Leeds, PhD
Brist.   Sr. Lectr.
Misztal, Barbara, MA Warsaw, PhD Warsaw
Prof.; Head*
Pilcher, Jane L., BSc Wales, PhD Wales   Sr.
Lectr.
Williams, John, BA Leic.   Sr. Lectr.
Other Staff: 4 Lectrs.; 1 Teaching Fellow
Research: sociological theory; sociology of body,
health, illness; sociology of children and
consumption; sociology of migration and
ethnicity; sociology of sport

SPECIAL CENTRES, ETC

American Studies, Centre for

Tel: (0116) 252 5009 Fax: (0116) 252 5213
E-mail: ljb11@le.ac.uk
Halliwell, Martin R., BA Exe., MA Exe., PhD
Nott.   Prof.; Dir.*
Other Staff: 1 Hon. Visiting Fellow
Research: gender, sexuality and race in US
literature and theory; modernism and the
city in culture; poetry, literature and society;
US film; US foreign policy, propaganda and
public diplomacy

Biological NMR Spectroscopy Centre

Tel: (0116) 252 2968 Fax: (0116) 223 1503
E-mail: gcr@le.ac.uk
Carr, Mark D., BSc Birm., DPhil Oxf.   Reader
Roberts, Gordon C. K., BSc Lond., PhD Lond.,
FRSChem, FMedSci   Prof.; Dir.*
Other Staff: 2 Lectrs.
Research: enzyme structure and function; nuclear
magnetic resonance (NMR) methods for
studying proteins; protein structure and
dynamics; structures of signalling proteins;
structures of target proteins for anti-bacterial
drug design

Cardiovascular Research Institute

Tel: (0116) 252 3182 Fax: (0116) 252 5847
E-mail: bw17@le.ac.uk
Williams, Bryan, BSc Lond., MB BS Lond., MD
Leic., FRCP   Prof., Medicine; Dir.*
Research: cardiovascular molecular genetics; ion
channel; vascular cell signalling

Diplomatic and International Studies, Centre for

Tel: (0116) 252 2797 Fax: (0116) 252 5082
E-mail: politics@le.ac.uk
Dumbrell, John, BA Camb., MA Keele, PhD Keele
Prof.; Dir.*

English Local History, Centre for

Tel: (0116) 252 2762 Fax: (0116) 252 5769
E-mail: elhinfo@le.ac.uk
Dyer, Christopher C., BA Birm., PhD Birm., FBA,
FSA, FRHistS   Prof., Regional and Local
History; Dir.*
Other Staff: 2 Univ. Fellows; 7 Hon. Visiting
Fellows
Research: identities and cultures in rural
communities; mediaeval rural economies
and landscapes; personal names and their
social and cultural significance; religion and
society in a local framework; settlement and
landscape

Environmental Research, Centre for (CERES)

E-mail: hb91@le.ac.uk
Balzter, Heiko, DrAgr Giessen   Prof.; Co-Dir.*
Pickerill, Jenny, BA Newcastle(UK), MSc Edin.,
PhD Newcastle(UK)   Co-Dir.*
Other Staff: 80 Academic and Res. Staff
Research: environmental futures; environmental
justice and equality; global energy security;

global environmental change; palaeo-
environmental change

History of Religious and Political Pluralism, Centre for the

Tel: (0116) 223 1899 Fax: (0116) 223 1899
E-mail: inparel@le.ac.uk
Bonney, Rev. Richard J., MA Oxf., DPhil Oxf.,
FRHistS   Prof.; Dir.*
Other Staff: 6 Hon. Visiting Fellows
Research: intercultural understanding;
international diplomacy, especially Indo-
Pakistan relations; international pluralism;
international security; world religions and
religious tension

Holocaust Studies, Stanley Burton Centre for

Tel: (0116) 252 2800 Fax: (0116) 252 3986
E-mail: history@le.ac.uk
Newman, Aubrey N., MA Glas., MA Oxf., DPhil
Oxf., FRHistS   Emer. Prof.; Assoc. Dir.
Szejnmann, Chris C. W., BA Lond., PhD Lond.
Reader; Dir.*
Other Staff: 2 Hon. Visiting Fellows
Research: Anglo-Jewry and the Holocaust;
Holocaust experiences in individual
European states; media studies (press and
radio); post-Holocaust experience
(restitution and resettlement); societies that
were destroyed

Postgraduate Medical Education, Centre for

Tel: (0116) 295 7639 Fax: (0116) 295 7640
1 Deputy Postgrad. Dean; 1 Assoc. Postgrad.
Dean; 1 Business Manager., Postgrad. Gen.
Practice Educn.; 2 Assoc. Advisers in Gen.
Practice; 6 Postgrad. Clin. Tutors
Vacant Posts: 1 Postgrad. Dean

Quebec Studies, Centre for

Tel: (0116) 252 2694 Fax: (0116) 252 3633
E-mail: cdr2@le.ac.uk
No staff at present

Research: art of Quebec; culture and society of
Quebec; literature of Quebec

Richard Attenborough Centre

Tel: (0116) 252 2455 Fax: (0116) 252 5165
E-mail: racentre@le.ac.uk
Milburn, Louisa J., BA Salf.   Dir.*
Other Staff: 1 Organising Tutor; 1 Univ.
Fellow

Sociology of Sport, Centre for the

Tel: (0116) 252 5929 Fax: (0116) 252 5720
E-mail: crss@le.ac.uk
Williams, John, BA Leic.   Sr. Lectr.; Dir.*
Research: sport, health, drugs, injury and sports
medicine; sport, violence and crowd
control; sports, careers and professionalism;
sports management; sports, race and
ethnicity

Space Research Centre

Tel: (0116) 252 3491 Fax: (0116) 252 2464
E-mail: rjd@star.le.ac.uk
Fraser, George W., BSc Aberd., PhD Leic.   Prof.,
Detector Physics; Dir.*
Research: bio-imaging; Earth observation science;
planetary science; X-ray and infrared
instrumentation for space astronomy

Tuscan Studies, Centre for

Tel: (0116) 252 2654 Fax: (0116) 252 3633
E-mail: tuscany@le.ac.uk
Ferzoco, George P., BA Tor., MA Trent   Lectr.;
Dir.*
Research: relations between Tuscany and the
anglophone world; Tuscan artistic, literary
and linguistic culture; Tuscan history and
society; Tuscan regional identity

University of Leicester Archaeological Services (ULAS)

Tel: (0116) 252 2848 Fax: (0116) 252 2614
E-mail: pnc3@le.ac.uk
Buckley, Richard J., BA Durh. Dir.*
Clay, Patrick N., BA Lanc., PhD Leic., FSA Dir.*
Research: archaeology of buildings; artefactual analysis; landscape archaeology; study of past environments; urban archaeology

Urban History, Centre for

Tel: (0116) 252 2378 Fax: (0116) 252 5769
E-mail: urbanhist@le.ac.uk
Rodger, Richard G., MA Edin., PhD Edin. Prof.; Dir.*
Other Staff: 1 Visiting Prof.; 1 Deputy Dir.; 1 Univ. Fellow; 4 Hon. Visiting Fellows
Research: European urban history; housing and urban planning since 1750; oral history in the twentieth century; urban culture and sociability; urban governance and power since 1700

Victorian Studies Centre

Tel: (0116) 252 3943 Fax: (0116) 252 2065
E-mail: vicstudies@le.ac.uk
Shattock, E. Joanne, BA New Br., MA Leeds, PhD Lond., Hon. DLitt New Br. Dir.*
Research: Dickens; literature and science; Victorian print culture; Victorian theatre; women's writing

CONTACT OFFICERS

Academic affairs. Academic Registrar: Williams, Katherine E., BA Reading (E-mail: registry@le.ac.uk)
Accommodation. Director of Residential and Conference Services: Stone, Frances (E-mail: accommodation@le.ac.uk)
Admissions (first degree). Principal Assistant Registrar (Admissions): Dnes, Jenny, BA Leic., MBA Aston (E-mail: admissions@le.ac.uk)
Admissions (higher degree). Principal Assistant Registrar (Graduate Office): Masterman, S. Louise, MA Manc. (E-mail: graduateoffice@le.ac.uk)
Adult/continuing education. Secretary (Adult/continuing education): (vacant) (E-mail: adulted@le.ac.uk)

Alumni. Graduate Relations Officer: Whitehurst, Kathryn J., BA Leic. (E-mail: kw42@le.ac.uk)
Archives. Archivist: Bettles, Mary E., BA Leic. (E-mail: meb16@le.ac.uk)
Careers. Head of Careers Service: Pennington, Martin J., BA Oxf. (E-mail: careers@le.ac.uk)
Conferences/corporate hospitality. Conference Sales and Marketing Manager: McRobbie, Sarah M. (E-mail: conferences@le.ac.uk)
Credit transfer. Principal Assistant Registrar (Admissions): Dnes, Jenny, BA Leic., MBA Aston (E-mail: admissions@le.ac.uk)
Distance education. Director of Distance Learning Administration: Christmas, David, BSc Warw., MBA Open(UK) (E-mail: graduate.office@le.ac.uk)
Equal opportunities. Head of Equal Opportunities and Staff Welfare: (vacant)
Estates and buildings/works and services. Director (Estates and buildings/works and services): Goffin, P. (E-mail: lmf8@le.ac.uk)
Examinations. Assistant Registrar (Examinations): Greenwood, Helen, BA Luton (E-mail: exams@le.ac.uk)
Finance. Director of Finance: Hunt, H. James, MA Oxf., MBA Warw.
General enquiries. Registrar and Secretary: Hall, David, BA (E-mail: registrar@le.ac.uk)
Health services. Director (Health services): Khunti, Prikash, MB ChB Dund.
Industrial liaison. Business Development Officer: Murray, Catherine M., BSc Salf. (E-mail: rbd@le.ac.uk)
International office. Director: Alexander, Suzanne, BA Birm., MBA Warw. (E-mail: international.office@le.ac.uk)
Language training for international students. Director of Languages Services Unit: Kenworthy, H. Martin, BA Leeds, MA Leeds (E-mail: mra@le.ac.uk)
Library (chief librarian). Librarian: Fyfe, Christine (E-mail: library@le.ac.uk)
Library (enquiries). Information Services Librarian: Rawlinson, Stephen, BSc S'ton. (E-mail: library@le.ac.uk)
Marketing. Marketing Director: Taylor, Richard, BA Durh. (E-mail: mrh18@le.ac.uk)
Minorities/disadvantaged groups. Head of Equal Opportunities and Staff Welfare: (vacant) (E-mail: mr20@le.ac.uk)

Minorities/disadvantaged groups. Head of Equal Opportunities and Staff Welfare: (vacant) (E-mail: mr20@le.ac.uk)
Ombudsman. Registrar and Secretary: Hall, David, BA (E-mail: registrar@le.ac.uk)
Personnel/human resources. Head of Personnel Office: Hall, Alison, BSc Liv., MA Leic., PhD Liv., FCIPD (E-mail: personnel@le.ac.uk)
Public relations. Director of Press and Public Relations: Mirza, Ather A., BA Leic. (E-mail: pressoffice@le.ac.uk)
Publications. Director of Press and Publications: Mirza, Ather A., BA Leic. (E-mail: pressoffice@le.ac.uk)
Research. Director (Research): Ward, David A., BSc Manc., PhD E.Anglia (E-mail: kamg1@le.ac.uk)
Safety. Director (Safety): Widdowson, David, BSc Newcastle(UK), PhD Sheff. (E-mail: pc22@le.ac.uk)
Scholarships, awards, loans. Assistant Registrar (Scholarships, awards, loans): Mann, Julia, BA Warw. (E-mail: registry@le.ac.uk)
Schools liaison. Senior Administrative Assistant (Schools liaison): Wetzig, Jacquelyn M. (E-mail: admissions@le.ac.uk)
Security. Security Officer: Monk, Ray (E-mail: rm72@le.ac.uk)
Sport and recreation. Manager (Sport and recreation): Hide, Colin P., BEd Warw., MA Birm. (E-mail: colin.hide@le.ac.uk)
Staff development and training. Director (Staff development and training): (vacant) (E-mail: sdu@le.ac.uk)
Student union. Union Manager: Kirk, Philip (E-mail: lusuweb@le.ac.uk)
Student welfare/counselling. Senior Student Welfare Officer: Taylor, Clare F., BA Leic. (E-mail: welfare@le.ac.uk)
Students from other countries. Director of the International Office: Alexander, Suzanne, BA Birm., MBA Warw. (E-mail: international.office@le.ac.uk)
Students with disabilities. Senior Student Welfare Officer: Taylor, Clare F., BA Leic. (E-mail: welfare@le.ac.uk)
Women. Head of Equal Opportunities and Staff Welfare: (vacant)

[Information supplied by the institution as at 29 January 2008, and edited by the ACU]

UNIVERSITY OF LINCOLN

Founded 1992

Member of the Association of Commonwealth Universities

Postal Address: Brayford Pool, Lincoln, England LN6 7TS
Telephone: (01522) 882000 **Fax:** (01522) 882088
URL: http://www.lincoln.ac.uk

VICE-CHANCELLOR*—Chiddick, Prof. David M., MSc Cran.IT, FRICS, FRSA
PRO-VICE-CHANCELLOR—Mannsaker, Frances, PhD Nott.
PRO-VICE-CHANCELLOR—Whittingham, Jim, PhD Sheff., BSc
PRO-VICE-CHANCELLOR—Saks, Prof. Mike, MA Kent, PhD Lond.
PRO-VICE-CHANCELLOR—Winston, Prof. Brian
UNIVERSITY REGISTRAR‡—(vacant)
DIRECTOR OF FINANCE—Avery, Stephen

GENERAL INFORMATION

History. The university was originally established as Hull School of Art (1861), later Humberside College of Higher Education (1982), and Humberside Polytechnic (1991). It achieved university status as the University of Humberside in 1992, was renamed

University of Lincolnshire and Humberside in 1996 and adopted its present name in 2001. It comprises one campus in Hull, three in Lincoln and a food science park in Holbeach.

Admission to first degree courses (see also United Kingdom Introduction). Through Universities and Colleges Admissions Service (UCAS). Minimum English language

requirements for international applicants: O Level/GCSE grade C, IELTS score 6.0, TOEFL score 550, TOEFL CBT score 215.

First Degrees (see also United Kingdom Directory to Subjects of Study) (* = with honours). BA, BA*, BSc, BSc*, LLB, LLB*.
Most courses last 3 years. Sandwich courses: 4 years.

Higher Degrees (see also United Kingdom Directory to Subjects of Study).

Master's. LLM, MA, MArch, MBA, MEd, MSc.

Admission. Applicants should normally hold an appropriate first degree with honours.

MA: also available by day release.

Length of course. Full-time: LLM, MA, MArch, MBA, MEd, MSc: 1 year. Part-time: LLM, MA, MArch, MBA, MEd: 1–3 years; MSc: 3 years.

Doctoral. DBA, EdD, PhD.

Admission. Applicants must normally hold a minimum of a second class honours degree or equivalent qualifications.

Length of course. Full-time: EdD: 1 year; PhD: 2–3 years. Part-time: EdD: 1–3 years; PhD: 4–6 years.

Libraries. Volumes: 250,000. Periodicals subscribed to: 1000.

FACULTIES/SCHOOLS

Art, Architecture and Design
Tel: (01522) 837177 Fax: (01522) 837155
Dean: Shacklock, Prof. Vincent

Business and Law
Tel: (01522) 886162 Fax: (01522) 886032
E-mail: lbs@lincoln.ac.uk
Dean: White, Don

Education Leadership, International Institute for (IIEL)
Tel: (01522) 886169 Fax: (01522) 886023
E-mail: fosullivan@lincoln.ac.uk
Dean: O'Sullivan, Fergus

Health, Life and Social Sciences
Tel: (01522) 886396 Fax: (01522) 886026
E-mail: rgoerisch@lincoln.ac.uk
Dean: McGaw, Prof. Brian

Media and Humanities
Tel: (01522) 886251 Fax: (01522) 886021
E-mail: rsherville@lincoln.ac.uk
Dean: McLaurin, Allen

Technology
Tel: (01522) 837381 Fax: (01522) 886974
E-mail: arixom@lincoln.ac.uk
Dean: Wilkinson, Prof. Graeme

ACADEMIC UNITS

Architecture
Tel: (01522) 837437 Fax: (01522) 837155
Arnold, Norman F. Sr. Lectr.
Chilton, John C., BSc Leeds, PhD CNAA Prof., Architectural Structures; Head*
Cottrell, Derek Sr. Academic
Earl, Andy Sr. Lectr.
Hay, Chris Sr. Lectr.
Hodges, David
Hyde, Phillip Sr. Lectr.
Locker, Pamela Sr. Lectr.
Lomholt, Jane Sr. Lectr.
Manoochehri, Jamileh Sr. Lectr.
Marquez, Carlos Sr. Lectr.
Matthews, Geoff Sr. Lectr.
Oakenfull, Michael Sr. Lectr.
O'Coill, Carl Sr. Lectr.
Sodagar, Behzad Sr. Lectr.
Squire, Paul Sr. Lectr.
Todd, David
Watt, Kathleen Sr. Lectr.
Wright, Richard Sr. Lectr.

Biological Sciences
Tel: (01522) 886396 Fax: (01522) 886026
E-mail: rgoerisch@lincoln.ac.uk
Baron, Mark Principal Lectr.
Birkett, Jason Lectr./Sr. Lectr.
Brown, Sarah Sr. Lectr.
Cooper, Jonathan Principal Lectr.
Cowell, Anthony Lectr./Sr. Lectr.
Curry, Mark Sr. Lectr.
Dixon, Ronald Principal Lectr.
Eady, Paul Sr. Lectr.

Fagbemi, Shamusi Sr. Lectr.
Gennard, Dorothy Principal Lectr.
Goodger, Simon Sr. Lectr.
Goodman, Adrian Lectr./Sr. Lectr.
Hall, Stephen Prof.; Head*
Locke, Nicholas Sr. Lectr.
Mills, Daniel Prof.
Morris, Anne Sr. Lectr.
Neville, Rachel Sr. Lectr.
Ruedisueli, Frank Sr. Lectr.
Smith, Peter Sr. Lectr.
Taylor, Tony Prof.
White, Peter Prof.

Corporate Strategy
Tel: (01522) 886162 Fax: (01522) 886032
E-mail: fcobaine@lincoln.ac.uk
Atherton, Andrew Prof., Entrepreneurship
Barnes, Ian Prof.; Head*
Blanchard, Kevin Sr. Lectr.
Clarke, Peter Sr. Lectr.
Flynn, John Sr. Lectr.
Gibbons, Stella Sr. Lectr.
Gray, David Sr. Lectr.
Harrison, Lynda Sr. Lectr.
Herron, Rebecca Sr. Lectr.
Howitt, Michael Sr. Lectr.
Landen, Ian Sr. Lectr.
Marchant, Alan Sr. Lectr.
McElwee, Ged Sr. Academic
Milner, Brian Principal Lectr.
Murphy, John Principal Lectr.
Murtagh, Thomas Sr. Lectr.
Myers, Malcolm Sr. Lectr.
Pliener, Martin Sr. Lectr.
Tether, Philip
Thompson, Timothy Sr. Lectr.
Varlow, Peter

Design
Tel: (01522) 837177 Fax: (01522) 837136
E-mail: jbird@lincoln.ac.uk
Atkinson-Dell, Peter Principal Lectr.
Bibby, Stewart Sr. Lectr.
Bramston, David Sr. Lectr.
Brown, Carol Principal Lectr.
Cheetham, Jonathon Sr. Lectr.
Diss, Daren Lectr./Sr. Lectr.
Dunne, Christopher Sr. Lectr.
Eastwood, Philip Sr. Lectr.
Elliott, Sarah Lectr./Sr. Lectr.
Etheridge, Judy Sr. Lectr.
Fabian, Timothy Sr. Lectr.
Finn, Mickey Sr. Lectr.
Franco, Omar Sr. Lectr.
Greenwood, John Sr. Lectr.
Healey, Michael Prof., Art and Design
Humphreys, Sarah Sr. Lectr.
Husband, Julie Sr. Lectr.
James, Keith Sr. Lectr.
Jeffery, Alan Sr. Lectr.
Lees, Heather Lectr./Sr. Lectr.
Lindenbaum, Ginny Sr. Lectr.
Lingwood, Gyles Lectr./Sr. Lectr.
Lock, Andrew Sr. Lectr.
Longworth, John Sr. Lectr.
Lord, John Sr. Lectr.
Maycroft, Neil Sr. Lectr.
McConachie, Robert Sr. Lectr.
McGurry, Judy Sr. Lectr.
Middleton, Paul Head*
Morley, Catherine Sr. Lectr.
Naylor, Maxine Prof.
Pemberton, Howard Sr. Lectr.
Puzzovio, Carolyn Principal Lectr.
Simpson, Neil Sr. Lectr.
Stocker, John Sr. Lectr.
Suckling, Roger Sr. Lectr.
Thomas, Alan Sr. Lectr.
Thomas, Susan Principal Lectr.
Tullett, Barrie Sr. Lectr.
Twells, Chloe Sr. Lectr.
Vickers, Richard, BA MSc Sr. Lectr., New Media
Waites, Ian Sr. Lectr.
Wolmark, Jenny Principal Lectr.

Educational Leadership, International Institute for
Tel: (01522) 886169 Fax: (01522) 886023
E-mail: fosullivan@lincoln.ac.uk
Bush, Tony Prof.
Dettman, Pamela Sr. Lectr.
Karran, Terence Sr. Academic
Lumby, Jacky Prof.
Morris, Aileen Sr. Lectr.
O'Sullivan, Fergus Dir.*
Scott, David, BA S'ton., MA Lond., PhD Warw. Prof.
Sood, Krishan Principal Lectr.
Wood, Linda Sr. Lectr.

Fine Art
Tel: (01522) 837177 Fax: (01522) 837155
E-mail: jbird@lincoln.ac.uk
Bingham, Jayne Head*
Charnley, Clare Sr. Lectr.
Edwards, Paul Lectr./Sr. Lectr.
Lamb, Francis
Miszewska, Anna Sr. Lectr.
O'Reilly, Oran
Phippard, Pat Sr. Lectr.
Plowman, John Sr. Lectr.
Ringe, Simon Sr. Lectr.

General Business and Law
Tel: (01522) 886162 Fax: (01522) 886032
E-mail: lbs@lincoln.ac.uk
Daglish, Andrew English Langs. Coordinator
Scott, Ian European Langs. Coordinator
White, Don Head*

Health and Social Care, School of
Tel: (01522) 886357 Fax: (01522) 886026
E-mail: ejubbs@lincoln.ac.uk
Bethell, Jackie Sr. Lectr.
Blackburn, Don Head*
Bower, Sue Sr. Lectr.
Clarke, Petra Sr. Lectr.
Clayton, John Principal Lectr.
Cobbold, Barbara Sr. Lectr.
Crawford, Karin Sr. Lectr.
Crimmens, David Principal Lectr.
Dagg, Jenny Sr. Lectr.
Davidson, Ian Sr. Lectr.
DeSiano-Plummer, Andy Sr. Lectr.
Flynn, Heather Sr. Lectr.
Franks, Paul Sr. Lectr.
Garvey, Sandra Sr. Lectr.
Golightly, Malcolm Head*
Griggs, Leonne Sr. Lectr.
Hine, Wendy Sr. Lectr.
Jarrell, Chris Sr. Lectr.
Khokher, Mohammed Sr. Lectr.
Kwhali, Josephine Sr. Lectr.
Lake, Margaret Sr. Lectr.
Lee, Philip Sr. Lectr.
McCavish, John Sr. Lectr.
Meng, Fanyi Sr. Lectr.
Ogley, Michael Sr. Lectr.
O'Sullivan, Terry Principal Lectr.
Page, Martin Sr. Lectr.
Petch, Anthony Sr. Lectr.
Rea, Carol Sr. Lectr.
Reilly, Ruth Co-ordinator, Continuing Professl. Devel.
Robertson, Colin Sr. Lectr.
Rogers, Jim Sr. Lectr.
Spencer, Rachel Sr. Lectr.
Stableford, Andrew Sr. Lectr.
Walker, Janet Sr. Lectr.
Wilkinson, Carol Principal Lectr.
Wilson, Lynne Sr. Lectr.

Human Resource Management
Tel: (01522) 886162 Fax: (01522) 886032
E-mail: lbs@lincoln.ac.uk
Agyeman, Samuel Sr. Lectr.
Brooke, Carole Reader
Currie, David Head*
Elsmore, Peter Principal Lectr.
Grimble, Maureen Sr. Lectr.
Johnson, Jennifer Lectr./Sr. Lectr.
Lamping, Tracy Sr. Lectr.
Loughlin, Linda Sr. Lectr.

Maksymiw, Wolodymir Sr. Lectr.
O'Brien, Paula Sr. Lectr.
Plumb, Kathleen Principal Lectr.
Thompson, Jane Sr. Lectr.
Valero-Silva, Nestor Sr. Lectr.

Journalism and Humanities

Tel: (01522) 886251 Fax: (01522) 886021
E-mail: amclaurin@lincoln.ac.uk
Adiseshiah, Sian Lectr./Sr. Lectr.
Byrne, Sandie Prof.
Dewerance, Peter Sr. Lectr.
Dixon, John Sr. Lectr.
Dubois, Diane Sr. Lectr.
Earley, Michael Prof., Drama
Gaughan, Michael Sr. Lectr.
Hildyard, Rupert Principal Lectr.
Hill, Kate Sr. Lectr.
Keeble, Richard Prof.
Kenyon, David Sr. Lectr.
Langran, Phillip Sr. Lectr.
Lewczuk, Alex A. Sr. Lectr.
Marlow, Chris Lectr./Sr. Lectr.
McLaurin, Allen Head*
Nayer, Bhaskaran Sr. Lectr.
Nield, Barbara Sr. Lectr.
Nuttall, Nicholas Sr. Lectr.
Ogunyemi, Olatunji Sr. Lectr.
Orange, Richard Sr. Lectr.
Packer, Ian Lectr./Sr. Lectr.
Pope, Steven Lectr./Sr. Lectr.
Redden, Guy Lectr./Sr. Lectr.
Redpath, Philip Sr. Lectr.
Russell, Bernie Sr. Lectr.
Shinner, Peter Lectr./Sr. Lectr.
Smejkalova, Jirina Sr. Lectr.
Swan, Philip Principal Lectr.
Tate, Alison Sr. Lectr.
Tulloch, John Prof.
Walker, Andrew Principal Lectr.
Welch, Catherine Lectr./Sr. Lectr.
Wilson, Deborah Sr. Lectr.
Ziegler, Harry Sr. Lectr.

Law

Tel: (01522) 886219 Fax: (01522) 886032
E-mail: bfitchett@lincoln.ac.uk
Barnes, Pam Principal Lectr.
Coggon, Brian Sr. Lectr.
Cutts, Lindsay Sr. Lectr.
Dennett, Anne Sr. Lectr.
Forbes, Malcolm Sr. Lectr.
Hall, Liz Sr. Lectr.
Porteous, Janette Sr. Lectr.
Ryland, Diane Sr. Lectr.
Stone, Prof. Richard Head*
Summan, Sandhla Sr. Lectr.
Whittle, Alan Principal Lectr.

Marketing

Tel: (01522) 886162 Fax: (01522) 886032
E-mail: lbs@lincoln.ac.uk
Ardley, Barry Sr. Lectr.
Chadd, Sara Sr. Lectr.
Cheeseman, Alison Sr. Lectr.
Corcoran, Andrew Sr. Lectr.
Cox, Val Head*
Davies, Frank Sr. Lectr.
DeBel, Marc Sr. Lectr.
Evans, David M. Sr. Lectr.
Evans, David P. Sr. Lectr.
Fan, Ying Principal Lectr.
Gannon, David Sr. Lectr.
Rahman, Mizanur Sr. Lectr.
Smith, Renate Sr. Lectr.
Taft, Malcolm Lectr./Sr. Lectr.
Taylor, Christopher Lectr./Sr. Lectr.
Taylor, Nick Principal Lectr.

Media Production

Tel: (01522) 886251 Fax: (01522) 886021
E-mail: jthompson@lincoln.ac.uk
Bellamy, Christine
Cairns, Barbara Head*
Cross, Simon Lectr./Sr. Lectr.
Forster, Marcella Lectr./Sr. Lectr.
Fowler, Ronald Lectr./Sr. Lectr.
Garland, Ros Sr. Lectr.

Harvey, Sylvia Prof.
Healy, Zara Lectr./Sr. Lectr.
Holden, John Sr. Lectr.
Kearns, Janice Lectr./Sr.Lectr.
Kendall, Neil Sr. Lectr.
Mason, Mike Sr. Lectr.
McKay, Andy Principal Lectr.
Morris, Nigel Sr. Lectr.
Nicholls, Tom Sr. Lectr.
O'Meara, Adam Sr. Lectr.
Reiners, Colin Principal Lectr.
Roach, Nancy Sr. Lectr.
Rudd, Bryan Sr. Lectr.
Sleight, David Sr. Lectr.
Sleight, Isabel Lectr./Sr. Lectr.
Tchernakova, Anna Sr. Lectr.
Verity, Adam

Policy Studies

Tel: (01522) 886084 Fax: (01522) 886026
E-mail: rgoerisch@lincoln.ac.uk
Bochel, Catherine Sr. Lectr.
Bochel, Hugh Prof.
Bond-Taylor, Sue Lectr./Sr. Lectr.
Bouandel, Youcef Sr. Lectr.
Briggs, Jacqueline Sr. Lectr.
Conversi, Daniele Sr. Lectr.
Foo, Yee Sr. Lectr.
Gordon, Janet Sr. Lectr.
Heslop, Joe Lectr./Sr. Lectr.
Jameson, Jill Sr. Lectr.
Jones, Kelvin Head*
Macdonald, Paul Sr. Lectr.
Maxwell, Maureen Sr. Lectr.
McCann, Liam Sr. Lectr.
Randerson, Claire Sr. Lectr.
Rust-Ryan, Alan Lectr./Sr. Lectr.
Somerville, Peter Prof.
Strange, Gerard Sr. Lectr.
Strudwick, Katie Sr. Lectr.
Walker, Carol Prof.

Psychology

Tel: (01522) 886396 Fax: (01522) 886026
E-mail: ejubbs@lincoln.ac.uk
Allinson, Lesley Sr. Lectr.
Bourke, Patrick Sr. Lectr.
Bromnick, Rachel Sr. Lectr.
Goddard, Paul Sr. Lectr.
Guo, Kun Sr. Lectr.
Hudson, John Sr. Lectr.
Hylton, Patrick Sr. Lectr.
Meints, Kerstin Sr. Lectr.
Pfeffer, Karen Sr. Lectr.
Robertson, Colin Sr. Lectr.
Slack, Jon Head*
Swallow, Brian Sr. Lectr.
van der Zee, Emile Principal Lectr.
Wilson, Garry Sr. Lectr.

Technology

Tel: (01522) 837381 Fax: (01522) 886974
E-mail: arixom@lincoln.ac.uk
Bird, Amanda Sr. Lectr.
Blaza, Sonia Sr. Lectr.
Cobham, David Sr. Lectr.
Doughty, Mark Sr. Lectr.
Farrall, Helen Sr. Lectr.
Garrigan, Brian Sr. Lectr.
Goodwin, Gerry Sr. Lectr.
Hamlin, John Sr. Lectr.
Hitchin, Linda Lectr./Sr. Lectr.
Hunter, Andrew Head*
Jacques, Kevin Sr. Lectr.
Lewak, John, MBA Sr. Lectr.
Packard, Paul Sr. Lectr.
Rank, Stephen Sr. Lectr.
Reeve, Paul Sr. Academic
Richardson, Philip Sr. Lectr.
Ross, Paul Sr. Lectr.
Shipley, Stephen Head, Media Technols.
Singer, George Sr. Lectr.
Spencer, Terence Principal Lectr.
Spilberg, Rose Sr. Lectr.
Williamson, Malcolm Sr. Lectr.

Tourism

Tel: (01522) 886395 Fax: (01522) 886032
E-mail: ahollick@lincoln.ac.uk
Bahaire, Tim Head*
Barnes, Pam Principal Lectr.
Bull, Adrian, BA Reading, PhD Griff. Principal Lectr.
Elliot-White, Martin Sr. Lectr.
Hughes, Heather Sr. Lectr.
Knight, Martin Sr. Lectr.
Lawson, Marie Sr. Lectr.
Rock, Paul Sr. Lectr.
Suddaby, Andrew Sr. Lectr.
Voase, Richard Sr. Lectr.
Wilson, Howard Principal Lectr.
Wright, Robin Sr. Lectr.

SPECIAL CENTRES, ETC

Enterprise and Entrepreneurial Development

Tel: (01522) 886927
Atherton, Andrew Dir.*

European Policy Research Centre

Tel: (01522) 886218
Barnes, Pam Dir.*

Food and Biological Sciences Research Centre

Tel: (01522) 886873
Taylor, Tony Dir.*

Graduate School

Tel: (01522) 886147
E-mail: gwilkinson@lincoln.ac.uk
Wilkinson, Prof. Graeme Dir.*

Health and Medical Psychology, Research Centre for

Tel: (01522) 886191
Slack, Jon Dir.*

Management Development, Hull Centre for

Tel: (01482) 311446 Fax: (01482) 311447
E-mail: ksanderson@lincoln.ac.uk
Collinson, Jill CIPD Programmes Coordinator
Dispenza, Vincenzo IMDP Programmes Coordinator
Nason, Francis J. Business Development and Corporate Programme

Policy Studies Research Centre

Tel: (01522) 886267
Somerville, Peter Dir.*

CONTACT OFFICERS

Academic affairs. University Registrar: (vacant)
Accommodation. Accommodation Manager: Ball, Michael (E-mail: mball@lincoln.ac.uk)
Admissions (first degree). Admissions and Customer Services Manager: Leggett, Christine (E-mail: admissions@lincoln.ac.uk)
Admissions (higher degree). Admissions and Customer Services Manager: Leggett, Christine (E-mail: admissions@lincoln.ac.uk)
Careers. Senior Careers Advisor: Jones, Mandy (E-mail: lhardman@lincoln.ac.uk)
Computing services. Director, Computing Services: Wheal, Adrian (E-mail: smurray@lincoln.ac.uk)
Conferences/corporate hospitality. Conference Officer: Bound, Maureen (E-mail: mbound@lincoln.ac.uk)
Estates and buildings/works and services. Director, Estates and Facilities: Mullaney, David (E-mail: crobertson@lincoln.ac.uk)
Finance. Director, Financial Services: Avery, Martin (E-mail: dshayler@lincoln.ac.uk)
General enquiries. Admissions and Customer Services Manager: Leggett, Christine (E-mail: enquiries@lincoln.ac.uk)
International office. Manager, International Recruitment: Mayer, Jacqueline (E-mail: jmayer@lincoln.ac.uk)

Library (chief librarian). Head of Learning Support: Anderson, Michelle (E-mail: phughes@lincoln.ac.uk)

Marketing. Director, Marketing: Cairns, Ian (E-mail: mmorgan@lincoln.ac.uk)

Personnel/human resources. Director, Human Resources: Taylor, Janet (E-mail: ldobricic@lincoln.ac.uk)

Public relations. Manager (Press and Media Relations): Ashberry, Jez (E-mail: jashberry@lincoln.ac.uk)

Quality assurance and accreditation. Head, Quality: Hanna, Jon (E-mail: quality@lincoln.ac.uk)

Safety. Health and Safety Manager: Wood, Rob (E-mail: rwood@lincoln.ac.uk)

Schools liaison. Education Liaison Manager: Raynes, Karen (E-mail: kraynes@lincoln.ac.uk)

Student welfare/counselling. Director, Student Services: Carey, Judith (E-mail: jcarey@lincoln.ac.uk)

Students with disabilities. Director, Student Services: Carey, Judith (E-mail: dart@lincoln.ac.uk)

[Information supplied by the institution as at 9 February 2005, and edited by the ACU]

UNIVERSITY OF LIVERPOOL

Founded 1903

Member of the Association of Commonwealth Universities

Postal Address: Liverpool, England L69 7ZX
Telephone: (0151) 794 2000 **Fax:** (0151) 708 6502
URL: http://www.liv.ac.uk

VICE-CHANCELLOR*—Newby, Sir Howard, CBE, KB, BA Essex, PhD Essex, Hon. DLitt CNAA, Hon. DLitt Portsmouth, Hon. DLitt S.Bank, Hon. DLitt Sur., Hon. DLitt Ulster

DEPUTY VICE-CHANCELLOR—Dockray, Prof. Graham J., BSc Nott., PhD Nott., FMedSci, Hon. FRCP

PRO-VICE-CHANCELLOR—Belchem, Prof. John C., BA Sus., DPhil Sus., FRHistS, FRSA

PRO-VICE-CHANCELLOR—Caldwell, Prof. John, BPharm Lond., PhD Lond., DSc Lond., FIBiol

PRO-VICE-CHANCELLOR—Saunders, Prof. Jon R., BSc Brist., PhD Brist.

CHIEF OPERATING OFFICER‡—Calvert, Ronald, BSc Newcastle(UK), MBA Newcastle(UK)

DIRECTOR OF FINANCE—Yuille, Michael G. S., BAcc Glas.

ACADEMIC SECRETARY—Jones, Catherine M., BA Liv.

DIRECTOR OF FACILITIES MANAGEMENT—Hackett, Patrick

DIRECTOR OF HUMAN RESOURCES—Rutherford, Susan J., BSc Leic.

GENERAL INFORMATION

History. The university was originally established in 1881 as University College, Liverpool, in response to a petition presented on behalf of the citizens of Liverpool, and gained university status in 1903.

Most of the university's buildings are located near the centre of Liverpool.

Admission to first degree courses (see also United Kingdom Introduction). Normally General Certificate of Education (GCE), A levels or equivalents (eg. International Baccalaureate, Malaysian STPM, Hong Kong A levels). Each course has its own formal entry requirements, which may include literacy and numeracy components. An international foundation year is available to students from countries whose high school graduation standard falls short of GCE A level. Candidates whose first language is not English must provide evidence of proficiency in English, such as the British Council IELTS test.

First Degrees (see also United Kingdom Directory to Subjects of Study). BA, BDS, BEng, BN, BSc, BTh, BVSc, LLB, MB ChB.

Length of course. Full-time: BN, LLB: 3 years; BA, BEng, BSc: 3–4 years; BDS: 5 years; BVSc, MB ChB: 5–6 years. Part-time: BA, BSc, LLB: 7 years.

Higher Degrees (see also United Kingdom Directory to Subjects of Study).

Master's. ChM, LLM, MA, MArch, MBA, MCD, MChOrth, MCommH, MDentSci, MDS, MIHR, MPhil, MRes, MSc.

Admission. Applicants for admission to master's degree courses must normally hold an appropriate first degree with at least second class honours; equivalent professional experience may be acceptable in some cases.

Length of course. Full-time: LLM, MA, MBA, MCommH, MDentSci, MPhil, MRes, MSc: 1 year; MCD, MIHR: 2 years. Part-time: LLM, MA, MBA, MPhil, MRes, MSc: 2 years; MDentSci: 2–6 years; MCD: 3 years. By distance learning: MBA, MSc: 1–6 years.

Doctoral. DClinPsychol, DEng, DLitt, DSc, DVSc, LLD, MD, PhD.

Admission. Applicants for admission to PhD must normally hold an appropriate first degree with at least second class honours or equivalent overseas qualification; equivalent professional experience may be acceptable in some cases. DEng, DLitt, DSc, DVSc, LLD: awarded on the basis of published work to graduates of this university of at least 7 years' standing.

Length of course. Full-time: MD: 1–6 years; PhD: 2 years; DClinPsychol: 3 years. Part-time: PhD: 4–7 years.

Language of Instruction. English. Intensive pre-sessional courses available through Applied English Language Studies Unit.

Libraries. Volumes: 1,860,000. Periodicals subscribed to: 7600. Special collections: Cunard Steamship Company; Gypsy (including archive of Gypsy Lore Society); John Wyndham (manuscripts including unpublished typescripts and letters); mediaeval and early Renaissance manuscripts; Science Fiction Foundation; social work (including Barnado's); Stapledon (life and works of Olaf Stapledon).

Statistics. Students (2005–2006): full-time 15,338 (7126 men, 8212 women); part-time 3458 (1439 men, 2019 women); international 1861 (1072 men, 789 women); undergraduate 14,248 (6546 men, 7702 women); master's 1314 (590 men, 724 women); doctoral 1328 (697 men, 631 women).

FACULTIES/SCHOOLS

Arts
Tel: (0151) 794 2458 Fax: (0151) 794 3646
E-mail: wilderc@liv.ac.uk
Dean: Hoey, Prof. Michael P., BA Lond., PhD Birm., AcSS
Sub-Dean: Wilde, Richard C., BA Nott.

Dental Sciences, School of
Tel: (0151) 706 5203 Fax: (0151) 706 5845
E-mail: deandent@liv.ac.uk

Dean: Pine, Prof. Cynthia M., CBE, BDS Manc., MBA Dund., PhD Manc., FDSRCS
School Administrator: James, David G., BA Brad.

Engineering
Tel: (0151) 794 4922 Fax: (0151) 794 3646
E-mail: steve.smitton@liv.ac.uk
Dean: Owen, Prof. Ieuan, BSc Wales, PhD Wales, FIMechE
Sub-Dean: Clarkson, Paul

Medicine
Tel: (0151) 706 4275 Fax: (0151) 706 5667
E-mail: deanmed@liv.ac.uk
Dean: Caldwell, Prof. John, BPharm Lond., PhD Lond., DSc Lond., FIBiol
Faculty Secretary: Smith, Stephen C., MA Camb.

Science
Tel: (0151) 794 3648 Fax: (0151) 794 3646
E-mail: clarkson@liv.ac.uk
Dean: Holloway, Prof. Stephen, BSc Leic., PhD Leic.
Sub-Dean: Clarkson, Paul

Social and Environmental Studies
Tel: (0151) 794 2427 Fax: (0151) 794 2465
E-mail: deanses@liv.ac.uk
Dean: Sadler, Prof. David, BA Durh., PhD Durh.
Sub-Dean: Wilde, Richard C., BA Nott.

Veterinary Science
Tel: (0151) 794 4797 Fax: (0151) 794 7279
E-mail: deanvets@liv.ac.uk
Dean: Trees, Prof. A. J. (Sandy), BVM&S Edin., PhD Edin.
Assistant Registrar: Jones, Sheila A., BA Sheff.

ACADEMIC UNITS

Archaeology, Classics and Egyptology, School of
Tel: (0151) 794 5044 Fax: (0151) 794 5057
E-mail: p.sweetingham@liv.ac.uk
Adams, Colin E. P., BA Belf., DPhil Oxf. Sr. Lectr.

Baird, Douglas D., MA Edin., PhD Edin.   Sr.
Lectr.
Barham, Lawrence S., BA Texas, MA Penn., PhD
Penn.   Prof.
Collier, Mark A., BA Lond., PhD Lond.   Sr. Lectr.
Eyre, Christopher J., MA Oxf., DPhil Oxf.   Prof.
Gibson, Bruce J., MA Oxf., DPhil Oxf.   Prof.
Gowlett, John A. J., MA Camb., PhD Camb.
Prof.
Harrison, Thomas E. H., BA Oxf., MA Oxf.,
DPhil Oxf.   Rathbone Prof., Ancient History
and Classical Archaeology; Head*
Jones, Fred M. A., BA Newcastle(UK), MA Leeds,
PhD St And.   Sr. Lectr.
Latham, Alf G., BSc Leeds, MSc Leeds, PhD McM.
Sr. Lectr.
Mee, Christopher B., BA Brist., PhD Lond.
Charles W. Jones Prof., Classical
Archaeology
Oliver, Graham J., BA Oxf., DPhil Oxf.   Sr.
Lectr.
Routledge, Bruce E., BA W.Laur., MA Tor., PhD
Tor.   Sr. Lectr.
Shaw, I. M. E., MA Camb., PhD Camb.   Sr.
Lectr.
Shaw, John, BSc Liv., PhD Liv.   Prof.
Sinclair, Anthony G. M., MA Camb., PhD Camb.
Sr. Lectr.
Slater, Elizabeth A., MA Camb., PhD Camb.
Garstang Prof., Archaeology
Snape, Steven R., BA Liv., PhD Liv.   Sr. Lectr.
Taylor, Joan J., BA Penn., PhD Camb.   John
Rankin Reader
Tuplin, Christopher J., MA Oxf., DPhil Oxf.
Prof.
Other Staff: 17 Lectrs.; 5 Res. Fellows; 4 Hon.
Sr. Fellows; 20 Hon. Res. Fellows
Research: archaeological science; archaeology of
human origins; archaeology of the
Mediterranean; Egyptology; Near Eastern
neolithic studies

Architecture, School of
Tel: (0151) 794 2606 Fax: (0151) 794 2605
E-mail: rufus@liv.ac.uk
Bandyopadhyay, Soumyen, BArch Calc., MArch
Liv., PhD Liv.   Sr. Lectr.
Brown, André G. P., MEng Liv.   Prof.
Carter, David J., MSc Manc., PhD Liv.   Reader
Dunster, David, BA Lond.   Roscoe Prof.,
Architecture
Gibbs, Barry M., BSc Sheff., MA Sheff., PhD Aston
Prof., Acoustics
Harris, Jonathan P., BA Sus., PhD CNAA   Prof.
Hopkins, Carl, BEng Salf., PhD H-W   Sr. Lectr.
Jackson, Neil M. T., PhD CNAA, FSA   Prof.
Kronenburg, Robert H., BA CNAA, MPhil Manc.,
PhD Liv.J.Moores   Prof.; Head*
Oldham, David J., MSc Manc., DPhil York(UK)
Prof., Building Engineering
Pepper, Simon M., PhD Essex, FSA, FRSA   Prof.
Sibley, Magda, BA Algiers, MArch Algiers, PhD
Sheff.   Sr. Lectr.
Other Staff: 1 Visiting Prof.; 7 Lectrs.; 1
Fellow; 1 Hon. Sr. Fellow; 3 Hon. Res.
Fellows
Research: contemporary design and technical
innovation; environmental engineering
(acoustics, lighting); history of art and
architecture

Biological Sciences, School of
Tel: (0151) 795 4400 Fax: (0151) 795 4414
E-mail: biolhos@liv.ac.uk
Atkinson, David, BSc Wales, PhD Wales   Sr.
Lectr.
Barraclough, Barry R., BSc Leeds, PhD Leeds
Reader
Bates, Andy D., BA Camb., PhD Nott.   Sr. Lectr.
Begon, Michael E., BSc Leeds, PhD Leeds   Prof.,
Ecology
Brophy, P. M., BSc Stir., PhD Wales   Reader
Caddick, Mark X., BSc Liv., PhD Newcastle(UK)
Reader
Cossins, Andrew R., BSc Durh., PhD Durh.
Prof., Animal Genomics
Dunbar, Robin I. M., BA Oxf., PhD Brist., FBA
Prof., Psychology

Edwards, Clive, BSc Wales, PhD Wales   Prof.,
Microbiology
Edwards, Steven W., BSc Wales, PhD Wales
Prof., Biochemistry; Head*
Fernig, David G., BSc Brist., PhD Nott.   Prof.
Frid, Christopher L. J., BSc Wales, MSc S'ton.,
PhD E.Anglia   Prof., Marine Biology
Hall, Neil, BSc Liv., PhD Liv.   Prof.
Hurst, Greg, BA Camb., PhD Camb.   Prof.
Jones, Meriel G., BSc Brist., MSc City(UK), PhD
Lond.   Sr. Lectr.
Jones, N. J., BSc Wales, PhD CNAA   Sr. Lectr.
Kemp, Stephen J., BSc Edin., PhD Edin.   Prof.,
Molecular Genetics
Lian, Lu-Yun, BSc W.Aust., MBA Open(UK), PhD
Warw.   Prof., Structural Biology
Marrs, Robert H., BA Stir., PhD Stir., DSc Stir.,
FIBiol   Bulley Prof., Applied Plant Biology
McCarthy, Alan J., BSc Bath, PhD Brad.   Prof.,
Microbiology
McLennan, Alexander G. (Sandy), BSc Glas.,
PhD Aberd., FIBiol   Prof., Biochemistry
Merry, Brian J., BSc Hull, MSc Leeds, PhD Hull
Reader
Middleton, D. A., BSc CNAA, DPhil Oxf.
Reader
Montagnes, David J. S., BSc Guelph, MSc Guelph,
PhD Br.Col.   Sr. Lectr.
Mortimer, A. Martin, BSc Wales, PhD Wales
Prof.
Moss, Brian, BSc Brist., PhD Brist., DSc Brist.,
FIBiol   Holbrook Gaskell Prof., Botany
Parker, Geoffrey A., BSc Brist., MA Camb., PhD
Brist., FRS   Derby Prof., Zoology
Rees, Huw H., BSc Wales, PhD Wales   Prof.,
Biochemistry
Rudland, Philip S., MA Camb., PhD Camb.,
FRCPath, FIBiol   Prof., Biochemistry
Saccheri, Ilik J., BSc Edin., PhD Lond.   Sr. Lectr.
Saunders, Jonathan R., BSc Brist., PhD Brist.
Prof., Microbiology
Speed, Mike P., MSc Leeds, PhD Leeds   Sr. Lectr.
Stanisstreet, Martin, BSc S'ton., PhD Brist.   Sr.
Lectr.
Thompson, David J., BA York(UK), DPhil
York(UK)   Prof.
Tomsett, A. Brian, BSc Sheff., PhD Camb.   Prof.,
Genetics
Turnbull, Jeremy E., BSc Wales, PhD Manc.
Prof.
Turner, Philip C., BSc Leeds, PhD Edin.   Sr.
Lectr.
White, Michael R. H., BA Oxf., PhD Lond.
Prof.
Wilkinson, Mark C., BSc Wales, PhD Wales   Sr.
Lectr.
Other Staff: 9 Visiting Profs.; 30 Lectrs.; 3
Fellows; 5 Univ. Teachers†; 1 Hon. Lectr.;
12 Hon. Sr. Fellows; 11 Hon. Res. Fellows
Research: behavioural ecology and evolutionary
psychology; conservation biology;
evolutionary biology; host-parasite biology;
marine and freshwater systems

Chemistry
Tel: (0151) 794 3572 Fax: (0151) 794 3588
E-mail: hodchem@liv.ac.uk
Aspinall, Helen C., BSc Lond., PhD Lond.   Sr.
Lectr.
Brust, Mathias, PhD Liv.   Prof.
Carnell, Andrew J., BSc Kent, PhD Exe.   Sr.
Lectr.
Cooper, Andrew I., BSc Nott., PhD Nott.   Prof.
Cooper, David L., BA Oxf., DPhil Oxf.   Reader
Cosstick, Richard, BSc Birm., PhD Birm.   Reader
Darling, George R., BSc Lond., PhD Lond.   Sr.
Lectr.
Evans, P. Andrew, BSc CNAA, PhD Camb.
Heath Harrison Prof., Organic Chemistry
Greeves, Nicholas, MA Camb., PhD Camb.   Sr.
Lectr.
Higgins, Simon J., BA S'ton., PhD S'ton.   Reader
Hodgson, Andrew, BA Camb., PhD Lond.   Prof.
Hofer, Werner A., MSc T.U.Vienna, PhD
T.U.Vienna   Prof.
Holloway, Stephen, BSc Leic., PhD Leic.   Prof.,
Chemical Physics
Iggo, J. A., BA Camb., PhD Camb.   Sr. Lectr.

Jones, Anthony C., BSc Manc., PhD Manc.,
FRSChem   Prof.
Kozhenikov, Ivan V., PhD DSc   Reader
Nichols, Richard J., BSc S'ton., PhD S'ton.   Prof.
O'Neil, Ian A., BSc Lond., PhD Lond.   Reader
O'Neill, Paul M., BSc Liv., PhD Liv.   Prof.
Persson, Mats, MSc Chalmers U.T., PhD Chalmers
U.T.   Prof.
Raval, Rasmita, BA Camb., PhD E.Anglia   Prof.
Rosseinsky, Matthew J., BA Oxf., DPhil Oxf.
Prof., Inorganic Chemistry
Stachulski, Andrew V., MA Camb., PhD Camb.,
FRSChem   Sr. Lectr.
Steiner, Alexander, PhD Gött.   Sr. Lectr.
Xiao, Jianliang, BSc Northwest(Xi'an), MSc Beijing,
PhD Alta.   Prof.
Other Staff: 7 Visiting Profs.; 11 Lectrs.; 2
Univ. Teachers; 4 Hon. Lectrs.; 9 Hon. Sr.
Fellows
Research: catalysis; inorganic, solid state and
polymeric materials; organic chemistry
(chemistry/biology interface); physical
chemistry and nanoscale science; surface
science

Civic Design
Tel: (0151) 794 3108 Fax: (0151) 794 3125
E-mail: sueedwds@liv.ac.uk
Batey, Peter W. J., BSc Sheff., MCD Liv., PhD
Liv., FRTPI, FRSA   Lever Prof., Town and
Regional Planning
Brown, Peter J. B., BEng Liv., MCD Liv., PhD
Liv.   Sr. Lectr., Transport Studies
Fischer, Thomas B., PhD Manc.   Reader
Kidd, Susan J., BA CNAA, MA CNAA   Sr. Lectr.
Lloyd, Michael G., BA Sheff., MSc Aberd.   Prof.,
Planning
Shaw, David P., BA Manc., PhD Wales   Sr.
Lectr.; Head*
Other Staff: 3 Lectrs.; 2 Fellows; 1 Univ.
Teacher†; 1 Hon. Sr. Fellow
Research: institutional capacity building and the
modernisation of planning practices;
methods for analysis, evaluation and impact
assessment

Computer Science
Tel: (0151) 794 3670 Fax: (0151) 794 3715
E-mail: generalenquiries@csc.liv.ac.uk
Bench-Capon, Trevor J. M., BA Oxf., MPhil
Oxf., DPhil Oxf.   Prof.; Head*
Coenen, Frans P., BSc CNAA, PhD CNAA   Sr.
Lectr.
Diaz, Bernard M., BSc Lond., PhD Lond.   Sr.
Lectr.
Dixon, Clare L., BSc Hull, MSc Manc., PhD Manc.
Sr. Lectr.
Dunne, Paul E., BSc Edin., PhD Warw.   Reader
Fisher, Michael D., BSc Manc., MSc Manc., PhD
Manc.   Prof.
Gasieniec, Leszek A., MA Warsaw, PhD Warsaw
Prof.
Goldberg, Leslie A., BA Rice, PhD Edin.   Prof.
Goldberg, P., BA Oxf., MSc Edin., MSc Paris XI,
PhD Edin.   Reader
Hustadt, Ullrich, DrIng Saar   Sr. Lectr.
Kowalski, Dariusz R., MSc Warsaw, PhD Warsaw
Sr. Lectr.
Leng, Paul H., BSc Lond., MSc Liv.   Prof., e-
Learning
McBurney, Peter J., BA Canberra, PhD Liv.   Sr.
Lectr.
van der Hoek, Wiebe, BSc Gron., PhD Utrecht
Prof.
Wolter, Frank, PhD F.U.Berlin   Prof.
Wooldridge, Michael J., BSc CNAA, PhD Manc.
Prof.
Other Staff: 1 Visiting Prof.; 15 Lectrs.; 1 Hon.
Lectr.; 3 Hon. Sr. Fellows
Research: agents; algorithmics and complexity
theory; computational biology; logic and
computation

Cultures, Languages and Area Studies, School of
Tel: (0151) 794 2775 Fax: (0151) 794 2785
E-mail: sml@liv.ac.uk
Rosenhaft, Eve, BA McG., PhD Camb.   Prof.;
Head*

French

Tel: (0151) 794 2741 Fax: (0151) 794 2357
E-mail: french@liv.ac.uk
Chadwick, Kay, BA Hull, MA Hull, PhD Hull
Sr. Lectr.
Croenen, Godfried, MA Ghent, PhD Ghent,
FRHistS Sr. Lectr.
Forsdick, Charles, BA Oxf., PhD Lanc. James
Barrow Prof.
Waller, Richard E. A., MA Oxf., DPhil Oxf. Sr.
Lectr.
Other Staff: 6 Lectrs.; 2 Tutors; 3 Hon. Sr.
Fellows; 1 Hon. Res. Fellow
Research: eighteenth-century studies; French
theatre, cinema and travel literature;
mediaeval studies; modern and
contemporary France; post-colonial
francophone studies

German

Tel: (0151) 794 2352 Fax: (0151) 794 2307
E-mail: german@liv.ac.uk
Rosenhaft, Eve, BA McG., PhD Camb. Prof.
Simpson, James, BA Liv., PhD Liv. Sr. Lectr.
Other Staff: 3 Lectrs.; 1 Tutor; 2 Hon. Sr.
Fellows; 2 Hon. Res. Fellows
Research: development of East and West
Germany since 1945; gender and women's
history; German cinema; post-1750 literary
and cultural studies; race and ethnicity
(including 'gypsy' studies)

Hispanic Studies

E-mail: lynnf@liv.ac.uk
Marfany, Joan-Luis, LicenFil&Let Barcelona, PhD
Barcelona Reader, Spanish and Catalan
Severin, Dorothy S., AM Harv., PhD Harv., FSA
Gilmour Prof., Spanish
Shaw, L., BA Salf., PhD Liv. Reader
Wright, Roger H. P., MA Oxf., BLitt Oxf., PhD
Liv. Prof., Spanish
Other Staff: 5 Lectrs.; 1 Tutor; 2 Univ.
Teachers; 2 Hon. Sr. Fellows
Research: Spanish, Catalan and Portuguese
literature; Spanish cinema; Spanish
linguistics/philology; Spanish-American and
Portuguese-African literature

Italian

Tel: (0151) 794 2352 Fax: (0151) 794 2307
1 Lectr.; 1 Univ. Teacher; 2 Hon. Sr. Fellows
Research: dialectology; language and nationalism;
linguistics/sociolinguistics

Latin American Studies

Tel: (0151) 794 3079 Fax: (0151) 794 3080
E-mail: smurph@liv.ac.uk
Fisher, John R., BA Lond., MPhil Lond., PhD Liv.,
FRHistS Prof., Latin American History
Rubenstein, Steven, BA Col., MA Col., PhD Col.
Reader
Taylor, Lewis, BA Sheff., BPhil Liv., PhD Liv.
Sr. Lectr.
Other Staff: 3 Lectrs.; 3 Fellows; 1 Univ.
Teacher†; 3 Hon. Sr. Fellows; 5 Hon. Res.
Fellows
Research: comparative American s udies;
economic history; linguistics and literature;
politics; social anthropology and sociology

University Languages Centre

Tel: (0151) 794 2731 Fax: (0151) 794 2748
E-mail: j.maher@liv.ac.uk
1 Lang. Adviser

Earth and Ocean Sciences

Tel: (0151) 794 5146 Fax: (0151) 794 5196
E-mail: h.kokelaar@liv.ac.uk
Boyle, Alan P., BSc Wales, MSc Oxf., PhD Wales,
FGS Sr. Lectr.
Elliott, Trevor, BSc Wales, DPhil Oxf. George
Herdman Prof., Geology
Flint, Steven S., BSc Aston, PhD Leeds Prof.
Holme, Richard T., BA Camb., SM M.I.T., PhD
Harv. Sr. Lectr.
Kokelaar, B. Peter, BSc Wales, MSc Oxf., PhD
Wales Reader

Kusznir, Nicholas J., BSc Durh., PhD Durh.
Prof., Geophysics
Leach, Harry, BSc Leeds, PhD Leeds Sr. Lectr.
Marshall, James D., BSc Sheff., PhD Leic. Prof.
Piper, John D. A., BSc Brist., PhD Lond. Reader
Preston, Martin R., BSc Liv., PhD Liv. Sr.
Lectr.
Prior, David J., BSc Wales, PhD Leeds Prof.;
Head*
Rietbrock, Andreas, DrRerNat Munich Reader
Shaw, John, BSc Liv., PhD Liv. Prof.
Thomas, Christine, BSc Marburg, MSc Erlangen-
Nuremberg, PhD Gött. Sr. Lectr.
van den Berg, C. M. G. (Stan), MSc Wageningen,
PhD McM. Prof.
Wheeler, John, BA Camb., PhD Leeds Prof.
Williams, Richard G., BSc Brist., MSc Lond., PhD
E.Anglia Prof.
Wolff, George A., BSc Brist., PhD Brist. Prof.,
Oceanography; Head*
Worden, Richard, BSc Manc., PhD Manc.
Reader
Other Staff: 20 Visiting Profs.; 4 Lectrs.; 5
Fellows; 12 Hon. Sr. Fellows; 1 Hon. Sr.
Res. Fellow; 41 Hon. Res. Fellows
Research: earth structure and geodynamics;
geomagnetism; microstructure, lithosphere
dynamics and deformation; oceans, climate
and life; stratigraphy, environments and
diagenesis

Engineering

Tel: (0151) 794 6801 Fax: (0151) 794 4930
E-mail: pgeng@liv.ac.uk
Al-Khalid, Hussain, BSc Baghdad, MSc Birm., PhD
Birm. Sr. Lectr.
Bacon, David J., PhD Lond., DSc Lond., FIMMM,
FIP Prof., Materials Science
Badcock, Kenneth, BSc Strath., DPhil Oxf. Prof.
Barakos, George N., MSc Ott., PhD Manc. Sr.
Lectr.
Blachut, Jan, PhD Cracow, DSc(Eng) Reader
Bleloch, Andrew L., PhD Camb. Reader
Bullough, Timothy J., BSc Brist., PhD Liv. Sr.
Lectr.
Burrows, Richard, BEng Liv., PhD Liv. Prof.,
Environmental Hydraulics
Cantwell, Wesley J., BSc S'ton., MSc Lond., PhD
Lond. Prof.
Chalker, Paul R., BSc Wales, PhD Wales Prof.
Chen, Daoyi, BEng Chongqing, MPhil Tsinghua,
PhD Tsinghua Prof., Maritime Civil
Engineering
Dearden, Geoff, MSc CNAA, PhD Liv. Sr. Lectr.
Escudier, Marcel P., PhD Lond., DSc Lond.,
FIMechE Harrison Prof.
Goodhew, Peter J., PhD Birm., DSc Birm., FIP,
FIMMM, FREng Henry Bell Wortley Prof.,
Materials Engineering
Guan, Z., PhD Brad., BEng Sr. Lectr.
Hedges, Terry S., MEng Liv. Sr. Lectr.
Hon, K. K. Bernard, MSc Birm., PhD Birm., FIEE
Prof., Manufacturing Systems
Johnson, Mark W., MA Camb., PhD Camb. Sr.
Lectr.
Millard, Steven G., BEng Leic., PhD Warw.
Prof.
Mines, Robert A. W., MSc Lond., DPhil Oxf.
Sr. Lectr.
Mottershead, John E., BSc CNAA, PhD CNAA,
DEng Liv., FIMechE Alexander Elder Prof.,
Applied Mechanics
Mountain, Linda J., BSc Leeds, MSc Leeds Sr.
Lectr.
Ouyang, Huajiang, BEng Dalian U.T., MEng
Dalian U.T., PhD Dalian U.T. Reader
Owen, Ieuan, BSc Wales, PhD Wales, FIMechE
Prof.
Padfield, Gareth D., BSc Lond., PhD Cran., FRAeS
James Bibby Prof., Aerospace Engineering;
Head*
Pond, Robert C., MSc Brist., PhD Brist., FIP
Prof.
Schleyer, Graham K., BSc Strath., PhD Strath.
Sr. Lectr.
Shenton, Andrew T., BSc Salf., PhD Salf. Sr.
Lectr.
Soutsos, Marios N., BEng Lond., PhD Lond.
Reader

Sutcliffe, Chris J., MEng Liv., PhD Liv. Sr.
Lectr.
Tatlock, Gordon J., BSc Brist., PhD Brist., FIP,
FIMMM Prof.
Walker, Daniel J., BA Oxf., PhD Lond. Sr.
Lectr.
Watkins, Kenneth G., BSc Wales, PhD Wales
Prof., Laser Engineering
Zhao, Yuyuan Y., BEng Dalian U.T., MSc Dalian
U.T., DPhil Oxf.
Other Staff: 15 Visiting Profs.; 13 Lectrs.; 1 Sr.
Fellow; 1 Visiting Sr. Fellow; 2 Sr. Res.
Fellows; 18 Fellows; 1 Visiting Fellow; 3
Res. Fellows; 5 Hon. Lectrs.; 20 Hon. Sr.
Fellows; 17 Hon. Res. Fellows
Research: construction and infrastructure;
dynamics and control; flight science and
technology; fluids engineering; functional
materials

Engineering, Electrical, and Electronics

Tel: (0151) 794 4539 Fax: (0151) 794 4540
E-mail: s.hall@liv.ac.uk
Bradley, James W., BSc Durh., MSc Cran., PhD
Manc. Prof., Plasma and Complex Systems
Eccleston, William, MSc Lond., PhD Lond., FIEE,
FREng Robert Rankin Prof., Electronic
Engineering
Hall, Stephen, BSc Liv., PhD Liv., FIEE Prof.;
Head*
Huang, Yi, BSc Wuhan, MSc Nanjing, DPhil Oxf.
Reader
Nandi, Asoke K., BSc Camb., PhD Camb., FIEE,
FIMA, FIP David Jardine Prof., Electrical
Engineering
Nicolau, Dan V., MEng Bucharest, MS Bucharest,
PhD Bucharest Prof., Bioengineering
Ralph, Jason F., BSc S'ton., DPhil Sus. Reader
Samsonov, Dmitry, MSc PhD Sr. Lectr.
Shen, Yaochun, BSc Nanjing, MSc Nanjing, PhD
Nanjing Sr. Lectr.
Smith, Jeremy S., BEng Liv., PhD Liv. Prof.
Song, Yong-Hua, BEng MSc PhD DSc, FREng,
FIEE, FRSA Prof., Electrical Engineering
Spencer, Joseph W., BEng Liv., PhD Liv.
Reader
Taylor, Stephen, BSc(Eng) Lond., MEng Liv.,
PhD Liv., FIEE Reader
Wu, Qing-Hua (Henry), MSc Huazhong U.S.T.,
PhD Belf., FIEE Prof., Electrical Engineering
Zhong, Qing-Chang, PhD Shanghai Jiaotong Sr.
Lectr.
Other Staff: 9 Visiting Profs.; 11 Lectrs.; 1
Fellow; 8 Hon. Sr. Fellows; 3 Hon. Sr. Res.
Fellows; 1 Hon. Fellow; 1 Hon. Res. Fellow
Research: bioMEMS, organic and silicon
electronics; intelligence engineering and
industrial automation; plasma and complex
systems; signal processing and
communications

English, School of

Tel: (0151) 794 2723 Fax: (0151) 794 2730
E-mail: englishgrad@liv.ac.uk
Baines, Paul T., BA Camb., PhD Brist. Prof.
Birch, Dinah L., BA Oxf., DPhil Oxf. Prof.,
English Literature
Burdett, Carolyn A., BA Sus., MA Sus., DPhil Sus.
Sr. Lectr.
Chapman, Siobhan R., BA Newcastle(UK), PhD
Newcastle(UK) Sr. Lectr.
Corcoran, Cornelius (Neil) D., BA Oxf., MA
Oxf., MLitt Oxf. King Alfred Prof., English
Literature
Davis, Philip M., BA Camb., PhD Camb. Prof.
Everest, Kelvin D., BA Reading, PhD Reading
Andrew Cecil Bradley Prof., Modern English
Literature
Hoey, Michael P., BA Lond., PhD Birm., AcSS
Baines Prof., English Language
John, Juliet V., BA Camb., PhD Lond. Reader
Rees-Jones, Deryn, BA Wales, MA Wales, PhD
Lond. Sr. Lectr.
Rudd, Gillian A., BA Oxf., DPhil York(UK) Sr.
Lectr.
Seed, David, MA Camb., MA Leic., PhD Hull
Prof.

Simms, Karl N., MA Camb., PhD S'ton. Sr. Lectr.

Thompson, Geoff R., MA Oxf., MA Leeds Sr. Lectr.

Walsh, Marcus, BPhil Oxf., MA Oxf., PhD Tor. Kenneth Allott Prof., English Literature

Watry, P. B., BA San Diego, DPhil Oxf. Prof.†

Other Staff: 3 Visiting Profs.; 13 Lectrs.; 4 Fellows; 1 William Noble Fellow; 1 Univ. Teacher; 1 Hon. Prof.; 5 Hon. Sr. Fellows; 2 Hon. Res. Fellows

Research: eighteenth-century, Romanticism and Victorian studies; medieval literature; modern and contemporary literature; Shakespeare and the Renaissance; textual editing and book history

Geography

Tel: (0151) 794 2874 Fax: (0151) 794 2866 E-mail: geography@liv.ac.uk

Bloemendal, Jan, BA Liv., PhD Liv. Sr. Lectr.

Bradshaw, Richard H. W., BA Camb., MA Camb., MA Trinity(Dub.), PhD Camb. Prof., Physical Geography

Chester, Rev. David K., BA Durh., PhD Aberd. Reader

Chiverrell, Richard C., BSc CNAA, MSc Wales, PhD Leeds Sr. Lectr.

Holdsworth, Clare M., BA Oxf., MSc Lond., PhD Liv. Reader

Hooke, Janet M. Prof.

Kulu, Hill, MSc Tartu, PhD Helsinki Sr. Lectr.

Lang, Andreas, PhD Heidel. Prof., Physical Geography; Head*

Morse, Andrew P., BSc CNAA, PhD Manc. Reader

North, Peter J., BA Warw., MA Brad., PhD Brist. Sr. Lectr.

Phillips, Richard, BSc Brist., MA Calif., PhD Br.Col. Sr. Lectr.

Plater, Andrew J., BSc Wales, PhD Nott. Reader

Sadler, David, BA Durh., PhD Durh. Prof., Economic Geography

Thomas, Geoffrey S. P., BSc Wales, PhD Wales Sr. Lectr.

Williamson, Paul, BA Leeds, PhD Leeds Sr. Lectr.

Woods, Robert I., MA Camb., DPhil Oxf., FBA, AcSS John Rankin Prof.

Other Staff: 12 Lectrs.; 1 Sr. Fellow; 2 Hon. Sr. Fellows; 1 Hon. Fellow

Research: palaeoecology; population, health and life course; sedimentary records of environmental change; sustainable ecosystems and societies (policy, practice and prediction)

History, School of

Tel: (0151) 794 2393 Fax: (0151) 794 2366 E-mail: history@liv.ac.uk

Ashworth, William J., BSc Plym., MA Kent, PhD Camb. Sr. Lectr.

Belchem, John C., BA Sus., DPhil Sus., FRHistS, FRSA Prof.

Booth, Paul H. W., BA Sheff., MA Liv., FRHistS Sr. Lectr.

Campbell, Alan B., MA Aberd., MA Warw., PhD Warw. Reader

Davies, Andrew M., BA Camb., PhD Camb. Sr. Lectr.

Dutton, David J., BA Lond., PhD Lond., FRHistS Prof.

Esdaile, Charles J., BA Lanc., PhD Lanc., FRHistS Prof.

Foley, Robert T., BA N.Y., MA N.Y., PhD Lond. Sr. Lectr.

Hoock, Holger, MA Freib., DPhil Oxf. Reader

Houlbrook, Matt, BA Camb., PhD Essex Sr. Lectr.

Hughes, Michael J., BA Reading, MSc Lond., PhD Lond. Prof.; Head*

Lee, W. Robert, MA Oxf., DPhil Oxf. Chaddock Prof., Economic and Social History

McLaren, Anne, MA Johns H., PhD Johns H. Sr. Lectr.

Resl, B., MPhil Vienna, DPhil Vienna Prof., Mediaeval History

Stafford, Pauline A., BA Oxf., DPhil Oxf., FRHistS Prof., Mediaeval History

Tadman, Michael, BA Warw., MA Birm., PhD Hull Sr. Lectr.

Other Staff: 1 Visiting Prof.; 19 Lectrs.; 5 Fellows; 2 Res. Fellows; 1 Sr. Lectr.†; 1 Hon. Lectr.; 9 Hon. Sr. Fellows; 3 Hon. Res. Fellows

Research: archive studies; British and European history; business and labour history; comparative industrialisation (social and demographic change); local, Irish and Manx history

Irish Studies, Institute of

Tel: (0151) 794 3831 Fax: (0151) 794 3836 E-mail: irish.studies@liv.ac.uk

Elliott, Marianne, OBE, BA Belf., DPhil Oxf., FRHistS, FBA Prof.; Head*

Urquhart, Diane L., BA Belf., MA Belf., PhD Belf. Sr. Lectr.

Other Staff: 2 Visiting Profs.; 4 Lectrs.; 1 Hon. Visiting Sr. Fellow; 4 Hon. Fellows; 1 Hon. Sr. Res. Fellow; 2 Hon. Res. Fellows

Research: cultural change in contemporary Ireland; gender; Northern Ireland/Ulster; regionalism; religion and identity in Ireland and its diasporas

Liverpool Law School

Tel: (0151) 794 2807 Fax: (0151) 794 2829 E-mail: clarek@liv.ac.uk

Arora, Anu, LLB Birm., PhD Birm. Prof.; Head*

Barr, Warren, LLB Reading, LLM Reading Sr. Lectr.

Beveridge, Fiona C., LLB Aberd., MPhil Nott. Prof.

Dougan, P. Michael, MA Camb., PhD Camb. Jean Monnet Prof., European Union Law

Glover-Thomas, Nicola E. D., LLB Wales, PhD Wales Reader

Halliday, Samantha L., LLB E.Anglia, PhD Sr. Lectr.

Harrington, John A., LLB Trinity(Dub.), BCL Oxf. Prof.

Jones, Michael A., BA Keele, LLM W.Ont., PhD Liv. Prof., Common Law

Lyon, Christina M., LLB Lond. Queen Victoria Prof.

McGoldrick, Dominic, LLB Nott., PhD Nott. Prof., Public International Law

Morris, Anne E., LLB Liv. Sr. Lectr.

Nott, Susan M., LLB Wales, BCL Durh. Sr. Lectr.

Pentassuglia, G., LLB Bari, PhD Bari Sr. Lectr.

Stalford, H. E., LLB Liv., PhD Sr. Lectr.

Thompson, W. Brian, LLB Belf., MLitt Oxf. Sr. Lectr.

Warburton, Jean, LLB Liv. Prof.†

Other Staff: 13 Lectrs.; 4 Univ. Teachers†; 2 Hon. Sr. Fellows; 1 Hon. Res. Fellow

Research: charity law; child law; feminist legal and socio-legal research; international, European and English law; medical law and bioethics

Management School

Tel: (0151) 794 3000 Fax: (0151) 794 3001 E-mail: s.isenberg@liv.ac.uk

Dalziel, Murray, MA PhD Head*

Accounting and Finance Division

Tel: (0151) 795 3610 Fax: (0151) 795 3001 E-mail: j.burnett@liv.ac.uk

Brookfield, David, BA Liv., DPhil Oxf. Sr. Lectr.

Ormrod, Phil, BCom Liv., MA Lanc. Sr. Lectr.; Head*

Other Staff: 6 Lectrs.; 1 Univ. Teacher†

Research: accounting and accountability (behavioural aspects, organisational aspects); finance and financial markets; financial contracting and corporate governance; financial reporting (including developing countries)

e-Business Division

Tel: (0151) 795 3609 Fax: (0151) 795 3666 E-mail: j.s.holbrook@liv.ac.uk

Drake, Paul R., BSc Wales, MSc Wales, PhD Wales Sr. Lectr.; Head*

Ismail, Hossam, BSc Ain Shams, PhD Birm. Sr. Lectr.

Kehoe, Dennis F., BSc(Eng) Lond., PhD Liv. Prof., Industrial Management

Other Staff: 1 Visiting Prof.; 6 Lectrs.

Research: e-business and information systems; operations and supply chain management

Economics Division

Tel: (0151) 795 3003 Fax: (0151) 795 3720 E-mail: h.bailey@liv.ac.uk

Bagust, Adrian, BSc Exe. Prof., Health Economics

Cook, Gary A. S., BA Leeds, MSc Warw., PhD Manc. Sr. Lectr.

Hojman, David E., BSc Chile, PhD Edin. Prof.

McCabe, Brendan P. M., BA Trinity(Dub.), MSc Lond., PhD Amst. Prof.

Sapsford, David R., BSc Leic., MPhil Leic., PhD Leeds Edward Gonner Prof., Applied Economics; Head*

Steffen, Frank, MA Hamburg, PhD Hamburg Sr. Lectr.

Other Staff: 4 Lectrs.; 1 Univ. Teacher

Research: econometrics; industrial organisation; international macroeconomics and financial economics; labour and development economics

Management Division

Tel: (0151) 795 3610 Fax: (0151) 795 3001 E-mail: j.burnett@liv.ac.uk

Antonacopoulou, Elena, BA Kent, MA Warw., PhD Warw. Prof., Organisational Behaviour

Drummond, Helga, BA Leeds, PhD Leeds Prof., Decision Sciences

Elliott, Dominic, BA Warw., MBA CNAA, PhD Durh. Prof., Business Continuity and Strategic Management; Head*

MacPherson, Allan M., MA Manc., MRes Manc., PhD Manc. Sr. Lectr.

McAllister, Laura J., BSc Lond., PhD Wales Prof., Governance

McNulty, Terence H., BA CNAA, PhD CNAA Prof., Management and Corporate Governance

Popp, Andrew D., BA Staffs., MA RCA, PhD Sheff. Sr. Lectr.

Southern, Alan, BA Lanc., MSc Manc., PhD Durh. Sr. Lectr.

Worthington, F. T., BA Lanc., MA Lanc., PhD Manc. Sr. Lectr.

Other Staff: 1 Visiting Prof.; 9 Lectrs.; 1 Univ. Teacher; 1 Hon. Reader; 2 Hon. Sr. Fellows

Research: entrepreneurship; football industries; organisational behaviour; public sector management and administration; risk and crisis management

Marketing and International Business Division

Tel: (0151) 795 3610 E-mail: j.burnett@liv.ac.uk

Baron, J. Steven, BSc Leeds, MSc Leeds, MSc Manc. Prof., Marketing

Hill, James J., BEd Belf., BA Ulster, MA Ulster, DPhil Ulster Prof., Entrepreneurship

Miller, Rory M., MA Camb., PhD Camb. Reader

Other Staff: 8 Lectrs.

Research: entrepreneurship/strategic marketing; foreign business in Latin America; tourism/services marketing; women in management

Mathematical Sciences

Tel: (0151) 794 4046 Fax: (0151) 794 4754 E-mail: bsms@liv.ac.uk

Bhansali, Rajendra J., BCom Bom., BSc Lond., PhD Lond. Prof.

Biktashev, Vadim N., BSc Moscow, MSc Moscow, PhD Moscow Prof.

Bowers, Roger G., BSc Lond., PhD Lond. Prof.

Chen, Anyue, MSc PhD Prof.

Chen, Ke, BSc *Dalian U.T.*, MSc *Manc.*, PhD *Plym.*, FIMA   Prof.
Clancy, Damian, BA *Camb.*, PhD *Nott.*   Reader
Faraggi, Alon E., BSc *Ben Gurion*, PhD *Texas A.& M.*   Prof.
Giblin, Peter J., BSc *Lond.*, PhD *Lond.*   Prof.
Goryunov, Victor V., PhD *Moscow*   Prof.
Gracey, John A., BA *Camb.*, PhD *Camb.*   Prof.
Hall, Toby, BA *Camb.*, PhD *Camb.*   Sr. Lectr.
Irving, Alan C., BSc *Glas.*, PhD *Durh.*, FIP   Prof.; Head*
Jack, D. Ian, BA *Camb.*, PhD *Camb.*   Prof.
Jones, D. R. Timothy, MA *Oxf.*, DPhil *Oxf.*, FIP   Prof.
Maz'ya, Vladimir, MS *Leningrad*, PhD *Moscow*, ScD *Leningrad*   Prof.†, Pure Mathematics
Michael, Christopher, MA *Oxf.*, DPhil *Oxf.*, FIP   Prof., Theoretical Physics
Morton, Hugh R., MA *Camb.*, PhD *Camb.*   Prof.
Movchan, Alexander, MSc *Leningrad*, PhD *Leningrad*   Prof., Applied Mathematics
Movchan, Natalia V., MSc *Leningrad*, PhD *Leningrad*   Reader
Nair, R. (Kit), BSc *Lond.*, MSc *Lond.*, PhD *Warw.*   Reader
Nikulin, Viacheslav V., MD *Moscow*, PhD *Russian Acad.Sc.*   Prof., Pure Mathematics
Piunovskiy, Aleksey B., MSc *Moscow State Inst.Electronic Technol.*, PhD *Moscow State Inst.Electronic Technol.*   Reader
Pukhilov, Prof. Alexsandr A. V., MSc *Moscow*, PhD *Moscow*   Prof.
Rakow, Paul E. L., BA *Camb.*, PhD *Camb.*   Sr. Lectr.
Rees, S. Mary, BA *Oxf.*, MSc *Oxf.*, PhD *Warw.*, FRS   Prof., Pure Mathematics
Vogt, A., PhD *Dortmund*   Prof.
Zakalyukin, Vladimir M., PhD *Moscow*   Prof.
Other Staff: 14 Lectrs.; 2 PPARC Res. Advanced Fellows; 1 Sr. Fellow; 1 Fellow; 1 Res. Fellow; 19 Hon. Sr. Fellows; 1 Hon. Sr. Visiting Fellow; 1 Hon. Visiting Fellow; 3 Hon. Res. Fellows
Research: algebra, number theory, analysis geometry and topology; applied mathematics, modelling and analysis; singularity theory; statistics, applied probability and operational research; theoretical physics (elementary particle theory)

Music, School of

Tel: (0151) 794 3096 Fax: (0151) 794 3141
   E-mail: music@liv.ac.uk
Cohen, Sara, BA *Sus.*, DPhil *Oxf.*   Reader
Kassabian, Anahid, BA *Fordham*, AM *Stan.*, PhD *Stan.*   James and Constance Alsop Prof.
Perrey, Beate J. E., MA *Kyoto*, PhD *Camb.*   Sr. Lectr.
Williamson, J. G. (Ian), MA *Glas.*, DPhil *Oxf.*   Prof.; Head*
Other Staff: 9 Lectrs.; 1 Sr. Fellow; 2 Hon. Sr. Fellows; 1 Hon. Res. Fellow
Research: contemporary and popular music; European music, 1850-1950; Italian Baroque music; music industries

Philosophy

Tel: (0151) 794 2787 Fax: (0151) 794 2789
   E-mail: philos@liv.ac.uk
Clark, Stephen R. L., MA *Oxf.*, DPhil *Oxf.*   Prof.
Dainton, Barry F., BSc *Lond.*, DPhil *Oxf.*   Prof.
Ganeri, Jonardon, BA *Camb.*, MPhil *Lond.*, DPhil *Oxf.*   Prof.
Gaskin, Richard M., MA *Oxf.*, BPhil *Oxf.*, DPhil *Oxf.*   Prof.
Howie, Gillian O., BA *Exe.*, PhD *Camb.*   Sr. Lectr.; Head*
McGhee, Michael J., BA *Lond.*, PhD *Lond.*   Sr. Lectr.
Other Staff: 6 Lectrs.; 1 Hon. Sr. Fellow; 1 Hon. Fellow; 7 Hon. Res. Fellows
Research: ancient and mediaeval philosophy; applied ethics; metaphysics; philosophy of mind; political philosophy/feminism

Physics

Tel: (0151) 794 3370 Fax: (0151) 794 3348
   E-mail: pjn@ns.ph.liv.ac.uk
Allport, Philip P., BSc *Lond.*, DPhil *Oxf.*, FIP   Prof.
Barrett, Steven D., BSc *E.Anglia*, PhD *E.Anglia*   Sr. Lectr.
Bowcock, Themis J. V., BA *Oxf.*, PhD *Lond.*   Prof.
Butler, Peter A., BSc *Lond.*, PhD *Liv.*   Prof.
Dainton, John B., MA *Oxf.*, DPhil *Oxf.*, FIP, FRS   Sir James Chadwick Prof., Experimental Physics
Fry, John R., MA *Oxf.*, PhD *Birm.*   Reader
Gamet, Ray, BSc *Liv.*, PhD *Liv.*   Reader
Goff, Jon P., MA *Camb.*, PhD *Camb.*   Sr. Lectr.
Greenshaw, Timothy J., BSc *Durh.*, PhD *Manc.*   Prof.
Herzberg, Rolf-Dietmar, BSc *Cologne*, PhD *Cologne*   Prof.
Hofer, Werner A., MSc *T.U.Vienna*, PhD *T.U.Vienna*   Prof.
Houlden, Michael A., BSc *Liv.*, PhD *Liv.*   Sr. Lectr.
Jackson, J. Neil, BSc *Liv.*, PhD *Liv.*, FIP   Reader
Klein, Max   Prof.
Klein, Uta, PhD   Sr. Lectr.
Lucas, Chris A., BSc *Leeds*, PhD *Edin.*   Reader
McGrath, Rónán J., BA *Trinity(Dub.)*, PhD *Trinity(Dub.)*, FIP   Prof.
Nolan, Paul J., BSc *Lond.*, PhD *Liv.*   Prof.; Head*
Page, Robert D., BA *Oxf.*, PhD *Birm.*   Reader
Touramanis, Christofas T., BSc *Salonika*, PhD *Salonika*   Reader
Weightman, Peter, BA *Keele*, PhD *Keele*, FIP   Prof.
Other Staff: 10 Visiting Profs.; 9 Lectrs.; 5 Sr. Res. Fellows; 6 Fellows; 1 Univ. Teacher; 7 Hon. Sr. Fellows; 4 Hon. Res. Fellows
Research: condensed matter physics; high-energy particle physics and accelerator science; medical imaging; nuclear structure physics; surface science

Politics and Communication Studies, School of

Tel: (0151) 794 2891 Fax: (0151) 794 3948
   E-mail: janv@liv.ac.uk
Corner, John R., MA *Camb.*, FRSA, AcSS   Prof.
Dolowitz, David P., BA *Puget Sound*, PhD *Strath.*   Reader
Femia, Joseph V., BA *Col.*, MPhil *Oxf.*, DPhil *Oxf.*   Prof.
Gavin, Neil T., MA *Glas.*, MSc *Lond.*, PhD *Lond.*   Sr. Lectr.
Gillespie, Richard H. C., BA *Liv.*, PhD *Liv.*   Prof., Politics
Hallam, Julia, BA *Strath.*, PhD *Warw.*   Sr. Lectr.
Miles, Lee S., BA *Lanc.*, MIS *Birm.*, PhD *Hull*   Prof.
Richardson, Kay P., BA *E.Anglia*, MA *Birm.*, PhD *Birm.*   Reader
Tonge, Jonathan, BA *CNAA*, MA *Hull*, PhD *W.England*   Prof., Politics; Head*
Other Staff: 7 Lectrs.; 1 Fellow; 4 Hon. Sr. Fellows; 3 Hon. Res. Fellows
Research: British/Irish/Caribbean/Latin American/European/Mediterranean politics; complexity research; film, television and new media; media and politics

Psychology

Tel: (0151) 794 2957 Fax: (0151) 794 2945
   E-mail: psychol@liv.ac.uk
Alison, Laurence, BSc *Lond.*, MSc *Sur.*, PhD *Liv.*   Prof.
Bennett, Kate M., BSc *Leic.*, PhD *Nott.*   Sr. Lectr.
Bertamini, Marco, Laurea *Padua*, MA *Virginia*, PhD *Virginia*   Sr. Lectr.
Browne, Kevin, BSc *Lond.*, MSc *Lond.Guild.*, MEd *Birm.*, PhD *Westminster*   Prof.
Canter, David V., BA *Liv.*, PhD *Liv.*, FBPsS, FAPA, AcSS   Prof.; Dir., Centre for Investigative Psychol.
Cole, Jon C., BSc *Leeds*, PhD *Leeds*   Reader

Donald, Ian, BA *CNAA*, MSc *Sur.*, PhD *Aston*   Prof.; Head*
Downes, John J., BSc *Liv.*, PhD *Liv.*   Reader
Goudie, Andrew J., BA *Oxf.*, MSc *Wales*, PhD *Liv.*   Reader
Halford, Jason C. G., BSc *Leeds*, PhD *Leeds*   Reader
Kirkham, Timothy C., BSc *Leeds*, PhD *Leeds*   Prof.
Latto, Richard M., MA *Camb.*, PhD *Camb.*, FBPsS   Sr. Lectr.
Lawson, Rebecca, BA *Camb.*, PhD *Birm.*   Sr. Lectr.
Meyer, Georg F., BA *Keele*, PhD *Keele*   Sr. Lectr.
Pine, Julian M., BA *Liv.*, PhD *Manc.*   Prof.
Rowland, Caroline F., BA *Manc.*, PhD *Nott.*   Sr. Lectr.
Stancak, Andrej, BSc *T.U.Kosice*, PhD *Prague*   Sr. Lectr.
Stott, Clifford, BSc *Plym.*, PhD *Exe.*   Sr. Lectr.
Thornton, Everard W., BSc *Durh.*, PhD *Durh.*   Sr. Lectr.
Wagstaff, Graham F., BA *Newcastle(UK)*, PhD *Newcastle(UK)*   Prof.
Wuerger, Sophie M., PhD *N.Y.*   Sr. Lectr.
Other Staff: 4 Visiting Profs.; 10 Lectrs.; 4 Fellows; 1 Hon. Sr. Fellow; 13 Hon. Res. Fellows
Research: cognitive science and cognitive neuroscience; health and applied social psychology; human psychopharmacology and eating behaviour; investigative and forensic psychology; vision and perception

Sociology and Social Policy, School of

Tel: (0151) 794 3009 Fax: (0151) 794 2997
   E-mail: fonty@liv.ac.uk
Ettorre, Elizabeth M., BA *Fordham*, PhD *Lond.*   Prof.
Evans, Karen F., MA(Econ) *Manc.*, PhD   Sr. Lectr.
Goldson, Barry, BA *Lanc.*, MA *Lanc.*, PhD *Liv.*   Prof.
King, David, BA *Lond.*, PhD *Essex*   Sr. Lectr.
Lavalette, Michael, MA *Glas.*, PhD *Paisley*   Sr. Lectr.
Miles, Steven, BA *Nott.Trent*, MA *Lanc.*, PhD *Hudd.*   Reader
Mythen, Gabe G., BA *Nott.*, MA *Warw.*, PhD *Nott.*   Sr. Lectr.
Petrie, Stephanie M., BA *Newcastle(UK)*, MSocSci *Birm.*   Sr. Lectr.
Roberts, Kenneth, BSc(Soc) *Lond.*, MSc(Econ) *Lond.*, FRHistS, AcSS   Prof.
Walklate, Sandra L., BA *Lanc.*, MLitt *Lanc.*   Eleanor Rathbone Prof., Sociology; Head*
Whyte, David, BA *R.Gordon*, PhD *Liv.J.Moores*   Reader
Other Staff: 3 Visiting Profs.; 12 Lectrs.; 3 Fellows; 1 Hon. Lectr.; 5 Hon. Res. Fellows
Research: crime, criminal justice and social control; culture, politics and identity; inclusion, exclusion and the city; policy, the lifecourse and welfare

MEDICINE

Tel: (0151) 706 4275 Fax: (0151) 706 5667
   E-mail: deanmed@liv.ac.uk

Biomedical Sciences, School of

Tel: (0151) 794 5455 E-mail: pickeia@liv.ac.uk
Burgoyne, Robert D., BSc *Birm.*, PhD *Birm.*, FMedSci   Prof.; Head*

Human Anatomy and Cell Biology, Division of

Tel: (0151) 794 5474 Fax: (0151) 794 5517
   E-mail: hacb@liv.ac.uk
Crompton, Robin H., BSc *Lond.*, AM *Harv.*, PhD *Harv.*   Prof.
Dangerfield, Peter H., MD *St And.*, PhD   Sr. Lectr.
Edgar, David H., BA *Oxf.*, DPhil *Oxf.*   Prof.
Gallagher, James A., BSc *Newcastle(UK)*, MSc *Aberd.*, PhD *Camb.*   Prof.; Head*
Gunther, Michael M., MSc PhD   Sr. Lectr.
Jarvis, Jonathan C., BSc *Lond.*, PhD *Lond.*   Reader

Jeffery, Nathan S., BSc *Tees.*, MSc *Oxf.*, PhD *Lond.* Sr. Lectr.

Marshall-Clarke, Stuart, PhD *Lond.* Sr. Lectr.

Moss, Diana J., BSc *Brist.*, PhD *Brist.* Sr. Lectr.

Quayle, John M., BSc *Newcastle(UK)*, PhD *Leic.* Sr. Lectr.

Quinn, John P., BSc *Glas.*, PhD *Glas.* Prof.

Simpson, Alec W. M., BSc *CNAA*, DPhil *Oxf.* Sr. Lectr.

Other Staff: 3 Lectrs.; 3 Fellows; 1 Sr. Lectr.†; 1 Univ. Teacher†; 1 Hon. Sr. Lectr.; 2 Hon. Lectrs.; 2 Hon. Sr. Fellows; 1 Hon. Res. Fellow

Research: evolutionary biology; musculoskeletal biology; neurobiology; stem cell biology; vascular biology

Pharmacology and Therapeutics, Division of

Tel: (0151) 794 5543 Fax: (0151) 794 5540
E-mail: b.k.park@liv.ac.uk

Back, David J., BSc *Liv.*, PhD *Liv.* Prof.

Craig, Alister G., BSc *Edin.*, PhD *Leic.* Prof., Molecular Biology and Genomes

Edwards, I. Geoffrey, BSc *Birm.*, PhD *Manc.* Sr. Lectr.

Green, T. P., BSc *Sheff.*, PhD *Sheff.* Sr. Lectr.

Haycox, Alan R., MA *Lanc.*, PhD *Lanc.* Sr. Lectr.

Khoo, Saye H., MA *Lond.*, PhD *Lanc.* Reader

Kitteringham, Neil R., BSc *Aberd.*, PhD *Aberd.* Sr. Lectr.

Naisbitt, Dean J., BSc *Liv.*, PhD *Liv.* Sr. Lectr.

O'Neill, Paul M., BSc *Liv.*, PhD *Liv.* Prof.

Park, B. Kevin, BSc *Liv.*, PhD *Liv.*, FMedSci Prof.; Head*

Pirmohamed, Munir, MB ChB *Liv.*, PhD *Liv.* Prof.

Walley, Thomas J., MB BCh BAO *N.U.I.*, MD *N.U.I.*, FRCP Glaxo Prof., Clinical Pharmacology

Other Staff: 2 Visiting Profs.; 5 Lectrs.; 1 Fellow; 3 Hon. Profs.; 2 Hon. Sr. Fellows; 5 Hon. Res. Fellows

Research: drug metabolism and adverse drug reactions; immunopharmacology and toxicology; pharmacology of HIV disease; proteomics; tropical pharmacology

Physiology, Division of

Tel: (0151) 794 5322 Fax: (0151) 794 5327
E-mail: s.wray@liv.ac.uk

Burdyga, T., BSc *Kiev*, PhD *Kiev*, DSc *Kiev* Reader

Burgoyne, Robert D., BSc *Birm.*, PhD *Birm.*, FMedSci Prof.

Clague, Michael, BSc *Exe.*, PhD *Essex* Prof.

Coulson, Judy M., BSc *Salf.*, PhD *Lond.* Sr. Lectr.

Dimaline, Rodney, BSc *Liv.*, PhD *Liv.* Prof.

Dockray, Graham J., BSc *Nott.*, PhD *Nott.*, FMedSci, Hon. FRCP Prof.

Gerasimenko, O. V., PhD *Moscow* Reader

Morgan, Alan, BSc *Liv.*, PhD *Liv.* Prof.

Petersen, Ole H., CBE, MD *Copenhagen*, FRS George Holt Prof.

Sanderson, C. M., BSc *Wales*, PhD *Sur.* Reader

Tepikin, Alexey, BSc *Moscow*, PhD *Kiev* Prof.

Varro, Andrea, MD *Szeged*, PhD *Bud.* Prof.

Wray, Susan C., BSc *Lond.*, PhD *Lond.*, FMedSci, FRCOG Prof.; Head*

Other Staff: 1 Visiting Prof.; 6 Lectrs.; 1 Univ. Teacher

Research: epithelial signalling; neuronal signalling; oncology and signalling; pathophysiology and signalling; signalling in smooth muscle

Cancer Studies, School of

Tel: (0151) 706 4170 Fax: (0151) 706 5826
E-mail: j.p.neoptolemos@liv.ac.uk

Neoptolemos, John P., MB BChir *Camb.*, MA *Camb.*, MD *Leic.*, FRCS Prof., Surgery; Head*

Other Staff: 2 Hon. Readers; 8 Hon. Sr. Lectrs.; 16 Hon. Lectrs.; 4 Hon. Res. Fellows; 64

Hon. Clin. Lectrs.

Haematology, Division of

Tel: (0151) 706 2000 Fax: (0151) 706 5810
E-mail: haem@liv.ac.uk

Cawley, John C., MB ChB *Leeds*, MD *Leeds*, PhD *Camb.*, FRCP, FRCPath Prof.; Head*

Clark, Richard E., MB BS *Lond.*, MA *Camb.*, MD *Lond.*, FRCP, FRCPath Prof.

Pettitt, Andrew R., BA *Camb.*, MB BChir *Camb.*, PhD *Liv.* Prof.

Toh, Cheng-Hock, MB ChB *Sheff.*, MD *Sheff.* Prof.

Zuzel, Mirko, MD *Zagreb* Prof.

Other Staff: 3 Lectrs.; 1 Hon. Lectr.; 1 Hon. Clin. Lectr.; 1 Hon. Res. Fellow

Research: chronic lymphoproliferative disorders; chronic myeloid leukaemia; vascular endothelium

Pathology

Tel: (0151) 706 4494 Fax: (0151) 706 5859
E-mail: phsmith@liv.ac.uk

Foster, Christopher S., BSc *Lond.*, MD *Lond.*, PhD *Lond.*, DSc *Lond.*, FRCPath George Holt Prof.; Head*

Gosden, Christine M., BSc *Edin.*, PhD *Edin.* Prof., Medical Genetics

Helliwell, Timothy R., MA *Camb.*, MD *Camb.*, FRCPath Reader

Ke, Youqiang, MB *Leeds*, DVSc *Leeds* Prof.

Nash, John R. G., BM BCh *Oxf.*, DPhil *Oxf.*, FRCPath Sr. Lectr.

Smith, Paul H., BSc *Liv.*, PhD *Liv.* Sr. Lectr.

Other Staff: 1 Lectr.; 2 Sr. Clin. Lectrs.

Research: borderline breast lesions; cancers of the prostate, head and neck; forensic pathology; lung, gastro-intestinal and uterine cervical neoplasia; ophthalmic wound repair

Surgery and Oncology, Division of

E-mail: y.e.cross@liv.ac.uk

Barr, Francis A., PhD Prof.

Boyd, Mark T., BSc *Lond.*, PhD *S'ton.* Reader

Costello-Goldring, E. M., BSc *N.U.I.*, PhD *N.U.I.* Sr. Lectr.

Field, John, BA BDS PhD, FRCPath Prof.

Frostick, Simon P., MA DM, FRCS Prof.

Ghaneh, Paula, MB ChB *Liv.* Sr. Lectr.

Green, John A., BSc MB ChB DM Sr. Lectr.

Greenhalf, Bill, BSc *Manc.*, PhD *Manc.* Sr. Lectr.

Jones, Terry M., BSc *Lond.*, MB BS *Lond.*, FRCSEd Sr. Lectr.

Neoptolemos, John P., MB BChir *Camb.*, MA *Camb.*, MD *Leic.*, FRCS Prof., Surgery; Head*

Raraty, Michael G. T., MB BS *Newcastle(UK)*, FRCS Sr. Lectr.

Shaw, Richard, MD Sr. Lectr.

Sibson, D. Ross, BSc PhD Prof.

Sutton, Robert, BA *Durh.*, MB BS *Lond.*, DPhil *Oxf.*, FRCS Prof.

Other Staff: 7 Lectrs.; 3 Hon. Res. Fellows

Research: cancer (clinical research, gene therapy, molecular diagnosis, molecular pathogenesis); pancreatitis (calcium signalling, clinical research, hereditary and familial pancreatitis)

Clinical Sciences, School of

Tel: (0151) 706 4284 Fax: (0151) 706 5668
E-mail: pickeia@liv.ac.uk

Winstanley, Peter A., MB ChB *Liv.*, MD *Liv.*, FRCP Head*

Other Staff: 14 Visiting Profs.; 8 Hon. Profs.; 3 Hon. Dirs.; 1 Hon. Dir., Clin. Studies; 3 Hon. Readers; 21 Hon. Sr. Lectrs.; 30 Hon. Lectrs.; 1 Hon. Sr. Fellow; 4 Hon. Sr. Res. Fellows; 38 Hon. Res. Fellows; 227 Hon. Clin. Lectrs.; 15 Hon. Clin. Tutors

Clinical Chemistry, Division of

Tel: (0151) 706 4232 Fax: (0151) 706 5813
E-mail: shenkin@liv.ac.uk

Diver, Michael J., MSc *W.Ont.*, PhD *Liv.* Sr. Lectr.

Fraser, William D., BSc *Glas.*, MB ChB *Glas.*, MD *Glas.*, FRCPath Prof.

Shenkin, Alan, BSc *Glas.*, MB ChB *Glas.*, PhD *Glas.*, FRCP, FRCPath Prof.; Head*

Research: endocrine and dietary factors associated with metabolic bone disease; micronutrient requirements in health and disease; pathophysiology of obesity; pepsin structure and function; reproductive endocrinology and biochemistry

Clinical Engineering, Division of

Tel: (0151) 706 5606 Fax: (0151) 706 5803
E-mail: clineng@liv.ac.uk

How, Thien V., BSc *Sus.*, PhD *Liv.* Sr. Lectr.

Hunt, John A., BSc *Trent*, PhD *Liv.* Reader

Rhodes, Nicolas P., BSc *Liv.*, PhD *Liv.* Sr. Lectr.

Williams, David F., BSc *Birm.*, PhD *Birm.*, DSc *Birm.*, FIMMM Prof.; Head*

Other Staff: 2 Lectrs.; 1 Sr. Lectr.†

Research: biocompatability; cardiovascular haemodynamics; tissue engineering

Clinical Science, Division of

Tel: (0151) 706 4008 Fax: (0151) 706 5884
E-mail: mleuwer@liv.ac.uk

Charters, Peter, BA *Open(UK)*, MB ChB *Liv.*, MD *Liv.*, FRCA Sr. Lectr.

Hart, George, MA *Camb.*, DM *Oxf.*, FRCP David A. Price Evans Prof.

Hunter, Jennifer M., MB ChB *St And.*, PhD *Liv.*, FRCA Prof.

Leuwer, Martin K., DrMed *Fran.*, DrMedHabil *Hanover Med.Sch.*, FRCA Prof.; Head*

Warenius, Hilmar M., MB BChir *Camb.*, MA *Camb.*, PhD *Camb.*, FRCR, FRCP Prof., Oncology Research

Welters, Ingeborg D. M.

Wilding, John P. H., BMed *S'ton.*, DM *S'ton.*, FRCP Prof., Medicine

Other Staff: 2 Lectrs.

Research: coagulation in sepsis; positive allosteric modulators of strychnine-sensitive glycine receptors; role of white adipose tissue in sepsis

Gastroenterology, Division of

Tel: (0151) 794 6822 E-mail: sscourt@liv.ac.uk

Bodger, Keith, MB ChB *Leeds*, MD *Leeds* Sr. Lectr.

Campbell, Barry J., BSc *Wales*, PhD *Liv.* Sr. Lectr.

Gerasimenko, O. V., PhD *Moscow* Reader

Pritchard, David M., BSc *Manc.*, MB ChB *Manc.*, PhD *Manc.* Sr. Lectr.

Rhodes, Jonathan M., MA *Camb.*, MD *Camb.*, FRCP Prof.

Watson, Alastair J. M., BA *Camb.*, MB BS *Lond.*, MD *Camb.*, FRCP, FRCPEd Prof.; Head*

Other Staff: 4 Lectrs.

Research: apoptosis/gastrin and gastrointestinal cancer; clinical studies in inflammatory bowel disease; colonic epithelial glycoconjugates; gut/mucosal interactions and intestinal disease

Infection and Immunity, Division of

Anderson, Marina, MB ChB *Edin.*, MSc *Manc.*, PhD *Manc.* Sr. Lectr.

Calverley, Peter M., MB ChB *Edin.*, FRCP, FRCPEd Prof., Rehabilitation Medicine

Goodson, N. J., MB ChB *Liv.*, PhD Sr. Lectr.

Moots, Robert J., BSc *Lond.*, MB BS *Lond.*, DPhil *Oxf.*, FRCP Prof.; Head*

Other Staff: 4 Lectrs.

Research: epidemiology of rheumatic diseases; immunotherapy in rheumatic diseases; innate immunity in autoimmune inflammatory diseases; role of rheumatic diseases and therapy in the development of cardiovascular disease; vascular physiology of systemic sclerosis and Raynaud's disease

Metabolic and Cellular Medicine, Division of

Daousi, Christina, MB ChB Sr. Lectr.

Gill, Geoffrey V., MA *Newcastle(UK)*, MSc *Newcastle(UK)*, MD *Newcastle(UK)*, FRCP Reader, Diabetes and Endocrinology

Grierson, Ian, BSc Glas., PhD Glas.   Prof.,
Ophthalmology
Griffiths, Richard P., BSc Lond., MD Lond., FRCS,
FRCPath   Prof.
Hiscott, Paul S., MB BS Lond., PhD Lond., FRCS,
FRCPath   Prof.
Jackson, Malcolm J., PhD Lond., DSc Sur.,
FRCPath   Prof., Cellular Pathophysiology;
Head*
Jagoe, R. T., MB BChir Camb., MA Camb., PhD
Newcastle(UK)   Sr. Lectr., Respiratory
Medicine
Kemp, Graham J., MA Oxf., DM Oxf.   Reader
McArdle, Anne, BSc Liv., PhD Liv.   Reader
Paraoan, Luminita, PhD Liv., BSc MSc   Sr.
Lectr.
Rustom, Rana, MD Liv., FRCP   Sr. Lectr.,
Transplant Nephrology
Trayhurn, Paul, BSc Reading, DPhil Oxf., DSc
Oxf., FRSEd   Prof., Nutritional Biology
Wilding, John P. H., BMed S'ton., DM S'ton.,
FRCP   Prof.
Williams, Rachel L., BSc Exe., MS Calif.   Sr.
Lectr.
Other Staff: 6 Lectrs.; 1 Sr. Fellow
Research: cell pathophysiology and intensive
care; human muscle research; obesity
biology; ophthalmology

Neuroscience, Division of

Tel: (0151) 529 5460 Fax: (0151) 525 3857
E-mail: p.bessant@liv.ac.uk
Baker, Guy A., MA Liv., PhD Liv.   Head*
Bubb, V. Jill, BSc Glas., BDS Glas., PhD Wash.
Sr. Lectr.
Hart, Ian K., BSc Glas., MB ChB Glas., PhD Lond.
Sr. Lectr.
Marson, A. G. (Tony), MB ChB Liv., MD Liv.
Reader
Nurmikko, Turo J., LicMed Turku, DMedSci
Tampere   Pain Relief Foundation Prof., Pain
Studies
Roberts, J. Neil, BSc Liv., MSc Aberd., PhD Wales
Prof.
Solomon, Tom, BA Oxf., MB BS Oxf., PhD,
FMedSci   Prof., Neurology
Other Staff: 1 Lectr.; 1 Clin. Lectrs.
Research: neuroimmunology and
neurophysiology; neurological infectious
diseases; neuropsychology and epilepsy;
neurorehabilitation; neurovascular research

Dental Sciences, School of

Tel: (0151) 706 5298 Fax: (0151) 706 5652
E-mail: dentenq@liv.ac.uk
Adams, Derek, MDS Liv., FDSRCSEd   Sr. Lectr.,
Dental Prosthetics
Alvesalo, Lasai, DDSc Sheff., LDS PhD   Prof.
Boyle, E. Liam, BSc BDS PhD   Sr. Lectr.
Brook, Alan H., BDS Lond., MDS Lond., FDSRCS
Prof., Paediatric Dentistry
Budenberg, Anne E., BDS   Sr. Lectr.
Carragher, Andrew O., BDS   Sr. Lectr.
Cooper, Nicholas, BDS   Sr. Lectr.
Dawson, Luke, BSc Liv., BDS Liv., PhD Liv.   Sr.
Lectr.
Higham, Susan M., BSc CNAA, PhD Liv.   Prof.,
Oral Biology
Lee, George T. R., MDS Liv., FDSRCPSGlas   Sr.
Lectr.
Mair, Lawrence H., BDS Liv., PhD Liv., FDSRCS
Sr. Lectr.
Manning, Christine J., BDS MPH   Sr. Lectr.
Pender, Neil, BDS Wales, MScD Wales, PhD,
FDSRCSEd   Prof.
Pine, Cynthia M., CBE, BDS Manc., MBA Dund.,
PhD Manc., FDSRCS   Prof., Dental Public
Health and Primary Dental Care
Preston, A. J., BDS Liv., PhD Liv., FDSRCS   Sr.
Lectr.
Risk, Janet M., BSc Liv., PhD Liv.   Sr. Lectr.
Smalley, J. W., BSc Liv., PhD Liv.   Sr. Lectr.
Smith, P. W.   Sr. Lectr.
Smith, Peter M., BSc Wales, PhD Lond.   Sr.
Lectr.
Thayer, Tom M. L., MDS Liv., BChD Liv., LDS
Liv., MSc, FDSRCSEd   Sr. Lectr.

Townsend, Grant C., BDS Adel., BScDent Adel.,
PhD Adel., DDSc Adel.   Prof.
Williams, Michael   Sr. Lectr.
Woodhead, Martin J.   Sr. Lectr.
Woolgar, Julia A., BDS Birm., PhD, FRCPath,
FDSRCS   Sr. Lectr.
Young, D. W. M.   Sr. Lectr.
Youngson, Callum C., BDS Dund., DDSc Leeds,
FDSRCS   Prof., Restorative Dentistry
Other Staff: 30 Lectrs.; 3 Tutors (Dent.
Therapy); 3 Dental Tutors†; 1 Sr. Clin.
Tutor; 5 Hon. Sr. Lectrs.; 15 Hon. Lectrs.; 1
Hon. Sr. Res. Fellow; 12 Hon. Clin. Lectrs.;
106 Hon. Clin. Tutors

Health Sciences, School of

Tel: (0151) 794 5799 E-mail: health@liv.ac.uk
Dickson, Rumona, BN Calg., MHSc McM.   Sr.
Lectr.
Robinson, Jude E., BA Durh., PhD Durh.   Sr.
Lectr.
Thornton, Eileen, BA Open(UK), MEd Liv.   Sr.
Lectr.; Head*
Walton, Julie M., MSc Liv.   Sr. Lectr.
Whittington, Richard, BA PhD   Reader
Other Staff: 1 Lectr.

Medical Imaging and Radiotherapy

Tel: (0151) 794 5805 Fax: (0151) 794 5751
E-mail: k.burgess@liv.ac.uk
Burgess, Kathryn, MMedSc Birm.   Head*
Scutt, N. Diane, MSc Liv., PhD Liv.   Sr. Lectr.
Sluming, Vanessa A., MSc Liv., PhD Liv.   Sr.
Lectr.
Other Staff: 9 Lectrs.; 2 Hon. Readers; 3 Hon.
Lectrs.; 13 Hon. Clin. Lectrs.
Research: application of Monte Carlo
simulations; breast imaging; human
reproduction; modelling of tumour control;
neurobiological systems and processes

Medical Statistics and Health Evaluation, Centre for

Tel: (0151) 794 5121
E-mail: k.forrest@liv.ac.uk
Gamble, Carrol   Sr. Lectr.
Lancaster, Gillian A., BSc Glam., MSc Leic., PhD
Lanc.   Sr. Lectr.
Tudur-Smith, Catrin   Sr. Lectr.
Williamson, Paula R., BSc Sheff., PhD Sheff.
Prof.; Dir.*
Other Staff: 4 Lectrs.
Research: clinical trials; metalysis; statistical
epidemiology; stereology; survival analysis

Nursing

Tel: (0151) 794 5684 Fax: (0151) 794 5719
E-mail: nursing@liv.ac.uk
Flynn, Maria, MSc Manc., PhD Liv.   Sr. Lectr.;
Head*
Perkins, Elizabeth S., BSc Hull, MSc Manc., PhD
Manc.   William Rathbone VI Prof.,
Community Nursing
Other Staff: 5 Lectrs.; 1 Univ. Teacher
Research: effectiveness of advanced nursing
roles; forensic mental health and violent
behaviour; service delivery and organisation

Occupational Therapy

Tel: (0151) 794 5716
E-mail: j.m.martin01@liv.ac.uk
Martin, Judith M., MEd Liv., PhD Lanc.   Sr.
Lectr.; Head*
Other Staff: 8 Lectrs.; 1 Univ. Teacher; 1 Hon.
Lectr.
Research: chronic pain; culture and health
services delivery; interprofessional
education in health care; occupational
therapy education; post-traumatic stress
disorder

Orthoptics

Tel: (0151) 794 5730 Fax: (0151) 794 5781
E-mail: m.g.stephenson@liv.ac.uk
Knox, Paul C., BSc Glas., PhD Glas.   Reader
Stephenson, M. Gail   Sr. Lectr.; Head*
Other Staff: 5 Lectrs.

Research: neuro-ophthalmology; oculomotor
control; sports vision; visual development

Physiotherapy

Tel: (0151) 794 5800 Fax: (0151) 794 5740
E-mail: jsharp@liv.ac.uk
Sharp, Jo, MSc Liv.   Lectr.; Head*
Other Staff: 9 Lectrs.; 1 Univ. Teacher†
Research: physiotherapy

Infection and Host Defence, School of

Hart, C. A. (Tony), BSc Lond., MB BS Lond., PhD
Lond., FRCPath   Prof.; Head*

Immunology, Division of

Tel: (0151) 706 4364 Fax: (0151) 706 5814
E-mail: immunology@liv.ac.uk
Christmas, Stephen E., MA Oxf., DPhil Oxf.   Sr.
Lectr.
Johnson, Peter M., MA Oxf., PhD Lond., DSc
Oxf., FRCPath   Prof., Reproductive
Immunology; Head*
Other Staff: 2 Lectrs.; 1 Hon. Visiting Prof.; 3
Hon. Res. Fellows; 1 Hon. Clin. Lectr.
Research: allergy; reproductive immunology;
tumour and transplantation immunology

Medical Microbiology and Genito-Urinary Medicine, Division of

Tel: (0151) 706 4381 Fax: (0151) 706 5805
E-mail: cahmm@liv.ac.uk
Blake, Neil W., BSc Edin., PhD Lond.   Sr. Lectr.
Cunliffe, Nigel A., BSc Liv., MB ChB Liv., PhD
Liv.   Sr. Lectr.
Ebrahimi, Bahram, BSc Lond., MSc Leeds, PhD
Edin.   Sr. Lectr.
Hart, C. A. (Tony), BSc Lond., MB BS Lond., PhD
Lond., FRCPath   Prof., Medical
Microbiology; Head*
Parry, Christopher M., BA Camb., MB BChir
Camb., FRCPath   Sr. Lectr.
Stewart, James P., BSc Edin., PhD Manc.   Prof.,
Molecular Virology
Wain, John   Sr. Lectr.
Winstanley, Craig, BSc Manc., PhD Wales   Sr.
Lectr.
Other Staff: 3 Visiting Profs.; 1 Lectr.; 6 Hon.
Sr. Lectrs.; 11 Hon. Lectrs.; 1 Hon. Sr.
Fellow; 4 Hon. Sr. Res. Fellows; 14 Hon.
Res. Fellows; 1 Hon. Visiting Fellow; 17
Hon. Clin. Lectrs.
Research: antimicrobials and antibiotic resistance;
gastrointestinal infections; infections in
intensive care; latent and persistent viral
infections; perinatal infections

Medical Education, School of

Tel: (0151) 706 4196 Fax: (0151) 706 5804
E-mail: w.a.skirrow@liv.ac.uk
Griffiths, Richard P., BSc Lond., MD Lond., FRCS,
FRCPath   Prof.; Acting Head*
Smith, John A., BSc Leeds, MSc Liv., PhD Lond.,
FIBiol   Sr. Lectr.
Taylor, Rev. David C. M., BSc Leeds, PhD Lond.
Sr. Lectr.
Other Staff: 1 Dir., Med. Studies; 5 Nurse
Tutors; 14 Univ. Community Clin.
Teachers†; 2 Hon. Sr. Lectrs.; 11 Hon.
Lectrs.; 1 Hon. Fellow; 155 Hon. Recog.
Teachers; 1 Hon. Clin. Lectr.; 13 Hon. Clin.
Tutors

Population, Community and Behavioural Studies, School of

Tel: (0151) 794 5597 Fax: (0151) 794 5604
E-mail: cfd@liv.ac.uk
Dowrick, Christopher F., BA Oxf., MB ChB
Manc., MSc Lond., MD Liv.   Prof.; Head*

Clinical Psychology, Division of

Tel: (0151) 794 5529 Fax: (0151) 794 5537
E-mail: psalmon@liv.ac.uk
Bogg, J., BA Lanc., MSc Manc., PhD Manc.   Sr.
Lectr.
Bramwell, Ros, BSc Manc., PhD Manc.   Sr.
Lectr.
Kinderman, Peter, BA Camb., MSc Leeds, PhD Liv.
Prof.; Head*

Lobban, Fiona, BA Oxf., PhD Manc.   Sr. Lectr.
McGuire, James, MA Glas., MSc Leeds, PhD Leic.   Prof.
Salmon, Peter, BA Oxf., MSc Leeds, DPhil Oxf.   Prof.
Sellwood, William, BSc Manc., MSc Manc., PhD Manc.   Sr. Lectr.
Young, Bridget, BA Sund., PhD Durh.   Sr. Lectr.
Other Staff: 3 Lectrs.; 1 Fellow; 2 Clin. Psychol. Advisers; 1 Univ. Teacher†; 3 Univ. Clin. Teachers; 3 Sr. Univ. Clin. Teachers†; 5 Hon. Lectrs.; 1 Hon. Res. Fellow
Research: offending behaviour; psychological aspects of physical health and illness; psychological processes in psychological disorders; psychopathology; reproductive health psychology/women's experience of the menstrual cycle

Primary Care

Brands, Martien, MD Amst., PhD Amst.   Sr. Lectr., Clinical Homeopathic Medicine
Bundred, Peter E., MB BS Lond., MD   Reader
Burns, Philip R., MB ChB Liv.   Sr. Lectr.
Dainty, Christine, BSc Liv.   Assoc Dir., Postgrad. Gen. Practice Educn.
Dowrick, Christopher F., BA Oxf., MB ChB Manc., MSc Lond., MD Liv.   Prof.; Head*
Fox, J. A., MB ChB Birm.   Assoc. Dir., Postgrad. Gen. Practice Educn.
Gabbay, Mark B., MB ChB Dund.   Sr. Lectr.
Howard, John C., BSc MB BS   Assoc. Dir., Gen. Practice Educn.
Kini, Kulai N., MB ChB Liv., FRCGP   Deputy Dir., Postgrad. Gen. Practice Educn.†
Lloyd-Williams, Mari A., MMedSci Leic., MD Leic.   Prof.
Mathie, Anthony G., MB BS Lond., FRCGP   Dir., Postgrad. Gen. Practice Educn.
Mellors, Arthur S., MB BS Newcastle(UK), FRCGP   Assoc. Dir., Gen. Practice Educn.
Other Staff: 2 Visiting Profs.; 4 Lectrs.; 2 Hon. Sr. Lectrs.; 13 Hon. Lectrs.; 1 Hon. Sr. Res. Fellow; 1 Hon. Visiting Sr. Fellow; 1 Hon. Fellow; 7 Hon. Res. Fellows
Research: health care education/sexual health; health technology; heart disease; psychosocial distress in primary care; user perspectives of health care

Psychiatry

Tel: (0151) 706 4149 Fax: (0151) 709 3765
E-mail: r.k.morriss@liv.ac.uk
Gowers, Simon G., BSc Lond., MB BS Lond., MPhil Lond.   Prof., Adolescent Psychiatry
Wilson, Kenneth C. M., MB ChB Liv., MPhil Lond.   Prof., Psychiatry of Old Age
Other Staff: 1 Visiting Prof.; 2 Lectrs.; 5 Hon. Sr. Lectrs.; 1 Hon. Sr. Res. Fellow; 3 Hon. Res. Fellows; 13 Hon. Clin. Lectrs.
Research: adult psychiatry; child and adolescent psychiatry; eating disorders; old age psychiatry; psychosis

Public Health

Tel: (0151) 794 5576 Fax: (0151) 794 5588
E-mail: depphenq@liv.ac.uk
Bruce, Nigel G., MB BS Lond., MSc Lond., MA Camb., PhD Lond.   Sr. Lectr.
Capewell, Simon J., MD Newcastle(UK), MSc Edin., FRCP   Prof., Clinical Epidemiology
Jacoby, A., BA Lond., PhD Newcastle(UK)   Prof., Medical Sociology
Maudsley, Gillian, MB ChB Liv., FRCPath   Sr. Lectr.
Platt, Mary Jane, MB BS Lond., MPH   Sr. Lectr.; Head*
Scott-Samuel, Alex J. R., MB ChB Liv., MCommH Liv.   Sr. Lectr.
Whitehead, Margaret M., BA York(UK), PhD Karolinska   W. H. Duncan Prof.
Williams, Evelyn M. I., MA Camb., MD Lond.   Sr. Lectr.
Other Staff: 4 Visiting Profs.; 4 Lectrs.; 1 Sr. Lectr.†; 1 Univ. Teacher†; 17 Hon. Lectrs.; 1 Hon. Sr. Fellow; 1 Hon. Sr. Res. Fellow; 7 Hon. Res. Fellows

Research: clinical epidemiology of chronic disease over the life course; practice and performance of local research ethics committees; psychological process and health; social context and consequences of ill health

Reproductive and Developmental Medicine, School of

Tel: (0151) 702 4100 Fax: (0151) 702 4024
E-mail: levans@liv.ac.uk
Neilson, James P., BSc Edin., MD Edin.   Prof.; Head*

Child Health

Tel: (0151) 252 5067 Fax: (0151) 228 5456
E-mail: m.saphier@liv.ac.uk
Carrol, Enitan D., MB ChB Aberd., MD Liv.   Sr. Lectr.
Jesudason, Edwin C., BA Camb., MB ChB Camb., FRCS   Sr. Lectr.
Losty, Paul D., MD Trinity(Dub.), FRCS   Prof.
Semple, Calum, BSc Lond., BM BCh Oxf., PhD Lond.   Sr. Lectr.
Smyth, Rosalind L., MB BS Lond., MA Camb., MD Camb., FMedSci   Brough Prof., Paediatric Medicine; Head*
Southern, Kevin W., MB ChB PhD   Sr. Lectr., Paediatric Respiratory Medicine
Other Staff: 1 Fellow; 4 Clin. Lectrs.; 1 Hon. Visiting Prof.; 2 Hon. Sr. Lectrs.; 8 Hon. Lectrs.; 1 Hon. Res. Fellow; 55 Hon. Clin. Lectrs.; 3 Hon. Clin. Tutors
Research: clinical genetics; infectious diseases; neonatology; paediatric respiratory medicine, cystic fibrosis and genetic disorders; paediatric surgery

Perinatal and Reproductive Medicine

Tel: (0151) 702 4100 E-mail: levans@liv.ac.uk
Alfirevic, Zarko, MD Zagreb, MRSci Zagreb   Prof.
Cooke, Richard W. I., MD Lond., FRCP   Prof., Neonatal Medicine
Ellis, Ian H., BSc Lond., MB BS Lond.   Sr. Lectr.
Neilson, James P., BSc Edin., MD Edin.   Prof.; Head*
Quenby, Siobhan M., MD Lond.   Sr. Lectr.
Turner, Mark, BSc St And., MB ChB Manc., PhD Manc.   Sr. Lectr.
Weeks, A. D., MB ChB Sheff., MD Leeds   Sr. Lectr.
Weindling, A. Michael, BSc Lond., MA Lond., MD Lond., FRCP   Prof.
Other Staff: 2 Lectrs.; 1 Fellow; 1 Hon. Sr. Lectr.; 40 Hon. Clin. Lectrs.; 4 Hon. Res. Fellows; 1 Hon. Fellow
Research: andrology; clinical epidemiology; foetomaternal and perinatal medicine; recurrent pregnancy loss; tropical obstetrics and gynaecology

VETERINARY SCIENCE

Tel: (0151) 794 4797 Fax: (0151) 794 7279
E-mail: deanvets@liv.ac.uk

Veterinary Clinical Science

Tel: (0151) 794 6026 Fax: (0151) 794 6028
E-mail: jyoung@liv.ac.uk
Winter, Agnes C., BVSc Liv., PhD Liv.   Sr. Lectr.; Head*
Other Staff: 1 Lectr.; 3 Hon. Sr. Fellows; 1 Hon. Fellow

Anaesthesia Division

Tel: (0151) 794 6076
Dugdale, Alexandra H. A., MA Camb., VetMB Camb.   Sr. Lectr.
Mosing, Martina, DrMedVet Vienna
Other Staff: 2 Lectrs.; 1 Resident; 3 Clin. Anaesthetists; 1 Hon. Lectr.; 1 Hon. Res. Fellow
Research: cardiovascular function and anaesthetics in horses and dogs; endotoxaemia in horses; molecular mechanisms of anaesthetic action; muscle changes in critical illness

Equine Division

Tel: (0151) 794 6073 Fax: (0151) 794 6034
E-mail: knotty@liv.ac.uk
Archer, D. C., BVMS Glas.   Sr. Lectr.
Clegg, Peter D., MA Camb., VetMB Camb., PhD Liv.   Prof.
Knottenbelt, Derek C., OBE, DVM&S Edin.   Prof.; Head*
Proudman, Christopher J., MA Camb., VetMB Camb., PhD Liv., FRCVS   Prof., Equine Studies
Singer, Ellen R., BA Penn., DVM Tufts, DVSc Guelph   Sr. Lectr.
Other Staff: 4 Lectrs.; 1 Clin. Dir.; 1 Sr. Fellow; 1 Practice Clinician; 1 Hon. Sr. Fellow; 1 Hon. Res. Fellow; 3 Interns
Research: aetiology and surgery of intestinal obstructions; endocrinology and seasonality in stallions; equine orthopaedics; equine parasitology and epidemiology; equine respiratory and alimentary tracts

Livestock Health and Welfare Division

Tel: (0151) 794 6029 Fax: (0151) 794 6065
E-mail: c.a.broadbent@liv.ac.uk
Baylis, Matthew, BA Oxf., DPhil Oxf.   Prof., Transmissible Spongiform Encephalopathy Epidemiology
Christley, Rob M., BVSc Syd., PhD Syd.   Sr. Lectr.
Cripps, Peter J., BSc Brist., BVSc Brist., MSc(Epid) Lond., PhD Brist.   Sr. Lectr.; Head*
Dobson, Hilary, PhD Liv., DSc Liv.   Prof., Veterinary Reproduction
Morgan, Kenton L., VetMB Camb., BA Camb., PhD Brist.   Prof., Epidemiology
Scudamore, James M., BSc Liv., BVSc Liv.   Prof.†
Smith, R. F., BSc Liv., BVSc Liv., PhD Liv.   Sr. Lectr.
Winter, Agnes C., BVSc Liv., PhD Liv.   Sr. Lectr.
Other Staff: 3 Visiting Profs.; 3 Lectrs.; 3 Sr. Res. Fellows; 2 Residents; 3 Practice Clinicians; 7 Hon. Lectrs.; 3 Hon. Sr. Fellows; 2 Hon. Res. Fellows
Research: cattle lameness; epidemiology; mastitis

Small Animal Division

Tel: (0151) 794 4290 Fax: (0151) 794 4304
E-mail: sah@liv.ac.uk
Blackwood, Laura, BVMS Glas., MVM Glas., PhD Glas.   Sr. Lectr., Small Animal Medicine
Carter, Stuart D., BSc Bath, PhD Bath, FRCPath   Prof.
Comerford, E. J. V., MVB   Sr. Lectr.
Dawson, Susan, BVMS Glas., PhD Liv.   Intervet Sr. Lectr.
Dukes-McEwan, Joanna, BVMS Glas., MVM Glas., PhD Edin.   Sr. Lectr.
Gaskell, Christopher J., BVSc Brist., PhD Brist.   Prof.
German, A. J., BVSc Brist., PhD Brist.   Royal Canin Sr. Lectr.
Innes, John F., BVSc Liv., PhD Brist.   Prof.; Head*
McConnell, J. F., BVM&S Edin.   Sr. Lectr.
McEwan, Neil A., BVM&S Edin., DVM Glas.   Sr. Lectr.
Nuttall, Timothy J., BSc Brist., BVSc Brist., PhD Edin.   Sr. Lectr.
Radford, A. D., BSc Liv., BVSc Liv., PhD Liv.   Sr. Lectr.
Other Staff: 2 Visiting Profs.; 7 Lectrs.; 5 Residents; 3 Clinicians (Small Animal Practice); 3 Clinician Teachers; 2 Hon. Lectrs.; 1 Hon. Res. Fellow; 1 Hon. Fellow; 3 Interns
Research: feline and canine virology; immunology of cat, dog and horse arthritides; small animal medicine and surgery; small animal nutrition

Veterinary Parasitology Unit

Tel: (0151) 705 3118 Fax: (0151) 705 8733
E-mail: jmr@liv.ac.uk
Trees, A. J. (Sandy), BVM&S Edin., PhD Edin.   Prof.

Williams, Diana J. L., BSc *Nott.*, PhD *Nott.*
Reader; Head*
Other Staff: 1 Visiting Prof.; 1 Lectr.; 2 Hon.
Res. Fellows
Research: coccidiosis immunology; immunity to
metacestodes; immunology and
epidemiology of bovine fasciolosis;
neospora; ovine toxoplasmosis

Veterinary Pathology

Tel: (0151) 794 4265 Fax: (0151) 794 4268
E-mail: m.bennett@liv.ac.uk
Bennett, Malcolm, BVSc *Liv.*, PhD *Liv.*, FRCPath
Prof.; Head*
Birtles, Richard, BSc *Leeds*, PhD *Open(UK)* Sr.
Lectr.
Bradbury, Janet M., MSc *St And.*, PhD *Liv.*
Prof.
Carter, Stuart D., BSc *Bath*, PhD *Bath*, FRCPath
Prof.
Gaskell, Rosalind M., BVSc *Brist.*, PhD *Brist.*
Prof.†
Jones, Richard C., PhD *Liv.*, DSc *Birm.*, FRCPath
Prof.
Kipar, Anja, DrMedVet *Giessen* Prof.
Scudamore, James M., BSc *Liv.*, BVSc *Liv.*
Prof.†
Wastling, Jonathan M., BSc *Keele*, PhD *Aberd.*
Reader
Wigley, Paul, BSc *Lond.*, PhD *Wales* Sr. Lectr.
Woldehiwet, Zerai, DVM *Salonika*, PhD *Edin.*
Reader
Other Staff: 7 Visiting Profs.; 10 Lectrs.; 8
Hon. Lectrs.; 7 Hon. Sr. Fellows; 11 Hon.
Res. Fellows
Research: comparative immunology;
immunogenetics; immunopathogenesis;
infectious diseases

Veterinary Preclinical Sciences

Tel: (0151) 794 4229 Fax: (0151) 794 4243
E-mail: r.g.cooke@liv.ac.uk
Beynon, Robert J., BSc *Wales*, PhD *Wales* Prof.,
Veterinary Basic Sciences
Cooke, Robert G., BSc *Liv.*, PhD *Liv.* Sr. Lectr.;
Head*
Hurst, Jane L., BSc *Birm.*, PhD *Birm.* William
Prescott Prof., Animal Science
Morris, Richard, BSc *Wales*, PhD *Leeds* Reader
Shirazi-Beechey, Soraya P., BS *Mich.*, PhD *Lond.*
Prof.
Stockley, P., BSc *Nott.*, PhD *Brist.* Sr. Lectr.
Thippeswamy, T., BVSc *B'lore.*, MVSc *B'lore.*,
PhD *Liv.* Sr. Lectr.
Vaillant, Camille R., BSc *Wales*, PhD *Liv.* Sr.
Lectr.
Wastling, Jonathan M., BSc *Keele*, PhD *Aberd.*
Reader
Other Staff: 4 Visiting Profs.; 5 Lectrs.; 1
Clinician Teacher; 2 Hon. Lectrs.; 3 Hon.
Sr. Fellows; 4 Hon. Res. Fellows
Research: gastroenterology; neurobiology;
protein structure and function

SPECIAL CENTRES, ETC

Advanced Internet Methods and Emergent Systems, Centre for

Tel: (0151) 795 0110 Fax: (0151) 795 0111
E-mail: contact@aimes.net
Kehoe, Dennis F., BSc(Eng) *Lond.*, PhD *Liv.*
Prof.; Dir.*
Research: 'grid' technology and applications to e-
commerce

Archive Studies, Centre for

Tel: (0151) 794 2390 Fax: (0151) 794 2366
E-mail: c.m.williams@liv.ac.uk
Buchanan, Alexandrina, BA MSc PhD Dir.*
Research: archives in the United Kingdom and
the government agenda; records and
information management

Cancer Tissue Bank

Tel: (0151) 705 4474 E-mail: rudland@liv.ac.uk
Rudland, Philip S., MA *Camb.*, PhD *Camb.*,
FRCPath, FIBiol Dir.*

Research: interdisciplinary collaboration in
oncology

Cell Imaging, Centre for

Tel: (0151) 795 4424 Fax: (0151) 795 4404
E-mail: mwhite@liv.ac.uk
White, Michael R. H., BA *Oxf.*, PhD *Lond.*
Dir.*
Research: real-time single cell imaging

Central and Eastern European Studies, Centre for

Tel: (0151) 794 2422 Fax: (0151) 794 2366
E-mail: swainnj@liv.ac.uk
Swain, Nigel J., MA *Camb.*, PhD *Camb.* Deputy
Dir.*
Research: identity of farming households; life
under the former socialist regimes; politics
of agricultural protection; rural
unemployment and rural regeneration;
socio-economic transformation

Charity Law Unit

Tel: (0151) 794 2931
E-mail: d.e.dennis@liv.ac.uk
Atkinson, Karen E. Acting Dir.*

Child, the Family and the Law, Centre for the Study of the

Tel: (0151) 794 3819 Fax: (0151) 794 2884
E-mail: c.m.lyon@liv.ac.uk
Lyon, Christina M., LLB *Lond.* Dir.*
Research: children and family law, policy and
practice

Clinical Tropical Medicine, Wellcome Trust Centre for Research in

Tel: (0151) 794 4221 Fax: (0151) 794 4222
E-mail: joanne.hollett@liv.ac.uk
Winstanley, Peter A., MB ChB *Liv.*, MD *Liv.*,
FRCP Dir.*
Research: public health needs of tropical
countries; tropical medicine

Cognitive Neuroscience Research Centre

Tel: (0151) 794 6954
E-mail: a.r.mayes@liv.ac.uk
Roberts, J. Neil, BSc *Liv.*, MSc *Aberd.*, PhD *Wales*
Dir.*
Research: amnesia; cognitive science; hearing
and speech/sensory integration; language
processing; neural mechanisms of human
attention

Comparative Infectious Diseases, Centre for

Tel: (0151) 794 6122 Fax: (0151) 794 6005
E-mail: richard.birtles@liv.ac.uk
Birtles, Richard, BSc *Leeds*, PhD *Open(UK)* Co-
Dir.*
Stewart, James P., BSc *Edin.*, PhD *Manc.* Co-
Dir.*
Research: interdisciplinary approaches to
infectious disease problems

Critical Incident Decision Making, Centre for

Tel: (0151) 794 6938 Fax: (0151) 794 6937
E-mail: l.j.alison@liv.ac.uk
Alison, Laurence, BSc *Lond.*, MSc *Sur.*, PhD *Liv.*
Prof.; Dir.*

English Language Unit

Tel: (0151) 794 2734 Fax: (0151) 794 2730
E-mail: english@liv.ac.uk
Thompson, Susan E., BA *Kent*, MA *Leeds*, PhD
Liv. Dir.*
Research: applied linguistics; discourse analysis;
language teaching and learning

Environmental Radioactivity Research Centre

Tel: (0151) 794 4020 Fax: (0151) 794 4061
E-mail: appleby@liv.ac.uk
Appleby, Peter G., BSc *Cant.*, BE *Cant.*, PhD
Cant. Dir.*

Research: dating of lake and estuarine sediments
and peat cores; erosion studies; monitoring
radioactive discharges; studies of Chernobyl
fallout

Europe in the World Centre

Tel: (0151) 794 2904 Fax: (0151) 794 3948
E-mail: ewc@liv.ac.uk
Miles, Lee S., BA *Lanc.*, MIS *Birm.*, PhD *Hull*
Prof.; Dir.*
Research: European models of constitutionalism
and democratic governance; European
Union (EU) monetary and cohesion
policies; media and communications;
migration and xenophobia; regional security
and EU borders

Health and Community Care Research Unit

Tel: (0151) 794 5503 Fax: (0151) 794 5258
E-mail: t.quillan@liv.ac.uk
Perkins, Elizabeth S., BSc *Hull*, MSc *Manc.*, PhD
Manc. Dir.*
Research: organisation and management of
health and social services; use and
experience of health and social care

Health Studies, Latin-American Centre for

Tel: (0151) 708 2222 Fax: (0151) 708 8733
E-mail: a.kroeger@liv.ac.uk
Kroeger, Prof. Axel, DrMed *Hamburg*, MSc *Lond.*,
PhD *Heidel.* Dir.*
Research: equity in health; health policies;
impact of health sector reforms on delivery
of public health programmes; management
of disease control programmes; quality
assurance in health

Impact Research Centre

Tel: (0151) 794 4874 Fax: (0151) 794 4892
E-mail: r.mines@liv.ac.uk
Cantwell, Wesley J., BSc *S'ton.*, MSc *Lond.*, PhD
Lond. Prof.; Dir.*
Research: explosion and impact loading of
structures; response of structural membranes
under large impact loads; structural
crashworthiness and transportation safety

Intelligent Monitoring Systems, Centre for

Tel: (0151) 794 4524 Fax: (0151) 794 4540
E-mail: joe@liv.ac.uk
Spencer, Joseph W., BEng *Liv.*, PhD *Liv.*
Reader; Dir.*

International and European Law Unit

Tel: (0151) 794 2812 Fax: (0151) 794 2884
E-mail: dmcg@liv.ac.uk
McGoldrick, Dominic, LLB *Nott.*, PhD *Nott.*
Prof., Public International Law; Dir.*

Magnetic Resonance and Image Analysis Research Centre

Tel: (0151) 794 5631 Fax: (0151) 794 5635
E-mail: sue1@liv.ac.uk
Roberts, J. Neil, BSc *Liv.*, MSc *Aberd.*, PhD *Wales*
Dir.*
Other Staff: 1 Hon. Sr. Res. Fellow
Research: functional magnetic resonance imaging
(MRI) of various perceptual and cognitive
functions; magnetic resonance spectroscopy;
peripheral vascular disease; stereological
estimation of the volume of structures; use
of computational methods to investigate
properties in the brain

Manx Studies, Centre for

Tel: (01624) 673074 Fax: (01624) 678752
E-mail: cms@liv.ac.uk
Mytum, Harold C. Dir.*
Research: Manx archaeology; Manx culture (art,
language, music); Manx environment; Manx
history; Manx politics, economics and
tourism

Materials and Catalysis, Liverpool Centre for
Rosseinsky, Matthew J., BA Oxf., DPhil Oxf.
  Prof., Inorganic Chemistry; Dir.*

Medical Technology Research Centre, Liverpool-Daresbury (Herald)
Tel: (01925) 603886 Fax: (01925) 603618
  E-mail: c.j.hall@dl.ac.uk
Hall, Chris J., BSc S'ton., PhD S'ton.   Dir.*
Research: use of iodising radiation for detecting
  disease

Medicine, Law and Bioethics, Institute of
Tel: (0151) 794 2302 Fax: (0151) 794 2311
  E-mail: imlab@liv.ac.uk
Halliday, Samantha L., LLB E.Anglia, PhD   Dir.*
Research: drug regulation; medical litigation;
  National Health Service (NHS) reforms and
  resource allocation; public health;
  reproductive medicine

Medieval Studies, Centre for
Tel: (0151) 794 2394 Fax: (0151) 794 2366
  E-mail: lcms@liv.ac.uk
Costambeys, Marios J., BA Lond., PhD Camb.
  Dir.*
Research: history and culture, c.300–c.1600, of
  North-West England, Wales, Europe, Near
  East and North Africa

Nanoscale Science, Centre for
Tel: (0151) 794 3493 Fax: (0151) 794 3588
  E-mail: drritson@liv.ac.uk
Brust, Mathias, PhD Liv.   Prof.; Dir.*
Research: biomedicine; functional materials;
  magnetic nanostructured materials;
  nanoelectronics; sensor technology

Popular Music, Institute of
Tel: (0151) 794 3101 Fax: (0151) 794 2566
  E-mail: ipm@liv.ac.uk
Cohen, Sara, BA Sus., DPhil Oxf.   Dir.*
Research: civic music policy initiatives; popular
  music, tourism and urban regeneration;
  popular music-making in Merseyside; urban
  shrinkage

Port and Maritime History, Centre for
Tel: (0151) 794 2413 Fax: (0151) 794 2425
  E-mail: w.r.lee@liv.ac.uk
Lee, W. Robert, MA Oxf., DPhil Oxf.   Dir.*
Research: changing structure of commerce and
  trade; dock management and ancillary
  occupations; Liverpool's merchant
  community 1851-1912; Merseyside's
  maritime history (social and community
  context)

Primary Science and Technology, Centre for Research in
Tel: (0151) 794 3270 Fax: (0151) 794 3271
  E-mail: ge02@liv.ac.uk
Russell, Terence J., BA MEd PhD   Dir.*
Research: assessing progress in science;
  curriculum development; e-learning and e-
  assessment; national test and task
  development; use of the Web and integrated
  digital television (iDTV) to support teaching
  and learning

Proudman Oceanographic Laboratory
Affiliated Institution
Tel: (0151) 795 4800 Fax: (0151) 795 4801
  E-mail: polenquiries@pol.ac.uk
Hill, Prof. A. Ed, MSc Wales, PhD Wales   Dir.*
Research: advanced numerical model
  development; changes in global and regional
  sea/land levels; continuous ocean
  measurement methods; function of shallow
  sea systems; sea level variability and
  extremes

Quaternary Environmental Research Centre
Tel: (0151) 794 3463 Fax: (0151) 794 3464
  E-mail: shaw@liv.ac.uk
Shaw, John, BSc Liv., PhD Liv.   Dir.*
Research: cavity detection and risk assessment;
  climatic change from magnetic
  measurements; environmental effects of
  magnetic fields; environmental monitoring
  instrumentation development; environmental
  pollution monitoring

Surface Science Research Centre
Tel: (0151) 794 3541 Fax: (0151) 794 3896
  E-mail: joyce@liv.ac.uk
Raval, Rasmita, BA Camb., PhD E.Anglia   Dir.*
Research: complex surface chemistry; gas-surface
  dynamics; nanotechnology; optical probes;
  physical and electronic structure

Sustainable Water, Integrated Management and Ecosystem Research Centre
Maltby, Edward, BSc Sheff., PhD Brist.   Dir.*

Time Series and Forecasting, Centre for
Tel: (0151) 794 4758 E-mail: sa17@liv.ac.uk
Bhansali, Rajendra J., BCom Bom., BSc Lond.,
  PhD Lond.   Co-Dir.*
McCabe, Brendan P. M., BA Trinity(Dub.), MSc
  Lond., PhD Amst.   Co-Dir.*

Tropical Medical Microbiology, Centre for
Tel: (0151) 706 4379 Fax: (0151) 706 5805
  E-mail: cmparry@liv.ac.uk
Shears, Paul, BSc Reading, MB BS Lond., MD Liv.
  Dir.*
Research: diseases in the tropics; epidemiology,
  clinical and genetic studies on antimicrobial-
  resistant bacteria; molecular epidemiology of
  enteric pathogens

Victorian Research, Gladstone Centre for
Tel: (0151) 794 2724 E-mail: j.johnv@liv.ac.uk
John, Juliet V., BA Camb., PhD Lond.   Dir.*
Research: interdisciplinary Victorian studies

CONTACT OFFICERS
Academic affairs. Academic Secretary: Jones,
  Catherine M., BA Liv.
  (E-mail: jonesc@liv.ac.uk)
Accommodation. Housing Manager: Kelley,
  Michael (E-mail: accommodation@liv.ac.uk)
Admissions (first degree). (International
  students) Director of International
  Recruitment and Relations: Quirk, John N.,
  BSc Staffs. (E-mail: irro@liv.ac.uk)
Admissions (first degree). (UK and EC
  students) Head of Service, University of
  Liverpool UK Student Recruitment Office:
  Brown, Claire E.
  (E-mail: ugrecruitment@liv.ac.uk)
Admissions (higher degree). (UK and EC
  students) Head of Postgraduate
  Recruitment: Gaynor, Glover M., BA Leeds
  (E-mail: pgrecruitment@liv.ac.uk)
Admissions (higher degree). (International
  students) Director of International
  Recruitment and Relations: Quirk, John N.,
  BSc Staffs. (E-mail: irro@liv.ac.uk)
Adult/continuing education. Director, Centre
  for Lifelong Learning: Merry, Anne M., BSc
  Hull, MSc Leeds, PhD Hull
  (E-mail: conted@liv.ac.uk)
Archives. University Archivist: Allan, Adrian
  R., BA Durh. (E-mail: archives@liv.ac.uk)
Careers. Director, Careers and Employability
  Service: Redmond, Paul, BA Manc., MA
  Manc., PhD Open(UK)
  (E-mail: careers@liv.ac.uk)
Computing services. Director, Computing
  Services: Stinson, Iain, BSc Lond., MSc Lond.,
  FBCS (E-mail: helpdesk@liv.ac.uk)

Consultancy services. Director, Business
  Gateway: Head, Rob
  (E-mail: business@liv.ac.uk)
Credit transfer. Director, Student
  Administration and Support Division:
  Knight, Heather (E-mail: knih1@liv.ac.uk)
Equal opportunities. Head, Diversity and
  Equality: Hewison, Frances M., BA Hull
  (E-mail: f.m.hewison@liv.ac.uk)
Estates and buildings/works and services.
  Director of Facilities Management: Hackett,
  Patrick (E-mail: patrick.hackett@liv.ac.uk)
Examinations. Head, Student Administration:
  Brookfield, David J., BSc CNAA, PhD Liv.
  (E-mail: examsenq@liv.ac.uk)
Finance. Director of Finance: Yuille, Michael
  G. S., BAcc Glas. (E-mail: findir@liv.ac.uk)
Industrial liaison. Director, Business Gateway:
  Head, Rob (E-mail: business@liv.ac.uk)
International office. Director of International
  Recruitment and Relations: Quirk, John N.,
  BSc Staffs. (E-mail: irro@liv.ac.uk)
Library (chief librarian). Librarian: Sykes,
  Philip, BA Oxf. (E-mail: p.sykes@liv.ac.uk)
Marketing. Research and Business Services:
  Harvey, Kerron A., BA York(UK), PhD Stir.
  (E-mail: respub@liv.ac.uk)
Minorities/disadvantaged groups. Head,
  Diversity and Equality: Hewison, Frances
  M., BA Hull (E-mail: f.m.hewison@liv.ac.uk)
Personnel/human resources. Director of
  Human Resources: Rutherford, Susan J., BSc
  Leic. (E-mail: jobs@liv.ac.uk)
Public relations. Media Relations Manager:
  Spark, Kate, BA Warw.
  (E-mail: kate.spark@liv.ac.uk)
Publications. Publications Manager: Elsworth,
  Suzanne
  (E-mail: suzanne.elsworth@liv.ac.uk)
Purchasing. Head of Procurement: Walton,
  Mark R., BA CNAA
  (E-mail: m.r.walton@liv.ac.uk)
Quality assurance and accreditation. Acting
  Director, Teaching Quality Support
  Division: McAleer, Liz, LLB Lond.
  (E-mail: tqsd@liv.ac.uk)
Research. Director, Research and Business
  Services: Carter, Ian, BSc Newcastle(UK), PhD
  Strath. (E-mail: orsil@liv.ac.uk)
Safety. Safety Adviser: Bowes, Christopher M.,
  BA Camb., PhD Lond.
  (E-mail: c.bowes@liv.ac.uk)
Scholarships, awards, loans. (Scholarships,
  awards) Student Administration and
  Support Division: Morton, Rebecca
  (E-mail: m.stephens@liv.ac.uk)
Scholarships, awards, loans. (Loans) Senior
  Student Financial Adviser: Christian, Linda
  S. (E-mail: l.s.christian@liv.ac.uk)
Schools liaison. Head of Schools and Colleges
  Relations: Todd, Christine E., BA Sur.
  (E-mail: ugrecruitment@liv.ac.uk)
Security. Security Manager: Wiggins, Paul
  (E-mail: paul.wiggins@liv.ac.uk)
Staff development and training. Training and
  Development Officer: Merritt, Tony
  (E-mail: training@liv.ac.uk)
Strategic planning. Director, Planning:
  Goddard, Vikki, BA Brad., MSocSc Birm.
  (E-mail: v.r.goddard@liv.ac.uk)
Student union. Chief Executive, Guild of
  Students: Robertson, Peter, BSc
  (E-mail: guild@liv.ac.uk)
Student welfare/counselling. Head of the
  Counselling Service: Sheehan, Karen J., BSc
  (E-mail: counserv@liv.ac.uk)
Students from other countries. International
  Students' Adviser: Haimes, Susan, BA Liv.
  (E-mail: ssrec@liv.ac.uk)
Students with disabilities. Welfare and
  Disability Adviser: Naylor, Beth
  (E-mail: disteam@liv.ac.uk)
University press. Publisher: Bloxsidge, Robin
  J. C., BA Liv. (E-mail: janmar@liv.ac.uk)

[Information supplied by the institution as at 30
November 2007, and edited by the ACU]

LIVERPOOL HOPE UNIVERSITY

Founded 2005

Postal Address: Liverpool, England L16 9JD
Telephone: (0151) 291 3000 Fax: (0151) 291 3100
URL: http://www.hope.ac.uk/

RECTOR AND CHIEF EXECUTIVE*—Pillay, Prof. Gerald J.

LIVERPOOL JOHN MOORES UNIVERSITY

Founded 1992

Member of the Association of Commonwealth Universities

Postal Address: Rodney House, 70 Mount Pleasant, Liverpool, England L3 5UX
Telephone: (0151) 231 2121
URL: http://www.livjm.ac.uk

VICE-CHANCELLOR AND CHIEF EXECUTIVE*—Brown, Prof. Michael A., CBE, DL, BSc Nott., PhD Nott., FIP, FRSA, FIMgt, FIET
PRO VICE-CHANCELLOR (INFRASTRUCTURE)—Bickerstaffe, J. Allan, FCIS
PRO VICE-CHANCELLOR (DEVELOPMENT)—Kenny, Steve A., BA Manc., MA Manc., MSc Manc.
PRO VICE-CHANCELLOR (DELIVERY)—Kelleher, Prof. Gerry, BSc Lond., PhD Leeds
PRO VICE-CHANCELLOR (MARKETING AND COLLABORATIVE PARTNERSHIPS)—Ibbs, Michele, BA Liv.
PRO VICE-CHANCELLOR (ADMINISTRATION) AND UNIVERSITY SECRETARY‡—Wild, Alison M.
FINANCE DIRECTOR—McClelland, Denise

GENERAL INFORMATION

History. The university was founded in 1823 as the Liverpool Mechanics' and Apprentices' Library. In 1970 many of the colleges formed in the intervening years were merged to become Liverpool Polytechnic, and in 1992 the university was given its current title.

Admission to first degree courses (see also United Kingdom Introduction). Through Universities and Colleges Admissions Service (UCAS). UK nationals: normally a minimum of 5 passes at General Certificate of Secondary Education (GCSE) including mathematics and English language, and 2 A levels or equivalent. International applicants: certified academic achievement equivalent to UK entry requirements. Where English is a second language: TOEFL score of 550–600, IELTS 6 or equivalent.

First Degrees (see also United Kingdom Directory to Subjects of Study). BA, BEd, BEng, BSc, LLB.
All courses are full-time and normally last 3 years. BEng/BA (business, computing and modern languages): 3 years plus 1 year placement in employment. Selected courses are available part-time.

Higher Degrees (see also United Kingdom Directory to Subjects of Study).
Master's. MA, MBA, MPhil, MSc.
Admission. Applicants to master's degree courses must normally hold a relevant first degree.
Length of course. Full-time: MA, MSc: 1 year; MPhil: 1–2 years; MBA: 2 years. Part-time: MA, MSc: 2–3 years; MPhil: 2–4 years; MBA: 4 years.
Doctoral. PhD.
Admission. For admission to PhD applicants must normally hold an appropriate master's degree with relevant research component.
Length of course. Full-time: PhD: 3 years. Part-time: PhD: 5 years.

Libraries. Volumes: 500,000. Periodicals subscribed to: 2500. Other holdings: 660,000 miscellaneous items.

FACULTIES/SCHOOLS

Business and Law
Tel: (0151) 231 3208 Fax: (0151) 709 5241
Dean: Kirkbride, Prof. James, LLB Leic., MPhil Leic., PhD Leeds Met.
Secretary: Gallagher, Karen

Education, Community and Leisure
Tel: (0151) 231 5240
Dean: Burton, Diana, BEng E.Anglia, MEng Birm., PhD Birm.
Secretary: Edge, Cherrill

Health and Applied Social Sciences
Tel: (0151) 231 4005 Fax: (0151) 258 1593
E-mail: health@livjm.ac.uk
Dean: Mazhindu, Prof. Godfrey, MSc Sur., PhD Reading
Secretary: Runacus, Alison

Media, Arts and Social Sciences
Tel: (0151) 231 5016
Dean: Webster, Prof. Roger J., BA Lond., MA Lond., PhD Lond.
Secretary: MacHenry, Patricia

Science
Tel: (0151) 231 2042
Dean: Wheeler, Prof. Peter, BSc Durh., PhD Durh.
Secretary: Prayle, Wendy

Technology and Environment
Tel: (0151) 231 2435 Fax: (0151) 231 2194
E-mail: d.meehan@livjm.ac.uk
Dean: Meehan, Prof. Diane, BSc Liv.J.Moores, PhD Liv.
Secretary: Reader, Gill

ACADEMIC UNITS
Arranged by Schools

Accounting, Finance and Economics
Tel: (0151) 231 3860 Fax: (0151) 707 0423
Bowdery, Angela, BSc Salf.   Principal Lectr.
Gardner, David N., BA Wolv., MSc Salf.   Dir.*
Padgett, Graham C., BA Wales, MA Manc. Principal Lectr.
Pegum, Roger H., BA Manc., MA Manc. Principal Lectr.
Pyke, Christopher J.   Principal Lectr.
Sargant, Christina M., BA Liv., MA Open(UK) Deputy Dir.
Smith, Stephen E., BA Essex, MA Essex, PhD Manc.   Principal Lectr.
Vane, Howard R., BA Liv., MA Manc.   Prof., Economics
Other Staff: 23 Lectr./Sr. Lectrs.; 1 Partnerships Manager

Applied Social and Community Studies
Brennan, Angela, LLB Liv.J.Moores, LLM Open(UK) Dir.*
Clifford, Derek J., BA Manc., MA Manc., PhD Manc.   Reader
Leather, Nicola C., BSc CNAA, MSc Bolton Inst. Asst. Dir.
Lyons, Christina M., MSc Manc.Met., PhD Manc.Met.   Principal Lectr.
Mayhew, John R., BSc Leeds, MSc Salf.   Head, Programmes
Medforth, Nick, BA Liv.J.Moores, MSc Bolton IHE Head, Cross Sch. Devel.
Tolan, Janet, BA Manc.   Principal Lectr.
Walton, Irene, BEd Manc., MSc Keele, PhD Liv.J.Moores   Head, Res.
Other Staff: 50 Lectr./Sr. Lectrs.; 4 Hon. Lectrs.

Art and Design, Liverpool School of
Tel: (0151) 231 5083 Fax: (0151) 231 5096
Barraclough, John H., BA Newcastle(UK) Principal Lectr.
Brown, Gary P., BA Portsmouth   Principal Lectr.
Chuhan, Jagjit   Prof., International Art
Clelland, Douglas J.   Prof., Architecture

Dawber, Martin, BA Liv.J.Moores, MA RCA
Principal Lectr.
Fallows, Colin, BA Liv.J.Moores   Prof., Sound
and Visual Art
Gant, Richard M., BA Nott.Trent, MA Manc.Met.,
MSc Manc.Met., PhD Liv.J.Moores   Principal
Lectr.; Head, Fine Art
Godfrey, Julia K.   Reader
Hardstaff, Stephen W., BA Portsmouth   Principal
Lectr.
Holt, Roy   Reader
MacDonald, Robert, BA PhD   Reader
Newton, John   Reader
Rees, David C., BA Manc.Met., MA RCA   Deputy
Dir.*
Smith, Merilyn M.   Prof., Fine Art
Wilson, Delphine, MA C.England   Principal
Lectr.
Wroot, Ian, BA Liv.   Principal Lectr.
Other Staff: 28 Lectr./Sr. Lectrs.; 1 Drawing
Co-ordinator; 4 Fractional Lectrs.†; 4
Lectrs.†
Vacant Posts: 1 Dir.*
Research: materiality and context in
contemporary art; trace memory

Biological and Earth Science

Tel: (0151) 231 2413 Fax: (0151) 207 3224
Aureli, Filippo, BSc Rome, PhD Utrecht   Reader
Brown, Richard, BSc Aberd., PhD Aberd.   Reader
Dickinson, Nicholas M., BSc Liv.J.Moores, PhD
Keele   Prof., Environmental Biology
Dowell, Simon D., BSc Exe., DPhil Oxf.   Dir.*
Feltham, Mark J., BSc Exe., PhD Stir.   Principal
Lectr.
Gonzalez, Silvia, BSc ME PhD   Reader
Haram, Owen J., BSc Liv., PhD Liv.   Principal
Lectr.
Hodkinson, Ian D., BSc Newcastle(UK), PhD Lanc.
Prof., Entomology and Animal Ecology
Lepp, Nicholas W., BSc Hull, PhD Hull   Prof.,
Plant Sciences
Mislom, Clare, BSc Durh., PhD Liv.   Principal
Lectr.
Sherwood, Graham J., BA Camb., PhD Wales
Academic Manager
Turner, Alan, BA Sheff., PhD Sheff., DSc Sheff.
Prof., Vertebrate Palaeontology
Young, Andrew J., BSc H-W, PhD Liv.   Prof.†,
Applied Plant Sciences
Other Staff: 16 Lectr./Sr. Lectrs.; 1 Postdoctoral
Res. Assoc.; 2 Res. Officers
Research: applied plant sciences; biodiversity and
evolution; biological anthropology

Biomolecular Sciences

Tel: (0151) 231 2233 Fax: (0151) 298 2821
E-mail: m.a.prosser@livjm.ac.uk
Billington, David, BSc Liv., PhD Newcastle(UK)
Prof., Medical Biochemistry
Bilton, Rodney F., BSc Durh., PhD Newcastle(UK)
Prof., Applied Biochemistry
Evans, E. Hilary, BSc Brist., PhD Brist.   Prof.,
Biochemistry; Dir.*
Phipps, David A., BSc Sheff., MSc Kent, PhD Kent
Deputy Dir.
Rahman, Khalid, BSc Liv.J.Moores, PhD Liv.J.Moores
Reader
Reed, Celia J., BSc Cape Town, PhD CNAA
Reader
Reynolds, Colin D., BSc Lond., MSc Lond., PhD
Liv.   Prof., Molecular Biophysics
Sands, Richard L., MSc Birm., PhD Birm.
Reader
Saunders, Venetia A., BSc Brist., PhD Brist.
Prof., Microbiology Genetics
Sharples, George P., BSc Liv., PhD Liv.   Reader
Whalley, Anthony J., BSc Liv., PhD Liv.   Prof.,
Mycology
Other Staff: 15 Lectr./Sr. Lectrs.; 1 Fractional
Lectr.†
Research: function of nucleo-proteins; structure
of chromoton

Built Environment

Tel: (0151) 231 3586 Fax: (0151) 709 4957
E-mail: bltadmissions@livjm.ac.uk
Alkhaddar, Rafid M., BSc Basrah, MSc Strath.,
PhD Strath.   Reader

Al-Nageim, Hassan K., BSc Baghdad, MSc Wales,
PhD H-W   Prof., Structural Engineering
Brown, Peter K.   Prof., Property Taxation
Couch, Christopher R., MSc Lond.   Prof.,
Urban Planning
Horgan, Bernice M., BE N.U.I., ME N.U.I.
Principal Lectr.; Head, Civil and
Environmental Engin.
Morley, David A., BSc Lond., MA Liv.   Deputy
Dir.
Riley, Michael L., BSc Salf., MSc H-W
Principal Lectr.; Dir.*
Ross, Andrew D., BSc Liv.J.Moores, MSc Salf.
Head of Construction Studies
Williams, Delyth W., BA Wales, LLB Liv.   Prof.,
Estate Management
Williams, Peter N., MSc Aston   Principal Lectr.
Wright, Linda P., BA Liv., MBA Liv.   Principal
Lectr.
Other Staff: 28 Lectr./Sr. Lectrs.; 1 Head,
External Affairs; 1 Academic Programmes
Manager; 1 Postdoctoral Researcher
Research: the importance of culture in
international business

Business Information

Tel: (0151) 231 3801 Fax: (0151) 707 0423
Ashcroft, Linda S., BA Liv., MA Liv.J.Moores
Reader
Barlow, Neil, BSc Liv.J.Moores, MPhil Liv.J.Moores,
PhD Liv.J.Moores   Head, Centre for
Automotive Sector Studies
Beckford, John, DPhil   Visiting Prof.†,
Management Cybernetics
Farrow, Anne J., BA Manc.Met., MA Liv.J.Moores
Principal Lectr.
Haynes, Douglas L., BSc Birm., MA Lanc.   Dir.*
Matthews, Graham, BA Nott., PhD Lough.
Prof., Information and Library Management
McClelland, Robert J., BSc Liv.J.Moores, MSc
Liv.J.Moores   Reader
Middleton, Sandra E. A., BA Open(UK), MSc
UMIST   Deputy Dir.
Mulhaney, Ann, BSc Liv.J.Moores   Principal
Lectr.
Yolles, Maurice, PhD Lanc.   Prof., Management
Systems
Other Staff: 19 Lectr./Sr. Lectrs.; 1 Sr.
Consultant†

Computing and Mathematical Sciences

Tel: (0151) 231 2267 Fax: (0151) 207 4594
E-mail: d.parker@livjm.ac.uk
Bamford, Carl, BA Camb., MA Camb., DPhil Sus.
Principal Lectr.
Duffy, Sandra P., BSc Wales   Principal Lectr.
El Rhalibi, Abdennour, BA Cons.Nat.Arts &
Métiers, Paris, MPhil Montpellier II   Principal
Lectr.
England, David, BSc Salf., MSc Strath., PhD Lanc.
Principal Lectr.
Hanneghan, Martin, BSc Liv.J.Moores, PhD
Liv.J.Moores   Principal Lectr.
Kelleher, Prof. Gerry, BSc Lond., PhD Leeds
Prof., Artificial Intelligence
Lisboa, Paulo, BSc Liv., PhD Liv.   Prof.,
Industrial Mathematics
Merabti, Madjid A., BSc Liv.J.Moores, MA Lanc.,
PhD Lanc.   Prof., Networked Systems; Dir.*
Moynihan, Edmund P., BSc Manc.   Reader
Pereira, Rubem, BEng Pontif.Rio de Janeiro, MSc
S.Bank, PhD Manc.Met.   Principal Lectr.
Pountney, David C., BSc Wales, PhD Wales
Principal Lectr.
Shi, Qi, BSc Dalian Maritime, MSc Dalian U.T.,
PhD Dalian U.T.   Reader
Taleb-Bendiab, Azzelarabe, BSc Liv., MSc Liv.,
PhD Liv.   Prof., Computing
Wade, Stuart J., BSc Salf., PhD Salf.   Reader
Willitts, John, BSc UMIST, MSc UMIST
Principal Lectr.
Other Staff: 35 Lectr./Sr. Lectrs.; 2 Res.
Fellows
Research: applied artificial intelligence

Education

Tel: (0151) 231 5425
Aiello, Michael, BA Liv., MSc Manc.Met., PhD
Manc.Met.   Head, Centre for Continual
Professional Devel.
Horsfall, Peter, BSc Liv.   Head, Centre for Sci.,
Technol. and Art
Johnston, Kate, BSc Leic., MEd Leeds   Principal
Lectr.
King, Patricia M., BSc Manc., MEng Liv.
Principal Lectr.
Murphy, Janet I., BSc UMIST   Head, Centre for
Educn.
Peel, Jennifer, BA Birm., MEd Loyola(La.), PhD
Nott.   Principal Lectr.
Yorke, Mantz   Prof., Higher Education
Other Staff: 27 Lectr./Sr. Lectrs.; 3 Programme
Managers; 1 Hon. Lectr.
Vacant Posts: Dir.*

Engineering

Tel: (0151) 231 2011 Fax: (0151) 2073460
E-mail: s.j.thornton-newby@livjm.ac.uk
Alexander, Graham I., MSc UMIST, PhD UMIST
Principal Lectr.
Barclay, Ian, MSc Lough.   Prof., Technology
Bartlett, Rebecca, BSc Leeds, PhD Manc.
Principal Lectr.
Burton, David R., BSc Liv.J.Moores, PhD
Liv.J.Moores   Prof., Engineering Science
Colquhoun, Gary J., MSc Liv.J.Moores, PhD
Liv.J.Moores   Reader
Douglas, Steven S., BSc Liv.J.Moores, MSc
Liv.J.Moores, PhD Liv.J.Moores   Principal Lectr.
Ellis, David L., BSc Liv.J.Moores, PhD Liv.J.Moores
Principal Lectr.
Gilmartin, Michael J., BEng Liv., PhD Liv.J.Moores
Reader
Gomm, James B., BEng Liv.J.Moores, PhD
Liv.J.Moores   Reader
Harvey, David M., BSc Liv.J.Moores, PhD
Liv.J.Moores   Prof., Electronic Engineering
Jenkinson, Ian D., BSc Newcastle(UK), MSc Liv.,
PhD Liv.J.Moores   Dir.*
Jones, Ian S., BSc Manc., PhD Manc.   Reader
Jones, Karl O., BEng Liv.J.Moores, PhD Liv.J.Moores
Principal Lectr.
Kaldos, Andrew, PhD Bud.   Reader
Lalor, Michael, BSc Liv., PhD Liv.   Prof.,
Engineering Optics
Levi, Emil, BSc Novi Sad, MSc Belgrade, PhD
Belgrade   Prof., Electric Machines and Drives
Morgan, Roger, BA Camb., PhD Camb.   Prof.,
Electronic Engineering
Otterson, Paul, BSc Liv.J.Moores, MSc Liv.J.Moores,
PhD Liv.J.Moores   Principal Lectr.
Rothwell, Glynn, BSc UMIST, PhD Liv.J.Moores
Principal Lectr.
Shaw, Michael, BEng Liv.J.Moores, PhD Liv.J.Moores
Deputy Dir.
Wall, Alan D., BSc Liv.J.Moores, MSc Lanc.
Reader
Wang, Jin Q., BEng Dalian U.T., MSc
Newcastle(UK), PhD Newcastle(UK)   Prof.,
Marine Technology
Williams, David, BEng Liv., PhD Liv.   Prof.,
Control Systems
Williams, Vincent J., BSc Wales, LLB Lond., MSc
Brad.   Principal Lectr.
Woolley, Neil H., BSc Manc., MSc Manc., PhD
Manc.   Reader
Yu, Dingli, BEng Harbin, MEng Jilin, PhD
Coventry   Reader
Zhang, Jian, BSc Xi'an Jiaotong, PhD Liv.   Prof.,
Microelectronics
Other Staff: 33 Lectr./Sr. Lectrs.; 2 Res.
Fellows; 1 EDC Centre Manager; 2 Engin.
Officers
Research: control engineering; electric machines
and drives; e-technology and commerce;
marine and offshore technology;
mechanical engineering and manufacturing

Languages

Tel: (0151) 231 3836 Fax: (0151) 231 3433
E-mail: l.archibald@livjm.ac.uk
Archibald, Linda, BA Stir., PhD Stir.   Prof.;
Dir.*

Haworth, William J., BA Durh., MSc Aston
  Principal Lectr.
Hill, Susan J., BSc Lanc.   Principal Lectr.
Luukko-Vinchenzo, Leila H., MA Munich, DPhil
  Munich   Deputy Dir.
Shepherd, Martine T., MSc Salf.   Deputy Dir.
Whitehead, Margaret M., BA Sheff., MA Lond.
  Principal Lectr.
Other Staff: 20 Lectr./Sr. Lectrs.; 7 Fractional
  Lectrs.†

Law

Tel: (0151) 231 3912
Ball, Christine, LLB Liv.J.Moores   Principal Lectr.
Brooman, Simon D., LLB Liv.J.Moores   Principal
  Lectr.
Cooke, Peter J., LLB Leeds, MPhil CNAA   Prof.,
  Common Law
de Cruz, Stephen P., LLB Sing., LLM
  Newcastle(UK), PhD Wales   Prof.
Evans, Roger J., BSc Wales, MA Warw., PhD
  Birm.   Prof.; Dir.*
Hardy, Sarah, LLB Wales, MA Warw.   Principal
  Lectr.
Jones, Dick P., LLB Lond., MA CNAA   Reader
Mair, George I. U., MA Glas., MSc Strath., PhD
  Lond.   Prof., Criminal Justice
Rawstorne, Shirley, MA Lanc.   Principal Lectr.
Selfe, David W., BA Lanc., MPhil Lanc.   Deputy
  Dir.
Other Staff: 31 Lectr./Sr. Lectrs.

Management

Tel: (0151) 231 3417 Fax: (0151) 707 0423
Balchin, Alistair J., BSc Hull, MBA Durh.
  Principal Lectr.
Douglas, Alex, BA Open(UK), MBA Napier, PhD
  QM Edin.   Reader
Harrison, Patricia A., MA Bourne.   Principal
  Lectr.
Lindsay, Keith W., BA Cape Town, PhD
  Liv.J.Moores   Deputy Dir.
Meehan, John P., BA Manc.Met., MSc Salf.
  Principal Lectr.
Moogan, Yvonne J., BSc Hull, MSc Salf., PhD
  Manc.Met.   Principal Lectr.
Mouzughi, Yusra, BA Lond., MBA H-W
  Principal Lectr.
Naylor, John B., BA Camb., MA Liv.   Principal
  Lectr.
Reed, John, BSc Newcastle(UK), MSc York(UK)
  Principal Lectr.
Simmons, John A., BA Manc.Met., MA
  Liv.J.Moores, PhD Liv.J.Moores
Vaughan, John W., LLB Manc., LLM Manc.
  Dir.*
Williamson, Peter M., BSc Manc., MSc Manc.
  Principal Lectr.
Other Staff: 22 Lectr./Sr. Lectrs.; 1 Comml.
  and Devel. Manager; 1 SME Workforce
  Devel. Co-ordinator

Media, Critical and Creative Arts

Tel: (0151) 231 5006 Fax: (0151) 231 5049
E-mail: mcca@livjm.ac.uk
Ashplant, Timothy G., BA Oxf., DPhil Sus.
  Reader
Borthwick, Stuart, BA CNAA, PhD Liv.J.Moores
  Principal Lectr.
Cusick, Edmund, MA Aberd., DPhil Oxf.
  Principal Lectr.
Frost, Chris, MA Lanc.   Prof., Journalism
Graham, Elspeth, BA Manc., MA Manc., PhD
  Manc.   Reader
Jones, Judith, BA Open(UK), MA Manc.Met.
  Principal Lectr.
Llewellyn, D. Llew J., MA Leeds, DEd Leeds
  Principal Lectr.
Long, Trevor S., BA Manc., MA Liv.   Principal
  Lectr.
Moody, Nickianne A., BA Warw., MPhil Warw.
  Principal Lectr.
Newman, Jenny, BA Liv., BPhil Liv., PhD Liv.
  Reader
Norquay, Glenda, MA Edin., PhD Edin.   Prof.,
  Scottish Literary Studies

Price, Joanna H., BA York(UK), MA Sus., DPhil
  Sus.   Principal Lectr.
Smyth, Gerrard A. M., BA Lanc., MA Lanc., PhD
  Staffs.   Reader
Spargo, Tamsin E. M., BA Wales, PhD Wales
  Reader; Dir.*
Other Staff: 1 Visiting Prof.; 41 Lectr./Sr.
  Lectrs.; 1 Lectr.†
Research: script adaptation

Nursing and Primary Care Practice

Congdon, Shirley, BSc Tees., MA Durh.   Asst.
  Dir., Undergrad./Postgrad. Studies
Firby, Patricia A., MSc Sur.   Dir.*
Jinks, Annette M., BA Open(UK), MA Keele, PhD
  Manc.   Prof.; Head, Inst. for Clin. Nursing
Jones, Colin, BA Manc., PhD Liv.J.Moores
  Principal Lectr.
Laing, Michelle, BSc Liv.J.Moores, MBA Liv.J.Moores
  Principal Lectr.
Mazhindu, Debbie M., BA Portsmouth, DPhil Sus.
  Principal Lectr.
McMurchie, Colin, BA MSc   Principal Lectr.
Simpson, George, BEd Bolton IHE, MSc Liv.
  Principal Lectr.
Stitt, Pauline, BSc Manc.Met., MBA Keele   Asst.
  Dir., Curric.
Welsh, Ian, BEd Bolton IHE   Principal Lectr.
Other Staff: 54 Lectr./Sr. Lectrs.; 1 Practice
  Devel. Co-ordinator; 1 Hon. Lectr.

Outdoors, Leisure and Food

Tel: (0151) 231 5280
Hackett, Allen F., BSc Leeds, MPhil Leeds, PhD
  Newcastle(UK)   Reader
Huddart, David, BA Reading, PhD Reading   Prof.,
  Quaternary and Environmental Science
Jepson, Margaret B., BEd Leeds, MA Lanc.
  Programme Manager, Consumer Studies
Maxwell, Sheila M., BSc Liv., MSc Liv., PhD Liv.
  Prof., Biochemical Nutrition
Prisk, Elaine M., BSc Leeds, MSc Liv.   Dir.*
Stott, Timothy A., BSc Wales, PhD Stir.   Reader
Other Staff: 15 Lectr./Sr. Lectrs.; 1 Res. Co-
  ordinator; 2 Researchers; 1 Deputy
  Programme Leader; 1 Indust. Liaison Tutor

Pharmacy and Chemistry

Tel: (0151) 231 2248 Fax: (0151) 231 2170
Armstrong, David J., BSc Brist., PhD Brist.
  Reader
Cronin, Mark T. D., BSc Liv.J.Moores, PhD
  Liv.J.Moores   Reader
Ford, James L., BSc CNAA, PhD CNAA   Dir.*
Heaton, C. Alan, PhD Durh.   Prof.
Morris, Harold, BSc Salf., PhD Salf.   Reader
Mottram, David R., BPharm Wales, PhD Wales
  Prof., Pharmacy Practice
Rostron, Christopher, BSc Manc., PhD Aston
  Academic Manager
Rowe, Philip H., BSc Reading, MSc Leeds, PhD Liv.
  Reader
Other Staff: 24 Lectr./Sr. Lectrs.; 2 Teacher
  Practitioners; 2 Res. Officers; 4 Hon. Lectrs.
Research: drug design and discovery; medicinal
  chemistry

Physical Education, Sports and Dance

Tel: (0151) 231 5279
Brooks, Pauline, BA Lough., MA Temple   Head,
  Centre for Dance
Hatfield, Susan C., BEd Liv.J.Moores   Academic
  Manager
Shenton, Patricia A., MEd Liv., MSc Nott.   Dir.*
Vickerman, Philip B., BSc Open(UK), MEd
  Liv.J.Moores, PhD Leeds   Head, Centre for
  Sport
Other Staff: 18 Lectr./Sr. Lectrs.
Research: exercise activity in children's health

Psychology

Tel: (0151) 231 4106 Fax: (0151) 231 4245
E-mail: psychology@livjm.ac.uk
Fisk, John E., BSc Lond., MA Georgetown, PhD
  Lond.   Reader
James, Pamela E., BSc Leeds, PhD Liv.   Prof.,
  Counselling Psychology

Lancaster, Brian L., BSc Manc., MSc Manc., PhD
  Liv.J.Moores   Principal Lectr.; Academic
  Manager
Tattersall, Andrew J., BSc Wales, DPhil Oxf.
  Prof.; Dir.*
Other Staff: 20 Lectr./Sr. Lectrs.
Research: cognition, development and
  educational psychology; consciousness and
  transpersonal psychology; human factors
  and applied cognitive psychology;
  psychology and health

Public Health, Centre for

Tel: (0151) 231 4510 Fax: (0151) 231 4515
  E-mail: info@cph.org.uk
Adams, Nicola, BSc Ulster, PhD Ulster   Head,
  Centre for Res. in Health Care
Bellis, Mark A., BSc Manc., PhD Manc.   Dir.*
Crossley, Michele, BA Manc., PhD Open(UK)
  Prof., Social Work
Glenn, Sheila, BSc Lond., PhD Lond.   Prof.,
  Applied Development Psychology
Lyons, Mary, BSc Manc., MPH Liv.   Principal
  Lectr.
McVeigh, James, MSc Liv.J.Moores   Head,
  Substance Use
Money, Michael C., BA Sheff., MA Sheff., PhD
  Liv.   Principal Lectr.
Perkins, Clare, BA Lond., MSc Lond.   Deputy
  Dir.
Springett, Rosemary J., BA Leeds, MA Leeds, PhD
  Leeds   Prof., Health Promotion
Other Staff: 7 Lectr./Sr. Lectrs.; 3 Sr. Res.
  Fellows; 1 Alcohol Res. Manager; 1
  Environmental Public Health Specialist; 1
  Postgrad. Res. Tutor; 2 Hon. Lectrs.

Social Science

Tel: (0151) 231 2121
Boothby, John, BA Manc., PhD Manc.   Reader
Cook, Ian G., BSc Aberd., PhD Nott.   Prof.,
  Human Geography
Davies, Robert S. W., BSc Brist., PhD Liv.J.Moores
  Prof., History
Edwards, Margaret M., BA Liv.J.Moores, PhD Lanc.
  Dir.*
Francis, Andrew J., BA Lond., MSc Lond.
  Principal Lectr.
Gill, Peter, BSc Lond., MA Essex   Reader
Hall, Gill, BA Lanc., MA Lanc.   Principal Lectr.
Herson, John D., BA Oxf., MSc Lond.   Principal
  Lectr.
Hull, Andrew P., BA Portsmouth, PhD Liv.J.Moores
  Reader
Mannin, Michael L., BSc Lond., MA Kent
  Principal Lectr.
Nightingale, Martin, BSc Brist., PhD Brist.
  Principal Lectr.
Sim, Joseph, BA Stir., MSc Stir., PhD Stir.
  Prof., Criminology
Tombs, Stephen P., BA Wolv., MA Manc.   Prof.,
  Sociology
Other Staff: 15 Lectr./Sr. Lectrs.; 1 Res. Officer

Sports and Exercise Science

Tel: (0151) 231 4321 Fax: (0151) 231 4353
Atkinson, Gregory, BSc Liv.J.Moores, PhD
  Liv.J.Moores   Prof., Chronobiology and
  Exercise
Cable, Nigel T., BSc Liv.J.Moores, PhD W.Aust.
  Dir.*
El-Sayad, Mahmoud S., BSc Helwan, MSc Helwan,
  PhD Salf.   Prof., Applied Physiology
George, Keith, BSc Liv.J.Moores, MSc Belf., MSc
  Qu., PhD Manc.Met.   Principal Lectr.
Gilbourne, Dave, BA Lond., MSc Lond.   Deputy
  Head
Goldspink, David F., BSc Newcastle(UK), PhD
  Newcastle(UK), DSc Newcastle(UK)   Prof., Cell
  and Molecular Sports Science
Lake, Mark J., BSc Lough., MSc Penn., PhD Guelph
  Reader
Lees, Adrian, BSc Leeds, PhD Leeds   Prof.,
  Biomechanics
MacLaren, Donald P. M., BSc Liv., MSc Salf.,
  PhD Liv.J.Moores   Prof., Sports Nutrition

Reilly, Thomas P., BA N.U.I., MSc Lond., PhD
CNAA   Dir., Res.
Scott, Mark A., BSc Manc.Met., PhD Manc.Met.
Reader
Stratton, Gareth, MPhil Exe., PhD Liv.J.Moores,
BHum   Reader, Paediatric Exercise Science
Waterhouse, Jim M., BA Oxf., DPhil Oxf.
Prof., Biological Rhythms
Williams, Andrew M., BSc Manc.Met., PhD Liv.
Prof.
Other Staff: 11 Lectr./Sr. Lectrs.; 3 Res.
Fellows

SPECIAL CENTRES, ETC

Astrophysics Research Institute

Tel: (0151) 231 2919 Fax: (0151) 231 2921
E-mail: admin@astro.livjm.ac.uk
Bode, Michael F., BSc Leeds, PhD Keele   Prof.
Carter, David, BA Oxf., MA Oxf., PhD Camb.
Prof., Observational Astronomy
Collins, Christopher A., BSc Lond., BA Lond.,
PhD Lond.   Prof., Cosmology
Steele, Iain A., BSc Leic., PhD Leic.   Reader
Other Staff: 4 Lectr./Sr. Lectrs.; 4 Res. Fellows
Research: hot star environments; observational
cosmology; star formation properties

Digital Content, International Centre for (ICDC)

Tel: (0151) 231 5129 Fax: (0151) 231 5132
E-mail: icdcadmissions@livjm.ac.uk
Robertshaw, Simon, MA RCA   Prof., Digitial
Media; Dir.*
Other Staff: 2 Lectr./Sr. Lectrs.; 2 Res. Officers;
1 Bus. Devel. Officer; 1 Incubation Manager

Lairdside Maritime Centre

Tel: (0151) 647 0494 Fax: (0151) 647 0498
E-mail: lairdside@livjm.ac.uk
Russ, Philip, BSc Lond., MSc Manc.   Dir.*
Other Staff: 2 Lectrs.; 1 Bus. Devel. Manager; 1
Tech. Support Officer

Urban Affairs, European Institute of

Tel: (0151) 231 5172 Fax: (0151) 708 0650
E-mail: j.parry@livjm.ac.uk
Evans, Stephen R., BA Oxf., MA Oxf., MCD Liv.,
PhD Liv.   Reader
Meegan, Richard, BSc Wales, MSc Reading
Reader
Parkinson, Michael, CBE, BA Liv., MA Manc.
Prof.; Head*
Russell, Hilary   Prof., Urban Policy
Other Staff: 1 Res. Fellow

CONTACT OFFICERS

Academic affairs. Director of Teaching and
Learning Innovation: Margham, J. Phil
(E-mail: j.p.margham@livjm.ac.uk)

Accommodation. Assistant Residence Manager:
Lyons, Jackie (E-mail: j.lyons@livjm.ac.uk)
Admissions (higher degree). Postgraduate
Registrar: Ward, Sue
(E-mail: s.p.ward@livjm.ac.uk)
Adult/continuing education. Director of
Teaching and Learning Innovation:
Margham, J. Phil
(E-mail: j.p.margham@livjm.ac.uk)
Alumni. Director of Advancement: Beesley,
Paul (E-mail: p.beesley@livjm.ac.uk)
Archives. Director of Learning and
Information Services: Melling, Maxine
(E-mail: m.melling@livjm.ac.uk)
Careers. Manager, Personal and Career
Development Team: James, Chris
(E-mail: c.p.james@livjm.ac.uk)
Computing services. Director of Computing
and Information Services: Wrightson, Jim
(E-mail: j.r.wrightson@livjm.ac.uk)
Consultancy services. Reachout Manager:
Leyland, Chris
(E-mail: c.leyland@livjm.ac.uk)
Credit transfer. Director of Teaching and
Learning Innovation: Margham, J. Phil
(E-mail: j.p.margham@livjm.ac.uk)
Development/fund-raising. Director of
Advancement: Beesley, Paul
(E-mail: p.beesley@livjm.ac.uk)
Equal opportunities. Senior Adviser, Equality
and Policy Development: Anwar, Naseem
(E-mail: n.anwar@livjm.ac.uk)
Estates and buildings/works and services.
Director of Property Services: Connell, Joe
(E-mail: j.connell@livjm.ac.uk)
Finance. Director of Financial Services:
McClelland, Denise
(E-mail: d.mcclelland@livjm.ac.uk)
General enquiries. Manager, Resources and
Secretariat: Grimes, Chris
(E-mail: c.grimes@livjm.ac.uk)
Health services. Director of Corporate
Services: Kerrigan, Brian
(E-mail: b.a.kerrigan@livjm.ac.uk)
Industrial liaison. Reachout Manager:
Leyland, Chris
(E-mail: c.leyland@livjm.ac.uk)
International office. Head of International
Recruitment: Seavor, Gill
(E-mail: g.seavor@livjm.ac.uk)
Library (chief librarian). Director of Learning
and Information Services: Melling, Maxine
(E-mail: m.melling@livjm.ac.uk)
Library (enquiries). Director of Learning and
Information Services: Melling, Maxine
(E-mail: m.melling@livjm.ac.uk)
Marketing. Corporate Communications
Manager: Martin, Janet
(E-mail: j.martin@livjm.ac.uk)
Minorities/disadvantaged groups. Senior
Adviser, Equality and Policy Development:

Anwar, Naseem
(E-mail: n.anwar@livjm.ac.uk)
Personnel/human resources. Director of
Personnel: Lloyd, Julie
(E-mail: j.lloyd@livjm.ac.uk)
Public relations. Corporate Communications
Manager: Martin, Janet
(E-mail: j.martin@livjm.ac.uk)
Publications. Corporate Communications
Manager: Martin, Janet
(E-mail: j.martin@livjm.ac.uk)
Purchasing. Purchasing Services Manager:
McDonald, Shaun
(E-mail: s.p.mcdonald@livjm.ac.uk)
Quality assurance and accreditation. Director
of Quality Support: Miller, Anne
(E-mail: a.m.miller@livjm.ac.uk)
Research. Head of Research: Young, Prof.
Andrew J., BSc H-W, PhD Liv.
(E-mail: a.j.young@livjm.ac.uk)
Safety. Senior Health and Safety Officer: Jones,
Terry (E-mail: t.l.jones@livjm.ac.uk)
Scholarships, awards, loans. Director of
Student Services: Saunders, Peter
(E-mail: p.j.saunders@livjm.ac.uk)
Security. Security Manager: Shackleton, Steve
(E-mail: s.shackleton@livjm.ac.uk)
Sport and recreation. Lecturer in Sports
Development: Nixon, Sarah
(E-mail: s.nixon@livjm.ac.uk)
Staff development and training. Manager,
Staff Development Centre: Box, Meriel
(E-mail: m.box@livjm.ac.uk)
Student union. Senior Manager (Student
Union): Smith, Nick
(E-mail: lsunsmit@livjm.ac.uk)
Student welfare/counselling. Director of
Student Services: Saunders, Peter
(E-mail: p.j.saunders@livjm.ac.uk)
Students from other countries. Director of
Languages: Seavor, Gill
(E-mail: g.seavor@livjm.ac.uk)
Students with disabilities. Senior Adviser,
Equality and Policy Development: Anwar,
Naseem (E-mail: n.anwar@livjm.ac.uk)
University press. Corporate Communications
Manager: Martin, Janet
(E-mail: j.martin@livjm.ac.uk)
Women. Senior Adviser, Equality and Policy
Development: Anwar, Naseem
(E-mail: n.anwar@livjm.ac.uk)

CAMPUS/COLLEGE HEADS

Liverpool Institute of Performing Arts,
Mount Street, Liverpool L1 9HF. (Tel:
(0151) 330 3000; Fax: (0151) 330 3131)
Chief Executive: Featherstone-Witty, Mark

[Information supplied by the institution as at 21
February 2005, and edited by the ACU]

UNIVERSITY OF LONDON

Founded 1836

Member of the Association of Commonwealth Universities

Postal Address: Senate House, Malet Street, London, England WC1E 7HU
Telephone: (020) 7862 8000 **Fax:** (020) 7862 8358
URL: http://www.lon.ac.uk

VICE-CHANCELLOR*—Davies, Sir Graeme, BE NZ, MA Camb., PhD NZ, ScD Camb., Hon. LLD Liv., Hon. LLD Strath.,
Hon. DMet Sheff., Hon. DSc Nott., Hon. DEng Manc.Met., Hon. DUniv Glas., Hon. DUniv Paisley, Hon. DSc Ulster,
FREng, FRSEd, FIMechE, Hon. FRSNZ, Hon. FTCL, Hon. FRCPSGlas
DEPUTY VICE-CHANCELLOR—Smith, Prof. Adrian, BA Lond., MA Oxf., MSc PhD, FIMA, FRS
PRO-VICE-CHANCELLOR (MEDICINE)—Farthing, Prof. Michael J. G., MD DSc(Med), FRCP, FMedSci
PRO-VICE-CHANCELLOR—Mann, Prof. Nicholas, CBE, MA Camb., PhD Camb., Hon. DLitt Warw., FBA
DIRECTOR OF ADMINISTRATION AND CLERK OF THE COUNCIL‡—Swarbrick, Catherine M., BA Lond.
DIRECTOR OF FINANCE—Cryer, Richard, MA, FCA

GENERAL INFORMATION

History. The university was constituted by
royal charter in 1836 as a body empowered to
grant degrees to students of approved
institutions after examination. In 1900 the
university was reconstituted: institutions were
admitted as schools of the university and it
thus became a teaching as well as an
examining university. It is now a federation of
colleges and institutes which teach for and
award degrees of the University of London.
The university also offers a number of its
degrees and other awards by distance learning
through its external system.

The university precinct is situated in
Bloomsbury, central London. Apart from Royal
Holloway (Surrey), almost all the colleges and
institutes are located within a 5km radius of
Bloomsbury.

Admission to first degree courses (see also
United Kingdom Introduction). Through
Universities and Colleges Admissions Service
(UCAS). Course requirements are set by the
colleges themselves: see individual entries,
below.

First Degrees (see also University of London
Directory to Subjects of Study). BA, BD, BDS,
BEd, BEng, BMedSci, BMus, BSc, BSc(Econ),
BVetMed, LLB, MB BS, MEng, MPharm, MSci.

Most first degrees may also be taken by
part-time study.

Length of course. Full-time: BA, BD, BEd, BEng,
BMedSci, BMus, BSc, BSc(Econ), LLB: 3 years;
MEng, MPharm, MSci: 4 years; BDS, BVetMed:
5 years; MB BS: 5–6 years. By distance learning:
BA, BD, BSc, BSc(Econ), LLB: 3–8 years.

Higher Degrees (see also University of
London Directory to Subjects of Study).

Master's. LLM, MA, MArch, MBA, MClinDent,
MDS, MEd, MFA, MMus, MPA, MPH, MPhil,
MPhilStud, MRes, MS, MSc, MTcg, MTh,
MVetMed.

Most master's degrees may also be taken by
part-time study.

Length of course. Full-time: LLM, MA, MArch,
MBA, MEd, MMus, MRes, MSc, MTh,
MVetMed: 1 year; MClinDent, MDS, MFA,
MPA, MPhil, MPhilStud, MS: 2 years. By distance
learning: LLM, MA, MBA, MSc: 2–5 years;
MClinDent: 4 years.

Doctoral. DClinPsy, DEdPsy, DHC, DMin,
DPsychotherapy, DrClinMed, DrPH, DVetMed,
EdD, EngD, MD, MD(Res), PhD.

Research degrees and specialist doctorates
may also be taken by part-time study.

Length of course. Full-time: DrClinMed,
DVetMed, MD, MD(Res), PhD: 2 years;
DClinPsy, DEdPsy, DPsychotherapy, DrPH,
EdD, EngD: 3 years. Part-time: DMin: 5–6 years.

Libraries. Volumes: 2,000,000. Periodicals
subscribed to: 5295.

Statistics. Students (2005–2006): distance
education/external 36,000.

COLLEGES, INSTITUTES, ETC, OF THE UNIVERSITY OF LONDON

The teaching and research work of the
University is carried out in (1) colleges of the
University each controlled by its own
governing body; (2) and (3) institutes
established and controlled by the University.

(1) Colleges of the University
Birkbeck, University of London, p 1776
Central School of Speech and Drama p 1780
Courtauld Institute of Art, p 1780
Goldsmiths, University of London, p 1781
Heythrop College, p 1783
Institute of Cancer Research, p 1784
Institute of Education, p 1786
King's College London, p 1787
London Business School, p 1797
London School of Economics and Political
Science, p 1799
London School of Hygiene and Tropical
Medicine, p 1803
Queen Mary, University of London, p 1805
Royal Academy of Music, p. 1806
Royal Holloway, University of London, p 1807
Royal Veterinary College, p 1812
St George's, University of London, p 1813
School of Oriental and African Studies, p 1814
School of Pharmacy, p 1818
University College London, p 1819

(2) Institutes, p 1820
University of London Institute in Paris
University Marine Biological Station, Millport

(3) School of Advanced Study, p 1820
Institute for the Study of the Americas
Institute of Advanced Legal Studies
Institute of Classical Studies
Institute of Commonwealth Studies
Institute of English Studies
Institute of Germanic and Romance Studies
Institute of Historical Research

Institute of Musical Research
Institute of Philosophy
Warburg Institute

CONTACT OFFICERS

Accommodation. Head of Housing Services:
Miller, Robert, BSc MA
(E-mail: housing@london.ac.uk)
Archives. University Archivist: Temple,
Richard, BA Oxf., MA Lond.
Careers. Careers Group, University of London:
Martin, Anne-Marie, BSc MSc
(E-mail: directors.office@careers.lon.ac.uk)
Computing services. Director, University of
London Computer Centre: Rippon, David,
BSc Lond., PhD Lond.
Distance education. Director, External and
Internal Student Administration: McConnell,
J. A., BA Lond., MA Brun.
(E-mail: enquiries@external.lon.ac.uk)
Estates and buildings/works and services.
Director of Estates and Facilities: Perham,
Julian, MBA, FRICS
Examinations. Director, External and Internal
Student Administration: McConnell, J. A.,
BA Lond., MA Brun.
(E-mail: enquiries@external.lon.ac.uk)
Finance. Director of Finance: Cryer, Richard,
MA, FCA
General enquiries. Head, Information Centre:
Harris, Joanne (E-mail: enquiries@lon.ac.uk)
Library (chief librarian). Director, University
of London Research Library Services:
Pearson, David, MA, FSA, FCLIP
(E-mail: david.pearson@london.ac.uk)
Personnel/human resources. Director of
Human Resources: Frost, Kim B., BA Oxf.,
MA Oxf., MLit Oxf., FCIPD
Public relations. Head of Communications:
Rai, Binda (E-mail: binda.rai@london.ac.uk)
Publications. Central Secretariat: Cushion,
Collette
(E-mail: centralsecretariat@london.ac.uk)
Scholarships, awards, loans. Head of
Academic Office: Johnson, Susan E.
Schools liaison. University Entrance
Requirements Adviser: Hurford, Susan, BA
Staff development and training. Staff
Development and Human Resources
Manager: Small, Susan A., MSc, FCIPD

[Information supplied by the institution as at 4 August
2006, and edited by the ACU]

UNIVERSITY OF LONDON : DIRECTORY TO SUBJECTS OF STUDY

The table below shows which of the institutions indicated provide facilities for study and/or research in the subjects named. In the case of related subject areas which have been grouped together (eg Botany/Plant Science), it should be borne in mind that one or more of the subjects may be offered by the institution concerned.

For further information about the individual subjects taught at each institution, please refer to the *Index to Subjects of Study* at the end of the Yearbook, but for full details about subjects/courses offered at universities and university colleges in the Commonwealth each institution's own official publications must be consulted. U = may be studied for first degree course; M = may be studied for master's degree course; D = research facilities to doctoral level; X = all three levels (UMD).

	Birkbeck	Central Sch. of Speech & Drama	Courtauld Inst. of Art	Goldsmiths	Heythrop	Hygiene & Tropical Med.	I. for the Study of the Americas	Inst. of Advanced Legal Studies	Inst. of Cancer Research	Inst. of Classical Studies	Inst. of Commonwealth Studies	Inst. of English Studies	Inst. of Germanic & Romance Studies	Inst. of Historical Research	King's	London Business Sch.	LSE	Royal Acad. of Music	Royal Holloway	Royal Veterinary	SOAS	Sch. of Pharmacy	St George's	U. of Lond. Inst. in Paris	Warburg Inst.	London: external programme
Accountancy/Accounting	U														D		X		D							U
Administration/Administrative Studies															U											
African Languages/Studies											MD										X					
Agriculture/Agricultural Science																										M
American Studies	M			UD			MD								X											
Anatomical Science/Anatomy															X								D			
Ancient Indian History and Culture																					X					
Animal Science/Husbandry/Production																				X						M
Anthropology/Folklore				X			MD										X				X					
Applied Physics																			U							
Arabic																					X					
Archaeology	X														X				UD		X					
Architecture																					X					
Area Studies				M			MD								MD		MD				X					
Art, Fine				X																						
Art, History of	X		X	X																	X					
Artificial Intelligence															MD											
Arts Management	M	M																								
Arts and Culture	X	M													MD											
Asian/Pacific Studies											D										X					
Astronomy/Astrophysics/Space Science																			UD							
Australian Studies											D				MD											
Banking/Finance	X															M	X		X		MD					UM
Behavioural Sciences				MD											MD		X		UD							M
Bengali																					X					
Biochemistry	X								D						X				UD			D	D			
Bioinformatics	MD														MD				M				U			
Biology	X														X				X							
Biology Molecular	X								D										UD				D			
Biomedical Sciences	U								D						X				UD			D	U			
Biophysics	MD														X											
Biostatistics															D											
Biotechnology									D										UD							
Botany/Plant Science																			D							
Buddhist Studies																					X					
Business Administration																			UD		MD					M

	Birkbeck	Central Sch. of Speech & Drama	Courtauld Inst. of Art	Goldsmiths	Heythrop	Hygiene & Tropical Med.	I. for the Study of the Americas	Inst. of Advanced Legal Studies	Inst. of Cancer Research	Inst. of Classical Studies	Inst. of Commonwealth Studies	Inst. of English Sudies	Inst. of Germanic & Romance Studies	Inst. of Historical Research	King's	London Business Sch.	LSE	Royal Acad. of Music	Royal Holloway	Royal Veterinary	SOAS	Sch. of Pharmacy	St George's	U. of Lond. Inst. in Paris	Warburg Inst.	London: external programme
Business Computing																										U
Business/Commerce	M														MD				X		M					UM
Canadian Studies							M				D															
Caribbean Studies							MD				D															
Catholicism					M																X					
Chemistry	X								D						MD				MD			D				
Child Health															MD											
Child Welfare															MD											
Child and Family Psychology	MD														MD											
Child/Youth Studies															M											
Chinese/Chinese Studies																					X					
Civil Care/Security												MD														
Classics/Greek/Latin/Ancient History	X									D					X				X							U
Cognitive Science				MD											M				D							
Commonwealth Studies	M										D	M														
Communication Sciences																					MD					
Communication/Journalism/Media Studies	X			X													MD		X		X					
Communications/Information Management																	MD		X							U
Community Health															M											
Community Studies	UM			X																						
Computer Science	X			X											X				X							U
Conservation Studies	X																									M
Corporate Governance	M																									
Counselling	M			X																						
Creative Writing	M	M		MD															X							
Criminal Justice/Public Policy															MD											
Criminology				MD											M		MD									
Cultural Heritage														M												
Cultural Studies	X			X	M									M	MD											
Defence Studies															MD											
Dentistry															X											M
Dermatology															M											
Design		X		X																						
Development Studies	M			M			MD				MD				X		MD		MD		X					M
Drama/Theatre/Dance/Performing Arts	UM	X		X											M				X					MD		
E-Business	M																		D							

	Birkbeck	Central Sch. of Speech & Drama	Courtauld Inst. of Art	Goldsmiths	Heythrop	Hygiene & Tropical Med.	I. for the Study of the Americas	Inst. of Advanced Legal Studies	Inst. of Cancer Research	Inst. of Classical Studies	Inst. of Commonwealth Studies	Inst. of English Sudies	Inst. of Germanic & Romance Studies	Inst. of Historical Research	King's	London Business Sch.	LSE	Royal Acad. of Music	Royal Holloway	Royal Veterinary	SOAS	Sch. of Pharmacy	St George's	U. of Lond. Inst. in Paris	Warburg Inst.	London: external programme
E-Commerce	M																		MD							
Ecology															MD				D							
Economic History							M										X		UD							
Economic Planning and Development							M																			
Economics	X			U			MD										X		X		X					UM
Economics Agricultural/Agribusiness																										M
Education		UM		X											X									M		
Education Adult	X														M											
Education Distance																					M					M
Education Extension	MD																									
Education Secondary															M											
Electronics															X											
Engineering															X											
Engineering Communications/ Telecommunications															X											
Engineering Electrical/Electronic															X											
Engineering Mechanical/Production															X											
Engineering Medical															M											
English	X			X								MD			X				X					D		U
English as a Second Language																					UM					
Entomology																			D							
Environmental Geosciences	U														MD											
Environmental Health															M											
Environmental Management	X																									
Environmental Science/Studies	X						M								X		X		X							M
Ethics	M														MD											
Ethics, Law and Governance	M														MD											
Ethnicity/Multiculturalism	MD						MD																			
Ethnomusicology																			M		X					
European Studies	M			X									MD		X		MD		X							
Film/Photography/Television/Animation	X			X									M						X		X					
Food Science/Nutrition/Home Science/Dietetics															X											
Forensic Science															MD				D							
French/French Studies	X			UD									MD		X				X		U			X		U
Gandhian Studies																					X					
Genetics															X				UD							
Geographic Information Systems/Geomatics	M														MD											

	Birkbeck	Central Sch. of Speech & Drama	Courtauld Inst. of Art	Goldsmiths	Heythrop	Hygiene & Tropical Med.	I. for the Study of the Americas	Inst. of Advanced Legal Studies	Inst. of Cancer Research	Inst. of Classical Studies	Inst. of Commonwealth Studies	Inst. of English Studies	Inst. of Germanic & Romance Studies	Inst. of Historical Research	King's	London Business Sch.	LSE	Royal Acad. of Music	Royal Holloway	Royal Veterinary	SOAS	Sch. of Pharmacy	St George's	U. of Lond. Inst. in Paris	Warburg Inst.	London: external programme
Geography	X														X		X		X		U					U
Geology/Earth Sciences/Atmospheric Studies	X																		X							
German/Germanic Studies	X			X									MD		X				X							U
Gerontology	MD														MD											
Ghanaian Languages																					X					
Global Studies	MD						M				MD				MD											
Greek, Modern/Greek Studies															X				X							
Gujarati																					X					
Health Education	M														M											M
Health Sciences/Studies															X		MD		M				D	MD		M
Health and Social Care															MD											
Health/Hospital Administration																			UM							
Hebrew/Semitic Studies																					X					
Hindi																					X					
History	X		X	M			MD				D			MD	X		X		X		X				MD	U
History/Philosophy of Science															M		M									
Human Biology															UD											
Human Genetics															MD											
Human Movement/Kinesiology/Biomechanics																			MD							
Human Resource Development																	M									
Human Rights/Globalisation	M						MD				MD				M		M									
Immunology/Infection/Immunity															MD											
Indian Languages																					X					
Indian Literature																					X					
Indonesian																					X					
Industrial Relations/Personnel/HRM	X														MD		X									M
Industrial and Organisation Psychology															M											
Information Science/Studies/Systems	X		UD														MD		X							U
Information Technology															MD											
International Business	M														MD						MD					
International Finance																					MD					
International Finance Economics																					MD					
International Relations/Studies	M						MD				MD				MD		X		X		MD					U
Islamic/Middle Eastern Studies	M																		D		X					
Italian													MD						X							U
Jainism																					X					

	Birkbeck	Central Sch. of Speech & Drama	Courtauld Inst. of Art	Goldsmiths	Heythrop	Hygiene & Tropical Med.	I. for the Study of the Americas	Inst. of Advanced Legal Studies	Inst. of Cancer Research	Inst. of Classical Studies	Inst. of Commonwealth Studies	Inst. of English Sudies	Inst. of Germanic & Romance Studies	Inst. of Historical Research	King's	London Business Sch.	LSE	Royal Acad. of Music	Royal Holloway	Royal Veterinary	SOAS	Sch. of Pharmacy	St George's	U. of Lond. Inst. in Paris	Warburg Inst.	London: external programme
Japanese/Japanese Studies	MD																				X					
Jewish Studies															M						X					
Kiswahili/Swahili																					X					
Korean/Korean Studies																					X					
Land Management/Rehabilitation	MD																									
Language Teaching/Learning															MD						MD					
Language and Communication															MD											
Languages, Modern	X		X										MD		X		U		X		X					U
Law Business/Commercial/Economic/Industrial								D													X					
Law Employment/Labour																					X					
Law Environmental																					X					
Law Intellectual Property/Copyright																					X					
Law International/Comparative/Trade								D													X					
Law Property/Construction/Housing															MD											
Law/Legal Studies	X		M					MD			MD				X		X				X					UM
Linguistics/Translation	X		MD												MD						X					
Literature, Comparative															X						MD					
Malay Language/Studies																					X					
Malayalam																					X					
Management	X														X		X		X		X					UM
Management Information Systems																	M									
Marketing																			UD							
Materials Science	MD																									
Mathematics	X														X		X		X							
Mechatronics															X											
Mediaeval Studies	M														MD				X							
Medical Ethics	M														M											
Medicine, Obstetrics and Gynaecology															MD											
Medicine, Oncology/Cancer studies									M						D											
Medicine, Paediatric															MD											
Medicine, Palliative															MD											
Medicine/Surgery						M									X								X			
Mediterranean Studies															MD											
Microbiology/Medical Microbiology	UM					D									X				D	X		D	MD			
Migration, Refugee and Diaspora Studies							MD																			
Mobile Communications/Telecommunications															M											

	Birkbeck	Central Sch. of Speech & Drama	Courtauld Inst. of Art	Goldsmiths	Heythrop	Hygiene fit. & Tropical Med.	I. for the Study of the Americas	Inst. of Advanced Legal Studies	Inst. of Cancer Research	Inst. of Classical Studies	Inst. of Commonwealth Studies	Inst. of English Sudies	Inst. of Germanic & Romance Studies	Inst. of Historical Research	King's	London Business Sch.	LSE	Royal Acad. of Music	Royal Holloway	Royal Veterinary	SOAS	Sch. of Pharmacy	St George's	U. of Lond. Inst. in Paris	Warburg Inst.	London: external programme
Multimedia	U																		U							
Museum Studies				M																						
Music				X											X			X	X		X					
Music Jazz																		UM								
Music Technology		UM																								
Nanotechnology															MD				M							
Neuroscience															X								D			
Nigerian Languages																					X					
Nursing/Midwifery															X									U		
Occupational Health/Therapy	MD																									
Operational Research/Operations Management	M																									
Pacific Islands Studies																							D			
Pakistan Studies											D										X					
Palaeography															D				D		MD					
Palaeontology/Palaeobiology																			D							
Parasitology																			D							
Peace/War Studies															X						X					
Persian																					X					
Pharmacology									D						X								D	D		
Pharmacy/Pharmaceutical Science															X							X				
Philosophy	X				X										X		X				MD					U
Physics	U								D						X				X							
Physiology															X				U				D			
Physiotherapy															UM									UD		
Planning/Landscape Studies																	MD									
Politics/Political Science/Government																	X				X					
Population Studies/Demography																	X									
Portuguese/Portugese Studies	U			U									M		X											
Psychiatry															MD											
Psychology	X			X											MD		X		X					D		M
Psychotherapy	MD		MD												M											
Public Administration	M																X		X							
Public Health/Population Health															M								D			
Public Sector Management	M														MD											
Punjabi																					X					
Radiography/Diagnostic Technology/MRI																								U		

	Birkbeck	Central Sch. of Speech & Drama	Courtauld Inst. of Art	Goldsmiths	Heythrop	Hygiene & Tropical Med.	I. for the Study of the Americas	Inst. of Advanced Legal Studies	Inst. of Cancer Research	Inst. of Classical Studies	Inst. of Commonwealth Studies	Inst. of English Studies	Inst. of Germanic & Romance Studies	Inst. of Historical Research	King's	London Business Sch.	LSE	Royal Acad. of Music	Royal Holloway	Royal Veterinary	SOAS	Sch. of Pharmacy	St George's	U. of Lond. Inst. in Paris	Warburg Inst.	London: external programme
Radiology															MD											
Rehabilitation Medicine/Therapy/Science															UD											
Religion/Theology	MD			D	X										X						X					U
Risk Management															MD		M									
Rural Studies/Development							MD												MD		X					M
Sanskrit/Pali/Prakrit/Vedic Studies																					X					
Sinhala																					X					
Social Policy	UM						MD										X		D							
Social Work/Studies				X											M		X		X							
Sociology	X			X			MD										X		D		MD					U
Sound Recording/Design		UM																								
Spanish/Hispanic/Latin American Studies	X			X			MD						MD		X				X							U
Statistics/Actuarial Science	X																X		U							
Sustainable Communities															MD											
Sustainable Development							MD												M							M
Tamil																					X					
Teacher Training				UM											M											
Telugu																					MD					
Textiles/Fibre Science/Technology				X																						
Thai/Thai Studies																					X					
Tibetan/Tibetan Studies																					X					
Tourism/Hospitality/Leisure/Recreation															M											
Toxicology															D								D			
Turkish/Turkish Studies															U						X					
United States Studies	M			U			MD																			M
Urban Studies																MD	MD									
Urdu																					X					
Vedas/Vedic																					X					
Veterinary Science																				X						M
Visual Arts	X	UM	X										M													
Women's/Gender Studies	M		MD				D						MD				X		MD		MD					
Youth and Community Development		UM													M											
Zoology																			UD							
Zulu																					X					

COLLEGES OF THE UNIVERSITY

BIRKBECK, UNIVERSITY OF LONDON

Founded 1926

Postal Address: Malet Street, Bloomsbury, London, England WC1E 7HX
Telephone: (020) 7631 6000 **Fax:** (020) 7631 6270
URL: http://www.bbk.ac.uk

MASTER*—Latchman, Prof. David S., MA PhD DSc, FRCPath
VICE-MASTER—Dewe, Prof. Philip, BCom *Well.*, MSc *Lond.*, PhD *Lond.*
PRO-VICE-MASTER (LEARNING AND TEACHING)—Frosh, Prof. Stephen, BA *Sus.*, MPhil *Lond.*, PhD *Lond.*
PRO-VICE-MASTER (RESEARCH)—Macmillan, Prof. Fiona, BA *NSW*, LLB *NSW*, LLM *Lond.*
PRO-VICE-MASTER (WIDENING PARTICIPATION AND COMMUNITY PARTNERSHIPS)—Annette, Prof. John, BA *Fordham*,
    PhD *Lond.*, FRSA
DEAN—Barnes, Prof. Paul, BSc *Brist.*, PhD *Camb.*, DSc *Lond.*
SECRETARY AND CLERK TO THE GOVERNORS‡—Harrison, Keith, BA
REGISTRAR—Harwood, B. A., BSc PhD, FRSA
DIRECTOR OF FINANCE—Westley, Peter, BA *Lond.*
LIBRARIAN—Payne, Philip, BA CN*AA*

GENERAL INFORMATION

History. The college was established by George Birkbeck in 1823 as the London Mechanics' Institution, and incorporated as a college of the University of London in 1926.
It is located in Bloomsbury, central London.

Admission to first degree courses (see also United Kingdom Introduction). Applicants under 21: recognised school-leaving or professional qualification. Applicants over 21 do not require formal qualifications or equivalent. All applicants must show evidence of the right to work in the UK; international students living in the UK on a student or a visitor's visa are not eligible to enrol as part-time students. Students whose first language is not English will be asked to demonstrate competence in the English language (eg IELTS score of 6.5; TOEFL (550)(or 237 on computer); AEB test in English for educational purposes (4)).

First Degrees (see also University of London Directory to Subjects of Study). BA, BSc, BSc(Econ), LLB.
    Length of course. Part-time: LLB: 3–4 years; BA, BSc, BSc(Econ): 4 years.

Higher Degrees (see also University of London Directory to Subjects of Study).
    Master's. MA, MFA, MPhil, MRes, MSc, MSc(Res).
    Admission. Applicants for admission to master's degrees should hold a good first degree in a relevant subject or equivalent professional qualification or experience.
    Length of course. Full-time: MA, MRes, MSc, MSc(Res): 1 year; MFA, MPhil: 2 years. Part-time: MA, MRes, MSc, MSc(Res): 2 years; MPhil: 3 years.
    Doctoral. DPsychotherapy, PhD.
    Length of course. Full-time: PhD: 2–3 years. Part-time: PhD: 3–4 years; DPsychotherapy: 4 years.

Libraries. Volumes: 364,102. Periodicals subscribed to: 4285. Other holdings: 17,000 electronic journals. Special collections: David Bohm Papers (theoretical physics).

Income (2005–2006). Total, £62,418,000.

Statistics. Students (2005–2006): full-time 680; part-time 6557; undergraduate 4077 (1933 men, 2144 women); master's 2541 (1162 men, 1379 women); doctoral 628 (336 men, 292 women).

FACULTIES/SCHOOLS

Arts
Tel: (020) 7631 6794 Fax: (020) 7323 3902
    E-mail: office@fac-arts.bbk.ac.uk
Dean: Innis, Matthew, BA *Camb.*, MA *Camb.*, PhD *Camb.*, FRHistS
Administrative Officer: Adams, Claire, BA *ANU*, BCom *ANU*, MA *NSW*

Continuing Education
Tel: (020) 7631 6633 Fax: (020) 7631 6688
    E-mail: info@bbk.ac.uk
Dean: Annette, Prof. John, BA *Fordham*, PhD *Lond.*, FRSA
Personal Assistant: Kitteringham, Elaine, BA *Kent*

Science
Tel: (020) 7631 6215 Fax: (070) 9239 0140
    E-mail: c.bray@bbk.ac.uk
Dean: Walker, Stephen F., BSc *Brist.*, PhD *Lond.*
Personal Assistant: Bray, Catherine, BSc *Lond.*, MSc *Lond.*

Social Sciences
Tel: (020) 7631 6722 Fax: (020) 7631 6727
    E-mail: k.mather@bbk.ac.uk
Dean: Johnson, Roger, BSc *Wales*, PhD *Lond.*, FBCS
Personal Assistant: Mather, Katarzyna, MSc MRes

ACADEMIC UNITS
Arranged by Schools

Biological and Chemical Sciences
Tel: (020) 7631 6238 Fax: (020) 7631 6246
    E-mail: d.witten@bbk.ac.uk
Bettinelli, Marco, BSc PhD   Visiting Prof., Chemistry
Blaney, W. M., MSc *Lond.*, PhD *Lond.*, FRES   Emer. Prof., Insect Physiology
Carless, Howard A. J., MA *Oxf.*, DPhil *Oxf.*, FRSChem   Sr. Lectr., Chemistry
Coast, Geoffrey M., BSc *Lond.*, PhD *Lond.*   Reader, Comparative Endocrinology; Head*
Collins, Peter M., PhD *Lond.*, DSc *Lond.*   Lectr.†; Emer. Prof., Organic Chemistry
Davies, David B., BSc *Edin.*, PhD *Essex*   Prof., Chemistry
Goldsworthy, Graham J., BSc *Sheff.*, PhD *Sheff.*, FIBiol, FRES   Prof., Biology
Hounsell, Elizabeth F., BSc *Sus.*, PhD *Lond.*, FRSChem   Prof., Biological Chemistry
Ingrouille, Martin, BSc *Aberd.*, PhD *Leic.*   Sr. Lectr., Biology

Mantle, Peter G., BSc *Lond.*, PhD *Lond.*, DSc *Lond.*   Visiting Prof., Biology
Nicklin, Jane L., BSc *Brist.*, PhD *Brist.*   Sr. Lectr., Biology
Shaw, Robert A., PhD *Lond.*, DSc *Lond.*, Hon. Dr *Toulouse*, FRSChem   Emer. Prof., Chemistry
Simmonds, Monique S. J., BSc *Leeds*, PhD *Lond.*   Visiting Prof., Biology
Veselkov, Alexei, BSc *Moscow*, PhD *Moscow*, DrSci   Visiting Prof., Chemistry
Wiedemann, Hans G., MSc *Rostock*, PhD *Berne*   Visiting Prof., Chemistry
Other Staff: 10 Lectrs. (Biology 4, Chemistry 6); 2 Researchers; 2 Emer. Readers
Research: analytical chemistry; computational chemistry; insect science; organic and bio-organic chemistry; plant taxonomy and molecular systematics

Computer Science and Information Systems
Tel: (020) 7631 6700 Fax: (020) 7631 6727
    E-mail: enquiries@dcs.bbk.ac.uk
Fenner, Trevor, MA *Camb.*, PhD *Lond.*   Sr. Lectr., Computer Science
Johnson, Roger, BSc *Wales*, PhD *Lond.*, FBCS   Reader, Computer Science
King, Peter J. H., MSc *Lond.*, FBCS   Emer. Prof., Computer Science
Kontoghiorghes, Erricos, BSc *Lond.*, PhD *Lond.*   Visiting Prof.
Levene, Mark, BSc *Auck.*, PhD *Lond.*   Prof., Computer Science
Loizou, George, BA *Lond.*, PhD *Lond.*   Emer. Prof., Mathematics of Computation
Magoulas, George, BEng *Patras*, PhD *Patras*   Reader, Computer Science
Martin, Nigel, BSc *Lond.*, MSc *Lond.*, PhD *Lond.*   Sr. Lectr., Computer Science
Maybank, Stephen, BA *Camb.*, PhD *Lond.*   Prof., Computer Science
Mirkin, Boris, PhD *Saratov*, DSc *Moscow*   Prof., Computer Science
Poulovassilis, Alex, MA *Camb.*, MSc *Lond.*, PhD *Lond.*   Prof., Computer Science
Roussos, George, BSc *Athens*, MSc *Manc.*, PhD *Lond.*   Sr. Lectr., Computer Science
Sharman, Geoff C. H., BSc *S'ton.*, PhD *S'ton.*   Visiting Prof.
Wood, Peter, BSc *Cape Town*, MSc *Cape Town*, PhD *Tor.*   Sr. Lectr., Computer Science; Head*
Zakharyaschev, Michael, BSc *Moscow*, MSc *Moscow*, PhD *Novosibirsk*   Prof., Computer Science
Other Staff: 10 Lectrs.; 8 Researchers; 3 Teaching Assts.

Research: bioinformatics; computational intelligence; databases and knowledge bases; information management and web technologies; neutral nets and evolutionary computation

Continuing Education

Tel: (020) 7631 6633 Fax: (020) 7631 6688
E-mail: info@bbk.ac.uk
Annette, John, BA *Fordham*, PhD *Lond.*, FRSA Prof., Citizenship and Lifelong Learning
Brah, Avtar, BSc *Calif.*, MSc *Wis.*, PhD *Brist.* Prof., Sociology
Caldwell, Raymond, BA *Mass.*, MBA *Manc.*, PhD *Lond.* Reader, Organisational Change
Clarke, Richard, BSc *Wales*, MTech *Brun.*, FLS Sr. Lectr., Conservation and Science Studies
Griffith-Dickson, Gwen, BD *Lond.*, PhD *Lond.* Reader, Religion and Philosophy
Jackson, Susan, BA *Open(UK)*, MA *Kent*, PhD *E.Lond.* Sr. Lectr., Lifelong Learning and Citizenship; Head*
Jamieson, Anne, MA *Copenhagen*, MSc *Lond.* Sr. Lectr., Gerontology
Wood, Mary, BA *Manc.*, PhD *Lond.* Reader, European Cinema
Other Staff: 21 Lectrs.; 1 Academic Fellow; 3 Lectrs.†; 15 Assoc. Lectrs.†
Research: contemporary art history; environmental policy, politics and management; football culture and society; lifelong learning and citizenship; social theory and life course development

Crystallography

Tel: (020) 7631 6800 Fax: (020) 7631 6803
E-mail: m.austin@bbk.ac.uk
Barnes, Paul, BSc *Brist.*, PhD *Camb.*, DSc *Lond.* Prof., Applied Crystallography
Blundell, Sir Tom, BA *Oxf.*, DPhil *Oxf.*, Hon. DSc *Edin.*, Hon. DSc *E.Anglia*, FRS Visiting Prof.
Borkakoti, Neera, MSc *Lond.*, PhD *Lond.* Visiting Prof.
Catlow, C. R., BA *Oxf.*, DPhil *Oxf.* Visiting Prof.
Cernik, R. J., BSc *Wales*, PhD *Wales* Visiting Prof.
Cockcroft, J., MA *Oxf.*, DPhil *Oxf.* Sr. Lectr.
de Leeuw, N. H., BSc *Open(UK)*, PhD *Bath* Reader, Computational Materials Science
Goodfellow, Julia M., CBE, BSc *Brist.*, PhD *Open(UK)*, FIBiol, FRSA, FMedSci Visiting Prof.
Goodfellow, Peter, BSc *Brist.*, DPhil *Oxf.* Visiting Prof.
Jaenicke, Rainer, DrPhilNat Visiting Prof.
Keep, Nicholas, BA *Camb.*, MA *Camb.*, PhD *Camb.* Reader, Structural Biology
Lindley, Peter F., BSc *Brist.*, PhD *Brist.* Visiting Prof.
Mackay, Alan L., BA BSc MA PhD DSc, FRS Emer. Prof.
McDonald, N. Q., BSc *Lond.*, PhD *Lond.* Prof.†, Structural Biology
Moss, David S., BSc *Lond.*, PhD *Lond.* Sr. Res. Fellow; Prof., Biomolecular Structure
Murray-Rust, P., MA *Oxf.*, DPhil *Oxf.* Visiting Prof.
Pitts, J. E., BSc *Sus.*, PhD *Lond.* Sr. Lectr.
Saibil, Helen R., BSc *McG.*, PhD *Lond.*, FRS Bernal Prof., Structural Biology
Sgouros, J. Visiting Prof.
Slingsby, Christine, BSc *Liv.*, DPhil *Oxf.* Reader, Protein Structure
Waksman, Gabriel, PhD *Paris*, FRS Prof.†, Structural Molecular Biology; Head*
Wallace, Bonnie A., BS *Rensselaer*, MPhil *Yale*, PhD *Yale*, DSc *Lond.*, FIBiol Prof.
Wernisch, L., PhD *F.U.Berlin* Prof., Computational Biology
Other Staff: 1 Emer. Reader; 2 Lectrs.; 1 Sr. Res. Fellow; 43 Researchers
Research: bioinformatics; cell signalling proteins; computer modelling of bone materials; electron microscopy; protein crystallography

Earth Sciences

Tel: (020) 7679 7333 Fax: (020) 7679 2867
E-mail: s.jenkins@bbk.ac.uk
Bristow, Charlie S., BSc *Sheff.*, PhD *Leeds* Reader, Sedimentology; Head*
Downes, Hilary, BSc *Durh.*, MSc *Calg.*, PhD *Leeds* Prof., Geochemistry
Roberts, Gerald P., BSc *Wales*, PhD *Durh.* Sr. Lectr., Geology
Temple, John T., MA *Camb.*, PhD *Camb.*, ScD *Camb.* Emer. Prof., Geology
Other Staff: 4 Lectrs.
Research: earthquake studies; igneous petrology and geochemistry; planetary geology; sedimentology and environmental geochemistry; stratigraphy and palaeontology

Economics, Mathematics and Statistics

Tel: (020) 7631 6401 Fax: (020) 7631 6416
E-mail: j.obrien@bbk.ac.uk
Aksoy, Yunus, BA *Bosphorus*, PhD *Leuven* Sr. Lectr., Economics
Baxter, Brad, BA *Camb.*, PhD *Camb.* Sr. Lectr., Financial Mathematics
Brummelhuis, Raymond, PhD *Amst.* Prof., Mathematical Finance
Driffill, E. John, MA *Camb.*, PhD *Prin.* Prof., Economics
Evans, Suzanne P., BSc *W.Aust.*, MSc *Sus.*, PhD *Lond.* Sr. Lectr., Statistics
Garrett, Anthony, BSc *Wales*, MSc *S'ton.*, PhD *Lond.* Reader, Economics
Geman, Hélyette, MSc *Éc.Normale Sup., Paris*, MSc *M.I.T.*, PhD *Paris VI*, PhD *Paris I* Prof., Mathematical Finance
Kapur, Sandeep, BA *Delhi*, PhD *Camb.* Reader, Economics
Psaradakis, Zacharias, BA *Athens*, MA *Athens*, PhD *S'ton.* Prof., Econometrics
Sabourian, Hamid, BA *Camb.*, MSc *Lond.*, PhD *Camb.* Prof., Economics
Satchell, Steve E., PhD *Lond.*, PhD *Camb.* Visiting Prof.
Sibert, Anne, BA *Carnegie-Mellon*, MSc *Carnegie-Mellon*, PhD *Carnegie-Mellon* Prof., Economics; Head*
Smith, Ron P., BA *Camb.*, PhD *Camb.* Prof., Applied Economics
Snower, Dennis J., MA *Oxf.*, PhD *Prin.* Prof., Economics (on leave)
Sola, Martin, BSc *Republic(Montevideo)*, MSc *Argentina Macroecon.*, MSc *S'ton.*, PhD *S'ton.* Prof., Economics
Tinsley, Peter, BA *Hobart(N.Y.)*, MA *Prin.*, PhD *Prin.* Prof., Economics
Wright, Stephen, MA *Camb.* Reader, Economics
Zoega, Gylfi, BA *Iceland*, MA *Col.*, MPhil *Col.*, PhD *Col.* Prof.†, Economics
Other Staff: 13 Lectrs.; 1 Res. Fellow
Research: applied statistics and multivariate analysis; econometrics; finance; international economics; mathematical finance (risk analysis and numerical computation)

English and Humanities

Tel: (020) 7631 6070 Fax: (020) 7631 6072
E-mail: office@eng.bbk.ac.uk
Armstrong, Isobel, BA *Leic.*, PhD *Leic.*, FRSA Emer. Prof., English
Baron, Michael, BA *Lond.*, PhD *Lond.* Sr. Lectr., English
Bown, Nicola, BA *N.Lond.*, MA *Sus.*, DPhil *Sus.* Sr. Lectr., Victorian Studies
Brooker, Joe, BA *E.Anglia*, MA *E.Anglia*, PhD *Lond.* Sr. Lectr., Modern and Contemporary Literature
Celyn Jones, Russell, MA *Iowa* Prof., Creative Writing
Clark, Sandra S., BA *Lond.*, PhD *Lond.* Sr. Res. Fellow; Prof., Renaissance Literature
Clucas, Stephen, BA *Wales*, PhD *Kent* Sr. Lectr.
Connor, Steven K., BA *Oxf.*, DPhil *Oxf.* Prof., Modern Literature and Theory
Craciun, Adriana, MA *Puget Sound*, PhD *Calif.*, BA Reader, Romantic Literature and Culture

Dobson, Michael, DPhil *Oxf.*, BA MA Prof., Shakespeare Studies
Finlay, Alison, BA *Melb.*, DPhil *Oxf.* Reader, Mediaeval English and Icelandic Literature; Head*
Fraser, Hilary, BA *Leic.*, DPhil *Oxf.* Geoffrey Tillotson Prof., Nineteenth-Century Studies
Hardy, Barbara, MA *Lond.*, DUniv *Open(UK)*, FRSL Emer. Prof., English Literature
Healy, Thomas F., BA *Reading*, PhD *Lond.*, FRSA Prof., Renaissance Studies
Inglesfield, Robert, MA *Camb.*, PhD *Camb.* Sr. Lectr., English
Ledger, Sally, BA *Lond.*, DPhil *Oxf.* Prof., Nineteenth-Century Literature
Leslie, Esther, BA *Sus.*, DPhil *Sus.* Prof., Political Aesthetics
Luckhurst, Roger, BA *Hull*, MA *Sus.*, PhD *Hull* Sr. Lectr., English
Msiska, Mpalive, BA *Malawi*, MA *Alta.*, PhD *Stir.* Sr. Lectr.
Mudford, Peter, BA MLitt Emer. Prof., English
Rowe, William, BA *Oxf.*, PhD *Lond.* Anniversary Prof., Poetics
Segal, Lynne, BA *Syd.*, PhD *Syd.* Anniversary Prof., Psychology and Gender Studies
Slater, Michael, MA *Oxf.*, DPhil *Oxf.* Emer. Prof., Victorian Literature
Swain, Rob, BSc *S.Bank* Sr. Lectr., Theatre Directing
Watts, Carol, MA *Warw.*, DPhil *Oxf.* Sr. Lectr., English
Wiseman, Susan, BA *Camb.*, PhD *Lond.* Reader, Early Modern Literature and Culture
Other Staff: 9 Lectrs.; 1 Academic Fellow
Research: literary and cultural theory; mediaeval literature and culture; modern and post-modern periods; Old English; Romantic and Victorian studies

Geography

Tel: (020) 7631 6473 Fax: (020) 7631 6498
E-mail: secretary@geography.bbk.ac.uk
Brooks, Susan, BA *Camb.*, PhD *Camb.* Sr. Lectr.
Callingham, Martin, BSc *Sheff.*, MSc Visiting Prof.
Damesick, Peter, MA *Camb.*, PhD *Camb.* Visiting Prof.
Frost, Martin, BA *Lond.*, MSc *Lond.*, PhD *Lond.* Reader
Hepworth, Mark, PhD *Tor.* Visiting Prof.
Horn, Diane, BA *William & Mary*, MA *Westchester*, DPhil *Oxf.* Sr. Lectr.
Jones, Andrew, MA *Brist.*, MSc *Brist.*, PhD *Camb.* Sr. Lectr.; Head*
Shepherd, John W., BSc(Econ) *Lond.*, MSc *Lond.*, PhD *Lond.*, FRICS, FRSA Prof.
Other Staff: 3 Lectrs.; 2 Res. Officers; 2 Assoc. Res. Fellows
Research: coastal geomorphology and policy; geographical information systems and geographical database development; globalisation and development; regional planning; social and urban geography

History, Classics and Archaeology

Tel: (020) 7631 6299 Fax: (020) 7631 6552
E-mail: admin@history.bbk.ac.uk
Arnold, John, BA *York(UK)*, DPhil *York(UK)* Reader, Mediaeval History
Bourke, Joanna, BA *Auck.*, MA *Auck.*, PhD *ANU*, FRHistS Prof., History
Dench, Emma, MA *Oxf.*, DPhil *Oxf.* Prof., Ancient History
Edwards, Catharine, MA *Camb.*, PhD *Camb.* Prof., Ancient History and Culture
Feldman, David M., MA *Camb.*, PhD *Camb.*, FRHistS Reader, Modern British History
Figes, Orlando, BA *Camb.*, PhD *Camb.* Prof., History
Hamilton, Marybeth, BA *Calif.*, MA *Prin.*, PhD *Prin.*, FRHistS Sr. Lectr., American History
Harding, Vanessa A., MA *St And.*, PhD *St And.*, FRHistS Reader, London History
Henderson, John, BA *Lond.*, PhD *Lond.* Wellcome Reader, History of Medicine

Hobsbawm, Eric J. E., CH, MA Camb., PhD Camb., Hon. PhilDr Stockholm, Hon. DHL Chic., Hon. LittD E.Anglia, Hon. DLitt Lond., Hon. PhD Col., FBA   Emer. Prof., Economic and Social History

Hunter, Michael C. W., MA Camb., DPhil Oxf., FRHistS, FSA   Prof., History

Innes, Matthew, BA Camb., MA Camb., PhD Camb., FRHistS   Prof., History

Pick, Daniel M., MA Camb., PhD Camb., FRHistS   Prof., Cultural History

Riall, Lucy J., BSc(Econ) Lond., MSc Lond., PhD Camb.   Reader, Modern European History

Sengoopta, Chandak, MD Calc., MA Cornell, PhD Johns H.   Reader, History of Medicine and Science

Shimazu, Naoko, BA Manit., MPhil Oxf., DPhil Oxf., FRHistS   Sr. Lectr., Japanese History

Swann, Julian, BA Lanc., PhD Camb.   Reader; Head*

Trentmann, Frank, BA Harv., MA Harv., PhD Harv.   Prof., Modern British History

Wachsmann, Nik, PhD Lond., BA   Sr. Lectr., Modern European History

Other Staff: 1 Emer. Reader; 14 Lectrs.; 1 Leverhulme Trust Fellow; 4 Res. Fellows

Research: archaeology of cult and ritual, death and burial; British social, cultural and political history since 1400; cultural and social history of ancient Greece, the Hellenistic world and ancient Italy and Rome; history of ideas from sixteenth to eighteenth centuries; Italian, French and Russian history

History of Art, Film and Visual Media

Tel: (020) 7631 6110 Fax: (020) 7631 6107
E-mail: office@hist-art.bbk.ac.uk

Allen, Brian, MA Lond., PhD Lond.   Visiting Prof.

Ames-Lewis, Francis A., BSc St And., MA Lond., PhD Lond.   Emer. Prof.; Sr. Res. Fellow

Christie, Ian, BA Belf., MA Oxf., FBA   Anniversary Prof., Film and Media History

Coombes, Annie E., BA E.Anglia, PhD E.Anglia, FRAI   Prof., Material and Visual Culture; Head*

Draper, Peter, MA Camb., FSA   Visiting Prof.

Gronberg, Tag, MA Camb., PhD Open(UK)   Reader, History of Art and Design

Hatt, Michael, PhD   Visiting Prof.

Mulvey, Laura, BA Oxf.   Prof., Film Studies

Nead, Lynda, BA Leeds, PhD Lond.   Pevsner Prof., History of Art

Pointon, Marcia, PhD   Visiting Prof.

Shaw-Miller, Simon, BA Brighton, PhD Essex   Sr. Lectr., History of Art

Steer, John R., BA Lond., MA Oxf., Hon. DLitt St And., FSA   Emer. Prof.

Vaughan, William H. T., BA Lond., PhD Lond., FRSA   Emer. Prof.

Warner, Marina, MA Lond.   Visiting Prof.

Wyver, John   Visiting Prof.

Other Staff: 8 Lectrs.; 1 Lectr.†

Research: art and music; digital media and critical theory; Italian late mediaeval and Renaissance art and patronage; mediaeval architecture; museology

Languages, Linguistics and Culture

Tel: (020) 7631 6117 Fax: (020) 7383 3729
E-mail: apli@sllc.bbk.ac.uk

Andermann, Jens, MA F.U.Berlin, DPhil F.U.Berlin   Sr. Lectr., Spanish

Dewaele, Jean-Marc, LicPhilRom Brussels, LicD Brussels, DèsL Brussels   Reader, French and Applied Linguistics

Howells, Robin J., BA Qld., PhD Lond.   Prof., French

Kraniauskas, John, BA CNAA, MA Sus., PhD Lond.   Sr. Lectr., Spanish

Li Wei, BA Beijing Normal, MA Newcastle(UK), PhD Newcastle(UK)   Prof., Applied Linguistics

Lorch, Marjorie, BA Wash., PhD Boston   Sr. Lectr., Applied Linguistics

Rowe, William, BA Oxf., PhD Lond.   Anniversary Prof., Poetics

Sewell, Penelope M., LèsL Aix-Marseilles, MA Essex   Sr. Lectr., French

Short, Ian, BA Lond., PhD Lond., FSA   Emer. Prof.

Walker, John, MA Camb., PhD Camb.   Sr. Lectr., German; Head*

Zhu Hua, BSc Beijing, MA Beijing Normal, PhD Newcastle(UK)   Sr. Lectr., Applied Linguistics

Other Staff: 1 Emer. Reader; 24 Lectrs. (Applied Linguistics 2, Brazilian 1, French 6, German 6, Japanese 2, Luso-Brazilian Studies 1, Spanish 6)

Research: applied linguistics (including bilingualism, linguistic analysis, psycholinguistics and neurolinguistics, second language acquisition, sociolinguistics); French, German, Japanese and Spanish language and literature, thought and cultural history

Law

Tel: (020) 7631 6507 Fax: (020) 7631 6506
E-mail: admin@law.bbk.ac.uk

Aristodemou, Maria, LLB Brist., LLM Camb.   Sr. Lectr.

Bowring, Bill, BA Kent   Prof.

Diamantides, Marinos, LLM Lanc., PhD Lond., BA   Sr. Lectr.

Douzinas, Costas, BA Athens, LLB Athens, LLM Lond., PhD Lond.   Prof.

Everson, Michelle, LLB Exe., PhD European Univ.Inst.   Prof.

Fitzpatrick, Peter, LLB Qld., LLM Lond.   Anniversary Prof.†

Gearey, Adam, BA York(UK), MA Sheff., PhD Lond.   Reader

Hanafin, Patrick, BA Limerick, PhD Dublin City   Reader

Macmillan, Fiona, BA NSW, LLB NSW, LLM Lond.   Corporation of London Prof.

McAuslan, J. Patrick W., MBE, BA Oxf., BCL Oxf.   Prof.†

Monk, Daniel, LLB Warw., LLM Lond.   Sr. Lectr.

Moran, Leslie, LLB Sheff., MA Sheff., PhD Lanc.   Prof.

Mulcahy, Linda, LLB S'ton., LLM Lond., PhD N.Lond.   Prof., Law and Society; Head*

Perry-Kessaris, Amanda, LLB S'ton., LLM S'ton., PhD Lond.   Sr. Lectr.

Reece, Helen, LLB Lond., MSc Lond.   Reader

Schütz, Anton, JD Vienna   Sr. Lectr.

Tuitt, Patricia, BA N.Lond., LLM Lond.   Reader

Valier, Claire, BA Lond., MPhil Camb., PhD Camb.   Sr. Lectr.

Other Staff: 5 Lectrs.

Research: intellectual property; international economic law; language and law; legal theory; public law

Management and Organizational Psychology

Tel: (020) 7631 6772 Fax: (020) 7631 6769
E-mail: orgpsych@bbk.ac.uk

Andersen, H. Birgitte, BEc Aalborg, MEc Reading, PhD Reading   Reader, Management

Archibugi, Daniele, DPhil Sus., Dott Rome   Prof., Innovation, Governance and Public Policy

Bachmann, Reinhard, BA Erlangen-Nuremberg, PhD Dortmund   Reader, Management

Briner, Rob, BA Hull, MSc Durh., PhD Sheff.   Prof., Organisational Psychology

Dewe, Philip, BCom Well., MSc Lond., PhD Lond.   Prof., Organisational Behaviour

Guest, David E., BA Birm., PhD Lond.   Visiting Prof.

Kelly, John, BSc Sheff., PhD Lond.   Prof., Industrial Relations; Head*

Kidd, Jennifer M., BA Keele, PhD CNAA   Reader, Organisational Psychology

Konzelmann, Suzanne, BA Trin.Coll.(Washington), MA S.Carolina, PhD Notre Dame(Ind.)   Reader, Management

Lawton Smith, Helen, BSc Lond., DPhil Oxf.   Reader, Management

Liefooghe, Andreas P. D., BSc Sur., MSc Lond., PhD Sur.   Sr. Lectr., Organisational Psychology

Mabey, Christopher, BA Reading, PhD Brun.   Reader, Organisational Psychology

Mackenzie Davey, Kate, BSc Lond., MSc Manc., PhD Manc.   Sr. Lectr., Organisational Psychology

Nielsen, Klaus, BA Copenhagen, MSc Copenhagen   Sr. Lectr., Management

Oughton, Christine P., BA E.Anglia, PhD Camb.   Prof., Management

Padayachee, Vishnu, BCom Durban-W., MCom Durban-W., PhD Natal   Visiting Prof.

Swann, Peter, MA St And., MSc Brist., PhD Lond.   Visiting Prof.

Symon, Gillian, MA Edin., MSc Sheff., PhD Sheff.   Sr. Lectr., Organisational Psychology

Trenberth, Linda, BEd Massey, MA Well., PhD Massey   Sr. Lectr., Management

Trim, Peter, BSc E.Lond., MBA City(UK), MSc Cran., MEd Camb., PhD Cran., FRSA   Sr. Lectr., Management

Wilkinson, Frank, BA Camb., MA Camb., PhD Camb.   Visiting Prof.

Xiaming Liu, PhD Strath.   Prof., International Business

Other Staff: 16 Lectrs.; 1 Teaching Fellow; 2 Teaching Assts.; 1 Emer. Reader (Occupational Psychology)

Research: e-commerce; human resource management; industrial economics and strategy; organisation studies and organisational sociology; technology development and organisational change

Philosophy

Tel: (020) 7631 6383 Fax: (020) 7631 6564
E-mail: office@philosophy.bbk.ac.uk

Dupré, John A., BA Oxf., MA Oxf., DPhil Oxf., PhD Camb.   Visiting Prof.

Fricker, Miranda, BA Oxf., MA Kent, DPhil Oxf.   Sr. Lectr.

Gemes, Ken, BA Syd., PhD Pitt.   Sr. Lectr.

Grayling, Anthony, BA Lond., MA Sus., DPhil Oxf.   Prof., Applied Philosophy

Guttenplan, Samuel D., BA C.C.N.Y., DPhil Oxf.   Prof.

Hornsby, Jennifer, BA Oxf., MPhil Lond., PhD Camb.   Prof.

James, Susan, BA Camb., MA Camb., PhD Camb.   Prof.; Head*

Janaway, Christopher, BA Oxf., DPhil Oxf.   Visiting Prof.

MacBride, Fraser L., BA Camb., MPhil Lond., PhD Lond.   Reader

Price, Anthony, BA Oxf., BPhil Oxf.   Reader

Rumfitt, Ian, BA Oxf., MA Oxf., DPhil Oxf.   Prof.

Smith, Barry C., MA Glas., PhD Edin.   Sr. Lectr., Theoretical Linguistics

Sturgeon, Scott, BA Texas, MA Arizona, PhD Arizona   Reader

Wiggins, David, MA Oxf., FBA   Visiting Prof.

Other Staff: 4 Lectrs.; 1 Sr. Res. Fellow

Research: ancient philosophy; ethics; logic, language, metaphysics; Nietzsche; philosophy of science

Politics and Sociology

Tel: (020) 7631 6789 Fax: (020) 7631 6787
E-mail: j.halstead@bbk.ac.uk

Ashenden, Samantha, BA Kingston(UK), MPhil Camb., PhD Lond.   Sr. Lectr., Sociology

Bacon, Edwin, BA Sheff., MSocSc Birm., PhD Birm.   Reader, Comparative Studies

Coole, Diana, BA Wales, MSc Lond., PhD Tor.   Prof., Political and Social Theory

Jenkins, Robert, BA *Harv.*, DPhil *Sus.* Prof., Political Science (on leave)

Kassim, Hussein, BA *Oxf.*, MPhil *Oxf.*, DPhil *Oxf.* Sr. Lectr., Politics; Head*

Kaufmann, Eric, BA *W.Ont.*, MSc *Lond.*, MRes *Lond.*, PhD *Lond.* Sr. Lectr.

Lovenduski, Joni, BSc *Lough.*, MA *Manc.*, PhD *Lough.* Anniversary Prof., Politics

Mabbett, Deborah, BA *Well.*, DPhil *Oxf.* Reader, Politics

Singh, Robert, BA *Oxf.*, DPhil *Oxf.* Prof., Politics

Tompson, W. J., BA *Emory*, DPhil *Oxf.* Prof., Political Economy

Zubaida, Sami D., BA *Hull*, MA *Leic.* Emer. Prof., Sociology

Other Staff: 6 Lectrs.

Research: civil society and the state; comparative public policy; European politics; gender; modern British politics and society

Psychology

see also Management and Orgnl. Psychol.

Tel: (020) 7631 6207 Fax: (020) 7631 6312
E-mail: g.cason@bbk.ac.uk

Barnes, Jacqueline, BSc *Lond.*, MSc *Wis.*, PhD *Lond.* Prof.

Belsky, Jay, BA *Vassar*, MS *Cornell*, PhD *Cornell* Prof.

Cooper, Richard, BMath *Newcastle(NSW)*, PhD *Edin.* Reader, Cognitive Science

Csibra, Gergely, MSc *E.L.Bud.*, PhD *E.L.Bud.* Prof.

Derakhshan, Naz, BSc *Lond.*, PhD *Lond.* Sr. Lectr.

Dick, Fred, BMus *Minn.*, PhD *Calif.* Sr. Lectr.

Eimer, Martin, PhD *Bielefeld* Prof.

Frosh, Stephen, BA *Sus.*, MPhil *Lond.*, PhD *Lond.* Prof.

Green, Simon E., BSc *Wales*, PhD *Lond.* Sr. Lectr.

Johnson, Mark, BSc *Edin.*, PhD *Camb.* Prof.

Mareschal, Denis, BA *Camb.*, MA *Queb.*, DPhil *Oxf.* Prof.

Marslen-Wilson, William D., BA *Oxf.*, PhD *M.I.T.*, FBA Visiting Prof.

Melhuish, Edward, BSc *Brist.*, PhD *Lond.*, FRSA, FBPsS Prof.

Müller, Hermann J., PhD *Durh.* Prof.†, Cognitive Psychology

Richards, Anne, BSc *Leic.*, PhD *Leic.* Reader

Segal, Lynne, BA *Syd.*, PhD *Syd.* Anniversary Prof., Psychology and Gender Studies

Shepherd, Alex, BA *Syd.*, MSc *Syd.*, PhD *Camb.* Sr. Lectr.

Smith, Jonathan A., BA *Camb.*, MSc *Sus.*, DPhil *Oxf.* Reader

Thomas, Michael, BSc *Exe.*, MSc *Birm.*, DPhil *Oxf.* Reader, Cognitive Neuropsychology

Usher, Marius, BSc *Haifa*, MSc *Tel-Aviv*, PhD *Tel-Aviv* Prof.

Walker, Stephen F., BSc *Brist.*, PhD *Lond.* Sr. Lectr.

Other Staff: 5 Lectrs.; 2 Res. Fellows; 71 Researchers; 1 Emer. Reader; 2 Sr. Lectrs.†

Research: cognitive psychology; cognitive psychophysiology; helping behaviour and human rights, early childcare, infancy; perceptual and cognitive development; social identities in adolescence, parenting, adoptive identities

SPECIAL CENTRES, ETC

Analytical Science, Centre for

Tel: (020) 7079 0799
E-mail: e.hounsell@bbk.ac.uk

Hounsell, Elizabeth F., BSc *Sus.*, PhD *Lond.*, FRSChem Prof.; Dir.*

Brain and Cognitive Development, Centre for

Tel: (020) 7631 6585 Fax: (020) 7631 6587
E-mail: m.johnson@psych.bbk.ac.uk

Johnson, Mark, BSc *Edin.*, PhD *Camb.* Prof.; Dir.*

British Film and Television Studies, Arts and Humanities Research Board Centre for

Tel: (020) 7631 6196 Fax: (020) 7631 6107
E-mail: a.jones@bbk.ac.uk

Christie, Ian, BA *Belf.*, MA *Oxf.*, FBA Anniversary Prof.; Dir.*

Canadian Studies, Centre for

Tel: (020) 7631 6132 Fax: (020) 7383 3729
E-mail: i.sachdev@bbk.ac.uk

Sachdev, I., BSc *Brist.*, PhD *McM.* Dir.*

Children, Family and Social Issues, Institute for the Study of

Tel: (020) 7631 0833 Fax: (020) 7323 4738
E-mail: m.lewis@bbk.ac.uk

Belsky, Jay, BA *Vassar*, MS *Cornell*, PhD *Cornell* Prof.; Dir.*

Contemporary Poetics Research Centre

Tel: (020) 7631 6143 Fax: (020) 7631 6072
E-mail: w.rowe@bbk.ac.uk

Rowe, William, BA *Oxf.*, PhD *Lond.* Anniversary Prof.; Dir.*

Crime Informatics, Centre for

Tel: (020) 7631 6709

Johnson, Roger, BSc *Wales*, PhD *Lond.*, FBCS Co-Dir.*

King, Peter J. H., MSc *Lond.*, FBCS Emer. Prof.; Co-Dir.*

Cultures of Consumption

Tel: (020) 7079 0601
E-mail: s.nixon@bbk.ac.uk

Trentmann, Frank, BA *Harv.*, MA *Harv.*, PhD *Harv.* Prof.; Dir.*

European Protected Areas Research, Centre for

Tel: (020) 7679 1048 Fax: (020) 7631 6679
E-mail: cepar@bbk.ac.uk

Clark, Julian, MA *Oxf.*, MSc *Lond.*, PhD *Lond.* Co-Dir.*

Clarke, Richard, BSc *Wales*, MTech *Brun.*, FLS Co-Dir.*

Football Governance Research Centre

Tel: (020) 7631 6768 Fax: (020) 7631 6872
E-mail: c.oughton@bbk.ac.uk

Oughton, Christine P., BA *E.Anglia*, PhD *Camb.* Prof.; Dir.*

Interlanguage Studies, Centre for

Tel: (020) 7631 6170
E-mail: r.brown@bbk.ac.uk

Dewaele, Jean-Marc, LicPhilRom *Brussels*, LicD *Brussels*, DèsL *Brussels* Dir.*

Lifelong Learning, Birkbeck Institute of

Tel: (020) 7631 6625
E-mail: r.clarke@bbk.ac.uk

Jackson, Susan, BA *Open(UK)*, MA *Kent*, PhD *E.Lond.* Dir.*

London Knowledge Laboratory

Tel: (020) 7631 6705 E-mail: ap@dcs.bbk.ac.uk

Poulovassilis, Alex, MA *Camb.*, MSc *Lond.*, PhD *Lond.* Prof.; Dir.*

Mutuality Research Centre

Tel: (020) 7631 6768
E-mail: c.oughton@bbk.ac.uk

Oughton, Christine P., BA *E.Anglia*, PhD *Camb.* Prof.; Dir.*

Natural Environment, Bloomsbury Institute for the

Jointly with University College London

Tel: (020) 7631 6480 Fax: (020) 7916 7565
E-mail: d.horn@bbk.ac.uk

Horn, Diane, BA *William & Mary*, MA *Westchester*, DPhil *Oxf.* Dir.*

Nineteenth-Century Studies, Centre for

Tel: (020) 7631 6083
E-mail: s.ledger@bbk.ac.uk

Fraser, Hilary, BA *Leic.*, DPhil *Oxf.* Geoffrey Tillotson Prof.; Co-Dir.*

Ledger, Sally, BA *Lond.*, DPhil *Oxf.* Co-Dir.*

Psychosocial Studies, Centre for

Tel: (020) 7631 6535
E-mail: p.fonseca@bbk.ac.uk

Frosh, Stephen, BA *Sus.*, MPhil *Lond.*, PhD *Lond.* Prof.; Dir.*

Robert Boyle Project, The

Tel: (020) 7631 6283

Hunter, Michael C. W., MA *Camb.*, DPhil *Oxf.*, FRHistS, FSA Prof.; Dir.*

Scientific Analysis for the Preservation of Cultural Heritage, Centre for

Tel: (020) 7631 0792
E-mail: m.odlyha@bbk.ac.uk

Odlyha, Marianne, BA *Adel.*, BSc *Adel.*, MSc *Adel.*, PhD *Lond.* Dir.*

South East Regional Research Laboratory

Tel: (020) 7631 6483 Fax: (020) 7631 6498
E-mail: j.shepherd@bbk.ac.uk

Shepherd, John W., BSc(Econ) *Lond.*, MSc *Lond.*, PhD *Lond.*, FRICS, FRSA Prof.; Dir.*

Structural Molecular Biology, Institute of

Tel: (020) 7631 6830 Fax: (020) 7631 6803
E-mail: t.hoe@ismb.lon.ac.uk

Waksman, Gabriel, PhD *Paris*, FRS Prof.; Dir.*

Theoretical Physics Research Unit

Tel: (020) 7631 6347, 7631 6289

Hiley, Basil J., BSc *Lond.*, PhD *Lond.* Prof.†

Vasari Centre for Digital Art History

Tel: (020) 7631 6197
E-mail: n.lambert@bbk.ac.uk

Allen, Mike, BA MA PhD Dir.*

CONTACT OFFICERS

Academic affairs. Pro-Vice-Master for Learning and Teaching: Frosh, Prof. Stephen, BA *Sus.*, MPhil *Lond.*, PhD *Lond.*

Admissions (first degree). (Contact the registry) (E-mail: admissions@bbk.ac.uk)

Admissions (higher degree). (Contact the registry) (E-mail: admissions@bbk.ac.uk)

Adult/continuing education. Information Co-ordinator: (vacant) (E-mail: info@bbk.ac.uk)

Alumni. Relations Officer: Archer, Alison, MA *Edin.* (E-mail: alumni@bbk.ac.uk)

Computing services. Director, Central Computing Services: Gill, Jasbir S., BSc *Hull*, MSc *City(UK)*, PhD *Durh.* (E-mail: ccs-helpdesk@bbk.ac.uk)

Conferences/corporate hospitality. Conference Manager (Acting): Rennie, Beatrice

Development/fund-raising. Head, Development and Alumni: Murphy, Anna, BA *Brist.* (E-mail: a.murphy@bbk.ac.uk)

Estates and buildings/works and services. Director, Estates and Facilities: Cowling, Philip, BSc *Manc.*

Examinations. Assistant Registrar (Examinations): Barnes, Jacqueline A. (E-mail: examinations@bbk.ac.uk)

Finance. Director of Finance: Westley, Peter, BA *Lond.*

General enquiries. Secretary and Clerk to the Governors: Harrison, Keith, BA (E-mail: info@bbk.ac.uk)

Industrial liaison. Head of Business Relations: Lawrence, Helen, BA Oxf.
(E-mail: h.lawrence@bbk.ac.uk)

International office. International Students Officer: Tupper, David, BA Newcastle(UK)
(E-mail: d.tupper@bbk.ac.uk)

Library (chief librarian). Librarian: Payne, Philip, BA CNAA
(E-mail: library-help@bbk.ac.uk)

Marketing. Head, Marketing and Recruitment: Law, Monica

Personnel/human resources. Director of Human Resources: Patel, Naina, BA Nott.Trent
(E-mail: humanresources@bbk.ac.uk)

Public relations. Director of External Relations: King, Tricia, BA York(UK), FRSA

Publications. Publications and Marketing Officer: Dodsworth, Lucy, BSc Exe.

Quality assurance and accreditation. Academic Quality Assurance Officer: Cutter, Sandra, BA Essex

Safety. Health and Safety and Radiation Protection Officer: McCartney, Tom, BSc CNAA, MA Lond.

Scholarships, awards, loans. Student Financial Support Manager: Murch, Jeanette, MA RCA

Staff development and training. Staff Development Manager: Johnston, Wendy,

BSc City(UK), MA Middx.
(E-mail: humanresources@bbk.ac.uk)

Students from other countries. International Students Officer: Tupper, David, BA Newcastle(UK) (E-mail: d.tupper@bbk.ac.uk)

Students with disabilities. Disability Service Manager: Pimm, Mark, MA Glas.
(E-mail: disability@bbk.ac.uk)

[Information supplied by the institution as at 7 December 2006, and edited by the ACU]

CENTRAL SCHOOL OF SPEECH AND DRAMA

Founded 1906

Postal Address: The Embassy Theatre, Eton Avenue, Swiss Cottage, London, England NW3 3HY
Telephone: (020) 7722 8183 **E-mail:** enquiries@cssd.ac.uk
URL: http://www.cssd.ac.uk/

PRINCIPAL*—Henderson, Gavin, CBE
DIRECTOR OF QUALITY‡—Cookson, Linda
DEPUTY PRINCIPAL—Scully, Debbie
HEAD OF FINANCE AND ESTATES—Lowe, Joseph

GENERAL INFORMATION

History. The school was founded in 1906 by Elsie Fogarty.
It is located in north London.

Admission to first degree courses. Admission varies for each course. Details available at www.cssd.ac.uk.

First Degrees (see also University of London Directory to Subjects of Study). BA.
Length of course. Full-time: BA: 3 years.

Higher Degrees (see also University of London Directory to Subjects of Study).
Master's. MA, MPhil.
Not all master's degree courses are available part-time.

Length of course. Full-time: MA, MPhil: 1 year.
Part-time: MA, MPhil: 2 years.
Doctoral. PhD.

Libraries. Volumes: 35,000. Periodicals subscribed to: 52. Special collections: International Centre for Voice; Audrey Laski.

[Information supplied by the institution as at 12 June 2006, and edited by the ACU]

COURTAULD INSTITUTE OF ART

Founded 1932

Postal Address: Somerset House, Strand, London, England WC2R 0RN
Telephone: (020) 7848 2777 **Fax:** (020) 7848 2410
URL: http://www.courtauld.ac.uk

DIRECTOR*—Swallow, Deborah, PhD Camb.
DEPUTY DIRECTOR—Green, Prof. Christopher K., MA Camb., MA Lond., PhD
SECRETARY AND REGISTRAR‡—Arthur, Michael, LLB LLM
ACADEMIC REGISTRAR—Walker, Rose J., MA Oxf., MA Lond., PhD
DIRECTOR OF FINANCE—Hefford, Terry R., MBA

GENERAL INFORMATION

History. The institute was founded in 1932.
Is it located at Somerset House on the Strand.

Admission to first degree courses (see also United Kingdom Introduction). Through Universities and Colleges Admissions Service (UCAS).

First Degrees (see also University of London Directory to Subjects of Study). BA.
Length of course. Full-time: BA: 3 years.

Higher Degrees (see also University of London Directory to Subjects of Study).
Master's. MA, MPhil.

Admission. Directly through the Institute.
Length of course. Full-time: MA: 1 year.
Doctoral. PhD.
Admission. Directly through the Institute.
Length of course. Full-time: PhD: 3 years. Part-time: PhD: 7 years.

ACADEMIC UNITS
Art, History of

Tel: (020) 7848 2777 Fax: (020) 7848 2410
Arscott, Caroline, PhD Sr. Lectr.
Behr, Shulamith, PhD Sr. Lectr.
Burnstock, Aviva, PhD Sr. Lectr.; Head, Conservation and Technol.

Cannon, Joanna, PhD Reader
Cather, Sharon, MA PhD Sr. Lectr.
Crossley, B. Paul, MA Camb., PhD, FSA Prof.
Eastmond, Antony D., MA PhD Reader
Green, Christopher K., MA Camb., MA Lond., PhD Prof.
Hills, Paul, MA PhD Prof.
House, John P. H., MA PhD Prof.
Koerner, Joseph L., MA PhD Prof.
Lowden, John H., MA PhD Prof.
Ribeiro, Aileen, PhD Prof.
Rubin, Pat L., MA PhD Prof.
Scott, Katie, BA MA PhD Reader
Solkin, David H., MA PhD Prof.
Stallabrass, Julian, MA PhD Sr. Lectr.
Wilson, Sarah, PhD Reader
Woodall, Joanna W., MA PhD Sr. Lectr.
Other Staff: 8 Lectrs.

Dress, History of

Tel: (020) 7848 2636 Fax: (020) 7848 2410
Ribeiro, Aileen, PhD   Prof.
Other Staff: 1 Reader†

Paintings, Conservation of

Tel: (020) 7848 2191 Fax: (020) 7848 2878
Burnstock, Aviva, PhD   Sr. Lectr.; Head,
   Conservation and Technol.

Wall Paintings, Conservation of

Tel: (020) 7848 2848
   E-mail: david.park@courtauld.ac.uk
Park, David, MA, FSA   Dir.*

CONTACT OFFICERS

General enquiries. (Contact the Academic
   office - postgraduate admissions)
   (E-mail: pgadmissions@courtauld.ac.uk)

General enquiries. (Contact the Academic
   Office - undergraduate admissions)
   (E-mail: ugadmissions@courtauld.ac.uk)

[*Information supplied by the institution as at 5 April
2006, and edited by the ACU*]

GOLDSMITHS, UNIVERSITY OF LONDON

Founded 1890

Associate Member of the Association of Commonwealth Universities

Postal Address: New Cross, London, England SE14 6NW
Telephone: (020) 7919 7171 **Fax:** (020) 7919 7113
URL: http://www.goldsmiths.ac.uk

WARDEN*—Crossick, Prof. Geoffrey J., MA *Camb.*, PhD *Lond.*, FRHistS
PRO-WARDEN (ACADEMIC)—Carr, Prof. Helen, BA *Brist.*, MA *Essex*, PhD *Essex*
PRO-WARDEN (RESEARCH)—McVeigh, Prof. Simon W., MA *Oxf.*, DPhil *Oxf.*
PRO-WARDEN (STUDENTS)—Stables, Prof. Kay, BEd *RCA*, MA *RCA*
REGISTRAR AND SECRETARY‡—Jones, Hugh
DIRECTOR OF RESOURCES AND PLANNING—Turner, Ian C., BA *S.Bank*
HEAD OF FINANCE—Douglas, Barry, BA *Liv.*
ACADEMIC REGISTRAR—Godman, Catherine, BA *W.Ont.*, MA *Qu.*
DIRECTOR OF CONTINUING EDUCATION AND HEAD OF PROFESSIONAL AND COMMUNITY EDUCATION—Mayo, Prof.
   Marjorie, BA *Oxf.*, MSc *Lond.*, PhD
DIRECTOR OF INFORMATION SERVICES AND LIBRARIAN—Pateman, Joan G., BSc *Montr.*

GENERAL INFORMATION

History. Originally founded by the
Worshipful Company of Goldsmiths in 1891,
Goldsmiths College was established in 1904. In
1977, it amalgamated with Rachel McMillan
and St Gabriel's colleges. It became a school of
the University of London in 1988 and was
granted its Royal Charter in 1990. In 2006, it
was renamed Goldsmiths, University of
London.
   It is located in southeast London.

Admission to first degree courses (see also
United Kingdom Introduction). Through
Universities and Colleges Admissions Service
(UCAS). Postgraduate and part-time degrees:
through the Registry Admissions Office. Home
students: 2 passes at General Certificate of
Education (GCE) A level, or 1 pass at A level
and 2 at AS level, or 4 passes at AS level.
Scottish Certificate of Education, Advanced
GNVQ (Level 3) and BTEC National and
Higher National Certificates and Diplomas also
accepted. Overseas students: qualifications
equivalent to those listed above, plus General
Certificate of Secondary Education (GCSE) or
GCE O level English language (grade C or
above), or IELTS score 6.5, or TOEFL score
580 (including minimum 4.5 in the test of
written English).

First Degrees (see also University of London
Directory to Subjects of Study). BA*, BAEd*,
BMus*, BSc*.
   Extension degree courses (incorporating a
year's foundation studies), courses
incorporating design and/or a European
language: 4 years full-time.
   Length of course. Full-time: BA*, BAEd*, BMus*,
BSc*: 3 years. *Part-time:* BA*, BAEd*, BMus*,
BSc*: 4 years.

Higher Degrees (see also University of
London Directory to Subjects of Study).
   Master's. MA, MMus, MPhil, MRes, MSc.
   Admission. Applicants for admission to
master's degrees should normally hold an

appropriate first degree with at least second
class honours.
   Length of course. Full-time: MA, MMus, MRes,
MSc: 1 year; MPhil: 2–4 years. *Part-time:* MA,
MMus, MRes, MSc: 2 years; MPhil: 3–6 years.
   Doctoral. PhD.
   Admission. PhD: applicants should hold an
appropriate master's degree or appropriate first
degree with at least upper second class
honours.
   Length of course. Full-time: PhD: 2–4 years. *Part-
time:* PhD: 3–6 years.

Libraries. Volumes: 250,000. Periodicals
subscribed to: 1200. Special collections: School
Practice (teaching practice).

ACADEMIC UNITS
Anthropology

Tel: (020) 7919 7800 Fax: (020) 7919 7813
   E-mail: anthropology@gold.ac.uk
Alexander, Catherine   Sr. Lectr.
Besson, Jean, MA *Edin.*, PhD *Edin.*   Reader
Caplan, A. Patricia, BA *Lond.*, MA *Lond.*, PhD
   Lond.   Emer. Prof.
Cassidy, Rebecca   Sr. Lectr.
Cohn, Simon   Sr. Lectr.
Day, Sophie E., BA *Camb.*, MA *Stan.*, PhD *Lond.*
   Prof.; Head*
Goddard, Victoria   Sr. Lectr.
Hart, Keith   Prof.
Morris, Brian   Emer. Prof.
Nelson, Nici M., MA *Col.*, PhD, FRAI   Emer.
   Prof.; Visiting Res. Fellow
Nugent, Stephen L., BA *Reed*, PhD   Prof.
Pine, Frances   Sr. Lectr.
Other Staff: 7 Lectrs.; 3 Postdoctoral Fellows; 8
   Visiting Fellows

Computing

Tel: (020) 7919 7850 Fax: (020) 7919 7853
   E-mail: maths-comp-studies@gold.ac.uk
Bishop, Mark   Reader
Blackwell, Tim   Lectr.; Dir., Undergrad.
   Studies
Casey, Michael   Prof.
d'Inverno, Mark   Prof.

Edmonds, Ernest   Prof.
Fol Leymarie, Frederic   Prof.
Jefferies, Janis K., BA *Kent*   Prof.
Latham, William   Prof.
Wiggins, Geraint   Prof.
Zimmer, Robert, MA *Col.*, MPhil *Col.*, PhD *Col.*
   Prof.; Head*
Other Staff: 11 Lectrs.; 7 Visiting Tutors

Goldsmiths Digital Studios

Jefferies, Janis K., BA *Kent*   Prof.; Artistic Dir.*
Other Staff: 24 Staff Members

Design

Tel: (020) 7919 7788 Fax: (020) 7919 7797
   E-mail: design@gold.ac.uk
Backwell, John   Des. and Technol. Programme
   Leader; Deputy Head
Bowers, John   Prof.; Res. Fellow
Gaver, Bill   Prof.
Kimbell, Richard A., BEd *Lond.*, MPhil *Lond.*
   Prof.
Rosenberg, Terry   Lectr.; Head*
Stables, Kay, BEd *RCA*, MA *RCA*   Prof.
Wood, John B.   Prof.
Other Staff: 12 Lectrs.; 3 Res. Fellows; 3
   Visiting Tutors

Technology Education Research Unit

Kimbell, Richard A., BEd *Lond.*, MPhil *Lond.*
   Prof.; Dir.*
Stables, Kay, BEd *RCA*, MA *RCA*   Prof.

Drama

Tel: (020) 7919 7414 Fax: (020) 7919 7413
   E-mail: drama@gold.ac.uk
Gordon, Robert J., MA *Natal*   Prof.
Lidstone, Gerald   Head*
London, John   Reader
Shevtsova, Maria, BA *Syd.*, PhD *Syd.*   Prof.
Other Staff: 8 Lectrs.; 1 AHRC Creative and
   Performing Arts Fellow

Educational Studies

see also Professl. and Community Educn.

Tel: (020) 7919 7300 Fax: (020) 7919 7313
   E-mail: educ-studies@gold.ac.uk
Adams, Jeff   Programme Co-ordinator

Atkinson, Dennis, PhD S'ton.   Prof.; Head*
Boorman, Dave   Sr. Lectr.
Chitty, Clyde, BA Leic., PhD Lond.   Prof.
George, Rosalyn P., BEd Lond., MA Lond.
   Reader
Gregory, Evelyn E., BA Wales(Swansea), PhD Lond.
   Prof.
Harris, Veronica, BA Lond.   Sr. Lectr.
Miller, Soo   Lectr.; Deputy Head
Paechter, Carrie, BA Camb., MEd Lond., PhD
   Lond.   Prof.
Rogers, Maggie, MA RCA   Sr. Lectr.
Smart, Lez   Programme Head
Other Staff: 23 Lectrs.; 2 Tutors; 1 Lectr.†

English and Comparative Literature

Tel: (020) 7919 7430 Fax: (020) 7919 7453
   E-mail: english@gold.ac.uk
Anim-Addo, Joan   Sr. Lectr.
Baldick, C. G., BA Oxf., DPhil Oxf.   Prof.
Blamires, Alcuin, BA Oxf., MPhil Oxf.   Prof.
Boldrini, Lucia, PhD Leic., PhD   Sr. Lectr.
Canova-Green, Marie Claude, BA Paris III, MA
   Paris III, PhD Paris III   Reader, French
Carr, Helen, BA Brist., MA Essex, PhD Essex
   Emer. Prof.
Cohen, J.   Reader
Dooley, M.   Sr. Lectr.
Downie, J. Alan, BA Newcastle(UK), MLitt
   Newcastle(UK), PhD Newcastle(UK)   Prof.
Dunwoodie, P., BA Edin., MA Edin., PhD Edin.
   Prof.; Head*
Greenlaw, L.   Sr. Lectr.
Kramer, Andreas, MA Mün., PhD Mün.   Sr.
   Lectr.
Krause, F.   Sr. Lectr.
McDonald, R.   Reader
Moore-Gilbert, Bart, MA DPhil   Prof.
Morrison, B.   Prof.
Natarajan, U.   Sr. Lectr.
Sokol, B. Jerry, BSc Col., MA Col., MPhil Col.,
   PhD Col.   Emer. Prof.
Other Staff: 14 Lectrs.; 1 Postdoctoral Fellow;
   1 Lectr.†

History

Tel: (020) 7919 7490 Fax: (020) 7919 7398
   E-mail: history@gold.ac.uk
Alexander, Sally, BA Lond.   Prof.; Head*
Broadhead, Philip J., BA Leeds, PhD Kent,
   FRHistS   Sr. Lectr.
Caygill, Howard, BSc Brist., MA Sus., DPhil Sus.
   Prof.
Jones, Helen, BA Lond., MA Lond., PhD   Sr.
   Lectr.
Keown, Damien, BA Lanc., DPhil Oxf.   Prof.
Killingray, David, BSc(Econ) PhD, FRHistS
   Emer. Prof.
Other Staff: 5 Lectrs.; 1 Lectr./Sr. Tutor; 6
   Visiting Tutors

Language Studies Centre

Tel: (020) 7919 7763 Fax: (020) 7919 7403
   E-mail: englang-unit@gold.ac.uk
Turner, Joan, MA Edin.   Sr. Lectr.; Head*
Other Staff: 8 Lectrs.

Media and Communications

Tel: (020) 7919 7600 Fax: (020) 7919 7616
   E-mail: media-comms@gold.ac.uk
Ahmed, Sara   Prof., Race and Cultural Studies
Berry, Chris   Prof., Film and Television Studies
Blackman, Lisa, BSc E.Lond., PhD Lond.   Sr.
   Lectr.
Couldry, Nick   Prof.
Crook, Tim   Sr. Lectr.
Curran, James P., BA   Prof.
Davis, Aeron   Sr. Lectr.
Fenton, Natalie   Sr. Lectr.
Freedman, Des   Sr. Lectr.
Gaber, Ivor   Emer. Prof., Broadcast Journalism
Kember, Sarah, BA Oxf., MA Sus., DPhil Sus.
   Reader
Lee-Wright, Peter   Sr. Lectr.
McRobbie, Angela, MA Glas.   Prof.
Morley, David G., BSc Kent, PhD Kent   Prof.
Ossman, Susan   Sr. Lectr.

Phillips, Angela   Sr. Lectr.
Stanton, Gareth   Sr. Lectr.; Head*
Zylinska, Joanna   Sr. Lectr.
Other Staff: 11 Lectrs.

Music

Tel: (020) 7919 7640 Fax: (020) 7919 7644
   E-mail: music@gold.ac.uk
Baily, John S., BA Oxf., DPhil Sus., PhD Belf.
   Prof., Musicology
Cottrell, Stephen   Lectr.; Deputy Head
Dickinson, Peter   Emer. Prof.
Glasser, Stanley   Visiting Prof.
Halstead, Jill   Sr. Lectr.
Hirshberg, Jehoash   Visiting Prof.
Ivashkin, Alexander V., BMus Gnesinz, MMus
   Gnesinz, PhD Gnesinz   Prof., Performance
   Studies
McVeigh, Simon W., MA Oxf., DPhil Oxf.
   Prof.
Musgrave, Michael   Visiting Prof.
Negus, Keith, BA Middx., PhD S.Bank   Prof.
Potter, Keith, BMus Birm., MA Cardiff   Sr.
   Lectr.; Head*
Redgate, Roger   Sr. Lectr.
Other Staff: 6 Lectrs.; 5 Visiting Fellows; 2
   Visiting Tutors; 15 Visiting Tutors/Lectrs.†

Afghanistan Music Unit

Baily, John S., BA Oxf., DPhil Sus., PhD Belf.
   Prof.; Dir.*

Politics

Tel: (020) 7919 7741 Fax: (020) 7919 7743
   E-mail: politics@gold.ac.uk
Dutton, Michael   Prof.
Grayson, Richard   Lectr.; Head*
Heidensohn, Frances M., BA Lond.   Emer. Prof.
Levy, Carl J., BA Lond., MA Lond., PhD Lond.
   Reader
Martin, James   Sr. Lectr.
Menz, George   Sr. Lectr.
Rao, Nirmala, BA Delhi, MA J.Nehru U., MPhil
   J.Nehru U., PhD Lond.   Prof.
Other Staff: 3 Lectrs.; 1 Lectr./Sr. Tutor; 12
   Visiting Tutors

Governance and Democracy, Research Unit in

Lawson, George   Dir.*

Professional and Community Education

Tel: (020) 7919 7200 Fax: (020) 7919 7223
   E-mail: pace@gold.ac.uk
Bernard, Claudia A., MA Middx.   Sr. Lectr.
Dryden, Windy, BSc Lond., MSc Warw., PhD
   Lond., FBPsS   Prof.
Evans, Norman   Visiting Prof.
Gilroy, Andrea, BA Kent, DPhil Sus.   Sr. Lectr.
Mayo, Marjorie, BA Oxf., MSc Lond., PhD
   Prof.
Pearson, G., BA Camb., MA   Prof.
Platt, Leonard H., BA N.Lond., PhD Lond.   Sr.
   Lectr.; Head*
Waller, Diane E., OBE, MA RCA, DPhil Sus.
   Prof.
Other Staff: 5 Lectrs.; 2 Sr. Tutors; 1 Visiting
   Res. Fellow; 1 Hon. Res. Fellow

Psychology

Tel: (020) 7919 7870 Fax: (020) 7919 7873
   E-mail: psychology@gold.ac.uk
Bhattacharya, Joydeep   Reader
Blumberg, Herb H., MA Johns H., PhD Johns H.
   Reader
Bond, Frank, BA S.Calif., MSc Lond., PhD Lond.
   Prof.
Davidoff, Jules, BSc Lond., PhD Wales, DSc Lond.,
   FBPsS   Prof.
Davies, Martin F., BA Camb., PhD   Sr. Lectr.
Fletcher, Clive   Prof.
French, Christopher C., BA Manc., PhD Leic.,
   FBPsS   Prof.
Gruzelier, John   Prof. Fellow
Heaton, Pam   Sr. Lectr.
Hill, Elisabeth   Sr. Lectr.
Pickering, Alan, BA Camb., PhD Manc.   Prof.;
   Head*

Powell, Jane H., BA Oxf., MPhil Lond., PhD Lond.
   Prof.
Pring, Linda, BSc Newcastle(UK), PhD   Prof.
Richardson-Klavehn, Alan, BA Oxf., MA PhD
   Reader
Smith, Peter, BA PhD, FBPsS   Prof.
Valentine, Tim, BSc Manc., PhD Nott.   Prof.
Velmans, Max L., BSc Syd., PhD, FBPsS   Emer.
   Prof.
Other Staff: 13 Lectrs.; 7 Visiting Fellows/
   Researchers

Anomalistic Psychology Research Unit

French, Christopher C., BA Manc., PhD Leic.,
   FBPsS   Prof.; Head*

School and Family Studies, Unit for

Smith, Peter, BA PhD, FBPsS   Prof.; Head*
Other Staff: 2 Visiting Res. Fellows

Sociology

Tel: (020) 7919 7707 Fax: (020) 7919 7713
   E-mail: sociology@gold.ac.uk
Adkins, Lisa   Prof.
Alexander, Jeff   Prof.
Alleyne, Brian   Sr. Lectr.
Back, Leslie, BSc Lond., PhD Lond.   Prof.
Bell, Vikki H., BA Camb., PhD Edin.   Reader
Bhatt, Chetan, BA Camb., PhD Lond.   Prof.
Filmer, Paul A., BA Nott.   Sr. Lectr.
Keith, Michael, BA Oxf., DPhil Oxf.   Prof.
Knowles, Caroline   Prof.
Lury, Celia, BA York(UK), MA Manc., PhD Manc.
   Prof.; Head*
Michael, Mike, BA Oxf., PhD Durh.   Prof.
Nash, Kate, BSc City(UK), PhD Essex   Sr. Lectr.
Oswell, David   Sr. Lectr.
Puwar, Nirmal   Reader
Seidler, Vic J. J., BA Oxf., MPhil Kent   Prof.
Silverman, David   Emer. Prof.
Simone, Abdou Maliq   Prof.
Skeggs, Bev   Prof.
Wakeford, Nina   Reader
Other Staff: 12 Lectrs.; 1 Res. Fellow

Visual Arts

Tel: (020) 7919 7671 Fax: (020) 7919 7673
   E-mail: visual-arts@gold.ac.uk
Barnett, Pennina, BA Leeds, MA Middx.   Sr.
   Lectr.
Beattie, Basil   Emer. Reader
Craig-Martin, Michael   Emer. Prof.
De Ville, Nick, BA Newcastle(UK)   Prof.; Dir.,
   Res.; Head*
Falconbridge, Brian   Prof.
Fisher, Sam   Sr. Lectr.
Hemsworth, Gerald   Prof., Fine Art
Jefferies, Janis K., BA Kent   Prof.; Head*
Mabb, David, BA MA   Sr. Lectr.
Malik, Suhail   Sr. Lectr.
Other Staff: 20 Lectrs.

Visual Cultures

Butt, Gavin   Sr. Lectr.
Düttman, Alexander   Prof.
Prendeville, Brendan   Sr. Lectr.
Rogoff, Irit, BA Jerusalem, MA Lond., PhD Lond.
   Prof.
Weizman, Eyal   Prof.
Other Staff: 9 Lectrs.; 2 Res. Fellows; 18
   Visiting Fellows

SPECIAL CENTRES, ETC

Arts and Learning, Centre for the

Adams, Jeff   Programme Co-ordinator
Atkinson, Dennis, PhD S'ton.   Prof.; Head*
Dash, Paul   Lectr.; Deputy Head
Other Staff: 6 Lectrs.

Caribbean Studies, Centre for

Anim-Addo, Joan   Sr. Lectr.; Dir.*

Cognition, Computation and Culture, Centre for

Davidoff, Jules, BSc Lond., PhD Wales, DSc Lond.,
   FBPsS   Prof.; Head*

Contemporary Music Cultures, Centre for (CCMC)

Baily, John S., BA *Oxf.*, DPhil *Sus.*, PhD *Belf.*   Prof.; Head*
Negus, Keith, BA *Middx.*, PhD *S.Bank*   Prof.; Deputy Head

Cultural Studies, Centre for

Fuller, Matthew   Reader
Hutnyk, John, BA *Deakin*, PhD *Melb.*   Reader; Acad. Dir.
Koepping, Klaus P.   Visiting Prof.
Lash, Scott M., BA *Mich.*, MA *Northwestern*, PhD *Lond.*   Prof.; Dir.*
Vergès, Françoise, BA *Calif.State*, MA *Calif.*, PhD *Calif.*   Reader
Other Staff: 4 Lectrs.

Invention and Social Progress, Centre for the Study of (CSISP)

Warner, Nathalie   Administrator*

Research Architecture, Centre for

Weizman, Eyal   Dir.*

Russian Music, Centre for (CRM)

Ivashkin, Alexander V., BMus *Gnesinz*, MMus *Gnesinz*, PhD *Gnesinz*   Prof.; Dir.*

Textiles, Constance Howard Resource and Research Centre in

Jefferies, Janis K., BA *Kent*   Prof.; Head*

Urban and Community Research, Centre for

Hewitt, Roger L., BA PhD   Prof.; Sr. Res. Assoc.; Deputy Head
Keith, Michael, BA *Oxf.*, DPhil *Oxf.*   Prof.; Head*
Mayo, Marjorie, BA *Oxf.*, MSc *Lond.*, PhD   Reader
Other Staff: 1 Lectr.; 1 Lectr./Sr. Res. Assoc.; 1 Res. Fellow; 2 Res. Assocs.

Visual Anthropology, Centre for

Nugent, Stephen L., BA *Reed*, PhD   Prof.; Dir.*

CONTACT OFFICERS

Academic affairs. Academic Registrar: Godman, Catherine, BA *W.Ont.*, MA *Qu.* (E-mail: registry@gold.ac.uk)
Accommodation. Accommodation Officer: Reck, Sarah, BA *Leeds* (E-mail: accommodation@gold.ac.uk)

Admissions (first degree). Head of Recruitment and Admissions: Fox, Geraint, BA (E-mail: admissions@gold.ac.uk)
Admissions (higher degree). Head of Recruitment and Admissions: Fox, Geraint, BA (E-mail: admissions@gold.ac.uk)
Adult/continuing education. Director of Continuing Education and Head of Professional and Community Education: Mayo, Prof. Marjorie, BA *Oxf.*, MSc *Lond.*, PhD
Alumni. Development/Alumni Manager: Clarke, Stephen, BA (E-mail: goldsoc@gold.ac.uk)
Careers. Head of Careers: Francis, Anne (E-mail: careers@gold.ac.uk)
Computing services. Director of Information Technology: El Haddadeh, Basem (E-mail: computer-services@gold.ac.uk)
Conferences/corporate hospitality. Conference Services Manager: Heaton, James (E-mail: conference-services@gold.ac.uk)
Credit transfer. Head of Recruitment and Admissions: Fox, Geraint, BA
Credit transfer. Head of Examinations and Archives: Beevers, Pamela M., BA *Open(UK)*, MA
Development/fund-raising. Development/Alumni Manager: Clarke, Stephen, BA (E-mail: goldsoc@gold.ac.uk)
Equal opportunities. Deputy Head of Personnel: May, Johanna K., BA (E-mail: personnel@gold.ac.uk)
Estates and buildings/works and services. Facilities Manager: Gamble, Diana (E-mail: estates@gold.ac.uk)
Examinations. Head of Examinations and Archives: Beevers, Pamela M., BA *Open(UK)*, MA
Finance. Head of Finance: Douglas, Barry, BA *Liv.* (E-mail: finance@gold.ac.uk)
General enquiries. Registrar and Secretary: Jones, Hugh
Health services. Medical Officer: MacFarlane, A. E., MB BS
International office. International Enquiries Officer: Bradley, Neil (E-mail: international-office@gold.ac.uk)
Library (chief librarian). Director of Information Services and Librarian: Pateman, Joan G., BSc *Montr.* (E-mail: library@gold.ac.uk)
Library (enquiries). Assistant Librarian: Houston, Sally (E-mail: library@gold.ac.uk)

Marketing. Head of Communications and Publicity: Annand, Vicky, BA (E-mail: ext-comms@gold.ac.uk)
Minorities/disadvantaged groups. Deputy Head of Personnel: May, Johanna K., BA (E-mail: personnel@gold.ac.uk)
Personnel/human resources. Head of Personnel: Letham, Robert, BA (E-mail: personnel@gold.ac.uk)
Public relations. Head of Communications and Publicity: Annand, Vicky, BA (E-mail: ext-comms@gold.ac.uk)
Publications. Head of Communications and Publicity: Annand, Vicky, BA (E-mail: ext-comms@gold.ac.uk)
Purchasing. Purchasing Officer: Ishmael, Kalam (E-mail: finance@gold.ac.uk)
Quality assurance and accreditation. Head of Quality: Thussu, Liz (E-mail: l.thussu@gold.ac.uk)
Research. Pro-Warden (Research): McVeigh, Prof. Simon W., MA *Oxf.*, DPhil *Oxf.* (E-mail: research-office@gold.ac.uk)
Safety. Safety Officer: Robson, Gordon
Scholarships, awards, loans. Administrative Assistant (Fees and Awards Office): Smith, John H., BA
Schools liaison. FE Schools Liaison Officer: Uddin, Suman
Security. College Superintendent: Sellar, Janet
Staff development and training. Head of Staff Development: Collins, Steve (E-mail: steve.collins@gold.ac.uk)
Student union. General Manager (Student Union): Hyde, Matthew (E-mail: gcsu@gold.ac.uk)
Student welfare/counselling. Senior Counsellor, Medical Centre: Denby, Veronica
Student welfare/counselling. President, Students' Union Welfare and Academic Affairs: Leary, Peter
Students from other countries. International Enquiries Officer: Bradley, Neil (E-mail: international-office@gold.ac.uk)
Students with disabilities. Administrative Assistant (Accommodation/Timetabling): Francis, Kay L.
Women. Deputy Head of Personnel: May, Johanna K., BA (E-mail: personnel@gold.ac.uk)

[*Information supplied by the institution as at 25 June 2007, and edited by the ACU*]

HEYTHROP COLLEGE

Founded 1926

Postal Address: Kensington Square, London, England W8 5HQ
Telephone: (020) 7795 6600 **Fax:** (020) 7795 4200 **E-mail:** enquiries@heythrop.ac.uk
URL: http://www.heythrop.ac.uk

PRINCIPAL*—McDade, Rev. John, BD *Lond.*, MA *Oxf.*, PhD *Edin.*
VICE-PRINCIPAL—Vardy, Peter, BA MTh PhD, FCA
DIRECTOR OF ADMINISTRATION‡—Smith, Alan
ACADEMIC REGISTRAR—Clarkson, Annabel
LIBRARIAN—Pedley, Rev. Christopher, BA(Econ) BA MTh ThM MA
DIRECTOR OF FINANCE—Tinley, Wayne, BCom

GENERAL INFORMATION

History. The college was originally established in 1614 in Louvain, Belgium for the education of English Jesuits. During the wars that followed the French revolution it relocated to various sites in Britain. It was founded under its present name upon moving to Heythrop, Oxfordshire in 1926. The college

moved to London in 1970, and in 1971 became one of the colleges of the University of London.
It is located in Kensington Square, London.

Admission to first degree courses (see also United Kingdom Introduction). Through Universities and Colleges Admissions Service (UCAS). Applicants require General Certificate

of Education (GCE) A levels or vocational qualifications, or must have completed an access course. Applicants whose first language is not English must have an English language test certificate at an acceptable level.

First Degrees (see also University of London Directory to Subjects of Study). BA.
Length of course. Full-time: BA: 3 years. Part-time: BA: 6 years.

Higher Degrees (see also University of London Directory to Subjects of Study).

Master's. MA, MPhil, MTh.

Admission. Applicants for admission to master's degree courses should hold a first degree and (in some instances) a professional qualification. Applicants whose first language is not English must have an English language test certificate at an acceptable level.

Length of course. Full-time: MA, MTh: 1 year; MPhil: 2 years. *Part-time:* MA, MTh: 2–3 years; MPhil: 3–4 years.

Doctoral. PhD.

Length of course. Full-time: PhD: 3 years. *Part-time:* PhD: 6 years.

Libraries. Volumes: 250,000. Periodicals subscribed to: 400. Special collections: pre-1501 books.

ACADEMIC UNITS

Pastoral and Social Studies

Tel: (020) 7795 4230

Callaghan, Rev. Brendan, MA MPhil MTh   Sr. Lectr.

Hoose, Bernard, BA(Ph) STB STL STD   Sr. Lectr.

Lonsdale, David, MA MTh   Sr. Lectr.

Sweeney, Rev. James, BD BA MTh PhD   Sr. Lectr.; Head*

Other Staff: 6 Lectrs.; 2 Visiting Lectrs.

Research: faith engagement in public life; health and wellbeing of the human person; life and witness of the church; retrieving resources for Christian life and spirituality

Philosophy

Tel: (020) 7795 4208

Caruana, Rev. Louis, BSc MA STL PhD   Sr. Lectr.

Gallagher, Rev. Peter, MA PhD   Lectr.; Head*

Lacewing, Michael, BA BPhil PhD   Sr. Lectr.

Law, Stephen, BSc BPhil DPhil   Sr. Lectr.

Vardy, Peter, BA MTh PhD, FCA   Sr. Lectr.

Other Staff: 8 Lectrs.

Research: history of philosophy; metaphysics and philosophy of science; philosophy of mind and psychology; philosophy of religion; philosophy of values

Theology

Tel: (020) 7795 4236

Jeffers, Rev. Ann, PhD N.U.I., LicTh   Sr. Lectr.

Kirwan, Rev. Michael, BD MA PhD   Lectr.; Head*

Price, Rev. Richard M., BD Lond., MA Oxf., MTh Lond., DPhil Oxf.   Sr. Lectr.

Other Staff: 8 Lectrs.; 6 Visiting Lectrs.

Research: church history and Biblical studies; inter-faith relations; systematic theology

SPECIAL CENTRES, ETC

Christianity and Interreligious Dialogue, Centre for

Tel: (020) 7795 4258

O'Mahoney, Anthony, BA MA MPhil   Lectr.; Dir.*

Other Staff: 1 Projects Administrator

Religious Ethics and Public Life, Heythrop Institute for

Tel: (020) 7795 4231

Carroll, Rev. Anthony, BSc BD MPhil PhD   Assoc. Dir.

Cowley, Catherine, MA PhD   Assoc. Dir.

Hanvey, Rev. James, BA MTh DPhil   Lectr.; Dir.*

Riordan, Rev. Patric, BA BPhil BD MA DPhil   Assoc. Dir.

CONTACT OFFICERS

Academic affairs. Dean, Undergraduate Studies: Burns, Elizabeth, BD PhD (E-mail: e.burns@heythrop.ac.uk)

Academic affairs. Dean, Postgraduate Studies: Lonsdale, David, MA MTh (E-mail: d.lonsdale@heythrop.ac.uk)

Admissions (first degree). Assistant Registrar: Charles, Antony, BA (E-mail: a.charles@heythrop.ac.uk)

Admissions (higher degree). Academic Registrar: Clarkson, Annabel (E-mail: a.clarkson@heythrop.ac.uk)

Alumni. Alumni Secretary: Conlon, James (E-mail: heythrop.association@ heythrop.ac.uk)

Computing services. IT Administrator and Web Developer: Davies, Sophie, BA MCSc (E-mail: s.davies@heythrop.ac.uk)

Library (chief librarian). Librarian: Pedley, Rev. Christopher, BA(Econ) BA MTh ThM MA (E-mail: c.pedley@heythrop.ac.uk)

Library (enquiries). Morgan, Michael, BA Warw. (E-mail: m.morgan@heythrop.ac.uk)

Marketing. Secretary to the Principal: Crimmins, Judith, MA (E-mail: j.crimmins@heythrop.ac.uk)

Quality assurance and accreditation. Quality and Research Co-ordinator: Powell, Kathryn, BA MA (E-mail: k.powell@heythrop.ac.uk)

Research. Quality and Research Co-ordinator: Powell, Kathryn, BA MA (E-mail: k.powell@heythrop.ac.uk)

Student welfare/counselling. Student Support Co-ordinator: McLoughlin, Dominic, BA MSc (E-mail: d.mcloughlin@heythrop.ac.uk)

[*Information supplied by the institution as at 15 January 2008, and edited by the ACU*]

INSTITUTE OF CANCER RESEARCH

Founded 1909

Postal Address: 123 Old Brompton Road, London, England SW7 3RP
Telephone: (020) 7532 8133 **Fax:** (020) 7370 5261
URL: http://www.icr.ac.uk

CHIEF EXECUTIVE OFFICER*—Rigby, Prof. P. W. J., BA *Camb.*, PhD *Camb.*, FMedSci
SECRETARY‡—Kipling, J. M., FCA
DIRECTOR OF FINANCE—Whitehead, Andrew A.
ACADEMIC DEAN—Horwich, Prof. A., MB BS *Lond.*, PhD *CNAA*, FRCR, FMedSci, FRCP

GENERAL INFORMATION

History. Established in 1909, the institute was originally founded as the Cancer Hospital Research Institute by the Cancer Hospital, now known as the Royal Marsden NHS Trust.

It is located on two sites in Chelsea and Sutton.

Higher Degrees (see also University of London Directory to Subjects of Study).

Master's. MSc.

Admission. Applicants for admission to Master's programmes should hold a first degree in science or medicine from a UK university or equivalent international qualification. Priority will be given to Specialist Registrars in Oncology in NHS Deanery higher medical training.

Length of course. Full-time: MSc: max. 4 years.

Doctoral. PhD.

Admission. Applicants for admission to PhD should have an appropriate upper second class honours degree or above, an appropriate

master's degree, or an overseas qualification of equivalent standard.

Length of course. Full-time: PhD: 4 years. *Part-time:* PhD: 6 years.

Libraries. Volumes: 15,000. Periodicals subscribed to: 5000. Special collections: Historical.

Academic Year (2007–2008). 1 September–31 August:

Income (2005–2006). Total, £60,236,000.

Statistics. Staff (2006–2007): 914 (583 academic, 331 non-academic). Students (2006–2007): full-time 220 (94 men, 126 women); part-time 156 (65 men, 91 women); international 54 (29 men, 25 women); master's 186 (80 men, 106 women); doctoral 190 (79 men, 111 women).

ACADEMIC UNITS

Biochemistry

Tel: (020) 7352 8171 Fax: (020) 7351 3785 E-mail: anne.mcgowan@icr.ac.uk

Dowsett, M., BSc *Lond.*, PhD *Lond.*   Prof., Biochemical Endocrinology; Head*

Other Staff: 33 Staff Members

Research: hormone-related cancers; improving the use of biomarkers in cancer patients

Breakthrough Toby Robins Breast Cancer Research Centre

Includes Cell Biology and Experimental Pathology

Tel: (020) 7153 5317 Fax: (020) 7153 5340 E-mail: janine.harris@icr.ac.uk

Ashworth, A., BSc *Lond.*, PhD *Lond.*   Team Leader, Gene Function; Prof., Molecular Biology; Dir.*

Crook, T. R., BSc *Lond.*, PhD *Lond.*, MB BS   Team Leader, Cancer Genetics and Epigenetics

Dowsett, M., BSc Lond., PhD Lond. Prof.; Team Leader, Molecular Endocrinol. and Breakthrough Translational Res.

Isacke, C. M., BA Oxf., DPhil Oxf. Prof.; Team Leader, Molecular Cell Biology

Linardopoulos, S., PhD Kandy Team Leader, Cancer Drug Target Discovery

Meier, P., PhD Zür. Team Leader, Apoptosis

Reis-Filho, J., PhD Minho Team Leader, Molecular Pathol.

Smalley, M., BA Oxf., PhD Lond. Team Leader, Mammary Stem Cells

Zvelebil, M. J., BSc Sus., PhD Lond. Team Leader, Cancer Information

Other Staff: 90 Staff Members

Cancer Genetics

Tel: (020) 8643 8901 Fax: (020) 8643 0257
E-mail: fiona.harvey@icr.ac.uk

Eeles, R., MA Camb., MB BS Lond., PhD, FRCR, FRCP Team Leader, Cancer Genetics and Clin. Oncology

Houlston, R., BSc Lond., MSc Lond., MD Lond., PhD Lond., FRCP, FRCPath Team Leader, Cancer Genetics and Population Genetics; Prof., Molecular Genetics

Rahman, N., BM BCh Oxf., MA Oxf., PhD Lond., FRCP Prof.; Team Leader, Cancer Genetics and Clin. Genetics; Head*

Stratton, M. R., BA Oxf., MB BS Lond., PhD Lond. Prof.; Team Leader, Cancer Genetics

Other Staff: 60 Staff Members

Research: mapping, identification, characterisation and clinical application of genes that are mutated in human cancer

Cancer Research UK Clinical Magnetic Resonance Research Group

Tel: (020) 8661 3701 Fax: (020) 8661 0846
E-mail: chris.croucher@icr.ac.uk

deSouza, N. M., MD, FRCP, FRCR Reader, Imaging

Leach, M. O., BSc Sur., MSc Birm., PhD Birm., FMedSci, FIP, FIPEM Prof., Physics Applied to Medicine; Head*

Other Staff: 25 Staff Members

Research: hyperpolarised gas; MR as a method of screening for breast cancer; MR imaging and spectroscopy in improved cancer diagnosis, staging and assessment of cancer; MR imaging and spectroscopy in the assessment of novel cancer therapeutics; MR imaging and spectroscopy methodology

Cancer Therapeutics

Includes Cancer Research UK Centre for Cancer Therapeutics

Tel: (020) 8722 4301 Fax: (020) 8722 4324
E-mail: pam.stevens@icr.ac.uk

Aherne, G. Wynne, BSc Wales, PhD Lond. Team Leader, Analyt. Technol. and Screening

Blagg, J., BA Oxf., DPhil Oxf. Head of Chem.; Team Leader, Medicinal Chem.

Collins, I., PhD Camb. Team Leader, Medicinal Chem.

Eccles, S. A., BSc Manc., MSc Lond., PhD Lond. Team Leader, Tumour Biol. and Metastis; Reader, Experimental Oncology

Garrett, M. D., BSc Leeds, PhD Lond. Team Leader, Cell Cycle Control

Hoelder, S., PhD Team Leader, Medicinal Chem.

Jones, K., MA Camb., PhD Camb., FRSChem Team Leader, Medicinal Chem.; Prof., Synthetic Chemistry

Judson, I. R., BA Camb., MB Camb., MB BChir Camb., MD Camb., FRCP Prof., Clinical Pharmacology

Linardopoulos, S., PhD Kandy Team Leader, Target Discovery and Apoptosis

McDonald, E., BSc Lond., PhD Liv. Team Leader, Medicinal Chem.

Springer, C. J., BSc Lond., PhD Lond. Team Leader, Gene and Oncogene Targeting; Prof., Molecular Pharmacology

Workman, P., BSc Leic., PhD Leeds, FIBiol, FMedSci Dir. and Team Leader, Signal Transduction and Molecular Pharmacol.; Prof., Pharmacology and Therapeutics; Head*

Other Staff: 170 Staff Members

Research: anti-cancer drug development; gene therapy

Cell and Molecular Biology

Includes Cancer Research UK Centre for Cell and Molecular Biology

Tel: (020) 7352 9772 Fax: (020) 7352 5630
E-mail: annette.argent@icr.ac.uk

Harrington, K., BSc MB BS, FRCR Leader, Targeted Therapy Team

Katan, M., BSc Belgrade, MSc Belgrade, PhD Glas. Leader, Lipid Signalling Team; Reader, Biochemistry

Lamb, R. F., BSc Glas., PhD Glas. Leader, Cell Regulation Team

Marais, R. M., BSc Lond., PhD Lond. Prof.; Leader, Signal Transduction Team

Marshall, C. J., MA Camb., DPhil Oxf., FRS Leader, Oncogene Team; Prof., Cell Biology; Chairman*

Mittnacht, S., MSc Heidel., PhD Heidel. Leader, Antioncogene Team; Reader, Cancer Biology

Weston, K. M., BSc Brist., PhD Camb. Sr. Tutor; Leader, Nuclear Oncogene Team

Willison, K. R., BSc Sus., PhD Camb. Prof.; Leader, Protein Folding Team

Other Staff: 53 Staff Members

Research: gene therapy for cancer; molecular dissection of cancer genes and cell signalling pathways

Clinical Trials and Statistics

Tel: (020) 8722 4013 Fax: (020) 8770 7876
E-mail: debbie.mills@icr.ac.uk

Bliss, J. M., BSc Birm., MSc Leic. Dir., Clin. Trials; Prof., Statistics

Hall, E., BSc Brist., MSc S'ton., PhD Lond. Deputy Dir.

Other Staff: 50 Staff Members

Research: design, initiation, conducting and analysis of clinical cancer trials

Epidemiology

Includes Department of Health Cancer Screening Evaluation Unit

Tel: (020) 8643 8901 Fax: (020) 8770 7876
E-mail: margaret.snigorska@icr.ac.uk

Melia, J. W., BA Camb., PhD Lond. Team Leader, Cancer Screening and Epidemiology

Moss, S. M., BSc Brist., MSc Exe., PhD Lond. Reader, Epidemiology

Peto, J., MA Oxf., MSc Prof., Epidemiology

Swerdlow, A., BA Camb., BM BCh Oxf., MA Oxf., DM Oxf., DPhil Oxf. Prof.; Head*

Other Staff: 44 Staff Members

Research: breast cancer aetiology; cancer genetics; cervical neoplasia and viral infection; industrial epidemiology; the aetiology of childhood cancers and leukaemias

Gene Function and Regulation

Tel: (020) 7352 8133 Fax: (020) 7352 0272
E-mail: marjorie.kipling@icr.ac.uk

Bruno, L., PhD Basle Immunol. Team Leader, Stem Cell Biol.

Rigby, P. W. J., BA Camb., PhD Camb., FMedSci Prof., Developmental Biology; Head*

Swain, A., PhD Boston Team Leader, Gene Function/Sexual Devel.

Other Staff: 16 Staff Members

Research: cell lineage specification; cell-cell interactions during development and organogenesis; developmental biology; organogenesis; regulation of cell proliferation

Haemato-Oncology

Fax: (020) 8722 4074
E-mail: barbara.deverson@icr.ac.uk

Davies, F. E., MB BCh Cardiff, MD Cardiff Sr. Lectr., Haematology

Greaves, M. F., BSc Lond., PhD Lond., FRS Prof., Cell Biology; Head*

Matutes, E., MD Barcelona, PhD Lond., FRCPath Reader, Haematology

Morgan, G. J., BSc Cardiff, MB BCh Cardiff, PhD Lond., FRCP, FRCPath Prof., Haematology

Zelent, A., BA Rutgers, PhD C.U.N.Y. Reader, Molecular Genetics

Other Staff: 34 Staff Members

Research: aetiological, genetic and biochemical mechanisms underlying the development of haematological malignancies

Medicine Section and Cancer Research UK Department of Medical Oncology

Tel: (020) 8661 3539 Fax: (020) 8661 3541
E-mail: linda.readings@icr.ac.uk

Banerji, U., MB BS Calicut, MD Bom., PhD Lond. Luck-Hille Clin.Sr. Lectr.; Team Leader, Pharmacodynamics

Brown, R., BSc PhD Team Leader, Epigenetics; Prof., Translational Oncology

de Bono, J. S., MB ChB Glas., PhD Glas., FRCP Team Leader, Drug Evaluation

Jackman, A. L., PhD Lond. Prof., Biochemistry

Kaye, S., BSc Lond., MD Lond., FRCP, FRCR, FRSEd, FMedSci Prof., Drug Development; Head*

Other Staff: 25 Staff Members

Research: clinical assessment of novel molecular-targetted drugs in cancer

Molecular Carcinogenesis

Tel: (020) 8643 8901 Fax: (020) 8770 7290
E-mail: christine.bell@icr.ac.uk

Cooper, C. S., BSc Warw., PhD Birm., DSc Warw., FMedSci Prof.; Head*

Goodwin, G. H., BSc Lond., MSc Lond., PhD Lond. Reader, Biochemistry

Phillips, D. H., BA Oxf., PhD Lond., DSc Oxf., FRCPath Prof., Environmental Carcinogenesis

Shipley, J. M., BSc S'ton., PhD Lond. Reader, Molecular Cytogenetics

Other Staff: 39 Staff Members

Research: microarray technology; the application of molecular biological technologies to clinical problems; using recombinant DNA technology to identify cancer-causing genes (oncogenes)

Paediatric Oncology

Tel: (020) 8661 3498 Fax: (020) 8661 3617
E-mail: regan.barfoot@icr.ac.uk

Jones, C., PhD Team Leader, Paediatric Molecular Pathol. Team

Pearson, A., MB BS MD DCH, FRCP, FRCPCH Prof.; Jt. Head*

Pritchard-Jones, K., BM BCh Oxf., MA Oxf., PhD CNAA, FRCPEd Prof., Childhood Cancer Biology; Team Leader*

Other Staff: 24 Staff Members

Research: cancer biology of childhood cancers; drug development in childhood cancers; function of specific genes in childhood cancers; genetic make-up of cancer cells; molecular pathology of childhood cancers

Physics

Tel: (020) 8642 6011 Fax: (020) 8643 3812
E-mail: marion.barrell@icr.ac.uk

Bamber, J. C., BSc Kent, MSc Lond., PhD Lond. Team Leader, Ultrasound and Optical Imaging

Darambara, D., BSc PhD Hon. Fac.; Team Leader, Multi-Modality Molecular Imaging

Evans, P. M., BSc Aston, DPhil Oxf. Reader, Radiation Physics

Flux, G., BSc PhD Hon. Fac.; Team Leader, Targeted Radionuclide Therapy

Partridge, M., BSc PhD Team Leader, Radiotherapy Physics

ter Haar, G. R., MA Oxf., MSc Aberd., PhD Lond., DSc Oxf., FIPEM Reader, Therapeutic Ultrasound

Webb, S., BSc Lond., PhD Lond., DSc Lond., FRSA Prof., Radiological Physics; Head*

Other Staff: 79 Staff Members

Research: biologically targeted radionuclide therapy; conformal and stereotactic radiotherapy; portal imaging; positron emission tomography; radiopharmaceutical development

Radiotherapy

Tel: (020) 8642 6011 Fax: (020) 8643 8809
E-mail: chris.martin@icr.ac.uk
Brada, M., BSc Brist., MB ChB Brist., FRCR, FRCP   Prof.; Hon. Consultant
Dearnaley, D. P., MA Camb., MB BChir Camb., MD Camb., FRCP, FRCR   Prof.; Hon. Consultant
Horwich, A., MB BS Lond., PhD CNAA, FRCR, FMedSci, FRCP   Prof.; Head*
Huddart, R., BM BCh Oxf., PhD Lond., FRCR   Reader
Yarnold, J. R., BSc Lond., MB BS Lond., FRCR   Prof.; Hon. Consultant
Other Staff: 28 Staff Members; 2 Hon. Consultants
Research: deletion size in mutations of human tumour cells; individualism of radiotherapy; molecular mechanisms of radiosensitivity; radiosensitivity and recovery in human tumour cell lines; repair of DNA damage measured in single cells using single-cell gel electrophorosis (SCGE)

Structural Biology

Tel: (020) 7153 5443 Fax: (020) 7153 5457
E-mail: sonia.malkani@icr.ac.uk
Barford, D., BSc Brist., DPhil Oxf., FRS, FMedSci   Section Co-Chair; Prof., Molecular Biology
Bayliss, R., MA Camb., PhD   Team Leader, Mitotic Regulation

Morris, E., BA Camb., PhD Lond.   Team Leader, Structural Electron Microscopy
Pearl, L. H., BSc Lond., PhD Lond., FMedSci   Section Co-Chairman; Prof., Protein Crystallography
Wilson, J., BSc Leeds, PhD Durh.   Team Leader, Chromatin Regulation
Other Staff: 48 Staff Members
Research: DNA damage recognition and repair; RNA interference; signal transduction; targeted protein destruction; transcriptional regulation

CONTACT OFFICERS

Academic affairs. Registrar: Pittam, B., PhD
(E-mail: barbara.pittam@icr.ac.uk)
Academic affairs. Academic Dean: Horwich, Prof. A., MB BS Lond., PhD CNAA, FRCR, FMedSci, FRCP (E-mail: dean@icr.ac.uk)
Admissions (higher degree). Research degrees (Admissions): Robinson, C.
(E-mail: catherine.robinson@icr.ac.uk)
Admissions (higher degree). Taught Masters (Admissions): Feasey, M.
(E-mail: margherita.feasey@icr.ac.uk)
Computing services. Information Technology Director: Harrington, Jeremy
(E-mail: jeremy.harrington@icr.ac.uk)
Development/fund-raising. General Manager, Fundraising: Provin, J., MA
(E-mail: jennifer.provin@icr.ac.uk)
Equal opportunities. Director of Human Resources: Scivier, C., MSc, FCIPD
(E-mail: cathy.scivier@icr.ac.uk)
Estates and buildings/works and services. Director of Facilities: Surridge, S., BSc
(E-mail: steve.surridge@icr.ac.uk)

Finance. Director of Finance: Whitehead, Andrew A.
(E-mail: andrew.whitehead@icr.ac.uk)
General enquiries.
(E-mail: switchbd@icr.ac.uk)
Library (enquiries). Librarian: Jenkins, Barry
(E-mail: sutlib@icr.ac.uk)
Personnel/human resources. Director of Human Resources: Scivier, C., MSc, FCIPD
(E-mail: cathy.scivier@icr.ac.uk)
Public relations. Director of Communications: Cardoe, N., BDS
(E-mail: nicky.cardoe@icr.ac.uk)
Quality assurance and accreditation. Scientific Secretary and Registrar: Pittam, B., PhD (E-mail: barbara.pittam@icr.ac.uk)
Research. Scientific Secretary and Registrar: Pittam, B., PhD
(E-mail: barbara.pittam@icr.ac.uk)
Safety. Chief Health and Safety Officer: Walford, C., MSc
(E-mail: clare.walford@icr.ac.uk)
Security. Director of Facilities: Surridge, S., BSc (E-mail: steve.surridge@icr.ac.uk)
Staff development and training. Development and Training Manager: Walford, N.
(E-mail: neil.walford@icr.ac.uk)
Strategic planning. Director of Corporate Development: Provin, J., MA
(E-mail: jennifer.provin@icr.ac.uk)

[*Information supplied by the institution as at 4 October 2007, and edited by the ACU*]

INSTITUTE OF EDUCATION

Founded 1902

Associate Member of the Association of Commonwealth Universities

Postal Address: 20 Bedford Way, London, England WC1H 0AL
Telephone: (020) 7612 6000 **Fax:** (020) 7612 6126
URL: http://www.ioe.ac.uk

DIRECTOR*—Whitty, Prof. Geoffrey J., MA Camb., MA Lond., DLit(Ed) Lond., Hon. DEd W.England, FRSA, FCT, AcSS
DIRECTOR OF ADMINISTRATION‡—Morris, Bryn
FINANCE OFFICER—McDonald, Marcus G., BSc Leic., MA Lond.
ACADEMIC REGISTRAR—Loughran, Loreto, PhD
HEAD OF INFORMATION SERVICES—Peters, Anne, BA Mich.State

KING'S COLLEGE LONDON

Founded 1829

Associate Member of the Association of Commonwealth Universities

Postal Address: Strand, London, England WC2R 2LS
Telephone: (020) 7836 5454
URL: http://www.kcl.ac.uk

PRINCIPAL*—Trainor, Prof. Richard H., BA *Brown*, MA *Oxf.*, MA *Prin.*, DPhil *Oxf.*, FRHistS, AcSS, FKC
HEAD OF ADMINISTRATION AND COLLEGE SECRETARY‡—Creagh, Ian, BA *NSW*, MA *Lond.*
VICE-PRINCIPAL (RESEARCH)—Freedman, Sir Lawrence, CBE, BA(Econ) *Manc.*, BPhil *York(UK)*, DPhil *Oxf.*, FBA, FKC
VICE-PRINCIPAL (STUDENTS)—Whitfield, Prof. Philip, MA *Camb.*, PhD *Camb.*, FKC
VICE-PRINCIPAL (ARTS AND SCIENCES)—Hoggart, Prof. Keith, BSc *Salf.*, MSc *Salf.*, PhD *Lond.*, FKC
VICE-PRINCIPAL (HEALTH)—Lechler, Prof. Robert, PhD *Lond.*, FRCP, FRCPath, FMedSci
DIRECTOR OF EMPLOYEE RELATIONS, VICE-PRINCIPAL AND COLLEGE SECRETARY EMERITUS—Musselwhite, Harry T., BA *Lond.*, FKC
DIRECTOR OF FINANCE—Large, Stephen
ASSISTANT PRINCIPAL (ESTATES)—Bushnell, Prof. Colin J., BSc *Lond.*, PhD *Lond.*, FKC
DEAN—Burridge, Rev. Richard A., MA *Oxf.*, PhD *Nott.*, FKC

GENERAL INFORMATION

History. The college, one of the two founding colleges of the University of London, was established in 1829 by King George IV and the Duke of Wellington. The college merged with King's College School of Medicine and Dentistry in 1983, Queen Elizabeth College and Chelsea College in 1985, the Institute of Psychiatry in 1997, and the United Medical and Dental Schools of Guy's and St Thomas' (UMDS) in 1998. The Florence Nightingale School of Nursing and Midwifery is directly descended from the world's first professional school of nursing, founded by Florence Nightingale at St Thomas' Hospital in 1860. Since 1996, through its department of defence studies, the college has provided education and training at the Joint Services Command and Staff College at Shrivenham, Wiltshire.

It is based on five campuses, all located in or near central London.

Admission to first degree courses (see also United Kingdom Introduction). Through Universities and Colleges Admissions Service (UCAS).

First Degrees (see also University of London Directory to Subjects of Study). BA, BDS, BEng, BMus, BSc, BSc(Eng), LLB, MB BS, MEng, MPharm, MSci.
Length of course. Full-time: BA, BEng, BMus, BSc, BSc(Eng), LLB: 3 years; MEng, MPharm, MSci: 4 years; BDS, MB BS: 4–6 years.

Higher Degrees (see also University of London Directory to Subjects of Study).
Master's. LLM, MA, MClinDent, MMus, MPH, MPhil, MRes, MS, MSc.
Admission. Admission requirements vary for each programme. Prospective students should consult the university's prospectus for information. Applicants for research degrees should normally hold at least an upper second class honours degree. Taught master's degrees: a first degree from a recognised university. Equivalent qualifications are considered.
Length of course. Full-time: LLM, MA, MMus, MPH, MRes, MSc: 1 year; MClinDent: 2–3 years; MPhil: 3–4 years. Part-time: LLM, MA, MMus, MPH, MRes, MSc: 2 years; MClinDent: 4 years; MPhil: 7–8 years. By *distance learning*: MSc: 2–4 years; MA: 3–6 years.
Doctoral. DClinPsy, DHC, DMin, EdD, MD, MD(Res), PhD.
Length of course. Full-time: DClinPsy: 3 years. Part-time: DHC, EdD: 4 years; DMin: 5 years.

Language of Instruction. English. English language courses available.

Libraries. Volumes: 1,000,000. Periodicals subscribed to: 3000. Other holdings: 4,000,000 archival documents; 500 e-books; 5000 e-journals.

Academic Awards (2006–2007). 461 awards ranging in value from £20 to £17,800.

Academic Year (2007–2008). Three terms: 24 September–14 December; 7 January–20 March; 21 April–6 June.

Income (2006–2007). Total, £407,081,000.

Statistics. Staff (2006): 5156 (2826 academic, 2330 non-academic). Students (2005–2006): full-time 15,178 (6024 men, 9154 women); part-time 3876 (1281 men, 2595 women); international 3918 (1702 men, 2216 women); distance education/external 235 (126 men, 109 women); undergraduate 13,683 (4800 men, 8883 women); master's 4049 (1906 men, 2143 women); doctoral 1557 (725 men, 832 women).

FACULTIES/SCHOOLS

Biomedical and Health Sciences, School of
Tel: (020) 7848 6979 Fax: (020) 7848 6394
Head: Morris, Prof. Roger, BSc *ANU*, DPhil *Oxf.*

Dental Institute
Tel: (020) 7188 7188 Fax: (020) 7188 1159
Head: Wilson, Prof. Nairn, CBE, BDS *Edin.*, MSc *Manc.*, PhD *Manc.*, FDSRCSEd, FKC

Humanities, School of
Tel: (020) 7848 2350 Fax: (020) 7848 2415
Head: Thompson, Prof. Ann R., BA *Lond.*, PhD *Lond.*

Law, School of
Tel: (020) 7836 5454 Fax: (020) 7848 2465
Head: Plant, Prof. Lord Raymond, BA *Lond.*, PhD *Hull*

Medicine, School of
Tel: (020) 7848 6971 Fax: (020) 7848 6969
Head: Greenough, Prof. Anne, MB BS *Lond.*, MD *Camb.*, FRCP

Nursing and Midwifery, Florence Nightingale School of
Tel: (020) 7848 4698 Fax: (020) 7848 3555
Head: Rafferty, Prof. Anne-Marie, BSc *Edin.*, MPhil *Nott.*, DPhil *Oxf.*

Physical Sciences and Engineering, School of
Tel: (020) 7848 2267/8 Fax: (020) 7848 2766
Head: Yianneskis, Prof. Michael, BScTech *Manc.*, MSc *Lond.*, PhD *Lond.*, FIEE, FKC

Psychiatry, Institute of
Tel: (020) 7848 0154 Fax: (020) 7848 0664
Dean: McGuffin, Prof. Peter, MB ChB *Leeds*, PhD *Lond.*, FRCP, FRCPsych, FMedSci

Social Science and Public Policy, School of
Tel: (020) 7848 1495 Fax: (020) 7848 2984
Head: Dandeker, Prof. Christopher, BSc *Leic.*, PhD *Leic.*

ACADEMIC UNITS
Biomedical and Health Sciences, School of
Tel: (020) 7848 2484, 7848 5454 Fax: (020) 7848 2285

Anatomy and Human Sciences
Tel: (020) 7848 6400 Fax: (020) 7848 6399
Brooks, Robert F., BSc *Lond.*, PhD *Lond.*   Sr. Lectr.
Buckland-Wright, J. Christopher, BSc *Lond.*, PhD *Lond.*, DSc *Lond.*   Prof.
Coen, Clive W., BA *Oxf.*, MA *Oxf.*, DPhil *Oxf.*   Prof.
Cohen, James, BSc *Glas.*, PhD *Lond.*   Prof.
Drescher, Uwe, PhD   Sr. Lectr.
Eickholt, Britta, PhD *Lond.*   Sr. Lectr.
Ellis, Harold, DM *Oxf.*, MCh *Oxf.*, FRSChem   Emer. Prof.
Fraser, Lynn R., BA *Colorado*, MPhil *Yale*, PhD *Yale*   Prof.
Gahan, Peter B., BSc *Lond.*, PhD *Lond.*   Emer. Prof.
Gordon-Weeks, Phillip R., PhD *Lond.*, BSc   Prof.
Graham, Anthony, BSc *Glas.*, PhD *Lond.*   Prof.
Guthrie, Sarah C., BA *Camb.*, MA *Lond.*, PhD *Lond.*   Prof.
Houart, Corinne, BSc *Brussels*, PhD *Brussels*   Sr. Lectr.
Hunter, Alistair, BSc *Aberd.*, PhD *Open(UK)*   Sr. Lectr.
Jones, Gareth E., BSc *Lond.*, PhD *Glas.*   Prof.
Lumsden, Andrew G. S., BA *Oxf.*, MA *Oxf.*, PhD *Lond.*, FRS, FKC, FMedSci   Prof.
Maden, Malcolm, BSc *Birm.*, PhD *Birm.*   Prof.
Mason, Ivor J., BA *Oxf.*, PhD *Lond.*, FIBiol   Prof.
O'Byrne, Kevin T., BSc *Lond.*, PhD *Brist.*   Sr. Lectr.
Older, John, MB BS *Lond.*, BDS *Lond.*, FRCS
Pizzey, John, BSc *Sus.*, PhD *Lond.*   Sr. Lectr.
Sales, Gillian D., BSc *Lond.*, PhD *Lond.*   Sr. Lectr.
Standring, Susan M., BSc *Lond.*, PhD *Lond.*, DSc *Lond.*   Prof.; Head*
Stolkin, Colin, BM BCh *Oxf.*, MA *Oxf.*   Sr. Lectr.

Biochemistry

Tel: (020) 7848 6766

Abuknesha, Ramadan R., BSc PhD   Sr. Lectr.
Ballard, Clive, MB ChB Leic., MMedSci Birm., MD Leic.   Wolfson Prof., Age Related Diseases
Brown, Paul R., PhD Lond., BSc   Sr. Lectr.
Cammack, Richard, MA Camb., PhD Camb., ScD Camb.   Prof.
Conte, Maria R., PhD Naples   Sr. Lectr.
Dingwall, Colin, BSc Newcastle(UK), PhD Camb. Prof.
Doherty, Patrick, BSc Lond., PhD Lond.   Prof.; Dir., Wolfson Centre for Age Related Diseases
Eagles, Peter A. M., BSc Sheff., DPhil Oxf.   Sr. Lectr.
Ellis, Peter   Sr. Lectr., Nutritional Sciences
Evans, Robert, BA Oxf., PhD Brist.   Reader, Nutritional Sciences
Francis, Paul T., BSc PhD   Reader, Wolfson Centre for Age Related Diseases
Garlick, Pamela B., BA Oxf., DPhil Oxf., MA Sr. Lectr.
Gould, Hannah, BA Radcliffe, MA Radcliffe, PhD Harv.   Prof., Randall Div.
Hogstrand, Christer, BS Gothenburg, PhD Gothenburg   Prof.
Irving, Malcolm, MA Camb., MSc Lond., PhD Lond., FKC, FRS   Prof.
Kelly, Francis J. (Frank), BSc Belf., PhD Belf. Prof.
McKie, Andrew   Sr. Lectr., Nutritional Sciences
Minger, Stephen, BA Minn., MS Albert Einstein Coll.of.Med, PhD Albert Einstein Coll.of.Med   Sr. Lectr., Wolfson Centre for Age Related Diseases
Nikolova, Penka, PhD Wat.   Sr. Lectr.
Panaretou, Barry   Sr. Lectr.
Papachristodoulou, Despina, BSc Lond., MSc Lond., PhD Lond.   Sr. Lectr.
Price, Robert G., PhD Wales, DSc Wales   Prof.
Quinn, Peter J., BAgrSc Melb., MSc Syd., PhD Syd., DSc Lond.   Prof.
Rattray, Marcus A. N., BSc PhD   Sr. Lectr.
Ross-Murphy, Simon B., BSc Manc., PhD Essex Prof.
Sanderson, Mark R., BSc E.Anglia, PhD Lond. Reader
Simpson, Robert   Sr. Lectr., Nutritional Sciences
Staines, Norman A., BSc Edin., PhD Edin.   Prof.
Sturzenbaum, Stephen, BSc Cardiff, PhD Cardiff
Sutton, Brian J., MA Oxf., DPhil Oxf.   Prof.
Tear, Guy, BSc Camb., MA Camb., PhD Camb. Prof.; Head*
Trentham, David R., BA Camb., PhD Camb., FRS Prof.
Whitfield, P. J., MA Camb., PhD Camb., FKC Prof.
Williams, Robert, BSc Leeds, PhD Leeds   Sr. Lectr.
Research: biophysics; cell biology; genetics; neuroscience; protein structure

Forensic Science and Drug Monitoring

Tel: (020) 7352 3838 Fax: (020) 7351 2591

Cowan, David A., BPharm Lond., PhD Lond., FRPharmS   Prof.; Dir.*
Daniel, Barbara, BSc Lond., PhD Lond.   Sr. Lectr.
Jickells, Susan, BSc Reading, MSc Lond., PhD Leeds Sr. Lectr.
Kicman, Andrew, BSc Lond., PhD Lond.   Sr. Lectr.
Research: analytical science; analytical toxicology; DNA analysis; fingerprint chemistry; sports doping

Nutrition and Dietetics

Tel: (020) 7848 4383

Baldwin, Christine, BSc Lond.
Emery, P. W., MA Camb., MSc Lond., PhD Lond. Prof.; Head*
Geissler, Catherine, BDS Edin., MS Calif., PhD Calif.   Emer. Prof.
Leeds, Anthony R., MSc Middx., MB BS, FIBiol Sr. Lectr.
Marshall, John, BSc PhD   Prof.

Nelson, M., BSc Montr., MSc Lond., PhD Reader
Preedy, Victor R., BSc Lond., PhD DSc, FIBiol, FRCPath   Prof.
Reidlinger, Dianne, BAppSc Qld., MND Deakin
Sanders, Tom A. B., BSc Lond., PhD Lond., DSc Lond.   Prof.
Sharp, Paul, PhD Lond., BSc   Sr. Lectr.
Stanford, Miles R., BChir MA MSc, FRCS Prof.
Thomas (Vlitos), Jane, BSc Lond., MMedSci Nott. Sr. Lectr.
Research: alcohol; inflammatory bowel disease; iron; lipids; nutrition

Pharmacology and Therapeutics

Tel: (020) 7848 6400 Fax: (020) 7848 6399

Aaronson, Philip I., BA PhD   Reader
Avrikan, Metin, BSc Bath, PhD Bath, DSc Bath Prof.
Bevan, Stuart   Prof.
Brain, Susan D., PhD Lond., BSc MA   Prof.
Cox, Helen M., BA S'ton., BSc S'ton., PhD S'ton. Prof.
Curtis, Michael J., BSc Lond., PhD Col.   Reader
Docherty, Reginald J., BSc Edin., PhD Edin.   Sr. Lectr.
Doherty, Patrick, BSc Lond., PhD Lond.   Prof.
Gibson, Alan, BSc Glas., PhD Glas., FKC   Sr. Lectr.; Head*
Halliday, John, BSc Edin., PhD Edin.   Sr. Lectr.
Jenner, Peter G., BPharm Lond., PhD Lond., DSc Lond., FRPharmS, FKC   Prof.
Kentish, Jonathan C., MA Oxf., PhD Lond. Prof.
Malcangio, Marzia, BSc Florence, PhD Florence Sr. Lectr.
McFadzean, Ian, BSc Strath., PhD Camb.   Sr. Lectr.
Page, Clive, BSc Lond., PhD Lond.   Prof.
Paterson, Stewart, BSc Glas., PhD Aberd.   Sr. Lectr.
Spina, Domenico, BSc W.Aust., PhD W.Aust. Reader
Research: asthma and chronic obstructive pulmonary disease (COPD); inflammation; neurodegenerative diseases; neuropharmacology; vascular biology

Pharmacy

Tel: (020) 7848 4783 Fax: (020) 7848 4800

Bansal, Sukhi, BSc Strath., PhD Strath.   Sr. Lectr.
Barlow, David, BSc Lond., MSc Lond., PhD Lond. Sr. Lectr.
Drake, A. F., MSc E.Anglia, PhD E.Anglia   Sr. Lectr.
Forbes, Ben, BPharm Lond., PhD Strath.   Sr. Lectr.
Greene, R., BPharm Nott., MSc Bath, PhD Lond. Sr. Lectr.
Hider, Robert C., BSc Lond., PhD Lond., FRSChem, FKC   Prof.
Houghton, Peter J., BPharm Lond., PhD Lond., FRPharmS, FRSChem   Prof.
Hylands, Peter   Sr. Lectr.; Head*
Lawrence, M. Jayne, BSc CNAA, PhD Manc. Prof.
Marriott, C., PhD CNAA, DSc CNAA, FRPharmS, FRSChem   Prof.
Martin, Gary, BPharm Nott., PhD Nott.   Prof.
Paine, Alan, BSc Lond., PhD Lond., DSc Lond., FIBiol, FRCPath   Prof.
Timbrell, J., BSc PhD DSc, FRSChem   Prof.
Whittlesea, Cate M. C., BSc Brighton, MSc Wales, PhD Lond.   Sr. Lectr.
Other Staff: 1 Sr. Teaching Fellow
Research: drug delivery; medicinal chemistry; molecular genetics; natural products; pharmacology

Physiology

Tel: (020) 7848 6373 Fax: (020) 7848 6399

Abbot, N. Joan, MA Camb., PhD Camb.   Prof.
Begley, David, BSc Edin., MSc Lond., PhD Lond. Sr. Lectr.
Ernsting, John, BSc Lond., MB BS Lond., PhD Lond., FRCP   Visiting Prof.
Francis, Paul T., BSc PhD   Sr. Lectr.

Fraser, Paul A., BSc Edin., MSc Lond., PhD Lond. Sr. Lectr.
Harridge, Stephen S. D. R., PhD   Prof.
Knight, Derek E., MSc Lond., PhD Lond.   Reader
Linden, Roger, BDS Brist., PhD Brist.   Prof.
Mann, Giovanni E., BSc Wash., MSc Lond., PhD Prof.
McMahon, Stephen B., BSc PhD   Prof.
Pearson, Jeremy D., BA Oxf., MA Camb., MA Oxf., PhD Camb., FMedSci   Prof.
Pini, Adrian P. J., MSc PhD   Sr. Lectr.
Preston, Jane E., BSc Lond., MSc Lond., PhD Lond. Sr. Lectr.
Shah, Ajay M., MB ChB Wales, MD Wales, FRCP, FMedSci   Prof., Cardiology
Shattock, Michael J., BSc Lond., PhD Lond., FESC Prof.
Simons, Timothy J. B., MA Camb., PhD Camb. Sr. Lectr.
Smith, I. Christopher S., BSc Sus., MSc Lond., PhD Lond.   Sr. Lectr.
Thompson, Ian   Prof.
Thompson, Stephen, BSc PhD   Sr. Lectr.
Tonge, David A., BSc S'ton., MPhil Sus., PhD Lond.   Sr. Lectr.
Tribe, Rachel, BSc Sheff., PhD Lond.
Ward, Jane, BSc Manc., MB ChB Manc., PhD Lond.   Sr. Lectr.
Ward, Jeremy P. T., BSc Lond., PhD Lond. Prof.; Head*
Research: cardiovascular and oxidant stress; endocrinology and reproduction; human and applied physiology; muscle function; pulmonary circulation

Physiotherapy

Tel: (020) 7848 6338 Fax: (020) 7848 6399

Beith, Iain, MSc Sur., PhD Lond.   Sr. Lectr.
Hilton, Ros, PhD Sur., BSc   Sr. Lectr.
Hurley, Mike, PhD Lond.   Prof.
Kitchen, Sheila, MSc Sur., PhD Lond.   Prof.; Head*
Morrissey, Matt, BSc Ill., MSc Stan., PhD Boston Sr. Lectr.
Newham, Di, PhD Lond.   Prof.
White, Claire, BSc Lond., MSc Lond., PhD Lond. Sr. Lectr.
Research: development and ageing; human function; rehabilitation

Reproduction and Endocrinology

Tel: (020) 7188 3639 Fax: (020) 7620 1227

Howell, Simon L., BSc Lond., PhD Lond., DSc Lond., FKC   Prof.
Jones, Peter M., BSc Coventry, PhD Lond.   Prof.
Milligan, Stuart R., MA Oxf., DPhil Oxf.   Prof.
Persaud, Shanta J., BSc Lond., PhD Lond. Reader
Pickup, John C., MA Oxf., BM BCh Oxf., DPhil Oxf., BA, FRCPath   Reader
Poston, Lucilla, PhD Lond., FRCOG   Prof.; Head*
Sugden, David, BSc Leeds, PhD CNAA   Reader
Research: diabetes; endocrinology; maternal health; obstetrics; reproduction

Dental Institute

Tel: (020) 7188 7188 Fax: (020) 7188 1159

Wilson, Nairn, CBE, BDS Edin., MSc Manc., PhD Manc., FDSRCSEd, FKC   Prof.; Head*

Conservative Dentistry

Banerjee, Avijit, BDS Lond., MSc Lond., PhD Lond., FDSRCS   Sr. Lectr.
Mannocci, Francesco, MD Pisa, DDS Pisa, PhD Lond.   Sr. Lectr.
Pitt Ford, Thomas R., BDS Lond., PhD Lond., FDSRCS   Prof.
Woolford, Mark, BDS Lond., PhD Dund., FDSRCS Sr. Lectr.; Head*
Research: biomaterials; carniology; endodontics; novel restorative treatment

Craniofacial Development

Dietrich, Susanne, PhD Heidel.   Reader
Francis-West, Philippa, BA Camb., PhD Lond. Prof.
Green, Jeremy, BA Camb., PhD Lond.   Sr. Lectr.

Grigoradis, Agamemnon, BSc Tor., MSc Tor., PhD Tor. Reader
Meredith Smith, Moya, BSc Lond., PhD Lond., DSc Lond. Prof.
Sharpe, Paul, BA York(UK), PhD Sheff. Prof.; Head*
Streit, Andrea, PhD Heidel. Reader
Tucker, Abigail, BA Oxf., DPhil Oxf. Sr. Lectr.
Research: bone; developmental biology; regenerative medicine and dentistry

Dental Materials

Curtis, Richard, BSc Manc., PhD Lond. Sr. Lectr.
Deb, Sanjukta, BSc Delhi, MSc Delhi, PhD Delhi Sr. Lectr.
Di Silvio, Luciana, BSc Lond., PhD Lond. Sr. Lectr.
Sherriff, Martyn, BSc Lond., PhD Lond. Reader
Watson, Timothy F., BSc Lond., BDS Lond., PhD Lond., FDSRCS Prof.; Head*
Research: biomaterials; biomimetics; biophotonics; imaging; medical metallurgy

Dental Public Health

Bedi, Raman, BDS Brist., MSc Manc., DDS Brist., DSc Brist., FDSRCS Prof.
Donaldson, Ana, BSc Valle, MSc Virginia Polytech., PhD Maryland Reader
Gallagher, Jennifer, BDS Belf., MSc Lond., PhD Lond., FDSRCS Sr. Lectr.
Newton, Jonathan, BA Liv., PhD Liv. Prof.; Head*
Research: health services research; psychology; public health

Fixed and Removable Prosthodontics

Bartlett, David, BDS Birm., PhD Lond., FDSRCSEd Prof.; Head*
Cabot, Lyndon, BDS Wales, MSc Lond., MA Open(UK) Sr. Lectr.
Clark, Robert, BDS Lond., PhD Lond., FDSRCPSGlas Prof.
Fenlon, Michael, BDentSc Trinity(Dub.), PhD Lond., FDSRCSEd Reader
Packer, Mark, BDS Lond., MPhil Lond., FDSRCS Sr. Lectr.
Radford, David R., BDS Lond., PhD Lond., FDSRCS Sr. Lectr.
Research: prosthodontic design; tooth wear

Flexible Learning in Dentistry, Centre of

Millar, Brian, BDS Dund., PhD Lond., FDSRCS Sr. Lectr.
Reynolds, Patricia, MB BS Lond., BDS Lond., MA Open(UK), PhD Lond., FDSRCS Prof.; Head*
Research: distance learning; education; haptics; International Virtual Dental School (IVIDENT); novel educational technologies

Microbiology

Beighton, David, BSc Melb., PhD Melb. Prof.
Lax, Alistair J., BSc Glas., PhD Lond. Prof.; Head*
Wade, William G., BSc E.Anglia, MSc Wales, PhD Wales Prof.
Wood, Ann, BSc Lond., PhD Lond. Sr. Lectr.
Research: bacterial toxins; microbial ecology; microbial physiology; molecular cellular microbiology

Oral Immunology

Ivanyi, Juraj, MD Prague, PhD Prague Prof.
Kelly, Charles, BSc Brist., PhD Brist. Prof.; Head*
Lehner, Thomas, CBE, BDS Lond., MB BS Lond., MD Lond., FDSRCS, FRCPath, FKC Prof.
Research: microbicides; mucosal immunology; tuberculosis; vaccines

Oral Medicine

Challacombe, Stephen J., BDS Lond., PhD Lond., FDSRCS, FRCPath Prof.
Setterfield, Jane, BDS Lond., MB BS Lond. Sr. Lectr.
Warnakulasuriya, Kasturi, OBE, BDS Ceyl., PhD Glas., DSc S.Lanka, FDSRCS Prof.; Head*
Research: candida infections; dermatology; mucosal biology; oral cancer

Oral Pathology

Harrison, John D., BDS Lond., PhD Lond., FDSRCS, FRCPath Reader
Morgan, Peter, BSc Lond., BDS Lond., PhD Lond., FDSRCS, FRCPath Prof.
Odell, Edward, BDS Lond., MSc Lond., PhD Lond., FDSRCSEd, FRCPath Prof.; Head*
Proctor, Gordon, BSc Brad., PhD Sheff. Prof.
Tavassoli, Mahvash, BSc Sus., MA Brighton, DPhil Sus. Prof.
Research: oral cancer; oral physiology; salivary research

Oral Surgery

McGurk, Mark, MB ChB Sheff., BDS Sheff., MD Sheff., FRCS, FDSRCPSGlas Prof.
Partridge, Maxine, BDS Brist., PhD Lond., FDSRCS, FRCPath Prof.
Renton, Tara, BDS Lond., MSc Melb., PhD Lond., FDSRCS Prof.; Head*
Research: imaging; oral cancer; pain

Orthodontics

Breckon, Jeremy J., BDS Lond., MSc Lond., PhD Lond., FDSRCS Sr. Lectr.
Cobourne, Martyn, BDS Lond., MSc Lond., PhD Lond., FDSRCSEd Sr. Lectr.
Derringer, Kathryn, BDS Liv., MSc Lond., PhD Lond., FDSRCPSGlas Sr. Lectr.
Hill, Peter, BSc Glas., BDS Glas., MSc Glas., PhD Lond., FDSRCPSGlas Sr. Lectr.
McDonald, Fraser, BDS Birm., MSc Lond., PhD Lond., FDSRCS, FFDRCSI Prof.; Head*
Research: clinical orthodontics; developmental biology

Paediatric Dentistry

Roberts, Graham, BDS Lond., MDS Lond., MPhil Lond., PhD Lond., FDSRCS Prof.; Head*
Sheehy, Evelyn, BDentSc Trinity(Dub.), PhD Lond., FDSRCSEd Sr. Lectr.
Research: bacteraemia in dentistry

Periodontology

Booth, Veronica, BDS Edin., MSc Lond., PhD Lond. Sr. Lectr.
Hasan, Adam, BSc Lond., BDS Lond., PhD Lond., FDSRCS Sr. Lectr.
Ide, Mark, BDS Lond., MSc Lond., PhD Lond., FDSRCS Sr. Lectr.; Head*
Palmer, Richard, BDS Lond., PhD, FDSRCS Prof.
Soory, Menaka, BDS S.Lanka, PhD Lond., FDSRCS Sr. Lectr.
Watts, Trevor, BDS Manc., MDS Manc., PhD Manc., FDSRCPSGlas Sr. Lectr.
Wilson, Ronald, PhD Lond. Sr. Lectr.
Research: clinical periodontology; dental implants; periodontal and systemic disease; periodontal microbiology and immunology

Primary Dental Care

Dunne, Stephen M., BDS Lond., PhD Lond., FDSRCS Prof.; Head*
Millar, Brian, BDS Dund., PhD Lond., FDSRCS Sr. Lectr.
Wilson, Nairn, CBE, BDS Edin., MSc Manc., PhD Manc., FDSRCSEd, FKC Prof.
Research: clinical trials; dental materials

Radiology

Ng, Suk, BSc Manc., BDS Manc., PhD Manc., FDSRCS Sr. Lectr.
Whaites, Eric, BDS Lond., MSc Lond., FDSRCSEd Sr. Lectr.; Head*
Research: imaging

Sedation and Special Care

Fiske, Janice, MBE, BDS Lond., MPhil Lond., FDSRCS Sr. Lectr.
Research: dental treatment for elderly; special needs

Humanities, School of

American Studies

Tel: (020) 7848 2315 Fax: (020) 7848 2001
E-mail: american-studies@kcl.ac.uk
Bush, Clive, BA Lond., MPhil Lond., PhD Lond. Emer. Prof.

Castillo, Susan, BA MPhil PhD Prof.
Howard, John, BA MA PhD Prof.
Marshall, Alan, BA York(UK), DPhil York(UK) Head*
Springer, Kimberley, BA Emory, MA Emory, PhD Emory Reader
Zamir, Shamoon, BA Lond., MA Lond., PhD Lond. Reader
Other Staff: 2 Lectrs.
Research: African American studies; American art and literature; American civil and natural history; queer studies; the built environment

Byzantine and Modern Greek Studies

Tel: (020) 7848 2343 Fax: (020) 7848 2545
E-mail: bmgs@kcl.ac.uk
Beaton, Roderick McL., MA Camb., PhD Camb. Koraes Prof.
Georgakapoulou, Alexandra, BA Athens, PhD Edin. Reader
Herrin, J. E., MA Camb., PhD Birm., BA Prof.
Ricks, David B., BA Lond., MA Oxf., PhD Lond. Sr. Lectr.
Roueché, Charlotte M., MA Camb. Prof., Classical and Byzantine Greek; Head*
Other Staff: 3 Lectrs.
Research: Byzantine history; language and literature; modern Greek history

Classics

Tel: (020) 7848 2343 Fax: (020) 7848 2545
E-mail: classics@kcl.ac.uk
Arafat, Karim, MA Oxf., DPhil Oxf. Reader
Bowden, Hugh, MA Oxf., DPhil Oxf. Sr. Lectr.
D'Alessio, Giambattista, DottLett Pisa Prof., Greek Language and Literature
Fitzgerald, William, BA Oxf., PhD Prin. Prof., Latin Language and Literature
Ganz, David, BA Oxf., DPhil Oxf. Prof., Palaeography
Herrin, J. E., MA Camb., PhD Birm., BA Prof., Late Antique and Byzantine Studies
Lada-Richards, Ismene, BA Athens, PhD Camb. Reader
Mayer, Roland G. M., BA Calif., MA Camb., PhD Camb. Prof.
Morgan, Catherine A., MA Camb., PhD Camb. Prof., Classical Archaeology (on leave)
Mouritsen, Henrik, BA Odense, PhD Copenhagen Reader
Rathbone, Dominic W., MA Camb., PhD Camb. Prof., Ancient History
Roueché, Charlotte M., MA Camb. Prof., Classical and Byzantine Greek
Silk, Michael S., MA Camb., PhD Camb. Prof., Greek Language and Literature
Trapp, Michael B., MA Oxf., DPhil Oxf. Prof.; Head*
Other Staff: 8 Lectrs.; 3 Res. Fellows
Research: archaeology; Greek and Roman culture; Greek and Roman history; Greek language, literature and thought; Latin language, literature and thought

English Language and Literature

Tel: (020) 7848 2185 Fax: (020) 7848 2257
E-mail: englishdepartment@kcl.ac.uk
Brant, Clare, MA Oxf., DPhil Oxf. Reader
Ganz, David, BA Oxf., DPhil Oxf. Prof.
Hurwitz, Brian, BA Camb., MB BS Lond., MA Lond., MSc Lond., MD Lond., FRCP, FRCGP D'Oyly Carte Prof. of Arts, Medicine and the Arts
Kirkland, Richard, BA Nott., MA Belf., PhD Belf. Reader
Lees, Clare, BA Leeds, MA Leeds, PhD Liv. Prof.
McDonagh, Josephine, BA Wales, MA S'ton., PhD S'ton. Reader
McMullan, Gordon, BA Birm., MA Kansas, DPhil Oxf., FRSA Reader
Nokes, David L., MA Camb., PhD Camb., FRSL Prof.
Ormond, Leonee, BA Oxf., MA Birm. Prof.
Pettitt, Claire, BA Camb., DPhil Oxf. Reader
Read, Alan, BA Exe., PhD George Washington Prof.
Ruvani, Ranasinha Sr. Lectr.

Salih, Sarah Sr. Lectr.
Saunders, Max, BA *Camb.*, MA *Camb.*, AM *Harv.*, PhD *Camb.* Prof.
Stokes, John, BA *Reading*, PhD *Reading* Prof.
Thompson, Ann R., BA *Lond.*, PhD *Lond.* Prof.
Turner, Mark, BA *Syd.*, MA *Lond.*, PhD *Lond.* Reader; Head*
Other Staff: 9 Lectrs.
Research: contemporary literary theory; post-colonialism; study of theatrical performance; theory and practice of biography; writing and the visual arts

Film Studies

Tel: (020) 7848 2315 Fax: (020) 7848 2001
E-mail: film-studies@kcl.ac.uk
Betz, Mark, BA *Manit.*, MA *Manit.*, PhD *Roch.* Sr. Lectr.
Cooper, Sarah, BA *Camb.*, MPhil *Camb.*, PhD *Camb.* Sr. Lectr.
Dyer, Richard, MA *St And.*, PhD *Birm.* Prof.
Shiel, Mark, BA *Trinity(Dub.)*, PhD *Lond.* Sr. Lectr.
Vincendeau, Prof. Ginette, Lic *Paris III*, PhD *E.Anglia* Prof.; Head*
Other Staff: 1 Lectr.
Research: cultural approaches to film; European cinema; film theory

French

Tel: (020) 7848 2404 Fax: (020) 7848 2720
Callinicos, Alex, MA *Oxf.*, DPhil *Oxf.* Prof.
ffrench, R. Patrick, BA *Lond.*, PhD *Lond.* Reader
Gaunt, Simon B., BA *Warw.*, PhD *Warw.* Prof.
Green, Anne, MA *Aberd.*, PhD *Camb.* Sr. Lectr.
Harrison, Nicholas, BA *Camb.*, PhD *Camb.* Prof.; Head*
McIlvanney, Siobhan, MA *Glas.*, DPhil *Oxf.* Sr. Lectr.
Pratt, Karen E., BA *Oxf.*, MA *Oxf.*, PhD *Reading* Sr. Lectr.
Wolfreys, James, BA *Liv.*, PhD *Liv.* Sr. Lectr.
Other Staff: 4 Lectrs.
Research: French literary studies; French politics and history; French postcolonial studies; French visual culture; modern French thought

German

Tel: (020) 7848 2124 Fax: (020) 7848 2089
Adler, J. D., PhD Emer. Prof.
Bell, Matthew, MA *Oxf.*, DPhil *Oxf.* Prof.
Brady, Martin, MA *St And.*, PhD *Lond.* Sr. Lectr.
Jones, Martin, MA *Oxf.* Sr. Lectr.
Palmowski, Jan, BA *York(UK)*, DPhil *Oxf.* Sr. Lectr.
Pott, Sandra, DrPhil *Giessen* Prof.
Weninger, Robert, DPhil *Fran.* Prof.; Head*
White, John, BA *Leic.*, MA *Alta.*, PhD *Lond.* Emer. Prof.
Yeandle, David, MA *Camb.*, PhD *Camb.* Prof.
Other Staff: 3 Lectrs.
Research: German culture; German linguistics; German literary theory; German politics and history; German thought and philosophy

History

Tel: (020) 7848 1078 Fax: (020) 7848 2052
Bowden, Hugh, MA *Oxf.*, DPhil *Oxf.* Sr. Lectr.
Burns, R. Arthur, MA *Oxf.*, DPhil *Oxf.* Prof.; Head*
Carpenter, David, MA *Oxf.*, DPhil *Oxf.*, FRHistS Prof.
Goldgar, Anne, AM *Harv.*, PhD *Harv.* Reader (on leave)
Gowing, Laura, BA *Oxf.*, PhD *Lond.* Reader
Jordanova, Ludmilla, MA *Camb.*, MA *Essex*, PhD *Camb.* Prof.
Lovell, Stephen, BA *Camb.*, MA *Lond.*, PhD *Lond.* Reader
McBride, Ian, MA *Lond.*, PhD *Lond.* Sr. Lectr.
McLean, David, BA *Hull*, MA *Camb.*, PhD *Camb.* Prof.
Nelson, Janet L., DBE, BA *Camb.*, PhD *Camb.*, FBA, FRHistS, FKC Prof.

Porter, Andrew N., MA *Camb.*, PhD *Camb.*, FRHistS Rhodes Prof.
Stockwell, Sarah, BA *Camb.*, DPhil *Oxf.* Sr. Lectr.
Vinen, Richard, MA *Lond.*, PhD *Lond.* Reader
Other Staff: 11 Lectrs.
Research: cultural history; imperial history; intellectual history (political ideas); nationalism and national identity; women, gender and sexuality

Music

Tel: (020) 7848 2029 Fax: (020) 7848 2326
Benjamin, George, BA *Camb.* Prof.
Chua, Daniel K. L., BA *Camb.*, MPhil *Camb.*, PhD *Camb.* Prof.
Deathridge, John, BA *Oxf.*, MA *Oxf.*, DPhil *Oxf.* Prof.; Head*
Eisen, Cliff, BA *Tor.*, MA *Tor.*, PhD *Cornell* Prof.
Fend, Michael, PhD *T.U.Berlin* Sr. Lectr.
Keeley, Robert, BA *Oxf.* Sr. Lectr.
Leech-Wilkinson, Daniel, MMus *Lond.*, PhD *Camb.* Prof.
Milstein, Silvana, BMus *Glas.*, MPhil *Camb.*, PhD *Camb.* Sr. Lectr.
Parker, Roger, BMus *Lond.*, MMus *Lond.*, PhD *Lond.* Prof.
Trendell, David, BA *Oxf.* Sr. Lectr.
Wintle, Christopher S., BA *Oxf.*, BMus *Oxf.* Sr. Lectr.
Other Staff: 2 Lectrs.
Research: music history; music theory; musical analysis; opera studies; performance practice

Philosophy

Tel: (020) 7873 2231 Fax: (020) 7873 2270
Adamson, Peter Sr. Lectr.
Gaita, Raimond J., MA *Melb.*, PhD *Leeds* Prof.
Hopkins, Glen, AB *Harv.*, BA *Camb.*, PhD Reader
Hughes, Christopher, BA *Wesleyan*, PhD *Pitt.* Reader
Kempson, Ruth, BA *Birm.*, MA *Lond.*, PhD *Lond.*, FBA Prof.
Lappin, Shalom, BA *Tor.*, MA *Brandeis*, PhD *Brandeis* Prof.
McCabe, Mary-Margaret, MA *Camb.*, PhD *Camb.* Prof.
Milton, John R., BA *Camb.*, MA *Camb.*, PhD *Camb.*, DPhil *Oxf.* Prof.
Papineau, David, BSc *Natal*, PhD *Camb.* Prof.; Head*
Pink, Thomas, BA *Camb.*, PhD *Camb.* Reader
Sainsbury, R. Mark, MA *Oxf.*, DPhil *Oxf.*, FKC, FBA Prof.
Segal, Gabriel, BA *Lond.*, BPhil *Oxf.*, PhD *M.I.T.* Prof.; Head*
Travis, Charles, BA *Calif.*, PhD *Calif.* Prof.
Other Staff: 8 Lectrs.
Research: ancient philosophy; epistemology and metaphysics; ethics; history of mediaeval/modern philosophy; philosophy of mind, psychology

Portuguese and Brazilian Studies

Tel: (020) 7848 2507 Fax: (020) 7848 2787
Bethencourt, Francisco, BA *Lisbon*, MA *Lisbon*, PhD *Florence* Prof.; Head*
Chabal, Patrick E., BA *Harv.*, MPhil *Col.*, PhD *Camb.* Prof. (on leave)
Cohen, Rip, BA *Calif.*, MA *Calif.*, PhD *Calif.* Reader
Naro, Nancy, BS *Chic.*, MS *Chic.*, PhD *Chic.* Reader
Newit, Malyn Prof.
Perkins, Juliet, BA *Lond.*, PhD *Lond.* Sr. Lectr.
Treece, David, BA *Liv.*, PhD *Liv.* Prof.
Other Staff: 3 Lectrs.
Research: cultural and intellectual history; history of the Portuguese-speaking world; nationalism and identity politics in Portugal; Portuguese literature; Romance and Portuguese languages

Spanish and Spanish American Studies

Tel: (020) 7848 2205 Fax: (020) 7848 2207
Archer, Robert, BA *Durh.*, DPhil *Oxf.*, FAHA Prof.; Head*
Boyle, Catherine, BA *Strath.*, MA *Liv.*, PhD *Liv.* Reader
Butt, J. W., MA *Camb.*, DPhil *Oxf.*, PhD Emer. Prof.
Ife, Barry W., BA *Lond.*, PhD *Lond.*, FKC Emer. Prof.
Moreira-Rodriquez, Antonia Sr. Lectr.
Muñoz, Daniel Sr. Lectr.
Rebaza-Soraluz, Luis, BA *Pontif.Peru*, MA *Maryland*, PhD *Maryland* Sr. Lectr.
Sage, Jack Emer. Prof.
Weiss, Julian, BA *Lond.*, DLitt *Oxf.* Prof.
Other Staff: 7 Lectrs.
Research: Latin American studies; mediaeval and golden age; modern peninsular Spanish studies

Theology and Religious Studies

Tel: (020) 7848 2339 Fax: (020) 7848 2255
Al-Rasheed, Madawi, BA *Salf.*, MPhil *Camb.*, PhD *Camb.* Prof., Anthropology
Antognazza, Maria Rosa, PhD Reader
Byrne, Peter A., BA *York(UK)*, BPhil *Oxf.* Prof., Ethics and Philosophy of Religion
Davies, Oliver, BA *Oxf.*, DPhil *Oxf.* Prof., Christian Doctrine; Head*
Sedmak, Clemens, DPhil *Innsbruck* Prof., Moral and Social Theology
Other Staff: 13 Lectrs.
Research: Christian ethics (including medical ethics); history of religions; Old and New Testament; philosophy of religion; systematic theology

Law, School of

E-mail: enq.genlaw@kcl.ac.uk
Aplin, Tanya, BA *W.Aust.*, LLB *W.Aust.*, BCL *Oxf.*, DPhil *Oxf.* Sr. Lectr.
Bercusson, Brian, LLB *Lond.*, LLM *McG.*, PhD *Camb.* Dir., Res. Students; Prof., European Social and Labour Law
Biondi, Andrea, LLM *Florence*, MA *Florence*, PhD *Florence* Prof., European Union Law
Blackburn, Robert, BA *Leeds*, MSc *Lond.*, PhD *Leeds*, LLD *Leeds*, FRHistS Dir., Centre of British Constitutional Law and History (CBCLH); Prof., Constitutional Law
Bowling, Benjamin, BA *Manc.Met.*, PhD *Lond.* Dir., Criminological Studies; Prof., Criminology and Criminal Studies
Brownsword, Roger, LLB *Lond.* Prof., Regulation and Technology
Chambers, Robert, BEd *Alta.*, LLB *Alta.*, DPhil *Oxf.* Prof.
Chowdry, Monica, LLB *Lond.*, LLM *Lond.* Sr. Lectr.
Coyle, Andrew, BA *Open(UK)*, PhD *Edin.*, FKC Prof., Prison Studies
Dalhuisen, Jan, LLM *Calif.*, MagJur *Amst.*, DrJuris *Amst.* Prof., Financial Law
Douglas-Scott, Sionaidh, BA *Lond.*, LLM *Lond.* Prof.
Dworkin, Gerald, LLB *Nott.* Emer. Prof.
Eeckhout, Piet, Lic *Ghent*, PhD *Ghent* Dir., LLM Programme; Prof., European Law
Ewing, Keith, LLB *Edin.*, PhD *Camb.* Prof., Public Law
Glover, Jonathan, MA *Oxf.*, BPhil *Oxf.* Dir., Centre of Medical Law and Ethics (CMLE); Prof., Ethics
Green, Penelope, BA *ANU*, MQual *W.Aust.*, MPhil *Camb.*, PhD *Camb.* Sr. Lectr.; Dir., Res. Students
Guest, Anthony, CBE, QC, MA *Oxf.*, FBA, FKC Emer. Prof., English Law
Henderson, Jane, LLB *Lond.*, LLM *Lond.* Sr. Lectr., Laws of Eastern Europe
Hooley, Richard, BA *Camb.*, MA *Camb.* Prof., Commercial and Banking Law
Hough, Michael J. M., MA *Oxf.* Dir., Inst. for Criminal Policy Res. (ICPR); Prof., Criminal Policy
Jacobs, Sir Francis, QC, MA *Oxf.*, DPhil *Oxf.* Prof., European Law

Jones, Alison, BA Camb., BCL Oxf.   Prof.
Juss, Satvinder, BA Wolv., PhD Camb.   Prof.
Keller, Perry, BA Br.Col., LLB York(Can.), LLM Harv.   Sr. Lectr.
Lewis, Penney, SB M.I.T., LLB Tor., MA Lond., LLM Col.   Prof.
Llewelyn, David, LLB S'ton., BCL Oxf.   Prof.
Lomnicka, Eva, LLB Camb., MA Camb.   Prof., Intellectual Property Law
Macklem, Timothy, BA Car., LLB Ott., BCL Oxf., DPhil Oxf.   Prof.; Deputy Head
Marks, Susan, BA Syd., LLB Syd., LLM Camb., PhD Camb.   Prof., Public International Law
McColgan, Aileen, BA Camb., LLM Edin.   Prof., Human Rights Law
Mellows, Anthony, TD, BD Lond., PhD Lond., LLD Lond.   Emer. Prof.
Mitchell, Charles, BA Oxf., LLM Lond., PhD Lond.   Prof.
Mitchell, Paul, BA Oxf., DPhil Oxf.   Sr. Lectr.
Müllerson, Rein, LLD Moscow   Prof., International Law
Norrie, Alan, LLB Edin., MA Sheff., PhD Dund.   Prof., Criminal Law and Criminal Justice
Ogowewo, Tunde, LLB Benin, LLM Lond., PhD Lond.   Sr. Lectr.
O'Higgins, Paul, BA Trinity(Dub.), LLB Trinity(Dub.), MA Camb., MA Trinity(Dub.), LLD Trinity(Dub.), PhD Camb.   Emer. Prof.
Penner, James, BEd Alta., LLB Alta., DPhil Oxf.   Prof.
Phillips, John, BA Camb., MA Camb., LLM Qld., PhD Qld.   Prof., English Law
Plant, Lord Raymond, BA Lond., PhD Hull   Prof., Jurisprudence and Political Philosophy; Head*
Player, Elaine, BSc Lond.   Reader
Richardson, Genevra, CBE, LLB Lond., LLM Lond.   Prof.
Scott, Rosamund, BA ANU, BA Oxf., PhD Lond.   Prof.
Stanton-Ife, John, LLB Lond., LLM Tor., BCL Oxf., PhD European Univ.Inst.   Sr. Lectr.
Steiner, Eva, DrJur Paris X   Sr. Lectr., French Law
Türk, Alexander, MA Augsburg, PhD Lond., LLM   Sr. Lectr.
Vogel, Mary, BSFS Georgetown, MCP Harv., PhD Harv.   Reader
Whish, Richard, BA Oxf., BCL Oxf.   Prof.
Wintemute, Robert, BA Alta., LLB McG., BCL McG., DPhil Oxf.   Prof., Human Rights Law
Yeung, Karen, LLB Melb., BComMkt Melb., BCL Oxf., DPhil Oxf.   Prof.
Other Staff: 16 Lectrs.; 1 Lektor (German Law); 24 Visiting Profs.
Research: constitutional affairs and history; criminal law and prison studies; European law; issues of human rights and civil liberties; medical law and ethics

Nursing and Midwifery, Florence Nightingale School of

Tel: (020) 7848 4698

Ageing and Health

Fitzpatrick, Joanne, BSc Ulster, PhD Lond.   Sr. Lectr.
Roberts, Julia, BSc Hull, MA Lond., PhD Lond.   Sr. Lectr.

Health and Social Care Research

Cowley, Sarah, BA Open(UK), PhD Brighton   Prof.
Griffiths, Peter D., BA Sus., PhD Lond.   Prof.
Humphrey, Charlotte, BA Brist., MSc Lond.   Prof.
Norman, Ian J., BA Keele, MSc Edin., PhD Lond.   Prof.
Rafferty, Anne-Marie, BSc Edin., MPhil Nott., DPhil Oxf.   Prof.; Head*
Ream, Emma, BSc Lond., MSc Lond., PhD Lond.   Sr. Lectr.
Richardson, Alison, BN Wales, MSc Lond., PhD Lond.   Prof.
Sandall, Jane, BSc Lond., MSc Lond., PhD Sur.   Prof.

Wainwright, Steven P., BSc Hull, MSc Lond., PhD Lond.   Sr. Lectr.
Williams, Clare, BSc Sur., MSc Lond., PhD Sur.   Reader

Health Policy Evaluation

Young, Ruth, BA Manc., PhD Liv.   Reader

Interpersonal Studies and Health Promotion

Tel: (020) 7848 5261
Cooper, Serena, BSc Lond., MSc Lond.   Prof.; Clin. Dean*

Midwifery and Women's Health Studies

Tel: (020) 7848 5207
Hammett, Pauleene, BSc Lond.   Sr. Lectr.; Head*

Nursing Studies

Tel: (020) 7872 3024 Fax: (020) 7872 3219
Norman, Ian J., BA Keele, MSc Edin., PhD Lond.   Prof.
Richardson, Alison, BN Wales, MSc Lond., PhD Lond.   Prof.
While, Alison, BSc S'ton., MSc CNAA, PhD Lond.   Prof.

Philosophy and Practice of Nursing

Tel: (020) 7848 5112
Chan, Wai Cheng, BEd S.Bank   Principal Lectr.
Mingay, Julia, BSc Cant., MSc City(UK)   Sr. Lectr.; Head*
Smith, Sue, BSc Manc.   Sr. Lectr., Child Branch

Primary and Intermediate Care

Barribball, Louise, BA Kent, PhD Lond.   Sr. Lectr.
Bliss, Julie, BSc Manc., MSc Manc.   Sr. Lectr.
Edwards, Margaret, BA Lond., MSc Lond., PhD Lond.   Sr. Lectr.
While, Alison, BSc S'ton., MSc CNAA, PhD Lond.   Prof.
Research: chronic illness care and symptom alleviation; health care workforce; women's and family health

Specialist Care

Richardson, Alison, BN Wales, MSc Lond., PhD Lond.   Prof.

Physical Sciences and Engineering, School of

Bioinformatics, Centre for

Tel: (020) 7848 2318 Fax: (020) 7848 2766
Ouzounis, Christos, BSc Salonika, MSc York(UK), PhD York(UK)   Prof.; Head*
Other Staff: 1 Lectr.
Research: bioinformatics

Computer Science

Tel: (020) 7848 2145 Fax: (020) 7848 2851
Cooper, Colin, PhD Lond.   Reader
Crochemore, Maxine, PhD Rouen   Prof.
Degtyarev, Anatoli, PhD Ukr.Natnl.Acad.Scis.   Sr. Lectr.
Fernández, Maribel, PhD Paris   Reader; Dir., Undergrad. Programmes
Gabbay, Dov M., BSc Jerusalem, MSc Jerusalem, PhD Jerusalem   Augustus De Morgan Prof.
Ginzburg, Jonathan, BSc Jerusalem, PhD Stan.   Sr. Lectr.
Gold, Nicolas, BSc Durh., PhD Durh.   Sr. Lectr.
Harman, Mark, PhD Lond.   Prof.; Dir., Centre for Res.on Evolution Search and Testing
Iliopoulos, Costas S., BSc Athens, MSc Warw., PhD Warw.   Prof.; Dir., MSc Programmes; Head, Algorithm Design Group
Jones, Andrew, PhD Birm.   Prof.; Head*
Kurucz, Agi, PhD Bud.   Sr. Lectr.
Lano, Kevin C., PhD Brist.   Reader
Luck, Michael, BSc Lond., PhD Lond.   Prof.
Overill, Richard E., BSc Leic., PhD Leic., FIMA   Sr. Lectr.
Radzik, Tomasz, MSc Warsaw, PhD Stan.   Reader
Steinhöfel, Kathleen, PhD T.U.Berlin   Sr. Lectr.
Other Staff: 9 Lectrs.

Research: algorithms; bioinformatics; logic, language and computation; software engineering; theory of computing

Engineering, Division of

Tel: (020) 7848 2437 Fax: (020) 7848 2932
Aghvami, Hamid, BSc Teheran, PhD Lond., MSc, FIEE   Prof.; Dir., Centre for Telecommunication Res.
Althoefer, Kaspar, PhD Lond.   Sr. Lectr.
Balabani, Stavroula, PhD Lond.   Sr. Lectr.
Clode, Michael P., PhD Lond., FIMMM   Sr. Lectr.
Cvetkovic, Zoran, MPhil Col., PhD Calif.   Reader; Dir., Centre for Digital Signal Processing Res.
Dai, Jian, BSc Shanghai Jiaotong, PhD Salf.   Prof.
Fenner, David, PhD Lond.   Sr. Lectr.
Ghavami, Mohammad, BE Isfahan, ME Isfahan, PhD Teheran   Reader; Head, Ultra Wideband Communications Group
Lee, Kalok, BEng CNAA, MSc Lond., PhD Lond.   Reader
Mannan, Samjid, BA Oxf., PhD S'ton.   Reader
Miodownik, Mark, BA Oxf., DPhil Oxf.   Reader; Head, Materials Res. Group
Nakhai, Mohammad R., BSc Sharif, MSc Sharif, PhD Lond.   Sr. Lectr.
Papadakis, George, PhD Athens   Sr. Lectr.
Seneviratne, Lakmal D., BSc Lond., PhD Lond.   Prof.; Dir., Centre for Mechatronics and Manufacturing Systems; Head*
Yianneskis, Michael, BScTech Manc., MSc Lond., PhD Lond., FIEE, FKC   Prof.
Other Staff: 17 Lectrs.
Research: digital signal processing; fluids; materials; mechatronics; telecommunications

Mathematics

Tel: (020) 7848 2216 Fax: (020) 7848 2017
Burns, David, PhD Camb.   Prof.
Bushnell, Colin J., BSc Lond., PhD Lond., FKC   Prof.
Coolen, Anthonius C. C., MSc Utrecht, PhD Utrecht   Prof.
Davies, E. Brian, MA Oxf., DPhil Oxf., FRS, FKC   Prof.
Diamond, Fred, PhD Prin.   Prof.
Harvey, William J., BSc Birm., PhD Birm.   Reader
Howe, Paul S., BSc Manc., PhD Lanc.   Prof.
Hughston, Lane P., DPhil Oxf., FIMA   Prof.
Kuehn, Reimer, PhD Kiel   Reader
Landau, Lawrence J., BS Troy, MA Calif., PhD Calif.   Reader
Papadopoulos, Georgios, PhD Lond.   Prof.
Pistorious, Martijn, PhD Utrecht   Reader
Pressley, Andrew N., BA Oxf., MSc Oxf., DPhil Oxf.   Prof.; Head*
Recknagel, Andreas, PhD Bonn   Reader
Rogers, F. Alice, MA Camb., PhD Lond.   Prof.
Safarov, Yuri, PhD Leningrad, DSc Russian Acad.Sc.   Prof.
Scott, Simon, DPhil Oxf.   Reader
Shargorodsky, Eugene, PhD Tbilisi   Reader
Shaw, William, DPhil Oxf.   Prof.
Silvester, John, PhD Lond.   Sr. Lectr.
Sollich, Peter, MPhil Camb., PhD Edin.   Prof.
Solomon, David, PhD Brown   Reader
Watts, Gerard, PhD Camb.   Reader
West, Peter C., BSc Lond., PhD Lond., FRS   Prof.
Other Staff: 10 Lectrs.
Research: disordered systems and neural networks; financial mathematics and applied probability; number theory; theoretical physics

Physics

Tel: (020) 7848 2155 Fax: (020) 7873 2420
Davies, Gordon, PhD Lond., DSc Lond., FIP   Prof.
De Vita, Alessandro, PhD Keele, PhD Milan   Reader
Green, Mark, BSc Manc.Met., PhD Lond.   Sr. Lectr.
Kantorovitch, Lev, PhD Latvia   Reader

Mainwood, Alison, BSc Brist., DPhil Oxf., FIP Prof.
Mavromatos, Nikolaos, DPhil Oxf., FIP Reader
Michette, Alan G., BSc Lond., PhD Lond., FIP Prof.; Coordinator, MRes Teaching
Molteni, Carla, PhD Milan Reader
Morrison, Graeme, PhD Glas., FIP Sr. Lectr.
Richards, David R., PhD Camb., FIP Prof.; Head*
Sakelleriadou, Maria, PhD Tufts Reader
Sarkar, Sarben, PhD Lond. Prof.
Other Staff: 5 Lectrs.; 1 Sr. Res. Fellow
Research: ab initio modelling; astrophysics; biophotonics; nanotechnology; optical microscopy

Psychiatry, Institute of

Biostatistics and Computing
Everitt, Brian S., MSc Prof.
Landau, Sabine, PhD Nott. Sr. Lectr.; Head*
Research: methods and behavioural research; missing data; multilevel modelling; multivariate statistical methods; structural equation modelling

Child and Adolescent Psychiatry
Bolton, Patrick, BSc Lond., MB BS Lond., MA Camb., PhD Camb., FRCPsych Prof., Child and Adolescent Psychiatry
Ford, Tamsin J., MSc Lond., PhD Lond., MB BS MRCP Sr. Lectr.
Goodman, Robert N., MA Camb., BM BCh Oxf., PhD Camb., FRCPsych Prof., Brain and Behavioural Medicine
Maughan, Barbara, BA MSc PhD Prof.
Rubia, Katya, BA Madrid, PhD Munich Reader, Cognitive Neuroscience
Scott, Stephen B. C., MB BChir Camb., BSc, FRCP, FRCPsych Consultant Child and Adolescent Psychiatrist; Prof., Child Health and Behaviour
Simonoff, Emily A., BA Harv., MD Prof.
Taylor, Eric A., MA Camb., MB BChir Camb., FRCP, FRCPsych, FMedSci Prof.
Research: Attention-Deficit Hyperactivity Disorder (ADHD)/early onset of psychosis; functional imaging, neuropsychology; intellectual disability/autism spectrum; Obsessive-Compulsive Disorder (OCD); parenting and anti-social behaviour

Clinical Neuroscience
Al-Chalabi, Ammar, MB ChB Leic., PhD Lond., FRCP Sr. Lectr.
Barker, Gareth J., BSc Nott., PhD Nott. Prof., Magnetic Resonance Physics
Ffytche, Dominic H., BSc MB BS Sr. Lectr.
Finnerty, Gerald T., BA Camb., PhD Lond., MB BS, FRCP Sr. Lectr., Neuroscience
Gallo, Jean-Marc, MSc Poitiers, PhD Poitiers Sr. Lectr.
Hughes, Richard A. C., MD, FRCP, FMedSci Prof., Neuroimmunology
Leigh, P. Nigel, BSc Lond., MB BS Lond., PhD Lond., FRCP, FMedSci Prof., Neurodegenerative Disorders
Meldrum, Brian S., MA Camb., MB BChir Camb. Emer. Prof., Experimental Neurology
Miller, Christopher, BSc Wales, PhD Prof., Molecular Neuroscience
Richardson, Mark, BM BCh Oxf., MA Camb., PhD Lond., FRCP Prof.
Ridsdale, Leone L., MD MSc PhD, FRCPCan, FRCGP, FRCP Reader/Sr. Lectr., Neurology and General Practice
Simmons, Andy, BSc Lond., MSc Aberd., PhD Lond. Sr. Lectr., Imaging Sciences
Zelaya, Fernando O., BSc Lanc., PhD Nott. Sr. Lectr., MR Imaging of Brain Function
Research: epilepsy; head injury; neurodegeneration; neuroimaging; stroke

Forensic Mental Health
Blackwood, Nigel J., MA Camb. Sr. Lectr., Forensic Psychiatry
Davison, Sophie E., BA Camb., MB BChir Camb., MA Camb., MPhil Sr. Lectr.

Fahy, Thomas, MPhil MD Prof., Forensic Mental Health
Hodgins, Sheilagh, BSc McG., MSc McG., PhD McG. Prof.
Johns, Andrew Sr. Lectr.
Young, Susan J., BSc Sur., PhD Lond. Sr. Lectr., Forensic Clinical Psychology
Research: management of violence; persistent violence neurobiology; psychopathy and neurobiology; schizophrenia and violence (aetiology and treatment)

Health Service and Population Research
Banerjee, Subrata, MB BS Lond. Prof.
Beecham, Jennifer, BA PhD Reader
Bhugra, Dinesh, MB BS Poona, MPhil Leic., MA Lond., PhD Lond. Prof., Mental Health and Cultural Diversity
Bouras, Nicandros, MD PhD, FRCPsych Sr. Lectr.
Byford, Sarah, BSc Brun., MSc York(UK) Sr. Lectr.
Churchill, Rachel C., BSc Lond., MSc Lond., PhD Lond. Sr. Lectr., Psychiatric Epidemiology
Craig, Thomas K. J., MB BS PhD, FRCPsych Prof.
Dewey, Michael E., BA Hull, PhD Liv. Sr. Lectr.
Gray, Richard J., BSc Lond., MSc Lond., PhD Lond. Sr. Lectr.
Howard, Louise, MB BS Lond., MSc Lond., MPhil Lond., PhD Lond. Sr. Lectr.
Jenkins, Rachel, MD, FRCPsych, FAPA Prof.; Dir., WHO Collaborating Centre
Knapp, Martin R., BA Sheff., MSc Lond., PhD Kent Prof., Health Economics
Leese, Morven, BSc Strath., MSc Lond., MSc Lond., PhD Lond. Reader
Macdonald, Alastair J. D., MB ChB MD, FRCPsych Prof.
Mann, Anthony H., MA Camb., MD BChir Camb., MPhil, FRCPsych, FRCP Prof., Epidemiological Psychiatry
Manthorpe, Jill, BA York(UK), MA Hull Prof., Social Work
McCrone, Paul, BA CNAA, MSc Lond., PhD Lond. Reader
Moran, Paul, BSc Lond., MB BS Lond., MSc Lond., MRCP Lond., MD Lond. Clin. Sr. Lectr.
Murray, Joanna, BA Reading Sr. Lectr.
Patel, Anita, BSc Lond., MSc York(UK), PhD Lond. Sr. Lectr.
Prince, Martin, BA MB BChir MSc Prof.
Rushton, Alan B., BA Manc., PhD Lond. Reader
Shaw, Christopher, MB ChB Otago, MD Otago, FRCP, FRACP Prof., Neurology
Slade, Mike, BA Open(UK), BSc Warw., MSc Warw., PsychD Sur., PhD Lond. Reader
Szmukler, George, MB BS Melb., MD Melb., FRCPsych Prof.
Thornicroft, Graham, BA Camb., MB, FRCPsych, FMedSci Prof., Community Psychiatry
Tylee, Andre, MB BS Lond., MD Lond., FRCGP Prof., Primary Care Mental Health
Wykes, Til I. R., BSc Nott., MPhil Lond., DPhil Sus. Prof.
Research: mental health economics evaluation; mental health policy; mental health services research; public mental health research; service user research

Neurodegeneration Research, MRC Centre for
Anderton, Brian H., BSc PhD, FMedSci Prof., Neuroscience
Banerjee, Subrata, MB BS Lond. Prof.
Barker, Gareth J., BSc Nott., PhD Nott. Prof., Magnetic Resonance Physics
Brown, Richard G., BA MPhil PhD Prof., Neuropsychology and Clinical Neuroscience
Buckley, Noel J., BA Camb., MA Camb., PhD Lond. Prof., Molecular Neurobiology
Cooper, Jonathan D., PhD Reader
Finnerty, Gerald T., BA Camb., PhD Lond., MB BS, FRCP Sr. Lectr.
Gallo, Jean-Marc, MSc Poitiers, PhD Poitiers Sr. Lectr.
Giese, Peter K. P., PhD E.T.H.Zürich Prof., Neurobiology

Hanger, Diane P., BSc Leeds, PhD Lond. Sr. Lectr., Neuroscience
Hirth, Frank, PhD Basle Sr. Lectr.
Howard, Robert J., MB MA Sr. Lectr.
Lovestone, Simon, BSc Sheff., BM S'ton., MPhil Prof., Old Age Psychiatry
Miller, Christopher, BSc Wales, PhD Prof., Molecular Neuroscience
Powell, John F., MA Oxf., DPhil Oxf. Sr. Lectr.
Price, Jack, PhD Lond. Prof., Neuroscience
Shaw, Christopher, MB ChB Otago, MD Otago, FRCP, FRACP Prof., Neurology
Soriano Castell, Salvador, PhD Sr. Lectr.
Williams, Brenda P., BSc Warw., PhD Lond. Sr. Lectr., Neural Stem/Progenitor Cells
Williams, Steven C. R., BSc Lough., PhD Lough. Prof., Imaging Sciences

Neuroscience
Brammer, Michael J., BSc Leeds, PhD Leeds Prof.
Campbell, Iain C., PhD DSc Prof., Neurochemical Pharmacy
Hanger, Diane P., BSc Leeds, PhD Lond. Sr. Lectr., Neuroscience
Makoff, Andrew, BA Camb., PhD Leeds Sr. Lectr.
Stephenson, John D., BSc PhD Sr. Lectr.
Research: learning and memory; mechanism of neurodegenerative diseases; neural gene expression; neural stem cell biology; neurobiology of psychosis

Psychological Medicine and Psychiatry
Aitchison, Katherine J., BA Oxf., MA Oxf., BM BCh PhD Sr. Lectr.
Arranz, Maria J., BSc Balearic Is., MSc Balearic Is., PhD Lond. Sr. Lectr., Clinical Neuropharmacology
Basoglu, Metin, MD PhD Sr. Lectr.
Bouras, Nicandros, MD PhD, FRCPsych Sr. Lectr.
Chalder, Trudie, MSc Lond., PhD Lond. Prof., Cognitive Behavioural Psychotherapy
Cleare, Anthony, BSc MB BS PhD Reader
Collier, David A., BSc Sheff., PhD Lond. Prof., Neuropsychiatric Genetics
Craig, Thomas K. J., MB BS PhD, FRCPsych Prof.
David, Anthony, MD, FRCP, FRCPsych Prof.
Davies, Teifion W., MB BS Lond., BSc Lond., PhD Lond. Sr. Lectr.
Dazzan, Paola, MSc PhD Sr. Lectr.
Edwards, Griffith, DM Oxf., DSc Lond., FRCP, FRCPsych, FMedSci Emer. Prof.
Eisler, Ivan, BA Oxf., MA Oxf., PhD Lond. Reader, Family Psychology and Family
Farrell, Michael, MB BCh BAO Trinity(Dub.) Sr. Lectr.
Fear, Nicola, BSc Lond., MSc Lond., DPhil Oxf. Sr. Lectr., Military Epidemiology
Fearon, Paul, MSc Lond., PhD Lond., MB BCh BAO Sr. Lectr.
Frangou, Sophia, MB BS Athens, MSc Lond., PhD Lond. Reader, Psychosis
Gaughran, Fiona P., MB BCh BAO Sr. Lectr.
Greenberg, Neil, BSc BM MMedSc Sr. Lectr.
Hotopf, Matthew, BSc MB BS MSc PhD Prof.
Howard, Robert J., MB MA Sr. Lectr.
Ismail, Khalida, BSc Manc., MSc Exe., PhD Harv., BM BCh Sr. Lectr., Liaison Psychiatry
Jenkins, Hugh, BA BPhil Sr. Lectr.
Jones, Edgar, MA Oxf., DPhil Oxf., PhD Lond., FRHistS Prof., Military Psychiatry
Kopelman, Michael D., BA MB BS PhD, FBPsS, FRCPsych Prof.
Lader, Malcolm H., OBE, BSc MD PhD, FRCPsych Emer. Prof., Clinical Psycho-Pharmacy
Lintzeris, Nicholas, BMedSci MB BS PhD
Lovestone, Simon, BSc Sheff., BM S'ton., MPhil Prof., Old Age Psychiatry
Makoff, Andrew, BA Camb., PhD Leeds Sr. Lectr.
Mann, Anthony H., MA Camb., MD BChir Camb., MPhil, FRCPsych, FRCP Prof.
Marks, Isaac M., MD Cape Town, FRCPsych Prof., Experimental Psychpathology

Marks, Maureen N., BA Well., DPhil Sus.   Sr.
Lectr.
Marsden, John R., BSc Lond., MSc Cran., PhD
Cran.   Sr. Lectr., Addictive Behaviour
Mataix-Cols, David, BSc Barcelona, PhD Barcelona
Sr. Lectr.
McGuire, Philip, BSc Edin., MB ChB Edin., PhD
Lond.   Prof., Psychiatric and Cognitive
Neuroscience
McLoughlin, Declan M., PhD Lond.   Sr. Lectr.,
Old Age Psychiatry
Murphy, Declan, MB BS MD   Prof.
Murray, Robin M., MPhil Lond., MD Glas., FKC,
FRCP, FRCPsych, FMedSci   Prof.
O'Keane, Veronica, MB N.U.I., PhD
Trinity(Dub.), FRCPI   Sr. Lectr.
Pariante, Carmine, MD Sacred Heart(Milan), PhD
Lond.   Reader
Phillips, Mary L., MB BChir Camb., MA Camb.,
MD Camb.   Prof., Neuroscience and
Emotion
Ramirez, Amanda-Jane, BSc MB BS MD,
FRCPsych   Prof., Liaison Psychiatry
Rona, Roberto J., PhD Lond., FFPHM   Prof.,
Public Health
Schmidt, Ulrike, MD PhD   Prof.
Schumann, Gunter, MD   Prof., Addiction
Biology
Shergill, Sukhwinder, BSc MB BS PhD   Reader
Shitij, Kapur, MB BS PhD, FBPsS, FRCPsych
Prof.
Stapleton, John A., BSc Herts., MSc Sus.   Sr.
Lectr.
Stolerman, Ian P., BPharm Lond., PhD Lond.
Prof., Behavioural Pharmacology
Strang, John, MB BS MD, FRCPsych   Prof.,
Addictions
Treasure, Janet L., BSc Lond., MB BS Lond., PhD
Lond.   Prof., Eating Disorders
Weinman, John A., BA PhD DSc, FBPsS   Prof.
Wessely, Simon, MA Camb., BM BCh Oxf., MSc
Lond., MD Lond., FRCP, FRCPsych, FMedSci
Prof., Epidemiology and Liaison Psychiatry
Wolff, Kim, BSc MSc PhD   Head, Taught
Postgrad. Studies; Sr. Lectr., Addictions
Other Staff: 1 Clin. Lectr.
Research: alcoholism; causes of schizophrenia;
drug abuse; military health; treatment of
anorexia

Psychology

Bolton, Derek, BA Camb., MPhil Camb., PhD
Camb.   Prof.
Chadwick, Oliver, BA MS MSc PhD   Sr. Lectr.
Clark, David M., MA Oxf., MPhil Lond., DPhil
Oxf., FBA, FMedSci, FKC   Prof.
Ehlers, Anke, PhD Tübingen, DrRerNatHabil
Marburg   Prof.
Garety, Philippa A., MA MPhil MA(Ed) PhD,
FBPsS   Prof.
Goldstein, Laura H., BSc MPhil PhD   Reader
Grunfeld, Beth, PhD   Sr. Lectr.
Gudjonsson, Gisli H., BSc Brun., MSc Sur., PhD
Sur.   Prof., Forensic Psychology
Hemsley, David R., MA MPhil PhD, FBPsS
Prof., Abnormal Psychology
Hirsch, Colette R., BSc DClinPsy PhD   Sr.
Lectr.
Hunter, Myra S., BA PhD   Prof.
Kuipers, Elizabeth A., BSc Brist., MSc Birm., PhD
Lond., FBPsS   Prof.
Kumari, Veena, BA MA PhD   Prof.
Marteau, Theresa M., BSc MSc PhD, FMedSci
Prof.
Morris, Robin G., MA Oxf., PhD Camb., BA Oxf.,
MSc   Prof.
Peters, Emmanuelle R., BSc MSc PhD   Sr.
Lectr.
Salkovskis, Paul, BSc MPhil PhD, FBPsS   Clin.
Dir., Centre for Anxiety Disorders and
Trauma; Prof., Clinical Psychology and
Applied Science
Wilson, Glenn D., MA Cant., PhD   Reader
Research: anxiety and health disorders;
neuropsychology; psychopathology in
children; psychosis; trauma

Social, Genetic and Developmental Psychiatry Centre

Asherson, Philip, MB BS Lond., PhD Wales
Prof., Molecular Psychiatry
Ball, David, BM BCh Oxf., MA Oxf., PhD Lond.
Sr. Lectr.
Caspi, Avshalom, BA Calif., MA Cornell, PhD
Cornell, FBA, FMedSci   Prof., Social/
Personality Psychology
Craig, Ian, BSc Liv., MA Oxf., PhD Liv.   Prof.
Dunn, Judith F., BA Camb., PhD Camb., FBA,
FKC, FMedSci   Prof.
Eley, Thalia, MA Camb., PhD Lond.   Sr. Lectr.
Farmer, Anne E., MB ChB Leeds, MD Leeds,
FRCPsych   Prof., Psychiatric Nosology
Happe, Francesca, BA Oxf., PhD Lond.   Sr.
Lectr.
Kuntsi, Jonna, BSc Lond., MSc Lond., PhD Lond.
Sr. Lectr.
Leff, Julian P., MD, FRCPsych   Emer. Prof.,
Social and Transcultural Psychiatry
Lewis, Cathryn M., BA Oxf., MSc Sheff., PhD
Sheff.   Reader, Genetic Epidemiology
Li, Tao, BM W.China Med.Scis., PhD Lond., MD
W.China Med.Scis.   Sr. Lectr., Psychiatric
Genetics
McGuffin, Peter, MB ChB Leeds, PhD Lond.,
FRCP, FRCPsych, FMedSci   Prof.,
Psychiatric Genetics
Moffitt, Terrie E., BA N.Carolina, MA S.Calif.,
PhD S.Calif., FBA, FMedSci   Prof., Social
Behaviour and Development Psychology
Plomin, Robert, BA Chic., PhD Texas, FKC, FBA,
FMedSci   Prof., Behavioural Genetics
Rijsdijk, Fruhling V., MSc Amst., PhD Amst.   Sr.
Lectr., Statistical and Behavioural Genetics
Rutter, Michael, KBE, MD Birm., FRCP,
FRCPsych, FRS, FBA, FKC, FMedSci   Prof.,
Developmental Psychopathology
Schalkwyk, Leonard C., BSc Alta., PhD Dal.
Reader, Functional Genomics
Research: anxiety and depression; autism; genes,
environment and development;
hyperactivity; learning disabilities

Social Science and Public Policy, School of

Tel: (020) 7848 1495 Fax: (020) 784 2984
E-mail: christophe.dandecker@kcl.ac.uk
Dandeker, Christopher, BSc Leic., PhD Leic.
Prof.; Head*

Defence Studies

Located at Joint Services Command and Staff
College (JSCSC), and RAF Cranwell

Tel: (01793) 788746 Fax: (01793) 788295
Barr, Niall, PhD St And.   Reader
Chin, Warren, PhD Lond.   Sr. Lectr.
Dorman, Andrew, PhD Birm.   Sr. Lectr.
Foot, Peter, PhD Edin.   Sr. Lectr.
Gearson, John, PhD Lond.   Reader
Gooderson, Ian, PhD Lond.   Sr. Lectr.
Gordon, Andrew, PhD Lond.   Reader
Goulter, Christina, PhD Lond.   Sr. Lectr.
Griffin, Stuart, PhD Birm.   Sr. Lectr.; Deputy
Dean, Academic Studies (JSCSC)
Hayward, Joel, PhD Kent   Sr. Lectr.; Dean,
Royal Air Force College, Cranwell
Jackson, Ashley, DPhil Oxf.   Sr. Lectr.
Jordan, David, PhD Birm.   Sr. Lectr.
Kelly, Saul, PhD Lond.   Reader
Kennedy, Gregory, PhD Alta.   Prof.
Lane, Ann, PhD Lond.   Reader
McCartney, Helen, PhD Camb.   Sr. Lectr.
Park, William, MA Lond.   Sr. Lectr.
Rohan, Sally, PhD Wolv.   Sr. Lectr.
Sanders, Deborah, PhD Wales   Sr. Lectr.
Till, Geoffrey, PhD Lond., FKC   Prof.
Utting, Catherine, PhD Leeds   Sr. Lectr.
Uttley, Matthew, PhD Lanc.   Prof.; Dean,
Academic Studies (JSCSC); Head*
Research: international studies; military studies;
policy studies

Education and Professional Studies

Tel: (020) 7848 3167 Fax: (020) 7872 3182
Abbott, Chris D., BA Open(UK), MA Lond., PhD
Lond.   Sr. Lectr.

Adey, Philip, BSc Lond., PhD Lond.   Emer. Prof.
Adler, Jillian, BSc Witw., MEd Witw., PhD Witw.
Prof.
Archer, Louise, BA Kent, PhD Lond.   Reader
Askew, Michael, BSc Sheff., MA Lond., PhD Lond.
Prof.
Barnes, Philip, MA Hull, MTh Belf., PhD
Trinity(Dub.)   Sr. Lectr.
Black, Paul J., BSc Manc., PhD Camb.   Emer.
Prof.
Brown, Margaret L., MA Camb., PhD Lond., EdD
Kingston(UK), FKC   Prof.
Coben, Diana C., BA Manc., PhD Kent   Reader
Cox, Margaret J., BSc Lond., PhD Lond.   Emer.
Prof.
Cribb, Alan, BA S'ton., PhD Manc.   Prof.
Dillon, Justin, BSc Manc., MA Lond., PhD Lond.
Sr. Lectr.
Duncan, Peter, BA Hull, MSc S.Bank, PhD Lond.
Sr. Lectr.
Fortune, Alan, BSc Reading, MSc Edin.   Sr. Lectr.
Gewirtz, Sharon, BA Manc., PhD Lond.   Prof.
Harris, Roxy, MA Dund., MEd Dund., PhD Lond.
Sr. Lectr.
Hodgen, Jeremy, BA Camb., MSc S.Bank, PhD
Lond.   Sr. Lectr.
Jones, Jane, MA Lond., PhD Lond.   Sr. Lectr.
Kanes, Clive, BSc ANU, DPhil ANU   Sr. Lectr.
Kutnick, Peter, BA Oakland, MSc Lond., PhD Lond.
Prof.
Leung, Constant, BA Coventry, MA Lanc., PhD
Westminster   Prof.
Maguire, Margaret M., MA Lond., PhD Lond.
Prof.
Marshall, Bethan-Jane, BA Nott., MA Lond., PhD
Lond.   Sr. Lectr.
May, John, BSc Lond., MPhil Lond.   Sr. Lectr.
Osborne, Jonathan, BSc Brist., MSc Lond., PhD
Lond.   Prof.; Head*
Rampton, Ben M. B. H., BA York(UK), MA Lond.,
PhD Lond.   Prof.
Roberts, Celia, BA   Reader
Street, Brian V., BA Oxf., DPhil Oxf.   Prof.
Walker, Andrew G., BA Hull, MSc Salf., PhD
Lond.   Prof.
Ward, Peter, BA Durh., MA Birm., PhD Lond.
Sr. Lectr.
Watson, Deryn M., MA Camb., PhD Lond.
Emer. Prof.
Webb, Mary, BSc Sheff., MSc City(UK), PhD
Open(UK)   Sr. Lectr.
Wright, Andrew, BA Lond., MA Lond., PhD Lond.
Sr. Lectr.
Research: language and literacy; mathematics,
science and technology education;
psychology and cognitive processes; public
policy research; theology, religion and
culture

Geography

Tel: (020) 7848 2599 Fax: (020) 7848 2287
Baas, Andreas, BSc Amst., MSc Amst., PhD S.Calif.
Sr. Lectr.
Baker, Kathy, BSc Lond., PhD Lond.   Sr. Lectr.
Bark, Anthony, BSc S'ton., PhD Lond.   Sr. Lectr.
Bryant, Raymond, BA Vic.(BC), MA Car., PhD
Lond.   Reader
Butler, Tim S. C., BA Essex, MA Essex, PhD
Open(UK)   Prof.; Head*
Demeritt, David, BA Maine(USA), MSc
Maine(USA), PhD Br.Col.   Prof.
Drake, N. A., BSc Plym., PhD Reading   Reader
Green, David, BA Camb., PhD Camb.   Reader
Grimmond, C. Susan, BSc Otago, MSc Br.Col.,
PhD Br.Col.   Prof.
Gurnell, Angela M., BSc Exe., PhD Exe., DSc Exe.
Prof.
Hamnett, C., BSc Lond.   Prof.
Hoggart, Keith, BSc Salf., MSc Salf., PhD Lond.
Prof.
Imrie, Rob, BA Sus., MPhil Reading, PhD Wales
Prof.
Lees, Loretta, BA Belf., PhD Edin.   Reader
Lofstedt, Ragnar, BA Calif., MA Clark, PhD Clark
Prof.
Malamud, Bruce, BA Reed, PhD Cornell   Reader
McGregor, Glenn, BSc Auck., MSc Auck., PhD NZ
Prof.

Mulligan, Mark, BSc Brist., PhD Lond. Reader
Newson, Linda A., BA Lond., PhD Lond., FKC, FBA Prof.
Pelling, Mark A., BA Hull, MSc H-W, PhD Liv. Reader
Potts, Deborah H., BSc Lond., PhD Lond. Sr. Lectr.
Raco, Mike, BA Lond., PhD Lond. Sr. Lectr.
Redclift, M. R., BA Sus., DPhil Sus. Prof.
Robinson, Vaughan, MA Oxf., DPhil Oxf. Prof.
Thornes, J., BSc Lond., MSc McG., PhD Lond. Emer. Prof.
Wiltshire, Richard J., BSc Lond., MA York(Can.), PhD Lond. Sr. Lectr.
Wooster, Martin J., BSc Brist., MSc Lond., PhD Open(UK) Prof.
Research: cities; environment, politics and development; environmental monitoring and modelling; hazards, vulnerability and risks

Gerontology, Institute of

Tel: (020) 7848 3035
Biggs, Simon, BSc Lond., PhD Lond. Prof.; Dir.*
Glaser, Karen F., BA Mich., MA Texas, MSc Lond., PhD Mich. Sr. Lectr.
Lowton, Karen, BSc Kingston(UK), MSc Lond., PhD Lond. Sr. Lectr.
Tinker, Anthea, BCom Birm., PhD Lond. Emer. Prof.
Research: biological ageing; material environment and its relation to ageing interests; psychological and social aspects of ageing; social and economic situations and population change; the individual, service providers and the state

Management

Tel: (020) 7848 4254 Fax: (020) 7848 4254
Bach, Stephen B., BA Leeds, MA Warw., PhD Warw. Reader
Brouthers, Keith B., BS Clarion, MBA Auburn, DBA U.S.Internat. Prof.
Deery, Stephen, BEc Monash, MCom Melb., PhD La Trobe Prof.
Edwards, Tony, BA Liv., MSc Warw., PhD Coventry Reader
Eng, Teck Yong, BSc Sur., MSc Manc., PhD Manc. Sr. Lectr.
Fulop, Naomi, BSc Brist., MA Harv., PhD Lond. Prof.
Guest, David, BA Birm., PhD Lond. Prof.
Heath, Christian, BA Manc., MA Manc., PhD Manc. Prof.; Head*
Hindmarsh, Jon, BA Sheff., MSc Sur., PhD Sur. Sr. Lectr.
Jackson, Gregory, BA Wis., PhD Col. Sr. Lectr.
Laughlin, Richard C., MSocSc Birm., PhD Sheff. Prof.
Lewis, Paul, MA Camb., MPhil Camb., PhD Camb. Sr. Lectr.
Lockwood, Graeme, LLB CNAA, PhD Lond. Sr. Lectr.
Luff, Paul, BSc York(UK), PhD Sur. Reader
Peccei, Riccardo, BA Harv., DPhil Oxf. Prof.
Piesse, Jenifer, BA Col., MA Col., MSc Lond., PhD Lond. Prof.
Pratten, Stephen, BA CNAA, MPhil Camb., PhD Camb. Sr. Lectr.
Rosenthal, Patrice E., BA Houston, MSc Lond., PhD Lond. Sr. Lectr.
Ryan, Paul, BA Lond., MSc Lond., PhD Harv. Prof.
Soin, Kim, BA Wales, MA Wales, PhD Sheff.Hallam Sr. Lectr.
Strange, Roger N., BSc Birm., MSc Lond., MPhil Lond. Sr. Lectr.
Sturges, Jane, MA Oxf., MBA Cran., PhD Cran. Sr. Lectr.
Walsh, Prof. Janet, BA Leeds, MA Warw., PhD Warw. Prof.
Wolf, Alison, MA Oxf., MPhil Oxf. Sir Roy Griffiths Prof., Public Sector
Research: accounting and accountability; human resource management and employment relations; international business and comparative management; public services

and management; work, interaction and technology

War Studies

Tel: (020) 7848 2178 Fax: (020) 7848 2026
Berdal, Mats, BSc Lond., BPhil Oxf. Prof.
Betz, David, BA Car., MA Car., PhD Glas. Sr. Lectr.
Bowen, Wyn, PhD Birm. Prof.
Dandeker, Christopher, BSc Leic., PhD Leic. Prof.
Dockrill, Saki, BA Kyoto, MA Sus., PhD Lond. Prof.
Farrell, Theo, BA Trinity(Dub.), MA Trinity(Dub.), PhD Brist. Prof.
Freedman, Sir Lawrence, CBE, BA(Econ) Manc., BPhil York(UK), DPhil Oxf., FBA, FKC Prof.
Frost, Mervyn, BA Stell., MA Stell., DPhil Oxf., DPhil Stell. Prof., International Relations; Head*
Gow, James, BA Lanc., PhD Lond. Prof.
Holden-Reid, Brian, BA Sus., MA Sus., PhD Lond., FRHistS Prof.
Honig, Jan, Drs Amst., PhD Lond. Sr. Lectr.
Jabri, Vivienne, BSc Lond., MA Kent, PhD City(UK) Prof.
James, Alan, BA Alta., MA Alta., PhD Manc. Sr. Lectr.
Karsh, Efraim, BA Jerusalem, MA Tel-Aviv, PhD Tel-Aviv Prof.
Lambert, A., LLB Lond., MA Lond., PhD Lond., FRHistS Prof.
Maiolo, Joseph, BA Tor., MA Tor., PhD Lond. Sr. Lectr.
Neumann, Peter, MA F.U.Berlin, PhD Lond. Sr. Lectr.
Paskins, Barrie A., MA Camb., PhD Camb. Sr. Lectr., Ethical Aspects of War
Philpott, William, MA Oxf., DPhil Oxf. Sr. Lectr.
Rainsborough, Michael L. R. S., BSc Wales, MA Lond., PhD Lond. Prof.
Sabin, Philip A. G., MA Camb., PhD Lond. Prof.
Sayigh, Yezid, BSc Beirut, PhD Lond. Prof.
Stone, John, BSc York(UK), MSc Wales, PhD Wales Sr. Lectr.
Young, Ken G., BSc Lond., MSc Lond., PhD Lond., AcSS Prof.
Research: international studies; military studies; policy studies

MEDICINE, SCHOOL OF

Tel: (020) 7848 6971 Fax: (020) 7848 6969

Asthma, Allergy and Lung Biology

Beavil, Andrew, BSc Lond., PhD Lond. Sr. Lectr.
Corrigan, Christopher, BA Oxf., MB BS Lond., MSc Oxf., PhD Lond. Prof.
Greenough, Anne, MB BS Lond., MD Camb., FRCP Prof.
Hawrylowicz, Catherine M., BSc Sheff., PhD Sheff. Sr. Lectr.
Hirst, Stuart, BSc Portsmouth, PhD Lond. Reader
Lack, Gideon, MA Oxf., MB BCh Oxf., FRCPCH Prof.
Lee, Tak Hong, MA Camb., MD Camb., MB BChir, FRCP Prof.; Head*
Moxham, John, MB BS Lond., MD Lond., FRCP Prof.
Noble, Alistair, BSc Lond., PhD Lond. Sr. Lectr.
O'Connor, Brian, MB BCh Sr. Lectr.
Rona, Roberto J., PhD Lond., FFPHM Prof.
Santis, George, MB ChB MD Sr. Lectr.
Spina, Domenico, BSc W.Aust., PhD W.Aust. Reader
Staynov, Dontcho Z., MSc PhD Sr. Lectr.
Sun, Ying, MSc Jilin, MD Jilin, PhD Lond. Sr. Lectr.
Ward, Jeremy P. T., BSc Lond., PhD Lond. Prof.
Research: airway inflammation and remodelling; IgE structure, function and regulation; prevention of allergy, asthma and chronic respiratory morbidity; risk factors for the development of life-threatening asthma in childhood; therapy

Cancer Studies

Barber, Linda, BSc Bath, PhD Lond. Sr. Lectr.
Camplejohn, Richard S., BSc MSc PhD Sr. Lectr.
Farzaneh, Farzin, BSc Aberd., MSc Aberd., DPhil Sus., FRCPath Prof.
Fentiman, Ian S., MB BS Lond., MD Lond., FRCS Prof.
Gäken, Johannes A., BSc Nijmegen, MSc Nijmegen, PhD Sus. Sr. Lectr.
Harding, Richard, BSc Brun., MSc Lond., PhD Lond. Sr. Lectr.
Higginson, Irene, BMedSci Nott., BM BS Nott., PhD Lond. Prof.
Holmberg, Lars, PhD Uppsala, MD Prof.
Moller, Henrik, BA Copenhagen, MSc Copenhagen, DM Copenhagen Prof.
Morris, Jonathan, BSc Sus., MPhil Camb., PhD Camb. Sr. Lectr.
Mufti, Ghulam J., MB BS J&K, DM S'ton., FRCPath Prof.; Head*
Ng, Tony C., MB ChB Aberd., PhD Lond. Prof.
Nicholson, Linda Sr. Lectr.
Parker, Peter J., BA Oxf., DPhil Oxf., FRS Prof.
Pinder, Sarah E., MB ChB Manc., FRCPath Prof.
Purushotham, Anand D., MB BS Madr., MD Glas., FRCSEd Prof.
Richards, Michael A., MB BChir MA MD, FRCP Prof.
Spicer, James, MB BS Lond., MA Oxf., PhD Lond. Sr. Lectr.
Tavares, Ignatius A. F., BSc S'ton., PhD S'ton. Sr. Lectr.
Thomas, Shaun N. S. B., BA Camb., MA Camb., PhD Lond. Sr. Lectr.
Turner-Stokes, Lynne, MB BS Lond., MA Oxf., DM Oxf., FRCP Prof.
Wade, Derick T., MA Camb., MB BCh Camb., MD Camb., FRCP Prof.
Research: cancer cell biology and imaging; cancer epidemiology; haemato-oncology; palliative care, policy and rehabilitation; tumour biology

Cardiovascular Medicine, Division of

Aaronson, Philip I., BA PhD Reader
Authi, Kalwant S., BSc Birm., MSc Lough., PhD Lough. Sr. Lectr.
Avrikan, Metin, BSc Bath, PhD Bath, DSc Bath Prof.
Brain, Susan D., PhD Lond., BSc MA Prof.
Cave, Alison C., BSc Lond., PhD Lond. Sr. Lectr.
Chowienczyk, Philip J., BSc MB BS Prof.
Curtis, Michael J., BSc Lond., PhD Col. Reader
Eaton, Philip, BSc Lond., DPhil Sus. Reader
Ehler, Elisabeth, MSc Salzburg, PhD Salzburg Sr. Lectr.
Ferro, Albert, BSc Lond., PhD Camb., FRCP Sr. Lectr.
Fraser, Paul A., BSc Edin., MSc Lond., PhD Lond. Sr. Lectr.
Gautel, Mathias S., MD Heidel. Prof.
Gnudi, Luigi, PhD Milan, FRCP Sr. Lectr.
Hill, Jonathan, MB ChB Edin., MA Camb. Sr. Lectr.
Kalra, Lalit, MB BS All India IMS, MD All India IMS, MD Lond., PhD Lond., FRCP Prof.
Kentish, Jonathan C., MA Oxf., PhD Lond. Prof.
Mann, Giovanni E., BSc Wash., MSc Lond., PhD Lond. Prof.
Marber, Michael S., BSc Lond., MB BS Lond., PhD Lond., FRCP Prof.; Head*
Pearson, Jeremy D., BA Oxf., MA Camb., MA Oxf., PhD Camb., FMedSci Prof.
Redwood, Simon R., MB BS Lond., MD Lond., FRCP Sr. Lectr.
Ritter, James M., BA Oxf., BM BCh Oxf., MA Oxf., DPhil Oxf., FRCP Prof.
Shah, Ajay M., MB ChB Wales, MD Wales, FRCP, FMedSci Prof.
Shanahan, Catherine M., BSc Adel., PhD Adel. Prof.
Shattock, Michael J., BSc Lond., PhD Lond., FESC Prof.
Smith, Alberto, BSc Trent, PhD Lond. Sr. Lectr.
Viberti, Giancarlo, MD Milan, FRCP Prof.

Xu, Qingbo, MB BS *Qingdao Sci.&Technol.*, MD *Innsbruck*, PhD *Peking*   Prof.
Research: cardiac myostructure, hypertrophy, remodelling and protection; cellular signalling; vascular risk, remodelling stem cells, inflammation

Gene and Cell Based Therapy

Alluvihare, Varuna R., BSc *Lond.*, MB BS *Lond.*, PhD *Camb.*   Sr. Lectr.
Amiel, Stephanie A., BSc *Lond.*, MB BS *Lond.*, MD, FRCP   Prof., Diabetic Medicine
Banga, Jasvinder-Paul, BSc *Lond.*, PhD *Lond.*   Reader
Bomford, Adrian, BSc MD, FRCP   Reader
Fabre, John W., BMedSc *Melb.*, MB BS *Melb.*, PhD *Melb.*   Prof.
Gnudi, Luigi, PhD *Milan*, FRCP   Sr. Lectr.
Harrison, Phillip M., BSc *Lond.*, MB BS *Lond.*, PhD *Lond.*, MD   Sr. Lectr.
Hendry, Bruce M., BA *Camb.*, BM BCh *Oxf.*, MD *Camb.*, PhD *Camb.*, FRCP   Prof., Renal Medicine
Huang, Guo Cai, BSc *Fujian Normal*, MSc *Fujian Normal*, PhD *Lond.*   Sr. Lectr.
Hughes, Robin D., BSc *Sus.*, PhD *Lond.*   Sr. Lectr.
Ma, Yun, MD *Capital Med.Scis.*, PhD *Lond.*   Sr. Lectr.
McGregor, Alun M., MA *Camb.*, MB BChir *Camb.*, MD *Camb.*, FRCP, FKC   Prof.
Menzel, Stephan, MD *Greifswald*   Sr. Lectr.
Mieli-Vergani, Giorgina, MD *Milan*, PhD *Lond.*, FRCP   Prof., Paediatric Hepatology
Rees, David C., MB BS *Lond.*, MA *Camb.*   Sr. Lectr.
Sheerin, Neil S., BSc *Lond.*, MB BS *Lond.*, PhD *Lond.*   Sr. Lectr.
Thein, Swee Lay, MB BS *Malaya*, DSc *Malaya*, FRCP, FRCPath   Prof.; Head*
Thompson, Richard J., BA *Oxf.*, BM BCh *Oxf.*   Sr. Lectr.
Tredger, Michael, BSc *Liv.*, PhD *Sur.*   Sr. Lectr.
Vergani, Diego, MD *Milan*, PhD *Lond.*, FRCP, FRCPath   Prof., Liver Immunopathology
Viberti, Giancarlo, MD *Milan*, FRCP   Prof.
Wendon, Julia A., MB ChB *Dund.*, FRCP   Sr. Lectr.
Research: autoimmune diseases of the liver, pancreas and thyroid; cell transplantation and metabolic studies; cholestasis and bile formation; renal epothelial cells and gene therapy

Genetics and Molecular Medicine, Division of

Antoniou, Michael, BA *Oxf.*, PhD *Reading*   Reader
Barker, Jonathan N. W. N., BSc MB BS, FRCP   Prof.
Bates, Gillian P., BSc *Sheff.*, MSc *Lond.*, PhD *Lond.*   Prof.
Grimwade, David J., BA *Oxf.*, MB BS *Lond.*, PhD *Lond.*   Sr. Lectr.
Hamilton, Andrew J., BSc MSc PhD   Prof.
Hawk, John   Prof.
Lewis, Cathryn M., BA *Oxf.*, MSc *Sheff.*, PhD *Sheff.*   Reader
Mathew, Christopher G., BSc *S.Af.*, PhD *Lond.*, FRCPath   Prof.
McFadden, John P., BM   Sr. Lectr.
McGrath, John A., MB BS MD   Prof.
Nestle, Frank, MD *Würzburg*   Prof.
Oakey, Rebecca, BSc *Brist.*, DPhil *Oxf.*   Sr. Lectr.
Roberts, Roland, BA *Oxf.*, PhD *Lond.*   Sr. Lectr.
Seller, Rev. Mary J., BSc *Lond.*, PhD *Lond.*, DSc *Lond.*   Reader
Smith, Catherine H., MB BS MD   Sr. Lectr.
Solomon, Ellen, BSc PhD, FKC   Prof.; Head*
Spector, Timothy D., MB BS *Lond.*, MSc *Lond.*, MD *Lond.*, FRCP   Prof.
Trembath, Richard, BSc *Lond.*, MB BS, FRCP, FMedSci   Prof.
Weale, Michael E., BSc *S'ton.*, MSc *Reading*, PhD *S'ton.*   Sr. Lectr.
Whittaker, Sean J., MB ChB *Manc.*, MD *Manc.*, FRCP   Sr. Lectr.
Young, Anthony R., BSc MSc PhD   Prof.

Research: genetics and skin sciences; medical and molecular genetics

Imaging Sciences, Division of

Tel: (020) 7188 5441 Fax: (020) 7188 5442
Adam, Andreas, MB BS, FRCP, FRCR   Prof.
Beerbaum, Philipp, MD *Cologne*   Sr. Lectr.
Blower, Philip J., BA *Camb.*, DPhil *Sus.*   Prof.
Clarke, Susan E. M., MB BS   Sr. Lectr.
Fogelman, Ignac, BSc *Glas.*, MB ChB *Glas.*, MD *Glas.*, FRCP   Prof.
Garlick, Pamela B., BA *Oxf.*, DPhil *Oxf.*, MA   Sr. Lectr.
Greil, Gerald, MD *T.U.Munich*   Sr. Lectr.
Marsden, Paul K., BA MSc PhD   Sr. Lectr.
Mullen, Gregory E. D., BSc *Kent*, PhD *Kent*   Sr. Lectr.
O'Doherty, Michael J., BA *Camb.*, MB BS *Lond.*, MA *Camb.*, MD *Lond.*, MSc *Lond.*   Sr. Lectr.
Padayachee, Soundrie, BSc PhD   Sr. Lectr.
Penney, Graeme P., BSc *Durh.*, PhD *Lond.*   Sr. Lectr.
Razavi, Reza, MD *Lond.*   Prof.
Schaeffter, Tobias, PhD *Bremen*   Prof.
Tabakov, Slavik, MSc *T.U.Sofia*, PhD *Plovdiv*, FIPEM   Reader
Research: clinical pet centre; interdisciplinary medical imaging group; interventional radiology; nuclear medicine and osteoporosis

Immunology, Infection and Inflammatory Disease, Division of

Tel: (020) 7188 3078 Fax: (020) 7188 3075
Cason, John, BSc *Lond.*, MPhil *Lond.*, PhD *Lond.*   Sr. Lectr.
Choy, Ernest H. S., MD *Wales*, FRCP   Sr. Lectr.
Corrigall, Valerie, BSc *Edin.*, PhD *Lond.*   Sr. Lectr.
De Bari, Cosimo, MD PhD   Sr. Lectr.
Dunn-Walters, Deborah K., BSc *Coventry*, PhD *Sur.*   Sr. Lectr.
Easterbrook, Phillipa J., BSc MB BChir   Prof.; Head*
French, Gary L., BSc MB BS MD, FRCP, FRCPath   Prof.
Gregson, Norman A., BSc PhD   Reader
Hayday, Adrian C., BSc *Camb.*, PhD *Lond.*, FKC   Prof.
Hendry, Bruce M., BA *Camb.*, BM BCh *Oxf.*, MD *Camb.*, PhD *Camb.*, FRCP   Prof.
Hernandez Fuentes, Maria, MD *Madrid*, PhD *Alcalá*   Sr. Lectr.
Hughes, Richard A. C., MD, FRCP, FMedSci   Prof.; Head, Neurosciences
John, Susan, BSc *Lond.*, PhD *Lond.*   Sr. Lectr.
Kingsley, Gabrielle H., BSc *Brist.*, MB ChB *Brist.*, PhD *Lond.*, FRCP   Reader
Klavinskis, Linda, PhD *Lond.*   Sr. Lectr.
Lechler, Robert, PhD *Lond.*, FRCP, FRCPath, FMedSci   Prof.
Lombardi, Giovanna, BSc *Rome*, PhD *Rome*   Reader
Lord, Graham, BA *Camb.*, MB BChir *Camb.*, PhD *Sur.*   Prof.
Lucas, Sebastian B., BM BCh *Oxf.*, MA *Oxf.*, BA, FRCP, FRCPath   Prof., Histopathology
Malim, Michael H., BSc *Brist.*, DPhil *Oxf.*   Prof.
Mills, Kerry R., BSc MB BS MA PhD, FRCP   Prof.
Mitchell, Graham H., BSc *Exe.*, PhD *Lond.*   Reader
Murphy, John, BSc *N.U.I.*, PhD *N.U.I.*   Sr. Lectr.
Noble, Alistair, BSc *Lond.*, PhD *Lond.*   Sr. Lectr.
Peakman, Mark, BSc *Lond.*, MB BS *Lond.*, MSc *Lond.*, PhD *Lond.*   Prof.
Peters, Barry S., MB BS *Lond.*, MD *Lond.*, FRCP   Sr. Lectr.
Philpott-Howard, John N., MB BCh *Wales*   Sr. Lectr.
Richardson, Mark, BM BCh *Oxf.*, MA *Camb.*, PhD *Lond.*, FRCP   Sr. Lectr.
Robson, Michael G., BA *Oxf.*, MB BS *Lond.*, PhD *Lond.*   Sr. Lectr.
Sacks, Steven H., BSc MB ChB PhD, FRCP   Prof.; Head, Renal Medicine

Scott, David L., BSc *Leeds*, MD *Leeds*, FRCP   Prof.
Sharief, Mohammed, MB ChB MPhil PhD   Sr. Lectr.
Shaw, Christopher, MB ChB *Otago*, MD *Otago*, FRCP, FRACP   Prof.
Sheerin, Neil S., BSc *Lond.*, MB BS *Lond.*, PhD *Lond.*   Sr. Lectr.
Spencer, Jo M., BSc *Manc.*, PhD *Lond.*   Reader
Taams, Leonie S., BSc *Utrecht*, MSc *Utrecht*, PhD *Utrecht*   Sr. Lectr.
Thompson, Stephen, BSc PhD   Sr. Lectr.
Tree, Tim, BSc *Lond.*, PhD *Lond.*   Sr. Lectr.
Vaughan, Robert W., BA *Camb.*, MA *Camb.*, MSc *Lond.*, PhD *Lond.*, FRCPath   Sr. Lectr.
Vyakarnum, Annapurna   Sr. Lectr.
Wong, Wilson, BSc *Lond.*, MB BS *Lond.*   Sr. Lectr., Renal Medicine
Zhou, Wuding, PhD *Lond.*, MB   Sr. Lectr.
Research: HIV/GU medicine; immunology; infectious diseases; renal medicine; rheumatology

Medical Education, Division of

Tel: (020) 7188 3739 Fax: (020) 7188 3737
Brown, Alun, BSc PhD   Sr. Lectr.
Clayden, Graham, MB BS *Lond.*, MD *Lond.*, FRCP, FRCPCH   Reader
Garlick, Pamela B., BA *Oxf.*, DPhil *Oxf.*, MA   Sr. Lectr.
Gill, Elaine, BA *Lond.*, PhD *Lond.*   Sr. Lectr.
Graham, Helen, MB ChB *Manc.*, FRCGP   Sr. Lectr.
Lucas, Sebastian B., BM BCh *Oxf.*, MA *Oxf.*, BA, FRCP, FRCPath   Prof.
Moreland, Barbara H., BSc *Lond.*, PhD *Lond.*   Sr. Lectr.
Phillips, Richard J. W., BM BCh *Oxf.*, MA *Camb.*   Sr. Lectr.
Philpott-Howard, John N., MB BCh *Wales*   Sr. Lectr.
Poston, Robin N., MD *Camb.*, MB BChir MA, FRCPath   Sr. Lectr.
Rees, P. John, MA *Camb.*, MD *Camb.*   Prof.; Head*
Stephenson, Anne E., MB ChB *Otago*, PhD *Otago*   Sr. Lectr.
Tilzey, Anthea J., MA *Oxf.*, MB BS *Lond.*, FRCP   Sr. Lectr.
Treacher, David, BA *Oxf.*, MB BS *Lond.*, FRCP   Sr. Lectr.

SPECIAL CENTRES, ETC

Australian Studies, Menzies Centre for

Tel: (020) 7240 0220 Fax: (020) 7240 8292
Bongiorno, Frank, BA *Melb.*, PhD   Sr. Lectr.
Bridge, Prof. Carl R., BA *Syd.*, PhD *Flin.*, FRHistS   Prof.; Head*
Other Staff: 1 Lectr.
Research: Australian colonial literary culture; Australian film; Australian history; Australian politics; Australia's media industries

Biomedicine and Society, Centre for (CBAS)

Prainsack, Barbara, MA *Vienna*, DPhil *Vienna*   Sr. Lectr.
Salter, Brian, BA *Sus.*, MA *Sus.*, DPhil *Sus.*   Prof.
Wainwright, Steven P., BSc *Hull*, MSc *Lond.*, PhD *Lond.*   Prof.
Williams, Claire, BSc *Sur.*, MSc *Lond.*, PhD *Sur.*   Prof.

British Constitutional Law and History, Centre for (CBCLH)

Blackburn, Robert, BA *Leeds*, MSc *Lond.*, PhD *Leeds*, LLD *Leeds*, FRHistS   Prof., Constitutional Law; Dir.*

Child Studies Programme

Driscoll, Jennifer, BA *Camb.*, MA *Lond.*   Dir.*

Computing in the Humanities, Centre for

Beacham, Richard, BA *Yale*   Prof.
Deegan, Marilyn, BA *Manc.*, BSc *Manc.*, PhD *Manc.*   Prof.

Lavagnino, John, BA Harv. Sr. Lectr.
McCarty, Willard, BA Reed, MA Portland, PhD Tor. Reader
Short, Harold, BA Lond. Prof.; Dir.*
Research: computer aided mapping; digital technologies and scholarship; textual scholarship; 3D visualisation

Construction Law and Dispute Resolution, Centre for (CCLDR)

Britton, Philip, LLB S'ton., BCL Oxf. Dir.*
Capper, Phillip, BA Durh., MA Oxf. Nash Prof. of Engineering Law
Uff, John F., QC, BSc Lond., PhD Lond., FICE, FREng, FKC Emer. Prof.
Other Staff: 1 Visiting Prof.; 2 Visiting Sr. Lectrs.; 3 Visiting Lectrs.; 2 Visiting Res. Fellows

Construction Law and Management, Centre for

Tel: (020) 7848 2685 Fax: (020) 7848 0210

Crime and Justice Studies, Centre for (CCJS)

Garside, Richard, BA Nott. Dir.*

Criminal Justice Research, Institute for (ICPR)

Turnbull, Paul, BA N.Lond., MSc S.Bank Sr. Res. Fellow; Deputy Dir.
Other Staff: 4 Sr. Res. Fellows; 3 Res. Fellows

Dentistry, Centre of Flexible Learning in

Tel: (020) 848 1517 Fax: (020) 848 1366
Millar, Brian, BDS Dund., PhD Lond., FDSRCS Sr. Lectr.
Reynolds, Patricia, MB BS Lond., BDS Lond., MA Open(UK), PhD Lond., FDSRCS Prof.; Head*

English Language Teaching Centre

Tel: (020) 7848 1600 Fax: (020) 7848 1601
McDermott, Nina, BA Leeds, MA Manc. Dir.*

European Law, Centre of (CEL)

Biondi, Andrea, LLM Florence, MA Florence, PhD Florence Prof., European Union Law
Eeckhout, Piet, Lic Ghent, PhD Ghent Prof.; Dir., LLM Programme; Dir.*
Türk, Alexander, MA Augsburg, PhD Lond., LLM Sr. Lectr.

Human Rights, British Institute of (BIHR)

Ghose, Katie, BA Oxf., MA Calif. Dir.*

Learning and Teaching, King's Institute of (KILT)

Tel: (020) 7848 3329 Fax: (020) 7848 3253
Hay, David, BSc Lond., DPhil Oxf. Sr. Lectr.
Kinchin, Ian, BSc Lond., MPhil Lond., PhD Sur. Sr. Lectr.
Lomas, Laurie, BA Kent, MA Kent, PhD Kent Sr. Lectr.
Lygo-Baker, Simon, BA MA Sr. Lectr.

Medical Law and Ethics, Centre for (CMLE)

Glover, Jonathan, MA Oxf., BPhil Oxf. Prof., Ethics; Dir.*
Lewis, Penney, SB M.I.T., LLB Tor., MA Lond., LLM Col. Prof.
Scott, Rosamund, BA ANU, BA Oxf., PhD Lond. Prof.
Other Staff: 2 Lectrs.

Mediterranean Studies, Centre for

Tel: (020) 7848 2535 Fax: (020) 7848 2325
E-mail: rory.miller@kcl.ac.uk
Karsh, Efraim, BA Jerusalem, MA Tel-Aviv, PhD Tel-Aviv Prof.; Head*
Miller, Rory, BA Trinity(Dub.), MA Lond., PhD Lond. Sr. Lectr.

Prison Studies, International Centre for (ICPS)

Allen, Rob, MA MSc Dir.*
Coyle, Andrew, BA Open(UK), PhD Edin., FKC Prof.
Other Staff: 1 Sr. Res. Fellow; 1 Res. Officer; 1 Res. Assoc.

Risk Management, Centre for

Tel: (020) 7848 2102 Fax: (020) 7848 1214
E-mail: kcrm@kcl.ac.uk
Fairman, Robyn, BSc Lond. Reader
Ragnar, Lofstedt, BA Calif., MA Calif., PhD Clark Prof.
Rogers, Brooke, BA Rollins, PhD Lond.
Rothstein, Henry, BSc Brist., MSc Sus., DPhil Sus. Deputy Dir.
Yapp, Charlotte, BSc Lond., LLM Wales, PhD Lond.

Social Care Workforce Research Unit

Manthorpe, Jill, BA York(UK), MA Hull Prof.

Technology, Law, Ethics and Society, Centre for (TELOS)

Brownsword, Roger, LLB Lond. Prof.; Dir.*
Yeung, Karen, LLB Melb., BComMkt Melb., BCL Oxf., DPhil Oxf. Prof.

CONTACT OFFICERS

Academic affairs. Academic Registrar and Deputy College Secretary: Salter, Brian E., BSc Leeds, FKC
Accommodation. Assistant Director of Services for Students: Parry, Angela, BSc(Econ) Wales
Admissions (first degree). (Contact the Admissions Tutor of the relevant academic department)
Admissions (higher degree). (Contact the Admissions Tutor of the relevant academic department)
Adult/continuing education. Professor (Education and Professional Studies): Osborne, Prof. Jonathan, BSc Brist., MSc Lond., PhD Lond.
Alumni. Head of Alumni: Garner, Jennifer, BA Queens, N.Y., MA Chatham

Archives. Director of Archive and Information Management: Methven, Patricia J., BA Lond. (E-mail: archives.web@kcl.ac.uk)
Careers. Head, Careers Advisory Service: Owen, Jenny, BSc Bath (E-mail: careers@kcl.ac.uk)
Computing services. Chief Information Officer and College Librarian: Stanton, Karen, BA Sheff. (E-mail: iss-admin@kcl.ac.uk)
Conferences/corporate hospitality. Head, Conference and Residential Lettings: Booth, Alison, BA
Credit transfer. Deputy Registrar: Placito, Hilary, BA Exe., MA Lond.
Development/fund-raising. Director of Development: Peters, Gemma, BA Sus. (E-mail: devofficemanager@kcl.ac.uk)
Equal opportunities. Director, Equality and Diversity: Wainwright, Virginia, BA Sus., BArch Strath., MSc Strath. (E-mail: equality@kcl.ac.uk)
Estates and buildings/works and services. Director, Estates: Caldwell, Ian, BSc BArch (E-mail: estates.help@kcl.ac.uk)
Examinations. Senior Assistant Registrar: Connor, Kathryn (E-mail: exams.office@kcl.ac.uk)
Finance. Director of Finance: Large, Stephen
Health services. Senior College Medical Officer: Chase, Derek, MB BChir MA, FRCGP
International office. International Officer: Wheeler, Jo, BA Warw., PhD Warw.
Library (chief librarian). Chief Information Officer and College Librarian: Stanton, Karen, BA Sheff. (E-mail: iss-admin@kcl.ac.uk)
Marketing. Managing Director, King's College London Business: Campbell, Alison, PhD
Personnel/human resources. Director of Human Resources: Dempster, Brent, BSocSci Natal
Public relations. Director, Communications: Coe, Christopher, BA Kent (E-mail: pr@kcl.ac.uk)
Purchasing. Director of Procurement: Wrigg, James, BSc Lough. (E-mail: james.wrigg@kcl.ac.uk)
Quality assurance and accreditation. Deputy Registrar: Placito, Hilary, BA Exe., MA Lond. (E-mail: qualityassurance-office@kcl.ac.uk)
Research. Senior Assistant Registrar: Sainsbury, Nicola, BA E.Anglia, MA Lond.
Safety. College Safety Officer: (vacant)
Staff development and training. Senior Training Officer: (vacant), MBE
Staff development and training. Staff Development Officer: Mayhew, Roger, BSc Lond.
Student welfare/counselling. Director of Student Services: Conlon, Ann, BEd Leeds, MA Herts.

[Information supplied by the institution as at 2 October 2007, and edited by the ACU]

LONDON BUSINESS SCHOOL

Founded 1965

Associate Member of the Association of Commonwealth Universities

Postal Address: Regent's Park, London, England NW1 4SA
Telephone: (020) 7000 7000 **Fax:** (020) 7000 7001
URL: http://www.london.edu

DEAN*—Buchanan, Robin W. T., MBA *Harv.*
DEPUTY DEAN (FACULTY)—Peterson, Prof. Randall, BS *Minn.*, MA *Minn.*, PhD *Calif.*
DEPUTY DEAN (PROGRAMMES)—Birkinshaw, Prof. Julian, BSc *Durh.*, MBA *W.Ont.*, PhD *W.Ont.*
SECRETARY‡—Frost, Richard

GENERAL INFORMATION

History. The school was founded in 1965 and was granted its Royal Charter in 1986.

Higher Degrees (see also University of London Directory to Subjects of Study).
Master's. MBA, MSc.
Admission. Applicants for admission to master's degree courses must hold a good Graduate Management Aptitude Test (GMAT) score, have work experience and management potential.
Length of course. Full-time: MBA: 1½–2 years; MSc: 2 years. Part-time: MBA, MSc: 2 years.
Doctoral. PhD.
Length of course. Full-time: PhD: 4–5 years.

FACULTIES/SCHOOLS

Executive Education
Tel: (020) 7000 7373
   E-mail: rsimpson@london.edu
Associate Dean: Simpson, Rory
Assistant: Highton, Lesley

Executive MBA Programme
Tel: (020) 7000 7460
   E-mail: lhoffman@london.edu
Associate Dean: Hoffman, Lynn

Finance Programmes Office
Tel: (020) 7000 7571
   E-mail: jsmiti@london.edu
Associate Dean: Vinck, Sabine

MBA Programme
Tel: (020) 7000 7521 Fax: (020) 7000 7501
   E-mail: ghowells@london.edu
Acting Associate Dean: Howells, G.
Associate Dean: Tyler, J.

PhD Programme/Research
Fax: (020) 7000 8960
   E-mail: rvipond@london.edu
Chair, PhD Programme: Hardie, Bruce G., BComm *Auck.*, MComm *Auck.*, MA *Penn.*, PhD *Penn.*
Director, Academic Affairs: Vipond, Rosemary, BA *Leeds*, PhD *Leeds*

Sloan Fellowships Masters Programme
Tel: (020) 7000 7460
   E-mail: lhoffman@london.edu
Director: (vacant)
Associate Dean: Hoffman, Lynn

ACADEMIC UNITS
Arranged by Subject Areas

Accounting
Tel: (020) 7000 8122
   E-mail: bsalas@london.edu
Amir, Eli, BA *Tel-Aviv*, MA *Calif.*, PhD *Calif.* Prof.; Head*
Franco, Francesca, BS *Bocconi*, PhD *Penn.*   Asst. Prof.

Kraft, Arthur, BBA *Mich.*, MAcc *Mich.*, PhD *Chic.*   Asst. Prof.
Likierman, Andrew, MA *Oxf.*   Prof., Management Practice
Shivakumar, Lakshmanan, BCom *Madr.*, MBA *Vanderbilt*, PhD *Vanderbilt*   Assoc. Prof.
Talmor, Eli, BSc *Haifa*, PhD *N.Carolina*   Prof.
Tamayo, Ane, BSc *Basque*, MSc *H-W*, MPhil *City(UK)*, MS *Roch.*, PhD *Roch.*   Asst. Prof.
Urcan, Oktay, PhD *Texas*, BA   Asst. Prof.
Vasvari, Florin, MA *Tor.*, PhD *Tor.*   Asst. Prof.
Other Staff: 1 Visiting Prof.; 3 Teaching Fellows

Economics
Tel: (020) 7000 8417
   E-mail: hgeorge@london.edu
Benoit, Jean-Pierre, BA *Yale*, PhD *Stan.*   Prof.
Coeurdacier, Nicolas, BSc *Ecole Poly.(Palaiseau)*, ME PhD   Asst. Prof.
Henry, Emeric, BA *Paris IX*, MA *École Nat.Stat.& l'Admin.Écon.*, MA *Stan.*, PhD *Stan.*   Asst. Prof.
Ottaviani, Marco, BA *Bocconi*, PhD *M.I.T.*   Prof.
Portes, Richard, BA *Yale*, MA *Oxf.*, DPhil *Oxf.* Prof.
Rey, Helene, MS *Stan.*, PhD *Lond.*   Prof.
Scott, Andrew, MA *Oxf.*, MSc *Lond.*, DPhil *Oxf.* Prof.
Waverman, Leonard, BComm *Tor.*, MA *Tor.*, PhD *M.I.T.*   Prof.; Head*
Other Staff: 1 Emer. Prof.; 1 Visiting Prof.; 1 Res. Fellow

Entrepreneurship
Tel: (020) 7000 8183
   E-mail: cbarry@london.edu
Hay, Michael, BA *York(UK)*, DPhil *York(UK)* Prof., Management Practice
Khavul, Susanna, BA *Calif.*, DBA *Boston*   Asst. Prof.
Mullins, John, BA *Lehigh*, MBA *Stan.*, PhD *Minn.* Assoc. Prof., Management Practice; Head*
Other Staff: 3 Teaching Fellows; 2 Visiting Staff; 3 Adjuncts

Finance
Tel: (020) 7000 8202
   E-mail: skeenan@london.edu
Acharya, Viral, BTech *IIT Bombay*, PhD *N.Y.* Prof.
Basak, Suleyman, BSc *Lond.*, MS *Carnegie-Mellon*, PhD *Carnegie-Mellon*   Assoc. Prof.
Chernov, Mikhail, BS *Moscow*, MS *Moscow*, PhD *Penn.*   Assoc. Prof.
Cocco, Joao, Lic *C.U.Portugal*, MA *Harv.*, PhD *Harv.*   Asst. Prof.
Cooper, Ian A., MA *Camb.*, MBA *N.Carolina*, PhD *N.Carolina*   Prof.
Cornelli, Francesca, Laurea *Bocconi*, MA *Harv.*, PhD *Harv.*   Prof.
Dimson, Elroy, BA *Newcastle(UK)*, MCom *Birm.*, PhD *Lond.*   Prof.
Dow, James C. F., BA *Camb.*, MA *Camb.*, PhD *Prin.*   Prof.; Head*
Franks, Julian R., BA *Sheff.*, MBA *Col.*, PhD *Lond.* Prof.
Gala, Vito, BA *Bocconi*, MBA *Chic.*, PhD *Chic.* Asst. Prof.

Gomes, Francisco, BA *New Lisbon*, MA *Harv.*, PhD *Harv.*   Asst. Prof.
Gromb, Denis, PhD *École Poly.(Palaiseau)*   Assoc. Prof.
Johnson, Timothy, SB *M.I.T.*, MS *Col.*, MBA *Col.*, PhD *Chic.*   Asst. Prof.
Julio, Brandon, BA *Brigham Young*, MS *S.Carolina*, PhD *Ill.*   Asst. Prof.
Lochstoer, Lars, SivIng *Norwegian U.S.T.*, PhD *Calif.*   Asst. Prof.
Makorov, Igor, MS *Moscow*, PhD *M.I.T.*, MA   Asst. Prof.
Malloy, Christopher, BA *Yale*, MBA *Chic.*, PhD *Chic.*   Asst. Prof.
Naik, Narayan, BTech *IIT Bombay*, PhD *Duke* Assoc. Prof.
Pavlova, Anna, MSc *Moscow*, PhD *Penn.*, MA Asst. Prof.
Plantin, Guillaume, BA *École Poly.(Palaiseau)*, MSc *École Nat.Stat.& l'Admin.Écon.*, PhD *Toulouse* Asst. Prof.
Schaefer, Stephen M., MA *Camb.*, PhD *Lond.* Prof.
Servaes, Henri, BS *European Univ.Inst.*, BBA *European Univ.Inst.*, MSIA *Purdue*, PhD *Purdue* Prof.
Uppal, Raman, BA *Delhi*, MA *Penn.*, MBA *Penn.*, PhD *Penn.*   Prof.
Vig, Vikrant, BS *Delhi*, MS *Ill.*, MBA *Ill.*, MIF *Ill.*, PhD *Col.*   Asst. Prof.
Volpin, Paolo, BA *Bocconi*, MA *Harv.*, PhD *Harv.* Assoc. Prof.; J. P. Morgan Chase Res. Fellow
Other Staff: 3 Emer. Profs.; 4 Visiting Profs.

Management Science and Operations
E-mail: ewelch@london.edu
Bunn, Derek W., MA *Camb.*, MSc *Lond.*, PhD *Lond.*   Prof.
De Miguel, Angel V., MSc *Madrid*, MS *Stan.*, PhD *Stan.*   Asst. Prof.
Degraeve, Zeger, BS *Ghent*, MBA *Leuven*, PhD *Chic.*   Prof.
Fridgeirsdottir, Kristin, CS *Iceland*, MS *Stan.*, PhD *Stan.*   Asst. Prof.
Masini, Andrea, MS *Rome*, MS *Europ.Inst.Bus.Admin.*, PhD *Europ.Inst.Bus.Admin.* Asst. Prof.
Stefanescu, Catalina, BSc *Bucharest*, MS *Cornell*, PhD *Cornell*   Asst. Prof.
Tsikriktsis, Nikolaos, BSc *Salonika*, MBA *Boston*, DBA *Boston*   Asst. Prof.
Voss, Chris, BSc *Lond.*, MSc *Lond.*, PhD *Lond.* Foundation Prof., Technology Management and Learning
Weber, Bruce, MA *Wharton*, PhD *Wharton* Prof.; Head*
Other Staff: 2 Visiting Profs.; 1 Emer. Prof.; 1 Exec. Fellow; 2 Adjuncts

Marketing
Tel: (020) 7000 8627
   E-mail: cayton@london.edu
Bertini, Marco, BA *Melb.*, BCom *Melb.*, MBA *Navarra*, DBA *Harv.*   Asst. Prof.
Goldstein, Daniel, BS *Wis.*, PhD *Chic.*   Asst. Prof.
Hardie, Bruce G., BComm *Auck.*, MComm *Auck.*, MA *Penn.*, PhD *Penn.*   Assoc. Prof.
Kumar, Nirmalya, BComm *Calc.*, MComm *Shiv.*, MBA *Ill.*, PhD *Northwestern*   Prof.

Roberts, John, BA *Melb.*, MComm *Melb.*, MSc *Mass.*, PhD *Mass.*   Prof. (joint appointment with the University of New South Wales)
Tavassoli, Nader, BA *Syr.*, MBA *Syr.*, MPhil *Col.*, PhD *Col.*   Assoc. Prof.
Vilcassim, Naufel, BSc *S.Lanka*, MBA *Texas*, PhD *Cornell*   Prof.
Other Staff: 2 Emer. Profs.; 1 Visiting Prof.; 1 Sr. Fellow; 1 Exec. Fellow

Organisational Behaviour

Tel: (020) 7000 8910
  E-mail: cmadden@london.edu
Cohen, Lisa, MBA *Duke*, PhD *Calif.*   Asst. Prof.
Conger, Jay, BA *Dartmouth*, MBA *Virginia*, PhD *Harv.*   Prof.
Earley, P. Christopher, BA *Knox(Ill.)*, MA *Ill.*, PhD *Ill.*   Prof.
Goffee, Rob, BA *Kent*, PhD *Kent*   Prof.; Head*
Gratton, Lynda C., BA *Liv.*, PhD *Liv.*   Assoc. Prof., Management Practice
Inesi, Ena, BSE *Duke*, PhD *Stan.*   Asst. Prof.
Ku, Gillian, AB *Harv.*, MS *Northwestern*, PhD *Northwestern*   Asst. Prof.
Mainemelis, Charalampos, BS *Salonika*, MBA *San Francisco*, PhD *Case W.Reserve*   Asst. Prof.
Moon, Henry, BS *Maryland*, MA *Oklahoma*, PhD *Mich.State*   Assoc. Prof.
Moore, Celia, BA *McG.*, MPA *Col.*, PhD *Tor.*   Asst. Prof.
Moynihan, Lisa, BA *Mt.Holyoke*, MA *Col.*, PhD *Cornell*   Asst. Prof.
Narasimhan, Anand, BE *BITS*, PhD *Vanderbilt*, MBA   Asst. Prof.
Nicholson, Nigel, BA *Wales*, PhD *Wales*, FBPsS   Prof.
Ormiston, Margaret, BA *Calif.*, MS *Calif.*, PhD *Calif.*   Asst. Prof.
Peterson, Randall, BS *Minn.*, MA *Minn.*, PhD *Calif.*   Prof.
Pillutla, Madan, BE *BITS*, MBA *Ill.*, PhD *Br.Col.*   Assoc. Prof.
Smith, Brent, BA *Tulsa*, MA *Maryland*, PhD *Maryland*   Assoc. Prof.
Thau, Stefan, MSc *Mannheim*, PhD *Gron.*   Asst. Prof.
Other Staff: 1 Emer. Prof.; 7 Visiting Profs.; 1 Res. Fellow; 2 Res. Assts.; 2 Adjunct Profs.

Strategic and International Management

E-mail: joconnor@london.edu
Birkinshaw, Julian, BSc *Durh.*, MBA *W.Ont.*, PhD *W.Ont.*   Prof.
Fernandez-Mateo, Isabel, BA *Carlos III(Madrid)*, MSc *Barcelona*, PhD *M.I.T.*   Asst. Prof.
Jacobides, Michael, BSc *Athens*, MA *Wharton*, PhD *Wharton*   Asst. Prof.
Kyle, Margaret, BS *Cornell*, PhD *M.I.T.*   Asst. Prof.
Lee, Brandon, MS *Cornell*, PhD *Cornell*   Asst. Prof.

Markides, Constantinos, BA *Boston*, MA *Boston*, MBA *Harv.*, DBA *Harv.*   R. P. Bauman Prof.; Head*
Mors, Louise, MA *Boston*, MBE *Norwegian Sch.Management*, PhD *Europ.Inst.Bus.Admin.*
Mylonadis, Yiorgos, BA *American Coll., Greece*, MA *Calif.*, PhD *M.I.T.*   Asst. Prof.
Puranam, Phanish, BE *Delhi*, MIB *Indian Inst.Foreign Trade*, MA *Wharton*, PhD *Wharton*   Asst. Prof.
Reitzig, Marcus, BS *Constance*, MS *Kiel*, MBR *Munich*, PhD *Munich*   Asst. Prof.
Sorenson, Olav, AB *Harv.*, PhD *Stan.*   Prof.
Sosa, Lourdes, BS *Monterrey Inst.Technol.*, PhD *M.I.T.*   Asst. Prof.
Sull, Don, AB *Harv.*, MBA *Harv.*, DBA *Harv.*   Assoc. Prof., Management Practice
Vermeulen, Godefriedus, MA *Tilburg*, PhD *Tilburg*   Assoc. Prof.
Weber, Bruce, MA *Wharton*, PhD *Wharton*   Assoc. Prof.
Yip, George, BA *Camb.*, MA *Camb.*, MBA *Cran.*, MBA *Harv.*, DBA *Harv.*   Prof.
Other Staff: 1 Visiting Prof.; 1 Res. Fellow; 3 Teaching Fellows; 3 Adjunct Profs.

SPECIAL CENTRES, ETC

Aditya V Birla India Centre

E-mail: sstorfjell@london.edu
Kumar, Nirmalya, BComm *Calc.*, MComm *Shiv.*, MBA *Ill.*, PhD *Northwestern*   Prof.; Co-Dir.*
Puranam, Phanish, BE *Delhi*, MIB *Indian Inst.Foreign Trade*, MA *Wharton*, PhD *Wharton*   Asst. Prof.; Co-Dir.*

BNP Paribas Hedge Fund Centre

E-mail: bnpparibashfc@london.edu
Naik, Narayan, BTech *IIT Bombay*, PhD *Duke*   Assoc. Prof.; Dir.*

Corporate Governance, Centre for

E-mail: jgrant@london.edu
Franks, Julian R., BA *Sheff.*, MBA *Col.*, PhD *Lond.*   Prof.; Dir.*

Management Innovation Lab

Tel: (020) 7000 8818
  E-mail: fhussan@london.edu
Birkinshaw, Julian, BSc *Durh.*, MBA *W.Ont.*, PhD *W.Ont.*   Dir.*

Marketing, Centre for

Fax: (020) 7000 8627
  E-mail: cayton@london.edu
Kumar, Nirmalya, BComm *Calc.*, MComm *Shiv.*, MBA *Ill.*, PhD *Northwestern*   Dir.*

Private Equity Institute

Tel: (020) 7000 8127
  E-mail: knemoto@london.edu

Acharya, Viral, BTech *IIT Bombay*, PhD *N.Y.*   Prof.; Academic Dir.*

Technology, Institute of

Tel: (020) 7000 8167
  E-mail: scurrall@london.edu
Currall, Steve, BA *Baylor*, MSc *Lond.*, PhD *Cornell*   Faculty Dir.*

Women in Business, Lehman Brothers Centre for

E-mail: lwalker@london.edu
Gratton, Lynda C., BA *Liv.*, PhD *Liv.*   Assoc. Prof., Management Practice; Exec. Dir.*

CONTACT OFFICERS

Academic affairs. Director, Academic Affairs: Vipond, Rosemary, BA *Leeds*, PhD *Leeds* (E-mail: rvipond@london.edu)
Alumni. Director, London Business School Alumni Association: Seedsman, Sarah (E-mail: sseedsman@london.edu)
Careers. Director, Career Services: Morgan, Dianne (E-mail: dmorgan@london.edu)
Computing services. Director, Information Systems: Altendorff, Russell, BA *Westminster* (E-mail: raltendorff@london.edu)
Development/fund-raising. Associate Dean for External Relations: (vacant) (E-mail: aantoniades@london.edu)
Finance. Chief Financial Officer and Treasurer: Webster, Catherine (E-mail: cwebster@london.edu)
General enquiries. Secretary: Frost, Richard (E-mail: rfrost@london.edu)
Library (enquiries). Head of Library: Edwards, Helen (E-mail: hedwards@london.edu)
Personnel/human resources. Director, Human Resources: Willat, Philip (E-mail: pwillat@london.edu)
Public relations. Director, Communications and Corporate Marketing: Lane, David (E-mail: dlane@london.edu)
Research. Director, Academic Affairs: Vipond, Rosemary, BA *Leeds*, PhD *Leeds* (E-mail: rvipond@london.edu)
Security. Head of Management Services: Humphries, Paul, BSc *S.Bank*, MBA *Lond.* (E-mail: phumphries@london.edu)
Staff development and training. Faculty Development Advisor: Morrison, Philippa, BA *CNAA*, MA *Antioch* (E-mail: pmorrison@london.edu)

[Information supplied by the institution as at 25 September 2007, and edited by the ACU]

LONDON SCHOOL OF ECONOMICS AND POLITICAL SCIENCE

Founded 1895

Associate Member of the Association of Commonwealth Universities

Postal Address: Houghton Street, London, England WC2A 2AE
Telephone: (020) 7405 7686 **Fax:** (020) 7242 0392
URL: http://www.lse.ac.uk

DIRECTOR*—Davies, Sir Howard, MA Oxf., MSc Stan.
PRO DIRECTOR, PLANNING AND RESOURCES—Gaskell, G. D., BSc Lond., PhD Lond.
PRO DIRECTOR, TEACHING AND LEARNING—Hartley, Prof. J. M., BA Lond., PhD Lond., FRHistS
PRO DIRECTOR, RESEARCH AND EXTERNAL RELATIONS—Worthington, Prof. S. E., BSc ANU, LLB Qld., LLM Melb., PhD Camb.
SECRETARY‡—Hall, A. N. P., BA
ACADEMIC REGISTRAR—Underwood, S., MA Oxf.
FINANCE OFFICER—Farrell, A.
LIBRARIAN—Sykes, J. M., MA Glas., MLitt Glas.

GENERAL INFORMATION

History. The school was founded in 1895 by Sydney and Beatrice Webb following a bequest from Henry Hunt Hutchinson, a member of the Fabian Society. It is located in central London.

Admission to first degree courses (see also United Kingdom Introduction). Through Universities and Colleges Admissions Service (UCAS). General Certificate of Education (GCE) A level passes in 3 subjects with high grades. There are specific requirements for each degree course. Other qualifications are also accepted.

First Degrees (see also University of London Directory to Subjects of Study). BA, BSc, LLB.
LLB with French law: 3 years plus 1 year studying abroad.
Length of course. Full-time: BA, BSc, LLB: 3 years.

Higher Degrees (see also University of London Directory to Subjects of Study).
Master's. LLM, MA, MBA, MPA, MPhil, MRes, MSc.
Admission. Applicants for admission to master's degree courses must normally hold an appropriate first degree with at least second class honours. MPhil: appropriate master's degree or, exceptionally, a very good appropriate first degree
Length of course. Full-time: LLM, MA, MSc: 1 year; MRes: 1–2 years; MPA: 2 years; MPhil: 2–4 years. Part-time: LLM, MA, MSc: 2 years; MPhil: 2–4 years.
Doctoral. PhD.
Admission. PhD: applicants should have an appropriate master's degree or, exceptionally, a very good appropriate first degree.
Length of course. Full-time: PhD: 2–4 years. Part-time: PhD: 2–4 years.

Libraries. Volumes: 4,000,000. Periodicals subscribed to: 10,000. Special collections: Beveridge (working papers); Gladstone (election addresses); Liberal Party (archives); pamphlets (rare political material); Shaw (personal collection); Webbs' Passfield papers (founders' personal collections); world-wide governments (official statistics).

FACULTIES/SCHOOLS

Graduate School
Tel: (020) 7955 7160 Fax: (020) 7955 6137
E-mail: graduate-school@lse.ac.uk
Dean: Fulbrook, J., LLB Exe., LLM Harv., PhD Camb.

Undergraduate Studies
Tel: (020) 7955 7124 Fax: (020) 7955 6368
Dean: Hoffman, M. J., MA Mass., MSc Lond.

ACADEMIC UNITS

In addition to the following, a large number of fixed-term occasional research and teaching appointments are made from year to year.

Accounting and Finance
Tel: (020) 7955 7324 Fax: (020) 7955 7420
E-mail: o.raie@lse.ac.uk
Anderson, R. W., MA Mich., PhD Mich. Prof., Finance; Head*
Bhattacharya, S., BSc Delhi, PhD Mass. Prof., Finance
Bhimani, A., BSc Cornell, MBA Cornell, PhD Lond. Reader
Bromwich, M., BSc(Econ) Lond. Prof., Accounting and Financial Management
Connor, G., BA(Econ) Georgetown, MA(Econ) Yale, PhD Yale Reader
Danielsson, J., PhD Duke Reader
Faure-Grimaud, A., BA Limoges, MA Limoges, PhD Toulouse Prof., Finance
Horton, J., MPhil Wales, PhD Sr. Lectr.
Macve, R. H., BA Oxf., MA Oxf., MSc Lond., FCA Prof., Accounting
Miller, P., BSc CNAA, PhD Lond. Prof., Management Accounting
Noke, C. W., MA Oxf., MSc Lond., FCA Sr. Lectr., Accounting
Power, M. K., MA Oxf., MPhil Camb., PhD Camb. Prof.
Rahi, R., BA Panjab, MA S.Fraser, PhD Stan. Reader
Vayanos, D. Prof., Finance
Webb, D. C., BA Manc., MA Manc., PhD Lond. Prof., Finance
Other Staff: 13 Lectrs.; 1 Tutorial Fellow
Research: developments in accounting and financial practices; financial accounting innovations and security prices; measurement and control of financial instruments; social/organisational context of accounting practices

Anthropology
Tel: (020) 7955 7202 Fax: (020) 7955 7603
E-mail: (Departmental Manager) y.hinrichsen@lse.ac.uk
Astuti, R., Laurea Siena, MSc PhD Reader
Fuller, C. J., MA Camb., PhD Camb. Prof.
Harris, O. H. Prof.; Head*
James, D., BA Witw., MA Witw., PhD Witw. Reader
Moore, H. L., BA Durh., PhD Lond. Prof.
Mundy, M., BA Oxf., MA Col., PhD Camb. Sr. Lectr.
Parry, J. P., BA Camb., PhD Camb. Prof.
Peabody, N., AB Harv., AM Harv., PhD Harv.
Stafford, C. L., BA Texas, MSc Lond., PhD Lond. Sr. Lectr.
Other Staff: 5 Lectrs.; 2 Res Fellows
Research: anthropological contributions to theories of cognition; anthropology of religion; combining ethnography and

general theory; integration of anthropology and history; non-European field

Economics
Tel: (020) 7955 7545 Fax: (020) 7831 1840
E-mail: (Departmental Administrator) j.law@lse.ac.uk
Barr, N., MSc(Econ) Calif., PhD Calif., FRSA Prof., Public Economics
Belenzon, S., MA(Econ)
Besley, T., BA Oxf., MA Oxf., MPhil Oxf., DPhil Oxf., FBA Prof.
Bray, M. M., BA Camb., MPhil Oxf., DPhil Oxf. Reader
Burgess, R., BSc Edin., MSc Oxf., DPhil Oxf. Reader
Caselli, F., Laurea Bologna, PhD Harv. Prof.
Cowell, F. A., MA Camb., PhD Camb. Prof.
Dougherty, C. R. S., MA Camb., MA Harv., PhD Harv. Sr. Lectr.
Felli, L., PhD M.I.T. Reader
Fernandez, R., MA Col., PhD Prof.
Ghatak, M., BSc Calc., MA Delhi, PhD Harv. Reader
Hajivassiliou, V. A., BSc Mass., MSc Mass., PhD Mass. Reader
Hardman Moore, J. H., BA Camb., MSc PhD Prof., Economic Theory
Hidalgo, F. J., Lic Madrid, MSc(Econ) PhD Prof., Econometrics
Leape, Prof. J. I., AB Harv., BA Oxf., PhD Harv. Sr. Lectr.
Linton, O., BSc Calif., MSc Calif., PhD Calif. Prof.
Manning, A., BA Camb., DPhil Oxf. Prof.
Marin, A. M., BSc Lond., MSc Lond., PhD M.I.T. Sr. Lectr.
Pesendorfer, M., PhD Northwestern Prof.
Piccione, M., MSc Lond., PhD N.Y. Prof.
Pischke, S., MA(Econ) N.Y.State, PhD Prin. Prof.
Pissarides, C. A., MA Essex, PhD Prof.
Prat, A., Laurea Turin, PhD Stan. Prof.
Quah, D., PhD Harv. Prof.; Head*
Robinson, P. M., BSc ANU, MSc ANU, PhD ANU Tooke Prof., Economic Science and Statistics
Schankerman, M., MA Harv., PhD Harv. Reader
Sutton, J., BSc Trinity(Dub.), MSc Trinity(Dub.), PhD Sheff. Prof.
Van Reenan, J., BA Camb., MSc(Econ) Lond., PhD Lond. Prof.
Venables, A. J., BPhil Oxf., MA Camb., DPhil Oxf. Prof., International Economics
Whitehead, C. M. E., OBE, BSc(Econ) Lond., PhD Lond. Prof., Housing
Other Staff: 17 Lectrs.; 1 Res. Officer; 18 Tutorial Fellows
Research: development economics; economics of industry; welfare state

Geography and Environment
Tel: (020) 7955 7587 Fax: (020) 7955 7412
E-mail: e.gasgoyne@lse.ac.uk
Chant, S. H., BA Camb., PhD Lond. Reader
Cheshire, P. C., BA Camb. Prof.

Corbridge, S. E., BA Camb., PhD Camb.   Prof., Human Geography
Gordon, I., BA Oxf.   Prof., Human Geography
Jones, G. A., BSc Camb., PhD Camb.   Sr. Lectr.
Neumayer, E., MSc PhD   Prof.
Overman, H., BSc(Econ) Brist., MSc PhD   Reader
Perrons, D. C., BSc Brist., MSc Westminster, MSc Brighton, PhD Brist.   Sr. Lectr.
Pratt, A. C., BSc Hudd., PhD Exe.   Sr. Lectr.
Rees, Prof. J., CBE, BSc Lond., MPhil Lond., PhD Lond.   Prof.
Rodriguez-Pose, A., BA Madrid, MA Brussels, PhD Florence   Sr. Lectr.; Head*
Rydin, Y. J., BA Camb., PhD   Sr. Lectr.
Storper, M. C., BA Calif., MA Calif., PhD Calif.   Prof.
Thornley, A. J., BA Manc., MSc(Econ) Lond., PhD Lond.   Sr. Lectr.
Other Staff: 7 Lectrs.; 2 Res. Officers
Research: economic performance and regulation; geographical information systems; planning and regulation; social institutions of economic transformation and environmental policy; urban and social geography and economic geography of private and state enterprises

Government

Tel: (020) 7955 7204 Fax: (020) 7831 1707
   E-mail: (Departmental Administrator)
   n.boyce@lse.ac.uk
Balfour, S., BA MA PhD   Prof., Contemporary Spanish Studies
Barker, R. S., BA Camb., PhD Lond.   Reader
Bose, S., BA Amherst, MA Col., MPhil Col., PhD Col.   Reader
Breuilly, J., BSc York(UK), PhD York(UK)   Prof.; Chair, Nationalism and Ethnicity
Coleman, J., BA Yale, MPhil Yale, PhD Yale   Prof., Ancient and Mediaeval Political Thought
Dimitrov, V., BA Camb., PhD Camb.   Sr. Lectr.
Dowding, K. M., BA Keele, DPhil Oxf.   Prof., Public Choice and Public Policy
Dunleavy, P. J., MA Oxf., DPhil Oxf.   Prof.
Fabre, C., DPhil Oxf.   Sr. Lectr.
Gray, J. N., BA Oxf., MA Oxf., DPhil Oxf.   Sch. Prof., European Thought
Held, D., BSc UMIST, MSc M.I.T., PhD M.I.T.   Prof., Political Science
Hix, S., BSc Lond., MSc Lond., PhD European Univ.Inst.   Sr. Lectr.
Hopkin, J., BSc Lond., MSc Lond., PhD European Univ.Inst.   Sr. Lectr.
Hughes, J. R., BA Belf., PhD Lond.   Sr. Lectr., Comparative Politics
Hutchinson, D. J. S., MA Edin., PhD   Sr. Lectr.
Kaldor, Mary H., CBE, BA Oxf., MA Oxf.   Prof.
Kelly, P. J., BA York(UK), MA York(UK), PhD Lond.   Prof.
List, C., BA Oxf., MPhil Oxf., DPhil Oxf.   Reader
Page, E. C., BA Kingston(UK), MSc Strath., PhD Strath.   Prof.
Panizza, F. E., BA Republic(Montevideo), MA Essex, DPhil   Sr. Lectr.
Philip, G. D. E., BA Oxf., DPhil Oxf.   Reader, Comparative and Latin American Politics; Head*
Ringmar, E., BA Stockholm, MA Yale, MPhil Yale, PhD Yale, DPhil Uppsala   Sr. Lectr.
Schonhardt-Bailey, C., BA Idaho, MA Calif., PhD Calif.   Sr. Lectr.
Other Staff: 8 Lectrs.; 2 Res. Officers; 3 Tutorial Fellows
Research: ancient and mediaeval political thought; interaction of economics and politics; local government; politics of nationalism and ethnic conflicts; worldwide politics

History, Economic

Tel: (020) 7955 7084 Fax: (020) 7955 7730
   E-mail: (Departmental Administrator)
   l.sampson@lse.ac.uk
Austin, G., BA Camb., PhD Birm.   Sr. Lectr.
Deng, K., BA Beijing, PhD La Trobe   Reader

Epstein, S., MA Siena, PhD Camb.   Prof.; Head*
Howlett, P., BA Warw., MPhil Camb., PhD Camb.   Sr. Lectr.
Hunt, E. H., BSc(Econ) PhD   Sr. Lectr.
Hunter, J. E., BA Sheff., DPhil Oxf.   Prof., Japanese Economic and Social History
Lewis, C. M., BA Exe., PhD Lond.   Sr. Lectr., Latin American Economic History
Morgan, M. S., BSc Lond., PhD Lond.   Prof.
Other Staff: 6 Lectrs.; 2 Res. Officers
Research: economic history of the less developed world; international economic history of the twentieth century; performance and structure of modern business

History, International

Tel: (020) 7955 7548 Fax: (020) 7955 6800
   E-mail: (Departmental Administrator)
   d.frini@lse.ac.uk
Ashton, N. J., MA Camb., PhD Camb.   Sr. Lectr.
Best, A., BA Leeds, PhD   Sr. Lectr.
Boyce, R. W. D., BA W.Laur., MA PhD   Sr. Lectr.
Hartley, J. M., BA Lond., PhD Lond., FRHistS   Prof.
Hochstrasser, T., MA Camb., PhD Camb.   Sr. Lectr.
Knox, B. M. B., BA Harv., MA Yale, PhD Yale   Stevenson Prof.
Ludlow, N. P., MA Oxf., DPhil Oxf.   Sr. Lectr.
Prazmowska, A.-J., BA Birm., PhD Lond.   Sr. Lectr.
Preston, P., MA Oxf., MA Reading, DPhil Oxf., FRHistS   Principe de Asturias Prof., Contemporary Spanish Studies
Rodriguez-Salgado, M. J., BA Durh., PhD Hull   Prof.
Rubies, J., Lic Barcelona, PhD Camb.   Sr. Lectr.
Schulze, K. E., BA Maine(USA), MPhil Oxf., DPhil Oxf.   Sr. Lectr.
Sked, A., MA Glas., DPhil Oxf.   Sr. Lectr.
Stevenson, D., MA Camb., PhD Camb.   Prof.
Westad, O. A., Cand Oslo, Mag Oslo, PhD N.Carolina   Prof.; Head*
Other Staff: 4 Lectrs.; 1 Res. Officer; 4 Tutorial Fellows
Research: British political history; foreign policy of USA; foreign policy/domestic history in Europe; international politics of the Middle East and East Asia; international/European history from 1200 onwards, including Russian and Soviet history

International Relations

Tel: (020) 7955 7404 Fax: (020) 7955 7446
   E-mail: (Departmental Administrator)
   h.parker@lse.ac.uk
Alden, C., BA MA PhD   Sr. Lectr.
Brown, C. J., BSc Lond., PhD Kent   Prof.; Head*
Buzan, B., BA Br.Col., PhD Lond.   Prof.
Coker, C., MA Camb., DPhil Oxf.   Prof.
Cox, M., BA Reading   Prof.
Economides, S., BSocSc Birm., MSc PhD   Sr. Lectr.
Halliday, F. P., BA Oxf., MSc Lond., PhD Lond.   Prof.
Hughes, C. R., BA MA MSC PhD   Sr. Lectr.
Hutchings, K. J., BSc Brist., MA Sus., PhD   Reader
Kent, C. J., MA Aberd., PhD Aberd.   Reader
Sally, M. R., BSc Lond., MSc Lond., PhD Lond.   Sr. Lectr.
Sims, N. R. A., BSc(Econ) Lond.   Reader
Smith, K., BA Wellesley, MA Johns H., PhD   Sr. Lectr.
Stasavage, D., BA PhD   Reader
Walter, A. R., BA W.Aust., MPhil Oxf., DPhil Oxf.   Sr. Lectr.
Wilson, P., BA Keele, MSc S'ton., PhD   Sr. Lectr.
Other Staff: 8 Lectrs.; 1 Res. Officer
Research: international theory, revolutions, nationalism and modernity; issues of gender; methodology, conflict and analysis

Law

Tel: (020) 7955 7278 Fax: (020) 7955 7366
   E-mail: (Departmental Administrator)
   j.m.whyte@lse.ac.uk

Baldwin, G. R., LLB Edin., PhD Edin.   Prof.
Barron, A., LLB Trinity(Dub.), LLM Harv.   Sr. Lectr.
Benjamin, J. H., BA Camb., PhD Lond.   Reader
Beyani, C., LLB Zambia, LLM Zambia, DPhil Oxf.   Sr. Lectr.
Black, J. M., BA Oxf., DPhil Oxf.   Sr. Lectr.
Bradley, D. C., LLB Manc.   Reader
Cass, D., LLM Harv., SJD Harv.   Sr. Lectr.
Chalmers, D., BA Oxf.   Reader
Chinkin, C. M., LLB Lond., LLM Lond., LLM Yale, PhD Syd.   Prof., International Law
Collins, H. G., BA Oxf., BCL Oxf., LLM Harv.   Prof.; Head*
Davies, P. L., MA Oxf., LLM Lond., LLM Yale   Cassel Prof., Commercial Law
Finch, V. M. I., BA CNAA, LLM Lond.   Reader
Greenwood, C. J., BA Camb., LLB Camb.   Prof., International Law
Hadjiemmanuil, C., LLB LLM PhD   Sr. Lectr.
Jacob, J. M., LLB Lond.   Reader
Lacey, N. M., LLB Oxf., BCL Oxf.   Prof., Criminal Law
Loughlin, M., LLB Lond., LLM Warw., LLM Harv.   Prof.
Murphy, W. T., BA Camb., MA Camb.   Prof.
Peay, J. V., BSc Lond., PhD Lond.   Prof.
Pottage, R. A., LLB Edin., LLM Lond.   Reader
Redmayne, M., LLB Birm., PhD Birm.   Sr. Lectr.
Reiner, R., BA Camb., MSc Brist., PhD Brist.   Prof., Criminology
Roberts, S. A., LLB Lond., PhD Lond.   Prof.
Roxan, I., BA Tor., LLB York(Can.), MPhil Camb., PhD Camb.   Sr. Lectr.
Scott, C. D., BA York(UK), PhD E.Anglia   Reader
Simpson, G., LLM Br.Col., SJD Mich.   Reader
Simpson, R. C., LLM Lond.   Reader
Worthington, S. E., BSc ANU, LLB Qld., LLM Melb., PhD Camb.   Prof.
Other Staff: 8 Lectrs.; 1 Res. Officer
Research: alternative dispute resolution; EC and EU law; reform of civil and criminal procedure; regulation of financial markets and utilities

Management

Industrial Relations

Tel: (020) 7955 7026 Fax: (020) 7955 7424
   E-mail: (Departmental Administrator)
   g.suo@lse.ac.uk
Ashwin, C. S. J., BA CNAA, MSc PhD   Reader
Coyle-Shapiro, J. A., BCom Trinity(Dub.), MBS Trinity(Dub.), DBS PhD   Reader
Frege, C. M., BA Freib., MSc PhD   Reader
Hyman, R., BA Oxf., DPhil Oxf.   Prof.; Head*
Marsden, D., BA Oxf., MA Leeds, PhD Aix-Marseilles II   Prof.
Metcalf, D., MA Manc., PhD Lond.   Prof.
Other Staff: 9 Lectrs.
Research: impact of unions on labour productivity; links between industrial relations and economic performance; privatisation and industrial relations; profit-related pay; role of union officials/shop stewards

Information Systems

Tel: (020) 7955 7655 Fax: (020) 7955 7385
   E-mail: (Departmental Administrator)
   c.a.edwardes@lse.ac.uk
Angell, I. O., BSc Wales, PhD Lond.   Prof.
Avgerou, C., BSc Athens, MSc Lough.   Sr. Lectr.
Backhouse, J. P., BA Exe., MSc Lond., PhD Lond.   Sr. Lectr.
Cornford, A., BSc(Econ) Lond., MSc Lond., PhD Lond.   Sr. Lectr.
Kallinikos, J., BSc Aalborg, MSc Aalborg, PhD Aalborg   Reader
Liebenau, J. M., BA Roch., MA Penn., PhD Penn.   Sr. Lectr.
Madon, S., BA CNAA, MSc CNAA, PhD   Sr. Lectr.
Smithson, S. C., BSc(Econ) Lond., MSc Lond., PhD Lond.   Sr. Lectr.
Sorensen, C., BSc Aalborg, MSc Aalborg, PhD Aalborg   Sr. Lectr.

Whitley, E. A., BSc(Econ) Lond., PhD Lond. Reader

Willcocks, L. Head*

Other Staff: 4 Lectrs.; 1 Res. Officer

Research: implementation of IS in organisations; information systems security; inter-organisational systems and electronic commerce; IS in developing countries; public sector computing

Managerial Strategy and Economics Group

Tel: (020) 7955 7920 Fax: (020) 7955 6887
E-mail: (Departmental Administrator) d.g.peppiat@lse.ac.uk

Barzelay, M., AB Stan., MPPM Yale, PhD Yale Reader

De Meza, D., BSc Lond., MSc Lond. Eric Sosnow Prof., Management; Head*

Mulford, M., BA Nebraska, MA N.Y., MSc Oregon, PhD Oregon Sr. Lectr.

Rothe, J., MSc PhD Deputy Dir.

Other Staff: 7 Lectrs.

Research: economic implications of profit sharing; entrepreneurship; management in the public sector; management of international organisations; market for corporate control

Operational Research

Tel: (020) 7955 7653 Fax: (020) 7955 6885
E-mail: (Departmental Administrator) b.mowlam@lse.ac.uk

Appa, G. M., BSc Lond., MSc Lond., PhD Lond. Reader

Bevan, G., MA MTech Prof.; Head*

Howard, J. V., MA Camb., MSc Newcastle(UK), PhD Brist. Sr. Lectr.

Williams, H. P., BA Camb., MA Camb., PhD Leic. Prof.

Other Staff: 7 Lectrs.; 2 Res. Officers

Research: mathematical modelling using combinatorial optimisation and mathematical programming; problem structuring methods; systems dynamics, environmental management and analysis

Mathematics

Tel: (020) 7955 7732 Fax: (020) 7955 6877
E-mail: (Departmental Administrator) d.scott@lse.ac.uk

Alpern, S. R., AB Prin., PhD N.Y. Prof.

Anthony, M. H. G., BSc Glas., PhD Lond. Prof.; Head*

Biggs, N. L., BA Camb., DSc Lond. Prof.

Brightwell, G., BA Camb., PhD Camb. Prof.

Ostoja-Ostaszewski, A. J., BSc Lond., PhD Lond. Sr. Lectr.

Von Stengel, B., MSc Texas, DSc Passau Reader

Other Staff: 4 Lectrs.; 1 Tutor

Research: applications of mathematics in social sciences; combinatorics and game theory; discrete and applicable mathematics; graph and computational learning theories; pure mathematics

Media and Communications

Tel: (020) 7955 6107 Fax: (020) 7955 7248
E-mail: (Departmental Administrator) c.l.bennett@lse.ac.uk

Beckett, C. Dir., POLIS

Cammaerts, B., MA Brussels, PhD Sikkim-Manipal Sr. Lectr.

Livingstone, S., BSc Lond., DPhil Oxf. Dir., Grad. Studies

Mansell, R., BA Manit., MSc Lond., MA S.Fraser Head*

Orgad, S., BA Jerusalem, MSc Lond., PhD Lond. Sr. Lectr.

Rantanen, T., LicSc Helsinki, MSc Helsinki, DocSci Helsinki Sr. Lectr.

Scammell, M., PhD Lond. Sr. Lectr.

Tambini, D., PhD European Univ.Inst. Sr. Lectr.

Von Stengel, B., MSc Texas, DSc Passau Reader

Other Staff: 1 Sr. Res. Fellow; 1 Res. Assoc.; 1

Visiting Res. Assoc.

Social Psychology, Institute of

Tel: (020) 7955 7714 Fax: (020) 7955 7565
E-mail: (Institute Administrator) d.linehan@lse.ac.uk

Bauer, M. W., LicPhil Berne, PhD Lond. Sr. Lectr.

Campbell, C. M., BA Natal, MA Natal, PhD Brist. Prof.

Franks, B., BSc Edin., MSc Edin., PhD Edin. Sr. Lectr.

Gaskell, G. D., BSc Lond., PhD Lond. Prof.

Humphreys, P. C., BSc Lond., PhD Lond. Prof.

Jovchelovitch, S., BSc Pontif.R.G.do Sul, MSc Pontif.R.G.do Sul, PhD Sr. Lectr.

Stockdale, J. E., BSc Lond., PhD Lond. Sr. Lectr.

Other Staff: 4 Lectrs.; 2 Res. Officers

Research: history of psychology as social science; new media; psychology of gender; public understanding of science and technology; social representations of economic/political change

Philosophy, Logic and Scientific Method

Tel: (020) 7955 7340 Fax: (020) 7955 6845
E-mail: (Departmental Administrator) r.matthams@lse.ac.uk

Bovens, L., MA Leuven, PhD Minn. Prof.

Bradley, R. W., BA Witw., MSc Lond., PhD Chic. Reader; Head*

Cartwright, N. L. D., BSc Pitt., PhD Ill. Prof.

Howson, C., BSc(Econ) Prof., Philosophy of Science

Worrall, J., BSc(Econ) Lond., PhD Lond. Prof.

Other Staff: 4 Lectrs.

Research: evidence/testing in science; free will and determinism; holism; nature of mind; reductionism

Social Policy

Incorporating Population Studies

Tel: (020) 7955 7345 Fax: (020) 7955 7415
E-mail: (Departmental Administrator) j.wilkes@lse.ac.uk

Dean, H., BTech Brun., MA Brun., PhD Kent Sr. Lectr.

Gjonca, A., PhD Lond., BSc MSc Sr. Lectr., Demography

Hall, A. L., BA Sheff., MPhil Glas., PhD Glas. Reader, Social Planning in Developing Countries

Hills, J., MA Camb., MSocSc Birm. Prof.

Howell, J. A. Prof.

Knapp, M. R. J., BA Sheff., MSc Kent, PhD Kent Prof.

Le Grand, J., BA Sus., PhD Penn. Richard Titmuss Prof., Health Policy

Lewis, D., BA Camb., PhD Bath Reader

Lewis, J. Prof.

Mangen, S., BSc Ulster, MA Sus., PhD Sr. Lectr.

McGuire, A., BSc(Econ) H-W, MLitt Aberd., PhD Aberd. Prof.; Head*

Mossialos, E., BSc Athens, MD Athens, PhD Athens Prof., Health Policy

Munro, E., BA Exe., MSc PhD Reader

Murphy, M. J., BA Camb., BPhil York(UK) Prof.

Newburn, T., BSc Leic., PhD Leic. Prof.

Piachaud, D. F. J., BA Oxf., MPA Mich. Prof.

Power, A. E., MBE, MA Wis., PhD Lond. Prof.

Rumgay, J. A., BA Reading, MA E.Anglia, PhD Lond. Sr. Lectr.

Other Staff: 16 Lectrs.; 4 Res. Officers

Research: crime and deviance; de-institutionalisation and community care; economic impact of social security; finance and management of health care; population studies and management of housing

Sociology

Tel: (020) 7955 7305 Fax: (020) 7955 7405
E-mail: (Departmental Administrator) j.i.lorinstein@lse.ac.uk

Alexander, C. Sr. Lectr.

Dodd, N., BSc Camb., PhD Camb. Sr. Lectr.

Foster, J., BSc PhD Sr. Lectr.

Franklin, S. Prof.

Frisby, D. Prof.

Gilroy, P. Anthony Giddens Prof., Social Theory

Hobbs, D., PhD Lond., PhD Sur. Prof.; Head*

Humphrey, N., PhD Camb. Prof.

Husbands, C. T., BA(Econ) Manc., MA Chic., PhD Chic. Reader

Hutter, B., BA Oxf., DPhil Oxf. Peacock Prof., Risk Management

McGovern, O., BSocSc N.U.I., MBS N.U.I., DPhil Oxf. Sr. Lectr.

Rock, P. E., BSc(Soc) Lond., DPhil Oxf. Prof.

Rose, N., BA Sus., MSc Sus., DPhil Sus. Prof.; Convener*

Slater, D. R., BA Camb., PhD Camb. Reader

Tavernor, R. Prof.

Other Staff: 5 Lectrs.; 6 Res. Officers

Research: criminology, deviance and regulation; modern Darwinism and psychoanalysis; politics, ethnicity and racism; religion and contemporary cults; sex and gender

Statistics

Tel: (020) 7955 7731 Fax: (020) 7955 7416
E-mail: (Departmental Administrator) l.s.watkin@lse.ac.uk

Dassios, A., BA Camb., MSc Lond., PhD Lond. Reader

Knott, M., BSc(Econ) Lond., PhD Lond. Sr. Lectr.

Norberg, R., CandAct Oslo, CandReal Oslo, DrPhil Oslo Prof.

Skrondal, A. Prof.

Smith, L. A., BS Flor., MA Col., MPhil Col., PhD Col. Reader

Tong, H., BSc Manc., MSc Manc., PhD Manc. Prof.

Wynn, H., BSc Lond., MA Lond., PhD Lond. Prof.

Yao, Q., BSc Southeast(Nanjing), MSc Southeast(Nanjing), PhD Wuhan Prof.; Head*

Other Staff: 8 Lectrs.; 2 Res. Officers

Research: latent variable modelling and time series; regression diagnostics and optimal experimental design; robustness; survey sampling; use of computers in stochastic modelling and simulation

SPECIAL CENTRES, ETC

Asia Research Centre

Tel: (020) 7955 7583 Fax: (020) 7955 7591
E-mail: arc@lse.ac.uk

Harriss, J. C., MA Camb., PhD E.Anglia Prof.; Dir.*

Hussain, S. A., BA Karachi, MA Karachi, BPhil Oxf., BLitt Oxf. Deputy Dir.

Research: collaborative research by Asia experts covering the regions from South and South East to East Asia

Business History Unit

Tel: (020) 7955 7109 Fax: (020) 7955 6861
E-mail: (Administrative Assistant) s.copeland@lse.ac.uk

Gourvish, T. R., BA Lond., PhD Lond., FRHistS Dir.*

Other Staff: 1 Res. Officer

Research: banking projects; genesis of business leaders; international bibliography of business history; multi-national corporations; pharmaceutical, chocolate and brewing industrial history

Civil Society, Centre for

Tel: (020) 7955 7205, 7955 7375 Fax: (020) 7955 6039
E-mail: (Centre Administrator) i.j.schieman@lse.ac.uk

Howell, J. A. Prof.; Dir.*

Other Staff: 3 Lectrs.; 1 Res. Officer

Research: contributions of community organisations; governing bodies in local voluntary agencies; improving effectiveness of small voluntary agencies; international comparisons of issues facing non-governmental organisations (NGOs); organisational issues in religious congregations

Criminology, Mannheim Centre for

Tel: (020) 7955 7344
E-mail: d.downes@lse.ac.uk
Downes, D. M., BA Oxf., PhD Lond.   Prof.;
Dir.*
Other Staff: 1 Res. Officer
Research: comparative sentencing and penal
policy in Britain and the Netherlands; crime
and employment; criminal justice process
and policy; theories of crime and
delinquency

Development Studies Institute (DESTIN)

Tel: (020) 7955 7424 Fax: (020) 7955 6844
E-mail: (Departmental Administrator)
s.davies@lse.ac.uk
Allen, T., BA Lanc., MA Manc., PhD Manc.
Reader
Barnett, Tony, BA Hull, MA(Econ) Manc., PhD
Manc.   ESRC Prof. Res. Fellow
Beall, J. D., BA Natal, MA Natal, PhD Lond.
Reader; Head*
Dyson, T. P. G., BSc Lond., MSc Lond.   Vice-
President; Prof.
Francis, E., BA Oxf., MSc Lond., DPhil Oxf.   Sr.
Lectr.
Kaldor, Mary H., CBE, BA Oxf., MA Oxf.
Prof., Global Governance
Keen, D., BA Camb., DPhil Oxf., MSc   Reader,
Complex Emergencies (on leave)
Putzel, J., BA McG., MA McG., DPhil Oxf.
Reader
Saith, A., BA Delhi, MA Delhi, PhD Camb.   Prof.
Wade, R., BA Well., DPhil Sus.   Prof., Politics
of Development
Weinhold, D., BSc Wis., PhD Calif.   Sr. Lectr.
Other Staff: 3 Lectrs.; 1 Sr. Visiting Res.
Fellow; 1 Res. Fellow; 3 Tutorial Fellows
Research: policy-related development studies

Discrete and Applicable Mathematics, Centre for

Tel: (020) 7955 7732 Fax: (020) 7955 6877
E-mail: (Administrator) d.scott1@lse.ac.uk
Brightwell, G., BA Camb., PhD Camb.   Dir.*
Research: artificial neural networks; complexity
theory; discrete probabilistic analysis;
mathematics in finance; theory of economic
forecasting

Economic and Related Disciplines, Suntory and Toyota International Centres for (STICERD)

Tel: (020) 7955 6699 Fax: (020) 7242 2357
E-mail: (Departmental Administrator)
a.swain@lse.ac.uk
Besley, T., BA Oxf., MA Oxf., MPhil Oxf., DPhil
Oxf., FBA   Prof.; Dir.*
Other Staff: 6 Res. Officers
Research: analysis of social exclusion;
distributional analysis; economic
organisation and public policy; economics
of industry; Japanese studies

Economic Performance, Centre for (CEP)

Tel: (020) 7955 7596 Fax: (020) 7955 6848
E-mail: (Administrators) g.lodge@lse.ac.uk,
m.o'brien@lse.ac.uk
Freeman, R. B., BA Harv., PhD Harv.   Prof.
Layard, P. R. G., BA Camb., MSc(Econ) Lond.
Prof.
Metcalf, D., MA Manc., PhD Lond.   Prof.
Van Reenan, J., BA Camb., MSc(Econ) Lond.,
PhD Lond.   Prof.; Dir.*
Other Staff: 6 Res. Officers
Research: global economies; labour markets;
national economy

Economics and Finance in South Africa, Centre for Research into (CREFSA)

Tel: (020) 7955 7280 Fax: (020) 7955 6954
E-mail: crefsa@lse.ac.uk
Leape, Prof. J. I., AB Harv., BA Oxf., PhD Harv.
Dir.*
Other Staff: 1 Res. Officer

Research: foreign exchange policy;
macroeconomic and financial issues in South
Africa; regional economic integration in
Development Community; role of
international finance in South Africa;
structure of South African financial system

Educational Research, Centre for

Tel: (020) 7955 7809 Fax: (020) 7955 7733
E-mail: (Office Manager) j.wilkes@lse.ac.uk
West, A., BA Lond., PhD Lond.   Dir.*
Other Staff: 3 Res. Officers
Research: curricula and examinations in Europe;
educational reforms; European and
international issues; European education and
training indicators; funding of education
and schools admissions

European Institute

Tel: (020) 7955 6780 Fax: (020) 7955 7546
E-mail: (Departmental Administrator)
n.hume@lse.ac.uk
Balfour, S., BA Trinity(Dub.), MA Lond., PhD Lond.
Reader, Contemporary Spanish Studies
Barr, N., MSc(Econ) Calif., PhD Calif., FRSA
Prof.
Chalmers, D., BA Oxf.   Reader
Economides, S., BSocSc Birm., MSc PhD   Sr.
Lectr.
Featherstone, K., BA Essex, MA Essex, PhD Manc.
Eleftherios Venizelos Prof.
Hancké, B., Lic Brussels, PhD M.I.T.   Reader
Leonardi, R., BA Calif., MA Johns H., PhD Ill.
Jean Monnet Sr. Lectr.
Preston, P., MA Oxf., MA Reading, DPhil Oxf.,
FRHistS   Prof.; Chairman*
Sasse, G., PhD   Sr. Lectr.
Other Staff: 6 Lectrs.; 1 Teaching Fellow
Research: contemporary Greek studies;
contemporary Spanish studies; economic
and social cohesion laboratory; ethnicity and
nationalism; forum for European philosophy

Financial Markets Group

Tel: (020) 7955 7891 Fax: (020) 7852 3580
E-mail: fmg@lse.ac.uk
Webb, D. C., BA Manc., MA Manc., PhD Lond.
Prof.; Dir.*
Other Staff: 17 Sr. Res. Assts.
Research: corporate finance; efficiency of
financial markets/asset pricing; market
microstructure; regulation of financial
markets; sources of shocks to the economy

Gender Institute

Tel: (020) 7955 7602 Fax: (020) 7955 6408
E-mail: (Centre Administrator)
h.johnstone@lse.ac.uk
Perrons, D. C., BSc Brist., MSc Westminster, MSc
Brighton, PhD Brist.   Sr. Lectr.; Dir.*
Phillips, A., BSc Brist., MSc City(UK), PhD
City(UK)   Sr. Lectr./Prof.
Other Staff: 2 Lectrs.; 4 Res. Fellows; 2
Tutorial Fellows
Research: analysis of gender in social sciences;
gender, violence and conflict; health and
social capital; households, family and work;
social identities and citizenship

Global Governance, Centre for the Study of

Tel: (020) 7955 7583 Fax: (020) 7955 7591
E-mail: (Centre Administrator)
j.otoadese@lse.ac.uk
Held, D., BSc UMIST, MSc M.I.T., PhD M.I.T.
Graham Wallas Prof., Political Science; Co-
Dir.*
Kaldor, Mary H., CBE, BA Oxf., MA Oxf.
Prof.; Co-Dir.*
Research: global civil society; globalisation and
global governance; human rights;
peacekeeping and humanitarian assistance;
reform of the UN

Greater London Group

Tel: (020) 7955 6522 Fax: (020) 7387 9152
E-mail: lselondon@lse.ac.uk
Travers, A. J., BA Lond.   Dir.*

Research: government and economy of London
and south east England

Information Systems Integrity Group

Tel: (020) 7955 7968
E-mail: (Administrator) e.s.peel@lse.ac.uk
Angell, I. O., BSc Wales, PhD Lond.   Prof.
Backhouse, J. P., BA Exe., MSc Lond., PhD Lond.
Dir.*
Other Staff: 1 Visiting Fellow
Research: analysis of responsibility; management
of information security; management policy
and analysis; risk to computer systems; use
of information in organisations

International Studies, Centre for

Tel: (020) 7955 7683
E-mail: (Administrative Assistant)
p.hodges@lse.ac.uk
Kent, J., MA Aberd., PhD Aberd.   Reader,
International Relations; Chair*

Language Studies Centre

Tel: (020) 7955 7043 Fax: (020) 7955 6847
E-mail: j.heyworth@lse.ac.uk
Byrne, N., MA Oxf.   Dir.*
Coca, M., BA Oviedo, MA   Lang. Co-ordinator
Didiot-Cook, H., MA Brun.   Lang. Co-
ordinator
Hernandez-Martin, L.   Modern Foreign Langs.
Asst. Co-ordinator
Küllman-Lee, A., MA Cologne, MSc   Lang. Co-
ordinator
McGarvey, M., MA Sus., MSc S.Bank   Lang. Co-
ordinator
Sobolev, O., BA Nantes, MSc Leningrad, MA Sus.,
PhD Moscow, DPhil   Lang. Co-ordinator
Research: general and historical linguistics and
stylistics; study of literature from
sociological viewpoint; usage of taught
languages

LSE Health

Tel: (020) 7955 7540 Fax: (020) 7955 6803
E-mail: (Research Administrator)
d.nicolaou@lse.ac.uk
Bevan, G., MA Oxf., MTech Oxf.   Reader
Forder, J., BSc Bath, MSc York(UK)   Deputy Dir.
Gjonca, A., PhD Lond., BSc MSc   Sr. Lectr.
Knapp, M. R. J., BA Sheff., MSc Kent, PhD Kent
Prof.; Dir., PSSRU
Le Grand, J., BA Sus., PhD Penn.   Chairman
McGuire, A., BSc(Econ) H-W, MLitt Aberd., PhD
Aberd.   Prof.
Mossialos, E., BSc Athens, MD Athens, PhD Athens
Brian Abel-Smith Prof., Health Policy; Dir.*
Oliver, A., BA E.Anglia, MSc York(UK)   Deputy
Dir.
Robinson, R.   Prof.
Other Staff: 4 Lectrs.; 5 Res. Fellows; 13 Res.
Officers
Research: comparative health studies; health
economics; health services; health
technology assessment; public health

LSE Housing

Tel: (020) 7955 6872 Fax: (020) 7955 6571
E-mail: (General Secretary) l.lane@lse.ac.uk
Power, A. E., MBE, MA Wis., PhD Lond.   Co-
ordinator*
Other Staff: 5 Res. Officers
Research: development of local housing
companies; European difficult-to-let estates;
methods for improving low-income
communities; problems with urban housing
areas; riots in the 1990s

Methodology Institute

Tel: (020) 7955 7639 Fax: (020) 7955 7005
E-mail: (Institute Administrator) v.grey-
edwards@lse.ac.uk
Bauer, M. W., LicPhil Berne, PhD Lond.   Sr.
Lectr.
Gaskell, G. D., BSc Lond., PhD Lond.   Dir.*
Mulford, M., BA Nebraska, MA N.Y., MSc Oregon,
PhD Oregon   Sr. Lectr.
Other Staff: 5 Lectrs.

Research: cognitive survey laboratory; judgement, decision-making and theory; multilevel modelling of family planning; public understanding of science; quality indicators for qualitative research

Personal Social Services Research Unit

Tel: (020) 7955 6238 Fax: (020) 7955 6131
  E-mail: (Administrator) a.mehta3@lse.ac.uk
Knapp, M. R. J., BA *Sheff.*, MSc *Kent*, PhD *Kent*
  Dir.*
Research: community care; criminal justice services; housing; in-patient health care; the voluntary sector

Philosophy of the Natural and Social Sciences, Centre for the

Tel: (020) 7955 6365 Fax: (020) 7955 6869
  E-mail: philcent@lse.ac.uk
Cartwright, N. L. D., BSc *Pitt.*, PhD *Ill.*   Chair;
  Prof., Philosophy
Cronin, H., BA *Manc.Met.*, MSc *Lond.*, PhD *Lond.*
  Visiting Fellow; Co-Dir.*
Montuschi, E., BA *Pavia*, MPhil *Pavia*, DPhil *Oxf.*
  Deputy Dir.
Redhead, M. G., PhD *Lond.*   Prof.; Co-Dir.*
Other Staff: 1 Staff Member
Research: Darwin at LSE; economics and human values; measurement in physics and economics; the Goldsmith Project; travel and tourism

Population Investigation Committee

Tel: (020) 7955 7666 E-mail: pic@lse.ac.uk
Shepherd, A.   General Secretary
Research: demographic questions

CONTACT OFFICERS

Academic affairs. Academic Registrar: Underwood, S., MA *Oxf.*
Accommodation. Head of Residential Services: Tymms, D. S., BA *N.Lond.*
Admissions (first degree).
  (E-mail: stu.rec@lse.ac.uk)

Admissions (higher degree).
  (E-mail: stu.rec@lse.ac.uk)
Adult/continuing education. Project Administrator: Harrison, J.
Alumni. Director, Alumni Relations: Horton, M., BA *Kent State*, MA *Kent State*
Archives. Archivist: Donnelly, S., BA *Durh.*
Careers. Director (Careers): Sandford, F.
Computing services. Network Manager: Barker, M.
Conferences/corporate hospitality. Conference Manager: Ward, W.
Conferences/corporate hospitality. Events Manager: Revel, A.
Consultancy services. Corporate Relations Director: Lennert, F.
Development/fund-raising. Director of Development and Alumni Relations: Blair., M.
Distance education. Programme Director (External Study): Gosling, R. A., BSc *Lond.*, MSc *Lond.*
Estates and buildings/works and services. Estates Officer: Kudlicki, C.
Examinations. Administrative Officer, Examinations: Aristides, P.
Finance. Finance Officer: Ferguson, M.
General enquiries. Secretary and Director of Administration: Hall, A. N. P., BA
Health services. Health Services Director (St Philips Medical Centre): Niadoo, R. O. M., BSc MB BS DCH
Health services. Convenor, LSE Health Service: Kelt, J., BSc *Edin.*, MB ChB *Edin.*, MPhil *Glas.*
Industrial liaison. Corporate Relations Director: Lennert, F.
International office. Head of Recruitment and Admissions: Baldwin, Catherine
  (E-mail: c.r.baldwin@lse.ac.uk)
Language training for international students. Director of Language Studies: Byrne, N., MA *Oxf.*
Library (chief librarian). Librarian: Sykes, J. M., MA *Glas.*, MLitt *Glas.*

Library (enquiries). Deputy Librarian: Wade, M., BA *Lond.*
Marketing. Head of Public Relations: Annett, D., BA *CNAA*
Personnel/human resources. Head of Personnel: Johns, A., MA *Oxf.*
Public relations. Head of Public Relations: Annett, D., BA *CNAA*
Publications. (Academic) Head of Academic Publishing: Friedgood, B. S., BA *Lond.*, MA *Lond.*
Purchasing. Purchasing Manager: Newson, M., BA
Quality assurance and accreditation. Teaching Quality Assurance Consultant: Husbands, C. T., BA(Econ) *Manc.*, MA *Chic.*, PhD *Chic.*
Research. Corporate Relations Director: Lennert, F.
Scholarships, awards, loans. Senior Administrator (Scholarships. Awards, Loans): Zalega, D.
Schools liaison. Head of Recruitment and Admissions: Baldwin, Catherine
  (E-mail: stu.rec@lse.ac.uk)
Security. House Manager: Taffs, B. N.
Sport and recreation. Head of Residential Services: Tymms, D. S., BA *N.Lond.*
Staff development and training. Head of Staff Development Unit: Connelley, C.
Strategic planning. Executive Officer: Barclay, G.
Student welfare/counselling. Student Counsellor: Shorrock, A.
Students from other countries. Head of Recruitment and Admissions: Baldwin, Catherine
Students with disabilities. Disabilities Adviser: Jameson, J.

[Information supplied by the institution as at 17 September 2007, and edited by the ACU]

LONDON SCHOOL OF HYGIENE AND TROPICAL MEDICINE

Founded 1899

Postal Address: Keppel Street, London, England WC1E 7HT
Telephone: (020) 7636 8636 **Fax:** (020) 7436 5389
URL: http://www.lshtm.ac.uk

DIRECTOR*—Haines, Prof. Sir Andrew, MB BS MD, FRCP, FRCGP, FFPH, FMedSci
SECRETARY AND REGISTRAR‡—Surridge, Wendy S., BA *Reading*, MA *Lond.*
DEPUTY SECRETARY (PLANNING AND RESOURCES)—Benson, Richard, BA *Oxf.*
DEAN OF STUDIES—Huttly, Sharon R. A., BSc *Exe.*, MSc *Reading*, MA *Lond.*
HEAD OF DEPARTMENT OF EPIDEMIOLOGY AND POPULATION HEALTH—Rodrigues, Prof. Laura, MSc PhD
HEAD OF DEPARTMENT OF INFECTIOUS AND TROPICAL DISEASES—Croft, Prof. S. L., BSc *Durh.*, PhD *Liv.*
HEAD OF DEPARTMENT OF PUBLIC HEALTH AND POLICY—Mills, Prof. Anne J., CBE, MA *Oxf.*, PhD

GENERAL INFORMATION

History. The school was originally established as the London School of Tropical Medicine in 1899. An institute of state medicine to be called the School of Hygiene was recommended in 1921 and a united school was established in 1924 and opened in 1929.
  The school is located in central London.

Higher Degrees (see also University of London Directory to Subjects of Study).
  Master's. MPhil, MSc.
  Admission. Applicants for admission to higher degree courses should hold a first degree with at least second class honours from a UK university, or an overseas qualification of an equivalent standard in an appropriate subject, or another appropriate qualification (eg

registrable qualification in medicine, dentistry or veterinary studies; master's degree; other professional qualification). Applicants whose first language is not English or whose university studies were not conducted in English will be required to take an approved English language test.
  Length of course. Full-time: MSc: 1 year; MPhil: 3 years. Part-time: MSc: 2 years; MPhil: 6 years.
  By distance learning: MSc: 2–5 years.
  Doctoral. DrPH, PhD.
  Length of course. Full-time: DrPH, PhD: 3 years.
  Part-time: DrPH: 4 years; PhD: 6 years.

Libraries. Volumes: 74,000. Periodicals subscribed to: 763. Special collections: international public health; tropical medicine; Sir Patrick Manson (archives); Sir Ronald Ross (archives).

Academic Year (2007–2008). Three terms: 24 September–14 December; 7 January–20 March; 21 April–19 September. Calendar year courses terminate on 19 September 2008.

Income (2006–2007). Total, £67,297,000.

Statistics. Staff (2006–2007): 849 (464 academic, 385 non-academic). Students (2006–2007): full-time 575; part-time 245; international 381; distance education/external 1922; master's 575; doctoral 338.

ACADEMIC UNITS

Epidemiology and Population Health

Tel: (020) 7927 2482 Fax: (020) 7436 4230
  E-mail: diana.harte@lshtm.ac.uk
Alexander, N. D. E., BA PhD   Reader
Altman, D. G., BSc DSc   Hon. Prof.

Ashworth-Hill, A., BSc PhD   Emer. Prof., Community Nutrition
Bartlett, C. L. R., MB BS MSc   Hon. Prof.
Beral, V., MB BS MD, FRCP, FRCOG, FFPH, FMedSci   Hon. Prof.
Brown, D. W. G., MB BS MSc, FRCPath   Hon. Prof.
Campbell, Oona M. R., BS Beirut, MSc Johns H., PhD Johns H.   Prof., Epidemiology and Reproductive Health
Carpenter, J. R., BSc MSc DPhil   Sr. Lectr.
Carpenter, R. G., MA PhD   Hon. Prof.
Cheung, Y., PhD   Sr. Lectr.
Clarke, L., BSc MSc   Sr. Lectr.
Clayton, T., BSc MSc   Sr. Lectr.
Cleland, J. G., MA Camb.   Prof., Medical Demography
Coleman, M. P., BA Oxf., BM BCh Oxf., MSc Lond.   Prof., Epidemiology and Vital Statistics
Cook, L. W., BA   Hon. Prof.
Cousens, S. N., MA Camb.   Prof., Epidemiology and Medical Statistics
Crampin, A. C., MB ChB MSc   Sr. Lectr.
Cutts, F., MB ChB MSc MD, FFPH   Hon. Prof.
Dangour, A. D., MSc PhD   Sr. Lectr.
Darbyshire, J., OBE, MB ChB MSc, FRCP   Hon. Prof.
Davey Smith, G., MA MSc MD   Hon. Prof.
DeStavola, B. L., MSc PhD   Reader
dos Santos Silva, Isobel M., MD Lisbon, MSc   Prof., Epidemiology
Doyle, Patricia E., BSc Sur., MSc PhD   Prof.
Dunnell, K., BSc MA   Hon. Prof.
Ebrahim, S., BM BS MSc DM, FRCP, FFPH   Prof., Public Health
Edmond, K. M., MB BS MSc PhD, FRCPCH, FAFPHM   Sr. Lectr.
Edwards, P. J., BSc PhD   Sr. Lectr.
Elbourne, D., BSc Lond., MSc Lond., PhD Lond.   Prof., Health Care Evaluation
Evans, S. J., BA Keele, MSc Lond.   Prof. Fellow
Fielding, K. L., BSc MSc PhD   Sr. Lectr.
Filippi, V., PhD   Sr. Lectr.
Filteau, S., BSc MSc PhD   Prof., International Nutrition
Fine, P. E. M., AB Prin., MSc Penn., PhD Penn., VMD Penn.   Prof., Communicable Diseases Epidemiology
Fletcher, Astrid E., BA Newcastle(UK), PhD   Prof., Epidemiology and Ageing
Fox, A. J., BSc PhD   Hon. Prof.
French, N., PhD   Reader (based in Malawi)
Frost, C. D., BA MA   Reader
Ghani, A., MA MSc PhD   Reader
Gill, O. P. N., MB BCh BAO MSc DCH, FFPH   Hon. Prof.
Glynn, J., BM BCh MA MSc PhD   Reader
Goldblatt, P., BSc MSc PhD   Hon. Prof.
Goldstein, H., BSc   Hon. Prof.
Grosskurth, H., MD PhD   Prof., Epidemiology and International Health
Grundy, E. M. D., MA MSc PhD   Prof., Demographic Gerontology
Hargreaves, J., BSc MSc PhD   Sr. Lectr.
Harpham, T., BA PhD   Hon. Prof.
Hayes, R. J., MSc Edin.   Prof., Epidemiology and International Health
Higgins, C. D., BSc MSc   Sr. Lectr.
Huttly, Sharon R. A., BSc Exe., MSc Reading, MA Lond.   Reader
Jaffar, S., MSc PhD   Reader
James, P., BSc MB BS, FRCP, FRCPEd, FRSEd, FRSA, FRCGP   Hon. Prof.
Johnson, A. M., MA Camb., BA MB BS MSc MD   Hon. Prof.
Jones, B., BSc MSc PhD   Hon. Prof.
Kapiga, S., MD MPH ScD   Sr. Lectr.
Kenward, M. G., BSc MSc PhD   SmithKline Beecham Prof., Biostatistics
Kirkwood, B. R., MA Camb., MSc   Prof., Epidemiology and International Health
Kleinschmidt, I., BSc MSc PhD   Sr. Lectr.
Lanata, C., MD MPP   Hon. Prof.
Leon, D., BA Camb., PhD   Prof., Epidemiology
Lilford, R. J., PhD, FRCOG, FRCO   Hon. Prof.
Maconochie, N. E. S., BA MSc PhD   Sr. Lectr.
Mangtani, P., BSc MB BS MSc MD   Sr. Lectr.

Marshall, T. F. de C., BA Camb., MSc Essex   Sr. Lectr.
Massad, E., BSc MD   Hon. Prof.
Mayhew, S., BA MA PhD   Sr. Lectr.
McKeigue, P., MA MB BChir MSc PhD   Hon. Prof.
McPherson, K., MA Camb., PhD   Hon. Prof.
Meade, T. W., CBE, DM, FRS, FRCP   Emer. Prof.
Metz, D., BSc Lond., MSc Lond., PhD Lond.   Hon. Prof.
Miller, E., BSc MB BS   Hon. Prof.
Milligan, P., BSc MSc PhD   Reader
Moller, H., BA BSc MSc DM, FFPH   Prof., Cancer Epidemiology
Morison, L. A., BSc MA   Sr. Lectr.
Mulholland, K.   Prof., Infectious Disease Epidemiology
Nicoll, A. G., MB ChB MA MSc   Hon. Prof.
Noah, N. D., MB BS, FRCP   Emer. Prof., Public Health
Nunn, A. J., BSc MSc   Hon. Prof.
Patel, V., MB BS MSc PhD   Prof., International Mental Health
Peto, J.   Prof., Cancer Epidemiology
Pfeiffer, D. U., DrMedVet Giessen, PhD Giessen   Hon. Prof.
Pocock, S. J., BA Camb., MSc PhD   Prof., Medical Statistics
Prentice, A. M., BSc PhD   Prof., International Nutrition
Rachet, B., MD PhD   Sr. Lectr.
Roberts, I. G., MB BCh PhD   Prof., Epidemiology and Public Health
Rodrigues, Laura, MSc PhD   Prof., Infectious Disease Epidemiology; Head*
Roman, E., BSc PhD   Hon. Prof.
Ronsmans, C., MD DPH   Reader
Ross, D. A., MB BCh Wales, MA Wales, MSc Oxf.   Prof., Epidemiology and International Public Health
Sasieni, P. D., BA MS PhD   Hon. Prof.
Schellenberg, D. M., BSc MB BS PhD   Prof., Malaria and International Health
Serjeant, G. R., BA MB BChir MA MD, FRCP   Hon. Prof.
Simpson, D., OBE   Hon. Prof.
Smeeth, L., MB ChB MSc DCH PhD   Prof., Clinical Epidemiology
Swerdlow, A. J., MA Camb., PhD Glas., DM Oxf.   Hon. Prof.
Thomas, S. M., MB BS MSc   Sr. Lectr.
Timaeus, I., MA Camb., MSc(Econ) PhD   Prof., Demography
Todd, J. E., BA MSc   Sr. Lectr.
Uauy, R., MD PhD   Prof., Public Health Nutrition
Victora, C. G., PhD Lond.   Hon. Prof.
Wang, D., BA MSc PhD   Sr. Lectr.
Waterlow, J., MD ScD, FRS, FRCP   Emer. Prof., Human Nutrition
Weiss, H. A., BSc MSc DPhil   Sr. Lectr.
Whittaker, J. C., BSc PhD   Prof., Genetic Epidemiology and Statistics
Wilesmith, J. W., BA MSc   Hon. Prof.
Zaba, B. W., BSc Lond., MSc Lond.   Reader
Other Staff: 46 Lectrs.; 56 Res. Fellows

Infectious and Tropical Diseases

Tel: (020) 7927 2637 Fax: (020) 7637 4314
E-mail: helen.edwards@lshtm.ac.uk
Ackers, J. P., MA Oxf., MSc Lond., DPhil Oxf.   Emer. Prof., Postgraduate Education in Public Health
Addington, W. W., MD MPH, FRCP   Hon. Prof.
Aunger, R., PhD   Sr. Lectr.
Bailey, R., BA Oxf., BM S'ton., PhD Lond.   Prof., Tropical Medicine
Baker, D. A., PhD   Reader
Bancroft, G. J., BSc W.Aust., PhD   Reader
Behrens, R. H., BSc MB ChB MD, FRCP   Sr. Lectr.
Bickle, Q. D., BA Oxf., MSc PhD   Reader
Bloomfield, S., BPharm PhD   Hon. Prof.
Borriello, S. P., BSc PhD   Hon. Prof.

Bradley, D. J., MB BChir Camb., MA Camb., DM Oxf., FIBiol, FRCPath, FRCP   Emer. Prof., Tropical Hygiene
Brooker, S. J., BA DPhil   Reader
Brown, M., BA BM BCh PhD   Sr. Lectr.
Brugha, R. F., MB MSc MD   Hon. Prof.
Bryceson, D. D. M., BA MD, FRCP   Emer. Prof., Medical Entomology
Butterworth, A. E., BA MB BCh MA PhD   Hon. Prof.
Cairncross, A. M., MA Camb., PhD   Prof., Environmental Health
Chandaramohan, D., MB BS MSc PhD   Reader
Chiodini, P., BSc MB BS PhD, FRCP   Hon. Prof.
Clark, C. G., BSc PhD   Reader
Clements, A. N., BSc PhD   Emer. Prof., Medical Entomology
Conway, D. J., BSc PhD   Reader
Cookson, B., BDS MB BS MSc, FRCPath   Hon. Prof.
Corbett, E. L., BA MB BChir PhD   Reader
Crawford, D., MB BS MD DSc PhD, FRCPath   Hon. Prof.
Croft, S. L., BSc Durh., PhD Liv.   Prof., Parasitology; Head*
Curtis, C. F., BA PhD   Emer. Prof., Medical Entomology
Curtis, V. A., BEng MSc PhD   Sr. Lectr.
Davies, C. R., MA MSc DPhil   Reader
De Cock, K. M., MD Brist.   Hon. Prof.
Dessens, J., MSc PhD   Sr. Lectr.
Dockrell, Hazel M., BA Trinity(Dub.), PhD   Prof., Immunology
Doherty, T. F., MB ChB MD   Sr. Lectr.
Dorrell, N., BPharm PhD   Sr. Lectr.
Dougan, G., BSc DPhil   Hon. Prof.
Drakeley, C. J., MBiol PhD   Sr. Lectr.
Drasar, B., BSc PhD DSc, FRCPath   Emer. Prof., Bacteriology
Elliott, A., BA Camb., MB BS Lond., MA Camb., PhD Camb.   Reader
Farrar, J.   Hon. Prof.
Foster, A., OBE, MD Birm.   Prof., International Eye Health
Gilbert, C., MB ChB MSc MD, FRCO   Reader
Godfrey-Faussett, P., BA Oxf., MB BS   Prof., Infectious Diseases and International Health
Gompels, U. A., BA Rutgers, MSc Chic., PhD Camb.   Reader
Grant, A., MSc   Reader
Greenwood, B. M., BA Lond., MB Lond., MA Lond.   Manson Prof., Clinical Tropical Medicine
Gudlavalleti, M. V. S., MD MSc   Sr. Lectr.
Harries, A. D., BA MB BChir MA MD, FRCP   Hon. Prof.
Hasan, R., BSc MB BS MSc PhD, FRCPath   Hon. Prof.
Hawkes, S. J., BSc MB BS PhD   Sr. Lectr.
Hay, R., BA BM BCh, FRCP   Hon. Prof.
Hill, D. R., BA MD   Hon. Prof.
Holland, M. J., BSc MSc PhD   Sr. Lectr.
Horn, D., BSc PhD   Sr. Lectr.
Horton, R. C., BSc MB ChB, FRCP   Hon. Prof.
Hussain, R., BSc MSc PhD, FRCPath   Hon. Prof.
Johnson, G. J., MB BChir MA MD, FRCO, FRCS   Hon. Prof.
Karlyshev, A., BSc MA PhD   Sr. Lectr.
Kelly, J. M., BSc Glas., PhD   Prof., Molecular Biology
Kuper, H. E., BA PhD ScD   Sr. Lectr.
Lawn, S. D., BMedSci MB BS MD   Reader
Lines, J. D., BSC MSc PhD   Reader
Lockwood, D. N. J., BSc Birm., MB ChB Birm.   Prof., Tropical Medicine
Mabey, D. C. W., BM BCh Oxf., MA   Prof., Communicable Diseases
Mayaud, P., MD   Reader
McAdam, K. P. W. J., MB BChir Camb., MA Camb., FRCP   Emer. Prof., Clinical Tropical Medicine
McNerney, R., PhD   Sr. Lectr.
Miles, M. A., PhD DSc   Prof., Medical Protozoology
Miller, R., MB BS, FRCP   Hon. Prof.

Parry, E. H. O., OBE, MD, FRCPath, FWACP   Hon. Prof.

Peters, W., MD DSc, FRCP   Hon. Prof., Medical Protozoology

Porter, J. D. H., MB BS MPH   Prof., International Health

Raynes, J. G., BSc PhD   Sr. Lectr.

Reyburn, H., MB BS MSc   Sr. Lectr.

Ribeiro, J., MD PhD   Hon. Prof.

Riley, E. M., BVSc BSc PhD   Prof., Infectious Disease Immunology

Roberts, C., BSc Liv., MD Liv.   Hon. Prof.

Roper, C., BSc PhD   Sr. Lectr.

Rowland, M., BSc MSc PhD   Reader

Roy, P., MSc PhD   Prof., Virology

Schaible, U. E., BSc PhD   Prof., Immunology

Schellenberg, D. M., BSc MB BS PhD   Prof., Malaria and International Health

Schellenberg, J. R., BA MSc PhD   Reader

Spratt, B. G., BSc PhD   Hon. Prof.

Staedke, S. G., BS MD   Sr. Lectr.

Steward, M. W., PhD Leeds, DSc, FRCPath   Emer. Prof., Immunology

Sutherland, C. J., BSc MPH PhD   Sr. Lectr.

Targett, G. A. T., BSc Nott., PhD DSc   Emer. Prof., Immunology of Protozoal Diseases

Taylor, Martin G., BSc Brist., MSc Brun., PhD DSc   Emer. Prof., Medical Helminthology

Titball, R. W., BSc PhD   Hon. Prof.

Tomkins, A., MB BS, FRCP, FRCPCH   Hon. Prof.

Varma, M. G. R., BSc PhD DSc, FIBiol   Emer. Prof., Medical Protozoology

Von Seidlein, L., MB BCh MSc PhD   Sr. Lectr.

Warhurst, D. C., BSc Leic., PhD Leic., DSc Lond., FRCPath   Emer. Prof., Protozoan Chemotherapy

Watson-Jones, D., BA BM BCh MSc   Sr. Lectr.

Weiss, R. A., BSc PhD, FRCPath   Hon. Prof.

Wellems, T., BSc MD PhD   Hon. Prof.

Whittle, H. C., BSc MB BS, FRCP   Hon. Prof.

Whitty, C. J. M., BA BM BCh MSc   Prof., International Health

Wren, B. W., BSc PhD   Prof., Microbial Pathogenesis

Zambon, M., BSc BM BCh PhD, FRCPath   Hon. Prof.

Other Staff: 34 Lectrs.; 52 Res. Fellows

Public Health and Policy

Tel: (020) 7927 2432 Fax: (020) 7436 3611   E-mail: wendy.knowles@lshtm.ac.uk

Acharya, A., BA MSc PhD   Sr. Lectr.

Anderson, S. C., BSc MA PhD   Sr. Lectr.; Assoc. Dean of Studies

Anionwu, E. N., CBE, PhD   Hon. Prof.

Armstrong, B., BSc Lond., MSc Lond., PhD Lond.   Reader

Berridge, V. S., BA PhD, FRHistS   Prof., History

Black, N. A., MD Birm.   Prof., Health Services Research

Bonell, C., PhD   Sr. Lectr.

Browne, J. P., BA PhD   Sr. Lectr.

Cairns, J., MA CNAA, MPhil CNAA, DMS CNAA   Prof., Health Economics

Coker, R., MB BS MSc MD, FRCP   Reader

Cookson, B., BS MA MPH PhD   Hon. Prof.

Crisp, Lord N.   Hon. Prof.

Dowie, J. A., BA MA PhD   Emer. Prof., Health Impact Analysis

Edwards, N., BA MBA   Hon. Prof.

Fletcher, A. C., MA Camb., MSc Aston, PhD Aston   Sr. Lectr.

Fulop, N. J., PhD   Hon. Prof.

Geissler, W. P., MSc MPhil PhD   Sr. Lectr.

Gilmore, A. B., MB BS MSc, FFPH   Sr. Lectr.

Gilson, L. J., BA Oxf., MA E.Anglia, PhD Lond.   Prof., Health Policy and Systems

Glasier, A., BSc MB ChB MD, FRCOG   Hon. Prof.

Gorsky, M., MBA PhD   Sr. Lectr.

Green, J. M., BSc MSc PhD   Reader

Hamlin, C. S., BA MA PhD   Hon. Prof.

Hanson, K. G., BA MPhil PhD SD   Sr. Lectr.

Kessel, A., BSc MB BS MPhil MSc PhD   Hon. Prof.

Klein, R., CBE, MA PhD   Hon. Prof.

Koh, Y. M., MB BS MBA MSc DCH   Hon. Prof.

Kumaranayake, L., BA MA PhD   Sr. Lectr.

Lamping, Donna L., BA Harv., PhD Harv.   Reader

Lee, K., BA MPA MA DPhil   Reader

Lewin, S., BSc(Med) MSc MB ChB   Sr. Lectr.

Macgregor, S., MA PhD, FRSA   Emer. Prof., Social Policy

Mackenbach, J., MD PhD   Hon. Prof.

Mays, N. B., BA Oxf.   Prof., Health Policy

McKee, C. M., CBE, MB BCh BAO Belf., MD Belf., MSc   Prof., European Public Health

McPake, B., BA PhD   Hon. Prof.

Mills, Anne J., CBE, BA Oxf., PhD   Prof., Health Economics and Policy; Head*

Morris, J., CBE, MA MD DSc DPH, FFPH, FRCP   Emer. Prof.

Morris, Sir Peter, MB BS MA PhD DSc, FRCS, FACS, FRS, FAMS, FRCP, FMedSci   Hon. Prof.

Nanchahal, Kiran, BA MSc   Sr. Lectr.

Nolte, E., MPH PhD   Sr. Lectr.

Normand, C., BA DPhil, FFPH   Hon. Prof.

Peckham, S., BSc MA(Econ)   Sr. Lectr.

Petticrew, M., BA PhD   Prof., Public Health Evaluation

Pool, R., BA MA PhD   Sr. Lectr.

Rafferty, A. M., BSc Edin., MPhil Nott., DPhil Oxf.   Hon. Prof.

Reeves, B. C., MSc DPhil   Hon. Prof.

Rhodes, T., BSc MSc PhD   Prof., Public Health Sociology

Roberts, J. A., MSc PhD   Emer. Prof.

Sanders, D. M., MB ChB   Hon. Prof.

Sanderson, C. F. B., MA Oxf., MSc Camb., PhD Camb.   Reader

Simpson, D., OBE   Hon. Prof.

Smith, R. D., BA MSc PhD   Prof., Health Systems Economics

Smith, R. S. W., BSc Edin.   Hon. Prof.

Sondorp, E., MD MPH   Sr. Lectr.

Stephens, C., MSc PhD   Sr. Lectr.

Stimson, G. V., BSc MSc PhD   Hon. Prof.

Tennison, B. R., MB BChir MA MSc PhD, FIMA, FFPH   Hon. Prof.

Thom, B., BSc MA PhD   Hon. Prof.

Thorogood, N., BA PhD   Sr. Lectr.

Townsend, J. L., BSc MSc PhD   Emer. Prof.

Troop, P., CBE, MA Camb., MB ChB MSc   Hon. Prof.

van der Meulen, J. H. P., PhD   Reader

Vaughan, J. P., CBE, MD, FRCPEd   Emer. Prof., Health Care Epidemiology

Walt, Gill, BSc PhD   Emer. Prof., International Health Policy

Watts, C., BA MSc PhD   Prof., Gender Violence and Health

Wellings, K., BA Lond., MA Lond., MSc Lond.   Prof., Sexual and Reproductive Health

Wilkinson, P., MSc   Reader

Wiseman, V., BSc MPhil   Sr. Lectr.

Other Staff: 46 Lectrs.; 45 Res. Fellows

CONTACT OFFICERS

Academic affairs. Director: Haines, Prof. Sir Andrew, MB BS MD, FRCP, FRCGP, FFPH, FMedSci (E-mail: andy.haines@lshtm.ac.uk)

Admissions (higher degree). Deputy Registrar: Shanley, Paul (E-mail: paul.shanley@lshtm.ac.uk)

General enquiries. Secretary and Registrar: Surridge, Wendy S., BA Reading, MA Lond. (E-mail: wendy.surridge@lshtm.ac.uk)

Library (chief librarian). Head of Library Services: Lloyd, C., BA MA MCLIP (E-mail: caroline.lloyd@lshtm.ac.uk)

Research. Deputy Director (Research): Dockrell, Prof. Hazel M., BA Trinity(Dub.), PhD

Scholarships, awards, loans. Deputy Registrar: Shanley, Paul

Students from other countries. Deputy Registrar: Shanley, Paul

[Information supplied by the institution as at 20 February 2008, and edited by the ACU]

QUEEN MARY, UNIVERSITY OF LONDON

Founded 1934

Associate Member of the Association of Commonwealth Universities

Postal Address: Mile End Road, London, England E1 4NS
Telephone: (020) 7975 5555 **Fax:** (020) 7882 3703
URL: http://www.qmul.ac.uk

PRINCIPAL*—Smith, Prof. Adrian F. M., BA Lond., MSc Lond., MA Camb., MA Oxf., PhD Lond., FIMA, FRS, FIP
VICE-PRINCIPAL AND WARDEN OF ST BARTHOLOMEW'S AND THE ROYAL LONDON SCHOOL OF MEDICINE AND
DENTISTRY—Wright, Prof. Sir N. A., MA MD PhD DSc, FRCS, FRCPath, FMedSci
VICE-PRINCIPAL (NHS LIAISON)—Kopelman, Prof. Peter G., MD, FRCP
VICE-PRINCIPAL (SCIENCE AND ENGINEERING)—MacCallum, Prof. M. A. H., MA Camb., PhD Camb., FIP, FRAS
VICE-PRINCIPAL (HUMANITIES AND LAW)—Ogden, Prof. Philip E., BA Durh., DPhil Oxf.
VICE-PRINCIPAL (ACADEMIC POLICY)—Olver, Prof. A. D., BSc Leeds, PhD Leeds, FIEE, FREng
VICE-PRINCIPAL (STRATEGIC DEVELOPMENT)—Williams, Prof. David M., BDS MSc PhD, FRCPath, FDSRCS
ACADEMIC REGISTRAR AND SECRETARY TO COUNCIL‡—Holiday, Peter G., BA Leeds, PhD Leeds
DIRECTOR OF ACADEMIC INFORMATION SERVICES—Murphy, Brian, BA

ROYAL ACADEMY OF MUSIC

Founded 1822

Postal Address: Marylebone Road, London, England NW1 5HT
Telephone: (020) 7873 7373 **Fax:** (020) 7873 7374
URL: http://www.ram.ac.uk

PRINCIPAL*—Freeman-Attwood, Prof. Jonathan, BMus MPhil
VICE-PRINCIPAL AND DIRECTOR OF STUDIES—Freeman-Attwood, Prof. Jonathan, BMus Lond., MPhil Lond.,
Hon. FRAM
DIRECTOR OF FINANCE AND PERSONNEL‡—Whitehouse, Jan, Hon. FRAM

GENERAL INFORMATION

History. The Academy was founded in 1822 and is the second oldest music conservatoire in Europe. It was admitted as a full college of the University of London in 1999.

It is located on the Marylebone Road in central London.

Admission to first degree courses (see also United Kingdom Introduction). Application is based primarily on performance audition where applicants should display professional performing potential. Applicants should also hold two General Certificate of Education (GCE) A level passes, or equivalent, and show competence in English language (minimum International English Language Testing Service (IELTS) 6.5–7).

First Degrees (see also University of London Directory to Subjects of Study). BMus.
Length of course. Full-time: BMus: 4 years.

Higher Degrees (see also University of London Directory to Subjects of Study).
Master's. MMus, MPhil.
Admission. Applicants for admission to higher degrees must normally hold an appropriate first degree and possess a level of performance equivalent to a recognised music diploma. MMus: minimum 7.0 IELTS score.
Length of course. Full-time: MMus: 1–2 years.
Part-time: MPhil: 1–2 years.
Doctoral. PhD.

Libraries. Volumes: 125,000. Special collections: Sir Arthur Sullivan; Sir Henry Wood (orchestral music); English Bach Society; R. J. S. Stevens; David Munrow; Robert Spencer; Foyle Menhuin.

Academic Year (2007–2008). Three terms: 10 September–30 December; 7 January–14 March; 7 April–26 June.

ACADEMIC UNITS
Brass
Tel: (020) 7873 7320 E-mail: brass@ram.ac.uk
Watson, Prof. James, FRAM   Head*

Choral Conducting
Tel: (020) 7873 7405
E-mail: choraldirection@ram.ac.uk
Russill, Patrick, MA, Hon. FRAM   Head*

Classical Accordion
Tel: (020) 7873 7380
E-mail: accordion@ram.ac.uk
Murray, Owen Head*

Composition
Tel: (020) 7873 7379
E-mail: composition@ram.ac.uk
Cashian, Phillip Head*

Conducting
Tel: (020) 7873 7405
E-mail: conducting@ram.ac.uk
Metters, Colin Head*

Guitar
Tel: (020) 7873 7380 E-mail: guitar@ram.ac.uk
Lewin, Michael Head*

Historical Performance
Tel: (020) 7873 7379
E-mail: historical.perf@ram.ac.uk
Cummings, Laurence, MA, FRCO   Head*

Jazz
Tel: (020) 7873 7379 E-mail: jazz@ram.ac.uk
Presencer, Gerard   Head*

Keyboard
Tel: (020) 7873 7405
E-mail: keyboard@ram.ac.uk
Elton, Christopher, FRAM   Prof.; Head*

Musical Theatre
Tel: (020) 7873 7483 E-mail: mth@ram.ac.uk
Hammond, Mary, FRAM   Head*

Organ
Tel: (020) 7873 7405 E-mail: organ@ram.ac.uk
Titterington, David, MA Hon. DMus,
Hon. FRCO   Head*

Strings
Tel: (020) 7873 7395
E-mail: strings@ram.ac.uk
Strange, David, FRAM   Prof.; Head*

Timpani and Percussion
Tel: (020) 7873 7320
E-mail: percussion@ram.ac.uk
Percy, Neil   Head*

Vocal Studies
Tel: (020) 7873 7384 E-mail: voice@ram.ac.uk
Wildman, Mark, FRAM, FRSA   Head*

Woodwind
Tel: (020) 7873 7320
E-mail: woodwind@ram.ac.uk
Bragg, Keith   Head*

CONTACT OFFICERS
Academic affairs. Head of Undergraduate Programmes: Summerly, Jeremy, MA MMus (E-mail: j.summerly@ram.ac.uk)
Accommodation. Estates Manager: Smith, Peter (E-mail: estates@ram.ac.uk)
Admissions (first degree). Admissions Officer: Kemp-Luck, Edward, MA, FRCO (E-mail: registry@ram.ac.uk)
Admissions (higher degree). Admissions Officer: Kemp-Luck, Edward, MA, FRCO (E-mail: registry@ram.ac.uk)
Archives. Librarian: Adamson, Kathryn (E-mail: library@ram.ac.uk)
Computing services. IT Manager: Meaney, Chris (E-mail: c.meaney@ram.ac.uk)
Conferences/corporate hospitality. Estates Manager: Smith, Peter (E-mail: estates@ram.ac.uk)
Credit transfer. Academic Services Officer: Watts, Claire, BA (E-mail: registry@ram.ac.uk)
Development/fund-raising. Director of Development: McCormack, Carol (E-mail: c.mccormack@ram.ac.uk)
Equal opportunities. Director of Finance and Personnel: Whitehouse, Jan, Hon. FRAM
Estates and buildings/works and services. Estates Manager: Smith, Peter (E-mail: estates@ram.ac.uk)
Examinations. Examinations Officer: Moloney, Sharon (E-mail: registry@ram.ac.uk)

Finance. Financial Controller: Cherry, Michael (E-mail: finance@ram.ac.uk)
General enquiries. Estates Manager: Smith, Peter (E-mail: estates@ram.ac.uk)
Health services. Counsellor: Singer, Dani (E-mail: counselling@ram.ac.uk)
Industrial liaison. Director of Finance and Personnel: Whitehouse, Jan, Hon. FRAM (E-mail: j.whitehouse@ram.ac.uk)
International office. Personal Assistant to the Vice-Principal: McKiernan, Kate (E-mail: k.mckiernan@ram.ac.uk)
Language training for international students. Head of English Language Unit: Dormer, Mairin (E-mail: registry@ram.ac.uk)
Library (chief librarian). Librarian: Adamson, Kathryn (E-mail: library@ram.ac.uk)
Library (enquiries). Librarian: Adamson, Kathryn (E-mail: library@ram.ac.uk)
Marketing. Press and Publicity Officer: Craik, Peter (E-mail: publicity@ram.ac.uk)
Minorities/disadvantaged groups. Registrar and Projects Manager: White, Philip, FRAM (E-mail: registry@ram.ac.uk)
Personnel/human resources. Head of Human Resources: Edwards, Juliet (E-mail: j.edwards@ram.ac.uk)
Public relations. Director of Finance and Personnel: Whitehouse, Jan, Hon. FRAM (E-mail: j.whitehouse@ram.ac.uk)
Purchasing. Director of Finance and Personnel: Whitehouse, Jan, Hon. FRAM (E-mail: j.whitehouse@ram.ac.uk)
Quality assurance and accreditation. Academic Secretary: Jury, Catherine (E-mail: c.jury@ram.ac.uk)
Research. Head of Postgraduate Programmes: Glauert, Amanda, MA PhD (E-mail: a.glauert@ram.ac.uk)
Safety. Estates Manager: Smith, Peter (E-mail: estates@ram.ac.uk)
Scholarships, awards, loans. Registrar and Projects Manager: White, Philip, FRAM (E-mail: registry@ram.ac.uk)
Schools liaison. Registrar (Schools Liaison): White, Philip, FRAM (E-mail: registry@ram.ac.uk)
Security. Estates Manager: Smith, Peter (E-mail: estates@ram.ac.uk)
Staff development and training. Head of Human Resources: Edwards, Juliet (E-mail: j.edwards@ram.ac.uk)
Strategic planning. Principal: Price, Prof. Sir Curtis, KBE, AM Harv., PhD Harv., Hon. FRAM, FKC (E-mail: c.price@ram.ac.uk)
Student union. Students' Union President: Holloway-Nahum, Aaron (E-mail: a.holloway-nahum@ram.ac.uk)
Student welfare/counselling. Counsellor: Singer, Dani (E-mail: counselling@ram.ac.uk)
Students from other countries. Overseas Liaison Officer: Biddlecombe, George, MA PhD (E-mail: g.biddlecombe@ram.ac.uk)
Students with disabilities. Counsellor: Singer, Dani (E-mail: counselling@ram.ac.uk)
University press. Press and Publicity Officer: Craik, Peter (E-mail: p.craik@ram.ac.uk)

[*Information supplied by the institution as at 3 September 2007, and edited by the ACU*]

ROYAL HOLLOWAY, UNIVERSITY OF LONDON

Founded 1886

Postal Address: Egham, Surrey, England TW20 0EX
Telephone: (01784) 434455 **Fax:** (01784) 437520
URL: http://www.rhul.ac.uk

PRINCIPAL*—Hill, Prof. Stephen R., BA Oxf., MSc Lond., PhD Lond.
VICE-PRINCIPAL (ACADEMIC AFFAIRS)—Kemp, Prof. Rob A., BSc Reading, MSc Qu., PhD Lond.
VICE-PRINCIPAL (COMMUNICATION, ENTERPRISE, RESEARCH)—Sweeney, David G., BSc Aberd.
VICE-PRINCIPAL (PLANNING AND RESOURCES)—(vacant)
HEAD OF REGISTRY‡—McGeevor, Philip A., BScEcon Wales, PhD Wales
DIRECTOR OF RESOURCES AND COLLEGE SECRETARY—Ross, J. Jane, BSc S'ton.
DIRECTOR OF FINANCES—Robinson, Graeme, BSc
DIRECTOR OF INFORMATION SERVICES—Gerrard, Sarah, BA Sus., MCLIP Sus.

GENERAL INFORMATION

History. The college was established in 1985 by the merger of Royal Holloway College (founded 1886) and Bedford College (1849). It is located in Egham, Surrey.

Admission to first degree courses (see also United Kingdom Introduction). Through Universities and Colleges Admissions Service (UCAS). Minimum requirements: passes in 2 subjects at General Certificate of Education (GCE) A level or 1 A level and 2 AS levels or equivalent. Equivalent international qualifications are also accepted.

First Degrees (see also University of London Directory to Subjects of Study). BA, BMus, BSc, MSci.
Length of course. Full-time: BA, BMus, BSc: 3 years; MSci: 4 years. Part-time: BA: 6 years.

Higher Degrees (see also University of London Directory to Subjects of Study).
Master's. MA, MBA, MMus, MPhil, MSc, MSc(Econ).
Length of course. Full-time: MA, MBA, MMus, MSc, MSc(Econ): 1 year; MPhil: 2 years. Part-time: MA, MMus, MSc, MSc(Econ): 2 years; MPhil: 4 years.
Doctoral. DClinPsy, PhD.
Length of course. Full-time: DClinPsy, PhD: 3 years. Part-time: PhD: 6 years.

Language of Instruction. English. Pre-sessional English language courses of 4 weeks and 8 weeks are available in July and August prior to the start of a full programme. In-sessional English language courses are available throughout the academic year.

Libraries. Volumes: 538,307. Periodicals subscribed to: 8146. Other holdings: 7460 e-journals subscribed to. Special collections: Coton collection (ballet); early printed books; Gay Sweatshop Theatre Company archives; Half Moon Theatre Company archives; Herringham collection (archives); Dom Anselm Hughes collection (music); institutional archives of Royal Holloway and Bedford Colleges and personal papers of staff associated with them; Sir Alfred Sherman papers; Victorian novels; Busk collection (history of science); Dawson collection; Oliver collection; private press titles; rare books; Sargant Benson botanical collection; south-east Asia geology collection; T. E. Lawrence collection; Tuke Italian collection; women's collection.

Academic Awards (2005–2006). 192 awards ranging in value from £300 to £11,880.

Statistics. Students (2005–2006): full-time 6913 (2884 men, 4029 women); part-time 887 (381 men, 506 women); international 1565 (726 men, 839 women); undergraduate 5723 (2303 men, 3420 women); master's 1178 (516 men, 662 women); doctoral 870 (417 men, 453 women).

FACULTIES/SCHOOLS

Arts
Tel: (01784) 414147 E-mail: m.ross@rhul.ac.uk
Dean: Davies, Máire C., BA Lond.
Secretary: Ross, Maureen

Graduate School
Tel: (01784) 414147 E-mail: m.ross@rhul.ac.uk
Dean: Nichols, Gary J., BSc Lond., PhD Camb.
Secretary: Ross, Maureen

History and Social Sciences
Tel: (01784) 414147 E-mail: m.ross@rhul.ac.uk
Dean: (vacant)
Secretary: Ross, Maureen

Science
Tel: (01784) 414147 E-mail: m.ross@rhul.ac.uk
Dean: Beesley, Philip W., BSc S'ton., PhD S'ton.
Secretary: Ross, Maureen

ACADEMIC UNITS

Biological Sciences, School of
Tel: (01784) 443559 Fax: (01784) 434326
E-mail: j.a.reid@rhul.ac.uk
Angus, Robert B., MA Oxf., DPhil Oxf., DSc Lond.   Sr. Lectr.
Beesley, Philip W., BSc S'ton., PhD S'ton.   Reader
Bögre, Laszlo, MD Agric.Univ.Gödöllö, PhD Agric.Univ.Gödöllö   Prof.
Bolwell, G. Paul, MA Oxf., DPhil Oxf.   Prof.
Bowyer, John R., MA Camb., PhD Brist.   Prof.
Bramley, Peter M., BSc Wales, PhD Wales   Prof.; Head*
Catchpole, Clive K., BSc Nott., PhD Nott.   Prof.
Credland, Peter F., BSc Nott., PhD Nott.   Sr. Lectr.
Crompton, Mark R., BSc Oxf., PhD Lond.   Sr. Lectr.
Cutting, Simon M., BSc Manc., DPhil Oxf.   Prof.
Davies, Dewi R., BSc Liv., PhD Lond.   Sr. Lectr.
Devlin, Paul, BSc Reading, PhD Leic.   Sr. Lectr.
Devoto, Alessandra, MSc Rome, PhD Rome   Sr. Lectr.
Dey, Prakash M., MSc Ban., PhD Ban., PhD Lond.   Reader
Dickson, J. George, BSc Strath., PhD Lond.   Prof.; Dir., Res.
Duden, Rainer, MSc Heidel., PhD Heidel.   Prof.
Empson, Ruth, BSc Oxf., PhD Lond.   Sr. Lectr.
Ford, Thomas, BSc Manc., PhD Manc.   Sr. Lectr.
Gange, Alan, BSc Lond., PhD Lond.   Sr. Lectr.
Jansen, Vincent, PhD Ley.   Prof.
Lewis, John W., BSc Wales, PhD Wales   Prof.
Morritt, David, BSc Brist., PhD Brist.   Sr. Lectr.
Rider, Christopher C., BSc Sheff., PhD Sheff.   Sr. Lectr.
Shaw, Paul, BSc Wales, PhD Wales   Sr. Lectr.
Soloviev, Mikhail, PhD Russian Acad.Sc.   Sr. Lectr.
Stead, Anthony D., BSc Wales, PhD Wales   Sr. Lectr.
Tovar, Jorge, BSc Mexico Natnl., PhD Lond.   Reader
Other Staff: 4 Lectrs.
Research: aquatic ecology and toxicology; developmental biology; environmental entomology; neurobiology; plant, cell and molecular biology

Classics
Tel: (01784) 443417 Fax: (01784) 439855
E-mail: m.scrivner@rhul.ac.uk
Alston, Richard, BA Leeds, PhD Lond.   Prof.
Claridge, Amanda, BA Lond.   Sr. Lectr.
Hall, Edith, MA Oxf., DPhil Oxf.   Prof.
Hawley, Richard, MA Oxf., DPhil Oxf.   Sr. Lectr.
Kahane, Ahuvia, BA Tel-Aviv, DPhil Oxf.   Prof.
Lowe, Nick J., MA Camb., PhD Camb.   Sr. Lectr.
Pakkanen, Jari, MA Helsinki, DPhil Helsinki   Sr. Lectr.
Powell, Jonathan, DPhil Oxf.   Prof.; Head*
Rankov, N. Boris, MA Oxf., DPhil Oxf.   Prof.
Rubinstein, Lene, MA Copenhagen, PhD Camb.   Reader
Sheppard, Anne, MA Oxf., DPhil Oxf.   Sr. Lectr.
Spentzou, Efi, BA Salonika, MSt Oxf., DPhil Oxf.   Sr. Lectr.
Other Staff: 1 Lectr.; 3 Res. Fellows
Research: archaeology and history; classical archaeology; Greek and Latin literature; Greek philosophy; Greek, Roman and early Byzantine history

Computer Science
Tel: (01784) 443421 Fax: (01784) 439786
E-mail: depsec@cs.rhul.ac.uk
Chervonenkis, Alexey Y., BSc Moscow, PhD Moscow   Prof.†
Cohen, David A., BA Oxf., DPhil Oxf.   Prof.
Gammerman, Alex J., BSc St.Petersburg, PhD St.Petersburg   Prof.
Gutin, Z. Gregory, PhD Tel-Aviv, BSc   Prof.
Johnstone, Adrian I. C., BSc Lond., PhD Lond.   Sr. Lectr.
Luo, Zhaohui, BSc Changsha I.T., MSc Changsha I.T., PhD Edin.   Prof.
Murtagh, Fionn, BA Trinity(Dub.), BAI Trinity(Dub.), MSc Trinity(Dub.), PhD Paris   Prof.; Head*
Scott, Elizabeth A., BSc Manc., DPhil Oxf.   Sr. Lectr.
Shafer, Glenn, BA Prin., PhD Prin.   Prof.†
Solovyev, Victor V., BSc Novosibirsk, PhD Novosibirsk   Prof.
Stathis, Kostas, BSc Newcastle(UK), MSc ICL, PhD ICL   Sr. Lectr.
Vapnik, Vladimir N., BSc Moscow, DSc Moscow   Prof.†
Vovk, Vladimir G., BSc Moscow, PhD Moscow   Prof.
Watkins, Christopher J. C. H., MA Camb., PhD Camb.   Sr. Lectr.
Yeo, Anders, BSc Odense, MSc Odense, PhD Odense   Sr. Lectr.
Other Staff: 7 Lectrs.; 1 Res. Fellow; 2 Temp. Lectrs.

Research: bioinformatics; distributed architecture, vision and signal processing; machine learning; theory of computing

Drama and Theatre

Tel: (01784) 443922 Fax: (01784) 431018
E-mail: drama@rhul.ac.uk
Bartlett, Neil, MA Oxf. Hon. Prof.
Bradby, David H., MA Oxf., PhD Glas. Prof.
Bratton, Jacky S., MA Oxf., DPhil Oxf. Res. Prof.†
Bush-Bailey, Gilli, BA Kingston(UK), PhD Lond. Sr. Lectr.; Dir., Grad. Studies
Cave, Richard A., MA Camb., PhD Camb. Prof.
Cohen, Matthew I., AB Harv., PhD Yale Sr. Lectr.
Dymkowski, Christine, MA Oxf., MA Leeds, AB Bryn Mawr, PhD Virginia Prof.
Gilbert, Helen, BA Br.Col., PhD Qld. Prof.; Dir., Res.
Hall, Edith, MA Oxf., DPhil Oxf. Res. Prof., Drama and Classics
Holmes, Jonathan, BA Birm., MPhil Birm., PhD Birm. Sr. Lectr.
Howard, Pamela, FRSA Hon. Prof.
Kustow, Michael, MA Oxf. Hon. Prof.
Nicholson, Helen, BA Lond., PhD Warw. Sr. Lectr.
Normington, Katie, BA Exe., MA S.Carolina, PhD Exe. Sr. Lectr.
Rebellato, Dan A., BA Brist., PhD Lond. Sr. Lectr.
Schafer, Elizabeth J., BA Lond., MA Birm., PhD Lond. Prof.
Umewaka, Naohiko, BA Sophia, PhD Lond. Hon. Prof.
Wiles, David, BA Camb., PhD Brist. Prof.; Head*
Other Staff: 8 Lectrs.; 4 Postdoctoral Res. Fellows; 1 Sr. Lectr.†; 25 Temp. Lectrs.
Vacant Posts: 1 Lectr.
Research: Indonesian theatre; modern drama; theatre history; theatre practice; women's theatre

Economics

Tel: (01784) 443383 Fax: (01784) 439534
E-mail: s.hallam@rhul.ac.uk
Anderberg, Dan, BA Lund, PhD Lund Sr. Lectr.
Chevalier, Arnaud, BA Angers, MSc Birm., PhD Birm. Sr. Lectr.
Dolton, Peter, BA Essex, MA Warw., PhD Camb. Prof.
Engelmann, Dirk, BSc Gött., PhD Humboldt Reader
Frank, Jeff, BA Reed, PhD Yale Prof.
Heyes, Anthony, MA Camb., PhD McG. Prof.
Lagerloef, Johan, BA Stockholm, PhD Stockholm Sr. Lectr.
Lavy, Victor, BA Jerusalem, MA Chic., PhD Chic. Prof.
Mandler, Michael, BA Swarthmore, MPhil Camb., PhD Yale Prof.
Marrese, Michael, MA Penn., PhD Penn. Hon. Prof.
Moav, Omer, BA Jerusalem, MSc Jerusalem, PhD Jerusalem Prof.
Mountford, Andrew, BA Camb., PhD Brown Sr. Lectr.
Munro, Alistair, BA Warw., MPhil Oxf., DPhil Oxf. Prof.
Normann, Hans T., PhD European Univ.Inst., MA Prof.
Seltzer, Andrew, BA Colby, MS Ill., PhD Ill. Prof.; Head*
Sentance, Andrew, MSc Lond., PhD Lond. Hon. Prof.
Spagat, Michael, BA Northwestern, PhD Harv. Prof.
Wadsworth, Jonathan, BSc Hull, PhD Lond. Reader
Other Staff: 7 Lectrs.
Research: economic theory; experimental economics; financial and industrial economics; labour economics; political economy

English

Tel: (01784) 443214 Fax: (01784) 479059
E-mail: english-department@rhul.ac.uk
Armstrong, Timothy D., BA NZ, MA NZ, PhD Lond. Prof.
Boehmer, Elleke, BA S.Af., MPhil Oxf., DPhil Oxf. Hildred Carlisle Prof.
Carson, Christie, BA Canberra, MA Tor., PhD Glas. Sr. Lectr.
Davenport, W. Anthony, MA Lond. Emer. Prof.
Dzelzainis, Martin, MA Camb., PhD Camb. Prof.
Eaglestone, Robert, MA S'ton., PhD Wales Sr. Lectr.
Fernie, Ewan, MA Edin., PhD St And. Sr. Lectr.
Field, Rosalind, MA Camb., DPhil York(UK) Reader
Gibson, Andrew W., MA Oxf., BPhil Oxf. Prof.
Gould, Warwick, BA Qld., FRSL, FRSA Prof.
Hampson, Robert G., MA Tor., PhD Lond., FRSA Prof.; Head*
Hawley, Judith V., DPhil Oxf. Sr. Lectr.
Kennedy, Ruth, MA Brist., PhD Brist. Sr. Lectr.
Motion, Andrew, MA Oxf., MLitt Oxf., FRSL, FRSA Prof.
Neville, Jennifer L., MA Tor., PhD Camb. Sr. Lectr.
Roberts, Adam, MA Aberd., PhD Camb. Reader
Ryan, Kiernan, MA Camb., PhD Amst., FRSL, FRSA Prof.
Varty, Anne, MA Glas., DPhil Oxf. Sr. Lectr.
Other Staff: 9 Lectrs.
Research: eighteenth-, nineteenth- and twentieth-century literature; mediaeval literature; modernism and post-modernism; Shakespeare and the Renaissance

European Studies

Tel: (01784) 443669 Fax: (01784) 479052
E-mail: a.pym@rhul.ac.uk
Wright, Joanne, BA MLitt PhD Prof.
Other Staff: 1 Lectr.; 3 Staff Members
Research: European international relations; European terrorism, Nato and the CFSP; international and European police co-operation; police reform in Northern Ireland; state and sub-state security

Geography

Tel: (01784) 443563 Fax: (01784) 472836
E-mail: geography@rhul.ac.uk
Coope, Russell, BSc Manc., MSc Manc., PhD Birm., DSc Birm. Hon. Prof.
Crang, Philip, BA Camb., PhD Camb. Prof.; Dir., MA Cultural Geog.
Cresswell, Tim, BA Lond., MS Wis., PhD Wis. Prof.
Derbyshire, Edward, BA Keele, MSc McG., PhD Monash Hon. Prof.
Desai, Vandana, BA Bom., BSL Poona, MPA Liv., DPhil Oxf. Sr. Lectr.
Dodds, Klaus J., BSc Brist., PhD Brist. Prof.
Driver, Felix, MA Camb., PhD Camb. Prof.; Head*
Elias, Scott, BSc Colorado, PhD Colorado Reader; Dir., MSc Quaternary Sci.
French, Peter, BSc Kingston(UK), PhD Reading Sr. Lectr.
Gamble, Clive, BA Camb., PhD Camb. Prof.
Gilbert, David M., MA Camb., DPhil Oxf. Prof.; Dir., MA Cultural Geog.
Kemp, Rob A., BSc Reading, MSc Qu., PhD Lond. Prof.
Lowe, J. John, MA St And., PhD Edin. Prof.
McGregor, Duncan F. M., BSc Edin., PhD Edin. Sr. Lectr.
Minca, Claudio, Laurea Trieste Prof.
Rose, James, BA Leic. Prof.
Simon, David, BA Reading, BA Cape Town, DPhil Oxf. Prof.
Stringer, Chris, BSc Lond., PhD Brist. Hon. Prof.
Unwin, P. Timothy H., MA Camb., PhD Durh. Prof.; Dir., Grad. Studies
Willis, Katie, BA Oxf., DPhil Oxf. Sr. Lectr.; Co-ordinator, Undergrad. Admissions

Other Staff: 6 Lectrs.; 8 Res. Fellows; 5 Hon. Res. Fellows; 9 Hon. Assocs.
Research: development and environment in the Third World; geopolitics and the sustainable environment; quaternary studies; social and cultural geography

Geology

Tel: (01784) 443581 Fax: (01784) 471780
E-mail: info@gl.rhul.ac.uk
Alderton, David H. M., BSc Lond., PhD Lond. Sr. Lectr.
Batt, Geoffrey E., BSc Otago, PhD ANU Sr. Lectr.
Blundell, Derek J., BSc Birm., PhD Lond. Emer. Prof.
Bosence, Daniel W. J., BSc Reading, PhD Reading Emer. Prof.
Chaloner, William G., BSc Reading, PhD Reading, FRS Emer. Prof.; Hon. Fellow
Collinson, Margaret, BSc Wales, PhD Lond. Prof.
Crane, Peter, BSc Reading, PhD Reading Hon. Prof.
Ebinger, Cynthia, BSc Duke, PhD M.I.T./W.H.O.I. Prof.
Elders, Christopher F., BA Oxf., DPhil Oxf. Sr. Lectr.; Dir., MSc Basin Evolution and Dynamics
Fowler, C. Mary R., BA Camb., MA Camb., PhD Camb. Prof., Geophysics; Head*
Hall, Robert, BSc Lond., PhD Lond. Prof.
Hossack, Jake, BSc Edin., PhD Edin., FGS Hon. Prof.
King, Martin, BA Oxf., MA Oxf., DPhil Oxf. Dir., MSc Environmental Analysis and Assessment
Kucera, Michal, BSc Prague, MSc Prague, PhD Gothenburg Hon. Prof.
Mattey, David P., BA Camb., PhD Lond. Prof.
McClay, Kenneth R., BSc Adel., MSc Lond., PhD Lond., FGS Prof.; Dir., MSc Tectonics
Menzies, Martin A., BSc Aberd., PhD Camb. Lyell Prof., Geochemistry
Naldrett, Anthony J., BA Camb., MA Camb., MSc Qu., PhD Qu. Hon. Prof.
Nichols, Gary J., BSc Lond., PhD Camb. Sr. Lectr.
Nisbet, Euan G., BA Camb., MA Camb., PhD Camb. Foundation Prof.
Roberts, David G., BSc Manc., DSc Manc. Hon. Prof.
Scott, Andrew C., BSc Lond., PhD Lond., DSc Lond., FGS Prof.
Thirlwall, Matthew F., MA Oxf., PhD Edin. Prof.
Walsh, J. Nicholas, BSc Lond., PhD Lond. Sr. Lectr.
Waltham, David, BSc Leic., PhD Lond. Reader
Other Staff: 3 Lectrs.; 3 Res. Officers; 4 Hon. Res. Fellows; 6 Hon. Res. Assocs.
Research: ancient and modern earth systems; geochemistry; tectonics and basins

Health and Social Care

Tel: (01784) 443681 Fax: (01784) 439248
E-mail: s.m.sweet@rhul.ac.uk
Barn, Ravinder, BA C.England, PhD Warw. Prof.
Bifulco, Antonia, BA Lond., PhD Lond. Prof.
Denney, David, BSocSc Birm., MA Warw., PhD Kent Prof.
Gabe, Jonathan, BSocSc Birm., PhD Birm. Prof.
Nicolson, Paula, BSc Wales, MSc Sur., PhD Lond. Head*
Other Staff: 1 Res. Prof.; 8 Lectrs.; 5 Res. Fellows
Vacant Posts: 1 Sr. Lectr.; 2 Lectrs.
Research: child care, child protection, abuse; children and social exclusion; health care organisation and chronic illness; mental health; violence and risk directed towards social care staff

History

Tel: (01784) 443639 Fax: (01784) 433032
E-mail: jane.page@rhul.ac.uk
Ansari, Humayan K., BSc Lond., MA Lond., MPhil Lond., PhD Lond. Prof.

Ansari, Sarah, BA Lond., MA Lond., PhD Lond.
Sr. Lectr.
Barron, Caroline M., MA Oxf., PhD Lond., FSA,
FRHistS Prof.
Blake, Hugo McK., MA Camb., PhD Lanc.
Reader
Burgess, Clive, MA Oxf., DPhil Oxf., FSA Sr.
Lectr.
Cavallo, Sandra, PhD Lond. Reader
Cesarani, David, MA Oxf., DPhil Oxf. Prof.
Champion, Justin A. I., BA Camb., PhD Camb.,
FRHistS Prof.; Head*
Claeys, Gregory R., MA Camb., PhD Camb.
Prof.
Corfield, Penelope J., MA Oxf., PhD, FRHistS
Prof.
Croft, J. Pauline, MA Oxf., DPhil Oxf., FSA,
FRHistS Prof.
Graham, Helen E., BA Lond., DPhil Oxf. Prof.
Harris, Jonathan, BA Lond., MA Lond., PhD Lond.
Sr. Lectr.
Horden, Peregrine, MA Oxf. Reader
Kirk, John, BA Newcastle(UK), PhD Newcastle(UK)
Prof.
Martin, Vanessa, BA Lond., MA Lond., PhD Lond.,
FRHistS Prof.
Phillips, Jonathan P., BA Keele, PhD Lond. Prof.
Robinson, Francis C. R., MA Camb., PhD Camb.,
FRHistS Prof.
Saul, Nigel E., MA Oxf., DPhil Oxf. Prof.
Stone, Dan, BA Oxf., MA Oxf., DPhil Oxf. Prof.
Vickery, Amanda, BA Lond., PhD Lond. Reader
Worden, Blair, MA Camb., PhD Camb., DPhil,
FBA Prof.
Other Staff: 12 Lectrs.
Research: ancient history; early modern history;
extra-European history; mediaeval history;
modern history

Information Security

Tel: (01784) 443101 Fax: (01784) 430766
E-mail: p.stoner@rhul.ac.uk
Beker, Henry, BA Open(UK), BSc Lond., PhD Lond.
Visiting Prof.
Blackburn, Simon, BSc Brist., DPhil Oxf. Prof.
Ciechanowicz, Zbigniew (Chez), BSc Lond.,
PhD Lond. Reader
Diffie, Whitfield, BSc M.I.T., DrScTechn
E.T.H.Zürich Visiting Prof.
Ganley, Hilary, BSc Lond., MSc Lond. Distance
Learning Co-ordinator
Gollmann, Dieter, PhD Linz Visiting Prof.
Holloway, Chris Visiting Prof.
Martin, Keith, BSc Glas., PhD Lond. Reader
Mayes, Keith, BSc Bath, PhD Bath Dir., Smart
Card Centre
Murphy, Sean, BA Oxf., PhD Bath Prof.
Paterson, Kenny, BSc Glas., PhD Lond. Prof.
Piper, Fred C., BSc PhD, FIMA Prof.*; Dir.*
Walker, Michael, BSc Lond., PhD Lond. Prof.
Walton, Richard, CB, BA Open(UK), BSc Nott.,
PhD Nott., FIMA Visiting Prof.
Wild, Peter R., BSc Adel., PhD Lond. Prof.;
Dir.*
Wolthusen, Stephen, PhD T.U.Darmstadt
Other Staff: 5 Lectrs.; 1 Sr. Visiting Fellow; 3
Consultants

Management, School of

Tel: (01784) 443780 Fax: (01784) 439854
E-mail: management-school@rhul.ac.uk
Barnes, David, BSc MBA PhD Sr. Lectr.
Brown, Donna, BSc Lond., MSc Lond., PhD Lond.
Sr. Lectr.
Brown, Rajeswary, MA Lond., PhD Lond.
Reader
Chong, Derrick, PhD Sr. Lectr.
Clark, Ed, BSc S'ton., PhD Glas. Reader
Cutler, Anthony J., BSc Lond., PhD Prof.
Davison, Jane, BA MA PhD, FCA Sr. Lectr.
Dyerson, Romano, BA PhD Sr. Lectr.
Exworthy, Mark, PhD Sr. Lectr.
Faulkner, David, MA Oxf., DPhil Oxf., BSc
Prof.
Ferlie, Ewan, BA Kent, PhD Kent Prof.; Dir.*
Fitzgerald, Robert, BA Lond., PhD Lond. Reader
Gabriel, Yiannis, BScEng MSc PhD Prof.
Gamble, Jos, BA Lond., PhD Lond. Reader

Gold, Michael, BA PhD Sr. Lectr.
Hackley, Chris, BSc Strath., PhD Strath. Prof.
Harindranath, G., BA Madr., MA J.Nehru U., PhD
Lond. Sr. Lectr.
Haunschild, Axel, MSc Hamburg, PhD Hamburg
Sr. Lectr.
Jashapara, Ashok, BScEng MBA DBA PhD Sr.
Lectr.
Johal, Sukhdev, BSc Reader
Lam, Alice, BScEng Lond., MA Lond., PhD Lond.
Prof.
Liston-Heyes, Catherine, BA Ott., MA McG.,
PhD McG. Reader
McSweeney, Brendan, BComm PhD Prof.
Napier, Chris, BA MA MSc, FCA Prof.
Newell, Sue, BSc Wales, PhD Wales Visiting
Prof.
Ozcan, Gul Berna, BSc MSc PhD Sr. Lectr.
Pilkington, Alan, BEng CNAA, PhD Aston Sr.
Lectr.
Popp, Andrew, BA MA PhD Sr. Lectr.
Rosenberg, Duska, BA Zagreb, MA Reading, PhD
Brun. Prof.
Saeedi, Masoud, MSc PhD Sr. Lectr.
Smith, Chris, PhD Brist., BA Prof.
Tan, Hui, BA Bath, MA Bath, PhD Bath Sr.
Lectr.
Unerman, Jeffrey, BA MSc PhD Prof.
Other Staff: 15 Lectrs.; 5 Teaching/Res. Assocs.
Research: accounting, finance and economics;
management information systems and
technology management; marketing and
strategy; organisational studies and human
resource management; public services
management

Mathematics

Tel: (01784) 443101 Fax: (01784) 430766
E-mail: p.stoner@rhul.ac.uk
Beker, Henry, BA Open(UK), BSc Lond., PhD Lond.
Hon. Visiting Prof.
Blackburn, Simon, BSc Brist., DPhil Oxf. Prof.;
Head*
Bowen, Kenneth C., BA Oxf., PhD Lond.
Visiting Prof.
Crampton, Jason, BSc Lond., MSc Lond., PhD
Lond.
Damerell, Mark, MA Camb., PhD Camb. Co-
ordinator, Maths. for Applications
Davies, Christine M., BSc Lond., PhD Lond. Sr.
Lectr.
Desmedt, Yvo, PhD Leuven Hon. Visiting Prof.
Diffie, Whitfield, BSc M.I.T., DrScTechn
E.T.H.Zürich Visiting Prof.
Elsholtz, Christian, PhD T.H.Darmstadt Sr. Lectr.
Essam, John W., BSc PhD Emer. Prof.
Farmer, Christine M., MA Oxf., DPhil Oxf. Sr.
Lectr.
Galbraith, Steven D., BCMS Waik., MS Georgia
I.T., DPhil Oxf. Reader
Godolphin, Edward J., MSc Wales Reader
Gollmann, Dieter, PhD Linz Hon. Visiting
Prof.
Harman, Glyn, BSc Lond., PhD Lond., DSc Wales
Prof.
Martin, Keith, BSc Glas., PhD Lond. Reader;
Course Dir., MSc Secure Electronic Comm.
Mayes, Keith, BSc Bath, PhD Bath Dir., Smart
Card Centre
McKee, James, MA Camb., PhD Camb. Sr.
Lectr.
Mitchell, Chris, BSc Lond., PhD Lond., FIMA
Prof.
Mota-Furtado, Francisca, BSc Lisbon, PhD Brussels
Reader
Murphy, Sean, BA Oxf., PhD Bath Prof.
O'Mahony, Patrick F., BSc N.U.I., MS Chic., PhD
Chic. Prof.
Paterson, Kenny, BSc Glas., PhD Lond. Prof.
Piper, Fred C., BSc PhD, FIMA Prof.
Schack, Rüdiger, Maîtrise Grenoble, PhD Munich
Prof.
Sheer, Andrew, MA Camb., PhD Camb. Sr.
Lectr.
Walker, Michael, BSc Lond., PhD Lond. Prof.
Walton, Richard, CB, BA Open(UK), BSc Nott.,
PhD Nott., FIMA Visiting Prof.
Wild, Peter R., BSc Adel., PhD Lond. Prof.;
Dir., Grad. Studies

Other Staff: 14 Lectrs.; 1 Sr. Visiting Fellow; 1
Hon. Course Dir.; 1 Hon. Res. Assoc.
Research: algebra; discrete mathematics and its
applications; information security and
cryptography; number theory; statistics and
probability

Media Arts

Tel: (01784) 443734 Fax: (01784) 443832
E-mail: mediaarts@rhul.ac.uk
Capon, Susanna, BA Lond. Dir., MA Producing
Film and Television; Head*
Clayton, Sue Sr. Lectr.; Dir., MA
Screenwriting for TV and Film (Retreat
Programme)
Ellis, John C. P., BA Camb., MA Birm. Prof.
Hill, John, MA Glas., PhD York(UK) Prof.;
Head, Res.
Leigh, Jacob, BA Warw., MA E.Anglia, PhD
E.Anglia Admissions Tutor
Merck, Mandy, BA Smith, BA Oxf. Prof.; Dir.,
MA Gender and Sexuality on Screen; Dir.,
Postgrad. Studies (Res.)
Quick, John, BA Exe. Sr. Lectr.; Dir., MA
Documentary by Practice; Dir., Postgrad.
Studies (Taught)
Rogers, Susan Sr. Lectr.; Dir., MA Feature
Film Screenwriting
Other Staff: 13 Lectrs.; 9 Temp. Lectrs.
Research: American and European cinema; film
and video production; gender, sexuality and
cinema; independent film-making;
screenwriting

**Modern Languages, Literatures and
Cultures, School of**

Tel: (01784) 414310 Fax: (01784) 470180
E-mail: modlangadmin@rhul.ac.uk

French

Davis, Colin, BA Oxf., DPhil Oxf. Prof.
Harvey, Ruth, BA Lond., PhD Lond. Reader
Landick, Marie, BA Lond., PhD Lond. Sr. Lectr.
O'Brien, John P., BA Camb., MA Camb., DPhil
Oxf. Prof.
Robertson, Eric, MA Aberd., PhD Aberd. Sr.
Lectr.
Thompson, Hannah A., BA Camb., MPhil Camb.,
PhD Camb. Sr. Lectr.
Williams, James, BA Lond., PhD Lond. Prof.
Other Staff: 5 Lectrs.; 2 Hon. Res. Fellows; 3
Temp. Lectrs.
Research: eighteenth-, nineteenth- and twentieth-
century literature; linguistics; mediaeval
literature; Renaissance literature; visual arts
and literature

German

Bowie, Andrew S., BA Camb., MA E.Anglia, PhD
E.Anglia Prof.
Davies, Máire C., BA Lond. Sr. Lectr.
Longerich, Peter, MA Munich, DPhil Munich,
DrPhilHabil T.U.Munich Prof., Modern
German History
Vilain, Robert L., MA Oxf., DPhil Oxf. Prof.,
German and Comparative Literature
White, I. Ann, BA Lond., PhD Lond. Sr. Lectr.;
Head*
Other Staff: 2 Lectrs.; 1 Res. Fellow
Research: modern German literature; philosophy
and thought; twentieth-century German
history

Hispanic Studies

Lee Six, Abigail, BA Camb., PhD Camb. Prof.;
Head*
Pym, Richard, BA Exe., MA Lond., PhD Lond.
Sr. Lectr.
Vilaseca, David, LicFil Barcelona, MA Indiana, PhD
Lond. Prof.
Wright, Sarah, BA Strath., PhD Camb. Sr. Lectr.
Other Staff: 1 Lectr.; 1 Temp. Lectr.

Italian

Everson, Jane E., MA Edin., DPhil Oxf. Prof.;
Head*
Gundle, Stephen, BA Liv., MA N.Y.State, PhD
Camb. Prof.

Suvini-Hand, Vivienne, BA Trinity(Dub.), DPhil Oxf.   Reader

Tosi, Arturo F., DottLett Padua, PhD Lond.   Prof.

Other Staff: 3 Lectrs.

Research: art and society; contemporary Italian studies; Dante; modern Italian literature; Renaissance studies

Music

Tel: (01784) 443540 Fax: (01784) 439441
E-mail: music@rhul.ac.uk

Beckles Willson, Rachel, MMus Glas., PhD Lond. Sr. Lectr.

Brown, Julie, BA Melb., MMus Lond., PhD Lond. Sr. Lectr.

Cashian, Philip, BMus Durh., DMus Durh. Reader

Charlton, David, BA Nott., DPhil Camb.   Prof.

Cook, Nicholas J., MA Camb., PhD Camb.   Prof.

Dack, James, BA Liv., BMus Liv., PhD Liv.   Sr. Lectr.; Head*

Ellis, Katharine, BA Oxf., DPhil Oxf.   Prof.

Leach, Elizabeth E., MA Oxf., MMus Lond., DPhil Oxf.   Sr. Lectr.

Levi, Erik W., BA Camb., BPhil York(UK) Reader

Lock, Brian, BA E.Anglia, MPhil Camb.   Sr. Lectr.

Ramnarine, Tina K., MMus Edin., DPhil Manc. Reader

Rink, John, AB Prin., MMus Lond., PhD Camb. Prof.

Samson, Jim, BMus Belf., MMus Wales, PhD Wales, FBA   Prof.

Stobart, Henry, MPhil Camb., PhD Camb.   Sr. Lectr.

Wathey, Andrew B., MA Oxf., DPhil Oxf., FRHistS, FSA   Prof.

Other Staff: 4 Emer. Profs.; 1 Visiting Prof.; 1 Academic Fellow; 1 Composer-in-Residence; 3 Lectrs.; 8 Postdoctoral Res. Fellows; 1 Visiting Lectr.

Research: composition; ethnomusicology; performance studies; social, political and institutional history of music; theory and analysis

Physics

Tel: (01784) 443448 Fax: (01784) 472794
E-mail: physics@rhul.ac.uk

Antonov, Vladimir, MSc Moscow, PhD Russian Acad.Sc.   Reader

Blair, Grahame A., BA Oxf., DPhil Oxf.   Prof.

Cowan, Brian P., BSc Sus., DPhil Sus.   Prof.; Head*

Cowan, Glen D., BS Calif., MA Calif., PhD Calif. Sr. Lectr.

Davies, E. Roy, MA Oxf., DPhil Oxf., DSc Lond. Prof.

Flockton, Stuart, BSc Liv., PhD Liv.   Sr. Lectr.

Green, Michael G., BSc Nott., PhD Lond.   Prof.

Grosche, F. Malte, BA Camb., PhD Camb. Reader

Lea, Michael J., BA Oxf., PhD Lanc.   Prof.

Lusher, Christopher P., BA Camb., MA Camb., DPhil Sus.   Sr. Lectr.

Meeson, Philip, BSc Manc., DPhil Sus.   Reader

Moore, A. Moreton, MA Camb., MSc Brist., PhD Brist., DSc Lond.   Prof.

Nicholls, James T., MA Camb., PhD M.I.T.   Sr. Lectr.

Petrashov, Victor, MSc Moscow, PhD U.S.S.R.Acad.Sc.   Prof.

Saunders, John, BA Oxf., DPhil Sus.   Prof.

Sosnin, Igor, MSc Moscow, PhD Russian Acad.Sc. Sr. Lectr.

Stewart, Noel M., BSc Belf., PhD   Sr. Lectr.

Teixeira-Dias, Pedro, BSc Coimbra, PhD Heidel. Sr. Lectr.

Other Staff: 3 Lectrs.; 1 Sr. Lectr.†

Research: low-temperature physics; nanophysics and nanotechnology; particle physics; signal processing and machine vision

Politics and International Relations

Tel: (01784) 443149 Fax: (01784) 434375
E-mail: spsadmin@rhul.ac.uk

Chadwick, Andrew, BA Birm., MSc Lond., PhD   Sr. Lectr.; Head*

Drewry, Gavin R., BSc(SocialSciences) S'ton. Prof.

Edwards, John R., BSc Bath   Prof.

Haines, Steven, LLM Lond., MA Aberd., PhD Aberd.   Sr. Lectr.

Rumford, Chris, MSc Lond., PhD City(UK)   Sr. Lectr.

Seglow, Jonathan, BA Oxf., MSc Lond., PhD Manc.   Sr. Lectr.

Other Staff: 4 Lectrs.

Research: international relations; politics, public administration and governance

Psychology

Tel: (01784) 443526 Fax: (01784) 434347
E-mail: psy-enquiries@rhul.ac.uk

Andrews, Bernice, BA Lond., PhD Lond.   Prof.

Bradley, Clare, BSc Lond., PhD Nott., FBPsS Prof.

Brown, Gary, BA Penn., MSc Penn., PhD Calif. Dir., Res.

Brysbaert, Marc, MA Leuven, PhD Leuven   Prof.

Cinnirella, Marco, BSc Lond., PhD Lond.   Sr. Lectr.

Eysenck, Michael W., BA Lond., PhD Lond. Prof.

Funnell, Elaine, BA Reading, PhD Reading   Emer. Prof.

Glover, Scott, BSc Leth., PhD Alta.   Sr. Lectr.

Hammett, Stephen, BSc Wales, PhD Wales   Sr. Lectr.

Langdon, Dawn, MA Oxf., MPhil Lond., PhD Lond.   Reader; Academic Dir.

Leman, Patrick, MA Oxf., PhD Camb.   Sr. Lectr.

Loewenthal, Catherine M., BSc Lond., PhD Lond. Prof.

MacLeod, Andrew, MA Aberd., PhD Camb. Prof.

Pincus, Tamar, MSc Lond., MPhil Camb., PhD Lond.   Reader

Ramnani, Narender, BSc Lond., PhD Lond. Reader

Rastle, Kathleen, BA Calif., PhD Syd.   Prof.

Smith, Andrew T., BSc Durh., MSc Qld., PhD Keele   Prof.

Valentine, Elizabeth R., BA Lond., PhD Lond. Prof.

Walker, Robin, BSc Newcastle(UK), PhD Durh. Prof.

Wilding, John, MA Oxf., PhD Lond.   Emer. Prof.

Woodcock, Alison, BA Reading, PhD Reading   Sr. Lectr.

Zanker, Johannes M., PhD Tübingen   Prof., Neuroscience; Head*

Other Staff: 5 Lectrs.; 1 Clin. Lectr.

Research: clinical psychology; cognitive psychology; developmental psychology; perception; social psychology

SPECIAL CENTRES, ETC

Bedford Centre for the History of Women

Tel: (01784) 414098 Fax: (01784) 435841
E-mail: bedford.centre@rhul.ac.uk

Vickery, Amanda, BA Lond., PhD Lond.   Dir.*

Biomedical Sciences Centre

Cutting, Simon M., BSc Manc., DPhil Oxf. Head*

Chemical and Bioanalytical Sciences, Centre for

Bramley, Peter M., BSc Wales, PhD Wales Head*

Clinical Psychology Research Group

Tel: (01784) 443526 Fax: (01784) 434347
E-mail: psy-enquiries@rhul.ac.uk

Andrews, Bernice, BA Lond., PhD Lond.   Prof.

Berger, Michael, BA Lond., PhD Lond., FBPsS Prof.

Brown, Gary, BA Penn., MSc Penn., PhD Calif. Sr. Lectr.; Dir., Res.

Eysenck, Michael W., BA Lond., PhD Lond. Prof.

Langdon, Dawn, MA Oxf., MPhil Lond., PhD Lond.   Sr. Lectr.

Loewenthal, Catherine M., BSc Lond., PhD Lond. Prof.

MacLeod, Andrew, MA Aberd., PhD Camb. Prof.

Other Staff: 1 Clin. Lectr.; 3 Clin. Tutors

Research: eating disorders; post-traumatic stress disorder; role of early experience; social and cognitive factors in anxiety and depression; unconscious processes and defence mechanisms

Cognitive Psychology Research Group

Brysbaert, Marc, MA Leuven, PhD Leuven   Prof.

Eysenck, Michael W., BA Lond., PhD Lond. Prof.

Funnell, Elaine, BA Reading, PhD Reading   Emer. Prof.

Glover, Scott, BSc Leth., PhD Alta.   Sr. Lectr.

Rastle, Kathleen, BA Calif., PhD Syd.   Sr. Lectr.

Valentine, Elizabeth R., BA Lond., PhD Lond. Emer. Prof.

Wilding, John, MA Oxf., PhD Lond.   Emer. Prof.

Other Staff: 1 Lectr.

Research: autobiographical memory; exceptional memory abilities; use of computers to remedy learning disabilities; working memory

Computer Learning Research Centre

Tel: (01784) 414024 Fax: (01784) 436332
E-mail: clrc@cs.rhul.ac.uk

Chervonenkis, Alexey Y., BSc Moscow, PhD Moscow   Prof.

Gammerman, Alex J., BSc St.Petersburg, PhD St.Petersburg   Prof.; Dir.*

Levin, Leonid A., MS Moscow, PhD Moscow   Hon. Visiting Prof.

Murtagh, Fionn, BA Trinity(Dub.), BAI Trinity(Dub.), MSc Trinity(Dub.), PhD Paris Prof.

Rissanen, Jorma, PhD Helsinki   Hon. Visiting Prof.

Shafer, Glenn, BA Prin., PhD Prin.   Hon. Visiting Prof.

Solomonoff, Ray J., MSc Chic.   Hon. Prof.

Vapnik, Vladimir N., BSc Moscow, DSc Moscow Prof.

Vovk, Vladimir G., BSc Moscow, PhD Moscow Prof.

Research: computational finance; machine learning

Defects in Solids Research Group

Moore, A. Moreton, MA Camb., MSc Brist., PhD Brist., DSc Lond.   Prof.

Rice-Evans, Peter, BSc Exe., MBA Col., DSc PhD Emer. Prof.

Stewart, Noel M., BSc Belf., PhD   Sr. Lectr.

Research: positrons; x-ray topography

Developing Areas Research, Centre for (CEDAR)

Desai, Vandana, BA Bom., BSL Poona, MPA Liv., DPhil Oxf.   Sr. Lectr.

Dodds, Klaus J., BSc Brist., PhD Brist.   Reader

McGregor, Duncan F. M., BSc Edin., PhD Edin. Sr. Lectr.

Simon, David, BA Reading, BA Cape Town, DPhil Oxf.   Prof.

Unwin, P. Timothy H., MA Camb., PhD Durh. Prof.

Willis, Katie, BA Oxf., DPhil Oxf.   Sr. Lectr.

Other Staff: 2 Lectrs.

Developmental Psychology Research Group

Funnell, Elaine, BA Reading, PhD Reading   Prof.

Leman, Patrick, MA Oxf., PhD Camb.   Sr. Lectr.

Rastle, Kathleen, BA Calif., PhD Syd.   Prof.

Other Staff: 1 Lectr.

Research: attentional deficits; development of memory skills; intergenerational processes; language acquisition in normal and deaf children; reading and dyslexia

Discrete Mathematics and its Applications Research Group

Blackburn, Simon, BSc Brist., DPhil Oxf.   Prof.
Elsholtz, Christian, PhD T.H.Darmstadt   Sr. Lectr.
Essam, John W., BSc PhD   Emer. Prof.
Mitchell, Chris, BSc Lond., PhD Lond., FIMA   Prof.
Murphy, Sean, BA Oxf., PhD Bath   Prof.
Piper, Fred C., BSc PhD, FIMA   Prof.
Walker, Michael, BSc Lond., PhD Lond.   Prof.
Wild, Peter R., BSc Adel., PhD Lond.   Prof.
Other Staff: 3 Lectrs.

English Subject Centre

Tel: (01784) 443221 Fax: (01784) 470684
E-mail: esc@rhul.ac.uk
Carson, Christie, BA Canberra, MA Tor., PhD Glas.   CETL Liaison Officer
Gibson, Jonathan, BA Oxf., PhD Lond.   Academic Co-ordinator
King, Nicole, BA Prin., MA Penn., PhD Penn.   Academic Co-ordinator
Knights, Ben, BA Oxf., PhD Camb.   Prof.; Natnl. Teaching Fellow; Dir.*
Other Staff: 1 Manager; 1 Learning Technologist

Health Psychology Research Group

Bradley, Clare, BSc Lond., PhD Nott., FBPsS   Prof.
Pincus, Tamar, MSc Lond., MPhil Camb., PhD Lond.   Reader
Woodcock, Alison, BA Reading, PhD Reading   Sr. Lectr.
Other Staff: 1 Lectr.
Research: development and evaluation of patient-reported outcomes; psychological factors in diabetes and chronic pain; psychological stress and chronic illness; self-efficacy and health

Hellenic Institute

Tel: (01784) 443086 Fax: (01784) 433032
E-mail: j.chrysostomides@rhul.ac.uk
Chrysostomides, Julian, MA BLitt   Dir.*

Humanities and Arts Research Centre (HARC)

Tel: (01784) 443532 Fax: (01784) 439441
E-mail: jim.samson@rhul.ac.uk
Samson, Jim, BMus Belf., MMus Wales, PhD Wales, FBA   Prof.; Dir.*

Language Centre

Tel: (01784) 443829 Fax: (01784) 477640
E-mail: language-centre@rhul.ac.uk
Simon, Sheryl   Dir.*
Other Staff: 16 Teaching Staff

Lifespan Research Group

Bifulco, Antonia, BA Lond., PhD Lond.   Dir.*

Low Temperature Research Physics

Cowan, Brian P., BSc Sus., DPhil Sus.   Prof.
Lea, Michael J., BA Oxf., PhD Lanc.   Prof.
Lusher, Christopher P., BA Camb., MA Camb., DPhil Sus.   Sr. Lectr.
Meeson, Philip, BSc Manc., DPhil Sus.   Reader
Saunders, John, BA Oxf., DPhil Sus.   Prof.
Other Staff: 1 Lectr.

Nanophysics and Nanotechnology Group

Moore, A. Moreton, MA Camb., MSc Brist., PhD Brist., DSc Lond.   Prof.
Petrashov, Victor, MSc Moscow, PhD U.S.S.R.Acad.Sc.   Prof.
Other Staff: 3 Lectrs.; 3 Res. Officers

Neuropsychology Research Group

Funnell, Elaine, BA Reading, PhD Reading   Prof.
Glover, Scott, BSc Leth., PhD Alta.   Sr. Lectr.
Ramnani, Narender, BSc Lond., PhD Lond.   Reader
Research: acquisition of motor memory; processing of error feedback and reward and social cognition of action; brain mechanisms that underlie cognitive controls of action;

dementia; functions of the frontal lobes; motor control, TMS, visual processing

Number Theory Group

Elsholtz, Christian, PhD T.H.Darmstadt   Sr. Lectr.
Galbraith, Steven D., BCMS Waik., MS Georgia I.T., DPhil Oxf.   Reader
Harman, Glyn, BSc Lond., PhD Lond., DSc Wales   Prof.; Dir.*
McKee, James, MA Camb., PhD Camb.   Sr. Lectr.
Other Staff: 1 Hon. Res. Assoc.
Research: additive and multiplicative number theory; Diophantine approximation; exponential sums; metric number theory; sieve methods

Particle Physics, Centre for

Blair, Grahame A., BA Oxf., DPhil Oxf.   Prof.
Cowan, Glen D., BS Calif., MA Calif., PhD Calif.   Sr. Lectr.
Green, Michael G., BSc Nott., PhD Lond.   Prof.
Strong, John A., BSc Lond., PhD Lond.   Emer. Prof.
Other Staff: 2 Lectrs.; 1 PPARC Fellow; 6 Postdoctoral Res. Assocs.

Plant Molecular Sciences, Centre for

Bögre, Laszlo, MD Agric.Univ.Gödöllö, PhD Agric.Univ.Gödöllö   Head*

Public Services Organisations, Centre for (CPSO)

Exworthy, Mark, PhD   Sr. Lectr.
Ferlie, Ewan, BA Kent, PhD Kent   Prof.; Dir.*
Other Staff: 3 Res. Assts.

Quantum Dynamics Group

Mota-Furtado, Francisca, BSc Lisbon, PhD Brussels   Reader
O'Mahony, Patrick F., BSc N.U.I., MS Chic., PhD Chic.   Prof.; Dir.*
Schack, Rüdiger, Maîtrise Grenoble, PhD Munich   Prof.
Other Staff: 1 Lectr.
Research: atoms in strong magnetic and electric fields; probability in quantum mechanics; quantum chaos; quantum trajectory methods and quantum state diffusion; theoretical atom physics

Quaternary Research, Centre for

Derbyshire, Edward, BA Keele, MSc McG., PhD Monash   Visiting Prof.
Elias, Scott, BSc Colorado, PhD Colorado   Reader; Acting Dir.*
Gamble, Clive, BA Camb., PhD Camb.   Prof.
Hodgkins, Richard, BSc Oxf., PhD Camb.   Sr. Lectr.
Kemp, Rob A., BSc Reading, MSc Qu., PhD Lond.   Prof.
Lowe, J. John, MA St And., PhD Edin.   Prof.
Rose, James, BA Leic.   Prof.
Other Staff: 1 Lectr.; 1 Dorothy Hodgkin Res. Fellow

Social and Cultural Geography Research Group

Crang, Philip, BA Camb., PhD Camb.   Prof.
Dodds, Klaus J., BSc Brist., PhD Brist.   Reader
Driver, Felix, MA Camb., PhD Camb.   Prof.
Gilbert, David M., MA Camb., DPhil Oxf.   Reader
Imrie, Rob F., BA Sus., MPhil Reading, PhD Wales   Prof.
Till, Karen, BA Calif., PhD Wis.   Sr. Lectr.
Unwin, P. Timothy H., MA Camb., PhD Durh.   Prof.
Willis, Katie, BA Oxf., DPhil Oxf.   Sr. Lectr.
Other Staff: 1 Lectr.; 2 Hon. Res. Assocs.

Social Psychology Research Group

Andrews, Bernice, BA Lond., PhD Lond.   Prof.
Cinnirella, Marco, BSc Lond., PhD Lond.   Sr. Lectr.
Leman, Patrick, MA Oxf., PhD Camb.   Sr. Lectr.
Loewenthal, Catherine M., BSc Lond., PhD Lond.   Prof.

Other Staff: 1 Lectr.
Research: group processes; patriotism; social identity; social support; violence and victimisation

Sustainability, Centre for Research into (CRIS)

Dyerson, Romano, BA PhD   Sr. Lectr.
Liston-Heyes, Catherine, BA Ott., MA McG., PhD McG.   Reader
Matten, Dirk, PhD Düsseldorf   Prof.; Dir.*
Unerman, Jeffrey, BA MSc PhD   Prof.
Other Staff: 2 Lectrs.

Victorian Studies, Centre for

Tel: (01784) 443664
Cowling, Mary, BA Leeds, PhD Leeds   Curator*

Vision and Signal Processing Research Group

Davies, E. Roy, MA Oxf., DPhil Oxf., DSc Lond.   Prof.
Flockton, Stuart, BSc Liv., PhD Liv.   Sr. Lectr.
Other Staff: 1 Res. Assoc.
Research: adaptive algorithms in food inspection; advanced image filtering techniques; intrinsic circuit evolution using programmable analogue arrays; signal processing; use of x-rays to detect foreign bodies in food

Vision Research Group

Glover, Scott, BSc Leth., PhD Alta.   Sr. Lectr.
Hammett, Stephen, BSc Wales, PhD Wales   Sr. Lectr.
Smith, Andrew T., BSc Durh., MSc Qld., PhD Keele   Prof.
Walker, Robin, BSc Newcastle(UK), PhD Durh.   Prof.
Zanker, Johannes M., PhD Tübingen   Prof.
Other Staff: 1 Lectr.
Research: brain imaging studies (fMRI); early mechanisms of vision and interrelation between perception and eye movements; eye movement; psychophysical investigations; psychophysics and computational modelling of the human visual system

CONTACT OFFICERS

Academic affairs. Academic Registrar: McGeevor, Philip A., BScEcon Wales, PhD Wales (E-mail: p.mcgeevor@rhul.ac.uk)
Accommodation. Accommodation Office Manager (Acting): Vardaki, Maria (E-mail: accommodation@rhul.ac.uk)
Admissions (first degree). Head of Admissions: Billington, Karl (E-mail: admissions@rhul.ac.uk)
Admissions (higher degree). Head of Admissions: Billington, Karl (E-mail: admissions@rhul.ac.uk)
Alumni. Head of Alumni Relations and Development: Gallagher, Kristen (E-mail: alumni@rhul.ac.uk)
Archives. Archivist: Sugar, Nicky (E-mail: archives@rhul.ac.uk)
Careers. Head of Careers Service: Wilson, Elizabeth (E-mail: v.laverlack@rhul.ac.uk)
Computing services. Director of Information Services: Gerrard, Sarah, BA Sus., MCLIP Sus. (E-mail: d.turner@rhul.ac.uk)
Conferences/corporate hospitality. Facilities Management Director: Bland, Stephen (E-mail: sales-office@rhul.ac.uk)
Consultancy services. Director of Research and Enterprise: Greenwood, Tony (E-mail: alice.eden@rhul.ac.uk)
Credit transfer. Admissions Administrator: Moore, Simon (E-mail: simon.moore@rhul.ac.uk)
Equal opportunities. Personnel Officer: Bonelli, Lorna (E-mail: equal-opps-advisor@rhul.ac.uk)
Estates and buildings/works and services. Facilities Management Director: Bland, Stephen

(E-mail: fmcustomerservices-nonresidential@rhul.ac.uk)

Finance. Director of Finances: Robinson, Graeme, BSc
(E-mail: marilyn.odell@rhul.ac.uk)

General enquiries. Head of External Relations: Clark, Chris
(E-mail: external-relations@rhul.ac.uk)

Health services. Sister in Charge: Daniels, Hilary (E-mail: healthcentre@rhul.ac.uk)

Industrial liaison. Director of Research and Enterprise: Greenwood, Tony
(E-mail: alice.eden@rhul.ac.uk)

International office. Head of EILO (Education and International Liaison Office): Butler, Nick, MA Camb.
(E-mail: liaison-office@rhul.ac.uk)

Language training for international students. Director of Language Centre: Simon, Sheryl
(E-mail: language-centre-support staff@rhul.ac.uk)

Library (enquiries). Librarian and Acting Director of Information Services: Gerrard, Sarah, BA Sus., MCLIP Sus.
(E-mail: library@rhul.ac.uk)

Minorities/disadvantaged groups. Training and Consultancy Manager, Centre for Ethnic Minority Studies: Jackson, June, BA Portsmouth (E-mail: j.jackson@rhul.ac.uk)

Personnel/human resources. Head of Personnel: Grimmer, John, BA
(E-mail: m.ashburner@rhul.ac.uk)

Public relations. Press and Public Relations Officer (Acting): Uttley, Anne
(E-mail: external-relations@rhul.ac.uk)

Publications. Publications and Web Manager: Uttley, Anne (E-mail: a.uttley@rhul.ac.uk)

Purchasing. Puchasing Manager: Fielding, Susan (E-mail: s.fielding@rhul.ac.uk)

Quality assurance and accreditation. Assistant Registrar (Faculty of History and Social Sciences): Rayner, Jean
(E-mail: s.hordern@rhul.ac.uk)

Quality assurance and accreditation. Assistant Registrar (Faculty of Arts): Sendall, Anna
(E-mail: anna.sendall@rhul.ac.uk)

Quality assurance and accreditation. Assistant Registrar (Faculty of Science): Elbourn, Alex (E-mail: sue.fairbrother@rhul.ac.uk)

Research. Deputy Head (Research): Patel, Hitesh (E-mail: lotte.bon@rhul.ac.uk)

Safety. Safety Officer: Fisk, Richard
(E-mail: karen.kingsley@rhul.ac.uk)

Scholarships, awards, loans. International Programmes Co-ordinator: Mann, Inderjit
(E-mail: inderjit.mann@rhul.ac.uk)

Schools liaison. Head of EILO (Education and International Liaison Office): Butler, Nick, MA Camb. (E-mail: liaison-office@rhul.ac.uk)

Security. Security Manager: Bathews, Tony
(E-mail: a.bathews@rhul.ac.uk)

Sport and recreation. Sports Centre Manager: Clark, Jon (E-mail: sportscentre@rhul.ac.uk)

Staff development and training. Staff Development Officer: Oke, Sue
(E-mail: sue.oke@rhul.ac.uk)

Strategic planning. Vice-Principal: Wathey, Prof. Andrew B., MA Oxf., DPhil Oxf., FRHistS, FSA
(E-mail: principalpa@rhul.ac.uk)

Student union. President (Student Union): Harris, Greg
(E-mail: reception@su.rhul.ac.uk)

Student welfare/counselling. Head of Student Services: Butler, Christopher, BA MA
(E-mail: counselling@rhul.ac.uk)

Students from other countries. Overseas Student Adviser: Watkins, Angela
(E-mail: angela.watkins@rhul.ac.uk)

Students with disabilities. Senior Educational Support Officer: Macleod, Sarah
(E-mail: educational-support@rhul.ac.uk)

[*Information supplied by the institution as at 26 July 2006, and edited by the ACU*]

ROYAL VETERINARY COLLEGE

Founded 1791

Postal Address: Royal College Street, London, England NW1 0TU
Telephone: (01707) 666333
URL: http://www.rvc.ac.uk

PRINCIPAL*—McKellar, Prof. Quintin A., PhD Glas., BVMS DVM, FIBiol, FRSEd
VICE-PRINCIPAL (TEACHING)—May, Prof. S. A., VetMB Camb., MA Camb., PhD DVR, FRCVS
VICE-PRINCIPAL (STRATEGIC DEVELOPMENT)—Howard, Prof. Colin R., BSc Durh., MSc Birm., DSc Birm., PhD, FRCPath, FIBiol
VICE-PRINCIPAL (RESEARCH)—Elliott, J., MA Camb., VetMB Camb., PhD Camb.
SECRETARY AND REGISTRAR‡—Smith, Alan N., MA Oxf., BPhil Newcastle(UK)

GENERAL INFORMATION

History. The college was founded in 1791 and became a college of the University of London in 1949.
It is located on two campuses, in central London and in Hertfordshire.

Admission to first degree courses (see also United Kingdom Introduction). Through Universities and Colleges Admission Service (UCAS). Good General Certificate of Education (GCE) A level passes in 3 subjects including biology and chemistry, or equivalent qualifications.

First Degrees (see also University of London Directory to Subjects of Study). BSc, BVetMed.
Length of course. Full-time: BSc: 3 years; BVetMed: 5–6 years.

Higher Degrees (see also University of London Directory to Subjects of Study).
Master's. MPhil, MSc.
Admission. Applicants for admission to higher degrees should possess a good first degree in a relevant subject.
Length of course. Full-time: MSc: 1 year; MPhil: 2 years. Part-time: MSc: 2 years; MPhil: 4 years. By distance learning: MSc: 2–5 years.
Doctoral. DVetMed, PhD.
Length of course. Full-time: DVetMed, PhD: 3 years. Part-time: DVetMed, PhD: 4–6 years.

Libraries. Volumes: 35,000. Periodicals subscribed to: 360. Other holdings: 2000

online periodicals. Special collections: historical (veterinary medicine and surgery).

ACADEMIC UNITS
Pathology and Infectious Diseases

Tel: (01707) 666572 Fax: (01707) 661464
E-mail: sporter@rvc.ac.uk

Biggs, P. M., CBE, PhD Brist., Hon. DVM Munich, Hon. DSc, FRCPath, FIBiol, FRCVS, FRS   Visiting Prof.
Bridger, Janice C., BSc Brist., PhD Reading   Sr. Lectr.
Brownlie, J., BVSc Brist., PhD Reading, FRCPath   Prof., Veterinary Pathology
Collins, M., BSc Wales, PhD Wales   Sr. Lectr., Immunology and Infection
Fox, M. T., BVetMed Lond., PhD Lond.   Sr. Lectr.
Howard, Colin R., BSc Durh., MSc Birm., DSc Birm., PhD, FRCPath, FIBiol   Prof., Microbiology and Parasitology
Jacobs, D. E., BVMS Glas., PhD Glas., FRCVS, FRCPath   Prof., Veterinary Parasitology
Patterson-Kane, J., BVSc Massey, PhD   Sr. Lectr., Anatomic Pathology
Russell, P. H., BVSc Brist., MSc Stir., PhD Glas.   Reader
Rycroft, A. N., BSc Leeds, PhD Leeds   Sr. Lectr.
Smyth, J. B. A., MVB MSc PhD   Sr. Lectr.
Stoker, N., BSc PhD   Prof., Molecular Bacteriology
Werling, D. H. A., DMV PhD   Sr. Lectr., Immunology of Infectious Disease
Williams, A. E., BVMS Glas., PhD Camb.   Prof.; Head*

Other Staff: 8 Lectrs.; 11 Res. Assocs.; 1 Reader†; 1 Hon. Lectr.; 1 Temp. Lectr.
Research: bacteriology; immunology; parasitology; virology

Veterinary Basic Sciences

Tel: (020) 7468 5200 Fax: (020) 7388 1027
E-mail: ataylor@rvc.ac.uk

Abayasekara, Robert, BSc Lond., PhD Lond.   Sr. Lectr.
Baxter, Gary F., BSc PhD   Sr. Lectr.
Botham, Kathleen M., BSc Liv., PhD Liv., DSc Liv.   Reader
Chantler, P. D., BSc Lond., PhD Lond., DSc Lond.   Prof., Veterinary Molecular and Cellular Biology
Cunningham, Fiona M., BSc Lond., PhD Lond.   Sr. Lectr.
Dhoot, G. J., BSc Birm., PhD Birm., DSc Birm.   Reader
Elliott, J., MA Camb., VetMB Camb., PhD Camb.   Prof., Veterinary Pharmacology
Goodship, A. E., BVSc Brist., PhD Brist.   Prof.
Lees, P., CBE, BPharm Lond., PhD Lond., Hon. Dr Ghent, FIBiol   Prof., Veterinary Pharmacology
Loughna, P. T., BSc Liv., PhD Hull   Sr. Lectr.
Michell, R., BSc Lond., BVetMed Lond., PhD Lond., FRSA   Visiting Prof., Applied Physiology and Comparative Medicine
Patel, K., BSc PhD   Reader
Pitsillides, A., BSc PhD   Sr. Lectr.
Price, J., BSc BVSc PhD   Sr. Lectr.
Scaramuzzi, R. J., BSc Syd., PhD Syd.   Prof., Veterinary Physiology

Stickland, Neil C., BSc PhD Prof., Veterinary Anatomy; Head*

Wathes, D. Claire, BSc Birm., PhD Nott., DSc Brist. Prof., Veterinary Reproduction

Watson, P. F., BSc Lond., BVetMed Lond., PhD Syd., DSc Prof., Reproductive Cryobiology

Wheeler-Jones, C., BSc PhD Sr. Lectr.

Wilson, A., BSc BVMS PhD Sr. Lectr.

Other Staff: 12 Lectrs.; 3 Res. Fellows; 32 Res. Assocs.; 1 Temp. Lectr.

Research: biology of bone and connective tissue; muscle biology; reproductive biology; vascular biology and inflammation

Veterinary Clinical Sciences

Tel: (01707) 666281 Fax: (01707) 666274
E-mail: jjones@rvc.ac.uk

Abbott, K. A., BVSc MVS PhD Sr. Lectr.

Bedford, P. G. C., BVetMed Lond., PhD Lond., FRCVS Emer. Prof., Veterinary Opthalmology

Binns, M. Prof.

Boswood, A., VetMB MA Sr. Lectr.

Brockman, D. J., BVSc Sr. Lectr.

Church, D. B., BVSc PhD Prof., Small Animal Studies; Head*

Clarke, Kathleen W., MA Camb., VetMB Camb., DVetMed Lond. Sr. Lectr.

Firth, E. C., BSc MSc PhD Visiting Prof.

Fishwick, J. C., VetMB MA Sr. Lectr.

Garden, O. A., BSc BVetMed PhD Sr. Lectr.

Gilbert, R. J., BPharm Lond., MPharm Lond., PhD Lond., FRPharmS, FRCPath, FIBiol Visiting Prof.

Gregory, N. G., BSc PhD Prof., Animal Welfare Physiology

Gregory, S., BVetMed PhD Sr. Lectr.

Hughes, D. Sr. Lectr.

Johnston, A. M., BVMS Edin., DVetMed Lond., FRCVS Prof., Veterinary Public Health

Lamb, C. R., VetMB MA Sr. Lectr.

Lloyd, D. H., BVetMed Lond., PhD Lond., FRCVS Prof.

Luis Fuentes, V., VetMB MA PhD Sr. Lectr.

May, S. A., VetMB Camb., MA Camb., PhD DVR, FRCVS Prof.

Pead, M. J., BVetMed PhD Sr. Lectr.

Pfeiffer, D. U., DrVetMed PhD Prof., Veterinary Epidemiology

Piercy, R. J., VetMB MA Sr. Lectr.

Sheldon, I. M., BVSc PhD Sr. Lectr.

Slater, J. Prof., Equine Clinical Studies

Smith, R. K. W., MA VetMB PhD Prof.

Varma, M. G. R., DSc, FIBiol Visiting Res. Prof., Entomology

Other Staff: 29 Lectrs.; 1 Res. Assoc.; 10 Temp. Lectrs.

Research: large animals; small animals

CONTACT OFFICERS

Academic affairs. Principal and Dean: McKellar, Prof. Quintin A., PhD Glas., BVMS DVM, FIBiol, FRSEd (E-mail: principal@rvc.ac.uk)

Accommodation. Head, Building Services and Facilities: Solman, Clive (E-mail: csolman@rvc.ac.uk)

Admissions (first degree). Head of Admissions: Harley, Simon (E-mail: sharley@rvc.ac.uk)

Admissions (higher degree). Head of Graduate School: Hamblin, Anne S., BSc E.Anglia, PhD Lond. (E-mail: ahamblin@rvc.ac.uk)

Adult/continuing education. Director, Lifelong Learning Unit: Silva-Fletcher, Ayona (E-mail: asilvafletcher@rvc.ac.uk)

Careers. Academic Registrar: Clark, Julie, PhD (E-mail: jclark@rvc.ac.uk)

Computing services. IT Manager: Marriott, Adam (E-mail: amarriott@rvc.ac.uk)

Consultancy services. Principal and Dean: McKellar, Prof. Quintin A., PhD Glas., BVMS DVM, FIBiol, FRSEd (E-mail: principal@rvc.ac.uk)

Equal opportunities. Human Resources Manager: (vacant)

Estates and buildings/works and services. Head, Building Services and Facilities: Solman, Clive (E-mail: csolman@rvc.ac.uk)

Examinations. Examinations Officer: Turner, Angela (E-mail: aturner@rvc.ac.uk)

Finance. Finance Officer: Blennerhassett, Reggie, BSc MBA, FRSA

General enquiries. Secretary/Registrar: Smith, Alan N., MA Oxf., BPhil Newcastle(UK) (E-mail: ansmith@rvc.ac.uk)

Health services. Occupational Health Advisor: Shaw, Sue (E-mail: sshaw@rvc.ac.uk)

Industrial liaison. Human Resources Manager: (vacant)

International office. Academic Registrar: Clark, Julie, PhD (E-mail: jclark@rvc.ac.uk)

Library (chief librarian). Librarian: Jackson, Simon, MA (E-mail: s.jackson@rvc.ac.uk)

Minorities/disadvantaged groups. Human Resources Manager: (vacant)

Personnel/human resources. Human Resources Manager: (vacant)

Purchasing. Head, Building Services and Facilities: Solman, Clive (E-mail: csolman@rvc.ac.uk)

Quality assurance and accreditation. Quality Assurance Manager: Pomerantz, Eve, BA Brighton (E-mail: qamanager@rvc.ac.uk)

Research. Vice-Principal (Research): Elliott, J., MA Camb., VetMB Camb., PhD Camb. (E-mail: jelliot@rvc.ac.uk)

Safety. Safety Officer: Stodulski, George, BSc (E-mail: gstoduls@rvc.ac.uk)

Scholarships, awards, loans. Academic Registrar: Clark, Julie, PhD (E-mail: jclark@rvc.ac.uk)

Schools liaison. Project Director, Widening Participation: Parry, Jon, BA (E-mail: jparry@rvc.ac.uk)

Security. Head, Building Services and Facilities: Solman, Clive (E-mail: csolman@rvc.ac.uk)

Sport and recreation. Clubs and Societies Officer: Akroyd, Rosie (E-mail: susports@rvc.ac.uk)

Staff development and training. Human Resources Manager: (vacant)

Student union. Student Union President: Gill, Mark (E-mail: supresident@rvc.ac.uk)

Student welfare/counselling. Academic Registrar: Clark, Julie, PhD (E-mail: jclark@rvc.ac.uk)

Students from other countries. Academic Registrar: Clark, Julie, PhD (E-mail: jclark@rvc.ac.uk)

Students with disabilities. Student Disability Officer: Tynan, Anne, BA (E-mail: atynan@rvc.ac.uk)

Women. Human Resources Manager: (vacant)

CAMPUS/COLLEGE HEADS

Hawkshead Campus, Hawkshead House, Hawkshead Lane, North Mymms, Hatfield, Herts; Fax: (01707) 652090) Secretary and Registrar: Smith, Alan N., MA Oxf., BPhil Newcastle(UK)

[Information supplied by the institution as at 1 March 2005, and edited by the ACU]

ST GEORGE'S, UNIVERSITY OF LONDON

Founded 1751

Postal Address: Cranmer Terrace, London, England SW17 0RE
Telephone: (020) 8672 9944 **Fax:** (020) 8725 3426
URL: http://www.sgul.ac.uk

PRINCIPAL*—Kopelman, Prof. Peter, MB BS MD, FRCP
VICE-PRINCIPAL—Horton, Prof. Roger
VICE-PRINCIPAL (TEACHING AND LEARNING)—Hilton, Prof. Sean
VICE-PRINCIPAL (RESEARCH)—(vacant)
DIRECTOR OF ADMINISTRATION‡—Duffy, John
ACADEMIC REGISTRAR—Jones, Hugh
ACTING DIRECTOR OF FINANCE—Smith, Mike

GENERAL INFORMATION

History. The school was founded in 1751 as part of St George's Hospital, Hyde Park Corner. Since 1976 it has been located in Tooting, southwest London.

Admission to first degree courses (see also United Kingdom Introduction). Through Universities and Colleges Admissions Service (UCAS).

First Degrees (see also University of London Directory to Subjects of Study). BSc, MB BS.
Length of course. Full-time: BSc: 3 years; MB BS: 5 years.

Higher Degrees (see also University of London Directory to Subjects of Study).
Master's. MPhil, MSc.
Length of course. Full-time: MSc: 1 year; MPhil: 2 years. Part-time: MSc: 2 years; MPhil: 4 years.
Doctoral. PhD.

Length of course. Full-time: PhD: 3 years. Part-time: PhD: 6 years.

Libraries. Volumes: 42,000. Periodicals subscribed to: 3500. Special collections: history of St George's Hospital and the School.

FACULTIES/SCHOOLS

Medicine and Biomedical Sciences

Dean: Brown, Prof. Nigel, BSc Leeds, PhD Sur.

ACADEMIC UNITS

Arranged by Divisions unless otherwise
indicated

Basic Medical Sciences

Brown, Nigel, BSc *Leeds*, PhD *Sur.*   Prof.;
Head*
Mason, Helen   Sr. Lectr.; Postgrad. Studies Co-
ordinator

Cardiac and Vascular Sciences

Baboonian, Christina, PhD *Lond.*   Sr. Lectr.;
Postgrad. Studies Co-ordinator
Camm, John, BSc *Lond.*, MB BS *Lond.*, MD *Lond.*,
FRCP, FRCPEd, FAHA, FESC, FAMS, FACC
Prudential British Heart Foundation Prof.,
Clinical Cardiology; Head*

Cellular and Molecular Sciences

Griffin, George E., BSc *Lond.*, MB BS *Lond.*, PhD
Hull, FRCP   Prof., Infectious Diseases and
Medicine; Head*
Warburton, Michael J., BSc *Wales*, PhD *Manc.*
Postgrad. Studies Co-ordinator; Sr. Lectr.,
Cellular Pathology

Clinical Developmental Sciences

Carter, Nicholas D., BSc *Lond.*, PhD *Lond.*
Prof.; Head*
Michael, Anthony   Postgrad. Studies Co-
ordinator

Community Health Sciences

Jones, Ian, BA *Wales*, MSc *Lond.*, PhD *Lond.*
Prof.; Postgrad. Studies Co-ordinator
Strachan, David, MB ChB *Edin.*, MSc *Lond.*
Prof.; Head*

Health and Social Care Sciences, Faculty of

Ellison, George T. H.   Prof.; Postgrad. Studies
Co-ordinator
Ross, Fiona   Prof.; Head*

Mental Health Sciences

Hughes, Patricia   Prof.; Head*
Stone, Patrick   Sr. Lectr.; Postgrad. Studies Co-
ordinator

CONTACT OFFICERS

Accommodation. Residential Services Officer:
Gunputrav, Laura
(E-mail: l.gunputrav@sgul.ac.uk)
Admissions (first degree). (MB BS) Assistant
Registrar (Undergraduate Admissions):
Persaud, Caroline A.
(E-mail: adm-med@sgul.ac.uk)
Admissions (higher degree). Assistant
Registrar (Postgraduate Degrees): Dacey,
Caroline(E-mail: adm-med@sgul.ac.uk)
Alumni. Alumni Relations Officer: Conneely,
Chris(E-mail: c.conneely@sgul.ac.uk)
Archives. Library Services Manager: Logan-
Bruce, Maina(E-mail: c.conneely@sgul.ac.uk)
Computing services. Computer Services
Manager: Iveson, David
(E-mail: d.iveson@sgul.ac.uk)
Estates and buildings/works and services.
Estates and Facilities Manager: Williams,
Vaughan(E-mail: v.williams@sgul.ac.uk)
Examinations. Examinations Officer: Gillard,
Elaine(E-mail: e.gilliard@sgul.ac.uk)
Finance. Deputy Director of Finance: Smith,
Mike(E-mail: msmith@sgul.ac.uk)
General enquiries. Director of Administration:
Duffy, John
Health services. Director, Staff and Student
Health Service: Mitchell-Heggs, Nita, MB
BS, FRCP

International office. Assistant Registrar
(Undergraduate Admissions): Persaud,
Caroline A. (E-mail: c.persaud@sgul.ac.uk)
Library (chief librarian). Library Services
Manager: Logan-Bruce, Maina
(E-mail: liblearn@sgul.ac.uk)
Marketing. Public Relations Officer: Griffiths,
Emma
Personnel/human resources. Head of
Personnel: Ball, Frank C., MA *Oxf.*
(E-mail: personnel@sgul.ac.uk)
Public relations. Public Relations Officer:
Griffiths, Emma
Publications. Public Relations Officer:
Griffiths, Emma
Purchasing. Supplies Officer: Umaria Gomes,
Hasmita
Quality assurance and accreditation. Deputy
Head of Planning and Secretariat Office:
Baldwinson, Derek
(E-mail: d.baldwinson@sgul.ac.uk)
Safety. Safety Officer: (vacant)
Schools liaison. Assistant Registrar
(Undergraduate Admissions): Persaud,
Caroline A. (E-mail: adm-med@sgul.ac.uk)
Security. Estates and Facilities Manager:
Williams, Vaughan
(E-mail: v.williams@sgul.ac.uk)
Staff development and training. Head of
Personnel: Ball, Frank C., MA *Oxf.*
(E-mail: personnel@sgul.ac.uk)
Student union. President of the Student
Union: Bamford, Richard
Student welfare/counselling. Student
Counsellor: Taggart, John
(E-mail: counselling@sgul.ac.uk)

[*Information supplied by the institution as at 3 April
2006, and edited by the ACU*]

SCHOOL OF ORIENTAL AND AFRICAN STUDIES

Founded 1916

Associate Member of the Association of Commonwealth Universities

Postal Address: Thornhaugh Street, Russell Square, London, England WC1H 0XG
Telephone: (020) 7637 2388 **Fax:** (020) 7436 3844
URL: http://www.soas.ac.uk

DIRECTOR AND PRINCIPAL*—Webley, Prof. Paul, BSc *Lond.*, PhD *Lond.*
PRO-DIRECTOR—Robb, Prof. Peter G., BA *Well.*, PhD *Lond.*
REGISTRAR AND SECRETARY‡—Page, Sharon, BA *Open(UK)*
DEPUTY SECRETARY—Halliday, Jo, BA *Warw.*, MA *Lond.*

GENERAL INFORMATION

History. The school was founded in 1916 as
the School of Oriental Studies and adopted its
present name in 1938.
It is located in Bloomsbury, central London.

Admission to first degree courses (see also
United Kingdom Introduction). Through
Universities and Colleges Admissions Service
(UCAS).

First Degrees (see also University of London
Directory to Subjects of Study). BA, BSc, LLB.
Length of course. Full-time: BA, BSc, LLB: 3–4
years.

Higher Degrees (see also University of
London Directory to Subjects of Study).
Master's. LLM, MA, MMus, MPhil, MSc.
Admission. Applications to master's degrees
and doctorates are made to the school's
registry.

Length of course. Full-time: LLM, MA, MMus,
MSc: 1 year; MPhil: 3 years. Part-time: LLM,
MA, MMus, MSc: 2–3 years.
Doctoral. PhD.
Length of course. Full-time: PhD: 3 years.

Libraries. Volumes: 1,200,000. Periodicals
subscribed to: 4400.

FACULTIES/SCHOOLS

Arts and Humanities

Tel: (020) 7898 4020 Fax: (020) 7898 4699
E-mail: artsandhumanities@soas.ac.uk
Dean: Brown, Prof. Ian G., BA *Brist.*, MA *Lond.*,
PhD *Lond.*

Languages and Cultures

Tel: (020) 7898 4404 Fax: (020) 7898 4399
E-mail: languagesandcultures@soas.ac.uk
Dean: Hutt, Prof. Michael J., BA *Lond.*, PhD
Lond.

Law and Social Sciences

Tel: (020) 7898 4477 Fax: (020) 7898 4559
E-mail: lawandsocialsciences@soas.ac.uk
Dean: Craven, Prof. Matthew, BA *Nott.*, LLM
Nott., PhD *Nott.*

ACADEMIC UNITS

Africa, Languages and Cultures of

Tel: (020) 7898 4404 Fax: (020) 7898 4399
E-mail: languagesandcultures@soas.ac.uk
Furniss, Graham L., BA *Lond.*, PhD *Lond.*   Prof.,
African Languages and Literature
Jaggar, Philip J., BA *Lond.*, MA *Calif.*, MPhil
Lond., PhD *Calif.*   Prof., West African
Linguistics
Marten, Lutz, MA *Lond.*, PhD *Lond.*   Sr. Lectr.,
Southern African Languages
Other Staff: 8 Lectrs.; 2 Lectors; 1 Res. Fellow;
1 Prof. Res. Assoc.; 4 Res. Assocs.
Research: African Islamic culture and tradition;
broadcast culture in Africa; descriptive and
comparative linguistics of African
languages; gender and history in the

African novel; media for development in contemporary Africa

Anthropology and Sociology

Tel: (020) 7898 4020 Fax: (020) 7898 4699
E-mail: anthropology@soas.ac.uk
Campbell, John R., BSc Oregon, MA N.Y., DPhil Sus. Sr. Lectr., Anthropology of Development, East Africa
Fardon, Richard O., BSc(Econ) Lond., PhD Lond. Prof., West African Anthropology; Co-Convenor*
Marchand, Trevor M. J., BSc Lond., PhD Lond. Sr. Lectr., Social Anthropology (Near and Middle East)
Martinez, Dolores P., BA Chic., DPhil Oxf. Sr. Lectr., Anthropology of Japan
Mosse, David, BA Oxf., DPhil Oxf. Prof., Social Anthropology, India
Osella, Caroline, BA Lond., PhD Lond. Reader, Anthropology of South Asia
Peel, John D. Y., MA Oxf., PhD Lond., DLit Lond., FBA Prof., African Anthropology and Sociology; Co-Convenor*
Pottier, Johan P. J., BA Sus., DPhil Sus. Prof., African Anthropology
West, Harry, BA Virginia, MA Wis., PhD Wis. Reader, Social Anthropology (Mozambique)
Other Staff: 5 Prof. Res. Assocs.; 1 Visiting Reader; 10 Lectrs.; 6 Res. Assocs.
Research: anthropology and history; anthropology of development; anthropology of religion; theory in anthropology; visual anthropology and anthropology of media

Art and Archaeology

Tel: (020) 7898 4020 Fax: (020) 7898 4699
E-mail: artarch@soas.ac.uk
Behrens-Abouseif, Doris, BA Hamburg, PhD Hamburg, DrHabil Freib. Nasser Khalili Prof., Islamic Art and Archaeology
Carpenter, John T., BA Notre Dame(N.Y.), MA Col., PhD Col. Reader, Japanese Art
Contadini, Anna, Laurea Venice, PhD Lond. Reader, Art and Archaeology of Islam
King, Geoffrey R. D., MPhil Lond., PhD Lond., FSA Reader, Islamic Art and Archaeology
Moore, Elizabeth H., BA Pomona, PhD Lond. Sr. Lectr., South East Asian Art
Screech, Timon, MA Oxf., AM Harv., PhD Harv. Prof., Japanese Art
Wang, Tao, BA Yunnan, PhD Lond. Sr. Lectr., Chinese Archaeology
Other Staff: 8 Lectrs.; 5 Prof. Res. Assocs.; 7 Res. Assocs.
Research: architecture in religious and court contexts; arts of Africa and the African diaspora; arts of China, Japan and Korea; Buddhist and Hindu art and archaeology; Islamic art and pre-Islamic architecture

China and Inner Asia, Languages and Cultures of

Tel: (020) 7898 4404 Fax: (020) 7898 4399
E-mail: languagesandcultures@soas.ac.uk
Fuehrer, Bernhard, BA Natnl.Taiwan, PhD Vienna Reader; Chair*
Hockx, Michel, PhD Ley., Drs Ley. Prof., Chinese
Lo, Andrew H.-B., MA Prin., PhD Prin. Sr. Lectr., Chinese
Other Staff: 5 Lectrs.; 1 Sr. Lector; 4 Lectors
Research: classical Chinese (aesthetics, games, literature, philosophy, poetry); modern Chinese (fiction, languages, literary criticism, poetry, society); Tibetan architecture and language

Development Studies

Tel: (020) 7898 4477 Fax: (020) 7898 4559
E-mail: lawandsocialsciences@soas.ac.uk
Achcar, Gilbert, BA Lyons, BA Lebanese, MA Lebanese, PhD Paris VIII Prof., Development and International Politics
Bernstein, Henry, MA Camb., MSc Lond. Prof., East and South Africa
Cramer, Christopher, BA Camb., PhD Camb. Prof., Development Economics

Goodhand, Jonathan, BA Birm., MSc Manc., PhD Manc. Sr. Lectr., Development Practice (South and Central Asia)
Kandiyoti, Deniz, BA Paris IV, MSc Lond., PhD Lond. Reader, Middle East and Central Asia
Lerche, Jens, MA Copenhagen, PhD Copenhagen Sr. Lectr., South Asia; Chair*
Saad-Filho, Alfredo, PhD Lond. Prof., Political Economy of Development
Other Staff: 10 Lectrs.; 5 Prof. Res. Assocs.
Research: agrarian political economy; development aid and non-government organisations (NGOs); gender dynamics in development; governance and institutions; rural labour markets, inequality and development

Economics

Tel: (020) 7898 4477 Fax: (020) 7898 4559
E-mail: lawandsocialsciences@soas.ac.uk
Ash, Robert F., BA Lond., MSc(Econ) Lond., PhD Lond. Prof., China and Taiwan
Booth, Anne, BA Well., PhD ANU Prof., South East Asia
Fine, Ben J., BA Oxf., BPhil Oxf., PhD Lond. Prof., Southern Africa
Harrigan, Jane, BA Oxf., MPhil Camb., PhD Reader
Karshenas, Massoud, BSc(Econ) Lond., MSc(Econ) Lond., PhD Camb. Prof., Middle East
Khan, Mushtaq, BA Oxf., MPhil Camb., PhD Camb. Prof., South and East Asia
Lapavitsas, Costas, BSc(Econ) Lond., MSc(Econ) Lond., PhD Lond. Reader, Japan
Lo, Dic, BSc(Econ) Chinese HK, MA E.Anglia, PhD Leeds Sr. Lectr., China
Nissanke, Machiko K., MSc Moscow, MSc(Econ) Lond., PhD Lond. Prof., Africa and Asia; Chair*
Smith, Graham, BA Durh., MA Warw., PhD Manc. Sr. Lectr., Econometrics
Other Staff: 3 Prof. Res. Assocs.; 10 Lectrs.; 1 Res. Assoc.; 1 Teaching Fellow
Research: economics of development and growth; financial economics; labour, employment and human resource development; political economy

Financial and Management Studies, Centre for (CeFiMs)

Tel: (020) 7898 4477 Fax: (020) 7898 4559
E-mail: cefims@soas.ac.uk
Ash, Robert F., BA Lond., MSc(Econ) Lond., PhD Lond. Prof., China and Taiwan
Dorward, Andrew Prof., Development Economics
Fattouh, Bassam, BA Beirut, MSc Lond., PhD Lond. Reader, Middle East
Harris, Laurence, BSc(Econ) Lond., MSc(Econ) Lond. Prof., Economics; Chair*
Howe, Christopher, MA Camb., PhD Inst.Soc.Stud.(The Hague) Prof., Chinese Business and Management
Scaramozzino, Pasquale, Laurea Rome, MSc(Econ) Lond., PhD Lond. Reader, Economics
Sun, Laixiang, BSc Peking, MSc Peking, PhD Inst.Soc.Stud.(The Hague) Prof., Chinese Business and Management
Other Staff: 3 Prof. Res. Assocs.; 2 Visiting Profs.; 14 Lectrs.; 3 Assoc. Members; 1 Res. Fellow; 1 Res. Assoc.

History

Tel: (020) 7898 4020 Fax: (020) 7898 4699
E-mail: history@soas.ac.uk
Ahuja, Ravi, PhD Heidel. Prof., Modern South Asia
Brown, Ian G., BA Brist., MA Lond., PhD Lond. Prof., South East Asian Economic History
Clarence-Smith, William G., MA Camb., PhD Lond. Prof., Asian and African Economic History
Dikötter, Frank, BA Geneva, MA Geneva, PhD Lond. Prof., Modern Chinese History
Fortna, Ben, BA Yale, MA Col., PhD Chic. Sr. Lectr., Modern Middle East

Hawting, Gerald R., BA Lond., PhD Lond. Prof., Near and Middle Eastern History; Chair*
McCaskie, Tom, MA Camb., PhD Camb. Prof., Africa
Powell, Avril A., BA Camb., PhD Lond. Reader, South Asian History
Robb, Peter G., BA Well., PhD Lond. Prof., History of India
Tomlinson, Tom, MA Camb., PhD Camb. Prof., Economic History
Other Staff: 5 Prof. Res. Assocs.; 13 Lectrs.; 1 Sr. Res. Fellow; 2 Res. Fellows; 6 Res. Assocs.; 1 Assoc. Member
Research: economic history; gender history; history of empire, colonialism and decolonisation; history of ideas; history of medicine and science

Japan and Korea, Languages and Cultures of

Tel: (020) 7898 4404 Fax: (020) 7898 4399
E-mail: languagesandcultures@soas.ac.uk
Breen, John L., MA Camb., PhD Camb. Sr. Lectr., Japanese
Dodd, Stephen H., BA Oxf., MA Col., PhD Col. Sr. Lectr., Japanese; Chair*
Gerstle, Andrew, BA Col., MA Waseda, PhD Harv. Prof., Japanese Studies
Yeon, Jae Hoon, BA Seoul, MA Seoul, PhD Lond. Reader, Korean Language and Literature
Other Staff: 1 Sr. Lector; 5 Lectrs.; 3 Lectors; 2 Res. Assocs.

Law, School of

Tel: (020) 7636 4477 Fax: (020) 7419 4559
E-mail: lawandsocialsciences@soas.ac.uk
Baderin, Mashood, LLB Nigeria, LLM Nott., PhD Nott. Prof., Islamic Law
Banda, Fareda, LLB Z'bwe., DPhil Oxf. Reader, Africa
Craven, Matthew, BA Nott., LLM Nott., PhD Nott. Prof., Public International Law
Cullett, Phillippe, LLM Lond., MA Lond., JSD Stan. Reader, International Environmental Law
Harding, Andrew J., MA Oxf., LLM Sing., PhD Monash Prof., South East Asia
Huxley, Andrew, MA Oxf., BCL Oxf. Sr. Lectr., South East Asian Law
Lau, Martin W., MA Lond., PhD Lond. Reader, South Asia; Chair*
Likosky, Michael, BA Vassar, DPhil Oxf., JSD Yeshiva Reader, International Economic Law
Menski, Werner F., MA Kiel, PhD Lond. Prof., South Asia
Muchlinski, Peter, LLB Lond., LLM Camb. Prof., International Commercial Law
Palmer, Michael J. E., LLB Camb., BSc(Econ) Lond., MA Lond., LLD Lond. Prof., China
Welchman, Lynn, MA Camb., PhD Lond. Sr. Lectr., Islamic and Middle Eastern Law
Other Staff: 3 Visiting Profs.; 11 Lectrs.; 1 Visiting Lectr.; 6 Prof. Res. Assocs.; 4 Res. Assocs.; 1 Teaching Fellow
Research: development and pluralism; globalisation, governance and transition; human rights and environment; international law and institutions; legal systems of the developing world

Linguistics

Tel: (020) 7898 4404 Fax: (020) 7898 4399
E-mail: languagesandcultures@soas.ac.uk
Austin, Peter, PhD ANU, BA Dir., Hans Rausing Endangered Langs. Project; Marit Rausing Prof., Field Linguistics
Charette, Monik, MA Queb., MA McG., PhD McG. Sr. Lectr.
Ingham, Bruce, BA Lond., PhD Lond. Prof., Arabic Dialect Studies
Li, Defeng, PhD Alta. Reader, Translation Studies
Sells, Peter, BA Liv., PhD Mass. Prof.
Other Staff: 2 Prof. Res. Assocs.; 4 Lectrs.; 1 Visiting Fellow; 5 Res. Assocs.
Research: automatic multi-lingual speech recognition; computational linguistics, formal semantics and formal syntax; cross

linguistic vowel perception; English Lakota dictionary project; phonology and morphology of Altaic languages

Music

Tel: (020) 7898 4020 Fax: (020) 7898 4699
E-mail: music@soas.ac.uk
Howard, Keith D., BA CNAA, MA Durh., PhD Belf., FRSA   Prof., East Asia
Hughes, David, MA Camb., MPhil Yale, PhD Mich.   Sr. Lectr., Ethnomusicology; Chair*
Lansdale, Janet, MA Leeds, PhD Leeds   Prof., Dance
Widdess, Richard A., MusB Camb., MA Camb., MA Lond., PhD Camb.   Prof., Ethnomusicology of South Asia
Wright, Owen, BA Leic., BA Lond., PhD Lond.   Prof., Musicology of the Middle East
Other Staff: 4 Lectrs.; 5 Res. Fellows; 10 Res. Assocs.
Research: ethnomusicology; music traditions of Asia and Africa

Near and Middle East, Languages and Cultures of the

Tel: (020) 7898 4404 Fax: (020) 7898 4399
E-mail: languagesandcultures@soas.ac.uk
Abdel-Haleem, Muhammad A. S., BA Cairo, PhD Camb.   King Fahd Prof., Islamic Studies
George, Andrew R., BA Birm., PhD Birm.   Prof., Babylonian; Chair*
Hafez, Sabry, MA Cairo, PhD Lond.   Prof., Modern Arabic
Hewitt, B. George, MA Camb., PhD Camb., FBA   Prof., Caucasian Languages
Ingham, Bruce, BA Lond., PhD Lond.   Prof., Arabic Dialect Studies
Kennedy, Hugh, PhD Camb.   Prof., Arabic
Ouyang, Wen-Chin, BA Al-Fateh, BED Al-Fateh, MA Col., MPhil Col., PhD Col.   Sr. Lectr., Arabic Literature
Parfitt, Tudor V., MA Oxf., DPhil Oxf.   Prof., Modern Jewish Studies
Rona, Bengisu, BA Istanbul, PhD Lond.   Sr. Lectr., Turkish Studies
Shindler, Colin, BSc Leic., MSc Lond., PhD Middx.   Sr. Lectr., Israeli and Modern Jewish Studies
Sims-Williams, Nicholas J., MA Camb., PhD Camb., FBA   Prof., Iranian and Central Asian Studies
Sperl, Stefan, BA Oxf., PhD Lond.   Sr. Lectr., Arabic
Zebiri, Katharine P., BA Lond., PhD Lond.   Sr. Lectr., Arabic
Other Staff: 5 Prof. Res. Assocs.; 1 Visiting Reader; 2 Sr. Lectors; 8 Lectrs.; 3 Lectors; 1 Sr. Visiting Lectr.; 2 Res. Fellows; 5 Res. Assocs.
Research: Arabic and Persian language, literature and culture; classical and modern Islamic studies; deciphering Bactrian documents (pre-Islamic Afghanistan); modern Hebrew, Israeli culture and Yiddish language; Ottoman and modern Turkish language and literature

Political Studies and International Studies

Tel: (020) 7898 4477 Fax: (020) 7898 4559
E-mail: lawandsocialsciences@soas.ac.uk
Adamson, Fiona, BA Stan., MA Col., PhD Col.   Sr. Lectr., International Relations
Chan, Stephen, BA Auck., MA Auck., MA Lond., PhD Kent   Prof., International Relations
Hopgood, Stephen, BSc Brist., DPhil Oxf.   Sr. Lectr., International Politics
Ismail, Salwa, BA Cairo, MA McM., PhD McG.   Reader, Comparative and International Politics
Kong, Tat Yan, BA Newcastle(UK), MPhil Oxf., DPhil Oxf.   Sr. Lectr., Politics and Development Studies
Saez, Lawrence, BA Calif., MALD Fletcher, MA Chic., PhD Chic.   Sr. Lectr., Comparative and International Politics
Springborg, Robert, BA St.Paul(Minn.), MA Stan., PhD Stan.   Prof., Middle Eastern Studies

Strauss, Julia C., BA Connecticut Coll., MA Calif., PhD Calif.   Sr. Lectr., Chinese Politics
Tripp, Charles R. H., BA Oxf., MSc Lond., PhD Lond.   Prof., Middle East
Young, Tom, BSc(Soc) Lond., MA Lond., PhD Lond.   Sr. Lectr., Southern Africa
Other Staff: 1 Prof. Res. Assoc.; 9 Lectrs.; 4 Res. Assocs.; 1 Res. Fellow
Research: identity and modernity; international politics; politics and development; regional relations in Asia and Africa; state and society

Religions, Study of

Tel: (020) 7898 4020 Fax: (020) 7898 4699
E-mail: religions@soas.ac.uk
Barrett, Timothy H., MA Camb., PhD Yale   Prof., History of Chinese Religion
Gifford, Paul, BA Well., MLitt Oxf.   Prof., African Christianity
Hezser, Catherine, DrTheol Heidel., PhD Jewish Theol.Sem.   Prof., Jewish Studies
Pagel, Ulrich, BA Lond., PhD Lond.   Lectr., Language and Religion in Tibet and Middle Asia; Chair*
Shackle, Christopher, BA Oxf., BLitt Oxf., PhD Lond., FBA   Prof., Sufism, Islam and Sikhism
Skorupski, Tadeusz, LTh Pontif.U.S.Th.Aq., PhD Lond.   Reader, Buddhist Studies
Other Staff: 1 Visiting Prof.; 7 Prof. Res. Assocs.; 12 Lectrs.; 13 Res. Assocs.; 2 Assoc. Members; 1 Res. Fellow
Research: contemporary religions from Asia and Africa; gender and religions in Asia and Africa; religious beliefs and practices; religious scriptures of Asia and Africa

South Asia, Languages and Cultures of

Tel: (020) 7898 4044 Fax: (020) 7898 4399
E-mail: languagesandcultures@soas.ac.uk
Dwyer, Rachel M. J., BA Lond., MPhil Oxf., PhD Lond.   Prof., Indian Studies
Hutt, Michael J., BA Lond., PhD Lond.   Prof., Nepali and Himalayan Studies
Radice, William, MA Oxf., DPhil Oxf.   Sr. Lectr., Bengali
Rosenstein, Lucy, BA Lond., MA Lond., PhD Lond.   Sr. Lectr., Hindi
Shackle, Christopher, BA Oxf., BLitt Oxf., PhD Lond., FBA   Prof., Modern Languages of South Asia
Söhnen-Thieme, Renate, DrPhil Mainz   Sr. Lectr., Sanskrit
Other Staff: 4 Lectrs.; 4 Lectors; 4 Res. Assocs.; 1 Visiting Fellow
Research: film and popular culture; oral folk literature and performance; text-based research on religion; translations of South Asian literature

South East Asia and the Islands, Languages and Cultures of

Tel: (020) 7898 4044 Fax: (020) 7898 4399
E-mail: languagesandcultures@soas.ac.uk
Braginsky, Vladimir I., PhD Moscow, DLit Moscow   Prof., Languages and Literatures of South East Asia
Harrison, Rachel V., BA Lond., PhD Lond.   Sr. Lectr., Thai Cultural Studies
Healy, Dana, PhD Prague   Sr. Lectr., Vietnamese
Kratz, E. Ulrich, DrPhil Fran.   Prof., Indonesian and Malay
Smyth, David A., BA Lond., PhD Lond.   Sr. Lectr., Thai; Chair*
Watkins, Justin, BA Leeds, MA Lond., PhD Lond.   Sr. Lectr., Burmese (Myanmar)
Other Staff: 1 Lectr.; 2 Lectors; 5 Res. Assocs.
Research: South East Asian languages and literatures in their traditional, modern, written and oral forms (Burmese, Cambodian, Indonesian, Malay, Tagalog, Thai, Vietnamese)

SPECIAL CENTRES, ETC

African Studies, Centre of

Tel: (020) 7898 4370 Fax: (020) 7898 4369
E-mail: cas@soas.ac.uk
Cramer, Christopher, BA Camb., PhD Camb.   Chair*
Other Staff: 1 Prof. Res. Assoc.; 6 Res. Assocs.
Research: environmental and farming systems (management and impact); ethnography, anthropology, social and economic history; language and the arts in Africa; political economy, law and the state; rural and urban systems and development

Brunei Gallery

Tel: (020) 7898 4023 Fax: (020) 7898 4046
E-mail: gallery@soas.ac.uk
Hollingworth, John, BA Brighton   Exhibitions Manager

Buddhist Studies, Centre of

Tel: (020) 7898 4775 Fax: (020) 7898 4699
E-mail: ts1@soas.ac.uk
Skorupski, Tadeusz, LTh Pontif.U.S.Th.Aq., PhD Lond.   Reader; Dir.*
Research: Buddhism

Chinese Art, Percival David Foundation of

Tel: (020) 7387 3909 Fax: (020) 7383 5163
Pierson, Stacey, MA Lond., BA   Curator*
Other Staff: 1 Asst. Curator

Chinese Studies, Centre of

Tel: (020) 7898 4893 Fax: (020) 7898 4498
E-mail: centres@soas.ac.uk
Tao, Wang, BA Yunnan, PhD Lond.   Sr. Lectr., Chinese Archaeology; Chair*
Other Staff: 2 Prof. Res. Assocs.; 2 Res. Assocs.
Research: contemporary economic, political and social issues; law and foreign relations

Contemporary Central Asia and the Caucasus, Centre of

Tel: (020) 7898 4893 Fax: (020) 7898 4489
E-mail: centres@soas.ac.uk
Dave, Bhavna, MA Bom., PhD Syr.   Lectr., Politics of Central Asia; Chair*
Other Staff: 2 Res. Assocs.

Cross-Cultural Music and Dance Performance, AHRB Research Centre for

Tel: (020) 7898 4515 Fax: (020) 7898 4519
E-mail: musicanddance@soas.ac.uk
Howard, Keith D., BA CNAA, MA Durh., PhD Belf., FRSA   Reader, East Asia; Dir.*

Development Policy and Research, Centre of

Tel: (020) 7898 4473 Fax: (020) 7898 4559
E-mail: rj1@soas.ac.uk
McKinley, Terry, BA San Diego, MA Calif., PhD Calif.   Dir.*
Other Staff: 2 Res. Officers
Research: economic and social effects of drugs in the sub-Saharan region; labour standards and trade union rights in the world trading system; post-apartheid NGO work in southern Africa; problems of conflict-affected countries; social impact of structural adjustment

East Asian Law, Centre of

Tel: (020) 7419 7645 Fax: (020) 7898 4559
Palmer, Michael J. E., LLB Camb., BSc(Econ) Lond., MA Lond., LLD Lond.   Prof.; Dir.*
Other Staff: 1 Prof. Res. Assoc.; 1 Res. Assoc.
Research: administrative law; civil law and civil procedure; family mediation; foreign trade law

Eastern and Orthodox Christianity, Centre of

E-mail: eh9@soas.ac.uk
Hunter, Erica, PhD Melb.   Chair*

Endangered Languages Documentation Programme (ELDP)

Tel: (020) 7898 4703 Fax: (020) 7898 4199
E-mail: eldp@soas.ac.uk
Furniss, Graham L., BA Lond., PhD Lond.   Prof., African Language Literature; Chair*
Oatey, Kathryn, BA E.Anglia   Manager, Documentation Programme
Other Staff: 3 Res. Grants/Support Officers

Ethnic Minority Studies, Centre of

Tel: (020) 7898 4477 Fax: (020) 7898 4559
Menski, Werner F., MA Kiel, PhD Lond.   Prof., South Asia
Other Staff: 3 Res. Assocs.

Food Studies, Centre for

E-mail: hw1@soas.ac.uk
West, Harry, BA Virginia, MA Wis., PhD Wis. Reader, Social Anthropology; Chair*

Gender and Religions Research, Centre for

Tel: (020) 7898 4020 Fax: (020) 7898 4699
E-mail: artsandhumanities@soas.ac.uk
Hawthorne, Sian, PhD Lond.   Chair*

International Foundation Courses and English Language Studies (IFCELS)

Tel: (020) 7898 4800 Fax: (020) 7898 4809
E-mail: ifcels@soas.ac.uk
Yates, Susan E., BA Lond.   Head*
Other Staff: 20 Engl. Teachers; 16 Subj. Teachers†

International Law and Colonialism, Centre of

E-mail: mc7@soas.ac.uk
Craven, Matthew, BA Nott., LLM Nott., PhD Nott. Prof., International Law; Chair*
Other Staff: 1 Prof. Res. Assoc.

International Studies and Diplomacy, Centre of

Tel: (020) 7898 4840 Fax: (020) 7898 4559
E-mail: cisd@soas.ac.uk
Kong, Tat Yan, BA Newcastle(UK), MPhil Oxf., DPhil Oxf.   Chair; Sr. Lectr., Politics and Development Studies
Plesch, Dan, BA Nott., PhD Keele   Dir.*
Other Staff: 6 Lectrs.; 1 Prof. Res. Assoc.; 9 Res. Assocs.

Islamic and Middle Eastern Law, Centre of

Tel: (020) 7898 4477 Fax: (020) 7898 4559
E-mail: lawandsocialsciences@soas.ac.uk
Edge, Ian, LLB Camb., MA Camb.   Co-Dir.*
Foster, Nicholas, MA Camb.   Co-Dir.*
Other Staff: 1 Res. Assoc.
Research: comparative developments in Islamic personal status law; constitutional law and courts; human rights and law; rule of law in the Arab and Islamic world; Shari'a and legislation

Islamic Studies, Centre of

Tel: (020) 7898 4325 Fax: (020) 7898 4379
E-mail: cis@soas.ac.uk
Abdel Haleem, Muhammad A. S., BA Cairo, PhD Camb.   Prof.; Dir.*
Other Staff: 1 Prof. Assoc.; 4 Res. Assocs.
Research: classical and contemporary Islamic moral and political thought; Islamic legal and theological texts; prophetic Hadith (contents, style, translation); the Qu'ran (contents, language, style); translations and interpretations

Jaina Studies, Centre for

E-mail: pf8@soas.ac.uk
Flugel, Peter, MA Mainz, DPhil Mainz   Chair*

Japan Research Centre

Tel: (020) 7898 4892 Fax: (020) 7898 4489
E-mail: centres@soas.ac.uk
Screech, Timon, MA Oxf., AM Harv., PhD Harv. Prof., History of Art; Chair*
Other Staff: 1 Prof. Res. Assoc.; 8 Res. Assocs.
Research: humanities (art history, history, linguistics, literature, music, religion); social science (anthropology, economics, geography, law, politics)

Japanese Arts and Cultures, Sainsbury Institute for the Study of

Carpenter, John T., BA Notre Dame(N.Y.), MA Col., PhD Col.   Head, London Office; Reader, History of Japanese Art
Rousmaniere, Nicole C., BA Harv., PhD Harv. Dir.*
Other Staff: 1 Asst. Dir.; 2 Visiting Fellows

Japanese Religions, Centre for the Study of

E-mail: ld16@soas.ac.uk
Dolce, Lucia, Laurea Venice, MA Venice, PhD Ley. Sr. Lectr., Japanese Religion and Japanese; Chair*

Jewish Studies, Centre for

Tel: (020) 7898 4350 Fax: (020) 7898 4349
E-mail: cjs@soas.ac.uk
Parfitt, Tudor V., MA Oxf., DPhil Oxf.   Reader; Chair*
Research: history, languages and literatures of Jews of Asia and Africa; the State of Israel; Yiddish language and literature

Korean Studies, Centre of

Tel: (020) 7898 4893 Fax: (020) 7898 4489
E-mail: centres@soas.ac.uk
Karlsson, Anders, MA Stockholm, PhD Stockholm Chair*
Other Staff: 1 Prof. Res. Assoc.; 1 Res. Assoc.
Research: art history; economics; ethnomusicology; history; linguistics

Language Centre

Tel: (020) 7898 4858 Fax: (020) 7898 4889
E-mail: languages@soas.ac.uk
Sachdev, Itesh, BSc Brist., PhD McM.   Dir., CETL
Zhang, Xinsheng, BA Shandong, MA E.China Normal, PhD Nott.   Head*
Other Staff: 100 Lang. Teaching Staff

Law and Conflict, Centre of

Tel: (020) 7898 4477 Fax: (020) 7898 4559
E-mail: lawandsocialsciences@soas.ac.uk
Jenkins, Catherine, MA Oxf., LLM Lond., DèsL Aix-Marseilles III   Chair*

Law, Human Rights and Peace Building in the Middle East, Sir Joseph Hotung Research Project in

Tel: (020) 7898 4561 E-mail: is17@soas.ac.uk
Scobbie, Iain, LLB Edin., LLB Camb., PhD Camb. Prof., Public International Law; Dir.*
Other Staff: 2 Res. Fellows; 1 Res. Assoc.

London Middle East Institute

Tel: (020) 7898 4442 Fax: (020) 7898 4329
E-mail: lmei@soas.ac.uk
Springborg, Robert, BA St.Paul(Minn.), MA Stan., PhD Stan.   Dir.*
Other Staff: 10 Res. Assocs.; 1 Prof. Res. Assoc.
Research: Caucasus, Central Asia, Middle East and North Africa (archaeology, anthropology, economics, geography including water issues, history, law, linguistics, literature, music, politics)

Media and Film Studies, Centre for

Tel: (020) 7898 4422 E-mail: as98@soas.ac.uk
Sreberny, Annabelle, MA Camb., PhD Col., FRSA Prof., Global Media and Communications
Other Staff: 3 Sr. Lectrs.; 13 Assoc. Members; 1 Prof. Res. Assoc.; 3 Res. Assocs.

Migration and Diaspora Studies, Centre for

E-mail: pr1@soas.ac.uk
Raman, Parvathi, BA Lond., PhD Lond.   Lectr., Social Anthropology; Chair*

Music and Dance Performance Research, Centre for

E-mail: kh@soas.ac.uk
Howard, Keith D., BA CNAA, MA Durh., PhD Belf., FRSA   Prof., Music; Dir.*

South Asian Studies, Centre of

Tel: (020) 7898 4892 Fax: (020) 7898 4489
E-mail: bm10@soas.ac.uk
Sinha, Subir, BA Delhi, MA Northwestern, PhD Northwestern   Chair*
Other Staff: 1 Res. Assoc.
Research: life histories in South Asia and the South Asian diaspora; literary criticism in South Asian languages; modern South Asian history; modern South Asian societies

South East Asian Studies, Centre of

Tel: (020) 7898 4893 Fax: (020) 7898 4489
Murtagh, Ben, BA Lond., MA Lond., PhD Lond. Lectr., Indonesian and Malay; Chair*
Other Staff: 3 Prof. Res. Assocs.; 7 Res. Assocs.
Research: Buddhism; economics and geography (agriculture, biogeography, poverty measurement, sustainable development); history (Burmese and Indonesian economies, Vietnam war); linguistics and traditional and modern literatures; music, art and archaeology (Buddhist art, Javanese music, remote sensing)

Taiwan Studies, Centre of

E-mail: lawandsocialsciences@soas.ac.uk
Ash, Robert F., BA Lond., MSc(Econ) Lond., PhD Lond.   Prof., Economics of China; Chair*
Other Staff: 1 Lectr.; 1 Res. Assoc.

CONTACT OFFICERS

Accommodation. Accommodation Officer: (vacant)
(E-mail: student@shaftesburyhousing.org.uk)
Admissions (first degree). Deputy Registrar (Undergraduate): Page, Nicholas J., BA S'ton. (E-mail: registrar@soas.ac.uk)
Admissions (higher degree). Deputy Registrar (Postgraduate): Radford, Pam, BA Lond. (E-mail: registrar@soas.ac.uk)
Alumni. Director of Development and Alumni Affairs: McWilliams, Fiona
(E-mail: fm3@soas.ac.uk)
Archives. Archivist: Rayner, Susannah, BA Lond., MA Lond.
(E-mail: docenquiry@soas.ac.uk)
Careers. Head of Careers Service: Huns, Emily, BA Lond. (E-mail: careers@soas.ac.uk)
Computing services. Information Technology Manager: Raggett, Malcolm, MSc Bath
(E-mail: helpdesk@soas.ac.uk)
Credit transfer. Registrar: Harvey, Terry, BSc CNAA (E-mail: registrar@soas.ac.uk)
Development/fund-raising. Development Manager, Major Gifts: Wilson, Abby
(E-mail: aw49@soas.ac.uk)
Distance education. CeFiMs Distance Learning Deputy Registrar: Wood, Greg
(E-mail: gw15@soas.ac.uk)
Estates and buildings/works and services. Building Services Manager: Poulson, Richard, BA Lond., MSc CNAA
(E-mail: rp2@soas.ac.uk)
Examinations. Assistant Registrar (Examinations): Cerny, Marcus
(E-mail: mc69@soas.ac.uk)
Finance. Director of Finance: Appleby, Graeme, BSc(Econ) Lond.
(E-mail: ga12@soas.ac.uk)
International office. Head of Student Recruitment: Butler, Nick, BA Camb., MA Camb., MA Lanc. (E-mail: study@soas.ac.uk)
Language training for international students. Head, International Foundation Courses and

English Language Studies (IFCELS): Yates, Susan E., BA Lond. (E-mail: sy1@soas.ac.uk)

Library (chief librarian). Head, Library Services: (vacant) (E-mail: ap45@soas.ac.uk)

Marketing. Head of Marketing: Sherry, Michael (E-mail: ms71@soas.ac.uk)

Personnel/human resources. Human Resources Director: Mitchell, Peter, BA Leic., MA Westminster (E-mail: pm30@soas.ac.uk)

Public relations. Press and Information Officer: O'Shea, Mary (E-mail: mo2@soas.ac.uk)

Publications. Book Production Officer: Osmond, Andrew (E-mail: ao1@soas.ac.uk)

Purchasing. Purchasing Manager: (vacant)

Quality assurance and accreditation. Registrar: Harvey, Terry, BSc CNAA (E-mail: registrar@soas.ac.uk)

Safety. Safety Officer: Alderton, Heidi (E-mail: healthandsafety@soas.ac.uk)

Scholarships, awards, loans. Scholarships Officer: Sales Fernandez, Alicia, BA L&H (E-mail: as100@soas.ac.uk)

Schools liaison. Widening Participation Coordinator: De La Coudray, Marva (E-mail: mc86@soas.ac.uk)

Security. Central Services Manager: Rhys, Deborah S. (E-mail: dr@soas.ac.uk)

Staff development and training. Staff Development Manager: Yeo, Serena, BA Hull, MA Birm. (E-mail: sy3@soas.ac.uk)

Student welfare/counselling. Senior Student Counsellor: Barty, Alison, MA Oxf. (E-mail: welfare@soas.ac.uk)

Students from other countries. International Officer: Barton, Amanda (E-mail: study@soas.ac.uk)

Students with disabilities. Student Welfare Officer: Davis, Zoe (E-mail: zd@soas.ac.uk)

[Information supplied by the institution as at 23 January 2008, and edited by the ACU]

SCHOOL OF PHARMACY

Founded 1842

Postal Address: 29-39 Brunswick Square, London, England WC1N 1AX
Telephone: (020) 7753 5800 **Fax:** (020) 7278 0622 **E-mail:** postmaster@pharmacy.ac.uk
URL: http://www.pharmacy.ac.uk

DEAN*—Smith, Prof. Anthony, BPharm Bath, PhD Bath
CLERK TO THE COUNCIL AND SECRETARY‡—Axe, Julian C., BSc Edin., DPhil York(UK), FRSA
REGISTRAR—Stone, Margaret L., BSc Georgetown, JD Georgetown
FINANCE OFFICER—Day, John, BSc
SCHOOL LIBRARIAN—Wake, Michelle, BA MA

GENERAL INFORMATION

History. The school was founded in 1842 by the Royal Pharmaceutical Society of Great Britain, and remained a college of the society until 1949. In 1925, it was admitted as a school of the University of London; in 1949, it became an independent grant-aided institution of the University; and in 1952, it was granted a Royal Charter. It moved into its present building, in central London, in 1960.

The School is located in Brunswick Square, Tavistock Square and Russell Square.

Admission to first degree courses (see also United Kingdom Introduction). Through Universities and Colleges Admissions Service (UCAS). Entrance requirements: 3 General Certificate of Education (GCE) A levels, including chemistry and at least one further science subject. Other equivalent qualifications may be accepted. All applicants must demonstrate proficiency in the English language.

First Degrees (see also University of London Directory to Subjects of Study). MPharm.
Length of course. Full-time: MPharm: 4 years.

Higher Degrees (see also University of London Directory to Subjects of Study).
Master's. MSc.
Admission. Applicants for admission to MSc must normally hold a first degree in a relevant subject with at least second class honours.
Length of course. Full-time: MSc: 1 year. Part-time: MSc: 1–3 years.
Doctoral. PhD.
Admission. PhD: applicants should have a first degree in a relevant subject (not necessarily pharmacy) with at least upper second class honours.
Length of course. Full-time: PhD: 3 years. Part-time: PhD: 5 years.

Libraries. Volumes: 500,000. Periodicals subscribed to: 250.

Academic Awards (2007–2008). 3 awards each with a min. value of £12,400.

Academic Year (2007–2008). Three terms: 1 October–8 December; 7 January–14 March; 17 April–20 June.

Income (2006–2007). Total, £16,900,000.

Statistics. Staff (2007–2008): 248 (122 academic, 126 non-academic). Students (2005–2006): full-time 828 (295 men, 533 women); part-time 367 (69 men, 298 women); international 225 (75 men, 150 women); undergraduate 695 (247 men, 448 women); master's 400 (81 men, 319 women); doctoral 100 (36 men, 64 women).

ACADEMIC UNITS

Pharmaceutical and Biological Chemistry

Tel: (020) 7753 5883 Fax: (020) 7753 5964 E-mail: sylvia.alban@pharmacy.ac.uk
Griffiths, William, BSC PhD   Reader
Munday, Mike R., BSc Oxf., MSc Oxf., DPhil Oxf.   Sr. Lectr.
Neidle, Stephen, BSc Lond., PhD Lond., DSc Lond.   Prof.
Searcey, Mark, BSc Lough., PhD Herts.   Sr. Lectr.
Stephenson, F. Anne, MA Camb., MSc Lond., PhD Bath   Prof.
Thurston, David E., BSc Portsmouth, PhD Portsmouth   Prof.; Head*
Other Staff: 5 Lectrs.; 18 Res. Fellows
Research: drug actions; drug discovery; drug receptors

Pharmaceutics

Tel: (020) 7753 5870 Fax: (020) 7753 5942 E-mail: catherine.baumber@pharmacy.ac.uk
Beezer, Anthony, BA PhD DSc, FRSChem Prof.†
Brocchini, Steve J., BA Reed, PhD Mich.   Sr. Lectr., Chemistry and Drug Delivery
Buckton, Graham, BPharm PhD DSc, FRPharmS Prof.
Hadgraft, Jonathan, DSc Oxf., FRSChem   Prof.
Taylor, Kevin M. G., BPharm Wales, PhD Wales   Prof.; Head*
Taylor, Peter W., PhD Lond.   Reader
Uchegbu, Ijeoma   Prof.
Other Staff: 8 Lectrs.; 14 Res. Fellows

Research: inhalation science; materials science; microbiology; novel drug delivery systems; pharmaceutical technology

Pharmacology

Tel: (020) 7753 5900 Fax: (020) 7753 5902 E-mail: vicky.welsh@pharmacy.ac.uk
Constanti, Andy, BSc CNAA, PhD   Reader
Fowler, Les J., BSc Wales, PhD Wales   Sr. Lectr.
Harvey, Robert J., BSc York(UK), PhD Camb.   Prof.
Jovanovic, Jasmina, BSc PhD   Sr. Lectr.
Lever, Rebecca, MPharm Lond., PhD Lond.   Sr. Lectr.
Pearce, Brian, BSc CNAA, PhD Open(UK)   Sr. Lectr.; Head*
Thomson, Alexandra M., BSc Lond., PhD Brist.   Wellcome Prof.
Whitton, Peter S., BSc CNAA, MSc Strath., PhD Glas.   Sr. Lectr.
Other Staff: 3 Lectrs.; 5 Res. Fellows
Research: regulation and function of the nervous system; synaptic and neuronal circuit function and dysfunction

Practice and Policy

Tel: (020) 7874 1270 Fax: (020) 7387 5693 E-mail: julie.bennet@pharmacy.ac.uk
Barber, Nicholas D., BPharm PhD   Prof.; Head*
Bates, Ian P., BPharm MSc   Sr. Lectr.
Smith, Felicity J., BPharm MA PhD   Reader
Taylor, David G., BSc   Prof.
Other Staff: 4 Lectrs.; 5 Res. Fellows
Research: interactions between medicine, individuals and society; risk associated with medicine use

SPECIAL CENTRES, ETC

Drug Delivery Research, Centre for

Tel: (020) 7753 5820 Fax: (020) 7753 5820 E-mail: julie.zirngast@pharmacy.ac.uk
Alpar, Oya, BSc Ankara, PhD   Prof.; Head*
Kostaleros, Kostas, BSc PhD   Sr. Lectr.
Other Staff: 3 Res. Fellows
Research: lipid-based vesicles and liposomes; natural and synthetic macromolecules; targeted delivery systems; therapeutic peptides and proteins; vaccines

Paediatric Pharmacy Research, Centre for

Tel: (020) 7753 5933 Fax: (020) 7753 5977
E-mail: ian.wong@pharmacy.ac.uk
Wong, Ian, BSc *Sund.*, MSc *Manc.*, PhD *Manc.*
Prof.; Head*
Other Staff: 5 Res. Fellows
Research: optimising the use of paediatric medicines; paediatric medicines, their formulation, delivery, monitoring and use; training healthcare professionals in the use of paediatric medicines

Pharmaceutical Analysis, Centre for

Tel: (020) 7753 5929 Fax: (020) 7753 5929
E-mail: tony.moffat@pharmacy.ac.uk
Jee, Roger D., BSc PhD   Sr. Lectr.
Moffat, Tony, BPharm PhD DSc, FRPharmS, FRSChem   Prof.; Head*
Watt, Robert A., BSc *Aberd.*, PhD   Sr. Lectr.
Other Staff: 1 Res. Fellow
Research: discovery, development and application of analytical methods and techniques; knowledge development and problem-solving skills in pharmaceutical analysis; training pharmacists and chemists

Pharmacognosy and Phytotherapy, Centre for

Tel: (020) 7753 5846 Fax: (020) 7753 5909
E-mail: phyto@pharmacy.ac.uk
Gibbons, Simon, BSc *Kingston(UK)*, PhD *Strath.*
Prof.
Heinrich, Michael E., MA PhD   Prof.; Head*
Tasdemir, Deniz   Sr. Lectr.
Other Staff: 3 Lectrs.; 3 Res. Fellows
Research: bioactive natural products from marine and terrestrial sources; food and medicines used in circum-Mediterranean countries; quality of herbal medical products

Toxicology, Centre for

Tel: (020) 7753 5811 Fax: (020) 7753 5811
Kortenkamp, Andreas, BSc *Mün.*, PhD *Bremen*
Sr. Lectr.
Other Staff: 1 Lectr.; 2 Res. Fellows
Research: anti-tumour agents; combination effects of mixtures of environmental pollutants with endocrine-disrupting properties; novel drug carrier and aplastic anaemia

CONTACT OFFICERS

Academic affairs. Dean: Smith, Prof. Anthony, BPharm *Bath*, PhD *Bath*
(E-mail: registry@pharmacy.ac.uk)
Academic affairs. Registrar: Stone, Margaret L., BSc *Georgetown*, JD *Georgetown*
(E-mail: registry@pharmacy.ac.uk)
Accommodation. Accommodation Officer: (vacant) (E-mail: registry@pharmacy.ac.uk)
Accommodation. Assistant Secretary (Accommodation): Green, Elisabeth, BA *S'ton.*, MSc *Lond.*
(E-mail: liz.green@pharmacy.ac.uk)
Admissions (first degree). Deputy Registrar: (vacant) (E-mail: registry@pharmacy.ac.uk)
Admissions (higher degree). Registry Officer: Dave, Sudershana, BSc *Lond.*
(E-mail: msc@pharmacy.ac.uk)
Alumni. Alumni Officer: Davenport, Zoe
(E-mail: zoe.davenport@pharmacy.ac.uk)
Archives. School Librarian: Wake, Michelle, BA MA (E-mail: library@pharmacy.ac.uk)
Careers. Registrar: Stone, Margaret L., BSc *Georgetown*, JD *Georgetown*
(E-mail: registry@pharmacy.ac.uk)
Computing services. Computer Unit Supervisor: Florence, Graham
(E-mail: cu@lsop.ac.uk)
Conferences/corporate hospitality. Administrator (Accommodation): Sheaves, Mark
(E-mail: mark.sheaves@pharmacy.ac.uk)
Consultancy services. Technology Transfer Officer: Lindsay, Bill, BSc *CNAA*, MSc *Durh.*, PhD *Durh.*
(E-mail: bill.lindsay@pharmacy.ac.uk)
Credit transfer. Registrar: Stone, Margaret L., BSc *Georgetown*, JD *Georgetown*
(E-mail: registry@pharmacy.ac.uk)
Equal opportunities. Personnel Officer: Lindsay, Joanna
(E-mail: personnel@pharmacy.ac.uk)
Examinations. Registrar: Stone, Margaret L., BSc *Georgetown*, JD *Georgetown*
(E-mail: registry@pharmacy.ac.uk)
Finance. Finance Officer: Day, John, BSc
(E-mail: john.day@pharmacy.ac.uk)
General enquiries. Clerk to the Council and Secretary: Axe, Julian C., BSc *Edin.*, DPhil *York(UK)*, FRSA
(E-mail: julian.axe@pharmacy.ac.uk)

International office. International Officer: Vepa, Arvind
(E-mail: arvind.vepa@pharmacy.ac.uk)
Library (chief librarian). School Librarian: Wake, Michelle, BA MA
(E-mail: library@pharmacy.ac.uk)
Personnel/human resources. Personnel Officer: Lindsay, Joanna
(E-mail: personnel@pharmacy.ac.uk)
Purchasing. Procurement Officer: Cadman, David, BSc
(E-mail: dave.cadman@pharmacy.ac.uk)
Quality assurance and accreditation. Registrar: Stone, Margaret L., BSc *Georgetown*, JD *Georgetown*
(E-mail: registry@pharmacy.ac.uk)
Research. Assistant Registrar: Dave, Sudershana, BSc *Lond.*
(E-mail: phd@pharmacy.ac.uk)
Safety. School Safety Officer: Marley, Derek
(E-mail: derek.marley@pharmacy.ac.uk)
Scholarships, awards, loans. Registrar: Stone, Margaret L., BSc *Georgetown*, JD *Georgetown*
(E-mail: registry@pharmacy.ac.uk)
Schools liaison. Outreach Officer: Wilgoss, Amanda, BSc *Lond.S.Bank*, PhD *Lond.*
(E-mail: registry@pharmacy.ac.uk)
Security. Assistant Secretary (Security): Green, Elisabeth, BA *S'ton.*, MSc *Lond.*
(E-mail: liz.green@pharmacy.ac.uk)
Strategic planning. Clerk to the Council and Secretary: Axe, Julian C., BSc *Edin.*, DPhil *York(UK)*, FRSA
(E-mail: julian.axe@pharmacy.ac.uk)
Student union. Student Union Liaison Officer: Sheaves, Mark
(E-mail: mark.sheaves@pharmacy.ac.uk)
Student welfare/counselling. Registrar: Stone, Margaret L., BSc *Georgetown*, JD *Georgetown*
(E-mail: registry@pharmacy.ac.uk)
Students from other countries. Registrar: Stone, Margaret L., BSc *Georgetown*, JD *Georgetown* (E-mail: registry@pharmacy.ac.uk)
Students with disabilities. Senior Lecturer: Jee, Roger D., BSc PhD
(E-mail: roger.jee@pharmacy.ac.uk)
University press. Assistant Secretary (University Press): Green, Elisabeth, BA *S'ton.*, MSc *Lond.*
(E-mail: liz.green@pharmacy.ac.uk)

[Information supplied by the institution as at 15 October 2007, and edited by the ACU]

UNIVERSITY COLLEGE LONDON

Founded 1826

Associate Member of the Association of Commonwealth Universities

Postal Address: Gower Street, London, England WC1E 6BT
Telephone: (020) 7679 2000 **Fax:** (020) 7679 7920
URL: http://www.ucl.ac.uk

PRESIDENT AND PROVOST*—Grant, Prof. Malcolm J., CBE, LLB *Otago*, MA LLM *Otago*, LLD *Otago*, Hon. LLD *Otago*, AcSS
VICE-PROVOST‡—Gallyer, Marilyn J., BA
VICE-PROVOST—Delpy, Prof. David T., BSc DSc, FIP, FRS
VICE-PROVOST—Worton, Prof. Michael J., MA *Edin.*, PhD *Lond.*
VICE-PROVOST—Frackowiak, Prof. Richard S. J., MB BChir MA MD DSc, FRCP
VICE-PROVOST—Spyer, Prof. K. Michael, BSc Hon. MD PhD DSc
PRO-PROVOST—Davies, Prof. Wendy E., BA *Lond.*, PhD *Lond.*, FBA, FSA, FRHistS
PRO-PROVOST—Lord, Prof. Alan R., BSc *Hull*, PhD *Hull*, FGS
PRO-PROVOST—Norse, Prof. David, BSc PhD
PRO-PROVOST—Treleaven, Prof. Philip C., BTech *Brun.*, MSc *Manc.*, PhD *Manc.*

INSTITUTES

UNIVERSITY OF LONDON INSTITUTE IN PARIS

Postal Address: Senate House, Malet Street, London, England WC1E 7HU
Paris address: 11 rue de Constantine, 75340-Paris Cedex 07, France; tel: (1) 4411 7383-4; fax: (1) 4411 7382
URL: http://www.ulip.lon.ac.uk
Director*—Shepheard, David
Associate Director—Jordan, Shirley, BA Hull, PhD Hull
Associate Director—Kahane, Prof. Ahuvia, MA Oxf., DPhil Oxf.
Head of Academic Department—Hussey, Andrew, BA Manc., MPhil Manc., PhD Manc.
Administrative Officer, Student and Academic Services‡—Miller, Claire

History. The institute was founded in 1894 as 'La Guilde Franco-Anglaise'. In 1927, it was attached to the University of Paris and became known as the Institut Britannique de Paris. It was incorporated into the University of London in 1969, and changed its name to the University of London Institute in Paris in 2005.
It is located on the Esplanade des Invalides in central Paris.

Admission to first degree courses (see also United Kingdom Introduction). By interview and language test.

First Degrees (see also University of London Directory to Subjects of Study). BA.
Length of course. Full-time: BA: 3 years.

Higher Degrees (see also University of London Directory to Subjects of Study).
Master's. MA, MPhil.
PhD: applicants should have a first degree in a relevant subject (not necessarily pharmacy) with at least upper second class honours.
Length of course. Full-time: MA: 1 year; MPhil: 2 years.
Doctoral. PhD.
Length of course. Full-time: PhD: 3 years. Part-time: PhD: 6 years.

Language of Instruction. French and English.

Libraries. Volumes: 16,000. Periodicals subscribed to: 27. Special collections: Granville Barker (1930s Shakespeare studies); Ellen Gendron (French theatre ephemera from 1970).

Academic Year (2007–2008). Two semesters: 1 October–14 December; 7 January–21 March.

ACADEMIC UNITS
French and Comparative Studies
French and English
Tel: (1) 4411 7383
  E-mail: french@ulip.lon.ac.uk

Milne, Anna-Louise, BA Oxf., MPhil Col., PhD Col. Sr. Lectr.
Rollet, Brigitte, LèsL Paris, MèsL Paris, Dr3rdCy Paris Sr. Lectr.
Sadler, Michael, MA Oxf., DPhil Oxf. Sr. Lectr.
Ward, Dunstan, BA Cant., MA Cant. Prof.
Williamson, Elaine, BA Birm., MèsL Paris, PhD Birm. Prof.
Other Staff: 6 Lectrs.; 9 Tutors

CONTACT OFFICERS
Academic affairs. Administrative Officer, Student and Academic Services: Miller, Claire
General enquiries. Secretary: Duperray, Catherine (E-mail: french@ulip.lon.ac.uk)

[*Information supplied by the institution as at 16 October 2007, and edited by the ACU*]

UNIVERSITY MARINE BIOLOGICAL STATION, MILLPORT

Postal Address: Millport, Isle of Cumbrae, Scotland KA28 0EG
Telephone: (01475) 530581-2 *Fax:* (01475) 530601
Director*—Ormond, Rupert

SCHOOL OF ADVANCED STUDY

SCHOOL OF ADVANCED STUDY

Founded 1994
Postal Address: Senate House, Malet Street, London, England WC1E 7HU
Telephone: (020) 7862 8659 *Fax:* (020) 7862 8657
  E-mail: deans.office@sas.ac.uk
  URL: http://www.sas.ac.uk
Dean*—Floud, Prof. Sir Roderick
Secretary and Senior Administrator‡—Mallard, Sally

History. Created in 1994, the school supports the work of the following research institutes in humanities and social sciences: Institute of Advanced Legal Studies, Institute of Classical Studies, Institute of Commonwealth Studies, Institute of English Studies, Institute of Germanic and Romance Studies, Institute of Historical Research, Institute of Musical Research, Institute of Philosophy, Institute for the Study of the Americas and Warburg Institute.
The school is located in Bloomsbury, central London.

Higher Degrees (see also University of London Directory to Subjects of Study).
Master's. MA, MSc.
Admission. Applicants should normally hold a first degree with at least second class honours (or equivalent overseas qualification) in an appropriate subject.
Length of course. Full-time: MA, MSc: 1 year. Part-time: MA, MSc: 2 years.
Doctoral. MPhil, PhD.
Admission. Applicants should normally hold a first degree with at least upper second class honours (or equivalent overseas qualification) in an appropriate subject.

Length of course. Full-time: MPhil: 2 years; PhD: 3 years. Part-time: MPhil: 4 years; PhD: 6 years.

Libraries. Volumes: 1,217,194. Periodicals subscribed to: 7023. Other holdings: 26,731 serial titles; 187,047 micro-forms; 842 archives.

Academic Awards (2006–2007). 3 awards ranging in value from £13,990 to £17,690.

CONTACT OFFICERS
General enquiries. Secretary and Senior Administrator: Mallard, Sally
(E-mail: deans.office@sas.ac.uk)

[*Information supplied by the institution as at 12 November 2007, and edited by the ACU*]

INSTITUTE FOR THE STUDY OF THE AMERICAS

Postal Address: Senate House, Malet Street, London, England WC1E 7HU
Telephone: (020) 7862 8870 *Fax:* (020) 7862 8886
  E-mail: americas@sas.ac.uk
  URL: http://americas.sas.ac.uk/
Director*—Molyneux, Prof. Maxine, BA Essex, PhD Essex
Deputy Director—Morgan, Prof. Iwan, BA Wales, PhD Lond.
Administrative Manager‡—Perkins, Karen, BA Qld., MA Bond

History. The institute was established in August 2004 as the result of the merger between the Institute of Latin American Studies and the Institute of United States Studies, both of which were established in 1965. It is a member institute of the university's School of Advanced Study.

It is located in Bloomsbury, London, close to the main University of London complex.

Higher Degrees (see also University of London Directory to Subjects of Study).
Master's. MA, MPhil, MSc.
Admission. Applicants for admission to master's degrees must normally hold an appropriate first degree from a UK university with at least second class honours, or an equivalent overseas qualification.
Length of course. Full-time: MA, MSc: 1 year; MPhil: 3 years. Part-time: MA, MSc: 2 years; MPhil: 6 years.
Doctoral. PhD.
Admission. PhD candidates must normally hold a master's degree in a relevant subject.
Length of course. Full-time: PhD: 4 years. Part-time: PhD: 6 years.

Language of Instruction. English. Some optional course components may require proficiency in Spanish or Portuguese.

Libraries. Volumes: 24,868. Periodicals subscribed to: 100. Special collections: Latin American political pamphlets/archives; microMACRO video (sustainable energy development); Nissa Torrents video.

Academic Awards (2006–2007). 21 awards ranging in value from £100 to £17,950.

Income (2006–2007). Total, £1,309,008.

Statistics. Staff (2006–2007): 20 (13 academic, 7 non-academic). Students (2006–2007): full-time 52 (24 men, 28 women); part-time 34 (18 men, 16 women); international 17 (6 men, 11 women); distance education/external 3 (1 man, 2 women); master's 69 (33 men, 36 women); doctoral 18 (9 men, 9 women).

ACADEMIC UNITS

Latin American/United States/ Comparative American Studies

Dunkerley, James, BA York(UK), DPhil Oxf. Prof.

Middlebrook, Kevin Reader, Latin American Politics

Molyneux, Maxine, BA Essex, PhD Essex Prof., Sociology

Morgan, Iwan, BA Wales, PhD Lond. Prof., United States Studies

Other Staff: 1 Sr. Lectr.; 3 Lectrs.; 2 Res. Fellows

Research: Canadian studies; Caribbean studies; Latin American history, politics, economics and sociology; United States history, politics and sociology

CONTACT OFFICERS

Admissions (higher degree). Postgraduate Administrator: Hughes, Kalinda (E-mail: kalinda.hughes@sas.ac.uk)

Finance. Finance and Resources Officer: Murphy, Mark

General enquiries. Administrative Manager: Perkins, Karen, BA Qld., MA Bond

Library (enquiries). United States Studies Librarian: Colvin, Shereen

Library (enquiries). Latin American Studies Librarian: Anderson, Christine (E-mail: latam.lib@sas.ac.uk)

Marketing. Marketing Officer: Gillespie, Agnieszka

[Information supplied by the institution as at 26 September 2007, and edited by the ACU]

INSTITUTE OF ADVANCED LEGAL STUDIES

Postal Address: Charles Clore House, 17 Russell Square, London, England WC1B 5DR

Telephone: (020) 7862 5800 Fax: (020) 7862 5850

E-mail: ials@sas.ac.uk

URL: http://www.ials.sas.ac.uk

Director*—Sherr, Prof. Avrom, LLB Lond., PhD Warw.

Librarian and Associate Director—Winterton, J. R., BA Kent, LLB Lond.

Administrator‡—Niven, Peter, LLB Edin.

History. The institute was established in 1947.

It is located in central London.

Higher Degrees (see also University of London Directory to Subjects of Study).

Master's. MA.

Admission. Applicants must have a first or second class degree in a relevant subject. Applicants with relevant experience and skill may also be considered.

Length of course. Full-time: MA: 1 year. Part-time: MA: 2 years.

Doctoral. PhD.

Admission. PhD candidates must normally hold a UK first degree with at least second class honours, an equivalent overseas qualification or equivalent relevant experience.

Length of course. Full-time: PhD: 2 years. Part-time: PhD: 4 years.

Libraries. Volumes: 264,000. Periodicals subscribed to: 2400. Special collections: Commonwealth law (including Commonwealth Law Library of the Foreign and Commonwealth Office); public and private law; UK and European law.

ACADEMIC UNITS

Advanced Legal Studies

Alexander, S. K., BA Cornell, PhD Lond. Sr. Res. Fellow, International Finance Regulation

Henning, J. J., BIur OFS, LLB OFS, LLD OFS Sr. Res. Fellow, Comparative Corporate Law

Sherr, A. H., LLB Lond., PhD Warw. Woolf Prof., Legal Education

Xanthaki, H., LLB Athens, MJur Durh., PhD Durh. Sr. Lectr., Legislative Studies

Other Staff: 3 Res. Fellows

Research: company and partnership law; comparative law; economic crime; financial services regulation; legal education and the legal profession

CONTACT OFFICERS

General enquiries. Administrator: Niven, Peter, LLB Edin. (E-mail: peter.niven@sas.ac.uk)

[Information supplied by the institution as at 21 July 2005, and edited by the ACU]

INSTITUTE OF CLASSICAL STUDIES

Postal Address: Senate House, Malet Street, London, England WC1E 7HU

Telephone: (020) 7862 8700 Fax: (020) 7862 8722 URL: http://icls.sas.ac.uk/

Director—Edwards, Prof. Michael J., BA Lond., PhD Lond.

Secretary‡—Krzyszkowska, Olga H., BA Mich., MA Camb., PhD Brist.

Librarian—Annis, C. H., BA

[Information supplied by the institution as at 21 August 2007, and edited by the ACU]

INSTITUTE OF COMMONWEALTH STUDIES

Founded 1949

Postal Address: 28 Russell Square, London, England WC1B 5DS

Telephone: (020) 7862 8844 Fax: (020) 7862 8820

E-mail: ics@sas.ac.uk

URL: http://www.sas.ac.uk/ commonwealthstudies

Director*—Crook, Prof. Richard, BA Durh., MA Durh., PhD Lond.

Administrative Manager‡—Stewart, Alison, BA Melb., MA Melb.

Information Resources Manager—Clover, David, BA MA

History. The institute was established by the University of London in 1949.

It is located in central London.

Higher Degrees (see also University of London Directory to Subjects of Study).

Master's. MA, MPhil, MSc.

Admission. Applicants for admission to master's degree courses must normally hold a first degree with at least upper second class honours or equivalent qualification.

Length of course. Full-time: MA, MPhil, MSc: 1 year. Part-time: MA, MPhil, MSc: 2 years.

Doctoral. PhD.

Length of course. Full-time: PhD: 4 years. Part-time: PhD: 6 years.

Libraries. Volumes: 176,000. Periodicals subscribed to: 900. Special collections: archival collections; political party, trades union and pressure group materials; West India Committee.

ACADEMIC UNITS

Commonwealth Studies

Tel: (020) 7862 8829 Fax: (020) 7862 8813 E-mail: ics@sas.ac.uk

Crook, Richard, BA Durh., MA Durh., PhD Lond. Emeka Anyaoku Prof. in Commonwealth Studies

Holland, Robert F., MA Oxf., DPhil Oxf. Prof., Imperial and Commonwealth History

Jones, Peris, BA E.Anglia, PhD Lough.

Manor, James, BA Yale, DPhil Sus. Emeka Anyaoku Prof.

Melchiorre, Angela, Laurea Milan, MA Padua

Shaw, Tim, BA Sus., MA E.Af., PhD Prin. Emer. Prof., Commonwealth Governance and Development

Twaddle, Michael J., BA Camb., PhD Reader

Vlcek, William, PhD Lond.

Waldorf, Lars, BA Harv., JD Harv.

Other Staff: 2 Res. Fellows

Research: colonial/imperial history including decolonisation, modern African and Caribbean history; globalisation, human security and human development; politics and international affairs (conflict, migration and ethnicity) and accommodation in the new states of the Commonwealth, nationalism; specialist areas (Australia, East Africa, English-speaking Caribbean, Mediterranean (especially Cyprus), Southern Africa, South Asia, West Africa)

SPECIAL CENTRES, ETC

International Human Rights, Centre for

Waldorf, Lars, BA Harv., JD Harv. Dir.*

CONTACT OFFICERS

Admissions (higher degree). Graduate Student Officer: (vacant)

Finance. Finance and Resources Officer: Kaur-Hunjan, Jasvinder

General enquiries. Administrative Manager: Stewart, Alison, BA Melb., MA Melb. (E-mail: alison.sterwart@sas.ac.uk)

Public relations. Events and Publicity Officer: Rutt, Troy

[Information supplied by the institution as at 5 February 2008, and edited by the ACU]

INSTITUTE OF ENGLISH STUDIES

Postal Address: Room 304 Senate House, Malet Street, London, England WC1E 7HU

Telephone: (020) 7862 8675 Fax: (020) 7862 8720

E-mail: ies@sas.ac.uk

URL: http://www.sas.ac.uk/ies

Director*—Gould, Prof. Warwick, BA Qld., FRSL, FRSA leave

Academic Programme Coordinator—Baron, Michael, BA Lond., PhD Lond.

Administrative Secretary‡—Grubb, Joanne

Finance Officer and MA Administrator—Bettocchi, Francesca

Centre for Manuscript and Print Studies Administrator—Vitello, Gina

Publications and Research Officer and Administrator to The Bibliographical Society—Van Mierlo, Wim

History. Previously established as the Centre for English Studies in 1991, and a programme of the School of Advanced Study since 1994, the Institute was established in January, 1999.

It is located in Bloomsbury, central London.

Higher Degrees (see also University of London Directory to Subjects of Study).

Master's. MA, MPhil.

Admission. Applicants for admission must normally hold a good first degree with honours.

Length of course. Full-time: MA: 1 year. Part-time: MA: 2 years.

Doctoral. PhD.

Length of course. Full-time: PhD: 3 years. Part-time: PhD: 6 years.

ACADEMIC UNITS

English Studies

Eliot, Prof. Simon, BA Sus., MA Sus., PhD Lond. Dir., MA in Hist. of the Book*

Msiska, Mpalive-Hangson, BA Malawi, MA Alta., PhD Stir. Dir., MA in National and Internat. Literatures in Engl.*

Other Staff: 2 Course Tutors; 17 Sr. Res. Fellows; 27 Visiting Res. Fellows; 36 Assoc. Fellows

SPECIAL CENTRES, ETC

Manuscript and Print Studies, Centre for

Tel: (020) 7862 8676 Fax: (020) 7862 8120

Gould, Prof. Warwick, BA Qld., FRSL, FRSA Dir.* (on leave)

CONTACT OFFICERS

Finance. Finance Officer: Bettocchi, Francesca
General enquiries. Administrative Secretary: Grubb, Joanne

[Information supplied by the institution as at 27 July 2005, and edited by the ACU]

INSTITUTE OF GERMANIC AND ROMANCE STUDIES

Founded 1989

Postal Address: Senate House, Malet Street, London, England WC1E 7HU
Telephone: (020) 7862 8677 Fax: (020) 7862 8672
E-mail: igrs@sas.ac.uk
URL: http://igrs.sas.ac.uk/
Director*—Segal, Prof. Naomi
Administrative Secretary‡—Lambeth, Rosemary

History. The Institute was established in 2004 following the merger of the Institute of Germanic Studies and the Institute of Romance Studies.

Higher Degrees (see also University of London Directory to Subjects of Study).
Master's. MA, MPhil, MRes.
Length of course. Full-time: MA, MPhil, MRes: 1 year. Part-time: MA, MRes: 2 years.
Doctoral. PhD.
Length of course. Full-time: PhD: 3 years.

Libraries. Volumes: 100,000. Special collections: Friedrich Gundolf.

Statistics. Staff (2006–2007): 9 (6 academic, 3 non-academic). Students (2006–2007): total 24.

ACADEMIC UNITS

Germanic and Romance Studies

Chiari, Eleanor Res. Training Co-ordinator; Convenor, Italian
Liebscher, Martin Co-ordinator, Ingeborg Bachmann Centre for Austrian Lit.
Pizzi, Katia Convenor, Res. Training Programme; Lectr., Italian
Rye, Gill Reader; Convenor, MA in Cultural Memory
Segal, Naomi Prof.; Dir.*
Weiss-Sussex, Godela Sr. Lectr., Germanic Studies

[Information supplied by the institution as at 15 August 2007, and edited by the ACU]

INSTITUTE OF HISTORICAL RESEARCH

Postal Address: Senate House, North Block, Malet Street, London, England WC1E 7HU
Telephone: (020) 7862 8740 Fax: (020) 7862 8745
E-mail: ihr@sas.ac.uk
URL: http://www.history.ac.uk
Director*—Taylor, Prof. Miles
Institute Administrator‡—Walters, E. M., BA Sheff.
Librarian—Lyons, R., BA York(UK)
Development Officer—Waterman, M., BA Conn., BS Conn., MA Lond.
Head of Publications—Winters, J. F., MA Oxf., PhD Lond.

History. The Institute was founded in 1921. It is located in Senate House near Russell Square.

Higher Degrees (see also University of London Directory to Subjects of Study).
Master's. MA, MPhil.
Admission. Applicants must normally hold a 2:1 (or higher) honours degree or equivalent professional qualification. Other qualifications may be considered.
Length of course. Full-time: MA: 1 year. Part-time: MA: 2 years.
Doctoral. PhD.
Admission. A good first class degree and preferably a master's degree.
Length of course. Full-time: PhD: 3 years. Part-time: PhD: 6 years.

Libraries. Volumes: 170,000. Periodicals subscribed to: 300. Other holdings: printed primary sources for the mediaeval and modern history of The British Isles and Western Europe.

Academic Year (2007–2008). Three terms: 1 October-14 December; 7 January–14 March; 14 April–13 June.

Income (2006–2007). Total, £3,455,408.

Statistics. Staff (2007–2008): 61 (22 academic, 39 non-academic). Students (2007–2008): full-time 23 (12 men, 11 women); part-time 23 (10 men, 13 women); international 8 (7 men, 1 woman); master's 14 (6 men, 8 women); doctoral 32 (17 men, 15 women).

ACADEMIC UNITS

Contemporary British History, Centre for

Tel: (020) 7862 8802 Fax: (020) 7862 8812
E-mail: ccbhinfo@sas.ac.uk
Cannadine, D. N., MA Camb., DPhil Oxf., FBA Queen Elizabeth the Queen Mother Chair, British History
Kandiah, M. D., BA Vic.(Tor.), MA Exe., PhD Exe. Sr. Lectr.
Roberts, R., BA Lond., PhD Camb. Dir.*
Thane, P. M., MA Oxf., PhD Lond. Leverhulme Prof.
Other Staff: 1 Deputy Dir.; 2 Officers (History and Policy); 1 ESRC Res. Officer

Metropolitan History, Centre for

Tel: (020) 7862 8790 Fax: (020) 7862 8793
E-mail: ihrcmh@sas.ac.uk
Davies, M. P., MA Oxf., DPhil Oxf. Dir.*
Keene, Derek J., MA Oxf., DPhil Oxf., FRHistS Leverhulme Prof., Comparative Metropolitan History
Moore, J. R., BA Oxf., PhD Manc. Deputy Dir.
Other Staff: 4 Res. Staff

Victoria County History

Tel: (020) 7862 8790 Fax: (020) 7862 8793
E-mail: ihrcmh@sas.ac.uk
Beckett, J. V., BA Lanc., PhD Lanc. Dir.*
Thacker, A. T., MA Oxf., DPhil Oxf. Exec. Editor
Williamson, E., BA Lond. Reader
Other Staff: 24 Res. Staff

CONTACT OFFICERS

Conferences/corporate hospitality.
Conference Administrator: Jordan, S., BA Lond. (E-mail: ihr.events@sas.ac.uk)
General enquiries. Institute Administrator: Walters, E. M., BA Sheff. (E-mail: ihr@sas.ac.uk)
Library (chief librarian). Librarian: Lyons, R., BA York(UK)
Publications. Head of Publications: Winters, J. F., MA Oxf., PhD Lond.

[Information supplied by the institution as at 20 November 2007, and edited by the ACU]

INSTITUTE OF MUSICAL RESEARCH

Founded 2005

Postal Address: Senate House, Malet Street, London, England WC1E 7HU
Telephone: (020) 7664 4865 Fax: (020) 7664 4867
E-mail: music@sas.ac.uk
URL: http://www.music.sas.ac.uk
Director*—Ellis, Prof. Katharine, BA Oxf., DPhil Oxf.
Administrator‡—James, Valerie, MA Oxf., MLitt Oxf.

[Information supplied by the institution as at 13 August 2007, and edited by the ACU]

INSTITUTE OF PHILOSOPHY

Founded 2005

Postal Address: Senate House, Malet Street, London, England WC1E 7HU
Telephone: (020) 7862 8683
E-mail: philosophy@sas.ac.uk
URL: http://www.philosophy.sas.ac.uk
Director—Smith, Prof. Barry C.
Administrator‡—Ali, Shahrar, BA Lond., MPhil Lond., PhD Lond.
Deputy Director—Smith, Barry C., BA Glas., PhD Edin.

WARBURG INSTITUTE

Postal Address: Woburn Square, London, England WC1H 0AB
Telephone: (020) 7862 8949 Fax: (020) 7862 8955
E-mail: warburg@sas.ac.uk
URL: http://warburg.sas.ac.uk
Director*—Hope, Prof. Charles, DPhil Oxf., MA
Secretary and Registrar‡—Pollard, Anita C., BA
Librarian—Kraye, Jill, BA Calif., MA Col., MPhil Col., PhD Col.
Curator of Photographic Collection—McGrath, Prof. Elizabeth, MA Glas., PhD, FBA

History. The institute was developed from the library of Professor A. M. Warburg (1866–1929) of Hamburg. It was transferred to England in 1933 and incorporated in the University of London in 1944.

Higher Degrees (see also University of London Directory to Subjects of Study).

Master's. MA, MPhil.

Admission. Applicants for admission must normally hold an appropriate first degree with at least upper second class honours. MA: reading knowledge of Latin and one modern European language (Italian is the most relevant) is required.

Length of course. Full-time: MA: 1 year; MPhil: 2 years. Part-time: MPhil: 4–5 years.

Doctoral. PhD.

Admission. Usually via MPhil programme.

Length of course. Full-time: PhD: 3 years. Part-time: PhD: 5–6 years.

Libraries. Volumes: 350,000. Other holdings: 3000 journal titles; 300,000 photographic items.

Academic Awards (2006–2007). 12 awards ranging in value from £1600 to £3800.

Academic Year (2007–2008). Three terms: 1 October–7 December; 7 January–14 March; 21 April–27 June.

Statistics. Students (2006–2007): full-time 14 (8 men, 6 women); part-time 1 (1 woman); international 7 (4 men, 3 women); master's 7 (5 men, 2 women); doctoral 8 (3 men, 5 women).

ACADEMIC UNITS

Classical Tradition

Burnett, C. S. F., BA *Camb.*, PhD *Camb.*, FBA Prof., History of Islamic Influences in Europe

Hope, Charles, DPhil *Oxf.*, MA Prof., History of the Classical Tradition

Kraye, Jill, BA *Calif.*, MA *Col.*, MPhil *Col.*, PhD *Col.* Prof., History of Renaissance Philosophy

McGrath, Elizabeth, MA *Glas.*, PhD, FBA Prof., History of Art

Other Staff: 2 Lectrs.

Research: interdisciplinary study of the classical tradition (influence of the ancient world on all aspects of European culture and intellectual history, especially the Renaissance)

CONTACT OFFICERS

General enquiries. Secretary and Registrar: Pollard, Anita C., BA

[Information supplied by the institution as at 7 November 2007, and edited by the ACU]

LONDON METROPOLITAN UNIVERSITY

Member of the Association of Commonwealth Universities

Postal Address: 31 Jewry Street, London, England EC3N 2EY
Telephone: (020) 7423 0000 **E-mail:** admissions@londonmet.ac.uk
URL: http://www.londonmet.ac.uk

VICE-CHANCELLOR AND CHIEF EXECUTIVE*—Roper, Brian A., BSc(Econ) *Wales*, MA(Econ) *Manc.*, Hon. DUniv
DEPUTY VICE-CHANCELLOR (ACADEMIC)—Aylett, Bob
DEPUTY VICE-CHANCELLOR (RESEARCH AND DEVELOPMENT)—(vacant)
REGISTRAR‡—McParland, John
DIRECTOR OF FINANCE—Nelson, Pam

GENERAL INFORMATION

History. The university was created by the merger on 1 August 2002 of London Guildhall University and the University of North London.

It is located at two major campuses: the London City campus in the City and Aldgate area, and the London North campus in Islington.

Admission to first degree courses (see also United Kingdom Introduction). Through Universities and Colleges Admissions Service (UCAS). Minimum of 2 GCE A level passes plus 2 other subjects at GCSE grade C, or 3 A level passes plus 1 other subject at GCSE grade C; or a minimum of 30 points at higher level International Baccalaureate; or equivalent qualifications.

First Degrees (see also United Kingdom Directory to Subjects of Study). BA, BEng, BSc, LLB.
Length of course. Full-time: BA, BEng, BSc, LLB: 3 years. Part-time: BA, BEng, BSc, LLB: 4 years.

Higher Degrees (see also United Kingdom Directory to Subjects of Study).
Master's. LLM, MA, MBA, MPhil, MRes, MSc.
Length of course. Full-time: LLM, MA, MBA, MRes, MSc: 1 year; MPhil: 2–3 years. Part-time: LLM, MA, MRes, MSc: 2 years; MBA: 2½ years; MPhil: 3–5 years.
Doctoral. PhD.
Length of course. Full-time: PhD: 2–5 years. Part-time: PhD: 3–8 years.

Libraries. Volumes: 801,300. Periodicals subscribed to: 4300. Special collections: Women's library; TUC library; Workers' Educational Association.

Academic Awards (2005–2006). 60 awards ranging in value from £2000 to £9000.

ACADEMIC UNITS

Accounting, Banking and Financial Services

Tel: (020) 7320 1538 Fax: (020) 7320 1557
Morgan, Bob Head*
Research: accounting; business information systems; financial services; quantitative methods

Applied Social Sciences

Tel: (020) 7133 5019 Fax: (020) 7133 5203
Gabriel, John Prof.; Head*
Research: child and women abuse studies; community health; social work; sociology; urban development

Architecture and Spatial Design

Tel: (020) 7133 2199 Fax: (020) 7133 2039
Mull, Robert Head*
Research: architecture; architecture and interior design; low energy architecture

Art, Media and Design, Sir John Cass Department of

Tel: (020) 7320 2800 Fax: (020) 7320 2833
Falconbridge, Brian Head*
Research: design and technology; film and broadcast production; jewellery; media and communications; silversmithing

Business and Service Sector Management

Tel: (020) 7133 3016 Fax: (020) 7133 3076
Morgan, Bob Head*
Research: business studies; hospitality management; leisure and tourism; marketing and purchasing; transport and consultancy

Computing, Communications Technology and Mathematics

Tel: (020) 7320 1700 Fax: (020) 7320 1717
Naylor, Jeff Head*
Research: communications technology and mathematical sciences; informatics and multimedia technology; operational research and probabilistic methods; statistics

Economics, Finance and International Business

Tel: (020) 7320 3005 Fax: (020) 7320 1414
Harper, Barry Head*
Research: business economics; economics and finance; international business law

Education

Tel: (020) 7133 2661 Fax: (020) 7133 2628
Gallacher, Roddy Head*
Research: education; information technology learning exchange; teacher training

Health and Human Sciences

Tel: (020) 7133 2115 Fax: (020) 7133 2184
Bointon, Brian Head*
Research: biological and applied sciences; chemical sciences; dietetics and food; health and sports science; nutrition

Humanities, Arts and Languages

Tel: (020) 7133 2578 Fax: (020) 7133 1234
Pike, Sue Head*
Research: English and creative writing; film; open language programmes; theatre and performing arts; translation and language studies

Law, Governance and International Relations

Tel: (020) 7320 4900 Fax: (020) 7320 4925
Ostmann, Connie Head*
Research: European studies; law; politics

London Metropolitan Polymer Centre

Tel: (020) 7133 2247 Fax: (020) 7133 2184
O'Brien, Mike Head*
Research: design with modern materials; plastic product design and manufacture; polymer technology; rubber technology; sports technology

Management and Professional Development

Tel: (020) 7320 1587 Fax: (020) 7320 1585
Inglis, Andy Head*
Research: accounting; banking and insurance; credit management; human resource management; organisation and employment studies

Psychology

Tel: (020) 7320 1067 Fax: (020) 7320 1236
Millar, Stuart Prof.; Head*
Research: counselling; forensic psychology; health psychology; occupational psychology; professional conversion psychology

SPECIAL CENTRES, ETC

Applied Mathematics and Coastal Studies, Centre for

Tel: (020) 7320 1728
E-mail: ulf.ehrenmark@londonmet.ac.uk
Ulf, Ehrenmark Prof.

Architecture Research Institute

Tel: (020) 7133 2485
E-mail: f.beigel@londonmet.ac.uk
Beigel, Florian Prof.

Brain Chemistry and Human Nutrition, Institute of

Tel: (020) 7133 2926
E-mail: m.crawford@londonmet.ac.uk
Crawford, Michael Prof.

Child and Woman Abuse Studies Unit (CWASU)

Tel: (020) 7133 5014
E-mail: cwasu@londonmet.ac.uk
Kelly, Liz, CBE Prof.

Cities Institute

Tel: (020) 7133 3028
E-mail: cities@londonmet.ac.uk
Evans, Graeme Prof.

Comparative European Survey Data, Centre for

Tel: (020) 7320 1140
E-mail: r.topf@londonmet.ac.uk
Topf, Richard Prof.

Consumer Sciences, Education and Policy Unit (CONSEP)

Tel: (020) 7133 2233
E-mail: m.kitson@londonmet.ac.uk
Kitson, Mike

Culture, Tourism and Development, International Institute for (IICTD)

Tel: (020) 7133 3035
E-mail: iictd@londonmet.ac.uk
Parravicini, Paola

Environmental and Social Studies in Ageing, Centre for (CESSA)

Tel: (020) 7133 5082
E-mail: l.kellaher@londonmet.ac.uk
Kellaher, Leonie

Equality Research in Business, Centre for (CERB)

Tel: (020) 7133 3033
E-mail: f.colgan@londonmet.ac.uk
Colgan, Fiona

Ethnicity and Gender, Centre for Research in

Tel: (020) 7133 2767
E-mail: i.gedalof@londonmet.ac.uk
Crowley, Helen
Gedalof, Irene

European Human Rights Advocacy Centre (EHRAC)

Tel: (020) 7133 5111
E-mail: pleach@londonmet.ac.uk
Leach, Philip

European Transformations, Institute for the Study of (ISET)

Tel: (020) 7133 2912
E-mail: iset@londonmet.ac.uk
Hickman, Mary J. Prof.

Financial Regulation Studies, Centre for

Tel: (020) 7320 1596
E-mail: p.tyldesley@londonmet.ac.uk
Tyldesley, Peter J.

Fine Art, Centre for

Tel: (020) 7320 1905
E-mail: i.robertson@londonmet.ac.uk
Robertson, Ian

Food Analysis Unit

Tel: (020) 7133 2272
E-mail: b.boniton@londonmet.ac.uk
Bointon, Brian

Gender Studies, Centre for

Tel: (020) 7320 1024
E-mail: c.midgley@londonmet.ac.uk
Midgley, Clare

Health Policy, Institute of

Tel: (020) 7133 2141
E-mail: c.branfordwhite@londonmet.ac.uk
Branford-White, Christopher Prof.

Human Rights and Social Justice, Research Institute on

Tel: (020) 7133 5132
E-mail: b.bowring@londonmet.ac.uk
Bowring, Bill Prof.

IMPACT

Involving Mathematics with Parents, Children and Teachers

Tel: (020) 7133 2617
E-mail: l.taylor@londonmet.ac.uk
Alexander, Patricia
Taylor, Lin

Intelligent Systems Research Centre

Tel: (020) 7320 3109
E-mail: h.kazemian@londonmet.ac.uk
Kazemian, Hassan

International Capital Markets, Centre for

Tel: (020) 7320 3079
E-mail: n.sarantis@londonmet.ac.uk
Sarantis, Nick Prof.

International Commercial Law, City Centre for

Tel: (020) 7320 1531
E-mail: c.chatterjee@londonmet.ac.uk
Chatterjee, Charles Prof.

International Transport Management, Centre for

Tel: (020) 7320 1669
E-mail: leggate@londonmet.ac.uk
Leggate, Heather

Irish Studies Centre

Tel: (020) 7133 2913
E-mail: mary.hickman@londonmet.ac.uk
Hickman, Mary J. Prof.

Language and Culture, Centre for Research

Tel: (020) 7320 1232
E-mail: t.pooley@londonmet.ac.uk
Pooley, Tim

Learning Technology Research Institute

Tel: (020) 7314 4301
E-mail: t.boyle@londonmet.ac.uk
Boyle, Tom Prof.

Leisure and Tourism Studies, Centre for (CELTS)

Tel: (020) 7133 3035
E-mail: iictd@londonmet.ac.uk
Parravicini, Paola

London European Research Centre

Tel: (020) 7133 2392
E-mail: m.newman@londonmet.ac.uk
Newman, Mike Prof.

London Metropolitan University Microwaves

Tel: (020) 7133 2511
E-mail: b.virdee@londonmet.ac.uk
Virdee, Bal

Low Energy Architecture Research Unit (LEARN)

Tel: (020) 7133 2178
E-mail: michael.wilson@londonmet.ac.uk
Wilson, Mike Prof.

Management Research Centre

Tel: (020) 7133 3032
E-mail: l.holmes@londonmet.ac.uk
Holmes, Len

Marketing Communications, Centre for Research in

Tel: (020) 7320 1577
E-mail: r.bennett@londonmet.ac.uk
Bennet, Roger

New Musical Instruments, Centre for (CNMI)

Tel: (020) 7320 1841
E-mail: l.jones@londonmet.ac.uk
Jones, Lewis

Policy Studies in Education, Institute for (IPSE)

Tel: (020) 7133 2649
E-mail: ipse@londonmet.ac.uk
Ross, Alistair Prof.

Primary Health and Social Care, Centre for

Tel: (020) 7133 5098
E-mail: f.couling@londonmet.ac.uk
Couling, Frank

Social and Evaluation Research, Centre for

Tel: (020) 7320 1276
E-mail: b.hall@londonmet.ac.uk
Hall, Brian

Statistics, Operational Research and Probabilistic Methods Research Centre

Tel: (020) 7133 7051
E-mail: r.gilchrist@londonmet.ac.uk
Gilchrist, Bob Prof.

Trade Union Studies, Centre for

Tel: (020) 7133 5206
E-mail: m.davis@londonmet.ac.uk
Davis, Mary Prof.

Transport Research Consultancy (TRAC)

Tel: (020) 7314 4213
E-mail: trac@londonmet.ac.uk
Shaw, Steve

Ukraine Centre

Tel: (020) 7133 2762
E-mail: m.bojcun@londonmet.ac.uk
Bojcun, Marko

Working Lives Research Institute

Tel: (020) 7607 2789
E-mail: s.jefferys@londonmet.ac.uk
Jefferys, Steve Prof.

[Information supplied by the institution as at 16 May 2006, and edited by the ACU]

LONDON SOUTH BANK UNIVERSITY

Founded 1892

Member of the Association of Commonwealth Universities

Postal Address: 103 Borough Road, London, England SE1 0AA
Telephone: (020) 7815 7815 **Fax:** (020) 7815 8273
URL: http://www.lsbu.ac.uk

VICE-CHANCELLOR AND CHIEF EXECUTIVE*—Hopkin, Prof. Deian R., BA *Wales*, PhD *Waik.*, Hon. DLitt *Glam.*, FRHistS, FRSA, Hon. FUWA
PRO-VICE-CHANCELLOR—Cardew, Philip, BA PhD
PRO-VICE-CHANCELLOR—McCaffery, Peter, BA MSc(Econ) PhD, FCMI, FCIPD
PRO-VICE-CHANCELLOR—Wilkinson, Mike, MA PhD
UNIVERSITY SECRETARY AND CLERK TO THE BOARD OF GOVERNORS‡—Stephenson, K., LLB MA
DIRECTOR OF FINANCE—Flatman, Richard, BA, FCA

GENERAL INFORMATION

History. The university was originally established as Borough Polytechnic Institute in 1892 and became the Polytechnic of the South Bank in 1970. It was granted university status in 1992.

It is located in central London.

Admission to first degree courses (see also United Kingdom Introduction). Through Universities and Colleges Admissions Service (UCAS).

First Degrees (see also United Kingdom Directory to Subjects of Study) (* = with honours). BA*, BEng*, BSc*, LLB*.

Length of course. Full-time: BSc*, LLB*: 3 years; BA*: 3–4 years; BEng*: 4 years. *Part-time:* LLB*: 4 years; BA*, BSc*: 5 years.

Higher Degrees (see also United Kingdom Directory to Subjects of Study).

Master's. MA, MBA, MPhil, MSc.

Length of course. Full-time: MA, MBA, MSc: 1 year; MPhil: 2 years. *Part-time:* MA, MBA, MSc: 2 years; MPhil: 4 years.

Doctoral. PhD.

Length of course. Full-time: PhD: 3 years. *Part-time:* PhD: 6 years.

Libraries. Volumes: 400,000.

FACULTIES/SCHOOLS

Arts and Human Sciences

Tel: (020) 7815 5741 Fax: (020) 7815 5799
Exec. Dean: Molan, Mike, BA LLM

Business, Computing and Information Management

Tel: (020) 7815 7805 Fax: (020) 7815 8250
Exec. Dean: Houzer, Jane, BA MSc(Econ)

Engineering, Science and the Built Environment

Tel: (020) 7815 7290 Fax: (020) 7815 6134
Exec. Dean: Bhamidimarri, Prof. Rao, BSc MTech PhD, FRSA

Health and Social Care

Tel: (020) 7815 8000 Fax: (020) 7815 8099
Exec. Dean: Sines, Prof. D., BSc PhD, FRCN

ACADEMIC UNITS

Accounting and Finance

Fax: (020) 7815 7793
Adomako, Joe, BSc MSc   Sr. Lectr.
Balachandran, Bala, BA LLB MBA MA   Sr. Lectr.
Batchelor, Denise, BA MA PhD   Reader
Blowes, Peter, BSc(Econ)   Principal Lectr.
Boatman, Iain, BSc MA   Principal Lectr.
Chambers, Andrew, BA, FCA, FBCS, FRSA   Deloitte Prof., Internal Auditing

D'Silva, Kenneth, BCom MSc PhD, FCA   Principal Lectr.
Griffiths, Howard, BSc(Econ) MSc(Econ) PhD   Sr. Lectr.
Kennedy, Michael, BA MBA, FBCS   Prof.; Head*
Khan, Yousuf, BA MSc MSc(Finance)   Sr. Lectr.
Kilmister, Tony, BA MA   Sr. Lectr.
Knight, Michael, BA MSc, FCA   Principal Lectr.
Kumar, Shashi, BSc MA MBA MSc   Sr. Lectr.
Lawrence, Mary, BSc   Principal Lectr.
Lee, Vijay, BA(Econ) MA(Econ) MBA   Principal Lectr.
Mandal, Ajjay, BA MA   Sr. Lectr.
McCarthy, Barry, BA   Sr. Lectr.
Moore-Williams, Sarah, BA
O'Connor, Steve, BA   Sr. Lectr.
Pingue, Ivor, BA MA   Sr. Lectr.
Rooks, Jonathan, BSc MSc   Sr. Lectr.
Scott, Libby, MSc   Sr. Lectr.
Scott, Nigel, MBA
Syer, John, MBA   Sr. Lectr.
Tanner, Jennie, MA DPhil DBA   Sr. Lectr.
Valiente, Carolina, BSc MPhil PhD   Sr. Lectr./Reader
Wilkinson, Andrew, BA MA   Sr. Lectr.
Williams, Steve, BA *Liv.*, MPhil *Liv.*   Sr. Lectr.
Wolstenholme, Eric, BSc MTech PhD   Prof., Business

Allied Health Professions

Ahmed-Landeryou, Musharrat, BSc BSc   Sr. Lectr., Occupational Therapy
Angell-Wells, Cheryl, BSc MSc   Sr. Lectr., Occupational Therapy
Baillie, Lesley, BA MSc PhD   Principal Lectr., Clinical Skills Development
Beale, Sophia, BSc   Sr. Lectr., Diagnostic Radiogaphy
Beanlands, Clare, MSc   Sr. Lectr., Occupational Therapy
Beckwith, Sally, MSc   Sr. Lectr., Occupational Therapy Studies
Beecraft, Susan, BEd MSc   Sr. Lectr., Occupational Therapy
Benwell, Martin, BA PhD   Sr. Lectr., Diagnostic Radiography
Bowler, Trish   Sr. Lectr., Occupational Therapy
Carpenter, Keith   Sr. Lectr., Perioperative Practice
Caunce, Maria, BSc PhD   Sr. Lectr., Occupational Therapy
Curtis, Kate, BSc   Sr. Lectr., Diagnostic Radiography
Eakin, Pamela, BA BA DPhil   Prof., Occupational Therapy
Ford, Rachel, BSc   Sr. Lectr., Diagnostic Radiography/Clinical Ultrasound
Forte, Anna, MSc   Sr. Lectr., Occupational Therapy
Fowler, Patricia S., BSc MMed   Course Dir., Radiography; Sr. Lectr., Diagnostic Imaging
Francis-Wright, Mark, BSc MEd   Sr. Lectr., Occupational Therapy

Hall, Anne, BA MSc   Sr. Lectr., Occupational Therapy
Henderson, Ian, MSc   Principal Lectr., Diagnostic Therapy
Holder-Powell, Heather, MSc PhD   Principal Lectr., Physiotherapy
Hughes, Jerry, BSc MSc   Sr. Lectr., Diagnostic Imaging-Radiography
Ilott, Lorraine   Sr. Lectr., Perioperative Practice
Keane, Peter A., MA MEd   Sr. Lectr., Diagnostic Radiography
Kent, Jacqueline   Sr. Lectr.
Lageard, Peter, MSc   Sr. Lectr.
Lovegrove, Mary, MSc   Prof., Education and Development; Head*
Maddex, Susan, BSc MSc   Sr. Lectr., Clinical Assistant Practice
Mahoney, Christine, BSc   Sr. Lectr., Perioperative Practice
Malik, Yasmeen, BSc MSc   Sr. Lectr., Radiotherapy
Maris-Shaw, Sarah   Sr. Lectr., Occupational Therapy
Moura, Walkira, MA   Sr. Lectr., Occupational Therapy
Parker, Elizabeth   Sr. Lectr., Clinical Ultrasound
Peterson-McKinney, Christine, BSc MScOT   Sr. Lectr., Occupational Therapy
Savill, Roger   Sr. Lectr., Diagnostic Radiography
Scotter, Judy, BA MSc   Sr. Lectr.; Course Dir., Clin. Asst. Practice
Sherwood, Wendy, MSc   Sr. Lectr., Occupational Therapy
Sinclair, Noreen, BSc MA   Principal Lectr., Radiotherapy
Stewart, Penny, BSc   Sr. Lectr., Occupational Therapy
Stewart-Lord, Adele, BRad MSc MBA   Sr. Lectr., Radiotherapy
Summerfield-Mann, Lynn, MSc   Principal Lectr., Occupational Therapy
Vawda, Shaheda, BA   Sr. Lectr., Occupational Therapy
Wheeler, Helen, MSc   Sr. Lectr., Occupational Therapy
Williams, Miriam, MSc   Sr. Lectr.
Woodhouse, Emily, BSc MSc   Sr. Lectr.
Wright, Deborah, MA   Sr. Lectr.; Course Dir., Occupational Therapy
Zahedi, Homa, MSc   Sr. Lectr., Occupational Therapy

Applied Science

Fax: (020) 7815 7999
Bartlett, I., BSc MSc   Sr. Lectr.
Beeby, A. N., BSc *Salf.*, PhD *Leic.*   Principal Lectr.
Bent, H., BS   Sr. Lectr.
Best, R. J., BSc *Lond.*, PhD *Lond.*   Principal Lectr.
Bowtell, Joanna, PhD
Brennan, A. M., BSc MSc PhD, FLS   Sr. Lectr.
Byford, Michael, PhD
Cadbury, R. G., BA MEng   Principal Lectr.
Chaplin, M. F., BSc PhD, FRSChem   Prof.

Clark, A. D., MA *Camb.*, PhD *Camb.* Principal Lectr.
Cook, David, PhD Sr. Lectr.
Davis, J., BSc PhD Prof.
Diaz, Pedro, PhD Sr. Lectr.
Dunne, L., BSc MSc PhD Prof.
Gergely, Laszlo, PhD Sr. Lectr.
Hibbs, M., BSc PhD Principal Lectr.
Hunter, S., BA MPhil Sr. Lectr.
Larkai, S., BSc PhD Sr. Lectr.
Maidment, M., BSc PhD Sr. Lectr.
Man, D., BSc MSc Sr. Lectr.
Morgan, N., BSc *Wales*, PhD *Brist.* Sr. Lectr.
Nolan, P. F. Prof.
Ojinnaka, C., BSc MSc PhD Sr. Lectr.
Orrin, J. E., BSc PhD Sr. Lectr.
Park, Sophie Sr. Lectr.
Piccirillo, Clara Sr. Lectr.
Qubian, A., PhD Sr. Lectr.
Richmond, Larry, PhD
Seeley, P. J., BSc PhD Sr. Lectr.
Spears, K., BSc MSc Principal Lectr.
Steele, C., BSc MSc PhD Sr. Lectr.
Willson, Hannah

Architecture, Division of

Allison, Peter Principal Lectr.
Andrews, Deborah, PhD Sr. Lectr.
Bayldon, Norman Sr. Lectr.; Professl. Placement Co-ordinator
Bowkett, Steve, BA MA Sr. Lectr.
Davies, Paul, BA Sr. Lectr.
Dowlen, Chris Reader
Evans, Michael Sr. Lectr.
Glanville, Rosemary, BA MA Dir., Medical Architecture Res. Unit; Course Dir., MA/ Postgrad. Diploma in Health Bldgs.
Howe, John RIBA Prof.
Jones, Tim M., MA *RCA* Sr. Lectr.
Kane, Mike, BA Sr. Lectr.
Kudic, Lilly Sr. Lectr.
Melvin, Jeremy P., BSc MSc Sr. Lectr.
Parine, Nick I., BSc MSc(Arch) PhD Sr. Lectr.
Pople, Nic Sr. Lectr.
Robbins, Michael W., MA *RCA* Sr. Lectr.
Rooney, Mary-Jane, BSc Sr. Lectr.
Thompson, Glen
Ward, Seamus Sr. Lectr.
Welsh, Mischa

Arts, Media and English

Aziz, Tahera, BA MB BS Sr. Lectr.
Banatvala, Jonathan, MA Course Dir., Theatre Practice, Creative Producing
Daniels, Terri, PhD Course Dir., Media and Society, Media Studies
Deacon, Robin, MA Course Dir., Drama and Performance Studies
Dewdney, Andrew, MA Prof., Media and Society; Head*
Domizio, Ricardo, MA MRes Course Dir., Film Studies
Elliott, Chris, MA Course Dir., Film and Video
Foster, Gill, MA Sr. Lectr., Drama and Performance Studies
Hammond, Philip, PhD Reader, Media and Communications
Harvey, Colin, BA Course Dir., Game Cultures
Kerr-Pertic, Suzy, MFA Principal Lectr.
Kinsman, Margaret, MA Sr. Lectr., English Studies
Luppa, Iris, PhD Sr. Lectr., Film
Maraschin, Donatella, PhD Sr. Lectr.; Course Dir., Writing for Media
Muir, Pauline, MA Course Dir., Arts Management; Sr. Lectr., Arts Management
Owen, Jennifer, PhD Deputy Head; Principal Lectr., Media Studies
Randell, Justin, BA Sr. Lectr., Sonic Media
Reading, Anna, PhD Programme Dir., MA Creative Media Arts; Reader, Cultural Theory
Rietveld, Hillegonda, PhD Course Dir., Sonic Media; Reader, Cultural Studies
Roush, Paula, MSc Sr. Lectr.
Rubinstein, Daniel, MA Sr. Lectr.; Course Dir., Digital Photography

Scafe, Suzanne, PhD Field Co-ordinator, English Studies
Sluis, Katrina, BA Course Dir., Digital Media Arts
Smith, Simon, BA Course Dir., Creative Writing and English
Tarrant, Patrick, PhD Sr. Lectr., Digital Film and Video
Other Staff: 2 Lectrs.

Business and International Studies

Fax: (020) 7815 7865
Ardy, Brian, BSc(Econ) MA MPhil Reader; Course Dir., MSc Internat. Bus.
Behennah, Mike Course Dir.
Burke, Jeff Course Dir.
Clemson, David Sr. Lectr.; Course Dir.
Cullen, John Sr. Lectr., Information Management
Desta, Amare Sr. Lectr.; Res. Scholar
Elci, Ceyhun Sr. Lectr., Economics
Freeman, Steve Course Dir.; Sr. Lectr., Economics
Green, Peter Course Dir., MSc Internat. Bus.; Principal Lectr., Economics and Finance
Grimwade, Nigel Emer. Prof., Applied Economics
Ietto-Gillies, Grazia Course Dir.; Prof., Applied Economics
Kahl, Jo Emer. Prof., Modern Languages
Koch, K., PhD Visiting Prof., Modern Languages
Lane, Vic Visiting Prof.
Luke, Peter Sr. Lectr.
Moss, Damian Sr. Lectr.
Scott, Anne-Marie Sr. Lectr.; Course Dir.; Programme Dir., Business
Snaith, Jim Head*
Tallent, Greg Sr. Lectr., Business Computing
Tetteh, Godwin Sr. Lectr.
Wolstenholme, Susie Course Dir.
Wood, Michael Sr. Lectr., Economics
Zanfei, Antonello Visiting Prof., International Business
Other Staff: 1 Lectr.; 3 Lectrs.†

Economics

Fax: (020) 7815 7793
Cox, H., BA MSc PhD Prof.
Grimwade, N. S., BA MA Principal Lectr.; Head*
Lintott, J., BA *Camb.*, MSc *Lond.*, PhD *Lond.* Sr. Lectr.
Lloyd, J. H., MA *Leeds*, MTech *Brun.* Principal Lectr.
Prevezer, M., BA MA MSc(Econ) PhD
Saad-Filho, A., BSc MSc(Econ) PhD Sr. Lectr.
Thomas, P., BA BSocSc Sr. Lectr.
Toporowski, J. M. Reader
Wood, M. L., BA MA(Econ) Sr. Lectr.
Other Staff: 2 Lectrs.

Education

Beg, Sid Sr. Lectr.
Britton, Alison, BA *E.Anglia*, MA *York(Can.)* Reader; Course Dir., Programme for Learning and Teaching in Higher Educn.
Burns, Jean, MA Principal Lectr.; Deputy Head
Coles, Jane, MA Head of Initial Teacher Training
Cowley, Richard, BSc Sr. Lectr.
Daniels, Karen, MSc Course Dir.
Horner, Chris, EdD Sr. Lectr., English (Primary)
Inman, Sally, MSc Prof.; Head*
Lerman, Steve, BSc MSc PhD Prof.
March, Caty, BA Sr. Lectr.
McCormack, Pip Sr. Lectr.
Meadows, John, BSc MA Sr. Lectr.; Course Dir.
Norman, Angela, MSc Sr. Lectr.; Course Dir.
Parkinson, Alan, BEd *Belf.*, MA *Lond.*, PhD Sr. Lectr.
Preston, Margaret, MA Sr. Lectr.
Rea, Val Sr. Lectr.
Ryf, Victoria, MA Sr. Lectr.

Strachan, Glenn Co-Dir., Educn. for Sustainability
Tizzard, Julia, BA Sr. Lectr.
Wade, Ros Course Dir., Educn. for Sustainability
Winbourne, Peter, MA Reader; MA Course Dir.
Other Staff: 2 Lectrs.

Engineering, Electrical, Computer and Communications

Fax: (020) 7815 7599
Alford, N. McN., BSc PhD Prof., Physical Electronics
Bao, Ya Course Dir.
Bezahov, Goran, PhD Sr. Lectr.
Bridge, Prof. B., BSc DSc, FIP, FIEE Head*
Centenu, Anthony Sr. Lectr.
Chen, Shuwu, PhD Sr. Lectr.
Dimitriou, Stavros Sr. Lectr.
Dudley-McEvoy, Sandra Sr. Lectr.
Fradkin, L. Ju, MSc PhD Reader
Howson, A., BSc Sr. Lectr.
Imhof, R. E., BSc PhD, FIEE, FIP Prof., Electrical Engineering
Kaye, R., BSc PhD Principal Lectr.
Klimo, P., MSc PhD Sr. Lectr.
Lunn, C., MSc Sr. Lectr.
Mukherjee, D., BSc MTech PhD Principal Lectr.
Nyerges, G., BSc MSc Sr. Lectr.
Pekris, J., BSc MSc Sr. Lectr.
Pervez, A., BSc *Pesh.*, BSc *Salf.*, MSc *Essex*, PhD *Lond.* Sr. Lectr.
Pettitt, R., BSc PhD Sr. Lectr.
Ponugubati, Manoj Sr. Lectr.
Poole, Marlene, PhD
Protheroe, D. W., BSc PhD Sr. Lectr.
Reehal, H. S., BSc PhD Reader, Thin Film Technology
Ridler, P., BSc *Wales*, MSc *Lond.*, PhD *Brun.* Sr. Lectr.
Sattar, T., BSc PhD Principal Lectr.
Shirkoohi, G. H., MSc PhD Sr. Lectr.
Siyau, Ming Fei, PhD Sr. Lectr.
Viscardi, K., BA Sr. Lectr.
Webster, N., BSc PhD Sr. Lectr.
Zhang, Jian Gwo Sr. Lectr.
Zhao, Zhanfan, PhD Sr. Lectr.
Other Staff: 1 Lectr.

Engineering Systems

Fax: (020) 7815 7699
Ajmal, A., MSc *Manc.*, PhD *Manc.*, BSc Sr. Lectr.
Bao, Yuqing, PhD Reader
Burgess, N. J., PhD Sr. Lectr.
Dance, Stephen, PhD Course Dir.
Datoo, M., PhD Course Dir.
Day, A. R., BEng Sr. Lectr.
Dunn, Alan, PhD Sr. Lectr.
Dwyer, T. C., BSc Sr. Lectr.
Ezugwu, E. O., MSc PhD Reader
Fuad, A. H., BEng MEng Sr. Lectr.
Gawne, D. T., BSc PhD, FIMMM Prof.
Goss, Victor, PhD Course Dir.
Gunn, Michael, PhD Prof., Geotechnical Engineering
Hardy, D. J., MPhil PhD Sr. Lectr.
Karayiannis, T. G., BSc PhD Prof., Heat Transfer
Kraincenic, Ivana, PhD Course Dir.
Lawner, Harry Course Dir.
Lowry, Gordon, PhD Reader; Course Dir.
Maidment, G. Course Dir.
Mavroulidou, Maria, PhD Sr. Lectr.
Missenden, J. F., BSc PhD Sr. Lectr.
Mitchell, Steven Sr. Lectr.
Perea, Esther Sr. Admissions Tutor; Course Dir.
Roberts, Tony Course Dir.
Rotter, K. R., BA MA MSc, FIMarEST Sr. Lectr.
Shield, Bridget M., BSc MSc PhD Prof.
Smith, Kenneth Programme Dir., Civil Engin.
Terry, A. V., MSc *Cran.*IT Principal Lectr.
Vary, Stephen Sr. Lectr.
Yiakoumetti, K., BSc MSc Sr. Lectr.

Vacant Posts: Head*

Human Resources and Management

Bagley, Denise Principal Lectr.; Programme Dir., HRM
Bell, George, BA BSc(Econ) MSc Sr. Lectr.; Course Dir., MBA
Briggs, Nick, BSc BSc MSc Sr. Lectr.; Course Dir., MA Management
Crummie, Milo, BA Principal Lectr.; Head*
Garner, Stephanie, MBA Sr. Lectr.
George, Helen, MSc
Gordon, Gloria, MBA PhD Sr. Lectr.
Hack-Polay, Dieu, BA MA EdD PhD Sr. Lectr.
Knapp, Colin, BSc MA Principal Lectr.
Mullen, Fiona, BA Sr. Lectr.
Murdoch, Sheena, BA MSc PhD Sr. Lectr.
Murdock, Alex, BSc MA MSc MBA Prof.
Myers, Piers, BA MA MA Sr. Lectr.
Oldfield, Chrissie, BA MA LLM Sr. Lectr.
Rae, Jan, BEd MSc DBA Sr. Lectr.
Shaw, Elizabeth, BSc MBA Sr. Lectr., Management
Somers, Alibeth, BA MPA Sr. Lectr.
Summers, Andrew, MSc Sr. Lectr.
Tandoh, John, BA MSc MA Sr. Lectr.
Vass, Cheryl-Anne Sr. Lectr.
Woods, Declan, MBA Dir., Coaching Programmes
Other Staff: 1 Lectr.; 6 Visiting Lectrs.; 9 Lectrs.†; 1 Course Dir.†

Information Systems and Information Technology

see also Software Development and Computer Networking
Fax: (020) 7815 7499
Ait-Braham, Aziz, BSc MSc PhD Sr. Lectr.
Barikzai, Safia Sr. Lectr.
Bradley, Mike, BA MSc Sr. Lectr.
Chang, Jeffery, BSc MPhil PhD Principal Lectr.
Chen, Daqing, BSc MPhil PhD Sr. Lectr.
Flynn, Val, PhD Sr. Lectr.
Ge, Jianmin Prof.
Hughes, Alun, BEd MSc
Inman, Dave, MSc MSc PhD Reader
Linecar, Peter, BSc MSc Sr. Lectr.; Head*
Long, Allen Prof.
Patel, Dillip, MSc PhD Prof.
Patel, Shushma, BSc PhD Prof.
Phillips, Nigel, MSc Principal Lectr.
Scott, Mike Sr. Lectr.
Ubakanma, George, MSc Sr. Lectr.
Other Staff: 3 Lectrs.†

Law

Fax: (020) 7815 7793
Andronicou, Louise, MA Sr. Admissions Tutor; Principal Lectr.
Aquino, Tracey, LLB Sr. Lectr.
Bain, William, LLM Sr. Lectr.
De Freitas, Jerry, LLM MA Sr. Lectr.
Jeeves, Mic, LLB Principal Lectr.; Course Dir.
Koo, John, MA Principal Lectr.
Lever, Jeffrey, MA Sr. Lectr.; Course Dir.
Moran, Gaye, LLB Sr. Lectr.
Mylonaki, Emmanouela, PhD Course Dir.
Rodney, Mike, MA Sr. Lectr.
Shepherd, Chris, LLB Sr. Lectr.
Stylianou, Katherine, LLM Sr. Lectr.
Thatcher, Caron, LLB Sr. Lectr.; Course Dir.
Tiagi, Nina, LLM Sr. Lectr.
Unger, R. A. D., LLB Sr. Lectr.; Head*

Marketing and Strategy

Fax: (020) 7815 7793
Aston, Helen, BSc Sr. Lectr.
Barker, Beverly, MSc Sr. Lectr.
Bennett, Dag, MBA PhD Sr. Lectr.
Boukersi, Lakhdar, BA MBA PhD Principal Lectr.
Campayne, Carol, BA MBA
Capper, David, PhD Sur., BA MSc Sr. Lectr.
Fisher, Laurence, MSc Sr. Lectr.
Fitzgerald, Felicity, BSocSci Sr. Lectr.
Gadman, Leslie, MA PhD Sr. Lectr.

Godfrey, Mel, MBA MA Principal Lectr.; Programme Dir., Marketing
Graham, Charles, BA MA Sr. Lectr.
Hirst, Alan, MSc Sr. Lectr.
John, Robin, BSc(Econ) MA(Econ) MBA Principal Lectr.; Head*
Lloyd, Bruce, BSc MSc PhD Prof., Strategic Management
Peleg, Anita, BSc MBA Sr. Lectr.
Roberts, Kim, BA MA Sr. Lectr.
Other Staff: 1 Lectr.; 5 Visiting Lectrs.; 1 Visiting Fellow; 1 Res. Fellow; 6 Lectrs.†

Mathematics, Statistics and Foundation Studies

Abram, Martin, BSc Sr. Lectr.
Burrell, Phillip, BSc MSc PhD Principal Lectr.
Connies-Laing, Helen, BA MA Sr. Lectr., English Lang. Section; Course Dir.
Darlington, Keith, BSc Sr. Lectr.
Dhesi, Gurjeet, BSc MA PhD Sr. Lectr.
Fogerty, Terry Emer. Prof.
Jennings, Sylvia, BSc MSc PhD Sr. Lectr.
Langley, Gail, BA MA Sr. Lectr.
Norman, Les, BSc Principal Lectr.
Olanrewaju, Emmanuel, BSc MEd Sr. Lectr., Quantitative Studies
Rose, Lee, BSc MSc MBA PhD Head*
Rutherford, Carrie, BSc PhD Sr. Lectr.
Selig, Jon, BSc PhD Sr. Lectr.
Warwick, Jon, BSc PhD FIMA Prof., Educational Development
Other Staff: 6 Lectrs.†

Mental Health and Learning Disabilities

Bedford, Lesley Sr. Lectr.
Blaney, Rachel Principal Lectr.
Burke, Tina, LLB BSc MSc Sr. Lectr.
Currid, Thomas, BSc Sr. Lectr.
Gale, Cathy Sr. Lectr.
Gordon, Jane, BSc Sr. Lectr.
Gunnoo, Vedan Sr. Lectr.
Howard, Mark, BSc MSc Sr. Lectr.
Jupp, Sharon, BSc MSc Sr. Lectr.
Kemp, Philip, BSc MSc Principal Lectr.
Lee, Richard, BSc MSc Sr. Lectr.
Leiba, Tony, BA MSc MPhil PhD Prof., Educational Development
Lynch, Jonathon Sr. Lectr.
Mallikaaratchi, Wijaya, MSc MEd Sr. Lectr.
Murray, Rosaleen Sr. Lectr.
Pennington, Jenni, BSc Sr. Lectr.
Rooks, Jenni, BSc MSc Sr. Lectr.
Simpson, Clive, BSc Sr. Lectr.
Smith, Stephen, MSc Sr. Lectr.
Sooboodoo, Enkanah, BEd MA Head*
Webley-Brown, Carol, BSc Sr. Lectr.
Weinstein, Jenny, BA BPhil MSc Principal Lectr.
Other Staff: 1 Lectr.

Primary and Social Care

Ahuja, Jaya Sr. Lectr., Pharmaco Therapeutics
Barratt, Julian Sr. Lectr.
Boran, Sue, BSc MSc Sr. Lectr.
Brodie, Sarah Sr. Lectr.
Campbell-King, Iain Sr. Lectr.
Colquhoun, Andrea Sr. Lectr.
Couchman, W. A. Emer. Prof., Social Work
David, Ami Visiting Prof., Primary Care
Fairbrass, Lesley Sr. Lectr., Community Health Care
Forbes-Buford, Janice Dir., Changing Workforce Centre
Goodyer, Annabel Sr. Lectr.; Social Work Course Dir.
Hack, Angie Sr. Lectr.
Hafford-Letchfield, Trish Sr. Lectr., Social Work
Harriss, Angie Reader
Higgins, Martyn Sr. Lectr., Social Work
Higgs, Alison Sr. Lectr.
Jameson, Maxine Sr. Lectr.
Johnson, Wendy Sr. Lectr.
Kennington, Gail Course Dir.
Lask, Sandra Sr. Lectr., Health Promotion
Leonard, Kate, BA MA Course Dir., Interprofessl. Practice Teaching Course

Macdonough, John Sr. Lectr.
Maclaine, Katrina Principal Lectr.
Nelson, Anna Sr. Lectr.
O'Connor, Louise Sr. Lectr., Social Work
Popple, Keith Prof., Social Work
Power, Joy Sr. Lectr.
Sanders, Jan Sr. Lectr., sanderje@lsbu.ac.uk
Saunders, Mary, BA MSc Head*
Spatcher, Pat Sr. Lectr., Social Work
Stark, Rose Sr. Lectr.
Stubbs, Karen Project Manager Primary Care
Sykes, Susie Sr. Lectr.
Taylor, Lynda Sr. Lectr., Infection Control Nursing
Taylor, Vicki Sr. Lectr.
Thei, Penny Sr. Lectr.
Tragen, Amanda Sr. Lectr.
Ward, Beth Sr. Lectr.
Ward, Helen Sr. Lectr.
Ward, Valerie Sr. Lectr., Health Protection
Whittaker, Andrew Sr. Lectr., Social Work
Wilks, Tom Sr. Lectr., Social Work
Willis, Annaliese Sr. Lectr.
Wills, Jane Reader

Property, Surveying and Construction

Fax: (020) 7815 6134
Adriaanse, John S., LLB Sr. Lectr.
Atkinson, Andy K., MSc PhD, FRICS Sr. Lectr.
Bayyati, Ali Course Dir., Foundation Degree
Bourne, Ian Course Dir., Property Management and Surveying
Burgess, Graham Course Dir., Construction Management
Dunkeld, Malcolm, BSc MSc Sr. Lectr.
Farshchi, Mahtab Course Dir., Property Develop. and Planning
Fong, D. Sr. Lectr.
Gonzalez, Carlos Sr. Lectr.
Gu, Guowei, PhD Sr. Lectr.
Haywood, P. G., BSc MSc Sr. Lectr.
James, Darren Course Dir., Built Environment
Knowles, J. B., BSc Principal Lectr.
Lake, Martin G., BSc Deputy Head
Multescu, Gheorge Sr. Lectr.
Naoum, S. G., BSc MSc PhD Sr. Lectr.
Page, Mark W., BA MA PhD Sr. Lectr.
Parine, Nick I., BSc MSc(Arch) PhD Sr. Lectr.
Pearson, Steve H., BSc MSc, FRICS Principal Lectr.
Powell, Chris J., BArch BSc Principal Lectr.
Rapley, Nigel Sr. Lectr.
Robinson, Herbert, PhD Course Dir., Quantity Surveying
Salzman, Diego, PhD Sr. Lectr.
Symonds, B. C., MSc Lond., FRICS Principal Lectr.; Head*
Tweedy, Keith Sr. Lectr.
Other Staff: 3 Lectrs.†

Psychology

Albery, Ian, PhD Prof.
Barker, Meg, PhD Sr. Lectr.
Brown, Janice, PhD Sr. Lectr.
Henry, Lucy, PhD Reader
Katz, Hillary, PhD Sr. Lectr.
Newton, Elizabeth, PhD Sr. Lectr.
Niazi, Asli, PhD Sr. Lectr.
Reavey, Paula, PhD Sr. Lectr.
Ridley, Anne, PhD Sr. Lectr.
Rycroft, Nicola, PhD Sr. Lectr.
Smith-Spark, James, PhD Sr. Lectr.
Sterling, Christopher, PhD Principal Lectr.; Head*
Stone, Tony, MSc Principal Lectr.
Wilcock, Rachel, PhD Sr. Lectr.
Other Staff: 1 Lectr.; 2 Res. Fellows

Social and Policy Studies

Alexander, Claire Sr. Lectr.
Atkinson, Hugh P., PhD Scheme Dir., Politics
Bailey, Bill Sr. Lectr.
Beaumont, Caitriona, BA PhD Sr. Lectr., History
Bosco, Andrea, MA Prof., European Integration
Budd, Adrian M., PhD Subject Leader, Politics

Callender, Claire, BA PhD   Prof., Social Policy
De Zoysa, Richard, MSc *Lond.*, MA *Lond.*, BSc
    Sr. Lectr., Politics
Edwards, Dave, BA   Deputy Head; Course
    Dir., Sociology
Farnsworth, Kevin, BA PhD   Sr. Lectr., Social
    Policy
Feldman, Rayah   Sr. Lectr.; Course Dir., Social
    Sci.
Fooks, Gary, PhD   Sr. Lectr., Criminology
Goulbourne, Harry, BA DPhil   Prof.,
    Sociology
Grier, Tom, BSc   Principal Lectr., Politics
Hudson, Kate J., PhD   Head*
Kibreab, Gaim, PhD   Prof.; Course Dir., MSc
    Refugee Studies
Marlow, Laurence A., BSc *Lond.*, MA *Warw.*,
    PhD *Warw.*
Matthews, Roger   Prof., Criminology
Parker, Jenneth, BA MSc   Course Dir.
Phellas, Constantinos   Sr. Lectr., Sociology
Pine, Lisa N., BA PhD   Sr. Lectr., History
Rogers, Antoine, MSc   Subject Leader; Course
    Dir., Childhood and Family Studies
Rooke, Richard, PhD   Course Dir.; Pathway
    Leader, Politics
Silvestri, Marisa, PhD   Course Dir.,
    Criminology
Sumner, Andrew, PhD   Sr. Lectr.
Takhar, Shaminder, PhD   Sr. Lectr.; Subject
    Leader
Taylor, John G., BA *Sus.*, MA *City(UK)*, PhD
    City(UK)   Course Dir., MSc Development
    Studies; Prof., Politics
Tucker, Colin, BSc   Course Dir., Pol.
Van Dyke, Ruth, PhD   Sr. Lectr.
Wade, Ros, BSc MSc   MSc Course Dir.
Other Staff: 1 Res. Fellow; 1 Res. Scholar; 2
    Lectrs.†

Software Development and Computer Networking

see also Information Systems and Information
    Technology
Abdallah, Ali, BSc MSc DPhil   Prof.,
    Computing
Adeboye, Kemi, BSc MSc   Sr. Lectr.; Course
    Dir.
Banissi, Ebad, BSc MSc PhD   Reader
Benjamin, Elroy, BSc MSc MPhil   Sr. Lectr.
Blair, Allan, BA   Principal Lectr.
Bush, Martin, BSc PhD   Principal Lectr.
Campbell, Phillip, MSc   Sr. Lectr.
Carden, Paul, MSc   Sr. Lectr.
Chalk, Bernard, BSc   Sr. Lectr.
Culwin, Fintan, BSc PhD, FBCS   Prof.; Head*
Devai, Frank, MSc PhD   Sr. Lectr.
Edmonds, Ian, BSc   Sr. Lectr.
Faulkner, Christine, BA   Reader

Hayton, Clive, BA MSc   Principal Lectr.
Josephs, Mark, BSc MSc DPhil, FBCS   Dir.,
    Institute for Computing Res.; Prof.,
    Computing
Protheroe, Dave, BSc PhD   Principal Lectr.;
    Course Dir., Computing
Rosner, Peter, BSc MSc   Sr. Lectr.

Urban, Environmental and Leisure Studies

Adams, Neil, MA   Course Dir.
Askew, Alison, MA   Sr. Lectr.
Harpham, Trudy, PhD   Prof., Urban
    Development and Policy
Hollins, Margaret, LLM   Deputy Head,
    Planning
Hunte, Claudette   Course Dir.
Isaacs, Edward, MA   Course Dir.
Jarvis, Robert K., PhD   Co-ordinator, Urban
    Design
Leary, Michael, MA   Course Dir.
Lyons, Michal, PhD   Prof., Urban
    Development
Madeddu, Manuela, PhD   Sr. Lectr.
Morad, Munir, PhD   Prof.; Head*
Noussia, Antonia, PhD   Course Dir.
Paice, Diane L., BA   Course Dir.
Pinch, Philip L., PhD   Course Dir.
Richards, Ruth   Subject Leader, Housing and
    Planning
Tyler, Duncan, PhD   Sr. Lectr.
Vickery, Lynn, MA   Sr. Lectr.
Want, Philip, MA   Course Dir.
Winter, Alan J., MA   Development Co-
    ordinator
Other Staff: 1 Lectr.; 5 Visiting Fellows

SPECIAL CENTRES, ETC

Language Centre

Bellas, Stephen   Principal Lectr.; Dir.*
Other Staff: 9 Lectrs.†; 2 Tutors†

Learning and Literacy Unit

Chanda, Noyona   Dir., Numeracy Division
Cooper, Ross   Dir., Dyslexia and Literacy
    Division
Held, Madeline   Dir.*
Rees, Shan   Dir., Community and Workforce
    Division
Savitzky, Foufou   Dir., Family Learning
    Division
Smith, Linda   Course Dir.
Sunderland, Helen   Dir., ESOL Division
Other Staff: 1 Lectr.; 4 Tutors; 11 Trainers; 1
    Numeracy Professional; 2 ESOL
    Professionals; 1 Sr. Project Manager; 1
    Project Manager; 1 Co-ordinator

National Bakery School

Durman, Jenny   Sr. Lectr.
Marchant, John   Head*
Other Staff: 5 Lectrs.; 1 Hon. Visiting Fellow

RCN Development Centre

Crichton, Nicola   Principal Lectr., Research
Garvey, Anne   Head*

CONTACT OFFICERS

Accommodation. Accommodation Office
    Manager: Thomas, Dawn
    (E-mail: thomasdc@lsbu.ac.uk)
Admissions (first degree). Head of UK
    Recruitment: Milne, Rebecca
    (E-mail: milner@lsbu.ac.uk)
Archives. Director of Archives, Records and
    Information Access: Kwafo-Akoto, Kate
    (E-mail: kwafoak@lsbu.ac.uk)
Careers. Head of Careers Service: Short, Jayson
    (E-mail: jaysons@lsbu.ac.uk)
Computing services. Director of Information
    Communication Technology: Adamek,
    Wojtek(E-mail: adamekw@lsbu.ac.uk)
Estates and buildings/works and services.
    Interim Director, Estates and Facilities:
    James, Terry(E-mail: jamest3@lsbu.ac.uk)
Finance. Director of Finance: Flatman,
    Richard, BA, FCA
International office. Head (International
    office): Wilson, Mark
    (E-mail: wilsonmo@lsbu.ac.uk)
Library (chief librarian). Director, Centre for
    Learning Support and Development: Hall,
    Robert (E-mail: r.hall@lsbu.ac.uk)
Marketing. Head of Marketing Services Unit:
    Pearce, David
    (E-mail: david.pearce@lsbu.ac.uk)
Marketing. Director of External Relations and
    Communications: Jenkins, Beth
    (E-mail: beth.jenkins@lsbu.ac.uk)
Personnel/human resources. Head, Human
    Resources: Boyce, Katie, MA
Quality assurance and accreditation. Head of
    Quality Unit: Burns, Tony, PhD
    (E-mail: burnspa@lsbu.ac.uk)
Research. Head, Research and Business
    Development: Tinley, E., BSc PhD
    (E-mail: tinleye@lsbu.ac.uk)
Sport and recreation. Academy Director:
    Powlesland, Andrew
    (E-mail: powlesa@lsbu.ac.uk)

[*Information supplied by the institution as at 8 January
2008, and edited by the ACU*]

LOUGHBOROUGH UNIVERSITY

Founded 1966

Member of the Association of Commonwealth Universities

Postal Address: Loughborough, England LE11 3TU
Telephone: (01509) 263171 **Fax:** (01509) 223900
URL: http://www.lboro.ac.uk

VICE-CHANCELLOR*—Pearce, Prof. Shirley, CBE, BA Oxf., MPhil Lond., PhD Lond.
DEPUTY VICE-CHANCELLOR—Halliwell, Prof. Neil A., BSc Liv., PhD Liv., DSc S'ton., FREng, FIMechE, FIP
PRO-VICE-CHANCELLOR (TEACHING)—Bell, Prof. Morag, BA Nott., DPhil Oxf.
PRO-VICE-CHANCELLOR (RESEARCH)—Golding, Prof. Peter, BSc Lond., MA Essex
CHIEF OPERATING OFFICER‡—Spinks, Will
DIRECTOR OF FINANCE—Wiggans, Rachel, MA Camb.
LIBRARIAN—Morley, Mary D., BA Nott.

GENERAL INFORMATION

History. The university was established as Loughborough College of Technology in 1952 and incorporated as a university in 1966. In 1998 Loughborough College of Art and Design merged with the university. The university is a partner in the Peterborough Higher Education Project Company.

It is located in the East Midlands.

Admission to first degree courses (see also United Kingdom Introduction). For the purpose of its general entrance requirements the university recognises all General Certificate of Education (GCE) A level and AS level subjects. Many overseas qualifications are also accepted.

First Degrees (see also United Kingdom Directory to Subjects of Study). BA, BEng, BSc, MChem, MComp, MEng, MMath, MPhys.
Length of course. Full-time: BA, BEng, BSc: 3–4 years; MChem, MComp, MEng, MMath, MPhys: 4–5 years.

Higher Degrees (see also United Kingdom Directory to Subjects of Study).
Master's. MA, MBA, MDes, MPhil, MSc.
Length of course. Full-time: MA, MDes, MSc: 1 year; MPhil: max. 2 years. Part-time: MA, MBA, MSc: 2–8 years; MPhil: max. 3 years. By distance learning: MA, MSc: 2–8 years.
Doctoral. PhD.
Length of course. Full-time: PhD: max. 3 years. Part-time: PhD: max. 5 years.

Language of Instruction. English. Ten-week and five-week intensive English language course before the start of the academic session; two-week study skills course and a one-week pre-sessional course.

Libraries. Volumes: 500,000. Periodicals subscribed to: 10,000.

Academic Awards (2007–2008). 150 awards ranging in value from £500 to £3000.

Academic Year (2007–2008). Two semesters: 1 October–8 February; 11 February–20 June. Summer session: July–September.

Income (2005–2006). Total, £166,000,000.

Statistics. Staff (2006–2007): 3036 (1553 academic, 1483 non-academic). Students (2006–2007): full-time 12,627; part-time 2062; international 2309; undergraduate 10,886; master's 2740; doctoral 1063.

FACULTIES/SCHOOLS
Engineering
Tel: (01509) 227508 Fax: (01509) 227502
Dean: Rothberg, Prof. Steve, BSc S'ton., PhD S'ton., FIMechE

Science
Tel: (01509) 222880 Fax: (01509) 223940
Dean: Parsons, Prof. Kenneth, BSc Lough., PhD S'ton., FErgS

Social Sciences and Humanities
Tel: (01509) 228901
Dean: Kavanagh, Prof. Terence, MDes RCA, FRSA

ACADEMIC UNITS
Art and Design, Loughborough University School of
Tel: (01509) 228903 Fax: (01509) 228902
E-mail: j.b.white@lboro.ac.uk
Archer, Michael, BA   Sr. Lectr.
Atkin, John, BA CNAA, MA RCA   Reader
Edwards, Clive, MA RCA, PhD RCA   Reader
Kavanagh, Terence, MDes RCA, FRSA   Prof., Design
Meskimmon, Marsha, BA Leic., PhD Leic.   Reader, Art History and Theory; Dir.*
Wells, Paul, BA CNAA, MLitt Reading, PhD Reading   Prof., Animation
Other Staff: 38 Lectrs.
Research: art, craft and design history, practice and theory; gallery of the future

Business School
Tel: (01509) 223393 Fax: (01509) 223960-1
E-mail: postmaster@bsb.lboro.ac.uk
Ackers, Peter, MA Oxf., MA Warw., MPhil CNAA, PhD CNAA   Prof., Industrial Relations and Labour History
Arnold, John, BSc Nott., PhD Sheff.   Prof., Organisational Behaviour
Boocock, Grahame, BA Sheff., MA Manc.   Sr. Lectr.
Buck, Trevor, BCom Liv., MA Liv.   Prof., International Business
Cadogan, John, BSc Wales, MPhil Wales, PhD Wales   Prof., Marketing
Calvert, John, BSc Durh., MSc Warw., MSc Hull, PhD Lough.   Sr. Lectr.
Cheyne, Alistair, BA Nott., MA St And., PhD Lough.   Sr. Lectr.
Chivers, Geoff, BSc Birm., PhD Birm., FRSA   Emer. Prof.
Cohen, Laurie, BA Colgate, MA Sheff.Hallam, PhD Sheff.Hallam   Prof., Organisation Studies
Daniels, Kevin, BSc Liv., PhD Cran.   Prof., Organisational Psychology
Davidson, Ian, MA Oxf., PhD Brist., FCA   Prof., Accounting and Finance; Dir.*
de Jonge, Jan, MSc Maastricht, PhD Maastricht   Visiting Prof.
Diamantopoulos, Adamantios, BSc H-W, MSc H-W, PhD Strath.   Visiting Prof.
Dobson, Paul, BA CNAA, MSc Lond., PhD Lond., FRSA   Prof., Competition Economics
Doherty, Neil, BSc Lough., MSc Birm., PhD Brad.   Prof., Information Management
Fitzgerald, Lin, BA Essex   Prof., Management Accounting

Forbes, William, BA Keele, MSocSci Birm., MA Warw., PhD Newcastle(UK)   Prof., Accounting and Finance
Gerstner, Eitan, BA Haifa, MA Calif., PhD Calif.   Prof., Marketing and Retail
Gregory, Geoff, MA MS MSc PhD   Emer. Prof.
Hart, Cathryn, BA CNAA, MA CNAA   Sr. Lectr.
Hislop, Donald, BSc Paisley, MSc Edin., PhD Edin.   Sr. Lectr.
Howcroft, Barry, BA Wales, MSc Wales   Prof., Retail Banking
King, Malcolm, MA Oxf., DPhil Oxf., FIMA   Prof., Management Sciences
Korczynski, Marek, BA Liv., MA Warw., PhD Warw.   Prof., Sociology of Work
Lawrence, Peter, BA Lond., MA Essex   Emer. Prof.
Li, Baibing, BSc Yunnan, MSc Shanghai Jiaotong, PhD Shanghai Jiaotong   Reader, Business Statistics and Management Science
Liu, Jiyin, PhD Nott., BEng MSc   Prof., Operations Management
Loan-Clarke, John, BA CNAA, MSc UMIST   Sr. Lectr.
Loucopoulos, Pericles, BSc Reading, MSc CNAA, PhD Manc.   Prof., Information Systems
Lui, Xiaohui, BSc Beijing, MPhil Beijing, PhD Birm.   Sr. Lectr.
Lyytinen, Kalle, MSc PhD   Visiting Prof.
Mantrala, Murali, BSc Delhi, MBA Minn., PhD Northwestern   Visiting Prof.
McAuley, Laurie, BA Open(UK), MSc Lough., PhD Lough.   Reader, Management Accountancy
Okunev, John, MSc NE, BSc PhD   Visiting Prof.
Pond, Keith, BSc Brad., MPhil Lough.   Sr. Lectr.
Rafiq, Mohammed, BA(Econ) Essex, MBA Brad., PhD Brad.   Reader, Retail and Marketing
Raman, Kalyan, BSc Madr., MSc Madr., PhD Dallas   Prof., Marketing
Rolland, Colette, PhD   Visiting Prof.
Schaufeli, Wilmar, BA Gron., MA Gron., PhD Gron.   Visiting Prof.
Seal, Will, BA Reading, BPhil York(UK), PhD Nott.Trent   Prof., Accounting
Seaton, Jonathan, BA Newcastle(UK), MA Essex, MPhil Essex, PhD Manc.   Reader, Business Economics
Shattacherjee, Debashish, PhD Ill., BA MA   Visiting Prof.
Sizer, John, CBE, BA Nott., DLitt Lough., Hon. DScEcon Hull, FRSA, FCMI   Emer. Prof.
Smith, Gareth, BA Essex, MSc Warw., FRSA   Sr. Lectr.
Sohal, Amrik, BEng Brad., MBA Brad., PhD Brad.   Visiting Prof.
Souchon, Anne, BA Coventry, MSc Strath., PhD Wales   Reader, Marketing
Tippett, Mark, BCom Newcastle(UK), PhD Edin.   Prof., Accounting and Finance
Travers, Cheryl, BSc Lanc., MSc Open(UK), MSc UMIST   Sr. Lectr.
Tyler, Melissa, BSc Birm., PhD Derby   Sr. Lectr.
Walker, Mike, BA Oxf., MPhil Oxf., DPhil Oxf.   Visiting Prof.

Welch, William, BSc Lough., MSc Lond., PhD Lond. Visiting Prof.

Wilkinson, Adrian, BSc Lond., MSc Lond., PhD Durh. Prof., Human Resource Management

Wilson, John, BSc Glas., MSc Sus., DPhil Sus., FIMA Prof., Operational Research

Wilson, Richard M. S., BCom Leeds, BA Open(UK), BPhil Open(UK), BSc Open(UK), MEd Open(UK), MSc Brad., FCMI, FRSA, FCIM Emer. Prof.

Other Staff: 28 Lectrs.; 7 Res. Assocs.

Research: accounting and finance management; banking and finance; European business; management sciences; retail management

Chemistry

Tel: (01509) 222592 Fax: (01509) 223925
E-mail: chemistry@lboro.ac.uk

Allin, Steven, BSc Liv., PhD Liv. Reader, Organic Chemistry

Bethell, Donald, BSc Lond., PhD Lond. Visiting Prof.

Bowman, Russell, BSc Cape Town, PhD Alta., FRSChem Prof., Organic Chemistry

Creaser, Colin, BSc Kent, PhD Kent, FRSChem Prof., Analytical Chemistry

Dann, Sandra, BSc S'ton., PhD S'ton. Sr. Lectr.

Dawkins, John, BSc Birm., PhD Birm., DSc Birm., FRSChem Emer. Prof.

Flanagan, Robert, BSc Lond., PhD Lond., FRSChem Visiting Prof.

Fletcher, Stephen, BSc Newcastle(UK), PhD Newcastle(UK), FRSChem Head of Section; Prof., Physical Chemistry

Heaney, Harry, BA Keele, DSc Keele, PhD Manc., FRSChem Emer. Prof.

Jones, Ray, MA Camb., PhD Camb., FRSChem Prof., Organic and Biological Chemistry

Kelly, Paul F., BSc Lond., PhD Lond. Sr. Lectr.

Marples, Brian, BSc Leeds, PhD Leeds, DSc Leeds, FRSChem Emer. Prof.

McKee, Vickie, BSc Belf., PhD Belf. Head of Section; Prof., Inorganic Chemistry

Miller, James, MA Camb., PhD Camb., FRSChem Emer. Prof.

Mortimer, Roger, BSc Lond., PhD Lond., FRSChem Reader, Physical Chemistry

Nelson, Jane, BSc Belf., MSc Belf., PhD Belf., FRSChem Visiting Prof.

Page, Philip, CB, BSc Lond., PhD Lond., FRSChem Prof., Organic Chemistry

Pritchard, Gareth, BSc Lond., PhD Wales Sr. Lectr.

Sharp, Barry, BSc Lond., PhD Lond., FRSChem Sr. Lectr.

Smith, Roger, BSc Manc., MSc Manc., PhD ANU, FRSChem Head of Section; Prof., Analytical Chemistry

Thomas, Paul, BSc Manc., PhD UMIST Prof., Analytical Chemistry

Warwick, Peter, BA Open(UK), MSc Lough., PhD Lough., FRSChem Prof., Environmental Radiochemistry; Head*

Weaver, George, BSc St And., PhD Edin. Sr. Lectr.

Wilkinson, Frank, BSc Sheff., MA Oxf., PhD Sheff., FRSChem Emer. Prof.

Other Staff: 10 Lectrs.; 1 Sr. Fellow; 3 Res. Fellows; 3 Visiting Lectrs.; 3 Hon. Res. Fellows

Research: analytical; environmental; inorganic and structural; organic and biomedical; physical

Computer Science

Tel: (01509) 222681 Fax: (01509) 211586
E-mail: p.j.holligan@lboro.ac.uk

Acar, Serpil, BS Middle East Tech., MS Middle East Tech., MSc Lough., PhD Lough. Sr. Lectr.

Alty, James, BScEng Lond., PhD Liv., FIEE, FBCS Emer. Prof.

Bez, Helmut, BSc Wales, MSc Oxf., DPhil Oxf. Reader

Chung, Paul W. H., BScEng Lond., PhD Edin., FBCS Prof.; Head*

Connolly, John, MA Camb., PhD Reading Sr. Lectr.

Dawson, Chris, BSc Lough., PhD Lough. Sr. Lectr.

Dawson, Ray, BSc Nott., MPhil Nott. Sr. Lectr.

Edirisinghe, Eran, BScEng Moratuwa, MSc Lough., PhD Lough. Sr. Lectr.

Hinde, Chris, BSc Brist., PhD Brun. Sr. Lectr.

Phillips, Iain, BSc Manc., PhD Manc., FBCS Sr. Lectr.

Singh, Sameer, BEng BIT(Ranchi), MSc Warw., PhD W.England, FRSS Dir., Res. School of Informatics; Prof., Autonomous Systems

Yang, Shuang-Hua, BSc China Petroleum, MSc China Petroleum, PhD Zhejiang Prof., Networks and Control

Other Staff: 11 Lectrs.; 2 Univ. Teachers; 3 Visiting Fellows

Research: artificial intelligence/knowledge-based systems; computer graphics; database technology; human-computer interfaces; intelligent information management and retrieval

Design and Technology

Tel: (01509) 222652 Fax: (01509) 223999
E-mail: s.e.green@lboro.ac.uk

Bhamra, Tracy, BSc CNAA, MSc Brad., PhD Manc.Met., FRSA Reader, Sustainable Design

Brittan, Ken W., BSc Nott., PhD Lond. Emer. Prof.

Campbell, Ian, BSc Brun., MSc Warw., PhD Nott. Reader, Computer-Aided Product Design

Denton, Howard, BEd Lough., MPhil Lough., PhD Lough. Sr. Lectr.

Dewberry, Emma, BSc Napier Sr. Lectr.

Evans, Mark, BEd CNAA, MA CNAA, PhD Lough. Sr. Lectr.

Hodgson, Tony, MSc Lough. Sr. Lectr.; Head*

Ireson, Gren, BA Open(UK), MEd Durh., PhD Lough. Sr. Lectr.

Norman, Eddie, MA Oxf., MSc Cran.IT, PhD Lough. Sr. Lectr.

Porter, Mark, BSc Lough., PhD Lough., FErgS Prof., Design Ergonomics

Porter, Samantha, BSc Lough., PhD Nott., FErgS Sr. Lectr.

Roberts, Philip H., MA(Ed) S'ton., PhD S'ton. Visiting Prof.

Wormald, Paul, BSc Brist., MDes RCA Sr. Lectr.

Other Staff: 10 Lectrs.; 5 Res. Assocs.; 6 Visiting Lectrs.; 1 Visiting Fellow

Research: design education; design ergonomics; hand performance; vehicle ergonomics

Economics

Tel: (01509) 222729 Fax: (01509) 223910
E-mail: a.j.potter@lboro.ac.uk

Green, Christopher, BA Oxf., MSc Yale, MPhil Oxf., MPhil Yale, PhD Yale Prof., Banking and Finance

Hall, Max, BA Nott., PhD Nott. Prof., Banking and Financial Regulation

Leger, Lawrence, BA Sus., MPhil Lond., MComm NSW, PhD W.Ont. Sr. Lectr.

Llewellyn, David, BSc(Econ) Lond., FRSA Prof., Money and Banking

Maunder, Peter, BA Exe., MSc Nott. Sr. Lectr.

Mills, Terence, BA Essex, MA Warw., PhD Warw. Prof., Applied Statistics and Econometrics

Pentecost, Eric, BA CNAA, MA Warw., PhD Lond. Prof.

Piga, Claudio, BA Sassari, MSc Turin, PhD Rome, DPhil York(UK) Reader

Poyago-Theotoky, Joanna, BSc Athens, MSc Brist., PhD Brist. Prof., Microeconomics

Simper, Richard, BA Sheff., PhD Sheff. Sr. Lectr.

Turner, Paul, BA Warw., BSc Open(UK), MA Warw., PhD Warw. Reader

Weyman-Jones, Tom, BSc(Econ) Lond., MSc(Econ) Lond., PhD Melb. Prof., Industrial Economics; Head*

Other Staff: 10 Lectrs.

Research: economics of law and regulation; finance, money and international banking; labour markets and industrial organisation; macroeconomics and exchange rates; time series and financial econometrics

Engineering, Aeronautical and Automotive

Tel: (01509) 223413 Fax: (01509) 223946
E-mail: s.boyd@lboro.ac.uk

Andrews, John, BSc CNAA, PhD CNAA Prof., Risk and Reliability Analysis

Best, Matthew, BEng Lough., PhD Lough. Sr. Lectr.

Callow, Geoff, BSc(Eng) S'ton., MSc S'ton., MBA Aston Indust. Prof.

Carrotte, Jonathan, BTech Lough., PhD Lough. Reader

Chen, Rui, BEng Tianjin, PhD Lough. Sr. Lectr.

Chen, Wen-Hua, BEng Jiangsu U.S.T., MSc Northeastern(Shenyang), PhD N.E.Tech.(Shenyang) Sr. Lectr.

Henshaw, Michael, BSc Hull, MBA L&H, PhD Hull Dir., Nectise Programme; Prof., Systems Engineering

Horner, Jane, BSc Brun., MSc S'ton., PhD S'ton., FIMechE Sr. Lectr.

Krylov, Victor, MSc Moscow, PhD Moscow, DSc Moscow Prof., Acoustics and Vibration

Loughlan, Joseph, BSc Strath., MSc Strath., PhD Strath., FRAeS Prof., Aerospace Structures

Lucas, Gordon, MSc Cran., PhD Lough., FIMechE Emer. Prof., Automotive Engineering

McGuirk, Jim, BSc Lond., MSc Lond., PhD Lond., DSc, FRAeS, FREng Prof., Aerodynamics

Page, Gary, BSc S'ton., PhD Lond. Sr. Lectr.

Parry-Jones, Richard, BSc Salf., Hon. DTech Lough. Indust. Prof.

Passmore, Martin, BTech Lough., PhD Lough., FIMechE Sr. Lectr.

Peat, Keith S., MSc Manc., PhD Manc. Reader

Render, Peter M., BTech Lough., PhD Cran.IT Sr. Lectr.

Stevens, Stanley J., MSc Nott., PhD Lough. Emer. Prof., Aeronautical Propulsion

Stobart, Richard K., MA, FIMechE Ford Prof., Automotive Engineering

Thring, Robert, BSc Reading, PhD Reading, FIMechE Prof., Fuel Cell Engineering; Head*

Wang, Simon, BSc(Eng) Tsinghua, MSc Tsinghua, PhD Tsinghua, PhD Birm. Sr. Lectr.

Zhiyin Yang, BSc Northwestern P.U.(Xi'an), PhD Sheff. Sr. Lectr.

Other Staff: 10 Lectrs.; 1 Sr. Visiting Fellow; 1 Sr. Res. Fellow; 1 Res. Fellow

Research: systems engineering

Engineering, Chemical

Tel: (01509) 222532 Fax: (01509) 223923
E-mail: cgadmin@lboro.ac.uk

Brewis, Neville, BSc UMIST, MSc UMIST, FIChemE Visiting Prof., Pharmaceutical Engineering

Chamberlain, Geoff, BSc Wales, PhD Wales Visiting Prof., Process Safety

Cumming, Iain, BTech Lough., PhD Lough. Sr. Lectr.

Hall, Alan, BSc Leeds, PhD, FIChemE Visiting Prof., Product Engineering

Hankinson, Geoff, BSc Leeds, PhD Leeds Prof., Safety Engineering

Hewitt, Chris, BSc Lond., PhD Birm., FIBiol Prof., Pharmaceutical Engineering

Holdich, Richard, BSc Birm., PhD Exe. Prof.

Kletz, Trevor, OBE, DSc Lough., FREng, FIChemE, FRSChem Visiting Prof., Process Safety

Lydon, Richard, BSc N.Lond. Visiting Prof., Seperation Processes

Nagy, Zoltan, BS Cluj, MS Cluj, PhD Cluj Sr. Lectr.

Nassehi, Vahid, MSc Tehran, MSc Wales, PhD Wales Visiting Prof., Computational Modelling

Rielly, Chris D., BSc Lond., MA Lond., PhD Lond. Prof.

Saha, Basudeb, BTech Calc., ME IISc., PhD Bom. Sr. Lectr.

Shama, Gilbert, BSc Manc., MSc Birm., PhD Lond. Sr. Lectr.

Stapley, Andrew, MA Camb., MEng Camb., PhD Camb. Sr. Lectr.

Starov, Victor M., MSc Moscow, PhD Moscow, DSc Moscow Prof.

Tarleton, Steve, BEng Liv., PhD Exe. Sr. Lectr.

Wakeman, Richard, BSc UMIST, MSc UMIST, PhD UMIST, FREng, FIChemE Prof.; Head*

Other Staff: 4 Lectrs.

Research: environmental process engineering; food engineering and biotechnology; particle technology; plant engineering; reaction engineering and transfer processes

Engineering, Civil and Building

Tel: (01509) 222884 Fax: (01509) 223980
E-mail: j.e.hull@lboro.ac.uk

Anumba, Chimay, BSc Leeds, PhD Leeds, FICE, FIStructE, FCIOB Prof., Construction Engineering and Informatics

Austin, Simon, BSc Lough., PhD Lough. Prof., Structural Engineering

Banyard, John, BSc(Eng), FREng, FICE Royal Academy of Engin. Visiting Prof.

Bouchlaghem, Dino, PhD UMIST Prof., Architectural Engineering

Bristow, Abigail, BSc(Econ) Wales, MA Leeds, PhD Newcastle(UK) Prof., Transport Studies

Carillo, Patricia, BSc WI, MSc Lough., PhD Lough., FCIOB Prof., Strategic Management in Construction

Chandler, Jim, BSc Newcastle(UK), PhD Lond., FRICS Sr. Lectr.

Dainty, Andrew R. J., BSc Glam., PhD Lough. Prof., Construction Sociology

Dickens, John, BSc Manc. Sr. Lectr.

Dixon, Neil, BSc CNAA, PhD Kingston(UK), FGS Prof., Geotechnical Engineering

Edwards, David J., BSc Wolv., PhD Wolv. Sr. Lectr.

El-Hamalawi, Ashraf, BEng Camb., PhD Camb. Sr. Lectr.

Enoch, Marcus, BEng Nott., MSc(Eng) Leeds, PhD Open(UK) Sr. Lectr.

Fleming, Paul, BEng Leeds, PhD Lough. Sr. Lectr.

Gibb, Alistair, BSc Lough., PhD Lough. Prof., Construction Engineering Management

Gillingwater, David, MSc(Econ) Lond., PhD Lond. Sr. Lectr.

Hassan, Tarek, BSc Lough., MSc Lough., PhD Lough. Sr. Lectr.

Holmes, Mike, BSc Royal Academy of Engin. Visiting Prof.

Ison, Stephen, BA Liv., MA Leeds, PhD Lough. Prof., Transport Policy

Loveday, Dennis L., BSc Aston, PhD Aston Eon/ Royal Acad. of Engin. Res. Chair, Low Carbon Energy Technol.; Prof., Building Physics

McCaffer, Ron, BSc Strath., PhD Lough., DSc Strath., FICE, FCIOB Prof., Construction Management

Pasquire, Christine, BSc CNAA, PhD Lough., FRICS Sr. Lectr.

Pitfield, David E., BSc Brist., PhD Stir. Sr. Lectr.

Price, Andrew D. F., BSc CNAA, PhD Lough., FCIOB Prof., Project Management

Raoof, Mohammed, BSc(Eng) Lond., MSc Lond., PhD Lond., DSc(Eng) Lond., FICE, FIStructE Prof., Structural Engineering

Robins, Peter J., BSc Nott., PhD Nott. Sr. Lectr.

Sander, Graham, BSc Griff., PhD Griff. Reader, Water Engineering

Shiono, Koji, BSc Lond., MSc Salf., PhD Birm. Prof., Environmental Hydrodynamics

Thorpe, Anthony, BSc Nott., MSc Lough., PhD Lough., FICE, FCIOB, FBCS Prof., Construction Information Technology; Head*

Twigg, David, BSc CNAA, MSc Oxf., PhD Newcastle(UK) Sr. Lectr.

Wheatley, Andrew D., BSc Aston, PhD Aston, FICE Prof., Water Technology

Wright, Jonathan, BTech Lough., PhD Lough. Prof.

Other Staff: 13 Lectrs.; 1 Sr. Tutor

Research: airport planning; building services; construction engineering management; European construction; water and waste engineering

Engineering, Electronic and Electrical

Tel: (01509) 228100 Fax: (01509) 222854
E-mail: r.e.lander@lboro.ac.uk

Bateman, Steve, BSc Lough., PhD Lough., FIEE Visiting Prof.

Blackledge, Jonathan, BSc Lond., PhD Lond., FIMA, FIP, FIEE, FBCS, FRSS Visiting Prof.

Brown, John, FIP Visiting Prof.

Chambers, Jonathon, BSc PhD Prof., Communications and Signal Processing

Chouliaras, Vassilios, BSc H-W, MSc UMIST Sr. Lectr.

Cowan, Colin, BSc Edin., PhD Edin., FIEE Visiting Prof.

Datta, Sekharjit, BSc Calc., MSc Lond., PhD Lond., FIETE Reader

Dixon, Roger, BEng Lanc., MSc Lanc., PhD Lanc. Sr. Lectr.

Dwyer, Vincent M., BA Camb., DPhil York(UK) Sr. Lectr.

Edwards, Rob, PhD Sheff. Sr. Lectr.

Feresidis, Alexandros, BSc Salonika, MSc Leeds, PhD Lough. Sr. Lectr.

Flint, James, MEng Lough., PhD Lough. Sr. Lectr.

Freris, Leon L., BSc Lond., MSc Lond., PhD Lond., FIEE Visiting Prof.

Gardner, David, OBE, BTech, FRAeS Visiting Prof.

Goodall, Roger M., MA Camb., PhD Lough., FIEE, FIMechE Prof., Control Systems Engineering

Gottschalg, Ralph, MSc Lough., PhD Lough. Sr. Lectr.

Gregory, Keith, BSc Aston, MSc Aston, PhD Lough. Sr. Lectr.

Kalawsky, Roy, BSc Hull, MSc Hull, PhD Hull, FRSA Prof., Human-Computer Integration

Kettleborough, J. Gordon, BSc CNAA, MSc Aston Sr. Lectr.

Kong, Michael, BSc Zhejiang, MSc Zhejiang, PhD Liv. Prof., Bioelectrics Engineering

Lambotharan, Sangarapillar, BEng PhD Visiting Prof.

Levis, Alexander H., AB Ripon, BS M.I.T., SM M.I.T., ME M.I.T., ScD M.I.T., MA Visiting Prof.

Lindsay, Neil, BSc PhD Visiting Prof.

Manning, Carl D., BSc Aston, MSc Birm., PhD Birm. Sr. Lectr.

Mulvaney, David, BSc Leeds, PhD Leeds Sr. Lectr.

Novac, Bucur, MSc Bucharest, PhD Bucharest Sr. Lectr.

Parish, David, BSc Liv., PhD Liv. Prof., Communication Networks

Siemieniuch, Carys, BA Manc., MSc Lough. Sr. Lectr.

Smith, Ivor R., BSc Brist., PhD Brist., DSc Brist., FIEE, FREng Prof., Electrical Power Engineering

Spyt, Tom, MD, FRCSGlas, FRCS, FRCSEd Visiting Prof.

Thwaites, Mike, BSc Salf., PhD Salf., FIP Visiting Prof.

Tiwari, Ayodhya, BSc Garh., MSc Roor., PhD IIT Delhi Prof., Renewable Energy Systems

Vadher, Von, BSc Aston, MPhil Lond., MBA Lough., PhD Lough., FRSA Sr. Lectr.

Vardaxoglou, Yiannis, BSc Kent, PhD Kent Prof., Wireless Communications; Head*

Volakis, John, MSc Ohio State, PhD Ohio State, FIEEE Visiting Prof.

Watson, Simon, BSc Lond., PhD Edin. Sr. Lectr.

Woodhead, Mike, BSc Salf., MSc Salf. Prof., Systems Engineering

Woodward, Bryan, BSc Lond., MSc Lond., PhD Lond., DSc Lough., FIEE, FRGS Prof., Underwater Acoustics

Other Staff: 13 Lectrs.; 2 Sr. Res. Fellows; 5 Visiting Fellows; 1 Teaching Fellow; 1 EPSRC Advanced Fellow

Vacant Posts: 1 Prof. (Photovoltaic Sys.)

Research: circuits, systems and control; communications and signal processing; electronic devices/systems, advanced control, photonics; microwaves, wireless communications, networks, underwater communications; power and renewable energy

Engineering, Mechanical and Manufacturing, Wolfson School of

Tel: (01509) 222913 Fax: (01509) 223979
E-mail: k.p.white@lboro.ac.uk

Acar, Memis, BS Middle East Tech., MSc Manc., PhD Lough., FIMechE Sr. Lectr.

Ashcroft, Ian, BSc Lough., DPhil Oxf., FIMechE Sr. Lectr.

Babitsky, Vladimir, PhD Moscow, DSc Moscow Prof., Dynamics

Backhouse, Christopher J., BSc Durh., MSc CNAA, PhD CNAA, FIEE, FIMechE Prof., Product Innovation

Bell, Bob, BSc(Tech) Manc., MSc(Tech) Manc., PhD Manc., DSc Manc., FIEE Emer. Prof.

Bouazza-Marouf, Kaddour, BSc Newcastle(UK), PhD Newcastle(UK), FIMechE Sr. Lectr.

Burns, Neil D., BSc Brun., PhD Lough., FIMechE Prof., Manufacturing Systems

Caine, Mike, BSc Lough., PhD Birm. Prof., Sports Technology and Innovation

Case, Keith, BSc Nott., PhD Nott., FErgS, FBCS Prof., Computer Aided Engineering

Clegg, Allen, BSc Lough., MSc Lough., MBA Lough., PhD Lough., FIMMM Sr. Lectr.

Conway, Paul P., BEng Ulster, MSc Lough. Prof., Manufacturing Processes

Coupland, Jeremy M., BSc Exe., PhD S'ton. Prof., Applied Optics

Dent, John Emer. Prof.

Dickens, Phill, BSc CNAA, PhD Aston, FIMechE Prof., Manufacturing Technology

Dowson, Duncan, CBE, BSc Leeds, PhD Leeds, DSc Leeds, Hon. DEng Chalmers U.T., Hon. DSc I.N.S.A.Lyons, Hon. DSc Liège, Hon. DEng Wat., Hon. DEng Brad., Hon. DEng Leeds, Hon. DSc Lough., FRS, FREng, FIMechE, FRSA, FASME External Prof., Tribology

Edwards, John, BSc Leic., PhD Lough. Sr. Lectr.

Fukuda, Toshio, MSc Tokyo, DrEng Tokyo Visiting Prof.

Garner, Colin, BTech Lough., BEng Lough., PhD Lough. Perkins Prof./Royal Academy of Engin. Prof., Applied Thermodynamics

Goosey, Martin, PhD CNAA, FIMMM Visiting Prof.

Hague, Richard, BEng Brad., PhD Nott. Prof., Innovative Manufacturing

Halliwell, Neil A., BSc Liv., PhD Liv., DSc S'ton., FREng, FIMechE, FIP Prof., Optical Engineering

Harding, Jenny, BA Open(UK), MSc De Mont., PhD Lough. Sr. Lectr.

Hargrave, Graham, BSc Leeds, PhD Leeds Prof., Optical Diagnostics

Harland, Andy, BEng Lough., PhD Lough. Sr. Lectr.

Harris, Russell, BEng Nott., PhD Lough. Sr. Lectr.

Harrison, Rob, BTech Lough., PhD Lough. Sr. Lectr.

Hopkinson, Neil, BEng Nott., PhD De Mont. Sr. Lectr.

Huntley, Jon, BA Camb., MA Camb., PhD Camb., FIP Prof., Applied Mechanics

Hutt, David, BSc Lond., PhD Lond. Sr. Lectr.

Jackson, Mike, BSc Salf., MSc Lough., PhD CNAA, FIMechE Sr. Lectr.

Jones, Roy, BTech Lough., PhD CNAA Dunlop Slazenger Prof., Sports Technology

Kallenbach, Eberhard, DSc T.H.Ilmenau, PhD T.H.Ilmenau Visiting Prof.

Kelly, Patrick, MSc Brad., PhD Brad. Visiting Prof.

Kerr, David, BSc CNAA, MSc CNAA, PhD Lough. Sr. Lectr.

Kesy, Andrzej, BSc Lodz, MSc Lodz, PhD Lodz Visiting Prof.

Kesy, Zbigniew, BSc Lodz, MSc Lodz, PhD Lodz Visiting Prof.

King, Paul, BTech Lough. Sr. Lectr.

Lawrence, Jonathan, BEng Brad., PhD UMIST Sr. Lectr.

Liu, Changqing, BEng Nanjing, MSc Chinese Acad.Sc., PhD Hull Sr. Lectr.

Liu, Johan, MSc Stockholm, PhD Stockholm Visiting Prof.

Malalasekera, Weeratunge, BSc(Eng) Peradeniya, PhD Lond. Sr. Lectr.

Morgan, Terry, MSc, FIEE, FREng Visiting Prof.

Nurse, Andrew, BEng Sheff., PhD Sheff. Sr. Lectr.

Parkin, Rob, BSc Leic., PhD CNAA, FIMechE, FIEE, FRSA Prof., Mechatronics; Head*

Pendlebury, Bob, BSc Leeds, FIMechE Visiting Prof., Principles of Engineering Design

Petzing, Jon, BEng Lough., PhD Lough. Sr. Lectr.

Preston, Mike, MTech Lough., PhD Lough., FIMechE Emer. Prof.

Rahimifard, Shahin, BSc CNAA, MSc Lough., PhD Lough. Sr. Lectr.

Rahnejat, Homer, MSc Lond., PhD Lond. Prof., Dynamics

Rothberg, Steve, BSc S'ton., PhD S'ton., FIMechE Prof., Vibration Engineering

Schaffer, Graham, BSc Cape Town, MSc Cape Town, PhD Birm. Visiting Prof.

Seaman, Matthew, MSc, FIMechE, FIEE Emer. Prof.

Silberschmidt, Vadim, PhD Perm State Prof., Mechanics of Materials

Snowdon, Ken, PhD Leeds Visiting Prof., Engineering Design for Sustainable Development

Soar, Rupert, BSc Nott., MSc Nott., PhD De Mont. Sr. Lectr.

Stevens, Tony, BSc Lond. Visiting Prof., Principles of Engineering Design

Sutton, Phil, BSc S'ton., PhD S'ton. Visiting Prof., Signal Processing

Szmelter, Joanna, MSc Warsaw, PhD Swansea Sr. Lectr.

Taylor, Doug, BTech PhD, FREng, FIMechE Visiting Prof., Thermofluids

Theodossiades, Stephanos, MBA Lough., PhD Salonika Sr. Lectr.

Tyrer, John R., MSc Cran.IT, PhD Lough., FIMechE Sr. Lectr.

Versteeg, Henk, Ing Amst., MEng Cran. Sr. Lectr.

Vitols, Ray, MTech PhD DTech, FIMechE, FTI, FRSA Emer. Prof.

West, Andy, BSc Leeds, PhD Leeds, FIMechE Sr. Lectr.

Weston, Richard, BSc Lond., PhD S'ton., FIEE ICL Prof., Flexible Automation

Whalley, David, BSc Lough., MPhil Lough., FIMechE Sr. Lectr.

Wickens, Alan, OBE, BSc(Eng) Lond., DSc Lough., FIMechE, FREng, FRS, FIEE Visiting Prof., Dynamics

Wildman, Ricky, BSc Manc., PhD Birm. Sr. Lectr.

Williams, David J., BSc Manc., PhD Camb., DSc UMIST, FIMechE, FIEE, FREng Visiting Prof., Healthcare Engineering

Wright, Paul, BSc Birm., PhD Birm., FASME Visiting Prof.

Young, Bob, BSc Dund., PhD Lough. Sr. Lectr.

Other Staff: 12 Lectrs.; 1 Principal Univ. Teacher; 1 Sr. Res. Fellow; 6 Res. Fellows; 2 Univ. Teachers; 5 Visiting Fellows; 1 Hon. Fellow

Research: information and simultaneous engineering; manufacturing organisation; manufacturing processes; manufacturing systems integration

English and Drama

Tel: (01509) 222969 Fax: (01509) 269994
E-mail: p.higgs@lboro.ac.uk

Chatterjee, Sudipto, BA MA MA PhD Sr. Lectr.

Ebbatson, Roger, BA Sheff., MA Sheff., MPhil Lond. Prof., English Studies

Egan, Gabriel, BA Birm., MA Birm., PhD Birm. Sr. Lectr.

Freeman, Nick, BA Leeds, MA Brist., PhD Brist. Sr. Lectr.

Hobby, Elaine, BA Birm., MA Essex, PhD Birm. Prof., Seventeenth Century Studies; Head*

Jarvis, Brian, BA Keele, MA Keele, PhD Keele Sr. Lectr.

Lucas, John, BA Reading, PhD Reading, FRSA Emer. Prof., English

Overton, William, MA Camb., MA Johns H., PhD Camb. Prof., Literature

Shaw, Marion, BA Hull, PhD Hull Prof., English

Wolfreys, Julian, BA Sus., MA Sus., DPhil Sus. Prof., Modern Literature and Culture

Wood, Nigel, BA Oxf., MA Indiana, PhD Durh. Prof., Literature

Other Staff: 14 Lectrs.

Research: contemporary women's drama; creative writing; semiotics of drama; seventeenth-century women's writing; twentieth-century women's writing

Geography

Tel: (01509) 222794 Fax: (01509) 223930
E-mail: geography@lboro.ac.uk

Anderson, John, BA Durh., PhD Lond. Prof., Physical Geography

Bell, Morag, BA Nott., DPhil Oxf. Prof., Cultural Geography

Bullard, Joanna, MA Edin., PhD Sheff. Reader, Aeolian Geomorphology

Hodgkins, Richard, MA Oxf., PhD Camb. Sr. Lectr.

Holloway, Sarah, BA Sheff., PhD Sheff. Reader, Human Geography

Hubbard, Philip, BA Birm., PhD Birm. Prof., Urban Social Geography

Reid, Ian, BA Hull, PhD Hull, FRGS Prof., Physical Geography; Head*

Rendell, Helen, BSc Nott., PhD Lond. Prof., Physical Geography

Rice, Stephen, BA Oxf., MSc Br.Col., PhD Br.Col. Reader, River Science

Skelton, Tracey, BA Oxf., PhD Newcastle(UK) Prof., Critical Geographies

Slater, David, BA Durh., PhD Lond. Prof., Human Geography

Taylor, Peter, BA Liv., PhD Liv. Prof.

Wood, Paul, BSc Lough., PhD Birm. Sr. Lectr.

Other Staff: 12 Lectrs.; 1 Res. Assoc.

Research: development studies; fluvial, littoral and aeolian sedimentology; global, social and economic geography; historical, political and cultural geography; river ecology

Human Sciences

see also Special Centres, etc.

Tel: (01509) 223036 Fax: (01509) 223940-1
E-mail: w.m.pilkington@lboro.ac.uk

Bogin, Barry, BA Temple, MA Temple, PhD Temple Reader

Cameron, Noel, BEd Nott., MSc Lough., PhD Lond., FIBiol Prof., Human Biology

Griffiths, Paula, BSc S'ton., PhD S'ton. Sr. Lectr.

Gyi, Diane, MSc Lough., PhD Lough. Sr. Lectr.

Haslam, Roger, BSc Lough., PhD Lough., FErgS Prof., Health and Safety Ergonomics; Head*

Havenith, George, BSc Utrecht, MSc Utrecht, PhD Nijmegen Prof., Environmental Physiology and Ergonomics

Hignett, Sue, BSc Sheff., MSc Nott., PhD Nott. Sr. Lectr.

Hogervorst, Eef, MSc Maastricht, PhD Maastricht Prof., Psychology

Horne, Jim, BSc Lond., MSc Aston, PhD Aston, DSc Lond., FBPsS, FIBiol Prof., Psychophysiology

Mansfield, Neil, BEng S'ton., PhD S'ton. Sr. Lectr.

Mastana, Sarabjit, BSc Panjab, MSc Panjab, MPhil Camb., PhD Newcastle(UK) Sr. Lectr.

Morgan, Kevin, BSc Ulster, PhD Edin. Prof., Gerontology

Parsons, Kenneth, BSc Lough., PhD S'ton., FErgS Prof., Environmental Ergonomics

Reyner, Louise, BSc CNAA, PhD Lough. Sr. Lectr.

Other Staff: 14 Lectrs.

Research: ergonomics; human biology; human psychology

Information Science

Tel: (01509) 223052 Fax: (01509) 223053
E-mail: dis@lboro.ac.uk

Beckford, John, PhD Visiting Prof.

Borgman, Christine L., BA Mich., MLS Pitt., PhD Stan. External Prof.

Damodaran, Leela, BTech Brun. Prof., Participative Design and Change Management

Feather, John P., MA Camb., BLitt Oxf., MA Oxf., PhD Lough., FCLIP, FRSA Prof., Library and Information Studies

Goulding, Anne, BA Leeds, MA Sheff., PhD Sheff. Reader

Harrison, Janet, BA CNAA, PhD Lough. Sr. Lectr.

Hayes, Robert, BA MA PhD Visiting Prof.

Hepworth, Mark, BA Lond., MSc Sheff., PhD Sheff. Sr. Lectr.

Jackson, Tom, BSc Lough., PhD Lough. Sr. Lectr.

Matthews, Graham, BA Nott., PhD Lough. Prof., Information Management

McKnight, Cliff, BTech Brun., PhD Brun. Prof.

Meadows, Jack, MA Oxf., MSc Lond., DPhil Oxf., FIP, FCLIP Emer. Prof.

Morris, Anne, BSc Lough., MSc Lough., PhD Lough. Prof.

Muir, Adrienne, MA MSc PhD Sr. Lectr.

Oppenheim, Charles, BSc Manc., PhD Manc., FCLIP, FRSA, Hon. FCLIP Prof.; Head*

Rowland, Fytton, MA Camb., PhD Camb., FCLIP Sr. Lectr.

Stephens, Derek, MSc Lough., PhD Lough. Sr. Lectr.

Sturges, Paul, BA Leic., MA Lough., PhD Lough., FCLIP Prof., Library Studies

Summers, Ron, BSc CNAA, MSc City(UK), PhD City(UK) Prof.

Other Staff: 10 Lectrs.; 1 Sr. Res. Fellow; 1 Consulting Sr. Res. Fellow; 2 Res. Assocs.; 2 Sr. Visiting Fellows

Research: information handling; information management; information technology; library systems

Library and Information Statistics Unit

Tel: (01509) 223070 Fax: (01509) 223072
E-mail: lisu@lboro.ac.uk

Creaser, Claire, BSc Kent Sr. Statistician; Dir.*

Other Staff: 2 Res. Assocs.

Research: collection and analysis of library statistics; public, academic and special libraries

Mathematical Sciences

Tel: (01509) 222861 Fax: (01509) 223969
E-mail: h.naylor@lboro.ac.uk

Bolsinov, Alexey, BSc Moscow, PhD Moscow Reader

Dullin, Holger R., PhD Bremen Sr. Lectr.

Ferapontov, Eugene V., PhD Moscow Reader

Griffiths, Jerry, BSc Wales, PhD Wales, FIP Prof., Applied Mathematics

Grimshaw, Roger H. J., BSc Auck., MSc Auck., PhD Camb., FAA Prof.

Groves, Mark, MA Oxf., DPhil Oxf. Prof.

Harrison, Martin C., BSc Sheff., MSc Sheff., PhD Sheff. Sr. Lectr.

Hoenselaers, Cornelius A., DSc Hiroshima, Dr Munich Reader

Hudson, Robin, BA Oxf., DPhil Oxf. Visiting Prof.

Kenny, Stephen, BSc Lond., PhD Camb. Sr. Lectr.

Linton, Christopher, BA Oxf., PhD Brist., FIMA Prof., Applied Mathematics; Head, Applied Mathematics*

Ma, Zhi-Ming, PhD Chinese Acad.Sc. Visiting Prof.

McIver, Maureen, BSc Brist., PhD Brist. Reader

McIver, Philip, BSc Liv., PhD Liv. Prof., Applied Mathematics

Neishtadt, Anatoly, PhD Moscow Prof., Applied Mathematics

Ruijsenaars, Simon, BSc Ley., PhD Ley. Visiting Prof.

Smith, Roger, BSc Manc., PhD Manc. Prof., Mathematical Engineering

Thiele, Uve, PhD *T.U.Dresden*   Reader
Veselov, Alexander, PhD *Moscow*, DSc *Moscow*
   Prof., Mathematics
Wallace, Prof. Sir David, CBE, BSc *Edin.*, PhD
   Edin., Hon. DEng *H-W*, Hon. DSc *Edin.*, FRS,
   FRSEd, FIP, FREng   Visiting Prof.
Ward, Joseph, BSc *Lond.*, PhD *Lond.*   Sr. Lectr.
Zhao, Huaizhong, BSc *Shandong*, MSc *Beijing*,
   PhD *Warw.*   Prof., Mathematics
Other Staff: 13 Lectrs.; 9 Res. Fellows; 1
   Visiting Fellow
Research: computational PDEs and mathematical
   modelling; control theory, reliability and
   optimisation; integrable systems, inverse
   problems and relativity; non-linear
   dynamics and mathematical biology; waves
   and environmental fluid dynamics

Physics

Tel: (01509) 228409 *Fax:* (01509) 223986
   E-mail: m.mckenzie@lboro.ac.uk
Abrikosov, Alexei, PhD *Moscow*, DSc *Moscow*, FRS
   Visiting Prof.
Alexandrov, Alexandre, BSc *Moscow*, PhD
   Moscow, ScD *Moscow*, FIP   Prof., Theoretical
   Physics
Brakvovsky, Alex, BSc *Moscow*, MSc *Moscow*, PhD
   Moscow   Visiting Prof.
Brown, Jane, MA *Camb.*, PhD *Camb.*, FIP
   Visiting Prof.
Cropper, Mike, BSc *York(UK)*, PhD *Warw.*   Sr.
   Lectr.
Emmony, David, BSc *Leic.*, PhD *Strath.*   Emer.
   Prof.
Kabanov, Viktor, BSc *Moscow*, MSc *Moscow*, PhD
   Moscow   Visiting Prof.
Khomskii, Daniel, MS *Moscow*, PhD *Moscow*
   Prof., Novel Material
Kornilovich, Pavel, BSc *Moscow*, MSc *Moscow*,
   PhD *Lond.*   Visiting Prof.
Kugel, Klim, BSc *Moscow*, MSc *Moscow*, PhD
   Moscow   Visiting Prof.
Kürten, Karl, BSc *Cologne*, MSc *Cologne*, PhD
   Cologne   Visiting Prof.
Kusmartsev, Feodor, MS *Moscow*, PhD *Russian
   Acad.Sc.*, FIP   Prof., Condensed Matter
   Theory; Head*
Neumann, Klaus, DrRerNat *T.H.Aachen*, FIP   Sr.
   Lectr.
Parry, David J., BSc *Wales*, PhD *Wales*   Sr.
   Lectr.
Phillips, Nick, BSc *Lond.*, FIP   Emer. Prof.
Rakhmanov, Alexander, BSc *Moscow*, MSc
   Moscow, PhD *Moscow*   Visiting Prof.
Rashba, Emmanuel, BSc *Kiev*, MSc *Kiev*, PhD *Kiev*
   Visiting Prof.
Röseler, Jörg, DrRerNat   Visiting Prof.
Swallowe, Gerry, PhD *Camb.*, BA   Sr. Lectr.
Wallace, Prof. Sir David, CBE, BSc *Edin.*, PhD
   Edin., Hon. DEng *H-W*, Hon. DSc *Edin.*, FRS,
   FRSEd, FIP, FREng   Visiting Prof.
Walls, Mike, BSc *Aston*, PhD *Aston*   Visiting
   Prof.
Zavaritsky, Vladimir, BSc *Moscow*, MSc *Moscow*,
   PhD *Moscow*   Visiting Prof.
Ziebeck, Kurt, BSc *Salf.*, PhD *Salf.*, FIP   Prof.
Other Staff: 6 Lectrs.; 1 EPSRC Adv. Res.
   Fellow; 3 Res. Fellows; 1 Sr. Visiting
   Fellow; 1 Res. Assoc.
Research: electromagnetism; environmental
   science; laser technology; optics and
   thermal physics

Politics, International Relations and European Studies

Tel: (01509) 222991 *Fax:* (01509) 223917
   E-mail: p.a.dainty@lboro.ac.uk
Allen, David, BSc *S'ton.*, MSc *S'ton.*   Prof.,
   European and International Politics; Head*
Berry, Dave, BA *Oxf.*, MA *Sus.*, DPhil *Sus.*   Sr.
   Lectr.
Byrne, Paul, BA *Essex*, MA *Sheff.*, PhD *Lough.*   Sr.
   Lectr.
Drake, Helen, BSc *Sur.*, MA *Cran.*, PhD *Aston*
   Sr. Lectr.
Hantrais, Linda, BA *Lond.*, PhD *Flin.*   Prof.,
   European Social Policy

Hocking, Brian, BA *Brist.*, MA *Leic.*, PhD *Lond.*,
   FRSA   Prof., International Relations
Kinna, Ruth, BA *Lond.*, DPhil *Oxf.*   Sr. Lectr.
Knight, Robert, BA *Camb.*, PhD *Lond.*   Sr. Lectr.
Leaman, Jeremy, BA *Liv.*, PhD *Liv.*   Sr. Lectr.
Lloyd, Moya, BA *Warw.*, PhD *Warw.*   Sr. Lectr.
Smith, Michael, MA *Camb.*, MA *Sus.*   Jean
   Monnet Prof., European and International
   Politics
Threlfall, Monica, BA *Oxf.*, MA *Leeds*   Sr. Lectr.
Webber, Mark, BA *Warw.*, MSocSci *Birm.*, PhD
   Birm.   Sr. Lectr.
Other Staff: 7 Lectrs.; 6 University Teachers
Research: contemporary European politics and
   political thought; European society and
   culture; European Union international
   policies; European Union policymaking;
   recent European history

Polymer Technology and Materials Engineering, Institute of

Tel: (01509) 222231 *Fax:* (01509) 223949
   E-mail: m.gilbert@lboro.ac.uk
Bao, Xujin, PhD *Northumbria*, BSc MEng   Sr.
   Lectr.
Binner, Jon, BSc *Leeds*, PhD *Leeds*, FIMMM
   Prof., Ceramic Materials; Dir.*
Faulkner, Roy, BSc *Leeds*, PhD *Camb.*, DSc *Leeds*,
   FIMMM   Prof., Physical Metallurgy
Gabe, David, BSc *Wales*, PhD *Sheff.*, DMet *Sheff.*,
   FIMMM   Emer. Prof.
Gilbert, Marianne, BSc *Aston*, PhD *Aston*,
   FRSChem, FIMMM   Prof., Polymer
   Technology
Harper, John, BSc(Eng) *S'ton.*, MSc *Leeds*   Sr.
   Lectr.
Haworth, Barry, BSc *Newcastle(UK)*, MSc
   Newcastle(UK)   Sr. Lectr.
Heath, Richard, MSc *Lough.*, PhD *Lough.*   Sr.
   Lectr.
Higginson, Rebecca, BSc(Eng) *Swansea*, PhD
   Birm.   Sr. Lectr.
Hourston, Douglas, BSc *Glas.*, PhD *Edin.*,
   FRSChem   Prof., Polymer Technology
Mascia, Leno, BSc *CNAA*, PhD *Aston*, FIMMM
   Reader
Menzies, Ian, BSc *St And.*, MBA *CNAA*, PhD
   Lond., DSc *Manc.*, FIMgt, FIMMM   Emer.
   Prof.
Rastogi, Sanjay, BSc MSc PhD   Prof., Polymer
   Technology
Song, Mo, BSc *Lanc.*, MSc *Lanc.*, PhD *Lanc.*
   Reader
Thomas, Noreen, MA *Camb.*, PhD *Camb.*   Sr.
   Lectr.
Thomson, Rachel, MA *Camb.*, PhD *Camb.*
   Prof., Materials Engineering
Wilcox, Geoffrey, BSc *Nott.*, MPhil *Lough.*, PhD
   Lough.   Sr. Lectr.
Wu, Houzheng, DPhil *Oxf.*, BEng MPhil   Sr.
   Lectr.
Other Staff: 4 Lectrs.; 1 Sr. Res. Fellow; 2 Res.
   Fellows; 16 Res. Assocs.; 3 Sr. Visiting
   Fellows; 1 Visiting Fellow
Research: ceramics; polymer science and
   technology; power and aerospace materials;
   rubber processing; surface and interface
   engineering

Social Sciences

Tel: (01509) 223365 *Fax:* (01509) 223944
   E-mail: l.m.dutton@lboro.ac.uk
Antaki, Charles, BA *Newcastle(UK)*, PhD *Sheff.*
   Prof., Language and Psychology
Bagilhole, Barbara, BA *Nott.*, PhD *Nott.*   Prof.,
   Social Policy and Equal Opportunities
Bean, Philip, BSc(Soc) *Lond.*, MSc(Econ) *Lond.*,
   PhD *Nott.*   Emer. Prof., Criminology
Billig, Michael G., BA *Brist.*, PhD *Brist.*   Prof.
Cramer, Duncan, BSc *Lond.*, PhD *Lond.*   Prof.,
   Psychological Health
Deacon, David, BA *CNAA*, MA *Leic.*   Reader
Demaine, Jack, BA *Liv.*, PhD *Liv.*   Sr. Lectr.
Downey, John, BA *Camb.*, MA *Camb.*, PhD *Camb.*
   Sr. Lectr.
Edwards, Derek, BA *Sus.*, DPhil *Sus.*   Prof.,
   Psychology

Farrell, Graham, BSc *Manc.*, PhD *Manc.*   Prof.,
   Criminology
Gane, Michael J., BA *Leic.*, PhD *Lond.*   Prof.,
   Sociology
Golding, Peter, BSc *Lond.*, MA *Essex*   Prof.,
   Sociology
Hepburn, Alexa, MA *Glas.*, PhD *Glas.*   Sr. Lectr.
Howitt, Dennis, BTech *Brun.*, DPhil *Sus.*, FBPsS
   Reader
Kniveton, Bromley, BA *Belf.*, PhD *Nott.*   Sr.
   Lectr.
Lister, M. Ruth A., CBE, BA *Essex*, MA *Sus.*,
   Hon. LLD *Manc.*, FRSA   Prof., Social Policy
McGuigan, Jim, BSc *Brad.*, MPhil *Leeds*, PhD *Leic.*
   Prof., Cultural Analysis
Murdock, Graham, BSc(Soc) *Lond.*, MA *Sus.*
   Reader
O'Neill, Maggie, BEd *Staffs.*, PhD *Staffs.*   Sr.
   Lectr.
O'Reilly, Karen, BA *Essex*, PhD *Essex*   Reader
Pickering, Michael, BA *Essex*, MA *Leeds*, PhD
   Leeds   Reader
Pink, Sarah, BA *Kent*, MA *Manc.*, PhD *Kent*   Sr.
   Lectr.
Potter, Jonathan, BA *Liv.*, MA *Sur.*, DPhil
   York(UK)   Prof., Discourse Analysis
Radley, Alan, BTech *Brun.*, PhD *Lond.*   Prof.,
   Social Psychology
Saukko, Paula, MSocSc *Tampere*, PhD *Ill.*   Sr.
   Lectr.
Smith, Dennis, BA *Camb.*, MSc *Lond.*, PhD *Leic.*
   Prof., Sociology; Head*
Stephens, Michael, BSc(Econ) *Wales*, DPhil *Oxf.*
   Sr. Lectr.
Stokoe, Elizabeth, MA *Leic.*, PhD *Leic.*   Reader
Ward, Harriet, MA *St And.*, PhD *Brist.*   Prof.,
   Child and Family Research
Wilkinson, Susan, BSc *Leic.*, FBPsS   Prof.,
   Feminism and Health Studies
Wring, Dominic, BA *Camb.*, PhD *Camb.*   Sr.
   Lectr.
Other Staff: 11 Lectrs.
Research: communication and media studies;
   social policy; social psychology; sociology

Sports and Exercise Sciences

Tel: (01509) 223283 *Fax:* (01509) 223971
   E-mail: j.e.godwin@lboro.ac.uk
Armour, Kathy, BEd *Lond.*, MA *Lond.*, PhD *S'ton.*
   Reader
Atkinson, Michael, BA *Wat.*, MA *McM.*, PhD
   Calg.   Sr. Lectr.
Bairner, Alan, MA *Edin.*, PhD *Hull*   Prof., Sport
   and Social Theory
Biddle, Stuart, BEd *Lough.*, MSc *Penn.State*, PhD
   Keele   Prof., Exercise and Sport Psychology
Bishop, Nicolette, BSc *Birm.*, PhD *Birm.*   Sr.
   Lectr.
Boobis, Leslie, MB ChB MD, FRCSEd   Visiting
   Prof.
Bull, Fiona, BEd *Exe.*, MSc *Lough.*, PhD *W.Aust.*
   Reader
Cale, Lorraine, BSc *Lough.*, MSc *Calif.*, PhD *Lough.*
   Sr. Lectr.
Cushion, Christopher, BSc *Brun.*, PhD *Brun.*   Sr.
   Lectr.
Downward, Paul, BA *Staffs.*, MA *Manc.*, PhD
   Leeds   Sr. Lectr.
Evans, John, BEd *Reading*, MA *Lond.*, PhD *Lond.*
   Prof., Sociology of Education and Physical
   Education
Ferguson, Richard, BSc *Birm.*, MPhil *Birm.*, PhD
   Manc.Met.   Sr. Lectr.
Gleeson, Mike, BSc *Birm.*, PhD *C.Lancs.*   Prof.,
   Exercise Biochemistry
Hardman, Adrianne, MSc *Salf.*, PhD *Lough.*
   Emer. Prof.
Harris, Jo, BA *Open(UK)*, MA *Birm.*, PhD *Lough.*
   Sr. Lectr.
Harwood, Christopher, BSc *Lough.*, MSc *Lough.*,
   PhD *Lough.*   Sr. Lectr.
Henry, Ian, BA *Stir.*, MSc *Lough.*, PhD *Lough.*
   Prof., Leisure Policy and Management
Houlihan, Barrie, BA *Liv.*, MSc *Salf.*, PhD *Salf.*
   Prof., Sport Policy
Jowett, Sophia, BSc *Athens*, MPhil *Lough.*, PhD
   Exe.   Sr. Lectr.
King, Mark, BSc *Lough.*, PhD *Lough.*   Sr. Lectr.

Maguire, Joseph, BEd Lond., PhD Leic.   Prof.,
   Sociology of Sport
Malcolm, Dominic, BA Nott., MA Leic., PhD Leic.
   Sr. Lectr.
Maughan, Ron, BSc Aberd., PhD Aberd.   Prof.,
   Sport and Exercise Nutrition
Meeusen, Romain, MSc Brussels, PhD Brussels
   Visiting Prof.
Nevill, Mary, BSc Lough., MSc Lough., PhD Lough.
   Sr. Lectr.
Nimmo, Myra A., BSc Glas., PhD Glas.   Prof.,
   Exercise Physiology; Head*
Pain, Matthew T. G., BSc Leic., MSc Birm., PhD
   Penn.State   Sr. Lectr.
Shirreffs, Susan, BA Aberd., PhD Aberd.   Sr.
   Lectr.
Spray, Christopher, BA Staffs., PhD Exe.   Sr.
   Lectr.
Stensel, David, MSc Lough., PhD Lough., BA   Sr.
   Lectr.
Tolfrey, Keith, BA Exe., MPhil Exe., PhD
   Manc.Met.   Sr. Lectr.
Tolfrey, Vicky, BSc Manc.Met., PhD Manc.Met.
   Sr. Lectr.
Waring, Michael, BEd Leeds, MSc Lough., PhD
   Lough.   Sr. Lectr.
White, Anita, MA Sus., PhD N.Colorado   Visiting
   Prof.
Williams, Clyde, BSc Wales, MSc Wash., PhD
   Aberd.   Prof., Sports Science
Yeadon, Fred, MA Camb., PhD Lough.   Prof.,
   Computer Simulation in Sport
Other Staff: 15 Lectrs.; 1 Sr. Res. Fellow; 3
   Res. Fellows; 1 University Teacher; 18 Res.
   Assocs.; 2 Sr. Visiting Fellows; 2 Visiting
   Fellows
Research: health science; recreation and leisure
   studies; sport and human performance;
   sports science; teacher education

SPECIAL CENTRES, ETC

Advanced Virtual Reality Research Centre

Kalawsky, Roy, BSc Hull, MSc Hull, PhD Hull,
   FRSA   Prof.; Dir.*

Automotive Management, Centre for

Reed, Gary, BEd Nott.Trent   Dir., Res.
Saker, Jim, BSc Wales, MSc Manc.   Prof.; Dir.*
Other Staff: 1 Ford Fellow

Child and Family Research, Centre for (CCFR)

Ward, Harriet, MA St And., PhD Brist.   Prof.;
   Dir.*
Other Staff: 3 Res. Fellows; 5 Res. Assocs.; 3
   Visiting Fellows

Communications Research Centre

Billig, Michael G., BA Brist., PhD Brist.   Prof.;
   Co-Dir.*
Golding, Peter, BSc Lond., MA Essex   Prof.; Co-
   Dir.*

Criminology and Criminal Justice, Midlands Centre for

Farrell, Graham, BSc Manc., PhD Manc.   Dir.*
Pease, Ken, MA Manc., PhD Manc.   External
   Prof.
Prins, Herschel, MPhil Leic., Hon. DSc Lough.
   External Prof.

Development Engineering, Institute of

Including Water, Engineering and
   Development Centre (WEDC)
Smout, Ian, BA Camb., MSc Reading, FICE   Dir.*
Sohail, Mohammed, BEng Lough., MSc Lough.,
   PhD Lough.   Prof., Sustainable Infrastructure
Other Staff: 2 Sr. Programme Managers

Disability Sport, Peter Harrison Centre for

Black, Ken, BA Glas.   Dir.*

Engineering Centre for Excellence in Teaching and Learning (engCETL)

Dickens, John, BSc Manc.   Dir.*
Other Staff: 3 Res. Assocs.

Environmental Studies, Centre for

Warwick, Peter, BA Open(UK), MSc Lough., PhD
   Lough., FRSChem   Prof.; Dir.*

Ergonomics and Safety Research Institute (ESRI)

Tel: (01509) 283300 Fax: (01509) 283360
   E-mail: enquire@ice.co.uk
Gale, Alastair, BA Durh., PhD Durh.   Prof.;
   Head, Applied Vision Centre
Haines, Victoria, BSc Lough.   Head, Applied
   Ergonomics Centre
Richardson, John, BA Wales, MSc Cran.   Dir.*
Thomas, Peter, BSc York(UK)   Prof.; Head,
   Vehicle Safety Res. Centre
Other Staff: 30 Res. Staff; 6 Sr. Visiting Fellows
Research: consumer products; occupational
   ergonomics; transport ergonomics; vehicle
   safety

European Construction Institute

Csotie, Imrie   Chairman*
McCaffer, Ron, BSc Strath., PhD Lough., DSc
   Strath., FICE, FCIOB   Finance Dir.;
   Chairman*
Storey, Robert   Chairman*

Gymnastics Research, Centre for

Yeadon, Fred, MA Camb., PhD Lough.   Prof.;
   Dir.*

Hazard and Risk Management, Centre for

Tel: (01509) 222158 Fax: (01509) 223991
   E-mail: j.bostock@lboro.ac.uk
Hancock, Charles, MSc Sur.   Programme Dir.
Mulhall, Tom, BA Open(UK), MSc Leic.   Dir.,
   Security Programmes
Walker, Deborah, BSc S'ton., MSc Leeds
Wenham, David, BSc S'ton., MSc Strath., PhD
   Birm.   Dir., Postgrad. Programmes
Other Staff: 1 Lectr.
Research: hazardous waste management;
   healthcare risk management; investigatory
   management; occupational health and safety;
   security management

Innovative and Collaborative Engineering, Centre for (CICE)

Anumba, Chimay, BSc Leeds, PhD Leeds, FICE,
   FIStructE, FCIOB   Prof.; Dir.*
Bouchlaghem, Dino, PhD UMIST   Prof.;
   Deputy Dir.
Thorpe, Anthony, BSc Nott., MSc Lough., PhD
   Lough., FICE, FCIOB, FBCS   Prof.; Deputy
   Dir.

Innovative Manufacturing and Construction Research Centre

Dickens, Phill, BSc CNAA, PhD Aston, FIMechE
   Prof.; Dir.*

Loughborough Materials Characterisation Centre (LMCC)

Hall, David, BSc CNAA, MSc Manc.   Dir.*
Other Staff: 4 Tech. Dirs.

Mathematics Education Centre

Croft, Tony, BSc Leeds, MPhil Leeds, PhD Keele,
   FIMA   Dir.*
Harrison, Martin C., BSc Sheff., MSc Sheff., PhD
   Sheff.   Sr. Lectr.
Mustoe, Leslie, BSc Birm., MSc Essex, PhD Lough.
   Sr. Lectr.
Ward, Joseph, BSc Lond., PhD Lond.   Sr. Lectr.
Other Staff: 2 Asst. Dirs.; 1 Lectr.; 1 Res.
   Fellow; 1 Visiting Fellow; 2 Univ. Teachers

Mobile Communications Research, Centre for

Edwards, Rob, PhD Sheff.   Sr. Lectr.
Flint, James, MEng Lough., PhD Lough.   Sr.
   Lectr.

Vardaxoglou, Yiannis, BSc Kent, PhD Kent
   Dir.*
Volakis, John, MSc Ohio State, PhD Ohio State,
   FIEEE   Visiting Prof.
Other Staff: 1 Lectr.

Olympic Studies and Research, Centre for

Henry, Ian, BA Stir., MSc Lough., PhD Lough.
   Prof.; Dir.*

Physical Activity and Health, British Heart Foundation National Centre for

Bull, Fiona, BEd Exe., MSc Lough., PhD W.Aust.
   Co-Dir.*
McGeorge, Sonia, BSc Lough.   Co-Dir.*

Professional and Management Development Centre

Smith, Alison, BA Essex   Deputy Dir.
Whittaker, John, BA(Econ) Manc., MA Manc.,
   FCA   Dir.*

Renewable Energy Systems Technology, Centre for

Freris, Leon L., BSc Lond., MSc Lond., PhD Lond.,
   FIEE   Visiting Prof.
Gottschalg, Ralph, MSc Lough., PhD Lough.   Sr.
   Lectr.
Tiwari, Ayodhya, BSc Garh., MSc Roor., PhD IIT
   Delhi   Prof.
Watson, Simon, BSc Lond., PhD Edin.   Sr.
   Lectr.; Acting Dir.*
Other Staff: 1 Visiting Fellow

Social Policy, Centre for Research in (CRSP)

France, Alan, BA Sheff., PhD Sheff.   Dir.*
Middleton, Sue, BSc(Econ) Lond.   Res. Dir.
Other Staff: 1 Asst. Dir.; 6 Res. Fellows; 10
   Res. Assocs.; 3 Visiting Fellows

Sport and Leisure Policy, Institute of

Downward, Paul, BA Staffs., MA Manc., PhD
   Leeds   Dir.*

Sports Technology Institute

Caine, Mike, BSc Lough., PhD Birm.   Prof.;
   Dir.*
Harland, Andy, BEng Lough., PhD Lough.   Sr.
   Lectr.
Jones, Roy, BTech Lough., PhD CNAA   Dunlop
   Slazenger Prof., Sports Technology
Other Staff: 2 Lectrs.

Systems Engineering Innovation Centre

Kalawsky, Roy, BSc Hull, MSc Hull, PhD Hull,
   FRSA   Prof.; Technical Head*
Other Staff: 29 Researchers

Teacher Education Unit

Cale, Lorraine, BSc Lough., MSc Calif., PhD Lough.
   Sr. Lectr.
Harris, Jo, BA Open(UK), MA Birm., PhD Lough.
   Head*
Ireson, Gren, BA Open(UK), MEd Durh., PhD
   Lough.   Sr. Lectr.
Waring, Michael, BEd Leeds, MSc Lough., PhD
   Lough.   Sr. Lectr.
Other Staff: 3 Lectrs.; 1 Univ. Teacher

Youth Sport, Institute of

Nevill, Mary, BSc Lough., MSc Lough., PhD Lough.
   Dir.*

CONTACT OFFICERS

Academic affairs. Academic Registrar:
   Nutkins, Jennifer C., BA Camb., PhD Camb.
Accommodation. Student Accommodation
   Officer: Henson, Elaine
Admissions (first degree). Senior Assistant
   Registrar (Admissions (first degree): Jones,
   Howard, JP, BA Exe.
Admissions (higher degree). Assistant
   Registrar (Admissions (higher degree -

research)): Vale, Brigette, BA Lond., DPhil York(UK)

Alumni. Alumni Officer: Johnson, Marilyn

Archives. Archivist: Clark, Jenny, BA Brist.

Careers. Director (Careers): Jones, Jennifer, BA Exe.

Computing services. Director (Information Technology): Richards, Philip, MA Oxf., DPhil Oxf.

Conferences/corporate hospitality. Director (Conferences/corporate hospitality): Brown, Malcolm

Development/fund-raising. Director of Development: Walker, Jon, BSc Lough.

Equal opportunities. Equal Opportunities Officer: Mansell, Lesley, BA Leic.

Estates and buildings/works and services. Director, Estates Organisation: Hill, Roy

Examinations. Examinations Officer: Hollingsworth, Mark, BA Liv., MA Nott., PhD Nott.

Finance. Director of Finance: Wiggans, Rachel, MA Camb.

Health services. University Medical Officer: Bhojani, Asghar, MB BS Newcastle(UK)

International office. Director, International Office: Westaway, Tony, BA Durh., MSc Warw.
(E-mail: international-office@lboro.ac.uk)

Language training for international students. Director, English Language Study Unit: Ellis, Jane, BSc Birm.

Library (chief librarian). Librarian: Morley, Mary D., BA Nott.

Marketing. Director of Marketing: Cairns, Ian

Minorities/disadvantaged groups. Equal Opportunities Officer: Mansell, Lesley, BA Leic.

Personnel/human resources. Personnel Officer: Cole, Patrick, BSc Lond.

Public relations. Publicity Director: Baldwin, Hannah, BA Lond.

Publications. Publicity Director: Baldwin, Hannah, BA Lond.

Purchasing. Head of Purchasing: Burton, Tim

Research. Research Manager: Townsend, Peter, BA Brad.

Safety. Health, Safety and Environment Officer: Moore, Catherine, BSc Lough.

Scholarships, awards, loans. Scholarships and Bursaries Officer: Ashby, Martine, BA Lough.

Schools liaison. Schools Liaison Officer: Cook, Eleanor, BA Nott., MA Nott.

Security. Security Manager: Kennedy, Roger

Staff development and training. Director (Professional Development): Wilson, Andrew, BSc Brist., PhD Brist.

Strategic planning. Planning Director: Hannah, Fidelma, BA York(UK)

Student union. President (Student Union): Gerty, David

Student welfare/counselling. Director, University Counselling Service: Bell, Jennifer, BA Manc.

Students with disabilities. Director (Students with disabilities): Kirby, James, BA C.England, MA S'ton.

University press. Director, Audio Visual Services: Mumford, Anne, BSc Leic., PhD Leic.

[Information supplied by the institution as at 11 September 2007, and edited by the ACU]

UNIVERSITY OF MANCHESTER

Founded 1824

Member of the Association of Commonwealth Universities

Postal Address: Oxford Road, Manchester M13 9PL
Telephone: (0161) 306 6000 **Fax:** (0161) 275 2300
URL: http://www.manchester.ac.uk

PRESIDENT AND VICE-CHANCELLOR*—Gilbert, Prof. Alan D., AO, BA ANU, MA ANU, DPhil Oxf., Hon. DLitt Tas., Hon. LLD McG., FASSA

VICE-PRESIDENT (COMMUNICATIONS AND EXTERNAL RELATIONS)—Layzell, Prof. Paul, BA Manc., MSc Manc., PhD Manc., FBCS

VICE-PRESIDENT (INNOVATION AND ECONOMIC DEVELOPMENT)—Coombs, Prof. Rod, BSc Kent, MSc Manc., PhD Manc.

VICE-PRESIDENT (RESEARCH)—Rothwell, Prof. Dame Nancy, DBE, BSc Lond., PhD Lond., DSc Lond.

VICE-PRESIDENT (TEACHING AND LEARNING)—Munn, Prof. Bob, BSc Brist., PhD Brist., DSc Manc., FIP, FRSChem

REGISTRAR‡—Mackie, Dugald, MA Edin., FRSA

DIRECTOR OF FINANCE—Hope-Terry, Geoffrey

MANCHESTER METROPOLITAN UNIVERSITY

Founded 1970

Member of the Association of Commonwealth Universities

Postal Address: All Saints, Manchester, England M15 6BH
Telephone: (0161) 247 2000 **Fax:** (0161) 247 6390 **E-mail:** enquiries@mmu.ac.uk
URL: http://www.mmu.ac.uk

VICE-CHANCELLOR*—Brooks, Prof. John S., BSc Sheff., PhD Sheff., DSc, FIP

DEPUTY VICE-CHANCELLOR—Plumb, Prof. B., MSc

FINANCIAL DIRECTOR—Grant, L., MBA

DEPUTY VICE-CHANCELLOR (RESEARCH AND DEVELOPMENT)—Lister, Prof. Paul, MSc PhD, FIEE

DIRECTOR OF HUMAN RESOURCES—Hemus, Gill

UNIVERSITY SECRETARY AND CLERK TO THE BOARD OF GOVERNORS‡—Hughes, K.

REGISTRAR—Gwyn, Arnold

GENERAL INFORMATION

History. The university was originally established as Manchester Polytechnic in 1970 and became an independent corporate body in 1989. It obtained university status in 1992 and amalgamated with Crewe and Alsager College of Higher Education in the same year.

Admission to first degree courses (see also United Kingdom Introduction). Through Universities and Colleges Admissions Service (UCAS).

First Degrees (see also United Kingdom Directory to Subjects of Study). BA, BEd, BEng, BSc, LLB.

Higher Degrees (see also United Kingdom Directory to Subjects of Study).
Master's. MA, MBA, MChem, MEd, MEng, MPhil, MSc, MSci.
Doctoral. PhD.

Libraries. Volumes: 841,000. Periodicals subscribed to: 4113. Other holdings: 6500

electronic periodical titles. Special collections: North West film archive; book design (including artists' books and Victorian ephemera); gallery.

FACULTIES/SCHOOLS

Art and Design
Tel: (0161) 247 1713 Fax: (0161) 247 6361
E-mail: artdes.fac@mmu.ac.uk
Dean: Wayman, Prof. Maureen
Faculty Secretary: Foote, S., BSc(Econ)

Business School
Tel: (0161) 247 3703 Fax: (0161) 247 6350
Dean: Morris, Prof. Huw
Faculty Registrar: Legge, N.

Food, Clothing and Hospitality Management
Tel: (0161) 247 2616 Fax: (0161) 247 6395
E-mail: hollings-fac@mmu.ac.uk
Dean: Murray, Prof. R., BSc PhD
Faculty Secretary: Austin, Maureen

Health, Social Care and Education
Tel: (0161) 247 2001 Fax: (0161) 247 6327
E-mail: commstud.fac@mmu.ac.uk
Dean: Ramprogus, Prof. V. K., BA MSc PhD
Faculty Secretary: Thorley, A.

Humanities, Law and Social Science
Tel: (0161) 247 1749 Fax: (0161) 247 6308
E-mail: humanities-fac@mmu.ac.uk
Dean: Holmes, Prof. Ann, BA MPhil
Faculty Secretary: Ford, Pauline, BA MSc

MMU Cheshire
Tel: (0161) 247 5182 Fax: (0161) 247 6371
Dean: Dunn, Dennis, JP, BA
Faculty Secretary: Legge, Hilary

Science and Engineering
Tel: (0161) 247 1783 Fax: (0161) 247 6315
Dean: Neal, Prof. Maureen, BSc PhD
Faculty Secretary: Austin, Maureen

ACADEMIC UNITS

Accounting and Finance Division
Tel: (0161) 247 3759 Fax: (0161) 247 6303
Alali, J. Sr. Lectr.
Arkwright, A. Sr. Lectr.
Ashworth, D. Principal Lectr.
Brander-Brown, J. C. F. Sr. Lectr.
Christian, J. Sr. Lectr.
De Silva, H. Sr. Lectr.
Guthrie, C. Sr. Lectr.
Helps, Lynda C. Sr. Lectr.
Holt, G. J. Principal Lectr.
Keenan, J. Sr. Lectr.
Lee-Faulkner, R. Sr. Lectr.
Leigh, B. Sr. Lectr.
Maguire, K. Sr. Lectr.
Marland, P. Sr. Lectr.
McKeon, P. Principal Lectr.
Mounsey, B. Sr. Lectr.
Princep, O. Sr. Lectr.
Rattenbury, J. N. Sr. Lectr.
Rodda, N. G. Sr. Lectr.
Scott, N. Sr. Lectr.
Scott, S. Sr. Lectr.
Smyth, S. Sr. Lectr.
Somerfield, A. Sr. Lectr.
Sweeting, R. C. Prof.; Exec. Head*
Townsley, J. Sr. Lectr.
Walker, C. Sr. Lectr.
Watson, M. H. Sr. Lectr.
Wayte, K. Sr. Lectr.
Williamson, T. Sr. Lectr.
Woollard, D. Sr. Lectr.
Wynne, J. Sr. Lectr.

Architecture, Manchester School of
Tel: (0161) 247 6950 Fax: (0161) 247 6810
E-mail: msa@mmu.ac.uk
Brook, R. Sr. Lectr.
Canniffe, E. Principal Lectr.

Chung, M. Sr. Lectr.
Dargavel, R. Sr. Lectr.
Dernie, D. Prof.; Head*
Epolito, G. Sr. Lectr.
Jefferies, T. E. Sr. Lectr.
Keeffe, Greg Principal Lectr.
McGonigal, E. Sr. Lectr.
McKennan, G. T. Sr. Lectr.
Pugh, C. L. Principal Lectr.
Stone, Sally H. Sr. Lectr.
Tyson, N. Sr. Lectr.
White, S. Sr. Lectr.
Other Staff: 6 Lectrs.

Art, School of
see also Contemporary Arts, and Hist. of Art and Des.
Tel: (0161) 247 1705 Fax: (0161) 247 6393
E-mail: artdes@mmu.ac.uk
Beadle, J. Sr. Lectr.
Biddulph, J. Sr. Lectr.
Brake, J. Sr. Lectr.
Brown, J. K. Principal Lectr.
Butler, J. Sr. Lectr.
Dolphin, T. F. Sr. Lectr.
Dowling, N. C. Principal Lectr.
Dunbar, T. Principal Lectr.
Eve, A. Sr. Lectr.
Fleming, C. N. Sr. Lectr.
Gawin, G. P. Sr. Lectr.
Hall, S. Sr. Lectr.
Hawley, S. Prof.; Head*
Johnson, B. Sr. Lectr.
Johnson, L. J. Sr. Lectr.
Jones, A. Sr. Lectr.
Jones, C. J. Sr. Lectr.
Jones, H. Sr. Lectr.
Limon, D. F. Sr. Lectr.
Magee, J. P. Sr. Lectr.
Moritz, C. Sr. Lectr.
Mytton, M. Sr. Lectr.
Orobiej, W. M. Sr. Lectr.
Osbaldeston, D. Sr. Lectr.
Parry, G. Sr. Lectr.
Posada, M. Sr. Lectr.
Ratcliffe, A. Sr. Lectr.
Rawlinson, I. Sr. Lectr.
Robb, W. Sr. Lectr.
Shirley, D. Sr. Lectr.
Spencer, B. R. Sr. Lectr.
Sweet, D. Sr. Lectr./Principal Lectr.
Vickers, J. Sr. Lectr.
White, J. Sr. Lectr.
Zapp, A. Sr. Lectr.
Other Staff: 3 Lectrs.

Biological Sciences
Tel: (0161) 247 1234 Fax: (0161) 247 6325
Ahmed, N. Sr. Lectr.
Ainley, C. Sr. Lectr.
Barnett, Ann Sr. Lectr.
Bohme, K. T. Sr. Lectr.
Chapman, J. Sr. Lectr.
Craig, G. D. Sr. Lectr.
Cresswell, N. Principal Lectr.
Dawson, Maureen M. Sr. Lectr.
Dempsey, M. J., BSc Liv., MSc Portsmouth, PhD Portsmouth Sr. Lectr.
Fielding, A. Sr. Lectr.
Gaffney, J. J. Sr. Lectr.
Gilmore, W. S. Prof.; Head*
Goldspink, C. R. Sr. Lectr.
Graham, I. Principal Lectr.
Gregson, Olga Sr. Lectr.
Gross, T. S. Principal Lectr.
Hayes, M. Sr. Lectr.
Hick, V. Sr. Lectr.
Hughes, H. Sr. Lectr.
Hughes, N. Sr. Lectr.
Hume, K. I. Principal Lectr.
Jones, C. Sr. Lectr.
Jones, M. J. Sr. Lectr.
Kay, I. S. Sr. Lectr.
Kumar, Patricia M. Reader
Lace, L. Sr. Lectr.
Looker, T., BSc PhD Prof.
McLaughlin, N. J. Sr. Lectr.

Nayagam, S. Sr. Lectr.
Overfield, Joyce A. Sr. Lectr.
Seal, L. H. Sr. Lectr.
Smith, C. A. Sr. Lectr.
Stevens-Wood, B. Sr. Lectr.
Sullivan, M. Sr. Lectr.
Verran, Joanna Prof. (Microbiology)
Whalley, W. M. Sr. Lectr.
Willcox, J. Sr. Lectr.

Business and Management Studies
Tel: (0161) 247 5022 Fax: (0161) 247 6378
E-mail: busman.ca@mmu.ac.uk
Broomfield, C. Sr. Lectr.
Coles, S. Sr. Lectr.
Curtis, S. Sr. Lectr.
Cuthbert, P. Sr. Lectr.
Fisher, R. Principal Lectr.
Gallimore, K. Sr. Lectr.
Grant, M. J. Sr. Lectr.
Hall, L. Sr. Lectr.
Jazayeri-Dezfuli, S. Sr. Lectr.
Knibbs, A. Sr. Lectr.
Leece, D. Prof.; Head*
Liu, J. Sr. Lectr.
Lovatt, C. Sr. Lectr.
McLean, J. Sr. Lectr.
Morris, J. Sr. Lectr.
Muir, J. Sr. Lectr.
O'Leary, B. J. Sr. Lectr.
Ormrod, N. G. Sr. Lectr.
Owen, A. S. Sr. Lectr.
Peet, S. T. Sr. Lectr.
Potter, S. A. Sr. Lectr.
Pratten, J. Principal Lectr.
Schofield, S. Sr. Lectr.
Spowage, R. Sr. Lectr.
Stevenson, D. Sr. Lectr.
Williams, J. A. Sr. Lectr.
Wright, D. Principal Lectr.

Business Information Technology and Management Science Division
Tel: (0161) 247 3809 Fax: (0161) 247 6317
Avery, J. D. Principal Lectr.
Bainbridge, S. F. Sr. Lectr.
Buehring, A. Sr. Lectr.
Bull, C. M. Sr. Lectr.
Carroll, A. Sr. Lectr.
Davidson, C. R. Sr. Lectr.
Endlar, L. D. Sr. Lectr.
Faraj, I. Sr. Lectr.
Harris, W. J. Sr. Lectr.
Jackson, A. B. Sr. Lectr.
Jayaratna, N. Prof.; Exec. Head*
Johnson, R. Sr. Lectr.
Jones, L. Sr. Lectr.
Lester, G. C. Sr. Lectr.
McLean, R. Sr. Lectr.
McQuater, R. Sr. Lectr.
Meldrum, M. C. R. Principal Lectr.
Mole, G. Principal Lectr.
Morris, M. Sr. Lectr.
Pagano, R. Sr. Lectr.
Parry, E. Sr. Lectr.
Paucar-Caceres, A. L. Sr. Lectr.
Petty, R. Sr. Lectr.
Salazar, A. Sr. Lectr.
Scown, P. J. Sr. Lectr.
Sheard, V. Principal Lectr.
Stubbs, M. A. Principal Lectr.
Tebboune, S. Sr. Lectr.
Tucker, D. E. Sr. Lectr.
Weaver, C. R. Sr. Lectr.
Other Staff: 1 Prof.; 1 Sr. Res. Fellow; 3 Res. Assocs.

Chemistry and Materials
Tel: (0161) 247 1437 Fax: (0161) 247 6357
Allen, N. S. Prof.
Birkett, P. Sr. Lectr.
Clemens, M. Sr. Lectr.
Cole, D. Sr. Lectr.
Cole, M. Sr. Lectr.
Dickinson, J. M. Principal Lectr.
Ding, J. Sr. Lectr.
Dolphin, G. P. Sr. Lectr.
Doyle, A. Sr. Lectr.

D'Silva, C. Sr. Lectr.
Edge, M. Reader
Gilbert, M. Sr. Lectr.
Gough, P. Sr. Lectr.
Horne, S. Sr. Lectr.
Hughes, A. Sr. Lectr.
Johnson, D. Principal Lectr.
Lees, G. L. Principal Lectr.
Maryan, C. Principal Lectr.
McCormick, P. Sr. Lectr.
McLean, Megan M. Sr. Lectr.
Monk, P. M. Sr. Lectr.
Murphy, B. P. Principal Lectr.
Nicholas, G. A. Sr. Lectr.
Rego, C. A. Sr. Lectr.
Smith, Paul Sr. Lectr.
Wardle, B. Sr. Lectr.
Other Staff: 1 Lectr.

Clothing Design and Technology

Tel: (0161) 247 2645 Fax: (0161) 247 6329
Ball, Christina S. Sr. Lectr.
Barlow, Delma Sr. Lectr.
Barnes, Liz Sr. Lectr.
Batson, Batson Sr. Lectr.
Bond, T. D. Sr. Lectr.
Bouvier, George, BA MSc Sr. Lectr.
Cadman, Barbara A. Sr. Lectr.
Chadwick, Nicola Sr. Lectr.
Chen, Terence Sr. Lectr.
Culliney, Claire Sr. Lectr.
Fairclough, Dorothy Sr. Lectr.
Fairhurst, Catherine L. Head*
Hayes, S. G. Sr. Lectr.
Iwanow, Heather Sr. Lectr.
Jefferson, Aileen Sr. Lectr.
Jeffrey, M. Principal Lectr.
Jones, Jacqueline L. Sr. Lectr.
Lea-Greenwood, Jacquetta G. Sr. Lectr.
Malone, Maria Sr. Lectr.
McTurk, Clare Sr. Lectr.
Mee, Christine Sr. Lectr.
Mitchell, Anita Sr. Lectr.
Norman, Debra L. Sr. Lectr.
Otieno, Rose Sr. Lectr.
Peers, Angela C. Principal Lectr.
Power, Jess Sr. Lectr.
Reilly, F. P. Sr. Lectr.
Rowe, Helen D. Principal Lectr.
Ruckman, Ji-Young Reader
Tate, Muriel A. Sr. Lectr.
Twine, C. Sr. Lectr.
Tyler, D. J. Sr. Lectr.
Wallace, Thomasina D. Sr. Lectr.
Other Staff: 5 Lectrs.; 1 Res. Staff

Combined Studies Scheme

Tel: (0161) 247 1460 Fax: (0161) 247 6336
Hughes, N. Principal Lectr.
Latham, A. Sr. Lectr.
Moore, K. J. Prof.; Head*
Nejad, L. Principal Lectr.

Computing and Mathematics

Tel: (0161) 247 1500 Fax: (0161) 247 6337
Bandar, Z. Reader
Brindle, G. J. Sr. Lectr.
Cameron, R. J. Sr. Lectr.
Causon, D. Prof.; Head*
Cherry, R. I. Sr. Lectr.
Costen, N. Sr. Lectr.
Crockett, K. Sr. Lectr.
Ellis, N. S. Principal Lectr.
Fakas, G. Sr. Lectr.
Gerber, L. Sr. Lectr.
Hancox, M. P. Principal Lectr.
Hicks, Helen C. Sr. Lectr.
Hoad, J. E. Sr. Lectr.
Li, B. Sr. Lectr.
Lynch, S. Sr. Lectr.
Marsden, P. J. Sr. Lectr.
McKenna, P. Sr. Lectr.
Miller, R. K. Principal Lectr.
Mingham, C. G. Reader
Nisbet, A. Sr. Lectr.
O'Shea, J. D. Sr. Lectr.
Quick, Pamela Sr. Lectr.

Quigley, P. Sr. Lectr.
Ryan, Julie Sr. Lectr.
Rybakov, V. Sr. Lectr.
Saberton, R. Principal Lectr.
Saunders, R. Reader
Scallan, Anthony J. Sr. Lectr.
Shani, N. Sr. Lectr.
Shea, B. L. Sr. Lectr.
Shen, H. Prof.
Slack, R. S. Sr. Lectr.
Stanton, M. Sr. Lectr.
Thorpe, J. C. Sr. Lectr.
Waraich, M. Sr. Lectr.
Wendl, B. A. Principal Lectr.
Whiteley, D. Sr. Lectr.
Whittaker, N. Sr. Lectr.
Wiseman, A. N. Sr. Lectr.
Yates, K. Sr. Lectr.
Other Staff: 9 Lectrs.

Contemporary Arts

see also Art, Sch. of

Tel: (0161) 247 5305 Fax: (0161) 247 6377
Allsopp, R. Principal Lectr.
Armstrong, J. A. Sr. Lectr.
Blain, M. A. Sr. Lectr.
Brodie, D. Sr. Lectr.
Cacalano, V. Sr. Lectr.
Chamberlain-Duerden, R. S. Sr. Lectr.
Chatwin, P. Sr. Lectr.
Deeney, J. Sr. Lectr.
Drakopoulou, A. Sr. Lectr.
Egan, K. Sr. Lectr.
Fairhall, A. Sr. Lectr.
Fisher, A. Prof.; Head*
Francis, R. Sr. Lectr.
Graham, R. Sr. Lectr.
Kinghorn, S. Sr. Lectr.
Linden, J. L. Sr. Lectr.
Lland, M. Sr. Lectr.
MacDonald, A. Sr. Lectr.
Mackenzie, N. K. Sr. Lectr.
McVittie, F. E. Sr. Lectr.
Mitchison, L. Sr. Lectr.
Nelson, R. A. Prof.
Reilly McVittie, N. O. Sr. Lectr.
Saddington, R. J. Sr. Lectr.
Shrubsole, A. G. Sr. Lectr.
Stanier, P. Sr. Lectr.
Stevens, B. A. Sr. Lectr.
Turner, Jane C. Sr. Lectr.
Webb, J. Sr. Lectr.
Other Staff: 6 Researchers

Design, School of

see also Hist. of Art and Des.

Tel: (0161) 247 1705 Fax: (0161) 247 6393
E-mail: artdes@mmu.ac.uk
Billson, N. Sr. Lectr.
Blakey, Sharon Sr. Lectr.
Brooker, G. Sr. Lectr.
Brown, M. R. Sr. Lectr.
Cahill, C. Sr. Lectr.
Canning-Smith, H. E. Principal Lectr.
Cooper, H. J. Sr. Lectr.
Cowland, T. Sr. Lectr.
Crow, D. Prof.; Head*
Curran, F. Sr. Lectr.
Cuthbert, V. Sr. Lectr.
Felcy, H. Sr. Lectr.
Finlay, R. J. Sr. Lectr.
Fisher, L. Sr. Lectr.
Glennon, S. Sr. Lectr.
Grant, N. O. Principal Lectr.
Grimshaw, D. Sr. Lectr.
Gristwood, E. Sr. Lectr.
Gristwood, Lenore Sr. Lectr.
Hargreaves, J. B. Sr. Lectr.
Harrison, J. Sr. Lectr.
Hartley, K. Sr. Lectr.
Hewitt, J. Sr. Lectr.
Holmes, A. M. Sr. Lectr.
Holtom, Teresa Sr. Lectr.
Hurlstone, N. Sr. Lectr.
Langdown, A. L. Sr. Lectr.
McCullough, I. Sr. Lectr.
McErlain, A. J. Sr. Lectr.

McFadyen, J. Principal Lectr.
McNulty, S. Sr. Lectr.
Miller, M. K. Sr. Lectr.
Mills, D. W. Sr. Lectr.
Morfill, S. Sr. Lectr.
O'Neill, C. J. Sr. Lectr.
Platt, S. Sr. Lectr.
Roberts, I. D., MDes RCA   Principal Lectr.
Russell, A. P. Sr. Lectr.
Scholey, S. E. Sr. Lectr.
Setterington, L. Sr. Lectr.
Shaw, A. M. Sr. Lectr.
Squires, T. M. Principal Lectr.
Taylor, M. Sr. Lectr.
Tebbit, J. Sr. Lectr.
Welsh, A. Sr. Lectr.
Worth, S. G. Sr. Lectr.
Wright, I. M. Sr. Lectr.
Other Staff: 4 Lectrs.

Economics

Tel: (0161) 247 3890 Fax: (0161) 247 6302
E-mail: d.sutcliffe@mmu.ac.uk
Albertson, K. Principal Lectr.
Askew, R. P. Sr. Lectr.
Cleeve, E. Sr. Lectr.
Dearden, S. J. Sr. Lectr.
Evans, Susan T. Sr. Lectr.
Gibbard, K. M. Sr. Lectr.
Khan, J. Sr. Lectr.
Leslie, D. Res. Prof.
Ndhlovu, T. P. Sr. Lectr.
Steedman, Ian Res. Prof.
Tinsdale, K. P. Princ. Lectr.
Tomkins, Judith M. Reader
Triantafillou, P. Sr. Lectr.
Vint, John Prof.; Head*
Zhang, W. Sr. Lectr.
Zis, G. Res. Prof.
Other Staff: 3 Lectrs.
Research: development economics; exchange rate
   analysis; history of economic thought/
   political economy; labour economics;
   microeconomic theory

Education, Institute of

Abbott, Lesley Prof.
Aitken, Susan Sr. Lectr.
Ariza, Pura Sr. Lectr.
Askew-Clough, R. Sr. Lectr.
Baker, W. Sr. Lectr.
Barnes, Jayne Sr. Lectr.
Barnes, R. F. Sr. Lectr.
Barron, I. Principal Lectr.
Bates, J. E. Sr. Lectr.
Batsleer, Janet R. Sr. Lectr.
Bermingham, Susan Sr. Lectr.
Bielby, Colin Sr. Lectr.
Binns, B. Sr. Lectr.
Bowen, P. Sr. Lectr.
Boys, R. A. Sr. Lectr.
Brady, Anthony Sr. Lectr.
Brown, A. M. Principal Lectr.
Browne, Karen Sr. Lectr.
Butcher, Valerie Sr. Lectr.
Capener, Judy Sr. Lectr.
Chambers, Chris Sr. Lectr.
Cleall-Hill, M. J. Sr. Lectr.
Comrie, C. Sr. Lectr.
Cooper, W. J. Sr. Lectr.
Coulbeck, J. Sr. Lectr.
Curtis, T. Sr. Lectr.
Devlin, L. M. Sr. Lectr.
Dickinson, Paul Sr. Lectr.
Duffy, Karen Sr. Lectr.
Eade, F. Principal Lectr.
Ellis, S. W. Sr. Lectr.
Evans, William Sr. Lectr.
Fasciato, Melanie Sr. Lectr.
Fenton, D. Sr. Lectr.
Green, Janet Principal Lectr.
Haldane, M. J. Sr. Lectr.
Hall, N. Prof.
Hanley, Una M. Sr. Lectr.
Haworth, Avril Sr. Lectr.
Heaton, D. Sr. Lectr.
Heywood, D. S. Sr. Lectr.
Hodson, Elaine Sr. Lectr.

Hollis, M. J. Sr. Lectr.
Holmes, Rachel Sr. Lectr.
Hoodless, Patricia A. Sr. Lectr.
Hunt, Sarah Sr. Lectr.
John, Jill V. Sr. Lectr.
Jolley, Rowena D. Sr. Lectr.
Jones, A. Dean*
Jones, Elizabeth Sr. Lectr.
Jones, P. S. G. Sr. Lectr.
Jones, R. J. Sr. Lectr.
Joyce, Marie Sr. Lectr.
Judge, Brenda Sr. Lectr.
Kelly, Kathleen Sr. Lectr.
Kenny, Stephanie E. Sr. Lectr.
Kirk, Katherine Sr. Lectr.
Lancaster, L. G. Sr. Lectr.
Leigh-Baker, P. Sr. Lectr.
Lewis, S. E. Sr. Lectr.
Leyland, Deborah Sr. Lectr.
Maclure, Maggie Prof.
Macrory, Geraldine F. Principal Lectr.
Maxfield, A. Sr. Lectr.
McCreery, E. Sr. Lectr.
McPeake, J. C. Sr. Lectr.
Micklewright, A. Sr. Lectr.
Mills, B. A. Principal Lectr.
Mimnagh, J. Sr. Lectr.
Moorcroft, R. Principal Lectr.
Moore, Lynda Principal Lectr.
Morley, J. W. Principal Lectr.
Mulligan, A. Sr. Lectr.
Naftalin, I. H. Sr. Lectr.
Opie, Clive Head, Educn. Centres
Packham, Carol Sr. Lectr.
Page, C. Sr. Lectr.
Palmer, Sandra Sr. Lectr.
Parker, J. Sr. Lectr.
Patterson, R. Sr. Lectr.
Pearce, Catherine Sr. Lectr.
Phethean, Peter Sr. Lectr.
Pickard, A. J. Principal Lectr.
Poulter, Anthony Sr. Lectr.
Powell, John Sr. Lectr.
Rainer, J. A. Sr. Lectr.
Roberts, I. M. Sr. Lectr.
Robinson, J. F. Principal Lectr.
Robson, C. Sr. Lectr.
Ronan, Alison Sr. Lectr.
Roscoe, C. Sr. Lectr.
Rowlands, M. A. Sr. Lectr.
Rudd, A. Sr. Lectr.
Ryan, Julie Sr. Lectr.
Savage, John Sr. Lectr.
Sayers, S. Sr. Lectr.
Schostak, John Prof.
Selby, D. B. Sr. Lectr.
Shallcross, A. G. Sr. Lectr.
Sidley, M. J. Sr. Lectr.
Sinclair, Yvonne Sr. Lectr.
Smith, Amanda Dir., Science Learning Centre NW
Smith, D. W. Sr. Lectr.
Smith, John Sr. Lectr.
Smith, Kim E. Sr. Lectr.
Somekh, Bridget Prof.
Spink, E. Sr. Lectr.
Stark, S. Principal Lectr.
Steel, Ben Sr. Lectr.
Stronach, Ian Prof.
Sugarman, I. Sr. Lectr.
Sweasey, Penny Principal Lectr.
Symes, Elizabeth Sr. Lectr.
Torrance, Harry Prof.; Head, Res. and Scholarly Activity
Tyler, Stephen Sr. Lectr.
Walker, K. Sr. Lectr.
Warburton, Terence Principal Lectr.
Whitehead, A. G. Sr. Lectr.
Willcock, Pamela H. Sr. Lectr.
Wood, D. J. Sr. Lectr.
Woods, Jane Sr. Lectr.
Wright, Sue Sr. Lectr.
Other Staff: 1 Lectr.; 9 Res. Fellows; 3 Res. Assocs.

Engineering and Technology

Tel: (0161) 247 1632 Fax: (0161) 247 1633
Ainscough, J. Principal Lectr.
Allwork, J. B. Sr. Lectr.
Anani, Nader Sr. Lectr.
Bowring, N. Sr. Lectr.
Brookes, D. S. Principal Lectr.
Cusworth, S. Sr. Lectr.
Deloughry, R. J. Sr. Lectr.
Foulger, M. Sr. Lectr.
Fowler, M. Sr. Lectr.
Hall, B. Sr. Lectr.
Hartley, T. Sr. Lectr.
Holland, D. Sr. Lectr.
Hurst, Ken Prof.; Head*
Iwnicki, S. D. Principal Lectr.
Ji, H. Sr. Lectr.
Kennedy, I. Sr. Lectr.
Knotts, R. Sr. Lectr.
Lakkas, V. Sr. Lectr.
Latif, M. N. Sr. Lectr.
Lo, Hong R. Sr. Lectr.
Manning, W. Sr. Lectr.
McCann, W. J. Sr. Lectr.
Nixon, S. A. Sr. Lectr.
Ponciano, J. Principal Lectr.
Ponnapalli, P. V. S. Sr. Lectr.
Poole, S. Sr. Lectr.
Ross, J. S. Sr. Lectr.
Samosa, M. D. Sr. Lectr.
Slaouti, A. Sr. Lectr.
South, G. E. Principal Lectr.
Southall, D. Sr. Lectr.
Taylor, H. Sr. Lectr.
Thomson, M. Principal Lectr.
Travis, L. Sr. Lectr.
Twigg, P. Sr. Lectr.
Verwer, A. A. Principal Lectr.
Ward, A. J. Sr. Lectr.
Watson, R. Sr. Lectr.
Wormald, P. Sr. Lectr.
Other Staff: 1 Lectr.

English

Tel: (0161) 247 1732 Fax: (0161) 247 6345
E-mail: english-hums@mmu.ac.uk
Arrowsmith, P. Sr. Lectr.
Berry, L. Sr. Lectr.
Bertram, V. Sr. Lectr.
Biswell, A. Principal Lectr.
Blake, L. Sr. Lectr.
Bradshaw, M. Principal Lectr.
Burke, L. Sr. Lectr.
Byrne, E. Sr. Lectr.
Coupe, L. H. Sr. Lectr.
Edwards, J. Principal Lectr.
Liggins, E. Sr. Lectr.
Louvre, A. Principal Lectr.
Maclachlan, S. Sr. Lectr.
Magrs, P. Sr. Lectr.
McGowan, Kathleen A. Sr. Lectr.
Michelis, A. Sr. Lectr.
Moor, A. Sr. Lectr.
Nicholson, H. Sr. Lectr.
Powell, C. A. Sr. Lectr.
Roberts, M. S. Sr. Lectr.
Roy, Jacqueline Sr. Lectr.
Schmidt, M. Prof.
Taylor, J. Sr. Lectr.
Zlosnik, Sue, BSc MA PhD Prof.; Head*
Other Staff: 5 Lectrs.
Research: critical theory including post-colonial theory, gender and queer theory, continental philosophy, psychoanalytical theory, myth and eco-criticism; cultural studies in film, television, history of popular print; Romanticism and Victorian literature; twentieth-century poetry; twentieth-century world literatures, especially American, Canadian and Caribbean

Environmental and Geographical Sciences

see also Sports and Environmental Sci.
Tel: (0161) 247 1600 Fax: (0161) 247 6318
Allman, W. R. Sr. Lectr.
Binnie, J. Sr. Lectr.

Caporn, S. J. M. Principal Lectr.
Chipman, P. Sr. Lectr.
Dobson, M. K. Sr. Lectr.
Drew, I. Sr. Lectr.
Dunleavy, P. J. Principal Lectr.
Edensor, T. Sr. Lectr.
Gibson, Christine S. Principal Lectr.
Hooker, J. Prof.; Head*
Hoon, S. R. Reader
Hooper, P. D. Sr. Lectr.
Howell, R. J. Sr. Lectr.
Lageard, J. Sr. Lectr.
Lambrick, D. B. Principal Lectr.
Langan, A. M. Sr. Lectr.
Marsden, S. Sr. Lectr.
Paget, G. E. Sr. Lectr.
Perry, C. Reader
Price, E. A. C. Sr. Lectr.
Raper, D. Prof.
Ratcliffe, G. Principal Lectr.
Smith, G. R. Sr. Lectr.
Thomas, A. Sr. Lectr.
Watson, A. F. R. Sr. Lectr.
Wheater, C. P. Principal Lectr.
Young, C. Sr. Lectr.
Other Staff: 7 Lectrs.

Exercise and Sport Science

Tel: (0161) 247 5472 Fax: (0161) 247 6375
Ashford, D. G. Sr. Lectr.
Atkin, I. Sr. Lectr.
Baltzopoulos, V. Prof.
Bell, B. Sr. Lectr.
Bell, T. C. Sr. Lectr.
Boyd, C. Sr. Lectr.
Burden, A. M. Principal Lectr.
Daniels, J. Sr. Lectr.
Day, D. Sr. Lectr.
De Haan, A. Prof.
Degens, H. Principal Lectr.
Dulla, J. R. Sr. Lectr.
Eaves, S. Sr. Lectr.
Fazackerley, F. Sr. Lectr.
Fenoglio, R. A. Sr. Lectr.
Fowler, N. E. Head*
Gold, J. Sr. Lectr.
Heap, A. R. Sr. Lectr.
Holmes, P. Sr. Lectr.
Jepson, S. Sr. Lectr.
Jones, D. Prof.
Jones, S. Sr. Lectr.
Keil, D. Sr. Lectr.
Lee, P. H. Principal Lectr.
Loram, I. Reader
Lowe, M. J. Sr. Lectr.
Maganaris, C. Prof.
Marple-Horvat, D. Reader
McEwan, I. M. Sr. Lectr.
McGuire, B. H. Sr. Lectr.
Moore, P. Sr. Lectr.
Morse, C. Sr. Lectr.
Narici, M. Prof.
Payton, C. Sr. Lectr.
Pheasey, C. Sr. Lectr.
Pickford, G. Sr. Lectr.
Pinner, S. Sr. Lectr.
Richards, P. Sr. Lectr.
Rittweger, J. Prof.
Roach, N. K. Sr. Lectr.
Sargeant, A. J. Prof.
Savelsbergh, G. Prof.
Slattery, M. Sr. Lectr.
Smith, N. C. Principal Lectr.
Stewart, C. Prof.
Taylor, W. G. Sr. Lectr.
Wallace, C. Sr. Lectr.
Williams, A. G. Sr. Lectr.
Other Staff: 1 Lectr.; 9 Res. Staff

Food and Tourism Management

Tel: (0161) 247 2682 Fax: (0161) 247 6331
Ainsworth, P. A. Principal Lectr.
Ansari, Khalid Sr. Lectr.
Bayliss, P. A. Sr. Lectr.
Bramfit, Jean Sr. Lectr.
Branston, Caroline Sr. Lectr.
Briggs, D. J. Sr. Lectr.

Clayson, Anne Sr. Lectr.
Eddy, S. Sr. Lectr.
Feeney, Catherine Sr. Lectr.
Fenby, J. Principal Lectr.
Gavin-Pitt, Jill Sr. Lectr.
Gillibrand, Gervase Sr. Lectr.
Gomes, F. H. Sr. Lectr.
Hill, D. J. Sr. Lectr.
Hill, Elizabeth Sr. Lectr.
Hobson, J. R., MSc Manc.Met. Sr. Lectr.
Holgate, D. J. Sr. Lectr.
Hollingsworth, Andrew Principal Lectr.
Hughes, H. L. Prof.
Ineson, Elizabeth M. Sr. Lectr.
Jeffrey, M. Acting Head*
Jung, Timothy Sr. Lectr.
Kershaw, Joanna L., BSc Leeds, PhD Leeds Sr.
  Lectr., Food Science and Technology
Knowles, Timothy Principal Lectr.
McDowall, F. W. Sr. Lectr.
Miller, Amanda Principal Lectr.
Mitchell, Christopher Sr. Lectr.
Moody, R. Prof.; Head*
Moravej, Haleh Sr. Lectr.
Palin, M. G. Sr. Lectr.
Patel, Ajay Sr. Lectr.
Peel, R. J. Sr. Lectr.
Ralston, Rita B. Sr. Lectr.
Ramsden, R. Sr. Lectr.
Rhoden, Steven Sr. Lectr.
Seeley, Colin Sr. Lectr.
Sheffield, Brian Sr. Lectr.
Shelton, D. R. Sr. Lectr.
Simms, I. D. Principal Lectr.
Smith, Richard Sr. Lectr.
Stone, Christopher Sr. Lectr.
Symon, Neil Sr. Lectr.
Theodore, J. A. Sr. Lectr.
Thomas, A. S. Sr. Lectr.
Turner, Anne Sr. Lectr.
Turner, Stephen Sr. Lectr.
Walters, Paul Sr. Lectr.
Wong, J. H. Sr. Lectr.
Wood, Julie Sr. Lectr.
Other Staff: 8 Lectrs.

Health, Psychology and Social Change, School of

Tel: (0161) 247 2517 Fax: (0161) 247 6328
Blampied, A. Sr. Lectr.
Bowden, Louise Sr. Lectr.
Campbell, W. H.
Canham, Judith Sr. Lectr.
Carey, Neil Sr. Lectr.
Chatterton, Hilary Sr. Lectr.
Davis, Julie Sr. Lectr.
Diack, Garry Sr. Lectr.
Dunn, Joanna Principal Lectr.
Edmondson, David Sr. Lectr.
Fitzpatrick, Marilyn Sr. Lectr.
Gardner, Ali Sr. Lectr.
Hayes, D. Sr. Lectr.
Hodgkiss, P. Sr. Lectr.
Jones, R. Sr. Lectr.
Jones, Susan G. Sr. Lectr.
Kenny, Stephanie E. Sr. Lectr.
Manson, Doreen E. Sr. Lectr.
Marsden, Janet E. Sr. Lectr.
McGoun, C. Sr. Lectr.
McLaughlin, Kenneth Sr. Lectr.
Mills, Pauline Sr. Lectr.
Mitchell, Duncan Prof.
Nesbitt, S. M. Sr. Lectr.
Presho, Margaret Sr. Lectr.
Renwick, Penny Dir.*
Sargeant, A. V. Sr. Lectr.
Shacklady, Carol Sr. Lectr.
Taylor, Carol Sr. Lectr.
Thomas, Ruth Sr. Lectr.
Weston, Helen Sr. Lectr.
Wilkins, P. Sr. Lectr.

History and Economic History

Tel: (0161) 247 1730 Fax: (0161) 247 6398
  E-mail: hist-hums@mmu.ac.uk
Adams, A. J., BA Leic., PhD Leic. Acting Head*
Ayers, Patricia, BA Liv. Sr. Lectr.

Danks, Catherine J., BA Manc., MA Essex Sr.
  Lectr.
Davies, S. J., MA St And., PhD St And. Sr. Lectr.
Fenemore, M. Sr. Lectr.
Kidd, A. J., MA Manc., PhD Manc. Prof.
Kirk, N., BA Birm., MA Warw., PhD Pitt. Prof.
Mason, J. J., BA Leic. Sr. Lectr.
Nicholls, D., MA Kent, PhD Kent Prof.
Oates, R. Sr. Lectr.
Phillips, G. Principal Lectr.
Tebbutt, M. Sr. Lectr.
Turner, B. C., MSc(Econ) Lond. Sr. Lectr.
Willmot, L. Sr. Lectr.
Wilson, E. R., BA York(UK), MSc Birm. Sr.
  Lectr.
Wyke, T. J., MBE, BA York(UK) Sr. Lectr.
Research: environmental history; Manchester
  comparative regional history; nineteenth-
  and twentieth-century labour history;
  nineteenth-century British political, social
  and economic history; women's history

History of Art and Design

see also Art, Sch. of, and Des., Sch. of
Ackroyd, C. Sr. Lectr.
Barber, F. C. Sr. Lectr.
Booth, P. Sr. Lectr.
East, H. Sr. Lectr.
Faulkner, S. Sr. Lectr.
Hamilton, R. A. Sr. Lectr.
Howard, M. J. Sr. Lectr.
Huxley, D. W. Sr. Lectr.
James, D. Sr. Lectr.
Ormrod, J. M. Sr. Lectr.
Sharp, M. E. Sr. Lectr.
Tilson, R. P. Sr. Lectr.
Other Staff: 3 Lectrs.

Human Resource Management and Organisational Behaviour Division

Tel: (0161) 247 3957 Fax: (0161) 247 6304
Abedin, S. Sr. Lectr.
Alker, L. Sr. Lectr.
Atkinson, C. Sr. Lectr.
Clark, B. Sr. Lectr.
Doyle, A. J. Sr. Lectr.
Homan, G. Principal Lectr.
Huang, Q. Sr. Lectr.
Jackson, M. G. Sr. Lectr.
Jenner, S. Sr. Lectr.
Lucas, R. E. Prof.
Lupton, B. Principal Lectr.
Mathieson, A. H. Sr. Lectr.
Mead, P. Principal Lectr.
Nabi, G. Sr. Lectr.
Rowe, A. Sr. Lectr.
Sandiford, P. Sr. Lectr.
Scutt, C. N. Sr. Lectr.
Shaw, S., BA MSc Exec. Head*
Taylor, S. Sr. Lectr.
Vyas-Brannick, A. Sr. Lectr.
Warren, R. C. Principal Lectr.
Other Staff: 1 Lectr.

Information and Communications

Tel: (0161) 247 6144 Fax: (0161) 247 6351
  E-mail: infcomms-hums@mmu.ac.uk
Brophy, P. Prof.
Cawood, J. Principal Lectr.
Dawson, C. Sr. Lectr.
Delbridge, R. Sr. Lectr.
Eskins, R. Sr. Lectr.
Fisher, Shelagh M. Reader
French, S. Sr. Lectr.
Geekie, G. Sr. Lectr.
Glass, N. R. Sr. Lectr.
Hartley, Dick J. Prof., Information Science;
  Head*
Hornby, Sue Sr. Lectr.
Hynes, D. Sr. Lectr.
Johnson, F. C. Sr. Lectr.
Kendall, Margaret Sr. Lectr.
Lambert, J. S. Sr. Lectr.
Simpson, J. M. Principal Lectr.
Willson, J. P. Principal Lectr.
Other Staff: 6 Res. Staff

Research: access to electronic information;
  information management (performance
  indicators); social informatics

Interdisciplinary Studies

Tel: (0161) 247 5373 Fax: (0161) 247 6374
  E-mail: humanities.ca@mmu.ac.uk
Bolland, W. J. Sr. Lectr.
Bottomley, M. A. Sr. Lectr.
Bourne-Day, J. Sr. Lectr.
Churchill, H. L. Sr. Lectr.
Crehan, A. S. Sr. Lectr.
Eastwood, I. W. Principal Lectr.
Fair, A. Sr. Lectr.
Hackney, M. Sr. Lectr.
Haire, A. Sr. Lectr.
Hamilton, Cynthia A. Sr. Lectr.
Hutchinson, P. Sr. Lectr.
Issitt, Mary A. Sr. Lectr.
Jones, D. W. Sr. Lectr.
Kim, J. Sr. Lectr.
Kinmond, K. S. Sr. Lectr.
Lee-Treweek, G. Principal Lectr.
Lofkin, M. Sr. Lectr.
Loughlin, M. Principal Lectr.
Lund, N. Sr. Lectr.
McCulloch, F. Sr. Lectr.
Morrison, A. A. Principal Lectr.
Oakley, L. Sr. Lectr.
Parsons, K. Sr. Lectr.
Peart, R. Sr. Lectr.
Piper, J. S., BA Essex, PhD Keele Head*
Reichenfeld, L. Sr. Lectr.
Roberts, D. Sr. Lectr.
Sears, J. A. Sr. Lectr.
Webster, D. C. H. Principal Lectr.
West-Burnham, Jocelyn M. Principal Lectr.
Other Staff: 1 Lectr.

Languages

Tel: (0161) 247 3923 Fax: (0161) 247 6323
  E-mail: languages-hums@mmu.ac.uk
Belkacemi, C. Principal Lectr.
Corkill, D. Prof.
Fieldhouse, Liliane S. Sr. Lectr.
Godsland, S. Sr. Lectr.
Hand, D. Sr. Lectr.
Handley, Sharon Head*
Herhoffer, B. L. Principal Lectr.
Herrero, C. Principal Lectr.
Jones, C. Sr. Lectr.
Leonardo, L. Sr. Lectr.
Mcgowan, Nicoletta Sr. Lectr.
Puig, M. I. Sr. Lectr.
Reilly, M. Sr. Lectr.
Samely, Ursula Sr. Lectr.
Screech, M. Sr. Lectr.
Sheppard, G. Sr. Lectr.
Smyth, E. Reader
Vanderschelden, Isabelle Sr. Lectr.
Vié, C. Sr. Lectr.
Research: computer- and Web-assisted language
  learning; contemporary Spanish fiction and
  popular culture; European crime fiction;
  French literary and cultural studies;
  integration of Spain and Portugal into the
  European Union

Law

Tel: (0161) 247 3049 Fax: (0161) 247 6309
  E-mail: a.a.law@mmu.ac.uk
Amos, D. Principal Lectr.
Barden, M. Head*
Billington, M. Sr. Lectr.
Cairns, W. Sr. Lectr.
Costello, N. Sr. Lectr.
Delany, Linda M. Principal Lectr.
Dent, H. Sr. Lectr.
Downs, C. Sr. Lectr.
Doyle, Kathleen M. Principal Lectr.
Fairhurst, Joy M. Sr. Lectr.
Gibb, T. A. Principal Lectr.
Grout, T. J. Sr. Lectr.
Higgins, Catherine A. Sr. Lectr.
Higgins, E. Principal Lectr.
Horton, B. Sr. Lectr.
Hughes, Diane B. Principal Lectr.
Jones, Lynda A. Sr. Lectr.

Kabishi, A. Sr. Lectr.
Kemble, M. J. Sr. Lectr.
Krawczyk, M. Sr. Lectr.
Latham, M. Reader
Lauterberg, D. Sr. Lectr.
Lee, R. Sr. Lectr.
Lewthwaite, D. Sr. Lectr.
Lipkin, H. Sr. Lectr.
Little, C. Principal Lectr.
Lund, C. Sr. Lectr.
Lunn, J. Sr. Lectr.
Matthews, J. Sr. Lectr.
Maynard, Fiona Sr. Lectr.
McKeon, R. C. Sr. Lectr.
Okojie, P. D. Sr. Lectr.
Panther, J. Sr. Lectr.
Russell, C. Sr. Lectr.
Singleton, R. J. Sr. Lectr.
Spilsbury, S. Principal Lectr.
Sutton, R. Sr. Lectr.
Tansinda, F. Sr. Lectr.
Tatham, L. Principal Lectr.
Taylor, S. Sr. Lectr.
Ward, C. Sr. Lectr.
Whittle, S. T., OBE Reader
Wrigley, L. Sr. Lectr.

Marketing and Retail Division

Tel: (0161) 247 3986 Fax: (0161) 247 6305
Ashford, R. Exec. Head*
Ashworth, C. A. Sr. Lectr.
Bakewell, C. J. Sr. Lectr.
Bennison, D. J. Prof.
Betts, P. B. Principal Lectr.
Bird, D. Sr. Lectr.
Brook, P. A. Sr. Lectr.
Byrne, A. Sr. Lectr.
Elphick, S. Sr. Lectr.
Grime, I. Principal Lectr.
Hall, A. E. Sr. Lectr.
Hines, A. A. Prof.
Humphreys, R. Sr. Lectr.
Leaver, D. Sr. Lectr.
Moss, D. Principal Lectr.
Muskett, D. Principal Lectr.
Pal, J. W. Sr. Lectr.
Pioch, E. A. Sr. Lectr.
Powell, M. J. H. Sr. Lectr.
Quinn, L. Sr. Lectr.
Rees, P. L. Principal Lectr.
Schmidt, R. Principal Lectr.
Talwar, V. Sr. Lectr.
Tonge, J. Sr. Lectr.
Varley, P. Sr. Lectr.
Whitehead, Maureen B. Sr. Lectr.

Politics and Philosophy

Tel: (0161) 247 3436 Fax: (0161) 247 6312
E-mail: pol-phil-hums@mmu.ac.uk
Archer, C. Res. Prof.
Barberis, J. P. Prof.
Barik, A. Sr. Lectr.
Bennett, R. J. Sr. Lectr.
Cammack, P. Prof.
Carr, F. T. Sr. Lectr.
Garfield, M. J. Principal Lectr.
Gibbons, J. P. Sr. Lectr.
Haase, U. M. Sr. Lectr.
Hodge, Joanna Prof.
Hurst, S. Sr. Lectr.
Lievesley, G. A. Sr. Lectr.
Mather, J. Sr. Lectr.
McHugh, J. Principal Lectr.
Nugent, N. Prof.
Townshend, J. Reader
Tyldesley, M. G. Sr. Lectr.
Other Staff: 3 Lectrs.
Research: European, British and American
politics; European, British and American
security studies

Sociology

Tel: (0161) 247 3021 Fax: (0161) 247 6321
E-mail: sociology-hums@mmu.ac.uk
Arun, S. Sr. Lectr.
Banks, M. O. Sr. Lectr.
Bell, D. Sr. Lectr.
Calvey, D. Sr. Lectr.
Ellingworth, D. Sr. Lectr.
Francis, D. W. Sr. Lectr.
Goodrum, Alison Sr. Lectr.
Hepworth, Frances A. Sr. Lectr.
Hodgkinson, D. L. Sr. Lectr.
Jacobs, Susie M., BA Antioch, MSc(Econ) Lond.,
DPhil Sus. Reader
Johnson, W. Sr. Lectr.
Jones, H. Sr. Lectr.
Joyce, P. Sr. Lectr.
Kennedy, P. T. Reader
Laverick, W. Sr. Lectr.
Leach, B. T., BA(Econ) MSc Head*
Lund, B. Principal Lectr.
Marr, E. A. Principal Lectr.
Massey, J. Sr. Lectr.
Milestone, K. Sr. Lectr.
Mythen, G. Principal Lectr.
Nasir, S. Sr. Lectr.
O'Connor, M. J. Reader
Pollack, G. P. S. Principal Lectr.
Randall, D. Sr. Lectr.
Scott, J. Sr. Lectr.
Tate, S. Sr. Lectr.
Turvey, Peta M. Sr. Lectr.
Walklate, S. Prof.
Wowk, Maria T. Sr. Lectr.
Other Staff: 2 Lectrs.
Research: cybersociety and sociology of the
Internet; ethnography of organisations;
social inclusions and exclusions; sociology
of gender and society; urban and popular
culture

Strategy, Entrepreneurship and International Business Division

Tel: (0161) 247 3824 Fax: (0161) 247 6307
Barrett, S. Sr. Lectr.
Bishop, C. Sr. Lectr.
Dawson, C. Sr. Lectr.
El-Sa'id, H. K. Sr. Lectr.
Filiou, D. Sr. Lectr.
Forbes, C. A. Sr. Lectr.
Fraser, N. Sr. Lectr.
Golesorkhi, S. Sr. Lectr.
Horsburgh, S. Exec. Head*
Howe, A. Sr. Lectr.
Hunt, W. J. Sr. Lectr.
Jeremy, D. J. Prof.
Jones, D. Sr. Lectr.
Kokkalis, P. Sr. Lectr.
Kuznetsova, O. Sr. Lectr.
Marsden, A. Sr. Lectr.
Mitton, A. E. Sr. Lectr.
Palowski, H. T. Sr. Lectr.
Pedley, M. C. Sr. Lectr.
Sheard, V. Principal Lectr.
Taylor, D. W. Sr. Lectr.
Tuselmann, H. J. Prof.
Tweedale, G. Reader
Walley, E. E. Sr. Lectr.
Wang, Z. Sr. Lectr.
Windrum, P. Reader
Other Staff: 1 Lectr.

SPECIAL CENTRES, ETC

Art and Design, Manchester Institute for Research and Innovation in (MIRIAD)

Aulich, J. Reader
Bennis, E. M. Principal Lectr.
Bezzant, J. Sr. Lectr.

Hewitt, J. Sr. Lectr.
Hyatt, J., BA Prof.; Head*
Roberts, I. D., MDes RCA Principal Lectr.
Other Staff: 11 Res. Staff

Enterprise, Centre for

Jones, O. E. Prof., Innovation and
Entrepreneurship; Dir.*
Other Staff: 9 Res. Staff

Library and Information Management, Centre for Research in

Tel: (0161) 247 6142 Fax: (0161) 247 6979
Brophy, P. Prof.; Head*
Other Staff: 7 Researchers

Policy Modelling, Centre for

Fax: (0161) 247 6802
Moss, S. Prof.; Head*
Other Staff: 4 Res. Staff

CONTACT OFFICERS

Academic affairs. Registrar: Gwyn, Arnold
Accommodation. Head of Student Services:
Aynsley Smith, S.
Careers. Head of Student Services: Aynsley
Smith, S.
Computing services. Head of Information
Systems: Niman, J. N.
Consultancy services. Director of Research
Development: Gilroy, Prof. P. D.
Estates and buildings/works and services.
Head of Estate Planning Services: Atkins, J.
Finance. Financial Director: Grant, L., MBA
General enquiries. University Secretary and
Clerk to the Board of Governors: Hughes,
K.
International office. International Recruitment
Officer: Corley, Frances
(E-mail: intoff@mmu.ac.uk)
Library (chief librarian). Librarian: Gill, Barry
(E-mail: g.r.barry@mmu.ac.uk)
Minorities/disadvantaged groups. Principal
Lecturer (Minorities/disadvantaged groups):
Avari, B.
Personnel/human resources. Director of
Human Resources: Hemus, Gill
(E-mail: g.hemus@mmu.ac.uk)
Quality assurance and accreditation. Head of
Academic Standards: Lloyd, P.
Research. Director of Research Development:
Gilroy, Prof. P. D.
Safety. Health and Safety Advisor: Gibb, A.
Schools liaison. External Liaison Co-ordinator:
McGrath, S.
Sport and recreation. Head of Student
Services: Aynsley Smith, S.
Staff development and training. Development
and Training Manager: Simpson, B. N.
(E-mail: b.simpson@mmu.ac.uk)
Student welfare/counselling. Head of Student
Services: Aynsley Smith, S.
Students from other countries. Head of
Student Services: Aynsley Smith, S.
Students with disabilities. Head of Student
Services: Aynsley Smith, S.

[Information supplied by the institution as at 17
December 2007, and edited by the ACU]

MIDDLESEX UNIVERSITY

Founded 1973

Member of the Association of Commonwealth Universities

Postal Address: Building 4, North London Business Park, Oakleigh Road South, London, England N11 1QS
Telephone: (020) 8411 5555 **Fax:** (020) 8411 5649 **E-mail:** admissions@mdx.ac.uk
URL: http://www.mdx.ac.uk

VICE-CHANCELLOR*—Driscoll, Prof. Michael J., BA, FRSA
DEPUTY VICE-CHANCELLOR AND DEPUTY CHIEF EXECUTIVE DIRECTOR, MIDDLESEX UK—Goulding, Prof. Ken, BSc
   Lond., PhD Brad., Hon. DSc W.England, FIBiol
DEPUTY VICE-CHANCELLOR AND DIRECTOR, MIDDLESEX INTERNATIONAL—Butland, Terry, BA Camb., MA Camb., PhD
   Bath, FRSA
ASSISTANT VICE-CHANCELLOR, FINANCE DIRECTOR AND DIRECTOR, MIDDLESEX BUSINESS SERVICES—Keen, Melvyn,
   MA, FCA
PRO VICE-CHANCELLOR (PROJECTS) AND DIRECTOR OF DEVELOPMENT STRATEGY—Hardy, Prof. Dennis, BA Exe., MA
   Exe., PhD Lond., FRTPI, FRSA
ASSISTANT VICE-CHANCELLOR AND DIRECTOR, RESEARCH—Ahmad, Prof. Waqar

GENERAL INFORMATION

History. The university's origins date from the nineteenth century with the foundation of St Katherine's College (1878) (now the Tottenham Campus) and Hornsey College of Arts and Crafts (1882). It was established as Middlesex Polytechnic in 1973 and gained university status in 1992.
   It is located on a number of campuses in north London.

Admission to first degree courses (see also United Kingdom Introduction). The university accepts AS levels in combination with 2 or more A levels (or with 1 A level considered on an individual basis) or equivalent. UCAS tariff used wherever possible. Special procedures for mature students.

First Degrees (see also United Kingdom Directory to Subjects of Study) (* = with honours). BA, BA*, BSc, LLB.
   Length of course. Full-time: BA, BA*, BSc, LLB: 3 years. Part-time: BA, BA*, BSc, LLB: 5 years. By distance learning: BA, BA*, BSc: 5–7 years.

Higher Degrees (see also United Kingdom Directory to Subjects of Study).
   Master's. BPhil, MA, MBA, MEd, MFA, MPhil, MProf, MSc.
   Admission. Candidates must hold a first degree.
   Length of course. Full-time: MA, MBA, MSc: 1 year; MFA, MPhil: 2 years. Part-time: MA, MBA, MProf, MSc: 2–3 years; MPhil: 3 years; MFA: 3–4 years. By distance learning: MSc: 2–3 years; MA: 2–4 years; MProf: 3–4 years.
   Doctoral. DLitt, DProf, DSc, DTech, EngD, LLD, PhD.
   Admission. Candidates must hold a Masters degree.
   Length of course. Full-time: DLitt, DProf: 2 years; PhD: 3 years. Part-time: DLitt, DProf: 3 years; PhD: 6 years. By distance learning: PhD: 6 years.

Libraries. Volumes: 750,000. Periodicals subscribed to: 3000. Other holdings: 28,000 audio and video tapes; 9175 CDs; 10,000 music scores. Special collections: Silver Studio (late nineteenth-/early twentieth-century decorative art and design); Museum of Domestic Design and Architecture (MODA); Runnymede Trust library and archive; Black Theatre Forum archive; Bernie Grant collection; Lesbian and Gay Newsmedia archive.

FACULTIES/SCHOOLS

Arts, School of
Tel: (020) 8411 5461
   E-mail: g.parker@mdx.ac.uk
Dean: Parker, Prof. Gabrielle, LèsL MèsL PhD
Secretary: Lear, Judith

Business School
Tel: (020) 8411 5834 Fax: (020) 8411 6011
   E-mail: d.parker@mdx.ac.uk
Dean: Parker, Prof. Dennis, BA PhD, FRGS
Secretary: Jones, Anna

Computing Science, School of
Tel: (020) 8411 5176 Fax: (020) 8411 6411
   E-mail: cswebmaster@mdx.ac.uk
Dean: (vacant)
Secretary: Purser-Marsh, Marilyn

Health, and Social Sciences, School of
Tel: (020) 8411 5543
   E-mail: m.house@mdx.ac.uk
Dean: House, Prof. Margaret, MA PhD
Secretary: Jarvis, Kate

Lifelong Learning and Education, School of
Tel: (020) 8411 5386
   E-mail: r.tufnell@mdx.ac.uk
Dean: Tufnell, Prof. Richard, BSc Lond., PhD Warw.
Secretary: Gurney, Helen

ACADEMIC UNITS
Arranged by Schools

Arts
Tel: (020) 8411 5035 Fax: (020) 8440 9541
Armes, Roy, BA PhD   Prof., Film
Bannerman, Chris   Prof., Dance
Bird, Jon, BA   Prof., Art and Critical Theory
Bridger, Michael, MusB MA MEd PhD   Prof., Music
Conway, David, MA PhD   Prof., Philosophy
Curtis, Barry, MA   Prof.; Dir., Res. and Postgrad. Studies
Durant, Alan, MA PhD   Prof., English Studies
Düttman, Alexander G., MA DPhil   Prof., Modern European Philosophy
Furnham, David, BSc MA   Reader, Media Arts
Guille, Jackie   Prof.; Dir., Curric., Learning and Quality
Hardy, Dennis, BA Exe., MA Exe., PhD Lond., FRTPI, FRSA   Prof., Utopian History
Hope Mason, John, MA PhD   Reader, Intellectual History (on leave)
Hutton, Sarah, PhD   Reader, Renaissance Studies
Jones, Huw, BSc MSc   Prof., Lansdown Centre for Electronic Arts, Computer Graphics
Malmkjaer, Kirsten, BA PhD   Dir., Centre for Res. in Translation; Prof., Translation Studies
Mulhern, Francis, MA PhD   Prof., Critical Studies
Osborne, Peter, BSc MA DPhil   Prof., Modern European History
Overy, Paul, BA MA   Reader, History and Theory of Modernism
Parker, Gabrielle, LèsL MèsL PhD   Prof., French; Dean*
Rifkin, Adrian   Prof., Visual Culture and Media
Rubin, Leon, BA MA   Prof., Drama and Theatre Arts
Thompson, Jon   Res. Prof., Fine Arts
Tickner, Lisa, BA PhD   Prof., Art History
Research: electronic arts; international affairs; modern European philosophy; practical philosophy

Business School
Tel: (020) 8411 5834 Fax: (020) 8411 6011
Barrett, Brenda, BA MA PhD   Emer. Prof., Law
Boddy, Clive R., MA, FCIM   Assoc. Prof., Marketing
Clark, Ephraim, BA PhD   Prof., Finance
Clay, Heather, LLB MA   Dir., Curric., Learning and Quality (Undergrad. Programmes)
Crilly, Tony, BSc MSc PhD   Reader, Mathematical Sciences
Evans, Jeff, BSc MSc PhD   Reader, Adults' Mathematical Learning
Ghobadian, Abby, BSc MSc MBA PhD DSc   Prof., Manufacturing and Operations Strategy
Haggar, Anthony, BA   Assoc. Prof., Strategic Management
Hopkins, Michael, BSc MSc PhD   Assoc. Prof., Corporate Responsibility and Business Performance
James, Philip, BA MPhil   Prof., Employment Relations
Jarrett, David, BSc MSc   Reader, Statistics
Lewis, David, LLB MA   Prof., Employment Law
Liu, Jonathan, BSc MBA   Prof., Chinese Management
Mark, Annabelle, BA MSc PhD   Prof., Healthcare Organisation
Mayo, Andrew, BSc(Eng) MSc(Eng), FRSA, FCIPD   Visiting Prof., Human Capital Management
Miles, Derek, BA MA   Assoc. Prof.
Morton, Clive, OBE, PhD, FIMgt, FRSA   Visiting Prof.
North, David, BA(Econ) PhD   Prof., Regional Development
O'Regan, Nicholas, BA MSc MBA PhD   Prof., Strategy
Parker, Dennis, BA PhD, FRGS   Prof.; Dean*
Redwood, John, MA DPhil   Assoc. Prof.
Sargeant, Malcolm, BA PhD   Reader, Employment Law
Shepherd, Ifan   Prof., Geo Business
Stainer, Alan, MSc PhD, FRSA   Emer. Prof.
Weldon, John, LLB LLM   Dir., Curric., Learning and Quality (Postgrad. Programmes)
Wood, Geoffrey, BA MA PhD   Dir., Res.; Prof., Comparative Human Resource Management

Wright, Chris, BSc PhD, FIMA   Prof.; Head, Transport Management Res. Centre

Yao, Shujie, BSc MA PhD   Prof., Economics

Research: accounting and finance; economics; human resource management; law; management

Computing Science

Tel: (020) 8411 5180 *Fax*: (020) 8411 6411
E-mail: cswebmaster@mdx.ac.uk

Abdel-Moteleb, Abou-Bakr, BSc MSc   Sr. Lectr.

Abeysinghe, Geetha, BSc MSc PhD   Sr. Lectr.

Adams, Ray, BSc PhD   Sr. Lectr.

Alty, James, BSc PhD, FIEE   Prof.†

Amaldi-Trillo, Paola, BSc MSc PhD   Sr. Lectr.

Bakry, Walaa, BSc MSc   Dir., Bus. Devel.

Bavan, Siri, BSc MSc PhD   Principal Lectr.

Belavkin, Roman, BSc MSc PhD   Sr. Lectr.

Bornat, Richard, BSc MSc   Prof.

Burbidge, Steve, BSc MSc   Sr. Lectr.

Busia, Yaw, BSc MSc PhD   Sr. Lectr.

Butterworth, Richard, BSc PhD   Sr. Lectr.

Censlive, Michael, BSc MSc PhD   Sr. Lectr.

Chera, Pav, BSc PhD   Sr. Lectr.

Colson, Robert, BSc MSc PhD   Sr. Lectr.

Comley, Richard, BSc PhD   Prof.

Currie, Edward, BSc MSc   Principal Lectr.

Dalcher, Darren, MSc PhD   Prof.

Duncker-Gassen, Elke, MA PhD   Sr. Lectr.

Duquenoy, Penny, BA PhD   Sr. Lectr.

Evans, Carl, BSc MSc PhD   Principal Lectr.

Fields, Bob, BSc MSc DPhil   Principal Lectr.

Gao, Xiaohong, BSc MSc PhD   Sr. Lectr.

Gemikonakli, Orhan, BEng MSc PhD   Principal Lectr.

George, Carlisle, BSc BVc LLM PhD   Sr. Lectr.

Georgiadou, Elli, BA   Principal Lectr.

Gledhill, Richard, BSc MSc   Principal Lectr.

Hanson, Owen, MA MSc PhD   Prof.

Harvey, Pirkko, BSc MA   Principal Lectr.; Dir., Natnl. Centre for Project Management

Hasan, Usama, MA MSc PhD   Sr. Lectr.

Huyck, Christian, BS AB MS PhD   Principal Lectr.

Jabbar, Muthana, BSc MSc PhD   Sr. Lectr.

Katsriku, Ferdinand, BSc MSc PhD   Sr. Lectr.

Kindberg, Chris, BA LLB MSc MSc(Eng)   Sr. Lectr.; Acting DCLQ

Lasebae, Aboubaker, BASc MSc PhD   Sr. Lectr.

Lawrence, Dave, BSc PhD   Sr. Lectr.

Lehman, Manny, BSc DSc PhD, FREng, FACM, FBCS, FIEE, FIEEE   Prof.

Luo, Yuan, BEng MEng PhD   Sr. Lectr.

Milankovic-Atkinson, Maya, BSc MSc MBA   Principal Lectr.

Mitchell, Ian, BSc PhD   Sr. Lectr.

Moseley, Ralph, BA MSc PhD   Sr. Lectr.

Murphy, Alan, BA MA MSc   Dir., Curric., Learning and Quality

Nistazakis, Emmanouil, BEng MSc MBA PhD   Sr. Lectr.

Passmore, Peter, BSc MSc PhD   Sr. Lectr.

Pearson, Russell, BEd BSc MSc, FRSA   Principal Lectr.

Perera, Vincent   Sr. Lectr.

Platts, John, BA MSc   Sr. Lectr.

Rahanu, Harjinder, BSc PhD   Sr. Lectr.

Rahman, Shahedur, BSc MSc PhD   Sr. Lectr.

Raineri, Gianni, BA   Sr. Lectr.

Revell, Norman, MA Oxf., FRSA   Prof.

Reynolds, Carl, MSc   Sr. Lectr.

Sadler, Chris, BSc MSc   Principal Lectr.

Sanders, Carl, MA   Sr. Lectr.

Sandhu, Kulwant, BSc MSc   Sr. Lectr.

Sheriff, Mohamed, BSc MSc PhD   Sr. Lectr.

Smith-Atakan, Serengul, BSc MSc PhD   Sr. Lectr.

Springett, Mark, BSc MSc PhD   Sr. Lectr.

Stokes, Elizabeth, BSc   Sr. Lectr.

Swift, John, BSc MSc   Sr. Lectr.

Tavakol, Soheyla, BA MA   Sr. Lectr.

Tully, Colin, MA Camb., FBCS   Prof.; Dir., Res. and Postgrad. Studies

Turner, David, BA MA DPhil, FBCS, FRSA   Prof.

Vincent, Hugh, BSc MSc MPhil   Sr. Lectr.

Ward, Patricia, BSc MSc   Sr. Lectr.

White, Anthony, BSc(Eng) MSc PhD, FIMechE, FRAS, FIEE   Prof.

Whitney, Gill, BSc MSc   Sr. Lectr.

Wong, William, BCom PhD   Prof.

Woodman, Mark, BSc PhD   Prof.

Woof, Gerry, BSc MSc   Sr. Lectr.

Wu, Wendy, BSc *Wuhan Hydraulic & Electr.Eng.*, PhD *Ulster*   Head, Internat. Devel.

Other Staff: 4 Emer. Profs.; 12 Visiting Profs.; 7 Lectrs.; 1 Academic Registrar; 3 Visiting Academics; 3 Sr. Res. Fellows; 4 Res. Fellows; 2 Researchers; 2 Principal Lectrs.†; 4 Sr. Lectrs.†; 3 Hon. Profs.

Vacant Posts: Dean*

Research: adaptive systems; human-computer interaction; modern IT-based business systems; systems failures

Health and Social Sciences

Tel: (020) 8411 6640 *Fax*: (020) 8411 6299

Anthony, Stewart   Head, Centre for Environment and Safety Management for Bus.

Beaumont, Richard, BA   Dir., Bus. Devel.

Burgoyne, Bernard   Head, Centre for Psychoanalysis

Caldwell, Kay   Head, Inst. of Nursing and Midwifery

Cockerton, Tracey, BSc MSc PhD   Assoc. Dir.

Foster, John   Head, Centre for Mental Health Res. and Devel.

House, Margaret, MA PhD   Prof.; Dean*

Iles, Ray, BSc MSc PhD   Dir., Res. and Postgrad. Studies

Mirza, Heidi Safia   Prof.; Head, Centre for Racial Equality Studies

Papadopoulos, Rena   Head, Centre for Transcultural Studies in Health

Penning-Rowsell, Edmund, BSc *Lond.*, MA *CNAA*, PhD *Lond.*   Head, Flood Hazard Res. Centre

Rounce, Katherine   Head, Work Based Learning

Thom, Betsy   Head, Soc. Policy Res. Centre

Traynor, Michael   Prof.; Head, Centre for Evidence in the Practice Disciplines

Walsh, Donal, BA MA MBA   Dir., Resources and Admin.

Watt, John   Head, Decision Analysis and Risk Management

Williams, Jan, BA MSc   Dir., Curric., Learning and Quality

Other Staff: 8 Academic Group Chairs

Lifelong Learning and Education

Tel: (020) 8411 6537 *Fax*: (020) 8411 6147

Cave, John, BEd *Lond.*, MSc *Lond.*, MA *Lond.*   Prof., Technology Education

Corner, Trevor E., MSc *Edin.*, PhD *Glas.*   Dir., Res. and Postgrad. Studies; Res. Prof., Education

Newby, Peter, BA *Exe.*, PhD *Exe.*   Prof., Education Development in Higher Education

Stephenson, John, BSc DPhil   Prof., Learner-Managed Learning

Tufnell, Richard, BSc *Lond.*, PhD *Warw.*   Prof., Design and Technology; Dean*

Research: arts, language and learning; higher education; learner-managed learning; primary education; technology education

CONTACT OFFICERS

Academic affairs. Academic Registrar: Davis, Colin, BSc (E-mail: c.davis@mdx.ac.uk)

Accommodation. Head of Accommodation Service: McCarney, Celine (E-mail: c.mccarney@mdx.ac.uk)

Admissions (first degree). Admissions Enquiries: Curry, Rosie (E-mail: admissions@mdx.ac.uk)

Admissions (higher degree). Head of Admissions Enquiries: Drinkwater, David (E-mail: admissions@mdx.ac.uk)

Alumni. Head, Alumni Relations: Aristidou, Maria (E-mail: m.aristidou@mdx.ac.uk)

Careers. University Co-ordinator for Careers Advisory Service: Farrar, Elspeth (E-mail: e.farrar@mdx.ac.uk)

Computing services. Head, Computing and Communication Systems Services: Vickers, Paula (E-mail: p.vickers@mdx.ac.uk)

Equal opportunities. Equal Opportunities Manager: Hancock, Susanna (E-mail: s.hancock@mdx.ac.uk)

Estates and buildings/works and services. Head, Facilities Management Services: Northey, Kirsty (E-mail: k.northey@mdx.ac.uk)

Examinations. Assistant Academic Registrar (Assessment Procedures): Hicks, Anna (E-mail: a.hicks@mdx.ac.uk)

Finance. Head, Financial Services: Meagher, Lesley (E-mail: l.meagher@mdx.ac.uk)

International office. Director, International Education: Gladstone, Joel (E-mail: internat@mdx.ac.uk)

Language training for international students. Head, Languages Centres and Audio-Visual Services: Rees Smith, John, MA *Oxf.*, PhD *Lond.* (E-mail: j.rees-smith@mdx.ac.uk)

Library (chief librarian). University Librarian and Head, Learning Resources: Marsterson, William, MA *Oxf.*, MA *Sheff.* (E-mail: w.marsterson@mdx.ac.uk)

Personnel/human resources. Head, Human Resource Services: Cheetham, Ian (E-mail: i.cheetham@mdx.ac.uk)

Public relations. Director of Communication: Owens, Marie (E-mail: m.owens@mdx.ac.uk)

Publications. Corporate Communications Manager: Nelson, Yolande (E-mail: y.nelson@mdx.ac.uk)

Quality assurance and accreditation. Head of Quality Assurance and Audit Service: Wing, Michael A., MSc PhD (E-mail: m.wing@mdx.ac.uk)

Research. Research Officer: Mayor, Jennifer, BA *CNAA*, MPhil *Open(UK)*, PhD *CNAA* (E-mail: j.mayor@mdx.ac.uk)

Safety. Health and Safety Manager: King, Vincent (E-mail: vincent1@mdx.ac.uk)

Scholarships, awards, loans. Student Financial Support Manager: Carter, Roslyn (E-mail: r.carter@mdx.ac.uk)

Schools liaison. Head, UK/EU Recruitment: Bentley, Yvonne (E-mail: y.bentley@mdx.ac.uk)

Sport and recreation. Head, Sports and Recreation: Parker, Mel (E-mail: m.parker@mdx.ac.uk)

Staff development and training. Staff Development Manager: Roberts, Heather (E-mail: h.roberts@mdx.ac.uk)

Strategic planning. Head, Planning and Development Services: Pelan, Steve (E-mail: s.pelan@mdx.ac.uk)

Student union. Student Union General Manager: Yeganeh, Farzaneh (E-mail: f.yeganeh@mdx.ac.uk)

Students from other countries. International Student Co-ordinator: Struwe, Christine (E-mail: c.struwe@mdx.ac.uk)

University press. Managing Director, MU Press: Sivak, John (E-mail: j.sivak@mdx.ac.uk)

[*Information supplied by the institution as at 11 March 2005, and edited by the ACU*]

NAPIER UNIVERSITY

Founded 1992

Member of the Association of Commonwealth Universities

Postal Address: 219 Colinton Road, Edinburgh, Scotland EH14 1DJ
Telephone: (0131) 444 2266 **Fax:** (0131) 455 6333 **E-mail:** info@napier.ac.uk
URL: http://www.napier.ac.uk

PRINCIPAL AND VICE-CHANCELLOR*—Stringer, Prof. Joan K., CBE, BA Keele, PhD Keele, Hon. DLitt Keele, FRSA, FRSEd
UNIVERSITY SECRETARY‡—Webber, Gerry C., BA Wales, MBA Open(UK), DPhil Oxf.
ACTING VICE-PRINCIPAL (RESEARCH AND KNOWLEDGE TRANSFER)—Mackenzie, Prof. Robin
VICE-PRINCIPAL (ACADEMIC DEVELOPMENT)—Easy, P., BA PhD, FRSA
VICE-PRINCIPAL (ACADEMIC QUALITY AND CUSTOMER SERVICE)—Rees, J., BSc PhD, FRSS

GENERAL INFORMATION

History. The university was originally established in 1964 as Napier Technical College and merged with Edinburgh College of Commerce in 1974 to become Napier College of Commerce and Technology. It became a polytechnic in 1987 and a university in 1992. It merged with the Borders and Lothian Colleges of Nursing and Midwifery in 1996.

It is located in the south and west of the city of Edinburgh, and also has campuses in Livingston and Melrose.

Admission to first degree courses (see also United Kingdom Introduction). Through Universities and Colleges Admissions Service (UCAS) or, for BN applicants, through Centralised Applications to nursing and midwifery Training Clearing House (CATCH).

First Degrees (see also United Kingdom Directory to Subjects of Study). BA, BDes, BEng, BMus, BN, BSc, LLB.
Length of course. Full-time: BA, BDes, BEng, BMus, BN, BSc, LLB: 4 years. Part-time: BA, BDes, BEng, BMus, BN, BSc, LLB: 6 years. By distance learning: BA, BDes, BEng, BMus, BN, BSc, LLB: 4–8 years.

Higher Degrees (see also United Kingdom Directory to Subjects of Study).
Master's. MA, MBA, MSc.
Admission. Applicants are expected to hold an appropriate first degree with honours.
Length of course. Full-time: MA, MBA, MSc: 1½ years. Part-time: MA, MBA, MSc: 3 years. By distance learning: MA, MBA, MSc: 5 years.
Doctoral. MPhil, PhD.
Length of course. Full-time: MPhil: 2 years; PhD: 3 years. Part-time: MPhil: 3 years; PhD: 5 years. By distance learning: MPhil: 3–5 years; PhD: 5–7 years.

Libraries. Volumes: 451,732. Periodicals subscribed to: 7185. Special collections: Edward Clark (printing from fifteenth century); war poets (Sassoon and Owen).

Academic Year (2007–2008). Three semesters: 1 October–26 January; 4 February–31 May; 2 June–13 September.

Statistics. Staff (2006–2007): 1692 (879 academic, 813 non-academic). Students (2006–2007): full-time 9775 (4828 men, 4947 women); part-time 4227 (1546 men, 2681 women); international 2750 (1442 men, 1308 women); distance education/external 1103 (479 men, 624 women); undergraduate 11,434 (5041 men, 6393 women); master's 2382 (1215 men, 1167 women); doctoral 186 (118 men, 68 women).

FACULTIES/SCHOOLS

Engineering, Computing and Creative Industries
Tel: (0131) 455 2472 Fax: (0131) 455 2400
E-mail: s.cairncross@napier.ac.uk
Dean (Acting): Cairncross, S., BSc Strath., BEng Strath., PhD Napier

Health, Life and Social Sciences
Tel: (0131) 455 5707 Fax: (0131) 455 5624
E-mail: m.prowse@napier.ac.uk
Dean: Prowse, Prof. Morag, BEd BSc MSc PhD
Secretary: Gilliam, Lou Ann

Napier University Business School
Tel: (0131) 455 4332 Fax: (0131) 455 4479
E-mail: g.stonehouse@napier.ac.uk
Dean: Stonehouse, Prof. George
Secretary: Lally, Mary

ACADEMIC UNITS

Accounting and Economics
Tel: (0131) 455 4405 Fax: (0131) 455 4506
E-mail: business@napier.ac.uk
Adams, J., BA CNAA   Prof.
Bate, J. B., MA Edin.   Sr. Lectr.
Falconer, S., MA MSc   Sr. Lectr.
Gao, S., BA Xi'an Jiaotong, MA Xi'an Jiaotong, PhD Rotterdam   Prof.
Gardner, P., BSc   Sr. Lectr.
Goldfinch, J. M., MA Oxf., PhD Strath.   Sr. Lectr.
Hughes, M., BSc Edin., PhD Napier   Sr. Lectr.
Juleff, L., BSc   Sr. Lectr.
Marek, S. A., MSc Napier, FCIS   Sr. Lectr.
Pettigrew, M., BA MSc   Sr. Lectr.
Troy, John, BA Strath., MSc Wales   Head*
Windram, B., BCom   Sr. Lectr.
Other Staff: 1 Reader; 34 Lectrs.
Research: auditing; corporate governance; development economics; entrepreneurial economics; risk management

Computing
Tel: (0131) 455 2700 Fax: (0131) 455 2727
E-mail: computing.enquiries@napier.ac.uk
Barclay, K. A., BSc H-W, MSc   Sr. Lectr.
Benyon, D., BSc Essex, MSc Warw., PhD Open(UK)   Prof.
Buchanan, W. J., BSc Napier, PhD Napier   Prof.
Bucker, K., BA Reading   Sr. Lectr.
Cowan, J. B., BSc St And.   Sr. Lectr.
Davenport, E., MA Edin., MLitt Edin., MSc Strath., PhD Strath., FIInfSc   Prof.
Hall, H., BA Birm., MA C.England   Reader
Hart, E., BA Oxf., MSc Edin., PhD Edin.   Reader
Kennedy, J. B., BSc CNAA, MPhil CNAA   Prof.
Kerridge, J., BSc Wales, MSc UMIST, PhD UMIST   Prof.
McEwan, T., BSc St And., MSc Napier   Sr. Lectr.
Rankin, R. C., BSc Glas.   Sr. Lectr.; Head*
Ritchie, B. D., BSc Manc., MSc Cran.IT   Sr. Lectr.
Ross, P., MA Camb., MSc Lond., PhD Lond.   Prof.
Smyth, M., BA Belf., PhD Lough.   Sr. Lectr.
Turner, P., BA Durh., MSc Newcastle(UK), PhD Durh.   Sr. Lectr.
Turner, S., BSc Wales, MSc Lough., PhD Open(UK)   Sr. Lectr.
Varey, A., BSc Brist., MSc H-W   Sr. Lectr.
Other Staff: 36 Lectrs.; 4 Res. Fellows
Research: database and object systems; distributed systems and mobile agents; emergent computing; human-computer interaction; social informatics

Creative Industries
Fax: (0131) 455 6193
Atton, C., MA Edin., MA Leic., PhD Napier   Reader
Baker, C., BA Hull, MA Derby, PhD Sund.   Sr. Lectr.
Davismoon, S., BA S'ton., PhD Edin.   Sr. Lectr.
MacLeod, C.   Sr. Lectr.
MacPherson, R., BA Stir., MLitt Stir.   Sr. Lectr.; Acting Head*
McCleery, A., MA St And., MLitt Stir., PhD St And.   Prof.
McGrath, R., MA Leeds, PhD Middx., BA   Sr. Lectr.
Sellors, P., BA Tor., MA N.Y., PhD N.Y.   Sr. Lectr.
Turner, M., PhD RCA   Prof.
Weir, G.   Sr. Lectr.
Other Staff: 56 Lectrs.; 3 Res. Fellows
Research: book research; colour; communication research; digital media; information society studies

Engineering and the Built Environment
Fax: (0131) 455 2239
Addison, P., MEng PhD   Prof.
Almaini, A. E., BSc Lond., PhD Lough., FIEE   Prof.
Barker, D., BTech Brad., MSc Salf.   Reader
Barker, M. B., BSc Liv., MBA Edin., PhD Brun.   Dir., Commercial Devel.; Reader, Polymer Engineering
Binnie, T. D., BSc H-W, PhD H-W   Reader
Deakin, I. M.   Sr. Lectr.
Fairfield, C., BEng PhD   Reader
Goodwin, R., BSc Strath., PhD Edin.   Sr. Lectr.
Gupta, N., BSc UMIST, PhD UMIST   Sr. Lectr.
Hajto, J., BSc Debrecen, MSc Debrecen, PhD Debrecen, DSc Edin., FIP   Prof.
Hay, N. C., BSc H-W, PhD CNAA   Sr. Lectr.
Hunt, I., BSc H-W, MSc H-W   Prof.; Head*
Kermani, A., BSc Tees., MSc Tees., PhD Tees.   Prof.
Khalaf, F., BEng Edin., MSc Edin., PhD Edin.   Reader
Kubie, J., BSc Lond., PhD Aston, DSc(Eng) Lond., FIMechE   Prof.
MacCallum, M., BSc Bolton, MBA Napier   Sr. Lectr.
McLeod, I., MPhil Napier   Sr. Lectr.
Muneer, T., BEng Osm., PhD R.Gordon   Prof.
Rae, G. D., BSc Strath.   Sr. Lectr.
Reid, D. B., BSc Edin., MSc H-W, PhD Napier   Sr. Lectr.
Roberts, D., BSc Glas., PhD Durh.   Sr. Lectr.
Saleh, W., BEng Cairo, MSc Cairo, PhD Newcastle(UK)   Sr. Lectr.
Sharp, J., BSc H-W, MSc H-W, FIEE   Reader
Sloan, B., MPhil Salf., Hon. DSc Vilnius T.U., FRICS, FRSA   Prof.
Smith, G. J., BSc Edin.   Sr. Lectr.
Smith, I., BEng H-W, PhD H-W   Sr. Lectr.
Stupart, A., BSc Edin., MPhil H-W   Sr. Lectr.
Wamuziri, S., BSc(Eng) UMIST, MSc UMIST, MBA Edin., PhD UMIST, FRSA   Sr. Lectr.; Dir., Postgrad. Studies
Wan, C., BSc Glas., MSc Napier, PhD Napier   Sr. Lectr.

Other Staff: 46 Lectrs.; 11 Res. Fellows

Research: acoustics and building performance; construction management; geotechnical engineering; transport planning and engineering; urban planning

Health and Social Sciences

Tel: (0131) 455 6014 Fax: (0131) 455 6306
E-mail: h.wollman@napier.ac.uk
Brennan, M., PhD *Edin.*   Sr. Lectr.
Grieco, M., DPhil *Oxf.*   Prof.
Harden, J., BA *Glas.*, PhD *Strath.*   Sr. Lectr.
Irvine, L., MSc *Edin.*   Sr. Lectr.
Laybourn, P. K., MA *Dund.*, PhD *Dund.*   Sr. Lectr.
McCleery, A., MA *St And.*, MLitt *Stir.*, PhD *St And.*   Prof.
Stradling, S., PhD *Newcastle(UK)*   Prof.
Wollman, H., BA *Oxf.*, BPhil *Oxf.*   Head*
Other Staff: 37 Lectrs.
Research: nationalism; population geography and migration; psychology of facial recognition; social and psychological aspects of transport; sociology of families and childhood

Law

Tel: (0131) 455 4566 Fax: (0131) 455 4369
E-mail: j.mcdowall@napier.ac.uk
Ashton, C., LLB MAEd   Head*
Grier, N., LLB *Edin.*, MA *Oxf.*
McManus, F., LLB *Edin.*, MLitt *Edin.*   Prof.
Other Staff: 11 Lectrs.
Research: environmental law; European law; human rights; public law

Life Sciences

Tel: (0131) 455 2376 Fax: (0131) 455 2291
E-mail: g.knox@napier.ac.uk
Beswick, P. H., BSc *Brun.*, PhD *Brun.*   Sr. Lectr.; Acting Head*
Bryce, C. F. A., BSc *Glas.*, PhD *Glas.*, FIBiol, FRSChem   Prof.
Christofi, N., BSc *Dund.*, PhD *Dund.*   Prof.
Davison, R., BSc *Glas.*, PhD *Glas.*   Prof.
Fernandes, T., BSc *New Lisbon*, MSc *Aberd.*, PhD *Aberd.*   Reader
Foley, S., BSc *N.U.I.*, PhD *N.U.I.*   Sr. Lectr.
Mincher, D., BSc *Brad.*, PhD   Reader
Smith, K., BSc *Napier*, PhD   Sr. Lectr.
Stone, V., BSc *Leeds*, PhD *Birm.*   Prof.
Strathie, E., BSc *Lough.*   Sr. Lectr.
Tett, P., MA *Camb.*, PhD *Glas.*   Prof.
Other Staff: 62 Lectrs.
Research: anti-cancer drug design and delivery; applied microbiology and biotechnology (bioremediation and biosensor development, exploitation of metabolic diversity of rhodococci); aquatic and terrestrial environmental biology of organisms/ecosystems; biomedicine (toxins, occupational and environmental air pollution, reproductive biology, diabetes, glycobiology)

Management

Tel: (0131) 455 4534 Fax: (0131) 455 4369
E-mail: e.horobin@napier.ac.uk
Bryans, P., BA *Lanc.*, MSc(Econ) *Lond.*   Sr. Lectr.
Cowe, A., BA *H-W*, MBA *Glas.*, FCIS   Sr. Lectr.
D'Annunzio-Green, N., BA *Napier*, MSc *Stir.*   Sr. Lectr.
Francis, H., BSc *Edin.*, PhD *De Mont.*, FCIPD   Sr. Lectr.
Laing, S., BA *Napier*, MSc *Stir.*   Sr. Lectr.
Lannon, R., BA *Napier*, MPhil *Napier*   Sr. Lectr.
MacKerron, G., BSc *Napier*, MBA *Warw.*   Sr. Lectr.
Masson, R. J., BSc *Glas.*   Sr. Lectr.
Sharkey, G., MA *Dund.*, MBA *Strath.*   Sr. Lectr.
Watson, A., BA *Strath.*, MSc *Strath.*, PhD *Napier*   Sr. Lectr.; Head*
Other Staff: 23 Lectrs.
Research: case study; diversity study; employee relations; human resources development; workplace learning

Marketing, Tourism and Languages

Tel: (0131) 455 4386 Fax: (0131) 455 4540
E-mail: business@napier.ac.uk
Barron, P., MSc *Strath.*, PhD *Qld.*   Reader
Drummond, G., BSc *H-W*, MBA *H-W*   Sr. Lectr.
Ensor, J. G., BA *Staffs.*, MBA *Cran.*, DBA *Nott.Trent*   Head*
Fischer, Mary, MA *St And.*, PhD *St And.*   Sr. Lectr.; Languages
Leask, A., MA *Aberd.*, MSc *Strath.*   Sr. Lectr.
Mouat, K., BA *CNAA*, MA *Manc.Met.*   Sr. Lectr.
Revuelta, J., BA MBA   Sr. Lectr.
Sutherland, R., BA *Hull*, MSc *Napier*   Sr. Lectr.
Thomson, J. R., BA *S'ton.*, MBA *Strath.*   Sr. Lectr.
Other Staff: 1 Reader; 32 Lectrs.
Research: critical research in tourism; cultural awareness; festival and event management planning; heritage and visitor attraction management; language teaching and learning

Nursing, Midwifery and Social Care

Tel: (0131) 536 5302 Fax: (0131) 536 5631
E-mail: s.muirhead@napier.ac.uk
Alder, E. M., BSc *Aberd.*, PhD *Edin.*   Res. Prof.
Brown, N., PhD *Lanc.*   Sr. Lectr.
Clinkscale, H., BSc *Napier*, MSc *Edin.*   Sr. Lectr.
Donaldson, J., BN *Glas.*, MN *Glas.*, PhD *Glas.*   Sr. Lectr.
Elliott, L., MA *Glas.*, PhD *Glas.*   Prof.
Forrest, S., MPhil *Edin.*   Sr. Lectr.
Kennedy, C., BA *G.Caledonian*, PhD *QM Edin.*   Reader
Kilbride, L., MEd *Edin.*   Sr. Lectr.
Leadbeater, V., BA *Open(UK)*   Sr. Lectr.
MacMillan, M., BA *Open(UK)*, PhD *Edin.*   Sr. Lectr.
Matthews-Smith, G., PhD *Napier*   Sr. Lectr.
McCann, E., MSc *Lond.*, PhD *Lond.*   Sr. Lectr.
McFarlane, Wai Choo, BEd *CNAA*, MA *Reading*   Sr. Lectr.
McIntosh, Iain   Head*
Neades, B., BN *Wales*, MPhil *Glas.*, PhD *Napier*   Sr. Lectr.
Philip, M., MBA *Napier*, MSc *Stir.*   Sr. Lectr.
Raab, G., BSc *Edin.*, MSc *Edin.*, PhD *Edin.*   Prof.
Sheard, H., MSc *Edin.*   Sr. Lectr.
Waugh, A., BSc *Edin.*, MSc *Edin.*   Sr. Lectr.
Other Staff: 117 Lectrs.
Research: acute and emergency nursing; care of older people; ethical issues in healthcare; nursing education and leadership; skin care in cancer

CONTACT OFFICERS

Academic affairs. Vice-Principal (Academic Development): Easy, P., BA PhD, FRSA
(E-mail: p.easy@napier.ac.uk)
Accommodation. Head of Residential Accommodation Service: Crocker, H., MA *St And.* (E-mail: h.crocker@napier.ac.uk)
Admissions (first degree). Admissions Officer: Smith, D.
(E-mail: registry.admissions@napier.ac.uk)
Admissions (higher degree). Admissions Officer: Smith, D.
(E-mail: registry.admissions@napier.ac.uk)
Adult/continuing education. Director, Educational Development Services: Percival, Prof. Fred, BSc *Glas.*, PhD *Glas.*
(E-mail: f.percival@napier.ac.uk)
Alumni. Development Officer, Alumni: Fleming, J. (E-mail: j.fleming@napier.ac.uk)
Careers. Head of Careers: Barbour, Kay
(E-mail: k.barbour@napier.ac.uk)
Computing services. Director of Communications and Information Technology Services: Dean, Paul, BSc *Birm.*, MSc *Birm.* (E-mail: p.dean@napier.ac.uk)
Conferences/corporate hospitality. Conference Services Manager: Crocker, H., MA *St And.* (E-mail: h.crocker@napier.ac.uk)
Consultancy services. Director, Knowledge Transfer and Commercialisation Services: McGuckin, B.
(E-mail: b.mcguckin@napier.ac.uk)
Development/fund-raising. Development Director: Cairney, K.
(E-mail: k.cairney@napier.ac.uk)
Distance education. Director, Educational Development Services: Percival, Prof. Fred, BSc *Glas.*, PhD *Glas.*
Estates and buildings/works and services. Director of Facilities: Hughes, P.
(E-mail: p.hughes@napier.ac.uk)
Examinations. Registry Operations Manager: McElone, L.
(E-mail: registry.exams@napier.ac.uk)
Finance. Director of Finance: Gibson, E.
(E-mail: e.gibson@napier.ac.uk)
General enquiries. University Secretary: Webber, Gerry C., BA *Wales*, MBA *Open(UK)*, DPhil *Oxf.* (E-mail: r.hall@napier.ac.uk)
Industrial liaison. Director, Knowledge Transfer and Commercialisation Services: McGuckin, B.
(E-mail: b.mcguckin@napier.ac.uk)
International office. Head of International Recruitment and Support: Brady, Peter
(E-mail: intoffice@napier.ac.uk)
Library (enquiries). Chief Librarian/Director of Learning Information Services: Pinder, C. J., BA *CNAA*, MLib *Wales*, FCLIP
(E-mail: c.pinder@napier.ac.uk)
Marketing. Acting Director of Marketing and Communications: Tierney, C.
(E-mail: c.tierney@napier.ac.uk)
Ombudsman. University Secretary: Webber, Gerry C., BA *Wales*, MBA *Open(UK)*, DPhil *Oxf.* (E-mail: g.c.webber@napier.ac.uk)
Personnel/human resources. Director of Human Resources: Caygill, B.
(E-mail: b.caygill@napier.ac.uk)
Public relations. Acting Director of Marketing and Communications: Tierney, C.
(E-mail: c.tierney@napier.ac.uk)
Publications. Acting Director of Marketing and Communications: Tierney, C.
(E-mail: c.tierney@napier.ac.uk)
Purchasing. Head of Procurement: Campbell, D. (E-mail: d.campbell@napier.ac.uk)
Quality assurance and accreditation. Head of Quality Enhancement Services: Sibbald, A.
(E-mail: a.sibbald@napier.ac.uk)
Research. University Director of Research: Woodward, Diana
(E-mail: d.woodward@napier.ac.uk)
Safety. Safety Adviser: Young, Liz, BSc *Napier*
(E-mail: l.young@napier.ac.uk)
Security. Facilities Service Manager: McEvoy, Laurence (E-mail: l.mcevoy@napier.ac.uk)
Staff development and training. Head of Corporate Staff Development: Meighan, Jill, MA (E-mail: j.meighan@napier.ac.uk)
Student union. President (Student Union): Simm, A. (E-mail: a.simm@napier.ac.uk)
Student welfare/counselling. Director of Student Services: Davidson, D. C.
(E-mail: d.davidson@napier.ac.uk)
Students from other countries. Head of International Recruitment and Support: Brady, Peter (E-mail: intoffice@napier.ac.uk)
Students with disabilities. Special Needs Co-ordinator: Robinson, Jacky
(E-mail: j.robinson@napier.ac.uk)

CAMPUS/COLLEGE HEADS

Craighouse Campus, Craighouse Road, Edinburgh EH10 5LG. (Tel: (0131) 455 6280; Fax: (0131) 455 6195) Campus Principal: Rees, J., BSc PhD, FRSS
Craiglockhart Campus, 219 Colinton Road, Edinburgh EH14 1DJ. (Tel: (0131) 455 4616) Campus Principal: Stonehouse, Prof. George
Merchiston Campus, 10 Colinton Road, Edinburgh EH10 5DT. (Tel: (0131) 455 2412; Fax: (0131) 455 2294) Campus Principal: Cairncross, S., BSc *Strath.*, BEng *Strath.*, PhD *Napier*

[Information supplied by the institution as at 3 December 2007, and edited by the ACU]

UNIVERSITY OF NEWCASTLE UPON TYNE

Founded 1963

Member of the Association of Commonwealth Universities

Postal Address: Newcastle upon Tyne, England NE1 7RU
Telephone: (0191) 222 6000 **Fax:** (0191) 222 6229 **E-mail:** postmaster@ncl.ac.uk
URL: http://www.ncl.ac.uk

VICE-CHANCELLOR*—Brink, Prof. Christopher, PhD Camb., DPhil Jo'burg., FRSSAf
DEPUTY VICE-CHANCELLOR—Goddard, Prof. John B., OBE, BA Lond., PhD Lond.
PRO-VICE-CHANCELLOR (TEACHING AND LEARNING)—Ritchie, Prof. Ella, BA Lanc., PhD Lond.
PRO-VICE-CHANCELLOR (EXTERNAL AFFAIRS AND RESEARCH LIAISON)—Page, Prof. T. F., MA Camb., PhD Camb., FIMMM
PRO-VICE-CHANCELLOR (PLANNING AND RESOURCES)—Stevenson, Prof. A., BSc Lond., PhD Lond.
PRO-VICE-CHANCELLOR (STRATEGIC DEVELOPMENT)—Young, Prof. M.
REGISTRAR‡—Hogan, J. V.
BURSAR—Farnhill, H. B.
LIBRARIAN AND KEEPER OF THE PYBUS COLLECTION—Graham, Thomas W.

GENERAL INFORMATION

History. The university was established in 1963.

It is located in the centre of Newcastle upon Tyne in the north-east of England.

Admission to first degree courses (see also United Kingdom Introduction). Through Universities and Colleges Admissions Service (UCAS). The university recognises a wide range of qualifications, including Business and Technology Education Council (BTEC) certificates and diplomas, advanced level General National Vocational Qualifications (GNVQ), Open University credits, International Baccalaureate, and certain access courses.

First Degrees (see also United Kingdom Directory to Subjects of Study). BA, BArch, BDS, BEng, BMedSci, BMus, BSc, LLB, MB BS, MChem, MEng, MMath, MMathStat, MPhys.

Length of course. Full-time: BMedSci: 1 year; BArch: 2–3 years; BMus: 2–4 years; LLB: 3 years; BA, BEng, BSc: 3–4 years; MChem, MMath, MMathStat, MPhys: 4 years; MEng: 4–5 years; MB BS: 4–6 years; BDS: 5 years.

Higher Degrees (see also United Kingdom Directory to Subjects of Study).

Master's. BPhil, LLM, MA, MArch, MBA, MEd, MFA, MIHSc, MLA, MLitt, MMus, MPhil, MRes, MSc, MTP, MTPE.

Admission. Applicants for admission to higher degree courses must normally hold a good first degree in a relevant subject. Other qualifications and relevant professional experience are considered.

MLA, MTP: may also be taken 9 months full-time plus 21 months part-time. BPhil: may also be taken 1 year part-time, following on from a certificate.

Length of course. Full-time: BPhil, LLM, MA, MBA, MEd, MLitt, MMus, MPhil, MRes, MSc, MTP: 1 year; MLA: 1¾ years; MFA, MIHSc, MTPE: 2 years. Part-time: MArch: 1½ years; MTP: 1¾ years; LLM, MA, MEd, MLitt, MMus, MPhil, MSc: 2 years; MBA: 2–2½ years.

Doctoral. DBA, DClinPsychol, DDS, DEdPsy, DEng, DLitt, DSc, EdD, LLD, MD, PhD.

Admission. Applicants for admission to DLitt, LLD, DEng or DSc must hold a degree of this university (or a degree of the University of Durham, provided that they matriculated in the Newcastle Division of that university before 1 August 1963), or be a full-time member of the academic staff.

Integrated PhD: 3–7 years. DEng, DLitt, DSc, LLD: awarded on published work.

Length of course. Full-time: DDS, MD: 2–3 years; DBA, DClinPsychol, EdD, PhD: 3 years. Part-time: DClinPsychol: 2–4 years; DDS, DEdPsy, EdD, MD: 4 years; DBA, PhD: 5 years.

Libraries. Volumes: 1,000,000. Periodicals subscribed to: 5000. Other holdings: 3000 full-text electronic journals. Special collections: Pybus collection; Walton library (medical and health); Gertrude Bell collection.

Income (2006–2007). Total, £317,316,000.

Statistics. Staff (2006–2007): 4796 (2182 academic, 2614 non-academic). Students (2005–2006): total 17,784.

FACULTIES/SCHOOLS

Humanities and Social Sciences
Tel: (0191) 222 7479 Fax: (0191) 222 5503
Acting Pro-Vice-Chancellor (Humanities and Social Sciences): Docherty, Prof. Gerard
Secretary and Head of Administration: Stafford, Christine, BA Lanc.

Medical Sciences
Tel: (0191) 222 7005 Fax: (0191) 222 8908
Pro-Vice-Chancellor (Medical Sciences): James, Prof. Oliver F. W., BM BCh Oxf., MA Oxf., FRCP
Secretary and Head of Administration: Hammond, Vanessa A., BSc Brist., BSc Newcastle(UK)

Science, Agriculture and Engineering
Tel: (0191) 222 5839 Fax: (0191) 222 8713
Pro-Vice-Chancellor (Science, Engineering and Agriculture): Hinton, Prof. O. R.
Secretary and Head of Administration: Young, A. G.

ACADEMIC UNITS
Arranged by Schools unless otherwise indicated

Agriculture, Food and Rural Development
Tel: (0191) 222 5955 Fax: (0191) 222 7811
Younger, A. Sr. Lectr.; Head*

Architecture, Planning and Landscape
Tel: (0191) 222 5831 Fax: (0191) 222 6115
Shaw, T. Sr. Lectr.; Head*

Arts and Cultures
Tel: (0191) 222 6000
Stone, P. G. Sr. Lectr.; Head*

Biology
Tel: (0191) 222 6269 Fax: (0191) 222 5228
Goodfellow, M. Prof.; Head*

Business School
Tel: (0191) 222 6790 Fax: (0191) 222 8131
E-mail: unbs@ncl.ac.uk
Leopold, J. W. Prof., Human Resources Management; Acting Dir.*

Chemical Engineering and Advanced Materials
Tel: (0191) 222 7266 Fax: (0191) 222 5292
Bull, S. J. Prof., Surface Engineering; Head*

Civil Engineering and Geosciences
Tel: (0191) 222 6323 Fax: (0191) 222 6502
Parker, D. Prof.; Head*

Computing Science
Tel: (0191) 222 7972 Fax: (0191) 222 8232
E-mail: computing.science@ncl.ac.uk
Lee, P. A. Prof.; Head*

Education, Communication and Language Sciences
Tel: (0191) 222 8170
Robson, S. Sr. Lectr.; Head*

Electrical, Electronic and Computer Engineering
Tel: (0191) 222 7340 Fax: (0191) 222 8180
E-mail: enquiries@eece.ncl.ac.uk
Sharif, B. S. Prof., Digital Communications; Head*

English Literature, Language and Linguistics
Tel: (0191) 222 7625 Fax: (0191) 222 8708
Richards, J. T. Reader, Early Modern Literature; Head*

Geography, Politics and Sociology
Tel: (0191) 222 6359 Fax: (0191) 222 5421
Gillespie, A. E. Sr. Lectr., Communications Geography; Head*

Historical Studies
Tel: (0191) 222 7844
E-mail: historical@ncl.ac.uk
Boulton, J. P. Prof.; Head*

Marine Science and Technology
Tel: (0191) 222 6718 Fax: (0191) 222 5491
Birmingham, R. W. Prof., Small Craft Design; Head*

Mathematics and Statistics
Tel: (0191) 222 7233 Fax: (0191) 222 8020
E-mail: maths.pub@ncl.ac.uk
Robertson, A. G. Prof.; Head*

Mechanical and Systems Engineering
Tel: (0191) 222 6163 Fax: (0191) 222 8600
Appleby, J. C. Sr. Lectr.; Head*

Modern Languages
Tel: (0191) 222 7441 Fax: (0191) 222 5442
Andersen, E. A. Sr. Lectr.; Head*

Natural Sciences

Tel: (0191) 222 7102 Fax: (0191) 222 6929
Lloyd, J. Sr. Lectr.; Head*

Newcastle Law School

Tel: (0191) 222 7624 Fax: (0191) 212 0064
E-mail: newcastle.law-school@ncl.ac.uk
Wilton, A. M. Sr. Lectr.; Head*

Psychology

Tel: (0191) 222 6269 Fax: (0191) 222 5228
Hurlbert, A. C. Prof., Visual Neuroscience;
Interim Head*

MEDICAL SCIENCES

Tel: (0191) 222 7005 Fax: (0191) 222 8908

Biomedical Sciences

Tel: (0191) 222 8200 Fax: (0191) 222 8900
Calvert, J. E. Prof.; Head*

Clinical and Laboratory Sciences

Tel: (0191) 222 7084
Reynolds, N. J. Prof.; Head*

Clinical Medical Sciences

Tel: (0191) 222 7149 Fax: (0191) 222 0723
Day, C. P. Prof., Liver Medicine; Head*

Dental Sciences

Tel: (0191) 222 8347 Fax: (0191) 222 6137
Seymour, R. A. Prof.; Head*

Medical Education Development

Tel: (0191) 222 5020 Fax: (0191) 222 5016
E-mail: medev@ncl.ac.uk
Hammond, G. R. Prof.; Head*

Neurology, Neurobiology and Psychiatry

Tel: (0191) 222 6648 Fax: (0191) 222 5227
Ingram, C. D. Prof., Psychobiology; Head*

Surgical and Reproductive Sciences

Tel: (0191) 222 7157
Lennard, T. W. J. Prof., Breast and Endocrine
Surgery; Head*

SPECIAL CENTRES, ETC

Ageing and Health, Institute for

Tel: (0191) 256 3828 Fax: (0191) 256 3011
Kirkwood, T. B. L. Prof.; Dir.*

**Arts, Social Sciences and Humanities,
Newcastle Institute for the**

Tel: (0191) 222 8679
Powrie, P. P. Prof.; Dir.*

Bacterial Cell Biology, Centre for

Tel: (0191) 222 8126
Errington, J. Prof.; Dir.*

Cancer Research, Northern Institute for

Tel: (0191) 246 4300 Fax: (0191) 246 4301
Calvert, A. H. Prof.; Clin. Dir.
Craft, Prof. Sir A. Dir.*
Hall, A. G. Prof.; Scientific Dir.

**Catalysis and Intensified Processing,
Research Centre in**

North, M. Prof.; Jt. Dir.*

**Cell and Molecular Biosciences, Institute
for**

Tel: (0191) 222 8126 Fax: (0191) 222 7424
Errington, J. Prof.; Dir.*

Cellular Medicine, Institute of

Tel: (0191) 222 3874
Jones, D. Prof.; Dir.*

**Environment and Sustainability, Institute
for Research on**

Tel: (0191) 246 4949 Fax: (0191) 246 4998
E-mail: ires@ncl.ac.uk
O'Donnell, A. G. Prof.; Dir.*

Global Urban Research Unit

Tel: (0191) 222 5900 Fax: (0191) 222 6008
E-mail: guru@ncl.ac.uk
Hillier, J. S. Dir.*

Health and Society, Institute of

Donaldson, C. Prof.; Dir.*

History of Medicine, Centre for the

Powrie, P. P. Prof.; Dir.*

Human Genetics, Institute of

Tel: (0191) 241 8616 Fax: (0191) 241 8666
Burn, J. Prof.; Med. Dir.
Strachan, T. Prof.; Scientific Dir.

Informatics Research Institute

Tel: (0191) 246 4938 Fax: (0191) 222 4905
E-mail: iri-enquiries@ncl.ac.uk
Harrison, M. D. Dir.*

**Knowledge, Innovation, Technology and
Enterprise, Centre for**

Tel: (0191) 243 0800
Charles, D. R. Prof.; Dir.*

Learning and Teaching, Centre for

Tel: (0191) 222 6943 Fax: (0191) 222 8170
E-mail: clt@ncl.ac.uk
Leat, D. Reader; Dir.*

**Linguistics and Language Sciences,
Centre for Research in**

Tel: (0191) 222 8790
Myles, Florence Prof.; Dir.*

**Nanoscale Science and Technology,
Institute for**

Tel: (0191) 222 8665
Snowdon, K. J. Res. Devel. Prof.; Dir.*

Neuroscience, Institute of

Tel: (0191) 222 6968 E-mail: ion@ncl.ac.uk
Hurlbert, A. C. Prof.; Jt. Dir.*
Ingram, C. D. Prof.; Jt. Dir.*

North East England Stem Cell Institute

Tel: (0191) 241 8657
Hutchison, C. Chair, Executive
Whitaker, M. Chair, Board

Policy and Practice, Institute for

Tel: (0191) 222 5037 Fax: (0191) 232 9259
Charles, D. R. Prof.; Dir.*

**Policy, Ethics and Life Sciences Research
Centre**

Tel: (0191) 241 8614 Fax: (0191) 243 8233
E-mail: peals@ncl.ac.uk
Haimes, E. V. Prof.; Exec. Dir.*

**Railway Research, Newcastle Centre for
(NewRail)**

Tel: (0191) 222 5821 Fax: (0191) 222 5821
E-mail: newrail@ncl.ac.uk
Robinson, M. Prof.; Dir.*

Rural Economy, Centre for

Tel: (0191) 222 6623 Fax: (0191) 222 5411
E-mail: cre@ncl.ac.uk
Ward, N. Prof.; Dir.*

Software Reliability, Centre for

Tel: (0191) 222 7997 Fax: (0191) 222 8788
E-mail: csr@ncl.ac.uk
Anderson, T. Prof.; Dir.*

**Stem Cell Biology and Developmental
Genetics, Centre for**

Tel: (0191) 241 8616 Fax: (0191) 241 8666
Strachan, T. Dir.*

**Urban and Regional Development
Studies, Centre for**

Tel: (0191) 222 8016 Fax: (0191) 232 9259
Coombes, M. G. Exec. Dir.*
Goddard, John B., OBE, BA Lond., PhD Lond.
Hon. Dir.*

CONTACT OFFICERS

Academic affairs. Head of Service, Quality in
Learning and Teaching: Wiles, K.
(E-mail: development@ncl.ac.uk)
Accommodation. Accommodation Manager,
Accommodation Services: Robinson, V.
(E-mail: accommodation-
enquiries@ncl.ac.uk)
Admissions (first degree). Admissions Officer:
Hind, K. A. (E-mail: enquiries@ncl.ac.uk)
Admissions (higher degree). Admissions
Officer: Hind, K. A.
(E-mail: enquiries@ncl.ac.uk)
Alumni. Head of Service/Director of
Development, Development and Alumni
Relations Office: Clubley, J.
(E-mail: alumni-office@ncl.ac.uk)
Careers. Director, Careers: Keeley, N. P.
(E-mail: careers@ncl.ac.uk)
Computing services. Director, Information
Systems and Services: Hopkins, P. J.
(E-mail: helpline@ncl.ac.uk)
Conferences/corporate hospitality.
Conference Co-ordinator: McGhie, J.
(E-mail: conference-team@ncl.ac.uk)
Consultancy services. Director of Business
Development and Regional Affairs:
Robertson, D.
(E-mail: business.directorate@ncl.ac.uk)
Credit transfer. Director, Marketing and
Communications Directorate: Braiden, L.
Development/fund-raising. Head of Service/
Director of Development, Development and
Alumni Relations Office: Clubley, J.
(E-mail: alumni-office@ncl.ac.uk)
Equal opportunities. Equal Opportunities
Adviser: Bullimore, J.
Estates and buildings/works and services.
Director of Estates: Rogers, C. L.
(E-mail: estates-customer-services@ncl.ac.uk)
Examinations. Assistant Registrar
(Examinations): Brierley, L.
Finance. Bursar: Farnhill, H. B.
General enquiries. Registrar: Hogan, J. V.
Industrial liaison. Director of Business
Development and Regional Affairs:
Robertson, D.
(E-mail: business.directorate@ncl.ac.uk)
International office. Head, International
Office: Terry, J.
Library (chief librarian). Librarian and
Keeper of the Pybus Collection: Graham,
Thomas W. (E-mail: library@ncl.ac.uk)
Library (enquiries). Librarian and Keeper of
the Pybus Collection: Graham, Thomas W.
(E-mail: library@ncl.ac.uk)
Marketing. Director, Marketing and
Communications Directorate: Braiden, L.
Personnel/human resources. Director of
Human Resources: Johnston, V. S.
(E-mail: hr@ncl.ac.uk)
Public relations. Press and Communications
Officer: Warwicker, M. J.
(E-mail: press.office@ncl.ac.uk)
Publications. Senior Publications Officer:
Suddes, M. (E-mail: publications@ncl.ac.uk)
Purchasing. Purchasing Manager: Addison, N.
I.
Quality assurance and accreditation. Head of
Service, Quality in Learning and Teaching:
Wiles, K. (E-mail: development@ncl.ac.uk)
Research. Director of Business Development
and Regional Affairs: Robertson, D.
(E-mail: business.directorate@ncl.ac.uk)
Safety. Head of Safety: Theobald, Vincent P.
(E-mail: safety-office@ncl.ac.uk)
Scholarships, awards, loans. Scholarships
Officer: Darling, V. M.
(E-mail: admissions-enquiries@ncl.ac.uk)

Schools liaison. Director, Marketing and Communications Directorate: Braiden, L. (E-mail: sro.enquiries@ncl.ac.uk)

Security. Estate Security Manager: Westwater, G. S. A. (E-mail: estates@ncl.ac.uk)

Sport and recreation. Director, Centre for Physical Recreation and Sport: Blackburn, C. (E-mail: physical-recreation-sport@ncl.ac.uk)

Staff development and training. Assistant HR Director (Development), Human Resources: Clark, J. (E-mail: hr@ncl.ac.uk)

Student union. (Contact the Communications Officer, Student Union) (E-mail: union.society@ncl.ac.uk)

Student welfare/counselling. Head, Student Wellbeing Service: Jennis, R. (E-mail: student.welfare@ncl.ac.uk)

Students from other countries. Head, International Office: Terry, J.

Students with disabilities. Head, Disability Support: Chilton, Prof. S. M. (E-mail: disability.support@ncl.ac.uk)

[Information supplied by the institution as at 11 March 2008, and edited by the ACU]

UNIVERSITY OF NORTHAMPTON

Founded 2005

Postal Address: Park Campus, Boughton Green Road, Northampton, England NN2 7AL
Telephone: (01604) 735500
URL: http://www.northampton.ac.uk/

RECTOR*—Tate, Ann

UNIVERSITY OF NORTHUMBRIA AT NEWCASTLE

Founded 1992

Member of the Association of Commonwealth Universities

Postal Address: Ellison Building, Ellison Place, Newcastle upon Tyne, England NE1 8ST
Telephone: (0191) 232 6002 **Fax:** (0191) 227 4017
URL: http://www.northumbria.ac.uk

VICE-CHANCELLOR AND CHIEF EXECUTIVE*—Wathey, Prof. Andrew B., MA Oxf., DPhil Oxf., FRHistS FSA FRSA
DEPUTY VICE-CHANCELLOR (RESOURCES) AND DIRECTOR OF FINANCE—Chesser, David, BSc
DEPUTY VICE-CHANCELLOR (LEARNING AND TEACHING)—Mahoney, Prof. Craig, BEd MA PhD
DEPUTY VICE-CHANCELLOR (STUDENT AND STAFF AFFAIRS)—Slee, Prof. Peter, BA PhD, FRHistS
DEPUTY VICE-CHANCELLOR (RESEARCH AND ENTERPRISE)—Strike, Prof. Peter
UNIVERSITY SECRETARY‡—Bott, Richard A., BSc(Econ) MSc, FCIS
ACADEMIC REGISTRAR—Kelly, Paul, BSc MSc

GENERAL INFORMATION

History. The university was originally established as Newcastle upon Tyne Polytechnic by the amalgamation in 1969 of the College of Art and Industrial Design, Municipal College of Commerce, and Rutherford College of Technology. It was later amalgamated with City College of Education (1974), Northern Counties College of Education (1976), and with Bede, Newcastle and Northumbria College of Health Studies (1995). University status was achieved under its present name in 1992.

Admission to first degree courses (see also United Kingdom Introduction). Through Universities and Colleges Admissions Service (UCAS).

First Degrees (see also United Kingdom Directory to Subjects of Study). BA, BEng, BSc, LLB, MChem, MEng.
Length of course. Full-time: BA, BEng, BSc: 3 years; LLB: 3–4 years; MChem: 4 years. Part-time: BEng, LLB: 4 years; BSc: 4–5 years; BA: 4–6 years.

Higher Degrees (see also United Kingdom Directory to Subjects of Study).
Master's. LLM, MA, MEd, MPhil, MSc.
Length of course. Full-time: LLM, MEd, MSc: 1 year; MA: 1–2 years. Part-time: LLM, MEd: 2 years; MSc: 3 years. By distance learning: LLM: 2 years.

Doctoral. PhD.
Length of course. Part-time: PhD: 4–7 years.

Libraries. Volumes: 500,000. Other holdings: 21,000 e-journals. Special collections: European Documentation Centre, which receives one copy of all official EU documents direct from Brussels or Luxembourg.

Academic Year (2007–2008). Two semesters: 18 September–30 May. Summer session: 2 June–19 September.

Income (2006–2007). Total, £165,000,000.

Statistics. Staff (2006–2007): 3242 (1286 academic, 1956 non-academic). Students (2006–2007): full-time 21,251; part-time 8250; international 3317; distance education/external 1449; undergraduate 18,875; master's 4750; doctoral 351.

ACADEMIC UNITS
Applied Sciences

Tel: (0191) 227 4453 Fax: (0191) 227 4561
E-mail: et.admissions@northumbria.ac.uk
Mennell, Julie, BSc PhD   Prof.; Dean*
Research: analytical chemistry; biomedical science; chemical reaction mechanisms and dynamics; environmental chemistry; geography and environmental management

Arts and Social Sciences

Tel: (0191) 227 3196 Fax: (0191) 227 3632
E-mail: ar.admissions@northumbria.ac.uk
Dobbs, Lynn, BA MA   Prof.; Dean*
Research: art practice and art history; literature and language; media and culture; politics and history; sociology and criminology

Built Environment

Tel: (0191) 227 4553 Fax: (0191) 227 4561
E-mail: et.admissions@northumbria.ac.uk
Hodgson, Steve, BSc   Dean*
Research: construction management; regeneration and conservation; sustainable cities; sustainable development

Computing, Engineering and Information Sciences

Tel: (0191) 227 4453 Fax: (0191) 227 4561
E-mail: et.admissions@northumbria.ac.uk
Sambell, Alistair, BSc DPhil   Prof.; Dean*
Research: computer engineering, software engineering, knowledge management; design, manufacturing, mechanical and materials engineering; mathematics, database; optical communications, microwave engineering, digital signal processing and control; renewable energy, photovoltaic, energy systems, power engineering

Design

Tel: (0191) 227 4913 Fax: (0191) 227 4655
E-mail: ar.admissions@northumbria.ac.uk
More, James, BA, FRSA   Prof.; Dean*

Research: fashion design; fashion marketing; graphic design; industrial design; three-dimensional design

Health, Community and Education Studies

Tel: (0191) 215 6006 Fax: (0191) 215 6015
E-mail: hs.admissions@northumbria.ac.uk
Stephens, Royston, BA MA PhD   Prof.; Dean*
Research: disability; older people; practice development; primary education; women's health

Law, School of

Tel: (0191) 227 4494 Fax: (0191) 227 4557
E-mail: ss.admissions@northumbria.ac.uk
Kenny, Phillip, LLB LLM   Prof.; Dean*
Research: commercial law; employment law; human rights law; legal information; property law

Newcastle Business School

Tel: (0191) 227 4433 Fax: (0191) 227 3893
E-mail: nb.admissions@northumbria.ac.uk
Croney, Paul, BA MA   Prof.; Dean*

Psychology and Sport Sciences

Tel: (0191) 227 3571 Fax: (0191) 227 3190
E-mail: ar.admissions@northumbria.ac.uk
Briggs, Pamela, BA PhD   Prof.; Dean*
Research: cognition and communication; cognitive neuroscience; nutrition, brain, performance; sports science

CONTACT OFFICERS

Academic affairs. Registrar: Kelly, Paul, BSc MSc (E-mail: paul.kelly@northumbria.ac.uk)
Accommodation. Student Accommodation Manager: Nicolls, Valerie (E-mail: valerie.nicolls@northumbria.ac.uk)
Admissions (first degree). Admissions Manager: Clift, Miriam (E-mail: miriam.clift@northumbria.ac.uk)
Admissions (higher degree). (Contact the assistant registrar of the relevant school)
Admissions (higher degree). Admissions Manager: Clift, Miriam (E-mail: miriam.clift@northumbria.ac.uk)
Adult/continuing education. Access Programmes Manager: Harrison, Judith (E-mail: judith.harrison@northumbria.ac.uk)

Alumni. Alumni Liaison Officer: Heath, Natalie (E-mail: natalie.heath@northumbria.ac.uk)
Archives. University Secretary: Bott, Richard A., BSc(Econ) MSc, FCIS (E-mail: richard.bott@northumbria.ac.uk)
Careers. Head of Careers Service: Riddick, Ed, BA MSc (E-mail: ed.riddick@northumbria.ac.uk)
Computing services. Director of Information Services: Woodhouse, Jed (E-mail: jed.woodhouse@northumbria.ac.uk)
Consultancy services. Director of Northumbria Commercial Enterprises: Hackney, Tony (E-mail: tony.hackney@northumbria.ac.uk)
Credit transfer. Central Contract: Ashdown, Enid (E-mail: enid.ashdown@northumbria.ac.uk)
Examinations. Academic Registrar: Kelly, Paul, BSc MSc (E-mail: paul.kelly@northumbria.ac.uk)
Finance. Deputy Vice-Chancellor (Resources) and Director of Finance: Chesser, David, BSc (E-mail: david.chesser@northumbria.ac.uk)
General enquiries. Academic Registrar: Kelly, Paul, BSc MSc (E-mail: paul.kelly@northumbria.ac.uk)
Health services. Director of Student Services: Groves, Shelagh, BA (E-mail: shelagh.groves@northumbria.ac.uk)
International office. Director of International Office: Purves, Joanne (E-mail: joanne.purves@northumbria.ac.uk)
Library (chief librarian). Director of Library and Learning Services: Core, Prof. Jane, BA MLib MCLIP (E-mail: jane.core@northumbria.ac.uk)
Library (enquiries). Library Customer Service Manager: McBride, Vivien (E-mail: vivien.mcbride@northumbria.ac.uk)
Marketing. Director of Marketing and Recruitment: Watts, Chris (E-mail: chris.watts@northumbria.ac.uk)
Personnel/human resources. Director of Human Resources: Curran, Clare, FCIPD (E-mail: clare.curran@northumbria.ac.uk)
Public relations. Director of Public Relations and Communications: Figgis, Sean (E-mail: sean.figgis@northumbria.ac.uk)
Publications. Senior Publications Officer: Bradley, Claire (E-mail: claire2.bradley@northumbria.ac.uk)

Purchasing. Deputy Expenditure Manager (Procurement): Foster, Katrina (E-mail: katrina.foster@northumbria.ac.uk)
Quality assurance and accreditation. Registrar: Kelly, Paul, BSc MSc (E-mail: paul.kelly@northumbria.ac.uk)
Research. Director of Research, Regional and European Affairs: MacNamara, Oisin, BSc PhD (E-mail: oisin.macnamara@northumbria.ac.uk)
Safety. Environmental Manager: Hall, Tim (E-mail: tim.hall@northumbria.ac.uk)
Scholarships, awards, loans. Welfare Senior Adviser: Wooden, Barbara, MA (E-mail: barbara.wooden@northumbria.ac.uk)
Schools liaison. Education Liaison Manager: Urquhart, Norma, BSc (E-mail: norma.urquhart@northumbria.ac.uk)
Security. Security Manager: Blanchflower, George (E-mail: george.blanchflower@northumbria.ac.uk)
Sport and recreation. Director of Sport: Elvin, Ian, BEd MSc (E-mail: ian.elvin@northumbria.ac.uk)
Staff development and training. Senior HR Manager (Training and Development): McDonald, Louise (E-mail: louise.mcdonald@northumbria.ac.uk)
Strategic planning. Director of Corporate Planning: Wilson, Val (E-mail: val.wilson@northumbria.ac.uk)
Student union. President (Student Union): Farr, Martin (E-mail: martin.farr@northumbria.ac.uk)
Student welfare/counselling. Director of Student Services: Groves, Shelagh, BA (E-mail: shelagh.groves@northumbria.ac.uk)
Students from other countries. Director of International Development: Purves, Joanne (E-mail: joanne.purves@northumbria.ac.uk)
Students with disabilities. Head of Disabilities Service: Newton, Karen (E-mail: karen.newton@northumbria.ac.uk)
University press. Managing Editor: Peden-Smith, Andrew (E-mail: andrew.peden-smith@northumbria.ac.uk)

[Information supplied by the institution as at 25 September 2007, and edited by the ACU]

UNIVERSITY OF NOTTINGHAM

Founded 1881

Member of the Association of Commonwealth Universities

Postal Address: University Park, Nottingham, England NG7 2RD
Telephone: (0115) 951 5151 **Fax:** (0115) 951 3666
URL: http://www.nottingham.ac.uk

VICE-CHANCELLOR*—Greenaway, Prof. David, BSc(Econ) Lond., MCom Liv., DLitt Nott.
PRESIDENT OF THE COUNCIL—Hamill, K., BA, FCA
VICE-PRESIDENT OF THE COUNCIL—McNamara, M., BA MA
PRO-VICE-CHANCELLOR—Birch, Prof. D. J., LLB Nott.
PRO-VICE-CHANCELLOR—Greenaway, Prof. D., BSc(Econ) Lond., MCom Liv., DLitt Nott.
PRO VICE-CHANCELLOR—Grierson, Prof. D., OBE, BSc E.Anglia, PhD Edin., DSc Nott., Hon. DSc Toulouse, FIBiol, FRS
PRO VICE-CHANCELLOR—Sewell, Prof. H. F., MB ChB Leic., BDS Birm., MSc Birm., PhD Birm., Hon. DDS Hon. DSc, FRCP, FRCPath, FMedSci
PRO VICE-CHANCELLOR—Tallack, Prof. D. G., MA Sus., DPhil Sus.
REGISTRAR‡—Greatrix, Paul
CHIEF FINANCIAL OFFICER—Beeby, D. A., BSc Manc., FCA
CHIEF INFORMATION OFFICER—Stanton, K. A., BA MEd
VICE-PRESIDENT, UNIVERSITY OF NOTTINGHAM MALAYSIA CAMPUS—Atkin, Prof. B. P., BSc Liv., PhD Liv., FGS

GENERAL INFORMATION

History. The university was established as University College, Nottingham in 1881. It moved to its present site on the outskirts of Nottingham in the 1920s and received its Royal Charter as the University of Nottingham in 1948.

Admission to first degree courses (see also United Kingdom Introduction). Through Universities and Colleges Admissions Service (UCAS).

First Degrees (see also United Kingdom Directory to Subjects of Study). BA, BArch, BEd, BEng, BM BS, BMedSci, BMus, BN, BPharm, BPhil(Ed), BSc, BTh, LLB, MEng, MMath, MNurse, MPharm, MSci.
  Length of course. Full-time: BEd: 1 year; BEng, LLB: 3 years; BA, BSc: 3–4 years; MEng, MMath, MNurse, MPharm, MSci: 4 years; BM BS, BMedSci: 5 years; BArch: 6 years. Part-time: BA, BEd, BEng, BSc, LLB, MEng, MMath, MNurse, MPharm, MSci: max. 7 years.

Higher Degrees (see also United Kingdom Directory to Subjects of Study).
  Master's. AMusD, AMusM, LLM, MA, MArch, MBA, MDiv, MEd, MMedSci, MPH, MPhil, MRes, MSc, MSW, MTh.
  Admission. Application for postgraduate courses should be made through the university's admissions office.
  Length of course. Full-time: LLM, MA, MArch, MBA, MMedSci, MPhil, MRes, MSc: 1 year. Part-time: LLM, MA, MArch, MBA: 2 years; MPhil, MRes, MSc: 2–4 years.
  Doctoral. DArch, DBA, DD, DLitt, DM, DMus, EdD, LLD, PhD.
  Length of course. Full-time: DArch: 2 years; DBA, EdD, PhD: 4 years. Part-time: EdD: 4 years; PhD: 7 years.

Libraries. Volumes: 1,000,000. Periodicals subscribed to: 5000.

FACULTIES/SCHOOLS

Arts
Tel: (0115) 951 5809 Fax: (0115) 951 5814
Dean: Currie, Prof. G. P., BSc Lond., PhD Lond., FAHA

Education
Tel: (0115) 951 4433 Fax: (0115) 846 6455
Dean: Hall, C. A., BA Nott., PhD Nott.

Engineering
Tel: (0115) 951 3770 Fax: (0115) 951 3881
Dean: Rudd, Prof. C. D., BSc CNAA, PhD Nott., DSc Nott., FIMMM, FIMechE

Graduate School
Tel: (0115) 951 4689
Dean: Heywood, Prof. P. M., MA Edin., MSc(Econ) Lond., PhD Lond.

Law and Social Sciences
Tel: (0115) 846 6693 Fax: (0115) 846 6667
Dean: Ennew, Prof. C., BA Camb., PhD Nott., FRSA

Medicine and Health Sciences
Tel: (0115) 974 1380 Fax: (0115) 970 9922
Dean: Stephenson, Prof. T. J., BSc Brist., BM BCh Oxf., DM Nott., FRCP, FRCPCH

Science
Tel: (0115) 951 6121 Fax: (0115) 951 6168
Dean: Buttery, Prof. P. J., BSc Manc., PhD Manc., DSc Nott.

ACADEMIC UNITS
Arranged by Schools

American and Canadian Studies
Tel: (0115) 951 4261 Fax: (0115) 951 4270
  E-mail: american-enquiries@nottingham.ac.uk
Ashworth, J., BA Lanc., MLitt Lanc., DPhil Oxf. Prof., American History
Billingham, S. E., BA Car., MA Qu., PhD Qu. Sr. Lectr.
Boyle, P. G., MA Glas., PhD Calif. Sr. Lectr.
Jones, M. C., BA Sus., DPhil Oxf. Prof., American Foreign Relations
King, R. H., BA N.Carolina, MA Yale, PhD Virginia Prof., American Intellectual History
Ling, P. J., BA Lond., MA Lond., PhD Keele Reader, American Studies
Messent, P. B., MA Manc., PhD Nott. Prof., Modern American Literature
Monteith, S., BA E.Anglia, PhD Nott. Reader, American Studies
Murray, D. J., BA Lond., PhD Lond. Prof., American Literature and Culture
Newman, J. A., MA Edin., MA Edin., PhD Camb. Prof., American Studies; Head*
Pearson, R. E., BA Duke, MPhil Yale, PhD N.Y. Prof., Film Studies
Tallack, D. G., MA Sus., DPhil Sus. Prof., American Studies
Thompson, G., BA E.Anglia, MA E.Anglia, PhD Nott.Trent Sr. Lectr.
Walsh, M., MA St And., AM Smith, PhD Wis., FRHistS Prof., American Economic and Social History
Other Staff: 8 Lectrs.; 1 Sp. Lectr.
Research: America, Canada, transnationalism and globalisation; contemporary America and cultural studies; literary studies; native peoples, slavery, race, immigration and ethnicity; the American South and civil rights

Biosciences
Tel: (0115) 951 6400 Fax: (0115) 951 6350
2 Sp. Profs.; 2 Sp. Lectrs.; 1 Chief Exper. Officer

Agricultural and Environmental Sciences, Division of
Tel: (0115) 951 6100 Fax: (0115) 951 6060
  E-mail: sheila.northover@nottingham.ac.uk
Alderson, P. G., BSc Nott., PhD Alta. Sr. Lectr.
Azam-Ali, S. N., BSc Wales, MSc Nott., PhD Nott. Reader, Agronomy
Colls, J. J., BSc Lond., PhD Camb. Reader
Crout, N. M. J., BSc Exe., PhD Birm. Prof., Environmental Modelling
Garnsworthy, P. C., BSc(Agr) Aberd., PhD Aberd. Sr. Lectr.
Holdsworth, M. J., BSc Leic., PhD Nott. Prof., Crop Science
Laybourn-Parry, J., BSc Reading, MSc Wales, PhD Stir., DSc Reading Prof., Environmental Biology
Ramsden, S. J., BSc Newcastle(UK), PhD Nott. Sr. Lectr.
Seabrook, M. F., BSc Reading, PhD Reading Prof., Rural Economy
Sinclair, K. D., BSc Aberd., PhD Aberd. Sr. Lectr.
Webb, Robert, BSc Nott., PhD Nott. Prof., Animal Science; Head*
Wiseman, J., BSc Wales, PhD Nott. Prof., Animal Production
Young, S. D., BSc Aberd., PhD Aberd. Sr. Lectr.
Other Staff: 14 Sp. Profs.; 7 Lectrs.; 11 Sp. Lectrs.; 1 Chief Exper. Officer; 1 Sr. Res. Officer; 1 Res. Fellows
Research: animal production science; crop science; environmental science; rural resources management and economics

Animal Physiology, Division of
Tel: (0115) 951 6301 Fax: (0115) 951 6302
  E-mail: monica.bagshaw@nottingham.ac.uk
Campbell, K. H., BSc Lond., DPhil Sus. Prof., Animal Development
Clarke, R. W., BSc Manc., PhD Lond. Sr. Lectr.
Flint, A. P. F., BSc St And., PhD Brist., DSc Brist., FIBiol Prof., Animal Physiology; Head*
Hunter, M. G., BSc Strath., PhD Edin. Prof., Reproductive Physiology
Luck, M. R., BSc Nott., MSc Leeds, PhD Leeds Sr. Lectr.
Mann, G. E., BSc Edin., PhD Edin. Sr. Lectr.
Other Staff: 2 Sp. Profs.; 1 Lectr.; 1 Sp. Lectr.; 4 Res. Fellows
Research: applied bioethics; integrated systems biology; mammalian reproductive physiology; spinal neuron transmission

Food Sciences, Division of

Tel: (0115) 951 6141 Fax: (0115) 951 6142
E-mail: lynne.moseley@nottingham.ac.uk
Connerton, I., BSc *Warw.*, MSc *Warw.*, PhD *Warw.* Northern Foods Prof., Food Safety
Dodd, C. E. R., BSc *Leic.*, PhD *Leic.* Reader
Farhat, I., MSc *Nantes*, PhD *Nott.* Sr. Lectr.
Harding, S. E., MA *Oxf.*, PhD *Leic.*, DSc *Oxf.* Prof., Physical Biochemistry
Hill, P. J., BSc *Manc.*, PhD *Nott.* Sr. Lectr.
Hill, S. E., BSc *Lond.*, PhD *Lough.* Sr. Lectr.
Mitchell, J. R., BSc *Newcastle(UK)*, PhD *Nott.* Prof., Food Technology
Rees, C. E. D., BA *Oxf.*, PhD *Leic.* Sr. Lectr.
Taylor, A. J., BSc *Wales*, PhD *Wales* Prof., Flavour Technology; Head*
Waites, W. M., BSc *Newcastle(UK)*, PhD *Sheff.* Emer. Prof., Food Microbiology
Other Staff: 5 Sp. Profs.; 4 Lectrs.; 4 Sp. Lectrs.; 12 Res. Fellows; 1 Temp. Lectr.
Research: spectroscopic, rheological and ultracentrifugation studies

Nutritional Sciences, Division of

Tel: (0115) 951 6121 Fax: (0115) 951 6122
E-mail: rosemary.reid@nottingham.ac.uk
Bardsley, R. G., BSc *Manc.*, PhD *Manc.* Sr. Lectr.
Buttery, P. J., BSc *Manc.*, PhD *Manc.*, DSc *Nott.* Prof., Applied Biochemistry; Head*
Langley Evans, S. C., BSc *Lond.*, PhD *S'ton.* Reader
Salter, A. M., BSc *Leic.*, PhD *Lond.* Prof., Nutritional Biochemistry
Tucker, G. A., BSc *E.Anglia*, PhD *E.Anglia* Prof., Plant Biochemistry
Other Staff: 1 Sp. Prof.; 6 Lectrs.; 6 Sp. Lectrs.; 1 Chief Exper. Officer; 1 Sr. Exper. Officer; 1 Res. Fellow
Research: diet and health (including food allergies); fat and lean deposition in animals; foetal programming by maternal nutrition; meat and plant product quality; nutrient-gene interactions

Plant Sciences, Division of

Tel: (0115) 951 6327 Fax: (0115) 951 6334
E-mail: jackie.humphreys@nottingham.ac.uk
Bennett, M. J., BSc *UMIST*, PhD *Warw.* Prof.
Black, C. R., BSc *Aberd.*, PhD *Aberd.* Prof., Environmental Plant Physiology
Cocking, E. C., BSc *Brist.*, PhD *Brist.*, DSc *Brist.*, FRS Emer. Prof., Botany
Dickinson, M. J., BSc *Liv.*, PhD *E.Anglia* Sr. Lectr., Molecular Plant Pathology
Grierson, D., OBE, BSc *E.Anglia*, PhD *Edin.*, DSc *Nott.*, Hon. DSc *Toulouse*, FIBiol, FRS Prof., Plant Physiology
Power, J. B., BSc *Nott.*, PhD *Nott.* Reader, Plant Biotechnology
Pyke, K., BSc *Bath*, PhD *E.Anglia* Sr. Lectr., Plant Cell Biology
Roberts, J. A., BA *Oxf.*, PhD *Camb.* Prof., Plant Biology; Head*
Rossall, S., BSc *Stir.*, PhD *Stir.* Sr. Lectr., Plant Pathology
Taylor, I. B., BSc *CNAA*, PhD *Wales* Reader, Plant Genetics
Wilson, Z. A., BSc *Nott.*, PhD *Nott.* Sr. Lectr., Plant Molecular Biology
Other Staff: 13 Sp. Profs.; 4 Lectrs.; 2 Sp. Lectrs.; 2 Res. Officers
Research: arabidopsis genomic resources; plant molecular and cell biology; plant responses to environmental stresses; plant-microbe interactions; transgenic plant technologies

Built Environment

Tel: (0115) 951 3134 Fax: (0115) 951 3159
E-mail: sbe@nottingham.ac.uk
Dernie, D., MA Reader; Co-Dir., Archit. Res.
Farmer, G., BA Sr. Lectr.; Dir., Diploma Course
Ford, B. H., MA *RCA* Prof., Bio-Climatic Architecture; Head*
Hale, J., BArch *Bath*, BSc *Bath*, MSc *Penn.*, FRSA Sr. Lectr.; Co-Dir., Archit. Res.

Heath, T. P., BA *Manc.*, BArch *Nott.*, MA *Nott.*, PhD *Nott.* Sr. Lectr.; Dir., Inst. of Archit.
Oc, T., BArch *Middle East Tech.*, MCP *Middle East Tech.*, MA *Chic.*, PhD *Penn.* Prof., Urban Design and Planning
Riffat, S. B., BSc *Oxf.*, MSc *Oxf.*, DPhil *Oxf.*, DSc *Oxf.*, FIMechE ICI Klea Prof., Sustainable Energy Systems
Shao, L., BSc *Beijing*, PhD *Sheff.* Reader
Wilson, R., BSc *H-W*, PhD *H-W* Sr. Lectr.
Yan, Y., BSc *Jilin*, MSc *Shanghai*, PhD *Lond.* Sr. Lectr.
Other Staff: 5 Sp. Profs; 19 Lectrs.; 2 Sp. Lectrs
Research: building and environmental services; history of architecture, architectural/critical theory; renewable energy and heat powered cycles; sustainable cities and building reuse; urban revitalisation and urban design

Chemistry

Tel: (0115) 951 3500 Fax: (0115) 951 3555
E-mail: chemistry-enquiries@nottingham.ac.uk
Althorpe, S. C., MA *Camb.*, PhD *Camb.* Reader; Royal Soc. Univ. Res. Fellow
Anderson, J. C., BSc *Lond.*, PhD *Lond.*, FRSChem Prof., Chemistry
Champness, N. R., BSc *S'ton.*, PhD *S'ton.* Prof., Chemistry
Clark, J. S., BSc *Edin.*, PhD *Camb.* Prof., Chemistry
Garner, C. D., BSc *Nott.*, PhD *Nott.*, FRSChem, FRS Prof., Biological Inorganic Chemistry
George, M. W., BSc *Nott.*, PhD *Nott.* Prof.
Harrison, P. G., PhD *Lond.*, DSc *Lond.* Reader, Inorganic Chemistry
Hayes, C. J., BSc *Nott.*, PhD *Nott.* Reader, Organic Chemistry
Hey, M. J., BSc *Leeds*, MSc *Leeds*, PhD *Nott.* Sr. Lectr., Physical Chemistry
Hirst, J. D., BA *Oxf.*, PhD *Lond.* Prof., Computational Chemistry
Howdle, S. M., BSc *Manc.*, PhD *Nott.* Prof., Inorganic Chemistry
Hubberstey, P., BSc *Nott.*, PhD *Nott.*, FRSChem Reader, Inorganic Chemistry
Jones, R. G., BSc *E.Anglia*, PhD *Camb.*, FIP Prof.
Lygo, B., BSc *Lond.*, PhD *Lond.* Prof., Organic Chemistry
McCoustra, M. R. S., BSc *H-W*, PhD *H-W* Reader, Chemical Physics
Moody, C., BSc *Liv.*, PhD *Liv.*, DSc *Lond.*, FRSChem Sir Jesse Boot Prof., Organic Chemistry
Pattenden, G., PhD *Lond.*, DSc *Lond.*, FRS, FRSChem Prof., Organic Chemistry
Poliakoff, M., CBE, MA *Camb.*, PhD *Camb.*, FRS Prof.
Powis, I., MA *Oxf.*, DPhil *Oxf.* Prof., Chemical Physics
Reid, K. L., BSc *Sus.*, DPhil *Sus.* Reader, Physical Chemistry
Sarre, P. J., BSc *Sus.*, PhD *S'ton.*, FRSChem, FRAS Prof., Chemistry and Molecular Astrophysics
Schröder, M., BSc *Sheff.*, PhD *Lond.*, FRSChem, FRSEd Prof., Inorganic Chemistry; Head*
Searle, M. S., MA *Oxf.*, PhD *Lond.*, FRSChem Prof., Biological Chemistry
Simpkins, N. S., BSc *Lond.*, PhD *Lond.* Prof.
Soultanas, P., BSc *Sheff.*, PhD *Sheff.* Reader, Chemical Biology
Stace, A. J., BA *Essex*, PhD *Essex*, FRSChem, FRS Prof., Physical Chemistry
Thomas, N. R., BSc *S'ton.*, PhD *S'ton.* Sr. Lectr.
Titman, J. J., MA *Camb.*, PhD *Camb.* Reader, Physical Chemistry
Wheatley, R. J., BA *Camb.*, PhD *Camb.* Reader, Theoretical Chemistry
Woodward, S., BSc *Sheff.*, PhD *Sheff.* Reader, Organic Chemistry
Wright, T. G., BSc *S'ton.*, PhD *S'ton.*, FRSChem Reader, Physical Chemistry
Other Staff: 6 Sp. Visiting Profs.; 6 Lectrs.; 4 Sp. Visiting Lectrs.; 4 Advanced Fellows; 4 Res. Officers; 2 Exper. Officers; 2 Temp. Lectrs.

Computer Science and Information Technology

Tel: (0115) 951 4251 Fax: (0115) 951 4254
E-mail: csit-enquiries@nottingham.ac.uk
Ashman, H. L., BA *Flin.*, BSc *Adel.*, PhD *RMIT* Sr. Lectr.
Backhouse, R. C., BA *Camb.*, PhD *Lond.* Prof., Computing Science
Bai, L., BSc *Siping*, MSc *Lanzhou* Sr. Lectr.
Benford, S. D., BSc *Nott.*, PhD *Nott.* Prof., Collaborative Computing
Brailsford, D. F., BSc *Lond.*, PhD *Lond.*, FBCS Dunford Prof., Computer Science
Burke, E. K., BEd *Leeds*, MSc *Leeds*, PhD *Leeds* Prof., Computer Science
Elliman, D. G., BSc *Nott.*, PhD *Nott.* Prof., Applied Computing
Ford, P. H., MA *Camb.*, FBCS Prof., Information Technology and Computing Practice; Head*
Greenhalgh, C. M., BA *Camb.*, PhD *Nott.* Prof., Computer Science
Higgins, C. A., BTech *Brad.*, MSc *Manc.*, PhD *CNAA* Sr. Lectr.
Hutton, G. M., BSc *Glas.*, PhD *Glas.* Sr Lectr.
Kendall, G., BSc *UMIST*, PhD *Nott.* Sr. Lectr.
Krasnogor, N., Licence *La Plata*, PhD *W.England*
Petrovic, S., BSc *Belgrade*, MSc *Belgrade*, PhD *Belgrade* Sr. Lectr.
Pridmore, T. P., BSc *Warw.*, PhD *Sheff.* Sr. Lectr.
Qiu, G., BSc *China U.Electronic S.T.*, PhD *China U.Electronic S.T.* Reader, Visual Information Processing
Rodden, T., BSc *Strath.*, PhD *Lanc.* Prof., Computer Science
Other Staff: 13 Lectrs.

Informatics Institute of Information Technology

Tel: (0115) 951 3345
No staff at present

Economics

Tel: (0115) 951 5620 Fax: (0115) 951 4159
E-mail: economics-enquiries@nottingham.ac.uk
Appleton, S. M., BA *Oxf.*, MA *Warw.*, DPhil *Oxf.* Sr. Lectr.
Bleaney, M. F., BA *Camb.*, PhD *Camb.* Prof.
Bougheas, S., BBA *American Coll., Greece*, MA *Penn.State*, PhD *Penn.State* Sr. Lectr.
Cornes, R. C., BSc *S'ton.*, MSc *S'ton.*, PhD *ANU* Prof., Economic Theory
Cubitt, R., BA *Oxf.*, MPhil *Oxf.*, DPhil *Oxf.* Prof., Economics and Decision Research
Dasgupta, I., BSc *Calc.*, MA *J.Nehru U.*, PhD *Calif.* Sr. Lectr.
Disney, R. F., BA *Camb.*, MA *Sus.* Prof., Labour Economics
Duncan, A. S., BA *Manc.*, DPhil *York(UK)* Prof., Microeconometrics
Falvey, R. E., BA *Cant.*, MA *Cant.*, MA *Roch.*, PhD *Roch.* Prof., International Trade
Gaechter, S., MA *Vienna*, PhD *Zür.* Prof., Psychology of Economic Decision Making
Greenaway, D., BSc(Econ) *Lond.*, MCom *Liv.*, DLitt *Nott.* Prof.
Guariglia, A., Laurea *Rome*, PhD *Boston* Sr. Lectr.
Hine, R. C., BA *Lond.*, MSc *Nott.* Reader, European Economics
Humphrey, S. J., BA *E.Anglia*, MA *E.Anglia*, PhD *E.Anglia* Sr. Lectr.
Kim, T., BA *Yonsei*, MA *Yonsei*, PhD *Calif.* Sr. Lectr.
Leybourne, S. J., BSc *Leeds*, MSc *Lond.*, PhD *Leeds* Prof., Econometrics
Lloyd, T. A., BSc *Newcastle(UK)*, PhD *Nott.* Sr. Lectr.
Milner, C. R., BA *Leic.*, MSc *Lough.* Prof., International Economics; Head*
Mizen, P., BScEcon *Wales*, PhD *Lough.* Reader
Morgan, C. W., BA *Exe.*, PhD *Nott.* Sr. Lectr.
Morrissey, W. O., BA *Trinity(Dub.)*, MSc *Bath*, PhD *Bath* Prof., Development Economics
Nelson, D. R., BA *Ohio*, MA *N.Carolina*, PhD *N.Carolina* Leverhulme Prof.

Newbold, P., BSc(Econ) Lond., PhD Wis.   Prof., Econometrics

Reed, G. V., BSc Nott.   Reader

Sefton, M., BA Camb., PhD Iowa   Reader

Seidmann, D. J., BA Oxf., MSc Lond., PhD Lond.   Prof., Economic Theory

Starmer, C. V., BA Birm., MA E.Anglia, PhD E.Anglia   Prof., Experimental Economics

Upward, R., BA Brist., MPhil Oxf., PhD Manc.   Sr. Lectr.

Whynes, D. K., BA York(UK), BPhil York(UK), MLitt St And.   Prof., Health Economics

Wright, P. W., BSc Brist., MSc Warw., PhD Warw.   Sr. Lectr.

Other Staff: 1 Visiting Prof.; 2 Sp. Profs.; 14 Lectrs.; 7 Res. Fellows; 1 Sr. Lectr.†

Research: econometrics (time series analysis and forecasting); economic development (infrastructure and institutions in export promotion); international trade (impact of globalisation on labour markets); macroeconomics (exchange rate and interest rate policies); microeconomics (ethics and welfare economics, social choice)

Education

Tel: (0115) 951 4543 Fax: (0115) 846 6600
E-mail: education-enquiries@nottingham.ac.uk

Atkin, C., BEd Hudd., MA De Mont., PhD Nott.   Sr. Lectr.

Coyle, D., BEd Nott., MEd Leic., PhD Nott.   Sr. Lectr.

Crook, C., BSc Wales, PhD Camb.   Reader, ICT in Education

Dale, M. B., BA Nott., PhD Nott.   Sr. Lectr.

Day, C. W., MA Sus., DPhil Sus., Hon. PhD Linköping   Prof.

Ellison, L., MSc CNAA   Sr. Lectr.

Gates, P., BSc UMIST, MA Open(UK), MSc UMIST, PhD Nott.   Sr. Lectr.

Hadfield, M. P., BSc S'ton., PhD Nott.Trent   Sr. Lectr.

Hall, C. A., BA Nott., PhD Nott.   Sr. Lectr.; Head*

Hall, C. J., BA Lond., MA Nott., PhD Nott.   Sr. Lectr.

Harris, P. D., BSc Lond., PhD Lond.   Sr. Lectr.

Harrison, C., BA Leeds, MPhil Nott., PhD Nott.   Prof., Literacy Studies in Education

Hedge, P. A., BA Keele, MA Essex, PhD Warw.   Sr. Lectr.

Hobson, A. J., BA Lanc., MA York(UK), MEd Leeds, PhD Leeds   Sr. Lectr.

Joyes, G., BEd Nott., PhD Nott.   Sr. Lectr.

Leicester, M., BA Wales, MEd Manc., PhD Manc.   Prof.†, Learning and Teaching

Marcombe, D., BA York(UK), PhD Durh.   Sr. Lectr.

McGrath, I., BA Camb., MA Camb., MLitt Edin., PhD Edin.   Sr. Lectr.

McGrath, S. A., BA Oxf., MSc Edin., PhD Edin.   Reader, Organisation and Management of Post-School Education

Morgan, W. J., BA Wales, MEd Wales, PhD Nott.   Prof., Comparative Education

Murphy, Roger J. L., BSc St And., PhD St And.   Prof.

Newton, L. R., BSc Leic., MA Open(UK), PhD Leic.   Sr. Lectr.

Olleson, Philip J., MA Camb., PhD Nott.   Prof., Historical Musicology

Preston, P. J. D., BA Nott., MA Nott., FRSA   Sr. Lectr.

Sammons, P. M., BSocSci Brist., PhD CNAA   Prof.

Sinclair, B. B., BA Bath, MA Lond., PhD Nott.   Sr. Lectr.

Speight, S. J., BA Manc., MA Nott., PhD Nott.   Sr. Lectr.

Thomson, P. L., PhD Deakin   Prof., School Leadership/School Improvement

Wallis, J. V., BA Birm., MA Birm., PhD Nott.   Sr. Lectr.

Other Staff: 30 Sp. Profs.; 19 Lectrs.; 22 Sp. Lectrs.; 10 Res. Fellows; 19 Lectrs.†; 4 Res. Fellows†

Research: comparative education; continuing education; human relations; lifelong learning; literacy studies

Engineering, Chemical, Environmental and Mining

Tel: (0115) 951 4081 Fax: (0115) 951 4115
E-mail: scheme.enquiries@nottingham.ac.uk

Atkin, B. P., BSc Liv., PhD Liv., FGS   Prof.

Azzopardi, B. J., BTech Brad., PhD Exe., FIChemE   Lady Trent Prof., Chemical Engineering

Cloke, M., BSc Nott., PhD Nott., FIChemE   Sr. Lectr.

Denby, B., BSc Nott., PhD Nott.   Prof., Minerals Computing

Edwards, J. S., BSc Nott., PhD Nott.   Sr. Lectr.

Hilal, N., BEng Al-Baath, MSc Wales, PhD Wales, FIChemE   Reader, Chemical Engineering

Lowndes, I. S., BSc St And., MSc Nott., PhD Nott.   Sr. Lectr.

Miles, N. J., BSc Leeds, PhD Nott.   Prof., Minerals Processing Engineering; Head*

Nathanial, P. C., BA Camb., MA Camb., MSc Lond., PhD Lond., FGS   Sr. Lectr.

Reddish, D. J., BSc Nott., PhD Nott.   Sr. Lectr.

Snape, C. E., BSc Leeds, PhD Leeds, FRSEd   Prof., Chemical Engineering and Chemical Technology

Wilson, J. A., BSc Nott., PhD Nott.   Sr. Lectr.

Other Staff: 9 Sp. Profs.; 13 Lectrs.; 10 Indust. Fellows; 2 Exper. Officers

Research: mining technology (after-use, design, environmental, geotechnics, safety); multiphase flow (gas-solid, solid-liquid, gas-liquid); process engineering (minerals, chemical and environmental engineering processes)

Engineering, Civil

Tel: (0115) 951 3907 Fax: (0115) 951 3898
E-mail: civeng-enquiries@nottingham.ac.uk

Airey, G. D., BSc Cape Town, MSc Pret., PhD Nott.   Reader

Brown, S. F., OBE, BSc Nott., PhD Nott., DSc Nott., FICE, FREng   Prof.

Collop, A. C., BEng Greenwich, PhD Camb.   Prof.

Dawson, A. R., BA Lanc., MSc Lond., FGS   Sr. Lectr.

Dodd, N., BSc Lond., PhD Brist.

Dodson, A. H., BSc Nott., PhD Nott., DSc Nott., FRAS, FRIN, FICE, FIAG   Prof., Geodesy; Head*

Elliot, K. S., BTech Brad., PhD Nott.   Sr. Lectr.

Mawdesley, M. J., BSc Nott., PhD Nott.   Sr. Lectr.

McDowell, G. R., MA Camb., PhD Camb.   Reader

Moore, T., BSc Nott., PhD Nott., FRAS   Prof., Satellite Navigation

Owen, J. S., BEng Brist., PhD Brist.   Sr. Lectr.

Reddish, D. J., BSc Nott., PhD Nott.   Sr. Lectr.

Tizani, W., BSc Leeds, MSc Leeds, PhD Brad.   Sr. Lectr.

Wright, N. G., BSc Brist., PhD Leeds   Reader, Environmental Fluid Mechanics

Yu, H., BE Shijiazhuang, MSc Lond., DPhil Oxf., DSc Newcastle(UK)   Prof., Geotechnical Engineering

Other Staff: 8 Sp. Profs.; 8 Lectrs.; 9 Res. Fellows; 11 Indust. Fellows; 6 Res. Assocs.; 1 Chief Exper. Officer; 2 Sr. Exper. Officers; 1 Exper. Officer

Research: computational mechanics; construction management; pavements/geotechnics; structural engineering; surveying

Engineering, Electrical and Electronic

Tel: (0115) 951 5600 Fax: (0115) 951 5616
E-mail: eee-enquiries@eee.nottingham.ac.uk

Asher, G. M., BSc Bath, PhD Bath   Prof., Electrical Drives and Control

Benson, T. M., BSc Sheff., PhD Sheff.   Prof., Opto-Electronics

Bradley, K. J., BEng Sheff., PhD Sheff.   Sr. Lectr.

Challis, R. E., BSc Lond., FIEE, FIP   Prof., Electronic Instrumentation; Head*

Christopoulos, C., MSc Sus., DPhil Sus.   Prof., Electrical Engineering

Clare, J. C., BSc Brist., PhD Brist.   Prof., Power Electronics

Cross, T. E., BSc Wales, PhD Wales   Sr. Lectr.

Crowe, J. A., BSc S'ton., DPhil Oxf.   Sr. Lectr.

Hayes-Gill, B. R., BSc Nott., PhD Nott.   Sr. Lectr.

Jakeman, Eric, BSc Birm., PhD Birm., FIP, FRS   Prof., Applied Statistical Optics

Larkins, E. C., BS Cornell, MS Stan., PhD Stan.   Prof., Opto-electronics

See, C. W., BSc Lond., PhD Lond.   Sr. Lectr.

Sewell, P. D., BSc Bath, PhD Bath   Reader

Somekh, M. G., MA Oxf., PhD Lanc.   Prof., Optical Engineering

Sumner, M., BEng Leeds, PhD Nott.   Sr. Lectr.

Thomas, D. W. P., BSc Lond., MPhil Sheff., PhD Nott.   Sr. Lectr.

Tuck, B., BSc Lond., PhD Lond., DSc Lond., FIP, FIEE   Prof., Physical Electronics Instrumentation

Walker, J. G., BSc Lond., PhD Lond.   Reader

Wheeler, P. W., BEng Brist., PhD Brist.   Sr. Lectr.

Other Staff: 2 Sp. Profs.; 8 Lectrs.; 2 Advanced Fellows; 2 Indust. Fellows

Research: electromagnetic modelling; optical engineering for materials characterisation; optoelectronic devices; power electronics; statistical electromagnetic scattering

Engineering, Mechanical, Materials and Manufacturing

Tel: (0115) 951 4001 Fax: (0115) 951 4000
E-mail: school4m-enquiries@nottingham.ac.uk

Aroussi, A., BSc CNAA, PhD CNAA   Sr. Lectr.

Becker, A. A., BSc(Eng) Lond., PhD Lond., FIP, FIMechE   Prof., Mechanical Engineering

Brooks, R., BSc Leeds, PhD Camb.   Sr. Lectr.

Brown, P. D., BSc Durh., PhD Durh.   Reader

Choi, K.-S., BSc Tottori, MSc Tottori, MBA Brun., PhD Cornell   Reader

Choy, K.-L., BScEd Malaya, DPhil Oxf.   Prof., Materials

Everitt, N., BSc Bath, DPhil Oxf.   Sr. Lectr.

Fox, C. H. J., BSc Newcastle(UK), PhD Newcastle(UK)   Prof., Applied Dynamics

Garvey, S. D., PhD Aston, BEng   Prof., Dynamics

Gindy, N. N. Z., BSc Mansourah, MSc Aston, PhD Aston   Prof., Advanced Manufacturing Technology

Grant, D. M., BSc York(UK), PhD Open(UK)   Prof., Materials Science

Haslegrave, Christine M., BSc Brist., MSc Birm., PhD Nott.   Sr. Lectr.

Hyde, T. H., BSc Aston, MSc Aston, PhD Nott., DSc Nott., FIMMM, FIMechE, FREng   Prof.; Head*

Jones, I. A., BSc Manc., BEng Manc., MBA Nott., PhD Nott.   Sr. Lectr.

Kennedy, A. R., BEng Lond., PhD Camb.   Sr. Lectr.

Liu, G., PhD UMIST, MEng   Sr. Lectr.

Long, A. C., BSc Warw., MSc Lough., PhD Nott.   Prof., Mechanics of Materials

Mather, J. S. B., BSc Manc., PhD Manc.   Sr. Lectr.

McCartney, D. G., MA Oxf., DPhil Oxf.   Prof., Materials Processing

McColl, I. R., BSc Hull, PhD Nott.   Sr. Lectr.

McNally, D. S., BSc Exe., PhD Exe.   Sr. Lectr.

McWilliam, S., BSc Durh., MSc Cran.IT, PhD S'ton.   Sr. Lectr.

Noble, B., BSc Nott., PhD Nott., FIMMM   Reader, Materials Analysis

Pashby, I. R., BMet Sheff., PhD Sheff.   Prof., Manufacturing Processes

Pickering, S. J., BSc Nott., PhD Nott.   Sr. Lectr.

Popov, A. A., MEng Sofia, MSc Sofia, PhD Sofia   Sr. Lectr.

Power, H., PhD Iowa, BEng MSc   Prof., Computational Fluid Dynamics

Ratchev, S. M., MEng T.U.Varna, PhD Moscow   Sr. Lectr.

Rudd, C. D., BSc *CNAA*, PhD *Nott.*, DSc *Nott.*, FIMMM, FIMechE Prof., Mechanical Engineering

Seddon, A. B., BSc *Nott.*, MPhil *CNAA*, PhD *CNAA* Prof., Inorganic Materials

Shayler, P. J., MSc *Birm.*, PhD *Birm.*, FIMechE Ford Prof.

Shipway, P. H., MA *Camb.*, PhD *Camb.* Reader, Surface Engineering

Standring, P. M., BSc *Nott.*, PhD *Nott.* Sr. Lectr.

Warrior, N. A., BSc *CNAA*, PhD *Nott.* Sr. Lectr.

Williams, E. J., BSc(Eng) *Lond.*, PhD *Lond.* Sr. Lectr.

Wilson, J. R., BTech *Lough.*, MSc *Lough.*, PhD *Birm.* Prof., Occupational Ergonomics

Wykes, Catherine, BSc *N.U.I.*, PhD *Edin.* Sr. Lectr.

Other Staff: 5 Sp. Profs.; 10 Lectrs.; 13 Indust. Fellows; 1 Temp. Lectr.

Research: component design and integrity; experimental/computational fluid mechanics; internal combustion engine; Rolls Royce technology centre

English Studies

Tel: (0115) 951 5900 Fax: (0115) 951 5924
E-mail: english-undergrad@nottingham.ac.uk

Carter, R. A., BA *Leeds*, MA *Birm.*, PhD *Birm.*, FRSA Prof., Modern English Language

Dillon, J., MA *Oxf.*, DPhil *Oxf.* Prof., Drama

Dörnyei, Z., MA *Bud.*, PhD *Bud.* Prof., Psycholinguistics

Guy, J. M., BA *Birm.*, PhD *Birm.* Prof., Victorian Studies

Hammond, B., MA *Edin.*, DPhil *Oxf.* Prof., English Literature

Head, D., MA *Ulster*, PhD *Warw.* Prof., Modern Literature

Herman, Vimala V., BA *Madr.*, MA *Madr.*, PhD *Exe.* Reader, Linguistics and Literary Studies

Jesch, Judith, BA *Durh.*, PhD *Lond.*, FSA, FRHistS Prof., Viking Studies

Marsden, R. C. J., BA *York(UK)*, PhD *Camb.* Sr. Lectr., Old English Language and Literature

Parsons, D., BA *Lond.*, MA *Nott.*, PhD *Camb.* Reader, Name-Studies

Sanders, J., MA *Camb.*, MA *Warw.*, PhD *Warw.* Prof., English Literature

Schmitt, N., BA *Gonzaga*, MEd *Temple*, MPhil *Wales*, PhD *Nott.* Reader, Applied Linguistics

Stockwell, P. J., BA *Liv.*, PhD *Liv.* Prof., Literary Linguistics

Turville-Petre, T. F. S., MA *Oxf.*, BLitt *Oxf.*, FRHistS Prof., Mediaeval English Literature

Other Staff: 1 Sp. Prof.; 15 Lectrs.; 2 Res. Fellows; 1 Lectr.†

Research: applied linguistics; literature post-1500 (D H Lawrence, literature and culture); mediaeval language and literature (Old and Middle English, Old Norse); modern English language (language, culture and discourse)

English Language Education, Centre for

Tel: (0115) 951 4405 Fax: (0115) 951 4992

Hughes, R. B., BA *Oxf.*, MSc *Oxf.*, DPhil *Oxf.* Dir.*

Other Staff: 1 Temp. Lectr.

Geography

Tel: (0115) 951 5428 Fax: (0115) 951 5249
E-mail: geogenquiries@nottingham.ac.uk

Bradshaw, R. P., BA *Keele*, PhD *Keele* Sr. Lectr.

Clarke, M. L., BSc *Sus.*, MSc *Lond.*, PhD *Leic.* Reader, Environmental Change

Clifford, N. J., BA *Camb.*, MA *Camb.*, PhD *Camb.* Prof., Physical Geography

Crewe, L. J., BA *Leeds*, PhD *Leeds* Prof., Human Geography

Daniels, S. J., MA *St And.*, MSc *Wis.*, PhD *Lond.* Prof., Cultural Geography

Dugdale, R. E., BSc *Nott.*, PhD *Nott.* Sr. Lectr.

Endfield, G. H., BSc *Liv.*, MSc *Liv.*, PhD *Sheff.* Sr. Lectr.

Haines-Young, R. H., BSc *Sus.*, MA *Nott.*, PhD *Lond.*, FRICS Prof., Environmental Management

Heffernan, M. J., BSc *Wales*, PhD *Camb.* Prof., Historical Geography

Jewitt, S. L., BA *Camb.*, MA *Camb.*, MA *Syr.*, PhD *Camb.* Sr. Lectr.

Lavers, C. P., BSc *Lond.*, PhD *Nott.* Sr. Lectr.

Leyshon, A., BA *Wales*, PhD *Wales* Prof., Economic and Social Geography

Mather, P. M., OBE, MA *Camb.*, PhD *Nott.* Prof., Geographical Information Science

Matless, D. S., BA *Nott.*, PhD *Nott.* Prof., Cultural Geography

Metcalfe, S. E., BA *Camb.*, MA *Camb.*, DPhil *Oxf.* Prof., Earth and Environmental Dynamics

Nathanial, P. C., BA *Camb.*, MA *Camb.*, MSc *Lond.*, PhD *Lond.*, FGS Sr. Lectr.

O'Hara, S. L., BSc *Liv.*, MSc *Alta.*, DPhil *Oxf.* Prof.

Priestnall, G., BSc *Durh.*, PhD *Nott.* Sr. Lectr.

Samers, M. E., BA *Clark*, MS *Wis.*, DPhil *Oxf.* Sr. Lectr.

Seymour, S. M., BA *Nott.*, PhD *Nott.* Sr. Lectr.

Smallman-Raynor, M., BA *Camb.*, MA *Camb.*, PhD *Camb.* Prof., Analytical Geography

Steven, M. D., BSc *McG.*, MSc *Reading*, PhD *Nott.* Prof., Environmental Remote Sensing

Thorne, C. R., BSc *E.Anglia*, PhD *E.Anglia* Prof., Physical Geography

Watkins, C., BSc *Lond.*, PhD *Nott.* Prof., Rural Geography; Head*

Other Staff: 12 Sp. Profs.; 8 Lectrs.; 4 Sp. Lectrs.; 2 Sr. Res. Fellows; 4 Res. Fellows; 7 Res. Assocs.

Research: cultural and historical geography; environmental change and biogeography; geographical information science; new economic geographies; process and applied geomorphology

History

Tel: (0115) 951 5928 Fax: (0115) 951 5948
E-mail: jane.mcveagh@nottingham.ac.uk

Balzaretti, R., BA *Lond.*, PhD *Lond.* Sr. Lectr.

Barrow, J. S., MA *St And.*, DPhil *Oxf.*, FRHistS, FSA Reader, Mediaeval Church History

Beckett, J. V., BA *Lanc.*, PhD *Lanc.*, FRHistS, FSA Prof., English Regional History

Booth, A., BA *Lanc.*, PhD *Lanc.* Reader

Ellis, Joyce M., MA *Oxf.*, DPhil *Oxf.* Sr. Lectr.

Geary, R. J., MA *Camb.*, PhD *Camb.* Prof., Modern History

Heywood, C. M., BA *Reading*, PhD *Reading* Reader, Modern French History

Meller, Helen E., BA *Brist.*, PhD *Brist.*, FRHistS Prof., Urban History

Townsend, S. C., BA *Staffs.*, PhD *Sheff.*, FRHistS Sr. Lectr.

Wrigley, C. J., BA *E.Anglia*, PhD *Lond.*, LittD *E.Anglia*, FRHistS Prof., Modern British History

Young, J. W., BA *Nott.*, PhD *Camb.* Prof., International History; Head*

Other Staff: 1 Sp. Prof.; 10 Lectrs.; 3 Sp. Lectrs.

Research: European middle ages; international labour history; medical history; modern British and Russian history; urban history

Humanities

Tel: (0115) 951 4766 Fax: (0115) 951 5887
E-mail: joan.leake@nottingham.ac.uk

Ford, G. A., BA *Trinity(Dub.)*, PhD *Camb.* Prof.; Head*

Archaeology

Tel: (0115) 951 4820 Fax: (0115) 951 4812

Cavanagh, W. G., MA *Edin.*, PhD *Lond.*, FSA Prof., Aegean Prehistory; Head*

Forbes, H. A., BA *Camb.*, PhD *Penn.* Sr. Lectr.

Henderson, J., BA *Belf.*, PhD *Brad.*, FSA Prof., Archaeological Science

Laing, L., MA *Edin.*, PhD *Liv.* Sr. Lectr.

Pearce, M. J., MA *Lanc.*, PhD *Lanc.* Sr. Lectr.

Poulter, A. G., BA *Birm.*, MA *Birm.*, PhD *Lond.*, FSA Prof., Late Roman and Early Byzantine Archaeology

Wilson, R. J. A., MA *Oxf.*, MA *Trinity(Dub.)*, DPhil *Oxf.*, FSA Prof.

Other Staff: 3 Lectrs.; 2 Sp. Lectrs.; 2 Res. Assocs.; 1 Res. Officer

Research: early copper mining in Italy; glass production in Islamic Syria; prehistoric burial practices in Greece; Roman rural landscapes in Sicily; transition from late antiquity (Bulgaria)

Art History

Tel: (0115) 951 3185 Fax: (0115) 951 3194
E-mail: margaret.boyd@nottingham.ac.uk

Alfrey, N., MA *Edin.*, MA *Lond.* Sr. Lectr.

Callen, A. E., MA *Leic.*, PhD *Lond.* Prof., Visual Culture

Cullen, F. M., PhD *Yale*, MA Sr. Lectr.; Head*

Other Staff: 3 Lectrs.

Classics

Tel: (0115) 951 4800 Fax: (0115) 951 4811
E-mail: classics@nottingham.ac.uk

Hodkinson, Stephen J., BA *Manc.*, PhD *Camb.* Prof., Ancient History

Lee, A. D., BA *Syd.*, PhD *Camb.* Sr. Lectr.

Rich, J. W., MA *Oxf.*, MPhil *Oxf.*, PhD *Nott.* Reader; Head*

Roy, J., MA *Edin.*, MA *Camb.*, PhD *Camb.* Reader, Greek History

Salmon, J. B., MA *Oxf.*, DPhil *Oxf.* Sr. Lectr.

Sommerstein, A. H., MA *Camb.*, PhD *Camb.* Prof., Greek

Other Staff: 1 Sp. Prof.; 5 Lectrs.; 3 Sp. Lectrs.

Research: Greek and Roman historiography; Greek and Roman social history; Greek drama; history of slavery; late antiquity

Music

Tel: (0115) 951 4755
E-mail: sally.britten@nottingham.ac.uk

Cooke, M. J., MA *Camb.*, MPhil *Camb.*, PhD *Camb.* Prof.

Sackman, N., BMus *Nott.*, MA *Leeds*, DMus *Nott.* Reader, Composition; Head*

Wright, P. A., BA *Oxf.*, BMus *Oxf.*, MA *Nott.*, PhD *Nott.* Reader

Other Staff: 2 Sp. Profs.; 3 Lectrs.; 1 Sp. Lectr.

Philosophy

Tel: (0115) 951 5850 Fax: (0115) 951 5840
E-mail: philosophy-enquiries@nottingham.ac.uk

Clark, M., MA *Oxf.* Prof.; Head*

Corazza, E., LèsL *Geneva*, MA *Indiana*, DèsL *Geneva* Sr. Lectr.

Currie, G. P., BSc *Lond.*, PhD *Lond.*, FAHA Prof.

Mumford, S. D., BA *CNAA*, MA *Leeds*, PhD *Leeds* Reader

Noordhof, P. J. P., BA *Oxf.*, PhD *Lond.* Reader

Other Staff: 5 Lectrs.; 2 Sp. Lectrs.; 1 Res. Fellow

Research: Indian philosophy of language and epistemology; metaphysics (causation, laws and dispositions); mind (consciousness, intentionality and mental causation); moral psychology (irrationality, compassion and friendship); philosophy of law (punishment, self-defence and responsibility)

Theology

Tel: (0115) 951 5852 Fax: (0115) 951 5887
E-mail: mary.elmer@nottingham.ac.uk

Bell, Rev. R. H., BSc *Lond.*, MA *Oxf.*, PhD *Lond.*, DrTheol *Tübingen* Sr. Lectr.

Casey, P. M., BA *Durh.*, PhD *Durh.* Prof., New Testament Languages and Literature

Ford, G. A., BA *Trinity(Dub.)*, PhD *Camb.* Prof.

Goddard, H. P., MA *Oxf.*, PhD *Birm.* Prof., Christian-Muslim Relations; Head*

Goodchild, P., MA *Camb.*, MA *Lanc.*, PhD *Lanc.* Sr. Lectr.

Other Staff: 1 Sp. Prof.; 3 Lectrs.; 3 Sp. Lectrs.; 1 Hon. Res. Fellow

Research: biblical theology (Jesus, Paul, Old Testament); hermeneutics (biblical, literary, philosophical, theological); historical theology (modern, puritan, Reformation); languages; religions (ancient and modern Judaism/Islam)

Law

Tel: (0115) 951 5700 Fax: (0115) 951 5696
E-mail: law-enquiries@nottingham.ac.uk
Arrowsmith, S. L., BA Oxf., DJur York(Can.) Prof., Public Procurement Law
Bailey, Stephen H., LLB Camb., MA Camb. Prof., Public Law
Bartlett, P., BA Tor., LLB York(Can.), MA Tor., PhD Lond.   Sr. Lectr.
Bennett, H. N., LLB Lond., LLM Lond., MenD Paris I   Hind Prof., Commercial Law
Birch, D. J., LLB Nott.   J. C. Smith Prof.
Bowman, M. J., LLB Nott.   Sr. Lectr.
Cartwright, P. R., LLB Hull, MPhil Wales, PhD Wales   Prof., Consumer Protection Law
Cryer, R., LLB Wales, LLM Nott., PhD Nott.   Sr. Lectr.
Davies, P. G. G., LLB Essex, LLM Nott.   Sr. Lectr.
Davis, C. J., LLB Nott., PhD Nott.   Sr. Lectr.
Fawcett, J. J., LLB Nott., PhD Brist.   Prof., International Commercial Law
Fraser, D., LLB Laval, LLB Dal., LLM Yale   Prof., Law and Social Theory
Gravells, N. P., MA Oxf.   Prof., English Law
Hervey, T. K., LLB Glas., PhD Sheff.   Prof.
Kenner, J. J., LLB Lond., LLM Lond.   Sr. Lectr.
Kritsiotis, D., LLB Wales, LLM Camb.   Reader, Public International Law
McCorquodale, R. G., BEc Syd., LLB Syd., LLM Camb.   Prof., International Law and Human Rights; Head*
Moloney, N., LLM Harv., LLB   Prof., Capital Markets Law
Mowbray, A. R., LLB Warw., PhD Edin.   Prof., Public Law
Murphy, M. T., BCL N.U.I., LLM Camb.   Prof., Law and Critical Theory
O'Flaherty, M., BCL N.U.I., BPh Greg., STB Greg., MA Amst., MPhil Amst.   Reader, Human Rights
Roberts, P., BCL Oxf., MA Oxf., MPhil Camb.   Prof., Criminal Jurisprudence
Rotherham, C., LLB Cant., LLM Yale, PhD Camb.   Prof.
Sandland, R. P. W., BA Kent, MPhil Camb.   Sr. Lectr.
Simester, A. P., BCom Auck., LLB Auck., DPhil Oxf.   Prof., Legal Philosophy
Todd, S. M. D., LLB Sheff., LLM Sheff., LLD Kent   Prof., Common Law
Torremans, P. L. C., LLM Leic., PhD Leic.   City Solicitors Educational Trust Prof., Intellectual Property
Van Zyl Smit, D., BA Stell., LLB Stell., PhD Edin.   Prof., Comparative and International Penal Law
White, N. D., MA Oxf., PhD Nott.   Prof., International Organisations
Other Staff: 5 Sp. Profs.; 14 Lectrs.; 2 Teaching Fellows
Research: commercial law; criminal law and evidence; human rights; international law; public law

Mathematical Sciences

Tel: (0115) 951 3851 Fax: (0115) 951 3837
E-mail: general-enquiries@maths.nottingham.ac.uk
Armour, E. A. G., BSc Edin., PhD Camb.   Prof., Applied Mathematics
Ball, F. G., BSc Manc., DPhil Oxf.   Prof., Applied Probability
Barrett, J. W., BA Camb., PhD Lond.   Reader, Applied Mathematics
Belavkin, V. P., MSc Moscow, PhD Moscow, DSc Moscow   Prof., Applied Mathematics
Billingham, J., BA Camb., PhD E.Anglia   Prof., Theoretical Mechanics
Byrne, H. M., MA Camb., MSc Oxf., DPhil Oxf.   Prof., Mathematical Medicine
Coombes, S., BSc Exe., PhD Lond.   Reader, Mathematical Neuroscience

Creagh, S. C., BSc N.U.I., PhD Calif.   Sr. Lectr.
Cremona, J. E., BA Oxf., DPhil Oxf.   Prof., Pure Mathematics
Dryden, I. L., BSc Nott., PhD Leeds   Prof., Statistics
Faulkner, T. R., BSc Liv., PhD Liv., FIMA   Sr. Lectr.
Feinstein, J. F., BA Camb., PhD Leeds   Sr. Lectr.
Fesenko, I. B., BSc St.Petersburg, PhD St.Petersburg   Prof., Pure Mathematics
Hibberd, S., BSc Brist., MSc Manc., PhD Brist., FIMA   Sr. Lectr.
Hoffman, D. W., PhD Calif.   Head, Pure Maths. Div.; Prof., Pure Mathematics
Hopcraft, K. I., BSc Sus., PhD Lond.   Sr. Lectr.
Jaroszkiewicz, G. A., BSc Edin., PhD Camb.   Sr. Lectr.
Jensen, O. E., MA Camb., PhD Camb.   Head, Appl. Maths. Div.; Prof., Applied Mathematics
King, J. R., MA Camb., DPhil Oxf.   Prof., Theoretical Mechanics
Langley, J. K., BA Leeds, MSc Lond., PhD Lond.   Prof., Mathematics
Le, H., BA Xi'an Jiaotong, MSc Xi'an Jiaotong, PhD Camb.   Reader, Probability
Lindsay, J. M., BSc Lond., PhD Nott.   Reader, Pure Mathematics
Litton, C. D., BSc Birm., PhD Lanc.   Sr. Lectr.
Louko, J. M. T., MPhil Helsinki, PhD Helsinki   Sr. Lectr.
Matthews, P. C., MA Camb., PhD Camb.   Reader, Applied Mathematics
O'Neill, P. D., BSc Nott., PhD Nott.   Sr. Lectr.
Owen, M. R., BSc Warw., PhD Warw.   Reader, Applied Mathematics
Parry, G. P., BSc Wales, PhD Camb.   Reader, Theoretical Mechanics
Riley, D. S., BSc Hull, PhD Hull   Prof., Applied Mathematics; Head*
Tanner, G., PhD Freib.   Reader, Applied Mathematics
Tew, R. H., MA Oxf., DPhil Oxf.   Sr. Lectr.
Wattis, J. A. D., MA Oxf., MSc Oxf., PhD H-W   Sr. Lectr.
Wood, A. T. A., BA Camb., PhD Open(UK)   Head, Stats. Div.; Prof., Statistics
Woodall, D. R., MA Camb., PhD Nott.   Reader, Pure Mathematics
Other Staff: 3 Sp. Profs.; 14 Lectrs.; 4 Sp. Lectrs.; 8 Res. Fellows
Research: algebra and discrete mathematics; applied non-linear mathematics; mathematical medicine; number theory and arithmetic geometry; statistics and applied probability

Modern Languages

Tel: (0115) 951 5799 Fax: (0115) 846 7309
E-mail: modern-languages-enquiries@nottingham.ac.uk
Hewitt, Nicholas, BA Hull, PhD Hull   Prof.; Head*

French

Tel: (0115) 951 5873 Fax: (0115) 951 4998
E-mail: french@nottingham.ac.uk
Bamforth, S. J., BA Durh., PhD Durh.   Prof., Renaissance Studies
Chapman, Rosemary A., MA Reading, PhD Exe.   Reader, French and Canadian Studies
Francis, R. A., MA Oxf., BLitt Oxf., PhD Nott.   Prof., Eighteenth-Century French Literature; Head*
Hewitt, Nicholas, BA Hull, PhD Hull   Prof.
Hitchcott, N., BA Lond., PhD Lond.   Sr. Lectr.
Hutton, M. A., MA St And., MLitt Oxf.   Sr. Lectr.
Johnson, C. M., BA Lond., PhD Camb.   Prof.
Knight, Diana M., MA Warw., PhD Warw.   Prof.
Ridon, J., LèsL Paris, Maîtrise Paris, PhD Ill.   Sr. Lectr.
Still, Judith M., BA Lond., MSc Lond., PhD Lond.   Prof., French and Critical Theory
Other Staff: 2 Sp. Profs.; 8 Lectrs.; 3 Lecteurs/ Lectrices; 1 Hon. Res. Fellow

Research: critical theory; French and Francophone literature (middle ages to present)

German

Tel: (0115) 951 5815 Fax: (0115) 951 5812
Giles, S. R., MA Camb., PhD E.Anglia   Prof., German Studies and Critical Theory
Göettsche, D., DPhil Mün.   Prof.
Oergel, M., MA Hamburg, PhD E.Anglia   Sr. Lectr.
Woods, R. A., BA Reading, MA Lond., DPhil Oxf.   Prof.; Head*
Other Staff: 1 Sp. Prof.; 4 Lectrs.; 3 Lektors; 1 Tutor†
Research: mediaeval German literature; minority stereotyping in German literature; national identity in modern Germany; recent women's writing in Germany; the new right in Germany

Hispanic and Latin American Studies

Tel: (0115) 951 5800 Fax: (0115) 951 5814
E-mail: jane.kerrigan@nottingham.ac.uk
Kapcia, A. M., BA Lond., PhD Lond.   Prof., Latin American History
McGuirk, B. J., MA Glas., BPhil Oxf., DPhil Oxf.   Prof., Romance Literatures and Literary Theory; Head*
Millington, M. I., BA Camb., MA Camb., PhD Camb.   Prof., Latin American Studies
Other Staff: 6 Lectrs.; 1 Visiting Lectr. (Brazilian Studies); 1 Lang. Instr. (Spanish); 3 Lectors/Lectrices†

Russian and Slavonic Studies

Tel: (0115) 951 5824 Fax: (0115) 951 5834
E-mail: slavonic.studies@nottingham.ac.uk
Dobrenko, E., BA Odessa, PhD Odessa   Prof., Russian Studies
Luker, N. J. L., MA Oxf., PhD Nott.   Sr. Lectr.
Marsh, Cynthia E. A., BA Nott., MA Lond., PhD Lond.   Sr. Lectr.
Milne, Lesley, BA Camb., PhD Camb.   Prof., Slavonic Studies; Head*
Norris, D. A., BA Lond., PhD Nott.   Sr. Lectr.
Rosslyn, Wendy A., BA Lond., MPhil Lond., PhD Nott.   Prof., Russian Literature
Other Staff: 1 Sp. Lectr.; 6 Lectrices; 1 Teaching Fellow
Research: identity and modernity in the Balkans; Maxim Gorky; Russian women poets and translators; Slovene language: reference grammar; Soviet prose (including Bukhov, Kharms, Zoschenko)

Nottingham University Business School

Tel: (0115) 846 6602 Fax: (0115) 846 6667
E-mail: business-enquiries@nottingham.ac.uk
Bacon, N. A., BA CNAA, PhD Sheff.   Prof., Human Resource Management
Ball, A., BA CNAA   Sr. Lectr., Accounting and Finance
Barnatt, C. J., BA Nott.   Sr. Lectr., Computing and Organisations
Berry, R. H., BSc(Econ) Lond., MSc Lond., PhD Warw.   Boots Prof., Accounting and Finance
Binks, M. R., BA Durh., PhD Nott.   Prof., Entrepreneurial Development
Bruce, A. C., MA St And., PhD H-W   Prof., Decision and Risk Analysis; Head*
Coupland, C., BSc Derby, PhD Nott.   Sr. Lectr., Organisational Behaviour
Crane, A., BSc Warw., PhD Nott.   Prof., Business Ethics
Currie, G., BSc Aston, MSc Aston, PhD Nott.   Prof., Public Sector Management
Devlin, J., BSc Lough., PhD Nott.   Reader, Marketing
Diacon, S. R., BSc Nott., PhD Nott.   Worshipful Company of Insurers Prof., Insurance Management
Dowd, K., BA Sheff., MA W.Ont., PhD Sheff.   Prof., Financial Risk Management
Drake, L. M., BA Essex, MA Essex   Swiss Re Prof., Management Risk

Ebrahim, M., BTech *Kharagpur*, MS *Penn.*, MBA *Wis.*, DBA *S.Illinois*   Prof., Financial Economics

Ennew, C., BA *Camb.*, PhD *Nott.*, FRSA   Prof., Marketing

Fenn, P. T., BA *Lanc.*, BPhil *York(UK)*   Norwich Union Prof., Insurance Studies

Gow, I., MA *Edin.*, PhD *Sheff.*, FRSA   Prof., Asian Business

Hasseldine, D. J., BCom *Cant.*, MCom *Cant.*, MBus *Indiana*, PhD *Indiana*   Prof., Accounting and Taxation

Haynes, M. L., BA *Lanc.*, MSc *Warw.*, PhD *Nott.*   Sr. Lectr., Industrial Economics

Hibbert, S. A., BA *Stir.*, PhD *Stir.*   Sr. Lectr., Marketing

Hoffman, J. R., BSc *Sur.*, MA *E.Anglia*, PhD *E.Anglia*   Sr. Lectr., Economics

Hoque, D. K., BSc *Lond.*, PhD *Lond.*   Sr. Lectr., Human Resource Management

Huang, J., LLB *Warw.*, MBA *Warw.*, PhD *Warw.*   Sr. Lectr., Information Technology/Strategy

Humphreys, M., BSc *Leeds*, MBA *Nott.*, PhD *Nott.*   Sr. Lectr., Organisational Behaviour

Jenkins, M., BA *Hudd.*, MSc *Cran.*, PhD *Cran.*   Prof., Competitive Strategy

Lindeloff, P., MSc *Gothenburg*, PhD *Gothenburg*   Sr. Lectr., Enterprise and Innovation

Lockett, A. D., BA *Manc.*, MSc *UMIST*, PhD *Nott.*   Reader, Strategy

MacCarthy, B. L., BA *Open(UK)*, PhD *Brad.*, FIEE, FIMA   Prof., Operations Management

Moon, J. W., BA *Exe.*, PhD *Exe.*   Prof., Corporate Social Responsibility

Newton, D., BSc *Nott.*, MBA *Manc.*, PhD *Salf.*   Prof., Accounting and Finance

O'Brien, C., OBE, BSc *Leeds*, DrHC *Cluj-Napoca*   Cripps Prof., Production Engineering

Owen, D. L., BA *Kent*   Prof., Social and Environmental Accounting

Paton, D., BSc *Lond.*, MA *Warw.*, PhD *Lond.*   Prof., Industrial Economics

Patriotta, G., PhD *Warw.*   Sr. Lectr., Organisational Behaviour and Human Resource Management

Pawar, K., BSc *CNAA*, MSc *Aston*, PhD *Aston*   Prof., Operations Management

Sinclair, M. T., BA *Reading*, MA *Reading*, PhD *Reading*   Prof., Economics of Tourism

Smith, A. P., BSc *Brad.*, MSc *Reading*, PhD *Stir.*   Sr. Lectr., Marketing

Sorwar, G., BSc *Lond.*, MSc *Lond.*, PhD *Lond.*   Sr. Lectr., Finance

Soulsby, A. M., BA *CNAA*, MA *De Mont.*, MBA *Nott.*   Sr. Lectr., Organisational Behaviour

Starkey, K. P., BA *Sheff.*, BSc *Lond.*, PhD *Aston*   Prof., Management and Organisational Learning

Swann, P., OBE, MA *St And.*, MSc *Brist.*, PhD *Lond.*   Prof., Industrial Economics

Tannock, J. D., BSc *Nott.*, PhD *CNAA*   Reader, Quality and Operations Management

Tempest, S., BA *Nott.Trent*, MBA *Nott.*, PhD *Nott.*   Sr. Lectr., Strategic Management

Thompson, R. S., BSc *Hull*, MA *Newcastle(UK)*, PhD *Newcastle(UK)*   Prof., Strategic Management

Tynan, A. C., BSc *Sur.*, PhD *Strath.*   Prof., Marketing

Ucbasaran, D., BA *Nott.*, MA *Nott.*, PhD *Nott.*   Sr. Lectr., Entrepreneurship

Wastell, D. G., BSc *Durh.*, PhD *Durh.*   Prof., Information Systems

Watson, T., BA *Lond.*, MSc *Lough.*, PhD *Nott.*   Prof., Organisational Behaviour

Westhead, P., BA *Wales*, PhD *Wales*   Prof., Entrepreneurship

Winklhofer, A. M., PhD *Wales*   Reader, Marketing

Woods, M., BCom *Liv.*, MSc *Lond.*   Sr. Lectr., Accounting and Finance

Wright, D. M., BA *CNAA*, MA *Durh.*, PhD *Nott.*, FRSA   Prof., Financial Studies

Other Staff: 30 Sp. Profs.; 31 Lectrs.; 9 Sp. Lectrs.; 10 Teaching Fellows/Univ. Teachers

Research: corporate and social responsibility; entrepreneurship, marketing and industrial economics; insurance and risk management; organisational behaviour and human resource management; strategy and information systems

Christel DeHaan Tourism and Travel Research Institute

Tel: (0115) 846 6606 Fax: (0115) 846 6612
E-mail: ttri@nottingham.ac.uk

Ennew, C., BA *Camb.*, PhD *Nott.*, FRSA   Prof., Marketing

Sinclair, M. T., BA *Reading*, MA *Reading*, PhD *Reading*   Prof., Economics of Tourism; Dir.*

Other Staff: 1 Sp. Prof.; 3 Lectrs.; 2 Res. Fellows; 1 Res. Assoc.

Research: tourism and sustainability; tourism business; tourism impacts; tourism management; tourism marketing

Pharmacy

Tel: (0115) 951 5100 Fax: (0115) 951 5102
E-mail: pharmacy-enquiries@nottingham.ac.uk

Alexander, M., BSc *Sheff.*, PhD *Sheff.*   Reader

Anderson, C. W., BPharm *Wales*, PhD *Lond.*   Prof., Social Pharmacy

Barrett, D. A., BSc *Lond.*, PhD *Birm.*   Sr. Lectr.

Briggs, D., BSc *Durh.*, PhD *Durh.*, DSc *Durh.*   Prof.†, Surface Chemical Analysis

Chan, W. C., BPharm *Lond.*, PhD *Nott.*   Sr. Lectr.

Davies, M. C., BSc *CNAA*, PhD *Lond.*   Prof., Biomedical Surface Chemistry

Emsley, J., BSc *Nott.*, PhD *Lond.*   Reader

Falcone, F., MSc PhD   Sr. Lectr.

Garnett, M. C., BSc *Wales*, PhD *Lond.*   Sr. Lectr.

Heery, D., BSc MSc PhD   Prof., Pharmaceutical Systems Biology

Laughton, C. A., MA *Oxf.*, DPhil *Oxf.*   Reader

Melia, C. D., BSc *CNAA*, PhD *Nott.*   Sr. Lectr.

Pritchard, D., BSc *Wales*, MSc *Birm.*, PhD *Birm.*   Prof., Immunoparasitology

Roberts, C. J., BSc *Lond.*, PhD *Lond.*   Prof., Pharmaceutical Nanotechnology

Shakesheff, K., BPharm *Nott.*, PhD *Nott.*   Prof., Advanced Drug Delivery

Stevens, Malcolm F. G., OBE, BPharm *Nott.*, PhD *Nott.*, DSc *Nott.*, FRSChem   Prof., Experimental Cancer Chemotherapy

Tendler, S. J. B., BSc *Manc.*, PhD *Aston*, FRPharmS, FRSChem   Prof., Biophysical Chemistry; Head*

Williams, P. M., BPharm *Nott.*, PhD *Nott.*   Reader, Theoretical Biophysics

Willis, A., BSc *Kent*, PhD *Lond.*   Prof., Cancer Cell Biology

Other Staff: 9 Sp. Profs.; 1 Assoc. Sr. Lectr.; 14 Lectrs.; 15 Sp. Lectrs.; 13 Visiting Lectrs.; 5 Teacher Practitioners; 1 Sr. Res. Officer

Research: advanced drug delivery; analytical bioscience; biophysics and surface analysis; medicinal chemistry and structural biology; molecular and cellular science

Physics and Astronomy

Tel: (0115) 951 5183 Fax: (0115) 951 5180

Aragon-Salamanca, A., BSc *Madrid*, PhD *Durh.*   Reader, Astronomy

Benedict, K. A., BSc *Lond.*, PhD *S'ton.*   Sr. Lectr.

Beton, P. H., BA *Camb.*, PhD *Manc.*   Prof., Physics; Head*

Bowley, R. M., BA *Camb.*, PhD *Camb.*   Prof., Physics

Bowtell, R. W., BA *Camb.*, PhD *Nott.*   Prof., Physics

Coles, P., MA *Camb.*, DPhil *Sus.*, FRAS   Prof., Astrophysics

Copeland, E. J., BSc *Lond.*, PhD *Newcastle(UK)*   Prof., Physics

Dunn, J. L., BSc *Liv.*, PhD *Nott.*   Reader, Theoretical Physics

Eaves, L., CBE, MA *Oxf.*, DPhil *Oxf.*   FRS   Lancashire-Spencer Prof., Physics

Foxon, C. T., BSc *Lond.*, PhD *Lond.*   Prof., Physics

Fromhold, T. M., BSc *Durh.*, PhD *Nott.*   Prof., Physics

Gallagher, B. L., BSc *Leeds*, PhD *Leeds*   Prof., Physics

Gowland, P. A., BSc *Lond.*, MSc *Lond.*, PhD *Lond.*   Prof.

Horsewill, A. J., BSc *Sheff.*, PhD *Sheff.*   Reader, Experimental Physics

Kent, A. J., BSc *Lond.*, PhD *Lond.*   Reader, Experimental Physics

King, P. J., MA *Oxf.*, DPhil *Oxf.*   Prof., Experimental Physics

Maddox, S. J., BA *Camb.*, PhD *Camb.*   Reader, Astronomy

Maxwell, K. J., BSc *Belf.*, DPhil *Oxf.*   Sr. Lectr.

Mellor, C. J., BSc *Birm.*, PhD *Birm.*   Sr. Lectr.

Merrifield, M. R., BA *Oxf.*, AM *Harv.*, PhD *Harv.*   Prof., Astronomy

Moriarty, P. J., BSc PhD   Prof., Experimental Physics

Morris, P. G., MA *Camb.*, PhD *Nott.*   Prof.

Owers-Bradley, J. R., BSc *Sus.*, DPhil *Sus.*   Reader, Experimental Physics

Other Staff: 3 Sp. Profs.; 12 Lectrs.; 3 Res. Fellows; 2 Res. Officers; 2 Sr. Exper. Officers

Research: condensed matter theory; low-dimensional semiconductor structures; nanoscience and technology; nitride semiconductors (growth and properties); nuclear magnetic resonance (imaging, spectroscopy and microscopy)

Politics

Tel: (0115) 951 4862 Fax: (0115) 951 4859
E-mail: politics@nottingham.ac.uk

Aldrich, R. J., BA *Manc.*, MLitt *Aberd.*, PhD *Camb.*   Prof.

Bieler, A., MA *Manc.*, PhD *Warw.*   Sr. Lectr.

Cowley, P. J., BSc *Brun.*, MA *Hull*   Reader, Parliamentary Government

Danchev, A., BA *Oxf.*, PhD *Lond.*   Prof.

Denham, A. R. J., BA *CNAA*, MA *Kent*, PhD *S'ton.*   Reader, Government

Forbes, I. G., BA *Adel.*, MA *Adel.*, PhD *E.Anglia*, FRSA   Prof.

Heywood, P. M., MA *Edin.*, MSc(Econ) *Lond.*, PhD *Lond.*   Sir Francis Hill Prof., European Politics

Humphrey, M. I., BSc *Bath*, MPhil *Oxf.*, DPhil *Oxf.*   Sr. Lectr.

Pierson, C. C., MA *Camb.*, PhD *Camb.*   Prof.; Head*

Rawnsley, G. D., BA *Leeds*, PhD *Leeds*   Sr. Lectr.

Rees, G. W., BA *Lanc.*, MSc *S'ton.*, PhD *S'ton.*   Reader

Sargisson, L. M., BA *Keele*, PhD *Keele*   Sr. Lectr.

Tormey, S. F., BA *Wales*, PhD *Wales*   Sr. Lectr.

Other Staff: 12 Lectrs.; 1 Sp. Res. Fellow†

Research: Asia-Pacific (civil society, politics and media); comparative politics; Europe (defence, economic and monetary union, integration); international relations; political theory

Psychology

Tel: (0115) 951 5361 Fax: (0115) 951 5324
E-mail: enquiries@psychology.nottingham.ac.uk

Ainsworth, S. E., BSc *Portsmouth*, MSc *Sus.*, PhD *Nott.*   Sr. Lectr.

Cassaday, H. J., BA *Oxf.*, PhD *Lond.*   Sr. Lectr.

Clarke, D. D., MA *Camb.*, MA *Oxf.*, PhD *Camb.*, DPhil *Oxf.*, FBPsS   Prof.; Head*

Ferguson, E., BSc *York(UK)*, PhD *Nott.*   Prof., Health Psychology

Jackson, S. R., BA *Open(UK)*, PhD *Camb.*   Prof., Cognitive Neuroscience

Ledgeway, T., BA *Nott.*, PhD *Nott.*   Sr. Lectr.

McGraw, P., BSc *Glas.*, PhD *Glas.*   Reader

Mitchell, P. L., BA *Liv.*, PhD *Liv.*   Prof., Developmental Psychology

Moran, P. M., BA *N.U.I.*, PhD *N.U.I.*   Reader

O'Malley, Claire E., BA *Leeds*, PhD *Leeds*   Prof., Learning Sciences

Paus, T., MD *Brno*, PhD *Prague*   Prof., Developmental Cognitive Neuroscience

Rorden, C. R., BA *Calif.*, PhD *Camb.*   Reader, Cognitive Neuroscience

Schurmann, M., MD *Marburg*, PhD *T.H.Aachen*
    Reader
Stevens, R. G., BTech *Brun.*, DPhil *Oxf.*   Sr.
    Lectr.
Sunderland, A., BSc *Aberd.*, MPhil *Glas.*, PhD
    Brun.   Reader
Underwood, G. J., BSc *Lond.*, PhD *Sheff.*, DSc
    Lond., FBPsS   Prof., Cognitive Psychology
Wood, D. J., BA *Nott.*, PhD *Nott.*   Prof.
Other Staff: 19 Lectrs.
Research: cognitive and applied psychology;
    cognitive and behavioural neuroscience;
    developmental and educational psychology;
    psychology of health and risk

Sociology and Social Policy

Tel: (0115) 951 5234 Fax: (0115) 951 5232
    E-mail: socspa@nottingham.ac.uk
Aldridge, Alan E., BA *Oxf.*, BPhil *Oxf.*, PhD *Nott.*
    Reader
Aldridge, Meryl E., BScEcon *Wales*, MA *Essex*,
    PhD *Nott.*   Reader, Sociology of News
    Media
Cope, Stephen, BA *Coventry*, MSc(Econ) *Lond.*,
    PhD *Lond.*   Sr. Lectr.
Evetts, Julia E., BA(Econ) *Sheff.*, PhD *Nott.*
    Prof., Sociology; Head*
Fitzpatrick, Tony, BA *Hull*, MA *Hull*, PhD *Edin.*
    Reader, Social and Political Thought
Lymbery, Mark R., BA *Kent*, MA *Leic.*, MPhil
    Leic.   Sr. Lectr.
Manning, Nick P., MA *Camb.*, MPhil *York(UK)*,
    PhD *Kent*   Prof., Social Policy and Sociology
Murphy, Elizabeth A., MA *St And.*, MSc
    Open(UK), PhD *S'ton*.   Prof., Medical
    Sociology
O'Connell Davidson, Julia N., BSc *Bath*, PhD
    Brist.   Prof., Sociology
Parker, Gillian, BA *Liv.*, PhD *Birm.*   Prof.,
    Health and Social Care
Pascall, Gillian, MA *Oxf.*, PhD *Nott.*   Prof.,
    Social Policy
Pilnick, Alison, BPharm *Nott.*, MA *Nott.*, PhD
    Nott.   Sr. Lectr.
Schneider, Justine, MSc *Oxf.*, MSc *Sur.*, PhD *Kent*
    Prof., Mental Health and Social Care
Shaw, Ian, BA *York(UK)*, DPhil *York(UK)*   Prof.,
    Health Policy
Song, Lina, BA *Amoy*, DPhil *Oxf.*   Reader
Stevenson, Nick, BA *Keele*, PhD *Camb.*   Reader,
    Cultural Sociology
Talbot, Colin L., MSc *S.Bank*, PhD *Lond.*   Prof.,
    Public Policy
Walker, Robert L., MSc(Econ) *Lond.*, PhD *Lond.*,
    BSocSci, FRSA   Prof., Social Policy
Wilson, A. Kate, BA *Oxf.*   Prof., Social Work
Other Staff: 6 Lectrs.; 2 Visiting Lectrs.; 9 Res.
    Fellows
Research: culture and citizenship; gender issues
    (domestic violence, family policy, housing,
    welfare theory); health and social care;
    international social policy; professions
    (international regulation, occupations,
    professional work)

MEDICINE AND HEALTH SCIENCES

Tel: (0115) 974 1380 Fax: (0115) 970 9922

Biology

Tel: (0115) 970 9398 Fax: (0115) 970 9906
    E-mail: biology@nottingham.ac.uk
Archer, D. B., MA *Camb.*, PhD *Camb.*   Prof.,
    Microbial Biochemistry
Armour, J. A., BM BCh *Oxf.*, MA *Camb.*, PhD
    Leic.   Prof., Human Genetics
Avery, S., BSc *Dund.*, PhD *Dund.*   Sr. Lectr.
Barnard, C. J., BSc *Liv.*, DPhil *Oxf.*   Prof.,
    Animal Behaviour
Behnke, J. M., BSc *S'ton.*, PhD *Lond.*   Prof.,
    Experimental Parasitology
Bell, D. R., BSc *Sur.*, PhD *Lond.*   Reader,
    Molecular Toxicology
Bradley, J. E., BSc *Hull*, PhD *Lond.*   Prof.,
    Parasitology
Brook, J. D., BSc *Manc.*, PhD *Edin.*   Prof.,
    Human Genetics; Head*
Brookfield, J. F. Y., BA *Oxf.*, PhD *Lond.*   Prof.,
    Evolutionary Genetics

Brown, W. R. A., BA *Camb.*, DPhil *Oxf.*
    Reader
Clarke, B. C., MA *Oxf.*, DPhil *Oxf.*, FRS   Emer.
    Prof., Genetics
Crittenden, P. D., BSc *Lond.*, PhD *Sheff.*   Sr.
    Lectr.
De-Pomerai, D. I. M., BSc *Edin.*, PhD *Lond.*   Sr.
    Lectr.
Duce, I. R., BSc *Wales*, PhD *Wales*   Sr. Lectr.
Gilbert, F. S., BA *Camb.*, PhD *Camb.*   Sr. Lectr.
Glass, R. E., BSc *Manc.*, PhD *Edin.*   Prof.,
    Molecular Biology
Hewitt, J. E., BA *Oxf.*, PhD *Camb.*   Prof.,
    Mammalian Genetics
Johnson, A. D., BA *C.U.N.Y.*, PhD *Purdue*
    Reader, Molecular Embryology
Lloyd, R. G., BSc *Brist.*, DPhil *Sus.*, FRS   Prof.
Lowe, K. C., BSc *Leeds*, MA *Camb.*, PhD *Camb.*,
    FIBiol   Reader
Sablitzky, F., PhD *Cologne*   Prof.
Scotting, P. J., BSc *Warw.*, PhD *Lond.*   Sr. Lectr.
Sharp, P. M., BSc *Edin.*, PhD *Edin.*   Prof.
Sockett, R. E., BSc *Leeds*, PhD *Lond.*   Reader,
    Bacterial Genetics
Usherwood, P. N. R., BSc *Wales*, PhD *Glas.*
    Prof. Emer., Zoology
Other Staff: 3 Sp. Profs.; 7 Lectrs.; 5 Sp.
    Lectrs.; 1 Res. Fellow; 1 Indust. Fellow
Research: animal behaviour and ecology; human
    genetics; molecular toxicology; parasite
    biology and immunogenetics; population
    and evolutionary genetics

Biomedical Sciences

Tel: (0115) 970 9480 Fax: (0115) 970 9259
    E-mail: hazel.binks@nottingham.ac.uk
Alexander, S. P. H., BSc *Bath*, PhD *Brist.*   Sr.
    Lectr.
Bates, T. E., BSc *Sheff.*, PhD *Lond.*   Sr. Lectr.
Bennett, A. J., BSc *Nott.*, PhD *Cran.IT*   Sr. Lectr.
Bennett, G. W., MSc *Lond.*, PhD *Lond.*   Reader,
    Neuropharmacology
Bennett, T., BSc *Nott.*, PhD *Melb.*   Prof.,
    Physiology
Billett, M. A., BSc *Brist.*, PhD *Brist.*   Sr. Lectr.
Brown, A. M., BSc *Dund.*, PhD *Manc.*   Sr. Lectr.
Brown, S., BSc *Nott.*, PhD *Nott.*   Sr. Lectr.
Chapman, V., BSc *Lond.*, PhD *Lond.*   Reader,
    Neuroscience
Clothier, BSc *Lond.*, PhD *E.Anglia*   Reader
Dunn, W. R., BSc *Glas.*, PhD *Glas.*   Reader,
    Cardiovascular Sciences
Ebling, F. J. P., BSc *Brist.*, PhD *Edin.*   Reader
Fone, K. C. F., BSc *Liv.*, PhD *Liv.*   Reader,
    Neuroscience and Neuropharmacology
Fry, J. R., BSc *Sur.*, PhD *Sur.*   Reader,
    Molecular Toxicology
Gardiner, Sheila M., BSc *Nott.*, PhD *Nott.*, DSc
    Nott.   Prof., Cardiovascular Physiology
Greenhaff, P. L., BSc *Salf.*, PhD *Aberd.*   Prof.,
    Muscle Metabolism
Hill, S. J., BSc *Brist.*, PhD *Camb.*   Prof.,
    Molecular Pharmacology
Kendall, D. A., BPharm *Nott.*, PhD *CNAA*
    Prof., Cellular Pharmacology; Head*
Leach, L., BSc *Lond.*, PhD *Lond.*   Sr. Lectr.
Macdonald, I. A., BSc *Lond.*, PhD *Lond.*   Prof.,
    Metabolic Physiology
Marsden, C. A., BSc *Lond.*, MSc *S'ton.*, PhD *S'ton.*,
    DSc *S'ton.*   Prof., Neuropharmacology
Mason, R., BSc *S'ton.*, PhD *Keele*   Sr. Lectr.
Mayer, R. J., BSc *Birm.*, PhD *Birm.*, DSc *Nott.*,
    FRCPath   Prof., Molecular Cell Biology
Mayhew, T. M., BA *Oxf.*, PhD *Sheff.*   Prof.,
    Human Morphology
McLaughlin, D. P., BSc *Glas.*, PhD *Glas.*   Sr.
    Lectr.
Middleton, B., MA *Camb.*, PhD *Camb.*   Sr.
    Lectr.
Monkhouse, W. S., MB BChir *Camb.*, MA *Camb.*,
    PhD *Nott.*   Sr. Lectr.
Murphy, S., BSc *Lond.*, MSc *Lond.*, PhD *Open(UK)*
    Prof., Neuroscience and Pharmacology
O'Shea, P. S., BSc *Brist.*, PhD *Brist.*   Prof.,
    Biophysics and Biomaterials
Parker, T. L., BSc *Wales*, PhD *Wales*   Sr. Lectr.
Pillay, T. S., MB ChB *Natal*, PhD *Camb.*, FRCPath
    Sr. Lectr.

Pratten, M. K., BSc *Sheff.*, PhD *Sheff.*   Sr. Lectr.
Ralevic, V., BSc *Bath*, PhD *Lond.*
Randall, M. D., BA *Camb.*, MPhil *Camb.*, PhD
    Camb.   Sr. Lectr.
Ray, D. E., BSc *Lond.*, PhD *Lond.*
Rennie, M. J., BSc *Hull*, MSc *Manc.*, PhD *Glas.*
    Prof.
Shaw, P. E., BSc *Heidel.*, PhD *Heidel.*   Prof.,
    Biochemistry
White, D. A., BSc *Birm.*, PhD *Birm.*, DSc *Nott.*
    Reader, Medical Biochemistry
Wilson, V. G., BSc *Aston*, PhD *Aston*   Reader
Other Staff: 6 Sp. Profs.; 13 Lectrs.; 9 Sp.
    Lectrs.

Community Health Sciences

Tel: (0115) 846 6901 Fax: (0115) 846 6904

Epidemiology and Public Health, Division of

Tel: (0115) 970 9330 Fax: (0115) 970 9316
    E-mail: pat.drane@nottingham.ac.uk
Britton, J. R., BSc *Lond.*, MSc *Lond.*, MD *Lond.*,
    FRCP   Prof., Epidemiology; Head*
Byass, P., BSc *Nott.*, MSc *CNAA*, PhD *Nott.*   Sr.
    Lectr.
Fogarty, A., DM MSc   Clin. Sr. Lectr.
Hubbard, R., BSc *Lond.*, MSc *Lond.*, DM *Nott.*
    Reader, Clinical Epidemiology
Logan, R. F. A., BSc *Edin.*, MB ChB *Edin.*, MSc
    Lond., FRCP   Prof., Clinical Epidemiology
Madeley, R. J., MB BS *Lond.*, MSc *Lond.*, DM
    Nott.   Prof., Community Medicine and
    Epidemiology
Muir, K. R., BSc *CNAA*, PhD *Birm.*   Prof.,
    Epidemiology
Wilkinson, R. G., BSc *Lond.*, MA *Penn.*, MMedSci
    Nott.   Prof., Social Epidemiology
Other Staff: 1 Sp. Prof.; 4 Lectrs.; 1 Clin.
    Reader; 1 Clin. Sr. Lectr.; 1 Clin. Lectr.

Physiotherapy, Division of

Tel: (0115) 840 4880 Fax: (0115) 840 4893
Mockett, S. P., MPhil *Nott.*   Sr. Lectr.; Deputy
    Head
Pope, G. D., MPhil *Nott.*   Sr. Lectr.; Head*
Other Staff: 10 Lectrs.; 4 Clin. Link Tutors; 3
    Lectrs./Practitioners†

Primary Care, Division of

Tel: (0115) 970 9387 Fax: (0115) 970 9389
    E-mail: allison.green@nottingham.ac.uk
Anderson, C., MB BChir *Camb.*, MA *Camb.*   Sr.
    Lectr.
Avery, A. J., BMedSci *Sheff.*, MB ChB *Sheff.*
    Prof., Primary Health Care; Head*
Churchill, R. D., BM BS *Nott.*, BMedSci *Nott.*,
    BSc *Sur.*, MSc *Sur.*   Sr. Lectr.
Coleman, T., MB BCh *Leeds*, MD *Leic.*   Sr. Lectr.
Coupland, C. A. C., BSc *Exe.*, MSc *Reading*   Sr.
    Lectr.
Faull, C. M., BMedSci *Newcastle(UK)*, MB BS
    Newcastle(UK), MD *Newcastle(UK)*, FRCP   Sr.
    Lectr.
Fortnum, Heather M., BM BS *Nott.*, BMedSci
    Nott., DM *Nott.*   Sr. Lectr.
Hampshire, A. J., BM BS *Nott.*, BMedSci *Nott.*,
    MEd *Nott.*   Sr. Lectr.
Hippisley-Cox, J., MB ChB *Sheff.*, DM   Prof.,
    Clinical Epidemiology
Kai, J. P., MB BS *Newcastle(UK)*, MD
    Newcastle(UK), FRCGP   Prof., General
    Practice
Kendrick, D., DM *Nott.*, BM   Sr. Lectr.
Pringle, M. A. L., CBE, MD *Lond.*, FRCGP, FRCP
    Prof.
Silcocks, P. B. S., BM BCh *Oxf.*, BSc *Brist.*, MSc
    Lond., FFPHM, FRCPath   Sr. Lectr.
Other Staff: 22 Lectrs.

Psychiatry, Division of

Tel: (0115) 993 4512 Fax: (0115) 955 5352
Bradshaw, C. M., BSc PhD, FBPsS   Prof.,
    Neuropsychology
Davies, S., MB ChB *Manc.*, MBA *Nott.*   Sr. Lectr.
Doody, G. A., MB BS *Lond.*, MPhil *Edin.*, MD
    Edin.   Sr. Lectr.

Duggan, C., BSc N.U.I., MD PhD, FRCPsych
Prof., Forensic Mental Health

Garrud, P., BA Oxf., MA Oxf., DPhil Oxf. Sr.
Lectr.

Glazebrook, C. P., BA Newcastle(UK), PhD Nott.
Reader, Health Psychology

Healy, E., MB BCh BAO Trinity(Dub.) Sr. Lectr.

Hollis, Chris P., BSc Lond., MB BS Lond., PhD
Lond. Prof., Child and Adolescent
Psychiatry; Head*

Jackson, G. M., BA Open(UK), BEd Reading, PhD
Sheff. Reader

Jones, R. G., MB ChB Manc., DPM, FRCPsych
Sr. Lectr., Old Age Psychiatry

Leask, S. J., MB BCh Camb., MA Camb., MD
Nott. Sr. Lectr.

Liddle, P. F., BM BCh Oxf., PhD Flin. Prof.,
Psychiatry

Middleton, H. C., MA Camb., MD Camb. Sr.
Lectr.

Park, S. B. G., BA Camb., BM BCh Oxf. Sr.
Lectr.

Other Staff: 1 Lectr.; 3 Clin. Lectrs.

Rehabilitation and Ageing, Division of

Tel: (0115) 970 9408 Fax: (0115) 942 3618
E-mail: joanna.zuranska@nottingham.ac.uk

Clegg, J. A., BSc Aberd., PhD Nott. Sr. Lectr.

Gladman, J. R. F., BSc Birm., MB ChB Birm.
Reader

Phillips, M. F., BSc Wales, BCh Wales, MD Wales,
MB Sr. Lectr.

Standen, P. J., BSc Lond., PhD Leic. Prof.,
Health Psychology and Learning Disabilities;
Head*

Walker, M. F., MPhil Nott., PhD Nott. Sr.
Lectr.

Ward, Christopher D., MB BChir Camb., MD
Camb. Prof., Rehabilitation Medicine

Other Staff: 2 Lectrs.; 1 Clin. Lectr.

Human Development

Tel: (0115) 970 9240 Fax: (0115) 970 9234

Shaw, R. W., MB ChB Birm., MD Birm.,
FRCOG, FRCS Prof.; Head*

Child Health, Division of

Tel: (0115) 970 9255 Fax: (0115) 970 9382

Choonara, I. A., MB ChB Liv., MD Liv. Prof.

Khan, R. N., BSc Greenwich, PhD Oxf. Sr. Lectr.

Loughna, P. V., MD Lond., FRCOG Sr. Lectr.

Marlow, N., BA Oxf., MB BS Lond., MA Oxf.,
DM Oxf. Prof., Neonatal Medicine

McIntyre, J. W., BSc Liv., MB ChB Nott., DM
Nott. Sr. Lectr.

Polnay, L., BSc Lond., MB BS Lond. Prof.,
Community Paediatrics

Rutter, N., BA Camb., MB BChir Camb. Prof.,
Paediatric Medicine

Shaw, R. W., MB ChB Birm., MD Birm.,
FRCOG, FRCS Prof., Obstetrics and
Gynaecology

Stephenson, T. J., BSc Brist., BM BCh Oxf., DM
Nott., FRCP, FRCPCH Prof., Child Health

Symonds, I. M., BM BS Nott., DM Nott. Sr.
Lectr.

Symonds, M. E., BSc Nott., PhD Reading
Reader, Foetal Nutrition and Developmental
Physiology; Head*

Thornton, J. G., MB ChB Leeds, MD Leeds,
FRCOG Prof., Obstetrics and Gynaecology

Vloeberghs, M. H., MD Brussels Sr. Lectr.

Walker, D. A., BMedSci Nott., BM BS Nott.
Reader, Paediatric Oncology

Whitehouse, W. P., BSc Lond., MB BS, FRCP,
FRCPCH Sr. Lectr.

Other Staff: 1 Sp. Prof. (Paed. Audiol.); 2 Sp.
Sr. Lectrs.; 4 Lectrs.

Midwifery, Division of

Tel: (0115) 919 4411 Fax: (0115) 970 0878
E-mail: midwifery-
enquiries@nottingham.ac.uk

Fraser, D. M., MPhil Nott., PhD Nott., BEd
Prof.; Head*

Other Staff: 16 Midwife Teachers; 3 Midwife
Practitioners/Teachers

Obstetrics and Gynaecology, Division of

Tel: (0115) 970 9240 Fax: (0115) 970 9034

Atiomo, W., MB BS Ib., MD Plym. Sr. Lectr.

Broughton Pipkin, Fiona, MA Oxf., DPhil Oxf.,
FRCOG Prof., Perinatal Physiology

Campbell, B. K., BScAgr Syd., PhD Syd. Reader

James, D. K., MA Camb., MD Camb., FRCOG
Prof., Foeto-Maternal Medicine

Johnson, I. R., BSc Lond., MB BS Lond., DM
Nott., FRCOG Prof.; Head*

Maynard, P. V., BSc Wales, PhD Wales Sr.
Lectr.

Perkins, Alan C., BSc Coventry, MSc Leeds, PhD
Nott. Prof., Medical Physics

Ramsay, M. M., BA Camb., MB BChir Camb.,
MA Camb., MD Camb. Sr. Lectr.

Robinson, G., BSc Belf., PhD Belf. Sr. Lectr.

Young, L. E., BSc Aberd., PhD Aberd. Reader,
Molecular Embryology

Other Staff: 3 Sp. Profs.; 4 Lectrs.; 1 Res.
Fellow; 3 Clin. Specialists

Medical and Surgical Sciences

Tel: (0115) 875 4520 Fax: (0115) 970 0739
E-mail: smss-enquiries@nottingham.ac.uk

Academic Radiology, Division of

Tel: (0115) 970 9121 Fax: (0115) 970 9140
E-mail: radiology-
enquiries@nottingham.ac.uk

Auer, D. P., MD Munich Head*

Morgan, P. S., BSc Cant., MSc Lond., PhD Nott.
Sr. Lectr.

Other Staff: 1 Res. Staff

Academic Rheumatology

Tel: (0115) 840 4733 Fax: (0115) 840 4732
E-mail: joanna.ramowski@nottingham.ac.uk

Doherty, M., MA Camb., MD Camb., FRCP
Prof.

Walsh, D. A., PhD Sr. Lectr.

Zhang, W., BSc Sichuan, MSc Sichuan, PhD Nott.
Sr. Lectr.

Other Staff: 5 Res. Staff

Anaesthesia and Intensive Care, Division of

Tel: (0115) 970 9229
E-mail: anaesthesia-
enquiries@nottingham.ac.uk

Aitkenhead, A. R., BSc Edin., MD Edin., FRCA
Prof.; Head*

Hardman, J. G., BM BS Nott., BSc Nott.,
FANZCA, FRCA Sr. Lectr.

Mahajan, R. P., MB BS Meerut, MD, FFARCSI
Reader

Other Staff: 1 Lectr.

Breast Surgery, Division of

Tel: (0115) 962 7951 Fax: (0115) 840 2618
E-mail: breast-surgery-
enquiries@nottingham.ac.uk

Cheung, K. L., MB BS HK, DM Nott., FRCSEd,
FHKAM, FACS Sr. Lectr.

Robertson, J. F. R., BSc Glas., MB ChB Glas.,
MD Glas., FRCSGlas Prof., Surgery; Head*

Other Staff: 2 Lectrs.; 3 Res. Staff

Cardiovascular Medicine, Division of

Tel: (0115) 970 9346 Fax: (0115) 970 9384
E-mail: jacqui.emerson@nottingham.ac.uk

Gray, D., BMedSci Nott., BM BS Nott., MPH
Nott., DM Nott., FRCP Reader, Medicine

Heptinstall, S., MBE, BSc Newcastle(UK), PhD
Newcastle(UK) Prof., Thrombosis and
Haemostasis

Wilcox, R. G., BSc Lond., MB BS Lond., DM
Nott., FRCP Prof.; Acting Head*

Other Staff: 1 Res. Staff

Clinical Neurology, Division of

Tel: (0115) 924 9924 Fax: (0115) 970 9738
E-mail: neurology-
enquiries@nottingham.ac.uk

Constantinescu, C., MD Boston, PhD Penn.
Head*

Other Staff: 2 Res. Staff

Dermatology Unit

Tel: (0115) 924 9924 Fax: (0115) 970 9003
E-mail:
margaret.whittingham@nottingham.ac.uk

Williams, H. C., BSc Lond., MB BS Lond., MSc,
FRCP Prof., Dermato-Epidemiology

Other Staff: 9 Res. Staff

Gastrointestinal Surgery, Division of

Tel: (0115) 970 9245 Fax: (0115) 970 9428
E-mail: surgery-enquiries@nottingham.ac.uk

Larvin, M., BSc Lond., MD Leeds, FRCS Prof.,
Surgery

Lobo, D., MB BS B'lore., MS Panjab, DM Nott.,
FRCS

Lund, J., BMedSci Nott., BM BS Nott., DM Nott.,
FRCS

Rowlands, B. J., MB BS Lond., MD Sheff., FRCS,
FACS, FRCSI, FRCSEd, FRCPSGlas Prof.;
Head*

Scholefield, J. H., ChM Liv., FRCSEd, FRCS
Prof., Surgery

Watson, S. A., BSc Leeds, PhD Nott. Prof., Pre-
Clinical Oncology

Other Staff: 1 Sp. Prof.; 1 Lectr.; 2 Sp. Lectrs.;
2 Res. Staff

Ophthalmology, Division of

Amoaku, Wilfred M., MB ChB Ghana, PhD Belf.,
FRCS Sr. Lectr., Ophthalmology and
Visual Sciences

Dua, H. S., MB BS Lond., PhD Nag., MS MD
Prof., Ophthalmology and Visual Sciences;
Head*

Other Staff: 1 Sp. Prof.; 2 Lectrs.

Orthopaedic and Accident Surgery, Division of

Tel: (0115) 970 9407 Fax: (0115) 849 3282
E-mail: joanne.burkitt@nottingham.ac.uk

Bayston, R., MMedSci Sheff., MSc Lond., PhD
Sheff., FRCPath Sr. Lectr.

Scammell, Bridget E., MB ChB Birm., DM S'ton.,
FRCS, FRCSEd Reader, Orthopaedic
Surgical Sciences; Head*

Wallace, W. A., MB ChB St And., FRCS, FRCSEd
Prof.

Other Staff: 4 Sp. Profs.; 2 Sp. Lectrs.; 2 Res.
Staff

Otorhinolaryngology, Division of

Tel: (0115) 924 9924 Fax: (0115) 970 9748
E-mail: otorhinolaryngology-
enquiries@nottingham.ac.uk

Birchall, J. P., MD Newcastle(UK), FRCS Prof.;
Head*

O'Donoghue, G. M., MB BCh BAO N.U.I.,
MCh, FRCSI, FRCS Prof., Neurotology

Other Staff: 1 Sp. Prof.; 1 Sp. Lectr.

Respiratory Medicine, Division of

Tel: (0115) 840 4772 Fax: (0115) 840 4771
E-mail: deborah.smith@nottingham.ac.uk

Britton, J. R., BSc Lond., MSc Lond., MD Lond.,
FRCP Prof., Epidemiology

Knox, A. J., MB ChB Edin., DM Nott., FRCP
Prof.

Lewis, S. A., BSc Nott., MSc Leic., PhD Nott.
Reader, Medical Statistics

Pang, L., BMed Chongqing, MSc Chongqing, PhD
Nott. Sr. Lectr.

Tattersfield, Anne E., OBE, MD Newcastle(UK),
FRCP Prof.; Head*

Other Staff: 1 Sp. Prof.; 1 Lectr.; 2 Sp. Lectrs.;
10 Res. Staff

Stroke Medicine, Division of

Tel: (0115) 875 4513 Fax: (0115) 875 4506
E-mail: stroke-medicine@nottingham.ac.uk

Bath, P. M. W., MD Lond., FRCP Stroke
Association Prof.; Head*

Other Staff: 2 Res. Staff

Therapeutics and Molecular Medicine, Division of

Tel: (0115) 970 9905 Fax: (0115) 875 4595
E-mail: louise.sabir@nottingham.ac.uk
Hall, I. P., BA Oxf., BM BCh Oxf., MD, FRCP
Prof., Molecular Medicine; Head*
Johnson, S. R., BSc DM Sr. Lectr.
Rubin, P. C., MA Camb., DM Oxf., FRCP Boots
Prof.
Other Staff: 2 Lectrs.

Vascular Medicine, Division of

Tel: (01332) 254966 Fax: (01332) 254968
Donnelly, R., MB ChB Birm., MD Birm., PhD
Glas., FRCP, FRACP Prof.; Head*
Manning, G., MPhil Coventry, PhD Nott. Sr.
Lectr.

Wolfson Digestive Diseases Centre

Tel: (0115) 924 9924 Fax: (0115) 942 2232
E-mail: rosemary.dainty@nottingham.ac.uk
Atherton, J. C., MD Prof.; Head*
Hawkey, C. J., DM Oxf., FRCP Prof.,
Gastrointestinal and Liver Medicine
Mahida, Y. R., MB ChB Liv., MD Liv. Prof.,
Medicine
Ragunath, K., MB BS Madr., MD Madr. Sr.
Lectr.
Spiller, R. C., MD, FRCP Prof.
Other Staff: 4 Lectrs.; 13 Res. Staff

Molecular Medical Sciences

Tel: (0115) 924 9924 Fax: (0115) 970 9233
E-mail: mol-enquiries@nottingham.ac.uk
Research: allergy (dust mite allergens,
immunomodulation); bacterial
pathogenicity (communication and
signalling, methicillin resistance,
staphylococcal and E. coli infections);
genetics (bacterial, human/eukaryotic,
population/evolutionary); oncology
(angiogenesis, stem cell transplantation)

Clinical Chemistry, Division of

Tel: (0115) 970 9166 Fax: (0115) 970 9467
Kalshekar, N., MSc Birm., MD Birm., FRCPath
Prof.; Head*
Morgan, K., BSc Bath, PhD Wales Reader,
Human Molecular Genetics
Other Staff: 1 Sr. Clin. Lectr.

Clinical Oncology, Division of

Tel: (0115) 962 7927 Fax: (0115) 962 7923
E-mail: catherine.douglas-
morgan@nottingham.ac.uk
Durrant, L. G., BSc Manc., PhD Manc. Prof.,
Cancer Immunotherapy
Martin, S. G., BSc Glas., MSc St And., PhD Lond.
Sr. Lectr.
Patel, P., MB BS Lond., PhD Lond., FRCP Prof.;
Head*
Other Staff: 1 Lectr.; 1 Clin. Reader; 1 Clin.
Lectr.

Haematology, Division of

Tel: (0115) 962 7708 Fax: (0115) 962 7742
E-mail: gholling@ncht.org.uk
Russell, N. H., MD Liv., FRCP, FRCPath Prof.;
Head*
Other Staff: 1 Lectr.; 2 Sr. Clin. Lectrs.

Microbiology and Infectious Diseases, Division of

Tel: (0115) 970 9162
E-mail: elaine.richards@nottingham.ac.uk
Ala'Aldeen, D. A., MB ChB Baghdad, MSc Lond.,
PhD Lond. Prof., Clinical Microbiology
Ball, J. K., BSc CNAA, PhD Warw. Sr. Lectr.
Finch, R. G., MB ChB Birm., FRCP, FRCPath,
FFPM Prof., Infectious Diseases
Irving, W. L., MB BChir Camb., MA Camb., PhD
Lond., FRCPath Prof., Virology
James, R., BSc Lond., PhD Lond. Prof.,
Microbiology; Head*

Other Staff: 1 Sp. Prof.; 3 Lectrs.; 1 Sr. Res.
Fellow; 3 Sr. Clin. Lectrs.

Molecular and Clinical Immunology, Division of

Tel: (0115) 970 9162
E-mail: elaine.richards@nottingham.ac.uk
Powell, R. J., MB BS Lond., DM Nott., FRCP,
FRCPath Prof., Clinical Immunology and
Allergy
Robins, R. A., BPharm Nott., PhD Nott. Reader
Sewell, H. F., MB ChB Leic., BDS Birm., MSc
Birm., PhD Birm., Hon. DDS Hon. DSc,
FRCP, FRCPath, FMedSci Prof.,
Immunology
Shakib, F., BSc Baghdad, PhD Birm. Prof.,
Experimental Allergy; Head*
Tighe, P. J., BSc Nott., PhD Nott. Sr. Lectr.
Todd, I., MA Oxf., PhD Lond. Sr. Lectr.
Other Staff: 1 Sp. Prof.; 1 Lectr.; 1 Sp. Lectr.;
1 Clin. Lectr.

Pathology, Division of

Tel: (0115) 970 9169 Fax: (0115) 970 4852
Ellis, I. O., BMedSci Nott., BM BS Nott., FRCPath
Prof., Cancer Pathology
Lowe, J., BMedSci Nott., BM BS Nott., DM Nott.,
FRCPath ILTM Prof., Neuropathology
Other Staff: 1 Sp. Prof. (Tumour Pathol.); 2
Sp. Sr. Lectrs. (Histopathol.)†

Nursing

Tel: (0115) 924 9924 Fax: (0115) 849 3238
E-mail: nursing-enquiries@nottingham.ac.uk
Allcock, Nicholas A., BSc Sur., PhD Nott. Sr.
Lectr.
Anderson, Martin, BA MSc PhD Sr. Lectr.
Arthur, Anthony J., BA E.Lond., PhD Leic. Sr.
Lectr.
Aston, Liz, BSc Open(UK), MRes Sr. Health
Lectr.
Avis, Mark, BA Lond., MSc CNAA Reader
Barker, Janet, BSc PhD Sr. Health Lectr.
Bath-Hextall, Fiona, BSc PhD Sr. Lectr.
Chambers, Derek, BEd PhD Sr. Health Lectr.
Chapple, Mary, MA Lond. Sr. Lectr.
Collier, Jacqueline, BSc Lough., MSc Leic., PhD
Lough. Prof., Health Services Research
Cook, Elaine, BA MSc Sr. Health Lectr.
Cox, Karen, BSc Lond., PhD Nott. Prof., Cancer
and Palliative Care; Head*
Crawford, Paul, BA Birm., PhD Birm. Sr. Lectr.
Davis, Peter, MBE, BEd MA Sr. Health Lectr.
Drake, Mary, BA Open(UK), MBA Lough. Sr.
Health Lectr.
Hall, Carol, BSc PhD Sr. Health Lectr.
Hart, Elizabeth A., BA Keele, PhD Lond. Sr.
Lectr.
Howard, David, MEd Nott.Trent, PhD Nott.Trent
Sr. Health Lectr.
James, Veronica C., MA Aberd., PhD Aberd.
Prof.
Kitching, David, BSc Leeds, MBA Nott. Sr.
Health Lectr.
Middleton, Chris, MA Nott.Trent Sr. Health
Lectr.
Mitchell, Gail, MA Keele Sr. Health Lectr.
Moxham, Eric, MEd Nott., MPhil Nott. Sr.
Health Lectr.
Narayanasamy, Aru, BA MSc MPhil PhD Sr.
Health Lectr.
Owen, Sara, BA E.Lond., BEd S.Bank, PhD Nott.
Reader
Penney, Viv, BSc Lough., MA Lough. Sr. Health
Lectr.
Plant, Nigel, LLB Nott.Trent Sr. Health Lectr.
Porock, Davina, BAppSci W.Aust., MSc Curtin,
PhD E.Cowan Prof., Nursing Practice
Rush, Brenda, BA MSc Sr. Health Lectr.
Wharrad, Heather J., BSc Aston, PhD Nott. Sr.
Lectr.
Other Staff: 5 Sp. Profs.; 29 Lectrs.; 128
Health Lectrs.; 1 Principal Res. Fellow; 1 Sr.
Res. Fellow; 13 Res. Assocs.
Vacant Posts: 2 Profs.; 1 Sr. Lectr./Lectr.; 3
Lectrs./Health Lectrs.

Research: cancer and palliative care; child and
maternal health; education and health
informatics; mental health

SPECIAL CENTRES, ETC

Asia-Pacific Studies, Institute of

Tel: (0115) 951 4862 Fax: (0115) 951 4859
Rawnsley, G. D., BA Leeds, PhD Leeds Dir.*

Building Technology, Institute of

Riffat, S. B., BSc Oxf., MSc Oxf., DPhil Oxf., DSc
Oxf., FIMechE Prof.; Dir.*

Cell Signalling, Institute of

Tel: (0115) 919 4440 Fax: (0115) 919 4493
Hill, S. J., BSc Brist., PhD Camb. Prof.; Head*
Murphy, S., BSc Lond., MSc Lond., PhD Open(UK)
Prof., Neuroscience and Pharmacology
Pillay, T. S., MB ChB Natal, PhD Camb., FRCPath
Sr. Lectr.
Other Staff: 2 Lectrs.; 2 Chief Experimental
Officers; 1 Independent Res. Fellows; 1
Wellcome Trust Res. Career Dev. Fellow

Conflict and Security Law, Centre for

Tel: (0115) 951 5700 Fax: (0115) 951 5696
White, N. D., MA Oxf., PhD Nott. Prof.,
International Organisations

Contemporary Chinese Studies, Institute of

Tel: (0115) 846 6322 Fax: (0115) 846 6324
E-mail: chinese.studies@nottingham.ac.uk
Marton, A. M., BSc Br.Col., MA Vic.(BC), PhD
Br.Col. Dir.*
Sargeson, S. A., BA Murd., PhD Murd. Sr. Lectr.
Sheehan, J., BA Camb., PhD Lond. Sr. Lectr.
Other Staff: 1 Lectr.

Corporate Social Responsibility, International Centre for

Tel: (0115) 846 6976 Fax: (0115) 846 6667
E-mail: iccsr@nottingham.ac.uk
Chapple, W., BA Nott., PhD Nott. Co-Dir.*
Crane, A., BSc Warw., PhD Nott. Prof.,
Business Ethics
Moon, J. W., BA Exe., PhD Exe. Prof.; Co-
Dir.*
Owen, D. L., BA Kent Prof., Social and
Environmental Accounting
Research: business ethics; corporate social
responsibility and comparative business
systems; corporate social responsibility and
governance; economics of corporate social
responsibility; theories of corporate social
responsibility

Critical Theory and Cultural Studies, Postgraduate School of

Tel: (0115) 951 4850 Fax: (0115) 951 4827
E-mail: critical-theory-
enquiries@nottingham.ac.uk
Daly, M. M., MA Glas., DPhil Oxf. Dir.*
Simons, J. H., BA Manc., MA Jerusalem, PhD
Jerusalem Sr. Lectr.

D. H. Lawrence Research Centre

Preston, P. J. D., BA Nott., MA Nott., FRSA
Dir.*

Decision Research and Experimental Economics, Centre for (CeDEx)

Starmer, C. V., BA Birm., MA E.Anglia, PhD
E.Anglia Prof.; Dir.*

Economic Development and International Trade, Centre for Research in

Morrissey, W. O., BA Trinity(Dub.), MSc Bath,
PhD Bath Prof.; Dir.*

Economic Modelling, Experian Centre for

Fax: (0115) 951 4159
E-mail: economics@nottingham.ac.uk
Disney, R. F., BA Camb., MA Sus. Prof.; Dir.*

Other Staff: 1 Res. Fellow
Research: corporate finance; economics of credit markets; household debt

Engineering Surveying and Space Geodesy, Institute of

E-mail: iessg@nottingham.ac.uk

Bingley, R. M., BEng Nott., PhD Nott.   Sr. Lectr.

Dodson, A. H., BSc Nott., PhD Nott., DSc Nott., FRAS, FRIN, FICE, FIAG   Prof., Geodesy

Moore, T., BSc Nott., PhD Nott., FRAS   Prof., Satellite Navigation; Dir.*

Roberts, G. W., BEng Nott., PhD Nott.   Sr. Lectr.

Smith, M. J., BSc Lond., MSc Lond., PhD Lond., FRICS   Sr. Lectr.

Other Staff: 4 Sp. Profs.; 1 Lectr.; 4 Sp. Lectrs.; 3 Sr. Res. Fellows; 3 Res. Fellows; 3 Res. Assocs.; 1 Principal Res. Officer; 2 Exper. Officers; 1 Lectr.†

Research: remote measurement systems (environmental and engineering applications); satellite navigation systems

Enterprise and Innovation, University of Nottingham Institute for (UNIEI)

Tel: (0115) 846 6609 Fax: (0115) 846 6650
E-mail: unieienquiries@nottingham.ac.uk

Binks, M. R., BA Durh., PhD Nott.   Prof.; Dir.*

Enterprise Systems Research, Centre for

Tel: (0115) 846 6687 Fax: (0115) 846 6667
E-mail: cesr@nottingham.ac.uk

Huang, J., LLB Warw., MBA Warw., PhD Warw.   Sr. Lectr., Information Technology/Strategy; Dir.*

Research: customer relationship management; enterprise knowledge management; enterprise resource planning systems; enterprise systems in the public sector; retailing and future technology

Environmental Law, Centre for

Tel: (0115) 951 5700 Fax: (0115) 951 5696

Davies, P. G. G., LLB Essex, LLM Nott.   Dir.*

Environmental Management, Centre for

Haines-Young, R. H., BSc Sus., MA Nott., PhD Lond., FRICS   Prof.; Dir.*

Environmental Science Institute

Laybourn-Parry, J., BSc Reading, MSc Wales, PhD Stir., DSc Reading   Dir.*

Europe Asia Business Research, Centre for

Tel: +603 2148 0171 Fax: +603 245 7297
E-mail: amy.justin@unim.nottingham.ac.uk

Gow, I., MA Edin., PhD Sheff., FRSA   Prof., Asian Business; Co-Dir.*

Kuk, G., BA Leeds, PhD Nott.   Deputy Dir.

Other Staff: 1 Assoc. Prof.; 4 Res. Fellows; 6 Researchers

Research: Asian economic development; corporate social responsibility in Asia; electronic government; foreign direct investment; open source software and entrepreneurship

European Governance, Centre for

Tel: (0115) 951 4862 Fax: (0115) 951 4859
E-mail: catherine.fieschi@nottingham.ac.uk

No staff at present

Film Studies, Institute of

Tel: (0115) 951 4261 Fax: (0115) 951 4270

Pearson, R. E., BA Duke, MPhil Yale, PhD N.Y.   Prof.

Other Staff: 5 Lectrs.

Research: contemporary Hollywood; film and television audiences; film and television industries; media and memory/history

Genetics, Biorisks and Society, Institute for the Study of

Dingwall, R. W. J., MA Camb., PhD Aberd.   Prof., Sociology; Dir.*

Martin, P. A., BA Camb., MSc S.Bank, DPhil Sus.   Sr. Lectr.

Genetics, Institute of

Tel: (0115) 849 3263 Fax: (0115) 970 9906
E-mail: genetics-enquiries@nottingham.ac.uk

Archer, D. B., MA Camb., PhD Camb.   Prof., Microbial Biochemistry

Armour, J. A., BM BCh Oxf., MA Camb., PhD Leic.   Prof., Human Genetics

Avery, S., BSc Dund., PhD Dund.   Sr. Lectr.

Brook, J. D., BSc Manc., PhD Edin.   Prof., Human Genetics; Dir.*

Brookfield, J. F. Y., BA Oxf., PhD Lond.   Prof., Evolutionary Genetics

Brown, W. R. A., BA Camb., DPhil Oxf.   Reader

Clarke, B. C., MA Oxf., DPhil Oxf., FRS   Emer. Prof.

Crittenden, P. D., BSc Lond., PhD Sheff.   Sr. Lectr.

De-Pomerai, D. I. M., BSc Edin., PhD Lond.   Sr. Lectr.

Hewitt, J. E., BA Oxf., PhD Camb.   Prof., Mammalian Genetics

Johnson, A. D., BA C.U.N.Y., PhD Purdue   Reader, Molecular Embryology

Kalshekar, N., MSc Birm., MD Birm., FRCPath   Prof.

Lloyd, R. G., BSc Brist., DPhil Sus., FRS   Prof.

Lowe, K. C., BSc Leeds, MA Camb., PhD Camb., FIBiol   Reader

Morgan, K., BSc Bath, PhD Wales   Reader, Human Molecular Genetics

Morgan, L. J., MB ChB Sheff., MD Nott.   Sr. Lectr.

Sablitzky, F., PhD Cologne   Prof.

Scotting, P. J., BSc Warw., PhD Lond.   Sr. Lectr.

Sharp, P. M., BSc Edin., PhD Edin.   Prof.

Sockett, R. E., BSc Leeds, PhD Lond.   Reader, Bacterial Genetics

Young, L. E., BSc Aberd., PhD Aberd.   Reader, Molecular Embryology

Other Staff: 5 Lectrs.; 4 Res. Fellows

Research: developmental genetics and gene control; fungal biology and genetics; human genetics; molecular microbiology and genome dynamics; population and evolutionary genetics

Globalisation and Economic Policy, Leverhulme Centre for Research on

Fax: (0115) 951 5552
E-mail: sue.berry@nottingham.ac.uk

Greenaway, D., BSc(Econ) Lond., MCom Liv., DLitt Nott.   Prof.; Dir.*

Research: China and the world economy; globalisation and labour markets; globalisation, productivity and technology; trade theory and methodology

Hearing Research, Medical Research Council Institute of

Tel: (0115) 922 3431 Fax: (0115) 951 8503
E-mail: enquiries@ihr.mrc.ac.uk

Hall, D., BSc Brun., PhD Birm.

Krumbholz, K., PhD Munich

Moore, D., BSc Monash, PhD Monash   Dir.*

Palmer, A. R., BSc Birm., PhD Keele   Asst. Dir.; Sp. Prof., Neuroscience

Sumner, C. J., BEng Lond., MSc Lond., PhD Lond.

Thomas, S., PhD St And., BSc

Other Staff: 9 Scientists

Human Rights Law Centre

Tel: (0115) 846 6309 Fax: (0115) 846 6579

Harris, D., CMG, LLM Lond., PhD Lond.   Co-Dir.*

O'Flaherty, M., BCL N.U.I., BPh Greg., STB Greg., MA Amst., MPhil Amst.

Humanities Research Centre

Tel: (0115) 951 4838 Fax: (0115) 951 4818

Geary, R. J., MA Camb., PhD Camb.   Prof.; Dir.*

Industrial Mathematical Modelling, Centre for

Tel: (0115) 951 3846 Fax: (0115) 951 3837
E-mail: john.billingham@nottingham.ac.uk

Billingham, J., BA Camb., PhD E.Anglia   Prof., Theoretical Mechanics; Dir.*

Other Staff: 3 Profs.; 3 Sr. Lectrs.; 3 Lectrs.

Research: acoustic electromagnetism and superconductivity; fluid and plasma dynamics; heat and mass transport (reaction-diffusion theory); semiconductor and optoelectronic devices; solid mechanics (composites and fibre-reinforced materials)

Infections, Immunity and Inflammation, Institute of

Tel: (0115) 846 7950 Fax: (0115) 846 7951
E-mail: diane.mitchell@nottingham.ac.uk

Camara Garcia, M. M., BSc Madrid, PhD Leic.   Sr. Lectr.

Minton, N. P., BSc Wales, PhD Wales   Prof., Applied Molecular Microbiology

Williams, P., BPharm Nott., PhD Aston   Dir.*

Other Staff: 3 Lectrs.; 2 Sr. Res. Fellows

Learning and Teaching in Higher Education, Institute of Research into (IRLTHE)

Tel: (0115) 951 4498 Fax: (0115) 951 4475
E-mail: carole.mallia@nottingham.ac.uk

Murphy, Roger J. L., BSc St And., PhD St And.   Prof.; Dir.*

Other Staff: 2 Sr. Lectrs.; 1 Res. Fellow

Research: e-learning; problem-based learning; visual learning

Macromolecular Hydrodynamics, National Centre for (BBSRC/EPSRC)

Harding, S. E., MA Oxf., PhD Leic., DSc Oxf.   Prof., Physical Biochemistry; Dir.*

Rowe, A. J., MA Camb., PhD Camb.   Special Prof., Biomolecular Technology

Other Staff: 1 Lectr.; 2 Res. Fellows

Management Buy-Out Research, Centre for

Tel: (0115) 951 5493 Fax: (0115) 951 5204
E-mail: karen.tune@nottingham.ac.uk

Burrows, A., BA Oxf., MBA Nott.   Dir.*

Wright, D. M., BA CNAA, MA Durh., PhD Nott., FRSA   Prof.

Other Staff: 2 Res. Fellows

Research: international dimensions of entrepreneurial management; management buy-outs and buy-ins; private equity and venture capital; serial entrepreneurs and business angels; university spin-outs

Materials Technology, University of Nottingham Institute for

Grant, D. M., BSc York(UK), PhD Open(UK)   Prof.; Dir.*

Mathematical Medicine, Centre for

Tel: (0115) 951 3852 Fax: (0115) 951 3837
E-mail: helen.byrne@nottingham.ac.uk

Byrne, H. M., MA Camb., MSc Oxf., DPhil Oxf.   Prof.; Dir.*

Other Staff: 7 Profs.; 4 Readers; 4 Sr. Lectrs.; 9 Postdoctoral Res. Fellows

Research: epidemic modelling and statistical shape analysis; physiological fluid mechanics and biomechanics; signalling in biological networks; theoretical neuroscience; tumour and tissue growth and development biology

Mediaeval Studies, Institute for

Balzaretti, R., BA Lond., PhD Lond.   Sr. Lectr.

Mixed Reality Laboratory

Tel: (0115) 846 6780 Fax: (0115) 846 6416
E-mail: hazel@cs.nott.ac.uk
Benford, S. D., BSc Nott., PhD Nott.   Prof.;
Dir.*
Greenhalgh, C. M., BA Camb., PhD Nott.   Prof.,
Computer Science
Rodden, T., BSc Strath., PhD Lanc.   Prof.,
Computer Science

Modern Cultural Studies, Institute of

Hewitt, Nicholas, BA Hull, PhD Hull   Dir.*

Nottingham Arabidopsis Stock Centre

May, S., BSc Sus., DPhil Sus.   Dir.*

Occupational Ergonomics, Institute for

Tel: (0115) 951 4041 Fax: (0115) 846 6771
Wilson, J. R., BTech Lough., MSc Lough., PhD
Birm.   Dir.*
Other Staff: 2 Lectrs.; 7 Sr. Consultants/
Consultants/Researchers

Optimisation Laboratory, Interdisciplinary

Burke, E. K., BEd Leeds, MSc Leeds, PhD Leeds
Prof.; Dir.*

Public Leadership and Management, Centre for

Tel: (0115) 846 6674 Fax: (0115) 846 6667
E-mail: susan.morgan@nottingham.ac.uk
Boyett, I., MBA Nott., PhD Sheff.Hallam   Co-
Dir.*
Currie, G., BSc Aston, MSc Aston, PhD Nott.
Prof., Public Services Management; Co-Dir.*
Humphreys, M., BSc Leeds, MBA Nott., PhD Nott.
Sr. Lectr., Organisational Behaviour
Research: knowledge management in the NHS;
public/private initiatives and de-regulation;
role of leadership in education; role of
middle managers in the public sector;
teamworking within the Inland Revenue

Public Procurement Group

Tel: (0115) 951 5700 Fax: (0115) 951 5696
Arrowsmith, S. L., BA Oxf., DJur York(Can.)
Dir.*

Quality in the Global Supply Chain, Centre for

Tel: (0115) 951 4023 Fax: (0115) 951 3800
E-mail: james.tannock@nottingham.ac.uk
Tannock, J. D., BSc Nott., PhD CNAA   Reader,
Quality and Operations Management; Dir.*
Research: quality management in the developing
world

Risk and Insurance Studies, Centre for

Tel: (0115) 846 6607 Fax: (0115) 846 6684
E-mail: cris@nottingham.ac.uk
Diacon, S. R., BSc Nott., PhD Nott.   Worshipful
Company of Insurers Prof., Insurance
Management
Dowd, K., BA Sheff., MA W.Ont., PhD Sheff.
Prof., Financial Risk Management
Drake, L. M., BA Essex, MA Essex   Swiss Re
Prof., Management of Risk
Fenn, P. T., BA Lanc., BPhil York(UK)   Norwich
Union Prof., Insurance Studies
O'Brien, C., BA Camb., MA Camb., FIA   Dir.*
Other Staff: 3 Lectrs.
Research: liability and liability insurance;
mortality, pensions and annuities; pricing in
and performance of insurance companies;
risk management and demand for insurance;
risk management in financial institutions

Russian and East European Studies, Nottingham Institute of (NIREES)

Swain, A., BA Durh., PhD Durh.   Dir.*
Other Staff: 1 Lectr.

Slavery, Institute for the Study of

Geary, R. J., MA Camb., PhD Camb.   Prof.;
Dir.*

Sustainable Energy Technology, Institute for (ISET)

Tel: (0115) 951 3157 Fax: (0115) 951 3159
E-mail: saffa.riffat@nottingham.ac.uk
Riffat, S. B., BSc Oxf., MSc Oxf., DPhil Oxf., DSc
Oxf., FIMechE   Prof.; Dir.*
Smith, Shaun, BSc Nott.Trent, PhD Nott.   Indust.
and Res. Liaison Manager
Wilson, R., BSc H-W, PhD H-W   Sr. Lectr.;
Co-Dir.
Other Staff: 4 Lectrs.; 5 Res. Fellows
Vacant Posts: 2 Lectrs.
Research: photovoltaic energy; renewable energy;
solar thermal energy; sustainable
technology; wind turbines

Treaty Centre

Tel: (0115) 951 5700 Fax: (0115) 951 5696
Bowman, M. J., LLB Nott.   Dir.*

Trent Research and Development Support Unit (RDSU)

Tel: (0115) 970 9765 Fax: (0115) 970 9766
E-mail: joanne.elliott@nottingham.ac.uk
Fortnum, Heather M., BM BS Nott., BMedSci
Nott., DM Nott.   Sr. Lectr.; Dir.*
Other Staff: 3 Lectrs.; 1 Sr. Lectr.†; 3 Res.
Fellows†; 1 Hon. Res. Fellow

University of Nottingham Tax Research Institute

Tel: (0115) 951 5279 Fax: (0115) 846 6667
E-mail: john.hasseldine@nottingham.ac.uk
Hasseldine, D. J., BCom Cant., MCom Cant.,
MBus Indiana, PhD Indiana   Prof., Accounting
and Taxation
Other Staff: 3 Lectrs.
Research: economic and behavioural effects of
tax; national and international comparisons;
tax compliance; tax policy evaluation; tax
practice and administration

Urban Culture, Centre for

Meller, Helen E., BA Brist., PhD Brist., FRHistS
Prof.; Dir.*

Urban Planning, Institute of

Tel: (0115) 951 4132 Fax: (0115) 951 3159
E-mail: sbe@nottingham.ac.uk
Oc, T., BArch Middle East Tech., MCP Middle East
Tech., MA Chic., PhD Penn.   Prof.; Dir.*
Other Staff: 1 Sr. Lectr.; 1 Lectr.
Research: ageing population in the city; city
living; safer cities; urban design

Visual Culture, Nottingham Institute for Research in (NIRV)

Callen, A. E., MA Leic., PhD Lond.   Prof.; Dir.*

Work, Health and Organisations, Institute of (I-WHO)

Tel: (0115) 846 7523 Fax: (0115) 846 6625
E-mail: i-who@nottingham.ac.uk
Borrill, C., BSc S'ton., MSc Lond., PhD Brad.   Sr.
Lectr.
Cox, T. R., CBE, BSc Nott., PhD Nott., FBPsS,
FRSA, Hon. FErgS   Prof., Organisational
Psychology; Dir.*
Griffiths, A. J., BA Hull, MSc Nott., PhD Nott.
Deputy Dir.; Prof., Occupational Health
Psychology
Haslam, C. O., BSc Lond., PhD Nott.   Prof.,
Health Psychology
Leather, P. J., BA Lanc., MA Lanc., PhD Lanc.
Reader
Lincoln, N., BSc Wales, MSc Leeds, PhD Lond.,
FBPsS   Acting Deputy Dir.; Prof., Clinical
Psychology
Richards, J., BA Open(UK), MA Oxf., MBA Nott.
Sp. Prof.
Other Staff: 8 Lectrs.; 1 Teaching Fellow; 3
Res. Fellows

CONTACT OFFICERS

Academic affairs. Academic Secretary: Hart,
Alan, BA Keele
(E-mail: alan.hart@nottingham.ac.uk)

Accommodation. Accommodation Services
Manager: Walker, Lynne
(E-mail: lynne.walker@nottingham.ac.uk)
Admissions (first degree). Head of
Admissions Office: Thompson, Caryl, BA
MA
(E-mail: caryl.thompson@nottingham.ac.uk)
Admissions (higher degree). Head of
Admissions Office: Thompson, Caryl, BA
MA
(E-mail: caryl.thompson@nottingham.ac.uk)
Alumni. Head of Alumni Team: Scott-Mitchell,
Katrine, BA Bourne.
(E-mail: linda.prince@nottingham.ac.uk)
Archives. Keeper of the Manuscripts and
Special Collections: Johnston, D. B., BA
Trinity(Dub.), PhD Trinity(Dub.)
(E-mail: dorothy.johnstone@
nottingham.ac.uk)
Careers. Director, Centre for Career
Development: Thorne, Martin E., MA Edin.
(E-mail: martin.thorne@nottingham.ac.uk)
Computing services. Chief Information
Officer: Stanton, K. A., BA MEd
Consultancy services. Director, Research
Innovation Services: Masterman, Richard J.
W., BA Lond., BSc Lond., MA CNAA, PhD Nott.
(E-mail: richard.masterman@
nottingham.ac.uk)
Credit transfer. Head of Student Registry:
Slater, A. J., BMus Nott.
(E-mail: alison.slater@nottingham.ac.uk)
Development/fund-raising. Director,
Development Office: (vacant)
Equal opportunities. Head, Employment
Services: Kaur, Jaspal, BSc MSc
(E-mail: jaspal.kaur@nottingham.ac.uk)
Estates and buildings/works and services.
Director of Estate Management: Jagger, C.
H., BSc Warw.
(E-mail: chris.jagger@nottingham.ac.uk)
Examinations. Assessment Manager:
Mienczakowski, Sandra, BA
(E-mail: sandra.mienczakowski@
nottingham.ac.uk)
Finance. Finance Director: Wynne-Jones, M.,
BSc Warw.
(E-mail: martin.wynne-
jones@nottingham.ac.uk)
General enquiries. Registrar: Greatrix, Paul
(E-mail: registrar@nottingham.ac.uk)
International office. Director, International
Office: Raimo, Vincenzo
(E-mail: vincenzo.raimo@nottingham.ac.uk)
Library (chief librarian). Assistant Director,
Research and Learning Resources Division:
Pinfield, S. J., MA Camb., MA Lond.
Marketing. Marketing Director: Longden, T. J.,
BA Sheff.
(E-mail: tim.longden@nottingham.ac.uk)
Minorities/disadvantaged groups. Head,
Employment Services: Kaur, Jaspal, BSc MSc
(E-mail: jaspal.kaur@nottingham.ac.uk)
Ombudsman. Registrar: Greatrix, Paul
(E-mail: registrar@nottingham.ac.uk)
Personnel/human resources. Director of
Human Resources: Lee, Richard A., BSc
Nott., FCIPD
(E-mail: richard.lee@nottingham.ac.uk)
Public relations. Director of Public Affairs:
Ray, Jonathan
Publications. Director of Public Affairs: Ray,
Jonathan
Purchasing. Commercial Director: Ward,
Graham
Quality assurance and accreditation. Deputy
Director, Academic Office: Dowling,
Robert, BA Oxf.
(E-mail: robert.dowling@nottingham.ac.uk)
Research. Director, Research Innovation
Services: Masterman, Richard J. W., BA
Lond., BSc Lond., MA CNAA, PhD Nott.
(E-mail: richard.masterman@
nottingham.ac.uk)
Safety. Safety and Radiation Protection Officer:
Sutherland, J. A., BSc Nott., PhD E.Anglia
(E-mail: john.sutherland@nottingham.ac.uk)

Scholarships, awards, loans. Registrar: Greatrix, Paul
(E-mail: registrar@nottingham.ac.uk)

Schools liaison. Marketing Manager: Grindrod, E. M., BA Sheff.
(E-mail: liz.grindrod@nottingham.ac.uk)

Security. Chief Security Officer: Stevens, G.
(E-mail: gary.stevens@nottingham.ac.uk)

Sport and recreation. Director of Physical Recreation: Williams, V. P., BEd Nott.
(E-mail: vaughan.williams@nottingham.ac.uk)

Staff development and training. Director of Training and Staff Development: Burns, D. A., BA Sheff., MSc Leic.
(E-mail: david.burns@nottingham.ac.uk)

Student union. President (Student Union)
(E-mail: president@osn1.nottingham.ac.uk)

Student welfare/counselling. Head of Student Services: Dollery, R. J., MA Sheff.
(E-mail: robin.dollery@nottingham.ac.uk)

Students from other countries. Head of International Student Support: Ward,

Christine, BA Nott., MEd Nott.
(E-mail: christine.ward@nottingham.ac.uk)

Students with disabilities. Officer for Disability Issues: Sanders, E. J., BSc Monash
(E-mail: ellen.sanders@nottingham.ac.uk)

[Information supplied by the institution as at 21 March 2005, and edited by the ACU]

NOTTINGHAM TRENT UNIVERSITY

Founded 1992

Member of the Association of Commonwealth Universities

Postal Address: Burton Street, Nottingham, England NG1 4BU
Telephone: (0115) 941 8418
URL: http://www.ntu.ac.uk

VICE-CHANCELLOR*—Gorman, Prof. Neil T., BVSc Liv., PhD Camb., Hon. DVMS, FRCVS
SENIOR PRO-VICE-CHANCELLOR (ACADEMIC DEVELOPMENT AND RESEARCH)—Jones, Prof. Peter
PRO-VICE-CHANCELLOR—Hastings, Prof. Nigel, BTech Lond., MSc Lond.
PRO-VICE-CHANCELLOR—Barnett, Prof. Yvonne
PRO-VICE-CHANCELLOR—Lewis, Prof. Simon
PRO-VICE-CHANCELLOR—Mason, Prof. David
DIRECTOR OF ORGANISATIONAL DEVELOPMENT AND BUSINESS IMPROVEMENT—Fowler, Francesca
COMMERCIAL DIRECTOR—Smith, Garry
POLICY AND STRATEGY ANALYST—Whiteley, Jayne
CHIEF FINANCIAL AND OPERATIONS OFFICER—Jackson, Stephen
DIRECTOR OF FINANCE—Lacey, James
REGISTRAR‡—Samson, David, BA MBA
HEAD OF LIBRARY AND INFORMATION SERVICES—McKnight, Sue

GENERAL INFORMATION

History. The institution was established as Trent Polytechnic in 1970 and acquired university status in 1992.

The university consists of two main sites: City Campus, close to Nottingham, and Clifton Campus, about four miles from the city centre. There is a subsidiary site at Brackenhurst, fifteen miles away.

Admission to first degree courses (see also United Kingdom Introduction). Through Universities and Colleges Admissions Service (UCAS). Two General Certificate of Education (GCE) A level passes and 3 General Certificate of Secondary Education (GCSE) or GCE O level passes; or 3 GCE A level passes and 1 GCSE or GCE O level pass; Scottish Certificate of Education (SCE) with 5 passes (3 at Higher grade) or 4 passes (all at Higher grade); Ordinary National Certificate or Diploma (ONC/OND); Business and Technology Education Council (BTEC) National Certificate or Diploma; Scottish Vocational Educational Council (SCOTVEC); advanced General National Vocational Qualifications (GNVQ); kitemarked access course. International applicants: Republic of Ireland Leaving Certificate, International or European Baccalaureate.

First Degrees (see also United Kingdom Directory to Subjects of Study). BA, BEd, BEng, BSc, LLB, MChem, MEng, MPhys.
Courses last 3-4 years.

Higher Degrees (see also United Kingdom Directory to Subjects of Study).
Master's. LLM, MA, MBA, MPhil, MSc.
Doctoral. PhD.

Libraries. Volumes: 428,000. Periodicals subscribed to: 2400.

Statistics. Staff (2006–2007): 928 (928 academic). Students (2006–2007): undergraduate 20,100 (9045 men, 11,055 women).

FACULTIES/SCHOOLS
Animal, Rural and Environmental Sciences
Tel: (01636) 817099 Fax: (01636) 815404
E-mail: are.enquiries@ntu.ac.uk
Dean: Saint, Prof. Jenny
Administrator to the Dean: Wibberley, Lynn

Architecture, Design and the Built Environment
Dean: Kennedy, Prof. Gordon M., MA CNAA

Art and Design
Tel: (0115) 948 6404 Fax: (0115) 948 6403
E-mail: artanddesign@ntu.ac.uk
Dean: Priest, Ann
Faculty Administrative Officer: Newton, Tracey

Arts and Humanities
Tel: (0115) 848 3136 Fax: (0115) 848 6632
E-mail: hum.undergrad@ntu.ac.uk
Dean: Howarth, Prof. Marianne S., BA Hull, MPhil Nott.
Faculty Administrative Officer: Henson, Joanne

Education
Tel: (0115) 848 8917 Fax: (0115) 848 6747
E-mail: edu.admin@ntu.ac.uk
Dean: Scott, Gill

Nottingham Business School
Tel: (0115) 941 8418
E-mail: nbs.enquiries@ntu.ac.uk
Dean: Yazdani, Prof. Baback
Faculty Administrative Officer: Jones, Emily

Nottingham Law School
Tel: (0115) 848 4498 Fax: (0115) 848 6512
E-mail: nls.enquiries@ntu.ac.uk

Dean: Gaines, Keith
Faculty Administrative Officer: Jones, Emily

Science and Technology
Tel: (0115) 848 6638 Fax: (0115) 848 6636
E-mail: ruth.hickling@ntu.ac.uk
Dean: Fazackerley, Pauline L., BSc Liv., MSc Oxf.
Faculty Administrative Officer: Pugh, Mary

Social Sciences
Dean: Pole, Prof. Chris

ACADEMIC UNITS
Accounting and Finance
Tel: (0115) 941 8418 Fax: (0115) 848 6512
E-mail: nbs.enquiries@ntu.ac.uk
Abdo, H., PhD Sr. Lectr.
Ball, G. R., BSc PhD Sr. Lectr.
Barker, I., BA Oxf. Sr. Lectr.
Boot, L., BSc Nott. Sr. Lectr.
Bowler, D. Sr. Lectr.
Bowler, I. Sr. Lectr.
Challenor, J. R., MEd Warw. Sr. Lectr.
Greenhalgh, K., BSc Sr. Lectr.
Hancox, S., BA Nott. Sr. Lectr.
Harradine, D. Sr. Lectr.
Hunt, C., BSc E.Anglia Sr. Lectr.
Hunt, S. P., BSc(Econ) Sr. Lectr.
Isaaks, C. M., BSc(Econ) Lond. Sr. Lectr.
Jones, M. Sr. Lectr.
Kellett, S., BA CNAA Sr. Lectr.
Knight, C., BA Nott. Sr. Lectr.
Lovejoy, P. D., MA Oxf. Sr. Lectr.
Malde, S., BSc Keele Sr. Lectr.
Mehari, T. Sr. Lectr.
Molthan-Hill, P. Sr. Lectr.
Oakes, R. J., FCA Sr. Lectr.
Pearson, J. M., BSc Manc., MA(Econ) Manc. Principal Lectr.
Sanderson, P. Principal Lectr.
Sargent, B. A., BA CNAA Sr. Lectr.
Slaich, V., BA N.Lond. Sr. Lectr.
Other Staff: 1 Res. Fellow

Research: effects of advertising on firm performance; efficiency of financial and betting markets

Animal, Rural and Environmental Sciences

Alder, Andrew   Programme Leader
Bettison, Tina   Sr. Lectr.
Bottom, Sarah   Programme Leader
Canton, Tina   Sr. Lectr.
Chiarrella, Sally   Sr. Lectr.
Clarkson, John   Sr. Lectr./Lectr.
Cox, Helen   Sr. Lectr.
Dando, Stephen   Programme Leader
Davey, Neville   Sr. Lectr./Lectr.
Davies, Julia   Acad. Team Leader
Dyson, Ruth   Sr. Lectr.
Edwards, Matthew   Programme Leader
Ellis, Andrea   Sr. Lectr.
Gentle, Louise   Programme Leader
Godby, Steven   Sr. Lectr./Lectr.
Hall, Carol   Programme Leader
Heckford, Sarah   Programme Leader
Heneghan, Dominic   Sr. Lectr./Lectr.
Hodgett, Margaret   Sr. Lectr.
Hopegood, Lyn   Sr. Lectr.
Jukes, David   Programme Leader
McPherson, Valerie   Sr. Lectr.
Midgley, Nick   Programme Leader
Owen, Heather   Acad. Team Leader
Oxenbury, Mark   Programme Leader
Poulson, Sara   Sr. Lectr./Lectr.
Ray, Nick   Programme Leader
Ruedisueli, Nicola   Programme Leader
Shelbourne, Graham   Programme Leader
Stapleton, John   Sr. Lectr.
Starbuck, Gareth   Programme Leader
Thomas, Caroline   Sr. Lectr./Lectr.
Tomlinson, Sarah   Sr. Lectr.
Varley, Anne   Programme Leader
Walker, Christine   Programme Leader
Wall, Rob   Sr. Lectr./Lectr.
Walton, Cheryl   Sr. Lectr.
Would, Joan   Sr. Lectr.
York, Samantha   Programme Leader

Arts, Humanities and Language Education

Tel: (0115) 848 8917
   E-mail: edu.admin@ntu.ac.uk
Adcock, L. M.   Sr. Lectr.
Bradley, D.   Sr. Lectr.
Corden, R. E., PhD *Keele*   Prof.
Disney, A. C., BA *Open(UK)*, MPhil *Nott.*   Sr. Lectr.
Greenaway, S. E.   Sr. Lectr.
Harris, A. C.   Sr. Lectr.
Paramore, J.   Sr. Lectr.
Posnett, C.   Acad. Team Leader
Spavin, S., BEd *Hull*, MEd *Leic.*   Principal Lectr.
Toft, H. M.   Sr. Lectr.
Warren, K.   Sr. Lectr.

Biomedical and Natural Sciences

Tel: (0115) 848 6638 Fax: (0115) 848 6636
   E-mail: sci.enquiries@ntu.ac.uk
Ahmed, S. I., BSc *Bhagal.*, MSc *Patna*, PhD *Leic.*   Sr. Lectr.
Ball, G. R., BSc PhD   Sr. Lectr.
Bates, R. F. L., PhD *Leeds*   Sr. Lectr.
Beardah, C. C., BSc *Nott.*, MSc *Manc.*, PhD *Manc.*   Principal Lectr.
Beattie, R. C., PhD *Durh.*   Principal Lectr.
Bencsik, M., PhD *Nott.*   Sr. Lectr.
Billett, E. E., BSc *Wales*, DPhil *Oxf.*   Reader
Birkett, J. W.   Sr. Lectr.
Bonner, P. L. R., BSc *Sus.*, PhD *CNAA*   Sr. Lectr.
Brindley, G., BSc *Wales*, PhD *Wales*   Sr. Lectr.
Butler, D., BA *Sheff.*, MSc *Wales*   Principal Lectr.
Cartledge, T. G., BSc *Wales*, PhD *Wales*   Sr. Lectr.
Cave, G.   Sr. Lectr.
Compton, G. J., BSc *E.Anglia*, PhD *Birm.*   Sr. Lectr.
Creaser, C. S., BSc *Kent*, PhD *Kent*   Prof.

Darlison, M. G., BSc *Birm.*, MSc *Warw.*, PhD *Warw.*   Prof.
Davis, J.   Reader
Dickenson, J., BSc *Lanc.*, PhD *Lanc.*   Sr. Lectr.
Dodi, I. A., MSc *Lond.*, PhD *Lond.*   Prof.
Fairhurst, D. J., BSc *Lond.*, PhD *Edin.*   Sr. Lectr.
Forsythe, S. J., PhD *Newcastle(UK)*   Reader
Freeman, F. M., BSc *Nott.Trent*, PhD *Open(UK)*   Sr. Lectr.
Frost, M. G., BSc *Nott.*, MSc *Nott.*, PhD *Lough.*   Principal Lectr.
Gao, F., BSc *Wuhan*, MSc *Dalian U.T.*, PhD *Lough.*   Reader
Godden, D. H., DPhil *Oxf.*   Sr. Lectr.
Halfpenny, J. C., BSc *Lanc.*, PhD *Lanc.*   Principal Lectr.
Hanley, Q., BA *Reed*, PhD *Arizona*   Sr. Lectr.
Hargreaves, A., PhD *CNAA*   Sr. Lectr.
Hearn, J., BSc *Edin.*, MSc *Brist.*, PhD *Brist.*   Reader
Hix, G.   Sr. Lectr.
Hughes, C. E., PhD *Nott.*   Principal Lectr.
Hughes, D. C., BSc *Manc.*, PhD *Sur.*   Lectr./Sr. Lectr.
Hyland, P., BSc *Ulster*, MRes *Ulster*, PhD *Ulster*   Sr. Lectr.
Kirk, S. H., BSc *Birm.*, PhD *Nott.*   Principal Lectr.
Lloyd Mills, C., BSc *Liv.*, PhD *S'ton.*   Sr. Lectr.
MacFarlane, N. A. A., BSc *Aberd.*, PhD *Stir.*   Assoc. Dean
Mangiapane, E. H., BSc *Birm.*, PhD *Birm.*   Sr. Lectr.
McHale, G., BSc *Nott.*, PhD *Nott.*   Prof.
Minshull, C.
Mireylees, S. E., BSc *Sheff.*, PhD *Manc.*   Principal Lectr.
Neal, D. B., BSc PhD   Sr. Lectr.
Newton, M. I., BSc MSc PhD   Sr. Lectr.
Osborough, C. D., BSc *Nott.*, MSc *Lough.*   Lectr./Sr. Lectr.
Patel, S., LLB LLM
Perry, C. C., MA *Oxf.*, DPhil *Oxf.*   Prof.
Pyatt, F. B., BSc *Wales*, PhD *Wales*, FLS   Prof.
Redfern, P., PhD *Wales*   Principal Lectr.
Rees, Robert C., BSc *Sur.*, PhD *Sheff.*   Prof.; Dean*
Sivasubramaniam, S. D., BSc *Nott.*, PhD *Nott.*   Sr. Lectr.
Stockenhuber, M., BSc PhD   Sr. Lectr.
Terrell-Nield, C. E., PhD *Manc.*   Principal Lectr.
Turner, R. J., BSc *Sur.*, PhD *Nott.*   Prof.
Verderio-Edwards, E.   Sr. Lectr.
Wallace, R. G., BSc *S'ton.*, PhD *CNAA*   Principal Lectr.
Wallis, J. D., MA *Oxf.*, DPhil *Oxf.*   Prof.
Other Staff: 2 Lectrs.
Research: bioinformatics; biomolecular and microbial analysis; cell biology and pathology; environmental quality and management; neuroscience, pharmacology and toxicology

Broadcasting and Journalism

Tel: (0115) 848 5806 Fax: (0115) 848 5859
Adams, Catherine C.   Lectr./Sr. Lectr.
Ball, Amanda J.   Lectr./Sr. Lectr.
Choudhary, Barnie   Lectr./Sr. Lectr.
Fleming, Carole A.   Lectr./Sr. Lectr.
Hemmingway, Emma L.   Lectr./Sr. Lectr.
Matthews, Jo M.   Lectr./Sr. Lectr.
Staniforth, Robin   Acad. Team Leader
Tatman, Jeremy   Lectr./Sr. Lectr.
Ventre, Richard I.   Lectr./Sr. Lectr.
Welford, Dave   Lectr./Sr. Lectr.

Building and Environmental Health

Tel: (0115) 848 6011 Fax: (0115) 848 6064
   E-mail: env.admissions@ntu.ac.uk
Blake, R. N. E., PhD *Lond.*   Sr. Lectr.
Carter, W. G., MSc *Manc.*   Principal Lectr.
Charlett, A. J., BA MPhil   Principal Lectr.
Chartlett, A. J., BA BPhil   Acting Head*
Darkwa, K., MSc *Cran.IT*, BEng PhD   Sr. Lectr.
Fewkes, A., BSc *CNAA*, MSc *CNAA*, MPhil *CNAA*   Sr. Lectr.
Frampton, D. I., BA *Open(UK)*, MSc *CNAA*   Principal Lectr.

George, B. W., BSc *Aston*, MSc *Lond.*   Principal Lectr.
Gregg, T. R., MPhil   Sr. Lectr.
Hardy, P. A.   Sr. Lectr.
Houldsworth, H. K., BA MPhil   Principal Lectr.
Hurst, A. G., MSc *Reading*, MBA   Sr. Lectr.
Lyons, P. E., BEd *Hull*   Sr. Lectr.
Maguire, Kevin J. P., BA *Open(UK)*, BSc *E.Anglia*, MSc *CNAA*   Sr. Lectr.
McCarthy, Ann, MA *Lough.*   Sr. Lectr.
McGrath, P. T., BSc *Manc.*, MSc *Manc.*   Sr. Lectr.
Orchard, K. J., BSc *CNAA*, MSc *Lough.*   Sr. Lectr.
O'Rourke, A., BSc *Leeds*, PhD   Sr. Lectr.
Paddock, Paul B., BSc *Nott.*, MPhil *CNAA*, MBA   Principal Lectr.
Pritchard, C., BA   Sr. Lectr.
Ramsay-Dawber, P. J., BSc *CNAA*, MBA *CNAA*   Sr. Lectr.
Trevorrow, A., MPhil   Sr. Lectr.
Woollard, A., BEng *Liv.*, MA *S'ton.*   Sr. Lectr.
Other Staff: 1 Res. Fellow
Research: construction companies (water recycling, corporate performance); housebuilding (structural defects, rectification, warranties, standardisation); thermal energy technology for sustainable development; urban regeneration (land use change, airfields); water management (rainwater, grey water)

Business and Technology in Education

Tel: (0115) 848 8917
   E-mail: edu.admin@ntu.ac.uk
Bindon, A. E., BEd *Sheff.*   Sr. Lectr.
Boulton, H. E.   Learning and Teaching Co-ordinator
Bradshaw, P. R.   Sr. Lectr.
Browne, A. J., BEd *CNAA*   Sr. Lectr.
Cooper, A. S., BSc *Lond.*, MEd *CNAA*   Sr. Lectr.
Dransfield, R. B. W., BSc *Wales*   Sr. Lectr.
Howkins, S., MEd *Nott.*   Sr. Lectr.
Lightfoot, N. J.   Principal Lectr.
Mitchell, D. R., MEd *Nott.*   Acad. Team Leader
Needham, D.   Sr. Lectr.
Rothwell, F. M.   Sr. Lectr.
Vanhegan, J. S., MEd *CNAA*   Sr. Lectr.
Other Staff: 2 Sr. Technicians; 1 Sr. Technician Co-ordinator

Business Information Systems

Tel: (0115) 848 4488 Fax: (0115) 848 6512
   E-mail: nbs.enquiries@ntu.ac.uk
Castell, A. M., BSc *E.Lond.*, MSc *Lough.*   Principal Lectr.
Currie, M. J., BA *Humb.*, MA *Hull*   Sr. Lectr.
Edwards, K., BSc *CNAA*   Sr. Lectr.
Gazely, A. M., BSc *Open(UK)*, BA *Manc.*, PhD *Lough.*   Sr. Lectr.
Graves, Robert, BA MSc   Head*
McAdam, D. R., BA *Essex*, MSc *Sus.*, MSc *CNAA*   Sr. Lectr.
Mutch, A. F., LLB *Dund.*, MA *Manc.*, PhD *Manc.*   Principal Lectr.
Pybus, E. J., BA *Lond.*, MA *Nott.*   Sr. Lectr.
Tranter, S.   Sr. Lectr.
Walker, S.   Lectr./Sr. Lectr.
Whiston, I. C.   Sr. Lectr.
Williams, V. A., BSc *Newcastle(UK)*, MA   Sr. Lectr.
Other Staff: 1 Lectr.

Chemistry and Physics

Tel: (0115) 848 6638 Fax: (0115) 848 6636
Bottrill, S. J., BSc *Coventry*, MEd *Nott.*   Sr. Lectr.
Braithwaite, A., BSc *Lough.*, PhD *Manc.*   Sr. Lectr.
Coffey, M., BSc PhD   Sr. Lectr.
Coutts, I. G. C., BSc *Aberd.*, PhD *Aberd.*   Sr. Lectr.
Creaser, C. S., BSc *Kent*, PhD *Kent*   Prof.; Head*
Crookes, J. N., BSc *Birm.*, PhD *Nott.*   Principal Lectr.
Fowell, J. C. T., BSc *Nott.*, PhD *Nott.*   Sr. Lectr.

Halfpenny, J. C., BSc Lanc., PhD Lanc.
Principal Lectr.
Hearn, J., BSc Edin., MSc Brist., PhD Brist.
Reader
Hill, R., BSc Lond., PhD Lond. Principal Lectr.
Jackson, E., BSc Durh., PhD Durh. Sr. Lectr.
Matharu, A. S., BSc CNAA, PhD CNAA Sr.
Lectr.
McHale, G., BSc Nott., PhD Nott. Sr. Lectr.
McKenzie, N. L., BSc Lond. Sr. Lectr.
Moss, K., BSc Manc., PhD Manc. Sr. Lectr.
Neal, D. B., BSc PhD Sr. Lectr.
Newton, M. I., BSc MSc PhD Sr. Lectr.
Percival, C., BSc PhD Sr. Lectr.
Perry, C. C., MA Oxf., DPhil Oxf. Sr. Lectr.
Rowan, S. M., BSc Sheff., MSc Durh. Principal
Lectr.
Stockenhuber, M., BSc PhD Sr. Lectr.
Turner, R. J., BSc Sur., PhD Nott. Sr. Lectr.
Wallace, R. G., BSc S'ton., PhD CNAA Sr. Lectr.
Wallis, J. D., MA Oxf., DPhil Oxf. Prof.
Woolley, R. G., MA Oxf., DPhil Oxf., ScD Camb.
Prof.
Other Staff: 2 Lectrs.
Research: analytical science; archaeometry and
art conservation; medical and materials
imaging; organic/inorganic/physical
chemistry; soft matter physics

Communications, Culture and Media Studies

Tel: (0115) 848 3136 Fax: (0115) 848 6632
Bailey, Olga G. Lectr./Sr. Lectr.
Braber, Natalie Lectr./Sr. Lectr.
Chadder, Viv A. M., BA Reading, MA Brun.
Lectr./Sr. Lectr.
Connell, Matt R. Lectr./Sr. Lectr.
Cummings, Louise Reader, Linguistics
Dawson, Alex Lectr./Sr. Lectr.
Edley, Nigel, PhD Lough. Lectr./Sr. Lectr.
Hardman, Dean Lectr./Sr. Lectr.
Hollows, Joanne K., BSc Salf., MA Lond.
Reader
Jones, Steven L. Lectr./Sr. Lectr.
Kidner, David W., PhD Lond. Lectr./Sr. Lectr.
Lodziak, Conrad M. J., MEd N.Carolina, PhD
N.Carolina Lectr./Sr. Lectr.
Morrish, Liz C. E., BA Leeds, PhD Leeds Lectr./
Sr. Lectr.
Murray, Russell S. Lectr./Sr. Lectr.
Needham, Gary W. Lectr./Sr. Lectr.
O'Shaughnessy, Martin P., BA Birm., MA Queb.,
PhD CNAA Reader, Film Studies
Simons, Iain Principal Lectr.
Stone, Georgia, BA CNAA Lectr./Sr. Lectr.
Taylor, Ben C. Principal Lectr.
Turnbull, Neil R. Lectr./Sr. Lectr.
Wittel, Andreas J. Lectr./Sr. Lectr.
Woods, David J., BA Manc., PhD Nott. Lectr./
Sr. Lectr.
Other Staff: 1 Sr. Res. Fellow; 2 Res. Fellows;
1 Res. Asst.

Computing

Tel: (0115) 848 6866 Fax: (0115) 848 6518
Al-Dabass, D., BSc Lond., PhD CNAA Principal
Lectr.
Allen, T., BA Open(UK), MSc Nott., PhD Nott.
Sr. Lectr.
Allison, I. K., BSc CNAA Sr. Lectr.
Bargiela, A., MSc Silesia, PhD Durh. Prof.
Battersby, A., BSc Salf., MSc Herts. Sr. Lectr.
Bidwell, L. M., BSc Sus., MSc Sheff. Sr. Lectr.
Bowden, P. R., BSc Nott., BSc Lond., MSc Nott.
Sr. Lectr.
Brown, D. J., MEng Nott., PhD Nott. Sr. Lectr.
Cant, R. J., BSc Manc., PhD Lond. Sr. Lectr.
Claramunt, C., MSc Lausanne, PhD
Evett, L. J., BSc CNAA, PhD Brist. Sr. Lectr.
Fazackerley, Pauline L., BSc Liv., MSc Oxf.
Acting Head*
Halstead, P., BSc Manc., MPhil CNAA Sr. Lectr.
Hibberd, R. B., BEd CNAA, MSc Sheff.Hallam
Sr. Lectr.
King, S. J., MSc CNAA Sr. Lectr.
Langensiepen, C., BSc Manc., PhD Manc. Sr.
Lectr.

McDonald, P. W., BSc CNAA, MSc CNAA Sr.
Lectr.
Newman, F. T., BSc Leic., BA Leic., DPhil Oxf.
Principal Lectr.
Orton, P. A., BSc Sus., PhD CNAA Sr. Lectr.
Osman, T., BSc Donetsk T.U., MSc Nott.Trent, PhD
Nott.Trent Sr. Lectr.
O'Sullivan, S. D., BA Lond. Sr. Lectr.
Palmer-Brown, D. P., BSc Leeds, MSc CNAA, PhD
Nott. Sr. Lectr.
Poliakoff, J., BA Camb., PhD Nott.Trent Sr.
Lectr.
Powell, H. M., BEng Sheff., PhD Sheff. Sr.
Lectr.
Sherkat, N., BEng Nott., PhD Nott.Trent Reader
Smith, J. R., BSc Wales, MPhil Nott. Sr. Lectr.
Smith, P. A., BSc Nott., PhD Nott. Sr. Lectr.
Thomas, P. D., BSc Wales, MSc Lough., PhD
Lough. Prof.
Other Staff: 1 Lectr.
Research: network simulation and modelling;
pattern and handwriting recognition; real
time machine control

Criminology, Public Health and Policy Studies

Ahearne, Mike, BA MA Lectr./Sr. Lectr.
Bowpitt, Graham, BScEcon PhD Lectr./Sr.
Lectr.
Buckley, Sian Lectr./Sr. Lectr.
Chan, Chak Kwan Lectr./Sr. Lectr.
Chubbock, Natasha Lectr./Sr. Lectr.
Crowther-Dowey, Chris, BA Hull, MA Leic., PhD
Sheff. Lectr./Sr. Lectr.
Fuller, F. A., BSc Nott.Trent Lectr./Sr. Lectr.
Gibson, Linda, BA MA PhD Lectr./Sr. Lectr.
Gillespie, Terry Lectr./Sr. Lectr.
Harrison, Tim D. Lectr./Sr. Lectr.
Hodgson, Phil, BA MPhil MBA PhD Lectr./Sr.
Lectr.
Hopkins Burke, Kristan, BSc MSc Lectr./Sr.
Lectr.
Hopkins Burke, Roger Principal Lectr.
Hunter, James Lectr./Sr. Lectr.
Lane, Gill Lectr./Sr. Lectr.
Long, Matt Lectr./Sr. Lectr.
Love, Kevin Lectr./Sr. Lectr.
Lyons, Andrea Lectr./Sr. Lectr.
Maguire, Kevin J. P., BA Open(UK), BSc E.Anglia,
MSc CNAA Lectr./Sr. Lectr.
McCarthy, Ann, MA Lough. Lectr./Sr. Lectr.
Moore, Roger Lectr./Sr. Lectr.
Paddock, Paul B., BSc Nott., MPhil CNAA, MBA
Principal Lectr.
Shaw, Mandy Lectr./Sr. Lectr.
Sparrow, Paul Acad. Team Leader
Sutton, Andy, BA MPhil Lectr./Sr. Lectr.
Sutton, Mike Reader
Tseloni, Andromachi, BA Athens Econ.&Bus., MA
Athens Econ.&Bus., PhD Manc. Prof.
Wane, Philip Lectr./Sr. Lectr.
White-Sansom, Lorna Lectr./Sr. Lectr.
Other Staff: 1 Researcher; 1 Postgrad.
Researcher

Design

Tel: (0115) 848 6404 Fax: (0115) 848 6403
Barnes, A., BA Nott.Trent Sr. Lectr.
Briggs, P. M., BA CNAA Sr. Lectr.
Colwell, A., BA CNAA, MA C.England Sr. Lectr.
Crabbe, A., MA Essex Sr. Lectr.
Crisp, Alan Sr. Lectr.
Cross, D., BA CNAA, MA RCA Sr. Lectr.
Hardy, C., BSc Nott., MBA Brighton Sr. Lectr.
Hebbditch, N., BA CNAA, MA Nott.Trent Sr.
Lectr.
Higgins, I. K., BA CNAA Sr. Lectr.
Johnson, P., MA CNAA Sr. Lectr.
Kennedy, Gordon M., MA CNAA Prof.; Head*
Lester, P., BA CNAA Sr. Lectr.
McCullagh, Joe, BA Nott.Trent, MA Westminster
Sr. Lectr.
McLennan, Jane, BA Kingston(UK) Sr. Lectr.
Pepin, Michelle, BA Sr. Lectr.
Reavley, G., BA CNAA, MA Nott. Sr. Lectr.
Rutherford, Steve, BA Tees., MSc Lough. Sr.
Lectr.

Senter, T. A., BA Newcastle(UK), MPhil Nott. Sr.
Lectr.
Simpson, K., BA CNAA Sr. Lectr.
Solomonides, Alan, BEd Sr. Lectr.
Taylor, B. M., MA CNAA Principal Lectr.
Treweek, Chris, MA Open(UK) Principal Lectr.
Varley, T., MA CNAA Sr. Lectr.
Walker, S., BA Nott., MA Nott. Sr. Lectr.
Ward, K. A. Sr. Lectr.
Research: designed environment; digital imagery;
history of design; product design and
evaluation

Economics

Tel: (0115) 941 8418
E-mail: nbs.enquiries@ntu.ac.uk
Ackrill, R. Sr. Lectr.
Cooke, A. J., BA Nott., MSc York(UK), PhD Nott.
Sr. Lectr.
Cuestas, J. Sr. Lectr.
Dobson, C. Reader
Dobson, S. Prof.
Faria, J. Prof.
Garratt, D. Sr. Lectr.
Harrison, B., BA Nott., MA Sheff. Sr. Lectr.
Heasell, S. L., BA CNAA Sr. Lectr.
Jones, R., BA CNAA, MSc(Econ) Lond. Sr.
Lectr.
Le, H. Sr. Lectr.
McCann, M. Sr. Lectr.
Philp, B. Sr. Lectr.
Quinn, P. A., MA Essex Sr. Lectr.
Swift, S. B., MA Leic. Sr. Lectr.
Vaughan Williams, L., BSc Wales, PhD Nott.Trent
Sr. Lectr.
Wu, Z. Reader

Education and Professional Studies

Tel: (0115) 848 8917 Fax: (0115) 848 6747
Atkins, E. J. Principal Lectr.
Brown, V. Sr. Lectr.
Burbanks, Y. S. Sr. Lectr.
Bushnell, R. C., BSc Durh. Sr. Lectr.
Chantrey Wood, K. Sr. Lectr.
Clague, E. J. Sr. Lectr.
Flint, K. J. Sr. Lectr.
Goepel, J. Sr. Lectr.
Graves, R. P. Sr. Lectr.
Kontogianni, M. Sr. Lectr.
Oldfield, B. Sr. Lectr.
Peart, S. Sr. Lectr.
Richards, G. F. Principal Lectr.
Robinson, D. C. Sr. Lectr.
Scruton, J. P. Sr. Lectr.
Simmons, S. Sr. Lectr.
Smith, P. D. Principal Lectr.
Sutcliffe-Binns, S. A. Sr. Lectr.
Turner, M. E. Sr. Lectr.
Voice, B. J. Principal Lectr.
Wallace, S. E., PhD Sheff. Reader
Walsh, M. T. Sr. Lectr.
Wells, F. I. Sr. Lectr.
Woods, A. M. Academic Team Leader

Education, Continuing

Atkins, E. J. Principal Lectr.
Clague, E. J. Principal Lectr.
Flint, K. J. Sr. Lectr.
Howard, S. Sr. Lectr.
Peart, S. Sr. Lectr.
Toft, H. M. Sr. Lectr.
Wallace, S. E., PhD Sheff. Reader

EFL/TESOL

Tel: (0115) 848 6156 Fax: (0115) 848 6513
Ataker, Lezli E. Lectr./Sr. Lectr.
Hassett, Donald V. Acad. Team Leader
Head, Katie M. Lectr./Sr. Lectr.
Humphrey, Donna L. C., BA Leeds Lectr./Sr.
Lectr.
McCall, Christine Lectr./Sr. Lectr.
Schmitt, Diane R. Lectr./Sr. Lectr.
Spencer, Sheila M., BA Lond., MEd Manc.
Lectr./Sr. Lectr.
Taylor, Linda H., MA Birm. Lectr./Sr. Lectr.
Other Staff: 7 Lectrs.

Engineering, Civil and Structural

Tel: (0115) 848 6011 Fax: (0115) 848 6450
   E-mail: env.admissions@ntu.ac.uk
Abbiss, J. C., BSc Nott., MSc Newcastle(UK)   Sr.
   Lectr.
Braithwaite, R. P., BSc Leeds   Sr. Lectr.
Breach, M. C., MA Camb., MSc Oxf., FRAS,
   FRICS   Principal Lectr.
Cowley, J. A., BSc Birm.   Sr. Lectr.
Daffern, C., BSc Nott., MPhil Nott.   Sr. Lectr.
Davison, M., BSc Nott., PhD Nott.   Sr. Lectr.
Dixon, N., BSc CNAA, PhD CNAA, FGS   Reader
Djerbib, Y., BEng Sheff., MEng Sheff., PhD Sheff.
   Sr. Lectr.
Goodall, G., MSc Birm.   Sr. Lectr.
Greenwood, J., BSc(Eng) Lond., MEng McM.,
   FGS   Sr. Lectr.
Hawkins, R. K., MSc Sur., PhD Nott., FICE
   Prof.; Head*
Hoppitt, J. W., BSc Nott.   Principal Lectr.
Jefferson, I., BEng Lough., PhD Lough.   Sr. Lectr.
Johnson, D., BSc Lond., MSc Manc., PhD CNAA,
   FIStructE   Principal Lectr.
Joynes, H. W., BSc Leeds, PhD Leeds   Sr. Lectr.
Krylov, V. V., MSc Moscow, PhD Moscow, DSc
   Moscow   Prof.
Roodbaraky, K., BSc CNAA, PhD Nott.   Sr.
   Lectr.
Rosenbaum, M. S., BSc Lond., PhD Lond., FGS
   Prof.
Sane, K. A., BSc CNAA, MSc Nott.Trent   Sr.
   Lectr.
Sargent, P. T. H., BEng Sheff.   Sr. Lectr.
Shapley, M. J., BSc Wales, BA Open(UK), MSc
   Birm.   Sr. Lectr.
Sholji, I. H., BSc Lond., PhD Lond.   Sr. Lectr.
Waltham, A. C., BSc Lond., PhD Lond.   Sr. Lectr.
Wright, D.   Sr. Lectr.
Wright, S., BSc CNAA   Sr. Lectr.
Other Staff: 7 Lectrs.†
Research: acoustics (train-generated ground
   vibrations); environmental engineering
   (water treatment and small-scale
   hydropower); geohazards (collapsible soils,
   ground subsidence, hazard mapping,
   landfill caping and lining systems, slope
   stability); structures (finite element analysis,
   structural defects); surveying
   (gyrotheodolite azimuth deterioration)

Engineering, Electrical and Electronic

Tel: (0115) 848 2799 Fax: (0115) 848 6567
   E-mail: eee-dept@ntu.ac.uk
Clark, S., MA Camb., PhD CNAA   Sr. Lectr.
Cranton, W. M., BSc Sur., PhD Brad.   Sr. Lectr.
Evans, J. P. O., BSc CNAA, PhD Nott.Trent   Sr.
   Lectr.
Germon, R. K., BSc Sheff., PhD Nott.Trent   Sr.
   Lectr.
Kansara, M., BSc Lond., MPhil Lond.   Sr. Lectr.
Kaye, W. K., BSc Nott.Trent   Sr. Lectr.
Mendenhall, P. C., BSc CNAA, MSc Aston   Sr.
   Lectr.
Mias, C., BEng Bath, PhD Camb.   Sr. Lectr.
Moore, P. W., BSc CNAA, MSc Nott.   Sr. Lectr.
Morley, D., BSc Wales, MSc Wales, PhD Wales
   Principal Lectr.
O'Neill, B. C., BA Trinity(Dub.), BAI Trinity(Dub.),
   PhD Liv.   Reader
Patterson, E. B., BSc CNAA, PhD Nott.Trent
   Principal Lectr.
Redgate, J. S., BSc CNAA   Sr. Lectr.
Robinson, M., BSc Salf., MSc Manc., PhD Leeds
   Prof.
Thomas, C. B., BSc Wales, MSc Wales, PhD Bath
   Prof.; Head*
Williams, A. A., BA Oxf., PhD Nott.Trent   Sr.
   Lectr.
Other Staff: 1 Sr. Res. Fellow; 2 Res. Fellows;
   2 Principal Lectrs.†; 3 Sr. Lectrs.†
Research: display technology (electroluminescent
   for flat-screen displays); electronic systems
   (networking hardware solutions for parallel
   systems); renewable energy
   (microhydropower for developing
   countries); three-dimensional imaging
   (stereoscopic imaging and metrology
   systems)

Engineering, Mechanical and Manufacturing

Tel: (0115) 848 2799 Fax: (0115) 848 6567
Ashforth-Frost, S. A., BEng Nott.Trent, PhD
   Nott.Trent   Reader
Codman, A. C., BEng Manc.   Sr. Lectr.
Crisp, A. R., MPhil Nott.Trent   Sr. Lectr.
Dobbins, B. N., BSc CNAA, MPhil CNAA   Sr.
   Lectr.
Drysdale, J., BSc CNAA   Sr. Lectr.
Fuller, F. A., BSc Nott.Trent   Sr. Lectr.
Gao, F., BSc Wuhan, MSc Dalian U.T., PhD Lough.
   Sr. Lectr.
Gentle, C. R., PhD Lond.   Prof., Mechanical
   Engineering
Gildersleeve, M. J., MPhil CNAA, PhD Leeds   Sr.
   Lectr.
Goodson, R. A. H., MEng CNAA   Sr. Lectr.
Harrison, Tim D.   Sr. Lectr.
Hewitt, I., BSc CNAA, MSc CNAA   Sr. Lectr.
Hicking, P., BSc CNAA   Sr. Lectr.
Higginson, M., MSc Lough.   Sr. Lectr.
Hull, J. B., BEng Liv., MMet Sheff., PhD Sheff.
   Prof.; Head*
Ianakiev, A., BEng Sofia, MSc Sofia, PhD Lond.
   Sr. Lectr.
Jambunathan, K., BSc Wales, PhD CNAA,
   FIMechE   Res. Co-ordinator; Prof., Heat
   Transfer/Fluid Flow
Jeffery, G. S. B., BSc Lond., MPhil Nott.   Sr.
   Lectr.
Jones, A. R., BEng Sheff., PhD Sheff.   Sr. Lectr.
Kennedy, S., BSc Brad., MSc Lough., PhD Lough.
   Sr. Lectr.
Lacey, M. R., BSc CNAA, PhD CNAA   Sr. Lectr.
Lai, E., BSc Lond., PhD Camb.   Sr. Lectr.
McGraw, K. L.   Sr. Lectr.
Sims, R., BSc Leeds   Sr. Lectr.
Sivayoganathan, K., PhD Birm.   Sr. Lectr.
Stratton, R., BSc Nott., MSc Warw.   Sr. Lectr.
Su, D., MSc Strath., PhD Strath.   Reader
Swannell, M. J., BSc CNAA, PhD CNAA
   Principal Lectr.; Fac. Teaching-Learning Co-
   ordinator
Swetnam, D., BSc Wales, MSc Cran.IT, PhD
   Cran.IT   Sr. Lectr.; Industrial Placement
   Tutor
Tranfield, G., BSc Birm., PhD Warw.   Sr. Lectr.
Turner, M., BSc Nott., PhD Nott.   Sr. Lectr.
Turner, T. S., BSc Manc., PhD Nott.   Sr. Lectr.
Ward, H., BSc   Sr. Lectr.
Yan, Y. Y., BSc MSc PhD   Sr. Lectr.
Yusuf, Y., BEng MSc PhD   Sr. Lectr.
Research: advanced technical ceramics;
   biomechanics; heat transfer and fluid flow;
   manufacturing automation

English

Tel: (0115) 848 3136 Fax: (0115) 848 6632
Belbin, David   Lectr./Sr. Lectr.
Byron, Catherine M., MA Oxf., MPhil Oxf.
   Lectr./Sr. Lectr.
Coleman, David   Lectr./Sr. Lectr.
Cordle, Daniel F.   Lectr./Sr. Lectr.
Joyce, Graham W.   Reader
Leonard, Philip C.   Reader
Lock, Georgina K.   Sr. Lectr.
Murphy, Michael   Lectr./Sr. Lectr.
Ouditt, Sharon A., BA Warw., MA York(UK),
   PhD Leic.   Reader
Smith, Peter J., BA Lanc., MA Lanc., PhD Leic.
   Reader, Renaissance Literature
Solanki, Mahendra   Lectr./Sr. Lectr.
Thompson, Carl E.   Lectr./Sr. Lectr.
van Loon, J., BA Rotterdam, MA Car., PhD Lanc.
   Sr. Lectr.
Ward, Abigail   Lectr./Sr. Lectr.
Yousaf, Naheem   Acad. Team Leader
Other Staff: 5 Res. Fellows; 1 Res. Asst.
Research: critical social theory; inter-cultural
   pragmatics relating to business discourse;
   literary recovery research and radical texts;
   media and cultural studies; post-colonial
   studies

Fashion, Textiles and Applied Design

Tel: (0115) 848 6404 Fax: (0115) 848 6403
Allen, D. P.   Reader
Arthur, Les, MA CNAA   Sr. Lectr.
Bartholomew, J.   Sr. Lectr.
Briggs-Goode, A.   Sr. Lectr.
Brown, D. H. G.   Sr. Lectr.
Brown, E.   Sr. Lectr.
Bunce, G.   Sr. Lectr.
Bushby, M.   Sr. Lectr.
Byrne, K.   Sr. Lectr.
Challendar, C., MA   Sr. Lectr.
Danjoux, M., BA   Sr. Lectr.
Francis, N.
Goulding, R., BA   Sr. Lectr.
Goworek, H.
Harrigan, K.   Sr. Lectr.
Holbrook, K.   Sr. Lectr.
Jones, C. A., BA CNAA, MDes RCA   Sr. Lectr.
Keen, S. P.   Principal Lectr.
Kenny, H.
Knox, A.   Sr. Lectr.
McNabb, S.
Philips, P., MA RCA   Principal Lectr.
Pinches, J. L., BA CNAA, MDes RCA   Principal
   Lectr.
Proctor, G.   Sr. Lectr.
Robinson, J.   Sr. Lectr.
Rundle, T.
Somerville, T.   Sr. Lectr.
Sparkes, B. M., MA RCA   Principal Lectr.
Staples, G.
Townsend, K.   Sr. Lectr.
Warde, L.
Watson, Y.   Sr. Lectr.
Wilson, D.
Other Staff: 1 Lectr.
Research: computer clothing research; design
   culture and technology; design of materials;
   structure, pattern and colour

Guidance, Youth Studies and Youth Justice (GYS)

Allen, Ann, BA Sheff.   Head*
Bower, Mark   Sr. Lectr.
Fletcher-Morgan, Charlotte, BA MA   Sr. Lectr.
Gee, Ricky   Sr. Lectr.
Hardy, Jackie, BA MA   Sr. Lectr.
McFadden, Jo   Sr. Lectr.
Murphy, Sam   Principal Lectr.
Owen, Anne, BA   Sr. Lectr.
Palmer, Vicky, BA MA   Sr. Lectr.
Reed, Helen   Sr. Lectr.
Scott, Frances   Sr. Lectr.
Vesey, Angela   Sr. Lectr.

History, Heritage and Geography

Tel: (0115) 848 3136 Fax: (0115) 848 6632
Black, R. Graham   Reader
Brown, Angela, BA Wales   Acad. Team Leader
Burch, Stuart J.   Lectr./Sr. Lectr.
Dingsdale, Alan, BA Durh., PhD Leeds   Principal
   Lectr.
Gould, Kevin C.   Lectr./Sr. Lectr.
Graham, David T., BA MSc PhD   Lectr./Sr.
   Lectr.
Hayes, Nick J., BA Open(UK), PhD Open(UK)
   Lectr./Sr. Lectr.
Lambert-Hurley, Siobhan   Lectr./Sr. Lectr.
Moses, Gary W., BA CNAA   Lectr./Sr. Lectr.
Newstead, Clare   Lectr./Sr. Lectr.
Pearce, Adrian J.   Lectr./Sr. Lectr.
Phelps, Angela R., BA Hull, MSocSc Birm., PhD
   Hull   Principal Lectr.
Rowbotham, Judith D., BA Wales, PhD Wales
   Reader
Skinner, Deborah S.   Lectr./Sr. Lectr.
Smith, Amanda J.   Lectr./Sr. Lectr.
Stankley, Neville N.   Lectr./ Sr. Lectr.
Tivers, Jacky   Lectr./ Sr. Lectr.

Human Resource Management

Tel: (0115) 941 8418
   E-mail: nbs.enquiries@ntu.ac.uk
Barton, H.   Head*
Best, W., BA Nott.Trent, PhD Nott.Trent   Sr.
   Lectr.
Bryson, C., MSc Stir.   Sr. Lectr.

Caven, V.   Lectr./Sr. Lectr.
Doughty, D. A., BA CNAA   Principal Lectr.
Downes, B.   Sr. Lectr.
Fisher, C. M., BA Camb., MA Camb., PhD Camb.
   Prof.
Harris, L. M., MA Lough., PhD   Prof.
Hay, A., PhD   Sr. Lectr.
Keegan, A.   Sr. Lectr.
King, D.   Sr. Lectr.
Kirk, S., BA Nott.Trent, MA Nott.Trent   Sr. Lectr.
Lawley, S.   Sr. Lectr.
Leinster, J.   Sr. Lectr.
Leverment, Y., MA Lough.   Sr. Lectr.
MacKay, C.   Sr. Lectr.
Sacks, R.   Lectr./Sr. Lectr.
Samra-Fredericks, D.   Reader
Sempick, A.   Sr. Lectr.
Simpson, S.   Lectr./Sr. Lectr.
Snook, J.   Sr. Lectr.
Stevens, P.   Sr. Lectr.
Tansley, C., MA CNAA, PhD   Prof.
Taylor, B., BA N.Y., MScEd N.Y.   Sr. Lectr.
Tietze, S.   Prof.
Tuckman, A., BA Hull, PhD Hull   Sr. Lectr.
Walsh, D. A., BA Nott.   Principal Lectr.
Watling, D.   Sr. Lectr.
Webb, J.   Principal Lectr.
Whiteland, P.   Sr. Lectr.
Whittall, M.   Sr. Lectr.
Williams, H.   Lectr./Sr. Lectr.
Other Staff: 1 Res. Fellow; 2 Visiting Res.
   Fellows
Research: changing employment policies and
   practices; international and comparative
   industrial relations; managerial behaviour
   and strategic direction; models and
   concepts of human resource development
   (academic and practitioner perspectives);
   organisation and management in post-
   communist society

Information Management and Systems

Tel: (0115) 941 8418
   E-mail: nbs.enquiries@ntu.ac.uk
Antill, L.   Sr. Lectr.
Buglear, J., BA CNAA, MSc Hull   Lectr./Sr.
   Lectr.
Castell, A. M., BSc E.Lond., MSc Lough.
   Principal Lectr.
Cramphorn, C.   Sr. Lectr.
Currie, M. J., BA Humb., MA Hull   Sr. Lectr.
Edwards, K., BSc CNAA   Sr. Lectr.
Gazely, A. M., BSc Open(UK), BA Manc., PhD
   Lough.   Sr. Lectr.
Knox, K.   Sr. Lectr.
McAdam, D. R., BA Essex, MSc Sus., MSc CNAA
   Sr. Lectr.
Mutch, A. F., LLB Dund., MA Manc., PhD Manc.
   Sr. Lectr.
Orley, J.   Sr. Lectr.
Pybus, E. J., BA Lond., MA Nott.   Sr. Lectr.
Sloper, J.   Sr. Lectr.
Tranter, S.   Sr. Lectr.
Walker, S.   Lectr./Sr. Lectr.
Whiston, I. C.   Sr. Lectr.
White, D.   Sr. Lectr.
Williams, V. A., BSc Newcastle(UK), MA   Sr.
   Lectr.
Woodhouse, P.   Sr. Lectr.

Joint Honours and Childhood Studies

Tel: (0115) 848 8917 Fax: (0115) 848 6747
Goepel, J.   Sr. Lectr.
Greenaway, S. E.   Sr. Lectr.
Kontogianni, M.   Sr. Lectr.
Lightfoot, N. J.   Principal Lectr.
Mackintosh, C.   Sr. Lectr.
Scruton, J. P.   Sr. Lectr.
Simmons, S.   Sr. Lectr.

Land-Based Studies

Tel: (01636) 817099
Butcher, D. P.   Head*
Davies, J. H.   Sr. Lectr.
Dellar, R. L.   Sr. Lectr.
Dixon, M. A.   Sr. Lectr.
Owen, H.   Sr. Lectr.
Royle, C.   Sr. Lectr.

Saint, J. A.   Principal Lectr.
Shelbourne, G. J.   Sr. Lectr.
Walker, C.   Sr. Lectr.
Whitley, E. J.   Sr. Lectr.
Other Staff: 3 Lectrs.; 1 Lectr.†

Language and International Studies

Tel: (0115) 848 3136 Fax: (0115) 848 6632
Allwood, Gill, BA Lough., PhD Lough.   Reader
Carbayo-Abengozar, Mercedes   Lectr./Sr. Lectr.
Cervato, Emanuela, BA Hull   Sr. Lectr.
Cole, Katrin C.   Lectr./Sr. Lectr.
Dutt, Sagarika   Lectr./Sr. Lectr.
Fanjul-Fanjul, M. C.   Lectr./Sr. Lectr.
Farrands, C. E. H., MSc Wales   Principal Lectr.
Funamoto, T.   Lectr./Sr. Lectr.
Fysh, P. M., PhD CNAA   Lectr./Sr. Lectr.
Gutierrez-Almarza, Gloria   Lectr./Sr. Lectr.
Hughes, Neil, BA S.Bank, MA Liv.   Principal
   Lectr.
Leahy, Christine B. L., MA   Lectr./ Sr. Lectr.
Lesport-Hall, Lya   Lectr./Sr. Lectr.
Mao, Lingling   Lectr./ Sr. Lectr.
Marklew, Anny   Lectr./Sr. Lectr.
McCaffrey, Enda V., MA Trinity(Dub.), PhD Col.
   Lectr./Sr. Lectr.
Norris, Jenny   Project Co-ordinator
Paleari, Gabriele   Lectr./Sr. Lectr.
Reynolds, Chris   Lectr./Sr. Lectr.
Rigby, Olga   Lectr./Sr. Lectr.
Ross-Waddell, Cathy A.   Lectr./Sr. Lectr.
Santamaria, Mirella P.   Lectr./Sr. Lectr.
Smith, Roy, BA CNAA, MSc S'ton., PhD S'ton.
   Principal Lectr.

Marketing, Retail and Operations

Tel: (0115) 941 8418
   E-mail: nbs.enquiries@ntu.ac.uk
Albery, D.   Lectr./Sr. Lectr.
Allen, A.   Sr. Lectr.
Brittain, P.   Sr. Lectr.
Disney, J.   Sr. Lectr.
Foster, C.   Sr. Lectr.
Harden, G.   Sr. Lectr.
Hiller, A.   Sr. Lectr.
Oxborrow, L.   Sr. Lectr.
Pick, P. A., MSc Nott.Trent   Sr. Lectr.
Reeve, A.   Sr. Lectr.
Sharp, H.   Sr. Lectr.
Stratton, R., BSc Nott., MSc Warw.   Sr. Lectr.
Sullivan, M.   Sr. Lectr.; Head*
Vickerstaff, A., BA   Sr. Lectr.
Whysall, P. T., PhD Nott.   Prof.
Woodall, A.   Sr. Lectr.
Other Staff: 1 Lectr.

Mathematics, Statistics and Operational Research

Tel: (0115) 848 6885 Fax: (0115) 848 2998
Applebaum, D. B., MSc St And., PhD Nott.
   Acting Head*
Barnett, V., BSc MSc PhD DSc, FLS   Prof.; Sr.
   Res. Fellow
Baxter, M. J., BSc Birm., PhD Edin.   Reader
Baylis, D. J., BSc Lond., DPhil Sus.   Sr. Lectr.
Beardah, C. C., BSc Nott., MSc Manc., PhD Manc.
   Sr. Lectr.
Bland, J. A., BSc Reading, PhD E.Anglia   Principal
   Lectr.
Bootyman, D. J., BSc Hull, MSc Warw., MSc
   Brad., PhD Leeds   Sr. Lectr.
Brindley, G., BSc Wales, PhD Wales   Sr. Lectr.
Buglear, J., BA CNAA, MSc Hull   Sr. Lectr.
Coelho, Z., PhD Warw.   Sr. Lectr.
Crabb, D., BEd MSc PhD   Sr. Lectr.
Davies, N., PhD Nott.   Reader/Prof.
Dixon, P. B., BSc St And., MSc Lond.   Principal
   Lectr.
Frost, M. G., BSc Nott., MSc Nott., PhD Lough.
   Principal Lectr.
Gough, J. E., BSc N.U.I., MSc N.U.I., PhD N.U.I.
   Sr. Lectr.
Hood, D. J., BSc Leic., PhD Lough.   Principal
   Lectr.
Hudson, R. L., BA Oxf., DPhil Oxf.   Prof.; Sr.
   Res. Fellow

Jumarhon, B., BSc Tsinghua, PhD Strath.   Sr.
   Lectr.
Kolokoltsov, V., PhD Moscow   Reader
Lightfoot, J. B., MSc Nott.   Sr. Lectr.
Lincoln, J. A. P., BSc Brad.   Sr. Lectr.
Marriott, J. M., BSc Sus., MSc Lond., PhD Nott.
   Principal Lectr.
McCollin, C., BSc Birm., MSc Brad., PhD CNAA
   Sr. Lectr.
Nikolov, H., MSc Belorussian State, PhD Moscow
   Sr. Lectr.
Payne, B. J., BSc Nott.Trent, PhD Nott.Trent   Sr.
   Lectr.
Sackfield, A., PhD Lond.   Reader
Salagean, A., MSc PhD   Sr. Lectr.
Schilling, R. L., PhD Erlangen   Sr. Lectr.
Wallace, S. G., BSc Newcastle(UK)   Sr. Lectr.
Webb, J. N., BSc Durh., PhD Durh.   Sr. Lectr.
Williams, H. C., MA Oxf., MSc Nott.   Sr. Lectr.
Other Staff: 1 Sr. Res. Fellow; 1 Res. Fellow

Maths Science and Sport Education

Tel: (0115) 848 8917 Fax: (0115) 848 6747
Ballard, D. H.   Sr. Lectr.
Cassidy, M. D.   Sr. Lectr.
Cotton, T. J. W.   Reader
Delaney, K. C., BSc Brist., MPhil S'ton.   Sr.
   Lectr.
Dibley, C.   Sr. Lectr.
Gibbons, C. P., BA Newcastle(UK), MA Nott.Trent
   Sr. Lectr.
Hindley, D. J.   Acad. Team Leader
Lee, J. B., BEd Nott., MPhil Nott.Trent   Sr. Lectr.
Mace, J. A.   Sr. Lectr.
Mackintosh, C.   Sr. Lectr.
Ovens, P. J., BSc Leeds, MEd Manc., PhD E.Anglia
   Principal Lectr.
Patmore, F. Mark   Project Co-ordinator
Pawluch, D. C. T., BA Leic.   Principal Lectr.
Williamson, D. C., BSc Oregon, MEd Missouri
   Principal Lectr.
Zaman, F.   Sr. Lectr.
Other Staff: 1 Sr. Technician

Nottingham Law School

Tel: (0115) 848 4498 Fax: (0115) 848 6512
   E-mail: nls.enquiries@ntu.ac.uk
Allen, N., BA Nott.Trent   Sr. Lectr.
Alonzi, A., BA   Sr. Lectr.
Avis, H., LLB   Sr. Lectr.
Baggaley, J., BA Camb., MA Camb.   Sr. Lectr.
Baseley, A., LLB Nott.   Sr. Lectr.
Bell-Boulé, A., LLB Nott.   Sr. Lectr.
Berry, E., LLB Nott.   Sr. Lectr.
Boyes, S., LLB Nott.   Sr. Lectr.
Boylan-Kemp, J., LLB Nott.Trent   Sr. Lectr.
Bramham, J., BA Lanc.   Sr. Lectr.
Brealey, A. C., LLB S'ton.   Sr. Lectr.
Brooks, S., LLB Nott.Trent   Principal Lectr.
Burdette, D. A., BIuris S.Af., LLB S.Af., LLD Pret.
   Prof.
Cassady, S., BA   Sr. Lectr.
Chadwick, E., BA N.Carolina, LLM Nott., PhD
   Nott.   Sr. Lectr.
Ching, J.   Reader
Clarke, S. C., BA Nott.   Principal Lectr.
Costello, G., LLB Liv.   Assoc. Dean
Cranny, A.   Sr. Lectr.
Critchley, E., BA Oxf.   Sr. Lectr.
Cunningham, F., MA Edin., LLM Cardiff   Head,
   Professnl. Div.
Cunningham, G., LLB Nott.   Principal Lectr.
Cutts, N., LLB   Sr. Lectr.
Davidson, A., LLB Leic.   Principal Lectr.
Davies, A., LLB   Principal Lectr.
Davies, J.   Sr. Lectr.
Davies, P.   Principal Lectr.
Donnelly, A., LLB Sheff.   Sr. Lectr.
Duxbury, R. M. C., LLB Leeds   Principal Lectr.
Edwards, H.   Course Leader/Principal Lectr.
Evans, A., BA   Sr. Lectr.
Ferris, G., LLB Nott.   Sr. Lectr.
Field, J. R., LLB Hull   Sr. Lectr.
Fox, I.   Sr. Lectr.
Garwood-Gowers, A., PhD De Mont., LLB   Sr.
   Lectr.
Goodall, C., LLB Nott.   Sr. Lectr.
Grant, J., LLB Leic.   Sr. Lectr.

Grignon, N., LLB Leic. Sr. Lectr.
Hamilton, N., BA CNAA Sr. Lectr.
Hankey, M., BA Sr. Lectr.
Hargreaves, S., PhD Sr. Lectr.
Harris, B., BALaw LLM
Harris, D., BJuris Oxf., MJuris Sr. Lectr.
Harrison, A., LLB Sheff. Sr. Lectr.
Harrison, N., LLB Liv. Sr. Lectr.
Henderson, P. Principal Lectr.
Henham, R. J., LLB Keele, MA Keele, MPhil Nott.
    Sr. Lectr.
Heppell, T., LLB Sr. Lectr.
Hodgson, J. S., MA Camb., LLM Camb.
    Principal Lectr.
Holloway, J., BLaws Principal Lectr.
Holmewood, M. Sr. Lectr.
Hooper, J. M., LLB Leeds Principal Lectr.
Hosking, A., BA Lond. Sr. Lectr.
Hudson, H., LLB Coventry Principal Lectr.
Huxley-Binns, R., LLB Lanc. Sr. Lectr.
Ireton, E., BSc Lond. Sr. Lectr.
Jarman, J., BA Sr. Lectr.
Johansen, K., LLB Brist. Sr. Lectr.
Johnson, N., BA Exe. Sr. Lectr.
Johnson, P., LLB Kingston(UK) Sr. Lectr.
Karat, P., BA Oxf. Sr. Lectr.
Kenny, D., LLB Sr. Lectr.
Kirk, E. C., LLB Nott. Sr. Lectr.
Klisz, M., BA Sr. Lectr.
Knott, P. M., LLB Newcastle(UK) Exec. Dir.
Latham, A. J., LLB Brist. Principal Lectr.
Launchbury, T., LLB Nott., LLM Nott. Sr. Lectr.
Lewis, T., BA Oxf. Sr. Lectr.
Lloyd-Davies, P., LLM Lond. Sr. Lectr.
Lowe, S., BSc Principal Lectr.
Lucas, N., LLB Sheff., LLM Leic. Sr. Lectr.
Macgregor, L., LLB Exe. Sr. Lectr.
Maksymiw, M., LLB Manc. Sr. Lectr.
Manning, R., LLB Leic. Sr. Lectr.
Martin, T., BA Sr. Lectr.
McLaughlin, S., LLB Leeds, LLM Sr. Lectr.
McTigue, P., BSocSci Sr. Lectr.
Miller, S. E., LLB Manc. Principal Lectr.
Mills, K., BLaw Liv. Sr. Lectr.
Millward, M. R., BA Oxf. Sr. Lectr.
Moffatt, P., BLaw Lond. Sr. Lectr.
Morton, S. G. C., LLB Lond. Sr. Lectr.
Murray, J., LLB Leic., PhD Leic. Sr. Lectr.
Murray, R., LLB Sr. Lectr.
Nicholson, A., LLB LLM Sr. Lectr.
Pacey, J., LLB LLM MBA Sr. Lectr.
Parry, R., LLB Sheff., LLM Newcastle(UK), PhD
    Manc. Prof.
Parsons, S., MA Oxf. Sr. Lectr.
Pegg, S., LLB Nott.Trent, PhD Nott.Trent Sr.
    Lectr.
Piggott, A. Sr. Lectr.
Rawlinson, V., LLB Leeds Met. Sr. Lectr.
Rea, T., LLB Brist., LLM Sr. Lectr.
Rodgers, L., LLB BASocSci Sr. Lectr.
Rushby, A., LLB Sheff.Hallam Sr. Lectr.
Russell, S., LLB Sr. Lectr.
Savage, A., MLaw Camb. Sr. Lectr.
Seneviratne, M. Head of ALS
Shone, L. Sr. Lectr.
Smith, C. Sr. Lectr.
Smith, J. D., LLB CNAA Sr. Lectr.
Sood, U. R., LLB Nott., MPhil Nott. Sr. Lectr.
Spearing, F. E., LLB Birm. Sr. Lectr.
Stephens, J. Sr. Lectr.
Stobart, T. Sr. Lectr.
Stretch, R. Sr. Lectr.
Sumpton, M. Sr. Lectr.
Taberham, J. Sr. Lectr.
Taylor, H. Sr. Lectr.
Taylor, I. Sr. Lectr.
Tegerdine, E. Sr. Lectr.
Thornton, L., LLB Manc. Dir., Undergrad.
    Programmes
Tingle, J. H., BA CNAA, MEd Birm. Sr. Lectr.
Trickett, L., MA Leic. Sr. Lectr.
Turner, C., BSc Sr. Lectr.
Turner, H. Sr. Lectr.
Twycross, H. C., BA CNAA Sr. Lectr.
Wainwright, J. A., BA Nott. Sr. Lectr.
Wakefield, J., BA Keele Acad. Team Leader
Walters, A., BA Camb. Prof., Corporate and
    Insolvency Law

Walters, T., LLB MA Visiting Prof.
Walters, T., BScEc Aberd.
West, M. Sr. Lectr.
Wheat, V. K., BA Reading Sr. Lectr.
White, R. D., BA CNAA Course Dir.
Wilson, G., BJuris Oxf. Reader
Wong, R., LLB Derby, MSc Lough., LLM Sheff.,
    PhD Sr. Lectr.
Wootton, S. Sr. Lectr.
Worsfold, A. Sr. Lectr.

Nottingham Technology Education Development Group

Tel: (0115) 848 2912 Fax: (0115) 848 6485
Batchelor, M. C., BEd Lough. Head*
Harrison, G. B., MA Camb. Prof.

Politics and Sociology

Darko, Natalie Lectr./Sr. Lectr.
Fitzgerald, Tony Lectr./Sr. Lectr.
Fraser, Ian, MA Edin., MA York(UK), PhD Warw.
    Lectr./Sr. Lectr.
Gann, Rose Acad. Team Leader
Goatcher, Jeff, PhD Lectr./Sr. Lectr.
Haselden, Karl Lectr./Sr. Lectr.
Keenan, Will Lectr./Sr. Lectr.
Lee, Deborah, BA Warw., MA Warw., PhD
    Warw. Lectr./Sr. Lectr.
McKay, Joanna, BA MSc(Econ) PhD Lectr./Sr.
    Lectr.
O'Neill, Michael Reader
Simon, Rick, BA Nott., MA CNAA, PhD Birm.
    Lectr./Sr. Lectr.
Wilde, Larry, BA Liv., PhD Liv. Prof.
Wright, Cecile Prof.
Other Staff: 1 Lectr.; 1 Project Officer
Research: British politics and administration
    (Conservative Party, information and
    government); comparative politics
    (environmental politics, election rhetoric);
    political theory (Hegel and Marx studies,
    needs and ethics)

Primary Teacher Education

Tel: (0115) 848 8917 Fax: (0115) 848 6747
Brown, V. Sr. Lectr.
Paramore, J. Sr. Lectr.

Secondary Teacher Training

Adcock, L. M. Sr. Lectr.
Ballard, D. H. Sr. Lectr.
Boulton, H. E. Learning and Teaching Co-
    ordinator
Harris, A. C. Sr. Lectr.

Social Work, Human Services and Counselling

Bardouille, Deborah, BA Sr. Lectr.
Barnard, Adam, BA MA PhD Sr. Lectr.
Baugh, Andy, BSc Bath, MPhil York(UK) Sr.
    Lectr.
Beart, Kirsty, MSc Sr. Lectr.
Boyd, Fiona Sr. Lectr.
Hallam, Bridget, BA MSc Sr. Lectr.
Harling, Martyn Sr. Lectr.
Jenkins, Anne, BSc Lond. Principal Lectr.
John-Baptiste, Catherine, BSc Sr. Lectr.
Liggett, Ann Principal Lectr.
Peach, Jeremy Acad. Team Leader
Raithby, Michelle, BSc Lond., MSc Oxf.
    Principal Lectr.
Sheppard, Mark Practice Learning
    Development Officer
Smith, Jo Sr. Lectr.
Ward, Jo, BA MA Programme Leader
Whitehead, Graham Sr. Lectr.
Wild, Jim Sr. Lectr.

Strategic Management and International Business

Tel: (0115) 941 8418
    E-mail: nbs.enquiries@ntu.ac.uk
Barley, G., MBA Brad. Sr. Lectr.
Brown, M. Sr. Lectr.
Fredericks, J. R., BA CNAA Sr. Lectr.
Helienek, E., MA Brno, MBA Nott.Trent, PhD
    Sofia, PhD Sr. Lectr.
Hodgkinson, M. Prof.

Ibrahim, G.
Mercado, S. A., BA Nott.Trent, MA Nott.Trent,
    PhD Nott.Trent Head*
Murphy, M. J., MPhil Nott. Sr. Lectr.
Neshamba, F., BSc Z'bwe.Open, PhD Cran.
Shackley, M. L., PhD S'ton. Prof.
Slater, K., MPhil Nott. Sr. Lectr.
Smith, D. Prof.; Dir., Res.
Teng, W. Sr. Lectr.
Welton, R. Sr. Lectr.
Winfield, F. M., BA CNAA Sr. Lectr.

Surveying

Tel: (0115) 848 2522 Fax: (0115) 848 6507
Beynon, N. J., BA Nott., MA Lond. Principal
    Lectr.
Butler, I., BSc MA Sr. Lectr.
Collins, P. R., MSc Principal Lectr.
Corner, R. B. Sr. Lectr.
Cudworth, A. L., MPhil, FRICS Sr. Lectr.
Fleming, D. N., BSc CNAA, MBA Principal
    Lectr.
Gallimore, P., MA PhD, FRICS Prof.; Head*
Griffiths, P. A. Sr. Lectr.
Hawkins, P. R., MSc Sheff.Hallam Sr. Lectr.
Hogg, K. I., BSc CNAA, FRICS Sr. Lectr.
Holden, P. Sr. Lectr.
Lane, J. H. Sr. Lectr.
Mansfield, John, BSc MSc Sr. Lectr.
Massey, R., MSc Aston Sr. Lectr.
Moohan, J. A. J., MA Prof.
Morledge, R., MSc H-W, FRICS Prof.
Noor-Mohamed, B., BSc CNAA, MBA Sr.
    Lectr.
Reyers, John, BSc Sr. Lectr.
Rowe, D. G. Sr. Lectr.
Royston, P. J., BSc City(UK), MBA City(UK)
    Principal Lectr.
Shaw, S. B., BA, FRICS Sr. Lectr.
Stafford, K. D., FRICS Principal Lectr.
Trow, P. S. Sr. Lectr.
Tyler, S. B., BSc Lough., MBA Lough., FRICS
    Principal Lectr.
Wetton, B. W., BA S'ton., MA S'ton. Principal
    Lectr.
Wiltshaw, D. G., BSc MSc Reader
Winfield, R., FRICS Principal Lectr.
Yarwood, C. P. D., MA, FRICS Sr. Lectr.
Other Staff: 1 Res. Lectr.; 16 Lectrs.†
Research: construction procurement (appropriate
    strategies for clients); contaminated land
    (economics and policy evaluation); real
    estate decision-making behaviour

Visual Arts

Tel: (0115) 848 6088 Fax: (0115) 848 6403
Abbott, F. J., BA Hull Sr. Lectr.
Birringer, Johannes
Brown, Andrew Sr. Lectr.
Cummins, S.
Davey, R.
Flint, R. Sr. Lectr.
Franks, M.
Higgins, D.
Ingram, T. Sr. Lectr.
Jones, C. A., BA CNAA, MDes RCA Sr. Lectr.
Lee, J. Sr. Lectr.
Lewis, S., MFA Reading Prof.; Head*
Lycouris, S., PhD Sur. Sr. Lectr.
Maier, D. Sr. Lectr.
Mottram, J. Prof.
Newling, J. B., BA CNAA, MA CNAA, MPhil
    CNAA Prof.
Shave, T. Prof.
Shaw, L. Sr. Lectr.
Sprawson, D. H., BA CNAA, MFA Reading Sr.
    Lectr.
Other Staff: 2 Lectrs.; 1 Principal Res. Fellow
Research: digital imaging photography; film and
    video; fine art and documentary
    photography; live art and live art archiving;
    performance

SPECIAL CENTRES, ETC

Automotive Industries Management, Centre for

Tel: (0115) 848 4056 Fax: (0115) 848 6037
E-mail: diane.seymour@ntu.ac.uk
Cooke, P. N. C.   Prof.; Head*

Corporate Business Unit

Tel: (0115) 848 6418 Fax: (0115) 848 6037
E-mail: cbu@ntu.ac.uk
Clewes, Debbie   Sr. Lectr.
Cobbold, Nigel   Sr. Lectr.
Hall, Rachael, BA *Leeds*, MSc *Nott.Trent*   Sr. Lectr.
Harris, Lynette   Dir., Human Resources Professl. Devel.
Jukes, Brian   Sr. Lectr.
Knowles, Vanessa, MA *Nott.Trent*   Sr. Lectr.
Prince, Chris   Dir.*
Tranter, S.   Sr. Lectr.

Growing Businesses, Centre for

Tel: (0115) 848 6128 Fax: (0115) 848 6130
E-mail: vivien.flynn@ntu.ac.uk
Llewelyn, T., BSc(Econ) *Lond.*   Sr. Lectr.
Neshamba, F., BSc *Z'bwe.Open*, PhD *Cran.*   Sr. Lectr.
Rae, D., BA *Brist.*, MEd *Sheff.*   Sr. Lectr.
Vyakanam, V., MBA *Cran.*, PhD *Cran.*   Prof., Enterprises; Dir.*
Other Staff: 2 Res. Fellows

International Business Centre

Tel: (0115) 948 6417 Fax: (0115) 950 5048
E-mail: ewa.helienek@ntu.ac.uk
Love, C.   Co-ordinator*

Quality Unit

Tel: (0115) 848 6830 Fax: (0115) 848 6420
E-mail: sarah.dossor@ntu.ac.uk
Disney, J., BSc *Nott.*, PhD *Nott.Trent*   Sr. Lectr.
Drake, P., BSc *Leeds*   Sr. Lectr.

Tew, R. E., BSc *CNAA*, MA *Lanc.*   Principal Lectr.
Woodall, T., BA *Nott.Trent*   Sr. Lectr.

CONTACT OFFICERS

Computing services. Head, Computing Services: Griffiths, I. D., BSc *Wales*
Finance. Chief Financial and Operations Officer: Jackson, Stephen
General enquiries. Registrar: Samson, David, BA MBA
Library (chief librarian). Head of Library and Information Services: McKnight, Sue
Marketing. Head of Integrated Marketing: Scarborough, Jane (E-mail: marketing@ntu.ac.uk)
Public relations. Director of Corporate Affairs: Spencer, Jennifer, BSc
Research. Director of Research: Joyner, Prof. R. W., BSc PhD DSc, FRSChem

[*Information supplied by the institution as at 24 September 2007, and edited by the ACU*]

OPEN UNIVERSITY

Founded 1969

Member of the Association of Commonwealth Universities

Postal Address: Walton Hall, Milton Keynes, England MK7 6AA
Telephone: (01908) 274066
URL: http://www.open.ac.uk

VICE-CHANCELLOR*—Gourley, Prof. Brenda M., MBL *S.Af.*, Hon. LLD *Nott.*, FRSA
SECRETARY‡—Woodburn, A. Fraser, BSc *Edin.*
PRO-VICE-CHANCELLOR (CURRICULUM AND AWARDS)—Kirkpatrick, Prof. Denise, BEd MEd DPhil
PRO-VICE-CHANCELLOR (LEARNING TECHNOLOGIES AND TEACHING)—Tait, Prof. Alan, MA *Camb.*, MA *Lond.*
PRO-VICE-CHANCELLOR (STRATEGY, PLANNING AND EXTERNAL AFFAIRS)—Vincent, Prof. David, BA PhD, FRSA, FRHistS
PRO-VICE-CHANCELLOR (RESEARCH)—Heywood, Prof. Brigid, BSc *Liv.*, PhD *Liv.*
DIRECTOR (STUDENTS)—Swann, Will S., BA
FINANCE DIRECTOR—Hedges, Miles, MA, FCA, FRSA

GENERAL INFORMATION

History. The university was established in 1969. It is an international university providing part-time higher education to the United Kingdom, the European Union and elsewhere overseas.

Its central offices are located in Milton Keynes, 80km north-west of London.

Admission to first degree courses (see also United Kingdom Introduction). Those resident in the UK/other parts of the EU/other areas where the university has agreed to register students are eligible for admission. There are no formal academic entry requirements. Students must normally be aged 18 or over.

First Degrees (see also United Kingdom Directory to Subjects of Study) (* = with honours). BA, BA*, BSc, BSc*, MEng, MMaths.

All courses are part-time and are assessed on a credit points rating (usually 60 or 30 points per course). Minimum requirements for a first degree are 360 credit points at specific levels. First degree master's: minimum 480 credit points. Most students study at the rate of 60 credit points a year.

Higher Degrees (see also United Kingdom Directory to Subjects of Study).
Master's. BPhil, MA, MBA, MPhil, MSc.
Admission. Direct applicants for admission to master's degree courses should normally hold a good first degree with honours; entry to master's degrees by coursework is also possible via a relevant diploma of the university.

Master's degrees normally require 180 credit points; entrants with university diploma (certain courses): 120 points.
Doctoral. DLitt, DSc, PhD.
DLitt, DSc: by published work.

Libraries. Periodicals subscribed to: 2400. Other holdings: 180,000 books and microforms; 150,000 non-book materials.

FACULTIES/SCHOOLS

Arts

Tel: (01908) 652479 Fax: (01908) 653750
E-mail: arts-faculty-enquiries@open.ac.uk
Dean: Rowland, Prof. David E., MA *Camb.*, PhD *Camb.*
Senior Faculty Administrator: Robertson, Hilary

Education and Language Studies (FELS)

Tel: (01908) 653299 Fax: (01908) 858429
E-mail: fels-dean@open.ac.uk
Dean and Director: Ding, Sharon, BA *Nott.*, PhD *Nott.*
Senior Faculty Administrator: Abbott, Justine

Educational Technology, Institute of

Tel: (01908) 653536 Fax: (01908) 654173
E-mail: iet@open.ac.uk
Acting Director: Taylor, Josie, DPhil *Sus.*, BA
Senior Faculty Administrator: Weaver, Amanda

Health and Social Care

Tel: (01908) 653743 Fax: (01908) 654124
E-mail: hsc-faculty-enquiries@open.ac.uk

Dean: Reveley, Prof. Shirley, BA *Open(UK)*, MA *Lanc.*, PhD *Lanc.*
Senior Faculty Administrator: Brett, Dympna

Mathematics, Computing and Technology

Tel: (01908) 653241 Fax: (01908) 652140
E-mail: maths-faculty-enquiries@openmail.ac.uk
Dean: Earl, Prof. Christopher, BA *Oxf.*, MSc *Oxf.*, PhD *Open(UK)*
Senior Faculty Secretary: Ogden, Liz

Open University Business School

Tel: (01908) 655888 Fax: (01908) 655898
E-mail: oubs-ilgen@open.ac.uk
Dean: Fleck, Prof. James, BSc *Edin.*, MA *Edin.*, MSc *Edin.*
Director of Planning and Resources: Green, Geoff

Science

Tel: (01908) 653993 Fax: (01908) 652559
E-mail: science-webmaster@openmail.open.ac.uk
Dean and Director of Studies: Potts, Philip, BSc *Leeds*, PhD *Leeds*, DSc *Open(UK)*
Faculty Administrator: Findlay, Roy

Social Sciences

Tel: (01908) 654431 Fax: (01908) 654488
E-mail: social-science-enquiries@open.ac.uk
Dean: Meill, Prof. Dorothy
Senior Faculty Administrator: Henderson, Michelle

ACADEMIC UNITS

Note—The academic staff of the university are organised into faculties but not into departments. The disciplines listed below represent the general subject interests of the staff concerned.

Art History

Tel: (01908) 652479 Fax: (01908) 653750
E-mail: arts-arthistory-gen-enquiries@open.ac.uk

Benton, Tim, BA Camb., MA Lond.   Prof.
Harrison, Charles, BA Camb., MA Camb., PhD Lond.   Prof.
King, Catherine E., BA Lond., MPhil Lond., PhD E.Anglia   Prof.
Norman, Diana, BA Lond., MA Lond., PhD Open(UK)   Sr. Lectr.
Perry, Gill, BA Sus., DPhil Sus.   Sr. Lectr.; Head*
Walsh, Linda, BA Lond., PhD Sheff.   Sr. Lectr.
Wood, Paul, MA Lond.   Sr. Lectr.
Other Staff: 6 Lectrs.

Biological Sciences

Tel: (01908) 653225 Fax: (01908) 654167
E-mail: h.j.holden@open.ac.uk

Datta, Saroj, BSc Glas., PhD Camb.   Sr. Lectr.
Davey, Basiro C., BSc Lond., PhD Lond.   Sr. Lectr.
Gillman, Michael P., BSc Sus., PhD S'ton.   Sr. Lectr.
Green, Alison   Sr. Lectr.
Halliday, Tim R., MA Oxf., DPhil Oxf.   Prof.
Hirst, Mark C., BSc Manc., PhD Edin.   Sr. Lectr.
Loughlin, Jane   Sr. Lectr.
MacQueen, Hilary, BSc Sheff., PhD Edin.   Sr. Lectr.
Male, David, BA Camb., PhD Lond.   Prof.; Head*
Mileusnic, Radmila, BSc Belgrade, MSc Belgrade, DrSc Belgrade   Sr. Lectr.
Pond, Caroline, MA Oxf., DPhil Oxf.   Prof.
Robinson, David J., BSc Newcastle(UK), PhD Nott.   Sr. Lectr.
Romero, Ignacio, BSc Valencia, PhD Lond.   Sr. Lectr.
Roth, Ilona A., MA Oxf., DPhil Oxf.   Sr. Lectr.
Saffrey, M. Jill, BSc Lond., PhD Lond.   Sr. Lectr.
Saunders, Robert D., BSc Edin., PhD Edin.   Reader
Silvertown, Jonathan W., BSc Sus., DPhil Sus.   Prof.
Stewart, Mike G., BSc Belf., PhD Belf.   Prof.
Thomas, Jeffrey N., BSc Birm., PhD Birm.   Sr. Lectr.
Toates, Fred M., DSc City(UK), DPhil Sus.   Reader
Other Staff: 10 Lectrs.; 10 Res. Fellows

Chemistry

Tel: (01908) 653226 Fax: (01908) 858327
E-mail: s.hegarty@open.ac.uk

Bennett, Stuart W., BSc Sus., DPhil Sus.   Sr. Lectr.
Berry, Frank J., BSc Lond., PhD Lond., DSc Lond.   Prof.
Iley, Jim N., BSc Lond., PhD Lond.   Sr. Lectr.
Moore, Elaine, MA Oxf., DPhil Oxf.   Sr. Lectr.
Mortimer, Michael, BSc Lond., PhD Leeds   Sr. Lectr.
Roberts, David R., MSc E.Anglia, MA Camb., PhD E.Anglia   Sr. Lectr.; Head*
Smart, Lesley E., BSc S'ton., PhD S'ton.   Sr. Lectr.
Taylor, Peter G., BSc E.Anglia, PhD E.Anglia   Prof.
Xu, Yao Z., BSc Hangzhou, PhD Shanghai   Sr. Lectr.
Other Staff: 5 Staff Tutors; 3 Res. Fellows

Classics

Tel: (01908) 653247 Fax: (01908) 653750
E-mail: arts-classics-gen-enquiries@open.ac.uk

Emlyn-Jones, Christopher, BA Birm., PhD Birm.   Sr. Lectr.

Hardwick, Lorna, BA Sus., MA Sus., PhD City(UK)   Prof.
Huskinson, Janet, MA Camb., PhD Camb.   Sr. Lectr.
James, Paula, BA S'ton., PhD S'ton.   Sr. Lectr.; Head*
Perkins, Philip, BA Lond., PhD Lond.   Sr. Lectr.
Other Staff: 3 Lectrs.; 2 Staff Tutors; 1 Res. Fellow; 4 Res. Assocs.; 2 Project Officers

Communication and Systems

Tel: (01908) 655561 Fax: (01908) 653718
E-mail: a.a.ibbotson@open.ac.uk

Alexander, Gary R., BS Col., PhD Purdue   Sr. Lectr.
Armson, R., BSc Newcastle(UK), PhD Open(UK)
Bell, S., BA E.Anglia, MPhil City(UK), PhD E.Anglia   Sr. Lectr.
Bettley, Alison, BSc Durh., MBA Open(UK), PhD Open(UK)   Sr. Lectr.
Bissell, Chris, MA Camb., PhD Open(UK), FIEE   Prof.
Blackmore, C., BSc E.Anglia   Sr. Lectr.
Chapman, David A., MA Oxf., MSc Aston, PhD Open(UK)   Sr. Lectr.
Fortune, Joyce, BSc Lough., PhD Nott.   Sr. Lectr.; Head*
Heap, Nick W., BSc CNAA, PhD Open(UK)   Sr. Lectr.
Holwell, S., BComm MSc PhD   Sr. Lectr.
Hughes, John, BA S'ton., DPhil Oxf.   Sr. Lectr.
Ison, Ray L., BScAgr Syd., PhD Qld.   Prof., Systems
Martin, Glyn, BSc Lond.   Head*
Martin, J. N. T., BSc Edin., MA Edin., PhD Lond.   Sr. Lectr.
Meade, Mike L., BScTech UMIST, PhD Reading, FIEE   Sr. Lectr.
Monk, John, BSc(Eng) Lond., PhD Warw., FBCS, FIEE   Prof.
Morris, R. M., BA Oxf., MA Oxf., PhD Reading   Sr. Lectr.
Naughton, J. J., BE N.U.I., MA Camb.   Sr. Lectr.
Peters, G., BSc Lough., MSc Sus.   Prof.
Spear, R., BSc(Eng) Lond., MA Lanc.   Sr. Lectr.
Other Staff: 32 Lectrs.; 4 Res. Fellows
Research: change management in manufacturing; ethical manufacturing; organisational learning; project management; systems failures (including information systems)

Computing

Tel: (01908) 653037 Fax: (01908) 652140
E-mail: mcs-computer-department@open.ac.uk

Barroca, Leonor, LicEng C.U.Portugal, MSc Oxf., PhD S'ton.   Sr. Lectr.
Bowers, David S., MA Camb., PhD Camb.   Sr. Lectr.
Cooke, I., BSc Lond., MSc Salf., PhD Lond.   Sr. Lectr.; Staff Tutor, Mathematics and Computing
De Roeck, Anne N., LicGermFil Leuven, MSc Essex   Prof.; Dir., Curriculum
Griffiths, Robert W., BA CNAA, MSc CNAA   Sr. Lectr.
Ince, Darrel C., BSc Wales, PhD Wales, FBCS   Prof.; Head*
Meehan, Anthony, BSc CNAA   Sr. Lectr.
Minocha, Shailey, BE Delhi, PhD IIT Delhi   Sr. Lectr.
Morse, David, BSc York(UK), DPhil York(UK)   Sr. Lectr.
Nuseibeh, Bashar A., BSc Sus., MSc Lond., PhD Lond., FBCS   Prof.; Dir., Res.
Petre, Marian, BA Penn., PhD Lond.   Reader
Quinn, Brendan, BSc Manc., BA Camb., MSc Sheff.   Sr. Lectr.
Robinson, Hugh M., BA Keele, MSc Lond., PhD CNAA   Sr. Lectr.
Scott, Donia, BA Hollins, MSc Sus., DPhil Sus.   Prof.
Sharp, Helen C., MSc Lond., PhD Lond.   Sr. Lectr.
Thomas, Peter G., BSc Leic., MSc Dund., PhD Dund.   Sr. Lectr.
Wermelinger, Michel, LicEng New Lisbon, MSc New Lisbon, PhD New Lisbon   Sr. Lectr.

Woodroffe, Mark, BA Liv., MSc Essex, MBA Open(UK), PhD Essex   Sr. Lectr.
Other Staff: 20 Lectrs.; 2 Res. Fellows; 8 Staff Tutors
Vacant Posts: 1 Lectr.
Research: cross-cutting themes (ubiquitous computing, GRID computing, security); human-computer interaction (usability, user-interface design, e-business, social aspects); informatics education (automatic assessment, mobile learning, empirical studies); intelligent systems (natural language processing, AI, robotics); software engineering (empirical studies, design, requirements)

Design, Development, Environment and Materials

Tel: (01908) 652944 Fax: (01908) 654052
E-mail: s.e.butler@opcn.ac.uk

Barratt, Rod S., BSc Birm., PhD Birm., FRSChem   Sr. Lectr.
Boyle, Godfrey   Sr. Lectr.
Burnley, Stephen, BSc Newcastle(UK), PhD Newcastle(UK)   Sr. Lectr.
Chataway, Joanna, BA Colorado, MPhil Sus., PhD Open(UK)   Prof.
Cross, Nigel G., BSc Bath, MSc Manc., PhD Manc.   Prof.
Demaid, Adrian, BSc Aston, MPhil CNAA   Sr. Lectr.
Dewberry, Emma   Sr. Lectr.
Dixon, John C., MA Oxf., PhD Reading, FIMechE, FRAeS   Sr. Lectr.
Edwards, Lyndon, MA Oxf., DPhil Oxf., FIMMM   Prof.; Head*
Elliott, David A., BSc Lond., PhD Lond.   Prof.
Endean, Mark H., BSc Lough.   Sr. Lectr.
Fitzpatrick, M. E., MA Camb., PhD Camb.   Sr. Lectr.
Garner, Steven W., BA CNAA, MPhil Lough., PhD Lough.   Sr. Lectr.
Hanlon, Joseph, BA M.I.T., PhD Tufts   Sr. Lectr.
Johnson, Hazel, BA Lond., MSc Lond., PhD Open(UK)
Johnson, Jeffrey H., BA Essex, PhD Essex, FIMA, FBCS   Prof., Complexity Science and Design; Head*
Lewis, Peter R., BSc Manc., PhD Manc.   Sr. Lectr.
Mohan, Giles, BA Manc., PhD Liv.   Sr. Lectr.
Nesaratnam, Suresh T., BSc(Eng) Lond., MSc Birm., PhD Birm.   Sr. Lectr.
Plumbridge, Bill J., MSc Manc., MA Camb., PhD Manc., FIMMM   Prof.
Porteous, Andrew, BSc H-W, MEng Dartmouth, DEng Dartmouth, FIMechE   Emer. Prof.
Potter, Stephen, BSc Lond., PhD Open(UK)   Sr. Res. Fellow
Roy, Robin, BSc Manc., MSc Manc., PhD Manc.   Prof.
Sharp, David B., BSc Edin.   Sr. Lectr.
Wield, David V., BSc Lond., MSc Lond., PhD Lond.   Prof.
Wilson, Gordon A., BSc Leeds, PhD Leeds   Sr. Lectr.
Other Staff: 22 Lectrs.; 9 Res. Fellows
Research: fatigue and fracture; forensic engineering; lead-free solders; plasma processing; residual stress measurement

Earth Sciences

Tel: (01908) 653012 Fax: (01908) 655151
E-mail: earth-sciences-hod@open.ac.uk

Blake, Steve, BSc St And., PhD Lanc.   Sr. Lectr.
Burton, Kevin W., BSc Lond., PhD Lond.   Prof.
Coe, Angela L., BSc Durh., DPhil Oxf.   Sr. Lectr.
Harris, Nigel B. W., MA Camb., PhD Camb., FGS   Prof.
Kelley, Simon P., PhD Lond., FGS   Head*
Rothery, David A., BA Camb., MA Camb., PhD Open(UK), FGS   Sr. Lectr.
Rymer, Hazel, BSc Reading, PhD Open(UK)   Sr. Lectr.
Self, Stephen, BSc Leeds, PhD Lond., FGS   Prof.
Sheldon, Peter R., BSc Durh., PhD Camb., FGS, FLS   Sr. Lectr.

Skelton, Peter W., BSc Brist., DPhil Oxf., FGS
Sr. Lectr.
Spicer, Robert A., BSc Lond., MA Oxf., PhD
Lond., FGS Prof.
Other Staff: 9 Lectrs.; 2 Sr. Res. Fellows; 4
Staff Tutors; 1 Sr. Project Officer; 5 Project
Officers; 12 Res. Fellows; 8 Visiting Staff
Research: environmental change in earth history;
isotope geochemistry and earth systems;
volcano dynamics

Economics

Tel: (01908) 654437 Fax: (01908) 654488
E-mail: a.lexton@open.ac.uk
Anand, Paul, PhD Reader; Head*
Brown, Vivienne, BSc Lond., MSc Lond., PhD
Lond. Prof.
Dawson, Graham, BA Oxf., PhD Sr. Lectr.
Himmelweit, Susan, BA Camb., PhD Camb.
Prof.
Mackintosh, Maureen, BA Oxf., DPhil Sus.
Prof.
Mazzucato, Mariana, BA Tufts, PhD New
Sch.Soc.Res.(N.Y.) Sr. Lectr.
Simonetti, Roberto, PhD Sr. Lectr.
Trigg, Andrew, BA Manc., PhD Liv. Sr. Lectr.
Other Staff: 1 Lectr.; 4 Staff Tutors; 2 Res.
Fellows

Education and Language Studies, Faculty of (FELS)

Tel: (01908) 652896 Fax: (01908) 858429

Childhood Development and Learning, Centre of

Tel: (01908) 653295 Fax: (01908) 858868
E-mail: fels-chdl-admin@open.ac.uk
Barnes, Peter R. W., BA Nott., MPhil Nott. Sr.
Lectr.; Dir.*
Faulkner, Dorothy, BA Stir., DPhil Oxf. Sr.
Lectr.
Hammersley, Martyn, BSc Lond., MA(Econ)
Manc., PhD Manc. Prof.
Kehily, Mary Jane, BA CNAA, MSocSci Birm.,
PhD Lond. Sr. Lectr.
Lewis, Vicky A., BA Oxf., MA Oxf., DPhil Oxf.
Prof.
Littleton, Karen S., BSc York(UK), DPhil York(UK)
Sr. Lectr.
Messer, David J., BSc Reading, PhD Strath. Prof.
Oates, John, BTech Brun. Sr. Lectr.
Woodhead, Martin, MA Manc., MA Leic., PhD
Open(UK) Prof., Childhood Studies
Other Staff: 4 Lectrs.; 1 Res. Fellow

Curriculum and Teaching Studies, Centre of

Tel: (01908) 652897 Fax: (01908) 654841
E-mail: d.cowling@open.ac.uk
Cable, Caroline, BA Exe. Sr. Lectr.
Craft, Anna, MA Camb., MA Lond. Sr. Lectr.
Griffith, Peter, MA Camb., MA Lond., FRSA Sr.
Lectr.
Hall, Kathy, BA PhD Prof.
McCormick, Robert, BSc CNAA, MA Leeds, PhD
Open(UK), FRSA Prof.
Miller, Linda K., MA Lond., MPhil Herts., PhD
Herts. Sr. Lectr.
Murphy, Patricia F., BSc Manc. Reader
Ralston, John, BEd Sr. Lectr.
Soler, Janet M., BA Massey, MPhil Massey, PhD
Otago Sr. Lectr.
Twining, Peter, BA Sus., PhD Open(UK) Sr.
Lectr.
Other Staff: 9 Lectrs.; 2 Res. Fellows
Research: assessment policy and practice;
learning and childhood; literacy and
language policy and practice; science,
technology and ICT policy and practice;
teaching for creativity

Educational Policy, Leadership and Lifelong Learning, Centre for

Tel: (01908) 652901 Fax: (01908) 654841
Anderson, Lesley, BA Essex, MSc Warw., EdD
Leic. Sr. Lectr.
Arthur, Eleonore, MSc MIL PhD Sr. Lectr.

Bennett, Nigel, MA Camb., MA Lanc., PhD Brun.
Sr. Lectr.; Dir.*
Cartwright, Marion, BA Lond., MA Open(UK)
Sr. Lectr.; Staff Tutor, OU in the S. W.
Harrison, Roger, MA St And. Sr. Lectr.
Kydd, Lesley, BA Ulster, MEd Glas. Sr. Lectr.
Newton, Wendy, BSc Wales, MA Nott. Sr.
Lectr.
Preedy, Maggie, BA E.Anglia, MA Sus., PhD
Open(UK), FRSA Sr. Lectr.
Other Staff: 4 Lectrs.; 2 Res. Fellows; 1 Staff
Tutor
Research: creative teaching and learning;
educational partnerships; non-formal and
informal learning; school leadership and
leadership development; work-related
learning

Language and Communications, Centre for

Tel: (01908) 652900 Fax: (01908) 654111
Coffin, Caroline, BA Liv., MAppLing Macq.,
MEdAdmin NSW, PhD NSW Sr. Lectr.
Cook, Guy W. D., MA Camb., MA Lond., PhD
Leeds, FRSA Prof.
Hewings, Ann, BSc S'ton., MPhil Birm., PhD
Birm. Sr. Lectr.
Lillis, Theresa, BA Leeds, MAppLing Sheff., MPhil
N.U.I., PhD Sheff.Hallam Sr. Lectr.
Maybin, Janet, BA Durh., MA Sus., PhD Open(UK)
Sr. Lectr.
Swann, Joan, BA Manc., MA Reading Sr. Lectr.;
Dir.*
Other Staff: 7 Lectrs.
Research: academic literacy; children's language;
educational dialogue; language and identity;
professional discourse

Languages, Department of

Tel: (01908) 652223 Fax: (01908) 652187
E-mail: fels-dol-admin@open.ac.uk
Adams, Helga L., MA CNAA Sr. Lectr.
Baumann, Uwe, MA Keele, MBA Open(UK) Sr.
Lectr.
Coleman, James A., BA Exe., MA Exe., PhD
Portsmouth, FRSA, FIL Prof.
Garrido, Cecilia, BA Colombia Natnl., MA Inst.Caro
y Cuervo Sr. Lectr.
Hampel, Regine, MA Tübingen, PhD Tübingen
Sr. Lectr.
Hauck, Mirjam C., MAAppLing Heidel. Sr.
Lectr.
Hurd, Stella, BA S'ton., MA Wolv. Sr. Lectr.
Lamy, Marie-Noëlle, LèsL Paris IV, Maîtrise Paris
IV Sr. Lectr.; Dir.*
Murphy, Linda, MA Wales, EdD Open(UK) Sr.
Lectr.
Nicolson, Margaret, MA Glas., MPhil Stir. Sr.
Lectr.
Other Staff: 29 Lectrs.; 12 Staff Tutors

Research and Development in Teacher Education, Centre of

Tel: (01908) 652391 Fax: (01908) 652218
E-mail: fels-crete-admin@open.ac.uk
Banks, Frank, BA York(UK), MA(Ed) Open(UK),
FRSA Sr. Lectr.; Dir.*
Burgess, Hilary, MA Lond., PhD Open(UK) Sr.
Lectr.
Butcher, John, BA CNAA, MA Keele, MA(Ed)
Open(UK), EdD Open(UK) Sr. Lectr.
Deane, Michele, LèsL Paris IV, MèsL Nantes Sr.
Lectr.
Fairlamb, Linda, BA CNAA, MA(Ed) Open(UK),
EdD Open(UK) Sr. Lectr.
Haggarty, Linda, BSc Liv., DPhil Oxf. Sr. Lectr.
Hutchinson, Steven, BMus Cardiff, MA(Ed) Birm.
Sr. Lectr.
Moon, Robert E., MA Warw., DPhil Sus. Prof.
Storey, Anne, BA Hull, MA Nott., PhD Nott.,
MBA Sr. Lectr.
Other Staff: 8 Lectrs.; 7 Staff Tutors; 3 Project
Officers
Research: comparative studies of teacher
education in Europe; development of
teachers' professional knowledge; new
models of teacher education with specific
reference to Sub-Saharan African countries;

teacher education; use of ICTs in
professional development

Geography

Tel: (01908) 654456 Fax: (01908) 654488
E-mail: j.f.smith@open.ac.uk
Allen, John, BA Kent Prof., Economic
Geography
Blowers, Andy T., BA Durh., MLitt Durh. Prof.
Brook, Chris, MA Exe., PhD Exe., BA Sr. Lectr.
Hetherington, Kevin, BA Leeds, PhD Lanc. Prof.
Humphreys, David, BA Kent, PhD Lond. Sr.
Lectr.
Massey, Doreen B., BA Oxf., MA Penn. Prof.
Pile, Steve J., BSc Lond., MA Lond., PhD Lond.
Sr. Lectr.
Pryke, Michael, BSc Lond., PhD Open(UK) Sr.
Lectr.
Robinson, Jenny, BA Durban-W., MA Durban-W.,
PhD Lond. Sr. Lectr.
Rose, Gillian, BA Camb., PhD Lond. Prof.
Sarre, Philip V., BSc S'ton., MA Calif., PhD Brist.
Sr. Lectr.
Other Staff: 6 Lectrs.; 3 Staff Tutors; 5 Res.
Fellows

Government

Tel: (01908) 654435 Fax: (01908) 654488
E-mail: politics-enquiries@open.ac.uk
Bromley, Simon J., BA Camb., PhD Camb. Sr.
Lectr.
Heffernan, Richard, BA Lond., PhD Lond.
Reader
Lewis, Paul G., BSocSc Birm., PhD Birm.
Reader
Prokhovnik, Raia, BA NSW, MSc Lond., PhD
Lond. Sr. Lectr.
Saward, Michael J., BA ANU, PhD Essex Prof.;
Head*
Smith, Mark J., BA Liv., MA Essex, PhD Sus. Sr.
Lectr.
Thompson, Grahame F., MA Leic., PhD Birm.
Prof.
Other Staff: 3 Lectrs.
Research: challenging contemporary political
ideas; global, regional and national
governance

Health and Social Care, Faculty of

Tel: (01908) 653743 Fax: (01908) 654124
E-mail: b.morris@open.ac.uk
Aldgate, Jane, OBE, MA Edin., MA Oxf., PhD
Edin. Prof., Social Care
Atkinson, Dorothy, BA Leeds, MPhil S'ton., PhD
Open(UK) Prof., Learning Disabilities
Baker, Chris, BSc Wales, MSc Brist. Sr. Lectr.
Beaumont, Kythé, BA CNAA, MA Leeds Sr.
Lectr.
Bornat, Joanna, BA Leeds, PhD Essex Prof., Oral
History
Brigham, Lindsay, BA Open(UK), MA
Newcastle(UK) Sr. Lectr.
Cull, Lesley-Anne, BA City(UK), MA City(UK)
Sr. Lectr.; Head*
Douglas, Jenny, BSc Warw., MSc Leeds, MA
Warw., PhD Warw. Sr. Lectr.
Dowling, Monica, BA Herts., PhD Sheff. Prof.,
Social Work
Eby, Maureen, BA Maryland, PhD Birm. Sr.
Lectr.
Fletcher, Anne, BA Lond., MPhil Birm. Sr.
Lectr.
Gibb, Jan, BA Open(UK), MA Sus. Sr. Lectr.
Heller, Tom, MB BS Lond. Sr. Lectr.
Katz, Jeanne, BA Brandeis, BA Haifa(Technion),
MSc Lond., PhD Warw. Sr. Lectr.
Lloyd, Cathy, BA E.Lond., PhD Lond. Sr. Lectr.
McDonagh, Linda, MSc Brist. Sr. Lectr.
Northedge, Andy, BSc Durh., MPhil Lond. Sr.
Lectr.
O'Malley, Marion, BA Lond., BA Open(UK), MA
Open(UK) Sr. Lectr.
Peace, Sheila M., BA Wales, PhD Wales Sr.
Lectr.
Reveley, Shirley, BA Open(UK), MA Lanc., PhD
Lanc. Prof., Nursing; Head*
Reynolds, Jill, BSc Brist., MSc Brist. Sr. Lectr.

Roche, Jeremy, BA *Kent*, MPhil *Camb.*   Sr. Lectr.

Rogers, Anita, BA *McG.*, MEd *Vic.(BC)*   Sr. Lectr.

Seden, Janet, BA *Warw.*   Sr. Lectr.

Shakespeare, Pam, BA *Sus.*, MA *Sus.*, PhD *Open(UK)*   Sr. Lectr.

Stainton-Rogers, Wendy, BSc *Brist.*, MPhil *Reading*, PhD *Open(UK)*   Prof.

Other Staff: 62 Lectrs./Staff Tutors; 10 Res. Fellows

History and European Humanities

Tel: (01908) 653266 Fax: (01908) 653750
E-mail: arts-history-gen-
   enquiries@open.ac.uk

Aldgate, A., MA *Edin.*, PhD *Edin.*   Reader

Donnachie, Ian, MA *Glas.*, MLitt *Strath.*, PhD *Strath.*   Staff Tutor; Reader

Emsley, C., BA *York(UK)*, MLitt *Camb.*, FRHistS   Prof.

Grell, O. P., PhD   Reader

King, P. J. R., BA *Kent*, BPhil *Exe.*, PhD *Camb.*   Prof.

Laurence, E. Anne, BA *York(UK)*, DPhil *Oxf.*   Prof., History

Mombauer, A., PhD   Sr. Lectr.

O'Day, M. Rosemary, BA *York(UK)*, PhD *Lond.*, FRHistS   Prof.; Head*

Waites, B. A., BA *Lond.*, PhD *Open(UK)*   Sr. Lectr.

Other Staff: 4 Lectrs.; 3 Staff Tutors

History of Science, Technology and Medicine

Tel: (01908) 858356 Fax: (01908) 653750
E-mail: arts-history-sci-tech-gen-
   enquiries@open.ac.uk

Chant, Colin, BA *Keele*, PhD *Keele*   Sr. Lectr.

Elmer, Peter, BA *Wales(Swansea)*, PhD *Wales(Swansea)*   Sr. Lectr.; Staff Tutor

Moore, James R., MDiv *Trinity Evang.Div.Sch.(Ill.)*, PhD *Manc.*   Reader

Roberts, Gerrylynn, BA *Vassar*, PhD *Johns H.*   Sr. Lectr.; Head*

Other Staff: 2 Lectrs.; 1 Staff Tutor; 1 Res. Fellow

Literature

Tel: (01908) 652092 Fax: (01908) 653750
E-mail: arts-lit-enquiries@open.ac.uk

Allen, Richard F., BA *Lond.*, PhD *Lond.*   Sr. Lectr.

Anderson, Linda A., BA *Belf.*, PhD *Lanc.*   Reader

Gupta, Suman, BA *Delhi*, MA *Delhi*, MPhil *Delhi*, DPhil *Oxf.*   Sr. Lectr.

Johnson, David W., BA *Cape Town*, LLB *Cape Town*, MA *Cape Town*, DPhil *Sus.*   Sr. Lectr.

Nasta, Susheila M., BA *Kent*, MA *Kent*, DLitt *Kent*, FRSA   Reader

Owens, Bob, BA *Ulster*, PhD *Open(UK)*   Prof., English Literature; Head*

Prescott, Lynda S., BA *Nott.*, PhD *Open(UK)*   Sr. Lectr.

Walder, Dennis J., BA *Cape Town*, BCom *Cape Town*, MA *Edin.*, MLitt *Edin.*, PhD *Edin.*   Prof.

Watson, Nicola J., BA *Oxf.*, MPhil *Oxf.*, DPhil *Oxf.*   Sr. Lectr.

Other Staff: 8 Lectrs.; 1 Sr. Res. Fellow; 2 Res. Fellows

Research: book history, bibliography and textual editing; Charles Dickens; colonial and post-colonial literatures in English; Daniel Defoe; sixteenth- to twentieth-century English literature

Management, School of

Tel: (01908) 655888 Fax: (01908) 655898

Barden, Miceal, LLB *Hull*, LLM *Lond.*   Group Regional Manager

Bolleurs, Nikki, BSocSc *Cape Town*, MBA *Stell.*   Dir., Teaching and Learning

Dixon, Keith, BA *CNAA*, PhD *Massey*   Lectr.; Dir., Master's Programme

Fenton-O'Creevey, Mark, BA *Warw.*, MBA *Lond.*, PhD *Lond.*   Sr. Lectr.; Dir., Programmes and Curric.

Fleck, James, BSc *Edin.*, MA *Edin.*, MSc *Edin.*   Prof.; Dir. of Studies; Head*

Green, Mike, BA *Oxf.*, MBA *Open(UK)*   Lectr.; Dir., Internat. Partnerships

Harris, Richard, BSc *Sur.*, MBA *Open(UK)*   Dir., Resources and Planning

Hollier, Joanne, BEd *Brist.*, MBA *W.England*   Group Regional Manager

Lucas, Mike, BSc *Salf.*, MA *Keele*   Lectr.; Dir., Undergrad. Bus. and Management Programme

McMahon, Carmel, BSc *Belf.*, MBA *Open(UK)*   Group Regional Manager

Quintas, Paul, BSc *Brad.*, MSc *Sus.*   Dir., Res.

Slade, John, BA *Reading*, MBA *Open(UK)*   Group Regional Manager

Slapper, Gary, LLB *Lond.*, LLM *Lond.*, PhD *Lond.*   Prof.; Dir., Law Programme

Financial Management, Centre for

Tel: (01908) 655879
E-mail: c.playle@open.ac.uk

Frecknall-Hughes, Jane, MA *Oxf.*   Prof.

Rutterford, Janette, BSc *Lond.*, MSc *Oxf.*, MBA *Lond.*, PhD *Lond.*   Prof.

Upton, Martin, BA *E.Anglia*, MA *E.Anglia*, MPhil *Leeds*   Head*

Walton, Peter, BA *Kingston(UK)*, MSc *Lond.*, PhD *Lond.*   Prof.

Wheatcroft, Richard, MA *Oxf.*, MBA *Lond.*   Sr. Lectr.

Other Staff: 6 Lectrs.

Research: decision-making in a financial and accounting context

Human Resource and Change Management, Centre for

Tel: (01908) 655882
E-mail: k.l.mccerfferty@open.ac.uk

Ball, Kirstie, BA *Birm.*, MSc *Birm.*, PhD *Aston*   Sr. Lectr.

Billsberry, Jon, BA *Manc.*, MBA *Birm.*, PhD *Nott.*   Sr. Lectr.

Edwards, Charles, BA *York(UK)*, MBA *Birm.*   Sr. Lectr.

Fenton-O'Creevey, Mark, BA *Warw.*, MBA *Lond.*, PhD *Lond.*   Sr. Lectr.

Henry, Jane, BA *Manc.*   Sr. Lectr.; Head*

Holti, Richard, BA *Camb.*, MSc *Lond.*, PhD *Lond.*   Sr. Lectr.

Lewis, Jenny, BSc *City(UK)*, PhD *Open(UK)*   Sr. Lectr.

Salaman, Graeme, BA *Leic.*, PhD *Camb.*   Prof.

Storey, John, BA *Hull*, MSc(Econ) *Lond.*, PhD *Lanc.*   Prof.

Other Staff: 7 Lectrs.; 1 Res. Fellow

Research: changing forms of work organisations; human resource management (HRM) in wider economic, political and social context; managerial strategies and processes relating to work and organisations

Innovation, Knowledge and Enterprise, Centre for

Tel: (01908) 655872
E-mail: b.a.ridgway@open.ac.uk

Daniel, Elizabeth, BSc *Manc.*, MBA *Lond.*, PhD *Manc.*   Prof.

Gray, Colin, BA *Syd.*, MSc(Econ) *Lond.*, PhD *Lond.Guild.*   Prof.

Little, Steve, BSc *Aston*, MSc *Aston*, PhD *RCA*   Sr. Lectr.; Head*

Quintas, Paul, BSc *Brad.*, MSc *Sus.*   Prof.

Ray, Tim, BTech *Brad.*, MSc *Lond.*, PhD *Manc.Met.*   Sr. Lectr.

Tyler, Sheila, BSc *York(UK)*, PhD *Open(UK)*   Sr. Lectr.

Other Staff: 3 Lectrs.

Research: interaction between knowledge generation and innovation within firms and across organisational and functional boundaries (international issues)

Law, Centre for

Bright, Keren, BEd *Brist.*, MA *Lond.*   Sr. Lectr.

Howells, Carol, LLB *Trent*, MA *Sheff.*   Sr. Lectr.

Slapper, Gary, LLB *Lond.*, LLM *Lond.*, PhD *Lond.*   Prof.; Dir.*

Other Staff: 4 Lectrs.

Research: criminal justice (young offenders and corporate crime); criminal law; legal theory and philosophy; the English legal system; white collar, corporate and international financial crime

Public Leadership and Social Enterprise, Centre for

Tel: (01908) 659289
E-mail: j.connell@open.ac.uk

Budd, Leslie, BA *Brad.*, MSc *Brad.*, MSc *Sus.*   Reader

Cornforth, Chris J., BSc *Exe.*, MA *RCA*   Sr. Lectr.

Edwards, Charles, BA *York(UK)*, MBA *Birm.*   Sr. Lectr.

Holloway, Jacky, BSc *Lond.*, BA *Open(UK)*, PhD *Open(UK)*   Sr. Lectr.; Head*

Mordaunt, Jill, BA *Durh.*, PhD *Edin.*

Paton, Rob, BA *Oxf.*, MA *Penn.*   Prof., Social Enterprise

Vangen, Siv, BA *Strath.*, MSc *Strath.*, PhD *Strath.*   Sr. Lectr.

Other Staff: 3 Lectrs.; 1 Res. Fellow

Research: aspects of regional economic policy; corporate universities in public and private contexts; governance in public and non-profit contexts; partnerships and collaborations, especially cross-sectorally; performance measurement in and of social enterprises

Strategy and Marketing, Centre for

Tel: (01908) 654753 Fax: (01908) 655898
E-mail: j.swallow@open.ac.uk

Carrigan, Marylyn, BA *Strath.*, PhD *Birm.*   Sr. Lectr.

Dibb, Sally, BSc *Manc.*, MSc *Manc.*, PhD *Warw.*   Prof.

Hinton, Matthew, BSc *Kingston(UK)*, PhD *Cran.*   Sr. Lectr.

Lindridge, Andrew, BSc *Kingston(UK)*, PhD *Cran.*   Sr. Lectr.

Margolis, Judith, BA *Middx.*, MBA *Herts.*, FCIM   Sr. Lectr.; Head*

Meadows, Maureen, BA *Oxf.*, MSc *Warw.*   Sr. Lectr.; Head*

O'Sullivan, Terry, BA *Oxf.*, PhD *Newcastle(UK)*   Sr. Lectr.

Segal-Horn, Susan, BA *Essex*, MA *Sus.*   Prof.

Smith, Anne, BSc *Manc.*, MSc *Manc.*, PhD *Manc.*   Reader

Stapleton, Tony, BA *Camb.*, PhD *Camb.*   Sr. Lectr.

Viney, Howard, BSc *Brun.*, MBA *Sheff.*, PhD *Middx.*   Sr. Lectr.

Wright, Alexis, MA *Nott.*, PhD *Nott.*   Sr. Lectr.

Other Staff: 5 Lectrs.

Mathematics and Statistics

Tel: (01908) 653580 Fax: (01908) 652140
E-mail: mcs-applied-enquiries@open.ac.uk

Allen, Barbara, BEd *Birm.*, MEd *Coventry*   Sr. Lectr.

Bromilow, T. Mick, BA *Oxf.*, MA *Oxf.*, MSc *Oxf.*, DPhil *Oxf.*   Sr. Lectr.; Head*

Critchley, Frank, MA *Camb.*, DPhil *Oxf.*   Prof.

Ekins, Judy, BSc *Sus.*, BA *Open(UK)*, MBA *Open(UK)*, PhD *St And.*   Sr. Lectr.

Farrington, Paddy, MA *Aberd.*, MSc *Oxf.*, MSc *Lond.*, PhD *Leeds*   Prof.

Garthwaite, Paul, MA *Oxf.*, MSc *Wales*, PhD *Wales*   Prof.

Goldrei, Derek C., MA *Oxf.*, MSc *Oxf.*   Sr. Lectr.

Gower, John, BA *Camb.*   Prof.

Grannell, Michael J., BSc *Lond.*, PhD *Lond.*   Prof.; Res. Fellow

Gray, Jeremy J., MSc *Warw.*, MA *Oxf.*, PhD *Warw.*   Prof.

Griggs, Terry S., BSc *Lond.*, MSc *Lond.*, MPhil *Lond.*   Prof.; Res. Fellow

Grimm, Uwe   Reader

Holroyd, Fred C., MA *Oxf.*, DPhil *Oxf.*   Sr. Lectr.

Jones, M. Chris, BSc Bath, PhD Bath   Prof.
Jordan, Camilla   Sr. Lectr.
Martin, I., BSc Lanc., MSc Oxf.   Sr. Lectr.
Mason, John H., MSc Tor., PhD Wis.   Prof.
McConway, Kevin J., BA Open(UK), BA Camb., MSc Lond., PhD Lond.   Sr. Lectr.
Mestel, Ben   Sr. Lectr.
Newton, John E., BSc Durh., MSc Newcastle(UK)   Sr. Lectr.
O'Neil, Toby   Sr. Lectr.
Richards, Derek, BSc Lond., PhD Lond.   Prof.
Rippon, Phil J., MA Camb., MSc Lond., PhD Lond.   Sr. Lectr.
Rowley, Chris A., MA Oxf., DPhil Oxf.   Sr. Lectr.
Simpson, Mike, BA Lond., MSc Lond.   Sr. Lectr.
Siran, Jozef   Prof.
Stallard, Gwyneth M., BA Camb., PhD Lond.   Sr. Lectr.
Thorpe, Mike, MA Camb., PhD Birm.   Sr. Lectr.
Trapp, John, MA Camb., PhD Camb.   Sr. Lectr.
Umerski, Andrey   Sr. Lectr.
Webb, Bridget   Sr. Lectr.
Wilkinson, Michael, BSc Leeds, PhD Brist.   Prof.
Wilson, Robin J., MA Oxf., PhD Penn.   Prof.
Other Staff: 19 Lectrs.; 6 Staff Tutors; 3 Res. Fellows
Research: applications of quantum mechanics; inverse problems in biomagnetism; numerical analysis; statistical physics; theory of crystalline and aperiodic materials

Music
Tel: (01908) 653280 Fax: (01908) 653750
E-mail: arts-music-enquiries@open.ac.uk
Burrows, Donald J., MA Camb., PhD Open(UK)   Prof.
Clayton, Martin, MA Lond., PhD Lond.   Sr. Lectr.
Mateer, David, BMus Belf., MMus Lond., PhD Belf.   Sr. Lectr.
Richards, Fiona, BA Durh., MMus Lond., PhD Birm.   Lectr.; Head*
Samuels, Robert, BA Camb., MA Camb., MPhil Camb., PhD Camb.   Sr. Lectr.
Other Staff: 5 Lectrs.; 1 Staff Tutor; 1 Res. Fellow; 3 Res. Assocs.

Philosophy
Tel: (01908) 659214 Fax: (01908) 653750
E-mail: arts-philosophy-enqs@open.ac.uk
Belshaw, Christopher D., BA York(UK), PhD Calif.   Sr. Lectr.
Chappell, Timothy   Prof.
Chimisso, Christina   Sr. Lectr.
Matravers, Derek, BA Lond., PhD Camb.   Sr. Lectr.
Price, Carolyn S., BA Oxf., BPhil Oxf.   Lectr.; Head*
Warburton, Nigel, BA Brist., PhD Camb.   Sr. Lectr.
Other Staff: 2 Lectrs.; 2 Staff Tutors

Physics and Astronomy
Tel: (01908) 653229 Fax: (01908) 654192
E-mail: t.j.moore@open.ac.uk
Bolton, John P. R., BSc Leeds, DPhil Sus.   Sr. Lectr.
Braithwaite, Nicholas St J., BSc Manc., MA Oxf., MSc Oxf., DPhil Oxf.   Prof.
Broadhurst, David J., MA Oxf., DPhil Sus.   Reader
Freake, Stuart M., MA Camb., PhD Camb.   Sr. Lectr.; Dir., Teaching
Haswell, Carol A., BA Oxf., PhD Texas   Sr. Lectr.
Jones, Barrie W., BSc Brist., PhD Brist.   Prof.
Kolb, Ulrich C., PhD Munich   Sr. Lectr.
Lambourne, Robert J. A., BSc Lond., PhD Lond.   Sr. Lectr.; Head*
Mackintosh, Raymond S., MSc Auck., PhD Calif.   Sr. Lectr.; Dir., Res.
Mason, Nigel J., OBE, BSc Lond., PhD Lond., DSc Lond.   Prof.
Norton, Andrew, BSc Leic., PhD Leic.   Sr. Lectr.
Ross, Shelagh M., BSc Kent, PhD Kent   Sr. Lectr.
Swithenby, Prof. Stephen J., MA Oxf., DPhil Oxf.   Sr. Lectr.

Other Staff: 5 Lectrs.; 6 Res. Fellows

Psychology
Tel: (01908) 654515 Fax: (01908) 654488
E-mail: psychology-enquiries@open.ac.uk
Brace, Nicola, BSc E.Lond., PhD E.Lond.   Sr. Lectr.
Gellatly, Angus R. H., MA Dund., PhD Lond.   Prof.; Head*
Hollway, Wendy, BA Sheff., PhD Lond.   Prof.
Le Voi, Martin E., BA Camb., PhD Lond.   Sr. Lectr.
Phoenix, Ann A., MA St And., PhD Lond.   Prof., Social and Developmental Psychology
Pike, Graham E., BA Westminster, PhD Westminster   Sr. Lectr.
Roth, Ilona A., MA Oxf., DPhil Oxf.   Sr. Lectr.
Wetherell, Margaret, BA Auck., PhD Auck.   Prof.
Other Staff: 8 Lectrs.; 6 Staff Tutors; 3 Res. Staff
Research: applied psychology; cognitive psychology; discourse psychology; forensic psychology; psycho-social psychology

Religious Studies
Tel: (01908) 652032 Fax: (01908) 653750
E-mail: arts-rel-studies-res-enquiries@open.ac.uk
Beckerlegge, Gwilym, MA Oxf., MA Lanc., PhD Lanc.   Sr. Lectr.; Staff Tutor
Bowman, Marion, BA Lanc., MA Nfld., PhD Glam.   Sr. Lectr.
Parsons, Gerald, BA Wales   Sr. Lectr.
Wolffe, John R., MA Oxf., DPhil Oxf.   Prof.
Other Staff: 2 Lectrs.; 1 Staff Tutor

Science Education, Centre for
Tel: (01908) 653993 Fax: (01908) 652559
E-mail: science-faculty-enquiries@open.ac.uk
Solomon, Joan, BA Camb., PhD Lond.   Visiting Prof.
Thomas, Jeffrey N., BSc Birm., PhD Birm.   Sr. Lectr.; Head*
Whitelegg, Elizabeth, BSc Nott., MA Open(UK)   Sr. Lectr.
Other Staff: 1 Lectr.; 2 Res. Fellows

Social Policy Discipline
Tel: (01908) 654530 Fax: (01908) 654488
E-mail: social-policy-enquiries@open.ac.uk
Carabine, Jean, MA Brad., PhD Sheff.   Sr. Lectr.
Clarke, John, BSc Aston, MA Birm.   Prof.
Cochrane, Allan, BA Oxf., PhD Open(UK)   Prof.
Fink, Janet, BA Essex, MA Essex, PhD Essex   Sr. Lectr.
Hughes, Gordon, BSc Leic., MPhil Leic., MSocSc Birm., PhD Open(UK)   Prof.
Langan, Mary, MA Essex   Sr. Lectr.
Muncie, John, BSc Leic., PhD Leic.   Prof.
Newman, Janet, BA PhD   Prof.
Silva, Elizabeth   Sr. Lectr.
Other Staff: 4 Lectrs.; 5 Staff Tutors

Sociology Discipline
Tel: (01908) 654457 Fax: (01908) 654488
E-mail: m.c.freeman@open.ac.uk
Bennett, Tony, BA Oxf., MA Oxf., PhD Sus.   Prof.; Head*
Collins, Richard, BA York(UK), MA Warw., PhD Strath., DSc Lond.   Prof.
du Gay, Paul, MA Durh., PhD Open(UK)   Prof.
Evans, Jessica, MA Sus.   Sr. Lectr.
Finnegan, Ruth, BA Oxf., DPhil Oxf., FBA   Emer. Prof.
Gillespie, Marie, MA Lond., PhD Brun.   Sr. Lectr.
Mackay, Hugh, BSc Wales, PhD Wales   Sr. Lectr.; Staff Tutor
Murji, Karim, BA Essex, MSc Lond., PhD Sur.   Sr. Lectr.
Thompson, Kenneth A., BA Leic., DPhil Oxf.   Prof.
Watson, Diane, BA Open(UK), PhD Nott.   Sr. Lectr.; Staff Tutor
Watson, Sophie, BA Sus., PhD Lond.   Prof.

Woodward, Kath, MA Sheff., PhD Sheff.   Sr. Lectr.
Other Staff: 6 Lectrs.; 5 Staff Tutors; 1 Sr. Res. Fellow
Research: culture/media industries and policy; media, culture and identities, culture and governance; race and ethnicity studies; sociology of economic life; sociology of everyday life

SPECIAL CENTRES, ETC

Charles Booth Research Centre
Social History
O'Day, M. Rosemary, BA York(UK), PhD Lond., FRHistS   Dir.*

Earth, Planetary, Space and Astronomical Research, Centre for
Spicer, Robert A., BSc Lond., MA Oxf., PhD Lond., FGS   Dir.*

Educational Technology, Institute of
Tel: (01908) 655581 Fax: (01908) 654173
Chambers, Eleanor A., BA Leic., MA Lond.   Prof., Humanities Higher Education
Goodfellow, Robin, BEd Keele, MSc Kingston(UK), PhD Open(UK)   Sr. Lectr.
Grant, Janet R., BA Sus., MSc Lond., PhD Lond.   Prof.
Henry, Jane, BA Manc.   Sr. Lectr.
Hodgson, Barbara K., BSc Lond., MSc Essex, PhD Warw.   Sr. Lectr.
Joinson, Adam N., BSc Lond., PhD Herts.   Sr. Lectr.
Jones, Ann C., BA Sheff., PhD Open(UK)   Sr. Lectr.
Kirkup, Gillian E., BEd Lond., BA Open(UK), MPhil CNAA   Sr. Lectr.
Kirkwood, Adrian, BA Lond., MEd Manc.   Sr. Lectr.
Kukulska-Hulme, Agnes M., MA Warsaw, PhD Aston   Sr. Lectr.
Lea, Mary R., BA Leic., MA Sus.   Sr. Lectr.
Mason, Robin D., BA Tor., MA Wis., PhD Open(UK)   Prof.
McAndrew, Patrick, BA Oxf., MA Oxf., PhD H-W   Sr. Lectr.
McKee, Anne C., BA Belf., MA E.Anglia, PhD E.Anglia   Sr. Lectr.
Richardson, John T. E., BA Oxf., DPhil Sus.   Prof.
Scanlon, Eileen, BSc Glas., PhD   Prof.
Taylor, Josie, DPhil Sus., BA   Acting Dir.*
Thorpe, Mary S., MA Camb.   Prof.
Weller, Martin J., BSc CNAA, MSc Kingston(UK), PhD Tees.   Sr. Lectr./Prof.
Whitelock, Denise M., BSc Sheff., MEd Lond., PhD Lond.   Sr. Lectr.
Other Staff: 10 Lectrs.; 4 Sr. Res. Fellows; 7 Res. Fellows

Knowledge Media Institute
Tel: (01908) 653800 Fax: (01908) 653169
E-mail: kmi@open.ac.uk
Eisenstadt, Marc, BA Wash., PhD San Diego   Prof.; Chief Scientist
Motta, Enrico, BSc Pisa, PhD Open(UK)   Prof.; Sr. Res. Fellow; Dir.*
Scott, Peter   Dir.*
Other Staff: 3 Sr. Res. Fellows; 16 Res. Fellows
Vacant Posts: 1 Reader/Sr. Lectr.; 1 Res. Fellow
Research: artificial intelligence; human-computer interaction; knowledge management; knowledge technologies; ontological engineering

Planetary Space Sciences Research Institute
Tel: (01908) 655808 Fax: (01908) 655667
E-mail: psri@open.ac.uk
Cockell, Charles, BSc Brist., DPhil Oxf., FRAS, FRGS   Prof.
Gilmour, Iain, BSc St And., PhD Camb.   Sr. Lectr.; Assoc. Dean
Grady, Monica, BSc Durh., PhD Camb., FRAS   Prof.

Green, Simon F., BSc *St And.*, PhD *Leic.*, FRAS
Sr. Lectr.; Dir., Postgrad. Studies
Pillinger, Colin T., BSc *Wales*, PhD *Wales*, DSc
Brist., FRAS, FRS, FGS   Prof.; Head*
Wright, Ian P., BSc *Birm.*, PhD *Camb.*, FRAS
Sr. Res. Fellow; Deputy Head
Zarnecki, John C., BA *Camb.*, PhD *Lond.*, FRAS
Prof.; Dir., Res.
Other Staff: 1 Prof.; 2 Lectrs.; 1 Sr. Res.
Fellow; 20 Res. Fellows
Research: astrobiology; interplanetary dust and
its effects; interstellar grains; large scale
planetary impacts; solar system evolution

CONTACT OFFICERS

Estates and buildings/works and services.
Director (Estates and buildings/works and
services): Burrell, Alan, BPharm
(E-mail: estates-directorate@open.ac.uk)
Finance. Finance Director: Hedges, Miles, MA,
FCA, FRSA
General enquiries. Secretary (General
enquiries): Woodburn, A. Fraser, BSc *Edin.*
(E-mail: sec-gen@open.ac.uk)
Marketing. Marketing and Customer
Development Director: Andrew, D.
Personnel/human resources. Director
(Personnel/human resources): Holt, Nigel
Public relations. Director (Communications
Group): Prior, Derek, MA, FRSA
(E-mail: communications@open.ac.uk)
Student union. General Manager, Open
University Students' Association: de Haney,
Trudi, MA *Warw.*
(E-mail: ousa-ps-admin@open.ac.uk)

CAMPUS/COLLEGE HEADS

Region 01: London, 1–11 Hawley Crescent,
Camden Town, London, England NW1

8NP. (Tel: (020) 7485 6597; Fax: (020)
556 6196; E-mail: r01@open.ac.uk)
Regional Director: Mayes, Rosemary, BA
Open(UK)
Region 02: South, Foxcombe Hall, Boars Hill,
Oxford, England OX1 5HR. (Tel: (01865)
327000; Fax: (01865) 736288;
E-mail: r02@open.ac.uk) Acting Regional
Director: Cohen, Celia, BSc(Econ)
Region 03: South West, 4 Portwall Lane,
Bristol, England BS1 6ND. (Tel: (0117) 929
9641; Fax: (0117) 925 5215;
E-mail: r03@open.ac.uk) Regional Director:
Brightman, Linda, BA *Open(UK)*
Region 04: West Midlands, 66 High Street,
Harborne, Birmingham, West Midlands,
England B17 9NB. (Tel: (0121) 426 1661;
Fax: (0121) 427 9484;
E-mail: r04@open.ac.uk) Regional Director:
Rookes, Mike, BA
Region 05: East Midlands, Clarendon Park,
Clumber Avenue, Sherwood Rise,
Nottingham, England NG5 1AH. (Tel:
(0115) 962 5451; Fax: (0115) 971 5575;
E-mail: r05@open.ac.uk) Regional Director:
Lammie, Gordon A., MA *Camb.*
Region 06: East Anglia, Cintra House, 12
Hills Road, Cambridge, England CB2 1PF.
(Tel: (01223) 364721; Fax: (01223)
355207; E-mail: r06@open.ac.uk) Regional
Director: Wildman, Helen
Region 07: Yorkshire, 2 Trevelyan Square,
Boar Lane, Leeds, England LS1 6ED. (Tel:
(0113) 244 4431; Fax: (0113) 234 1862;
E-mail: r07@open.ac.uk) Regional Director:
Berry, Nick, BA(Econ)
Region 08: North West, 351 Altrincham
Road, Sharston, Manchester, England M22

4UN. (Tel: (0161) 998 7272; Fax: (0161)
945 3356; E-mail: r08@open.ac.uk)
Regional Director: Brady, Linda
Region 09: North, Eldon House, Regent
Centre, Regent Farm Road, Gosforth,
Newcastle upon Tyne, England. (Tel:
(0191) 284 1611; Fax: (0191) 284 6592;
E-mail: r09@open.ac.uk) Regional Director:
Knight, David
Region 10: Wales, 24 Cathedral Road, Cardiff,
Wales CF1 9SA. (Tel: (029) 2039 7911;
Fax: (029) 2022 7930;
E-mail: r10@open.ac.uk) Welsh Director:
Graham, Heather, PhD
Region 11: Scotland, 10 Drumsheugh
Gardens, Edinburgh, Scotland EH3 7QJ.
(Tel: (0131) 226 3851; Fax: (0131) 220
6730; E-mail: r11@open.ac.uk) Scottish Dir.:
Syme, Peter W., MA *Camb.*
Region 12: Northern Ireland, 40 University
Road, Belfast, Northern Ireland BT7 1SU.
(Tel: (028) 9024 5025; Fax: (028) 9023
0565; E-mail: r12@open.ac.uk) Regional
Director: Hamilton, Rosemary K., CBE, BSc
Belf., PhD *Belf.*
Region 13: South East, St James's House, 150
London Road, East Grinstead, West Sussex,
England RH19 1HG. (Tel: (01342) 327821;
Fax: (01342) 317411;
E-mail: r13@open.ac.uk) Regional Director:
Gray, Liz, BA *York(UK)*

[*Information supplied by the institution as at 17 March
2008, and edited by the ACU*]

UNIVERSITY OF OXFORD

Member of the Association of Commonwealth Universities

Postal Address: University Offices, Wellington Square, Oxford, England OX1 2JD
Telephone: (01865) 270000 **Fax:** (01865) 270708 **E-mail:** information.officer@admin.ox.ac.uk
URL: http://www.ox.ac.uk

VICE-CHANCELLOR*—Hood, John A., BE *Auck.*, MPhil *Oxf.*, PhD *Auck.*, Hon. LLD *Auck.*, Hon. PhD *Peking*, Hon. LLD
Br.Col., Hon. PhD *Korea*, Hon. FIPENZ, FNZIM
PRO-VICE-CHANCELLOR (DEVELOPMENT AND EXTERNAL AFFAIRS)—Dellandrea, Jon S., BA *Tor.*, MA *Tor.*, EdD *Tor.*
PRO-VICE-CHANCELLOR (EDUCATION)—Fallaize, Prof. Elizabeth A., MA *Exe.*, MA *Oxf.*, PhD *Exe.*
PRO-VICE-CHANCELLOR (PERSONNEL AND EQUAL OPPORTUNITIES)—Caldicott, Dame Fiona, DBE, BM BCh *Oxf.*, MA
Oxf., Hon. MD *Oxf.*, Hon. DSc *Oxf.*, FRCPsych, FRCP, FRCPI, FRCGP
PRO-VICE-CHANCELLOR (PLANNING AND RESOURCES)—Monaco, Prof. Anthony P., AB *Prin.*, MD *Harv.*, PhD *Harv.*
PRO-VICE-CHANCELLOR (RESEARCH)—McKendrick, Prof. Ewan G., LLB *Edin.*, MA *Oxf.*
REGISTRAR‡—Maxton, Julie K., LLB *Lond.*, LLM *Cant.*, PhD *Auck.*
DIRECTOR OF FINANCE AND SECRETARY OF THE CHEST—Kerr, Giles, BA *York(UK)*, FCA
SECRETARY OF FACULTIES AND ACADEMIC REGISTRAR—Sibly, Michael D., MA *Camb.*

GENERAL INFORMATION

History. There is no clear date of foundation
for the university, but teaching existed at
Oxford in some form in 1096 and developed
rapidly from 1167, when Henry II banned
English students from attending the University
of Paris. The oldest colleges—University,
Balliol and Merton—were founded between
1249 and 1264.
The university is located in the city of
Oxford, about 90km north-west of London.

Admission to first degree courses (see also
United Kingdom Introduction). For students
from the United Kingdom, entry is through
the Universities and Colleges Admissions
Service (UCAS) and the university's individual
colleges and halls. Enquiries should be directed
to the Undergraduate Admissions Office,
University Offices, Wellington Square, Oxford,
England OX1 2JD. Selection procedures for

international students do not differ, though
some earlier closing dates may apply, and all
candidates are considered on the basis of their
academic record and potential.

First Degrees (see also United Kingdom
Directory to Subjects of Study). BA, BFA, BM
BCh, MBioChem, MChem, MCompSci,
MEarthSc, MEng, MMath, MMathCompSci,
MMathPhil, MPhys, MPhysPhil.
Length of course. Full-time: BFA: 3 years; BA:
3–4 years; MBioChem, MChem, MCompSci,
MEarthSc, MEng, MMath, MMathCompSci,
MMathPhil, MPhys, MPhysPhil: 4 years; BM
BCh: 6 years.

Higher Degrees (see also United Kingdom
Directory to Subjects of Study).
Master's. BCL, BD, BMus, MBA, MFA, MJur,
MLitt, MPhil, MSc, MSt, MTheol.
Admission. Applicants for admission to higher
degrees must normally hold a first degree with
upper second class honours, or equivalent.

Length of course. Full-time: BMus, MBA, MFA,
MSc, MSt: 1 year; BCL, MJur: 1–2 years; BD,
MLitt, MPhil, MTheol: 2 years. Part-time:
MTheol: 3–4 years.
Doctoral. DPhil.
Length of course. Full-time: DPhil: 3–4 years.

Libraries. Volumes: 11,000,000. Periodicals
subscribed to: 59,000. Special collections:
many special collections.

Academic Year (2007–2008). Three terms:
7 October–1 December; 13 January–8 March;
20 April–14 June.

Income (2006–2007). Total, £609,000,000.

Statistics. Staff (2005–2006): 8570 (4285
academic, 4285 non-academic). Students
(2006–2007): full-time 19,993 (10,709 men,
9284 women); international 4929; undergraduate-

12,106 (6371 men, 5735 women).

FACULTIES/SCHOOLS

Humanities, Division of
Tel: (01865) 270559 Fax: (01865) 270553
Head: Shuttleworth, Sally A., BA York(UK), PhD Camb. (S.Ann.)
Secretary: Gambles, Peter R.

Mathematical and Physical Sciences, Division of
Tel: (01865) 282570 Fax: (01865) 282571
E-mail: enq@mps.ox.ac.uk
Head: Halliday, Prof. Alexander N., BSc Newcastle(UK), PhD Newcastle(UK) (S.Hug.)
Secretary: Robertson, Mary Ann

Medical Sciences, Division of
Tel: (01865) 221689 Fax: (01865) 750750
E-mail: enquiries@medsci.ox.ac.uk
Head: Fleming, Kenneth A., MB ChB Glas., MA Oxf., DPhil Oxf. (Gre.)
Secretary: Bryan, David E. H., MA Oxf., DPhil Oxf.

Social Sciences, Division of
Tel: (01865) 270254 Fax: (01865) 270554
Head: (vacant) (S.Cat.)
Secretary: Shaikh, Saira J., BSc Lond., PhD Lond.

ACADEMIC UNITS

Anthropology, Social and Cultural, Institute of
Tel: (01865) 274670 Fax: (01865) 274630
Banks, Marcus J., MA Camb., MA Oxf., PhD Camb., DPhil Oxf.   Prof., Visual Anthropology (Wolfs.)
Barnes, Robert H., BLitt Oxf., DPhil Oxf.   Prof., Social Anthropology (S.Ant.)
Harris, Clare, BA Camb., MA Lond., PhD Lond.   Reader, Visual Anthropology (Magd.)
James, Wendy R., BLitt Oxf., MA Oxf., DPhil Oxf.   Prof., Social Anthropology (S.Cross)
Parkin, David J., BA Lond., MA Oxf., PhD Lond., FBA   Prof.; Head* (All S.)
Ulijaszek, Stanley J., BSc Manc., MSc Lond., PhD Lond.   Prof., Human Ecology (S.Cross)
Vertovec, Steven, MA Santa Barbara, DPhil Oxf.   Prof., Transnational Anthropology (Linac.)
Whitehouse, Harvey, BA Lond., PhD Camb.   Prof., Social Anthropology (Magd.)

Archaeology
Tel: (01865) 278240 Fax: (01865) 278254
Barton, R. Nicholas E., BA Birm.   Prof. (Hert.)
Gosden, Christopher H., BA Sheff., MA Oxf., PhD Sheff.   Prof., European Archaeology (Keb.)

Hamerow, Helena, BA Wis., MA Oxf., DPhil Oxf.   Prof. (S.Cross)
Hedges, Robert E. M., MA Camb., MA Oxf., PhD Camb., DPhil Oxf.   Prof. (S.Cross)
Lock, Gary R., BA Leic., PhD CNAA   Prof.; Head* (Kell.)
Mayhew, Nick J., MA Oxf., DLitt Oxf.   Prof., Numismatics and Monetary History (S.Cross)
Mitchell, Peter J., MA Camb., DPhil Oxf.   Prof., African Archaeology (S.Hug.)
Pollard, A. Mark, BA York(UK), DPhil York(UK)   Edward Hall Prof., Archaeological Science (Linac.)
Ramsey, Christopher B., MA Oxf., DPhil Oxf.   Prof., Archaeological Science
Robinson, Mark A., PhD Lond.   Prof., Environmental Archaeology
Vickers, Michael M., BA Wales, DLitt Wales   Prof. (Jes.)

Area Studies, Interdisciplinary
Tel: (01865) 284991 Fax: (01865) 284992
Anderson, David M., BA Sus., PhD Camb.   Prof., African Politics (S.Ant.)
Beinart, William, BA Cape Town, MA Lond., MA Oxf., PhD Lond.   Rhodes Prof., Race Relations (S.Ant.)
Corbett, Jennifer M., BA ANU, MA Oxf.   Reader, Economy of Japan (S.Ant.)
Davis, Christopher M., BA Harv., MSA George Washington, PhD Camb.   Reader, Command and Transition Economics (Wolfs.)
Goodman, Roger J., BA Durh., MA Oxf., DPhil Oxf.   Nissan Prof., Modern Japanese Studies; Head* (S.Ant.)
Shue, Vivienne B., BA Vassar, PhD Harv.   Prof., Study of Contemporary China (S.Ant.)
Thorp, T. Rosemary, MA Oxf.   Reader, Economics of Latin America (S.Ant.)

Biochemistry
Tel: (01865) 275263 Fax: (01865) 275259
E-mail: admin@bioch.ox.ac.uk
Armitage, Judith P., BSc Lond., MA Oxf., PhD Lond.   Prof. (Mert.)
Bell, Stephen D., BSc Glas., PhD Glas.   Prof., Microbiology (Wadh.)
Butters, Terry C., BSc Lond., MPhil CNAA, PhD Open(UK)   Reader, Glycobiology
Campbell, Iain D., BSc St And., MA Oxf., PhD St And.   Prof., Structural Biology (S.Joh.)
Dwek, Raymond A., BSc Manc., MSc Manc., MA Oxf., DPhil Oxf., DSc Oxf., FRS   Prof., Glycobiology (Exet.)
Endicott, Jane A., MA Oxf., PhD Tor.   Prof., Structural Biology (S.Cross)
Ferguson, Stuart J., MA Oxf., DPhil Oxf.   Prof. (S.Edm.)
Handford, Penelope A., BSc S'ton., MA Oxf., PhD S'ton.   Prof. (S.Cat.)

Hodgkin, Jonathan A., BA Oxf., PhD Camb.   Prof., Genetics (Keb.)
Johnson, Dame Louise N., DBE, BSc Lond., MA Oxf., PhD Lond., FRS   David Phillips Prof., Molecular Biophysics (Corp.)
Lea, Susan M., MA Oxf., DPhil Oxf.   Reader, Structural Biology (S.Hild.)
Mahadevan, Louis C., BSc Delhi, MSc Lond., PhD Lond.   Prof. (Trin.)
Nasmyth, Kim, BA York(UK), PhD Edin.   Whitley Prof.; Head* (Trin.)
Noble, Martin E. M., BA Camb., PhD Heidel.   Prof., Structural Biology
Platt, Frances M., BSc Lond., PhD Bath   Reader, Glycobiology
Reid, Kenneth B. M., BSc Aberd., MA Oxf., PhD Aberd., FRS, FMedSci   Prof., Immunochemistry (Gre.)
Rudd, Pauline M., BSc Lond., PhD Open(UK)   Reader, Glycobiology
Sansom, Mark S. P., MA Oxf., DPhil Oxf.   Prof., Molecular Biophysics (Ch.Ch.)
Sherratt, David J., BSc Edin., MA Oxf., PhD Edin., FRS   Iveagh Prof., Microbiology (Linac.)
Watts, Anthony, BSc Leeds, MA Oxf., PhD Leeds, DSc Oxf.   Prof. (S.Hug.)
Whitby, Matthew C., BSc Exe., PhD Nott.   Prof., Molecular Genetics
Yudkin, Michael D., MA Camb., MA Oxf., PhD Camb., DPhil Oxf.   Prof. (Kell.)

Chemistry
Tel: (01865) 275990 Fax: (01865) 275905
Anderson, Harry L., MA Oxf., PhD Camb.   Prof. (Keb.)
Armstrong, Fraser A., BSc Leeds, MA Oxf., PhD Leeds   Prof. (S.Joh.)
Atkins, Peter W., BSc Leic., MA Oxf., PhD Leic.   Prof. (Linc.)
Battle, Peter D., BSc Brist., MA Oxf., DPhil Oxf.   Prof. (S.Cat.)
Bayley, J. Hagan P., MA Oxf., PhD Harv.   Prof., Chemical Biology (Hert.)
Beer, Paul D., BSc Lond., MA Oxf., PhD Lond.   Prof. (Wadh.)
Brouard, Mark, MA Oxf., DPhil Oxf.   Prof. (Jes.)
Brown, John M., BA Camb., MA Oxf., PhD Camb., DPhil Oxf.   Prof. (Exet.)
Clary, David D., BSc Sus., PhD Camb., ScD Camb., FRS, FRSChem   Prof. (Magd.)
Compton, Richard G., MA Oxf., DPhil Oxf.   Prof. (S.Joh.)
Davies, Stephen G., MA Oxf., DPhil Oxf., DSc Paris   Waynflete Prof.; Chairman* (Magd.)
Davis, Ben G., MA Oxf., DPhil Oxf.   Prof. (Pemb.)
Dilworth, Jonathan R., MA Oxf., DPhil Sus., DSc Sus.   Prof. (S.Ann.)
Donohoe, Timothy J., BSc Bath, DPhil Oxf.   Prof. (Magd.)
Edwards, Peter P., BSc Salf., PhD Salf.   Prof., Inorganic Chemistry (S.Cat.)
Egdell, Russell G., MA Oxf., DPhil Oxf.   Prof., Inorganic Chemistry (Trin.)
Fleet, George W. J., MA Camb., PhD Camb.   Prof. (S.Joh.)
Foord, John S., MA Camb., MA Oxf., PhD Camb.   Prof. (S.Cat.)
Gouverneur, Veronique E. B. M., PhD Louvain   Reader (Mert.)
Green, Jennifer C., MA Oxf., DPhil Oxf.   Prof. (S.Hug.)
Hancock, Gus, MA Trinity(Dub.), MA Camb., MA Oxf., PhD Camb.   Prof. (Trin.)
Hodgson, David M., BSc Bath, PhD S'ton.   Prof. (Oriel)
Hore, Peter J., MA Oxf., DPhil Oxf.   Prof., Physical Chemistry (Corp.)
Howard, Brian J., MA Camb., MA Oxf., PhD S'ton.   Prof. (Pemb.)
Klein, Jacob, MA Camb., PhD Camb.   Dr Lee's Prof. (Exet.)
Logan, David E., MA Camb., MA Oxf., PhD Camb.   Coulson Prof., Theoretical Chemistry (Univ.)
Manolopoulos, David E., BA Camb., PhD Camb.   Prof., Theoretical Chemistry (S.Edm.)

The abbreviation in brackets after a teacher's name denotes the college of which the teacher is a present member or fellow. The names of the colleges are indicated by abbreviations as follows:

All S.	All Souls College	Oriel	Oriel College
Ball.	Balliol College	Pemb.	Pembroke College
Bras.	Brasenose College	Qu.	Queen's College
Camp.	Campion Hall	Reg.P.	Regent's Park College
Ch.Ch.	Christ Church	S.Ann.	St Anne's College
Corp.	Corpus Christi College	S.Ant.	St Antony's College
Exet.	Exeter College	S.Ben.	St Benet's Hall
Gre.	Green College	S.Cat.	St Catherine's College
Greyf.	Greyfriars	S.Cross	St Cross College
Harris	Harris Manchester College	S.Edm.	St Edmund Hall
Hert.	Hertford College	S.Hil.	St Hilda's College
Jes.	Jesus College	S.Hug.	St Hugh's College
Keb.	Keble College	S.Joh.	St John's College
Kell.	Kellogg College	S.Pet.	St Peter's College
L.M.H.	Lady Margaret Hall	Som.	Somerville College
Linac.	Linacre College	Templ.	Templeton College
Linc.	Lincoln College	Trin.	Trinity College
Magd.	Magdalen College	Univ.	University College
Mansf.	Mansfield College	Wadh.	Wadham College
Mert.	Merton College	Wolfs.	Wolfson College
New	New College	Worc.	Worcester College
Nuff.	Nuffield College	Wycl.H.	Wycliffe Hall

Mingos, D. Michael P., BSc Manc., MA Oxf., DPhil Sus., FRS, FRSChem   Prof. (S.Edm.)
Moloney, Mark G., BSc Syd., PhD Syd.   Reader (S.Pet.)
Mountford, Philip, BSc CNAA, MA Oxf., DPhil Oxf.   Prof. (S.Edm.)
O'Hare, Dermot M., MA Oxf., DPhil Oxf.   Prof. (Ball.)
Redfield, Christina, BA Wellesley, MA Harv., PhD Harv.   Reader, Molecular Sciences (Wolfs.)
Richards, W. Graham, CBE, MA Oxf., DPhil Oxf., DSc Oxf.   Prof. (Bras.)
Schofield, Christopher J., BSc Manc., MA Oxf., DPhil Oxf.   Prof. (Hert.)
Softley, Timothy P., MA Oxf., PhD S'ton.   Prof., Chemical Physics (Mert.)
Thomas, Robert K., MA Oxf., DPhil Oxf.   Reader; Aldrichian Praelector (Univ.)

Classics, Faculty of

Tel: (01865) 288391 Fax: (01865) 288386
Bowie, Ewen L., MA Oxf.   Prof., Classical Languages and Literature (Corp.)
Cameron, Averil M., DBE, MA Oxf., PhD Lond., FBA, FSA   Prof., Late Antique and Byzantine History (Keb.)
Feeney, Dennis, BA Auck., MA Auck., DPhil Oxf.   Corpus Christi Prof., Latin Language and Literature (Corp.)
Harrison, Stephen J., MA Oxf., DPhil Oxf.   Prof., Classical Languages and Literature (Corp.)
Howgego, Christopher J., MA Oxf., DPhil Oxf.   Prof., Greek and Roman Numismatics (Wolfs.)
Hutchinson, Gregory O., MA Oxf., MPhil Oxf., DPhil Oxf.   Prof., Greek and Latin Languages and Literature (Exet.)
Jenkyns, Richard H. A., MA Oxf., MLitt Oxf.   Prof., Classical Tradition (L.M.H.)
Kurtz, Donna C., BA Cinc., MA Yale, DPhil Oxf.   Prof., Classical Art (Wolfs.)
Leigh, Matthew G. L., MA Oxf., DPhil Oxf.   Prof. (S.Anne)
Lemos, Irene S., DPhil Oxf.   Reader, Classical Archaeology (Mert.)
Pelling, Christopher B. R., MA Oxf., DPhil Oxf.   Regius Prof., Greek (Ch.Ch.)
Smith, Roland R. R., CBE, MA Oxf., MPhil Oxf., DPhil Oxf., FBA   Lincoln Prof., Classical Art and Archaeology (Linc.)
Taplin, Oliver P., MA Oxf., DPhil Oxf.   Prof. (Magd.)
Willi, Andreas J., LicPhil Basle, LicPhil Frib., DPhil Oxf.   Diebold Prof., Comparative Philology (Worc.)
Wilson, Andrew I., MA Oxf., DPhil Oxf.   Prof., Archaeology of the Roman Empire (All S.)

Computing Laboratory

Tel: (01865) 273838 Fax: (01865) 273839
E-mail: enquiries@comlab.ox.ac.uk
Abramsky, Samson, MA Camb., PhD Lond.   Christopher Strachey Prof., Computing (Wolfs.)
Bird, Richard S., MA Camb., MA Oxf., PhD Lond.   Prof., Computing Science (Linc.)
Cameron, Stephen A., BA Edin., MA Oxf., PhD Edin.   Reader (Keb.)
Davies, Jim W. M., MA Oxf.   Prof., Software Engineering (Kell.)
de Moor, Oegerikus, MSc Utrecht, MA Oxf., DPhil Oxf.   Prof. (Magd.)
Gavaghan, David J., BSc Durh., MSc Oxf., PhD Durh.   Prof., Computational Biology (New)
Gibbons, Jeremy   Reader, Software Engineering (Kell.)
Giles, Michael, BA Camb., MA Oxf., PhD M.I.T.   Rolls Royce Reader; Prof., Scientific Computing
Gottlob, Georg, PhD T.U.Vienna   Prof., Computing Science (S.Ann.)
Hauser, Raphael A., MSc Cornell, PhD Cornell   Reader, Mathematical Programming (Pemb.)

Jeavons, Peter G., MSc Leic., MA Oxf., PhD Lond.   Prof., Computer Science (S.Ann.)
Kwiatkowska, Marta Z., BSc Cracow, MSc Cracow, PhD Leic.   Prof., Computing Systems (Trin.)
Melham, Thomas F., BSc Calg., PhD Camb.   Prof., Computer Science (Ball.)
Ong, C. H. Luke, MA Camb., PhD Lond.   Prof., Computer Science (Mert.)
Pulman, Stephen G., BA Lond., MA Essex, PhD Essex, FBA   Prof., Computational Linguistics (Som.)
Roscoe, A. William, MA Oxf., DPhil Oxf.   Prof., Computing Science; Dir.* (Univ.)
Sueli, Endre E., MSc Belgrade, MA Oxf., PhD Belgrade   Prof., Numerical Analysis (Linac.)
Trefethen, L. Nick, AB Harv., MS Stan., MA Oxf., PhD Stan.   Prof., Numerical Analysis (Ball.)
Wathen, Andy J., MA Oxf., PhD Reading   Reader, Numerical Analysis (New)

Continuing Education

Tel: (01865) 270360 Fax: (01865) 270309
E-mail: enquiries@conted.ox.ac.uk
Dawkins, C. Richard, MA Oxf., DPhil Oxf., DSc Oxf.   Charles Simonyi Reader; Prof., Public Understanding
Thomas, Geoffrey P., BSc Wales, MA Oxf., PhD Camb.   Dir.* (Kell.)

Drawing and Fine Art, Ruskin School of

see also Oriental Sudies, Fac. of

Tel: (01865) 276940 Fax: (01865) 276949
Archer, Michael G., BA Camb., MEd Manc.   Head*
Catling, Brian D., MA RCA, MA Oxf.   Prof., Fine Art (Linac.)
Chevska, Maria, MA Oxf.   Prof., Fine Art (Bras.)
Wentworth, Richard, MA Lond.   Prof., Fine Art (S.Edm.)

Earth Sciences

Tel: (01865) 272000 Fax: (01865) 272072
E-mail: enquiries@earth.ox.ac.uk
Brasier, Martin D., BSc Lond., MA Oxf., PhD Lond.   Prof., Palaeobiology (S.Edm.)
Das, Shamita, MS Boston, MSc Calc., MA Oxf., ScD M.I.T.   Prof. (Gre.)
England, Philip C., BSc Brist., MA Oxf., DPhil Oxf.   Prof., Geology; Head* (Exet.)
Fraser, Don G., BSc Edin., MA Oxf., DPhil Oxf.   Prof. (Worc.)
Halliday, Alexander N., BSc Newcastle(UK), PhD Newcastle(UK)   Prof., Geochemistry (S.Hug.)
Henderson, Gideon M., PhD Camb.   Prof. (Univ.)
Hesselbo, Stephen P., BSc Aberd., PhD Brist.   Prof., Stratigraphy (S.Pet.)
Parsons, Barry E., MA Camb., MA Oxf., PhD Camb.   Prof., Geodesy and Geophysics (S.Cross)
Siveter, Derek J.   Reader
Watts, Anthony B., BSc Lond., MA Oxf., PhD Durh.   Prof., Marine Geology and Geophysics (Wolfs.)
Woodhouse, John H., BSc Brist., MA Camb., MA Oxf., PhD Camb., DPhil Oxf.   Prof., Geophysics (Worc.)

Economics

see also Internat. Devel.

Tel: (01865) 271089 Fax: (01865) 271094
E-mail: reception@economics.ox.ac.uk
Allen, Robert C., MA Oxf.   Prof., Recent Social and Economic History (Nuff.)
Allsopp, Christopher J., BPhil Oxf., MA Oxf.   Reader, Economic Policy (New)
Anand, Sudhir, BPhil Oxf., MA Oxf., DPhil Oxf.   Prof., Quantitative Economic Analysis (S.Cat.)
Collier, Paul, MA Oxf., DPhil Oxf.   Prof. (S.Ant.)
Davis, Christopher M., BA Harv., MSA George Washington, PhD Camb.   Reader, Command and Transition Economics (Wolfs.)
Fafchamps, Marcel, MA Oxf., PhD Calif.   Prof., Development Economics (Mansf.)

Graddy, Katherine, BS(BA) Tulane, MBA Col., PhD Prin.   Prof., Applied Economics (Exe.)
Greenhalgh, Christine A., MSc Lond., MA Oxf., PhD Prin.   Reader (S.Pet.)
Harley, C. Knick, BA Wooster, MA Harv., PhD Harv.   Prof., Economic History (S.Ant.)
Hendry, David F., MA Aberd., MA Oxf., MSc Lond., PhD Lond.   Prof.; Head* (Nuff.)
Joshi, Vijay R., MA Oxf.   Reader (Mert.)
Keller, R. Godfrey, MSc Lond., PhD Lond.   Prof., Microeconomic Theory
Klemperer, Paul D., MBA Stan., MA Camb., MA Oxf.   Edgeworth Prof. (Nuff.)
Knight, John B., MA Camb., MA Oxf.   Prof. (S.Edm.)
Malcomson, James M., MA Camb., MA Harv., MA Oxf., PhD Harv.   Prof. (All S.)
Mayhew, Ken, MSc(Econ) Lond., MA Oxf.   Reader (Pemb.)
Muellbauer, John N. J., MA Calif., PhD Calif.   Prof. (Nuff.)
Mukerji, Sujoy, BSc Calc., MA Delhi, PhD Yale   Prof. (Univ.)
Neary, J. Peter, BA N.U.I., BPhil Oxf., MPhil Oxf.   Prof. (Mert.)
Nielsen, Bent, PhD Copenhagen   Reader, Econometrics (Nuff.)
Offer, Avner, BA Jerusalem, MA Oxf., DPhil Oxf.   Chichele Prof., Economic History (All S.)
Quah, John K.-H., BSc Sing., PhD Calif.   Prof., Economic Theory (S.Hug.)
Roberts, Kevin W. S., BA Essex, MA Oxf., DPhil Oxf.   Sir John Hicks Prof. (Nuff.)
Shephard, Neil, BA York(UK), MSc Lond., PhD Lond.   Prof. (Nuff.)
Venables, Anthony J., BA Camb., BPhil Oxf., DPhil Oxf.   BP Prof. (New)
Vickers, John S., MA Oxf., MPhil Oxf., DPhil Oxf.   Drummond Prof., Political Economy (All S.)
Vines, David A., BA Melb., MA Camb., MA Oxf., PhD Camb., DPhil   Prof., Economics (Ball.)
Young, H. Peyton   James Meade Prof. (Nuff.)
Research: econometric computing; econometric modelling (computer automation, modelling selection, modelling theory); economic forecasting; macroeconomics (consumption, inflation, money, unemployment); UK economic history since 1870

Education

Tel: (01865) 274023 Fax: (01865) 274027
E-mail: general.enquiries@edstud.ox.ac.uk
Furlong, John, BA CNAA, MA Camb., PhD City(UK)   Prof., Educational Studies; Dir.* (Gre.)
Macaro, Ernesto, BA Kent, MA Warsaw   Reader, Applied Linguistics and Second Language Acquisition (Worc.)
Marsh, Herbert W., BA Indiana, MA Calif., PhD Calif., DSc W.Syd.   Prof. (S.Cross)
Nunes, Terezinha, BSc Minas Gerais, MA C.U.N.Y., PhD C.U.N.Y.   Prof. (Harris)
Phillips, David G., BA Lond., MA Oxf., DPhil Oxf.   Prof., Comparative Education (S.Edm.)
Sylva, Kathy D., BA Harv., MA Oxf., MA Harv., PhD Harv.   Prof., Educational Psychology (Jes.)
Walford, Geoffrey, BSc Kent, BSc Open(UK), MA Oxf., MA Lond., MSc Open(UK), MPhil Oxf., PhD Kent   Prof., Education Policy (Gre.)
Watson, Anne, BA Open(UK), MA Oxf., DPhil Oxf.   Reader, Mathematics Education (Linac.)

Engineering Science

Tel: (01865) 273000 Fax: (01865) 273010
Banares-Alcantara, Rene, BSc Mexico, MS Carnegie-Mellon, PhD Carnegie-Mellon   Reader (New)
Borthwick, Alistair G. L., BEng Liv., MA Oxf., PhD Liv.   Prof. (S.Edm.)
Brady, Sir Mike, MSc Manc., MA Oxf., PhD ANU, FREng   BP Prof., Information Engineering (Keb.)
Buckley, C. Paul, MA Oxf., DPhil Oxf.   Prof. (Ball.)

Clarke, David W., MA Oxf., DPhil Oxf., FRS, FREng   Prof., Control Engineering (New)

Cocks, Alan C. F., BSc Leic., PhD Camb.   Prof., Materials Engineering (S.Ann.)

Cui, Zhanfeng, MA Oxf., MSc Dalian U.T., PhD Dalian I.T., BSc   Donald Pollock Prof., Chemical Engineering (Hert.)

Daniel, Ronald W., BSc Brun., MA Oxf., MA Camb., PhD Camb.   Prof. (Bras.)

Darton, Richard, BSc Birm., PhD Camb.   Prof.; Head* (Keb.)

Dexter, Arthur L., MA Oxf., DPhil Oxf.   Prof. (Worc.)

Duncan, Stephen R., MA Camb., MSc Lond., PhD Lond.   Reader (S.Hug.)

Dunne, Fionn P. E., BSc Brist., MA Oxf., PhD Sheff.   Prof. (Hert.)

Eatock Taylor, W. Rodney, MS Stan., PhD Stan., MA Camb., MA Oxf.   Prof., Mechanical Engineering (S.Hug.)

Edwards, David J., MA Oxf., MSc Brist., PhD Brist.   Prof. (Wadh.)

Efstathiou, H. Janet, MA Oxf., PhD Durh.   Reader (Pemb.)

Elston, Stephen J., BSc Exe., PhD Exe.   Prof. (S.Joh.)

Field, Robert W., MA Camb., PhD Camb.   Reader (Ball.)

Hills, David A., MA Oxf., PhD CNAA   Prof. (Linc.)

Houlsby, Guy T., MA Camb., MA Oxf., PhD Camb.   Prof., Civil Engineering (Bras.)

Ireland, Peter T., MA Oxf., DPhil Oxf.   Prof. (S.Ann.)

Korsunsky, Alexander M., BSc Moscow, MSc Moscow, DPhil Oxf.   Prof. (Trin.)

Kouvaritakis, Basil, MA Oxf., MSc Manc., PhD Manc.   Prof. (S.Edm.)

Ligrani, Phillip, BS Texas, PhD Stan.   Donald Schultz Prof., Turbomachinery (S.Cat.)

McFadden, Peter D., BE Melb., MA Oxf., PhD Melb.   Reader (Jes.)

Murray, David W., MA Oxf., DPhil Oxf.   Prof. (S.Ann.)

Noble, J. Alison, MA Lond., PhD Lond.   Prof. (Wolfs.)

Nowell, David, BA Camb., MA Oxf., DPhil Oxf.   Prof. (Ch.Ch.)

O'Brien, Dominic C., BA Camb., PhD Camb.   Reader (Bal.)

Probert Smith, Penelope J., MA Camb., MA Oxf., PhD Camb.   Reader (L.M.H.)

Raynes, Edward P., MA Oxf., MA Camb., PhD Camb.   Prof., Opto-electronic Engineering (S.Cross)

Reid, Ian D., BSc W.Aust., MA Oxf., DPhil Oxf.   Reader (Exe.)

Roberts, Stephen J., MA Oxf., DPhil Oxf.   Prof. (Some.)

Smith, Paul W., BSc Lond., MSc S'ton., PhD Lond.   Reader (Pemb.)

Stone, C. Richard, MA Camb., MA Oxf., DPhil Oxf.   Prof. (Som.)

Tarassenko, Lionel, MA Oxf., DPhil Oxf.   Prof., Electrical and Electronic Engineering (S.Joh.)

Taylor, Paul H., MA Camb., PhD Camb.   Prof. (Keb.)

Ventikos, Ioannis, PhD T.U.Athens   Reader (Wadh.)

Williams, Martin S., BSc Brist., PhD Brist.   Reader (New)

Wilson, Tony, MA Oxf., DPhil Oxf.   Prof. (Hert.)

Zavatsky, Amy B., BSc Penn., MA Oxf., DPhil Oxf.   Reader (S.Edm.)

Zisserman, Andrew P., MA Oxf., MA Camb., PhD Camb.   Prof.

Research: chemical engineering (bioremediation, membrane separation, tissue engineering); civil engineering (coastal engineering, geotechnics, structural dynamics); electrical engineering (communications, control engineering, optoelectronics, signal processing); information engineering (computer vision, medical image analysis, robotics); mechanical engineering (aero-thermodynamics, combustion, offshore structures, structural integrity)

English

Tel: (01865) 271055 Fax: (01865) 271054
E-mail: english.office@e11.ox.ac.uk

Achinstein, Sharon, AB Harv., PhD Prin.   Reader, English Renaissance Studies (S.Edm.)

Bradshaw, John D., BA Newcastle(UK), MA Oxf., DPhil Oxf.   Prof. (Worc.)

Bush, Ron L., BA Penn., MA Oxf., MA Camb., PhD Prin.   Drue Heinz Prof., American Literature (S.Joh.)

Butler, I. Christopher, MA Oxf.   Prof. (Ch.Ch.)

Cameron, Deborah J., BA Newcastle(UK), MLitt Oxf.   Rupert Murdoch Prof., Language and Communication (Worc.)

Coleman, John S., BA York(UK), MA Oxf., DPhil York(UK)   Dir., Phonetics Lab.; Reader, Phonetics (Wolfs.)

Cunningham, Valentine D., MA Oxf., DPhil Oxf.   Prof. (Corp.)

Giles, Paul, MA Oxf., DPhil Oxf.   Prof., American Literature (Linac.)

Gill, Stephen C., BPhil Oxf., MA Oxf., PhD Edin.   Prof. (Linc.)

Gillespie, Vincent A., MA Oxf., DPhil Oxf.   Tolkien Prof., Mediaeval Language and Literature (L.M.H.)

Godden, Malcolm R., MA Camb., MA Oxf., PhD Camb.   Rawlinson and Bosworth Prof., Anglo-Saxon (Pemb.)

Hanna, Ralph, AB Amherst, MA Yale, PhD Yale   Prof., Palaeography (Keb.)

Kelly, John S., MA Trinity(Dub.), MA Oxf., PhD Camb., DPhil Oxf.   Prof. (S.Joh.)

Lee, Hermione, MA Oxf., MPhil Oxf., FBA   Goldsmiths' Prof., English Literature (New)

Maguire, Laurie E., BA Lond., MA Birm., PhD Lond.   Reader (Magd.)

Mapstone, Sally L., MA Oxf., DPhil Oxf.   Reader, Older Scottish Literature (S.Hild.)

McCabe, Richard A., BA Trinity(Dub.), MA Oxf., MA Camb., PhD Camb.   Prof. (Mert.)

McDonagh, Josephine, BA Wales, MA S'ton., PhD S'ton.   Prof., Victorian Literature (Linac.)

Mugglestone, Lynda, MA Oxf., DPhil Oxf.   Prof., History of English (Pemb.)

Newlyn, Lucy A., MA Oxf., DPhil Oxf.   Prof. (S.Edm.)

Norbrook, David G. E., MA Aberd., DPhil Oxf.   Merton Prof., English Literature (Mert.)

O'Donoghue, Heather, MA Oxf., MPhil Oxf., DPhil Oxf.   Vigfusson-Rausing Reader, Ancient Icelandic Literature and Antiquities (Linac.)

Ricks, Christopher, BLitt Oxf., MA Oxf.   Prof., Poetry (Ball.)

Romaine, Suzanne, AB Bryn Mawr, MA Oxf., MLitt Edin., PhD Birm.   Merton Prof., English Language (Mert.)

Stafford, Fiona, BA Leic., MA Oxf., DPhil Oxf.   Reader (Some.)

Sutherland, Kathryn, MA Oxf., DPhil Oxf.   Prof., Bibliography and Textual Criticism (S.Ann.)

Womersley, David J., MA Camb., PhD Camb.   Thomas Warton Prof., English Literature (S.Cat.)

Wu, Duncan, MA Oxf., DPhil Oxf.   Prof. (S.Cat.)

Geography and the Environment

Tel: (01865) 285070 Fax: (01865) 275885
E-mail: enquiries@geog.ox.ac.uk

Banister, David, BA Nott., PhD Leeds   Reader, Transport Studies (S.Ann.)

Barry, Andrew M., BA Camb., DPhil Sus.   Reader (S.Cat.)

Boardman, John, BA Keele, BSc Lond., PhD Lond.   Reader, Geomorphology and Land Degradation (Gre.)

Clark, Gordon L., BEc Monash, MA Monash, MA Oxf., PhD McM.   Halford Mackinder Prof.; Head* (S.Pet.)

Liverman, Diana M., BA Tor., MA Tor., PhD Calif.   Dir., Environmental Change Inst.; Prof., Environmental Science (Linac.)

McDowell, Linda M., BA Camb., MPhil Lond., PhD Lond.   Prof., Human Geography (S.Joh.)

Swyngedouw, Erik A. M., MA Leuven, MA Oxf., PhD Johns H.   Prof. (S.Pet.)

Thomas, David S. G., MA Oxf., DPhil Oxf.   Prof. (Hert.)

Viles, Heather A., MA Oxf., DPhil Oxf.   Reader, Geomorphology (Worc.)

Whatmore, Sarah, BA Lond., MPhil Lond., PhD Lond., DSc Brist.   Prof., Environment and Public Policy

Whittaker, Rob J., BSc Hull, MSc Wales, MA Oxf., PhD Wales   Prof., Biogeography (S.Edm.)

Willis, Katherine J., BSc S'ton., PhD Camb.   Prof., Long-Term Ecology (Jes.)

History

see also Econ.

Tel: (01865) 615000 Fax: (01865) 250704

Blair, William J., MA Oxf.   Prof., Mediaeval History and Archaeology (Qu.)

Brigden, Susan E., BA Manc., MA Oxf., PhD Camb.   Reader (Linc.)

Brockliss, Laurence W. B., MA Camb., MA Oxf., PhD Camb., DPhil Oxf.   Prof., Early Modern French History (Magd.)

Brown, Judith M., MA Camb., MA Oxf., PhD Camb., DPhil Oxf., FRHistS   Beit Prof., History of British Commonwealth (Ball.)

Carwardine, Richard J., MA Oxf., DPhil Oxf.   Rhodes Prof., American History (S.Cat.)

Clunas, Craig, BA Camb., PhD Lond.   Prof., History of Art (Trin.)

Corsi, Pietro, DPhil   Prof., History of Science (Linac.)

Evans, Robert J. W., MA Camb., MA Oxf., PhD Camb., DPhil Oxf., FBA   Regius Prof. (Oriel)

Foster, Roy F., MA Trinity(Dub.), MA Oxf., PhD Trinity(Dub.), DPhil Oxf., FRHistS, FBA   Carroll Prof., Irish History (Hert.)

Gildea, Robert N., MA Oxf., DPhil Oxf.   Prof., Modern History (Worc.)

Harris, José F., MA Camb., MA Oxf., PhD Camb., FBA   Prof. (S.Cat.)

Harrison, Mark, DPhil Oxf.   Dir., Wellcome Unit for the Hist. of Med.; Prof., History of Medicine (Gre.)

Humphries, Katherine J., MA Camb., MA Cornell, PhD Cornell   Prof., Economic History (All S.)

Kemp, Martin J., MA Oxf., MA Camb., FBA   Head, Dept. of Hist. of Art; Prof., History of Art (Trin.)

Knight, Alan, MA Oxf., DPhil Oxf.   Prof., History of Latin America (S.Ant.)

Langford, Paul, MA Oxf., DPhil Oxf., FBA   Prof. (Linc.)

Maclean, Ian W. F., MA Oxf., DPhil Oxf.   Prof., Renaissance Studies (All S.)

Pelling, Margaret H., MA Oxf., MLitt Oxf., LittD Melb.   Reader, Social History of Medicine (Linac.)

Roper, Lyndal A., BA Melb., PhD Lond.   Prof., Early Modern History (Ball.)

Service, Robert J., MA Camb., PhD Essex   Prof., Russian History (S.Ant.)

Sharpe, Richard, MA Camb., MA Oxf., PhD Camb., FSA, FRHistS   Prof., Diplomatic (Wadh.)

Slack, Paul A., MA Oxf., DPhil Oxf., FBA   Prof., Early Social Modern History

Strachan, Huw F. A., MA Camb., PhD Camb.   Chichele Prof., History of War (All S.)

Washbrook, David A., MA Camb., MA Oxf., PhD Camb., DPhil Oxf.   Reader, Modern South Asian History (S.Ant.)

Wickham, Christopher J., BA Oxf., DPhil Oxf.   Chichele Prof., Medieval History (All S.)

History, Ancient

see also Classics, Fac. of

Tel: (01865) 288391 Fax: (01865) 288386

Bowman, Alan K., MA Tor., PhD Tor.   Camden Prof. (Bras.)

Lane Fox, Robin J., MA Oxf.   Reader (New)

Parker, Robert C. T., MA Oxf., DPhil Oxf.   Wykeham Prof. (New)

International Development

Queen Elizabeth House

Tel: (01865) 281800 Fax: (01865) 281801

Adam, Christopher S., MA St And., MA Oxf., MPhil Oxf., DPhil Oxf.   Reader, Economics for Development (S.Cross)

Castles, Stephen, MA Sus., DPhil Sus.   Prof., Migration and Refugee Studies (Gre.)

Chatty, Dawn, MA Inst.Soc.Stud.(The Hague), PhD Calif.   Reader, Forced Migration (S.Cross)

Dercon, Stefan, BPhil Leuven, MA Oxf., MPhil Oxf., DPhil Oxf.   Prof., Development Economics (Wolfs.)

Fitzgerald, Edmund V. K., MA Oxf., PhD Camb.   Prof., International Development (S.Ant.)

Gibney, Matthew J., BEc Monash, MPhil Camb., PhD Camb.   Reader, Politics and Forced Migration (Linac.)

Gooptu, Nandini, MA Calc., PhD Camb.   Reader, South Asian Studies (S.Ant.)

Harriss-White, Barbara, MA Camb., MA Oxf., PhD E.Anglia   Prof., Development Studies; Dir.* (Wolfs.)

Stewart, Frances J., DPhil Oxf.   Prof., Development Economics (Som.)

Thorp, T. Rosemary, MA Oxf.   Reader, Economics of Latin America (S.Ant.)

Wood, Adrian J. B., MA Camb., PhD Camb.   Prof. (Wolfs.)

Law

Tel: (01865) 271490 Fax: (01865) 271493
E-mail: lawfac@law.ox.ac.uk

Armour, John H., BCL Oxf., MA Oxf., LLM Yale   Lovells Prof., Law and Finance (Oriel)

Ashworth, Andrew J., BCL Oxf., LLB Lond., DCL Oxf., PhD Manc., FBA   Vinerian Prof., English Law (All S.)

Briggs, Adrian, BCL Oxf., MA Oxf.   Prof., Private International Law (S.Edm.)

Bright, Susan J., BCL Oxf., MA Oxf.   Prof., Land Law (New)

Burrows, Andrew S., BCL Oxf., LLM Harv., MA Oxf.   Norton Rose Prof., Commercial and Financial Law (S.Hug.)

Cartwright, John, BCL Oxf., MA Oxf.   Reader, Law of Contract (Ch.Ch.)

Chen-Wishart, Mindy, BA Otago, LLB Otago, LLM Otago   Reader, Contract Law (Mert.)

Craig, Paul P., BCL Oxf., MA Oxf.   Prof., English Law (S.Joh.)

Davies, Anne C. L., MA Oxf., DPhil Oxf.   Reader, Public Law. (Bras.)

Endicott, Timothy, AB Harv., LLB Tor., MPhil Oxf., DPhil Oxf.   Prof., Legal Philosophy; Dean* (Ball.)

Finnis, John M., LLB Adel., MA Oxf., DPhil Oxf.   Prof., Law and Legal Philosophy (Univ.)

Fredman, Sandra D., BCL Oxf., MA Oxf.   Prof. (Exet.)

Freedland, Mark R., LLB Lond., MA Oxf., DPhil Oxf.   Prof., Employment Law (S.Joh.)

Freedman, Judith A., MA Oxf.   KPMG Prof., Taxation (Worc.)

Galligan, Denis J., LLB Qld., BCL Oxf., MA Oxf.   Dir., Centre for Socio-Legal Studies; Prof., Socio-Legal Studies (Wolfs.)

Gardner, John B., BCL Oxf., MA Oxf., DPhil Oxf.   Prof., Jurisprudence (Univ.)

Getzler, Joshua S., BA ANU, LLB ANU, DPhil Oxf.   Reader, Legal History (S.Hug.)

Green, Leslie, BA Qu., MPhil Oxf., DPhil Oxf.   Prof., Philosophy of Law (Ball.)

Horder, Jeremy C. N., LLB Hull, BCL Oxf., MA Oxf., DPhil Oxf.   Prof., Criminal Law (Worc.)

Hoyle, Carolyn E., BA Kent, MA Oxf., DPhil Oxf.   Reader, Criminology (Gre.)

Loader, Ian, LLB Sheff., MSc Camb., PhD Edin.   Dir., Centre for Criminology; Prof., Criminology (All S.)

Lowe, A. Vaughan, LLB Wales, LLM Wales, MA Camb.   Chichele Prof., Public International Law (All S.)

McBarnet, Doreen J., CBE, MA Glas., PhD Glas.   Prof., Socio-Legal Studies (Wolfs.)

McCrudden, J. Christopher, LLB Belf., LLM Yale, MA Oxf., DPhil Oxf.   Prof., Human Rights Law (Linc.)

McKendrick, Ewan G., LLB Edin., MA Oxf.   Prof., English Private Law (L.M.H.)

Prentice, Dan D., LLB Belf., MA Oxf., JD Chic.   Allen and Overy Prof., Corporate Law (Pemb.)

Roberts, Julian V., MA Oxf., PhD Tor.   Prof., Criminology (Worc.)

Sarooshi, Dan, BComm NSW, LLB NSW, LLM Lond., PhD Lond.   Prof., Public International Law (Qu.)

Sirks, A. J. Boudewijn, LLM Ley., PhD Amst.   Regius Prof., Civil Law (All S.)

Talmon, Stefan, MA Oxf., LLM Oxf., DPhil Oxf.   Reader, Public International Law (S.Ann.)

Varese, Federico, MA Camb., DPhil Oxf.   Prof., Criminology (Linac.)

Vaver, David, BA Auck., LLB Auck., MA Oxf., JD Chic.   Prof., Intellectual Property and Information Technology (S.Pet.)

Vogenauer, Stefan, MJur Oxf.   Prof., Comparative Law (Bras.)

Weatherill, Stephen R., MA Camb., MSc Edin., MA Oxf.   Jacques Delors Prof., European Community Law (Som.)

Whittaker, Simon J., BCL Oxf., MA Oxf., DPhil Oxf.   Prof., European Comparative Law (S.Joh.)

Wyatt, Derrick A., LLB Camb., BCL Oxf., MA Camb., MA Oxf., JD Chic.   Prof. (S.Edm.)

Zedner, Lucia H., BA York(UK), MA Oxf., DPhil Oxf.   Prof., Criminal Justice (Corp.)

Zuckermann, Adrian A. Z., LLB Jerusalem, LLM Jerusalem   Prof., Civil Procedure (Univ.)

Linguistics and Philology, Centre for

Tel: (01865) 280400 Fax: (01865) 280412
E-mail: enquiries@ling-phil.ox.ac.uk

Dalrymple, Mary E., BA Cornell, MA Texas, PhD Stan.   Prof., Linguistics (Linac.)

Management Studies

Said Business School

Tel: (01865) 288800 Fax: (01865) 288805
E-mail: enquiries@sbs.ox.ac.uk

Barron, David N., BA Camb., MA Cornell, PhD Cornell   Reader, Organisational Sociology (Jes.)

Chapman, Chris, BSc Lond., MSc Lond., PhD Lond.   Reader, Accounting (Linac.)

Dopson, Sue E., BSc Leic., MSc Lond., PhD Leic.   Reader, Organisational Behaviour (Templ.)

Earl, Michael J., BA Newcastle(UK), MSc Warw., MA Oxf.   Prof., Information Management (Templ.)

Empson, Laura, BSc Lond., MBA Lond., MPhil Lond., PhD Lond.Bus.   Reader, Management of Professional Service Firms (S.Ann.)

Holt, Douglas B., AB Stan., MBA Chic., PhD Northwestern   L'Oreal Prof., Marketing (Worc.)

Hopwood, Anthony G., BSc Lond., MBA Chic., PhD Chic.   American Standard Companies Prof., Operations Management (Ch.Ch.)

Jenkinson, Tim J., BA Camb., AM Penn., MPhil Oxf., DPhil Oxf.   Prof., Finance (Keb.)

Kessler, Ian J., BA Manc., MA Warw., PhD Warw.   Reader, Employment Relations (Temp.)

Mayer, Colin P., MA Oxf., MPhil Oxf., DPhil Oxf.   Peter Moores Prof.; Peter Moores Dean* (S.Edm.)

Morris, Timothy J., BA Camb., MSc Lond., PhD Lond.   Prof. (Templ.)

Morrison, Alan D., MSc Lond., PhD Lond.   Reader, Finance (Mert.)

Noe, Thomas H., MBA Texas, PhD Texas   Ernest Butten Prof. (Ball.)

Powell, Thomas C., MPhil N.Y., PhD N.Y.   Prof., Strategy (S.Hug.)

Rayner, Steve F., BA Kent, PhD Lond.   Prof., Science and Civilisation

Romero-Morales, Maria D., MSc Seville, PhD Rotterdam   Reader, Operations Research (S.Cross)

Sako, Mari, MSc Lond., MA Johns H., PhD Lond.   Peninsular and Oriental Steam Navigation Company Prof. (Templ.)

Scott, Linda, MA Texas, MBA S.Methodist, PhD Texas   Reader, Marketing (Temp.)

Sussman, Owen, BA Jerusalem, MA Jerusalem, PhD Jerusalem   Reader, Finance (Wadh.)

Taylor, James W., MA Camb., MSc Lanc., PhD Lond.Bus.   Reader, Decision Science (S.Cross)

Vulkan, Nir, BSc Tel-Aviv, PhD Lond.   Reader, Business Economics (Worc.)

Westbrook, Roy K., BA Leic., PhD Lond.   Prof., Operations Management (S.Hug.)

Whittington, Richard C., MA Oxf., MBA Aston, PhD Manc.   Prof., Strategic Management (New)

Woolgar, Stephen W., MA Camb., PhD Camb.   Prof., Marketing (Gre.)

Materials

Tel: (01865) 273700 Fax: (01865) 273789
E-mail: enquiries@materials.ox.ac.uk

Briggs, G. Andrew D., MA Oxf., PhD Camb.   Prof., Nanomaterials (S.Ann.)

Cerezo, Alfred, MA Oxf., DPhil Oxf.   Prof. (Wolfs.)

Cockayne, David J. H., BSc Melb., MSc Melb., MA Oxf., DPhil Oxf.   Prof., Physical Examination of Materials (Linac.)

Grant, Patrick S., MA Oxf., DPhil Oxf.   Cookson Prof., Materials Science (S.Cat.)

Grovenor, Christopher R. M., MA Oxf., DPhil Oxf.   Prof.; Head* (S.Ann.)

Hutchinson, John L., BSc Glas., PhD Glas.   Reader (Wolfs.)

Jenkins, Michael L., BSc Brist., DPhil Oxf.   Reader (Wolfs.)

Kirkland, Angus I., MA Camb., PhD Camb.   Prof. (Linac.)

Pettifor, David G., CBE, BSc Witw., MA Oxf., PhD Camb.   Isaac Wolfson Prof., Metallurgy (S.Edm.)

Roberts, Steve G., BA Camb., MA Oxf., PhD Camb.   Prof., Materials (S.Cross)

Smith, George D. W., MA Oxf., DPhil Oxf.   Prof., Nanomaterials (S.Ann.)

Sykes, John M., MA Camb., MA Oxf., PhD Camb.   Reader (Mansf.)

Wilshaw, Peter R., BA Camb., MA Oxf., DPhil Oxf.   Reader (S.Ann.)

Mathematical Sciences

Tel: (01865) 273525 Fax: (01865) 273583

Ball, Sir John M., MA Oxf., MA Camb., DPhil Sus., FRS   Sedleian Prof., Natural Philosophy (Qu.)

Batty, Charles J. K., MA Oxf., MSc Oxf., DPhil Oxf.   Prof., Analysis (S.Joh.)

Candelas, Philip, MA Camb., MA Oxf., DPhil Oxf.   Rouse Ball Prof. (Wadh.)

Chapman, S. Jonathan, MA Oxf., DPhil Oxf.   Prof., Mathematics and its Applications (Mansf.)

du Sautoy, Marcus P. F., MA Oxf., DPhil Oxf.   Prof. (All S.)

Etheridge, Alison M., MA Oxf., DPhil Oxf.   Prof., Probability (Magd.)

Flynn, Eugene V., BA Otago, PhD Camb.   Prof. (New)

Haydon, Richard G., MA Camb., MA Oxf., PhD Camb.   Prof. (Bras.)

Heath-Brown, D. Roger, MA Camb., MA Oxf., PhD Camb., DPhil Oxf., FRS   Prof., Pure Mathematics (Worc.)

Hitchin, Nigel J., MA Oxf., DPhil Oxf., FRS   Savilian Prof., Geometry (New)

Joyce, Dominic D., MA Oxf., DPhil Oxf.   Prof. (Linc.)

Kirwan, Frances C., MA Camb., MA Oxf., DPhil Oxf.   Prof. (Ball.)

Lackenby, Marc, MA Camb.   Prof.,
Mathematics (S.Cath.)

Lyons, Terry J., MA Camb., MA Oxf., DPhil Oxf.,
FRS   Wallis Prof. (S.Ann.)

Maini, Philip K., MA Oxf., DPhil Oxf.   Prof.,
Mathematical Biology (Bras.)

Mason, Lionel J., MA Oxf., DPhil Oxf.   Prof.
(S.Pet.)

Priestley, Hilary A., MA Oxf., DPhil Oxf.   Prof.
(S.Ann.)

Rouquier, Raphael, PhD Paris VII   Waynflete
Prof., Pure Mathematics (Magd.)

Scott, Alexander D., MA Camb., PhD Camb.
Prof., Mathematics (Mert.)

Segal, Daniel, MA Camb., MSc Lond., PhD Lond.,
DSc Manc.   Prof. (All S.)

Tillman, Ulrike L., BA Brandeis, PhD Stan.   Prof.
(Mert.)

Tod, K. Paul, MA Oxf., MSc Oxf., DPhil Oxf.
Prof., Mathematical Physics (S.Joh.)

Vaughan-Lee, Michael R., MA Oxf., DPhil Oxf.
Prof. (Ch.Ch.)

Wilkie, Andrew J., MSc Lond., MA Oxf., PhD
Lond.   Prof., Mathematical Logic (Wolfs.)

Wilson, John S., MA Camb., PhD Camb., ScD
Camb.   Prof. (Univ.)

Witelski, Thomas P., PhD Cal.Tech.   Reader
(S.Cat.)

Woodhouse, Nicholas M. J., MSc Lond., MA
Oxf., PhD Lond.   Reader; Chairman*
(Wadh.)

Zhou, Xunyu, BSc Fudan, PhD Fudan   Prof.,
Mathematical Finance (S.Hug.)

Zilber, Boris, MSc Novosibirsk, MA Oxf., DSc
Leningrad   Prof., Mathematical Logic (Mert.)

Research: algebra; industrial and financial
applications; mathematical biology; pure
and applied analysis; pure geometry and
physical applications

Modern Languages, Faculty of

Tel: (01865) 270750 Fax: (01865) 270757
E-mail: enquiries@mod-langs.ox.ac.uk

Bethea, David M., BA Washington & Lee, MS
Georgetown, PhD Kansas   Prof., Russian
Studies (Wadh.)

Charles-Edwards, Thomas M. O., MA Oxf.,
DPhil Oxf., FBA   Jesus Prof., Celtic (Jes.)

Cooper, Richard A., MA Oxf., DPhil Oxf.
Prof., French (Bras.)

Cronk, Nicholas E., MA Oxf., DPhil Oxf.   Prof.,
French Literature (S.Edm.)

Earle, Thomas F., MA Oxf., DPhil Oxf.   King
John II Prof., Portuguese Studies (S.Pet.)

Engel, Manfred, DPhil Erlangen-Nuremberg
Taylor Prof., German Language and
Literature

Fallaize, Elizabeth A., MA Exe., MA Oxf., PhD
Exe.   Prof., French (S.Joh.)

Fiddian, Robin W., MA Edin., MA Oxf., PhD
Edin.   Prof., Spanish (Wadh.)

Howells, Christina M., BA Lond., MA Oxf., PhD
Lond.   Prof., French (Wadh.)

Jefferson, Ann M., MA Oxf., DPhil Oxf.   Prof.,
French Literature (New)

Kelly, Catriona H. M., MA Oxf., DPhil Oxf.
Prof., Russian (New)

Lauxtermann, Marc D., PhD Amst.   Bywater
and Sotheby Prof., Byzantine and Modern
Greek Language and Literature (Exe.)

Leeder, Karen J., MA Oxf., DPhil Oxf.   Reader,
German (New)

Maiden, Martin D., MA Oxf., MPhil Camb., PhD
Camb.   Prof., Romance Languages (Trin.)

McGuinness, Patrick R. A., MA Camb., MA
York(UK), DPhil Oxf.   Reader, French and
Comparative Languages (S.Ann.)

McLaughlin, M. L., MA Glas., MA Oxf., DPhil
Oxf.   Fiat-Serena Prof., Italian Studies
(Ch.Ch.)

Palmer, Nigel F., MA Oxf., DPhil Oxf.   Prof.,
German Mediaeval and Linguistic Studies
(S.Edm.)

Parish, Richard J., MA Oxf., DPhil Oxf.   Prof.,
French (S.Cat.)

Pearson, Roger A. G., MA Oxf., DPhil Oxf.
Prof., French (Qu.)

Robertson, Ritchie N. N., MA Edin., MA Oxf.,
DPhil Oxf.   Prof., German (S.Joh.)

Sheringham, Michael H. T., BA Kent, PhD Kent
Marshal Foch Prof., French Literature (All
S.)

Viala, Alain B. J., MA Oxf.   Prof., French
Literature (L.M.H.)

Volfing, Annette M., MA Oxf., DPhil Oxf.
Reader (Oriel)

Watanabe-O'Kelly, Helen, MA N.U.I., MA Oxf.,
DPhil Basle   Prof., German Literature (Exe.)

Williamson, Edwin H., MA Edin., PhD Edin.
King Alfonso XIII Prof., Spanish Studies
(Exe.)

Zancani, Diego, MA Oxf.   Prof., Italian (Ball.)

Zorin, Andrei L., MA Moscow, PhD Moscow
Prof., Russian (New)

Music

Tel: (01865) 276125 Fax: (01865) 276128

Clarke, Eric F., BA Sus., MA Sus., PhD Exe.
Heather Prof. (Wadh.)

Cross, Jonathan G. E., BA Brist., PhD Lond.
Prof., Musicology (Ch.Ch.)

Dreyfus, Laurence, BA Yeshiva, PhD Col.   Prof.
(Magd.)

Franklin, Peter R., BA York(UK), MA Oxf., DPhil
York(UK)   Prof. (S.Cat.)

Johnson, Julian M., BA Plym., MA Sus., DPhil
Sus.   Reader (S.Ann.)

Rees, Owen L., MA Oxf., DPhil Oxf.   Reader
(Qu.)

Senici, Emanuele, PhD Cornell   Reader,
Musicology (S.Hug.)

Wollenberg, Susan L. F., MA Oxf., DPhil Oxf.
Reader (L.M.H.)

Oriental Studies, Faculty of

Tel: (01865) 278200 Fax: (01865) 278190
E-mail: orient@orinst.ox.ac.uk

Allan, James W., MA Oxf., DPhil Oxf.   Prof.,
Eastern Art (S.Cross)

Baines, John R., MA Oxf., DPhil Oxf.   Prof.,
Egyptology (Qu.)

Goodman, Martin D., MA Oxf., DPhil Oxf.
Prof., Jewish Studies (Wolfs.)

Herzig, Edmund, MA Camb., DPhil Oxf.
Masoumeh and Fereydoon Soudavar Prof.,
Persian Studies (Wadh.)

Holes, Clive D., MA Oxf., MA Birm., PhD Camb.,
DPhil Oxf.   Khalid bin Abdullah Al Saud
Prof., Contemporary Arab World (Magd.)

Johns, Jeremy, MA Oxf., DPhil Oxf.   Prof., Art
and Archaeology of the Islamic
Mediterranean (Wolfs.)

Minkowski, Christopher Z., AB Harv., PhD Harv.
Boden Prof., Sanskrit (Ball.)

O'Hanlon, Polly, MA Camb., PhD Lond.   Prof.,
Indian History and Culture (S.Cross)

Rawson, Dame Jessica M., CBE, DBE, MA Oxf.,
MA Camb., DLitt Oxf., LittD Camb., FBA
Prof., Chinese Art and Archaeology (Mert.)

Robinson, Chase F., BA Brown, PhD Harv.
Prof., Islamic History (Wolfs.)

Sanderson, Alexis G. J. S., MA Oxf.   Spalding
Prof., Eastern Religions and Ethics (All S.)

Savage-Smith, Emilie, BA De Pauw, MA Wis.,
PhD Wis.   Prof., History of Islamic Science
(S.Cross)

Smith, Mark J., MA Oxf., PhD Chic.   Prof.,
Egyptology (Univ.)

Sullivan, Peter D., BSc Manc., MB ChB Manc.,
DM Manc.   Reader (Magd.)

Van De Mieroop, Marc G. J., MA Yale, PhD Yale
Prof., Assyriology (Wolfs.)

Van Gelder, Gerard J. H., MA Oxf.   Laudian
Prof., Arabic (S.Joh.)

Van Lint, Theo M., MA Ley., PhD Ley.
Calouste Gulbenkian Prof., Armenian
Studies (Pemb.)

Williamson, Hugh G. M., MA Camb., PhD
Camb., DD Camb., DD Oxf.   Regius Prof.,
Hebrew (Ch.Ch.)

Oxford Internet Institute

Tel: (01865) 287210 Fax: (01865) 287211
E-mail: enquiries@oii.ox.ac.uk

Dutton, William H., BA Missouri, MA N.Y., PhD
N.Y.   Prof., The Internet and Society; Dir.*
(Ball.)

Margetts, Helena Z., BSc Brist., MSc Lond., PhD
Lond.   Prof., Society and the Internet
(Mansf.)

Zittrain, Jonathan, BSc Yale, MPA Harv., JD Harv.
Prof., Internet Governance and Regulation
(Keb.)

Philosophy

Tel: (01865) 276926 Fax: (01865) 276932
E-mail: enquiries@philosophy.ox.ac.uk

Broome, John R., BA Camb., MA Oxf., MA Lond.,
PhD M.I.T.   White's Prof., Moral
Philosophy (Corp.)

Brown, Harvey R., BSc Cant., MA Oxf., PhD
Lond.   Prof. (Wolfs.)

Charles, David O. M., BPhil Oxf., MA Oxf.,
DPhil Oxf.   Prof. (Oriel)

Davies, Martin K., BA Monash, BPhil Oxf., DPhil
Oxf.   Wilde Prof., Mental Philosophy
(Corp.)

Halbach, Volker   Reader (New)

Hawthorne, John, BA Manc., PhD Syr.
Waynflete Prof., Metaphysical Philosophy
(Magd.)

Irwin, Terence H., PhD Prin.   Prof., Ancient
Philosophy (Keb.)

Moore, Adrian W., MA Camb., MA Oxf., DPhil
Oxf.   Prof. (S.Hug.)

Saunders, Simon W., MA Oxf., PhD Lond.
Reader, Philosophy of Physics (Linac.)

Savulescu, Julian, BMedSc Monash, MB BS
Monash, PhD Monash   Uehiro Prof., Applied
Ethics (S.Cross)

Williamson, Timothy, MA Oxf., DPhil Oxf.
Wykeham Prof., Logic (New)

Physics

Tel: (01865) 272200 Fax: (01865) 272400

Abraham, Douglas B., MA Camb., MA Oxf., PhD
Camb., DSc   Prof., Statistical Mechanics
(Wolfs.)

Allison, Wade W. M., MA Camb., MA Oxf.,
DPhil Oxf.   Prof. (Keb.)

Andrews, David G., MA Camb., MA Oxf., PhD
Camb., DPhil Oxf.   Prof. (L.M.H.)

Ardavan, Arzhang, BA Oxf., DPhil Oxf.   Prof.
(Magd.)

Barnett, John J., MA Camb., DPhil Oxf.   Reader

Barr, Giles D., MA Oxf., DPhil Oxf.   Reader
(Magd.)

Binney, James J., MA Oxf., DPhil Oxf., FRS
Prof. (Mert.)

Blundell, Katherine M., MA Oxf., PhD Camb.
Reader (S.Joh.)

Blundell, Stephen J., MA Camb., PhD Camb.
Prof. (Mansf.)

Boothroyd, Andrew T., BA Camb., MA Oxf.,
PhD Camb.   Prof. (Oriel)

Burrows, Philip N., MA Oxf., DPhil Oxf.   Prof.,
Accelerator Physics (Jes.)

Cavalleri, Andrea, PhD Pisa   Prof. (Mert.)

Chalker, John T., MA Camb., MA Oxf., DPhil
Oxf.   Prof. (S.Hug.)

Close, Frank, OBE, BSc St And., DPhil Oxf.
Prof., Theoretical Physics (Exe.)

Cobb, John H., MA Oxf., DPhil Oxf.   Reader

Cooper, Susan, BA Colby, MA Oxf., PhD Calif.
Prof., Experimental Physics (S.Cat.)

Cooper-Sarkar, Amanda M., MA Oxf., DPhil Oxf.
Reader (S.Hil.)

Davies, Roger L., BA Lond., PhD Camb.   Philip
Wetton Prof., Astrophysics; Chair* (Ch.Ch.)

Devenish, Robin C. E., MA Camb., MA Oxf.,
PhD Camb., DPhil Oxf.   Prof. (Hert.)

Essler, Fabian, MA N.Y., PhD N.Y.   Prof.
(Worc.)

Ewart, Paul, BSc Belf., MA Oxf., PhD Belf.   Prof.
(Worc.)

Ferreira, Pedro G.   Reader (Oriel)

Foot, Christopher J., MA Oxf., DPhil Oxf.   Prof.
(S.Pet.)

Foster, Brian, OBE, BA Lond., DPhil Oxf.   Prof.,
Experimental Physics (Ball.)

Glazer, A. Michael, BSc St And., MA Camb., MA
Oxf., PhD Lond.   Prof. (Jes.)

Harnew, Neville, BSc Sheff., MA Oxf., PhD Lond.
Prof. (S.Ann.)

Hooker, Simon, MA Oxf., DPhil Oxf. Reader (Mert.)

Irwin, Patrick G. J., MA Oxf., DPhil Oxf. Reader (S.Ann.)

Jelley, Nicholas A., MA Oxf., DPhil Oxf. Prof. (Linc.)

Johnson, Neil F., BA Camb., MA Harv., PhD Harv. Prof. (Linc.)

Jones, Jonathan A., MA Oxf., DPhil Oxf. Prof. (Bras.)

Jones, Michael E., MA Camb., PhD Camb. Prof., Experimental Cosmology

Jordan, Carole, MA Oxf., PhD Lond., FRS Prof. (Som.)

Kraus, Hans A. P., DrRerNat Munich Prof. (Corp.)

March-Russell, John, MA Oxf. Prof. (New)

Miller, Lance, BA Leic., PhD Camb. Reader (S.Cat.)

Nicholas, Robin J., MA Oxf., DPhil Oxf. Prof. (Univ.)

Peach, Ken, BSc Edin., PhD Edin. Prof.

Podsiadlowski, Philip, PhD M.I.T. Prof. (S.Edm.)

Rawlings, Steve G., MA Camb., PhD Camb. Prof. (S.Pet.)

Read, Peter L., BSc Birm., MA Oxf., PhD Camb. Prof. (Trin.)

Renton, Peter B., BSc Liv., PhD Liv. Prof.

Roche, Pat F., BSc Lond., MA Oxf., PhD Lond. Prof. (Hert.)

Ross, Graham G., BSc Aberd., MA Oxf., PhD Durh., FRS Prof. (Wadh.)

Ryan, John F., BSc Edin., MA Oxf., PhD Edin. Prof. (Ch.Ch.)

Sarkar, Subir, BSc Kharagpur, MSc Kharagpur, MA Oxf., PhD Bom. Prof. (Linac.)

Sherrington, David, BSc Manc., MA Oxf., PhD Manc., FRS Wykeham Prof. (New)

Silk, Joseph I., MA Camb., MA Oxf., PhD Harv. Savilian Prof., Astronomy (New)

Silver, Joshua D., MA Oxf., DPhil Oxf. Prof. (New)

Steane, Andrew M., MA Oxf., DPhil Oxf. Prof. (Exe.)

Taylor, Fred W., BSc Liv., MA Oxf., DPhil Oxf. Halley Prof., Atmospheric Physics (Jes.)

Taylor, Robert A., MA Oxf., DPhil Oxf. Reader (Qu.)

Turberfield, Andrew J., MA Oxf., MA Camb., DPhil Oxf. Prof. (Magd.)

Walmsley, Ian A., BSc Lond., PhD Roch. Hooke Prof., Experimental Physics (S.Hug.)

Wark, Justin S., MA Oxf., PhD Lond. Prof. (Trin.)

Weber, Alfons J. G., DrRerNat Aix-la-Chapelle Reader (S.Ann.)

Weidberg, Anthony R., BSc Lond., MA Oxf., PhD Camb., DPhil Oxf. Reader (S.Joh.)

Wheater, John F., MA Oxf., DPhil Oxf. Reader (Univ.)

Yassin, G., BSc MSc PhD Reader

Yeomans, Julia M., MA Oxf., DPhil Oxf. Prof. (S.Hil.)

Plant Sciences

Tel: (01865) 275000 Fax: (01865) 275074
E-mail: reception@plants.ox.ac.uk

Dickinson, Hugh G., MA Oxf., PhD Birm., DSc Birm. Sherardian Prof., Botany (Magd.)

Gurr, Sarah J., BSc Lond., PhD Lond. Prof., Molecular Plant Pathology (Some.)

Harber, Nicholas P., MD Camb., PhD Camb. Sibtorpian Prof. (S.Joh.)

Langdale, Jane A., BSc Bath, PhD Lond. Prof., Plant Development (Qu.)

Pannell, John R., BSc Syd., MA Oxf., DPhil Oxf. Reader, Plant Evolutionary Biology (Wolfs.)

Ratcliffe, R. George, MA Oxf., DPhil Oxf. Prof. (New)

Scotland, Robert W., BSc Lond., PhD Lond. Reader, Systemic Botany (Linac.)

Smith, J. Andrew C., MA Camb., MA Oxf., PhD Glas. Prof. (Magd.)

Politics and International Relations

Tel: (01865) 278700 Fax: (01865) 278725

Bermeo, Nancy, BA Mt.Holyoke, PhD Yale Nuffield Prof., Comparative Government (Nuff.)

Bogdanor, Vernon B., MA Oxf. Prof., Politics and Government (Bras.)

Busch, Andreas C., MA Heidel., DPhil Heidel. Reader (Hert.)

Caplan, Richard D., BA McG., MPhil Camb., PhD Lond. Prof., International Relations (Linac.)

Capoccia, Giovanni, BA Rome, MA Rome, PhD Florence Prof., Comparative Politics (Corp.)

Ceadel, Martin E., MA Oxf., DPhil Oxf. Prof. (New)

Cohen, Gerald A., BA McG., BPhil Oxf., MA Oxf., FBA Chichele Prof., Social and Political Theory (All S.)

Deighton, Anne F., MA Reading, PhD Reading Reader, European Politics (Wolfs.)

Duch, Raymond M., MA Roch., PhD Roch. Prof., Quantitative Political Science (Nuff.)

Evans, Geoffrey A., BA Sus., MA Oxf., MPhil Oxf., DPhil Oxf. Prof., Sociology of Politics (Nuff.)

Foot, Rosemary J., MA Oxf., PhD Lond., FBA Prof., International Relations (S.Ant.)

Freeden, Michael S., BA Jerusalem, MA Oxf., DPhil Oxf. Prof. (Mansf.)

Hood, Christopher C., BA York(UK), BLitt Glas., DLitt York(UK) Gladstone Prof., Government (All S.)

Khong, Yuen Foong, BA Claremont, PhD Harv. Prof., International Relations (Nuff.)

King, Desmond S., BA Trinity(Dub.), MA Northwestern, PhD Northwestern Andrew W. Mellon Prof., American Government (Nuff.)

Macfarlane, S. Neil, AB Dartmouth, MA Oxf., MPhil Oxf., DPhil Oxf. Lester B. Pearson Prof., International Relations; Head* (S.Ann.)

Mattli, Walter, MA N.Y., PhD Chic. Prof., International Political Economy (S.Joh.)

McLean, Iain S., MA Oxf., DPhil Oxf. Prof., Politics (Nuff.)

McNay, Lois, MA Sus., MA Oxf., PhD Camb., DPhil Oxf. Reader, Politics (Som.)

Miller, David L., DPhil Oxf. Prof., Political Theory (Nuff.)

Roberts, Sir Adam, MA Oxf., FBA Montague Burton Prof., International Relations (Ball.)

Robertson, David B., MA Oxf., PhD Essex Prof. (S.Hug.)

Rueda, F. David, MSc Lond., PhD Cornell Prof., Comparative Politics (Mert.)

Ryan, Alan J., MA Oxf., DLitt Oxf., FBA Prof. (New)

Shlaim, Avi, BA Camb., MSc(Econ) Lond., MA Oxf., PhD Reading Prof.; Alastair Buchan Reader, International Relations

Tsang, Steve Y.-S., BA HK, MA Oxf., DPhil Oxf. Reader (S.Ant.)

Ware, Alan J., MA Oxf., DPhil Oxf. Prof. (Worc.)

Welsh, Jennifer, BA Sask., MA Oxf., DPhil Oxf. Prof., International Relations (Som.)

Wright, Jonathan R. C., MA Oxf., DPhil Oxf. Prof., International Relations (Ch.Ch.)

Zielonka, Jan A., PhD Warsaw Prof. (S.Ant.)

Social Policy and Social Work

Tel: (01865) 270325 Fax: (01865) 270324

Buchanan, Ann H., MA Oxf., MSc Bath, PhD S'ton. Prof., Social Work (S.Hil.)

Coleman, David A., MA Lond., MA Oxf., PhD Lond. Prof., Demography (Qu.)

Kemp, Peter A., BSc S'ton., MPhil Glas., DPhil Sus. Barnett Prof., Social Policy (S.Cross)

Noble, Michael W. J., CBE, MA Oxf. Prof., Social Policy (Gre.)

Ringen, Stein, MA Oslo, MA Oxf., DPhil Oslo Prof., Sociology and Social Policy (Gre.)

Seeleib-Kaiser, Martin, PhD Munich Reader, Comparative Social Policy and Politics (Gre.)

Smith, George A. N., BPhil Oxf., MA Oxf. Reader, Social Policy; Head* (S.Edm.)

Walker, Robert L., BSocSci Brist., MSc Lond., PhD Lond. Prof., Social Policy (Gre.)

Sociology

Tel: (01865) 281740 Fax: (01865) 286171
E-mail: enquiries@sociology.ox.ac.uk

Evans, Geoffrey A., BA Sus., MA Oxf., MPhil Oxf., DPhil Oxf. Prof. (Nuff.)

Gallie, Duncan I. D., MSc Lond., MA Oxf., DPhil Oxf. Prof. (Nuff.)

Gambetta, Diego, MA Oxf., PhD Camb. Prof. (All S.)

Gershuny, Jonathan, BSc Lough., MSc Strath., DPhil Sus. Prof. (S.Hug.)

Harper, Sarah, MA Oxf., DPhil Oxf. Prof., Gerontology (Nuff.)

Heath, Anthony F., PhD Camb. Prof.; Head* (Nuff.)

Snijders, Thomas A. B., MSc Gron., PhD Gron. Prof., Statistics in the Social Sciences (Nuff.)

Statistics

Tel: (01865) 272860 Fax: (01865) 272595
E-mail: info@stats.ox.ac.uk

Clifford, Peter, BSc Lond., MA Oxf., PhD Calif. Reader, Mathematical Statistics (Jes.)

Donnelly, Peter J., BSc Qld., MA Oxf., DPhil Oxf. Prof., Statistical Science (S.Ann.)

Griffiths, Robert C., BSc Syd., PhD Syd. Prof., Mathematical Genetics (L.M.H.)

Hein, Jotun J., Lic Aarhus Prof., Bioinformatics (Univ.)

Lauritzen, Steffen L., MSc Copenhagen, DPhil Copenhagen, DSc Copenhagen Prof. (Jes.)

McDiarmid, Colin J. H., BSc Edin., MA Oxf., MSc Oxf., DPhil Oxf. Prof., Combinatronics; Head* (Corp.)

Reinert, Gesine D., PhD Zür. Prof. (Keb.)

Ripley, Brian D., MA Camb., MA Oxf., PhD Camb. Prof., Applied Statistics (S.Pet.)

Silverman, Bernard W., BTh S'ton., MA Oxf., MA Camb., DPhil Oxf., PhD Camb., DSc Camb., FRS Prof. (S.Pet.)

Theology

see also Oriental Studies, Fac. of

Tel: (01865) 270790 Fax: (01865) 270795

Adams, Marilyn M., AB Ill., ThM Princeton Theol.Sem., PhD Cornell Regius Prof., Divinity (Ch.Ch.)

Barton, John, MA Oxf., DPhil Oxf., DLitt Oxf. Oriel and Laing Prof., Interpretation of Holy Scripture (Oriel)

Biggar, Nigel J., PhD Chic. Regius Prof., Moral and Pastoral Theology (Ch.Ch.)

Day, John, MA Oxf., MA Camb., DPhil Oxf., PhD Camb. Prof., Old Testament Theology (L.M.H.)

Fiddes, Rev. Paul S., MA Oxf., DPhil Oxf. Prof., Systematic Theology (Regent's Park)

Foot, Sarah R., MA Camb., PhD Camb. Regius Prof., Ecclesiastical History (Ch.Ch.)

Harrison, Peter, BSc Qld., BA Qld., MA Yale, PhD Qld. Andreas Idreos Prof., Science and Religion (Harris)

Leftow, Brian, BA Grove City, MA Yale, MPhil Yale, PhD Yale Nolloth Prof., Philosophy of the Christian Religion (Oriel)

MacCulloch, Diarmaid N. J., MA Oxf., PhD Camb., DPhil Oxf., DD Oxf., FBA Prof., History of the Church (S.Cross)

Maltby, Rev. Judith D., BA Ill., PhD Camb. Reader, Ecclesiastical History (Corp.)

McGrath, Alister E., MA Oxf., DPhil Oxf., DD Oxf. Prof., Historical Theology (Wycl.H.)

Pattison, George L., BD Edin., MA Edin., PhD Durh. Lady Margaret Prof., Divinity (Ch.Ch.)

Rowland, Christopher C., MA Camb., MA Oxf., PhD Camb., DPhil Oxf. Dean Ireland's Prof., Exegesis of Holy Scripture (Qu.)

Tuckett, Christopher M., MA Oxf., MA Camb., PhD Lanc. Prof., New Testament Studies (Wolfs.)

Zoology

Tel: (01865) 271234 Fax: (01865) 310447
Alphey, Luke S., MA Camb., PhD Dund.
Reader, Genetics
Cavalier-Smith, Thomas, PhD Lond. Prof.,
Evolutionary Biology
Dawkins, C. Richard, MA Oxf., DPhil Oxf., DSc
Oxf. Prof., Public Understanding of
Science (New)
Dawkins, Marian E. S., MA Oxf., DPhil Oxf.
Prof., Animal Behaviour (Som.)
Gardner, Sir Richard L., MA Camb., MA Oxf.,
PhD Camb., FRS Henry Dale Royal Soc.
Res. Prof. (Ch.Ch.)
Grafen, Alan, MA Oxf., MPhil Oxf., DPhil Oxf.
Prof., Theoretical Biology (S.Joh.)
Graham, Christopher F., MA Oxf., DPhil Oxf.,
FRS Prof., Animal Development (S.Cat.)
Guilford, Tim C., MA Oxf., DPhil Oxf. Prof.,
Animal Behaviour (Mert.)
Gupta, Sunetra, AB Prin., MA Oxf., PhD Lond.
Prof., Theoretical Epidemiology (Linac.)
Harvey, Paul, BA York(UK), MA Oxf., DPhil
York(UK), DSc Oxf., FRS Prof.; Head* (Jes.)
Holland, Peter W. H., MA Oxf., PhD Lond., DSc
Reading Linacre Prof. (Linac.)
Kacelnik, Alex, LicCienBiol Buenos Aires, MA
Oxf., DPhil Oxf. Prof., Behavioural Ecology
(Pemb.)
Kennedy, W. Jim, BSc Lond., MA Oxf., PhD Lond.
Prof., Natural History (Kell.)
Krebs, Lord, MA Oxf., DPhil Oxf., FRS Prof.
(Jes.)
Macdonald, David W., MA Oxf., DPhil Oxf.
Prof., Wildlife Conservation (L.M.H.)
Maiden, Martin C. J., BSc Reading, PhD Camb.
Prof., Molecular Epidemiology
May, Lord, PhD Syd. Royal Society Res. Prof.
McLean, Angela R., MA Oxf., PhD Lond. Prof.,
Mathematical Biology (S.Cat.)
Rambaut, A., DPhil Oxf. Reader, Evolutionary
Biology (Bras.)
Randolph, Sarah E., MA Oxf., PhD Lond. Prof.,
Parasite Ecology (Oriel)
Rogers, David J., MA Oxf., DPhil Oxf. Prof.,
Ecology (Gre.)
Sheldon, Ben C., BA Camb., PhD Sheff. Luc
Hoffman Prof., Field Ornithology (Wolfs.)
Shotton, David M., MA Camb., PhD Camb.
Reader, Image Bioinoformatics (Wolfs.)
Speight, Martin R., BSc Wales, MA Oxf., DPhil
York(UK) Reader, Entomology (S.Ann.)
Research: animal welfare (particularly in relation
to food production and animal rearing
practice); conservation biology and
management of natural resources;
epidemiology of infectious disease
(including viral spread through human,
farmed and wildlife fauna); evolution
(including genome projects, palaeontology,
and the use of fossil DNA); stem cell
research and animal development

MEDICAL SCIENCES, DIVISION OF

Tel: (01865) 221689 Fax: (01865) 750750
E-mail: enquiries@medsci.ox.ac.uk

Anaesthetics

Tel: (01865) 224770 Fax: (01865) 794191
Hahn, Clive E. W., MA Oxf., MSc Sheff., DPhil
Oxf. Prof.; Head* (Gre.)
McQuay, Henry J., MA Oxf., BM Oxf. Nuffield
Prof., Clinical Anaesthetics (Ball.)
Sear, John W., BSc Lond., MA Oxf., MB BS Lond.,
PhD Lond., FFARCS Prof. (Gre.)
Tracey, Irene M. C., MA Oxf., DPhil Oxf.
Nuffield Prof., Anaesthetic Science (Pemb.)

Cardiovascular Medicine

Tel: (01865) 220257 Fax: (01865) 768844
Bhattacharya, Shoumo, MSc Lond., MD Delhi
Prof.
Casadei, Barbara S. Prof. (Qu.)
Channon, Keith M., BSc Manc., MB ChB Manc.,
MD Manc. Prof. (L.M.H.)
Farrall, Martin Prof., Cardiovascular Genetics
(Keb.)
Neubauer, Stefan, MD Würzburg Prof. (Ch.Ch.)

Watkins, Hugh C., BSc Lond., MB BS Lond., MA
Oxf., PhD Lond. Field Marshal Alexander
Prof.; Head* (Exet.)

Clinical Laboratory Sciences

Tel: (01865) 220559 Fax: (01865) 220524
Bell, John I., KB, BSc Alta., MA Oxf., DM Oxf.
Regius Prof. (Magd.)
Boultwood, Jacqueline, BSc Wales, PhD Wales
Reader, Molecular Haematology
Ferguson, David J. P., DSc Strath. Prof.,
Ultrastructural Morphology
Gatter, Kevin C., BM Oxf., MA Oxf., DPhil Oxf.
Prof., Pathology; Head* (S.Joh.)
Gibbons, Richard J., BM Oxf., MA Oxf., DPhil
Oxf. Reader, Clinical Genetics (Gre.)
Higgs, Douglas, MB BS Lond. Prof.,
Haematology
La Thangue, Nicholas B., BSc Birm., MSc
Reading, PhD Lond. Prof. (Linac.)
Mason, David Y., DM Oxf. Prof., Cellular
Pathology (Pemb.)
McKenna, William G., BSc Edin., MD Albert
Einstein Coll.of.Med, PhD Albert Einstein Coll.of.Med
Prof., Radiation Oncology and Biology
(Wolfs.)
Murphy, M. F. G., MD Lond. Reader,
Epidemiology
Old, John M., BSc Liv., PhD Liv. Reader,
Haematology
Wainscoat, James S., MB ChB Liv., MSc Birm.
Prof., Haematology
Watt, Suzanne, BSc Lond., PhD Lond. Reader,
Haematology
Wilkie, Andrew O. M., MA Camb., MA Oxf.,
DM Oxf. Nuffield Prof., Pathology

Medicine, Clinical

Tel: (01865) 857621 Fax: (01865) 857623
Altman, Douglas G., BSc Bath, DSc Lond. Prof.,
Statistics in Medicine
Armitage, J. Reader, Clinical Epidemiology
Bowness, Persephone, BA Camb., MB BChir
Lond., DPhil Oxf. Reader, Immunology
(Magd.)
Cerundolo, Vincenzo, MA Oxf. Prof.,
Immunology (Mert.)
Clark, Ann, BSc Lond., PhD Lond. Reader,
Diabetic Medicine
Conlon, Christopher P., BA Oxf., MD Lond.
Reader, Infectious Diseases and Tropical
Medicine (Oriel)
Cookson, William O. C., MB BS W.Aust., MD
W.Aust., DPhil Oxf. Prof., Genetics (Gre.)
Darby, Sarah C., BSc Lond., MSc Birm., PhD Lond.
Prof., Medical Statistics (Gre.)
Davies, Robert J. O., MD S'ton. Reader,
Respiratory Medicine
Enver, Tariq, BSc Lond., PhD Lond. Prof.,
Molecular Haematology
Frayn, Keith N., BA Camb., PhD Lond. Prof.,
Human Metabolism (Gre.)
Fugger, Lars, MD Copenhagen, PhD Copenhagen,
DMSc Copenhagen Prof., Neuroimmunology
(Oriel)
Gauguier, Dominique Prof., Mammalian
Genetics
Gibbons, Geoff F., BSc Leic., MSc Wales, PhD
Liv. Prof., Human Metabolism
Hill, Adrian V. S., MA Oxf., DPhil Oxf., DM Oxf.
Prof., Human Genetics (Exet.)
Holman, Rury, MB ChB Brist. Prof., Diabetic
Medicine (Gre.)
Jacobsen, Sten E., MD Bergen, PhD Bergen Anne
T. and Robert M. Bass Prof., Developmental
and Stem Cell Biology (Medicine) (S.Cross)
Jewell, Derek P., BM Oxf., MA Oxf., DPhil Oxf.
Prof., Gastroenterology (Gre.)
Jones, E. Yvonne Prof., Protein
Crystallography
Karpe, Fredrik Reader, Metabolic Medicine
Marsh, Kevin Prof., Tropical Medicine
Matthews, David R., BM Oxf., MA Oxf., DPhil
Oxf. Prof., Diabetic Medicine (Harris)
McCarthy, Mark, MB BChir Camb., MA Camb.,
MD Camb. Robert Turner Prof., Diabetic
Medicine (Gre.)

Monaco, Anthony P., AB Prin., MD Harv., PhD
Harv. Prof., Human Genetics
Newbold, Christopher I., MA Camb., MA Oxf.,
PhD Camb., DPhil Oxf. Prof., Tropical
Medicine (Gre.)
Nosten, Francois Prof., Tropical Medicine
Novak, Bela, MS T.U.Budapest, MS E.L.Bud., PhD
T.U.Budapest, PhD E.L.Bud. Prof., Integrative
Systems Biology (Mert.)
Ogg, G. S., BA Oxf., BM Oxf., DPhil Oxf.
Reader, Cutaneous Immunology (Ch.Ch.)
Peto, Sir Richard, MSc Lond., MA Camb., MA
Oxf., FRS Co-Dir., Clinical Trials Service
Unit and Epidemiological Studies Unit;
ICRF Prof., Medical Statistics and
Epidemiology (Gre.)
Peto, Tim E. A., BM Oxf., MA Oxf., DPhil Oxf.
Prof., Medicine
Phillips, Rodney E., MA Oxf., MD Melb., MB BS,
FRACP Prof. (Wolfs.)
Pugh, Christopher W., BM Oxf., MA Oxf., DPhil
Oxf. Prof., Renal Medicine (Gre.)
Rajagopalan, Bheeshma, BM Oxf., MA Oxf.,
DPhil Oxf. Reader (Ball.)
Ratcliffe, Peter J., BA Camb., MB BChir Camb.,
MA Oxf., MD Camb., FRS Nuffield Prof.;
Head* (Jes.)
Rorsman, Patrik, KandMed Uppsala, PhD Uppsala
Prof., Diabetic Medicine (Harr.)
Rowland-Jones, Sarah, MA Oxf., DPhil Oxf.
Prof., Immunology (Ch.Ch.)
Stammers, David K. Prof., Structural Biology
Stradling, J. R., BSc Lond., MB BS Lond., MA Oxf.
Prof., Respiratory Medicine
Stuart, D. I., BSc Lond., MA Oxf., PhD Brist.
MRC Prof., Biochemistry (Hert.)
Thakker, Rajesh V., MA Camb., MB BChir
Camb., MD Camb. May Prof. (Som.)
Townsend, Alain R. M., MB BS Lond., MA Oxf.,
PhD Lond. Prof., Molecular Immunology
(Linac.)
Warrell, David A., MA Oxf., DSc Oxf., DM Oxf.,
FRCP Prof., General Medicine (S.Cross)
Wass, John A. H., BM BCh Oxf., MA Oxf., DM
Oxf. Prof., Endocrinology (Gre.)
White, Nick J. Prof., Tropical Medicine
Wojnarowska, Fenella, BM BCh Oxf., MSc Oxf.,
MA Oxf. Prof., Dermatology (Som.)
Wordsworth, B. Paul, MB BS Lond., MA Oxf.
Prof., Rheumatology (Gre.)

Medicine, Molecular

Tel: (01865) 222443 Fax: (01865) 222737
Fugger, Lars, MD Copenhagen, PhD Copenhagen,
DMSc Copenhagen Prof., Clinical
Immunology
McMichael, Andrew J., MB BChir Camb., MA
Camb., PhD CNAA Dir., Weatherall Inst. of
Molecular Med.; Prof., Molecular Medicine
(Corp.)

Neurology, Clinical

Tel: (01865) 231909 Fax: (01865) 231914
Beeson, David M. W., MA Camb., PhD Lond.
Prof., Neuroscience
Donaghy, Michael J., MB BS Lond., PhD Camb.
Reader (Gre.)
Ebers, George C., MD Tor. Action Res. Prof.
(S.Edm.)
Esiri, Margaret M., DM Oxf., MA Prof.,
Neuropathology (S.Hug.)
Flint, Jonathan, BA Oxf., BM BCh Oxf.
Michael Davys Prof., Neuroscience (Mert.)
Jezzard, Peter, BSc Manc., PhD Camb. Herbert
Dunhill Prof., Neuro-Imaging (Univ.)
Matthews, Paul M., MA Oxf., MD Stan., DPhil
Oxf. Prof., Neurology (S.Edm.)
Rothwell, Peter M., MB ChB Edin., MD Edin.,
PhD Edin. Prof.
Vincent, Angela C., MB BS Lond., MA Oxf., MSc
Lond., MSt Prof., Clinical
Neuroimmunology; Head* (Som.)
Wade, D. T., MD Camb. Prof., Neurological
Disability
Willcox, H. Nick A., MB BChir Camb., PhD
Camb. Prof., Neurosciences

Obstetrics and Gynaecology

Tel: (01865) 221008 Fax: (01865) 769141

Kehoe, Sean T., MB BCh BAO Trinity(Dub.), BA Trinity(Dub.), MD Trinity(Dub.)   Prof., Gynaecological Cancer (S.Pet.)

Kennedy, S. H., MA Oxf., MD Lond.   Reader; Head* (Gre.)

Mackenzie, Ian Z., MA Oxf., MD Brist., DSc Oxf.   Reader (S.Hug.)

Mardon, Helen J., MA Oxf., DPhil Oxf.   Prof., Reproductive Science (S.Cat.)

Poulton, Joanna   Prof., Mitochondrial Genetics (L.M.H.)

Redman, Christopher W. G., MB BChir Camb., BM Oxf., MA Oxf., MA Camb.   Clin. Prof., Obstetric Medicine (L.M.H.)

Rees, C. Margaret P., BSc Lond., MB BS Lond., DPhil Oxf.   Reader, Reproductive Medicine (S.Hil.)

Sargent, Ian L., BSc Wales, MA Oxf., PhD Lond.   Prof., Reproductive Science (Mansf.)

Oncology, Medical

Tel: (01865) 226184 Fax: (01865) 226179

Elliott, T. J., PhD S'ton.   Prof., Immunology (Ball.)

Ganesan, Trivadi S., MB BS Madr., MD Madr., PhD Lond.   Reader, Medical Oncology

Harris, Adrian L., BSc Liv., MB ChB Liv., MA Oxf., DPhil Oxf., FRCP   Cancer Research Prof., Clinical Oncology (S.Hug.)

Ophthalmology

Tel: (01865) 248996 Fax: (01865) 794508

Foster, Russell G., BSc Brist., PhD Brist.   Prof., Circadian Neuroscience; Head* (Bras.)

Harding, John J., BA Camb., PhD Lond.   Prof., Ocular Biochemistry

Osborne, Neville N., BSc Lond., MA Oxf., PhD St And.   Prof., Ocular Neurobiology (Gre.)

Research: cataract protection and biochemical changes; retinal diseases and treatment; tear diseases and dry eye

Orthopaedic Surgery

Tel: (01865) 227374 Fax: (01865) 737640

Athanasou, Nicholas A., MB BS Syd., MD Syd., PhD Lond.   Prof., Osteoarticular Pathology

Brown, Matthew A., MB BS Syd., FRACP   Prof., Musculoskeletal Science (S.Pet.)

Bulstrode, Christopher J. K., BM Oxf., MA Oxf., FRCS   Prof. (Gre.)

Carr, Andrew J., MB ChB Brist., ChM Brist.   Nuffield Prof. (Worc.)

Fairbank, Jeremy C. T., MD Camb.   Prof., Spinal Surgery

Murray, David, MD Lond., MA Oxf.   Prof.

Russell, R. Graham, MA Camb., PhD Leeds, FRCP, FRCPath   Norman Collison Prof., Musculoskeletal Sciences; Head* (S.Pet.)

Willett, Keith M., MB BS Lond.   Prof., Orthopaedic Trauma Medicine (Wolfs.)

Paediatrics

Tel: (01865) 221077 Fax: (01865) 220479

Kwiatkowski, Dominic P., MB BS Lond., MA Oxf.   Prof., Tropical Paediatrics (S.Joh.)

Moxon, E. Richard, BA Camb., MB BChir Camb., MA Camb., MA Oxf.   Action Res. Prof.; Head* (Jes.)

Pollard, A. J., BSc Lond., MB BS Lond., PhD Lond.   Reader, Paediatric Infection and Immunity

Wilkinson, Andrew R., MB ChB Birm., MA Oxf., FRCP   Prof. (All S.)

Pathology, Sir William Dunn School of

see also Clin. Lab. Scis.

Tel: (01865) 275500 Fax: (01865) 275501

Barclay, A. Neil, MA Oxf., DPhil Oxf.   Prof., Molecular Immunology (Oriel)

Brownlee, George G., MA Camb., MA Oxf., PhD Camb., DPhil Oxf., FRS   E. P. Abraham Prof., Chemical Pathology (Linc.)

Cobbold, Stephen P., PhD Camb.   Reader, Cellular Immunology (Ch.Ch.)

Cook, Peter R., MA Oxf., DPhil Oxf.   E. P. Abraham Prof., Cell Biology (Linc.)

Errington, Jeff, BSc Newcastle(UK), MA Oxf., PhD CNAA   Prof., Microbiology (Magd.)

Greaves, David R., BSc Lond., PhD Lond.   Reader, Molecular Pathology (Exe.)

Griffiths, Gillian M.   Prof., Experimental Pathology

Hale, Geoff, BA Camb., PhD Camb.   Prof., Therapeutic Immunology

James, William S., BSc Birm., MA Oxf., DPhil Oxf.   Prof., Virology (Bras.)

MacPherson, Gordon G., BM Oxf., MA Oxf., DPhil Oxf.   Reader, Experimental Pathology (Oriel)

Proudfoot, Nicholas J., BSc Lond., MA Oxf., PhD Camb.   Brownlee-Abraham Prof., Molecular Biology (Linc.)

Sattenau, Quentin J.   Prof., Immunology (Magd.)

van der Merwe, P. Anton, MB ChB Cape Town, BSc Cape Town, PhD Cape Town   Prof., Molecular Immunology

Waldmann, Hermann, MB Camb., BM Oxf., MA Camb., MA Oxf., PhD Camb., DPhil Oxf., FRS   Prof.; Head* (Linc.)

Pharmacology

Tel: (01865) 271850 Fax: (01865) 271853
E-mail: info@pharm.ox.ac.uk

Bolam, J. Paul, BSc Brist., PhD Brist.   Prof., Anatomical Neuropharmacology

Galione, Anthony G., BSc Open(UK), MA Camb., PhD Camb.   Prof.; Head* (L.M.H.)

Greenfield, Baroness Susan, MA Oxf., DPhil Oxf.   Prof. (Linc.)

Sharp, Trevor, MA Oxf.   Reader

Sim, Edith, BSc Edin., MA Oxf., DPhil   Prof. (S.Pet.)

Terrar, Derek A., BSc Lond., MA Oxf., PhD Lond.   Prof., Cardiac Electrophysiology (Worc.)

Pharmacology, Clinical

Tel: (01865) 224482 Fax: (01865) 224538

Aronson, Jeff K., MB ChB Glas., MA Oxf., DPhil Oxf.   Reader (Gre.)

Kerr, David J., CBE, BSc Glas., MSc Glas., MD Glas., PhD Glas., DSc Glas., FRCP   Rhodes Prof., Therapeutic Sciences and Clinical Pharmacology; Head* (Corp.)

Seymour, Leonard W., BSc Manc., PhD Keele   Prof., Genetic Therapy

Talbot, Denis C., BSc Liv., MB BChir Camb., PhD Lond.   Reader, Medical Oncology

Research: adverse drug reactions; cation transport abnormalities in disease; clinical pharmacokinetics; clinical trials in cancer, especially colorectal cancer

Physiology, Anatomy and Genetics

Tel: (01865) 272500 Fax: (01865) 272469
E-mail: enquiries@physiol.ox.ac.uk

Ashcroft, Frances M., MA Oxf., MA Camb., DPhil Oxf., PhD Camb.   Prof. (Trin.)

Ashley, Christopher C., BSc Brist., MA Oxf., PhD Brist., DSc Oxf.   Prof. (Corp.)

Blackshaw, Susanna E., BSc Birm., PhD Birm.   Reader, Neurobiology (S.Hil.)

Clarke, Kieran, BSc Flin., PhD Qld.   Prof., Physiological Biochemistry

Davies, Kay E., CBE, DBE, MA Oxf., DPhil Oxf.   Dr Lee's Prof., Anatomy (Hert.)

Ellory, J. Clive, BSc Brist., MA Camb., MA Oxf., PhD Brist.   Prof. (Corp.)

King, Andrew J., BSc Lond., PhD Lond.   Prof., Neurophysiology (Linc.)

Miesenboeck, Gero, MD Innsbruck   Waynflete Prof. (Magd.)

Morris, John F., BSc Brist., MB ChB Brist., MD Brist., MA Oxf.   Prof., Human Anatomy (S.Hug.)

Parekh, Anant B., MA Oxf., DPhil Oxf.   Prof. (Exe.)

Parker, Andrew J., BA Camb., MA Oxf., PhD Camb., DPhil Oxf.   Prof. (S.Joh.)

Paterson, David J., MSc W.Aust., MA Oxf., DPhil Oxf.   Prof., Cardiovascular Physiology (Mert.)

Ponting, Christopher P.   Prof., Bioinformatics

Powell, Trevor, BSc Lond., MA Oxf., PhD Lond., PhD Houston, DSc Oxf.   Prof.; British Heart Foundation Winstone Reader, Cellular Cardiology (New)

Radda, Sir George, MA Oxf., DPhil Oxf.   Prof.; Head* (Mert.)

Robbins, Peter A., BM BCh Oxf., MA Oxf., DPhil Oxf.   Prof. (Qu.)

Sattelle, David B.   Prof., Molecular Neurobiology

Smith, Stephen M., DPhil Oxf.   Prof., Biomedical Engineering

Stein, John F., BSc Oxf., BM BCh Oxf., MA Oxf.   Prof. (Magd.)

Vaughan-Jones, Richard D., BSc Brist., MA Oxf., PhD Brist.   Prof., Cellular Physiology (Exet.)

Wilson, C., BM BCh Cape Town, MA Oxf., DPhil Oxf.   Reader, Molecular Genetics (S.Hug.)

Psychiatry

Tel: (01865) 223635 Fax: (01865) 793101

Bailey, Anthony J., BSc Lond., MB BS Lond.   Cheryl and Reece Scott Prof. (S.Joh.)

Burns, Thomas P., MB BCh Camb., MA Camb., MD Camb.   Prof.

Cowen, Philip J., MD Lond.   Prof., Psychopharmacology

Ebmeier, Klaus P., DM Aberd.   Prof., Old Age Psychiatry (Linac.)

Fairburn, Christopher J. A. G., MA Oxf., MPhil Edin., DM Edin.   Prof.

Geddes, John, MD Leeds   Prof., Epidemiological Psychiatry

Goodwin, Guy M., BM Oxf., MA Oxf., DPhil Oxf.   W. A. Handley Prof. (Mert.)

Harrison, Paul J., MA Oxf., DM Oxf.   Prof. (Wolfs.)

Hawton, Keith E., MB BChir Camb., MA Camb.   Prof. (Gre.)

Rogers, R. D., BA Lond., MSc Lond., PhD Camb.   Reader, Cognitive Psychiatry (Jes.)

Stein, Alan L., MB BCh Witw.   Prof., Child and Adult Psychiatry (Linac.)

Psychology, Experimental

Tel: (01865) 271444 Fax: (01865) 310447

Bishop, Dorothy V. M., MA Oxf., DPhil Oxf.   Prof., Developmental Neuropsychology (S.Hug.)

Braddick, Oliver J., MA Camb., PhD Camb.   Prof.; Head* (Magd.)

Martin, Rose M. A., MA Oxf., DPhil Oxf.   Prof., Abnormal Psychology (S.Edm.)

Nation, Kate A., BSc York(UK), PhD York(UK)   Prof. (S.Joh.)

Nobre, Anna C. de O., BA Mass., MS Yale, MPhil Yale, PhD Yale   Prof., Cognitive Neuroscience (New)

Parkes, Katharine R., MSc Lough., MA Oxf., MSc Oxf., PhD Lough.   Reader, Applied Psychology (Gre.)

Passingham, Richard E., MSc Lond., MA Oxf., PhD Lond.   Prof., Cognitive Neuroscience (Wadh.)

Plunkett, Kim R., BSc Lond., MSc Sus., MA Oxf., DPhil Sus.   Prof., Cognitive Neuroscience (S.Hug.)

Rawlins, J. Nicholas P., MA Oxf., DPhil Oxf.   Watts Prof. (Wolfs.)

Rogers, Brian J., BSc Brist., MA Oxf., PhD Brist.   Prof. (L.M.H.)

Rolls, Edmund T., MA Oxf., DPhil Oxf., DSc   Prof. (Corp.)

Spence, Charles J., PhD Camb.   Prof. (Some.)

Research: behavioural and cognitive neuroscience (brain mechanisms underlying perception, memory and emotion); cognitive development (development of perception and understanding in childhood); psychology of language (normal, developmental and abnormal language processing); sensory processes (psychological and neural processes of vision); social psychology (inter-group processes and social cognition)

Public Health and Primary Health Care

Tel: (01865) 226666 Fax: (01865) 226720

Austoker, Joan I., BSc Witw., MA Lond., PhD Lond. Reader (Gre.)

Beral, Valerie, MB BS Syd. Prof., Epidemiology (Gre.)

Brocklehurst, Peter Prof., Perinatal Epidemiology

Carpenter, Lucy M., BSc Exe., MSc Lond., PhD Lond. Reader, Statistical Epidemiology (Nuff.)

Chen, Z., MB BS Shanghai, MSc Shanghai Prof., Epidemiology (Gre.)

Collins, Rory E., MB Lond., MSc Oxf. Prof., Medicine and Epidemiology

Fitzpatrick, Raymond M., BA Oxf., MSc Lond., MA Oxf., PhD Lond. Prof. (Nuff.)

Glasziou, Paul P., BSc Qld., MB BS Qld., PhD Qld. Prof., Evidence-Based Medicine (Kell.)

Goldacre, Michael J., BM Oxf., MA Oxf. Prof., Public Health (Magd.)

Gray, Alastair M. Prof., Health Economics

Hope, R. Tony, BA Oxf., BM BCh Oxf., MA Oxf. Prof., Medical Ethics (S.Cross)

Jaffe, Harold W., AB Calif., MD Calif. Head*

Jenkinson, Crispen P., MA Oxf., DPhil Oxf. Prof., Health Services Research (Gre.)

Lancaster, Tim R., MB BS Lond., MSc Harv., MA Oxf. Reader, General Practice (S.Ann.)

Mant, David, MB ChB Birm., MA Camb., MSc Lond. Prof., General Practice (Kell.)

Neil, H. Andrew W., MB BChir Camb., PhD Birm. Prof., Clinical Epidemiology (Wolfs.)

Parker, Michael J., BSc Manc., BEd W.England, MPhil W.England, PhD Hull Prof., Bioethics (S.Cross)

Snow, R. W. Prof., Tropical Public Health

Stewart-Brown, Sarah L., BM Oxf., MA Oxf. Reader, Health Services Research

Venables, Kate M., BSc Lond., MSc Lond., PhD Lond. Reader, Occupational Medicine (S.Cross)

Yudkin, Pat L., MA Oxf., DPhil Oxf. Reader, Medical Statistics (S.Hug.)

Surgery

Tel: (01865) 221297 Fax: (01865) 765063

Austyn, Jonathan M., MA Oxf., DPhil Oxf. Prof., Immunobiology (Wolfs.)

Aziz, Tipu A., BSc Lond., MB BS Lond., MD Manc. Prof., Neurosurgery

Byrne, James V., MD Lond. Prof., Neuroradiology

Friend, Peter J., BA Camb., MB BChir Camb., MA Camb., MD Oxf., DM Oxf., FRCS Prof., Transplantation (Gre.)

Hands, Linda J., BSc Lond., MB BS Lond., MS Lond. Reader (Gre.)

Meakins, Jonathan L., BSc McG., MD W.Ont., DSc Cinc. Nuffield Prof.; Head* (Ball.)

Mortensen, Neil J., MB ChB Birm., MD Brist., FRCS Prof., Colorectal Surgery (Gre.)

Taggart, David P., PhD Strath., MD Glas. Prof., Cardiothoracic Surgery

Wood, Kathryn J., BSc Oxf., MA Oxf., DPhil Oxf. Prof., Immunology (Univ.)

SPECIAL CENTRES, ETC

Art and Archaeology, Ashmolean Museum of

Tel: (01865) 278000 Fax: (01865) 278018

Brown, Christopher P. H., MA Oxf., PhD Lond. Dir.* (Worc.)

History of Science, Museum of the

Tel: (01865) 277280 Fax: (01865) 277288

Bennett, Jim A., MA Oxf., PhD Camb. Dir.* (Linac.)

Natural History, University Museum of

Tel: (01865) 272950 Fax: (01865) 272970
E-mail: info@oum.ox.ac.uk

Kennedy, W. Jim, BSc Lond., MA Oxf., PhD Lond. Prof., Natural History; Dir.* (Kell.)

Pitt Rivers Museum

Tel: (01865) 270927 Fax: (01865) 270943
E-mail: prm@prm.ox.ac.uk

O'Hanlon, Michael D. P., MA Oxf., PhD Lond. Dir.* (Linac.)

ALL SOULS COLLEGE

Tel: (01865) 279379 Fax: (01865) 279299
E-mail: enquiries@all-souls.ox.ac.uk

Davis, John H. R., MA Oxf., PhD Lond., FBA Warden*

Lever, Sir Jeremy, KCMG, QC, MA Oxf. Sr. Dean

Seaman, Thomas W., BA Yale, MA Oxf., MBA Chic. Bursar

BALLIOL COLLEGE

Tel: (01865) 277777 Fax: (01865) 277803
E-mail: college.secretary@balliol.ox.ac.uk

Graham, Andrew W. M., MA Oxf. Master*

Trott, Nicola, DPhil Oxf. Sr. Tutor

Woodall, Carl V., BA Manc., BPhil Manc. Bursar

BLACKFRIARS

Tel: (01865) 278400 Fax: (01865) 278403

Edney, Rev. R. Mark W., MPhil Oxf. Bursar

Finn, Rev. Richard, MA Camb., MPhil Camb. Regent*

Minns, Very Rev. Denis, BA Melb., TheolM Melb.Div.Coll. Secretary of Studies

BRASENOSE COLLEGE

Tel: (01865) 277830 Fax: (01865) 277822
E-mail: college.office@bnc.ox.ac.uk

Cashmore, Roger J., MA Oxf., DPhil Oxf., FRS Principal*

Knowland, John S., MA Oxf., DPhil Oxf. Bursar

Stockley, Andrew, BA Cant., LLB Well., PhD Camb. Sr. Tutor

CAMPION HALL

Tel: (01865) 286100 Fax: (01865) 286148

L'Estrange, Rev. Peter, DPhil Oxf. Master*

Selwood, Peter Bursar

CHRIST CHURCH

Tel: (01865) 276150 Fax: (01865) 286588

Harris, John G., MA Oxf. Steward

Lewis, Very Rev. Christopher A., PhD Camb. Dean*

Simpson, Edwin J. F., BCL Oxf., MA Oxf. Sr. Censor

CORPUS CHRISTI COLLEGE

Tel: (01865) 276700 Fax: (01865) 276767

Hore, Peter J., MA Oxf., DPhil Oxf. Sr. Tutor

Lankester, Sir Tim, KCB, BA Camb., MA Yale President*

Ruck Keene, Ben C., JP, BA York(UK), MA Oxf. Bursar

EXETER COLLEGE

Tel: (01865) 279600 Fax: (01865) 279645
E-mail: academic.administrator@exeter.ox.ac.uk

Bennett, Eric M., MA Oxf., MA Glas. Home Bursar

Cairncross, Frances A., CBE, MAEcon Rhode I. Rector*

Hutchinson, Gregory O., MA Oxf., MPhil Oxf., DPhil Oxf. Sr. Tutor

GREEN COLLEGE

Tel: (01865) 274770 Fax: (01865) 274796

Bundy, Colin J., MPhil Oxf., DPhil Oxf. Warden*

Chambers, Gerald, MA Oxf. Domestic Bursar

Hsu, Elisabeth, MPhil Camb., PhD Camb. Academic Tutor

GREYFRIARS

Tel: (01865) 243694 Fax: (01865) 256750

Lawes, Richard, MB ChB Edin., MA Oxf., DPhil Oxf. Sr. Tutor

Reynolds, Carol Bursar

Richardson, Nicholas, BPhil Oxf., MA Oxf., DPhil Oxf. Warden*

HARRIS MANCHESTER COLLEGE

Tel: (01865) 271006 Fax: (01865) 271012
E-mail: enquiries@hmc.ox.ac.uk

Duffell, Annette, BEd Birm. Bursar

Smith, Lesley J., BSc Lond., MSc Lond., MA Oxf., DPhil Oxf. Sr. Tutor

Waller, Rev. Ralph, BD Lond., MTh Nott., MA Oxf., PhD Lond. Principal*

HERTFORD COLLEGE

Tel: (01865) 279400 Fax: (01865) 279437

Baker, Peter R., MA Reading, MA Oxf. Bursar

Day, William A., MA Camb., PhD Carnegie-Mellon Sr. Tutor

Landers, John M., MA Oxf., PhD Camb., FRHistS Principal*

JESUS COLLEGE

Tel: (01865) 279700 Fax: (01865) 279687
E-mail: enquiries@jesus.ox.ac.uk

Krebs, Lord, MA Oxf., DPhil Oxf., FRS Principal*

Patell, Shahpur, PhD Camb. Home Bursar

Sherwood, Jane E., MA Oxf., DPhil Oxf. Sr Tutor

KEBLE COLLEGE

Tel: (01865) 272727 Fax: (01865) 272705
E-mail: enquiries@keble.ox.ac.uk

Boden, Roger J., MA Oxf. Bursar

Cameron, Averil M., DBE, MA Oxf., PhD Lond., FBA, FSA Warden*

Mazey, Sonia P., BA Leic., MPhil Oxf., DPhil Oxf. Sr. Tutor

KELLOGG COLLEGE

Tel: (01865) 270383 Fax: (01865) 270314
E-mail: college.office@kellogg.ox.ac.uk

Flood, Raymond G., BSc Belf., MA Oxf., MSc Oxf., PhD Sr. Tutor

Hawkins, Angus B., BA Reading, MA Oxf., PhD Lond., FRHistS Bursar

Thomas, Geoffrey P., BSc Wales, MA Oxf., PhD Camb. President*

LADY MARGARET HALL

Tel: (01865) 274300 Fax: (01865) 274313
E-mail: lodge@lmh.ox.ac.uk

Lannon, Frances, MA Oxf., DPhil Oxf., FRHistS Principal*

Robson, Mark H., MA Oxf., MPhil Oxf. Treasurer

Spensley, M. Fiona, BA Warw., PhD Open(UK) Sr. Tutor

LINACRE COLLEGE

Tel: (01865) 271650 Fax: (01865) 271668
E-mail: college.secretary@linacre.ox.ac.uk

Brown, Nicholas D., BA Camb., MSc Aberd., DPhil Oxf. Sr. Tutor

Reid, Alison A., MA Finance Bursar

Slack, Paul A., MA Oxf., DPhil Oxf., FBA Principal*

LINCOLN COLLEGE

Tel: (01865) 279800 Fax: (01865) 279802
E-mail: info@lincoln.ox.ac.uk

Knowles, Timothy M., MA Oxf. Bursar

Langford, Paul, MA Oxf., DPhil Oxf., FBA
Rector*

MAGDALEN COLLEGE

Tel: (01865) 276000 Fax: (01865) 276030
Clary, David D., BSc Sus., PhD Camb., ScD
Camb., FRS, FRSChem   President*
Pobjoy, Mark, MA Oxf., DPhil Oxf.   Sr. Tutor
Young, Charles G., MA Oxf., MBA Harv.   Sr.
Bursar

MANSFIELD COLLEGE

Tel: (01865) 270999 Fax: (01865) 270970
E-mail: admissions@mansfield.ox.ac.uk
Kennedy, Philip A. M., BA Manc., PhD S'ton.
Sr. Tutor
Walford, Diana M., CBE, BSc Liv., MB ChB Liv.,
MSc Lond., MD Liv., FRCP, FRCPath
Principal*
Waterman, Steve R., MA Oxf., MEd Nott.
Bursar

MERTON COLLEGE

Tel: (01865) 276310 Fax: (01865) 276361
Paxton, Catherine, BA Oxf., DPhil Oxf.   Sr.
Tutor
Rawson, Dame Jessica M., CBE, DBE, MA Oxf.,
MA Camb., DLitt Oxf., LittD Camb., FBA
Warden*
Webb, Clifford R., MA Oxf., MLitt Edin.
Bursar

NEW COLLEGE

Tel: (01865) 279555 Fax: (01865) 279590
Griffith, Mark S., MA Oxf., DPhil Oxf.   Sr.
Tutor
Palfreyman, David, LLB Oxf.Brookes, MBA Aston,
MA Oxf.   Bursar
Ryan, Alan J., MA Oxf., DLitt Oxf., FBA
Warden*

NUFFIELD COLLEGE

Tel: (01865) 278500 Fax: (01865) 278621
E-mail: college.secretary@nuf.ox.ac.uk
Evans, Geoffrey A., BA Sus., MA Oxf., MPhil
Oxf., DPhil Oxf.   Sr. Tutor
Hughes, Gwilym F., MA Camb., MA Oxf., MDA
Cran.   Bursar
Nickell, Stephen, CBE, BA Camb., MSc Lond.,
FBA   Warden*

ORIEL COLLEGE

Tel: (01865) 276555 Fax: (01865) 791823
MacPherson, George G., BM Oxf., MA Oxf.,
DPhil Oxf.   Sr. Tutor
Morris, Sir Derek, MA Oxf., DPhil Oxf.
Provost*
Stephenson, E. Wilf, MA Camb.   Bursar

PEMBROKE COLLEGE

Tel: (01865) 276444 Fax: (01865) 276418
Church, John E., MA Oxf.   Bursar
Eekelaar, John M., LLB Lond., BCL Oxf., MA
Oxf., FBA   Sr. Tutor
Henderson, Giles, CBE, BA Witw., BCL Oxf.,
MA Oxf.   Master*

QUEEN'S COLLEGE

Tel: (01865) 279120 Fax: (01865) 790819
Budd, Sir Alan, BSc Lond., MA Oxf., PhD Camb.,
DPhil Oxf.   Provost*
Irving-Bell, Linda, MA Oxf., DPhil Oxf.   Home
Bursar
Neumann, Peter M., OBE, MA Oxf., DPhil Oxf.,
DSc Oxf.   Sr. Tutor

REGENT'S PARK COLLEGE

Tel: (01865) 288120 Fax: (01865) 288121
Bradshaw, Rev. Timothy, MA Oxf., PhD Nott.
Sr. Tutor
Ellis, Robert A., MA Oxf., DPhil Oxf.
Principal*
Harper, David A., BSc Warw.   Bursar

SOMERVILLE COLLEGE

Tel: (01865) 270600 Fax: (01865) 270620
E-mail: secretariat@somerville.ox.ac.uk
Caldicott, Dame Fiona, DBE, BM BCh Oxf., MA
Oxf., Hon. MD Oxf., Hon. DSc Oxf.,
FRCPsych, FRCP, FRCPI, FRCGP   Principal*
MacManaway, Norma, MA Oxf.   Sr. Tutor
Morton, Helen, MA Camb., MSc Boston
Treasurer

ST ANNE'S COLLEGE

Tel: (01865) 274800 Fax: (01865) 274899
Gardam, Tim D., MA Camb.   Principal*
Jackson, Martin L., OBE, MA Oxf.   Bursar
Mullen, Anne, BA Strath., MA Oxf., DPhil Oxf.
Sr. Tutor

ST ANTONY'S COLLEGE

Tel: (01865) 284700 Fax: (01865) 274526
MacMillan, Margaret, BA Tor., BPhil Oxf., DPhil
Oxf.   Warden*
Robins, Philip, MA Manc., PhD Exe.   Sr. Tutor
Taylor, Allan, BA Brist., MA Oxf.   Bursar

ST BENET'S HALL

Tel: (01865) 280556 Fax: (01865) 280792
Bhattacharji, Santha, PhD Brist.   Sr. Tutor
Chamberlain, Leo, MA   Bursar; Master*

ST CATHERINE'S COLLEGE

Tel: (01865) 271700 Fax: (01865) 271768
Ainsworth, Roger W., MA Oxf., DPhil Oxf.
Master*
Bennett, James L., BA Reading, MA Oxf.   Home
Bursar
Thompson, Colin P., MA Oxf., DPhil Oxf.   Sr.
Tutor

ST CROSS COLLEGE

Tel: (01865) 278490 Fax: (01865) 278484
E-mail: college.secretary@stx.ox.ac.uk
Deutsch, Jan-Georg, MA Hanover, PhD Lond.   Sr.
Tutor
Doherty, Maureen P., BA Lanc., MA Open(UK),
MA Oxf.   Bursar
Goudie, Andrew S., MA Camb., MA Oxf., PhD
Camb., DPhil Oxf., DSc Oxf.   Master*

ST EDMUND HALL

Tel: (01865) 279000 Fax: (01865) 279090
E-mail: college.secretary@seh.ox.ac.uk
Ferguson, Stuart J., MA Oxf., DPhil Oxf.   Sr.
Tutor
Mingos, D. Michael P., BSc Manc., MA Oxf.,
DPhil Sus., FRS, FRSChem   Principal*
Parkin, Ernest J., MA Virginia, PhD Rensselaer
Home Bursar

ST HILDA'S COLLEGE

Tel: (01865) 276884 Fax: (01865) 276816
E-mail: college.office@st-hildas.ox.ac.uk
Berry, Richard L., BSc Durh.   Bursar
Forbes, Sheila, CBE, MA Oxf.   Principal*
Yeomans, Julia M., MA Oxf., DPhil Oxf.   Sr.
Tutor

ST HUGH'S COLLEGE

Tel: (01865) 274900 Fax: (01865) 274912
Dilnot, Andrew, CBE, MA Oxf.   Principal*
Emerson, Elizabeth J., MA Camb., MPhil Camb.,
PhD Camb.   Sr. Tutor
Kerr, Mary A.   Bursar

ST JOHN'S COLLEGE

Tel: (01865) 277300 Fax: (01865) 277435
E-mail: college.office@sjc.ox.ac.uk
Boyce, Anthony J., MA Oxf., DPhil Oxf.
Principal Bursar
Ostle, Robin C., MA Oxf., DPhil Oxf.   Sr. Tutor
Scholar, Sir Michael, CB, KCB, MA Camb., PhD
Camb.   President*

ST PETER'S COLLEGE

Tel: (01865) 278900 Fax: (01865) 278855
Gordon, Richard, MA Aberd., MBA Edin.   Bursar
Silverman, Bernard W., BTh S'ton., MA Oxf.,
MA Camb., DPhil Oxf., PhD Camb., DSc Camb.,
FRS   Master*
Southworth, Eric, MA Camb.   Sr. Tutor

ST STEPHEN'S HOUSE

Tel: (01865) 247874 Fax: (01865) 794338
Boxall, Ian K., MA Oxf., MPhil Oxf.   Sr. Tutor
Smith, Michele   Bursar
Ward, Rev. Robin   Principal*

TEMPLETON COLLEGE

Tel: (01865) 422500 Fax: (01865) 422501
E-mail: enquiries@templeton.ox.ac.uk
Earl, Michael J., BA Newcastle(UK), MSc Warw.,
MA Oxf.   Dean*
Kessler, Ian J., BA Manc., MA Warw., PhD Warw.
Sr. Tutor
Pritchard, Glyn, MA Oxf., FCA   Treasurer and
Chief Financial Officer

TRINITY COLLEGE

Tel: (01865) 279900 Fax: (01865) 279911
Keling, John J.   Domestic Bursar
Roberts, Sir Ivor, KCMG, MA Oxf.   President*
Watt, Trudy A., BA Open(UK), MSc Sheff.Hallam,
MA Oxf., DPhil Oxf.   Sr. Tutor

UNIVERSITY COLLEGE

Tel: (01865) 276602 Fax: (01865) 276790
E-mail: college.office@univ.ox.ac.uk
Crawford, Elizabeth J., BA CNAA, MA Oxf.
Domestic Bursar
Knowland, Anne M., MA Oxf.   Sr. Tutor

WADHAM COLLEGE

Tel: (01865) 277900 Fax: (01865) 277937
Chalmers, Sir Neil, BA Oxf., PhD Camb.
Warden*
Linieres-Hartley, Pauline A., BA C'dia.
Domestic Bursar
Mawson, Caroline S., DPhil Oxf.   Sr. Tutor

WOLFSON COLLEGE

Tel: (01865) 274100 Fax: (01865) 274125
Francis, Martin J. O., MA Oxf., DPhil Oxf.   Sr.
Tutor
Lee, Hermione, CBE, MA Oxf., MPhil Oxf., FBA
FRSL President*
Palmer, Stephen C., CBE, MA Camb., PhD Camb.
Bursar

WORCESTER COLLEGE

Tel: (01865) 278300 Fax: (01865) 278369
Dyer, Stephen D., MA Oxf.   Domestic Bursar
Lunn, A. Daniel, MA Oxf., DPhil Oxf.   Sr.
Tutor
Smethurst, Richard G., MA Oxf.   Provost*

WYCLIFFE HALL

Tel: (01865) 274200 Fax: (01865) 274215
E-mail: enquiries@wycliffe.ox.ac.uk
Boyce, Lyn M.   Bursar
Southwell, Rev. Peter J. M., MA *Oxf.*   Sr. Tutor
Turnbull, Rev. Richard D., BA *Reading*, BA *Durh.*,
PhD *Durh.*   Principal*

CONTACT OFFICERS

Academic affairs. Registrar: Maxton, Julie K.,
LLB *Lond.*, LLM *Cant.*, PhD *Auck.*
Accommodation. Accommodation Officer:
Jacobs, Sue V.
(E-mail: accommodation.office@
admin.ox.ac.uk)
Admissions (first degree). Director, Oxford
Colleges Admissions Office: Nicholson,
Mike, BA *Sheff.*
(E-mail: undergraduate.admissions@
admin.ox.ac.uk)
Admissions (higher degree). Head, Graduate
Office: Griffiths, Stella
(E-mail: graduate.admissions@
admin.ox.ac.uk)
Adult/continuing education. Director,
Continuing Education: Thomas, Geoffrey P.,
BSc *Wales*, MA *Oxf.*, PhD *Camb.*
(E-mail: enquiries@conted.ox.ac.uk)
Alumni. Secretary, Oxford University Society:
Kenny, Lady Nancy
(E-mail: enquiries@ousoc.ox.ac.uk)
Archives. Keeper of the Archives: Bailey,
Simon, BA *Warw.*
(E-mail: enquiries@oua.ox.ac.uk)
Careers. Director, Careers Service: (vacant)
(E-mail: postmaster@cas.ox.ac.uk)
Computing services. Director, Computing
Services: Lee, Stuart D., BA *Keele*, MA *Lond.*,
PhD *Lond.* (E-mail: enquiries@oucs.ox.ac.uk)
Development/fund-raising. Director,
Development: Cunningham, Sue, MA *Oxf.*
(E-mail: enquiries@devoff.ox.ac.uk)
Estates and buildings/works and services.
Director, University Estates: Wood, Jennifer
G., BSc *Manc.*, MSc *Lough.*
Examinations. Head of Examinations and
Assessment: Gurm, Bulvinder
Finance. Director of Finance and Secretary of
the Chest: Kerr, Giles, BA *York(UK)*, FCA
(E-mail: university.chest@admin.ox.ac.uk)
General enquiries. Information Officer:
Woodcock, Clare, BA *Hull*, MA *Sheff.*
(E-mail: information.officer@
admin.ox.ac.uk)
International office. International Officer:
Potts, Beverly A., MSc *Wales*
(E-mail: international.office@admin.ox.ac.uk)
Library (chief librarian). Director of
University Library Services and Bodley's
Librarian: Thomas, Sarah E., AB *Smith*, MS
Simmons, PhD *Johns H.*
(E-mail: enquiries@bodley.ox.ac.uk)
Personnel/human resources. Head, Personnel
Services: Whiteley, Jeremy D., MA *Camb.*,
MA *Oxf.*, PhD *Camb.*, DPhil *Oxf.*
(E-mail: personnel.services@admin.ox.ac.uk)
Public relations. Director, Public Affairs:
Harris, Jeremy M., MA *Camb.*
Publications. Head of Publications: Brunner-
Ellis, Anne, BA *E.Anglia*
(E-mail: publications@admin.ox.ac.uk)
Purchasing. Head, Purchasing: Bowen, Mark
Research. Director, Research Services:
Swafford, Glenn, BA *Well.*, MA *La Trobe*, PhD
Flin.
(E-mail: research.services@admin.ox.ac.uk)
Safety. Safety Officer: Bowker, Keith W., PhD
Leic., MA
Schools liaison. Schools and Colleges Liaison
Manager: Teulon, Paul, MA *Camb.*
(E-mail: undergraduate.admissions@
admin.ox.ac.uk)
Staff development and training. Director,
Institute for the Advancement of University
Learning: Gibbs, Prof. Graham P., BSc
City(UK) (E-mail: services@learning.ox.ac.uk)

Student union. President, Student Union:
McCluskey, Martin, BA *Oxf.*
(E-mail: info@ousu.org)
Student welfare/counselling. Head of
Counselling: Bell, Elsa I., MA
(E-mail: reception@counserv.ox.ac.uk)
Students from other countries. International
Officer: Potts, Beverly A., MSc *Wales*
(E-mail: international.office@admin.ox.ac.uk)
Students with disabilities. Head, Equal
Opportunities: Cooke, Felicity
University press. Secretary and Chief
Executive: Reece, Henry, BA *Brist.*, MA *Oxf.*,
DPhil *Oxf.* (E-mail: enquiry@oup.co.uk)

CAMPUS/COLLEGE HEADS

All Souls College, Oxford, England OX1 4AL.
(Tel: (01865) 279379; Fax: (01865)
279299;
E-mail: enquiries@all-souls.ox.ac.uk)
Warden: Davis, Prof. John H. R., MA *Oxf.*,
PhD *Lond.*, FBA
Balliol College, Oxford, England OX1 3BJ.
(Tel: (01865) 277777; Fax: (01865)
277803;
E-mail: college.secretary@balliol.ox.ac.uk)
Master: Graham, Andrew W. M., MA *Oxf.*
Blackfriars, 64 St Giles, Oxford, England OX1
3LY. (Tel: (01865) 278400; Fax: (01865)
278403) Regent: Finn, Rev. Richard, MA
Camb., MPhil *Camb.*
Brasenose College, Oxford, England OX1 4AJ.
(Tel: (01865) 277830; Fax: (01865)
277822;
E-mail: college.office@bnc.ox.ac.uk)
Principal: Cashmore, Prof. Roger J., MA
Oxf., DPhil *Oxf.*, FRS
Campion Hall, Oxford, England OX1 1QS.
(Tel: (01865) 286100; Fax: (01865)
286148) Master: L'Estrange, Rev. Peter,
DPhil *Oxf.*
Christ Church, Oxford, England OX1 1DP.
(Tel: (01865) 276150; Fax: (01865)
286588) Dean: Lewis, Very Rev.
Christopher A., PhD *Camb.*
Corpus Christi College, Oxford, England OX1
4JF. (Tel: (01865) 276700; Fax: (01865)
276767) President: Lankester, Sir Tim,
KCB, BA *Camb.*, MA *Yale*
Exeter College, Oxford, England OX1 3DP.
(Tel: (01865) 279600; Fax: (01865)
279645; E-mail: academic.administrator@
exeter.ox.ac.uk) Rector: Cairncross, Frances
A., CBE, MAEcon *Rhode I.*
Green College, Oxford, England OX2 6HG.
(Tel: (01865) 274770; Fax: (01865)
274796) Warden: Bundy, Colin J., MPhil
Oxf., DPhil *Oxf.*
Greyfriars, Oxford, England OX4 1SB. (Tel:
(01865) 243694; Fax: (01865) 256750)
Warden: Richardson, Nicholas, BPhil *Oxf.*,
MA *Oxf.*, DPhil *Oxf.*
Harris Manchester College, Oxford, England
OX1 3TD. (Tel: (01865) 271006; Fax:
(01865) 271012;
E-mail: enquiries@hmc.ox.ac.uk) Principal:
Waller, Rev. Ralph, BD *Lond.*, MTh *Nott.*,
MA *Oxf.*, PhD *Lond.*
Hertford College, Oxford, England OX1 3BW.
(Tel: (01865) 279400; Fax: (01865)
279437) Principal: Landers, John M., MA
Oxf., PhD *Camb.*, FRHistS
Jesus College, Oxford, England OX1 3DW.
(Tel: (01865) 279700; Fax: (01865)
279687; E-mail: enquiries@jesus.ox.ac.uk)
Principal: Krebs, Lord, MA *Oxf.*, DPhil *Oxf.*,
FRS
Keble College, Oxford, England OX1 3PG.
(Tel: (01865) 272727; Fax: (01865)
272705; E-mail: enquiries@keble.ox.ac.uk)
Warden: Cameron, Averil M., DBE, MA
Oxf., PhD *Lond.*, FBA, FSA
Kellogg College, 1 Wellington Square,
Oxford, England OX1 2JA. (Tel: (01865)
270383; Fax: (01865) 270314;
E-mail: college.office@kellogg.ox.ac.uk)
President: Thomas, Geoffrey P., BSc *Wales*,
MA *Oxf.*, PhD *Camb.*

Lady Margaret Hall, Oxford, England OX2
6QA. (Tel: (01865) 274300; Fax: (01865)
274313; E-mail: lodge@lmh.ox.ac.uk)
Principal: Lannon, Frances, MA *Oxf.*, DPhil
Oxf., FRHistS
Linacre College, Oxford, England OX1 3JA.
(Tel: (01865) 271650; Fax: (01865)
271668;
E-mail: college.secretary@linacre.ox.ac.uk)
Principal: Slack, Paul A., MA *Oxf.*, DPhil
Oxf., FBA
Lincoln College, Oxford, England OX1 3DR.
(Tel: (01865) 279800; Fax: (01865)
279802; E-mail: info@lincoln.ox.ac.uk)
Rector: Langford, Prof. Paul, MA *Oxf.*, DPhil
Oxf., FBA
Magdalen College, Oxford, England OX1
4AU. (Tel: (01865) 276000; Fax: (01865)
276030) President: Clary, Prof. David D.,
BSc *Sus.*, PhD *Camb.*, ScD *Camb.*, FRS,
FRSChem
Mansfield College, Oxford, England OX1 3TF.
(Tel: (01865) 270999; Fax: (01865)
270970;
E-mail: admissions@mansfield.ox.ac.uk)
Principal: Walford, Diana M., CBE, BSc *Liv.*,
MB ChB *Liv.*, MSc *Lond.*, MD *Liv.*, FRCP,
FRCPath
Merton College, Oxford, England OX1 4JD.
(Tel: (01865) 276310; Fax: (01865)
276361) Warden: Rawson, Dame Jessica
M., CBE, DBE, MA *Oxf.*, MA *Camb.*, DLitt
Oxf., LittD *Camb.*, FBA
New College, Oxford, England OX1 3BN. (Tel:
(01865) 279555; Fax: (01865) 279590)
Warden: Ryan, Prof. Alan J., MA *Oxf.*, DLitt
Oxf., FBA
Nuffield College, Oxford, England OX1 1NF.
(Tel: (01865) 278500; Fax: (01865)
278621;
E-mail: college.secretary@nuf.ox.ac.uk)
Warden: Nickell, Stephen, CBE, BA *Camb.*,
MSc *Lond.*, FBA
Oriel College, Oxford, England OX1 4EW.
(Tel: (01865) 276555; Fax: (01865)
791823) Provost: Morris, Sir Derek, MA
Oxf., DPhil *Oxf.*
Pembroke College, Oxford, England OX1
1DW. (Tel: (01865) 276444; Fax: (01865)
276418) Master: Henderson, Giles, CBE, BA
Witw., BCL *Oxf.*, MA *Oxf.*
Queen's College, Oxford, England OX1 4AW.
(Tel: (01865) 279120; Fax: (01865)
790914) Provost: Budd, Sir Alan, BSc *Lond.*,
MA *Oxf.*, PhD *Camb.*, DPhil *Oxf.*
Regent's Park College, Oxford, England OX1
2LB. (Tel: (01865) 288120; Fax: (01865)
288121) Principal: Ellis, Robert A., MA
Oxf., DPhil *Oxf.*
Somerville College, Oxford, England OX2
6HD. (Tel: (01865) 270600; Fax: (01865)
270620;
E-mail: secretariat@somerville.ox.ac.uk)
Principal: Caldicott, Dame Fiona, DBE, BM
BCh *Oxf.*, MA *Oxf.*, Hon. MD *Oxf.*, Hon. DSc
Oxf., FRCPsych, FRCP, FRCPI, FRCGP
St Anne's College, Oxford, England OX2 6HS.
(Tel: (01865) 274800; Fax: (01865)
274899) Principal: Gardam, Tim D., MA
Camb.
St Antony's College, Oxford, England OX2
6JF. (Tel: (01865) 284700; Fax: (01865)
274526) Warden: MacMillan, Margaret, BA
Tor., BPhil *Oxf.*, DPhil *Oxf.*
St Benet's Hall, 38 St Giles, Oxford, England
OX1 3LN. (Tel: (01865) 280556; Fax:
(01865) 280792) Master: Chamberlain,
Leo, MA
St Catherine's College, Oxford, England OX1
3UJ. (Tel: (01865) 271700; Fax: (01865)
271768) Master: Ainsworth, Roger W., MA
Oxf., DPhil *Oxf.*
St Cross College, Oxford, England OX1 3LZ.
(Tel: (01865) 278490; Fax: (01865)
278484;
E-mail: college.secretary@stx.ox.ac.uk)
Master: Goudie, Andrew S., MA *Camb.*, MA
Oxf., PhD *Camb.*, DPhil *Oxf.*, DSc *Oxf.*

St Edmund Hall, Oxford, England OX1 4AR. (Tel: (01865) 279000; Fax: (01865) 279090; E-mail: college.secretary@seh.ox.ac.uk) Principal: Mingos, Prof. D. Michael P., BSc Manc., MA Oxf., DPhil Sus., FRS, FRSChem

St Hilda's College, Oxford, England OX4 1DY. (Tel: (01865) 276884; Fax: (01865) 276816; E-mail: college.office@st-hildas.ox.ac.uk) Principal: Forbes, Sheila, CBE, MA Oxf.

St Hugh's College, Oxford, England OX2 6LE. (Tel: (01865) 274900; Fax: (01865) 274912) Principal: Dilnot, Andrew, CBE, MA Oxf.

St John's College, Oxford, England OX1 3JP. (Tel: (01865) 277300; Fax: (01865) 277435; E-mail: college.office@sjc.ox.ac.uk) President: Scholar, Sir Michael, CB, KCB, MA Camb., PhD Camb.

St Peter's College, Oxford, England OX1 2DL. (Tel: (01865) 278900; Fax: (01865) 278855) Master: Silverman, Bernard W.,

BTh S'ton., MA Oxf., MA Camb., DPhil Oxf., PhD Camb., DSc Camb., FRS

St Stephen's House, 16 Marston Street, Oxford OX4 1JX. (Tel: (01865) 247874; Fax: (01865) 794338) Principal: Ward, Rev. Robin

Templeton College, Oxford, England OX1 5NY. (Tel: (01865) 422500; Fax: (01865) 422501; E-mail: enquiries@templeton.ox.ac.uk) Dean: Earl, Prof. Michael J., BA Newcastle(UK), MSc Warw., MA Oxf.

Trinity College, Oxford, England OX1 3BH. (Tel: (01865) 279900; Fax: (01865) 279911) President: Roberts, Sir Ivor, KCMG, MA Oxf.

University College, Oxford, England OX1 4BH. (Tel: (01865) 276602; Fax: (01865) 276790; E-mail: college.office@univ.ox.ac.uk) Master: (vacant)

Wadham College, Oxford, England OX1 3PN. (Tel: (01865) 277900; Fax: (01865)

277937) Warden: Chalmers, Sir Neil, BA Oxf., PhD Camb.

Wolfson College, Oxford, England OX2 6UD. (Tel: (01865) 274100; Fax: (01865) 274125) President: Lee, Hermione, CBE, MA Oxf., MPhil Oxf., FBA FRSL

Worcester College, Oxford, England OX1 2HB. (Tel: (01865) 278300; Fax: (01865) 278369) Provost: Smethurst, Richard G., MA Oxf.

Wycliffe Hall, Oxford, England OX2 6PW. (Tel: (01865) 274200; Fax: (01865) 274215; E-mail: enquiries@wycliffe.ox.ac.uk) Principal: Turnbull, Rev. Richard D., BA Reading, BA Durh., PhD Durh.

[Information supplied by the institution as at 23 September 2007, and edited by the ACU]

OXFORD BROOKES UNIVERSITY

Founded 1992

Member of the Association of Commonwealth Universities

Postal Address: Headington Campus, Gipsy Lane, Oxford, England OX3 0BP
Telephone: (01865) 741111 **Fax:** (01865) 483073
URL: http://www.brookes.ac.uk

VICE-CHANCELLOR*—Beer, Prof. Janet P., BA Reading, MA Warw., PhD Warw.
DEPUTY VICE-CHANCELLOR—Wend, Petra, PhD Leeds
DEPUTY VICE-CHANCELLOR AND REGISTRAR‡—Knight, Rex, MA Camb.
PRO-VICE-CHANCELLOR (RESEARCH)—Woodhouse, Prof. Diana, BA CNAA, PhD CNAA
PRO VICE-CHANCELLOR (EXTERNAL AFFAIRS)—Raftery, Prof. John, BSc N.U.I., PhD Liv., FRICS
DIRECTOR OF FINANCE—Large, Paul
CLERK TO THE BOARD OF GOVERNORS—Knight, Rex, MA Camb.
DIRECTOR OF LEARNING RESOURCES—Workman, Helen M., BSc Birm., MA Sheff., PhD Open(UK)

GENERAL INFORMATION

History. The university was established in 1992 when Oxford Polytechnic achieved university status and is named in honour of John Brookes, a former principal.

It is located on three campuses: Headington, 1.5km east of Oxford city centre, Harcourt Hill, 2km west of the city centre, and Wheatley, 8km from the outskirts of Oxford.

Admission to first degree courses (see also United Kingdom Introduction). Through Universities and Colleges Admissions Service (UCAS). General academic requirements: acceptable passes in 5 subjects in General Certificate of Secondary Education (GCSE) or General Certificate of Education (GCE) including 2 at A level, or 4 subjects at GCSE or GCE including 3 at A level.

First Degrees (see also United Kingdom Directory to Subjects of Study). BA, BEng, BSc, LLB.

Programmes are taught on a modular basis, and most courses last 3 to 4 years full-time or up to 8 years part-time.

Length of course. Full-time: BA, LLB: 3 years; BSc: 3–4 years; BEng: 4 years. Part-time: BA, BEng, BSc: 5–8 years.

Higher Degrees (see also United Kingdom Directory to Subjects of Study).

Master's. LLM, MA, MBA, MEng, MPhil, MSc.
Admission. Normal entry requirements for master's degrees: honours degree, postgraduate diploma or equivalent professional qualification. MPhil: first or second class UK honours degree or equivalent.

Length of course. Full-time: LLM, MA, MBA, MEng, MSc: 1 year; MPhil: 2 years. Part-time: LLM, MA, MBA, MEng, MSc: 2 years; MPhil: 3 years.

Doctoral. EdD, PhD.
Admission. PhD: candidates should have an appropriate master's degree (including research training and research project); PhD by published work: at least 5 years' relevant postgraduate experience.

Length of course. Full-time: PhD: 3 years. Part-time: EdD: 2–5 years; PhD: 4 years.

Language of Instruction. English. The International Centre for English Language Studies provides a range of support and preparation classes for students whose first language is not English.

Libraries. Volumes: 463,000. Periodicals subscribed to: 2150. Special collections: Andre Deutsch; Dorset House archive (occupational therapy); Fuller (catering, cookery, gastronomy); Harold Fullard (atlases); medical sciences video archive; Museum of Modern Art, Oxford (exhibition catalogues); National Brewing Library; Oxfordshire Society of Architects; publishing in Africa; Charles Webster Welfare (20th century medical history); Jane Grigson (cookery, gastronomy).

Academic Year (2008–2009). Two semesters: 15 September–22 December; 29 January–15 May.

Income (2005–2006). Total, £124,711,000.

Statistics. Staff (2007): 2916 (1263 academic, 1653 non-academic). Students

(2005–2006): full-time 12,693; part-time 6075; international 2314; undergraduate 13,647; master's 4449; doctoral 435.

FACULTIES/SCHOOLS

Arts and Humanities, School of
Tel: (01865) 484129 Fax: (01865) 483791
E-mail: ah@brookes.ac.uk
Dean: Fitzsimmons, Prof. Linda, BA Hull
Personal Assistant to Dean/School Administrator: Perridge, Rhian

Built Environment, School of
Tel: (01865) 483202/483684 Fax: (01865) 483410 E-mail: be@brookes.ac.uk
Dean: Raftery, Prof. John, BSc N.U.I., PhD Liv., FRICS
School Administrator: Bartlett, Sue

Business School
Tel: (01865) 485908 Fax: (01865) 485830
E-mail: business@brookes.ac.uk
Dean: Langford, Prof. David, BA York(UK), MA York(UK), DPhil York(UK)
Personal Assistant to Dean: Bartholomew, Laura

Education, Westminster Institute of
Tel: (01865) 488600 Fax: (01865) 488666
E-mail: wioe@brookes.ac.uk
Dean: Langford, Prof. David, BA York(UK), MA York(UK), DPhil York(UK)
Personal Assistant to Dean: Chagouri, Debbie

Health and Social Care, School of
Tel: (01865) 482600 Fax: (01865) 482775
E-mail: shc@brookes.ac.uk
Dean: Girvin, June, MSc Cardiff

Head, School Support Services: Brockington, Karen

Life Sciences, School of

Tel: (01865) 483600 Fax: (01865) 483242
    E-mail: lifesciences1@brookes.ac.uk
Dean: King, Prof. Linda A., BSc Liv., DPhil Oxf.
School Administrator/Manager: Hobbs, John

Social Sciences and Law, School of

Tel: (01865) 483950 Fax: (01865) 483937
    E-mail: ssl@brookes.ac.uk
Dean: Elsom, Prof. Derek M., BSc Birm., MSc Birm., PhD CNAA
Personal Assistant to Dean/Senior School Administrator: Iliffe, Jane

Technology, School of

Tel: (01865) 483500 Fax: (01865) 483637
    E-mail: cms@brookes.ac.uk
Dean: Morrey, Denise, BA Camb., MA Camb., PhD Oxf.Brookes
Administration Manager: Flint, Sue

ACADEMIC UNITS

Accounting, Governance and Information Management

Tel: (01865) 485908
    E-mail: business@brookes.ac.uk
Diggle, Graham, BA Reading, PhD Reading   Acting Head, Acctg. and Finance
Duhan, Stephen, MA Camb., MBA Warw.   Acting Head, Acctg., Governance and Information Management
Spira, Laura, BA Manc., PhD Oxf.Brookes   Prof.; Acting Head, Corporate Governance
Other Staff: 1 Prof.; 25 Lectrs.; 17 Assoc. Lectrs.
Research: accounting; corporate governance; information systems strategy for small and medium enterprises (SMEs); international accounting and risk; social responsibility

Anthropology and Geography

Tel: (01865) 483950 Fax: (01865) 483937
    E-mail: ssl@brookes.ac.uk
McDonaugh, Chris, MA Oxf., MLitt Oxf., DPhil Oxf.   Head*
Other Staff: 5 Profs.; 4 Readers; 1 Principal Lectr.; 3 Sr. Lectrs.; 2 Lectrs.; 2 Res. Fellows
Research: environmentalism; human evolution; primatology; social anthropology of Japan and South Asia; urban geography

Architecture

Tel: (01865) 483200 Fax: (01865) 483298
    E-mail: arch@brookes.ac.uk
Swenarton, Mark, BA Oxf., MA Sus., PhD Lond., FRSA, FRHistS   Prof.; Head*
Other Staff: 5 Profs.; 20 Res. Staff; 30 Teaching Staff
Research: architectural history; architectural technology; development and emergency practice; sustainable architecture; sustainable cities

Arts: Fine Art, Film Studies and Music

Tel: (01865) 484959 E-mail: art@brookes.ac.uk
Howard, Janice, BA Oxf., MA Lond.   Principal Lectr.; Head*
Other Staff: 13 Lectrs.; 2 Fellows; 4 Specialist Technicians
Research: contemporary art; contextual art practices; post-colonialism, globalisation and photographic theory of electroacoustic composition; social sculpture; sound, live art and digital art practices

Computing and Electronics

Tel: (01865) 484500 Fax: (01865) 484545
    E-mail: wfc@brookes.ac.uk
Clocksin, William, BA Evergreen, MA Oxf., MA Camb., PhD Camb.   Prof.; Head*
Other Staff: 7 Profs.; 36 Lectrs.; 9 Res. Fellows

Research: applied formal methods; biomedical engineering; computer vision; medical instrumentation; multiservice systems

Economics and Strategy

Tel: (01865) 485908
    E-mail: business@brookes.ac.uk
Wildish, Clive, BA Warw., MBA Brad.   Head*
Other Staff: 2 Profs.; 26 Lectrs.; 18 Assoc. Lectrs.
Research: business history (entrepreneurship and outsourcing/offshoring); cost benefit analysis (CBA) of fiscal welfare weights and the political economy of the East Asian region; international economics/economic development (foreign investment, international trade, role of exchange rates)

Education, Westminster Institute of

Tel: (01865) 488600 Fax: (01865) 488666
    E-mail: wioe@brookes.ac.uk

Initial Teacher Training and Continuing Professional Development

Teacher and Professional Development
Tel: (01865) 488502
Whitehead, Phil, BEd Lanc., MEd Manc.   Head*
Other Staff: 3 Profs.; 58 Lectrs.
Research: creativity in science; mathematics education; primary geography; school governor initial teacher education (ITE) training; supporting trainees in challenging circumstances

Learning Sciences and Human Development

Tel: (01865) 488272
Hinton, Perry, BA Warw., BSc Lond., DPhil Oxf.   Head*
Other Staff: 1 Prof.; 26 Lectrs.
Research: childhood studies; communication and media; education; linguistics; philosophy

Lifelong Learning and Access

Tel: (01865) 488272
Gibson, William, BA Wales, MA Wales, PhD Middx., DLitt Wales   Prof.; Head*
Other Staff: 1 Prof.; 35 Lectrs.
Research: academic English skill acquisition; coaching and mentoring; ecclesiastical history; religion, learning and spirituality; work-based learning

Engineering

Tel: (01865) 483500 Fax: (01865) 483637
    E-mail: technology@brookes.ac.uk

Engineering, Mechanical

Durodola, John, BSc Ib., MSc Ib., PhD Lond.   Head*
Other Staff: 3 Profs.; 22 Lectrs.; 5 Res. Fellows
Research: acoustics and vehicle engineering; electronics; joining technology; stress and materials analysis; vibration

Joining Technology Research Centre

Hutchinson, Alan, BSc Portsmouth, PhD Dund.   Prof.; Head*
Other Staff: 1 Lectr.; 1 Res. Fellow
Research: aerospace research; automotive research; construction; materials and surfaces

English

Tel: (01865) 484329
    E-mail: english@brookes.ac.uk
Marshall, Gail, BA MA PhD   Head*
Other Staff: 3 Profs.; 13 Lectrs.
Research: contemporary fiction; modernism and women writers; post-colonial theories and literature; Romantic literature; textual analysis, intervention and parody

Environment and Conservation

Tel: (01865) 483240 Fax: (01865) 483242
    E-mail: lifesciences1@brookes.ac.uk
Thurling, David J., BA Camb., MA Camb., MSc Wales, PhD Leic.   Head of Programme*

Research: biology; invertebrate ecology and biogeography; spatial ecology and land use

Health and Social Care

Tel: (01865) 482600 Fax: (01865) 482775
    E-mail: shsc@brookes.ac.uk

Continuing Professional Development

E-mail: programmesshsc@brookes.ac.uk
Atkins, Sue, MSc Manc.   Programme Leader, UK Collaborative
Davis, Sally, MSc Lond.   Programme Leader, Public Health, Primary Care and Rehabilitation
Ewens, Ann, BSc Leeds, MA S'ton., PhD Reading   Dir.*
Gottwald, Mary, BA MA   Programme Leader, Management and Educn.
Lansdown, Gail, MSc Exe.   Programme Leader, Internat. Collaboration
Roberts, Dave, MSc Oxf.Brookes   Programme Leader, Cancer and Palliative Care
Walthall, Helen, BSc E.Lond., PhD Oxf.Brookes   Programme Leader, Critical and Advanced Practice
Other Staff: 35 Lectrs.

Health and Social Care Research Directorate

E-mail: programmesshsc@brookes.ac.uk
Boulton, Mary, BA Tor., PhD Lond.   Prof.; Dir.*
Other Staff: 6 Profs.; 7 Fellows
Research: health and social policy; primary care; public health; rehabilitation, mobility and movement science

Placement Learning Unit

Tel: (01865) 485253 Fax: (01865) 485500
    E-mail: programmesshsc@brookes.ac.uk
Khan, Sarah, BA Oxf.Brookes   Placement Leader, Adult Nursing
Lloyd-Jones, Netta   Head, Professnl. Practice Educn.*

Pre-Qualifying Learning and Development

Health and Social Care
Tel: (01865) 486200
    E-mail: programmesshsc@brookes.ac.uk
Beale, Hilary, BSc S'ton., MA Oxf.Brookes   Programme Leader, Social Work
Bostwick, Juliet, BSc C.England, MSc Birm.   Programme Leader, Adult Nursing
Bower, Heather, MA Warw.   Programme Leader, Midwifery and Post-Experience Midwifery
Conway, Nigel, BA Oxf.Brookes   Programme Leader, Operating Dept. Practice
Feaver, Sally, BA Oxf.Brookes, MA Oxf.Brookes   Programme Leader, Occupnl. Therapy
Freeman-May, Andrew, BA Oxf.Brookes   Programme Leader, Paramedic Studies
Kirk, Laurence, BSc Westminster   Programme Leader, Osteopathy
Scrivener, Neville, MA Portsmouth   Programme Leader, Mental Health
Sharman, Graham   Dir.*
Westcott, Liz, MSc Lond.   Dir.*
Winter, Julia, BSc Manc., MSc Manc.   Programme Leader, Children's Nursing
Zaagman, Peter, MSc Portsmouth   Programme Leader, Disability Nursing
Other Staff: 95 Lectrs.

History

Tel: (01865) 483722
    E-mail: kjohnson@brookes.ac.uk
Kilday, Anne-Marie, MA St And., PhD Strath.   Principal Lectr.; Head*
Other Staff: 7 Profs.; 18 Lectrs.
Research: citizenship; crime and punishment; medicine; nationhood and identity; the empire

History of Art

Tel: (01865) 484329
    E-mail: arthistory@brookes.ac.uk
Mount, Harry, BA Camb., MA Chic., PhD Camb.   Principal Lectr.; Head*

Other Staff: 6 Lectrs.

Research: eighteenth-century British painting; gender in architecture; Italian Renaissance art; twentieth-century art in Europe and the US

Hospitality, Leisure and Tourism Management

Tel: (01865) 485908
E-mail: business@broookes.ac.uk
Sloan, Donald, BSc *Strath.*   Head*
Other Staff: 1 Prof.; 22 Lectrs.; 10 Assoc. Lectrs.

Research: customer satisfaction; entrepreneurship; environmental management and sustainability; internationalisation; profit planning and performance measurement

Human Biology, Food Science and Nutrition

Tel: (01865) 483240 Fax: (01865) 483242
E-mail: lifesciences1@brookes.ac.uk
Craven, Richard P., BSc *Sheff.*, PhD *Sheff.*   Head of Programme*

Research: exercise and sports science; movement science and rehabilitation; nutrition and food science

Human Resource Management and Operational Behaviour

Tel: (01865) 485908
E-mail: business@brookes.ac.uk
Bassett-Jones, Nigel, BA *Leeds*, MBA *Aston* Head*
Other Staff: 4 Profs.; 23 Lectrs.; 19 Assoc. Lectrs.

Research: diversity management; employment relations dynamics of organisational life (justice, trust); implications of public sector procurement; organisational leadership and change; unionisation of migrant workers

International Relations, Politics and Sociology

Tel: (01865) 483950 Fax: (01865) 483937
E-mail: ssl@brookes.ac.uk
Axford, Barrie, BA *Reading*, MA *Reading*   Prof.; Head*
Other Staff: 3 Profs.; 1 Reader; 9 Sr. Lectrs.; 1 Lectr.

Research: critical international students; democracy and democratisation; globalisation and global governance; social inclusion and exclusion

Law

Tel: (01865) 484931 Fax: (01865) 484930
E-mail: pglaw@brookes.ac.uk
Dean, Meryll, BA *CNAA*, LLM *Camb.*   Prof.; Head*
Other Staff: 2 Profs.; 4 Readers; 1 Principal Lectr.; 14 Sr. Lectrs.; 1 Res. Fellow
Research: comparative law; international law; Japanese law

Marketing and Operations Management

Tel: (01865) 485908
E-mail: business@brookes.ac.uk
Whyatt, Georgina, BA *Leeds*, MBA *Oxf.Brookes* Head*
Other Staff: 1 Prof.; 23 Sr. Lectrs.; 20 Assoc. Lectrs.

Research: consumer loyalty; customer relationships; electronic marketing and online purchasing; giving experience gifts; strategic and services marketing

Modern Languages

Tel: (01865) 483920
E-mail: languages@brookes.ac.uk
Hill, Irene, BA *Oxf.Brookes*, MèsL *Orléans*   Head*
Other Staff: 2 Profs.; 20 Lectrs.
Research: Austrian and German literature; city in contemporary literature, film and art; contemporary French and Francophone fiction; French theatre; Spanish fiction

Molecular and Cell Biology

Tel: (01865) 483240 Fax: (01865) 483242
E-mail: lifesciences1@brookes.ac.uk
No staff at present

Research: biofilm development; insect virology; plant cell biology and microscopy; plant mineral relations; repair of ultraviolet-(UV) induced DNA damage in micro-organs

Planning

Tel: (01865) 483400 Fax: (01865) 483559
E-mail: planning@brookes.ac.uk
Butina Watson, Georgia, BA *Zagreb*, MA *Virginia Polytech.*, PhD *CNAA*   Prof.; Head*
Other Staff: 5 Profs.; 5 Fellows; 30 Teaching Staff
Research: impact assessment; planning policy; planning theory and history; urban design and conservation; urban policy and management

Psychology

Tel: (01865) 483771 Fax: (01865) 483887
E-mail: psychology@brookes.ac.uk
Harris, Margaret, BSc *Lond.*, PhD *Lond.*, FBPsS Prof.; Head*
Other Staff: 1 Prof.; 2 Emer. Profs.; 2 Readers; 1 Principal Lectr.; 9 Sr. Lectrs.; 2 Lectrs.
Research: connectionist modelling; normal and abnormal cognition; qualitative methods; social and health psychology; typical and atypical development

Publishing

Tel: (01865) 484992
E-mail: publishing@brookes.ac.uk
Phillips, Angus, BA *Oxf.*, MBA *Warw.*   Head*
Other Staff: 17 Lectrs.
Research: culture and history of publishing; international, strategy, policy and development studies

Real Estate and Construction

Tel: (01865) 484326 Fax: (01865) 483927
E-mail: drec@brookes.ac.uk
Dent, Peter, BA *Open(UK)*, MSocSc *Birm.*   Head*
Other Staff: 3 Profs.; 24 Teaching Staff
Research: knowledge transfer in the construction industry; land markets and emerging economies; low-cost housing; sustainable property development; valuation

SPECIAL CENTRES, ETC

Conservation, Environment and Development, Anthropology Centre for (ACCEnD)

Tel: (01865) 483950 E-mail: ssl@brookes.ac.uk
No staff at present

Research: changing countryside in Europe; food; human-wildlife interaction; primate conservation; social anthropology of environmental conservation

Democracy Studies, Centre for

Tel: (01865) 483924
E-mail: gkbrowning@brookes.ac.uk
No staff at present

Research: significance of democracy and democratisation

English Language Studies, International Centre for

Tel: (01865) 483874 Fax: (01865) 484377
E-mail: ic@brookes.ac.uk
Ansell, Mary Anne, BA *Sus.*, MA *Lond.*, MA *Reading*   Academic Devel. Dir.; Head*
Other Staff: 42 Staff Members

Europe Japan Research Centre

Tel: (01865) 483922
E-mail: jhendry@brookes.ac.uk
20 Staff Members

Health, Medicine and Society, Past and Present, Centre for

Teaching staff are drawn from the History department.
Tel: (01865) 483489
E-mail: medhist@brookes.ac.uk
King, Steven, BA *Kent*, PhD *Liv.*   Prof.; Asst. Dean; Dir.*
Research: social history of medicine (Africa, Britain, Europe, South America and South Asia, 1700-2000)

Historical and Cultural Research, Institute for

Academics are employed within the Publishing department.
Tel: (01865) 483665
E-mail: ihrc@brookes.ac.uk
Jay, Liz, MA *Oxf.*, MPhil *Oxf.*, DPhil *Oxf.*   Prof.; Assoc. Dean; Dir.*
Research: historical and cultural studies

Legal Research and Policy Studies, Centre for

Tel: (01865) 484931
E-mail: pglaw@brookes.ac.uk
Vickers, Lucy, BA *Camb.*, MA *Camb.*, PhD *Oxf.Brookes*   Reader, Law; Dir.*
Research: implementation of policy by government and its agencies; interrelationship between politicians, judges and citizens in policy formulation

Modern and Contemporary Poetry, Research Centre for

Tel: (01865) 484308
E-mail: rbuxton@brookes.ac.uk
Buxton, Rachel, BA MSt   Dir.*
Research: British, Irish, American and post-colonial twentieth- and twenty-first-century poetry in English

Publishing Studies, Oxford International Centre for

Academics are employed within the Publishing department.
Tel: (01865) 484992
E-mail: r.ockwell@brookes.ac.uk
Phillips, Angus, BA *Oxf.*, MBA *Warw.*   Dir.*
Research: culture and history of publishing; international publishing; publishing development; publishing strategy and policy

Sustainable Development, Oxford Institute for

Tel: (01865) 483430
E-mail: oisd@brookes.ac.uk
Dixon, Tim., BA *Leeds*, PhD *Reading*   Prof.; Dir.*
Other Staff: 65 Res. Staff
Research: architecture, culture and technology; environmental assessment and spatial planning; sustainable urban environments; urban design; urban policy and international development

Urban Design, Joint Centre for

Tel: (01865) 483200 Fax: (01865) 483298
E-mail: jcud@brookes.ac.uk
Butina Watson, Georgia, BA *Zagreb*, MA *Virginia Polytech.*, PhD *CNAA*   Prof.; Dir.*
Other Staff: 3 Profs.; 1 Fellow; 8 Teaching Staff
Research: construction of local and regional identity; designing out crime; privatising the public realm; regeneration of social housing; traffic and pedestrian movement

CONTACT OFFICERS

Accommodation. Senior Housing Officer: Eadie, Helen
(E-mail: accomm@brookes.ac.uk)
Admissions (first degree). Head of Admissions: Daniels, H. Krys
(E-mail: admissions@brookes.ac.uk)
Admissions (higher degree). Head of Admissions: Daniels, H. Krys
(E-mail: admissions@brookes.ac.uk)

Adult/continuing education. Head, Adult/ Continuing Education: Whitehead, Phil, BEd *Lanc.*, MEd *Manc.*
(E-mail: wioe@brookes.ac.uk)

Alumni. Events Officer: Hill, Beth, BA *C&GCHE*
(E-mail: bhill@brookes.ac.uk)

Alumni. Senior Alumni Officer: Butcher, Ceri
(E-mail: cebutcher@brookes.ac.uk)

Archives. Director of Learning Resources: Workman, Helen M., BSc *Birm.*, MA *Sheff.*, PhD *Open(UK)*
(E-mail: h.workman@brookes.ac.uk)

Careers. Head (Careers): Froud, Lorna
(E-mail: lhfroud@brookes.ac.uk)

Computing services. Director of Learning Resources: Workman, Helen M., BSc *Birm.*, MA *Sheff.*, PhD *Open(UK)*
(E-mail: h.workman@brookes.ac.uk)

Conferences/corporate hospitality. Conference Co-ordinator: Fletcher, Phillipa
(E-mail: pfletcher@brookes.ac.uk)

Credit transfer. Head of Admissions: Daniels, H. Krys (E-mail: hkdaniels@brookes.ac.uk)

Development/fund-raising. Development Director: Steadman, Ian
(E-mail: isteadman@brookes.ac.uk)

Equal opportunities. Equal Opportunities and Diversity Manager: Holliday, Michelle
(E-mail: mholliday@brookes.ac.uk)

Estates and buildings/works and services. Director of Estates and Facilities Management: King, Ian
(E-mail: ikking@brookes.ac.uk)

Examinations. Head of Examination and Conferment Unit: Burrell, Philippa
(E-mail: pburrell@brookes.ac.uk)

Finance. Director of Finance and Legal Services: Large, Paul
(E-mail: pjlarge@brookes.ac.uk)

General enquiries. Head of Student Liaison Enquiry Centre: Churchley, Hilary
(E-mail: query@brookes.ac.uk)

Health services. Head of Student Services: Cooper, Keith H.
(E-mail: khcooper@brookes.ac.uk)

Library (chief librarian). Head of Academic Library Services: Haines, Jan
(E-mail: jan.haines@brookes.ac.uk)

Minorities/disadvantaged groups. Equal Opportunities and Diversity Manager: Holliday, Michelle
(E-mail: mholliday@brookes.ac.uk)

Personnel/human resources. Head of Personnel/Human Resources: Price, Bob
(E-mail: bprice@brookes.ac.uk)

Public relations. Head of Public Relations: Penney, David
(E-mail: dpenney@brookes.ac.uk)

Purchasing. Purchasing Manager: Bacon, Nigel
(E-mail: nbacon@brookes.ac.uk)

Research. Director of Research and Business Development: Francis, John
(E-mail: jfrancis@brookes.ac.uk)

Safety. Safety Officer: McGill, Tim
(E-mail: trmcgill@brookes.ac.uk)

Security. Director of Estates and Facilities Management: King, Ian
(E-mail: ikking@brookes.ac.uk)

Sport and recreation. Director (Sport and recreation): Dodwell, Mark E. J.
(E-mail: mdodwell@brookes.ac.uk)

Staff development and training. Development Officer: Rust, Chris
(E-mail: crust@brookes.ac.uk)

Student union. President (Students' Union): Kyuchokova, Antoinette
(E-mail: iconobsu@brookes.ac.uk)

Student welfare/counselling. Head of Student Services: Cooper, Keith H.
(E-mail: khcooper@brookes.ac.uk)

Students from other countries. International Students' Adviser: Cammack, Freda
(E-mail: isas@brookes.ac.uk)

Students with disabilities. Disabled Students' Adviser: Shreir, Gill
(E-mail: gshreir@brookes.ac.uk)

[Information supplied by the institution as at 21 January 2008, and edited by the ACU]

UNIVERSITY OF PLYMOUTH

Founded 1989

Member of the Association of Commonwealth Universities

Postal Address: Drake Circus, Plymouth, Devon, England PL4 8AA
Telephone: (01752) 600600 **Fax:** (01752) 232293 **E-mail:** postmaster@plymouth.ac.uk
URL: http://www.plym.ac.uk

VICE-CHANCELLOR*—Purcell, Prof. Wendy M., BSc *Plym.*, PhD *Herts.*
DEPUTY VICE-CHANCELLOR (ACADEMIC)—Beveridge, Prof. M. C., BA PhD
DEPUTY VICE-CHANCELLOR (ACADEMIC)—(vacant)
DEPUTY VICE-CHANCELLOR AND DIRECTOR OF CORPORATE FINANCE—Raikes, G., MBE, BA, FCIS
UNIVERSITY SECRETARY AND ACADEMIC REGISTRAR‡—Hopkinson, J., LLB
PRO VICE-CHANCELLOR (RESEARCH)—Newstead, Prof. Steve, BA PhD
PRO VICE-CHANCELLOR—(vacant)
PRO VICE-CHANCELLOR—Watkins, Prof. M. J., PhD
DIRECTOR OF ACADEMIC PLANNING AND DEVELOPMENT—Stephenson, D., BSc PhD
HEAD OF THE GRADUATE SCHOOL—Fuller, Prof. M. P., BSc PhD
DEAN OF STUDENTS—Jellings, A., BSc PhD
DIRECTOR OF PERSONNEL AND DEVELOPMENT—Buckley, R. D., FCIS

GENERAL INFORMATION

History. The university was created by the merger of Plymouth Polytechnic, Rolle College in Exmouth, Exeter College of Art and Design and Seale-Hayne Agricultural College. Subsequently Tor and South West College of Health and the School of Podiatry have been incorporated into the university.

Admission to first degree courses (see also United Kingdom Introduction). Through Universities and Colleges Admissions Service (UCAS) or, for nursing and midwifery applications, through Nursing Midwifery Admissions Service (NMAS). Normal minimum requirements are passes in 3 General Certificate of Secondary Education (GCSE) subjects, and 2 General Certificate of Education (GCE) A levels or 2 Advanced General National Vocational Qualifications (GNVQs). Alternatively, a good Business and Technology Education Council (BTEC) National Certificate or National Diploma may be accepted. Technology and science candidates offering a BTEC National Certificate or Diploma should

have merit passes in 3 to 5 level III units in subjects relevant to the programme to be undertaken.

First Degrees (see also United Kingdom Directory to Subjects of Study). BA, BEd, BEng, BSc, LLB, MChem, MEng, MMath.
Programmes usually last 3 years full-time or 4 years on a sandwich basis.

Higher Degrees (see also United Kingdom Directory to Subjects of Study).
Master's. MA, MBA, MD, MEd, MPhil, MS, MSc.
Admission. Applicants for admission to higher degree courses must normally hold a degree or equivalent qualification from an approved UK or overseas university.
Doctoral. DClinPsy, DLitt, DSc, DTech, LLD, PhD.

Language of Instruction. English. Pre-sessional courses available for one or two months in the summer.

Libraries. Volumes: 537,400. Periodicals subscribed to: 4372. Other holdings: 13,500

e-journals. Special collections: Ronald Duncan (literature).

Income (2005–2006). Total, £142,277,000.

Statistics. Staff (2005–2006): 3571 (968 academic, 2603 non-academic). Students (2005–2006): full-time 17,682 (8056 men, 9626 women); part-time 11,275 (3041 men, 8234 women); international 1101 (645 men, 456 women); undergraduate 23,609 (8983 men, 14,626 women); master's 1142 (486 men, 656 women); doctoral 570 (265 men, 305 women).

FACULTIES/SCHOOLS

Arts
Tel: (01392) 475022 Fax: (01392) 475012
Acting Dean: Coslett, D. L., BA MA
Secretary: Wells, Y.
Faculty Business Manager: Hurrell, C., BA MSC

Education
Tel: (01395) 255301 Fax: (01395) 253303
E-mail: education.enq@plymouth.ac.uk

Dean: (vacant)
Personal Assistant: Arthur, K.
Faculty Business Manager: Braund, P. I., MBA

Health and Social Work

Tel: (01752) 233198 Fax: (01752) 233829
E-mail: healtheducation@plymouth.ac.uk
Acting Dean: Clibbens, Prof. J. S., BA BSc PhD
Personal Assistant: Marshall, S.
Faculty Business Manager: Stenhouse, R. C.,
MA MBA

Peninsula Medical School

Tel: (01752) 437444 Fax: (01752) 517842
E-mail: pmsenq@pms.ac.uk
Dean: Tooke, Sir John E., KBE, MA MSc BM
BCh DM DSc, FRCP
Personal Assistant: Smith, J.
Faculty Business Manager/School Secretary and
Head of Administration: Lindsay, C. A., MA
Sus., BA MSC

Science

Tel: (01752) 233093 Fax: (01752) 233095
E-mail: science@plymouth.ac.uk
Dean: Williamson, Prof. R., BSc PhD
Personal Assistant: Higman, L.
Faculty Business Manager: Mushens, C., BA
MSC

Social Science and Business

Tel: (01752) 232800 Fax: (01752) 232853
E-mail: ssb.enquiry@plymouth.ac.uk
Dean: Chandler, E. J., BA PhD
Secretary: Hill, H.
Faculty Business Manager: Stonefield, D., BA
MSC

Technology

Tel: (01752) 233300 Fax: (01752) 233310
E-mail: technology@plymouth.ac.uk
Dean: James, Prof. M. N., PhD Camb., BSc,
FIMMM
Personal Assistant: Ley, K.
Faculty Business Manager: Tilley, S.

University of Plymouth Colleges

Tel: (01752) 232334 Fax: (01752) 232369
E-mail: itunbridge@plymouth.ac.uk
Dean: Tunbridge, I. P., OBE, BSc PhD
Personal Assistant: Schofield, C.
Head of Faculty Administration: Stringer, M.

ACADEMIC UNITS

Applied Psychosocial Studies, School of

Alexander, S. E., BSc MSc   Sr. Lectr.
Baynes, P. E.   Sr. Lectr., Social Work
Burt, S. J., MSc   Sr. Lectr.; Deputy Head
Butler, A., MA   Sr. Lectr., Social Work
Carberry, A. P., BSc MA   Placement Co-
ordinator
Cassidy, T. E., BA MSc   Sr. Lectr., Mental
Health
Cattani, A., PhD   Sr. Lectr., Psychology
Chung, M. C., BA PhD   Reader, Psychology
Clack, E., BSc   Sr. Lectr., Nursing (Mental
Health)
Clibbens, J. S., BA BSc PhD
Dallos, A. R., MSc   Programme Dir., Clin.
Psychol.
Deakin, H. G., BEd MSc   Acting Principal
Lectr., Psychological Interventions/Clinical
Leadership
Elliot, T.   Sr. Lectr., Social Work
Farrand, P. A., BA PhD   Sr. Lectr., Health
Studies
Fisher, T. B., MPhil   Sr. Lectr., Nursing
(Mental Health)
Ford, D. J., BA MSc   Sr. Lectr., Social Work
Garrard, D., BA   Sr. Lectr., Social Work
Giarchi, G. G., BA MA PhD   Prof., Social Care
Studies
Gilbert, A. P., BA MSc PhD   Deputy Head
Gleeson, K., BA PhD   Res. Dir.
Hagley, A. C., BSc MSc   Sr. Lectr., Nursing
(Mental Health)

Haigh, D. E., BSc   Sr. Lectr., Nursing (Mental
Health)
Hampton, J., BSc MSc   Sr. Lectr., Social Work
Harrison, G., MSc PhD   Sr. Lectr., Social
Work
Hay, W. T., BA MPhil PhD   Sr. Lectr., Social
Work
Heath, V. A., BSc MSc   Principal Lectr.
Hickman, C. L., BA   Sr. Lectr., Social Work
Horton, V. M.   Sr. Lectr., Social Work
Janitsch, P. C. W., BEd   Sr. Lectr.
Johnstone, L. C., MA   Reader; Academic Dir.
Jordan, W. J., MA   Prof.
Kirsch, I., BA MA PhD   Chair, Psychol.
Kroll, B. A., BA   Principal Lectr.
Ley, T. C., BSc   Sr. Lectr.
Linsley, S., BSc   Sr. Lectr., Mental Health
Nursing
Madge, G. C.   Sr. Lectr., Social Work
Mann, J., BA MA   Sr. Lectr., Social Work
Miles, A. G., MBA   Locality Academic Dir.,
Cornwall
Morris, R. C., BA PhD   Course Dir.
Pankhurst, K., BSc MA   Sr. Lectr., Nursing
(Learning Disability)
Peacham, C. E., MSc   Sr. Lectr., Mental Health
Nursing
Perry, J. L. W., BSc   Sr. Lectr., Mental Health
Phillips, C., BA MA PhD   Sr. Lectr., Social
Work
Radford, S., BSc PhD   Assoc. Dir.
Rawlinson, J. W., MN   Sr. Lectr., Nursing
(Mental Health)
Reid, F. J., PhD   Dir., Taught Programmes;
Acting Head*
Ringer, I. A., BA   Sr. Lectr., Nursing (Mental
Health)
Russell, G. C., BSc MPhil   Sr. Lectr., Health
Psychology
Sheppard, M. G., BSc MA PhD   Prof., Social
Work
Wallace, S. D., BA MSc PhD   Principal Lectr.
Watts, A. M., BA   Scheme Leader, Health
Studies Modular Scheme
Welbourne, P. A., BSc MA MSc   Sr. Lectr.,
Social Work
Wilkinson, J. M., MSc   Sr. Lectr., Nursing
(Adult)
Williams, S. D., MA PhD   Combined
Programme Manager; Sr. Lectr., Social
Work
Williamson, G. M., MEd   Sr. Lectr., Nursing
(Mental Health)
Woodcock, J., BA MSc   Sr. Lectr., Social Work
Other Staff: 1 Lectr.; 4 Lectrs./Tutors; 1
Teaching Fellow; 2 Res. Fellows; 1 Clin. Sr.
Lectr.; 2 Clin. Lectrs./Tutors; 2 Clin. Res.
Tutors
Vacant Posts: 1 Principal Lectr.; 1 Sr. Lectr.
Research: communication in health; family and
well-being; implementing evidence based
healthcare; psychological aspects of health
and well-being; user involvement

Architecture and Design, School of

Tel: (01752) 233600 Fax: (01752) 233634
Adams, B. C., BA MA   Sr. Lectr., Three-
Dimensional Design
Aldrich, A., BA   Sr. Lectr.
Blackburn, S. P., BSc   Sr. Lectr., Rural
Resource Management
Fraquelli, R., BSc   Head, Three-Dimensional
Des.
Mackie, M. M., MPhil   Sr. Lectr., Architecture
Sara, R. J., BA PhD   Sr. Lectr., Architecture
Stevenson, M. L.   Head*
Watson, L. L., BSc BA   Principal Lectr.,
Architecture
Willey, D. S., BA PhD   Principal Lectr.,
Architecture
Other Staff: 10 Lectrs.
Research: architectural conservation; built
environment (environmental performance,
energy, conservation); CAD/rapid
prototyping; design innovation
(architecture, product design, designer-
maker); sustainable building (earthen
architecture, humane architecture)

Art and Performance, School of

Tel: (01392) 475022 Fax: (01392) 475021
Bennett, S., BA   Principal Lectr., Fine Art
Blackshaw, G., BA MPhil PhD   Sr. Lectr., Art
History and Visual Studies
Clucas, G., BA PhD   Sr. Lectr., Fine Art
Collins, J. M., BA MA   Sr. Lectr., Art History
Coslett, D. L., BA MA   Head*
Danvers, T. J.   Deputy Head
Dudley, E. H., BA   Sr. Lectr., Design History
Enright, T. J., BA MA   Sr. Lectr., Theatre and
Performance
Graham, J. F., BA MA PhD   Sr. Lectr., Art
History
Hall, C. M., BEd MEd   Sr. Lectr., Theatre and
Performance Studies
Jones, P. C., BA   Sr. Lectr., Graphic
Communication with Typography
Klunder, A., BA   Sr. Lectr., Design and Visual
Studies
Macleod, K. A., BA MEd   Sr. Lectr., History of
Art
Miles, M., BA PhD   Reader, Art and Design
Pay, P. R., PhD   Sr. Lectr., Combined Studies
Potter, A., BA   Sr. Lectr., Illustration
Power, P. I., BA   Head, Fine Art
Pratt, S. R., BSc PhD   Principal Lectr., Art
History
Prettejohn, E. F., BA MA PhD   Prof., Modern
Art
Smiles, S. A., BA MA PhD   Prof., Art History
Smith, A. J.   Subject Leader, Graphic Des.
Thorpe, S., BA   Sr. Lectr., Painting and
Printmaking
Virtue, J. A.   Prof., Painting and Printmaking
Way, R. M., BA   Sr. Lectr., Theatre and
Performance Art
Other Staff: 1 Reader; 8 Sr. Lectrs.; 1 Lectr.; 1
Archit. Historian
Research: city cultures (identity, representation,
power, hope); history of art, architecture
and design; natural world (recording and
representation); professional practice in art
and design; theatre and performance
(embodiment and identity)

Art History

Tel: (01392) 475055
E-mail: s.smiles@plymouth.ac.uk
Research: art, architecture and design from the
eighteenth- to the twentieth-century;
European and American depiction of non-
Western cultures; investigations of romantic
art; reinterpretation of Victorian art and
aestheticism; role of art in the construction
of national and group identities

Biological Sciences, School of

Tel: (01752) 232900 Fax: (01752) 232970
Attrill, M. J., BSc PhD   Prof., Marine and
Estuarine Ecology
Beal, J. D., BA PhD   Sr. Lectr., Microbiology
Bilton, D. T., BA MA PhD   Sr. Lectr., Ecology
Bishop, J. D. D., BSc PhD   Reader, Marine
Bioscience
Blackshaw, R. P., BSc PhD   Prof., Agricultural
Zoology
Bradley, G., PhD   Sr. Lectr., Microbiology
Brooks, P. H., BSc PhD   Prof.; Head*
Brown, M. T., BSc PhD   Principal Lectr.,
Marine Biology
Cotton, P. A., BSc PhD   Sr. Lectr., Ecology
Davies, S. J., BSc MSc PhD   Reader
Donkin, M. E., BSc PhD   Principal Lectr.
Eddison, J. C., BSc PhD   Principal Lectr.
Foey, A. D., BSc PhD   Sr. Lectr., Immunology
Foggo, A., BA MA DPhil   Sr. Lectr., Ecology
Fox, S. W., BSc MA   Sr. Lectr., Biomedical
Science
Franco, M. G., BSc MSc PhD   Sr. Lectr.,
Ecology
Galloway, T. S., BSc PhD   Reader,
Biochemistry
Gaudie, D., BSc PhD   Sr. Lectr., Genetics
Gilpin, M. L., BSc PhD   Sr. Lectr., Molecular
Genetics
Gresty, K. A., BSc PhD   Sr. Lectr.
Handy, R. D., BSc PhD   Principal Lectr.

Hanley, M. E., BSc MSc PhD Sr. Lectr., Terrestrial Ecology

Jha, A. N., BSc MSc PhD Principal Lectr., Genotoxicology

Jones, M. B., BSc PhD DSc Prof., Marine Biology

Kirk, J. A., BSc PhD Principal Lectr.

Kudi, A. C., MSc PhD Sr. Lectr., Animal Production

Kuri-Hernandez, V. M., PhD Sr. Lectr., Food Quality

Lane, S. D., BSc PhD Principal Lectr.; Programme Co-ordinator

Margerison, J. K., BSc PhD Sr. Lectr., Dairy and Animal Nutrition

Moody, A. J., BSc PhD Sr. Lectr., Biochemistry

Munn, R. D., BSc PhD Principal Lectr.

Orr, R. M., BSc PhD Sr. Lectr.

Parkinson, R. J., BSc MSc PhD Principal Lectr., Soil Sciences

Pearce, J., BSc PhD Sr. Lectr.

Price, D. J., BSc MSc PhD Sr. Lectr., Genetics

Ramsay, P. M., BSc PhD Sr. Lectr., Ecology

Rees, G. A., BSc PhD Sr. Lectr., Human Nutrition

Rundle, S. D., BSc PhD Sr. Lectr., Freshwater Ecology

Samuel, A. M., BSc Sr. Lectr., Crop Production

Sloman, K. A., BSc PhD Sr. Lectr., Marine and Freshwater Biology

Spicer, J. I., BSc PhD Reader

Thomas, C. F. G., BSc MSc PhD Sr. Lectr., Invertebrate Ecology

Thompson, R. C., BSc PhD Sr. Lectr., Marine Bethnic Ecology

Thompson, S. W. N., BSc PhD Principal Lectr., Biomedical Sciences

Uttley, M. G., BA DPhil Assoc. Head

Votier, S. C., BSc PhD Sr. Lectr., Marine Ecology

Wigham, G. D., BSc PhD Principal Lectr.; Academic Subject Leader

Williams, E. N., BA MA PhD Principal Lectr., Ecology

Other Staff: 2 Lectrs.; 3 Res. Fellows

Research: ecotoxicology and stress biology; food, nutrition and health; marine biology and ecology; terrestrial ecology

Computing, Communications and Electronic Engineering, School of

Tel: (01752) 232541 Fax: (01752) 232540

Ali Abu-Rgheff, M., BSc PhD Sr. Lectr.

Ascott, R., BA Prof., Technoetic Arts

Barlow, G. N. D., BSc MSc PhD Sr. Lectr., Computing

Barlow, I. M., BA MSc Sr. Lectr., Communication Engineering

Beck, M. A., BA BSc MSc Sr. Lectr.

Belpaeme, T., MSc PhD Sr. Lectr., Intelligent and Autonomous Control Systems

Brooke, P. J., BA MA DPhil Sr. Lectr.

Bugmann, G. V. F., PhD Reader

Cangelosi, A., PhD Reader, Artificial Intelligence and Cognition

Culverhouse, P. F., BA MPhil PhD Principal Lectr.

Davey, P. J., BEng PhD Sr. Lectr.

Dowland, P. S., BSc PhD Sr. Lectr.

Dyke, P. P. G., BSc PhD Prof.; Head*

Filmore, P. R., BSc MBA PhD Sr. Lectr., Electrical and Electronic Engineering

Furnell, S. M., BSc PhD Reader

Geroimenko, V. A., PhD DSc Reader, Computing

Hamer, C. F., BSc Teaching Fellow

Hawley, R. J., BA Sr. Lectr., Computing and Information Science

Ifeachor, E. C., BSc MSc PhD Wandel and Goltermann Prof., Intelligent Electronic Systems

Jenkins, D. F. L., BSc MSc PhD Sr. Lectr.

Johnson, C. A., BSc MSc PhD Principal Lectr.

Knahl, M. H., BSc PhD Sr. Lectr.

Linford, R. S., BSc MSc Deputy Head, Computing

Livingstone, D., BA MA Sr. Lectr.

Mayne, F., BSc Sr. Lectr., Computing

Merritt, R. J., BSc Sr. Lectr., Computing

Miranda, E. R., BSc MSc PhD Reader, Artificial Intelligence and Music

Mushens, B. G., BSc MSc Undergrad. Programme Dir.

Outram, N. J., BEng PhD Sr. Lectr., Biomedical Informatics and E-Health

Pan, G., BEng PhD Sr. Lectr.

Panina, L. V., PhD Prof.

Phillips, M. L., BA MA Subject Leader, Interactive Media

Phippen, A. D., BSc PhD Sr. Lectr.

Punt, M., BA MA PhD Reader, Digital Art and Technology

Rees, R. A. Sr. Lectr.

Reeve, C. D., BSc PhD Programme Manager, BSc

Robinson, P., BSc MEng PhD Principal Lectr., Robotics and Industrial Automation

Speed, C. J., BA Sr. Lectr., Interactive Multimedia

Squire, M. L. Sr. Lectr., Computing

Stamp, A. C., BSc MSc Sr. Lectr., Communication Engineering

Stuart, E. J., BSc PhD Sr. Lectr., Computing

Sturley, C. R., BSc Sr. Lectr., Computing

Subramaniam, P. R., MSc Sr. Lectr., Systems Analysis Methods

Tomlinson, M., BSc PhD Prof., Res.

Wang, X. Sr. Lectr., Computer Networks

Other Staff: 2 Assoc. Sr. Lectrs.; 8 Lectrs.; 3 Res. Fellows; 7 Res. Assts.; 1 Sch. Recruitment Manager

Research: communications research; interactive intelligent systems; network research; robotics; signal processing and multimedia communications

Earth, Ocean and Environmental Sciences, School of

Tel: (01752) 233000 Fax: (01752) 233035

Abbott, V. J., MSc PhD Sr. Lectr., Hydrographic Surveying

Anderson, M. W., BSc PhD, FGS Principal Lectr., Structural Geology

Andrew, K. N., BSc PhD Sr. Lectr., Environmental Analytical Chemistry

Barlow, M. J., BSc MSc Sr. Lectr., Sports Science in the Marine Environment

Bass, S. J., BSc MSc PhD Sr. Lectr., Marine Physical Science

Belt, S. T., BSc DPhil Prof.

Bull, J. N., BSc Principal Lectr., Pollution Ecology

Crichton, T. F. N., BSc Sr. Lectr., Navigation/Hydrography

Davidson, M. A., BSc Principal Lectr., Physical Oceanography

Diver, W. L., BSc MSc Principal Lectr., Geology

Evans, E. H., BSc PhD Reader

Findlay, M. M., BSc MSc PhD Principal Lectr.

Fitzsimmons, M. F., BSc PhD Sr. Lectr., Organic Geochemistry

Foulkes, M. E., PhD Sr. Lectr., Environmental Chemistry

Glegg, Gillian A., BSc PhD Principal Lectr., Marine Management

Hart, M. B., BSc DSc PhD Prof., Micropalaeontology

Hooper, J. B., MSc Assoc. Head

Huntley, D. A., BA MA PhD Prof.; Head*

Jones, G. E., BSc Sr. Lectr., Hydrography

Jones, P., MSc PhD Principal Lectr.

Lavender, S. J., BSc PhD Sr. Lectr., Geomatics

Lohan, M., BSc MSc PhD Sr. Lectr., Biogeochemistry and Environmental Analytical Chemistry

Lowry, R. B., BSc PhD Teaching Fellow

Maskall, J. E., BA MSc PhD Sr. Lectr., Land Remediation/Reclamation

Masse, G. G., PhD Sr. Lectr., Petroleum and Environmental Chemistry

Matthews, G. P., BSc MA Reader, Applied Physical Chemistry

Mee, L. D., BSc PhD Prof., Marine and Coastal Policy

Miles, J. R., BSc PhD Principal Lectr., Marine Sports Science

Millward, G. E., MSc PhD Prof., Marine Chemistry

Morris, A. J. D., BSc MSc PhD Sr. Lectr., Geological Sciences

Nimmo, M., BSc PhD Principal Lectr., Environmental Chemistry

Nimmo Smith, M., BSc PhD Sr. Lectr., Marine Physics

O'Hare, T. J., MA MSc PhD Dir., Undergrad. Programmes

O'Sullivan, P. E., BA DPhil Principal Lectr., Environmental Science

Pollard, C. D., BSc MSc Sr. Lectr., Marine Studies

Price, G. D., BSc MSc PhD Sr. Lectr., Environmental Geology

Richards, J. P., BSc MSc PhD Sr. Lectr., Environmental Science

Rieuwerts, J. S., BSc MSc PhD Sr. Lectr., Environmental Science

Rodwell, L. D., BSc MSc PhD Sr. Lectr., Environmental and Natural Resource Economics

Rowland, Steve J., BSc PhD Prof., Organic Geochemistry

Russell, P. E., BSc PhD Reader

Scott, S. C., BA PhD Principal Lectr.

Searle, T. J., BSc PhD Sr. Lectr., Marine Science and Technology

Shapiro, G. I., MSc PhD DSc Prof., Physical Oceanography

Smart, C. W., BSc PhD Sr. Lectr., Palaeontology

Stevens, T. F., BSc MSc PhD Sr. Lectr., Marine and Coastal Ecosystem-Based Management

Stewart, I. S., BSc PhD Sr. Lectr., Geodynamics

Stokes, M. R., BSc PhD Sr. Lectr., Geological Sciences

Taylor, G. K., BSc PhD Principal Lectr.

Trier, C. J., BSc PhD Sr. Lectr., Environmental Sciences

Turner, A., BSc PhD Sr. Lectr., Environmental Sciences

Watkinson, M. P., BSc PhD Sr. Lectr., Petroleum Geology

Wilkins, C., BSc MSc PhD Sr. Lectr., Economic Geology

Witt, N. A. J., BSc PhD Principal Lectr., Navigation Systems

Wood, N. L. H., BSc MSc Sr. Lectr., Meteorology

Worsfold, P. J., BSc MSc PhD DSc Prof., Analytical Chemistry

Other Staff: 1 Assoc. Principal Lectr.; 1 Assoc. Sr. Lectr.; 7 Lectrs.; 18 Res. Fellows; 1 Teaching Fellow

Research: coastal and continental shelf physical oceanography; coastal and ocean policy; palaeoenvironments, palaeomagnetism and geodynamics; petroleum geochemistry and environmental analytical chemistry; speciation and environmental analysis

Chemical Sciences, Centre for

Tel: (01752) 233013 Fax: (01752) 233035
E-mail: s.rowland@plymouth.ac.uk

Rowland, Steve J., BSc PhD Prof., Organic Geochemistry; Head*

Research: biogeochemistry and environmental analytical chemistry; environmental and fluid modelling; petroleum and environmental geochemistry; speciation and environmental analysis

Education, Faculty of

Tel: (01752) 233190 Fax: (01752) 233194

Bayliss, P. J., BSc MEd PhD Sr. Lectr., Post-16 Education and Training

Bennett, R. J., BEd Sr. Lectr., Partnership and Information Communication Technology

Berry, J. S., BSc PhD Prof., Mathematics Education

Burghes, D. N., BSc PhD   Prof.

Burnett, J. V., MEd   Programme Dir., Steiner-Waldorf Educn.

Caldock, S. J., BSc   Sr. Lectr., Primary Science Education

Carrington, V. M., BEd PhD   Prof.; Assoc. Dean, Teaching and Learning

Chilcott, E., BA MA   Sr. Lectr., Post Compulsory Education (PCET)

Cutting, R., BA PhD   Sr. Lectr., Environmental Studies

Dowdall, C. A., BA   Sr. Lectr., Language and Literacy Education

Dyer, A. J., BSc MPhil   Assoc. Dir., Centre for Sustainable Futures

Exley, S., BA   Sr. Lectr., Post Compulsory Education (PCET)

Fallows, M. D., BSc MSc   Principal Lectr., Academic Standards

Friend, M., BA MA   Sr. Lectr., Art and Design Education

Gabriel, N. R., BA DPhil   Sr. Lectr., Early Childhood Studies

Gale, K. J., BA MA   Sr. Lectr., Post-16 Education

Gatrell, M. J., MEd   Sr. Lectr., Mathematics Education

Gelder, U. I., BA PhD   Sr. Lectr., Early Childhood Studies

Gibson, S., BA MPhil PhD   Sr. Lectr., Education Studies (Disability and Inclusion)

Gompertz, S. B., BSc   Sr. Lectr., Science Education

Hannan, A. W., MA PhD   Prof.

Hayes, D., BSc MEd PhD   Reader

Hindle, M., MA   Sr. Lectr., Mathematics Education

Howarth, S., MA   Principal Lectr.

Hull, P. J., BSc   Sr. Lectr., Music in the Expressive Arts

Kelly, P. A., BA MEd PhD   Sr. Lectr., Learning Communities

Knowler, H. L., BEd   Sr. Lectr.

Lambert-Heggs, W., BSc   Sr. Lectr., Post Compulsory Education

Lawson, H. A., BA MA PhD   Principal Lectr.

Lee, C. G., BEd MEd PhD   Dir., Continuing Professional Devel.

Lewis, J. P., BEd MEd   Principal Lectr.

MacKenzie, R. N., BPhil MPhil PhD   Principal Lectr.; Chair, Contextual Studies in Educn.

Macleod-Johnstone, E. E., BA   Sr. Lectr., Post-16 Education

Markham, T. D., BEd   Sr. Lectr.; Academic Support Tutor

Martin, K. E., BA MEd   Programme Dir., Post-16 Educn. and Training

Martin, W. E., BSc MSc   Sr. Lectr., Post-16 Education

McBurnie, W., MA   Principal Lectr.

McQueen, T. J., BA   Sr. Lectr., Post-16 Education and Training

Mepham, T. M., BA   Sr. Lectr., Steiner Waldorf Education

Murphy, M., BEd MA   Sr. Lectr.

Nichol, J. D., BA PhD   Prof.

Noon, P. D., BA BEd MA   Sr. Lectr., Information and Communication Technology in Education

Norman, P. R., BA MBA   Sr. Lectr.

Pagett, L. M., BEd MEd   Sr. Lectr., Language and Literacy

Parker, M. C., BA   Sr. Lectr.

Parker-Rees, R., BA MPhil   Principal Lectr., Early Childhood Studies

Pittman, M., BEd MPhil   Sr. Lectr.

Pratt, N. M., BA   Principal Lectr.; Programme Dir., PGCE

Rea, A. T., BA MA   Sr. Lectr.

Reynolds, D., BSc   Prof.

Rogers, S. J., BA PhD   Sr. Lectr., Early Childhood Studies

Roscorla, R. B.   Sr. Lectr.

Rose, J. A., BA MA PhD   Sr. Lectr.; Academic Support Tutor

Savage, J. E., BEd PhD   Sr. Lectr., Early Childhood Studies

Selby, D. E., BA PhD   Prof., Education for Sustainability

Sharma, B., MA   Sr. Lectr., Jazz Studies/Contemporary World Music

Smith, R. M.   Sr. Lectr., Mathematics

Smith, V. M., BA PhD   Sr. Lectr., Early Childhood Studies

Taylor, G. T., BA MEd PhD   Dir., Continuing Professional Devel.

Teagle-McQueen, G. L., BSc MEd   Sr. Lectr., Post-16 Education and Training

Townsend, M. T., BA   Sr. Lectr., Information and Computer Technology Education

Tucker, V. J.   Sr. Lectr., Post Compulsory Education

Waters-Adams, S. L., BSc MPhil PhD   Principal Lectr., Science Education

Wheeler, S., BSc   Sr. Lectr., Information and Computer Technology

Willan, J. E. A., BEd MEd   Sr. Lectr., Early Childhood Education

Woods, M. S.   Sr. Lectr., Primary Mathematics Education

Woods, P. E., BA MPhil PhD   Prof.

Wright, D. L., BSc MA   Dir., Undergrad. and Initial Teacher Educn.

Zaman, F. F., BSc   Sr. Lectr., Primary Science Education

Other Staff: 1 Assoc. Principal Lectr.; 9 Assoc. Sr. Lectrs.; 3 Lectrs.; 1 Res. Fellow

Research: core curriculum (literacy, maths and science); early childhood studies; higher education values; inclusion and special educational needs; values, citizenship and global education

E-Health Research Group

Tel: (01752) 233886
E-mail: r.jones-5@plymouth.ac.uk
Research: e-health technology

Engineering, School of

Tel: (01752) 233664 Fax: (01752) 232638

Azizi, F., MSc PhD   Sr. Lectr., Geomechanics

Barlow, J. W., BSc   Sr. Lectr., Stress Analysis

Bell, M. A., BEng MSc   Principal Lectr.

Borthwick, M. F.   Sr. Lectr., Civil Engineering

Bullock, G. N., BSc PhD   Prof., Civil and Coastal Engineering

Chadwick, A. J., BSc MSc PhD   Prof., Coastal Engineering

Dai, Y. M., BEng PhD   Sr. Lectr., Marine Technology

De Wilde, P. J. C. J., MSc PhD   Sr. Lectr., Sustainable Construction

Donohoe, S. W., BSc LLB LLM MSc   Sr. Lectr.

Dyson, P. K., BSc MSc PhD   Sr. Lectr., Marine Technology

Easterbrook, D. J., BSc   Sr. Lectr., Civil and Structural Engineering

Goodhew, S. M. R., BSc MSc PhD   Sr. Lectr., Building

Grieve, D. J., BSc PhD   Deputy Head

Grove, S. M., BSc MPhil PhD   Sr. Lectr.

Hall, W., BEng PhD   Sr. Lectr., Design, CAD and CAE

Holgate, P. R.   Sr. Lectr., Land Management

Hunt, A. C., BSc PhD   Sr. Lectr.

Miles, M. E., BSc MPhil   Sr. Lectr., Mechanical Engineering

Otta, A. K., MA PhD   Sr. Lectr., Coastal Engineering

Paterson, T., BSc   Sr. Lectr., Mechanical Engineering

Plane, D. C., BSc PhD   Sr. Lectr., Engineering Materials

Rafiq, M. Y., BSc MSc PhD   Sr. Lectr., Civil and Structural Engineering

Reeve, D. E., BSc PhD   Prof., Coastal Dynamics

Riley, M. J., BSc PhD   Prof.; Head*

Simmonds, D. J., BA MSc PhD   Sr. Lectr., Coastal Engineering

Singh, M. M., BA MSc PhD   Sr. Lectr.

Steuwer, A., MPhil PhD   Sr. Lectr.

Summerscales, J., BSc MSc PhD   Reader, Composites Engineering

Sutton, R., BEng(Tech) MEng PhD, FIMechE, FIEE   Prof., Control Systems Engineering; Head*

Turpin-Brooks, S. D., BSc MPhil   Sr. Lectr., Building Surveying

Wigginton, M., BA MA   Prof.

Zou, Q., PhD   Sr. Lectr., Coastal Engineering

Other Staff: 2 Res. Fellows; 1 Res. Project Manager

Research: coastal engineering and dynamics; engineering management in construction and manufacturing; innovative structures, composites and materials; marine and industrial dynamics; sustainable building (technology, construction and design)

Geography, School of

Tel: (01752) 233053 Fax: (01752) 233054

Bailey, I. G., BA MSc PhD   Principal Lectr., Human Geography

Brassley, P. W., BSc PhD   Sr. Lectr.

Brayshay, V. M., BA PhD   Reader

Charlton, C. A., BA   Principal Lectr.

Charman, D. J., BSc PhD   Prof.

Croot, D. G., BA PhD   Teaching Fellow

Essex, S. J., BA PhD   Principal Lectr.

Gehrels, W., BSc PhD   Reader, Sea-Level Studies

Gibb, R. A., BSc DPhil   Reader, Geographical Sciences

Hodder, R. N. W., BA MPhil PhD   Reader

Kent, M., BA MSc PhD   Prof., Biogeography

Masselink, M., BSc PhD   Reader, Coastal Geomorphology

Mather, A. E., BSc PhD   Principal Lectr., Physical Geography

Newnham, R. M., BSc MSc PhD   Reader

Petticrew, E. L., BSc MSc PhD   Sr. Lectr., Physical Geography

Rahman, S., BSc MSc PhD   Sr. Lectr., Rural Development

Roberts, C. N., BA PhD   Prof.; Head*

Sims, P. C., BSc MSc   Deputy Head

Ternan, J. L., BA PhD   Reader, Geography

Warren, M. F., BSc MSc   Dir., Rural Futures

Whitehead, I. R., MA MSc   Principal Lectr., Estate Management

Williams, A. G., MSc PhD   Reader, Soil and Water Management

Williams, J. J., BSc PhD   Sr. Lectr., Physical Geography

Wilson, G. A., MA PhD   Prof., Human Geography

Wise, M., BA MA DPhil   Principal Lectr., Political Geography

Yarwood, R. B., BA PhD   Sr. Lectr., Human Geography

Other Staff: 2 Lectrs.; 1 Res. Fellow

Research: biogeography and environmental management; developing areas; European economic and social change; quaternary environments; rural economy and society

Health Professions, School of

Tel: (01392) 219774 Fax: (01392) 435357

Abey, S., BSc   Sr. Lectr., Podiatry

Achilles, A., BSc   Principal Lectr.; Head of Programmes, Podiatry

Bishop, G. R., MA   Head, Occupational Therapy

Bruce, M. A., BSc MPhil   Sr. Lectr.

Collard, K., BSc MSc PhD   Head, Medical Services

de Looy, A. E., BSc PhD   Prof.; Head of Programmes, Dietetics

Dominey, M. E., MSc   Scheme Co-ordinator, Pre-Registration Midwifery

Doris, F. E., MEd   Head, Allied Health Professions and Midwifery

Drew, J. M., BSc MEd   Sr. Lectr.

Fisher, M. L., BSc   Sr. Lectr., Health Studies and Midwifery

Gunn, H. J.   Sr. Lectr., Physiotherapy

Haas, B. M., BA BSc   Head of Programmes, Physiotherapy

Hough, A. D.   Sr. Lectr., Physiotherapy

Hughes, J. L., BA MSc   Sr. Lectr.

Hunter, H. D., BSc MSc   Sr. Lectr.,
Physiotherapy
Hurst, J. E., MSc   Sr. Lectr.
James, A., BSc MSc   Sr. Lectr., Midwifery
Johnson, S. C., MSc   Sr. Lectr.
Leigh, A.   Sr. Lectr.
Leverett, C., BSc MSc   Sr. Lectr., Podiatry
Lewy, L., BSc MA   Principal Lectr.,
Interprofessional Learning
Llywelyn, D. E. M., BSc   Sr. Lectr., Midwifery
McGahey, T. A.   Sr. Lectr., Physiotherapy
Morris, J. M., BSc PhD   Principal Lectr.,
Health Studies Research
Mounter, C. R., BEd   Principal Lectr.
Nicholls, L. C., BA MSc   Sr. Lectr., Midwifery
Parkin, T. A., BA   Sr. Lectr., Diatetics Practice
Paul, B. A., BSc   Deputy Head
Redwood, R. A., BSc MA   Sr. Lectr./
Practitioner, Midwifery
Roberts, A. E., MSc PhD   Sr. Lectr.
Russell, F. J., BSc   Sr. Lectr.
Sheaff, W. R., BA PhD   Prof., Health Services
Research
Taylor, C. E., BA MSc   Sr. Lectr., Occupational
Therapy
Thoburn, A., BSc   Sr. Lectr., Health Studies/
Midwifery
Useh, U., BSc MEd PhD   Sr. Lectr.,
Physiotherapy
Wells, T. J., MA   Sr. Lectr., Midwifery
Wright, L., BSc   Sr. Lectr., Health Studies/
Midwifery
Other Staff: 10 Sr. Lectrs.; 8 Lectrs.
Research: communication in health; family and
well-being; implementing evidence based
healthcare; psychological aspects of health
and well-being; user involvement

Humanities, School of

Tel: (01392) 475009 *Fax*: (01392) 475012
Bennett, G. H., BA PhD   Head*
Caleshu, A. P., BA MA PhD   Sr. Lectr., English
and Creative Writing
Christofides, R., BA PhD   Sr. Lectr., English
Education
Daybell, J. R. T., BA MA PhD   Sr. Lectr., Early
Modern History
Farr, S. E., BA MA   Sr. Lectr., English
Jacobs, M. E., BA MA   Sr. Lectr.
Jefferys, K., BA PhD   Prof.; Deputy Head
Lawley, P. A., BA PhD   Sr. Lectr., English
Lopez, A. C., BA PhD   Prof., Poetry
Moore, D. R., MA PhD   Sr. Lectr., English
Peel, R. W., BEd MA PhD   Principal Lectr.;
Integrated Masters Programme/MA Co-
ordinator
Smart, N., BA PhD   Sr. Lectr., History
Smith, A. K., BA MA PhD   Sr. Lectr., English
Tingle, E., BA DPhil   Sr. Lectr., Early Modern
History
Williams, R. J., BA PhD   Sr. Lectr., History
Other Staff: 4 Lectrs.
Research: creative writing; critical writing in
English literature; eighteenth-century
history and literature; modern Anglo-
American political and military history
writing; modern music and culture

English and Creative Writing

Tel: (01752) 238131 *Fax*: (01752) 238102
E-mail: t.lopez@plymouth.ac.uk
Research: contemporary poetry; early modern
literature; eighteenth century and
Romanticism; modern drama; modernism
and postmodernism

History

Tel: (01752) 238122
E-mail: k.jefferys@plymouth.ac.uk
Research: British and American biographies of
the twentieth century; British government
and politics during the inter-war years;
British military history since 1914; crime
and popular culture in eighteenth- and
nineteenth-century England; political
history of the USA since 1914

Mathematics and Statistics, School of

Tel: (01752) 232720 *Fax*: (01752) 232780
Aron, A., MSc PhD   Reader, Continuum
Mechanics
Cai, Y., BSc MSc PhD   Sr. Lectr., Statistics
Christopher, C. J., BA PhD   Sr. Lectr.,
Mathematics
Clinton, N. C., BSc MSc   Sr. Lectr.,
Mathematics
Crocker, G. R., BSc PhD   Sr. Lectr., Statistics
Davies, J. M., BSc PhD   Sr. Lectr.,
Mathematics
Eales, J. D., MSc PhD   Sr. Lectr., Statistics
Graham, D., BSc PhD   Principal Lectr.
Graham, E., BSc PhD   Sr. Lectr.
Heinzl, T.   Sr. Lectr., Theoretical Physics
Henley, W. E., BA MSc PhD   Sr. Lectr.,
Statistics
Huggett, S. A., BSc MSc DPhil   Reader,
Mathematical Physics
James, P. W., BSc PhD   Prof.; Deputy Head
Lavelle, M. J., BSc PhD   Principal Lectr.
McMullan, D., BSc PhD   Reader
Moyeed, R. A., BSc MSc PhD   Sr. Lectr.,
Operational Research
Sanders, H. P., BSc   Sr. Lectr., Statistics
Shaw, S. R., BSc MSc PhD   Sr. Lectr.
Stander, J., MA PhD   Principal Lectr.
Watkins, A. J., BSc DPhil   Principal Lectr.;
Faculty Franchise Manager
Wilton, D. T., BA MSc MSc DPhil   Head*
Wright, D. E., BSc MSc PhD   Reader, Applied
Statistics
Yu, K., BSc MPhil PhD   Sr. Lectr., Statistics
Other Staff: 2 Res. Fellows
Research: applied fluid dynamics; biostatistics
and epidemiology; mathematics education;
particle physics; theoretical magnetic
recording

Media and Photography, School of

Tel: (01392) 475222 *Fax*: (01392) 475234
Grant, J. M., BA   Sr. Lectr., Visual Arts
Hilton, D. E., BA MA   Sr. Lectr., Media Arts
Honeywill, P. W. N., BA   Sr. Lectr., Visual
Arts
Lewin, A., BA MA   Sr. Lectr., Visual Arts
Morstang, H. C., BA MA   Sr. Lectr.,
Photography
Nicol, E. J.   Head*
Rodrigues, C. A. J., BA   Sr. Lectr., Media
Southam, J. V.   Reader, Photography
Stancer, P. P., BA MA   Sr. Lectr., Electronic
Media
Standing, S. P., BA PhD   Deputy Head
Wells, E. Y., BSc MA   Principal Lectr., Media
Arts
Other Staff: 3 Assoc. Sr. Lectrs.; 3 Lectrs.
Research: European project (land and water);
experimental film and video; independent
film in the South West; media arts;
photographic arts (landscape and
evironment)

Neuroscience

Centre for Theoretical and Computational
Neuroscience
Borisyuk, R., BSc MSc PhD   Prof.,
Computational Neuroscience
Denham, M. J., BSc PhD   Prof., Adaptive and
Neural Computation
Harris, C. M., BSc MA MSc PhD   Prof.
Other Staff: 3 Res. Fellows

Nursing and Community Studies, School of

Tel: (01752) 233795 *Fax*: (01752) 233829
Bennallick, M., BSc MSc   Sr. Lectr., Health
Studies (Adult)
Borlase, J., MSc   Sr. Lectr.
Bradbury, M. C., BSc MSc   Sr. Lectr., Nursing
(Adult)
Cadman, C., MEd   Sr. Lectr.
Campbell, H. B., BA MSc   Macmillan Sr.
Lectr., Macmillan
Chambers, M. A., BSc MSc   Academic Lead,
Child Health

Clay, G., BA MSc   Sr. Lectr., Health Studies
(Adult Community)
Coleman, C. L., BSc   Sr. Lectr., Nursing
(Adult)
Cooper, S. J. R., BA PhD   Sr. Lectr., Nursing
Studies
Cornock, M. A., BA BSc   Academic Lead, Law
in Health Care
Doman, M. J., BA MSc   Sr. Lectr.
Dryden, R. J., BSc MSc   Sr. Lectr., Health
Studies (Adult)
Earl, D. N., BSc   Sr. Lectr., Nursing (Adult)
Gillard, M. R., MSc   Sr. Lectr., Nursing
(Adult)
Goodman, L. S. B., BSc MSc   Sr. Lectr., Health
Studies (Adult)
Green, G. H., BSc MSc   Sr. Lectr., Nursing
(Adult)
Griffith, J., MSc   Sr. Lectr., Nursing (Adult)
Grigg, E., BA MA   Sr. Lectr., Nursing (Adult)
Hambridge, K., BSc MSc   Sr. Lectr., Nursing
(Adult)
Hanks, C. M., BSc MSc   Academic Lead,
Health Studies, Care of Older People
Haydon, J. C., MSc   Sr. Lectr., Nursing
(Adult)
Hennessy, C. H., BA MA PhD   Chair, Public
Health and Ageing
Hide, K. M., BSc MEd   Sr. Lectr., Operating
Department Practice
Humphreys, A. J., PhD   Deputy Head, Pre-
registration
Hyde, V. M., MSc   Academic Lead, Primary
Care
Jenkin, A. M., BSc   Sr. Lectr., Health Studies
Jenkinson, T. P., BSc MSc   Sr. Lectr., Nursing
(Adult)
Jones, S. E., MSc   Sr. Lectr., Nursing
Kane, A. L., BSc   Sr. Lectr., Nursing (Adult)
Keitley, N.   Sr. Lectr., Operating Department
Practice
Kelsey, J. A., BA BSc MSc   Student Co-
ordinator
Kerslake, D. H., BSc   Sr. Lectr.
Kevern, J. J., BSc MSc   Sr. Lectr.
McConnon, A. M. G., BPhil   Sr. Lectr.,
Nursing (Adult)
McEwing, G. A., MSc   Sr. Lectr., Paediatric
Nursing
Millward, J. M., BA   Sr. Lectr., Nursing
(Adult)
Murray, J. K., BA   Sr. Lectr./Practitioner,
Health Studies
Nelmes, P., BSc MSc   Sr. Lectr., Critical Care
Nursing
Nesbitt, A., BA BSc MSc   Sr. Lectr., Health
Studies
Nichols, A. T., MA   Sr. Lectr., Nursing Studies
Pooler, J. K.   Sr. Lectr., Primary Care/Public
Health
Proctor-Childs, T. G., BSc   Sr. Lectr., Nursing
(Adult)
Pufahl, E., BSc   Sr. Lectr., Nursing (Adult)
Richardson, J., BSc PhD   Reader, Nursing and
Health Studies
Skirton, H., MSc PhD   Reader, Health Genetics
Slade, D. R., BSc   Sr. Lectr., Nursing (Adult)
Strange, F., BSc MA   Sr. Lectr., Nursing
Studies
Temple, J. A., MA   Primary Lead, Adult Pre-
registration Competency Curriculum
Thornton-Parr, D. J., BSc MA   Sr. Lectr.,
Nursing (Adult)
Twose, S. J., MSc   Locality Academic Dir.
Wade, M., BSc   Sr. Lectr., Health Studies/
Nursing and Midwifery
Waring, A. M., BA MSc   Sr. Lectr., Health
Studies and Nursing (Adult)
Watts, A. M., BA   Sr. Lectr., Nursing (Adult)
Webb, C., BA MSc PhD   Prof., Health Studies
White, S. J., MSc   Sr. Lectr., Nursing (Adult)
Williamson, G. M., MA   Sr. Lectr., Nursing
(Adult)
Wilson, G. J., BSc MSc   Sr. Lectr.
Winfield, L., BSc MSc   Sr. Lectr., Nursing
(Adult)
Woodward, V. A., BSc   Sr. Lectr., Community
Work and Social Policy

Wright, E. M., BA MSc   Sr. Lectr., Cancer
Education
Young, K. M., MSc   Sr. Lectr., Nursing
(Adult)
Other Staff: 6 Sr. Lectrs.; 2 Lectrs.; 1 Res.
Fellow; 1 Student Co-ordinator; 2 Clin.
Facilitators
Research: communication in health; family and
well-being; implementation of evidence
based healthcare; professional and
employment issues; user involvement

Peninsula Medical School

Tel: (01752) 238000 Fax: (01752) 238001
Bakheit, A. M., MSc PhD   Prof., Neurological
Rehabilitation
Barton, A. G., BA MA PhD   Principal Lectr.,
Healthcare Research Methodology
Bishop, J. P., BSc MSc   Principal Lectr.,
Medical Ethics and Law
Bleakley, A. D., BSc DPhil   Principal Lectr.,
Clinical Education
Bligh, J. G., BSc MMEd MD, FRCGP   Prof.,
Inst. of Clin. Educn.
Bristow, D. R., BSc MPhil PhD   Dir.,
Academic Studies; Reader, Pharmacology
and Clinical Education
Campbell, J. L., BSc   Chair, General Practice
and Primary Care
Cooper, N. A., BSc MEd   Pathway Lead, MSc
Clin. Educn.
Demaine, A. G., BSc PhD   Prof., Biomolecular
and Cellular Sciences
Elzubeir, M. A., BA PhD   Dir., Problem Based
Learning
Hanemann, C. O., PhD   Assoc. Lectr.; Chair,
Clinical Neurobiology
Hobart, J. C., BSc PhD   Sr. Lectr., Clinical
Neuroscience
Logan, G. S., MB ChB MSc MSc, FRCPCH
Dir., Health and Soc. Care Res.; Prof.,
Paediatric Epidemiology
Macleod, K., BA MD, FRCP, FRCPEd   Dir.,
Clin. Studies
Oldham, J., BSc BSc   Sr. Lectr./Assoc. Lectr.
Pinching, A. J., BM BCh MA DPhil, FRCP
Prof.; Assoc. Dean (Cornwall)
Sneyd, J. R., BA MA MB BChir MD, FRCA
Assoc. Dean; Prof., Anaesthesia
Somerville, M., PhD   Dir., Public Health
Learning
Stein, K., MSc   Dir., Peninsula Technol.
Group; Sr. Lectr., Public Health
Strobel, S., MD PhD, FRCP   Dir., Postgrad.
Clin. Educn.; Chair, Peninsula Postgrad.
Health Inst.
Sweeney, K. G., MA MPhil   Module Leader
Wilkin, T. J.   Prof., Endocrinology and
Metabolism
Yang, B. M., MSc   Sr. Lectr., Molecular
Medicine
Zajicek, J. P., BA MA PhD   Prof., Clinical
Neuroscience
Other Staff: 1 Academic Fellow; 13 Res.
Fellows; 1 Resource Centre Manager; 1 Sr.
Clin. Tutor; 10 Clin. Skills Tutors; 6 Clin.
Facilitators; 4 Community Clin. Teachers
Research: cardiovascular; community health and
health services; diabetes and metabolism;
molecular genetics; neuroscience

Plymouth Business School

Tel: (01752) 232800 Fax: (01752) 232853
E-mail: enquiry@pbs.plym.ac.uk
Agarwal, S. J., BA PhD   Principal Lectr.,
Tourism Management
Aulakh, G. S., BSc MSc PhD   Sr. Lectr., Rural
Development
Badger, B. A., BSc   Principal Lectr.
Bell, D. E., BA MA   Head of English Lang.
Centre; Principal Lectr., English as a Foreign
Language
Bell, P. R., BA MA PhD   Principal Lectr.
Bishop, D. C., BA PhD   Sr. Lectr., Modern
Languages
Boston, J. A., BA   Sr. Lectr.; Co-ordinator,
Taught Postgrad. Programmes

Brand, S. J., BA PhD   Principal Lectr.,
Economics
Brooks, N. R., BSc   Sr. Lectr.
Busby, G. D., BA MSc   Sr. Lectr., Tourism
Management
Butel, L. H., BA MA   Sr. Lectr., Corporate
Strategy
Butts, S., BA MA PhD   Sr. Lectr., Tourism
Management
Challacombe, J. A.   Sr. Lectr., Maritime Studies
and International Logistics
Chaston, I., BSc MBA PhD   Prof., Marketing
and Entrepreneurship
Cook, A. P., BA MA PhD   Sr. Lectr.,
Manpower Studies
Curtis, A. J., BSc PhD   Sr. Lectr., Business
Policy and International Business
De Andres Martinez, C., BA MBA PhD   Sr.
Lectr., Operations Management
Dinwoodie, M., MA MEd PhD   Principal
Lectr.
Driver, C., BA MBA PhD   Sr. Lectr.,
Operations Management
Dyke, E. G. L., BSc MSc   Sr. Lectr., Financial
Accounts
Edwards, P. H., BA   Sr. Lectr., Modern
Languages
El Refaie, E., MEd PhD   Sr. Lectr., Languages
for Business (German)
Fisher, S. J., BSc   Sr. Lectr.
Garland, D. Y., BA MPhil   Sr. Lectr.
Gervais-Le Garff, M., MA PhD   Deputy Dir.
Gibson, P., MEd   Sr. Lectr., Hospitality
Management
Gripaios, P. A., BA MSc   Prof., Applied
Economics
Guijarro-Fuentes, P., BA PhD   Sr. Lectr.,
Spanish
Head, D. W., BA MA MPhil   Prof.; Dir.*
Hope, J. E., BA MA DPhil   Sr. Lectr., Modern
Languages
Kaler, J. H., BA MA   Principal Lectr., Business
Ethics and Governance
Kyaw, K., MSc PhD   Sr. Lectr., Finance
Lean, J. W. L., BA PhD   Sr. Lectr., Strategic
Management
Leat, M. J., BSc MSc   Head, Subject Group,
Human Res. Management
Leybourne, S. A., BSc PhD   Sr. Lectr., Human
Resource Management
Lowes, R., BA MEd   Sr. Lectr., English as a
Foreign Language (EFL)
Masterson, D., BA MEd   Sr. Lectr., English as
a Foreign Language (EFL)
McIntyre, J., MSc   Teaching Fellow
McVittie, E., BA PhD   Head, Subject Group,
Economics
Mishra, A., BA MA PhD   Sr. Lectr., Strategic
Management
Moizer, J. D., MSc PhD   Sr. Lectr., Business
Operations and Strategy
Nicholas, P. A., BA BSc BPhil MSc   Sr. Lectr.,
Economics
O'Mahoney, K. P., BSc   Sr. Lectr., Accounting
and Finance
Padfield, D. R.   Sr. Lectr., Languages
Pearson, E., BSc MA   Sr. Lectr., Manpower
Studies
Pointon, J., BA BSc PhD   Prof., Finance
Rainbow, S. W., BA MSc   Acting Deputy Dir.
Roe, M. S., BA MSc PhD   Prof., Transport
Shepherd, D. B., BSc MSc   Co-ordinator,
Taught Programmes/HND and Degree
Smith, D., BSc MBA   Sr. Lectr., Business
Operations Strategy
Song, D. J., BSc   Sr. Lectr., Business
Management and Marketing
Stacey, S. G., BA MA   Sr. Lectr., International
Logistics
Towler, M. J., BSc MA PhD   Sr. Lectr.,
Operations Management and Business
Decision Making
Turner, D. M., BA   Sr. Lectr., Hospitality
Management
Villoria-Nolla, M. T., BA MA   Sr. Lectr.,
Spanish
Wang, A., BSc   Sr. Lectr., Economics

Ward, T., BSc MEng   Sr. Lectr., International
Port Management
Whisker, P. M., BSc PhD   Sr. Lectr.,
Economics
White, J. E., BA   Sr. Lectr., Marketing
Williams, J. E. M., BA PhD   Sr. Lectr.,
Marketing
Winch, G. W., BSc PhD   Prof., Business
Analysis
Wright, P. G., BSc MSc   Principal Lectr.,
International Shipping and Logistics
Other Staff: 2 Assoc. Sr. Lectrs.; 14 Lectrs.; 1
Teraching Fellow; 1 Quality Assurance Co-
ordinator
Research: corporate finance; human resource and
organisational studies; organisational
learning; regional economics; tourism and
hospitality management

Psychology, School of

Tel: (01752) 233157 Fax: (01752) 233176
Andres-Benito, P., MSc PhD   Sr. Lectr.
Auburn, T., BSc MSc PhD   Sr. Lectr.
Benenson, J., BSc PhD   Reader
Chung, M. C., BA PhD   Principal Lectr.
Coventry, K. R., BSc PhD   Reader
Edworthy, J., BA PhD   Prof., Applied
Psychology
Ellis, R. C., BA BSc PhD   Principal Lectr.
Evans, J. S. B. T., BSc PhD   Head*
Gee, P., BSc PhD   Sr. Lectr.
Handley, S. J., BSc PhD   Reader
Hellier, E. J., BSc PhD   Reader
Hyland, M. E., BSc PhD   Prof., Health
Psychology
Jacobs, P. A., BSc MSc   Sr. Lectr.,
Occupational/Organisational Psychology
Markovits, H., BSc MSc   Prof.
Mazzoni, G., BA PhD   Reader
Parmentier, F. B. R., PhD   Sr. Lectr.
Perfect, T. J., BSc PhD   Prof., Experimental
Psychology
Reid, F. J., PhD   Dir., Taught Programmes
Rose, D. H., BSc PhD   Sr. Lectr.
Roser, M., MA PhD   Sr. Lectr.
Schnall, S., BA MA PhD   Sr. Lectr.
Verde, F. F.   Sr. Lectr.
Walsh, C., BA PhD   Sr. Lectr.
Wyer, N. A., MA PhD   Sr. Lectr.
Other Staff: 4 Lectrs.; 7 Res. Fellows
Research: applied psychology and human factors;
cognitive psychology and cognitive
neuropsychology; developmental
psychology; health psychology; psychology
of vision and action

Sociology, Politics and Law, School of

Tel: (01752) 233275 Fax: (01752) 233206
Anderson, A., BA PhD   Principal Lectr.
Annison, C. J., BA PhD   Deputy Head
Asthana, S., BA PhD   Prof., Health Policy
Barton, A. J., BA MSc PhD   Sr. Lectr.,
Criminal Justice Studies
Cappi, P. A., LLB LLM   Sr. Lectr., Law
Childs, P. A., BA MA   Sr. Lectr., Law
Clark, A. G., LLB PhD   Principal Lectr., Law
Coomber, R. P., BA MSc PhD   Principal Lectr.,
Sociology
Cordell, K., BSc PhD   Principal Lectr., Politics
Corrigan, O. P., BA PhD   Sr. Lectr., Sociology
Cunliffe, S. A., BA PhD   Principal Lectr.,
Politics
David, M., BSc MA PhD   Sr. Lectr., Sociology
Davies, R. J., MA DPhil   Sr. Lectr.,
International Relations
Dunne, G. A., BA PhD   Sr. Lectr., Sociology
Gilling, D. J., BA PhD   Principal Lectr.,
Criminal Justice Studies
Gray, P. M., MA PhD   Principal Lectr.,
Criminal Justice Studies
Green, A. J., BA PhD   Sr. Lectr., Research
Methods
Harris, C. E., LLB LLM   Sr. Lectr., Law
Heristchi, C., BA PhD   Sr. Lectr., International
Relations
Hull, C. W., LLB LLM   Sr. Lectr., Law
Hyde, M. B., BA PhD   Principal Lectr., Social
Policy

Letherby, G., BA PhD   Prof., Sociology
Lowther, J., LLB LLM   Sr. Lectr., Law
Mawby, R. I., BA MSc PhD   Prof.,
 Criminology and Criminal Justice
Meethan, K., BA PhD   Principal Lectr.,
 Sociology
Payne, S. J., LLB   Head*
Peterson, A. R., BA MA PhD   Prof., Sociology
Rallings, C., BA MSc PhD   Prof., Politics
Sellick, J., LLB LLM   Sr. Lectr., Law
Sheaff, M. J., BA MA PhD   Sr. Lectr.,
 Sociology
Shears, P. G., BA LLB LLM   Dir., Professional
 Legal Studies
Stevenson, K. A., LLB PhD   Sr. Lectr., Law
Sundaram, J. N., LLM   Sr. Lectr., Maritime
 Law
Sutton, C. D., BSc MSc   Sr. Lectr.
Tamaki, T., BA MSc PhD   Sr. Lectr.,
 International Relations
Tant, A. P., BA PhD   Sr. Lectr., Politics
Thrasher, M. A. M., BA PhD   Prof., Politics
Williams, M., BA MSc   Prof., Social Research
 Methodology
Wilton, J. F., BA MA PhD   Sr. Lectr., Politics
Other Staff: 2 Assoc. Sr. Lectrs.; 8 Lectrs.; 3
 Res. Fellows
Research: electoral studies; European politics and
 political systems; international relations and
 peace-building; law and criminal justice;
 sociology of health, exclusion and work

Teaching and Learning Development

Brown, A., BEd MScN   Head, Advisory
 Services
Burkill, S. M., BA   Head, Educnl. Devel.
Fitzgerald, V., BA   Head, Access and
 Widening Participation
Lintern, M. A., BSc MSc   Head, Learning
 Devel. and Guidance
Sterling, S. R., BSc PhD   Principal Lectr.;
 Schumacher Reader
West, R. L., BA MA PhD   Sr. Lectr.
Other Staff: 1 Devel. Advisor (Res.); 1 Devel.
 Advisor (Learning); 1 Co-ord., Widening
 Participation; 1 Music Tutor; 2 Educnl.
 Developers
Vacant Posts: 1 Sr. Lectr.; 1 Resource Devel.
 Officer

SPECIAL CENTRES, ETC

Adaptive Behaviour and Cognition Research Group

Tel: (01752) 232559
 E-mail: a.cangelosi@plymouth.ac.uk
Research: categorical perception and language;
 cognitive and neural modelling; evolution of
 language and cognition; symbol grounding
 and embodied cognition; synthetic brain
 imaging

Ageing, Research into

Tel: (01752) 238810
 E-mail: catherine.hennessy@plymouth.ac.uk
Research: social and healthcare issues for older
 people

Anaesthesia Research Group

Tel: (01752) 238010 Fax: (01752) 238001
 E-mail: pamela.frost@pms.ac.uk
Research: acute and chronic pain; effects of
 carbon monoxide on the heart; effects of
 hyperbaric oxygen on blood components;
 pharmacokinetics and pharmacodynamics;
 structure and function of human cilia

Analytical Chemistry, Centre for Research in

Tel: (01752) 233038 Fax: (01752) 233039
 E-mail: echarles@plymouth.ac.uk
Hill, S. J., BSc PhD   Head*
Other Staff: 15 Staff Members

Applied Health Genetics Group

Tel: (01823) 366911 Fax: (01823) 366901
 E-mail: heather.skirton@plymouth.ac.uk
Research: information and support for parents
 making decisions on antenatal screening for
foetal abnormality; interactive emotional
 tools in genetics for midwives; needs and
 coping strategies of people who care for a
 family member with Huntington's disease;
 perception of causes and prevention of birth
 defects; web-based learning tools for health
 professionals

Architecture and the Built Environment

includes Centre for Earthen Architecture

Tel: (01752) 233610
 E-mail: rachel.sara@plymouth.ac.uk
Research: architectural conservation; architectural
 education; architectural history; humane
 architecture; sustainable settlements and
 technology

Auditory Cognition Group

Tel: (01752) 233138
 E-mail: j.edworthy@plymouth.ac.uk
Research: applying visual cognition models to
 auditory cognition; relationship between
 audition and action; role of semantics and
 acoustics in sound representation

Biogeochemistry and Environmental Analytical Chemistry (BEACh)

Tel: (01752) 233048
 E-mail: miranda.keith-roach@plymouth.ac.uk
Research: atmospheric trace element transport
 and biogeochemistry; biogeochemistry of
 nutrients, trace elements and anthropogenic
 radionuclides; coastal and oceanic iron
 cycling; ecosystem functioning; elemental
 speciation

Catchment and Coastal Environments Group

Tel: (01752) 233061 Fax: (01752) 233054
 E-mail: m.kent@plymouth.ac.uk
Research: coastal processes and ecosystems,
 particularly those characteristics of muddy,
 sandy and gravel coasts and estuaries;
 environmental degradation; hydrological
 processes linked to soil water movement
 and catchment sediment dynamics; plant
 ecology and biogeography

Cell and Molecular Biology Research Group

Tel: (01392) 262944 Fax: (01392) 403027
 E-mail: jackie.whatmore@pms.ac.uk
Research: cancer biology; neuroscience; vascular
 biology

Child Health Group

Tel: (01392) 403146 Fax: (01932) 403158
 E-mail: john.tripp@pms.ac.uk
Research: behaviourally effective sex and
 relationships education; contraception and
 reproductive health in the UK; family
 breakdown and parental support; managing
 diabetes for young people; perinatal and
 early chidhood deaths

Childhood, Studies of

Tel: (01395) 255402 Fax: (01395) 255303
 E-mail: r.parker-rees@plymouth.ac.uk
Research: child protection; education; play; social
 policy; sociology

Clinical Microvascular Research Group

Tel: (01392) 403064 Fax: (01392) 403027
 E-mail: tina.lewis@pms.ac.uk
Research: disease states; ethnic differences in
 microvascular function; genetics and
 vascular function; normal physiology;
 vascular permeability

Clinical Neurobiology Research Group

Tel: (01752) 437418
 E-mail: oliver.hanemann@pms.ac.uk
Research: brain tumours; cytoskeletal function;
 motor neurone disease; neuronal migration

Clinical Neurology Research Group

Tel: (01752) 315250
 E-mail: cannabis-trial@pms.ac.uk
Research: epidemiology of multiple sclerosis; use
 of cannabinoids in multiple sclerosis

Coastal Engineering Research Group

Tel: (01752) 233680 Fax: (01752) 232638
 E-mail: a.chadwick@plymouth.ac.uk
Chadwick, A. J., BSc MSc PhD   Prof.; Head*
Other Staff: 4 Sr. Lectrs.; 3 Res. Fellows; 2 Sr.
 Managers; 5 Staff Members
Research: coastal and estuarine processes; flood
 and coastal protection; flood risk;
 morphodynamics; sediment dynamics

Coastal Processes Research Group

Tel: (01752) 232416 Fax: (01752) 232406
 E-mail: alex.nimmo.smith@plymouth.ac.uk
Research: boundary layer dynamics and
 turbulence; coastal process modelling;
 coastal systems; cohesive and non-cohesive
 sediment dynamics; natural coastlines,
 beaches and estuaries

Cognitive and Behavioural Neurology Research Group

Tel: (01392) 208581
 E-mail: amy.norris@pms.ac.uk
Research: impairment of memory in epilepsy;
 neurological and conceptual basis of
 consciousness; neuropsychiatry;
 spinocerebellar ataxia type 8; visual imagery
 deficits

Cognitive and Neural Systems Modelling Research Group

Tel: (01752) 232559
 E-mail: a.cangelosi@plymouth.ac.uk
Research: computational neuroscience;
 connectionist (neural network) cognitive
 modelling

Communication and Learning Technologies Team

Tel: (01752) 232532
 E-mail: n.witt@plymouth.ac.uk
Research: online delivery of continuing
 professional development for marine
 engineers; student progress and transfers;
 web accessibility

Communications Group

Tel: (01752) 233513 Fax: (01752) 232512
 E-mail: mosa@plymouth.ac.uk
Research: advanced modulation and coding
 techniques; code division multiple access
 and spread spectrum technigues; mobility
 schemes and network protocols in 3G
 wireless communication networks and
 beyond; multimedia communications in 3G
 wireless networks and beyond; smart
 antenna and software radio for future land
 mobile communication systems

Complementary Medicine Group

Tel: (01392) 424989 Fax: (01392) 427562
 E-mail: edzard.ernst@pms.ac.uk
Research: acupuncture for osteoarthritis;
 acupuncture in alcohol dependence; herbal
 remedies for chronic obstructive pulmonary
 disease, allergic rhinitis and sinusitis;
 progressive muscle relaxation for
 performance anxiety; t'ai chi for chronic
 conditions

Computer Music Research, Interdisciplinary Centre for

Tel: (01752) 232532
 E-mail: eduardo.miranda@plymouth.ac.uk
Research: computer-aided musical composition;
 generative music; interaction and control;
 robotics and music; software sound
 synthesis

Corporate Finance Group

Tel: (01752) 232865
 E-mail: john.pointon@plymouth.ac.uk
Research: corporate performance; European
 finance; small-firm finance; stochastic
 modelling; tax harmonisation

Crime, Deviance and Society Programme

Tel: (01752) 233208
E-mail: r.mawby@plymouth.ac.uk
Research: local community justice policies

Critical Spaces

Tel: (01392) 254370
E-mail: m.f.miles@plymouth.ac.uk
Research: built and social architectures of alternative settlements; digital curating; digital deconstructions of authorship; reconsidering Lefebvre; sites of social memory

Curriculum, Pedagogy and Educational Change

Tel: (01752) 235521
E-mail: john.berry@plymouth.ac.uk
Research: computers and hand-held technology; environmental education; innovative pedagogy in science teaching; science education and spirituality; student beliefs and perceptions of mathematics

Darwin Innovation and the Creative Industries

Tel: (01392) 475101
E-mail: jeremy.diggle@plymouth.ac.uk

Development and Disability Research Group

Tel: (01752) 233143
E-mail: john.clibbens@plymouth.ac.uk
Research: developmental disabilities

Digital Art and Technology, Institute of (i-DAT)

Tel: (01752) 232549 Fax: (01752) 232540
E-mail: m.phillips@plymouth.ac.uk

Ecotoxicology and Stress Biology Research Centre

Tel: (01752) 232904 Fax: (01752) 232970
E-mail: t.galloway@plymouth.ac.uk
Research: ecotoxicology; molecular and cell biology; physiology and behaviour; regeneration and repair

Emergency, Critical and Intensive Care Group

Tel: (01752) 233864
E-mail: simon.cooper@plymouth.ac.uk
Research: auditory alarms; paediatric studies; resuscitation and emergency care

Endocrinology and Metabolism Research Group

Tel: (01752) 792552 Fax: (01752) 792471
E-mail: linda.voss@pms.ac.uk
Research: pre-diabetes

Engineering Management Group

Tel: (01752) 232573 Fax: (01752) 232646
E-mail: s.goodhew@plymouth.ac.uk
Research: efficient building and constructions; manufacturing and business systems; new building

Environmental and Fluid Modelling Group

Tel: (01752) 233021
E-mail: p.matthews@plymouth.ac.uk
Research: behaviour of pollutants and nutrients in soil; development of environmentally benign catalysts; modelling of high-performance filters for environmental, industrial and medical applications; modelling of processes involved in the production of high-performance carbonate-based paper coatings; void structure and pore-fluid modelling software

Environmental Building and Construction Group

Tel: (01752) 232573 Fax: (01752) 232646
E-mail: m.riley@plymouth.ac.uk
Research: construction education; cultural elements of construction teams; sustainable construction

Epidemiology and Public Health Group

Tel: (01392) 406751 Fax: (01392) 406767
E-mail: alison.hurst@pms.ac.uk
Research: early disability in middle-aged and elderly people; policy issues in the evaluation of genetic tests for complex conditions; role of genetic markers in ageing

European Studies Research Group (ESRG)

Tel: (01752) 232891
E-mail: pedro.guijarro@plymouth.ac.uk
Research: European culture and society; language and identity; transnational communication in the European context

Food, Nutrition and Health Research Group

Tel: (01752) 233365
E-mail: s.davies@plymouth.ac.uk
Research: animal health; animal nutrition; aquaculture; crop physiology; dietetics

Geodynamics and Palaeomagnetism Research Group

Tel: (01752) 233120 Fax: (01752) 233117
E-mail: a.morris@plymouth.ac.uk
Research: active tectonics, earthquake hazards and risk; engineering geology and landslide risk assessment; magmatism and volcanism; structural controls on mineral resources; tectonic processes at plate boundaries

Geomatics Research Group

Tel: (01752) 232460 Fax: (01752) 232406
E-mail: s.lavender@plymouth.ac.uk
Research: application of earth observation data to climate change; development of renewable energy in the south-west United Kingdom; ecological and biological variability within the Celtic shelf-sea and Atlantic ecosystems; new visualisation techniques to improve the provision of hydrographic data; prediction of pollutant fluxes and environment vulnerability in the UK coastal zone

Governance Network

Tel: (01752) 233274
E-mail: john.dixon@plymouth.ac.uk
Research: governance of business; governance of communities; governance of public sector organisations; governance of the individual; governance of the non-profit sector

Health and Psychology Research

Tel: (01752) 233157
E-mail: m.hyland@plymouth.ac.uk
Research: evaluation of self-help for mild to moderate mental health problems; health of older women; placebo response and hypnosis; post-traumatic stress; psychological aspects of complementary and alternative medicine (CAM) including spirituality

Health Complexity Group

Tel: (01392) 264916 Fax: (01392) 264714
E-mail: susanne.hughes@pms.ac.uk
Research: achieving sustainable change

Health Group

Tel: (01752) 233220 Fax: (01752) 233202
E-mail: a.peterson@plymouth.ac.uk
Research: auto-ethnography and health; clinical trials; ethnicity in the NHS; evaluation of local health interventions; evidence-based public health

Hepatology Research Group

Tel: (01752) 792725 Fax: (01752) 792240
E-mail: matthew.cramp@phnt.swest.nhs.uk
Research: hepatitis C virus infection

Human Centred Systems Design Research Group

Tel: (01752) 232551
E-mail: f.reid@plymouth.ac.uk
Research: multimedia learning environments; support of engineering applications; support of health care teams; work systems in organisations

Human Factors Group

Tel: (01752) 233174
E-mail: e.hellier@plymouth.ac.uk
Research: computer-mediated design-support systems used by engineering and architectural design teams; design, evaluation and psychological relevance of visual and auditory warnings; how people understand and react or respond to warnings and risk information; medical risk information and patient safety and the presentation of civil and environmental risk information to the general public; psychological impact of mobile text messaging by teenagers and young adults

Human Resource Management and Organisation Studies Group

Tel: (01752) 232849
E-mail: mike.leat@plymouth.ac.uk
Research: human resources development; international comparative studies; organisational analysis; organisational learning; team working

Hypoglycaemia Research Group

Tel: (01392) 403081 Fax: (01392) 403027
E-mail: kenneth.macleod@pms.ac.uk
Research: accident rates in diabetes; counter-regulatory responses to hypoglycaemia in people with reactive hypoglycaemia; counter-regulatory/cognitive response to hypoglycaemia in type-2 diabetes; frequency of hypoglycaemia in diabetics

Immunology Research Group

Tel: (01752) 792417
E-mail: edward.kaminski@phnt.swest.nhs.uk
Research: autoimmunity; chimerism in bone marrow transplantation; human leukocyte antigen (HLA) and disease associations; transplantation immunology; tumour immunology

Inclusive Education and Stability Research Group

Tel: (01752) 255493
E-mail: jenny.lowe@plymouth.ac.uk
Research: behaviour management; curriculum reform on global education principles in Kazakhstan and central Asia; holistic vision of professional practice and educational change; special education needs and disability; transient families

Inflammation and Musculoskeletal Diseases Research Group

Tel: (01392) 262929 Fax: (01392) 262926
E-mail: paul.winyard@pms.ac.uk
Research: inflammation and vascular dysfunction; nervous system mechanisms of musculoskeletal pain and dysfunction

Information Storage Technology, Centre for Research in

Tel: (01752) 232570
E-mail: d.mapps@plymouth.ac.uk
Mapps, D. J., BEng PhD, FIP, FIEEE   Prof.; Head*
Other Staff: 3 Principal Lectrs.; 3 Sr. Lectrs.; 2 Lectrs.
Research: disk-head flying height modelling; multi-level turbo codes for magnetic recording; multi-track thin film write-read-

write head; spin transport in nanoscale thin film devices; ultra high-density optical recording

Interactive Intelligent Systems, Centre for

Tel: (01752) 232532
E-mail: eduardo.miranda@plymouth.ac.uk
2 Principal Lectrs.; 5 Sr. Lectrs.; 2 Profs.; 2 Readers
Research: design of innovative computing and IT systems requiring different approaches to systems architecture and interaction; interactions between humans and machines

International Shipping and Logistics, Centre for

Tel: (01752) 232412 Fax: (01752) 232249
E-mail: m.roe@plymouth.ac.uk
Research: Greece as a logistics gateway to south-eastern Europe and the Black Sea; international logistics and the role of shipping and ports; international supply-chain management in developing and transitional economies; logistics developments and policy in the EU, eastern Europe and the Far East; maritime, logistics and transport policy in eastern Europe

International Studies and Development Research Group

Tel: (01752) 233073
E-mail: r.gibb@plymouth.ac.uk
Research: globalisation, development and transformation; security, peacekeeping and humanitarianism

Land/Water and the Visual Arts

Tel: (01752) 238155 Fax: (01752) 238151
E-mail: e.wells@plymouth.ac.uk
Research: landscape studies

Language and Cognitive Development Group

E-mail: caroline.floccia@plymouth.ac.uk
Research: development of language and higher order cognitive processes such as reasoning and judgement; how children acquire the sound system of their native language, link sound to meaning and develop a representation of underlying syntax; role of pragmatics in the development of children's understanding of scalar terms

Law Group

Tel: (01752) 232844
E-mail: p.childs@plymouth.ac.uk
Research: business regulation (including consumer and employment law); corporate governance; environmental law

Learning and Teaching Group

Plymouth Business Group
Tel: (01752) 238440 Fax: (01752) 232862
E-mail: m.stone-2@plymouth.ac.uk
Research: generic business and management education; tourism and hospitality management education

Local Government Chronicle Elections, Centre for Research in

Tel: (01752) 233207 Fax: (01752) 232785
E-mail: d.cole@plymouth.ac.uk
Rallings, C., BA MSc PhD   Prof.; Co-Dir.*
Thrasher, M. A. M., BA PhD   Prof.; Co-Dir.*
Research: active civic participation; geography of turnout; local election results; metropolitan observatory; women in local politics

Long-Term Conditions and Rehabilitation Research Group

Tel: (01752) 238835 Fax: (01752) 233890
E-mail: jenny.freeman@plymouth.ac.uk
Research: diabetes; neurological (multiple sclerosis, stroke); respiratory diseases (chronic lung disease of prematurity)

Marine and Coastal Policy Research Group

Tel: (01752) 232463 Fax: (01752) 232406
E-mail: g.glegg@plymouth.ac.uk
Research: improved assessment; improvement of environmental education; management techniques and tools; participatory processes, policy and law; understanding global and regional pressures

Marine and Industrial Dynamic Analysis Group (MIDAS)

Tel: (01752) 232425 Fax: (01752) 232638
E-mail: r.sutton@plymouth.ac.uk
Sutton, R., BEng(Tech) MEng PhD, FIMechE, FIEE   Head*
Other Staff: 2 Principal Lectrs.; 2 Sr. Lectrs.; 1 Sr. Manager
Research: advanced control systems engineering theory; artificial intelligence; dynamics; industrial dynamics; multi-sensor data fusion

Marine Biology and Ecology Research Centre (MBERC)

Tel: (01752) 232967 Fax: (01752) 232970
E-mail: s.rundle@plymouth.ac.uk
Research: aquatic biodiversity and ecology; behavioural ecology; conservation biology and pollution; developmental plasticity and ecophysiology; global climate change

Marine Institute

Tel: (01752) 232407 Fax: (01752) 232406
E-mail: l.stott@plymouth.ac.uk
Research: biogeochemistry; dynamics, engineering and coastal change; marine biosciences and ecosystem dynamics; marine policy and maritime affairs

Marketing Strategy and Consumer Behaviour

Tel: (01752) 232821 Fax: (01752) 232249
E-mail: jasmine.williams@plymouth.ac.uk
Research: change management; enterprise; European studies; international business; regional economics

Mathematics Research Groups

Tel: (01752) 232721 Fax: (01752) 232780
E-mail: d.mcmullan@plymouth.ac.uk
Research: applied mathematics; industrial and engineering mathematics; particle physics; pure mathematics

Memory Group

Tel: (01752) 233157 Fax: (01752) 233362
E-mail: t.perfect@plymouth.ac.uk
Research: autobiographical memory and false memory; long-term memory and eyewitness memory; repetition priming; spatial memory; working memory and inhibitory function in memory

Mental Health Research Group

Plymouth
Tel: (01392) 475143
E-mail: p.farrand@plymouth.ac.uk
Research: primary care mental health; psychological interventions; self-help

Mental Health Research Group

Peninsula Medical School
Tel: (01392) 403462 Fax: (01392) 403445
E-mail: c.v.owens@exeter.ac.uk
Research: doctor-patient communication in the treatment of schizophrenia; identifying suicide hotspots; impact of post-modern cultural change on mental health service delivery; mental health needs of released prisoners; user and carer involvement in care planning

Meta.art Research Group

E-mail: robert.pepperell@plymouth.ac.uk
Research: metaphysical aspects of art and creative practice

Methodological Innovations Research Group

Tel: (01752) 233283
E-mail: m.williams@plymouth.ac.uk
Research: innovative methods and good methodological practice; sustainable research culture

Molecular Genetics Research Group

Tel: (01392) 402983 Fax: (01392) 403027
E-mail: a.t.hattersley@ex.ac.uk
Research: developmental eye movement disorders; developmental spinal disorders; familial hypoglycaemia; monogenic diabetes; permanent neonatal diabetes

Molecular Medicine Research Group

Tel: (01752) 437413
E-mail: andy.demaine@pms.ac.uk
Research: 'initiator' and 'progressor' genes for diabetic nephropathy; maternal factors influencing early childhood growth and implications for diabetes; molecular and cellular basis of stress and implications for disease; role of angiogenic factors in tumour and angiogenesis (renal cell carcinoma) and diabetic microvascular complications; role of pro-and anti-inflammatory mediators in acute allograft rejection and endothelial cell dysfunction

Network Research Group

Tel: (01752) 233521
E-mail: s.furnell@plymouth.ac.uk
Furnell, S. M., BSc PhD   Reader; Head*
Other Staff: 6 Sr. Lectrs.; 2 Lectrs.
Research: information system security; Internet and World Wide Web technologies and applications; mobile applications and services

Neurological Rehabilitation Research Group

Tel: (01752) 272481
E-mail: magid.bakheit@pcs-tr.swest.nhs.uk
Research: impairment of language function after stroke and its treatment; laboratory gait analysis; locomotor disability (study of muscle spasticity); use of botulinum toxin in neurological disease

Obesity and Lifestyle Research Group

Tel: (01752) 238817 Fax: (01752) 238873
E-mail: anne.delooy@plymouth.ac.uk

Organisational Learning and Health Sector Management, Group for

Tel: (01752) 232810
E-mail: ian.chaston@plymouth.ac.uk
Research: building learning partnerships; electronic mechanisms for learning; learning communities; learning in technology transfer; performance of firms

Palaeontology and Palaeoenvironments, Centre for

Tel: (01752) 233119 Fax: (01752) 233117
E-mail: g.price@plymouth.ac.uk
Research: biostratigraphy; ecology/palaeoecology; micropalaeontology; palaeobiology; palaeoceanography

Particle Physics Theory Group

Tel: (01752) 232721 Fax: (01752) 232780
E-mail: dmcmullan@plymouth.ac.uk
McMullan, D., BSc PhD   Head*
Other Staff: 1 Principal Lectr.; 2 Sr. Lectrs.
Research: quantum chromodynamics; strong sub-nuclear interaction

Performance and Reliability of Structures and Materials Research Group (PRISM)

Tel: (01752) 233300 Fax: (01752) 232632
E-mail: m.james@plymouth.ac.uk
Research: advanced composites manufacture; mechanical engineering and manufacture; rheology and fluid dynamics; structural

integrity and health monitoring; structures/ conceptual modelling

Petroleum and Environmental Geochemistry Research Group (PEGG)

Tel: (01752) 233013 Fax: (01752) 233035
E-mail: s.rowland@plymouth.ac.uk
Research: characterisation and geochemical fate of highly branched isoprenoids (HBIs); characterisation of the unresolved complex mixture (UCM) of hydrocarbons in petroleum feedstocks; environmental toxicology of petroleum hydrocarbons; origins and fate of organic nitrogen compounds from natural and sewage-related sources in the environment; uses of electrospray ionisation multistage mass spectrometry to identify polar environmental and geological chemicals

Philosophy in Art, Unit for the Study of (USOPIA)

Tel: (01392) 475101
E-mail: jeremy.diggle@plymouth.ac.uk
Research: philosophies in art

Planetary Collegium

Tel: (01752) 232532
E-mail: r.ascott@plymouth.ac.uk
Research: advancement of emergent art and architectural forms; science, technology and consciousness; telematic, interactive and technoetic media

Plymouth International Studies Centre (PISC)

Tel: (01752) 233204 Fax: (01752) 233206
E-mail: andrea.teti@plymouth.ac.uk
Research: international relations and human geography (construction and representation of security and developmental issues in the context of debates on globalisation); security and development, social justice and political identity

Plymouth Sustainable Architecture Research Unit (PSARU)

Tel: (01752) 233602
E-mail: m.wigginton@plymouth.ac.uk
Research: building metabolism; glass and glazing technologies; intelligent and interactive facade; very low energy architecture

Policy and Governance in Europe Group

Tel: (01752) 233781 Fax: (01752) 233054
E-mail: geoff.wilson@plymouth.ac.uk
Research: European integration and identity; multifunctional rural spaces in Europe; policy in Europe

Preventative and Supportive Care Programme

Tel: (01752) 233810
E-mail: catherine.hennessy@plymouth.ac.uk
Research: applied health genetics; limiting conditions; older adults

Primary Care Group

Tel: (01752) 764230 Fax: (01752) 764234
E-mail: julie.orr@pms.ac.uk
Research: acupuncture; financial assessment; mental health needs of released prisoners (role of the probation service); out-of-hours healthcare for cancer patients; suicide and self-harm prevention

Professional and Higher Education

Tel: (01395) 255368
E-mail: a.hannan@plymouth.ac.uk
Research: mentoring and supervision; partnerships and e-learning; policy and practice of teacher education; quality enhancement; widening participation

Professional and Organisational Issues Research Group

Tel: (01392) 475155
E-mail: ruth.endacott@plymouth.ac.uk
Research: health systems organisation and management; identifying risk of deterioration; preparing the future workforce

Quaternary Environments Group

Tel: (01752) 233065
E-mail: c.n.roberts@plymouth.ac.uk
Research: holocene sea-level change; palaeoecology and carbon cycling; peat and palaeoclimate; quaternary environmental change in New Zealand; testate amoebae and environmental change

Research and Development Support Unit

Tel: (01752) 315112
E-mail: susan.anderson@phnt.swest.nhs.uk
Research: housing and health; service organisation; women's reproductive health

Research and Innovation

Tel: (01752) 233411 Fax: (01752) 233411
Chudley, J., BSc PhD   Dir.*

Robotics and Intelligent Systems Group

Tel: (01752) 232566 Fax: (01752) 232540
E-mail: g.bugmann@plymouth.ac.uk
Bugmann, G. V. F., PhD   Prof.; Head*
Other Staff: 1 Principal Lectr.; 3 Sr. Lectrs.
Research: artificial vision sensing; biologically inspired control; human-robot interaction; intelligent, multi-agent behaviour; natural language interfaces

Science Education, Institute for (ISE)

Tel: (01752) 233015 Fax: (01752) 233035
E-mail: d.harwood@plymouth.ac.uk
Harwood, D. J., BSc PhD   Dir.*

Science, Risk and Representation Group

Tel: (01752) 233234
E-mail: a.anderson@plymouth.ac.uk
Research: construction of genetic risk; environmental risk and the media; genetics and gender; media portrayals of genetics/ biotechnologies; reproductive genetics

Shelf Sea Oceanography and Meteorology Research Group

Tel: (01752) 232470
E-mail: clare.oneill@plymouth.ac.uk
Research: comparative analysis of water mass distribution and circulation in semi-enclosed seas (White Sea and Irish Sea); dense water overflows off continental shelves (cascading); meso-scale physical and biogeochemical processes in coastal waters of the Russian Arctic; morphodynamics of estuarine systems in the UK (Teignmouth and Humber); recent/current climate of Greenland and relation with ice sheet mass balance

Signal Processing and Multimedia Communications Group

Tel: (01752) 232677
E-mail: cindy.goh@plymouth.ac.uk
Ifeachor, E. C., BSc MSc PhD   Prof., Intelligent Medical Systems; Head*
Other Staff: 1 Sr. Lectr.
Research: audio signal processing; biomedical informatics; multimedia communications over IP networks

Small Business and Enterprise Strategy Group

Tel: (01752) 232837
E-mail: phil.megicks@plymouth.ac.uk
Research: employee development; enhancement of small firms' performance through processes including computer-based modelling; entrepreneurial marketing;

formation of strategic alliances or networks and e-commerce

Social and Public Policy Group

Tel: (01752) 233246
E-mail: a.barton@plymouth.ac.uk
Research: governance; identity; pensions; poverty and inequality; risk

Social Evaluation, Research and Development Group (SERD)

Tel: (01752) 233268
E-mail: m.sheppard@plymouth.ac.uk
Research: adults and adult services; intervention with children and families; social exclusion; social work theory, knowledge and education

Social Psychology Group

Tel: (01752) 233134 Fax: (01752) 233362
E-mail: natalie.wyer@plymouth.ac.uk
Research: applied social psychology (human communication, group interaction and social influence); discursive social psychology (examination of social actions accomplished in discourse with emphasis on institutional contexts); emotions (influences of emotion on social cognition and memory, humour, stress and the regulation of negative emotions); social cognition (stereotyping and prejudice, motivational and cognitive influence on social judgement and behaviour)

Social Research and Regeneration Unit

Tel: (01752) 232747 Fax: (01752) 233813
E-mail: m.darch@plymouth.ac.uk
Research: applied social research; emerging social issues; labour market; market trends; role of work

SOLON Project

Society, Order, Law, Offences, Notoriety
Tel: (01752) 233689
E-mail: kim.stevenson@plymouth.ac.uk
Research: law and history; society and law

South West Economy Centre

Tel: (01752) 232827 Fax: (01752) 232247
E-mail: peter.gripaios@plymouth.ac.uk
Gripaios, P. A., BA MSc   Dir.*
Other Staff: 3 Principal Lectrs.; 2 Lectrs.; 1 Res. Asst.
Research: cluster evaluation; convergence; policy evaluation; regional modelling; sector studies

Speciation and Environmental Analysis Research Group (SEA)

Tel: (01752) 233040 Fax: (01752) 233040
E-mail: hevans@plymouth.ac.uk
Research: chemical and biological metrology using isotope dilution analysis and elemental tagging of molecules for protein quantitation; speciation analysis in the marine, estuarine and freshwater environments; uptake and bioavailability of trace elements and environmental pollutants

Statistics Group

Tel: (01752) 232726 Fax: (01752) 232780
E-mail: r.moyeed@plymouth.ac.uk
Research: biostatistics and epidemiology; computational statistics; environmental statistics; image analysis; non-parametric statistics

Strategic Management and Business Modelling Group

Tel: (01752) 233350
E-mail: jonathon.lean@plymouth.ac.uk
Research: application of system dynamics and system thinking to inform policy and management decision making; decision analysis; performance measurement; role of management information systems in decision support; small business strategy

Structures and Materials, Plymouth Research Institute for (PRISM)

Tel: (01752) 232650 Fax: (01752) 232650
E-mail: jsummerscales@plymouth.ac.uk
Summerscales, J., BSc MSc PhD   Head*
Other Staff: 5 Principal Lectrs.; 11 Sr. Lectrs.; 1 Lectr.; 2 Sr. Managers
Research: agronomy for natural fibre, generic waste management; fatigue (modelling, microscopy, spectroscopy); fibre-reinforced polymer composites design and manufacture; renewable energy generation systems and optimisation; rheology and computational fluid dynamics

Structures/Conceptual Modelling Group

Tel: (01752) 232662 Fax: (01752) 232638
E-mail: m.rafiq@plymouth.ac.uk
Rafiq, M. Y., BSc MSc PhD   Head*
Other Staff: 2 Sr. Lectrs.; 1 Sr. Manager
Research: application of adaptive and evolutionary search and optimisation techniques in building design; efficient building and constructions; improvement of the design process in line with the Eagan Report; novel and efficient decision support tools for design; visualisation of search and solution spaces

Sustainable Building Group

Tel: (01752) 233692 Fax: (01752) 232638
E-mail: sgoodhew@plymouth.ac.uk
Goodhew, S. M. R., BSc MSc PhD   Head*
Other Staff: 1 Reader; 1 Principal Lectr.; 3 Sr. Lectrs.; 1 Res. Fellow; 2 Sr. Managers
Research: listing process and building condition; sustainable building materials (production and use); sustainable buildings in use; sustainable composites and life cycle assessments; thermal and moisture performance of buildings

Teaching and Learning, Centre of Excellence in

Lea, S. J., BA MA MSc PhD   Prof.; Dir., Placement Learning in Health and Soc. Care
Selby, D. E., BA PhD   Prof.; Dir., Sustainable Futures
Stone, M. A., BA MSc   Dir., Higher Educn. Learning Partnerships (HELP)
Weaver, R. S., BA PhD   Dir., Experimental Learning

Teaching Mathematics, Centre for

Mathematics Education
Tel: (01752) 232772 Fax: (01752) 232780
E-mail: egraham@plymouth.ac.uk
Graham, E., BSc PhD   Head*
Other Staff: 1 Lectr.; 1 Sr. Manager; 1 Res. Asst.; 1 Lectr.†
Research: conceptual understanding in the teaching and learning of mechanics; philosophy of mathematics and education; teaching and learning; the influence of images and beliefs on student motivation and attitudes to learning; use of technology in the teaching and learning of mathematics

Terrestrial Ecology Research Group

Tel: (01752) 232913 Fax: (01752) 232970
E-mail: p.ramsay@plymouth.ac.uk
Research: biodiversity, conservation and sustainable management of the world's highest woodlands (Polylepis forest in the Andes of southern Peru); conservation of Euphrasia vigursii, an endemic plant of southwestern England; habitat complexity and biodiversity; novel composting techniques; plant functional types and mountain vegetation in Picos de Europa, Spain

Theatre and Performance Group

Tel: (01395) 255415
E-mail: r.mock@plymouth.ac.uk
Research: constructing performance texts and scores (playwriting, choreography, and devising processes); cultural identities in performance; interdisciplinary and cross-artform performance practice; the body in performance (dance-theatre, physical theatre); women's theatre and performance practice

Thinking and Language, Centre for

Tel: (01752) 233175
E-mail: clare.walsh@plymouth.ac.uk
Research: child language; decision making; human reasoning in both adults and children; hypothesis testing; probability judgement

Tourism and Hospitality Management Team

Tel: (01752) 238421
E-mail: s.agarwal@plymouth.ac.uk
Research: literary tourism; tourism and culture; tourism and local economic development; tourism and social exclusion; tourism innovations in a rural context

Vision and Action Research Group

Tel: (01752) 233140
E-mail: r.ellis@plymouth.ac.uk
Research: relations between visual objects and action; use of artificial neural networks in automating aspects of expert visual clarifications

CONTACT OFFICERS

Accommodation. Student Accommodation Manager: Simpson, M., BSc
(E-mail: m.simpson@plymouth.ac.uk)
Admissions (first degree). University Admissions Officer: Todd, C.
(E-mail: c.todd@plymouth.ac.uk)
Admissions (higher degree). Senior Administrator: Rivas, C., BSc MSc PhD
(E-mail: c.rivas@plymouth.ac.uk)
Alumni. Marketing Officer (Alumni): Liddington, R.
(E-mail: r.liddington@plymouth.ac.uk)
Careers. Head of Learning Development and Guidance: Lintern, M. A., BSc MSc
(E-mail: careers@plymouth.ac.uk)
Computing services. Director of Information and Learning Services: Holland, P. C., BA
(E-mail: p.holland@plymouth.ac.uk)
Credit transfer. Assistant University Secretary: Chapman, J. M., BA
(E-mail: j.chapman@plymouth.ac.uk)
Examinations. Assistant University Secretary: Chapman, J. M., BA
(E-mail: j.chapman@plymouth.ac.uk)
Finance. Deputy Vice-Chancellor and Director of Corporate Finance: Raikes, G., MBE, BA, FCIS
(E-mail: graham.raikes@plymouth.ac.uk)
Health services. Head of Advisory Services: Brown, A., BEd MScN
(E-mail: a.brown@plymouth.ac.uk)
International office. Director of International Office: Ingram, Peter, BSc MSc
(E-mail: intoff@plymouth.ac.uk)
Library (chief librarian). Director of Information and Learning Services: Holland, P. C., BA
(E-mail: p.holland@plymouth.ac.uk)
Library (enquiries). Head of Customer Services: Holland, P. C., BA
(E-mail: libraryservices@plymouth.ac.uk)
Marketing. Director of Marketing and Communications: Griffiths, J. P., BSc
(E-mail: j.p.griffiths@plymouth.ac.uk)

Personnel/human resources. Director of Personnel and Development: Buckley, R. D., FCIS (E-mail: personnel@plymouth.ac.uk)
Public relations. Head of Communications: Farrell, C. S., BA
(E-mail: c.s.farrell@plymouth.ac.uk)
Publications. Head of Communications: Farrell, C. S., BA
(E-mail: c.s.farrell@plymouth.ac.uk)
Quality assurance and accreditation. Head, Quality Support Unit: Jennett, S., BA MA
(E-mail: s.jennett@plymouth.ac.uk)
Safety. Safety Officer: Morton, D., BA
(E-mail: d.morton@plymouth.ac.uk)
Scholarships, awards, loans. Assistant Registrar (Student Funding): Morgan, G. R., BA (E-mail: g.morgan@plymouth.ac.uk)
Schools liaison. Schools and Colleges Liaison Officer: Ayer, N., BA
(E-mail: n.ayer@plymouth.ac.uk)
Security. Security Operations Manager: Harrison, P.
(E-mail: p.d.harrison@plymouth.ac.uk)
Sport and recreation. Head of Sport and Recreation: Coulton, L.
(E-mail: l.coulton@plymouth.ac.uk)
Staff development and training. Training Manager: Kan, J.
(E-mail: staffdevelopment@plymouth.ac.uk)
Staff development and training. Development Officer, Educational Developer: Carkett, R., BSc (E-mail: r.carkett@plymouth.ac.uk)
Student welfare/counselling. Head of Advisory Services: Brown, A., BEd MScN
(E-mail: a.brown@plymouth.ac.uk)
Students from other countries. Director of International Office: Ingram, Peter, BSc MSc
(E-mail: p.ingram@plymouth.ac.uk)
Students with disabilities. Head of Disability ASSIST Services: Waterfield, J. H., MEd
(E-mail: j.waterfield@plymouth.ac.uk)

CAMPUS/COLLEGE HEADS

Bicton College. (Tel: (01395) 562300; Fax: (01395) 567502) Principal: Sadler, P., BEd MA
City of Bristol College, Brunel Centre, Ashley Down Road, Bristol BS7 9BU. (Tel: (0117) 904 5000; Fax: (0117) 949 6648; E-mail: keith.elliott@cityofbristol.ac.uk) Principal: Elliott, K., BSc MSc
Cornwall College. (Tel: (01209) 611611; Fax: (01209) 611612) Principal: Latham, J.
East Devon College. (Tel: (01884) 235200; Fax: (01884) 235262) Principal: Edwards, M.
Exeter College. (Tel: (01392) 205222; Fax: (01392) 210282) Principal: Atkins, R.
Highlands College. (Tel: (01534) 608608; Fax: (01534) 608600) Principal: Sallis, E., BSc(Econ) MA(Soc) MA PhD
North Devon College. (Tel: (01271) 345291; Fax: (01271) 388121) Principal: Dodd, D., MSc
Penwith College. (Tel: (01736) 335000; Fax: (01736) 335100) Principal: Andruszko, R.
Plymouth College of Further Education. (Tel: (01752) 385300; Fax: (01752) 385098) Principal: Gillespie, V.
Somerset College of Arts and Technology. (Tel: (01823) 366366; Fax: (01823) 366418) Principal: Scott, A., BA, FRSA
South Devon College. (Tel: (01803) 540540; Fax: (01803) 540541) Principal and Chief Executive: Maxwell, H.
Truro College. (Tel: (01872) 267000; Fax: (01872) 267100) Principal: Burnett, J.
Weymouth College. (Tel: (01305) 208801; Fax: (01305) 208734) Principal: Moore, S., BA MSc

[Information supplied by the institution as at 15 August 2006, and edited by the ACU]

UNIVERSITY OF PORTSMOUTH

Founded 1992

Member of the Association of Commonwealth Universities

Postal Address: University House, Winston Churchill Avenue, Portsmouth, England PO1 2UP
Telephone: (023) 9284 8484 **Fax:** (023) 9284 3082 **E-mail:** admissions@reg.port.ac.uk
URL: http://www.port.ac.uk

VICE-CHANCELLOR*—Craven, Prof. John A. G., BA Camb., MA Camb., Hon. DSc Tech.U.Malaysia
PRO-VICE-CHANCELLOR—Arrell, David J., BSc St And., MSc Oxf., PhD St And.
PRO-VICE-CHANCELLOR—Bunting, Rebecca, MA Lond.
PRO-VICE-CHANCELLOR—Turner, Prof. John D., BSc Reading, PhD Reading
CLERK TO THE BOARD OF GOVERNORS AND UNIVERSITY SECRETARY—Hartley, Sally, BA Wales(Swansea)
DIRECTOR OF FINANCE—Woollard, Emma

GENERAL INFORMATION

History. Originally established in 1869 as Portsmouth and Gosport School of Science and Arts, the university was inaugurated in 1992.
The main campus is situated in the centre of Portsmouth.

Admission to first degree courses (see also United Kingdom Introduction). Through Universities and Colleges Admissions Service (UCAS). Minimum requirement: 2 GCE/VCE A level passes and 3 General Certificate of Secondary Education (GCSE) subjects at grade C or above in differing subjects. Some courses will require students to have more than the minimum entry requirements including qualifications in specific subjects. International Applicants whose first language is not English will be required to demonstrate a suitable level of proficiency in the language.

First Degrees (see also United Kingdom Directory to Subjects of Study). BA, BEng, BSc, LLB, MEng, MPharm.
Extended BA, BEng, BSc: 4 years full-time or 5 years sandwich.
Length of course. Full-time: BA, BEng, BSc, LLB: 3 years; MEng, MPharm: 4 years.

Higher Degrees (see also United Kingdom Directory to Subjects of Study).
Master's. LLM, MA, MArch, MBA, MPhil, MS, MSc.
Admission. Applicants for admission to master's degrees must normally hold an appropriate first degree with at least second class honours.
Length of course. Full-time: MArch: 0½ years; LLM, MA, MBA, MSc: 1 year; MPhil, MS: 2 years. Part-time: LLM, MA, MBA, MSc: 2–3 years; MPhil, MS: 3 years.
Doctoral. DBMS, DChiro, DMedImaging, DNursing, DPharm, DSW, MD, PhD.
Admission. Applicants for admission to doctoral degrees should hold an appropriate master's degree (which must have included research training) or other equivalent qualifications or professional experience.
Length of course. Full-time: MD: 2 years; PhD: 3 years. Part-time: DBMS, DChiro, DMedImaging, DNursing, DPharm, DSW: 3–5 years; MD: 4 years; PhD: 6 years.

Libraries. Volumes: 397,884. Periodicals subscribed to: 17,684. Other holdings: 1500 audio-visual items. Special collections: European Documentation Centre; Statistics; Law.

Academic Year (2007–2008). Three terms; two semesters: Term dates: 1 October–14 December; 7 January–14 March; 31 March–6 June. Semester dates: 1 October–8 February; 11 February–6 June.

Statistics. Staff (2007): 3355 (1508 academic, 1847 non-academic). Students (2007): full-time 14,577 (8082 men, 6495

women); part-time 5050 (2364 men, 2686 women); international 1877; undergraduate 15,573 (8230 men, 7343 women); master's 3486 (1880 men, 1606 women); doctoral 526 (313 men, 213 women).

FACULTIES/SCHOOLS

Creative and Cultural Industries
Tel: (023) 9284 5452 Fax: (023) 9284 5192
E-mail: simon.claridge@port.ac.uk
Dean: Claridge, Simon, BSc CNAA, PhD CNAA

Humanities and Social Sciences
Tel: (023) 9284 6012 Fax: (023) 9284 6254
E-mail: david.russell@port.ac.uk
Dean: Russell, David, BA Manc., MSc Lond.

Portsmouth Business School
Tel: (023) 9284 4058 Fax: (023) 9284 4059
E-mail: ann.ridley@port.ac.uk
Dean: Ridley, Ann, BA Witw., LLB Lond., LLM Lond.

Science
Tel: (023) 9284 3007 Fax: (023) 9248 3335
E-mail: david.hughes@port.ac.uk
Dean: Hughes, David J., BSc Leic., PhD Manc., FGS

Technology
Tel: (023) 9284 2012 Fax: (023) 9284 2584
E-mail: timothy.goodhead@port.ac.uk
Dean: Goodhead, Timothy, BA Nott., MSc Reading, MPhil Reading, MSc Portsmouth

ACADEMIC UNITS

Accounting and Law
Tel: (023) 9284 4095 Fax: (023) 9284 4037
Al-Hawamdeh, Ahmed, LLB Jordan, LLM Aberd., PhD Leic.   Sr. Lectr.
Andrew, Peter, MBA Portsmouth, PhD Lond.   Sr. Lectr.
Baden-Powell, Imogen, BA Oxf., MA Oxf., LLM Lond.   Sr. Lectr.
Bennett, Michael, BA CNAA, LLM Lond., PhD S'ton.   Principal Lectr.
Bevington, Alexandra, BA Kent   Sr. Lectr.
Bowhill, Bruce N., BSc Bath, MBA Portsmouth   Principal Lectr.
Callaghan, Clare, BCom N.U.I., MSc S'ton.   Head*
Carney, Damian, BA Lond., PhD Sheff.   Sr. Lectr.
Conrad, Lynne, BA CNAA, MA Essex, PhD Essex   Principal Lectr.
Davey-Evans, Sue, BA CNAA   Sr. Lectr.
Daynes, Arief, BA Auck., MA Auck., PhD Well.   Sr. Lectr.
Dockery, Everton, BA CNAA, MA Leic., PhD Essex   Sr. Lectr.
Gillies, Annette, MBA Portsmouth   Sr. Lectr.
Graham, Alan, BA Oxf., MA Oxf., FCA   Sr. Lectr.
Hicks, James R., BSc Stan., MSc Stan., DPhil Oxf.   Sr. Lectr.
Hines, Anthony C., BSc Bath, MSc Wales   Principal Lectr.

Major, Robert, BSc Sheff.   Sr. Lectr.
Maniruzzaman, Munir, PhD Camb.   Prof., International and Business Law
Page, Michael J., BA Camb., MA Camb., PhD S'ton., FCA   Halpern and Woolf Prof., Accounting
Sekhon, Piratpal, BA Nott.Trent   Sr. Lectr.
Sparrow, Claire, MA St And.   Sr. Lectr.
Strevens, Caroline, LLB Exe.   Principal Lectr.
Toon, Ian, BSc Portsmouth   Sr. Lectr.
Welch, Roger D., LLB Lond., LLM Lond., MPhil Lond.   Principal Lectr.
Willett, Caroline, BA Birm.   Principal Lectr.
Yarr, Margaret, BSc Open(UK)   Sr. Lectr.
Other Staff: 4 Assoc. Sr. Lectrs.; 3 Lectrs.
Research: corporate governance and financial regulation; employment and industrial relations law; financial reporting; international business law

Architecture, School of
Tel: (023) 9284 2083 Fax: (023) 9284 2087
Baker, Kate   Principal Lectr.
Blott, Dan, BArch CNAA   Sr. Lectr.
Cole, Pamela, BA CNAA   Sr. Lectr.
Farrelly, Lorraine, BA CNAA   Principal Lectr.
Hodson, Peter, BA Virginia, MA Virginia   Sr. Lectr.
Mesher, Lynne, BA Wales   Sr. Lectr.
Pearce, Martin L., BA CNAA   Principal Lectr.
Teeling, Catherine, BA Oxf.Brookes, MSc E.Lond.   Sr. Lectr.
Tuson, Elizabeth-Marie, BArch Glas., MArch Glas., PhD Portsmouth   Sr. Lectr.
Wakefield, Tod, BA CNAA   Head*
Weguelin-Yearley, Mary, BA Kent   Principal Lectr.
Yearley, David, BA CNAA   Assoc. Sr. Lectr.
Other Staff: 4 Assoc. Sr. Lectrs.

Art, Design and Media, School of
Tel: (023) 9284 3801 Fax: (023) 9284 3808
Balogh, Eva, BA Portsmouth   Sr. Lectr.
Batey, Jackie, BA Brighton, MA Brighton, PhD Brighton   Assoc. Sr. Lectr.
Bridge, David, MA Brighton   Sr. Lectr.
Bromwich, Hans, BA CNAA, MDes RCA   Sr. Lectr.
Bull, Stephen, BA Sur., MA Sur.   Sr. Lectr.
Cavusoglu, Ergin, MA Lond.   Sr. Lectr.
Clarke, Simon, BA Newcastle(UK)   Principal Lectr.
Coleman, Heather, BA CNAA   Assoc. Sr. Lectr.
Coleman, Robert, MA Portsmouth   Sr. Lectr.
Dauppe, Michèle-Anne, BA Sheff.Hallam, MA Leeds   Principal Lectr.
Denham, Andrew, BA Liv., MA Middx.   Sr. Lectr.
Devine, Ken, BA CNAA, MA Brighton   Principal Lectr.
Garcia, David   Prof., Design/Digital Cultures
Golya, Christopher, BA CNAA   Sr. Lectr.
Hakim-Dowek, Leslie, BA CNAA   Assoc. Sr. Lectr.
Harrison, Judy, BA CNAA, MA RCA   Principal Lectr.
Harvey, Edward   Sr. Lectr.
Hayworth, Roger   Sr. Lectr.

Houghton, Sarah, BA Portsmouth, MA Portsmouth
Sr. Lectr.
Jenkins, David, BA CNAA, MA Manc.Met.
Principal Lectr.
Kochberg, Searle, BSc Lond., MA CNAA, MA
Lond. Sr. Lectr.
Lamburn, Louise Sr. Lectr.
Matheson, Iacob, BA CNAA Sr. Lectr.
Milligan, Barbara, BA Leeds Head*
Molyneux, John, BA S'ton., PhD S'ton. Sr.
Lectr.
Newland, Paul, BArch CNAA, PhD CNAA Sr.
Lectr.
Noble, Susan, BA CNAA, MA Brighton Sr. Lectr.
O'Neill, Maureen, BA CNAA, MA Brighton Sr.
Lectr.
Palacios, Eva, BA Westminster Sr. Lectr.
Povey, Martin, BSc Wolv. Sr. Lectr.
Sonnet, Esther, BA CNAA, MA Nott., PhD Nott.
Principal Lectr.
Sparshott, Ingrid, BA CNAA Sr. Lectr.
Tidbury, Roger, MSc Bourne. Sr. Lectr.
Toal, Damian, BA Brighton Assoc. Sr. Lectr.
Way, Mark Sr. Lectr.
Wright, Robert, MA Brighton Sr. Lectr.
Young, Jane, BA Brist., MA Brighton Sr. Lectr.
Other Staff: 6 Assoc. Sr. Lectrs.; 6 Lectrs.; 2
Assoc. Lectrs.
Research: creative industries and cultural policy;
multi-sensory interactive environments;
narrative, memory and identity; negotiating
cultural boundaries and territories; web-
based knowledge management

Biological Sciences, School of

Tel: (023) 9284 2033 Fax: (023) 9284 2070
E-mail: bioadmin@port.ac.uk
Armbruster, Scott, BA Calif., MSc Calif., PhD
Calif. Prof., Ecology and Evolution
Cragg, Simon M., BSc Wales, PhD Wales, FLS,
FIWSc Principal Lectr.
Farnham, Bill F., BSc Liv., MSc Wales, PhD
CNAA, FLS Sr. Lectr.
Firman, Keith, BSc Hull, PhD Newcastle(UK)
Reader, Molecular Biotechnology
Gowers, Darren, BSc S'ton., PhD S'ton. Sr.
Lectr.
Greenwood, Richard, BSc Birm., PhD CNAA
Prof.
Guille, Matthew, BSc Lond., PhD Lond. Head*
Hebbes, Tim, BSc CNAA, PhD CNAA Sr. Lectr.
Kneale, Geoff, BSc Leeds, PhD Leeds Prof.;
Assoc. Dean (Research)
May, Eric, BSc Dund., PhD Dund. Reader,
Microbiology
McClellan, James A., BSc Edin., PhD Leeds Sr.
Lectr.
Mitchell, Julian I., BSc Liv., PhD Liv. Sr. Lectr.
Myers, Fiona, BSc CNAA, PhD Portsmouth Sr.
Lectr.
Peterkin, John H., BSc Liv., PhD Sheff. Sr.
Lectr.
Pickford, Andrew, DPhil Oxf. Sr. Lectr.
Powling, Andrew H., BSc Sheff., MSc Sheff., PhD
Constance Sr. Lectr.
Scarlett, Garry, BSc CNAA, PhD Portsmouth Sr.
Lectr.
Schubert, Frank, BSc Kiel, PhD Heidel. Sr. Lectr.
Sharpe, Colin, MA Oxf., DPhil Oxf. Sr. Lectr.
Thorne, Alan, BSc CNAA, PhD CNAA Reader,
Biochemistry
Waring, Colin, BSc Aberd., PhD H-W Sr. Lectr.
Watson, Gordon, BSc Newcastle(UK), PhD St And.
Sr. Lectr.
Other Staff: 1 Lectr.; 3 Sr. Res. Fellows; 6 Res.
Fellows; 6 Res. Assocs.; 1 Sr. Experimental
Officer
Research: biomolecular structure (protein-nucleic
acid interactions); biotechnology
(molecular design, nanotechnology, natural
products); chromatin and molecular
embryology; environmental biology
(environmental monitoring, microbiology,
pollution); marine biology (algae, fish
biology, invertebrates)

Computing, School of

Tel: (023) 9284 6403 Fax: (023) 9284 6364
E-mail: hos.comp@port.ac.uk
Adams, Carl, MSc S'ton., PhD S'ton. Principal
Lectr.
Adda, Mo, MSc Boumerdes, PhD Sur. Principal
Lectr.
Allan, G. W., BSc Reading, MA(Ed) Portsmouth,
PhD Portsmouth Sr. Lectr.
Anderson, C. David, BA Belf., PhD Belf.
Principal Lectr.
Bednar, Peter, BSc Lund, MPhil Lund Sr. Lectr.
Bennett, Alex, BA Lanc., MSc Portsmouth Sr.
Lectr.
Beresford, Roger A., BSc Lond., PhD S'ton.
Principal Lectr.
Bramer, Max A., BSc S'ton., PhD Open(UK),
FBCS, FIEE, FRSA Prof., Information
Technology
Briggs, Jim S., BA York(UK), DPhil York(UK)
Principal Lectr.
Chandler, Jane M., BSc Brun., MSc CNAA
Principal Lectr.
Crellin, Jonathan, BA Open(UK), PhD Open(UK)
Principal Lectr.
Delve, Janet, BSc Lond., MSc Lond., PhD Middx.
Principal Lectr.
Dingley, Kate, BSc Bourne., PhD Portsmouth Sr.
Lectr.
Duke-Williams, Emma, BSc Durh., MSc
Portsmouth Sr. Lectr.
Early, Gordon H., BSc CNAA Sr. Lectr.
Fitch, Tineke, MSc Portsmouth, PhD Portsmouth
Sr. Lectr.
Fletcher, Angela, BA CNAA, BSc Open(UK), MSc
CNAA Sr. Lectr.
Gegov, Alexander, BSc T.U.Sofia, MSc T.U.Sofia,
PhD Bulgarian Acad.Sc., DSc Bulgarian Acad.Sc.
Sr. Lectr.
Gnanayutham, Paul, BSc Greenwich, MSc
Lond.Guild. Sr. Lectr.
Hart, Penny, BA Oxf., MA Oxf., MSc Portsmouth
Sr. Lectr.
Hennell, Cheryl, MSc CNAA Sr. Lectr.
Jerrams-Smith, Jennifer, BSc Lond., MSc Birm.,
PhD Birm. Principal Lectr.
Jordanov, Ivan, MSc T.U.Sofia, PhD T.U.Sofia, BSc
Sr. Lectr.
Katos, Vasilios, MEng Thrace, MBA Keele, PhD
Aston Sr. Lectr.
King, Terry, BSc Manc., MSc Brad. Principal
Lectr.
Lester, C., BSc Hull, MSc Essex, PhD Lond.
Principal Lectr.
Millard, Peter, BSc Leic., MSc CNAA Sr. Lectr.
Moulton, Michael, BSc Portsmouth, MBA
Portsmouth Sr. Lectr.
Peart, Amanda, BSc Portsmouth Sr. Lectr.
Poole, Matthew, BSc Wales, PhD Wales Sr.
Lectr.
Poyner, Arthur, BSc Reading Sr. Lectr.
Rosbottom, J., BEd Manc., MEd Liv., MSc Lond.
Principal Lectr.
Tan, Jiacheng, BSc Jilin, MSc Xidian, PhD De
Mont. Sr. Lectr.
Topp, Robert G., BSc CNAA Principal Lectr.
Ward, Shelley, BSc Portsmouth Sr. Lectr.
Wilson, Annette, BSc CNAA Head*
Wilson, Steve, BSc CNAA Principal Lectr.
Other Staff: 1 Sr. Res. Fellow; 1 Assoc. Prof.; 1
Assoc. Lectr.
Research: complexity in system design; computer
vision; data mining and categorisation;
distributed systems; intelligent agents and
belief systems

Creative Arts, Film and Media, School of

Tel: (023) 9284 6132 Fax: (023) 9284 6132
Allen, Dave, BEd S'ton., MPhil CNAA, PhD S'ton.
Head*
Billingham, Peter, BA Open(UK), MA Leeds, PhD
Leeds Reader, Drama and Performance
Buckley, Reka, BA Lond., MA Lond., PhD Lond.
Sr. Lectr.
Burrows, George, BMus Birm., MLitt
Newcastle(UK) Sr. Lectr.
Caro, John, BA Northumbria, MA York(Can.) Sr.
Lectr.

Ede, Laurie, BA CNAA, PhD Portsmouth Sr.
Lectr.
Forster, Laurel, BA S'ton., MA Sus., DPhil Sus.
Sr. Lectr.
Garland, David, BA Exe. Sr. Lectr.
Geraghty, Lincoln, BA Lanc., MA Nott., PhD
Nott. Sr. Lectr.
Harper, Stephen, MA Glas., PhD Glas. Sr.
Lectr.
Harper, Susan, BA Reading, MA CNAA, MPhil
Reading, PhD CNAA Prof., Film History
Jagger, Colin, BMus Manc., MM Cinc. Sr.
Lectr.; Dir., Music
McDonald, Paul, BA Reading, PhD Warw. Prof.,
Film and TV Studies
North, Sam, BA Cape Town, MA L&H Sr. Lectr.
O'Shea, Barry, BA Open(UK), PhD Open(UK) Sr.
Lectr.
Shaw, Deborah, BA CNAA, MA Leeds Sr. Lectr.
Smith, Justin, BA Kent, MA Open(UK) Sr. Lectr.
Symonds, Dominic, BA Lond., MA Lond. Sr.
Lectr.
Tester, Keith, BSc CNAA, PhD Leeds Prof.,
Social Theory
Wooldridge, Patricia, BA Lond., MA Lond. Sr.
Lectr.
Other Staff: 3 Lectrs.; 2 Assoc. Sr. Lectrs.; 1
Assoc. Lectr.; 2 Tutors

Creative Technologies

Tel: (023) 9284 6404 Fax: (023) 9284 6350
Bain, Andrew Sr. Lectr.
Billinge, David J., BA Lond., MSc CNAA, PhD
Portsmouth, FRSA Principal Lectr.
Bown, Gary, BSc CNAA, MSc Portsmouth FRSA
Principal Lectr.
Eglin, Roger, PhD Lond. Sr. Lectr.
Eyles, Mark Sr. Lectr.
Grigg, Robert, BSc Griff. Sr. Lectr.
Hand, Stephen C., BSc S'ton., PhD S'ton.
Principal Lectr.; Head*
Heal, Brian W., BSc CNAA, MPhil CNAA
Principal Lectr.
Jeffcote, Rod, BTech Brad., MSc Sus. Principal
Lectr.
Kalus, A., BSc CNAA, MSc CNAA Sr. Lectr.
Krokos, Mel, MSc Lond., PhD Lond. Sr. Lectr.
Latif, Ahmed Sr. Lectr.
Maniar, Nipan, BSc Gujar., MSc Portsmouth Sr.
Lectr.
Newman, Ken, MA Griff., MEd Deakin Sr.
Lectr.
Pettitt, Jules, MA Portsmouth Sr. Lectr.
Pinchbeck, Daniel, MSc Essex Sr. Lectr.
Reeve-Baker, Denis, BA Open(UK) Sr. Lectr.
Sambrook, Claire Sr. Lectr.
Stevens, Brett, BSc Portsmouth, MSc Portsmouth,
PhD Portsmouth Sr. Lectr.
Villez, Pere, BSc Sus. Sr. Lectr.
Watts, Charlie Assoc. Sr. Lectr.
Other Staff: 3 Lectrs.
Research: applications of computer animation
and digital media video; computer games;
mobile technology and largescale 3D
visualisation; music and technology; web
based technologies

**Earth and Environmental Sciences,
School of**

Tel: (023) 9284 2258-9 Fax: (023) 9284 2244
E-mail: janet.woodford@port.ac.uk
Dewdney, Christopher, BSc Warw., PhD Lond.
Reader, Theoretical Physics
Fones, Gary, BSc CNAA, MSc S'ton., PhD C.Lancs.
Sr. Lectr.
Fowler, Michael, BSc Brist., MSc Birm., PhD
Lond. Sr. Lectr.
Giles, David P., BSc CNAA, FGS Principal
Lectr.
Hendry, James, BA Camb., PhD Liv. Sr. Lectr.
Koor, Nicholas, BSc CNAA, MSci Lond., FGS
Sr. Lectr.
Loydell, David, BSc Wales, PhD Wales Sr.
Lectr.
Martill, David, BSc Leic., PhD Leic. Reader,
Palaeobiology
Poulsom, Andrew J., BSc CNAA, MSc Lond. Sr.
Lectr.

Proykova, Yana, BSc Moscow, PhD Moscow   Sr. Lectr.

Solana, Carmen, BSc Madrid, PhD Madrid   Sr. Lectr.

Strachan, Robin, BSc Wales, PhD Keele   Head, Earth Sciences*

Teeuw, Richard, BSc Nott., PhD Stir.   Sr. Lectr.

Walton, Nicolas R. G., BSc Leeds, MSc Oxf., FGS   Principal Lectr.

Whalley, John S., BSc Leic., MSc Lond., FGS   Principal Lectr.

Whitworth, Malcolm, MSc Keele, MSc Durh., PhD Portsmouth   Sr. Lectr.

Other Staff: 1 Lectr.; 1 Res. Fellow; 1 Res. Assoc.

Research: applied geosciences; crustal evolution; human impact on the aquatic environment; materials in the environment; palaeobiology

Economics

Tel: (023) 9284 4094 Fax: (023) 9284 4037

Asteris, Mike, BSc Lond., MSc Birm., PhD Brun.   Principal Lectr.

Bibby, Dave, BA Wales, MA McM., MSc Strath., EdD Lond.   Principal Lectr.; Head*

Collins, Alan O. M., BSc Brad., MSc Salf.   Prof.

Fysh, David, BA CNAA, MSc Lond.   Sr. Lectr.

Gausden, Robert, BA CNAA, MA Manc.   Sr. Lectr.

Ghulam, Yaseen, BA B.Zak., MA Islamia, Bahawal., MAS Karachi   Sr. Lectr.

Grainger, Jeff S., BA CNAA, MA Essex   Principal Lectr.

Hallett, Mary E., BSc Lond., MPhil CNAA   Sr. Lectr.

Heather, Ken F., BSc S'ton.   Principal Lectr.

Jaffry, Shabbar, BA Islamia, Bahawal., MSc Quaid-i-Azam, MAppSc Karachi, PhD Portsmouth   Reader

Judge, Guy, BA Warw., MA Warw.   Principal Lectr.

Murphy, F. P. (Barry), BCom N.U.I., MEconSc N.U.I., MSc Lond.   Sr. Lectr.

Reid, Chris, BA CNAA, PhD Portsmouth   Principal Lectr.

Rich, Judith, BA Monash, MEc Monash, PhD Monash   Principal Lectr.

Smith, G. A. E. (Sandy), BA CNAA, MPhil Glas.   Sr. Lectr.

Snell, Martin C., MA Edin., DPhil York(UK)   Principal Lectr.

Thorpe, Andy T., BSc CNAA, MA Sus., PhD Lond.   Reader, Development Economics

Whitmarsh, David T., BA Exe., MA Exe., PhD Portsmouth   Prof., Marine Resource Management

Other Staff: 3 Lectrs.; 1 Assoc. Sr. Lectr.; 1 Res. Fellow

Research: business economics; development economics; local and regional economics; social and urban economics

Education and Continuing Studies, School of

Tel: (023) 9284 5204 Fax: (023) 9284 5365

Betts, Penny, BA Portsmouth, MA Portsmouth   Sr. Lectr.

Briddick, Colin, BEd S'ton., MAS Brun.   Sr. Lectr.

Chalke, Joy, BEd CNAA   Sr. Lectr.

Coeshott, Mike, BA Warw., MAEd S'ton.   Sr. Lectr.; Head*

Edwards, F. John, BA Wales, MSc Oxf.   Sr. Lectr.

Hawkins, Gillian, BA CNAA   Sr. Lectr.

Holloway, David, BA Sheff., MA E.Anglia, PhD Portsmouth   Principal Lectr.

Neanon, Chris, BEd S'ton., MA S'ton.   Sr. Lectr.

Parfect, Susan, BA S'ton., PhD S'ton.   Sr. Lectr.

Porter, Andrew, BA Exe.   Sr. Lectr.

Rea, Priscilla, BA Open(UK)   Sr. Lectr.

Riordan, Tanya, BA CNAA, MEd S'ton.   Sr. Lectr.

Stittrich-Lyons, Helga, BSc Portsmouth   Sr. Lectr.

Wood, Jane, BA Birm.   Sr. Lectr.

Other Staff: 1 Assoc. Sr. Lectr.; 1 Assoc. Lectr.

Engineering, Civil

Tel: (023) 9284 2424 Fax: (023) 9284 2521

Collings, Andrew, MPhil Sur., PhD Auck.   Sr. Lectr.

Fox, Dominic, BSc CNAA, PhD Portsmouth   Head*

Lee, Brian, BSc Leic., PhD Leic.   Prof.

Nassif, Ayman, BEng Assiut, PhD Lond.   Sr. Lectr.

Otter, Robert A., BSc Birm., PhD Portsmouth   Principal Lectr.

Ponterosso, Pasquale, BEng S'ton., MSc Lond., PhD Portsmouth   Sr. Lectr.

Sangha, Chander M., BSc St And., PhD Dund., FGS   Principal Lectr.

Tutesigensi, Apollo, BSc Mak., MSc Leeds, PhD Leeds   Sr. Lectr.

Walden, Philip J., BSc CNAA   Principal Lectr.

Watson, Paul, BSc Lond., PhD Lond.   Sr. Lectr.

Williams, John, BSc CNAA, PhD Portsmouth   Principal Lectr.

Other Staff: 1 Res. Fellow

Research: construction management; environmental engineering (landfill processes, wastewater treatment); material properties (aggregate replacement, concrete technology); novel IT applications in civil engineering; wind engineering and disaster risk management

Engineering, Electronic and Computer

Tel: (023) 9284 2179 Fax: (023) 9284 2561

Aljareh, Salem, BSc Garyounis   Sr. Lectr.

Alkadhimi, Khalil I., BSc CNAA, MEng Sheff., PhD Sheff.   Principal Lectr.

Azzi, Djamel, BSc Constantine, MSc UMIST, PhD UMIST   Principal Lectr.

Cripps, Martin D., BSc(Eng) S'ton., PhD Lond.   Prof., Information Engineering

Dunn, Victor, MSc S'ton.   Sr. Lectr.

Filip, Miodrag, BEng Belgrade, PhD CNAA   Principal Lectr.; Head*

Geddes, E. John, BA Oxf., PhD Leic.   Principal Lectr.

Gremont, Boris, BEng Coventry, PhD Coventry   Sr. Lectr.

Haynes, Barry P., BSc CNAA, MSc CNAA, PhD Portsmouth   Principal Lectr.

Hewitt, Alan, BA York(UK), MSc S'ton., PhD CNAA   Sr. Lectr.

Khusainov, Rinat, PhD N.U.I.   Sr. Lectr.

Liu, Ying, BSc Chongqing, PhD Strath.   Sr. Lectr.

Margrave, Frank, BEng Manc.Met.   Sr. Lectr.

Ndzi, David, BSc Keele, PhD Portsmouth   Sr. Lectr.

Nguyen, Chi, BSc Harv.   Sr. Lectr.

Papademetriou, Rallis C., MSc Patras   Principal Lectr.

Parchizadeh, G., BSc Wales, MSc Wales   Principal Lectr.

Pritchard, Clifford, BSc Salf., MSc Manc., PhD Manc.   Sr. Lectr.

Savage, Nicholas, BEng Portsmouth   Sr. Lectr.

Tawfik, Abdul N., BEng CNAA, PhD CNAA   Principal Lectr.

Vuksanovic, Branislav, MSc S.Bank, PhD Hudd.   Sr. Lectr.

Yang, Linda, BSc N.Jiaotong, MEng Beijing, PhD Peking   Sr. Lectr.

Zhou, Shikun, BSc Zhejiang, MPhil De Mont., PhD De Mont.   Sr. Lectr.

Other Staff: 3 Lectrs.

Research: artificial intelligence (AI) systems; building comfort management systems; communication system design; radiowave propagation and channel modelling; robotics

Engineering, Mechanical and Design

Tel: (023) 9284 2610 Fax: (023) 9284 2351

Alani, Amir, BSc E.Lond., MSc Montpellier, PhD Montpellier   Head*

Bennett, Nicholas G., BSc Bath, MBA Open(UK), FIMechE   Prof.; Dir., Regional Centre for Manufacturing Indust.

Cawte, Howard, BSc CNAA, PhD CNAA   Principal Lectr.

Foster, John V., BSc CNAA   Principal Lectr.; Head*

Gilbert-Wood, Colin   Sr. Lectr.

Graham-Jones, Jasper, BEng Nott.Trent, MSc Brun., PhD S'ton.   Sr. Lectr.

Hicks, Peter, BA Oxf., MA Oxf.   Principal Lectr.

Hogan, Vince, BSc CNAA   Principal Lectr.

Hughes, Vince, BSc CNAA, MSc CNAA, PhD Portsmouth   Principal Lectr.

Little, Andrew P. F., BSc City(UK), PhD Portsmouth, FIMechE   Principal Lectr.

Oliver, Terry, BSc CNAA, DEd Donetsk T.U.   Principal Lectr.

Onuh, Spencer, BEng Ilorin, MEng Ilorin, MA Portsmouth, PhD Liv.   Sr. Lectr.

Popov, Ivan, MSc Roussé T.I., PhD Roussé T.I.   Sr. Lectr.

Prichard, B. L., BSc Manc., MSc Cran., PhD S'ton.   Sr. Lectr.

Richardson, Mel, MBE, BSc Brun., PhD Brun., FRSChem, FRSA, FIMMM   Prof., Manufacturing

Sanders, David A., BA Open(UK), BSc CNAA, MBA Open(UK), PhD CNAA, FIEE, FIMechE   Reader, Systems and Knowledge Engineering

Shen, Wei Qin, BEng Shanghai, MPhil Shanghai, PhD Shanghai   Reader, Impact Engineering

Taylor, Robin, BSc CNAA, MPhil CNAA   Sr. Lectr.

Tong, Jie, BSc Shenyang Mech.& Electr., MSc Shenyang Mech.& Electr., PhD Sheff.   Prof., Mechanical Engineering

Waite, Mike L., BSc CNAA, MPhil CNAA   Principal Lectr.

Zhang, Zhong Yi, BSc Sichuan, MSc Sichuan, PhD Lough.   Sr. Lectr.

Zhao, Li Guo, BEng Xi'an Jiaotong, PhD Xi'an Jiaotong   Sr. Lectr.

Other Staff: 1 Lectr.; 1 Sr. Res. Fellow; 3 Res. Fellows

Research: energy and environment; manufacturing engineering; materials and structural integrity; systems engineering

Environmental Design and Management, School of

Tel: (023) 9284 2918 Fax: (023) 9284 2913

Aygen, Zeynep, MA Mimar Sinan, PhD Istanbul   Sr. Lectr.

Blackledge, Michael J., FRICS   Sr. Lectr.

Chapman, G. Keith, BSc Aston, FCIOB   Principal Lectr.

Douvlou, Elena, MArch Sheff., PhD Sheff.   Sr. Lectr.

Edwards, Victoria, OBE, BSc Reading, MSc Cant., PhD Reading, FRICS   Principal Lectr.

Lee, Rosalind M., LLB Sheff., MA Sheff.   Sr. Lectr.

Packer, Andrew D., BSc CNAA, MA Open(UK)   Head*

Pitchforth, Steven J., BA CNAA, MSc Sur.   Sr. Lectr.

Tyrrell, Roger, BA CNAA   Principal Lectr.

Waterson, Geoffrey, LLB Essex, LLM Wales, MA S'ton.   Principal Lectr.

Whiting, David, BSc CNAA   Sr. Lectr.

Wooldridge, Jonathan, BSc Open(UK), MSc Open(UK)   Sr. Lectr.

Other Staff: 2 Assoc. Sr. Lectrs.

Research: health and occupational safety; heritage, leisure and tourism; maritime and heritage and integrated coastal zone management; property management, surveying and development; sustainable design

Geography

Tel: (023) 9284 2507 Fax: (023) 9284 2512

Bray, Malcolm, BSc Sheff., PhD Lond.   Sr. Lectr.

Collier, Peter, BSc Newcastle(UK), PhD Aston   Principal Lectr.

Ekinsmyth, Carol, BA Leic., PhD Leic.   Sr. Lectr.

Farres, Paul, BSc Reading, PhD Reading   Principal Lectr.

Fontana, Dominic, BA CNAA, PhD Portsmouth   Sr. Lectr.

Healey, Richard G., MA Camb., PhD Camb. Prof.

Inkpen, Robert, BA Oxf., PhD Lond.   Principal Lectr.

Leonard, Simon, BA CNAA, MSc Lond., PhD Lond.   Head*

Pearson, Alastair, BA Leeds, PhD Portsmouth Principal Lectr.

Pepin, Nicholas, BSc Durh., PhD Durh.   Sr. Lectr.

Ryder, Andrew, BA Conn., DPhil Oxf.   Sr. Lectr.

Southall, Humphrey, BA Camb., PhD Camb. Reader

Twigg, Lizbeth, BA CNAA, PhD Lond.   Principal Lectr.

Other Staff: 1 Lectr.; 1 Res. Fellow; 1 Res. Assoc.

Research: contemporary and historical geographic information system (GIS); economy and society; environmental change; geography of health

Health Sciences and Social Work, School of

Tel: (023) 9284 5240 Fax: (023) 9284 5326
E-mail: pimhs.enquiries@port.ac.uk

Adrian-Harris, Derek, TD, BA Open(UK), MPhil Bath   Head, Centre for Radiography Educn.

Armstrong, Lisa, BA Open(UK), MSc S'ton.   Sr. Lectr.

Bartholomew, Jeannette, BSc Lond., PhD CNAA   Head*

Blane, Shelley, BSc Herts., MSc Lond.   Sr. Lectr.

Bown, Kim, BSc CNAA, MSc S'ton., MA Portsmouth   Sr. Lectr.

Cassidy, Mark, BSc Birm., MSci Portsmouth   Sr. Lectr.

Castle, Alan, BEd S'ton., MA S'ton., PhD S'ton. Principal Lectr.

Chaplen, Carol   Sr. Lectr.

Clarke, Harold, MEd Brun.   Sr. Lectr.

Dean, Taraneh, BSc Wales, MEd Lond.   Prof., Health Sciences

Delf, Penny, BSc Portsmouth, MSc Portsmouth   Sr. Lectr.

Elsbury, Sally, BSc Portsmouth, MA Portsmouth   Sr. Lectr.

Evered, Helen, MSc Portsmouth   Principal Lectr.

Gardiner, Martyn, BSc Leic., PhD Leic.   Sr. Lectr.

Givati, Assaf, MA Maastricht   Sr. Lectr.

Halson-Brown, Susan, MSc Portsmouth   Sr. Lectr.

Harper, Michael, BSc Portsmouth   Sr. Lectr.

Harvey, Paul, BSc Portsmouth   Sr. Lectr.

Hatton, Kieron, BA CNAA, MSc Brist., PhD Portsmouth   Principal Lectr.

Joyce, Penny, BA Portsmouth, MA Portsmouth Principal Lectr.

Kilburn, Sally, BSc Lond., PhD Lond.   Principal Lectr.

Leadbetter, Christine, BSc Sur., MSc Portsmouth   Sr. Lectr.

Oakley, Jason, BSc CNAA, MSc Portsmouth   Sr. Lectr.

Reynolds, Lesley-Jane, BSc Wales, PhD Bath Prof., Education for Health and Society

Rogers, Teri, BA CNAA, MSc Portsmouth   Sr. Lectr.

Ryder, Isobel, MSc Portsmouth   Sr. Lectr.

Sander, Ruth, BA Open(UK), MSc Lond.   Sr. Lectr.

Saunders, Mary, BSc De Mont., PhD Wales   Sr. Lectr.

Shepherd, Peter, BSc Portsmouth, MSc S'ton.   Sr. Lectr.

Slack, Edward, MSc S'ton.   Sr. Lectr.

Turner, Louise, MSc Lond., PhD Lond.   Sr. Lectr.

Vassallo, Maxine   Sr. Lectr.

Williams, Andrew   Sr. Lectr.

Other Staff: 7 Assoc. Sr. Lectrs.; 2 Lectrs.; 1 Assoc. Lectr.; 1 Sr. Res. Fellow; 2 Res. Fellows; 2 Res. Assocs.

Research: allergy; evaluation of radiography practice; gerontology; knowledge management; patient participation

Human Resource and Marketing Management

Tel: (023) 9284 4060 Fax: (023) 9284 4037

Adam-Smith, Derek W., BTech Brun., MA Warw.   Head*

Anderson, Valerie, BA Sheff., MEd Sheff., PhD Open(UK)   Principal Lectr.

Banks, Gerry, MPhil CNAA   Principal Lectr.

Brown, Emma, BSc Sur., PhD Sur.   Sr. Lectr.

Brown, Jill, BA S'ton., MA Greenwich   Assoc. Principal Lectr.

Carberry, Mary, BA Ulster, PhD De Mont.   Sr. Lectr.

Chapleo, Christopher, BA Brun., MA CNAA   Sr. Lectr.

Chapman, Thomas, BA Bourne., MSc Bourne.   Sr. Lectr.

Christy, Gillian, BA Camb., MA Camb., MA S'ton.   Principal Lectr.

Christy, Richard H., BA Camb., MA Camb., MBA City(UK)   Principal Lectr.

Dace, Roger W., BA CNAA, MBA Aston   Sr. Lectr.

Dossor, Penny, BA Strath.   Sr. Lectr.

Fill, Christopher Y., BA CNAA, MSc Warw., FCIM   Principal Lectr.

French, Raymond D., BA Essex, PhD CNAA Principal Lectr.

Gilbert, Alan, BSc S'ton.   Principal Lectr.

Gilmore, Sarah, BA Essex, PhD Portsmouth   Sr. Lectr.

Goss, Fiona, BA Portsmouth   Principal Lectr.

Hall, David, BSc Wales, PhD Wales   Sr. Lectr.

Howe-Walsh, Liza, BA Portsmouth, MA Portsmouth   Sr. Lectr.

Karas, Judi, BA N.Lond., MA N.Lond.   Sr. Lectr.

Lockyer, Lynne C., MA Portsmouth   Sr. Lectr.

Lowman, Mark, BSc Sur., MBA Warw., PhD S'ton.   Sr. Lectr.

Pilbeam, Stephen P., MSc Portsmouth, FCIPD Principal Lectr.

Rayner, Charlotte, PhD UMIST   Prof., Human Resource Management

Rees, Gary, BSc Wales, MBA City(UK), FCIPD, FRSA   Principal Lectr.

Rogers, Beth, BA Warw., MBA Cran.IT   Sr. Lectr.

Rumbles, Sally, MSc Portsmouth   Sr. Lectr.

Scott, Peter, BA CNAA, MSc Manc., PhD Bath Sr. Lectr.

Thomas, Rob, BA Warw., MA Warw.   Principal Lectr.

Trott, Paul, BSc CNAA, PhD Cran.   Principal Lectr.

Wheeler, Colin, BA Newcastle(UK), MA Lanc. Prof., Marketing

Williams, David, BA Open(UK), MBA Open(UK), DEd S'ton.   Sr. Lectr.

Williams, Stephen, BA CNAA, PhD Sund. Principal Lectr.

Other Staff: 1 Lectr.; 1 Sr. Assoc. Lectr.; 1 Assoc. Lectr.; 1 Res. Assoc.

Research: entrepreneurship, innovation and enterprise; human resource management (HRM) and organisation studies; marketing (communications, direct, e-marketing, services); sales management

Languages and Area Studies, School of

Tel: (023) 9284 6100 Fax: (023) 9284 6040

Ainslie, Marie, BA CNAA, MA Portsmouth   Sr. Lectr.

Arrebola-Sanchez, Miguel, MA Portsmouth   Sr. Lectr.

Bryant, Janet, BA Reading, MA Reading   Sr. Lectr.

Chafer, Tony, BA Nott., MA Reading, MA Lond., LèsL Nantes, PhD Lond.   Prof., Contemporary French Area Studies

Clark, Rose, BA York(UK), MA Lanc.   Sr. Lectr.

Cleminson, Ralph, BA Oxf., DPhil Oxf.   Prof., Slavonic Studies

Coverdale-Jones, Patricia, BA Keele, MA Hull Sr. Lectr.

Edmondson, Lesley, BA CNAA, MA Portsmouth Sr. Lectr.

Evans, Martin, BA Sus., DPhil Sus.   Prof., Contemporary European History

Godin, Emmanuel, MA Inst.Nat.Poly.Grenoble Principal Lectr.

Gould, Bob, BA CNAA, MA Sus.   Principal Lectr.

Gronow, Gillian, BA Oxf., MEd Wales   Sr. Lectr.

Hand, Penelope, BA Lond., MA Lond.   Sr. Lectr.

Hitchcock, Richard, BA E.Anglia, MA E.Anglia Sr. Lectr.

Hughes, Felicity, BA CNAA, MPhil Reading   Sr. Lectr.

Humphreys, Peter, BA CNAA, MA Lond.   Sr. Lectr.

Jeffcote, Caterina, BA CNAA, MA Sur.   Assoc. Sr. Lectr.

Kemble, Ian, BSc Sur.   Principal Lectr.

Knischewski, Gerd, MA CNAA, MA Bochum   Sr. Lectr.

Marten-Finnis, Susanne, PhD Tübingen   Prof., Applied Linguistics

Matear, Ann, BA Manc., MA Liv., PhD Liv. Principal Lectr.

McCullagh, Marie, BA CNAA, MA Sund.   Sr. Lectr.

McEwan, Maggi, BA CNAA   Sr. Lectr.

Mitchell, Samia, LES Oran, MES Rouen   Sr. Lectr.

Naysmith, John, BA Stir., MEd Lond.   Head*

O'Sullivan, Carol, BA Trinity(Dub.), MPhil Camb., PhD Camb.   Sr. Lectr.

Oughton, Sabrea, BA Toulouse, MA Toulouse   Sr. Lectr.

Parkes, Genevieve, MèsL Nancy   Sr. Lectr.

Pickett-Rose, Lorraine, BA CNAA, MA Portsmouth   Sr. Lectr.

Poulsom, Dorothy, BA CNAA, MA Portsmouth   Sr. Lectr.

Rastall, Paul, BA Oxf., PhD St And.   Principal Lectr.

Rodriguez De Cespede, Begona, BA Malaga, BA Portsmouth, MA Portsmouth   Sr. Lectr.

Saraceni, Mario, PhD Nott.   Sr. Lectr.

Syngellakis, Anna, LLB Athens, LLM Lond., MA Rutgers, MPhil S'ton., PhD Portsmouth Principal Lectr.

Waterhouse, Eleanor, BA Hull   Sr. Lectr.

Watkins, Peter, BA Sheff., MA Portsmouth   Sr. Lectr.

Williams, Patrick, BA Nott., PhD Lond.   Sr. Lectr.

Winkfield, Elke, MA Trier   Sr. Lectr.

Wrigglesworth, John, BA Warw., MA Sheff.Hallam   Sr. Lectr.

Wright, Sue, PhD   Prof., Language Learning and Linguistics

Other Staff: 4 Lectrs.; 8 Lectors; 3 Sr. Tutors; 5 Tutors; 1 Res. Fellow

Research: area studies; cultures of memory and identity; European social and cultural theory; film and media; languages across borders

Mathematics

Tel: (023) 9284 6367 Fax: (023) 9284 6364

Barrett, J. David, BSc(Tech) Wales, MPhil CNAA   Sr. Lectr.

Beullens, Patrick, MSci Leuven, MSc Leuven, PhD Leuven   Sr. Lectr.

Burbanks, Andrew, BSc Lough., PhD Lough.   Sr. Lectr.

Davies, H. Barrie, BSc Wales, MSc Oxf. Principal Lectr.

Elliott, Graham, BSc Lond., MSc Lond., PhD Lond. Principal Lectr.

Heal, Ann, BSc CNAA   Sr. Lectr.

Higgins, Bernard, BSc CNAA   Sr. Lectr.

Jones, Dylan, BSc S'ton., PhD Portsmouth Principal Lectr.

Makroglou, Athena, BSc Athens, MSc Manc., PhD Manc.   Sr. Lectr.

McCabe, E. Michael, BSc Sus., DPhil Sus. Principal Lectr.

Message, Fiona, BSc Bath   Assoc. Sr. Lectr.

Nesteruk, Alexei, MSc St.Petersburg, PhD St.Petersburg   Sr. Lectr.

Osbaldestin, Andrew, BSc Nott., PhD Nott. Prof., Applied Mathematics; Head*

Pevy, Lynn, BSc Durh.   Sr. Lectr.

Salt, David W., BSc Lond., MSc Lond., PhD Lond., FRSS   Principal Lectr.
Tamiz, Mehrdad, BSc Lond., PhD Brun.   Prof., Operational Research
Research: biostatistics; mathematics education; nonlinear dynamics; numerical analysis; operations research and financial mathematics

Pharmacy and Biomedical Sciences, School of

Tel: (023) 9284 3596 Fax: (023) 9284 2165
E-mail: sharon.dickson@port.ac.uk
Ball, Karen, BSc Kingston(UK), PhD Kingston(UK)   Sr. Lectr.
Banting, Lee, BSc Reading, PhD CNAA   Sr. Lectr.
Beech, Iwona, BSc Warsaw, MSc Warsaw, MSc Lond., PhD CNAA   Reader, Applied Environmental Microbiology
Brown, David T., BPharm Bath, PhD Nott.   Prof., Pharmacy Practice
Brown, James, BSc CNAA, PhD Aston   Principal Lectr.
Butt, Arthur, BSc Liv., MPhil Lond., PhD Lond.   Prof., Biomedical Sciences and Pharmacology
Campbell, Sheelagh, BSc Lond., PhD CNAA   Principal Lectr.
Chopra, Mridula, BSc Strath., MSc Strath., PhD Strath.   Sr. Lectr.
Clark, Peter J., BSc CNAA   Sr. Lectr.
Cox, Paul A., BSc Lond., PhD Keele   Principal Lectr.
Ebenezer, Ivor S., BSc CNAA, PhD Newcastle(UK)   Principal Lectr.
Gibbs, Roslyn, BSc CNAA, PhD CNAA   Principal Lectr.
Gorecki, Dariuz C., MD Warsaw, PhD Warsaw   Reader, Molecular Medicine
Hardman, John S., BSc Leeds, PhD Leeds, FRSChem, FIP   Principal Lectr.
Hull, Helen, BSc Portsmouth, MSc Portsmouth   Sr. Lectr.
Hunt, Adrian J., BSc CNAA, PhD   Principal Lectr.
Laight, David, BSc Bath, PhD Bath   Sr. Lectr.
Mason, Tim G., BSc Kent, MSc Warw., PhD CNAA   Sr. Lectr.
Mernagh, Darren, BSc Portsmouth, PhD Portsmouth   Principal Lectr.
Mills, Graham A., BSc S'ton., BA Portsmouth, MA Portsmouth, PhD S'ton.   Reader, Environmental Chemistry
Mills, Jeremy, BSc CNAA, PhD Lond.   Sr. Lectr.
Norris, Michael, BSc Wales, MSc Wales, PhD Wales   Principal Lectr.
Ockwell, Clare, BSc Portsmouth   Sr. Lectr.
Oliver, Geoffrey W. O., BSc S'ton., PhD S'ton.   Principal Lectr.
Pilkington, Geoffrey, BSc CNAA, MPhil Lond., PhD Lond., FIBiol   Prof., Pharmacy
Portlock, Jane, BPharm Wales, PhD Wales   Assoc. Principal Lectr.
Rennison, Susan, MSci Portsmouth   Sr. Lectr.
Saunders, Kay, PhD W.England   Sr. Lectr.
Sautreau, Asmita, BSc CNAA, PhD CNAA   Principal Lectr.
Shute, Janis, BSc Reading, PhD Reading   Reader, Pharmacology
Tsibouklis, John, BSc CNAA, MSc Lond., PhD CNAA   Reader, Polymer Science
Van der Merwe, Susanna, BSc Potchef., MSc Potchef., PhD Potchef.   Sr. Lectr.
Warren, Nicholas, BSc Brighton   Sr. Lectr.
Watson, Paul, BSc CNAA, MSc Brun.   Sr. Lectr.
White, Godfrey L., BSc Birm., PhD Birm.   Sr. Lectr.
Wilkinson, Myra, MSc Portsmouth   Principal Lectr.
Wong, John C. L., BSc HK, MPhil HK, PhD Monash   Head*
Other Staff: 3 Lectrs.; 2 Sr. Res. Fellows; 2 Res. Fellows; 5 Res. Assocs.
Research: biomaterials and drug delivery; microbiology and natural product chemistry; molecular design electrochemistry; molecular medicine; pharmacy practice

Professionals Complementary to Dentistry, School of

Tel: (023) 9284 5281 Fax: (023) 9284 5236
E-mail: spcd.enquiries@port.ac.uk
Hartridge, Sarah, BSc Brist., PhD Brist., FRCS   Clinical Dir.
Holmes, Sara, BSc Portsmouth, MA Portsmouth   Head*
Ormes, Kate, BDA   Dentist
Phillips, Sheila   Principal Lectr.
Weld, John, BDS Birm.   Clinical Dir.
Other Staff: 8 Tutors

Psychology

Tel: (023) 9284 6313 Fax: (023) 9284 6300
E-mail: frances.hayes@port.ac.uk
Akehurst, Lucy, BSc Portsmouth, PhD Portsmouth   Sr. Lectr.
Bard, Kim A., BA Wheaton(Mass.), MA Georgia State, PhD Georgia State   Reader, Comparative Developmental Psychology
Blank, Hartmut, PhD Constance   Sr. Lectr.
Cherryman, Julie, BSc Portsmouth, PhD Portsmouth   Principal Lectr.
Costall, Alan, BSc Wales, PhD Birm.   Prof., Theoretical Psychology
Fluck, Michael J., BSc Wales, PhD Nott.   Principal Lectr.
Hillstrom, Anne, BSc Virginia, MSc Johns H., PhD Johns H.   Sr. Lectr.
Hoskins, Sherria, BSc Plym., PhD Plym.   Sr. Lectr.
Kadar, Endre, BA Bud., MA Bud., MA Conn., PhD Conn.   Sr. Lectr.
Linnell, Margaret, BSc Portsmouth, PhD Portsmouth   Sr. Lectr.
Morris, Paul H., BSc S'ton., PhD S'ton.   Sr. Lectr.
Nee, Claire, BA N.U.I., PhD N.U.I.   Sr. Lectr.
Needs, Adrian, BA Cardiff, DPhil York(UK)   Principal Lectr.
Nunkoosing, Karl K., BA Open(UK), EdD E.Anglia   Principal Lectr.
Ost, James, BA Portsmouth, PhD Portsmouth   Sr. Lectr.
Reddy, Vasudevi, BA Osm., MA Osm., PhD Edin.   Reader, Developmental and Cultural Psychology; Head*
Sinha, Christopher, BA Sus., PhD Utrecht   Prof., Psychology of Language
Turner, Mark, BSc CNAA, MSc CNAA, PhD S'ton.   Sr. Lectr.
Van Laar, Darren L., BSc CNAA, MSc York(UK), PhD Lond.   Principal Lectr.
Vrij, Aldert, BA Amst., MA Amst., PhD Amst.   Prof., Social Psychology
Wilson, Clare, BSc Otago, PhD Otago   Reader, Forensic Psychology
Zinken, Joerg, MA Bielefeld, PhD Bielefeld   Sr. Lectr.
Other Staff: 2 Assoc. Sr. Lectrs.; 2 Lectrs.; 4 Res. Fellows; 3 Res. Assocs.
Research: cognitive development; emotions in human and non-human species; forensic psychology; human-machine interfaces and ecological psychology; language, culture and mind

Social, Historical and Literary Studies, School of

Tel: (023) 9284 2173 Fax: (023) 9284 2174
Andress, David, BA York(UK), DPhil York(UK)   Reader, Modern European History
Beaven, Bradley, BA CNAA, MA Warw., PhD De Mont.   Principal Lectr.
Blackmore, Martin, BA Portsmouth, MSc Portsmouth, PhD Portsmouth   Sr. Lectr.
Bowers-Bridge, Margaret, BA E.Anglia, MA Alta., PhD Kent   Sr. Lectr.
Bradshaw, Yvonne, BA CNAA, MA Portsmouth, PhD Portsmouth   Sr. Lectr.
Bruley, Susan, BSc Lond., MSc Lond., PhD Lond.   Sr. Lectr.
Callan, Theresa, BA Belf., PhD Belf.   Principal Lectr.
Carpenter, David, BA Lond., MA Lond.   Principal Lectr.
Carr, Fergus, BA Hull, MSc Lond.   Head*

Davis, John, BA Sus., MA Essex, PhD Essex   Assoc. Head (Quality)
Finn, Daniel, BA Warw., PhD Birm.   Prof., Social Policy
Flenley, Paul, MA St And., PhD Birm.   Principal Lectr.
Giddey, Martin N., MA CNAA   Sr. Lectr.
Kaiser, Wolfram, PhD Hamburg   Prof., European Studies
McNulty, Eugene, BEd Belf., MA Kent, PhD Kent   Sr. Lectr.
McSorley, Kevin, BSc Sheff., MA York(UK)   Sr. Lectr.
McVeigh, Paul, BA Leeds, PhD Leeds   Sr. Lectr.; Assoc. Head (Curriculum)
Mitchell, Mark, BA Leeds, MSc Lond.   Principal Lectr.
Nicol, Bran, MA Dund., PhD Lanc.   Sr. Lectr.
North, Nancy, BA Leic., MA CNAA, PhD Lond.   Principal Lectr.
Paice, Rosamund, MA Camb., MA Manc., PhD Manc.   Sr. Lectr.
Peggs, Kay, BSc CNAA, MSc Sur., PhD Sur.   Principal Lectr.
Price, Bronwen, BA Wales, PhD Wales   Principal Lectr.
Pulham, Patricia, BA Lond., MA Lond., PhD Lond.   Sr. Lectr.
Rau, Petra, MA Munich, PhD E.Anglia   Sr. Lectr.
Smart, Barry, BSc Lond., PhD Sheff.   Prof., Sociology
Thomas, James H., BA Lond., PhD S'ton., FRHistS   Principal Lectr.
Tickell, Alex, BA Leeds, MA Leeds, PhD Leeds   Sr. Lectr.
Walinski-Kiehl, Robert, BA CNAA, MPhil CNAA   Sr. Lectr.
Warren, Diane, BA Nott., MPhil Glas., PhD Nott.   Principal Lectr.
Other Staff: 1 Assoc. Lectr.; 4 Lectrs.; 4 Res. Fellows
Research: cultural values and European social theory; film and media; nation and identity, and social and historical change; politics and policy making; women's and gender studies

Sport and Exercise Science

Tel: (023) 9284 2640 Fax: (023) 9284 2641
Ball, Nicholas, BSc Portsmouth   Sr. Lectr.
Eglin, Clare, BSc Sheff., PhD Sheff.   Sr. Lectr.
Hencken, Clare, BA Exe., MSc Alabama, PhD Alabama   Sr. Lectr.
Hughes, Christopher, BEd CNAA   Sr. Lectr.
Iggleden, Colin, BSc Portsmouth   Sr. Lectr.
Rees, Alun, BSc CNAA, MPhil Portsmouth   Head*
Scurr, Joanna, BA S'ton., PhD S'ton.   Sr. Lectr.
Thelwell, Richard, BSc S'ton., PhD S'ton.   Principal Lectr.
Tipton, Michael, BEd Keele, MSc Lond., PhD Lond.   Prof., Human and Applied Physiology
Weston, Neil, BSc Glas., MSc S'ton.   Sr. Lectr.
White, Colin, BSc Kent, MSc CNAA   Sr. Lectr.
Other Staff: 3 Lectrs.; 1 Res. Fellow; 3 Res. Assocs.
Research: altitude physiology; biomechanics of sport; sports psychology; survival in the sea; thermal physiology

Strategy and Business Systems

Tel: (023) 9284 4067 Fax: (023) 9284 4037
Akers-Smith, Lynn, MSc Herts.   Sr. Lectr.
Borodzicz, Edward, BSc Brun., MA Kent, PhD Lond.   Prof., Risk and Crisis Management
Botten, Neil J., MA Oxf., MSc Sus.   Principal Lectr.
Brocklehurst, Fiona, BSc Wales, MSc Portsmouth   Sr. Lectr.
Capon, Nicholas C., BSc Nott., MBA Portsmouth   Principal Lectr.
Daly, John, BSc Lond., MSc Cran., MBA Lond.   Principal Lectr.
Foley, Andrea, BA Warw., MSc Portsmouth   Sr. Lectr.
Greswell, Tammi, BEng CNAA, PhD Plym.   Sr. Lectr.
Hoecht, Andreas H., MA Hamburg, MSc Reading, PhD Bud.   Sr. Lectr.

Jepson, Barry, BSc CNAA, MSc S'ton.   Sr. Lectr.

Noble, Richard, BSc Dund., MA Portsmouth
Principal Lectr.

Perrins, Andrew, MEd S'ton., MSc Portsmouth
Sr. Lectr.

Povey, Barry, MSc CNAA, MPhil Brighton
Assoc. Sr. Lectr.

Read, Martin J., BA CNAA, MSc Birm., MBA
Portsmouth, PhD Glam.   Head*

Reed, Deborah, BSc Sur., MA S'ton., PhD
W.England   Principal Lectr.

Roberts, Martyn, BA CNAA, MSc Leic.
Principal Lectr.

Rodgers, Cheryl, BA Leeds, MSc Cran.IT, DPhil
Sus.   Principal Lectr.

Smith, David M., BSc Lond., MBA Wales   Sr.
Lectr.

Starkey, David, BEng S'ton., MBA Portsmouth   Sr.
Lectr.

Walton, John A., BA CNAA, MBA Sheff.   Sr.
Lectr.

Welch, Christine, BA Open(UK), MSc City(UK)
Sr. Lectr.

Wilson, Laura, MSc G.Caledonian   Sr. Lectr.

Wood, Michael J., BSc Sus., MSc Sus., DPhil Oxf.
Principal Lectr.

Xu, Mark, BA Beijing, MA Beijing, MSc C.Lancs.,
PhD Open(UK)   Principal Lectr.

Other Staff: 1 Assoc. Sr. Lectr.; 2 Lectrs.; 1
Res. Fellow

Research: enterprise and innovation; operations
management; quality management; strategic
management

SPECIAL CENTRES, ETC

Cosmology and Gravitation, Institute of

Tel: (023) 9284 5151 Fax: (023) 9284 5626

Bruni, Marco, BSc Rome, MSc Trieste, PhD Trieste
Sr. Lectr.

Crittenden, Robert, PhD Penn.   Reader,
Cosmology/Gravitational Physics

Maartens, Roy, BSc Cape Town, PhD Cape Town
Prof., Cosmology; Head*

Nichol, Robert, BSc Manc., PhD Edin.   Prof.,
Astrophysics

Wands, David, BA Camb., DPhil Sus., FIP, FRAS
Prof., Cosmology

Other Staff: 1 Lectr.; 4 Res. Fellows; 2 Res.
Assocs.; 2 Postdoctoral Res. Assocs.

Research: black hole and stellar perturbations;
gravity waves; inflation and the early
universe; string cosmology and brane-
worlds; structure formation in the universe

Criminal Justice Studies, Institute of

Tel: (023) 9284 3926 Fax: (023) 9284 3933

Aleem, Azeem, BSc Portsmouth, MSc Portsmouth
Sr. Lectr.

Bretherick, Diana, BA CNAA, MA Middx.   Sr.
Lectr.

Brooks, Graham, BA CNAA, MPhil Camb.   Sr.
Lectr.

Button, Mark, BA Exe., MA Warw.   Assoc.
Head (Curriculum)

Carson, David, BA Belf.   Reader, Law and
Behavioural Sciences

Charman, Sarah, BA Wales, MA Wales
Principal Lectr.

Clements, Philip, BA CNAA, MEd Brun., DEd
Brun.   Principal Lectr.

Creaton, Jane, LLB Warw., MSc Edin.   Assoc.
Head (Quality)

Davis, Helen, BA Brighton, MA Sus.   Sr. Lectr.

Ellis, Thomas, BA CNAA, MSc Brist.   Principal
Lectr.

Hall, Nathan, BSc Brun., MSc Portsmouth   Sr.
Lectr.

Hayden, Carol, BA Sus., MA Sus., PhD Portsmouth
Reader, Applied Social Research

Heath, Bernadette, MSci Liv.J.Moores   Sr. Lectr.

Jacobs, Marc, LLB Manc.Met., MA Brun.   Sr.
Lectr.

Johnston, Les, BA Liv., PhD Liv.   Prof.,
Criminology

Jones, John, MPhil Portsmouth   Sr. Lectr.

Loveday, Barry, BA Lanc., MPhil Glas.   Reader,
Criminal Justice

Milne, Rebecca, BSc CNAA, PhD Portsmouth
Principal Lectr.

Nash, Mike R., BA CNAA, MPhil S'ton., PhD
Portsmouth   Principal Lectr.; Deputy Dir.

Norman, Paul, BA Sus., MA Reading, DPhil Sus.
Principal Lectr.

Pakes, Francis, PhD Ley.   Principal Lectr.

Pycroft, Aaron, MA CNAA   Sr. Lectr.

Savage, Stephen, BA Liv., PhD Liv.   Prof.,
Criminology; Dir.*

Scurlock, William, BSc Wales   Sr. Lectr.

Silverstone, Daniel, BA Lond., PhD Lond.   Sr.
Lectr.

Skinner, Caroline, BSc Brist.   Sr. Lectr.

Smith, Geoffrey, BSc Wales, MSc Leic., PhD S'ton.
Sr. Lectr.

Tapley, Jacqueline, BSc Open(UK), MSc S'ton.,
PhD S'ton.   Sr. Lectr.

Watson, Aileen, BA Leeds, MA Keele   Sr. Lectr.

Williams, Andrew, BA Reading, MA Brist., PhD
Reading   Sr. Lectr.

Winstone, Jane, BA Open(UK), MA Brun.
Principal Lectr.

Other Staff: 4 Lectrs.; 3 Sr. Res. Fellows; 1 Res.
Fellow; 3 Sr. Univ. Tutors; 6 Univ. Tutors

Research: criminal investigation; miscarriages of
justice; police governance; private security;
professional cultures in criminal justice

Economics and Management of Aquatic Resources, Centre for the (CEMARE)

Tel: (023) 9284 4082 Fax: (023) 9284 4614

Bjorndal, Trond, PhD Br.Col.   Prof.,
Economics; Dir.*

Other Staff: 5 Sr. Res. Fellows; 1 Res. Fellow;
2 Res. Assocs.

Research: aquaculture economics; aquatic
resource economics and management;
coastal zone management; fisheries
economics and management

Molecular Design, Centre for

Tel: (023) 9284 3612 Fax: (023) 9284 3722

Whitley, David, BSc Warw., PhD S'ton.   Dir.*

Other Staff: 1 Sr. Res. Fellow

Technology Faculty Office

Tel: (023) 9284 3101 Fax: (023) 9284 3030

Bishop, John, BEng CNAA, MSc Portsmouth,
FIMechE   Dir., Learning at Work

Williams, Roy, BA Stell., MPhil CNAA, PhD
Witw.   Sr. Lectr.

CONTACT OFFICERS

Academic affairs. Academic Registrar: Rees,
Andrew, BA CNAA
(E-mail: andy.rees@port.ac.uk)

Accommodation. Director of Campus Services:
Webster, Michelle
(E-mail: michelle.webster@port.ac.uk)

Admissions (first degree). Assistant Academic
Registrar (Admissions): Thomson, Briony,
BA Open(UK)
(E-mail: briony.thomson@port.ac.uk)

Admissions (higher degree). Assistant
Academic Registrar (Admissions):
Thomson, Briony, BA Open(UK)
(E-mail: briony.thomson@port.ac.uk)

Adult/continuing education. Head of Centre
for Continuing Studies: Coeshott, Mike, BA
Warw., MAEd S'ton.
(E-mail: mike.coeshott@port.ac.uk)

Alumni. Alumni Officer: Higgins, Lucy
(E-mail: lucy.higgins@port.ac.uk)

Careers. Head of Careers: Townsin, Guy, BA
Keele (E-mail: guy.townsin@port.ac.uk)

Computing services. Director of Information
Services: Minter, Andrew, BSc Warw.

Credit transfer. Academic Registrar: Rees,
Andrew, BA CNAA
(E-mail: andy.rees@port.ac.uk)

Estates and buildings/works and services.
Director of Estates: Cardy, Andrew, FCIOB
(E-mail: andrew.cardy@port.ac.uk)

Examinations. Deputy Academic Registrar:
Giles, Christine, BSc CNAA, MSc Portsmouth
(E-mail: christine.giles@port.ac.uk)

Finance. Director of Finance: Woollard, Emma
(E-mail: emma.woollard@port.ac.uk)

General enquiries. Academic Registrar: Rees,
Andrew, BA CNAA
(E-mail: andy.rees@port.ac.uk)

International office. International Director:
Docherty, Joseph, MA St And., MSc Bath
(E-mail: joe.docherty@port.ac.uk)

Library (chief librarian). University Librarian:
Bonar, Ian, BSc Edin.
(E-mail: ian.bonar@port.ac.uk)

Marketing. Director of Marketing: Pulvertaft,
Sally, BSc CNAA, MBA Edin.
(E-mail: sally.pulvertaft@port.ac.uk)

Ombudsman. Clerk to the Board of
Governors: Hartley, Sally, BA Wales
(E-mail: sally.hartley@port.ac.uk)

Personnel/human resources. Director of
Personnel Services: Boam, John
(E-mail: john.boam@port.ac.uk)

Public relations. Public Relations Manager:
Stanford, Anne
(E-mail: anne.stanford@port.ac.uk)

Publications. Corporate Communications
Manager: Brookes, Claire, BA Portsmouth
(E-mail: claire.brookes@port.ac.uk)

Purchasing. Purchasing Manager: Fenton,
Douglas (E-mail: doug.fenton@port.ac.uk)

Quality assurance and accreditation. Pro-
Vice-Chancellor (Academic): Bunting,
Rebecca, MA Lond.
(E-mail: rebecca.bunting@port.ac.uk)

Research. Director of Research: Rogers, Prof.
David, BA Open(UK), MPhil CNAA
(E-mail: david.rogers@port.ac.uk)

Safety. Health and Safety Adviser: Denholm,
Ian (E-mail: ian.denholm@port.ac.uk)

Scholarships, awards, loans. Head of Student
Finance: Hawkins, Mary, BA CNAA
(E-mail: mary.hawkins@port.ac.uk)

Schools liaison. Head of Marketing Services:
Burrill, Anne, BA C&GCHE
(E-mail: anne.burrill@port.ac.uk)

Staff development and training. Training and
Development Manager, Personnel Services:
Amor, Linda, BA Leeds
(E-mail: linda.amor@port.ac.uk)

Student welfare/counselling. Head of
Counselling Service: Barden, Nicola
(E-mail: nicola.barden@port.ac.uk)

Students from other countries. General
Manager: Taylor, Susan
(E-mail: susan.taylor@port.ac.uk)

Students with disabilities. Disability Co-
ordinator: Belcher, Robert G., BSc CNAA,
MSc Lond., FRICS
(E-mail: bob.belcher@port.ac.uk)

University press. Printing and Photographic
Services Manager: Brookes, Claire, BA
Portsmouth (E-mail: claire.brookes@port.ac.uk)

[Information supplied by the institution as at 30 October
2007, and edited by the ACU]

QUEEN MARGARET UNIVERSITY

Founded 1999

Member of the Association of Commonwealth Universities

Postal Address: Queen Margaret University Drive, Musselburgh, East Lothian, Scotland EH21 6UU
Telephone: (0131) 474 0000 **Fax:** (0131) 474 0001 **E-mail:** admissions@qmu.ac.uk
URL: http://www.qmu.ac.uk

PRINCIPAL AND VICE-CHANCELLOR*—Cohen, Prof. Anthony P., CBE, BA S'ton., MSc S'ton., PhD S'ton., Hon. DSc Edin., FRSEd
VICE PRINCIPAL (ACADEMIC STRATEGY)—Kirk, Prof. David, BSc MPhil, FIFST
VICE PRINCIPAL (STRATEGIC PROJECTS)—Marshall, Rosalyn, BSc Dund.
DIRECTOR, REGISTRY AND SECRETARIAT/ACADEMIC REGISTRAR‡—Hynd, Irene, MA
DIRECTOR OF FINANCE—McCabe, Liam

GENERAL INFORMATION

History. The institution was established in 1875 as Edinburgh School of Cookery and renamed the Edinburgh College of Domestic Science in 1930. It was awarded university college status in February 1999, and full university status in 2007. The university recently moved to a new purpose-built campus at Craighall on the outskirts of Edinburgh.

Admission to first degree courses (see also United Kingdom Introduction). Through Universities and Colleges Admissions Service (UCAS).

First Degrees (see also United Kingdom Directory to Subjects of Study) (* = with honours). BA*, BSc*.
Length of course. Full-time: BA*, BSc*: 3–4 years. Part-time: BA*, BSc*: max. 9 years.

Higher Degrees (see also United Kingdom Directory to Subjects of Study).
Master's. MA, MBA, MFA, MPhil, MSc.
Length of course. Full-time: MA, MBA, MFA, MSc: 1 year; MPhil: 2 years. Part-time: MA, MBA, MFA, MSc: 2–3 years; MPhil: 4 years. By distance learning: MA, MBA, MFA, MSc: 2–3 years.
Doctoral. PhD.
Length of course. Full-time: PhD: 3 years. Part-time: PhD: 8 years.

Libraries. Volumes: 122,000. Periodicals subscribed to: 1270. Other holdings: 1780 audio-visual items.

FACULTIES/SCHOOLS
Business and Arts
E-mail: rkerley@qmu.ac.uk
Vice Principal, International Strategy and Commercialisation: Kerley, Prof. Richard, BA
Executive Assistant: Wallace, Ruth

Health and Social Sciences
E-mail: agilloran@qmu.ac.uk
Vice Principal, Research Development: Gilloran, Prof. Alan, MA PhD
Executive Assistant: Wallace, Ruth

ACADEMIC UNITS
Arranged by Schools

Business and Enterprise
Donnelly, Mike   Prof.; Dean of Sch.*
Hood, Susan   School Manager

Drama and Creative Industries
Dunn, David   Dean of Sch.*
Watson, Sheena   School Manager

Health Sciences
Donaghy, Marie, BA PhD   Prof.
Thomson, Gillian   School Manager

International Health and Development, Institute for
Tel: (0131) 317 3571 Fax: (0131) 317 3494
E-mail: int-health@qmu.ac.uk
McPake, Barbara, BA PhD   Prof.; Dir.*
Research: health systems (organisational studies); international ageing (prospective policy analysis, cultural constructions of ageing, health promotion for active ageing); policy analysis of poverty reduction strategies (coping and resilience); refugees, displacement and psychosocial interventions; reproductive health (HIV/AIDS, maternal health)

Social Sciences, Media and Communication
Cnossen, Christine, PhD   Dean of Sch.*
Twaddell, Kath   School Manager

SPECIAL CENTRES, ETC

Academic Practice, Centre for (CAP)
Morss, Kate, BSc PhD   Dir.*

Educational Resource Centre
Bain, J.   Supervisor*

CONTACT OFFICERS
Academic affairs. Vice Principal of Learning, Teaching and Assessment: Kirk, Prof. David, BSc MPhil, FIFST (E-mail: dkirk@qmu.ac.uk)
Accommodation. Hospitality Manager: O'Connell, Siobhan (E-mail: soconnell@qmu.ac.uk)
Admissions (first degree). Head of Admissions: Parratt, Margaret (E-mail: admissions@qmu.ac.uk)
Admissions (higher degree). Head of Admissions: Parratt, Margaret (E-mail: admissions@qmu.ac.uk)
Adult/continuing education. Head of Admissions: Parratt, Margaret (E-mail: admissions@qmu.ac.uk)
Alumni. Head of Development: Telfer, Lesley (E-mail: ltelfer@qmu.ac.uk)
Careers. Careers Officer: Cox, Lorna (E-mail: lcox@qmu.ac.uk)
Careers. Careers Officer: Pollock, Marion (E-mail: mpollock@qmu.ac.uk)
Computing services. Information Technology Manager: Graham, Dave (E-mail: dgraham@qmuc.ac.uk)

Development/fund-raising. Head of Development: Telfer, Lesley (E-mail: ltelfer@qmu.ac.uk)
Distance education. School Officer, Business and Enterprise: Wilson, Christine (E-mail: cwilson@qmu.ac.uk)
Equal opportunities. Director of Human Resources: Wright, Dorothy, LLB (E-mail: dwright@qmu.ac.uk)
Estates and buildings/works and services. Director, Estates and Facilities: Scott, Steve, BSc (E-mail: sscott@qmu.ac.uk)
Examinations. Examinations Officer: Morgan, Heather (E-mail: hmorgan@qmu.ac.uk)
Finance. Head of Finance: Cutt, Malcolm, LLB (E-mail: mcutt@qmu.ac.uk)
General enquiries. Vice Principal (Strategic Projects): Marshall, Rosalyn, BSc Dund. (E-mail: sbuchan@qmu.ac.uk)
International office. Head of International Office: (vacant)
Library (chief librarian). University Librarian: Rowley, Jo (E-mail: jrowley@qmu.ac.uk)
Library (enquiries). University Librarian: Rowley, Jo (E-mail: jrowley@qmu.ac.uk)
Marketing. Marketing and Communications Manager: Scott, Jane (E-mail: jscott@qmu.ac.uk)
Personnel/human resources. Director of Human Resources: Wright, Dorothy, LLB (E-mail: dwright@qmu.ac.uk)
Public relations. Marketing and Communications Manager: Scott, Jane (E-mail: jscott@qmu.ac.uk)
Publications. Marketing and Communications Manager: Scott, Jane (E-mail: jscott@qmu.ac.uk)
Purchasing. Head of Finance: Cutt, Malcolm, LLB (E-mail: mcutt@qmu.ac.uk)
Research. Vice Principal, Research Development: Gilloran, Prof. Alan, MA PhD (E-mail: agilloran@qmu.ac.uk)
Research. Dean of Research: Hardcastle, Prof. William, MA Qld., PhD Edin. (E-mail: whardcastle@amu.ac.uk)
Safety. Health and Safety Officer: Allen, Les (E-mail: lallen@qmu.ac.uk)
Security. Head Housekeeper/Bursar: Glennie, Gail (E-mail: gglennie@qmu.ac.uk)
Sport and recreation. Sports Supervisor: McHenry, Tony (E-mail: tmchenry@qmu.ac.uk)
Student welfare/counselling. Student Counsellor: Kelly, Frances (E-mail: fkelly@qmu.ac.uk)
Students from other countries. Head of International Office: (vacant)
Students with disabilities. Student Disability and Financial Advisor: Jebb, Jo (E-mail: jjebb@qmu.ac.uk)

[Information supplied by the institution as at 8 November 2007, and edited by the ACU]

UNIVERSITY OF READING

Founded 1926

Member of the Association of Commonwealth Universities

Postal Address: Whiteknights, PO Box 217, Reading, Berkshire, England RG6 6AH
Telephone: (0118) 987 5123 **Fax:** (0118) 931 4404
URL: http://www.reading.ac.uk

VICE-CHANCELLOR*—Marshall, Prof. Gordon R., CBE, BA Stir., DPhil Oxf., FBA
PRO-VICE-CHANCELLOR—Berry, Prof. Dianne C., BSc CNAA, DPhil Oxf.
PRO-VICE-CHANCELLOR—Stychin, Prof. Carl F., BA Alta., LLB Tor., LLM Col.
PRO-VICE-CHANCELLOR—Robson, Prof. R. L., BA York(UK), PhD Wales
PRO-VICE-CHANCELLOR—Downes, Prof. Tony A., BA Oxf., BCL Oxf.
PRESIDENT OF THE COUNCIL—Ford, T. G., FRSA
TREASURER—Fisher, Christopher
DIRECTOR OF STUDENT SERVICES‡—Watts, William D., BSc Lond.
DIRECTOR OF ACADEMIC SERVICES—Hodgson, Keith N., BA Leic.
LIBRARIAN—Munro, Julia, BSc Lond., MSc City(UK), MBA Reading
DIRECTOR OF INFORMATION SERVICES—Haworth, Annette E., MA Oxf., FBCS, FRSA
DIRECTOR OF FINANCE AND CORPORATE SERVICES—Savage, David C. L., BA Lond.

GENERAL INFORMATION

History. The university was originally established in 1892 as an extension college of the University of Oxford. It gained independent status in 1926.

The main campus is located 2.5km from Reading town centre, and 64km west of London.

Admission to first degree courses (see also United Kingdom Introduction). Through Universities and Colleges Admissions Service (UCAS). Two General Certificate of Education (GCE) A levels or the approved equivalent. Matriculation requirements may be waived for students over 21.

First Degrees (see also United Kingdom Directory to Subjects of Study) (* = with honours). BA*, BA(Ed)*, BEng*, BSc*, LLB*, MChem*, MDes*, MEng*, MMath*, MPharm*, MPhys*.

Length of course. Full-time: BA*, BEng*, BSc*, LLB*: 3–4 years; BA(Ed)*, MChem*, MDes*, MMath*, MPharm*: 4 years; MEng*, MPhys*: 4–5 years. Part-time: BA*: 5–7 years.

Higher Degrees (see also United Kingdom Directory to Subjects of Study).

Master's. LLM, MA, MBA, MFA, MMus, MPhil, MRes, MSc.

Admission. Applicants for admission to master's degrees and doctorates must normally hold a good first degree in an appropriate subject. Postgraduate applications are made directly to the faculty concerned.

Length of course. Full-time: LLM, MBA, MMus, MRes: 1 year; MA, MSc: 1–2 years; MFA: 2 years; MPhil: 2–3 years. Part-time: LLM, MMus: 2 years; MA, MSc: 2–5 years; MPhil: 3–6 years. By distance learning: MBA: 3–6 years.

Doctoral. DLitt, DSc, LLD, PhD.

Length of course. Full-time: PhD: 3–4 years. Part-time: PhD: 4–6 years.

Libraries. Volumes: 1,074,297. Periodicals subscribed to: 3742. Other holdings: 71 databases on CD-ROM. Special collections: Samuel Beckett Papers; records of British Publishing and Printing; the Astor Papers; Huntley & Palmers; Peek Frean; Finzi book room; Finzi music.

FACULTIES/SCHOOLS

Arts and Humanities

Tel: (0118) 378 8063 Fax: (0118) 378 6658
E-mail: fasug@reading.ac.uk,
faspg@reading.ac.uk
Dean: Walker, Prof. S. F., BA Reading, PhD Reading
Sub Dean: Trethewy, N. G., MA Dund.

Economic and Social Sciences

Tel: (0118) 378 8061 Fax: (0118) 931 0748
E-mail: fasug@reading.ac.uk,
faspg@reading.ac.uk
Dean: Pemberton, Prof. James, MA Camb., PhD Camb.
Sub Dean: Ashton, D., BA Lanc., MA Lanc., DPhil Oxf.

Life Sciences

Tel: (0118) 378 8370 Fax: (0118) 935 2063
E-mail: sciug@reading.ac.uk,
scipg@reading.ac.uk
Dean: Williams, Prof. Christine M., BSc Lond., PhD Lond.
Sub Dean: Adams, Sally

Science

Tel: (0118) 378 8342 Fax: (0118) 975 5509
E-mail: sciug@reading.ac.uk,
scipg@reading.ac.uk
Dean: Porter, Prof. D., BSc Wales, PhD Leic.
Sub Dean: Adams, Sally

ACADEMIC UNITS

Agriculture, Policy and Development, School of

Tel: (0118) 378 8471 Fax: (0118) 935 2421
E-mail: sapdstudentoffice@reading.ac.uk
Ellis, R. H., BSc Wales, PhD Reading   Head*

Agricultural and Food Economics

Tel: (0118) 378 7429 Fax: (0118) 975 6467
E-mail: aesadept@reading.ac.uk
Balcombe, Kelvin G., BCom Auck., MCom Auck., PhD Lond.
Bennett, Richard M., BSc Reading, MSc Oxf., PhD Reading   Sr. Lectr.
Holloway, Garth J., BCom(Ag) Lincoln(UK), MSc Guelph, PhD Purdue   Reader
Swinbank, Alan, BSc Reading, MA McM., PhD Lond.   Prof.
Tiffin, J. Richard, BSc Newcastle(UK), PhD Lond.   Reader; Head*
Traill, W. Bruce, BSc Glas., PhD Cornell   Prof.
Other Staff: 4 Lectrs.; 3 Res. Fellows; 2 Visiting Res. Fellows; 3 Res. Fellows†; 1 Hon. Fellow
Research: agricultural and food economics and policy; consumer food choice and marketing; food and agricultural competitiveness and globalisation; international development and rural livelihoods; production and environmental economics

Agricultural Strategy, Centre for

Tel: (0118) 931 8152 Fax: (0118) 935 3423
E-mail: casagri@reading.ac.uk
Swinbank, Alan, BSc Reading, MA McM., PhD Lond.   Prof.; Dir.*

Tranter, R. B., BSc Reading   Dep. Dir.
Other Staff: 1 Sr. Res. Fellow; 1 Res. Fellow; 1 Res. Officer†
Research: developments in agricultural and food industries and the countryside

Agriculture

Bryant, M. J., BSc(Agric) Nott., PhD Liv.   Sr. Lectr.; Head*
Ellis, R. H., BSc Wales, PhD Reading   Prof.
Givens, D. I., BSc Newcastle(UK), PhD Newcastle(UK)   Prof.; Dir., Centre for Dairy Res. (CEDAR); Dir., Nutritional Scis. Res. Unit (NSRU)
Gooding, Mike J., BSc CNAA, PhD Wolv.   Sr. Lectr.
James, A. D., BA Oxf., PhD   Sr. Lectr.
Rehman, T., BSc W.Pak.Ag., MSc W.Pak.Ag., PhD   Sr. Lectr.
Wheeler, T. R., BSc Keele, MSc Reading, PhD Reading   Reader; Dir., Plant Environment. Lab.
Other Staff: 5 Lectrs.; 3 Principal Res. Fellows; 7 Sr. Res. Fellows; 2 Sr. Visiting Res. Fellows; 17 Res. Fellows; 3 Visiting Res. Fellows; 1 Hon. Principal Res. Fellow; 3 Hon. Sr. Res. Fellows; 1 Hon. Res. Fellow
Research: agri-environmental research; animal science; crop science; dairy research; veterinary epidemiology and economics

Agri-Environmental Research, Centre for

Tel: (0118) 378 8938 Fax: (0118) 935 2421
Mortimer, S. R., BSc Lond., PhD Camb.   Asst. Dir.
Norris, K. J., BSc Wales, DPhil Oxf.   Dir.*

International Development and Applied Economics, Graduate Institute of

Tel: (0118) 378 8119 Fax: (0118) 926 1244
E-mail: ird@reading.ac.uk
Garforth, C. J., MA Camb., PhD Camb.   Prof.; Dir.*
Shankar, B., BA Madr., MA J.Nehru U., MA N.Y.State, PhD Ill.
Research: international changes in public and private service provision; natural resource livelihood development; nature of civil society and governance

Arts and Communication Design, School of

Taylor, L. J., MA Lond.   Sr. Lectr.; Head*

Film, Theatre and Television

Tel: (0118) 378 8878 Fax: (0118) 378 8873
E-mail: film.drama@reading.ac.uk
Bignell, J. C., MA Camb., MA Sus., DPhil Sus.   Reader; Head*
Bull, J. S., BA Wales   Prof.
Hillier, J. M., BA Oxf.   Sr. Lectr.
Pye, D., BA Reading   Sr. Lectr.

Taylor, L. J., MA Lond. Sr. Lectr.
Other Staff: 7 Lectrs.; 1 Res. Fellow
Research: critical, theoretical and historical
studies of film, theatre and television;
methodologies of performance analysis;
practical work as a form of critical enquiry;
relationships between film, theatre and
television

Fine Art

Tel: (0118) 931 8051 Fax: (0118) 926 2667
E-mail: fineart@reading.ac.uk
Buckley, Stephen, BA Durh., MFA Reading Prof.
Clausen, S., MA Lond. Reader
Dronsfield, J. L., BA St.Martin's, MA RCA, PhD
Kingston(UK) Reader
Edmond, T. A., BA CNAA Sr. Lectr.
Russell, J., BA St.Martin's, MA Lond., PhD
Kingston(UK)
Other Staff: 3 Lectrs.; 1 Reader†; 5 Lectrs.†; 1
Hon. Fellow
Research: contemporary art

Typography and Graphic Communication

Tel: (0118) 378 8081 Fax: (0118) 935 1680
E-mail: typography@reading.ac.uk
Dyson, M. C., BA Reading, PhD Reading Sr.
Lectr.
Eliot, S. J., BA Sus., MA Sus., PhD Lond. Prof.†
Luna, P., BA Reading Prof.; Head*
Mosley, J., MA Camb. Prof.†
Stiff, P., BA Reading Reader
Unger, Gerard Prof.†
Walker, S. F., BA Reading, PhD Reading Prof.
Other Staff: 1 Lectr.; 1 AHRB Creative Arts
Fellow; 5 Lectrs.†
Research: history of typography, book design
and letterforms; information design;
theoretical issues in typography

Biological Sciences, School of

Tel: (0118) 378 8093 Fax: (0118) 378 8902
Andrews, S. C., BSc Sheff., PhD Sheff. Reader
Battey, N. H., BSc Wales, PhD Edin. Prof.;
Head of Sch.*
Bisby, F. A, BA Oxf., DPhil Oxf., FLS Prof.
Bisgrove, R. J., BSc Reading, MLA Mich. Sr.
Lectr.
Bohning, D., DrRerNat Prof.
Callaghan, A., BSc CNAA, PhD Lond. Sr. Lectr.
Cook, J., BA Oxf., PhD Lond. Prof.
Darbre, P. D., BSc Birm., PhD Camb. Sr. Lectr.
Dennett, M. D., BSc Lond., MSc Reading, PhD
Reading, DSc Birm. Reader; Dir., Teaching
and Learning; Head, Plant Scis.
Dunwell, J. M., BA Oxf., PhD E.Anglia Prof.
Froud-Williams, R. J., BSc Reading, PhD Reading
Sr. Lectr.
Gibbins, J. M., BSc Reading, PhD Reading Reader
Hadley, P., BSc Wales, PhD Wales Prof.
Hatcher, P. E., BA Oxf., PhD Oxf.Brookes Dir.,
Teaching and Learning
John, P., BSc Lond., PhD Lond. Prof.
Jones, I. M., BSc Warw., PhD Warw. Prof.,
Virology
Kimber, A. C., BSc Hull, MSc Sheff., PhD Hull
Reader; Head, Applied Stats.
Knight, P. G., BSc Wales, MSc Birm., PhD Reading
Prof., Reproductive Biology
Leake, D. S., BSc Birm., PhD Camb. Reader
Lowry, P. J., BSc Leeds, PhD Leeds, DSc Leeds,
FIBiol Prof., Biochemistry and Physiology
MacIntyre, S., BSc Glas., PhD Br.Col.
Okamura, B., BSc Montr., PhD Calif. Reader
Pagel, M., BA Wash., PhD Wash. Prof.,
Evolutionary Biology
Patel, K., BSc Kent, PhD Lond. Prof.
Poole, P. S., BSc Murd., PhD Murd. Prof.,
Microbial Biology
Robson, R. L., BA York(UK), PhD Wales Head
of Res.; Prof., Microbiology
Savva, Demetris, BSc Lond., PhD Lond. Sr.
Lectr.; Dir. Teaching and Learning
Shaw, M. W., BA Camb., MSc Newcastle(UK), PhD
E.Anglia Reader
Sibly, R. M., MA Oxf., DPhil Oxf. Prof.,
Behavioural Ecology

Strange, P. G., MA Camb., PhD Camb. Prof.,
Neuroscience
Todd, S. C., BSc Warw., MSc Reading, PhD Reading
Watson, Kimberley, BSc Qu., MSc Qu., DPhil
Oxf. Reader, Structural Biology
Wilkinson, Michael J., BSc Leic., PhD Leic., FLS
Reader, Plant Genetics
Other Staff: 20 Lectrs.; 9 Sr. Res. Fellows; 38
Postdoctoral Res. Fellows; 13 Visiting Res.
Fellows; 1 Reader†; 3 Lectrs.†; 2 Hon.
Lectrs.; 11 Hon. Fellows; 2 Hon. Res.
Fellows
Research: microbiology; molecular and cell
biology; zoology

Plant Sciences

Tel: (0118) 378 8163 Fax: (0118) 378 8160
E-mail: plantsci@reading.ac.uk
Research: crop ecology and climatology; crop
physiology and biochemistry; ecology;
genetics, plant breeding and crop evolution;
plant pathology

Quantitative Biology and Applied Statistics

Tel: (0118) 378 8022 Fax: (0118) 975 3169
E-mail: appstats@reading.ac.uk
Research: medical statistics; statistical genetics;
statistical modelling

Statistical Services Centre

Tel: (0118) 378 8025 Fax: (0118) 975 3169
E-mail: statistics@reading.ac.uk
Allan, E. F., BSc Glas., MSc Reading Dir.*
Stern, R. D., BSc Sus., MSc Sus., PhD Reading,
Hon. DSc Colombo Chief Biometrician
Wilson, I. M., BSc St And., MSc Wales Spec.
Adviser
Other Staff: 2 Principal Statisticians; 3 Sr.
Statisticians; 1 Statistician; 2 Visiting
Fellows

Business

University of Reading Business School
Tel: (0118) 378 8226 Fax: (0118) 975 0236
E-mail: business@reading.ac.uk
Hendry, John, BA Camb., MA Camb., MSc Lond.,
PhD Lond. Head of Sch.*

Economics

Tel: (0118) 987 5123
E-mail: b.l.sofocli@rdg.ac.uk
Burke, S. P., BA Lanc., MA Warw., PhD Reading
Sr. Lectr.
Casson, M. C., BA Brist. Prof.
D'Arcy, P. E., BA N.U.I., MA N.U.I. Sr. Lectr.
Della Giusta, M., BSc Venice, MSc Reading, PhD
Reading Sr. Lectr.
Evans, A. W., BA Lond., PhD Lond., FCA Prof.
Kalyuzhnova, Y., MSc Kazakh State, MA PhD
Sr. Lectr.
Kambhampati, U. S., BA Camb., MPhil Camb.,
PhD Camb. Reader; Head*
McQueen, M., BScEcon Wales, MA Sus. Sr.
Lectr.
Meen, G. P., OBE, BA Reading, MSc Lond., PhD
Lond. Prof.
Narula, R., BEng Rutgers, MBA Rutgers, PhD
Rutgers Prof.
Patterson, K. D., BA Essex, BPhil Oxf. Prof.
Pavelin, S., BA E.Anglia, MA E.Anglia, PhD
E.Anglia Reader
Pearce, R. D., BA Reading Reader
Pemberton, James, MA Camb., PhD Camb.
Prof.
Other Staff: 15 Lectrs.; 3 Res. Fellows; 2
Visiting Res. Fellows; 1 Hon. Fellow
Research: econometrics; environmental
economics; international business; real
estate; urban and regional economics

Euro-Asian Studies, Centre for

Tel: (0118) 931 6205 Fax: (0118) 931 6274
E-mail: e.macdonald@reading.ac.uk
Kalyuzhnova, Y., MSc Kazakh State, MA PhD
Dir.*
Waters, C. P. M., BA Tor., LLB Qu., LLM McG.,
DCL McG. Deputy Dir.

Research: economics, politics and diplomacy in
transition

ICMA Centre

Business School for Financial Markets
Tel: (0118) 378 8239 Fax: (0118) 931 4741
E-mail: admin@icmacentre.reading.ac.uk
Alexander, C., BSc Sus., MSc Lond., PhD Essex
Prof.
Board, J., BA Newcastle(UK), PhD Newcastle(UK)
Prof., Finance; Dir.*
Brooks, C., BA Reading, PhD Reading Prof.
Neftci, S., BA Ankara, PhD Minn. Prof.
Nelson, P., MA Camb. Prof.
Scott-Quinn, B. S., BA CNAA, MAcc Glas.
Prof., Investment Banking; Chairman*
Skinner, F., BCom Nfld., MBA Tor., PhD Tor.
Reader
Sutcliffe, C., BA Reading Prof.
Ward, C., MA Camb., MA Exe., PhD Reading
Prof.
Ziemba, W., BSChE Mass., MBA Calif., PhD Calif.
Prof.
Other Staff: 6 Lectrs.; 2 Teaching Fellows
Research: international securities, investment,
banking

Management

Tel: (0118) 378 8069 Fax: (0118) 378 6229
E-mail: p.e.wylie@reading.ac.uk
Basu, A., BA Delhi, MPhil Camb., PhD Camb.
Sr. Lectr. (on leave)
Booth, S. A., BA Leeds, PhD Reading Sr. Lectr.;
Head*
Cooper, J., BA Reading, MSc Lond. Sr. Lectr.
Godley, A., BSc(Econ) Lond., PhD Lond.
Reader; Dir. of Teaching and Learning
Hendry, John, BA Camb., MA Camb., MSc Lond.,
PhD Lond. Prof.
King, Z., BA Camb., PhD Lond. Sr. Lectr.
Meyer, K. F. E., MSc Gött., PhD Lond. Prof.
Miskell, P., BA Wales, MA Wales, PhD Wales
Mol, M., MSc Rotterdam, PhD Rotterdam Sr.
Lectr.
Scott, P., BA York(UK), MSc Lond., DPhil Oxf.
Reader
Other Staff: 11 Lectrs.
Research: attitudes to accounting data and
variations in corporate financial reporting;
dynamics and evolution of industrial
districts or clusters; leadership and business
strategy; organisational behaviour and
corporate culture; small business
development and entrepreneurship

Real Estate and Planning

Tel: (0118) 378 8175 Fax: (0118) 378 8172
E-mail: rep@reading.ac.uk
Allmendinger, P. M., BSc H-W, BSc Oxf.Brookes,
FRGS Prof., Planning
Ball, M. J., BSc S'ton., MSc Lond., PhD Lond.
Prof., Urban and Property Economics
Baum, A. E., BSc(EstMan) MPhil PhD, FRICS
Prof.†, Land Management
Byrne, P. J., BA Manc. Prof., Real Estate
Dynamics
Crosby, N., PhD Reading Prof., Land
Management; Head*
Doak, A. J., BA Lond., MPhil Lond. Sr. Lectr.
Gibbard, R., BSc Reading Sr. Lectr.
Gibson, Virginia A., BA W.Ont., MSc Sr.
Lectr., Land Management
Hart, D. A., BA Colorado, MA Exe., PhD Lond.
Reader
Lizieri, C. M., BA Oxf., PhD Lond. Prof., Real
Estate Finance
Matysiak, G. A., MSc Lond.Guild. Prof.†, Real
Estate Investment
McAllister, P., BA Kent, MPhil Reading, MPhil
Camb.
Parker, G., BSc E.Lond., MPhil Lond., PhD Brist.
Sr. Lectr.
Rowley, A. R., MA(UrbDes) Manc. Sr. Lectr.
Other Staff: 4 Lectrs.; 5 Visiting Fellows; 1
British Property Fed. Visiting Fellow; 1
Lectr.†; 1 Sr. Visiting Fellow†
Research: corporate real estate management;
property valuation and appraisal; real estate

finance; rural property; town and country planning

Chemistry, Food Biosciences and Pharmacy, School of

Tel: (0118) 378 8703
Marston, G., MA Oxf., DPhil Oxf.   Sr. Lectr.; Head*

Biotechnology Education, National Centre for

Tel: (0118) 378 8934
Madden, Dean, BSc Wales, Dr Gothenburg   Jt. Dir.*
Schollar, John, BSc Lond., Dr Gothenburg   Jt. Dir.*
Other Staff: 1 Project Manager; 2 Tech. Staff

Chemistry

Tel: (0118) 378 8447 Fax: (0118) 378 6331
   E-mail: chemistry@reading.ac.uk
Almond, M. J., BSc Reading, DPhil Oxf.   Sr. Lectr.; Head*
Cardin, C. J., MA Oxf., MA Trinity(Dub.), DPhil Sus.   Reader
Cardin, D. J., BSc Sus., MA Trinity(Dub.), DPhil Sus.   Prof., Inorganic Chemistry
Colquhoun, H. M., MA Camb., PhD Lond., FRSChem   Prof.
Cramer, R. K.
Hamley, I. W., BSc Reading, PhD S'ton.   Diamond Prof., Physical Chemistry
Harwood, L. M., BSc Manc., MSc Manc., MA Oxf., PhD Manc., FRSChem   Prof., Organic Chemistry
Hayes, W. C., BSc Nott.Trent, PhD Birm.
Held, G. F. K., PhD T.U.Munich
Hibble, S. J., MA Oxf., DPhil Oxf.
Hollins, P., MA Camb., PhD Lond.   Reader
Marston, G., MA Oxf., DPhil Oxf.   Sr. Lectr.
Osborn, H. M. I., BA Oxf., PhD Brist.   Reader
Sweeney, J. B., BSc Lond., DPhil Oxf.   Reader
Tsang, S. C. E., BSc Lond., PhD Reading   Reader
Other Staff: 7 Lectrs.; 2 Sr. Res. Fellows; 7 Visiting Fellows; 1 NERC Advanced Fellow; 1 Tutorial Fellow
Research: atmospheric chemistry, spectroscopy and kinetics; catalysis and surface science; chemistry at the biological interface; structural and computational chemistry; synthetic chemistry

Food Biosciences

Tel: (0118) 378 8700 Fax: (0118) 378 0080
   E-mail: food@reading.ac.uk
Gibson, G. R., BSc Dund., PhD Dund.   Prof.
Gordon, M. H., MA Oxf., DPhil Oxf.   Sr. Lectr.
Gosney, M. A., MB ChB Liv., MD Liv., FRCP   Prof.
Grandison, A. S., BSc Liv., PhD Liv.   Sr. Lectr.
Jukes, D. J., BSc Birm., MSc Leeds, PhD Reading   Sr. Lectr.
Lewis, M. J., MSc Birm., PhD Birm.   Sr. Lectr.
Lovegrove, J. A., PhD Sur., BSc
Mackey, B. M., BSc Brun., PhD Leic.
Minihane, A. M., BSc N.U.I., PhD N.U.I.
Mottram, D. S., BSc Leeds, PhD Leeds   Prof.
Niranjan, K., BChemEng Bom., MChemEng Bom., PhD Bom.   Sr. Lectr.
Rastall, R. A., BSc Greenwich, PhD Greenwich   Sr. Lectr.; Head*
Rowland, I., BSc Lond., PhD Lond.   Hugh Sinclair Prof., Human Nutrition
Williams, Christine M., BSc Lond., PhD Lond.   Prof.
Yaqoob, P., MA Oxf., DPhil Oxf.
Other Staff: 9 Lectrs.; 3 Sr. Res. Fellows; 21 Res. Fellows; 9 Lectrs.†; 3 Hon. Fellows
Research: biotechnology; food chemistry and biochemistry; food microbial sciences; food processing sciences; human nutrition

Pharmacy, School of

Tel: (0118) 378 5394 Fax: (0118) 378 6562
Alexander, A. M., BPharm Aston, MSc Aston, MSc Open(UK), PhD Aston, FRPharmS
Brooks, G., BPharm Lond., PhD Lond., FAHA   Prof.; Head*

Denicolo, Pam, BA Open(UK), PhD Sur.   Reader; Dir., Postgrad. Educn.
Osborn, H. M. I., BA Oxf., PhD Brist.   Reader; Dir., Pharmaceutical Chem.
Strange, P. G., MA Camb., PhD Camb.   Dir., Pharmacol.; Prof., Neuroscience
Williams, A. C., BSc CNAA, PhD Brad., FRSChem   Prof.; Dir., Res.; Dir., Pharmaceutics
Williamson, E. M., BScPharm Lond., PhD Lond., FLS   Prof.; Dir., Pharmacy Practice
Other Staff: 11 Lectrs.

Construction Management and Engineering, School of

Tel: (0118) 378 8201 Fax: (0118) 931 3856
Anumba, C. J., BSc Jos, PhD Leeds, DSc Lough., DrHC T.H.Delft   Prof.
Awbi, H. B., BSc Manc., MSc Manc., PhD CNAA   Sr. Lectr.
Chaplin, C. R., MA Camb., PhD Camb., FRSA   Prof., Engineering Science
Clements-Croome, D. J., BSc Aston, MSc Lond., PhD Lough., FRSA, FIP, FICE   Prof., Construction Engineering
Cook, G. K., BSc Aston, PhD Sur., FRSA   Sr. Lectr.
Flanagan, R., MSc Aston, PhD Aston, FICE, FRICS   Prof.
Gray, C., MPhil Reading   Prof.
Green, S. D., BSc Birm., MSc H-W, PhD Reading   Prof.
Hughes, W. P., BSc Manc., PhD CNAA   Head*
Jeronimidis, G., DottChim Rome   Prof.
Lansley, Peter R., BSc Leic., MSc Newcastle(UK), PhD Reading   Prof.
Shipworth, D. T., BA(Arch) Deakin, BArch Deakin, PhD Melb.
Whyte, J., MA Camb., PhD Lough.
Other Staff: 13 Lectrs.; 2 Visiting Sr. Res. Fellows; 25 Res. Staff; 1 Adjunct Prof.; 3 Lectrs.†
Research: construction management; inclusive environments; sustainable technologies; sustainable urban environments

Biomimetics, Centre for

Tel: (0118) 378 8585 Fax: (0118) 931 3327
   E-mail: biomimetics@reading.ac.uk
Jeronimidis, G., DottChim Rome   Prof.; Dir.*
Other Staff: 1 Lectr.; 4 Res. Staff
Research: the abstraction of good design from nature

Continuing Education, School of

Tel: (0118) 378 8347 Fax: (0118) 378 6539
   E-mail: cont-ed@reading.ac.uk
Cottingham, M. L., BA Claremont Teachers
O'Callaghan, J. Brian, BA Manc., PhD Manc.   Head*
Woodman, P. E., BA N.U.I., MAppSci Glas., PhD Reading
Other Staff: 5 Lectrs.

Education, Institute of

Tel: (0118) 378 8811 Fax: (0118) 935 2080
   E-mail: b.little@reading.ac.uk
Croll, Paul, BA York(UK), MSc Strath.   Prof.
Edwards, V., BA Reading, PhD Reading   Prof.
Fidler, F. B., BSc Lond., MSc Sheff., MA Lanc., PhD Sheff.   Prof.
Goodwyn, A. C., BA Reading, MA Leic.   Head*
Kempe, A. J., BEd Nott., MEd Exe.   Sr. Lectr.
Malvern, David D., MA Oxf.   Prof.
McCrum, E. M., BA Kent, MA Cant.CC
Parsons, M. L., BA Open(UK), PhD Reading   Sr. Lectr.
Rassool, Naz, BEd CNAA, MA Lond., PhD Lond.   Reader
Richards, B. J., BA Wales, MEd Brist., PhD Brist.   Prof.
Smith, I. F.   Sr. Lectr.
Stainthorp, R., BA Nott., BSc Lond., MSc Lond., PhD Lond.
Other Staff: 22 Lectrs.; 3 Sr. Lectrs.†; 2 Lectrs.†; 5 Hon. Fellows

Research: educational research methods; international and comparative education; language and literacy education; music education; school improvement, leadership and management

Engineering, Systems, School of

Tel: (0118) 378 8601 Fax: (0118) 975 1994
Alexandrov, V. N., MSc Moscow, PhD Sofia   Prof.
Baker, M., BSc Cardiff, PhD Cardiff   Prof.
Becerra, V. M., BEng Simón Bolívar, MSc Middx., PhD City(UK)   Reader
Bowen, J. W., BSc Lond., PhD Lond.   Sr. Lectr.
Ferryman, J. M., BSc Reading, PhD Reading   Sr. Lectr.
Guy, C. G., BSc Durh., FIEE   Sr. Lectr.; Sch. Dir. of Teaching and Learning; Head of Sch.*
Harwin, W. S., MA Camb., MSc Strath., PhD Camb.   Reader
McCrindle, R. J., BSc Liv., MSc Warw., PhD Durh.   Sr. Lectr.
McKee, G. T., BSc Manc., PhD Manc.   Sr. Lectr.
Megson, G. M., BSc Leeds, PhD Lough.   Prof.
Mitchell, R. J., BSc Reading, PhD Reading, FIEE   Sr. Lectr.
Nasuto, S. J., PhD Reading, MSc   Reader
Ruiz, V., BSc Rouen, MSc Rouen, PhD Rouen   Sr. Lectr.
Sharkey, P. M., BSc(Eng) Trinity(Dub.), MA Trinity(Dub.), PhD Strath.   Prof.
Sherratt, R. S., BEng CNAA, MSc Salf., PhD Salf.   Sr. Lectr.
Sun, L., BSc Staffs., MSc Staffs., PhD Staffs.   Sr. Lectr.
Warwick, K., BSc Aston, PhD Lond., DSc Lond., DrSc Prague, FIEE   Prof.
Williams, S. A., BSc Lough., PhD Lough., FBCS   Sr. Lectr.
Zheng, F.-C., BEng Harbin, MEng Harbin, PhD Edin.   Prof.
Other Staff: 16 Lectrs.; 1 Sr. Res. Fellow; 3 Res. Fellows; 7 Lectrs.†

English and American Literature, School of

Tel: (0118) 378 8361 Fax: (0118) 378 6561
   E-mail: english@reading.ac.uk
Brauner, D., MA Camb., PhD Lond.   Sr. Lectr.
Brown, C. C., BA Reading, PhD Reading   Prof.; Co-Dir., Renaissance Texts Res. Centre
Bullen, J. B., MA Camb., MA Oxf., PhD Camb.   Prof.
Donnell, A. J., BA Warw., PhD Warw.
Eliot, S. J., BA Sus., MA Sus., PhD Lond.   Dir. of Res.; Prof., Publishing and Printing History
Hardman, C. B., MA Oxf., BLitt Oxf.   Sr. Lectr.
Hardman, P. M., BA E.Anglia, BLitt Oxf.   Sr. Lectr.
Harvey, G. M., BA Hull, PhD Hull, FRSA   Sr. Lectr.; Head*
Heale, E. M., BA Warw., PhD Lond.   Sr. Lectr.
Ioppolo, G. J., BA Calif., MA Calif., PhD Calif.
Lesnik-Oberstein, K. B., MA Brist., MA V.U.Amst., PhD Brist.   Sr. Lectr.
Lyle, C. D., BLitt Oxf., MA Oxf.   Sr. Lectr.
McDonald, R. D. A., BA N.U.I., MA N.U.I., MSt Oxf., DPhil Oxf.   Sr. Lectr.
O'Callaghan, M., BA Melb., DPhil Oxf.   Reader
Parrinder, J. P., MA Camb., PhD Camb.   Prof.
Woodman, T. M., MA Oxf., MPhil Oxf., PhD Yale   Sr. Lectr.
Other Staff: 13 Lectrs.; 1 Assoc. Lectr.; 2 Lectrs.†; 3 Hon. Fellows
Research: children's literature; contemporary literature; mediaeval and Renaissance literature; romantic poetry and prose; Victorian literature

Health and Social Care, School of

Tel: (0118) 931 8853 Fax: (0118) 935 2080
   E-mail: r.adby@reading.ac.uk
Connelly, J., MB BS Newcastle(UK), MSc Lond., MBA Leeds, FFPHM   Prof.
Courtenay, M., BSc Reading, PhD Reading   Prof.
Keene, Jan, BA Sus., PhD Wales   Prof.; Dir., Res.

Oliver, D., MB BChir Camb., MA Oxf.   Sr. Lectr.

Quinn, A., BA Melb.   Sr. Lectr.

Victor, C., BA Wales(Swansea), MPhil Nott., PhD Wales   Head*

Other Staff: 6 Lectrs.; 4 Res. Fellows; 10 Lectrs.†

Research: bereavement and palliative care; crisis intervention; mental health social work; school refusal; therapeutic child care

Human and Environmental Sciences, School of

Fax: (0118) 931 0279
   E-mail: shes@reading.ac.uk
Mithen, S. J., BA Sheff., MSc York(UK), PhD Camb., FSA   Prof.; Head of Sch.*

Archaeology

Tel: (0118) 378 8132 Fax: (0118) 378 6718
   E-mail: archaeology@reading.ac.uk
Astill, G. G., BA Birm., PhD Birm., FSA   Prof.
Bell, M. G., BSc Lond., PhD Lond., FSA   Prof.
Black, S., BSc Aberd., PhD Lanc., FGS   Sr. Lectr.
Bradley, R. J., MA Oxf., FSA   Prof.
Chapman, R. W., MA Camb., PhD Camb., FSA   Prof.; Head*
Creighton, J. D., BA Durh., PhD Durh.   Sr. Lectr.
Dark, S. P., MA Camb., DPhil Oxf.   Sr. Lectr.
Fulford, Michael G., BA S'ton., PhD S'ton., FBA, FSA   Prof.
Gilchrist, Roberta, BA York(UK), DPhil York(UK), FSA   Prof.
Mithen, S. J., BA Sheff., MSc York(UK), PhD Camb., FSA   Prof.
Other Staff: 9 Lectrs.; 1 Assoc. Lectr.; 3 Res. Fellows; 1 Hon. Res. Fellow

Research: geoarchaeology; mediaeval monasticism and buildings archaeology; prehistoric hunters and gatherers; social archaeology; urbanism

Geography

Tel: (0118) 378 8733 Fax: (0118) 975 5865
   E-mail: geography@reading.ac.uk
Bowlby, Sophia R., BA Camb., MSc Northwestern, PhD Northwestern   Sr. Lectr.
Coleman, M. L., BSc Lond., MSc Leeds, PhD Leeds   Prof., Sedimentary Geochemistry
Foot, D. H. S., BSc Wales   Sr. Lectr.
Griffiths, G. H., BA Camb., PhD Aston   Sr. Lectr.
Howard, A., BSc Leeds, PhD Leeds   Sr. Lectr.
Johnes, P. J., BSc CNAA, DPhil Oxf.   Prof.†
Morse, S., BSc Wales, MSc Reading, PhD Reading, PhD S'ton.   Head*
Potter, R. B., BSc Lond., PhD Lond.   Prof.
Skeffington, R., BSc Sus., PhD Dund.   Prof.†
White, K., BSc CNAA, PhD Reading   Sr. Lectr.
Whitehead, P. G., BSc Lough., MSc Manc., PhD Camb.   Prof.
Other Staff: 6 Lectrs.; 2 Res. Scientists; 1 Sr. Lectr.†; 1 Lectr.†

Research: aquatic environments; geographies of development; landscape and landform change; political and cultural geography; tourism

Soil Science

Tel: (0118) 378 6557 Fax: (0118) 378 6660
   E-mail: s.m.hawthorne@reading.ac.uk
Collins, C., BSc Wales, PhD Lond.   Reader
Hodson, M., BA Oxf., PhD Edin., FGS   Reader
Nortcliff, S., BA Brist., PhD E.Anglia   Prof.; Head*
Robinson, J. S., BSc Newcastle(UK), PhD Newcastle(UK)   Sr. Lectr.
Other Staff: 3 Lectrs.; 1 Visiting Fellow; 6 Res. Fellows; 1 Sessl. Lectr.†

Research: agriculture and soils; contaminated soils and remediation; environmental management; soil processes; soil spatial analysis

Humanities, School of

Tel: (0118) 378 8325

Atkin, N. J., BA Lond., PhD Lond., FRHistS   Sr. Lectr.; Head of Sch.*

Classics

Tel: (0118) 931 8420 Fax: (0118) 931 6661
   E-mail: classics@reading.ac.uk
Duff, T. E., MA Camb., PhD Camb.   Reader
Goff, B. E., MA Camb., PhD Cornell   Sr. Lectr.
King, H., BA Lond., PhD Lond.   Reader; Head*
Knight, G. R., BA Oxf., MA Reading, PhD Reading   Sr. Lectr.
Rajak, Tessa, MA Oxf., DPhil Oxf.   Prof., Ancient History
Rutherford, I. C., MA Oxf., DPhil Oxf.   Prof.
Smith, A. C., BA Dartmouth, PhD Yale   Sr. Lectr.
Vasunia, P., BA Pomona, PhD Stan.   Reader
Wallace-Hadrill, A. F., MA Oxf., DPhil Oxf.   Prof. (on leave)
Other Staff: 6 Lectrs.; 2 Hon. Fellows

Research: gender and the classical tradition; Greek lyric poetry; Hellenistic Judaism; papyrology and philology; Roman social history

History

Tel: (0118) 378 8147 Fax: (0118) 378 6440
   E-mail: history@reading.ac.uk
Atkin, N. J., BA Lond., PhD Lond., FRHistS   Sr. Lectr.
Grant, L., MA St And., MA Lond., PhD Lond.   Prof.
Hoyle, R. W., BA Birm., DPhil Oxf., FRHistS   Prof.
Lawrence, A., MA Camb., MA Lond., PhD Lond.   Sr. Lectr.
Murphy, P. V., BA Oxf., DPhil Oxf.   Reader
Parish, H., MA St And., DPhil Oxf., FRHistS   Head*
Tallett, F., JP, BA PhD   Sr. Lectr.
Taylor, S. J. C., MA Camb., PhD Camb., FRHistS   Reader
West, E., BA Liv., MA Manc., PhD Liv.
Other Staff: 10 Lectrs.; 1 Assoc. Lectr.; 2 Hon. Visiting Fellows; 3 Hon. Res. Fellows

Research: American history; economic history (agricultural and local communities); European history (France and Germany); mediaeval history (England, France and Germany); religious history (the Church of England, witchcraft in the Middle Ages)

History of Art

see also Fine Art

Tel: (0118) 931 8890 Fax: (0118) 931 8918
   E-mail: arthistory@rdg.ac.uk
Davies, P., BA Reading, MA Lond., PhD Lond.   Reader
Gruetzner-Robins, A. E., BA Tor., MA Lond., PhD Lond.   Reader
Lee, S., BA Reading, PhD Reading   Sr. Lectr.
Malvern, S. B., BA Reading, PhD Reading   Lectr.; Head*
Robertson, E. Clare, MA Oxf., MPhil Lond., PhD Lond.   Reader
Other Staff: 1 Lectr.; 1 Assoc. Lectr.

Research: British artists and the First World War; European and American hospital architecture; Michele Sanmichele; Paolo Veronese; Walter Sickert

Medieval Studies, Graduate Centre for

Tel: (0118) 931 8148
   E-mail: gcms@reading.ac.uk
Grant, L., MA St And., MA Lond., PhD Lond.   Dir.*
Other Staff: 22 Lectrs.

Research: mediaeval studies, literature, history

Philosophy

Fax: (0118) 378 5123
   E-mail: philosophy@reading.ac.uk
Borg, E. G. N., BA Lond., MPhil Lond., PhD Lond.   Prof.
Cottingham, John G., MA Oxf., DPhil Oxf.   Prof.; Dir. of Res.
Dancy, Jonathan, BPhil Oxf., MA Oxf.   Prof.
Hooker, Bradford W., BA Prin., DPhil Oxf.   Prof.
Oderberg, David S., BA Melb., LLB Melb., DPhil Oxf.   Prof.

Preston, John M., BA N.Lond., BPhil Oxf., MSc Essex, DPhil Oxf.   Sr. Lectr.
Stratton-Lake, Philip J., BA Essex, PhD Essex   Sr. Lectr.; Head*
Strawson, Galen J., MA Camb., DPhil Oxf.   Prof.
Other Staff: 3 Lectrs.; 2 Tutors†

Research: contemporary moral theory; early modern philosophy; ethics; philosophy (language, science)

Languages and European Studies, School of

Tel: (0118) 378 8123 Fax: (0118) 378 6797
   E-mail: languages@reading.ac.uk
Tucker, G. H., MA Camb., PhD Camb.   Prof.; Head of Sch.*

Applied Linguistics

Tel: (0118) 378 8141 Fax: (0118) 975 3365
   E-mail: slals@reading.ac.uk
Huang, Y., BA Nanking, MA Nanking, PhD Camb., DPhil Oxf.   Prof., Theoretical Linguistics
Spelman Miller, K. E., BA Manc., MA Reading, PhD Reading   Sr. Lectr.
Tonkyn, A., BA Natal, MA Oxf., MA Reading   Head*
Other Staff: 5 Lectrs.; 1 Res. Fellow; 3 Visiting Res. Fellows

Research: accents and dialects; acquisition of language; applied linguistics; discourse; English for academic purposes

French Studies

Tel: (0118) 378 8121 Fax: (0118) 378 8122
   E-mail: french@reading.ac.uk
Bryden, M., BA Reading, MA Salf., PhD Reading   Prof.
Félix, J. M., Dr E.H.E.S.S., Paris   Reader; Head*
Knapp, A. F., BA Camb., DPhil Oxf.   Sr. Lectr.
Le Saux, F. H. M., LèsL Lausanne, MA Wales, DèsL Lausanne   Sr Lectr.
Noble, P. S., MA Camb., PhD Lond.   Prof.
Segal, N. D., MA Camb., PhD Lond.   Visiting Prof.
Tucker, G. H., MA Camb., PhD Camb.   Prof.
Other Staff: 4 Lectrs.; 2 Visiting Res. Fellows; 2 Hon. Fellows

Research: contemporary and mediaeval French history; film studies; literature; politics

German Studies

Tel: (0118) 378 8331 Fax: (0118) 378 8333
   E-mail: german@reading.ac.uk
Roe, I. F., BA Durh., PhD Durh.   Sr. Lectr.; Head*
Other Staff: 2 Lectrs.; 1 Res. Fellow; 2 Hon. Fellows

Research: German literature; German mass media; mediaeval German history and culture; political issues in Germany since 1945

Italian Studies

Tel: (0118) 378 8400 Fax: (0118) 378 6797
   E-mail: italian@reading.ac.uk
Duggan, C. J. H., BA Oxf., DPhil Oxf.   Prof.; Acting Head*
Robey, D. J. B., MA Oxf.   Prof.†
Vinall, Shirley W., MA Oxf., MA Reading, PhD   Sr. Lectr.
Wagstaff, C. G., BA Oxf.   Sr. Lectr.
Other Staff: 4 Lectrs.; 4 Hon. Fellows

Research: film studies; Italian history and politics; Italian women's studies; literature

Law, School of

Tel: (0118) 378 6568 Fax: (0118) 975 3280
   E-mail: law@reading.ac.uk
Auchmuty, R., BA ANU, LLB Lond., LLM Lond., PhD ANU   Prof.
Buckley, R. A., MA Oxf., DPhil Oxf.   Prof.
Cooke, E. J., MA Oxf., LLM Reading   Prof.†; Dir., Centre for Property Law
Crabb, B. S. L., LLB Wales, LLM Lond.   Sr. Lectr.
Downes, Tony A., BA Oxf., BCL Oxf.   Prof.
Ghandhi, P. R., MA Oxf., LLM Lond.   Prof.
Hilson, C. J., MA Camb., PhD Sheff.   Reader

Kleinhans, M.-M., BA McG., BCL McG., LLB McG., PhD Lond. Sr. Lectr.

Leopold, Patricia M., LLB Belf., LLM Exe. Sr. Lectr.; Head*

McNamara, L., BEc Monash, LLB Syd., PhD Syd. Reader

Newdick, C., BA CNAA, LLM Lond. Reader

Smith, P. F., MA Oxf., BCL Oxf. Reader

Stychin, Carl F., BA Alta., LLB Tor., LLM Col. Prof.

Other Staff: 12 Lectrs.

Research: European Community law; human rights; medical law; property law; public law

Mathematics, Meteorology and Physics, School of

Belcher, S. E., BA Camb., PhD Camb. Reader; Head of Sch.*

Data Assimilation Centre

Ehrendorfer, M., MSc Vienna, PhD Vienna Prof.; Dir.*

Nichols, Nancy K., BA Harv., DPhil Oxf. Prof.†, Applied Mathematics

O'Neill, A., MA Oxf., PhD Prof.

Other Staff: 3 Res. Fellows

Environmental Systems Science Centre

Tel: (0118) 931 7765 Fax: (0118) 931 6413
E-mail: admin@mail.nerc-essc.ac.uk

Bengtsson, L., BSc Uppsala, MSc Uppsala, PhD Stockholm Prof.†

Gurney, R. J., BSc Lond., PhD Brist. Dir.*

Haines, K., BA Camb., PhD Lond. Prof.

Pentreath, R. J., BSc Lond., PhD Auck., DSc Lond. Prof.†

Slingo, A., BSc S'ton., PhD Camb. Prof.; Deputy Dir.

Wadge, G., BSc Lond., PhD Lond. Prof. Res. Fellow

Other Staff: 1 Principal Res. Fellow; 4 Sr. Res. Fellows; 1 Sr. Sci. Officer; 1 Visiting Fellow; 7 Res. Fellows; 1 Reader/Principal Res. Fellow†

Research: computer science techniques applied to environmental processes; modelling of environmental sciences; remote sensing

Global Atmospheric Modelling, NCAS Centre for

Tel: (0118) 378 8315 Fax: (0118) 378 8316

Slingo, J. M., BSc Brist., PhD Brist. Principal Res. Fellow; Dir.*

Other Staff: 40 Res. Fellows

Research: Atlantic and European global atmospheric modelling; tropical global atmospheric modelling; understanding climate change; upper atmosphere

Mathematics

Tel: (0118) 378 8996 Fax: (0118) 931 3423
E-mail: maths@reading.ac.uk

Bunce, L. J., BSc Wales, BSc Reading, MSc Oxf., PhD Reading Reader

Chandler-Wilde, S., BSc Lond., MSc Newcastle(NSW), PhD Brad. Prof., Applied Mathematics; Head*

Glaister, P., BSc Reading, MSc Reading, PhD Reading Sr. Lectr.

Kondratiev, Y. G., MSc Kiev, PhD Kiev, DSc Kiev Prof.

Likhtman, A., BSc Moscow, PhD Moscow Prof.

Matsen, M. W., BSc S.Fraser, PhD Guelph Prof.

Needham, David J., BSc Leeds, PhD Leeds Prof., Applied Mathematics

Nichols, Nancy K., BA Harv., DPhil Oxf. Prof.†, Applied Mathematics

Porter, D., BSc Wales, PhD Leic. Prof., Applied Mathematics

Stirling, D. S. G., BSc Glas., PhD Edin. Sr. Lectr.

Sweby, P. K., BSc Brist., PhD Reading Sr. Lectr.

Williams, G. D., MA Oxf., MSc Oxf., DPhil Oxf. Sr. Lectr.

Other Staff: 11 Lectrs.; 4 Res. Fellows; 2 Visiting Res. Fellows

Research: applied analysis; combinatorics; fluid mechanics; functional analysis; numerical analysis

Meteorology

Tel: (0118) 378 8954 Fax: (0118) 378 2604
E-mail: infosec@met.reading.ac.uk

Arnell, N., BSc S'ton., PhD S'ton. Prof.; Dir., Walker Inst.

Belcher, S. E., BA Camb., PhD Camb. Reader

Craig, G. C., BSc Tor., MSc Tor., PhD Tor. Reader

Ehrendorfer, M., MSc Vienna, PhD Vienna Prof.

Gray, L. J., BSc S'ton., PhD Reading Prof./ Principal Res. Fellow

Gray, S. L., BA Camb., PhD Reading Sr. Lectr.

Gregory, J. M., MA Oxf., PhD Birm. Prof.

Grimes, D. I. F., BSc Sheff., PhD Open(UK) Sr. Lectr.

Harrison, R. G., MA Camb., PhD Lond. Reader

Highwood, E. J., BSc Manc., PhD Reading Sr. Lectr.

Hogan, R. J., BSc Leic., PhD Reading Reader

Hoskins, Prof. Sir. B. J., CBE, KBE, MA Camb., PhD Camb., FRS Royal Soc. Res. Prof.

Illingworth, Anthony J., BA Camb., PhD Camb., DSc Manc. Prof.

James, Rev. I. N., BSc Leeds, PhD Manc. Prof.

O'Neill, A., MA Oxf., PhD Prof.

Shine, K. P., BSc Lond., PhD Edin. Prof.; Head*

Slingo, J. M., BSc Brist., PhD Brist. Prof./ Principal Res. Fellow

Sutton, R. T., BSc Camb., DPhil Oxf. Prof.

Other Staff: 4 Lectrs.; 1 Sr. Teaching Fellow; 24 Res. Fellows; 4 Hon. Fellows

Research: atmospheric chemistry; climate change; computational fluid dynamics; urban and boundary layer meteorology; weather systems

Physics

Tel: (0118) 378 8543 Fax: (0118) 975 0203
E-mail: physicsadmissions@reading.ac.uk

Blackman, J. A., BA Oxf., DPhil Oxf. Prof.

Dunn, D., BSc Birm., PhD Birm. Sr. Lectr.

Frasinski, L. J., PhD Cracow, FIP Reader

Hatherly, P. A., BSc Reading, PhD Reading Dir., Teaching and Learning Programme

Macdonald, J., BSc Lond., MSc Lond., PhD Reading Sr. Lectr.

Mitchell, G. R., MSc CNAA, PhD CNAA, FIP Prof.

Stewart, R. J., BSc Reading, PhD Reading Reader; Deputy Dir., J. J. Thompson Phys. Lab.; Head*

Wright, A. C., PhD Brist., DSc Brist. Prof.

Other Staff: 2 Lectrs.; 2 Sr. Res. Fellows; 4 Res. Fellows; 1 Principal Sci. Officer; 1 Sr. Sci. Officer; 3 Hon. Fellows

Research: applied optics; atomic and molecular physics; condensed matter physics; polymer physics

Politics and International Relations, School of

Tel: (0118) 378 8377
E-mail: spirs@reading.ac.uk

Giddings, P. J., MA Oxf., DPhil Oxf. Sr. Lectr.; Head*

Political and International Studies, Graduate Institute of

Tel: (0118) 378 8378 Fax: (0118) 975 7442
E-mail: gipis@reading.ac.uk

Sloan, G. R., BA Keele, PhD Keele Dir.*

Research: government; international studies; political theory

Politics and International Relations

Tel: (0118) 378 8501 Fax: (0118) 975 3833
E-mail: politics@reading.ac.uk

Casal, E. P., BA Madrid, MA Madrid Reader

Cromartie, A. D. T., BA Camb., PhD Camb. Reader

Giddings, P. J., MA Oxf., DPhil Oxf. Sr. Lectr.

Gray, C. S., BA Manc., DPhil Oxf. Prof.

Heuser, D. G. B., BA Lond., MA Lond., DPhil Oxf., Dr Marburg Prof.

Lester, J. P., BSc Brad., PhD Hull Sr. Lectr.

Lord, C. J., BA Oxf., PhD Lond. Prof.

McKinnon, C., BA Lond., MA Lond., PhD Lond. Reader

Woodward, P. R., BA S'ton., MA Essex, PhD Reading Prof.; Head*

Other Staff: 7 Lectrs.; 2 Res. Fellows; 4 Visiting Res. Fellows; 3 Assoc. Staff

Research: comparative government/area studies; international relations; political theory

Sociology

Tel: (0118) 378 8519 Fax: (0118) 931 8922

Hamilton, M. B., BScEcon Wales, MPhil Reading, PhD Reading Sr. Lectr.

Schweber, L., BA Harv., PhD Prin. Reader; Head*

Other Staff: 2 Lectrs.

Research: development and migration; social networks

Psychology and Clinical Language Sciences, School of

Tel: (0118) 378 8523 Fax: (0118) 378 6604
E-mail: psychology@reading.ac.uk

Beaman, C. P., BSA Wales, MSc Wales, PhD Wales Sr. Lectr.

Berry, Dianne C., BSc CNAA, DPhil Oxf. Prof.

Cooper, P. J., BA Cape Town, DPhil Oxf. Prof.

Edwards, S. I., MSc Lond., PhD Reading Sr. Lectr.

Ellis, J. A., BSc Lond., PhD Camb. Sr. Lectr.; Head*

Fearon, P., BA Camb., PhD Lond., DClinPsy Wales

Gaffan, Elizabeth A., MA Oxf., DPhil Oxf. Reader

Glennerster, A., MB BChir Camb., MA Camb., DPhil Oxf. Reader

Harris, J. P., BA Camb., BA Reading, PhD CNAA Prof.

McKenna, F. P., BSc Glas., PhD Lond. Prof.

Murray, Lynne, MA Edin., PhD Edin. Prof.

Riddell, P. M., BSc Glas., MSc Lond., DPhil Oxf. Sr. Lectr.

Saddy, D., BA S.Fraser, MA Ott., PhD M.I.T. Prof.

Shafran, R., BA Oxf., PhD Lond. Prof.

Other Staff: 19 Lectrs.; 14 Res. Staff; 3 Visiting Fellows; 1 Sci. Officer; 6 Lectrs.†; 8 Res. Fellows

Research: cognitive psychology; developmental psychology; human skills and information processing; neurochemistry of behaviour; visual psychophysics

SPECIAL CENTRES, ETC

Language and Literacy, National Centre for

Tel: (0118) 378 8820 Fax: (0118) 378 6801
E-mail: ncll@reading.ac.uk

Edwards, V., BA Reading, PhD Reading Prof.; Dir.*

Mesoscale Meteorology, Met Office Joint Centre for

Tel: (0118) 378 8954 Fax: (0118) 378 8905
E-mail: infosec@met.rdg.ac.uk

Browning, Keith A., BSc Lond., PhD Lond., FRS Prof.

Illingworth, Anthony J., BA Camb., PhD Camb., DSc Manc. Prof.; Group Leader, Radar

Research: local and regional atmospheric phenomena

Music Education, International Centre for Research in

Tel: (0118) 931 8821

Cox, G. S. A., MA Nfld., PhD Reading Dir.*

Spatial and Real Estate Economics, Centre for

Tel: (0118) 378 8230 Fax: (0118) 378 6533

D'Arcy, P. E., BA N.U.I., MA N.U.I. Sr. Lectr.

Evans, A. W., BA Lond., PhD Lond., FCA Prof.

Meen, G. P., OBE, BA Reading, MSc Lond., PhD Lond. Prof.

Other Staff: 2 Lectrs.; 1 Sr. Visiting Res. Fellow; 2 Visiting Res. Fellows

CONTACT OFFICERS

Academic affairs. Director of Academic Services: Hodgson, Keith N., BA *Leic.* (E-mail: k.n.hodgson@reading.ac.uk)

Accommodation. Accommodation Officer: Dickinson, Kay, BSc *Brist.* (E-mail: accommodation@reading.ac.uk.)

Admissions (first degree). Academic Registrar: Kishore, Laura, BA *Reading* (E-mail: l.j.kishore@reading.ac.uk)

Admissions (higher degree). Academic Registrar: Kishore, Laura, BA *Reading* (E-mail: l.j.kishore@reading.ac.uk)

Adult/continuing education. Head, School of Continuing Education: O'Callaghan, J. Brian, BA *Manc.*, PhD *Manc.* (E-mail: cont-ed@reading.ac.uk.)

Alumni. Head of Alumni Relations: O'Neill, T., BSocSc *Birm.* (E-mail: alumni@reading.ac.uk.)

Archives. Keeper of Archives: (vacant) (E-mail: library@reading.ac.uk.)

Careers. Director of Careers Advisory Service: Widdows, C., BA *Leeds* (E-mail: careers@reading.ac.uk.)

Computing services. Director of IT Services: Roch, D. Michael, BA *Open(UK)* (E-mail: d.m.roch@reading.ac.uk)

Consultancy services. Director of Research and Enterprise Services: Gillham, David, BSc *Reading*, PhD *Bath* (E-mail: res@reading.ac.uk)

Credit transfer. Academic Registrar: Kishore, Laura, BA *Reading* (E-mail: information@reading.ac.uk.)

Development/fund-raising. Head of Development: Wood, A. (E-mail: alumni@reading.ac.uk)

Estates and buildings/works and services. Director of Facilities Management: Robbins, Colin (E-mail: c.robbins@reading.ac.uk)

Examinations. Assistant Registrar: Swanson, Keith, BA *York(UK)*, MA *York(UK)* (E-mail: examinations@reading.ac.uk.)

Finance. Director of Finance: Savage, David C. L., BA *Lond.* (E-mail: finance-help@reading.ac.uk.)

General enquiries. Director of Student Services: Watts, William D., BSc *Lond.* (E-mail: communications@reading.ac.uk)

Health services. Director of Health Service: Johnston, Elizabeth M., MB ChB *Glas.*

International office. Director of International Office: Nunnerley, C., MA *Edin.* (E-mail: intoff@reading.ac.uk)

Library (chief librarian). Librarian: Munro, Julia, BSc *Lond.*, MSc *City(UK)*, MBA *Reading* (E-mail: library@reading.ac.uk)

Marketing. Head of Marketing: Wilstead, Anne, BA *Reading* (E-mail: a.wilstead@reading.ac.uk)

Personnel/human resources. Director of Human Resources: Brady, John, BA *Belf.*, MA *Herts.* (E-mail: humanresources@reading.ac.uk.)

Public relations. Director of Development and External Affairs: Horan, Shaun (E-mail: communications@reading.ac.uk)

Purchasing. Purchasing Manager: Jeffries, Lisa (E-mail: purchasing@reading.ac.uk.)

Quality assurance and accreditation. Director of Quality Support: Stannard, D. A., BA *Durh.* (E-mail: k.h.hodgson@reading.ac.uk)

Research. Pro-Vice-Chancellor: Berry, Prof. Dianne C., BSc *CNAA*, DPhil *Oxf.* (E-mail: res@reading.ac.uk.)

Safety. Safety Officer: Simpson, Moira, MA (E-mail: safety@reading.ac.uk.)

Scholarships, awards, loans. Student Financial Support: James, A., BA *Leeds*, MA *Leeds* (E-mail: a.s.james@reading.ac.uk)

Schools liaison. Director of Student Recruitment and Schools Liaison: Singleton, Carey, BA *Lanc.* (E-mail: schools.liaison@reading.ac.uk.)

Security. Security Services Manager: Mills, Maureen (E-mail: securitycontrol@reading.ac.uk.)

Sport and recreation. Director of Sport and Recreation: Akhurst, Iain

Student welfare/counselling. Head of Counselling: Purcell, V., BSc *Oxf.Brookes*, MSc *E.Lond.* (E-mail: intoff@reading.ac.uk.)

Students from other countries. Director of International Office: Nunnerley, C., MA *Edin.* (E-mail: intoff@reading.ac.uk.)

Students with disabilities. Disability Officer: French, K., BA *Keele* (E-mail: k.a.french@reading.ac.uk)

[Information supplied by the institution as at 9 November 2007, and edited by the ACU]

ROBERT GORDON UNIVERSITY

Founded 1992

Member of the Association of Commonwealth Universities

Postal Address: Schoolhill, Aberdeen, Scotland AB10 1FR
Telephone: (01224) 262000 **Fax:** (01224) 263000 **E-mail:** admissions@rgu.ac.uk
URL: http://www.rgu.ac.uk

CHANCELLOR—Wood, Sir Ian, CBE, BSc LLD DBA DTech
PRINCIPAL*—Pittilo, Prof. R. Michael, BSc *Strath.*, PhD *CNAA*, FIBiol, FLS
DIRECTOR OF FINANCE—Briggs, Patricia, MA, FCA
DIRECTOR OF HUMAN RESOURCES—Briggs, David, BSc MSc
VICE PRINCIPAL—Harper, Prof. John, BSc PhD, FRSChem
VICE PRINCIPAL—Robertson, Prof. Peter, BSc DPhil, FRSChem
VICE PRINCIPAL—Cormack, Shona, MA MSc
DIRECTOR OF INFORMATION TECHNOLOGY—McCreath, Andrew, BSc MSc

GENERAL INFORMATION

History. Established in 1750 as a hospital to educate scholars, The Robert Gordon's Hospital became The Robert Gordon's College in 1881. In 1903 it was accorded the status of Central Institution as a Higher Technical College, and in 1965 it became The Robert Gordon's Institute of Technology. In 1992, following the Further and Higher Education Act, the institute was awarded the title of The Robert Gordon University.

The university has two campuses in the city of Aberdeen, which lies in the north-east Grampian region of Scotland: one in the city centre at Schoolhill; and the Garthdee campus on the southern side of the city, near the banks of the River Dee.

Admission to first degree courses (see also United Kingdom Introduction). Through Universities and Colleges Admissions Service (UCAS).

First Degrees (see also United Kingdom Directory to Subjects of Study) (* = with honours). BA, BA*, BDes*, BEng, BEng*, BSc, BSc*, LLB, LLB*, MEng, MPharm.
Length of course. Full-time: BA, BEng, BSc: 3 years; BA*, BDes*, BEng*, LLB, LLB*, MPharm: 4 years; BSc*, MEng: 4–5 years.

Higher Degrees (see also United Kingdom Directory to Subjects of Study).
Master's. LLM, MA, MBA, MPA, MPhil, MSc.
Length of course. Full-time: LLM, MA, MBA, MPA, MSc: 1 year; MPhil: max. 3 years. Part-time: MA, MBA, MPA, MSc: 2 years; LLM: 2–3 years; MPhil: 4 years. By *distance learning*: MBA, MPA, MSc: 2 years; LLM: 2–3 years; MPhil: 2½ years.
Doctoral. PhD.
Length of course. Full-time: PhD: 3 years. Part-time: PhD: 6 years.

Language of Instruction. English. Pre-sessional, pre-entry and in-sessional programmes available.

Libraries. Volumes: 255,877. Periodicals subscribed to: 1902. Other holdings: 4939 electronic periodicals. Special collections: local architecture and landscape design.

Statistics. Staff (2006–2007): 1489 (661 academic, 828 non-academic). Students (2005–2006): full-time 8652; part-time 4666; international 1477; undergraduate 9065; master's 4019; doctoral 220.

FACULTIES/SCHOOLS

Aberdeen Business School
Tel: (01224) 263550 Fax: (01224) 263838
E-mail: j.dey@rgu.ac.uk
Dean: Marcella, Prof. Rita C., MA PhD, FCMI
Secretary: Dey, Jean

Design and Technology
Tel: (01224) 263750 Fax: (01224) 263757
E-mail: c.black@rgu.ac.uk
Dean: Watson, Prof. John
Secretary: Black, Christine

Health and Social Care
Tel: (01224) 263050 Fax: (01224) 263053
E-mail: s.barnett@rgu.ac.uk

Dean: Maehle, Prof. Valerie A., MEd PhD
Secretary: Barnett, Susan

ACADEMIC UNITS

Arranged by Schools

Aberdeen Business School

Tel: (01224) 263800 Fax: (01224) 263838
E-mail: abs-enquiries@rgu.ac.uk
Arnell, P. D. Sr. Lectr.
Barnes, R. W. Sr. Lectr.
Bonney, N. L. Prof.; Sr. Res. Fellow
Connon, J. Sr. Lectr.
Coram, A. B. T. Prof., Political Economy
Cruickshank, D. M. Sr. Lectr.
Donaldson, W. G. Prof., Marketing
Duncan, J. E. Sr. Lectr.
Gammie, E. B. Prof.; Sr. Lectr.
Gammie, R. P. Assoc. Head of Dept.
Gibbons-Wood, D. Sr. Lectr.
Greenwood, J. Jean Monnet Prof., European Public Policy
Hamilton, M. Assoc. Head of Dept.
Hill, M. M. Sr. Lectr.
Johnson, I. Head of Dept.
Kirkham, L. M. Prof., Accountancy
Mackay, A. M. L. Sr. Lectr.
MacTaggart, D. C. Sr. Lectr.
Marcella, Rita C., MA PhD, FCMI Prof.; Head*
Mason, T. G. Sr. Lectr.
Middlemiss, G. Sr. Lectr.
Newton, R. Assoc. Head of Dept.
Nisbet, D. J. Sr. Lectr.
Raj, M. Abtrust Prof., International Finance
Royle, J. M. Sr. Lectr.
Smart, P. J. Sr. Lectr.
Strachan, V. M. Assoc. Head of Dept.
Taylor, J. Sr. Lectr.
Tourish, D. J. Prof., Communications
Turnbull, A. A. Sr. Lectr.
Wallace, R. M. M. Prof., Law
Other Staff: 4 Readers; 111 Lectrs.; 3 Sr. Res. Fellows; 1 Teaching Fellow
Research: accounting and finance; business management and human resource management; communication and languages; economics and public policy; information and management, law and marketing

Applied Social Studies

Tel: (01224) 263200 Fax: (01224) 263222
E-mail: kath.sharp@rgu.ac.uk
Cox, D. E. H. Sr. Lectr.
Gibson, A. Sr. Lectr.
Keenan, C. G. Sr. Lectr.
Lishman, Joyce, MA Oxf., PhD Prof.; Head*
McLean, T. Assoc. Head
Munro, N. Sr. Lectr.
Other Staff: 30 Lectrs.; 1 Devel. Worker; 1 Res. Fellow; 3 Res. Assts.
Research: community care and residential child care; evaluation of social work and services; occupational stress and psychology; professional ethics; volunteering and volunteers

Architecture, Scott Sutherland School of

Tel: (01224) 263700 Fax: (01224) 263535
E-mail: p.morrison@rgu.ac.uk
Gordon, D. I. Sr. Lectr.
Lonsdale, W. G. Sr. Lectr.
Martin, P. J. Sr. Lectr.
McClean, D. E. D. Head*
Other Staff: 4 Readers; 24 Lectrs.; 1 Sr. Res. Fellow; 4 Res. Fellows
Research: building performance; history and theory of architecture; rural studies; technology and environmental design; urban design

Art, Gray's School of

Tel: (01224) 263602 Fax: (01224) 263609
E-mail: a.young@rgu.ac.uk
Campbell, C. A. Sr. Lectr.
Cordiner, S. B. Assoc. Head
MacDonald, S. Head*

Smith, Lenny Sr. Lectr.
Other Staff: 4 Readers; 35 Lectrs.; 1 Sr. Res. Fellow; 3 Res. Fellow; 1 Teaching Fellow
Research: collaborative and interdisciplinary practices in the visual arts; critical and contextual research related to practice; environmental/sustainable practice; interpretative research methodologies; new technologies

Computing

Tel: (01224) 262700 Fax: (01224) 262727
E-mail: office@comp.rgu.ac.uk
Allison, I. Head*
Arana, I. Sr. Lectr.
Brown, D. F. Sr. Lectr.
Davidson, D. G. Assoc. Head
Lowit, P. J. Sr. Lectr.
McCall, J. A. W. Sr. Lectr.
McDermott, R. J. Sr. Lectr.
Tyler, J. E. M. Sr. Lectr.
Watt, S. N. K. Sr. Lectr.
Other Staff: 32 Lectrs.; 1 Sr. Res. Fellow; 2 Res. Fellows
Research: biomedical computing and personalisation agents; computer graphics and image processing; knowledge-based systems and intelligent technologies; mathematical sciences and statistical process control; specification and implementation of programming languages

Engineering

Tel: (01224) 262400 Fax: (01224) 262444
E-mail: info@eng.rgu.ac.uk
Adam, A. E. T. Sr. Lectr.
Aust, C. Sr. Lectr.
Bradley, R. Prof.; Sr. Lectr.
Brown, A. W. Sr. Lectr.
Butler, R. A. Sr. Lectr.
Croft, M. B. Academic Project Manager
Edward, N. S. Sr. Lectr.
Fraser, M. I. Sr. Lectr.
Gow, K. S. Sr. Lectr.
Maxwell, G. M. Assoc. Head
Power, L. J. Sr. Lectr.
Robertson, Peter, BSc DPhil, FRSChem Prof., Energy and Environmental Engineering
Sethuraman, S. K. Sr. Lectr.
Siddiqui, A. M. Sr. Lectr.
Steel, I. Head*
Teperek, R. J. Sr. Lectr.
Other Staff: 4 Readers; 15 Lectrs.; 3 Sr. Res. Fellows; 17 Res. Fellows
Research: computational intelligence; condition monitoring and non-destructive testing; environmental engineering; high-performance networks; optoelectronics and renewable energy

Health Sciences

Tel: (01224) 263252 Fax: (01224) 263290
E-mail: e.e.smith@rgu.ac.uk
Caldwell, J. Sr. Lectr.
Duthie, J. Sr. Lectr.
Hancock, E. I. Head*
MacSween, A. Sr. Lectr.
Stewart, A. Sr. Lectr.
Other Staff: 1 Reader; 20 Lectrs.; 1 Res. Fellow; 1 Clin. Tutor
Research: cancer; cardiovascular conditions; children's and women's services; elderly people; mental health

Life Sciences

Tel: (01224) 262800 Fax: (01224) 262828
E-mail: m.stewart@rgu.ac.uk
Belton, E. A. Sr. Lectr.
Emmison, N. Sr. Lectr.
Melvin, Maureen, BSc PhD Prof.; Head*
Morrisson, A. R. Assoc. Head
Ratcliffe, B. Assoc. Head
Wahle, K. Res. Prof.
Other Staff: 3 Readers; 12 Lectrs.; 2 Res. Fellows
Research: analytical, medical and bio-organic chemistry; biomedical sciences;

environmental biotechnology; nutrition and food sciences; optoelectronics

Nursing and Midwifery

Tel: (01224) 262906 Fax: (01224) 262630
E-mail: s.cumming@rgu.ac.uk
Banks, D. Sr. Lectr.
Gass, J. P. Sr. Lectr.
Gass, L. E. Sr. Lectr., Practice Development
Gibb, S. J. Sr. Lectr.
Grundy, M. Sr. Lectr.
Guthrie, C. Sr. Lectr.
Mackenzie, J. M. Sr. Lectr.
McKay, A. R. D. Sr. Lectr.
McLennan, A. M. Sr. Lectr.
Milne, A. Sr. Lectr.
Parry, Jennie, BA MSc Head*
Taylor, R. F. Sr. Lectr.
Wilcock, S. E. Assoc. Head
Wilson, A. J. Sr. Lectr.
Other Staff: 57 Lectrs.; 1 Res. Fellow
Research: clinical skills and shared learning; evaluation of nurse-led minor injury treatments; health care for elderly people; hospital-at-home, evening services and homeless people; nurse-led support for post-natal depression

Pharmacy

Tel: (01224) 262501 Fax: (01224) 262555
E-mail: j.lowe@rgu.ac.uk
Bell, J. H. Sr. Lectr.
Cairns, D. Assoc. Head
Cunningham, I. T. S. Sr. Lectr.
Durham, D. G. Sr. Lectr.
Handsford, D. Sr. Lectr.
Healey, Terry, BSc PhD Prof.; Head*
Knott, R. N. Sr. Lectr.
Lamb, A. J. Sr. Lectr.
Macmanus, S. M. Sr. Lectr.
McCaig, D. J. Sr. Lectr.
Munday, D. L. Sr. Lectr.
Pfleger, D. E. Sr. Lectr.
Stewart, D. C. Sr. Lectr.
Wainwright, C. Res. Prof.
Other Staff: 1 Reader; 19 Lectrs.; 3 Res. Fellows
Research: biomedical sciences; drug development; microbiology and antibacterial agents; pharmaceutical care; pharmaceutical public health

SPECIAL CENTRES, ETC

E-Learning, Department of (DeL)

Tel: (01224) 262232 Fax: (01224) 262231
E-mail: i.gordon@rgu.ac.uk
James, Sarah Acting Dir.*
Other Staff: 1 Business Manager; 1 Distance Learning Devel. Manager; 1 Project Devel. Officer; 1 Online Course Devel. Advisor; 5 Web Technologists; 1 Web Developer
Research: developing e-business online; e-business training online; online learning for people with disabilities; virtual learning space

Interdisciplinary Studies, Centre for

Tel: (01224) 262041
Miller, A. J. Dir.*

Learning and Teaching, Centre for Enhancement of (CELT)

Tel: (01224) 263341 Fax: (01224) 262231
E-mail: a.t.davidson@rgu.ac.uk
Davidson, Alan Dean*
Other Staff: 1 Audiovisual and Digital Imaging Manager; 1 Video and Multimedia Production Manager; 1 Project Manager; 1 Sr. Educnl. Devel. Officer; 2 Educnl. Devel. Officers; 2 Lectrs.; 1 Teaching Fellow
Research: staff development in communication and IT; teaching and learning in Scottish higher education institutions

Nurse Practice Research, Centre for

Tel: (01224) 262647 E-mail: b.west@rgu.ac.uk
West, B. J. M. Dir.*

Tourism, Scottish Centre of

Tel: (01224) 263036 Fax: (01224) 263038
Martin, A   Dir.*

Univation Ltd

Training consultancy

Tel: (01224) 263320 Fax: (01224) 263323
E-mail: univation@rgu.ac.uk
Campbell, Ian   Managing Dir.*
Other Staff: 2 Programme Co-ordinators; 6
Business Devel. Execs.; 2 Business Devel. Co-
ordinators; 6 Consultants; 2 Project
Engineers; 1 Asst. Project Civil Engineer; 7
Project Officers; 1 Course Developer; 3
Lectrs. (on contract)

Viscom (Aberdeen) Ltd

Multimedia and video production

Tel: (0845) 345 1987
E-mail: bruce@viscom-aberdeen.ltd.uk
Milne, Bruce   Gen. Manager/Head of
Production*
Other Staff: 1 Multimedia Co-ordinator; 1
Multimedia Author

CONTACT OFFICERS

Academic affairs. Academic Registrar:
Douglas, Hilary J.
(E-mail: academic.affairs@rgu.ac.uk)
Accommodation. Accommodation and
Catering Services Manager: Webster, Ian C.
(E-mail: accommodation@rgu.ac.uk)
Admissions (first degree). Student Admissions
Manager (Acting): Kay, Sheila
(E-mail: admissions@rgu.ac.uk)

Alumni. Alumni Officer: Brown, Jenny
(E-mail: alumni@rgu.ac.uk)
Careers. Student Services Manager: Buchanan,
Christine (E-mail: careers@rgu.ac.uk)
Computing services. Shared Services Manager
of IT Services: Glennie, Peter E. P.
(E-mail: adviser@rgu.ac.uk)
Development/fund-raising. Research Projects
Officer: Thomas, Radha
(E-mail: r.thomas@rgu.ac.uk)
Estates and buildings/works and services.
Estates Director: Lane, Fiona
(E-mail: f.lane@rgu.ac.uk)
Examinations. Administration Officer:
Maxwell, Sandra
(E-mail: academic.affairs@rgu.ac.uk)
Finance. Finance Manager: Telford, Mike
(E-mail: m.telford@rgu.ac.uk)
Industrial liaison. Managing Director,
Univation Ltd: Campbell, Ian
(E-mail: univation@rgu.ac.uk)
International office. International Programmes
Manager: Morris, Giles P.
(E-mail: international@rgu.ac.uk)
Library (chief librarian). Director of
Knowledge and Information Services:
Munro, Carole (E-mail: library@rgu.ac.uk)
Marketing. Marketing Manager UK: Bowden,
Kate (E-mail: c.l.bowden@rgu.ac.uk)
Personnel/human resources. Director of
Human Resources: Briggs, David, BSc MSc
(E-mail: d.briggs@rgu.ac.uk)
Public relations. Press Officer: Haddock, Gail
(E-mail: newsdesk@rgu.ac.uk)
Purchasing. Procurement Officer: Keith,
Stephen, MA (E-mail: s.keith@rgu.ac.uk)
Research. Research and Commercialisation
Support Officer: Gillibrand, Emma
(E-mail: innovation@rgu.ac.uk)

Safety. Occupational Health and Safety
Manager: Clark, Angus
(E-mail: s.w.marshall@rgu.ac.uk)
Scholarships, awards, loans. Student Finance
and Information Manager: Mair, Colin
(E-mail: studentfinance@rgu.ac.uk)
Schools liaison. Schools Liaison Officer: Clark,
Alison (E-mail: a.clark@rgu.ac.uk)
Security. Ancillary Services Officer: Kaye, Ian
A. (E-mail: i.kaye@rgu.ac.uk)
Sport and recreation. Student Association
Administrator: Bainbridge, Audrey
(E-mail: a.bainbridge@rgu.ac.uk)
Staff development and training. Employee
Development Adviser: Aberdein, Catherine
(E-mail: c.h.aberdein@rgu.ac.uk)
Student union. General Manager: Collie,
Michelle (E-mail: m.collie@rgu.ac.uk)
Student welfare/counselling. Student Welfare
Adviser: McIntosh, Margaret
(E-mail: m.mcintosh@rgu.ac.uk)
Student welfare/counselling. Student Services
Manager: Buchanan, Christine
(E-mail: c.buchanan@rgu.ac.uk)
Students from other countries. European
Officer: Forsyth, Marlene
(E-mail: m.forsyth@rgu.ac.uk)
Students with disabilities. Adviser for
Students with Disabilities: Davidson,
Annette (E-mail: disability@rgu.ac.uk)
University press. Head of Communications:
Shackleton, Jonathan, MA
(E-mail: newsdesk@rgu.ac.uk)

[Information supplied by the institution as at 20
September 2007, and edited by the ACU]

ROEHAMPTON UNIVERSITY

Founded 2000

Member of the Association of Commonwealth Universities

Postal Address: Roehampton Lane, London, England SW15 5PJ
Telephone: (020) 8392 3000 **E-mail:** enquiries@roehampton.ac.uk
URL: http://www.roehampton.ac.uk

VICE-CHANCELLOR*—O'Prey, Prof. Paul G., PhD Brist.
PRO-RECTOR (ACADEMIC)—Weston, Peter, BA Lond., MA Exe., PhD Exe.
PRO-RECTOR (INNOVATION)—Guzkowska, Myszka, TD, BSc Lond., MSc Oxf., MBA Henley, DPhil Oxf., FRSA
PRO-RECTOR (EXTERNAL PARTNERSHIPS)—Briggs, Peter, BSc Sus., DPhil Sus., Hon. DSc Leic., FRSA
PRO-RECTOR (SERVICES)—Roberts, Trish, BSc Lond., MUP Ill., PhD Reading, FRSA
DIRECTOR OF FINANCIAL STRATEGY—Attwell, Simon
DIRECTOR OF HUMAN RESOURCES—Fairfoul, Helen, BA Birm., MBA Open(UK)
DIRECTOR OF MARKETING, RECRUITMENT AND ADMISSIONS—King, Tricia, BA York(UK)
ACADEMIC SECRETARY‡—Skinner, Andrew, BSc Lond.

ROYAL COLLEGE OF ART

Founded 1896

Member of the Association of Commonwealth Universities

Postal Address: Kensington Gore, London, England SW7 2EU
Telephone: (020) 7590 4444 **Fax:** (020) 7590 4500 **E-mail:** admissions@rca.ac.uk
URL: http://www.rca.ac.uk

RECTOR AND VICE-PROVOST*—Frayling, Prof. Sir Christopher, KBE, MA Camb., PhD Camb.
DIRECTOR OF ADMINISTRATION‡—Philpott, Garry S., BA Open(UK)

ROYAL WELSH COLLEGE OF MUSIC AND DRAMA

Postal Address: Castle Grounds, Cathays Park, Cardiff, Wales CF10 3ER
Telephone: (029) 2034 2854 **Fax:** (029) 2039 1304
URL: http://www.rwcmd.ac.uk

PRINCIPAL*—Boulding, Hilary
DIRECTOR OF RESOURCES AND ADMINISTRATION‡—James, Dorothy

UNIVERSITY OF ST ANDREWS

Founded 1413

Member of the Association of Commonwealth Universities

Postal Address: College Gate, St Andrews, Fife, Scotland KY16 9AJ
Telephone: (01334) 476161 **Fax:** (01334) 462570
URL: http://www.st-and.ac.uk

PRINCIPAL AND VICE-CHANCELLOR*—Lang, Brian A., MA Edin., PhD Edin.
DEPUTY PRINCIPAL AND MASTER OF THE UNITED COLLEGE‡—Brown, Prof. Keith M., MA Glas., PhD Glas., FRHistS
PRINCIPAL OF ST. MARY'S COLLEGE—Hart, Prof. Trevor A., BA Durh., PhD Aberd.
QUAESTOR AND FACTOR—Watson, Derek
VICE-PRINCIPAL (GOVERNANCE AND PLANNING)—Piper, Prof. R. A., BA Calif., BD Lond., PhD Lond.
VICE-PRINCIPAL (LEARNING AND TEACHING)—Winn, Prof. P., BA Hull, PhD Hull
VICE-PRINCIPAL (RESEARCH)—Miller, Prof. A., BSc Edin., PhD Bath
VICE-PRINCIPAL (EXTERNAL RELATIONS)—Magee, S. R., MA St And., MSc Edin.
PROCTOR AND PROVOST—Smith, C., BSc Liv., PhD Liv.

GENERAL INFORMATION

History. The university was founded in 1413 and is the oldest university in Scotland and the third oldest in the United Kingdom.

It is located in St Andrews on the east coast of Scotland about 72km north of Edinburgh and 21km south of Dundee.

First Degrees (see also United Kingdom Directory to Subjects of Study). BEng.

Higher Degrees (see also United Kingdom Directory to Subjects of Study).
Master's. BD, MA, MChem, MEng, MLitt, MMath, MPhil, MPhys, MRes, MSc, MSci, MTheol.
Doctoral. DLang, EngDoc, PhD.

Statistics. Staff (2006): 2068 (500 academic, 1568 non-academic). Students (2005–2006): full-time 1583 (941 men, 642 women); part-time 383 (65 men, 318 women); international 347 (187 men, 160 women); distance education/external 57 (19 men, 38 women); undergraduate 6295 (2572 men, 3723 women); master's 303 (152 men, 151 women); doctoral 1818 (944 men, 874 women).

FACULTIES/SCHOOLS

Arts
Tel: (01334) 462139/4 Fax: (01334) 462144
E-mail: faculty@st-andrews.ac.uk
Dean: Milne, Lorna, MA St And., PhD Auck.
Secretary: Forrester, M.

Divinity
Tel: (01334) 462139/4 Fax: (01334) 462144
E-mail: faculty@st-andrews.ac.uk
Dean: Aguilar, M. I., BA Chile, STB Leuven, MA Leuven, MA Lond., PhD Lond.
Secretary: Smith, D.

Medicine
Tel: (01334) 463597 Fax: (01334) 463482
E-mail: medical.dean@st-andrews.ac.uk

Dean: MacDougall, Prof. H., MB ChB St And.
Secretary: Dye, S.

Science
Tel: (01334) 462137 Fax: (01334) 462144
E-mail: faculty@st-andrews.ac.uk
Dean: Tobin, A. K., BSc Newcastle(UK), PhD Newcastle(UK)
Secretary: Pogorzelec, W.

ACADEMIC UNITS
Arranged by Schools

Art History
Tel: (01334) 462400 Fax: (01334) 462401
E-mail: art.history@st-andrews.ac.uk
Carradice, I. A., BA Liv., PhD St And., FSA Prof.
Carruthers, V. A., BA Manc.   Sr. Lectr.; Head*
Cassidy, Brendan F., MA Edin., PhD Camb. Reader
Fawcett, Prof. R., BA E.Anglia, PhD E.Anglia Prof.
Humfrey, P. B., BA Trinity(Dub.), MA Lond., PhD Lond.   Prof.
Lodder, Christina A., BA York(UK), MA Sus., DPhil Sus., FRSEd   Prof.
Normand, T. A., BA CNAA, PhD Durh.   Sr. Lectr.
Smith, G., MA St And., MFA Prin., PhD Prin. Prof.
Walker, D. M.   Emer. Prof.
Other Staff: 7 Lectrs.

Biology
Tel: (01334) 463501 Fax: (01334) 463600
E-mail: biology@st-andrews.ac.uk
Abbott, R. J., BSc Wales, DPhil Oxf.   Prof.
Boyd, I. L., BSc Aberd., DSc Aberd.   Prof.
Brierley, A., BSc Wales, PhD Liv.   Reader
Burchell, Brian, BSc St And., PhD Dund.   Hon. Prof.
Cottrell, Glen, BSc S'ton., DSc S'ton.   Emer. Prof.
Cramb, G., BSc Edin., PhD Edin.   Sr. Lectr.
Cresswell, W., BA Camb., PhD Edin.   Reader
Elliott, R., BSc Sur., DPhil Oxf.   Reader

Fedak, M. A., BA New Br., MA Duke, PhD Duke Prof.
Graves, J. A., BA Arkansas, MLitt St And.   Sr. Lectr.
Griffiths, R., BSc Wales, PhD Wales   Sr. Lectr.
Gunn-Moore, F., BSc Edin., PhD Camb.   Sr. Lectr.
Gust, G., PhD Kiel, MS   Hon. Prof.
Hammond, P. S., BA York(UK), DPhil York(UK) Reader
Harwood, J., BSc Lond., PhD W.Ont.   Prof.
Hazon, N., BSc Manc., PhD Sheff.   Reader
Heitler, W. J., BA Oxf., DPhil Oxf.   Reader
Ingledew, W. J., BA York(UK), PhD Brist.   Sr. Lectr.
Johnston, I. A., BSc Hull, PhD Hull, FRSEd Prof.
Kemp, G. D., BSc St And., PhD St And.   Sr. Lectr.
Kinghorn, J. R., BSc Strath., PhD Glas.   Sr. Lectr.
Laland, K., BSc S'ton., PhD Lond.   Reader
Lipworth, B. J., BSc MB ChB MD, FRCP   Hon. Prof.
Magurran, A. E., BSc Ulster, DPhil Ulster   Prof.
Meagher, T. R., BA S.Florida, PhD S.Florida Prof.
Milner, M. J., BSc Leic., DPhil Sus.   Sr. Lectr.
Northridge, S., MA Oxf., MSc York(UK)   Sr. Lectr.
Paterson, D. M., BSc Glas., PhD Bath   Prof.; Head*
Pippard, M. J., BSc MB ChB, FRCP, FRCPEd, FRCPath   Hon. Prof.
Ramsay, Rona R., BSc Edin., MA Camb., PhD Camb.   Reader
Randall, R. E., BSc Leeds, PhD Leeds   Prof.
Ritchie, M. G., BSc Edin., PhD E.Anglia   Prof.
Ryan, M. D., BSc Lond., MSc Lond., PhD Leic. Reader
Sillar, K. T., BSc Glas., PhD St And.   Prof.
Slater, P. J. B., BSc Edin., PhD Edin., DSc Edin., FRSEd, FIBiol   Kennedy Prof., Natural History
Smith, V. J., BSc Wales, PhD Wales   Reader
Sommerville, J., BSc Edin., PhD Edin.   Sr. Lectr.
Struthers, A. D., BSc MB ChB MD, FRCP Hon. Prof.
Taylor, Gary L., BSc Lond., PhD Lond.   Prof.

Tobin, A. K., BSc *Newcastle(UK)*, PhD *Newcastle(UK)*   Reader
Todd, C. D., BSc *Leeds*, PhD *Leeds*   Prof.
Unkles, S., BSc *Glas.*, PhD *St And.*   Prof.
White, M. F., BSc *Aberd.*, PhD *Edin.*   Prof.
Willmer, P. G., MA *Camb.*, PhD *Camb.*   Prof.
Wray, J. L., BSc *Birm.*, PhD *Birm.*   Hon. Prof.
Other Staff: 2 Sr. Teaching Fellows; 73 Res. Fellows; 4 Teaching Fellows

Chemistry

Tel: (01334) 463800 Fax: (01334) 463808
    E-mail: chemistry@st-and.ac.uk
Aitken, R. A., BSc *Edin.*, PhD *Edin.*   Sr. Lectr.
Baddeley, C., BA *Camb.*, MA *Camb.*, PhD *Camb.*   Reader
Botting, N., BSc *Lond.*, PhD *Lond.*   Sr. Lectr.
Bruce, P. G., BSc *Aberd.*, PhD *Aberd.*, FRSChem, FRSEd   Prof.
Buck, M.   Reader
Cole-Hamilton, D. J., BSc *Edin.*, PhD *Edin.*, FRSChem, FRSEd   Irvine Prof.
David, W. I. F., BA *Oxf.*, MA *Oxf.*, DPhil *Oxf.*   Hon. Prof.
Ferguson, G., BSc PhD DSc   Hon. Prof.
Gerber, C.   Hon. Prof.
Glidewell, C., MA *Camb.*, PhD *Camb.*, ScD *Camb.*, FRSEd   Reader
Haehner, G., PhD *Heidel.*   Reader
Howard, P., MA   Hon. Prof.
Iqbal, A., MSc *Dhaka*, DrRerNat *T.H.Aachen*   Hon. Prof.
Irvine, John T. S., BSc *Edin.*, DPhil *Ulster*   Prof.
Kamer, P., MSc *Utrecht*, PhD *Utrecht*   Prof.
Lightfoot, P., BA *Oxf.*, DPhil *Oxf.*   Reader
Lloyd, D., DSc *St And.*   Hon. Prof.
Morris, R. E., MA *Oxf.*, DPhil *Oxf.*   Prof.
Naismith, J. H., BSc *Edin.*, PhD *Manc.*   Prof.
O'Hagan, D., BSc *Glas.*, PhD *Glas.*, DSc *S'ton.*   Prof.
Philp, D., BSc *Aberd.*, PhD *Birm.*   Reader
Richardson, N. V., BA *Oxf.*, DPhil *Oxf.*   Prof.; Head*
Richens, D. T., BSc *Manc.*, MSc *Manc.*, PhD *Manc.*   Sr. Lectr.
Slawin, A., BSc *Lond.*, PhD *Lough.*   Prof.
Tooze, R.   Hon. Prof.
Walton, J. C., DSc *Sheff.*, PhD *St And.*, FRSEd   Prof.
Westwood, N., BA *Oxf.*, DPhil *Oxf.*   Reader
Woollins, J. D., BSc *E.Anglia*, PhD *E.Anglia*   Prof.
Wright, P. A., BA *Camb.*, PhD *Camb.*   Reader
Zhou, W., BSc *Fudan*, PhD *Camb.*   Reader
Other Staff: 4 Lectrs.; 1 Teaching Fellow; 70 Res. Fellows; 1 Hon. Reader; 2 Hon. Sr. Lectrs.; 3 Hon. Lectrs.

Classics

Tel: (01334) 462600 Fax: (01334) 462602
    E-mail: classics@st-andrews.ac.uk

Ancient History

Tel: (01334) 462613
Craik, E., MA *St And.*, MLitt *Camb.*   Hon. Prof.
Dickie, M.   Hon. Prof.
Harries, Jill D., MA *Oxf.*, DPhil *Oxf.*   Prof.
Henry, A.   Hon. Prof.
Smith, C. J., BA *Oxf.*, MA *Oxf.*, DPhil *Oxf.*   Prof.
Woolf, G. D., BA *Oxf.*, MA *Oxf.*, PhD *Camb.*   Prof.; Head*
Other Staff: 1 Hon. Sr. Lectr.

Greek

Tel: (01334) 462617
Halliwell, Francis S., MA *Oxf.*, DPhil *Oxf.*   Prof.
Hesk, J., BA PhD   Sr. Lectr.
Konig, J., BA *Camb.*, MPhil *Camb.*, DPhil *Oxf.*   Sr. Lectr.

Latin (Humanity)

Gratwick, A. S., MA *Camb.*, DPhil *Oxf.*   Prof.
Hine, H. M., MA *Oxf.*, DPhil *Oxf.*   Scotstarvit Prof.

Pollman, K. F. L., MA *Bochum*, PhD *Bochum*   Prof.
Rees, R., BA *Camb.*, PhD *Kent*   Reader
Other Staff: 1 Sr. Lectr.; 6 Lectrs.; 2 Res. Fellows; 2 Teaching Fellows

Computer Science

Tel: (01334) 463253 Fax: (01334) 463278
    E-mail: enquiries@dcs.st-and.ac.uk
Allison, C., MA MSc   Sr. Lectr.
Bhatti, S., BEng PhD   Prof.
Dearle, A., BSc PhD   Prof.
Dyckhoff, R., BA *Camb.*, DPhil *Oxf.*   Sr. Lectr.
Gent, I., MA *Camb.*, MSc *Edin.*, PhD *Warw.*   Reader
Hammond, K., BSc PhD   Reader
Kirby, G., BSc *St And.*, PhD *St And.*   Sr. Lectr.
Linton, S. A., BA *Camb.*, PhD *Camb.*   Sr. Lectr.
Morrison, R., BSc *Strath.*, MSc *Glas.*, PhD   Prof.; Head*
Sommerville, J. F., BSc *Strath.*, MSc *St And.*, PhD *St And.*   Prof.
Other Staff: 10 Lectrs.; 17 Res. Fellows; 2 Hon. Readers; 1 Hon. Lectr.; 1 Teaching Fellow

Divinity

Tel: (01334) 462850 Fax: (01334) 462852
    E-mail: divinity@st-andrews.ac.uk
Aguilar, M. I., BA *Chile*, STB *Leuven*, MA *Leuven*, MA *Lond.*, PhD *Lond.*   Reader
Begbie, J., BA *Edin.*, BD *Aberd.*, PhD *Aberd.*   Hon. Prof.
Bradley, I., BA *Oxf.*, BD *St And.*, MA *Oxf.*, DPhil *Oxf.*   Reader
Brown, D., MA *Oxf.*, PhD *Kent*   Prof.
Davila, J., BA *Harv.*, MA *Harv.*, PhD *Harv.*   Prof.
Esler, P. F., BA *Syd.*, LLB *Syd.*, LLM *Syd.*, DPhil *Oxf.*   Prof.
Green, J.   Hon. Prof.
Hall, S., BA *Oxf.*   Prof.
Hart, Trevor A., BA *Durh.*, PhD *Aberd.*   Prof.; Head*
Kerr, S., BA *Oxf.*   Hon. Prof.
Lang, B., DrTheol *Tübingen*, DrHabil *Freib.*   Hon. Prof.
Piper, R. A., BA *Calif.*, BD *Lond.*, PhD *Lond.*   Prof., New Testament Language and Literature
Torrance, A. J., MA *Edin.*, BD *Aberd.*, DrTheol *Erlangen-Nuremberg*   Prof.
Witherington, B.   Hon. Prof.
Other Staff: 1 Sr. Lectr.; 5 Lectrs.; 2 Res. Fellows; 3 Hon. Lectrs.; 1 Hon. Res. Fellow; 2 Hon. Chaplains

Economics and Finance

Tel: (01334) 462420 Fax: (01334) 462444
    E-mail: econsec@st-and.ac.uk
Beath, J. A., MA *Penn.*, MA *Camb.*, MA *St And.*, MPhil *Lond.*   Prof.
Evans, G., BA *Oxf.*, MA *Calif.*, PhD *Calif.*   Prof.
Fitzroy, F. R., BA *Lond.*, MSc *Aberd.*, PhD *Heidel.*   Prof.
Jin, J.   Sr. Lectr.
La Manna, Manfredi M. A., DottScEc *Siena*, MSc *Lond.*, PhD *Lond.*   Reader
McCrory, J. R., BSc *St And.*, MA *Essex*, PhD *Essex*   Prof.
Mitra, K., BSc *Cornell*, MA *Calc.*, PhD *Cornell*   Prof.
Nolan, C., BA *Strath.*, MSc *Lond.*   Prof.
Reid, G. C., MA *Aberd.*, MSc *S'ton.*, PhD *Edin.*, FRSA   Prof.
Shea, Gary S., BA *Indiana*, PhD *Wash.*   Reader
Sutherland, A. J., BA *E.Anglia*, MA *Warw.*, PhD *Warw.*   Prof.
Thomas, J., BA *Camb.*, MPhil *Oxf.*, DPhil *Oxf.*   Hon. Prof.
Ulph, D., MA *Glas.*, BLitt *Oxf.*   Prof.; Head*
Other Staff: 19 Lectrs.

English

Tel: (01334) 462666 Fax: (01334) 462655
    E-mail: english@st-andrews.ac.uk
Alexander, M. J., MA *Oxf.*   Hon. Prof.
Burnside, J., BA   Reader

Crawford, R., MA *Glas.*, DPhil *Oxf.*, FRSEd   Prof.
Dunn, D. E., BA *Hull*, LLD *Dund.*, DLitt *Hull*, FRSL   Prof.
Herbert, M., BA *Cape Town*, BLitt *Oxf.*, MA   Sr. Lectr.
Hutson, L., BA *Oxf.*, DPhil *Oxf.*   Prof.
Jamie, K., MA *Edin.*   Reader
Jamison, K. R., BA *Calif.*, MA *Calif.*, PhD *Calif.*   Hon. Prof.
Johnson, I., BA *Oxf.*, DPhil *Oxf.*, PhD *Brist.*   Sr. Lectr.
Jones, C., BA *Lond.*, MA *Belf.*, PhD *St And.*   Sr. Lectr.
MacLachlan, C. J. M., MA *Edin.*, PhD *Edin.*   Sr. Lectr.
Mallett, P. V., MA *Camb.*   Sr. Lectr.
Murphy, A., MA *Brandeis*, PhD *Brandeis*, BA   Prof.
Murray, B., BPhil *St And.*, MA *St And.*, PhD *Camb.*   Sr. Lectr.
Parry, P., BA *Brist.*, MA *Birm.*   Sr. Lectr.
Plain, G., MA *Camb.*, PhD *Newcastle(UK)*   Reader
Rhodes, N. P. P., BA *Oxf.*, DPhil *Oxf.*   Prof.
Roe, N. H., MA *Oxf.*, DPhil *Oxf.*   Prof.; Head*
Sellers, Susan C., BA *Kent*, MA *Lond.*, PhD *Lond.*   Prof.
Stabler, J., BA *Stir.*, MPhil *Stir.*, PhD *Glas.*   Reader
Warner, M. S., MA   Hon. Prof.
Other Staff: 10 Lectrs.; 2 Teaching Fellows; 2 Hon. Sr. Lectrs.; 2 Hon. Lectrs.; 1 Res. Assoc.

Geography and Geosciences

Tel: (01334) 463940 Fax: (01334) 463949
    E-mail: gg@st-andrews.ac.uk
Alsop, G. I., BSc *Liv.*, PhD *Durh.*   Sr. Lectr.
Austin, W. E. N., BSc *Lond.*, MSc *Wales*, PhD *Wales*   Reader
Ballantyne, C. K., MA *Glas.*, MSc *McM.*, PhD *Edin.*, DSc *St And.*   Prof.
Bates, R., BSc *Edin.*, PhD *Wales*   Sr. Lectr.
Benn, D. I., BSc *Leic.*, PhD *St And.*   Reader
Bird, M., BSc *ANU*, PhD *ANU*   Prof.
Bowring, S. A., PhD   Hon. Prof.
Boyle, P. J., BA *Lanc.*, PhD *Lanc.*   Prof.; Head*
Chappel, B.   Hon. Prof.
Doherty, Joe M., BA *N.U.I.*, MSc *Penn.State*, PhD *Lond.*   Prof.
Donaldson, C. H., BSc PhD, FRSEd   Reader
Fallick, A. E., BSc PhD, FRSA, FRSEd   Hon. Prof.
Flowerdew, R., BA *Oxf.*, PhD *Northwestern(Wis.)*   Prof.
Gordon, J. E., MA PhD   Hon. Prof.
Graham, E. F., MA *St And.*, PhD *Durh.*   Reader
London, L.   Hon. Prof.
McManus, J., BSc *Lond.*, PhD *Lond.*, DSc *Dund.*, FRSEd   Emer. Prof.
Oliver, G. J. H., BSc *Sheff.*, PhD *Otago*   Reader
Prave, A. R., BS *Indiana*, MS *Penn.State*, PhD *Penn.State*   Reader
Robinson, G.   Hon. Prof.
Stephens, W. E., BSc *Wales*, PhD *Wales*   Sr. Lectr.
Walden, J., BA *Wolv.*, PhD *Wolv.*   Sr. Lectr.
Warren, C.   Sr. Lectr.
Other Staff: 12 Lectrs.; 18 Res. Fellows; 1 Hon. Sr. Lectr.; 2 Hon. Lectrs.

History

Tel: (01334) 462900 Fax: (01334) 462927
    E-mail: history@st-andrews.ac.uk
20 Lectrs.; 8 Res. Fellows; 2 Hon. Readers; 5 Hon. Sr. Lectrs.; 4 Hon. Lectrs.; 7 Hon. Res. Fellows

History, Mediaeval

Tel: (01334) 463308 Fax: (01334) 462914
    E-mail: medhist@st-andrews.ac.uk
Andrews, F., BA PhD   Reader
Bartlett, R. J., MA *Camb.*, DPhil *Oxf.*, FRHistS   Prof.
Given-Wilson, C. J., MA PhD   Prof.
Hudson, J. G. H., MA *Tor.*, MA *Oxf.*, DPhil *Oxf.*   Prof.
Kennedy, H. N., BA *Camb.*, PhD *Camb.*   Prof.

Magdalino, P., BA Oxf., DPhil Oxf.   Prof.
Maxwell, G., MA, FSA   Hon. Prof.

History, Modern

Tel: (01334) 462923 Fax: (01334) 462927
E-mail: modhist@st-andrews.ac.uk
Ansari, A., PhD Lond., BA MA   Reader
Bentley, Michael J., BA Sheff., PhD Camb.,
    FRHistS   Prof.
De Groot, G. J., BA Whitman, PhD Edin., FRHistS
    Prof.
Gordon, B., MA Dal., PhD St And., BA, FRHistS
    Reader
Hammer, P. E. J., BA Auck., MA Auck., PhD
    Camb.   Sr. Lectr.
Houston, R. A., PhD Camb., MA, FRHistS, FAE
    Prof.
MacKenzie, J.   Hon. Prof.
Muller, F., DPhil   Sr. Lectr.
Pettegree, A. D. M., BA Oxf., MA Oxf., DPhil
    Oxf., FRHistS   Prof.; Head of Sch.*
Scott, H. M., MA Edin., PhD Lond., FRHistS
    Prof.
Scott, T.   Hon. Prof.
Vysny, M. P., BA Nott., PhD Manc.   Sr. Lectr.

History, Scottish

Tel: (01334) 462890 Fax: (01334) 462927
E-mail: scottish@st-andrews.ac.uk
Allan, D., MA Edin., PhD Camb., FRHistS
    Reader
Brown, Keith M., MA Glas., PhD Glas., FRHistS
    Prof.
Brown, M., MA St And., PhD St And.   Reader
Knox, W. W., MA Edin., PhD Edin.   Sr. Lectr.
Mason, R. A., MA Edin., PhD Edin., FRHistS
    Prof.

Middle Eastern Studies

Tel: (01334) 463632 Fax: (01334) 462914
E-mail: arabic@st-andrews.ac.uk
Hoyland, R., BA MA DPhil   Reader

International Relations

Tel: (01334) 462938 Fax: (01334) 462937
E-mail: intrel@st-andrews.ac.uk
Anderson, J., BSc Lond., MSc Lond., PhD Lond.
    Prof.
Cummings, S. N.   Sr. Lectr.
Fawn, R.   Sr. Lectr.
Fierke, K., BA Minn., PhD Minn.   Sr. Lectr.
Hayden, J. P., BA Pret., MA Pret., PhD Pret.   Sr.
    Lectr.
Hinnebusch, R., BA Duquesne, MA Pitt., PhD Pitt.
    Prof.
Imber, M. F., BSc Lond., PhD S'ton.   Sr. Lectr.
Lang, A., BA Baltimore, MA Baltimore, PhD
    Baltimore   Sr. Lectr.
Rengger, N. J., BA Durh., PhD Durh.   Prof.
Richmond, O. P., BA Kent, MA Kent, PhD Kent
    Prof.
Schmid, A. P.   Prof.
Taylor, I, C., BA MPhil DPhil   Prof.
Taylor, M., BA Liv., PhD Liv.   Prof.
Walker, W. B., BSc Edin., MSc Essex   Prof.
Watson, A. M. S., MA Aberd., MSc Glas., PhD
    Dund.   Sr. Lectr.; Head*
Williams, A. J., BA Keele   Prof.
Other Staff: 11 Lectrs.; 2 Res. Fellows; 1
    Teaching Fellow

Management

Tel: (01334) 462800 Fax: (01334) 462812
E-mail: management.school@st-
    andrews.ac.uk
Alvesson, M.   Hon. Prof.
Bebbington, J., BCom NZ, PhD Dund.   Prof.
Beech, P. N. H., BSc MA   Prof.
Burt, E., BA Strath., PhD Strath.   Sr. Lectr.
Carter, C., BA Bourne., MSc Aston, PhD Aston   Sr.
    Lectr.
Check-Teck, F.   Hon. Prof.
Davies, H. T. O., BA Camb., MSc Sus., PhD Dund.
    Prof.
Desmond, J., BA PhD   Reader
Gray, R., BSc Hull, PhD Glas.   Prof.
Grinyer, P., MA PhD   Prof. Emer.
Littler, C., BSc PhD   Prof.

McKiernan, P., BA CNAA, MA Lanc., PhD Sur.
    Prof.; Head*
McKinlay, A., BA CNAA, DPhil Oxf.   Prof.
McMillan, D., BA Wales, MSc Wales, PhD Wales
    Prof.
Mueller, F., MA Oxf., MSc Oxf., DPhil Oxf.
    Prof.
Parker, L. D.   Hon. Prof.
Scott, J. T., MA Lanc., PhD Hull   Sr. Lectr.
Tavakoli, M., BSc Natnl.Iran, MSc Wales(Swansea),
    PhD Exe.   Reader
Tinker, T.   Hon. Prof.
Townley, B., BA Lanc., MSc Lond., PhD Lond.
    Prof.
Wilson, J., BA Abertay, MPhil Wales, PhD Wales
    Prof.
Other Staff: 7 Lectrs.; 4 Res. Fellows; 3
    Teaching Fellows; 2 Hon. Res. Fellows

Mathematics and Statistics

Tel: (01334) 462344 Fax: (01334) 463748
E-mail: enq.am@mcs.st-andrews.ac.uk
Bell, G. E., BTech Brun., PhD Brun.   Sr. Lectr.
Bingham, R., BSc MSc DPhil   Hon. Prof.
Blyth, T. S., DèsSc Paris, DSc, FRSEd, FIMA
    Emer. Prof., Pure Mathematics
Borchers, D. L., BA Cape Town, BSc Cape Town,
    PhD Cape Town   Reader
Buckland, S. T., BSc S'ton., MSc Edin., PhD Aberd.
    Prof., Statistics
Cairns, R. A., BSc Glas., PhD Glas.   Prof.
Campbell, C. M., MA Edin., MSc McG., PhD
    Reader
Campbell, W. R.   Hon. Prof.
Craik, A. D. D., BSc St And., PhD Camb.   Emer.
    Prof.
Dritschel, D. G., BSc   Prof.
Falconer, K. J., MA Camb., PhD Camb.   Prof.,
    Pure Mathematics
Grundy, R. E., BSc Lond., PhD Lond.   Sr. Lectr.
Harrison, R. A., BSc PhD   Hon. Prof.
Hood, A. W., BSc PhD   Prof.; Head*
Jupp, P. E., BA Camb., PhD Camb.   Reader
Kemp, Cecil D., BSc Brist., PhD Brad.   Hon.
    Prof.
Lashmore-Davies   Hon. Prof.
McCabe, J. H., BTech Brun., PhD Brun.   Sr.
    Lectr.
Neukirch, T., MSc Bochum, PhD Bochum   Reader
O'Connor, J. J., BA Oxf., DPhil Oxf.   Sr. Lectr.
Olsen, L., PhD Northwestern(Louisiana)   Reader
Priest, E. R., BSc Nott., MSc Leeds, PhD Leeds,
    FRSEd, FRSL   Prof., Theoretical Solar
    Physics
Roberts, B., BSc Hull, PhD Sheff.   Prof.
Robertson, E. F., MSc Warw., PhD Warw., BSc
    Prof.
Ruskuc, N., BA Novi Sad, PhD St And.   Prof.
Sanderson, J. J., BSc Birm., PhD Manc.   Hon.
    Prof.
Wright, A. N., BSc Brist., PhD Lond.   Reader
Other Staff: 12 Lectrs.; 23 Res. Fellows; 2
    Hon. Readers; 2 Hon. Sr. Lectrs.; 2 Hon.
    Lectrs.; 1 Hon. Res. Fellow

Modern Languages

Tel: (01334) 463670 Fax: (01334) 463677
E-mail: modlangs@st-andrews.ac.uk
18 Lectrs.; 3 Teaching Fellows; 1 Hon. Reader;
    1 Hon. Sr. Lectr.

French

Tel: (01334) 463647
Culpin, D. J., BA Brist., MA Brist., MèsL Bordeaux
    III, PhD Brist.   Sr. Lectr.
Gifford, P. P. D., MA Camb., Dr3rdCy Toulouse,
    DèsL Toulouse   Prof.
Lodge, Raymond A., BA Manc., PhD Manc.
    Prof.
Milne, Lorna, MA St And., PhD Auck.   Sr. Lectr.
Other Staff: 4 Lectrs.; 1 Teaching Fellow

German

Tel: (01334) 463655
Chambers, H. E., MA Glas., PhD Glas.   Prof.
Other Staff: 5 Lectrs.; 2 Teaching Fellows

Italian

Tel: (01334) 463678
Ferguson, R. G., MA Glas., BPhil St And.   Prof.;
    Head. of Sch.*
Other Staff: 3 Lectrs.; 2 Teaching Fellows

Russian

Tel: (01334) 462949 Fax: (01334) 462959
E-mail: russian@st-andrews.ac.uk
Press, Jeffrey I., BA Lond., PhD Lond.   Prof.
Pugh, Stefan M., BA Duke, MA Yale, PhD
    N.Carolina   Reader
Other Staff: 3 Lectrs.; 1 Hon. Sr. Lectr.

Spanish

Tel: (01334) 462961 Fax: (01334) 462959
Bentley, B. P. E., MA St And.   Sr. Lectr.
Dennis, Nigel R., BA Camb., MA Camb., PhD
    Camb.   Prof.
Fowler, W. M., BA Brist., PhD Brist.   Reader
San Roman, G. F., BA Nott., PhD Camb.   Sr.
    Lectr.
Other Staff: 4 Teaching Fellows

Philosophical and Anthropological
Studies

Tel: (01334) 462486 Fax: (01334) 462485
E-mail: philosophy@st-andrews.ac.uk
16 Lectrs.; 4 Teaching Fellows; 6 Res. Fellows

Film Studies

Tel: (01334) 467473
Iordanova, D., BA PhD   Prof.

Logic and Metaphysics

Clark, P. J., BSc Manc., MSc Lond., PhD Lond.
    Reader; Head*
Hawley, K., MSc Lond., MPhil Camb., PhD Lond.
    Sr. Lectr.
Priest, G., BA Camb., MSc Lond., PhD Lond.
    Prof. Fellow
Read, S. L., BA Keele, MSc Brist., DPhil Oxf.
    Reader
Shapiro, S., BA Case W.Reserve, MA Buffalo, PhD
    Buffalo   Prof. Fellow
Wright, C. J. G., BPhil Oxf., MA Camb., MA
    Oxf., PhD Camb., DLitt Oxf.   Prof.

Philosophy, Moral

Broadie, S. J., BPhil Oxf., MA Oxf.   Prof.
Brown, J. A., BA Oxf., BPhil Oxf., DPhil Oxf.
    Prof.
Gaut, B., BA Oxf., MA Prin., PhD Prin.   Sr.
    Lectr.
Haldane, J. J., BA CNAA, BA Lond., PhD Lond.
    Prof.
Harris, M.   Sr. Lectr.
Mulgan, T., BA Otago, BPhil Oxf.   Prof.
Nolan, D., BA PhD   Prof.
Skorupski, J. M., MA Camb., PhD Camb., FRSEd
    Prof.
Toren, C., BSc Lond.Inst., PhD Lond.Inst.   Prof.

Social Anthropology

Tel: (01334) 462977
Dilley, R. M., BSc CNAA, DPhil Oxf.   Reader
Gow, P., BA Kent, PhD   Prof.
Overing, Joanna A., BA Conn., MA Conn., PhD
    Brandeis   Emer. Prof.
Platt, Tristan, MA Oxf.   Reader
Rapport, N. J., BA Camb., MA Camb., PhD Manc.
    Prof.; Dir., Centre for the Anthropol. Study
    of Knowledge and Ethics
Riches, D. J., MA Camb., PhD Lond.   Sr. Lectr.

Physics and Astronomy

Tel: (01334) 463103 Fax: (01334) 463104
E-mail: physics@st-andrews.ac.uk
Allen, J. W., BA Camb., MA Camb.   Hon. Prof.
Bonnell, I. A., MSc Montr., PhD Montr.   Prof.
Cameron, Andrew C., BA Camb., PhD Camb.
    Prof.
Cornwell, J. F., BSc Lond., PhD Lond., FRSEd
    Hon. Prof., Theoretical Physics
Davis, J. S., BSc Calif., PhD Calif.   Prof.
Dholakia, Kishan, BA Camb., MSc   Prof.

Driver, S. P., BSc PhD   Reader
Dunn, M. H., BA Camb., PhD St And., FRSEd
   Prof.
Greaves, J. S., BA PhD   Reader
Green, A., BA Camb., DPhil Oxf.   Reader
Grigera, S. A., MA La Plata, PhD Cuyo   Reader
Horne, Keith D., BA Cal.Tech., PhD Cal.Tech.
   Prof.
Jardine, M. M., BSc St And., PhD St And.
   Reader
Krauss, T. F., PhD Glas.   Prof.
Lee, S. L., BSc Nott., PhD Birm.   Prof.; Head*
Leonhardt, U., PhD   Prof.
MacKenzie, A. P., BSc Edin., PhD Camb.   Prof.
McGill, N. C., BSc St And., PhD St And.   Sr.
   Lectr.
Miller, A., BSc Edin., PhD Bath   Prof.
Pickard, C., BA Camb., PhD Camb.   Reader
Riedi, P. C., MSc Lond., PhD S'ton.   Hon. Prof.
Samuel, I., BA Camb., MA Camb.   Prof.
Sibbett, W., BSc Belf., PhD Belf.   Prof.
Sinclair, B. D., BSc St And., PhD St And.   Reader
Smith, G. M., BSc York(UK), MSc St And., PhD St
   And.   Reader
Wan, K. K., BSc St And., PhD St And.   Reader
Zhao, H.   Reader
Other Staff: 8 Lectrs.; 49 Res. Fellows; 4 Hon.
   Readers; 1 Hon. Sr. Lectr.; 7 Hon. Lectrs.

Psychology

Tel: (01334) 462157 Fax: (01334) 463042
   E-mail: psych@st-andrews.ac.uk
Anderson, M. C., MSc Ghent, PhD Ghent   Prof.
Brown, V. J., BSc Lond., PhD Camb.   Prof.;
   Head*
Byrne, R. W., BA Camb., PhD Camb.   Prof.
Gomez, J. C., MA   Reader
Harris, J., BSc Lond., DPhil Oxf.   Prof.
Heely, D.   Hon. Prof.
Jeeves, M.   Emer. Prof.
Johnson, R. S.   Hon. Prof.
Lee, Terrance R., MA Camb., PhD Camb.   Hon.
   Prof.
MacLeod, M.   Prof.
Milner, A. D., MA PhD, FRSEd   Hon. Prof.
Perrett, D. I., DPhil Oxf., BSc   Prof.
Quinn, J. G., BA Stir., DPhil Sus.   Sr. Lectr.
Reicher, S. D., BSc Brist., PhD Brist.   Prof.
Sprenglemeyer, R.   Reader
Whiten, D. A., BSc Sheff., PhD Brist., FBPsS,
   FBA, FRSEd   Prof.
Winn, P., BA Hull, PhD Hull   Prof.
Zuberbuhler, K., MA Penn., MSc Zür., PhD Penn.
   Reader
Other Staff: 13 Lectrs.; 25 Res. Fellows; 3
   Teaching Fellows; 1 Hon. Sr. Lectr.; 3 Hon.
   Res. Fellows

Sport and Exercise

Tel: (01334) 462190 Fax: (01334) 462182
Stewart, S., BA Ulster, MSc Lough.   Dir.*
Other Staff: 1 Teaching Fellow

SPECIAL CENTRES, ETC

Advanced Materials, St Andrews' Centre for

Tel: (01334) 463817 Fax: (01334) 463808
   E-mail: chemistry@st-andrews.ac.uk
Baddeley, C., BA Camb., MA Camb., PhD Camb.
   Reader
Bruce, P. G., BSc Aberd., PhD Aberd., FRSChem,
   FRSEd   Prof.
Cole-Hamilton, D. J., BSc Edin., PhD Edin.,
   FRSChem, FRSEd   Prof.
Irvine, John T. S., BSc Edin., DPhil Ulster   Prof.
Lee, S. L., BSc Nott., PhD Birm.   Prof.
Lightfoot, P., BA Oxf., DPhil Oxf.   Reader
Morris, R. E., MA Oxf., DPhil Oxf.   Prof.
Richardson, N. V., BA Oxf., DPhil Oxf.   Prof.
Riedi, P. C., MSc Lond., PhD S'ton.   Hon. Prof.
Wright, S. P. A., BA Camb., PhD Camb.   Reader
Zhou, W., BSc Fudan, PhD Camb.   Reader

Ancient Systems of Knowledge (Logos), Centre for the Study of

Tel: (01334) 462600 Fax: (01334) 462602
   E-mail: classics@st-andrews.ac.uk
Konig, J., BA Camb., MPhil Camb., DPhil Oxf.
   Sr. Lectr.
Woolf, G. D., BA Oxf., MA Oxf., PhD Camb.
   Prof.; Dir.*
Other Staff: 3 Assoc. Staff

Arché: Centre for the Philosophy of Logic, Language, Mathematics and Mind

Tel: (01334) 462459 Fax: (01334) 462485
   E-mail: arche@st-andrews.ac.uk
Broadie, S. J., BPhil Oxf., MA Oxf.   Prof.;
   Assoc. Dir.
Greenough, P.   Assoc. Dir.
Smith, M.   Exec. Dir.
Wright, C. J. G., BPhil Oxf., MA Camb., MA
   Oxf., PhD Camb., DLitt Oxf.   Prof.; Dir.*
Other Staff: 4 Res. Fellows
Vacant Posts: 6 Prof. Fellows

Biomolecular Sciences, Centre for

Tel: (01334) 463401 Fax: (01334) 462595
   E-mail: mew@st-andrews.ac.uk
Botting, N., BSc Lond., PhD Lond.   Sr. Lectr.
Elliott, R., BSc Sur., DPhil Oxf.   Prof.
Griffiths, R., BSc Wales, PhD Wales   Sr. Lectr.
Iggo, R., BSc Brist., PhD Lond.   Prof.
Ingledew, W. J., BA York(UK), PhD Brist.   Sr.
   Lectr.
Kemp, G. D., BSc St And., PhD St And.   Sr.
   Lectr.
Naismith, J. H., BSc Edin., PhD Manc.   Prof.
O'Hagan, D., BSc Glas., PhD S'ton., DSc Glas.
   Prof.
Philp, D., BSc Aberd., PhD Leeds   Prof.
Ramsay, Rona R., BSc Edin., MA Camb., PhD
   Camb.   Reader
Randall, R. E., BSc Leeds, PhD Leeds   Prof.
Ryan, M. D., BSc Lond., MSc Lond., PhD Leic.
   Reader
Taylor, Gary L., BSc Lond., PhD Lond.   Prof.;
   Dir.*
Other Staff: 48 Res. Fellows; 1 Hon. Lectr.

Computational Algebra, Centre for Interdisciplinary Research in

Tel: (01334) 462344 Fax: (01334) 463748
   E-mail: enq.am@st-andrews.ac.uk
Linton, S. A., BA Camb., PhD Camb.   Dir.*
Robertson, E. F., MSc Warw., PhD Warw., BSc
   Prof.; Assoc. Dir.
Ruskuc, N., BA Novi Sad, PhD St And.   Prof.
Other Staff: 16 Teaching Staff; 5 Res. Fellows

Ecological and Environmental Modelling, Centre for Research into

Tel: (01334) 461842 Fax: (01334) 461800
   E-mail: rhona@mcs.st-andrews.ac.uk
Buckland, S. T., BSc S'ton., MSc Edin., PhD Aberd.
   Prof.
Dritschel, D. G., BSc   Prof.
Falconer, K. J., MA Camb., PhD Camb.   Prof.
Hammond, P.
Harwood, J., BSc Lond., PhD W.Ont.   Prof.;
   Dir.*
Johnston, I. A., BSc Hull, PhD Hull, FRSEd
   Prof.
Magurran, A. E., BSc Ulster, DPhil Ulster   Prof.
Other Staff: 11 Res. Fellows

Environmental History, Centre for

Tel: (01334) 462910 Fax: (01334) 463334
   E-mail: envhist@st-andrews.ac.uk
Clark, J. F. M.   Lectr.; Dir.*
Smout, T. C., CBE, MA Camb., PhD Camb.,
   FRSEd, FBA   Emer. Prof.
Other Staff: 2 Res. Fellows

Ethics, Philosophy and Public Affairs, Centre for

Tel: (01334) 462486 Fax: (01334) 462485
   E-mail: cppa@st-andrews.ac.uk
Haldane, J. J., BA CNAA, BA Lond., PhD Lond.
   Prof.
Shapiro, S., BA Case W.Reserve, MA Buffalo, PhD
   Buffalo   Prof. Fellow
Other Staff: 22 Members

European Cultural Identity Studies, Institute of

Tel: (01334) 463646 Fax: (01334) 463677
   E-mail: modlangs@st-andrews.ac.uk
Chambers, H. E., MA Glas., PhD Glas.   Prof.,
   German
Gifford, P. P. D., MA Camb., Dr3rdCy Toulouse,
   DèsL Toulouse   Dir.*
Other Staff: 26 Staff Members

Film Studies, Centre for

Iordanova, D., BA PhD   Prof.

Gatty Marine Laboratory

Tel: (01334) 463441 Fax: (01334) 463443
   E-mail: biology@st-andrews.ac.uk
Boyd, I. L., BSc Aberd., DSc Aberd.   Prof.
Fedak, M. A., BA New Br., MA Duke, PhD Duke
   Prof.
Hammond, P. S., BA York(UK), DPhil York(UK)
   Prof.
Johnston, I. A., BSc Hull, PhD Hull, FRSEd
   Dir.*
Magurran, A. E., BSc Ulster, DPhil Ulster   Prof.
Paterson, D. M., BSc Glas., PhD Bath   Prof.
Todd, C. D., BSc Leeds, PhD Leeds   Prof.
Other Staff: 3 Readers; 3 Lectrs.; 3 Res.
   Fellows

Housing Research, Centre for

Tel: (01334) 463911 Fax: (01334) 463949
   E-mail: gg@st-andrews.ac.uk
Doherty, Joe M., BA N.U.I., MSc Penn.State, PhD
   Lond.   Dir. (St. Andrews)*
Edgar, W. M.   Hon. Sr. Lectr.; Dir. (Dundee)*
Other Staff: 2 Res. Fellows

Indigenous American Studies, Centre for

Tel: (01334) 462977 Fax: (01334) 462985
   E-mail: socanth@st-andrews.ac.uk
Gow, P., BA Kent, PhD   Prof.
Overing, Joanna A., BA Conn., MA Conn., PhD
   Brandeis   Emer. Prof.; Dir.*
Platt, Tristan, MA Oxf.   Reader; Dir.*
Other Staff: 16 Fellows; 13 Res. Fellows

Industry Enterprise Finance and the Firm, Centre for Research into

Tel: (01334) 462438 Fax: (01334) 462444
   E-mail: gp8@st-andrews.ac.uk
Beath, J. A., MA Penn., MA Camb., MA St And.,
   MPhil Lond.   Prof.
Fitzroy, F. R., BA Lond., MSc Aberd., PhD Heidel.
   Prof.
Ulph, D., MA Glas., BLitt Oxf.   Prof.
Other Staff: 2 Readers; 7 Lectrs.; 6 Res.
   Fellows

Language and Linguistics, Institute for

Tel: (01334) 463670 Fax: (01334) 463677
   E-mail: saills@st-andrews.ac.uk
Lodge, Raymond A., BA Manc., PhD Manc.
   Prof.; Dir.*
Press, Jeffrey I., BA Lond., PhD Lond.   Prof.,
   Russian
Other Staff: 22 Staff Members

Middle East, Central Asia and the Caucasus Studies, Institute of

Tel: (01334) 463308 Fax: (01334) 463334
   E-mail: history@st-andrews.ac.uk
Ansari, A., PhD Lond., BA MA   Prof.; Dir.*
Hinnebusch, R., BA Duquesne, MA Pitt., PhD Pitt.
   Prof.

Pharmacoeconomics Research Centre

Tel: (01334) 462810 Fax: (01334) 462812
   E-mail: mt@st-andrews.ac.uk
Tavakoli, M., BSc Natnl.Iran, MSc Wales(Swansea),
   PhD Exe.   Dir.*
Other Staff: 4 Res. Fellows

Photonics Innovation Centre (PIC)

Tel: (01334) 467315 Fax: (01334) 467313
   E-mail: pic@st-andrews.ac.uk
Dunn, M. H., BA Camb., PhD St And., FRSEd
   Prof.; Jt. Dir.*
Sibbett, W., BSc Belf., PhD Belf.   Prof.; Jt. Dir.*
Other Staff: 6 Res. Fellows

Public Policy and Management, Centre for

Tel: (01334) 462878 Fax: (01334) 462812
   E-mail: bl12@st-andrews.ac.uk
Davies, H. T. O., BA Camb., MSc Sus., PhD Dund.
   Prof.; Jt. Dir.*
Other Staff: 7 Staff Members

Reformation Studies Institute

Tel: (01334) 462903 Fax: (01334) 462927
   E-mail: refinst@st-andrews.ac.uk
Gordon, F. B., BA St And., MA St And., PhD St
   And.   Prof.
Pettegree, A. D. M., BA Oxf., MA Oxf., DPhil
   Oxf., FRHistS   Prof.; Dir.*
Other Staff: 10 Staff Members; 4 Hon. Staff

Russian, Soviet and East European Studies, Centre for

Tel: (01334) 462952 Fax: (01334) 462959
   E-mail: fn4@st-andrews.ac.uk
Lodder, Christina A., BA York(UK), MA Sus.,
   DPhil Sus., FRSEd   Prof., Art History
Nethercott, F., BA Oxf., PhD Paris   Dir.*
Press, Jeffrey I., BA Lond., PhD Lond.   Prof.,
   Russian
Other Staff: 10 Staff Members

Scottish Studies Institute

Tel: (01334) 462666 Fax: (01334) 462655
   E-mail: english@st-andrews.ac.uk
Brown, Keith M., MA Glas., PhD Glas., FRHistS
   Prof., Scottish History
Crawford, R., MA Glas., DPhil Oxf., FRSEd
   Prof., English
Dunn, D. E., BA Hull, LLD Dund., DLitt Hull,
   FRSL   Prof.; Dir.*
Mason, R., MA Middx., PhD Edin.   Prof.
Other Staff: 4 Staff Members

Scottish Writing Centre

Tel: (01334) 462666 Fax: (01334) 462665
   E-mail: english@st-andrews.ac.uk
Crawford, R., MA Glas., DPhil Oxf., FRSEd
   Prof.; Dir.*

Social Learning and Cognitive Evolution

Tel: (01334) 462073 Fax: (01334) 463024
   E-mail: psychology@st-andrews.ac.uk
Byrne, R. W., BA Camb., PhD Camb.   Prof.,
   Psychology
Laland, K., BSc S'ton., PhD Lond.   Prof.
Perrett, D. I., DPhil Oxf., BSc   Prof.,
   Psychology

Slater, P. J. B., BSc Edin., PhD Edin., DSc Edin.,
   FRSEd, FIBiol   Prof., Biology
Whiten, D. A., BSc Sheff., PhD Brist., FBPsS,
   FBA, FRSEd   Prof., Psychology; Co-
   ordinator*
Other Staff: 2 Visiting Fellows; 5 Staff
Members

Terrorism and Political Violence, Centre for the Study of

Tel: (01334) 462938 Fax: (01334) 462937
   E-mail: cstpv@st-andrews.ac.uk
Schmid, A. P.   Prof.
Taylor, M., BA Liv., PhD Liv.   Prof.
Wilkinson, P., MA Wales   Prof.
Other Staff: 2 Sr. Res. Assocs.; 3 Hon. Fellows

Theology, Imagination and the Arts, Institute for

Tel: (01334) 462850 Fax: (01334) 462030
   E-mail: divinity@st-andrews.ac.uk
Begbie, J., BA Edin., BD Aberd., PhD Aberd.
   Prof.
Hart, Trevor A., BA Durh., PhD Aberd.   Prof.;
   Dir.*
Other Staff: 1 Res. Fellow; 1 Hon. Lectr.

CONTACT OFFICERS

Academic affairs. Master: Brown, Prof. Keith
   M., MA Glas., PhD Glas., FRHistS
   (E-mail: master@st-andrews.ac.uk)
Accommodation. Director, Residential and
   Business Services: Smith, R. G., MBA
   (E-mail: rbs.director@st-andrews.ac.uk)
Admissions (first degree). Director,
   Admissions: Disbury, A., BA Leeds
   (E-mail: admissions@st-andrews.ac.uk)
Admissions (higher degree). Director,
   Admissions: Disbury, A., BA Leeds
   (E-mail: pgadmissions@st-andrews.ac.uk)
Adult/continuing education. Director, Centre
   for Continuing Education: Rougvie, A., BSc
   H-W, MA Open(UK)
   (E-mail: fch@st-andrews.ac.uk)
Alumni. Alumnus Relations Officer:
   Cartwright, E.
   (E-mail: ec3@st-andrews.ac.uk)
Archives. Keeper of University Muniments:
   Reid, N. H., MA Edin., PhD Edin.
   (E-mail: norman.reid@st-andrews.ac.uk)
Careers. Director, Careers Advisory Service:
   Brown, P. (E-mail: cas@st-andrews.ac.uk)
Consultancy services. Director of Research
   and Enterprise Services: Chirnside, E., BSc
   PhD (E-mail: ec36@st-andrews.ac.uk)
Development/fund-raising. Director of
   Fundraising and Alumni Relations:
   Frankland, Sarah
Development/fund-raising. Director of
   Operations and Donor Relations: Taylor,
   Louise (E-mail: develop@st-andrews.ac.uk)
Equal opportunities. Director of Human
   Resources: Stewart, M. A.
   (E-mail: mas1@st-andrews.ac.uk)
Estates and buildings/works and services.
   Acting Director, Estates and Buildings:
   Maguire, John
   (E-mail: jgm10@st-andrews.ac.uk)
Examinations. Examinations Officer: Foldiak,
   P., MSc Bud., PhD Camb.
   (E-mail: peter.foldiak@st-andrews.ac.uk.)

Finance. Quaestor and Factor: Watson, Derek
   (E-mail: quaestor@st-andrews.ac.uk)
General enquiries. Deputy Principal: Brown,
   Prof. Keith M., MA Glas., PhD Glas., FRHistS
   (E-mail: deputyprincipal@st-andrews.ac.uk)
Health services. Occupational Health Adviser:
   Clark, A. (E-mail: ajc30@st-andrews.ac.uk)
Industrial liaison. Director of Research and
   Enterprise Services: Chirnside, E., BSc PhD
   (E-mail: ec36@st-andrews.ac.uk)
International office. Director, Admissions:
   Disbury, A., BA Leeds
   (E-mail: intoff@st-andrews.ac.uk)
Library (chief librarian). Director of the
   University Library: Purcell, J.
   (E-mail: library@st-andrews.ac.uk)
Minorities/disadvantaged groups. Director of
   Student Support Services: Ritchie, A., MA
   Aberd. (E-mail: ajr7@st-andrews.ac.uk)
Personnel/human resources. Director of
   Human Resources: Stewart, M. A.
   (E-mail: mas1@st-andrews.ac.uk)
Publications. Publications Officer: Lind, L., BA
   Newcastle(UK)
   (E-mail: publications@st-andrews.ac.uk)
Purchasing. Director, Residential and Business
   Services: Smith, R. G., MBA
   (E-mail: purchase@st-andrews.ac.uk)
Quality assurance and accreditation. Director
   LTSU/Director of Academic Audit: Piper,
   Prof. R. A., BA Calif., BD Lond., PhD Lond.
   (E-mail: learning@st-andrews.ac.uk)
Research. Vice-Principal (Research): Miller,
   Prof. A., BSc Edin., PhD Bath
   (E-mail: vpres@st-andrews.ac.uk)
Safety. Safety Adviser: Clark, A.
   (E-mail: ajc30@st-andrews.ac.uk)
Scholarships, awards, loans. Director of
   Student Support Services: Ritchie, A., MA
   Aberd. (E-mail: ajr7@st-andrews.ac.uk)
Schools liaison. Director, Admissions:
   Disbury, A., BA Leeds
   (E-mail: srm1@st-andrews.ac.uk)
Security. Acting Director, Estates and
   Buildings: Maguire, John
   (E-mail: jgm10@st-andrews.ac.uk)
Sport and recreation. Director of Physical
   Education: Scott, J., BA Birm., MA Birm.
   (E-mail: mrf@st-andrews.ac.uk)
Staff development and training. Director of
   Human Resources: Stewart, M. A.
   (E-mail: staff.development@st-
   andrews.ac.uk)
Student union. Secretary to the University
   Court: (vacant)
   (E-mail: secretary@st-andrews.ac.uk.)
Student welfare/counselling. Director of
   Student Support Services: Ritchie, A., MA
   Aberd. (E-mail: ajr7@st-andrews.ac.uk)
Students from other countries. Director,
   Admissions: Disbury, A., BA Leeds
   (E-mail: srm1@st-andrews.ac.uk)
Students with disabilities. Director of Student
   Support Services: Ritchie, A., MA Aberd.
   (E-mail: ajr7@st-andrews.ac.uk)
Women. Director of Human Resources:
   Stewart, M. A.
   (E-mail: mas1@st-andrews.ac.uk)

[Information supplied by the institution as at 19
December 2007, and edited by the ACU]

UNIVERSITY OF SALFORD

Founded 1967

Member of the Association of Commonwealth Universities

Postal Address: Salford, Greater Manchester, England M5 4WT
Telephone: (0161) 295 5000 **Fax:** (0161) 295 5999
URL: http://www.salford.ac.uk

VICE-CHANCELLOR*—Harloe, Prof. Michael H., BA Oxf., MA Oxf., PhD Essex
PRO-VICE-CHANCELLOR—Barrett, Prof. Peter S., MSc Brun., PhD CNAA
PRO-VICE-CHANCELLOR—Garrity, Michael, OBE, BEd Manc., MSc Brist., MA Manc.
PRO-VICE-CHANCELLOR—Hanstock, H. Jane, BA Leeds, MèsL Paris XII
PRO-VICE-CHANCELLOR—Powell, Prof. James A., OBE, BSc Manc., MSc Manc., PhD Salf.
REGISTRAR AND SECRETARY‡—Graves, Adrian, BA Adel., DPhil Oxf., FRHistS

GENERAL INFORMATION

History. The university was established in 1967. It was previously founded as the Royal Salford Technical Institute in 1896.

It is located 2.5km from the centre of Manchester.

Admission to first degree courses (see also United Kingdom Introduction). UK students apply through: Universities and Colleges Admissions Service (UCAS); Social Work Admissions System (SWAS); Nursing and Midwifery Admissions System (NMAS). International students should contact the university's International Office.

First Degrees (see also United Kingdom Directory to Subjects of Study). BA, BEng, BSc, MChem, MEng, MPhys.

Courses may include additional optional placement years.

Length of course. Full-time: BA, BSc, MChem, MPhys: 3–4 years; BEng, MEng: 4 years. *Part-time:* BA, BSc, MChem: 5 years; BEng: 5–6 years.

Higher Degrees (see also United Kingdom Directory to Subjects of Study).

Master's. MA, MBA, MPhil, MRes, MSc.

Admission. Applicants for admission to master's degrees must normally hold a good honours degree, or equivalent qualification.

Length of course. Full-time: MA, MBA, MRes, MSc: 1 year. *Part-time:* MA, MBA, MRes, MSc: 2 years. *By distance learning:* MA, MSc: 2 years.

Doctoral. PhD.

Language of Instruction. English. English summer school and preliminary-year English courses are available.

Libraries. Volumes: 623,154. Periodicals subscribed to: 2270.

Statistics. Students (2005–2006): full-time 14,049; part-time 4673; international 2000; undergraduate 15,480; master's 1088.

FACULTIES/SCHOOLS

Arts, Media and Social Sciences
Tel: (0161) 295 2345 Fax: (0161) 295 2348
E-mail: j.a.flynn@salford.ac.uk
Dean: Longhurst, Prof. Brian J., BA Lanc., PhD Lanc.

Business and Informatics
Tel: (0161) 295 5359 Fax: (0161) 295 3173
E-mail: a.swann@salford.ac.uk
Dean: Roberts, Prof. Carole A., BSc S'ton., MSc Birm.

Health and Social Care
Tel: (0161) 295 2367 Fax: (0161) 295 2368
E-mail: j.hinsley@salford.ac.uk
Dean: Howard, Prof. Rona, MEd Manc.

Science, Engineering and Environment
Tel: (0161) 295 5502 Fax: (0161) 295 4382
E-mail: s.herbertson@salford.ac.uk
Dean: Donnelly, Prof. Stephen E., BSc Liv., MSc Sus., PhD Salf.

ACADEMIC UNITS
Arranged by Schools

Art and Design
Tel: (0161) 295 6140 Fax: (0161) 835 2453
E-mail: artdes-admissions@salford.ac.uk
Davey, Caroline, BSc Leeds, MSc UMIST, PhD UMIST   Sr. Lectr.
Evans, Martyn, BA Sus., MA Manc.Met.   Sr. Lectr.
Fuchs, Mathias   Sr. Lectr.
Howe, J. Nigel, BA CNAA   Head*
Leighton, Debra, BA CNAA, MA Lincoln(UK)   Sr. Lectr.
Novak, John   Sr. Lectr.
O'Brien, Mark, BA Sheff., MA Lond.   Sr. Lectr.
Rivlin, Chris, BA CNAA, PhD CNAA   Prof. Fellow
Sermon, Paul, BA Wales, MA Reading   Sr. Lectr.
Sherrington, Sue, BA CNAA   Sr. Lectr.
Sterry, Patricia, BA CNAA, PhD Manc.Met.   Sr. Lectr.
Thomas, Angharad, BSc Lond., MA CNAA   Sr. Lectr.
Williams, Alex J., BSc Leeds, MA Lond., PhD Strath.   Prof. Fellow
Other Staff: 16 Staff Members

Community, Health Sciences and Social Care
Tel: (0161) 295 2426 Fax: (0161) 295 2427
E-mail: e.higginbotham@salford.ac.uk
Beverley, Audrey, BA Leic., MA Brad.   Sr. Lectr.
Cassidy, Simon, BSc Bolton Inst., MPhil Bolton Inst.   Sr. Lectr.
Chrysanthou, Marc, BA CNAA, MLitt Oxf.   Sr. Lectr.
Coldridge, Elizabeth, BA Essex   Sr. Lectr.
Duerden, Tim   Programme Leader
Dugdill, Lindsey, BA Oxf., MA Oxf., MPhil Nott., PhD Liv.   Sr. Lectr.
Eachus, Peter, BSc Wales, MSc Manc., PhD Manc.   Sr. Lectr.
Harrison, Philomena
Hicks, Stephen, BA Birm., MA Manc., PhD Manc.   Sr. Lectr.
Hill, Andrew, BA Lanc.   Sr. Lectr.
Jones, Julie, BSc Salf., MSc Salf.   Sr. Lectr.
Kniveton, Karen, BA Nott.   Head*
Lawson, John, BA Open(UK), MA Warw.   Sr. Lectr.
McLaughlin, Hugh   Sr. Lectr.
Mello-Baron, Samantha, MA Manc.   Sr. Lectr.
Murphy, Michael F., BA Keele   Sr. Lectr.
Myers, John S., BA Manc., MA Manc.   Sr. Lectr.
Pashley, Christopher, BSc Nott., MSc Manc.   Sr. Lectr.
Pugh, Stephen E., BSc Manc., MA Nott.   Sr. Lectr.
Rimmer, Annette   Sr. Lectr.

Shardlow, Steven M., BA Oxf., MA Oxf., MSc Oxf.   Prof.
Sudbery, John, BA Camb., MA Camb., MPhil Sheff.   Sr. Lectr.
Taylor, Carolyn P., BA Warw., MA Warw.   Sr. Lectr.
Thompson, Sheila M., BA Sus.   Sr. Lectr.
Weinberg, Ashley, BSc Manc., MSc Sheff., PhD Manc.   Sr. Lectr.
Wilson, Paul S., BSc Liv., MSc Liv.   Sr. Lectr.
Other Staff: 1 Lectr.; 16 Staff Members; 1 Sr. Lectr.†

Computing, Science and Engineering
Tel: (0161) 295 3223 Fax: (0161) 295 5575
E-mail: enquiries@cse.salford.ac.uk
Addyman, Anthony M., MSc Manc.   Sr. Lectr.
Amini, Siamak, BSc Manc., MSc Manc., PhD Manc.   Prof., Mathematics
Angus, James A. S., BSc Kent, PhD Kent   Prof.
Antonacopoulos, A.   Sr. Lectr.
Atcliffe, Phillip   Sr. Lectr.
Boag, Neil, BSc Lond., PhD Brist.   Sr. Lectr.
Bradbury, Peter, BSc   Sr. Lectr.
Caldwell, Darwin G., BSc Hull, PhD Hull   Prof.
Cooper, Graham S., BSc Liv., MSc Salf., PhD Salf.   Prof.
Cox, Trevor J., BSc Birm., PhD Salf.   Prof.
Davies, William, BSc Salf., PhD Salf.   Sr. Lectr.
Donnelly, Stephen E., BSc Liv., MSc Sus., PhD Salf.   Prof.
Eustace, David, BSc Brist., MSc Aston   Sr. Lectr.
Ford, Roger R., BSc Lond., PhD Lond.   Prof.
Henson, Ralph R., BA Warw., MSc Salf.   Sr. Lectr.
Hill, Arthur   Prof.
Hill, Stephen L., BSc Manc., PhD Manc.   Sr. Lectr.
Howard, David, BSc Brun., PhD Bath   Prof.
Jackson, Robert P., BSc   Prof.
James, Brian W., MSc St And., PhD Salf.   Sr. Lectr.
Johnston, Leslie J., BSc Lond., PhD Lond.   Reader
Jones, Anthony H., PhD Salf.   Sr. Lectr.
Jouri, Walid, PhD Liv.   Sr. Lectr.
Keeler, Graham   Sr. Lectr.
Kilcoyne, Susan   Prof.
Lam, Yui Wai, BSc HK, PhD Birm.   Prof.
Laws, Elizabeth M., BSc Lond., PhD Salf.   Prof. Fellow
Laws, Gordon T., BSc Lond., MSc Sheff., PhD Salf.   Sr. Lectr.
Linge, Nigel, BSc Salf., PhD Salf.   Prof.; Head*
McDonald, Graham   Reader
Melbourne, Clive, BEng Sheff., PhD Sheff.   Prof.
Meziane, Farid   Sr. Lectr.
Moorhouse, Andrew   Reader
Morrison, Ian, BSc Brist., PhD Newcastle(UK)   Reader
Nasr, Ghasem   Sr. Lectr.
Newton, David   Sr. Lectr.
Pemble, Martyn E., BSc S'ton., PhD S'ton.   Prof.
Pilkington, Richard D., BSc Salf., PhD Salf.   Sr. Lectr.
Ritchings, Richard T., BSc Manc., PhD Manc.   Prof.
Roberts, David   Reader

Rogerson, Graham A., BSc Leic., MSc E.Anglia, PhD E.Anglia   Prof.
Shen, Tiehan, PhD Camb., BSc   Reader
Silver, Jane   Prof. Fellow
Takruri-Rizk, Haifa   Sr. Lectr.
Vadera, Sunil, BSc Salf., MSc Manc., PhD Manc. Prof.
Van den Berg, Jacob A., PhD Salf.   Prof.
Other Staff: 1 Lectr.; 1 Hon. Visiting Fellow

Construction and Property Management

Tel: (0161) 295 4600 Fax: (0161) 295 5011
E-mail: enquiries-scpm@salford.ac.uk
Alexander, Keith, BSc Manc., BArch Manc. Prof.
Al-Shawi, Mustapha, BSc Basrah, MSc Ohio, PhD Leeds   Prof.
Amaratunga, Dilanthi   Dir., Postgrad. Res. Studies
Aouad, Ghassan, BSc Beirut, MSc Lough., PhD Lough.   Prof.; Head*
Baldry, David, MSc Aston   Sr. Lectr.
Barrett, Peter S., MSc Brun., PhD CNAA   Prof.
Brandon, Peter S., MSc Brist., DSc Brist.   Prof.
Curwell, Stephen R., BSc Belf., MSc Belf.   Prof.
Eaton, David, BSc Salf., MSc H-W, PhD Salf. Sr. Lectr.
Fernando, Terence, BSc S.Lanka, MSc Manc., PhD Manc.   Prof.
Khosrowshahi, Farzad, BSc Wales, MSc Wales, PhD S.Bank   Prof.
Koskela, Lauri   Prof.
Lees, Melvyn, BSc Salf.   Sr. Lectr.
Marvin, Simon   Prof.
McDermott, Peter
Newton, Rita, MEd Manc.   Sr. Lectr.
Ormerod, Marcus   Prof.
Ruddock, Leslie, BA CNAA, MSc Salf., PhD Salf. Prof.
Sexton, Martin G.   Sr. Lectr.
Tah, Joseph   Prof.

English, Sociology, Politics and Contemporary History

Tel: (0161) 295 3597 Fax: (0161) 295 5511
E-mail: s.vaughan@salford.ac.uk
Bagnall, G., BSc Salf., PhD Salf.   Sr. Lectr.
Bellaby, Paul, BA Camb., MA Camb., PhD Camb. Prof.
Birkbeck, Christopher, BA Oxf., MA Oxf., PhD Wales
Bull, Martin J., BA Nott., MA Oxf., PhD Florence Prof.
Buse, Peter, BA Alta., MA Cardiff, PhD Cardiff Sr. Lectr.
Callick, Paul, BA CNAA, MA Kent   Sr. Lectr.
Cooper, Andrew, BA Leeds, PhD S'ton.   Head*
Crawford, Garry, BSc Salf., PhD Salf.   Sr. Lectr.
Evans, Jocelyn, BA Manc., PhD Florence   Sr. Lectr.
Fielding, Stephen J., BA Camb., PhD Warw.   Sr. Lectr.
Flynn, Robert, BA Sus., MA Kent   Prof.
Garrard, John A., BA Keele, MA Manc.   Sr. Lectr.
Harding, Alan P., BA Middx., MSc Lond., DPhil Oxf.   Prof.
Harrison, Edward D. R., MA Oxf.   Sr. Lectr.
Maidment, Brian E., BA Wales, MA Wales, PhD Leic.   Prof.
May, Tim P., BSc Lond., MSc Sur., PhD Plym. Prof.
Newall, James L., BA E.Anglia, MSc Lond., PhD Florence   Reader
Powell, Susan, BA Lond., PhD Lond.   Sr. Lectr.
Rowland, Antony C., BA Hull, MA Leeds   Sr. Lectr.
Smith, Gregory W. H., BSc Salf., PhD Salf. Reader
Ward, Stephen J.   Sr. Lectr.
Other Staff: 2 Lectrs.; 1 Tutor

Environment and Life Sciences

Tel: (0161) 295 5796 Fax: (0161) 295 5141
E-mail: info-els@salford.ac.uk
Bisby, Roger H., BSc Nott., PhD Nott.   Prof.
Butler, John, BSc CNAA, PhD CNAA   Sr. Lectr.
Chappell, Adrian, BSc CNAA, PhD Lond.   Sr. Lectr.

Collier, Christopher G., BSc Lond.   Prof.
Collins, David N., BA Camb., MA Camb., MA Oxf., PhD Nott., DSc Manc.   Prof.
Craig, Phillip S., BSc Leeds, MSc Liv., PhD Melb. Prof.
Danson, F. Mark, BSc Sheff., PhD Sheff.   Prof.
Davies, David H., BSc Aston, MSc Lond., PhD Salf. Sr. Lectr.
Ford, Norma J., BSc Salf.   Sr. Lectr.
Foster, Howard A., BSc Leeds, PhD Leeds   Sr. Lectr.
Heath, Stephen, BSc Manc., MSc Liv., PhD Liv. Sr. Lectr.
Hemmings, Martin, MA Oxf.   Sr. Lectr.
Heritage, George, BSc E.Anglia, PhD E.Anglia   Sr. Lectr.
Hide, G., BSc Edin., PhD Edin.   Prof.
Hodgson, Kenneth, BSc Salf., MSc Wash.   Sr. Lectr.
Hutchinson, Simon M., BSc Liv., PhD Liv.   Sr. Lectr.
Ingram, George A., BSc Sheff., MSc Salf., PhD Salf.   Sr. Lectr.
James, Philip, PhD Wales   Sr. Lectr.
Knowles, Richard D., BA Newcastle(UK), PhD Newcastle(UK)   Prof.
Miller, Christopher E., BSc Lond., PhD Lond. Prof.
Morgan, Christopher G., MA Oxf., DPhil Oxf. Prof.
Murphy, Rosemary G., BSc Belf., PhD Manc. Sr. Lectr.
Rennie, Denise M., BSc Strath.   Sr. Lectr.
Rogan, Michael T., BSc Belf., PhD Keele   Sr. Lectr.
Steele, Andrew, BSc CNAA, MSc Hull   Prof.
Storey, David M., MSc Salf., PhD Salf., FIBiol Prof.; Head*
Thomas, Emrys W., BSc Wales, DPhil Oxf.   Sr. Lectr.
Todd, Stephen, BSc Manc., MSc Leeds, PhD Salf. Sr. Lectr.
Other Staff: 24 Lectrs.; 11 Res. Fellows/Res. Assts.

Health Care Professions

Tel: (0161) 295 2211 Fax: (0161) 295 2432
E-mail: healthcare@salford.ac.uk
Barlow, Alison, MSc Manc.   Sr. Lectr.
Bowker, Peter, BSc Salf., PhD Salf.   Prof.
Braid, Sue, MSc Manc.   Sr. Lectr.
Butler, Marie, MA Salf.   Sr. Lectr.
Chesney, Margaret, MSc Sur.   Sr. Lectr.
Choucri, Lesley, BSc Hudd.   Sr. Lectr.
Crofts, Gillian, MSc Liv.   Sr. Lectr.
Eaton, Carena, BSc CNAA   Sr. Lectr.
Eyres, Renata D., MSc   Sr. Lectr.
Hatcher, Julian O., MPhil Salf.   Sr. Lectr.
Heath, Glyn, BSc E.Anglia, PhD   Sr. Lectr.
Hogg, Peter, BSc CNAA, MPhil   Prof.
Hollingworth, Linda, MSc   Sr. Lectr.
Howard, Rona, MEd Manc.   Prof., Health Care Education
Hurst, Barbara, MEd   Sr. Lectr.
Hutchins, Stephen, MSc   Sr. Lectr.
Kay, Stephen, BSc MSc PhD   Prof.
Mackay, Stuart, MSc Sur.   Sr. Lectr.
Martin, Rachel, MSc   Sr. Lectr.
Matthews, Helen, BSc MSc   Sr. Lectr.
Matthews, Martyn, BSc Brighton   Sr. Lectr.
McCourt, Francis, BA Open(UK), MSc Salf.   Sr. Lectr.
McKenna, Jacqueline, BSc Salf.   Sr. Lectr.
Moore, Lynne, BA(Soc) Open(UK), MEd York(UK) Sr. Lectr.
Nightingale, Julie M., MSc   Sr. Lectr.
Niven, Deborah, MSc   Dir., Occupnl. Therapy
Norton, Sue, BSc Open(UK)   Sr. Lectr.
Robinson, Leslie, MSc Lanc.   Sr. Lectr.
Smith, Christine, MSc Newcastle(UK)   Sr. Lectr.
Supyk, Joanne, MSc   Sr. Lectr.
Taylor, Jacqueline, BSc Leic.   Sr. Lectr.
Wilkinson, Joseph J., MSc   Sr. Lectr.
Other Staff: 45 Lectrs.

Languages

Tel: (0161) 295 5990 Fax: (0161) 295 5335
E-mail: enquiries-languages@salford.ac.uk
Ania, Gillian, BA Leeds, MA Hull, PhD Hull   Sr. Lectr.
Blakemore, Diane, BA Well., PhD Lond.   Prof.
Bromby, Susan M., BA Lond., MEd Manc.   Sr. Lectr.
Carr, Myriam S., Lic Lyons, Maîtrise Paris, PhD Paris   Reader
Dickins, James, BA Camb., MA Camb., PhD H-W Sr. Lectr.
Gregory, Abigail, BSc Aston, PhD Aston   Sr. Lectr.
Hanstock, H. Jane, BA Leeds, MèsL Paris XII   Sr. Lectr.
Hoffmann, Charlotte, MA Reading   Reader
Hollis, Anthony, BA Newcastle(UK), MLitt Newcastle(UK)   Sr. Lectr.
Jarvis, Huw A., BA CNAA   Sr. Lectr.
Keiger, John F. V., PhD Camb.   Prof.
Mailhac, J. P., PhD Salf.   Sr. Lectr.
Rowlett, Paul, BA Brad., MA York(UK), PhD Salf. Sr. Lectr.
Salama-Carr, Myriam   Prof.
Tomlinson, Philip, BA Liv., PhD Liv.   Prof.; Head*
Towell, Richard J., MA Aberd., PhD Salf.   Prof.
Watson, Janet, BA Exe., PhD Lond.   Prof.
Wigmore, Juliet, BA Lond., MA Kent, MPhil Lond. Sr. Lectr.
Zemke, Uwe J., BA Hull, PhD Camb.   Sr. Lectr.

Media, Music and Performance

Tel: (0161) 295 6000 Fax: (0161) 295 6023
E-mail: a.vowles@salford.ac.uk
Cook, Ron, BA Manc., MA Manc.   Prof.
Denning, Walter, BSc Reading   Sr. Lectr.; Head*
Dewhurst, Robin, MA CNAA   Sr. Lectr.
Dixon, Stephen R., BA Manc., MA Middx.   Sr. Lectr.
Gill, Tom, MA Dund.   Sr. Lectr.
Graham, Peter, BMus Edin.   Reader
King, David, BA Pacific Union   Prof.
Knudsen, Erik   Sr. Lectr.
McKay, George   Prof.
Muir, Colin, BA Ulster, MFA Conn., MFA Temple Sr. Lectr.
Oliver, Mary, BA Nott., MA Manc.Met.   Sr. Lectr.
O'Reilly, Carole, BA N.U.I., MA N.U.I.   Sr. Lectr.
Palmer, Gareth E., BA Sund., PhD Stir.   Sr. Lectr.
Peters, Lloyd, BA Manc.   Sr. Lectr.
Scott, Derek, BA Hull, MMus Hull, PhD Hull Prof.
Whiteley, Sheila, BA Open(UK), PhD Open(UK) Prof.
Williams, Alan   Sr. Lectr.
Willis, Andrew, BA CNAA, MA CNAA   Sr. Lectr.

Nursing

Tel: (0161) 295 2999 Fax: (0161) 295 2963
E-mail: a.e.gallacher@salford.ac.uk
Ashton, Elizabeth, BSc Hudd., MAEd Open(UK) Sr. Lectr.
Baker, Deborah   Prof.
Beswick, Sandra, BA Open(UK), MA   Sr. Lectr.
Cappleman, Julia, BSc Salf.   Sr. Lectr.
Chadwick, Ruth H., BA Manc., MSc Manc.   Sr. Lectr.
Darvill, Angela, BSc Salf., MSc   Sr. Lectr.
Devitt, Patrick, BA Warw., MSc Hudd.   Sr. Lectr.
Dickinson, Phyllis, BA C.Lancs., LLM Liv.   Sr. Lectr.
Fallon, Deborah, BSc Hudd., MA Lanc.   Sr. Lectr.
Grant, Janice M., BSc Manc.Met., MSc Salf.   Sr. Lectr.
Haigh, Carol   Sr. Lectr.
Hastings-Asatourian, Barbara, BA Manc., MSc Salf.   Sr. Lectr.
Hogg, Christine, BSc Wales, MSc Manc.   Sr. Lectr.
Holland, Katherine, BSc Manc.Met., MSc Keele Prof.

Horrocks, Stephen, BA Manc., MPhil Manc., PhD Durh.   Sr. Lectr.
Howe, Paula D., BA Manc., MSc Salf.   Sr. Lectr.
Hynes, Celia, MSc Sheff., MA Sheff.   Sr. Lectr.
Jenkins, Imelda, BSc C.Lancs.   Sr. Lectr.
Jenkins, Jane, BA Manc., MSc Manc.   Sr. Lectr.
Johnson, Martin, MSc Manc., PhD Manc.   Prof.
Lee, Nancy, BA C.Lancs., MA Leeds, PhD Salf.   Sr. Lectr.
Leyden, Marguerita, BEd Manc., MEd Manc.   Sr. Lectr.
Livesley, Joan, BSc Hudd.   Sr. Lectr.
Long, Anthony J., BSc Hudd., MA Manc., PhD Manc.   Sr. Lectr.
McCartney, William, BSc Manc.Met., MA Manc.   Sr. Lectr.
McLoughlin, Moira, BSc Salf.   Sr. Lectr.
McMahon, Maureen, BSc Manc., MSc Manc.Met., MA Open(UK)   Sr. Lectr.
Mitchell, Mark, BA Open(UK), MSc Manc.   Sr. Lectr.
Murray, Cyril J., BA Manc., MSc Salf.   Sr. Lectr.
Neville, Lillian, MA Manc.   Sr. Lectr.
Ryan, Julia, BA Manc., MA Keele   Sr. Lectr.
Sharples, Naomi   Sr. Lectr.
Staniland, Karen, BSc Salf., MSc Salf.   Sr. Lectr.
Wild, Jill, MBA CNAA   Sr. Lectr.; Head*
Wild, Karen, MA Manc.   Sr. Lectr.

Salford Business School

Tel: (0161) 295 2938
   E-mail: t.libby@salford.ac.uk
Adam, Alison E., BSc Edin., PhD Sheff.   Prof.
Anderson, Gregory L., BA York(UK), MA Lanc., PhD Lanc.   Sr. Lectr.
Arnold, Glen C., BSc Cardiff, PhD Lough.   Prof.
Baker, Rose D., MA Camb., PhD Camb.   Prof.
Basden, Andrew, BSc S'ton., PhD S'ton.   Sr. Lectr.
Bell, Frances   Sr. Lectr.
Carroll, Anita, BA Sheff.   Sr. Lectr.
Cleary, Richard, BEd Hull, MSc Salf.   Sr. Lectr.
Collins, Peter H. D., BA Camb., BA Oxf., MA Oxf.   Prof., Public Policy
Conway, Anthony, BA CNAA, MSc Manc.   Sr. Lectr.
Coulburn, Mike   Head, Sch. of Acctg., Econ. and Management Sci.
Crabtree, Helen, BSc Warw.   Sr. Lectr.
Crosbie, Mike   Sr. Lectr.
Dangerfield, Brian C., BScEcon Wales, PhD Salf.   Prof.
Darlington, Ralph, BA CNAA, MA Warw., PhD Warw.   Sr. Lectr.
Davies, John, BSc Salf., MSc Salf., PhD Salf.   Sr. Lectr.
Dobson, John R., BA Liv., MA Warw.   Head, Sch. of Management
Doran, Edward J., BA Open(UK), MSc Salf., PhD Salf.   Sr. Lectr.
Ferneley, Elaine H.   Sr. Lectr.
Forrest, David K., BA Liv., MA Manc., PhD W.Ont.   Reader
Fox, Roland P., BA Manc., MA Manc.   Sr. Lectr.
Harding, Mike, BA CNAA, MSc Salf.   Sr. Lectr.
Hayes, Helen   Sr. Lectr.
Ingham, Barbara M., BA Manc., MSc Lond., PhD Salf.   Reader
Jones, Margaret, BA Sheff.   Sr. Lectr.
Kane, Kevin, MSc Sheff.   Sr. Lectr.
Kerfoot, Russell, MA Manc.Met.   Sr. Lectr.
Kidger, Peter J., BA Sheff.   Sr. Lectr.; Head, Sch. of Leisure, Hospitality and Food Management
Kirkham, John A., BScTech Wales, MSc Warw.   Sr. Lectr.
Kobbacy, Khairy, MSc Strath., PhD Bath   Prof.
Larmouth, John   Prof.
Light, Brian A., BA Leeds, MSc Lanc.   Sr. Lectr.
Lister, Roger, PhD Salf.   Prof.
Lucas, John, BA Lanc., MBA Open(UK), MSc Lond.   Sr. Lectr.; Deputy Dir., Centre for Gambling and Commercial Gaming
Moran, Timothy, MSc Sheff.   Sr. Lectr.
Mulhall, Jean, MSc Manc.   Sr. Lectr.
Mulkeen, James, BSc Manc.   Sr. Lectr.
Percy, David F., BSc Lough., PhD Liv., FIMA   Sr. Lectr.

Procter, Chris, BSc Wales, MSc UMIST   Sr. Lectr.
Rae, John M., BSc Salf., MA Newcastle(UK), DPhil York(UK)   Sr. Lectr.
Roberts, Carole A., BSc S'ton., MSc Birm.   Prof.
Ross, Judith, LLB Birm., LLM Lond.   Sr. Lectr.
Rudder, Harold E., MSc Sheff.   Sr. Lectr.
Schofield, Peter, PhD Manc.   Sr. Lectr.
Sharifi, Sedigheh, MSc Aston, PhD Aston   Sr. Lectr.
Sharp, John M., BEng Brad., PhD Brad.   Prof.
Southan, John M., BTech Lough.   Sr. Lectr.
Spedding, Paul, MA Camb., MSc Salf.   Sr. Lectr.
Swift, Jonathan S., BA CNAA, MSc UMIST, MA Liv., PhD Liv.   Sr. Lectr.
Taylor, Eunice, BSc Reading, PhD Brad.   Prof.
Wang, Wen Bin, PhD Salf.   Sr. Lectr.
Warnaby, Gary C., BA Newcastle(UK), MSc Salf.   Sr. Lectr.
Whittaker, Phillip, MA Oxf.   Sr. Lectr.
Wieteska, Paul, BSc Lond., MSc Lond.   Sr. Lectr.
Wilson, Francis, BA Liv., MA Sheff.   Sr. Lectr.
Wilson, John   Prof.; Head*
Wood, W. Graham, BSc Wales   Sr. Lectr.

Salford Law School

Alcock, Alistair R., MA Camb.   Prof.
Cooper, Simon, LLB Manc.Met., MA Leeds   Sr. Lectr.
Howes, Victoria S., BSc Kiev, MA Salf., MEd Manc.   Sr. Lectr.
James, Mark D., LLB Leeds, PhD Anglia Ruskin   Sr. Lectr.

SPECIAL CENTRES, ETC

Academic Enterprise

Tel: (0161) 295 3000 Fax: (0161) 295 4256
   E-mail: ae@salford.ac.uk
Wood, Laurie, BA CNAA, PhD   Prof.; Dir.*

Bioscience Research Institute

Tel: (0161) 295 4912 Fax: (0161) 295 5210
   E-mail: r.h.bisby@salford.ac.uk
Bisby, Roger H., BSc Nott., PhD Nott.   Dir.*

Built and Human Environment, Research Institute for the

Tel: (0161) 295 4600 Fax: (0161) 295 5011
   E-mail: scpm@salford.ac.uk
Ruddock, Leslie, BA CNAA, MSc Salf., PhD Salf.   Prof.; Dir.*

Creative Arts and Sciences, Adelphi Research Institute for

Tel: (0161) 295 6146
   E-mail: n.j.edwards@salford.ac.uk
Cooper, Rachel   Prof.; Dir.*

European Studies Research Institute

Tel: (0161) 295 5614 Fax: (0161) 295 2818
   E-mail: d.hughes1@salford.ac.uk
Keiger, John F. V., PhD Camb.   Prof.; Dir.*

Gambling, Centre for the Study of

Tel: (0161) 295 6299 Fax: (0161) 295 2130
   E-mail: k.milhench@salford.ac.uk
Collins, Peter H. D., BA Camb., BA Oxf., MA Oxf.   Prof., Public Policy

Health and Social Care Research, Institute for

Tel: (0161) 295 7016 Fax: (0161) 295 2241
   E-mail: d.livesay@salford.ac.uk
Holland, Katherine, BSc Manc.Met., MSc Keele   Prof.; Acting Dir.*

Informatics Research Institute

Tel: (0161) 295 5292
Rezgui, Yacine, PhD Paris   Prof.; Dir.*

Management and Management Sciences Research Institute

Tel: (0161) 295 4369 Fax: (0161) 295 4947
   E-mail: s.j.sharples@salford.ac.uk
Kobbacy, Khairy, MSc Strath., PhD Bath   Prof.; Dir.*

Materials Research, Institute for

Tel: (0161) 295 5432 Fax: (0161) 295 5147
   E-mail: d.k.ross@salford.ac.uk
Huglin, Malcolm B., BSc Liv., DSc Liv., FRSChem   Prof.
Ross, D. Keith, MA Camb., MSc Birm., PhD Birm., DSc Birm.   Prof.; Dir.*

Regional Language Network

Tel: (0161) 295 3006 Fax: (0161) 295 5135
   E-mail: info@rln-northwest.com
Sousa, Cristina   Dir.*

Research and Graduate College

Tel: (0161) 295 5839 Fax: (0161) 295 5526
   E-mail: p.s.barrett@salford.ac.uk
Barrett, Peter S., MSc Brun., PhD CNAA   Dir.*

Social, Cultural and Policy Research, Institute for

Tel: (0161) 295 5876 Fax: (0161) 295 0460
   E-mail: m.byrne@salford.ac.uk
Flynn, Robert, BA Sus., MA Kent   Prof.; Dir.*

Sustainable Urban and Regional Futures, Centre for (SURF)

Tel: (0161) 295 4018 Fax: (0161) 295 5880
   E-mail: p.allen@salford.ac.uk
Harding, Alan P., BA Middx., MSc Lond., DPhil Oxf.   Prof.; Co-Dir.*
Marvin, Simon   Prof.; Co-Dir.*
May, Tim P., BSc Lond., MSc Sur., PhD Plym.   Prof.; Lead Dir.*

Virtual Environments, Centre for

Tel: (0161) 295 2916 Fax: (0161) 295 8196
   E-mail: l.m.piper@salford.ac.uk
Fernando, Terence, BSc S.Lanka, MSc Manc., PhD Manc.   Prof.

CONTACT OFFICERS

Accommodation. Accommodation Officer: Kirby, S. G., BSc Nott., PhD Nott.
   (E-mail: s.kirby@salford.ac.uk)
Admissions (first degree). Admissions Officer: Haran, Joanna
   (E-mail: j.haran@salford.ac.uk)
Admissions (higher degree). Admissions Officer: Hamada, Rosie
   (E-mail: pgadmissions-extrel@salford.ac.uk)
Adult/continuing education. Director of Education Development Unit: Cove, Geoff, BA Manc. (E-mail: g.c.cove@salford.ac.uk.)
Careers. Head of Careers: Ireland, Peter
   (E-mail: p.ireland@salford.ac.uk.)
Computing services. Executive Director, Knowledge and Information Management: Lewis, Anthony M., BA Lanc., MSc Birm.
   (E-mail: a.m.lewis@salford.ac.uk.)
Estates and buildings/works and services. Director of Estates and Buildings: Eastham, Rod, MSc Salf., PhD Salf.
   (E-mail: r.a.eastham@salford.ac.uk.)
Finance. Director of Finance: Corner, Raymond A.
   (E-mail: r.corner@salford.ac.uk.)
General enquiries. Registrar
   (E-mail: w.quilliam@salford.ac.uk)
International office. Head of International Office: Gerrard, Piera
   (E-mail: intoff@salford.ac.uk)
Library (enquiries). Executive Director, Knowledge and Information Management: Lewis, Anthony M., BA Lanc., MSc Birm.
   (E-mail: helpdesk-isd@salford.ac.uk)
Marketing. Head of Marketing and Communications: Blackburn, Mark, BA Lanc.
   (E-mail: m.blackburn@salford.ac.uk.)
Personnel/human resources. Director of Personnel: Watkinson, Keith
   (E-mail: personnel@salford.ac.uk.)
Public relations. Press Officer: Conway, Rachel, BA Leic.
   (E-mail: r.conway@salford.ac.uk.)
Purchasing. University Purchasing Manager: Brewer, Peter, BA E.Anglia
   (E-mail: p.brewer@salford.ac.uk.)

Safety. Director of Occupational Hygiene and Safety Services: Meachin, Tony
(E-mail: t.meachin@salford.ac.uk.)
Schools liaison. Head of Education Liaison Services: Hallows, Clare, BA Birm., MEd Birm. (E-mail: c.hallows@salford.ac.uk.)
Security. Chief Security Officer: Shutt, Mark
(E-mail: m.shutt@salford.ac.uk)

Student union. President: Snowden, Andrew
(E-mail: president-ussu@salford.ac.uk)
Student welfare/counselling. Welfare and Education Officer: Mold, Matthew
(E-mail: welfare-ussu@salford.ac.uk)
Students from other countries. Head of International Office: Gerrard, Piera
(E-mail: intoff@salford.ac.uk)

Students with disabilities. Equalities Co-ordinator: Pile, Arron
(E-mail: equalities-academic@salford.ac.uk.)

[Information supplied by the institution as at 5 July 2006, and edited by the ACU]

UNIVERSITY OF SHEFFIELD

Founded 1905

Member of the Association of Commonwealth Universities

Postal Address: Sheffield, England S10 2TN
Telephone: (0114) 222 2000 **Fax:** (0114) 222 1234
URL: http://www.sheffield.ac.uk

VICE-CHANCELLOR*—Burnett, Prof. Keith, CBE, BA Oxf., DPhil Oxf., FRS, FIP
PRO-VICE-CHANCELLOR—Beaulieu, Prof. M., BA McM., PhD City(UK), FCLIP
PRO-VICE-CHANCELLOR—Crook, Prof. A. D. H., BA Brist., MPhil Lond., PhD Sheff.
PRO-VICE-CHANCELLOR—Fleming, Prof. P. J., BSc Belf., PhD Belf., FIEE
PRO-VICE-CHANCELLOR—Tomlinson, Prof. G. R., BSc Aston, MSc Aston, PhD Salf., DSc Manc., FREng, FIMechE, FRSA, FRAeS
PRO-VICE-CHANCELLOR—White, Prof. P. E., BA Oxf., DPhil Oxf.
TREASURER—Staniforth, A. M. C., BA Manc., FCA
REGISTRAR AND SECRETARY‡—Fletcher, D. E., BA Sheff., PhD Sheff.
LIBRARIAN—Lewis, M. J., MA Camb.

GENERAL INFORMATION

History. The university's origins can be traced back to the foundation of Sheffield School of Medicine in 1828. In 1897 the University College of Sheffield was created by the amalgamation of the school of medicine with Firth College (founded 1879) and Sheffield Technical School (1884). The university was granted its charter in 1905.

Admission to first degree courses (see also United Kingdom Introduction). Through Universities and Colleges Admissions Service (UCAS). International applicants: certificates/diplomas satisfying matriculation requirements in country of origin will be considered on an individual basis, provided they reach the level of attainment required by the university.

First Degrees (see also United Kingdom Directory to Subjects of Study). BA, BA(Law), BDS, BEng, BMedSci, BMinTheol, BMS, BMus, BSc, BScTech, LLB, MB ChB, MChem, MEng, MMath, MPhys.
The university operates a modular structure for most of its degree programmes.
Length of course. Full-time: BMus, LLB: 3 years; BA, BA(Law), BEng, BMedSci, BSc: 3–4 years; MChem, MEng, MMath, MPhys: 4 years; BDS: 5 years; MB ChB: 5–6 years.

Higher Degrees (see also United Kingdom Directory to Subjects of Study).
Master's. LLM, MA, MArch, MArchStudies, MBA, MD, MDS, MEd, MMedSci, MMet, MMinTheol, MMus, MPhil, MSc, MSc(Eng), MSc(Res).
Admission. Applicants for admission to master's degree courses must normally hold an appropriate first degree with at least second class honours.
Length of course. Full-time: LLM, MBA, MMus, MSc, MSc(Res): 1 year; MA, MArch, MArchStudies, MMet, MSc(Eng): 1–2 years; MMedSci: 1–3 years; MPhil: 2 years. Part-time: MArchStudies, MMus: 2 years; MMet, MSc(Eng): 2–3 years; MA, MEd, MSc: 2–4 years; MMedSci: 2–5 years; LLM: max. 3 years; MPhil: 4 years. By distance learning: MA, MSc:

1–4 years; MMedSci: 2–3 years; MEd: 2–4 years.
Doctoral. DClinPsy, EdD, PhD.
Admission. PhD: candidates for admission must hold a first degree with at least upper second class honours.
Length of course. Full-time: DClinPsy, EdD: 3 years; PhD: 3–4 years. Part-time: PhD: 6 years.

Language of Instruction. English. Preparatory courses and English language support classes available for international students.

Libraries. Volumes: 1,400,000. Other holdings: 60,000 maps.

FACULTIES/SCHOOLS

Architectural Studies
Tel: (0114) 222 6911 Fax: (0114) 279 8276
E-mail: j.alsop@shef.ac.uk
Dean: Sharples, Prof. S., BSc Nott., PhD Sheff.
Secretary: Alsop, J. K., BA Sheff.

Arts
Tel: (0114) 222 0574 Fax: (0114) 222 0588
E-mail: alison.griffin@shef.ac.uk
Dean: Hookway, Prof. C. J., BPhil E.Anglia, MA Oxf., PhD Camb.
Secretary: Griffin, A., BA Exe.

Engineering
Tel: (0114) 222 5134 Fax: (0114) 222 5661
E-mail: a.d.isaac@shef.ac.uk
Dean: Niranjan, Prof. M., BSc Peradeniya, MEE T.U.Eindhoven, PhD Camb.
Secretary: Isaac, A. D., BSc Sheff., MSc Sheff.

Law
Tel: (0114) 222 6829 Fax: (0114) 222 6832
E-mail: s.hardcastle@shef.ac.uk
Dean: White, Prof. N. D., BA Oxf., MA Oxf., PhD Nott.
Secretary: Hardcastle, S. J., BA York(UK), MA York(UK)

Medicine
Tel: (0114) 271 3115 Fax: (0114) 271 3960
E-mail: r.b.ward@shef.ac.uk

Dean: Hutchinson, Prof. A., MB BS Newcastle(UK), FRCGP, FFPHM

Pure Science
Tel: (0114) 222 6546 Fax: (0114) 276 6515
E-mail: a.symington@shef.ac.uk
Dean: Nicolson, Prof. R. I., MA Camb., MSc Sus., PhD Camb.
Secretary: Symington, A., BSc Newcastle(UK)

Social Sciences
Tel: (0114) 222 6445 Fax: (0114) 226 8125
E-mail: l.manley@shef.ac.uk
Dean: Marsh, Prof. P., BSc(SocSc) S'ton., MPhil S'ton.
Secretary: Gascoyne, A., BSc Salf.

ACADEMIC UNITS

Animal and Plant Sciences
Tel: (0114) 222 0123 Fax: (0114) 222 0002
E-mail: animal.plant@shef.ac.uk
Beerling, D. J., BSc Wales, PhD Wales   Prof., Palaeontology
Birkhead, T. R., DSc Newcastle(UK), DPhil Oxf., FRS   Hon. Curator, Alfred Denny Museum; Prof., Zoology
Boots, M. R. J., BSc Leeds, PhD Liv.   Reader
Burke, T. A., BSc Wales, PhD Nott.   Prof., Molecular Ecology
Butlin, R. K., BA Camb., PhD Nott.   Prof., Evolutionary Biology
Callaghan, T. V., BSc Manc., PhD Birm., DSc Manc., Hon. FilDr Lund   Prof.; Dir., Sheffield Centre for Arctic Ecol.
Fleming, A. J., BA Camb., PhD Camb.   Prof., Plant Sciences
Gaston, K. J., BSc Sheff., DPhil York(UK)   Prof., Biodiversity and Conservation
Hatchwell, B. J., BSc Brist., PhD Sheff.   Reader
Leake, J. R., BSc Brist., PhD Sheff.   Sr. Lectr.
Leegood, R. C., MA Camb., PhD Camb.   Prof., Plant Biochemistry
Maltby, L. L., BSc Newcastle(UK), PhD Glas.   Prof., Environmental Biology
Osborn, A. M., BSc Sheff., PhD Liv.   Sr. Lectr.
Press, M. C., BSc Lond., PhD Manc.   Prof., Physiological Ecology; Head*
Quick, W. P., BSc Essex, PhD Sheff.   Prof., Plant Physiology

Ratnieks, F. L. W., BSc Ulster, MS Cornell, PhD Cornell Prof., Apiculture
Read, D. J., BSc Hull, PhD Hull, FRS Prof., Plant Sciences
Rees, M., BSc Lond., PhD Lond. Prof., Plant Ecology
Rolfe, S. A., BSc Lond., PhD Camb. Sr. Lectr.
Scholes, J. D., BSc Wales, PhD Wales Prof., Plant and Microbial Science
Siva-Jothy, M. T., BSc Lond., DPhil Oxf. Reader
Snook, R. R., BSc Mich., PhD Arizona Sr. Lectr.
Warren, P. H., BSc Wales, DPhil York(UK) Sr. Lectr.
Wellman, C. H., BSc S'ton. Sr. Lectr.
Wheeler, B. D., BSc Durh., PhD Durh. Reader
Woodward, F. I., BA Camb., MA Camb., PhD Lanc., FLS Prof., Plant Ecology
Other Staff: 5 Lectrs.; 2 Emer. Profs. Assoc.; 50 Res. Contract Staff; 8 Independent Res. Fellows; 3 Teaching Fellows; 2 Hon. Sr. Lectrs.; 3 Hon. Res. Assocs.
Research: aquatic ecology; behavioural ecology; metabolic and molecular biology; plant and fungal ecophysiology

Archaeology

Tel: (0114) 222 2900 Fax: (0114) 272 2563
E-mail: archaeology@shef.ac.uk
Barrett, J. C., BSc Wales, DLitt Wales, FSA Prof.; Head*
Bennet, D. J., BA Camb., MA Camb. Prof.
Carroll, M., BA Brock, MA Indiana, PhD Indiana Sr. Lectr.
Chamberlain, A. T., BSc Liv., PhD Liv., MSc S'ton. Reader
Charles, M. P., BSc Wales, PhD Lond. Sr. Lectr.
Day, P. M., BA S'ton., PhD Camb. Sr. Lectr.
Dennell, R. W., MA Camb., PhD Camb. British Academy Res. Prof.
Hadley, D. M., BA Hull, PhD Birm. Sr. Lectr.
Halstead, P. L. J., MA Camb., PhD Camb. Reader
Jackson, C. M., BA Lanc., MA Brad., PhD Brad. Sr. Lectr.
Jones, G. E. M., BSc Wales, MPhil Camb., PhD Camb. Prof.
Moreland, J. F., BA Sheff., PhD Sheff. Reader
Parker Pearson, M. G., BA S'ton., PhD Camb., FSA Prof.
Pettitt, P. B., BA Birm., MA Lond., PhD Camb. Sr. Lectr.
Zvelebil, M., BA Sheff., PhD Camb., FSA Prof.
Other Staff: 8 Lectrs.; 3 Teaching Fellows; 1 Res. Assoc.; 1 Postdoctoral Res. Fellow; 2 Res. Officers; 2 Res. Contract Staff; 1 Hon. Reader; 10 Hon. Lectrs.; 3 Hon. Res. Assocs.
Research: archaeomaterials; environmental archaeology and palaeoeconomy; landscape archaeology; osteology, palaeopathology and funerary archaeology

Architecture

Tel: (0114) 222 0399 Fax: (0114) 279 8276
E-mail: p.hodgkinson@shef.ac.uk
Blundell Jones, P., MA Camb. Prof.
Chiles, P. A., BA Portsmouth Sr. Lectr.
Hunt, A., FIStructE Visiting Prof.
Kang, J., BArch Tsinghua, MArch Tsinghua, PhD Camb. Prof.
Lawson, B. R., MSc Aston, PhD Aston, FRSA Prof.
Light, R. D., BA CNAA Sr. Lectr.
Peng, C., MSc Strath., PhD Edin. Sr. Lectr.
Pitts, A. C., BScTech Sheff., PhD Sheff. Sr. Lectr.
Plank, R. J., BSc Birm., PhD Birm. Prof.; Head*
Popovic, O., BSc Skopje, MSc Skopje, PhD Nott. Sr. Lectr.
Sharples, S., BSc Nott., PhD Sheff. Prof.
Till, J., MA Camb. Prof.
Torrington, J. M., BA Nott., BArch Nott. Sr. Lectr.
Ward, I. C., BSc Strath. Reader; Dir., Building Energy Analysis Unit
Wigglesworth, S., MA Camb. Prof.†
Other Staff: 11 Lectrs.; 8 Res. Contract Staff
Research: architectural humanities; architectural processes; architectural science and technology

Biblical Studies

Tel: (0114) 222 0508 Fax: (0114) 222 0500
E-mail: bibs@shef.ac.uk
Alexander, Canon L. C. A., MA Oxf., DPhil Oxf. Prof.
Edelman, D. J. V., BA Smith, MA Chic., PhD Chic. Reader
Exum, J. C., BA Wake Forest, MA Col., MPhil Col., PhD Col. Prof.
Okland, J., PhD Oslo Sr. Lectr.
Pyper, H. S., BSc Edin., BD Glas., PhD Glas. Sr. Lectr.
Whitelam, K. W., BD Manc., PhD Manc. Prof.; Head*
Other Staff: 2 Lectrs.; 2 Res. Assocs.
Research: biblical ethics; biblical interpretation; feminist biblical criticism; interpretation of the Dead Sea Scrolls; social world of the New Testament

Chemistry

Tel: (0114) 222 9300 Fax: (0114) 222 9346
E-mail: chemistry@shef.ac.uk
Armes, S. P., BSc Brist., PhD Brist. Prof.
Brammer, L., BSc Brist., PhD Brist. Reader
Coldham, I., MA Camb., PhD Camb. Reader
Devonshire, R., BSc Durh., PhD Newcastle(UK), FRSChem Sr. Lectr.
Fairclough, J. P. A., BSc Birm., PhD Birm. Sr. Lectr.
Fowler, P. W., BSC Sheff., PhD Sheff. Prof.
Grasby, J. A., BSc Birm., PhD S'ton. Reader
Harrity, J. P. A., BSc Strath., PhD Strath. Sr. Lectr.
Haynes, A., BSc Exe., PhD Nott. Sr. Lectr.
Hippler, M. F. A., PhD H-W Sr. Lectr.
Hunter, C. A., BA Camb., PhD Camb. Prof.
Jackson, R. F. W., BA Camb., PhD Camb. Prof., Synthetic Chemistry; Head*
Jones, S., BSc S'ton., PhD Wales Sr. Lectr.
Leggett, G. J., BSc UMIST, PhD UMIST Prof., Nanoscale Analytical Science
Mann, B. E., MA Oxf., DPhil Oxf., DSc Oxf. Prof.
McLeod, C. W., BSc Edin., PhD Lond. Prof.
Morris, M. J., BSc Brist., PhD Brist. Sr. Lectr.
Pickup, B. T., BSc Manc., PhD Manc. Prof.; Dir. of Studies
Rimmer, S., BSc UMIST, PhD Lond. Reader
Ryan, A. J., OBE, BSc Manc., PhD Manc. Prof., Physical Chemistry
Swanson, L., BSc H-W, PhD H-W Sr. Lectr.
Twyman, L. J., BSc Lond., PhD Kent Sr. Lectr.
Ward, M. D., BA Camb., PhD Camb. Prof., Inorganic Chemistry
Williams, N. H., BA Camb., PhD Camb. Sr. Lectr.
Winter, M. J., BSc Brist., PhD Brist. Sr. Lectr.
Other Staff: 8 Lectrs.; 2 Sr. Experimental Officers; 2 Experimental Officers; 1 Res. Officer; 47 Res. Contract Staff; 1 Hon. Reader
Research: biologically active compounds; catalysis by metal complexes; new materials; reaction mechanisms; the search for selectivity and new methodologies

Computer Science

Tel: (0114) 222 1800 Fax: (0114) 222 1810
E-mail: dept@dcs.shef.ac.uk
Brown, G. J., BSc CNAA, PhD Sheff. Sr. Lectr.
Ciravegna, F., BSc Turin, PhD Turin Prof.
Clayton, R., BSc Durh., PhD Newcastle(UK) Sr. Lectr.
Cooke, M. P., BSc Manc., PhD Sheff. Prof.
Cowling, A. J., BSc Leeds, PhD Leeds Sr. Lectr.
Derrick, J., BSc Nott., DPhil Oxf. Prof.
Gaizauskas, R., BA Ott., MA Sus., DPhil Sus. Prof.
Gheorge, M., BSc Bucharest, PhD Bucharest Sr. Lectr.
Green, P. D., BSc Reading, PhD Keele Prof.; Head*
Guthrie, L., BS New Mexico State, MS New Mexico State, PhD New Mexico State Sr. Lectr.
Hepple, M., BSc Sheff., MSc Edin., PhD Edin. Reader

Holcombe, W. M. L., MSc Sheff., PhD Leeds Prof.
Manson, G. A., BSc Strath., PhD Strath., MSc Manc. Sr. Lectr.
Moore, R. K., BA Essex, MSc Essex, PhD Essex Prof.
Niranjan, M., BSc Peradeniya, MEE T.U.Eindhoven, PhD Camb. Prof.
Sharkey, A. J. C., BA Exe., PhD Essex Sr. Lectr.
Sharkey, N., BA Exe., PhD Exe. Prof.
Simons, A. J. H., MA Camb., PhD Sheff. Sr. Lectr.
Smallwood, R. H., BSc Lond., MSc Lanc., PhD Sheff., FREng, FIEE, FIP, Hon. FRCP Prof.
Walker, M., BA Calif., MSc Stan., MA Penn., PhD Penn. Prof.
Watt, A. H., BSc Nott. Reader
Winkler, J., BSc Lond., PhD Lond. Sr. Lectr.
Other Staff: 11 Lectrs.; 40 Res. Contract Staff
Research: computer speech and hearing; computer-aided software engineering (CASE) tools for parallel systems; natural language processing; neural networks; object-oriented programming

East Asian Studies, School of

Tel: (0114) 222 8400 Fax: (0114) 222 8432
E-mail: seas@shef.ac.uk
Bramall, C., MA Camb., PhD Camb. Sr. Lectr.
Dobson, H., BA Leeds, MA Leeds, PhD Sheff. Sr. Lectr.
Grayson, J. H., BA Rutgers, MA Col., MDiv Duke, PhD Edin. Prof.
Hook, G. D., BA Br.Col., MA Br.Col., LLD Chuo Prof.
Wright, T., BA Camb., PhD Camb. Prof., Chinese; Head*
Other Staff: 14 Lectrs.; 6 Teaching Fellows; 1 Hon. Lectr.
Research: international relations; language; literature; politics; society

Economics

Tel: (0114) 222 3398 Fax: (0114) 222 3458
E-mail: econ@shef.ac.uk
Brown, S., BA Hull, MA Warw., PhD Lough. Prof.
Dickerson, A. P., BA Durh., MA Warw., PhD Warw. Prof.
Dietrich, M., BA CNAA, MA Sus., DPhil Sus. Sr. Lectr.
McIntosh, S., BA Leic., MSc Warw., PhD Lond. Reader
Mosley, P., BA Camb., MA Essex, PhD Camb. Prof.
Roberts, J. R., BA CNAA, MA Leeds, PhD Leeds Prof.
Taylor, K. B., BA Staffs., MA Staffs., PhD Open(UK) Reader
Tsuchiya, A., BL Kyoto, MA Kyoto, MEcon Kyoto, PhD Kyoto Sr. Lectr.
Other Staff: 11 Lectrs.
Research: applied economics and econometrics; economic theory; industrial organisation and public sector economics; international and development economics; political economy

Education

see also Lifelong Learning, Inst. of

Tel: (0114) 222 8087 Fax: (0114) 279 6236
E-mail: education@shef.ac.uk
Billington, T., MEd Exe., MEd Manc., MSc Manc.Met. Sr. Lectr.
Brooks, R. G., MA Camb., MA Essex, PhD Leeds Prof.
Carr, W., BA Warw., MA Warw. Prof.; Head*
Hannon, P. W., BSc Liv., BA Liv., PhD Manc. Prof.
Harris, S. M. F., MA Aberd., PhD Nott. Sr. Lectr.
Marsh, J. A., BA Sheff., MEd Sheff., PhD Sheff. Sr. Lectr.
Moore, M. P., BA Newcastle(UK), MSc Lond., PhD Greenwich Sr. Lectr.
Nixon, J. D., BA Oxf., MA Lond., PhD E.Anglia Prof.
Parry, G. W., BA CNAA, PhD City(UK) Prof.

Skelton, A. M., BEd *Leeds*, MPhil *Bath*, PhD *Nott.* Sr. Lectr.

Wellington, J. J., BSc *Brist.*, MA *Lond.*, PhD *Sheff.* Prof.

Other Staff: 15 Lectrs.; 2 Sr. Res. Fellows; 1 Visiting Sr. Fellow; 4 Teaching Fellows; 8 Res. Contract Staff; 1 Hon. Emer. Prof.; 8 Hon. Lectrs.; 7 Hon. Tutors

Research: educational policy; literacy; post-compulsory education and training; professional development; special/inclusive education

Engineering, Automatic Control and Systems

Tel: (0114) 222 5250 Fax: (0114) 222 5661
E-mail: acse@shef.ac.uk

Allerton, D. J., BSc *CNAA*, PhD *Camb.*, FIEE Prof.

Alleyne, H. S. K., BSc *Lond.*, MSc *WI*, PhD *WI* Reader

Balikhin, M. A., BSc *Moscow*, PhD *Moscow* Sr. Lectr.

Banks, S. P., MSc *Sheff.*, PhD *Sheff.* Prof.

Billings, S. A., BEng *Liv.*, DEng *Liv.*, PhD *Sheff.*, FIEE Prof.

Daley, S., BSc *C.Lancs.*, PhD *Leeds* Prof.

Fleming, P. J., BSc *Belf.*, PhD *Belf.*, FIEE Prof.

Harrison, R. F., BSc *S'ton.*, PhD *S'ton.* Reader

Kadirkamanathan, V., BA *Camb.*, MA *Camb.*, PhD *Camb.* Reader

Mahfouf, M., MPhil *Sheff.*, PhD *Sheff.* Prof.

Morris, A. S., BEng *Sheff.*, PhD *Sheff.* Sr. Lectr.

Owens, D. H., BSc *Lond.*, PhD *Lond.*, FIEE, FIMechE, FIMA Prof.; Head*

Rossiter, J. A., MA *Oxf.*, DPhil *Oxf.* Reader

Thompson, H. A., BSc *Wales*, PhD *Wales* Prof. Assoc.

Tokhi, M. O., BSc *Kabul*, PhD *H-W* Reader

Other Staff: 5 Lectrs.; 1 Sr. Experimental Officer; 24 Res. Contract Staff; 3 Hon. Lectrs.; 1 Hon. Res. Fellow

Research: automation and systems architectures; intelligent and adaptive sytems; non-linear systems and signal processing

Engineering, Chemical and Process

Tel: (0114) 222 7500 Fax: (0114) 222 7501
E-mail: chemeng@shef.ac.uk

Allen, R. W. K., MSc *Manc.*, PhD *McG.*, FREng, FIChemE Prof.

Biggs, C., BEng *Qld.*, PhD *Qld.* Sr. Lectr.

Edyvean, R. G. J., BSc *Wales*, MSc *Portsmouth*, PhD *Newcastle(UK)*, FIMMM, FIBiol Reader

Ewan, B. C., BSc *Glas.*, PhD *Glas.* Sr. Lectr.

Hounslow, M. J., BEng *Adel.*, PhD *Adel.*, FREng Prof.; Head*

MacInnes, J. M., BSc *Calif.*, MSc *Calif.*, PhD *Manc.* Sr. Lectr.

Nasserzadeh-Sharifi, V. N., BEng *Sheff.*, PhD *Sheff.* Prof.

Priestman, G. H., BScTech *Sheff.*, PhD *Sheff.*, FREng Sr. Lectr.

Ristic, R. I., MSc *Belgrade*, PhD *Belgrade* Reader

Salman, A. D., BSc *Baghdad*, PhD *Bud.* Reader

Styring, P., BSc *Sheff.*, PhD *Sheff.* Sr. Lectr.

Wright, P. C., BE *Syd.*, ME *W'gong.*, PhD *Syd.* Prof.

Zimmerman, W. B. J., BSE *Prin.*, MSc *Stan.* Prof.

Other Staff: 6 Lectrs.; 1 Teaching & Res. Fellow; 9 Res. Contract Staff; 1 Co-ordinator (Design Teaching)

Research: environmental engineering; incineration and combustion; process innovation and intensification; process safety and loss prevention

Engineering, Civil and Structural

Tel: (0114) 222 5783 Fax: (0114) 222 5700
E-mail: civil@shef.ac.uk

Ashley, R. M., BSc *Greenwich*, MPhil *Greenwich* Prof.

Askes, H., MSc *T.H.Delft*, PhD *T.H.Delft* Prof.

Banwart, S. A., BSc *Iowa*, MSc *Iowa*, PhD *E.T.H.Zürich* Prof.

Brownjohn, J., BSc *Brist.*, PhD *Brist.* Prof.

Burgess, I. W., BA *Camb.*, PhD *Lond.* Prof.; Head*

Cripps, J. C., BSc *Aston*, MSc *Durh.*, PhD *Durh.*, FGS Sr. Lectr.

Davison, J. B., BEng *Sheff.*, PhD *Sheff.* Sr. Lectr.

Gilbert, M., BEng *Sheff.*, PhD *Manc.* Sr. Lectr.; EPSRC Advanced Fellow

Harris, R. C., BSc *Nott.*, MSc *Newcastle(UK)* Hon. Visiting Prof.

Hird, C. C., MA *Camb.*, PhD *Manc.* Sr. Lectr.

Hyde, A. F. L., BSc *Nott.*, PhD *Nott.* Reader

Lerner, D. N., BA *Camb.*, MSc *Lond.*, PhD *Birm.*, DSc *Birm.*, FREng, FICE, FGS Prof.

Pavic, A., MSc *Belgrade*, PhD *Sheff.* Prof.

Pilakoutas, K., BSc *Lond.*, PhD *Lond.* Prof.; EPSRC Advanced Fellow

Saul, A. J., BEng *Liv.*, PhD *H-W* Prof.

Waldron, P., BSc *Nott.*, PhD *Lond.* Prof.

Other Staff: 12 Lectrs.; 1 Visiting Lectr.; 27 Res. Contract Staff; 1 Course Co-ordinator

Research: civil engineering dynamics; concrete engineering; geotechnical engineering; numerical modelling; steel and composite structures

Engineering, Electronic and Electrical

Tel: (0114) 222 5355 Fax: (0114) 222 5143
E-mail: c.e.potts@shef.ac.uk

Allinson, N. M., BEng *Brad.*, MSc *Camb.*, FIEE Prof.

Atallah, K., PhD *Sheff.* Sr. Lectr.

Benaissa, M., PhD *Newcastle(UK)* Sr. Lectr.

Bingham, C., BEng *Sheff.*, MSc *Sheff.*, PhD *Cran.* Sr. Lectr.

Chambers, B., BEng *Sheff.*, PhD *Sheff.*, DEng *Sheff.*, FIEE Prof.

Cook, G. G., BSc *Hull*, PhD *Sheff.* Reader

Cullis, A. G., MA *Oxf.*, DPhil *Oxf.*, DSc *Oxf.*, FIP, FIMMM, FRSChem, FRS Prof.

David, J. P. R., BEng *Sheff.*, PhD *Sheff.* Prof.

Hogg, R. A., BSc *Nott.*, PhD *Sheff.* Sr. Lectr.

Houston, P. A., BSc *Strath.*, PhD *Strath.*, FIEE Prof.; Head*

Howe, D., BTech *Brad.*, MSc *Brad.*, PhD *S'ton.*, FREng Prof.

Jewell, G. W., BEng *Sheff.*, PhD *Sheff.* Reader

Langley, R. J., BSc *Kent*, PhD *Kent* Prof.

Parbrook, P. J., BSc *Strath.*, PhD *Strath.* Reader

Rodenberg, J. M., BSc *Exe.*, PhD *Camb.*, FIP Prof.

Seed, N. L., BEng *Sheff.*, PhD *Sheff.* Sr. Lectr.

Stone, D. A., BEng *Sheff.*, PhD *Liv.* Sr. Lectr.

Tennant, A., BEng *Sheff.*, PhD *Sheff.* Sr. Lectr.

Tozer, R. C., BEng *Sheff.*, MEng *Sheff.*, PhD *Sheff.* Sr. Lectr.

Walther, T., DPhys *Aix-la-Chapelle*, PhD *Camb.* Sr. Lectr.

Wang, J. B., BEng *Jiangsu U.S.T.*, MEng *Jiangsu U.S.T.*, PhD *E.Lond.* Sr. Lectr.

Zhu, Z. Q., BEng *Zhejiang*, MSc *Zhejiang*, PhD *Sheff.* Prof.

Other Staff: 6 Lectrs.; 3 Sr. Res. Scientists; 5 Sr. Experimental Officers; 2 Res. Fellows; 38 Res. Contract Staff

Research: communications and radar; electrical machines and drives; electronic systems; medical electronics; micro-electromechanical systems

Engineering, Materials

Tel: (0114) 222 5467 Fax: (0114) 222 5943
E-mail: c.a.plant@shef.ac.uk

Gibb, F. G. F., BSc *St And.*, PhD *St And.*, FGS Prof.

Gibbs, M. R. J., BSc *Sheff.*, PhD *Camb.*, FIP Prof.

Hand, R. J., MA *Camb.*, MEd *Sheff.*, PhD *Camb.* Sr. Lectr.

Harding, J., BA *Camb.*, PhD *Camb.*, FIP Prof.

Haycock, J. W., BSc *Newcastle(UK)*, PhD *Newcastle(UK)* Sr. Lectr.

Inkson, B. J., BA *Camb.*, MA *Camb.*, PhD *Camb.* Sr. Lectr.

Jones, F. R., PhD *Keele*, FRSChem, FIMMM Prof.

Mac Neil, S., BSc *Aberd.*, PhD *Sheff.* Prof., Tissue Engineering

Matthews, A., BSc *Salf.*, PhD *Salf.*, FIMMM, FIMechE, FIEE Prof.

McArthur, S. L., MEngSci *NSW*, PhD *NSW* Sr. Lectr.

Milestone, N. B., BSc *Well.*, MSc *Well.*, PhD *Well.*, DSc *Well.*, FNZIC Sr. Lectr.

Moebus, G., DPhys *Stuttgart*, PhD *Stuttgart* Sr. Lectr.

Ojovan, M. I., MSc *Moscow*, PhD *Moscow*, DSc *Moscow* Reader

Palmiere, E. J., BSc *Pitt.*, MSc *Pitt.*, PhD *Pitt.* Sr. Lectr.

Parker, J. M., MA *Camb.*, PhD *Camb.*, FIMMM Reader

Rainforth, W. M., BMet *Sheff.*, PhD *Leeds* Prof.

Reaney, I. M., BSc *Manc.*, MSc *Manc.*, PhD *Manc.*, FIP Reader

Schrefl, T., DrTechn *T.U.Vienna* Prof.

Sinclair, D. C., BSc *Aberd.*, PhD *Aberd.* Reader

Tsakiropoulos, P., DEng *T.U.Athens*, MMet *Sheff.*, PhD *Sheff.* Prof.

Ungar, G., BSc *Zagreb*, PhD *Brist.* Prof.

West, A. R., BSc *Wales*, PhD *Aberd.*, DSc *Aberd.*, FIMMM, FRSChem, FRSEd Prof.; Head*

Other Staff: 6 Visiting Profs.; 10 Lectrs.; 2 Sr. Res. Fellows; 2 Sr. Experimental Officers; 46 Res. Contract Staff; 1 Innovation Fellow; 1 Hon. Reader; 1 Hon. Sr. Lectr.; 4 Hon. Lectrs.

Research: ceramics and glasses; metallic and magnetic materials; polymers and polymer matrix composites

Engineering, Mechanical

Tel: (0114) 222 7700 Fax: (0114) 222 7890
E-mail: me-enquiries@shef.ac.uk

Beck, S. M., BSc *Bath*, PhD *Sheff.* Sr. Lectr.

Boller, C., DrIng *T.U.Darmstadt* Prof.

Brown, M. W., MA *Camb.*, PhD *Camb.* Prof.

Dwyer-Joyce, R., BEng *Lond.*, PhD *Lond.* Sr. Lectr.

Hodzic, A., PhD *Canberra* Sr. Lectr.

Johnson, A. R., BEng *Sheff.*, PhD *Hull*, FIMechE Sr. Lectr.

Nicolleau, F. C. G. A., PhD *Lyons* Sr. Lectr.

Qin, N., PhD *Glas.* Prof.

Soutis, C., BSc *Camb.*, MSc *Camb.*, PhD *Camb.*, FIMMM, FRAeS Prof.

Stanway, R., BSc *Manc.*, MSc *Sus.*, DPhil *Sus.*, FIMechE Reader

Staszewski, W. J., BSc *T.U.Poznan*, MSc *T.U.Poznan*, PhD *Manc.*, DSc *Gdansk* Prof.

Tomlinson, G. R., BSc *Aston*, MSc *Aston*, PhD *Salf.*, DSc *Manc.*, FREng, FIMechE, FRSA, FRAeS Prof.

Wilson, C. W., PhD *Leeds* Prof.

Worden, K., BSc *York(UK)*, PhD *H-W*, FIMA Prof.

Yates, J. R., MA *Camb.*, MSc *Cran.IT*, PhD *Sheff.* Prof.; Head*

Other Staff: 12 Lectrs.; 1 Res. Fellow; 1 Teaching Fellow; 49 Res. Contract Staff; 1 Hon. Lectr.

Research: computer analysis using numerical methods; computer-aided design and computer-aided manufacturing; engineering dynamics; experimental stress analysis; materials and tribology

English, School of

English Language and Linguistics

Tel: (0114) 222 0210 Fax: (0114) 222 0240
E-mail: e.f.bradley@shef.ac.uk

Beal, J. C., BA *Newcastle(UK)*, PhD *Newcastle(UK)* Prof.

Dabrowska, E., MA *Gdansk*, MPhil *Glas.*, PhD *Gdansk* Reader

Duffield, N. G., BA *Camb.*, MA *Lond.*, PhD *Loyola(Calif.)* Prof.

Fitzmaurice, S., BA *Rhodes*, MPhil *Camb.*, PhD *Camb.* Prof.

Hallett, N., BA *Kent*, DPhil *York(UK)* Sr. Lectr.

Jones, M. H., MA *Camb.*, PhD *CNAA* Sr. Lectr.

Linn, A. R., MA *Camb.*, MPhil *Camb.*, PhD *Camb.* Prof.; Head*

Other Staff: 7 Lectrs.; 2 Tutors

Research: cultural tradition, sociolinguistics; dialect study; history of English; history of linguistics; mediaeval language and literature

English Literature

Tel: (0114) 222 8480 Fax: (0114) 222 8481
E-mail: english@shef.ac.uk
Adamson, S., MA Camb. Prof.
Campbell, M. J. B., BA Trinity(Dub.), PhD Camb. Sr. Lectr.
Falconer, R. A. E., BA Yale, BA Oxf., DPhil Oxf. Sr. Lectr.
Gray, F. B., MA Hull Sr. Lectr.
Karlin, D., BA Camb., MA Camb., PhD Camb. Prof.
Nicholson, S., BA Exe., MA Lanc., PhD Leeds Reader
Owen, S. J., BA Oxf., MA Leeds, PhD Leeds Reader
Piette, A., BA Camb., MA Camb., PhD Camb. Prof.
Rayner, J. R., BA Sheff., MA Sheff., PhD Sheff. Sr. Lectr.
Shellard, D. M., MA Oxf., DPhil Oxf. Prof.; Head*
van Oostrum, D., BA Central Wash., MA Gron., PhD Texas Sr. Lectr.
Vice, S., MA Camb., DPhil Oxf. Prof.
Other Staff: 14 Lectrs.; 2 Res. Assocs.; 3 Teaching Fellows
Research: American studies; early modern period; literary biography; modern and contemporary literature; nineteenth-century literature and culture

French

Tel: (0114) 222 4386 Fax: (0114) 275 1198
E-mail: k.southern@shef.ac.uk
Ainsworth, P. F., BA Manc., MA Manc., Dr3rdCy Paris III, FRHistS Prof.
Austin, G. N., BA Oxf., PhD Leeds Sr. Lectr.
Eley, P. A., MA Oxf., MEd Sheff., PhD Wales Reader
McCallam, D., BA CNAA, MA Warw., MPhil Camb., PhD Camb. Sr. Lectr.
Simons, P. C., BA Camb., MA Camb., PhD Sheff. Sr. Lectr.
Walker, D. H., BA Liv., PhD Liv. Prof.; Head*
Windebank, J. E., BSc Aston, PhD Bath Sr. Lectr.
Other Staff: 5 Lectrs.; 5 Lecteurs; 1 Res. Fellow; 3 Hon. Res. Profs.
Research: mediaeval and Renaissance studies; nineteenth-century poetry; surrealism; the contemporary novel; the Enlightenment

Geography

Tel: (0114) 222 7900 Fax: (0114) 279 7912
E-mail: geography@shef.ac.uk
Armstrong, H. W., BA Sheff., MA Lond. Prof.; Head*
Bateman, M. D., BSc Lond., DPhil Sus. Sr. Lectr.
Bigg, G. R., BSc Adel., PhD Adel. Prof.
Bryant, R. G., BSc Reading, PhD Reading Sr. Lectr.
Clark, C. D., BSc Wales, PhD Edin. Reader
Dorling, D. F. L., BSc Newcastle(UK), PhD Newcastle(UK) Prof.
Gregson, N. A., BA Durh., PhD Durh. Prof.
Hodson, A. J., BSc S'ton., PhD S'ton. Sr. Lectr.
Jackson, P. A., BA Oxf., DPhil Oxf. Prof., Human Geography
Parsons, A. J., BA Sheff., MSc Sheff., PhD Reading Prof.
Pattie, C. J., BSc Glas., PhD Sheff. Prof.; Head*
Rigby, J. E., BSc Newcastle(UK), MSc Edin., PhD Lanc. Sr. Lectr.
Sporton, D. S., BA Sheff., PhD Sheff. Sr. Lectr.
Twyman, K. C., BSc Newcastle(UK), PhD Sheff. Sr. Lectr.
Wainwright, J., BA Brist., PhD Brist. Prof.
White, P. E., BA Oxf., DPhil Oxf. Prof.
Wise, S. M., BSc Brist. Sr. Lectr.
Other Staff: 13 Lectrs.; 5 Res. Contract Staff; 1 Teaching Fellow; 1 DTI Academy Fellow

Research: economic and political geography; environmental change and drylands; environmental hydrology and fluvial geomorphology; geographic information systems in human geography; social geography

Germanic Studies

Tel: (0114) 222 4396 Fax: (0114) 222 2160
E-mail: germanicstudies@shef.ac.uk
de Berg, H., MA Ley., PhD Ley. Reader
Newton, G., BA Liv., PhD Liv. Prof.
Perraudin, M. F., MA Camb., PhD Birm. Prof.; Head*
Vismans, R., BA V.U.Amst., MA Manc., PhD V.U.Amst. Sr. Lectr.
Weinert, R., MA Edin., PhD Edin. Sr. Lectr.
Other Staff: 5 Lectrs.; 2 Lectors (German); 1 Lector (Dutch); 1 Lector (Swedish)
Research: Ernst Jünger; German Romanticism; Heine and Nietzsche; political extremist literature in the Weimar Republic; the Thingspiel

Hispanic Studies

Tel: (0114) 222 4398 Fax: (0114) 222 0561
E-mail: c.a.marsh@shef.ac.uk
Brooksbank-Jones, A., BA Wales, PhD Nott. Hughes Prof.
Davies, R., MA Oxf., DPhil Oxf. Sr. Lectr.
Deacon, A., BA S'ton., PhD Trinity(Dub.) Prof.
Johnson, P. L., MA Oxf., DPhil Oxf. Sr. Lectr.
Swanson, P., BA Liv., PhD Edin. Prof.; Head*
Trippett, A. M., BA Lond., PhD Lond. Sr. Lectr.
Wood, D., BA Exe., PhD Exe. Sr. Lectr.
Other Staff: 3 Lectrs.; 1 Lectora (Catalan); 1 Leitora (Portuguese); 2 Tutors; 2 Tutors (Catalan); 1 Tutor (Hispanic Studies); 1 Hon. Prof.; 1 Hon. Res. Fellow
Research: Catalan; early modern literature; eighteenth-century studies; Peruvian and Uruguayan studies; translation studies

History

Tel: (0114) 222 2555 Fax: (0114) 278 8304
E-mail: history@shef.ac.uk
Baycroft, T. P., BA Mt.All., PhD Camb. Sr. Lectr.
Braddick, M. J., BA Camb., PhD Camb., FRHistS Prof.
Cook, R. J., BA Warw., DPhil Oxf. Prof.
Greengrass, M., BA Oxf., DPhil Oxf., FRHistS, FSA Prof.
Kershaw, Sir I., KBE, BA Liv., DPhil Oxf., FBA Prof., Modern History
Martin, D. E., BSc Hull, PhD Hull Sr. Lectr.
Milton, A., BA Camb., MA Camb., PhD Camb., FRHistS Reader
Moore, R. G., BA Manc., PhD Manc. Reader
Phimister, I. P., BA Nott., BA Rhodesia, DPhil Rhodesia Prof., International History
Shoemaker, R. B., BA Oregon, PhD Stan., FRHistS Prof.; Head*
Staub, M. H., LèsL Paris I, MA Paris X, PhD Paris X Prof.
Thurlow, R. C., BA York(UK), MA Sus. Sr. Lectr.
Vincent, M. M. T., BA Oxf., DPhil Oxf., FRHistS Sr. Lectr.
Other Staff: 13 Lectrs.
Research: American history; early modern studies; European history; mediaeval studies; modern British history

Information Studies

Tel: (0114) 222 2630 Fax: (0114) 278 0300
E-mail: dis@shef.ac.uk
Bath, P. A., BSc Wales, MSc Sheff., PhD Sheff. Sr. Lectr.
Corrall, S. M., MA Camb., MBA Sus., MSc S'ton., FCLIP Prof.
Eaglestone, B. M., BSc Staffs., PhD Hudd. Sr. Lectr.
Ford, N. J., BA Leeds, MA Sheff. Reader
Gillet, V. J., BA Camb., MSc Sheff., PhD Sheff. Sr. Lectr.
Levy, P., BA Birm., MA Warw., MA Sheff. Sr. Lectr.

Sanderson, M., BSc Glas., PhD Glas. Sr. Lectr.
Saunders, W. L., CBE, MA Camb., Hon. LittD Sheff., FLA, FCLIP, FCP Emer. Prof.
Webber, S., BA Kent, FCLIP Sr. Lectr.
Whittaker, S. J., BA Camb., PhD St And. Prof.
Willett, P., MA Oxf., MSc Sheff., PhD Sheff., DSc Sheff., FCLIP Prof.; Head*
Other Staff: 8 Lectrs.; 9 Res. Contract Staff; 1 Hon. Lectr.; 1 Hon. Res. Fellow
Research: information management; librarianship; networked work and learning; public library services

Journalism Studies

Tel: (0114) 222 2500 Fax: (0114) 222 2530
E-mail: journalism@shef.ac.uk
Cole, P., MA Camb. Prof.; Head*
Conboy, M., BA Durh., MA Lond., PhD Lond. Reader
Foster, J. D., BA Sheff. Sr. Lectr.
Harcup, T., BA Leeds Met. Sr. Lectr.
Harrison, J. L., BA CNAA, PhD Sheff. Prof.
Negrine, R., BA Kent, PhD Leic. Prof.
Other Staff: 8 Lectrs.; 3 Hon. Fellows
Research: journalism, law and ethics; media coverage and understanding of science; media violence; sport and the media

Landscape

Tel: (0114) 222 0600 Fax: (0114) 275 4176
E-mail: landscape@shef.ac.uk
Dee, C., BA CNAA, MA Sheff. Sr. Lectr.
Dunnett, N. P., BSc Brist., MSc Lond., PhD Sheff. Sr. Lectr.
Hitchmough, J. D., BSc Bath, PhD Bath Prof.
Lange, E., MDes Harv., DIng T.U.Berlin, PhD E.T.H.Zürich Prof.
Selman, P. H., BSc E.Anglia, MSc H-W, PhD Stir. Prof.; Head*
Swanwick, C. A., BA York(UK), MSc Lond. Prof.
Woolley, H. E., BSc Newcastle(UK), BPhil Newcastle(UK) Sr. Lectr.
Woudstra, J., MA York(UK), PhD Lond. Sr. Lectr.
Other Staff: 4 Lectrs.
Research: landscape design; landscape management

Law

Tel: (0114) 222 6771 Fax: (0114) 222 6832
E-mail: law@shef.ac.uk
Baker, E., BA Nott., MPhil Camb. Sr. Lectr.
Bottoms, A. E., MA Oxf., MA Camb., PhD Sheff. Prof., Criminology
Bradgate, J. R., MA Camb. Prof., Commercial Law
Crow, I. D., BA Keele, MSc Lond. Reader
de Lacy, J., LLB Sheff., PhD Sheff., DPhil Oxf. Sr. Lectr.
Firth, C. G., LLB Sheff. Sr. Lectr.
French, D., LLM Nott., PhD Wales, LLB Sr. Lectr.
Holdaway, S. D., BA Lanc., PhD Sheff. Prof., Sociology; Head*
Jefferson, M., MA Oxf., BCL Oxf. Sr. Lectr.
Llewelyn, M. S. M., LLB Wales, PhD Wales Reader, Intellectual Property Law
Merrills, J. G., BCL Oxf., MA Oxf. Prof., International Law
Plomer, A., BA Lanc., LLB Manc., MA Lanc., PhD Lanc. Prof.
Shapland, J. M., MA Oxf., DPhil Oxf. Prof., Criminal Justice
Townend, D. M. R., LLB Sheff., DPhil Oxf. Sr. Lectr.
White, N. D., BA Oxf., MA Oxf., PhD Nott. Prof., International Law
Williams, C., LLB Newcastle(UK) Reader
Wykes, M., BA Sheff.Hallam, PhD Sheff. Sr. Lectr.
Other Staff: 29 Lectrs.; 5 Res. Assocs.; 2 Sr. Univ. Teachers; 4 Teaching Fellows
Research: biotechnological law and ethics; commercial law studies; criminological and legal research; international, comparative and European law; socio-legal studies

Leisure Management

Tel: (0114) 222 2181 Fax: (0114) 222 3348
E-mail: leisure.mgt@shef.ac.uk
Taylor, P. D., BA Warw., MA Leeds, MBA CNAA
Prof.; Dir.*
Other Staff: 2 Lectrs.
Research: innovation in leisure industries;
internationalisation in leisure industries;
leisure and urban regeneration; sustainable
development in leisure industries;
understanding the leisure consumer

Lifelong Learning, Institute for

see also Educn.

Tel: (0114) 222 7000 Fax: (0114) 222 7001
E-mail: till@shef.ac.uk
Webb, S. C., BA Leic., PhD Manc. Prof.; Dir.*
Other Staff: 4 Lectrs.; 3 Tutor Co-ordinators; 1
Res. Contract Staff
Research: adult education; energy studies; field
archaeology; geology; local history

Management School

Tel: (0114) 222 3346 Fax: (0114) 222 3348
E-mail: sums@shef.ac.uk
Adcock, C. J., BSc S'ton., PhD S'ton. Prof.
Birkin, F. B., BSc Lond. Sr. Lectr.
Cullen, J. Prof.
Fletcher, D., BA Nott., PhD Nott. Sr. Lectr.
Frecknall-Hughes, J., MA Oxf., PhD Leeds Sr.
Lectr.
Georgen, M., BSc Brussels, DPhil Oxf. Prof.
Glaister, K. M., BA Leic., MA Lanc., MBA Brad.
Prof.
Heald, D. E. A., BA Leic. Prof.
Hodges, R., FCA Prof.
Huggins, R., BA Kent, MSc Wales, PhD Wales
Sr. Lectr.
Johnson, P., BA Sheff., MSc CNAA, MSc
Open(UK), PhD Sheff.Hallam Prof.
Koh, S. C. L., BEng Herts., PhD Herts. Sr. Lectr.
Lewis, L. A., BA CNAA, MPhil CNAA Sr. Lectr.
Macdonald, S., MA Camb., PhD Newcastle(UK)
Prof.
Mellahi, K., BA Algiers, PhD Nott. Prof.
Musson, G., BA Sheff., PhD Sheff. Sr. Lectr.
Nichols, G., BA Durh., MSc Strath., MSc Lough.,
PhD Sheff. Sr. Lectr.
O'Sullivan, C. N., BA Limerick, PhD Nott. Prof.
Pittaway, L., BA Hudd., PhD Newcastle(UK) Sr.
Lectr.
Richbell, S. M., BScEcon Wales, MScEcon Wales
Sr. Lectr.
Simpson, M., MSc Brist., MBA Sheff., PhD Aston
Sr. Lectr.
Tylecote, A. B., BA Oxf., BPhil Oxf., MA Sus.,
PhD Sheff. Prof.
Williams, C. C., BSc CNAA, MPhil Birm. Prof.
Wood, G. T., BA Cape Town, MA Cape Town, PhD
Rhodes Prof.
Wright, P. W., MA Camb., Drs Amst. Reader
Other Staff: 18 Lectrs.; 1 Res. Assoc.; 1 Sr.
Teaching Fellow; 5 Teaching Fellows; 2
Lectrs.†
Research: accounting and finance; human
resource management and organisational
behaviour; information management;
marketing; operations management and
operational research

Mathematics and Statistics, School of

Tel: (0114) 222 3802 Fax: (0114) 222 3809
E-mail: maths@shef.ac.uk
Thompson, M. J., MA Camb., PhD Camb., FRAS
Prof.; Chair*

Applied Mathematics

Tel: (0114) 222 3731 Fax: (0114) 222 3739
E-mail: appliedmaths@shef.ac.uk
Mole, N., BA Camb., PhD Reading Sr. Lectr.
Ohkitani, K., BA Kyoto, MSc Kyoto, DSc Kyoto
Prof.
Quegan, S., BA Warw., MSc Warw., PhD Sheff.
Prof.
Rees, J. M., BSc Leeds, PhD Leeds Sr. Lectr.
Ruderman, M. S., MSc Moscow, PhD Russian
Acad.Sc. Reader

Thompson, M. J., MA Camb., PhD Camb., FRAS
Prof.; Head*
von Fay-Siebenbürgen, R., MSc Bud., MA Bud.,
PhD Leuven, CSc Hungarian Acad.Sc. Prof.
Winstanley, E., BA Oxf., DPhil Oxf. Sr. Lectr.
Wyatt, L. R., BSc Manc., MSc Brist., PhD S'ton.
Prof.
Zinober, A. S. I., MSc(Eng) Cape Town, PhD
Camb. Prof.
Other Staff: 6 Lectrs.; 1 Sci. Officer; 7 Res.
Contract Staff; 3 Hon. Res. Fellows; 1
Temp. Lectr.
Research: control theory and optimisation;
mathematical biology; numerical analysis;
remote sensing; theoretical physics

Probability and Statistics

Tel: (0114) 222 3751 Fax: (0114) 222 3759
E-mail: statistics@shef.ac.uk
Anderson, C. W., MA Camb., MSc Lond., PhD
Lond. Prof.
Applebaum, D. B., MA St And., MSc Nott., PhD
Nott. Prof.
Biggins, J. D., MA Camb., MSc Oxf., DPhil Oxf.
Prof.; Head*
Blackwell, P. G., BSc Warw., PhD Nott. Prof.
Fieller, N. R. J., MA Camb., MSc Birm., PhD Hull
Sr. Lectr.
O'Hagan, A., BSc Lond., PhD Lond. Prof.
Other Staff: 5 Lectrs.; 1 Independent Res.
Worker; 1 Computing Officer; 5 Res.
Contract Staff; 1 Hon. Res. Assoc.
Research: applied probability and stochastic
processes; computational inference; images
analysis and design; medical and
environmental statistics; spatial statistics

Pure Mathematics

Tel: (0114) 222 3761 Fax: (0114) 222 3769
E-mail: puremaths@shef.ac.uk
Bavula, V. V., MS Kiev, DrSci Kiev Taras Scevchenko
Reader
Bridgeland, T., BA Camb., PhD Edin. Reader
Dixon, P. G., MA Camb., PhD Camb., ScD Camb.
Reader
Dummigan, N. P., BA Oxf., PhD Harv. Sr.
Lectr.
Greenlees, J. P. C., MA Camb., PhD Camb.
Prof.; Head*
Jarvis, A. F., MA Camb., PhD Camb. Sr. Lectr.
Jordan, D. A., BSc Belf., PhD Leeds Prof.
Mackenzie, K. C. H., BSc Monash, PhD Monash
Reader
Moerdijk, I., Drs Amst., PhD Amst. Prof.
Sharp, R. Y., MA Oxf., DPhil Oxf. Prof.
Snaith, V. P., MSc Warw., MA Camb., PhD
Warw., ScD Camb. Prof.
Strickland, N. P., MA Camb., PhD Manc. Prof.
Whitehouse, S. A., BSc Warw., MSc Warw., PhD
Warw. Sr. Lectr.
Other Staff: 4 Lectrs.; 4 Res. Assocs.; 3 Hon.
Lectrs.
Research: algebraic topology; differential
geometry; functional analysis; number
theory; ring theory

Music

Tel: (0114) 222 0470 Fax: (0114) 222 0469
E-mail: music@shef.ac.uk
Davidson, J. W., BA CNAA, MA City(UK), PhD
City(UK) Prof.
Dibben, N. J., BSc City(UK), MA City(UK), PhD
Sheff. Sr. Lectr.
Hill, P. H. A. W., MA Oxf. Prof., Musical
Performance
Killick, A. P., BMus Edin., MA Hawaii, PhD
Wash. Sr. Lectr.
Moore, A. J., BSc Birm., MA Birm., PhD Birm.
Sr. Lectr.
Nicholson, G., BA York(UK), DPhil York(UK)
Sr. Lectr.; Head*
Pitts, S. E., BA York(UK), PhD Sheff. Sr. Lectr.
Simeone, N., BMus Manc. Prof.
Stock, J. P. J., MA York(UK), PhD Belf. Reader
Other Staff: 2 Lectrs.; 2 AHRC Res. Fellows; 1
AHRC Creative & Performing Arts Fellow; 1
DTI Academy Fellow

Research: opera; popular music of the eighteenth
and nineteenth centuries; psychology of
music; sixteenth- and seventeenth-century
English music; twentieth-century piano
music

Philosophy

Tel: (0114) 222 0571 Fax: (0114) 222 0588
E-mail: philosophy@shef.ac.uk
Hale, R., BA St And., BPhil St And., FRSEd Prof.
Hookway, C. J., BPhil E.Anglia, MA Oxf., PhD
Camb. Prof.
Hopkins, R., MA Camb., MPhil Lond., PhD Camb.
Prof.
Keefe, R., BA Camb., MPhil Camb., PhD Camb.
Sr. Lectr.
Laurence, S., BA Bates, MA Arizona, PhD Rutgers
Sr. Lectr.
Lenman, J., BA Oxf., PhD St And. Sr. Lectr.
Makin, S. A. R., MA Edin., PhD Camb. Sr.
Lectr.
Olson, E., BA Reed, PhD Syr. Reader
Owens, D. J., BA Camb., BPhil Oxf., DPhil Oxf.
Prof.
Saul, J. M., BA Roch., MA Prin., PhD Prin. Prof.
Stern, R., BA Camb., MA Camb., PhD Camb.
Prof.
Wenar, L., BA Stan., PhD Harv. Reader
Other Staff: 5 Lectrs.; 1 Hon. Assoc.; 1 Temp.
Lectr.
Research: aesthetics; ancient philosophy; ethics
and political philosophy; metaphysics and
epistemology; philosophy of mind and
language

Physics and Astronomy

Tel: (0114) 222 3519 Fax: (0114) 222 3555
E-mail: l.simmons@shef.ac.uk
Booth, C. N., BA Camb., PhD Camb. Sr. Lectr.
Cartwright, S. L., BSc Glas., PhD Glas. Sr.
Lectr.
Cockburn, J. W., BSc Lanc., PhD Camb. Prof.
Crowther, P. A., BSc Lond., PhD Lond. Prof.
de Grijs, R., MSc Gron., PhD Gron. Sr. Lectr.
Dhillon, V. S., BSc Sus., MSc Lond., DPhil Sus.,
FRAS Reader
Fox, A. M., BA Oxf., MA Oxf., DPhil Oxf.
Reader
Geoghegan, M., MA Oxf., MSc Birm., PhD Camb.
Sr. Lectr.
Golestanian, R., BSc Tehran, MSc Zanjan, PhD
Zanjan Reader
Hughes, D. W., BSc Birm., DPhil Oxf., FIP,
FRAS Prof.
Jones, R. A. L., MA Camb., PhD Camb. Prof.
Lidzey, D. G., BSc Birm., PhD Birm. Reader
Mowbray, D. J., BA Oxf., DPhil Oxf. Prof.
Richardson, T., BSc Durh., DPhil Oxf. Sr. Lectr.
Roszkowski, L., MSc Warsaw Prof.
Searle, T. M., BSc Lond., PhD Lond. Reader
Skolnick, M. S., BA Oxf., DPhil Oxf. Prof.,
Experimental Condensed Matter
Spooner, N. J. C., BSc S'ton., PhD Lond. Prof.
Tadhunter, C. N., BSc Sus., DPhil Sus. Prof.;
Head*
Thompson, L. F., BSc Sheff., PhD Sheff. Sr.
Lectr.
Tovey, D. R., BA Oxf., PhD Sheff. Sr. Lectr.
Whittaker, D. M., BA Oxf., DPhil Oxf. Reader
Other Staff: 7 Lectrs.; 3 Res. Fellows; 30 Res.
Contract Staff; 1 Hon. Lectr.
Research: high energy particle physics;
magnetism and magnetic materials; opto-
electronic properties of semiconductor low
dimensional structures; space physics;
theoretical condensed matter physics

Politics

Tel: (0114) 222 1700 Fax: (0114) 222 1717
E-mail: politics@shef.ac.uk
Bache, I., BA Leeds, MA Sheff., PhD Sheff. Sr.
Lectr.
Flinders, M. V., BA Lough., PhD Sheff. Sr. Lectr.
Gamble, A. M., BA Camb., PhD Camb., MA Durh.
Prof.
Geddes, A. P., BA Oxf., PhD Lough. Prof.
Grugel, J. B., BA Liv., PhD Liv. Prof.

Harrison, G., BSc Lond., MA Leeds, PhD Staffs.
Sr. Lectr.
Hobson, J. M., BA Herts., MSc Lond., PhD Lond.
Prof.
Kenny, M. H., BA Camb., MA Manc., PhD Manc.
Prof.; Head*
Ludlam, S. G. P., BA Sheff., PhD Sheff. Sr.
Lectr.
Payne, A. J., BA Camb., PhD Manc. Prof.
Richards, D., BA Essex, MSc Lond., PhD Strath.
Reader
Smith, M. J., BA Essex, MA Essex, PhD Essex
Prof.
Taylor, A. J., BA Manc., PhD Sheff. Prof.
Vickers, R. M., BA Warw., PhD Warw. Sr.
Lectr.
Vincent, A. W., BA Exe., PhD Manc. Prof.
Waylen, G. N. A., BA Manc., PhD CNAA Sr.
Lectr.
Other Staff: 6 Lectrs.; 2 Hon. Profs.
Research: democratisation; international political
economy; political parties; political theory,
political thought; public policy

Psychology

Tel: (0114) 222 6559 Fax: (0114) 276 6515
E-mail: psychology@shef.ac.uk
Armitage, C. J., BA Wales, PhD Leeds Sr. Lectr.
Blades, M., BA Sheff., MA Camb., PhD Sheff. Sr.
Lectr.
Dean, P., MA Camb., DPhil Oxf. Prof.
Eiser, C., BSc Brist., PhD Brist. Prof.
Eiser, J. R., MA Oxf., PhD Lond. Prof.; Head*
Gurney, K., BSc Sus., MSc Brun., PhD Brun. Sr.
Lectr.
Hardy, G., BA Sheff., MSc Sheff., PhD Leeds
Prof., Clinical Psychology
Harris, P., BSc Lond., PhD Lond. Sr. Lectr.
Hockey, G. R. J., BSc Leic., PhD Camb. Prof.
Nicolson, R. I., MA Camb., MSc Sus., PhD Camb.
Prof.
Norman, P. D., BSc Lanc., PhD Lanc. Sr. Lectr.
Overton, P., BA Sheff., PhD Sheff. Sr. Lectr.
Parsons, L. M., BA Calif., PhD Calif. Prof.
Pascalis, O., BSc Aix-Marseilles I, MSc Aix-Marseilles
I, PhD Aix-Marseilles I Sr. Lectr.
Porrill, J., BA Camb., PhD Sheff. Reader
Prescott, A. J., MA Edin., MSc Aberd., PhD Sheff.
Sr. Lectr.
Redgrave, P., BA Hull, MSc Hull, PhD Hull
Prof.
Sheeran, P., BA Trinity(Dub.), MA Trinity(Dub.)
Prof.
Siegal, M., BA McG., MEd Harv., DPhil Oxf., DSc
Oxf. Prof.
Slade, P., BSc Nott., MSc Leeds, PhD Sheff. Prof.,
Clinical Psychology
Stone, J. V., BSc Manc., MSc Sus., DPhil Sus.
Reader
Turpin, G. C. H., BSc Lond., MPhil Lond., PhD
S'ton., FBPsS Prof.; Dir., Clin. Psychol. Unit
Other Staff: 11 Lectrs.; 5 Lectrs. in Clin.
Psychol.; 2 Res. Fellows; 1 Sr. Exper.
Officer; 24 Res. Contract Staff; 1 Practice
Dir.; 1 Consultant Clin. Psychologist; 3 Sr.
Clin. Tutors; 5 Clin. Tutors; 2 Hon. Profs.;
1 Hon. Prof. Assoc.; 1 Hon. Reader; 6 Hon.
Lectrs.; 8 Hon. Lectrs. in Clin. Psychol.; 13
Hon. Res. Assocs. in Clin. Psychol.; 46
Hon. Teachers in Clin. Psychol.
Research: clinical psychology; developmental
psychology; occupational psychology; social
and health psychology

Russian and Slavonic Studies

Tel: (0114) 222 7400 Fax: (0114) 222 7416
E-mail: russian-slavonic@shef.ac.uk
Bermel, N., BA Yale, MA Calif., PhD Calif.
Reader
Brandist, C., MA Sus., DPhil Sus. Reader
Leatherbarrow, W. J., MA Exe. Prof.
Reid, S. E., BA Leeds, MA Penn., PhD Penn. Sr.
Lectr.
Shepherd, D. G., MA Oxf., PhD Manc. Prof.
Other Staff: 1 Lector; 1 AHRB Res. Assoc.
Research: Bakhtin studies; Dostoevsky studies;
nineteenth- and twentieth-century Russian

literature; Russian language; Slavonic
languages and linguistics

Sociological Studies

Tel: (0114) 222 6400 Fax: (0114) 276 8125
E-mail: sociological.studies@shef.ac.uk
Deacon, R., BA Lond., MPhil Kent Prof. Assoc.
Hockey, J. L., BA Durh., PhD Durh. Prof.
Horwath, J. A., BA Brad. Sr. Lectr.
James, A. L., BA Hull, PhD Hull Prof., Social
Work
James, A., BA Durh., PhD Durh. Prof.,
Sociology
Jenkins, R. P., BA Belf., PhD Camb. Prof.,
Sociology; Head*
Marsh, P., BSc(SocSc) S'ton., MPhil S'ton. Prof.,
Child and Family Welfare
Norris, C. A., BA Sus., MSc Sur., PhD Sur.
Prof., Sociology
Phillips, D. R., BA E.Anglia, MPhil York(UK) Sr.
Lectr.
Roche, M. C., BSc(Econ) Lond., PhD Lond.
Reader
Walker, A. C., BA Essex, DLitt Essex Prof.,
Social Policy
Other Staff: 14 Lectrs.; 1 Dir. (Res. Training
Program); 2 Lectrs.†; 7 Hon. Assocs.; 2
Hon. Res. Fellows
Research: changes in society; citizenship and
social integration; participation and power
in health, social service and criminal justice
services

Town and Regional Planning

Tel: (0114) 222 6180 Fax: (0114) 272 2199
E-mail: planning@shef.ac.uk
Abram, S., BSc Manc., MEng Manc., MSt Oxf.,
DPhil Oxf. Sr. Lectr.
Booth, P. A., MA Camb., MA Sheff., PhD Sheff.
Reader
Campbell, H. J., BA Durh., MA Sheff., PhD Sheff.
Prof.; Head*
Crook, A. D. H., BA Brist., MPhil Lond., PhD
Sheff. Prof.
Dabinett, G. E., BSc H-W, MSc Camb. Reader
Gough, A. J., BA Oxf., MPhil Lond., DPhil Oxf.
Sr. Lectr.
Henneberry, J. M., MA Camb., MA Sheff., FRICS
Prof.
Huxley, M. E., BA ANU, MA Melb., PhD
Open(UK) Sr. Lectr.
Jackson, K., BSc Sheff., PhD Aberd. Sr. Lectr.
Watkins, C. A., BA Strath., PhD Paisley Reader
Other Staff: 6 Lectrs.; 1 Visiting Res. Fellow; 1
Postdoctoral Teaching Fellow; 1 Hon. Sr.
Lectr.
Research: information management; local
economic development and housing;
planning systems (theory and practice)

DENTAL SCHOOL

Tel: (0114) 271 7807 Fax: (0114) 279 7050
E-mail: dental.genenquiries@shef.ac.uk
Walsh, T. F., BDS Lond., MSc Lond., DDS Birm.,
FDSRCS Dean of Sch.*

Adult Dental Care

Including Mechanics, Materials and Prosthetics
Tel: (0114) 271 7984 Fax: (0114) 266 5326
E-mail: j.newstead@shef.ac.uk
Griffiths, G. S., BDS Wales, MScD Wales, PhD
Lond., FDSRCSEd Prof.
Hatton, P. V., BSc CNAA, PhD Sheff.Hallam
Prof.
Martin, N., BDS Liv., PhD Liv. Sr. Lectr.
Rawlinson, A., BChD Leeds, MDS Sheff.,
FDSRCSEd Prof.
van Noort, R., BSc Sus., DPhil Sus., FRSA
Prof.; Head*
Walsh, T. F., BDS Lond., MSc Lond., DDS Birm.,
FDSRCS Prof.
Other Staff: 2 Lectrs.; 3 Res. Contract Staff; 3
Dental Instrs.; 1 Sr. Clin. Lectr.; 5 Clin.
Lectrs.; 2 Clin. Lectrs.†; 1 Hon. Sr. Lectr.; 5
Hon. Sr. Clin. Lectrs.; 1 Hon. Clin. Lectr.; 3
Hon. Teachers; 23 Hon. Clin. Teachers

Research: clinical services and standards; dental
biomaterials, dental materials and dental
technology; dental education science

Oral and Maxillofacial Surgery

Tel: (0114) 271 7849 Fax: (0114) 271 7863
E-mail: judy.smith@shef.ac.uk
Boissonade, F. M., BDS Birm., PhD Brist. Prof.
Brook, I. M., BDS Liv., MDS Sheff., PhD Sheff.,
FDSRCS Prof.; Deputy Dean of Sch.
Loescher, A. R., BDS Birm., MB ChB Sheff., PhD
Birm., FDSRCS Reader
Robinson, P. P., BDS Sheff., DSc Sheff., PhD
Brist., FDSRCS Prof.; Res. Dean of Sch.
Smith, K. G., BDS Newcastle(UK), PhD Sheff.,
FDSRCS Head*
Thornhill, M., BDS Lond., MSc Lond., PhD Lond.,
FDSRCS Prof.
Other Staff: 1 Lectr.; 1 Res. Assoc.; 2 Res.
Contract Staff; 3 Clin. Lectrs.; 7 Hon. Sr.
Clin. Lectrs.; 3 Hon. Teachers; 18 Hon.
Clin. Teachers
Research: development of oral biological
evaluation of medical materials; nerve
injuries and repair

Oral Health and Development

Tel: (0114) 271 7885 Fax: (0114) 271 7843
E-mail: adc@shef.ac.uk
Deery, C., BDS Edin., MSc Brist., PhD Dund.
Prof.
Farthing, P., BSc Edin., BDS Edin., PhD Edin.
Reader
Lennon, M., BDS Liv. Prof.
Robinson, P. G., BDS Lond., LDS Lond., MSc
Lond., PhD Lond., FRACDS Prof.; Res. Dean
of Sch.
Rodd, H. D., BDS Brist., PhD Sheff., FDSRCS
Reader
Other Staff: 5 Lectrs.; 2 Res. Assocs.; 1 Sr.
Clin. Lectr.; 1 Clin. Lectr.; 1 Clin. Lectr.†; 8
Hon. Sr. Clin. Lectrs.; 5 Hon. Clin. Lectrs.;
1 Hon. Teacher; 8 Hon. Clin. Teachers
Research: normal and abnormal dental growth
and development

Oral Pathology

Tel: (0114) 271 7951 Fax: (0114) 271 7894
E-mail: c.ballantyne@shef.ac.uk
Craig, G. T., BDS Sheff., PhD Sheff., FDSRCS,
FRCPath Reader; Clin. Dean of Sch.
Douglas, C. W. I., BSc Birm., PhD Birm. Prof.
Farthing, P., BSc Edin., BDS Edin., PhD Edin.
Reader
Speight, P. M., BDS Manc., PhD Dund.,
FDSRCPSGlas, FDSRCS, FRCPath Prof.;
Head*
Other Staff: 3 Lectrs.; 5 Sr. Tech. Staff; 1 Sr.
Clin. Lectr.; 1 Sr. Clin. Lectr.†; 1 Hon. Clin.
Teacher
Research: diagnostic oral histopathology; electron
microscopy; histochemistry;
immunocytochemistry; stereology

HEALTH AND RELATED RESEARCH, SCHOOL
OF

Tel: (0114) 222 5454 Fax: (0114) 272 4095
E-mail: scharr.reception@shef.ac.uk
Akehurst, R. L., BSc(Econ) Lond. Dean*

General Practice and Primary Care,
Institute of

Tel: (0114) 271 5917 Fax: (0114) 242 2136
E-mail: gpreception@shef.ac.uk
Campbell, M. J., BA York(UK), MSc Edin., PhD
Edin. Prof., Medical Physics with an
interest in Primary Care Res.
Julious, S. A., BSc Manc., MSc Reading Sr. Lectr.
Other Staff: 1 Lead Lectr.; 8 Lectrs.; 3 Sr. Res.
Fellows; 5 Res. Fellows; 9 Res. Assocs.; 1
Academic Training Fellow; 140 Gen.
Practice Tutors; 6 Lectrs.†; 1 Hon. Sr.
Lectr.; 4 Hon. Lectrs.; 3 Hon. Res. Fellows
Research: educational innovations; mental health;
organisation of primary health care team;
use of IT

Health Economics and Decision Science

Tel: (0114) 222 0175
E-mail: j.e.brazier@shef.ac.uk
Akehurst, R. L., BSc(Econ) Lond. Prof.
Brazier, J. E., BA Exe., MSc York(UK), PhD Sheff. Prof.
Dixon, S., BSc S'ton., MSc York(UK) Sr. Lectr.
Ellis, L. B., BA Sheff.Hallam, MSc Sheff.Hallam, PhD Sheff. Sr. Lectr.
Walters, S. J., BSc Keele, MSc Leic. Sr. Lectr.
Other Staff: 2 Lectrs.; 2 Sr. Res. Fellows; 8 Res. Fellows; 7 Res. Assocs.; 3 Sr. OR Analysts; 1 Hon. Prof.; 3 Hon. Sr. Res. Fellows; 1 Hon. Res. Fellow
Research: economic evaluations of purchasing health care; health care policy studies; health care resource allocation decisions

Health Services Research

Tel: (0114) 222 0750 Fax: (0114) 222 0749
E-mail: j.willoughby@shef.ac.uk
Fox, N. J., BSc Brist., MSc(Econ) Lond., PhD Warw. Reader
Nicholl, J. P., BA Brist., MSc CNAA Prof.; Dir., Med. Care Res. Unit
Parry, G., BSc Reading, MSc S'ton., PhD Dund. Reader
Shipton, G. A., BA Nott. Sr. Lectr.
Other Staff: 7 Lectrs.; 2 Sr. Res. Fellows; 8 Res. Fellows; 1 MRC Res. Fellow; 13 Res. Assocs.; 3 Clin. Sr. Lectrs.; 1 Clin. Res. Fellow; 1 Hon. Sr. Res. Fellow; 1 Hon. Res. Fellow
Research: aspects of primary care; services for acute illness

Information Resources

Tel: (0114) 222 5420
E-mail: info@trentrdsu.org.uk
Booth, A., BA Wales Reader; Dir.*
Other Staff: 1 Information Services Manager; 5 Information Officers
Research: systematic reviews for health care interventions

Mental Health

Tel: (0114) 222 0786
E-mail: s.b.proctor@shef.ac.uk
Parry, G. D., BA Manc., PhD Sheff., FBPsS Prof., Applied Psychological Therapies
Tantam, D. J. H., BA Oxf., BA Open(UK), BM BCh Oxf., MA Oxf., MPH Harv., PhD Lond., FRCPsych Prof., Psychotherapy; Dir.*
Other Staff: 1 Prof. Assoc.; 1 Lectr.; 2 Res. Fellows; 1 Res. Assoc.; 1 Hon. Reader; 6 Hon. Res. Fellows
Research: clinical risk assessment; dissociative disorders; Munchhausen by proxy syndrome; personality disorder; the establishment of an international forensic database

Public Health

Tel: (0114) 222 0811 Fax: (0114) 222 0791
E-mail: c.grinold@shef.ac.uk
Goyder, E., MA Camb., MB BChir Camb., MD Leic. Sr. Lectr.
Hutchinson, A., MB BS Newcastle(UK), FRCGP, FFPHM Prof.; Dir.*
Research: promoting public health at local, national and international levels

MEDICINE AND BIOMEDICAL SCIENCES, SCHOOL OF

Tel: (0114) 271 3349 Fax: (0114) 271 3030
E-mail: v.bathe-taylor@shef.ac.uk
Weetman, A. P., BMedSc Newcastle(UK), MD Newcastle(UK), DSc Newcastle(UK), FRCP, FRCPEd, FMedSci Sir Arthur Hall Prof., Medicine; Dean*

Ageing, Sheffield Institute for Studies on

Tel: (0114) 222 6270 Fax: (0114) 222 6230
E-mail: c.l.tingle@shef.ac.uk
Gott, C. M., BA Oxf., PhD Sheff. Sr. Lectr.
McKee, K. J., BSc Stir., PhD Stir. Sr. Lectr.

Parker, S. G., MB BS Newcastle(UK), MD Newcastle(UK), FRCP Prof., Health Care for Elderly People; Dir.*
Philp, I., MB ChB Edin., MD Edin., FRCP, FRCPEd Marjorie Coote Prof., Health Care for Elderly People
Warnes, A. M., BA Hull, PhD Salf. Prof., Social Gerontology
Research: elderly homeless; geriatric assessment; health services for older patients; osteoporosis; palliative care

Biomedical Science

Tel: (0114) 222 2320 Fax: (0114) 276 5413
E-mail: bmsoffice@shef.ac.uk
Atkinson, M. E., BSc Birm., PhD Sheff. Prof.
Furley, A. J. W., BSc Edin., PhD Lond. Sr. Lectr.
Grundy, D., BSc Lond., PhD Dund. Prof.
Holley, M. C., BSc Newcastle(UK), DPhil Oxf. Prof.
Ingham, P. W., MA Camb., DPhil Sus., FIBiol, FRS, FMedSci Prof.; Chairman*
Placzek, M., BSc Edin., PhD Lond. Prof.
Rashbass, P., BA Camb., MA Camb., MB BChir Camb. Sr. Lectr.
Robson, L., BSc Leeds, PhD Leeds Sr. Lectr.
Seward, E. P., BSc McG., MPhil Camb., PhD Camb. Sr. Lectr.
Smythe, C., BA Trinity(Dub.), PhD Trinity(Dub.) Prof.; Head*
Smythe, E., BA Trinity(Dub.), PhD Trinity(Dub.) Prof.
Strutt, D. I., BA Camb., MA Camb., PhD Camb. Prof.
Warren, M. A., BSc Aston, PhD Aberd. Sr. Lectr.
Whitfield, T., MA Camb., PhD Camb. Sr. Lectr.
Winder, S., BSc Brun., PhD Reading Prof.
Other Staff: 8 Lectrs.; 1 Sr. Experimental Officer; 1 Res. Fellow; 44 Res. Contract Staff; 1 Hon. Reader
Research: anatomy; cell biology; developmental biology; neurobiology; physiology

Clinical Sciences, Division of (North)

Tel: (0114) 226 6976 Fax: (0114) 261 9587
E-mail: r.metcalfe@shef.ac.uk
Hellewell, P. G., BSc Lond., PhD Camb. Dir. of Div.*

Cardiovascular Science

Tel: (0114) 226 6976 Fax: (0114) 261 9587
Chan, P., MA Camb., MChir Camb., FRCS Reader
Crossman, D. C., BSc Lond., MB BS Lond., MD Lond., FRCP Prof., Cardiology; Section Head*
Dear, T. N., BSc Adel., PhD Syd. Prof., Gene Targeting
Francis, S. E., BSc CNAA, PhD Manc. Sr. Lectr.
Hellewell, P. G., BSc Lond., PhD Camb. Prof., Vascular Biology
Michaels, J. A., BA Camb., BM BCh Oxf., MA Oxf., MA Camb., MB BChir Camb., MChir Camb., FRCS Hon. Prof.
Newman, C. H., MB BS Lond., MA Camb., PhD Camb. Sr. Lectr.
Pockley, A. G., BSc Sheff., PhD CNAA Prof., Immunobiology
Shackley, P., BA York(UK), MSc York(UK), PhD Sheff. Sr. Lectr.
Storey, R. F., BSc York(UK), BM S'ton., MD Nott. Sr. Lectr.
Thomas, S. M., MB BS Lond., MSc Sheff., FRCR Sr. Lectr.
Research: biology of blood vessels; immunobiology (heat shock proteins); vascular disease

Human Metabolism

Fax: (0114) 256 0458
Eastell, R., BSc Edin., MB ChB Edin., MD Edin., FRCPEd, FRCP, FRCPI, FRCPath Prof., Bone Metabolism
Haylor, J., BPharm Wales, PhD Birm. Sr. Lectr.
Heller, S. R., MB BChir Camb., MA Camb., DM, FRCP Reader

McCloskey, E. V., BA Trinity(Dub.), MB BCh Trinity(Dub.), MD Sheff. Sr. Lectr.
Newell-Price, J., BA Camb., MB BChir Camb., MA Camb. Sr. Lectr.
Ong, A., BA Oxf., BM BCh Oxf., MA Oxf., DM Oxf., FRCP Reader
Powers, H. J., BSc Leic., PhD Lond. Prof., Nutritional Biochemistry
Ross, R. J. M., MD Lond., FRCP Prof., Endocrinology; Section Head*
Watson, P. F., BSc Sheff., PhD Sheff. Sr. Lectr.
Weetman, A. P., BMedSc Newcastle(UK), MD Newcastle(UK), DSc Newcastle(UK), FRCP, FRCPEd, FMedSci Sir Arthur Hall Prof., Medicine
Other Staff: 5 Lectrs.; 15 Res. Assocs./Fellows; 23 Clin. Res. Fellows
Research: bone metabolism; diabetes and endocrinology; human nutrition; nephrology; skin

Clinical Sciences, Division of (South)

Tel: (0114) 271 3017 Fax: (0114) 271 1711
E-mail: l.henery@shef.ac.uk
Hamdy, F. C., MD Sheff., FRCS Prof.; Dir.*

Anaesthesia, Academic Unit of

Tel: (0114) 271 2510 Fax: (0114) 271 3771
E-mail: j.heppenstall@shef.ac.uk
Ross, J., MB ChB Edin., FRCA Sr. Lectr.
Other Staff: 1 Lectr.; 1 Res. Assoc.
Research: anaesthetics; microcirculation

Bone Biology, Academic Unit of

Tel: (0114) 271 2475 Fax: (0114) 271 1711
E-mail: b.j.price@shef.ac.uk
Croucher, P. I., BSc Wales, PhD Wales Prof., Bone Biology; Head*
Skerry, T., BVetMed Lond., PhD Lond., FRCVS Prof., Orthopaedic Biology
Smallwood, R. H., BSc Lond., MSc Lanc., PhD Sheff., FREng, FIEE, FIP, Hon. FRCP Prof.
Other Staff: 1 Sr. Res. Scientist; 2 Res. Fellows
Research: bone biology; bone disease; osteoblast biology and bone formation

Child Health, Academic Unit of

Tel: (0114) 271 7228 Fax: (0114) 275 5364
E-mail: m.g.hargan@shef.ac.uk
Bishop, N. J., MD Manc., FRCPCH Prof., Paediatric Bone Disease; Head*
Taylor, C. J., MD Liv., FRCP Prof., Paediatric Gastroenterology
Wales, J. K. H., MA Oxf., DM Oxf., FRCP Sr. Lectr.
Other Staff: 2 Lectrs.; 4 Res. Staff; 4 Res. Contract Staff; 2 Clin. Lectrs.; 2 Clin. Res. Fellows
Research: educational methods; genetic disorders in childhood; inflammation and cell injury; physiological measurement

Clinical Pharmacology, Academic Unit of

Tel: (0114) 271 2863 Fax: (0114) 226 1348
E-mail: p.rayner@shef.ac.uk
Jackson, P. R., MB ChB Sheff., MA Oxf., PhD Sheff., FRCP Reader
Lennard, L., BSc Sheff., PhD Sheff. Reader
Lennard, M. S., MSc Birm., PhD Sheff. Reader
Peachell, P. T., BSc Lond., PhD Lond. Sr. Lectr.
Rostami-Hodjegan, A., PharmD Tabriz, PhD Sheff. Reader
Tucker, G. T., BPharm Lond., PhD Lond., FRCA, FRCP Prof., Molecular Pharmacology and Pharmacogenetics; Head*
Other Staff: 2 Lectrs.; 2 Res. Contract Staff; 2 Sr. Clin. Lectrs.
Research: clinical pharmacology; clinical trials and therapeutics; drug metabolism; immunopharmacology

Medical Physics and Clinical Engineering

Tel: (0114) 271 2688 Fax: (0114) 271 3403
E-mail: m.beckett@shef.ac.uk
Barber, D. C., BA Camb., MSc Lond., MSc Lanc., PhD Sheff. Prof. Assoc.
Brown, B. H., BSc Lond., PhD Sheff., FIP, FIEE Prof., Medical Physics

Griffiths, P. D., MB ChB Manc., FRCR   Prof.;
   Head*
Hose, D. R., BSc Manc., PhD UMIST   Sr. Lectr.
Lawford, P. V., BSc Sheff., PhD Sheff.   Sr. Lectr.
Other Staff: 1 Lectr.; 2 Res. Staff
Research: bioprostheses; electrical impedance
   spectroscopy; impedance imaging;
   predictive modelling

Ophthalmology and Orthoptics, Academic Unit of

Tel: (0114) 271 2713 Fax: (0114) 276 6381
Buckley, D., BSc Birm., PhD Sheff.   Sr. Lectr.
Davis, H.   Sr. Lectr.
Firth, A. Y., MSc Wales   Sr. Lectr.
Rennie, I. G., MB ChB Glas., FRCSEd   Prof.,
   Ophthalmology; Head*
Other Staff: 7 Lectrs.
Research: absence of binocular vision; ocular
   melanoma; opiates and orthoptics

Radiology, Academic Unit of

Tel: (0114) 271 2587 Fax: (0114) 272 4760
   E-mail: radiology@shef.ac.uk
Griffiths, P. D., MB ChB Manc., FRCR   Prof.;
   Head*
Paley, M. N. J., BSc Nott., PhD Nott., FIP
   Prof., M R Physics
Thomas, S. M., MB BS Lond., MSc Sheff., FRCR
   Sr. Lectr.
Whitby, E., BSc Manc., MB ChB Manc., PhD
   Sheff.   Sr. Lectr.
Wild, J. M., MA Camb., MMedSci Sheff., PhD
   Edin.   Sr. Lectr.
Other Staff: 1 Lectr.; 1 Res. Staff; 1 Sr. Clin.
   Lectr.
Research: human neuro-imaging; hyperpolised
   gas MRI (magnetic resonance imaging) of
   lungs; maternal foetal and neonatal
   imaging; MR physics and engineering

Reproductive and Developmental Medicine

Tel: (0114) 226 8317 Fax: (0114) 226 1074
   E-mail: d.m.swain@shef.ac.uk
Fraser, R. B., MD Sheff., FRCOG   Reader
Ledger, W. L., BM BCh Oxf., MA Oxf., DPhil
   Oxf., FRCOG   Prof.; Head*
Pacey, A., BSc Hull, PhD St And.   Sr. Lectr.
Other Staff: 2 Lectrs.; 2 Sr. Clin. Lectrs.; 1
   Clin. Res. Fellow; 1 Clin. Lectr.
Research: human fertility and infertility

Sports Medicine, Academic Unit of

Tel: (0114) 267 8889 Fax: (0114) 267 2050
   E-mail: scsm@shef.ac.uk
Rolf, C. G., MD Umeå, PhD Umeå   Prof.
Research: sports medicine; sports medicine
   education

Supportive Care, Academic Unit of

Tel: (0114) 271 3992 Fax: (0114) 271 3991
   E-mail: pallmed@shef.ac.uk
Ahmedzai, S. H., BSc Manc., MB ChB Manc.,
   FRCPGlas, FRCP   Prof.; Head*
Noble, W., MB ChB Sheff., MD Sheff.   Sr. Lectr.
Other Staff: 1 Res. Staff

Surgical Oncology, Academic Unit of

Tel: (0114) 271 3326 Fax: (0114) 271 3314
   E-mail: a.duffes@shef.ac.uk
Brown, N. J., BSc Sheff., PhD Sheff.   Prof.
Kanthou, C., BScBiol Lond., MPhil Lond., PhD
   Lond.   Sr. Lectr.
Reed, M. W. R., BMedSci Sheff., MB ChB Sheff.,
   MD Sheff., FRCS   Prof., Surgery; Head*
Tozer, G., BSc Keele, MSc Lond.   Prof., Cancer
   Research
Other Staff: 4 Lectrs.; 4 Res. Staff; 1 Sr. Clin.
   Lectr.

Urology, Academic Unit of

Tel: (0114) 271 2154 Fax: (0114) 271 2268
   E-mail: c.stenton@shef.ac.uk
Eaton, C. L., BSc St And., PhD Wales   Sr. Lectr.
Hamdy, F. C., MD Sheff., FRCS   Prof.
Rosario, D. J. P., MB ChB Sheff., MD Sheff.,
   FRCS   Sr. Lectr.

Other Staff: 2 Lectrs.; 2 Res. Staff
Research: bladder cancer; prostate cancer

Genomic Medicine, Division of

Tel: (0114) 271 2055 Fax: (0114) 271 3943
   E-mail: c.vielle@shef.ac.uk
Duff, Sir G. W., KBE, BM BCh Oxf., MA Oxf.,
   PhD Lond., FRCPEd   Prof.; Dir. of Div.*
Hancock, B. W., MD Sheff., FRCP, FRCPEd,
   FRCR   Deputy Clin. Dir. of Div.; YCR
   Prof., Clinical Oncology
Peake, I. R., BSc Liv., PhD Liv., FRCPath
   Deputy Non-Clin. Dir. of Div.; Sir Edward
   Mellanby Prof., Molecular Medicine

Functional Genomics

Tel: (0114) 271 2085
Barber, C. M., BM BS Nott., BMedSci Nott.   Sr.
   Lectr.
Bingle, C. D., BSc Brad., PhD Lond.   Sr. Lectr.
Buttle, D. J., BSc E.Anglia, PhD Camb.   Reader
Dobson, P. R. M., BSc Strath., PhD Lond.   Sr.
   Lectr.
Dockrell, D., MB ChB Trinity(Dub.)   Sr. Lectr.
Dower, S. K., MA Oxf., DPhil Oxf.   Prof.,
   Molecular Immunology; Head*
Eley, A. R., MSc Sheff.Hallam, PhD Nott.   Sr.
   Lectr.
Fishwick, D., MB ChB Manc., MD Manc., FRCP
   Reader
Heath, A. W., BSc Sheff., PhD Sheff.   Reader
Jennings, R., BSc Birm., PhD WI   Emer. Prof.
Qwarnström, E. E., PhD Lund   Prof., Cell
   Biology
Read, R. C., BMedSci Sheff., MB ChB Sheff., MD
   Sheff.   Prof., Infectious Diseases
Renshaw, S. A., BM BCh Oxf., MA Camb., PhD
   Sheff.   Sr. Lectr.
Sabroe, I., BSc Lond., MB BS Lond., PhD Lond.
   Reader
Sayers, J. R., BSc Birm., PhD Birm.   Prof.
Thomas, M. S., BSc S'ton., PhD S'ton.   Sr. Lectr.
Whyte, M. K. B., BSc Lond., MB BS Lond., PhD
   Lond., FRCP   Prof., Respiratory Medicine
Other Staff: 5 Lectrs.; 14 Res. Assocs./Fellows

Genetics and Informatics

Tel: (0114) 271 2085
Cannings, C., BSc Lond., PhD Lond.   Prof.,
   Mathematics and Informatics; Head*
Cork, M. J., BSc St And., MB BChir Camb., PhD
   St And.   Reader
Daly, M. E., BSc N.U.I., PhD N.U.I.   Sr. Lectr.
di Giovine, F. S., MD Florence, PhD Edin.   Sr.
   Lectr.
Goodeve, A. C., BSc Sheff., PhD Sheff.   Reader
Hampton, K. K., BSc Leeds, MD Leeds   Sr. Lectr.
Makris, M., MA Oxf., MD Sheff.   Reader
Nicklin, M., BA Camb., PhD Camb.   Sr. Lectr.
Peake, I. R., BSc Liv., PhD Liv., FRCPath   Sir
   Edward Mellanby Prof., Molecular Medicine
Wilson, A. G., MB BCh Belf.   Reader
Woodruff, P. W. R., MB BS Newcastle(UK), PhD
   Lond.   Academic/Clin. Prof., Psychiatry
Other Staff: 15 Lectrs.; 9 Res. Assocs./Fellows;
   7 Res. Nurses

Neurosciences

Tel: (0114) 271 2085
Azzouzz, M., MSc Aix-Marseilles, PhD Aix-
   Marseilles, BSc   Prof.
Bandmann, O., MD Munich, PhD Munich   Sr.
   Lectr.
Hunter, M. D., MB ChB Sheff.   Sr. Lectr.
McDermott, C. J., MB ChB Leeds, PhD Sheff.   Sr.
   Lectr.
Parks, R., BA Dickinson Coll., MA Wheaton(Ill.),
   MA Chic., MS Miami(Fla.), PhD Miami(Fla.),
   PsyD Miami(Fla.)   Sr. Lectr.
Reuber, M., MD Cologne, PhD Bonn
Shaw, P. J., MB BS Newcastle(UK), MD
   Newcastle(UK)   Prof., Neurology; Head*
Spence, S. A., BSc Lond., MB BS Lond., MD Lond.
   Prof., General Adult Psychiatry
Woodruff, P. W. R., MB BS Newcastle(UK), PhD
   Lond.   Academic/Clin. Prof., Psychiatry

Other Staff: 7 Lectrs.; 15 Res. Assocs./Fellows;
   2 Res. Nurses; 4 Clin. Lectrs.

Oncology and Pathology

Tel: (0114) 271 2085
Coleman, R. E., MB BS Lond., MD Lond., FRCP,
   FRCPEd   Prof., Medical Oncology
Cox, A., BA Camb., PhD Lond.   Sr. Lectr.
Cross, S. S., BSc Lond., MB BS Lond., MD Sheff.
   Reader
Hancock, B. W., MD Sheff., FRCP, FRCPEd,
   FRCR   YCR Prof., Clinical Oncology
Holen, I., BSc Oslo, MSc Oslo   Sr. Lectr.
Ince, P., BSc Newcastle(UK), MB BS Newcastle(UK),
   MD Newcastle(UK), FRCPath   Prof.,
   Neuropathology
Lewis, C. E., BSc Reading, DPhil Oxf.   Prof.;
   Head*
Meuth, M., BSc Purdue, PhD M.I.T.   Prof.,
   Cellular Genetics; Section Head*
Robinson, M. H., MB BChir Camb., MA Camb.,
   MChir Camb., MD Camb., FRCP, FRCR
   Reader
Wells, M., BSc Manc., MD Manc., FRCPath
   Prof., Gynaecological Pathology
Wharton, S. B., BSc Lond., MB BS Lond., MSc
   Camb.   Sr. Lectr.
Woll, P. J., BMedSci Newcastle(UK), MB BS
   Newcastle(UK), PhD Lond., FRCP   Prof.,
   Medical Oncology
Other Staff: 6 Lectrs.; 23 Res. Assocs./Fellows;
   24 Res. Sisters/Nurses

Human Communication Sciences

Tel: (0114) 222 2418 Fax: (0114) 273 0547
   E-mail: hcs@shef.ac.uk
Brumfitt, S. M., MPhil Sheff.   Sr. Lectr.
Cowell, P. E., BA Boston, MS Conn., PhD Conn.
   Sr. Lectr.
Howard, S. J., BA Leeds, BSc Leeds, MA Leeds, PhD
   Sheff.   Sr. Lectr.
Perkins, M. R., BA Leeds, MA Leeds, PhD Wales
   Prof.
Stackhouse, R. J., BSc Lond., PhD Lond.   Prof.
Varley, R., BSc Newcastle(UK), MA Sheff., PhD
   Sheff.   Reader
Wells, W. H. G., BA Oxf., MA Oxf., DPhil
   York(UK)   Prof.; Head*
Other Staff: 9 Lectrs.; 2 Res. Contract Staff; 2
   Clin. Tutors; 5 Hon. Lectrs.
Research: clinical communication studies;
   language and communication impairment
   in children

Medical Education, Academic Unit of

Tel: (0114) 271 5943 Fax: (0114) 271 4896
   E-mail: g.hible@shef.ac.uk
Bax, N. D. S., BSc Lond., MB BS Lond., PhD
   Sheff., FRCP, FRCPEd   Head*
Stark, P., BA Leeds Met., PhD Leeds   Sr. Lectr.
Other Staff: 3 Academic-Related Staff
Research: assessment of clinical competence;
   clinical teaching; community-based
   education; curriculum management IT
   systems

Molecular Biology and Biotechnology

Tel: (0114) 222 2722 Fax: (0114) 222 2800
   E-mail: mbb@shef.ac.uk
Anderson, R. W., BSc Leic., PhD Leic.   Sr. Lectr.
Artymiuk, P. J., BA Oxf., DPhil Oxf.   Prof.
Bullough, P. A., BSc Lond., PhD Camb.   Prof.
Ford, G. C., BA Oxf., DPhil Oxf.   Reader
Foster, S. J., BSc Liv., PhD Camb.   Prof.
Gilmour, D. J., BSc Glas., PhD Glas.   Sr. Lectr.
Goldman, A. S., BSc Lond., PhD Birm.   Sr. Lectr.
Gray, J. E., BSc Liv., PhD Nott.   Reader
Green, J., BSc Hull, PhD Hull   Reader
Helm, B. A., BSc Lond., PhD Lond.   Sr. Lectr.
Hornby, D. P., BSc Sheff., PhD Sheff.   Prof.
   Assoc.
Horton, P., BA York(UK), DPhil York(UK), DSc
   York(UK)   Prof.
Hunter, C. N., BSc Leic., PhD Brist.   Prof.
Kelly, D. J., BSc Bath, PhD Warw.   Prof.
Moir, A., BSc Aberd., PhD Edin.   Sr. Lectr.

Moore, H. D. M., BSc Reading, PhD Reading
Prof.
Partridge, L. J., BSc Birm., MSc Birm., PhD Birm.
Sr. Lectr.
Piper, P., BSc Brist., PhD Camb. Prof.
Poole, R. K., BSc Wales, PhD Wales, DSc Wales
Prof.
Rafferty, J. B., BSc Sheff., PhD Leeds Reader
Rice, D. W., BA Oxf., DPhil Oxf. Prof.;
Chairman*
Sudbery, P. E., BSc Leic., PhD Leic. Sr. Lectr.
Turner, G., BSc Wales, PhD Wales Prof.
Wainwright, M., BSc Nott., PhD Nott. Sr.
Lectr.
Waltho, J. P., BSc Durh., PhD Camb. Prof.
Watts, D. J., MA Camb., PhD Brist. Sr. Lectr.
Williamson, M. P., BA Camb., PhD Camb. Prof.
Wilson, S. A., BSc Lond., PhD Lond. Sr. Lectr.
Other Staff: 4 Lectrs.; 3 Sr. Experimental
Officers; 2 Independent Res. Workers; 3
Hon. Lectrs.; 3 Hon. Assocs.; 41 Res.
Contract Staff
Research: biomolecular research; biotechnology
and cell culture; molecular cell biology and
development; photosynthesis

NURSING AND MIDWIFERY, SCHOOL OF

Tel: (0114) 222 9711 Fax: (0114) 222 9712
E-mail: m.d.ashton@shef.ac.uk
Watson, R., BSc Edin., PhD Sheff., FIBiol, FRSA
Prof.; Dir., Grad. Sch. of Nursing

Acute and Critical Care Nursing

Hancock, P. K., BEd Hudd., MEd Sheff. Sr.
Nursing Lectr.
Platt, J., BSc CNAA, MSc Sheff. Sr. Nursing
Lectr.
Other Staff: 19 Lectrs.; 26 Nursing Lectrs.; 6
Lectr. Practitioners
Research: ethics; health policy; new nursing
roles; nurse education

Community, Ageing and Rehabilitation

Chilvers, J. R., BSc CNAA, MA Sheff. Sr.
Nursing Lectr.
Davies, S., BSc S'ton., MSc Sur., PhD Sheff. Sr.
Lectr.
Frogatt, K., BSc Durh., PhD S.Bank Sr. Lectr.
Gerrish, K., BN Wales, MSc Manc. Prof.,
Nursing Practice Development
Glossop, D., BA Open(UK), MSc Leeds Met. Sr.
Nursing Lectr.
Harrison, J., BA Open(UK), MMedSci Sheff. Sr.
Nursing Lectr.
Hayter, M., BA Sheff.Hallam, MMedSci Sheff., PhD
Sheff. Sr. Lectr.
Higginbottom, G., MBE, BA Sheff.Hallam, PhD
Sheff.Hallam Sr. Lectr.
Ingleton, C., BEd CNAA, MA Leeds, PhD Sheff.
Reader; Head*
James, J., MA Lond. Sr. Lectr.
Jones, D., OBE, BEd Wales, FRCN Emer. Prof.
Kershaw, B., DBE, MSc Manc., Hon. LLD Manc.,
FRCN Prof.
Marr, A., MA CNAA Sr. Nursing Lectr.
Marvell, G., BA CNAA, MSc Leeds Sr. Nursing
Lectr.
Nolan, M. R., BEd Wales, BSc Wales, MSc Wales,
PhD Wales Prof., Gerontological Nursing
Payne, S., BA Exe., PhD Exe. Prof., Palliative
Care Nursing
Penhale, B., BA Nott., MSc Lond. Sr. Lectr.
Procter, P., MSc Brun. Reader
Salway, S., BA Oxf., MSc Lond., PhD Lond. Sr.
Lectr.
Saverimoutou, J., BA CNAA Sr. Nursing Lectr.
Schofield, K. A., PhD Wales Sr. Lectr.
Seymour, J. E., BA Exe., MA CNAA, PhD Sheff.
Sr. Lectr.
Sykes, P., BSc CNAA Sr. Nursing Lectr.
Winterburn, S., BSc Liv. Sr. Univ. Teacher
Other Staff: 30 Lectrs.; 15 Nursing Lectrs.; 4
Lectr. Practitioners; 1 Res. Practitioner; 10
Researchers
Research: elderly people and carers in different
cultures; health promotion; lay health
beliefs; primary care; public health

Mental Health and Learning Disability

Brooker, C. G. D., BA Lond., MSc City(UK), PhD
Manc. Prof., Mental Health
Bush, J., BA CNAA, MA York(UK) Sr. Nursing
Lectr.
Dowd, C., MSc CNAA Sr. Lectr.
Flynn, M., BA Manc., PhD Manc. Sr. Lectr.
Goward, P., MSc CNAA Sr. Nursing Lectr.
Grant, G. W. B., BSc Manc., MSc UMIST, PhD
UMIST Prof., Cognitive Disability
Martin, C. R., BSc Lond., PhD Sur. Sr. Lectr.
Matanga, R., BSc CNAA, MA Leeds Sr. Nursing
Lectr.
Ramcharan, P., BSc Salf., PhD Manc. Reader
Repper, J. M., BA CNAA, MPhil Nott.Trent, PhD
Manc. Reader
Richardson, M., BEd CNAA, MSc CNAA Sr.
Nursing Lectr.; Head*
Other Staff: 12 Lectrs.; 15 Nursing Lectrs.
Research: advocacy and empowerment; stress,
coping and trauma; suicide; therapeutic
interventions

Midwifery and Child Health Nursing

Blackett, A., BSc Birm., PhD Leeds Sr. Lectr.
Curtis, P., BA CNAA, MA Leeds, PhD Manc. Sr.
Lectr.
Walker, A. J., BEd CNAA Sr. Midwifery Lectr.
Other Staff: 3 Lectrs.; 8 Nursing Lectrs.; 11
Midwifery Lectrs.; 3 Researchers
Research: family trauma; history of midwifery;
neonatal and infant care

SPECIAL CENTRES, ETC

Advanced Electrical Machines and Drives, Rolls-Royce University Technology Centre for

Tel: (0114) 222 5854 Fax: (0114) 222 5196
E-mail: j.gawthorpe@shef.ac.uk
Howe, D., BTech Brad., MSc Brad., PhD S'ton.,
FREng Prof.; Dir.*

Advanced Magnetic Materials and Devices, Sheffield Centre for

Tel: (0114) 222 5467 Fax: (0114) 222 5943
E-mail: c.a.plant@shef.ac.uk
Gibbs, M. R. J., BSc Sheff., PhD Camb., FIP
Dir.*
Other Staff: 1 Deputy Dir.
Research: novel and improved magnetic
materials

Advanced Manufacturing Research Centre

with Boeing
Tel: (0114) 222 1747 Fax: (0114) 222 7678
E-mail: k.ridgway@shef.ac.uk
Allen, A. P., MBA Sheff. Commercial Dir.*
Ridgway, K., OBE, BSc UMIST, MSc Salf., PhD
Manc., FREng Prof.; Res. Dir.*
Other Staff: 1 Chairman; 8 Project Managers;
15 Res. Assocs.
Research: advanced manufacturing for the
aerospace industry and related high
technology industries

Advanced Research in Identification Science, Centre for (ICARIS)

Tel: (0114) 222 5414
E-mail: n.allinson@shef.ac.uk
Allinson, N. M., BEng Brad., MSc Camb., FIEE
Network Co-ordinator*
Research: novel interdisciplinary research in
human identification

Aegean Archaeology, Centre for

Tel: (0114) 222 5103 Fax: (0114) 272 2563
E-mail: archaeology@shef.ac.uk
Bennet, J., BA Camb., MA Camb., PhD Camb.
Prof.; Dir.*

Antibody Resource Centre

Tel: (0114) 222 7480 Fax: (0114) 222 7843
E-mail: arc@shef.ac.uk
Brouwer, G. J., BSc Lond., BVetMed Lond.
Tech. Dir.*

Smith, S., BSc CNAA, PhD Sheff. Tech.
Manager
Research: production of monoclonal antibodies
by biotechnological means

Archaeological Research and Consultancy Service

Tel: (0114) 222 5106 Fax: (0114) 279 7158
E-mail: j.symonds@shef.ac.uk
Symonds, J., BA Sheff., FSA, FRAI Exec. Dir.*
Other Staff: 2 Asst. Dirs.; 7 Advisory Staff
Research: dendrochronology; environmental
science; field services; human remains;
materials science

Arctic Ecology, Sheffield Centre for

Tel: (0114) 222 6102 Fax: (0114) 268 2521
E-mail: t.v.callaghan@shef.ac.uk
Callaghan, T. V., BSc Manc., PhD Birm., DSc
Manc., Hon. FilDr Lund Prof.; Dir.*
Research: Fennoscandian sub-Arctic and high
Arctic Svalbard

Bakhtin Centre

Tel: (0114) 222 7415 Fax: (0114) 222 7416
E-mail: bakhtin.centre@shef.ac.uk
Shepherd, D. G., MA Oxf., PhD Manc. Prof.;
Dir.*
Other Staff: 1 Reader; 2 Hon. Res. Fellows
Research: Bakhtin's work; his circle; related
critical, cultural, linguistic and literary
theory

Bayesian Statistics in Health Economics, Centre for

Tel: (0114) 222 3754 Fax: (0114) 222 3759
E-mail: chebs@shef.ac.uk
O'Hagan, A., BSc Lond., PhD Lond. Dir.*
Other Staff: 1 Res. Assoc.
Research: Bayesian statistical methods for
economic evaluation of health technologies;
design of cost-effectiveness studies;
quantifying uncertainty in cost-effectiveness
analyses and economic models

Bible in the Modern World, Centre for the Study of the

Tel: (0114) 222 0508 Fax: (0114) 222 0507
E-mail: j.c.exum@shef.ac.uk
Exum, J. C., BA Wake Forest, MA Col., MPhil
Col., PhD Col. Prof.; Dir.*
Other Staff: 2 Co-Dirs.; 1 Res. Assoc.
Research: contemporary impact of the Bible

Bioinformatics and Computational Biology, Centre for

Tel: (0114) 222 1832 Fax: (0114) 222 1810
Cannings, C., BSc Lond., PhD Lond. Prof.; Dir.*
Other Staff: 1 Deputy Dir.

Biomaterials and Tissue Engineering, Centre for

Tel: (0114) 222 1832 Fax: (0114) 222 1810
E-mail: r.vannoort@shef.ac.uk
Mac Neil, S., BSc Aberd., PhD Sheff. Prof.; Dir.*
Research: elucidating materials-tissue
interactions; new materials and coatings

Biomolecular Research, The Krebs Institute for

Tel: (0114) 222 2750 Fax: (0114) 222 2850
E-mail: d.rice@shef.ac.uk
Rice, D. W., BA Oxf., DPhil Oxf. Prof.; Dir.*
Research: activity of biological enzymes,
antibodies, gene repressors, hormones

Biotechnological Law and Ethics, Sheffield Institute of (SIBLE)

Tel: (0114) 222 6716 Fax: (0114) 222 6886
E-mail: d.beyleveld@shef.ac.uk
Beyleveld, D., BSc Witw., MA Camb., PhD
E.Anglia Prof.; Dir.*
Other Staff: 1 Asst. Dir.; 2 Deputy Dirs.
Research: ethical and legal issues raised by
developments in biotechnology

Cancer Studies, Institute for

Tel: (0114) 271 2237 Fax: (0114) 271 3515
E-mail: m.meuth@shef.ac.uk
Meuth, M., BSc Purdue, PhD M.I.T.   Dir.*

Catchment Science, Centre for

Tel: (0114) 222 5743 Fax: (0114) 222 5701
E-mail: d.n.lerner@shef.ac.uk
Lerner, D. N., BA Camb., MSc Lond., PhD Birm.,
DSc Birm., FREng, FICE, FGS   Prof.; Dir.*
Research: novel interdisciplinary solutions to
support sustainable management of
freshwater ecosystems

Cement and Concrete, Centre for

Tel: (0114) 222 5065 Fax: (0114) 222 5700
E-mail: k.pilakoutas@shef.ac.uk
Pilakoutas, K., BSc Lond., PhD Lond.   Manager
Waldron, P., BSc Nott., PhD Lond.   Prof.; Dir.*
Other Staff: 1 Manager
Research: durability problems; introduction of
new materials; performance of concrete and
concrete structures

Childhood and Youth, Centre for the Study of

Tel: (0114) 222 6434 Fax: (0114) 276 8125
E-mail: a.p.france@shef.ac.uk
France, A. P., BA Sheff., PhD Sheff.   Dir.*

Cognitive Studies, Hang Seng Centre for

Tel: (0114) 222 0570 Fax: (0114) 222 0588
E-mail: hangseng@shef.ac.uk
Botterill, G., MA Oxf., BPhil Oxf.   Co-Dir.*
Laurence, S., BA Bates, MA Arizona, PhD Rutgers
Co-Dir.*
Research: collaborative research involving
philosophy, psychology and speech science

Control and Systems Engineering, Rolls-Royce University Technology Centre in

Tel: (0114) 222 5233 Fax: (0114) 222 5661
E-mail: p.fleming@shef.ac.uk
Fleming, P. J., BSc Belf., PhD Belf., FIEE   Prof.;
Dir.*
Other Staff: 1 Deputy Dir.; 2 Res. Contract
Staff
Research: control systems and embedded
software

Criminological Research, Centre for

Tel: (0114) 222 6859 Fax: (0114) 222 6832
E-mail: criminology@shef.ac.uk
Norris, C. A., BA Sus., MSc Sur., PhD Sur.
Deputy Dir.
Shapland, J. M., MA Oxf., DPhil Oxf.   Prof.;
Dir.*
Research: criminology and criminal justice

Design, BAe Systems/Rolls-Royce University Technology Partnership for

Tel: (0114) 222 3249 Fax: (0114) 272 7206
E-mail: c.clegg@shef.ac.uk
Clegg, C. W., BA Newcastle(UK), MSc Brad., FBPsS
Dir.*
Research: maximisation of human creativity and
innovation in engineering design processes

Developmental Genetics, Centre for

Including MRC Intercellular Signalling Group

Tel: (0114) 222 2320 Fax: (0114) 276 5413
E-mail: bmsoffice@shef.ac.uk
Ingham, P. W., MA Camb., DPhil Sus., FIBiol,
FRS, FMedSci   Prof.; Dir.*
Other Staff: 1 Lectr.; 1 Sr. Res. Fellow; 1 Sr.
Fellow; 13 Univ. Staff; 1 Clin. Scientific
Fellow
Research: cell signalling; development and
disease; gene expression; organogenesis;
tissue morphogenesis

Dutch Studies, Centre for

Tel: (0114) 222 4919
Vismans, R., BA V.U.Amst., MA Manc., PhD
V.U.Amst.   Dir.*
Research: culture of the Low Countries

Earth Observation Science, Sheffield Centre for

Tel: (0114) 222 3803 Fax: (0114) 222 3809
E-mail: sceos@shef.ac.uk
Quegan, S., BA Warw., MSc Warw., PhD Sheff.
Prof.; Dir.*
Other Staff: 1 Deputy Dir.
Research: theory, methodology, application of
remote sensing

English Cultural Tradition, National Centre for

Tel: (0114) 222 6296 E-mail: j.lowe@shef.ac.uk
Beal, J. C., BA Newcastle(UK), PhD Newcastle(UK)
Dir.*
Other Staff: 1 Asst. Dir.; 1 Archivist
Research: English folklore; modern English usage

European Social and Cultural Studies Centre (ESCUS)

Tel: (0114) 222 6447 Fax: (0114) 222 6133
E-mail: escus@shef.ac.uk
Roche, M. C., BSc(Econ) Lond., PhD Lond.
Dir.*
Research: interdisciplinary research (humanities,
sciences, social sciences)

Freemasonry, Centre for Research into

Tel: (0114) 222 9890 Fax: (0114) 222 9894
E-mail: crf@shef.ac.uk
Prescott, A., BA Lond., PhD Lond.   Prof.; Dir.*
Research: historical, social and cultural impact of
freemasonry

Gender Studies in Europe, Centre for

Tel: (0114) 222 4392 Fax: (0114) 222 2160
E-mail: c.bland@shef.ac.uk
Bland, C., BA Wales, PhD Wales   Lectr.; Dir.*
Research: gender issues in European context

Glass Research, Centre for

Tel: (0114) 222 5467 Fax: (0114) 222 5943
E-mail: p.f.james@shef.ac.uk
Hand, R. J., MA Camb., MEd Sheff., PhD Camb.
Co-Dir.*
Parker, J. M., MA Camb., PhD Camb., FIMMM
Co-Dir.*
Research: coatings; photonic glasses; predictive
modelling of glass properties

Health Information Management Research, Centre for

Tel: (0114) 222 2636 Fax: (0114) 278 0300
E-mail: p.a.bath@shef.ac.uk
Bath, P. A., BSc Wales, MSc Sheff., PhD Sheff.
Acting Dir.*
Other Staff: 1 Deputy Dir.
Research: information-related activities of
National Health Service purchasers,
providers and consumers

Humanities Research Institute

Tel: (0114) 222 9890 Fax: (0114) 222 9894
E-mail: hri@shef.ac.uk
Greengrass, M., BA Oxf., DPhil Oxf., FRHistS,
FSA   Prof.; Dir.*
Other Staff: 13 Res. Staff
Research: application of new technology to text-
and image-based research

III-V Semiconductors, EPSRC Central Facility for

Tel: (0114) 222 5180 Fax: (0114) 272 5413
E-mail: c.e.potts@shef.ac.uk
Houston, P. A., BSc Strath., PhD Strath., FIEE
Prof.; Co-Dir.*
Skolnik, M. S., BA Oxf., DPhil Oxf.   Prof.; Co-
Dir.*

Other Staff: 3 Sr. Res. Scientists; 8 Res. Assocs.;
1 RAE Res. Fellow; 3 Other Academic Staff
Research: next-generation III-V semiconductor
materials and devices

Immobilisation Science Laboratory

Tel: (0114) 222 6028 Fax: (0114) 222 5943
E-mail: j.w.roberts@shef.ac.uk
Milestone, N. B., BSc Well., MSc Well., PhD
Well., DSc Well., FNZIC   Acting Dir.*
Other Staff: 1 Tech. Manager
Research: immobilisation of radioactive and toxic
waste streams

Informatics Collaboratory for Social Sciences (ICOSS)

Tel: (0114) 222 8340 Fax: (0114) 222 8341
E-mail: icoss@shef.ac.uk
Beaulieu, M., BA McM., PhD City(UK), FCLIP
Prof.; Dir.*
Other Staff: 5 Res. Leaders
Research: social science research to inform social
policy

International Drylands Research, Sheffield Centre for

Tel: (0114) 222 7900 Fax: (0114) 279 7912
E-mail: d.s.thomas@shef.ac.uk
Bateman, M. D., BSc Lond., DPhil Sus.   Acting
Dir.*
Research: past, present and future environmental
changes in drylands

Kroto Research Institute

Tel: (0114) 222 7445 Fax: (0114) 222 5701
E-mail: george.rees@shef.ac.uk
Tomlinson, G. R., BSc Aston, MSc Aston, PhD
Salf., DSc Manc., FREng, FIMechE, FRSA,
FRAeS   Prof.; Dir.*
Other Staff: 1 Business Devel. Manager
Research: multidisciplinary research
(environmental engineering, future
generation materials, nanotechnology, tissue
engineering)

Language, Speech and Hearing, Institute of

Tel: (0114) 222 1800 Fax: (0114) 222 1810
E-mail: ilash@dcs.shef.ac.uk
Wilks, Y., BA Camb., MA Camb., PhD Camb.
Prof.; Dir.*
Research: artificial intelligence; auditory
modelling; computational psychology;
natural language processing; neural
networks

Leisure Industries Research Centre

Tel: (0114) 222 2186 Fax: (0114) 222 3348
E-mail: leisure.mgt@shef.ac.uk
Gratton, C., BA Manc., MA Manc., PhD Manc.
Prof.; Co-Dir.*
Taylor, P. D., BA Warw., MA Leeds, MBA CNAA
Co-Dir.*
Research: nature of competitive advantage in
leisure industries

Luxembourg Studies, Centre for

Tel: (0114) 222 4396 Fax: (0114) 222 2160
E-mail: g.newton@shef.ac.uk
Newton, G., BA Liv., PhD Liv.   Prof.; Dir.*
Research: language and literature of Luxembourg

Materials Damping Technology, Rolls-Royce University Technology Centre in

Tel: (0114) 222 7882 Fax: (0114) 222 7890
E-mail: g.balikhin@shef.ac.uk
Tomlinson, G. R., BSc Aston, MSc Aston, PhD
Salf., DSc Manc., FREng, FIMechE, FRSA,
FRAeS   Prof.; Dir.*
Other Staff: 1 Deputy Dir.; 1 Sr. Researcher
Research: adhesives; hard ceramic coatings; novel
damping materials; viscoelastic materials
applications

Microstructural and Mechanical Process Engineering, Institute for (IMMPETUS)

Tel: (0114) 222 6018 Fax: (0114) 222 6015
E-mail: immpetus@shef.ac.uk
Rainforth, W. M., BMet *Sheff.*, PhD *Leeds*   Prof.; Dir.*
Research: process planning and control; steels, aluminium and nickel-based alloys

Nineteenth-Century Studies, Centre for

Tel: (0114) 222 4396 Fax: (0114) 222 2160
E-mail: m.f.perraudin@shef.ac.uk
Perraudin, M. F., MA *Camb.*, PhD *Birm.*   Prof.; Dir.
Research: Europe and America, 1789-1914

Political Economy Research Centre

Tel: (0114) 222 0660 Fax: (0114) 222 1717
E-mail: perc@shef.ac.uk
Harrison, G., BSc *Lond.*, MA *Leeds*, PhD *Staffs.*   Co-Dir.*
Ludlam, S. G. P., BA *Sheff.*, PhD *Sheff.*   Co-Dir.*
Other Staff: 1 Deputy Dir.; 1 Researcher
Research: current transformation of the world economy

Political Parties, Institute for the Study of

Tel: (0114) 222 1702 Fax: (0114) 222 1717
E-mail: c.s.j.lees@shef.ac.uk
Lees, C. S. J., BA *Thames V.*, MA *Essex*, PhD *Birm.*   Dir.*

Political Theories and Ideologies, Centre for

Tel: (0114) 222 1691 Fax: (0114) 273 9769
E-mail: politics@shef.ac.uk
Vincent, A. W., BA *Exe.*, PhD *Manc.*   Prof.; Dir.*
Research: changing role and nature of ideologies in politics; ideological framework for formulating public policies; political ideologies in political studies

Public Library and Information in Society, Centre for

Tel: (0114) 222 2653 Fax: (0114) 278 0300
E-mail: b.train@shef.ac.uk
Train, B., BA *Hull*, MA *Sheff.*   Dir.*
Other Staff: 1 Prof.; 1 Res. Assoc.
Research: public library services

Robert Hill Institute

Tel: (0114) 222 4189 Fax: (0114) 272 8697
E-mail: p.horton@shef.ac.uk
Horton, P., BA *York(UK)*, DPhil *York(UK)*, DSc *York(UK)*   Dir.*
Research: photosynthesis in plants and micro-organisms

Sheffield Polymer Centre

Tel: (0114) 222 9537 Fax: (0114) 222 9346
E-mail: polymers@shef.ac.uk
Hunt, B. J., MSc *Lanc.*, PhD *Lanc.*   Asst. Dir.
Ryan, A. J., OBE, BSc *Manc.*, PhD *Manc.*   Prof.; Dir.*
Other Staff: 1 Gen. Manager; 3 Assoc. Dirs.
Research: applications of polymers in high technology areas; polymer science and engineering

Sheffield University Waste Incineration Centre (SUWIC)

Tel: (0114) 222 7518 Fax: (0114) 222 7501
E-mail: v.n.sharifi@shef.ac.uk
Sharifi, V. N., BEng *Sheff.*, PhD *Sheff.*   Dir.
Swithenbank, J., BSc *Birm.*, PhD *Sheff.*, FREng   Chairman*
Research: new techniques for controlling pollutant from incinerators

Signal Processing in Neuroimaging and Systems Neuroscience, Centre for (SPiNSN)

Tel: (0114) 222 6511 Fax: (0114) 276 6515
Zheng, Y., BEng *Sheff.*, PhD *Sheff.*   Dir.*
Other Staff: 2 Co-Dirs.
Research: signal processing and data analysis

South East Europe Research Centre

Tel: (30) 2310 253477 Fax: (30) 2310 253478
Deacon, B., BSc *Lond.*, MPhil *Kent*   Assoc. Prof.; Assoc. Dir.
Strong, D., BSc *Boston*, MSc *Boston*, PhD *Boston*   Dir.*
Research: support of stable and peaceful development of South East Europe

Steel Construction, Academy for

Tel: (0114) 222 0303 Fax: (0114) 279 8276
E-mail: r.j.plank@shef.ac.uk
Plank, R. J., BSc *Birm.*, PhD *Birm.*   Head*
Research: connections; environmental issues; fire engineering

Stem Cell Biology, Centre for

Tel: (0114) 222 1082
E-mail: stemcell@shef.ac.uk
Andrews, P. W., BSc *Leeds*, DPhil *Oxf.*   Prof.; Co-Dir.*
Moore, H. D. M., BSc *Reading*, PhD *Reading*   Prof.; Co-Dir.*
Research: stem cell technology

Terrestrial Carbon Dynamics, Centre for

Tel: (0114) 222 3803 Fax: (0114) 222 3809
E-mail: ctcd@shef.ac.uk
Quegan, S., BA *Warw.*, MSc *Warw.*, PhD *Sheff.*   Dir.*
Woodward, F. I., BA *Camb.*, MA *Camb.*, PhD *Lanc.*, FLS   Prof.; Deputy Dir.
Research: analysis of carbon cycle uncertainty; carbon budget, land ecosystems and satellite biomass data and climate change

Underground Science, Institute for

Tel: (0114) 222 4351 Fax: (0114) 222 3555
Spooner, N. J. C., BSc *S'ton.*, PhD *Lond.*   Dir.*
Research: dark matter and neutrino physics at the Boulby underground laboratory

Urban and Regional Policy Research Institute

Tel: (0114) 222 7900 Fax: (0114) 279 7912
E-mail: h.armstrong@shef.ac.uk
Armstrong, H. W., BA *Sheff.*, MA *Lond.*   Co-Dir.*
Henneberry, J. M., MA *Camb.*, MA *Sheff.*, FRICS   Co-Dir.*
Research: contemporary regional and urban policy analysis

Well-being in Public Policy, Centre for

Tel: (0114) 222 5454 Fax: (0114) 272 4095
E-mail: wellbeing@shef.ac.uk
Dolan, P. H. R., BSc *Wales(Swansea)*, MSc *York(UK)*, DPhil *York(UK)*

Work Psychology, Institute of

Tel: (0114) 222 3271 Fax: (0114) 272 7206
E-mail: iwp@shef.ac.uk
Clegg, C. W., BA *Newcastle(UK)*, MSc *Brad.*, FBPsS   Prof.; Deputy Dir.
Wall, T. D., BA *Nott.*, PhD *Nott.*, FBPsS   Prof.; Dir.*
Warr, P. B., MA *Camb.*, PhD *Sheff.*, FBPsS   Emer. Prof.
Wood, S. J., BSc *Aston*, PhD *Manc.*   Prof.; Deputy Dir.
Other Staff: 16 Res. Contract Staff
Research: psychological causes of effectiveness and mental health at work

Workplace Health, Centre for

Tel: (0129) 821 8447 E-mail: cwh@hsl.gov.uk
Fishwick, D., MB ChB *Manc.*, MD *Manc.*, FRCP   Dir.*

CONTACT OFFICERS

Academic affairs. Academic Secretary: O'Donovan, J. B., BSc *Lond.*, MSc *Newcastle(UK)*, PhD *Newcastle(UK)* (E-mail: academic.sec@shef.ac.uk)
Accommodation. Director, Accommodation and Campus Services: McGrath, P. A., MBA *Sheff.Hallam* (E-mail: c.elliss@shef.ac.uk)
Admissions (first degree). Director (Admissions): Kingston, A., BA *Essex*, MSc *Lond.* (E-mail: study@shef.ac.uk)
Admissions (higher degree). Director (Admissions): Kingston, A., BA *Essex*, MSc *Lond.*
Adult/continuing education. Director, Institute for Lifelong Learning: Webb, Prof. S. C., BA *Leic.*, PhD *Manc.* (E-mail: till@shef.ac.uk)
Alumni. Director of Development and Alumni Relations Office: Stevenson, M. R., BA *Durh.*, MA *Durh.* (E-mail: development@shef.ac.uk)
Archives. Records Officer: Zawadzki, M. B., BSc *Wales* (E-mail: m.zawadzki@shef.ac.uk)
Careers. Director of Careers Service: Fish, S. J., BSc *Brad.* (E-mail: a.hutchinson@shef.ac.uk)
Computing services. Head of Corporate Information and Computing Services: Sexton, C. E., BSc *Sheff.*, PhD *Sheff.* (E-mail: cics@shef.ac.uk)
Conferences/corporate hospitality. Director, Accommodation and Campus Services: McGrath, P. A., MBA *Sheff.Hallam* (E-mail: l.j.carroll@shef.ac.uk)
Equal opportunities. Director of Human Resource Management: Valerio, R. A., BA *Sheff.*
Estates and buildings/works and services. Director of Estates: Cameron, N., BSc *Strath.*, BArch *Strath.* (E-mail: estates-help@shef.ac.uk)
Examinations. Head of Registry Services: Hall, E. J., BA *Sheff.* (E-mail: j.hardy@shef.ac.uk)
Finance. Director of Finance: Rabone, R., BSc *Lond.* (E-mail: finance@shef.ac.uk)
General enquiries. Registrar and Secretary: Fletcher, D. E., BA *Sheff.*, PhD *Sheff.*
Health services. Director of University Health Service: King, J. A., MB ChB *Sheff.* (E-mail: health.service@shef.ac.uk)
Industrial liaison. Director of Business Development Services: Handscombe, R. D., BSc *Lond.*, PhD *Lond.* (E-mail: r.d.handscombe@shef.ac.uk)
International office. Director of International Office: Wells, G., MA *Leic.*, BA (E-mail: international@shef.ac.uk)
Language training for international students. Director, English Language Teaching Centre: Gresham, J. D., BA *Lond.*, MA *Leeds* (E-mail: elt@shef.ac.uk)
Library (chief librarian). Librarian: Lewis, M. J., MA *Camb.* (E-mail: library@shef.ac.uk)
Marketing. Head of Marketing: Chafer, J., BSc *Brad.* (E-mail: marketing@shef.ac.uk)
Minorities/disadvantaged groups. Assistant Director: Green, D. G. M., BEd *Lond.*, MEd *Wales* (E-mail: m.g.evans@shef.ac.uk)
Personnel/human resources. Director of Human Resource Management: Valerio, R. A., BA *Sheff.* (E-mail: hr-enq@shef.ac.uk)
Public relations. Director of Public Relations: Pyle, J. C., BA *Manc.*, MA *Manc.*, MA *Sheff.* (E-mail: j.pyle@shef.ac.uk)
Publications. Publications Manager: Fylan, E. M. M., BA *Birm.* (E-mail: marcoms@shef.ac.uk)
Purchasing. Director of Procurement: South, S. L. (E-mail: procurement@shef.ac.uk)
Research. Head (Research): Fulton, S., BA *Sheff.* (E-mail: research.office@shef.ac.uk)
Safety. Director of Safety Services: Thomas, D. G., BSc *Wales* (E-mail: safety@shef.ac.uk)

Schools liaison. Head of Outreach and Access: Fowler, D., BA Humb.
(E-mail: d.fowler@shef.ac.uk)

Security. Head of Security: Mole, B. L.
(E-mail: a.j.morton@shef.ac.uk)

Sport and recreation. Director of Sport and Recreation Services: Baker, T., BEd Lond., MSc U.S.Sports Acad.
(E-mail: l.murphy@shef.ac.uk)

Staff development and training. Senior Human Resources Adviser: Beesley, J., BA Hull (E-mail: sdu.places@shef.ac.uk)

Strategic planning. Head, Corporate Planning Office: Baines, C. E., BSc CNAA, PhD Nott.

Student union. Manager (Student Union): Blomfield, P. (E-mail: union@shef.ac.uk)

Student welfare/counselling. Director of Student Services: West, A., BA Manc., PhD Manc. (E-mail: s.ibbotson@shef.ac.uk)

Student welfare/counselling. Associate Director of University Counselling Service: Phillips, A., BA Hull, MA Lanc.
(E-mail: ucs@shef.ac.uk)

Students from other countries. Assistant Director: Green, D. G. M., BEd Lond., MEd Wales
(E-mail: international.students@shef.ac.uk)

Students with disabilities. Assistant Director: Green, D. G. M., BEd Lond., MEd Wales
(E-mail: m.g.evans@shef.ac.uk)

Women. Director of Human Resource Management: Valerio, R. A., BA Sheff.
(E-mail: hr-enq@shef.ac.uk)

[Information supplied by the institution as at 20 November 2007, and edited by the ACU]

SHEFFIELD HALLAM UNIVERSITY

Founded 1992

Member of the Association of Commonwealth Universities

Postal Address: City Campus, Howard Street, Sheffield, England S1 1WB
Telephone: (0114) 225 5555 **Fax:** (0114) 225 3398
URL: http://www.shu.ac.uk

VICE-CHANCELLOR*—Jones, Prof. Philip A., LLM Lond., MA Essex
PRO-VICE-CHANCELLOR (ACADEMIC DEVELOPMENT)—Hawkes, Prof. Colin, BSc PhD
PRO-VICE-CHANCELLOR (RESEARCH AND BUSINESS DEVELOPMENT)—Anderson, Prof. Bob, BSc MA PhD
UNIVERSITY SECRETARY‡—Colson, Tom
DIRECTOR OF FINANCE—Severs, Philip

UNIVERSITY OF SOUTHAMPTON

Founded 1952

Member of the Association of Commonwealth Universities

Postal Address: Highfield, Southampton, England SO17 1BJ
Telephone: (023) 8059 5000 **Fax:** (023) 8059 3939
URL: http://www.soton.ac.uk

VICE-CHANCELLOR*—Wakeham, Prof. William A., BSc Exe., PhD Exe., DSc Exe., FREng, FIP, FIChemE, FIEE
DEPUTY VICE-CHANCELLOR—Nelson, Prof. Philip A., BSc S'ton., PhD S'ton.
DEPUTY VICE-CHANCELLOR—Thomas, Prof. Caroline, BSc(Econ) Lond., PhD Lond.
SENIOR DEPUTY VICE-CHANCELLOR—Wheeler, Prof. Adam A., BSc E.Anglia, PhD E.Anglia
REGISTRAR AND CHIEF OPERATING OFFICER‡—Higman, Simon
DIRECTOR OF FINANCE—Ace, Malcolm J., MA Oxf.

GENERAL INFORMATION

History. The university's origins date from 1862 when the Hartley Institution was founded in central Southampton, the result of a benefaction by local philanthropist Henry Robinson Hartley. Renamed Hartley University College, it moved to the present Highfield Campus in 1919, and was granted its charter in 1952. The university merged with Winchester School of Art in 1996, with La Sainte Union College in 1997 and with the Textile Conservation Centre in 1998.

Admission to first degree courses (see also United Kingdom Introduction). Through Universities and Colleges Admissions Services (UCAS). Candidates with current UK qualifications must satisfy the relevant faculty and specific course requirements. Certain non-UK qualifications are acceptable including: Irish Leaving Certificate, International Baccalaureate, European Baccalaureate, etc. Mature candidates not possessing any formal qualifications may be admitted provided they

can submit evidence of previous serious study and demonstrate the capacity to pursue the proposed course. Candidates whose first language is not English must reach a satisfactory standard in an approved test in English.

First Degrees (see also United Kingdom Directory to Subjects of Study). BA, BEng, BM, BMid, BN, BSc, LLB, MEng, MMath, MPhys.
Length of course. Full-time: BEng, BMid, BN: 3 years; BA, BSc, LLB: 3–4 years; MEng, MMath, MPhys: 4 years; BM: 5 years. Part-time: BMid, BN: 5 years; BA, BSc: 5–8 years.

Higher Degrees (see also United Kingdom Directory to Subjects of Study).
Master's. LLM, MA, MA(Ed), MBA, MMaths, MMus, MPhil, MRes, MSc, MSc(Ed).
Admission. Applicants for admission to master's degrees must normally hold an appropriate first degree with at least second class honours.
Length of course. Full-time: LLM, MA, MA(Ed), MBA, MMus, MRes, MSc, MSc(Ed): 1 year;

MPhil: 3 years; MMaths: 4 years. Part-time: LLM, MA, MA(Ed), MBA, MMus, MRes, MSc, MSc(Ed): 2 years; MPhil: 5 years.
Doctoral. DBA, DCP, DEd, DL, DLitt, DM, DMus, DSc, LLD, PhD.
Admission. PhD: appropriate master's degree.
Length of course. Full-time: DM, DSc, LLD: 2 years; DCP, PhD: 3 years; DBA, DEd, DL: 4 years. Part-time: DSc, LLD: 3 years; DM: 4 years; DBA, DCP, DEd, DL, PhD: 6 years.

Language of Instruction. English. Intensive remedial courses available prior to the beginning of each academic year.

Libraries. Volumes: 1,690,000. Periodicals subscribed to: 6500. Special collections: Ford (official papers); Hartley (military, political, official and diplomatic papers, including those of the first Duke of Wellington, third Viscount Palmerston and Earl Mountbatten of Burma); National Oceanographic Library (marine science); Parkes (material relating to Jewish communities, Anglo-Jewish archive collections).

Academic Year (2007–2008). Two semesters: 4 October–2 February; 3 February–21 June. Summer session: 23 June–3 October.

Income (2005–2006). Total, £310,608,000.

Statistics. Staff (2005–2006): 4991 (2300 academic, 2691 non-academic). Students (2005–2006): full-time 17,818; part-time 4352; international 2412; undergraduate 16,679; master's 3559; doctoral 1932.

FACULTIES/SCHOOLS

Engineering, Science and Mathematics

Tel: (023) 8059 4184 Fax: (023) 8059 4182
E-mail: cp8@soton.ac.uk
Dean: Kilburn, Prof. Jeremy D., MA Camb., PhD Camb.

Law, Arts and Social Sciences

Tel: (023) 8059 3265 Fax: (023) 8059 8540
E-mail: mmurphy@soton.ac.uk
Dean: Foskett, Prof. N. H., MA Oxf., PhD

Medicine, Health and Life Sciences

Tel: (023) 8059 6702 Fax: (023) 8059 4481
E-mail: rmt@soton.ac.uk
Dean: Williams, Prof. David M., MSc PhD

ACADEMIC UNITS

Archaeology

Avenue Campus

Tel: (023) 8059 4439 Fax: (023) 8059 3032
E-mail: arch@soton.ac.uk
Adams, Jonathan R., BA Durh., DPhil Stockholm Reader
Arnold, Dana R., BA Lond., MSc Lond., PhD Lond., FRSA Prof.
Champion, Timothy C., MA Oxf., DPhil Oxf., FSA Prof.
Curry, Anne, FRHistS Prof.
Dix, Justin, MA PhD Sr. Lectr.
Hamilakis, Y., BA Crete, MSc Sheff., PhD Sheff. Sr. Lectr.
Hinton, David A., MA Oxf., FSA Prof.
Johnson, M. H., MA PhD, FSA Prof.; Head of Discipline*
Keay, Simon J., BA Lond., PhD Lond. Prof.
Leech, Roger H., MA Brist., PhD Brist. Visiting Prof.
Marshall, Yvonne M., BA Otago, MA Auck., PhD S.Fraser Sr. Lectr.
McGrail, Sean, BA Brist., MA Oxf., PhD Lond., DSc Oxf., FSA Visiting Prof.
Moser, Stephanie A., BA PhD Prof.
Peacock, David P. S., BSc St And., PhD St And., FSA Emer. Prof.
Sofaer, J. R., BA PhD Sr. Lectr.
Sparkes, Brian A., BA Lond., PhD Lond. Emer. Prof.
Wheatley, David W., BSc Wales, MSc S'ton., PhD S'ton. Sr. Lectr.
Other Staff: 12 Lectrs.; 2 Res. Fellows; 2 Visiting Fellows
Research: applied archaeological analysis; archaeology of hominid evolution; art and representation; cultural and economic integration in the Roman world; maritime archaeology and coastal communities

Art, School of

Winchester Campus

Fax: (023) 8059 6901
E-mail: artsrec@soton.ac.uk
Makhoul, Bashir, BA MA PhD Prof.; Head*

Contemporary Studies

Hon, Gordon, BA MRes Lectr.; Head of Subject Area*

Fine Art

Tel: (023) 8059 6985
E-mail: n.j.sweed@soton.ac.uk
Cooper, Stephen, BA MA Head of Subject Area*

Daniel, Marko, BA MA PhD Sr. Lectr.; Dir., Grad. Sch.
Ferry, David, BA CNAA, FRSA Sr. Lectr.
Gibbons, John, BA CNAA Prof.; Deputy Head of Sch., Res.
Harland, Beth, BA RCA, MA RCA Sr. Lectr.; Dir., MA Studies
Huddleston, Rob, MA RCA Deputy Head of Sch., Collaborative
Taylor, Brandon, BA Brist., MLitt Edin., PhD Lond. Prof.
Whittaker, Paul, BA RCA, MA RCA, PhD RCA Sr. Lectr.; Deputy Head of Sch., Educn.
Other Staff: 5 Lectrs.
Research: commitment to visual cultural research in its broadest terms; creative integrity of the individual; development of cross-disciplinary research projects; individual research projects at international and national level; studio-based PhD programmes

Graphic Arts

D'Souza, Ed, MA Programme Leader*
Other Staff: 2 Lectrs.

Textile Conservation Centre

Tel: (023) 8059 7100 Fax: (023) 8059 7101
E-mail: tccuk@soton.ac.uk
Brooks, Mary, MA Camb. Reader
Eastop, Diana, BA MA Sr. Lectr.
Hayward, Maria, BA MA PhD Reader; Head of Subject Area*
Hoare, Nell, MBE, BA S'ton. Dir.*
Rowe, Amber, BA Head, Conservation Services
Wyeth, Paul, MA Camb., PhD Sr. Lectr.
Other Staff: 4 Lectrs.; 3 Res. Fellows; 1 Sr. Conservator; 4 Conservators
Research: conservation science including deterioration of fibres; interventive and preventative conservation; modern textile materials including smart and techno fibres; object-based research (English pre-Reformation textiles, English seventeenth-century embroidery)

Textiles

Tel: (023) 8059 6966
Hemmings, Jessica, BA MA PhD Programme Leader
Padovani, Clio, BA RCA, MA RCA Sr. Lectr.; Dir., Undergrad. Studies
Other Staff: 7 Lectrs.

Biological Sciences

Tel: (023) 8059 7747 Fax: (023) 8059 7779
E-mail: mas2@soton.ac.uk
Shepherd, D., BSc Manc., PhD UMIST Prof.; Head*

Biochemistry and Molecular Biology

Tel: (023) 8059 4338 Fax: (023) 8059 4459
E-mail: biochem@soton.ac.uk
Akhtar, M., MSc Punjab, PhD Lond., FRS Emer. Prof.
Anthony, C., PhD Reading, DSc Reading Emer. Prof.
Barton, C. H., BSc Nott., PhD Sheff. Reader
Cooper, J. B., BSc PhD Reader
East, J. M., BSc CNAA, PhD Open(UK) Reader
Fox, K. R., MA Camb., PhD Camb. Prof.; Head*
Gore, M. G., BSc Wales, PhD E.Anglia Prof.
Keevil, C. W., BSc Birm., PhD Birm. Prof.
Lee, A. G., MA Camb., PhD Camb. Prof.
O'Connor, C. D., MSc Lond., PhD Liv. Prof.
O'Connor, Vincent M., BSc Reading, PhD Lond. Sr. Lectr.
Sale, G. J., BSc S'ton., PhD S'ton. Sr. Lectr.
Shoolingin-Jordan, P. M., PhD S'ton., FRSChem Prof.
Smyth, N., BVSc PhD Reader
Terry, Matthew J., BSc PhD Sr. Lectr.
Wilton, D. C., BSc S'ton., PhD S'ton. Prof.
Wood, S. P., BSc Wales, DPhil Sus. Prof.

Research: mechanistic enzymology; membrane structure and function; molecular cell biology; nucleic acid sequence recognition; protein structure and function

Biodiversity and Ecology

Tel: (023) 8059 4341 Fax: (023) 8059 4559
E-mail: ecology@soton.ac.uk
Allen, J. A., BSc Edin., PhD Edin. Sr. Lectr.; Head of Discipline and Dir, Educn.*
Doncaster, C. P., BSc E.Anglia, DPhil Oxf. Sr. Lectr.
Goulson, D., BA Oxf., PhD Oxf.Brookes Reader
Jackson, Chris W., BSc Wales, PhD Lond. Sr. Lectr.
Maclean, N., BSc Edin., PhD Edin., FIBiol Emer. Prof.
Poppy, G. M., BSc Lond., DPhil Oxf., FIBiol p
Restartits, William, BA MA MS PhD Reader
Sleigh, M. A., PhD Brist., DSc Brist., FIBiol Emer. Prof.
Taylor, G., BSc Lanc., PhD Lanc. Prof.
Research: biodiversity and ecology from an evolutionary perspective and in applied environmental research; organisms from the individual to the community

Cell Sciences

Tel: (023) 8059 4431 Fax: (023) 8059 4459
E-mail: cellsci@soton.ac.uk
Chad, J. E., BSc S'ton., PhD S'ton. Sr. Lectr.
Dixon, M. S., BSc Sus., PhD Lond. Sr. Lectr.
Fleming, T. P., BSc Wales, PhD CNAA Prof.
Hall, J. L., BSc Lond., DPhil Oxf. Emer. Prof.
Holden-Dye, L. M., BSc Wales, PhD S'ton. Prof.
Newland, P. L., BSc Glas., PhD Glas. Reader
Perry, V. H., BA Oxf., MA Oxf., DPhil Oxf. Prof.
Shepherd, D., BSc Manc., PhD UMIST Prof.; Head*
Walker, R. J., PhD S'ton., DSc, FIBiol Emer. Prof.
Wheal, H. V., BSc S'ton., PhD S'ton. Prof.
Williams, Lorraine E., BSc Bath, PhD S'ton. Sr. Lectr.
Other Staff: 10 Lectrs.; 40 Res. Fellows
Research: genes and development (drosophila neurogenesis, epithelial differentiation, mammalian blastocyst); neuroscience (calcium imaging, caenorhabditis elegans neuromuscular model, central nervous system neuroinflammation, epilepsy); plant cell biology (lignification, membrane transport, pathogen resistance, phytochromes); receptor pharmacology (immunopharmacology, peptide receptors, proteinase inhibitors, pulmonary disease)

Chemistry

Tel: (023) 8059 3333 Fax: (023) 8059 3781
E-mail: chem@soton.ac.uk
Attard, George S., BSc Warw., PhD S'ton. Prof.
Bartlett, Philip N., BA Oxf., PhD Lond., FRSChem Prof.; Deputy Head, Res.
Birkin, P. R., BSc PhD Sr. Lectr.
Brown, R. C. D., BSc PhD Sr. Lectr.
Brown, Tom, BTech Brad., PhD Brad. Prof.
Danopoulos, Andreas A., BSc Athens, PhD Athens Prof.
Denuault, Guy, MST Bordeaux, PhD S'ton. Sr. Lectr.
Dyke, John M., BSc Wales, PhD Brist., FRSChem Prof.
Essex, Jonathon W., BA Oxf., MA Oxf., DPhil Oxf. Reader
Evans, John, BSc Lond., PhD Camb. Prof.; Head*
Frey, Jeremy G., MA Oxf., DPhil Oxf. Prof.
Gale, P. A., MA DPhil, FRSChem Prof.
Ganesan, A., BSc NU Singapore, PhD Calif. Reader
Grossel, Martin C., BSc Lond., MA Oxf., PhD Lond. Prof.
Harrowven, David C., BSc S'ton., PhD S'ton. Prof.
Hayden, Brian E., BSc Brist., PhD Brist. Prof.
Howard, Alan G., BSc Brist., MSc Brist., PhD Brist. Sr. Lectr.

Hursthouse, Michael B., BSc *Lond.*, PhD *Lond.*
  Prof.
Kilburn, Jeremy D., MA *Camb.*, PhD *Camb.*
  Prof.
Levason, William, BSc *Manc.*, PhD *Manc.*   Prof.
Levitt, Malcolm H., DPhil *Oxf.*, BA   Prof.
Linclau, B., Lic PhD   Sr. Lectr.
Luckhurst, Geoffrey R., BSc *Hull*, PhD *Camb.*
  Emer. Prof.
Ogden, J. Steven, MA *Camb.*, PhD *Camb.*
  Reader
Owen, John R., BSc *Lond.*, PhD *Lond.*   Prof.
Pletcher, Derek, BSc *Sheff.*, PhD *Sheff.*   Prof.
Raja, R., MSc PhD   Sr. Lectr.
Reid, Gillian, BSc *Edin.*, PhD *Edin.*   Prof.
Russell, A. E., BSc *Mich.*, PhD *Utah*   Prof.
Turner, David L., MA *Oxf.*, DPhil *Oxf.*   Reader
Weller, Mark T., MA *Oxf.*, DPhil *Oxf.*   Prof.
Whitby, Richard J., BA *Camb.*, PhD *Leeds*   Prof.
Other Staff: 8 Lectrs.; 1 Royal Society Res.
  Fellow; 51 Res. Fellows; 14 Visiting Profs.;
  5 Visiting Lectrs.; 5 Visiting Res. Fellows
Research: atmospheric chemistry; biological and
  biophysical chemistry; electrochemistry;
  structural chemistry; synthetic organic
  chemistry

Civil Engineering and the Environment

Tel: (023) 8059 4651 Fax: (023) 8067 7519
  E-mail: civilenv@soton.ac.uk
Bahaj, A. S., BSc *S'ton.*, PhD *S'ton.*   Prof.
Banks, C. J., BSc *Salf.*, DPhil *York(UK)*   Prof.
Butterfield, R., BSc(Eng) *Lond.*, DSc *S'ton.*
  Emer. Prof.
Chaplin, J. R., BSc *Brist.*, PhD *Brist.*, FICE   Prof.
Clayton, C. R. I., BSc *Lond.*, MSc *Lond.*, PhD *Sur.*,
  FICE   Prof.
Haq, N., BSc *Rajsh.*, MSc *Rajsh.*, PhD *S'ton.*   Sr.
  Lectr.
Hounsell, N. B., BSc *Aston*, MSc *S'ton.*, PhD *S'ton.*
  Reader
Lee, M. M. K., JP, BSc *Birm.*, PhD *Birm.*   Prof.
McDonald, M., BSc *Newcastle(UK)*, PhD *S'ton.*
  Prof.
Moy, S. S. J., BSc *Nott.*, PhD *Nott.*   Prof.
Muller, G., PhD   Sr. Lectr.
Nicholls, R. J., BSc *S'ton.*, PhD *S'ton.*   Prof.;
  Dir., Res.
Osborne, P. E., BSc DPhil   Sr. Lectr.
Powrie, W., MA *Camb.*, MSc *Lond.*, PhD *Camb.*,
  FICE   Prof.; Head*
Preston, J. M., BA PhD   Prof., Rail Transport
Richards, D. J., BEng *Lond.*, PhD *Lond.*   Sr.
  Lectr.
Shaw, Peter S., BSc MSc PhD   Sr. Lectr.
Tanton, T. W., BSc *Hull*, PhD *S'ton.*   Prof.
Williams, I. D., BSc PhD   Sr. Lectr.; Dir.,
  Educn.
Other Staff: 13 Lectrs.; 9 Sr. Res. Fellows; 27
  Res. Fellows; 6 Visiting Profs.; 1 Sr. Lectr.†
Research: coastal engineering; geotechnics;
  hydraulics; transportation; waste
  management

Education

Tel: (023) 8059 3475 Fax: (023) 8059 3556
  E-mail: educate@soton.ac.uk
Bhatti, Ghazala, BA MA PhD   Sr. Lectr.
Bhopal, Kalwant, BA MSc PhD   Reader
Bourne, Jill M., BA *Liv.*, PhD *S'ton.*   Prof.; Dep.
  Head, Res.
Clarke, Gill, MBE, BEd MA(Ed) PhD   Reader
Dyke, Martin, BA MSc PhD   Sr. Lectr.
Foskett, N. H., MA *Oxf.*, PhD   Prof.
Foskett, Rosalind, BA *Oxf.*, MA *Oxf.*   Assoc.
  Dean
Fuller, Alison, BA PhD   Prof.
Grace, Marcus, BSc MSc PhD   Sr. Lectr.
Grenfell, M. J., BA *Lond.*, MA *Lond.*, PhD   Prof.
Jones, Keith, BSc MSc MA(Ed)   Sr. Lectr.
Kelly, Tony, BSc MSc MPhil   Prof.
Kinchin, Gary, BEd MA PhD   Sr. Lectr.;
  Deputy Head, Educn.
Lumby, Jacky, BA MA PhD   Prof.
Nind, Melanie, BEd PhD   Prof.; Deputy Head,
  Res.
Polley, M. R., BA *Wales*, PhD *Wales*   Sr. Lectr.

Ratcliffe, Mary, BSc *UMIST*, MSc *Sur.*, PhD *S'ton.*,
  FRSChem   Prof.; Head*
Seale, Jane, BSc PhD   Sr. Lectr.
Taylor, John, BA MA PhD   Prof.
Weare, Katherine, BA *Kent*, MA *Lond.*, PhD *S'ton.*
  Prof.
Other Staff: 21 Lectrs.; 27 Teaching Fellows
Research: institutional and professional
  development; pedagogy and curriculum;
  post-compulsory education and training

Electronics and Computer Science

Tel: (023) 8059 2909 Fax: (023) 8059 2978
  E-mail: mm2@ecs.soton.ac.uk
Al-Hashimi, Bashir M., BSc *Bath*, MSc *Wales*,
  PhD *York(UK)*   Prof., Electronics and
  Computer Engineering
Ashburn, Peter, BSc *Leeds*, PhD *Leeds*, FIEE
  Prof., Microelectronics
Bagnall, D. M., BEng PhD   Sr. Lectr.
Baumberg, Jeremy J., BA *Camb.*, DPhil *Oxf.*, FIP
  Prof., Astronomy Physics
Beeby, S. P., BEng PhD   Sr. Lectr.
Berners-Lee, Tim, FRS, FREng, FRSA   Prof.
Brown, Andrew D., BSc *S'ton.*, PhD *S'ton.*, FIEE
  Prof., Electronics
Bullock, S., BA DPhil   Sr. Lectr.
Butler, Michael J., BA *Trinity(Dub.)*, MSc *Oxf.*,
  DPhil *Oxf.*   Prof., Computer Science
Carr, Leslie A., BSc *S'ton.*, PhD *S'ton.*   Sr. Lectr.
Carter, John N., BA *Trinity(Dub.)*, PhD *S'ton.*   Sr.
  Lectr.
Chappell, P. H., BSc PhD   Sr. Lectr.
Chen, Guanghui (George), BEng *Xi'an Jiaotong*,
  MSc *Xi'an Jiaotong*, PhD *Strath.*   Reader
Chen, Sheng, BEng *China Petroleum*, PhD *City(UK)*
  Prof.
Crowder, Richard M., BSc *Leic.*, PhD *Leic.*   Sr.
  Lectr.
Damper, Bob, BSc *Salf.*, MSc *Lond.*, PhD *Lond.*,
  FIEE   Prof.
de Groot, C. H., MSc PhD   Sr. Lectr.
DeRoure, David C., BSc *S'ton.*, PhD *S'ton.*
  Prof., Computer Science
Fischer, B., MSc PhD   Sr. Lectr.
French, M. C., MA PhD   Sr. Lectr.
Garratt, P. W., BSc PhD   Sr. Lectr.
Glaser, Hugh W., BSc *Lond.*   Reader
Gravell, Andrew M., BA *Camb.*, PhD *S'ton.*   Sr.
  Lectr.
Gunn, Steve R., BEng *S'ton.*, PhD *S'ton.*   Prof.
Hall, Wendy, CBE, BSc *S'ton.*, MSc *Lond.*, PhD
  S'ton., FBCS, FIEE, FREng, FCGI   Prof.,
  Computer Science
Hanzo, Lajos, MSc *Bud.*, PhD *Bud.*, FIEE   Prof.,
  Communications
Harnard, Stevan R., BA *McG.*, MA *McG.*, MA
  Prin., PhD *Prin.*   Prof., Cognitive Sciences
Harris, Chris J., BSc *Leic.*, MA *Oxf.*, PhD *S'ton.*,
  DSc *S'ton.*, FIEE, FREng   Emer. Prof.
Henderson, P., BSc *Manc.*, MSc *Newcastle(UK)*,
  PhD *Newcastle(UK)*   Prof., Computer Science
Hey, Tony J. G., CBE, BA *Oxf.*, MA *Oxf.*, DPhil
  Oxf., FREng   Emer. Prof.
Hughes, John F., BSc *Wales*, PhD *Wales*   Emer.
  Prof.
Jennings, Nick R., BSc *Exe.*, PhD *Lond.*, FBCS
  ECCAI Fellow; Prof., Computer Science
Kazmierski, T. J., MSc PhD   Sr. Lectr.
Kraft, M., PhD   Sr. Lectr.
Lewin, P. L., BSc PhD   Reader
Lewis, Paul H., BSc *Lond.*, PhD *Lond.*   Prof.
Luck, M. M., BSc *Lond.*, PhD *Lond.*   Prof.
Maharatna, K., BSc MSc PhD   Sr. Lectr.
Marques-Silva, J. P., BSc PhD   Prof.
Martinez, K., BSc *Reading*, PhD *Essex*   Sr. Lectr.
Melvin, T., BSc PhD   Reader
Mizuta, H., BSc PhD   Prof., Nanoelectronics
Moreau, Luc A.V., PhD *Liège*   Prof., Electronics
  and Computer Science
Morgan, Hywel, BSc *Wales*, PhD *Wales*   Prof.,
  Bioelectronics
Newson, Trevor P., MA *Oxf.*, DPhil *Oxf.*   Sr.
  Lectr.
Nicole, Denis A., MA *Camb.*, PhD *S'ton.*
  Reader
Nixon, Mark S., BSc *Reading*, PhD *Reading*   Prof.
Nunn, Dave, BA *Oxf.*, MSc *McG.*, PhD *Lond.*
  Prof.

Parker, Greg J., BSc *Sus.*, PhD *Sur.*, FIP   Prof.
Payne, David N., BSc *S'ton.*, PhD *S'ton.*, FRS
  Prof., Photonics
Prügel-Bennett, Adam, BSc *S'ton.*, PhD *Edin.*
  Reader
Rapisada, P., MSc PhD   Sr. Lectr.
Rathke, J., BA DPhil   Sr. Lectr.
Redman-White, Bill, BSc *Exe.*, MSc *S'ton.*, PhD
  S'ton.   Prof., Integrated Circuit Design
Reeve, Jeff S., BSc *Cant.*, MSc *NZ*, PhD *Alta.*   Sr.
  Lectr.
Rogers, Eric T. A., BSc *Belf.*, MEng *Sheff.*, PhD
  Sheff.   Prof., Control Systems Theory and
  Design
Ross, J. Neil, BSc *St And.*, PhD *St And.*   Sr.
  Lectr.
Rutt, Harvey N., BSc *S'ton.*, PhD *S'ton.*, FIP
  Prof., Infra-red Science and Technology;
  Head*
Sassone, V., MSc PhD   Prof., Formal Methods
Schraefel, Monica M. C., BA *Winn.*, MA
  Vic.(BC), PhD *Vic.(BC)*   Sr. Lectr.
Shadbolt, Nigel R., BA *Newcastle(NSW)*, PhD
  Edin.   Prof., Artificial Intelligence
Smith, Peter G. R., MA *Oxf.*, DPhil *Oxf.*   Prof.
Swingler, S. G., BA *Lanc.*, PhD *Lanc.*   Prof.,
  Transmission Asset Engineering
Sykulski, Jan K., MSc *Lodz*, PhD *Lodz*, FIEE, FIP
  Prof., Applied Electromagnetics
Vaughan, Alun S., BSc *Reading*, PhD *Reading*
  Prof.
Wald, M., BA MA PhD   Sr. Lectr.
Watson, R. A., BA MSc PhD   Sr. Lectr.
White, Neil M., BSc *CNAA*, PhD *S'ton.*, FIP, FIEE
  Prof., Intelligent Sensor Systems
White, S. A., BSc PhD   Sr. Lectr.
Wilkinson, James S., BSc *Lond.*, PhD *Lond.*, FIEE
  Prof., Optoelectronics
Wills, G. B., BEng PhD   Sr. Lectr.
Wilson, P. R., BEng *H-W*, MBA *Edin.*, PhD *S'ton.*
  Sr. Lectr.
Yang, L. L., BSc MEng PhD   Reader
Zaluska, Ed, BSc *S'ton.*, FIEE   Sr. Lectr.
Zwolinski, Mark, BSc *S'ton.*, PhD *S'ton.*   Prof.
Other Staff: 28 Lectrs.; 2 Teaching Fellows; 15
  Sr. Res. Fellows; 64 Res. Fellows; 23
  Visiting Profs.; 10 Emer. Profs.
Research: declarative systems and software
  engineering; electrical power engineering;
  image, speech and intelligent systems/
  communications; intelligence, agents,
  media; microelectronics/electronic systems
  design

Engineering Sciences

Tel: (023) 8059 2839 Fax: (023) 8059 5167
  E-mail: mfa@soton.ac.uk
Price, W. G., BSc *Wales*, PhD *Wales*, DSc *Lond.*,
  FREng, FRS   Prof.; Head*
Other Staff: 34 Lectrs.; 4 Sr. Res. Fellows; 22
  Res. Fellows; 13 Visiting Profs.; 3 Visiting
  Readers; 3 Visiting Sr. Lectrs.; 2 Visiting
  Lectrs.

Aeronautics and Astronautics

Tel: (023) 8059 4887 Fax: (023) 8059 3058
  E-mail: hsp@soton.ac.uk
Aglietti, G. S., Dott Ing PhD   Sr. Lectr.
Castro, I. P., MA MSc PhD, FRAeS   Prof.,
  Experimental Fluid Dynamics
Chernyshenko, S., PhD DSc   Prof., Fluid
  Dynamics
Coleman, G. N., MSc PhD   Reader, Fluid
  Dynamics
Gabriel, S. B., BSc PhD   Prof.
Newman, S. J., MSc PhD, FIMA   Sr. Lectr.
Roberts, G. T., BSc PhD   Prof.
Sandham, N. D., BSc MS PhD   Prof.,
  Aerospace Engineering
Swinerd, G. G., BSc PhD, FRAS   Reader,
  Astronautics
Tatnall, A. R. L., BSc PhD   Sr. Lectr.
Tutty, O. R., MSc PhD, FIMA   Prof., Fluid
  Mechanics
Zhang, X., BSc PhD   Prof., Aerodynamics
Research: aerodynamics and flight mechanics;
  astronautics

Engineering, Materials

Tel: (023) 8059 2871 Fax: (023) 8059 3016
E-mail: gs3@soton.ac.uk
Browne, M., BSc PhD   Reader, Biomaterials
 Science
Chambers, Alan R., BSc Birm., PhD Birm.   Sr.
 Lectr.
Langdon, T. G., BSc PhD DSc   Res. Prof.,
 Materials Science
Markvart, Tomas, BSc Birm., PhD Birm.
 Reader, Electronic Materials
Mellor, Brian G., MA Camb., PhD Camb.   Sr.
 Lectr.
Reed, Phillippa A. S., BA Camb., PhD Camb.
 Prof., Structural Materials
Sinclair, I., BA PhD   Prof.
Spearing, S. Mark, MA PhD   Prof.; Deputy
 Head
Starink, Marco J., PhD T.H.Delft   Prof.
Willoughby, A. F. W., BSc(Eng) Lond., PhD
 Lond.   Emer. Prof.
Research: aerospace and automative materials;
 functional materials; surface engineering

Engineering, Mechanical

Tel: (023) 8059 4632 Fax: (023) 8059 3230
E-mail: dla@soton.ac.uk
Atkinson, J. K., BSc Essex, PhD S'ton.   Reader
Barrett, D. S., BSc MB BS, FRCS   Prof.,
 Orthopaedic Engineering
Bhaskar, A., PhD Camb.   Sr. Lectr.
Calvert, J. R., BA Camb., PhD Camb.   Dir.,
 Educn.
Chipperfield, A. J., BSc Wales, PhD Sheff.   Sr.
 Lectr.
Cox, S. J., BSc S'ton., PhD S'ton.   Prof.,
 Computational Methods
Fangohr, H., PhD   Sr. Lectr.
Hill, M., BSc S'ton.   Reader, Electromechanical
 Systems
Holmes, R., BSc(Eng) Lond., PhD Lond.,
 DSc(Eng) Lond., FIMechE   Visiting Prof.
Keane, A. J., MSc Lond., MA Oxf., PhD Brun.
 Prof., Computational Engineering
Luo, K. H., BEng Camb., PhD Camb.   Prof.,
 Energy Systems
McBride, J. W., BSc S'ton., PhD CNAA   Prof.,
 Electro-Mechanical Engineering
Nair, P. B., BTech PhD   Sr. Lectr.
Richardson, R. N., BSc(Eng) Lond., DPhil Oxf.
 Sr. Lectr.
Scanlan, J. P., PhD   Prof., Design
Sharkh, S. M., BEng PhD   Sr. Lectr.
Stephen, N. G., BTech Lough., PhD Exe.   Prof.,
 Structural Mechanics
Syngellakis, S., MSE Prin., MA Prin., PhD Prin.
 Sr. Lectr.
Taylor, M., BEng MSc PhD   Prof.,
 Bioengineering Science
Veres, S. M., MSc PhD   Prof., Autonomous
 Control Systems
Walsh, F. C., BSc MSc PhD   Prof.,
 Electromechanical Engineering
Yang, Y., BSc PhD   Prof., Cryogenics and
 Applied Conductivity
Research: biomedical science (biomechanics,
 biomedical fluid mechanics); computational
 mechanics (design, design optimisation,
 structural mechanics); electro-mechanical
 engineering (instrumentation, metrology,
 robotics, sensors (thick film)); thermo-fluid
 engineering (biomedical fluid mechanics,
 computational fluid dynamics, cryogenics,
 pipe freezing, tribology)

Ship Science

Tel: (023) 8059 2316 Fax: (023) 8059 3299
E-mail: w.g.price@ship.soton.ac.uk
Barton, J. M., BSc Salf., PhD Manc.   Prof.,
 Experimental Mechanics
Griffiths, G., BA MSc   Prof., Underwater
 Systems Engineering
Hearn, G. E., BSc Bath, MSc Sheff.   Prof., Ocean
 Engineering Science
Hudson, D. A., BEng PhD   Sr. Lectr.
Price, W. G., BSc Wales, PhD Wales, DSc Lond.,
 FREng, FRS   Prof.; Head*

Shenoi, R. A., BTech Kharagpur, PhD Strath.
 Prof., Lightweight Composite Structures
Temarel, P., MSc Lond., PhD Lond.   Deputy
 Head; Prof., Hydroelasticity
Turnock, S. R., MA Camb., SM M.I.T., PhD   Sr.
 Lectr.
Wilson, P. A., BSc Leic.   Prof., Ship Dynamics
Xing, J. T., MEngSc Tsinghua, DEngSc   Prof.,
 Applied Mechanics
Research: fluid-structure interactions

English

Avenue Campus

Tel: (023) 8059 3410 Fax: (023) 8059 2859
E-mail: jej1@soton.ac.uk
Bending, Stephen, PhD   Sr. Lectr.
Bygrave, Stephen, BA Camb., PhD Camb.
 Reader
Clery, Emma, BA PhD   Prof.
Glover, David, MA Manit., PhD Sheff.   Sr. Lectr.
Hammond, Mary, BA MA PhD   Sr. Lectr.
Hanson, Clare, BA MA PhD   Prof.
King, Ros, BA   Prof.
Marsh, Nicola, BA PhD   Sr. Lectr.
McDonald, Gail, BA MA PhD   Sr. Lectr.
McGavin, John, MA Edin., PhD Edin.   Sr. Lectr.
Middleton, Peter L., BA Oxf., PhD Sheff.   Prof.;
 Head*
Millett, Bella, MA Oxf., DPhil Oxf.   Reader
Peacock, John, BA Syd., BLitt Oxf.   Sr. Lectr.
Williams, Linda, BA Sus., DPhil Sus., MA   Sr.
 Lectr.
Other Staff: 12 Lectrs.; 2 Res. Fellows; 3
 Teaching Fellows
Research: critical and cultural theory (cultural
 poetics, modernism); diaspora, post-
 colonial and Jewish studies; eighteenth-
 century studies (women's writing); film
 and visual studies; mediaeval studies

Film Studies

Avenue Campus

Tel: (023) 8059 2256 Fax: (023) 8059 3288
Bergfelder, Tim, MA E.Anglia, PhD E.Anglia
 Prof.
Donnelly, Kevin   Reader
Dunn, David, BA PhD   Sr. Lectr.
Hammond, Mike, PhD   Sr. Lectr.
Mazdon, Lucy, BA Birm., MA Warw., PhD S'ton.
 Sr. Lectr.
Williams, Linda, BA Sus., DPhil Sus., MA   Prof.
Other Staff: 4 Lectrs.
Research: American cinema; British cinema;
 European cinema; television; transnational
 cinemas

Geography

Tel: (023) 8059 2215 Fax: (023) 8059 3295
E-mail: geog@soton.ac.uk
Atkinson, Peter M., BSc Nott., PhD Sheff.   Prof.;
 Head*
Barber, Keith E., BSc Brist., PhD S'ton.   Prof.
Brown, Tony, BSc PhD   Prof.
Carling, Paul A., BSc Leic., PhD Wales(Swansea)
 Prof.
Dawson, Terry, BSc MSc PhD   Prof.
Dearing, John, BSc PhD   Prof.
Edwards, Mark, BSc MSc PhD   Prof.
Faggian, Allessandra, BSc MSc PhD   Reader
Hart, Jane K., BSc Reading, PhD E.Anglia   Reader
Martin, David J., BSc Brist., PhD Wales   Prof.
Milton, Edward J., BSc Exe., PhD Reading   Prof.
Moon, Graham, BA PhD   Prof.
Pinch, Steven P., BA Sus., MSc(Econ) Lond., PhD
 Lond.   Prof.
Sear, David A., BSc Sur., PhD Newcastle(UK)
 Prof.
Sunley, Peter J., MA Camb., PhD Camb.   Prof.
Wrigley, Neil, BA Wales, PhD Camb., DSc Brist.
 Prof.
Other Staff: 2 Emer. Profs.; 14 Lectrs.; 4
 Visiting Profs.; 2 Visiting Readers
Research: economy, culture, space;
 environmental processes and change;
 remote sensing and spatial analysis

Health Professions and Rehabilitation Sciences

Tel: (023) 8059 2142 Fax: (023) 8059 5301
E-mail: sotpadm@soton.ac.uk
Ashburn, Ann, MPhil Lough., PhD S'ton.   Prof.,
 Rehabilitation
Barnit, Rosemary, BSc MSc PhD   Visiting Prof.
Burridge, Jane, PhD S'ton.   Sr. Lectr.
Collier, Richard, MSc Lond.   Sr. Lectr.
Conway, Joy, MSc S'ton., PhD S'ton.   Reader
Ellis-Hill, Caroline, MSc PhD   Sr. Lectr.
Griffith, Jackie G., MSc   Head of
 Physiotherapy
Kersten, Paula, MSc S'ton., PhD S'ton.   Sr.
 Lectr.; Head, Postgrad. Studies
Potter, Julia, BSc PhD   Sr. Lectr.
Potter, Michael, BA Open(UK), MSc Lond.   Sr.
 Lectr.; Head of Podiatry; Deputy Head
Waters, Bernadette, MA Westminster   Sr. Lectr.;
 Head of Occupnl. Therapy
Other Staff: 44 Lectrs.; 4 Sr. Res. Fellows; 4
 Res. Fellows
Research: acute management; rehabilitation
 (living with disability, movement disorders
 and falls)

History

Avenue Campus

Tel: (023) 8059 2157 Fax: (023) 8059 3458
E-mail: history@soton.ac.uk
Arnold, Dana R., BA Lond., MSc Lond., PhD
 Lond., FRSA   Prof.
Bernard, George W., MA Oxf., DPhil Oxf.,
 FRHistS   Prof.
Cornwall, J. Mark, BA Leeds, PhD Leeds   Prof.;
 Head of Discipline*
Curry, Anne E., MA PhD   Deputy Head; Prof.,
 Medieval History
Ernst, Waltraud, PhD Lond.   Reader
Golding, Brian J., MA Oxf., DPhil Oxf., FRHistS
 Reader
Gregor, Neil, BA Exe., PhD Exe.   Reader
Kushner, Anthony R. W., BA Sheff., MA Conn.,
 PhD Sheff.   Marcus Sief Prof.
Levene, Dan, BA PhD   Sr. Lectr.
Levene, Mark, BA Warw., DPhil Oxf.   Reader
McDermid, J., MA Lond., MA Glas., PhD Lond.,
 PhD Glas.   Sr. Lectr.
Oldfield, John R., MA Camb., PhD Camb.   Sr.
 Lectr.
Oliver, Kendrick, BA Reading, PhD Lond.   Sr.
 Lectr.
Pearce, Sarah J., BA PhD   Sr. Lectr.
Schloer, Joachim   Prof.
Skinner, Patricia, MPhil Birm., PhD Birm.
 Reader
Smith, A., BA Kent, MA Kent, PhD Kent   Sr.
 Lectr.
Stoyle, Mark, BA S'ton., DPhil Oxf.   Prof.
Talbot, Ian, BA MA PhD   Prof., Modern
 British History
Other Staff: 11 Lectrs.
Research: early modern British and Dutch
 history; Jewish history (ancient and
 modern); mediaeval political and
 ecclesiastical history; modern history
 (Britain, France, Germany, India); US
 history, 1850–present

Law

Tel: (023) 8059 3632 Fax: (023) 8059 3024
E-mail: lawhos@soton.ac.uk
Baatz, Y., BA Oxf.   Prof.
Betlem, G., LLM LLD   Prof., European Law
Conte, A., LLB LLM PhD   Reader
Debattista, C., LLD Malta, MA Oxf.   Dir., Inst.
 of Maritime Law; Prof., Commercial Law
Edwards, J., LLB LLM MSc   Prof., Information
 Technology Law
Fionda, J. A., LLB S'ton., PhD S'ton.   Sr. Lectr.;
 Dir., Inst. of Criminal Justice
Ganz, Gabriele, LLM Lond.   Emer. Prof.
Gaskell, N. J. J., LLB Hull   Prof., Maritime and
 Commercial Law
Hannigan, Brenda M., MA Trinity(Dub.), LLM
 Harv.   Prof., Corporate Law
Hopkins, N. P., LLB Lond.   Sr. Lectr.; Assoc.
 Dean (Undergrad.)

Jackson, D. C., MA Oxf., BCL Oxf., LLD S'ton. Emer. Prof.
Lee, N. J., LLB S'ton.   Prof.; Head*
Meredith, A. P. K., LLB Edin., PhD Camb. Reader; Deputy Head, Educn.
Merkin, R., LLB Wales, LLM Lond.   Prof.
Montgomery, Jonathan, BA Camb., LLM Camb. Deputy Head (Res.); Prof., Health Care Law
Nazzini, R., PhD Lond., LLD PhD   Reader
Nield, S., LLB   Sr. Lectr.
Rutherford, A. F., BA Durh.   Emer. Prof.
Saxby, S. J., BA Kent, PhD S'ton.   Deputy Head, Res.; Prof., Information Technology Law
Sparkes, P., LLB Exe.   Prof.
Steele, Jennifer C., BA Oxf., LLM Brist.   Prof.
Tsimplis, M. N., BSc LLM PhD   Sr. Lectr.
Wikeley, N. J., MA Camb.   Prof.
Other Staff: 14 Lectrs.; 1 Sr. Res. Fellow; 4 Visiting Profs.
Research: criminal justice; maritime law

Management

Tel: (023) 8059 7677 Fax: (023) 8059 3844
   E-mail: mgtmail@soton.ac.uk
Ashleigh, Melanie, BSc PhD   Sr. Lectr.
Bennell, Julia, BSc PhD   Sr. Lectr.
Brailsford, Sally, BSc Lond., MSc S'ton., PhD S'ton. Sr. Lectr.
Brannen, Peter, BA Manc.   Visiting Prof.
Casson, Peter, MSc Lond., PhD Brun.   Sr. Lectr.
Chapman, Chris B., BASc Tor., MSc Birm., PhD Visiting Prof., Management Science
Choudhry, Taufiq, BSc MA PhD   Prof., Finance
Clarke, Nicholas, BSc MSc PhD   Sr. Lectr.
Connell, Con N. A. D., BSc Lond., MSc Aston, PhD   Prof.
Goddard, Andrew R., BSc Manc., PhD S'ton. Prof., Accounting
Haigh, Matthew, BCom MCom PhD   Sr. Lectr.
Halldorsson, Arni, BSc MSc PhD   Sr. Lectr.
Harris, Lisa, MBA PhD   Sr. Lectr.
Holland, Kevin, BA   Prof., Accounting
Hulbert, Bev, MBA PhD   Sr. Lectr.
Johnson, Johnnie E. V., BSc Manc., PhD   Prof., Decision and Risk Analysis
Klein, Jonathan H., MSc Sus., PhD Lond.   Sr. Lectr.
Lamming, Richard, BSc Aston, DPhil Sus.   Prof.; Dir.*
Macbeth, Douglas K., BSc MSc   Prof.
Marti, John, BSc MBA PhD   Sr. Lectr.
Martin, Roderick, MA Oxf., DPhil Oxf., DLitt Oxf.   Visiting Prof.
Nisar, Tahir, BA MA MPhil PhD   Reader
Patton, Dean, BA PhD   Sr. Lectr.
Schwartz, Mirela, BSc PhD   Sr. Lectr.
Targett, David, MA PhD   Visiting Prof.
Taylor, John, BA MA PhD   Prof., Higher Education Management and Policy
Thomas, Lyn, MA Oxf., DPhil Oxf.   Prof., Management Science
Ward, Stephen C., BSc Nott., MSc Lond., PhD Prof.
Warren, Lorraine, BSc MSc PhD   Sr. Lectr.
Werner, Richard, BSc Lond., MPhil Oxf., DPhil Oxf.   Prof., International Banking
Wilkinson, Charles, BSc Lough., MA Lanc., PhD Lanc.   Dir., MBA Programme
Williams, Terry M., MA MSc PhD   Prof.
Wolfe, Simon S. J., BA MSc PhD   Sr. Lectr.
Woodward, David, BA York(UK), MSc Brad., MBA Open(UK)   Reader
Other Staff: 17 Lectrs.; 3 Teaching Fellows; 3 Emer. Profs.; 11 Visiting Profs.
Research: accounting; banking and finance; information management/systems science; management science; organisational behaviour and human resource management (HRM)

Mathematics

Tel: (023) 8059 5155 Fax: (023) 8059 5147
   E-mail: school@maths.soton.ac.uk
Anderson, James W., BA Georgia, PhD N.Y.State Sr. Lectr.; Deputy Head, Educn.
Andersson, Nils, BSc Uppsala, PhD Uppsala Prof., Applied Mathematics

Brodzki, J., MSc DPhil   Sr. Lectr.
Cheng, R. C. H., MA PhD   Prof., Operational Research
Chillingworth, David R. J., BA Camb., PhD Camb.   Sr. Lectr.
Craine, Robert E., BSc Manc., PhD Manc., FIMA Sr. Lectr.
d'Alessandro, G., PhD   Sr. Lectr.
d'Inverno, Raymon A., MA Oxf., MSc Lond., PhD Lond.   Emer. Prof.
Fitt, Alistair D., MA Oxf., MSc Oxf., DPhil Oxf. Prof., Applied Mathematics; Head*
Fliege, J., PhD   Prof., Operational Research
Forster, Jonathan J., BA Camb., PhD Nott. Deputy Head (Res.); Prof., Statistics
Gundlach, C. J., PhD   Reader
Harper, P. R., BSc MSc PhD   Sr. Lectr.
Howls, Christopher J., BSc Brist., PhD Brist.   Sr. Lectr.
Jones, Gareth A., MA Oxf., DPhil Oxf.   Prof., Pure Mathematics
Kennedy, Gerard, BSc Strath., PhD Manc.   Sr. Lectr.
Kimber, A., BSc MSc PhD   Reader
Koeck, Bernhard, PhD Regensburg   Reader
Lewis, Susan M., MSc Lond., PhD S'ton.   Prof., Statistics
Liu, Wei, BSc Fudan, PhD Bath   Prof., Statistics
Michailidis, G.   Sr. Lectr., Obstetrics/Gynaecology
Niblo, Graham A., BSc Reading, MSc Lond., PhD Liv.   Prof., Pure Mathematics
Please, Colin P., BSc S'ton., MSc Oxf., DPhil Oxf. Prof., Applied Mathematics
Potts, Christopher N., BSc Manc., MSc Hull, PhD Birm.   Prof., Operational Research
Prescott, Philip, BSc Lond., PhD Lond.   Prof., Statistics
Renshaw, J. H., BSc PhD   Sr. Lectr.
Roehrie, G., MA PhD   Prof., Pure Mathematics
Sahu, S. K., BSc MStat PhD   Sr. Lectr.
Singerman, David, BSc Birm., PhD Birm.   Prof., Pure Mathematics
Sluckin, Timothy J., BA Camb., PhD Nott. Prof., Applied Mathematical Physics
Vickers, James A. G., BA Oxf., DPhil York(UK) Prof., Applied Mathematics
Wheeler, Adam A., BSc E.Anglia, PhD E.Anglia Prof., Industrial Applied Mathematics
Xu, H., PhD   Sr. Lectr.
Other Staff: 17 Lectrs.; 7 Res. Fellows; 6 Emer. Profs.
Research: applied mathematics (biomathematics, general relativity, industrial mathematics, mathematical physics); operational research (discrete and continuous optimisation, healthcare modelling, scheduling, simulation, stochastic and fractal processes); pure mathematics (algebra, algebraic K-theory, geometric group theory, non-linear dynamics, topology); statistics (Bayesian inference, design of experiments, non-parametric and robust estimation, sample surveys, simultaneous inference)

Modern Languages

Avenue Campus
Tel: (023) 8059 3974 Fax: (023) 8059 3288
   E-mail: smlinfo@soton.ac.uk
Blue, George, MA   Sr. Lectr.; Head of Educn.
Jenkins, Jennifer, BA PhD   Prof.
Mitchell, Rosamond F., BA Trinity(Dub.), MSc Edin., PhD Stir.   Prof.; Dir., Centre for Appl. Lang. Res.
Orr, Mary, PhD   Prof.
Reiter, Andrea, MA PhD   Sr. Lectr.
Other Staff: 12 Lectrs.; 1 Teaching Fellow

French

Tel: (023) 8059 2256
Day, L., BA Birm., PhD Birm.   Sr. Lectr.
Kelly, M. H., BA Warw., MBA S'ton., PhD Warw. Prof.; Head*
Research: cultural studies (French and Francophone cinema, Liberation period); language studies (French language and linguistics); literary studies (nineteenth- and twentieth-century literature and

thought); social, political and historical studies (French foreign policy, women in politics)

German

Tel: (023) 8059 2256
Meinhof, U. H., MA T.U.Munich, DPhil Sus. Prof.
Stevenson, P. R. A., BA Oxf., MA Reading, PhD S'ton.   Prof.
Research: cultural studies (German cinema and German/Turkish literature); language studies (sociolinguistics of German); literary studies (nineteenth- and twentieth-century German and Austrian literature)

Language Study, Centre for

Tel: (023) 8059 3977 Fax: (023) 8059 3849
   E-mail: clsmail@soton.ac.uk
Wright, V. M., BA MA(Ed)   Dir.*
Research: applied linguistics; assessment; language and politics; learner autonomy; writing in a foreign language

Spanish, Portuguese and Latin American Studies

Tel: (023) 8059 2256
Dore, E., BA Vassar, PhD Col.   Prof.
Labanyi, J., MA   Prof.†
Mar-Molinero, F. C., BA Birm., MA(Ed) S'ton., PhD   Prof.
Research: language studies (language and nationalism, language policy, sociolinguistics); Latin America and the Caribbean (literature and popular culture, modern history); literary studies (literature of Spain, Portugal and Latin America); social and political studies (modern Spanish and Latin American history)

Music

Tel: (023) 8059 3425 Fax: (023) 8059 3197
   E-mail: musicbox@soton.ac.uk
Brooks, Laura J., MA C.U.A., PhD C.U.A. Reader
Drabkin, William M., BA Cornell, MFA Prin., PhD Prin.   Reader
Everist, Mark E., MMus Lond., DPhil Oxf. Prof.; Head*
Finnissy, Michael   Prof.
Nicholls, David, MA Camb., PhD Camb.   Prof.
Other Staff: 14 Lectrs.
Research: composition; early music; jazz and popular music; music and multimedia; performance

National Oceanography Centre, Southampton

Tel: (023) 8059 5106 Fax: (023) 8059 5107
   E-mail: jmj4@soc.soton.ac.uk
Hill, A. E., BSc MSc PhD   Prof.; Dir.*
Other Staff: 2 Res. Fellows; 5 Hon. Visiting Profs.; 11 Hon. Fellows
Research: marine and earth science; mathematical modelling; ocean engineering; remote sensing

National Marine Facilities Division

Tel: (023) 8059 6012 Fax: (023) 8059 6295
   E-mail: p.stone@soc.soton.ac.uk
Griffiths, G., BA MSc   Head, Underwater Systems Lab.
Lewis, Commodore David, CBE   Head of Div.*
West, G., BSc   Head, UKORS
Other Staff: 1 Sr. Res. Fellow; 3 Res. Fellows; 40 Staff Members

NERC Strategic Research Division

Tel: (023) 8059 6434 Fax: (023) 8059 6204
   E-mail: l.allen@noc.soton.ac.uk
Billett, D. S. M., BSc PhD   Principal Scientist
Bryden, Harry L., AB Dartmouth, PhD M.I.T. Prof.
Burkhill, P. H., BSc PhD   Prof.; Head, George Deacon Division*
German, C. R., MBE, MA PhD   Prof.

Guymer, T. H., BSc MSc Sr. Principal Scientist
Killworth, P. D., BA MA PhD Prof.
Pollard, R. T., BSc PhD Prof.
Taylor, Peter K., BSc PhD Sr. Lectr.
Weaver, P. P. E., BSc PhD DSc, FGS Prof.; Head*
Other Staff: 16 Sr. Res. Fellows; 22 Res. Fellows; 51 Staff Members
Research: climate; global ocean circulation; hydrography; ocean modelling; satellite remote sensing

Ocean and Earth Science

see also National Oceanography Centre, Southampton

Tel: (023) 8059 2011 Fax: (023) 8059 3052
E-mail: soes@soc.soton.ac.uk
Achterberg, E. P., MSc PhD Prof.
Amos, Carl L., BSc Wales, PhD Lond. Prof.
Andrews, J. R., BSc PhD Sr. Lectr.
Bryden, Harry L., AB Dartmouth, PhD M.I.T. Prof.
Bull, Jon, BSc Durh., PhD Edin. Prof.; Deputy Head, Res.
Croudace, Ian, BSc Liv., PhD Birm. Sr. Lectr.
Dix, Justin K., BSc Dund., PhD St And. Sr. Lectr.
Harding, Ian C., BSc Nott., PhD Camb. Sr. Lectr.
Hawkins, Lawrence E., BSc Exe., MSc S'ton., PhD S'ton. Sr. Lectr.
Henstock, T. J., BA PhD Sr. Lectr.
Holligan, Patrick M., MA Camb., PhD Leeds Emer. Prof.
Jensen, Antony C., PhD S'ton., BA Sr. Lectr.
Kemp, Alan E. S., BA Cant.CCC, PhD Edin. Prof.
Marshall, John E. A., BA Camb., PhD Brist., FGS Prof.
Mills, Rachel A., BSc S'ton., PhD Camb. Sr. Lectr.; Deputy Head, Educn. Devel.
Minshull, Timothy A., MA Camb., MSc Durh., PhD Camb. Prof.; Head, Educn. Policy
Palike, H., BA MSc PhD Reader
Palmer, M. R., BSc PhD Prof.
Purdie, Duncan, BSc Wales, PhD Wales Reader
Roberts, Andrew P., BSc Well., PhD Well. Prof.; Head*
Roberts, Stephen, BSc Wales, PhD Open(UK), FGS Reader
Robinson, Ian S., MA Camb., PhD Warw. Prof.
Rohling, Eelco, BSc Utrecht, MSc Utrecht, PhD Utrecht Prof.
Sheader, Martin, BSc Newcastle(UK), PhD Newcastle(UK) Sr. Lectr.
Sinha, Martin, BSc Liv., PhD Camb. Prof.
Statham, Peter J., BSc Nott., PhD S'ton. Prof.
Stow, Dorrik A. V., MA Camb., PhD Dal., FGS Prof.
Taylor, R. N., BSc PhD Sr. Lectr.
Teagle, D. A. H., BSc MSc PhD Prof.
Tyler, Paul A., BSc Wales, PhD Wales, DSc Wales Prof., Deep-Sea Biology
Tyrell, L. R., BSc MSc PhD Reader
Williams, John, BSc Wales, PhD Liv. Sr. Lectr.
Wilson, Paul A., BA Manc., MS Louisiana State, PhD Camb. Prof.
Other Staff: 14 Lectrs.; 2 Teaching Fellows; 11 Sr. Res. Fellows; 17 Res. Fellows; 6 Emer. Profs.; 2 Visiting Profs.; 3 Visiting Fellows
Research: hydrothermal processes and ocean/crust interaction; marine biodiversity and population dynamics; ocean circulation and climate; sedimentary dynamics and diagenetic processes; upper ocean processes and biogeochemistry

Optoelectronics Research Centre

Tel: (023) 8059 3150 Fax: (023) 8059 3142
E-mail: light@orc.soton.ac.uk
Brocklesby, Bill S., BA DPhil Res. Reader
Clarkson, Andy, PhD Prof., Advanced Solid State Sources
Dakin, John P., BSc PhD Prof., Optical Sensors and Instrumentation

Eason, Robert W., BSc Lond., DPhil York(UK) Prof., Nonlinear and Microstructured Optical Materials
Hewak, D., BSc MSc PhD Prof.
Ibsen, M., MSc Res. Reader
Jeong, Y., PhD Res. Reader
Kazansky, Peter G., MSc PhD Prof., Physical Optics
Melvin, T., BSc PhD Res. Reader
Newson, Trevor P., MA Oxf., DPhil Oxf. Sr. Lectr.
Nilsson, Johan, PhD Prof., High Power Fibre Lasers
Payne, David N., BSc S'ton., PhD S'ton., FRS Prof., Photonics; Dir.*
Petropolous, P., PhD Res. Reader.
Richardson, David J., BSc PhD Deputy Dir.; Prof., Advanced Fibre Technologies and Applications
Rutt, Harvey N., BSc S'ton., PhD S'ton., FIP Deputy Dir.; Prof., Infrared Science and Technology
Shepherd, D. P., PhD Res. Reader
Smith, Peter G. R., MA Oxf., DPhil Oxf. Res. Prof.
Wilkinson, James S., BSc Lond., PhD Lond., FIEE Prof.
Zervas, Mikhail N., MSc PhD Prof.
Zheludev, N. I., BSc Moscow, PhD Moscow, DSc Moscow Prof.
Other Staff: 1 Lectr.; 2 Principal Res. Fellows; 18 Sr. Res. Fellows; 32 Res. Fellows

Philosophy

Avenue Campus

Tel: (023) 8059 3400 Fax: (023) 8059 3344
E-mail: ww@soton.ac.uk
Collier, Andrew S., BA Lond., MPhil Lond. Prof.
Gemes, Kenneth, BA PhD Reader
Janaway, Christopher, MA DPhil Prof.
McManus, Dennis, BA MPhil PhD Reader
Monk, Ray, BA York(UK), BLitt Oxf. Prof.
Neill, Alex, BA S'ton., MA Alta., PhD Camb. Sr. Lectr.; Head*
Pugmire, David, MA Sr. Lectr.
Ridley, Aaron, BA York(UK), PhD Camb. Prof.
Other Staff: 4 Lectrs.
Research: analytic aesthetics and the history of aesthetics; the character of practical reason and ethical deliberation; Wittgenstein and his place in twentieth-century philosophy

Physics and Astronomy

Tel: (023) 8059 2088 Fax: (023) 8059 3910
E-mail: cs@phys.soton.ac.uk
Barnes, K. J., BSc Lond., PhD Lond., FIP Emer. Prof.
Baumberg, J., BA Camb., DPhil Oxf. Prof.
Charles, P. A., BSc Lond., MA Oxf., PhD Lond. Prof.
Coe, M. J., BSc Lond., PhD Lond. Prof.; Head*
de Carlos, B., MSc PhD Sr. Lectr.
de Groot, P. A. J., MSc T.H.Delft, PhD Leuven Prof.
Dean, A. J., BSc S'ton., PhD S'ton. Prof.
Evans, N. J., PhD Prof.
Fender, R., BSc PhD Prof.
Flynn, J. M., BA Camb., PhD Harv., FIP Reader
Hanna, David C., BA Camb., PhD, FIP Prof.
Harley, R. T., MA Oxf., DPhil Oxf. Prof.
Kaczmarek, M., PhD Sr. Lectr.
Kaiser, C., BSc PhD Reader
Kavokin, A., MSc PhD Prof.
King, S. F., BSc Leeds, PhD Manc. Prof.
Knigge, C., BSc DPhil Reader
Lanchester, B. S., MSc PhD Prof.
Lanchester, Peter C., BSc Monash, PhD Monash Sr. Lectr.
Lockwood, M., BSc Exe., PhD Exe. Prof.
McHardy, I. M., BSc Lond., PhD Camb. Prof.
Moretti, S., MSc PhD Reader
Morris, T. R., BA Camb., PhD S'ton. Prof.; Deputy Head, Academic
Rainford, B. D., MA Oxf., DPhil Oxf. Prof.
Risbeth, H., BA PhD ScD Emer. Prof.
Ross, D. A., BA Oxf., DPhil Oxf., FIP Reader
Sachrajda, C. T. C., BSc Sus., PhD Lond., FIP, FRS Prof.; Deputy Head (Res.)

Smith, D. C., BA DPhil Reader
Tropper, A. C., MA Oxf., DPhil Oxf. Prof.
Warner, B., PhD Prof.
Watson, J. H. P., BSc Liv., PhD Tor. Prof. Emer.
Other Staff: 11 Lectrs.; 24 Res. Fellows; 1 Visiting Prof.
Research: astrophysics; high energy particle physics; laser physics and optoelectronics; quantum and functional matter (magnetism, superconductivity, liquid crystal, semiconductor laser spectroscopy, photonic crystals); solar terrestrial physics

Psychology

Tel: (023) 8059 2619 Fax: (023) 8059 4597
E-mail: tb@soton.ac.uk
Adams, W., BSc PhD Sr. Lectr.
Bradley, Brendan P., MA Camb., MSc Aberd., PhD Lond., FBPsS Prof.; Co-Dir., DClinPsychol Programme
Coleman, P. G., MA Oxf., PhD Lond., FBPsS Prof.
Donnelly, Nick, BA PhD Reader; Head*
Dror, Itiel, BA Ben Gurion, MA Harv., PhD Harv. Sr. Lectr.
Elliott, Peter, BA MSc Co-Dir., DClinPsychol Programme; Sr. Lectr., Clinical Psychology
Glautier, Steven, PhD S'ton. Sr. Lectr.
Higham, Philip, BSc PhD Reader
Ingham, Roger, BSc Lond., DPhil Oxf. Prof.
Liossi, Christina, BA MSc MPhil DPsych Sr. Lectr.
Liversedge, Simon, BSc PhD Prof.
Mogg, Karin, BSc MA MSc PhD Prof.; Wellcome Trust Sr. Res. Fellow
Moss-Morris, Rona, BSc MSc PhD Reader
Remington, Bob, BSc Exe., PhD Exe., FBPsS Prof.
Sedikides, Constantine, BA MA PhD Prof.
Sonuga-Barke, Edmund, BSc Wales, PhD Exe. Prof.
Stevenage, Sarah, BSc PhD Sr. Lectr.
Stevenson, Jim, BA Oxf., MSc Sus., PhD Sur. Prof.
Stratford, Bob, BA Sheff., PhD, FBPsS Sr. Lectr.
Wildschut, Tim, BA MA PhD Sr. Lectr.
Yardley, Lucy, BSc S'ton., MSc S'ton., PhD S'ton. Prof.; Head*
Other Staff: 21 Lectrs.; 1 Sr. Res. Fellow; 11 Res. Fellows; 4 Hon. Profs.
Research: abnormal and clinical psychology; cognitive psychology; developmental psychology; educational and social psychology; neuropsychology

Social Sciences

Tel: (023) 8059 3968 Fax: (023) 8059 2954
E-mail: socsci@soton.ac.uk
Falkingham, J. C., BSc(Econ) Lond., MSc Lond. Prof.; Deputy Head (Res. and Enterprise)
McGrew, Anthony, BSc S'ton., PhD S'ton. Prof.; Head*
Mizon, G. E., MA Oxf., MSc(Econ) Lond., PhD Lond. Emer. Prof., Econometrics
Smith, P., BA Warw., PhD Birm. Sr. Lectr.; Deputy Head, Educn.

Economics, Division of

Tel: (023) 8059 2537 Fax: (023) 8059 3858
E-mail: econ@soton.ac.uk
Aldrich, J., BA Sus., MSc Lond. Reader
Gervais, M., MA PhD Reader
Hillier, G. H., BEc Penn., PhD Penn. Prof., Econometrics
Kugler, M., MSc PhD Reader
Lu, M., BSc Shanghai, MSc S'ton., PhD S'ton. Sr. Lectr.
Mason, R. A., BA Camb., MPhil Camb., PhD Camb. Prof.
Mateos-Planas, X., MA PhD Reader
O'Brien, R., BSc(Econ) Lond. Sr. Lectr.
Pitarakis, J.-Y., Lic Paris II, Maîtrise Paris II, MA Boston, PhD Boston Reader
Podivinsky, J., MSc PhD Sr. Lectr.
Rodriguez-Mora, S., MSc PhD Prof.
Sauer, R., BSc PhD Prof.

Schluter, C., BSc(Econ) Lond., MSc(Econ) Lond., PhD Lond.   Reader
Seccia, G., MA PhD   Reader
Smith, P., BA Warw., PhD Birm.   Sr. Lectr.
Valentinyi, A., PhD European Univ.Inst.   Prof.
Wahba, J., MA PhD   Reader
Other Staff: 14 Lectrs.; 1 Visiting Prof.; 3 Profs.†; 1 Teaching Fellow
Research: applied and theoretical econometrics; environmental and resource economics; industrial organisation; labour economics; macroeconomics

Politics and International Relations, Division of

Tel: (023) 8059 4746 Fax: (023) 8059 3276
   E-mail: politics@socsci.soton.ac.uk
Armstrong, C., BSc MSc PhD   Sr. Lectr.
Bentley, R. K., BA MSc PhD   Sr. Lectr.
Craig, C., BA MA PhD   Prof., Politics and International Relations
Evans, Anthony J., BA E.Anglia, MSc S'ton., PhD Aberd.   Reader
Freedman, J., BA MSc PhD   Reader
Gregory, Frank E. C., BA Brist., MSc(SocSci) Prof.
Howlett, Darryl, BA E.Anglia, MA Lanc., PhD S'ton.   Sr. Lectr.
Mason, Andrew, BA Brist., MA Minn., DPhil Oxf.   Head of Div.; Prof., Political Theory
McGrew, Anthony, BSc S'ton., PhD S'ton.   Prof., International Relations
Newton, Kenneth, BA Exe., PhD Camb.   Prof., Comparative Politics and Policy
Owen, David, BA Durh., PhD Durh.   Prof.
Simpson, John, OBE, MSc(Econ) Lond., PhD S'ton.   Dir., Mountbatten Centre for Internat. Studies; Prof., International Relations
Smith, Graham M., BSc(Chem) Brad., MSc Manc., PhD S'ton.   Prof., Politics
Stoker, G., BA PhD   Prof., Governance
Thomas, Caroline, BSc(Econ) Lond., PhD Lond.   Prof., Global Politics
Other Staff: 4 Lectrs.; 2 Emer. Profs.
Research: citizenship and governance; comparative politics; global politics; political theory; security studies

Social Statistics, Division of

Tel: (023) 8059 2527 Fax: (023) 8059 3846
   E-mail: socstats@soton.ac.uk
Berrington, A., BA Oxf., MSc Lond.   Sr. Lectr.
Brown, J. J., BSc MSc PhD   Sr. Lectr.
Falkingham, J. C., BSc(Econ) Lond., MSc Lond.   Prof.
Hinde, P. R. A., MA Camb., PhD Sheff.   Sr. Lectr.
Madise, Nyovani, BSc Malawi, MSc S'ton., PhD S'ton.   Reader
Matthews, Zoe, BSc Sheff., MSc Newcastle(UK), PhD S'ton.   Reader
Micklewright, J., BA Exe., PhD Lond.   Prof.
Ní Bhrolcháin, Máire, BA Trinity(Dub.), MSc Trinity(Dub.), PhD S'ton.   Prof., Demography
Skinner, C. J., BA Camb., MSc Lond., PhD S'ton.   Prof.
Smith, P. W. F., BSc Lanc., MSc Sheff., PhD Lanc.   Prof.; Head of Div.*
Other Staff: 5 Lectrs.
Research: demography; living standards; official statistics; sample surveys; statistical modelling

Social Work Studies, Division of

Tel: (023) 8059 2629 Fax: (023) 8059 4800
   E-mail: gms1@socsci.soton.ac.uk
Fook, J., MSW Syd., BSW   Prof.; Head of Div.*
Ford, P. K., MA   Sr. Lectr.
McAuley, M. C., MSc Oxf., BA PhD   Prof.
Powell, Jackie, MA Oxf.   Prof.
Ruch, G., MA MSc PhD   Sr. Lectr.
Warren-Anderson, C., BA MPhil   Sr. Lectr.
Other Staff: 7 Lectrs.; 3 Sr. Res. Fellows; 3 Res. Fellows
Research: ageing and end of life studies; child welfare and kinship care; methodologies for practice, research and education

Sociology and Social Policy

Tel: (023) 8059 2602
   E-mail: chann@socsci.soton.ac.uk
Bridgen, P., BA MSc PhD   Sr. Lectr.
Causer, G. A., BA Reading, BPhil York(UK)   Sr. Lectr.
Crow, G. P., BA Oxf., MA Essex, PhD Essex   Prof.
Graham, D., BA MA   Sr. Lectr.
Halford, S. J., BA Sus., MA Sus., DPhil Sus.   Prof., Sociology
Harris, B. J., MA Camb., PhD Lond.   Prof., History of Social Policy; Head of Div.*
Heath, S. J., BSc Brist., PhD Lanc.   Prof.
Leonard, P., BA MA(Ed) PhD   Sr. Lectr.
McGhee, D., BSc MA PhD   Reader, Sociology
Meyer, T., PhD F.U.Berlin   Sr. Lectr.
Mohan, J., BA PhD   Prof., Social Policy
Roth, S., MA PhD   Sr. Lectr.
Sweetman, P., BA MA PhD   Sr. Lectr.
Ungerson, C., BA Oxf., MSc Lond., PhD Kent   Emer. Prof.
Other Staff: 9 Lectrs.; 1 Teaching Fellow; 1 Res. Fellow
Research: family, community and identity; gender, work and the public sector; historical social policy and demography; qualitative methodologies

Sound and Vibration Research, Institute of

Tel: (023) 8059 2294 Fax: (023) 8059 3190
   E-mail: mzs@isvr.soton.ac.uk
Allen, Robert, BSc PhD   Prof., Biodynamics and Control
Astley, R. Jeremy, BSc Cant., MSc Cant., PhD Brist.   Prof., Computational Acoustics
Barney, A., BSc MSc PhD   Sr. Lectr.
Brennan, Michael J., BA Open(UK), MSc S'ton., PhD S'ton.   Prof., Engineering Dynamics
Davies, Peter O. A. L., BE Syd., PhD Cant.   Emer. Prof.
Elliott, Stephen J., BSc Sur., PhD Sur.   Prof., Adaptive Systems; Dir.*
Fahy, Francis J., BSc Lond., PhD   Emer. Prof., Engineering Acoustics
Ferguson, N. S., BSc PhD   Sr. Lectr.
Frampton, K. D., BSc MSc PhD   Reader
Gardonio, Paolo, LaurIngMecc Polytech.Milan, PhD Polytech.Milan   Prof.
Griffin, Michael J., BSc S'ton., PhD S'ton.   Prof., Human Factors
Hammond, Joseph K., BSc S'ton., PhD S'ton.   Emer. Prof., Signal Analysis
Holland, K. R., BSc PhD   Sr. Lectr.
Humphrey, Victor, BSc PhD   Prof., Acoustics
James, C. J., BElecEng PhD   Reader
Jones, C. J. C., BSc PhD   Reader
Joseph, Phillip F., BSc York(UK), MSc S'ton., PhD S'ton.   Sr. Lectr.
Leighton, Timothy G., MA Camb., PhD Camb.   Prof., Ultrasonics and Underwater Acoustics
Lutman, Mark E., BSc S'ton., PhD S'ton.   Prof., Audiology
Mace, Brian R., MA DPhil   Prof., Structural Dynamics
Morfey, Christopher L., BA Camb., MSc PhD   Emer. Prof., Biomechanics
Nelson, Philip A., BSc S'ton., PhD S'ton.   Prof., Acoustics; Head*
Petyt, Maurice, MSc Hull, PhD   Emer. Prof.
Simpson, D. M., BSc PhD   Sr. Lectr.
Thompson, David J., MA PhD   Prof., Railway Noise and Vibration
Waters, T. P., BSc PhD   Sr. Lectr.
White, Paul R., BSc S'ton., PhD S'ton.   Prof., Static Signal Processing
Wright, M. C. M., BEng PhD   Sr. Lectr.
Other Staff: 15 Lectrs.; 3 Teaching Fellows; 6 Sr. Res. Fellows; 15 Res. Fellows; 5 Visiting Profs.
Research: dynamics (condition monitoring, vehicle noise and vibration); fluid dynamics and acoustics (aeroacoustics, bioacoustics, electroacoustics, hydroacoustics, vibroacoustics); human sciences (audiology, human response to sound and vibration); signal processing and control (active

control, biomedical signal processing, underwater systems)

MEDICINE, SCHOOL OF

Tel: (023) 8079 6581 Fax: (023) 8079 4760
   E-mail: apc@soton.ac.uk
Cameron, Iain T., BSc Edin., MB ChB Edin., MD Edin., MA Camb., FRCOG   Head*
Elliott, T. J., BA PhD   Dir., Res.
Iredale, John P. I., BSc MB BS PhD   Prof.
Stephens, Chris, MB BS DCH   Prof.; Dir., Educn.

Cancer Sciences Division

Tel: (023) 8079 5150 Fax: (023) 8079 5152
   E-mail: oncology@soton.ac.uk
Al-Shamkhani, A., BSc PhD   Reader, Immunology
Eccles, D. M., MB ChB MD   Clin. Prof., Cancer Genetics
Glennie, M. J., BSc PhD   Dir. of Div.*
Griffiths, D. M., MS, FRCS   Sr. Lectr., Paediatric Surgery
Hamblin, T. J., MB ChB Brist., DM   Prof., Immunohaematology
Harrison, C. J., BSc PhD   Hon. Prof., Cancer Science Cytogenics
Johnson, C. D., MChir Camb., FRCS   Reader, Surgery
Johnson, P. W. M., MA Camb., MD Camb.   Cancer Res. UK Prof., Medical Oncology
Kohler, J. A., MB ChB Brist.   Sr. Lectr., Paediatric Oncology
Lucassen, A. M., BMedSci MB BS DPhil   Clin. Sr. Lectr., Clinical Genetics
Murray, N., BM   Cancer Research UK Clin. Sr. Lectr., Medical Oncology
Nugent, Karen, MD, FRCS   Clin. Sr. Lectr., Surgery
Orchard, K., MB BS PhD   Sr. Lectr., Haematology
Ottensmeier, C. H., MD Mün., PhD S'ton.   Cancer Research UK Clin. Sr. Lectr.
Packham, G., BSc Leeds, PhD Lond.   Cancer Research UK Prof., Experimental Oncology
Primrose, J. N., MD Glas., MB ChB, FRCS   Prof., Surgery
Quarantino, S., MD Palermo, PhD Palermo   Reader
Smith, D., BM BS Nott., MD Nott.   Clin. Sr. Lectr., Anaesthetics
Stevenson, F. K., MSc DPhil, FRCPath   Prof., Immunology
Other Staff: 3 Lectrs.; 15 Sr. Res. Fellows
Research: DNA vaccine development; immunogenic glycopeptide (MHC class I complexes); mechanisms of MoAb immunotherapy

Clinical Neurosciences Division

Tel: (023) 8059 7804 Fax: (023) 8059 7803
   E-mail: cns@soton.ac.uk
Baldwin, D., MB BS Lond.   Reader, Psychiatry
Belli, A., MD, FRCS   Sr. Lectr., Neurosurgery
Bridges, L.   Sr. Lectr., Neuropathology
Gray, W. P., MD, FRCSI, FRCS   Prof., Neurosurgery
Hill, C. M., BM   Sr. Lectr., Community Child Health
Holmes, C., BSc ChB   Prof., Biological Psychiatry
Kaube, H.   Prof., Neurology
Kennedy, C. R., BA BS MD, FRCPCH   Reader, Community Child Health
Kingdon, D., MD, FRCPsych   Prof., Mental Health Care Delivery
Lees, P. D., MB ChB MS, FRCS   Sr. Lectr., Neurosurgery
Lotery, A. J., MB BCh MD   Prof., Ophthalmology
Nicoll, J. A.R., BSc MB ChB MD, FRCPath   Prof., Neuropathology; Dir.*
Peveler, R., BA Oxf., DPhil Oxf.   Prof., Liaison Psychiatry
Pringle, A., BSc PhD   Sr. Lectr., Neurosciences
Sinclair, J. M. A., BSc MSc MB BS DPhil   Sr. Lectr., Psychiatry

Sundstrom, L. E., BA DPhil   Prof., Neurosciences

Other Staff: 1 Sr. Res. Fellow

Research: genetic determinants of outcome in head injury; inflammatory responses during brain damage; ischaemic brain damage; mechanisms and pathology of neurodegeneration

Community Clinical Sciences Division

Tel: (023) 8024 1050 Fax: (023) 8070 1125
E-mail: ccsdiv@soton.ac.uk

Coggon, David N. M., MA PhD DM, FRCP   Hon. Prof., Occupational and Environmental Medicine

Coleman, P. G., MA Oxf., PhD Lond., FBPsS   Prof., Psychogerontology

Dunn, N., MA Camb., DM S'ton., MSc   Sr. Lectr., Primary Medical Care

George, S. L., MB BS Lond., MSc Lond.   Reader, Public Health Medicine

Kendrick, Anthony, MB BS Lond., MD Lond., BSc, FRCGP   Prof., Primary Care; Dir.*

Lewith, G. T., MA MB BChir   Reader, Complimentary Medicine

Little, P., BA MSc MD   Prof., Primary Medical Care

Moore, M.   Sr. Lectr., Primary Medical Care

Mullee, M. A.   Sr. Lectr., Medical Statistics

Pickering, R., MSc PhD   Sr. Lectr., Medical Statistics

Roderick, P. J., BSc Camb., MB BS Lond., MSc Lond.   Sr. Lectr., Public Health Medicine

Williamson, I. G., MB ChB Edin., MD Edin., FRCSEd   Sr. Lectr., Primary Care

Other Staff: 10 Sr. Res. Fellows; 1 Clin. Lectr.; 1 Clin. Scientist/Hon. Reader

Research: common mental health problems; design and delivery of health care; occupational and environmental medicine

Developmental Origins of Health and Disease Division

Tel: (023) 8079 8421 Fax: (023) 8078 6933

Anderson, Frazer H., MB ChB Edin.   Sr. Lectr., Geriatric Medicine

Arden, N. K., MB BS MSc MD   Reader, Rheumatology

Byrne, C. D. T., PhD, FRCP   Prof., Endocrinology

Calder, P. C., BSc PhD DPhil   Prof., Nutritional Immunology

Cameron, Iain T., BSc Edin., MB ChB Edin., MD Edin., MA Camb., FRCOG   Prof., Obstetrics and Gynaecology

Clarke, N. M. P., ChM, FRCS   Prof., Orthopaedic Surgery

Cooper, C., MA DM, FRCP   Hon. Prof., Rheumatology

Dennison, E. M., MB BChir MA MSc DPhil   Reader, Rheumatology

Elia, M., BSc MB ChB MD, FRCP   Prof., Clinical Nutrition and Metabolism

Fall, C. H. D., MB ChB BSc DM, FRCP, FRCPCH   Prof., Paediatric Epidemiology

Godfrey, K. M., BM PhD   Prof., Epidemiology and Human Development

Green, L. R., BSc PhD   Sr. Lectr.

Grimble, R. F., BSc Wales, PhD Wales   Prof., Nutrition

Hanson, M., MA DPhil, FRCOG   Prof., Cardiovascular Sciences; Dir.*

Holt, R. I. G., PhD   Reader, Endocrinology

Jackson, A. A., CBE, BA Camb., MB BChir Camb., MD Camb., FRCP   Prof., Nutrition

Jackson, P. C., BSc PhD, FIP   Reader, Medical Physics and Bioengineering

Margetts, B. M., BSc W.Aust., MSc Lond., PhD W.Aust.   Prof., Public Health Nutrition

Michailidis, G.   Sr. Lectr., Obstetrics/Gynaecology

Oreffo, R. O., BSc   Prof., Orthopaedic Surgery

Roach, H. I., BA MSc PhD   Reader, Orthopaedic Surgery

Roberts, G. C., MA MSc DM   Reader, Child Health

Shearman, C., BSc MB BS MS, FRCS   Prof., Vascular Surgery

Stroud, M. A., BSc MB BS MD, FRCP   Sr. Lectr., Human Nutrition

Wootton, S. A., BSc PhD   Sr. Lectr., Human Nutrition

Other Staff: 5 Lectrs.; 8 Sr. Res. Fellows; 2 Clin. Lectrs.; 2 Hon. Sr. Lectrs.; 1 Hon. Non-Clin. Scientist/Statistician

Research: corticosteroid therapy and fracture risk; early development and the metabolic syndrome X; epidemiology of osteoporotic fracture; epidemiology, pathophysiology and prevention of osteoporosis; programming of laer life osteoporosis

Human Genetics Division

Tel: (023) 8079 6421 Fax: (023) 8079 4264
E-mail: hgenq@soton.ac.uk

Collins, A. R., BSc MSc PhD   Prof., Genetic Epidemiology and Bioinformatics

Cross, N. C., MA PhD   Prof.

Hanley, N. A., MB ChB PhD   Prof., Endocrinology

Temple, I. K., MB ChB, FRCP   Prof., Medical Genetics

Townsend, P. A.   Reader

Wilson, D. I., BA MB BS PhD, FRCP   Prof., Human Developmental Genetics; Dir.*

Other Staff: 3 Lectrs.; 6 Sr. Res. Fellows; 1 Principal Res. Fellow

Research: cytogenetics and molecular genetics; genetic epidemiology and bio-informatics; human developmental genetics; molecular genetic epidemiology and cardiovascular genetics; studies in fragile X and autism

Infection, Inflammation and Repair Division

Tel: (023) 8079 5026 Fax: (023) 8050 1761

Arshad, S. H.   Reader, Allergy

Benyon, C., BA PhD   Sr. Lectr., Medicine

Christodoulides, M.   Sr. Lectr.

Church, M. K., MPharm Wales, PhD CNAA, DSc S'ton.   Prof., Experimental Immunopharmacology

Clarke, I. N., BSc Leeds, PhD Warw.   Prof., Virology

Clough, G. F., BSc PhD   Reader

Collins, J. E., BSc PhD   Sr. Lectr.

Davies, D., PhD   Prof., Cell and Molecular Biology

Djukanovic, Ratko, MSc Belgrade, MD Belgrade   Prof., Respiratory Medicine

Faust, S.   Sr. Lectr., Child Health

Friedmann, P. S., BA Camb., MB BChir Camb., MD Camb.   Prof., Dermatology; Dir.*

Gallagher, P. J., MD PhD   Reader, Pathology

Healy, E., BA MB BCh BAO PhD   Prof., Dermatology

Heckels, J. E., BSc Newcastle(UK), PhD Newcastle(UK)   Prof., Molecular Microbiology

Holgate, Stephen T., BSc Lond., MD Lond., DSc Lond., FRCP   Prof., Immunopharmacology

Hossain, P. N., MB ChB PhD   Sr. Lectr., Ophthalmology

Howarth, Peter H., BSc Lond., MB BS Lond., DM, FRCP   Reader, Medicine

Khakoo, S. I.   Prof., Hepatology

Lucas, J.   Sr. Lectr., Child Health

Patel, Rajul, MB ChB Sheff.   Sr. Lectr., Genito-Urinary Medicine

Pender, S. L., BSc PhD   Sr. Lectr.

Postle, A. D., BSc PhD   Prof., Developmental Biochemistry

Roche, W. R., MB ChB BAO N.U.I., BSc N.U.I., MD N.U.I., FRCPath   Prof., Pathology

Rosenberg, W. M. C., MB BS Lond., MA Camb., DPhil Oxf.   Reader, Medicine

Sampson, A. P., MA PhD   Reader

Sheron, N., MD Sheff., FRCP   Sr. Lectr., Medicine

Walls, Andrew F., BSc Aberd., PhD Lond.   Reader, Medicine

Warner, J. A.   Reader, Allergy and Immunology

Other Staff: 5 Lectrs.; 1 Principal Res. Fellows; 3 Sr. Res. Fellows

Research: environmental influences on development of allergy; foetal sensitisation to aeroallergens; melanocortin-1 receptor variants in skin cancer; molecular and cellular mechanisms of peanut allergy; prophylaxis of allergic disease

Management, Information and Computing Division

Tel: (023) 8079 6566 Fax: (023) 8079 4460
E-mail: icd@soton.ac.uk

Bryant, T. N., BSc PhD   Sr. Lectr., Biocomputation

Medical Education Division

Tel: (023) 8059 4556 Fax: (023) 8059 4159

Briggs, R. S. J., MB BS Lond., MSc Lond., FRCP   Prof., Geriatric Medicine

Dunn, N., MA Camb., DM S'ton., MSc   Sr. Lectr., Primary Medical Care

Fenwick, A., BA MSc PhD   Sr. Lectr., Medical Ethics and Education

Field, J., BM BCh Oxf., BA   Sr. Lectr., Primary Medical Care

Hill, F. J., BA MA(Ed) PhD   Sr. Lectr.; Dir.*

Kendall, K., BA MA PhD   Sr. Lectr., Sociology as applied to Medicine

Lueddeke, G. R., BA MEd PhD   Sr. Lectr.

Noble, A. R., BSc S'ton., PhD S'ton.   Sr. Lectr., Physiology

Roberts, H. C., BSc MB ChB   Sr. Lectr., Geriatric Medicine

Skidmore, J. R., MB ChB PhD   Sr. Lectr., Anatomical Science

Stephens, C. R., MB BS   Sr. Lectr., Primary Care

Stones, R. W., MD   Sr. Lectr., Obstetrics and Gynaecology

Thavarajar, M., BDS BMedSci PhD   Sr. Lectr., Anatomical Sciences

Winyard, G., CBE, FRCP   Hon. Visiting Prof.; Regional Postgrad. Dean, Med. Studies

Other Staff: 5 Lectrs.; 5 Hon. Profs.; 2 Hon. Readers; 39 Hon. Sr. Lectrs.; 49 Hon. Clin. Sr. Lectrs.

Nursing and Midwifery

Tel: (023) 8059 7979 Fax: (023) 8059 7900
E-mail: uossonam@soton.ac.uk

Addington-Hall, Julia, BA PhD   Prof., End of Life Care

Barrett, Chris, BSc PhD   Sr. Lectr.

Brown, Janice, BSc PhD   Sr. Lectr.

Buckingham, Sylvia, BEd MSc   Sr. Lectr.

Cluett, Elizabeth, MSc PhD   Sr. Lectr.

Colley, Sue, MA EdD   Dir., Professional and External Liaison

Corner, Jessica, BSc Lond., PhD Lond.   Prof., Cancer and Palliative Care

Duke, Sue, BSc MSc   Sr. Lectr.

Fader, Mandy, BSc PhD   Reader

Foster, Claire, BSc MSc PhD   Reader

Gerard, Karen, BA MSc PhD   Reader

Getliffe, Kathy, BSc Sur., MSc Qld., PhD Sur.   Prof., Nursing

Glasper, E. Alan, BA CNAA, PhD   Prof., Nursing Studies

Gobbi, Mary, MA PhD   Sr. Lectr.

Green, Sue, BSc Sheff., MMedSci Sheff., PhD Leeds   Sr. Lectr.

Jackson, Pamela, BSc MSc   Sr. Lectr.

Jowett, Rosalind   Dir., Education

Knowles, Helena, BSc MPhil   Sr. Lectr.

Lathlean, Judith, BSc Cardiff, MA Brun., DPhil Oxf.   Prof., Health Research

Latter, Sue, BSc Lond., PhD Lond.   Reader

Lattimer, Val, MA(Ed) S'ton., PhD S'ton.   Prof., Health Services Research

le May, Andree, BSc Lond., PhD Lond.   Prof., Nursing

Macleod Clark, Jill, DBE, BSc Lond., PhD Lond.   Prof.; Head*

Marjoram, Barbara, MA   Sr. Lectr.

Meakin, Stephanie, BA BSc MA   Sr. Lectr.

Owens, Kathleen, MSc   Sr. Lectr.

Pogson, Delia, MSc CNAA, MPhil S'ton.   Sr. Lectr.

Pope, Catherine, BA PhD   Reader

Reading, Sheila, BSc MSc Sr. Lectr.
Rogers, Lynda, BA MA PhD Sr. Lectr.
Rushforth, Helen, BA PhD Sr. Lectr.
Sque, Magaret, BSc Sur., PhD S'ton. Sr. Lectr.
Tee, Steve, BA Portsmouth, MA S'ton. Sr. Lectr.
Voegli, David, BSc PhD Sr. Lectr.
Walsh, Bronagh, BSc PhD Sr. Lectr.
Webster, Brian, BA Portsmouth Sr. Lectr.
Other Staff: 107 Lectrs.; 6 Sr. Res. Fellows; 5 Res. Fellows
Research: cancer, palliative and end of life care; health services research linked to innovations in care delivery and professional development; living with chronic health needs

CONTACT OFFICERS

Academic affairs. Director of Student Services: Phillips, M., BSc MA(Ed)
  (E-mail: mp5@soton.ac.uk)
Accommodation. Accommodation Officer: Cliburn, M., BA Wales, MA Wales
  (E-mail: m.p.cliburn@soton.ac.uk)
Admissions (first degree). Head of Registry Services: Heathcote, Z., MA Edin.
  (E-mail: asm3@soton.ac.uk)
Admissions (higher degree). Head of Registry Services: Heathcote, Z., MA Edin.
  (E-mail: asm3@soton.ac.uk)
Alumni. Alumni Officer: Chillingworth, S., BA S'ton. (E-mail: sc18@soton.ac.uk)
Archives. Archivist and Head of Special Collections: Woolgar, C., BA S'ton., PhD Durh. (E-mail: c.m.woolgar@soton.ac.uk)
Careers. Director, Careers Advisory Service: Collins, A., BA Plym., MSc Open(UK)
  (E-mail: a.collins@soton.ac.uk)
Computing services. Director (Information Systems Services): Tebbett, Ian, BSc PhD
  (E-mail: p.j.hancock@soton.ac.uk)
Conferences/corporate hospitality. Conference Manager: Wootten, Rachel, BA Hull (E-mail: conferences@soton.ac.uk)
Consultancy services. Director, Innovation and Research Support: Raven, A. P., BSc Manc., MSc Oxf., DPhil Oxf.
  (E-mail: t.raven@soton.ac.uk)

Credit transfer. Acting Head, Learning and Teaching Enhancement Unit: Giles, Ian, BSc PhD (E-mail: jb1@soton.ac.uk)
Development/fund-raising. Senior Development Officer: Glasspool, Steve
  (E-mail: s.w.glasspool@soton.ac.uk)
Equal opportunities. Head of Staff Diversity: Kerridge-Poonia, Kamaljit
Estates and buildings/works and services. Director, Estates and Buildings: Monaghan, Kevin, BSc (E-mail: kpm@soton.ac.uk)
Examinations. Student Operations Manager: (vacant), MA(Ed) S'ton.
  (E-mail: j.lupton@soton.ac.uk)
Finance. Director, Finance: Ace, Malcolm J., MA Oxf. (E-mail: m.j.ace@soton.ac.uk)
General enquiries. Registrar and Chief Operating Officer: Higman, Simon
  (E-mail: sh@soton.ac.uk)
Health services. Partner, University Health Service: (vacant)
Industrial liaison. Director, Innovation and Research Support: Raven, A. P., BSc Manc., MSc Oxf., DPhil Oxf.
  (E-mail: t.raven@soton.ac.uk)
International office. Head: Doyle, J. A., BA Trinity(Dub.), MBA S'ton.
  (E-mail: ednfairs@soton.ac.uk)
Library (chief librarian). Librarian: Brown, M. L., MA Camb., PhD Camb.
  (E-mail: mlb@soton.ac.uk)
Library (enquiries). Assistant Librarian, Enquiry Service: Boagey, P. W., MSc Brist.
  (E-mail: libenqs@soton.ac.uk)
Marketing. Director, Corporate and Marketing Services: (vacant)
  (E-mail: j.m.mccaig@soton.ac.uk)
Minorities/disadvantaged groups. Head of Staff Diversity: Kerridge-Poonia, Kamaljit
Personnel/human resources. Director, Human Resources: Strike, A. J., MSc Portsmouth (E-mail: a.j.strike@soton.ac.uk)
Public relations. Director, Media Relations: Waring, Steve, BEd Liv., MA(Ed) S'ton.
  (E-mail: swaring@soton.ac.uk)
Purchasing. Manager, Purchasing Services: Candy, J. (E-mail: jtc2@soton.ac.uk)

Quality assurance and accreditation. Acting Head, Learning and Teaching Enhancement Unit: Giles, Ian, BSc PhD
Research. Director, Innovation and Research Support: Raven, A. P., BSc Manc., MSc Oxf., DPhil Oxf. (E-mail: t.raven@soton.ac.uk)
Safety. Safety Adviser: Booker, M. D., BSc Birm., MSc Lond.
  (E-mail: m.d.booker@soton.ac.uk)
Schools liaison. Head of UK Office: Kennett, Richard, BSc Salf., MA(Ed) S'ton.
  (E-mail: rjck@soton.ac.uk)
Security. Chief Security Officer: Jackson, Gary, MA Lond. (E-mail: g.k.jackson@soton.ac.uk)
Sport and recreation. Director, Sport and Recreation: Barber, Laurence, BEd Sus., MA(Ed) S'ton. (E-mail: lb1@soton.ac.uk)
Staff development and training. Training and Development Manager: Cooper, A., BSc CNAA (E-mail: c.a.cooper@soton.ac.uk)
Strategic planning. Director, Corporate and Marketing Services: (vacant)
  (E-mail: j.m.mccaig@soton.ac.uk)
Student union. Permanent Secretary: Clegg, G. R. (E-mail: g.r.clegg@soton.ac.uk)
Student welfare/counselling. Assistant Director, Student Support: Partington, Kevin
  (E-mail: tm7@soton.ac.uk)
Students from other countries. Adviser to International Students: Cooke, E. C., MSc Lond. (E-mail: ecc@ecs.soton.ac.uk)
Students with disabilities. Head of Disability Service: Henry, Sarah, BA MSc
  (E-mail: enable@soton.ac.uk)
Women. Head of Staff Diversity: Kerridge-Poonia, Kamaljit

CAMPUS/COLLEGE HEADS

Winchester School of Art, Park Avenue, Winchester, England SO23 8DL. (Tel: (023) 8059 6900; Fax: (023) 8059 6901; E-mail: b.makhoul@soton.ac.uk) Head: Makhoul, Prof. Bashir, BA MA PhD

[Information supplied by the institution as at 29 November 2007, and edited by the ACU]

SOUTHAMPTON SOLENT UNIVERSITY

Postal Address: East Park Terrace, Southampton, Hampshire, England SO14 0YN
Telephone: (023) 8031 9000 **Fax:** (023) 8033 4161 **E-mail:** enquiries@solent.ac.uk
URL: http://www.solent.ac.uk

VICE-CHANCELLOR*—(from 1 August 2007) Gore, Prof. Van

STAFFORDSHIRE UNIVERSITY

Founded 1992

Member of the Association of Commonwealth Universities

Postal Address: College Road, Stoke-on-Trent, England ST4 2DE
Telephone: (01782) 294000 **Fax:** (01782) 295799 **E-mail:** postmaster@staffs.ac.uk
URL: http://www.staffs.ac.uk

VICE-CHANCELLOR*—King, Prof. Christine E., CBE, BA Birm., MA Birm., PhD CNAA, Hon. DLitt Birm., FRHistS, FRSA
UNIVERSITY SECRETARY‡—Sproston, Kenneth B. G.
DEPUTY VICE-CHANCELLOR—O'Brien, Susan, BA PhD
DEPUTY VICE-CHANCELLOR—Richards, Paul, BA, FRSA
DIRECTOR OF FINANCE—Starkie, Ian D., BA Sheff.
DEAN OF STUDENTS AND ACADEMIC REGISTRAR—Francis, Francesca, BA Leic.
DIRECTOR OF LIBRARY AND LEARNING RESOURCES—Hart, Elizabeth, BA Leic., FLA

UNIVERSITY OF STIRLING

Founded 1967

Member of the Association of Commonwealth Universities

Postal Address: Stirling, Scotland FK9 4LA
Telephone: (01786) 473171 **Fax:** (01786) 463000
URL: http://www.stir.ac.uk

PRINCIPAL AND VICE-CHANCELLOR*—Hallett, Prof. Christine M., MA Camb., PhD Lough., FRSEd
SENIOR DEPUTY PRINCIPAL—Keeble, Prof. N. H., BA Lampeter, DPhil Oxf., DLitt Stir., FRSEd, FRHistS, FRSA
DEPUTY PRINCIPAL—Burt, Prof. S. L., BA Oxf., PhD Stir.
DEPUTY PRINCIPAL—Jarvie, G., BEd Exe., MA Qu., PhD Leic.
DEPUTY PRINCIPAL—Simpson, Prof. I. A., BSc Strath., PhD Strath.
UNIVERSITY SECRETARY‡—Clarke, Kevin J., BA Stir.
ACADEMIC REGISTRAR—Morrow, J. F., MA Edin.
DIRECTOR OF INFORMATION SERVICES AND UNIVERSITY LIBRARIAN—Kemp, P., MA Camb., PhD Camb.

GENERAL INFORMATION

History. The university was established in 1967.

It is located in central Scotland, 5km north of Stirling and 50km from Edinburgh.

Admission to first degree courses (see also United Kingdom Introduction). BA, BAcc, BSc, LLB: through Universities and Colleges Admissions Service (UCAS); other programmes: direct to university.

First Degrees (see also United Kingdom Directory to Subjects of Study) (* = with honours). BA, BA*, BAcc, BAcc*, BM, BN, BSc, BSc*, LLB.

BA, BAcc, BSc: also available part-time.
Length of course. Full-time: BA, BAcc, BSc: 3 years; BA*, BAcc*, BSc*, LLB: 4 years. Part-time: BM, BN: 4 years.

Higher Degrees (see also United Kingdom Directory to Subjects of Study).

Master's. MBA, MEd, MgMg, MLitt, MN, MPhil, MRes, MSc.

Length of course. Full-time: MBA, MEd, MLitt, MPhil, MRes, MSc: 1 year. Part-time: MPhil, MSc: 2 years; MBA, MEd, MLitt, MRes: 2½ years. By distance learning: MEd, MSc: 2–5 years; MBA: 2¼ years; MgMg, MN: 4–6 years.

Doctoral. DASR, DBA, DM, DN, EdD, PhD.

Length of course. Full-time: PhD: 3 years; DASR, DBA, DM, DN, EdD: 3–4 years. Part-time: DASR, DBA, DM, DN, EdD, PhD: 4–6 years.

Academic Year (2007–2008). Two semesters: 10 September–17 December; 11 February–31 May.

Statistics. Students (2006–2007): full-time 8150; part-time 2250; international 2000; distance education/external 300; undergraduate 8250; master's 1600; doctoral 500.

FACULTIES/SCHOOLS

Arts
Tel: (01786) 467490 Fax: (01786) 451335
Head: McKean, Prof. R. B., MA Glas., PhD E.Anglia, FRHistS
Secretary: Robertson, E.

Human Sciences
Tel: (01786) 467595 Fax: (01786) 467641
Head: Timms, Prof. D. W. G., BA Camb., PhD Camb.
Secretary: Morris, S.

Management
Tel: (01786) 467278 Fax: (01786) 467279
Head: Ball, Prof. Rob, MA Oxf., MSc Birm., PhD Stir.
Secretary: Malone, C.

Natural Sciences
Tel: (01786) 467750 Fax: (01786) 466896
Head: Sommerville, Prof. C., BA Stir., PhD Stir.
Secretary: Alexander, V.

ACADEMIC UNITS

Accounting and Finance
Tel: (01786) 467280 Fax: (01786) 467308
E-mail: accountancy@stir.ac.uk
Campbell, K., MA Glas., PhD Glas.   Sr. Lectr.
Evans, L., MA Edin., PhD Reading   Prof.
Fraser, I. A. M., MA Glas.   Prof.
Goodacre, A., BSc Exe., PhD Exe.   Prof.; Head*
Kabir, R. M., BA Dhaka, MA Leuven, PhD Maastricht   Prof.
McInnes, W. M., MSc Durh., PhD Glas., FRSA   Prof.
Stopforth, D. P., PhD Glas.   Prof.
Veld, C. H., MA Tilburg, MFE Tilburg, PhD Tilburg   Prof.
Other Staff: 7 Lectrs.; 1 Sr. Teaching Fellow
Research: auditing; financial reporting and finance; taxation

Applied Social Science
Tel: (01786) 467691 Fax: (01786) 467689
E-mail: jgc2@stir.ac.uk
Anderson, I., BSc St And., DPhil York(UK)   Sr. Lectr.
Birchall, R. J., BA Oxf., MA York(UK), DPhil York(UK)   Prof.
Bowes, A. M., BA Durh., PhD Durh., FRAI   Prof.
Cavanagh, K., BA Stir., MA Warw., MSc Stir., PhD Manc.   Sr. Lectr.
Daniel, B., MA St And., PhD Edin.   Prof.
Eley-Morris, S., BA Manc., MSc Stir., PhD Glas.   Sr. Lectr.
Ferguson, I., LLB Glas., MSc G.Caledonian, PhD Glas.   Sr. Lectr.
Gayle, V., BA CNAA, MA Lanc., PhD Sund.   Sr. Lectr.
Innes, A., BA Stir., MSc Stir., PhD Brad.   Sr. Lectr.
Maxwell, M., MA Edin., PhD Edin.   Reader
McIntosh, I., MA Glas., PhD Manc.   Sr. Lectr.
Murray, C., MA St And., MSc Stir.   Sr. Lectr.
Robertson, D. S., MA Aberd., PhD Glas.   Sr. Lectr.; Head
Rowlings, C., BA York(UK)   Prof.; Dir., Soc. Work Educn.
Rummery, K., LLB Kent, MA Kent, PhD Birm.   Prof.
Satsangi, M., MSc Stir., MPhil Glas., PhD   Sr. Lectr.
Tombs, J., MA Glas., PhD Edin.   Prof.
Other Staff: 12 Lectrs.; 2 Sr. Teaching Fellows; 2 Sr. Res. Fellows; 5 Teaching Fellows; 9 Res. Fellows; 2 Hon. Profs.; 3 Hon. Sr. Lectrs.; 1 Hon. Sr. Res. Fellow; 4 Hon. Res. Fellows
Research: care and protection (children, young people); dementia; social care and health; social exclusion and marginalisation

Aquaculture, Institute of
Tel: (01786) 467878 Fax: (01786) 472133
Adams, A., BSc Glas., PhD Glas.   Prof.
Bell, J. G., BSc Edin., PhD Stir.   Sr. Lectr.
Bell, M. V., BSc Leeds, PhD Leeds   Reader
Ferguson, H. W., BVM&S Edin., PhD Stir., FRCPath   Prof.
George, S. G., BSc Leeds, MPhil Leeds, PhD Leeds   Prof.
Jauncey, K., BSc Wales, PhD Aston   Sr. Lectr.
Little, D. C., BSc Liv., MSc Stir., PhD Stir.   Sr. Lectr.
MacIntosh, D. J., BSc Aberd., PhD Malaya   Sr. Lectr.
McAndrew, B. J., BSc Wales, PhD Wales   Prof.
Muir, J. F., BSc Edin., PhD Strath.   Prof.
Penman, D. J., BSc Edin., PhD Wales   Sr. Lectr.
Richards, R. H., MA Camb., VetMB Camb., PhD Stir., FIBiol   Prof.; Head*
Ross, L. G., BSc CNAA, PhD Stir.   Prof.
Sommerville, C., BA Stir., PhD Stir.   Prof.
Teale, A. J., BA Camb., MA Camb., VetMB Camb., MSc Edin., PhD Edin.   Prof.
Telfer, T. C., BSc H-W, PhD H-W   Sr. Lectr.
Tocher, D. R., BSc Edin., PhD Edin.   Sr. Lectr.
Turnbull, J. F., BVMS Edin., MSc Stir., PhD Stir.   Sr. Lectr.
Wootten, R., BSc Lond., BA Open(UK), PhD Lond.   Sr. Lectr.; Deputy Dir.
Other Staff: 6 Lectrs.; 4 Postdoctoral Res. Fellows; 13 Res. Fellows; 2 Teaching Fellows; 2 Postdoctoral Scientists; 1 Postdoctoral Researcher; 1 Res. Assoc.
Research: aquaculture systems; disease; environment; genetics and reproduction; nutrition

Biological and Environmental Sciences, School of
Tel: (01786) 467755-6 Fax: (01786) 464994
Davidson, D. A., BSc Aberd., PhD Sheff., FRSEd   Prof.
Gilvear, D. J., BSc S'ton., PhD Lough.   Reader
Goulson, D., BSc Oxf., PhD Oxf.Brookes   Prof.; Head*
Grieve, I. C., BSc Glas., PhD Brist.   Sr. Lectr.
Hopkins, D. W., BSc CNAA, PhD Newcastle(UK), FIBiol   Prof.
Moffatt, I., BSc Lond., MSc Newcastle(UK), PhD Newcastle(UK), FRGS   Sr. Lectr.
Salt, C. A., DrRerNat F.U.Berlin   Sr. Lectr.
Simpson, I. A., BSc Strath., PhD Strath.   Prof.
Tipping, R. M., BSc Hull, PhD CNAA   Sr. Lectr.
Tyler, A. N., BSc Birm., MSc Dund., PhD Glas.   Sr. Lectr.
Willby, N. J., BSc Liv., PhD Liv.   Sr. Lectr.
Wookey, P., BSc Exe., PhD Lanc.   Reader
Wyman, M., BSc Lond., PhD Lond.   Sr. Lectr.
Other Staff: 7 Lectrs.; 1 Sr. Teaching Fellow; 1 Sr. Res. Fellow; 2 Teaching Fellows; 3 Res. Fellows; 1 Academic Fellow; 4 Postdoctoral Res. Fellows/Assts.; 4 Hon. Profs.; 1 Hon. Sr. Res. Fellow; 4 Hon. Lectrs.
Research: climatic and hydrological variability; ecology and wildlife epidemiology; land

resources; landscape change; molecular life sciences

Computing Science and Mathematics

Tel: (01786) 467421 Fax: (01786) 464551
Clark, R. G., BSc St And., PhD Dund.   Sr. Lectr.; Head*
Graham, B. P., BA Flin., PhD Qld.   Reader
Hussain, A., BEng Strath., PhD Strath.   Sr. Lectr.
Kleczkowski, A., MSc T.U.Cracow, PhD T.U.Cracow   Sr. Lectr.
Magill, E., BSc UMIST, MSc UMIST, PhD Strath., FIETE   Prof.
Norman, R. A., BSc Liv., PhD Liv.   Sr. Lectr.
Shankland, C. E., BSc Glas., PhD Glas.   Sr. Lectr.
Smith, L. S., BSc Glas., PhD Glas.   Prof.
Turner, K. J., BSc Glas., PhD Edin.   Prof.
Other Staff: 7 Lectrs.; 2 Teaching Fellows; 5 Res. Fellows; 1 Hon. Prof.
Research: algebraic graph theory; applied artificial intelligence; mathematical ecology; neural computing; persistent systems

Economics

Tel: (01786) 467470 Fax: (01786) 467469
E-mail: econ@stir.ac.uk
Bell, D. N. F., MA Aberd., MSc Lond., PhD Strath., FRSEd   Prof.
Blanchflower, D., BA Leic., PhD Lond.   Prof.
Dow, S. C., MA St And., MA Manit., PhD Glas.   Prof.
Ghosh, D., MA Calc., MSocSc Birm., PhD Stir.   Sr. Lectr.
Hanley, N. D., BA Stir., PhD Newcastle(UK)   Prof.
Hart, Robert A., BA Liv., MA Liv., FRSA   Prof.; Head*
King, D. N., MA Oxf., DPhil York(UK)   Prof.
Ruffell, R. J., MA Camb., PhD Brist.   Sr. Lectr.
Other Staff: 5 Lectrs.; 1 Res. Assoc.
Research: economic thought; finance; labour economics

Education, Institute of

Tel: (01786) 467600 Fax: (01786) 467633
Allan, J. E., BEd CNAA, PhD Stir.   Prof.
Boreham, N., BA Nott., MA Nott., MPhil Nott., PhD Manc.   Prof.
Canning, R., BA H-W, MA Brighton, PhD Aberd.   Sr. Lectr.
Cope, P. A., BSc Aberd., PhD Belf.   Prof.
Edwards, R. G., BA CNAA, PhD Kent   Prof.; Head*
Field, J., BA Portsmouth, PhD Warw.   Prof.
McNally, J. G., BSc Glas., MEd Stir.   Sr. Lectr.
Morgan-Klein, B., BA Stir.   Sr. Lectr.
Nicoll, K., BEd Edin., MPH Dund., PhD Technol.Syd.   Sr. Lectr.
Oberski, I., MSc Amst., PhD Stir.   Sr. Lectr.
Osborne, M. J., BSc Reading, PhD Lond.   Prof.
Plowman, L., BA E.Anglia, PhD Brighton   Prof.
Priestly, M. R., BA Manc., MEd Leeds   Sr. Lectr.
Reeves, Carol J., BA Keele, MPhil E.Anglia, PhD Strath.   Sr. Lectr.
Other Staff: 14 Lectrs.; 4 Sr. Teaching Fellows; 1 Sr. Res. Fellow; 13 Teaching Fellows; 9 Res. Fellows; 2 Hon. Profs.; 1 Hon. Lectr.; 1 Hon. Teaching Fellow
Research: curriculum, teaching and learning; policy into practice; practitioner thinking and development

English Studies

Tel: (01786) 467495 Fax: (01786) 466210
E-mail: engl1@stir.ac.uk
Byron, G., BA Calg., MA Calg., PhD Alta.   Prof.
Drakakis, J., BA Wales, MA Wales, PhD Leeds   Prof.
Evans, R., BA Manc., MA Manc., PhD Leeds   Prof.; Head*
Keeble, N. H., BA Lampeter, DPhil Oxf., DLitt Stir., FRSEd, FRHistS, FRSA   Prof.
Richards, D., MA Lond., MA Lond., MA Camb., PhD Camb.   Prof.
Sowerby, R. E., MA Camb., PhD Camb.   Sr. Lectr.

Watson, R. B., MA Aberd., PhD Camb., FRSEd   Prof.
Wheatcroft, A. J. M., MA Camb.   Sr. Lectr.
Other Staff: 7 Lectrs.; 1 Sr. Teaching Fellow; 1 Teaching Fellow; 1 Postdoctoral Fellow; 1 Res. Fellow
Research: computational and descriptive linguistics; early modern studies; modern writing; Scottish literature

Film and Media Studies

Tel: (01786) 467520 Fax: (01786) 466855
Blain, N. A., BA Stir., PhD Strath.   Prof.; Head*
Izod, K. John, BA Leeds, PhD Leeds   Prof.
Kilborn, R. W., BA Nott., MA Lond., MPhil Nott.   Sr. Lectr.
MacDonald, M. N., MA Aberd., PhD Camb.   Reader
Meech, P. H., BA Wales, MA Manc., MA Leic.   Sr. Lectr.
Other Staff: 9 Lectrs.; 1 Sr. Teaching Fellow; 6 Teaching Fellows; 8 Hon. Profs.; 4 Hon. Lectrs.
Research: cultural policy; media and national identity; media systems; screen interpretation; sociology of journalism

History

Tel: (01786) 467580 Fax: (01786) 467581
Bebbington, D. W., MA Camb., PhD Camb., FRHistS   Prof.
Hopkinson, M. A., MA Camb., PhD Camb.   Reader
Hutchison, I. G. C., MA Aberd., PhD Edin., FRHistS   Reader
Law, R. C. C., BA Oxf., PhD Birm., FRHistS, FBA, FRSEd   Prof.
Oram, R. D., MA St And., PhD St And.   Sr. Lectr.
Peden, G. C., MA Dund., DPhil Oxf., FRHistS, FRSEd   Prof.
Penman, M., MA St And., PhD St And.   Sr. Lectr.
Rapport, M. G., MA Edin., PhD Brist., FRHistS   Sr. Lectr.
Smyth, J. J., MA Glas., PhD Edin.   Sr. Lectr.; Head*
Stachura, P. D., MA Glas., PhD E.Anglia, DLitt Stir., FRHistS   Prof.
Other Staff: 7 Lectrs.; 1 Hon. Prof.; 3 Hon. Lectrs.; 1 Hon. Sr. Res. Fellow
Research: African history; British history; continental European history; Scottish history; social history

Environmental History, Centre for

Ross, A., MA Aberd., PhD Aberd.   Commercial Manager

Languages, Cultures and Religions, School of

Tel: (01786) 467530 Fax: (01786) 466088
Duncan, A. B., MA Aberd., PhD Aberd.   Sr. Lectr.
Ezra, E., BA Calif., MA Cornell, PhD Cornell   Sr. Lectr.
Fitzgerald, T. F., BA Lond., MSc Lond., PhD Lond.   Reader
Flood, G., BA Lanc., MA Lanc., PhD Lanc.   Prof.
Ginger, A., MA Oxf., DPhil Oxf.   Prof., Hispanic Studies; Head*
Kidd, W., MA Glas., PhD Stir.   Reader
Murdoch, B. O., BA Exe., PhD Camb., LittD Camb., FRHistS   Prof.
Murphy, D. F., MA PhD   Sr. Lectr.
Other Staff: 8 Lectrs.; 1 Visiting Lectr.; 1 Hon. Prof.

Law, School of

Tel: (01786) 467280 Fax: (01786) 467308
Busby, N. E., BA Westminster, PhD Glas.   Sr. Lectr.
Davidson, F., LLB Dund., PhD Dund.   Prof.; Head*
Goodall, K. E., MA Edin., LLB Edin., MSc Edin., PhD Belf.   Sr. Lectr.
Little, G. F. M., PhD Edin.   Prof.

McArdle, D. A., LLB Wales, PhD Manc.Met.   Sr. Lectr.
Sutherland, E. E., LLB Glas., LLM Br.Col.   Prof.
Other Staff: 2 Lectrs.; 3 Teaching Fellows

Management

Tel: (01786) 467311 Fax: (01786) 467329
Baldry, C. J., BSc S'ton., MSc Lond., PhD Durh., FRSA   Prof
Ball, Rob, MA Oxf., MSc Birm., PhD Stir.   Prof.
Bowers, J. A., BA Camb., MA Lanc.   Prof.
Curry, A. C., BA Nott., MPhil Nott., MBA Stir.   Sr. Lectr.
Fincham, R., BSc Exe., MA Exe., PhD Lond.   Prof.
Forbes, T. M., BA G.Caledonian, PhD Glas.   Sr. Lectr.
Hallier, J. P., BA CNAA, MSc CNAA, PhD CNAA   Sr. Lectr.
Mould, G. I., BA Sheff., MSc Aston   Sr. Lectr.
Stewart, P., BSc Leic., PhD Leeds   Prof.
Other Staff: 10 Lectrs.; 6 Sr. Teaching Fellows; 1 Teaching Fellow; 2 Hon. Profs.
Vacant Posts: Head*
Research: human resource management; organisational management and change; public sector management

Marketing

Tel: (01786) 467380 Fax: (01786) 467745
Broadbridge, A. M., BA Stir., MA Kent   Sr. Lectr.
Brownlie, D. B. T., BSc Strath.   Prof.
Burt, S. L., BA Oxf., PhD Stir.   Prof.
Connell, J. J., BA Plym., MA Exe., PhD Plym.   Sr. Lectr.
Davies, B. K., BA Exe., PhD Wales   Sr. Lectr.
Fillis, I. R., BSc Glas., MA Ulster, PhD Stir.   Sr. Lectr.
Kent, R. A., BSc S'ton., MA Essex, MSc Strath.   Sr. Lectr.
McAuley, A., BA Nott., PhD Nott.   Prof.; Head*
Page, S. J., BA Staffs., PhD Leic., FRSA   Prof.
Young, J. A., BSc Aberd., PhD CNAA   Prof.
Other Staff: 5 Lectrs.; 1 Teaching Fellow
Research: consumer, social and macromarketing; innovation; internationalisation

Retail Studies, Institute for

Tel: (01786) 467386 Fax: (01786) 465290
Dawson, J. A., BSc Lond., MPhil Lond., PhD Nott.   Prof.
Freathy, J. P., MA Warw., PhD Manc.   Prof.
Other Staff: 1 Res. Fellow

Social Marketing, Institute for

Hastings, G., BSc Newcastle(UK), PhD Strath.   Prof.; Dir.*
Stead, M., BA Lond.   Deputy Dir.
Other Staff: 3 Sr. Researchers; 3 Res. Officers; 1 Res. Fellow

Nursing and Midwifery

Tel: (01786) 466340 Fax: (01786) 466344
Angus, N. J., BN Glas., MN Glas.   Lectr.; Assoc. Head, Highland Campus
Bugge, C., BN Glas., MSc Glas., PhD Aberd.   Sr. Lectr.
Dalgleish, L., BSc Qld., PhD Qld.   Prof., Decision Making
Kearney, N., MSc Glas.   Prof., Cancer Care Nursing
Niven, C. A., BSc Stir., PhD Stir.   Prof.
Paley, J., MA Camb.   Sr. Lectr.
Sharkey, S., BA E.Anglia, PhD E.Anglia   Sr. Lectr.
Smith, A., BA MA   Sr. Teaching Fellow; Head, Undergrad. Studies; Assoc. Head, Western Isles Campus
Starrs, T. A., MSc Edin.   Prof.; Head*
Stoddard, K. M., BA Stir., MSc Stir., PhD Stir.   Sr. Teaching Fellow; Dir., Educn.; Assoc. Head, Stirling Campus
Watterson, A. E., BA Nott., PhD Brist.   Dir., Res.; Prof., Health Effectiveness
Wyke, S., BSc Lond., PhD Newcastle(UK), FRCGP   Prof., Health and Social Care

Other Staff: 12 Lectrs.; 1 Sr. Res. Fellow; 6 Sr.
Teaching Fellows; 15 Res. Fellows; 37
Teaching Fellows; 2 Hon. Profs.; 1 Hon. Sr.
Lectr.; 2 Hon. Lectrs.
Research: health care ethics; pain

Philosophy

Tel: (01786) 467555 Fax: (01786) 451335

Duff, R. A., BA Oxf., FBA, FRSEd   Prof.; Head*
Millar, A., MA Edin., PhD Camb., FRSEd   Prof.
Milne, P., BSc Edin., MSc Lond., PhD Lond.   Prof.
Sullivan, P. M., BA Leeds, BPhil Oxf., MA Oxf.,
DPhil Oxf., FRSEd   Prof.
Wheeler, M. W., BA Sus., DPhil Sus.   Reader
Other Staff: 5 Lectrs.; 1 RCUK Acad. Fellow; 1
Hon. Res. Fellow
Research: history of philosophy; legal, moral and
social philosophy; philosophy of language;
philosophy of mind

Politics

Tel: (01786) 467568 Fax: (01786) 466266

Baumeister, A. T., BSc Brad., MA York(UK),
DPhil York(UK)   Sr. Lectr.
Ingle, S., BA Sheff., MA Sheff., PhD Well.   Emer.
Prof.
Lynch, P., BA Strath., PhD Lond.   Sr. Lectr.
Shaw, E. D., BA Sheff., MPhil Leeds, PhD Manc.
Sr. Lectr.
Timmins, G., BA Portsmouth, MPhil Glas., PhD
Hudd.   Prof.; Head*
Other Staff: 1 Teaching Fellow; 2 Hon.
Researchers
Research: citizenship and the liberal state;
democracy; political parties and strategies;
politics of war and peace; territorial politics

Psychology

Tel: (01786) 467640 Fax: (01786) 467641

Anderson, J. R., BSc Stir., PhD Stir.   Reader
Buchanan-Smith, H. M., BSc St And., PhD St
And., FBPsS   Prof.
Doherty-Sneddon, G. M., BSc Glas., PhD Glas.
Sr. Lectr.
Donaldson, D. I., BSc Manc., PhD St And.   Sr.
Lectr.
Dow, M., MA Aberd., MPhil Edin., PhD Glas.   Jt.
Course Dir.
Dudchenko, P., BS Columbus State, MA Columbus
State, PhD Columbus State, FBPsS   Sr. Lectr.
Fryer, D. M., BA Lond., MA Lond., PhD Edin.
Prof.
Hancock, P. J. B., MA Oxf., MSc Brun., PhD Stir.
Sr. Lectr.
Lee, P., BA Calif., PhD Camb.   Prof.; Head*
Lieberman, D. A., BA Col., PhD Brown   Sr.
Lectr.
Little, A., BSc Durh.   Reader
O'Carroll, R., BSc Edin., MPhil Edin., PhD Edin.
Prof.
O'Connor, R. C., BSc Belf., PhD Belf.   Reader
Swanson, V., BA Leic., PhD Stir.   Sr. Lectr.
Watt, Roger J., BA Camb., PhD Keele, FRSEd
Prof.
Wilson, J. T. L., BA Stir., PhD Stir.   Prof.
Other Staff: 12 Lectrs.; 1 Sr. Teaching Fellow;
6 Res. Fellows; 2 Teaching Fellows; 1
Postdoctoral Res. Fellow; 1 Sr. Clin. Res.
Fellow; 5 Hon. Profs.; 2 Hon. Lectrs.; 2
Hon. Sr. Res. Fellows; 9 Hon. Res. Fellows
Research: clinical and health psychology;
comparative and developmental psychology;
neural computation and neuroscience;
neuropsychology; perception

Sports Studies

Tel: (01786) 466901 Fax: (01786) 466919
E-mail: ews1@stir.ac.uk

Coalter, J. A., BSc N.Lond., MSc Lond., PhD Leeds
Met.   Prof.
Galloway, S., BSc Glas., MPE New Br., PhD Aberd.
Sr. Lectr.
Jarvie, G., BEd Exe., MA Qu., PhD Leic.   Prof.
Morrow, S., BA H-W   Sr. Lectr.; Head*
Vamplew, W., BSc S'ton., PhD Edin., FRSA,
FRHistS   Prof.
Other Staff: 5 Lectrs.; 3 Sr. Teaching Fellows;
1 Teaching Fellow; 2 Res. Fellows; 2 Hon.
Profs.; 1 Hon. Res. Fellow

SPECIAL CENTRES, ETC

Alliance for Self Care Research

Wyke, S., BSc Lond., PhD Newcastle(UK), FRCGP
Prof., Health and Social Care; Dir.*
Other Staff: 2 Res. Fellows

Cancer Care Research Centre

Kearney, N., MSc Glas.   Prof.; Dir.*
Other Staff: 5 Sr. Res. Fellows; 7 Res. Fellows

Crime and Justice Research, Scottish Centre for

2 Sr. Res. Fellows; 2 Res. Fellows

Dementia Services Development Centre

Tel: (01786) 467740-1 Fax: (01786) 466846
Andrews, J., MA Glas., MA Nott.   Prof.; Dir.*
Chapman, A. J., BA Open(UK), MEd   Assoc.
Dir., Educn. and Training
Cunningham, C., MSc Stir.   Assoc. Dir., Health
and Social Care
Research: social research into dementia

Health Qwest

Dalgleish, L., BSc Qld., PhD Qld.   Prof.,
Decision Making
Other Staff: 1 Res. Fellow

Information on Language Teaching and Research, Scottish Centre for

McKinstry, R., BA Belf., MEd Stir., MLitt Stir.
Deputy Dir.; Head, Professnl. Services
McPake, J. M., BA Oxf., MA Lond.   Dir.*
Other Staff: 2 Professnl. Services Officers

Lifelong Learning, Centre for Research in

Boreham, N., BA Nott., MA Nott., MPhil Nott.,
PhD Manc.   Prof.
Canning, R., BA H-W, MA Brighton, PhD Aberd.
Sr. Lectr.
Edwards, R. G., BA CNAA, PhD Kent   Prof.
Field, J., BA Portsmouth, PhD Warw.   Prof.
Morgan-Klein, B., BA Stir.   Sr. Lectr.; Depute
Dir.
Nicoll, K., BEd Edin., MPH Dund., PhD
Technol.Syd.   Sr. Lectr.
Osborne, M. J., BSc Reading, PhD Lond.   Prof.;
Dir.*
Other Staff: 5 Lectrs.; 1 Teaching Fellow; 4
Res. Fellows

MacRobert Arts Centre

Tel: (01786) 467155 Fax: (01786) 451369
Moran, Liz E., BA Strath.   Dir.*

Nursing, Midwifery and Allied Health Professions Research Unit

Niven, C. A., BSc Stir., PhD Stir.   Prof.,
Nursing and Midwifery Studies; Dir.*

Other Staff: 1 Programme Co-ord.; 1 Res.
Midwife; 2 Postdoctoral Res. Fellows; 1
Clin. Res. Fellow

Stirling Aquaculture

Bostock, J. C., BSc Wales, MSc Stir.   Sr.
Consultant*

CONTACT OFFICERS

Academic affairs. Academic Registrar:
Morrow, J. F., MA Edin.
Accommodation. Head, Residential Services:
Broadfoot, C. W.
Admissions (first degree). Head of Student
Recruitment and Admissions: Cockbain, Ian
Admissions (higher degree). Head of Student
Recruitment and Admissions: Cockbain, Ian
Adult/continuing education. FE/HE and
Continuing Education Co-ordinator:
Bradley, J., BA Strath.
Careers. Senior Careers Advisor: Campbell, J.,
BA Liv.
Computing services. Assistant Director
(Computing services): Osborne, Tony
Credit transfer. Undergraduate Admissions
Officer: Davidson, Kate, MA Edin.
Equal opportunities. University Secretary:
Clarke, Kevin J., BA Stir.
Estates and buildings/works and services.
Director of Estates and Campus Services:
Plouviez, Karen, BSc Reading
Examinations. Examinations Officer: Halliday,
Ronald, MA Edin., MLitt Stir.
Finance. Director of Finance: Gordon, John S.
General enquiries. University Secretary:
Clarke, Kevin J., BA Stir.
International office. Senior International
Officer: Christie, N., MA St And.
(E-mail: international@stir.ac.uk)
Library (chief librarian). Director of
Information Services and University
Librarian: Kemp, P., MA Camb., PhD Camb.
Personnel/human resources. Director of
Human Resources: McCrindle, Martin, BSc
St And.
Publications. Publications Manager: Tabel, H.,
BA Lanc., MSc Napier
Quality assurance and accreditation.
Academic Registrar (Registry and
Governance Services): Morrow, J. F., MA
Edin.
Safety. Safety Adviser: Duckett, David C., BSc
Wales
Scholarships, awards, loans. Assistant
Registrar (Head of Recruitment and
Admissions): Cockbain, Ian
Schools liaison. Assistant Registrar (Head of
Recruitment and Admissions): Cockbain,
Ian
Security. Director of Estates and Campus
Services: Plouviez, Karen, BSc Reading
Sport and recreation. Director of Sports
Development: Bilsborough, Peter, BEd Leeds,
MEd Manc., MLitt Stir.
Staff development and training. Director of
Training and Development: Willis, V., BA
Open(UK)
Student union. (Contact the President, Stirling
University Students' Association)
Students from other countries. Senior
International and Study Abroad Officer:
Niven, S. J., BSc Stir., MSc Edin.

[Information supplied by the institution as at 21
September 2007, and edited by the ACU]

UNIVERSITY OF STRATHCLYDE

Founded 1964

Member of the Association of Commonwealth Universities

Postal Address: McCance Building, 16 Richmond Street, Glasgow, Scotland G1 1XQ
Telephone: (0141) 552 4400 **Fax:** (0141) 552 0775
URL: http://www.strath.ac.uk

PRINCIPAL AND VICE-CHANCELLOR*—Hamnett, Prof. Andrew, MA Oxf., DPhil Oxf., Hon. DSc T.U.Lodz, FRSChem, FRSEd
VICE-PRINCIPAL—Love, Prof. James, BA MSc PhD
PRO-VICE-PRINCIPAL—Miller, Prof. Kenneth, LLB LLM PhD
DEPUTY PRINCIPAL—Condie, Prof. Rae E., BSc BA MSc MA(Ed) PhD
DEPUTY PRINCIPAL—Ferguson, Prof. Allister I., BSc St And., MA Oxf., PhD St And., FRSEd, FIP
DEPUTY PRINCIPAL—Hughes, Anne, MPhil
DEPUTY PRINCIPAL—McDonald, Prof. James R., BSc MSc PhD
SECRETARY TO THE UNIVERSITY‡—West, Peter W. A., OBE, MA St And., DUniv DPhil
LIBRARIAN AND HEAD OF INFORMATION RESOURCES DIRECTORATE—Law, Prof. Derek G., MA DUniv, FIInfSc, FRSEd, FLA, FKC

GENERAL INFORMATION

History. Originally founded as Anderson's Institution in 1796, the University of Strathclyde received its Royal Charter in 1964.
It has two campuses (John Anderson and Jordanhill), both located in Glasgow.

Admission to first degree courses (see also United Kingdom Introduction). Through Universities and College Admissions Service (UCAS). Four or five subjects at SQA Higher level or equivalent are required. Proficiency in mathematics and English must also be shown. Applicants whose first language is not English must provide evidence of proficiency; IELTS and TOEFL are acceptable qualifications.

First Degrees (see also United Kingdom Directory to Subjects of Study) (* = with honours). BA, BA*, BEd*, BEng, BEng*, BSc, BSc*, LLB, LLB*, MEng, MPharm, MSci.
Length of course. Full-time: BA, BEng, BSc, LLB: 3 years; BA*, BEd*, BEng*, BSc*, LLB*, MPharm: 4 years; MEng, MSci: 5 years. Part-time: BA: 6 years; BA*: 8 years.

Higher Degrees (see also United Kingdom Directory to Subjects of Study).
Master's. LLM, MBA, MLitt, MPhil, MSc.
Admission. Applicants should have a good honours degree of an approved university or equivalent qualification.
Length of course. Full-time: LLM, MBA, MLitt, MPhil, MSc: 1 year. Part-time: LLM, MLitt, MPhil, MSc: 2 years; MBA: 3 years.
Doctoral. DBA, PhD.
Admission. Applicants should normally have a first or second class honours degree of a British university or equivalent qualification.
Length of course. Full-time: DBA, PhD: 3 years. Part-time: DBA, PhD: 4 years.

Libraries. Volumes: 551,000. Periodicals subscribed to: 4000. Special collections: Fleck Library (chemistry); Royal Scottish Geographical Society Library; Dictionary of National Biography Library.

Academic Year (2007–2008). Two semesters: 28 September–25 January; 28 January–6 June.

Income (2006). Total, £191,054,000.

Statistics. Students (2006): total 29,000.

FACULTIES/SCHOOLS

Education
Tel: (0141) 950 3243 Fax: (0141) 950 3166
E-mail: contact-facultyofeducation@strath.ac.uk

Dean: Bourne, Prof. Jill, BA PhD
Faculty Officer: Dougall, Lorna, BSc

Engineering
Tel: (0141) 548 4172 Fax: (0141) 552 5860
E-mail: contact-facultyofengineering@strath.ac.uk
Dean: Grant, Prof. Colin D., BSc PhD, FIChemE, FRSA
Faculty Officer: Bridgeford, Susan, MA MBA

Law, Arts and Social Sciences
Tel: (0141) 553 4171 Fax: (0141) 552 5860
E-mail: contact-facultyofarts@strath.ac.uk
Dean: Hutton, Prof. Neil, MA PhD
Faculty Officer: Dallat, Bronagh, BSc MBA

Science
Tel: (0141) 548 4173 Fax: (0141) 552 5860
E-mail: contact-facultyofscience@strath.ac.uk
Dean: Furman, Prof. Brian L., BPharm Lond., PhD, FRPharmS
Faculty Officer: McGrath, James S., MA PhD

Strathclyde Business School
Tel: (0141) 548 4170 Fax: (0141) 552 5860
E-mail: contact-facultyofbusiness@strath.ac.uk
Dean: Harvey, Prof. Charles, BSc PhD, FRHistS
Faculty Officer: Livingston, Roderick, BSc, FRSA, FCIS

ACADEMIC UNITS

Accounting and Finance
Tel: (0141) 548 3261 Fax: (0141) 552 3547
E-mail: contact-accfin@strath.ac.uk
Byrne, Alistair, BA   Sr. Lectr.
Capstaff, John, BA BPhil MSc   Sr. Lectr.
Ciancanelli, Penelope, BA MA PhD   Sr. Lectr.
Cooper, Christine, BA MSc   Prof., Accounting
Davies, John R., BSc Lond., MBA Mich.   Prof.
Fletcher, Jonathon, MA MSc PhD   Prof.
Marshall, Andrew P., BA   Prof.; Head*
McColgan, Patrick, BA   Sr. Lectr.
Smith, Julia, BCom PhD   Reader
Thomson, Ian, BA   Sr. Lectr.
Other Staff: 2 Visiting Profs.; 7 Lectrs.
Research: capital markets research; corporate finance research; critical accounting theory; financial asset pricing

Architecture
Tel: (0141) 548 3023 Fax: (0141) 552 3997
E-mail: contact-architecture@strath.ac.uk
Bridges, H. Alan, MSc PhD   Prof.
Charley, Jonathan, BA MSc PhD   Sr. Lectr.
Chase, Scott, BSc MA PhD   Sr. Lectr.
Frey, Hildebrand W., PhD   Sr. Lectr.
Grant, P. Michael, BSc PhD   Sr. Lectr.; Head*
Grierson, David, BSc BArch PhD   Sr. Lectr.
Howieson, Stirling, BArch MPhil   Sr. Lectr.
Platt, Christopher   Sr. Lectr.

Yaneske, Paul P., BSc Leeds, PhD Leeds   Sr. Lectr.
Other Staff: 7 Visiting Profs.; 8 Lectrs.
Research: computer-aided design education and training; environmental design and research; facilities management; production of architecture, theory and history; safety and environmental management

Bioengineering Unit
Tel: (0141) 548 3780 Fax: (0141) 552 6098
E-mail: contact-bioeng@strath.ac.uk
Black, Richard, BSc PhD   Sr. Lectr.
Connolly, Patricia, BSc PhD, FIEE   Prof.
Conway, Bernard A., BSc PhD   Prof.
Gaylor, John D. S., BSc PhD   Reader
Gourlay, Terry, PhD   Prof.
Grant, M. Helen, BSc Aberd., PhD Aberd.   Prof.
Nicol, Alexander C., BSc PhD   Prof.; Head*
Rowe, Philip, BSc PhD   Prof.
Other Staff: 4 Visiting Profs.; 3 Lectrs.
Research: cell tissue and organ engineering (artificial organs); rehabilitation engineering (biomechanics, movement disorders, prosthetics and orthotics)

Chemistry, Pure and Applied
Tel: (0141) 548 2019 Fax: (0141) 548 4288
E-mail: contact-chemistry@strath.ac.uk
Armstrong, David R., DSc Newcastle(UK), PhD Newcastle(UK)   Sr. Lectr.
Berlouis, Leonard E. A., BSc PhD   Reader
Cormack, Peter, BSc PhD   Sr. Lectr.
Davidson, Christine, BSc PhD   Sr. Lectr.
Dufton, Mark, BA PhD   Sr. Lectr.
Dunkin, Ian R., BSc Birm., PhD Birm., FRSChem   Reader
Fraser, Jim   Prof.
Gibson, Colin L., BSc PhD   Sr. Lectr.
Gibson, Lorraine, BSc PhD   Sr. Lectr.
Graham, Duncan, BSc PhD   Prof.
Halling, Peter J., BA PhD   Prof., Biocatalyst Science
Kennedy, Alan, BSc PhD   Sr. Lectr.
Kerr, William J., BSc PhD   Prof.
Liggat, John, BSc PhD   Sr. Lectr.
Linacre, Adrian M. T., BSc DPhil   Sr. Lectr.
Littlejohn, David, BSc PhD, FRSChem   Philips Prof.; Head*
Mills, Andrew, BSc PhD   Prof.
Moore, Barry D., BSc PhD   Reader
Mulvey, Robert E., BSc PhD   Prof., Inorganic Chemistry
Murphy, John, BSc PhD DSc   Merck Pauson Prof.
NicDaeid, Niamh, BSc BA PhD   Sr. Lectr.
Percy, Jonathan, BSc PhD   Prof., Synthetic Chemistry
Pethrick, Richard A., BSc Lond., PhD Salf., DSc Salf., FRSChem, FRSEd   Prof.
Reglinski, John, BSc Dund., PhD St And.   Reader
Sherrington, David C., BSc Liv., PhD Liv., FRSChem, FRSEd   Prof., Polymer Chemistry

Skabara, Peter J., BSc PhD   Prof., Materials
   Chemistry
Spicer, Mark D., BSc PhD   Sr. Lectr.
Suckling, Colin J., PhD DSc, FRSChem, FRSEd
   Freeland Prof.
Other Staff: 5 Visiting Profs.; 9 Lectrs.; 1 Res.
   Officer
Research: clean technologies for synthesis for the
   twenty-first century; crystal growth,
   engineering and chemistry; organic
   synthesis and synthetic methods; polymer
   chemistry; surface-enhanced Raman
   spectroscopy

Childhood and Primary Studies

Tel: (0141) 950 3342 Fax: (0141) 950 3151
   E-mail: contact-primaryed@strath.ac.uk
Allan, James G., BA   Sr. Lectr.
Brownlow, Margaret, MA   Sr. Lectr.
Christie, Donald, BA   Prof.
Deuchar, Ross, BEd MSc PhD   Sr. Lectr.
Dunlop, Aline-Wendy, MEd   Prof.
Ellis, Sue, BA MSc   Reader
Gavienas, Eleanor, MSc   Sr. Lectr.
Grogan, Deirdre   Sr. Lectr.
Hughes, Anne, MPhil   Sr. Lectr.
Keith, Lynda, MA Glas.   Sr. Lectr.
Lee, Peter, MEd   Dir., Childhood and
   Families: Res. and Develop. Centre
Lindsay, Joyce   Head*
Logue, Jennifer, MSc   Sr. Lectr.
McGregor, Anne S., BEd BA MEd   Sr. Lectr.
McNaughton, Marie-Jeanne, BEd   Sr. Lectr.
Munn, Penelope, PhD   Reader
Semple, Sheila, MA MPhil   Reader
Smyth, Geraldine, MA MAA EdD   Reader
Other Staff: 2 Visiting Profs.; 24 Lectrs.
Research: attitudes in environmental studies and
   environmental education; bilingual learners
   in the early stages; diagnostic assessment in
   mathematical problem-solving; nature of
   school experience in teacher education
   institutions; probationer support/mentoring
   of beginning teachers

Computer and Information Sciences

Tel: (0141) 548 3522 Fax: (0141) 552 5330
   E-mail: enquiries@cis.strath.ac.uk
Burton, Paul F., BA MA MPhil, FIInfSc, FCLIP
   Sr. Lectr.
Chowdhury, Gobinda, BSc BLISc MLISc PhD
   Sr. Lectr.
Connor, Richard, BSc PhD   Prof.
Crestani, Fabio, MSc Padua, MSc Glas., PhD Glas.
   Prof.
Dunlop, Mark, BSc PhD   Sr. Lectr.
Ferguson, John D., BSc MSc PhD   Sr. Lectr.
Fox, Maria, BA MSc PhD   Prof.; Head*
Gibb, Forbes, BA   Prof.
Goldfinch, Paul, MA Oxf., MSc Essex, MSc Edin.
   Sr. Lectr.
Levine, John, MA MPhil PhD   Sr. Lectr.
Long, Derek, MA DPhil   Reader
McGettrick, Andrew D., BSc Glas., PhD Camb.
   Prof., Computer Science
McInnes, John A., BSc Lond., PhD Lond.   Sr.
   Lectr.
Revie, Crawford, BSc MSc   Reader
Roper, Marc, BSc PhD   Reader
Ruthven, Ian, BSc MSc PhD   Sr. Lectr.
Wilson, John N., BSc MEd MSc   Sr. Lectr.
Wood, Murray I., BSc PhD   Sr. Lectr.
Other Staff: 14 Lectrs.
Research: advanced databases, transparent
   telepresence work; algorithms, problems
   and empirical studies; marketing, pricing
   and value of information and information
   services; multilingual information retrieval,
   interface design and evaluation, decision
   support; video compression

Creative and Aesthetic Studies

Tel: (0141) 950 3476 Fax: (0141) 950 3314
   E-mail: contact-appliedarts@strath.ac.uk
Byrne, Charles   Sr. Lectr.
Hewitt, Allan   Lectr.; Head*
Sheridan, Mark, BMus   Sr. Lectr.
Other Staff: 5 Lectrs.

Curricular Studies

Tel: (0141) 950 3243 Fax: (0141) 950 3166
   E-mail: facultyofeducation@strath.ac.uk
Boyd, Brian, MA MEd PhD   Prof.
Chambers, Paul, BSc   Sr. Lectr.
De Cecco, G. R. John, BA   Sr. Lectr.
Forrest, Joan, MA(Ed)   Sr. Lectr.
Gray, Iain A. S., MA MSc   Sr. Lectr.
Grieve, Ann, BEd PhD   Lectr.; Dir., Professnl.
   Develop. Unit
Hillis, Peter L. M., MA PhD   Prof.
Lawson, John   Sr. Lectr.
Maitles, Henry   Sr. Lectr.; Head*
Mclaren, Susan V., BA   Sr. Lectr.
Munro, Robert, MA   Reader
Reid, Brian M., BA   Sr. Lectr.
Robertson, A. G. Boyd, MA   Reader
Souter, Nicholas T., BSc   Sr. Lectr.
Tierney, Daniel, BA   Reader
Welsh, Anne, MA   Sr. Lectr.
Wilson, Mona, BEd   Sr. Lectr.
Winch, John R., BSc   Sr. Lectr.
Other Staff: 15 Lectrs.
Research: cultural contrasts; drugs education;
   health education in secondary schools;
   language education; professional
   development

Design, Manufacture and Engineering Management

Tel: (0141) 548 2839 Fax: (0141) 552 0557
   E-mail: contact-dmem@strath.ac.uk
Anthony, Jiju   Prof.
Bititci, Umit S., MSc PhD   Prof.
Corney, Jonathan   Prof.
Duffy, Alexander H. B., BSc PhD   Prof.
Ion, William J., BSc   Sr. Lectr.; Head*
MacBryde, Jillian, BSc PhD   Sr. Lectr.
Mair, Gordon M., BSc   Sr. Lectr.
Qin, Yi, BEng MEng PhD   Sr. Lectr.
Yan, Xiu, BEng PhD   Sr. Lectr.
Other Staff: 9 Visiting Profs.; 7 Lectrs.
Research: design principles, methods and tools;
   intelligent design support; manufacturing
   systems; transparent telepresence

Economics

Tel: (0141) 548 3842 Fax: (0141) 552 5589
   E-mail: contact-economics@strath.ac.uk
Darby, Julia, MSc MSc   Reader
Fingleton, Bernard   Prof.
Holden, Darryl R., BSc MA   Sr. Lectr.
Koop, Gary, BA MA PhD   Prof.
Love, James, BA MSc PhD   Prof.
McGregor, Peter G., BA Stir., MSc Stir.   Prof.,
   Regional Economics
Perman, Roger J., BA MSc   Reader
Scouller, John, BA   Sr. Lectr.
Swales, J. Kim, BA Camb.   Prof.
Tole, Lise, PhD   Sr. Lectr.
Turner, Karen, BA MSc PhD   Sr. Lectr.
Wooton, Ian, MA MPhil PhD   Prof.; Head*
Wright, Robert   Prof.
Other Staff: 2 Visiting Profs.; 6 Lectrs.
Research: business and industrial economics;
   econometrics; law and economics;
   macroeconomics and international
   economics; regional economics and
   development economics (including
   environmental health economics)

Educational and Professional Studies

Tel: (0141) 950 3368 Fax: (0141) 950 3367
   E-mail: eps@strath.ac.uk
Anderson, Carolyn, BA MPhil   Sr. Lectr.
Baldry, Heather   Sr. Lectr.
Baron, Stephen   Prof.
Bryce, Thomas G. K., BSc MEd PhD   Prof.
Clark, Kathleen A., MSc   Sr. Lectr.
Condie, Rae E., BSc BA MSc MA(Ed) PhD
   Prof.
Connelly, Graham, BEd MEd   Sr. Lectr.
Cooper, Mick, BA DPhil   Prof.
Cornwell, David G., MA   Sr. Lectr.
Elliott, Robert   Prof.
Fagan, Geoff, MA   Sr. Lectr.
Finlay, Ian, BA MA   Sr. Lectr.
Finn, Gerard P. T., BSc PhD   Prof.

Gordon, Andrew T., BA MBA   Sr. Lectr.
Halliday, John S., BA MEd PhD   Prof.
Hamill, Paul, BA MEd   Sr. Lectr.
Hewitt, Carol M., MA MEd   Sr. Lectr.
Hough, Michael T., MA   Sr. Lectr.
Johnson, Andrew, BPhil   Sr. Lectr.
Kennedy, Aileen, BEd MEd   Sr. Lectr.
Kirkwood, Margaret J., BSc MEd PhD   Reader
Lowit, Anja   Sr. Lectr.
Mackenzie, Catherine, MEd   Reader
MacLellan, Euphemia M., BA PhD   Prof.
McAteer, Erica   Sr. Lectr.
McCartney, Elspeth, BSc MEd   Sr. Lectr.
McLaren, David, MA MEd PhD   Sr. Lectr.
McLarty, Marion M., BA MA   Sr. Lectr.
Murray, Rowena, MA Glas., PhD Penn.   Reader
Nicholson, Anne, MBA   Sr. Lectr.
Rowlands, Clive J., BA MEd   Prof.; Head*
Sercombe, Howard, BA BD PhD   Prof.
Smith, Iain R. M., BSc MEd   Sr. Lectr.
Soden, Rebecca, BA MEd PhD   Reader
Stalker, Kirsten   Reader
Wallace, David   Sr. Lectr.
Other Staff: 20 Lectrs.
Research: curriculum studies and pedagogy;
   educational effectiveness and school
   management; quality in education; social
   contexts of education and allied professions

Engineering, Chemical and Process

Tel: (0141) 548 2361 Fax: (0141) 552 2302
   E-mail: contact-chemeng@strath.ac.uk
Cousins, Roderick B., BSc   Sr. Lectr.
Grant, Colin D., BSc PhD, FIChemE, FRSA
   Roche Prof.
Hall, Peter J., BSc Durh., MLitt Newcastle(UK),
   PhD Newcastle(UK)   Prof.
Larsen, Vidar F., BSc PhD   Sr. Lectr.
Muir, David M., BSc Glas., PhD   Sr. Lectr.
Mulheran, Paul   John Anderson Res. Sr. Lectr.
Postlethwaite, Bruce E., BSc PhD   Sr. Lectr.
Schaschke, Carl J., BSc PhD   Reader; Head*
Shilton, Simon J., BSc PhD   Sr. Lectr.
Other Staff: 3 Lectrs.
Research: biochemical engineering; biomedical
   engineering; membrane technology; process
   cybernetics

Engineering, Civil

Tel: (0141) 548 4352 Fax: (0141) 553 2066
   E-mail: contact-civeng@strath.ac.uk
Beverland, Iain, BSc PhD   Sr. Lectr.
Booth, Peter, BA   Sr. Lectr.
Copeland, Graham J. M., MA Camb., MSc Wales,
   PhD Liv.   Reader
Dyer, Mark, BSc BEng DPhil   Prof.; Head*
Grimason, Anthony, BSc PhD   Sr. Lectr.
Joao, Elsa   Sr. Lectr.
Karstunen, Minna, MSc PhD   Reader
Lunn, Rebecca, BA MA MSc PhD   Sr. Lectr.
Tanyimboh, Tiku T., MEng PhD   Sr. Lectr.
Other Staff: 7 Visiting Profs.; 7 Lectrs.
Research: construction management;
   environmental health; geotechnical and
   highway engineering; structural
   engineering; water engineering and
   environmental management

Engineering, Electronic and Electrical

Tel: (0141) 548 2097 Fax: (0141) 552 2487
   E-mail: contact-eee@strath.ac.uk
Andonovic, Ivan, BSc PhD   Prof., Broadband
   Networks
Ault, Graham, PhD   Sr. Lectr.
Bell, Keith, BEng PhD   Sr. Lectr.
Bullinger, Eric   Sr. Lectr.
Burt, Graeme, BEng PhD   Reader
Chapman, Roy, MSc Newcastle(UK)   Sr. Lectr.
Crichton, Bruce H., BSc Edin., PhD   Sr. Lectr.
Cruden, Andrew, BEng MSc PhD   Sr. Lectr.
Culshaw, Brian, BSc Lond., PhD Lond.   Prof.,
   Opto-Electronics
Dunlop, John, MSc Wales, PhD Wales   Prof.,
   Electronic Systems
Durrani, Tariq S., BSc Karachi, BSc Dacca, MSc
   S'ton., PhD S'ton., FREng, FIEEE, FIEE, FRSEd
   Prof., Signal Processing
Finney, Stephen   Sr. Lectr.

Fouracre, Richard A., BSc Birm., MSc Aston, PhD
Reader
Gachagan, Anthony, BSc PhD   Sr. Lectr.
Given, Martin J., BSc PhD   Sr. Lectr.
Glover, Ian   Reader
Grimble, Michael J., BA Open(UK), DSc CNAA,
MSc Birm., PhD Birm., FIEE   Prof., Control
Hamilton, David J., BSc   Sr. Lectr.
Harle, David, BSc PhD   Sr. Lectr.
Hayward, Gordon, BSc Glas., MSc PhD   Prof.,
Ultrasonics
Infield, David   Prof.
Irvine, James, BEng PhD   Reader
Johnstone, Walter, BSc PhD   Prof.
Judd, Martin, PhD   Sr. Lectr.
Katebi, Mohammed R., BSc Shiraz, MSc Manc.,
PhD Manc.   Reader
Leithead, William E., BSc Edin., PhD Edin.
Prof.
Lo, Kwok Lun, MSc Manc., PhD Manc.   Prof.,
Power Systems
MacGregor, Scott J., BSc PhD   Prof.
Marshall, Stephen, BSc Nott., PhD   Prof.
McArthur, Stephen, BEng PhD   Prof.; Head*
McDonald, James R., BSc MSc PhD   Rolls-
Royce Prof., Power Systems
Michie, Walter   Sr. Lectr.
Moore, Philip, BEng PhD
Siew, Wah Hoon, BSc MBA PhD   Reader
Soraghan, John J., MEng Trinity(Dub.), PhD
Prof.
Stewart, George S., BSc Glas., PhD Glas.
Reader
Stewart, Robert W., BSc PhD   Prof.
Stimpson, Brian P., BEng Lond., PhD Liv.   Sr.
Lectr.
Uttamchandani, Deepak G., BEng A.Bello, MSc
Lond., PhD Lond.   Prof.
Weiss, Stephan   Reader
Williams, Barry, BSc BEng MSc PhD   Prof.
Other Staff: 15 Visiting Profs.; 9 Lectrs.
Research: broadband communications; electrical
materials; high-voltage technologies; mobile
communications; power systems

Engineering, Mechanical

Tel: (0141) 548 4815 Fax: (0141) 552 5105
E-mail: contact-mecheng@strath.ac.uk
Banks, William M., BSc MSc PhD   Prof.,
Advanced Materials
Boyle, James T., BSc PhD   Prof., Mechanics of
Materials
Carus, David A., MSc PhD   Sr. Lectr.
Clarke, Joseph A., BSc PhD   Prof.
Counsell, John, BA PhD   Prof., Energy
Utilisation
Craighead, Ian A., BSc PhD   Sr. Lectr.
Gorman, Daniel, BSc PhD DSc   Prof.,
Mechanical Engineering
Grant, Andrew D., BSc PhD   Sr. Lectr.
Johnstone, Cameron M., MSc   Sr. Lectr.
Mackenzie, Donald, BSc PhD   Reader; Head*
Mackenzie, Peter, BSc PhD   Sr. Lectr.
McInnes, Colin, BSc DPhil DSc, FREng, FRSEd
Prof.
Mclaren, Andrew J., BEng PhD   Sr. Lectr.
McLean, Robert, BSc MPhil   Sr. Lectr.
Nash, David H., BSc MSc PhD   Reader
Reese, Jason, BSc MSc DPhil   Prof.
Rhodes, James, BSc PhD   Prof., Mechanics of
Materials
Spathopoulos, Michael, MSc PhD   Sr. Lectr.
Stack, Margaret, BE MSc PhD   Prof.,
Mechanical Engineering
Stickland, Matthew, MSc PhD   Sr. Lectr.
Strachan, Paul A., BSc MSc PhD   Sr. Lectr.
Thomason, James, PhD   Prof.
Trendafilova, Irina, MSc PhD   Sr. Lectr.
Walker, Colin A., BSc Glas., PhD Glas.   Reader
Wood, James, BSc PhD   Sr. Lectr.
Other Staff: 2 Visiting Profs.; 8 Lectrs.
Research: experimental mechanics; materials and
metallurgy; pressure systems and
computational mechanics; strength of
components and structures; system
dynamics and control

English Studies

Tel: (0141) 548 3711 Fax: (0141) 552 3493
E-mail: contact-english@strath.ac.uk
Elphinstone, Margaret N., BA   Prof., Writing
Fabb, Nigel, BA Camb., PhD M.I.T.   Prof.,
Literary Linguistics
Furniss, Thomas E., MA S'ton., BA PhD   Sr.
Lectr.
Goldie, David, MA DPhil   Sr. Lectr.
Hammill, Faye   Sr. Lectr.
Hope, Jonathan, BA PhD   Reader; Head*
Kinloch, David   Reader
McNair, Brian, MA MPhil PhD   Prof.
Montgomery, Martin, BA Birm., MA Birm., PhD
Strath.   Reader
Sawday, Jonathan, BA PhD, FRSA   Prof.
Thorne, Alison, BA PhD   Sr. Lectr.
Wicomb, Zoe, BA MLitt PhD   Prof.
Other Staff: 6 Lectrs.
Research: creative writing; literary linguistics;
literature and cultural identity; Renaissance
studies

Entrepreneurship at Strathclyde, Hunter Centre for

Tel: (0141) 548 3482 Fax: (0141) 552 7602
E-mail: huntercentre@strath.ac.uk
Bottomley, Colin, MSc DMS   Sr. Lectr.
Carter, Sarah, BA PhD   Prof.
Cooper, Sarah, BA PhD   Sr. Lectr.
Levie, Jonathan, BSc MSc PhD   Sr. Lectr.
Mason, Colin, MA PhD   Prof.; Head*
Other Staff: 1 Lectr.
Research: entrepreneurial dynamics, resources
and education

Geography and Sociology

Tel: (0141) 548 3606 Fax: (0141) 552 7857
E-mail: contact-geography@strath.ac.uk
Boyle, Mark, BSc PhD   Sr. Lectr.
Clark, Colin, BA MA PhD   Sr. Lectr.
Hollier, Graham P., BA MA PhD   Sr. Lectr.
Miller, David, BSc PhD   Prof.; Head*
Pacione, Michael, MA Dund., PhD Dund.   Prof.
Rogerson, Robert J., BSc Glas., PhD Lond.   Sr.
Lectr.
Other Staff: 3 Visiting Profs.; 8 Lectrs.
Research: environmental implications of
sustainable development; social and
economic structuring of the city

Government

Tel: (0141) 548 4004 Fax: (0141) 552 5677
E-mail: contact-government@strath.ac.uk
Carman, Christopher Jarl, Policy Change
Cram, Laura, BA MSc PhD   Reader
Curtice, John, BA Oxf., MA Oxf.   Prof.
Eschle, Catherine, BSc MSc DPhil   Sr. Lectr.
Hogwood, Brian W., BA Keele, PhD Keele   Prof.,
Politics
Judge, David, BA Exe., PhD Sheff.   Prof.; Head*
Mitchell, James, MA Aberd., DPhil Oxf.   Prof.
Newey, Glen, BA Camb., MA York(UK), DPhil
York(UK)   Reader
Padgett, Stephen, BA York(UK), PhD Kent   Prof.
Rudig, Wolfgang, DP F.U.Berlin, PhD Manc.
Reader
Shephard, Mark P., BA MA PhD   Sr. Lectr.
Other Staff: 5 Lectrs.
Research: crime, deviance and violence; local
governance; public employment; public
policy; social movements and collective
action

History

Tel: (0141) 548 2206 Fax: (0141) 552 8509
E-mail: contact-history@strath.ac.uk
Adams, Simon, BA MA MPhil   Reader
Brown, David, BA MA PhD   Sr. Lectr.
Ellis, Mark, MA PhD   Sr. Lectr.
Finlay, Richard J., BA PhD   Prof.; Head*
Fischer, Conan, BA MA DPhil   Prof., Modern
European History
Heimann, Mary, BA DPhil   Sr. Lectr.
Macinnes, Allan   Prof.
McIvor, Arthur J., BA PhD   Reader
Mills, James, MA PhD   Sr. Lectr.
Young, John R., MA PhD, FRHistS   Sr. Lectr.

Other Staff: 1 Visiting Prof.; 5 Lectrs.
Research: modern Scottish history; social history;
urban history

Hospitality and Tourism Management

Tel: (0141) 548 3941 Fax: (0141) 552 2870
E-mail: htm@strath.ac.uk
Baum, Thomas G., BA Wales, MA CNAA, MPhil
CNAA, PhD Strath.   Prof., International
Hospitality Management
Butler, Richard   Prof.
Lynch, Paul, BA MBA PhD   Reader
MacLellan, Lachlan R., MA MSc   Sr. Lectr.
Morrison, Alison J., BA MSc PhD   Prof.;
Head*
Nickson, Dennis P., BA PhD   Reader
Other Staff: 10 Visiting Profs.; 7 Lectrs.
Research: human resource management in
hospitality and tourism; Scottish tourism;
small business management and
entrepreneurship; strategy and marketing in
hospitality and tourism; tourism in
developing countries

Human Resource Management

Tel: (0141) 548 3287 Fax: (0141) 552 3581
E-mail: contact-hrm@strath.ac.uk
Cunningham, Ian, BA   Sr. Lectr.
Gennard, John, BA(Econ) Sheff., MA(Econ)
Manc.   IPM Prof.
Gibb, Stephen J., BA MSc PhD   Sr. Lectr.
Gilbert, Kay, BA MSc   Sr. Lectr.
Moore, Christopher B., BA Leeds   Sr. Lectr.
Newsome, Kirsty, BA MA PhD   Sr. Lectr.
Nickson, Dennis P., BA PhD   Reader
Scholarios, Dora M., MA PhD   Reader
Taylor, Philip, MA MPhil   Prof.
Thompson, Paul, BA PhD   Prof.,
Organisational Analysis; Head*
Warhurst, Chris, BA PhD   Prof.
Watson, Aileen C., BA   Sr. Lectr.
Other Staff: 1 Visiting Prof.; 4 Lectrs.
Research: information and communication
technologies; labour market issues;
organisational behaviour; public policy and
public management

Law School

Tel: (0141) 548 3738 Fax: (0141) 553 1546
E-mail: contact-law@strath.ac.uk
Barton, Karen, BSc   Sr. Lectr.
Blackie, John W. G., BA Camb., LLB Edin.
Prof., Scots Law
Clark, Bryan, BA LLM PhD   Sr. Lectr.
Colston, Catherine, LLB LLM   Sr. Lectr.
Halliday, Simon   Prof.
Hamilton, Jennifer M., LLB LLM   Sr. Lectr.
Hutton, Neil, MA PhD   Prof.
Lloyd, Ian J., LLM Exe., LLB PhD   Prof.,
Computer Law
Maharg, Paul, LLB Glas., MA Glas., PhD Edin.
Prof.
Mcdiarmid, Claire, LLB LLM PhD   Sr. Lectr.
Miller, Kenneth, LLB LLM PhD   Prof.
Nicolson, Donald J., BA LLB PhD   Prof.
Norrie, Kenneth M., LLB Dund., PhD Aberd.
Prof.
O'Donnell, Therese, LLB MLitt   Sr. Lectr.
Paterson, Alan A., LLB Edin., DPhil Oxf.   Prof.
Piacentini, Laura   Reader
Poustie, Mark R., LLB MA   Prof.; Head*
Robson, Peter W., LLB St And., PhD   Prof.,
Social Welfare Law
Rodger, Barry J., LLB LLM   Prof.
Ross, Jennifer M., LLB MA   Sr. Lectr.
Scoular, Jane, LLB MA   Sr. Lectr.
Susskind, Richard   Prof.
Tata, Cyrus, BA MA   Sr. Lectr.
Other Staff: 6 Visiting Profs.; 5 Lectrs.
Research: environmental law; race discrimination
within the industrial tribunal system;
Scottish child law; sentencing information
system

Management

Tel: (0141) 548 4170 Fax: (0141) 552 5860
E-mail: admissions@gsb.strath.ac.uk
Andrews, Tim   Sr. Lectr.

Bolton, Sharon   Prof.
Burt, George, BA MBA   Sr. Lecter.
Eden, Colin, BSc PhD   Prof., Management
   Science
Huxham, Christine S., BSc MSc DPhil   Prof.
Mcgaughey, Sara   Prof., International Business
Scullion, Hugh, MA MA PhD   Prof.,
   International Business
Sillince, John   Prof.
Simpson, Barbara, BSc MSc PhD   Sr. Lecter.
Other Staff: 12 Visiting Profs.; 6 Lecters.
Research: behavioural decision-making; financial
   analysis in the stock market; sales and sales
   management practices; user input to
   organisational decision-making

Management Science

Tel: (0141) 548 3613 Fax: (0141) 552 6686
   E-mail: contact-mansci@strath.ac.uk
Ackermann, Frances, BA W.Aust., PhD   Prof.
Bedford, Tim, BSc MSc PhD   Prof.
Belton, Valerie, BSc Durh., MA Lanc., PhD Camb.
   Prof.
Howick, Susan, BSc MSc PhD   Sr. Lecter.
Macbryde, Jillian, BSc PhD   Sr. Lecter.
Quigley, John, BMath PhD   Sr. Lecter.
Van der Meer, Robert, CandEcon MSc   Sr.
   Lecter.
Walls, Lesley, BSc PhD   Prof.; Head*
Whalley, Jason, BA MA PhD   Sr. Lecter.
Other Staff: 3 Visiting Profs.; 3 Lecters.
Research: computer-supported group and
   individual decisions support systems;
   operational research to support decision-
   making; organisational implications of
   information systems

Marketing

Tel: (0141) 548 3734 Fax: (0141) 552 2802
   E-mail: contact-marketing@strath.ac.uk
Bernard, Kenneth N., MA   Sr. Lecter.
Ennis, Sean, BSc MBS MA PhD   Sr. Lecter.
Finch, John   Prof.
Grant, Ian, BCom MSc   Sr. Lecter.
Hamill, James, BSc PhD   Reader
Hart, Susan, BA PhD   Prof.
Hewer, Paul, BA MA DPhil   Sr. Lecter.
Hogg, Gillian, MA PhD   Prof.
Ibeh, Kevin, BSc MSc MBA PhD   Prof.
Paliwoda, Stanley, BA MSc PhD   Prof.
Shaw, Eleanor, MA PhD   Sr. Lecter.
Shiu, Edward, BSc MSc   Sr. Lecter.
Tagg, Stephen K., BSc PhD   Sr. Lecter.
Wagner, Beverly A.   Sr. Lecter.
Walsh, Gianfranco, MPhil PhD   Prof.
Wilson, Alan, BSc MBA PhD   Prof.; Head*
Other Staff: 1 Visiting Prof.; 7 Lecters.
Research: international business development and
   strategy; international marketing; inward
   investment; marketing of social issues and
   the social issues of marketing; supply chain
   management

Mathematics

Tel: (0141) 548 3721 Fax: (0141) 552 8657
   E-mail: contact-mathematics@strath.ac.uk
Ainsworth, Mark, BSc PhD   Prof.
Coles, Christopher, BA DPhil PhD   Sr. Lecter.
Davies, Penny J., BA MSc PhD   Sr. Lecter.
Davydov, Oleg, MS PhD   Reader
Duffy, Brian, MA MSc PhD   Sr. Lecter.
Grinfield, Michael, BSc MA PhD   Sr. Lecter.
Higham, Desmond J., BSc MSc PhD   Prof.
Lamb, Wilson, BSc PhD   Sr. Lecter.
MacKenzie, John A., BSc DPhil   Sr. Lecter.
McBride, Adam C., BSc Edin., PhD Edin., DSc
   Edin.   Prof.
McGhee, Desmond, BSc PhD   Sr. Lecter.
McKay, Geoffrey, BSc PhD   Sr. Lecter.
McKee, J. C. St. C. Sean, BSc St And., MA Oxf.,
   PhD Dund., DSc, FIMA, FRSEd   Prof.
Mottram, Nigel, BA PhD   Reader
Mulholland, Anthony J., BSc MSc PhD   Sr.
   Lecter.
Murdoch, A. Ian, MA Oxf., MS Pitt., PhD Pitt.
   Prof.
Osipov, Mikhail, PhD DSc   Prof., Applied
   Mathematics

Parkes, John, MA PhD   Sr. Lecter.
Ramage, Alison, BSc PhD   Reader
Sonnet, Andre, DrRerNat   Sr. Lecter.
Stewart, Iain W., MA Glas., PhD H-W   Prof.
Tweddle, Ian, BSc Glas., PhD Glas.   Reader
Wilson, Stephen K., BA MSc DPhil   Prof.;
   Head*
Other Staff: 4 Visiting Profs.; 3 Lecters.
Research: boundary integral methods and
   evolution processes; continuum modelling
   of anisotropic fluids; numerical analysis of
   nonlinear differential equations

Modern Languages

Tel: (0141) 548 3406 Fax: (0141) 552 4979
   E-mail: contact-modlang@strath.ac.uk
Cooke, Philip E., MA PhD   Sr. Lecter., Italian
Dickson, Michèle, Licence   Sr. Lecter., French
Dickson, Sheila, MA PhD   Sr. Lecter., German
Farrell, Joseph, MA Glas.   Prof., Italian; Head*
Macklin, John, BA PhD   Prof.
Millan, C. Gordon, MA Edin., PhD Edin.   Prof.,
   French
Morris, Alan I., MA St And., PhD St And.   Sr.
   Lecter., French
Rodero, Jesus, BA MA PhD   Sr. Lecter.
Stewart, Miranda M., BA PhD   Sr. Lecter.,
   Spanish
Wilkin, Andrew, BA Manc.   Sr. Lecter., Italian
Other Staff: 3 Lecters.; 1 Hon Res. Fellow
Research: contemporary German and German-
   Swiss literature; legacy of the Italian
   resistance movement; nineteenth- and
   twentieth-century French aesthetics;
   nineteenth- and twentieth-century Spanish
   prose fiction; Russian, Slavonic and Baltic
   linguistics

Naval Architecture and Marine Engineering

Tel: (0141) 548 4094 Fax: (0141) 552 2879
   E-mail: dept@na-me.ac.uk
Barltrop, Nigel, BSc, FICE   Prof.
Das, Purnendu K., BE ME PhD   Prof.
Day, Alexander H., BSc MSc PhD   Sr. Lecter.
Huang, Shan, BSc MPhil PhD   Sr. Lecter.
Lee, Byung S., BSc Seoul, MSc Strath., PhD Strath.
   Sr. Lecter.
Sayer, Philip G., BSc Manc., PhD Manc.   Reader
Turan, Osman, BSc MSc PhD   Sr. Lecter.
Varyani, Kamlesh S., MEng DEng   Sr. Lecter.
Vassalos, Dracos, BSc PhD   Prof.; Head*
Zhou, Peilin, BSc MSc PhD   Prof.
Other Staff: 5 Visiting Profs.; 4 Lecters.
Research: stability and safety of ships; surface
   support for subsea operations

Pharmacy and Biomedical Sciences, Strathclyde Institute of

Tel: (0141) 548 2125 Fax: (0141) 552 2562
Alexander, James, BSc Glas., PhD Glas.   Prof.
Anderson, John G., BSc PhD   Prof.
Boyter, Anne, BSc MSc   Sr. Lecter.
Carter, Katherine, BSc PhD   Sr. Lecter.
Coggans, Niall, BA   Sr. Lecter.
Connolly, John, BSc PhD   Sr. Lecter.
Converse, Carolyn A., ScB Brown, PhD Harv.
   Sr. Lecter.
Coombs, Graham H., BSc PhD, FRSEd   Prof.;
   Head*
Dempster, John   Sr. Lecter.
Eccleston, Gillian M., BSc PhD   Prof.
Ellis, Elizabeth, BSc PhD   Sr. Lecter.
Flint, David, BSc PhD   Prof.
Florence, Alastair J., BSc PhD   Sr. Lecter.
Furman, Brian L., BPharm Lond., PhD,
   FRPharmS   Prof.
Gray, Alexander I., BSc Trinity(Dub.), MA
   Trinity(Dub.), PhD   Reader
Halbert, Gavin W., BSc PhD   Prof.
Harnett, William, BSc Glas., PhD Glas.   Prof.
Harvey, Alan L., BSc PhD   Prof.
Harvey, Linda M., BSc PhD   Sr. Lecter.
Hudson, Steve, BPharm Nott., MPharm Brad.
   Prof.
Hunter, Iain S., BSc PhD   Prof., Molecular
   Microbiology
Johnson, James, BPharm PhD   Sr. Lecter.

Kane, Kathleen A., BSc Edin., PhD Edin.   Prof.
Kennedy, Charles, BSc PhD   Reader
Lutz, Eve, BSc PhD   Sr. Lecter.
Macaluso, Andrea   Sr. Lecter.
Mackay, Simon, BPharm PhD   Prof.
Mccarron, John, BSc PhD   Prof.
McNeil, Brian, BSc PhD   Prof.
Mullen, Thomas D., BSc PhD   Sr. Lecter.
Nimmo, Myra, BSc PhD DSc   Prof.
Paterson, Alistair, BSc Edin., PhD Lond.   Sr.
   Lecter.
Piggott, John R., BA Camb., MSc Leeds, PhD
   Reading   Reader
Plevin, Robin, BSc PhD   Prof.
Pratt, Judith, BSc Reading, PhD Lond.   Prof.
Prior, Christopher, BSc PhD   Sr. Lecter.
Pyne, Nigel J., BSc Birm., PhD Manc.   Prof.
Pyne, Susan, BSc PhD   Prof.
Roberts, Craig W., BSc PhD   Reader
Rowan, Edward G., BSc PhD   Sr. Lecter.
Skellern, Graham G., BSc CNAA, PhD   Reader
Stimson, William H., BSc St And., PhD St And.,
   FIBiol, FRSEd   Prof.
Wadsworth, Roger M., BPharm Lond., PhD
   Strath., DSc Strath.   Prof.
Watson, David G., BSc Leic., PhD Lond.   Reader
Watson-Craik, Irene A., BSc Glas., PhD   Sr.
   Lecter.
Wiese, Martin   John Anderson Res. Sr. Lecter.
Wilson, Clive G., BSc CNAA, PhD Sur.   Prof.
Other Staff: 20 Visiting Profs.; 29 Lecters.
Research: biochemical, drug delivery and
   formulation; mitogen, stress-activated and
   NFkB kinase cascades; myocardial
   ischaemia/reperfusion; nucleotidases
   released by stimulation of sympathetic
   nerves; roles of ion channels and receptors
   in control of cell excitability and synaptic
   transmission

Physics

Tel: (0141) 548 3363 Fax: (0141) 552 2891
   E-mail: contact-physics@strath.ac.uk
Badnell, Nigel, BSc PhD   Prof.
Barnett, Stephen M., BSc Lond., PhD Lond.,
   FRSEd   Prof., Quantum Optics
Bingham, Robert, BSc MSc DPhil   Prof.
Birch, David J. S., BSc Manc., PhD Manc., FIP
   Prof., Photophysics; Head*
Brown, Ronal, BSc PhD   Sr. Lecter.
Cross, Adrian, BSc PhD   Reader
Cunningham, Alexander, BSc Edin., PhD
   Reader
Ferguson, Allister I., BSc St And., MA Oxf., PhD
   St And., FRSEd, FIP   Prof., Photonics
Galster, Wilfried, PhD   Reader
Han, Thomas, BSc MSc PhD   Sr. Lecter.
Jaroszynski, Dino A., BSc PhD   Prof.
Jeffers, John, BSc PhD   Reader
Langford, Nigel, BSc PhD   Reader
Lockerbie, Nicholas A., BSc Nott., PhD Nott.
   Reader
Martin, Robert W., MA DPhil   Prof.
O'Donnell, Kevin P., BSc Glas., PhD Trinity(Dub.)
   Prof., Semiconductor Spectroscopy
Oppo, Gian-Luca, PhD Florence   Prof.,
   Computational and Nonlinear Physics
Papoff, Francesco, MSc PhD   Sr. Lecter.
Phelps, Alan D. R., MA Camb., DPhil Oxf., FIP
   Prof., Plasma Physics
Riis, Erling, MSc Aarhus, PhD Aarhus   Prof.
Rolinski, Olaf, MSc PhD   Sr. Lecter.
Ruddock, Ivan S., BSc Belf., PhD Lond.   Reader
Trager-Cowan, Carol, BSc MSc PhD   Sr. Lecter.
Wynne, Klaas, MSc PhD   Reader
Other Staff: 10 Visiting Profs.; 5 Lecters.
Research: atomic, molecular and plasma physics;
   computational non-linear and quantum
   optics; laser science; photonics; structural
   studies and dynamics

Prosthetics and Orthotics, National Centre for Training and Education in

Tel: (0141) 548 3298 Fax: (0141) 552 1283
   E-mail: contact-prosthetics@strath.ac.uk
Condie, Elizabeth   Reader
Dykes, William G.   Sr. Lecter.
Figgins, Elaine, BSc   Reader

McHugh, Brendan, BEng PhD   Sr. Lectr.
Meier, Magrit-Regula, PhD   Dir., Res.
Sexton, Sandra, BSc   Dir.*
Simpson, David, BSc MSc   Sr. Lectr.
Other Staff: 2 Visiting Profs.; 9 Lectrs.
Research: insole design and its effect on interface pressure with neuropathic diabetic feet; investigation of dynamic pressures at the interface between trans-tibial prosthetic sockets and the stump; measurement of the movement of the femur within the socket of a trans-femoral amputee; novel socket-shaping techniques for use in low-income countries

Psychology

Tel: (0141) 548 2700 Fax: (0141) 552 4001
    E-mail: contact-psychology@strath.ac.uk
Baxter, James, MA PhD   Sr. Lectr.
Boyle, James M. E., BSc Glas.   Reader
Davies, John B., BA PhD   Prof.
Durkin, Kevin, BEd PhD   Prof.
Fisher, Stephen G., BSc   Sr. Lectr.
Grealy, Madeleine, BSc MPhil PhD   Sr. Lectr.
Kelly, Steve, BSc PhD   Sr. Lectr.
Obonsawin, Marc C., BA BSc MSc PhD   Sr. Lectr.
Sanford, Alison, MA PhD   Sr. Lectr.
Thomson, James A., MA Edin., PhD Edin.   Prof.; Head*
Warden, David A., BA Belf., PhD Lond.   Reader
Woolfson, Lisa, BSc PhD   Reader
Other Staff: 6 Lectrs.
Research: applied social psychology; developmental and educational psychology; interactive learning; neuropsychology; road user behaviour

Social Work

Tel: (0141) 950 3380 Fax: (0141) 950 3474
    E-mail: contact-socialwork@strath.ac.uk
Ballantyne, Neil, BSc   Sr. Lectr.
Cameron, Kathryn, MA LLB   Sr. Lectr.
Campbell, John W. S., MA   Sr. Lectr.; Course Dir.
Hill, Malcolm   Prof.
Kendrick, Andrew, MA PhD   Prof., Residential Child Care; Head*
Nellis, Mike, BEd MSc PhD   Prof.
Other Staff: 13 Lectrs.
Research: children's needs: valuing diversity; comparative study in residential childcare; learning technology and social work education; students with dyslexia

Sport, Culture and the Arts

Tel: (0141) 950 3460 Fax: (0141) 950 3132
    E-mail: contact-sportstudies@strath.ac.uk
Clarke, Peter T., MEd MPhil   Sr. Lectr.
Coutts, Glen, BA   Reader
Dougall, Paul, BA BA(Ed) PhD   Sr. Lectr.
Forsyth, Stuart, BEd MA   Sr. Lectr.
Green, Brian N., BEd MSc   Sr. Lectr.
McWilliam, Angus A., BSc PhD   Sr. Lectr.; Head*
Mutrie, Nanette, PhD   Prof.
Rowe, David A., BEd MSc PhD   Sr. Lectr.
Other Staff: 1 Visiting Prof.; 9 Lectrs.
Research: applied physiology; outdoor and environmental education

Statistics and Modelling Science

Tel: (0141) 548 3805 Fax: (0141) 552 2079
    E-mail: contact-stams@strath.ac.uk
Allardice, Gwendolyn, BSc MSc PhD   Sr. Lectr.
Gettinby, George C., BSc Belf., DPhil Ulster   Prof., Statistics
Greenhalgh, David, MA PhD   Reader
Gurney, William S. C., BSc Brist., PhD Brist.   Prof., Mathematical Biology
Mao, Xuerong, MSc PhD   Prof.
McKenzie, Edward, MSc Glas., PhD   Reader; Head*
Reid, Stuart W. J., BVMS PhD   Prof., Veterinary Informatics and Epidemiology
Robertson, Chris, BSc MSc PhD   Prof.
Rotondo, Dino, BSc PhD   Sr. Lectr.
Smith, Kevin, BSc PhD   Sr. Lectr.

Spickett, Corinne, BSc MA DPhil   Sr. Lectr.
Stevens, Howard, BPharm PhD, FRSChem   Prof.
Tettey, Justice N. A., BSc MSc PhD   Sr. Lectr.
Thomson, Alison, BSc MSc PhD   Sr. Lectr.
Van Der Walle, Christopher, BPharm PhD   Sr. Lectr.
Wiese, Martin   John Anderson Res. Sr. Lectr.
Zuyev, Sergei, MSc PhD   Reader
Other Staff: 4 Visiting Profs.; 2 Lectrs.
Research: epidemiology; machine learning; mathematical ecology; spatial processes; statistical inference

SPECIAL CENTRES, ETC

European Policies Research Centre

Tel: (0141) 548 3672 Fax: (0141) 548 4898
    E-mail: contact-eprc@strath.ac.uk
Bachtler, John, BA   Prof.
Yuill, Douglas, MA MPhil   Prof.; Dir.*
Other Staff: 1 Visiting Prof.; 2 Sr. Res. Fellows
Research: EU structural and cohesion policies; European competition policy and subsidy discipline; internationalisation and European integration; regional development policies of Western European countries; regional restructuring and technology transfer

Forensic Science, Centre for

Tel: (0141) 548 2100
    E-mail: lorraine.stewart@strath.ac.uk
Fraser, Jim   Prof.; Dir.*
Linacre, Adrian M. T., BSc DPhil   Sr. Lectr.
NicDaeid, Niamh, BSc BA PhD   Sr. Lectr.
Other Staff: 2 Lectrs.

Lifelong Learning, Centre for

Tel: (0141) 548 4287 Fax: (0141) 553 1270
    E-mail: learn@cll.strath.ac.uk
Hart, Lesley A., MBE   Dir.*
McKechnie, Brian, MA MSc   Manager, Sr. Studies Inst.
Thomson, Raymond, BA MA DMus PhD   Deputy Dir.; Head, Open Studies
Other Staff: 6 Co-ordinators

Professional Legal Studies, Centre for

Tel: (0141) 548 3049 E-mail: ptllb@strath.ac.uk
Maharg, Paul, LLB Glas., MA Glas., PhD Edin.   Prof.
Paterson, Alan A., LLB Edin., DPhil Oxf.   Prof.; Dir.*
Sochart, Elise A., BA   Deputy Dir.
Watson, Robert, BA LLM   Dir., Resources
Other Staff: 4 Visiting Profs.

Public Policy, Centre for the Study of

Tel: (0141) 548 3217 Fax: (0141) 552 4711
    E-mail: contact-cspp@strath.ac.uk
Rose, Richard, BA Johns H., DPhil Oxf., FBA   Prof.; Dir.* (Politics of Public Policy)
Other Staff: 1 Visiting Prof.

Scottish Economy, Fraser of Allander Institute for Research on the

Tel: (0141) 548 3958 Fax: (0141) 552 8347
    E-mail: fraser@strath.ac.uk
Swales, J. Kim, BA Camb.   Prof.; Res. Dir.*
Research: modelling regional economies; short-term movements in economic activity

Scottish Institute for Residential Child Care

National Office
Tel: (0141) 950 3683 Fax: (0141) 950 3681
    E-mail: sircc@strath.ac.uk
Davidson, Jennifer   Dir.*
Other Staff: 4 Lectrs.

Scottish Local Authorities Management Centre

Tel: (0141) 548 4143 Fax: (0141) 552 6587
    E-mail: victoria.mackenzie@strath.ac.uk
Mair, Colin, BA   Dir.*
Other Staff: 2 Lectrs.

Research: appraisal practices in local government; councillor turnover; local government's relations with its customers; management of fragmentation in local government; pay and reward systems in local government

Strathclyde Science and Technology Forum

Tel: (0141) 548 3105 Fax: (0141) 548 3597
    E-mail: ann.morrow@strath.ac.uk
Brown, Douglas, MPhil PhD   Dir.*

CONTACT OFFICERS

Academic affairs. Head, Academic Office: Kochanowska, R.
    (E-mail: r.kochanowska@mis.strath.ac.uk)
Accommodation. Director of Residence and Catering: Cook, Robert J.
    (E-mail: student.accommodation@strath.ac.uk)
Admissions (first degree). Head of Schools and Colleges Liaison Service: Wright, Zane
    (E-mail: scls@strath.ac.uk)
Admissions (higher degree). Head, International and Graduate Office: Stewart, Michelle
    (E-mail: international@mis.strath.ac.uk)
Adult/continuing education. Director, Centre for Lifelong Learning: Hart, Lesley A., MBE
    (E-mail: learn@cll.strath.ac.uk)
Alumni. Head, Alumni and Development: Shepherd, Frances
    (E-mail: alumni@mis.strath.ac.uk)
Archives. Archivist: Harrison, Margaret
    (E-mail: archives@strath.ac.uk)
Careers. Director (Careers): Graham, Barbara
    (E-mail: yourcareer@strath.ac.uk)
Computing services. Director of IT Services: Brough, Stuart
    (E-mail: helpdesk@strath.ac.uk)
Consultancy services. Director of Research and Consultancy Services: McBeth, David, BSc PhD (E-mail: rcs@strath.ac.uk)
Development/fund-raising. Head, Alumni and Development: Shepherd, Frances
    (E-mail: alumni@mis.strath.ac.uk)
Estates and buildings/works and services. Director of Estates Management: Roddick, Graham (E-mail: g.roddick@mis.strath.ac.uk)
Examinations. Head, Registry: Williamson, Craig
    (E-mail: c.williamson@mis.strath.ac.uk)
Finance. Director of Finance: Coyle, David
    (E-mail: d.coyle@strath.ac.uk)
General enquiries. Secretary to the University: West, Peter W. A., OBE, MA St And., DUniv DPhil (E-mail: p.west@mis.strath.ac.uk)
Health services. Medical Adviser to the University: Boyle, Iain T., BSc MB ChB, FRCP, FRCPGlas
    (E-mail: occupationalhealth@strath.ac.uk)
Industrial liaison. Director of Research and Consultancy Services: McBeth, David, BSc PhD (E-mail: rcs@strath.ac.uk)
International office. Head, International and Graduate Office: Stewart, Michelle
    (E-mail: igo@strath.ac.uk)
Library (chief librarian). Librarian and Head of Information Resources Directorate: Law, Prof. Derek G., MA DUniv, FIInfSc, FRSEd, FLA, FKC (E-mail: library@strath.ac.uk)
Marketing. Director of Marketing and Communications: Taylor, Adam J.
    (E-mail: corporatecomms@strath.ac.uk)
Personnel/human resources. Director of Human Resources: Sutherland, William M.
    (E-mail: humanresources@mis.strath.ac.uk)
Public relations. Head, Communications: Hunt, Suzanne
    (E-mail: corporatecomms@strath.ac.uk)
Publications. Head, Communications: Hunt, Suzanne
    (E-mail: corporatecomms@strath.ac.uk)
Purchasing. Procurements Officer: McAllister, Shaun
    (E-mail: shaun.mcallister@strath.ac.uk)

Quality assurance and accreditation. Head, Academic Office: Kochanowska, R. (E-mail: r.kochanowska@mis.strath.ac.uk)

Research. Director of Research and Consultancy Services: McBeth, David, BSc PhD (E-mail: rcs@strath.ac.uk)

Safety. Safety Officer: Thompson, Suzanne, BSc (E-mail: safety@strath.ac.uk)

Scholarships, awards, loans. Finance Officer: MacKenzie, Roddy (E-mail: r.mackenzie@mis.strath.ac.uk)

Schools liaison. Head of Schools and Colleges Liaison: Wright, Zane (E-mail: scls@strath.ac.uk)

Security. Security Services Manager: Nimmo, David W. (E-mail: d.nimmo@strath.ac.uk)

Sport and recreation. Head of Centre for Sport and Recreation: Sturrock, Niall (E-mail: n.sturrock@strath.ac.uk)

Staff development and training. Director, Centre for Academic Practice: Gordon, Prof. George, MA Edin., PhD (E-mail: g.gordon@strath.ac.uk)

Student welfare/counselling. Director of Student Affairs: Martin, John W. F. (E-mail: j.martin@mis.strath.ac.uk)

Students from other countries. Head, International and Graduate Office: Stewart, Michelle (E-mail: igo@strath.ac.uk)

Students with disabilities. Head of Disability Service: Simpson, Anne, OBE (E-mail: disabilityservice@strath.ac.uk)

[Information supplied by the institution as at 2 October 2007, and edited by the ACU]

UNIVERSITY OF SUNDERLAND

Founded 1992

Member of the Association of Commonwealth Universities

Postal Address: Edinburgh Building, Chester Road, City Campus, Sunderland, England SR1 3SD
Telephone: (0191) 515 2000 **Fax:** (0191) 515 2044 **E-mail:** postmaster@sunderland.ac.uk
URL: http://www.sunderland.ac.uk

VICE-CHANCELLOR AND CHIEF EXECUTIVE*—Fidler, Prof. Peter, MBE, MSc Salf.
DEPUTY VICE CHANCELLOR—Brown, Prof. Jeff R., BSc MSc PhD, FRPharmS, FRSChem, FIBiol
PRO-VICE-CHANCELLOR—Bell, Bob, BSc
PRO-VICE-CHANCELLOR—Burns, Ian
SECRETARY‡—Pacey, John D., LLB

UNIVERSITY OF SURREY

Founded 1966

Member of the Association of Commonwealth Universities

Postal Address: Guildford, Surrey, England GU2 7XH
Telephone: (01483) 689905 **Fax:** (01483) 683948 **E-mail:** information@surrey.ac.uk
URL: http://www.surrey.ac.uk

VICE-CHANCELLOR AND CHIEF EXECUTIVE*—Snowden, Prof. Christopher M., BSc MSc PhD, FREng, FIEE, FIEEE, FRS, FCGI, FIET
DEPUTY VICE-CHANCELLOR—Turner, Prof. J. A., MA DPhil, FRHistS
PRO-VICE-CHANCELLOR (TEACHING AND LEARNING)—Airey, Prof. David W., BA Lond., MSc Strath., FRSA, FTS
PRO-VICE-CHANCELLOR (STAFF DEVELOPMENT)—(vacant)
PRO-VICE-CHANCELLOR (RESEARCH AND ENTERPRISE)—Evans, Prof. Barry G., BSc Leeds, PhD Leeds, FIEE, FRSA, FREng
PRO-VICE-CHANCELLOR—Weiss, Prof. Bernard L., BSc Newcastle(UK), PhD Newcastle(UK), DSc, FIEE, FIP
UNIVERSITY SECRETARY AND CLERK TO THE COUNCIL‡—Strawson, James W. A., MA MSc
DIRECTOR OF CORPORATE SERVICES—Melly, Greg K., MBA
DIRECTOR OF EXTERNAL ACADEMIC RELATIONS—Harding, John E., BSc MSc PhD, FIStructE, FICE

GENERAL INFORMATION

History. The university was originally established as Battersea Polytechnic Institute in 1891, subsequently designated Battersea College of Advanced Technology, and was incorporated by royal charter in 1966.

The university is located near Guildford town centre.

Admission to first degree courses (see also United Kingdom Introduction). Through Universities and Colleges Admissions Service (UCAS). The university's general entrance requirement must be satisfied, as well as particular requirements for the chosen course. The university accepts a range of educational qualifications as satisfying the minimum general entrance requirement.

First Degrees (see also United Kingdom Directory to Subjects of Study). BA, BEng,

BMus, BSc, LLB, MChem, MEng, MMath, MPhys.

Courses normally last 3 years full-time, or 4 years including 1 year professional/research-based placement. Some science or engineering programmes offer an additional foundation year. BA/BSc in combined studies: part-time self paced courses.

Length of course. Full-time: BA, BEng, BMus, BSc, LLB: 3–4 years; MMath, MPhys: 4 years; MChem, MEng: 4–5 years.

Higher Degrees (see also United Kingdom Directory to Subjects of Study).

Master's. LLM, MA, MBA, MMus, MPhil, MSc.

Admission. Applicants for admission to master's degrees must normally hold an appropriate first degree with at least second class honours, or an equivalent overseas qualification; non-graduates with appropriate professional or other qualifications may also be admitted.

Master's degree courses normally last 1 year full-time or up to 6 years part-time. MPhil: 21 months full-time or 33 months part-time.

Length of course. Full-time: MMus, MSc: 1 year; MPhil: 2 years. Part-time: MA, MBA, MMus: 2 years; MSc: 2–3 years; MPhil: 3 years. By *distance learning:* LLM: 2 years.

Doctoral. DLitt, DSc, EdD, EngD, PhD, PsychD.

Admission. PhD: applicants should hold an appropriate master's degree; EdD: master's degree and minimum 4 years' relevant experience; PsychD: first degree in psychology with at least upper second class honours, and relevant experience.

PhD, EdD: 33 months full-time or 45 months part-time; PsychD: 33 months full-time or up to 60 months part-time; EngD: 45 months full-time. DLitt, DSc: awarded on published work to graduates of this university of minimum 10 years' standing.

Length of course. Full-time: PhD, PsychD: 3 years; EngD: 4 years. *Part-time:* PsychD: 4–5 years; PhD: 5 years.

Libraries. Volumes: 550,000. Periodicals subscribed to: 2060. Other holdings: 10,000 electronic journals; 250 electronic databases; 30,000 e-books. Special collections: European Documentation Centre; National Resource Centre for Dance; E. H. Shepard.

FACULTIES/SCHOOLS

Arts, Communications and Humanities

Tel: (01483) 686200 Fax: (01483) 686201
Head: Lutzeier, Prof. Peter R., MLitt Oxf., DPhil Stuttgart, DrHabil Berl.
Manager: Grimmer, Ruth N., BSc Lond., MBA Reading

Biomedical and Molecular Sciences, School of

Tel: (01483) 689721 Fax: (01483) 576978
E-mail: bio@surrey.ac.uk
Dean: Robertson, Prof. W. R., BSc PhD, FRCPath
School Manager: Arendell, Brian

Electronics and Physical Sciences, School of

Tel: (01483) 686110 Fax: (01483) 534139
E-mail: information@eim.surrey.ac.uk
Head: Weiss, Prof. Bernard L., BSc Sur., PhD Sur., DSc Sur., FIEE, FIP
Manager: Clapham, Mike J.

Engineering, School of

Tel: (01483) 686292 Fax: (01483) 686601
E-mail: eng@surrey.ac.uk
Head: Smith, Prof. Paul A., MA Camb., PhD Camb., FIMMM
Manager: Millington, Anthony H., BSc(Eng) Lond., FIMechE

Health and Medical Sciences, European Institute of

Tel: (01483) 686700
Head: Pope, Prof. Rosemary, BSc Lond., PhD
Manager: Gilbert, Ken

Human Sciences, School of

Tel: (01483) 686900 Fax: (01483) 686901
E-mail: d.williams@surrey.ac.uk
Head: Emler, Prof. Nicholas, BSc S'ton., MA Oxf., PhD Lond., FBPsS
School Manager: Carruthers, Graham H.

Management, School of

Tel: (01483) 686300 Fax: (01483) 686301
E-mail: management@surrey.ac.uk
Head: O'Keefe, Prof. Robert M., BA Lanc., PhD S'ton.
School Manager: Styche-Patel, Heather, BSc Sur., MBA

Postgraduate Medical School

Tel: (01483) 688500 Fax: (01483) 688501
E-mail: pgms-pgadmin@surrey.ac.uk
Head: Myint, Prof. Steven, MB BS MD

ACADEMIC UNITS

Biomedical and Molecular Sciences, School of

Tel: (01483) 689721 Fax: (01483) 576978
E-mail: smbs@surrey.ac.uk
Adams, Martin R., BSc Warw., MSc Manc., PhD Manc. Reader
Bishop, Jacqueline A., BSc Sur., PhD Sur. Sr. Lectr.
Bushell, Michael E., BSc Lond., PhD Kent Prof., Microbial Physiology
Butterworth, Peter H. W., BSc Liv., PhD Liv., FIBiol Prof., Molecular Biology
Carter, Michael J., BA Oxf., PhD Camb. Reader, Virology
Clifford, Michael N., BSc Reading, PhD Strath. Prof., Food Safety

Dale, Jeremy W., BSc Lond., PhD Lond. Prof., Molecular Microbiology
Danil de Namor, Angela F., BSc Natnl.Santiago, PhD Sur., FRSChem Prof.
Dijk, Derk-Jan, BSc Gron., MSc Gron., PhD Gron. Reader, Physiology
Foster, Russell G., BSc DPhil Visiting Prof.
Gibson, Gordon G., BSc Glas., PhD Lond., DSc Lond., FRCPath Prof., Molecular Toxicology
Gillies, Duncan G., BSc Lond., PhD Lond. Reader
Goldfarb, Peter S. G., BSc Aberd., PhD Lond., FRCPath Prof., Molecular Biology
Griffin, Bruce A., BSc CNAA, PhD Aberd. Reader, Nutritional Metabolism
Hamerton, Ian, BSc Sur., PhD Sur., FRSChem Sr. Lectr.
Hay, John N., BSc Edin., PhD Edin., FRSChem Prof.
Heyes, David M., BSc Brist., PhD Manc., DSc Brist., FRSChem Prof.
Hinton, Richard H., BA Camb., PhD Sur., FIBiol, FRSChem, FRCPath Reader, Cell Pathology
Hourani, Susanna M. O., BA Camb., PhD Lond. Reader
Howell, Nazlin K., BSc Nott., PhD Nott., FRSChem, FRSA Reader, Food Science
Howland, Roger J., BSc Hull, PhD Hull Sr. Lectr., Physiology
Howlin, Brendan J., BSc Essex, PhD Essex Sr. Lectr.
Islam, M. Saiful, BSc Lond., PhD Lond. Reader
Jones, John R., PhD Wales, DSc Wales, FRSChem Prof., Radiochemistry
Jones, Robin S., BSc Wales, PhD Wales, FRSChem Sr. Lectr.
Kitchen, Ian, BSc CNAA, PhD Lond. Prof., Neuropharmacology
Lewis, David F. V., BSc Sur., MSc Sur., PhD Sur. Reader, Toxicology
Lynch, James M., BTech Lough., PhD Lond., DSc Lond., FIBiol, FRSA Prof., Biotechnology
McFadden, Johnjoe J., BSc Lond., PhD Lond. Prof., Molecular Genetics
Millward, D. Joe, PhD WI, DSc Wales Prof., Nutrition
Morgan, Jane B., MSc Lond., PhD Lond. Reader, Childhood Nutrition
Morgan, Linda M., BSc Brist., MSc Sur., PhD Lond. Reader, Nutritional Endocrinology
Povey, David C., MSc Sur., PhD Sur. Sr. Lectr.
Reynolds, Lesley-Jane, BSc PhD Sr. Lectr.
Robertson, W. R., BSc PhD, FRCPath Prof.; Head*
Sammes, Peter G., BSc Lond., PhD Lond., DSc Lond., FRSChem Prof., Organic Chemistry
Sanders, Peter G., BSc Lond., PhD Glas. Sr. Lectr.
Sermon, Paul A., BSc Wales, PhD Brist., DSc Brist. Prof., Physical Chemistry
Skene, Debra J., BPharm Rhodes, MSc Rhodes, PhD S.Af.Med. Reader, Neuroendocrinology
Slade, Robert C. T., BA Oxf., MA Oxf., DPhil Oxf., FRSChem, FIMMM Prof., Inorganic Chemistry
Stevens, Gary C., PhD Lond. Sr. Res. Fellow; Dir., Polymer Res. Centre
Stevenson, Derek, PhD Sur. Sr. Lectr.
Symons, Andrew M., BSc Bath, PhD Bath Sr. Lectr.
Wang, Timothy W., MB BChir Camb., PhD Camb., PhD Open(UK) Sr. Lectr.
Ward, Neil I., MSc NZ, PhD NZ Sr. Lectr.
Wright, John W., MB BS Lond., MSc Sur. Reader, Metabolic Medicine
Other Staff: 3 Prof. Res. Fellows; 19 Lectrs.; 4 Sr. Dieticians/Tutors; 3 Sr. Tutors; 28 Res. Fellows; 24 Res. Officers; 2 Sr. Exper. Officers; 5 Exper. Officers
Research: chemical and analytical sciences (supramolecular and biomolecular chemistry, materials chemistry); integrative physiology sciences (molecular toxicology, neuroendocrinology, pharmacology, human psychopharmacology); microbial sciences (functional genomics, microbial physiology and ecology, molecular microbiology); nutrition and food safety

Computing

Tel: (01483) 686058 Fax: (01483) 686051
E-mail: cs@surrey.ac.uk
Browne, Antony, BSc Liv., MSc S.Bank, PhD S.Bank Sr. Lectr.
Ho, Anthony T. S., MSc Lond., PhD Lond., FIEE Prof., Multimedia Security
Krause, Paul J., PhD Exe., FIMA Res. Prof., Software Engineering
Peel, Roger, BSc Sur., MA Sur., PhD Sur. Sr. Lectr.
Schneider, Steve, BA Oxf., MSc Oxf., DPhil Oxf., FBCS Prof.; Head*
Other Staff: 10 Lectrs.; 6 Res. Officers
Research: biologically inspired modelling and applications; digital watermarking; form-mail methods and security; neural computing; software systems

Culture, Media and Communication Studies

Tel: (01483) 686222 Fax: (01483) 686201
E-mail: j.blows@surrey.ac.uk
Anderman, Gunilla M., FilMag Stockholm, PhD Lond. Prof., Translation Studies
Barta, P., BA Bud., MA Ill., PhD Ill. Prof., Russian and Cultural Studies
Corbett, Greville G., BA Birm., MA Birm., PhD Birm., FBA Prof., Linguistics and Russian Language
Hughes, Helen A., BA Lond., PhD Lond. Sr. Lectr.
Lutzeier, Peter R., MLitt Oxf., DPhil Stuttgart, DrHabil Berl. Prof., German
Marquiz-Reiter, Rosina, MA Sur., PhD Sheff., BSc Sr. Lectr.
Merricks, Linda, BSc Sus., DPhil Sus. Head*
Munday, Jeremy, BA Camb., MEd Liv., PhD Brad. Sr. Lectr.
Rogers, Margaret A., BA Birm., MA Kent, PhD Sur. Reader
Other Staff: 7 Lecteurs; 4 Lektor/Lektorinnes; 5 Sr. Tutors; 6 Tutors; 4 Res. Fellows
Research: applied linguistics; cultural studies; lexicology; linguistics, sociolinguistics and pragmatics; literature and visual media

Dance

Tel: (01483) 686500 Fax: (01483) 686501
E-mail: dance@surrey.ac.uk
Dodds, Sherril, BA Manc.Met., MA Sur., PhD Sur. Sr. Lectr.
Johnson-Jones, Jean, BA Ill., MA Ill. Tutor; Dir., Labanotation Inst.
Kane, Angela, MA City(UK), PhD Kent Sr. Lectr.; Head*
Lansdale, Janet, MA Leeds, PhD Leeds, FRSA Prof.; Dir. of Res.
Poesio, Giannandrea, MA Florence, PhD Sur. Sr. Lectr.
Other Staff: 7 Lectrs.; 2 Res. Fellows; 2 Tutors
Research: choreography and performance (practice-based research); critical theory, dance analysis and history; cultural studies, post-colonial theory and ethnography

Economics

Tel: (01483) 686920 Fax: (01483) 689548
E-mail: economics@surrey.ac.uk
Bag, Parimal, BSc MA PhD Prof.
Bird, Graham R., MA Camb., PhD Sur. Prof.
Gage, Heather, BA Reading, MSc Reading Sr. Lectr.
Hawdon, David, MSc(Econ) Lond. Sr. Lectr.
Hunt, Lester C., BSc Lough., MA Essex Prof.; Head*
Ingram, Peter, BA Kent, MSc Lond. Sr. Lectr.
Levine, Paul, BSc Manc., MSc(Econ) Lond., PhD Manc. Prof.
Pierse, Richard, BA Oxf., MSc(Econ) Lond. Reader
Rickman, Neil, BA Durh., MA(Econ) McG., PhD McG. Foundation Fund Lectr.; Reader
Temple, P. A., MA Camb., MA(Econ) Manc. Sr. Lectr.
Wall, John R., BA Essex, MA CNAA Sr. Tutor; Deputy Head

Witt, Robert J., BSc CNAA, MSc Wales, MA Essex, PhD Essex   Sr. Lectr.

Other Staff: 10 Lectrs.; 1 Res. Fellow

Research: energy economics (energy demand modelling and policy analysis); health and other interdisciplinary research (crime and unemployment, health economics and health services, political economy); international economics (arms trade, developing and emerging countries, European integration, IFIs, technology transfer); macroeconomics, mathematical economics and econometrics (dynamic optimisation, finite sampling properties of estimators, theory of growth)

Engineering, Chemical and Process

Tel: (01483) 686292 Fax: (01483) 686581

Kirkby, Norman F., BSc Nott., PhD Camb.   Sr. Lectr.

Kokossis, Antonis C., PhD Prin., FIChemE   Prof., Process Systems Engineering Optimisation

Millington, C. Alan, BSc Lond., PhD Sur.   Sr. Lectr.

Sharif, Adel, BSc Baghdad, MSc Wales, PhD Wales   Reader, Chemical and Process Engineering

Thorpe, Rex, MA Camb., MEng Camb., PhD Camb.   Prof., Multiphase Engineering

Tüzün, Ugur, BSc Leeds, PhD Camb., FIChemE, FRSA   Dir., Res.; Prof., Process Engineering; Head of Discipline*

Other Staff: 2 Lectrs.; 5 Res. Fellows; 1 Sr. Exper. Officer; 1 Exper. Officer

Research: environmental systems engineering (environmental bio-separations, environmental process technology, sustainable development); multi-phase engineering (heat and mass transfer, multi-phase simulations, multi-phase transport); particulate technology (DEM simulations, nano-technology, power handling, tomography); process systems engineering and optimisation (process optimisation logistics of supply chain management)

Engineering, Civil

Tel: (01483) 686292 Fax: (01483) 450984

Chryssanthopoulos, Marios K., BSc Newcastle(UK), PhD Lond., SM, FICE, FIStructE   Prof., Structural Systems

Clarke, Brian A., MSc Lond.   Sr. Lectr.

Hollaway, Leonard C., BSc(Eng) Lond., MSc(Eng) Lond., PhD Lond., FICE   Prof., Composite Structures

Huxley, Michael A., BSc Sur., FRSA   Univ. Dir.

Jiang, Jia-Quin, BSc Lond., PhD Lond.   Reader, Environmental Engineering

Lawson, Mark, BSc(Eng) Lond., PhD Salf.   Prof., Construction Systems

Lloyd, Barry J., BSc Leeds, MPhil Reading, PhD Sur.   Prof., Environmental Health Engineering

Matthews, Marcus C., BSc CNAA, MSc Birm., PhD Sur., FGS   Sr. Lectr., Geotechnics

Mulheron, Michael, BSc Sur., PhD Sur.   Sr. Lectr.

Nooshin, Hoshyar, BSc Teheran, PhD Lond., FIStructE   Prof., Space Structures

Onoufriou, Toula, BSc(Eng) Lond., PhD Lond.   Reader, Structural Engineering

Ouki, Sabeha K., MSc Penn., PhD Penn.   Reader, Environmental Engineering

Parke, Gerald A. R., BSc CNAA, MSc(Eng) City(UK), PhD Glas., FIStructE, FICE   Head of Discipline; Prof., Structural Engineering

Toy, Norman, BSc(Eng) City(UK), PhD City(UK), FRAeS   Prof., Fluid Mechanics

Woods, Richard I., BSc CNAA, PhD Sur.   Sr. Lectr.

Other Staff: 6 Lectrs.; 5 Res. Fellows; 1 Sr. Tutor; 1 Tutor; 1 Sr. Exper. Officer

Research: construction materials (new materials for construction, repair and remediation of stone and concrete); environmental health engineering (air, water and ground pollution, water quality, water treatment

and distribution systems for industrialised and developing countries)

Engineering, Mechanical, Biomedical, Materials and Aerospace

Tel: (01483) 686292 Fax: (01483) 306039

Baker, Mark, BSc Kent, PhD Sur.   Sr. Lectr.

Chew, John W., DPhil Sus., FRAeS, FASME   Dir., Fluids and Systems Res. Centre; Prof., Mechanical Engineering

Crocombe, Andrew D., BSc(Eng) Brist., PhD Brist., FIMechE   Head of Discipline; Prof., Structural Mechanics

Driscoll, John, BSc Aston, PhD Aston, FIMechE   Sr. Lectr.

Ewins, David J., BSc Bath, PhD Bath   Reader, Biomedical Engineering

Gillan, Mark, BEng Belf., PhD Belf., FRAeS   Prof., Aerospace Engineering

Goringe, Michael J., MA Camb., PhD Camb., FIMMM, FRSA   Prof., Materials

Hancock, Philip E., BSc(Eng) Lond., PhD Lond.   Sr. Lectr.

Hughes, Michael P., MEng Wales, PhD Wales   Reader, Biomedical Engineering

Lekakou, Constantina, PhD Lond.   Sr. Lectr.

Ogin, Steven L., BSc Manc., PhD Camb.   Reader

Parker, Graham A., BSc Birm., PhD Birm., FIMechE   Prof., Mechanical Engineering

Robins, Alan G., BSc Lond., PhD Lond., FRSA   Res. Prof., Environmental Fluid Mechanics

Rockliff, Nicole J., BSc Adel., PhD Camb., FIMA   Sr. Lectr.

Smith, Paul A., MA Camb., PhD Camb., FIMMM   Prof., Composite Materials

Tsakiropoulos, Panos, MMet Sheff., PhD Sheff., DEng T.U.Athens   Prof., Metallurgy

Wahab, Magd-El-Din A., BSc Cairo, MSc Cairo, PhD Leuven   Sr. Lectr.

Watts, John F., BSc Sur., PhD Sur., DSc, FIP, FIMMM   Dir., Materials, Surfaces and Struct. Systems Res. Centre; Prof., Materials Science

Whiting, Mark J., BEng Sur., PhD Sur.   Sr. Lectr.

Xu, Wei, BEng Tsinghua, PhD Birm.   Sr. Lectr.

Yeomans, Julie A., MA Camb., PhD Camb.   Reader, Ceramics

Other Staff: 4 Lectrs.; 15 Res. Fellows; 2 Sr. Tutors; 1 Sr. Exper. Officer; 3 Exper. Officers

Research: ceramic materials (ceramic-matrix composites, ceramics, functional materials); composites (polymer matrix, fibre reinforced materials for engineering structures, processing and process modelling); physical and process metallurgy (microstructures, modelling, phase equilibria, processing, transformations, metal-matrix composites); surface and interface reactions (surface characterisation and reaction kinetics in technology, adhesives, surface engineering)

Health and Medical Sciences, European Institute of

Tel: (01483) 686700 Fax: (01483) 686701   E-mail: recruitment@surrey.ac.uk

Bryan, Karen, BSc Newcastle(UK), PhD Newcastle(UK)   Head, Res.; Prof., Clinical Practice

Buckle, Peter, BSc Leic., MSc Lond., PhD Cran.IT   Head, Ergonomics; Prof., Health Ergonomics

Cowie, Helen, MA Glas., MSc Birm., PhD Lond.   Dir., UK Observatory for the Pomotion of Non-Violence; Prof., Mental Health and Youth

Edgar, Jen, MMedSci Birm., PhD Lond.   Dir., Studies for Occupnl. Health and Safety

Faithfull, Sara, BSc Sur., MSc Lond., PhD Lond.   Dir. of Studies

Hawkins, Leslie H., BSc Sur., PhD Sur.   Dir., Robens Centre for Occupnl. Health; Sr. Lectr., Physiology

Hunt, Geoffrey P., BSc Wales, MLitt Edin., PhD Wales   Prof., Philosophy of Care

Pope, Rosemary, BSc Lond., PhD   Prof.

Rhodes, Alison, MSc Sur.   Dir. of Studies, Teaching and Learning

Robbins, Ian, BSc Lond., MSc Leeds, PsychD Sur.   Prof., Mental Health Practice

Ryle, Susan R., BSc Sur., MA Brighton   Head, Postgrad. Educn.

Smith, Pam, BNurs Manc., MSc Lond., PhD Lond.   Prof., Nurse Education

Snowden, Lynette, BA Lond., MSc City(UK)   Head, Professl. Preparation

Stubbs, David A., BEd Lough., PhD Sur.   Prof., Ergonomics

Volante, Margaret, BSc Aberd., MSc Sur.   Head, Learning and Educn.

Vydelingum, Vasso, BSc Sur., PhD S'ton.   Dir. of Studies (MSc Advanced Practice)

Other Staff: 1 Reader; 3 Sr. Lectrs.; 74 Lectrs./Tutors; 2 Sr. Res. Fellows; 2 Res. Fellows

Research: advanced clinical practice; education and professional ethics; health policy and health informatics; nursing and healthcare; public health

Law

Tel: (01483) 686220 Fax: (01483) 686208   E-mail: law-ug@surrey.ac.uk

Benny, Richard, BA CNAA, LLB CNAA, MA Leeds, LLM Brist.   Sr. Lectr.

Malcolm, Rosalind, LLB Lond.   Univ. Dir.

Upex, Robert V., MA Camb., LLM Camb., FRSA   Prof.; Head*

Other Staff: 6 Lectrs.

Research: employment law; environmental law; EU law

Management, School of

Tel: (01483) 686300 Fax: (01483) 686301   E-mail: management@surrey.ac.uk

Airey, David W., BA Lond., MSc Strath., FRSA, FTS   Prof., Tourism Management

Arnold, Steve, BSc Tor., MBA Tor., PhD Tor.   Visiting Prof.

Bell, James R., BA CNAA, MBA Brighton   Sr. Lectr.; Dir., Undergrad. Studies

Bridgeman, John S., CBE   Visiting Prof.

Chen, Jean, BSc Nankai, PhD Lanc.   Sr. Lectr.

Cramp, Derek G.   Visiting Prof.

Crossman, Alf, MA Brun., FCIPD   Sr. Lectr.

Desombre, Terence, MSc Sur., PhD Reading   Dir., Postgrad. Studies; Prof., Healthcare Management

Dowell, Phillip, BDS Lond., MScD Wales, FICD   Visiting Prof.

Ekinci, Yuksel, BA MSc MA PhD   Sr. Lectr.

Eves, Anita, BSc Reading, PhD Reading   Sr. Lectr.

Gilbert, David, BA Lond., MA CNAA, PhD Sur.   Dir., DBA; Prof., Marketing

Gore, Julie, BSc Hudd., BPS Oxf.Brookes, PhD Oxf.Brookes   Sr. Lectr.

Goss, David, BA PhD   Prof.

Gray, David, BSc Lond., MA Leeds, MSc Sur., PhD Sur.   Sr. Lectr.

Gregory, Josie, BA Open(UK), PhD Sur.   Sr. Lectr.

Hales, Colin, BA Camb., MA Kent, PhD Kent   Prof., Organisational Behaviour

Halliday, Susan, BA MA MBA PhD   Sr. Lectr.

Ibbott, Christopher J., MTech Brun., DBA Brun., FIEE, FBCS   Visiting Prof.

Jones, Peter L. M., BA Open(UK), MBA Lond., PhD Sur.   Prof., Productions and Operations Management

Karim, Rifaat A. A., BSc Khart., MSocSc Birm., PhD Bath   Visiting Prof.

Kirby, David, BA Durh., PhD Durh.   Prof., Entrepreneurship

Lockwood, Andrew J., BSc Sur., PhD Sur.   Prof., Hospitality Management

Louvieris, Panos, BSc Manc., MSc UMIST, MBA Birm., PhD UMIST   Sr. Lectr.

Lowe, Michelle, BA Birm., PhD Camb.   Prof., Retail Management

Lumbers, Margaret, BSc Birm., PhD Sur.   Sr. Lectr.

Massay, Anne, BSc MSc PhD   Prof.

Miller, Graham, BSc MSc PhD   Sr. Lectr.

Moore, Christopher, MA Glas., MBA Stir., PhD Stir.   Visiting Prof.

Norris, Steven, BA MPhil PhD   Visiting Prof.

O'Keefe, Robert M., BA Lanc., PhD S'ton.   Prof., Information Management; Head*

Parker, Alan, BSc Sur., Hon. BDA   Visiting Prof.

Riley, Michael J., MA Sus., PhD Essex   Prof., Organisational Behaviour

Sadler-Smith, Eugene, BSc Leeds, PhD Birm.   Prof., Management Development and Organisational Behaviour

Seltsihas, Philip, BSc MSc PhD   Sr. Lectr.

Skinner, Frank, BCom MBA PhD   Prof.

Somerville, Hugh, BSc Edin., PhD Sheff.   Visiting Prof.

Song, Hiayan, PhD G.Caledonian, BA(Econ)   Prof., Economics

Swindels, Matthew, BSc MBA   Visiting Prof.

Szivas, Edit, BSc Bud., MSc Sur., PhD Sur.   Sr. Lectr.

Todeva, Emanuela, PhD Sofia   Sr. Lectr.

Tosey, Paul C., BSc Bath, MSc Bath, PhD Bath, FRSA   Sr. Lectr.

Tribe, John, BSc MA PhD   Prof.

Van der Heijden, Hans, BSc MSc PhD   Prof.

Werthner, Hannes, MSc T.U.Vienna, PhD T.U.Vienna   Visiting Prof.

Yacoumis, John, BA Manc., MSc Sur.   Visiting Prof.

Other Staff: 1 Reader; 34 Lectrs.; 2 Sr. Tutors; 6 Tutors

Research: enterprise and strategy; finance and financial management; health care management; hospitality and food management; information management

Mathematics and Statistics

Tel: (01483) 689634 Fax: (01483) 686071
E-mail: mathsinfo@eim.surrey.ac.uk

Aston, Philip J., BSc Brun., PhD Brun.   Reader; Head*

Bartuccelli, Michele V., MSc Calabria, PhD T.U.Denmark   Reader

Bridges, Thomas J., BSc Rhode I., MSc Texas, MA Penn., PhD Penn.   Prof., Mathematics

Bruin, Henk, MSc T.H.Delft, PhD T.H.Delft, FRSA   Reader

Deane, Jonathan H. B., BA Oxf., PhD Sur.   Sr. Lectr.

Derks, Gianne L. A., BA T.U.Eindhoven, MSc T.U.Eindhoven, PhD T.H.Twente   Sr. Lectr.

Gourley, Stephen A., BA Oxf., MSc Bath, PhD Bath   Sr. Lectr.

Hoyle, R., BA Camb., MA Camb., PhD Camb.   Sr. Lectr.

Hydon, Peter E., BSc Bath, PhD Camb.   Reader

Melbourne, Ian, BSc Warw., MSc Warw., PhD Warw.   Prof., Mathematics

Roberts, R. Mark, BA Oxf., PhD Liv.   Prof., Mathematics

Roulstone, I., BSc Lond., DPhil Oxf., FRAS, FIMA   Reader

Sandstede, B., MSc Heidel., PhD Stuttgart   Prof., Mathematics

Young, Karen D., BSc Lond., PhD Lond.   Sr. Lectr.

Other Staff: 5 Lectrs.; 1 Res. Fellow

Research: dynamical systems and ergodic theory; dynamics of patterns; geometrical fluid dynamics; geometry and mechanics; mathematical biology

Music and Sound Recording

Tel: (01483) 686500 Fax: (01483) 686501
E-mail: music@surrey.ac.uk

Downes, Stephen C., BA Exe., MMus Lond., PhD Lond.   Sr. Lectr.

Fisher, David M., MA Camb.   Univ. Dir.; Head, Sound Recording

Forbes, Sebastian, MA Camb., MusD Camb., FRSA   Prof.; Dir., Music

Mark, Christopher, BA S'ton., PhD S'ton.   Sr. Lectr.

Messenger, Thomas, BMus Glas., PhD Wales   Univ. Dir.

Moore, Allan, BA S'ton., MMus Sur., PhD Sur.   Prof.; Dir., Res. Studies in Music; Head*

Rumsey, Francis, BMus Sur., MMus Sur., PhD Sur.   Reader; Dir., Res. Studies in Sound Recording

Other Staff: 5 Lectrs.; 2 Res. Fellows; 3 Tutors

Research: analysis and aesthetics of nineteenth- and twentieth-century music; composition and contemporary music performance; critical musicology; measurement, characterisation and analysis of sound; popular music

Physics

Tel: (01483) 686780 Fax: (01483) 686781
E-mail: physics@surrey.ac.uk

Adams, Alfred R., PhD Leic., DSc Leic., FIP, FRS   Prof.

Al-Khalili, Jameel S., BSc Sur., PhD Sur.   Sr. Lectr.

Allam, Jeremy, BA Oxf., MA Oxf., PhD Sur.   Prof.

Bacon, Richard A., MSc Lond., PhD Sur.   Sr. Lectr.

Clough, Anthony S., BSc Lond., PhD Lond., FIP   Prof.

Faux, David A., BSc Nott., MSc Birm., PhD Birm.   Sr. Lectr.

Gelletly, William, OBE, PhD Edin., FIP   Prof.

Gilboy, Walter B., BSc Leeds, PhD Leeds, FIP   Sr. Lectr.

Hess, Ortwin, BACH Erlangen-Nuremberg, PhD T.U.Berlin   Prof.

Hosea, Thomas J., PhD Edin.   Sr. Lectr.

Lancefield, David, BSc CNAA, MSc CNAA, PhD Sur.   Sr. Lectr.

McDonald, Peter J., PhD Nott.   Sr. Lectr.

Morton, Edward J., BSc Lond., PhD Lond.   Sr. Lectr.

Regan, Patrick H., BSc Liv., DPhil York(UK), FIP   Sr. Lectr.

Spyrou, Nicholas M., MPhil Lond.   Prof.

Thompson, Ian J., MSc Massey, PhD Auck.   Prof.

Tostevin, Jeffrey A., PhD   Prof.

Walker, Philip M., MA Camb., PhD ANU   Prof.; Head*

Other Staff: 4 Readers; 9 Lectrs.; 1 Exper. Officer; 28 Res. Fellows/Res. Assts.

Research: condensed matter physics (magnetic resonance imaging (MRI), ellipsometry, microscopy of heterogeneous materials); ion-beam analysis (high-precision elemental profiling in materials); nuclear physics (halo nuclei, nuclear structures, radioactive beams); optoelectronic devices (semiconductor lasers, blue to mid-infrared, strain); radiation imaging (X-ray imaging, medical physics, radiation detectors)

Political, International and Policy Studies

Tel: (01483) 686220 Fax: (01483) 686191
E-mail: pips@surrey.ac.uk

Flood, Christopher G., MA Edin., MA Reading, DPhil Oxf.   Prof., European Studies

Holford, John, BA Oxf., MSc Sur., PhD Edin.   Prof., Adult Education; Head*

Jarvis, Peter, BA(Econ) Sheff., BD Lond., MSocSc Birm., PhD Aston, Hon. DPhil Helsinki, FRSA   Prof., Continuing Education

Olssen, Mark E. H., BA Otago, PhD Otago   Reader

Other Staff: 3 Lectrs.; 2 Sr. Tutors; 2 Res. Officers

Research: citizenship and policy studies; educational policy and politics; European politics; political theory

Psychology

Tel: (01483) 689436 Fax: (01483) 689553
E-mail: p.yehia@surrey.ac.uk

Barrett, Martyn D., MA Camb., DPhil Sus.   Prof.

Brown, Jennifer M., BA Reading, PhD Sur.   Prof., Forensic Psychology

Coyle, Adrian, BA N.U.I., PhD Sur.   Sr. Lectr.

Davies, Ian R., BSc Brist.   Prof.

Davis, Alyson, BSc Sus., PhD Birm.   Sr. Lectr.

de Bruyn, Bart, MA Leuven, PhD Leuven   Reader

Emler, Nicholas, BSc S'ton., MA Oxf., PhD Lond., FBPsS   Prof., Social Psychology

Everatt, John M., BSc Northumbria, PhD Nott.   Sr. Lectr.

Fife-Schaw, Christopher R., BSc Newcastle(UK), MSc Strath., PhD Sheff.   Sr. Lectr.; Head*

Groeger, John A., BA N.U.I., MA N.U.I., PhD Belf.   Prof., Cognitive Psychology

Hampson, Sarah E., BA Exe., PhD Exe.   Prof., Psychology and Health

John, Mary, BSc Liv., MSc E.Lond.   Sr. Lectr.

Lyons, Evanthia, BSc Lond., MSc Lond., PhD Lond.   Sr. Lectr.

Millward-Purvis, Lynne J., BA Exe., PhD Kent   Sr. Lectr.

Milton, Martin J., BA S.Af., MA Lond., PsychD Lond.   Sr. Lectr.

Ogden, Jane, BSc Sus., PhD Lond.   Prof., Health Psychology

Rose, David, BSc Brist., PhD Camb.   Reader

Shepherd, Richard, BSc Wales, MA Camb., PhD S'ton.   Prof.

Simpson, Peter J., BSc Leeds, MA Camb., DPhil Sus.   Sr. Lectr.

Sowden, Paul T., BSc Sur., PhD Sur.   Sr. Lectr.

Sterr, Annette, PhD Constance   Prof., Cognitive Neuroscience and Neuropsychology

Uzzell, David L., BA Liv., MSc Lond., PhD   Prof., Environmental Psychology

Vetere, Arlene, BSc S'ton., PhD S'ton.   Sr. Lectr.

Zijlstra, Fred, MSc Gron., PhD I.M.S., Delft   Prof., Occupational and Organisational Psychology

Other Staff: 3 Prof. Tutors; 15 Lectrs.; 4 Sr. Res. Fellows; 27 Res. Fellows; 1 Sr. Academic Tutor; 1 Academic Tutor; 1 Res. Tutor; 2 Sr. Clin. Tutors; 2 Clin. Tutors; 2 Clin. Liaison Tutors

Research: cognitive and social development in infancy, childhood and adolescence; health psychology, clinical, psychotherapeutic and counselling psychology; perception and cognition (visual and auditory, linguistic and pictorial/spatial); social psychology (identity processes, social representations, risk perception and communication, social cognition and behaviour, discourse analysis and decision making, leadership)

Sociology

Tel: (01483) 686970 Fax: (01483) 686971
E-mail: sociology@surrey.ac.uk

Alexander, Victoria D., AB Prin., AM Stan., PhD Stan.   Sr. Lectr.

Arber, Sara L., MSc Lond., PhD   Prof.

Bulmer, Martin I. A., BSc Lond., PhD Lond.   Prof.

Burningham, Katherine A., BSc S'ton., MSc Sur., PhD Sur.   Sr. Lectr.

Cooper, Geoffrey, BA Lond., PhD Open(UK)   Sr. Lectr.; Head*

Davidson, Kate, BSc Sur., PhD Sur.   Sr. Lectr.

Fielding, Jane L., BSc Sus., DPhil Sus.   Sr. Lectr.

Fielding, Nigel G., BA Sus., MA Kent, PhD Lond.   Prof.

Gilbert, G. Nigel, MA Camb., PhD Camb.   Prof.

Hine, Christine, BA Oxf., MSc York(UK), DPhil York(UK)   Sr. Lectr.

Innes, Martin, BA Lond., MSc Lond., PhD Lond.   Sr. Lectr.

Moran-Ellis, Jo M., BSc City(UK), MSc Sur.   Sr. Lectr.

Sturgis, Patrick, BA Liv., MSc Lond., PhD Lond.   Sr. Lectr.

Tarling, Roger, PhD Lond.   Prof.

Wakefield, Nina, BA Camb., DPhil Oxf.   Reader

Other Staff: 7 Lectrs.; 16 Res. Fellows

Research: age, generation and health; crime and criminal justice; culture and identity; developments in methodology; science and technological studies

SPECIAL CENTRES, ETC

Adult and Continuing Education

Tel: (01483) 686222 Fax: (01483) 686171
E-mail: ace@surrey.ac.uk

Merricks, Linda, BSc Sus., DPhil Sus.   Head of Div.*

Other Staff: 10 Tutors

Communications Systems Research, Centre for

Tel: (01483) 689844 Fax: (01483) 686011
E-mail: ccsr@ee.surrey.ac.uk
Evans, Barry G., BSc *Leeds*, PhD *Leeds*, FIEE, FRSA, FREng   Alec Harley Reeves Prof., Information Systems Engineering; Dir.*
Kondoz, Ahmet M., BSc *Birm.*, MSc *Essex*, PhD *Sur.*   Prof.
Pavlou, George, PhD *Lond.*   Racal Prof., Information Technology
Sun, Zhili, BSc *Lanc.*, PhD *Lanc.*   Reader
Sweeney, Peter, MA *Oxf.*, PhD *Camb.*   Reader
Tafazolli, Rahim, BSc *Bath*, MSc *Lond.*, PhD *Sur.*   Prof., Mobile Communications
Other Staff: 4 Lectrs.; 32 Res. Fellows
Research: communications networking; mobile cellular and satellite communications; multimedia systems

Environmental Strategy, Centre for

Tel: (01483) 686670 Fax: (01483) 686671
E-mail: m.a.ellis@surrey.ac.uk
Azapagic, Adisa, BSc *Tulsa*, MSc *Tulsa*, PhD *Sur.*   Prof., Sustainable Engineering
Burningham, Katherine A., BSc *S'ton.*, MSc *Sur.*, PhD *Sur.*   Sr. Lectr.
Chenoweth, Jonathan, BPD *Melb.*, PhD *Melb.*
Clift, Roland, CBE, BA *Camb.*, MA *Camb.*, PhD *McG.*, FREng, FIChemE, FRSA   Prof., Environmental Technology; Dir.*
Cowell, Sarah J., BSc *Leeds*, MSc *Tor.*, PhD *Sur.*   Sr. Lectr.
Duff, Charles, BSc MBA   RA Visiting Prof.
Eghali, Lucia, BSc MSc EngD
France, Christopher, BSc *Salf.*, MSc *Manc.*, PhD *UMIST*, FRSA   Sr. Lectr.
Jackson, Tim, MA *Camb.*, MA *W.Ont.*, PhD *St And.*, FRSA   Prof., Sustainable Development
Jefferis, Stephan, MA *Camb.*, MEng *Camb.*, MSc *Lond.*, PhD *Lond.*, FICE, FGS   Prof., Civil Engineering
Mulugetta, Yacob, BA MSc PhD
Wehrmeyer, Walter C. H., MA *Kent*, PhD *Kent*   Sr. Lectr.
Other Staff: 3 Lectrs.; 6 Res. Fellows; 1 Res. Officer; 1 Exper. Officer
Research: ecological economics and ethics; life cycle and systems analysis (company environmental performance); management of risks by public and private sector organisations

Ergonomics, Robens Centre for

Tel: (01483) 689209 Fax: (01483) 689971
E-mail: s.pedley@surrey.ac.uk
Pedley, S., BSc *Manc.*, PhD *Manc.*   Dir.*
Research: analytical expertise, training, laboratory development and management; development of monitoring programmes and monitoring for management; groundwater quality monitoring; product development; recreational water quality modelling

Health Ergonomics, Robens Centre for (RCHE)

Tel: (01483) 689213 Fax: (01483) 689395
E-mail: d.whyndham@surrey.ac.uk
Buckle, Peter, BSc *Leic.*, MSc *Lond.*, PhD *Cran.IT*   Dir.*
Research: ergonomics interventions in work systems; improving performance and wellbeing; work system interventions to reduce accidents, pain and sickness absence

Healthcare Workforce Research Centre (HWRC)

Tel: (01483) 684631 Fax: (01483) 682541
E-mail: wendy.knibb@surrey.ac.uk
Bryan, Karen, BSc *Newcastle(UK)*, PhD *Newcastle(UK)*   Dir.*
Research: promoting health in the workplace; technological advances for e-health and patient safety; workforce development to achieve new forms of service delivery

Human Psychopharmacology Research Unit

Tel: (01483) 686797 Fax: (01483) 686798
Hindmarch, Ian, BSc *Leeds*, PhD *Leeds*, FBPsS   Prof.; Dir.*
Other Staff: 1 Sr. Res. Fellow; 18 Res. Officers

Ion Beam Applications, Surrey Centre for Research in (SCRIBA)

Tel: (01483) 686090 Fax: (01483) 534139
E-mail: scriba-info@surrey.ac.uk
Cowern, Nicholas E. B., BA *Oxf.*, MA *Oxf.*, DPhil *Oxf.*   Prof., Nanoscale Materials Processing
Forbes, Richard G., PhD *Camb.*, DSc *Aston*, FIEE, FIP   Reader
Hemment, Peter L. F., BSc *City(UK)*, PhD *Reading*, DSc *City(UK)*, FIP, FIEE   Prof. Res. Fellow
Homewood, Kevin P., BSc *Newcastle(UK)*, PhD *Manc.*   Prof., Semiconductor Optoelectronics
Kirkby, Karen J., BSc *Leic.*, PhD *CNAA*   Sr. Lectr.
Reed, Graham T., BSc *Sur.*, PhD *Sur.*   Prof., Optoelectronics
Sealy, Brian J., BSc *Sur.*, PhD *Sur.*, DSc *Sur.*, FIP, FIEE   Prof., Solid State Devices and Ion Beam Technology
Shannon, John M., BTech *Brun.*, PhD *Sur.*, DSc *Brun.*, FIP, FREng   Prof. Res. Fellow
Silva, S. Ravi, BA *Camb.*, MA *Camb.*, PhD *Camb.*   Prof., Solid State Electronics
Webb, Roger P., BSc *Salf.*, PhD *Salf.*   Reader; Acting Dir.*
Weiss, Bernard L., BSc *Newcastle(UK)*, PhD *Newcastle(UK)*, DSc, FIEE, FIP   Prof., Microelectronics
Other Staff: 3 Lectrs.; 2 Sr. Res. Fellows; 15 Res. Fellows
Research: III-V and amorphous semiconductors; ion implantation technologies for silicon

Language Centre

Tel: (01483) 686222 Fax: (01483) 689505
E-mail: g.oneill@surrey.ac.uk
Dlaska, Andrea, MA *Innsbruck*, PhD *Innsbruck*   Dir.*
Other Staff: 3 Sr. Tutors; 11 Tutors
Research: action research and materials development in English and foreign languages; e-learning; English literature; intercultural communication in language teaching; language teacher training

Microwave and Systems Research Group

Tel: (01483) 686080 Fax: (01483) 686081
E-mail: l.tumility@surrey.ac.uk
Aitchison, Colin S., BSc, FIEE   Prof.
Free, Charles E., BSc *Aston*, MSc *Aston*, PhD *Brun.*   Sr. Lectr.
Jefferies, David J., MA *Oxf.*, MS *Stan.*, PhD *Stan.*   Sr. Lectr.
Robertson, Ian D., BSc *Lond.*, PhD *Lond.*   Prof., Microwave Subsystems Engineering; Head*
Rogers, Alan J., MA *Camb.*, PhD *Lond.*, FIP, FIEE   Prof.
Underhill, Michael J., MA *Oxf.*, PhD *Sur.*, FIEE, FRSA, FREng   Prof.
Other Staff: 20 Researchers
Research: millimetre-wave circuits and systems; Monolithic Microwave Integrated Circuits (MMICs)

Nursing and Midwifery Education, Centre for Research in

Tel: (01483) 683120 Fax: (01483) 686711
E-mail: centre-rnme@surrey.ac.uk
Smith, Pam, BNurs *Manc.*, MSc *Lond.*, PhD *Lond.*   Dir.*
Research: development in practice; education for practice; innovation and research in practice

Nursing Ethics, International Centre for (ICNE)

Tel: (01483) 682978
E-mail: v.tschudin@surrey.ac.uk
Tschudin, Verena   Dir.*
Research: ethics; healthcare philosophy; law; professional and organisational accountability; professional regulation

Policy and Change, Centre for

Tel: (01483) 683137
E-mail: alan.smith@surrey.ac.uk
McNair, Stephen, BA *York(UK)*, MA *Kent*   Prof., Education
Middlehurst, Robin, BA *Lanc.*, MPhil *Reading*, FRSA   Prof., Higher Education; Dir.*
Research: higher education; older workforce; public policy (education and training)

Surrey Space Centre

Tel: (01483) 686020 Fax: (01483) 686021
Hodgart, Stephen, MA *Camb.*, PhD *Sur.*   Reader
Palmer, Philip L., BSc *Leic.*, PhD *Camb.*   Reader
Sweeting, Martin N., OBE, BSc *Sur.*, PhD *Sur.*, FREng, FRS, FIEE, FRAeS   Prof., Satellite Engineering; Dir.*
Underwood, Craig I., BSc *York(UK)*, PhD *Sur.*   Sr. Lectr.
Vladimirova, Tanya, MSc MEng PhD   Sr. Lectr.
Other Staff: 3 Lectrs.
Research: low-cost micro-minisatellite spacecraft engineering

Vision, Speech and Signal Processing, Centre for

Tel: (01483) 686030 Fax: (01483) 686031
Chilton, Edward H. S., BSc *Manc.*, MSc *Cran.IT*, PhD *Sur.*   Sr. Lectr.
Illingworth, John, BSc *Birm.*, DPhil *Oxf.*, FIEE   Prof.
Kittler, Josef V., MA *Camb.*, PhD *Camb.*, ScD *Camb.*, FREng   Prof., Machine Intelligence; Dir.*
Mokhtarian, Farzin, BES *Johns H.*, MSc *Br.Col.*, PhD *Br.Col.*   Sr. Lectr.
Petrou, Maria, BSc *Salonika*, PhD *Camb.*   Prof.
Other Staff: 6 Lectrs.; 1 EPSRC Advanced Res. Fellow; 11 Res. Fellows
Research: developing methodology and algorithms, for image processing, pattern recognition and computer vision

CONTACT OFFICERS

Academic affairs. Registrar: Beardsley, Peter W., BA *Lond.*, FRSA
(E-mail: p.beardsley@surrey.ac.uk)
Accommodation. Director of Accommodation and Conference Services: Paxton, Richard
Admissions (first degree). Undergraduate Admissions Officer: Pike, Shirley, BA *Open(UK)* (E-mail: admissions@surrey.ac.uk)
Admissions (higher degree). Assistant Registrar (Postgraduate Admissions): Homer, Andrew, BA *Wales*, PhD *Luton*
(E-mail: pg.admissions@surrey.ac.uk)
Alumni. Alumni Officer: Cohen, Jane
(E-mail: j.cohen@surrey.ac.uk)
Careers. Head of Service and Senior Careers Adviser: Clark, Russ M., BSc *Brist.*, MSc *S'ton.*, PhD *Lond.*
(E-mail: careers@surrey.ac.uk)
Computing services. Director, IT Services: Burden, Michael J., BSc *Brist.*
(E-mail: m.burden@surrey.ac.uk)
Conferences/corporate hospitality. Conference Manager: Jeanes, Michael
(E-mail: conferences@surrey.ac.uk)
Credit transfer. Deputy Academic Registrar (Academic Standards): Watson, Anthony C., BSc *Lond.*
Development/fund-raising. Development Director: Donnelly, Neal
(E-mail: development@surrey.ac.uk)
Estates and buildings/works and services. Director of Estates and Facilities Management: Caleb, Derry A., BSc *CNAA*
Examinations. University Examinations Officer: Wodgett, Karl, BA *Exe.*, MA *Exe.*
Finance. Director of Finance: Knapp, Anthony J. (E-mail: v.crawshaw@surrey.ac.uk)

Health services. Student Medical Officer: Carr-
Bains, Stephen, MB BChir MA
(E-mail: s.carr-baines@surrey.ac.uk)

International office. Director of International
Office and Dean of Overseas Students:
Brown, Gwyn, BSc S'ton., PhD S'ton.
(E-mail: internationaladmin@surrey.ac.uk)

Library (chief librarian). Director of Library
Services: Savidge, Jane C., BA Wales, MA
Wales, MA Sheff.
(E-mail: library-enquiries@surrey.ac.uk)

Marketing. Director of Marketing and Public
Affairs: (vacant)
(E-mail: information@surrey.ac.uk)

Personnel/human resources. Director of
Human Resources: Behagg, Alan, MA Oxf.,
MBA (E-mail: humanresources@surrey.ac.uk)

Public relations. Head of Communications
and Public Affairs: Somerville, Todd
(E-mail: t.somerville@surrey.ac.uk)

Publications. Director of Marketing and Public
Affairs: (vacant)
(E-mail: information@surrey.ac.uk)

Quality assurance and accreditation. Deputy
Academic Registrar (Academic Standards):
Watson, Anthony C., BSc Lond.

Research. Postgraduate Officer (Research
higher degrees): Homer, Andrew, BA Wales,
PhD Luton
(E-mail: pg.admissions@surrey.ac.uk)

Research. Strategic Planning and Resource
Allocation: Butterworth, Prof. Peter H. W.,
BSc Liv., PhD Liv., FIBiol

Safety. University Safety Adviser: Curnock,
Peter (E-mail: safety@surrey.ac.uk)

Scholarships, awards, loans. Deputy Academic
Registrar (Student Administration): Fice,
Graham, BA Exe., MSc CNAA
(E-mail: g.fice@surrey.ac.uk)

Security. Chief Security Officer: Jakeman,
Barry
(E-mail: security-advisors@surrey.ac.uk)

Sport and recreation. Director, University
Centre for Sport and Recreation: Hitchcock,
Barry G. (E-mail: d.p.brown@surrey.ac.uk)

Staff development and training. Staff
Development Manager and Personnel
Officer: (vacant)
(E-mail: personnel@surrey.ac.uk)

Strategic planning. Director of Planning:
Gunn, Robert I., BEng W.Aust., MEngSc
W.Aust., MSc Lond.Bus.
(E-mail: r.gunn@surrey.ac.uk)

Students from other countries. Director of
International Office and Dean of Overseas
Students: Brown, Gwyn, BSc S'ton., PhD
S'ton. (E-mail: g.brown@surrey.ac.uk)

Students with disabilities. Disability Co-
ordinator: Beaumont, John
(E-mail: j.beaumont@surrey.ac.uk)

University press. Bookshop Manager: Newby,
James (E-mail: bookshop@surrey.ac.uk)

[Information supplied by the institution as at 11 May
2006, and edited by the ACU]

UNIVERSITY OF SUSSEX

Founded 1961

Postal Address: Sussex House, Falmer, Brighton, England BN1 9RH
Telephone: (01273) 606755 **Fax:** (01273) 678335
URL: http://www.sussex.ac.uk

VICE-CHANCELLOR*—Farthing, Prof. Michael, DSc MD, FRCP
REGISTRAR AND SECRETARY‡—Harvey, Philip K., BSc CNAA, PhD Durh.

SWANSEA UNIVERSITY

Prifysgol Abertawe

Founded 1920

Member of the Association of Commonwealth Universities

Postal Address: Singleton Park, Swansea, Wales SA2 8PP
Telephone: (01792) 205678 **Fax:** (01792) 295655
URL: http://www.swansea.ac.uk

VICE-CHANCELLOR*—Davies, Prof. Richard B., MA Camb., MSc Birm., PhD Brist.
PRO-VICE-CHANCELLOR—Baylis, Prof. J., BA Wales, MScEcon Wales, PhD Wales, DLitt
PRO-VICE-CHANCELLOR—Weatherill, Prof. N. P., PhD S'ton., DSc S'ton., FIMA, FRAeS
PRO-VICE-CHANCELLOR—Williams, Prof. R. W., MA Oxf., DPhil Oxf.
REGISTRAR‡—Townsend, Prof. P., BSc Wales, PhD Wales, DSc Wales
LIBRARIAN—West, C. M., MA Nott.
DIRECTOR OF FINANCE—Gough, P. R. C., BSc Brist.

GENERAL INFORMATION

History. The university was originally
established in 1920 as University College of
Swansea, a constituent college of the
University of Wales. On 1 September 2007,
Swansea University became an independent
university.

It is located on the south coast of Wales.

Admission to first degree courses (see also
United Kingdom Introduction). Through
Universities and Colleges Admissions Service
(UCAS). General Certificate of Education (GCE)
or General Certificate of Secondary Education
(GCSE) pass in English language or Welsh
language and at least 2 passes at GCE A level
or 1 pass at A level and 2 at AS level.

Equivalent qualifications (such as International
or European Baccalaureate, Business and
Technology Education Council (BTEC) exams)
are acceptable.

First Degrees (see also United Kingdom
Directory to Subjects of Study). BA, BEng, BSc,
BScEcon, LLB, MChem, MEng, MMath, MPhys.
Length of course. Full-time: BA, BEng, BSc,
BScEcon, LLB: 3 years; MChem, MEng, MMath,
MPhys: 4 years.

Higher Degrees (see also United Kingdom
Directory to Subjects of Study).
Master's. MA, MAEd, MBA, MPhil, MRes,
MSc, MScEcon.
Admission. Applicants for admission to
master's degree courses should hold a first

degree with at least second class honours.
International candidates should also meet
English language requirements (eg IELTS score
of 6.0-7.0 or TOEFL score of 550-590).
Length of course. Full-time: MA, MAEd, MBA,
MPhil, MRes, MSc, MScEcon: 1 year. Part-time:
MA, MAEd, MBA, MPhil, MRes, MSc,
MScEcon: 2 years.
Doctoral. EngD, PhD.
Length of course. Full-time: PhD: 3 years; EngD:
4 years. Part-time: PhD: 5 years.

Language of Instruction. English. Students
may sit exams in Welsh in some subject areas.

Libraries. Volumes: 804,000. Periodicals
subscribed to: 7112. Other holdings: 25,000
microforms, videos, CD-Roms. Special

collections: South Wales coalfield collection (trade union activity); Rush Rhees (Wittgenstein studies); John Loder (civil aviation); Llewellyn bequest (antiquarian Welsh language and history); Salmon pamphlets (nineteenth-century education).

FACULTIES/SCHOOLS

Arts
Head: Williams, Prof. K. M., BA *Keele*, MSc(Econ) *Lond.*

Business and Economics
Head: Henley, Prof. A. G., BA *Nott.*, MA *Warw.*, PhD *Warw.*

Engineering
E-mail: s.j.hardy@swansea.ac.uk
Head: Weatherill, Prof. N. P., PhD *S'ton.*, DSc *S'ton.*, FIMA, FRAeS

Environment and Society
Head: Barnsley, Prof. M. J., BA *Reading*, PhD *Reading*

Health Science
E-mail: m.isaac@swansea.ac.uk
Head: Hopkins, A., BEd *Wales*

Human Sciences
Head: Reed, Prof. P., BSc *Leeds*, DPhil *York(UK)*

Humanities
Head: Thompson, Prof. N. W., MA *St And.*, MSc *Belf.*, PhD *Camb.*

Law
Head: Davies, Prof. I. R., LLB *Camb.*, LLM *Wales*, PhD *Wales*

Medicine
Head: Hopkin, Prof. J. M., MSc MA MD, FRCP

Physical Sciences
Head: Charlton, Prof. M., BSc *Lond.*, PhD *Lond.*

ACADEMIC UNITS

Adult Continuing Education
University Department
Tel: (01792) 295786 Fax: (01792) 295751
E-mail: adult.education@swansea.ac.uk
Elliott, J. S., BA *Open(UK)*, MPhil *CNAA*   Sr. Lectr.
Trotman, C., BSc *Wales*, PhD *Wales*   Sr. Lectr.; Head*
Walters, P. J., BSc *Durh.*, PhD *Durh.*   Sr. Lectr.
Other Staff: 5 Lectrs.; 5 Tutors
Research: community-based adult education; research and evaluation in lifelong learning; women and continuing education

American Studies
Tel: (01792) 295305 Fax: (01792) 295719
E-mail: b.evans@swansea.ac.uk
French, W. G., BA *Penn.*, MA *Texas*, PhD *Texas*   Hon. Prof.
Melling, P. H., BA *Manc.*, PhD *Manc.*   Reader
Roper, J. R., BA *Oxf.*, PhD *Kent*   Reader; Head*
Other Staff: 5 Lectrs.; 1 Tutor
Research: Americanisation of culture; literature, history and politics

Biological Sciences, School of
Tel: (01792) 295361 Fax: (01792) 295447
E-mail: s.v.walmsley@swansea.ac.uk
Ashby, J., BSc *Lond.*, PhD *Lond.*, FRCS   Hon. Prof.
Bayne, B. L., BSc *Wales*, PhD *Wales*, FIBiol   Hon. Prof.
Bell, R. M.   Hon. Prof.
Berry, M. S., BSc *Wales*, MSc *Birm.*, PhD *Brist.*   Sr. Lectr.
Brain, P. F., BSc *Hull*, PhD *Hull*, FIBiol   Prof.
Butt, T. M., BSc *Brist.*, PhD *Brist.*   Sr. Lectr.
Dyson, P. J., BSc *E.Anglia*, PhD *Glas.*   Sr. Lectr.
Flynn, K. J., BSc *Wales*, PhD *Wales*   Prof.

Hays, G. C., BSc *S'ton.*, PhD *Aberd.*   Sr. Lectr.
Hayward, P. J., BSc *Reading*, PhD *Wales*, DSc *Wales*   Sr. Lectr.
Hipkin, C. R., BSc *Wales*, PhD *Wales*   Sr. Lectr.
Jones, D. H., MA *Camb.*, MPhil *Camb.*, PhD *Camb.*   Sr. Lectr.
Newton, R. P., BSc *Liv.*, PhD *Liv.*, DSc *Liv.*, FRSChem   Prof., Biochemistry
Parry, J. M., BSc *Lond.*, PhD *Liv.*, DSc *Liv.*   Prof.
Ratcliffe, N. A., BSc *Wales*, PhD *Wales*, DSc *Wales*, FIBiol   Prof.
Rowley, A. F., BSc *Wales*, PhD *Wales*, DSc *Wales*   Prof., Immunology; Head*
Shackley, S. E., BSc *Wales*, PhD *Wales*   Sr. Lectr.
Shestakov, S. V., MD *Moscow*, PhD *Moscow*, DrSci *Moscow*   Hon. Prof.
Skibinski, D. O. F., BSc *Lond.*, PhD *Camb.*, FIBiol   Prof., Evolutionary Biology
Smith, C. J., BSc *Wales*, PhD *Wales*   Sr. Lectr.
Stirton, C., MSc *Natal*, PhD *Cape Town*, FLS   Hon. Prof.
Tweats, D. J., BSc *Sheff.*, PhD *Lond.*, FIBiol, FRCP   Hon. Prof.
Wainwright, S. J., BSc *Sheff.*, PhD *Leeds*   Sr. Lectr.
Walton, T. J., BSc *Liv.*, PhD *Liv.*   Sr. Lectr.
Other Staff: 4 Lectrs.; 6 Hon. Lectrs.
Research: biochemistry; biomedical and physiological research; ecological research; marine and environmental biology; molecular genetics

Chemistry
Tel: (01792) 295506 Fax: (01792) 295747
E-mail: cmdept@swansea.ac.uk
Brenton, A. G., BSc *Wales*, PhD *Wales*   Prof.
Cadogan, Sir John, CBE, PhD *Lond.*, DSc *Lond.*, FRSChem, FKC, FRS   Hon. Prof.
Evans, D., MSc *Manc.*, PhD *Manc.*   Hon. Prof.
Mason, R. S., BSc *Birm.*, PhD *Birm.*   Sr. Lectr.
Smith, K., MSc *Manc.*, PhD *Manc.*, FRSChem   Prof.; Head*
Ward, R. S., MA *Camb.*, PhD *Camb.*, FRSChem   Reader
Other Staff: 4 Lectrs.; 3 Hon. Lectrs.; 2 Hon. Res. Fellows
Research: chromatographic analysis; gas phase ion chemistry; heterocyclic chemistry; natural products; synthetic reactions and reagents

Classics and Ancient History
Tel: (01792) 295187 Fax: (01792) 295739
E-mail: a.b.lloyd@swansea.ac.uk
Davies, C., BA *Wales*, MPhil *Oxf.*, DLitt *Wales*   Prof.
Gill, D. W. J., BA *Newcastle(UK)*, DPhil *Oxf.*, FSA   Sr. Lectr.
Herrmann, F.-G., BA *Camb.*, PhD *Edin.*   Sr. Lectr.
Lloyd, A. B., BA *Wales*, MA *Oxf.*, DPhil *Oxf.*, FSA   Prof.; Head*
Morgan, J. R., BA *Oxf.*, DPhil *Oxf.*   Sr. Lectr.
Owens, E. J., MA *Sheff.*, PhD *Sheff.*   Sr. Lectr.
Other Staff: 2 Lectrs.; 1 Lectr.†; 1 Hon. Res. Fellow
Research: Egyptology; Greek and Roman history; historiography; the ancient novel

Computer Science
Tel: (01792) 295393 Fax: (01792) 295708
E-mail: csdept@swansea.ac.uk
Chen, M., BSc *Fudan*, PhD *Wales*   Prof.
Grant, P. W., BSc *Manc.*, DPhil *Oxf.*   Sr. Lectr.
Moller, F. G., BSc *Br.Col.*, MMath *Wat.*, PhD *Edin.*   Prof.
Mosses, P. D., BA *Oxf.*, MSc *Oxf.*   Prof.
Thimbleby, H. W., BSc *Lond.*, MSc *Lond.*, PhD *Lond.*   Prof.
Tucker, J. V., BA *Warw.*, MSc *Brist.*, PhD *Brist.*, FBCS   Prof.; Head*
Webster, M. F., MSc *Manc.*, PhD *Wales*   Prof.
Other Staff: 8 Lectrs.; 2 Hon. Lectrs.; 1 Hon. Res. Fellow
Research: algebraic and logical methods for computing systems; computer graphics and visualisation; scientific computation for non-Newtonian fluid mechanics

Economics
Tel: (01792) 295168 Fax: (01792) 295872
E-mail: ecdept@swansea.ac.uk
Arabsheibani, G., BA *Trent*, MSc *Lond.*, PhD *Lond.*   Sr. Lectr.; Postgrad. Admissions Tutor
Blackaby, D. H., BA *Wales*, MA(Econ) *Manc.*, PhD *Manc.*   Prof.; Head*
Cook, S., BA *Lond.*, MSc *S'ton.*, DPhil *Oxf.*   Sr. Lectr.
Hopkin, Sir Brian   Hon. Prof. Fellow
Lawler, P., MA(Econ) *Manc.*, PhD *Manc.*   Reader
Murphy, P. D., BSc(Econ) *Hull*, MA *Sheff.*   Prof.
Sloane, P. J., BA *Sheff.*, PhD *Strath.*   Prof.
Speight, A. E. H., BA *Essex*, MSc *Lond.*, PhD *Lond.*   Prof.
Treble, J. G., BA *Wales*, MA *Essex*, PhD *Northwestern*   Prof.
Other Staff: 6 Lectrs.; 1 Hon. Lectr.
Research: business economics; industrial organisation; labour economics; macro-economic theory and policy

Engineering, School of
Tel: (01792) 295514 Fax: (01792) 295676
E-mail: eng.enquiries@swansea.ac.uk
Alberry, P. J., BSc *Sheff.*, PhD *Sheff.*, FIMMM   Hon. Prof.
Arnold, J. C., MA *Camb.*, PhD *Camb.*   Sr. Lectr.
Atkinson, B., BSc *Birm.*, PhD *Manc.*   Hon. Prof.
Bache, M. R., BA *Keele*, PhD *Keele*   Reader
Board, K., PhD *Wales*, DSc *Wales*   Prof.
Bonet, J., BSc *Wales*, PhD *Wales*   Prof.
Brown, S. G. R., BSc *Wales*, PhD *Wales*, FIMMM   Sr. Lectr.
Claypole, T. C., BSc(Eng) *Lond.*, PhD *Wales*   Sr. Lectr.
Clement, R. M., BSc *Wales*, PhD *Wales*   Innovation Prof.
Conder, J. R., MA *Camb.*, PhD *Camb.*, FRSChem   Sr. Lectr.
Cross, M., BSc PhD   Prof.
Elmirghani, J. M. H., BSc *Khart.*, PhD *Hudd.*   Prof.
Evans, R. W., BSc *Wales*, PhD *Wales*, FIMMM   Prof.
Evans, W. J., BSc *Wales*, PhD *Wales*, FIMMM   Prof.
Feng, Y., BSc *Shanxi*, PhD *Beijing*   Sr. Lectr.
Gethin, D. T., BSc *Wales*, PhD *Wales*   Prof.
Hardy, S. J., JP, BSc *CNAA*, PhD *Nott.*, FIMechE   Reader
Hassan, O., MBE, BSc *Damascus*, MSc *Wales*, PhD *Wales*   Prof.
Hayes, C. R., BSc MSc PhD
Hurst, R. C., MSc *Manc.*, PhD *Manc.*   Hon. Prof.
Isaac, D. H., BSc *Brist.*, PhD *Brist.*, FIMMM   Reader
Jack, K. H., MSc *Durh.*, PhD *Camb.*, ScD *Camb.*, FRSChem, FRS   Hon. Prof.
King, J. E., MA *Camb.*, PhD *Camb.*, FIMMM   Hon. Prof.
Lees, A. W., BSc *Manc.*, PhD *Manc.*   Prof.
Lewis, R. W., PhD *Wales*, DSc *Wales*, FREng, FICE   Prof.
Lovitt, R. W., BSc *CNAA*, PhD *Wales*   Sr. Lectr.
Luxmoore, A. R., MSc *Leeds*   Sr. Lectr.
Mason, J. S. D., BSc *CNAA*, MSc *Sur.*, PhD *Sur.*   Sr. Lectr.
Mawby, P. A., BSc *Leeds*, PhD *Leeds*   Prof.
McCowen, A., BSc *Lond.*, PhD *Leeds*   Reader
McMurray, H. N., BSc *Wales*, PhD *Wales*   Sr. Lectr.
Morgan, K., PhD *Brist.*, DSc *Brist.*, FIMA, FREng, FICE   Prof.
Owen, D. R. J., PhD *Northwestern*, DSc *Wales*, FICE, FREng   Prof.
Pande, G. N., BTech *Kharagpur*, PhD *Wales*, DSc *Wales*   Prof.
Peric, D., PhD *Wales*   Prof.
Randle, V., BSc *Wales*, PhD *Wales*, DSc *Wales*, FIMMM   Prof.
Rees, P., BSc PhD   Prof.
Rodd, M. G., MSc(Eng) *Cape Town*, PhD *Cape Town*, FIEE   Hon. Prof.

Sienz, J., BEng *CNAA*, MSc *Wales*, PhD *Wales*, DPhil   Sr. Lectr.
Spittle, J. A., BSc *Birm.*, PhD *Birm.*, FIMMM   Reader
Towers, M. S., MSc *Manc.*, PhD *Manc.*   Sr. Lectr.
Tucker, P. G., BEng DPhil   Prof.
Viswanathan, R., BSc *Madr.*, ME *Flor.*, PhD *Carnegie-Mellon*   Hon. Prof.
Wardle, A. P., BSc *Wales*, PhD *Wales*, FIChemE   Sr. Lectr.
Weatherill, N. P., PhD *S'ton.*, DSc *S'ton.*, FIMA, FRAeS   Prof.; Head*
Wilks, S. P., BSc *Wales*, PhD *Wales*   Prof.
Williams, P. R., BSc *Wales*, PhD *Wales*   Prof.
Wilshire, B., OBE, PhD *Wales*, DSc *Wales*, FREng, FIMMM   Prof.
Wood, R. D., MSc *Wales*, PhD *Wales*   Sr. Lectr.
Worsley, D. A., BSc *Wales*, PhD *Wales*   Sr. Lectr.
Xiao, R. Y., MSc *Nott.*, PhD *Nott.*   Sr. Lectr.
Other Staff: 16 Lectrs.; 1 EPSRC Advanced Res. Fellow; 6 Tutors; 3 Hon. Lectrs.
Research: atomic force microscopy; biochemical engineering; complex fluids processing; computer-aided process engineering; discrete element

English Language and Literature

Tel: (01792) 295926 Fax: (01792) 295761
E-mail: g.wasinak@swansea.ac.uk
Davies, S., BA MA PhD   Dir., Creative Writing MA
Franklin, C., BA *Lond.*, MA *Wales*, PhD *Wales*   Reader
Goodby, J., BA *Hull*, MA *Leeds*, PhD *Leeds*   Sr. Lectr.
Hardy, B., MA *Lond.*   Hon. Prof.
Heilmann, A. B., MA PhD   Sr. Lectr.
Penhallurick, R. J., BA *Wales*, MA *Leeds*, PhD *Wales*   Sr. Lectr.
Pursglove, G., BA *Oxf.*, BLitt *Oxf.*   Reader
Reeve, N. H., MA *Camb.*   Sr. Lectr.
Thomas, M. W., BA *Wales*, FBA   Prof.
Turner, J. F., BA *Camb.*, PhD *Camb.*   Sr. Lectr.
Other Staff: 5 Lectrs.; 1 Hon. Res. Fellow
Research: linguistics and sociolinguistics; Scottish and Irish literature; Welsh writing in English

European Business Management, School of

Tel: (01792) 295601 Fax: (01792) 295626
Adams, M. B., BA *Wales*, MSc *Wales*, PhD *Massey*   Prof.
Beynon-Davies, P., BSc *Camb.*, PhD *Wales*   Reader
Bischoff, E., MSc *Wales*, PhD *Wales*   Prof.
Buckle, M. J., BA *CNAA*, MSc *Warw.*, PhD *CNAA*   Sr. Lectr.
Henley, A. G., BA *Nott.*, MA *Warw.*, PhD *Warw.*   Prof.
Jacobs, G. C., BA *Lond.*, PhD *Wales*   Prof.
Luintel, K. B., MPhil *Glas.*, PhD *Glas.*, BA BL MA   Prof.
Probert, E. J., BSc *Lond.*, MSc *Wales*, PhD *Wales*   Sr. Lectr.
Reynolds, N. L., BSc *Wales*, MPhil *Wales*, PhD *Wales*   Sr. Lectr.
Simintiras, A. C., BA(Econ) *Salonika*, MBA *New Haven Coll.*, PhD *CNAA*   Prof.; Head*
Watkins, A. J., MSc *Leeds*, PhD *Leeds*   Sr. Lectr.
Williams, M. D., BSc *Wales*, MEd *Camb.*, PhD *Sheff.*   Sr. Lectr.
Other Staff: 13 Lectrs.; 3 Lectrs.†; 2 Hon. Res. Fellows
Research: financial innovation and risk management; globalisation, organisational behaviour and environmental management; information systems; logistics and scheduling; marketing

French

Tel: (01792) 295968 Fax: (01792) 295978
E-mail: french@swansea.ac.uk
Connon, D. F., BA *Liv.*, PhD *Liv.*   Reader
Harrow, S. R., MA *Edin.*, PhD *Edin.*   Sr. Lectr.
Rodgers, C., PhD *E.Anglia*   Sr. Lectr.

Rothwell, A. J., MA *Oxf.*, DPhil *Oxf.*   Prof.; Head*
Rothwell, W.   Prof.
Other Staff: 4 Lectrs.
Research: European literatures; French politics and literature; literary translation; seventeenth- and eighteenth-century drama; translation with language technology

Geography

Tel: (01792) 295228 Fax: (01792) 295955
E-mail: ggenquirie@swansea.ac.uk
Barnsley, M. J., BA *Reading*, PhD *Reading*   Prof.; Head*
Bromley, R. D. F., MA *Camb.*, PhD *Wales*   Sr. Lectr.
Davies, W. K. D., MA *Wales*, PhD *Wales*   Hon. Prof.
Doel, M. A., BSc *Brist.*, PhD *Brist.*   Prof.
Gruffudd, R. P., BSc *Lough.*, PhD *Lough.*   Sr. Lectr.
Halfacree, K. H., BSc *Brist.*, PhD *Lanc.*   Sr. Lectr.
Los, S. O., MSc *Amst.*, PhD *Amst.*   Sr. Lectr.
Luckman, A., BSc *York(UK)*, PhD *York(UK)*   Sr. Lectr.
Matthews, J. A., BSc *Lond.*, PhD *Lond.*   Prof.
McCarroll, D., BA *Sheff.*, PhD *Wales*   Reader
Murray, T., BSc *Wales*, PhD *Wales*   Prof.
Nestje, A., BSc *Bergen*, PhD *Bergen*   Hon. Prof.
North, P. J. R., BA DPhil   Sr. Lectr.
Robinson, Vaughan, MA *Oxf.*, DPhil *Oxf.*   Prof., Human Geography
Shakesby, R. A., BA *CNAA*, PhD *Edin.*   Sr. Lectr.
Street-Perrott, F. A., MA *Colorado*, MA *Oxf.*, MA *Camb.*, PhD *Camb.*   Prof.
Thomas, C. J., BSc *Wales*, PhD *Nott.*   Sr. Lectr.
Walsh, R. P. D., MA *Camb.*, PhD *Camb.*   Prof.
Other Staff: 6 Lectrs.; 1 Sr. Lectr.†
Research: environmental monitoring; geographical information systems; land surface processes and management; migration; retail geography

German

Tel: (01792) 295170 Fax: (01792) 295710
E-mail: e.s.parker@swansea.ac.uk
Basker, D. R., BA *Manc.*, PhD *Wales*   Sr. Lectr.
Cheesman, C. T., BA *Oxf.*, DPhil *Oxf.*   Sr. Lectr.
Haines, B. A., BA *Lond.*, PhD *Lond.*   Sr. Lectr.
Jucker, R., PhD *Zür.*   Sr. Lectr.
Large, Duncan, MA *Oxf.*, DPhil *Oxf.*   Sr. Lectr.
Williams, R. W., MA *Oxf.*, DPhil *Oxf.*   Prof.; Head*
Other Staff: 2 Lectrs.
Research: European literatures; literary translation; nineteenth- and twentieth-century literature; translation with language technology

Health Science, School of

Tel: (01792) 295789 Fax: (01792) 295487
Borsay, A., BA *Wales*, MLitt *Oxf.*, DPhil *Wales*   Prof.
Coleman, M. R., MScEcon *Wales*   Sr. Lectr.
Davies, R. E., MA PhD   Sr. Lectr.
Delaney, C. W., MA *Iowa*, PhD *Iowa*   Hon. Prof.
Edwards, S. D., BA MPhil PhD   Reader
Evans, C. J., BSc *Wales*, PhD *Wales*   Sr. Lectr.
Fitzsimmons, D., BN PhD   Sr. Lectr.
Goldberg, C. B., MMS   Dir., Health Informatics Centre
Griffiths, L. J., BSc *Wales*, PhD *Wales*   Sr. Lectr.
Griffiths, P., BN *Wales*   Sr. Lectr.
Hughes, D. J., BA *Kent*, MA *Essex*, PhD *Wales*   Prof.
Hunter, B. J., BNurs *Manc.*, PhD *Wales(Swansea)*   Sr. Lectr.
Jordan, S. E., MB BCh *Wales*, PhD *W.England*   Sr. Lectr.
Koch, T., BA *Flin.*, PhD *Manc.*   Hon. Prof.
Lawton, V. M., MSc *Lond.*, PhD   Hon. Prof.
Mcnamee, M. J., PhD   Sr. Lectr.
Merrell, J. A., BSc *Lond.*, MSc *Manc.*, PhD *Manc.*   Prof.

Murphy, F. A., BN *Manc.*, MSc *Wales*   Sr. Lectr.
Pearson, N. A., BN *Wales*, MBA   Head of Studies (Post Registration Undergraduate); Contract Manager
Phillips, C. J., MSc *Wales*, PhD *Wales*   Reader
Philpin, S. M., BScEcon *Wales*   Sr. Lectr.
Rolfe, G., BSc *Sur.*, MA *S'ton.*, PhD *S'ton.*   Prof.
Tait, M. I., BSc *Dund.*, PhD *Edin.*   Sr. Lectr.
Thomas, J., MSc *Wales*   Sr. Lectr.
Watts, T., BA *Lond.*   Sr. Lectr.
Williams, A. M., MA *Br.Col.*, PhD *Manc.*   Prof.
Willshaw, P., BSc *Lond.*, PhD *Lond.*   Sr. Lectr.
Other Staff: 62 Lectrs.; 1 Sr. Tutor; 21 Tutors; 7 Hon. Sr. Lectrs.; 17 Hon. Lectrs.; 1 Hon. Res. Fellow
Research: delivery of health care; evaluation of health care; health care policy; philosophy of health care

Hispanic Studies

Tel: (01792) 513195 Fax: (01792) 295130
E-mail: hispanic@swansea.ac.uk
Gagen, D. H., BA *Manc.*   Res. Prof.
George, D. J., BA *Wales*, PhD *Wales*   Reader; Head*
Hall, J. B., TD, MA *Oxf.*, BPhil *Oxf.*   Sr. Lectr.
Other Staff: 3 Lectrs.
Research: European literatures; Latin-American literature; literary translation; translation with language technology; twentieth-century drama

History

see also Classics and Anc. Hist.

Tel: (01792) 295980 Fax: (01792) 295746
E-mail: j.toft@swansea.ac.uk
Clark, D. S. T., BA *Wales*, PhD *Camb.*, FRHistS   Prof.
Dunthorne, H. L. A., MA *Edin.*, PhD *Lond.*, FRHistS   Sr. Lectr.
France, J., BA *Nott.*, PhD *Nott.*, FRHistS   Prof.
Healey, D., MA *Lond.*, MA *Tor.*, PhD *Tor.*   Sr. Lectr.
Law, J. E., MA *St And.*, DPhil *Oxf.*, FRHistS   Reader
Lewis, J. J., BA *Lanc.*, PhD *Lanc.*   Sr. Lectr.
Morgan, K. O., MA *Oxf.*, DPhil *Oxf.*, DLitt *Oxf.*, FRHistS, FBA   Hon. Prof.
Spurr, J., MA *Oxf.*, DPhil *Oxf.*, FRHistS   Reader
Thompson, N. W., MA *St And.*, MSc *Belf.*, PhD *Camb.*   Prof.; Head*
Turner, D. M., BA MA DPhil   Sr. Lectr.
Whitehead, M., BA *Durh.*, PhD *Hull*   Prof.
Williams, C. M., PhD *Wales*, BA   Prof.
Other Staff: 8 Lectrs.; 3 Hon. Sr. Lectrs.; 3 Hon. Res. Fellows
Research: mediaeval history; modern British history; modern economic and social history; modern international history

Italian

Tel: (01792) 513538 Fax: (01792) 295919
Dunnage, J. M., BA MA PhD   Sr. Lectr.
Moss, H. K., BA *Hull*   Head*
Other Staff: 2 Lectrs.
Research: European literatures; literary translation; translation with language technology; twentieth-century language and literature

Law

Tel: (01792) 295831 Fax: (01792) 295855
Davies, I. R., LLB *Camb.*, LLM *Wales*, PhD *Wales*   Prof.; Head*
Jones, T. H., LLB *Birm.*, MPhil *Camb.*, PhD *Brun.*   Prof.
MacDonald, E. A.   Prof.
Perry, A., BA LLM   Sr. Lectr.
Snell, J.   Sr. Lectr.
Soyer, B., LLM PhD   Sr. Lectr.
Todd, P. N., MA *Oxf.*   Sr. Lectr.
Williams, M. L., BA *Camb.*, MA *Sus.*   Reader
Other Staff: 15 Lectrs.
Research: commercial law; family law; instalment credit law; medical law; shipping and international trade law

Mathematics

Tel: (01792) 295457 Fax: (01792) 295843
E-mail: mathematics@swansea.ac.uk
Beggs, E. J., MA DPhil
Clarke, F. W., BSc Birm., MSc Warw., PhD
Warw.   Reader
Davies, I. M., BSc H-W, PhD H-W, FIMA   Sr.
Lectr.
Dorlas, T. C., PhD Gron.   Hon. Prof.
Freidlin, M., MS Moscow, PhD Russian Acad.Sc.,
DSc Moscow   Hon. Prof.
Jacob, N., PhD Berl.   Prof.
Thomas, D. K., BSc Lond., PhD Lond., PhD Wales
Sr. Lectr.
Truman, A., MA Oxf., DPhil Oxf., FRSEd, FIMA
Prof.; Head*
Williams, D., BA Oxf., DPhil Oxf., FRS   Res.
Prof.
Wood, G. V., MA Camb., PhD Newcastle(UK)   Sr.
Lectr.
Other Staff: 5 Lectrs.; 1 Advanced Fellow; 2
Hon. Lectrs.
Research: algebraic topology; computation
mathematics; functional analyis; probability
theory and its applications; quantum
physics

Media Studies

Tel: (01792) 513375 Fax: (01792) 513453
E-mail: d.j.rideout@swansea.ac.uk
Hoskins, A. D., MA PhD   Sr. Lectr.
Williams, K. M., BA Keele, MSc(Econ) Lond.
Prof.; Head*
Other Staff: 4 Lectrs.; 1 Sr. Tutor; 1 Tutor
Research: media history; public and media
relations; screen studies

Philosophy

Tel: (01792) 295190 Fax: (01792) 295893
E-mail: h.baldwin@swansea.ac.uk
4 Lectrs.; 1 Hon. Lectr.; 3 Hon. Res. Fellows
Research: philosophy of logic and language;
philosophy of religion; Wittgenstein

Physics

Tel: (01792) 295849 Fax: (01792) 295324
E-mail: e.jones@swansea.ac.uk
Allton, C. R., BSc Qld., PhD ANU   Sr. Lectr.
Charlton, M., BSc Lond., PhD Lond.   Prof.;
Head*
Davies, A. J., BSc Wales, PhD Wales, FIP, FIEE
Res. Prof.
Dunbar, D. C., BSc Glas., PhD Glas.   Reader
Halliday, I. G., MA MSc PhD   Prof.
Hands, S. J., BA Camb., PhD Edin.   Reader
Hollowood, T. J., BA Oxf., PhD Durh.   Reader
Nunez, C.
Shore, G. M., BSc Edin., PhD Camb.   Prof.
Telle, H. H., MSc Cologne, PhD Cologne   Prof.†
Other Staff: 3 Lectrs.; 2 Hon. Res. Fellows; 4
Hon. Lectrs.
Research: experimental atomic and condensed
matter physics; laser physics; theoretical
particle physics

Politics and International Relations

Tel: (01792) 295303 Fax: (01792) 295716
E-mail: s.l.irving@swansea.ac.uk
Axtmann, R., MA PhD   Prof.
Baylis, J., BA Wales, MScEcon Wales, PhD Wales,
DLitt   Prof.; Head*
Bideleux, R. J., MA Edin.   Reader
Bradbury, J. P., BA Brist., PhD Brist.   Sr. Lectr.
Finlayson, A., BA Camb., PhD Wales   Sr. Lectr.
Sheehan, M., BSc PhD   Prof.
Taylor, R., MA Camb., PhD Lond., FRHistS
Prof., Politics and Russian Studies
Vali, A., BA Teheran, MA Keele, PhD Lond.   Sr.
Lectr.
Other Staff: 5 Lectrs.; 1 Hon. Res. Fellow
Research: contemporary political thought; history
of political thought; international politics;
Russian and East European politics

Psychology

Tel: (01792) 295280 Fax: (01792) 295679
E-mail: psy@swansea.ac.uk
Beaton, A. A., BA Wales, PhD Wales   Sr. Lectr.

Bennett, P., BA Plym., MSc Plym., PhD Birm.
Prof.
Benton, D., BSc Aston, PhD Birm.   Prof.
Blagrove, M. T., MA Camb., PhD Brun.   Reader
Clark, D. R., BSc CNAA, PhD Reading   Prof.
Corr, P. J. J., BSc PhD   Prof.
Hermann, D. J., BS PhD   Prof.
McDougall, S. J. P., MA Glas., PhD Lond.   Sr.
Lectr.
Reed, P., BSc Leeds, DPhil York(UK)   Prof.
Wood, R. L., BA Wales, PhD Leic., FBPsS   Prof.;
Head*
Other Staff: 10 Lectrs.; 1 Tutor; 2 Hon. Profs.;
4 Hon. Res. Fellows
Research: biological psychology; body rhythms
and shiftwork; occupational and applied
social psychology

Russian

Fax: (01792) 295710
Martin, D. W., MA Oxf., BLitt Oxf.   Lectr.;
Head*
Other Staff: 1 Tutor
Research: language and history of Russia

Russian and East European Studies, Centre of

Tel: (01792) 295630 Fax: (01792) 295716
Bideleux, R. J., MA Edin., MA Sus.   Head,
Russian Economic History*
Taylor, R., MA Camb., PhD Lond., FRHistS
Prof., Politics and Russian Studies
Other Staff: 1 Lectr.
Research: East-West relations; Soviet cinema;
transition to democracy since 1989

Social Sciences and International Development, School of

Tel: (01792) 513137 Fax: (01792) 295750
E-mail: c.cook@swansea.ac.uk
Barrow, C. J., BSc Hull, PhD Birm.   Sr. Lectr.
Blakemore, K. P., BA Hull, MSocSci Birm., PhD
Birm.   Sr. Lectr.
Byron, R. F., BA S.Calif., PhD Lond.   Prof.
Charles, N., BA Keele, PhD Keele   Prof.
Clarke, G., BA N.U.I., MSc Lond., PhD Lond.   Sr.
Lectr.
Colton, M. J., BA Keele, DPhil Oxf.   Prof.
Davies, C. A., BS Alabama, MS Mississippi, PhD
Duke   Sr. Lectr.
Drake, R. F., BSc Salf., MA Sheff., PhD Wales
Sr. Lectr.
Hughes-Freeland, F., BA Oxf., MA Lond., PhD
Lond.   Sr. Lectr.
Kenna, M. E., BA Lond., PhD Kent   Reader
Phillips, J. E.   Prof.
Price, N. L., BSc Wales, MA Reading
Raynor, P. C., MA Oxf., BPhil Exe., PhD Wales
Prof.
Rew, A. W., MA(Econ) Manc., PhD ANU   Prof.
Saha, S. K., MA Patna, PhD Wales   Sr. Lectr.
Sullivan, M. J., MA Oxf., PhD Wales   Prof.
Thomas, A. R., BA Camb., MA Lanc.   Prof.;
Head*
Townsend, P., BA Camb., PhD Essex   Hon. Prof.
Vanstone, M. T., BA Wales   Sr. Lectr.
Other Staff: 19 Lectrs.; 5 Tutors; 1 Hon. Lectr.;
7 Hon. Res. Fellows
Research: anthropology; applied social studies;
development policy and planning; social
policy; sociology

Sports Science

Tel: (01792) 295057 Fax: (01792) 513171
Watkins, J., BEd Liv., MA Leeds, PhD Leeds
Prof.; Head*
Other Staff: 6 Lectrs.; 2 Tutors†
Research: biomechanics, physiology and
psychology of sport

Swansea Clinical School

Tel: (01792) 513400 Fax: (01792) 513430
E-mail: medicine@swansea.ac.uk
Cheung, W. Y., BSc HK, MPhil HK, PhD Wales
Sr. Lectr.
Dodge, J. A., MD ChB Wales, FRCP   Hon.
Prof.

Gravenor, M. B., BA Camb., MSc Reading, DPhil
Oxf.   Sr. Lectr.
Hopkin, J. M., MSc MA MD, FRCP   Prof.;
Dir.*
Jenkins, G. J. S., BSc Wales, MB BCh Wales   Sr.
Lectr.
Kelly, S. L., BSc Wales, PhD Wales   Prof.
Shirakawa, T., MD Kyoto, PhD Osaka   Hon.
Prof.
Snooks, H. A., BSc Sur., PhD Sheff.   Sr. Lectr.
Thomas, G. A., BSc Bath, PhD Wales   Sr. Lectr.
Thornton, C. A., BA Tas., BSc Tas., DPhil S.Aust.
Sr. Lectr.
Westwood, O. M. R., BSc Sur., PhD Lond.   Sr.
Lectr.
White, J. O., BSc Lond., MSc Lond., PhD Lond.
Prof.
Other Staff: 8 Sr. Lectrs.; 8 Lectrs.; 9 Res.
Fellows; 5 Hon. Sr. Lectrs.
Research: clinical epidemiology; experimental
medicine; human cancer studies; primary
care; surgery in general

Welsh

Cymraeg
Tel: (01792) 295193 Fax: (01792) 295399
Ellis Evans, D., MA Wales, DPhil Oxf., FBA
Hon. Prof.
Johnston, D. R., BA Camb., PhD Wales   Prof.;
Head*
Rhys, R. G., BA Wales, MPhil Wales   Sr. Lectr.
Other Staff: 3 Lectrs.; 2 Tutors
Research: European literatures; literary
translation; popular eighteenth- and
nineteenth-century literature; socio-
linguistics and dialectology; translation with
language technology

SPECIAL CENTRES, ETC

Applied Language Studies, Centre for

Tel: (01792) 295391 Fax: (01792) 295641
E-mail: cals@swansea.ac.uk
Butler, C. S., MA Oxf., PhD Nott.   Hon. Prof.
Meara, P. M., BA Camb., MSc Sus., DPhil
York(UK)   Prof.
Milton, J. M., BA Liv., PhD Wales   Dir.*
Other Staff: 3 Lectrs.; 18 Tutors; 1 Hon. Lectr.
Research: lexical acquisition in a foreign
language; teaching English as a foreign
language

Public Policy Research, National Centre for

Tel: (01792) 295059 Fax: (01792) 513031
E-mail: ncpp@swansea.ac.uk
Sullivan, M. J., MA Oxf., PhD Wales   Prof.;
Head*
Other Staff: 1 Sr. Res. Fellow; 1 Res. Fellow
Research: political trends; social policy; social
trends

CONTACT OFFICERS

Academic affairs. Academic Registrar: Morris,
H. D. L., BA Wales, LLD Lond.
(E-mail: p.tweebeeke@swansea.ac.uk)
Accommodation. Accommodation Officer:
Barney, H., BA Wales
(E-mail: accommodation@swansea.ac.uk)
Admissions (first degree). Admissions Officer:
Williams, K. L., BA Lanc.
(E-mail: admissions@swansea.ac.uk)
Admissions (higher degree). Admissions
Officer: Williams, K. L., BA Lanc.
(E-mail: postgraduate.admissions@
swansea.ac.uk)
Adult/continuing education. Director of
Adult Education: Trotman, C., BSc Wales,
PhD Wales
(E-mail: adult.education@swansea.ac.uk)
Alumni. Alumni Officer: Newman, S. Y., BSc
Wales (E-mail: alumni@swansea.ac.uk)
Archives. Librarian: West, C. M., MA Nott.
Careers. Careers Director: Slater, F. W., BSc
Aberd., BA Open(UK)
(E-mail: careers@swansea.ac.uk)
Computing services. Librarian: West, C. M.,
MA Nott.

Conferences/corporate hospitality.
Conference Services Manager: Belcher, P.
(E-mail: conference@swansea.ac.uk)

Credit transfer. Academic Registrar: Morris,
H. D. L., BA *Wales*, LLD *Lond.*
(E-mail: p.tweebeeke@swansea.ac.uk)

Equal opportunities. Acting Personnel
Director: Williams, D. G., BSc *Wales*
(E-mail: personnel.mailbox@swansea.ac.uk)

Estates and buildings/works and services.
Director of Estates: Benson, D. G.

Examinations. Academic Registrar: Morris, H.
D. L., BA *Wales*, LLD *Lond.*
(E-mail: p.tweebeeke@swansea.ac.uk)

Finance. Director of Finance: Gough, P. R. C.,
BSc *Brist.*

General enquiries. Registrar: Townsend, Prof.
P., BSc *Wales*, PhD *Wales*, DSc *Wales*

Health services. Nurse Practitioner/
Administrator (Health Services): Anthony,
C.
(E-mail: occupational-health@swansea.ac.uk)

Industrial liaison. Commercial Manager: Day,
M. (E-mail: a.m.day@swansea.ac.uk)

International office. Dean of International
Affairs: McGann, O., BScEcon *Wales*, MBA
Wales (E-mail: international@swansea.ac.uk)

Language training for international students.
Director, Centre for Applied Language
Studies: Milton, J. M., BA *Liv.*, PhD *Wales*
(E-mail: cals@swansea.ac.uk)

Library (chief librarian). Librarian: West, C.
M., MA *Nott.*

Marketing. Director of Marketing: Mullin, C.,
BSc *Wales*, MSc *Newcastle(UK)*
(E-mail: marketing@swansea.ac.uk)

Personnel/human resources. Acting Personnel
Director: Williams, D. G., BSc *Wales*
(E-mail: personnel.mailbox@swansea.ac.uk)

Public relations. Public Relations Officer:
Jones, M. (E-mail: press@swansea.ac.uk)

Publications. Publications Officer: Clifton, R.
J., BSc *Wales*
(E-mail: publications@swansea.ac.uk)

Purchasing. Purchasing Officer: Caruana, J. R.
(E-mail: purchasing@swansea.ac.uk)

Quality assurance and accreditation. Assistant
Registrar (Quality assurance and
accreditation): Rees, L. J., BSc *Wales*, MSc
Calg.

Safety. Safety Officer: Davies, J.
(E-mail: safety@swansea.ac.uk)

Scholarships, awards, loans. Student Financial
Aid Officer: Hanford, J. D.
(E-mail: sfao@swansea.ac.uk)

Scholarships, awards, loans. (Scholarships)
Admissions Officer: Williams, K. L., BA
Lanc. (E-mail: admissions@swansea.ac.uk)

Schools liaison. Student Recruitment Officer:
Clark, B. M., BScEcon *Wales*
(E-mail: sro@swansea.ac.uk)

Security. Director of Estates: Benson, D. G.

Sport and recreation. Director of Physical
Recreation: Addicott, W. S., BA *Wales*, MEd
Liv.

Staff development and training. Staff
Development Officer: Sykes, R. N., BSc *Lond.*

Strategic planning. Strategic Planning Officer:
Britton, J. F., BSc *Wales*
(E-mail: j.britton@swansea.ac.uk)

Student union. Union Manager: Hilton, D.
(E-mail: superintendent@swansea.ac.uk)

Student welfare/counselling. Senior Student
Counsellor: Turner, R. S., BA *York(UK)*
(E-mail: r.s.turner@swansea.ac.uk)

Students from other countries. International
Student Advisor: Huws-Davies, S. Y.
(E-mail: international@swansea.ac.uk)

Students with disabilities. Assistant Disability
Officer: Jones, A. M., BSc *Middx.*
(E-mail: disability@swansea.ac.uk)

[*Information supplied by the institution as at 1 April
2005, and edited by the ACU*]

SWANSEA METROPOLITAN UNIVERSITY

Founded 1976

Postal Address: Mount Pleasant, Swansea, Wales SA1 6ED
Telephone: (01792) 481000 **Fax:** (01792) 481085 **E-mail:** enquiry@sihe.ac.uk
URL: http://www.sihe.ac.uk

PRINCIPAL AND CHIEF EXECUTIVE*—Warner, Prof. David, MA *Warw.*

UNIVERSITY OF TEESSIDE

Founded 1992

Postal Address: Middlesbrough, England TS1 3BA
Telephone: (01642) 218121 **Fax:** (01642) 342067
URL: http://www.tees.ac.uk

VICE-CHANCELLOR AND CHIEF EXECUTIVE*—Henderson, Prof. Graham, BSc *Coventry*, MSc *City(UK)*, FRSA
SECRETARY AND REGISTRAR‡—McClintock, J. M., BA *Trinity(Dub.)*, LLB *Trinity(Dub.)*, MA *Trinity(Dub.)*, LLM *Penn.*

THAMES VALLEY UNIVERSITY

Founded 1992

Postal Address: St Mary's Road, Ealing, London, England W5 5RF
Telephone: (020) 8579 5000 **Fax:** (020) 8566 1353 **E-mail:** learning.advice@tvu.ac.uk
URL: http://www.tvu.ac.uk

VICE-CHANCELLOR*—John, Prof. Peter D., BA MA MSc PhD
SECRETARY AND REGISTRAR‡—Dalton, Ann Marie

TRINITY COLLEGE, CARMARTHEN

Postal Address: Wales SA31 3EP
Telephone: (01267) 676767 **Fax:** (01267) 676766 **E-mail:** registry@trinity-cm.ac.uk
URL: http://www.trinity-cm.ac.uk

PRINCIPAL*—Hughes, Medwin, DPhil DPS, FRSA

UNIVERSITY OF ULSTER

Founded 1984

Member of the Association of Commonwealth Universities

Postal Address: Cromore Road, Coleraine, County Londonderry, Northern Ireland BT52 1SA
Telephone: 08 700 400 700 **Fax:** (028) 7032 4927
URL: http://www.ulster.ac.uk

VICE-CHANCELLOR*—Barnett, Prof. Richard R., BSc Salf., PhD Salf.
PRO-VICE-CHANCELLOR (COMMUNICATION AND INSTITUTIONAL DEVELOPMENT)—Allen, Prof. James M., BSc Belf.,
   PhD Belf., FIBiol
PRO-VICE-CHANCELLOR (ACADEMIC DEVELOPMENT AND STUDENT SERVICES)—Black, Prof. Norman D., BSc Belf., PhD
   Belf.
PRO-VICE-CHANCELLOR (RESEARCH AND INNOVATION)—Hannigan, Prof. Bernadette M., BA Trinity(Dub.), PhD N.U.I.
PRO-VICE-CHANCELLOR (TEACHING AND LEARNING)—McAlister, Prof. Denise A., BSc Belf., MSc Salf.
DIRECTOR OF PLANNING AND GOVERNANCE SERVICES‡—Aston, Irene, BSc Belf.
DIRECTOR OF FINANCE—Hope, Peter W., BA Stir., MBA Ulster, FCA
DIRECTOR OF INFORMATION SERVICES—Macartney, Nigel S., BA Camb., MA Camb., FRSA

GENERAL INFORMATION

History. The university was established in 1984 by the merger of the New University of Ulster (founded 1967) and Ulster Polytechnic (founded 1971). The university traces its origins back to the middle of the nineteenth-century with the foundation of the Belfast College of Art and Magee College.

It is a unitary institution with four campuses: Belfast; Coleraine, on the Causeway Coast; Jordanstown, on the shores of Belfast Lough; and Magee in Derry City/Londonderry.

Admission to first degree courses (see also United Kingdom Introduction). Through Universities and Colleges Admissions Service (UCAS). Further information on entry qualifications can be found online at http://prospectus.ulster.ac.uk

First Degrees (see also United Kingdom Directory to Subjects of Study). BA, BDes, BEng, BMus, BSc, LLB, MEng.

4- or 5-year programmes typically include 1 year's work placement or 1 year's study abroad.

Length of course. Full-time: BA, BDes, BEng, BMus, BSc, LLB: 3–4 years; MEng: max. 5 years. *Part-time:* BA, BDes, BEng, BMus, BSc, LLB: max. 5 years.

Higher Degrees (see also United Kingdom Directory to Subjects of Study).

Master's. LLM, MA, MBA, MBS, MDes, MFA, MMedSc, MMus, MPA, MPhil, MRes, MSc.

Admission. Applicants for admission to master's degree courses must normally hold an appropriate first degree with at least second class honours. Applicants for admission to the MBA must also have at least 3 years' relevant work experience.

Length of course. Full-time: LLM, MA, MBA, MBS, MDes, MRes, MSc: 1 year; MFA, MMedSc, MMus, MPA, MPhil: 2 years. Part-time: LLM, MA, MBA, MBS, MDes, MFA, MMedSc, MMus, MPA, MRes, MSc: max. 3 years; MPhil: max. 4 years.

Doctoral. DEng, DEnvSc, DMan, DMedSc, DMidSc, DNSc, DTech, EdD, MD, PhD.

Admission. Applicants must normally hold an appropriate first degree with at least second class honours. Applicants for admission to some doctoral programmes (eg. DMan) must have at least 3 years' relevant work experience.

Length of course. Full-time: DEng, DEnvSc, DMan, DMedSc, DMidSc, DNSc, DTech, EdD, MD, PhD: 3 years. Part-time: DEng, DEnvSc, DMan, DMedSc, DMidSc, DNSc, DTech, EdD, MD, PhD: max. 6 years.

Language of Instruction. English (except in some specialist language courses). Intensive pre-sessional courses available for international students.

Libraries. Volumes: 854,819. Periodicals subscribed to: 16,000. Other holdings: 22,000 micro-forms; 100,000 slides; 9500 audio and video tapes. Special collections: Henry Davis (early printed books); Henry Morris (Irish material); Irish Travellers; Magee (rare books); Diocese of Derry and Raphoe.

Academic Year (2007–2008). Three semesters: 24 September–25 January; 28 January–30 May; 21 July–12 September.

Income (2006–2007). Total, £174,393,000.

Statistics. Staff (2007): 3521 (1117 academic, 2404 non-academic). Students (2006): full-time 16,250; part-time 7011; international 2993.

FACULTIES/SCHOOLS

Art, Design and Built Environment
Tel: (028) 9036 6310 Fax: (028) 9036 6816
   E-mail: as.adair@ulster.ac.uk
Dean: Adair, Prof. Alastair S., BA Belf., PhD Reading, FRICS
Head of Faculty Administration: Wasson, Ruth, MA Ulster

Arts
Tel: (028) 7032 4517 Fax: (028) 7032 4925
   E-mail: arts@ulster.ac.uk
Dean: Welch, Prof. Robert W., BA N.U.I., MA N.U.I., PhD Leeds
Head of Faculty Administration: Kendall, Gary, BSc CNAA, MSc Aberd., MBA Ulster

Business and Management
Tel: (028) 9036 6351 Fax: (028) 9036 6805
   E-mail: business@ulster.ac.uk
Dean: Hutchinson, Prof. Robert W., BSc Ulster, MA Warw.
Head of Faculty Administration: O'Neill, Tom, BA Ulster, MA Ulster

Computing and Engineering
Tel: (028) 9036 6855 Fax: (028) 9036 6803
   E-mail: engineering@ulster.ac.uk
Dean: Millar, Prof. Richard, MA Camb., PhD Ulster
Head of Faculty Administration: Hunter, Nicholas D., BA Ulster

Life and Health Sciences
Tel: (028) 7032 4491 Fax: (028) 7032 4596
   E-mail: science@ulster.ac.uk
Dean: McKenna, Prof. Hugh P., BSc Ulster, PhD Ulster
Head of Faculty Administration: Chapman, Stephen, MA St And., MBA Ulster, FCA

Social Sciences
Tel: (028) 9036 6157 Fax: (028) 9036 8266
   E-mail: socsci@ulster.ac.uk
Dean: Moran, Prof. Anne, BEd Ulster, MSc Ulster, PhD Ulster
Head of Faculty Administration: Crean, Colm, BA Belf.

ACADEMIC UNITS
Arranged by Schools

Accounting
Tel: (028) 9036 6906 Fax: (028) 9036 8502
   E-mail: ka.greenan@ulster.ac.uk
Green, J. Peter, BA Ulster, PhD Ulster   Sr. Lectr.
Greenan, Kate, BSc Belf., MBA Belf.   Prof., Management Education; Head*
Kirk, Robert J., BSc Belf., FCA   Prof., Financial Accounting
Martin, Gary, BA Ulster, MSc Ulster   Sr. Lectr.
Patton, Ronnie, BA Belf., MBA Ulster   Sr. Lectr.
Rankin, Denis C., FCA   Sr. Lectr.
Wall, Anthony P., BA Ulster   Sr. Lectr.
Other Staff: 13 Lectrs.; 5 Asst. Lectrs.

Research: corporate governance; international finance reporting standards; private finance initiative; public sector accounting

Architecture and Design

Tel: (028) 9026 7252 Fax: (028) 9026 7356
E-mail: h.elkadi@ulster.ac.uk
Dass, Barbara, BA *Ulster*, PhD *Ulster*   Sr. Lectr.
Elkadi, Hisham, BScArch *Liv.*, PhD *Liv.*   Prof., Architecture; Head*
Other Staff: 6 Lectrs.; 2 Res. Fellows
Research: architecture of power; cultural impact of façade design; glass in architecture

Art and Design

Tel: (028) 9026 7243 Fax: (028) 9026 7356
E-mail: jai.montgomery@ulster.ac.uk
Aiken, Susan   Sr. Lectr.
Campbell, David, BA *Liv.*, MA *Leeds*   Reader
Doherty, Willie, BA *Ulster*, Hon. DLitt *Staffs.*   Prof., Video Art
Fiddis, Clive, BA *Ulster*   Sr. Lectr.
Fleming, Karen, BA *Ulster*, MEd *Ulster*   Reader
Fraser, Debbie, BA *Ulster*   Sr. Lectr.
Kelly, Liam, BA *Lond.*, PhD *Trinity(Dub.)*   Prof., Irish Culture
Lawrence, C. Norman   Sr. Lectr.
Mackel, Sean, BA *Ulster*   Sr. Lectr.
MacLennan, Alastair M., MFA *Chic.*   Prof., Fine Art
McClelland, Brian, MDes *RCA*, FRSA   Prof., Design
McGonagle, Declan, BA *Ulster*   Prof.
McIntyre, Mary, BA *Ulster*, MA *Ulster*   Reader
McLaughlin, Patricia B., BA *Surrey IAD*, MPhil *Ulster*   Sr. Lectr.
McMillan, John   Reader
Mey, Kerstin, MA *Humboldt*, PhD *Humboldt*   Prof., Fine Art
Montgomery, J. A. Ian, BA *Ulster*, PhD *Ulster*   Prof., Design; Head*
Moore, Michael, BA *N.U.I.*, MA *N.U.I.*   Reader
Morrow, Ruth R., BScArch *Dund.*   Prof., Architecture
Sander, Volker, MA *Berlin Coll.Arts*   Reader
Seawright, Paul, BA *Ulster*, PhD *Wales*   Prof., Photography
Wright, Terence V., MA *Lond.*, PhD *Lond.*   Reader
Other Staff: 36 Lectrs.; 24 Assoc. Lectrs.; 8 Res. Fellows
Research: constructed textiles; critical theory of art and design; design (fine and applied arts); visual communication

Biomedical Sciences

Tel: (028) 7032 3011 Fax: (028) 7032 4965
E-mail: nh.mcclenaghan@ulster.ac.uk
Abdel-Wahab, Yasser, MB BCh PhD   Sr. Lectr.
Anderson, Roger S., BSc *Wales*, MPhil *Wales*, PhD *Indiana*   Prof., Vision Science
Banat, Ibrahim, BSc *Kuwait*, PhD *Essex*   Prof., Microbiology
Bjourson, Anthony, MSc *Ulster*, PhD *Belf.*   Prof., Genomics
Dooley, James, BSc *N.U.I.*, PhD *Vic.(BC)*   Sr. Lectr.
Douglas, Pauline, BSc *Edin.*, MBA   Sr. Lectr.
Downes, C. Stephen, OBE, BA *Oxf.*, MA *Oxf.*, DPhil *Oxf.*   Prof., Cancer Biology
Dubitzky, Werner, MSc *F.H.Augsburg*, PhD *Ulster*   Prof., Bioinformatics
Flatt, Peter R., BSc *Aston*, PhD *Aston*   Prof., Biological and Biomedical Sciences
Gallagher, Alison M., BSc *Ulster*, MSc *Ulster*   Sr. Lectr.
Holscher, Christian, BSc *Kiel*, MSc *Tübingen*, PhD *Open(UK)*   Sr. Lectr.
Howard, C. Vyvyan, MB ChB *Liv.*, PhD *Liv.*   Prof., Bioimaging
Livingstone, M. Barbara E., BEd *Lond.*, MSc *Lond.*, PhD *Ulster*   Prof., Human Nutrition
Marchant, Roger, BSc *Lond.*, PhD *Lond.*, DSc *Lond.*, FIBiol   Prof., Biology
McClenaghan, Neville, BSc *Ulster*, PhD *Ulster*   Sr. Lectr.; Head
McDowell, D. Rod, BSc *Glas.*, MSc *Ulster*, DMedSc *Ulster*   Sr. Lectr.

McHale, Anthony P., BSc *N.U.I.*, PhD *N.U.I.*   Prof., Medical Biotechnology
McKelvey-Martin, Valerie J., BSc *Ulster*, PhD *Ulster*   Prof., Molecular Biosciences
McKeown, Stephanie R., BA *Oxf.*, MA *Oxf.*, PhD *Belf.*   Prof., Cancer Biology
McKerr, George, BSc *Belf.*, PhD *Belf.*   Sr. Lectr.
McKillop, Aine, BSc *Liv.*, MSc *Ulster*, PhD *Belf.*   Sr. Lectr.
McMullan, Geoffrey, BSc *Belf.*, PhD *Belf.*   Prof., Microbiology
McNulty, Helene M., BSc *Trinity(Dub.)*, PhD *Trinity(Dub.)*   Prof., Human Nutrition and Dietetics
Mitchell, Christopher, BSc *W.Aust.*, PhD *W.Aust.*   Sr. Lectr.
Mitchell, Peter, BSc *Edin.*, MSc *Calif.*   Sr. Lectr.
Moore, C. B. Tara, BSc *Belf.*, PhD *Belf.*   Sr. Lectr.
O'Connor, Jacqueline, BSc *Ulster*, PhD *Ulster*   Sr. Lectr.
O'Harte, Finbarr, BSc *Belf.*, PhD *Belf.*   Prof., Endocrinology and Metabolism
Pentieva, Krisitna, MD *Sofia Acad.Med.*, PhD *Sofia Acad.Med.*   Sr. Lectr.
Pierscionek, Barbara K., BSc *Melb.*, MBA *Brad.*, LLM *Leeds*, PhD *Melb.*   Prof., Optometry and Vision Science
Sarkar, Satyajit, BPharm *Dhaka*, MPharm *Dhaka*, PhD *Strath.*   Reader
Saunders, Kathryn, BSc *Wales*, PhD *Wales*   Sr. Lectr.
Singh, Poonam, BSc *Kanpur*, MSc *Kanpur*, PhD *Kanpur*   Sr. Lectr.
Smyth, W. Franklin, BSc *Belf.*, PhD *Belf.*, DSc *Belf.*   Prof., Bio-analytical Chemistry
Stewart-Knox, Barbara, BA *Belf.*, PhD *Belf.*   Sr. Lectr.
Strain, Sean J. J., BSc *Belf.*, BAgr *Belf.*, PhD *Belf.*   Prof., Human Nutrition
Walsh, Colum, BSc *Trinity(Dub.)*, PhD *Uppsala*   Sr. Lectr.
Ward, Mary, BSc *Trinity(Dub.)*, PhD *Ulster*   Sr. Lectr.
Welch, Robert W., BSc *Wales*, PhD *Wales*   Sr. Lectr.
Other Staff: 45 Lectrs.; 2 Sr. Res. Fellows; 11 Res. Fellows
Research: bioimaging; biomedical genomics; cancer and ageing; diabetes; microbial biotechnology

Built Environment

Tel: (028) 9036 6310 Fax: (028) 9036 6816
Ali, Faris, BEng *Baghdad*, MSc *Odessa*, PhD *Odessa*   Sr. Lectr.
Berry, James N., BSc *Belf.*, PhD *Belf.*   Prof., Urban Planning and Property Development
Delichatsios, Michael, BSc *Athens*, MSc *M.I.T.*, PhD *M.I.T.*   Prof., Fire Dynamics
Gray, Patrick F., BSc *CNAA*, MSc *Ulster*   Sr. Lectr.
Gunning, Joseph G., BSc *Belf.*, MSc *Belf.*, PhD *Ulster*   Sr. Lectr.
Harvey, Harold D., BSc *Aston*, MSc *Aston*, PhD *Ulster*   Sr. Lectr.
Heaney, George, MSc *H-W*   Sr. Lectr.
Hewitt, Neil J., BSc *Ulster*, PhD *Ulster*   Prof., Energy
Hine, Julian, BSc *H-W*, PhD *H-W*   Prof., Transport
Lyness, John F., BSc *Wales*, MSc *Wales*, PhD *Wales*   Reader
McCluskey, William J., PhD *Ulster*   Reader
McGreal, Stanley, BSc *Belf.*, PhD *Belf.*   Prof., Property Research
McLernon, Timothy, BSc *CNAA*, MA *York(UK)*   Sr. Lectr.
Molkov, Vladimir, MSc *Moscow*, DSc *Moscow*   Prof., Fire Safety Science
Myers, W. Robert C., BA *Open(UK)*, BSc *Belf.*, PhD *Belf.*   Reader
Nadjai, Ali, BEng *Annaba*, MSc *H-W*, PhD *Sheff.*   Prof., Fire Structural Engineering
Novozhilov, Vasily, PhD *Moscow*   Prof., Fire Dynamics
Paris, Christopher T., BA *S'ton*, PhD *ANU*   Prof., Housing

Parsa, Ali, MPhil *Newcastle(UK)*, PhD *Newcastle(UK)*   Prof., Urban Planning and Business Development
Strong, Alan, BSc *Belf.*   Sr. Lectr.
Woodside, Alan R., MPhil *CNAA*, FICE   Prof., Highway Engineering
Woodward, David H., BSc *Ulster*, PhD *Ulster*, DPhil   Reader
Yohanis, Yigsaw G., BSc *Haile Sellassie I*, MSc *Belf.*, PhD *Ulster*   Sr. Lectr.
Other Staff: 43 Lectrs.; 6 Res. Fellows
Research: fire safety; property and planning; sustainable energy engineering; transport

Business Organisation and Management

Tel: (028) 9036 8844 Fax: (028) 9036 8459
E-mail: ml.mchugh@ulster.ac.uk
Boyle, Emily J., BA *Belf.*, PhD *Belf.*   Sr. Lectr.
Heaton, Norma, BSc *UMIST*, MSc *Lond.*   Sr. Lectr.
Humphreys, Paul K., MEng *Belf.*, MBA *Ulster*, PhD *Belf.*   Prof., Operations Management
McHugh, Marie L., BA *Belf.*, MSc *Belf.*, PhD *Ulster*   Prof., Organisational Behaviour; Head*
O'Neill, Edel, BA *Ulster*, MSc *Ulster*   Sr. Lectr.
Preston, J. Alan, BSc *Belf.*, PhD *Belf.*   Sr. Lectr.
Pyper, Ian F., BTech *Lough.*, MSc *CNAA*   Sr. Lectr.
Thompson, John E., BSc *Ulster*, MSc *Durh.*   Sr. Lectr.
Other Staff: 15 Lectrs.
Research: human resource management; operations management; organisational culture, behaviour and change; supply chain management; total quality management

Business, Retail and Financial Services

Tel: (028) 7032 4371 Fax: (028) 7032 4910
E-mail: b.quinn@ulster.ac.uk
Bond, Derek, BSc *Ulster*, MSc *Manc.*   Sr. Lectr.
Boyle, Marie-Therese, BSc *Belf.*   Sr. Lectr.
Glass, J. Colin, BSc *Belf.*, MSc *Lond.*   Prof., Applied Financial Economics
Hamill, Philip, BA *Ulster*, MSc *Ulster*, PhD *Ulster*   Prof., Finance
Ibbotson, Patrick, BSc *Belf.*, MSc *Belf.*, MBA *Ulster*, PhD *Belf.*   Sr. Lectr.
Quinn, Barry, BA *Ulster*, PhD *Ulster*   Sr. Lectr.; Head*
Scharf, W. Fred, BA *Lond.*, MA *Ulster*   Sr. Lectr.
Other Staff: 18 Lectrs.
Research: cost function analysis; e-business; financial market analysis; income distribution; international retailing

Communication

Tel: (028) 9036 6605 Fax: (028) 9036 8251
Dickson, David A., BA *Belf.*, MA *Ulster*, PhD *Ulster*   Sr. Lectr.
Hargie, Owen D. W., BA *Belf.*, PhD *Ulster*   Prof., Communication
Hazlett, Diane, BSc *Ulster*, MSc *Ulster*, PhD *Ulster*   Sr. Lectr.
Henry, Alison, BA *York(UK)*, PhD *Ulster*   Prof., Linguistics
Irving, Pauline, BSc *Belf.*, MSc *Belf.*, MSc *Stir.*, PhD *Ulster*   Sr. Lectr.
Other Staff: 14 Lectrs.
Research: corporate communication; interpersonal communication; language and communication; organisation communication; theoretical linguistics

Computing and Information Engineering

Tel: (028) 7032 4440 Fax: (028) 7032 4916
E-mail: dw.bustard@ulster.ac.uk
Bustard, David W., BSc *Belf.*, MSc *Belf.*, PhD *Belf.*   Prof., Computing Science; Head*
McClean, Sally I., BA *Oxf.*, MA *Oxf.*, MSc *Wales*, PhD *Ulster*   Prof., Mathematics
McKinney, Martin E. T., BSc *Belf.*, MSc *Belf.*   Sr. Lectr.
McNeill, Michael, BSc *Bath*, DPhil *Sus.*   Sr. Lectr.
McSherry, David M. G., BSc *Belf.*, MSc *Belf.*, PhD *Belf.*   Sr. Lectr.

Morrow, Phillip J., BSc Belf., MSc Belf., PhD Belf. Sr. Lectr.

Parr, Gerard P., BSc Ulster, PhD Ulster Prof., Telecommunications

Scotney, Bryan W., BSc Durh., PhD Reading Prof., Informatics

Other Staff: 12 Lectrs.

Research: data mining; knowledge discovery in databases; knowledge engineering; requirements definition; software engineering

Computing and Intelligent Systems

Tel: (028) 7137 5605 Fax: (028) 7137 5254
E-mail: tm.mcginnity@ulster.ac.uk

Curran, Kevin, BSc Ulster, PhD Ulster Sr. Lectr.

Lunney, Tom F., BSc Belf., PhD Belf. Sr. Lectr.

Maguire, Liam, MEng Belf., PhD Belf. Prof., Computational Intelligence; Head*

McGinnity, T. Martin, BSc Ulster, PhD Durh., FIEE Prof., Intelligent Systems

McKevitt, Paul, BSc N.U.I., MSc New Mexico State, MEd Sheff., PhD Exe. Prof., Digital Multimedia

Prasad, Girijesh, BTech Calc., MTech Roor., PhD Belf. Sr. Lectr.

Sayers, Heather, BA Ulster, MSc Ulster, PhD Ulster Sr. Lectr.

Woods, Derek N., BA Open(UK) Sr. Lectr.

Other Staff: 19 Lectrs.; 2 Teaching Fellows

Research: bio-inspired systems; computational intelligence; embedded systems; intelligent multimedia; intelligent systems

Computing and Mathematics

Tel: (028) 9036 6126 Fax: (028) 9036 6068
E-mail: hg.mcallister@ulster.ac.uk

Adamson, Kenny A., BSc Belf., PhD Ulster Reader

Anderson, Terry J., BA Belf., PhD Belf. Prof., Interactive Computing

Azuaje, Francisco J., BSc Simón Bolívar, PhD Ulster Reader

Copeland, Christopher J., BSc Belf., MSc Belf. Sr. Lectr.

Farahmand, Kambiz, BSc Natnl.Iran, MSc Lond., PhD Lond. Prof., Mathematics

Glass, Derrick, BSc Ulster, MSc S'ton. Sr. Lectr.

Hanna, J. R. Paul, BSc Belf., PhD Belf. Sr. Lectr.

Houston, S. Kenneth, BSc Belf., PhD Belf., FIMA Prof., Mathematical Studies

Hull, M. Elizabeth C., BSc Belf., PhD Belf., FBCS Prof., Computing Science

Lundy, Patrick J., BSc Ulster, MSc Belf., PhD Ulster Sr. Lectr.

McAllister, H. Gerry, BSc Belf., PhD Ulster Prof., Computer Science; Head*

McCullagh, Paul, BSc Belf., PhD Belf. Sr. Lectr.

McLarnon, R. Duncan, BSc Belf., BA Open(UK) Sr. Lectr.

McTear, Michael F., BA Belf., MA Essex, PhD Ulster Prof., Knowledge Engineering

Mulvenna, Maurice, BSc Ulster, MPhil Ulster Sr. Lectr.

Nugent, Christopher, BEng Ulster, PhD Ulster Reader

Patterson, W. R. David, BSc Belf., MSc Ulster, PhD Ulster Sr. Lectr.

Shapcott, C. Mary, BSc Monash, MSc Monash Sr. Lectr.

Sweeney, Patrick J., BSc Ulster, MSc Belf. Sr. Lectr.

Wallace, Jonathan, BA Ulster, MSc Ulster Sr. Lectr.

Wang, Hui, BSc Jilin, MSc Jilin, PhD Ulster Reader

Wilkie, F. George, BSc Belf., PhD Belf. Sr. Lectr.

Other Staff: 30 Lectrs.; 11 Res. Fellows

Research: artificial intelligence (AI); computer science education; human-computer interaction; medical informatics; natural language processing

Creative Arts

Tel: (028) 7137 5133 Fax: (028) 7137 5473
E-mail: d.hunter1@ulster.ac.uk

Hunter, Desmond M., MA N.U.I., PhD N.U.I., FRCO Prof., Music; Head*

Hutton, Anthony, BDes Natnl.Coll.Art & Des., Dublin, MEd Ulster Sr. Lectr.

Lyons, Frank, BMus Ulster, PhD Ulster Sr. Lectr.

Magee, Justin, BA Coventry Sr. Lectr.

Moore, Paul, BA Ulster, PhD Ulster Sr. Lectr.

Upton, Carol-Anne, BA Lond. Prof., Drama

Other Staff: 18 Lectrs.; 1 Teaching Fellow

Research: composition; ethnomusicology; Irish and Northern Irish theatre; musicology; performance and performance practice

Economics and Politics

Tel: (028) 9036 6339 Fax: (028) 9036 6847
E-mail: mcm.roulston@ulster.ac.uk

Aughey, Arthur H., BA Belf., PhD Ulster Prof., Politics

Borooah, Vani K., BA Bom., MA Bom., PhD S'ton. Prof., Applied Economics

Geary, Frank, BA Belf. Prof., Economic History

Hainsworth, Paul A., BA Liv., PhD Brist. Sr. Lectr.

Kula, Erhun I., BSc Istanbul, MSc Wales, PhD Leic. Sr. Lectr.

McGregor, Patrick P. L., BA Belf., PhD Edin. Sr. Lectr.

Osmani, Siddiq R., BA Dhaka, MA Islam., MSc Lond., PhD Lond. Prof., Development Economics

Patterson, Henry H., BA Belf. Prof., Politics

Roulston, M. Carmel M., BA Belf., MA Lond. Sr. Lectr.; Head*

Smyth, Michael F., BA N.U.I., MSc Belf. Sr. Lectr.

Thain, Colin, BA Manc., PhD Manc., FRSA Prof., Politics

Tridimas, George, BA Athens, MPhil Oxf., DPhil Oxf. Prof., Political Economy

Other Staff: 8 Lectrs.

Research: comparative economic policy making; development economics; ethnic conflict; politics of Northern Ireland and Irish Republic; regional development, racism

Education

Tel: (028) 7032 4719 Fax: (028) 7032 4918
E-mail: r.pritchard@ulster.ac.uk

Austin, Roger, BA Manc., PhD Manc. Sr. Lectr.

Bleakley, Walter E., BA Open(UK), MSc Ulster Sr. Lectr.

Burgess, Barry R., BMus Belf., MA Ulster Sr. Lectr.

Dallat, John P., BEd Leeds, MA Ulster, PhD N.U.I. Sr. Lectr.

Griffiths, Sandra, BEd Belf., MEd Bath Sr. Lectr.

McAleavy, Gerry J., BA Belf., MEd Belf., PhD Ulster Prof., Further and Higher Education

McNair, Victor, BEd Belf., PhD Ulster Sr. Lectr.

Pritchard, Rosalind M. O., BA Trinity(Dub.), MA Ulster, PhD Ulster Prof.; Head*

Smith, Alan, BSc Ulster, PhD Ulster UNESCO Prof., Education for Pluralism, Human Rights and Democracy

Wilson, Derick, MBE, BSc Belf., PhD Ulster Sr. Lectr.

Other Staff: 25 Lectrs.; 7 Res. Fellows

Research: education for pluralism and democracy; inclusive learning and social policy; information and communications technology (ICT) for enhancing learning; teacher professional development and school organisation

Engineering, Electrical and Mechanical

Tel: (028) 9036 6278 Fax: (028) 9036 6356
E-mail: rb.clarke@ulster.ac.uk

Akay, Mustafa, BSc UMIST, PhD UMIST Sr. Lectr.

Anderson, John McC., MPhil Ulster, PhD Ulster Prof., Biomedical Engineering

Brown, Desmond, BSc Belf., PhD Belf. Sr. Lectr.

Clarke, Robin, BSc Belf., PhD Ulster, FIMechE Prof., Mechanical Engineering; Head*

Katzen, Sidney J., BSc Belf., MSc Belf., PhD Ulster Sr. Lectr.

Laverty, Seamus J., BSc Belf. Sr. Lectr.

Maguire, Paul D., BSc Belf., PhD Belf. Prof., Plasmas and Nanofabrication

McAdams, Eric T., BSc Ulster, MSc Ulster, PhD Leeds Prof., Bioengineering

McKeag, Denis, BSc Strath., PhD Belf. Prof., Product Development

McKeown, Robert, BSc Ulster Sr. Lectr.

McLaughlin, James A., BSc Ulster, PhD Ulster Prof., Advanced Functional Materials

Meenan, Brian, BSc Ulster, MSc Ulster, PhD Ulster Prof., Biomedical Materials

Owens, Frank J., BSc Belf., PhD Belf. Sr. Lectr.

Papakonstantinou, Pagona, BSc Salonika, MSc Belf., PhD Belf. Reader

Webb, J. Alan C., BSc Belf., PhD Belf. Sr. Lectr.

Other Staff: 22 Lectrs.

Research: bio-engineering; engineering design; manufacturing; nanotechnology; structural and functional materials

Environmental Sciences

Tel: (028) 7032 4428 Fax: (028) 7032 4911
E-mail: p,jordan@ulster.ac.uk

Breen, Colin, BA N.U.I., MPhil St And., PhD N.U.I. Sr. Lectr.

Cooper, Alan, BSc Wales, PhD Wales Sr. Lectr.

Cooper, Andrew, BSc Belf., MSc Natal, PhD Natal Prof., Coastal Studies

Day, Keith R., BSc Reading, MSc Lond., PhD Lond. Prof.

Eastwood, David A., BA Camb., MA Camb., PhD Camb., FLS Prof., Environmental Studies

Graham, Brian, BA Belf., PhD Belf. Prof., Geography

Griffiths, David, BSc Wales, PhD Wales Reader

Guyer, Claire, BSc E.Anglia, MA Wat. Sr. Lectr.

Jackson, Derek W., BSc Ulster, PhD Ulster Sr. Lectr.

Jordan, Philip, BSc Leeds, PhD Ulster Sr. Lectr.; Head*

McCabe, A. Marshall, BA Trinity(Dub.), PhD Trinity(Dub.), ScD Trinity(Dub.) Prof., Quaternary Science

McCloskey, John, BSc Belf., PhD Ulster Prof., Geophysics

Moore, Adrian, BSc Ulster, MSc Ulster, PhD Ulster Prof., Geographic Information Science

Poole, Michael, BA Nott., PhD Belf. Sr. Lectr.

Quinn, Rory, BSc N.U.I., MSc Durh., PhD S'ton. Sr. Lectr.

Rippey, Brian, BSc Belf., MSc Lond., PhD Ulster Reader

Rushton, Brian S., BSc Birm., DPhil York(UK) Prof., Botany

Steacy, Sandy, BS N.Carolina, PhD S.Calif. Reader

Wilson, Peter, BA Ulster, PhD Salf. Reader

Other Staff: 14 Lectrs.

Research: environmental science; geography; geophysics; marine archaeology; marine science

Health Sciences

Tel: (028) 9036 8418 Fax: (028) 9036 8419
E-mail: r.rogers@ulster.ac.uk

Bishop, Ronald H., BSc Lond., MSc Lond., PhD Lond. Sr. Lectr.

Bradley, Judy, BSc Ulster, PhD Ulster Sr. Lectr.

Byers, William, BSc Manc., PhD Manc., FRSChem Sr. Lectr.

Lennon-Fraser, Sheila, BSc Montr., MSc Lond., PhD Ulster Sr. Lectr.

Lowe-Strong, Andrea, BSc Ulster, PhD Ulster Sr. Lectr.

McClure, Patricia, BSc Ulster, MSc Ulster Sr. Lectr.

McDonough, Suzanne M., BPhysiotherapy N.U.I., PhD Newcastle(UK) Prof., Health and Rehabilitation

McDowell, David, PhD CNAA Prof., Food Studies

McIntyre, Irene, MSc Ulster Sr. Lectr.

Patterson, Aileen M., BA Open(UK), MSc Ulster Sr. Lectr.

Porter-Armstrong, Alison, BSc Ulster, PhD Ulster Sr. Lectr.

Thompson, Nuala, MSc Ulster Sr. Lectr.

Walsh, Deirdre, BPhysiotherapy N.U.I., PhD Ulster Prof., Rehabilitation Research

Winder, John, BSc Ulster, MSc Wales, PhD Ulster Sr. Lectr.

Other Staff: 62 Lectrs.

Research: cardiopulmonary and neurological rehabilitation; care-givers and community interventions; electrotherapy and complementary medicine; musculoskeletal and low back pain; pressure care

History and International Affairs

Tel: (028) 9032 4474 Fax: (028) 7032 4952
E-mail: t.okeeffe@ulster.ac.uk
Arthur, Paul J., BA Belf., MSSc Belf.   Prof., Politics
Blackstock, A. F., BA Belf., PhD Belf.   Reader
Crooke, Elizabeth, BA Trinity(Dub.), MPhil Camb., PhD Camb.   Sr. Lectr.
Emmerson, W. Anthony, BA Belf.   Sr. Lectr.
Garnham, Neal, BA Ulster, PhD Ulster   Sr. Lectr.
Hart, William, MA Glas., PhD Edin.   Sr. Lectr.; Head*
Jones, Greta J., BA Lond., PhD Lond., FRHistS   Prof., Social and Intellectual History
Kirby, Dianne, BA Hull, PhD Hull   Sr. Lectr.
Larres, K. W., BA Cologne, MA Cologne, PhD Cologne   Prof.
Loughlin, James P., BA CNAA, PhD Trinity(Dub.)   Reader
MacRaild, Donald M., BA Liv., PhD Sheff., FRHistS   Prof., History
O'Brien, M. Gerald R., MA N.U.I., PhD Camb.   Reader
O'Connor, P. Emmet J., MA N.U.I., PhD Camb.   Sr. Lectr.
Ryan, Stephen, BA Keele, PhD Lond.   Sr. Lectr.
Other Staff: 8 Lectrs.

Research: conflict management; contemporary history; ethnic conflict; Irish history and politics; social history

Hospitality and Tourism Management

Tel: (028) 7032 3999 Fax: (028) 7032 3997
E-mail: ae.murray@ulster.ac.uk
Boyd, Stephen, BA Belf., MA Regina, PhD W.Ont.   Prof., Tourism
Campbell, Lucia, MBA S.Bank   Sr. Lectr.
Fawcett, S. Lyn, BSc Sur.   Sr. Lectr.
McKenna-Black, Margaret A., BA CNAA, MSc Ulster   Sr. Lectr.
Murray, Agnes, BA Open(UK), MA Ulster   Sr. Lectr.
Murray, Anna E., BA Ulster, MBA Ulster   Prof., Hospitality Management; Head*
Quinn, Ursula M., BA Ulster, MPhil Ulster   Sr. Lectr.
Strugnell, Christopher, BSc Belf., PhD Belf., FRSA   Sr. Lectr.
Other Staff: 19 Lectrs.

Research: consumer studies; hospitality management; tourism management

International Business

Tel: (028) 7137 5321 Fax: (028) 7137 5323
E-mail: md.oreilly@ulster.ac.uk
Bell, James D., MA St And., MBA Belf., PhD Strath.   Prof., International Business Entrepreneurship
McCurry, Larry, BA Ulster, MBA Ulster   Sr. Lectr.
McIvor, Ronan, BA Ulster, MSc Ulster, PhD Ulster   Prof., Operations Management
O'Reilly, M. Dolores, BEd Belf., MA Ulster, PhD Sur.   Prof., International Business Strategy; Head*
Ward, John D., BA Lond., FCA   Prof., Taxation
Other Staff: 16 Lectrs.

Research: e-business; international business; marketing; small to medium-sized enterprises; taxation

Languages and Literature

Tel: (028) 7032 4636 Fax: (028) 7032 4962
E-mail: j.gillespie@ulster.ac.uk
Black, Stanley, BA Belf., PhD Belf.   Sr. Lectr.
Bradford, Richard W., BA Wales, DPhil Oxf.   Prof., Literary History and Theory
Connor, Ian D., MA E.Anglia, PhD E.Anglia   Sr. Lectr.
Davies, Paul, BA Camb., PhD Reading   Reader
Gargett, Graham, BA Reading, PhD Reading   Prof., French Culture and Ideas

Gillespie, John M., BA Belf., PhD Belf.   Prof., French Literature; Head*
Hughes, Art, BA Belf., MA Belf., MèsL Rennes, PhD Belf.   Sr. Lectr.
Jedrzejewski, Jan, MA Lodz, DPhil Oxf.   Prof., English and Comparative Literature
Kennedy-Andrews, Elmer, BA Belf., MA Belf., PhD Belf.   Prof., English
Kockel, Ullrich, BA Leeds, PhD Liv.   Prof., Ethnology and Folklife
Lazenbatt, William, BA Belf., PhD Belf.   Sr. Lectr.
Lillie, Elizabeth M., MA Trinity(Dub.), PhD Trinity(Dub.)   Prof., Language Learning and Teaching
Macklin, Gerald M., BA Belf., PhD Belf.   Sr. Lectr.
MacMathuna, Seamus, BA Belf., PhD Belf.   Prof., Irish
McKee, Jane, MA Trinity(Dub.), PhD Trinity(Dub.)   Sr. Lectr.
McMinn, Joseph M., MA N.U.I., PhD N.U.I.   Prof., Anglo-Irish Literature
Nic Craith, Máiréad, BA N.U.I., MA N.U.I., PhD N.U.I.   Prof., Irish Culture and Language
Ó'Corráin, Ailbhe, BA Belf., PhD Belf.   Prof., Modern Irish
Ò'Dochartaigh, Pól, BA Wales, BA Ulster, PhD Nott.   Prof., German
Ò'Murchú, Micheál, BA Belf., MPhil Ulster   Sr. Lectr.
Toner, Greg, BA Belf., MSc Belf., PhD Belf.   Prof., Irish Language and Literature
Other Staff: 34 Lectrs.

Research: English literature; French language, literature and history of ideas; German history and literature; Irish and Celtic language and literature; Irish cultural heritages

Law

Tel: (028) 9036 6346 Fax: (028) 9036 6847
E-mail: i.topping@ulster.ac.uk
Bell, Christine, BA Camb., LLM Harv.   Prof., International Law
Campbell, Colm, BCL N.U.I., PhD Belf.   Prof.
Castellino, Joshua, BComm Bom., MA Hull, PhD Hull   Prof.
Hegarty, Angela, LLB Belf., LLM Belf.   Sr. Lectr.; Head*
Iyer, Venkat, BSc Bom., LLB Bom., LLM Bom., LLM Belf., PhD Belf.   Sr. Lectr.
Kretzmer, David, LLB Jerusalem, LLM Jerusalem, JD York(Can.)   Prof.
Maxwell, Patricia, LLB Brist., LLM Belf.   Sr. Lectr.
Ní Aoláin, Fionnuala, LLB Belf., LLM Col., PhD Belf., JD Col.   Prof.
Topping, Ivan, LLB Belf., LLM Belf.   Sr. Lectr.
White, Ciaran, BCL N.U.I., LLM Belf.   Sr. Lectr.
Zacharopoulou, Amanda, LLB Belf., LLM Belf.   Sr. Lectr.
Other Staff: 10 Lectrs.

Research: emergency law and security; equality and socio-economic rights; medical law; peace processes; transitional justice and human rights

Marketing, Entrepreneurship and Strategy

Tel: (028) 9036 8992 Fax: (028) 9036 8146
E-mail: r.mcadam@ulster.ac.uk
Armstrong, Gillian, BA Ulster, PhD Ulster   Sr. Lectr.
Brown, Stephen, BA Belf., PhD Belf.   Prof., Marketing Research
Carson, David J., MBA Belf., PhD N.U.I.   Prof., Marketing
Farley, Heather, BA Ulster, MBA Ulster   Sr. Lectr.
Gilmore, Audrey, MA Ulster, PhD Ulster   Prof., Services Marketing
McAdam, Rodney, BSc Belf., MA Lanc., PhD Belf., PhD Ulster   Prof., Innovation Management; Head*
McMahon-Beattie, Una, BA Ulster, PhD Belf.   Sr. Lectr.
McNamee, Patrick B., BSc Belf., MPhil CNAA   Prof., International Business

O'Neill, Kenneth E., BSc Belf., Hon. DSc Natnl.& World Econ., Sofia   Prof., Entrepreneurship and Small Business Development
Stewart, Kate M., BA Ulster, PhD N.U.I.   Sr. Lectr.
Other Staff: 9 Lectrs.

Research: business improvement; small business entrepreneurship; web-based marketing

Media, Film and Journalism

Tel: (028) 7032 4176 Fax: (028) 7032 4925
E-mail: sj.edge@ulster.ac.uk
Edge, Sarah, BA Portsmouth, PhD Ulster   Sr. Lectr.; Head*
Ekins, Richard J., LLB Lond., PhD Chic.   Prof., Sociology and Cultural Studies
McLaughlin, Cahal, MA Lond., PhD Lond.   Sr. Lectr.
McLaughlin, Gregory, BA Ulster, PhD Glas.   Sr. Lectr.
McLoone, J. Martin, BA Trinity(Dub.), PhD Ulster   Prof., Media Studies
Messenger-Davies, Maire, BA Trinity(Dub.), PhD E.Lond.   Prof., Media Studies
Rossiter, Ned, BA E.Cowan, PhD E.Cowan   Sr. Lectr.
Willemen, Paul, PhD Middx.   Prof., Media Studies
Zdravkovic, Vladan, BA Belgrade, MA Belgrade, MSc Belgrade, PhD Belgrade   Reader
Other Staff: 11 Staff Members

Research: documentary, journalism and conflict reporting; film and television history; national cinema, television and cultural identity; photography, new media and digital cultures

Nursing

Tel: (028) 9036 8386 Fax: (028) 9036 8202
E-mail: o.barr@ulster.ac.uk
Barr, Owen G., BSc Ulster, MSc Ulster, PhD Ulster   Sr. Lectr.; Head*
Boore, Jennifer R. P., OBE, BSc Sur., PhD Manc.   Prof.
Coates, Vivien, BSc Newcastle(UK), MPhil Hull, PhD Ulster   Prof., Nursing Research
Curran, Carol, BSc Ulster, MSc Ulster, PhD Ulster   Prof.
Deeny, Patrick, BSc Ulster   Sr. Lectr.
Dolk, Helen, BA Oxf., PhD Louvain   Prof., Epidemiology
Fitzsimons, Donna, BSc Ulster, PhD Ulster   Reader
Fleming, Paul, BEd Belf., MSc Leeds Met., PhD Ulster   Sr. Lectr.
Hasson, Felicity, BA Ulster, MSc Ulster   Sr. Lectr.
Keeney, Sinead, BA Ulster, MRes Ulster, PhD Ulster   Sr. Lectr.
Kernohan, George, BSc CNAA, PhD Belf.   Prof., Health Science Research
Kirby, Carol, BSc Ulster   Sr. Lectr.
McCance, Tanya, BSc Ulster, MSc Ulster, PhD Ulster   Prof., Nursing Research and Practice Development
McConkey, Roy A., BA Belf., PhD Manc.   Prof., Learning Disability
McCormack, Brendan, DPhil Oxf.   Prof., Gerontological Nursing
Melby, Vidar, BSc Ulster, PhD Ulster   Sr. Lectr.
Parahoo, Kader, BSc CNAA, PhD Keele   Prof., Nursing Research
Poulton, Brenda, PhD Sheff.   Prof., Community Health Nursing
Sinclair, Marlene, BSc Ulster, PhD Belf.   Prof., Midwifery Research
Slevin, Eamonn, BSc Ulster, DNursSc Ulster   Reader
Other Staff: 81 Lectrs.; 3 Res. Fellows

Research: chronic illness; disaster relief nursing; health informatics; learning disabilities; multidisciplinary primary and community care

Policy Studies

Tel: (028) 7131 5203 Fax: (028) 7137 5286
E-mail: p.carmichael@ulster.ac.uk
Birrell, W. Derek, BSc Belf.   Prof., Social Administration and Policy

Carmichael, Paul, BA CNAA, PhD Strath. Prof., Government; Head*
Carswell, Leslie A., BSc Belf., MBA Ulster Sr. Lectr.
Erridge, Andrew F., BA Sus., MSc Lond. Prof., Public Policy and Management
Fee, Ruth, LLB Belf., MPhil Ulster Sr. Lectr.
Gray, Ann, BSc Ulster, PhD Ulster Sr. Lectr.
Heenan, Deirdre, BA Ulster, PhD Ulster Prof., Social Policy
Knox, Colin G., BA Ulster, MSc Lough., MSc Ulster, PhD Belf. Prof., Comparative Public Policy
Marnoch, Gordon, MA Aberd., PhD Hull Reader
O'Connor, Julia S., BSocSc N.U.I., MSocSc N.U.I., PhD Tor. Prof., Social Policy
Offer, John, BSc Keele, PhD Keele Prof., Social Theory and Policy
Osborne, Robert D., BA Belf., PhD Belf. Prof., Applied Policy Studies
Williamson, Arthur P., BA Trinity(Dub.), MLitt Trinity(Dub.), PhD Trinity(Dub.), MA Prof., Non-Profit Research
Other Staff: 6 Lectrs.; 2 Res. Fellows
Research: conflict resolution and community relations; education policy; equality and social inclusion; governance and devolution; voluntary action

Psychology

Tel: (028) 7032 4326 Fax: (028) 7032 4897
E-mail: r.wilson1@ulster.ac.uk
Adamson, Gary, BSc Ulster, PhD Ulster Sr. Lectr.
Bunting, Brendan, BSc Ulster, PhD Ulster Prof.
Cairns, S. E., BSc Belf., PhD Belf. Prof., Social Psychology
Giles, Melanie, BSc Ulster, MSc Sheff., PhD Ulster Sr. Lectr.
Harrison, Simon, BA McG., PhD ANU Reader
Keenan, Michael, BSc Ulster, PhD Ulster Sr. Lectr.
Leslie, Julian C. L., BA Oxf., MA Oxf., DPhil Oxf. Prof., Behavioural Psychology
Lewis, Christopher, BSc Ulster, PhD Ulster Reader
Liddell, Christine, BA Natal, PhD Lond. Prof.
Rae, Gordon, BSc Glas., PhD Aberd. Prof., Mathematical Psychology
Reinhardt-Rutland, Anthony, BSc Edin., PhD Ulster Reader
Shevlin, Mark, BSc Ulster, PhD Ulster Reader
Stringer, Maurice, BSc Ulster, PhD Ulster Prof., Social Psychology
Wilson, Ronnie, BSc Ulster, PhD Sheff. Prof.; Head*
Woodward, Roger J., BA Wales, MSc Stir. Sr. Lectr.
Other Staff: 23 Lectrs.; 3 Res. Assocs.
Research: applied behavioural analysis; peace and conflict; psychobiology and neuropsychology; psychology of health and illness; socialisation and child development

Sociology and Applied Social Studies

Tel: (028) 7137 5229 Fax: (028) 7137 5627
E-mail: ms.mccolgan@ulster.ac.uk
Campbell, Hugh, BA Belf., MA Belf. Sr. Lectr.
Griffiths, W. Huw, BA CNAA, MSc Wales Sr. Lectr.
Lundy, Patricia, BA Belf., PhD Belf. Sr. Lectr.
McColgan, Mary, BSc Belf., MSc Belf. Sr. Lectr.; Head*
McCready, Sam, BA Belf., MEd Manc. Sr. Lectr.
Rolston, William J., BSc Belf., PhD Belf. Prof., Sociology
Taylor, Brian J., BSc Brist., PhD Belf. Sr. Lectr.
Other Staff: 32 Lectrs.
Research: community conflict and social exclusion; community, youth and women's studies; comparative and historical sociology; identity, gender, ethnicity and social inequality; user perspectives and evidence-based practice in social work

Sports Studies

Tel: (028) 9036 8177 Fax: (028) 9036 6028
E-mail: mh.murphy@ulster.ac.uk
Brennan, Deirdre, BA Ulster, MA Ulster, PhD Ulster Sr. Lectr.
Darby, Paul, BA Ulster, PhD Ulster Sr. Lectr.
Davison, Gareth, BA Ulster, MSc Ulster, PhD Glam. Sr. Lectr.
Hassan, David, BA Ulster, MSc Ulster, PhD Ulster Sr. Lectr.
Murphy, Marie, BA Ulster, MSc Lough., PhD Lough. Sr. Lectr.; Head*
Wallace, Eric, BEd Belf., MA Calif., PhD Ulster Reader
Other Staff: 10 Lectrs.
Research: exercise and health; social science of sport; sports and exercise physiology; sports biomechanics

SPECIAL CENTRES, ETC

Access and Distributed Learning

Tel: (028) 9036 8027 Fax: (028) 9036 8634
Alexander, Sylvia, BSc Belf., MSc Ulster Dir.*

Art and Design Research Institute

Tel: (028) 9026 7258
Mey, Kerstin, MA Humboldt, PhD Humboldt Prof.; Dir.*

Biomedical Sciences Research Institute

Tel: (028) 7032 4121
Bjourson, Anthony, MSc Ulster, PhD Belf. Prof.; Dir.*

Built Environment Research Institute

Tel: (028) 9036 6566
McGreal, Stanley, BSc Belf., PhD Belf. Prof.; Dir.*

Business and Management Research Institute

Tel: (028) 9036 8410
Humphreys, Paul K., MEng Belf., MBA Ulster, PhD Belf. Prof.; Dir.*

Business Institute

Tel: (028) 9036 6417 Fax: (028) 9036 6843
McCoy, Jackie, BA Ulster, MA Lanc. Prof.; Head*

Computer Science Research Institute

Tel: (028) 7032 4648
Scotney, Bryan W., BSc Durh., PhD Reading Prof.; Dir.*

Environmental Science Research Institute

Tel: (028) 7032 4447
Day, Keith R., BSc Reading, MSc Lond., PhD Lond. Prof.; Dir.*

Health and Rehabilitation Sciences Research Institute

Tel: (028) 9036 6840
Winder, John, BSc Ulster, MSc Wales, PhD Ulster Sr. Lectr.; Dir.*

Humanities Research Institute

Tel: (028) 7032 4111
Ó'Dochartaigh, Pól, BA Wales, BA Ulster, PhD Nott. Prof.; Dir.*

International Conflict Research Centre (INCORE)

(Joint initiative with United Nations University)
Tel: (028) 7137 5500 Fax: (028) 7137 5510
Robinson, Gillian, BSocSc N.U.I., MSc Ulster, PhD Ulster Prof.; Dir.*

Irish and Celtic Research Institute

Tel: (028) 7032 4557
MacMathuna, Seamus, BA Belf., PhD Belf. Prof.; Dir.*

Irish Cultural Heritages, Academy for

Tel: (028) 7137 5519
Nic Craith, Máiréad, BA N.U.I., MA N.U.I., PhD N.U.I. Prof.; Dir.*

Media Research, Centre for

Tel: (028) 7032 4069
Messenger-Davies, Maire, BA Trinity(Dub.), PhD E.Lond. Prof.; Dir.*

Nanotechnology and Advanced Materials Institute

Tel: (028) 9036 8933
McLaughlin, James A., BSc Ulster, PhD Ulster Prof.; Dir.*

Nursing Research, Institute of

Tel: (028) 7032 4623
Parahoo, Kader, BSc CNAA, PhD Keele Prof.; Dir.*

Psychology Research Institute

Tel: (028) 7032 4693
Stringer, Maurice, BSc Ulster, PhD Ulster Prof., Social Psychology; Dir.*

Social and Policy Research Institute

Tel: (028) 9036 6159
Osbourne, Robert, BA Belf., PhD Belf. Prof.; Dir.*

Sport and Exercise Sciences Research Institute

Tel: (028) 9036 6535
Wallace, Eric, BEd Belf., MA Calif., PhD Ulster Reader; Dir.*

Transitional Justice Institute

Tel: (028) 7137 5333
Bell, Christine, BA Camb., LLM Harv. Prof., International Law; Dir.*
Campbell, Colm, BCL N.U.I., PhD Belf. Prof.; Assoc. Dir.
Ní Aoláin, Fionnuala, LLB Belf., LLM Col., PhD Belf., JD Col. Prof.; Dir.*

CONTACT OFFICERS

Academic affairs. Pro-Vice-Chancellor (Academic Development and Student Services): Black, Prof. Norman D., BSc Belf., PhD Belf. (E-mail: nd.black@ulster.ac.uk)
Admissions (higher degree). (Taught Programmes) Director of Student Marketing: Durkin, Mark, MA Ulster, PhD Lough. (E-mail: mg.durkin@ulster.ac.uk)
Admissions (higher degree). (Research programmes) Pro-Vice-Chancellor (Research and Innovation): Hannigan, Prof. Bernadette M., BA Trinity(Dub.), PhD N.U.I. (E-mail: bm.hannigan@ulster.ac.uk)
Adult/continuing education. Director, Access and Distributed Learning: Alexander, Sylvia, BSc Belf., MSc Ulster (E-mail: s.alexander@ulster.ac.uk)
Alumni. Director of Communication and Development: Taggart, Noreen, BA Belf. (E-mail: ner.taggart@ulster.ac.uk)
Computing services. Director of Information Services: Macartney, Nigel S., BA Camb., MA Camb., FRSA (E-mail: n.macartney@ulster.ac.uk)
Estates and buildings/works and services. Director of Physical Resources: Donnelly, Paddy (E-mail: ppg.donnelly@ulster.ac.uk)
Finance. Director of Finance: Hope, Peter W., BA Stir., MBA Ulster, FCA (E-mail: pw.hope@ulster.ac.uk)
Industrial liaison. Pro-Vice-Chancellor (Research and Innovation): Hannigan, Prof. Bernadette M., BA Trinity(Dub.), PhD N.U.I. (E-mail: bm.hannigan@ulster.ac.uk)
International office. Head, International Office: Reilly, Joan, BA CNAA (E-mail: e.j.reilly@ulster.ac.uk)
Library (enquiries). Director of Information Services: Macartney, Nigel S., BA Camb., MA Camb., FRSA (E-mail: n.macartney@ulster.ac.uk)
Personnel/human resources. Director of Human Resources: Magee, Ronnie, BA Wales (E-mail: r.magee@ulster.ac.uk)
Public relations. Director of Communication and Development: Taggart, Noreen, BA Belf. (E-mail: ner.taggart@ulster.ac.uk)

Quality assurance and accreditation. Pro-Vice-Chancellor (Teaching and Learning): McAlister, Prof. Denise A., BSc *Belf.*, MSc *Salf.* (E-mail: da.mcalister@ulster.ac.uk)

Research. Pro-Vice-Chancellor (Research and Innovation): Hannigan, Prof. Bernadette M., BA *Trinity(Dub.)*, PhD *N.U.I.* (E-mail: bm.hannigan@ulster.ac.uk)

Schools liaison. Head of Student Recruitment: Barnhill, Tony, BSc *Ulster*, PhD *Ulster* (E-mail: sda.barnhill@ulster.ac.uk)

Sport and recreation. Director (Sports Development and Services): Dobson, Nigel, BSc *Lough.*, PhD *Sheff.Hallam* (E-mail: n.dobson@ulster.ac.uk)

Strategic planning. Director, Corporate Planning and Governance Services: Aston, Irene, BSc *Belf.* (E-mail: ii.aston@ulster.ac.uk)

Student welfare/counselling. Pro-Vice-Chancellor (Academic Development and Student Services): Black, Prof. Norman D., BSc *Belf.*, PhD *Belf.* (E-mail: nd.black@ulster.ac.uk)

Student welfare/counselling. Pro-Vice-Chancellor (Communication and Institutional Development): Allen, Prof. James M., BSc *Belf.*, PhD *Belf.*, FIBiol (E-mail: jm.allen@ulster.ac.uk)

CAMPUS/COLLEGE HEADS

Belfast Campus, York Street, Belfast, County Antrim, Northern Ireland BT15 1ED. (Tel: (028) 9036 7330; Fax: (028) 9036 7339; E-mail: wm.clarke@ulster.ac.uk) Provost: Clarke, Prof. William C., BSc *Belf.*, MSc *Reading*

Coleraine Campus, Cromore Road, Coleraine, County Londonderry, Northern Ireland BT52 1SA. (Tel: (028) 7032 4300; Fax: (028) 7032 4936;

E-mail: aj.sharp@ulster.ac.uk) Provost: Sharp, Prof. Alan J., BA *Nott.*, PhD *Nott.*, FRHistS

Jordanstown Campus, Shore Road, Newtownabbey, County Antrim, Northern Ireland BT37 OQB. (Tel: (028) 9036 6533; Fax: (028) 9036 6827; E-mail: wm.clarke@ulster.ac.uk) Provost: Clarke, Prof. William C., BSc *Belf.*, MSc *Reading*

Magee Campus, Northlands Road, Londonderry, County Londonderry, Northern Ireland BT48 7JL. (Tel: (028) 7137 5268; Fax: (028) 7137 5631; E-mail: jm.allen@ulster.ac.uk) Provost: Allen, Prof. James M., BSc *Belf.*, PhD *Belf.*, FIBiol

[Information supplied by the institution as at 11 October 2007, and edited by the ACU]

UNIVERSITY OF WALES

Founded 1893

Member of the Association of Commonwealth Universities

Postal Address: University Registry, Cathays Park, Cardiff, Wales CF10 3NS
Telephone: (029) 2037 6999 **Fax:** (029) 2037 6980 **E-mail:** uniwales@wales.ac.uk
URL: http://www.wales.ac.uk

VICE-CHANCELLOR AND CHIEF EXECUTIVE*—Clement, Prof. Marc, BSc *Wales*, PhD *Wales*, FIETE
DIRECTOR OF RESOURCES—George, D. Ian, BScEcon *Wales*

GENERAL INFORMATION

History. The university was founded as a federal institution in 1893, bringing together three existing colleges: University College of Wales, Aberystwyth; University College of South Wales and Monmouthshire; and University College of North Wales in Bangor, and eventually comprising ten member institutions. Since September 2007 the university has ceased to be federal in nature, instead accrediting nine university institutions within Wales to award degrees.

The registry is located in the centre of Cardiff.

Admission to first degree courses (see also United Kingdom Introduction). All applications for admission should be referred to the individual institutions where study is to be undertaken.

First Degrees (* = with honours). BA*, BArch, BD*, BD*, BDS*, BEd*, BEng*, BMedSc*, BMid*, BMus*, BN*, BSc*, BScEcon*, BSD, BTh*, LLB*, MB BCh, MChem*, MEng*, MESci*, MMath*, MPhys*.

Most courses are modular and normally last 3 years full-time.

Higher Degrees.
Master's. LLM, LLM(Res), MA, MBA, MBL, MCh, MEd, MEnvSci, MFA, MMarSc, MMin, MMus, MPH, MPharm, MPhil, MRes, MSc, MScEcon, MTh.

Admission. Applications for admission to master's degrees must be of graduate equivalence as recognised by the university.

Doctoral. DBA, DBMS, DClinPsy, DCompSci, DCounsSci, DD, DDS, DDSc, DEdPsy, DLitt, DMin, DMus, DNursSci, DSc, DScEcon, DTourism, EdD, EngD, LLD, MD, PhD.

Admission. Applicants for admission to DBA, DBMS, DClinPsy, DCompSci, DCounsSci, DEdPsy, DMin, DNursSci, DTourism, EdD, EngD, PhD should have an appropriate first or master's degree. DD, DDSc, DLitt, DMus, DSc, DScEcon, LLD: awarded on published work.

Language of Instruction. English and, for some degrees, Welsh.

Academic Awards (2006–2007). 57 awards ranging in value from £25 to £23,002.

Income (2006–2007). Total, £9,400,000.

Statistics. Staff (2005–2006): 125 (65 academic, 60 non-academic).

ACADEMIC UNITS

Advanced Welsh and Celtic Studies, Centre for

At Aberystwyth

Tel: (01970) 631000 Fax: (01970) 639090
E-mail: cawcs@wales.ac.uk
Gruffydd, R. G., BA *Wales*, DPhil *Oxf.*, Hon. DLitt *Wales*, FBA   Prof. Emer.; Hon. Sr. Fellow
Jenkins, Geraint H., BA *Wales*, PhD *Wales*, DLitt *Wales*, FBA   Prof.; Dir.*
Other Staff: 1 Prof.; 1 Reader; 2 Sr. Fellows; 8 Res. Fellows; 1 Hon. Sr. Fellow; 1 Hon. Res. Fellow; 5 Hon. Fellows
Research: etymology and history of the Welsh language; language, literature and history of Celtic countries; mediaeval Welsh poetry; modern social history of Welsh language; Welsh place names

CONTACT OFFICERS

Academic affairs. Head of Academic Office: McInally, John H., BA *Wales*, MA *Birm.* (E-mail: academic@wales.ac.uk)

Computing services. Head, Administrative Computing Unit: Parry, Owen D., BSc *Sur.*, PhD *CNAA*

Estates and buildings/works and services. Director of Resources: George, D. Ian, BScEcon *Wales*

Examinations. Administrative Assistant (Records): Plumb, James I. R., BA *Wales* (E-mail: academic@wales.ac.uk)

Finance. Director of Resources: George, D. Ian, BScEcon *Wales*

General enquiries. Public Relations Officer: Childs, Jennifer, BA *Wales*

Personnel/human resources. Personnel and Training Officer: Cuthbert, Karin

Public relations. Public Relations Officer: Childs, Jennifer, BA *Wales*

Scholarships, awards, loans. Administrative Assistant (Scholarships and Awards): Plumb, James I. R., BA *Wales* (E-mail: awards@wales.ac.uk)

Staff development and training. Personnel and Training Officer: Cuthbert, Karin

University press. Director (University Press): Drake, Ashley, BA *Wales* (E-mail: press@press.wales.ac.uk)

[Information supplied by the institution as at 28 September 2007, and edited by the ACU]

UNIVERSITY OF WALES, LAMPETER

Founded 1822

Postal Address: Lampeter, Ceredigion, Wales SA48 7ED
Telephone: (01570) 422351 **Fax:** (01570) 423423 **E-mail:** t.roderick@lamp.ac.uk
URL: http://www.lamp.ac.uk

VICE-CHANCELLOR*—Pearce, Prof. Robert A., BCL Oxf., MA Oxf., Hon. LLD Buckingham
PRO-VICE-CHANCELLOR—Burnham, B. C., MA Camb., PhD Camb., FSA
REGISTRAR AND SECRETARY‡—Roderick, Thomas D., BA Lond., PhD Lond.
DIRECTOR OF FINANCE AND RESOURCES—Tobias, G., BA Glam.

GENERAL INFORMATION

History. The university was founded in 1822 as St David's College, and joined the University of Wales in 1971 as St David's University College. It gained its current name in 1996.

The university is located in the town of Lampeter, 25 miles south of Aberystwyth.

Admission to first degree courses (see also United Kingdom Introduction). Through Universities and Colleges Admissions Service (UCAS).

First Degrees (see also United Kingdom Directory to Subjects of Study). BA, BD, BTh.
Length of course. Full-time: BA, BD, BTh: 3 years. Part-time: BA, BD, BTh: 6–10 years. By distance learning: BA, BD, BTh: 6–10 years.

Higher Degrees (see also United Kingdom Directory to Subjects of Study).
Master's. MA, MPhil, MTh.
Length of course. Full-time: MA, MTh: 1 year; MPhil: 1–2 years. Part-time: MA, MTh: 2 years; MPhil: 2–4 years. By distance learning: MA, MTh: 2 years; MPhil: 2–4 years.
Doctoral. PhD.
Length of course. Full-time: PhD: 3 years. Part-time: PhD: 3–6 years. By distance learning: PhD: 3–6 years.

Language of Instruction. English, except in department of Welsh, where Welsh is the main language. Students may write exams in Welsh.

Libraries. Volumes: 215,000. Periodicals subscribed to: 1000. Special collections: Founders' library (pre-nineteenth-century).

FACULTIES/SCHOOLS

Humanities and Social Sciences, School of
Tel: (01570) 424962 Fax: (01570) 424987
E-mail: a.gardner@lamp.ac.uk
Head: O'Loughlin, T. J. J., PhD N.U.I., FRHistS

ACADEMIC UNITS

Archaeology and Anthropology
Tel: (01570) 424751 Fax: (01570) 424994
E-mail: a.mackie@lamp.ac.uk
Austin, D., BA S'ton., FSA   Prof.
Burnham, B. C., MA Camb., PhD Camb., FSA   Sr. Lectr.
Crowther, J., MA Camb., PhD Hull   Reader
Dransart, P., MSt Oxf., DPhil Oxf., FSA   Sr. Lectr.
Fleming, A., MA Camb., FSA   Prof.
Rainbird, P. S., BA Sheff., PhD Syd.   Sr. Lectr.; Head*
Walker, M. J. C., BA Oxf., MSc Calg., PhD Edin.   Prof.
Other Staff: 10 Lectrs.
Research: archaeological theory; human and physical geography; prehistoric, historic and mediaeval archaeology; social and environmental anthropology

Classics
Tel: (01570) 424723 Fax: (01570) 424995
E-mail: l.ayre@lamp.ac.uk
Wilson, J. P., BA Keele, PhD Lond.   Head*
Other Staff: 4 Lectrs.
Research: ancient history; classical philosophy and mythology; Renaissance Latin of the Americas

English
Tel: (01570) 424764 Fax: (01570) 424992
E-mail: b.doyle@lamp.ac.uk
Manning, J., MA Syd., PhD Edin.   Prof.
Marx, C. W., MA Tor., DPhil York(UK)   Sr. Lectr.; Head*
Other Staff: 5 Lectrs.
Research: American literature; English literature from the mediaeval period to the twentieth century; literature and the visual arts

Film/Media
Tel: (01570) 424790 Fax: (01570) 424993
E-mail: fms@lamp.ac.uk
Horrocks, S. L., MA Edin., MA Warw.   Head*
Other Staff: 4 Lectrs.
Research: British cinema; media literacy; southeast Asian cinema

History
Tel: (01570) 424872 Fax: (01570) 424998
E-mail: m.smith@lamp.ac.uk
Borsay, P. N., BA Lanc., PhD Lanc.   Prof.
Burton, J. E., BA Lond., DPhil York(UK), FSA   Reader
Eldridge, C. C., BA Nott., PhD Nott., FRHistS   Prof.
Smith, M. S., BA Lanc., PhD Lanc.   Sr. Lectr.; Head*
Research: history of the seventeenth century; mediaeval history; nineteenth- and twentieth-century British and European history

Management and Information Technology
Tel: (01570) 424727 Fax: (01570) 424994
E-mail: mit@lamp.ac.uk
Matera-Rogers, C. S., MBA Glam.   Head*
Venus, J. C., BSc Wales, PhD Wales   Sr. Lectr.
Other Staff: 4 Lectrs.
Research: enterprises and small business development

Philosophy
Tel: (01570) 424715 Fax: (01570) 424986
E-mail: philosophy@lamp.ac.uk
Cockburn, D. A., MA St And., DPhil Oxf.   Prof.
Wooding, J. M., BA Syd., PhD Syd.   Head*
Other Staff: 2 Lectrs.
Research: philosophy of the mind

Theology and Religious Studies
Tel: (01570) 424708 Fax: (01570) 424987
E-mail: m.ablett@lamp.ac.uk
Arthur, C., MA Edin., PhD Edin.   Sr. Lectr.
Badham, P. B. L., MA Oxf., MA Camb., PhD Birm.   Prof.
Cohn-Sherbok, D., MLitt Camb., PhD Camb.   Prof.
Izzidien, M. Y., BA Baghdad, PhD Manc.   Sr. Lectr.

Knight, F. M. R., BD Lond., MTh Lond., PhD Camb.   Sr. Lectr.; Head*
O'Loughlin, T. J. J., PhD N.U.I., FRHistS   Reader
Wooding, J. M., BA Syd., PhD Syd.   Sr. Lectr.
Yao, X., MA Peking, PhD Peking   Prof.
Other Staff: 16 Lectrs.
Research: Islamic studies; major world religions; New Testament and Christology; Old Testament and Jewish studies

Voluntary Sector Studies
Tel: (01570) 424785 Fax: (01570) 424990
E-mail: d.wilcox@lamp.ac.uk
Fisher, C. M., BSc Lond., PhD Wales   Head*
Other Staff: 4 Tutors

Welsh
Tel: (01570) 424754 Fax: (01570) 424996
E-mail: linda.jones@lamp.ac.uk
Cartwright, J., BA Wales, PhD Wales   Sr. Lectr.; Head*
Jones, C. M., BA Wales, PhD Wales   Sr. Lectr.
Thorne, D. A., BA Wales, MA Wales, PhD Wales   Prof.
Other Staff: 2 Lectrs.
Research: modern Welsh literature; Welsh linguistics and dialectology

CONTACT OFFICERS

Academic affairs. Registrar and Secretary: Roderick, Thomas D., BA Lond., PhD Lond. (E-mail: t.roderick@lamp.ac.uk.)
Accommodation. Accommodation Officer: Thomas, P. (E-mail: p.thomas@lamp.ac.uk.)
Admissions (first degree). Undergraduate Administrator: Jarman, R. C. (E-mail: admissions@lamp.ac.uk.)
Admissions (higher degree). Postgraduate Administrator: Holder, Mark (E-mail: pg-office@lamp.ac.uk.)
Alumni. Marketing and Recruitment Officer: Norris-Hill, J., BSc Lond., PhD Lond. (E-mail: alumni@lamp.ac.uk.)
Archives. Archivist: Yates, Nigel, BA Hull, MA Hull, PhD Hull, FRHistS (E-mail: n.yates@lamp.ac.uk.)
Careers. Careers Officer: Owen, H. L., BSc Wales, PhD Wales (E-mail: lyn.owen@lamp.ac.uk.)
Computing services. Management and Information Systems Co-ordinator: Thomas, J., BA Wales (E-mail: janice.thomas@lamp.ac.uk.)
Computing services. Director of Computing Services: Gibbs, S. J. P. (E-mail: s.gibbs@lamp.ac.uk.)
Credit transfer. Registrar and Secretary: Roderick, Thomas D., BA Lond., PhD Lond. (E-mail: t.roderick@lamp.ac.uk.)
Estates and buildings/works and services. Estates Manager: Rollason, A. (E-mail: a.rollason@lamp.ac.uk.)
Examinations. Registrar and Secretary: Roderick, Thomas D., BA Lond., PhD Lond. (E-mail: t.roderick@lamp.ac.uk.)
Finance. Director of Finance and Resources: Tobias, G., BA Glam. (E-mail: g.tobias@lamp.ac.uk.)
International office. Marketing and Recruitment Officer: Norris-Hill, J., BSc

Lond., PhD Lond.
(E-mail: j.norris-hill@lamp.ac.uk)

Library (chief librarian). Systems Librarian: Perrett, M. A., BA Camb.
(E-mail: m.perrett@lamp.ac.uk)

Marketing. Marketing and Recruitment Officer: Norris-Hill, J., BSc Lond., PhD Lond.
(E-mail: j.norris-hill@lamp.ac.uk)

Minorities/disadvantaged groups. Registrar and Secretary: Roderick, Thomas D., BA Lond., PhD Lond.
(E-mail: t.roderick@lamp.ac.uk.)

Public relations. Marketing and Recruitment Officer: Norris-Hill, J., BSc Lond., PhD Lond.
(E-mail: j.norris-hill@lamp.ac.uk)

Publications. Marketing and Recruitment Officer: Norris-Hill, J., BSc Lond., PhD Lond.
(E-mail: j.norris-hill@lamp.ac.uk)

Purchasing. Director of Finance and Resources: Tobias, G., BA Glam.
(E-mail: g.tobias@lamp.ac.uk)

Quality assurance and accreditation. Registrar and Secretary: Roderick, Thomas D., BA Lond., PhD Lond.
(E-mail: t.roderick@lamp.ac.uk.)

Research. Archivist: Yates, Nigel, BA Hull, MA Hull, PhD Hull, FRHistS
(E-mail: n.yates@lamp.ac.uk)

Safety. Estates Manager: Rollason, A.
(E-mail: a.rollason@lamp.ac.uk)

Scholarships, awards, loans. Registrar and Secretary: Roderick, Thomas D., BA Lond., PhD Lond. (E-mail: t.roderick@lamp.ac.uk)

Security. Estates Manager: Rollason, A.
(E-mail: a.rollason@lamp.ac.uk)

Sport and recreation. Estates Manager: Rollason, A. (E-mail: a.rollason@lamp.ac.uk.)

Strategic planning. Registrar and Secretary: Roderick, Thomas D., BA Lond., PhD Lond.
(E-mail: t.roderick@lamp.ac.uk.)

Student union. President of Students' Union
(E-mail: union@lamp.ac.uk)

Students from other countries. Registrar and Secretary: Roderick, Thomas D., BA Lond., PhD Lond. (E-mail: t.roderick@lamp.ac.uk.)

Students with disabilities. Student Support Officer: Wade, Victoria
(E-mail: v.wade@lamp.ac.uk.)

[Information supplied by the institution as at 16 March 2005, and edited by the ACU]

UNIVERSITY OF WALES INSTITUTE, CARDIFF

Founded 1996

Associate Member of the Association of Commonwealth Universities

Postal Address: Central Administration, Llandaff Campus, Western Avenue, Cardiff, Wales CF5 2SG
Telephone: (029) 2041 6070 **Fax:** (029) 2041 6286 **E-mail:** uwicinfo@uwic.ac.uk
URL: http://www.uwic.ac.uk

VICE-CHANCELLOR AND PRINCIPAL AND CHIEF EXECUTIVE*—Chapman, Prof. Antony J., BSc Leic., PhD Leic., Hon. DSc Leic., FBPsS, FRSA, FIWA
DIRECTOR OF OPERATIONS‡—Ackroyd, Pam, BA Newcastle(UK), MA Lanc., FRSA, FCIPD
PRO VICE-CHANCELLOR (LEARNING AND TEACHING)—Hare, Jacqui, BA Lanc., MA Lanc.
PRO VICE-CHANCELLOR (RESEARCH)—Brown, Prof. Robert, MDes RCA, BA, FRSA
DIRECTOR OF MARKETING AND STUDENT RECRUITMENT—Pugh, John, BEd Wales, MPhil Glam., PhD Wales
DIRECTOR OF FINANCE—Warren, Martin J., BSc Hull, FCA

GENERAL INFORMATION

History. The history of the institute can be traced back to 1865 when the School of Art was opened in Cardiff city centre. In 1976 the school merged with Cardiff Training College, Llandaff Technical College, and Cardiff College of Food, Technology and Commerce to form South Glamorgan Institute for Higher Education. The institute gained university status in 1996.

The institute is spread across four campuses around Cardiff city centre, South Wales.

Admission to first degree courses (see also United Kingdom Introduction). Through Universities and Colleges Admissions Service (UCAS).

First Degrees (see also United Kingdom Directory to Subjects of Study). BA, BSc.
Length of course. Full-time: BA, BSc: 3 years. Part-time: BA, BSc: 10 years.

Higher Degrees (see also United Kingdom Directory to Subjects of Study).
Master's. MA, MBA, MSc.
Admission. Applicants should complete an application form, available from the admissions office.
Length of course. Full-time: MA, MBA, MSc: 2 years. Part-time: MA, MBA, MSc: 5 years.

Libraries. Volumes: 255,000. Periodicals subscribed to: 1064.

Statistics. Students (2005-2006): full-time 7424 (3418 men, 4006 women); part-time 2518 (1366 men, 1152 women); international 1095 (730 men, 365 women); undergraduate 7505 (3396 men, 4109 women); master's 2222 (1257 men, 965 women); doctoral 215 (131 men, 84 women).

FACULTIES/SCHOOLS

Art and Design, School of

Tel: (029) 2041 6154 Fax: (029) 2041 6944
E-mail: artdesign@uwic.ac.uk
Dean: Kavanagh, Gaynor
Administrator: Makris, Kim

Education, School of

Tel: (029) 2041 7092 Fax: (029) 2041 6921
E-mail: education@uwic.ac.uk
Dean: Thomas, Paul, BMus Wales, MEd Wales
Administrator: Gardner, Bryn

Health Sciences, School of

Tel: (029) 2041 6890 Fax: (029) 2041 6985
E-mail: hss@uwic.ac.uk
Dean: Bowen, S. Maureen, BSc Wales, PhD Wales
Administrator: McMullan, Lorraine

Management, School of

Tel: (029) 2041 7136 Fax: (029) 2041 6940
E-mail: business@uwic.ac.uk
Dean: Newth, Mike, BSc Aberd., MSc CNAA
Administrator: Phillips, Jane

Sport, School of

Tel: (029) 2041 6591 Fax: (029) 2041 6589
E-mail: sport@uwic.ac.uk
Dean: Cobner, David E., BEd Wales, MA Leeds
Administrator: Forrester, Fran

ACADEMIC UNITS

Applied Sciences

Tel: (029) 2041 6830
E-mail: lmcmullan@uwic.ac.uk
Adams, Rachel A., BSc Wales, PhD Wales Sr. Lectr.
Allender, Vittoria L., BSc Wales, PhD Wales Sr. Lectr.

Ashmead, Bryan V., BSc Wales, PhD Wales Sr. Lectr.
Belcher, Paul C., BA Open(UK), MSc Brist. Principal Lectr.
Bowen, S. Maureen, BSc Wales, PhD Wales Head*
Burton, Neil, BSc Wales, PhD Wales Sr. Lectr.
Cooper, Rosemary A., BSc Wales, PhD Wales Principal Lectr.
Curnin, Andrew D., MPH Wales Sr. Lectr.
Eccles, Khwala S., MB ChB Baghdad, MSc Baghdad, PhD Wales Sr. Lectr.
Evans, Shelley-Ann, BSc Wales, PhD Wales Sr. Lectr.
Fairchild, Ruth, BSc Wales, PhD Wales Sr. Lectr.
Fielding, Louise M., BSc Reading, PhD Reading Sr. Lectr.
Foley, Paul, BSc Essex, PhD Sr. Lectr.
Giles, S. Helen, MPhil Wales Sr. Lectr.
Gilhooly, Gerard Sr. Lectr.
Griffith, C. J., BSc Liv., PhD Liv. Dir., Res. and Enterprise
Hayburn, G., MSc S.Bank, LLM De Mont. Sr. Lectr.
Hayward, A. Sr. Lectr.
Hicks, Sally, BSc Wales, PhD Wales Sr. Lectr.
Jones, Karin E., BSc Wales Sr. Lectr.
Jones, Ken P., MPhil Brun., PhD Brun. Reader; Principal Lectr.
Kanekanian, Ara, BSc Baghdad, MSc Reading, PhD Reading Principal Lectr.
Karani, George, MSc Nair., PhD Leeds Sr. Lectr.
Morgan, Hubert D. R., BSc Wales, PhD Wales Sr. Lectr.
Morgan, Julia G. Sr. Lectr.
Morris, R. H. Keith, BSc Wales, BA Open(UK), MSc CNAA, PhD Wales Reader
Munro, Robert I., BA Open(UK), PhD Dir., Learning and Teaching
Newberry, R. W., BSc Wales Sr. Lectr.
Noble, Teresa E., BSc Strath., MBA Glam. Sr. Lectr.

Peters, A. C., BSc *Wales*, PhD *Wales*   Dir., Res. and Grad. Studies
Powell, Colin, BSc(Tech) *Wales*   Sr. Lectr.
Redding, Peter, BSc *Rice*, MSc *Vanderbilt*   Sr. Lectr.
Rushmere, N. K., BSc *S'ton.*, PhD *Wales*   Sr. Lectr.
Thomas, A. W., BSc *Wales*, PhD *Wales*   Sr. Lectr.
Thornton, David, BSc *Leeds*, PhD *Wales*   Sr. Lectr.
Watkins, Peter J., BSc *CNAA*, PhD *Lond.*   Sr. Lectr.
Webb, Richard J., BSc *Liv.*, PhD *Wales*   Sr. Lectr.
Wildsmith, John D., BSc *CNAA*, MSc *Coventry*   Sr. Lectr.
Williams, Robert G., MEd *Wales*   Sr. Lectr.
Williams, Ronald J. H., BSc *Wales*, MSc *Wales*, PhD *Wales*   Sr. Lectr.
Other Staff: 1 Lectr.; 2 Staff Members

Art and Design, School of

Tel: (029) 2041 6647 Fax: (029) 2041 6944
    E-mail: artdesign@uwic.ac.uk
Beauchamp, Paul M.   Principal Lectr.
Butler, Susan, BA *Texas*, MA *Texas Christian*, PhD *Mass.*   Sr. Lectr.
Canavan, Keireine, BA *Liv.*, MA *RCA*, PhD *H-W*, MDes   Course Dir., BA Contemporary Textile Practice
Castle, Peter, BA *CNAA*   Sr. Lectr.
Cazeaux, Clive J., BA *CNAA*, MA *Wales*, PhD *Wales*   Reader
Coward, Timothy, MDes *RCA*   Dir., Res. and Grad. Studies
Cox, Richard, BA *MDA*   Sr. Lectr.
Crowther, Michael J.   Sr. Lectr.
Dineen, Ruth V., BEd *Wales*, BA *Reading*, MSc *Wales*   Sr. Lectr.
Done, Delyth E., BA *Wales*, MA *RCA*   Sr. Lectr.
Edge, K., BA *Leic.*   Sr. Lectr.
Gould, David P., MA *RCA*   Sr. Lectr.
Granjon, P.   Sr. Lectr.
Grove-White, Ann, BA *Reading*, MA *Middx.*   Sr. Lectr.
Hannay, Patrick J. S., MA   Sr. Lectr.; Course Dir.
Harris, H., BA *Keele*, MSc *Wales*   Sr. Lectr.
Hiscock, Karin A., BA *Bath*, MA *C.England*   Sr. Lectr.
Hose, Michael A., MDes *RCA*   Principal Lectr.; Dir., Res. and Enterprise
Hunt, Sue A., MA *CNAA*   Sr. Lectr.
Jackson, D. R., BA *Wales*   Sr. Lectr.
Keay-Bright, Wendy, BA *Wales*   Sr. Lectr.
Lawrence, Philipa, BA *RCA*, MA *RCA*   Sr. Lectr.
Long, Helen, BA *Lond.*, MA *E.Anglia*, PhD *Brighton*   Sr. Lectr.
McNorton, J. A., MEd *Wales*   Sr. Lectr.
Mitchell, R., DFA   Principal Lectr.
Moseley, J. Olwen, BA *CNAA*   Dir., Enterprise and Devel.
Neil, Stuart, BA *Wales*   Sr. Lectr.
Nicklin, R., BA *Wales*   Sr. Lectr.
Nicol, P., BA *Wales*   Sr. Lectr.
O'Neil, Christopher, BA *CNAA*, MA *RCA*   Head*
O'Reilly, P.   Sr. Lectr.
Pickles, Cherry, BA *Lond.*, BSc *Ulster*   Sr. Lectr.
Piper, Tom D., BFA *S.Dakota*, MFA *Mich.*   Sr. Lectr.
Shepherd, David J.   Sr. Lectr.
Shields, Susan S.   Sr. Lectr.
Short, C., BEd *Exe.*, MA *Essex*, PhD *Essex*   Sr. Lectr.
Stitt, A., BA *Ulster*   Sr. Lectr.
Taylor, Alison, BA *CNAA*   Sr. Lectr.
Watkins, Helen, BA *CNAA*, MA *RCA*   Sr. Lectr.
Weir, Ian P., BA *CNAA*, MA *W.England*   Sr. Lectr.
Young, Stephen   Principal Lectr.
Other Staff: 1 Lectr.; 1 Res. Fellow; 8 Staff Members

Business

Tel: (029) 2041 7136 Fax: (029) 2041 6940
    E-mail: business@uwic.ac.uk
Adlam, R., MSc *Wales*   Sr. Lectr.
Arthur, Leonard, BA *Durh.*   Dir., Res. and Enterprise
Avery, Ian A., BA *Wales*   Principal Lectr.
Ball, David, BSc *Lond.*, MSc *Aston*, PhD *Aston*   Sr. Lectr.
Barlow, Ann, BSc *Sus.*   Sr. Lectr.
Breverton, Terence, BA *Manc.*, MA *Lanc.*   Sr. Lectr.
Buckley, Paul, BSc *Salf.*, MSc *Sur.*
Catani, Nicole M., LèsL *Bordeaux*   Sr. Lectr.
Choo, Kok L., MBA *Wales*, EdD   Sr. Lectr.
Cleary, Pat, BSc *CNAA*   Sr. Lectr.
Collins, Jeff, BSc *Wales*, MSc *W.Ont.*, PhD *W.Ont.*   Sr. Lectr.
Croad, Jane L., BSc *Manc.*, MSc *Glam.*   Sr. Lectr.
Dakin, Terence A., MSc *Wales*   Principal Lectr.
Evans, Claire, BSc *Wales*   Sr. Lectr.
Gaunt, John N., BA *Wales*, MEd *Wales*, PhD   MBA Dissertation Co-ordinator
Georghiades, P., MSc *Wales*, PhD *Wales*   Sr. Lectr.
Gilhooly, Eileen, MBA *Glam.*   Sr. Lectr.
Godfrey, R. S., BA *Stir.*, MSc *Stir.*   Sr. Lectr.
Grub, J., MA *Cologne*, PhD *Cologne*   Sr. Lectr.
Gundermann, Marco, MA *F.U.Berlin*, MSocSc *Birm.*   Sr. Lectr.
Gunson, John, BA *Strath.*, MBA *Lausanne*   Sr. Lectr.
Hughes, K., BSc *Glam.*, PhD *Wales*
James, Malcolm D., BA   Sr. Lectr.
Johnston, Rebecca, BA *Wolv.*, MBA *Liv.*
Joice, P. Ann, BSc *CNAA*   Sr. Lectr.
Jones, Caroline, BSc *Wales*   Sr. Lectr.
Jones, Gareth R., BSc *Wales*, LLB *Wales*, MSc *Brist.*   Di Programme Dir.
Jones, Lawrence J., BSc *Wales*, MBA *Wales*   Sr. Lectr.
Jones, N., BA *W.England*   Sr. Lectr.
Joseph, Angela, BA *Manc.*, LLM *Leic.*   Sr. Lectr.
Keay-Bright, Wendy, BA *Wales*   Sr. Lectr.
Kelly, R. S., MBA *Wales*   Sr. Lectr.
Kemp, Raymond E., MBA *Open(UK)*   Sr. Lectr.
Kennedy, Barbara, BA *CNAA*, MA *Wales*
Koukouravas, Theodoros, BSc *Herts.*, MSc *Wales*   Dir. Teaching and Learning
Lewis, Trefor G., BA *Calif.*, MSc *Arizona*, MPhil *Wales*   Sr. Lectr.
Lloyd, David
Lowell, Jonathan, BA *Wales*, MBA *Wales*   Sr. Lectr.
Macdonald, Jeanne L., LèsL *Haute-Bretagne*   Sr. Lectr.
Marsh, Stephen J., BA *Open(UK)*   Sr. Lectr.
Neil, Stuart, BA *Wales*   Sr. Lectr.
Newth, Mike, BSc *Aberd.*, MSc *CNAA*   Head*
Norris-Jones, Lynne S., LLB *Glam.*, MA *Glam.*   Sr. Lectr.
Parry, Christopher T., BSc *CNAA*   Dir., Enterprise and Devel.
Pope, S. J., BA *Wales*   Sr. Lectr.
Samuel, Peter, MSc *Wales*   Sr. Lectr.
Scott-Cato, Molly
Screen, Allan D., BA *Wales*   Sr. Lectr.
Smith, Russell, BA *CNAA*, MA *Reading*, PhD *Open(UK)*   Sr. Lectr.
Tevar Terol, Esperanza, BA *Alicante*, MA *Wales*   Sr. Lectr.
Thorne, Simon
Waring, M. A., BA *Hudd.*   Sr. Lectr.
Williams, Alan, MBA *Wales*   Sr. Lectr.
Other Staff: 6 Lectrs.

Education, School of

Tel: (029) 2041 6461
    E-mail: education@uwic.ac.uk
Bartlett, Peter R., BSc *Leic.*   Sr. Lectr.
Carter, Peter G., MA *Wales*, MEd *Wales*   Sr. Lectr.
Challenger, S., BEd *Glam.*, MEd *Wales*   Sr. Lectr.
Cook, Martin J., MEd *Wales*, BEd   Sr. Lectr.
Cooke, Alan R., BSc *Wales*, PhD *Wales*   Sr. Lectr.

Curtis, Lorna, BA *Leic.*, BSc *Open(UK)*, MEd *Wales*   Sr. Lectr.
Dafydd, Sioned, BA *Wales*   Sr. Lectr.
Davies, Jason, BA   Sr. Lectr.
Davies, Jayne E.   Sr. Lectr.
Davies, Susan, BSc MA   Sr. Lectr.
Dodd, Graham, BSc *Tor.*, MEd *Sheff.*   Sr. Lectr.
Egan, David W., BA *Wales*, MA *Wales*   Head*
Evans, Hadyn, BSc *Wales*, MSc *Wales*, PhD *Wales*   Sr. Lectr.
Evans, Patricia, BEd *Wales*   Sr. Lectr.
Gadd, J., BEd *CNAA*   Sr. Lectr.
Geen, Arthur, BA *Wales*, MEd *Wales*, PhD *Wales*   Principal Lectr.
Haines, Graham A., BEd *Wales*, MEd *Wales*   Sr. Lectr.
Harris, Charles J., BA *Wales*, MEd *Nott.*, MPhil *Nott.*   Sr. Lectr.
Herrington, Paul, BA *CNAA*, MA *Wales*   Sr. Lectr.
Hughes, Ann, BEd *Wales*, MEd *Wales*   Dir., Enterprise and Devel.
Laugharne, Janet G., MA *Oxf.*, MPhil *Oxf.*, PhD *Wales*   Dir., Res. and Grad. Studies
Lewis, S. E., BA *CNAA*, MA *Wales*   Sr. Lectr.
Morgan, Georgina, BA *CNAA*, PhD *Wales*   Sr. Lectr.
Piacentini, Julie, BMus *Wales*   Sr. Lectr.
Pickin, M. G., MSc *Lond.*   Sr. Lectr.
Rawle, D. M., BA *Birm.*, MPhil *Wales*   Sr. Lectr.
Rees, Karen E., BA *Wales*   Sr. Lectr.
Richards, N. B., BA *Birm.*, MPhil *Wales*   Sr. Lectr.
Rowlands, Clive, BA   Sr. Lectr.
Stevens, Marie France, BA *Montpellier*
Strange, Keith, BSc(Econ) *Wales*, PhD *Wales*   Sr. Lectr.
Thomas, Paul, BMus *Wales*, MEd *Wales*   Dean*
Williams, D. T., BSc *Wales*, MEd *Wales*   Sr. Lectr.
Williams, Gill L., BA *Wales*, MBA *Glam.*
Williams, Sian R., BA *Wales*, PhD *Wales*   Sr. Lectr.
Winfield, Michelle, BA *CNAA*   Sr. Lectr.
Yu, Kin, BSc   Sr. Lectr.
Other Staff: 1 Lectr.; 4 Staff Members

Health and Social Sciences

Tel: (029) 2041 6890 Fax: (029) 2041 6985
    E-mail: hss@uwic.ac.uk
Alwyn, C., BSc *CNAA*, PhD *Wales*   Sr. Lectr.
Barasi, Mary E., BSc *Lond.*, BA *Open(UK)*, MSc *Lond.*   Principal Lectr.
Boorer, Malcolm, BA *York(UK)*, MA *Brun.*   Sr. Lectr.
Boswell, Catherine, BSc MSc   Sr. Lectr.
Brown, Glynis, MEd *Wales*   Sr. Lectr.
Burke, Eileen H., MSc *Lond.*   Sr. Lectr.
Collins, Veronica, BA *Durh.*, MSc(Econ) *Wales*   Sr. Lectr.
Cooper, Francesca J., BSc *Wales*   Sr. Lectr.
Daly, Annette, PhD *Belf.*   Sr. Lectr.
Daries, Hayley, BSc *W.Cape*, MSc *Cape Town*   Sr. Lectr.
Davies, Heulwen, BSc *CNAA*   Sr. Lectr.
Delaney, Calum, BA *Witw.*   Sr. Lectr.
Ellis, Sarah, BSc *Birm.*   Sr. Lectr.
Evans, Jeffrey, BA *Open(UK)*, MScEcon *Wales*   Sr. Lectr.
Finch, Susan E., BA *York(UK)*, MSc *Wales*   Sr. Lectr.
Frowen, Paul, MPhil *Wales*   Sr. Lectr.
Gallimore, Katherine, BSc   Sr. Lectr.
Harries, C.   Sr. Lectr.
Harris, Pamela J., BSc *Brist.*, MA *Nott.*, PhD *Nott.*   Head*
Harris, Philip E., BSc *Brist.*, MPhil *CNAA*   Sr. Lectr.
Harris, Rhiannon, BSc *Wales*, MSc *Wales*   Sr. Lectr.
Jenkins, Elaine, BA *Open(UK)*, MEd *Wales*   Sr. Lectr.
John, Bev, BA PhD   Sr. Lectr.
Lee, Jacqueline, BA *Sus.*   Sr. Lectr.
Lewis, Jeffrey   Sr. Lectr.
Lock, David, BA *Leic.*, MSc *Lough.*, MA *Brun.*   Sr. Lectr.
Mathieson, I., BSc *QM Edin.*   Sr. Lectr.

Miller, Dave, LLB   Sr. Lectr.
Millward, Liz, BA *Newcastle(UK)*, MA *Sheff.*   Sr. Lectr.
Munroe, Siân, MSc PhD   Principal Lectr.
Murray, Alison C., BSc *Lond.*, MPhil *Camb.*, PhD   Sr. Lectr.
Nicholls, Alison, BSc *Lond.*, MPhil *Wales*   Sr. Lectr.
Pandeli, Helen, MA *Camb.*, PhD *Camb.*   Sr. Lectr.
Protheroe, Amanda, BSc *Bath*   Sr. Lectr.
Roberts, Gwenda, BA *Reading*, MSc *Wales*   Sr. Lectr.
Robertson, Stewart, MA   Sr. Lectr.
Sander, Paul, BSc *Lond.*, MSc *Brun.*   Sr. Lectr.
Sanders, Lalage, BScEcon *Wales*, PhD *Wales*   Dir., Res. and Grad. Studies
Smith, Derek J., BSc *Lond.*   Sr. Lectr.
Thirlaway, Kathryn, BSc *Wales(Swansea)*, PhD *Wales(Swansea)*   Sr. Lectr.
Tyrrell, Wendy, MEd *Wales*   Sr. Lectr.; Dir., Res. and Enterprise
Upton, Dominic, BSc *Leic.*, MSc *Middx.*, PhD *Lond.*   Sr. Lectr.
Watt, Andrew, BSc *Ulster*, PhD *Wales*   Sr. Lectr.
Williams, Robert J., BA *Keele*, PhD *Keele*   Dir., Learning and Teaching
Other Staff: 11 Lectrs.

Hospitality, Tourism and Leisure Management, Welsh School of

Tel: (029) 2041 6425 E-mail: htl@uwic.ac.uk
Avery, Patricia M.   Sr. Lectr.
Botterill, T. David, BSc *Sur.*, MSc *Lough.*, PhD *Texas A.& M.*   Prof.; Dir., Res. and Grad. Studies
Bradshaw, Philip E.   Sr. Lectr.
Coleman, Philip D., BA *Open(UK)*   Sr. Lectr.; Dir., Learning and Teaching
Duggan, Sarah   Sr. Lectr.
Fallon, Julia M., BA *Brad.*, MBA *Wales*   Sr. Lectr.
Flynn, Michael J., BSc *Wales*, MBA *Wales*   Sr. Lectr.
Honey, Martin D., BA *Sur.*   Sr. Lectr.
Hunter-Powell, Patricia A., BA *Open(UK)*   Sr. Lectr.
Lord, J., BSc *Birm.*, MSc *Lough.*   Sr. Lectr.
Luther, Angela P., BA *Wales*   Sr. Lectr.
Moore, Stephen P., MA *Manc.Met.*, MSc *Manc.Met.*   Sr. Lectr.
Morgan, N., BA *Exe.*, PhD *Exe.*   Reader, Tourism Studies
Norman, K., MA *Oxf.*, MBA *Manc.*   Sr. Lectr.
Pepper, S. Alice, BA *Wales*   Sr. Lectr.
Pritchard, Annette, MScEcon *Wales*, PhD *Manc.Met.*   Reader, Tourism Studies
Ritchie, Caroline, BSc *Lond.*   Sr. Lectr.
Roberts, Andrew, BSc *Wales*   Sr. Lectr.
Savage, Timothy J., BSc *CNAA*, MSc *Lough.*   Sr. Lectr.
Sedgley, Diane Z., BA *CNAA*, MSocSci *Birm.*   Sr. Lectr.
Silk, T. Michael, MEd *Wales*   Sr. Lectr.
Snelgrove, M., BA *Wales*, MPhil *Wales*   Sr. Lectr.
Tresidder, F. Kenneth, BA *Lond.*   Principal Lectr.
Other Staff: 5 Staff Members

Lifelong Learning

Tel: (029) 2041 6571 Fax: (029) 2041 6715
E-mail: lll@uwic.ac.uk
Barclay, M., BA *CNAA*, MA *Wales*, MA(Ed) *Open(UK)*   Sr. Lectr.
Carter, Mary E., BSc *Birm.*, MA *Wales*   Sr. Lectr.
Mathias, J. G., MSc *S'ton.*   Sr. Lectr.
Newnham, R.   Sr. Lectr.
Rathkey, Michael, BSc *Wales*   Sr. Lectr.; Dir., Teaching and Learning
Sowden, C., BA *York(UK)*, MEd *Sheff.*   Sr. Lectr.
Treadwell, Peter J., BEd *Lough.*, MEd *Exe.*   Head*
Other Staff: 3 Staff Members

Product and Engineering Design

Tel: (029) 2041 6696 Fax: (029) 2041 6946
E-mail: ped@uwic.ac.uk
Barham, G.   Sr. Lectr.
Bichard, Simon H., BSc *CNAA*   Sr. Lectr.; Programme Dir.
Cousins, Simon E., BSc *S.Bank*   Sr. Lectr.; Course Dir.
Darlington, J. G., BA *Open(UK)*   Sr. Lectr.
Evans, Nicholas, BSc *Open(UK)*   Sr. Lectr.
Fathers, J., BA *CNAA*   Sr. Lectr.
Gill, S. J., BA *Northumbria*   Sr. Lectr.; Programme Dir.
Griffiths, R. S., BA *CNAA*   Sr. Lectr.; Dir., Enterprise and Devel.
Hann, Anne E., BSc *Wales*   Sr. Lectr.
Holifield, David M., BSc *Wales*   Dir., Res. and Grad. Studies
Jacklin, David A., BA *Open(UK)*   Sr. Lectr.
O'Connell, Michael, BSc *Lond.*   Sr. Lectr.; Dir., Learning and Teaching
Pole, Glyn, BSc *Wales*, MEng *Wales*   Sr. Lectr.
Rafik, Tahseen A., MSc *Baghdad*, PhD *CNAA*   Sr. Lectr.; Head*
Whyman, A., BSc *Wales*, BArch *Wales*, MA *Brist.*   Sr. Lectr.; Programme Dir.
Wilgeroth, Paul M., MSc *Lough.*   Sr. Lectr.; Programme Dir.
Other Staff: 1 Lectr.; 1 Staff Member

Sport, Physical Education and Recreation

Tel: (029) 2041 6591 Fax: (029) 2041 6589
E-mail: sport@uwic.ac.uk
Beynon, Carl, BA *Wales*, MSc *Wales*   Sr. Lectr.
Bolton, Nicola, MBA *Birm.*, PhD *Plym.*   Principal Lectr.
Cobner, David E., BEd *Wales*, MA *Leeds*   Head*
Cooper, Stephen M., BEd *Wales*, MA *Birm.*   Dir., Learning and Teaching
Davey, Christopher, BEd   Sr. Lectr.
Davies, Gwilym, BA *Wales*, MEd *Wales*, PhD *Wales*   Dir., Grad. Studies
Davies, Lyn, MBE, MA *Open(UK)*   Sr. Lectr.
Dawkins, N. T., MA *Wales*   Sr. Lectr.
Evans, Lynne, BA *Leeds*, MSc *Lakehead*, PhD *Wales*   Sr. Lectr.
Fenner, Anthony J.   Sr. Lectr.
Hanton, Sheldon   Principal Lectr.; Reader; Dir., Res.
Hare, D., BSc *Wales*, DPhil *York(UK)*   Principal Lectr.
Harris, John, BA *Wales*, PhD *Brun.*   Sr. Lectr.
Haworth, Christa, BA *CNAA*, MA *Wales*   Sr. Lectr.
Hughes, Michael G., BSc *Liv.*, MSc *Flor.*   Sr. Lectr.
Hughes, Mike D., BSc *Manc.*, PhD *Manc.*   Principal Lectr.
Hurl, Geraldine, MA *CNAA*   Sr. Lectr.
Irwin, G., BSc *Wales*   Sr. Lectr.
Jackson, Ceinwen B., BEd *Wales*   Sr. Lectr.
Jennings, Christopher W., BA *Wales*   Sr. Lectr.
Jones, Carwyn, BA *Wales*, MSc *Tees.*, PhD *Open(UK)*   Sr. Lectr.
Kingston, K. M., BA *Wales*, PhD *Wales*   Sr. Lectr.
Lancey, Keith W., BEd *Wales*, MA *Birm.*   Sr. Lectr.
Llewellyn, J., MSc   Sr. Lectr.
Longville, Julia, BEd *CNAA*   Sr. Lectr.
Miles, A. P., BSc *Liv.*, PhD *Liv.*   Principal Lectr.; Dir., Enterprise and Devel.
Morgan, K., BA *CNAA*   Sr. Lectr.
Mullen, R. H., BA *Wales*, MSc *Lough.*, PhD *Wales*   Sr. Lectr.
O'Donoghue, Peter, BSc *Ulster*, MSc *Ulster*, DPhil *Ulster*   Sr. Lectr.
Power, Sean, MA *W.Kentucky*   Dir., Athletics Academy
Rawlins, John, BEd *Wales*, MA *Wales*   Sr. Lectr.
Smith, Beverley A., MA *Wales*   Sr. Lectr.
Thomas, Non E., BA *Wales*   Sr. Lectr.
Tong, Richard J., BA *Wales*, MSc *Lough.*, PhD *Wales*   Principal Lectr.; Dir., Learning and Teaching
Wasley, David, MSc *Ill.*   Sr. Lectr.

Wilson, Cassie, BSc *Lough.*, PhD *Lough.*   Sr. Lectr.
Wiltshire, Huw D., BA *Wales*, MEd *Wales*   Sr. Lectr.
Other Staff: 3 Lectrs.; 5 Staff Members

SPECIAL CENTRES, ETC

Celtic Inspection Services Unit
Tel: (029) 2041 6513
E-mail: pthomas@uwic.ac.uk
Thomas, Paul, BMus *Wales*, MEd *Wales*   Head*

Manufacturing Advisory Service (MAS)
Tel: (029) 2041 7216 Fax: (029) 2041 6973
E-mail: pdr@uwic.ac.uk
No staff at present

National Indoor Athletics Centre
Tel: (029) 2041 6777 Fax: (029) 2041 6768
No staff at present

Performance Analysis, Centre for
Tel: (029) 2041 6523
E-mail: mdhughes@uwic.ac.uk
Hughes, Mike D., BSc *Manc.*, PhD *Manc.*   Dir.*

Podiatric Studies, Welsh Centre for (Soletek)
Tel: (029) 2041 6890 Fax: (029) 2041 6895
E-mail: soletek@uwic.ac.uk
No staff at present

Product Design and Development Research, National Centre for (PDR)
Tel: (029) 2041 7035 Fax: (029) 2041 6973
E-mail: pdr@uwic.ac.uk
No staff at present

CONTACT OFFICERS

Accommodation. Accommodation Services Manager: Spencer, Sarah (E-mail: accomm@uwic.ac.uk)
Admissions (first degree). Admissions Officer: Bowen, Lisa (E-mail: lbowen@uwic.ac.uk)
Admissions (higher degree). Admissions Officer: Wulff, Lydia (E-mail: lwulff@uwic.ac.uk)
Alumni. Alumni Officer: Norton, Kay (E-mail: knorton@uwic.ac.uk)
Careers. Careers Officer: Twyman, Alison (E-mail: careers@uwic.ac.uk)
Computing services. Head of IT Services: Cullinan, Sean (E-mail: isdhelpdesk@uwic.ac.uk)
Development/fund-raising. Director of Finance: Warren, Martin J., BSc *Hull*, FCA (E-mail: mjwarren@uwic.ac.uk)
Equal opportunities. Equality Development and Training Officer: O'Reilly, Allison (E-mail: aoreilly@uwic.ac.uk)
Estates and buildings/works and services. Estates Officer: Liddington, A. V. (E-mail: aliddington@uwic.ac.uk)
Finance. Director of Finance: Warren, Martin J., BSc *Hull*, FCA (E-mail: mjwarren@uwic.ac.uk)
General enquiries. (Contact UWIC General Enquiries)
International office. Head of International Marketing: Phillips, John (E-mail: overseas@uwic.ac.uk)
Ombudsman. Chairman, Board of Governors: Owen, John W.
Personnel/human resources. Head of Human Resources: Barrow, Jonathan (E-mail: humanresources@uwic.ac.uk)
Publications. Publications Officer: Walton, Ruth (E-mail: rwalton@uwic.ac.uk)
Purchasing. Purchasing Manager: Standfast, Peter (E-mail: purchasing@uwic.ac.uk)

Research. Pro Vice-Chancellor (Research): Brown, Prof. Robert, MDes *RCA*, BA, FRSA (E-mail: rbrown@uwic.ac.uk)

Safety. Health and Safety Advisor: Stuart, Anthony B. (E-mail: tstuart@uwic.ac.uk)

Schools liaison. Schools and Colleges Liaison Officer: Hughes, Ben (E-mail: schoolsofficer@uwic.ac.uk)

Sport and recreation. Facilities Manager: Rogers, Owen (E-mail: sfm@uwic.ac.uk)

Student union. General Manager (Student Union): Davies, Mike (E-mail: studentunion@uwic.ac.uk)

Student welfare/counselling. Head of Student Services: Ellis, David (E-mail: studentservices@uwic.ac.uk)

Students with disabilities. Head, Disability Department: Robson, Karen (E-mail: disability@uwic.ac.uk)

[Information supplied by the institution as at 9 May 2006, and edited by the ACU]

UNIVERSITY OF WALES, NEWPORT

Founded 1975

Postal Address: Caerleon Campus, PO Box 179, Newport, Wales NP18 3YG
Telephone: (01633) 432432 **Fax:** (01633) 432046 **E-mail:** uic@newport.ac.uk
URL: http://www.newport.ac.uk

VICE-CHANCELLOR*—Noyes, Peter, BSc *Lough.*, PhD *Lond.*
DEPUTY VICE-CHANCELLOR (ACADEMIC)—Carlisle, A., BA *Ulster*, MA *Lond.*
DEPUTY VICE-CHANCELLOR (LEARNING SUPPORT)—Rogers, Graham
PRO VICE-CHANCELLOR (RESOURCE PLANNING) AND DIRECTOR OF FINANCE—Jones, Denis, BSc *Wales*
PRO VICE-CHANCELLOR (REGIONAL AND INTERNATIONAL DEVELOPMENT)—O'Malley, Chris
PRO VICE-CHANCELLOR (HUMAN RESOURCES)—Edwards, Bethan, BA *CNAA*

GENERAL INFORMATION

History. The university college was founded in 1975 as Gwent College of Higher Education, with the merger of several specialist institutions. It became University of Wales College, Newport in 1996, and University of Wales, Newport in 2004.

It has two campuses, one in Caerleon and the other at Allt-yr-yn in Newport city centre.

Admission to first degree courses (see also United Kingdom Introduction). Through Universities and Colleges Admissions Service (UCAS). Passes in 2 subjects at General Certificate of Education (GCE) A Level or equivalent qualifications (including qualifications from overseas institutions) or experience.

First Degrees (see also United Kingdom Directory to Subjects of Study). BA, BEd, BEng, BSc.

Special BSc in education: 2 years (at least 1 year of higher education study required for entry).

Length of course. Full-time: BA, BEd, BEng, BSc: 3 years. Part-time: BA, BEd, BEng, BSc: 3–6 years.

Higher Degrees (see also United Kingdom Directory to Subjects of Study).

Master's. MA, MBA, MPhil, MSc, MScEcon.

Admission. Applicants for admission to master's degrees must normally hold an appropriate first degree awarded by a recognised institution. For applicants over 25, relevant experience may be accepted in place of a first degree.

Length of course. Full-time: MA, MBA, MSc, MScEcon: 1 year; MPhil: 1–3 years. Part-time: MA, MBA, MPhil, MSc, MScEcon: 3–5 years.

Doctoral. PhD.

Admission. Good honours degree.

Length of course. Full-time: PhD: 3–5 years. Part-time: PhD: 5–9 years.

Language of Instruction. English. Classes available for students needing help.

Libraries. Volumes: 150,000. Periodicals subscribed to: 1630. Other holdings: 40,000 art slides. Special collections: David Hurn (documentary photography); Primrose Hockey (local history); Stuart Piggott (archaeology);

Stuart Morgan (art); Newport Survey (photography).

Academic Year (2008–2009). Three terms: 29 September–19 December; 12 January–3 April; 20 April–5 June.

Income (2006–2007). Total, £39,279,000.

Statistics. Staff (2007): 694 (179 academic, 515 non-academic). Students (2007): full-time 3614; part-time 6200.

ACADEMIC UNITS

Art, Media and Design, School of

E-mail: uic@newport.ac.uk
Atkins, B. Sr. Lectr.
Ayisi, F., BA *Yaounde*, MA *Leeds*, MA *Hull* Sr. Lectr.
Bennewith, C., BA *Wales* Acting Head, Design
Bobby, P. Sr. Lectr.
Close, R. Sr. Lectr.
Conway, P. Sr. Lectr.
Corris, M., BA *N.Y.*, MFA *Maryland*, PhD *Lond.* Prof.
Cowan, P., MA *Glam.* Sr. Lectr.
Cunnick, G., BA *Nott.Trent* Acting Head, Art and Photography
Davis, P., MA *Wales* Sr. Lectr.
Davison, J., BA *Wales*, MA *Derby* Assoc. Dean, Acad. Devel. and Planning
Dee, I. Sr. Lectr.
Durden, M. Prof.
Evans, G. Course Leader
Furlong, R., BA *Anglia PU*, MA *Lond.* Sr. Lectr.
Graf, A., BA *Wales*, MSc *Edin.*, PhD *Edin.* Sr. Lectr.
Grant, K., BA *Sur.* Sr. Lectr.
Gravelle, A. M. Sr. Lectr.
Houtman, C., BA *Kent* Sr. Lectr.
Jackson, C., BA *Wales* Sr. Lectr.
Jeavons, E., BA *Wales* Sr. Lectr.
Ktori, A. Sr. Lectr.
Landen, C. Course Leader
Lawther, Derek Dean*
Little, E., BA *Colorado*, MFA *Colorado* Sr. Lectr.
Lyons, K., MFA *Yale* Sr. Lectr.
Manning, J., BA *Wales* Sr. Lectr.
Martin, A. Acting Sr. Lectr., Media
Mason, R., BA *CNAA*, MA *Arts(Lond.)* Sr. Lectr.
McCann, J. Dir., Res., Smart Clothes Wearable Technologies
Morgan, C., BA *Oxf.* Sr. Lectr.
Morris, B., BA *Nott.Trent*, MA *Wales* Sr. Lectr.

Morris, C., BA *Wales*, MA *RCA* Sr. Lectr.
Morris, P., MA *Lond.* Sr. Lectr.
Nelson, E. Sr. Lectr.
Newman, A., MA *CNAA* Sr. Lectr.
Nougarede, M. Sr. Lectr.
Orrillard, N., BA *Wales*, MA *Wales* Sr. Lectr.
Parsons, C., BA *CNAA* Sr. Lectr.
Penwarden, Charles, BA *Wales*, MA *CNAA* Sr. Lectr.; Foundation Studies Art and Des. Co-ordinator
Pritchard, Gary, BA *Wales*, MA *W.England*, PhD *Azusa Pacific* Assoc. Dean (Learning and Teaching)
Reas, P. Sr. Lectr.
Rees, S., BA *CNAA* Programme Leader
Ruethi, A. Sr. Lectr.
Sharrock, L. Sr. Lectr.
Smith, A., BA *Wales*, PhD *Glam.* Sr. Lectr.
Smith, David Assoc. Dean (Res. and Enterprises)
Surman, D., BA *Wales*, MA *Warw.* Sr. Lectr.
Trevelyan, H., BA *Camb.*, MA *Essex* Head, Internat. Film Sch., Wales
Vellani, S., BA *Manc.* Sr. Lectr.
Walker, I., BA *Manc.*, MA *Lond.*, DPhil *Sus.* Reader
Watkins-Hughes, P. Sr. Lectr.
Wooster, R., BA *Wales*, MA Sr. Lectr.
Other Staff: 1 Reader; 4 Lectrs.; 2 Sr. Res. Fellows; 2 Res. Fellows

Community and Lifelong Learning, Centre for

E-mail: uic@newport.ac.uk
Davies, M. Project Manager
Davies, Vivian P., BA *Kent*, BScEcon *Wales*, MA *Open(UK)* Dir.*
Dyson, T. Project Co-ordinator
Gass, Jeremy, BA *Brad.*, MA *Wales* Project Co-ordinator
O'Connell, C. Sr. Lectr.
Pinder, Janet, BA L-Action Res. Co-ordinator
Trippier, Paul, BA *Cardiff* Sr. Lectr.
Other Staff: 1 Lectr.; 5 Community Tutors; 6 Community Learning Devel. Officers; 1 Res. and Evaluation Officer; 7 Project Officers

Education, School of

E-mail: uic@newport.ac.uk
Allen, R. Sr. Lectr.
Benjamin, T., BEd *Wales* Programme Leader
Clarke, R. Programme Leader
Coffey, W., MA Programme Leader
Davies, A., BScEcon *Wales*, MA *Open(UK)* Programme Leader

Dodd, V. Sr. Lectr.
Edmunds, J. A., MEd *Wales* Sr. Lectr.
Egley, S., BA *Durh.*, MEd *Birm.*, PhD *Brist.*
  Programme Leader
Evans, T., BEd *Wales* Sr. Lectr.
Fear, A. D., BSc *Lond.*, MEd *Wales* Sr. Lectr.;
  Assoc. Dean (Res. and Enterprise)
Foulston, L., BA *Wales*, MA *Wales*, PhD *Wales*
  Sr. Lectr.
George, S., BEd *Wales* Programme Leader
Gray, M., PhD *Wales* Sr. Lectr.
Green, K. F., BSc *Kent*, PhD *Kent* Sr. Lectr.;
  Programme Leader
Heard, C. D., BEd *CNAA* Sr. Lectr.
Howell, R. C., MA *Lond.*, PhD *Lond.* Reader
Johnston, R. Sr. Lectr.
Jones, L., BSc *CNAA* Sr. Lectr.
Kelly, E. Sr. Lectr.
Kingdon, R., BEd *Wales*, MSc *Glam.* Sr. Lectr.
Kissock, J., BA *Camb.*, MA *Camb.*, PhD *Leic.* Sr.
  Lectr.
Kurzik, R. B., MEd *Wales* Sr. Lectr.
Lamb, E. Sr. Lectr.
Lawton, J. L., MEd *Wales* Sr. Lectr.; Subj.
  Leader
Lehal, B., BEd *Nott.Trent*, MBA *Nott.Trent* Sr.
  Lectr.
Lewis, R., BSc *C.Lancs.*, MSc *Wales* Sr. Lectr.
Lock-Lewis, R., BA *Wales*, MA Sr. Lectr.
Longman, D., MA *Sus.* Sr. Lectr.
McClachlan, C., BSc(Ed) *Exe.* Sr. Lectr.
Morgan Thomas, I., BA *Wales* Sr. Lectr.; Subj.
  Leader
Morris, K. P., BEd *Wales*, MPhil *Wales* Head,
  Initial Teacher Training
Newcomb, J. W., MA *Open(UK)*, EdD *Open(UK)*
  Sr. Lectr.
Oti, J., BEd *Cardiff*, PhD *Cardiff* Sr. Lectr.
Packer, R. Sr. Lectr.
Pagan, A. J., MEd *Wales* Sr. Lectr.
Peters, C. W., BSc *Wales*, PhD *Aston* Dean*
Peters, S., BEd *Cardiff* Sr. Lectr.
Petrie, L. G., BA *Open(UK)*, MA *Lond.* Sr. Lectr.;
  Subj. Leader
Roberts, J., BSc *Brad.*, MA *Wolv.* Assoc. Dean
  (Acad. Devel. and Planning)
Rowse, A., BSc(Ed) *Exe.* Sr. Lectr.
Ruhemann, L., MA *Manc.*, MA *Lond.*
  Programme Leader
Ryan, P. Sr. Lectr.
Sparks, J. M., BEd *Wales* Principal Lectr.;
  Head, Educn. and Humanities
Steer, S., MEd *Wales* Sr. Lectr.
Stubley, R., BA MA Sr. Lectr.
Tennant, D., BSc Sr. Lectr.
Williams, J., BEd *Wales*, MA *Wales* Sr. Lectr.
Williams, M., BSc(Econ) *Wales*, MBA *Wales* Sr.
  Lectr.
Wilson, S. Sr. Lectr.
Wilton-Jones, A. Sr. Lectr.
Woods, Nicola, BA *Roeh.*, MPhil *Oxf.*, DPhil *Oxf.*
  Assoc. Dean (Learning and Teaching)
Other Staff: 1 EFL Co-ordinator
Research: learning and teaching strategies;
  literacy

Health and Social Sciences, School of
E-mail: uic@newport.ac.uk
Brayford, J. Sr. Lectr.
Calder, G. Sr. Lectr.
Cowe, F., MA *Glas.* Assoc. Dean (Acad. Devel.
  and Planning)
Deering, J. Sr. Lectr.
Edwards, M. Sr. Lectr.
Faris, A. Sr. Lectr.
Greaux, V., BA *Wales* Sr. Lectr.
James, N. Sr. Lectr.
Jones, E. Sr. Lectr.
Kynnear, E. Sr. Lectr.
Lewis, N., BSc *Exe.*, MSc *Exe.*, PhD *Brist.* Head,
  Soc. Scis.
Lyons, A., BSc *Lanc.*, MSc *Sur.* Dean*
Matheson, H., BEd *Warw.*, MSc *Iowa*, PhD
  Springfield Head, Health
Morris, L. Sr. Lectr.
Nordcliffe, D. Principal Lectr.

Ross, S., BA *Strath.*, MSc *Sus.*, PhD *Strath.* Subj.
  Leader
Simmons, M., BA *Wales* Assoc. Dean
  (Learning and Teaching)
Smith, S., BA *Newcastle(UK)*, MSc *Oxf.*, PhD
  Warw. Reader
Spencer, L., BA *CNAA*, MA Sr. Lectr.
Spong, S., BA *Nott.*, MSc *Wales* Sr. Lectr.
Tagg, J. Sr. Lectr.
Thomas, A. Sr. Lectr.
Van Ooijen, E. Sr. Lectr.
Williamson, S. Sr. Lectr.
Other Staff: 1 Specialist Lectr.
Research: community justice; counselling;
  management of human services; political
  and applied philosophy; sports studies

Newport Business School
E-mail: uic@newport.ac.uk
Bamber, M. Sr. Lectr.
Baxter, D. Sr. Lectr.
Cole, S. M., BA *Open(UK)*, MBA *Open(UK)* Sr.
  Lectr.
Cook, C., MSc *Wales* Sr. Lectr.
Corner, A., PhD Head, Computing
Dahl, T., PhD Sr. Lectr.
Darwish, M. Sr. Lectr.
David, H. Sr. Lectr.
Davies, J., BScEcon *Warw.* Sr. Lectr.
Deacon, J., BSc *Wales*, MA *Glam.* Sr. Lectr.
Evans, D. S., BSc *Bath* Sr. Lectr.
Evans, M., BA *Lond.* Sr. Lectr.
Gaffney-Rhys, Ruth, LLB *Wales* Sr. Lectr.
Gilbert, N., BSc *Wales* Sr. Lectr.
Griffiths, L. G., FCA Head of Bus. Professions
Harris, J. Sr. Lectr.
Hayes, A., BA *Essex*, MSc *Brun.* Assoc. Dean
  (Learning and Teaching)
Hedderman, M. Sr. Lectr.
Janes, I., BScEcon Sr. Lectr.
Jones, A., BSc *CNAA*, MSc *Wales* Sr. Lectr.
Jones, C., BSc *Dund.* Sr. Lectr.
Jones, E. B., BSc *Wales*, MBA *Wales* Head, Bus.
  and Management
Jones, J., MBA *Wales* Sr. Lectr.
Lawson, R., MBA *Wales* Sr. Lectr.
Lee, S. Sr. Lectr.
Llewellyn, E., BSc *Wales* Sr. Lectr.
Marsh, Teresa Sr. Lectr.
McIntyre-Bhatty, Tim Dean*
Metcalfe, S., BA MA PhD Sr. Lectr.
Murphy, L., BSc *Wales*, MA *Wales*, MPhil
  Greenwich Sr. Lectr.
Mutter, K., BA *Wales* Sr. Lectr.
Orford, D., BScEcon *Wales*, MEd *Wales* Assoc.
  Dean (Acad. Devel. and Planning)
Reddy, M., BSc *Durh.*, MSc *UMIST*, PhD *Glam.*
  Sr. Lectr.
Robins, G. W., BSc *Wales*, MSc *Wales* Sr. Lectr.
Russell, G. K., BSc *Cant.*, MSc *Syd.*, PhD *Syd.*
  Sr. Lectr.
Salijeni, G. Sr. Lectr.
Sansom, J. W., BSc *CNAA*, MSc Sr. Lectr.
Seward, N., BSc *Leeds* Sr. Lectr.
Singh-Baicher, G., BSc *Jab.*, BEng *Nigeria*, MSc
  Leeds, PhD *Wales* Sr. Lectr.
Talbot, L. N., BA *Open(UK)*, MBA *Wales* Sr.
  Lectr.
Taylor, M. Sr. Lectr.
Tubb, C. Sr. Lectr.
Vidalis, S. Sr. Lectr.
Waythe, M. A., BSc *CNAA*, MSc *Lough.* Head
  of Engin.
Other Staff: 1 Lectr.
Research: industrial automation and IT strategies;
  innovation, creativity and enterprise;
  mechatronics; quality tools and techniques

CONTACT OFFICERS
Accommodation. Student Accommodation
  Manager: Powell, Helen
  (E-mail: helen.powell@newport.ac.uk)
Alumni. Alumni Officer: Jenkins, Carolyn
  (E-mail: carolyn.jenkins@newport.ac.uk)
Archives. Alumni Officer: Jenkins, Carolyn
  (E-mail: carolyn.jenkins@newport.ac.uk)

Careers. Head of Student Services: Wilson,
  Lawrence, BA *Leeds*
  (E-mail: lawrence.wilson@newport.ac.uk)
Computing services. Head of IT and Media
  Services: Webb, Michael, BSc *Exe.*
  (E-mail: michael.webb@newport.ac.uk)
Conferences/corporate hospitality.
  Conference and Events Manager: Manson,
  Morna
  (E-mail: conferencecentre@newport.ac.uk)
Consultancy services. Commercial Manager:
  Turnbull, Karen, BSc *Wales*, MBA
  (E-mail: ers@newport.ac.uk)
Development/fund-raising. Head of
  Development: Jarman, Penny, BA *Wales*
  (E-mail: penny.jarman@newport.ac.uk)
Equal opportunities. Equalities and Diversity
  Officer: Preece, Alison
  (E-mail: alison.preece@newport.ac.uk)
Estates and buildings/works and services.
  Director of Estates: Godber, Stephen, BSc
  Glam.
  (E-mail: stephen.godber@newport.ac.uk)
Finance. Director of Finance: Jones, Denis, BSc
  Wales (E-mail: denis.jones@newport.ac.uk)
Health services. Head of Student Services:
  Wilson, Lawrence, BA *Leeds*
  (E-mail: lawrence.wilson@newport.ac.uk)
Industrial liaison. Commercial Manager:
  Turnbull, Karen, BSc *Wales*, MBA
  (E-mail: ers@newport.ac.uk)
International office. Dean of International
  Affairs: Wood, Graham, BA *CNAA*, MA *Griff.*
  (E-mail: internationalaffairs@newport.ac.uk)
Language training for international students.
  Dean of International Affairs: Wood,
  Graham, BA *CNAA*, MA *Griff.*
  (E-mail: internationalaffairs@newport.ac.uk)
Library (chief librarian). Librarian: May,
  Lesley, BA *Lond.*
  (E-mail: lesley.may@newport.ac.uk)
Library (enquiries). Librarian: May, Lesley,
  BA *Lond.* (E-mail: lesley.may@newport.ac.uk)
Marketing. Director of Marketing and External
  Affairs: Murphy, Carolyn
  (E-mail: carolyn.murphy@newport.ac.uk)
Minorities/disadvantaged groups. Equalities
  and Diversity Officer: Preece, Alison
  (E-mail: alison.preece@newport.ac.uk)
Personnel/human resources. Director of
  Human Resources: Edwards, Bethan, BA
  CNAA
  (E-mail: bethan.edwards@newport.ac.uk)
Public relations. Director of Marketing and
  External Affairs: Murphy, Carolyn
  (E-mail: carolyn.murphy@newport.ac.uk)
Publications. Publications and Advertising
  Officer: Tilley, Sarah
  (E-mail: sarahtilley1@newport.ac.uk)
Purchasing. Director of Finance: Jones, Denis,
  BSc *Wales*
  (E-mail: denis.jones@newport.ac.uk)
Quality assurance and accreditation. Director
  of Quality Assurance and Enhancement:
  Stephens, Brent
  (E-mail: brent.stephens@newport.ac.uk)
Safety. Health and Safety Officer: Jones,
  Wayne, BSc *Open(UK)*
  (E-mail: wayne.jones@newport.ac.uk)
Scholarships, awards, loans. Head of Student
  Services: Wilson, Lawrence, BA *Leeds*
  (E-mail: lawrence.wilson@newport.ac.uk)
Schools liaison. Schools and Colleges Liaison
  Officer: Veasey, Sandra, BA *Glam.*
  (E-mail: sandra.veasey@newport.ac.uk)
Security. Director of Estates: Godber, Stephen,
  BSc *Glam.*
  (E-mail: stephen.godber@newport.ac.uk)
Sport and recreation. Sports Centre Manager:
  Statton, Ryan, BA *Wales*
  (E-mail: ryan.statton@newport.ac.uk)
Staff development and training. Associate
  Director, Organisational Design and
  Development: Stedman, Trudy
  (E-mail: trudy.stedman@newport.ac.uk)
Strategic planning. Head of Strategic
  Planning: Arnold, Ben

Student union. President, Students' Union:
Cargill, Andrew
(E-mail: studentsunion.president@
newport.ac.uk)
Student welfare/counselling. Head of Student
Services: Wilson, Lawrence, BA *Leeds*
Students from other countries. Dean of
International Affairs: Wood, Graham, BA

CNAA, MA *Griff.*
(E-mail: internationalaffaris@newpot.ac.uk)
Students with disabilities. Head of Student
Services: Wilson, Lawrence, BA *Leeds*
University press. Press and Communications
Officer: Mansell, Phil, MA *Wales*
(E-mail: pressandcoms@newport.ac.uk)

Women. Human Resources Officer: Faithfull,
Antonia, LLB *Wales*

[*Information supplied by the institution as at 17
December 2007, and edited by the ACU*]

UNIVERSITY OF WARWICK

Founded 1965

Member of the Association of Commonwealth Universities

Postal Address: Coventry, England CV4 7AL
Telephone: (024) 7652 3523 **Fax:** (024) 7646 1606
URL: http://www.warwick.ac.uk

VICE-CHANCELLOR*—Thrift, Prof. Nigel J., BA *Wales*, MA *Oxf.*, PhD *Brist.*, DSc *Brist.*, FBA, AcSS
DEPUTY VICE-CHANCELLOR—Palmer, Prof. Stuart B., BSc *Sheff.*, PhD *Sheff.*, DSc *Sheff.*, FIP, FREng
PRO-VICE-CHANCELLOR—Whitby, Prof. M., MA *Oxf.*, DPhil *Oxf.*
PRO-VICE-CHANCELLOR—Bassnett, Prof. Susan E., BA *Manc.*, PhD *Lanc.*
PRO-VICE-CHANCELLOR—Carter, Prof. Y., OBE, BSc *Lond.*, MB BS *Lond.*, MD *Lond.*, FRCGP, FMedSci
PRO-VICE-CHANCELLOR—Higgott, Prof. R. A., BA *CNAA*, MSc *Lond.*, PhD *Birm.*
PRO-VICE-CHANCELLOR—Smith, Prof. Mark E., BA *Camb.*, PhD *Warw.*
TREASURER—Woods-Scawen, B., DL, BA(Econ) *Sheff.*, MA *Warw.*, Hon. DUniv *C.England*, Hon. LLD *Birm.*, FCA,
FRSA
REGISTRAR‡—Baldwin, Jon F., BA *CNAA*, MBA *Open(UK)*, Hon. DLitt *UMIST*, FCIS, FRSA
LIBRARIAN—Bell, A., BA *E.Anglia*, MA *Sheff.*

GENERAL INFORMATION

History. The university was established in
1965.
It is located about 5km from the centre of
Coventry.

Admission to first degree courses (see also
United Kingdom Introduction). Through
Universities and College Admissions Service
(UCAS). Applicants must satisfy the general
entrance requirement. Equivalent overseas
qualifications are accepted. Applicants whose
first language is not English must demonstrate
competence in the English language.

First Degrees (see also United Kingdom
Directory to Subjects of Study). BA, BEng, BSc,
LLB, MB ChB, MChem, MEng, MMath,
MMathStat, MMORSE, MPhys.
Courses may also be taken part-time.
Length of course. Full-time: BA, BEng, BSc, LLB,
MChem, MEng, MMath, MMathStat, MMORSE,
MPhys: 3–4 years; MB ChB: 4–5 years.

Higher Degrees (see also United Kingdom
Directory to Subjects of Study).
Master's. LLM, MA, MBA, MClinSci, MHist,
MMedSci, MPA, MPhil, MRes, MS, MSc.
Admission. Applicants for admission to
master's degrees courses should normally hold
an appropriate first degree with at least second
class honours.
Length of course. Full-time: LLM, MA, MBA,
MPA, MSc: 1 year. Part-time: LLM: 2 years;
MClinSci: 2–8 years. By distance learning: MBA:
3½–8 years.
Doctoral. DClinPsych, DLitt, DSc, EdD, EngD,
LLD, MD, PhD.
Admission. DLitt, DSc, LLD: awarded on
published work.
Length of course. Full-time: DClinPsych, EdD,
PhD: 3 years; EngD: 4 years. Part-time: PhD: 5
years.

Libraries. Volumes: 1,000,000. Periodicals
subscribed to: 12,000. Special collections:
British Petroleum Company archives; corporate
information library (economics and
management); post-1945 German literature;

Modern Records Centre; political groups and
figures (including Frank Cowins, Richard
Crossman, Sir Victor Gollancz); trades union,
employers' and trade associations' records.

Academic Awards (2007–2008). 275
awards ranging in value from £10 to £11,500.

Academic Year (2007–2008). Three terms:
1 October–8 December; 7 January–15 March;
21 April–28 June. Summer session: 29
June–29 September.

Income (2006–2007). Total, £330,670,000.

Statistics. Students (2007–2008): full-time
16,646; international 4348; undergraduate
11,203.

FACULTIES/SCHOOLS

Arts
Tel: (024) 7652 4480 Fax: (024) 7652 8173
Chair: Hallamore Caesar, Prof. Ann, MA *Camb.*,
PhD *Lond.*

Medicine
Tel: (024) 7652 8101 Fax: (024) 7652 4649
Dean: Carter, Prof. Y., OBE, BSc *Lond.*, MB BS
Lond., MD *Lond.*, FRCGP, FMedSci

Science
Tel: (024) 7652 3096 Fax: (024) 7652 4225
Chair: Lamberts, Prof. Koen, BA *Leuven*, BSc
Leuven, MSc *Leuven*, PhD *Leuven*

Social Studies
Tel: (024) 7652 3284 Fax: (024) 7652 4241
Chair: Lindley, Prof. Robert, BSc *Lond.*, MSc
Lond., PhD *Warw.*

ACADEMIC UNITS
Biological Sciences
Staff holding joint appointments with
Walsgrave Hospital NHS Trust are
individually indicated
Tel: (024) 7652 3517 Fax: (024) 7652 3568
E-mail: chowes@bio.warwick.ac.uk
Anderson, E. C., MBioc *Oxf.*, PhD *Camb.*
Assoc. Prof.

Arumagam, P., BSc MSc PhD   Assoc. Prof.
Bland, R., BSc *Wales*, MPhil *Wales*, PhD *Birm.*
Assoc. Prof.
Boseley, P. G., BSc *Edin.*, PhD *Portsmouth*   Hon.
Prof.
Burgert, H. G., MSc *Tübingen*, PhD *Heidel.*
Assoc. Prof.
Carr, N. G., BSc *Leeds*, DPhil *Oxf.*   Emer. Prof.
Carré, I. A., BSc *Paris*, PhD *N.Y.*   Assoc. Prof.
Courtenay, O., BSc *Oxf.*, PhD *Lond.*   Assoc.
Prof.
Dale, Nicholas, BSc *Camb.*, PhD *Brist.*   Prof.
Dalton, Sir Howard, KBE, BSc *Lond.*, DPhil *Sus.*,
FRS   Prof.
Davey, John, BSc *Warw.*, PhD *Warw.*   Prof.
Dow, Crawford S., BSc *Edin.*, PhD *Warw.*
Assoc. Prof. (Reader)
Dowson, Christopher G., BSc *Bath*, PhD *Bath*
Prof.
Easton, Andrew J., BSc *Aberd.*, PhD *Glas.*   Prof.;
Head*
Ellis, R. J., BSc *Lond.*, PhD *Lond.*   Emer. Prof.
Evans, D. J., BSc *Dund.*, DPhil *Sus.*   Prof.
Flint, Ken P., BSc *Birm.*, PhD *Birm.*   Dir. of
Studies
Follett, Brian K., BSc *Brist.*, PhD *Brist.*, DSc
Wales, Hon. LLD *Wales*, Hon. DSc
Tech.U.Malaysia, FRS   Hon. Prof.
Freedman, Robert B., BSc *Oxf.*, DPhil *Oxf.*
Prof.
Frenguelli, B. G., BSc *Glas.*, PhD *Birm.*   Prof.
Frigerio, L., Laurea *Sacred Heart(Milan)*, PhD *Sacred
Heart(Milan)*   Assoc. Prof.
Fulop, V., BSc *Bud.*, PhD *Bud.*   Prof.
Green, A. K., BSc *Manc.*, PhD *Liv.*   Assoc. Prof.
Green, Laura E., BSc *Brist.*, MSc *Lond.*, PhD *Brist.*
Prof.
Hodgkin, M. N., BSc *Coventry*, PhD *Birm.*
Assoc. Prof.
Hodgson, David A., BSc *Warw.*, PhD *E.Anglia*
Prof.
Hulten, M. A., PhD *Stockholm*, MD, FRCPath
Hon. Prof.
Jennings, K. R., BA *Oxf.*, MA *Oxf.*, DPhil *Oxf.*
Emer. Prof.
Jones, Elizabeth A., BSc *Manc.*, DPhil *Oxf.*
Prof.
Keeling, M. J., BSc *Camb.*, PhD *Warw.*   Prof.
Kelly, D. P., BSc *Lond.*, PhD *Lond.*, DSc *Lond.*
Emer. Prof.

Leppard, Keith N., BA Oxf., PhD Lond.   Assoc. Prof. (Reader)
Lord, J. Michael, BSc Salf., PhD Brad.   Prof.
Mann, Nicholas H., BSc Liv., PhD Liv.   Prof.
Marriott, A. C., BA Camb., PhD Lond.   Assoc. Prof.
McCrae, Malcolm A., BSc Edin., PhD Glas.   Prof.
Medley, Graham F. H., BSc York(UK), PhD Lond.   Prof.
Millar, J. B. A., BSc Camb., PhD Lond.   Prof.
Moffat, K. G., BSc Reading, PhD Cran.IT   Assoc. Prof.
Morris, Alan G., BA Oxf., DPhil Oxf.   Assoc. Prof. (Reader)
Murrell, J. Colin, BSc S'ton., PhD Warw.   Prof.
Nokes, D. J., BSc Lond., PhD Lond.   Assoc. Prof. (Reader)
Norris, Paul R., BSc CNAA, PhD Lond.   Assoc. Prof. (Reader)
Old, Robert W., BA Camb., PhD Edin.   Assoc. Prof. (Reader)
Pankratov, Y., BSc Moscow, MSc Moscow, PhD Kiev   Assoc. Prof.
Pinheiro, T. J. T., Lic Coimbra, MSc Coimbra, DPhil Oxf.   Assoc. Prof.
Price, A. R. G., BSc Wales, PhD Wales   Assoc. Prof. (Reader)
Primrose, S., BSc Strath., PhD Calif.   Hon. Prof.
Pringle, C. R., BSc Glas., PhD Edin.   Emer. Prof.
Roberts, Lynne M., BTech Brad., PhD Brad.   Prof.
Robinson, Colin, BSc Edin., PhD Warw.   Prof.
Roper, D. I., BSc Wales, PhD Leic.   Assoc. Prof.
Scanlan, D. J., MSc Durh., PhD Warw.   Prof.
Scott, D., BSc Bath, PhD Bath   Assoc. Prof.
Scrivens, J. H., BSc Manc., MSc Manc., PhD Manc.   Prof.
Sheppard, C., BSc CNAA, PhD Durh.   Reader
Smith, C. J. I., BSc Brist., PhD Brist.   Assoc. Prof.
Squires, P. E., BSc Sheff., PhD Sheff.   Assoc. Prof.
Stanfield, Peter R., BA Camb., PhD Camb., ScD Camb.   Prof.
Wall, M. J., BPharm Lond., PhD Brist.   Assoc. Prof.
Wellington, Elizabeth M. H., BSc Liv., PhD Liv.   Prof.
Whittenbury, R., BSc Leeds, MSc Edin., PhD Edin.   Emer. Prof.
Wilson, T. M. A., BSc Edin., PhD Camb.   Prof.
Woodland, Hugh R., MA Oxf., DPhil Oxf.   Prof.
Other Staff: 8 Res. Fellows; 1 Assoc. Clin. Prof.; 1 Hon. Fellow
Research: cell and molecular development; ecosystems analysis and management; microbiology; molecular cell biology; molecular medicine

Chemistry

Tel: (024) 7652 3653 Fax: (024) 7652 4112
E-mail: c.a.m.billing@warwick.ac.uk
Bon, S. A. F., MSc T.U.Eindhoven, PhD T.U.Eindhoven   Assoc. Prof.
Bugg, Timothy D. H., BA Camb., PhD Camb.   Prof., Biological Chemistry
Challis, Gregory L., BSc Lond., DPhil Oxf.   Prof.
Clark, Andrew J., BSc Lond., PhD Lond.   Assoc. Prof.
Davis, P. J., BSc Lond., MSc Lond., PhD Lond.   Hon. Prof.
Deeth, Robert J., BSc Tas., PhD Camb.   Assoc. Prof. (Reader)
Derrick, Peter J., BSc Lond., PhD Lond., FIP, FRACI, FRSChem   Prof.
Drewello, Thomas, PhD T.U.Berlin   Assoc. Prof.
Haddleton, David M., BSc York(UK), DPhil York(UK), PhD York(UK)   Prof.
Jenkins, H. Donald B., BScTech Manc., DPhil Sus.   Prof.
Jones, T., BSc Liv., PhD Liv.   Prof.
Marsh, Andrew, BSc Lond., PhD Lond.   Assoc. Prof.
Roberts, P. D., BSc Durh., PhD Durh.   Hon. Prof.
Rodger, Alison, BSc Syd., MA Oxf., PhD Syd.   Prof.

Rodger, P. Mark, BSc Syd., PhD Syd.   Prof.
Rourke, Jonathan P., BSc Sheff., PhD Sheff.   Assoc. Prof.
Sadler, P. J., MA Oxf., DPhil Oxf., FRS, FRSEd   Prof.; Head*
Scott, Peter, BSc Salf., DPhil Oxf.   Prof.
Shipman, M., BSc Lond., PhD Lond.   Prof.
Taylor, Paul C., BSc Durh., PhD Durh.   Assoc. Prof. (Reader)
Taylor, Peter R., BSc Syd., PhD Syd.   Prof.
Unwin, Patrick R., BSc Liv., DPhil Oxf.   Prof.
Walsh, T. R., BSc Melb., PhD Camb.   Assoc. Prof.
Walton, R. I., BA Oxf., MA Oxf., PhD Reading   Assoc. Prof.
Wills, Martin, BSc Lond., DPhil Oxf.   Prof.
Other Staff: 3 Asst. Profs.; 1 Sr. Res. Fellow; 30 Res. Fellows; 2 Acad. Fellows; 2 Res. Officers
Research: analytical chemistry; biological chemistry; inorganic chemistry; organic chemistry; physical chemistry

Classics and Ancient History

Tel: (024) 7652 3023 Fax: (024) 7652 4973
E-mail: josie.brown@warwick.ac.uk
Butcher, K., BA Lond., PhD Lond.   Prof.
Cooley, A. E., MA Oxf., DPhil Oxf.   Assoc. Prof.
Davidson, James N., MA Oxf., MPhil Col., DPhil Oxf.   Reader
Ireland, Stanley, BA Hull, PhD Camb.   Assoc. Prof.
Laird, Andrew J. W., MA Lond., DPhil Oxf.   Prof.; Head*
Murray, Penny A., MA Camb., PhD Camb.   Assoc. Prof.
Swain, Simon C. R., MA Oxf., DPhil Oxf.   Prof.
Whitby, Michael L., MA Oxf., DPhil Oxf.   Prof.
Other Staff: 6 Asst. Profs.
Research: archaeology of the Black Sea coast; east Roman studies; Greek and Roman poetry and drama

Computer Science

Tel: (024) 7652 3193 Fax: (024) 7657 3024
E-mail: comp-sci@dcs.warwick.ac.uk
Anand, S. S., BA Delhi, MSc Belf., DPhil Ulster   Assoc. Prof.
Beynon, W. Meurig, BSc Lond., PhD Lond.   Assoc. Prof. (Reader)
Bhalerao, A. H., BSc Warw., PhD Warw.   Assoc. Prof.
Campbell-Kelly, Martin, BSc Manc., PhD CNAA   Prof.
Cristea, A. I., MEng Bucharest, PhD Tokyo   Assoc. Prof.
Czumaj, A., MSc Warsaw, PhD Paderborn   Prof.
Feng, J., BS Peking, MS Peking, PhD Peking   Prof.
Griffiths, N. E., BSc Warw., PhD Warw.   Assoc. Prof.
Jarvis, Stephen, BSc Lond., MSc Oxf., PhD Durh.   Assoc. Prof.
Joy, Mike S., MA Camb., PhD E.Anglia   Assoc. Prof.
Kalvala, S., MCA Hyd., MSc Calif., PhD Calif., BSc   Assoc. Prof.
Lazic, R. S., BA Oxf., DPhil Oxf.   Assoc. Prof.
Li, C. T., PhD Warw., BS MS   Assoc. Prof.
Martin, Graham R., BSc Lond., PhD Lond.   Assoc. Prof.
Matthews, S. G., BSc Lond., MSc Lond., PhD Warw.   Assoc. Prof.
Nagarajan, R., MS Delaware, PhD Lond.   Assoc. Prof.
Nudd, Graham R., BSc S'ton., PhD S'ton.   Prof.; Head*
Paterson, Mike S., MA Camb., PhD Camb.   Prof.
Peled, Doron, BSc MSc DSc   Prof.
Rajpoot, N. M., PhD Warw., BSc MSc   Assoc. Prof.
Russ, S. B., BSc Lond., MA Lond., PhD Open(UK)   Assoc. Prof.
Sinclair, J. E., BA Oxf., PhD Open(UK)   Assoc. Prof.
Tiskin, A., MSc Leningrad Inst.Technol., DPhil Oxf.   Assoc. Prof.

Wilson, Roland G., BSc Glas., PhD Glas.   Prof.; Head*
Other Staff: 4 Asst. Profs.
Research: applications; software; systems; theory

Economics

Tel: (024) 7652 3055 Fax: (024) 7652 3032
E-mail: a.simper@warwick.ac.uk
Arulampalam, S. Wiji, BSc(Econ) Lond., MSc Lond., PhD Lond.   Assoc. Prof.
Barankav, I., BA Lausanne, MSc Warw., PhD(Econ) Warw.   Assoc. Prof.
Blackorby, Charles, BA Harv., PhD Johns H.   Prof.
Bloch, F., MA Paris, PhD Penn.   Prof.
Boero, G., MA Warw., PhD Cagliari   Assoc. Prof.
Broadberry, Stephen N., BA Warw., DPhil Oxf.   Prof.
Cave, J. A. K., BSc Yale, MA Camb., PhD Stan.   Assoc. Prof.
Chatterji, S., BA Delhi, PhD N.Y.State   Prof.
Clements, Mike, BSc Brist., MSc York(UK), DPhil Oxf.   Prof.
Corradi, V., BA Milan, MA Calif., PhD Calif.   Prof.
Crafts, Nicholas F. R., BA Camb., FBA   Prof.
Dhillon, A., BA Delhi, MA Delhi, PhD   Assoc. Prof. (Reader)
Dutta, Bhaskar, BA Calc., MA Delhi, PhD Delhi   Prof.
Ellison, M., MPhil Oxf., PhD Florence   Prof.
Ghosal, Sayantan, BA Bom., MA Delhi, PhD Paris, PhD   Prof.
Gupta, B., BA Calc., MA Calc., MPhil J.Nehru U., DPhil Oxf.   Assoc. Prof.
Hammond, P., BA Camb., PhD Camb.   Prof.
Harrison, R. Mark, BA Camb., DPhil Oxf.   Prof.; Head*
Hart, O., BA Camb., MA Warw., PhD Prin.   Hon. Prof.
Ireland, Norman J., BSocSci Birm., MSocSc Birm., PhD Warw.   Prof.
Kanbur, R., BA Camb., MPhil Oxf., DPhil Oxf.   Hon. Prof.
Knight, K. G., BA Manc., MA(Econ) Manc.   Assoc. Prof.
Leech, Dennis, BA Manc., MA(Econ) Manc., PhD Warw.   Prof.
Lockwood, Ben, BA Sus., PhD Warw.   Prof.
Mani, A., BA Bom., PhD Boston   Assoc. Prof.
Mezzetti, C., BA Manc., MA(Econ) Manc., PhD ANU   Prof.
Miller, Marcus H., BA Oxf., MA Yale, PhD Yale   Prof.
Mukand, S., BA Delhi, MA(Econ) Delhi, PhD Boston   Prof.
Naylor, Robin A., BSc(Econ) Lond., MPhil Oxf., PhD Warw.   Prof.
Oswald, Andrew J., BA Stir., MSc Strath., DPhil Oxf.   Prof.
Perroni, Carlo, BSc(Econ) Genoa, PhD Pavia   Prof.
Pitt, M., BSc Brad., MSc Oxf., PhD Oxf.   Assoc. Prof.
Polemarchakis, H. M., AB Yale, PhD Harv.   Prof.
Pyatt, G., BA Manc., PhD Camb.   Hon. Prof.
Rankin, Neil, MA Oxf., DPhil Oxf.   Prof.
Redoano Coppede, M., MSc Warw., PhD Warw.   Assoc. Prof.
Round, Jeffrey I., BSc Nott., PhD Wales   Assoc. Prof. (Reader)
Scharf, Kimberley A., BA W.Ont., MA W.Ont., PhD Tor.   Assoc. Prof. (Reader)
Seade, J., BSc Mexico Natnl., MPhil Oxf., DPhil Oxf.   Hon. Prof.
Slade, Margaret, BA N.Y., MA Calif., PhD(Econ) Wash.   Prof.
Smith, J. C., BA Oxf., MPhil Camb., PhD Camb.   Assoc. Prof.
Smith, Jeremy P. D., BA(Econ) Manc., PhD ANU   Prof.
Stewart, Mark B., BA Warw., MSc(Econ) Lond.   Prof.
Taylor, Mark P., MA Oxf., MSc Lond., PhD Lond.   Prof.
Thomas, J. P., MA Camb., MPhil Oxf., DPhil Oxf.   Hon. Prof.

Walker, Ian, BA Liv., MA Warw.   Prof.

Wallis, K. F., BSc Manc., MScTech Manc., PhD Stan., FBA   Prof.

Waterson, Michael J., BA Warw., MSc Lond., PhD Warw.   Prof.

Whalley, John, BA Essex, MA Essex, PhD Yale Prof., Development Economics

Williamson, J. H., BSc(Econ) Lond., PhD Prin.   Hon. Prof.

Wooders, Myrna, BA Alta., PhD Minn.   Prof.

Zhang, Lei, BSc Peking, MSc Peking, MA Warw., PhD Warw.   Assoc. Prof.

Other Staff: 1 Assoc. Prof.; 11 Asst. Profs.

Research: econometrics; economic history; economic theory; industrial and labour economics; macroeconomics

Education, Institute of

Tel: (024) 7652 4122 Fax: (024) 7652 4177
E-mail: wie@warwick.ac.uk

Abbott, Ian D., BA Leic.   Assoc. Prof.

Allen, T., BA Leeds, PhD Leic.   Assoc. Prof.

Aubrey, C., BA Open(UK), BPhil(Ed) Birm., MEd Birm., PhD Hull   Prof.

Barnes, A., BA Nott., MA Nott., PhD Warw.   Assoc. Prof.

Briggs, Mary, BA Open(UK)   Assoc. Prof.

Brooks, V., BA Leeds, PhD Leic.   Assoc. Prof.

Bush, T., BSocSci Birm., MA Brun.   Prof.

Christensen, P., MSc Copenhagen, PhD Hull   Prof.

Coates, E. A., BA Open(UK), MPhil Birm.   Assoc. Prof.

Engestrom, Y.   Prof.

Everington, J., BA Lanc., MA Lanc., MEd Birm.   Assoc. Prof.

Francis, L., BA Oxf., BD Oxf., MA Oxf., MSc Lond., MTh Nott., PhD Camb., ScD Camb.   Prof.

Gleeson, Dennis, BSc Lond., MA Lond.   Prof.

Gray, Eddie M., BA Open(UK), MSc Lough., PhD Warw.   Assoc. Prof. (Reader)

Hammond, M., BA Warw., MEd Open(UK), PhD Sheff.   Assoc. Prof.

Harris, A., BA Wales, MEd Wales, PhD Bath   Prof.; Dir.*

Hartas, D., BA Ill., MEd Ill., PhD Ill.   Assoc. Prof.

Huddleston, Prue J., BA Lond., MEd Warw.   Prof.

Hunt, M. J., BA Lond.   Assoc. Prof.

Jackson, Robert M. D., BA Wales, MA Warw., PhD Warw.   Prof.

Johnston-Wilder, P. J., BA Camb., MSc Lond.   Assoc. Prof.

Johnston-Wilder, S.   Assoc. Prof.

Kumpulainen, K.   Prof.

Lee, N. M., BA Reading, MSc Bath, PhD Reading   Assoc. Prof.

Lindsay, Geoffrey A., BSc Durh., MEd Birm., PhD Birm., FBPsS   Prof.

Medwell, J., BA Reading, MEd Wales, PhD Exe.   Assoc. Prof.

Neelands, J., BEd Leic., MEd Leic., PhD Warw.   Reader

Neill, Sean R. St. J., BA Oxf., DPhil Oxf.   Assoc. Prof.

Nesbitt, Eleanor M., MA Camb., MPhil Nott., PhD Warw.   Prof.

Pritchard, A. M., BEd Warw., MSc Warw.   Assoc. Prof.

Prout, A., BA Keele, MA Keele, PhD Keele   Prof.

Ranson, S., BSc Lond., MA Reading, DSocSci Birm.   Prof.; Dir., Res. Students

Raper, G., BSc Durh., MSc Newcastle(UK), PhD Leeds   Dir., Undergrad. Studies

Shilvock, K. E., MA Warw.   Assoc. Prof.

Strand, S., BA Plym., PhD Plym.   Assoc. Prof. (Reader)

Tall, David O., MA Oxf., DPhil Oxf., PhD Warw.   Prof.

Trowsdale, J. A., BA Sheff.   Assoc. Prof.

Wilkie, C., MA S'ton., PhD Wales   Assoc. Prof.

Winston, J. A., BA Lond., MEd Exe., PhD Warw.   Assoc. Prof.

Wray, David J., BA Hull, MSc Lanc.   Prof.

Wyness, M., MA Edin., PhD Edin.   Assoc. Prof.

Other Staff: 12 Asst. Profs.; 5 Res. Fellows; 1 Res. Assoc.; 5 Sr. Teaching Fellows; 1 Teaching Fellow

Research: arts education; industry collaboration; mathematics education; primary education; special needs

Engineering, School of

Tel: (024) 7652 2135 Fax: (024) 7641 8922
E-mail: v.l.flower@warwick.ac.uk

Anderson, David, BSc Manc., PhD Manc., FIStructE, FICE   Prof.

Arunachalam, V. S., BSc Mys., MSc Saug., PhD Wales, Hon. DSc Indore, Hon. DLitt   Prof.

Bal, D. J., BSc CNAA, MSc UMIST   Assoc. Prof.

Banerji, S., BTech Kharagpur, MTech Kharagpur, PhD Manc.   Prof., Operations Management

Barnes, S., BSc CNAA, PhD Birm.   Assoc. Prof.; Dir., Indust. Programmes

Bhattacharyya, S. Kumar, CBE, KBE, BTech Kharagpur, MSc Birm., PhD Birm., Hon. DUniv Sur., Hon. DEng Tech.U.Malaysia, Hon. DBA HK Poly., FREng, FIEE   Prof.; Head, Warwick Manufacturing Group

Billson, D. R., BSc H-W, MSc H-W, PhD Warw.   Assoc. Prof.

Bradbury, K. S., BEng CNAA, MSc Herts.   Dir., Undergrad. Admissions

Bryanston-Cross, Peter J., BSc Aston, PhD Aston, FRAeS   Prof.

Chalmers, A. G., BSc Natal, BSc Rhodes, MSc Rhodes, PhD Brist.   Prof.

Chappell, M. J., BSc Warw., MSc Warw., PhD Warw.   Assoc. Prof.

Chetwynd, Derek G., BA Oxf., PhD Leic.   Prof.

Chung, Y. M., BSc Korea A.I.S.T., MSc Korea A.I.S.T., PhD Korea A.I.S.T.   Assoc. Prof.

Cole, M., PhD Coventry, BSc   Assoc. Prof.

Covington, J. A., BEng Warw., MRes Warw., PhD Warw.   Assoc. Prof.

Critoph, Robert E., BSc S'ton., PhD S'ton., DSc Warw.   Prof.

Davies, S. T., BSc Lond., PhD Lond.   Assoc. Prof.

Dover, R. A., BSc Manc., Hon. DSc Warw., FREng, FRSA   Indust. Prof.

Dowd, Amanda L., BSc Leic., PhD Leic.   Lectr.; Academic Dir., Grad. Studies

Eames, P., BSc Brist., MSc Cran.IT, PhD Cran.IT   Prof.

Er, A., MSc Birm., PhD Birm.   Assoc. Prof.

Ferrie, John, BSc Warw., EngD Warw.   Indust. Prof.

Flower, John O., BSc(Eng) Lond., PhD Lond., DSc Lond., FIEE, FIMarEST   Prof.

Gardner, Julian W., BSc Birm., PhD Camb., DSc Warw., FIEE   Prof., Electronic Engineering; Dean*

Godfrey, Keith R., BSc(Eng) Lond., PhD Lond., DSc Warw., FIEE   Prof.

Green, R. J., BSc UMIST, PhD Brad., FIEE   Head of Div., Electronic Engin.; Prof., Electronic Communication System

Guymer, I., BSc Lough., PhD Birm.   Prof.

Hines, Evor L., BSc CNAA, PhD Brad.   Reader

Hodge, C., BSc MSc, FIMarEST, FREng   Hon. Prof.

Huang, T., BSc Tianjin, MSc Tianjin, PhD Tianjin   Prof.

Hutchins, David A., BSc Aston, PhD Aston   Prof.

Iliescu, D. D., BSc Bucharest, PhD Warw.   Assoc. Prof.

Jennings, P. A., BA Oxf., EngD Warw.   Assoc. Prof.

Jones, R. Peter, BSc Sheff., MScTech Sheff., PhD Sheff., FIMA   Reader

Kerr, Robert M., BSc Chic., MSc Chic., PhD Cornell   Prof.

Kimber, P. J., BSc Warw.   Assoc. Prof.

Leeson, M. S., BSc Nott., BEng Nott., PhD Camb.   Assoc. Prof.

Lewis, Wanda J., BSc Opole, MSc Birm., PhD CNAA   Assoc. Prof. (Reader)

Liu, X., BSc Harbin, MSc Harbin, PhD Warw.   Assoc. Prof.

Mao, K., BSc Harbin, MSc Harbin, PhD Birm.   Assoc. Prof.

Mawby, P. A., BSc Leeds, PhD Leeds, FIEE, FIP   Prof.

McNulty, Sir Roy, CBE, BA Trinity(Dub.), BComm Trinity(Dub.)   Indust. Prof.

Mias, C., BEng Bath, PhD Camb.   Assoc. Prof.

Mottram, J. Toby, BSc Durh., PhD Durh.   Reader

Neailey, K., BSc Leeds, PhD Warw.   Assoc. Prof.

Purnell, P., BEng Exe., PhD Aston   Assoc. Prof.

Raja, V. H., BSc Coventry, MSc Tees., PhD Calif.   Prof. Fellow

Rakels, J. H., DrIng T.U.Eindhoven, PhD Warw.   Dir., Undergrad. Studies

Roy, Rajat, BSc Calc., MSc Birm.   Prof. Fellow

Ruffles, Philip C., BSc Brist., Hon. DEng Brist., Hon. DEng Birm., Hon. DEng Sheff., FREng, FIMechE, FRAeS   Hon. Prof.

Stocks, Nigel G., BSc Lanc., PhD Lanc.   Prof.

Storey, N., BSc S'ton., PhD S'ton.   Dir., Internat. Undergrad. Admissions

Tennant, C., BSc CNAA, MSc Warw., EngD Warw., FIMechE   Assoc. Prof.

Thomas, Peter J., PhD Gött.   Assoc. Prof. (Reader)

Thomas, T. H., BA Camb., PhD Warw.   Assoc. Prof.

Tjahjadi, T., BSc Lond., MSc UMIST, PhD UMIST   Assoc. Prof.

Veshagh, Ali, BSc Teheran, PhD Bath   Assoc. Prof.

Wallbank, James, BSc Wales, MSc Strath., PhD Birm.   Assoc. Prof.

Warry, Peter T., LLB Lond., MA Oxf., FIMechE, FIEE   Indust. Prof.

Young, K. W., BSc Nott., PhD Nott.   Reader

Zhao, C-Y, BEng Xi'an Jiaotong, PhD Xi'an Jiaotong   Assoc. Prof.

Other Staff: 15 Asst. Profs.; 5 Principal Res. Fellows; 6 Principal Teaching Fellows; 9 Principal Fellows; 27 Sr. Res. Fellows; 41 Sr. Teaching Fellows; 4 Sr. Fellows; 27 Res. Fellows; 1 Royal Society Res. Fellow; 4 Res. Assocs.; 2 Sr. Lectrs.†; 13 Asst. Profs.†; 1 Sr. Res. Fellow†; 31 Sr. Teaching Fellows†

Research: advanced materials assessment and characterisation; control engineering; development studies; electronics; fluid mechanics and aerodynamics

English and Comparative Literary Studies

Tel: (024) 7652 3323 Fax: (024) 7652 4750
E-mail: helen.j.taylor@warwick.ac.uk

Barry, E. C., BA York(UK), DPhil Oxf.   Assoc. Prof.

Bate, J., MA Camb., PhD Camb.   Prof.

Bates, C. T., BA Oxf., DPhil Oxf.   Assoc. Prof. (Reader)

Bell, Michael, BA Lond., PhD Lond.   Prof.

Britzolakis, C., BA Witw., MPhil Oxf., DPhil Oxf.   Assoc. Prof.

Clarke, E., BA Lond., DPhil Oxf.   Reader

Coe, J., BA Camb., PhD Warw.   Hon. Prof.

Dennis, Helen M., BA York(UK), DPhil York(UK)   Assoc. Prof.

Docherty, T., MA Glas., DPhil Oxf.   Prof.; Head*

Fletcher, A. J., BA Melb., BPhil Oxf.   Assoc. Prof.

Francis, E., BA S'ton., MA S'ton., PhD Liv.   Assoc. Prof.

Frith, G. M., BA Oxf., MA Warw., PhD Warw.   Assoc. Prof.

Grant, T., BA Camb., PhD Camb.   Assoc. Prof.

Howard, Antony, BA Warw., MA Tor.   Assoc. Prof.

Hulse, M. W., MA St And.   Assoc. Prof.

Kennedy, A. L., BA Warw.   Assoc. Prof.

Kooy, M. J., BA Redeemer UC, DPhil Oxf.   Assoc. Prof.

Labbe, J., BA Ohio, MA Penn., PhD Penn.   Prof.

Lazarus, Neil, BA Witw., MA Essex, PhD Keele   Prof.

Mack, P. W. D., MA Oxf., MPhil Lond., PhD Lond.   Prof.

Mason, E. J., BA Wales, MA Wales, PhD Warw.   Assoc. Prof.

Mee, J., BA Newcastle(UK), PhD Camb.   Prof.

Miéville, C., BA Camb., MSc Lond., PhD Lond.   Assoc. Prof.

Morley, D., BSc Brist.   Assoc. Prof.; Dir., Warwick Writing Programme

Mukherjee, U. P., BA Calc., MA Calc., MPhil Oxf., PhD Camb.   Assoc. Prof.

Mulryne, J. R., MA Camb., PhD Camb. Hon. Prof.

O'Brien, K., BA Oxf., DPhil Oxf. Prof.

Pamuk, O., BA Robert(Istanbul) Hon. Prof.

Parry, B., BSocSci Cape Town, BA Birm., MA Birm. Prof.

Rawson, C. J., MA Oxf., BLitt Oxf. Hon. Prof.

Rignall, J. M., MA Camb., DPhil Sus. Assoc. Prof. (Reader)

Rutter, C. C., BA Calif., MA Mich., PhD Mich. Prof.

Shapiro, S., BA Williams(Mass.), MA Yale, PhD Yale Assoc. Prof.

Sharpe, K., BA Oxf., MA Oxf., DPhil Oxf., FRHistS Hon. Prof.

Treglown, J. D., MA Oxf., BLitt Oxf., PhD Lond., FRSL Prof.

Uglow, J., BA Oxf., BLitt Oxf. Hon. Prof.

Varma, R., BA Delhi, MA Delhi, PhD Ill. Assoc. Prof.

Whitehead, C. A. R., BA Oxf., DPhil Oxf. Assoc. Prof.

Other Staff: 6 Asst. Profs.; 3 Royal Literary Fund Teaching Fellows; 2 Hon. Teaching Fellows

Research: literature in the English language from the Middle Ages to the present

English Language Teacher Education, Centre for

Tel: (024) 7652 3200 Fax: (024) 7652 4318
E-mail: celte@warwick.ac.uk

Kennedy, J., BEd Lond., MA Leic. Assoc. Prof.

Pinter, A. M., BA Bud., MA Warw., PhD Warw. Assoc. Prof.

Richards, K., BA Liv., MSc Aston, PhD Aston Assoc. Prof.

Rixon, S., BA Camb., MSc Edin. Assoc. Prof.

Smith, R., MA Oxf., MA Reading, PhD Edin. Assoc. Prof.

Spencer-Oatey, H., BA Durh., MEd Wales, PhD Lanc. Dir.*

Ushioda, E., BA Trinity(Dub.), MPhil Trinity(Dub.), PhD Trinity(Dub.) Assoc. Prof.

Wharton, S., BA Sheff., MA Lond., PhD Aston Assoc. Prof.

Other Staff: 2 Sr. Teaching Fellows; 1 Lang. Tutor

Research: language education policy; planning, grammar and discourse; testing and evaluation

Film and Television Studies

Tel: (024) 7652 3511 Fax: (024) 7652 4757
E-mail: t.a.bale@warwick.ac.uk

Arroyo, J. A. A., BA McG., MA E.Anglia Assoc. Prof.

Brunsdon, Charlotte M., BA Lond., PhD Birm. Prof.

Bruzzi, S., BA Manc., PhD Brist. Prof.; Head*

Burrows, J., BA Exe., MA E.Anglia, PhD E.Anglia Assoc. Prof.

Constable, C. A. E., BA Camb., MA York(UK), PhD Warw. Assoc. Prof.

Gallafent, E. C., BA S'ton., PhD S'ton. Assoc. Prof. (Reader)

Gundle, S. J., BA Liv., MA N.Y.State, PhD Camb. Prof.

Moseley, R. S., BA Warw., MA E.Anglia, PhD Warw. Assoc. Prof.

Phillips, A. W. E., BA Stir., MA Warw., PhD Warw. Assoc. Prof.

Pumphrey, M., BA Durh., MA Leic., PhD Iowa Assoc. Prof.

Other Staff: 1 Asst. Prof.

Research: European cinema and television; gender and ethnicity

French Studies

Tel: (024) 7652 3013 Fax: (024) 7652 4679
E-mail: s.howell@warwick.ac.uk

Ahearne, J. N., BA Oxf., DPhil Oxf. Assoc. Prof.; Head*

Astbury, K., BA Exe., PhD Exe. Sr. Lectr.

De Smet, Ingrid A. R., MA Leuven, PhD Camb. Assoc. Prof. (Reader)

Haigh, Samantha J., BA Birm., MA Nott., PhD Nott. Assoc. Prof.

Hampton, C. M., BA Durh., PhD Durh. Assoc. Prof.

Hand, S., BA Oxf., DPhil Oxf. Prof.

Hewlett, N. P., BA Sus., MA Essex, PhD Oxf.Brookes Prof.

Hill, Leslie J., MA Camb., PhD Camb. Prof.

Morrey, D., BA Warw., MA Warw., PhD Warw. Assoc. Prof.

Paterson, Linda M., MA Camb., PhD Camb. Prof.

Shields, James G., MA Glas., PhD Glas. Assoc. Prof. (Reader)

Other Staff: 3 Asst. Profs.; 1 Acad. Fellow

Research: cinema, politics and culture; francophone Caribbean writing; French literature, philosophy and critical theory

German Studies

Tel: (024) 7652 4419 Fax: (024) 7652 8173
E-mail: m.l.lucas@warwick.ac.uk

Allan, S. D., MA Camb., MPhil Camb., PhD Camb. Assoc. Prof.

Burns, Robert A., BA Birm., MA Warw., PhD Warw. Prof.; Head*

Carter, E. A., BA Birm., PhD Birm. Prof.

Jordan, J., PhD Warw. Assoc. Prof.

Lamb, Stephen J., BA Birm., MA Warw. Assoc. Prof.

Schmitz, H., MA Warw., PhD Warw. Assoc. Prof.

Other Staff: 2 Asst. Profs.; 3 Lectrs.; 1 Lang. Co-ord.

Research: German culture from 1870 to the present day

Health and Social Studies, School of

Tel: (024) 7657 4136 Fax: (024) 7652 4415
E-mail: p.j.glover@warwick.ac.uk

Blackburn, C., BA CNAA Assoc. Prof. (Reader)

Chand, A., BSc E.Lond., MASocWork E.Anglia Assoc. Prof.

Chung, D., BSW NE, MA NE, PhD Adel. Assoc. Prof. (Reader)

Dolan, A., BA Warw., PhD Warw. Assoc. Prof.

Galvani, S., MA Hull, PhD Hull Assoc. Prof.

Harris, J., BA CNAA, MA Warw., PhD Warw. Prof.

Harrison, C., BA CNAA, MA Warw., PhD Warw. Assoc. Prof.; Head*

Joly, Daniele, LèsL Paris, MèsL Paris, PhD Aston Prof.

Lewando-Hundt, G., MA Edin., MPhil Edin., PhD Warw. Prof.

Markham, W., BSc St And., MPhil Camb., PhD Birm. Assoc. Prof.

McLeod, E., BA Camb., PhD Warw. Assoc. Prof. (Reader)

Mullender, A. E., BA Sheff., MA Nott., PhD Warw., FRSA Prof.

Seers, K., BSc PhD Prof.

Tanner, D., BSc Birm., MSocSci Birm., PhD Warw. Assoc. Prof.

White, V., MA Warw., PhD Warw. Assoc. Prof.

Other Staff: 7 Sr. Res. Fellows; 8 Res. Fellows; 2 Marie Curie Res. Fellows

Research: community care; health-related behaviour; welfare of children and young people

History

Tel: (024) 7652 2080 Fax: (024) 7652 4451
E-mail: j.m.noonan@warwick.ac.uk

Arnold, D., BA Exe., DPhil Sus., FBA Prof.

Berg, Maxine L., BA S.Fraser, MA Sus., DPhil Oxf., FBA Prof.

Burnard, T. G., PhD Johns H. Prof.

Butters, Humfrey C., MA Oxf., DPhil Oxf., FRHistS Assoc. Prof. (Reader)

Capp, Bernard S., MA Oxf., DPhil Oxf., FRHistS Prof.

Earle, R. A., BA Bryn Mawr, MA Warw., MSc Warw., PhD Warw. Assoc. Prof. (Reader)

Fagge, R. J., BA Lond., PhD Camb. Assoc. Prof.

Finn, M. C., BSc Syr., MA Col., MPhil Col., PhD Col., FRHistS, FBA Prof.

Gerritsen, A., BA Ley., PhD Harv. Assoc. Prof.

Heuman, Gad J., BA Col., MA Yale, MPhil Yale, PhD Yale, FRHistS Prof.

Hindle, S., MA Minn., MA Camb., PhD Camb., FRHistS Prof.

Hodges, S., BA Brown, MA Chic., PhD Chic. Assoc. Prof.

Horn, G. R., BA Minn., PhD Mich. Assoc. Prof.

King, John P., MA Edin., DPhil Oxf. Prof.

Knights, M. J., BA Oxf., DPhil Oxf. Prof.

Kùmin, B., MA Berne, PhD Camb., FRHistS Assoc. Prof. (Reader)

Lockley, T. J., MA Edin., PhD Camb. Assoc. Prof.

Luddy, Mona, BEd Limerick, MA N.U.I., PhD N.U.I. Prof.

Major, P., BA Oxf., DPhil Oxf. Assoc. Prof.

Marland, H., BA Warw., MA Warw., PhD Warw. Prof.

Marshall, P., MA Oxf., DPhil Oxf. Prof.

McFarlane, Anthony J., BSc(Econ) Lond., PhD Lond. Prof.

Mick, C., MA Tübingen, DPhil Tübingen Assoc. Prof.

Molà, L., Laurea Venice, MA Johns H., PhD Johns H. Assoc. Prof.

Okey, Robin F. C., MA Oxf., DPhil Oxf., FRHistS Prof.

Read, Christopher J., BA Keele, MPhil Glas., PhD Lond., FRHistS Prof.

Richardson, S. A., BA Manc., MA Hull, PhD Leeds Assoc. Prof.

Roberts, P. W., BA Birm., MA Warw., PhD Birm., FRHistS Assoc. Prof.

Rose, S., PhD Northwestern Hon. Prof.

Steedman, Carolyn K., BA Sus., MLitt Camb., PhD Camb. Prof.

Thomson, Guy P. C., BSc(Econ) Lond., DPhil Oxf., FRHistS Assoc. Prof. (Reader)

Van Damme, S., PhD Paris IV Assoc. Prof.

Other Staff: 5 Asst. Profs.; 3 Res. Fellows; 1 Warwick Res. Fellow

Research: British, European and comparative American history, including social history and the history of medicine

History of Art

Tel: (024) 7652 3005 Fax: (024) 7652 3006
E-mail: history.of.art@warwick.ac.uk

Bourdua, L., BA McG., MLitt Lond., PhD Warw. Assoc. Prof.

Campbell, Louise E. M., BA Sus., MA Lond., PhD Lond. Assoc. Prof.

Hatt, M., BA Lond., PhD Lond. Prof.

Rosenthal, Michael J., BA Lond., MA Camb., PhD Lond. Prof.

Smith, P., BA Lond., PhD Lond. Prof.; Head*

Other Staff: 4 Asst. Profs.

Research: art and architecture of Western Europe; mediaeval art in the East and West; Venice

Italian

Tel: (024) 7652 4126 Fax: (024) 7652 8174
E-mail: j.f.williams@warwick.ac.uk

Burns, J., MA Oxf., MSt Oxf., DPhil Oxf. Assoc. Prof.

Gilson, Simon, BA Leeds, PhD Camb. Assoc. Prof. (Reader); Head*

Hallamore Caesar, Ann, MA Camb., PhD Lond. Prof.

Polezzi, L., MA Warw., PhD Warw. Assoc. Prof.

Other Staff: 1 Asst. Prof.; 2 Language Tutors

Research: narrative and theatre from the Middle Ages to the present day

Law

Tel: (024) 7652 3075 Fax: (024) 7652 4105
E-mail: lesley.morris@warwick.ac.uk

Adelman, S., BA Witw., LLB Witw., LLM Harv., PhD Warw. Assoc. Prof.

Alexander, S. K., BA Cornell, MPhil Camb., JD Minn., PhD Lond. Assoc. Prof.

Ali, S. S., BA Pesh., LLB Pesh., LLM Hull, MPolSc MPolSt Prof.

Baxi, Upendra, BA Gujar., LLB Bom., LLM Bom., LLM Calif., JSD Calif. Prof.

Beale, Hugh G., BA Oxf. Prof.

Bridges, Lee T., BA Dartmouth Prof.

Burridge, Roger H. M., LLB Birm.   Prof.;
Head*
Chan, W. M. F., LLB Auck., LLM Lond.   Assoc.
Prof.
Choo, A., BCom NSW, LLB NSW, DPhil Oxf.,
FTCL   Prof.
Dean, J., BA Oxf., LLM Manc., PhD Brun.
Assoc. Prof.
Faundez, Julio, LCJ Santiago(Chile), LLM Harv.,
SJD Harv.   Prof.
Guira, J., BA Flor., MA Flor., LLM Lond., JD Flor.
Assoc. Prof.
Hodgson, J. S., LLB Birm., PhD Birm.   Prof.
Leng, Roger, LLB Nott.   Reader
Luckhaus, L., LLB Warw., MA Sheff.   Assoc.
Prof.
McEldowney, John F., LLB Belf., PhD Camb.
Prof.
McMahon, K., BA Syd., LLB NSW, MA Syd., PhD
Syd.   Assoc. Prof.
Moffatt, G., LLB Warw., MA Warw.   Assoc.
Prof.
Nayar, R. J., LLB Leic., PhD Camb.   Assoc. Prof.
Neal, A., LLB Warw., LLM Lond., DGLS Stockholm
Prof.
O'Brien, W., BA N.Carolina, LLM Lond., JD Harv.
Assoc. Prof.
Paliwala, Abdul H., LLB Lond., PhD Lond.   Prof.
Patel, R., LLB N.Law Sch.India, LLM Warw., PhD
Warw.   Assoc. Prof.
Pogany, S. Istvan, LLB Edin., LLM Edin., PhD Exe.
Prof.
Probert, R., BA Oxf., LLM Lond.   Assoc. Prof.
Raffield, P., LLB Wales, PhD Lond.   Assoc. Prof.
Rogowski, R., LLM Wis., DrIur Florence   Reader
Salter, D., LLB Birm.   Assoc. Prof. (Reader)
Snape, E. J., MA Oxf.   Assoc. Prof.
Stevens, D. E., LLB Hull   Assoc. Prof.
Stewart, Ann, LLB Leic., MJur Birm.   Assoc.
Prof. (Reader)
Toner, H., BA Camb., LLM Lond., DPhil Oxf.
Assoc. Prof.
Wakefield, J., BA Newcastle(UK), LLM Lond., PhD
Lond.   Assoc. Prof.
Watt, G., BA Oxf.   Assoc. Prof. (Reader)
Williams, A., LLM Brist., PhD Warw.   Assoc.
Prof.
Other Staff: 7 Asst. Profs.; 1 Sr. Res. Fellow; 1
Teaching Fellow; 2 Res. Fellows; 1 Socio-
Legal Res. Fellow
Research: social and theoretical contexts of the
operation of legal rules and institutions;
UK, European and international law

Mathematics

Tel: (024) 7652 4661 Fax: (024) 7652 4182
E-mail: g.c.copeland@maths.warwick.ac.uk
Baesens, C., MSc Brussels, PhD Brussels   Assoc.
Prof.
Barkley, D., BS C.U.A., MA Texas, PhD Texas
Prof.
Bowditch, B. H., BA Camb., PhD Warw.   Prof.
Burroughs, N. J., BA Camb., PhD Camb.   Prof.
Cohen, J., BSc Hull, PhD Hull, DSc Birm.   Hon.
Prof.
Cremona, J. E., BA Oxf., DPhil Oxf.   Prof.
Earle, C., BA Swarthmore, MA Harv., PhD Harv.
Hon. Prof.
Elliot, C. M., BSc Birm., MSc Oxf., DPhil Oxf.
Prof.
Elworthy, K. David, MA Oxf., DPhil Oxf.   Prof.
Epstein, A., AB Harv., AM Harv., PhD C.U.N.Y.
Assoc. Prof.
Friesecke, Gero, MSc H-W, PhD H-W   Prof.
Gelfreich, V., PhD St.Petersburg   Assoc. Prof.
(Reader)
Gray, J., MSc Warw., PhD Warw.   Hon. Prof.
Holt, Derek F., BA Oxf., MSc Oxf., DPhil Oxf.
Prof.
Jones, John D. S., BSc Manc., MSc Oxf., DPhil
Oxf.   Prof.
Keeling, M. J., BSc Camb., PhD Warw.   Prof.
Kerr, Robert M., BSc Chic., MSc Chic., PhD
Cornell   Prof.
Kirkilionis, M., PhD Heidel.   Assoc. Prof.
Korchagina, I. N., PhD Ohio State   Assoc. Prof.
Kotecky, R., FRS   Prof.
Kozlovski, O., MS Moscow, PhD Amst.   Assoc.
Prof. (Reader)

Krammer, D., PhD Utrecht   Assoc. Prof.
Li, X-M, MSc Warw., PhD Warw.   Assoc. Prof.
MacKay, R., BA Camb., PhD Prin., FRS   Prof.
Maclagan, D., BSc Cant., PhD Calif.   Assoc.
Prof.
Manning, Anthony K., MA Camb., PhD Warw.
Assoc. Prof. (Reader)
Markovic, V., MS Belgrade, PhD Belgrade   Prof.
Markus, Lawrence, BS Chic., MS Chic., PhD Harv.
Hon. Prof.
Micallef, Mario J., BSc Sus., MS N.Y., PhD N.Y.
Assoc. Prof. (Reader)
Mond, David M. Q., BA Oxf., MA Col., PhD Liv.
Prof.
Moody, J. A., AB Prin., PhD Col.   Assoc. Prof.
Nazarenko, S. V., MS Russian Acad.Sc., MPTI
Russian Acad.Sc., PhD Russian Acad.Sc.   Prof.
Newell, A. C., BA Trinity(Dub.), MSc M.I.T., PhD
M.I.T.   Hon. Prof.
Plechac, P., MSc Prague, PhD Prague   Assoc.
Prof.
Priess, D., FRS   Prof.
Rawnsley, John H., BA Oxf., DPhil Oxf.   Prof.
Reid, Miles A., BA Camb., PhD Camb., FRS
Prof.
Robinson, J., BA Camb., PhD Camb.   Assoc.
Prof. (Reader)
Rourke, Colin P., MA Camb., PhD Camb.   Prof.
Rumynin, D., BSc Novosibirsk, MSc Novosibirsk,
PhD Mass.   Assoc. Prof.
Series, Caroline M., MA Oxf., AM Harv., PhD
Harv.   Prof.
Siksek, S., BA Oxf., PhD Exe.   Assoc. Prof.
(Reader)
Sparrow, C., BSc Camb., PhD Camb.   Prof.;
Head*
Stewart, Ian N., BA Camb., PhD Warw., FRS
Prof.
Stuart, A., BSc Brist., DPhil Oxf.   Prof.
Swinnerton-Dyer, Sir Peter, KBE, Hon. DSc
Warw., FRS   Hon. Prof.
Theil, F.   Assoc. Prof.
Topping, P., BA Camb., MSc Warw., PhD Warw.
Prof.
Tribe, R., BA Camb., PhD Br.Col.   Assoc. Prof.
Ueltschi, D., PhD Lausanne   Assoc. Prof.
Walters, Peter, BSc Birm., DPhil Sus.   Prof.
Zeeman, Sir Christopher, MA Camb., PhD
Camb., Hon. Dr Stras., Hon. DSc Hull,
Hon. DSc Warw., FRS   Hon. Prof.
Other Staff: 10 Asst. Profs.; 1 Warwick
Zeeman Lectr.; 1 Sr. Warwick Res. Fellow;
1 EPSRC Sr. Res. Fellows; 11 Res. Fellows;
2 Royal Soc. Res. Fellows; 2 EPSRC Adv.
Res. Fellows
Research: pure and applied mathematics

Philosophy

Tel: (024) 7652 3421 Fax: (024) 7652 3019
E-mail: l.d.hemsley@warwick.ac.uk
Ansell-Pearson, Keith, BA Hull, MA Sus., DPhil
Sus.   Prof.
Battersby, Christine, BA York(UK), DPhil Sus.
Reader
Beistegui, M. J. F., BA Paris, MA Paris, PhD
Assoc. Prof. (Reader)
Brewer, B., BA Oxf., BPhil Oxf., DPhil Oxf.
Prof.
Eilan, N. H., BA Jerusalem, BPhil Oxf., DPhil Oxf.
Prof.; Acting Head*
Hobbs, A. H., MA Camb., PhD Camb.   Assoc.
Prof.
Hoerl, C., BA Munich, MA Munich, MA Sus.,
DPhil Oxf.   Assoc. Prof.
Houlgate, Stephen, BA Camb., MA Camb., PhD
Camb.   Prof.
John, A. E., BA Yale, PhD Mich.   Assoc. Prof.
Luntley, Michael, BA Warw., BPhil Oxf., DPhil
Oxf.   Prof.; Head*
Miller, David W., MA Camb., MSc(Econ) Lond.
Reader
Peter, F., LicOec St.Gallen, PhD St.Gallen   Assoc.
Prof.
Poellner, P. A., MA Edin., DPhil Oxf.   Assoc.
Prof.
Roessler, J., MA Tübingen, DPhil Oxf.   Assoc.
Prof.
Smith, D., BA Oxf., DPhil Oxf.   Prof.

Soteriou, M., BA Lond., MPhil Lond., PhD Lond.
Assoc. Prof.
Williams, A. D., BA Oxf.   Prof.
Wood, David C., BA Manc., PhD Warw.   Hon.
Prof.
Other Staff: 4 Asst. Profs.; 1 Res. Fellow; 1
Teaching Fellow
Research: European philosophy; philosophy in
literature; philosophy of consciousness and
self-consciousness; philosophy of
psychiatry; political and social theory

Physics

Tel: (024) 7652 3965 Fax: (024) 7669 2016
E-mail: jan.spencer@warwick.ac.uk
Allen, M. P., MA Oxf., DPhil Oxf., FIP   Prof.
Arber, T. D., BSc Lond., PhD Lond.   Assoc. Prof.
Ball, Robin C., MA Camb., PhD Camb.   Prof.,
Theoretical Physics
Chapman, Sandra C., BSc Lond., PhD Lond.,
FRAS, FIP   Prof.
Cooper, Malcolm J., MA Camb., PhD Camb., FIP
Prof.; Head*
d'Ambrumenil, Nicholas H., MA Camb.,
DrRerNat T.H.Darmstadt   Assoc. Prof.
Dendy, Richard O., BA Oxf., DPhil Oxf.   Hon.
Prof.
Dixon, John M., BSc Nott., PhD Nott., DSc Nott.,
FIP, FIMA   Assoc. Prof. (Reader)
Dixon, S., BSc Oxf., PhD Warw.   Assoc. Prof.
Dowsett, Mark G., BSc Lond., PhD CNAA   Prof.
Harrison, P. F., BSc Brist., PhD Lond.   Prof.
Holland, Diane, MA Oxf., DPhil Oxf.   Assoc.
Prof. (Reader)
Kearney, Michael J., MA Oxf., PhD Warw., FIP,
FIEE   Hon. Prof.
Leadley, D. R., MA Oxf., DPhil Oxf.   Assoc.
Prof.
Lees, M. R., BSc Warw., MA Boston, PhD Lond.
Assoc. Prof. (Reader)
Marsh, T., MA Camb., PhD Camb.   Prof.
McConville, Christopher F., BSc Lanc., PhD
Warw., FIP, FRAS   Prof.
Mck., Paul D., BSc St And., DPhil Sus.   Prof.
Mouzykantskii, B., BSc Moscow, PhD Moscow
Assoc. Prof.
Nakariakov, V. M., PhD Gorky State   Prof.
Newton, M., BSc Warw., PhD Oxf.   Assoc.
Prof. (Reader)
Parker, E. H. C., BSc Lond., DPhil Sus.   Prof.,
Semi-conductor Physics
Robinson, James, BSc S'ton., PhD S'ton.   Assoc.
Prof.; Dir. of Studies
Roemer, R. A., PhD Utah   Assoc. Prof.
(Reader)
Smith, Mark E., BA Camb., PhD Warw.   Prof.
Staunton, Jane B., BSc Brist., PhD Brist.   Prof.
Thomas, Pamela A., BA Oxf., DPhil Oxf.   Prof.
Turner, M. S., BSc S'ton., PhD Camb.   Assoc.
Prof. (Reader)
Wilson, A. J., BSc Sus., PhD Sheff.   Prof.,
Medical Physics
Woodruff, D. Philip, BSc Brist., PhD Warw., DSc
Warw.   Prof.
Other Staff: 9 Asst. Profs.; 46 Res. Fellows; 1
RCUK Fellow
Research: astronomy; experimental solid state
physics; physics of materials; theoretical
condensed matter physics

Politics and International Studies

Tel: (024) 7652 3486 Fax: (024) 7652 4221
E-mail: charlotte.lewis@warwick.ac.uk
Aldrich, R., BA Manc., MLitt Aberd., PhD Camb.
Prof.
Allison, Lincoln R. P., MA Oxf.   Assoc. Prof.
(Reader)
Breslin, Shaun, BA Newcastle(UK), PhD
Newcastle(UK)   Prof.
Burnell, Peter J., BA Brist., MA Warw., PhD
Warw.   Prof.
Burnham, Peter, BA Warw., PhD Warw.   Prof.;
Head*
Christou, G., BA Sheff., MA Sheff., PhD Sheff.
Assoc. Prof.
Clayton, M., BA Oxf., DPhil Oxf.   Assoc. Prof.
Clift, B., BA Sheff., MA Sheff., PhD Sheff.   Assoc.
Prof.

Croft, S., BSc S'ton., MSc S'ton., PhD S'ton.   Prof.
Duclaud-Williams, R. H., BA Oxf., MA C.U.N.Y., DPhil Sus.   Assoc. Prof.
Ferdinand, C. I. P., BA Oxf., MSc(Econ) Lond., DPhil Oxf.   Assoc. Prof. (Reader)
Grant, Wyn P., BA Leic., MSc Strath., PhD Exe. Prof.
Higgott, R. A., BA CNAA, MSc Lond., PhD Birm. Prof.
Hughes, C. W., BA Sheff., MA Sheff., PhD Sheff. Assoc. Prof. (Reader)
Kelly, D., BA Sheff., MA Sheff., PhD Sheff. Assoc. Prof.
Kennedy-Pipe, C., BA Oxf., MA Oxf., PhD Oxf. Prof.
Kettell, S., BSc York(UK), MA York(UK), PhD Warw.   Assoc. Prof.
McCrisken, T., BA Kent, MA Wash.State, DPhil Sus.   Assoc. Prof.
Page, E., BA Sheff., MA Sheff., MA Essex, PhD Warw.   Assoc. Prof.
Rai, Shirin M., MA Delhi, PhD Camb.   Prof.
Reeve, Andrew W., MA Oxf., DPhil Oxf.   Prof.
Roberson, B., BA New Sch.Soc.Res.(N.Y.), MA Abilene, PhD Lond.   Assoc. Prof.
Rosamund, B. J., BA Manc., MA Manc., PhD Sheff.   Prof.
Scholte, J. A., BA Pomona, MA Sus., DPhil Sus. Prof.
Sinclair, T. J., BA Cant., MA Cant., DPhil York(UK)   Assoc. Prof.
Smith, Hazel, BA Essex, PhD Lond.   Prof.
Stone, D. L., BA Murd., MA ANU, PhD ANU Prof.
Watson, M., BSc Birm., MSc Birm., PhD Birm. Assoc. Prof. (Reader)
Williams, P. D., BSc Wales, MSc Wales, PhD Wales   Assoc. Prof.
Other Staff: 7 Asst. Profs.
Research: democratisation; international business history; international political economy; political theory; politics of environmental policy and sport

Psychology

Tel: (024) 7652 3096 Fax: (024) 7652 4225
E-mail: psychology@warwick.ac.uk
Boucher, J., BA Oxf., PhD Birm.   Hon. Prof.
Brown, Gordon D. A., MA Oxf., DPhil Sus. Prof.
Dunbar, G., MA Edin., PhD Edin.   Assoc. Prof.
Estes, Z., BSc Texas, MA Prin., PhD Prin.   Assoc. Prof.
Jones, Gregory V., MA Oxf., MA Camb., PhD Camb., DPhil Oxf.   Prof.
Kunar, M., BSc Birm., PhD Birm.   Assoc. Prof.
Lamberts, Koen, BA Leuven, BSc Leuven, MSc Leuven, PhD Leuven   Prof.; Head*
Maylor, Elizabeth A., BSc Durh., PhD Durh. Prof.
Mitra, S., AB Dartmouth, DPhil Conn.   Assoc. Prof.
Pickering, J. A., BSc Edin., DPhil Sus.   Assoc. Prof.
Robinson, E. J., BSc Lond., PhD Lond.   Prof.
Schlaghecken, F., MA Munich, DPhil Munich Assoc. Prof.
Skinner, M. R., BSc Brist., PhD Nott.   Assoc. Prof.
Stewart, N., BA Camb., PhD Warw.   Assoc. Prof. (Reader)
Tresilian, J., BSc Lond., PhD Edin.   Prof.
Watson, D. G., BSc Birm., MSc Birm., PhD Birm. Assoc. Prof. (Reader)
Wolke, D., PhD Lond.   Prof.
Other Staff: 4 Asst. Profs.; 5 Res. Fellows; 1 Hon. Sr. Clin. Lectr.
Research: cognitive, developmental and chemosensory psychology; philosophy of psychology; relationships support and health

Sociology

Tel: (024) 7652 3150 Fax: (024) 7652 3497
E-mail: j.i.tyrrell@warwick.ac.uk
Anderson, C.   Assoc. Prof. (Reader)
Archer, Margaret S., BSc(Soc) Lond., PhD Lond.

Beckford, James A., BA Reading, PhD Reading, DLitt Reading   Prof.
Bradby, H., BA Lond., MSc Lond., PhD Glas. Assoc. Prof.
Carpenter, M. J., BSc Lond., MA Warw., PhD Warw.   Reader
Carter, R., BSc Lond., MSocSci Birm., PhD Leic. Assoc. Prof.
Charles, N., BA Keele, PhD Keele   Prof.
Clarke, Simon R. C., BA Camb., PhD Essex Prof.
Dowler, E. A., MA Camb., MSc Lond., PhD Lond. Reader
Elger, Anthony J., BA Hull, PhD Durh.   Prof.
Fine, Robert D., BA Oxf., PhD Warw.   Prof.; Chair*
Fuller, Steve, BA Col., MPhil Camb., PhD Pitt. Prof.
Grant, C.   Assoc. Prof. (Reader)
Hoskins, A. D., BA Lanc., MA Lanc., PhD Lanc. Assoc. Prof.
Hughes, C., BA Warw., PhD Warw.   Prof.; Head*
Jones, C., BA Sus., PhD Lond.   Assoc. Prof.
Lambert, C., BA Birm., MSocSci Birm.   Assoc. Prof.
Lampard, R. J., BSc Durh., MSc S'ton., DPhil Oxf. Assoc. Prof.
Liddle, J. M., BA Manc., MPhil Lond.   Assoc. Prof.
Lovell, T. A., BA Leeds   Emer. Prof.
Mizen, P. A. J., BA Warw., PhD Warw.   Assoc. Prof.
Mukta, P., BA Edin., MA Edin., PhD Manc. Assoc. Prof.
Parker, A., BEd CNAA, MA Warw., PhD Warw. Assoc. Prof.
Phizacklea, Annie M., BA Exe., MA McM., PhD Exe.   Prof.
Pilkington, H., BA Camb., MSocSc Birm., PhD Birm.   Prof.
Ratcliffe, Peter B., BSc Lond., MSc Lond., PhD Warw.   Prof.
Steinberg, D. L., BA Calif., MA Kent, PhD Birm. Reader
Throsby, K., BA Oxf., MSc Lond., PhD Lond. Assoc. Prof.
Turner, D. S. C., BA Durh., PhD Lond.   Assoc. Prof.
Whiteside, N., BA Liv., PhD Liv.   Prof.
Williams, S. J., BA CNAA, MSc Lond., PhD Lond. Prof.
Wolkowitz, C., BA Mass., MA Sus., DPhil Sus. Assoc. Prof.
Wright, C., BA Durh., PhD Leeds   Assoc. Prof.
Other Staff: 2 Asst. Profs.; 5 Res. Fellows
Research: labour studies; political sociology; social and political thought; social theory and philosophy; sociologies of crime, education, gender, health, migration, race and racism, and religion

Statistics

Tel: (024) 7652 3066 Fax: (024) 7652 4532
E-mail: s.e.castle@stats.warwick.ac.uk
Assing, S., PhD Bielefeld   Assoc. Prof.
Copas, John B., BSc Lond., PhD Lond.   Prof.
Finkenstadt, B. F., MA Georgia, PhD   Assoc. Prof.
Firth, D., BA Camb., PhD Lond.   Prof.
Hobson, D., PhD Camb.   Assoc. Prof. (Reader)
Hutton, J. L., BSc Edin., PhD Lond.   Reader; Head*
Jacka, Saul D., MA Camb., PhD Camb.   Prof.
Kendall, Wilfred S., MA Oxf., MSc Oxf., DPhil Oxf.   Prof.
Kennedy, J. E., BSc Syd., MSc Syd., PhD Camb. Assoc. Prof.
Kolokolstov, V., PhD Moscow   Assoc. Prof. (Reader)
Lawrance, A. J., BSc Leic., PhD Leic.   Prof.
Reed, R. J., BSc Lond., PhD Durh.   Assoc. Prof.
Roberts, G. O., BA Oxf., PhD Warw.   Prof.
Shaw, J. E. H., BA Oxf., MSc Lond., PhD Nott. Assoc. Prof.
Smith, J. Q., BSc Nott., PhD Warw.   Prof.
Steel, M. F. J., MA Louvain, PhD Louvain   Prof.
Thonnes, E., MSc N.U.I., PhD Warw.   Assoc. Prof.

Warren, J., BA Camb., PhD Bath   Assoc. Prof.
Other Staff: 4 Asst. Profs.; 11 Res. Fellows
Research: Bayesian statistics; image analysis; numerical methods; probability theory and applications; socio-medical statistics

Theatre, Performance and Cultural Policy Studies, School of

Tel: (024) 7652 3020 Fax: (024) 7652 4446
E-mail: c.brennan@warwick.ac.uk
Beacham, Richard C., MFA Yale, DFA Yale Prof.
Bennett, Oliver, BA York(UK)   Prof.
Bilton, C. J., BA Camb., MA Warw., PhD Warw. Assoc. Prof.
Cousin, Geraldine, BA Exe., PhD Exe.   Assoc. Prof.
Davies, A., BA Lond.   Hon. Prof.
Davis, J., BA Oxf., MA Oxf., PhD Exe.   Head*
Eyre, Sir R., BA Camb.   Hon. Prof.
Haedicke, S., BA Wheaton(Ill.), MA Mich., PhD Mich.   Assoc. Prof.
Holdsworth, N., BA Lough., PhD Lough.   Assoc. Prof.
Hutchison, Y. A., BA Natal, MA Stell., PhD Stell. Assoc. Prof.
Kershaw, B. R., MA Hawaii, PhD Exe.   Prof.
Reinelt, J., PhD Stan.   Prof.
Scheer, E., BA Macq., PhD Macq.   Assoc. Prof.
Shewring, Margaret E., BA Birm., PhD Birm. Assoc. Prof.
Stafford-Clark, M., BA Trinity(Dub.)   Hon. Prof.
Vickery, J., BA E.Anglia, MA E.Anglia, PhD Essex Assoc. Prof.
White, T., BA CNAA, MA Lanc., PhD Warw. Assoc. Prof.
Whybrow, N., BA Leeds, MA Leeds, PhD Leeds Assoc. Prof.
Other Staff: 3 Asst. Profs.; 2 Sr. Teaching Fellows; 1 Teaching Fellow
Research: European cultural policy and administration; history of theatre; Third World theatre; twentieth-century performance theory and analysis

Translation and Comparative Cultural Studies, Centre for

Tel: (024) 7652 3655 Fax: (024) 7652 4468
E-mail: ctccs@warwick.ac.uk
Bassnett, Susan E., BA Manc., PhD Lanc.   Prof.
Dabydeen, David, MA Camb., PhD Lond.   Prof.
Gilmore, J. T., MA Camb., PhD Camb.   Assoc. Prof.
Kuhiwczak, P., MA Warsaw, PhD Warsaw Assoc. Prof.
Long, L., BA Leeds, PhD Warw.   Dir.*
Snell-Hornby, M., MA St And., DPhil Zür. Hon. Prof.
Weissbort, D., BA Camb., MA Camb.   Hon. Prof.
Other Staff: 1 Asst. Prof.; 1 Assoc. Fellow; 3 Teaching Fellows; 1 Hon. Fellow
Research: Caribbean studies; literary criticism; literature; translation in theory and practice

Warwick Business School

Tel: (024) 7652 4306 Fax: (024) 7652 3719
E-mail: enquiries@wbs.warwick.ac.uk
Abimbola, T., BA Ilorin, MBA San Diego, PhD Aston   Assoc. Prof.
Ahrens, T., BA CNAA, MSc Lond., PhD Lond. Prof.
Anderson-Gough, F., BA Leeds, PhD Leeds Assoc. Prof. (Reader)
Angwin, D. N., MA Camb., MPhil Camb., MBA Cran.IT, PhD Warw.   Assoc. Prof.
Arnott, F. D. C., BSc Sheff., MBA Manc., PhD Manc.   Assoc. Prof.
Arrowsmith, J., BA York(UK), MA Warw., PhD Manc.   Assoc. Prof.
Asmild, M., BSc Copenhagen, MSc Copenhagen, PhD Copenhagen Agric.   Assoc. Prof.
Bates, K., BA Nott., FCA   Assoc. Prof.
Bedell-Pearce, K., LLB Exe., MSc Warw.   Hon. Prof.
Benington, John, MA Camb.   Prof.
Bridgewater, S. H., BA Durh., MBA Warw., PhD Warw.   Assoc. Prof.

Brown, R. M., BA Nott.Trent, PhD Warw., FCA
Assoc. Prof.
Bryant, J. W., BSc Durh., MA Lanc., PhD Lanc.
Hon. Prof.
Bryer, Robert A., BA CNAA, MSc Warw., PhD
Warw. Prof.
Carey, A., BSc MBA Hon. Prof.
Carnall, C., BTech Lough., MSc Brad., PhD Henley,
FRSA Prof.
Cave, Martin, BA Oxf., BPhil Oxf., DPhil Oxf.
Prof.
Charlwood, A., BA Liv., MSc Lond., PhD Lond.
Assoc. Prof.
Chen, B., BSc Zhejiang, MSc Chinese Acad.Sc., PhD
Rotterdam Prof.
Clubb, C., BA Manc., MSc Lond., PhD Lond.
Prof., Accounting
Colling, T., BA CNAA, MA Warw., MA Leic. Sr.
Lectr.
Collinson, Simon, BA Leeds, MA Flor., DPhil Sus.
Prof.
Contu, A., MA Lanc., PhD UMIST, Laurea
Assoc. Prof.
Corbett, Martin J., BA Leeds, MA Lanc., PhD
Warw. Sr. Lectr.
Corea, S., BA Sing., MSc Hawaii, PhD Lond.
Assoc. Prof.
Croom, S., BA CNAA, MSc Warw., PhD Warw.
Assoc. Prof.
Crouch, C., BA Lond., DPhil Oxf. Prof.
Currie, W., BSc Kingston(UK), PhD Brun. Prof.
Dacko, S., BME Minn., MBA Minn., PhD Ill.
Assoc. Prof.
Davies, J., BA Kent, MA York(UK), DPhil York(UK)
Sr. Lectr.
Davies, R., BA Warw., MSc Birm., PhD S'ton.
Prof.
Deineko, V., PhD Kiev Sr. Lectr.
Dickens, Linda J., BA Kent, MA Warw. Prof.
du Gay, P., BA Durh., MA Durh., DPhil Open(UK)
Prof.
Dyson, Robert G., BSc Liv., PhD Lanc. Prof.
Edwards, Paul K., BA Camb., BPhil Oxf., DPhil
Oxf., FBA Prof.
Fletcher, C., PhD Wales, FBPsS Hon. Prof.
Franco, A., MSc Lanc., PhD Lond., BSc MBA
Assoc. Prof.
Fraser, S., LLB Glas., MSc Brist., PhD Warw.
Assoc. Prof.
Fryer, R. H., CBE, BA Camb., MA Camb.,
Hon. DLitt Staffs. Hon. Prof.
Geddes, Mike, BA S'ton., DPhil Sus. Prof.
Fellow
Gemmill, G., BSc Lond., MSc Reading, MA Mich.,
PhD Mich. Prof.
Gillespie, N., BA Qld., PhD Melb. Assoc. Prof.
Greene, A-M., BA Oxf., MA Warw., PhD Wolv.
Sr. Lectr.
Greene, F., BA Sheff., MPhil Sheff., PhD Durh.
Assoc. Prof.
Grey, C., BA Manc., PhD Manc. Prof.
Gulpinar, N., PhD Brun., BSc MSc Assoc. Prof.
Hall, J., OBE, MA Oxf. Hon. Prof.
Hall, M. J., BA York(UK), MA Warw. Prof.
Fellow
Hancock, P., BA Nott., MA Warw., PhD Keele
Assoc. Prof.
Harris, L. C., BSc Cardiff, PhD Cardiff Prof.
Hartley, J., BA Reading, PhD Manc. Prof.
Henderson, V., BA Syd., PhD Bath Assoc. Prof.
(Reader)
Heracleous, L., BSc Lanc., MPhil Camb., PhD
Camb. Prof.
Hodges, Stuart D., BSc S'ton., MSc S'ton., PhD
Lond., FIMA Prof.
Hoskin, Keith W., BA Oxf., MSc Penn., PhD Penn.
Prof.
Huang, J., LLB Natnl.Chengchi, MBA Exe., PhD
Warw. Assoc. Prof. (Reader)
Jin, X., MSc Xi'an Jiaotong, PhD Chinese Acad.Sc.,
PhD Xi'an Jiaotong, BSc Assoc. Prof.
Johnston, R., BSc Aston, PhD Warw. Prof.
Keep, E., BA Lond., MA(Econ) Manc., PhD Warw.
Prof. Fellow
Lane, N., BSc Wales, PhD Wales Sr. Lectr.
Langlands, Sir Alan, BSc Glas., FRCP Hon.
Prof.
Leighfield, J., MA Oxf., FBCS Hon. Prof.

Levy, M. S., BSc Lond., MSc Lond. Sr. Lectr.
Liff, Sonia T., BA Lanc., MSc Manc., PhD Manc.
Assoc. Prof. (Reader)
Lilford, R., MB PhD Hon. Prof.
Llewellyn, N., BA Nott.Trent, PhD Bourne.
Assoc. Prof.
Marginson, Paul, BA Camb., MA Warw., PhD
Warw. Prof.
Martin, A., MA Camb., PhD Warw. Assoc.
Prof.
Mawson, John, BSc Lond., MPhil Lond. Prof.
McDonald, M. H. B., MA MSc PhD DLitt, FRSA
Hon. Prof.
McGee, J., BA(Econ) Manc., PhD Stan. Prof.,
Strategic Management
Meardi, G., BSc Milan, MA Paris, PhD Florence
Assoc. Prof.
Merali, Y., BSc Lond., MSc Birm., MSc CNAA
Assoc. Prof.
Morgan, G., MA Camb., MA Essex Prof.
Morley, K., BSc Sur., MSc Aston, MBA Aston
Hon. Prof.
Morris, G., LLB Brist., PhD Camb. Hon. Prof.
Mumby-Croft, R., MA Warw. Prof. Fellow
Nandhakumar, J., BSc Brad., PhD Camb. Prof.
Neuberger, A., BA Camb., MBA Lond., PhD Lond.
Prof.
Newell, S., BSc Cardiff, PhD Cardiff Prof.
Oats, L., BBus W.Aust.I.T., PhD W.Aust. Assoc.
Prof. (Reader)
O'Brien, F. A., BSc Sur., MSc S'ton. Assoc. Prof.
Oomen, R., MA Gron., PhD Florence Assoc.
Prof.
Pézier, J., PhD Dartmouth Hon. Prof.
Piercy, N., BA H-W, MA Durh., PhD Wales,
DLitt H-W Prof.
Podinovski, Victor V., MSc Moscow, PhD Moscow
Assoc. Prof.
Purcell, J., MA Camb., MSc Lond., DLitt Oxf.
Prof.
Radnor, Z., BEng Nott., MSc Cran., PhD UMIST
Sr. Lectr.
Reed, A., CBE Hon. Prof.
Reimann, M., MSc Vienna, PhD Vienna Assoc.
Prof.
Robinson, Stewart, BSc Lanc., PhD Lanc. Prof.
Roos, G., MSc Chalmers U.T., MBA Hon. Prof.
Roper, S. N., BA Durh., MPhil Oxf., PhD Lond.
Prof.
Salmon, M., BA Essex, MA Lond. Prof.
Sarno, L., Laurea Salerno, MA Liv., PhD Liv., PhD
Salerno Prof.
Scarbrough, H., BA Durh., MBA Brad., PhD Aston
Prof.
Scarparo, S., BSc Cagliari, MA Bologna, PhD Edin.
Assoc. Prof.
Shah, Z., PhD Manc., BBA MBA Assoc. Prof.
Shale, E. A., BSc Warw., MSc Warw. Assoc.
Prof.
Silvestro, R. M., BA Warw., MBA Warw., PhD
Warw. Assoc. Prof.
Simkin, Lyndon P., BA Leic., PhD Brad. Assoc.
Prof. (Reader)
Simms, M., BSc UMIST, MA Warw., PhD Cardiff
Assoc. Prof.
Slack, Nigel D. C., BTech Brad., MSc Brad., PhD
Brun. A. E. Higgs Prof.
Spicer, A., BCom Otago, MBus Otago, PhD Melb.
Assoc. Prof.
Stern, P., BSc Sus., MSc Lond., PhD Lond. Assoc.
Prof.
Stoneman, Paul L., BA Warw., MSc(Econ) Lond.,
PhD Camb. Prof.
Storey, David J., BSc Hull, PhD Newcastle(UK)
Prof.
Stray, Stephanie J., BA York(UK), PhD Essex
Assoc. Prof.
Sturdy, A., BSc UMIST, PhD UMIST Prof.
Swan, Jacqueline A., BSc Sus., PhD Wales Prof.
Taylor, D., BA Strath. Hon. Prof.
Terry, Michael A., BSc Sus., MA Warw. Prof.
Thomas, Howard, BSc Lond., MSc Lond., MBA
Chic., PhD Brun. Prof.
Tompkins, R. G., BA Chic., MA Chic., MBA
Chic., PhD Warw. Hon. Prof.
Tritter, J., AB Chic., DPhil Sus. Prof. Fellow
Tsoukas, H., BSc Lond., MSc Lond., PhD Manc.
Prof.

van Batenburg, P. C., PhD Rotterdam Hon.
Prof.
Waine, P., BSc Brad. Hon. Prof.
Walley, P., BSc UMIST, BEng UMIST, MBA
Warw. Assoc. Prof.
Wang, Q., BSc Xi'an Jiaotong, PhD Warw. Assoc.
Prof.
Warhurst, Alyson, BSc Brist., MSc Sus., DPhil
Sus. Prof.
Webber, N., BSc Warw., MSc Oxf., PhD Lond.
Assoc. Prof. (Reader)
Wensley, J. Robin C., BA Camb., MSc Lond.,
PhD Lond. Prof.
Wilson, D. C., BA Leeds, MA Leeds, PhD Brad.
Prof.
Wongkaew, M., BA Chulalongkorn, MSc Lond.,
PhD Warw. Assoc. Prof.
Other Staff: 32 Asst. Profs.; 4 Lectrs.; 4
Principal Teaching Fellows; 6 Sr. Teaching
Fellows; 4 Teaching Fellows; 2 Principal
Res. Fellows; 3 Sr. Res. Fellows; 10 Res.
Fellows; 2 Sr. Res. Assocs.

Warwick Medical School

Tel: (024) 7657 5770 Fax: (024) 7652 4649
E-mail: wmsinfo@warwick.ac.uk

Abrahams, P., MB BS Hon. DO Lond., FRCSEd,
FRCR Prof., Anatomy
Ayres, J. Hon. Prof.
Barlow, J., BA Warw., MSc Oxf., DPhil Oxf.
Prof., Public Health in the Early Years
Blackburn, C., BA CNAA Assoc. Prof.
Bland, R., BSc Wales, MPhil Wales, PhD Birm.
Assoc. Prof.
Bridle, C., BSc Kent, MSc Kent, PhD Kent Assoc.
Prof.
Cappuccio, F. P., MB BS Naples, MD Naples, MSc
Lond., FRCP Cephalon Prof., Cardio
Medicine and Epidemiology
Carpenter, M. J., BSc Lond., MA Warw., PhD
Warw. Assoc. Prof.
Carter, Y., OBE, BSc Lond., MB BS Lond., MD
Lond., FRCGP, FMedSci Prof.; Dean*
Ceriello, A., MD Prof.
Collins, D. R., BSc Wales, PhD Aberd. Assoc.
Prof.
Cooke, M. W., MB ChB Birm., PhD Birm., FRCS
Prof., Emergency Care
Costa, M. L., MB BChir Camb., PhD C.England,
FRCS Assoc. Prof.
Dale, Jeremy, MB BS Lond., MA Camb., PhD
Lond., FRCGP Head, Health in the
Community; Prof., Primary Care
Dolan, A., BA Warw., PhD Warw. Assoc. Prof.
Dunn, A., BSc Portsmouth, MSc UMIST, PhD Birm.
Prof., Cancer Trials
Feelisch, M. Prof., Experimental Medicine and
Integrative Biology
Field, S., MB ChB MMed, FRCGP Hon. Prof.
Friede, T., PhD Heidel. Assoc. Prof.
Fulford, K. W. N., MA Camb., MD Camb., PhD
Lond., DPhil Oxf., FRCP Prof., Philosophy
and Mental Health
Grammatopoulos, D., BSc Salonika, MSc
Newcastle(UK), PhD Newcastle(UK) Prof.
Griffin, D., BM BCh Oxf., MA MPhil, FRCS
Prof., Trauma and Orthopaedic Surgery
Gullam, J. E., MB ChB Leic. Assoc. Prof.
Heginbotham, C., BSc Birm., MSc Essex, MA
Wales, MPhil Camb. Hon. Prof.
Hodgkin, M. N., BSc Coventry, PhD Birm.
Assoc. Prof.
Jackson, J. A., BA De Mont., PhD Leic. Assoc.
Prof.
Johnson, M. Hon. Prof.
Karteris, E. K., BSc Sur., MSc Brun., PhD Warw.
Assoc. Prof.
Keay, S. D., MB ChB Edin., MD Brist., FRCOG
Assoc. Prof.
Kidd, J., BSc Lond., PhD Lond. Reader,
Communication Skills
Kumar, S., MD Manc., FRCP Prof., Medicine,
Diabetes and Metabolism
Lamb, S., MSc Oxf., PhD Oxf. Prof.,
Physiotherapy and Rehabilitation
Lehnert, H., MD Mün. Prof., Medicine
Lewando-Hundt, G., MA Edin., MPhil Edin., PhD
Warw. Prof.

Markham, W., BSc St And., MPhil Camb., PhD Birm.   Assoc. Prof.

Matyka, K., MB BS Lond., MD Lond.   Assoc. Prof.

McTernan, P., BSc Keele, PhD Birm.   Assoc. Prof.

Meads, G., BA Oxf., MA Oxf., MSc(Tech) PhD   Visiting Prof.

Miller, M. A., BSc Lond., PhD Lond.   Assoc. Prof.

Morris, Alan G., BA Oxf., DPhil Oxf.   Reader

Murch, S., BSc Lond., MB BS Lond., PhD Lond., FRCP, FRCPCH   Prof., Paediatrics and Child Health

Nwokolo, C.   Hon. Prof.

Patel, V., BSc MB ChB MD, FRCP   Reader, Clinical Skills

Peile, Ed, EdD, FRCP, FRCGP, FRCPCH   Head, Div. of Med. Educn.; Assoc. Dean (Teaching)

Petersen, S. A., MA Camb., PhD Edin.   Hon. Prof.

Randeva, H., MB ChB Dund., PhD Warw., FRCP   Assoc. Prof.

Raymond, N. T., BA Nott., MSc Sheff.   Assoc. Prof.

Rodgers, C., MD   Assoc. Prof.

Saravanan, P.   Assoc. Prof.

Shmygol, A., MD Kiev, PhD Kiev   Assoc. Prof.

Singer, D., BMedBiol Aberd., MB ChB Aberd., MD Aberd., FRCP   Prof., Clinical Pharmacology

Singh, S., MB BS Jammu, MD Lond., DM Nott.   Prof., Social and Community Psychiatry

Spanswick, David C., BSc E.Anglia, PhD Birm.   Prof., Molecular Neurosciences

Spurgeon, P.   Prof., Health Services Management

Stallard, N., BA Camb., MSc Reading, PhD Reading   Prof., Medical Statistics

Stanfield, Peter R., BA Camb., PhD Camb., ScD Camb.   Prof.

Stewart Brown, S., BA Oxf., BM BCh Oxf., MA Oxf., PhD Brist., FFPHM, FRCP, FRCPCH   Prof.; Dir., Res.

Stranges, S., MB BS Naples, MD Naples, PhD Naples   Assoc. Prof.

Sturt, J., BA Oxf., PhD Brun.   Assoc. Prof.

Szczepura, Ala K., BA Oxf., DPhil Oxf.   Prof., Health Services Research

Thornalley, P., BSc UMIST, DPhil Oxf.   Prof., Systems Biology

Thornton, S., BM S'ton., DM S'ton.   Assoc. Dean, Res.; Prof., Obstetrics and Gynaecology

Thorogood, M., BSc Lond., PhD Lond.   Prof., Epidemiology

Underwood, M., MB ChB MSc Keele, MD Manc.   Prof., Primary Care Research

Vatish, M., MB BChir Camb., MA Oxf., DPhil Oxf.   Assoc. Prof.

Weich, S., BA MB BS MSc MD   Prof., Psychiatry

Williams, S., BA Wales, MPhil Wales, PhD Cardiff   Assoc. Prof.

Withnall, A., BA Sus., MA Sus., PhD Keele   Assoc. Prof.

Zammit, V. A., BSc Malta, MSc Malta, DPhil Oxf., DSc Oxf.   Dir., Clin. Sci.; Prof., Metabolic Chemistry

Zehnder, D., MB ChB Berne, MD Berne, PhD Birm.   Assoc. Prof.

Other Staff: 7 Asst. Profs.; 8 Sr. Teaching Fellows; 1 Teaching Fellow; 4 Principal Res. Fellows; 4 Sr. Res. Fellows; 32 Res. Fellows; 16 Assoc. Clin. Profs.; 1 Clin. Lectr.; 10 Clin. Res. Fellows; 6 Hon. Sr. Lectrs.; 10 Hon. Sr. Clin. Lectrs.

SPECIAL CENTRES, ETC

Advanced Materials, Centre for

Tel: (024) 7657 4803
 E-mail: d.holland@warwick.ac.uk
Holland, Diane, MA Oxf., DPhil Oxf.   Dir.*
Research: development of novel ceramics and glasses

Caribbean Studies, Centre for

Tel: (024) 7652 3443 Fax: (024) 7652 3443
 E-mail: caribbeanstudies@warwick.ac.uk
Burnard, T. G., PhD Johns H.   Prof.
Dabydeen, David, MA Camb., PhD Lond.   Prof.
Gilmore, J. T., MA Camb., PhD Camb.   Assoc. Prof.
Heuman, Gad J., BA Col., MA Yale, MPhil Yale, PhD Yale, FRHistS   Prof.
Jones, C., BA Sus., PhD Lond.   Assoc. Prof.; Dir.*
Other Staff: 3 Asst. Profs.
Research: Caribbean history and literary culture

Comparative American Studies

Tel: (024) 7652 2502
 E-mail: valerie.melling@warwick.ac.uk
Burnard, T. G., PhD Johns H.   Prof.
Earle, R. A., BA Bryn Mawr, MA Warw., MSc Warw., PhD Warw.   Assoc. Prof.
Fagge, R. J., BA Lond., PhD Camb.   Assoc. Prof.
Heuman, Gad J., BA Col., MA Yale, MPhil Yale, PhD Yale, FRHistS   Prof.
King, John P., MA Edin., DPhil Oxf.   Prof.
Lockley, T. J., MA Edin., PhD Camb.   Assoc. Prof.
McFarlane, Anthony J., BSc(Econ) Lond., PhD Lond.   Prof.
Thomson, Guy P. C., BSc(Econ) Lond., DPhil Oxf., FRHistS   Dir.*
Other Staff: 1 Asst. Prof.; 1 Principal Language Tutor; 5 Teaching Staff

Comparative Labour Studies, Centre for

Tel: (024) 7652 3091 Fax: (024) 7652 3497
 E-mail: a.j.elger@warwick.ac.uk
Elger, Anthony J., BA Hull, PhD Durh.   Dir.*

Corporate Citizenship Unit

Tel: (024) 7657 3131 Fax: (024) 7657 3177
 E-mail: a.warhurst@wbs.ac.uk
Warhurst, Alyson, BSc Brist., MSc Sus., DPhil Sus.   Prof.; Dir.*
Other Staff: 1 Assoc. Fellow
Research: corporate strategy and change in the public and private sectors

Cultural Policy Studies, Centre for

Tel: (024) 7652 3020 Fax: (024) 7652 4446
 E-mail: culturalpolicy@warwick.ac.uk
Belfore, E.   Assoc. Prof.
Bennett, Oliver, BA York(UK)   Dir.*
Bilton, C. J., BA Camb., MA Warw., PhD Warw.   Assoc. Prof.
Vickery, J., BA E.Anglia, MA E.Anglia, PhD Essex   Assoc. Prof.
Other Staff: 2 Sr. Teaching Fellows; 1 Teaching Fellow

Democratisation, Centre for the Study of

Tel: (024) 7652 3302 Fax: (024) 7652 4221
 E-mail: charlotte.lewis@warwick.ac.uk
Burnell, Peter J., BA Brist., MA Warw., PhD Warw.   Co-Dir*
Doorenspleet, R., BA Ley., MA Ley., PhD Ley.   Co-Dir.*
Research: economic, historical, legal, political and social dimensions of democratisation

East Roman Studies, Centre for Research in

Tel: (024) 7652 3023 Fax: (024) 7652 4973
 E-mail: s.c.r.swain@warwick.ac.uk
Swain, Simon C. R., MA Oxf., DPhil Oxf.   Prof.
Research: archaeology; economy; history; literature; religion

Education and Industry, Centre for

Tel: (024) 7652 3909 Fax: (024) 7652 3617
 E-mail: cei@warwick.ac.uk
Fiehn, J., BA Reading, MSc CNAA   Regional Dir.
Foweather, R., BEd Leic., MEd Warw.   Regional Dir.
Grewcock, C., BA York(UK), MA Leic.   Regional Dir.

Hoare, M., BA Essex, MA Open(UK), FRSA   Regional Dir.
Huddleston, Prue J., BA Lond., MEd Warw.   Dir.*
Muir, F., MA Lond., FRSA   Regional Dir.
Stagg, Peter, BSc Leeds, MA Lond.   Regional Dir.
Stanley, J., BA Oxf., MA Lond.   Regional Dir.
Other Staff: 2 Principal Res. Fellows; 1 Res. Fellow

Education in Development, International Centre for (INCED)

Tel: (024) 7652 3838 Fax: (024) 7652 4223
 E-mail: r.a.preston@warwick.ac.uk
Preston, R. A., BA Leeds, MA Leeds, PhD Leeds   Dir.*
Other Staff: 1 Deputy Dir.
Research: education and training in economic, political and social development, especially in developing countries

Educational Development, Appraisal and Research, Centre for (CEDAR)

Tel: (024) 7652 3638 Fax: (024) 7652 4472
 E-mail: j.p.mcelroy@warwick.ac.uk
Lindsay, Geoffrey A., BSc Durh., MEd Birm., PhD Birm., FBPsS   Prof.; Dir.*
Strand, S., BA Plym., PhD Plym.   Reader
Other Staff: 1 Principal Res. Fellow; 3 Sr. Res. Fellows; 1 Res. Fellow
Research: education and training

Employment Research, Institute for

Tel: (024) 7652 4127 Fax: (024) 7652 4241
 E-mail: ier@warwick.ac.uk
Bosworth, D. L., BA CNAA, MA Warw., PhD Warw.   Prof.
Elias, D. Peter B., BSc Manc., MA Sheff., PhD Calif.   Prof.
Lindley, Robert, BSc Lond., MSc Lond., PhD Warw.   Prof.; Dir.*
Purcell, K. G., BA Lond., MA Manc., PhD Manc.   Prof.
Wilson, R. A., BA Warw., MA Warw., PhD Warw.   Deputy Dir.
Other Staff: 1 Prof. Fellow; 6 Principal Res. Fellows; 2 Sr. Res. Fellows; 6 Res. Fellows; 3 Res. Assocs.
Research: developments in education, household, population and training behaviour; labour market

Ethnic Relations, Centre for Research in

Tel: (024) 7652 4869 Fax: (024) 7652 4324
 E-mail: c.e.oakman@warwick.ac.uk
Anwar, Mohammed, OBE, BA Punjab, MA Punjab, MA(Econ) Manc., PhD Brad.   Prof.
Joly, Daniele, LèsL Paris, MèsL Paris, PhD Aston   Prof.; Dir.*
Other Staff: 2 Jt. MA Course Convenors
Research: economic change and racial discrimination; ethnic mobilisation and nationalism; migration and citizenship

Financial Options Research Centre

Tel: (024) 7652 3606 Fax: (024) 7652 4167
 E-mail: s.d.hodges@warwick.ac.uk
Webber, N., BSc Warw., MSc Oxf., PhD Lond.   Dir.*
Research: derivative instruments and risk management

Fluid Dynamics Research Centre

Tel: (024) 7652 2200
 E-mail: peter.thomas@warwick.ac.uk
Thomas, Peter J., PhD Gött.   Dir.*

Globalisation and Regionalisation, Centre for the Study of

Tel: (024) 7657 2533 Fax: (024) 7657 2548
 E-mail: csgr@warwick.ac.uk
Scholte, J. A., BA Pomona, MA Sus., DPhil Sus.   Dir.*
Other Staff: 1 Prof. Fellow; 4 Res. Fellows; 1 Deputy Dir.
Research: causes and effects of the tendencies towards globalisation and regionalisation in the world political economy

Governance and Public Management, Institute of

Tel: (024) 7652 4505 Fax: (024) 7652 4410
    E-mail: igpm@warwick.ac.uk
Benington, John, MA Camb.   Prof.; Dir.*
Other Staff: 1 Principal Res. Fellow

Health, Institute of

Tel: (024) 7657 4098 Fax: (024) 7657 4101
    E-mail: k.van.rompaey@warwick.ac.uk
Bradby, H., BA Lond., MSc Lond., PhD Glas.   Co-Dir.*
Lewando-Hundt, G., MA Edin., MPhil Edin., PhD Warw.   Prof., Health and Social Services; Co-Dir.*

Humanities Research Centre

Tel: (024) 7652 3401 Fax: (024) 7657 2997
    E-mail: hrc@warwick.ac.uk
King, John P., MA Edin., DPhil Oxf.   Prof.; Dir.*

Industrial Relations Research Unit

Tel: (024) 7652 4268 Fax: (024) 7652 4184
    E-mail: v.j.jephcott@wbs.warwick.ac.uk
Edwards, Paul K., BA Camb., BPhil Oxf., DPhil Oxf., FBA   Prof.
Marginson, Paul, BA Camb., MA Warw., PhD Warw.   Dir.*†
Other Staff: 1 Sr. Res. Fellow; 1 Principal. Res. Fellow†
Research: employment relationships in Britain in the context of the internationalisation of the world economy

Legal Education, UK Centre for

Tel: (024) 7652 3117 Fax: (024) 7652 4105
    E-mail: hollie.wright@warwick.ac.uk
Varnava, T., BA Kent, MPhil Camb.   Assoc. Dir.
Webb, J., BA CNAA, LLM Warw., FRSA   Dir.*
Other Staff: 1 Information Manager; 1 Acad. Developer; 1 Vocational Educn. Developer

Legal Research Institute

Tel: (024) 7652 3215 Fax: (024) 7652 4105
    E-mail: lee.bridges@warwick.ac.uk
Bridges, Lee T., BA Dartmouth   Prof.; Dir.*

Local Government Centre

Tel: (024) 7657 2546 Fax: (024) 7657 2545
    E-mail: lgc@wbs.ac.uk
Geddes, Mike, BA S'ton., DPhil Sus.   Prof. Fellow
Hartley, J., BA Reading, PhD Manc.   Prof.
Mawson, John, BSc Lond., MPhil Lond.   Prof.; Dir.*
Other Staff: 2 Principal Res. Fellows; 1 Sr. Res. Fellow; 1 Res. Fellow; 1 Sr. Res. Assoc.
Research: local government economic, social and organisational strategies

Magnetic Resonance, Centre for

Tel: (024) 7652 3403
    E-mail: m.e.smith.1@warwick.ac.uk
Smith, Mark E., BA Camb., PhD Warw.   Dir.*

Management Under Regulation, Centre for

Tel: (024) 7652 4153 Fax: (024) 7652 4965
    E-mail: gill.allen@wbs.ac.uk
Cave, Martin, BA Oxf., BPhil Oxf., DPhil Oxf.   Prof.; Dir.*
Other Staff: 1 Sr. Res. Fellow; 1 Res. Fellow

Mass Spectrometry, Institute of

Tel: (024) 7652 3653 Fax: (024) 7652 3819
    E-mail: c.a.m.billings@warwick.ac.uk
Derrick, Peter J., BSc Lond., PhD Lond., FIP, FRACI, FRSChem   Prof., Chemistry; Dir.*

Mathematics Research Centre

Tel: (024) 7652 2681 Fax: (024) 7652 3548
    E-mail: mrc@maths.warwick.ac.uk
Reid, Miles A., BA Camb., PhD Camb., FRS   Prof.; Dir.*

New Technologies Research in Education, Centre for

Tel: (024) 7652 8352 Fax: (024) 7652 3834
    E-mail: centre@fcis1.wie.warwick.ac.uk
Kingston, Y., BEd Exe., MSc Warw.   Manager
Pratt, D. C., BSc Birm., MEd Warw., PhD Warw.   Dir.*

Philosophy and Literature, Centre for Research in

Tel: (024) 7652 3421 Fax: (024) 7652 3019
    E-mail: h.a.jones@warwick.ac.uk
Bell, Michael, BA Lond., PhD Lond.   Dir.*

Renaissance, Centre for the Study of

Tel: (024) 7652 4587 Fax: (024) 7657 2997
    E-mail: rssac@warwick.ac.uk
Clarke, E., BA Lond., DPhil Oxf.   Assoc. Dir.
De Smet, Ingrid A. R., MA Leuven, PhD Camb.   Dir.*
Hindle, S., MA Minn., MA Camb., PhD Camb., FRHistS   Dir.*
Lines, D.   Dir., Grad. Studies
Other Staff: 1 Assoc. Fellow; 1 Postdoctoral Fellow
Research: history, literature, theatre and art of Renaissance Europe (especially England, France and Italy)

Renaissance Elites and Court Cultures, AHRC Centre for the Study of

Tel: (024) 7652 4587 Fax: (024) 7657 2997
    E-mail: rssah@warwick.ac.uk
Hindle, S., MA Minn., MA Camb., PhD Camb., FRHistS   Dir.*

Risk Initiative and Statistical Consultancy Unit

Tel: (024) 7652 4553 Fax: (024) 7652 4532
    E-mail: riscu@warwick.ac.uk
Fenlon, J., MSc Manc.   Dir.*
Smith, J. Q., BSc Nott., PhD Warw.   Prof.
Other Staff: 2 Res. Fellows
Research: business risk perception

Safety and Well-Being, Centre for the Study of

Tel: (024) 7652 3174 Fax: (024) 7652 4415
    E-mail: k.j.peavoy@warwick.ac.uk
Chung, D., BSW NE, MA NE, PhD Adel.   Dir.*
Harrison, C., BA CNAA, MA Warw., PhD Warw.   Deputy Dir.

Scientific Computing, Centre for

Tel: (024) 7657 4111 Fax: (024) 7657 3133
    E-mail: csc-secretary@warwick.ac.uk
Roemer, R. A., PhD Utah   Dir.*

Small and Medium-Sized Enterprises, Centre for

Tel: (024) 7652 3741 Fax: (024) 7652 3747
    E-mail: david.storey@wbs.ac.uk
Storey, David J., BSc Hull, PhD Newcastle(UK)   Prof.; Dir.*
Other Staff: 1 Prof. Fellow

Social Theory Centre

Tel: (024) 7652 3114 Fax: (024) 7652 3497
    E-mail: d.c.s.turner@warwick.ac.uk
Rogowski, R., LLM Wis., DrIur Florence   Co-Dir.*
Turner, D. S. C., BA Durh., PhD Lond.   Co-Dir.*

Sport in Society, Centre for the Study of

Tel: (024) 7652 3065 Fax: (024) 7652 4221
    E-mail: andrew.parker@warwick.ac.uk
Parker, A., BEd CNAA, MA Warw., PhD Warw.   Dir.*
Research: history and politics of sport; legal intervention in sport; social and political theory; sports structures and organisation

Women and Gender, Centre for the Study of

Tel: (024) 7652 3600 Fax: (024) 7652 8178
    E-mail: christine.wilson@warwick.ac.uk
Charles, N., BA Keele, PhD Keele   Co-Dir.*
Steinberg, D. L., BA Calif., MA Kent, PhD Birm.   Co-Dir.*
Other Staff: 3 Asst. Profs.
Research: feminism; gender and development; science communications; sociology of literature and culture

CONTACT OFFICERS

Academic affairs. Registrar: Baldwin, Jon F., BA CNAA, MBA Open(UK), Hon. DLitt UMIST, FCIS, FRSA

Accommodation. Accommodation Manager: Scott, Matthew, BA CNAA (E-mail: accommodation@warwick.ac.uk)

Admissions (first degree). Director, Student Admissions and Recruitment: Wallis, Darren, BSc Lond., MSc Lond.

Adult/continuing education. Director, Centre for Lifelong Learning: Moseley, R., BSc Edin., MSc Sus., DPhil Sus. (E-mail: cll@warwick.ac.uk)

Alumni. Interim Director of Development and Alumni Relations: Rowley, I. P., BA Sheff. (E-mail: wga@warwick.ac.uk)

Archives. Archivist: (vacant) (E-mail: archives@warwick.ac.uk)

Careers. Director of Careers Advisory Service: (vacant) (E-mail: careers@warwick.ac.uk)

Computing services. Director of IT Services: Roberts, Mike (E-mail: helpdesk@warwick.ac.uk)

Conferences/corporate hospitality. Acting Director: Robinson, Alan M. (E-mail: conferences@warwick.ac.uk)

Development/fund-raising. Director of Major Gifts: McGrath, Mary, BSc Lond. (E-mail: wga@warwick.ac.uk)

Equal opportunities. Personnel Officer: Aspinall, L., BSc Hull

Estates and buildings/works and services. Director of Estates: Wilson, R. B., MBA Glas. (E-mail: enquire@estate.warwick.ac.uk)

Examinations. Assistant Registrar (Examinations Officer): Taylor, J. A., BA Leeds, MA Leeds, DPhil Oxf.

Finance. Finance Director: Drinkwater, R. A., BA Durh., FCA

General enquiries. Registrar: Baldwin, Jon F., BA CNAA, MBA Open(UK), Hon. DLitt UMIST, FCIS, FRSA

Health services. Medical Officer: Ballantine, R. J., MB BS (E-mail: uni.admin@gp-m86029.wmids.nhs.uk)

Industrial liaison. Industrial Development Officer: Bobe, M., BSc Portsmouth, PhD Portsmouth

International office. Director, International Office: (vacant) (E-mail: int.office@warwick.ac.uk)

Library (chief librarian). Librarian: Bell, A., BA E.Anglia, MA Sheff. (E-mail: library@warwick.ac.uk)

Marketing. Director of Communications: Rowley, I. P., BA Sheff. (E-mail: communications@warwick.ac.uk)

Ombudsman. Registrar: Baldwin, Jon F., BA CNAA, MBA Open(UK), Hon. DLitt UMIST, FCIS, FRSA

Personnel/human resources. Director, Human Resources and Commercial Services: Stephenson, Paul, BA Nott.

Public relations. Director of Communications: Rowley, I. P., BA Sheff.

Publications. Corporate Communications Manager: Warman, Roberta M., BA Oxf., PhD Lond.

Purchasing. Purchasing and Insurance Officer: Lightbown, M. J.

Quality assurance and accreditation. Senior Assistant Registrar: Salter-Wright, Y. A., BA C.U.A., MA Warw.

Research. Pro-Vice-Chancellor (Research): Jones, Prof. John D. S., BSc Manc., MSc Oxf., DPhil Oxf.

Safety. Director, Safety and Occupational Health Services: Veale, David R., BSc Birm., MSc Birm., PhD Birm.

Scholarships, awards, loans. Head of Student Finance: Bell, J., BA *CNAA*

Schools liaison. Recruitment Officer (Undergraduate): (vacant)
(E-mail: student.recruitment@warwick.ac.uk)

Security. Security Manager and Head of Ancillary Services: Farr, L. R.

Sport and recreation. Director of Physical Education and Sport: Monnington, Terence, MA *Birm.* (E-mail: fitness@warwick.ac.uk)

Staff development and training. Director, Learning and Development Centre: Bennett, Sue, BA *Reading*, FCIPD

Strategic planning. Registrar: Baldwin, Jon F., BA *CNAA*, MBA *Open(UK)*, Hon. DLitt *UMIST*, FCIS, FRSA

Student union. General Manager: Horton, Claire (E-mail: sunion@warwick.ac.uk)

Student welfare/counselling. Senior Tutor: Lamb, Stephen J., BA *Birm.*, MA *Warw.* (E-mail: advice@sunion.warwick.ac.uk)

Students from other countries. Director, International Office: (vacant)
(E-mail: int.office@warwick.ac.uk)

Students with disabilities. Disability Co-ordinator: Abson, J., BA *Brad.*, BSc *Brad.*, MA *Brad.*

[*Information supplied by the institution as at 4 February 2008, and edited by the ACU*]

UNIVERSITY OF THE WEST OF ENGLAND, BRISTOL

Founded 1992

Member of the Association of Commonwealth Universities

Postal Address: Frenchay Campus, Coldharbour Lane, Bristol, England BS16 1QY
Telephone: (0117) 965 6261 **Fax:** (0117) 328 2810
URL: http://www.uwe.ac.uk

VICE-CHANCELLOR*—West, Prof. Steven, BSc
DEPUTY VICE-CHANCELLOR—Cuthbert, Prof. R. E., MA MSc MBA
DIRECTOR OF FINANCE—Marshall, Bill, BA

GENERAL INFORMATION

History. The university was founded as Bristol Polytechnic in 1969 and gained university status in 1992.
It has four campuses, three in north Bristol and one in south Bristol, and an associate faculty at Hartpury College, Gloucester.

Admission to first degree courses (see also United Kingdom Introduction). Through Universities and Colleges Admissions Service (UCAS). Minimum international language qualifications are IELTS (6) or TOEFL (570).

First Degrees (see also United Kingdom Directory to Subjects of Study). BA, BEng, BSc, LLB, MEng.
Length of course. Full-time: BA, BEng, BSc, LLB: 3 years; MEng: 4 years. Part-time: BA, BEng, BSc, LLB, MEng: max. 5 years.

Higher Degrees (see also United Kingdom Directory to Subjects of Study).
Master's. LLM, MA, MBA, MPhil, MSc.
Length of course. Full-time: LLM, MA, MBA, MSc: 1 year; MPhil: 1½–3 years. Part-time: LLM, MA, MSc: 2–3 years; MBA: 2½ years; MPhil: 2½–4 years. By distance learning: MA, MSc: 2–3 years.
Doctoral. PhD.
Length of course. Full-time: PhD: 2–5 years. Part-time: PhD: 3–6 years.

Libraries. Volumes: 563,000. Periodicals subscribed to: 12,400.

Academic Year (2007–2008). Three terms: 24 September–21 December; 7 January–14 March; 7 April–27 June.

Statistics. Students (2006–2007): full-time 18,959; part-time 6640; international 1531; undergraduate 20,436.

ACADEMIC UNITS

Arranged by Faculties

Applied Sciences

Tel: (0117) 328 2967 Fax: (0117) 328 2904
E-mail: andrew.carter@uwe.ac.uk
Duffield, John, BSc PhD   Prof.; Dean (Acting)*

Art, Media and Design, Bristol School of

Tel: (0117) 966 0222 Fax: (0117) 328 4745
E-mail: amd.enquiries@uwe.ac.uk
Gough, Paul, MA PhD   Prof.; Dean*

Bristol Business School

Tel: (0117) 328 2247 Fax: (0117) 328 2289
E-mail: business@uwe.ac.uk
Gow, Ian   Dean*

Built Environment

Tel: (0117) 328 3020 Fax: (0117) 328 3002
E-mail: fbe.entry@uwe.ac.uk
Boddy, Martin, MA PhD   Prof.; Dean (Acting)*

Computing, Engineering and Mathematical Sciences

Tel: (0117) 328 3356 Fax: (0117) 328 3155
E-mail: cems.reception@uwe.ac.uk
Vinney, John, BEng PhD, FIMechE   Dean*

Education

Tel: (0117) 328 4151 Fax: (0117) 328 4108
E-mail: reception.edu@uwe.ac.uk
Ritchie, Ron, BSc PhD   Prof.; Dean*

Health and Social Care

Tel: (0117) 328 8534 Fax: (0117) 328 8412
E-mail: hsc.admissions@uwe.ac.uk
Foreman, Kevin, BSc PhD   Dean*

Humanities, Languages and Social Sciences

Tel: (0117) 328 2366 Fax: (0117) 328 2295
E-mail: hlss.admissions@uwe.ac.uk
Channon, Prof. Geoff, BSc PhD, FRHistS   Dean*

Law

Tel: (0117) 328 2604 Fax: (0117) 328 2268
E-mail: law@uwe.ac.uk
Bensted, Prof. A. R., BA LLM   Dean*

SPECIAL CENTRES, ETC

Aerospace Manufacturing Research Centre

Tel: (0117) 328 3500 Fax: (0117) 328 3636
E-mail: alexander.fanourakis@uwe.ac.uk
Jocelyn, Prof. A., BA   Dir.*

Aerospace Strategy Research Centre

Tel: (0117) 328 3630 Fax: (0117) 328 2295
E-mail: philip.lawrence@uwe.ac.uk
Lawrence, Prof. Philip, BA MA PhD, FRAeS   Dir.*

Air Quality Management Resource Centre

Tel: (0117) 328 3825 Fax: (0117) 328 2132
E-mail: aqmrc@uwe.ac.uk
Longhurst, Jim, BSc *Plym.*, MSc *Aston*, PhD *Birm.*, FRGS, FIEnvSc   Dir.*

Analytical, Materials and Sensors Science, Centre for Research in

Tel: (0117) 328 3815 Fax: (0117) 328 2904
Duffield, John, BSc PhD   Prof.; Dir.*

Appearance Research, Centre for

Tel: (0117) 328 3947 Fax: (0117) 328 3645
E-mail: laura.kingston@uwe.ac.uk
Rumsey, Prof. Nichola J., BSc MSc PhD   Dir.*

Biomedicine, Centre for Research in

Tel: (0117) 328 3954 Fax: (0117) 328 2132
E-mail: crib@uwe.ac.uk
Avent, Neil, BSc PhD   Dir.*

Bristol Robotics Laboratory

Tel: (0117) 328 2539 Fax: (0117) 328 3960
E-mail: chris.melhuish@uwe.ac.uk
Melhuish, Prof. Chris, BSc MSc PhD, FBCS   Dir.*

Child and Adolescent Health, Centre for

Tel: (0117) 328 8851
E-mail: nicola.eaton@uwe.ac.uk
Gray, S., MB ChB, FRCP, FFPHM   Prof.; Dir.*

Cities Research Centre

Tel: (0117) 328 3998 Fax: (0117) 328 3899
E-mail: jane.newton@uwe.ac.uk
Smith, Ian   Dir.*

Clinical and Health Services Research, Centre for

Tel: (0117) 328 8449 Fax: (0117) 328 8437
E-mail: selena.grey@uwe.ac.uk
Gray, S., MB ChB, FRCP, FFPHM   Prof.; Dir.*

Community Information Systems Centre

Tel: (0117) 328 3170 Fax: (0117) 328 3155
Stephens, Rob   Dir.*

Complex Cooperative Systems, Centre for

Tel: (0117) 328 3176 Fax: (0117) 328 3155
    E-mail: richard.mcclatchey@uwe.ac.uk
McClatchey, Prof. R. H., BSc PhD   Dir.*

Construction and Property Research Centre

Tel: (0117) 328 3102 Fax: (0117) 328 3899
    E-mail: jane.newton@uwe.ac.uk
Grimshaw, R., BA   Prof.; Dir.*

Education and Democracy, Centre for Research in

Tel: 0117 328 4258 Fax: 0117 328 4108
    E-mail: cred@uwe.ac.uk
Kushner, S.   Prof.; Dir.*

Employment Studies Research, Centre for

Tel: (0117) 328 3476 Fax: (0117) 328 3911
Tailby, Stephanie   Prof.; Dir.*

Engineering and Medicine Elastomers Research Centre

Tel: (0117) 328 2639 Fax: (0117) 328 3800
    E-mail: vince.coveney@uwe.ac.uk
Coveney, V., BA PhD   Dir.*

Environment and Planning, Centre for

Tel: (0117) 328 3102 Fax: (0117) 328 3899
    E-mail: jane.newton@uwe.ac.uk
Williams, Katie   Dir.*

Environmental Sciences, Centre for Research in

Tel: (0117) 328 3692 Fax: (0117) 328 2904
Longhurst, Jim, BSc Plym., MSc Aston, PhD
    Birm., FRGS, FIEnvSc   Prof.; Dir.*

Fine Print Research, Centre for

Tel: (0117) 328 4832 Fax: (0117) 328 4745
    E-mail: cfprinfo@uwe.ac.uk
Hoskins, Prof. S., MA RCA   Dir.*

Healthy Cities and Urban Policy, World Health Organisation Collaborating Centre for

Tel: (0117) 328 3258 Fax: (0117) 328 3899
    E-mail: hugh.barton@uwe.ac.uk
Barton, H., MPhil   Dir.*

Innovative Manufacturing and Machine Vision System, Centre for

Tel: (0117) 328 3578 Fax: (0117) 328 3636
    E-mail: melvyn.smith@uwe.ac.uk
Smith, M., BEng MSc PhD   Dir.*

Intelligent Autonomous Systems Engineering Laboratory

Tel: (0117) 328 2539 Fax: (0117) 328 3960
    E-mail: chris.melhuish@uwe.ac.uk
Melhuish, Prof. Chris, BSc MSc PhD, FBCS
    Dir.*

Learning and Workforce Research, Centre for

Tel: (0117) 328 8777
    E-mail: margaret.miers@uwe.ac.uk
Miers, M.   Dir.*

Legal Research, Centre for

Tel: (0117) 328 2899 Fax: (0117) 328 2268
Lloyd-Cape, E., BTech LLM   Prof.; Dir.*

Lifelong Learning and Education, Bristol Centre for Research in

Tel: (0117) 328 4241
Bathmaker, Ann-Marie   Prof.; Dir.*

Brine, Jacky   Prof.; Dir.*
James, David   Prof.; Dir.*

Linguistics, Bristol Centre for

Tel: (0117) 328 3278
Coates, Richard   Prof.; Dir.*

Local Democracy, Centre for

Tel: (0117) 328 8758 Fax: (0117) 328 8421
    E-mail: lesley.wright@uwe.ac.uk
Miller, C., BSc MSc PhD, FBCS   Prof.; Dir.*

Management Accounting Research, Bristol Centre for

Tel: (0117) 328 2293 Fax: (0117) 328 2289
    E-mail: robert.luther@uwe.ac.uk
Luther, Prof. R., BCom MA   Dir.*

Plant Science, Centre for Research in

Tel: (0117) 328 2149 Fax: (0117) 328 2904
Neill, Prof. S.   Dir.*

Psycho-Social Studies, Centre for

Tel: (0117) 328 2932 Fax: (0117) 328 2295
    E-mail: julia.long@uwe.ac.uk
Hoggett, Prof. P., BA   Dir.*

Public Health Research, Centre for Research in

Tel: (0117) 328 8836 Fax: (0117) 328 7534
    E-mail: emma2.griffin@uwe.ac.uk
Orme, J., BSc MSc   Dir.*

Regional History Centre

Tel: (0117) 328 4437 Fax: (0117) 328 4417
    E-mail: steve.poole@uwe.ac.uk
Poole, S.   Dir.*

Transport and Society, Centre for

Tel: (0117) 328 3219 Fax: (0117) 328 3899
    E-mail: jane.newton@uwe.ac.uk
Lyons, Prof. G.   Dir.*

Visual Arts Research in Place, Location and Context and Environment, Centre for

Tel: (0117) 328 4720 Fax: (0117) 328 4745
Gough, Paul, MA PhD   Prof.; Dir.*

CONTACT OFFICERS

Academic affairs. Academic Registrar:
    Harrison, Tessa
    (E-mail: tessa.harrison@uwe.ac.uk)
Accommodation. Accommodation Officer:
    Jowett, Vivienne
    (E-mail: accommodation@uwe.ac.uk)
Admissions (first degree). Admissions and
    International Recruitment: Francombe,
    Dianne (E-mail: admissions@uwe.ac.uk)
Admissions (higher degree). Admissions and
    International Recruitment: Francombe,
    Dianne (E-mail: admissions@uwe.ac.uk)
Alumni. Alumni Officer: Amphlett, Sarah
    (E-mail: alumni@uwe.ac.uk)
Careers. Careers Officer: Clarke, John
    (E-mail: careers@uwe.ac.uk)
Computing services. IT Services: Grive, Steve
    (E-mail: its.helpdesk@uwe.ac.uk)
Conferences/corporate hospitality. Sales and
    Marketing Manager: Bailey, Joanne
    (E-mail: joanne.bailey@uwe.ac.uk)
Consultancy services. Executive Director,
    Research, Business and Innovation: Hagen,
    Prof. S. (E-mail: crigs@uwe.ac.uk)
Estates and buildings/works and services.
    Estates Officer: Fell, John D., BA MBA
    (E-mail: john.fell@uwe.ac.uk)
Examinations. Academic Registrar: Harrison,
    Tessa (E-mail: tessa.harrison@uwe.ac.uk)

Finance. Director of Finance: Marshall, Bill
    (E-mail: finance@uwe.ac.uk)
General enquiries. Contact Marketing and
    Communications Office
    (E-mail: enquiries@uwe.ac.uk)
Industrial liaison. Executive Director,
    Research, Business and Innovation: Hagen,
    Prof. S. (E-mail: crigs@uwe.ac.uk)
International office. Head, Student Affairs:
    McGoldrick, Theresa
    (E-mail: uwe.international@uwe.ac.uk)
Language training for international students.
    Head, English as a Foreign Language and
    Linguistics: Mann, George
    (E-mail: george.mann@uwe.ac.uk)
Library (chief librarian). Head of Library
    Services: Rex, Cathy
    (E-mail: lib.enquiries@uwe.ac.uk)
Marketing. Head, Marketing and
    Communications: Hicks, Keith
    (E-mail: keith.hicks@uwe.ac.uk)
Personnel/human resources. Director of
    Personnel Services: Apperley, Ian
    (E-mail: personnel@uwe.ac.uk)
Public relations. Head, Marketing and
    Communications: Hicks, Keith
    (E-mail: keith.hicks@uwe.ac.uk)
Publications. Publications Officer: Guillaume,
    Josephine, BA
    (E-mail: josephine.guillaume@uwe.ac.uk)
Purchasing. Procurement Officer: Baker, Helen
    (E-mail: helen.baker@uwe.ac.uk)
Quality assurance and accreditation.
    Academic Registrar: Harrison, Tessa
    (E-mail: tessa.harrison@uwe.ac.uk)
Research. Executive Director, Centre for
    Research: Hagen, Prof. S.
    (E-mail: crigs@uwe.ac.uk)
Safety. Safety Officer: Champion, Robin
    (E-mail: robin.champion@uwe.ac.uk)
Scholarships, awards, loans. Enquiry and
    Admissions Service: Robinson, Kelly
    (E-mail: kelly.robinson@uwe.ac.uk)
Schools liaison. Enquiry and Admissions
    Service: Keith-Miller, Guy
    (E-mail: admissions@uwe.ac.uk)
Security. Security Services: Taylor, David
    (E-mail: david.taylor@uwe.ac.uk)
Sport and recreation. Physical Recreation:
    Vanstone, Stuart
    (E-mail: stuart.vanstone@uwe.ac.uk)
Staff development and training. Personnel
    Manager - Development Team:
    Fitzsimmons, Pam
Student union. General Manager (Student
    Union): Smith, Sarah-Jane
    (E-mail: union@uwesu.ac.uk)
Student welfare/counselling. Student
    Counsellor: Topham, Phil
    (E-mail: counselling@uwe.ac.uk)
Student welfare/counselling. Student Welfare
    Officer: (vacant) (E-mail: saws@uwe.ac.uk)
Students from other countries. Head, Student
    Affairs: McGoldrick, Theresa
    (E-mail: uwe.international@uwe.ac.uk)
Students with disabilities. Head, Disability
    Service: Huggins, Christine
    (E-mail: drc@uwe.ac.uk)
University press. Printing and Stationery
    Manager: (vacant)

CAMPUS/COLLEGE HEADS

Hartpury College, Hartpury House, Hartpury,
    Gloucester, England GL19 3BE. (Tel:
    (01452) 830065; Fax: (01452) 700629)
    Principal: Wharton, M.

[Information supplied by the institution as at 26
September 2007, and edited by the ACU]

UNIVERSITY OF THE WEST OF SCOTLAND

Founded 1992

Postal Address: Paisley, Renfrewshire, Scotland PA1 2BE
Telephone: (0141) 848 3000 **Fax:** (0141) 887 0812
URL: http://www.uws.ac.uk

PRINCIPAL AND VICE-CHANCELLOR*—McDaid, Prof. Seamus, MBA *Strath.*
UNIVERSITY SECRETARY‡—Alexander, Kenneth, BSc *Strath.*

UNIVERSITY OF WESTMINSTER

Founded 1992

Member of the Association of Commonwealth Universities

Postal Address: 309 Regent Street, London, England W1B 2UW
Telephone: (020) 7911 5000 **Fax:** (020) 7911 5103
URL: http://www.wmin.ac.uk

VICE-CHANCELLOR AND RECTOR*—(from 1 August 2007) Petts, Prof. Geoff E., BSc *Liv.*, PhD *S'ton.*, FRSA, FRGS
UNIVERSITY SECRETARY AND CLERK TO THE COURT‡—Mainstone, Carole, BA *Sheff.*, MA *Sheff.*, MBA *Brun.*
ACADEMIC REGISTRAR—Rugg, Evelyne, BA *Manc.*, Hon. FTCL
DIRECTOR OF FINANCE—Harding, Philip, BSc *Warw.*, MSc *Lond.*
PROVOST (CAVENDISH)—Tyler, Maud, BA *Lond.*, PhD *Camb.*
DEPUTY VICE-CHANCELLOR (INTERNAL AFFAIRS)—Tyler, Maud, BA *Lond.*, PhD *Camb.*
PROVOST (HARROW)—Phillips, Prof. Keith C., BSc *Camb.*, MA *Camb.*, PhD *Hull*
PROVOST (MARYLEBONE)—(vacant)
PROVOST (REGENT)—Blunden, Prof. Margaret, BA *Exe.*, MA *Exe.*, DPhil *Oxf.*
DEPUTY VICE-CHANCELLOR (EXTERNAL AFFAIRS)—Blunden, Prof. Margaret, BA *Exe.*, MA *Exe.*, DPhil *Oxf.*

UNIVERSITY OF WINCHESTER

Founded 1840

Postal Address: West Hill, Winchester, Hampshire, England SO22 4NR
Telephone: (01962) 841515 **Fax:** (01962) 842280
URL: http://www.winchester.ac.uk

VICE-CHANCELLOR*—Carter, Prof. Joy, BSC *Durh.*, PhD *Lanc.*

UNIVERSITY OF WOLVERHAMPTON

Founded 1992

Member of the Association of Commonwealth Universities

Postal Address: Wulfruna Street, Wolverhampton, England WV1 1SB
Telephone: (01902) 321000 **Fax:** (01902) 322680
URL: http://www.wlv.ac.uk

VICE-CHANCELLOR*—Gipps, Prof. Caroline V., BSc Brist., MSc Lond., PhD Lond., FRSA, AcSS
DEPUTY VICE-CHANCELLOR—Hurd, Prof. G., BA MSc MA
SENIOR PRO-VICE-CHANCELLOR AND DIRECTOR OF FINANCE—Sproston, G. S.
PRO-VICE-CHANCELLOR (STUDENT AFFAIRS)—Nelson, Jane C., BA
PRO-VICE-CHANCELLOR (EDUCATION PARTNERSHIPS)—Hampton, Sir Geoff, KBE, BEd MEd
PRO-VICE-CHANCELLOR (RESEARCH AND EXTERNAL DEVELOPMENT)—Bennett, Prof. G. F., BSc MBA PhD
PRO-VICE-CHANCELLOR (ACADEMIC)—Glen, Prof. S., MA(Ed) MA(Phil) PhD, FRSA
ACADEMIC REGISTRAR‡—Travill, Paul, BA

GENERAL INFORMATION

History. The university, established in 1992, was originally founded as Wolverhampton Polytechnic (1969).

The main campus is in Wolverhampton city centre; other campuses are on the outskirts of Wolverhampton (Compton Park Campus), and in Walsall and Telford. A hospital-based teaching centre affiliated to the school of health is situated in Burton upon Trent.

Admission to first degree courses (see also United Kingdom Introduction). Through Universities and Colleges Admissions Service (UCAS). The university accepts a wide range of entry qualifications.

First Degrees (see also United Kingdom Directory to Subjects of Study). BA, BEd, BEng, BSc, LLB.

Sandwich courses and courses including a year abroad: 4 years.

Length of course. Full-time: BEd: 3 years; BA, BEng, BSc: 3–4 years. Part-time: BA, BEng, BSc: 5–6 years. By distance learning: LLB: 4–6 years.

Higher Degrees (see also United Kingdom Directory to Subjects of Study).

Master's. LLM, MA, MBA, MMedSc, MPH, MPhil, MSc.

Admission. Applicants for admission to taught or research master's degree courses must normally hold a first degree with at least second class honours, or equivalent qualification.

MA, MSc: course lengths vary according to the subject studied. Some courses are available part-time only.

Length of course. Full-time: LLM, MBA, MPH, MSc: 1 year; MA: 1–2 years; MPhil: 1½–3 years. Part-time: LLM, MMedSc: 2 years; MBA, MPH: 2–3 years; MA, MSc: 2–5 years; MPhil: 2½–4 years.

Doctoral. DCounPsych, DLitt, DSc, DSocSc, PhD.

Admission. Applicants for PhD must have an appropriate master's degree. DLitt, DSocSc, DSc: awarded on published work.

PhD may be taken direct (2–5 years full-time, 3–6 years part-time) or via MPhil (2.75–5 years full-time, 3.75–6 years part-time).

Length of course. Full-time: PhD: 2–5 years. Part-time: DCounPsych: 3–5 years; PhD: 3–6 years.

Libraries. Volumes: 582,329. Periodicals subscribed to: 6548.

Academic Year (2007–2008). Three terms or two semesters: (terms) 17 September–14 December; 7 January–14 March; 31 March–23 May; (semesters) 24 September–14 December; 28 January–23 May.

Income (2006–2007). Total, £144,453,000.

Statistics. Staff (2006–2007): 2747 (915 academic, 1832 non-academic). Students (2006–2007): full-time 13,953 (5779 men, 8174 women); part-time 9607 (3734 men, 5873 women); international 3561 (1877 men, 1684 women); distance education/external 748 (311 men, 437 women); undergraduate 19,390 (7748 men, 11,642 women); master's 3917 (1613 men, 2304 women); doctoral 253 (152 men, 101 women).

FACULTIES/SCHOOLS

Applied Sciences, School of
Tel: (01902) 322667 Fax: (01902) 322714
E-mail: sas@wlv.ac.uk
Dean: Robotham, Prof. P., BSc PhD

Art and Design, School of
Tel: (01902) 321900 Fax: (01902) 321944
E-mail: sad@wlv.ac.uk
Dean: Conway, B., BA MA PhD

Business School
Tel: (01902) 321789 Fax: (01902) 321724
E-mail: wbsmarketing@wlv.ac.uk
Dean: Wilson, Prof. D., BA MBA PhD

Computing and Information Technology, School of
Tel: (01902) 321402 Fax: (01902) 321478
E-mail: scit@wlv.ac.uk
Dean: Moreton, Prof. R., BA MTech, FBCS

Education, School of
Tel: (01902) 322860 Fax: (01902) 323180
E-mail: sed-enquiries@wlv.ac.uk
Dean: Field, Prof. C., BA MA

Engineering and the Built Environment, School of
Tel: (01902) 322282 Fax: (01902) 322743
E-mail: sebe@wlv.ac.uk
Dean: Olomolaiye, Prof. P., BSc MSc PhD

Graduate School
Tel: (01902) 323313 Fax: (01902) 323316
E-mail: grads@wlv.ac.uk
Dean: Gilkison, Prof. J., BA MA PhD

Health, School of
Tel: (01902) 518600 Fax: (01902) 518660
E-mail: soh@wlv.ac.uk
Dean: Lang, Prof. L., PhD

Humanities, Languages and Social Science, School of
Tel: (01902) 322484 Fax: (01902) 322739
E-mail: shlss@wlv.ac.uk
Dean: Gwinnett, B., BA PhD

Learning and Teaching, Centre for Excellence in
Tel: (01902) 322361 Fax: (01902) 518539
E-mail: celt@wlv.ac.uk
Dean (Acting): Gale, H., BA MA

Legal Studies, School of
Tel: (01902) 321515 Fax: (01902) 323569
E-mail: sls@wlv.ac.uk
Dean: Mitchell, B., BA LLM

Sport, Performing Arts and Leisure, School of
Tel: (01902) 322898 Fax: (01902) 322894
E-mail: sspal@wlv.ac.uk
Dean: Pymm, J., BA MEd MPhil

CONTACT OFFICERS

Academic affairs. Pro-Vice-Chancellor (Academic): Glen, Prof. S., MA(Ed) MA(Phil) PhD, FRSA

Accommodation. Accommodation Operations Manager: Woolley, Rebecca (E-mail: becwoolley@wlv.ac.uk)

Admissions (first degree). Academic Registrar: Travill, Paul, BA

Admissions (higher degree). Academic Registrar: Travill, Paul, BA

Archives. Information and Records Manager: Young, Janette, BSc (E-mail: janette.young@wlv.ac.uk)

Careers. Head of Careers and Employment Services: Brandwood, Simon, BA MA (E-mail: s.brandwood@wlv.ac.uk)

Computing services. Director of IT Services: Range, Phil, BSc PhD (E-mail: phil.range@wlv.ac.uk)

Conferences/corporate hospitality. Catering and Operations Manager: Warrender, Susan, MBA (E-mail: s.j.warrender@wlv.ac.uk)

Consultancy services. Director of Business Development and Enterprise: Collins, Alan J., BEng PhD (E-mail: a.j.collins@wlv.ac.uk)

Credit transfer. Academic Registrar: Travill, Paul, BA

Development/fund-raising. Director of Business Development and Enterprise: Collins, Alan J., BEng PhD (E-mail: a.j.collins@wlv.ac.uk)

Equal opportunities. Equal Opportunities Co-ordinator: Dicker, Berry, BA MSc (E-mail: b.j.dicker@wlv.ac.uk)

Estates and buildings/works and services. Director of Facilities: Williams, Roger H., BSc (E-mail: rogerw@wlv.ac.uk)

Examinations. Academic Registrar: Travill, Paul, BA

Finance. Head of Finance: Hicks, Stephen, BSc (E-mail: s.r.hicks@wlv.ac.uk)

Industrial liaison. Director of Business Development and Enterprise: Collins, Alan J., BEng PhD (E-mail: a.j.collins@wlv.ac.uk)

International office. Director of International: Gittens, Jo, BSc MA (E-mail: j.gittens@wlv.ac.uk)

Language training for international students. International Development Manager: Richards, Jonathan, BA MBA (E-mail: jonathan.richards@wlv.ac.uk)

Library (chief librarian). Director of Learning and Information Services: Parsons, Fiona, BA MLib (E-mail: a.f.parsons@wlv.ac.uk)

Marketing. Director of Marketing and Communications: Ehsan, Ashar (E-mail: a.ehsan@wlv.ac.uk)

Minorities/disadvantaged groups. Equal Opportunities Co-ordinator: Dicker, Berry, BA MSc (E-mail: b.j.dicker@wlv.ac.uk)

Ombudsman. University Secretary: Lee, Tony, LLB (E-mail: a.w.lee@wlv.ac.uk)

Personnel/human resources. Head of Personnel: Williams, Roger J., BSc (E-mail: roger.williams@wlv.ac.uk)

Public relations. Media Relations Manager: Kilvert, Emma, BA (E-mail: e.kilvert@wlv.ac.uk)

Publications. Publications Manager: Scott, Charles, BA (E-mail: c.a.scott@wlv.ac.uk)

Purchasing. Purchasing Officer: Porter, Gordon (E-mail: g.porter@wlv.ac.uk)

Quality assurance and accreditation. Pro-Vice-Chancellor (Academic): Glen, Prof. S., MA(Ed) MA(Phil) PhD, FRSA

Research. Dean of Research and Graduate Studies: Gilkison, Prof. J., BA MA PhD (E-mail: j.gilkison@wlv.ac.uk)

Safety. Head of Risk, Safety and Health: Hedley-Smith, Martin, MBA (E-mail: mhs@wlv.ac.uk)

Scholarships, awards, loans. Head of Higher Education Advice and Guidance: Hall, Keith, BA (E-mail: keith.hall@wlv.ac.uk)

Schools liaison. Associate Dean for Education Partnerships: Hart, Ian, BA MA MEd (E-mail: ian.hart@wlv.ac.uk)

Security. Campus Operations Co-ordinator: McGloin, Trish, BA MBA (E-mail: t.mcgloin@wlv.ac.uk)

Sport and recreation. Director of Sports: Chamberlain, Mike, BSc (E-mail: m.chamberlain@wlv.ac.uk)

Staff development and training. Personnel Manager: Gordon, Neil, BA MA (E-mail: n.j.gordon@wlv.ac.uk)

Strategic planning. Pro-Vice-Chancellor (Student Affairs): Nelson, Jane C., BA (E-mail: j.c.nelson@wlv.ac.uk)

Student union. President (Student Union) (E-mail: su.president@wlv.ac.uk)

Students from other countries. Director of International: Gittens, Jo, BSc MA (E-mail: j.gittens@wlv.ac.uk)

Students with disabilities. Student Enabling Centre Manager: Williams-Findlay, Cindy, BA (E-mail: cindy@wlv.ac.uk)

University press. Media Relations Manager: Kilvert, Emma, BA (E-mail: e.kilvert@wlv.ac.uk)

Women. Equal Opportunities Co-ordinator: Dicker, Berry, BA MSc (E-mail: b.j.dicker@wlv.ac.uk)

[*Information supplied by the institution as at 30 January 2008, and edited by the ACU*]

UNIVERSITY OF WORCESTER

Founded 2005

Member of the Association of Commonwealth Universities

Postal Address: Henwick Grove, Worcester, England WR2 6AJ
Telephone: (01905) 855000 **E-mail:** study@worc.ac.uk
URL: http://www.worcester.ac.uk

VICE-CHANCELLOR AND CHIEF EXECUTIVE*—Green, Prof. David, BA Camb., MA Camb.
PRO-VICE-CHANCELLOR—Elkin, Prof. Judith, BA Open(UK), PhD C.England, FLA, FIInfSc, FCLIP
PRO-VICE-CHANCELLOR (RESOURCES/PLANNING)—Doughty, Martin, BA Oxf., PhD Lond.
REGISTRAR AND SECRETARY‡—Ryan, John, MLitt Birm.
DIRECTOR OF FINANCE—Finch, Pat
DIRECTOR OF REGIONAL AND INTERNATIONAL DEVELOPMENT—Baker, Susanne, BA CNAA, MA Westminster
DIRECTOR OF LIFELONG LEARNING—Elliott, Prof. Geoffrey, BA Lanc., MAEd Lanc., EdD Brist.
DIRECTOR OF QUALITY ASSURANCE—Stowell, Marie, BSc Leic., PhD Warw.
DIRECTOR OF INFORMATION LEARNING SERVICES—Hannaford, Anne, BA Kent
HEAD OF PERSONNEL—Slater, Gill, BSc Birm.

GENERAL INFORMATION

History. The university was first established as an Emergency Teacher Training College in 1947 and developed under the aegis of the University of Birmingham's department of education. From 1970 degrees were validated by the Council for National Academic Awards under the name of Worcester College of Higher Education, and in 1995 Herefordshire and Worcestershire College of Nursing and Midwifery was absorbed into the college. In 1997 the college gained degree-awarding powers and became known as University College Worcester. Full university status was achieved in 2005.

The university is located on a purpose-built campus close to Worcester city centre. Worcester is 50km south of Birmingham.

Admission to first degree courses (see also United Kingdom Introduction). Admission requirements vary according to the degree programme. Full details are available in the university's prospectus.

First Degrees (see also United Kingdom Directory to Subjects of Study). BA, BSc.
Length of course. Full-time: BA, BSc: 3 years. Part-time: BA, BSc: 6 years.

Higher Degrees (see also United Kingdom Directory to Subjects of Study).
Master's. MA, MPhil, MSc.
Admission. Applicants for admission to master's degree courses must hold a good honours degree in a relevant subject from a recognised institution of higher education.

Length of course. Full-time: MA, MSc: 1 year; MPhil: 2 years. Part-time: MA, MSc: 2 years; MPhil: 4 years.
Doctoral. PhD.
Admission. PhD: a good honours degree in a relevant subject from a recognised institution of higher education.
Length of course. Full-time: PhD: 3 years. Part-time: PhD: 6 years.

Statistics. Staff (2005–2006): 670 (300 academic, 370 non-academic).

ACADEMIC UNITS

Applied Sciences, Geography and Archaeology

Tel: (01905) 855224 E-mail: asga@worc.ac.uk
Evans, Nicholas, BSc Coventry, PhD Coventry Dir., Centre for Rural Res.
Fagg, John, BA Leic., PhD Leic. Head*
Herbert, Robert, BSc Lond., PhD Cardiff Head, Appl. Scis.
Maddock, Ian, BSc Lough., PhD Lough. Head, Centre for Fluvial Res.
McDougall, Derek, BSc Glas., PhD Glas. Head, Geog.
Other Staff: 14 Academic Staff

Arts, Humanities and Social Sciences

Tel: (01905) 855280 E-mail: ahss@worc.ac.uk
Broster, David, BA Portsmouth, MA Leeds Head, Partnerships
Gamble, Maureen, BA Sur., MA Worcester Head, Art, Des. and Drama
McNally, Paddy, BA Belf., PhD Belf. Head, Hist. and Sociol.

Pearson, Richard, BA Newcastle(UK), MA Nott., PhD Manc. Head*
Terry, Jill, BA CNAA, PhD Exe. Head, English and Lang. Studies
Webb, Jean, BA Reading, PhD Reading Prof.; Head, Centre for Res. in Children's Lit.
Other Staff: 30 Academic Staff

Education, Institute of

Tel: (01905) 855231
E-mail: education@worc.ac.uk
Bertram, Antony, BEd Birm., PhD Worcester Prof.; Dir., Centre for Res. in Early Childhood
Flint, David, BEd Manc., MA Birm. Head, Primary Educn.
Hodgson, Joseph, BA Open(UK), MA Worcester Head, Sub-Degree Programmes
Murray, Janet, BA Manc., MA Open(UK) Head, Early Childhood
Pascal, Christine, BA Lanc., PhD Birm. Prof.; Dir., Centre for Res. in Early Childhood
Pumphrey, Peter Hon. Prof.
Robertson, Christine, MA Manc.Met. Head*
Russel, Vince, BA Coventry, MA Warw. Head, Management, Leadership and Post-Compulsory Educn.
Sears, John, BEd Brist. Head, Secondary Educn.
Somervell, Hugh, BA Birm., PhD Wolv. Head, Educn. Studies
Other Staff: 66 Academic Staff

Health and Social Care, Institute of

Tel: (01905) 855282
E-mail: health@worc.ac.uk

Emberlin, Jean, BSc Lond., PhD Lond. Prof.;
Dir., Natnl. Pollen and Aerobiol. Res. Unit

Evans, Deborah, BA Wolv., PhD Wolv. Head,
Community and Soc. Welfare

Jones, Louise, BA Open(UK), MBA W.England
Head*

Quallington, Janet, BA CNAA, MA Keele Head,
Quality Assurance, Undergrad. and Pre-
Registration Curric. Devel.

Toner, Louise, MA Glas. Head, Continuing
Professl. Devel.

Upton, Dominic, BA Leic., PhD Lond. Prof.;
Head, Psychol. and Health Studies

Wright, Judith, BA Wales, MA Wales Head of
Nursing, Midwifery, Pre-Registration and
Emergency Care

Other Staff: 70 Academic Staff

Sport and Exercise Science, School of

Tel: (01905) 855525 E-mail: sport@worc.ac.uk

Armstrong, Malcolm, BA Liv., MA Liv. Head*

Bill, Karen, BEd Chichester, MA Lough. Head,
External Devels.

Donovan, Michael, BEd Manc., MA Warw.
Head, Resources

Hulse, Kate, BSc Lough., MSc Lough. Head,
Quality and Curriculum Devel.

Other Staff: 20 Academic Staff

Worcester Business School

Tel: (01905) 855279 E-mail: wbs@worc.ac.uk

Cox, Howard, BA Kingston(UK), PhD Lond.
Prof.; Head, Res.

Francis-Smythe, Janet, MSc Brist., PhD Manc.
Dir., Res. Centre for People at Work

Hunt, Marilyn, MA C.England Head,
Undergrad. Curric. Devel.

Maxfield, Timothy, BA Lanc., MSc Lanc. Head,
Bus. Devel.

Richardson, Mark, BSc Wales, MA C.England,
MPhil Wales Head*

Wright, Warren, BA C.England, MA Aston Head
of Resources

Other Staff: 21 Academic Staff

CONTACT OFFICERS

Development/fund-raising. Director of
Regional and International Development:
Baker, Susanne, BA CNAA, MA Westminster

Finance. Director of Finance: Finch, Pat

Personnel/human resources. Head of
Personnel: Slater, Gill, BSc Birm.

Quality assurance and accreditation. Director
of Quality Assurance: Stowell, Marie, BSc
Leic., PhD Warw.

[Information supplied by the institution as at 9 May
2006, and edited by the ACU]

UNIVERSITY OF YORK

Founded 1963

Postal Address: Heslington, York, England YO10 5DD
Telephone: (01904) 430000 **Fax:** (01904) 433433
URL: http://www.york.ac.uk

VICE-CHANCELLOR*—Cantor, Prof. Brian, BA Camb., MA Camb., PhD Camb., FIMMM, FIP, FREng
REGISTRAR AND SECRETARY‡—(until 31 December 2008) Neocosmos, Sally, BA Lough.

YORK ST JOHN UNIVERSITY

Founded 2006

Member of the Association of Commonwealth Universities

Postal Address: Lord Mayor's Walk, York, England YO31 7EX
Telephone: (01904) 876600 **Fax:** (01904) 670622 **E-mail:** d.willcocks@yorksj.ac.uk
URL: http://www.yorksj.ac.uk

VICE-CHANCELLOR*—Willcocks, Prof. Dianne, CBE, BSc Sur.
DEPUTY VICE-CHANCELLOR‡—Brown, Prof. David M

GENERAL INFORMATION

First Degrees. BA, BHSc, BSc.
Length of course. Full-time: BA, BHSc, BSc: 3
years. Part-time: BA, BHSc, BSc: 4–8 years.

Higher Degrees.
Master's. MA, MPhil, MSc.
Admission. Students enrolled on master's by
research degrees are registered for an award of
the University of Leeds.

Length of course. Full-time: MA, MPhil, MSc: 1
year. Part-time: MPhil: 2 years; MA, MSc: 2–5
years.
Doctoral. PhD.
Admission. PhD candidates are registered for
an award of the University of Leeds.
Length of course. Full-time: PhD: 3 years. Part-
time: PhD: 5 years.

Statistics. Students (2007): international 340;
distance education/external 61; undergraduate
4527; master's 901; doctoral 25.

FACULTIES/SCHOOLS

Arts
Dean: Purcell, Steve, BA CNAA, MA Leeds

Business and Communication
Dean: Mathers, Jackie, MBA Leeds

Education and Theology
Dean: Spindler, John, BA Open(UK), PhD Sheff.

Health and Life Sciences
Dean: Gacal, Pauline, BSc Tees., MA Leeds

WEST INDIES

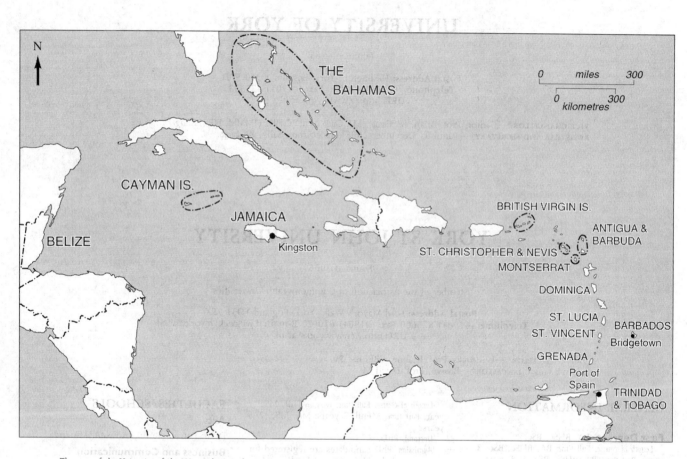

The seats of the University of the West Indies are shown in upper/lower case letters. States and Territories supporting the university are shown in capital letters

WEST INDIES: DIRECTORY TO SUBJECTS OF STUDY

The table below shows which subjects are available for study and/or research at the constituent campuses of the University of the West Indies. U = may be studied for first degree course; M = may be studied for master's degree course; D = research facilities to doctoral level; X = all three levels (UMD).

	West Indies	West Indies: Cave Hill	West Indies: Mona	West Indies: St Augustine
Accountancy/Accounting	UM	U	UM	UM
Administration/Administrative Studies		U	UM	U
Advertising				U
African Languages/Studies	X		U	U
Agricultural Extension and Education				X
Agriculture/Agricultural Science	X			X
Agronomy/Soil Science	X			X
Agrotechnology				U
Anaesthesia/Anaesthesiology	M		M	UM
Anatomical Science/Anatomy	MD		X	X
Animal Nutrition/Animal Physiology				U
Animal Science/Husbandry/Production				X
Anthropology/Folklore	U			
Applied Chemistry	X		MD	
Applied Physics			M	
Aquaculture/Fisheries/Marine Science	X		UM	X
Archaeology	MD		U	U
Art, Fine	M			UM
Arts General	D		X	M
Arts and Culture			M	U
Astronomy/Astrophysics/Space Science	M			X
Banking/Finance	UM		U	UM
Behavioural Sciences	UM		UM	X
Biochemistry	X		X	X
Bioengineering	X			
Biology	X	X	U	X
Biology Molecular	X			U
Biostatistics	M			
Biotechnology	X		MD	U
Botany/Plant Science	X		X	X
Building/Built Environment/Construction				UM
Business Administration	MD		UM	UM
Business Computing				U
Business Economics	U		X	UM
Business Information Systems			U	UM
Business/Commerce			UM	UM
Caribbean Studies		X	UM	X
Catholicism				U
Chemistry	X	X	X	X

	West Indies	West Indies: Cave Hill	West Indies: Mona	West Indies: St Augustine
Child Health	M		X	UM
Child Welfare			U	
Child and Family Psychology			UM	U
Child/Youth Studies				U
Communication Sciences	UM		UM	
Communication/Journalism/Media Studies	UM		X	U
Communications/Information Management			M	UM
Community Health	MD		UM	UM
Community Medicine	D		U	
Computer Science	X	X	X	X
Conservation Studies			M	
Consumer Studies				U
Counselling	M		M	
Creative Writing	M			UM
Criminology	X	U		X
Crop Science/Production	MD		UM	X
Cultural Studies	MD		MD	X
Curriculum and Assessment Studies			M	U
Deaf Studies	U			
Dentistry	X			UM
Design, Industrial				U
Development Studies	MD		X	
Drama/Theatre/Dance/Performing Arts	U			UM
E-Business				U
E-Commerce	M			U
Ecology	U		U	X
Economic History	UM	U		U
Economic Planning and Development	MD			
Economics	X	X	X	X
Economics Agricultural/Agribusiness	X			X
Education	X	X	X	X
Education Adult	D			
Education Primary	X			X
Education Special	X		U	
Educational Administration	M		UM	
Educational Psychology			UM	
Electronics	U		U	U
Emergency/Trauma Care Technology				M
Energy Studies	M			X

	West Indies	West Indies: Cave Hill	West Indies: Mona	West Indies: St Augustine
Engineering	X			X
Engineering Agricultural/Fisheries	X			UM
Engineering Business				UM
Engineering Chemical/Petrochemical/Process	X			X
Engineering Civil/Environmental/Structural	X			X
Engineering Communications/Telecommunications	M			X
Engineering Computer	X			X
Engineering Construction	MD			UM
Engineering Design				X
Engineering Electrical/Electronic	X			X
Engineering Environmental Geophysics				X
Engineering Geological				X
Engineering Industrial	UM			X
Engineering Information Technology				X
Engineering Instrumentation	UM			X
Engineering Management	M			X
Engineering Manufacturing	MD			U
Engineering Materials/Mineral Resources/Petroleum	M			X
Engineering Mathematical				X
Engineering Mechanical/Production	X			X
Engineering Metallurgical/Mining				X
Engineering Software				UM
English	X	X	X	X
Entomology				X
Entrepreneurship	U			
Environmental Management				U
Environmental Science/Studies	U		U	X
Epidemiology	MD		M	
Ergonomics				U
Ethics			UM	U
Ethics, Law and Governance	MD		MD	
Ethnomusicology				U
Film/Photography/Television/Animation	UM			U
Food Science/Nutrition/Home Science/Dietetics	X		MD	UM
French/French Studies	X	X	X	X
Genetics				U
Geographic Information Systems/Geomatics	M			
Geography	X		X	

	West Indies	West Indies: Cave Hill	West Indies: Mona	West Indies: St Augustine
Geology/Earth Sciences/Atmospheric Studies	X		X	X
Geophysics				X
Global Studies	M			
Health Education	M		M	
Health Sciences/Studies	U			X
Health/Hospital Administration			U	
Heritage Studies	M		M	
Hindi	U			U
History	X	X	X	X
Horticulture	U			UM
Hotel Management	U		U	U
Human Biology			U	
Human Resource Development	M		UM	
Immunology/Infection/Immunity	MD			
Industrial Chemistry	U			
Industrial Relations/Personnel/HRM	M	M	UM	UM
Information Science/Studies/Systems	X		X	UM
Information Technology	U			U
International Business	M			
International Finance				UM
International Marketing				UM
International Relations/Studies	X		U	X
Interpreting			M	
Japanese/Japanese Studies			U	
Labour Studies	U			U
Language Teaching/Learning	X		U	
Language and Communication	U		UM	
Languages, Modern	U		UM	U
Law Business/Commercial/Economic/Industrial				U
Law Employment/Labour	U			
Law International/Comparative/Trade	M		M	
Law/Legal Studies	X	X		UM
Library/Information Science	X		UM	
Linguistics/Translation	X	X	X	X
Literature, Comparative	X			
Livestock Science	MD			U
Management	X	X	M	UM
Management Information Systems	M		M	
Management, Hotel and Catering Technology			U	U

	West Indies	West Indies: Cave Hill	West Indies: Mona	West Indies: St Augustine
Marketing	U		UM	UM
Materials Science	U		UM	UM
Mathematics	X	X	X	X
Medical Physics	U			
Medicine, Obstetrics and Gynaecology	X		X	UM
Medicine, Orthopaedic	M		M	
Medicine, Otorhinolaryngology/Otolaryngology			UM	
Medicine, Paediatric	M		X	
Medicine/Surgery	X	X	X	X
Meteorology	X	X		
Microbiology/Medical Microbiology	X		X	UM
Migration, Refugee and Diaspora Studies	D		M	
Mobile Communications/Telecommunications				M
Multimedia			U	
Music	U		U	U
Music Education	U			U
Music Technology	U			U
Natural Resource Studies	MD	M	M	UM
Nursing Education/Administration			UM	
Nursing/Midwifery	UM		UM	U
Occupational Health/Therapy	X			
Oceanography/Oceanic Sciences	D			
Ophthalmology	M		M	
Pacific Islands Studies				UM
Parasitology	UM		UM	UM
Pastoral Studies				U
Pathology	MD		X	UM
Pharmacology	X		X	M
Pharmacy/Pharmaceutical Science	X			UM
Philosophy	X	X	X	U
Physical Education/Sports Science	U			U
Physics	X	X	X	X
Physiology	X		X	UM
Physiotherapy	U		U	
Planning/Landscape Studies	M			UM

	West Indies	West Indies: Cave Hill	West Indies: Mona	West Indies: St Augustine
Politics/Political Science/Government	X	X	X	X
Polymer Science				U
Population Studies/Demography	X		UM	U
Portuguese/Portugese Studies				U
Project Management				UM
Psychiatry	M		X	UM
Psychology	X	U	U	UM
Psychology Clinical	MD		M	UM
Public Administration	UM	X	UM	U
Public Health/Population Health	MD		M	
Public Relations				U
Public Sector Management	UM		M	U
Radiography/Diagnostic Technology/MRI	U		M	UM
Radiology			X	
Rehabilitation Medicine/Therapy/Science			X	
Religion/Theology	X	U	X	U
Rural Studies/Development				M
Sign Language	U			
Social Policy	X		X	UM
Social Work/Studies	X	U	UM	UM
Sociology	X	X	X	X
Spanish/Hispanic/Latin American Studies	X	X	X	X
Speech Science/Pathology/Therapy				U
Statistics/Actuarial Science	U		UM	X
Surveying/Quantity Surveying	MD			UM
Sustainable Development	MD		M	
Taxation				U
Teacher Training	M		UM	UM
Tourism/Hospitality/Leisure/Recreation	X	U	UM	U
Transport Studies				UM
Veterinary Science	X			UM
Visual Arts	U			U
Wildlife Management				M
Women's/Gender Studies	X	MD	X	X
Zoology	X		X	X

UNIVERSITY OF THE WEST INDIES

Founded 1948

Member of the Association of Commonwealth Universities

Postal Address: Mona, Kingston 7, Jamaica
Telephone: 927 1660-9 **Fax:** 977 1422 **E-mail:** oadmin@uwimona.edu.jm
URL: http://www.uwicentre.edu.jm

VICE-CHANCELLOR*—Harris, Prof. E. Nigel, BSc *Howard*, MPhil *Yale*, MD *Penn.*, DM *WI*, FACR
PRO-VICE-CHANCELLOR AND PRINCIPAL, CAVE HILL—Beckles, Prof. Hilary, BA *Hull*, PhD *Hull*
PRO-VICE-CHANCELLOR AND PRINCIPAL, MONA—Shirley, Prof. Gordon, BSc *WI*, MBA *Northwestern*, DBA *Harv.*
PRO-VICE-CHANCELLOR AND PRINCIPAL, ST. AUGUSTINE—Brereton, Prof. Bridget, BA *WI*, MA *Tor.*, PhD *WI*
PRO-VICE-CHANCELLOR (PLANNING AND DEVELOPMENT)—Tewarie, Bhoendradatt, BA *Northwestern*, MA *Chic.*, PhD *Penn.*
PRO-VICE-CHANCELLOR, GRADUATE STUDIES—Sankat, Prof. Clement, BSc *WI*, MSc *WI*, PhD *Guelph*
PRO-VICE-CHANCELLOR, RESEARCH—Hunte, Prof. Wayne, BSc *WI*, PhD *WI*
PRO-VICE-CHANCELLOR, UNDERGRADUATE STUDIES—Wint, Prof. Alvin, BSc *WI*, MBA *Northeastern*, DBA *Harv.*
PRO-VICE-CHANCELLOR, OPEN CAMPUS—Simmons-McDonald, Prof. Hazel, BA *WI*, MA(Ling) *Stan.*, MA *Stan.*, PhD *Stan.*
UNIVERSITY REGISTRAR‡—Iton, C. Williams, BSc *WI*, LLM *Essex*
DIRECTOR OF FINANCE/UNIVERSITY BURSAR—Bayley, Winston, BSc *Lond.*

GENERAL INFORMATION

History. The university was first established at Mona, Jamaica in 1948, as a college in special relationship with the University of London to serve the British territories in the Caribbean area. Campuses were later created at St Augustine, Trinidad (1960) and Cave Hill, Barbados (1963). In 1962 the university was granted its charter and became empowered to grant its own degrees.

The university is centered at the Mona Campus in Kingston (Jamaica), with campuses at Cave Hill (Barbados) and St Augustine (Trinidad and Tobago), and a recently established Open Campus to serve the UWI12 and the UWI Centres in the Campus countries. There are also twelve university centres spread throughout the English speaking Caribbean.

Admission to first degree courses. General requirement: passes in 2 subjects at GCE A level and acceptable passes (Grades I, II and III at the General Proficiency Level) in three further subjects at CXC or GCE O level or passes in 3 subjects at GCE A level and 1 further subject at CXC or GCE O level or equivalent qualifications.

First Degrees (see also West Indies Directory to Subjects of Study). BA, BEd, BPharm, BSc, DDS, DVM, LLB, MB BS.
Length of course. Full-time: BA, BEd, BPharm, BSc, LLB: 3 years; DDS, DVM, MB BS: 5 years.
Part-time: BA, BEd, BPharm, BSc, LLB: 6 years.

Higher Degrees (see also West Indies Directory to Subjects of Study).
Master's. DM, LLM, MA, MAEd, MBA, MEd, MPhil, MSc.
Admission. Applicants for admission to higher degree courses must hold at least a second class honours degree from an approved university or possess appropriate professional qualifications and experience.
Length of course. Full-time: LLM, MA, MBA: 1 year; MAEd, MEd, MSc: 1½ years; DM: 2 years; MPhil: 4 years. Part-time: LLM, MA, MBA: 2 years; MAEd, MEd, MSc: 2½ years; MPhil: 6 years.
Doctoral. MD, PhD.
Admission. PhD: master's degree by research (applicants without this qualification must first register for MPhil).
Length of course. Full-time: MD, PhD: 5 years. Part-time: MD, PhD: 7 years.

Libraries. Volumes: 1,001,644. Periodicals subscribed to: 17,092. Other holdings: 158 diskettes; 25,420 pamphlets; 10,590 vertical files; 790 cassettes; 40,539 microform; 3105 film/multimedia; 523 CDs; 1608 maps; 5042 photographs; 470 cassettes/videos. Special collections: West Indiana; MedCarib; Caribbean Disaster Information Network (CARDIN); Caribbean Environmental Database (CAREN); Caribbean Information System for Economic and Social Planning (CARISPLAN); West Indian; Dame Nita Barrow Papers; C. L. R. James; Capildeo Papers; Colonial Bank Correspondence; Dennis Mahabir; Earl Lovelace Manuscripts; Eric Williams Memorial; PAHO; Sam Selvon; Roy Prieswerk; West Indian Medical; William Young Diaries.

Academic Awards (2005–2006). 300 awards each with a min. value of US$1000.

Income (2005–2006). Total, J$13,508,540,000.

Statistics. Staff (2005–2006): 6270 (2037 academic, 4233 non-academic).

ACADEMIC UNITS

(C) = Cave Hill Campus; (M) = Mona Campus; (S) = St Augustine Campus

Continuing Studies, School of

Tel: (876) 927 1201 *Fax:* (876) 977 3443
E-mail: lifelong@uwimona.edu.jm
Longsworth, Luz, BA *WI*, MBA *WI*, MA *Qu.* Deputy Dir.
Other Staff: 12 Resident Tutors; 4 Tutors/Co-ordinators; 2 Programme Officers
Research: adult and continuing education, history in the West Indies; early childhood development, HIV/AIDS and the young child, child rights; gender studies, women in community development; labour studies and the role of women in trade unions; social work, professional standards, youth development

Education, Institute of

Tel: (876) 927 2431 *Fax:* (876) 927 2502
E-mail: halden.morris@uwimona.edu.jm
Evans, Hyacinth, BA *WI*, MEd *Ott.*, PhD *Calif.* Prof., Teacher Education
Griffith, Stafford, LLB *Lond.*, PhD *WI*, BA MEd Prof., Research, Measurement and Evaluation
Other Staff: 1 Sr. Lectr.; 10 Lectrs.; 1 Publications Officer
Research: best practices in educating student teachers and inducting new teachers; contextual issues and problems related to the school system; evaluation of educational innovation and development

Gender and Development Studies, Centre for

Tel: (876) 927 1913 *Fax:* (876) 927 1913
E-mail: cgd.rcu@uwimona.edu.jm
Bailey, Barbara, BSc *WI*, PhD *WI* Prof.; Regional Co-ordinator* (M)
Barriteau, Eudine, BSc *WI*, MPA *N.Y.*, PhD *Howard* Prof.; Head of Unit (C)
Dunn, Leith, BA *WI*, MSc *WI*, PhD *Lond.* Head of Unit (M)
Mohammed, Patricia, BA *WI*, MSc *WI*, PhD *Inst.Soc.Stud.(The Hague)* Prof.
Reddock, Prof. Rhoda, BSc *WI*, MSc *Inst.Soc.Stud.(The Hague)*, PhD *Amst.* Head of Unit (S)
Research: Caribbean women catalysts for change; gender imbalances at secondary and tertiary levels; gender socialisation, schooling and violence; gendered case study in natural resource management; root causes of gender-based violence

Social and Economic Studies, Sir Arthur Lewis Institute of

Tel: (246) 417 4476 *Fax:* (246) 424 7291
E-mail: salises@uwichill.edu.bb
Downes, Prof. Andrew S., BSc *WI*, MSc *WI*, PhD *Manc.* Univ. Dir.* (C)
Duncan, Prof. Neville, BSc *WI*, MSc *WI*, PhD *Manc.* Dir. (M)
Watson, Patrick, BCom *Leeds*, LèsEcon *Paris I*, MèsEcon *Paris I*, PhD *Paris I* Dir., St. Augustine
Other Staff: 2 Profs. Emer.; 1 Sr. Res. Fellow; 1 Sr. Fellow; 1 Sr. Librarian; 1 Librarian; 1 Data Bank Manager; 1 Publications Coordinator; 1 Temp. Res. Fellow
Research: alcohol consumption in Trinidad and Tobago; migration, family structures and morbidity from external causes; social protection and poverty eradication in St. Lucia

Sustainable Development, Institute for

Tel: 977 1659 *Fax:* 977 1658
E-mail: pvcresearch@admin.uwi.tt
Clayton, Anthony, MA *Edin.*, PhD *Edin.* Prof.
Hunte, Prof. Wayne, BSc *WI*, PhD *WI* Prof.; Head*
Other Staff: 1 Project Officer
Research: climate change; land, water and biodiversity resources conservation; sustainable energy; sustainable tourism; waste management

Tropical Medicine Research Institute (TMRI)

Tel: (876) 927 1884 *Fax:* (876) 977 0632
E-mail: tmru@uwimona.edu.jm
Forrester, Prof. Terrence, MB BS *WI*, MSc *WI*, DM *WI*, PhD *WI*, FRCPEd Dir.* (M)

Powell, Christine, BSc *WI*, MSc *WI*, PhD *WI*
  Sr. Lectr.
Reid, Marvin, MB BS *WI*   Dir., Sickle Cell
  Unit
Walker, Susan, BSc *Brist.*, MSc *Lond.*, PhD *Lond.*
  Prof.
Wilks, Rainford, MB BS *WI*, MSc *Lond.*, DM
  WI, FRCPEd   Prof.
Other Staff: 4 Profs.; 2 Sr. Lectrs.; 15 Lectrs.; 1
  Asst. Lectr.; 5 Res. Fellows; 2 Statisticians; 1
  Dir.; 1 Manager; 1 Deputy Manager; 1
  Systems Analyst; 1 Analyst Programmer; 1
  Project Coordinator; 3 Res Assts.; 5 Clin.
  Fellows; 5 Clin. Res. Fellows
Research: foetal origins of adult disease;
  malnutrition; molecular genetics; protein
  metabolism and immunity; salt sensitivity
  and hypertension

CONTACT OFFICERS

Academic affairs. (St Augustine) Deputy
  Principal: Kochhar, Prof. Gurmohan, BE
  Baroda, MS *Wis.*, PhD *WI*
  (E-mail: dprincipal@admin.net.ttor)
Academic affairs. (Mona) Deputy Principal:
  Pereira, Joseph, BA *WI*, MA *Qu.*
  (E-mail: joseph.pereira@uwimona.edu.jm)
Academic affairs. (Cave Hill) Deputy
  Principal: Moseley, Prof. Leo, BSc *WI*, MSc
  WI (E-mail: leo.moseley@cavehill.uwi.edu)
Accommodation. (Cave Hill) Campus
  Registrar: Wade, Jacqueline, JP, BA *WI*,
  MSc *Manc.*
  (E-mail: jacqueline.wade@cavehill.edu.bb)
Accommodation. (St Augustine) Assistant
  Registrar: Francis, Gene, BSc *WI*
  (E-mail: gfrancis@centre.uwi.tt)
Accommodation. (Mona) Deputy Estate
  Manager: Heron, Angela, BA *WI*, MSc *WI*
  (E-mail: angela.heron@uwimona.edu.jm)
Admissions (first degree). (St Augustine)
  Assistant Registrar: Brown, Patricia, BA *WI*
  (E-mail: aregsecr@sta.uwi.edu)
Admissions (first degree). (Cave Hill) Senior
  Assistant Registrar: Crichlow, Desmond R.,
  BSc *WI*, MSc *Keele*
  (E-mail: dcrichlow@uwichill.edu.bb)
Admissions (first degree). (Mona) Senior
  Assistant Registrar: Witter, Ann Marie, BA
  WI, MA *WI*
  (E-mail: admissns@uwimona.edu.jm)
Admissions (higher degree). (Mona) Senior
  Assistant Registrar: Miller, Barbara S., BA
  WI, MSc *WI*
  (E-mail: postgrad@uwimona.edu.jm)
Admissions (higher degree). (Cave Hill)
  Senior Assistant Registrar: Crichlow,
  Desmond R., BSc *WI*, MSc *Keele*
  (E-mail: dcrichlow@uwichill.edu.bb)
Admissions (higher degree). (St Augustine)
  Senior Assistant Registrar: Charles-Smythe,
  Deborah, BA *WI*, MSc *Lond.*
  (E-mail: gradstudies@sta.uwi.edu)
Adult/continuing education. (Resident in
  Jamaica) Deputy Director (School of
  Continuing Studies): Longsworth, Luz, BA
  WI, MBA *WI*, MA *Qu.*
  (E-mail: lus.longsworth@uwimona.edu.jm)
Archives. (Resident in Jamaica) Acting
  University Archivist: Georges, Jo-Ann, BA
  WI, MLS *Col.* (E-mail: jgeorges@recc.uwi.tt)
Careers. (Mona) Manager, Placement and
  Career Services: Henry, Merrit, BSc *WI*,
  MEd *WI*
  (E-mail: merrit.henry@uwimona.edu.jm)
Computing services. (Cave Hill) Acting Head:
  Gill, Patrick, BSc *WI*, MSc *Alta.*
  (E-mail: pgill@uwichill.edu.bb)
Computing services. (St Augustine) Technical
  Services Manager: Raghunanan, Marlon, BSc
  WI, MPhil *WI*
  (E-mail: mraghunanan@cits.uwi.tt)
Computing services. Chief Information
  Officer: Samuels, Carlton, BSc *WI*, MIS
  G.Mason
  (E-mail: carlton.samuels@uwimona.edu.jm)
Distance education. (Resident in Barbados)
  Director, Distance Education: Marshall, Prof.

B. Stewart, BA *York(UK)*, MPhil *Leeds*
  (E-mail: telecon@uwichill.edu.bb)
Estates and buildings/works and services.
  (Mona) Estate Manager: Sambo, Kathleen,
  BSc *WI*, MBA *Col.*
  (E-mail: kathleen.sambo@uwimona.edu.jm)
Estates and buildings/works and services. (St
  Augustine) Estate Manager: Nobbee,
  Kenrick A. W., BSc *Strath.*, MSc *Strath.*
Estates and buildings/works and services.
  (Cave Hill) Estate Manager: Warrington,
  Martin, BSc *Leeds*
  (E-mail: martin.warrington@
  cavehill.uwi.edu)
Examinations. (Cave Hill) Assistant Registrar
  (Examinations): Thorpe, Betty, BSc *WI*, MSc
  WI (E-mail: bthorpe@uwichill.edu.bb)
Examinations. (St Augustine) Senior Assistant
  Registrar (Examinations): George, Jessie-
  Ann, BA *Howard*, MEd *Howard*
  (E-mail: aregexam@centre.uwi.tt)
Examinations. (Mona) Senior Assistant
  Registrar (Examinations): Nelson, Cordel,
  BA *WI*
  (E-mail: cordel.nelson@uwimona.edu.jm)
Finance. (Resident in Jamaica) Director of
  Finance/University Bursar: Bayley,
  Winston, BSc *Lond.*
  (E-mail: winston.bayley@uwimona.edu.jm)
General enquiries. (Resident in Jamaica)
  University Registrar: Iton, C. Williams, BSc
  WI, LLM *Essex*
  (E-mail: clement.iton@uwimona.edu.jm)
Health services. (St Augustine) Medical
  Officer/Head, Health Service Unit: Singh,
  Neil, MB BS *WI*
  (E-mail: doctor@sta.uwi.edu)
Health services. (Mona) Director (Clinical
  Services, Health): Anglin Brown, Blossom,
  MB BS *WI*, MPH *WI*, DM *WI*
  (E-mail: blossom.anglinbrown@
  uwimona.edu.jm)
Industrial liaison. (Cave Hill) Senior Assistant
  Registrar: Brewster, Henri, BA *WI*, MA *Nott.*
  (E-mail: hbrewster@uwichill.edu.bb)
Industrial liaison. (St Augustine) Campus
  Registrar: Callaghan, Jeremy, BA *York(UK)*,
  MA *Reading* (E-mail: campreg@centre.uwi.tt)
Industrial liaison. (Mona) Senior Assistant
  Registrar: Eytle, Raymond, BSc *Cornell*
  (E-mail: raymond.eytle@uwimona.edu.jm)
Library (chief librarian). (St Augustine)
  University Librarian: Rouse-Jones, Prof.
  Margaret, BA *WI*, MA *Johns H.*, PhD *Johns H.*
  (E-mail: mrouse-jones@library.uwi.tt)
Library (enquiries). (Cave Hill, resident in
  Barbados) Campus Librarian: Lequay,
  Karen, BSc *WI*, MSc *S'ton.*, MSc *Lough.*
  (E-mail: klequay@uwichill.edu.bb)
Library (enquiries). (St Augustine) Campus
  Librarian: Rouse-Jones, Prof. Margaret, BA
  WI, MA *Johns H.*, PhD *Johns H.*
  (E-mail: mrouse-jones@library.uwi.tt)
Library (enquiries). (Cave Hill, resident in
  Barbados) Law Librarian: Newton, Prof.
  Velma E., BA *WI*, LLB *WI*, MA *WI*, FLA
  (E-mail: vnewton@uwichill.edu.bb)
Library (enquiries). (Mona, resident in
  Jamaica) Campus Librarian: Amenu-Kpodo,
  Norma, BA *Sask.*, BLS *Tor.*
  (E-mail: norma.amenukpodo@
  uwimona.edu.jm)
Marketing. (St Augustine) Business Officer: De
  Four-Gill, Dawn Marie, BSc *WI*, MBA
  City(UK) (E-mail: dmdefour@admin.uwi.tt)
Personnel/human resources. (Cave Hill)
  Senior Assistant Registrar: Brewster, Henri,
  BA *WI*, MA *Nott.*
  (E-mail: hbrewster@uwichill.edu.bb)
Personnel/human resources. (Mona) Senior
  Assistant Registrar (Appointments): Hall,
  Mabel, BA *WI*, MSc *WI*
  (E-mail: mabel.hall@uwimona.edu.jm)
Personnel/human resources. (Resident in
  Jamaica) Senior Assistant Registrar (Centre):
  Young, Pansy, BA *WI*, MSc *WI*
  (E-mail: pansy.young@uwimona.edu.jm)

Personnel/human resources. (St Augustine)
  Assistant Registrar: Francis, Gene, BSc *WI*
  (E-mail: gfrancis@sti.uwi.edu)
Public relations. (Cave Hill) Assistant
  Registrar: Lovell, Chelston, MA
  (E-mail: chelston.lovell@cavehill.uwi.edu)
Public relations. (Mona) Public Relations
  Officer: Edwards, Carroll, BA *WI*, MJ *Car.*
  (E-mail: carroll.edwards@uwimona.edu.jm)
Public relations. (St Augustine) Business
  Officer: De Four-Gill, Dawn Marie, BSc *WI*,
  MBA *City(UK)*
  (E-mail: dmdefour@admin.uwi.tt)
Publications. (St Augustine) Campus Co-
  ordinator, Board for Graduate Studies and
  Research: Baban, Prof. Abiodun Adesiyun,
  MPH *Minn.*, PhD *Minn.*
  (E-mail: postgradstudies@sta.uwi.edu)
Publications. (Mona) Jackson, Prof. Yevette,
  BSc *WI*, PhD *WI*
  (E-mail: postgrad@uwimona.edu.jm)
Publications. (Cave Hill) Pro-Vice-Chancellor:
  Hunte, Prof. Wayne, BSc *WI*, PhD *WI*
  (E-mail: gradstud@uwichill.edu.bb)
Purchasing. (Mona) Campus Bursar:
  Robinson, Elaine, BSc *WI*
  (E-mail: elaine.robinson@uwimona.edu.jm)
Purchasing. (Cave Hill) Campus Bursar:
  Webster, Maurice, MSc *Sheff.*
  (E-mail: mwebster@uwichill.edu.bb)
Purchasing. (St Augustine) Campus Bursar:
  Bada, Lylla, BA *Brist.*
  (E-mail: lbada@admin.uwi.tt)
Quality assurance and accreditation. Director,
  Quality Assurance and Accreditation: Wint,
  Prof. Alvin, BSc *WI*, MBA *Northeastern*, DBA
  Harv. (E-mail: alvin.wint@uwimona.edu.jm)
Safety. (Cave Hill) Campus Registrar: Wade,
  Jacqueline, JP, BA *WI*, MSc *Manc.*
  (E-mail: jacqueline.wade@cavehill.edu.bb)
Safety. (St Augustine Campus; resident in
  Trinidad) Campus Registrar: Callaghan,
  Jeremy, BA *York(UK)*, MA *Reading*
  (E-mail: campreg@centre.uwi.tt)
Scholarships, awards, loans. (St Augustine)
  Assistant Registrar, Scholarships and
  Awards: Brown, Patricia, BA *WI*
  (E-mail: aregsecr@centre.uwi.tt)
Scholarships, awards, loans. (Mona)
  Manager: Dickenson, Joy, MPSM *WI*
  (E-mail: outaward@uwimona.edu.jm)
Scholarships, awards, loans. (Cave Hill)
  Senior Assistant Registrar: Crichlow,
  Desmond R., BSc *WI*, MSc *Keele*
  (E-mail: dcrichlow@uwichill.edu.bb)
Security. Director, Security Services: Reid, Ora,
  BA *WI*, MA *Exe.*
Security. (Mona) Campus Registrar: Bell
  Hutchinson, Camille, BSc *WI*, MA(Ed) *WI*,
  PhD *WI* (E-mail: camille.bellhutchinson@
  uwimona.edu.jm)
Security. (St Augustine) Director, Security:
  Richardson, Wayne, JP, BA *WI*, LLB *Lond.*
  (E-mail: wrichardson@police.uwi.tt)
Sport and recreation. (Cave Hill) Director of
  Student Services (Sport and recreation):
  Yearwood, Harriet, BSc *Car.*, MSW *Car.*
  (E-mail: hyearwood@uwichill.edu.bb)
Sport and recreation. (St Augustine) Director,
  Sports and Physical Education: Gloudon,
  Iva, BSc *Ill.*, MSc *Ill.*, EdD *Mass.*
  (E-mail: igloudon@sta.uwi.edu)
Sport and recreation. (Mona) Director of
  Sports: Jackson, Grace, BA *Alabama*, MA
  Queens, N.Y.
  (E-mail: gjackson@uwimona.edu.jm)
Student welfare/counselling. (Cave Hill)
  Director of Student Services: Yearwood,
  Harriet, BSc *Car.*, MSW *Car.*
  (E-mail: hyearwood@uwichill.edu.bb)
Student welfare/counselling. (St Augustine)
  Director of Student Services (Student
  welfare/counselling): Charles, Deirdre, BSc
  WI, MSc *Warw.*, MBA *Massey*
Student welfare/counselling. (Mona)
  Director of Student Services: Reynolds,
  Thelora, JP, BA *WI*, MA *WI*, PhD *WI*
  (E-mail: thelora.reynolds@uwimona.edu.jm)

Students with disabilities. (Cave Hill)
Director of Student Services: Yearwood,
Harriet, BSc Car., MSW Car.
(E-mail: hyearwood@uwichill.edu.bb)
Students with disabilities. (Mona) Deputy
Principal: Pereira, Joseph, BA WI, MA Qu.
(E-mail: joseph.pereira@uwimona.edu.jm)
Students with disabilities. (St Augustine)
Director of Student Services (Student
welfare/counselling): Charles, Deirdre, BSc
WI, MSc Warw., MBA Massey
Students with disabilities. (Mona) Director of
Student Services: Reynolds, Thelora, JP, BA
WI, MA WI, PhD WI
(E-mail: thelora.reynolds@uwimona.edu.jm)
University press. (Resident in Jamaica)
Director (University Press): Speth, Linda,
BA Utah State, MA Utah State
(E-mail: lspeth@cwjamaica.com)

Women. (Mona, resident in Mona) Dunn,
Leith, BA WI, MSc WI, PhD Lond.
(E-mail: leith.dunn@uwimona.edu.jm)
Women. (Cave Hill, resident in Barbados)
Barriteau, Prof. Eudine, BSc WI, MPA N.Y.,
PhD Howard
(E-mail: ggender@cavehill.uwi.edu)
Women. (Mona, resident in Jamaica) Regional
Co-ordinator, Centre for Gender and
Development Studies: Bailey, Prof. Barbara,
BSc WI, PhD WI
(E-mail: barbara.bailey@uwimona.edu.jm)
Women. (St Augustine) Reddock, Prof. Rhoda,
BSc WI, MSc Inst.Soc.Stud.(The Hague), PhD
Amst. (E-mail: gender@cgds.uwi.tt)

CAMPUS/COLLEGE HEADS
University of the West Indies, Cave Hill
Campus. (Tel: (246) 417 4000; Fax: (246)
425 1327; E-mail: -

hbeckles@uwichill.edu.bb) Campus
Principal: Beckles, Prof. Hilary, BA Hull,
PhD Hull
University of the West Indies, Mona
Campus. (Tel: (876) 927 1660; Fax: (876)
927 0977;
E-mail: gordon.shirley@uwimona.edu.jm)
Campus Principal: Leo-Rhynie, Prof. Elsa,
CD, BSc Lond., PhD WI
University of the West Indies, St Augustine
Campus. (Tel: (868) 662 2002; Fax: (868)
663 9684; E-mail: princuwi@sta.uwi.edu)
Campus Principal: Tewarie, Bhoendradatt,
BA Northwestern, MA Chic., PhD Penn.

[Information supplied by the institution as at 2 November
2007, and edited by the ACU]

UNIVERSITY OF THE WEST INDIES, CAVE HILL CAMPUS

Founded 1963

Postal Address: PO Box 64, Bridgetown, Barbados
Telephone: 417 4000 **Fax:** 425 1327
URL: http://www.cavehill.uwi.edu

PRINCIPAL AND PRO-VICE-CHANCELLOR*—Beckles, Prof. Hilary McD., BA Hull, PhD Hull
DEPUTY PRINCIPAL—Moseley, Prof. L. Leo, PhD Wales, MSc
CAMPUS REGISTRAR‡—Wade, Jacqueline E., JP, MA Manc., BA
CAMPUS BURSAR—Webster, M. A. T., MSc Sheff.
CAMPUS LIBRARIAN—Lequay, Karen, MSc Lough., MSc S'ton., BSc
PUBLIC ORATOR—Fraser, Prof. Henry, BSc Lond., PhD Lond., MB BS, FRACP, FACP

ACADEMIC UNITS
Biological and Chemical Sciences
Tel: 417 4323 Fax: 417 4597
E-mail: bcs@uwichill.edu.bb
Carrington, C. M. Sean, BSc Edin., DPhil
York(UK)   Prof.
Chinnery, Louis E., BSc Ulster, DPhil Ulster   Sr.
Lectr.; Head*
Horrocks, Julia, BSc Reading, PhD   Prof.
Hunte, Wayne, BSc PhD   Prof.
Lavoie, Marc, BSc Montr., MSc Montr., PhD
Montr.   Prof.
Mathison, George, BSc Brist., PhD Nott.   Prof.
Emer.
Sutrina, Sarah, BA Colorado, PhD Johns H.   Sr.
Lectr.
Tinto, Winston, BSc PhD   Prof.
Other Staff: 4 Lectrs.; 4 Temp. Lectrs.
Vacant Posts: 2 Lectrs.

Chemistry
Kulikov, Sergei M., MS Novosibirsk, PhD Russian
Acad.Sc.   Sr. Lectr.
McDowell, Sean, PhD Camb., BSc   Prof.
Tinto, Winston, BSc PhD   Prof.
Other Staff: 3 Lectrs.
Vacant Posts: 3 Lectrs.

Computer Science, Mathematics and Physics
Tel: 417 4363 Fax: 417 4597
E-mail: cmp_staff@uwichill.edu.bb
Cadogan, Charles, BSc PhD   Prof. Emer.
Chaudhuri, Pranay, BSc Calc., BTech Calc.,
METelE Jad., PhD Jad.   Prof.; Head*
Chillumuntala, Jayaram, MSc And., PhD And.
Sr. Lectr.
Mahdi, Smail, BSc Constantine, PhD Montr.   Prof.
Peter, Hadrian, BSc Ohio, MSc Ohio, MS Ohio,
PhD Ohio   Sr. Lectr.
Schwartzman, Yefim, MA Voronezh, PhD Voronezh
Sr. Lectr.
Other Staff: 10 Lectrs.

Vacant Posts: 2 Lectrs.

Physics
Tel: 417 4366
Gibbs, Peter, MSc Guelph, BSc   Sr. Lectr.
Moseley, L. Leo, PhD Wales, MSc   Prof.
Ray, Tane, BSc Ill., PhD Boston   Sr. Lectr.
Singh, U., MS Delaware, PhD Delaware, BSc MPhil
Sr. Lectr.
Sodha, Janak, BSc Manc., MSc Manc., PhD Manc.
Sr. Lectr.
Other Staff: 2 Lectrs.

Economics
Tel: 417 4278 Fax: 417 4270
E-mail: economics@uwichill.edu.bb
Craigwell, Roland, MA Warw., PhD S'ton., BSc
Prof.
Downes, Andrew, BSc Manc., MSc Manc., PhD
Manc.   Prof.
Howard, Michael, BA MSc PhD   Prof.
Iyare, S. Osaretin, BA Minn., MA Sangamon, PhD
Durh.   Prof.; Head*
Mamingi, Nlandu, LicEcon Zaire, MA
Inst.Soc.Stud.(The Hague), MA N.Y.State, PhD
N.Y.State   Prof.
Whitehead, Judy A., MA Wat., PhD Edin., BA
Sr. Lectr.
Other Staff: 4 Lectrs.

Education, School of
Tel: 417 4426 Fax: 417 9615
E-mail: directorsoe@uwichill.edu.bb
Cobley, Alan G., BA Manc., MA York(UK), PhD
Lond.   Prof.; Temp. Dir.*
Griffith, Anthony, BA McG., BEd Qu., MA McG.,
MEd Tor.   Sr. Lectr.
Layne, Anthony, BEd Calg., MA Calg., PhD Calg.,
BA   Sr. Lectr.
Lewis, Clive, BSc C.Lancs., PhD C.Lancs.   Sr.
Lectr.
Richardson, Arthur G., BEd PhD   Prof.
Other Staff: 5 Lectrs.; 1 Res. Fellow

French and Spanish
Tel: 417 4405 Fax: 424 0634
E-mail: lll@uwichill.edu.bb
Almenas, Egberto, BA Ill., PhD Ill.   Sr. Lectr.
Bryce, Jane, BA Oxf., MA Essex, PhD O.Awolowo
Sr. Lectr.; Head*
Constant, Isabelle, MSc Paris III, PhD Arizona
Sr. Lectr.
Mabana, Kahiudi, BA Urbana, MA Frib., PhD
Sr. Lectr.
McWatt, Amparo, MPhil   Sr. Lectr.
Other Staff: 4 Lectrs.

Government, Sociology and Social Work
Tel: 417 4289 Fax: 417 4270
E-mail: gsswork@uwichill.edu.bb
Belle, G. A., PhD Manc., MSc   Sr. Lectr.,
Political Science
Karch Brathwaite, Cecilia, BA Calif., BSc N.U.I.,
MS Calif., DSc Rutgers   Sr. Lectr.
Rock, Letnie F., BSW Windsor, MA NE, DP
Fordham, BA   Lectr.; Head*
Other Staff: 4 Lectrs.; 4 Temp. Lectrs.
Vacant Posts: 1 Lectr.

History and Philosophy
Tel: 417 4403 Fax: 424 0634
E-mail: history@uwichill.edu.bb
Cobley, Alan G., BA Manc., MA York(UK), PhD
Lond.   Prof.
Goodridge, Richard, MA Ib., PhD Ib., BA
Lectr.; Head*
Ochieng'Odhiambo, Frederick, BA Nair., MA
Nair., PhD Nair.   Sr. Lectr.
Watson, Karl, BA Flor., MA Flor., PhD Flor.   Sr.
Lectr.
Welch, Pedro, MSc Bath, BA PhD   Sr. Lectr.
Other Staff: 2 Lectrs.; 3 Temp. Lectrs.; 1
Temp. Asst. Lectr.

Language, Linguistics and Literature
Tel: (246) 417 4404 Fax: (246) 424 0634
E-mail: lll@uwichill.edu.bb
Best, Curwen, PhD Birm., BA MPhil   Sr. Lectr.

Bryce, Jane, BA Oxf., MA Essex, PhD O.Awolowo
Sr. Lectr.; Head*
Gibson, Kean A., BA Guy., DPhil York(UK) Sr.
Lectr.
O'Callaghan, Evelyn, BA N.U.I., MLitt Oxf. Sr.
Lectr.
Roberts, Peter A., BA MA PhD Prof.
Simmons-McDonald, Hazel C., PhD Stan., BA
Prof.
Wade, Carl, MA Stan., PhD Stan., BA Sr. Lectr.
Other Staff: 3 Lectrs.; 1 Temp. Lectr.

Law

Tel: 417 4215 Fax: 424 1788
E-mail: asthill@uwichill.edu.bb
Anderson, Winston, LLB Camb., PhD Camb.
Prof.
Antoine, Rose-Marie B., LLB Camb., LLM Camb.,
DPhil Oxf. Prof.
Berry, David S., BA Tor., LLM Qu., PhD Edin.
Sr. Lectr.
Burgess, Andrew D., LLM York(Can.), LLB
Prof.
Carnegie, A. Ralph, BA Lond., MA Oxf. Prof.
Emer.
Cumberbatch, Jefferson O'B., LLB Sr. Lectr.
Fiadjoe, Albert, LLB Ghana, LLM Lond., PhD Lond.
Prof.
Hall, Clifford, BA Camb., MA Cant., LLM Wales
Sr. Lectr.
Jackson, Leighton, LLM Syd., DJur York(Can.),
LLB Sr. Lectr.
Kaczorowska, Alina, BCL Poznan, PhD Nice
Prof.
Kodilinye, A. Gilbert, MA Oxf., LLM Lond.
Prof.
McIntosh, Simeon C., BA York(Can.), LLM Col.,
JD Prof.; Head*
Owusu, Sampson, LLB Ghana, LLM Lond. Sr.
Lectr.
Robinson, Tracy, BCL Oxf., LLM Yale, LLB Sr.
Lectr.
Other Staff: 3 Lectrs.; 1 Temp. Res. Fellow
Vacant Posts: 1 Sr. Lectr.; 1 Res. Fellow

Management Studies

Tel: 417 4295 Fax: 438 9167
E-mail: jrobinson@uwichill.edu.bb
Glidden, Priscilla, BA Mass., PhD M.I.T. Sr.
Lectr.
Khan, Jamal, MA Dacca, MPA Cinc., PhD Cinc.
Prof.
Nurse, Lawrence, MS Mass., DPhil Mass., BA
Sr. Lectr.
Punnett, Betty J., BA McG., MBA Marist, PhD
N.Y. Prof.
Robinson, C. Justin, MSc Florida Internat., PhD
Manc., BSc Lectr.; Head*
Other Staff: 11 Lectrs.; 7 Temp. Lectrs.

Resource Management and Environmental Studies, Centre for

Tel: 417 4317 Fax: 424 4204
E-mail: cermes@uwichill.edu.bb
Mahon, Robin, MSc Guelph, PhD Guelph, BSc
Prof.; Acting Dir.*
McConney, Patrick, BSc Wales, MES Dal., PhD
Br.Col. Sr. Lectr.
Nurse, Leonard, MSc Nfld., PhD McG., BSc Sr.
Lectr.
Oxenford, Hazel, BSc Exe., PhD WI Prof.
Other Staff: 2 Lectrs.
Vacant Posts: Dir.*

CLINICAL MEDICINE AND RESEARCH, SCHOOL OF

Tel: 429 5112 Fax: 429 6738
E-mail: scmr@uwichill.edu.bb

Clinical Medicine and Research, School of

Fraser, Henry, BSc Lond., PhD Lond., MB BS,
FRACP, FACP Prof.; Head*
Moseley, Harley S. L., FFARCS Prof.,
Anaesthesia
Nicholson, George, BA Oxf., MB BS Oxf., DM
Oxf. Prof. Emer.
Ortega-Benito, Jose Prof., Epidemiology
Prussia, Patsy R., MB BS DM Prof.,
Anatomical Pathology
Walrond, Errol, ChB, FRCS, FACS Prof. Emer.
Other Staff: 16 Lectrs.; 1 Temp. Lectr.
Vacant Posts: 1 Prof.

SPECIAL CENTRES, ETC

Caribbean Law Institute Centre

Tel: 417 4561 Fax: 424 1318
E-mail: clic@cavehill.uwi.edu
Anderson, Winston, LLB Camb., PhD Camb.
Prof.; Dir.*

Creative Imagination, Errol Barrow Centre for

Tel: 417 4776 Fax: 417 8903
E-mail: ebcci@uwichill.edu.bb
Yearwood, Gladstone L., BFA N.Y., MA Ohio,
PhD Ohio Dir.*
Other Staff: 1 Manager; 1 Temp. Lectr.
Vacant Posts: 6 Lectrs.

Cricket Research, C. L. R. James Centre for

Beckles, Prof. Hilary McD., BA Hull, PhD Hull
Dir.*
Other Staff: 1 Librarian
Vacant Posts: 1 Res. Fellow

Gender and Development Studies, Centre for

Tel: 417 4491 Fax: 424 3822
E-mail: gender@uwichill.edu.bb
Barriteau, Eudine, MPA N.Y., PhD Howard, BSc
Prof.
Other Staff: 1 Temp. Lectr.
Vacant Posts: 2 Lectrs.

International Trade Law, Policy and Services, Shridath Ramphal Centre for

Tel: 417 4584 Fax: 425 1348
E-mail: src@cavehill.uwi.edu
Nurse, Keith, BA W.Ont., PhD Dir.*
Other Staff: 1 Manager; 1 Programme Officer

Learning Resource Centre

Tel: 417 4200 Fax: 424 8944
E-mail: lrc@uwichill.edu.bb
Atherley, Patricia, MSc Sheff., BA Educnl.
Technologist
Watson, Elizabeth, MSc Long Island, BA Sr.
Librarian
Other Staff: 1 Instructional Devel. Specialist

Management Development, Centre for

Tel: 424 7731 Fax: 425 1670
E-mail: cmd@caribsurf.com
Comma, Jeannine L., MA George Washington, PhD
George Washington, BA Dir.*

Other Staff: 4 Co-ordinators

CONTACT OFFICERS

Accommodation. Campus Registrar: Wade,
Jacqueline E., JP, MA Manc., BA
(E-mail: jacqueline.wade@cavehill.uwi.edu)
Admissions (first degree). Temporary
Assistant Registrar (Admissions): Carter,
Rommell, MBA Hull, BA
(E-mail: rommell.carter@cavehill.uwi.edu)
Admissions (higher degree). Senior Assistant
Registrar (Graduate Studies): Carter-Payne,
Gail, BSc Lond., MBA H-W
(E-mail: gail.carter@cavehill.uwi.edu)
Adult/continuing education. Resident Tutor/
Organiser: Austin, Ian, MBA Virginia Polytech.,
BSc (E-mail: iaustin@uwichill.edu.bb)
Computing services. Director: Gill, Patrick St.
A., MSc Alta., BSc
(E-mail: computercentre@cavehill.uwi.edu)
Distance education. Director (Distance
education): Marshall, B. Stewart, BA
York(UK), MPhil Leeds, PhD C.Qld.
(E-mail: smarshall@uwichill.edu.bb)
Examinations. Assistant Registrar: Thorpe,
Betty, BSc MSc
(E-mail: betty.thorpe@cavehill.uwi.edu)
Finance. Campus Bursar: Webster, M. A. T.,
MSc Sheff.
(E-mail: maurice.webster@cavehill.uwi.edu)
General enquiries. Campus Registrar: Wade,
Jacqueline E., JP, MA Manc., BA
(E-mail: jacqueline.wade@cavehill.uwi.edu)
Health services. Director, Student Services:
Yearwood, Harriett, MSW Car., BSc
(E-mail: harriett.yearwood@
cavehill.uwi.edu)
Library (chief librarian). Campus Librarian:
Lequay, Karen, MSc Lough., MSc S'ton., BSc
(E-mail: karen.lequay@cavehill.uwi.edu)
Library (enquiries). Campus Librarian:
Lequay, Karen, MSc Lough., MSc S'ton., BSc
(E-mail: karen.lequay@cavehill.uwi.edu)
Marketing. Business Development Officer:
Johnson, Sonia R., MBA Miami(Fla.), BA
(E-mail: sjohnson@uwichill.edu.bb)
Personnel/human resources. Senior Assistant
Registrar (Personnel/human resources):
Walters, Kenneth, MA Manc., BA
(E-mail: kenneth.walters@cavehill.uwi.edu)
Personnel/human resources. Senior Assistant
Registrar (Personnel/human resources):
Brewster, Henri O., MA Nott., BA
(E-mail: henri.brewster@cavehill.uwi.edu)
Public relations. Communications Officer
(Public relations): Lovell, Chelston, MA Car.
(E-mail: chelston.lovell@cavehill.uwi.edu)
Purchasing. Campus Bursar: Webster, M. A.
T., MSc Sheff.
(E-mail: maurice.webster@cavehill.uwi.edu)
Security. Campus Registrar: Wade, Jacqueline
E., JP, MA Manc., BA
(E-mail: jacqueline.wade@cavehill.uwi.edu)
Sport and recreation. Director, Sports:
Butcher, Roland
(E-mail: rbutcher@uwichill.edu.bb)
Student welfare/counselling. Director,
Student Services: Yearwood, Harriett, MSW
Car., BSc (E-mail: harriett.yearwood@
cavehill.uwi.edu)

[Information supplied by the institution as at 24 January
2008, and edited by the ACU]

UNIVERSITY OF THE WEST INDIES, MONA CAMPUS

Founded 1948

Postal Address: Mona, St Andrew, Kingston 7, Jamaica
Telephone: (876) 927 1660-9 **Fax:** (876) 927 2765
URL: http://www.uwimona.edu.jm

PRINCIPAL AND PRO-VICE-CHANCELLOR*—Shirley, Prof. Gordon, BSc WI, MBA Harv., PhD Harv.
DEPUTY PRINCIPAL—Pereira, Joseph, BA WI, MA Qu.
CAMPUS REGISTRAR‡—Bell-Hutchinson, Camille, BSc WI, MA(Ed) WI, PhD WI
CAMPUS BURSAR—Robinson, Elaine, BSc(Econ) WI
CAMPUS LIBRARIAN—Amenu-Kpodo, Norma, BA Sask., BLS Tor.
PUBLIC ORATOR—Meeks, Prof. Brian W. E., BSc WI, MSc WI, PhD WI

GENERAL INFORMATION

History. The campus was established in 1948. It is located in Mona, Jamaica.

Admission to first degree courses. See under University of the West Indies, above.

First Degrees (see also West Indies Directory to Subjects of Study). BA, BEd, BMedSci, BSc, BScN, MB BS.
See also under University of the West Indies, above.
Length of course. Full-time: BEd: 2 years; BSc: 2–3 years; BA, BMedSci, BScN: 3 years; MB BS: 5 years. Part-time: BA: 4 years. By distance learning: BEd: 3 years; BSc: 4–6 years.

Higher Degrees (see also West Indies Directory to Subjects of Study).
Master's. DM, MA, MBA, MEd, MLS, MPH, MPhil, MSc.
See also under University of the West Indies, above.
Length of course. Full-time: DM, MA, MBA, MEd, MLS, MPH, MSc: 1 year; MPhil: 2 years. Part-time: DM, MA, MBA, MEd, MLS, MPH, MSc: 2 years; MPhil: 5 years. By distance learning: MEd, MSc: 3 years.
Doctoral. MD, PhD.
See also under University of the West Indies, above.
Length of course. Full-time: MD, PhD: 3 years. Part-time: MD, PhD: 7 years.

Libraries. Volumes: 393,313. Periodicals subscribed to: 5667. Other holdings: 504 videos; 7123 microfiches; 8750 microfilms. Special collections: West Indies Literarture Collection; Roger Mais Papers; Edward Seaga; Caribbean Voices; Thistlewood Papers.

Academic Awards (2006–2007). 652 awards ranging in value from J$25,000 to J$500,000.

Income (2006–2007). Total, J$9,116,373,000.

Statistics. Staff (2006–2007): 2172 (900 academic, 1272 non-academic). Students (2006–2007): full-time 7507 (2149 men, 5358 women); part-time 4477 (1321 men, 3156 women); international 105 (59 men, 46 women); distance education/external 1941 (409 men, 1532 women); undergraduate 11,759 (2987 men, 8772 women); master's 2521 (743 men, 1778 women); doctoral 528 (220 men, 308 women).

FACULTIES/SCHOOLS

Humanities and Education
Tel: (876) 977 3659 Fax: (876) 977 0622
E-mail: artsed@uwimona.edu.jm
Dean: Wilmot, Swithin R., BA WI, DPhil Oxf.
Secretary/Administrative Officer: Gordon-Clennon, Althea, BSc WI, MA Hull

Medical Sciences
Tel: (876) 927 2556 Fax: (876) 977 3470
E-mail: medsci@uwimona.edu.jm
Dean: McDonald, Prof. Archibald H., MB BS WI, DM WI, FRCSEd, FACS
Secretary/Administrative Officer: Simon, Donna, BSc WI, MBA WI

Pure and Applied Sciences
Tel: (876) 977 1785 Fax: (876) 927 1566
E-mail: fpas@uwimona.edu.jm
Dean: Young, Prof. Ronald E., BSc WI, MSc WI, PhD St And., leave
Secretary/Administrative Officer: Leighton, Carmen, BA WI

Social Sciences
Tel: (876) 977 0640 Fax: (876) 927 2163
E-mail: fsocsci@uwimona.edu.jm
Dean: Figueroa, Mark, BA WI, MSc WI, PhD Manc.
Secretary/Administrative Officer: McEwan, Peta-Gaye, BSc WI, MSc WI

ACADEMIC UNITS
Chemistry
Tel: (876) 977 1834 Fax: (876) 977 1835
E-mail: wwchem@uwimona.edu.jm
Bakir, Mohammed, BSc Birzeit, MSc N.Y.State, PhD Purdue   Prof.
Dasgupta, T. P., BSc Calc., MSc Bihar, DPhil Calc., FRSChem   Prof.
Ellis, H. A., BSc WI, PhD Leeds   Sr. Lectr.
Greenaway, Anthony M., BSc Cant., PhD Cant.   Sr. Lectr.
Jackson, Yvette A., BSc WI, PhD WI, FRSChem   Prof.
Jacobs, Helen M., BSc WI, PhD WI   Prof.
Kahwa, Ishenkumba A., BSc Dar., MSc Dar., PhD Louisiana State, FRSChem   Prof.; Head*
Lancashire, Robert J., BSc Monash, PhD Monash   Prof.
Mulder, Willem, BSc Ley., MSc Ley., PhD Utrecht   Sr. Lectr.
Pinnock, Willard, BSc WI, MSc WI, PhD Dund.   Sr. Lectr.
Reese, Paul B., BSc WI, DPhil Sus.   Prof.
Other Staff: 7 Lectrs.; 1 Engineer; 3 Temp. Asst. Lectrs.
Vacant Posts: 1 Sr. Lectr.; 3 Lectrs.
Research: chemical education and computer applications; environmental and industrial chemistry; materials synthesis, structure and physical behaviour; natural products isolation, characterisation and synthesis; reaction mechanisms

Community Health and Psychiatry
Tel: (876) 927 2476 Fax: (876) 977 6346
Bain, Brendan C., BSc WI, MB BS WI, MPH Boston, DM WI   Prof.
Eldemire-Shearer, Denise, CD, BA Bishop's, MB BS WI, PhD WI   Prof.; Head*
Hickling, Frederick W., BSc WI, MB BS WI, DM WI   Prof., Psychiatry
Jackson, Maria, BSc Pratt, MSc WI, PhD WI   Sr. Lectr.
La Grenade, Janet A., MB BS WI, MPH WI   Sr. Lectr.

McCaw-Binns, Affette, BA N.Y., MPH Tulane, PhD Brist.   Prof.
Paul, Tomlin, MB BS WI, MPH WI   Sr. Lectr.
Other Staff: 26 Lectrs.; 1 Asst. Lectr.; 2 Medical Officers
Research: ageing and ageing-related issues; HIV/AIDS; nutritional epidemiology; psychiatry (substance abuse, adolescent psychiatry, cultural therapy); reproductive health (maternal mortality, adolescent sexual health)

Economics
Tel: (876) 977 1188 Fax: (876) 977 1483
E-mail: econ@uwimona.edu.jm
Figueroa, Mark, BA WI, MSc WI, PhD Manc.   Sr. Lectr.
Ghartey, Edward E., BA Ghana, MA Acad., PhD Dal.   Sr. Lectr.
King, Damien, BSc York(Can.), MSc WI, PhD N.Y.   Sr. Lectr.
Kirton, Claremont D., BSc WI, MSc WI   Sr. Lectr.
Persaud, Wilberne H., BSc WI, MA Manc.   Sr. Lectr.
Witter, Michael P., BSc Ill., MSc Wis., PhD Wis.   Sr. Lectr.; Head*
Other Staff: 8 Lectrs.; 5 Asst. Lectrs.
Vacant Posts: 3 Profs.; 1 Sr. Lectr.; 1 Lectr.
Research: financial markets; fiscal policy; macroeconomic policy; remittances; trade and development

Education, Institute of
Tel: (876) 927 2431 Fax: (876) 927 2502
Davies, Rose, BA WI, PhD WI, MA   Sr. Lectr., Early Childhood Education
Evans, Hyacinth, BA WI, MEd Ott., PhD Calif.   Prof., Teacher Education
Miller, Errol, BSc WI, MA WI, PhD WI   Prof. Emer.
Morris, Halden, PhD S.Illinois   Sr. Lectr.; Head*
Tucker, Joan, MA WI   Sr. Lectr.
Other Staff: 10 Lectrs.
Research: biodiversity education in teachers' colleges; early childhood education; environmental education for sustainable development; HIV/AIDS and education (policy, practices and implications); teacher education and curriculum reform

Educational Studies
Tel: (876) 927 2130 Fax: (876) 977 0482
E-mail: des@uwimona.edu.jm
Bankay, Anne-Maria, BA WI, MA WI, MAEd Stan., PhD Stan.   Sr. Lectr.
Bryan, Beverley A., BA N.Lond., MA Lond., PhD Lond.   Sr. Lectr.; Head*
Ezenne, Augustine N., BSc Nigeria, LLB A.Bello, MEd A.Bello, PhD Wales   Sr. Lectr.
Jennings-Craig, Zellynne, BA Hull, MA Leeds, MEd Birm., PhD WI   Prof.
Jones, Sonia O., BSc Tuskegee, MEd Tuskegee, PhD Flor.   Sr. Lectr.
Soyibo, Kolawole, BScEd Lagos, MAEd Leeds, PhD Leeds   Prof.
Other Staff: 13 Lectrs.
Vacant Posts: 1 Prof.; 1 Sr. Lectr.; 1 Asst. Lectr.
Research: action research in educational administration; implementing curriculum

innovation; language and literacy in a
Creole speaking environment; leadership
and school improvement; Spanish language
teaching

Environment, Centre for the

Tel: (876) 702 4154 Fax: (876) 702 4152
E-mail: emu@uwimona.edu.jm
Thomas-Hope, Elizabeth M., MA *Aberd.*, MS
Penn.State, DPhil *Oxf.*   James Seivwright
Moss-Solomon (Sr.) Prof.; Dir.* (on leave)
Other Staff: 2 Res. Fellows
Research: environmental education;
environmental ethics and environmental
behaviour; integrated hazard mitigation;
urban environments, social issues and waste
management; watershed management and
the conservation of agro-biodiversity

Geography and Geology

Tel: (876) 927 2728 Fax: (876) 927 1566
E-mail: geoggeol@uwimona.edu.jm
Arimah, Benedict, BA *Lagos*, MA *Lagos*, PhD *Ib.*
Sr. Lectr.
Bailey, Wilma R., BA *Newcastle(UK)*, MA *Leic.*,
PhD *WI*   Prof.; Acting Head*
Barker, David, BSc *Wales*, PhD *Brist.*   Prof.
Jackson, Trevor A., BSc *WI*, MSc *WI*, PhD *WI*
Prof.
Mitchell, Simon F., BSc *Hull*, PhD *Liv.*   Sr.
Lectr.
Robinson, Edward, BSc *Birm.*, PhD *Lond.*   Emer.
Prof.; Dir., Marine Geol. Unit
Thomas-Hope, Elizabeth M., MA *Aberd.*, MS
Penn.State, DPhil *Oxf.*   Head* (on leave)
Other Staff: 6 Lectrs.; 1 Academic Co-
ordinator; 1 Museum Curator; 1 Temp.
Asst. Lectr.
Vacant Posts: 2 Profs.; 1 Lectr.; 1 Museum
Curator
Research: Caribbean international migration;
disaster management planning and landslide
mapping; modelling groundwater flow;
reproductive health in the Caribbean;
sedimentology and reef coral biodiversity

Earthquake Unit

Wiggins-Grandison, Margaret, BSc *WI*, MSc
Atlanta, DrSc *Bergen*   Res. Fellow,
Seismology; Head*
Other Staff: 1 Engineer; 1 Res. Fellow
Research: GPS measurement of strain
accumulation; Jamaica's crustal model;
Jamaica's seismicity and tectonics; seismic
hazard assessment, national and site
specific; seismic micro-zonation of urban
areas

Government

Tel: (876) 977 5935 Fax: (876) 977 1809
E-mail: govt@uwimona.edu.jm
Byron-Reid, Jessica M., BA *WI*, PhD *Geneva*   Sr.
Lectr.
Harriott, Anthony D., BA *WI*, PhD *WI*   Sr.
Lectr.
Jones, Edwin S., CD, OD, BScEcon *WI*, MSc
WI, PhD *Manc.*   Prof., Public
Administration
Lewis, Rupert C., BScEcon *WI*, MSc *WI*   Prof.
Meeks, Brian W. E., BSc *WI*, MSc *WI*, PhD *WI*
Prof.
Powell, Lawrence A., BA *Minn.*, PhD *M.I.T.*   Sr.
Lectr.
Rapley, John A., BA *Car.*, MA *Qu.*, PhD *Qu.*
Sr. Lectr.
Valcin, Raymond, MSc *Laval*   Sr. Lectr.
Vasciannie, Stephen C., BSc *WI*, BA *Oxf.*, LLM
Camb., DPhil *Oxf.*   Prof., International Law;
Head*
Other Staff: 8 Lectrs.; 4 Asst. Lectrs.
Vacant Posts: 1 Prof.; 1 Lectr.
Research: Caribbean political thought;
comparative politics; criminology;
international relations; public sector
management

History

Tel: (876) 927 1922 Fax: (876) 927 1999
E-mail: historyarch101@yahoo.co.uk
Bryan, Patrick, BA *WI*, MA *WI*, PhD *Lond.*
Prof.
Shepherd, Verene, BA *WI*, MPhil *WI*, PhD
Camb.   Prof.
Wariboko, Waibinte, BA *P.Harcourt*, PhD *Birm.*
Prof.
Other Staff: 2 Profs. Emer.; 5 Sr. Lectrs.; 6
Lectrs.; 3 Temp. Lectrs.
Research: Caribbean business history; Caribbean
cultural history; Caribbean economic
history; Caribbean social history; post-
slavery society and politics

Hotel and Tourism Management, UWI Centre for

Nassau, Bahamas

Tel: (242) 323 5714 Fax: (242) 325 3246
Figueroa, Mark, BA *WI*, MSc *WI*, PhD *Manc.*
Head*
Other Staff: 3 Lectrs.
Vacant Posts: 1 Prof.; 1 Lectr.
Research: restaurant, hotel and resort marketing;
sustainable tourism

Language, Linguistics and Philosophy

Tel: (876) 927 2743 Fax: (876) 927 3540
E-mail: lanlinph@uwimona.edu.jm
Bewaji, John A. I., BA *Ife*, MA *Ife*, PhD *Ib.*   Sr.
Lectr.
Brodber, Kathryn, BA *WI*, MPhil *WI*   Sr.
Lectr.; Head*
Devonish, Hubert S., BA *Guy.*, DPhil *York(UK)*
Prof.
Harding, Oswald, BA *McG.*, LLB *Lond.*, PhD *WI*
Sr. Lectr.
Kouwenberg, Silvia K., MA *Amst.*, PhD *Amst.*
Sr. Lectr.
Mervyn, Alleyne, BA *Lond.*, DU *Stras.*
Other Staff: 8 Lectrs.; 1 Asst. Lectr.; 3 Lectrs.†
Vacant Posts: 1 Prof.; 1 Sr. Lectr.; 1 Lectr.; 3
Instructors

Law

Tel: (876) 927 1855 Fax: (876) 927 1855
E-mail:
suzanne.ffolkesgoldson@uwimona.edu.jm
McKoy, Derrick V., LLB *WI*, LLM *Lond.*, MBA
Barry, DBA   Sr. Lectr.
Other Staff: 1 Lectr.
Research: financial services and financial crime;
institutional governance and ethics; money
laundering and terrorist financing control;
public sector management

Library and Information Studies

Tel: (876) 927 2944 Fax: (876) 970 4903
E-mail: dlis@uwimona.edu.jm
Durrant, C. Fay, BA *WI*, BLS *Tor.*, MLS *Syr.*
Prof.; Head*
Mohamedali, Ownali N., BA *Mak.*, MS(LS)
C.U.A., MA *Sheff.*   Sr. Lectr.
Shelley-Robinson, Cherrell V., BA *WI*, MLS
Rutgers, PhD *Tor.*   Sr. Lectr.
Other Staff: 2 Lectrs.; 1 Librarian
Research: Caribbean children's literature; e-
government and access to information;
information literacy; information services
for disabled persons; internet access policies
in libraries

Life Sciences

Tel: (876) 927 1202 Fax: (876) 977 1075
E-mail: lifesci@uwimona.edu.jm
Coates-Beckford, Phyllis, BSc *WI*, MSc *Lond.*,
PhD *Ill.*   Prof.
Garraway, Eric, BSc *WI*, PhD *WI*
Hyslop, Eric, BSc *Aberd.*, PhD *Open(UK)*   Sr.
Lectr.; Head*
Robinson, Ralph, BSc *Belf.*, PhD *Belf.*   Prof.
Webber, Dale, BSc *WI*, MSc *WI*, PhD *WI*   Sr.
Lectr.
Webber, Mona, BSc *WI*, MPhil *WI*, PhD *WI*
Sr. Lectr.

Wilson, Byron, BA *Calif.*, PhD
Trin.Coll.(Washington)
Other Staff: 10 Lectrs.; 2 Asst. Lectrs.
Research: agroforestry, plant physiology and
pathology; animal and plant taxonomy,
biodiversity and conservation; entomology,
pest management and pesticide fate and
impact; marine and freshwater ecology,
fisheries and aquaculture; medical/
veterinary helminthology and
epidemiology, antioxidants and muscle
development

Literatures in English

Tel: (876) 927 2217 Fax: (876) 970 4232
E-mail: liteng@uwimona.edu.jm
Chang, Victor, BA *WI*, MA *Alta.*, PhD *Qu.*   Sr.
Lectr.
Cooper, Carolyn J., BA *WI*, MA *Tor.*, PhD *Tor.*
Prof.
Edwards, Norval, BA *WI*, MA *York(Can.)*, PhD
York(Can.)   Sr. Lectr.
Forbes, Curdella, BA *WI*, MEd *Monash*, PhD *WI*
Sr. Lectr.
Lennard, John, BA *Oxf.*, MA *Wash.*, DPhil *Oxf.*
Prof.
Morrison, Anthea, BA *WI*, Maîtrise *Paris*,
Dr3rdCy *Paris*   Head*
Williams, David, BA *WI*, MA *WI*   Sr. Lectr.
Other Staff: 4 Lectrs.; 1 Lectr.†
Research: Caribbean and African/African
diaspora literatures; literature and gender;
popular culture and film studies; post-
colonial literatures and theories; science
fiction

Management Studies

Tel: (876) 977 3775 Fax: (876) 977 1605
E-mail: doms@uwimona.edu.jm
Chen, Gavin M., BA *Howard*, MA *Wash.*, PhD
Wash.   Sr. Lectr.
Crick, M. Anne, BSc *WI*, MS *Penn.*, PhD *Rutgers*
Sr. Lectr.; Head*
Daley, Jenifer, BSc *WI*, MSc *WI*, PhD *Cardiff*
Sr. Lectr.
Shirley, Gordon V., BSc *WI*, MBA *Harv.*, PhD
Harv.   Carlton Alexander Prof. (on leave)
Wint, Alvin G., BSc *WI*, MBA *Northeastern*, DBA
Harv.   Prof.
Other Staff: 23 Lectrs.; 2 Asst. Lectrs.
Vacant Posts: 1 Prof.; 2 Sr. Lectrs.; 1 Lectr.
Research: ethics in business; human resource
management and labour relations;
international business; migratory issues;
tourism

Mathematics and Computer Science

Tel: (876) 977 1810 Fax: (876) 977 1810
E-mail: michelle.leighton@uwimona.edu.jm
Rodkina, Alexandra E., MSc *Voronezh*, PhD DSc
Moscow   Prof.
Whyte, Winston, BSc *WI*, FIA   Sr. Lectr.
Young, Ronald E., BSc *WI*, MSc *WI*, PhD *St
And.*   Prof.; Acting Head* (on leave)
Zhang, Wen-Bin, MS *Ill.*, PhD *Ill.*   Prof.
Other Staff: 8 Lectrs.; 1 Res. Fellow
Vacant Posts: 3 Profs.; 1 Sr. Lectr.; 2 Lectrs.; 1
Asst. Lectr.
Research: amorphous computing; problems
related to Schur multiplication; vibration
protection in industry; visualisation through
obscuration noise using n-tuple technique

Media and Communication, Caribbean Institute of (CARIMAC)

Tel: (876) 977 2111 Fax: (876) 977 1597
E-mail: carimac@uwimona.edu.jm
Brown, W. Aggrey, CD, BA *Hamline*, MA *Prin.*,
PhD *Prin.*   Prof.
De Bruin, Marjan J. D., Drs *Amst.*   Sr. Lectr.;
Dir.*
Dunn, Hopeton, BA *WI*, MA *City(UK)*, PhD
City(UK)   Sr. Lectr.
Rowe, Yvette, BSc *Newcastle(UK)*   Sr. Lectr.
Other Staff: 8 Lectrs.; 1 Asst. Lectr.; 1 Sr.
Lectr.; 3 Adjunct Profs.; 60 Adjunct Lectrs.
Research: Caribbean visual media aesthetics;
children and media; community media,

crime, environmental reporting, gender and communication; health communication (HIV/AIDS); new media technologies

Medical Sciences, Basic

Tel: (876) 927 0586 Fax: (876) 977 3823
E-mail: wayne.mclaughlin@uwimona.edu.jm
Asemota, Helen N., BSc Benin, MSc A.Bello, PhD Benin Prof., Biochemistry
Fletcher, Cyril K., MB BS WI, FRCSEd Sr. Lectr., Anatomy
Guldner, Fritz H., DM F.U.Berlin, MD Monash Prof., Anatomy
McFarlane-Anderson, Norma D., BSc WI, PhD Lond. Prof., Biochemistry
McLaughlin, Wayne A., BSc Wat., PhD WI Sr. Lectr.; Head, Biochem. Section
Mills, James L., MD Düsseldorf, PhD WI Sr. Lectr., Physiology
Morrison, The Hon. Errol Y. St. A., OJ, MD Malta, MSc Lond., PhD WI, FRCPGlas, FACP Prof., Biochemistry (on leave)
Parshad, Omkar, BVSc&AH Punj.Ag., MSc Punj.Ag., PhD Punj.Ag. Prof., Physiology
Pearson, Andrew, BSc Leeds, PhD Leeds Sr. Lectr., Biochemistry
Ragoobirsingh, Dalip, BSc WI, MPhil WI, PhD WI Sr. Lectr., Biochemistry
Reid, Harvey L., BSc Lond., PhD Lond. Prof., Physiology
Simon, Oswald R., BSc Lond., MSc Lond., PhD Howard Sr. Lectr., Pharmacology; Head*
Wais, Allen C., BS Cornell, PhD Tufts Sr. Lectr., Biochemistry
Young, Lauriann, BSc WI, MPhil WI, PhD WI Sr. Lectr., Physiology
Young, Ronald E., BSc WI, MSc WI, PhD St And. Prof., Physiology (on leave)
Other Staff: 11 Lectrs.; 1 Asst. Lectr.; 2 Temp. Lectrs.
Vacant Posts: 2 Profs.; 1 Sr. Lectr.; 2 Lectrs.
Research: anti glaucoma drops; anti-inflammatory potential of compounds from Noni; biochemistry and molecular basis of human diseases; medicinal plant extracts for diabetes mellitus; strategies for production/storage/utilisation of tropical tuber crops

Medicine

Tel: (876) 927 1707
E-mail: medicine@uwimona.edu.jm
Barton, Everard N., BSc WI, MB BS Ib., DM WI, FACP, FRCP Prof.; Head*
Clarke, Tanya, MB BS
Collie, Charlton, MB BS
Denbow, Charles E., BSc WI, MB BS WI, DM WI, FACP, FRCP Prof.
East-Innes, Althea, MB BS WI
Gilbert, David, BSc WI, MB BS WI, DM
Hurlock, Lisa, MB BS WI, DM
Lee, Michael G., MB BS WI, DM WI, FRCPCan, FACP Prof.; Dir., Postgrad. Programme
Scott, Paul, MB BS WI, DM WI
Smith, Roger, MB BS WI, DM WI
Williams, Winston, MB BS WI, DM WI, FACP Sr. Lectr.
Wright-Pascoe, Rosemarie A., MB BS WI, DM WI, FACP, FACE, FRCPEd Sr. Lectr.
Other Staff: 19 Assoc. Lectrs.; 8 Hon. Lectrs.
Research: collagen vascular diseases; endocrinology (diabetes); immunogenetics; kidney diseases; natural products (cancer treatment from plants)

Microbiology

Tel: (876) 977 2947 Fax: (876) 977 1265
E-mail: micro@uwimona.edu.jm
Bodonaik, Nabin C., MB BS Madr., MD Madr. Sr. Lectr.
Lindo, John F., BSc WI, PhD WI Sr. Lectr.; Head*
Smikle, Monica P., BSc WI, MSc Amst., PhD WI Prof.
Other Staff: 6 Lectrs.; 1 Asst. Lectr.
Research: ESBL testing on Escherichia coli; molecular epidemiology of HIV/AIDS; occupational exposures and needle stick injury; strains on clostridium difficile

among hospitalised patients; susceptibility of isolates to tigecycline

Modern Languages and Literatures

Tel: (876) 927 2293 Fax: (876) 977 2215
E-mail: modlang@uwimona.edu.jm
Nzengou-Tayo, Marie-José, Mèsl Besançon, DèsL Lille Sr. Lectr., French; Head*
Pereira, Joseph, BA WI, MA Qu. Sr. Lectr., Spanish
Sanz, Ileana, BEd Havana, PhD Havana Sr. Lectr., Spanish
Williams, Claudette, BA WI, MA WI, PhD Stan. Sr. Lectr., Spanish
Other Staff: 5 Lectrs.; 3 Asst. Lectrs.; 3 Foreign Lang Instrs.; 15 Lectrs./Tutors†
Research: foreign language teaching and learning; Francophone literatures and cultures; Latin American and Afro-Hispanic literatures; translation theory and practice

Nursing, The UWI School of, Mona

Tel: (876) 970 3304 Fax: (876) 927 2472
E-mail: nursing@uwimona.edu.jm
Bennett, Joanna, BA Middx., PhD Herts. Sr. Lectr.
Hewitt, Hermi H., OD, BScN WI, MPH Tulane, PhD Iowa Sr. Lectr.; Dir.*
Other Staff: 9 Lectrs.; 7 Asst. Lectrs.
Research: asthma in Jamaica; HIV prevention; medication in mental health; nursing history; nursing migration in Jamaica

Obstetrics, Gynaecology and Child Health

Tel: (876) 927 1145 Fax: (876) 977 9397
E-mail: og@uwimona.edu.jm
Christie-Samuels, Celia, MB BS WI, DM WI Prof., Child Health
Fletcher, Horace M., BSc WI, MB BS WI, DM WI Prof., Obstetrics and Gynaecology; Head*
Frederick, Joseph, MB BS WI, DM WI Prof.
Kulkarni, Santosh K., MB BS WI, DM WI Sr. Lectr., Obstetrics and Gynaecology
Mullings, Anthony M., MB BS WI, MPH Miami(Fla.), DM WI Sr. Lectr., Obstetrics and Gynaecology
Pierre, Russell, MB BS WI, DM WI Sr. Lectr.
Pottinger, Audrey, BA Rutgers, MSc WI, PhD Aberd. Sr. Lectr.
Rattray, Carole A., MB BS WI, DM WI, DCH WI Sr. Lectr., Obstetrics and Gynaecology
Samms-Vaughan, Maureen, MB BS WI, DM WI, PhD Brist. Sr. Lectr., Child Health
Thame, Miverva, MB BS DM Sr. Lectr., Child Health
Other Staff: 7 Lectrs. (Child Health); 10 Lectrs. (Obstet. and Gynae.); 5 Assoc. Lectrs. (Obstet. and Gynae.); 1 Res. Fellow (Obstet. and Gynae.); 7 Lectrs. (Child Health)†
Vacant Posts: 2 Sr. Lectrs.
Research: anthropometry of mothers and infants; HIV (mother to child transmission); management and complications of uterine fibroids; pentavalent human reassortant rotavirus vaccine in healthy infants; twin birth study (best route of delivery)

Pathology

Tel: (876) 977 3942 Fax: (876) 977 1811
E-mail: pathology@uwimona.edu.jm
Bennett, Franklyn, BSc WI, MSc McG., PhD WI Prof.
Char, Gurendra, MD Ban., MB BS Prof.
Choo-Kang, Eric, MB BS WI, FRCPCan Sr. Lectr.
Coard, Kathleen, BSc Brist., MB BS WI, DM WI Prof.
Escoffery, Carlos T., BSc Brist., MB BS WI, DM WI Prof.; Head*
Hanchard, Barrie, MB BS Lond., FRCPCan Prof.
Shah, Dipak, MD Ban., DM WI, MB BS Prof.
Shirley, Suzanne E., MB BS WI, DM WI Sr. Lectr.
Wharfe, Gilian, MB BS WI, DM WI Sr. Lectr.

Williams, Elaine E., MB BS WI, DM WI Sr. Lectr.
Williams, Nadia P., MB BS WI, DM WI Sr. Lectr.
Other Staff: 8 Lectrs.
Research: cancer of breast, cervix, prostate and gastro-intestinal tract; HTLV-1 associated diseases; molecular pathology; neuropathology; perinatal/paediatric pathology

Physics

Tel: (876) 927 2480 Fax: (876) 977 1595
E-mail: physics@uwimona.edu.jm
Amarakoon, A. M. D., BSc S.Lanka, MSc Louisiana State, PhD Louisiana State Sr. Lectr.; Postgrad. Co-ordinator
Chen, Anthony, BSc Boston Coll., MA Harv., MSc Maryland, PhD WI Prof.†
Ponnambalam, Michael J., BSc Madr., MSc IIT Madras, PhD Illinois Tech.Inst. Sr. Lectr.; Undergrad. Co-ordinator
Skobla, Joseph, MSc T.U.Bratislava, PhD T.U.Bratislava, PhD Tor. Sr. Lectr.; Head*
Walwyn, Donald R., BSc WI, PhD WI Sr. Lectr.
Other Staff: 2 Sr. Lectrs.; 8 Lectrs.; 2 Asst. Lectrs.; 1 Prof.†
Research: climate studies; climate variability and climate change in the Caribbean; feasibility of green hybrid system; global positioning systems (GPS) error correction studies; renewable energy

Sociology, Psychology and Social Work

Tel: (876) 977 0315 Fax: (876) 927 9301
E-mail: socy@uwimona.edu.jm
Anderson, Patricia Y., BSc WI, MA Chic., PhD Chic. Prof.
Boxill, Ian O., BSc WI, MPhil WI, PhD Colorado State Prof.
Branche, Clement, BSc WI, MSc Lond. Sr. Lectr.; Head*
Headley, Bernard, AB Andrews, MA Howard, PhD Howard Prof.
Uche, Chukwudum, BSc Ife, MA Chic., PhD Chic. Prof.
Other Staff: 1 Sr. Lectr. (Sociology); 17 Lectrs. (Sociology); 14 Lectrs. (Psychology); 9 Lectrs. (Social Work)
Research: crime, urban development and impact on society; domestic violence and trauma in children; HIV/AIDS and implications for society; migration, the Caribbean diaspora and popular culture; poverty, community and development in the Caribbean

Surgery, Radiology, Anaesthesia and Intensive Care

Tel: (876) 927 1270 Fax: (876) 970 4302
E-mail: surradic@uwimona.edu.jm
Branday, Joseph M., MB BS WI, MS WI, FRCSEd, FACS Prof.
Carpenter, Reginald A., MB BChir Camb., MA Camb., FRCS, FRCSEd Prof. Emer.
Crandon, Ivor W., MB BS WI, BSc Windsor, FRCSEd Sr. Lectr.; Head*
Duncan, Newton D., MB BS WI, DM WI, FACS Sr. Lectr.
DuQuesnay, Denis R. L., MB BS WI, DM WI, FRCSEd, FACS Sr. Lectr.
Fletcher, Peter R., MB BS Lond., FACS, FRCSEd Prof.
McDonald, Archibald H., MB BS WI, DM WI, FRCSEd, FACS Prof.
Spencer, Howard W., MB BS WI, MPH WI, FRCSEd, FACS Prof. (on leave)
Other Staff: 20 Lectrs.; 24 Assoc. Lectrs.; 1 Hon. Prof.; 5 Hon. Assoc. Lectrs.
Vacant Posts: 1 Prof.
Research: breast cancer; colon cancer; prostate cancer; trauma care; trauma (risk factors associated with injuries)

SPECIAL CENTRES, ETC

Biotechnology Centre

Tel: (876) 977 1828 Fax: (876) 977 3331
E-mail: karen.levy@uwimona.edu.jm
Ahmad, Mohammed H., BSc Bhagal., MSc IARI, PhD IARI Prof.; Dir.*
Asemota, Helen N., BSc Benin, MSc A.Bello, PhD Benin Prof.
McLaughlin, Wayne A., BSc Wat., PhD WI Sr. Lectr.
Other Staff: 2 Lectrs.; 1 Asst. Lectr.; 1 Temp. Lectr.
Research: molecular biology of gemini viruses in Jamaica; molecular breeding of virus-resistant papaya; molecular pathology of diseases affecting citrus; somatic embryogenesis of tropical crops; tropical medicinal plants

Business, Mona School of

Tel: (876) 977 6035 Fax: (876) 977 4622
E-mail: msb@uwimona.edu.jm
Abrikian, Harry, BA WI, MIA Col., MBA Stan. Sr. Lectr.
Duggan, Evan, BSc WI, MBA Georgia State, PhD WI, PhD Georgia State Prof., Managment Information Systems
Dunn, Hopeton, BA WI, MA City(UK), DPhil City(UK) Dir., Telecom Policy and Management Unit
Ivey, Boswell, BSc WI, MBA WI, MBA Aston Sr. Lectr.
Robinson, Claude, BA Car., BJ Car. Sr. Lectr.
Ying, Neville, CD, BSc WI, MA Maryland, PhD Maryland Prof., Business Development; Acting Executive Dir.*
Other Staff: 6 Lectrs.; 1 Sr. Teaching Fellow; 16 UWI Adjunct Fac.; 19 Visiting Adjunct Fac.; 5 Visiting (Overseas) Fac. Profs.
Research: family and women-owned businesses; mobile opportunities (poverty and telephone access in Latin America and the Caribbean); WEF executive opinion survey

Caribbean Studies, Institute of (ICS)

Tel: (876) 977 1951 Fax: (876) 977 3430
E-mail: icsmona@uwimona.edu.jm
Cooper, Carolyn J., BA WI, MA Tor., PhD Tor. Prof., Literary and Cultural Studies; Dir.*
Other Staff: 4 Lectrs.
Research: Caribbean gender and sexuality (female sexuality); Caribbean religions, folk forms and pan-Africanism (Rastafari, Yoruba, revivalism, Kumina and liberation ideology); Jamaican gay space; postcolonial Caribbean culture; reggae and dancehall theory and popular culture

Communication for Development, Caribbean Centre for (CCCD)

Carr, Robert, MSW WI, BA PhD Sr. Lectr.; Dir.*

Environmental and Nuclear Sciences, International Centre for (ICENS)

Tel: (876) 927 1777 Fax: (876) 977 0768
E-mail: icens@uwimona.edu.jm
Grant, Charles, BSc Sur., MSc Sur. Head, Nuclear Analytical Lab.
Lalor, The Hon. Gerald C., OJ, CD, BSc WI, MSc WI, PhD Lond. Prof.; Head*
Preston, John, BSc WI Head, Info. Systems Unit
Rattray, Vaughn, BSc Birm., MSc Birm., PhD McG. Head, Solutions Analysis Lab.
Taylor, Gladstone, BSc McM., MSc Br.Col., PhD WI Head, Admin.
Thomas, Joan, BSc WI Head, Radiation Monitoring Unit
Other Staff: 1 Sr. Res. Fellow
Research: environmental geochemistry (heavy metals in soils, food and humans); food (transfer of elements from soils to food); health (effects of lead and cadmium)

Fertility Management Unit, Advanced Training and Research in

Tel: (876) 927 2481 Fax: (876) 927 0100
E-mail: atrfmu@uwimona.edu.jm
Frederick, Joseph, MB BS WI, DM WI Prof.; Dir.*
Other Staff: 2 Res. Fellows; 1 Jr. Res. Fellow
Research: contraceptive technology; infertility and assisted conception; knowledge, attitude and practice (reproductive health, HIV/AIDS and gender); minimally invasive surgery; reproductive health counselling

Gender and Development Studies, Mona Unit, Centre for (CGDS)

Tel: (876) 977 7365 Fax: (876) 977 9053
E-mail: cgdsmona@uwimona.edu.jm
Dunn, Leith L., BA WI, MSc WI, PhD Lond. Head*
Thomas-Hope, Elizabeth M., MA Aberd., MS Penn.State, DPhil Oxf. James Seivwright Moss-Solomon (Sr.) Prof., Environmental Management (on leave)
Other Staff: 2 Lectrs.
Research: gender and governance; gender and theology; gender, sexuality and HIV/AIDS; gender, work and human rights

Marine Sciences, Centre for (CMS)

Tel: (876) 927 1609 Fax: (876) 977 1033
E-mail: cms@uwimona.edu.jm
Webber, Dale, BSc WI, MSc WI, PhD WI Sr. Lectr.; Dir.*
Other Staff: 1 Lectr.
Research: Caribbean coastal marine productivity programme; Caribbean coastal scenarios modelling; coral reef monitoring for climate change; coral reef restoration by enhanced growth; enhancing coral reef fish habitat

Media, Caribbean Centre for Excellence in (CCEM)

James, Canute, BA WI, MPhil WI Sr. Lectr.; Head*

Natural Products Institute

Tel: (876) 970 2574 Fax: (876) 970 2574
E-mail: trevor.yee@uwimona.edu.jm
Delgoda, Thejani R., BSc PNG, DPhil Oxf. Res. Dir.
Yee, Trevor H., BSc WI, MBA Nova(Fla.), PhD WI Executive Dir.*
Other Staff: 1 Res. Fellow
Research: drug-herb interactions; local economic plant extracts (essential oils, biopesticides and biofertilisers); natural products interactions with cancer cell lines and P450 enzymes

Tropical Medicine Research Institute (TMRI)

Tel: (876) 977 6151 Fax: (876) 927 2984
E-mail: tmri@uwimona.edu.jm
Ali, Susanna, MB BS WI, DM WI Lectr.; Head, Clin. Services (Sickle Cell Unit)
Forrester, Terrence G., MB BS WI, MSc WI, DM WI, PhD WI, FRCPEd Prof.; Acting Dir., Tropical Metabolism Res. Unit; Dir.*
Powell, Christine A., BSc WI, MSc WI, PhD WI Sr. Lectr. (Epidemiology Research Unit)
Reid, Marvin, MB BS WI, PhD WI Sr. Lectr.; Dir., Sickle Cell Unit
Walker, Susan P., BSc Brist., MSc Lond., PhD Lond. Prof. (Epidemiology Research Unit)
Wilks, Rainford J., MB BS WI, MSc Lond., DM WI, FRCPEd Prof.; Dir., Epidemiol. Res. Unit
Other Staff: 1 Prof.; 9 Lectrs.; 3 Med. Lectrs.; 2 Asst. Lectrs.; 5 Lectrs./Clin. Fellows; 2 Statisticians/Lectrs./Asst. Lectrs.; 1 Res. Fellow; 4 Med. Res. Fellows; 1 Clin. Res. Fellow
Research: aggression in Jamaican children; cardiovascular risk factors in Jamaica; incidence of hypertension and diabetes in Jamaica; low birth weight and mental development; malnutrition and mental development

CONTACT OFFICERS

Admissions (first degree). Senior Assistant Registrar (Admissions (undergraduate degree)): Witter, Anne Marie, BA WI, MA WI
(E-mail: annmarie.witter@uwimona.edu.jm)
Admissions (higher degree). Senior Assistant Registrar, Graduate Studies and Research (higher degree): Miller, Barbara, BA WI, MSc WI
(E-mail: barbara.miller@uwimona.edu.jm)
Alumni. President, UWI Alumni Association (Jamaica Chapter): Marriott, Nadine, BSc WI (E-mail: uwiguild@kasnet.com)
Archives. Campus Records Manager: Black, Sonia, BA WI, MBA New Orleans
(E-mail: sonia.black@uwimona.edu.jm)
Careers. Student Services Manager (Careers and Job Placement): Henry, Merrit, BSc Lond., MEd WI
(E-mail: merrit.henry@uwimona.edu.jm)
Distance education. Campus Co-ordinator: Thompson, Derrick, BSc WI
(E-mail: uwidec@uwimona.edu.jm)
Estates and buildings/works and services. Estate Manager: Sambo, Kathleen, BSc WI, MBA Col.
(E-mail: kathleen.sambo@uwimona.edu.jm)
Examinations. Senior Assistant Registrar (Examinations): Nelson, Cordel, BA WI
(E-mail: cordel.nelson@uwimona.edu.jm)
Finance. Campus Bursar: Robinson, Elaine, BSc(Econ) WI
(E-mail: elaine.robinson@uwimona.edu.jm)
General enquiries. Campus Registrar: Bell-Hutchinson, Camille, BSc WI, MA(Ed) WI, PhD WI (E-mail: campusregistraroffice@uwimona.edu.jm)
Health services. Director Clinical Services, Health Centre: Anglin-Brown, Blossom, MB BS WI, DM WI, MPH WI
(E-mail: healthcr@uwimona.edu.jm)
Library (chief librarian). Campus Librarian: Amenu-Kpodo, Norma, BA Sask., BLS Tor.
(E-mail: mainlibrary@uwimona.edu.jm)
Personnel/human resources. Director, Human Resources Management: Hinds, Allister, BA WI, MA Dal., PhD Dal.
(E-mail: directorhrmd@uwimona.edu.jm)
Public relations. Public Relations Officer: Edwards, Carroll, BA WI, MJ Car.
(E-mail: proffice@uwimona.edu.jm)
Quality assurance and accreditation. Deputy Principal (Quality Assurance and Accreditation): Pereira, Joseph, BA WI, MA Qu.
(E-mail: joseph.pereira@uwimona.edu.jm)
Scholarships, awards, loans. Manager, Office of Student Financing: Dickenson, Joy, MPSM WI, FCA
(E-mail: stufinc@uwimona.edu.jm)
Sport and recreation. Student Services Manager (Sports): Jackson, Grace, BA Alabama, MA Queens, N.Y.
(E-mail: sports@uwimona.edu.jm)
Staff development and training. Manager, Instructional Development Unit: Allen, Beryl M., BA WI, MA WI, PhD Sur.
(E-mail: idu@uwimona.edu.jm)
Student welfare/counselling. Student Counsellor: Gordon-Stair, Angela, BSc WI, MAEd W.Carolina, PhD WI
(E-mail: counsel@uwimona.edu.jm)
Students with disabilities. Student Services Manager: O'Sullivan, Peter, BSc WI, MBA Barry
(E-mail: peter.osullivan@uwimona.edu.jm)
University press. General Manager, University Press: Speth, Linda, BA Utah, MA Utah
(E-mail: cuserv@cwjamaica.com)

[Information supplied by the institution as at 30 October 2007, and edited by the ACU]

UNIVERSITY OF THE WEST INDIES, ST AUGUSTINE CAMPUS

Founded 1960

Postal Address: St Augustine, Trinidad and Tobago
Telephone: 662 2002 **Fax:** 663 9684
URL: http://www.uwi.tt

ACTING CAMPUS PRINCIPAL AND PRO-VICE-CHANCELLOR*—Sankat, Prof. Clement, BSc *WI*, MSc *WI*, PhD *Guelph*
DEPUTY PRINCIPAL—Kochhar, Prof. G. S., BE *Baroda*, MS *Wis.*, PhD *WI*
PRO-VICE-CHANCELLOR (PLANNING AND DEVELOPMENT)—Tewarie, Bhoendradatt, BA *Northwestern*, MA *Chic.*, PhD *Penn.State*
PRO-VICE-CHANCELLOR (GRADUATE STUDIES)—Sankat, Prof. Clement, BSc *WI*, MSc *WI*, PhD *Guelph*
PRO-VICE-CHANCELLOR (RESEARCH)—Hunte, Prof. W., BSc *WI*, PhD *WI*
CAMPUS REGISTRAR‡—Callaghan, Jeremy, BA *York(UK)*, MA *Reading*
CAMPUS BURSAR—Bada, Lylla, BA *Brist.*
CAMPUS LIBRARIAN/UNIVERSITY LIBRARIAN—Rouse-Jones, Prof. Margaret, BA *WI*, MA *Johns H.*, PhD *Johns H.*

GENERAL INFORMATION

History. Originating in the Imperial College of Tropical Agriculture, St Augustine campus was established in 1960 as the second campus of the University of the West Indies.

It is located 15km east of Port of Spain, the capital of Trinidad and Tobago.

Admission to first degree courses. See under University of the West Indies, above.

First Degrees (see also West Indies Directory to Subjects of Study). BA, BEd, BSc, DDS, DVM, LLB, MB BS.
Length of course. Full-time: BEd: 2–5 years; LLB: 3 years; BSc: 3–4 years; BA: 3–6 years; DDS, DVM, MB BS: 5 years. *Part-time:* BSc: 3–7½ years; BA: 4–9 years; BEd: 5–7 years. *By distance learning:* BSc: 5 years.

Higher Degrees (see also West Indies Directory to Subjects of Study).
Master's. MA, MBA, MEd, MPhil, MSc.
Admission. Candidates must normally hold an appropriate first degree with at least second class honours in a relevant or analogous subject area, or a qualification accepted as equivalent.
Length of course. Full-time: MA: 1 year; MSc: 1–1½ years; MEd: 1¾ years; MBA: 2 years; MPhil: 2–4 years. *Part-time:* MA, MSc: 2 years; MEd: 3 years; MPhil: 3–6 years. *By distance learning:* MSc: 4 years.
Doctoral. DM, MD, PhD.
Admission. Candidates for doctoral degrees should hold a master's degree from an approved university, with a specialty in the relevant area of study. Other candidates are required to register for MPhil and then transfer or upgrade to PhD.
Length of course. Full-time: DM: 2–4 years; MD, PhD: 3–5 years. *Part-time:* PhD: 4–7 years.

Libraries. Volumes: 402,199. Periodicals subscribed to: 9908. Other holdings: 46,105 bound volumes of serials; 10,600 vertical files; 5078 photographs; 3419 film/multimedia; 1349 maps; 811 cassettes; 289 cassettes/ videos; 448 compact disks; 22,737 microforms. Special collections: Derek Walcott; Eric Williams Memorial; C. L. R. James.

FACULTIES/SCHOOLS

Engineering
Fax: 662 4414 E-mail: clem@eng.uwi.tt
Dean: Sankat, Prof. Clement, BSc *WI*, MSc *WI*, PhD *Guelph*
Administrative Officer: Sargeant, Carol, BSc *WI*, MSc *WI*

Humanities and Education
Tel: 645 5601 Fax: 645 5601
E-mail: fhesh@tstt.net.tt
Dean: Robertson, Ian, BA *WI*, PhD *WI*
Administrative Assistant (Humanities - Student and Staff Matters): Julien, A., BSc *WI*

Administrative Assistant (Education): Pamela, De Silva, BSc *WI*
Administrative Assistant (Humanities - Distance and Outreach): Berridge, M.
Administrative Assistant (Humanities - Buildings, Facilities, Maintenance and Postgraduate matters): Rogers, R., BA *WI*

Medical Sciences
Tel: 645 2640 Fax: 645 2544
E-mail: medsci@tstt.net.tt
Dean: Ramsewak, Prof. Samuel, MB BS *WI*, MD, FRCOG
Administrative Officer: Edoo, A., BA *Lock Haven*, MA *Johns H.*, MBA *WI*

Science and Agriculture
Tel: 662 5012 Fax: 663 9686
E-mail: fansuwi@tstt.net.tt
Dean: Narinesingh, Prof. Dyer, BSc *WI*, MSc *WI*, PhD *WI*
Senior Administrative Assistant: Sobers, M., BA *WI*

Social Sciences
Tel: 645 7004 Fax: 662 6295
E-mail: fss@fss.uwi.tt
Dean: Ghany, Hamid, BA *WI*, MA *Fordham*, PhD *Lond.*
Administrative Assistant (Acting): George, A., BSc *WI*

ACADEMIC UNITS

Agricultural Economics and Extension
Tel: 663 8355 Fax: 663 8355
E-mail: daee@fans.uwi.tt
9 Lectrs.
Vacant Posts: 1 Sr. Lectr.; 3 Lectrs.

Agricultural Economics
Pemberton, C. A., BSc *WI*, MSc *WI*, PhD *Manit.*
Sr. Lectr.
Singh, R. H., BSc *Manit.*, MSc *Manit.*, PhD *Manit.*
Sr. Lectr.; Head*
Other Staff: 6 Lectrs.
Research: food, economic analysis; technologies for farmer training using video and print media; technology transfer and trade liberalisation

Agricultural Extension
Seepersad, J., BSc *WI*, MSc *WI*, PhD *Manit.*   Sr. Lectr.
Other Staff: 3 Lectrs.
Research: extension policy analysis

Basic Health Sciences, School of
28 Lectrs.; 18 Assoc. Lectrs.; 1 Asst. Lectr.

Anatomy
Fax: 662 9148
McRae, Amanda, BSc *Alabama*, PhD *Lyons I*   Prof.
Odekunle, A., MB BS *Benin*, PhD *Sheff.*   Sr. Lectr.

Ovchinnikov, N. A., MD *Perm State Inst.Med.*, PhD *Perm State Inst.Med.*   Sr. Lectr.
Other Staff: 2 Lectrs.
Research: human anatomy (morphological investigations of the brain: normal/ pathological conditions)

Biochemistry
Tel: 662 1219 Fax: 662 9148
Alleyne, Trevor, BSc *Essex*, MSc *Essex*, PhD *Essex*   Sr. Lectr.
Ramdath, Dan, BSc *Tor.*, MSc *WI*, PhD *WI*   Prof.; Head, Pre-Clin. Scis.*
Other Staff: 1 Lectr.
Research: biochemistry (chronic disasters, including malnutrition)

Physiology
Fax: 662 9148
Addae, J., MB ChB *Ghana*, PhD *Lond.*   Prof.
Other Staff: 3 Lectrs.
Vacant Posts: 1 Prof.
Research: human physiology (normal biological macro- and microsystems)

Behavioural Sciences
Fax: 663 4948 E-mail: wrocke@fss.uwi.tt
15 Lectrs.; 3 Temp. Lectrs.; 4 Temp. Asst. Lectrs.

Political Sciences
Bissessar, Ann-Marie, BA *WI*, MSc *WI*, PhD *WI*   Sr. Lectr., Government
Ghany, Hamid, BA *WI*, MA *Fordham*, PhD *Lond.*   Sr. Lectr.; Head*
Premdas, R., MA *Ill.*, PhD *Ill.*, PhD *McG.*   Prof.
Ragoonath, B., BSc *WI*, MSc *WI*, PhD *WI*   Sr. Lectr.
Other Staff: 1 Lectr.; 3 Temp. Asst. Lectrs.
Vacant Posts: 1 Lectr.
Research: Caribbean politics; comparative and international politics; political theory and sociology; public policy and administration

Psychology/Sociology
E-mail: psychres@trinidad.net
8 Lectrs.; 1 Temp. Lectr.
Vacant Posts: 3 Lectrs.
Research: criminology; industrial sociology; social psychology; sociology of development; sociology of education and health

Social Work
E-mail: kvaltonen@fss.uwi.tt
Valtonen, K., MA *Aberd.*, MSW *Alabama*, PhD *Turku*   Sr. Lectr.; Head*
Other Staff: 5 Lectrs.; 1 Temp. Lectr.; 1 Temp. Asst. Lectr.
Research: children in care; developing the leadership potential of young females; domestic violence; household coping strategies; social services

Chemistry

Tel: 662 6013 Fax: 645 3771
  E-mail: chemistry@fsa.uwi.tt
Chan, W., BSc Lond., MSc Lond., PhD Lond.
  Prof. Emer.
Chang-Yen, I., BSc Guy., PhD Brist. Sr. Lectr.
Grierson, L., BSc Lond., PhD Lond. Lectr.;
  Head*
Hall, L., BSc WI, MSc WI, PhD WI Prof.
Maxwell, A., BSc WI, MSc WI, PhD Br.Col. Sr.
  Lectr.
Mootoo, Baldwin S., BSc Lond., MSc Lond., PhD
  WI Prof. Emer.
Narinesingh, Dyer, BSc WI, MSc WI, PhD WI
  Prof.
Pelter, Andrew, BSc Brist., PhD Brist., DSc Brist.
  Hon. Prof.
Singh, Gurdial, BSc Liv., PhD Manc. Prof.
Stephenson, D., BA York(UK), MPhil CNAA, PhD
  Lond. Sr. Lectr.
Other Staff: 6 Lectrs.; 1 Sr. Scientist; 1 Hon.
  Lectr.
Vacant Posts: 1 Sr. Lectr.; 2 Lectrs.
Research: analytical/environmental monitoring;
  biosensors; natural products from marine
  and terrestrial organisms; organic synthesis;
  supramolecular chemistry

Dentistry, School of

Fax: 645 3823 E-mail: dentsch@carib-link.net
Al-Bayaty, H. F., BDS Baghdad, MDSc Leeds, PhD
  Wales Sr. Lectr., Oral Biology
Paluri, Murti, BDS Calc., MDS Bom. Prof.;
  Head*
Other Staff: 16 Lectrs.; 1 Asst. Lectr.
Vacant Posts: 4 Profs.; 1 Lectr.
Research: adult dental health; child dental health;
  dental technology

Economics

Tel: 662 6555 Fax: 662 6555
  E-mail: deptecon@fss.uwi.tt
Farrell, T., BA McG., MA Cornell, PhD Cornell
  Sr. Lectr.
Pantin, D., BSc WI, MPhil Sus. Sr. Lectr.
Theodore, K., BA Lond., MSc Lond., PhD Boston
  Prof.; Head*
Watson, P., BCom Leeds, LèsEcon Paris, MèsEcon
  Paris, PhD Paris Sr. Lectr.
Other Staff: 6 Lectrs.; 3 Temp. Lectrs.; 1
  Temp. Asst. Lectr.; 1 Hon. Lectr.
Vacant Posts: 2 Sr. Lectrs.; 1 Lectr.
Research: applied econometrics; health
  economics; international trade;
  macroeconomics and microeconomics;
  sustainable development

Education, School of

Tel: 662 6615 Fax: 662 6615
  E-mail: head@educ.uwi.tt
Byron, M., BA WI, MAEd WI, PhD Ohio Sr.
  Lectr.
George, J., BSc WI, MEd Tor., MEd Qu., PhD
  WI Sr. Lectr.; Head*
Keller, C., BA WI, MA Stan. Sr. Lectr.
Quamina-Aiyejina, Lynda, BA Sr. Lectr.
Other Staff: 21 Lectrs.; 2 Res. Fellows; 1
  Librarian/Documentalist; 5 Temp. Lectrs.; 1
  Temp. Asst. Lectr.
Vacant Posts: 1 Prof.; 1 Sr. Lectr.; 4 Lectrs.
Research: gender relations in the school system;
  health and family life education; policy
  analysis and policy reform; science
  education in the lower secondary school;
  teacher education

Engineering, Chemical

Fax: 662 4414 E-mail: chemeng@eng.uwi.tt
Abder, Clyde, BSc WI, MS Penn. Sr. Lectr.
Aina, Adebayo, BSc Ib., MSc Ife, MBA Lagos,
  PhD Ife Prof.
Akingbala, J., BSc Ib., MSc Texas A.& M., PhD
  Texas A.& M. Prof.
Baccus-Taylor, G., BSc WI, MSc WI, MSCons
  Reading, PhD Wis. Sr. Lectr.
Dawe, Richard, BA Oxf., MA Oxf., DPhil Oxf.,
  FRSChem Prof.

Farabi, H., BSc Arya-Mehr, MSc Aston, PhD Aston
  Sr. Lectr.
Foley, M., BSc Qu., MSc Alta., PhD Qu. Sr.
  Lectr.
McGaw, D. R., BSc Wales, MSc Wales, PhD WI,
  FICE Prof. Emer.
Mellowes, W. A., BSc WI, MSc WI, PhD WI
  Prof.
Pilgrim, A., BSc WI, BSc(Eng) WI, PhD WI
  Sr. Lectr.; Head*
Richards, G. M., CM, MSc Manc., PhD Cant.
  Prof. Emer.
Thomas, S., BSc WI, MSc New Br., PhD McM.
  Sr. Lectr.
Other Staff: 7 Lectrs.; 2 Visiting Fellows; 16
  Lectrs.†
Vacant Posts: 1 Prof.; 1 Lectr.
Research: casing wear offshore and hydraulic
  fracturing; chemical processing; food
  sciences and technology; gas hydrate
  transportation for the Caribbean; sugar
  technology

Engineering, Civil and Environmental

Fax: 645 7691
  E-mail: civil.engineering@sta.uwi.edu
Charles, R. F., BSc WI, MPhil WI Sr. Lectr.
Dean, E. T. R., BA Camb., MA Camb., MBA
  Open(UK), MPhil Camb., PhD Camb. Sr.
  Lectr.
Imbert, I. D. C., ME N.U.I., PhD Prof. Emer.,
  Construction Engineering and Management
Lewis, T. M., BEng Liv., MEng Liv., MSc Stir.,
  PhD WI Prof.
Petersen, A., BSc Wales, PhD Portsmouth Sr.
  Lectr.
Phelps, H. O., BSc Wales, PhD Manc., FICE
  Prof. Emer.
Ramamurthy, K. N., BE Madr., MTech IIT
  Madras, PhD IIT Madras Sr. Lectr.
Shrivastava, Gyan, BTech IIT Delhi, MSc Lond.,
  MTech Kharagpur, PhD WI Sr. Lectr.; Head*
Venkobacher, C., BSc Madr., BTech IIT Madras,
  MTech IIT Kanpur, PhD IIT Kanpur Prof.
Other Staff: 11 Lectrs.; 1 Hon. Fellow
Vacant Posts: 1 Prof.; 1 Lectr.
Research: analysis and design of hydraulic
  systems; analysis and design of structures;
  disaster mitigation and management;
  environmental engineering; transport
  engineering

Engineering, Electrical and Computer

Fax: 662 4414
  E-mail: electrical.engineering@sta.uwi.edu
Copeland, Brian R., BSc WI, MSc Tor., PhD
  S.Calif. Prof.
Gift, S., BSc WI, PhD WI Prof.
Joshi, A., PhD Mumbai Sr. Lectr.
Julien, Kenneth, BSc Nott., PhD Br.Col., FIEEE,
  FIEE Prof. Emer.
Mallalieu, K., BSEE M.I.T., MSc Roch., PhD Lond.
  Sr. Lectr.; Head*
Sharma, C., BSc WI, MSc WI, PhD WI Sr.
  Lectr.
Other Staff: 8 Lectrs.; 2 Asst. Lectrs.; 5 Hon.
  Consultants; 1 Temp. Sr. Lectr.
Vacant Posts: 1 Prof.; 2 Sr. Lectrs.; 2 Lectrs.
Research: communication systems (network
  performance analysis and simulation,
  telecommunications innovations for
  developing countries, telecommunications
  policy and regulation for social inclusion,
  wireless communications for poverty
  alleviation); computer systems (high
  performance architecture, multimedia
  processing and archiving, reconfigurable
  computing, scholarship of teaching and
  learning); control systems (control using
  fuzzy logic and artificial intelligence (AI)
  concepts, development of interactive online
  control systems laboratories, robust control
  system design); energy systems (analysis
  and simulation of power systems, motor
  drive, techniques for the analysis of small
  electric grids, wind energy); reconfigurable
  embedded computing using field
  programmable gate array (FPGA)
  technology (computer-aided design (CAD)

tools for process control, linear integrated
  circuit application, multi-media signal
  processing, robotics, sound profile of the
  steel pan)

Engineering, Mechanical

Fax: 662 4414 E-mail: mecheng@eng.uwi.tt
Dumas, McD., BSc(Eng) WI, MS N.Y.State, MBA
  N.Y.State, PhD N.Y.State, FIMechE Sr. Lectr.
Ekwue, E. I., BEng Nigeria, MSc Cran., PhD Cran.
  Sr. Lectr.
Imbert, C. A. C., BSc(Eng) WI, MTech Brun.,
  PhD WI Prof.
Keshavan, S. Y., BE B'lore., ME IISc., PhD IISc.
  Sr. Lectr.
Kochhar, G. S., BE Baroda, MS Wis., PhD WI
  Prof.
Lau, S. M. J., BSc(Eng) WI, MEng Cornell, MSc
  WI Sr. Lectr.
Lewis, Winstin G., BScEng WI, MPhil WI, PhD
  Tech.UNS Sr. Lectr.; Head*
Narayan, C. V., MSc Guelph, PhD Mich., BSc
  Prof.
Persad, P., BSc WI, BSc(Eng) WI, PhD WI Sr.
  Lectr.
Pun, K., MSc Middx., MSc Sterling, MEd Manc.,
  MPhil City HK, PhD Middx. Prof.,
  Engineering, Industrial/Mechanical
Sankat, Clement, BSc WI, MSc WI, PhD Guelph
  Prof.
Other Staff: 5 Lectrs.; 11 Lectrs.†
Vacant Posts: 1 Prof.; 1 Sr. Lectr.; 1 Lectr.
Research: alternative energy technologies; food
  and agricultural engineering; industrial
  automation and engineering management
  systems; materials and manufacturing
  systems; thermodynamics, heat transfer and
  renewable energy resources

Environmental Studies

No staff at present
Research: soil classification; water quality

Food Production

Fax: 645 0479 E-mail: df@sta.uwi.edu
Ahmad, N., MSc Br.Col., PhD Nott. Prof. Emer.
Badrie, N., BSc WI, MSc WI, PhD WI Sr.
  Lectr.
Bekele, I., BSc Addis Ababa, MSc Reading, PhD
  Cornell Sr. Lectr.; Head*
Brathwaite, Richard A. I., BSc Poona, PhD
  Prof., Agronomy
Garcia, G., BSc WI, MSc WI, PhD WI Sr.
  Lectr.
Mohammed, M., BSc WI, MSc Guelph, PhD WI
  Sr. Lectr.
Rastogi, R. K., BVSc&AH GBP, MVSc GBP, PhD
  Minn. Sr. Lectr.
Robinson, D., BSc Reading, PhD Ulster Sr. Lectr.
Stone, R., BSc WI, MSc Guelph, PhD WI Sr.
  Lectr.
Wickham, Lynda, BSc WI, PhD WI Sr. Lectr.
Williams, H. E., MSc Wis., DVM Tor., PhD Edin.
  Prof. Emer.
Wilson, L. A., BSc Lond., MSc Lond., PhD Brist.
  Prof. Emer.
Wilson, M., BSc S'ton., PhD S'ton.
Other Staff: 5 Lectrs.; 1 Asst. Lectr.
Vacant Posts: 3 Profs.; 1 Sr. Lectr.

Geography

2 Sr. Lectrs.; 1 Lectr.
Vacant Posts: 1 Lectr.
Research: spatial and atmospheric sciences

History

Fax: 662 9684 E-mail: maria.peter@sta.uwi.edu
Brereton, Bridget, BA WI, MA Tor., PhD WI
  Prof.
Haraksingh, K., BA WI, LLB Lond., PhD Lond.
  Sr. Lectr.; Head*
Laurence, K. O., BA Camb., PhD Camb. Prof.
  Emer.; Co-ordinator, Archaeol. Centre
Pemberton, R., BA WI, MA WI, PhD WI Sr.
  Lectr.
Other Staff: 1 Visiting Prof.; 7 Lectrs.; 1
  Lectr.†; 2 Temp. Lectrs.; 1 Temp. Asst.
  Lectr.

Research: African history; American history; archaeology; Asian history; Caribbean/West Indian history

Law

Fax: 645 3232 E-mail: safiya@wow.net
Mendes, G., LLB WI Head*
Other Staff: 1 Lectr.
Vacant Posts: 1 Sr. Lectr.
Research: constitutional law; industrial relations law

Liberal Arts

Tel: 663 5059 Fax: 663 5059
    E-mail: libarts@carib-link.net
Singh, V., BA WI Head*
Other Staff: 10 Lectrs.; 2 Asst. Lectrs.; 2 Foreign Lang. Instrs.
Vacant Posts: 1 Sr. Lectr.; 2 Lectrs.

French

Carter, B., LèsL Besançon, MèsL Besançon, PhD WI Co-ordinator*
Walcott-Hackshaw, E., BA Boston, MA Boston, PhD Boston Co-ordinator*
Other Staff: 1 Lectr.; 1 Foreign Lang. Instr.
Research: contemporary Caribbean women writers; feminism; French language; life writing

Language and Linguistics

Cowie, Lancelot, BA WI, PhD WI Sr. Lectr.
Hodge, M., BA Lond., MPhil Lond. Sr. Lectr. (on leave)
Lalla, Barbara, BA WI, PhD WI Prof., Linguistics; Head*
Robertson, Ian, BA WI, PhD WI Sr. Lectr., Linguistics
Youssef, V., BA Reading, MA American(Cairo), PhD WI Sr. Lectr.
Other Staff: 6 Lectrs.; 1 Asst. Lectr.
Vacant Posts: 1 Sr. Lectr.; 1 Lectr.
Research: Caribbean dialectology; Creole linguistics; educational linguistics; issues in first and second language acquisition

Literatures in English

Aiyejina, F., BA Ife, MA Acad., PhD WI Sr. Lectr.
Rohlehr, D. F. G., BA Lond., PhD Birm. Prof.
Salick, R., BA Sir G.Wms., MA McG., PhD Manit. Sr. Lectr.
Singh, V., BA WI Sr. Lectr.
Other Staff: 2 Lectrs.
Vacant Posts: 1 Lectr.

Spanish Language

Cowie, Lancelot, BA WI, PhD WI Sr. Lectr.
Mansoor, R., BA Car., MA Car., PhD Laval Co-ordinator*
Other Staff: 1 Lectr.; 1 Asst. Lectr.; 1 Foreign Lang. Instr.
Research: Spanish language; Venezuelan literature; violence, narco-guerillas and narco-trafficking in Latin American literature

Life Sciences

Fax: 663 5241 E-mail: lifesci@fsa.uwi.tt
12 Lectrs.; 1 Asst. Lectr.; 2 Lectrs.†; 1 Curator
Vacant Posts: 1 Prof.; 3 Lectrs.

Biochemistry

Cockburn, B., BSc WI, PhD WI Subject Leader
Other Staff: 1 Lectr.; 1 Asst. Lectr.
Vacant Posts: 1 Lectr.
Research: biochemical and molecular basis of diabetes; enzymes of glucose metabolism

Plant Science

Duncan, J., BSc Lond., PhD St And. Prof. Emer., Botany
Sirju-Charran, G., BSc WI, PhD WI Sr. Lectr.; Head*
Spence, J. A., BSc Brist., PhD Brist. Prof. Emer., Botany
Umaharan, P., BSc Peradeniya, PhD WI Sr. Lectr.

Other Staff: 7 Lectrs.; 1 Temp Lectr.; 1 Curator
Research: entomology and plant pathology; general botany and ecology; plant and crop physiology; plant biotechnology; plant breeding

Zoology

Agard, J., BSc WI, MSc Manc., PhD WI Sr. Lectr.
Ramnarine, I., BSc WI, MSc Wales, MBA H-W, PhD WI Sr. Lectr.
Starr, C. K., BA Car., MA Kansas, PhD Georgia Sr. Lectr.
Other Staff: 4 Lectrs.; 1 Temp. Lectr.
Vacant Posts: 1 Prof.; 2 Lectrs.
Research: aquatic sciences and fisheries biology; management of wetlands and central ecosystems; parasitology; physiology and reproductive biology; terrestrial ecology and entomology

Management Studies

Fax: 662 1140 E-mail: deptmgmt@fss.uwi.tt
Arjoon, S., BSc Wat., MSc W.Ont. Sr. Lectr.; Head*
Baptiste, R., BA Howard, MA Howard, MSc Manc. Sr. Lectr.
Gayle, D., BA WI, MSc Lond., MA Calif., PhD Calif. Prof.
Ghosh, D., MBA Roch., PhD N.Y.State Prof.
Simms, E., BSc WI, MSc WI, MBA Ohio Sr. Lectr.
Other Staff: 10 Lectrs.
Vacant Posts: 1 Sr. Lectr.; 4 Lectrs.
Research: accounting (environmental accounting and reporting disclosure requirements); ethical considerations in business management; human resources management across cultures, organisational behaviour issues, selection and training; management information systems (qualitative issues); marketing (consumer behaviour, environmental and cultural dimensions of marketing, international marketing, service quality and customer satisfaction)

Mathematics and Computer Science

Fax: 645 7132 E-mail: dmcs@sta.uwi.edu

Vacant Posts: 1 Sr. Lectr.; 1 Lectr.
Research: electrostatics (magnets); fluid dynamics

Computer Science

Bernard, Margaret, BSc WI, MPhil WI, PhD WI Sr. Lectr.
Kalicharan, Noel, BSc WI, MSc Br.Col., PhD WI Sr. Lectr.
Mohan, Permanand, BSc WI, MSc Sask., PhD WI Sr. Lectr.
Nikov, Alexander, MSc Sofia, PhD Sofia, DrHabil Sr. Lectr.
Posthoff, Christian, DrRerNat Leip., DrIngHabil Prof.
Other Staff: 5 Lectrs.; 1 Asst. Lectr.
Research: artificial intelligence (AI); distributed computing; high performance computer (HPC); human computer interaction (HCI); logic functions and equations, Boolean modelling of discrete problems

Mathematics

Ali, Hydar, BA WI, MSc Lond., MPhil Sus., PhD WI Sr. Lectr.
Bhatt, Balswaroop, BSc Raj., MSc Raj., PhD Raj., FIMA Prof.
Farrell, Edward, BSc WI, MSc Wat., PhD Wat. Prof.
Ramkissoon, Harold, BSc WI, MSc Tor., PhD Calg. Prof., Applied Mathematics
Sahai, Ashok, MA Lucknow, PhD Lucknow Prof.
Wahid, Shanaz, BSc WI, MPhil WI, PhD WI Sr. Lectr.; Head*
Other Staff: 6 Lectrs.
Research: biostatistics; clinical research; electromagnetics/electromagnetism; statistics (tests of hypotheses); survival analysis

Medicine, School of

Fax: 663 983619 Lectrs.; 1 Temp. Lectr.
Vacant Posts: 2 Profs.; 1 Sr. Lectr.; 1 Lectr./Asst. Lectr.

Adult Medicine

Seemungal, T., BSc WI, MB BS WI, MSc WI, PhD Lond. Sr. Lectr.
Teelucksingh, S., MB BS WI, MBA WI, PhD Edin., FRCPEd Prof.; Head*
Other Staff: 12 Assoc. Lectrs.
Vacant Posts: 1 Prof.; Lectrs.

Anaesthetics and Intensive Care

Tel: 662 4030 Fax: 662 4030
Pitt-Miller, Phyllis, MB ChB Edin., FFARCS, FRCA Prof.
Other Staff: 3 Lectrs.; 9 Assoc. Lectrs.
Research: gender issues in medicine; intensive care; medical care

Child Health

Fax: 662 9596 E-mail: childhealth@ttst.com
Ali, Zulaika, MB BS WI, DM WI, DCH WI, FRCPCH Sr. Lectr.; Head, Clin. Med. Scis.
Omer, M., MB BCh Khart., FRCPEd, FRCP, FRCPCH Prof.; Head*
Other Staff: 3 Lectrs.; 2 Assoc. Lectrs.

Obstetrics and Gynaecology

Tel: 663 4319 Fax: 663 4319
    E-mail: obsgynfms@gmail.com
Bassaw, B., MB BS WI, FRCOG Sr. Lectr.
Gopeesingh, T. D., MB BS WI, MBA, FRCOG Sr. Lectr., Gynaecologic Oncology
Kuruvilla, A., MB BS WI, PhD Sr. Lectr.
Ramsewak, Samuel, MB BS WI, MD, FRCOG Prof.; Head*

Psychiatry

Hutchinson, G., BSc WI, MB BS WI, DM WI Sr. Lectr.
Maharajh, G., MB BS Sr. Lectr.
Other Staff: 3 Lectrs.; 6 Assoc. Lectrs.

Radiology and Nuclear Medicine

Fax: 662 7060
Khan, O., BSc Lond., MB BS Newcastle(UK), MSc Lond., PhD Lond. Sr. Lectr., Nuclear Medicine
Other Staff: 2 Lectrs.; 1 Assoc. Lectr.

Surgery

Tel: 663 4319 Fax: 663 4319
    E-mail: surgsci@tstt.net
Ali, Terry, MB BS WI, DM WI, FRCSEd Sr. Lectr.
Anatol, T., MB BCh N.U.I., FRCSEd, FRCSI Sr. Lectr., Paediatric Surgery
Butler, K. A., MB BS, FRCS, FACS Prof. Emer.
Cross, J., MB BCh, FRCSEd Prof. Emer., Neurosurgery
Naraynsingh, V., BSc Lond., MB BS WI, FRCSEd, FACS Prof.; Head*
Other Staff: 9 Lectrs.; 34 Assoc. Lectrs.; 1 Temp. Lectr.
Vacant Posts: 1 Sr. Lectr.
Research: ear, nose and throat (ENT) and general surgery; general orthopaedic and paediatric surgery

Para-Clinical Sciences

Tel: 663 3797 Fax: 663 3797
    E-mail: hdaisley_fma@hotmail.com
Jones-Lecointe, Altheia, BSc Lond., MB BS WI, PhD Lond. Head*
Other Staff: 14 Lectrs. (Community and Public Health 5, Microbiol. 1, Pathol. 4, Pharmacol. 1, Pharm. 3); 1 Asst. Lectr.
Vacant Posts: 2 Profs.; 1 Sr. Lectr.; 4 Lectrs.; 18 Assoc. Lectrs. (Community and Public Health 15, Microbiol. 1, Pathol. 2)
Research: community and public health, including dental health; microbiology;

pathology; pharmacology

Pathology/Microbiology

Daisley, H., BSc WI, MB BS WI, DM WI
Prof., Pathology
Ezenwaka, Chindum, BSc Ib., MSc Ib., MPhil
Ib., PhD Ib.   Sr. Lectr., Pathology
Jones-Lecointe, Altheia, BSc Lond., MB BS WI,
PhD Lond.   Sr. Lectr., Pathology
Monteil, Michele A., BSc Lond., MB BS WI, MSc
Lond., PhD Lond.   Sr. Lectr., Pathology
Orrett, Fitzroy, BSc MSc MB BS   Sr. Lectr.,
Microbiology
Other Staff: 5 Lectrs.; 3 Assoc. Lectrs.
Vacant Posts: 1 Prof.; 1 Sr. Lectr.; 1 Lectr.

Pharmacology

Tel: 663 8613 E-mail: pharmunit@yahoo.com
Pinto Pereira, Lexley, MB BS Bom., MD Bom.
Prof.
Other Staff: 3 Lectrs.
Vacant Posts: 1 Lectr.

Pharmacy Programme

Tel: 662 1472 Fax: 662 1472
E-mail: pharmacy@fms.uwi.tt
Gadad, Andanappa, MPharm   Prof.
Pillai, G., BPharm BITS, MPharm BITS, MSc
Br.Col., PhD Br.Col.   Prof., Pharmaceutics
Other Staff: 3 Lectrs.; 1 Asst. Lectr.

Public Health and Primary Care Unit

Tel: 645 2018 Fax: 645 5117
E-mail: publichealth@fms.uwi.tt
5 Lectrs.; 15 Assoc. Lectrs.
Research: community and public health,
including dental health

Physics

Fax: 662 9904 E-mail: physics@fans.uwi.tt
Achong, A., BSc WI, PhD WI   Lectr.; Head*
Knight, J. C., BSc WI, PhD Camb.   Sr. Lectr.
McDoom, I. A., BSc Lond., MSc WI, PhD WI
Sr. Lectr.
Saunders, R. McD., BSc WI, PhD Lond.   Prof.
Other Staff: 4 Lectrs.; 1 Asst. Lectr.
Research: astronomy (extragalactic and
theoretical); earth materials studies;
environmental physics; medical physics and
bioengineering; solar energy studies

Surveying and Land Information

Fax: 662 4414 E-mail: survey@eng.uwi.tt
Baban, S., BSc Baghdad, MSc Baghdad, PhD
E.Anglia, FGS, FRGS   Prof.
Brkovic, M. B., MSc Calif., PhD Belgrade   Prof.
Miller, Keith, BSc CNAA, PhD CNAA   Head*
Opadeyi, J., BSc Lagos, MBA WI, MSc Lagos,
MEng New Br., PhD New Br.   Sr. Lectr.
Other Staff: 6 Lectrs.; 4 Lectrs.†; 1 Temp.
Lectr.
Research: coastal zone and agriculture policy and
implementation; mapping and monitoring
of the environment, natural habitats and
the coastal zone using GIS; natural hazard
assessment and management; role of
physical planning and urban development
in the Caribbean; sustainable and improved
access to water and urban infrastructure

Veterinary Medicine, School of

Fax: 645 7428 E-mail: vetsch@tstt.net.tt
Adesiyun, A. A., DVM A.Bello, MPH Minn., PhD
Minn.   Prof., Veterinary Health; Dir.*
Adogwa, A. O., DVM A.Bello, LLB Lond., PhD
A.Bello   Sr. Lectr.
Bourne, G., BA Ohio, PhD Cinc.   Sr. Lectr.,
Veterinary Physiology
Cooper, J., FRCPath, FIBiol, FRCVS   Temp.
Prof.
Ezeokoli, Chukwudozie O., BS Cornell, DVM
Cornell, MS Kansas State, PhD Yale   Prof.;
Head, Distance Educn. and Outreach
Harewood, W., BSc WI, BVSc Qld., PhD Syd.
Lectr.
Isitor, G. N., MS Kansas, DVM A.Bello, PhD
A.Bello   Prof.

Molokwu, E. C., BS Tuskegee, MS Iowa, DVM
Tuskegee, PhD A.Bello   Sr. Lectr., Veterinary
Physiology
Offiah, Veronica, BSc Ib., MSc Ib., PhD Nigeria
Sr. Lectr.
Other Staff: 11 Lectrs.; 1 Asst. Lectr.; 1 Temp
Asst. Lectr.
Vacant Posts: 1 Prof.; 1 Lectr./Asst. Lectr.
Research: parasitology; pharmacology;
physiology; public health; veterinary
anatomy

SPECIAL CENTRES, ETC

Analytical Services Unit

Tel: 645 9632 Fax: 645 9632
E-mail: asu@tstt.net.tt
Eudeoxia, Guais, BSc WI, PhD WI   Head*
Research: agricultural and environmental
sampling and analysis

ANSA McAL Psychological Research
Centre

E-mail: dchadee@fss.uwi.tt
Chadee, D., BSc WI, PhD WI   Lectr.;
Manager*

Business Development Unit

Faculty of Science and Agriculture
Tel: 662 2686 Fax: 662 1182
E-mail: bdu@fans.uwi.tt
Narinesingh, Dyer, BSc WI, MSc WI, PhD WI
Prof.; Head*
Other Staff: 10 Lectrs.

Business, Institute of (IOB)

Tel: 645 6700 Fax: 662 1411
E-mail: corporate@uwi-iob.net
Balgobin, Rolph, BSc WI, EMBA WI, DBA Manc.
Sr. Lectr.; Exec. Dir.*
Gray, Michael, BScEcon WI   Programme Dir.
McDonald, Colin, BSc WI, MSc ITC (Netherlands),
PhD Gött.
Oakley, Mark, BSc Newcastle(UK), PhD Aston
Prof.; Academic Dir.
Research: corporate turnaround; financial services
and energy sectors; micro, small and
medium enterprises sector; sustainable
development; tourism

Caribbean Agricultural Research and
Development Institute

Tel: 645 1206 Fax: 645 6357
E-mail: hresources@cardi.org
Parham, Wendel, BSc WI, PhD NZ, MSc   Exec.
Dir.*
Research: agriculture and development

Caribbean Food and Nutrition Institute

Tel: 645 2917 Fax: 663 1544
E-mail: cfni@cablenett.net
Research: assessment of tertiary food safety
training needs in the English-speaking
Caribbean; knowledge and practices of
health care personnel in the area of
nutrition in the management of chronic
diseases; nutrition for HIV/AIDS treatment
and care

Caribbean Industrial Research Institute

Tel: 662 7161 Fax: 662 7177
E-mail: cariri@trinidad.net
Shah, L. Ali, BSc WI, MSc WI, MS Rutgers
Chief Executive Officer*
Research: development of quality management
systems; environmental engineering; food
and biotechnology; laboratory testing

Cocoa Research Unit

Tel: 662 8788 Fax: 662 8788
E-mail: cru@cablenett.net
Butler, D., BSc Nott., MSc Brist., PhD Brist.
Head*
Other Staff: 2 Res. Fellows
Vacant Posts: 1 Botanist/Collector
Research: cacao germplasm resistance to witches'
broom disease; collection, conservation,
characterisation, verification and evaluation

of cacao germplasm; germplasm
enhancement and distribution; disease
resistance in cacao and molecular markers;
molecular characterisation of the cocoa
germplasm; physical, chemical and
organoleptic parameters of fine and bulk
cocoa

Continuing Studies, School of (SCS)

Tel: 645 3029 Fax: 645 8270
E-mail: scscmpus@tstt.net.tt
Bernard, Lennox, BA WI, MEd Tor., PhD Sheff.
Sr. Lectr.; Resident Tutor; Head*

Creative and Festival Arts, Centre for

Tel: 663 2222 Fax: 663 2222
E-mail: festival@fhe.uwi.tt
Gibbons, R., BA WI, MPhil WI   Lectr.
Lyndersay, D., MA Vic.(BC), PhD Ib.   Sr. Lectr.
Sharma, S., MMus N.Illinois, BMus   Lectr.;
Head*
Other Staff: 5 Lectrs.; 1 Temp. Lectr.
Research: evolution of music cultures in Trinidad
and Tobago; folk religion and ritual;
indigenous cultural traditions; the Orisha
movement in Trinidad and Tobago;
transmission, retention and re-creation of
the Calypso

Criminology and Criminal Justice,
Centre for

Fax: 645 1020 E-mail: crimrd@trinidad.net
Deosaran, R., BSc Tor., MA Tor., PhD Tor.
Prof.; Head*
Research: civic attitudes, psychological capital
and school deviance; prison recidivism in
Trinidad and Tobago: reduction,
rehabilitation, reform and restorative justice;
reducing youth deviance in schools; social
psychology of fear of crime; youth crime:
psychological capital and relative deprivation
in the Caribbean

Distance Education, Centre for

Tel: 645 2995 Fax: 645 2424
E-mail: disted@tstt.net.tt
Kuboni, O., BA WI, MA C'dia., PhD Open(UK)
Campus Co-ordinator*
Other Staff: 1 Lectr.; 1 Telecommunicns.
Specialist; 1 Temp. Lectr.

Engineering Institute

Tel: 662 6267 Fax: 662 6267
E-mail: enginst@eng.uwi.tt
Rajpaulsingh, W., BSc WI, MPhil WI
Manager*

Field Station

Tel: 662 2750 Fax: 663 8689
E-mail: uss@tstt.net.tt
Ragoobarsingh, A., BSc WI, MPhil WI
Contract Officer*

Gender and Development Studies,
Centre for

E-mail: gender@cgds.uwi.tt
Reddock, Rhoda, BSc WI, MSc Inst.Soc.Stud.(The
Hague), PhD Amst.   Prof.; Head*
Other Staff: 1 Prof.; 1 Outreach and Res.
Officer
Research: autobiographies of women in science
in Trinidad and Tobago; gender differentials
in educational performance at the secondary
and tertiary levels in Trinidad and Tobago;
gender, science and technology; men and
masculinities; the making of feminisms in
the Caribbean

Instructional Development Unit

Tel: 663 9236 Fax: 662 0558
E-mail: idu@idu.uwi.tt
Edwards-Henry, Anna-May, BSc WI, MSc WI,
PhD WI   Programme Co-ordinator
Other Staff: 1 Educnl. Technologist

International Relations, Institute of

Fax: 663 9685 E-mail: iirt@sta.uwi.edu

Francis, Anselm, LLB Lond., LLM Lond. Sr. Lectr.

Girvan, Norman, BSc Lond., BSc WI, PhD Lond. Prof. Res. Fellow

Kirton, Raymond M., BA Guy., MSc Georgetown, PhD Texas Sr. Lectr.

Lewis, Vaughan, BA Manc., MA Manc., PhD Manc. Prof.

Nurse, Keith, BA W.Ont., PhD WI Sr. Lectr.

Ramsaran, Ramesh, BSc WI, MSc WI, PhD WI Prof.

Shaw, Timothy, BA Sus., MA E.Af., MA Prin., PhD Prin.

Other Staff: 2 Lectrs.; 2 Librarians

Research: international trade and finance; law of the sea; regional integration; security issues and conflict resolution; sustainable development

Language Learning, Centre for

Tel: 645 2278 Fax: 662 0758

E-mail: cll@fhe.uwi.tt

Carter, B., LèsL Besançon, MèsL Besançon, PhD WI Dir.*

Other Staff: 1 Asst. Lectr.; 1 Foreign Lang. Instr.

Vacant Posts: 1 Lectr.

Research: teaching of foreign languages in the secondary school system (Spanish, French, Hindi); teaching of Spanish to young children ages 6-10

Medical Sciences Education, Centre for

Tel: 645 8639 E-mail: cmse@tstt.net.tt

3 Lectrs.

Vacant Posts: 1 Prof./Head*; 1 Lectr.

Monetary Studies, Caribbean Centre for

Tel: 645 1174 Fax: 645 6017

E-mail: ccmsacad@fss.uwi.tt

Jackson, C., BSc WI, MSc WI, PhD Lond. Exec. Dir.; Head*

Other Staff: 2 Res. Fellows

Vacant Posts: 1 Dir.; 2 Res. Fellows; 1 Librarian

Research: banking activity and performance in the Caribbean; economic growth and development in the Caribbean; financial regulation in the Caribbean; mergers and acquisitions in the Caribbean; tax reform and financial development

National Herbarium

Tel: 645 3509 Fax: 663 9686

E-mail: trinherb@centre.uwi.tt

Comean, Yasmin, BSc WI Curator*

Seismic Research Unit

Tel: 662 4659 Fax: 663 9293

E-mail: uwiseismic@uwiseismic.com

Robertson, Richard, BSc WI, MPhil Leeds, PhD WI Head*

Other Staff: 6 Res. Fellows

Research: volcanological and seismological activity in the Eastern Caribbean region

Social and Economic Studies, Sir Arthur Lewis Institute of

Tel: 645 6329 Fax: 645 6329

E-mail: salises@fss.uwi.tt

Watson, P., BCom Leeds, LèsEcon Paris, MèsEcon Paris, PhD Paris Prof.; Dir.*

Other Staff: 3 Res. Fellows

Research: computable general equilibrium model of the Caribbean Community (CARICOM) region; computable general equilibrium model of Trinidad and Tobago; empirical Caribbean modelling with emphasis on the evaluation of economic policy; poverty and poverty reduction with special reference to the Caribbean; the hidden economy in the Caribbean region (size, causes, consequences)

Sports and Physical Education Centre

Tel: 645 9239 Fax: 645 9239

E-mail: info@spec.uwi.tt

Gloudon, Iva, BSc Ill., MSc Ill., EdD Mass. Dir.*

Sustainable Economic Development Unit

Tel: 662 9461 Fax: 662 9461

E-mail: sedu@fss.uwi.tt

Pantin, D., BSc WI, MPhil Sus. Sr. Lectr.; Co-ordinator*

Other Staff: 1 Res. Assoc.

CONTACT OFFICERS

Accommodation. Director, Student Services: Charles, Deidre, BSc WI, MSc Warw., MBA Massey

(E-mail: student.advisory@admin.uwi.tt)

Admissions (first degree). Assistant Registrar (Admissions): Brown, P., BA WI

(E-mail: admis@admin.uwi.tt)

Admissions (higher degree). Senior Assistant Registrar (Postgraduate Studies and Research): Charles-Smythe, Deborah, BA WI, MSc Lond.

(E-mail: postgrad@admin.uwi.tt)

Adult/continuing education. Resident Tutor (Adult/continuing education): Bernard, Lennox, BA WI, MEd Tor., PhD Sheff.

(E-mail: scscmpus@tstt.net.tt)

Alumni. Administrative Assistant (Alumni): Pierre, S., BSc WI

(E-mail: gog@admin.uwi.tt)

Archives. Record Manager: Georges, Jo-Ann, BA WI, MLS Col.

(E-mail: recordscentre@admin.uwi.tt)

Careers. Director, Student Services: Charles, Deidre, BSc WI, MSc Warw., MBA Massey

(E-mail: dcharles@admin.uwi.tt)

Development/fund-raising. Director, Business Development: Rampersad, D., MA Camb., DPhil Oxf.

(E-mail: development@admin.uwi.tt)

Distance education. Campus Co-ordinator: Kuboni, O., BA WI, MA C'dia., PhD Open(UK) (E-mail: disted@tstt.net.tt)

Estates and buildings/works and services. Estate Manager: Nobbee, Kenrick, BSc

Strath., MSc Strath.

(E-mail: worksstaff@works.uwi.tt)

Examinations. Senior Assistant Registrar (Examinations): George, Jessie-Ann, BA Howard, MEd Howard

(E-mail: exams@admin.uwi.tt)

Finance. Campus Bursar: Bada, Lylla, BA Brist.

(E-mail: bursar@admin.uwi.tt)

General enquiries. Director, Marketing and Communications: De Four-Gill, Dawn-Marie, BSc WI, MBA City(UK)

(E-mail: markcom@admin.uwi.tt)

Health services. Campus Doctor: Singh, N., MB BS WI (E-mail: nsingh@hsu.uwi.tt)

Library (chief librarian). Campus Librarian: Rouse-Jones, Prof. Margaret, BA WI, MA Johns H., PhD Johns H.

(E-mail: mainlib@library.uwi.tt)

Library (enquiries). Campus Librarian: Rouse-Jones, Prof. Margaret, BA WI, MA Johns H., PhD Johns H. (E-mail: mainlib@library.uwi.tt)

Marketing. Director, Marketing and Communications: De Four-Gill, Dawn-Marie, BSc WI, MBA City(UK)

(E-mail: markcom@admin.uwi.tt)

Purchasing. Campus Bursar: Bada, Lylla, BA Brist. (E-mail: bursar@admin.uwi.tt)

Scholarships, awards, loans. Director, Student Services: Mike, C., BSc WI, MBA H-W

(E-mail: student.advisory@admin.uwi.tt)

Scholarships, awards, loans. Assistant Registrar (Admissions): Brown, P., BA WI

(E-mail: admis@admin.uwi.tt)

Security. Director, Security: Richardson, Wayne, BA WI, LLB Lond.

(E-mail: wrichardson@police.uwi.tt)

Sport and recreation. Director, Sports and Physical Education Centre: Gloudon, Iva, BSc Ill., MSc Ill., EdD Mass.

(E-mail: info@spec.uwi.tt)

Strategic planning. Director, Planning and Development: Greaves, Carlyle, BS WI, LLM Essex, DM McG.

(E-mail: planning@admin.uwi.tt)

Student welfare/counselling. Director, Student Services: Charles, Deidre, BSc WI, MSc Warw., MBA Massey

(E-mail: student.advisory@admin.uwi.tt)

Student welfare/counselling. Student Counsellor: Jackman, A., BA Middx., MSc Lond. (E-mail: ajackman@hsu.uwi.tt)

Students from other countries. Co-ordinator, International Studies and Exchanges: Warner-Poon-Kwong, B., BSc WI, IMBA WI

(E-mail: bwarner@fss.uwi.tt)

Students from other countries. Assistant Registrar (Admissions): Brown, P., BA WI

(E-mail: admis@admin.uwi.tt)

Women. Head, Centre for Gender and Development Studies: Reddock, Prof. Rhoda, BSc WI, MSc Inst.Soc.Stud.(The Hague), PhD Amst. (E-mail: gender@cgds.uwi.tt)

[Information supplied by the institution as at 19 October 2007, and edited by the ACU]

ZAMBIA

Copperbelt University (p. 2005)   University of Zambia (p. 2006)

DIRECTORY TO SUBJECTS OF STUDY

The table below shows which subjects are available for study and/or research at the universities in Zambia. U = may be studied for first degree course; M = may be studied for master's degree course; D = research facilities to doctoral level; X = all three levels (UMD).

	Copperbelt	Zambia
Accountancy/Accounting	UM	
Administration/Administrative Studies	UM	X
Agriculture/Agricultural Science		U
Agronomy/Soil Science	U	M
Animal Science/Husbandry/Production		M
Applied Chemistry		UM
Applied Physics		UM
Architecture	U	
Banking/Finance	UM	
Behavioural Sciences	UM	
Biochemistry	U	
Biology	U	UM
Biophysics		UM
Biostatistics		UM
Biotechnology	U	
Botany/Plant Science	U	
Building/Built Environment/Construction	U	
Business Administration	UM	
Business Economics		UM
Business/Commerce	U	
Chemistry	U	UM
Communication/Journalism/Media Studies		UM
Community Health		UM
Community Medicine		UM
Community Studies		UM
Computer Science	U	UM
Conservation Studies	U	
Counselling		U
Criminal Justice/Public Policy		UM
Crop Science/Production	U	UM

	Copperbelt	Zambia
Dentistry		UM
Development Studies		X
Ecology	U	
Economic Planning and Development		X
Economics	UM	X
Economics Agricultural/Agribusiness		UM
Education		X
Education Adult		UM
Education Distance		X
Education Primary		X
Education Secondary		X
Education Special		X
Education Tertiary		X
Educational Administration		X
Educational Psychology		X
Electronics		X
Engineering	U	X
Engineering Chemical/Petrochemical/Process	U	
Engineering Civil/Environmental/Structural	U	
Engineering Computer	U	
Engineering Electrical/Electronic	U	
Engineering Instrumentation	U	
Engineering Manufacturing	U	
Engineering Metallurgical/Mining	U	
Engineering Software	U	
English		X
Environmental Health		X
Environmental Management		X
Environmental Science/Studies	U	X
Estate Management	U	

	Copperbelt	Zambia
Ethics, Law and Governance		X
Food Science/Nutrition/Home Science/Dietetics		UM
Geography		X
Geology/Earth Sciences/Atmospheric Studies	U	
Health Education		UM
Health Sciences/Studies		UM
History		X
Housing/Real Estate	U	
Human Biology		X
Human Movement/Kinesiology/Biomechanics		U
Industrial Relations/Personnel/HRM	UM	
Industrial and Organisation Psychology		U
Information Science/Studies/Systems	UM	
Information Technology	U	U
International Business		U
International Finance		U
International Marketing		U
Land Resource Science	U	
Language Teaching/Learning		X
Language and Communication	U	
Languages, Modern		X
Law Business/Commercial/Economic/Industrial		U
Law Civil		X
Law Property/Construction/Housing	U	
Law/Legal Studies		U
Management	UM	
Management Information Systems	U	
Marketing	UM	
Materials Science	U	
Mathematics	UM	X
Medicine, Obstetrics and Gynaecology		UM
Medicine, Orthopaedic		UM
Medicine, Paediatric		UM

	Copperbelt	Zambia
Medicine, Palliative		UM
Medicine/Surgery		U
Mobile Communications/Telecommunications	U	
Natural Resource Studies	U	
Nursing Education/Administration		UM
Nursing/Midwifery		UM
Pharmacy/Pharmaceutical Science		UM
Philosophy		X
Physical Education/Sports Science		UM
Physics		X
Physiotherapy		UM
Planning/Landscape Studies	U	
Plant Pathology	U	
Politics/Political Science/Government		X
Population Studies/Demography		X
Project Management	U	
Psychiatry		UM
Psychology		X
Psychology Clinical		UM
Public Administration		X
Remote Sensing	U	U
Rural Studies/Development		X
Social Work/Studies		X
Sociology		X
Surveying/Quantity Surveying	U	
Taxation		U
Teacher Training		X
Urban Studies	U	
Veterinary Science		UM
Wildlife Management	U	
Wood Science	U	
Zoology	U	

COPPERBELT UNIVERSITY

Founded 1987

Member of the Association of Commonwealth Universities

Postal Address: PO Box 21692, Kitwe, Zambia
Telephone: (02) 222066 **Fax:** (02) 228319 **E-mail:** info@cbu.ac.zm
URL: http://www.cbu.edu.zm

VICE-CHANCELLOR*—Musonda, Prof. Mutale M., BVM *Nair.*, PhD *Azabu*
DEPUTY VICE-CHANCELLOR—Beele, Ernest M., LLB *Zambia*, MA *Warw.*, LLM *Wis.*, PhD *Warw.*
REGISTRAR‡—Ilunga, A. M., BA *Zambia*
BURSAR—Musonda, F., FCIS
LIBRARIAN—(vacant)
DEAN OF STUDENTS—Chilufya, M. K., BA *Zambia*, MA(Ed) Trinity(Dub.)
CHIEF INTERNAL AUDITOR—Katongo, M.

GENERAL INFORMATION

History. The university was established in 1987.

Admission to first degree courses. General entrance requirements: minimum 5 passes in General Certificate of Education (GCE) exam, or credit passes in at least 5 subjects at Cambridge Overseas School Certificate level, or equivalent.

First Degrees (see also Zambian Directory to Subjects of Study). BAc, BArch, BBA, BEng, BSc.
  Length of course. Full-time: BAc, BBA: 4 years; BSc: 4–5 years; BArch, BEng: 5 years.

Higher Degrees (see also Zambian Directory to Subjects of Study).
  Master's. MBA.
  Admission. First degree in business administration, commerce, accounting or economics and three years work experience.
  Length of course. Full-time: MBA: 1½ years. Part-time: MBA: 2 years.

Libraries. Volumes: 35,000. Periodicals subscribed to: 148. Special collections: Zambiana (publications on Zambia or by Zambians; government documents; documents from international organisations (IMF, World Bank, UN Agencies etc.).

Income (2005–2006). Total, K49,500,000,000.

Statistics. Staff (2005–2006): 564 (185 academic, 379 non-academic). Students (2005–2006): full-time 3523 (2815 men, 708 women); part-time 186 (150 men, 36 women); master's 77 (63 men, 14 women).

FACULTIES/SCHOOLS

Built Environment, School of

Tel: (02) 225086 Fax: (02) 225086
  E-mail: sbe@cbu.ac.zm
Dean: Ngoma, G. C., BEng *Belf.*, MSc *Lough.*
Secretary: Mwangala, S.

Business, School of

Tel: (02) 227946 Fax: (02) 229354
  E-mail: deansb@cbu.ac.zm
Dean: Chama, S., BEng *Zambia*, MSc *Liv.*, PhD *Liv.*
Secretary: Chabala, B.

Natural Resources, School of

Tel: (02) 227946 E-mail: forestry@cbu.ac.zm
Dean: Chunda, E., BA(Educn) *Zambia*, MA *Wales*
Secretary: Muyunda, T. M.

Technology, School of

Tel: (02) 228212 Fax: (02) 228212
  E-mail: sot@cbu.ac.zm

Dean: Singh, I. S., BSc *Gorak.*, MSc *Ban.*, PhD *Ban.*
Secretary: Magaisa, E.

ACADEMIC UNITS

Accounting and Finance

Tel: (02) 228006 Fax: (02) 229354
  E-mail: deansb@cbu.ac.zm
Musokwa, P., BCom MACom   Head*
Other Staff: 5 Lectrs./Researchers

Architecture

Tel: (02) 225086 Fax: (02) 225086
  E-mail: sbe@cbu.ac.zm
Mabo, B., BArch *Zambia*, MArch T.U.Helsinki
  Head*
Other Staff: 5 Lectrs./Researchers

Building Science

Tel: (02) 225086 Fax: (02) 225086
  E-mail: sbe@cbu.ac.zm
Simushi, S., BSc *Zambia*, MSc *Lough.*   Head*
Other Staff: 6 Lectrs./Researchers

Business Administration

Tel: (02) 228006 Fax: (02) 229354
  E-mail: deansb@cbu.ac.zm
Mulambya, A., BA *Zambia*, MBA *Copperbelt*
  Head*
Other Staff: 15 Lectrs./Researchers

Computer Science

Tel: (02) 228212 Fax: (02) 228212
  E-mail: sot@cbu.ac.zm
Libati, H. M., BSc *T.H.Ilmenau*, MSc *T.H.Ilmenau*,
  PhD *Jena*   Head*
Other Staff: 15 Lectrs./Researchers
Research: delivery of the Internet to rural areas by satellite; network traffic monitoring; word processor development

Engineering, Chemical

Tel: (02) 228212 Fax: (02) 228212
  E-mail: sot@cbu.ac.zm
Maseka, K., BSc *Zambia*, MSc *Leeds*, PhD *Leeds*
  Head*
Other Staff: 15 Lectrs.
Research: water sector issues

Engineering, Civil, and Construction

Tel: (02) 223896 Fax: (02) 223896
  E-mail: sbe@cbu.ac.zm
Banda, D., BEng *Aberd.*, MSc *S'ton.*   Head*
Other Staff: 11 Lectrs.

Engineering, Electrical

Tel: (02) 228212 Fax: (02) 228212
  E-mail: sot@cbu.ac.zm
Kucheba, A. M., BEng *Zambia*, MEng *Zambia*
  Head*
Other Staff: 13 Lectrs./Researchers

Forest Resource Management

Tel: (02) 230923 E-mail: forestry@cbu.ac.zm
Njovu, C. Felix, BSc(Forestry) *Sokoine Ag.*,
  MSc(For) *Helsinki*   Head*
Other Staff: 12 Lectrs.
Research: management of Miombo woodlands

Wood Science and Technology

Tel: (02) 230923 E-mail: forestry@cbu.ac.zm
Malambo, Fabian M., BScFor *Dar.*, MSc *Wales*
  Head*
Other Staff: 4 Lectrs.
Research: bark harvesting

Mining

Tel: (02) 228212 Fax: (02) 228212
  E-mail: sot@cbu.ac.zm
Chulu, B., BSc *Zambia*, MSc *Colorado*   Head*
Other Staff: 11 Lectrs.

Planning

Tel: (02) 225086 Fax: (02) 225086
  E-mail: sbe@cbu.ac.zm
Okrah, J. A., MCP *Howard*   Head*
Other Staff: 8 Lectrs.

Postgraduate Studies

Tel: (02) 225434 E-mail: deansb@cbu.ac.zm
Taylor, T. K., BSc *Kumasi*, MSc DSc   Sr. Lectr.;
  Head*

Production Management

Tel: (02) 227946 Fax: (02) 229354
  E-mail: deansb@cbu.ac.zm
Banda, F., MSc(MechEng) *T.U.Sofia*   Head*
Mwila, Col. L., BSc *Zambia*, MSc *Zambia*   Head*
Other Staff: 8 Lectrs.

Real Estate Management

Tel: (02) 225086
Akakandelwa, N., BSc *Copperbelt*, MSc *Camb.*
  Head*
Other Staff: 7 Lectrs.

CONTACT OFFICERS

Academic affairs. Deputy Registrar (Academic Affairs): Chama, J. K.
  (E-mail: chamajk@cbu.ac.zm)
Accommodation. Accommodation Officer: Chilufya, M. K., BA *Zambia*, MA(Ed) Trinity(Dub.) (E-mail: mkchilufya@cbu.ac.zm)
Admissions (first degree). Deputy Registrar (Academic Affairs): Chama, J. K.
  (E-mail: chamajk@cbu.ac.zm)
Admissions (higher degree). Deputy Registrar (Academic Affairs): Chama, J. K.
  (E-mail: chamajk@cbu.ac.zm)
Adult/continuing education. Director, Centre for Lifelong Education: Mwila, Col. L., BSc *Zambia*, MSc *Zambia* (E-mail: clle@cbu.ac.zm)
Careers. Placement Officer: Chinyanta, P., BA *Zambia*
  (E-mail: patriciachinyanta@yahoo.com)

Computing services. Manager, Computer Centre: Khunga, B., BSc Zambia, MSc Essex (E-mail: khungab@cbu.ac.zm)

Estates and buildings/works and services. Director of Works: Ndhlovu, B. J., BEng Zambia (E-mail: bndhlovu@cbu.ac.zm)

Examinations. Deputy Registrar (Academic Affairs): Chama, J. K. (E-mail: chamajk@cbu.ac.zm)

Finance. Bursar: Musonda, F., FCIS (E-mail: musondaf@cbu.ac.zm)

General enquiries. Registrar: Ilunga, A. M., BA Zambia (E-mail: registrar@cbu.ac.zm)

Health services. Medical Officer: Simooya, O. O., BSc Zambia, MB ChB Zambia, MSc Ib. (E-mail: cbumed@zamnet.zm)

International office. Dean of Students: Chilufya, M. K., BA Zambia, MA(Ed) Trinity(Dub.) (E-mail: mkchilufya@cbu.ac.zm)

Library (chief librarian). Librarian: (vacant)

Marketing. Planning/Public Relations Officer: Chiyanika, R. M., BAEd Zambia (E-mail: tito@cbu.ac.zm)

Personnel/human resources. Deputy Registrar: Sheba, M. (E-mail: shebamk@cbu.ac.zw)

Public relations. Planning/Public Relations Officer: Chiyanika, R. M., BAEd Zambia (E-mail: tito@cbu.ac.zm)

Publications. Planning/Public Relations Officer: Chiyanika, R. M., BAEd Zambia (E-mail: tito@cbu.ac.zm)

Purchasing. Purchasing Officer: Chishimba, J. (E-mail: john.chishimba@cbu.ac.zm)

Safety. Director of Works: Ndhlovu, B. J., BEng Zambia (E-mail: bndhlovu@cbu.ac.zm)

Security. Chief Security Officer: Sendoi, J.

Sport and recreation. Sports Officer: Muyunda, J.

Staff development and training. Staff Development Officer: Chiyanika, R. M., BAEd Zambia (E-mail: tito@cbu.ac.zm)

Student welfare/counselling. Head, Counselling Unit: Chinyanta, P., BA Zambia (E-mail: patriciachinyanta@yahoo.com)

Student welfare/counselling. Head, Counselling Unit: Chinyanta, P., BA Zambia (E-mail: patriciachinyanta@yahoo.com)

[Information supplied by the institution as at 5 May 2006, and edited by the ACU]

UNIVERSITY OF ZAMBIA

Founded 1965

Member of the Association of Commonwealth Universities

Postal Address: PO Box 32379, Lusaka, Zambia
Telephone: (01) 293058 **Fax:** (01) 253952 **E-mail:** registrar@unza.zm
URL: http://www.unza.zm

VICE-CHANCELLOR*—Simukanga, Prof. Stephen, BMinSc Zambia, MMinSc Zambia, PhD Strath.
DEPUTY VICE-CHANCELLOR—Mwenya, Wilson N. M., BScAgric MSc PhD
REGISTRAR‡—Ng'andu, Alvert N., BEng Zambia, MSc Cran., PhD Nott.
BURSAR—Chitambala, Boniface M., BA
UNIVERSITY LIBRARIAN (ACTING)—Akakandelwa, A., BALS Zambia, MLIS Botswana, PhD Antwerp
DEAN OF STUDENTS—Chiboola, Hector, MA Reading

GENERAL INFORMATION

History. The university was established in 1965 by an Act of parliament.
Is is located about 7km east of Lusaka.

Admission to first degree courses. Applicants must hold passes at credit level in at least five subjects (in certain combinations) in the Zambian School Certificate (or Cambridge Overseas School Certificate) and passes in at least five subjects (in certain combinations) at GCE O Level; or passes in GCE A Level (a total of five subjects, which may include credits obtained at O Level); or a two-year diploma of this university or an institution in associate relationship with the university.
Other qualifications may be accepted, if approved by Senate.

Libraries. Volumes: 500,000. Periodicals subscribed to: 2700.

Statistics. Students (2007–2008): full-time 7984; part-time 161; distance education/external 1949; undergraduate 10,319; master's 284; doctoral 24.

FACULTIES/SCHOOLS

Agricultural Sciences

Tel: (01) 250587 E-mail: dean-agric@unza.zm
Dean: Lungu, Judith C. N., MSc Mass., PhD Manit.

Education

Tel: (01) 291381 E-mail: dean-edu@unza.zm
Dean: Chakanika, W., BA Hull, MA Hull

Engineering

Tel: (0211) 293792 Fax: (0211) 293792
E-mail: dean-eng@unza.zm
Dean: Wamukwambwa, C. K., MSc Bucharest, PhD Erlangen-Nuremberg

Humanities and Social Sciences

Tel: (01) 253827 E-mail: dean-hss@unza.zm
Dean: Phiri, Prof. Biszerk J., BA(Educn) Zambia, MA Sus., DPhil Sus.

Law

E-mail: dean-law@unza.zm
Dean: Munalula, Margaret M., LLB Zambia, LLM Zambia, MA Inst.Soc.Stud.(The Hague), JSD

Medicine

E-mail: deanmed@medicine.unza.zm
Dean: Mulla, Y., BSc Zambia, MB ChB Zambia, MChOrth Liv., MMed

Mines

Tel: (0211) 294086 Fax: (0211) 294086
E-mail: dean@mines.unza.zm
Dean: Kambani, S., BMinSc Zambia, MSc McG., PhD Montana

Natural Sciences

Tel: (01) 254406 Fax: (01) 254406
E-mail: dean-ns@unza.zm
Dean: Banda, S. F., BScEd Zambia, MSc Manc., PhD Manc.

Veterinary Medicine

Tel: (01) 254406 Fax: (01) 254406
E-mail: dean-vet@unza.zm
Dean (Acting): Phiri, G. K., DVM Leip., PhD Edin., MVSc

ACADEMIC UNITS

Adult Education and Extension Studies (AEES)

Tel: (01) 292702 Fax: (01) 292702
E-mail: aees.edu@edu.unza.zm
Chakanika, W., BA Hull, MA Hull   Head*
Mtonga, H. M., MEd PhD
Sibalwa, D., MEd Indiana, PhD Mich., BAEd

Agricultural Economics and Extension Education

Tel: (01) 295419
E-mail: ruralecon@agric.unza.zm
Kalinda, H. T., MSc Guelph, PhD Guelph   Head*
Maimbo, F., BA Zambia, MSc Zambia, MPhil Reading

Animal Science

Tel: (01) 295422 E-mail: animal@agric.unza.zm
Daura, M. T., MSc Kansas, PhD W.Virginia, BAgriSci   Head*
Lungu, Judith C. N., MSc Mass., PhD Manit.   Sr. Lectr.
Nyirenda, Drinah B., BAgricSc Zambia, MSc Zambia, PhD Calif.
Yambayamba, E. S. K., BAgricSc Zambia, MSc Alta., PhD Alta.

Biological Sciences

Tel: (01) 254406
E-mail: biology@natsci.unza.zm
Chidumayo, E. N., BSc MSc   Prof.
Kapooria, R. G., BSc Agra, MSc Agra, PhD Agra   Prof.
Mbata, K. J., BSc Iowa, PhD Iowa   Prof.
Mubila, Likezo, MSc Salf., PhD Liv., BScEd   Sr. Lectr.
Mumba, L. E., BSc Zambia, MSc Wales, PhD Camb.   Prof.
Mwauluka, K., BSc Lond., PhD Cant.   Prof.
Nkunika, P. O. Y., BSc Lond., MSc Lond., PhD   Sr. Lectr.
Zulu, J. N., BSc Zambia, PhD Lond.   Assoc. Prof.; Head*

Chemistry and Biochemistry

Tel: (01) 254406
E-mail: chemistry@natsci.unza.zm
Anekwe, G. E., BSc Cuttington, MSc Tuskegee, PhD N.Y.   Prof.
Banda, S. F., BScEd Zambia, MSc Manc., PhD Manc.   Sr. Lectr.

Belenavicius, K., MSc U.S.S.R.Acad.Sc., PhD
  U.S.S.R.Acad.Sc., DocenCiencias Kaunas   Prof.
Cernak, J., PhD Purkyne, MSc CSc   Prof.
Mbewe, B., MSc Sus., PhD Cape Town   Head*
Prakash, S., BSc Lucknow, MSc Lucknow, PhD
  Lucknow   Sr. Lectr.
Siamwiza, M. N., AB New Br., MSc M.I.T., PhD
  M.I.T.   Prof.

Crop Science

Tel: (01) 295655 Fax: (01) 295655
  E-mail: crop@agric.unza.zm
Deedat, Y., MSc Guelph, PhD Manit., BSc   Sr.
  Lectr.
Mwala, M. S., BAgrSc Zambia, MSc S.Dakota, PhD
  Missouri   Head*
Other Staff: 10 Lectrs.; 2 Res. Fellows

Development Studies

Tel: (01) 253827 E-mail: devstud@hss.unza.zm
Lipalile, M., BA Zambia, MA Inst.Soc.Stud.(The
  Hague)
Matenga, C. R., BA Zambia, MSc Edin.   Acting
  Head*
Wonani, C., BA Zambia, MA Inst.Soc.Stud.(The
  Hague)
Other Staff: 5 Lectrs.; 2 Res. Staff

Economic Studies

Tel: (01) 290475
  E-mail: economics@hss.unza.zm
Ndulo, M., BA Zambia, MA Ohio, PhD Mich.
  Prof.; Head*
Seshamani, V., BA Bom., MA Bom., MS Stan.
  Prof.
Other Staff: 7 Lectrs.

Educational Administration and Policy Studies (EAPS)

Tel: (01) 291381 E-mail: eaps.edu@unza.zm
Msango, H. J., MA Lond., BAEd   Head*
Other Staff: 4 Lectrs.; 4 Staff Devel. Fellows

Educational Psychology, Sociology and Special Education (EPSSE)

Tel: (01) 291381 Fax: (01) 291381
  E-mail: ochakulimba@edu.unza.zm
Chakulimba, Oswell, BAEd Zambia, MEd Harv.,
  PhD Tor.   Head*
Kalabula, Darlington, BAEd Zambia, MEd Birm.,
  PhD Birm.
Kapungulya, Paula P.
Other Staff: 11 Lectrs.

Engineering, Agricultural

Tel: (01) 253194
  E-mail: agriceng@eng.unza.zm
Lusambo, E., BEng Zambia, MSc Cran., PhD
  Newcastle(UK)   Head*
Simate, I. N., BEng Zambia, MSc Reading, PhD
  Newcastle(UK)   Sr. Lectr.
Other Staff: 3 Lectrs.; 2 Staff Devel. Fellows

Engineering, Civil

Tel: (01) 253194 E-mail: civil@eng.unza.zm
Mulenga, M. N., BEng Zambia, MSc Rutgers, PhD
  Alta.
Muya, M., BEng Zambia, MSc Lough., PhD Lough.
  Head*
Phiri, Z., BEng Zambia, MSc Leeds, PhD Kumamoto
Other Staff: 2 Lectrs.; 4 Staff Devel. Fellows

Engineering, Electrical and Electronic

Tel: (01) 253194 E-mail: elect@eng.unza.zm
Nyirenda, L. D., BEng Zambia, MSc Calif., PhD
  Calif.
Zulu, A. A., BEng Zambia, MSc H-W   Head*
Other Staff: 4 Lectrs.; 1 Res. Staff; 5 Staff
  Devel. Fellows

Engineering, Geomatic

E-mail: survey@eng.unza.zm
Zimba, R., BEng Zambia, MSc Cape Town   Head*
Other Staff: 6 Lectrs.; 2 Staff Devel. Fellows

Engineering, Mechanical

Tel: (01) 293791 Fax: (01) 293792
  E-mail: mechanical@eng.unza.zm
Chisale, P. C., PhD Kobe, MSc
Kanyanga, S. B., BEng Zambia, MSc Lond., PhD
  Sheff.   Prof.
Mwenda, H. M., BEng Zambia, MSc Strath., PhD
  Nott.
Siaminwe, L., BEng Zambia, MSc Lough., PhD
  Lough.   Head*
Wamukwamba, C. K., MSc Bucharest, PhD
  Erlangen-Nuremberg
Yamba, F. D., MSc Moscow, PhD Leeds   Prof.
Other Staff: 6 Lectrs.

Engineering, Mining

Tel: (01) 251672 Fax: (01) 294086
  E-mail: skambani@mines.unza.zm
Kambani, S., BMinSc Zambia, MSc McG., PhD
  Montana
Krishna, R., BEng Bihar, MPhil Nott., PhD Leeds
  Prof.
Mpande, M. M., BEng Zambia, MEng McG., PhD
  Leeds   Sr. Lectr.
Sinkala, T., BMinSc Zambia, MSc Luleå, PhD Luleå
  Head*
Other Staff: 2 Lectrs.; 2 Special Res. Fellows

Food Science and Technology

Tel: (01) 295141 Fax: (01) 295141
  E-mail: jshindano@agric.unza.zm
Lisulo-Mkandawire, Nyamba, BSc Zambia, MSc
  Ghent   Head*
Other Staff: 5 Lectrs.; 2 Special Res. Fellows

Gender Studies

Tel: (01) 291777
Raising, T., BA Amst., MA Amst., MA(Anthro)
  Amst., PhD Rotterdam   Head*
Other Staff: 2 Lectrs.

Geography

Tel: (01) 254406 Fax: (01) 253552
  E-mail: geog@natcsi.unza.zm
Kajoba, G. M., BA(Educn) Zambia, MA Arizona,
  MPhil Sus.   Sr. Lectr.
Mulenga, M. C., BAEd Zambia, MA Zambia, PhD
  Lond.   Head*
Sichingabula, H. M., BAEd Zambia, MSc S.Fraser,
  PhD S.Fraser   Sr. Lectr.
Singh, R. Y., BA Agra, MA Agra, PhD Ban.
Other Staff: 3 Lectrs.; 5 Special Res. Fellows; 2
  Staff Devel. Fellows

Geology

Tel: (01) 251672
  E-mail: geology@mines.unza.zm
Ahmed, A. H., BSc Khart., MSc Bucharest, PhD
  Bucharest   Head*
Nkhuwa, D. C. W., BSc Zambia, MSc T.H.Delft,
  PhD T.H.Aachen   Sr. Lectr.
Nyambe, I. A., BSc Zambia, MSc Windsor, PhD
  Ott.   Prof.
Tembo, F., BSc Zambia, MSc Zambia, PhD Gött.
  Sr. Lectr.
Other Staff: 2 Lectrs.; 2 Staff Res. Fellows

History

Tel: (01) 291777 E-mail: history@edu.unza.zm
Chondoka, A. Y., BA Zambia, MA Zambia, PhD
  Tor.   Sr. Lectr.
Krishna, K., PhD Patna, BA MA
Musambacime, M. C., BA Zambia, MA Wis.,
  PhD Wis.   Prof.
Musonda, F., MA Ghana, PhD Calif.   Sr. Lectr.
Phiri, B. J., BA Zambia, MA Zambia, PhD Dal.
  Sr. Lectr.
Siamwiza, B., BA Zambia, MA Zambia, PhD Camb.
  Sr. Lectr.; Head*
Other Staff: 7 Lectrs.; 2 Special Res. Fellows; 1
  Staff Devel. Fellow

In-Service Education and Advisory Services (ISEAS)

Tel: (01) 291381
  E-mail: iseas.edu@edu.unza.zm

Chishimba, C. P., BA Zambia, MEd Col., PhD Col.
  Prof.
Kakuwa, M, MA Havana   Head*
Other Staff: 2 Lectrs.; 1 Special Res. Fellow

Language and Social Science Education (LSSE)

Tel: (01) 291381 E-mail: lsse.edu@edu.unza.zm
Manchishi, Peter C., BA Besançon, MA Besançon,
  PhD Besançon   Sr. Lectr.
Milingo, Sr. Tomaida
Namafe, Charles M., MEd McG., PhD Lond.,
  BScEd   Sr. Lectr.
Sumbwa, George N., BAEd Zambia, MA Zambia
  Sr. Lectr.
Other Staff: 15 Lectrs.; 2 Staff Devel. Fellows

Law

Tel: (01) 290739 Fax: (01) 290733
  E-mail: deanlaw@law.unza.zm
Kulusika, S. E., LLB Khart., LLM Leip.   Sr. Lectr.
Munalula, Margaret M., LLB Zambia, LLM
  Zambia, MA Inst.Soc.Stud.(The Hague), JSD   Sr.
  Lectr.; Head*
Mvunga, P. M., LLB Zambia, LLM Harv., PhD
  Lond.   Prof.
Other Staff: 12 Lectrs.; 1 Res. Staff Member

Library Studies (LIS)

Tel: (01) 291361 Fax: (01) 291361
  E-mail: lis.edu@edu.unza.zm
Chifwepa, V., BALibSc W.Ont., MLIS Zambia,
  PhD Zambia   Sr. Lectr.
Mwacalimba, H., MSLS Syr.   Sr. Lectr.
Walusiku, L., BA Zambia, BALibSc Zambia,
  MALibSc Cape Town   Head*
Other Staff: 3 Lectrs.; 4 Staff Devel. Fellows

Literature and Languages

Tel: (01) 253827 E-mail: litlang@hss.unza.zm
Chanda, V. M., PhD Zaire   Prof., African
  Linguistics/General Linguistics
Hirst, S. B., MA Oxf., MA Essex, BA   Sr. Lectr.,
  English
Lyn, T., MA Essex   Sr. Lectr.
Mwape, F. A., BAEd Zambia, MA Zambia, PhD
  Lectr.; Head*
Sumaili, F. K. M., BA Zambia, MA N.Y.State, PhD
  N.Y.   Sr. Lectr.
Other Staff: 10 Lectrs.

Mass Communication

Tel: (01) 290035 Fax: (01) 290035
  E-mail: masscomm@hss.unza.zm
Makungu, K. M., MA Wales, BMC   Lectr.;
  Head*
Nkunika Billy, S., MFA   Sr. Lectr.
Other Staff: 8 Lectrs.

Mathematics and Science Education (MSE)

Tel: (01) 291381
  E-mail: mse.edu@edu.unza.zm
Hambokoma, Christopher, BScEd Zambia,
  MScEd Lond.   Sr. Lectr.; Head*
Kostyuk, Vasil, MSc Vinnitsa State T. U., PhD
  Kiev   Prof.
Other Staff: 4 Lectrs.; 1 Special Res. Fellows

Mathematics and Statistics

Tel: (01) 254406 E-mail: maths@natsci.unza.zm
Banda, B., BAEd Zambia, MSc Wales, PhD Iowa
  Lectr.; Head*
Jain, S., BA Delhi, MA Delhi, MPhil Delhi   Sr.
  Lectr.
Kunda, W., MSc Aston, PhD Hull, BSc   Sr.
  Lectr.
Ngwengwe, A., BSc Zambia, MSc Mass., PhD
  Cornell   Sr. Lectr.
Theo, D. D., BSc Zambia, MSc Wales, PhD Wales
  Prof.
Other Staff: 6 Lectrs.; 2 Special Res. Fellows; 4
  Staff Devel. Fellows

Metallurgy and Mineral Processing

Tel: (01) 251672 E-mail: metal@mines.unza.zm
Chama, C. C., BMinSc Zambia, MSc Penn.State, PhD Penn.State   Assoc. Prof.
Jere, E. H., BSc Rutgers, MSc Lehigh, PhD Lehigh   Sr. Lectr.
Lungu, C. V., BSc Birm., MSc Zambia   Acting Head*
Mwalula, J. B., PhD Ljubljana, BSc MSc MPhil   Sr. Lectr.
Nyirenda, R. L., BMinSc Zambia, MMinSc Zambia, PhD T.H.Delft   Sr. Lectr.
Simukanga, Stephen, BMinSc Zambia, MMinSc Zambia, PhD Strath.   Prof.
Witika, L. K., BSc Zambia, MSc Zambia, DSc Zambia   Sr. Lectr.
Other Staff: 1 Lectr.

Philosophy

Tel: (01) 253827 E-mail: phil@hss.unza.zm
Dillon-Mallone, C., LPh Greg., MSocSc Birm., PhD N.Y., BA   Prof.; Head*
Spiethenner, G., MA Graz, MSc Graz, MTheol Graz, PhD Graz   Sr. Lectr.
Other Staff: 5 Lectrs.; 1 Special Res. Fellow

Physics

Tel: (01) 254406
E-mail: physics@natsci.unza.zm
Husain, M. M., BSc Karachi, MSc Karachi, PhD Louvain   Sr. Lectr.
Jain, P. C., BSc Delhi, MSc Delhi, PhD Delhi   Prof.
Kaloyerou, P. N., BSc Salf., MSc Lond., PhD Lond.   Assoc. Prof.
Mweene, V. H., BSc Zambia, MSc Zambia, PhD Sur.   Lectr.; Head*
Singh, S., BSc Meerut, MSc Meerut, PhD Indore   Sr. Lectr.

Political and Administrative Studies

Tel: (01) 253827 E-mail: pas@hss.unza.zm
Bwalya, M. C., BA Syr., MA Syr., PhD E.Anglia
Kaela, L. C. W., BA Zambia, MSocSc Birm., PhD Boston
Momba, J. C., BA Zambia, MA Tor., PhD Tor.   Assoc. Prof.; Head*
Other Staff: 5 Lectrs.; 1 Special Res. Fellow; 1 Staff Devel. Fellow

Psychology

Tel: (01) 253827
E-mail: psychology@hss.unza.zm
Mwape, G., BA Zambia, MPhil Camb., MEd Zambia   Lectr.; Head*
Serpell, Prof. R., BA Oxf., DPhil Sus.   Prof.
Other Staff: 7 Lectrs.

Social Development Studies

Tel: (01) 253827 E-mail: sds@hss.unza.zm
Chikalanga, D., BA Zambia, MPhil Camb.
Kapungwe, A., BA Zambia, MA Ghana, MA Zambia, PhD Penn.   Sr. Lectr.
Lemba, M., BA Prin., MA Penn., PhD Penn.   Sr. Lectr.
Malungo, R. J. S., BA Zambia, MA Ghana, PhD Newcastle(NSW)   Sr. Lectr.; Head*
Matoka, P., BA Rhodes, PhD Warw.   Sr. Lectr.
Mukuka, L., BSW Zambia, MA Calif., MSc Col., PhD Calif.
Other Staff: 7 Lectrs.; 4 Staff Devel. Fellows

Soil Sciences

Tel: (01) 255421 Fax: (01) 295448
E-mail: soil@agric.unza.zm
Chishala, B. H., BSc Zambia, MSc Zambia, PhD Aberd.   Sr. Lectr.
Lungu, Obed I. M., BAgrSc Zambia, MSc Newcastle(UK), PhD Calif.   Assoc. Prof.
Phiri, E., BSc Zambia, MSc Ghent
Shitumbanuma, V., BSc Zambia, MSc Ghent   Sr. Lectr.
Yerokun, O. A., BSc Col., MSc Mich., PhD Mich.   Sr. Lectr.
Other Staff: 4 Lectrs.

Veterinary Medicine

Tel: (01) 293727 Fax: (01) 293727
E-mail: dean@vet.unza.zm

Biomedical Sciences

E-mail: biomed@vet.unza.zm
Chongo, K., BVetMed Zambia, MSc Sur., PhD Edin.   Head*
Siulapwa, N. J., MSc Newcastle(UK), PhD Wales   Sr. Lectr.
Other Staff: 4 Lectrs.; 1 Special Res. Fellow

Clinical Studies

E-mail: clinical@vet.unza.zm
Mwanza, A. M., DVM Havana, PhD   Sr. Lectr.
Nalubamba, K., BVetMed Zambia, MVetMed Zambia, PhD Edin.   Head*
Phiri, I. G. K., DVM Leip., MVSc F.U.Berlin, PhD Edin.   Sr. Lectr.
Other Staff: 4 Lectrs.; 4 Sr. Res. Fellows; 1 Special Res. Fellow; 3 Staff Devel. Fellows; 2 Clin. House Surgeons

Disease Control

E-mail: disease@vet.unza.zm
Mweene, A. D., BVetMed Zambia, MSc Sur., PhD Hokkaido   Sr. Lectr.; Head*
Nambota, A. M., DVM Leip., MSc Leip.   Sr. Lectr.
Pandey, G. S., BScAgr Agra, BVSc&AH Jab., MVSc Jab.   Prof.
Samui, K L., MScVM Kiev, MPVM Kiev, DVM Kiev, PhD Louisiana State   Assoc. Prof.
Syakalima, M. S., BVetMed Zambia, MSc Edin., PhD Hokkaido   Sr. Lectr.
Other Staff: 3 Lectrs.; 1 Special Res. Fellow

Paraclinical Studies

E-mail: paraclin@vet.unza.zm
Chitambo, H., BScAgric Zambia, MSc Wales, PhD Osaka   Sr. Lectr.
Hang'ombe, M. B., BVetMed Zambia, MVetMed Zambia   Sr. Lectr.; Head*
Other Staff: 3 Lectrs.; 2 Special Res. Fellows; 1 Staff Devel. Fellow

MEDICINE

E-mail: deanmed@medicine.unza.zm

Anatomy

E-mail: anatomy@medicine.unza.zm
Gabr, M. A. M., MB BCh Tanta, MD Assiut, PhD Cairo   Prof.
Karashani, J. T., MB ChB Mak., PhD Qu.   Prof.; Head*
Other Staff: 1 Lectr.

Community Medicine

Tel: (01) 254414
E-mail: community@medicine.unza.zm
Baboo, K. S., BSc Orissa Ag., MD Delhi, MB BS   Assoc. Prof.
Silwamba, G. B., MCommH Liv.   Lectr.; Head*
Siziya, S., BA(Educn) Zambia, MSc Lond., PhD Zambia   Assoc. Prof.
Other Staff: 6 Lectrs.; 2 Staff Res. Fellows; 2 Staff Devel. Fellows

Internal Medicine

Tel: (01) 250606
Atadzhanov, M., MD Tashkent, PhD Tashkent, DSc Tashkent   Prof.
Khare, Rekha, MB BS MD   Sr. Lectr.
Mwaba, P., MMed Lond., PhD Lond., BSc MB ChB   Head*
Other Staff: 7 Hon. Lectrs.

Medical Education

Banda, S. S., BSc Zambia, MB ChB Zambia, MMed Dund., MMedSc Glas., PhD Zambia   Lectr.; Head*
Other Staff: 1 Lectr.; 1 Lectr.†

Nursing, Post Basic

Tel: (01) 252453
E-mail: pbn@medicine.unza.zm
Mubita-Ngoma, Catherine A., MSc Lond., MCH Lond., BScN   Lectr.; Head*
Other Staff: 6 Lectrs.; 1 Staff Devel. Fellow; 1 Lectr.†

Obstetrics and Gynaecology

E-mail: obs@medicine.unza.zm
Kasonka, L., MD Zambia, MMed Zambia   Hon. Lectr.; Head*
Muparrakh, Zuparkhodjaeva, PhD Moscow, MSc   Sr. Lectr.
Other Staff: 7 Hon. Lectrs.

Paediatrics and Child Health

Tel: (01) 250530
E-mail: paed@medicine.unza.zm
Chintu, C., MD Tor., FRCPCan, FRCP   Prof.
Chomba, Elwyn N., MB ChB ChD   Sr. Lectr.
Shilalukey-Ngoma, Mary P., BSc MB ChB   Sr. Lectr.
Somwe Wa, S., MMed MD   Acting Head*
Other Staff: 2 Lectrs.; 11 Hon. Lectrs.

Pathology and Microbiology

Tel: (01) 252904
E-mail: path@medicine.unza.zm
Mudenda, V., MMedSc Belf., BSc MB ChB, FRCPath   Hon. Lectr.; Head*
Other Staff: 3 Lectrs.; 10 Hon. Lectrs.†

Pharmacy

Ewais, M. S., MB BCh Strath., PhD Strath.   Assoc. Prof.
Muungo, L. T. M., BPharm Aberd., PhD Aberd.   Lectr.; Head*
Other Staff: 1 Lectr.; 3 Lectrs.†

Physiological Sciences

E-mail: physio@medicine.unza.zm
Khare, A. K., MB BS Kanpur, MD Kanpur, PhD Bom.   Assoc. Prof.
Manakov, A. K., BSc Mys., MSc Mys., PhD Moscow   Prof.
Munalula-Kanyanda, Betty M., MSc Moscow, PhD S'ton.   Sr. Lectr.; Head*
Other Staff: 3 Lectrs.

Physiotherapy

Munalula-Kanyanda, Esther, BSc Stell., MSc Stell., PhD Stell.   Lectr.; Head*
Other Staff: 4 Lectrs.; 2 Staff Devel. Fellows; 1 Hon. Lectr.

Psychiatry

E-mail: psychiatry@medicine.unza.zm
Banda, M., BSc MMed   Lectr.; Head*
Haworth, A., MB BChir Camb., MA Camb., BA, FRCPsych   Prof.

Surgery

E-mail: surgery@medicine.unza.zm
Bowa, K., BSc Zambia, MB ChB Zambia, MSc MMed, FRCSGlas   Sr. Lectr.
Desai, G., MB BS, FRCSEd   Prof.; Head*
Labib, M., MB ChB Cairo, MD Cairo   Assoc. Prof.
Mulla, Y., BSc Zambia, MB ChB Zambia, MChOrth Liv., MMed   Assoc. Prof.
Munkonge, L., MB BS MD, FRCSGlas   Assoc. Prof.
Odimba, B. F. K., MSc MPH MD PhD   Prof.
Other Staff: 1 Lectr.; 15 Hon. Lectrs.; 1 Hon. Visiting Lectr.

SPECIAL CENTRES, ETC

Creative Arts, Centre for

Mapopa, M., BA Zambia, MA Ghana, PhD   Sr. Lectr.; Dir.*
Ngandu, J., BMusE Bard   Arts Manager*

Distance Education, Directorate of

Tel: (01) 290719 E-mail: dde@unza.zm
Chifwepa, V., BALibSc *W.Ont.*, MLIS *Zambia*,
PhD *Zambia*   Dir.*
Siaciwena, R. C. M., BA *Zambia*, MA *Lond.*, PhD
Wales   Assoc. Prof.

Economic and Social Research, Institute of

Tel: (0211) 294131

Kamwanga, J., BA *Zambia*, MA *ANU*, PhD *Lond.*
Kashoki, M. E., BA *C.U.A.*, MA *Baroda*, MA
Mich.State   Prof.
Macwang'i, M., MSc *Mich.*, MPH *Mich.*, PhD
N.Carolina
Mulenga, C., MSc *E.Anglia*, PhD *Wales*
Mutumba-Bull, Mainga, BA *Lond.*, PhD *Lond.*
Dir.*
Mwale, S., BALS *Zambia*, MCD *Zambia*
Mwanawina, I., BA *Zambia*, MA *E.Anglia*, PhD
Constance   Asst. Dir.
Mwesa, M. I., MA *Calif.*, MPhil *Calif.*, PhD *Calif.*
Ndubani, P., BSW *Zambia*, MSc *Stockholm*, PhD
Karolinska
Ngulube, T. J., BSc *Leeds*, MB ChB *Leeds*, MSc
Vermont, PhD *Leeds*
Wamulume, M., BSc *Zambia*, MSc *Conn.*
Zulu, R., BA *Zambia*, MA *Ghana*

Research and Postgraduate Studies, Directorate of

Tel: (0211) 290258
E-mail: director@drgs.unza.zm
Kanyanga, S. B., BEng *Zambia*, MSc *Lond.*, PhD
Sheff.   Assoc. Prof.; Dir.*
Ndubani, P., BSW *Zambia*, MSc *Stockholm*, PhD
Karolinska   Sr. Lectr.; Asst. Dir.

Technology Development Advisory Unit

E-mail: tdau@zamnet.zm
Tambatamba, Jonathan M., MSc *Moscow*, PhD
T.U.Eindhoven   Head*

CONTACT OFFICERS

Academic affairs. Deputy Registrar
(Academic): Simasiku, R. N., BA *Zambia*,
MA *Mak.* (E-mail: dregistrar-aca@unzca.zm)
Accommodation. Senior Assistant Dean of
Student Affairs: Ngwenya, M., BA *Zambia*
(E-mail: dean-students@unza.zm)
Alumni. Public Relations Officer: Kaunda,
Martina
Careers. Student Counsellor: Mseteka, N., BA
Zambia
Computing services. Director (Computing
services): Chinyama, C. C., BSc *Zambia*, MSc
Open(UK)
(E-mail: dcomputercentre@unza.zm)
Consultancy services. Deputy Vice-Chancellor:
Mwenya, Wilson N. M., BScAgric MSc PhD
Development/fund-raising. Bursar:
Chitambala, Boniface M., BA
(E-mail: bursar@unza.zm)
Estates and buildings/works and services.
Resident Engineer: Sibanyama, G.
Examinations. Deputy Registrar (Academic):
Simasiku, R. N., BA *Zambia*, MA *Mak.*
(E-mail: dregistrar-aca@unzca.zm)
Finance. Bursar: Chitambala, Boniface M., BA
(E-mail: bursar@unza.zm)
General enquiries. Registrar: Ng'andu, Alvert
N., BEng *Zambia*, MSc *Cran.*, PhD *Nott.*
(E-mail: registrar@unza.zm)
Health services. Medical Officer: Mooto, P.
(E-mail: clinic@admin.unza.zm)
Industrial liaison. Deputy Vice-Chancellor:
Mwenya, Wilson N. M., BScAgric MSc PhD
Library (chief librarian). University Librarian
(Acting): Akakandelwa, A., BALS *Zambia*,
MLIS *Botswana*, PhD *Antwerp*
(E-mail: librarian@unza.zm)
Marketing. Community Relations: Mulenga,
M., BA *Zambia*, MCD *Zambia*
(E-mail: pri@admin.unza.zm)
Public relations. Community Relations:
Mulenga, M., BA *Zambia*, MCD *Zambia*
(E-mail: pri@admin.unza.zm)

Purchasing. Purchasing Manager: Malundu, C.,
BA *Zambia* (E-mail: pmanager@unza.zm)
Research. Director, Directorate of Research and
Postgraduate Studies: Kanyanga, S. B., BEng
Zambia, MSc *Lond.*, PhD *Sheff.*
(E-mail: drgs@unza.zm)
Security. Chief Security Officer: Namushi, H.
N. (E-mail: security@admin.unza.zm)
Sport and recreation. Sports Officer: Nshimbi,
M.
Staff development and training. Staff
Development Officer: Mulenga, M.
(E-mail: sdf@unza.zm)
Strategic planning. Strategic Planning
Manager: Nkumbwa, K., BALS *Zambia*,
MDevSt *N.U.I.*
(E-mail: strategic-plan@unza.zm)
Student union. Secretary General: (vacant)
(E-mail: unzasu@unza.zm)
Student welfare/counselling. Senior
Counsellor: Chiboola, Hector, MA *Reading*
Students with disabilities. Senior Assistant
Dean of Student Affairs: Ngwenya, M., BA
Zambia (E-mail: dean-students@unza.zm)
University press. Acting Publisher: Kasankha,
S., BA(Educn) *Zambia*, MCD *Zambia*
(E-mail: press@admin.unza.zm)

CAMPUS/COLLEGE HEADS

Copperbelt Secondary Teachers' College,
Kitwe, Zambia. Principal: Sikazwe, A. K.,
BA(Educn) *Zambia*, MSc *N.Y.State*
George Benson Christian College,
Namwianga, Zambia. (Tel: (032) 324304)
Principal: Chona, F.
Nkrumah Secondary Teachers' College,
Kabwe, Zambia. (Tel: (05) 221525)
Principal: Mpundu, S. B.
Technical and Vocational Teachers' College,
Luanshya, Zambia. Principal: Zulu, G. D.

[*Information supplied by the institution as at 6 November
2007, and edited by the ACU*]

ZIMBABWE

See Appendix 1:
ACU Members of Former Commonwealth Countries

ZIMBABWE

See Appendix 1:
ACU Members of Former Commonwealth Countries

APPENDIX 1

ACU Members of Former Commonwealth Countries

Hong Kong (People's Republic of China) (p. 2012)

Zimbabwe (p. 2039)

HONG KONG

THE UNIVERSITIES OF HONG KONG

Information compiled by the University Grants Committee, Hong Kong as at March 2008

The University System

The University Grants Committee (UGC) is appointed by the Chief Executive of the Hong Kong Special Administrative Region (HKSAR) as the principal advisory committee on the developmental and funding needs of higher education institutions in the HKSAR. There are eight publicly funded higher education institutions under the aegis of UGC, namely City University of Hong Kong, Hong Kong Baptist University, Lingnan University, Chinese University of Hong Kong, Hong Kong Institute of Education, Hong Kong Polytechnic University, Hong Kong University of Science and Technology, and the University of Hong Kong. The UGC comprises eminent local and overseas academics and prominent lay members from the Hong Kong community. Other degree-awarding institutions outside the ambit of the UGC include the Open University of Hong Kong, the Hong Kong Academy for Performing Arts, and Hong Kong Shue Yan University.

All of the UGC-funded institutions are autonomous bodies, with the authority to grant degrees, and with their own ordinances and governing councils. Each institution determines its own establishment, governance, structure and operation. As the institutions are mainly supported by public funds, the UGC takes on the role of an intermediary, to ensure both academic freedom and autonomy for the institutions as well as public accountability and value for money. The UGC also has broad oversight responsibility in respect of the institutions' development, quality assurance and their general academic and administrative operations.

In January 2004, the UGC published its roadmap document *Hong Kong Higher Education—to make a difference, to move with the times,* in which it sets out its detailed thinking on how strategically to develop the Hong Kong higher education sector into an interlocking yet differentiated system, and to make Hong Kong the higher education hub of the region. In March 2004, the UGC published another major document *Hong Kong Higher Education—Integration Matters,* explaining in detail one of the UGC's major directions to promote deep collaboration among higher education institutions.

In 1988, the UGC assumed responsibility for administering research project funding provided separately by the Government. In 1991, a Research Grants Council was established, under the aegis of the UGC, to administer this funding and to advise on the development of research in the higher education sector of Hong Kong.

The UGC has been performing an important role in assuring the quality of higher education provision at the UGC-funded institutions through the conduct of various reviews in the past. Taking into account this valuable experience, together with the changing higher education landscape, the UGC decided to set up a Quality Assurance Council (QAC) under its aegis with a view to discharging a larger role in quality-related matters in respect of programmes offered at degree and above levels at the UGC-funded institutions. The new body was formed in April 2007 and has two primary roles: to undertake quality audits of the student learning experience at each of the eight UGC-funded institutions; and to promote quality assurance and enhancement, and the spread of good practice.

Academic Year

The academic year in Hong Kong begins in September/October and ends in May/June.

Language of Instruction

English and Chinese.

Pre-University Education

Primary and secondary education in Hong Kong is provided by government schools, aided schools (largely funded by the government but managed by voluntary bodies) and private schools. Currently, the primary curriculum lasts for six years, and secondary schools offer a five-year course leading to the Hong Kong Certificate of Education Examinations (HKCEE) and often run the two-year sixth form courses leading to the Hong Kong Advanced Level Examination (HKALE).

In May 2005, the Government announced the implementation of the new academic structure for senior secondary education (commonly referred to as '3+3+4') in September 2009. Under the '3+3+4', secondary students, after completing three years of junior and three years of senior secondary education, will take the Hong Kong Diploma of Secondary Education (HKDSE) Examination. Students who have attained the required standards may undertake a 4-year undergraduate programme at the UGC-funded institutions starting from the 2012–13 academic year. In this connection, all UGC-funded undergraduate programmes will extend their normal duration from three to four years starting with the 2012–13 academic year. The UGC attaches great importance to this fundamental change, and has been working closely with the Government and the institutions with a view to ensuring that the new undergraduate programmes deliver their full potential to enhance the higher education experience of our students.

Admission to First Degree Courses

Each UGC-funded institution has its own admission requirements. For local school leavers, whilst the results of the HKALE remain the major factor of consideration for admission, more emphasis has been put on achievements in non-academic aspects as well as performance in aptitude tests and interviews conducted by the institutions themselves. Applications from students with qualifications gained outside Hong Kong are considered individually, though entry to university courses requires the equivalent of matriculation.

The Early Admissions Scheme (EAS, or the former Advance Placement Scheme for Secondary Six Students) was first introduced in the 2002–03 academic year to allow a small number of outstanding local secondary school students to gain access to tertiary education a year earlier. Under the scheme, students must fulfil the admission requirements set by the institutions themselves which are mainly based on their results in the HKCEE.

Method of application. Applicants seeking admission to UGC-funded institutions with HKALE results should apply through the Joint University Programmes Admissions System (JUPAS). Applicants may choose up to 25 study programmes in order of preference. Each programme will then give the student a rating based on HKALE and HKCEE results, information contained on the application form, performance at interviews and during tests. Apart from the EAS, there are three other sub-systems under JUPAS, namely, the sub-system for applicants with a disability, the sub-system for school principal's nominations, and the self-recommendation scheme. These sub-systems are in place to facilitate institutions to consider applications for admission based on students' non-academic achievements/factors.

Applicants seeking admission with qualifications other than HKALE results should apply to the individual institutions directly outside JUPAS.

Finance

In Hong Kong, public funding accounts for some 80% of the institutions' operating budget in respect of UGC-funded activity (institutions have a growing percentage of self-financed activity). The UGC's assessment of the UGC-funded institutions' recurrent funding takes into account the relative cost weightings of different disciplines, programme levels (undergraduate, postgraduate, sub-degree), mode of study/tuition (eg full-time, part-time, sandwich), student numbers by categories, staff numbers and active research workers in each field.

Recurrent operating grants are normally allocated to institutions in the form of a block grant on a triennial basis. Separately, UGC also provides institutions with capital grants for approved capital works programmes of the institutions on a project basis.

The principle of public and financial accountability is emphasized in that the distribution of public funds is based on quality assurance outcomes in terms of teaching and research. In the 2001–04 triennium, the UGC introduced a Performance and Role-related Funding Scheme under which a portion of the recurrent funding was tied with institutions' performance against their respective roles. In order further to encourage institutions to adhere to their roles, a second round exercise of the scheme was conducted in 2004 to inform the funding allocation for institutions in the 2005–08 triennium. The size of funds involved was increased to around 10% of the recurrent funding requirement for all eight UGC-funded institutions.

Student finance. Tertiary students in Hong Kong are required to pay tuition fees. The current indicative tuition fee level has remained unchanged for several years and is currently set at HK$42,100 per academic year for full-time UGC-funded degree programmes. The Hong Kong Academy for Performing Arts follows the UGC in setting its tuition fees for sub-degree and degree programmes. For the master's degree programmes launched in 2006–07, a fee of HK$75,000 p.a. is charged. Operating on a self-financing basis, Chu Hai College for Higher Education, Hong Kong Shue Yan University and the Open University of Hong Kong tend to charge a slightly higher tuition fee as compared to publicly funded degree programmes.

In addition to the existing government grants and loans to means-tested students, a non-means-tested loan scheme was also introduced in 1998 to provide further financial assistance to students in need, in support of the promise that no student would be denied a place in higher education for want of financial resources.

Staff and Student Numbers

A total of about 72,600 students (in headcount terms) were taking publicly funded programmes at different levels at the eight UGC-funded institutions in the 2006–07 academic year. The student enrolments for sub-degree, undergraduate, taught postgraduate and research postgraduate programmes are respectively around 9700, 52,500, 4700 and 5700. The sub-degree sector is experiencing expansion in the recent years as the needs for higher education continue to rise in transforming Hong Kong into a knowledge-based economy. Non-local students are also on the rise: in the 2006–07 academic year there were about 6200 non-local students studying in Hong Kong. To further develop Hong Kong as a regional education hub, the government has decided further to relax the enrolment quota so that the UGC-funded institutions could recruit non-

local students on up to 20% of the approved student number targets for their undergraduate and taught postgraduate publicly funded programmes with effect from 2008–09.

In addition, all of the UGC-funded institutions have established community colleges or extension arms to provide quality programmes at various levels. Such programmes cater for both full-time students as well as providing continuing education and life-long learning courses for professional practice, retraining and self-development. Such programmes are usually self-financed.

In 2006–07, there were around 5800 full-time equivalent teaching staff at UGC-funded institutions.

The Open University of Hong Kong makes higher education opportunities available to all through a system of open access and distance education. In 2007–08, more than 17,000 students enrolled in its sub-degree, degree and postgraduate programmes. The Open University has also moved into 'face to face' full-time education as part of its move to position itself as a dual mode institution. In addition, distance higher education opportunities are also available through other overseas institutions and local continuing education organizations.

Further Information

University Grants Committee (UGC). *Facts and figures 2002*, report of the University Grants Committee. Hong Kong, 2003.
————————. *Facts and figures 2003*, report of the University Grants Committee. Hong Kong, 2004.
————————. *Facts and figures 2004*, report of the University Grants Committee. Hong Kong, 2005.
————————. *Facts and figures 2005*, report of the University Grants Committee. Hong Kong, 2006.
————————. *Facts and figures 2006*, report of the University Grants Committee. Hong Kong, 2007.
————————. *Higher education in Hong Kong—a report by the University Grants Committee.* Hong Kong, 1996.
————————. *Higher education in Hong Kong—report of the University Grants Committee.* Hong Kong, 2002.
————————. *Hong Kong higher education: integration matters.* Hong Kong, 2004.
————————. *Hong Kong higher education: to make a difference, to move with the times.* Hong Kong, 2004.
————————. *Report on the 1995–98 triennium.* Hong Kong, 1999.
————————. *Report on the 1998–2001 triennium.* Hong Kong, 2002.
————————. *Supplement to higher education in Hong Kong.* Hong Kong, 1999.
Hong Kong Special Administrative Region Government. *Annual Report of the Hong Kong Special Administrative Region Government.* (Chapter 10: Education). Hong Kong, 1998.
University Grants Committee website: http://www.ugc.edu.hk/

The Hong Kong Directory to Subjects of Study follows on p. 2016

The table below shows which of the institutions indicated provide facilities for study and/or research in the subjects named. In the case of related subject areas which have been grouped together (eg Botany/Plant Science), it should be borne in mind that one or more of the subjects may be offered by the institution concerned.

	Chinese U. of Hong Kong	Hong Kong	Open U. of Hong Kong
Accountancy/Accounting	X	X	UM
Administration/Administrative Studies	U	X	
Advertising	M		
Agriculture/Agricultural Science		X	
Agronomy/Soil Science		UM	
Agrotechnology		MD	
American Studies		X	
Anaesthesia/Anaesthesiology	MD	U	
Anatomical Science/Anatomy	X	X	
Animal Nutrition/Animal Physiology		X	
Animal Science/Husbandry/Production		X	
Anthropology/Folklore	X	UD	
Applied Chemistry	U	X	
Applied Physics	U	X	
Aquaculture/Fisheries/Marine Science		X	
Arabic		U	
Archaeology		U	
Architectural Design	UM	UM	
Architecture	X	X	
Area Studies		UD	
Art, Fine	UM	X	
Art, History of	X	X	
Arts Management	M		
Arts and Culture	M		
Arts, Graphic		X	
Asian/Pacific Studies		X	
Astronomy/Astrophysics/Space Science		X	
Audiology		MD	
Banking/Finance	X	X	UM
Behavioural Sciences		X	
Biochemistry	X	X	
Bioengineering		X	
Bioethics		U	
Bioinformatics		X	
Biology	X	X	
Biology Molecular	X	X	
Biomedical Sciences	X	X	
Biostatistics	M	MD	
Biotechnology	X	X	
Botany/Plant Science		X	

	Chinese U. of Hong Kong	Hong Kong	Open U. of Hong Kong
Buddhist Studies		X	
Building/Built Environment/Construction	M	X	
Business Administration	X	X	X
Business Economics	M		
Business Information Systems	UM	X	U
Business/Commerce	X	X	
Chemistry	X	X	
Child and Family Psychology	M		
Child/Youth Studies		X	
Chinese Language and Literature	X	X	U
Chinese/Chinese Studies	X	X	U
Cognitive Science		X	
Communication/Journalism/Media Studies	X	X	
Communications/Information Management	M	X	
Community Health	M	X	
Community Medicine	UM	X	
Computer Science	X	X	UM
Conservation Studies		X	
Corporate Governance			UM
Counselling	M	MD	
Creative Writing		X	
Criminal Justice/Public Policy		X	
Criminology		X	
Crop Science/Production		X	
Cultural Heritage		X	
Cultural Studies	X	UD	
Curriculum and Assessment Studies	M	D	M
Dentistry		X	
Dermatology		U	
Design, Industrial		X	
Development Studies		X	
Disaster/Emergency		U	
Drama/Theatre/Dance/Performing Arts	M		
E-Business	M	M	
E-Commerce	M	MD	UM
Ecology		X	
Economic History		X	
Economics	X	X	U
Education	X	X	X
Education Primary		X	U

TO SUBJECTS OF STUDY

For further information about the individual subjects taught at each institution, please refer to the *Index to Subjects of Study* at the end of the Yearbook, but for full details about subjects/courses offered by the universities in this directory each institution's own official publications must be consulted. U = may be studied for first degree course; M = may be studied for master's degree course; D = research facilities to doctoral level; X = all three levels (UMD). **Note**—The table only includes information provided by institutions currently in membership of the Association of Commonwealth Universities.

	Chinese U. of Hong Kong	Hong Kong	Open U. of Hong Kong
Education Secondary		X	U
Education Special		MD	
Educational Administration	M		
Educational Psychology	M	MD	
Electronics		UM	U
Emergency/Trauma Care Technology	MD	U	
Energy Studies		X	
Engineering		X	
Engineering Agricultural/Fisheries		X	
Engineering Architectural		U	
Engineering Automobile		X	
Engineering Biomedical	M	U	
Engineering Business		X	
Engineering Civil/Environmental/Structural		X	
Engineering Communications/Telecommunications	X	X	U
Engineering Computer	X	X	U
Engineering Construction		X	
Engineering Design	U	X	U
Engineering Electrical/Electronic	X	X	
Engineering Geological		UM	
Engineering Industrial		X	
Engineering Information Technology	X	X	
Engineering Management	X	X	
Engineering Manufacturing	X	X	
Engineering Materials/Mineral Resources/Petroleum		X	
Engineering Mechanical/Production	X	X	U
Engineering Medical		X	
Engineering Metallurgical/Mining		X	
Engineering Software		UM	
English	X	X	
English as a Second Language		X	
Entomology		MD	
Entrepreneurship		UD	
Environmental Geosciences		UM	
Environmental Management		U	UM
Environmental Science/Studies	X	X	U
Epidemiology	M		
Estate Management		X	
Ethics		U	
Ethnomusicology	MD		

	Chinese U. of Hong Kong	Hong Kong	Open U. of Hong Kong
European Studies	U	U	
Food Science/Nutrition/Home Science/Dietetics	UM	X	
Forensic Science		U	
Forestry		MD	
French/French Studies	U	U	
Genetics		X	
Genetics and Plant Breeding		X	
Geographic Information Systems/Geomatics	MD	X	
Geography	X	X	
Geology/Earth Sciences/Atmospheric Studies		X	
Geophysics		UM	
German/Germanic Studies	U	U	
Gerontology	M	M	
Health Education		D	
Health Sciences/Studies	UM	X	
Health and Social Care	M		
Health/Hospital Administration	M		
History	X	X	
History/Philosophy of Science		X	
Horticulture		MD	
Hotel Management	X		
Housing/Real Estate		X	
Human Biology		X	
Human Genetics		X	
Human Resource Development			M
Immunology/Infection/Immunity		X	
Industrial Hygiene and Safety			UM
Industrial Relations/Personnel/HRM	U	X	M
Industrial and Organisation Psychology	M		
Information Science/Studies/Systems	X	X	
Information Technology	M	MD	UM
Insurance	U	U	
International Business	UM		
International Relations/Studies		X	
Internet Computing/Technologies	U		
Italian	U	U	
Japanese/Japanese Studies	UM	X	
Laboratory Science Technology		U	
Land Management/Rehabilitation	U	UM	
Land Resource Science	U	MD	

	Chinese U. of Hong Kong	Hong Kong	Open U. of Hong Kong
Landscape Architecture		M	
Language Teaching/Learning	UM	UM	U
Language and Communication		U	
Languages, Modern	U		
Law Business/Commercial/Economic/Industrial	M	U	M
Law Employment/Labour		X	
Law Enforcement/Security Management			U
Law Environmental		M	
Law Intellectual Property/Copyright		X	
Law International/Comparative/Trade	M	X	
Law Legal Practice		X	
Law Property/Construction/Housing		X	
Law/Legal Studies	X	X	
Library/Information Science		X	
Linguistics/Translation	X	X	UM
Literature, Comparative		X	
Logic/Computation		MD	
Management	X	X	U
Management Information Systems	M		
Marketing	X	X	U
Materials Science	X	UM	
Mathematics	X	X	U
Mediaeval Studies		UM	
Medical Ethics		U	
Medicine, Alternative	M		
Medicine, Chinese	X	U	
Medicine, Obstetrics and Gynaecology	X	X	
Medicine, Oncology/Cancer studies	MD		
Medicine, Orthopaedic	X	X	
Medicine, Otorhinolaryngology/Otolaryngology		X	
Medicine, Paediatric	X	X	
Medicine, Palliative		U	
Medicine/Surgery	X	X	
Meteorology		U	
Microbiology/Medical Microbiology	X	X	
Mobile Communications/Telecommunications		X	
Musculoskeletal Studies		MD	
Music	X	X	
Music Pop		X	

	Chinese U. of Hong Kong	Hong Kong	Open U. of Hong Kong
Nanotechnology		X	
Natural Resource Studies	U		
Neuroscience	M	X	
Nursing/Midwifery	X	MD	U
Occupational Health/Therapy	M		UM
Operational Research/Operations Management		U	
Ophthalmology	X	U	
Optics/Photonics		U	
Optometry/Vision Science	X		
Palaeontology/Palaeobiology		U	
Parasitology		X	
Pathology	X	X	
Pharmacology	X	X	
Pharmacy/Pharmaceutical Science	X	MD	
Philosophy	X	X	
Physical Education/Sports Science	UM	X	
Physics	X	X	
Physiology	X	X	
Planning/Landscape Studies		X	
Plant Pathology		MD	
Popular Culture		UD	
Portuguese/Portugese Studies		U	
Product Design and Technology			U
Project Management		UM	
Property Economics		UM	
Psychiatry	X	X	
Psychology	X	X	
Psychology Clinical	MD	X	
Psychotherapy	M	UM	
Public Administration	X	X	U
Public Health/Population Health	MD	X	
Public Sector Management		X	
Radiography/Diagnostic Technology/MRI	MD	U	
Rehabilitation Medicine/Therapy/Science		U	
Religion/Theology	X	X	
Risk Management	UM		
Social Policy	M	X	
Social Work/Studies	X	X	
Sociology	X	X	

	Chinese U. of Hong Kong	Hong Kong	Open U. of Hong Kong
Spanish/Hispanic/Latin American Studies	U	U	
Speech Science/Pathology/Therapy		X	
Statistics/Actuarial Science	X	X	
Surveying/Quantity Surveying		UM	
Sustainable Development	M	U	
Taxation		UM	
Teacher Training	UM	X	
Thai/Thai Studies		U	

	Chinese U. of Hong Kong	Hong Kong	Open U. of Hong Kong
Tourism/Hospitality/Leisure/Recreation	X	X	
Toxicology		X	
Transport Studies		X	
Urban Studies		X	
Visual Arts		X	
Women's/Gender Studies	X	X	
Zoology		X	

CHINESE UNIVERSITY OF HONG KONG

Founded 1963

Member of the Association of Commonwealth Universities

Postal Address: Sha Tin, New Territories, Hong Kong
Telephone: 2609 8899 **Fax:** 2603 5115
URL: http://www.cuhk.edu.hk

VICE-CHANCELLOR*—Lau, Prof. Lawrence J., BS *Stan.*, MA *Calif.*, PhD *Calif.*, Hon. DSocSc *HKUST*, Hon. Doc *Soka*,
Hon. LLD *Waseda*, FES
PRO-VICE-CHANCELLOR—Young, Prof. Kenneth, BS *Cal.Tech.*, PhD *Cal.Tech.*
PRO-VICE-CHANCELLOR—Liu, Prof. P. W., AB *Prin.*, MA *Stan.*, MA(Ed) *Stan.*, PhD *Stan.*
PRO-VICE-CHANCELLOR—Cheng, Prof. Jack C. Y., MB BS *HK*, MD *Chinese HK*, FRCSEd, FRCSGlas, FACS, FRCSEd
PRO-VICE-CHANCELLOR—Ching, Prof. P. C., BEng *Liv.*, PhD *Liv.*, FIEE
ASSOCIATE PRO-VICE-CHANCELLOR—Hui, Prof. Michael K. M., BBA *Chinese HK*, PhD *Lond.*
ASSOCIATE PRO-VICE-CHANCELLOR AND REGISTRAR—So, Prof. Billy K. L., BA *Chinese HK*, MPhil *Chinese HK*, PhD *ANU*
TREASURER—Luk, Roger K. H., JP, BSocSc *HK*, MBA *Chinese HK*
SECRETARY‡—Leung, Jacob S. K., BSocSc *HK*, MDiv *S.Baptist Theol.Sem.*
LIBRARIAN—Storey, C., BA *Leeds*, MPhil *E.Anglia*, PhD *HK*, FCLIP
BURSAR—Chan, Terence C. W., BSocSc *HK*, FCA, FCA(Aust)
UNIVERSITY DEAN OF STUDENTS—Ho, P. P., MA *Edin.*, PhD *Lond.*

GENERAL INFORMATION

History. Established in 1963, the university has its origin in three post-secondary colleges: New Asia College (founded in 1949), Chung Chi College (founded in 1951) and United College of Hong Kong (founded in 1956). Its fourth constituent, Shaw College, became operational in 1988. Morningside College and S. H. Ho College were established in 2006; and three more colleges, S. W. Chu College, Wu Yee College and Lee Woo Sing College, were approved in 2007.

Admission to first degree courses (see also Hong Kong Introduction). Hong Kong applicants: through Joint University Programmes Admissions System (JUPAS). Hong Kong Certificate of Education Examination (HKCEE) with 7 subjects (in one sitting) at grade E/level 2, including 2 languages (Chinese, English, French or German), and the Hong Kong Advanced Level Examination (HKALE) with grade E in advanced supplementary level (AS) Chinese language and culture and the use of English, and at least 2 A level subjects, or 1 A and 2 AS level subjects.
International and non-JUPAS local applicants: direct to the university. General Certificate of Education (GCE) with pass grades in 3 A level subjects (or 2 A levels plus 2 AS levels); or International Baccalaureate Diploma; or other equivalent qualifications. Mainland Chinese Gao Kao candidates should apply through NCUES.

First Degrees (see also Hong Kong Directory to Subjects of Study). BA, BBA, BChiMed, BEd, BEd(ECE), BEng, BMedSc, BNurs, BPharm, BSc, BSSc, LLB, MB ChB.
BA part-time - 6 years: only offered for Music programme.
Length of course. Full-time: BMedSc: 1 year; BA, BBA, BEng, BPharm, BSc, BSSc: 3 years; BEd, BNurs, LLB: 4 years; BChiMed, MB ChB: 5 years. *Part-time:* BEd(ECE): 3 years; BA: 6 years.

Higher Degrees (see also Hong Kong Directory to Subjects of Study).
Master's. MA, MAcc, MArch, MBA, MChiMed, MClinPharm, MDiv, MEd, MFA, MFM, MHSc, MMus, MNurs, MOM, MPH, MPhil, MSc, MSSc, MSW.
Admission. Applicants for admission to master's degrees must normally hold an appropriate bachelor's degree with second class honours or above (or average grade B or above).
Master's degrees normally last 1–2 years full-time or 2–3 years part-time.

Length of course. Full-time: MA, MEd, MMus, MSc, MSSc: 1 year; MArch, MBA, MDiv, MFA, MHSc, MPhil, MSW: 2 years; MChiMed: 4 years. *Part-time:* MA, MAcc, MClinPharm, MEd, MFM, MMus, MNurs, MOM, MPH, MSc, MSSc: 2 years; MBA, MPhil, MSW: 3 years.
Doctoral. DMus, EdD, PhD, PsyD.
Admission. For admission to DMus, EdD, PhD: appropriate master's degree.
Length of course. Full-time: DMus, EdD, PhD: 3–4 years. *Part-time:* PsyD: 3 years; DMus, EdD, PhD: 4–5½ years.

Language of Instruction. English and Chinese.

Libraries. Volumes: 2,083,003. Periodicals subscribed to: 14,525. Other holdings: 137,209 audiovisual materials; 75,585 electronic journals; 387,538 microfilms; 13,215 CD-ROMs; 631 electronic databases. Special collections: rare books 1260–1795; modern Chinese drama (1930s and 1940s); Chinese overseas; history of medicine of Hong Kong, China and the Asia-Pacific region; Hong Kong Government documents; Hong Kong studies; Gao Xingjian.

Academic Awards (2006–2007). 2778 awards ranging in value from HK$200 to HK$391,389.

Income (2005–2006). Total, HK$3,795,700,000.

Statistics. Staff (2006–2007): 5796 (1284 academic, 4512 non-academic). Students (2006–2007): full-time 13,015 (6102 men, 6913 women); part-time 7108 (3264 men, 3844 women); undergraduate 10,224 (4759 men, 5465 women); master's 7036 (3328 men, 3708 women); doctoral 1126 (616 men, 510 women).

FACULTIES/SCHOOLS

Arts
Tel: 2609 7107 Fax: 2603 5621
E-mail: afo@arts.cuhk.edu.hk
Dean: Lee, Rev. Archie C. C., BA *Chinese HK*,
MDiv *Chinese HK*, PhD *Edin.*
Secretary: Chan, M. K., BSocSc *HK*

Business Administration
Tel: 2609 7785 Fax: 2603 5917
E-mail: bafac@cuhk.edu.hk
Dean: Lee, Prof. T. S., BSc *Chiao Tung*, MS *Chiao Tung*, MBA *Missouri*, PhD *Missouri*
Acting Secretary: Cheng, S. K., BSSc *Chinese HK*,
MA *Chinese HK*, MBA *Monash*

Education
Tel: 2609 6937 Fax: 2603 6129
E-mail: edu@fed.cuhk.edu.hk
Dean: Lee, Prof. John C. K., BA *HK*, MSc *Oxf.*,
MA(Ed) *Chinese HK*, PhD *Chinese HK*
Secretary: Lau, Pauline K. P., BBA *Chinese HK*

Engineering
Tel: 2609 8446 Fax: 2603 5701
E-mail: facultyoffice@ie.cuhk.edu.hk
Dean: Yum, Peter T. S., BS *Col.*, MS *Col.*, MPh
Col., PhD *Col.*
Secretary: Law, Doris S. L. Chu, BA *HK*,
MSocSc *HK*

Graduate School
Tel: 2609 8976 Fax: 2603 5779
E-mail: pgstudent@cuhk.edu.hk
Dean: Wong, W. S., BA *Yale*, MA *Yale*, MS
Harv., PhD *Harv.*, FIEEE

Law, School of
Tel: 2696 1095 Fax: 2294 2505
E-mail: law@cuhk.edu.hk
Director: McConville, Prof. M., LLB *Lond.*, PhD
Nott.
Planning Officer: Ying, Diana, MA *City HK*,
LLM *City HK*

Medicine
Tel: 2609 6891 Fax: 2603 5821
E-mail: faculty@med.cuhk.edu.hk
Dean: Fok, Prof. T. F., MB BS *HK*, MD *Chinese
HK*, FRCPEd, FRCPCH
Secretary: Siu, Alison S. M., BA *Chinese HK*, MSc
Edin., MEd *Edin.*

Science
Tel: 2609 6327 Fax: 2603 5156
E-mail: sfo@cuhk.edu.hk
Dean: Kwan, Prof. H. S., BSc *Chinese HK*, MPhil
Chinese HK, PhD *Calif.*
Secretary: Yang Ho, Angela, BA *Alta.*

Social Science
Tel: 3163 4096 Fax: 2603 6774
E-mail: ssinfo@cuhk.edu.hk
Dean: Lee, Prof. Paul S. N., BSSc *Chinese HK*,
MPhil *Chinese HK*, PhD *Mich.*
Secretary: Law, Joseph K. H., BSocSc *HK*,
MSocSc *HK*, MA *Chinese HK*

ACADEMIC UNITS

Accountancy, School of
Tel: 2609 7838 Fax: 2603 5114
E-mail: schoolacy@cuhk.edu.hk
Chung, Y. T., BCom *Edin.*, MBA *Indiana*, DBA
Indiana, FCA   Emer. Prof.
Fan, Joseph P. H., LLB *Natnl.Taiwan*, PhD *Pitt.*
Prof.

Wong, T. J., BA *Dickinson Coll.*, MBA *Calif.*, PhD *Calif.*   Prof.; Dir.*

Wu, W. Y., BEng *S.China U.T.*, MBA *C'dia.*, MSc *N.Y.*, MPhil *N.Y.*, PhD *N.Y.*   Prof.

Xie, James J. Z., MSc *Shanghai Jiaotong*, PhD *Br.Col.*   Prof.

Other Staff: 8 Assoc. Profs.; 6 Asst. Profs.; 3 Teaching Fellows; 1 Professl. Consultant; 1 Adjunct Prof.; 3 Adjunct Assoc. Profs.; 2 Hon. Profs.

Research: accounting issues in China and Asia; analytical modelling in accounting issues; corporate financial disclosure and policies; corporate governance; international capital markets and accounting issues

Anthropology

Tel: 2609 7670 Fax: 2603 5218
E-mail: anthropology@cuhk.edu.hk

Cheung, Sidney C. H., BA *Chiba*, MA *Osaka*, PhD *Osaka*   Prof.

Mathews, G. C., BA *Yale*, MA *Sch.Internat.Training(Vermont)*, MA *Cornell*, PhD *Cornell*   Prof.

Tan, C. B., BSocSc *Sci.U.Malaysia*, MA *Cornell*, PhD *Cornell*   Prof.; Chairman*

Other Staff: 3 Assoc. Profs.; 1 Asst. Prof.; 1 Res. Assoc.; 3 Adjunct Profs.; 2 Hon. Advisers

Research: cultural and ethnic identity; cultural heritage and tourism; food and culture; gender and culture; globalisation and culture

Architecture

Tel: 2609 6517 Fax: 2603 5267
E-mail: architecture@cuhk.edu.hk

Ho, P. P., MA *Edin.*, PhD *Lond.*   Prof.; Chairman*

Lee, Tunney F., BArch *Mich.*   Emer. Prof.

Lim, Bernard V. W. F., BA *HK*, BArch *HK*, MSc *HK*   Prof.

Ng, Y. Y., BArch *Manc.*, MBA *Warw.*, PhD *Camb.*   Prof.

Tsou, J. Y., BS *Chinese Culture*, MArch *Mich.*, PhD *Mich.*   Prof.

Other Staff: 8 Assoc. Profs.; 5 Asst. Profs.; 2 Professl. Consultants; 1 Res. Assoc.; 1 Visiting Scholar; 1 Adjunct Prof.; 2 Hon. Profs.

Research: Chinese architectural heritage; community participation; computation and simulation; environmental and sustainable design; housing innovations

Biochemistry

Tel: 2609 6359 Fax: 2603 7246
E-mail: biochemistry@cuhk.edu.hk

Chen, Z. Y., BSc *Henan Normal*, PhD *Mass.*   Prof.

Cheng, H. K., BSc *Chinese HK*, PhD *Lond.*   Prof.

Fong, W. P., BSc *Chinese HK*, PhD *Chinese HK*   Prof.

Fung, K. P., BSc *Chinese HK*, MPhil *Chinese HK*, PhD *HK*   Prof.; Chairman*

Ho, Walter K. K., AB *Calif.*, PhD *Calif.*   Res. Prof.

Kong, S. K., MSc *Salf.*, MBA *Strath.*, PhD *Chinese HK*   Prof.

Lee, C. Y., BSc *Br.Col.*, MSc *Br.Col.*, PhD *Br.Col.*   Emer. Prof.

Leung, K. N., BSc *Chinese HK*, PhD *ANU*   Prof.

Ma, Lin, BSc *W.China Union*, PhD *Leeds*   Emer. Prof.

Ng, T. B., BSc *HK*, MPhil *HK*, PhD *Nfld.*   Prof.

Shaw, P. C., BSc *Chinese HK*, MPhil *Chinese HK*, PhD *Lond.*   Prof.

Tsang, David S. C., BSc *McG.*, PhD *McG.*   Res. Prof.

Tsui, K. W., BSc *Chinese HK*, PhD *Chinese HK*   Prof.

Wang, J., PhD *Wis.*   Prof.

Waye, M. Y., BSc *W.Ont.*, PhD *Tor.*   Prof.

Other Staff: 9 Assoc. Profs.; 5 Asst. Profs.; 1 Res. Asst. Prof.; 4 Res. Assocs.; 3 Postdoctoral Fellows; 2 Visiting Scholars; 3 Adjunct Profs.; 1 Adjunct Asst. Prof.; 1 Hon. Prof.; 1 Hon. Assoc. Prof.; 1 Hon.

Asst. Prof.; 1 Hon. Sr. Res. Fellow; 1 Hon. Visiting Scholar

Biology

Tel: 2609 6348 Fax: 2603 5646
E-mail: bio@cuhk.edu.hk

But, Paul P. H., BSc *Chinese HK*, MBA *Chinese HK*, MA *Calif.*, PhD *Calif.*   Prof.

Chang, S. T., OBE, BSc *Natnl.Taiwan*, MS *Wis.*, PhD *Wis.*   Emer. Prof.

Chu, K. H., BA *Calif.*, PhD *M.I.T.*   Prof.

Fung, M. C., BSc *Chinese HK*, MPhil *Chinese HK*, PhD *ANU*   Prof.

Ge, W., BS *Nanjing*, MS *Chinese Acad.Sc.*, PhD *Alta.*   Prof.

Jiang, L., BS *S.China Agric.*, MS *Br.Col.*, PhD *S.Fraser*   Prof.

Kwan, H. S., BSc *Chinese HK*, MPhil *Chinese HK*, PhD *Calif.*   Prof.

Sun, Samuel S. M., BSc *HK*, BSc *Chinese HK*, MSc *HK*, PhD *Wis.*   Prof.

Thrower, L. B., BSc *Melb.*, MSc *Melb.*, PhD *Melb.*   Emer. Prof.

Wong, C. K., BSc *Tor.*, PhD *Tor.*, MSc *Ott.*   Prof.

Wong, P. K., BSc *Chinese HK*, MPhil *Chinese HK*, PhD *Calif.*   Prof.

Woo, Norman Y. S., BSc *HK*, PhD *HK*   Prof.; Chairman*

Other Staff: 7 Assoc. Profs.; 3 Asst. Profs.; 4 Res. Asst. Profs.; 1 Res. Assoc.; 2 Sr. Res. Fellows; 1 Res. Fellow; 9 Postdoctoral Fellows; 1 Res. Officer; 1 Visiting Scholar; 2 Adjunct Profs.; 5 Adjunct Assoc. Profs.; 3 Hon. Sr. Res. Fellows; 1 Hon. Visiting Scholar

Research: animal physiology, development, endocrinology and reproduction; environmental and marine biology; genetics and microbiology; genomics, proteomics and bioinformatics; plant molecular biology and biotechnology

Chemistry

Tel: 2609 6344 Fax: 2603 5057
E-mail: chemistry@cuhk.edu.hk

Au-Yeung, Steve C. F., BSc *S.Fraser*, PhD *McM.*   Prof.

Chan, Dominic T. W., BSc *Warw.*, PhD *Warw.*   Prof.

Chan, K. S., BSc *HK*, PhD *Chic.*   Prof.

Chow, H. F., BSc *Chinese HK*, MPhil *Chinese HK*, PhD *Camb.*, FRSChem   Prof.

Leung, W. P., BSc *Kent*, MSc *Sus.*, PhD *W.Aust.*, FRSChem   Prof.

Li, W. K., BS *Ill.*, MS *Mich.*, PhD *Mich.*   Emer. Prof.

Liu, Z., BS *Wuhan*, MS *Chinese Acad.Sc.*, PhD *W.Ont.*   Prof.

Mak, Thomas C. W., BSc *Br.Col.*, PhD *Br.Col.*   Wei Lun Res. Prof.

Ng, Dennis K. P., BSc *Chinese HK*, MPhil *Chinese HK*, DPhil *Oxf.*, FRSChem   Prof.

Shing, K. M., BSc *HK*, MSc *Lond.*, PhD *Lond.*, DSc *Lond.*, FRSChem   Prof.

Tam, S. W., OBE, JP, BSc *HK*, MSc *HK*, PhD *Nott.*, FRSChem   Emer. Prof.

Wong, Henry N. C., BSc *Chinese HK*, PhD *Lond.*, DSc *Lond.*, FRSChem   Prof.

Wu, C., BSc *China U.S.T.*, PhD *N.Y.*, FAPS   Prof.; Chairman*

Xie, Z., BS *Hangzhou*, MS *Shanghai Inst.Org.Chem.*, PhD *T.U.Berlin*   Prof.

Yu, Jimmy C. M., BS *St.Martin's*, PhD *Idaho*   Prof.

Other Staff: 2 Assoc. Profs.; 3 Asst. Profs.; 1 Res. Prof.; 2 Res. Asst. Profs.; 1 Teaching Fellow; 8 Postdoctoral Fellows; 7 Adjunct Profs.; 2 Adjunct Assoc. Profs.; 1 Hon. Prof.

Research: analytical chemistry (instrumental methods, nuclear magnetic resonance (NMR) spectroscopy and MS (mass spectroscopy)); computational chemistry (energetics, reactivities of molecular species, structures); materials/bio-related chemistry (inclusion compounds, macromolecules, polymeric nanoparticles); physical chemistry (frustrated total internal

reflection (FTIR), laser scattering, NMR, ultraviolet-visible (UV/VIS) spectroscopy); synthetic chemistry (bioactive, coordination, organic, organometallic, polymeric)

Chinese Language and Literature

see also Special Centres, etc (Chinese Studies, Institute of)

Tel: 2609 7074 Fax: 2603 6048
E-mail: chilan@cuhk.edu.hk

Chan, H. K., BA *Chinese HK*, MPhil *Chinese HK*, PhD *Chinese HK*   Prof.; Chairman*

Chang, S. H., BA *Chinese HK*, MA *Chinese HK*   Prof.

Cheung, Alex K. Y., BA *Natnl.Taiwan*, MA *Natnl.Taiwan*, PhD *Natnl.Taiwan*   Res. Prof.

Cheung, Samuel H. N., BA *Chinese HK*, MA *Chinese HK*, PhD *Calif.*   Prof.

Chiang, Y. H., BA *Chinese HK*, MPhil *Chinese HK*, PhD *Calif.*   Prof.

Dudbridge, G., BA *Camb.*, MA *Camb.*, MA *Oxf.*, PhD *Camb.*, FBA   ICS Visiting Prof.

Ho, C. W., BA *Chinese HK*, MPhil *Chinese HK*, PhD *Chinese HK*   Prof.

Jao, T. I., Hon. DrHumSc *École Pratique des Hautes Études*, Hon. DLitt *HK*, Hon. DLitt *Lingnan*, Hon. DLitt *Chinese HK*   Emer. Prof.

Lau, D. C., BA *HK*, MA *Glas.*, Hon. DLitt *HK*, Hon. LLD *Chinese HK*   Emer. Prof.

Wong, K. I., BA *Taiwan Normal*, MPhil *Chinese HK*, PhD *Chinese HK*   Prof.

Wong, Y. K., BA *Chinese HK*, MLet *Kyoto*, DLet *Kyoto*   Prof.

Zhang, J., BA *Anhui*, MA *Beijing Normal*, DLitt *Beijing Normal*   Prof.

Zhou, J. Y., BA *Kunming Teachers*, MA *Sichuan Normal*, MA *Prin.*, PhD *Prin.*, DLitt *Chinese Acad.Soc.Sc.*   Prof.

Other Staff: 2 Visiting Profs.; 3 Assoc. Profs.; 5 Asst. Profs.; 3 Hon. Profs.; 1 Hon. Res. Assoc.

Research: Chinese ancient documents; Chinese language and linguistics; classical Chinese literature; modern Chinese literature

Chinese Medicine, School of

Tel: 3163 4328 Fax: 2603 7203
E-mail: scm@cuhk.edu.hk

Che, C. T., BSc *Chinese HK*, MPhil *Chinese HK*, PhD *Ill.*   Prof.; Dir.*

Hu, S. Y., BA *Ginling*, MSc *Lingnan*, PhD *Harv.*   Hon. Prof.

Other Staff: 4 Visiting Profs.; 1 Asst. Prof.; 1 Res. Asst. Prof.; 3 Res. Assocs.; 2 Postdoctoral Fellows; 1 Visiting Scholar; 5 Professl. Consultants; 7 Adjunct Profs.; 1 Adviser/Adjunct Prof.; 5 Adjunct Assoc. Profs.; 3 Adjunct Asst. Profs.; 1 Hon. Prof.; 6 Hon. Visiting Profs.; 1 Hon. Assoc. Prof.; 1 Hon. Adviser/Hon. Visiting Prof.; 1 Hon. Professl. Consultant

Computer Science and Engineering

Tel: 2609 8440 Fax: 2603 5302
E-mail: dept@cse.cuhk.edu.hk

Cai, L., BSc *Zhejiang*, MSc *Vic.(BC)*, PhD *Tor.*   Prof.

Chan, L. W., BA *Camb.*, MA *Camb.*, PhD *Camb.*   Prof.

Chen, T. C., ScB *Brown*, MA *Duke*, PhD *Duke*, FIEEE   Emer. Prof.

Heng, P. A., BSc *NU Singapore*, MSc *Indiana*, MA *Indiana*, PhD *Indiana*   Prof.

Lee, Jimmy H. M., BMath *Wat.*, MMath *Wat.*, PhD *Vic.(BC)*   Prof.

Leong, Philip H. W., BSc *Syd.*, BE *Syd.*, PhD *Syd.*   Prof.

Leung, H. F., BSc *Chinese HK*, MPhil *Chinese HK*, PhD *Lond.*, FBCS   Prof.

Leung, K. S., BSc *Lond.*, PhD *Lond.*   Prof.

Lui, C. S., BSEE *Illinois Tech.Inst.*, MS *Illinois Tech.Inst.*, PhD *Calif.*   Prof.; Chairman*

Lyu, Michael R. T., BS *Natnl.Taiwan*, MSc *Calif.*, PhD *Calif.*, FIEEE   Prof.

Moon, Y. S., BSc *Manit.*, MSc *Tor.*, PhD *Tor.*   Prof.

Ng, K. W., MSc *Brad.*, PhD *Brad.*   Prof.

Wong, C. K., BA HK, MA Col., PhD Col., FIEEE, FACM   Emer. Prof.

Wong, T. T., BSc Chinese HK, MPhil Chinese HK, PhD Chinese HK   Prof.

Wu, Y. L., BS Florida Internat., MS Miami(Fla.), PhD Calif.   Prof.

Xu, L., BEng Harbin, MEng Tsinghua, DEng Tsinghua, FIEEE   Prof.

Other Staff: 8 Assoc. Profs.; 5 Asst. Profs.; 5 Postdoctoral Fellows; 2 Res. Assocs.; 1 Hon. Res. Assoc.

Research: database information systems; graphics and visualisation; networks and distributed systems; theoretical computer science; VSLI and computer-aided design (CAD) systems

Cultural and Religious Studies

Including Divinity School of Chung Chi College

Tel: 2609 6477 Fax: 2603 5280
E-mail: crsdept@cuhk.edu.hk

Lai, C. T., BA Chinese HK, MA Chic., PhD Chic., BD   Prof.

Lai, P. C., BA Chinese HK, MDiv Chinese HK, PhD Lond.   Prof.; Chairman*

Lee, Rev. Archie C. C., BA Chinese HK, MDiv Chinese HK, PhD Edin.   Prof.

Lo, L. K., BSc Natnl.Chung Hsing, MDiv Chinese HK, PhD Durh.   Prof.

Ng, Peter T. M., BA Chinese HK, MDiv Chinese HK, MA Lond., PhD Lond.   Prof.

Tam, W. L., BA Chinese HK, MA McM., PhD McM.   Prof.

Wong, Eric K. C., BA Chinese HK, MDiv Chinese HK, DTh Heidel.   Prof.

Other Staff: 6 Assoc. Profs.; 7 Asst. Profs.; 1 Res. Asst. Prof.; 2 Res. Assocs.; 3 Postdoctoral Fellows; 1 Adjunct Prof.; 3 Adjunct Asst. Profs.; 32 Hon. Res. Assocs.; 4 Hon. Visiting Scholars

Research: Biblical studies and Christian theology; Chinese Christianity; Chinese religions including Buddhism and Taoism; contemporary cultural and media studies; gender and culture

Curriculum and Instruction

Tel: 2609 6905 Fax: 2603 6724
E-mail: cri@fed.cuhk.edu.hk

Coniam, David J., BA S'ton., MA Birm., PhD Birm.   Prof.; Chairman*

Lam, C. C., BA HK, MA Lond., PhD Lond.   Prof.

Lee, John C. K., BA HK, MSc Oxf., MA(Ed) Chinese HK, PhD Chinese HK   Prof.

Lin, M. Y., BA HK, MPhil HK, PhD Tor.   Prof.

Wong, H. W., BSSc Chinese HK, MA(Ed) Chinese HK, EdD Calif.   Prof.

Wong, N. Y., BA HK, MA(Ed) Chinese HK, MPhil HK, PhD HK   Prof.

Other Staff: 9 Assoc. Profs.; 6 Asst. Profs.; 3 Adjunct Profs.; 7 Adjunct Assoc. Profs.; 3 Adjunct Asst. Profs.; 4 Hon. Asst. Profs.; 36 Hon. Professl. Consultants

Decision Sciences and Managerial Economics

Tel: 2609 7813 Fax: 2603 5104
E-mail: dse@cuhk.edu.hk

Cheung, W. M., BSc Natnl.Taiwan, MBA Rensselaer, PhD Rensselaer   Prof.; Chairman*

Du, Timon C. T., BS Natnl.Chung Hsing, MSE Arizona, PhD Arizona   Prof.

Fung, K. Y., BSSc Chinese HK, MA W.Ont., PhD W.Ont.   Prof.

Lai, Vincent S. K., BSSc Chinese HK, MBA Ohio, MS Arizona, PhD Texas   Prof.

Law, Japhet S., BA Texas, PhD Texas   Prof.

Lee, C. C., BA Tunghai, MBA Oklahoma City, PhD Penn.State   Prof.

Lee, T. S., BSc Chiao Tung, MS Chiao Tung, MBA Missouri, PhD Missouri   Prof.

Leung, Lawrence C. K., BSIE Northwestern, MS Virginia Polytech., PhD Virginia Polytech.   Prof.

Mok, Henry M. K., MA Tor., MSW Hawaii, MURP Hawaii, PhD Hawaii   Prof.

Ng, Linda F. Y., BS Northwestern(Oklahoma), MS Oklahoma State, PhD Oklahoma State   Prof.

Zhao, X., BS Nankai, MS Utah, MBA Utah, PhD Utah   Prof.

Other Staff: 4 Assoc. Profs.; 3 Asst. Profs.; 1 Professl. Consultant; 2 Postdoctoral Fellows; 4 Adjunct Profs.; 1 Adjunct Assoc. Prof.

Economics

Tel: 2609 8190 Fax: 2603 5805
E-mail: economics@cuhk.edu.hk

Chao, C. C., BC Chengchi, MA Natnl.Taiwan, PhD S.Illinois   Prof.

Chou, W. L., BA Fujen, MS Ill., PhD Ill.   Prof.

Lau, Lawrence J., BS Stan., MA Calif., PhD Calif., Hon. DSocSc HKUST, Hon. Doc Soka, Hon. LLD Waseda, FES   Ralph and Claire Landau Prof.

Li, H., BEcon S.China Agric., MS S.China Agric., PhD Stan.   Prof.

Liu, P. W., AB Prin., MA Stan., MA(Ed) Stan., PhD Stan.   Prof.

Sung, Y. W., BSocSc HK, PhD Minn.   Prof.; Chairman*

Tsui, K. Y., BA Tor., MA Tor., PhD Tor.   Prof.

Yang, Dennis T., BA Calif., PhD Calif.   Prof.

Yip, C. K., BSSc Chinese HK, MA(Econ) Penn.State, MA(Stat) Penn.State, PhD Penn.State   Prof.

Zhang, J., BSc Zhejiang, MA McM., PhD McM.   Prof.

Other Staff: 5 Assoc. Profs.; 6 Asst. Profs.; 1 Postdoctoral Fellow; 1 Hon. Res. Fellow

Research: econometrics; economy of Greater China; international trade and economic development; labour and family economics; macroeconomic theory

Educational Administration and Policy

Tel: 2609 6953 Fax: 2603 6761
E-mail: eapdept@cuhk.edu.hk

Chung, Stephen Y. P., JP, BA Oregon, MA Mich.State, MA Stan., PhD Stan.   Prof.

Lo, Leslie N. K., BA Oregon, MIA Col., EdD Col.   Prof.

Pang, S. K., BSc HK, MEd HK, PhD Newcastle(NSW)   Prof.

Tsang, W. K., BSSc Chinese HK, MPhil Chinese HK, PhD Chinese HK   Prof.

Walker, A. D., BEd NE, MEd Ill., PhD Ill.   Prof.; Chairman*

Other Staff: 4 Assoc Profs.; 3 Asst. Profs.; 1 Res. Assoc.; 3 Postdoctoral Fellows; 2 Professl. Consultants; 3 Adjunct Profs.; 1 Adjunct Assoc. Prof.

Research: economics and finance in education; education and societies in China; educational leadership and administration; educational policy analysis; school evaluation and improvement (school effectiveness)

Educational Psychology

Tel: 2609 6904 Fax: 2603 6921
E-mail: edpsy@fed.cuhk.edu.hk

Chan, David W. O., BA Brock, MA W.Ont., PhD W.Ont.   Prof.

Chang, L., BA Hebei, MS Calif., PhD Calif.   Prof.

Hau, K. T., BSc Chinese HK, MA(Ed) Chinese HK, PhD HK   Prof.; Chairman*

Leung, S. M., BS Ill., MS Ill., PhD Ill.   Prof.

Other Staff: 8 Assoc. Profs.; 2 Asst. Profs.; 1 Postdoctoral Fellow; 1 Adjunct Prof.; 3 Hon. Professl. Consultants

Research: educational assessment; gifted and talented education; psychological counselling and guidance; teacher development

Engineering

Tel: 2609 8446 Fax: 2603 5701
E-mail: facultyoffice@ie.cuhk.edu.hk

Kao, Charles K., CBE, BSc Lond., PhD Lond., Hon. DSc Chinese HK, Hon. DSc Sus., Hon. Doctorat Soka, Hon. DEng Glas., Hon. DSc Durh., Hon. DUniv Griff., Hon. DTE Padua, Hon. DSc Hull, Hon. DSc Yale, FREng, FRS, FIEEE, FIEE   Hon. Prof.

Other Staff: 2 Hon. Profs.

Engineering, Electronic

Tel: 2609 8274 Fax: 2603 5558
E-mail: dept@ee.cuhk.edu.hk

Cham, W. K., BSc Chinese HK, MSc Lough., PhD Lough.   Prof.

Chan, K. T., BSc HK, PhD Cornell   Prof.

Cheng, Michael K. K., BSc Lond., PhD Lond.   Prof.

Ching, P. C., BEng Liv., PhD Liv., FIEE   Prof.

Choy, C. S., BSc Manc., MSc Manc., PhD Manc.   Prof.

Ho, H. P., BEng Nott., PhD Nott.   Prof.

Lam, Y. W., BSc Lond., MSc Birm., PhD Manc., FIEE, FIP   Emer. Prof.

Meng, Max Q. H., BS Luoyang I.T., MEng Beijing I.T., PhD Vic.(BC)   Prof.

Ngan, K. N., BSc Lough., PhD Lough., FIEE, FIEEE, FIEAust   Prof.; Chairman*

Shu, Chester C. T., BSc HK, MS Col., PhD Col.   Prof.

Tsang, H. K., BA Camb., MA Camb., PhD Camb.   Prof.

Wang, William S. Y., BA Col., MA Mich., PhD Mich.   Res. Prof.

Wilson, I. H., BSc Reading, PhD Reading, FIP   Emer. Prof.

Wu, K. L., BS Nanjing Sci. & Tech., MEng Nanjing Sci. & Tech., PhD Laval   Prof.

Xu, J., BS Nanjing, MS Nanjing, DrRerNat Constance   Prof.

Zhang, Y., BSc Shandong, MSc Shandong, PhD New Br.   Prof.

Other Staff: 2 Assoc. Profs.; 4 Asst. Profs.; 2 Res. Assocs.; 17 Postdoctoral Fellows; 1 Visiting Scholar; 12 Adjunct Profs.; 1 Adjunct Assoc. Prof.; 3 Hon. Profs.; 2 Hon. Lectrs.; 2 Hon. Res. Fellows; 1 Hon. Professl. Consultant

Research: biomedical engineering; solid state and optoelectronics; speech and video technology; VLSI circuit design; wireless and microwave communications

Engineering, Information

Tel: 2609 8385 Fax: 2603 5032
E-mail: dept@ie.cuhk.edu.hk

Chen, L. K., BS Natnl.Taiwan, MS Col., PhD Col.   Prof.

Cheung, K. W., BSc(Eng) HK, MS Yale, PhD Cal.Tech.   Prof.

Chiu, D. M., BSc Lond., PhD Harv.   Prof.

Lee, T. T., BS Cheng Kung, MS Cleveland, MS N.Y.Polytech., PhD N.Y.Polytech., FIEEE   Prof.

Li, Robert S. Y., BS Natnl.Taiwan, PhD Calif.   Prof.

Liew, S. C., BS M.I.T., MS M.I.T., PhD M.I.T., FIEE   Prof.; Chairman*

Tang, X., BS China U.S.T., MS Roch., PhD M.I.T.   Prof.

Wei, Victor K. W., BS Natnl.Taiwan, PhD Hawaii   Prof.

Wing, O., BS Tennessee, MS M.I.T., EngScD Col., FIEEE   Emer. Prof.

Wong, P. C., BSc Chinese HK, MPhil Chinese HK, PhD Chinese HK   Prof.

Wong, W. S., BA Yale, MA Yale, MS Harv., PhD Harv., FIEEE   Prof.

Yeung, W. H., BS Cornell, MEng Cornell, PhD Cornell, FIEEE   Prof.

Yum, Peter T. S., BS Col., MS Col., MPh Col., PhD Col.   Prof.

Other Staff: 5 Assoc. Profs.; 6 Asst. Profs.; 3 Res. Assocs.; 2 Postdoctoral Fellows; 4 Adjunct Profs.; 1 Hon. Assoc. Prof.

Engineering, Mechanical, Automation and Computer-Aided

Tel: 2609 8337 Fax: 2603 6002
E-mail: dept@mae.cuhk.edu.hk

Chung, Ronald C. K., BSc(Eng) HK, MSEE S.Calif., PhD S.Calif.   Prof.

Du, R., MEng S.China Tech., PhD Mich.   Prof.

Huang, J., MEng Nanjing Sci. & Tech., PhD Johns H., FIEEE   Prof.

Hui, K. C., BSc(Eng) HK, PhD HK   Prof.

Kwong, C. P., MSc Lough., PhD Chinese HK, PhD City HK, FIEE   Prof.

Li, W. J., BS S.Calif., MS S.Calif., PhD Calif.
Prof.
Liu, Y., BEng Beijing I.T., MEng Osaka, PhD Tokyo
Prof.
Wang, J., BEng Dalian U.T., MEng Dalian U.T.,
PhD Case W.Reserve, FIEEE   Prof.
Wang, Michael Y., BS Xi'an Jiaotong, ME
Penn.State, PhD Carnegie-Mellon, FIEEE   Prof.
Xu, Y., BEng Zhejiang, MEng Zhejiang, PhD Penn.,
FIEEE   Prof.
Yam, Y., BSc Chinese HK, MSc Akron, MSc M.I.T.,
ScD M.I.T.   Prof.; Chairman*
Other Staff: 1 Assoc. Prof.; 1 Asst. Prof.; 1 Res.
Asst. Prof.; 3 Res. Assocs.; 2 Postdoctoral
Fellows; 1 Visiting Scholar
Research: manufacturing process and design;
micro-/nano-device fabrication and
application; robotics and visual-based
applications; smart materials and structures

Engineering, Systems, and Engineering Management

Tel: 2609 8313 Fax: 2603 5505
E-mail: dept@se.cuhk.edu.hk
Cai, X., BEng Harbin Shipbldg.Engin., MEng
Tsinghua, DEng Tsinghua   Prof.
Lam, K. P., BSc HK, MPhil Chinese HK, DPhil Oxf.
Prof.
Lam, W., BSc Chinese HK, MPhil Chinese HK, PhD
Wat.   Prof.
Leung, Janny M. Y., SB Harv., BA Oxf., PhD
M.I.T.   Prof.
Li, D., BSc Fudan, MEng Shanghai Jiaotong, PhD
Case W.Reserve   Prof.; Chairman*
Lum, Vincent Y. S., BAppSc Tor., MSc Wash.,
PhD Ill.   Emer. Prof.
Meng, Helen M. L., SB M.I.T., SM M.I.T., PhD
M.I.T.   Prof.
Wong, K. F., BSc Edin., PhD Edin.   Prof.
Yan, H., BEng Tsinghua, MEng Tsinghua, PhD Tor.
Prof.
Yao, David D. W., MSc Tor., PhD Tor., FIEEE
Prof.
Yu, Jeffrey X., BE Tsukuba, ME Tsukuba, PhD
Tsukuba   Prof.
Zhang, S., BS Fudan, MS Fudan, PhD Rotterdam
Prof.
Zhou, X., BS Fudan, DS Fudan, FIEEE   Prof.
Other Staff: 1 Visiting Prof.; 4 Assoc. Profs.; 4
Asst. Profs.; 9 Postdoctoral Fellows; 4 Sr.
Res. Fellows; 4 Visiting Scholars; 2 Adjunct
Profs.; 1 Hon. Prof.
Research: business information systems (core of
enterprise in knowledge-based society); e-
commerce systems (new paradigm for
doing business); financial engineering
(advanced technologies for financial
industries); logistics and supply chain
management (strategic/operational nexus of
global supply chain); operations research
(solution methodologies for making
optimal decisions)

English

Tel: 2609 7005 Fax: 2603 5270
E-mail: english@cuhk.edu.hk
Crisp, P. G., BA Trinity(Dub.), PhD Reading   Sr.
Lectr.
Gong, G., BA Mississippi, MA Mississippi, PhD
Purdue   Prof.
Jackson, B. J., BT St Thomas(NB), BA St
Thomas(NB), MEd Calg., PhD Tor.   Prof.
Parker, D. H., BA Adel., BA Flin., DPhil Oxf.
Prof.; Chairman*
Parkin, A. T. L., BA Camb., MA Camb., PhD Brist.
Emer. Prof.
Skehan, P., BA Keele, MA W.Ont., MA Paris III,
PhD Lond.   Prof.
Weiss, T., BA Colorado, MA Wis., PhD New Mexico
Prof.
Zhang, B., BA Liaoning, MA Guangzhou Foreign
Langs., PhD Alta.   Prof.
Other Staff: 4 Assoc. Profs.; 4 Asst. Profs.

English Language Teaching Unit

Tel: 2609 7465 Fax: 2603 5157
E-mail: eltu-info@cuhk.edu.hk
Curtis, Andy, BEd Sund., MA York(UK), PhD
York(UK)   Dir.*

Other Staff: 1 Res. Assoc.

Finance

Tel: 2609 7805 Fax: 2603 6586
E-mail: finance@baf.msmail.cuhk.edu.hk
Chan, W. S., BBA Chinese HK, MPhil Chinese HK,
MSc Temple, PhD Temple, FRSS, FSA   Prof.
Fan, Joseph P. H., LLB Natnl.Taiwan, PhD Pitt.
Prof.
Han, L. M., BS Fujen, MS Natnl.Taiwan, PhD Texas
Prof.
He, J., BS Heilongjiang, MS Shanghai Jiaotong, PhD
Penn.   Prof.
Lang, Larry H. P., BA Tunghai, MA Natnl.Taiwan,
MA Penn., PhD Penn.   Prof.
McGuinness, P. B., BA Newcastle(UK), MPhil
Camb., PhD Leeds   Prof.; Chairman*
Young, Leslie, BSc Well., MSc Well., DPhil Oxf.
Prof.
Zhang, H., BEng Tianjin, MBA McG., PhD McG.
Prof.
Other Staff: 10 Assoc. Profs.; 6 Asst. Profs.; 2
Professl. Consultants; 4 Adjunct Profs.; 1
Hon. Prof.

Fine Arts

Tel: 2609 7615 Fax: 2603 5755
E-mail: finearts@cuhk.edu.hk
Jao, T. I., Hon. DrHumSc École Pratique des Hautes
Études, Hon. DLitt HK, Hon. DLitt Lingnan,
Hon. DLitt Chinese HK   Wei Lun Hon. Prof.
Mok, Harold K. L., BA HK, MPhil HK, DPhil
Oxf.   Prof.
So, Jenny F. S., BA Swarthmore, MA Harv., PhD
Harv.   Prof.; Chairman*
Other Staff: 4 Assoc. Profs.; 1 Asst. Prof.; 1
Adjunct Prof.; 2 Hon. Profs.; 1 Hon. Assoc.
Research: ancient Chinese art (Neolithic to
Bronze Age); artistic and cultural exchange
between China and neighbours; history and
theory of Chinese painting and calligraphy;
Hong Kong and Asian art; western media,
abstract art and mixed media

Geography and Resource Management

Tel: 2609 6532 Fax: 2603 5006
E-mail: geography@cuhk.edu.hk
Fung, T., BA HK, MPhil HK, PhD Wat.   Prof.;
Chairman*
Lam, K. C., JP, BA HK, MPhil HK, PhD NE
Prof.
Leung, Y., BSSc Chinese HK, MA Colorado, MS
Colorado, PhD Colorado   Prof., Geography
Lin, H., MS Chinese Acad.Sc., MA N.Y.State, PhD
N.Y.State   Prof.
Shen, J., BS E.China Normal, MS E.China Normal,
PhD Lond., FRGS   Prof.
Yeung, Y. M., OBE, JP, BA HK, MA W.Ont.,
PhD Chic.   Emer. Prof.
Other Staff: 5 Assoc. Profs.; 3 Asst. Profs.; 1
Res. Assoc.; 1 Postdoctoral Fellow; 1
Adjunct Prof.; 1 Hon. Prof.; 1 Hon. Visiting
Scholar
Research: environmental studies (environmental
impact assessment (EIA), policy analysis,
resource management, sustainable
development); geographical techniques
(quantitative methods, urban and regional
analysis); geoinformation sciences
(geographic information systems (GIS),
geoinformatics, remote sensing, spatial
modelling); human and regional geography
(China, globalisation, population, urban
and regional development); physical
geography (climatology, geomorphology,
hydrology, pedology, quaternary studies)

Government and Public Administration

Tel: 2609 7530 Fax: 2603 5229
E-mail: gpadept@cuhk.edu.hk
Davis, M. C., BA Ohio State, LLM Yale, JD Calif.
Prof.
Kuan, H. C., LLB Chengchi, MA F.U.Berlin, PhD
Munich   Emer. Prof.
Li, L., BPhil Nankai, MPhil Nankai, MA Ohio State,
PhD Ohio State   Prof.

Preston, P. W., BA Leeds, PhD Leeds   Prof.;
Acting Chairman*
Wang, S., LLB Peking, MA Cornell, PhD Cornell
Prof.
Other Staff: 4 Assoc. Profs.; 4 Asst. Profs.

History

Tel: 2609 7117 Fax: 2603 5685
E-mail: history@cuhk.edu.hk
Choi, C. C., BA Natnl.Taiwan, MPhil Chinese HK,
DLitt Tokyo   Prof.
Chu, H. L., PhD Prin., MA Prin., BA MA   Prof.
Faure, D. W., BA HK, PhD Prin.   Prof.
Leung, Philip Y. S., BA Chinese HK, MPhil Chinese
HK, PhD Calif.   Prof.; Chairman*
So, Billy K. L., BA Chinese HK, MPhil Chinese HK,
PhD ANU   Prof.
Yip, H. M., BA Chinese HK, MA Calif., PhD Calif.
Prof.
Other Staff: 2 Visiting Profs.; 5 Assoc. Profs.; 1
Asst. Prof.; 1 Res. Assoc.; 2 Postdoctoral
Fellows; 1 Adjunct Prof.; 3 Adjunct Assoc.
Profs.; 8 Adjunct Asst. Profs.; 1 Hon. Prof.;
1 Hon. Asst. Prof.; 1 Hon. Sr. Res. Assoc.;
1 Hon. Res. Assoc.

Hotel and Tourism Management, School of

Tel: 2609 8590 Fax: 2603 7724
E-mail: htm@cuhk.edu.hk
Lau, K. N., BSSc Chinese HK, MA Georgia State,
PhD Purdue   Prof.
Lee, K. H., BCom Chinese HK, MCom Chinese HK,
PhD Northwestern   Prof., Marketing; Dir.*
Tse, Eliza C. Y., BS Utah State, MS Virginia
Polytech., PhD Virginia Polytech.   Prof.
Other Staff: 2 Assoc. Profs.; 3 Asst. Profs.; 1
Res. Assoc.; 1 Professl. Consultant; 2
Adjunct Profs.; 2 Adjunct Assoc. Profs.; 1
Hon. Prof.

Japanese Studies

Tel: 2609 6563 Fax: 2603 5118
E-mail: japanese-studies@cuhk.edu.hk
Lee, W. H., BA Tokyo Foreign, MIA Tsukuba, PhD
Tsukuba   Prof.; Chairman*
Mito, T., BA Internat.Christian(Tokyo), MIA
Tsukuba, PhD Tsukuba   Prof.
Other Staff: 2 Assoc. Profs.; 3 Asst. Profs.

Journalism and Communication, School of

Tel: 2609 7680 Fax: 2603 5007
E-mail: com@cuhk.edu.hk
Chan, J. M., BS Minn., PhD Minn., MPhil Chinese
HK   Prof.
Huang, Y. H., BA Fujan, MS Maryland, PhD
Maryland   Prof.
Lee, Paul S. N., BSSc Chinese HK, MPhil Chinese
HK, PhD Mich.   Prof.
Leung, Kenneth W. Y., MA Minn., PhD Minn.
Prof.
So, Clement Y. K., BSSc Chinese HK, MPhil
Chinese HK, PhD Penn.   Assoc. Prof.; Dir.*
Other Staff: 4 Assoc. Profs.; 6 Asst. Profs.; 3
Adjunct Asst. Profs.
Research: cultural phenomena in societies;
integrated marketing communication:
goodwill and image; international
communication and globalisation (trans-
border cross-cultural communication); new
media (digital media); the press and the
journalism industry

Law, School of

Tel: 2609 4316 Fax: 2994 2505
E-mail: law@cuhk.edu.hk
Hall, S., LLB Qld., LLM Technol.Syd., DPhil Oxf.
Prof.
Ling, B., LLB Peking, LLM Mich.   Prof.; Deputy
Dir.
McConville, M., LLB Lond., PhD Nott.   Simon F.
S. Li Prof.; Dir.*
Mercurio, B. C., BA Ohio Wesleyan, LLM NSW,
JD Case W.Reserve   Prof.
Pendleton, M. D., LLB Syd., LLM Lond.   Prof.

Williams, Sir D. G. T., QC, LLB Camb., MA Camb., LLM Calif., Hon. DLitt   Hon. Prof.

Wolff, L. C., DrIur Passau, DrHabil Passau   Prof.

Woolf, Lord, of Barnes, LLB Lond., Hon. LLD Buckingham, Hon. LLD Brist., Hon. LLD Lond., Hon. LLD Anglia PU, Hon. LLD Manc.Met., Hon. LLD Hull, Hon. LLD Cran., Hon. LLD Richmond, Hon. LLD Camb., Hon. LLD Oxf., Hon. LLD Exe., Hon. LLD Birm., Hon. LLD Wolv., Hon. FBA   Hon. Prof.

Yang, Sir T. L., JP, LLB Lond., Hon. LLD Chinese HK, Hon. DLitt HK, Hon. LLD HKPU   Hon. Prof.

Other Staff: 6 Assoc. Profs.; 5 Asst. Profs.; 2 Visiting Scholars; 7 Professl. Consultants; 1 Adjunct Prof.; 2 Hon. Visiting Scholars

Research: Chinese law and legal culture; criminal justice; English and Hong Kong common law; intellectual property rights; international law

Linguistics and Modern Languages

Tel: 2609 7911 Fax: 2603 7755
E-mail: lin@cuhk.edu.hk

Gu, Y., BA Xian Inst.Foreign Langs., MA Arizona State, MA Cornell, PhD Cornell   Prof.

Lee, Thomas H. T., BA Swarthmore, MA Calif., PhD Calif.   Prof.

Tang, Gladys W. L., BA HK, PhD Edin.   Prof.; Chairman*

Wang, William S. Y., BA Col., MA Mich., PhD Mich.   Res. Prof.

Yip, Virginia C. Y., BA Texas, MA Texas, MA S.Calif., PhD S.Calif.   Prof.

Other Staff: 1 Assoc. Prof.; 1 Asst. Prof.; 2 Postdoctoral Fellows; 2 Adjunct Profs.

Management

see also Decision Scis. and Managerial Econ.

Tel: 2609 7898 Fax: 2063 6840
E-mail: mgt@cuhk.edu.hk

Ahlstrom, D. C., BA N.Y., MPhil N.Y., MBA Hawaii, PhD N.Y.   Prof.

Cheung, Gordon W. H., BBA Chinese HK, PhD Virginia Polytech.   Prof.

Chow, Irene H. S., BA Chinese HK, MBA Georgia State, PhD Georgia State   Prof.

Hui, C., BA Greenville, MA Indiana, PhD Indiana   Prof.

Lau, C. M., BSSc Chinese HK, MBA Chinese HK, PhD Texas A.& M.   Prof.

Law, S. K., BBA Chinese HK, PhD Iowa, FAmPsyS   Prof.

Lu, Y., BEng Beijing I.T., PhD Aston, MBA   Prof.

Makino, S., BA Keio, MBA Keio, PhD W.Ont.   Prof.; Chairman*

Ngo, H. Y., BSSc Chinese HK, MA Chic., PhD Chic.   Prof.

Wong, C. S., BBA Chinese HK, PhD Purdue   Prof.

Other Staff: 1 Visiting Prof.; 4 Assoc. Profs.; 3 Asst. Profs.; 1 Postdoctoral Fellow; 2 Professl. Consultants; 3 Adjunct Profs.; 1 Hon. Prof.; 1 Hon. Res. Assoc.

Research: entrepreneurship; human resource management; international business; organisation behaviour; strategic management

Marketing

Tel: 2609 7809 Fax: 2603 5473
E-mail: mkt@cuhk.edu.hk

Chan, Andrew C. F., BBA Chinese HK, MBA Calif., PhD Chinese HK   Prof.

Hui, Michael K. M., BBA Chinese HK, PhD Lond.   Prof.

Jia, J., BS S.W.China Jiaotong, MS Shanghai Jiaotong, PhD Texas   Prof.

Lau, K. N., BSSc Chinese HK, MA Georgia State, PhD Purdue   Prof.

Lee, K. H., BCom Chinese HK, MCom Chinese HK, PhD Northwestern   Prof.

Mun, K. C., MA Freib., PhD Freib.   Emer. Prof.

Sin, Leo Y. M., BBA Chinese HK, MBA Texas, PhD Br.Col.   Prof.

Tse, C. B., BBA Chinese HK, LLB Wolv., MBA Chinese HK, MSocSc HK, PhD Massey   Prof.

Tung Ho, S. C., BBA Chinese HK, MBA Indiana   Prof.; Chair*

Other Staff: 5 Assoc. Profs.; 3 Asst. Profs.; 1 Postdoctoral Fellow; 1 Professl. Consultant; 2 Adjunct Profs.; 1 Hon. Prof.

Research: business negotiation; cross-cultural marketing; customer relations; marketing engineering; service marketing

Mathematics

Tel: 2609 7729 Fax: 2603 5154
E-mail: dept@math.cuhk.edu.hk

Chan, H. F., BSc Chinese HK, MSc N.Y., PhD N.Y.   Prof.

Chou, K. S., BSc Chinese HK, MSc Chinese HK, PhD N.Y.   Prof.

Lau, K. S., BSc Chinese HK, PhD Wash.   Prof.; Chairman*

Leung, N. C., MS Calif., PhD M.I.T.   Prof.

Luk, H. S., BA HK, MA Col., MPhil Col., PhD Col.   Prof.

Ng, K. F., MSc Wales, PhD Wales, DSc Wales   Res. Prof.

Tam, L. F., BSc Chinese HK, PhD Stan.   Res. Prof.

Wan, Tom Y. H., BSc Chinese HK, MSc Stan., PhD Stan.   Prof.

Wang, J., BS E.China Normal, MS E.China Normal, PhD Calif.   Prof.

Wei, J., BS Wuhan, PhD Minn.   Prof.

Xin, Z., BS Northwestern, MA Chinese Acad.Sc., PhD Mich.   William M. W. Mong Prof.

Zou, J., BS Jiangxi, MS Wuhan, PhD Chinese Acad.Sc.   Prof.

Other Staff: 2 Assoc. Profs.; 2 Asst. Profs.; 1 Visiting Scholar; 1 Postdoctoral Fellow

Research: algebra (algebraic geometry, commutative algebra, number theory); analysis (dynamical systems, functional and harmonic analysis, and wavelets, operator algebra, optimisation); applied analysis (applied partial differential equations, fluid dynamics, mathematical physics); computational mathematics (image processing, inverse problems, numerical analysis); geometric analysis (complex geometry, differential geometry, string theory)

Music

Tel: 2609 6510 Fax: 2603 5273
E-mail: music@cuhk.edu.hk

Chan, S. Y., BA Chinese HK, MA Pitt., PhD Pitt.   Prof.

Chan, Victor W. K., BA Chinese HK, DPhil York(UK)   Prof.

Cheong, W. L., BA Chinese HK, MPhil Camb., PhD Camb.   Prof.

Gwilt, D. W., MBE Camb., MusB Camb.   Emer. Prof.

Law, Daniel P. L., BA Chinese HK, MMus Northwestern, PhD Northwestern   Prof.

McClellan, M. E., BA Minn., MA N.Carolina, PhD N.Carolina   Assoc. Prof.; Chairman*

Olson, G. J., BA S.Calif., MA S.Calif., PhD S.Calif.   Prof.

Other Staff: 1 Assoc. Prof.; 1 Asst. Prof.; 1 Res. Assoc.; 2 Hon. Sr. Res. Fellows

Research: composition (western, Chinese instruments and voice); ethnomusicology (instrumental, operatic and ritual music of China); musicology (topics from sixteenth- to twentieth-century)

Philosophy

Tel: 2609 7135 Fax: 2603 5323
E-mail: philosophy@cuhk.edu.hk

Cheng, C. Y., BA Chinese HK, MA Chinese HK, PhD Chinese HK   Prof.

Cheung, C. F., BA Chinese HK, MPhil Chinese HK, DrPhil Freib.   Prof.; Chairman*

Kwan, T. W., BA Chinese HK, MPhil Chinese HK, DrPhil Bochum   Prof.

Lao, Y. W., BA Natnl.Taiwan   Tang Chun-I Visiting Prof.

Lau, K. Y., BA Chinese HK, PhD Paris I   Prof.

Li, H. L., BA Oxf., MA Oxf., MA Cornell, PhD Cornell   Prof.

Liu, S. H., BA Natnl.Taiwan, MA Natnl.Taiwan, PhD S.Illinois   Emer. Prof.

Liu, X., BA Inner Mongolian Normal, MA Peking, PhD Peking   Prof.

Shun, K. L., BA HK, BA Lond., BPhil Oxf., MPhil HK, PhD Stan.   Prof.

Wang, Q., BA Nanjing, MA Peking, PhD Tulane   Prof.

Other Staff: 1 Assoc. Prof.; 3 Asst. Profs.; 3 Res. Assocs.; 1 Hon. Assoc. Prof.

Research: applied ethics; Chinese philosophy and related areas; comparative philosophy; phenomenology; philosophy of language

Physics

Tel: 2609 6339 Fax: 2603 5204
E-mail: physics@cuhk.edu.hk

Chan, Y. W., BS Lingnan, MS Lingnan, PhD Calif.   Emer. Prof.

Ching, Emily S. C., BSc HK, MPhil Chinese HK, PhD Chic.   Prof.

Chiu, Willie L. S., ScD M.I.T., BS   Prof.

Chu, M. C., BSc Cal.Tech., PhD Cal.Tech.   Prof.

Hsu, B., OBE, JP, BSc Manc., PhD Manc., FIP   Emer. Prof.

Hui, P. M., BSc HK, MS Ohio State, PhD Ohio State   Prof.

Kui, H. W., BS Cal.Tech., PhD Harv.   Prof.

Lau, Leo W. M., BSc Chinese HK, PhD Br.Col.   Prof., Materials Science

Leung, P. T., BSc Chinese HK, MS Cal.Tech., PhD Chinese HK   Prof.

Lin, H. Q., BS China U.S.T., MS Iowa State, PhD Calif.   Prof.; Chairman*

Liu, K. L., BSc Chinese HK, MSc Tor., PhD Tor.   Prof.

Wong, H. K., BSc Chinese HK, MPhil Chinese HK, PhD Northwestern   Prof.

Xia, K., BS Lanzhou, MS Pitt., PhD Pitt.   Prof.

Xiao, X., BS China U.S.T., MA Calif., PhD Calif.   Prof.

Yang, C. N., BSc Kunming, PhD Chic., Hon. DSc Chinese HK   Hon. Prof.

Young, Kenneth, BS Cal.Tech., PhD Cal.Tech.   Prof.

Yu, K. W., BSc Chinese HK, MS Calif., PhD Calif.   Prof.

Other Staff: 6 Assoc. Profs.; 4 Asst. Profs.; 6 Res. Asst. Profs.; 9 Res. Assocs.; 2 Visiting Scholars; 7 Postdoctoral Fellows; 5 Adjunct Profs.; 2 Adjunct Asst. Profs.; 5 Hon. Profs.; 4 Hon. Res. Assocs.

Research: condensed matter physics; functional nanomaterials and their electronic structures; optical properties of semiconductors; optics and quantum information; turbulence and complex fluids

Psychology

Tel: 2609 6578 Fax: 2603 5019
E-mail: info@psy.cuhk.edu.hk

Bond, M., BA Tor., PhD Stan.   Res. Prof.; Emer. Prof.

Chan, Agnes S. Y., AB Mich., MSW Mich., AM Mich., PhD Calif.   Prof.

Chen, H. C., BA Fujen, MA Calif.State, PhD Kansas   Prof.

Cheung, Fanny M. C., OBE, JP, BA Calif., PhD Minn.   Prof.; Chair*

Leung, Patrick W. L., BSocSc HK, MSocSc HK, PhD Sheff.   Prof.

McBride, C. A., BA Oberlin, MA S.Calif., PhD S.Calif.   Prof.

Other Staff: 6 Assoc. Profs.; 5 Asst. Profs.; 1 Postdoctoral Fellow; 2 Professl. Consultants; 1 Adjunct Assoc. Prof.; 2 Adjunct Asst. Profs.; 1 Hon. Prof.

Research: clinical and health psychology; cognitive psychology and neuropsychology; developmental psychology; personality; social and industrial-organisational psychology

Science, Faculty of

Tel: 2609 6327 Fax: 2603 5156
E-mail: sfo@cuhk.edu.hk

Roberts, R. J., Hon. MD Bath, Hon. DSc Sheff., Hon. DSc Derby, Hon. DSc Chinese HK, BSc PhD, FRS   Hon. Prof.

Wuthrich, K., PhD Basle, Hon. DrUniv Siena, Hon. Dr Zür., Hon. Dr Lausanne, Hon. Dr Valencia, Hon. Dr Sheff., Hon. Dr Lond., Hon. Dr Pécs, Hon. FRCSEd, Hon. FRSCan, Hon. FAAAS, Hon. FNI   Prof.
Other Staff: 1 Res. Asst. Prof.

Social Work

Tel: 2609 7507 Fax: 2603 5018
E-mail: socialwork@cuhk.edu.hk
Lam, M. C., BSSc Chinese HK, MSW Minn., PhD S.Calif.   Prof.
Ma, L. C., BSocSc HK, MSocSc HK, PhD HK   Prof.
Mok, B. H., BSSc Chinese HK, MSW Hawaii, PhD S.Calif.   Prof.
Ngai, N. P., BSSc Chinese HK, LLB Peking, MSW HK, PhD Sheff.   Prof.
Shek, Daniel T. L., JP, BSocSc HK, PhD HK   Prof.
Tang, K. L., BSocSc HK, MSW HK, MSc Lond., LLB Lond., LLM Camb., PhD Calif.   Prof.; Chairman*
Wong, C. K., BSocSc HK, MSW HK, PhD Sheff.   Prof.
Other Staff: 2 Assoc. Profs.; 4 Asst. Profs.; 3 Res. Asst. Profs.; 5 Professl. Consultants; 1 Adjunct Prof.; 1 Hon. Res. Assoc.
Research: child and youth welfare; East Asian social welfare; family practice and counselling; human behaviour and social environment; social welfare indicators

Sociology

Tel: 2609 6604 Fax: 2603 5213
E-mail: sociology@cuhk.edu.hk
Cheung, Y. W., BSSc Chinese HK, MA McM., PhD Tor.   Prof.
Chiu, Stephen W. K., BSocSc HK, MA Prin., MPhil HK, PhD Prin.   Prof.
King, Ambrose Y. C., JP, BA Natnl.Taiwan, MPhil Natnl.Chengchi, MPhil Pitt., PhD Pitt., Hon. DLitt HKUST   Emer. Prof.
Lau, S. K., JP, BSocSc HK, PhD Minn.   Emer. Prof.
Lee, Rance P. L., OBE, JP, BSSc Chinese HK, PhD Pitt.   Prof.; Chairman*
Lui, T. L., BA HK, MPhil HK, MPhil Oxf., DPhil Oxf.   Prof.
Ting, K. F., BSSc Chinese HK, MPhil Chinese HK, PhD N.Carolina   Prof.
Other Staff: 3 Assoc. Profs.; 8 Asst. Profs.
Research: civil society; social class and mobility; social problems; sociology of education; work and globalisation

Sports Science and Physical Education

Tel: 2609 6089 Fax: 2603 5781
E-mail: sports@cuhk.edu.hk
Ha, Amy S. C., BA Fujen, MPE Springfield, PhD   Prof.
Hong, Y., MEd Beijing Phys.Educn.   Prof.; Chairman*
Hui, S. C., BPE Springfield, MSc Springfield, EdD Houston   Prof.
Wong, Stephen H. S., BEd Liv., MSc Lough., PhD Lough.   Prof.
Other Staff: 1 Asst. Prof.; 1 Dir., Phys. Educn. Unit; 3 Adjunct Profs.; 1 Res. Assoc.; 1 Hon. Prof.; 5 Hon. Professl. Consultants
Research: critical pedagogy and teacher development; health and performance-related physical fitness and activity; motivation in sport, exercise and rehabilitation; sports footwear and biomechanics of T'ai Chi; sports nutrition for health and performance

Statistics

Tel: 2609 7931 Fax: 2603 5188
E-mail: statdept@cuhk.edu.hk
Chan, N. H., BSc Chinese HK, PhD Maryland   Prof.; Chairman*
Cheung, S. H., BA C'dia., MA Georgia, MS Georgia, PhD Temple   Prof.
Gu, M., BS Fudan, MA Col., MPhil Col., PhD Col.   Prof.

Lee, C. M., BAppSc Technol.Syd., PhD Macq.   Prof.
Lee, S. Y., BSc Chinese HK, MA Calif., MSc Calif., PhD Calif.   Prof.
Li, K. H., BSc Chinese HK, MPhil Chinese HK, MSc Chic., PhD Chic.   Prof.
Poon, W. Y., BSc Chinese HK, MPhil Chinese HK, PhD Calif.   Prof.
Other Staff: 4 Assoc. Profs.; 3 Asst. Profs.; 1 Postdoctoral Fellow; 2 Visiting Scholars; 3 Adjunct Profs.; 1 Hon. Prof.
Research: computational statistics; signal processing; statistical finance; structural equation models; times series

Translation

Tel: 2609 7700 Fax: 2603 7843
E-mail: tra@cuhk.edu.hk
Chan, S. W., BA Chinese HK, PhD Lond.   Prof.
Fong, Gilbert C. F., BA Chinese HK, MA York(Can.), MA Tor., PhD Tor.   Prof.
Jin, Serena, OBE, MA Wash., Dr3rdCy Paris   Emer. Prof.
McDougall, B. S., BA Syd., MA Syd., PhD Syd.   Res. Prof.
Tung, Y. F., BA Natnl.Taiwan, MA Oregon, MA Oregon, PhD Harv.   Prof.
Wong, Laurence K. P., BA HK, MPhil HK, PhD Tor.   Prof.; Chairman*
Wong, W. C., BA HK, MPhil HK, PhD Lond.   Prof.
Other Staff: 2 Assoc. Profs.; 1 Asst. Prof.; 2 Adjunct Profs.
Research: bilingual laws in Hong Kong; Gao Xingjian project; parallel translation corpus; translation studies in China; translator training

MEDICINE

Tel: 2609 6891 Fax: 2603 5821
E-mail: faculty@med.cuhk.edu.hk
Hazlett, C. B., BEd Alta., MEd Alta., PhD Alta.   Prof., Medical Education
Ignarro, L. J., BA Col., PhD Minn., Hon. Doc Madrid, Hon. Doc Lund, Hon. Doc Ghent, Hon. Doc N.Carolina   Hon. Prof.
Kan, Y. W., MB BS HK, DSc HK, Hon. DSc HK, Hon. MD Cagliari, Hon. DSc Chinese HK, Hon. DSc Open HK   Hon. Prof.
Lau, Joseph W. Y., MB BS HK, MD Chinese HK, FRCSEd, FRCS, FRCSGlas, FRACS, FACS, Hon. FRACS   Prof., Surgery
Lo, Dennis Y. M., BM BCh Oxf., MA Camb., DPhil Oxf., DM Oxf., FRCPEd, FRCPath, FRCP   Li Ka Shing Prof.

Anaesthesia and Intensive Care

Tel: 2632 2735 Fax: 2637 2422
E-mail: ansoffice@cuhk.edu.hk
Chan, T. V., MB BS NSW, FANZCA   Clin. Prof.
Critchley, L. A. H., BMedSci Sheff., MB ChB Sheff., MD Sheff., FFARCSI   Prof.
Gin, Tony, BSc Cant., MB ChB Otago, MD Otago, FRCA, FANZCA   Clin. Prof.; Chairman*
Ho, Anthony M. H., MSc Stan., MD McM., FRCPCan   Clin. Prof.
Joynt, G. M., MB BCh Witw.   Clin. Prof.
Ngan Kee, W. D., BHB Auck., MB ChB Auck., MD Auck., FANZCA   Clin. Prof.
Other Staff: 1 Assoc. Prof.; 4 Visiting Scholars; 3 Clin. Assoc. Profs.; 2 Hon. Profs.

Anatomical and Cellular Pathology

Tel: 2632 3334 Fax: 2637 6274
E-mail: hkng@cuhk.edu.hk
Lo, K. W., BSc Chinese HK, MPhil Chinese HK, PhD Chinese HK   Prof.
Mac-Moune Lai, Fernand, MD Lyons, FRCPA   Clin. Prof.
Ng, H. K., MB ChB Edin., MD Chinese HK, FRCPA, FRCPath   Clin. Prof.; Chairman*
Ng, Margaret H. L., MB ChB Chinese HK, MBA Warw., MD Chinese HK, FRCPath   Clin. Prof.
To, K. F., MB ChB Chinese HK, FRCPA   Clin. Prof.
Wong, Nathalie, BSc Lond., MSc Lond., DPhil Oxf.   Prof.

Other Staff: 2 Asst. Profs.; 1 Postdoctoral Fellow; 3 Fellows; 1 Clin. Assoc. Prof.; 2 Clin. Asst. Profs.; 1 Hon. Prof.; 1 Hon. Res. Assoc.
Research: cancer genomics and epigenomics; hepatocellular carcinoma; medulloblastoma; multiple myeloma; nasopharyngeal carcinoma

Anatomy

Tel: 2609 6853 Fax: 2603 5031
E-mail: anatomy@cuhk.edu.hk
Chan, Franky L., BSc Chinese HK, PhD HK   Prof.
Chan, S. O., BSc Chinese HK, MPhil Chinese HK, DPhil Oxf.   Prof.
Chan, W. Y., BSc Chinese HK, MPhil Chinese HK, PhD Chinese HK   Prof.; Chairman*
Chow, Patricia P. H., BSc HK, PhD HK   Prof.
Lee, Kenneth K. H., BSc Aberd., PhD Glas.   Prof.
Liu, W. K., BSc Chinese HK, MPhil Chinese HK, DrRerNat Düsseldorf   Prof.
Yew, David T. W., BSc Chinese HK, PhD Wayne State, DrMed(habil) Rostock, DrScMed Rostock, FIBiol   Prof.
Other Staff: 3 Assoc. Profs.; 1 Res. Assoc.; 1 Postdoctoral Fellow; 1 Visiting Scholar; 4 Hon. Profs.; 5 Hon. Res. Assocs.; 1 Hon. Visiting Res. Assoc.; 1 Hon. Res. Fellow
Research: carcinogenesis and functions of sex glands; development and degeneration of retina; development, injury, ageing of nervous systems; embryonic development and stem cells in normal/abnormal pregnancies; muscular, immune and neuronal cells

Chemical Pathology

Tel: 2632 3338 Fax: 2636 5090
E-mail: waikeilam@cuhk.edu.hk
Chiu, Rossa W. K., MB BS Qld., PhD Chinese HK, FRCPA   Prof.
Lam, Christopher W. K., MSc Warw., PhD S'ton., FRSChem   Prof.; Chairman*
Lo, Dennis Y. M., BM BCh Oxf., MA Camb., DPhil Oxf., DM Oxf., FRCPEd, FRCPath, FRCP   Li Ka Shing Prof., Medicine
Tang, Nelson L. S., MB ChB Chinese HK, MD Chinese HK, FRCPA   Clin. Prof.
Other Staff: 2 Assoc. Profs.; 5 Postdoctoral Fellows; 1 Clin. Assoc. Prof.; 2 Clin. Asst. Profs.
Research: genetics of polygenic diseases; immunopathology of allergy and autoimmunity; molecular genetics of cancer; molecular tumour markers; non-invasive pre-natal diagnosis

Clinical Immunology Unit

Tel: 2632 2709 Fax: 2645 0856
E-mail: peggyfung@cuhk.edu.hk
Lam, Christopher W. K., MSc Warw., PhD S'ton., FRSChem   Prof.; Dir.*
Lim, P. L., BSc Adel., PhD Adel., FASM   Prof.
Other Staff: 1 Assoc. Prof.; 1 Postdoctoral Fellow

Clinical Oncology

Tel: 2632 2119 Fax: 2649 7426
E-mail: clo@cuhk.edu.hk
Chan, Anthony T. C., MB BS Lond., MD Chinese HK, FRCPEd   Clin. Prof.; Chairman*
Mok, Tony S. K., BMSc Alta., MD Alta., FRCPCan   Clin. Prof.
Yeo, Winnie, MB BS Lond., MD Chinese HK   Prof.
Other Staff: 1 Assoc. Prof.; 2 Asst. Profs.; 1 Postdoctoral Fellow; 1 Visiting Scholar; 2 Clin. Assoc. Profs.; 4 Hon. Profs.

Community and Family Medicine

Tel: 2252 8800 Fax: 2606 3500
E-mail: cfm@cuhk.edu.hk
Griffiths, S. M., OBE, BA Camb., MB BChir Camb., MSc Lond., FFPHM, FRCP, FDSRCS, FRCPEd   Clin. Prof., Public Health; Chairman*

Ho, Suzanne S. Y., BA Calif., MSc Brown, MPH Col., PhD NU Singapore, FACE   Prof.

Lee, Albert, MB BS Lond., MPH Chinese HK, FRACGP   Clin. Prof.

Lee, S. H., JP, MB BS HK, MD HK, FRCP, FFPHM   Emer. Prof.

Tang, J., MB Beijing Med., MSc Lond., PhD Lond.   Prof.

Wong, T. W., MB BS HK, MSc NU Singapore, FFPHM, FRCPGlas   Clin. Prof.

Yeoh, E. K., OBE, JP, MB BS HK, FRCPEd, FRCP, FRCPGlas, FRACP, FFPHM   Clin. Prof., Public Health

Yu, Ignatius T. S., MB BS HK, MPH Texas   Clin. Prof.

Zee, Benny C. Y., BSc Manit., MSc Manit., PhD Pitt.   Prof.

Other Staff: 1 Assoc. Prof.; 3 Asst. Profs.; 1 Visiting Prof.; 1 Clin. Assoc. Prof.; 3 Clin. Asst. Profs.; 2 Clin. Professl. Consultants; 2 Hon. Profs.; 1 Hon. Visiting Prof.; 1 Hon. Assoc. Prof.; 1 Hon. Res. Assoc.

Research: health care needs and services; health in the elderly population; nutritional epidemiology; occupational and environmental health; women's health

Diagnostic Radiology and Organ Imaging

Tel: 2632 2290 Fax: 2636 0012
    E-mail: radiology@med.cuhk.edu.hk

Ahuja, A. T., MB BS Bom., MD Bom., FRCR   Clin. Prof.; Chairman*

Antonio, G. E., BSc NSW, MB BS NSW   Prof.

Chu, Winnie C. W., MB ChB Chinese HK, FRCR   Prof.

Griffith, J. F., MB BCh N.U.I., BAO N.U.I., FRCR   Clin. Prof.

King, A. D., MB ChB Sheff., FRCR   Clin. Prof.

Lam, Wynnie W. M., MB BS HK, MD Chinese HK, FRCR   Clin. Prof.

Other Staff: 1 Asst. Prof.; 1 Visiting Scholar

Medicine and Therapeutics

Tel: 2632 3942 Fax: 2637 3852
    E-mail: alanfok@cuhk.edu.hk

Chan, Henry L. Y., MB ChB Chinese HK, MD Chinese HK, FRCPEd   Prof.

Chan, Julia C. N., MB ChB Liv., MD Liv., FRCPEd, FRCP   Clin. Prof.

Chan, K. L., MB ChB Chinese HK, MD Chinese HK   Clin. Prof.

Chan, Thomas Y. K., MB ChB Glas., PhD Chinese HK, MD Glas., FRCPEd, FRCP, FRCPGlas   Clin. Prof.

Cheng, Gregory, MD Tor., PhD Tor., FRCPCan   Clin. Prof.

Cockram, C. S., BSc Lond., MB BS Lond., MD Lond., FRCP, FRCPEd, FRACP   Clin. Prof., Medicine

Hui, David S. C., MB BS NSW, MD NSW, FRACP, FRCP, FRCPGlas, FRCPEd   Prof.

Kwok, Timothy C. Y., MB ChB Leic., MD Leic.   Prof.

Leung, W. K., MB ChB Chinese HK, MD Chinese HK   Clin. Prof.

Li, Edmund K. M., BS Loma Linda, MD East(Manila), FRCPCan, FRCP, FRCPEd, FACP   Clin. Prof.

Sung, Joseph Y., MB BS HK, MD Chinese HK, PhD Calg., FRCPEd, FRCP   Clin. Prof.; Chairman*

Szeto, C. C., MB ChB Chinese HK, MD Chinese HK   Clin. Prof.

Tomlinson, B., BSc Lond., MD Lond., FRCP, FRCPEd, FACP   Clin. Prof.

Wong, K. S., MB BS NSW, MHA NSW, MD NSW, FRCP   Clin. Prof.

Woo, Jean, MB BChir Camb., MA Camb., MD Camb., FRCPEd, FRCP, FRACP   Clin. Prof., Medicine

Yu, C. M., MB ChB Chinese HK, MD Chinese HK, FRACP   Clin. Prof.

Other Staff: 1 Res. Assoc. Prof.; 3 Asst. Profs.; 4 Res. Asst. Profs.; 6 Res. Assocs.; 5 Postdoctoral Fellows; 2 Visiting Scholars; 8 Clin. Assoc. Profs.; 1 Clin. Asst. Prof.; 1 Clin. Res. Fellow; 9 Hon. Profs.; 5 Hon. Res. Assocs.; 1 Hon. Visiting Scholar

Microbiology

Tel: 2632 3333 Fax: 2647 3227
    E-mail: microbiology@cuhk.edu.hk

Chan, Paul K. S., MB BS HK, MSc Lond., MD Chinese HK   Clin. Prof.

Chan, Raphael C. Y., BSc Calg., PhD Calg.   Sr. Lectr.; Acting Chairman*

Ip, Margaret, BM S'ton., MSc Lond., FRCPA, FRCPGlas   Clin. Prof.

Other Staff: 1 Assoc. Prof.; 1 Res. Asst. Prof.; 64 Postdoctoral Fellows; 1 Clin. Assoc. Prof.; 1 Clin. Asst. Prof.; 1 Hon. Res. Officer

Research: antibiotic resistance; infection control; mycobacteriology and mycology; pharmacokinetics and pharmacodynamics; virology

Nursing, Nethersole School of

Tel: 2609 6220 Fax: 2603 5269
    E-mail: nursing@cuhk.edu.hk

Chan, Sally W. C., BHS C.Sturt, MSN Edin., PhD Oxf.Brookes   Prof.

Courtney, M. D., BCom Griff., MHP NSW, PhD NE   Prof.

Lee, Diana T. F., MSc Edin., PhD Chinese HK   Prof., Clinical Nursing

Twinn, S. F., BA CNAA, PhD Lond.   Prof.; Dir.*

Other Staff: 8 Assoc. Profs.; 8 Asst. Profs.; 1 Res. Asst. Prof.; 2 Professl. Consultants

Research: cancer prevention and management; cardiovascular disease prevention and management; gerontology/long-term care; mental health

Obstetrics and Gynaecology

Tel: 2632 2806 Fax: 2636 0008
    E-mail: obsgyn@cuhk.edu.hk

Chung, Tony K. H., MB BS Syd., MD Chinese HK, FRACOG, FRCOG   Clin. Prof.; Chairman*

Haines, C. J., MB BS Adel., MD Chinese HK, FRACOG   Clin. Prof.

Lau, T. K., MB ChB Chinese HK, MD Chinese HK, MMed NU Singapore   Clin. Prof.

Rogers, M. S., MB ChB Birm., MD Chinese HK, FRCOG, FRCS   Clin. Prof.

Wong, Y. F., MD Shanghai 1st Med.Coll., MMedSc Shanghai 2nd Med.Coll., PhD Chinese HK   Res. Prof.

Yip, Alexander S. K., BSc Portland, MB ChB Chinese HK, MD Chinese HK   Clin. Prof.

Other Staff: 2 Assoc. Profs.; 3 Asst. Profs.; 1 Res. Assoc.; 1 Postdoctoral Fellow; 2 Clin. Assoc. Profs.; 1 Clin. Professl. Consultant; 2 Hon. Visiting Scholars

Research: developmental genomics and bioinformatics; molecular profiling of gynaecology cancer; non-invasive prenatal diagnosis and monitoring; signal transduction during spermatogenesis; urogynaecology and female pelvic medicine

Ophthalmology and Visual Sciences

Tel: 2762 3124 Fax: 2715 9490
    E-mail: med_dovs@cuhk.edu.hk

Congdon, N. G., AB Prin., MPhil Camb., MPH Johns H., MD Johns H.

Fan, Dorothy S. P., MB ChB Chinese HK, MSc Chinese HK, FRCSEd   Clin. Prof.

Lam, Dennis S. C., MB BS HK, MD Chinese HK, FRCSEd   Clin. Prof.; Chairman*

Pang, C. P., BSc Lond., DPhil Oxf.   Prof.

Tham, Clement C. Y., BM BCh Oxf., BA Camb., MA Camb., FRCSGlas   Clin. Prof.

Other Staff: 1 Assoc. Prof.; 1 Asst. Prof.; 1 Res. Assoc.; 7 Visiting Scholars; 2 Clin. Assoc. Profs.; 5 Clin. Asst. Profs.; 21 Hon. Profs.

Research: medical and surgical treatment of myopia (short-sightedness); molecular and genomic investigations of genetic eye diseases; ocular hypertension in children; photodynamic therapy, a new treatment modality for choroidal neovascularisation (CNV) and choroidopathy

Orthopaedics and Traumatology

Tel: 2632 2722 Fax: 2637 7889
    E-mail: dept@ort.cuhk.edu.hk

Chan, K. M., OBE, JP, MB BS HK, MCh Liv., FRCSEd, FRCSGlas, FACS   Clin. Prof.

Cheng, Jack C. Y., MB BS HK, MD Chinese HK, FRCSEd, FRCSGlas, FACS, FRCSEd   Clin. Prof.

Hung, L. K., MB BS HK, MChOrth Liv., FRCSEd, FRCSGlas   Clin. Prof.; Chairman*

Kumta, S. M., MB BS Bom., MS Bom., PhD Chinese HK   Clin. Prof.

Leung, K. S., MB BS HK, MD Chinese HK, FRCSEd   Clin. Prof.

Leung, P. C., OBE, JP, MB BS HK, MS HK, DSc Chinese HK, Hon. DSocSc HK, FRCSEd, FRACS   Emer. Prof.

Qin, L., BEd Beijing Phys.Educn., MEd Beijing Phys.Educn., PhD D.H.S.Cologne   Prof.

Other Staff: 1 Res. Asst. Prof.; 2 Postdoctoral Fellows; 3 Res. Assocs.; 1 Visiting Scholar; 1 Clin. Assoc. Prof.; 4 Hon. Profs.; 3 Hon. Res. Assocs.

Research: bone tumour and osteonecrosis; congenital disorders and scoliosis; musculoskeletal ageing; sports medicine and health promotion; tissue healing and biophysical interventions

Hong Kong Jockey Club Sports Medicine and Health Sciences Centre

Research: professional sports training; sports biomechanics and automation engineering; sports for health and physical fitness; sports medicine and traumatology; sports nutrition and physiology

Otorhinolaryngology, Head and Neck Surgery

Tel: 2632 3950 Fax: 2145 8876
    E-mail: ent@cuhk.edu.hk

Tong, Michael C. F., MB ChB Chinese HK, MD Chinese HK, FRCSEd   Prof.

van Hasselt, C. A., MB BCh Witw., MMed Witw., FCS(SA), FRCSEd, FRCS   Prof.; Chairman*

Other Staff: 2 Asst. Profs.; 2 Professl. Consultants; 1 Visiting Scholar; 1 Clin. Asst. Prof.; 1 Hon. Prof.

Paediatrics

Tel: 2632 2851 Fax: 2636 0020
    E-mail: paediatrics@cuhk.edu.hk

Fok, T. F., MB BS HK, MD Chinese HK, FRCPEd, FRCPCH   Clin. Prof.

Leung, T. F., MB ChB Chinese HK, MD Chinese HK, FRCPCH   Prof.

Li, Albert M. M. C., BSc Wales, MB BCh Wales   Prof.

Nelson, E. A. S., MB ChB Cape Town, MD Otago   Clin. Prof.

Ng, P. C., MB ChB Dund., MD Leeds, FRCPEd, FRCPCH, FRCP   Clin. Prof.; Chairman*

Sung, Rita Y. T., MB Natnl.Taiwan, MSc Wales, MD Wales, FRCP, FRCPCH   Clin. Prof.

Wong, W. K., BMSc Alta., MD Alta., MD Chinese HK, FRCPCan   Clin. Prof.

Other Staff: 1 Assoc. Prof.; 2 Res. Assocs.; 1 Postdoctoral Fellow; 3 Visiting Scholars; 1 Clin. Assoc. Prof.; 4 Hon. Profs.

Research: haemotology and oncology; immunology/infection; neonatal medicine; paediatric respirology; stem cells

Pharmacology

Tel: 2609 6820 Fax: 2603 5139
    E-mail: pharmacology@cuhk.edu.hk

Cho, C. H., BPharm Natnl.Def.Med.Center, Taiwan, PhD HK   Prof.; Chairman*

Jones, R. L., BPharm Lond., PhD Lond., DSc Lond.   Emer. Prof.

Lin, G., MSc Alta., PhD Sask., BSc   Prof.

Wise, H., BSc Brist., PhD Bath   Prof.

Yeung, John H. K., BSc Liv., PhD Liv.   Prof.

Other Staff: 4 Assoc. Profs.; 2 Res. Assocs.; 1 Adjunct Prof.; 1 Hon. Postdoctoral Fellow

Research: anti-emetic and gastro-intestinal pharmacology; anti-inflammatory pharmacology; cardiovascular pharmacology; molecular pharmacology of receptors; pharmacodynamics and pharmacokinetics

Pharmacy, School of

Tel: 2609 6860 Fax: 2603 5295
E-mail: pharmacy@cuhk.edu.hk
Chow, Albert H. L., BPharm Brad., MSc Tor., PhD Tor.   Prof.
Lee, Kenneth K. C., BSc Wash., MPhil Chinese HK, PhD Chinese HK   Prof.
Lee, Vincent H. L., BS Ferris, MS Wis., PhD Wis., Hon. DSc Lond.   Prof.; Dir.*
Other Staff: 3 Assoc. Profs.; 2 Asst. Profs.; 1 Teaching Fellow; 3 Res. Assocs.; 1 Adjunct Prof.
Research: medicinal and pharmaceutical chemistry; pharmaceutics and pharmaceutical technology; pharmacognosy and Chinese herbal medicine; pharmacokinetics, pharmacogenetics and pharmacogenomics; pharmacy practice and pharmacoeconomics

Physiology

Tel: 2609 6882 Fax: 2603 5022
E-mail: physiology@cuhk.edu.hk
Chan, H. C., BS Ill., PhD Ill.   Li Ka Shing Prof.
Huang, Y., BSc Shanghai 1st Med.Coll., MPhil Camb., PhD Camb.   Prof.
Leung, P. S., BS Natnl.Taiwan, PhD Belf.   Prof.
Tam, Michael S. C., BSc Tor., MSc Tor., PhD Tor.   Prof.; Chairman*
Wong, Patrick Y. D., MA Camb., PhD Camb., DSc Lond., ScD Camb., FIBiol, FRSChem   Res. Prof.; Emer. Prof.
Yao, X., BS Hangzhou, MS Chinese Acad.Sc., PhD N.Y.State   Prof.
Yung, W. H., BSc Chinese HK, MPhil Chinese HK, DPhil Oxf.   Prof.
Other Staff: 1 Assoc. Prof.; 1 Res. Assoc. Prof.; 1 Asst. Prof.; 1 Res. Asst. Prof.; 2 Res. Assocs.; 1 Teaching Fellow; 1 Postdoctoral Fellow; 1 Hon. Postdoctoral Fellow; 1 Hon. Visiting Scholar
Research: cardiovascular physiology and ion channels; central nervous system physiology and pathophysiology; epithelial transport and cellular physiology; molecular endocrinology and male reproductive physiology; respiratory physiology and renal/acid base physiology

Psychiatry

Tel: 2607 6026 Fax: 2667 1255
E-mail: psychiatry@cuhk.edu.hk
Chiu, Helen F. K., MB BS HK, FRCPsych   Clin. Prof.; Chair*
Lam, C. W., MB ChB Chinese HK   Clin. Prof.
Lee, S., MB BS HK   Clin. Prof.
Tang, W. K., MB ChB Chinese HK, MD Chinese HK   Prof.
Ungvari, G. S., MD Semmelweis, PhD Hungarian Acad.Sc., FRANZCP   Clin. Prof.
Wing, Y. K., MB ChB Chinese HK   Clin. Prof.
Other Staff: 1 Postdoctoral Fellow; 2 Clin. Assoc. Profs.; 2 Hon. Profs.

Public Health, School of

Tel: 2252 8488 Fax: 2145 7489
E-mail: info_sph@cuhk.edu.hk
Griffiths, S. M., OBE, BA Camb., MB BChir Camb., MSc Lond., FFPHM, FRCP, FDSRCS, FRCPEd   Clin. Prof.; Dir.*
Lau, Joseph T. F., BSSc Chinese HK, MA Calif., PhD Calif.   Prof.
Yeoh, E. K., OBE, JP, MB BS HK, FRCPEd, FRCP, FRCPGlas, FRACP, FFPHM   Clin. Prof.
Zee, Benny C. Y., BSc Manit., MSc Manit., PhD Pitt.   Prof.
Other Staff: 1 Visiting Prof.; 5 Asst. Profs.; 2 Res. Assocs.; 2 Postdoctoral Fellows; 1 Professl. Consultant; 2 Adjunct Profs.; 1 Adjunct Assoc. Prof.; 2 Clin. Asst. Profs.; 9 Hon. Profs.; 1 Hon. Assoc. Prof.; 1 Hon. Asst. Prof.; 1 Hon. Adviser

Research: biostatistics and epidemiology; family medicine and primary health care; health improvement; health systems policy and management; infectious diseases

Emerging Infectious Diseases, Stanley Ho Centre for

Tel: 2252 8812 Fax: 2635 4977
E-mail: ceid@med.cuhk.edu.hk
Kung, H. F., BS Natnl.Chung Hsing, PhD Vanderbilt   Prof., Virology
Lee, S. S., JP, MB BS HK, MD HK, FRCPA, FRCPGlas, FRCPEd   Clin. Prof., Infectious Diseases
Sung, Joseph Y., MB BS HK, MD Chinese HK, PhD Calg., FRCPEd, FRCP   Clin. Prof., Medicine and Therapeutics; Dir.*
Other Staff: 1 Assoc. Prof.; 1 Asst. Prof.; 2 Res. Asst. Profs.; 1 Postdoctoral Fellow; 3 Visiting Scholars; 1 Adjunct Asst. Prof.
Research: enteric infections (diagnostic and clinical management, epidemiology); HIV/AIDS (clinical science, cohort studies, epidemiology, social-behavioural science); influenza and respiratory infections (public health impacts, diagnostics, clinical management); tuberculosis (public health impacts, diagnostics, clinical management); viral hepatitis (epidemiology, genomic analysis, prevention effectiveness)

Surgery

Tel: 2632 2789 Fax: 2637 7974
E-mail: surgery@cuhk.edu.hk
Burd, D. A. R., MB ChB Aberd., MD Aberd., FRCSEd   Clin. Prof.
Chen, George G., MM Shanghai 2nd Med.Coll., PhD Glas., MB   Prof.
He, G. W., MB Anhui Med., MMEd Peking Union Med., PhD Monash, DSc Monash   Res. Prof.
Lai, Paul B. S., MB ChB Chinese HK, MD Chinese HK, FRCSEd   Clin. Prof.
Li, Arthur K. C., JP, BChir Camb., MA Camb., MD Camb., Hon. DSc Hull, Hon. DLitt HKUST, Hon. Doc Soka, Hon. LLD Chinese HK, FRCS, FRCSEd, FRACS, FACS, Hon. FRCSGlas, Hon. FRCSI, Hon. FACS   Emer. Prof.
Ng, K. W., MB ChB Chinese HK, MD Chinese HK, FRCSEd   Clin. Prof.
Poon, W. S., MB ChB Glas., FRCSGlas   Clin. Prof.
Underwood, M. J., MB ChB Leic., MD Leic., FRCSEd   Clin. Prof.
van Hasselt, C. A., MB BCh Witw., MMed Witw., FCS(SA), FRCSEd, FRCS   Clin. Prof., Otorhinolaryngology; Chairman*
Yeung, C. K., MB BS HK, MD Chinese HK, FRCSEd, FRCSGlas, FRACS   Clin. Prof.
Yip, Sidney K. H., MB BS HK, FRCSEd, FAMS   Prof.
Other Staff: 1 Asst. Prof.; 4 Res. Asst. Profs.; 8 Res. Assocs.; 3 Postdoctoral Fellows; 8 Visiting Scholars; 7 Clin. Assoc. Profs.; 2 Clin. Asst. Profs.; 1 Clin. Professl. Consultant; 5 Hon. Profs.; 2 Hon. Visiting Scholars

Accident and Emergency Medicine

Tel: 2632 1033 Fax: 2648 1469
E-mail: aemau@med.cuhk.edu.hk
Graham, C. A., MB ChB Glas., MPH Glas., FRCSEd, FRCSGlas   Prof.
Rainer, T. H., BSc Wales, MB BCh Wales, MD Wales   Assoc. Prof.; Dir.*
Other Staff: 1 Postdoctoral Fellow

SPECIAL CENTRES, ETC

Advanced Engineering, Shun Hing Institute of

Tel: 2609 8407 Fax: 2603 5024
E-mail: info@shiae.cuhk.edu.hk
Ching, P. C., BEng Liv., PhD Liv., FIEE   Dir.*

Advanced Integration Technology, CAS-CUHK Shenzen Institute of

Tel: 2680 3632 Fax: 2680 3632
E-mail: wt.feng@siat.ac.cn
Xu, Y., BEng Zhejiang, MEng Zhejiang, PhD Penn., FIEEE   Dir.*

Asia-Pacific Studies, Hong Kong Institute of

Tel: 2609 6740 Fax: 2603 5215
E-mail: hkiaps@cuhk.edu.hk
Lee, Paul S. N., BSSc Chinese HK, MPhil Chinese HK, PhD Mich.   Dir.*
Yeung, Y. M., OBE, JP, BA HK, MA W.Ont., PhD Chic.   Res. Prof.
Other Staff: 2 Assoc. Dirs.; 1 Res. Assoc. Prof.; 1 Res. Asst. Prof.; 1 Res. Officer; 6 Hon. Sr. Res. Fellows; 4 Hon. Res. Fellows; 1 Hon. Res. Assoc.

Biotechnology, Chinese University Institute of

Tel: 2603 5111 Fax: 2603 5012
E-mail: eidy@hkib.org.hk
Ho, Walter K. K., AB Calif., PhD Calif.   Dir.*
Other Staff: 1 Assoc. Dir.; 1 Res. Asst. Prof.

Business, Asia-Pacific Institute of

Tel: 2609 7473 Fax: 2603 5136
E-mail: apib@cuhk.edu.hk
Chang, Randall, BA Calif.State, MA Calif.State, PhD Claremont   Dir., Bus. Devel.
Lu, Y., BEng Beijing I.T., PhD Aston, MBA   Dir., Res. Devel.
Young, Leslie, BSc Well., MSc Well., DPhil Oxf.   Exec. Dir.*
Other Staff: 1 Sr. Operations Manager

China Studies, Universities Service Centre for

Tel: 2609 8762 Fax: 2603 5030
E-mail: usc@cuhk.edu.hk
Kuan, H. C., LLB Chengchi, MA F.U.Berlin, PhD Munich   Dir.*
Other Staff: 2 Asst. Dirs.; 1 Res. Assoc. Prof.; 2 Hon. Sr. Fellows; 2 Hon. Res. Fellows; 2 Hon. Res. Assocs.; 1 Hon. Consultant

Chinese Medicine, Institute of

Tel: 3163 4370 Fax: 2603 5248
E-mail: icm@cuhk.edu.hk
Fung, K. P., BSc Chinese HK, MPhil Chinese HK, PhD HK   Dir.*
Leung, P. C., OBE, JP, MB BS HK, MS HK, DSc Chinese HK, Hon. DSocSc HK, FRCSEd, FRACS   Dir.*
Woo, K. S., MB BS HK, MD HK, MMed NU Singapore, FRACP, FACC, FACP, FRCPEd   Res. Prof.
Other Staff: 2 Dep. Dirs.; 1 Sr. Res. Fellow; 5 Postdoctoral Fellows; 5 Res. Assocs.; 1 Visiting Scholar; 5 Hon. Advisers; 1 Hon. Assoc. Prof.; 1 Hon. Visiting Scholar

Chinese Studies, Chiang Ching-kuo Foundation Asia-Pacific Centre for

Tel: 2696 1710 Fax: 2603 5149
So, Billy K. L., BA Chinese HK, MPhil Chinese HK, PhD ANU   Dir.*
Other Staff: 2 Hon. Dirs.

Chinese Studies, Institute of

Tel: 2609 7394 Fax: 2603 5149
E-mail: ics@cuhk.edu.hk
Dudbridge, G., BA Camb., MA Camb., MA Oxf., PhD Camb., FBA   ICS Visiting Prof.
Jao, T. I., Hon. DrHumSc École Pratique des Hautes Etudes, Hon. DLitt HK, Hon. DLitt Lingnan, Hon. DLitt Chinese HK   Wei Lun Hon. Prof., Fine Arts
Lau, D. C., BA HK, MA Glas., Hon. DLitt HK, Hon. LLD Chinese HK   Hon. Prof.; Adviser
So, Jenny F. S., BA Swarthmore, MA Harv., PhD Harv.   Dir.*

Other Staff: 1 Hon. Prof. and Chief Editor; 1 Assoc. Prof.; 1 Res. Asst. Prof.; 1 Res. Assoc.; 2 Hon. Res. Fellows; 1 Hon. Res. Assoc.; 1 Hon. Sr. Res. Fellow; 1 Hon. Adviser

Art Museum

Tel: 2609 7416 Fax: 2603 5366
E-mail: artmuseum@cuhk.edu.hk
Lam, Peter Y. K., BA Lond. Dir.*
Other Staff: 1 Curator; 2 Hon. Res. Fellows; 1 Hon. Adviser

Chinese Ancient Text, Research Centre for

Tel: 2609 7381 E-mail: rccat@cuhk.edu.hk
Ho, C. W., BA Chinese HK, MPhil Chinese HK, PhD Chinese HK Dir.*
Other Staff: 1 Hon. Res. Assoc.
Research: Chinese ancient texts; Chinese lexicon (word usage); comparative study of Chinese ancient texts

Chinese Archaeology and Art, Centre for

Tel: 2609 7371 Fax: 2603 7539
E-mail: ccaa@cuhk.edu.hk
Tang, C., BA Chinese HK, MA Chinese HK, DLet Tokyo Dir.*
Other Staff: 3 Hon. Res. Fellows

Contemporary Chinese Culture, Research Centre for

Tel: 2609 7382 Fax: 2603 5202
E-mail: rcccc@cuhk.edu.hk
Jin, G. T. Res. Prof.; Dir.*
Other Staff: 2 Res. Assocs.; 5 Hon. Res. Fellows; 4 Hon. Res. Assocs.
Research: development of modern Chinese political concepts; foreign cultures in China; intellectual history of modern China; quantitative study of modern concepts and ideas

T. T. Ng Chinese Language Research Centre

Tel: 2609 7392 Fax: 2603 7989
E-mail: clrc@cuhk.edu.hk
Chang, S. H., BA Chinese HK, MA Chinese HK Dir.*

Translation, Research Centre for

Tel: 2609 7399 Fax: 2603 5110
E-mail: rct@cuhk.edu.hk
McDougall, B. S., BA Syd., MA Syd., PhD Syd. Acting Dir.*
Wong, W. C., BA HK, MPhil HK, PhD Lond. Dir.*
Other Staff: 1 Editor of Renditions; 1 Adviser; 1 Advisory Editor

Continuing and Professional Studies, School of

Tel: 2209 0299 Fax: 2739 2797
E-mail: scs@cuhk.edu.hk
Lee, Victor S. K., BSc Indiana, MSc Indiana, MBA Strath., PhD Lond., FAIM Dir.*
Other Staff: 1 Assoc. Dir.; 1 Res. Fellow; 1 Sr. Planning and Devel. Officer

Diabetes and Obesity, Institute of

Tel: 2632 1419 Fax: 2637 3929
E-mail: hkfrdd@med.cuhk.edu.hk
Chan, Julia C. N., MB ChB Liv., MD Liv., FRCPEd, FRCP Dir.*
Other Staff: 1 Assoc. Dir.

Digestive Disease, Institute of

Tel: 2632 2233 Fax: 2635 0075
E-mail: idd@med.cuhk.edu.hk
Sung, Joseph Y., MB BS HK, MD Chinese HK, PhD Calg., FRCPEd, FRCP Dir.*
Other Staff: 2 Res. Asst. Profs.; 2 Postdoctoral Fellows; 1 Visiting Scholar; 2 Hon. Visiting Scholars

East Asian Studies, Centre for

Tel: 3163 4392 Fax: 2994 3105
E-mail: ceas@cuhk.edu.hk
Dirlik, A., BS Robert(Istanbul), PhD Roch. Prof., Chinese Studies
Dudbridge, G., BA Camb., MA Camb., MA Oxf., PhD Camb., FBA ICS Visiting Prof.
Lee, Leo O. F., BA Natnl.Taiwan, MA Harv., PhD Harv. Prof.
So, Billy K. L., BA Chinese HK, MPhil Chinese HK, PhD ANU Acting Dir.*
Wang, William S. Y., BA Col., MA Mich., PhD Mich. Res. Prof.
Other Staff: 1 Asst. Dir.; 1 Asst. Prof.; 1 Hon. Dir.
Research: Chinese studies (culture, history, law, literature, society)

Economics and Finance, Centre of

Fan, Joseph P. H., LLB Natnl.Taiwan, PhD Pitt. Dir.*
Other Staff: 1 Assoc. Dir.; 2 Asst. Profs.; 1 Res. Asst. Prof.; 1 Postdoctoral Fellow; 2 Res. Assocs.

Economics, Institute of

Tel: 2609 8189 Fax: 2603 5805
E-mail: institute.econ@cuhk.edu.hk
Fung, K. Y., BSSc Chinese HK, MA W.Ont., PhD W.Ont. Co-Dir., Business Economics*
Sung, Y. W., BSocSc HK, PhD Minn. Co-Dir.*

Educational Research, Hong Kong Institute of

Tel: 2609 6999 Fax: 2603 6850
E-mail: hkier@cuhk.edu.hk
Lo, Leslie N. K., BA Oregon, MIA Col., EdD Col. Dir.*
Other Staff: 3 Assoc. Dirs.; 1 Postdoctoral Fellow; 7 Professl. Consultants; 21 School Devel. Officers; 1 Quality Project Officer; 1 Adjunct Asst. Prof.; 1 Hon. Prof.
Research: medium of instruction (English or Chinese) in Hong Kong's schools; monitoring quality of education in Hong Kong; principals' needs assessment and analysis; relationship between education and work in three regions of China; school self-evaluation and improvement

Health Sciences, Li Ka Shing Institute of

Tel: 3763 6003 Fax: 3763 6333
E-mail: lihs@cuhk.edu.hk
Lo, Dennis Y. M., BM BCh Oxf., MA Camb., DPhil Oxf., DM Oxf., FRCPEd, FRCPath, FRCP Dir.*
Research: cancer; cardiovascular research; diabetes; gastroenterology; molecular diagnosis

Hong Kong Cancer Institute

Tel: 2632 1037 Fax: 2649 7426
E-mail: yungchan@cuhk.edu.hk
Chan, Anthony T. C., MB BS Lond., MD Chinese HK, FRCPEd Dir.*

Housing Innovations, Centre for

Tel: 2994 0495 Fax: 2603 6515
E-mail: innovations@cuhk.edu.hk

Human Communicative Research, Institute of

Tel: 2632 3288 Fax: 2145 8876
E-mail: info@ihcr.cuhk.edu.hk
van Hasselt, C. A., MB BCh Witw., MMed Witw., FCS(SA), FRCSEd, FRCS Dir.*
Other Staff: 1 Assoc. Dir.

Humanities, Research Institute for the

Tel: 2609 8698 Fax: 2609 7722
E-mail: rihs@arts.cuhk.edu.hk
Leung, Philip Y. S., BA Chinese HK, MPhil Chinese HK, PhD Calif. Dir.*
Other Staff: 3 Assoc. Dirs.

Learning Enhancement and Research, Centre for

Tel: 2609 6201 Fax: 2603 6804
E-mail: clear@cuhk.edu.hk
Kember, D. R., BSc E.Anglia, MSc E.Anglia, PhD E.Anglia Prof.
McNaught, C. M., BSc Monash, MEd Monash, PhD Natal Prof.; Dir.*
Other Staff: 1 Asst. Prof.; 1 Res. Assoc.
Research: characterisation of motivation and motivating environments; higher education; innovative teaching and learning strategies in higher education; pedagogical applications of new technologies; web-supported learning designs

Mathematical Sciences, Institute of

Tel: 2609 8038 Fax: 2603 7636
E-mail: ims@ims.cuhk.edu.hk
Leung, N. C., MS Calif., PhD M.I.T. Prof.
Tam, L. F., BSc Chinese HK, PhD Stan. Res. Prof.
Xin, Z., BS Northwestern, MS Chinese Acad.Sc., PhD Mich. William M. W. Mong Prof.; Assoc. Dir.
Yau, S. T., PhD Calif., Hon. DSc Chinese HK, Hon. MA Harv., Hon. DSc Chiao Tung, Hon. DSc Tsinghua, Hon. DSc Macau, Hon. DSc Zhejiang, Hon. DSc HKUST, Hon. DSc Brooklyn Polytech., Hon. DSc Natnl.Taiwan, FAAAS Dir.*
Other Staff: 1 Res. Assoc.; 2 Postdoctoral Fellows; 2 Visiting Scholars

New Asia–Yale-in-China Chinese Language Centre

Tel: 2609 6727 Fax: 2603 5004
E-mail: clc@cuhk.edu.hk
Wu, W., BA Guangzhou Foreign Langs., MA Zhongshan, PhD Georgetown Dir.*

Optical Science and Technology, Institute of

Tel: 2609 8370 Fax: 2603 7210
E-mail: chinlon@ie.cuhk.edu.hk
Chan, K. T., BSc HK, PhD Cornell Dir.*
Other Staff: 1 Assoc. Dir.

Advanced Research in Photonics, Centre for

E-mail: chinlon@ie.cuhk.edu.hk
Chan, K. T., BSc HK, PhD Cornell Dir.*
Other Staff: 1 Assoc. Dir.

Optical Sciences, Centre of

Tel: 2609 6365 E-mail: hqlin@phy.cuhk.edu.hk
Lin, H. Q., BS China U.S.T., MS Iowa State, PhD Calif. Prof.; Acting Dir.*
Other Staff: 1 Assoc. Dir.

Plant Molecular Biology and Agricultural Biology, Institute of

Tel: 2609 8133 Fax: 2603 6382
E-mail: ipmbab@cuhk.edu.hk
Sun, Samuel S. M., BSc HK, BSc Chinese HK, MSc HK, PhD Wis. Dir.*
Other Staff: 1 Dep. Dir.; 3 Res. Asst. Profs.

Precision Engineering, Institute of

Tel: 2696 1079 Fax: 2603 6002
E-mail: pccheng@mae.cuhk.edu.hk
Du, R., MEng S.China Tech., PhD Mich. Dir.*
Other Staff: 1 Res. Fellow; 3 Postdoctoral Fellows; 5 Res. Assocs.

Science and Technology, Institute of

Tel: 2609 6354 Fax: 2603 5315
E-mail: kntsang@ie.cuhk.edu.hk
Wu, C., BSc China U.S.T., PhD N.Y., FAPS Dir.*

Materials Science and Technology Research Centre

Tel: 2609 8297 Fax: 2603 5558
E-mail: jbxu@ee.cuhk.edu.hk
Xu, J., BS Nanjing, MS Nanjing, DrRerNat Constance Dir.*

Other Staff: 1 Assoc. Dir.

Space and Earth Information Science, Institute of

Tel: 2609 6538 Fax: 2603 7470
E-mail: iseis@cuhk.edu.hk
Chiu, Willie L. S., ScD M.I.T., BS   Prof.
Lin, H., MS Chinese Acad.Sc., MA N.Y.State, PhD N.Y.State   Dir.*
Other Staff: 1 Assoc. Dir.; 1 Asst. Prof.; 2 Res. Asst. Profs.; 4 Postdoctoral Fellows; 1 Visiting Scholar
Research: cloud-prone and rainy area remote sensing; coastal environmental studies (water quality monitoring, disasters, oil); earth system sciences (global water, energy and biogeochemical cycles); oceanic sciences (ocean processes, atmosphere-ocean interaction); virtual geographic environments and geographical information systems (GIS)

Geoinformation Science, Joint Laboratory for

E-mail: jlgis@cuhk.edu.hk
Lin, H., MS Chinese Acad.Sc., MA N.Y.State, PhD N.Y.State   Dir.*
Other Staff: 1 Assoc. Dir.; 1 Postdoctoral Fellow; 1 Res. Assoc.

Sports Medicine and Sports Science, Hong Kong Centre for

Tel: 2646 1477 Fax: 2646 3020
E-mail: whoctr@cuhk.edu.hk
Chan, K. M., JP, OBE, MB BS HK, MChOrth Liv., FRCSEd, FRCSGlas, FACS   Dir.*

Supply Chain Management and Logistics, Li and Fung Institute of

Tel: 3163 4081 Fax: 3163 4081
E-mail: lf-scml@baf.msmail.cuhk.edu.hk
Cheung, W. M., BSc Natnl.Taiwan, MBA Rensselaer, PhD Rensselaer   Dir.*

Cyber Logistics Research Centre

E-mail: ccl@baf.msmail.cuhk.edu.hk
Cheung, W. M., BSc Natnl.Taiwan, MBA Rensselaer, PhD Rensselaer   Dir.*

Logistics Technologies and Supply Chain Optimisation, Centre for

Tel: 2609 8215 Fax: 2603 5505
E-mail: office@logitsco.cuhk.edu.hk
Yao, David D. W., MSc Tor., PhD Tor., FIEEE   Dir.*

Supply Chain and Logistics Management, Joint Research and Development Centre for

Tel: 2609 8468 Fax: 2603 5505
E-mail: slliu@se.cuhk.edu.hk
Yan, H., BEng Tsinghua, MEng Tsinghua, PhD Tor.   Dir.*

Supply Chain Management and Logistics, Centre for

Tel: 3163 4491 Fax: 3163 4492
E-mail: cscml@baf.msmail.cuhk.edu.hk
Zhao, X., BS Nankai, MS Utah, MBA Utah, PhD Utah   Dir.*

Supply Chain Management Research Centre

Tel: 3163 4491 Fax: 3163 4492
E-mail: scmrc@baf.msmail.cuhk.edu.hk
Yeung, Jeff H. Y., BSc Natnl.Cheng Kung, MS Houston, PhD Qld.UT   Dir.*
Other Staff: 1 Res. Assoc.

Theoretical Computer Science and Communications Institute

E-mail: itcsc@cuhk.edu.hk
Yao, Andrew C. C., BS Natnl.Taiwan, AM Harv., PhD Harv., PhD Ill., Hon. DSc City HK,

Hon. DEng HKUST, Hon. DSc Chinese HK, FACM, FAAAS   Dir.*
Other Staff: 2 Assoc. Dirs.

Theoretical Physics, Institute of

Tel: 2609 6339 Fax: 2603 5204
E-mail: itp@phy.cuhk.edu.hk
Yang, C. N., BSc Kunming, PhD Chic., Hon. DSc Chinese HK   Dir.*
Other Staff: 1 Assoc. Dir.

University General Education, Office of

Tel: 2609 7563 Fax: 2603 5398
E-mail: oge@cuhk.edu.hk
Cheung, C. F., BA Chinese HK, MPhil Chinese HK, DrPhil Freib.   Dir.*
Other Staff: 1 Visiting Prof.; 2 Assoc. Dirs.; 1 Asst. Registrar; 4 Module Dirs.

General Education, Research Centre for

Tel: 2609 8955 E-mail: rcge@cuhk.edu.hk
Cheung, C. F., BA Chinese HK, MPhil Chinese HK, DrPhil Freib.   Dir.*
Other Staff: 1 Assoc. Dir.

CONTACT OFFICERS

Academic affairs. Director of Registry Services: Ng, Eric S. P., BSc Dund., MA Dund., MTh Lond. (E-mail: aas@cuhk.edu.hk)
Admissions (first degree). Director of Admissions and Financial Aid: Chow, Grace M. Y. C., BSSc Chinese HK, LLB Manc.Met., MA HK, LLM HK (E-mail: ugadm@cuhk.edu.hk)
Admissions (higher degree). Senior Assistant Registrar: Lee, Joanna L. H., BSocSc HK (E-mail: gradschool@cuhk.edu.hk)
Adult/continuing education. Director, School of Continuing and Professional Studies: Lee, Victor S. K., BSc Indiana, MSc Indiana, MBA Strath., PhD Lond., FAIM (E-mail: scs@cuhk.edu.hk)
Alumni. Director, Alumni Affairs Office: Li, K. M., BA Chinese HK (E-mail: alumni@cuhk.edu.hk)
Careers. Director of Student Affairs: Leung, Timothy T. M., MEd N.Texas, PhD N.Texas (E-mail: career-plan@cuhk.edu.hk)
Computing services. Acting Director, Information Technology Services Centre: Leung, Philip K. H., BBA Chinese HK, MA HK Baptist (E-mail: itsc@cuhk.edu.hk)
Development/fund-raising. Director, Office of Institutional Advancement: Cheng, Ricky M. S., BS Calif.State Polytechnic (E-mail: oia@cuhk.edu.hk)
Estates and buildings/works and services. Director, Estates Management Office: Tam, Benny P. S., MBA HK (E-mail: emo@cuhk.edu.hk)
Estates and buildings/works and services. Director, Campus Development Office: Lim, David S. W., BA(ArchStudies) HK, BArch HK (E-mail: cdo@cuhk.edu.hk)
Examinations. Assistant Registrar: Chan, Aubrey, BSocSc HK, MA Chinese HK (E-mail: ugadmin@cuhk.edu.hk/ pgadmin@cuhk.edu.hk)
Finance. Bursar: Chan, Terence C. W., BSocSc HK, FCA, FCA(Aust)
General enquiries. University Secretary: Leung, Jacob S. K., BSocSc HK, MDiv S.Baptist Theol.Sem. (E-mail: secretary@cuhk.edu.hk)
Health services. Director, University Health Service: Fong, Ben Y. F., MB BS Syd., MPH Syd., FRACMA (E-mail: uhc@cuhk.edu.hk)
International office. Director, Office of Academic Links: Wu, Thomas W. O., BA HK, MBA HK (E-mail: oal@cuhk.edu.hk)

Library (chief librarian). Librarian: Storey, C., BA Leeds, MPhil E.Anglia, PhD HK, FCLIP (E-mail: library@cuhk.edu.hk)
Marketing. Director, Communications and Public Relations Office: Tsui, Amy Y. M., BSSc Chinese HK, MA Chinese HK (E-mail: ipro@cuhk.edu.hk)
Personnel/human resources. Director of Personnel: Lau, Sophie L. M. Kwok, BSocSc HK (E-mail: personnel-6@cuhk.edu.hk)
Public relations. Director, Communications and Public Relations Office: Tsui, Amy Y. M., BSSc Chinese HK, MA Chinese HK (E-mail: ipro@cuhk.edu.hk)
Publications. Director, Information Services Office: Cho, Tommy W. K., LLB Manc.Met., MA Penn., MA Northwest(Xi'an), LLM HK, BA (E-mail: iso@cuhk.edu.hk)
Purchasing. Senior Finance Manager: Yiu, Patrick K. C., BA HK (E-mail: yftang@cuhk.edu.hk)
Research. Director, Research Administration Office: Lam Yeung, Cecilia S. S., BA City HK, MPA HK
Safety. Safety Manager: Lam, S. K., BSc Chinese HK, MSc Lond. (E-mail: uls@cuhk.edu.hk)
Scholarships, awards, loans. Director of Student Affairs: Leung, Timothy T. M., MEd N.Texas, PhD N.Texas (E-mail: sfas@cuhk.edu.hk)
Security. Director, Security and Transport Office: Wong, P. N. (E-mail: security_unit@cuhk.edu.hk)
Sport and recreation. Director, Physical Education Unit: Lo, Y. C., BEd Taiwan Normal, MPE Springfield
Staff development and training. Training Manager, Personnel Office: Chow, Danniel W. W., BBA Chinese HK, MA Macq. (E-mail: personnel-6@cuhk.edu.hk)
Student welfare/counselling. Director of Student Affairs: Leung, Timothy T. M., MEd N.Texas, PhD N.Texas (E-mail: scds@cuhk.edu.hk)
Students from other countries. Director, Office of Academic Links: Wu, Thomas W. O., BA HK, MBA HK (E-mail: oal@cuhk.edu.hk)
University press. Director, The Chinese University Press: Gan, Q., BH Peking, MA Wash. (E-mail: cup@cuhk.edu.hk)

CAMPUS/COLLEGE HEADS

Chung Chi College. (Tel: 2609 6441; Fax: 2603 5440; E-mail: ccc@cuhk.edu.hk) Head of College: Leung, Prof. Philip Y. S., BA Chinese HK, MPhil Chinese HK, PhD Calif.
Morningside College. Master-Designate: Mirrlees, J. A., BA Camb., MA Edin., PhD Camb., Hon. DSSc Chinese HK
New Asia College. (Tel: 2609 7609; Fax: 2603 5418; E-mail: nao@nao.msmail.cuhk.edu.hk) Head of College: Wong, Prof. Henry N. C., BSc Chinese HK, PhD Lond., DSc Lond., FRSChem
S. H. Ho College. Master-Designate: Sun, Samuel S. M., BSc HK, BSc Chinese HK, MSc HK, PhD Wis.
Shaw College. (Tel: 2609 7355; Fax: 2603 5427; E-mail: shaw-college@cuhk.edu.hk) Head of College: Ching, Prof. P. C., BEng Liv., PhD Liv., FIEE
United College. (Tel: 2609 7579; Fax: 2603 7241; E-mail: unitedcollege@cuhk.edu.hk) Head of College: Fung, Prof. K. P., BSc Chinese HK, MPhil Chinese HK, PhD HK

[Information supplied by the institution as at 18 October 2007, and edited by the ACU]

UNIVERSITY OF HONG KONG

Founded 1911

Member of the Association of Commonwealth Universities

Postal Address: Pokfulam Road, Hong Kong
Telephone: 2859 2111 **Fax:** 2858 2549
URL: http://www.hku.hk

VICE-CHANCELLOR*—Tsui, Prof. Lap-Chee, OC, BSc *Chinese HK*, MPhil *Chinese HK*, PhD *Pitt.*, Hon. DCL *KCNS*,
    Hon. DSc *New Br.*, Hon. DSc *Chinese HK*, Hon. DSc *York(Can.)*, Hon. LLD *St FX*, FRS, FRSCan, FWIF, Hon. FRCP
DEPUTY VICE-CHANCELLOR—Wong, Prof. Richard Y. C., JP, AB *Chic.*, AM *Chic.*, PhD *Chic.*
PRO-VICE-CHANCELLOR—Lee, Prof. C. F., BSc(Eng) *HK*, MSc(Eng) *HK*, PhD *W.Ont.*, FICE, FEIC, FCAE
PRO-VICE-CHANCELLOR—Lee, Prof. Joseph H. W., BSc(Eng) *M.I.T.*, MSc *M.I.T.*, PhD *M.I.T.*
PRO-VICE-CHANCELLOR—Malpas, Prof. John G., BA *Oxf.*, MA *Oxf.*, MSc *Nfld.*, PhD *Nfld.*, DSc *Oxf.*
PRO-VICE-CHANCELLOR—Tam, Prof. Paul K. H., MB BS *HK*, ChM *Liv.*, FRCSEd, FRCSGlas, FRCSI, FRCPCH
TREASURER—Fan, Henry H. L., JP
REGISTRAR‡—Wai, Henry W. K., MA *HK*, FCIS
DIRECTOR OF FINANCE—Lam, Philip B. L.
LIBRARIAN—Ferguson, A. W., BA *Brigham Young*, MA *Wash.*, MLS *Wash.*, EdD *Col.*

GENERAL INFORMATION

History. The university was founded in 1911 and opened in 1912. Its history dates from the establishment of the College of Medicine in 1887.

It is located in Pokfulam.

Admission to first degree courses (see also Hong Kong Introduction). Hong Kong Certificate of Education Examination (HKCEE) grade E or above in at least seven subjects at the first and/or second attempt, six of which must be gained at one attempt, including English language (syllabus B), Chinese language or other language, and mathematics; and Hong Kong Advanced Level Exam (HKALE) with grade D or above in AS level use of English, grade E or above in AS Chinese language and culture, and grade E or above in two A level subjects. (The two A level subjects may be replaced by one A level and two AS subjects or by four AS subjects (other than use of English and Chinese language and culture). Candidates with other qualifications will be considered individually.

First Degrees (see also Hong Kong Directory to Subjects of Study). BA, BA(ArchStud), BAcc, BBA, BBA(Acc&Fin), BBA(IGBM), BBA(IS), BChinMed, BCJ, BCogSc, BDS, BEcon, BEcon&Fin, BEd, BEd(ITE), BEd(LangEd), BEd(LIS), BEng, BFin, BHousMan, BJ, BMS, BNurs, BPharm(ChinMed), BSc, BSc(ActuarSc), BSc(BioInf), BSc(BiomedSc), BSc(CSIS), BSc(Sp&HearSc), BSc(SSLM), BSc(Surv), BSocSc, BSW, BTCM, LLB, MB BS.

Joint degree courses: BBA(IS)/BEng(SE): 4 years; BBA(Law)/LLB, BEng(CivE-Law)/LLB, BSocSc(Govt&Laws)/LLB: 5 years.

Length of course. Full-time: BA, BA(ArchStud), BBA, BBA(Acc&Fin), BBA(IGBM), BCogSc, BEcon, BEcon&Fin, BEng, BFin, BJ, BSc, BSc(ActuarSc), BSc(BioInf), BSc(BiomedSc), BSc(CSIS), BSc(SSLM), BSc(Surv), BSocSc, BSW: 3 years; BBA(IS), BEd(LangEd), BNurs, BSc(Sp&HearSc), LLB: 4 years; BChinMed, BDS, BTCM, MB BS: 5 years. *Part-time:* BNurs: 2 years; BAcc, BEd(ITE), BEd(LIS): 3 years; BCJ, BEd: 4 years; BHousMan, BPharm(ChinMed): 4½ years; BTCM, BMS: 6 years; BChinMed: 6–10 years.

Higher Degrees (see also Hong Kong Directory to Subjects of Study).

Master's. IMBA, LLM, LLM(CFL), LLM(HR), LLM(ITL), MA, MA(AppliedLinguistics), MArch, MBA, MBuddhStud, MChinMed, MCL, MDS, MEcon, MEd, MFin, MGIS, MHousMan, MIPA, MJ, MLA, MMedSc, MNurs, MOrth, MPA, MPH, MPhil, MRes(Med), MS, MSc, MSc(Audiology), MSc(CompSc), MSc(Conservation), MSc(ConstProjectMan),

MScDMS, MSc(ECom&IComp), MSc(Eng), MScEng(EEE), MSc(EnvMan), MSc(IDM), MSc(ITE), MSc(LIM), MSc(RealEst), MSc(SportsScience), MSc(UrbanPlan), MSocSc, MStat, MSW, MUD.

MRes(Med): 1 year and 8 weeks full-time.

Length of course. Full-time: LLM(HR), MA, MBuddhStud, MCL, MJ, MMedSc, MPH, MRes(Med), MSc, MSc(Conservation), MSc(ConstProjectMan), MSc(RealEst), MScDMS, MUD: 1 year; IMBA, LLM, LLM(CFL), LLM(ITL), MBA, MEcon, MFin, MSc(CompSc), MSc(ECom&IComp), MSc(Eng), MSocSc: 1–2 years; MScEng(EEE): 1–3 years; MGIS: 1½ years; MArch, MIPA, MLA, MSc(Audiology), MSc(UrbanPlan), MSW: 2 years; MDS: 2–3 years; MOrth: 3 years. *Part-time:* MScEng(EEE): 1–3 years; LLM(HR), MA, MA(AppliedLinguistics), MBuddhStud, MChinMed, MCL, MEd, MGIS, MIPA, MJ, MMedSc, MNurs, MPA, MPH, MPhil, MSc, MSc(Conservation), MSc(EnvMan), MSc(IDM), MSc(SportsScience), MScDMS, MStat, MUD: 2 years; MSc(CompSc), MSc(ConstProjectMan), MSc(ECom&IComp), MSc(Eng), MSc(RealEst), MSocSc: 2–3 years; IMBA, LLM, LLM(CFL), LLM(ITL), MBA, MEcon, MFin, MSc(ITE), MSc(LIM): 2–4 years; MHousMan: 2½ years; MSc(UrbanPlan), MSW: 3 years; MDS: 3–4 years; MS: 5 years. *By distance learning:* MPhil: 3 years.

Doctoral. EdD, MD, PhD, PsyD, SJD.

Length of course. Full-time: PsyD: 2 years; PhD: 3–4 years; SJD: 3–5 years. *Part-time:* PsyD: 3 years; EdD: 4–6 years; PhD, SJD: 4½–6 years; MD: 5 years.

Language of Instruction. English, except for courses in Chinese and other languages.

Libraries. Volumes: 2,478,968. Periodicals subscribed to: 43,147. Other holdings: 1,772,684 non-print items. Special collections: Asian Development Bank depository; Chan Kwan-po; Eu Yan Sang; Hankow; Hong Kong Bank chairman's library; Hong Kong Company papers; Hong Kong stock market archives and artefacts; Hong Kong Tourism Board; Hung On-To Memorial Library; Lin Sheng-Shih; Sir Lindsay Ride; Luen Yick Hong; Morrison; Taiwan research materials; United Nations depository; United Nations Research Institute for Social Development (UNRISD); World Health Organization (WHO); World Trade Organization (WTO); European Documentation Centre depository; Doming Lam; Patten; Lo Hsing-lin (Chinese).

Academic Awards (2005–2006). 1000 awards ranging in value from HK$1000 to HK$100,000.

FACULTIES/SCHOOLS

Architecture

Tel: 2859 2149 Fax: 2857 2852
  E-mail: faculty@arch.hku.hk
Dean: Lerner, R., BArch *Cooper Union*, MArch *Harv.*, FAIA
Secretary: Chan, C., BA *Br.Col.*

Arts

Tel: 2859 2733 Fax: 2548 5231
  E-mail: artsfac@hku.hk
Dean: Louie, K. H., BA *Syd.*, MPhil *Chinese HK*, PhD *Syd.*, FAHA
Secretary: Shen, E. D., LLB

Business and Economics

Tel: 2241 5343 Fax: 2549 3735
  E-mail: info@fbe.hku.hk
Acting Dean: Wong, Prof. Richard Y. C., JP, AB *Chic.*, AM *Chic.*, PhD *Chic.*
Secretary: Tsui, Betty M. W., BSc(Econ) *Lond.*, MSc *Lond.*

Dentistry

Tel: 2859 0376 Fax: 2517 0544
  E-mail: dental@hkusua.hku.hk
Dean: Samaranayake, Prof. L. P., BDS *S.Lanka*, DDS *Glas.*, FRCPath
Secretary: Chan, Rupert K. Y., BA *HK*, MBA *Chinese HK*, FRSA

Education

Tel: 2859 2519 Fax: 2517 0075
  E-mail: edfac@hkucc.hku.hk
Acting Dean: Rao, Nirmala, BA *B'lore.*, MS *Tulane*, PhD *Tulane*
Secretary: Ngai, Annie Y. S., BA *HK*, MA *C&GCHE*

Engineering

Tel: 2859 2803 Fax: 2546 9142
  E-mail: enggfac@hkucc.hku.hk
Dean: Ng, Prof. T. S., BSc(Eng) *HK*, MEngSc *Newcastle(NSW)*, PhD *Newcastle(NSW)*, Hon. DEng *Newcastle(NSW)*, FIEE
Secretary: Lin, W. Y. L., BSocSc *HK*, MBA *Chinese HK*

Law

Tel: 2859 2953 Fax: 2559 5690
  E-mail: lawfac@hkusua.hku.hk
Dean: Chan, Prof. J. M. M., LLB *HK*, LLM *Lond.*
Secretary: Wong, Vivian T. V., BA *HK*, MPA *HK*

Medicine

Tel: 2819 9175 Fax: 2855 9742
  E-mail: medfac@hku.hk
Dean: Lam, Prof. S. K., OBE, MB BS *HK*, MD *HK*, FRCP, FRCPEd, FRCPGlas, FRACP, FACP
Secretary: Tang, Liza M., BSocSc *HK*

Science

Tel: 2859 2682 Fax: 2858 4620
  E-mail: science@hku.hk
Dean: Kwok, S., BSc McM., MSc Minn., PhD Minn.
Secretary: Tsang, Angela O. M., BSocSc HK

Social Sciences

Tel: 2859 8016 Fax: 2517 0806
  E-mail: socsc@hkucc.hku.hk
Acting Dean: Blowers, G. H., BSc Sheff., MPhil Sus., PhD HK
Secretary: Tsang, Amy W. C., BSc Aston, MSc Manc.

ACADEMIC UNITS

Architecture

Tel: 2859 2133 Fax: 2559 6484
  E-mail: dept@arch.hku.hk
Hui, D. C. K., BArch Cornell, MPhil Camb., PhD Camb. Assoc. Prof.
Lau, S. S. Y., BArch HK, MSc Lond. Assoc. Prof.
Lu, L. L., BArch Houston, MArch Yale Assoc. Prof.; Head*
Lung, D. P. Y., MBE, JP, BArch Oregon, MA Oregon, MArch Oregon Prof.
Matsuda, N., BFA Tokyo, MA RCA Assoc. Prof.
Other Staff: 10 Assoc. Profs./Lectrs.; 6 Asst. Profs./Lectrs.; 1 Res. Asst. Prof.; 1 Lectr.; 1 Postdoctoral Fellow; 1 Adjunct Prof.; 14 Hon. Profs.

Botany

Tel: 2299 0300 Fax: 2858 3477
  E-mail: botanya@hkucc.hku.hk
Chen, S. F., BSc S.China Tech., MEngSc Qld., PhD Qld. Assoc. Prof.; Acting Head*
Chye, Mee Len, BSc Malaya, PhD Melb. Assoc. Prof.
Ma, C. Y., MSc HK, MSc Br.Col., PhD Br.Col. Prof.
Other Staff: 4 Assoc. Profs./Lectrs.; 2 Asst. Profs./Lectrs.; 4 Hon. Profs.; 1 Hon. Assoc. Prof.; 1 Hon. Asst. Prof.

Business, School of

Tel: 2859 1000 Fax: 2858 5614
  E-mail: enquiry@business.hku.hk
Chang, Eric C., BS Natnl.Cheng Kung, MBA Wright, PhD Purdue Chair Prof., Finance; Dir.*
Chau, P. Y. K., BSSc Chinese HK, MBA Edin., PhD W.Ont. Prof.
Enright, M. J., AB Harv., MBA Harv., PhD Harv. Sun Hung Kai Properties Prof.
Farhoomand, A. F., BEng C'dia., MBA C'dia., PhD McG. Prof.
Lam, S. S. K., MSc Essex, PhD ANU Assoc. Prof.
Lau, Amy H. L., BAcc NU Singapore, MPA Texas Christian, PhD Wash. Chair Prof., Accounting
Ng, S. H., BSocSc HK, MSocSc HK, MSc Lond., PhD Lond. Reader
Pan, Y., BA Internat.Business & Econ., Beijing, MA Internat.Business & Econ., Beijing, MPhil Col., PhD Col. Assoc. Prof.
Tao, Z., BSc Fudan, MA Prin., PhD Prin. Assoc. Prof.
Tse, David K. C., BBA Chinese HK, MBA Calif., PhD Calif. Chair Prof., International Marketing
Wong, G. Y. Y., BSc HK, MBA Manc., PhD Brad. Assoc. Prof.
Other Staff: 1 Visiting Assoc. Prof.; 5 Assoc. Profs./Lectrs.; 6 Asst. Profs./Lectrs.; 1 Res. Asst. Prof.; 1 Lectr.; 1 Teaching Fellow; 5 Teaching Consultants; 1 Res. Assoc.; 5 Hon. Profs.; 1 Hon. Assoc. Prof.

Chemistry

Tel: 2859 7919 Fax: 2857 1586
  E-mail: chemmail@hkucc.hku.hk
Chan, G. K. Y., BSc Alta., MS Cornell, PhD Cornell Prof.

Che, C. M., BSc HK, PhD HK Dr. Hui-Wai-Haan Chair Prof.
Cheung, A. S. C., BSc Wat., PhD Br.Col. Sr. Lectr.
Lie Ken Jie, M. S. F., BSc HK, PhD St And., DSc St And., DSc HK, FRSChem Chair Prof.
Phillips, D. L., BS Iowa State, PhD Calif. Prof.; Head*
Wong, W. T., BSc HK, MPhil HK, PhD Camb., ScD Camb., FRSChem Prof.
Yam, Vivian W. W., BSc HK, PhD HK, FRSChem Chair Prof.
Yang, D., BSc Fudan, MA Col., PhD Prin. Prof.
Other Staff: 1 Distinguished Visiting Prof.; 5 Assoc. Profs./Lectrs.; 1 Assoc. Prof./Investigator; 4 Asst. Profs./Lectrs.; 10 Res. Asst. Profs.; 24 Res. Assocs.; 16 Postdoctoral Fellows; 3 Res. Officers; 4 Hon. Profs.; 13 Hon. Assoc. Profs.; 12 Hon. Asst. Profs.

Chinese

Tel: 2859 2426 Fax: 2858 1334
Chan, M. S., BA HK, MPhil HK, PhD ANU Assoc. Prof.
Ho, K. P., BA HK, MPhil HK, PhD HK Sr. Lectr.
Lee, K. S., BA HK, MPhil HK, PhD HK Prof.
Liu, M. W., BA HK, MPhil HK, PhD Calif. Prof.
Sin, C. Y., BA HK, MPhil HK, PhD HK Prof.; Head*
Other Staff: 13 Assoc. Profs.; 1 Lectr.; 1 Teaching Fellow; 2 Res. Officers; 16 Hon. Profs.; 3 Hon. Assoc. Profs.; 1 Hon. Asst. Prof.; 10 Hon. Lectrs.

Chinese Language Division

Si, C. M., BA Chinese HK, MA Chinese HK, DEd Beijing Normal Assoc. Prof.
Other Staff: 2 Lang. Instrs.; 1 Asst. Lang. Instr.; 14 Lang. Instrs.†

Comparative Literature

Tel: 2859 2769 Fax: 2857 7955
  E-mail: complit@hkucc.hku.hk
Cheung, E. M. K., BA HK, MA San Diego State, PhD Chinese HK Acting Head*
Tambling, J. C. R., BA York(UK), MPhil Nott., PhD Essex Prof.
Other Staff: 1 Assoc. Prof./Lectr.; 2 Asst. Profs./Lectrs.; 1 Res. Asst. Prof.; 1 Postdoctoral Fellow; 2 Hon. Profs.; 2 Hon. Assoc. Profs.

Computer Science

Tel: 2859 2180 Fax: 2559 8447
  E-mail: dept@csis.hku.hk
Cheung, D. W. L., BSc Chinese HK, MSc S.Fraser, PhD S.Fraser Assoc. Prof.; Head*
Chin, F. Y. L., BASc Tor., MSc Prin., MA Prin., PhD Prin., FIEE Chair Prof.
Lam, T. W., BSc Chinese HK, MS Wash., PhD Wash. Assoc. Prof.
Lau, F. C. M., BSc Acad., MMath Wat., PhD Wat. Assoc. Prof.
Tan, C. J., BSEE Seattle, MSEE Calif., DEng Col. Visiting IBM Chair Prof., E-Business Technology
Tse, T. H., MBE, BSc HK, MSc Lond., PhD Lond., FBCS, FIMA, FIMIS, FHKIE Assoc. Prof.
Other Staff: 2 Visiting Assoc. Profs.; 10 Assoc. Profs./Lectrs.; 3 Asst. Profs./Lectrs.; 2 Res. Asst. Profs.; 1 Lectr.; 1 Res. Assoc.; 2 Teaching Consultants; 10 Computer Officers; 10 Asst. Computer Officers; 4 Adjunct Profs.; 1 Hon. Prof.; 3 Hon. Assoc. Profs.; 10 Hon. Asst. Profs.; 3 Hon. Lectrs.; 2 Hon. Res. Assocs.

Earth Sciences

Tel: 2859 8062 Fax: 2517 6912
  E-mail: earthsci@hkusub.hku.hk
Aitchison, Jonathan C., BSc Otago, MSc Otago, PhD NE Prof.; Head*
Malpas, John G., BA Oxf., MA Oxf., MSc Nfld., PhD Nfld., DSc Oxf. Chair Prof.

Sun, M., BSc Beijing, MSc Br.Col., PhD Br.Col. Assoc. Prof.
Yim, W. W. S., BSc Lond., MPhil Lond., PhD Tas., DSc Lond., FGS Assoc. Prof.
Other Staff: 4 Assoc. Profs./Lectrs.; 2 Asst. Profs./Lectrs.; 1 Res. Asst. Prof.; 4 Hon. Profs.; 3 Hon. Assoc. Profs.; 5 Hon. Asst. Profs.; 2 Hon. Res. Assocs.

Ecology and Biodiversity

Tel: 2299 0600 Fax: 2517 6082
  E-mail: ecology@hkucc.hku.hk
Corlett, R. T., BA Camb., PhD ANU, FLS Assoc. Prof.
Dudgeon, D., BSc Newcastle(UK), PhD HK Prof.; Head*
Hyde, K. D., BSc Wales, MSc CNAA, PhD CNAA Assoc. Prof.
Williams, G. A., BSc Manc., PhD Brist. Assoc. Prof.
Other Staff: 3 Assoc. Profs./Lectrs.; 4 Asst. Profs./Lectrs.; 1 Res. Asst. Prof.; 1 Teaching Consultant; 6 Hon. Profs.; 3 Hon. Assoc. Profs.; 9 Hon. Asst. Profs.; 3 Hon. Res. Assocs.

Economics and Finance, School of

Tel: 2859 2192 Fax: 2548 1152
  E-mail: econ@hku.hk
Luk, Y. F., AB Chic., MA Cornell, PhD Cornell Dir.*
Shea, K. L., BSocSc HK, AM Wash., PhD Wash. Assoc. Prof.
Wong, Richard Y. C., JP, AB Chic., AM Chic., PhD Chic. Chair Prof.
Other Staff: 18 Assoc. Profs./Lectrs.; 2 Asst. Profs.; 3 Visiting Asst. Profs.; 7 Asst. Profs./Lectrs.; 2 Teaching Fellows; 5 Hon. Profs.; 1 Hon. Assoc. Prof.

Education, Faculty of

Tel: 2859 2519 Fax: 2517 0075
  E-mail: edfac@hku.hk
Andrews, S. J., MA Camb., MA Essex Assoc. Prof.
Bray, T. M., BA Newcastle(UK), MSc Edin., PhD Edin. Chair Prof.
Chan, C. K. K., BA HK, MEd Tor., MA Tor., PhD Tor. Assoc. Prof.
Cheng Kai Ming, JP, BSc HK, MEd HK, PhD Lond. Chair Prof.
Davison, C. M., BA Melb., BEd La Trobe, MEd Melb., PhD La Trobe Assoc. Prof.
Evers, C. W., BA Syd., BLitt NE, PhD Syd. Prof.
Law, Nancy W. Y., BSc HK, MPhil HK, PhD Lond. Prof.
Leung, Frederick K. S., BSc HK, MEd HK, PhD Lond. Assoc. Prof.
Postiglione, G. A., BS N.Y.State, PhD N.Y.State Assoc. Prof.
Rao, Nirmala, BA B'lore., MS Tulane, PhD Tulane Assoc. Prof.; Acting Dean*
Stimpson, P. G., BSc Brist., MSc Sheff., PhD Sheff. Assoc. Prof.
Tse, S. K., BA HK, MA(Ed) Chinese HK, MPhil HK, PhD Nott. Assoc. Prof.
Tsui, Amy B. M., BA HK, MA HK, PhD Birm. Prof.
Watkins, D. A., BSc Syd., MSc Melb., PhD ANU Prof.
Whitehill, Tara L., BA Oberlin, MS Col., PhD HK Assoc. Prof.
Yiu, Edwin, BAppSc Lincoln Inst., MPhil HK, PhD Qld. Assoc. Prof.
Other Staff: 1 Visiting Prof.; 30 Assoc. Profs./Lectrs.; 17 Asst. Profs./Lectrs.; 2 Res. Asst. Profs.; 4 Teaching Fellows; 20 Teaching Consultants; 5 Postdoctoral Fellows; 1 Clin. Instr.; 7 Hon. Profs.; 2 Hon. Assoc. Profs.; 129 Hon. Asst. Profs.; 2 Hon. Res. Assocs.

Information and Technology Studies, Division of

Tel: 2859 2550 Fax: 2517 7194
Law, Nancy W. Y., BSc HK, MPhil HK, PhD Lond. Prof.; Head*

Language and Literature, Division of

Tel: 2859 2531 Fax: 2858 5649

Andrews, S. J., MA Camb., MA Essex   Assoc. Prof.; Head*

Learning, Development and Diversity, Division of

Tel: 2859 2524 Fax: 2858 5649

Winter, S. J., BSc S'ton., MEd Exe., PhD HK   Assoc. Prof.; Head*

Policy, Administration and Social Sciences Education, Division of

Tel: 2859 2518 Fax: 2858 5649

Wong, K. C., BA Chinese HK, PhD Lond.   Assoc. Prof.; Head*

Science, Mathematics and Computing, Division of

Tel: 2857 8546 Fax: 2858 5649

Day, J. R., BSc E.Anglia, PhD E.Anglia   Assoc. Prof.; Head*

Speech and Hearing Sciences, Division of

Tel: 2859 0583 Fax: 2559 0060

Yiu, Edwin, BAppSc Lincoln Inst., MPhil HK, PhD Qld.   Assoc. Prof.; Head*

Engineering, Civil

Tel: 2859 2668 Fax: 2559 5337
E-mail: civdept@hkucc.hku.hk

Chandler, A. M., BSc(Eng) Lond., PhD Lond.   Prof.

Fang, H. H. P., BS Natnl.Taiwan, MS Roch., PhD Roch.   Chair Prof.

Kwan, A. K. H., BSc(Eng) HK, PhD HK   Prof.

Lee, C. F., BSc(Eng) HK, MSc(Eng) HK, PhD W.Ont., FICE, FEIC, FCAE   Chair Prof.

Lee, Joseph H. W., BSc(Eng) M.I.T., MSc M.I.T., PhD M.I.T.   Chair Prof.

Lee, P. K. K., MSc Sur., FIStructE, FICE   Assoc. Prof.; Head*

Lo, S. H., BSc(Eng) HK, MPhil HK, DrIng E.N.Ponts & Chaussées, Paris   Prof.

Tham, L. G., BSc(Eng) HK, PhD HK   Prof.

Wong, S. C., BSc(Eng) HK, MPhil HK, PhD Lond.   Assoc. Prof.

Other Staff: 11 Assoc. Profs./Lectrs.; 4 Asst. Profs.; 4 Res. Asst. Profs.; 1 Sr. Teaching Consultant; 1 Special Adviser; 7 Res. Assocs.; 3 Distinguished Adjunct Profs.; 15 Adjunct Profs.; 11 Adjunct Assoc. Profs.; 5 Hon. Profs.; 3 Hon. Asst. Profs.; 1 Hon. Sr. Lectr.; 2 Hon. Lectrs.

Engineering, Electrical and Electronic

Tel: 2859 7093 Fax: 2559 8738
E-mail: eee@eee.hku.hk

Chan, S. C., BSc(Eng) HK, PhD HK   Assoc. Prof.

Cheung, P. Y. S., BSc Lond., PhD Lond.   Assoc. Prof.

Ho, K. L., BSc(Eng) HK, MPhil HK, PhD Lond.   Assoc. Prof.

Hung, Y. S., BSc(Eng) HK, BSc HK, MPhil Camb., PhD Camb.   Assoc. Prof.

Lai, P. T., BSc(Eng) HK, PhD HK   Assoc. Prof.

Li, Victor O. K., BBS M.I.T., SB M.I.T., SMEE M.I.T., ScD M.I.T.   Chair Prof.

Ng, T. S., BSc(Eng) HK, MEngSc Newcastle(NSW), PhD Newcastle(NSW), Hon. DEng Newcastle(NSW), FIEE   Chair Prof.

Wu, Felix F., BS Natnl.Taiwan, MS Pitt., PhD Calif.   Chair Prof.

Yang, Edward S., BS Cheng Kung, MS Oklahoma State, PhD Yale   Chair Prof.

Other Staff: 1 Visiting Assoc. Prof.; 11 Assoc. Profs./Lectrs.; 1 Visiting Asst. Prof.; 10 Asst. Profs./Lectrs.; 2 Res. Asst. Profs.; 1 Sr. Teaching Consultant; 1 Sr. Computer Officer; 2 Teaching Consultants; 5 Hon. Profs.; 8 Hon. Assoc. Profs.; 1 Hon. Asst. Prof.; 5 Hon. Lectrs.

Engineering, Industrial and Manufacturing Systems

Tel: 2859 2583 Fax: 2858 6535
E-mail: imse@hku.hk

Chan, P. L. Y., BSc HK, PhD HK   Assoc. Prof.; Head*

Mak, K. L., MSc Salf., PhD Salf.   Prof.

Sculli, D., MSc Birm., FIMA   Sr. Lectr.

Other Staff: 6 Assoc. Profs./Lectrs.; 3 Asst. Profs./Lectrs.; 1 Res. Asst. Prof.; 1 Hon. Prof.; 2 Hon. Assoc. Profs.; 1 Hon. Asst. Prof.; 1 Hon. Lectr.

Engineering, Mechanical

Tel: 2859 2635 Fax: 2858 5415
E-mail: medept@hku.hk

Chwang, A. T., MSc Sask., PhD Cal.Tech., FIMechE   Chair Prof.

Duggan, B. J., BSc Aston, PhD Birm., DEng Birm., FIMMM   Chair Prof.

Lam, J., BSc Manc., MPhil Camb., PhD Camb., FIMA   Prof.

Ngan, A. H. W., BSc(Eng) HK, PhD Birm.   Assoc. Prof.

Soh, A. K., BEng Sing., PhD Sur.   Prof.

Sze, K. Y., BSc(Eng) HK, PhD HK   Assoc. Prof.

Tan, S. T., BSc Leeds, PhD Leeds, FIMechE   Prof.; Head*

Other Staff: 1 Visiting Assoc. Prof.; 14 Assoc. Profs./Lectrs.; 6 Asst. Profs./Lectrs.; 3 Res. Asst. Profs.; 1 Sr. Teaching Consultant; 2 Teaching Consultants; 12 Res. Assocs.; 12 Hon. Profs.; 2 Hon. Assoc. Profs.; 4 Hon. Asst. Profs.

English

Tel: 2859 8950 Fax: 2559 7139
E-mail: english@hkucc.hku.hk

Ashcroft, W. D., BA Syd., MA Syd., PhD ANU

Hutton, C. M., MA Col., MA Oxf., DPhil Oxf.   Assoc. Prof.; Head*

Kerr, D. W. F., MA Camb., PhD Warw.   Assoc. Prof.

Other Staff: 4 Assoc. Profs./Lectrs.; 6 Asst. Profs./Lectrs.; 1 Postdoctoral Fellow; 2 Hon. Profs.; 2 Hon. Assoc. Profs.; 4 Hon. Asst. Profs.

Fine Arts

Tel: 2859 7040 Fax: 2548 0987
E-mail: finearts@hkusua.hku.hk

Clarke, D. J., BA Lond., PhD Lond.   Assoc. Prof.; Head*

Wan, Q., BA Beijing, MFA Beijing, MA Kansas, PhD Kansas   Prof.

Other Staff: 1 Visiting Assoc. Prof.; 3 Assoc. Profs./Lectrs.; 1 Hon. Prof.; 2 Hon. Assoc. Profs.; 3 Hon. Asst. Profs.; 1 Hon. Lectr.

Geography

Tel: 2859 2836 Fax: 2559 8994
E-mail: geog@hkucc.hku.hk

Jim, C. Y., JP, BA HK, PhD Reading, FLS   Chair Prof.

Lai, Poh Chin, BES Wat., MA Wat., PhD Wat.   Sr. Lectr.

Lin, G. C. S., BSc Zhongshan, MSc Zhongshan, MA Akron, PhD Br.Col.   Assoc. Prof.; Head*

Peart, M. R., BA Manc., PhD Manc.   Assoc. Prof.

Sit, V. F. S., BA HK, MA HK, PhD Lond.   Prof.

Other Staff: 7 Assoc. Profs./Lectrs.; 1 Asst. Prof.; 1 Res. Asst. Prof.; 1 Postdoctoral Fellow; 4 Hon. Profs.; 2 Hon. Assoc. Profs.; 4 Hon. Asst. Profs.

History

Tel: 2859 2861 Fax: 2858 9755
E-mail: history@hkucc.hku.hk

Cunich, P. A., BA NE, MA Syd., PhD Camb.   Assoc. Prof.; Head*

Dikotter, F., BA Geneva, MA Geneva, PhD Lond., FRHistS   Prof.

Sabine, Maureen A., BA Fordham, MA Penn., PhD Penn.   Assoc. Prof.

Other Staff: 1 Visiting Assoc. Prof.; 2 Assoc. Profs./Lectrs.; 3 Asst. Profs./Lectrs.; 10

Hon. Profs.; 5 Hon. Assoc. Profs.; 2 Hon. Asst. Profs.; 3 Hon. Lectrs.; 3 Hon. Res. Assocs.

Japanese Studies

Tel: 2859 2879 Fax: 2548 7399
E-mail: jpstd@hkucc.hku.hk

Cave, P., BA Oxf., MPhil Oxf., DPhil Oxf.   Asst. Prof.; Head*

Refsing, K., BA Copenhagen, MA Copenhagen, PhD Copenhagen   Prof.

Other Staff: 3 Assoc. Profs./Lectrs.; 3 Asst. Profs./Lectrs.; 7 Lang. Instrs.; 1 Hon. Prof.; 2 Hon. Lectrs.; 2 Hon. Res. Assocs.

Law

see also Professl. Legal Educn.

Tel: 2859 2951 Fax: 2559 3543
E-mail: law@www.hku.hk

Chen, Albert H. Y., LLB HK, LLM Harv.   Prof.

Hannum, H., AB Calif., JD Calif.   Chair Prof.

Jackson, M. I., LLB Br.Col., LLM Br.Col.   Assoc. Prof.

Rwezaura, B. A., LLB Mak., LLM Harv., PhD Warw.   Sr. Lectr.

Other Staff: 21 Assoc. Profs.; 3 Teaching Fellows; 1 Postdoctoral Fellow; 3 Hon. Profs.

Linguistics

Tel: 2857 8286 Fax: 2546 4943
E-mail: linguist@hkucc.hku.hk

Luke, K. K., BA HK, MPhil York(UK), DPhil York(UK)   Sr. Lectr.

Matthews, S. J., BA Camb., MA S.Calif., PhD S.Calif.   Assoc. Prof.; Head*

Other Staff: 2 Visiting Profs.; 2 Assoc. Profs./Lectrs.; 1 Asst. Prof.; 1 Res. Asst. Profs.; 1 Teaching Fellow; 1 Hon. Prof.; 7 Hon. Asst. Profs.; 1 Hon. Lectr.

Mathematics

Tel: 2859 2250 Fax: 2559 2225
E-mail: math@hkucc.hku.hk

Cheung, W. S., BSc Chinese HK, AM Harv., MPhil Chinese HK, PhD Harv.   Assoc. Prof.; Head*

Chu, S. C. K., MS Cornell, MS Col., EngScD Col.   Sr. Lectr.

Lu, J. H., BS Beijing, PhD Calif.   Assoc. Prof.

Mok, Ngaiming, MA Yale, PhD Stan.   Chair Prof.

Tsang, K. M., BA HK, MA Prin., MPhil HK, PhD Prin.   Sr. Lectr.

Yu, J. T., BSc Anhui Educn., MSc China U.S.T., PhD Notre Dame(Ind.)   Assoc. Prof.

Other Staff: 3 Visiting Profs.; 16 Asst. Profs./Lectrs.; 1 Res. Asst. Prof.; 2 Postdoctoral Res. Fellows

Music

Tel: 2859 7045 Fax: 2858 4933
E-mail: okleung@hkucc.hku.hk

Chan, H. Y., BA Chinese HK, MMus Ill., DMA Ill.   Asst. Prof.; Head*

Chan, J. K. B., BMus N.S.W.Conservatorium, PhD HK   Assoc. Prof.

Other Staff: 1 Assoc. Prof./Lectr.; 3 Asst. Profs./Lectrs.; 1 Postdoctoral Fellow; 3 Lectrs.†; 2 Hon. Profs.; 1 Hon. Asst. Prof.

Philosophy

Tel: 2859 2796 Fax: 2559 8452
E-mail: philosophy@hku.hk

Hansen, C., BA Utah, PhD Mich.   Chair Prof.

Lau, J. Y. F., BA Oxf., PhD M.I.T.   Assoc. Prof.; Head*

Other Staff: 3 Assoc. Profs./Lectrs.; 4 Asst. Profs./Lectrs.; 1 Hon. Prof.; 1 Hon. Asst. Prof.

Physics

Tel: 2859 2359 Fax: 2559 9152
E-mail: physdept@hkucc.hku.hk

Beling, C. D., MA Oxf., PhD Lond.   Assoc. Prof.

Cheng, K. S., BSc *Chinese HK*, MPhil *Col.*, PhD *Col.*, FRAS Chair Prof.

Fung, S., BA *Oxf.*, MA *Oxf.*, DPhil *Oxf.*, DSc *Oxf.* Prof.

Gao, Ju, BSc *Beijing*, MSc *Chinese Acad.Sc.*, PhD *T.H.Twente* Assoc. Prof.

Wang, Jian, BSc *Beijing*, PhD *Penn.* Assoc. Prof.

Wang, Z. D., BS *China U.S.T.*, MS *Nanjing*, PhD *Nanjing* Prof.

Zhang, F. C., BSc *Fudan*, PhD *Virginia Polytech.* Chair Prof.; Head*

Other Staff: 2 Distinguished Visiting Profs.; 5 Assoc. Profs./Lectrs.; 6 Asst. Profs./Lectrs.; 5 Res. Asst. Profs.; 4 Res. Assocs.; 2 Postdoctoral Fellows; 11 Hon. Profs.; 1 Hon. Assoc. Prof.; 13 Hon. Asst. Profs.

Politics and Public Administration

Tel: 2859 2393 Fax: 2858 3550
E-mail: psdhku@hku.hk

Burns, J. P., BA *St.Olaf*, MA *Oxf.*, MA *Col.*, MPhil *Col.*, PhD *Col.* Chair Prof.

Chan, J. C. W., BSSc *Chinese HK*, MSc *Lond.*, DPhil *Oxf.* Assoc. Prof.

Cheung, P. T. Y., BSSc *Chinese HK*, MA *Indiana*, PhD *Wash.* Assoc. Prof.; Head*

Lam, W. F., BSSc *Chinese HK*, PhD *Indiana* Assoc. Prof.

Tang, J. T. H., BA *HK*, MPhil *Camb.*, PhD *Lond.* Assoc. Prof.

Other Staff: 1 Visiting Prof.; 3 Assoc. Profs./Lectrs.; 1 Visiting Asst. Prof.; 2 Asst. Profs./Lectrs.; 1 Teaching Fellow; 1 Hon. Prof.; 1 Hon. Assoc. Prof.; 1 Hon. Asst. Prof.; 1 Hon. Lectr.

Professional Legal Education

see also Law

Tel: 2859 2951 Fax: 2559 3543

Chow, Wilson W. S., LLB *HK*, LLM *HK* Assoc. Prof.; Head*

Halkyard, A. J., LLB *ANU*, LLM *Virginia* Prof.

Sherrin, C. H., LLB *Lond.*, LLM *Lond.*, PhD *Lond.* Chair Prof.

Wilkinson, R. M., BA *Camb.*, LLB *Camb.* Chair Prof.

Other Staff: 5 Assoc. Profs./Lectrs.; 2 Asst. Profs./Lectrs.; 5 Teaching Consultants; 46 Hon. Lectrs.

Psychology

Tel: 2859 2375 Fax: 2858 3518
E-mail: dpsychol@hkucc.hku.hk

Au, T. K. F., BA *Harv.*, PhD *Stan.* Chair Prof.

Blowers, G. H., BSc *Sheff.*, MPhil *Sus.*, PhD *HK* Sr. Lectr.

Hayes, A., BSc *W.Aust.*, PhD *W.Aust.* Assoc. Prof.; Head*

Ho, C. S. H., BSocSc *HK*, MSocSc *HK*, DPhil *Oxf.* Assoc. Prof.

Hui, H. C. C., BSocSc *HK*, MCS *China Grad.Sch.Theol.*, MA *Ill.*, PhD *Ill.* Sr. Lectr.

Lee, T. M. C., MSc *S'ton.*, MEd *Alta.*, PhD *Alta.* Assoc. Prof.

Spinks, J. A., BSc *Newcastle(UK)*, PhD *S'ton.* Prof.

Other Staff: 2 Assoc. Profs./Lectrs.; 6 Asst. Profs./Lectrs.; 2 Res. Asst. Profs.; 2 Teaching Consultants; 1 Postdoctoral Fellow; 10 Hon. Profs.; 30 Hon. Assoc. Profs.; 10 Hon. Asst. Profs.; 1 Hon. Sr. Res. Assoc.

Real Estate and Construction

see also Archit.

Tel: 2859 2128 Fax: 2559 9457
E-mail: reco@hkucc.hku.hk

Chau, K. W., BBuilding *HK*, PhD *HK* Chair Prof.

Fellows, R. F., BSc *Aston*, PhD *Reading* Assoc. Prof.

Ho, Daniel C. W., BSc *CNAA*, MBA *Chinese HK*, PhD *HK* Assoc. Prof.; Head*

Lai, Lawrence W. C., LLB *Lond.*, BSocSc *HK*, MSocSc *HK*, MTCP *Syd.*, PhD *HK* Prof.

McKinnell, K. G., BSc *CNAA*, MSc *Edin.*, MPhil *Aston* Assoc. Prof.

Rowlinson, S. M., BSc *Nott.*, MSc *Lond.*, PhD *Brun.* Prof.

Other Staff: 10 Assoc. Profs.; 2 Asst. Profs.; 4 Adjunct Profs.; 12 Hon. Profs.; 1 Hon. Assoc. Prof.

Social Work and Social Administration

Tel: 2859 2288 Fax: 2858 7604
E-mail: swsa@hkusua.hku.hk

Chan, Cecilia L. W., BSocSc *HK*, MSocSc *HK*, PhD *HK* Prof.

Chi, Iris, BSSc *Chinese HK*, MSW *San Diego State*, DSW *Calif.* Prof.

Chow, N. W. S., MBE, JP, BA *HK*, MA(Econ) *Manc.*, PhD *HK* Chair Prof.

Law, C. K., BSocSc *HK*, MBA *Chinese HK*, MSW *HK*, DSW *Calif.* Assoc. Prof.

Leung, J. C. B., BSocSc *HK*, MA *Brun.*, MA *HK*, PhD *HK* Assoc. Prof.; Head*

Other Staff: 1 Visiting Prof.; 9 Assoc. Profs./Lectrs.; 7 Asst. Profs./Lectrs.; 3 Teaching Consultants; 1 Field Instrucn. Co-ordinator; 10 Fieldwork Supervisors; 1 Res. Officer; 8 Hon. Profs.; 11 Hon. Assoc. Profs.; 36 Hon. Asst. Profs.; 11 Hon. Lectrs.; 1 Hon. Res. Assoc.

Sociology

Tel: 2859 2299 Fax: 2559 8044
E-mail: socidept@hkucc.hku.hk

Evans, G. R., BA *La Trobe*, MA *La Trobe*, PhD *La Trobe* Reader; Head*

Joe Laidler, K. A., BA *Calif.*, MA *Calif.*, PhD *Calif.* Assoc. Prof.

Kuah-Pearce, K. E., BA *Sing.*, PhD *Monash* Assoc. Prof.; Head*

Other Staff: 4 Assoc. Profs.; 1 Visiting Assoc. Prof.; 1 Assoc. Prof./Lectr.; 1 Visiting Asst. Prof.; 1 Asst. Prof./Lectr.; 3 Hon. Profs.; 3 Hon. Assoc. Profs.; 5 Hon. Asst. Profs.; 9 Hon. Lectrs.

Statistics and Actuarial Science

Tel: 2859 2466 Fax: 2858 9041
E-mail: saas@hku.hk

Fung, T. W. K., BSocSc *HK*, MSc *Lond.*, PhD *HK* Prof.

Lauder, I. J., BSc *Edin.*, MSc *Kent*, PhD *HK* Assoc. Prof.

Lee, S. M. S., BA *Camb.*, PhD *Camb.* Assoc. Prof.

Li, W. K., BSc *York(Can.)*, MA *York(Can.)*, PhD *W.Ont.* Chair Prof.; Head*

Ng, K. W., BSc *Chinese HK*, MSc *Alta.*, PhD *Tor.* Sr. Lectr.

Yip, P. S. F., BSc *Melb.*, PhD *La Trobe* Sr. Lectr.

Other Staff: 2 Assoc. Profs.; 4 Asst. Profs./Lectrs.; 1 Sr. Teaching Consultant; 4 Teaching Consultants; 8 Hon. Profs.

Zoology

Tel: 2299 0800 Fax: 2559 9114
E-mail: zoology@hkusua.hku.hk

Ko, R. C. C., BSc *Manit.*, MSc *Br.Col.*, PhD *Guelph* Chair Prof.

Lee, W. W. M., BSc *Wis.*, MPhil *Chinese HK*, PhD *HK* Prof.

Leung, F. C. C., BA *Calif.*, PhD *Calif.* Assoc. Prof.

Li, E. T. S., BSc *Tor.*, MSc *Tor.*, PhD *Tor.* Assoc. Prof.; Head*

Other Staff: 8 Assoc. Profs./Lectrs.; 2 Asst. Profs./Lectrs.; 1 Res. Asst. Prof.; 1 Res. Assoc.; 2 Hon. Profs.; 1 Hon. Assoc. Prof.; 3 Hon. Asst. Profs.; 1 Hon. Res. Assoc.

DENTISTRY

Tel: 2859 0376 Fax: 2517 0544
E-mail: dental@hkusua.hku.hk

Dentistry

Tel: 2859 0376 Fax: 2517 0544
E-mail: dental@hkusua.hku.hk

Cheung, L. K., BDS *Glas.*, PhD *HK*, FFDRCSI, FDSRCPSGlas, FRACDS Chair Prof., Oral and Maxillofacial Surgery

Chow, T. W., BDS *Lond.*, MSc *Lond.*, PhD *Lond.*, FDSRCSEd, FRACDS Assoc. Prof.

Corbet, E. F., BDS *N.U.I.*, FDSRCS, FFDRCSI Assoc. Prof.

Darvell, B. W., MSc *Wales*, PhD *Birm.*, FRSChem, FIMMM Prof.

Hagg, E. U. O., DDS *Lund*, OdontDr *Lund*, FDSRCSEd, FHKAM, FCDSHK Chair Prof., Orthodontics

Jin, L. J., MMedSc *Karolinska*, PhD *Beijing Med.*, OdontDr *Karolinska*, DDS Assoc. Prof.

King, N. M., BDS *Lond.*, MSc *Lond.*, PhD *HK* Prof.

Lo, E. C. M., BDS *HK*, MDS *HK*, PhD *HK* Assoc. Prof.

McMillan, A. S., BDS *Dund.*, PhD *Br.Col.*, FDSRCPSGlas, FDSRCSEd Chair Prof., Oral Rehabilitation

Newsome, P. R. H., BChD *Leeds*, MBA *Warw.*, PhD *Brad.*, FDSRCSEd Assoc. Prof.

Rabie, A. B. M., BDS *Cairo*, MS *Northwestern*, PhD *Northwestern* Assoc. Prof.

Samaranayake, L. P., BDS *S.Lanka*, DDS *Glas.*, FRCPath Chair Prof., Oral Microbiology

Samman, N., BDS *Syd.*, FDSRCS, FRCSEd Prof.

Other Staff: 7 Assoc. Profs./Lectrs.; 16 Asst. Profs./Lectrs.; 1 Res. Asst. Prof.; 1 Postdoctoral Fellow; 4 Tutors; 2 Instrs. (1 Dent. Technol.; 1 Dent. Surg. Assisting); 89 Lectrs.†; 1 Clin. Asst. Prof.; 3 Hon. Profs.; 8 Hon. Assoc. Profs.; 11 Hon. Asst. Profs.; 2 Hon. Res. Assocs.; 1 Hon. Clin. Prof.; 9 Hon. Clin. Assoc. Profs.; 25 Hon. Clin. Asst. Profs.; 1 Hon. Clin. Assoc.

MEDICINE

Tel: 2819 9175 Fax: 2855 9742
E-mail: medfac@hku.hk

Anaesthesiology

Tel: 2855 3303 Fax: 2855 1654
E-mail: anaes@hkucc.hku.hk

Irwin, M. G., MB ChB *Glas.*, FRCA Assoc. Prof.; Head*

Ng, Jacobus K. F., MB ChB *Chinese HK*, MBA *Hull*, FANZCA Assoc. Prof.

Other Staff: 2 Clin. Asst. Profs.; 2 Clin. Assocs.; 1 Hon. Assoc. Prof.; 4 Hon. Asst. Profs.; 19 Hon. Clin. Assoc. Profs.; 35 Hon. Clin. Asst. Profs.

Anatomy

Tel: 2819 9259 Fax: 2817 0857
E-mail: anatomy@hkucc.hku.hk

Chiu, J., BPharm *Taipei Med.Coll.*, MSc *Natnl.Taiwan*, PhD *Br.Col.* Assoc. Prof.

O, Wai-Sum, BSc *HK*, MPhil *HK*, PhD *Edin.* Assoc. Prof.

So, K. F., BA *Northeastern*, PhD *M.I.T.* Prof.; Head*

Tsao, G. S. W., BSc *Chinese HK*, PhD *Lond.* Prof.

Wong, Y. C., BSc *Nan.*, MSc *W.Ont.*, PhD *W.Ont.* Prof.

Other Staff: 5 Assoc. Profs./Lectrs.; 2 Asst. Profs./Lectrs.; 1 Res. Asst. Prof.; 2 Res. Assocs.; 2 Res. Officers; 4 Lectrs.†; 1 Teaching Consultant†; 6 Hon. Profs.; 2 Hon. Assoc. Profs.; 5 Hon. Asst. Profs.; 7 Hon. Res. Assocs.

Biochemistry

Tel: 2819 9241 Fax: 2855 1254
E-mail: biochem@hkusua.hku.hk

Cheah, Kathryn S. E., BSc *Lond.*, PhD *Camb.* Chair Prof.; Head*

Sham, M. H., BSc *Chinese HK*, MPhil *Chinese HK*, PhD *Cant.* Assoc. Prof.

Other Staff: 2 Assoc. Profs.; 1 Assoc. Prof./Lectr.; 7 Asst. Profs./Lectrs.; 1 Res. Asst. Prof.; 8 Res. Assocs.; 3 Teaching Consultants; 12 Hon. Profs.; 1 Hon. Reader; 1 Hon. Assoc. Prof.; 9 Hon. Asst. Profs.; 1 Hon. Res. Assoc.

Clinical Oncology

Tel: 2855 4352 Fax: 2872 6426

Wei, W. I., MB BS HK, MS HK, FRCS, FRCSEd., FACS   William Mong Prof., Otorhinolaryngology; Acting Head*

Other Staff: 3 Assoc. Profs./Lectrs.; 1 Res. Assoc.; 1 Hon. Prof.; 1 Hon. Asst. Prof.; 1 Hon. Clin. Prof.; 9 Hon. Clin. Assoc. Profs.; 7 Hon. Clin. Asst. Profs.

Community Medicine

Tel: 2819 9280 Fax: 2855 9528
E-mail: commed@hkucc.hku.hk

Hedley, A. J., JP, MB ChB Aberd., MD Aberd., Hon. MD Khon Kaen, BBS Aberd., FRCP, FRCPEd, FRCPGlas, FACE, FFPHM   Chair Prof.

Lam, T. H., MB BS HK, MSc Lond., MD HK, FFPHM, FRCPEd   Chair Prof.; Head*

Other Staff: 2 Assoc. Profs./Lectrs.; 4 Asst. Profs./Lectrs.; 1 Res. Asst. Prof.; 9 Res. Assocs.; 1 Res. Officer; 1 Teaching Consultant; 1 Postdoctoral Fellow; 1 Sr. Computer Officer; 7 Hon. Profs.; 13 Hon. Assoc. Profs.; 13 Hon. Asst. Profs.; 3 Hon. Lectrs.; 4 Hon. Res. Assocs.; 1 Hon. Clin. Prof.; 11 Hon. Clin. Assoc. Profs.; 5 Hon. Clin. Asst. Profs.

Behavioural Sciences, Unit for

Tel: 2819 9280 Fax: 2855 9528

Fielding, R., BA Lond., PhD Sheff.   Sr. Lectr.; Head*

Diagnostic Radiology

Tel: 2855 3307 Fax: 2855 1652
E-mail: irenel@hkucc.hku.hk

Wei, W. I., MB BS HK, MS HK, FRCS, FRCSEd, FACS   William Mong Prof., Otorhinolaryngology; Acting Head*

Other Staff: 1 Assoc. Prof./Lectr.; 2 Hon. Profs.; 3 Hon. Assoc. Profs.; 17 Hon. Clin. Assoc. Profs.; 25 Hon. Clin. Asst. Profs.

Medicine

Tel: 2855 4604 Fax: 2855 1143
E-mail: meddept@hkucc.hku.hk

Chan, D. T. M., MB BS HK, MD HK, FRCP, FRCPEd, FRCPGlas   Prof.

Chan, Vivian N. Y., BSc Lond., MSc Lond., PhD Lond., FRCPath, Hon. FRCP   Chair Prof., Molecular Medicine

Cheung, R. T. F., MB BS HK, PhD W.Ont., FRCP, FRCPEd, FRCPGlas   Assoc. Prof.

Epstein, R. J., MB BS Syd., MD Lond., PhD Camb., FRACP, FRCP   Prof.

Fung, P. C. W., BSc Tas., PhD Tas.   Chair Prof., Medical Physics

Ho, S. L., MD Wales, FRCP, FRCPEd, FRCPGlas   Assoc. Prof.

Ip, Mary S. M., MD HK, FRCPEd, FRCPGlas, FRCP   Prof.

Kung, Annie W. C., MB BS HK, MD HK, FRCPEd, FRCP   Prof.

Kwong, Y. L., MB BS HK, MD HK, FRCPEd, FRCPath   Prof.

Lai, C. L., MD HK, FRCPEd, FRCP, FRCPGlas, FRACP   Chair Prof., Medicine and Hepatology

Lai, K. N., MD HK, DSc HK, FRCPath, FRCPEd, FRCP, FRCPGlas, FRACP, FACP   Chair Prof., Nephrology; Head*

Lam, Karen S. L., MD HK, FRCPEd, FRCP, FRACP   Chair Prof.

Lam, W. K., MD HK, FRCP, FRCPEd, FRCPGlas, FRACP   Chair Prof., Respiratory Medicine

Lau, C. P., MB BS HK, MD HK, FRACP, FRCP, FRCPEd, FRCPGlas, FACP   Prof.

Lau, G. K. K., MB BS HK, MD HK   Assoc. Prof.

Lau, W. C. S., MB ChB Dund., MD Dund., FRCPEd, FRCPGlas, FRCP   Prof.

Liang, R. H. S., MD HK, FRCP, FRCPEd, FRCPGlas, FRACP   Chair Prof., Haematology and Oncology

Tan, Kathryn C. B., MB BCh Wales, MD Wales, FRCP, FRCPEd   Assoc. Prof.

Tse, H. F., MB BS HK, MD HK, FRCPEd   Assoc. Prof.

Wong, B. C. Y., MB BS HK, MD HK, FRCPEd, FRCPGlas   Assoc. Prof.

Yuen, R. M. F., MB BS HK, MD HK   Assoc. Prof.

Other Staff: 1 Assoc. Prof./Lectr.; 4 Asst. Profs./Lectrs.; 8 Res. Asst. Profs.; 10 Res. Assocs.; 1 Teaching Consultant; 1 Adjunct Assoc. Prof.; 1 Clin. Asst. Prof.; 8 Hon. Profs.; 8 Hon. Assoc. Profs.; 5 Hon. Asst. Profs.; 16 Hon. Res. Assocs.; 4 Hon. Clin. Profs.; 65 Hon. Clin. Assoc. Profs.; 33 Hon. Clin. Asst. Profs.; 3 Hon. Clin. Assocs.; 1 Hon. Clin. Res. Assoc.

Family Medicine Unit

Tel: 2518 5657 Fax: 2814 7475
E-mail: fmunit@hku.hk

Lam, Cindy L. K., MB BS HK, FRCGP   Assoc. Prof.

Lam, T. P., MB BS W.Aust., MFM Monash, PhD Syd., FRACGP   Assoc. Prof.

Other Staff: 1 Sr. Teaching Consultant; 1 Hon. Asst. Prof.; 24 Hon. Clin. Assoc. Profs.; 160 Hon. Clin. Asst. Profs.; 51 Hon. Clin. Tutors

Microbiology

Tel: 2855 4897 Fax: 2855 1241
E-mail: hkumicro@hkucc.hku.hk

Guan, Y., MD Jiangxi Med., MMedSc Peking Union Med., PhD HK   Assoc. Prof.

Ho, P. Lo, MB BS HK, FRCPA, FACP   Assoc. Prof.

Peiris, J. S. M., MB BS Ceyl., DPhil Oxf., FRCPath, FRS   Prof.

Woo, P. C. Y., MB BS HK   Assoc. Prof.

Yuen, K. Y., MB BS HK, MD HK, FRCPath, FRCPEd   Chair Prof.; Head*

Other Staff: 1 Assoc. Prof./Lectr.; 4 Asst. Profs./Lectrs.; 1 Res. Asst. Prof.; 1 Res. Officer; 1 Clin. Bacteriologist; 10 Hon. Profs.; 11 Hon. Assoc. Profs.; 12 Hon. Asst. Profs.; 1 Hon. Tutor; 1 Hon. Res. Assoc.; 1 Hon. Clin. Assoc. Prof.

Nursing Studies

Tel: 2819 2600 Fax: 2872 6079
E-mail: nursing@hkucc.hku.hk

Chan, S. S. C., MEd Manc., PhD HK   Assoc. Prof.; Head*

Sullivan, P. L., BSc Mt.St.Vin., MSc Boston, PhD Alta.   Prof.

Other Staff: 1 Assoc. Prof.; 5 Asst. Profs.; 8 Teaching Consultants; 4 Hon. Profs.; 1 Hon. Assoc. Prof.; 15 Hon. Asst. Profs.

Obstetrics and Gynaecology

Tel: 2855 4260 Fax: 2855 0947

Ho, P. C., MB BS HK, MD HK, FRCOG   Chair Prof.; Head*

Lao, Terence T. H., MB BS HK, MD HK, FRCOG   Prof.

Ngan, Hextan Y. S., MB BS HK, MD HK, FRCOG   Prof.

Tang, Grace W. K., MB BS HK, FRCOG   Prof.

Yeung, W. S. B., BSc HK, PhD HK   Prof.

Other Staff: 1 Asst. Prof./Lectr.; 1 Res. Asst. Prof.; 1 Res. Assoc.; 1 Clin. Assoc. Prof./Lectr.; 5 Clin. Asst. Profs./Lectrs.; 1 Hon. Prof.; 5 Hon. Asst. Profs.; 3 Hon. Clin. Profs.; 24 Hon. Clin. Assoc. Profs.; 37 Hon. Clin. Asst. Profs.

Orthopaedic Surgery

Tel: 2855 4254 Fax: 2817 4392
E-mail: orthol@hkucc.hku.hk

Cheung, K. M. C., MB BS Lond., FRCS   Assoc. Prof.

Chiu, P. K. Y., MB BS HK, FRCSEd   Assoc. Prof.

Chow, S. P., JP, MB BS HK, MS HK, FRCSEd, FACS   Chair Prof., Orthopaedics and Traumatology

Luk, K. D. K., MB BS HK, MChOrth Liv., FRCSEd, FRCSGlas, FRACS   Chair Prof.; Head*

Other Staff: 3 Assoc. Profs./Lectrs.; 1 Asst. Prof./Lectr.; 1 Res. Asst. Prof.; 1 Postdoctoral Fellow; 2 Hon. Profs.; 4 Hon. Asst. Profs.; 1 Hon. Res. Assoc.; 2 Hon. Clin. Profs.; 22 Hon. Clin. Assoc. Profs.; 63 Hon. Clin. Asst. Profs.; 5 Hon. Clin. Assocs.

Paediatrics and Adolescent Medicine

Tel: 2855 4482 Fax: 2855 1523

Cheung, P. T., MB BS HK, FRCPEd   Assoc. Prof.

Lau, Allan S. Y., BSc McG., MD McG., FRCPCan   Assoc. Prof.

Lau, Y. L., MB ChB Glas., MD Glas., FRCPEd, FRCP, FRCPCH   Chair Prof.; Head*

Low, L. C. K., BSc Glas., MB ChB Glas., FRCPEd, FRCP, FRCPGlas, FRCPCH   Prof.

Wong, Virginia C. N., MB BS, FRCPEd, FRCPCH   Prof.

Other Staff: 4 Assoc. Profs./Lectrs.; 3 Asst. Profs./Lectrs.; 1 Res. Asst. Prof.; 1 Teaching Consultant; 2 Res. Officers; 39 Hon. Assoc. Profs.; 12 Hon. Tutors; 2 Hon. Clin. Profs.; 44 Hon. Clin. Asst. Profs.

Pathology

Tel: 2855 4875 Fax: 2819 3859
E-mail: enquiry@pathology.hku.hk

Chan, K. W., MB BS HK, FRCPath   Sr. Lectr.

Chan, L. C., MB BChir Camb., MA Camb., PhD Lond., FRCP, FRCPath   Chair Prof.; Head*

Cheung, Annie N. Y., MB BS HK, MD HK, FRCPath   Prof.

Leung, S. Y., MB BS HK, MD HK, FRCPath, FRCPA   Assoc. Prof.

Ng, I. O. L., MB BS HK, MD HK, FRCPath   Prof.

Nicholls, J. M., MB BS Adel., FRCPA   Assoc. Prof.

Srivastava, G., BSc Punjab, MSc Punjab, PhD Adel.   Prof.

Wong, M. P., MB BS HK, MD HK, FRCPath, FRCPA   Assoc. Prof.

Other Staff: 3 Assoc. Profs./Lectrs.; 2 Asst. Profs./Lectrs.; 3 Res. Asst. Profs.; 3 Res. Assocs.; 2 Sr. Hospital Immunologists; 1 Sci. Officer; 1 Clin. Assoc. Prof.; 2 Sr. Clin. Pathologists; 5 Hon. Profs.; 8 Hon. Assoc. Profs.; 7 Hon. Asst. Profs.; 2 Hon. Clin. Profs.; 21 Hon. Clin. Assoc. Profs.; 17 Hon. Clin. Asst. Profs.

Pharmacology

Tel: 2819 9250 Fax: 2817 0859
E-mail: pharma@hkusua.hku.hk

Cho, C. H., BPharm Natnl.Def.Med.Center, Taiwan, PhD HK   Chair Prof.

Man, R. Y. K., BSc Manit., PhD Manit.   Chair Prof.; Head*

Vanhoutte, P. M. G. R., MS Ghent, MD Ghent, PhD Antwerp   Distinguished Visiting Prof.

Other Staff: 1 Assoc. Prof./Lectr.; 1 Asst. Prof./Lectr.; 2 Res. Asst. Profs.; 5 Hon. Profs.; 3 Hon. Assoc. Profs.; 4 Hon. Asst. Profs.

Physiology

Tel: 2819 9162 Fax: 2855 9730

Ballard, H. J., BSc Leeds, PhD Leeds   Assoc. Prof.

Chan, Y. S., BSc HK, PhD HK   Prof.

Lung, Mary A. K. Y., BSc HK, PhD HK   Assoc. Prof.

Shiu, S. Y. W., MB BS HK, DPhil Oxf.   Assoc. Prof.

Tang, F., BSc HK, MSc HK, PhD Hull   Prof.

Wong, T. M., BSc Chinese HK, MSc HK, PhD HK   Prof.; Head*

Other Staff: 5 Assoc. Profs./Lectrs.; 1 Res. Assoc.; 6 Hon. Profs.; 4 Hon. Assoc. Profs.; 3 Hon. Asst. Profs.; 2 Hon. Res. Assocs.

Psychiatry

Tel: 2855 4486 Fax: 2855 1345
E-mail: psychiat@hkucc.hku.hk
Chen, E. Y. H., MB ChB Edin., MA Oxf.   Assoc. Prof.
Lee, P. W. H., MSocSc HK, PhD HK   Prof.
Ng, M. L., MB BS HK, MD HK, FRCPsych   Prof.
Tang, S. W., MB BS HK, MBA Calif., PhD Tor., FRCPCan   Chair Prof.; Head*
Other Staff: 2 Visiting Profs.; 4 Asst. Profs./ Lectrs.; 1 Clin. Assoc. Prof.; 17 Hon. Profs.; 3 Hon. Assoc. Profs.; 13 Hon. Asst. Profs.; 1 Hon. Lectr.; 1 Hon. Clin. Prof.; 8 Hon. Clin. Assoc. Profs.; 27 Hon. Clin. Asst. Profs.

Surgery

Tel: 2855 4589 Fax: 2855 1897
E-mail: surgery@hkucc.hku.hk
Cheng, S. W. K., MB BS HK, MS HK, FRCSEd, FACS, FRCS   Prof.
Chu, K. M., MB BS HK, MS HK, FRCSEd, FACS   Assoc. Prof.
Fan, S. T., MB BS HK, MS HK, MD HK, PhD HK, FRCSGlas, FRCSEd, FACS   Sun Chieh Yeh Chair Prof., Hepatobiliary Surgery
Lo, C. M., MB BS HK, MS HK, FRCSEd, FRACS, FACS   Chair Prof.
Lo, C. Y., MB BS HK, MS HK, FRCSEd, FACS   Assoc. Prof.
Poon, R. T. P., MB BS HK, MS HK, FRCSEd, FACS   Assoc. Prof.
Tam, Paul K. H., MB BS HK, ChM Liv., FRCSEd, FRCSGlas, FRCSI, FRCPCH   Chair Prof., Paediatric Surgery
Wei, W. I., MB BS HK, MS HK, FRCS, FRCSEd, FACS   William Mong Prof., Otorhinolaryngology
Wong, J., BSc(Med) Syd., MB BS Syd., PhD Syd., Hon. MD Syd., FRACS, FRCSEd, FRCSGlas, Hon. FACS   Chair Prof.; Head*
Yuen, P. W., MB BS HK, MS HK, FRCSEd, FRCSGlas, FACS   Prof.
Other Staff: 2 Assoc. Profs./Lectrs.; 3 Asst. Profs./Lectrs.; 6 Res. Asst. Profs.; 1 Sr. Teaching Consultant; 9 Postdoctoral Fellows; 4 Res. Assocs.; 2 Res. Officers; 1 Clin. Prof.; 2 Clin. Asst. Profs.; 10 Hon. Profs.; 8 Hon. Asst. Profs.; 1 Hon. Res. Assoc.; 72 Hon. Clin. Assoc. Profs.; 56 Hon. Clin. Asst. Profs.; 6 Hon. Clin. Assocs.; 2 Hon. Clin. Res. Assocs.

SPECIAL CENTRES, ETC

Ageing, Sau Po Centre on

Tel: 2241 5524 Fax: 2540 1244
E-mail: ageing@hku.hk
Chow, N. W. S., MBE, JP, BA HK, MA(Econ) Manc., PhD HK   Acting Dir.*
Other Staff: 6 Assoc. Dirs.; 2 Hon. Assoc. Dirs.

American Studies, Centre of

Roberts, P. M., MA Camb., PhD Camb.   Hon. Dir.*
Other Staff: 2 Hon. Lectrs.

Anthropological Research, Centre for

Tel: 2859 2060 Fax: 2857 4074
Kuah-Pearce, K. E., BA Sing., PhD Monash   Hon. Academic Dir.*

Applied Spectroscopy and Analytical Sciences, Centre for

Chan, G. K. Y., BSc Alta., MS Cornell, PhD Cornell   Dir.*

Asia Case Research Centre

Farhoomand, A. F., BEng C'dia., MBA C'dia., PhD McG.   Dir.*
Other Staff: 1 Res. Officer; 6 Res. Assocs.

Asian Studies, Centre of

Tel: 2859 2460 Fax: 2559 3185
E-mail: casgen@hku.hk
Wong, S. L., JP, BSocSc HK, MPhil Chinese HK, BLitt Oxf., DPhil Oxf.   Dir.*
Other Staff: 4 Res. Asst. Profs.; 4 Distinguished Fellows; 2 Res. Assocs.; 1 Res. Officer; 1 Postdoctoral Fellow; 4 Hon. Profs.; 3 Hon. Assoc. Profs.; 2 Hon. Asst. Profs.; 58 Hon. Res. Fellows

Behavioural Health, Centre on

Tel: 2589 0500 Fax: 2816 6710
E-mail: bhealth@hku.hk
Chan, Cecilia L. W., BSocSc HK, MSocSc HK, PhD HK   Dir.*
Other Staff: 2 Asst. Profs./Lectrs.; 1 Sr. Consultant; 1 Centre Manager

Buddhist Studies, Centre of

Tel: 2241 5019 Fax: 2549 3040
E-mail: buddhism@hku.hk
Dhammajoti, K. L., MA Kelaniya, PhD Kelaniya   Prof.
Jing, Y., MA Kelaniya, MPhil Kelaniya, PhD Lond., BA   Dir.*
Other Staff: 1 Visiting Assoc. Prof.; 2 Visiting Asst. Profs.; 1 Res. Asst. Prof.; 5 Teaching Consultants; 1 Hon. Prof.; 1 Hon. Assoc. Prof.

Cardiovascular Science and Medicine, Institute of

Wong, T. M., BSc Chinese HK, MSc HK, PhD HK   Dir.*

China and Global Development, Institute for

Tang, J. T. H., BA HK, MPhil Camb., PhD Lond.   Hon. Dir.*
Other Staff: 3 Hon. Deputy Dirs.

China Development Studies, International Centre for

Zhao, S. X. B., BSc Sun Yat-Sen, MSc Chinese Acad.Sc., PhD Manc.   Dir.*
Other Staff: 2 Assoc. Dirs.

China Financial Research, Centre for

Song, F. M., BS Zhejiang, MS Huazhong U.S.T., MA Ohio State, PhD Ohio State   Dir.*

China Information Technology and Law Centre

Lee, A. S. C., LLB HK, BCL Oxf.   Co-Dir.*
Pun, K. H., BS HK, LLB Lond., LLM Lond., MS Ill., PhD Ill.   Co-Dir.*

Chinese Medicine, School of

Tong, Y., BTCM Shanghai Trad.Med.& Pharmacol., MMed Shanghai Trad.Med.& Pharmacol., DMed Shanghai Trad.Med.& Pharmacol.   Dir.*
Other Staff: 3 Assoc. Profs.; 1 Asst. Prof.; 7 Asst. Profs./Lectrs.; 1 Teaching Consultant; 1 Practitioner; 7 Hon. Profs.; 1 Assoc. Prof.; 1 Asst. Prof.

Civil Society and Governance, Centre for

Chan, J. C. W., BSSc Chinese HK, MSc Lond., DPhil Oxf.   Hon. Dir.*

Clinical Trials Centre

Tel: 2855 4664 Fax: 2974 1248
E-mail: ctcentre@hkucc.hku.hk
Karlberg, J. P. E., BSc Gothenburg, MD Gothenburg, PhD Gothenburg   Prof.; Dir.*
Other Staff: 5 Res. Officers; 2 Hon. Asst. Dirs.; 1 Hon. Prof.; 2 Hon. Assoc. Profs.; 2 Hon. Asst. Profs.; 1 Hon. Res. Assoc.; 1 Hon. Clin. Prof.; 4 Hon. Clin. Assoc. Profs.; 3 Hon. Clin. Asst. Profs.; 1 Hon. Clin. Res. Assoc.

Cognitive Science Centre

Hayes, A., BSc W.Aust., PhD W.Aust.   Hon. Dir.*

Communication Disorders, Centre for

McPherson, D. B., BA Syd., MEd Manc., PhD Qld.   Assoc. Prof.; Hon. Dir.*

Comparative and Public Law, Centre for

Tel: 2859 2965 Fax: 2549 8495
E-mail: fkleung@hku.hk
Fu, H., MA Tor., DJur York(Can.), LLB   Dir.*
Young, S. N. M., BArtsSc McM., LLB Tor., LLM Camb.   Deputy Dir.

Comparative Education Research Centre

Mason, M., BA Cape Town, MA Col., MEd Col., PhD Col.   Assoc. Prof.

Construct IT, Centre for

Tel: 2857 8628 Fax: 2540 1836
E-mail: cfhui@hku.hk
Rowlinson, S. M., BSc Nott., MSc Lond., PhD Brun.   Prof.; Dir.*

Criminology, Centre for

Tel: 2859 2114 Fax: 2975 4080
E-mail: crimctr@hkucc.hku.hk
Bacon-Shone, J. H., BSc Durh., MSc Lond., PhD Birm.   Acting Dir.*

Cyberport Institute of Hong Kong

Tel: 2857 3000 Fax: 2807 2054
E-mail: enquiry@cyber-i.hku.hk
Shen, S. M., BA HK, MSc Lond., PhD HK   Head*

E-Business Technology Institute

Tel: 2299 0505 Fax: 2299 0500
E-mail: info@eti.hku.hk
Tan, C. J., BSEE Seattle, MSEE Calif., DEng Col.   Dir.*
Other Staff: 3 Asst. Dirs.; 1 Sr. Manager; 1 Manager; 2 Sr. Computer Officers; 10 Computer Officers; 12 Asst. Computer Officers

E-Commerce Infrastructure Development, Centre for

Cheung, D. W. L., BSc Chinese HK, MSc S.Fraser, PhD S.Fraser   Dir.*
Lau, F. C. M., BSc Acad., MMath Wat., PhD Wat.   Deputy Dir.

Economic Research, Hong Kong Centre for

Tel: 2547 8313 Fax: 2548 6319
E-mail: hkcer@econ.hku.hk
Siu, Alan K. F., BA Brandeis, PhD Harv.   Exec. Dir.
Wong, Richard Y. C., JP, AB Chic., AM Chic., PhD Chic.   Dir.*

Economics and Business Strategy, Hong Kong Institute of

Tel: 2548 9300 Fax: 2548 3223
E-mail: info@hiebs.hku.hk
Siu, Alan K. F., BA Brandeis, PhD Harv.   Deputy Dir.
Wong, Richard Y. C., JP, AB Chic., AM Chic., PhD Chic.   Dir.*
Other Staff: 1 Asst. Prof.; 1 Res. Asst. Prof.; 1 Sr. Res. Assoc.; 5 Res. Assocs.; 1 Hon. Assoc. Prof.

Education in China, Wah Ching Centre of Research on

Cheung, K. W., BEd Lond., MA Lond., PhD Lond.   Dir.*

Educational Leadership, Centre for

Ng, H. M., BSc Chinese HK, PhD Birm.   Hon. Dir.*

Electric Vehicles, International Research Centre for

Chau, K. T., BSc(Eng) HK, MPhil HK, PhD HK   Dir.*

English Centre

Tel: 2859 2009 Fax: 2547 3409
E-mail: ecmail@hkucc.hku.hk
Lam, Agnes S. L., BA *Sing.*, MA *Sing.*, PhD *Pitt.*
Assoc. Prof.
Nunan, David C., BA *NSW*, MEd *Exe.*, PhD *Flin.*
Prof.; Dir.*
Other Staff: 1 Assoc. Prof./Lectr.; 1 Asst. Prof./
Lectr.; 1 Principal Lang. Instr.; 4 Sr. Lang.
Instrs.; 14 Lang. Instrs.; 9 Asst. Lang. Instrs.

Family Institute

Tel: 2859 5300 Fax: 2964 9475
E-mail: hkufi@hkusua.hku.hk
Lee, W. Y., BA *Chengchi*, MSW *Tor.*, PhD *Union Inst.(Ohio)*   Dir.*
Other Staff: 2 Assoc. Dirs.; 1 Sr. Teaching
Consultant

Genome Research Centre

Tel: 2819 9848 Fax: 2818 5653
E-mail: genome@hku.hk
Mak, W. W., BSc *Chinese HK*, MSc *Tor.*, PhD *Tor.*
Manager*
Other Staff: 2 Res. Asst. Profs.; 3 Affiliated
Scientists

Graduate School

Tel: 2559 3306 Fax: 2857 3543
E-mail: gradsch@hkucc.hku.hk
Burns, J. P., BA *St.Olaf*, MA *Oxf.*, MA *Col.*,
MPhil *Col.*, PhD *Col.*   Prof.; Assoc. Dean
Chin, F. Y. L., BASc *Tor.*, MSc *Prin.*, MA *Prin.*,
PhD *Prin.*, FIEE   Prof.; Assoc. Dean
Yeh, Anthony G. O., BA *HK*, MSc *Asian I.T.,
Bangkok*, MRP *Syr.*, PhD *Syr.*, FRTPI, FRAPI,
FCILT   Prof.; Dean*

Hong Kong Putonghua Education and Assessment Centre

Cheng Kai Ming, JP, BSc *HK*, MEd *HK*, PhD
Lond.   Chair Prof.; Hon. Dir.*

Human Performance, Institute of

Tel: 2817 9576 Fax: 2818 8042
E-mail: ihphku@hku.hk
Abernethy, B., BHMS(Ed) *Qld.*, PhD *Otago*
Prof.; Dir.*
Other Staff: 3 Asst. Dirs.; 1 Assoc. Prof./Lectr.;
5 Res. Asst. Profs.; 1 Sr. Phys. Educn.
Officer; 3 Phys. Educn. Officers; 1 Tutor; 2
Hon. Assoc. Profs.

Human Reproduction, Centre of

Tel: 2885 3402 Fax: 2817 5374
Lao, Terence T. H., MB BS *HK*, MD *HK*, FRCOG
Dir.*

Information Technology in Education, Centre for

Tel: 2857 8540 Fax: 2517 7194
E-mail: cite@hkucc.hku.hk
Law, Nancy W. Y., BSc *HK*, MPhil *HK*, PhD
Lond.   Prof.; Dir.*

International Financial Law, Asian Institute of

Tel: 2859 2491 Fax: 2549 8495
E-mail: fkleung@hku.hk
Arner, D. W., BA *Drury*, LLM *Lond.*, JD
S.Methodist   Dir.*
Hsu, B. F. C., BSc *Alta.*, LLM *Alta.*, MA *Oregon*,
PhD *Lond.*   Deputy Dir.
Lewis, D. J., AB *S.Calif.*, LLM *Lond.*, JD *Emory*
Deputy Dir.

Jockey Club Magnetic Resonance Imaging Centre

Tel: 2241 5681 Fax: 2540 6215
E-mail: info@mri.hku.hk
Yang, Edward S., BS *Cheng Kung*, MS *Oklahoma
State*, PhD *Yale*   Dir.*
Other Staff: 1 Visiting Assoc. Prof.

Journalism and Media Studies Centre

Tel: 2964 5733 Fax: 2858 8736
E-mail: jmsc@hku.hk
Chan, Yuen-Ying, BSocSc *HK*, MSSc *Chinese HK*
Freedom Forum Media Studies Fellow;
Nieman Fellow; Prof.; Dir.*
Plott, D. A., BA *Calif.*, MA *Harv.*, PhD *Harv.*
Deputy Dir.
Other Staff: 2 Asst. Profs./Lectrs.; 1 Sr.
Teaching Consultant; 3 Res. Assocs.; 1 Res.
Officer

Kadoorie Agricultural Research Centre

Tel: 2488 5060 Fax: 2488 5285
E-mail: karc@hkusua.hku.hk
Hills, P. R., BA *Lond.*, MA *York(Can.)*, PhD *Aston*
Prof.; Dir.*

Language Centre

Tel: 2859 2000 Fax: 2548 0487
E-mail: language@hkusua.hku.hk
Martin, Michael R., AB *Prin.*, MA *Harv.*, PhD
Harv.   Acting Dir.*
Other Staff: 2 Sr. Lang. Instrs.; 3 Lang. Instrs.;
4 Visiting Lang. Instrs.; 1 Teaching
Consultant; 7 Asst. Lang. Instrs.; 15 Lang.
Instrs.†

Liver Disease, Centre for the Study of

Liu, Y., MB BS *Shanghai Jiaotong*, PhD *Nott.*   Res.
Asst. Prof.; Dir.*

Marine Science, Swire Institute of

Tel: 2809 2179 Fax: 2809 2197
E-mail: swims@hkucc.hku.hk
Williams, G. A., BSc *Manc.*, PhD *Brist.*   Hon.
Dir.*
Other Staff: 2 Asst. Profs.; 3 Postdoctoral
Fellows

Mathematical Research, Institute of

Mok, Ngaiming, MA *Yale*, PhD *Stan.*   Hon.
Dir.*

Medical and Health Sciences Education, Institute of

Ip, Mary S. M., MD *HK*, FRCPEd, FRCPGlas,
FRCP   Dir.*
Patil, N. G., MBE, MB BS *Bom.*, MS *Bom.*,
FRCSEd   Deputy Dir.

Medical Ethics Unit

Hui, E. C., BA *Calif.*, MD *Br.Col.*, MTS *Br.Col.*,
PhD *Br.Col.*   Dir.*

Pasteur Research Centre

Tel: 2816 8403 Fax: 2872 5782
E-mail: hkuip@hkusua.hku.hk
Altmeyer, Ralf   Sci. Dir.*
Other Staff: 6 Postdoctoral Fellows

Poon Kam Kai Institute of Management

Tel: 2523 8878 Fax: 2523 7555
E-mail: admin@pkki.business.hku.hk
Wong, G. Y. Y., BSc *HK*, MBA *Manc.*, PhD *Brad.*
Assoc. Prof.; Exec. Dir.*
Other Staff: 1 Assoc. Prof.; 2 Asst. Profs.

Professional and Continuing Education, School of

Tel: 2975 5751 Fax: 2559 7528
E-mail: enquiry@hkuspace.hku.hk
Lee, Jane C. Y., BA *HK*, MSocSc *HK*, PhD *ANU*
Assoc. Dir.
Luk, Michael Y. L., BA *HK*, MPhil *HK*, PhD *Tor.*
Assoc. Prof.; Deputy Dir.
Shen, S. M., BA *HK*, MSc *Lond.*, PhD *HK*   Assoc.
Prof.; Deputy Dir.
Young, Enoch C. M., BSc *HK*, PhD *Brist.*, FRAS,
FCIM   Prof.; Dir.*
Other Staff: 14 Assoc. Profs. (Chinese Med.); 1
Visiting Assoc. Prof. (Chinese Med.); 4 Asst.
Profs. (Chinese Med.); 4 Lectrs. (Chinese
Med.); 3 Specialist Consultants (Chinese
Med.); 10 Tutors/Coll. Lectrs.; 4 Principal
Programme Dirs.; 24 Sr. Programme Dirs.; 3

Sr. Consultants; 3 Consultants; 1 Res.
Consultant; 20 Programme Dirs.; 1 Asst.
Programme Dir.; 20 Programme Managers;
18 Adjunct Profs.; 12 Adjunct Assoc. Profs.;
3 Hon. External Advisors; 8 Hon. Profs.; 11
Hon. Assoc. Profs./Sr. Lecrts.; 10 Hon. Asst.
Profs./Lectrs.

Social Sciences Research Centre

Tel: 2859 2412 Fax: 2858 4327
E-mail: hkussrc@hkucc.hku.hk
Bacon-Shone, J. H., BSc *Durh.*, MSc *Lond.*, PhD
Birm.   Dir.*
Other Staff: 3 Hon. Profs.; 1 Hon. Assoc. Prof.;
2 Hon. Asst. Profs.

Special Education, Centre for Advancement in

Lian, J. M., BEd *Natnl.Taiwan Normal*, MEd *Texas
Tech*, EdD *Texas Tech*   Hon. Dir.*

Suicide Research and Prevention, Hong Kong Jockey Club Centre for

Tel: 2241 5013 Fax: 2549 7161
E-mail: csrp@hku.hk
Yip, P. S. F., BSc *Melb.*, PhD *La Trobe*   Dir.*
Other Staff: 1 Trg. Consultant/Clin.
Psychologist

University Teaching, Centre for the Advancement of

Tel: 2859 8953 Fax: 2540 9941
E-mail: cauthku@hkucc.hku.hk
Johnston, D. J., BA *NE*, MEd *James Cook*, PhD
Curtin   Dir.*
Other Staff: 1 Asst. Prof./Lectr.; 1 Teaching
Consultant

Urban Planning and Environmental Management, Centre of

Tel: 2859 2721 Fax: 2559 0468
E-mail: cupem@hkusua.hku.hk
Hills, P. R., BA *Lond.*, MA *York(Can.)*, PhD *Aston*
Prof.; Dir.*
MacPherson, Kerrie L., BA *N.Y.State*, MA
N.Y.State, PhD *N.Y.State*   Assoc. Prof.
Yeh, Anthony G. O., BA *HK*, MSc *Asian I.T.,
Bangkok*, MRP *Syr.*, PhD *Syr.*, FRTPI, FRAPI,
FCILT   Prof.
Other Staff: 5 Assoc. Profs./Lectrs.; 1 Asst.
Prof./Lectr.; 2 Hon. Profs.; 21 Hon. Res.
Fellows

CONTACT OFFICERS

Academic affairs. Registrar: Wai, Henry W.
K., MA *HK*, FCIS (E-mail: afss@reg.hku.hk)
Admissions (first degree). Registrar: Wai,
Henry W. K., MA *HK*, FCIS
(E-mail: afss@reg.hku.hk)
Admissions (higher degree). Dean, Graduate
School (research curricula): Yeh, Prof.
Anthony G. O., BA *HK*, MSc *Asian I.T.,
Bangkok*, MRP *Syr.*, PhD *Syr.*, FRTPI, FRAPI,
FCILT (E-mail: gradsch@hku.hk)
Admissions (higher degree). Head, Research
Services Section, Registry (taught curricula):
Ng, E. S. P., BSc *Dund.*, MA *Dund.*, MTh *Lond.*
(E-mail: rss@reg.hku.hk)
Adult/continuing education. Director, School
of Professional and Continuing Education:
Young, Prof. Enoch C. M., BSc *HK*, PhD
Brist., FRAS, FCIM
(E-mail: enquiry@hkuspace.hku.hk)
Alumni. Director, Development and Alumni
Affairs Office: Tsui, Bernadette W. S., BA
HK, MPhil *HK* (E-mail: daao@www.hku.hk)
Archives. Registrar: Wai, Henry W. K., MA
HK, FCIS
Careers. Director, Careers Education and
Placement Centre: Li, Louisa W. T., BSocSc
HK (E-mail: cepc@hkucc.hku.hk)
Computing services. Director, Computer
Centre: Ng, N., MSc(Eng) *HK*, MASc *Br.Col.*,
PhD *Alta.* (E-mail: ccbox@hku.hk)
Consultancy services. Managing Director,
Versitech Ltd.: Li, Prof. Victor O. K., BBS

M.I.T., SB M.I.T., SMEE M.I.T., ScD M.I.T.
(E-mail: info@versitech.hku.hk)

Credit transfer. Registrar: Wai, Henry W. K.,
MA HK, FCIS (E-mail: afss@reg.hku.hk)

Development/fund-raising. Director,
Development and Alumni Affairs Office:
Tsui, Bernadette W. S., BA HK, MPhil HK
(E-mail: daao@www.hku.hk)

Distance education. Director, School of
Professional and Continuing Education:
Young, Prof. Enoch C. M., BSc HK, PhD
Brist., FRAS, FCIM
(E-mail: enquiry@hkupsace.hku.hk)

Estates and buildings/works and services.
Director of Estates: Wong, Kenneth P. K.,
BA Hawaii, BArch Br.Col.,
MSc(ConstProjectMan) HK
(E-mail: estates@hku.hk)

Examinations. Assistant Registrar (Academic):
Lai, C. K., BSSc Chinese HK, MAppSc C.Sturt
(E-mail: afss@reg.hku.hk)

Finance. Director of Finance: Lam, Philip B. L.
(E-mail: finance@fo.hku.hk)

General enquiries. Registrar: Wai, Henry W.
K., MA HK, FCIS

Health services. Director, University Health
Service: Chan, Kitty K. C., MB BS HK, MHP
NSW (E-mail: uhealth@hkusub.hku.hk)

International office. Assistant Registrar: Wan,
Katherine H. M., BA HK
(E-mail: exchange@reg.hku.hk)

Library (chief librarian). Librarian: Ferguson,
A. W., BA Brigham Young, MA Wash., MLS
Wash., EdD Col.
(E-mail: libadmin@hkucc.hku.hk)

Marketing. Director, Development and Alumni
Affairs Office: Tsui, Bernadette W. S., BA
HK, MPhil HK (E-mail: daao@www.hku.hk)

Personnel/human resources. Head, Staffing
Section, Registry: Koo, Yvonne Y., BA HK

Public relations. Director of Communications:
(vacant) (E-mail: eromail@reg.hku.hk)

Publications. Director of Communications:
(vacant) (E-mail: eromail@reg.hku.hk)

Purchasing. Director of Finance: Lam, Philip
B. L. (E-mail: finance@fo.hku.hk)

Research. Head, Research Services Section,
Registry: Ng, E. S. P., BSc Dund., MA Dund.,
MTh Lond. (E-mail: rss@reg.hku.hk)

Safety. Director of Safety: Mabbott, Derek J.,
BSc Sheff., PhD Sheff.

Scholarships, awards, loans. Registrar: Wai,
Henry W. K., MA HK, FCIS
(E-mail: afss@reg.hku.hk)

Schools liaison. Senior Assistant Registrar:
Wong, Isabella Y. S., BSc Jinan
(E-mail: chinaaff@www.hku.hk)

Sport and recreation. Director, Institute of
Human Performance: Abernethy, Prof. B.,
BHMS(Ed) Qld., PhD Otago
(E-mail: ihphku@hku.hk)

Staff development and training. Head,
Staffing Section, Registry: Koo, Yvonne Y.,
BA HK

Strategic planning. Pro-Vice-Chancellor:
Malpas, Prof. John G., BA Oxf., MA Oxf.,
MSc Nfld., PhD Nfld., DSc Oxf.

Student union. President, HKU Students'
Union: Lau, Fong
(E-mail: union@hkusua.hku.hk)

Student welfare/counselling. Dean of Student
Affairs: Chau, A. W. L., BSc(Eng) HK, MS
Wis., PhD Wis.

University press. Publisher: Day, C. L., MA
Oxf., MA Camb., PhD Stir.
(E-mail: hkupress@hkucc.hku.hk)

[Information supplied by the institution as at 9 June
2006, and edited by the ACU]

OPEN UNIVERSITY OF HONG KONG

Founded 1989

Member of the Association of Commonwealth Universities

Postal Address: 30 Good Shepherd Street, Homantin, Kowloon, Hong Kong
Telephone: 2711 2100 **Fax:** 2715 0760 **E-mail:** infoctr@ic.ouhk.edu.hk
URL: http://www.ouhk.edu.hk

PRESIDENT*—Leong, Prof. John C. Y., MB BS HK, FRCS, FRCSEd, FRACS, FHKAM
VICE PRESIDENT (ACADEMIC)—Wong, Prof. Danny S. N., BSc Calif.State, MSc Penn., PhD Penn.
VICE PRESIDENT (TECHNOLOGY AND DEVELOPMENT)—Leung, Prof. Chun-ming, BSc W.Mich., PhD Calif.
REGISTRAR‡—Lee, S. W., BSc Chinese HK, MPhil Chinese HK
LIBRARIAN—Mok, W. M., BSc Chinese HK
ACTING HEAD OF FINANCE—Tsui, Stephen H. M., BSSc Chinese HK

GENERAL INFORMATION

History. The university, formerly the Open
Learning Institute of Hong Kong, was
established in 1989. It was officially retitled
the Open University of Hong Kong in 1997.

Admission to first degree courses (see also
Hong Kong Introduction). There are normally
no academic requirements for most of the
distance learning courses. Applicants should be
17 years or above.

First Degrees (see also Hong Kong Directory
to Subjects of Study) (* = with honours).
BA*, BBA*, BComputing*, BECom*, BEd*,
BGS, BLang*, BNursing*, BSc*, BSocSc,
BSocSc*.
Bachelor of Language Studies (English)
(hons) and BEd (hons) offered as a double
degree (3-4 years full-time).
Length of course. Full-time: BA*, BBA*,
BComputing*, BLang*, BNursing*, BSc*,
BSocSc*: 3-4 years. By distance learning: BEd*:
3-6 years; BA*, BBA*, BComputing*, BECom*,
BGS, BLang*, BNursing*, BSc*, BSocSc,
BSocSc*: 3-8 years.

Higher Degrees (see also Hong Kong
Directory to Subjects of Study).
Master's. LLM, MBA, MECom, MEd, MHRM,
MPhil, MSc.
Admission. Applicants for admission to
master's degrees must normally hold an
appropriate first degree.

Length of course. Full-time: MBA: 2-3 years. By
distance learning: LLM, MBA, MECom, MEd,
MHRM, MSc: 2-5 years; MPhil: 3-6 years.
Doctoral. DBA, EdD.
Admission. Applicants for admission to
doctoral programmes must hold an appropriate
master's degree.
Length of course. By distance learning: DBA, EdD:
4-7 years.

Language of Instruction. English. Chinese is
used for some courses in business
administration, Chinese business law Chinese
humanities, Chinese language, literature and
translation, and education.

Libraries. Volumes: 120,000. Periodicals
subscribed to: 1060. Other holdings: electronic
library (17000 e-books and 15500 databases
and full-text journals). Special collections:
open distance education.

Academic Awards (2006-2007). 155
awards ranging in value from HK$2000 to
HK$22,500.

Income (2006-2007). Total,
HK$392,000,000.

Statistics. Staff (2006-2007): 480 (130
academic, 350 non-academic). Students
(2006-2007): full-time 2201 (1095 men,
1106 women); distance education/external
15,075 (7220 men, 7855 women);
undergraduate 12,387 (5839 men, 6548

women); master's 2660 (1357 men, 1303
women); doctoral 28 (24 men, 4 women).

FACULTIES/SCHOOLS

Arts and Social Sciences, School of
Tel: 2768 5721 Fax: 2391 3184
    E-mail: ass@ouhk.edu.hk
Dean: Tam, Prof. K. K., BA Chinese HK, MA Ill.,
    PhD Ill.
Secretary: Mak, Daise W. Y.

Business and Administration, School of
Tel: 2768 6940 Fax: 2391 9095
    E-mail: ba@ouhk.edu.hk
Dean: Ip, Prof. Y. K., BSc N.Y.State, MBA Indiana,
    PhD S.Carolina
Secretary: Au, Estella Y. L.

Education and Languages, School of
Tel: 2768 5807 Fax: 2395 4235
    E-mail: el@ouhk.edu.hk
Dean: Fung, Prof. Yvonne S. Y. H., BSc HK,
    MEd HK, PhD Nott.
Secretary: Wong, Anissa F. S.

Science and Technology, School of
Tel: 2768 6822 Fax: 2789 1170
    E-mail: sct@ouhk.edu.hk
Acting Dean: Ho, Prof. K. C., BSc Chinese HK,
    MSc Salf., PhD HK
Secretary: Wong, Winnie M. C.

ACADEMIC UNITS

Arranged by Schools

Arts and Social Sciences

Tel: 2768 5721 Fax: 2391 3184
E-mail: ass@ouhk.edu.hk
Cheuk, W. H., BSc Texas A.& M., MSc Texas A.& I., PhD Georgia   Assoc. Prof.
Cheung, W. K., PhD Beijing   Assoc. Prof.
Chiu, Y. L., BA Chinese HK, MPhil Chinese HK, PhD Kyoto   Assoc. Prof.
Han, Y., BA York(UK), PhD York(UK)   Assoc. Prof.
Lau, Raymond W. K., BSocSc HK, MBA HK, PhD HK   Assoc. Prof.
Lo, W. C., MA Georgia, PhD Georgia   Assoc. Prof.
So, W. C., BA HK, MPhil HK, PhD ANU   Prof.
Yeung, C. K., BA Chinese HK, MPhil Chinese HK, PhD ANU   Assoc. Prof.
Other Staff: 9 Asst. Profs.; 8 Lectrs.
Research: Chinese history, laws, literature and philosophy; communication and mass communication; economics, public administration, political science; linguistics and translation (Chinese and English); sociology, psychology, cultural studies

Business and Administration

Tel: 2768 6940 Fax: 2391 9095
E-mail: ba@ouhk.edu.hk
Au, Alan K.M., MBA Massey, MMS Waik., PhD Waik.   Assoc. Prof.
Chung, S. L., BSc HK, MS Ill., PhD Ill.   Assoc. Prof.
Ko, Anthony C. K., BSSc Chinese HK, MBA HK, PhD HK   Assoc. Prof.
Other Staff: 18 Asst. Profs.; 15 Lectrs.
Research: accounting; banking and finance; business information systems; international business; marketing and management

Education and Languages

Tel: 2768 5806 Fax: 2395 4235
E-mail: el@ouhk.edu.hk
Tang, Thomas K. W., BSc Lond., MEd HK, PhD HK   Assoc. Prof.
Other Staff: 7 Asst. Profs.; 4 Lectrs.
Research: adult and distance education; curriculum studies; educational psychology; language education; teacher education

Science and Technology

Tel: 2768 6822 Fax: 2789 1170
E-mail: sct@ouhk.edu.hk
Ho, K. C., BSc Chinese HK, MSc Salf., PhD HK   Prof.
Kwok, Paul C. K., BSc Essex, PhD Camb.   Assoc. Prof.
Lee, Joseph K. L., PhD Lingnan   Assoc. Prof.
Lui, Andrew K. F., BSc Syd., PhD ANU   Assoc. Prof.
Other Staff: 11 Asst. Profs.; 6 Lectrs.
Research: applied computer science and technology; computing in distance education; environmental science, biology and ecology; mathematics and statistics; nursing studies

SPECIAL CENTRES, ETC

Distance and Adult Learning, Centre for Research in

Tel: 2768 6420 Fax: 2396 5009
E-mail: cridal@ouhk.edu.hk
Yuen, K. S., BSc HK, MEd HK, PhD HK   Dir.*
Research: adult and distance education

Information Technology Unit

Tel: 2768 6522 Fax: 2762 7469
E-mail: itu@ouhk.edu.hk
Wong, C. Y., BE C.C.N.Y., MSc Syr.   Computer Centre Manager
Wong, Ernest K. K., BSc Chinese HK   Head*
Other Staff: 2 System Analysts; 19 Analyst Programmers

Professional and Continuing Education, Li Ka Shing Institute of

Tel: 3120 9988 Fax: 2381 8456
E-mail: lipace@ouhk.edu.hk
Lui, Prof. Y. H., BBA Chinese HK, MA Lanc., PhD Lanc.   Dir.*
Other Staff: 1 Asst. Prof.; 3 Lectrs.
Research: accounting; adult and continuing education; banking and finance; occupational health and safety; quality assurance in higher education

CONTACT OFFICERS

Academic affairs. Vice President (Academic): Wong, Prof. Danny S. N., BSc Calif.State, MSc Penn., PhD Penn.
(E-mail: po@ouhk.edu.hk)
Accommodation. Senior Estates Officer: Lam, Cybill M. L. Y. (E-mail: aau@ouhk.edu.hk)
Admissions (first degree). Senior Assistant Registrar (Admissions (first degree)): Watt, Wendy Y. H., BA HK, MA City HK
(E-mail: regadm@ouhk.edu.hk)
Adult/continuing education. Director, Li Ka Shing Institute of Professional and Continuing Education: Lui, Prof. Y. H., BBA Chinese HK, MA Lanc., PhD Lanc.
(E-mail: lipace@ouhk.edu.hk)
Archives. Librarian: Mok, W. M., BSc Chinese HK (E-mail: libwww@ouhk.edu.hk)
Computing services. Head, Information Technology: Wong, Ernest K. K., BSc Chinese HK (E-mail: itu@ouhk.edu.hk)
Consultancy services. Vice President (Academic): Wong, Prof. Danny S. N., BSc Calif.State, MSc Penn., PhD Penn.
(E-mail: po@ouhk.edu.hk)
Credit transfer. Senior Assistant Registrar: Watt, Wendy Y. H., BA HK, MA City HK
(E-mail: regaso@ouhk.edu.hk)
Development/fund-raising. Head (Public Affairs): Wong, Alex J. W., BA Chinese HK
(E-mail: pau@ouhk.edu.hk)

Estates and buildings/works and services. Senior Estates Officer: Lam, Cybill M. L. Y. (E-mail: aau@ouhk.edu.hk)
Examinations. Deputy Registrar: Hui, Sylvia W. L., BSocSc HK, MEd Sheff.
(E-mail: regexam@ouhk.edu.hk)
Finance. Acting Head of Finance: Tsui, Stephen H. M., BSSc Chinese HK
(E-mail: fu@ouhk.edu.hk)
General enquiries. Head (Public Affairs): Wong, Alex J. W., BA Chinese HK
(E-mail: infoctr@ic.ouhk.edu.hk)
Library (chief librarian). Librarian: Mok, W. M., BSc Chinese HK
(E-mail: libwww@ouhk.edu.hk)
Library (enquiries). Librarian: Mok, W. M., BSc Chinese HK
(E-mail: libwww@ouhk.edu.hk)
Marketing. Head (Public Affairs): Wong, Alex J. W., BA Chinese HK
(E-mail: pau@ouhk.edu.hk)
Personnel/human resources. Head (Human Resources): Fan, Jack, BA HK
(E-mail: hruwww@ouhk.edu.hk)
Public relations. Head (Public Affairs): Wong, Alex J. W., BA Chinese HK
(E-mail: pau@ouhk.edu.hk)
Publications. Publishing Manager: Chow, Linda K. B. I., BSc NSW
(E-mail: etp@ouhk.edu.hk)
Purchasing. Deputy Head (Finance): Tsui, Stephen H. M., BSSc Chinese HK
(E-mail: fu@ouhk.edu.hk)
Quality assurance and accreditation. Vice President (Academic): Wong, Prof. Danny S. N., BSc Calif.State, MSc Penn., PhD Penn.
(E-mail: po@ouhk.edu.hk)
Research. Director, Research Centre: Yuen, K. S., BSc HK, MEd HK, PhD HK
(E-mail: cridal@ouhk.edu.hk)
Scholarships, awards, loans. Senior Assistant Registrar (Scholarships, awards, loans): Watt, Wendy Y. H., BA HK, MA City HK
(E-mail: regsao@ouhk.edu.hk)
Staff development and training. Senior Executive Officer (Staff development and training): Shek, Vincent K. C., BA HK
(E-mail: hruwww@ouhk.edu.hk)
Student union. Senior Assistant Registrar (Student union): Watt, Wendy Y. H., BA HK, MA City HK
(E-mail: regsao@ouhk.edu.hk)
Student welfare/counselling. Senior Assistant Registrar (Student welfare/counselling): Watt, Wendy Y. H., BA HK, MA City HK
(E-mail: regsao@puhk.edu.hk)
Students with disabilities. Senior Assistant Registrar (Students with disabilities): Watt, Wendy Y. H., BA HK, MA City HK
(E-mail: regsao@puhk.edu.hk)
University press. Publishing Manager: Chow, Linda K. B. I., BSc NSW
(E-mail: etp@ouhk.edu.hk)

[Information supplied by the institution as at 11 September 2007, and edited by the ACU]

ZIMBABWE

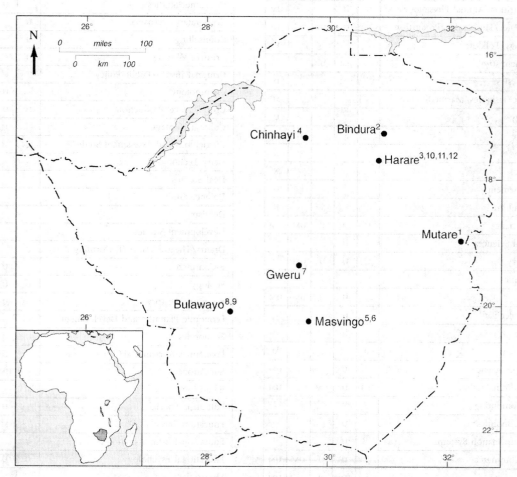

The places named are the seats of the university institutions numbered above

The table below shows which of the institutions indicated provide facilities for study and/or research in the subjects named. In the case of related subject areas which have been grouped together (eg Agronomy/Soil Science), it should be borne in mind that one or more of the subjects may be offered by the institution concerned.

	Africa	Bindura	Midlands State	N.U.S.T., Bulawayo	Zimbabwe
Accountancy/Accounting	U	U	U	U	U
Administration/Administrative Studies	UM		U		UM
Advertising		U			
African Languages/Studies	U		U		UM
Afrikaans/Dutch					U
Agricultural Extension and Education		U			M
Agriculture/Agricultural Science	UM	U	U		X
Agronomy/Soil Science	UM	U	U		X
Agrotechnology			U		
Anaesthesia/Anaesthesiology					M
Anatomical Science/Anatomy		U			UM
Animal Nutrition/Animal Physiology	U	U			UM
Animal Science/Husbandry/Production	U	U	U		U
Anthropology/Folklore					U
Applied Chemistry		UM	U		
Applied Physics		UM	U		D
Aquaculture/Fisheries/Marine Science	U				M
Archaeology					U
Architecture				U	
Art, History of					X
Arts General					X
Arts Management					U
Arts and Culture					X
Banking/Finance	U	U	U	UM	UM
Behavioural Sciences		U			
Biochemistry		U	U	UM	U
Bioinformatics	U				
Biology		U	U	UM	UM
Biology Molecular		U	U		
Biostatistics	U	U			
Biotechnology	M		U		M
Botany/Plant Science	U	U			UM
Business Administration	UM	U	UM		UM
Business Computing		U			
Business Economics		U			
Business Information Systems		U			
Business/Commerce		U	U	UM	UM
Chemistry		UM	U		UM

	Africa	Bindura	Midlands State	N.U.S.T., Bulawayo	Zimbabwe
Child Health	U				
Child and Family Psychology	U				M
Classics/Greek/Latin/Ancient History					U
Communication Sciences					UM
Communication/Journalism/Media Studies			U	U	UM
Communications/Information Management		U	U		UM
Community Health	U				
Community Medicine					UM
Computer Science	U	U	U	UM	U
Conservation Studies		U		U	
Consumer Studies		U			
Corporate Governance	U				M
Counselling	U				
Creative Writing	U				
Criminal Justice/Public Policy		U			M
Criminology		U			
Crop Science/Production	UM	U	U		U
Cultural Heritage					M
Curriculum and Assessment Studies	U	M			M
Dairy Technology					U
Deaf Studies					M
Defence Studies					U
Dentistry					U
Development Studies	U		U		
Drama/Theatre/Dance/Performing Arts	U		U		U
E-Commerce		U			
Ecology	U	U	U		
Economic History	U	U	U		UM
Economic Planning and Development		U			
Economics	U	U	U		UM
Economics Agricultural/Agribusiness	U	U			U
Education	U	UM	U	U	UM
Education Adult	M				
Education Special		U			U
Education Tertiary		M			
Educational Administration	U				M
Educational Psychology	U	U			M
Electronics		U			UM

TO SUBJECTS OF STUDY

For further information about the individual subjects taught at each institution, please refer to the *Index to Subjects of Study* at the end of the Yearbook, but for full details about subjects/courses offered at universities in the Commonwealth each institution's own official publications must be consulted. U = may be studied for first degree course; M = may be studied for master's degree course; D = research facilities to doctoral level; X = all three levels (UMD). **Note**—The table only includes information provided by institutions currently in membership of the Association of Commonwealth Universities.

	Africa	Bindura	Midlands State	N.U.S.T., Bulawayo	Zimbabwe
Engineering					UM
Engineering Agricultural/Fisheries					UM
Engineering Chemical/Petrochemical/Process				UM	
Engineering Civil/Environmental/Structural				UM	U
Engineering Communications/Telecommunications					M
Engineering Computer				UM	
Engineering Electrical/Electronic				UM	UM
Engineering Industrial				UM	
Engineering Manufacturing				M	M
Engineering Materials/Mineral Resources/Petroleum					M
Engineering Mechanical/Production					UM
Engineering Metallurgical/Mining					U
English			U		UM
English as a Second Language	U				
Entomology					UM
Entrepreneurship	U	U			
Environmental Health	U		U		U
Environmental Management	U	U			U
Environmental Science/Studies	U	U	U	U	
Epidemiology	U				M
Ethnicity/Multiculturalism	U				
Ethnomusicology	U				U
Fashion/Clothing					U
Food Science/Nutrition/Home Science/Dietetics			U		U
Forestry		UM			
French/French Studies	U	U			UM
Genetics	U				U
Genetics and Plant Breeding	U				
Geographic Information Systems/Geomatics	U	U	U		
Geography	U	UM	U		UM
Geology/Earth Sciences/Atmospheric Studies					U
German/Germanic Studies					U
Greek, Modern/Greek Studies					U
Health Education	U	U			U
Health Information	U				

	Africa	Bindura	Midlands State	N.U.S.T., Bulawayo	Zimbabwe
Health Sciences/Studies		U			
Health and Social Care	U				
Hebrew/Semitic Studies	U				
Health/Hospital Administration	U				
Heritage Studies					M
History	U		U		UM
History/Philosophy of Science					UM
Homeopathy	U				
Horticulture	U	U	U		
Hotel Management					UM
Human Biology		U			U
Human Resource Development	U				U
Human Resource Economics	M				
Human Rights/Globalisation	U		U		
Industrial Hygiene and Safety	M				
Industrial Relations/Personnel/HRM	U	U	U		U
Industrial and Organisation Psychology	U				M
Information Science/Studies/Systems	U		U	UM	
Information Technology	U				
International Business		U			
International Finance	U	U			
International Finance Economics	M	U			
International Marketing	U	U			
International Relations/Studies	M		U		UM
Internet Computing/Technologies		U			
Labour Studies		U			
Land Management/Rehabilitation		U	U		
Land Resource Science		U	U		
Language Teaching/Learning			U		
Languages, Modern	U		U		U
Law Business/Commercial/Economic/Industrial		U			
Law Civil					U
Law Employment/Labour		U			U
Law Enforcement/Security Management		U			
Law Intellectual Property/Copyright	M	U			
Law International/Comparative/Trade		U			
Law Legal Practice					U
Law Property/Construction/Housing		U			
Law/Legal Studies					U

	Africa	Bindura	Midlands State	N.U.S.T., Bulawayo	Zimbabwe
Library/Information Science				U	
Linguistics/Translation	U		U		
Literature, Comparative	U				
Livestock Science		U			
Management	U	U			U
Management Information Systems	U	U			
Management, Hotel and Catering Technology					M
Marketing	U	U	U	UM	U
Mathematics		UM	U	X	UM
Medicine, Obstetrics and Gynaecology					UM
Medicine, Paediatric					M
Medicine/Surgery					UM
Meteorology		U			M
Microbiology/Medical Microbiology		U		UM	U
Multimedia			U		
Museum Studies			U		
Music	U		U		UM
Music Education			U		
Music Technology			U		
Natural Resource Studies	U		U		
Nursing Education/Administration		U			UM
Nursing/Midwifery	U				UM
Occupational Health/Therapy					U
Operational Research/Operations Management	U				
Pastoral Studies	U				
Peace/War Studies	M				U
Pharmacology					U
Pharmacy/Pharmaceutical Science					U
Philosophy	U				UM
Physical Education/Sports Science		U			U
Physics		UM	U	UM	U

	Africa	Bindura	Midlands State	N.U.S.T., Bulawayo	Zimbabwe
Physiology					U
Physiotherapy					U
Planning/Landscape Studies					U
Plant Pathology	U				
Politics/Political Science/Government					UM
Population Studies/Demography	U				UM
Portuguese/Portugese Studies	U				U
Project Management	M				M
Psychiatry					M
Psychology	U	U			UM
Psychology Clinical					M
Public Administration					UM
Public Health/Population Health	M				M
Public Sector Management	M				
Radiography/Diagnostic Technology/MRI					U
Religion/Theology	U				UM
Remote Sensing	U				
Renewable Energy Studies					M
Risk Management	U				
Social Work/Studies					UM
Sociology	U	U			UM
Spanish/Hispanic/Latin American Studies					U
Statistics/Actuarial Science				U	UM
Surveying/Quantity Surveying				U	U
Taxation	U	U			
Teacher Training	U	U			M
Textiles/Fibre Science/Technology				U	U
Tourism/Hospitality/Leisure/Recreation					UM
Veterinary Science					UM
Wildlife Management	U	U	U		
Women's/Gender Studies	M				
Zoology					U

AFRICA UNIVERSITY

Founded 1992

Member of the Association of Commonwealth Universities

Postal Address: PO Box 1320, Mutare, Zimbabwe
Telephone: (020) 61611 **Fax:** (020) 61785 **E-mail:** registrar@africau.ac.zw
URL: http://www.africau.edu

VICE-CHANCELLOR*—Murapa, Prof. Rukudzo J., BA *Hamline*, MA *N.Illinois*, PhD *N.Illinois*, Hon. DHumL *Hamline*
DEPUTY VICE-CHANCELLOR—Mphuru, Prof. Athanasius N., BSc *Mak.*, MA *W.Virginia*, PhD *Dar.*
ASSOCIATE VICE-CHANCELLOR (INSTITUTIONAL DEVELOPMENT)—Salley, James H., BA *S.Carolina*, Hon. DHumLett *Claflin*
REGISTRAR‡—Chikange, Frank W., BScEd *Zambia*, MEd *Birm.*
LIBRARIAN—Pfukani, Bilha A., BA *Otago*
BURSAR—Chibanda, Ireen T., MBA *Z'bwe.*

GENERAL INFORMATION

Admission to first degree courses.
Zimbabwean applicants should possess 5 O-levels at grade C or above, including English language and mathematics, and 2 relevant A-level subjects, or equivalent recognised professional qualifications.

International applicants should possess qualifications acceptable for entry into accredited universities in their country of origin.

First Degrees (see also Zimbabwean Directory to Subjects of Study). BA, BAcc, BAEd, BASocSci, BBS, BD, BEd, BHSM, BScAgric, BScAgricEd, BSc-CIS, BScEcon, BScEd, BSN, BSocSc.

Length of course. Full-time: BEd, BSN: 2 years; BA, BASocSci, BD, BSocSc: 3 years; BScAgric: 3–4 years; BAcc, BAEd, BBS, BHSM, BScAgricEd, BScEcon, BScEd: 4 years.

Higher Degrees (see also Zimbabwean Directory to Subjects of Study).
Master's. EMBA, MA, MBA, MEd, MPH, MPSM, MSc, MTS.

Admission. Applicants for admission to higher degrees must normally hold an appropriate first degree recognised by Africa University Senate or an equivalent professional qualification obtained by formal study and examination.

Libraries. Volumes: 77,000. Periodicals subscribed to: 100. Other holdings: 1120 journals. Special collections: June Ammons Memorial (humanities); American Corners.

Statistics. Staff (2005–2006): 400 (60 academic, 340 non-academic). Students (2005–2006): total 1300.

FACULTIES/SCHOOLS

Agriculture and Natural Resources
Dean: Tagwira, Fanuel, BSc NUL, MSc *Reading*, PhD *Z'bwe.*

Education
Dean: Quarshie, James D., BEd *Alta.*, MEd *Alta.*, MA *Br.Col.*, PhD *Alta.*

Health Sciences
Dean: Fasan, Peter O., MB BS *Lond.*, MD *Lond.*, FRCPEd, FWACP

Humanities and Social Sciences
Dean: Chitepo, Thokozile A., BEdSc *Kenyatta*, MA *McG.*, PhD *McG.*

Management and Administration
Dean: Ilunga, Jean G., MA(Econ) *S.Illinois*, PhD *S.Illinois*, BS

Theology
Dean: Maenzanise, Rev. Dr. Beauty, STM *Drew*, MDiv *Drew*, MPhil *Drew*, PhD *Drew*, DTh *Z'bwe.*

ACADEMIC UNITS
Arranged by Faculties

Agriculture and Natural Resources
Tel: (020) 66965
   E-mail: deanfanr@africau.ac.zw
Chiteka, A., BScAgric *Rhodesia*, MS *Flor.*   Sr. Lectr.
Mashingaidze, K., BScAgric *Z'bwe.*, MPhil *Z'bwe.*, PhD *Mich.*   Sr. Lectr. (on leave)
Mtaita, T. A., BSc *Sokoine Ag.*, MSc *Lond.*   Sr. Lectr.
Muzorewa, E. I., BSc *Morningside*, MSc *Missouri*   Sr. Lectr.; Dir., Practical Agric.
Tagwira, Fanuel, BSc NUL, MSc *Reading*, PhD *Z'bwe.*   Assoc. Prof.; Head*
Other Staff: 10 Lectrs.

Education
Tel: (020) 66782 E-mail: deanfoe@africau.ac.zw
Quarshie, James D., BEd *Alta.*, MEd *Alta.*, MA *Br.Col.*, PhD *Alta.*   Assoc. Prof.; Head*
Other Staff: 6 Lectrs.

Health Sciences
Tel: (020) 61065
   E-mail: deanfms@africau.ac.zw
Fasan, Peter O., MB BS *Lond.*, MD *Lond.*, FRCPEd, FWACP   Assoc. Prof.; Head*
Krumme, Baerbel A., MSc *Heidel.*, MD *Liv.*, DrMed *Mün.*   Assoc. Prof.
Other Staff: 4 Lectrs.; 2 Visiting Scientists

Humanities and Social Sciences
Tel: (020) 68312
   E-mail: deanfhss@africau.ac.zw
Banfa, Stephen, BA *A.Bello*, MA *Birm.*, PhD *Birm.*   Sr. Lectr.
Chitepo, Thokozile A., BEdSc *Kenyatta*, MA *McG.*, PhD *McG.*   Sr. Lectr.; Head*
Dhliwayo, Kholisile D., BA *Bates*, MA *Penn.*, MPhil *Lond.*   Sr. Lectr.
Humbane, William, BA *Taylor*, MA *Ball*, EdD *Ball*   Sr. Lectr.
Machakanja, Isaac T., BA *Z'bwe.*, MA *Z'bwe.*, PhD *Fort Hare*   Sr. Lectr.
Other Staff: 11 Lectrs.

Management and Administration
Tel: (020) 66793
   E-mail: deanfma@africau.ac.zw
Ghumbo, A. Mhike, BA *Rhodesia*, MBA *Z'bwe.*   Sr. Lectr.
Ilunga, Jean G., MA(Econ) *S.Illinois*, PhD *S.Illinois*, BS   Sr. Lectr.; Head*
Mareya, L., BA *St.Olaf*, MA *St.Olaf*   Sr. Lectr.
Other Staff: 11 Lectrs.

Theology
Tel: (020) 66967 E-mail: deanfot@africau.ac.zw
Bakare, Bishop S., BEd *Birm.*, MA *Grad.Theol.Union*, DM *San Francisco Theol.Sem.*   Sr. Lectr.
Kurewa, J. Z., BA *Asbury*, BD *Garrett Theol.Sem.*, PhD *Northwestern*   Assoc. Prof.
Maenzanise, Rev. Dr. Beauty, STM *Drew*, MDiv *Drew*, MPhil *Drew*, PhD *Drew*, DTh *Z'bwe.*   Lectr.; Head*
Ndyabahika, J. F., MA *Trinity Evang.Div.Sch.(Ill.)*, MDiv *Trinity Evang.Div.Sch.(Ill.)*, MTh *Aberd.*, PhD *Cape Town*, DTh *Uganda Christian*   Sr. Lectr.
Zulu, E., BTh *S.Af.*, MTh *Stell.*, ThD *Stell.*   Sr. Lectr.
Other Staff: 3 Lectrs.

SPECIAL CENTRES, ETC

Peace, Leadership and Governance, Institute of
Tel: (020) 66788
   E-mail: iplgdirector@africau.ac.zw
Machakanja, P., BEd *Z'bwe.*, MEd *Z'bwe.*, MA *Brad.*, MPhil *Brad.*, PhD *Brad.*   Assoc. Dir.
Shankanga, A., BA *Zambia*, MEd *Alta.*, EDD *S.Calif.*   Interim Dir.*
Other Staff: 6 Lectrs.; 1 Tutor

CONTACT OFFICERS
Finance. Bursar: Chibanda, Ireen T., MBA *Z'bwe.*
Library (chief librarian). Librarian: Pfukani, Bilha A., BA *Otago*
   (E-mail: pfukanib@africau.ac.zw)
Public relations. Director, Information and Public Affairs: Stevens, A. M., BAA *Ryerson*
   (E-mail: dipa@africau.ac.zw)

[Information supplied by the institution as at 15 October 2007, and edited by the ACU]

BINDURA UNIVERSITY OF SCIENCE EDUCATION

Founded 2000

Member of the Association of Commonwealth Universities

Postal Address: Private Bag 1020, Bindura, Zimbabwe
Telephone: (071) 7621-4 **Fax:** (071) 7534 **E-mail:** info@buse.ac.zw
URL: http://www.buse.ac.zw

VICE-CHANCELLOR*—Tswana, Prof. Sam A., BSc *Wake Forest*, MSc *W.Kentucky*, PhD *Vanderbilt*
PRO-VICE-CHANCELLOR—(vacant)
REGISTRAR‡—(vacant)
BURSAR—Hadzirabwi, Norman, BAcc *Z'bwe.*
LIBRARIAN—Mhlanga, Audrey, BA *Guy.*, MLIS *McG.*

GENERAL INFORMATION

History. The university was established by an Act of Parliament in February 2000. It had since 1996 been a university college of the University of Zimbabwe.

It is situated in Bindura, 90km north-east of Harare.

Admission to first degree courses. Five GCE O-level passes including mathematics and English and 2 GCE A-levels in relevant subjects or equivalent. International applicants: equivalent qualifications accepted.

First Degrees (see also Zimbabwean Directory to Subjects of Study) (* = with honours). BAcc*, BAgSc*, BBS*, BComm*, BES*, BScComp*, BScEco*, BScEd*, BScEdH*, BScPSS*.

Length of course. Full-time: BAgSc*, BScEd*, BScPSS*: 3 years; BAcc*, BBS*, BComm*, BES*, BScComp*, BScEco*, BScEdH*: 4 years.

Higher Degrees (see also Zimbabwean Directory to Subjects of Study).

Master's. MSc, MScEd.

Applicants to MScEd and MSc should hold either a BScEd(Hons), BAgSc(Hons) or BES(Hons) with minimum 2:1, or BSc honours in natural sciences or other relevant qualification.

Length of course. Full-time: MSc, MScEd: 2 years.

Libraries. Volumes: 15,750. Periodicals subscribed to: 22. Other holdings: 116 student research projects; 235 maps.

Academic Year (2007–2008). Two semesters: 12 March–2 July; 20 August–4 December.

Statistics. Staff (2006–2007): 325 (175 academic, 150 non-academic). Students (2005–2006): undergraduate 1161 (930 men, 231 women); master's 20 (14 men, 6 women).

FACULTIES/SCHOOLS

Agriculture and Environmental Sciences

E-mail: catkatsvanga@buse.ac.zw

Executive Dean: Katsvanga, Cuthbert A. T., MSc *Voronezh Forestry Engin.*

Faculty Administrator: Matenga, Beauty, BEd *Z'bwe.*

Commerce

E-mail: lrunyowa@buse.ac.zw

Executive Dean: Runyowa, L., BA *S.Af.*, EMBA *NUST Bulawayo*

Faculty Administrator: Chikasa, Dzikamai, BEd *Z'bwe.Open*, MEd *Z'bwe.Open*

Science Education

E-mail: fased@buse.ac.zw

Executive Dean: Zengeya, Alfred, BA *Z'bwe.*, MEd *Z'bwe.*

Faculty Administrator: Chitera, Stennly G., BEd *Z'bwe.*

ACADEMIC UNITS

Accounting

E-mail: accounting@buse.ac.zw

Mudavanhu, V. K., BAEcon *Alig.*, MAEcon *Alig.* Chairperson*

Other Staff: 4 Lectrs.

Agricultural Economics and Management

E-mail: agricecon@buse.ac.zw

Mutenje, M. J., BSc *Z'bwe.*, MSc *Z'bwe.* Co-ordinator*

Other Staff: 2 Lectrs.

Research: agronomy, horticulture and extension; impact of HIV/AIDS on farming

Agricultural Education and Extension

E-mail: agricedu@buse.ac.zw

Gadzirayi, C. T., BEd *Z'bwe.*, MEd *Z'bwe.* Co-ordinator*

Other Staff: 2 Lectrs.

Research: ethnoveterinary education; management extension/education programmes; organic farming

Animal Science

E-mail: animalscience@buse.ac.zw

Mapiye, C., BSc *Z'bwe.*, MSc *Z'bwe.* Co-ordinator*

Other Staff: 2 Lectrs.

Biology

E-mail: biosciences@buse.ac.zw

Mundembe, R., BSc *Z'bwe.*, MPhil *Z'bwe.*, PhD *Z'bwe.* Chairperson*

Other Staff: 9 Lectrs.

Research: applied botany; microbiology of foods; molecular biology; reproductive health

Business Studies

E-mail: business@buse.ac.zw

Runyowa, L., BA *S.Af.*, EMBA *NUST Bulawayo* Chairperson*

Other Staff: 8 Lectrs.

Chemistry

E-mail: chemistry@mailhost.buse.ac.zw

Ngarivhume, T., LicEd *Havana*, MSc *Havana* Chairperson*

Other Staff: 11 Lectrs.

Research: analytical chemistry; atmospheric chemistry; environmental chemistry; nitric oxide trapping potential of copper (II) complexes; quality of rural drinking water

Computer Science

E-mail: compscience@buse.ac.zw

Mlambo, N., BScEd *Havana*, MSc *NUST Bulawayo* Chairperson*

Other Staff: 9 Lectrs.

Research: caching object-oriented paradigms; communication and networking; distributed databases; software development

Crop Science

E-mail: cropscience@buse.ac.zw

Chikuvire, J., BSc *Z'bwe.*, MPhil *Z'bwe.* Co-ordinator*

Other Staff: 3 Lectrs.

Research: agronomy; crop storage and processing; soil fertility; soil microbiology

Economics

E-mail: economics@buse.ac.zw

Mudavanhu, V. K., BAEcon *Alig.*, MAEcon *Alig.* Chairperson*

Other Staff: 6 Lectrs.

Education

E-mail: educ@buse.ac.zw

Zinyeka, G., BA *Z'bwe.*, MA *Z'bwe.* Chairperson*

Other Staff: 12 Lectrs.

Research: applied sociology; chemistry education; mathematics education; mentoring; physics education

Financial Intelligence

No staff at present

Fire Safety

No staff at present

Forestry Science

E-mail: forestry@buse.ac.zw

Katsvanga, Cuthbert A. T., MSc *Voronezh Forestry Engin.* Chairperson*

Other Staff: 3 Lectrs.

Research: ethnobotany and ethology; feed resources and animal nutrition; forest products; forestry and natural resources; solute movement in soils

Geography

E-mail: geo@mailhost.buse.ac.zw

Manatsa, D., MSc *St.Petersburg Polytech.U.* Chairperson*

Other Staff: 10 Lectrs.

Research: climate impact studies; hydrology; meteorology; population geography; urban housing

Health Sciences

E-mail: healthscience@buse.ac.zw

Katsinde, C. S., BSc *Z'bwe.*, MSc *Z'bwe.* Co-ordinator*

Other Staff: 2 Lectrs.

Horticulture

E-mail: horticulture@buse.ac.zw

Tigere, A., BSc *Z'bwe.*, MSc *Z'bwe.* Co-ordinator*

Other Staff: 2 Lectrs.

Research: adoption of agricultural technologies; plant propagation using tissue culture methods

Land Conservation and Reclamation

E-mail: landconserv@buse.ac.zw

Gotosa, J., BSc *Z'bwe.*, MSc *Nair.* Co-ordinator*

Other Staff: 4 Lectrs.

Research: community board natural resource management; vulnerability analysis and rural development; wood preservation

Mathematics

E-mail: maths@buse.ac.zw

Shateyi, S., BSc NUST *Bulawayo*, MSc *Z'bwe.* Chairperson*

Other Staff: 6 Lectrs.

Research: computer-aided learning time series; dynamic series; mathematics education; operations research

Physical Science and Sport Administration

No staff at present

Physics

E-mail: physics@mailhost.buse.ac.zw

Magama, Mike T., BSc *Z'bwe.*, MSc *Z'bwe.* Chairperson*

Other Staff: 9 Lectrs.

Research: electronic instrumentation; laser physics; physics education; solar physics

Police and Security Studies

E-mail: policesecurity@buse.ac.zw

Maunga, M. M., BSc *Ib.*, MA *Exe.* Co-ordinator*

Other Staff: 4 Lectrs.

Pollution Science

E-mail: pollution@buse.ac.zw

Kuvarega, A., BSc *Z'bwe.*, MSc *Z'bwe.* Co-ordinator*

Other Staff: 4 Lectrs.

Research: analytical chemistry

Wildlife and Rangeland Management

E-mail: wildlife@buse.ac.zw

Imbayarwo-Chikosi, V. E., BSc *Z'bwe.*, MSc *Malawi* Co-ordinator*

Other Staff: 4 Lectrs.

Research: animal breeding; human-environment relations; ruminant nutrition

CONTACT OFFICERS

Academic affairs. Vice-Chancellor: Tswana, Prof. Sam A., BSc *Wake Forest*, MSc *W.Kentucky*, PhD *Vanderbilt* (E-mail: satswana@buse.ac.zw)

Admissions (first degree). Deputy Registrar: Chitera, Stennly G., BEd *Z'bwe.*

Admissions (higher degree). Deputy Registrar: Chitera, Stennly G., BEd *Z'bwe.*

Archives. Librarian: Mhlanga, Audrey, BA *Guy.*, MLIS *McG.* (E-mail: amhlanga@buse.ac.zw)

Careers. Dean of Students: Makado, Retias K., BA *Z'bwe.*, MEd *Z'bwe.* (E-mail: rkmakado@buse.ac.zw)

Computing services. Information and Communication Technology Manager: Dube, Givemore, BSc *Z'bwe.*, MSc *NUST Bulawayo* (E-mail: gdube@buse.ac.zw)

Development/fund-raising. Director, Marketing and Communications: Gutura, James J., BSc *Z'bwe.*, MSc *Z'bwe.* (E-mail: jjgutura@buse.ac.zw)

Estates and buildings/works and services. Director of Works: Kuona, S. S., BSc *Z'bwe.* (E-mail: sskuona@buse.ac.zw)

Examinations. Deputy Registrar: Chitera, Stennly G., BEd *Z'bwe.*

Finance. Bursar: Hadzirabwi, Norman, BAcc *Z'bwe.* (E-mail: nhadzirabwi@buse.ac.zw)

General enquiries. Registrar: (vacant)

Health services. Sister-in-Charge: Masvaure, M. (E-mail: mmasvaure@buse.ac.zw)

Industrial liaison. Industrial Liaison Officer: Chikasa, Dzikamai, BEd *Z'bwe.Open*, MEd *Z'bwe.Open* (E-mail: dchikasa@buse.ac.zw)

Library (chief librarian). Librarian: Mhlanga, Audrey, BA *Guy.*, MLIS *McG.* (E-mail: amhlanga@buse.ac.zw)

Marketing. Director, Marketing and Communications: Gutura, James J., BSc *Z'bwe.*, MSc *Z'bwe.* (E-mail: jjgutura@buse.ac.zw)

Public relations. Director, Marketing and Communications: Gutura, James J., BSc *Z'bwe.*, MSc *Z'bwe.* (E-mail: jjgutura@buse.ac.zw)

Safety. Registrar: (vacant)

Schools liaison. Dean of Students: Makado, Retias K., BA *Z'bwe.*, MEd *Z'bwe.* (E-mail: rkmakado@buse.ac.zw)

Security. Security Officer: Muchena, K. C., BSc(Psych) *Z'bwe.* (E-mail: kcmuchena@buse.ac.zw)

Sport and recreation. Director of Sports: Muzuva, T., BEd *Z'bwe.* (E-mail: tmuzuva@buse.ac.zw)

Staff development and training. Acting Human Resources Director: Rumhuma, T. F., BBS *Z'bwe.*, MBA *Z'bwe.Open* (E-mail: tfrumhuma@mailhost.buse.ac.zw)

Student welfare/counselling. Dean of Students: Makado, Retias K., BA *Z'bwe.*, MEd *Z'bwe.* (E-mail: rkmakado@buse.ac.zw)

Students from other countries. Dean of Students: Makado, Retias K., BA *Z'bwe.*, MEd *Z'bwe.* (E-mail: rkmakado@buse.ac.zw)

Students with disabilities. Dean of Students: Makado, Retias K., BA *Z'bwe.*, MEd *Z'bwe.* (E-mail: rkmakado@buse.ac.zw)

[*Information supplied by the institution as at 15 October 2007, and edited by the ACU*]

CATHOLIC UNIVERSITY

Postal Address: Cranborne Avenue, Hatfield, P O Box CR 18443, Cranborne, Harare, Zimbabwe

VICE-CHANCELLOR*—Nondo, S. J., BA *S.Af.*, MA *Lond.*, MPhil *Rhodesia*

CHINHOYI UNIVERSITY OF TECHNOLOGY

Founded 2001

Postal Address: Off Harare - Chirundu Road, P Bag 7724, Chinhoyi, Zimbabwe
Telephone: (263) 0672 2203 **Fax:** (263) 0672 7214 **E-mail:** admin@cut.ac.zw
URL: http://www.cut.ac.zw

VICE-CHANCELLOR*—Simbi, Prof. David J., BSc(AppChem) *Portsmouth*, PhD *Leeds*, FZAS
REGISTRAR‡—Makunde, Jairos, BSc *Z'bwe.*, MEd *Z'bwe.*, MBA *Z'bwe.*

GREAT ZIMBABWE UNIVERSITY

Founded 2001

Postal Address: Old Morgenster Road, P O Box 1460, Masvingo, Zimbabwe
Telephone: (263) 396 5266 **Fax:** (263) 396 5275 **E-mail:** chempath@medsch.uz.ac.zw

VICE-CHANCELLOR*—Marima-Matarira, Hilda T., BSc *Zambia*, MSc *Warw.*, PhD *Edin.*
REGISTRAR‡—Kurebwa, Mercy, BA *Z'bwe.Open*, MA *Z'bwe.Open*

MASVINGO STATE UNIVERSITY

Founded 2002

Postal Address: P O Box 1235, Masvingo, Zimbabwe
Telephone: 039 63628 **Fax:** 039 65955

VICE-CHANCELLOR*—Maravanyika, Prof. O. E., MEd *Manc.*, DPhil *Z'bwe.*
DIRECTOR OF INFORMATION‡—Dzenga, W. S., BA *Z'bwe.*

MIDLANDS STATE UNIVERSITY

Founded 2000

Member of the Association of Commonwealth Universities

Postal Address: Private Bag 9055, Gweru, Zimbabwe
Telephone: (054) 60753 **Fax:** (054) 60311
URL: http://www.msu.ac.zw

VICE-CHANCELLOR*—Bhebe, Prof. Ngwabi M., BA *UBLS*, PhD *Lond.*
PRO-VICE-CHANCELLOR—Zvobgo, Prof. R. J., BA MA MPhil PhD
REGISTRAR‡—Gurira, G. T., BSc *Z'bwe.*, MPA *Z'bwe.*
BURSAR—Musasa, L. N., BAcc *Z'bwe.*
LIBRARIAN—Ndhlovu, S. N., BA *Z'bwe.*, MA *Lond.*
DEAN OF STUDENTS—Mkwananzi, T. N., BA *Lond.*
DEPUTY REGISTRAR—Mupfiga, E., BSc *Z'bwe.*, MSc

GENERAL INFORMATION

History. The university was established in 2000 by an act of parliament.

It is situated in Midlands Province, 265km from Harare, the capital of Zimbabwe.

Admission to first degree courses. Applicants must have good A level results or recognised professional qualifications.

First Degrees (see also Zimbabwean Directory to Subjects of Study). BA, BCom, BSc.

Length of course. Full-time: BA, BCom, BSc: 4 years.

Higher Degrees (see also Zimbabwean Directory to Subjects of Study).
Master's. MBA.
Length of course. Full-time: MBA: 2 years.

Libraries. Volumes: 50,841. Periodicals subscribed to: 74. Other holdings: audio-visual materials; government publications; international organizations publications; maps; pamphlets.

FACULTIES/SCHOOLS

Arts

Acting Executive Dean: Harford, Prof. C., BA *Carleton(Minn.)*, MA *Wis.*, PhD *Wis.*
Faculty Administrator: Baye, C., BEd *Z'bwe.*, MEd

Commerce

Tel: (054) 60464 Fax: (054) 60233
Executive Dean: Mbetu, K. C., BComm *S.Af.*
Faculty Administrator: Muchuchuti, K., BBS *Z'bwe.*, MBA *Z'bwe.*

Education

Executive Dean: Ndawi, Prof. O., BEd *Z'bwe.*, MEd *Z'bwe.*, PhD *Z'bwe.*
Faculty Administrator: Shoko, E. A., BA *Z'bwe.*

Natural Resource Management and Agriculture

Dean: Mugabe, F. T., BSc(Agric) *Z'bwe.*, MSc(Agric) *Z'bwe.*
Faculty Administrator: Kusema, L., BEd *Z'bwe.*

Science

Tel: (054) 60464
Executive Dean: Chawanda, A., BSc *Z'bwe.*, MSc *Z'bwe.*
Faculty Administrator: Rutunga, L., BSc *Z'bwe.*

Social Science

Tel: (054) 60331
Executive Dean: Gwatidzo, C. N., MA *Keele*
Faculty Administrator: Chifamba, K., BSc *Z'bwe.*

ACADEMIC UNITS

Accounting

Tel: (054) 60450
Mlambo, E. T., BBS *Z'bwe.*, FCIS Head*
Other Staff: 4 Lectrs.; 1 Staff Devel. Fellow
Research: financial management of rural district councils

African Languages and Literature

Tel: (054) 60450 Fax: (054) 60233
Viriri, A., BA *Z'bwe.*, MA *S.Af.* Acting Head*
Other Staff: 5 Lectrs.

Agronomy

Tel: (054) 60409
Makuvaro, V., BScAgric *Z'bwe.*, MScAgric *Z'bwe.* Head*
Other Staff: 3 Lectrs.

Applied Educational Foundations and Administration

Tel: (054) 60337
Chiromo, A. S., BEd *Z'bwe.*, MEd *Z'bwe.* Head*
Other Staff: 6 Lectrs.; 1 Staff Devel. Fellow

Archaeology, Museum Studies and Cultural Heritage

Mtombeni, N., MSc Acting Head*
Other Staff: 3 Lectrs.

Banking and Finance

Tel: (054) 60464
Sithole, S. T. M., BAcc *Z'bwe.* Head*
Other Staff: 1 Lectr.; 2 Staff Devel. Fellows

Biological Sciences

Tel: (054) 60337
Moyo, D. Z., BSc *Z'bwe.*, MPhil *Z'bwe.*, PhD *Z'bwe.* Head*
Other Staff: 5 Lectrs.
Research: environmental biotechnology; fowl immunology; veterinary parasitology

Business Management

Tel: (054) 60419
Ngwenya, F. J., BA *Wolv.*, MBA PhD Head*
Other Staff: 4 Lectrs.
Research: performance of manufacturing sector; project planning

Chemical Technology

Tel: (054) 60337 Fax: (054) 60233
Tinofireyi, N. W., BSc *Z'bwe.*, MSc *Z'bwe.* Head*
Other Staff: 4 Lectrs.; 1 Staff Devel. Fellow
Research: medicinal chemistry; mineral processing and refinery; pollution control

Computer Science and Information Systems

Tel: (054) 60337 Fax: (054) 60233
Mukwembi, A., MSc *Kharkov* Head*
Other Staff: 4 Lectrs.; 4 Staff Devel. Fellows

Economics

Tel: (054) 60450
Sunde, T., BSc(Econ) *Z'bwe.*, MSc *Z'bwe.* Head*
Other Staff: 6 Lectrs.
Research: effects of privatisation in Zimbabwe; international trade; investment economics

Educational Foundations Management and Curriculum Studies

Tel: (054) 60450
Jani, P. M., BA *Zambia*, MEd *Z'bwe.* Head*

Other Staff: 6 Lectrs.
Research: teacher education

English

Tel: (054) 60450
Javangwe, T., BA Z'bwe., MA(Eng) Z'bwe.
    Head*
Other Staff: 4 Lectrs.

Geography and Environmental Studies

Tel: (054) 60337
Mhlahlo, S. R., BA Lond., MA Lond.   Head*
Other Staff: 5 Lectrs.
Research: environmental impact assessment;
    impact of unemployment on environment

History and Development Studies

Tel: (054) 60450
Mashingaidze M, T., BA Z'bwe., MA Z'bwe.
    Head*
Other Staff: 4 Lectrs.; 1 Temp. Lectr.

Home Economics

Tel: (054) 60251
Makamure, C., BEd Z'bwe., MA Solusi   Head*
Other Staff: 2 Lectrs.

Horticulture

Tel: (054) 60404
Gomba, A., BScAgric Z'bwe., MSc Z'bwe.   Head*
Other Staff: 2 Lectrs.

Human Resources Management

Tel: (054) 60404
Mehlo, K. P., MA Panjab   Head*
Other Staff: 5 Lectrs.
Research: contract workers; impact of HIV/AIDS
    on productivity; trade union democracy

Land and Water Resources Management

Tel: (054) 60450
Kapenzi, A., BScAgric Z'bwe., MScAgric Cran.
    Head*
Other Staff: 4 Lectrs.
Research: catchment hydrology; environmental
    management; land reform programmes

Livestock and Wildlife Management

Tel: (054) 60337
Fushai, F., BScAgric Z'bwe., MSc(Agric) Natal
    Head*
Other Staff: 4 Lectrs.

Local Governance

Chakaipa, S., BA Z'bwe., MBA

Marketing

Fax: (054) 60233
Mupemhi, T. P., MBA Z'bwe.   Head*
Other Staff: 2 Lectrs.

Mathematics

Tel: (054) 60337 Fax: (054) 60233
Chinofunga, P. T., BSc Z'bwe., MSc Z'bwe.
    Head*
Other Staff: 6 Lectrs.

Media and Society Studies

Tel: (054) 60337 Fax: (054) 60233
Mandava, P., BA Z'bwe., MA Z'bwe.   Head*
Other Staff: 4 Lectrs.

Physics

Tel: (054) 60337 Fax: (054) 60233
Chiroro, A., BSc Z'bwe., MSc Z'bwe.   Head*
Other Staff: 3 Lectrs.
Research: laser technology; solar energy
    applications

Psychology

Ngwenya, F., BSc Z'bwe., MSc Z'bwe.
Other Staff: 1 Lectr.

Surveying and Geomatics

Tel: (054) 60337 Fax: (054) 60233
Njike, D., BSc Z'bwe., MSc Z'bwe.   Head*
Other Staff: 4 Lectrs.
Research: environmental information systems;
    spacial data infrastructures

Tourism and Hospitality Management

Tel: (054) 60210 Fax: (054) 60233
Nyahunzvi, BSc(Econ) Z'bwe., MSc Z'bwe.
    Head*
Other Staff: 4 Lectrs.
Research: tourism development

[Information supplied by the institution as at 13 June
2005, and edited by the ACU]

NATIONAL UNIVERSITY OF SCIENCE AND TECHNOLOGY, BULAWAYO

Founded 1990

Member of the Association of Commonwealth Universities

Postal Address: PO Box AC939, Ascot, Bulawayo, Zimbabwe
Telephone: (09) 282842 **Fax:** (09) 286903 **E-mail:** info@nust.ac.zw
URL: http://www.nust.ac.zw/

VICE-CHANCELLOR*—Ndlovu, Prof. Lindela R., BSc S.Leone, MSc Wales, PhD Guelph, FZAS
PRO-VICE-CHANCELLOR (ACADEMIC RESEARCH AND CONSULTANCY)—Sibanda, Prof. S., BSc CNAA, PhD Lond.
REGISTRAR (ACTING)‡—Phiri, Richmond, BA Lond., MA Reading
LIBRARIAN—Matsika, Katherine, BA Rhodesia
BURSAR—Sithole, Lameck, BAdmin Z'bwe., MBA Brun.

GENERAL INFORMATION

History. The university was established in
1990 and opened in 1991.
    It is located in the city of Bulawayo, in the
southwest of Zimbabwe.

Admission to first degree courses. Applicants
should normally hold the Cambridge School
Certificate exam or equivalent, with 5 O level
passes at grade C or above including English
language and mathematics, and either 2
relevant subjects at A level (for applied
sciences, architecture, commerce and quantity
surveying), or 3 relevant subjects at A level
(for engineering).

First Degrees (see also Zimbabwean
Directory to Subjects of Study) (* = with
honours). BArchSt*, BCom*, BEng*, BQSurv*,
BSc*.
    Length of course. Full-time: BCom*, BQSurv*,
BSc*: 4 years; BArchSt*, BEng*: 5 years.

Higher Degrees (see also Zimbabwean
Directory to Subjects of Study).
    Master's. MBA, MPhil, MSc.

Admission. Applicants for admission to
master's degrees must normally hold an
appropriate first degree or approved
equivalent.
    Doctoral. PhD.
    Admission. PhD: appropriate master's degree.

Academic Year (2008–2009). Two
semesters: August–December; January–May.

FACULTIES/SCHOOLS

Applied Sciences

Fax: (09) 286390 E-mail: fas@nust.ac.zw
Dean: Mwenje, E., BSc Z'bwe., PhD Birm.
Senior Assistant Registrar: Makoni, C. S., BA
    Rhodesia, MEd Z'bwe.

Commerce

E-mail: fcom@nust.ac.zw
Dean: Tadu, R., BCom NUST Bulawayo, MBA
    Nott.
Senior Assistant Registrar: Silamba, S., BSc
    Z'bwe.

Communication and Media Studies

E-mail: jms@nust.ac.zw
Dean: Hikwa, L., MA Lond., PhD
Senior Assistant Registrar: Mnkandla, V. A., BA
    Z'bwe., MPhil Z'bwe.

Industrial Technology

E-mail: fit@nust.ac.zw
Dean: Kuipa, P. K., MSc(Eng) Ivanovo, PhD Brad.
Senior Assistant Registrar: Dube, Vivian R.,
    MBA NUST Bulawayo, BSc

Medicine

Dean: Ndiweni, Nomathemba, BSc Z'bwe.,
    MPhil Camb., PhD Brist.
Senior Assistant Registrar: Bako, Catherine, BSc
    S.Af., MSc Z'bwe.

ACADEMIC UNITS

Accounting

E-mail: accountingdepartment@nust.ac.zw
Moyo, A. T. C., BCom Punjab, MCom Punjab,
    MBA Hull   Sr. Lectr.
Shumba, F., BSc MBA   Chairperson*
Other Staff: 6 Lectrs.

Architecture

E-mail: archqs@nust.ac.zw
Madaki, S. A., MSc(Arch) Kiev, PhD Kiev   Sr.
   Lectr.
Mutsambiwa, C.   Chairman*
Other Staff: 6 Lectrs.

Banking

E-mail: bankingdepartment@nust.ac.zw
Ndlovu, M. W., BCom NUST Bulawayo, MSc
   NUST Bulawayo   Chairman*
Other Staff: 6 Lectrs.

Basic Medical Sciences

Yahaya, B. C. Malango, BSc St And., MB ChB
   Z'bwe.   Chairman*
Other Staff: 4 Lectrs.

Biology and Biochemistry, Applied

E-mail: appliedbio@nust.ac.zw
Siwela, A. H., BAppSc RMIT, MPhil Z'bwe.
   Chairman*
Other Staff: 14 Lectrs.

Business, Graduate School of

E-mail: gsb@nust.ac.zw
Gwate-Hall, O., BBS Z'bwe., BCom Fort Hare
   Dir.*
Mtigwe, B., BCom Pret., BTech Z'bwe., MBA
   E.Cowan   Sr. Lectr.
Other Staff: 3 Lectrs.

Business Management

E-mail: busmgnt@nust.ac.zw
Dube, T., BTech Z'bwe., MSc Strath.   Chairman*
Other Staff: 11 Lectrs.

Chemistry, Applied

E-mail: appliedchemistry@nust.ac.zw
Parekh, Champaklal T., BSc Gujar., MSc Gujar.,
   MSc Manc., PhD Manc.   Chairman*
Other Staff: 4 Lectrs.

Clinical Practice and Patient Care

Cotton, Michael H., MB BS Lond., MA Oxf.,
   FRCS, FACS
Mgwenya, Solwayo, MB ChB Z'bwe.

Computer Science

E-mail: compscie@nust.ac.zw
Moyo, B., MSc NUST Bulawayo, Lic   Chairman*
Other Staff: 11 Lectrs.

Engineering, Chemical

Tel: (09) 475192 Fax: (09) 464363
   E-mail: chemeng@nust.ac.zw
Mudono, S., BSc(ChemEng) MSc(ChemEng)
   Chairman*
Other Staff: 3 Lectrs.

Engineering, Civil and Water

E-mail: civil@nust.ac.zw
Mutsvangwa, C., MSc Lough., MSc(Eng)
   Chairman*
Other Staff: 4 Lectrs.

Engineering, Electronic

Tel: (09) 475192 Fax: (09) 464363
   E-mail: electronic@nust.ac.zw
Collier, Michael, BA Camb., MA Camb., PhD HK,
   FIEE   Prof.
Mtunzi, B., BTech MSc   Chairman*
Other Staff: 4 Lectrs.

Engineering, Industrial and Manufacturing

E-mail: indeng@nust.ac.zw
Dlodlo, Z. B., MSc P.F.U., Moscow, PhD Liv.
   Chairman*
Mhlanga, S., BEng NUST Bulawayo, MSc Brun.
   Sr. Lectr.
Other Staff: 8 Lectrs.; 4 Engin. Instrs.; 2 Staff
   Devel. Fellows

Environmental Science and Health

E-mail: environ@nust.ac.zw
Zimba, M., BTech Pret., MIH Copenhagen
   Chairman*
Other Staff: 6 Lectrs.

Finance

E-mail: finance@nust.ac.zw
Bhala, R. M., BBS Z'bwe., MBL S.Af.
   Chairman*
Mutungwazi, BAEcon Punjab, MAEcon Punjab
   Sr. Lectr.
Other Staff: 4 Lectrs.; 1 Staff. Devel. Fellow

Forest Resources and Wildlife Management

Nyathi, P., BSc Dar., PhD Z'bwe., MSc
   Chairman*
Other Staff: 8 Lectrs.

Insurance and Actuarial Science

E-mail: insurance@nust.ac.zw
1 Lectr.; 2 Lectrs.†

Journalism and Media Studies

E-mail: jms@nust.ac.zw
Matenda, S., BSc Z'bwe., MA Z'bwe.   Chairman*
Other Staff: 5 Lectrs.; 3 Staff Devel. Fellows

Landscape Architecture and Urban Design

Murombe, M., BArch Bom.   Chairman*

Library and Information Science

E-mail: librarysciences@nust.ac.zw
Ngwenya, A. M. L., BA Tas., MEd Tas.
   Chairman*
Other Staff: 6 Lectrs.; 3 Staff. Devel. Fellows

Mathematics, Applied

E-mail: applied_maths@nust.ac.zw
Garira, W., BSc Z'bwe., MSc Brist., PhD Lond.
   Chairman*
Other Staff: 18 Lectrs.

Physics, Applied

E-mail: applied_physics@nust.ac.zw
Hlatywayo, D. J., BSc Zambia, PhD Uppsala
   Chairman*
Other Staff: 17 Lectrs.

Quantity Surveying

E-mail: qsurveying@nust.ac.zw
Gumbo, T., BSc Z'bwe., MSc Z'bwe.   Chairman*
Other Staff: 2 Staff Devel. Fellows

Records and Archives Management

Sibanda, Rosemary, BA Z'bwe., MLIS MBL
   Chairman*
Other Staff: 2 Lectrs.; 3 Staff Devel. Fellows

Social Medical Sciences

Chamisa, Judith A., BAdEd Z'bwe., MSc Z'bwe.
   Chairperson*
Other Staff: 3 Lectrs.

Sports Science and Coaching

Mugandani, S. C., BEd NUST Bulawayo, MEd
   NUST Bulawayo   Chairman*
Other Staff: 7 Lectrs.

Technical Teacher Education

E-mail: techteacher@nust.ac.zw
Sibanda, I. M., BSc Z'bwe., MA Lond., PhD Z'bwe.
   Chairman*
Other Staff: 5 Lectrs.

Textile Technology

E-mail: textile_tech@nust.ac.zw
Nkiwane, Londiwe, MA Gothenburg, PhD Leeds,
   MSc   Sr. Lectr.
Nyoni, A. B., MSc Leeds, PhD Leeds   Chairman*
Other Staff: 4 Lectrs.; 1 Res. Fellow

SPECIAL CENTRES, ETC

Continuing Education, Cemtre for

Mpofu, S., BAdmin Rhodesia, PhD Mich.State
   Dir.*

CONTACT OFFICERS

Academic affairs. Deputy Registrar (Academic
   affairs): Phiri, Richmond, BA Lond., MA
   Reading
Admissions (first degree). Senior Assistant
   Registrar: Mhlanga, F., BEd Z'bwe., MSc
   Z'bwe.
Admissions (higher degree). Senior Assistant
   Registrar: Mhlanga, F., BEd Z'bwe., MSc
   Z'bwe.
Careers. Director of Information and Public
   Relations: Moyo, Felix F., BA S.Af.
Computing services. Director, ICTS: Nyathi,
   T., BSc NUST Bulawayo, MSc NUST Bulawayo
Development/fund-raising. Industrial Liaison
   Officer: (vacant)
Estates and buildings/works and services.
   Director of Works and Estates: Maphosa,
   M., BSc Z'bwe., MBA NUST Bulawayo
Finance. Bursar: Sithole, Lameck, BAdmin
   Z'bwe., MBA Brun.
General enquiries. Registrar (Acting): Phiri,
   Richmond, BA Lond., MA Reading
Health services. Director of Student Health
   Services: (vacant)
Industrial liaison. Industrial Liaison Officer:
   Mhlanga, L., BA Z'bwe.
Library (chief librarian). Librarian: Matsika,
   Katherine, BA Rhodesia
Marketing. Director of Information and Public
   Relations: Moyo, Felix F., BA S.Af.
Personnel/human resources. Senior Assistant
   Registrar (Personnel/human resources):
   Bidi, Mavis, BAdmin Z'bwe., MBA Wales
Public relations. Director of Information and
   Public Relations: Moyo, Felix F., BA S.Af.
Publications. Chairman, Research Board: Read,
   Prof. J. S., BSc Natal, PhD Calif.
Purchasing. Bursar: Sithole, Lameck, BAdmin
   Z'bwe., MBA Brun.
Research. Director, Research and Innovation:
   Chimbari, J. M.
Safety. Registrar (Acting): Phiri, Richmond,
   BA Lond., MA Reading
Scholarships, awards, loans. Deputy Registrar
   (Scholarships, awards, loans): Phiri,
   Richmond, BA Lond., MA Reading
Schools liaison. Director of Information and
   Public Relations: Matshe, S. Priscillah, BSW
   Z'bwe.
Security. Registrar (Acting): Phiri, Richmond,
   BA Lond., MA Reading
Sport and recreation. Director of Sports:
   Muller, Berenice, LLB Z'bwe.
Staff development and training. Senior
   Assistant Registrar (Staff development and
   training): Bidi, Mavis, BAdmin Z'bwe., MBA
   Wales
Student union. President of Student
   Representative Council: Bomba, John
Student welfare/counselling. Dean of
   Students: Sifobela, Lobi, BA Birm., MA Birm.,
   PhD Lond.
Students from other countries. Dean of
   Students: Sifobela, Lobi, BA Birm., MA Birm.,
   PhD Lond.
Students with disabilities. Dean of Students:
   Sifobela, Lobi, BA Birm., MA Birm., PhD
   Lond.

[Information supplied by the institution as at 2 October
2007, and edited by the ACU]

SOLUSI UNIVERSITY

Founded 1994

Postal Address: PO Solusi, Bulawayo, Zimbabwe
Telephone: (09) 83226-8 **Fax:** (09) 83229 **E-mail:** solusi@esanet.zw

VICE-CHANCELLOR*—Maphosa, Prof. Norman, BA Z'bwe., MSc Z'bwe., PhD Z'bwe.
REGISTRAR‡—Sithole, Richard, BA Andrews, MA Andrews, MA Z'bwe.Open

WOMEN'S UNIVERSITY IN AFRICA

Founded 2002

Postal Address: Education Services Centre, P O Box MP 1222, Mount Pleasant, Harare, Zimbabwe
Telephone: (04) 333139 **Fax:** (04) 333154 **E-mail:** womunica@africaonline.co.zw
URL: http://www.womensuniversityinafrica.org

VICE-CHANCELLOR*—Sadza, Prof. Hope C., BSc Missouri, MA Missouri, PhD Z'bwe.
DIRECTOR OF FINANCE AND PLANNING‡—Mugari, Simplicius M. N., MSc Birm.

UNIVERSITY OF ZIMBABWE

Founded 1955

Member of the Association of Commonwealth Universities

Postal Address: PO Box MP 167, Mount Pleasant, Harare, Zimbabwe
Telephone: (04) 303211 **Fax:** (04) 333407 **E-mail:** postmaster@mango.apc.org
URL: http://www.uz.ac.zw

VICE-CHANCELLOR*—Nyagura, Prof. Levi M., BSc Lond., BSc Rhodesia, MSc S.Af., PhD S.Illinois
PRO-VICE-CHANCELLOR—Chivinge, Prof. O. A., BSc Ib., MSc Ib., DPhil Z'bwe.Open
REGISTRAR‡—Chevo, Sergeant M., BAdmin
LIBRARIAN—Mbambo, B. M., BSc(Soc) Z'bwe., MSc Botswana
BURSAR—Dhlamini, I. E., BBS Z'bwe.
SENIOR PROCTOR—Hamudikuwanda, H., BScAgric Rhodesia, MSc Cornell, PhD McG.

GENERAL INFORMATION

History. The university was originally founded as University College of Rhodesia and Nyasaland in 1955 and established as University of Rhodesia in 1971. It became known under its present name after independence.

It is located in the city of Harare.

Admission to first degree courses (see also Zimbabwean Introduction). O and A level with 5 passes (minimum 2 at A level) or 4 passes (minimum 3 at A level); candidates must also pass O level English language or equivalent. A number of international students with high academic qualifications may be admitted.

First Degrees (see also Zimbabwean Directory to Subjects of Study) (* = with honours). BA, BA*, BAcc*, BAdEd, BA(E&CS), BBS*, BBS&CompSc, BDS, BDS*, BEd, BMLS*, BNSc, BNSc*, BPharm*, BSc, BSc*, BScAgric*, BScAgricEng*, BScAgric(Mngt), BScAn*, BScEcon*, BScEng*, BScHP*, BScMining*, BScOT*, BScPolAd*, BScPsych*, BScPT*, BScRUP*, BScSoc*, BScTHM, BScVA*, BSE, BSurv*, BSW, BVSc, BVSc*, LLB*, MB ChB, MB ChB*.

Most degrees normally last 3 years.
Length of course. Full-time: BA(E&CS), BAdEd, BEd: 2 years; BA, BA*, BNSc*, BSc, BSc*,

BScAgric*, BScAgricEng*, BScEcon*, BScHP*, BScPolAd*, BScPsych*, BScSoc*: 3 years; BAcc*, BBS&CompSc, BBS*, BMLS*, BPharm*, BScEng*, BScMining*, BScOT*, BScPT*, BScRUP*, BScTHM, BSurv*, BSW, LLB*: 4 years; BDS, BDS*, BVSc, BVSc*, MB ChB, MB ChB*: 5 years. *Part-time:* BAdEd, BEd: 2–4 years; BAcc*: 4–8 years.

Higher Degrees (see also Zimbabwean Directory to Subjects of Study).
Master's. LLM, MA, MBA, MEd, MMEd, MPhil, MSc, MScTHM.
Admission. Applicants for admission to master's degrees must normally hold an appropriate first degree.
Length of course. Full-time: MSc: 1–2 years; MA, MEd: 2 years. *Part-time:* MBA, MScTHM: 2 years; MEd: 2–4 years; MMEd: 5 years.
Doctoral. DPhil.
Admission. DPhil: appropriate master's degree.
Length of course. Full-time: DPhil: 3 years. *Part-time:* DPhil: 4 years.

Language of Instruction. English. Remedial courses are available through the Communication Skills Centre.

Libraries. Volumes: 430,000. Special collections: Godlonton (Zimbabwe and Southern Africa); Doka (African languages);

Astor (American history); African writers (novels in English by Africans).

Statistics. Students (2005–2006): international 129 (78 men, 51 women); undergraduate 9967 (6773 men, 3194 women); master's 1345 (933 men, 412 women); doctoral 83 (61 men, 22 women).

FACULTIES/SCHOOLS
Agriculture
Tel: (04) 333880 E-mail: mutisi@agric.uz.ac.zw
Dean: Mutisi, C., BSc Reading, PhD Reading
Secretary: Chiwara, O., BSc(Econ) Z'bwe.

Arts
Tel: (04) 308296 E-mail: arts@arts.uz.ac.zw
Dean: Mashiri, P., BA Z'bwe., MPhil Z'bwe., DPhil Z'bwe.Open
Secretary: Masinire, A., BA(Gen) Z'bwe., MEd Z'bwe.

Commerce
Tel: (04) 333674
E-mail: dean@commerce.uz.ac.zw
Dean: Chikondo, J. T. M., MAcc Glas.
Secretary: Makusha, M., BSc(Psych) Z'bwe.

Education
Tel: (04) 303291 Fax: (04) 303291
E-mail: dean@education.uz.ac.zw

Dean: Dyanda, C., BEd Z'bwe., MEd Howard, PhD
Chic.
Secretary (Acting): Nyamunokora, S., BA
Z'bwe., MBA Z'bwe.

Engineering
Tel: (04) 303280
E-mail: deanchair@eng.uz.ac.zw
Dean: Nyemba, W., BScEng MSc
Secretary: Zisengwe, N., BScPsych Z'bwe.

Medicine
Tel: (04) 705155 Fax: (04) 724912
E-mail: aslatif@medsch.uz.ac.zw
Dean: Latif, A. S., MB ChB Birm., MD, FCP(SA)
Acting Secretary: Chitiyo, W. P., BA

Science
Tel: (04) 307130
E-mail: zengeni@science.uz.ac.zw
Dean: Zengeni, T. G., BSc Lond., MS Stan., PhD
Stan.
Secretary: Mangwanya, L., BSc(Soc) Z'bwe., MSc

Social Studies
Tel: (04) 333353 E-mail: dean@sociol.uz.ac.zw
Dean: Muzvidziwa, V. N., BScSoc Z'bwe.,
MScSoc Z'bwe., PhD Waik.
Secretary: Madzimure, O., BA Z'bwe.Open

Veterinary Science
Fax: (04) 333683
E-mail: vetscience@vet.uz.ac.zw
Dean: Mukaratirwa, Prof. S., MVSc Liv., PhD
Copenhagen, DVM
Secretary: Silamba, S., BA Rhodesia

ACADEMIC UNITS
Accountancy
Tel: (04) 333674 E-mail: tchitate@yahoo.co.uk
Hove, M. R., MA Sheff.   Sr. Lectr.
Paradza, P. P., BScEcon S.W.Missouri, MSc
S.W.Missouri   Chairman*
Other Staff: 6 Lectrs.

Adult Education
E-mail: adult@education.uz.ac.zw
Mashayamombe, F. E. N., BEd Z'bwe., MEd
Z'bwe.Open   Chairman*
Other Staff: 5 Lectrs.
Vacant Posts: 1 Lectr.

African Languages and Literature
E-mail: africanlangs@avu.org
Chimhundu, H., BA Z'bwe., DPhil Z'bwe.   Prof.
Hadebe, S., BA Z'bwe., MA Z'bwe., PhD Z'bwe.,
PhD Oslo   Sr. Lectr.; Chairman*
Kahari, G. P., BA Z'bwe., MA Z'bwe., DPhil Z'bwe.
Prof.
Mashiri, P., BA Z'bwe., MPhil Z'bwe., DPhil
Z'bwe.Open   Sr. Lectr.
Matambirofa, F., BA Z'bwe.Open, MA Z'bwe.Open,
PhD Z'bwe.
Matshakayile-Ndlovu, T., BA Lond., MPhil
Z'bwe.Open   Sr. Lectr.
Mguni-Gambahaya, Z., BA Z'bwe.Open, PhD Cape
Town   Sr. Lectr.
Other Staff: 8 Lectrs.; 3 Res. Fellows; 6 Temp.
Lectrs.

Agricultural Economics and Extension
E-mail: lrugube@yagric.uz.ac.zw
Rugube, L., BSc Idaho, MSc Idaho, PhD Manit.
Chairman*
Other Staff: 15 Lectrs.

Animal Science
E-mail: mpofu@agric.uz.ac.zw
Hamudikuwanda, H., BScAgric Rhodesia, MSc
Cornell, PhD McG.   Assoc. Prof.
Makuza, S. M., BScAgric Z'bwe., MSc Mich.State,
PhD N.Carolina State   Assoc. Prof., Animal
Breeding and Genetics; Chairman*
Mpofu, I. D. T., BSc Z'bwe., MSc Z'bwe., PhD
Pret.   Sr. Lectr.

Mugabe, P. H., BScAgric Z'bwe., MSc Reading,
PhD Texas A.& M.   Sr. Lectr.
Mutisi, C., BSc Reading, PhD Reading   Sr. Lectr.
Ngongoni, N. T., BScAgric Rhodesia, MSc Aberd.,
PhD Aberd.   Sr. Lectr.
Other Staff: 6 Lectrs.

Biochemistry
Tel: (04) 308047 Fax: (04) 308046
E-mail: muchiweti@medic.uz.ac.zw
Benhura, M. A., BSc UBLS, MSc Warw., PhD
Warw.   Assoc. Prof.
Gooch, J. A., BSc Lond., PhD Lond.   Sr. Lectr.
Hasler, Julie A., BSc Cape Town, PhD Cape Town
Assoc. Prof.
Muchuweti, M., BSc Z'bwe., DPhil Z'bwe.
Chairperson*
Sithole-Niang, I., BSc Lond., PhD Mich.State
Assoc. Prof.
Other Staff: 13 Lectrs.

Biological Sciences
E-mail: liviniab@yahoo.com
Feresu, Sarah, BSc CNAA, PhD Leic.   Assoc.
Prof.
Kativhu, S., DPhil Z'bwe.
Loveridge, J. P., BSc Lond., PhD Lond.   Prof.
Mabveni, A., BSc Z'bwe., MSc Calif., PhD Z'bwe.
Chairperson*
Magadza, C. H. D., BSc Lond., MPhil Lond., PhD
Auck.   Assoc. Prof.
Marshall, B. E., BSc Lond., MPhil Lond., PhD
Rhodes   Assoc. Prof.
Other Staff: 10 Lectrs.

Business Studies
E-mail: jzmushipe@commerce.uz.ac.zw
Muranda, Z., BBS Z'bwe.Open, MPhil Z'bwe.Open,
DPhil Z'bwe.   Sr. Lectr.
Mushipe, J. Z., BBA N.Carolina Central, MBA
N.Carolina   Chairman*
Other Staff: 11 Lectrs.

Chemistry
E-mail: chemdept@science.uz.ac.zw
Gurira, R. C., BSc Central State(Ohio), PhD
Penn.State   Sr. Lectr.
Nhamo, L. R. M., BSc Lond., PhD Lond.
Chairman*
Zaranyika, M. F., BSc Lond., PhD Boston   Prof.
Other Staff: 4 Lectrs.

Computer Science
E-mail: compscie@science.uz.ac.zw
Mazhindu-Shumba, R., BSc Z'bwe.Open, MSc
Manc., PhD Birm.   Lectr.; Chairman*
Other Staff: 13 Staff Members

Crop Science
E-mail: cropsci@uz.ac.zw
Chiduza, C., BScAgric Z'bwe., MPhil Z'bwe.,
DPhil Z'bwe.   Sr. Lectr.
Chivinge, O. A., BSc Ib., MSc Ib., DPhil
Z'bwe.Open   Prof.
Kageler, S. J., BSc Z'bwe., DPhil Z'bwe., MSc
Maasdorp, B. V., BScAgric Rhodesia, MPhil
Z'bwe., MAgric Qld.   Prof.
Madakadze, I. C., BScAgric Z'bwe., MSc Reading,
PhD Mich.
Mashingaidze, A. B., BSc Z'bwe.Open, MSc Iowa
State, PhD Wageningen   Sr. Lectr.; Chairman*
Other Staff: 11 Lectrs.

Curriculum and Arts Education
Maravanyika, O. E., MEd Manc., DPhil Z'bwe.Open
Assoc. Prof.
Mavhunga, P. J., BEd Z'bwe., MEd Z'bwe.
Chairman*
Moyana, R., BA Lincoln(Pa.), MA Westchester, MA
Z'bwe., DPhil Z'bwe.   Sr. Lectr.
Nyawaranda, V., BA Z'bwe., DPhil McG.   Sr.
Lectr.
Other Staff: 11 Lectrs.

Economic History
E-mail: econohist@arts.ac.zw
Mlambo, A. S., BA Cant., MA Lond., MA
Wesleyan, PhD Duke   Sr. Lectr.; Chairman*
Other Staff: 8 Lectrs.

Economics
E-mail: economics@sociol.uz.ac.zw
Matshe, I., MSc Sophia, MA Manc., PhD Manc.
Assoc. Prof.; Chairman*
Other Staff: 21 Lectrs.

Education, Teacher
E-mail: brschivore@yahoo.co.uk
Chisaka, B. C., BA Dar., MEd Z'bwe., DEd S.Af.
Sr. Lectr.
Chivore, B. R. S., BA Sus., MA Lond., PhD Lond.
Prof.
Munetsi, C., BSc Aston, MSc Iowa State   Sr.
Lectr.; Chairman*
Shumba, O., BEd Z'bwe.Open, MSc Iowa State, PhD
Iowa State   Assoc. Prof.
Other Staff: 9 Lectrs.

Education, Technical
E-mail: gweru@compcentre.uz.ac.zw
Kwaira, P., MA Linköping   Sr. Lectr.; Chairman*
Nherera, C. M., BEd Exe., MA Linköping, PhD
Lond.   Prof.
Other Staff: 13 Lectrs.

Educational Administration
E-mail: edadmin@education.uz.ac.zw
Jonga, W., MSc Z'bwe., BSc   Chairman*
Other Staff: 2 Lectrs.

Educational Foundations
Fax: (04) 335249
E-mail: edfoundzool@yahoo.com
Atkinson, N. D., BA Trinity(Dub.), MLitt
Trinity(Dub.), PhD Trinity(Dub.), PhD Lond.
Sr. Lectr.
Peresuh, M. N., MEd Manc., PhD Manc.   Assoc.
Prof.
Rinashe, H. M., BA Manc., MEd Manc.
Chairman*
Zindi, F., BEd Lond., MA Lond., PhD Lond.
Assoc. Prof.
Other Staff: 12 Lectrs.

Educational Technology, Centre for
Rwambiwa, J. P., BSc Lond., MEd Col., PhD Col.
Lectr.; Chairman*
Other Staff: 1 Lectr.

Engineering, Civil
Fax: (04) 303288
E-mail: salahuddin@eng.uz.ac.zw
Djifarova-Vassileva, L., MArch Sofia, PhD Sofia
Assoc. Prof.
Grant, M. P., BSc(Eng) Cape Town, MSc Birm.
Sr. Lectr.
Salahuddin, A., MSc N.Y., PhD Montr.   Sr.
Lectr.; Chairman*
Other Staff: 10 Lectrs.
Research: water resources management

Engineering, Electrical
Fax: (04) 303280 E-mail: chikuni@eng.uz.ac.zw
Chikuni, E., BEng S.Leone, MSc UMIST, PhD
Wales   Chairman*
Other Staff: 11 Lectrs.

Engineering, Mechanical
Fax: (04) 303280
Nyemba, W., BScEng MSc   Sr. Lectr.
Other Staff: 11 Lectrs.

Engineering, Metallurgical
E-mail: dsimbi@eng.uz.ac.zw
Dube, N., MSc Moscow Steel & Alloys, PhD Moscow
Steel & Alloys   Sr. Lectr.
Magombedze, C., BSc Z'bwe., MSc Exe.
Chairperson*
Simbi, D. J., BSc Portsmouth, PhD Leeds   Prof.

Other Staff: 5 Lectrs.

Engineering, Mining
Voss, J. G., MSc T.H.Aachen   Assoc. Prof.
Other Staff: 4 Lectrs.

English
see also Theatre Arts
Chivaura, V. G., BA Ib., MA N.Y.State, MPhil Ife, PhD N.Y.State
Gecau, K., BA E.Af., MA McM., PhD N.Y.State   Sr. Lectr.
Louw, W. E., BA Rhodes, MA Reading   Sr. Lectr.
Zhuwarara, R., BA Sheff., MA Sheff., PhD New Br.   Sr. Lectr.
Zimunya, M. B., BA Kent, MA Kent   Sr. Lectr.
Zinyemba, R., BA Rhodes, MPhil Wat., PhD Alta., MA   Chairman*
Other Staff: 10 Lectrs.

Geography
Fax: (04) 333 353
    E-mail: geography@arts.uz.ac.zw
Mazvimavi, D., BSc Z'bwe., MSc Brussels, DPhil ITC (Netherlands)
Mutambirwa, C. C., MA Penn., PhD W.Ont.   Prof.
Tevera, D. S., BA S.Leone, MA Qu., MPA Cinc., PhD Cinc.   Prof.
Zanamwe, L., BA Z'bwe., MA Leeds, PhD Leeds   Chairman*
Other Staff: 13 Lectrs.

Geoinformatics and Surveying
E-mail: ivan_m12@hotmail.com
Muzondo, I. F., BSc Z'bwe., MSc Z'bwe.   Chairman*
Other Staff: 3 Lectrs.

Geology
Tel: (04) 303557 E-mail: gchipari@yahoo.com
Blenkinsop, T. G., MA Oxf., MSc Lond., PhD Keele   Assoc. Prof.
Dirks, P., Drs Amst., PhD Melb.   Assoc. Prof.
Mapani, B., BSc Zambia, MSc Nancy II, PhD Melb.
Other Staff: 8 Lectrs.; 1 Res. Fellow; 2 Staff Devel. Fellows

History
see also Econ. Hist.
E-mail: history@arts.uz.ac.zw
Pwiti, G., BA Z'bwe., MPhil Camb., PhD Uppsala   Prof.
Zimudzi, T. B., BA Z'bwe., MA Z'bwe., MA   Chairman*
Other Staff: 8 Lectrs.

Law, Private
Fax: (04) 333567
    E-mail: amanase2@yahoo.com
Manase, A. J., BL Z'bwe.Open, LLB Z'bwe.Open, LLM Camb.   Sr. Lectr.; Chairman*
Ncube, W., BL Z'bwe.Open, LLB Z'bwe.Open, MPhil Z'bwe.Open   Assoc. Prof.
Other Staff: 2 Lectrs.

Law, Procedural
Fax: (04) 333554
    E-mail: rumbi317@yahoo.co.uk
Magade, E., BL Z'bwe., LLB Z'bwe., MPhil Z'bwe.   Sr. Lectr.; Chairman*
Other Staff: 5 Lectrs.

Law, Public
Fax: (04) 333556
    E-mail: lmadhuku@hotmail.com
Feltoe, G., BA Rhodes, LLB Lond., MPhil Kent   Assoc. Prof.
Madhuku, L., BL Z'bwe., LLB Z'bwe., LLM Camb., PhD Camb.   Chairman*
Other Staff: 3 Lectrs.

Linguistics
E-mail: linguistics@arts.uz.ac.zw
Gwete, W. B.   Chairperson*

Love, Alison, BA Brist., MA Z'bwe., MLitt Brist.   Assoc. Prof.
Mkanganwi, K. G., BA Lond., MPhil Lond.   Sr. Lectr.
Other Staff: 19 Lectrs.

Management
No staff at present

Mathematics
see also Sci. and Maths. Educn.
E-mail: stewart@maths.uz.ac.zw
Dzinotyiweyi, H. A. M., BSc Rhodesia, MSc Aberd., PhD Aberd.   Prof.
Hitchcock, A. G., BA Oxf., PhD Keele   Sr. Lectr.
Petrov, M. B., BSc Leningrad, MSc Leningrad, PhD Leningrad   Assoc. Prof.
Stewart, A. G. R., BSc Rhodes, MSc ANU, PhD ANU   Prof.; Chairman*
Other Staff: 10 Lectrs.

Medical Microbiology
Robertson, Valerie J., BSc Lond., MSc Lond., PhD Lond.   Sr. Lectr.
Tswana, S. A., BA N.Carolina, MSc W.Kentucky, PhD Vanderbilt   Assoc. Prof.; Chairman*
Other Staff: 6 Lectrs.

Modern Languages
E-mail: modlan@arts.uz.ac.zw
Wakerley, Veronique, BA Lond., MA Exe., PhD Lond.   Sr. Lectr.
Other Staff: 10 Lectrs.

Physics
Gwavava, O., BSc Z'bwe., DPhil Z'bwe.   Sr. Lectr.
Mathuthu, M., BSc Z'bwe., DPhil Z'bwe.   Sr. Lectr.
Olumekor, L., MSc Brun., PhD Brun.   Sr. Lectr.
Podmore, F., MA Camb., PhD Lond.   Sr. Lectr.
Selden, A. C., BA Oxf., PhD Lond.   Prof.
Zengeni, T. G., BSc Lond., MS Stan., PhD Stan.   Sr. Lectr.
Other Staff: 8 Lectrs.
Research: agricultural meteorology; applied physics; geophysics

Political and Administrative Studies
Fax: (04) 333353
    E-mail: eldred@sociol.uz.ac.zw
Makumbe, J. M., BA UBS, BAdmin Z'bwe., PhD Tas.   Sr. Lectr.
Masunungure, E., BAdmin Z'bwe., MPA Dal., MPhil Z'bwe.   Sr. Lectr.; Chairman*
Mukonoweshuro, E. G., BA Birm., MA Birm., PhD Birm.   Prof.
Patel, H. H., BSc Lond., MA Calif., PhD Calif.   Prof.
Sithole, M., BA Muskingum, MA Cinc., PhD Cinc.   Assoc. Prof.
Other Staff: 9 Lectrs.

Psychology
Muromo, T., BSc Z'bwe., MPhil Z'bwe.   Lectr.; Chairman
Other Staff: 7 Lectrs.

Religious Studies, Classics and Philosophy
E-mail: rscp@arts.uz.ac.zw
Chitando, E., DPhil Z'bwe.   Sr. Lectr.
Kurasha, J., BA York(Can.), MA Manit., MA Z'bwe., PhD Georgetown   Sr. Lectr.
Shoko, T., BA Z'bwe., MA Z'bwe., DPhil Z'bwe.   Chairman*
Other Staff: 18 Lectrs.

Rural and Urban Planning
E-mail: azimucha@sociol.uz.ac.zw
Kwangwama, N. A.   Chairman*
Mbara, T.
Other Staff: 9 Lectrs.

Science and Mathematics Education
Tel: (04) 308241
    E-mail: pngwazi@education.uz.ac.zw
Chagwedera, S. M., BScEd S.Leone, MS Penn.State, DEd Penn.State   Sr. Lectr.
Ngwazikana, P. S., BA Rhodesia, MA Alabama   Lectr.; Chairman*
Nyagura, Levi M., BSc Lond., BSc Rhodesia, MSc S.Af., PhD S.Illinois   Prof.
Other Staff: 12 Lectrs.

Sociology
E-mail: chair@sociol.uz.ac.zw
Bourdillon, M. F. C., LicPhil Heythrop, MPhil Oxf., DPhil Oxf.   Emer. Prof., Social Anthropology
Gaidzanwa, Rudo B., BSc Rhodesia, MA Inst.Soc.Stud.(The Hague)   Assoc. Prof.
Maphosa, F., PhD   Chairman*
Other Staff: 8 Lectrs.

Soil Science and Agricultural Engineering
E-mail: pnyamu@agric.uz.ac.zw
Mpepereki, S., BSc S.Leone, MSc N.Carolina, DPhil Z'bwe.Open, DPhil Z'bwe.   Assoc. Prof.
Nyamangara, J., BScAgric Z'bwe., MSc Aberd., DPhil Z'bwe.   Sr. Lectr.
Nyamugafata, P., BSc(Agric) Z'bwe., MSc Aberd.
Wuta, M., BSc Z'bwe., MSc Reading, PhD Edin.   Chairman*
Other Staff: 11 Lectrs.

Statistics
E-mail: chair@science.uz.ac.zw
7 Lectrs.

Theatre Arts
Zimunya, M. B., BA Kent, MA Kent   Sr. Lectr., English; Chairman*
Other Staff: 4 Lectrs.

MEDICINE
Tel: (04) 705155 Fax: (04) 724912
    E-mail: aslatif@medsch.uz.ac.zw

Anaesthetics
Chinyanga, H. M., MSc Jerusalem, MD Jerusalem, FRCPCan   Prof.
Chironga, M., MB ChB Z'bwe.Open, MMed Z'bwe.   Chairman*
Other Staff: 7 Lectrs.

Anatomy
Fax: (04) 333678
    E-mail: anatomy@medic.uz.ac.zw
Masanganise, R., MB ChB Z'bwe., FRCSEd   Sr. Lectr.
Mawera, G., MB ChB MMedSc   Sr. Lectr.; Chairman*
Other Staff: 5 Lectrs.

Chemical Pathology
Fax: (04) 703923
    E-mail: chempath@ecoweb.co.zw
Gomo, Z. A. R., BSc Sur., PhD Birm.   Prof.; Chairman*
Other Staff: 6 Lectrs.

Clinical Pharmacology
Fax: (04) 705581
Nhachi, C. F. B., BSc Aberd., MSc Lough., MSc Sur., PhD Lond.   Prof.; Chairman*
Nyazema, N. Z., BSc Ife, BSc Liv., PhD Liv.   Prof.
Other Staff: 3 Lectrs.

Community Medicine
Tel: (04) 791631 Fax: (04) 795835
    E-mail: mmarufu@medsch.uz.ac.zw
Matchaba-Hove, R. B., MB ChB MSc   Sr. Lectr.
Tshimanga, M., MD MPH   Sr. Lectr.
Woelk, G. B., BSc(Soc) Z'bwe.Open, MCommH Liv., PhD Wash.   Assoc. Prof.; Chairman*

Other Staff: 9 Lectrs.

Haematology

Tel: (04) 793185
Mandisodza, A., MSc Lectr.; Chairman*
Other Staff: 1 Lectr.

Histopathology

Makunike-Mutasa, R., MB ChB Z'bwe.,
MEdScience Chairperson*
Other Staff: 2 Lectrs.

Medical Laboratory Sciences

E-mail: pmason@healthnet.zw
Gwanzura, L., BSc Zambia, MPhil Z'bwe.,
MMedSc Utrecht, PhD Utrecht Prof.;
Chairman*
Mandisodza, A. R., BSc MSc Sr. Lectr.
Mason, Peter R., BA MSc PhD Prof.;
Chairman*
Simango, C., BSc MSc DPhil Sr. Lectr.
Other Staff: 4 Lectrs.

Medicine

Fax: (04) 251017
E-mail: medicine@healthnet.zw
Gangaidzo, T., BM BCh Oxf., MA Oxf. Assoc.
Prof.
Hakim, J. G., MB ChB Mak., MMed Nair.,
MMedSc Newcastle(UK), FRCP, FRCPEd
Assoc. Prof.; Chairman*
Matenga, J. A., FRCP Assoc. Prof.
Meikle, J., MB ChB Cape Town Assoc. Prof.
Ndhlovu, C. E., MMedSci, FRCP
Other Staff: 2 Lectrs.

Nursing Science

E-mail: nursing@medsch.uz.zw
Mapanga, K. G., PhD Chairman*
Other Staff: 9 Lectrs.

Obstetrics and Gynaecology

Tel: (04) 791631 Fax: (04) 794272
E-mail: obsgynpari@zol.co.zw
Chipato, T., MB ChB, FRCOG Sr. Lectr.
Chirenje, Z. M., BA Ohio, MD Liberia, FRCOG
Sr. Lectr.; Chairman*
Kasule, J., MB ChB Mak., MSc Lond., FRCOG,
FRCSEd Asst. Prof.
Other Staff: 10 Lectrs.; 2 Res. Fellows

Paediatrics and Child Health

E-mail: paediatrics@healthnet.zw
Bannerman, C., MB BS Lond. Sr. Lectr.
Chidede, O. S., MB ChB Birm. Sr. Lectr.
Choto, R. G. A. B., MD Lond., BA Sr. Lectr.
Kambarami, R. A., MB ChB Z'bwe. Chairman*
Nathoo, Kusum J., MB ChB Birm. Sr. Lectr.
Other Staff: 9 Staff Members

Pharmacy

Ball, D., BSc(Pharm) Natal, MSc Newcastle(UK),
PhD Newcastle(UK) Sr. Lectr.
Chagonda, L. S., BSc S.Leone, MSc Lough., PhD
Lough. Sr. Lectr.
Chagwedera, T. E., BSc S.Leone, MSc McG., PhD
Laval Assoc. Prof.
Gundidza, M. G., BSc Salf., MSc Strath., PhD
Nott. Assoc. Prof.
Munjeri, O. B., BPharm Sur., PhD Manc.
Lectr.; Chairman*
Other Staff: 2 Lectrs.

Physiology

E-mail: cmusabayane@hotmail.com
Mufunda, J., MB ChB Z'bwe.Open, PhD Mich.State
Assoc. Prof.
Parry, O., BSc Wales, PhD Wales Sr. Lectr.
Watt, A. J., BSc Aberd., PhD Aberd. Sr. Lectr.
Other Staff: 1 Lectr.

Psychiatry

Mutambirwa, J., BSc W.Ont., DPhil Z'bwe.Open
Sr. Lectr.; Chairman*

Sebit, M. B., MB ChB Cairo, MScMed Cairo, PhD
Nair. Sr. Lectr.
Other Staff: 4 Lectrs.

Rehabilitation

Tel: (04) 797800 Fax: (04) 797800
E-mail: rehab@medsch.uz.ac.zw
Madzivire, D., MSc N.Y. Sr. Lectr.;
Chairperson*
Other Staff: 6 Lectrs.; 5 Staff Members

Surgery

Fax: (04) 791995
E-mail: surgery@medsch.uz.ac.zw
Harid, A. C., MD Jerusalem, FACS Sr. Lectr.
Jonsson, K. M. D., PhD Prof.
Kalangu, K., MD Assoc. Prof.
Masanganise, R., MB ChB Z'bwe., FRCSEd Sr.
Lectr.
Mbuwayesango, B. A., MB ChB Z'bwe., MEd
Z'bwe. Chairman*
Muguti, G. I., MB BCh Rhodesia, MS Syd.,
FRCSEd, Hon. FRCS Prof.
Munyaradzi, O. M., MB ChB Natal, FRCSGlas,
FRCS Sr. Lectr.
Other Staff: 4 Lectrs.

VETERINARY SCIENCE

Fax: (04) 333683
E-mail: vetscience@vet.uz.ac.zw

Clinical Veterinary Studies

E-mail: clinvet@vet.uz.ac.zw
Bobade, P. A., MVM Glas., DVM Ib., PhD Ib.
Assoc. Prof.
Hill, F. W. Graham, BVetMed Lond., MA Melb.,
PhD Brist., DSc Z'bwe.Open Prof.
Stewart, R. J. E., BVSc Z'bwe., MVetSc Sask.
Chairman*
Other Staff: 10 Lectrs.

Paraclinical Veterinary Studies

Fax: (04) 333683
Bhebhe, E., BScAgric Z'bwe., MS Texas A.& M.,
PhD Texas A.& M.
Hove, T., MVSc Liv., PhD Copenhagen, DVM Sr.
Lectr.
Madekurozva, R. Chairperson*
Mohan, K., BVSc Panjab, PhD Mag. Prof.
Mukaratirwa, S., MVSc Liv., PhD Copenhagen,
DVM Prof.
Muvavarirwa, P., BVSc Z'bwe., MSc Sur. Sr.
Lectr.
Obwolo, M. J., BVM Nair., PhD Brist. Prof.
Other Staff: 2 Lectrs.; 1 Researcher

Preclinical Veterinary Studies

Fax: (04) 333683
E-mail: preclinical@vet.uz.ac.zw
Ruziwa, S. D., BVSc Z'bwe., MSc Edin.
Chairman*
Other Staff: 8 Lectrs.

SPECIAL CENTRES, ETC

Applied Social Sciences, Centre for

Tel: (04) 303306 Fax: (04) 307134
E-mail: cass@cass.org.zw
2 Lectrs.

Commercial Law Institute

Fax: (04) 304973
Tilbury, M. J., LLB Lond., BCL Oxf. Prof.; Dir.*
Other Staff: 2 Lectrs.

Computer Centre

Tel: (04) 307149 Fax: (04) 307149
E-mail: helpdesk@compcentre.uz.ac.zw
Hapanyengwi, G. T., BSc Z'bwe., MS Vanderbilt,
PhD Vanderbilt Dir.*

Continuing Health Education, Institute of

Tel: (04) 791631 Fax: (04) 724912, 704867
Nyazema, N. Z., BSc Ife, BSc Liv., PhD Liv.
Assoc. Prof.

Samkange, C. A., MA Birm., MB BChir Camb.,
FRCSEd Prof.
Other Staff: 1 Lectr.

Development Studies, Institute of

Fax: (04) 333341
E-mail: dpchimanikire@compcentre.uz.ac.zw
Chimanikire, Donald P., MA Kiev, MPhil PhD
Res. Fellow; Acting Dir.*
Moyo, S., BA S.Leone, MA PhD Assoc. Prof.
Other Staff: 2 Res. Fellows; 11 Staff Members

Development Technology Centre

Tel: (04) 334257 E-mail: rukuni@agric.uz.ac.zw
Rukuni, T., MSc Cran.IT Dir.*
Other Staff: 1 Lectr.

Electron Microscope Unit

E-mail: mufunda@physiol.uz.ac.zw
Mufunda, J., MB ChB Z'bwe.Open, PhD Mich.State
Acting Chairman*

Human Resources Research Centre

Tel: (04) 303271 Fax: (04) 302182
E-mail: f_zindi@hotmail.com
Zindi, F., BEd Lond., MA Lond., PhD Lond.
Prof.; Acting Dir.*

Legal Aid and Advice Scheme

Fax: (04) 304008 E-mail: vguni@law.uz.ac.zw
Guni, V. G., BALaw LLM DPhil Dir.*

Mining Research, Institute of

Tel: (04) 336416 Fax: (04) 336418
E-mail: imr@science.uz.ac.zw
Fernandes, T. R. C., BSc Lond., MPhil Z'bwe.Open
Prof.; Chairman*
Other Staff: 7 Lectrs.

Population Studies, Centre for

Tel: (04) 303211
E-mail: ravai@compcentre.uz.ac.zw
Marindo, R., PhD
Mhloyi, M., PhD Assoc. Prof.
Other Staff: 1 Lectr.

University Lake Kariba Research Station

Tel: (061) 3035 Fax: (061) 3035
E-mail: ulkrs@telco.co.zw
Chimbari, M. J., BSc NUL, PhD Copenhagen
Assoc. Prof.; Dir.*
Other Staff: 5 Res. Fellows

University Teaching and Learning Centre

E-mail: utlc@arts.uz.ac.zw
1 Sr. Res. Fellow
Vacant Posts: Dir.*

Women's Law Centre

Fax: (04) 745365-6
Stewart, Julie E., LLB Lond. Assoc. Prof.; Dir.*
Tsanga, A., LLB PhD Sr. Lectr.
Other Staff: 1 Lectr.

CONTACT OFFICERS

Academic affairs. Deputy Registrar
(Academic): Takawira, N., BA Z'bwe., MEd
(E-mail: ntakawira@esanet.zw)
Accommodation. Staff Development and
Welfare Officer: Mandizvidza, N. N., BA
Z'bwe.
Admissions (first degree). Senior Assistant
Registrar (Admissions (first degree)):
(vacant) (E-mail: maphosa@admin.com.zw)
Admissions (higher degree). Acting Assistant
Registrar (Admissions (higher degree)):
Lieto, J., BSc Z'bwe.
(E-mail: lietoj@admin.uz.ac.zw)
Adult/continuing education. Chairperson
(Adult/continuing education): Midzi, D.
D., BEd Z'bwe., MEd Manc.
(E-mail: ddmidzi@yahoo.com)
Alumni. Director, Public and International
Relations: Chihombori, D., MPA Z'bwe.,

BSc(PolAd) Z'bwe.
(E-mail: daniel@admin.uz.ac.zw)
Archives. Librarian: Mbambo, B. M., BSc(Soc)
Z'bwe., MSc Botswana
(E-mail: bmbambo@uzlib.uz.ac.zw)
Careers. Dean of Students: Mashiri, P., BA
Z'bwe., MPhil Z'bwe., DPhil Z'bwe.Open
(E-mail: pedzimash@yahoo.com)
Computing services. Deputy Bursar, Data
Processing: Ncube, F., BScCompSc NUST
Bulawayo (E-mail: fncube@admin.uz.ac.zw)
Consultancy services. Vice-Chancellor:
Nyagura, Prof. Levi M., BSc Lond., BSc
Rhodesia, MSc S.Af., PhD S.Illinois
(E-mail: lnyagura@admin.uz.ac.zw)
Credit transfer. Deputy Registrar (Academic):
Takawira, N., BA Z'bwe., MEd
(E-mail: ntakawira@esanet.zw)
Equal opportunities. Registrar: Chevo,
Sergeant M., BAdmin
(E-mail: registrar@admin.uz.ac.zw)
Estates and buildings/works and services.
Director (Estates and buildings/works and
services): Mhunduru, S.
(E-mail: works@admin.uz.ac.zw)
Examinations. Examinations Officer: Lieto, J.,
BSc Z'bwe. (E-mail: lietoj@admin.uz.ac.zw)
General enquiries. Registrar: Chevo, Sergeant
M., BAdmin
(E-mail: registrar@admin.uz.ac.zw)
Health services. Sister-in-Charge:
Makahamadze, V.
International office. Director, Public and
International Relations: Chihombori, D.,
MPA Z'bwe., BSc(PolAd) Z'bwe.
(E-mail: daniel@admin.uz.ac.zw)

Library (chief librarian). Librarian: Mbambo,
B. M., BSc(Soc) Z'bwe., MSc Botswana
(E-mail: bmbambo@uzlib.uz.ac.zw)
Marketing. Assistant to the Vice-Chancellor:
Mabeza, T. F., BA Z'bwe.
(E-mail: tmabeza@admin.uz.ac.zw)
Minorities/disadvantaged groups. Registrar:
Chevo, Sergeant M., BAdmin
(E-mail: registrar@admin.uz.ac.zw)
Ombudsman. Assistant Registrar: Ndoma, H.,
MPA Z'bwe., BSc
(E-mail: hndoma@admin.uz.ac.zw)
Personnel/human resources. Deputy Registrar
(Human Resources): Bhebhe, T. B., BA
Z'bwe., MEd Z'bwe.
(E-mail: tbhebhe@admin.uz.ac.zw)
Public relations. Assistant to the Vice-
Chancellor: Mabeza, T. F., BA Z'bwe.
(E-mail: tmabeza@admin.uz.ac.zw)
Publications. Publications Officer: Mtetwa, M.
S. (E-mail: mtetwam@admin.uz.ac.zw)
Purchasing. Buyer: (vacant)
Quality assurance and accreditation. Deputy
Registrar (Academic): Takawira, N., BA
Z'bwe., MEd (E-mail: ntakawira@esanet.zw)
Research. Senior Assistant Registrar: Makaza,
G., BAcc Z'bwe.
(E-mail: gmakaza@admin.uz.ac.zw)
Safety. Vice-Chancellor: Nyagura, Prof. Levi
M., BSc Lond., BSc Rhodesia, MSc S.Af., PhD
S.Illinois (E-mail: lnyagura@admin.uz.ac.zw)
Scholarships, awards, loans. Senior Assistant
Registrar (Scholarships, awards, loans):
Mawoza, M., BAdEd Z'bwe.
(E-mail: mawozam@admin.uz.ac.zw)

Schools liaison. Dean of Students: Mashiri, P.,
BA Z'bwe., MPhil Z'bwe., DPhil Z'bwe.Open
(E-mail: pedzimash@yahoo.com)
Security. Chief Security Officer: Tarambiwa,
M., BA Z'bwe.
(E-mail: tarambiwa@yahoo.com)
Sport and recreation. Sports Director:
(vacant)
Staff development and training. Staff
Development and Welfare Officer:
Bandama, G. F., BSc
(E-mail: gbandama@admin.uz.ac.zw)
Student union. Dean of Students: Mashiri, P.,
BA Z'bwe., MPhil Z'bwe., DPhil Z'bwe.Open
(E-mail: pedzimash@yahoo.com)
Student welfare/counselling. Dean of
Students: Mashiri, P., BA Z'bwe., MPhil
Z'bwe., DPhil Z'bwe.Open
(E-mail: pedzimash@yahoo.com)
Students from other countries. Deputy
Registrar (Academic): Takawira, N., BA
Z'bwe., MEd (E-mail: ntakawira@esanet.zw)
Students with disabilities. Co-ordinator,
Disabled Students: (vacant)
(E-mail: mundluli@yahoo.com)
University press. Director of Information and
Media: (vacant)
(E-mail: daniel@admin.uz.ac.zw)
Women. Registrar: Chevo, Sergeant M.,
BAdmin (E-mail: chevo@admin.uz.ac.zw)

[Information supplied by the institution as at 15 May
2006, and edited by the ACU]

ZIMBABWE OPEN UNIVERSITY

Founded 1999

Member of the Association of Commonwealth Universities

Postal Address: PO Box MP 1119, Mount Pleasant, Harare, Zimbabwe
Telephone: (04) 793002 **Fax:** (04) 251520 **E-mail:** information@zou.ac.zw
URL: http://www.zou.ac.zw/

VICE-CHANCELLOR*—Kurasha, Primrose, BBS Z'bwe., MBA Bridgeport, PhD Potchef.
PRO VICE-CHANCELLOR, ACADEMIC—Chimedza, Prof. Robert, PhD Mich.State
PRO VICE-CHANCELLOR, FINANCE AND ADMINISTRATION—Kaseke, Ruth, MBA Z'bwe.
REGISTRAR‡—Benza, Timothy E., MEd H-W
DIRECTOR, INFORMATION COMMUNICATION TECHNOLOGY—Kabanda, Gabriel, PhD
DIRECTOR, LIBRARY AND INFORMATION SYSTEMS—Maenzanise, Jasper L., BA Z'bwe., MIS S.Af.
DIRECTOR OF FINANCE—Ndekwere, Perpetual, MBA Z'bwe.
ACTING DEAN OF STUDENTS—Maunganidze, Davison, MSc Z'bwe.

GENERAL INFORMATION

History. The university's predecessor was the
Centre for Distance Education established in
1993, at the University of Zimbabwe.
Zimbabwe Open University was created from
the University College of Distance Education in
1999.
The main national centre is in Harare. The
university has ten regional centres representing
each of Zimbabwe's ten provinces.

Admission to first degree courses. General
entry requirements are five passes at GCE level,
including English. Some programmes (e.g.
agriculture and nursing science) may require a
diploma.

First Degrees (* = with honours). BA,
BAMS, BComA, BCom(B&F), BComF,
BComMkt, BEd, BMgt(HR), BMgt(ILR), BSc,
BSc(Psy), BSc(Psy)*, BSN.

Higher Degrees.
Master's. MBA, MEEAPPS.

Statistics. Students (2006–2007): total
21,423.

FACULTIES/SCHOOLS
Arts, Education and Humanities
Tel: (04) 251517 Fax: (040 251647
Acting Executive Dean: Chakanyuka, Shorai

Commerce and Law
Tel: (04) 793642 Fax: (04) 793678
Executive Dean: Magaramombe, Gideon, MSc

Science
Tel: (04) 795990 Fax: (04) 704167
Acting Executive Dean: Chitura, Miriam, MPH

ACADEMIC UNITS
Accounting
Eliachem, Shirichena, MBA   Chairperson*

Agriculture (Management)
Marume, U., MSc Z'bwe.   Programme Leader*

Arts
Muchena, Elliott, MA Sofia   Chairperson*

Banking and Finance
No staff at present

Business Administration, Master's in
Gona, F., MA Z'bwe.   Programme Leader*

Business Leadership
No staff at present

Counselling
Mafunga, B., MEd Z'bwe.   Programme Leader*

Educational Administration
Madziyire, Nelson C., MEd Z'bwe.Open   Subject
Co-ordinator

**Educational Administration, Planning
and Policy Studies**
Senah, A. K., MEd   Subject Co-ordinator*

**English and Communication, Applied
Linguistics and Literature in English**
Chitando, A., MA Z'bwe.   Programme Leader*

Geography and Environmental Studies

Sithde, N., MA   Programme Leader*

Health Science

Chitura, Miriam, MPH   Chairperson*

Human Resources

Bhobho, N., MBA   Programme Leader*

Instructional Technology

Vengesayi, Chesterfield K., MEd Z'bwe.Open
    Editor

Management and Business

Namusi, Cornelius, MPA Z'bwe.   Chairperson*

Marketing

Chitumba, R., MEcon Z'bwe., MSc   Programme
    Leader*

Physical Education and Sport

Kanhukamwe, Oliver, MEd   Programme
    Leader*

Postgraduate Studies

Chitumba, R., MA   Programme Leader
Jubenkanda, Roy, MA   Chairperson*

**Psychology, Special Education and
Counselling**

Chakachichi, D., MEd Z'bwe.   Programme
    Leader*

Religious Studies

Chirovamavi, M., MSc   Programme Leader*

Science, Mathematics and Technology

Graffen, Mutika   Programme Leader*

CONTACT OFFICERS

Academic affairs. Acting Registry Manager:
    Saumpindi, MA Z'bwe.
Alumni. Director, Information and Public
    Relations: Karonga-Mamire, Elizabeth, BA
International office. Chairman, International
    Relations and External Affairs: Chawawa,
    Morgen, DMin *Georgia State*
Library (chief librarian). Director, Library
    and Information Systems: Maenzanise,
    Jasper L., BA Z'bwe., MIS *S.Af.*
Marketing. Director: Mabika, O., BSc MBA

CAMPUS/COLLEGE HEADS

Bulawayo Region. (Tel: (09) 884053; Fax:
    (09) 70871) Regional Director: Ncube,
    Ndabezinhle J., MEd MBA DEd

Harare Region. (Tel: (04) 702762; Fax: (04)
    702703) Regional Director: Mutezo, Justina
    Z., BEd MSc
Manicaland Region. (Tel: (020) 67189; Fax:
    (020) 67196) Regional Director: Saruchera,
    Kenneth J., MEd
Mashonaland Central Region. (Tel: (071)
    7484; Fax: (071) 6653) Acting Regional
    Director: Majoni, Cuthbert, MEd
Mashonaland East Region. (Tel: (079) 22396;
    Fax: (079) 21570) Regional Director:
    Zinyama, M.
Mashonaland West Region. (Tel: (067)
    24050; Fax: (067) 23533) Regional
    Director: Nyajeka, Enock, MEd
Masvingo Region. (Tel: (039) 64965; Fax:
    (039) 64993) Regional Director: Chabaya,
    Raphinos A., MEd
Matabeleland North Region. (Tel: (09)
    60202; Fax: (09) 60197) Regional Director:
    Njini, Kalayi S., PhD *Lond.*
Matabeleland South Region. (Tel: (084)
    22965; Fax: (084) 22967) Regional
    Director: Nkala, Alan, MA
Midlands Region. (Tel: (054) 26002-3; Fax:
    (054) 26004) Regional Director:
    Mugwangi, Mberikunashe P., MEd

[*Information supplied by the institution as at 6 August
2007, and edited by the ACU*]

APPENDIX 2

INTER-UNIVERSITY BODIES

This section describes, for each of the Commonwealth countries that has one, the vice-chancellors' committee or corresponding body. The regional body for East Africa, and five provincial or inter-provincial bodies in Canada are also included here.

Universities Australia

GPO Box 1142, Canberra, ACT, Australia 2601
Street Address: Australian Universities Centre, 1 Geils Court, Deakin, ACT, Australia 2600
Telephone: (02) 6285 8100 **Fax:** (02) 6285 8211 **E-mail:** contact@universitiesaustralia.edu.au
URL: http://www.universitiesaustralia.edu.au

Chair—Larkins, Prof. Richard G., AO, BS *Melb.*, MD *Melb.*, PhD *Lond.*, Hon. LLD *Melb.*, FRACP, FRCP, FRCPI,
    FAMS, Hon. FRCP, Hon. FACP (Vice-Chancellor and President, Monash University)
Chief Executive Officer*—Withers, Glenn, AO, BEc *Monash*, AM *Harv.*, PhD *Harv.*, FASSA
Director, Policy and Analysis—Magarry, Angela, BHealthAdmin *NSW*, MPolSt *NSW*, FCHSE
Director, Communication and Government Relations—Harris, Rebecca, BA *Syd.*, PhD *W.Syd.*
Director, International Relations—Moore, Ainslie, BComms *Canberra*
Director, National Staff Development and Training Program—Scott, Susan, BA *Monash*, MEd(T&D) *NE*

Mission

Universities Australia is the peak industry body representing the
nation's universities and a global brand recognised for knowledge
excellence. Universities Australia will influence policy and advocate for
the benefit of all member universities. It will provide appropriate
collective services for members and will seek acceptance and respect by
stakeholders for performance of this role as the authoritative voice for
Australian universities.

Universities Australia will build constructive relationships across the
higher education sector, with governments, industry, professions and
the broader community nationally and internationally.

In general Universities Australia will reflect the values common to its
members. Universities Australia upholds the following key values:
Discover (Investigate, examine and analyse new and better ways of
helping universities contribute to national and global goals. Identify the
shared goals of members and articulate and promote them.); Learn
(Observe, organise and understand the environment around higher
education and aspire to deploy knowledge to advance the mission of
universities. Forge relationships to exchange knowledge that will
advance universities and their contributions.); Lead (Represent, unify
and support university members by influencing debates, inspiring
confidence in the sector, and enhancing the opportunities for
universities to fulfil their goals.)

Membership

Universities Australia represents 38 of Australia's universities in the
public interest, both nationally and internationally.

[Information supplied by the institution as at 19 May 2008, and edited by the ACU]

Association of Universities of Bangladesh

House No 47, Road 10/A, Dhanmondi R/A, Dhaka 1209, Bangladesh
Telephone: (02) 812 6101 **Fax:** (02) 812 6101 **E-mail:** aub@bangla.net

Chairman—Ahmed, Prof. M. Farid, MBA *Nagoya*, MCom *Dhaka*, PhD *Nagoya* (Vice-Chancellor, Bangladesh Open
    University)
Executive Secretary*—Saifuddin, Prof. Sheikh M., BA *Dhaka*, MA *Dhaka*

Mission

The aims of the Association are to foster and promote the cause of
higher education in Bangladesh, and to this end the Association
performs such things as are deemed fit to promote the interests and
well-being of the universities of Bangladesh.

Membership

The AUB comprises the following 28 public universities of Bangladesh:
University of Dhaka; University of Rajshahi; Bangladesh Agricultural
University; Bangladesh University of Science and Technology;
University of Chittagong; Jahangirnagar University; Islamic University
of Bangladesh; Shahjalal University of Science and Technology; Khulna
University; National University; Bangladesh Open University;
Bangabandhu Sheikh Mujibur Rahman Agricultural University;
Bangabandhu Sheikh Mujib Medical University; Sher-e-Bangla
Agricultural University; Patuakhali Science and Technology University;
Hajee Mohammad Danesh University of Science and Technology;
Mawlana Bhashani Science and Technology University; Dhaka U. E. T.;
Rajshahi U. E. T.; Bangladesh U. E. T.; Khulna U. E. T.; Chittagong U.
E. T.; Noakhali Science and Technology University; Jagannath
University; Comilla University; Jatio Kobi Kazi Nazrul Islam University;
Chittagong Veterinary and Animal Science University, Sylhet
Agricultural University.

A university is admitted to membership by a resolution adopted by
the Association. The private universities of Bangladesh are not eligible
for membership.Each university is represented by its vice-chancellor
and two other persons (usually deans of faculties and senior
professors), each to be nominated by the academic council of the
university for a period of two years. The term of office of the
president and treasurer expire with the calendar year.

[Information supplied by the institution as at 20 April 2008, and edited by the ACU]

Association of Universities and Colleges of Canada

350 Albert Street, Suite 600, Ottawa, Ontario, Canada K1R 1B1

Telephone: (613) 563 1236 **Fax:** (613) 563 9745 **E-mail:** info@aucc.ca **URL:** www.aucc.ca

Chair—Traves, Prof. Thomas D., BA Manit., MA York(Can.), PhD York(Can.), Hon. Dr Umeå (President and Vice-Chancellor, Dalhousie University)
President and Chief Executive Officer*—Morris, Claire, BA Tor., MSocWk Tor., Hon. LittD New Br., Hon. LLD T.Rivers

Mission

The association is the voice of Canada's universities. It represents 92 Canadian public and private not-for-profit universities and university degree level colleges.

Since 1911 the AUCC has provided strong and effective representation for its members, in Canada and abroad. Its mandate is to facilitate the development of public policy on higher education and to encourage co-operation among universities and governments, industry, communities, and institutions in other countries. Services to member universities are in three main areas: public policy and advocacy; communications, research and information sharing; scholarships and international programs.

Membership

Membership of the association ranges from small, undergraduate liberal arts institutions to large, urban multi-campus universities offering a broad selection of undergraduate, graduate and professional programmes.

The AUCC provides university leaders and their institutions with a supportive network as well as opportunities for collective action. Its links to member universities extend beyond university presidents to senior academic, administrative officers and faculty, either individually or through their own national organisations. Many of these national organisations are also AUCC associate members and share in a regular information exchange.

[Information supplied by the institution as at 23 April 2008, and edited by the ACU]

Association of Atlantic Universities

Suite 403, 5657 Spring Garden Road, Halifax, Nova Scotia, Canada B3J 3R4

Telephone: (902) 425 4230 **Fax:** (902) 425 4233 **E-mail:** info@atlanticuniversities.ca
URL: http://www.atlanticuniversities.ca

Chair—Fontain, Yvon, BScSoc Moncton, LLB Moncton, LLM Tor., MA Paris I
Executive Director*—Halpin, Peter

Mission

Established in 1964, the Association is a voluntary association of the universities and colleges in the Atlantic region and in the West Indies, which offer programmes leading to a degree or have degree-granting status.

The AAU represents the interests of universities across the region, ensuring public visibility for the important role they play in preparing future leaders of our communities, in path-breaking research and innovation, and in contributing to the economic prosperity of life in Atlantic Canada. It provides a forum where university executive heads reflect, consult and collaborate on all aspects of the whole university; define common objectives and positions; develop strategies to promote, collectively and co-operatively, the highest ideals of post-secondary education; and exercise leadership to promote the objectives of the collective.

Membership

The following 17 Atlantic universities and colleges, plus the University of the West Indies, are currently members of the Association: Acadia University, Atlantic School of Theology, Cape Breton University, Dalhousie University, Memorial University of Newfoundland, Mount Allison University, Mount Saint Vincent University, Nova Scotia Agricultural College, Nova Scotia College of Art and Design University, Saint Mary's University, St Francis Xavier University, St Thomas University, Université de Moncton, Université Sainte-Anne, University of King's College, University of New Brunswick, and University of Prince Edward Island. Each institution is represented by its executive head.

[Information supplied by the institution as at 6 August 2008, and edited by the ACU]

Conference of Rectors and Principals of Quebec Universities

500, rue Sherbrooke Ouest, Bureau 200, Montréal, Québec, Canada H3A 3C6
Street Address: Montréal, Québec, Canada

Telephone: (514) 288 8524 **Fax:** (514) 288 0554 **E-mail:** daniel.zizian@crepuq.qc.ca
URL: http://www.crepuq.qc.ca

President—Munroe-Blum, Heather, OC, BA McM., BSW McM., MSW *W.Laur.*, PhD *N.Carolina*, FRSCan (Principal and Vice-Chancellor, McGill University)
Director-General*—Zizian, Daniel, LicenDroit *Montr.*, MBA *Montr.*

Mission
The Conference's main objective is to provide a forum where university administrators can reflect, consult and collaborate on all aspects of university life, define common objectives and positions and develop strategies to preserve university autonomy and academic freedom and to enhance performance and quality. To support this effort, the CREPUQ staff carries out research and administers services for the benefit of its members.

Membership
All of Quebec's universities.

[Information supplied by the institution as at 30 April 2008, and edited by the ACU]

Council of Nova Scotia University Presidents

Suite 403, 5657 Spring Garden Road, Halifax, Nova Scotia, Canada B3J 3R4

Telephone: (902) 425 4230 **Fax:** (902) 425 4233

Chair*—Traves, Prof. Thomas D., BA *Manit.*, MA *York(Can.)*, PhD *York(Can.)*, Hon. Dr *Umeå* (President and Vice-Chancellor, Dalhousie University)

Mission
The objectives of the Council are: to work for the improvement of higher education in Nova Scotia; to exercise leadership in matters concerning post-secondary education; to promote co-operation and inter-university planning among those institutions listed in the membership; to be the channel of collective communication between the universities and the government, as well as between the universities and the Nova Scotia Advisory Board on Colleges and Universities and other bodies or individuals. The Council will make or recommend appointments to national, regional and provincial bodies as required.

Membership
The presidents of the 11 degree-granting institutions in Nova Scotia: Acadia University, Atlantic School of Theology, Cape Breton University, Dalhousie University, University of King's College, Mount Saint Vincent University, Nova Scotia Agricultural College, NSCAD University, Université Sainte-Anne, St Francis Xavier University and Saint Mary's University.

[Information supplied by the institution as at 20 May 2008, and edited by the ACU]

Council of Ontario Universities

180 Dundas Street West, 11th Floor, Toronto, Ontario, Canada M5G 1Z8
Telephone: (416) 979 2165 **Fax:** (416) 979 8635 **E-mail:** jgrass@cou.on.ca **URL:** http://www.cou.on.ca

Chair—George, Peter, CM, BA *Tor.*, MA *Tor.*, PhD *Tor.*, DLitt *Nipissing*, LLD *Tor.*, Hon. DU *Ott.*, Hon. DHC *Mexico Natnl.Polytech.* (President and Vice-Chancellor, McMaster University)
President and Chief Executive Officer*—Genest, Paul, BA *Guelph*, MA *Ott.*, MA *Johns H.*, PhD *Johns H.*

Mission
The Council is an advocacy, communications and research organisation representing the collective interests of its 18 member institutions and two associate members. It is the mandate of the Council to provide leadership on issues facing Ontario's provincially assisted universities, to promote the contribution of higher education to the province of Ontario, and to meet public policy expectations of greater accountability, financial self-reliance, diversity of educational opportunity, and responsiveness to education and marketplace needs, while supporting institutions' traditional rights of autonomy and self-regulation.

Membership
Eighteen universities and two associate members.

[Information supplied by the institution as at 28 April 2008, and edited by the ACU]

Council of Western Canadian University Presidents

Simon Fraser University, Burnaby, British Columbia, Canada V5A 1S6

Telephone: (778) 782 4641 **Fax:** (778) 782 4860 **E-mail:** stevensn@sfu.ca **URL:** http://www.sfu.ca/pres/

Chair*—Stevenson, Prof. Michael, BA *Witw.*, MA *Mich.*, PhD *Northwestern* (President and Vice-Chancellor, Simon Fraser University)

Mission
The Council provides a forum for communication among university presidents on common problems and to address issues in higher education that are unique to Western Canada.

Membership
The chief executive officers of university institutions in Western Canada: University of Alberta, Athabasca University (Alberta), Brandon University (Manitoba), University of British Columbia, University of Calgary (Alberta), Concordia University College of Alberta, Emily Carr University of Art and Design (British Columbia), First Nations University of Canada (Saskatchewan), University of the Fraser Valley (British Columbia), King's University College (Alberta), University of Lethbridge (Alberta), University of Manitoba, University of Northern British Columbia, University of Regina (Saskatchewan), Royal Roads University (British Columbia), Collège universitaire de Saint-Boniface (Manitoba), University of Saskatchewan, Simon Fraser University (British Columbia), Trinity Western University (British Columbia), Vancouver Island University (British Columbia), University of Victoria (British Columbia), University of Winnipeg (Manitoba).

[Information supplied by the institution as at 4 July 2008, and edited by the ACU]

Inter-University Council for East Africa

PO Box 7110, Kampala, Uganda
Street Address: East African Development Bank Building, Plot 4, Nile Avenue, Kampala, Uganda, East Africa

Telephone: (041) 256251-2 **Fax:** (041) 342007 **E-mail:** info@iucea.org **URL:** http://www.iucea.org/

Chairperson—Mbwette, Prof. Tolly S. A., BSc(Eng) *Dar.*, MSc *Dar.*, PhD *Lond.* (Vice-Chancellor, Open University of Tanzania)
Executive Secretary*—Nyaigotti-Chacha, Prof. Chacha, PhD *Yale*, BEd MA MPhil

Mission
The vision of the IUCEA is to become an effective regional advocate and catalyst for the strategic development and management of higher education in East Africa. Its mission is to co-ordinate, facilitate and encourage stakeholders so as to promote strategic, sustainable and competitive development of the higher education sector in East Africa.

Membership
IUCEA membership currently consists of 54 public and private universities and university colleges distributed within Kenya, Tanzania and Uganda. Members include the following: African Nazarene University, Ardhi University, University of Arusha, Bugema University, Busitema University, Busoga University, University of Dar es Salaam, Daystar University, University of Dodoma, Catholic University of Eastern Africa, University of Eastern Africa, Baraton, Egerton University, Gulu University, Hubert Kairuki Memorial University, International Medical and Technological University, Islamic University in Uganda, Jomo Kenyatta U. A. T., Kabarak University, Kampala University, Kampala International University, Kenya Methodist University, Kenyatta University, Kiriri Women's U. S. T., Kyambogo University, Lugazi University, Masinde Muliro U. S. T., Makerere University, Maseno University, Mbarara U. S. T., Mkwawa University, Moi University, Moshi University, Muhimbili University College of Health Sciences, Muslim University Morogoro, Mzumbe University, University of Nairobi, Ndejje University, Nkumbe University, Ruaha University, Open University of Tanzania, St. Augustine University of Tanzania, St. John's University, St. Paul University, Scott Theological College, Sokoine University of Agriculture, Strathmore University, Tumaini University, Uganda Christian University, Uganda Martyrs University, United States International University, State University of Zanzibar, Zanzibar University.

[Information supplied by the institution as at 25 April 2008, and edited by the ACU]

Vice Chancellors Ghana

PO Box 25, Legon, Accra, Ghana
Telephone: (021) 512415 **Fax:** (021) 512409 **E-mail:** vcg@ug.edu.gh

Chairman—Anamuah-Mensah, Prof. Jophus, BScEd *Cape Coast*, BSc(Chem) *Cape Coast*, MSc *Cape Coast*, MA *Br.Col.*, EdD *Br.Col.*
Executive Secretary*—Kaba, Peter, BA *Cape Coast*, MPhil *Devel.Studies(Ghana)*

Mission

The aim of the Committee, which came into being in 1965, is to provide a consultative forum for the heads of university institutions in Ghana to discuss and find solutions to problems of common interest to their institutions as well as build tertiary education capacity in Ghana. Decisions of the Committee are in the form of recommendations to the governing bodies of the member institutions. Its non-statutory status is being changed with its registration as a Trust and the appointment of Trustees.

Membership

The vice-chancellors of the six public universities are the members of the VCG and in attendance are the Registrars and Finance Officers of the six public universities i.e. University of Ghana, Legon, University of Cape Coast, University of Education, Winneba, University for Development Studies, Tamale, Kwame Nkrumah University of Science and Technology, Kumasi, University of Mines and Technology, Tarkwa.

[*Information supplied by the institution as at 17 October 2006, and edited by the ACU*]

Association of Indian Universities

AIU House, 16 Comrade Indrajit Gupta Marg (Kotla Marg), New Delhi 110 002, India
Telephone: (011) 2323 6105 **Fax:** (011) 2323 2131 **E-mail:** aiu@bol.net.in **URL:** http://www.aiuweb.org

President—Pathan, Prof. A. M., BSc *Karn.*, MSc *Karn.*, PhD *B'lore.* (Vice-Chancellor, Maulana Azad National Urdu University)
Secretary General*—Dongaonkar, Prof. Dayanand G., MB BS *Marath.*, MS(Ortho) *Mumbai*

Mission

The Association provides liaison between the universities and central and state governments and co-operates with other universities and bodies (national and international) in matters of common interest in the field of higher education. It also acts as the representative of Indian universities at various forums in India and abroad.

Membership

Indian universities, institutions 'deemed to be universities', and institutions of national importance; also universities from neighbouring countries as 'associate members' and inter-university organisations as 'associate organisations'. The present membership totals 286 (plus three associate members from Nepal, Mauritius and Bhutan).

[*Information supplied by the institution as at 25 April 2008, and edited by the ACU*]

New Zealand Vice-Chancellors' Committee

PO Box 11-915, Manners Street, Wellington, New Zealand
Street Address: 11th floor, 94 Dixon Street, Wellington
Telephone: (04) 381 8500 **Fax:** (04) 381 8501 **E-mail:** penny@nzvcc.ac.nz **URL:** http://www.nzvcc.ac.nz

Chair—Field, Prof. Roger J., BSc *Hull*, PhD *Hull* (Vice-Chancellor, Lincoln University)
Executive Director*—Fenwick, Penny R., MA *Cant.*

Mission

The Committee provides administrative machinery for the formulation and implementation of policies on any matters where collective action is considered to be to the advantage of the eight universities, both internally among themselves, and externally when a collective viewpoint is needed. The Committee is also a useful and important forum for the exchange of views on all aspects of university development. The Committee has statutory powers with respect to

quality assurance in universities, entrance to universities and administration of scholarships.

Membership

The vice-chancellors of the eight universities in New Zealand.

[*Information supplied by the institution as at 15 April 2008, and edited by the ACU*]

Committee of Vice-Chancellors of Nigerian Universities

PMB 12002, 3, Idowu Taylor Street, Victoria Island, Lagos 12022, Nigeria
Telephone: (01) 261 2425

Chairman—Nwanze, Prof. Emmanuel A. C., BSc *Ib.*, MSc *Warw.*, PhD *Warw.* (Vice-Chancellor, University of Benin)
Secretary-General*—Abdullahi, Prof. Musa, BA *A.Bello*, MA *Kent*, MA *Chic.*, PhD *Chic.*

Mission
The objectives of the Committee are: (a) to provide a focus of academic leadership through bold initiatives in higher education in Nigeria with particular reference to the roles of universities; (b) to act as a channel through which the joint opinion of Nigerian universities on any matter affecting higher education in Nigeria is expressed; (c) to study, comment and make recommendations on proposals, legislation, regulations or rules affecting universities in Nigeria; (d) to act as a bureau of information and to facilitate communication and mutual consultation among the universities; (e) to co-operate with organisations that have similar aims and objectives and to protect the interests of Nigerian universities; (f) to organise, sponsor or promote conferences, seminars, workshops, lectures, colloquia and symposia on

higher education, particularly in Nigeria; (g) to provide a platform for discussing common problems such as inter-university co-operation, administrative and academic practices, maintenance of academic standards, staff recruitment, physical exchange and student affairs; (h) to serve as a forum for collaboration with the National Universities Commission (NUC) and federal government on matters concerning university education; (i) to do all such other lawful things as are necessary for the attainment and furtherance of these objectives.

[Information supplied by the institution as at 24 November 2006, and edited by the ACU]

Vice-Chancellors' Committee of Pakistan

Sector H-9, Islamabad, Pakistan
Telephone: (051) 444 8369 **Fax:** (051) 925 7505 **E-mail:** chairman@hec.gov.pk **URL:** http://www.hec.gov.pk

Chairman—Siddiqi, Mazhar ul Haq, BA *Sindh*, MSc *Quaid-i-Azam* (Vice-Chancellor, University of Sindh)
Executive Director, Higher Education Commission*—Naqvi, Prof. S. Sohail H., BSc *Purdue*, MSc *Purdue*, PhD *Purdue*

Mission
The Committee is an advisory body for the promotion of higher education in Pakistan.

Membership
The vice-chancellors of all the 59 state-funded and 56 privately chartered universities/institutes of Pakistan are the members of the Committee.

[Information supplied by the institution as at 4 June 2008, and edited by the ACU]

Higher Education South Africa

PO Box 27392, Sunnyside, Pretoria, 0132 South Africa
Telephone: (012) 481 2842 **Fax:** (012) 481 2843 **E-mail:** admin@hesa.org.za **URL:** http://www.hesa.org.za

Chairperson—Eloff, Theuns, BA(Law) *Potchef.*, MA(Theology) *Potchef.*, PhD *Potchef.* (Vice-Chancellor, North-West University)
Chief Executive Officer*—Malaza, Prof. Duma, BSc *Fort Hare*, MSc *Brown*, PhD *Camb.*

Mission
HESA seeks to be the unified body of leadership in a transforming, dynamic and diverse system of higher education through: promoting and exercising proactive transformation, leadership and expertise for the sector and the country; addressing, through its members, national development imperatives; positioning higher education at the centre of knowledge production, research and development and innovation strategies; building and developing links with international organisations in higher education; and providing value-added services to its members.

Membership
Membership of the organisation is open to all South African public higher education institutions. Representation of these sectors had previously been through two statutory bodies, the South African Universities Vice-Chancellors Association (SAUVCA) for universities, and the Committee of Technikon Principals (CTP) for universities of technology (formerly technikons). HESA currently consists of the vice-chancellors of all 23 public higher education institutions within the borders of South Africa.

[Information supplied by the institution as at 25 April 2008, and edited by the ACU]

Committee of Vice-Chancellors and Directors (Sri Lanka)

University of Kelaniya, Dalugama, Kelaniya, Sri Lanka
Telephone: (01) 291 4474 **Fax:** (01) 291 1485 **E-mail:** academicest@kin.ac.lk

Chairman—Wijeyaratne, Prof. M. J. S., BSc *S.Lanka*, MSc Mich., PhD *S.Lanka*, FNAS(SL), FIBiol(SLanka) (Vice-Chancellor, University of Kelaniya, Sri Lanka)
Executive Secretary* —Ranasinghe, A. P., BSc *S.Lanka*, MSc Birm.

Mission

The principal aims of the Committee are: (a) to serve as an inter-university organisation; (b) to make recommendations to the University Grants Commission (UGC), in an advisory capacity, regarding the formulation and adoption of schemes of recruitment and promotion for all categories of staff and any other matters relating to the internal management of the universities; (c) to act as a bureau of information and to facilitate communication, co-ordination and consultation among universities; (d) to act as an intermediary between the universities and international universities and institutions in furtherance of common interests; (e) to act as the representative of the university system in Sri Lanka in international organisations; (f) to promote and safeguard the principle of university autonomy; (g) to promote, facilitate and monitor the maintenance of quality education in the university system in Sri Lanka; (h) to promote activities relating to staff development; (i) to advise the UGC on matters such as recruitment schemes, staff welfare, salaries and emoluments; (j) to co-ordinate and process applications for fellowships and scholarships referred to the committee by national and international agencies and donors, and to represent the universities' interests in the UGC committee on scholarships, fellowships and other awards; (k) to advise and assist universities on matters relating to student counselling, student participation in university governance, student welfare, careers guidance, bursaries, loans and other financial assistance to students; (l) to advise the UGC on matters of academic administration such as the rationalisation of university faculties, departments and courses; (m) to assist in securing the recognition in Sri Lanka and abroad of degrees, diplomas and other academic distinctions awarded by the universities and other higher education institutions; (n) to assist in the obtaining of information relating to degrees, diplomas, etc awarded by universities and other higher education institutions in Sri Lanka.

Membership

The vice-chancellors of the universities of Sri Lanka: Buddhist and Pali University (associate member); Buddhasravaka Bhiksu University (associate member); University of Colombo; Eastern University; University of Jaffna; University of Kelaniya; University of Moratuwa; Open University of Sri Lanka; University of Peradeniya; Rajarata University of Sri Lanka; University of Ruhuna; Sabaragamuwa University of Sri Lanka; South Eastern University of Sri Lanka; University of Sri Jayewardenepura; Wayamba University of Sri Lanka; University of the Visual and Performing Arts; and Uva Wellassa University of Sri Lanka.

[*Information supplied by the institution as at 21 April 2008, and edited by the ACU*]

Universities UK

Woburn House, 20 Tavistock Square, London, England WC1H 9HQ
Telephone: (020) 7419 4111 **Fax:** (020) 7388 8649 **E-mail:** info@universitiesuk.ac.uk
URL: http://www.universitiesuk.ac.uk

President—Trainor, Prof. Richard H., BA Brown, MA Oxf., MA Prin., DPhil Oxf., FRHistS, AcSS, FKC (Principal, King's College London)
Chief Executive* —Warwick, Baroness Diana, BA Lond., Hon. DLitt Brad., Hon. PhD Open(UK), Hon. PhD Lond., Hon. DUniv Open(UK), Hon. DSSc Lond., FRSA

Mission

The mission of Universities UK is to be the essential voice and the best support for a vibrant successful and diverse sector, to influence and create policy for higher education, and to provide an environment where the interests of its sector can flourish. UK Universities works to deliver its mission by: providing members with foresight on policy issues and helping them shape the agenda; mounting effective and timely advocacy campaigns on policy issues vital to the sector; promoting the achievements of the sector and thereby securing support for continued investment; being recognised as having excellent and effective communication with decision makers, stakeholders and the media, and with members and their institutions; collaborating with other sector bodies and where necessary coordinate sector-wide activities; regularly reviewing our effectiveness and organisation to ensure it remains fit for purpose, well managed and supportive of our staff.

Membership

Universities UK has 132 members and 5 associate members. All vice-chancellors or principals of the universities in the United Kingdom are eligible for membership.

[*Information supplied by the institution as at 5 August 2008, and edited by the ACU*]

APPENDIX 3

COMMONWEALTH OF LEARNING

Postal Address: 1055 West Hastings St, Suite 1200, Vancouver, British Columbia, V6E 2E9 Canada

Telephone: (604) 775 8200 **Fax**: (604) 775 8210 **E-mail**: info@col.org **WWW**: http://www.col.org
Chair of the Board of Governors—Whiteman, The Hon. Burchell, OJ
President and Chief Executive Officer*—Daniel, Sir John, BA Oxf., MA Sir G.Wms., DèsSc Paris XI, Hon. DLitt NS Open

Senior Staff

Alluri, Krishna, BSc Osm., BSc AP Ag., MSc AP Ag., PhD
  Philippines Educational Specialist, Food Security and
  Environment
Clarke-Okah, Willie, MA Brock, PhD McGill Education
  Specialist, Higher Education and Policy Development
Fehr, Helena M., BA Br.Col., MA S.Fraser Board Secretary and
  Gender Officer
Ferreira, Frances J. Education Specialist, Basic Education and
  Open Schooling
Kanwar, Prof. Asha S., MA Panjab, MPhil Panjab, DPhil Sus. Vice-
  President and Programme Dir.
Kapoor, Malay, BA Delhi, MA Delhi Human Resources and
  Contracts Manager
Kwan, Angela, BA Chinese HK, MBA Leic. Learning Manager,
  International Organisations
Lee, Anna Information Technology Manager
Lee, Raymond H., BA Br.Col. Accounting and Payroll Manager
Mackintosh, Wayne Education Specialist, eLearning and ICT
  Policy
Mallet, Joshua C., BEd Winneba, BA Benin Education Specialist,
  Learning and Livelihoods
McEachern, Doris B., BSc New Br. Dir., Finance, Administration
  and Human Resources
Munro, Tanyss Education Specialist, Governance
Pringle, Ian Education Specialist, Media
West, Paul G., MBA Dir., Knowledge Management and
  Information Technol.
Wilson, David R., BCom Br.Col. Communications Manager

Commonwealth Educational Media Centre for Asia (New Delhi)
Samdup, Pema E., PhD JNU Programme Officer
Sreedher, R. Dir.*
Tetri, Dalip K., BA Panjab, MA HP Head, Administration and
  Finance
Vemraju, Rukmini, BSc Baroda, MCJ Osm. Programme Officer

Profile

The Commonwealth of Learning (COL) was set up by
Commonwealth governments in September 1988, to promote
collaboration in distance education. In proposing the creation of
this new institution, heads of government stated that its
objectives would be to widen access to education, share
resources, raise educational quality, and support the mobility of
ideas, of teaching, of relevant research and of people. 'Our
long-term aim is that any learner, anywhere in the
Commonwealth, shall be able to study any distance teaching
programme available from any bona fide college or university in
the Commonwealth.'

The purpose of COL, as defined under its 'memorandum of
understanding', is to create and widen access to opportunities
for learning, by promoting co-operation between universities,
colleges and other educational institutions throughout the
Commonwealth, making use of the potential offered by
distance education and by the application of communication
technologies to education. The agency's activities aim to
strengthen member countries' capacities to develop the human
resources required for their economic and social development,
and give priority to those developmental needs to which
Commonwealth co-operation can apply.

The organisation has provided a wide range of services to
many Commonwealth countries, especially those that are less
well endowed, small and in great need of increasing
educational access to their people. These services have made a
significant impact in the orientation and thinking of policy-
makers in the area of educational provision. Through
demonstrations, advice, training and the exchange of materials
and information, COL has been able to sensitise educational
planners to the advantageous ways in which both tested and
emerging communication technologies can be applied to
enhance learning opportunities.

Background

Proposals for COL grew out of the work of the Commonwealth
Standing Committee on Student Mobility. The committee
realised that the rapid developments in communications
technology offered the potential for Commonwealth universities
and colleges to share their resources, and thus to complement
the established programmes of staff and student mobility. In
the light of the committee's reports, Commonwealth heads of
government in 1985 asked the Commonwealth secretary-
general to 'explore the scope for new Commonwealth
initiatives in open learning'. He, in turn, brought together a
group of eminent educators and others from across the
Commonwealth under the chairmanship of Lord Briggs of
Lewes. Their proposals for a Commonwealth institution to
promote co-operation in distance education were endorsed by
heads of government in 1987. Work on the detailed structure
of the new institution by a group chaired by Dr. J. S. Daniel,
led to the formal establishment of COL as an independent
international organisation by means of a 'memorandum of
understanding' between governments in September 1988.

COL is governed by a board of governors which is
representative of all parts of the Commonwealth. The
Commonwealth secretary-general and the president of COL sit
on the board as ex-officio members. The first chairman was the
Rt. Hon. Lord Briggs of Lewes. Professor James A. Maraj was
appointed in January 1989 as the founding president. In
January 1994, former president of York University (Canada),
Dr. H. Ian Macdonald, was appointed chairman, and in
September 1995 the former director of the Open Learning
Institute of Hong Kong (now the Open University of Hong
Kong) took up duties as president and chief executive officer.
On 28 April 2003, Mr. Lewis Perinbam was appointed chair of
COL's board of governors, COL's third chair. And on 1 June
2004, Sir John Daniel, former UNESCO Assistant Director
General for Education and Vice-Chancellor of the Open
University (UK), became COL's third president and chief
executive officer.

COL was launched with pledged funds from Commonwealth governments amounting to some £15 million for its first five years. In addition, the institution seeks funds from donor agencies of all kinds in order to finance individual projects and programmes. Canada, India, Nigeria, New Zealand, Britain and Australia continue to provide sustaining financial support, while about 30 other Commonwealth member states also contribute to core funding.

Activities

The fundamental mission of the COL is to promote the development of human resources through the application of distance teaching techniques and technologies, in response to the developmental needs of member countries – Open and Distance Learning for Development. The focus of COL's work is in developing Commonwealth countries. The organisation supports the development and use of the entire spectrum of communication technologies, from print materials to satellite transmission, in order to expand learning opportunities. Activities are principally in three areas.

First, COL encourages and arranges the sharing of distance-teaching materials and supports the development of new materials to meet identified educational needs. In these ways it assists institutions in extending the range of their courses, raising quality, and making more economic use of their resources.

Second, it helps to support institutions through staff training, improved communications, an information service about distance education, and programmes of evaluation and research.

Third, it plans to assist institutions to provide better services to students, improve study support systems, facilitate the

> The Commonwealth of Learning does not enrol individual students. It works with colleges and universities that can enrol students, and so enables these to tap into each other's resources. It does not teach students directly.

transfer of course credits between Commonwealth institutions and develop telecommunications networks.

COL's programmes cover open and distance learning (ODL) policy, systems development, applications and knowledge resources.

In seeking to achieve these goals, COL works closely with a range of institutions and organisations. It contracts out services as required, encouraging regional programmes, and seeks to pool and share techniques and distance-teaching experiences of benefit to all participating member countries.

Model-building is also an important aspect of COL's work. The Commonwealth Educational Media Centre for Asia (CEMCA), located in New Delhi, was established by COL in 1994 to promote co-operation and collaboration in technical applications among educational institutions and media organisations. It also serves as a regional resource centre, facilitating the exchange of audio/video productions. Work is progressing on the establishment of a similar centre for Africa.

Responding to other expressed needs, COL is developing distance education curriculum material in fields such as environmental engineering, technical/vocational education and training and teacher education—where existing materials are not available or not particularly suitable—and is developing copyright protocols for the transfer, use and adaptation of materials that do exist.

Headquarters

COL's headquarters is in Vancouver, Canada. Much of the institution's work is, however, decentralised. Thus, the development of materials is carried out largely by the staff of Commonwealth universities and colleges under contract. Its information services network draws on the strengths available from other institutions and databases.

COL also works regionally where it can, both through existing regional institutions and by itself promoting the development of regional activity where appropriate.

Further information

Information about the current activities of COL is available at www.col.org or from the communications office at the Vancouver address.

APPENDIX 4

COMMONWEALTH SCHOLARSHIP AND FELLOWSHIP PLAN

Origin

On the opening day of the Eighth Quinquennial Congress of Commonwealth Universities at Montreal in early September 1958, Sidney Smith, former president of the University of Toronto and then Canadian minister for external affairs, delivered a speech stressing the importance of developing educational links between Commonwealth countries. Later that month the Commonwealth Trade and Economic Conference met in the same city, and it was from that conference that there emerged the proposal to establish a new scheme of Commonwealth scholarships and fellowships. The purpose and operation of the scheme were elaborated at the First Commonwealth Education Conference, held at Oxford in July 1959, and the first Commonwealth Scholars took up their awards in 1960.

Aims

The Commonwealth Scholarship and Fellowship Plan (CSFP) was created to enable Commonwealth students of high intellectual promise to pursue studies in Commonwealth countries other than their own so that on their return home they could make a distinctive contribution to life in their own countries and to mutual understanding in the Commonwealth.

Operation

After a period of some decline in the 1990s, the number of host countries is once again increasing. Awards are currently on offer in Australia, Botswana, Canada, Ghana, India, Jamaica, Malaysia, Malta, Mauritius, New Zealand, South Africa, Trinidad and the United Kingdom, although in some cases awards are only available to citizens of certain countries. The sixteenth Conference of Commonwealth Education Ministers, which took place in Cape Town in December 2006, endorsed proposals for further expansion.

Between Commonwealth Education Conferences there is no single authority exercising central control over the Plan's operation. Each member country of the Commonwealth and each dependency or state associated with such a member has designated an agency (the 'Commonwealth Scholarship agency') which draws up the list of recommended candidates from its country and nominates them direct to the agency in the awarding country.

Agencies in countries offering awards have of course the dual function of nominating candidates to other awarding countries on the one hand; and of receiving nominations from other countries and selecting and placing candidates for its own awards.

The addresses of the Commonwealth Scholarship agencies are given below.

There are two main types of award: Commonwealth Scholarships and Commonwealth Fellowships.

Commonwealth Scholarships

These are intended mainly for postgraduate study by course work or research at university, or for clinical training in medicine. Awards are not for the purpose of acquiring professional qualifications. In addition, awards for undergraduate study can be made to students from countries in which there are no universities.

Each awarding country determines the value of its own awards and gives details in a prospectus which it circulates to the Commonwealth Scholarship agency inthe countries which are invited to nominate candidates. The following allowances are regarded as basic: fares to and from the awarding country for the Scholar (but not usually for spouse or dependants); approved fees; personal maintenance allowances; contributions towards apparatus and (if necessary) special clothing; contributions towards approved travel expenses within the awarding country. In some countries a marriage and child allowance may be paid.

An individual candidate must apply to the Commonwealth Scholarship agency in his/her own country (see list, below); awarding countries do not accept applications directly from candidates.

Scholarships may be held in any academic discipline, subject to such restrictions as the awarding or nominating countries may impose. A recent development, piloted in both Canada and the United Kingdom, has been the introduction of Commonwealth Scholarships by distance learning. These are restricted to specific master's degrees offered by a range of UK universities and have separate selection arrangements. Further information can be obtained from the relevant section of the CSFP website (see below).

Commonwealth Fellowships

Fellowships are offered primarily in the United Kingdom and are available each year to enable academic staff in universities in the developing Commonwealth to receive training and experience so as to increase their usefulness as teachers in their own universities. The Fellowships are primarily intended for fully qualified members of staff and not available for study towards a degree or diploma. The awards are for periods of study of six months.

Nomination for Commonwealth Fellowships should be initiated by the head of the candidate's university. Since 2002, the Professional Fellowships Programme has allowed those in key professions other than academic life to undertake short visits of approximately three months to the United Kingdom. Nominations for these awards are made by an appropriate host organisation in the UK.

Special categories of award

In the UK there are also a number of Commonwealth Scholarships available for work-related study by more junior university staff, which may include study for a higher degree in any academic discipline. These awards are intended to enhance the experience and training of locally-born members of staff in universities of developing Commonwealth countries.

In addition, the UK offers split-site scholarships, awarded for twelve months' research in the United Kingdom as part of a doctorate undertaken at a developing Commonwealth institution. Nomination for these awards should be initiated by the head of the candidate's university or by nominating agencies.

What the Plan has achieved

Over 25,000 individuals have now held awards under the Plan. The proportion of awards taken up by women has risen from 10% in 1962 to 43% in 2005–2006. The Plan has played a significant part in meeting the manpower needs of the developing countries of the Commonwealth, and has come to occupy an important role in the educational life of the Commonwealth. The impact of Scholars and Fellows in the development of their respective countries is graphically illustrated in a tracer study of UK award holders, conducted in 2000, and the first ever Directory of Commonwealth Scholars and

COMMONWEALTH SCHOLARSHIPS

The table below shows the number of awards (scholarships and fellowships) held by awarding country in the year 2005/06.

Home Country	Australia	Botsw.	Can.	Ind.	Jam.	Malaysia	Malta	Maurit.	NZ	Trin. & Tob.	UK	Total
ANGUILLA			1									1
ANTIGUA AND BARBUDA			1								1	2
AUSTRALIA											44	44
BAHAMAS			2			1						3
BANGLADESH			9	4		5			2		79	99
BARBADOS			2						1		3	6
BELIZE			1						1		1	3
BOTSWANA			3						1		14	18
BRUNEI DARUSSALAM						2						2
CAMEROON			3								8	11
CANADA				1		1			7		46	55
CAYMAN ISLANDS											1	1
CYPRUS			3						1		1	5
DOMINICA									2	1	2	5
FIJI			2						2		5	9
GAMBIA			1			2					7	10
GHANA			8	8					1		39	56
GRENADA			1									1
GUYANA			5	4					4		6	19
INDIA			19			1			1		140	161
JAMAICA			5						1		11	17
KENYA			3	10					2		144	159
LESOTHO			1								5	6
MALAWI			3						3		29	35
MALAYSIA			3								9	12
MALDIVES			5	9		2			2		5	23
MALTA			2			1					1	4
MAURITIUS			3	2					2		14	21
MONTSERRAT			2				1				1	4
MOZAMBIQUE											2	2
NAMIBIA				10		2					10	22
NEW ZEALAND			2								15	17
NIGERIA		1	13						1	1	42	58
PAKISTAN			7			3					55	65
PAPUA NEW GUINEA			1								4	5
SAINT LUCIA			3						5		3	11
SAINT VINCENT AND THE GRENADINES			3			1					1	5
SAMOA			1						1			2
SEYCHELLES											2	2
SIERRA LEONE			3						1		15	19
SINGAPORE			4								2	6
SOLOMON ISLANDS						1			1		1	3
SOUTH AFRICA		1	8						3		94	106
SRI LANKA			5	11					2		13	31
SWAZILAND			2			1					8	11
TANZANIA			5	13				1	2		62	83
TRINIDAD AND TOBAGO			3						3		8	14
UGANDA			5	1							25	31
UNITED KINGDOM	3		40	4	1				18			66
VIRGIN ISLANDS (BRITISH)			3								1	4
ZAMBIA			2	4		1					66	73
ZIMBABWE			3	2							9	14
Total	3	2	201	83	1	24	1	1	70	2	1,054	1,442

* UK awards to Australia are through the institution rather than the national agency.

Fellows, 1960–2002, published in 2003. It shows that the overwhelming majority have returned to their home countries, and provides literally hundreds of examples of alumni who have reached senior roles in all walks of life, including a significant number of Vice Chancellors and other heads of university institutions in different parts of the Commonwealth. This study is the first element in a wider programme to develop a Commonwealth-wide network of alumni, which has also resulted in the launch, in April 2000, of the CSFP Alumni Association. Further details of the Association are available from the CSFP website, or by email to alumni@cscuk.org.uk.

Further sources of information

Information about all awards offered throughout the Plan can be accessed on the CSFP website at www.csfp-online.org.

(*a*) Reports of the Commonwealth Education Conferences, the first of which was held in 1959 and thereafter at three-yearly intervals. (*b*) Reports on the Commonwealth Scholarship and Fellowship Plan issued by the Commonwealth Secretariat (frequency varies—annually until 1976 and since 1980 and trienially since 1993). The latest report covers the period from 2003–2006. (*c*) Annual Reports, where issued, of countries participating in the Plan, *e.g.* of the Commonwealth Scholarship Commission in the United Kingdom. The latest eight Reports of the Commission can be accessed on the CSFP website (details above).

Commonwealth Scholarship Agencies

Except where stated above candidates must apply to the agency in their own country and not to the agency in the awarding country. Agency addresses are listed below.

Anguilla: Department of Public Administration, Government of Anguilla, James Ronald Webster Building, PO Box 60, The Valley, Anguilla (Permanent Secretary)

Antigua: Ministry of Education, Government Complex, Queen Elizabeth Highway, St John's, Antigua and Barbuda, West Indies (Permanent Secretary)

Australia (developed countries): Development Implementation Branch IDP Education Australia Ltd., GPO Box 2006, Canberra, ACT 2601, Australia (Manager: Ms Anna Kent)

Australia (developing countries) Australian Agency for International Development (AusAID), GPO Box 887, Canberra, ACT 2601, Australia (Director General)

Bahamas: Ministry of Education and Culture, Scholarships and Loans Division, PO Box N3913, Nassau, NP, The Bahamas (Permanent Secretary)

Bangladesh: Ministry of Education, Building No. 6, 17th & 18th Floor, Bangladesh Secretariat, Dhaka, Bangladesh (Ms Syeda Salma Jafreen)

Barbados: Ministry of Education, Youth Affairs and Sports, 'The Elsie Payne Complex', Constitution Road, St Michael, Barbados (Permanent Secretary)

Belize: Office of Governance, First Floor, Administration Building, Belmopan, Belize, Central America (Permanent Secretary)

Bermuda: Ministry of Education and Development, PO Box HM 1185, Hamilton HM EX, Bermuda (Chief Education Officer)

Botswana: Department of Student Placement and Welfare, Ministry of Education, P/Bag 0079, Gaborone, Botswana (Secretary)

British Virgin Islands: Ministry of Education and Culture, BVI Government, Central Administration Complex, Road Town, Tortola, British Virgin Islands (Permanent Secretary)

Brunei Darussalam: Kementerian Pendidikan Ministry of Education, Bandar, Seri, Begawan BB3510, NEGARA, Brunei Darrusalam (Permanent Secretary)

Cameroon: Cameroon Commonwealth Scholarship Agency, Ministry of Higher Education, Department of Students' Assistance and University Welfare, PO Box 1457, Yaounde, Cameroon

Canada: Canadian Bureau for International Education, 220 Laurier Avenue West, Suite 1550, Ottawa, Ontario KIP 5Z9, Canada (Ms Jennifer Humphries)

Cayman Islands: Education Department, PO Box 910, George Town, Grand Cayman, Cayman Islands (Senior Education Officer)

Cyprus (Greek Cypriots): Cyprus State Scholarship Foundation, PO Box 23949, 1687, Nicosia, Cyprus (Secretary)

Cyprus (Turkish Cypriots): 3 Museum Street, PO Box 25654, 1387, Nicosia, Cyprus (Dilek Behcetogullany)

Dominica: Ministry of Education, Youth Affairs, Sports and Human Resource Development, Government Headquarters, Kennedy Avenue, Roseau, Dominica, West Indies (Permanent Secretary)

Falkland Islands: Education Department, Falkland Islands Government, Stanley Cottage, Ross Road, Stanley, Falkland Islands (Director of Education)

Fiji: Workforce Planning and Scholarship Unit, Public Service Commission, Berkeley Crescent, PO Box 2211, Government Buildings, Suva, Fiji (Secretary)

The Gambia: Scholarship Advisory Board, Department of State for Education, Willy Thorpe Place Building, Banjul, The Gambia (Mr Madi Jatta)

Ghana: Scholarships Secretariat, PO Box M-75, Ministry Branch Post Office, Accra, Ghana (Registrar)

Gibraltar: Department of Education and Training, 40 Town Range, Gibraltar (Director)

Grenada: Department of Human Resources, Prime Minister's Office, Botanical Gardens, Tanteen, St George's, Grenada (Permanent Secretary)

Guyana: For Permanent Secretary, Public Service Ministry, Training Division, Vlissengen Road and Durban Street, Georgetown, Guyana (Mr Artie Harricharan)

India (inward): Ministry of Human Resource Development, Department of Secondary Education & Higher Education, Government of India, New Delhi 110 001, India (Director (Scholarships))

India (outward): Indian Council for Cultural Relations, Bhavan, Indraprastha Estate, New Delhi 110 002, India (Director General)

India (UGC): University Grants Commisson, Bahadurshah Zafar Marg, New Delhi 110 002, India (Secretary)

Jamaica (inward): Cabinet Office, Public Sector Reform Unit, Corporate Management and Development Branch, Scholarships and Assistance Unit, JAMPRO Building, 2nd floor, 18 Trafalgar Road, Kingston 10, Jamaica (Director)

Jamaica (outward): Ministry of Education, 2 National Heroes Circle, PO Box 498, Kingston, Jamaica (Permanent Secretary)

Kenya: Ministry of Education, Science and Technology, Harambee Avenue, PO Box 30040, Nairobi, Kenya (Permanent Secretary)

Kiribati: Ministry of Education, Training and Technology, PO Box 263, Bikenibeu, Tarawa, Kiribati (Secretary)

Lesotho: The National Manpower Development Secretariat, PO Box MS 517, Maseru 100, Lesotho (Director)

Malawi: Department of Human Resource Management and Development, PO Box 30227, Lilongwe 3, Malawi (Secretary)

Malaysia: Public Service Department Malaysia, Training Division, Level 4-6, Block C1 and C2, Federal Government Administrative Centre, 62510 W.P. Putrajaya, Malaysia (Director)

Maldives: Department of External Resources, Ministry of Foreign Affairs, Male, Maldives (Director, Ms Arninath Didi)

Malta: Commonwealth Scholarships and Fellowships Board, Ministry of Education, Floriana, Malta (Secretary, Ms Annabelle Vassallo)

Mauritius: Ministry of Education and Human Resources, IVTB House, Pont Fer, Phoenix, Mauritius (Permanent Secretary)

Montserrat: Department of Administration, Government Headquarters, Brades, Montserrat, West Indies (Permanent Secretary)

Mozambique: Minister of Education and Culture, Maputo, Mozambique (Mr Miguel Inacio)

Namibia: Ministry of Education, POB 23053, Windhoek, Namibia (Permanent Secretary)

Nauru: Department of Education, Nauru, Central Pacific (Secretary)

New Zealand: New Zealand Vice-Chancellors' Committee, PO Box 11-915, 11th floor, 94 Dixon Street, Wellington 6034, New Zealand (Scholarships Manager, Ms Kiri Manuera)

Nigeria: Federal Scholarship Board, Federal Ministry of Education, Plot 245, Samuel Ademulegan Street, Wuse Zone 6, PMB 134, Garki-Abuja, FCT Nigeria (Deputy Director)

Pakistan: Ministry of Education, Islamabad, Pakistan (Deputy Educational Adviser (Scholarships))

Papua New Guinea: Department of Personnel Management, PO Box 519, Waigani, Papua New Guinea (Secretary)

Seychelles: Ministry of Education, Mont Fleuri, PO Box 48, Mahe, Seychelles (Principal Secretary (Education))

Sierra Leone: Ministry of Education Science and Technology, New England, Freetown, Sierra Leone (Chief Education Officer)

Singapore: Prime Minister's Office, Public Service Division, 100 High Street, #07-01, The Treasury, Singapore 179 434 (Permanent Secretary)

Solomon Islands: Ministry of Education and Human Resource Development, PO Box G28, Honiara, Solomon Islands (Permanent Secretary)

South Africa: Higher Education South Africa - HESA, PO Box 27392, Sunnyside, Pretoria 0132, South Africa (Ms Jana van Wyk)

Sri Lanka: Ministry of Education Higher Education Division, 18 Ward Place, Colombo 07, Sri Lanka (Secretary)

St Helena: Education Department, Jamestown, St Helena, South Atlantic Ocean (Chief Secretary, Mr John Styles)

St Kitts & Nevis: Establishment Division, Government of St Kitts & Nevis, Church Street, PO Box 186, Basseterre, St Kitts & Nevis, West Indies (Permanent Secretary)

St Lucia: Ministry of Education, Human Resource Development, Youth and Sports, Francis Compton Building, The Waterfront, Castries, St Lucia, West Indies (Dr Didacus Jules)

St Vincent and the Grenadines: Service Commissions Department, Ministerial Building, Halifax Street, Kingstown, St Vincent and the Grenadines, West Indies (Mr Bernard Morgan)

Swaziland: Swaziland Government, Ministry of Public Service and Information, PO Box 170, Mbabane, Swaziland (Principal Secretary)

Tanzania: Ministry of Science, Technology and Higher Education, PO Box 2645, Dar es Salaam, Tanzania (Permanent Secretary)

Tonga: Ministry of Education, Community Development & Training Centre, PO Box 161, Nuku'alofa, Tonga (Ms Ilaise Tongilava-Kupu)

Trinidad and Tobago: Ministry of Public Administration and Information, Scholarships and Advanced Training Section, National Library Building, Corner Hart and Abercromby Streets, Port of Spain, Trinidad and Tobago (Permanent Secretary)

Turks and Caicos: Staff Training Unit, South Base, Grand Turk, Turks and Caicos, West Indies (Training Manager)

Tuvalu: Personnel and Training Department, Office of the Prime Minister, Funafuti, Tuvalu (Deputy Secretary)

Uganda: The Central Scholarships Committee (CSC), Ministry of Education and Sports, Embassy House, PO Box 7063, Kampala, Uganda (Permanent Secretary)

United Kingdom: Commonwealth Scholarship Commission in the United Kingdom, Woburn House, 20-24 Tavistock Square, London WC1H 9HF, United Kingdom (Executive Secretary)

Vanuatu: Training and Scholarships Coordination Unit, Ministry of Education, PMB 9059, Port Vila, Vanuatu, South Pacific (Senior Scholarships Officer)

Western Samoa: Staff Training and Scholarships Committee, Ministry of Foreign Affairs, PO Box L1859, Apia, Western Samoa (Secretary)

Zambia: Bursaries Committee, Ministry of Education, PO Box 50093, Lusaka, Zambia (Secretary)

Zimbabwe: Ministry of Higher Education, PO Box UA275, Union Avenue, Harare, Zimbabwe (Secretary for Higher Education)

Information compiled by the secretariat of the Commonwealth Scholarship Commission in the United Kingdom as at 1 February 2007 and edited by the ACU

INDEXES

INDEX TO INSTITUTIONS

The contents of the Yearbook are listed at the beginning of each volume.

This is a selective index to institutions and organisations named in the Yearbook. Where appropriate, the letters a, b and c are used to indicate the first, second and third columns of each page, and the abbreviated name of the university in whose chapter a particular institution appears is included.

The index does not attempt to include all the references that there may be to every institution or organisation mentioned in the book. For example, references in 'national introductions' are not indexed.

Centres, institutes, etc, which form an integral part of a university are individually indexed only if they have a distinctive name. For example, there are index entries for the John Deutsch Institute for the Study of Economic Policy at Queen's University at Kingston (but not for its Centre for International Relations) and for the Scottish Inst. for Residential Child Care at the University of Strathclyde (but not for its Centre for the Study of Public Policy). However all colleges, centres, institutes, etc, which have an independent existence but are also constitutents of, or associated with, the universities are entered by name in this index, whether or not they have a distinctive title. Institutions affiliated to universities in Bangladesh, India and Pakistan are indexed only by locality, under 'Bangladesh colleges located at', 'Indian colleges located at', etc.

Chhatarpur 737c
Chhaygaon 747c
Chhindwara 737c
Chhota Udepur 751b
Chidambaram 827c
Chikhaldara 905a
Chikhali 905a
Chikiti 703b
Chikodi 813b
Chilakaluripet 665a
Chilumuru 665a
Chimakurthi 665a
Chincholi 755c
Chintalapudi 673b
Chirala 665a
Chirmiri 757c
Chitaguppa 755c
Chitayala 878b
Chittapur 755c
Chittiguduru 665a
Chittor 799c
Chittorgarh 860c
Chodavaram 673b
Chopda 869b
Chousala 733c
Choutuppal 878b
Chowari 768c
Chowdavaram 665a
Chunkankadai 857c
Chunni Kalan (Fatehgarh Sahib) 688b
Churachandpur 855c
Cochin 838b
Coimbatore 932c, 934a
Coondapur 844b
Courtallam 857c
Cuddalore 827c
Cumbum 665a, 861c
Cuttack 945c
Dabhoi 751b
Dabhra 757c
Daboh 802c
Dabok 860c
Dabra 802c
Dabugaon 703b
Dahihanda 905a
Dahiwel 869b
Dahod 751b, 918b
Dakha 884b
Dakor 751b
Dakshin 747c
Dalu 872c
Damoh 738a
Damua 738a
Dandeli 813c
Daramali 766b
Darapur 905a
Darsi 665a
Darwha 905a
Daryapur 905a
Dasuya 884b
Datia 802c
Daudhar (Moga) 688b
Daulatpur Chowk 768c
Debalpur 727a
Debari 860c
Deedwana 836b
Deenapur 665a
Deesa 766b
Degana 836b
Dehgam 751b
Dehradoon 910c
Dehri 768c
Delhi 759b
Demow 729c
Deogaon 733c
Deogarh 902b
Deogarh (Barkote) 902b
Deogarh (Budhapal) 902b
Deogarh (Kalla) 902b
Deogarh (Kansar) 902b
Deogarh (Passama) 902b
Deogarh (Reamal) 902b
Deoli 836b
Deomornoi 747c
Deoral 751b
Deori 738a
Deosar 687c
Dera Bassi 894b
Dera Bassi (Patiala) 688b
Dergaon 729c
Deshmukh 799c
Desuri 836b
Deulgaon Raja 905a
Devarapalli 673b
Devendra Nagar 738a
Deverkonda 878b
Devershigihalli 813c
Devgadh-Baria 751b
Devsthali 820a
Dhaba 905a

Dhahan Kaleran (Nawan Shahar) 688b
Dhakuakhana 729c
Dhaliara 768c
Dhama 902b
Dhamangaon 905a
Dhamnod 727a
Dhampur 841a
Dhand Dadwana (Kaithal) 820b
Dhandhuka 751b
Dhanera 766b
Dhanpuri 687c
Dhansura 766b
Dhar 727a
Dharamgarh 902b
Dharamjaygarh 757c
Dharamkot 884b
Dharampuri 727a
Dharamsala 768c
Dharangaon 869b
Dhari 910c
Dhariyavad 860c
Dharmanagar 943c
Dharmapuri 673b, 934a
Dharmpuri 805c
Dharni 905a
Dharugapuram 857c
Dharur 733c
Dharwad 813c
Dhekiajuli 747c
Dhemaji 729c
Dhenkanal 945c
Dhing 747c
Dholka 751c
Dhoraji 910c
Dhorimanna 836b
Dhrangadhra 910c
Dhrol 910c
Dhubri 747c
Dhudike 884b
Dhule 869b, 918c
Dhupdhara 747c
Dibrugarh 729c
Digapahandi 703b
Digboi 730a
Diggi Malpura 836b
Digras 905a
Dikrong 730a
Dindigul 861c, 830b, 934a
Diu 910c
Doboka 747c
Dolgoma 747c
Dondaicha 869b
Doom Dooma 730a
Doraha 884b
Draksharama 673b
Dudhnoi 747c
Duduka 902b
Duggirala 665a
Duliajan 730a
Dumiyani 910c
Dumpagadapa 673b
Dumrai 738a
Dungarpur 860c
Dunguripali 902b
Dura 703b
Dusarbid 905a
Dwarka 910c
Dwarka Tirumala 673b
East Godavari 799c
Edacochin 838b
Edat 809b
Edathala 838b
Edathua 838b
Edlapadu 665a
Edugundlapadu 665a
Elamanchili 673b
Ellenabad 820b
Eluru 673b
Erandol 869b
Ernakulam 838b
Erode 934a
Erumeli 838b
Etawah 718c
Etcherla 673b
Ettumanoor 838b
Faizpur 869b
Fakiragram 747c
Falna 836b
Faridabad 759b, 834a
Faridabad (Ballabgarh) 834b
Faridabad (Hodal) 834b
Faridabad (Hodel) 834b
Faridabad (Tigaon) 834b
Faridkot 688b, 894b
Faridpur 841a
Farrukhabad 718c
Fatehabad 820b
Fatehgarh Sahib 894b
Fatehnagar 860c
Fatehpur 718c

Fatehpur-Pundri 820b
Fatepura 751c
Fatikroy 943c
Fazilka 884c
Ferozepur 884c
Ferozepur Cantt 884c
Ferozepur City 884c
Gadag 813c
Gadikota 665a
Gadwal 878b
Gairatganj 701c
Gaisilate 902b
Gajapathinagaram 673b
Gajendragad 813c
Gajraula 841a
Gallegry 703b
Ganapavaram 673c
Gandepalli Mandal 673c
Ganderbal 816c
Gandhigram 830b
Gandhinagar 751c
Gangapur 733c
Gangapura 836b
Gangavathi 755c
Ganj Basoda 701c
Ganjam 703b
Gannavaram 665b
Gantyada 673c
Gargaon 730a
Garhakota 738a
Garhdiwala 884c
Garhshankar 884c
Gartad 869b
Garuvu 673c
Gauripur 747c
Gavrai 733c
Gazipur 718c
Gevrai 733c
Ghanpur 805c
Ghansawangi 733c
Gharaunda 820b
Gharghora 757c
Ghatanji 905a
Ghatol 860c
Ghatprabha 813c
Ghaziabad 759b
Ghess 902b
Ghilamora 730a
Ghumarwin 768c
Ghumusar Udayagiri 703b
Ghusiya 910c
Ghuwara 738a
Giddaluru 665b
Gidderbaha 884c
Girgadhada 910c
Goalpara 747c
Godavarikhani 805c
Godhara 766b
Godhra 751c, 918c
Gogunda 860c
Gohad 802c
Gohpur 747c
Gokak 813c
Gokarna 813c
Gokavaram 673c
Golaghat 730a
Gollalamamidada 673c
Gollaprolu 673c
Golokganj 747c
Gondal 910c
Gondala 703b
Goniana Mandi 894b
Gonikoppal 844b
Gopalapatnam 673c
Gopalapuram 673c
Gopaldham (Ta. Jasdan) 910c
Gopalpur (Ludhiana) 688b
Gopalpur-on-Sea 703b
Gopannapalem 673c
Goraimari 747c
Goreswar 747c
Gorpar 757c
Gossaigaon 747c
Gouripatnam 673c
Govindapalli 703b
Gozaria 766b
Gudari 703c
Guddimalani 836b
Gudigeri 813c
Gudivada 665b
Gudiyatham 827c
Gudlavalleru 665b
Gulabpura 836b
Gulbarga 755c
Guledgudda 813c
Guna 803a
Gungoti 733c
Gunnayyanagar 673c
Guntur 665b, 799c
Gunupur 703c

Gurandi 703c
Gurazala 665b
Gurdaspur 764c
Gurgaon 759b, 834b
Gurgaon (Budhera) 834b
Gurgaon (Farukh Nagar) 834b
Gurgaon (Firozpur Zhirka) 834b
Gurgaon (Jatauli-Hailey Mandi) 834b
Gurgaon (Manesar) 834b
Gurgaon (Nagina) 834b
Gurgaon (Panchgaon) 834b
Gurgaon (Sidhrawali) 834b
Gurgaon (Sohna) 834b
Gurh 687c
Guru Teg Bahadur Garh 884c
Gurumitkal 756a
Gurusar Sadhar 884c
Guwahati 747c
Gwalior 803a
Hagaribommanhalli 756a
Hajo 747c
Haleangady 844b
Haliyal 813c
Hallikhed 756a
Halol 751c
Halvad 910c
Hamirpur 714b, 768c
Hanamkonda 805c
Handwara 816c
Hangal 813c
Hansi 820b
Hanumana 687c
Harda 701c
Hardibazar 757c
Hardoi 718c
Hariana 884c
Haridwar 719a
Haripur 768c
Harpalpur 738a
Harrai 738a
Harsud 727a
Harugeri 813c
Hasoud 757c
Hatichong 747c
Hatidhura 747c
Hatta 738a
Hatundi 836b
Haunsbhavi 813c
Haveri 813c
Hebbal 814a
Hebri 844b
Heduva-Rajgar 766b
Himmatnagar 766b
Hinjilicut 703c
Hirakud 902b
Hiramandalam 673c
Hirekerur 814a
Hireroogi-Bolegaon 814a
Hisar 820b
Hisar (Agroha) 834b
Hittanahalli-Tanda 814a
Hiwarkhed 905a
Hiwra (Ashram) 905a
Hiyanglam 855c
Hiyangthang 855c
Hojai 747c
Holealur 814a
Honnavar 814a
Hoovinahadagali 756a
Horti 814a
Hoshangabad 701c
Hoshiarpur 688b, 884c
Hospet 756a
Howly 747c
Hubli 814a
Hukkeri 814a
Humnabad 756a
Hunasagi 756b
Hungund 814a
Huzoornagar 878b
Huzurabad 805c
Hyderabad 800a, 878b
Ibrahimpatnam 665b
Ichapuram 673c
Ichhawar 701c
Idar 766b
Ilkal 814a
Imphal 855c
Indi 814a
Indora 768c
Indore 727a, 918c
Inkollu 665b
Iragavaram 673c
Ismailabad (KKR) 820b
Israna (Panipat) 820b
Itanagar 872c
Itarsi 701c
Jabera 738a
Jadcherla 879a
Jafrabad 733c

Jagadhri 820b
Jagannathprasad 703c
Jagara 747c
Jagatsinghpur 946a
Jaggaiahpet 665b
Jaggampeta 673c
Jagiroad 747c
Jagraon 884c
Jagtial 805c
Jaijaipur 757c
Jaipatna 902b
Jaisalmer 836b
Jaisinagar 738a
Jaitaran 836b
Jaithane 869c
Jajpur 946a
Jalah 747c
Jalalabad 841a, 884c
Jalandhar 688b, 764c
Jalandhar Cantt 764c
Jalaun 714b
Jalgaon 869c, 918c
Jalgaon Jamod 905a
Jalna 733c
Jalore 836b
Jamadarhat 747c
Jami 673c
Jamjodhpur 910c
Jamkandoran 910c
Jamkhambhaliya 910c
Jamkhandi 814a
Jammikunta 805c
Jammu 797b
Jamnagar 910c
Jamner 869c
Jamugurihat 747c
Jandiala 764c
Janeh 687c
Jangaon 805c
Jangareddigudem 673c
Janjgir 757c
Jarud 905c
Jasapar (Ta. Jasdan) 910c
Jasdan 910c
Jashpurnagar 757c
Jatara 747c
Jawa 687c
Jayal 836b
Jaysinghnagar 687c
Jetpur 910c
Jewargi 756b
Jeypore 703c
Jhabua 727c
Jhadol 860c
Jhajjar 834b
Jhajjar (Badli) 834b
Jhajjar (Bahadurgarh) 834b
Jhajjar (Dubaldhan) 834b
Jhajjar (Dujana) 834b
Jhalod 751c
Jhanji 730a
Jhansi 714c, 719a
Jharsuguda 902b
Jharsuguda (Bijapali) 902b
Jharsuguda (H-Kantapali) 902b
Jharsuguda (Kirmira) 902b
Jharsuguda (Kulabira) 902b
Jharsuguda (Kumarbandh) 902b
Jharsuguda (Laikera) 902b
Jillellamudi 665b
Jind 820b
Jirania 943c
Jiribam 855c
Jiwan Nagar (Sirsa) 820b
Jobat 727c
Jodhpur Nadi (Morbi) 911a
Joginder Nagar 768c
Jogipet 879a
Jonai 730a
Jora 803a
Jorhat 730a
Jowai 872c
Junagadh 911a
Junagarh 902b
Junnerdeo 738a
Juria 747c
Kaalol (Panchmahal) 751c
Kabisuryanagar 703c
Kachla 841a
Kada 733c
Kadapa 800a
Kadayanallur 934a
Kadi 766b
Kaduthuruthy 838b
Kagwad 814b
Kaij 733c
Kaikachhar 757c
Kaikaluru 665b
Kailashahar 943c
Kaithal 820b

Kakanpur 751c
Kakching 855c
Kakching-Khunou 855c
Kakinada 673c
Kakkanadu 838b
Kala Amb. 768c
Kalabari 747c
Kalady 838c
Kalag 747c
Kalahandi 902b
Kalahandi (Belkhandi) 902b
Kalahandi (Biswanathpur) 902b
Kalahandi (Borda) 902b
Kalahandi (Dharamgarh) 902b
Kalahandi (Golamunda) 902b
Kalahandi (Kalampur) 902b
Kalahandi (Karlapara) 902b
Kalahandi (Koksara) 902b
Kalahandi (M. Rampur) 902b
Kalahandi (Risida) 902b
Kalairdia 747c
Kalamassery 838c
Kalamb 905b
Kalavai 827c
Kalgachia 747c
Kalghatgi 814b
Kalimela 703c
Kalka 820b
Kallakurichi 827c
Kallam 733c
Kallianpur 844b
Kallikulam 857c
Kalloli 814b
Kalluru 805c
Kalol, Gandhinagar 751c
Kalvad 911a
Kalyanpura 766b
Kamalanagar 756b
Kamalapur 756b
Kamalpur 943c
Kamareddy 879a
Kamargaon 905b
Kamatagi 814b
Kamavarapukota 673c
Kampli 756b
Kampur 747c
Kanagala 665b
Kanamaadagu 756b
Kancheepuram 827c, 934a
Kanchikacherla 665b
Kandhala Jattan 884c
Kandukuru 665b
Kandulapuram 665b
Kanglatongbi 855c
Kangpokpi 855c
Kangra 768c
Kanhangad 809b
Kanigiri 665b
Kanjirappally 838c
Kankroli 860c
Kannad 734a
Kannauj 719a
Kannur 809c
Kanod 860c
Kanpur City 719a
Kanpur (Dehat) 719a
Kanpur Nagar 719b
Kansa 766b
Kantabanji 902b
Kantamal 902b
Kantepudi 665b
Kanth 841a
Kanumalla 665b
Kanumolu 665b
Kanuru 800a
Kanyakumari 934b
Kapadwanj 751c
Kapasan 860c
Kapurthala 764c
Karaikal 887c
Karaikkal 948c
Karajgaon 905b
Karamsad 908c
Karamsar Rara Sahib 884c
Karanja (Lad) 905b
Karatagi 756b
Karera 803a
Kargil 816c
Karilcode 838c
Karimnagar 805c, 800a
Karkala 844b
Karlapalem 665b
Karnal 820b
Karpalli 800a
Karsog 768c
Kartarpur 765a
Karumathur 830b
Karur 705c
Karvi (Chitrakoot) 714c
Karwar 814b

Kasabel 757c
Kasaragod 809c
Kashinagar 703c
Kasibugga 673c
Kasrawad 727c
Kasuali 768c
Kateel 844b
Katghora 757c
Katipalla 844b
Kattappana 838c
Kaul 820b
Kaup 844b
Kaushambi 719b
Kavithi 673c
Kekri 836b
Kelambakkam 827c
Kelapur (Pandharkawada) 905b
Kendrapara 946a
Kendua 748a
Kendupadara 703c
Keroor 814b
Keru 836b
Kerwadi 814b
Keshali 738a
Keshod 911a
Keshpur 703c
Kesinga 902b
Khadki (BK) 905b
Khagarijan 748a
Khairabari 748a
Khairi 905b
Khajipalem 665b
Khallikote 703c
Khambhat 751c
Khambra (Jalandhar) 688b
Khamgaon 905b
Khammam 806a, 800a
Khanapur 814b
Khandadeuli 703c
Khandwa 727c
Khanna 884c
Khargone 727c
Khariar 902b
Kharkan (Hoshiarpur) 688c
Kharod 757c
Kharsia 757c
Kharupetia 748a
Kharwara 860c
Kheda 751c
Khedbrahma 766b
Kheralu 766b
Kherva 766b
Khetri 748a
Khilchipur 701c
Khinchan 836b
Khinwsar 836b
Khirkiya 701c
Khiroda 869c
Khliehriat 872c
Khowai 943c
Khultabad 734a
Khundrakpam 855c
Khurai 738a, 855c
Khurda 946b
Killanaikkarai 827c
Killianwali 884c
Kinana (Jind) 820b
Kishangarh 836b
Kishatwar 797c
Kittur 814b
Kodad 879a
Kodagu 844b
Kodaikanal 861c, 830b
Kodala 703c
Kodikurichi, Tenkasi 857c
Kodinar 911a
Koirengei 855c
Kokrajhar 748a
Kolanka 673c
Kolaras 803b
Kolenchery 838c
Kolhapur 918c
Kollipara 665b
Kolluru 665b
Komlathabi 855c
Kondanagula 879a
Kondapalli 665b
Kondapi 665b
Kongba 855c
Konkorada 703c
Konni 838c
Konthoujam 855c
Kookar 836b
Koppal 756b
Koraput 703c
Koratla 806a
Korba 757c
Kornepadu 665b
Korukonda 673c
Kota 757c

Kotabommali 673c
Kotananduru 673c
Kothagudem 806a
Kothamangalam 838c
Kothamba 751c
Kothapet 665b
Kothapet, Chirala 665b
Kothapeta 673c
Kothavalasa 673c
Kothuru 673c
Kotkapura 894b
Kotkhai 768c
Kotma 687c
Kotpad 703c
Kottan 884c
Kottayam 838c
Kottur 756b
Kotturu 673c
Kovilpatti 857c
Kovvada 800a
Kovvur 673c
Koyyalagudem 673c
Kozhencherry 838c
Krishna 800a
Krishnadevarayanagar 756b
Krishnai 748a
Krishnankoil 830b
Kshatriyabarpur 703c
Kuchaman City 836b
Kuchinda 902b
Kudachi 814b
Kudligi 756b
Kuknoor 756b
Kukshi 727c
Kukumseri 768c
Kulgam 816c
Kulhati 748a
Kullu 768c
Kumarakam 838c
Kumbakonam 705c
Kumbhari 905b
Kumbi 855c
Kumta 814b
Kundapur 844b
Kundgol 814b
Kundra 703c
Kunkury 757c
Kuntara 902b
Kupwara 816c
Kuravilangadu 838c
Kurha 905b
Kurichi 838c
Kuriuchipadi 827c
Kurnool 800a
Kurukshetra 820b
Kurwai 701c
Kusami 757c
Kushalgarh 860c
Kushalnagar 844b
Kushmunda 757c
Kustagi 756b
Kusumbha 869c
Kutch 918c
Kutch (Gujarat) 918c
Kuthuparamba (Kannur) 809c
Kutiyana 911a
Kuttikkanam 838c
Kuwarito 748a
Kuwaritol 748a
Kuzhithurai 857c
Kyamgeta 673c
Ladwa (Dhanora) 820b
Lahar 803b
Lahunipara 902b
Laida 902b
Lailunga 758a
Lakhanpur 758a
Lakhimpur 730b
Lakhimpur Kheri 719c
Lakhipur 748a
Lakhtar 911a
Lakshmeshwar 814b
Lalajando (Dharamgarh) 902b
Lalgaon 687c
Lalitpur 714c
Lanka 748a
Larambha 902b
Laxmanchanda 806b
Laxmipur 703c
Leh 816c
Lengtisinga 748a
Lilong 855c
Limbdi 911a
Limda 751c
Limkheda 751c
Linepada 703c
Lingasugur 756b
Loage 911a
Loch 748a
Lodhikheda 738a

Lohar Majra (KKR) 820b
Lohar Majra (Kurukshetra) 820b
Loisingha 902b
Lonar 905b
Loni (B.K.) 814b
Lopon 884c
Lormi 758a
Loundi 738a
Lucknow 719c
Ludhiana 688c, 884c
Lumding 748a
Lunawada 751c
Luwangsangbam 855c
Macherla 665b
Machhiwara 884c
Machilipatnam 665b
Madana (Gadh) 766b
Madanthyar 844b
Maddirala 665b
Madhira 806b
Madhya Pradesh 888a
Madikeri 844b
Madlauda (Panipat) 820b
Madurai 830b, 932c, 934b
Madurantakam 827c
Mahaboobnagar 800a, 879a
Mahabubabad 806b
Mahagaon 905b
Mahalingapur 814b
Mahamyahat 748a
Mahanandapur 703c
Maharajpur 738a
Mahe 888a
Mahemadavad 751c
Mahendraganj 872c
Mahilpur 884c
Mahoba 714c
Mahtoli 748a
Mahudha 751c
Maihar 687c
Mailam 827c
Mairang 872c
Majhauli 687c
Majuli 730b
Makavara Palem 673c
Makthal 879a
Malecruz 838c
Malegaon 905b
Malerkotla 894b
Malia Hatina 911a
Maliankara 838c
Malikipuram 673c
Malkanagiri 703c
Malkapur 905b
Malkhrouda 758a
Mallappally 838c
Malout Mandi 884c
Malpura 836b
Malthaun 738a
Malvan 751c
Mamallapuram 827c
Manana (Panipat) 820b
Mananthavady 809c
Manapparai 705c
Manarcadu 838c
Manavadar 911a
Manawar 727c
Mancherial 806b
Mandal 836b
Mandalgarh 836b
Mandapeta 673c
Mandasa 673c
Mandi 768c
Mandi Dabwali (Sirsa) 820b
Mandi Gobindgarh 894b
Mandi Gobindgarh (Fatehgarh Sahib) 688c
Mandia 748a
Mandideep 701c
Mandiphia 860c
Mandleshwar 727c
Mandvi 751c
Manendragarh 758a
Mangalagiri 665b
Mangalore 844b
Mangrol 911a
Mangrulpir 905b
Manikpur 748a
Manikwar 687c
Manimalakunnu 838c
Manipal 844c
Manjeswaram 809c
Manjlegaon 734a
Mankachar 748a
Mannaekhelli 756b
Mannanam 838c
Mannargudi 706a
Manora 905b
Mansa 751c, 894b
Mantha 734a
Manthani 806b

Manvi 756b
Maram 855c
Maregaon 905b
Margherita 730b
Mariagiri, Kaliakkavilai 857c
Mariani 730b
Maridhal 730b
Markapur 665c
Marriguda 879a
Martandam 857c
Martur 665c
Marwad 869c
Marwahi 758a
Marwar 836b
Maski 756b
Mastuana 894b
Masturi 758a
Masuda 836c
Matak Majri (Indri) 820b
Mathur 827c
Mauganj 687c
Mauranipur 714c
Mavli 860c
Mawkyrwat 872c
Mawsynram 872c
Mayabundar 888a
Mayang Imphal 855c
Mayiladuthurai 706a
Mazbat 748a
Medak 800a, 879a
Medarametla 665c
Meerganj 841a
Meghraj 766b
Mehgaon 803b
Mehkar 905b
Mehrauni 714c
Mehsana 766b, 918c
Meignanapuram 857c
Melaisivapuri 706a
Melaiyur 706a
Melaneelithanallur 857c
Melapalayam 857c
Melukavu 838c
Melur 830c
Melvisharam 827c
Mendarda 911a
Mendipathar 872c
Merta City 836c
Mhasadi 869c
Mhow 727c
Miryalguda 879a
Mirza 748a
Miyagam-Karjan 751c
Modasa 766c
Moga 688c, 884c
Mogalturu 673c
Mohali 894b
Mohali (Ropar) 688c
Mohana 703c
Mohindergarh 834b
Mohindergarh (Ateli) 834b
Mohindergarh (Kanina) 834b
Mohindergarh (Nangal Chaudhary) 834b
Mohindergarh (Narnaul) 834b
Mohna 803b
Moirabari 748a
Moirang 855c
Molagi 869c
Mongaldoi 748b
Mongsangei 855c
Moodabidri 844c
Moolamattom 838c
Moondwa 836c
Moothakunnam 838c
Moradabad 841a
Moran 730b
Morane 869c
Morar 803b
Morbi 911a
Moreh 855c
Morena 803b
Morigaon 748b
Morinda 894b
Morshi 905b
Morvad 766c
Motala 905b
Motbung 855c
Moti-Pavthi (Dahegam) 766c
Movva 665c
Mozari 905b
Mudalagi 814b
Muddebihal 814b
Mudhol 814b
Mukalmua 748b
Mukerian 884c
Muktainagar 869c
Mukteswaram 673c
Muktsar 688c, 885a
Mukutban 905b
Mulaguntapadu 665c

Mulawa 905b
Mulki 844c
Mullana (Ambala) 820b
Multai 701c
Mulug 806b
Mumbai 918c
Mummidivaram 673c
Munavalli 814b
Mundargi 814b
Mundgod 814b
Mundra 751c
Munganda 673c
Mungeli 758a
Mungwali 803b
Muniguda 703c
Munnar 838c
Munpur 751c
Murickassery 838c
Murtizapur 905b
Murum 734a
Musiri 706a
Muval 751c
Muvattupuzha 838c
Muzaffar Nagar 719c
Muzaffarnagar 719c
Mylavaram 665c
Nabarangapur 703c
Nabha 894b
Nadaun Hamirpur 768c
Nadiad 751c
Nadikudi 665c
Nagaon 869c
Nagapattinam 706a
Nagappattinam 934b
Nagaram 665c, 673c
Nagarbera 748b
Nagarjunanagar 665c
Nagarjunasagar 665c, 879a
Nagaur 836c
Nagercoil 857c
Nagina 841b
Nagod 687c
Nahan 768c
Naharkatiya 730b
Naidu Nagar 674a
Najibabad 841b
Nakhatrana 751c
Nakodar 765a
Nakrekal 879a
Nalagarh 768c
Nalatwad 814b
Nalbari 748b
Naldurg 734a
Nalgonda 800b, 879a
Nallajerla 674a
Nallapadu 665c
Nallur 857c
Nalogonda 800b
Namakkal 934b
Nambol 855c
Nambur 665c
Namrup 730b
Nandapur 703c
Nandgad 814b
Nandgaon Khandeswar 905b
Nandgaon Peth 905b
Nandigama 665c
Nandri 836c
Nandura Railway 905b
Nandurbar 869c, 918c
Naneola 820c
Nangal 894b
Nangal Kalan (Mansa) 688c
Nanguneri 857c
Naraingarh 820c
Narangwal 885a
Narasannapeta 674a
Narasapur 674a
Narasaraopet 665c
Narasimhapuram 674a
Narasingarh 701c
Narayanapuram 674a
Narayanpet 879b
Nardana 869c
Nardipur 766c
Naregal 814b
Narendrapur 703c
Nargund 814b
Narla 902b
Narsampet 806b
Narsaur 674a
Narsipatnam 674a
Narwana 820c
Nashik 918c
Nasik 918c
Nasirabad 836c
Nasrullah Ganj 701c
Naswadi 751c
Nathdwara 860c, 836c
Navagarh 758a

Navalgund 814b
Navan Shahar 836c
Navapur 869c
Nawabganj 841b
Nawan Shahar Doaba 765a
Nawanshahar 885a
Nawapara 902b
Nawapara (Komna) 902b
Naya Nangal 894b
Nayagarh 946b
Nazira 730b
Nedumkandam 838c
Nedumkunnam 838c
Neknoor 734a
Nelapadu 665c
Nellimarla 674a
Nellore 800b
Nepanagar 727c
Nerparsopant 905b
Nerwa 768c
Nesargi 814b
New Bhaitbari 872c
New Delhi 759b, 765b, 918c
New Vallabh Vidyanagr/Mogri 908c
Newai 836c
Neyveli 827c
Neyyoor 857c
Nial 894b
Nidadavole 674a
Nidadavoli 674a
Nidagundi 814b
Nidubrolu 665c
Nikashi 748b
Nilakottai 861c
Nileshwar 809c
Nimbaheda 860c
Ningthoukhong 855c
Nippani 814b
Nirmal 806b
Nitte 844c
Niwari 738b
Nizamabad 800b, 879b
Noida 759c
Nongpoh 872c
Nongstoin 872c
Nongtalang 872c
Nonoi 748b
Norawar 836c
North Lakhimpur 730b
North Paravur 838c
Nowgaon 738b
Nowgong 748b
Nurpur 768c
Nuvapada 703c
Nuwapara (Boden) 902b
Nuwapara (Golamunda) 902c
Nuzvid 665c
Obedullahganj 701c
Ode 751c
Odhan (Sirsa) 820c
Oinam 855c
Omerga 734a
Ongole 665c
Oomerabad 827c
Orai 714c
Orathanadu 706a
Osmanabad 734b
Ottanchatram 830c
Pachmarhi 701c
Pachmari 701c
Pachora 869c
Pachore 701c
Pachpedi 758a
Padampur 902c
Paderu 674a
Padiala 894c
Padmapur 703c
Paikamal 902c
Painavu 838c
Paithan 734b
Pal 870a
Palai 838c
Palakol 674a
Palakonda 674a
Palampur 768c
Palani 861c, 830c
Palanpur 766c
Palasar 766c
Palayamkottai 857c
Palem 879b
Palera 738b
Pali 758a, 836c
Palitana 918c
Pallivayal 809c
Paloncha 806b
Pamarru 665c
Pampady 838c
Pamuru 665c
Panchayat 674a
Panchkula 820c

Robert Cedergren Res. Centre, *Montr.* 421b
Robert Gordon Univ. 1910
Robert Hill Inst., *Sheff.* 1931a
Robert Menzies College, *Macq.* 92c
Robertson Centre for Biostatistics, *Glas.* 1671a
Robinson Coll., *Camb.* 1611c, 1613c
Roehampton Univ. 1912
Rogers Communicns.Centre, *Ryerson* 466b
Rolls-Royce Univ. Technol. Centre for Advanced Electr.
	Machines and Drives, *Sheff.* 1929b
Rolls-Royce Univ. Technol. Centre in Control and
	Systems Engin., *Sheff.* 1930a
Rolls-Royce Univ. Technol. Centre in Materials Damping
	Technol., *Sheff.* 1930c
Rollwala Computer Centre, *Gujar.* 750c
Roseworthy Campus, *Adel.* 31c
Ross Parsons Centre of Comml., Corporate and
	Taxation Law, *Syd.* 175a
Roy McKenzie Centre for the Study of Families, *Well.*
	1118b
Royal Academy of Music 1806
Royal Bank of Canada Centre for Risk Management, *Dal.*
	359c
Royal Coll. of Art 1912
Royal (Dick) Sch. of Vet. Studies, *Edin.* 1653a
Royal Holloway, Univ. of Lond. 1807
Royal Military Coll. of Canada 461
Royal Roads Univ. 461
Royal Vet. Coll. 1812
Royal Welsh Coll. of Music and Drama 1913
Ruhuna, Sri Lanka, Univ. of 1458
Ruskin Sch. of Drawing and Fine Art, *Oxf.* 1874b
Rutherford Coll., *Kent* 1717c
Ryerson Caribbean Res. Centre, *Ryerson* 466b
Ryerson Univ. 462

S. H. Ho Coll., *Chinese HK* 2029c
S. L. Trivedi Inst. of Pharm., *G.Ghasidas* 757b
S. N. D. T. Arts and Comm. Coll. for Women, Pune,
	SNDT 918a
S. N. D. T. Coll. of Arts and Smt. C. B. Coll. of Comm.
	and Econ. for Women, Mumbai, *SNDT* 918a
S. N. D. T. Coll. of Educn. for Women, Pune, *SNDT* 918b
S. N. D. T. Coll. of Home Sci., Pune, *SNDT* 917c, 918b
Sabaragamuwa Univ. of Sri Lanka 1460
Said Bus. Sch., *Oxf.* 1876b
Sainsbury Centre for Visual Arts, *E.Anglia* 1641b
Sainsbury Inst. for the Study of Japanese Arts and
	Cultures, *Lond.* 1817b
Sainsbury Res. Unit for the Arts of Africa, Oceania and
	the Americas, *E.Anglia* 1641a
Saint John Campus, *New Br.* 434c
Saint Paul Univ. 448
Saint-Boniface, Coll. Univ. de 400
Saint-Jean, Faculté, *Alta.* 302c
Sainte-Anne, Univ. 467
Salford, Univ. of 1918
Sambalpur Univ. 901
Sampurnanand Sanskrit U. 903
Sanjay Gandhi Postgrad. Inst. of Med. Scis. 903
Sant Gadge Baba Amravati Univ. 903
Sapporo Dental Coll., *Dhaka* 240c
Sardar Krushinagar Dantiwada Agric. Univ. 906
Sardar Patel Univ. 906
Sarojini Naidu Sch. of Performing Arts, Fine Arts and
	Communicn., *Hyd.* 769b, 770b
Saskatchewan, Univ. of 471
Satyabama Inst. of Sci. and Technol. 908
Sau Po Centre on Ageing, *HK* 2035a
Saurashtra Univ. 909
Saw Centre for Financial Studies, *NU Singapore* 1318b
Scarborough Campus, *Hull* 1700c
Scarborough Coll., *Tor.* 510b, 511c
Scarborough Sch. of Educn., *Hull* 1699b
School of —
	Oriental and African Studies 1814
	Pharm. 1818
	Planning and Archit., New Delhi 912
Schulich Sch. of Med., *W.Ont.* 547c
Schulich Sch. of Med. and Dent., *W.Ont.* 538a, 547b
Science Coll., *C'dia.* 348c
Scott Polar Res. Inst., *Camb.* 1607a
Scott Sutherland Sch. of Archit., *R.Gordon* 1911a
Scottish Agric. Coll., *Glas.* 1671c, *Edin.* 1654c
Scottish Borders Campus, *H-W* 1682c
Scottish Centre for Crime and Justice Res., *Stir.* 1943b
Scottish Centre for Info. on Lang. Teaching and Res., *Stir.*
	1943b
Scottish Econ. Res., *Abertay* 1539b
Scottish Informatics, Maths., Biol. and Stats., *Abertay*
	1539b
Scottish Inst. for Residential Child Care, *Strath.* 1948b
Scottish Inst. of Sustainable Technol., *H-W* 1682a
Scottish Local Authorities Management Centre, *Strath.*
	1948b
Scottish Manufacturing Inst., *H-W* 1682b
Scottish Univs. Environ. Res. Centre, *Glas.* 1671a
Seagram Sports Sci. Centre, *McG.* 384c
Sellenger Centre, *E.Cowan* 66c
Selwyn Coll., *Camb.* 1612a, 1613c

Shah Abdul Latif Univ, 1271
Shahabuddin Med. Coll., *Dhaka* 240c
Shaheed Zulfikar Ali Bhutto Inst. of Sci. and Technol.
	1272
Shaikh Zayed Islamic Res. Centre, *Karachi* 1254a
Shailesh J. Mehata Sch. of Management, *IIT Bombay* 779a
Shajalal Univ. of Sci. and Technol. 258
Shanmugha Arts, Sci., Technol. and Res. Acad. 913
Shaw Coll., *Chinese HK* 2029c
Sheffield Hallam Univ. 1932
Sheffield, Univ. of 1921
Sheldon Biotechnol. Centre, *McG.* 384c
Shepparton Campus, *La Trobe* 85c, *Melb.*, 112b
Sher-e-Bangla Agric. Univ. 258
Sher-e-Bangla Med. Coll., *Dhaka* 240c
Sher-e-Kashmir Univ. of Agric. Scis. and Technol. of
	Jammu 913
Sher-e-Kashmir Univ. of Agric. Scis. and Technol. of
	Kashmir 914
Sherbrooke, Univ. de 481
Sheth Damodardas Sch. of Commerce, *Gujar.* 749c
Shivaji Univ. 914
Shreemati Nathibai Damodar Thackersey Women's Univ.
	916
Shri Jagannath Sanskrit Vishvavidyalaya 919
Shri Lal Bahadur Shastri Rashtriya Sanskrit Vidyapeetha
	919
Shri Mata Vaishno Devi Univ. 920
Shridath Ramphal Centre for Internat. Trade Law, Policy
	and Services, *WI* 1993b
Shrivenham Site, *Cran.* 1630b, 1631c
Shun Hing Inst. of Advanced Engin., *Chinese HK* 2027b
Sidney Sussex Coll., *Camb.* 1612a, 1613c
Sido-Kanhu Murmu Univ. 920
Sierra Leone, Univ. of 1286
Sikkim-Manipal Univ. of Health, Med. and Technol. Scis.
	921
Simon Fraser Univ. 481
Simone de Beauvoir Inst., *C'dia.* 347a
Sindh Agric. Univ. 1277
Sindh, Univ. of 1273
Singapore Synchrotron Light Source, *NU Singapore* 1318c
Sir Arthur Lewis Inst. of Social and Econ. Studies, *WI*
	1990c, 2002b
Sir James Dunn Wildlife Res. Centre, *New Br.* 434b
Sir John Cass Dept. of Art, Media and Des., *Lond.Met.*
	1824b
Sir Joseph Hotung Res. Project in Law, Human Rights and
	Peace Building in the Middle East, *Lond.* 1817c
Sir Salimullah Med. Coll., *Dhaka* 240c
Sir Syed Univ. of Engin. and Technol. 1277
Sir Vithaldas Thackersey Coll. of Home Sci., Mumbai,
	SNDT 917c, 918b
Sir Wilfred Grenfell Coll., *Nfld.* 408b, 409c
Sir William Dunn Sch. of Pathol., *Oxf.* 1880a
SLOWPOKE Nuclear Res. Reactor, *Dal.* 360a
Social based Dental Coll., *Dhaka* 240c
Sokoine Univ. of Agric. 1485
Solomon Mahlangu Campus, *Sokoine Ag.* 1487c
Solusi Univ. 2049
Somerset Coll. of Arts and Technol., *Plym.* 1897c
Somerville Coll., *Oxf.* 1882b, 1883c
South Africa, Univ. of 1391
South African Bird Ringing Unit, *Cape Town* 1341c
South African Coll. of Music, *Cape Town* 1337c
South African Herbal Sci. and Medicine Instit., *W.Cape*
	1410a
South African Inst. for Agric. Extension, *Pret.* 1385c
South African National Bio-Informatics Instit., *W.Cape*
	1410a
South Auckland Clin. Sch., *Auck.* 1078a
South Australia, Univ. of 154
South Australian Centre for Econ. Studies, *Adel.* 30b
South Delhi Campus, *Delhi* 725c
South Devon Coll., *Plym.* 1897c
South Eastern Univ. of Sri Lanka 1461
South Pacific Regional Herbarium, *S.Pac.* 1423b
South Pacific, Univ. of 1421
Southampton Solent Univ. 1940
Southampton, Univ. of 1932
Southern Africa Labour and Devel. Res. Unit, *Cape Town*
	1341c
Southern Cross Univ. 155
Southern Queensland, Univ. of 158
Southwestern Ontario Res. Data Centre, *Wat.* 535c
Sree Chitra Tirunal Inst. for Med. Scis. and Technol. 922
Sree Sankaracharya Univ. of Sanskrit 923
Sri Chandrasekharendra Saraswathi Viswa Mahavidyalaya
	923
Sri Jayewardenepura, Sri Lanka, Univ. of 1462
Sri Krishnadevaraya Univ. 923
Sri Lanka, Cttee. of Vice-Chancellors and Dirs. 2062
Sri Lanka Inst. of Information Technol. 1465
Sri Padmavati Mahila Visvavidyalayam 924
Sri Palee Campus, *Colombo* 1440c
Sri Paramakalyani Centre for Environmental Scis., *M.Sund.*
	856c
Sri Ramachandra Dental Coll., *S.Ramachandra* 928c, 929c
Sri Ramachandra Univ. 926
Sri Sathya Sai Univ. 929

Sri Siddhendra Kalakshetram, Kuchipudi, *Potti ST* 889c
Sri Venkateswara Inst. of Med. Scis. 929
Sri Venkateswara Univ. 929
St Aidan's Coll., *Durh.* 1637a
St Albans, *Vic.(Aust.)* 189c
St Andrew's Coll., *Manit.* 400b
St. Andrews Coll., *Sask.* 480c
St Andrews, Univ. of 1913
St. Anne's Coll., *Oxf.* 1882b, 1883c
St Antony's Coll., *Oxf.* 1882b, 1883c
St. Augustine Campus (Trinidad) 1998
St Augustine Univ. of Tanzania 1484
St Augustine's Seminary, *Tor.* 511c
St. Benet's Hall, *Oxf.* 1882b, 1883c
St Catharine's Coll., *Camb.* 1612a, 1613c
St Catherine's Coll., *Oxf.* 1882b, 1883c
St Chad's Coll., *Durh.* 1637a
St Cross Coll., *Oxf.* 1882b, 1883c
St Cuthbert's Society, *Durh.* 1637b
St Edmund Hall, *Oxf.* 1882b, 1884a
St Edmund's Coll., *Camb.* 1612a, 1613c
St Francis Xavier Univ. 467
St George's, Univ. of Lond. 1813
St Hild and St Bede, Coll. of, *Durh.* 1637a
St Hilda's Coll., *Oxf.* 1882b, 1884a
St Hugh's Coll., *Oxf.* 1882c, 1884a
St John's Coll., *Camb.* 1612b, 1613c, *Durh.*, 1637b, *Manit.*,
	400c, *Oxf.*, 1882c, 1884a
St Joseph's Coll., *Alta.* 313c
St Mary's Coll., *Durh.* 1637b
St. Mary's Univ. 467
St Mary's Univ. Coll., *Belf.* 1564a, 1565c
St Michael's Coll., Univ. of 511
St Paul's Coll., *Manit.* 400c
St Paul's United Coll., *Wat.* 537c
St Peter's Coll., *Oxf.* 1882c, 1884a
St. Peter's Coll., *Sask.* 480c
St Stephen's Coll., *Alta.* 313c
St Stephen's House, *Oxf.* 1882c, 1884b
St Thomas Dept. of Christian Studies, *Madr.* 825c
St Thomas More Coll. 481
St. Thomas Univ. 470
Staffordshire, Univ. of 1940
Stanley Burton Centre for Holocaust Studies, *Leic.* 1750c
Stanley Ho Centre for Emerging Infectious Diseases,
	Chinese HK 2027b
Star Lake Field Station, *Manit.* 399b
State Coll. of Ayurveda, *Lucknow* 824c
Stellenbosch Inst. for Advanced Study, *Stell.* 1400a
Stellenbosch, Univ. of 1391
Stirling, Univ. of 1941
Stout Res. Centre for New Zealand Studies, *Well.* 1118c
Stranmillis Univ. Coll., *Belf.* 1564c, 1565c
Strathclyde Bus. Sch., *Strath.* 1946c
Strathclyde, Univ. of 1944
Strathfield Campus (Mount St. Mary), *Aust.Cath.* 35a
Strathmore Univ. 977
Subramania Bharthi Sch. of Tamil Lang. and Lit.,
	Pondicherry 887b
Sudbury, Univ. of 488
Suleman Dawood Sch. of Business, *Lahore MS* 1255a
Sultan Haji Omar Ali Saifudien Inst. of Islamic Studies,
	Brunei 266b
Sultan Hassanal Bolkiah Inst. of Educn., *Brunei* 266b
Sultan Idris Univ. of Educn. 1029
Sultan Iskandar Inst. of Urban Habitat and Highrise Bldg.,
	Tech.U.Malaysia 1035c
Sunbury, *Vic.(Aust.)* 189c
Sunderland, Univ. of 1949
Sunshine and Newport, *Vic.(Aust.)* 189c
Sunshine Coast, Univ. of the 158
Suntory and Toyota Internat. Centres for Econ. and
	Related Disciplines, *Lond.* 1802a
Surrey, Univ. of 1949
Sussex, Univ of 1954
Sustainable Tourism Co-op. Res. Centre, *Murd.* 133c
Svamy Vipulananda Inst. of Aesthetic Studies,
	Eastern(S.Lanka) 1442b
Swami Ramanand Teerth Marathwada Univ. 930
Swansea Clin. Sch., *Swansea* 1957b
Swansea Metropolitan Univ. 1958
Swansea Univ. 1954
Swaziland Inst. for Res. in Traditional Med., Medicinal and
	Indigenous Plants, *Swazi.* 1472a
Swaziland, Univ. of 1470
Swinburne, Sarawak Inst. of Technol., *Swinburne UT* 164c
Swinburne Univ. of Technol. 160
Swire Inst. of Marine Sci., *HK* 2036b
Sydney Conservatorium of Music, *Syd.* 165c
Sydney Internat. Campus (Postgrad.), *C.Qld.* 47c
Sydney Internat. Campus (Undergrad.), *C.Qld.* 47c
Sydney Regional Visualisation Lab., *Syd.* 177a
Sydney, Univ. of 164
Sydney, Univ. of Technol. 183
Sylhet Agric. Univ. 258
Symbiosis Internat. Univ. 931

T. T. Ng Chinese Lang. Res. Centre, *Chinese HK*
	2028a

INDEX TO SUBJECTS OF STUDY

This index includes a reference to all subjects of study as suggested by the names of all academic departments and sub-departments which appear under the heading 'Academic Units' in the university chapters. The letters a, b and c are used to indicate the first, second and third columns of each page, and the abbreviated name of the

university in whose chapter a particular subject of study appears is included (*example*: geography, *Adel.* 29c, *Panjab* 881b, *Well.* 1114c).

Separate references have been included to the component subjects mentioned in a department's name, eg a department called 'Accountancy and Finance' is indexed separately

under 'accountancy' and 'financial studies'. Multi-departmental faculty names (eg Medicine) and campus names are not indexed, but the subjects of study of their individual departments are included.

anatomy, veterinary, Ib. 1177c, Maid. 1192a, Mak. 1499a, Makurdi Ag. 1144b, Nair. 971b, Pret. 1384b, Sokoine Ag. 1486c, TN Vet. 936b, 936c
ancient studies, Stell. 1393a
andragogy, Montr. 415c
Anglo-Saxon, Camb. 1599a
animal production, AT Balewa 1138a, Abeokuta Ag. 1140c, Akure 1167c, Dschang 272c, Ebonyi State 1163b, Glas. 1669a, Makurdi Ag. 1143b, Nair. 971a, Olabisi Onabanjo 1204a, Pret. 1385a, Sokoine Ag. 1485c, Swazi. 1470c, TN Vet. 935c
animal sciences, Adel. 25a, Ambrose Alli 1145c, Arid Ag. 1235b, B'desh.Ag. 220b, B'thidasan. 704b, BSMR Ag. 218a, Bayero 1148c, Benin 1152c, Bindura 2044b, Calabar 1158c, Cape Coast 574c, Devel.Studies(Ghana) 577b, Eastern(S.Lanka) 1441b, Ghana 581b, Hyd. 769b, Ib. 1173a, Kwame NUST 587a, Leeds 1737b, M.Okpara, Umudike 1193c, MJP Rohil. 840b, Maid. 1190c, Mak. 1496a, Malawi 986a, Manit. 388a, Massey 1101a, McG. 385b, Moi 968b, Monash 114b, N-W(S.Af.) 1365b, NUL 980b, Namibia 1056a, Njala 1285b, Nott.Trent 1862a, O.Awolowo 1197b, P.Harcourt 1207a, Peradeniya 1452a, Pret. 1374a, Putra 1022a, Rivers SUST 1210b, Ruhuna 1458b, S.Pac. 1421b, Sask. 472b, Sheff. 1921c, Sokoine Ag. 1485c, Stell. 1393a, TN Vet. 936a, Uyo 1214a, Venda 1403b, W.Aust. 191b, Wales 1542a, Witw. 1411a, Yola 1170b, Z'bwe. 2050a, Zambia 2006c
animal sciences, companion, Glas. 1669a
animal studies, farm, Peradeniya 1456c, Pret. 1385a
animal studies, small, Liv. 1761c
anthropological language, Punjabi 891a
anthropology, Aberd. 1537a, Adel. 29b, Alta. 303b, And. 669c, Auck. 1067a, Belf. 1559a, Benin 1155c, Bourne. 1578c, Bran. 316b, Brist. 1583c, Brun. 1593c, Brunei 268b, C'dia. 347a, Calg. 323b, Camb. 1599a, 1599b, Cant. 1088c, Car. 341a, Chinese HK 2021a, Chitt. 228a, Dar. 1480c, Delhi 722a, Dhaka 233a, Dib. 728a, Dr HGV 736b, Durh. 1633a, Ebonyi State 1166b, G.Ghasidas 757a, Gauh. 744c, Glas. 1668b, Hyd. 769b, IIU Malaysia 1002c, Ib. 1173b, Jahang. 244c, Jo'burg. 1346a, Kannur 809a, Karn. 810b, 812a, Kent 1713b, KwaZulu-Natal 1351a, La Trobe 82c, 83a, Leth. 363c, Lond. 1781b, 1799b, 1815a, Lucknow 822b, Macq. 87a, Madr. 825a, Maid. 1192a, Malaya 1005a, Manip. 853c, Manit. 388b, McG. 368a, Melb. 102a, Moi 968c, Monash 120b, Montr. 411a, Mt.All. 427b, N.Azikiwe 1196a, NE Hill 871a, Nelson Mandela Met. 1363b, New Br. 429a, Nfld. 401a, O.Awolowo 1200c, Otago 1103c, Oxf.Brookes 1885a, Panjab 880c, Pondicherry 886a, Pret. 1374a, Rajsh. 252c, Rhodes 1388b, S.Fraser 486b, Samb. 901a, Sask. 477c, Sri Jay. 1464a, St And. 1915c, St Mary's(Can.) 468a, Syd. 166b, Tor. 490a, Trent 513b, Utkal 944a, Uyo 1216c, Venda 1404b, Vic.(BC) 517a, W.Aust. 195c, W.Cape 1406a, W.Laur. 556c, W.Ont. 538b, Waik. 1123b, Wales 1965a, Wat. 523c, Well. 1117c
anthropology, Chinese, Chinese HK 2021a
anthropology, physical, And. 672c, Jo'burg. 1349a
anthropology, social, Belf. 1559a, Brun. 1593c, Camb. 1599b, Cape Town 1338a, Dal. 355b, Guj.Vid. 753b, Kent 1713b, NUL 981b, Oxf. 1873a, Punjabi 893a, St And. 1915c, Witw. 1414c
aquaculture, Abeokuta Ag. 1141a, B'desh.Ag. 220b, Durh. 1633b, Makurdi Ag. 1143c, Malawi 986a, Rajsh. 254a, Stir. 1941c, TN Vet. 936a, Tas. 182b, Uyo 1215b, Wayamba 1467a
aquatic resources, C.Qld. 45c, Moi 969a
Arabic, Assam 682b, B'tullah.V. 700b, Ban. 690a, Bayero 1148c, Brunei 266c, Colombo 1437b, Delhi 722b, Dhaka 233a, Durh. 1635c, Eastern(S.Lanka) 1441b, Gauh. 745a, Ghana 583a, IIU Malaysia 999a, Islamia, Bahawal. 1248c, Islamic(B'desh.) 242c, JMI 793a, Karachi 1250b, Kashmir 815b, Leeds 1732c, Lucknow 822b, 823b, Madr. 825b, Maid. 1190c, Malaya 1005a, Maulana Azad Natnl.Urdu 858b, Osm. 873b, 875a, 875c, Punjabi 892b, Rajsh. 252c, Syd. 166b, VB 949c, 951a, W.Cape 1407b
Arabic literature, Durh. 1635c, Islamic(B'desh.) 242c
Arabic studies, Chitt. 228a, Engl.&Foreign Langs. 741a, Exe. 1655a, Ib. 1173a, Islamic Uganda 1494a, Malta 1040c, NU Malaysia 1015b, Peradeniya 1452a
archaeology, A.Nagar. 664a, And. 670b, B&P SLanka 1435a, Belf. 1558c, Birm. 1569c, Botswana 262a, Bourne. 1578c, Brist. 1583c, Calg. 323c, Camb. 1599b, Cape Town 1333a, Cardiff 1617c, Chinese HK 2021a, Cyprus 564b, Dar. 1479c, Drav. 740a, Durh. 1633a, Edin. 1647c, Exe. 1656b, Ghana 581c, Glas. 1663a, Ib. 1173b, Jahang. 244c, Karn. 811a, Kelaniya 1443c, Kent 1714b, La Trobe 80b, Leic. 1745b, 1745c, Leth. 364b, Liv. 1754c, Lond. 1777c, 1807c, 1815a, MP Bhoj 824b, Madr. 825a, Malta 1041b, Midlands State 2046b, Monash 117c, Nair. 976a, Nfld. 401a, Nott. 1853b, Oxf. 1873a, 1874a, Peradeniya 1452b, Potti ST 889a, Pret. 1374a, Reading 1908a, S'ton. 1933a, S.Fraser 482a, Sask. 472b, Sheff. 1922a, Sri Jay. 1463b, Syd. 166b, W.Aust. 195c, W.Laur. 557a, WI 1995b, Wales 1965a, Witw. 1413a, Worcester 1984b
archaeology, ancient Indian, APS 686c, Ban. 690a, Dr HGV 736b, Jiw. 801b, Kuruk. 818b, Lucknow 822a, Osm. 875b, Panjab 880c, Utkal 944a, VB 949c
archaeology, Australian indigenous, Monash 117b, W.Aust. 195c
archaeology, environmental, Leic. 1745c
archaeology, Near Eastern, Syd. 166b
archaeology, palaeochristian, Malta 1041b
architecture, AT Balewa 1138a, Adel. 25a, Ambrose Alli 1146a, And. 671a, Auck. 1067b, B'desh.Engin. 223b, Bath 1550a, Belf. 1560c, Bharati V. 707a, Botswana 261b, Camb. 1599c, Canberra 42a, Cape Town 1333a, Car. 335c, Cardiff 1614b, Chinese HK 2021a, Copperbelt 2005b, Cyprus 563a, Dal. 350a, Deakin 61c, E.Lond. 1642a, Edin. 1645a, GGS Indra. 758c, GND 762a, Greenwich 1675b, Guy. 593a, HK 2031a, IIU Malaysia 999a, JMI 793a, Jamaica UT 956a, Jo'burg. 1346a, Jomo K. 965c, Jos 1180a, Khulna 248b, Kingston(UK) 1717c, KwaZulu-Natal 1351a, Kwame NUST 587b, Lagos 1183c, Lahore UET 1240b, Lincoln(UK) 1752a, Liv. 1755a, Lond.Met. 1824b, Lond.S.Bank 1827a, Mak. 1496a, Malawi 988a, Malaya 1005a, Malta 1040c, Manc.Met. 1837a, Manipal 851a, Manit. 388b, McG. 368a, Mehran 1257a, Melb. 94c, Montr. 411a, N-WFP Eng. 1267b, N.Azikiwe 1195b, NED Eng. 1260a, NU Singapore 1305b, NUST Bulawayo 2048a, Nair. 972a, Nehru Tech. 799b, Nelson Mandela Met. 1360c, Newcastle(NSW) 141a, Newcastle(UK) 1846b, O.Awolowo 1197b, Olabisi Onabanjo 1204a, Oxf.Brookes 1885a, PNG Tech. 1282a, Plym. 1888b, Portsmouth 1898c, Potti ST 889a, Pret. 1374a, Putra 1022a, R.Gordon 1911a, Rivers SUST 1210c, Ryerson 462b, SMVD 920b, SPA Delhi 912a, Sheff. 1922a, Strath. 1944b, Syd. 166b, Tas. 182b, Tech.U.Malaysia 1030c, Tor. 490b, Ulster 1960a, Uyo 1214a, W.Aust. 191c, Wat. 524a, Well. 1113a, Witw. 1411b, Yola 1170b
architecture, interior, Monash 115a, Pret. 1374a, Well. 1113a
architecture, landscape, Adel. 25a, Greenwich 1675b, Leeds Met. 1740c, Lincoln(NZ) 1094b, Manit. 391c, Montr. 413b, NUST Bulawayo 2048b, Pret. 1374a, Putra 1026a, Ryerson 462b, SPA Delhi 912b, Sheff. 1924c, Tech.U.Malaysia 1034a, W.Aust. 191c, Wayamba 1467b, Well. 1113a
architecture, naval, B'desh.Engin. 225b, Glas. 1667c, Strath. 1947b
archive studies, Botswana 262c, E.Anglia 1639c, Glas. 1666b, Ib. 1174c, Liv. 1757a, Mak. 1498a, NUST Bulawayo 2048b, Sindh 1275a
area studies, Durh. 1634c, 1635a, Liv. 1755c, Oxf. 1873b, Portsmouth 1901b
art, Alta. 303b, Auck.UT 1081a, B&P SLanka 1435a, Ballarat 37a, Belf. 1564a, CSJ Maharaj 718a, Calg. 323c, Car. 336a, 336c, Coventry 1625b, Curtin 55a, E.Anglia 1641a, Edin. 1645a, Griff. 69b, Herts. 1683c, Hudd. 1691b, Hull 1698c, Kwame NUST 588c, Leeds Met. 1740b, Leth. 363c, Liv.J.Moores 1764c, Lond. 1815a, Lond.Met. 1824b, Lond.S.Bank 1827a, Lough. 1830b, Manc.Met. 1837b, 1838b, Manit. 388b, Melb. 102b, Nan.Tech. 1292b, Nelson Mandela Met. 1361a, Newcastle(UK) 1846b, Open Tanz. 1483b, Oxf.Brookes 1885a, Plym. 1888c, Portsmouth 1898c, Qu. 452a, R.Gordon 1911a, Reading 1905c, S'ton. 1933a, SNDT 916b, 917b, Salf. 1918b, Sask. 472b, Syd. 172b, Tas. 179a, Ulster 1960a, Uyo 1214b, W'gong. 206c, W.England 1980b, W.Syd. 202a, Wales 1540b, 1967a, 1969b, Witw. 1411b
art, African, Venda 1403a
art, applied, Ambrose Alli 1146c, Ban. 690a, Benin 1154b, Mak. 1498c, N.Azikiwe 1195c, Nehru Tech. 799a, R.Bhar. 894c
art, Chinese, Chinese HK 2023b
art, computer, Abertay 1538b, C'dia. 344a, FJ Women 1242c
art, contemporary, E.Cowan 64b, Leeds Met. 1741a, S'ton. 1933a, S.Fraser 483b, W.Syd. 202b
art, creative, Bran. 317a, Deakin 61c, Keele 1710c, Lagos 1184b, Liv.J.Moores 1766a, Maid. 1191a
art curatorship, Cant. 1087b, Wales 1540b
art, digital, C'dia. 344a, Lond. 1781c, Monash 120a, Syd. 166c, 168b
art, dramatic, Belf. 1564b, Brock 321a, Calabar 1159a, 1160c, Dal. 355b, Dar. 1479a, Ghana 583b, Hyd. 770b, Jos 1181a, Malawi 986c, O.Awolowo 1198a, Pondicherry 887a, Potti ST 889c, Uyo 1216c, Witw. 1411b
art, fine, Alta. 310a, Ambrose Alli 1146c, And. 670b, Assam 682c, Auck. 1071c, Benin 1154b, Bran. 317a, Bundel. 713b, Cant. 1087b, Cape Town 1335b, Chinese HK 2023b, Chitt. 229a, Dar. 1479a, Dhaka 235a, Eastern(S.Lanka) 1441c, FJ Women 1243a, Fort Hare 1344a, Gandh.Rural 743a, HK 2032b, Hyd. 770b, JMI 793c, Jo'burg. 1347b, Karn. 811b, Kelaniya 1444b, Kingston(UK) 1718c, Kuruk. 819a, Kwame NUST 588c, Leeds 1730c, Lincoln(UK) 1752c, MDU 832c, Malawi 986c, Massey 1097b, Monash 114a, 117a, Mt.All. 426c, N.Azikiwe 1195c, Newcastle(NSW) 141c, Nfld. 408c, O.Awolowo 1198c, Oxf. 1874b, Oxf.Brookes 1885a, P.Harcourt 1207c, Panjab 881b, Peradeniya 1454a, Punjabi 892a, Rajsh. 253c, Reading 1906a, Rhodes 1389a, S'ton. 1933a, Stell. 1394c, Tor. 493c, Uyo 1215b, Wales 1540b, Wat. 529b, Witw. 1411b
art, folk, Potti ST 889a
art, graphic, Ryerson 464c, VB 950b, Yaounde II 276c
art, industrial, Kwame NUST 588c, Mak. 1497a, Uyo 1215b
art, studio, C'dia. 347a, Nelson Mandela Met. 1363b
art, theory of, Cant. 1087b, Kent 1714a, Monash 114a, P.Harcourt 1208c, Syd. 166c
art, visual, Banasth. 699c, Brock 322b, C.Sturt 52b, E.Lond. 1642a, HP 768a, Kelaniya 1444b, Kent 1714a, La Trobe 83b, Lond. 1782c, M.Sukh. 860b, Monash 114a, Namibia 1057b, Nan.Tech. 1296a, Nfld. 408c, Nott.Trent 1866c, Ott. 444a, Pret. 1381b, Qld.UT 152c, Qu. 454a, Tas. 183a, Tor. 510b, Vic.(Aust.) 188a, Vic.(BC) 522b, W.Aust. 191c, W.Ont. 546b
artificial intelligence, Malaya 1005a, Malta 1041a
arts, Bharati V. 707a, C.Qld. 44c, Griff. 69c, Guy. 594b, La Trobe 78b, Lahore MS 1255b, Lanc. 1722a, Lond.Met. 1824b, Massey 1101b, Monash 114a, 114b, N.Azikiwe 1196b, Nair. 972a, Northumbria 1848c, Nott.Trent 1862a, Olabisi Onabanjo 1204c, Ryerson 462c, S.Cross 155c, Sindh 1274a, Strath. 1948a, Syd. 166c, 172b, Tripura 942c, Worcester 1984b, Z'bwe.Open 2053c
arts, critical, Liv.J.Moores 1766a
arts, performing, C.Sturt 52b, Dr HGV 737b, Jiw. 802b, Kelaniya 1444b, Kingston(UK) 1719b, Leeds Met. 1741b, Madurai K. 829b, Namibia 1057a, Nan.Tech. 1296a, Olabisi Onabanjo 1205a, Tas. 183a, Tor. 510b, Ulster 1962c
arts, plastic, Ban. 692c
Asian culture, Lond. 1815a, Nan.Tech. 1294c, W.Aust. 195c
Asian languages, Auck. 1067c, Lond. 1815a, Macq. 89b, Malaya 1005a, Nan.Tech. 1294c, Tas. 179b, Well. 1113b
Asian literature, Auck. 1067c
Asian studies, Adel. 29c, Camb. 1599c, Griff. 71c, La Trobe 82c, Lagos 1183c, Manit. 388b, Melb. 95a, Murd. 131c, S.Fraser 482a, St Mary's(Can.) 468a, Tas. 179b, Vic.(BC) 521a, W.Aust. 195c, Well. 1113b
Assamese, Dib. 728b, Gauh. 745a, 747a
assessment, Colombo 1436c, Namibia 1056b
astrology, Jiw. 802b
astronautics, S'ton. 1934c
astronomy, Birm. 1571c, Bran. 317c, Calg. 329a, Camb. 1599c, Cant. 1092a, Cape Town 1333b, Cardiff 1621b, Durh. 1636b, Glas. 1667c, Herts. 1688a, Leeds 1733c, Leic. 1749c, Lucknow 823b, Manit. 393a, Nott. 1855b, Nott.Trent 1862a, Open(UK) 1871a, Osm. 877a, S'ton. 1937b, Sheff. 1925c, St And. 1915c, St Mary's(Can.) 468a, Swinburne UT 161c, Tor. 490b, Vic.(BC) 521b, W.Ont. 545a
astrophysics, Delhi 724a, Durh. 1636b, Gauh. 746b, N-W(S.Af.) 1370a, Tor. 490b
atmospheric science, Alta. 304a, Dal. 354b, Durh. 1634b, Leeds 1728b, Madurai K. 828c, McG. 368b
audio-visual studies, Dr HGV 737b, YCM Open 953a
audiology, Alta. 309c, Auck. 1077b, KwaZulu-Natal 1358c, Manipal 845a, Montr. 418c, NU Malaysia 1018b, W.Aust. 191c, Witw. 1415a
auditing, Jo'burg. 1346a, Malaya 1007c, N-W(S.Af.) 1370c, Namibia 1056a, Pret. 1374b, Venda 1403a
Australian studies, Bond 39b, La Trobe 82c, Monash 117c, Sunshine Coast 159c, Syd. 167a
Australian studies, indigenous, Adel. 30b, C.Darwin 48a, E.Cowan 65b, Monash 117c, S.Cross 156c
automation, IISc. 774a
avian disease, TN Vet. 935a
avian science, Wayamba 1467b
aviation, Griff. 70a, Massey 1096b, Vic.(Aust.) 185c
Ayurved, Bharati V. 707a
Ayurveda, Manipal 849b
Ayurvijana, Tibetan, CIHTS 716b

bacteriology, Lond. 1814a
banking, Ambrose Alli 1146a, Calabar 1158c, Chitt. 228c, Colombo 1436c, Dhaka 233a, Ebonyi State 1163c, Ghana 581a, Jo'burg. 1346a, Lagos State 1188b, Lond.Met. 1824a, M.Sukh. 859b, Malaya 1007c, Malta 1041a, Massey 1097b, Midlands State 2046c, Murd. 130a, N-W(S.Af.) 1367c, N.Azikiwe 1195b, NUST Bulawayo 2048a, Nan.Tech. 1300c, Olabisi Onabanjo 1204a, Open HK 2038a, P.Harcourt 1207c, Pondicherry 886a, Rajsh. 253c, Rivers SUST 1210c, Technol.Maur. 1053c, Uyo 1214a, Wayamba 1467a, Yaounde II 276a, Z'bwe.Open 2053c
behaviour, animal, Belf. 1557b, Exe. 1658a
behaviour, organisational, Brock 320b, Glam. 1660c, Hull 1695c, Lond. 1798a, Manc.Met. 1840b, Sask. 475a, Swinburne UT 161a
behavioural sciences, Ballarat 37a, Devel.Studies(Ghana) 577c, Durh. 1633b, FJ Women 1242b, HK 2034a, Hudd. 1691c, Kwame NUST 589c, Leeds 1735a, Liv. 1760c, M.Gandhi 837b, Mak. 1498b, Melb. 102c, Moi 969c, N-W(S.Af.) 1369c, 1370c, Newcastle(NSW) 144c, Syd. 167a, WI 1998c
behavioural studies, Chinese HK 2024a, Monash 120b
Bengali, Assam 682b, Ban. 690a, 696c, Chitt. 228a, Dhaka 233a, Gauh. 745a, Islamic(B'desh.) 243a, Jahang. 245a, Kal. 807a, Karachi 1250c, R.Bhar. 894c, Rajsh. 252c, Tripura 942c, VB 949c
Bhaisjya Rasayan, Ban. 694c
Bhoti, HP 767b
Biblical studies, Exe. 1655c, Jo'burg. 1346a, Pret. 1374b, Sheff. 1922b, Syd. 170b
bio-energy, ANG Ranga Ag. 662c
bio-ethics, Dal. 356a, Monash 120a

land studies, Belf. 1557b, Camb. 1604b, Fort Hare 1344a, Kwame NUST 587b, Nair. 972b, Nott.Trent 1865a, PNG Tech. 1282c, Swazi. 1471b, WI 2001a
language modernisation, Potti ST 889b
language studies, Alagappa 667b, Aston 1544b, Athab. 314c, Auck.UT 1082c, B'desh.Ag. 221c, BITS 710c, Belf. 1559b, Bran. 317b, Brunei 267c, Buddha SK 1434b, Bundel. 713a, Calabar 1159c, Canberra 42b, Cant. 1087c, Cape Town 1336a, Cardiff 1617a, Curtin 56a, DAV 726a, Drav. 740b, 740c, E.Af.Baraton 964b, E.Anglia 1639c, Eastern(S.Lanka) 1441c, Ebonyi State 1165a, Edin. 1648c, 1649b, Engl.&Foreign Langs. 741b, Gauh. 747a, Ghana 582c, Glam. 1661a, Griff. 72a, Guy. 593c, H-W 1680c, Hull 1699a, Ib. 1173b, Islamic Uganda 1494b, Jiw. 802b, Jos 1180b, Keele 1710c, Kotelawala Defence 1448b, KwaZulu-Natal 1352c, 1358a, Leeds Met. 1743b, Liv. 1755c, Liv.J.Moores 1765c, Lond. 1778a, 1782a, 1811a, Lond.Met. 1824b, Maid. 1191c, Mak. 1497b, Malawi 986b, 987a, 988b, Manc.Met. 1840c, Massey 1099a, Melb. 99a, 99b, Moi 969a, Monash 118c, N-W(S.Af.) 1371a, N.Maharashtra 868b, NE 136b, 138b, NU Malaysia 1017b, Nelson Mandela Met. 1362a, New Br. 430a, 435a, Newcastle(NSW) 143b, Newcastle(UK) 1846c, Nott.Trent 1865b, Open HK 2038a, Open S.Lanka 1450a, Open(UK) 1869a, 1869b, Ott. 443c, PNG Tech. 1282c, Portsmouth 1901b, Potti ST 889b, Pret. 1373c, Putra 1026a, Qld.UT 149b, Rajsh. 254c, Rhodes 1389c, S'ton. 1936c, S.Leone 1287b, S.Pac. 1422b, SE(S.Lanka) 1461b, SMVD 920c, Salf. 1919c, Sask. 475a, Sindh 1275a, Sri Jay. 1463b, Stir. 1942b, Sunshine Coast 159a, Swinburne UT 161a, Uganda Christian 1503a, Ulster 1962a, Vic.(Aust.) 185b, W.England 1980b, W.Laur. 558b, W.Syd. 203b, WI 1992c, 1995b, 2000a, Waik. 1122a, Witw. 1413c, 1415a, Zambia 2007c
language studies, applied, Auck. 1067b, Car. 339b, Nelson Mandela Met. 1362b, Qu. 453b, Venda 1403b, Well. 1116a
language studies, modern, Alta. 307b, Ambrose Alli 1147a, B&P SLanka 1435b, Bath 1551c, Brock 321c, C'dia. 343b, CIHTS 716a, Cape Town 1336c, Chinese HK 2024a, Dhaka 237a, Exe. 1657b, Ghana 583a, Glas. 1667a, Kelaniya 1445b, Leeds 1732c, Leic. 1749c, Leth. 365b, Montr. 414b, Mt.All. 427a, Newcastle(UK) 1846c, Nott. 1854b, Ott. 443b, S'ton. 1936b, St And. 1915b, St Mary's(Can.) 469b, Stell. 1396b, Strath. 1947b, Swazi. 1471c, Tech.U.Malaysia 1034c, Trent 514b, W'gong. 208b, W.Ont. 544a, WI 1996b, Wales 1547a, Witw. 1414a, Z'bwe. 2051b
language teaching, Nott.Trent 1863c
languages, ancient, Pret. 1373c
laser science, Manipal 852b
Latin, Pret. 1373c, St And. 1914a, W.Cape 1407b
Latin American studies, Auck. 1071b, Brist. 1587a, Durh. 1636a, La Trobe 80b, Liv. 1756a, Lond. 1821a, Nott. 1854c, S'ton. 1936c, S.Fraser 485a, Wat. 534a
Latin studies, Durh. 1633c, Jo'burg. 1347c
laundry, SNDT 917c
law, A.Nagar. 664a, Aberd. 1536c, Abertay 1539a, Abia State 1137a, Adel. 27a, Alta. 306c, 307a, Annam. 681a, Assam 683a, Athab. 315a, Auck. 1072c, Auck.UT 1082c, B'tullah.V. 700c, Ban. 691c, Belf. 1559c, Berh. 702c, Bharati V. 707c, Bhutto IST 1272c, Birm. 1571b, Bond 40a, Botswana 262b, Bourne. 1579b, Brist. 1587b, Brun. 1595a, Bundel. 713a, C.Darwin 48b, Calabar 1159c, Calg. 328a, Camb. 1604c, Canberra 42c, Cant. 1092b, Car. 339b, Cardiff 1618a, Chinese HK 2023c, Chitt. 229c, Colombo 1437b, DAV 726b, Dal. 353b, Deakin 62a, Delhi 723b, Dhaka 236a, Dr HGV 737a, Durh. 1635b, E.Anglia 1639c, E.Cowan 65b, E.Lond. 1643a, Ebonyi State 1165a, Edin. 1648b, Exe. 1657b, Fort Hare 1344a, G.Caledonian 1673a, GGS Indra. 759a, GND 763a, 764a, 764b, Gauh. 746a, Ghana 582c, Glam. 1660c, Glas. 1666b, Griff. 72a, Gujar. 750a, Gulb. 754b, Guy. 593c, HK 2032c, HP 768a, Herts. 1686a, Hudd. 1693c, Hull 1697a, ICFAI 772b, IIU Malaysia 1001a, Islamia, Bahawal. 1249b, Islamic(B'desh.) 243c, JMI 794a, Jammu 796a, Jiw. 802b, Jo'burg. 1348a, Kakatiya 804b, Kannur 809b, Karn. 811a, Kashmir 815c, Keele 1710c, Kent 1715a, Kingston(UK) 1719a, Kuruk. 819a, KwaZulu-Natal 1353a, 1358a, Lanc. 1723a, Leeds 1731c, Leeds Met. 1741b, Leic. 1748c, Lincoln(UK) 1752c, 1753a, Liv. 1757b, Liv.J.Moores 1766a, Lond. 1778b, 1790c, 1800b, 1815c, Lond.Met. 1824b, Lond.S.Bank 1828a, Lucknow 823a, M.Sukh. 859b, MDU 833a, MJP Rohil. 840c, Macq. 89b, Madr. 826b, Mak. 1497b, Malawi 986c, Malaya 1008b, Malta 1042c, Manc.Met. 1840c, Manit. 391c, Maur. 1051c, McG. 372a, Melb. 99b, Monash 119a, Montr. 413b, Murd. 131a, N-W(S.Af.) 1366a, 1368c, N.Azikiwe 1195c, NALSAR 863b, NE 136c, NE Hill 871c, NU Malaysia 1017c, NU Singapore 1311c, Nair. 976a, Napier 1845a, Nelson Mandela Met. 1362b, New Br. 432b, Newcastle(NSW) 143c, Newcastle(UK) 1847a, Northumbria 1849a, Nott. 1854a, Nott.Trent 1865c, Open S.Lanka 1450b, Open Tanz. 1483b, Open(UK) 1870a, Osm. 874b, Otago 1106a, Oxf. 1876a, Oxf.Brookes 1886a, Panjab 881c, Plym. 1892c, Portsmouth 1898b, Punjabi 892b, Qld.UT 150c, Qu. 455c, RTM Nag. 898c, Rajsh. 255a, Reading 1908c, Rhodes 1390a, S'ton. 1935c, S.Cross 156c, S.Leone 1287b, S.Pac. 1422b, SGB Amravati 904a, SPMV 925a, Salf. 1920b, Samb. 901b, Sask. 475b, Saur. 910a, Sheff. 1924c, Shiv. 915a, Sindh 1275a, Stir. 1942b, Strath. 1946c, Sur. 1951c, Swansea 1956c, Swazi. 1471b, Swinburne UT 161a, Syd. 171a, TN Law 932b, Tas. 180a, Tor. 495c, Uganda Christian 1503a, Ulster 1962b, Utkal 944c, Vic.(Aust.) 186c, Vic.(BC) 520a, W'gong. 209a, W.Aust. 194c, W.England 1980b, W.Ont. 543a, W.Syd. 203b, WI 1993a, 1995b, 2000a, Waik. 1122a, Wales 1541c, 1547a, Warw. 1974c, Wat. 531a, Well. 1116a, Witw. 1413c, Zambia 2007c
law, adjective, Venda 1403b, W.Cape 1408a
law, administrative, Dar. 1479c
law and society studies, Stell. 1396b
law, business, Benin 1154c, Chinese HK 2023c, Curtin 55b, 60a, Ib. 1174c, Lagos State 1189a, Leeds Met. 1742a, Macq. 87b, Monash 114b, Murd. 130a, Nan.Tech. 1301a, O.Awolowo 1199b, Otago 1103b, Rivers SUST 1211a, Stir. 1942b, Syd. 167c, TN Law 932a, Yaounde II 276a
law, canon, Lond. 1784b, Malta 1043b
law, civil, Dar. 1479c, Malta 1042c, Ott. 442c
law, clinical, Venda 1403b
law, commercial, Ambrose Alli 1146c, Auck. 1068c, Bayero 1150a, Cape Town 1336a, Durh. 1635b, Jos 1180c, Lagos 1185b, Mak. 1497b, Malta 1042c, N-W(S.Af.) 1371a, N.Azikiwe 1195c, Nair. 976a, Namibia 1057a, Olabisi Onabanjo 1204c, Rivers SUST 1211a, WI 1995b, Well. 1113a
law, common, Dschang 273b, Islamic Uganda 1494b, Ott. 442c, Yaounde II 276a
law, community, N-W(S.Af.) 1367b, Yaounde II 276b
law, comparative, Mak. 1497b, Malta 1042c, Pret. 1378c, Venda 1403c, Yaounde II 276a
law, constitutional, Dar. 1479c, TN Law 932b
law, construction, Lond. 1796a
law, criminal, Cape Town 1334a, Dar. 1479c, Malta 1042c, N-W(S.Af.) 1366a, TN Law 932b, WI 1995b, Yaounde II 276a
law, economic, Chinese HK 2023c, Dar. 1480a
law, education, N-W(S.Af.) 1367c
law enforcement, Open HK 2038a
law, environmental, Kent 1715a, Macq. 88c, W'gong. 209a
law, European, Durh. 1635b, Kent 1715a, Malta 1042c
law, French, Dschang 273c, Sur. 1951c
law, German, Sur. 1951c
law, history of, Venda 1403c
law, indigenous, N-W(S.Af.) 1366a
law, industrial, Ambrose Alli 1146c, Lagos 1185b
law, intellectual property, TN Law 932b, WI 1995b
law, international, Ambrose Alli 1146c, Benin 1154c, Calabar 1160a, Cant. 1088b, 1092b, Dar. 1480a, Durh. 1635b, E.Lond. 1643a, Ib. 1174c, Kent 1715a, Lagos 1185b, Lagos State 1189a, Malta 1042c, N.Azikiwe 1195c, O.Awolowo 1199b, Rivers SUST 1211c, Sur. 1951c, TN Law 932b, Uyo 1215c, Venda 1404a, WI 1995b
law, international human rights, Durh. 1635b, WI 1995b
law, Islamic, Bayero 1150a, Islamic Uganda 1494b, NU Malaysia 1017b
law, labour, N-W(S.Af.) 1366a, Pret. 1378b
law, maritime, W'gong. 209a
law, medical, Kelaniya 1444b, Kent 1715a
law, mercantile, Pret. 1378b, Stell. 1395b, Venda 1403c, W.Cape 1407c
law, private, Ambrose Alli 1146c, Bayero 1150a, Benin 1154c, CUE Af. 962b, Calabar 1160a, Cape Town 1336b, Dschang 273c, Ib. 1174c, Jos 1180c, Lagos 1185c, Lagos State 1189a, Maid. 1191c, N.Azikiwe 1195c, NUL 981a, Nair. 976a, Namibia 1057a, O.Awolowo 1199b, Olabisi Onabanjo 1204c, Pret. 1378c, Rivers SUST 1211a, Stell. 1395c, Uyo 1215c, Venda 1403c, W.Cape 1408a, Yaounde II 276a, Z'bwe. 2051a
law, procedural, N-W(S.Af.) 1366a, NUL 981a, Namibia 1057a, Pret. 1378c, Z'bwe. 2051a
law, property, Ambrose Alli 1146c, Benin 1154c, Jos 1180c, Lagos 1185c, Lagos State 1189a, N.Azikiwe 1195c, Rivers SUST 1211a
law, public, Ambrose Alli 1146c, Bayero 1150b, Benin 1155a, CUE Af. 962c, Calabar 1160a, Cape Town 1336b, Dschang 273c, Ib. 1174c, Jos 1180c, Lagos 1185c, Lagos State 1189a, Macq. 90c, Maid. 1191c, Mak. 1497b, Malta 1042c, N-W(S.Af.) 1366a, N.Azikiwe 1195c, NUL 981a, Nair. 976a, Namibia 1057a, O.Awolowo 1199b, Olabisi Onabanjo 1205a, Pret. 1378c, Rivers SUST 1211c, 1212a, Stell. 1395c, Uyo 1215c, Venda 1404a, W.Cape 1408a, Yaounde II 276b, Z'bwe. 2051a
law, public international, N-W(S.Af.) 1366a, Yaounde II 276b
law, Roman, Stell. 1395c
law, Sharia, Maid. 1191c
law, Spanish, Sur. 1951c
law, trade, Durh. 1635b
leadership studies, Aust.Cath. 33b, 33c, 34b, 35b, Herts. 1686c, Jo'burg. 1348a, Lanc. 1723b, Lincoln(UK) 1752c, NE 137a, Nan.Tech. 1295c, Open(UK) 1870c, Vic.(BC) 518b
learning, Auck. 1069c, C.Qld. 45c, Edin. 1652c, Glam. 1660b, HK 2032a, Hull 1697b, Manit. 389b, Massey 1097a, Melb. 100a, Open(UK) 1869a, Oxf.Brookes 1885b, Portsmouth 1902b, Qld.UT 150c, Tor. 503c
learning development, Plym. 1893a
learning difficulties, Hudd. 1693b, Kent 1716a, Lond.S.Bank 1828b, Sheff. 1929b
learning, distance, Brock 321a
learning, lifelong, Cardiff 1618b, Colombo 1437a, Coventry 1628a, E.Anglia 1639b, Hull 1697b, Leic. 1749a, Middx. 1843b, Open(UK) 1869a, Oxf.Brookes 1885b, W.Syd. 204c, Wales 1540c, 1547a, 1968a, 1969c
learning, organisational, Melb. 96c
legal practice, Qld.UT 151a
legal studies, Durh. 1635b, GGS Indra. 759a, La Trobe 82c, Lond. 1821a, Malawi 986c, Murd. 131a, Sunshine Coast 159a, TN Law 932b, Vic.(Aust.) 188a, W'gong. 209a
leisure studies, Belf. 1564c, Bourne. 1580b, Brock 319c, C'dia. 345c, E.Cowan 65b, Griff. 73b, Liv.J.Moores 1766b, Lond.S.Bank 1829b, N-W(S.Af.) 1370b, Pret. 1374b, Salf. 1920a, Syd. 173a, Waik. 1123c, Wales 1968a, Wat. 533b
leprology, Manipal 845b
lexicography, Potti ST 889b
liberal studies, C.Sturt 52a, Chinese HK 2022b, Jamaica UT 956b, Newcastle(NSW) 143b, Open HK 2038a, S.Fraser 485a
library studies, Alta. 307a, And. 670b, Annam. 678b, 681a, Ban. 692a, Bayero 1150b, Botswana 262c, Bundel. 713a, CSJ Maharaj 718a, Delhi 723c, Dr BA Marath. 732c, Dr BRA Open 730c, Dr HGV 737a, Fort Hare 1344b, G.Ghasidas 757a, GND 763a, Gauh. 746b, Gujar. 750a, Gulb. 754b, I.Gandhi Nat.Open 786b, Ib. 1174c, Islamia, Bahawal. 1249b, Jammu 796a, Jiw. 802b, Karachi 1252a, Karn. 811a, Kashmir 816a, Kelaniya 1445a, Kuruk. 819a, Lucknow 823a, M'lore. 843b, M.Sukh. 860a, M.Sund. 856c, MCN Journ.& Comm. 841c, Madr. 826a, Maid. 1191c, Mak. 1497b, Malta 1043a, Manip. 854b, McG. 372b, Moi 969a, Montr. 413c, Mzuzu 990a, N.Azikiwe 1195c, N.Maharashtra 868c, NE Hill 871c, NUST Bulawayo 2048b, Osm. 875c, Panjab 881c, Pondicherry 886c, Punjabi 892b, R.Bhar. 895a, Rajsh. 255a, SGB Amravati 904a, SP 907b, Samb. 901b, Saur. 910a, Shiv. 915a, Sindh 1275a, Utkal 944c, Uyo 1215a, Vic.(Aust.) 188a, W.Cape 1408a, WI 1995b, YCM Open 953b, Zambia 2007c
life sciences, Assam 683a, Aston 1544c, Bundel. 713b, CSJ Maharaj 718a, Coventry 1627a, DAV 726b, Deakin 62a, Dib. 729a, Glam. 1660c, Glas. 1663a, Gujar. 750a, H-W 1680b, Herts. 1686b, I.Gandhi Nat.Open 786b, Keele 1710c, Kingston(UK) 1719a, La Trobe 81a, Liv. 1755a, M.Gandhi 837a, Manip. 854b, N.Maharashtra 868c, Napier 1845a, Newcastle(NSW) 143a, Qld.UT 151a, R.Gordon 1911b, Samb. 901c, Swinburne UT 162a, Tas. 182c, Tor. 510b, Tripura 943a, WI 1995b, 2000a
limnology, B'tullah.V. 700c
linguistics, Adel. 27a, Alta. 307a, And. 670b, Annam. 678c, Assam 683a, Auck. 1067b, Ban. 692a, Belf. 1558c, Benin 1155a, Berh. 702c, C'dia. 343b, Calabar 1160a, Calg. 328b, Camb. 1605a, Cant. 1087a, Car. 339b, Chinese HK 2024a, Dar. 1479b, Delhi 723c, Dhaka 236b, Dr HGV 737a, Drav. 739c, E.Anglia 1639c, Ebonyi State 1165a, Engl.&Foreign Langs. 741b, Gauh. 746b, Ghana 582c, Griff. 72a, Gujar. 750b, HK 2032c, Ib. 1174c, Islamic Uganda 1494b, Jo'burg. 1348a, Jos 1180b, Kashmir 816a, Kelaniya 1445a, KwaZulu-Natal 1352c, 1358a, La Trobe 78c, 79a, Lanc. 1723b, Leeds 1733a, Liv. 1756c, Lond. 1778a, 1815c, Lucknow 823b, Macq. 89c, Maid. 1191c, Malawi 986b, Manip. 854c, Manit. 391c, McG. 372b, Melb. 99b, Moi 969a, Monash 118c, Montr. 414a, N.Azikiwe 1196a, NE 136b, NE Hill 872a, Nair. 976a, Nfld. 404c, Osm. 876a, Ott. 442c, Oxf. 1876b, P.Harcourt 1208a, Pret. 1373c, Punjabi 891a, Reading 1908c, S.Fraser 485b, Sask. 475a, Stell. 1395c, Syd. 171b, Tor. 496a, Uyo 1215c, Vic.(BC) 520b, W.Aust. 194b, W.Cape 1408a, W.Syd. 203b, WI 1992c, 1995b, 2000a, Waik. 1122b, Wales 1547a, Well. 1116a, Z'bwe. 2051a
linguistics, applied, Bond 39b, Brock 320a, Brunei 267b, Melb. 99b, Pret. 1373c, Reading 1908c, Sur. 1950c, Waik. 1122b, Z'bwe.Open 2053c
linguistics, theoretical, C'dia. 345c
literacy studies, Auck. 1069b, KwaZulu-Natal 1352c, Malaya 1006b, Witw. 1412b
literary studies, Athab. 314c, Belf. 1559b, Calabar 1159b, Cyprus 564b, Dar. 1480a, Deakin 61c, E.Af.Baraton 964b, Edin. 1648c, KwaZulu-Natal 1353a, 1358a, M.Gandhi 838a, Mak. 1497b, Moi 969a, Monash 117a, NE Hill 871b, Nair. 976b, Open(UK) 1870a, P.Harcourt 1207c, Portsmouth 1902b, S.Pac. 1422b, Ulster 1962a, W.Laur. 558b, WI 1992c, Witw. 1412c, Zambia 2007c
literary studies, comparative, Car. 336c, Montr. 411c, N.Maharashtra 868b, Warw. 1973c
literary theory, Jo'burg. 1348a
literature, Cant. 1087b, Cape Town 1336a, E.Anglia 1640a, Gauh. 747a, Islamic Uganda 1494b, KwaZulu-Natal 1352c, 1358a, Monash 118c, Nelson Mandela Met. 1362a, New Br. 430a, Uganda Christian 1503a, Wales 1541a
literature, American, Reading 1907c
literature, modern, Brock 321c, Cape Town 1336c, Montr. 414b, Ott. 443b, Trent 514b, W.Ont. 544a, WI 1996b

INDEX TO RESEARCH INTERESTS

This index includes references to the research interests supplied under departments, sub-departments and special centres in the university chapters. The letters a, b and c are used to indicate the first, second and third columns of each page, and the abbreviated name of the university in whose chapter the subject appears is included (examples: ageing, Auck. 1073a; education, M.Gandhi. 838a).

In most cases, only a general indication of subject area is given. Note—Hyphenated words or phrases precede unhyphenated words in the alphabetical sort (examples: 'Canadian-USA relations' precedes 'Canadian art').

ecology, *Calabar* 1160c, *Gujar.* 750c, *Guy.* 593b, *Kelaniya*
1446c, *Lond.* 1807c, *N-W(S.Af.)* 1368b, *Plym.*
1895b, *Rivers SUST* 1211c, *Sheff.* 1922a,
Vic.(Aust.) 185b, *W.Aust.* 193c
ecosystems, *W.Aust.* 193c
ecosystems (assessment), *E.Cowan* 66b
ecosystems (dynamics), *W.Aust.* 200c
ecosystems (management), *E.Cowan* 66b
environment, *Ghana* 583b, *Reading* 1908a, *Stir.* 1941c
environment (human impact on), *Portsmouth* 1900a
health, *Jo'burg.* 1349a
management, *N-W(S.Af.)* 1368b
microbiology, *O.Awolowo* 1199c, *Tas.* 182b
organisms (biochemistry of), *Dar.* 1480c
organisms (health), *W.Laur.* 557a
organisms (physiology of), *Dar.* 1480c
parasitology, *Jo'burg.* 1349a
processes, *Griff.* 73c, *Lanc.* 1723a
resource(s) (economics), *Portsmouth* 1903b
resource(s) (management), *C.Qld.* 45c, *Portsmouth*
1903b
science (and palaeontology), *Deakin* 62a
sciences, *WI* 2000b
technology, *Tas.* 182b
toxicology, *Lond.* 1807c
Arabic
colleges, *Peradeniya* 1452a
culture, *Exe.* 1655a, *Ib.* 1173b
dictionary, *Bayero* 1148c
language, *Durh.* 1635c, *Exe.* 1655a, *Gauh.* 745a, *Ib.*
1173b, *Sindh* 1275a, *W.Cape* 1407b
law, *Lond.* 1817a
linguistics, *Durh.* 1635c, *Ib.* 1173b, *Leeds* 1732c, *Malta*
1040c
literature, *Durh.* 1635c, *Exe.* 1655a, *Gauh.* 745a, *Ib.*
1173b, *Malta* 1040c, *Sindh* 1275a
literature (Nigerian authorship), *Bayero* 1148c
literature (West African), *Ghana* 583c
studies, *Lond.* 1816a
arabidopsis, *Nott.* 1851a
archaeological
analysis (lipid residue), *Bran.* 317c
conservation, *Cardiff* 1618a
exploration (Upper Malwatu Oya), *Kelaniya* 1443c
field services, *Sheff.* 1929c
fieldwork, *Belf.* 1558c
heritage studies, *Kelaniya* 1443c
information systems, *Peradeniya* 1452a
investigations (of Esie stone), *O.Awolowo* 1202b
method, *W.Aust.* 195c
resource management, *Witw.* 1413a
science, *Cardiff* 1618a
sites (management of), *Macq.* 88c
theory, *W.Aust.* 195c, *Wales* 1965a
archaeology, *Auck.* 1067b, *Birm.* 1569b, *Cardiff* 1618a,
Cyprus 565b, *Dar.* 1479c, *Durh.* 1633b, *Ghana*
581c, *Karn.* 811a, *Lond.* 1807c, *MP Bhoj* 824b,
Manit. 388b, 389a, *McG.* 368a, *Melb.* 99a, *Montr.*
411a, *Wales* 1547a
Aboriginal, *E.Cowan* 65b
applied, *S'ton.* 1933a
classical, *Lond.* 1807c, *Peradeniya* 1452a
classical (in south Italy and Sicily), *La Trobe* 83c
environmental, *Birm.* 1569c, *Cyprus* 565b, *Leic.* 1745c,
S.Cross 156b, *Sheff.* 1922a
field, *Sheff.* 1925a
for children, *W.Aust.* 198c
for teachers, *W.Aust.* 198c
funerary, *Sheff.* 1922a
historical, *Glas.* 1663a, *Leic.* 1745c, *NU Singapore* 1315a,
Wales 1965a
in southwest Manitoba, *Bran.* 317c
mediaeval, *Cardiff* 1618a, *Reading* 1908a, *Wales* 1965a
of ancient Corinth, *La Trobe* 80c
of early Christian Rome, *La Trobe* 80b
of early mediaeval Rome, *La Trobe* 80b
of food, *Leic.* 1745c
of gender, *W.Aust.* 195c
of hunter-gatherers, *W.Aust.* 195c
of land use, *NE* 136b
of northwest Europe, *Kent* 1714b
prehistoric, *McG.* 368a, *Peradeniya* 1452b, *Wales* 1965a
protohistoric, *Peradeniya* 1452b
science-based, *Durh.* 1633b
scientific, *Glas.* 1663a
social, *Reading* 1908a
Syro-Palestinian, *Malta* 1040c
archaeomaterials, *Cape Town* 1333a, *Sheff.* 1922a
archaeometry, *Nott.Trent* 1863a
Archean terrains, *AT Balewa* 1138c
architectural
computation, *Chinese HK* 2021a
computer modelling, *Bath* 1553c
conservation, *Cape Town* 1333b, *Plym.* 1888b, 1893b
design, *Plym.* 1894c, *Qld.UT* 149c, *Wat.* 524a, *Winneba*
579c
design (contemporary), *Liv.* 1755a
design (environmental), *Chinese HK* 2021a
design (processes), *Well.* 1113a

design (sustainable), *Auck.* 1067c, *Chinese HK* 2021a,
Tas. 182b
development (and emergency practice), *Oxf.Brookes*
1885a
education, *Plym.* 1893b
engineering, *Bath* 1550b
forms (emergent), *Plym.* 1896a
history, *Bath* 1553c, *Cardiff* 1614b, *Cyprus* 563a,
KwaZulu-Natal 1351a, *Liv.* 1755a, *Malta*
1041a, *McG.* 368a, *Newcastle(NSW)* 141a,
Nott. 1851b, *Oxf.Brookes* 1885a, *Plym.* 1893b,
R.Gordon 1911a, *Wat.* 524a
history (nineteenth-century), *Cant.* 1087c
history (twentieth-century), *Cant.* 1087c
humanities, *Sheff.* 1922a
innovation (technical), *Liv.* 1755a
practice, *Cardiff* 1614b
practice (contemporary), *Cape Town* 1333b
processes, *Sheff.* 1922a
production (history), *Strath.* 1944c
production (theory), *Strath.* 1944c
representation (use of computers in), *Dal.* 350b
science, *Sheff.* 1922a
simulation, *Chinese HK* 2021a
studies (advanced), *Bath* 1550b
sustainability (environmental), *Newcastle(NSW)* 141a
technology, *Oxf.Brookes* 1885a, *Sheff.* 1922a
theory, *Auck.* 1067c, *Cardiff* 1614b, *McG.* 368b, *Montr.*
411b, *Newcastle(NSW)* 141a, *Nott.* 1851b,
R.Gordon 1911a, *Wat.* 524a
theory (contemporary), *Cape Town* 1333b
architecture, *Deakin* 61c, *Leeds Met.* 1740c, *Lond.Met.*
1824a, *Melb.* 95a, *Montr.* 419b, *Nan.Tech.*
1302b, *Syd.* 166c, *Tor.* 490b
and culture, *Oxf.Brookes* 1886c
and space, *Cyprus* 563a
and technology, *Oxf.Brookes* 1886c
city/civic, *Deakin* 61c
community participation in, *Chinese HK* 2021a
court, *Lond.* 1815a
design, *Monash* 115a, *Syd.* 166c
distributed, *Lond.* 1808a
eighteenth- to twentieth-century, *Plym.* 1888c
flood, *Manit.* 388b
gender in, *Oxf.Brookes* 1886c
history, *Leeds Met.* 1740c, *Plym.* 1888c
humane, *Plym.* 1893b
in community development, *Dal.* 350b
industrial, *C'dia.* 343a
interior, *Well.* 1113b, 1114b
low-energy, *Lond.Met.* 1824a
mediaeval, *McG.* 368b
post-mediaeval, *McG.* 368b
pre-Islam/Islamic, *Lond.* 1815a
religious, *Lond.* 1815a
social, *Cyprus* 563a
sustainable, *Oxf.Brookes* 1885a
sustainable tropical, *Putra* 1022a
technologically intelligent, *Cyprus* 563a
theology of, *Leeds Met.* 1740c
timber use in, *Tas.* 182b
urban, *Montr.* 411b
very low-energy, *Plym.* 1896a
archive/archival, *Ghana* 581c
administration, *Ib.* 1174c, *Wales* 1541c
record managment, *Ib.* 1174c
science, *Montr.* 413c
studies, *Liv.* 1757b, *Manit.* 391b
studies (African), *S.Leone* 1287b
system(s), *Monash* 127b
archives
computing for, *Glas.* 1666b
government agenda, *Liv.* 1762a
in the United Kingdom, *Liv.* 1762a
Arctic
archaeology, *Wat.* 524a
communities, *W.Laur.* 560b
culture, *Manit.* 392b
ecology, *Sheff.* 1929c
history, *Manit.* 392b
political development, *Manit.* 392b
Russian (coastal waters), *Plym.* 1896b
terrain, *Wat.* 535c
area studies, *Ib.* 1175b, *Portsmouth* 1901c, *Reading* 1909a
arid
ecophysiology, *Pret.* 1380a
Aristotelianism, *Dal.* 351a
Aristotle, *Herts.* 1689b
arms
control, *Manit.* 398c, *W.Laur.* 560b, *Wat.* 533a
proliferation, *Manit.* 398c
race (international), *Wat.* 532a
trade, *Wat.* 532a
arrhythmia, *Montr.* 419a
artefacts/artefactual
analysis, *Leic.* 1751a
in research, *Herts.* 1688c
arterial
disease, *Birm.* 1574c
arthritis, *Cardiff* 1620c, *E.Anglia* 1638c, *McG.* 380b

inflammatory (molecular basis of), *Auck.* 1076c
psoriatic, *KwaZulu-Natal* 1355b
rheumatic (genetics of), *KwaZulu-Natal* 1355b
rheumatoid, *Herts.* 1689a, *S.Ramachandra* 927c, 928c
rheumatoid (biochemical studies), *S.Ramachandra* 926b
rheumatoid (genetic studies), *S.Ramachandra* 926b
rheumatoid (management of), *S.Ramachandra* 926b
surgery, *Cape Town* 1340b
Arthurian
literature, *Wales* 1546c
artificial
cells, *McG.* 380a
intelligence, *Auck.* 1069a, *Azad J&K* 1237b, *Botswana*
261a, *Brist.* 1586a, *C'dia.* 344a, *Cant.* 1090a,
Curtin 55c, *DAV* 726a, *Dharmsinh Desai* 728a,
Exe. 1656a, *FJ Women* 1243a, *Ghulam IKIST*
1245c, *Griff.* 71c, *Gulb.* 754a, *Hudd.* 1692b,
J.Hamdard 791a, *Jo'burg.* 1347c, *La Trobe* 83c,
Lahore MS 1255c, *Leeds* 1728b, *Lough.*
1831b, *M.Sund.* 856b, 857b, *Manit.* 389b,
Melb. 97b, *NE* 136c, *NUST(P'stan.)* 1264a,
Open(UK) 1871c, *Plym.* 1895b, *Portsmouth*
1900b, *Punjabi* 891b, *SP* 907a, *Sheff.* 1930c,
Stell. 1394c, *Stir.* 1942a, *Tas.* 182b, *Ulster*
1961a, *Wat.* 526a, *Well.* 1116c
intelligence (and design), *Syd.* 175b
intelligence (and logic), *Cyprus* 563c, *ICL* 1702b
intelligence (applications), *Tas.* 179c
intelligence (applied), *Liv.J.Moores* 1765b
intelligence (technologies), *Glam.* 1660b
limbs (fabrication), *Sir Syed UET* 1277c
organs, *MDSU* 836a, *McG.* 380a
vision, *McG.* 382a
vision (sensing), *Plym.* 1896b
artistic
practice (as research), *Griff.* 74c
art(s), *Auck.UT* 1081b, *C.Sturt* 52c, *Deakin* 62b, *Herts.*
1689b, *Leth.* 365b, *Lond.* 1778a, *Qld.UT* 149c,
Sunshine Coast 159a
-making behaviour (collaborative processes in), *Hull*
1699a
abstract, *Chinese HK* 2023b
and representation, *S'ton.* 1933a
and technologies, *R.Gordon* 1911b
anthropology of, *C'dia.* 347a
applied, *Ulster* 1960a
appreciation, *NU Malaysia* 1020b
Canadian, *McG.* 368b
city/civic, *Deakin* 61c
collecting, *Kingston(UK)* 1718a
collecting (history of), *Birm.* 1569c
conservation, *Nott.Trent* 1863a, *Qu.* 452a
construction of national and group identities, *Plym.*
1888c
contemporary, *Auck.* 1067c, *Leeds Met.* 1740c,
Liv.J.Moores 1765a, *McG.* 368b, *Oxf.Brookes*
1885a, *Reading* 1906a
contemporary (practice), *Herts.* 1688c
contextual, *Oxf.Brookes* 1885a
creativity in the, *Nipissing* 437b
critical theory, *Ulster* 1960a
digital, *Monash* 120a, *Oxf.Brookes* 1885a
eighteenth- to twentieth-century, *Plym.* 1888c
electronic, *Middx.* 1842c, *Monash* 120a
emergent, *Plym.* 1896a
environmental studies, *Tas.* 183a
experimental, *W.Aust.* 191c
feminist theory and the, *Rhodes* 1389b
fine, *Herts.* 1684a, *Monash* 114a, 117b, *Qu.* 452a, *Ulster*
1960a
gallery (of the future), *Lough.* 1830b
history, *Adel.* 26c, *Griff.* 69c, *Herts.* 1684a, *Karn.* 811a,
Liv. 1755a, *Lough.* 1830b, *Manit.* 388b, *Montr.*
411b, 420b, *NU Singapore* 1311b, *Plym.*
1888c, *Qu.* 452a, *Wales* 1540b
history (contemporary), *Lond.* 1777a
in the classroom, *C'dia.* 343a
international, *Pret.* 1381b
live, *Nott.Trent* 1866c, *Oxf.Brookes* 1885a
live (archiving), *Nott.Trent* 1866c
management, *Deakin* 62a, *Qld.UT* 149b
materials, *Qu.* 452a
materials (local), *Winneba* 578c
media, *Plym.* 1891b
media (traditional), *Dar.* 1479b
metaphysical aspects of, *Plym.* 1895b
modern, *Auck.* 1067c, *McG.* 368b
nineteenth-century, *Auck.* 1067c, *Glas.* 1666b
oral, *Cape Coast* 575b
Pacific, *Cant.* 1087c, *Well.* 1113b
philosophies in, *Plym.* 1896a
philosophy of, *Auck.* 1074a
plastic, *Cape Town* 1335c
poetic, *Ib.* 1176a
practice (and research), *R.Gordon* 1911b
practice (contemporary), *Leth.* 363c, *Tas.* 179a
practice (environmental), *R.Gordon* 1911b
practice (sustainable), *R.Gordon* 1911b
romantic (investigations of), *Plym.* 1888c
seventeenth-century, *Glas.* 1666b

Cornish studies
  culture, *Exe.* 1658b
  education, *Exe.* 1658b
  history, *Exe.* 1658b
  territorial politics, *Exe.* 1658b
coronary
  prevention (in children), *Exe.* 1658b
coronary artery
  bypass, *S.Ramachandra* 926b
coronary heart disease, *Leic.* 1749c
  risk factors (genetic), *KwaZulu-Natal* 1354c
  risk factors (inter-generational), *Nan.Tech.* 1295c
coroners, *Nipissing* 437c
corporate
  accounting, *Aberd.* 1535a, *H-W* 1680c
  change (management), *Bath* 1556a
  communication, *DAV* 726b, *Ulster* 1960c
  communication (accountable), *G.Jamb.* 760b
  communication (strategy/ies), *Nan.Tech.* 1293c
  control, *Lond.* 1801a, *Syd.* 169c
  crime, *Open(UK)* 1870c
  culture, *Reading* 1906c, *S.Pac.* 1422b
  decision support systems, *Botswana* 262c
  ethics, *Bath* 1553c
  failure (prediction of), *Stell.* 1392c
  finance, *Adel.* 25b, *Birm.* 1567a, *C'dia.* 345b, *Durh.*
      1634a, *Exe.* 1658c, *Ghana* 581a, *H-W* 1680c,
      Inst.Bus.Man.(P'stan.) 1247c, *J.Hamdard* 791b,
      Lanc. 1721b, *Lond.* 1802b, *McG.* 382c, *Montr.*
      424c, *NU Singapore* 1318c, *Nan.Tech.* 1301a,
      1302a, *Nott.* 1859a, *Plym.* 1892c, *Strath.*
      1944b, *Swinburne UT* 161a
  finance (disclosure), *Chinese HK* 2021a
  finance (international), *Manit.* 388a
  governance, *Bath* 1556a, *Belf.* 1559c, *C.Sturt* 50c,
      Chinese HK 2021a, *Colombo* 1436c, *Deakin*
      61c, *Exe.* 1655b, *Griff.* 74a, 74c, *KwaZulu-*
      Natal 1351a, *Lahore MS* 1255b, *Lanc.* 1721b,
      Liv. 1757b, *McG.* 382c, *Melb.* 94b, *Monash*
      114a, *NU Malaysia* 1015b, *NU Singapore*
      1318b, *Nan.Tech.* 1300c, 1301a, *Napier*
      1844b, *Nott.* 1858c, *Oxf.Brookes* 1885a, *Plym.*
      1895a, *Portsmouth* 1898c, *Qld.UT* 149a, 149b,
      Syd. 169c, *Tas.* 179a, *Ulster* 1960a, *Vic.(Aust.)*
      186c, *W.Aust.* 192c, 198b
  governance (of regulated industries), *Bath* 1555b
  governance (regulation), *C.Sturt* 50c, *Griff.* 74a
  leadership, *Bath* 1556a
  management, *Montr.* 423c
  performance, *Herts.* 1689a, *Plym.* 1893c
  performance (management), *Monash* 125a
  performance measurement, *Belf.* 1559c
  policy, *Chinese HK* 2021a, *Karn.* 810c, *Lincoln(NZ)* 1094b
  regulation, *Monash* 114a
  reports/reporting, *Vic.(Aust.)* 185a
  responsibility, *Aberd.* 1535a, *Griff.* 74a, *Nott.* 1855a
  responsibility (social), *Bath* 1553c, *C.Sturt* 50c, *Leeds*
      Met. 1743b, *Nott.* 1858c
  responsibility (social, economics of), *Nott.* 1858c
  responsibility (social, in Asia), *Nott.* 1859a
  responsibility (social, theories of), *Nott.* 1858c
  social performance, *C'dia.* 346c
  strategy, *Montr.* 425a, *Warw.* 1978c
  turnaround, *WI* 2001b
corporations
  and society, *Bath* 1553c
  professional, *Tor.* 509c
corrosion, *Ghulam IKIST* 1246a, *IIT Bombay* 778c, *Monash*
      125b, *Pret.* 1376c, 1385c, *W.Aust.* 194a
  environmental (chemistry), *Calabar* 1159a
  high-temperature, *Auck.* 1070b
  inhibition, *MDSU* 835c
corruption, *Griff.* 74a, *KwaZulu-Natal* 1351c
  investigation, *Qld.UT* 150c
  prevention, *Pret.* 1385c
corsets
  eighteenth-century, *Dal.* 355b
corticosteroids, *Rhodes* 1390b
cosmetics, *Leeds* 1728a
cosmic ray physics, *N-W(S.Af.)* 1370a, *Tas.* 183a
cosmological
  structures (large-scale), *Swinburne UT* 162b
cosmology, *Cant.* 1092a, *Cape Town* 1336c, *Kelaniya*
      1445b, *Kent* 1714c, *KwaZulu-Natal* 1353c, *McG.*
      384c, *NE Hill* 872a, *Tor.* 508c, *Wat.* 531b
  observational, *Liv.J.Moores* 1767a
  string, *Portsmouth* 1903a
cost
  -effectiveness analysis (uncertainty in), *Sheff.* 1929c
  -effectiveness studies (design), *Monash* 121b, *Sheff.*
      1929c
  analysis, *Calabar* 1158b
  benefit analysis, *M'lore.* 843a, *Stell.* 1396a
  function analysis, *Ulster* 1960c
  management systems, *NE* 137a
costume
  design, *Leth.* 366a, *Melb.* 102b
  Egungun, *O.Awolowo* 1198c
cot death, *Monash* 122b

coude spectropolarimeter
  high resolution (development of), *Bran.* 317c
cough reflex, *Hull* 1698c
counselling, *Putra* 1023b
counselling/counsellors, *Abertay* 1539b, *Calabar* 1159b,
      Cape Coast 575a, *FJ Women* 1243a, *Griff.* 71b,
      Herts. 1688b, *Leic.* 1749a, *Lond.Met.* 1824c,
      Melb. 106c, *Monash* 126b, *NE* 136b, *Nan.Tech.*
      1296a, *Pret.* 1380b, *Stell.* 1400a, *Wales* 1970b
  coping mechanisms among, *KwaZulu-Natal* 1358b
  cross-cultural, *Canberra* 42b, *Stell.* 1397a
  discursive approaches to, *Waik.* 1121c
  in schools, *Aust.Cath.* 34b
  interactions (micro-analysis of), *Bond* 39a
  para-professional, *Bran.* 317a
  pastoral, *W.Laur.* 560a
  positive therapy, *Avina. Women* 685c
  psychology, *McG.* 370a, *New Br.* 430b
  studies, *Well.* 1115a
counter-terrorism
  politics of, *Monash* 125c
countryside, *Reading* 1905c
  European (changing), *Oxf.Brookes* 1886b
courts, *Manit.* 399b
  and crime, *E.Cowan* 65b
  and drug(s), *E.Cowan* 65b
  functions of, *Monash* 125c
  processes of, *Monash* 125c
covert
  operations, *New Br.* 434b
cowpeas, *Ebonyi State* 1164b
crafts
  contemporary, *Herts.* 1689a
  history of, *Lough.* 1830b
  manipulation, *Herts.* 1689a
  processes, *Herts.* 1689a
cranio-facial
  anomalies (aetiology of), *NU Singapore* 1315c
  anomalies (prevention of), *NU Singapore* 1315c
  morphology, *Adel.* 25c
  surgery, *KwaZulu-Natal* 1356b, *Stell.* 1399c, 1400a
craniosynostosis, *KwaZulu-Natal* 1356b
creative/creativity, *Avina. Women* 684c, *Cant.* 1086c, *Ib.*
      1174b, *La Trobe* 78c, *Montr.* 424c, *Qld.UT* 153a,
      Wales 1970b
  individual, *S'ton.* 1933b
  industries, *Murd.* 133a, *Portsmouth* 1899a, *Qld.UT* 152c,
      Waik. 1123b
  practice, *Canberra* 42a, *Waik.* 1123b
  practice (metaphysical aspects of), *Plym.* 1895b
  spaces, *Deakin* 61c
  thinking, *Malta* 1045b
credit
  functions of, *Dschang* 273a
  management, *Lond.Met.* 1824c
  markets (economics of), *Nott.* 1859a
  planning, *M'lore.* 843a
  risk management, *Malta* 1041a
Cree
  language, *Bran.* 317b
Creole
  languages (French-based), *Macq.* 89b
  linguistics, *Maur.* 1051c, *WI* 2000a
Creoles, *Auck.* 1071b
crime, *Birm.* 1572c, *Calabar* 1160b, *Cardiff* 1622c, *Durh.*
      1633a, *Hudd.* 1694b, *Lond.* 1801b, *Monash*
      120c, *Strath.* 1946b, *Tata Inst.Soc.Scis.* 939a, *WI*
      1996c, *Wales* 1547c, *Well.* 1118b
  and criminal justice, *Qld.UT* 150c, *Sur.* 1952c
  and delinquency (theories of), *Lond.* 1802a
  and employment, *Lond.* 1802a
  and popular culture (eighteenth-century), *Plym.* 1891a
  and popular culture (nineteenth-century), *Plym.* 1891a
  and punishment, *Cant.* 1087c
  and punishment (history of), *Tor.* 508c
  causes of, *W.Aust.* 198b
  control, *Hull* 1696a
  fear of, *WI* 2001c
  impact of (on society), *M.Sund.* 856b
  organised (investigation), *Qld.UT* 150c
  patterns (regional), *W.Aust.* 198b
  patterns (urban), *W.Aust.* 198b
  prevention, *Montr.* 419b, *Well.* 1117c
  reduction, *Leic.* 1747a
  sociology of, *NE* 137c, *Warw.* 1976b
  trans-national, *S.Fraser* 487a
  trends, *W.Aust.* 198b
  victims of, *Montr.* 412a
  violence, *W.Aust.* 198b
  white collar, *Open(UK)* 1870c
criminal
  behaviour, *Montr.* 412a, 419b
  investigation(s), *Portsmouth* 1903b
  justice, *Aberd.* 1536c, *Birm.* 1571b, *Cardiff* 1622c,
      Chinese HK 2024a, *Glas.* 1668b, *Herts.* 1688b,
      1688c, *Hull* 1696a, *Kent* 1715a, *KwaZulu-*
      Natal 1358a, *Lanc.* 1721c, *Leic.* 1749a, *Leth.*
      365b, *Monash* 117c, *Open(UK)* 1870c, *Plym.*
      1893a, *Qld.UT* 150c, *S'ton.* 1936a, *S.Cross*
      156c, *Sheff.* 1930a, *Wales* 1547c

justice (and rehabilitation), *NU Singapore* 1314b
justice (decision-making), *Griff.* 70b
justice (ethics), *C.Sturt* 52c
justice (indigenous), *Syd.* 175b
justice (policy, comparative), *S.Fraser* 487a
justice (process and policy), *Lond.* 1802a
justice (professional cultures in), *Portsmouth* 1903b
justice (reform), *Tor.* 508c
justice (sentencing), *Griff.* 70b
justice (sentencing, comparative), *Lond.* 1802a
justice (services), *Lond.* 1803a, *Sheff.* 1926b
justice (system), *M.Sund.* 856b, *Tas.* 180b
  procedure, *Cape Town* 1334a
  regulation, *Tor.* 508c
criminology, *Bath* 1553b, *Bayero* 1151a, *C.Sturt* 52a,
      Calabar 1160b, *Deakin* 62a, *Ebonyi State* 1165b,
      Glas. 1668b, *Ib.* 1175c, *Keele* 1712b, *Kent*
      1716a, *Lond.* 1801c, *Manit.* 394a, *Punjabi* 893a,
      Sheff. 1924c, 1930a, *Tas.* 180b, 180c, *W.Aust.*
      194c, *WI* 1995a, 1998c, *Wat.* 534a
  Canadian youth, *Bran.* 318a
  Chinese, *Bran.* 318a
  cultural, *Well.* 1117c
  ecological, *Cape Town* 1334a
  feminist, *Manit.* 398c
  historical, *Manit.* 398c
crisis
  intervention, *Reading* 1908a
  management, *Liv.* 1757c, *Wat.* 526b
critical enquiry, *Reading* 1906a
critical practice, *La Trobe* 84c
critical reflection, *La Trobe* 84c
critical risk, *Deakin* 62a
critical studies, *La Trobe* 78c
critical theory, *Cardiff* 1617b, *Exe.* 1656b, *La Trobe* 84a,
      Lond. 1778a, *Monash* 117a, 125a, *S'ton.* 1935b,
      Sheff. 1929c, *W.Aust.* 196a, *W.Ont.* 544a
  modern, *Cyprus* 564b
criticism, *M'lore.* 843a
  theory of, *Islamia, Bahawal.* 1249c
Croatian
  studies, *Macq.* 89b
Crohn's disease, *Qu.* 459a
cropping, *C.Sturt* 52c
crop(s), *Rivers SUST* 1212b
  biochemistry, *Reading* 1906b
  biotechnology of, *Bran.* 316c
  development, *Stell.* 1395b
  disease (bio-control of), *C.Sturt* 50b
  disease (management), *BSMR Ag.* 218c
  ecology, *Reading* 1906b
  environmental effects on, *Pret.* 1380a
  evolution, *Reading* 1906b
  for export, *Kwame NUST* 588c
  growth, *Stell.* 1395b
  husbandry, *VB* 949c
  hybrid technology, *BSMR Ag.* 218b
  improvement, *Avina. Women* 684b
  improvement (molecular), *BSMR Ag.* 218b
  management, *BSMR Ag.* 218a, *NE* 137b, *Pret.* 1380a
  management (cultural), *BSMR Ag.* 218c
  modelling, *Aberd.* 1534c
  Nigerian (lipids in), *O.Awolowo* 1199a
  nutrient management, *McG.* 381b
  nutrition, *Ib.* 1173a
  pathogens (resistance to), *Makurdi Ag.* 1143b
  pest control/biocontrol, *McG.* 381b
  physiology, *BSMR Ag.* 218a, 218b, *Ib.* 1173a, *Maur.*
      1050c, *Nair.* 971b, *Plym.* 1894b, *Reading*
      1906b, *VB* 950a, *WI* 2000b
  plantation, *Peradeniya* 1452c
  processing, *Bindura* 2044c, *Ib.* 1172c
  production, *Maur.* 1050c, *Melb.* 102a, *Rivers SUST*
      1211b, *Stell.* 1393a
  production (economics of), *BSMR Ag.* 217b
  production (technology), *Ebonyi State* 1164b
  protection, *Rivers SUST* 1211b, *Tas.* 179a
  rotation, *Adel.* 26a
  science, *Aberd.* 1534c, *Nott.* 1850c, *Reading* 1905c,
      W.Aust. 195b, *Wales* 1546c
  soil-machine-crop interaction, *McG.* 385c
  storage, *Bindura* 2044c, *Ib.* 1172c, *Peradeniya* 1453a
  systems, *Dschang* 273a, *Manit.* 393b
  systems (sustainable), *NE* 138a
  tropical (embryogenesis of), *WI* 1997a
  tropical (fermentation of), *Lagos* 1184a
  tropical (in vitro propagation of), *Jomo K.* 967a
  tropical (production strategies), *WI* 1996a
  tropical (storage of), *WI* 1996a
  tropical (strategic utilisation of), *WI* 1996a
cross-cultural
  communications, *Leeds Met.* 1743b, *NE* 137c
  health psychology, *Curtin* 58c
  issues, *La Trobe* 84b
  practice(s), *W.Aust.* 196b
  pragmatics, *Well.* 1116b
  studies, *Monash* 117b, 117c, 120c, 124b, 125a, 127c,
      128c, *Putra* 1025c, *Sindh* 1275c
crustal
  evolution, *Portsmouth* 1900a

policy (reform), WI 1999a
policy (studies in), Durh. 1634b
political, Ib. 1176a
population, Ebonyi State 1163c, Manip. 855a, Winneba 579a
post-compulsory, Lanc 1722a, 1722b, 1724c, S'ton. 1934b, Sheff. 1923a
post-fourteen, Leeds 1729a
post-secondary, Manit. 399a
postgraduate, Auck. 1079b
practice, Bayero 1149b, Lanc. 1724c, Sur. 1953b
practitioners, Vic.(Aust.) 185c
practitioners (thinking and development), Stir. 1942a
pre-school, Leeds 1729a, Newcastle(NSW) 145a
primary, Leeds 1729a, Middx. 1843b, Northumbria 1849a, Warw. 1973b
primary (learning and assessment in), Leeds Met. 1744a
primary (literacy), E.Cowan 65a
primary (partnership working), Hull 1699b
primary (resourcing), E.Cowan 65a
professional, Newcastle(NSW) 141a
psychology, DAV 726b
quality in, Strath. 1945c
quality of, S.Pac. 1423a
quality of (monitoring), Chinese HK 2028b
regulatory frameworks, Montr. 421a
relationships, Griff. 70c
religious, Cape Coast 576a, Cape Town 1338a, McG. 369c
religious (provision of resources for), Aust.Cath. 33c, 34c, 35c
religious (teacher education in), Aust.Cath. 33c, 34c, 35c
religious (teaching), Botswana 262b
religious (theory and practice of), Aust.Cath. 33c, 34c, 35c
remote, C.Sturt 52b
science, Aust.Cath. 35a, Cant. 1090a, Colombo 1438a, Durh. 1634b, Exe. 1656a, Leeds 1729a, Malta 1043b, McG. 369c, NE 138c, Open(UK) 1869a, Pret. 1375b, Putra 1023c, Qu. 453b, 453c, Rhodes 1389a, W.Ont. 541a, WI 1999a
science (and computers), Winneba 579b
science (and spirituality), Plym. 1894a
science (assessing progress in), Liv. 1763a
science (creativity in), Nan.Tech. 1295c, Oxf.Brookes 1885b
science (early years), Bran. 317c
science (innovative), Plym. 1894a
science (language in), Botswana 263a
social and cultural context of, Adel. 26b
social contexts of, Strath. 1945c
social outcomes of, Monash 125b
social (studies), Botswana 262b
social work, Strath. 1948a
sociology of, Auck.UT 1083b, Botswana 261b, Chinese HK 2025a, Gauh. 745c, Karn. 811c, KwaZulu-Natal 1354c, M.Sund. 857a, Macq. 88b, WI 1998c, Warw. 1976b
special, C.Sturt 52b
special/special needs, Birm. 1568a, Cape Coast 575a, Leeds 1729a, M.Gandhi 837b, MP Bhoj 824c, Melb. 100a, 105b, Monash 126b, NE Hill 872b, Nan.Tech. 1294c, Newcastle(NSW) 142b, 146a, Open S.Lanka 1449c, Plym. 1890b, Sheff. 1923a, W.Aust. 193b, Waik. 1121c, Warw. 1973b
special needs (and disability), Plym. 1894c
spiritual dimension in, Aust.Cath. 33c, 34c, 35c
sports, Putra 1024a
studies, Melb. 100a, Sunshine Coast 159a
systems, Montr. 412c
talented, Chinese HK 2022b
task development (national), Liv. 1763a
technology/ical, DAV 726b, FJ Women 1243a, McG. 369c, Middx. 1843b, Open(UK) 1869a, Pret. 1375b, 1386c, Rhodes 1389a, W.Ont. 541a, Winneba 579a, 579c
technology/ical transfer in, Botswana 261b
technology in, C.Sturt 51a
technology-enhanced, Maur. 1052c
tertiary (management), NE 138b
theatre in, Qu. 453b
training, Montr. 412c
transformational, Qu. 453b
upper secondary, Lanc. 1724c
values, Aust.Cath. 33c, 34c, NE Hill 872b, Punjabi 891c
values (in Singapore), Nan.Tech. 1295c
visual arts, Aust.Cath. 35b
vocational, Hudd. 1693a, Putra 1023c, Winneba 579a
widening access, Glas. 1663a
workplace, Montr. 412c
youth (non-formal), Botswana 260c
educational
administration, Botswana 261b, Chinese HK 2022b, DAV 726b, NE 137a, W.Aust. 193b
assessment, Cant. 1089c, Cape Coast 575a, Chinese HK 2022b, Exe. 1656a, Nan.Tech. 1296a, Pret. 1375b, Qu. 453c, S.Pac. 1423a, Waik. 1121a, 1124b, Winneba 579b
assessment (contexts), Belf. 1558a

assessment (culturally appropriate, in New Zealand), Waik. 1123a
assessment (digital formats of), E.Cowan 66c
assessment (in New Zealand), Waik. 1123a
assessment (international), Bath 1554a
assessment (national), Ib. 1178b
assessment (policy), Open(UK) 1869a
assessment (practice), Open(UK) 1869a
attainment, Bayero 1149b
broadcasting, M.Sund. 856b
change, Leeds Met. 1744a
computing, Aust.Cath. 35a
consultation, McG. 383b, Stell. 1400c
counselling, Newcastle(NSW) 145a, Stell. 1394a
counselling (psychological), Chinese HK 2022b
development, Leth. 364b, WI 1990b
development (influence of missionaries in), S.Leone 1287b
disadvantage (effects of), Cape Town 1341b
economics, Chinese HK 2022b
effectiveness, Strath. 1945c
environment(s), Montr. 412c
evaluation, Cant. 1089c, Colombo 1436c, Exe. 1658b, S.Pac. 1423a
films (production of), DAV 726c
finance, Chinese HK 2022b
foundations, Newcastle(NSW) 142b
guidance, Punjabi 891c, Stell. 1394a
guidance (psychological), Chinese HK 2022b
ideology, Stell. 1394a
innovation, WI 1990b
innovations (and research findings, dissemination of), McG. 383b
leadership, Botswana 261b, Chinese HK 2022b, Leeds Met. 1744a, Nott. 1860a, Rhodes 1389a, S.Cross 156a, Stell. 1393c, Waik. 1123a
leadership management, FJ Women 1243a
management, Aust.Cath. 33c, Birm. 1568a, Botswana 261b, Gauh. 745c, Gulb. 754a, Manip. 854b, Rhodes 1389a, SP 907a, Sindh 1274c, W.Aust. 193b, Winneba 580a
measurement, Colombo 1436c, Nan.Tech. 1296a
media, Melb. 99b, 102a, Qld.UT 152c
mentoring, Stell. 1400c
methods, Sheff. 1927c
needs, Exe. 1656a
organisation(s), Stell. 1394a
outcomes, Manit. 398c
partnerships, Open(UK) 1869b, Plym. 1896a
performance (indicators), Pret. 1376a
philosophy, E.Af.Baraton 964a
planning, McG. 383b, Qu. 453c, Sindh 1274c
policy, Birm. 1568a, Botswana 261b, Cape Town 1335b, Cyprus 564a, Lanc. 1722b, Pret. 1376a, Sheff. 1923a, Sur. 1952b, W.Ont. 541a, Wales 1541a, Well. 1115a
policy (-making), W.Aust. 193b
policy (analysis), Stell. 1394a, Waik. 1121c
policy (development), Stell. 1394a
policy (evaluation), Cape Town 1334c
policy (support), Cape Town 1334c
programme evaluation, Aust.Cath. 35b, Ib. 1178b, Qu. 453c
psychology, Colombo 1436c, Hull 1698c, Melb. 100a, Nan.Tech. 1296a, Qu. 453c
quality (assurance), Pret. 1375b, 1376a
reform, Lond. 1802b
reform (Sri Lankan), Peradeniya 1453a
research, C.Qld. 45b, 45c, Islamia, Bahawal. 1249a
research (methodology), W.Aust. 193b
research (methods), Reading 1907c
settings (complex, learning in), McG. 380a
standards, Winneba 579b
studies, Newcastle(NSW) 145b
supervision, E.Af.Baraton 964a
systems (evaluation of), Ib. 1178b
systems (in North-Eastern region (India)), NE Hill 871b
technology, Birm. 1568c, C'dia. 344b, Dib. 728c, Gulb. 754a, Melb. 99b, 102a, Nan.Tech. 1295a, SPMV 924c, Stell. 1393c
technology (and behavioural management), E.Cowan 66c
technology (and ethics), E.Cowan 66c
technology (and social interaction), E.Cowan 66c
technology (and teachers), E.Cowan 66c
technology (application(s) in remote learning), S.Pac. 1423b
technology (application(s) in remote teaching), S.Pac. 1423b
television, M.Sund. 856b
test development (national), Liv. 1763a
theory, Stell. 1394a
effluent
discharges (effects), Makurdi Ag. 1143c
industrial, Bayero 1151a
management, KwaZulu-Natal 1352a
treatment (cattle and swine), McG. 379c
treatment (plants), G.Jamb. 760b
Efutu
vowels (phonological analysis of), Winneba 579a

Egyptian archaeology, Macq. 89a, 91c
Egyptology, Auck. 1068c, Swansea 1955b
eighteenth-century
studies, Liv. 1757a, S'ton. 1935b, Stell. 1396b, Wales 1541a
elasticity, Glas. 1667a, M.Gandhi 838a
systems, Wat. 531b
elastin assembly, Syd. 172b
elderly people
and carers (in different cultures), Sheff. 1929a
and modernisation, Gandh.Rural 743c
care of, ICL 1706c, La Trobe 83c, Napier 1845b, Newcastle(NSW) 145c, Plym. 1896a, Qu. 458c
competence in, C'dia. 347c
disability in, Plym. 1894b
exploitation of (prevention of), S.Fraser 487b
falls/falling in, Hull 1699a, Tor. 509b, W.Laur. 558b
health care of, Edin. 1647b, Plym. 1893a, R.Gordon 1911c
health of, Chinese HK 2026a, Kwame NUST 590a, R.Gordon 1911b
health of (women), Plym. 1894b
healthcare of, Herts. 1689b
homeless, Sheff. 1927b
institutionalisation of, Wat. 530a
motivation, Bran. 318a
nursing care of, Edin. 1647b, Manit. 399a
nutrition in, Kwame NUST 590a, Makurdi Ag. 1144a
Parsi, Tata Inst.Soc.Scis. 939a
pharmacotherapeutics, Montr. 416c
problems of, SPMV 925b
psychiatric problems in, Kelaniya 1446b
psychiatry of, Liv. 1761a
rehabilitation of, Exe. 1658c
social issues, Plym. 1893a
victimisation of (prevention of), S.Fraser 487a
elections
observers of, Kingston(UK) 1720a
electoral
behaviour, W.Aust. 196a
geography, Plym. 1895a
politics, Exe. 1657a, Gauh. 746c, SP 907c
studies, Lanc. 1724a, Montr. 415b, Plym. 1893a
system(s), S.Pac. 1422a, Well. 1115b
electrical
drives, Liv.J.Moores 1765c, Sheff. 1923b
energy (conversion systems), Nan.Tech. 1297c
generation (distributed), Cant. 1086b
machines, Liv.J.Moores 1765c, S.Leone 1287a
plant condition monitoring, G.Caledonian 1673a
power, Belf. 1558b, Leic. 1747b
power (and control), C.Qld. 44c
power (systems), AT Balewa 1138b
power (technology), Cant. 1086b
transformers, Cant. 1086b
electricity
demand (management), Pret. 1386c
generation (photovoltaic), Malta 1045b
price modelling, Vic.(Aust.) 185c
supply (power systems), W.Aust. 198c
electro-acoustics, C'dia. 346b
electro-hydraulic power, Bath 1555a
electro-optics, Ghulam IKIST 1246a, W.Aust. 198c, Wat. 528a
electrobiotechnology, Waik. 1121b
electrocatalytic
reactions, Rhodes 1388c
electrochemistry/electrochemical, Bath 1550c, M'lore. 843a, Monash 115a, Putra 1022c, S'ton. 1934a
fundamentals, Pret. 1385c
molecular design, Portsmouth 1902a
sensors, Botswana 261a
electroluminescent display, SP 907a
electrolysers, W.Cape 1406b
electromagnetic(s)/electromagnetism, Lough. 1834a, Macq. 88c, NU Singapore 1319a, WI 2000b
acoustic, Nott. 1859c
applied, Manit. 390a, Maur. 1052a, W.Ont. 541c
compatibility, Bayero 1149c
computational, C'dia. 344c, Witw. 1412c
interference, Bayero 1149c
materials, Exe. 1658a
modelling, Nott. 1852c
power, C'dia. 344c
scattering (statistical), Nott. 1852c
systems, New Br. 431a
theory, S.Leone 1287b
electromaterials
applications, W'gong. 210c
characterisation of, W'gong. 210c
synthesis of, W'gong. 210c
electromechanical systems, Glas. 1665b, Sheff. 1923b
micro-, Belf. 1563c
micro- (manufacturing), H-W 1681c
micro- (packaging of), H-W 1681c
micro- (radio frequency), H-W 1681c
electromyography, Macq. 89a, W.Ont. 551b
electronic
circuits (component design), Pret. 1386b
circuits (high-frequency), Belf. 1558b

meat
  and fat quality, *Adel.* 30a
  freezing of, *Auck.* 1072a
  microbiology, *Pret.* 1377b
  non-conventional, *Jomo K.* 966c
  products, *Peradeniya* 1452a
  quality, *Lincoln(NZ)* 1094b, *Nott.* 1851a
  sciences, *Stell.* 1393a
  technology, *Arid Ag.* 1235b
mechanical
  behaviour (of very small systems), *McG.* 384a
  design, *Wat.* 528c
  systems, *C'dia.* 345a, *Nan.Tech.* 1299b
mechanics, *Sur.* 1952a, *W'gong.* 209c
  applied, *Cant.* 1090c, *Ib.* 1174a, *KwaZulu-Natal* 1352b,
      New Br. 431b, *Rivers SUST* 1211c
  biological, *ICL* 1701a
  classical, *N.Maharashtra* 868c
  computational, *ICL* 1703c, *Nan.Tech.* 1293b, 1299a,
      Nott. 1852b, *S'ton.* 1935a, *Strath.* 1946a,
      W'gong. 210b, *W.Aust.* 193c
  continuum, *Cape Town* 1336c, *Hull* 1697b, *Witw.* 1414b
  damage, *Syd.* 174c
  experimental, *Strath.* 1946a
  granular, *Kingston(UK)* 1718b
  particle, *Curtin* 56a
  quantum, *Griff.* 74c
  solid, *Auck.* 1071a, *Dal.* 352a, *E.Anglia* 1640b, *G.Jamb.*
      761a, *IIT Bombay* 779b, *Ib.* 1174a, *Nott.*
      1859c, *VB* 950c
  solid (body), *Wat.* 528c
  teaching and learning, *Plym.* 1897a
mechanisms, *Bayero* 1149c
mechatronics, *Cant.* 1090c, *Lanc.* 1722b, *Lond.* 1791c,
      Monash 116c, *Nan.Tech.* 1299c, *Pret.* 1376c,
      Swinburne UT 161c, *W.Aust.* 194a, *Wales* 1970b,
      Wat. 529a
  intelligent (automation and applications), *W'gong.* 208a
media, *Bayero* 1150b, *Birm.* 1573b, *Cant.* 1087b, *Cape Town*
      1335b, *Ghana* 582a, *Greenwich* 1677c, *Leeds*
      Met. 1741b, *Leic.* 1747c, *Montr.* 411c, *NE* 136a,
      Newcastle(NSW) 141c, *Open(UK)* 1871c,
      Oxf.Brookes 1885b, *Portsmouth* 1901c, 1902c,
      S'ton. 1934c, *Swinburne UT* 163c, *Wales* 1542b
  advertising (in Swaziland), *Swazi.* 1470c
  alternative, *Cant.* 1088b
  analysis, *S.Cross* 155c
  and communication(s), *Kelaniya* 1445a, *Lond.Met.*
      1824b, *Murd.* 133b
  and culture, *Murd.* 133b
  and history, *Nott.* 1859a
  and memory, *Nott.* 1859a
  and national identity, *Stir.* 1942b
  and policy (public), *Auck.UT* 1081b
  and political economy, *Cant.* 1088b
  and politics, *Cant.* 1088b, *Griff.* 70a, *Liv.* 1758b
  and society, *New Br.* 433b
  anthropology of, *Lond.* 1815a
  art, *Deakin* 61c
  audiences, *Leic.* 1749b
  broadcast, *Colombo* 1437b
  children's, *NE* 136a
  community, *C'dia.* 345c, *Cant.* 1088b, *Griff.* 69c
  content analysis, *M'lore.* 843b
  cult, *Brun.* 1597c
  culture, *W.Ont.* 543a
  development, *Rhodes* 1389c
  digital, *Napier* 1844c
  discourses, *Cant.* 1088b
  economics, *Nan.Tech.* 1293c
  education (global), *Waik.* 1123b
  effects, *Leic.* 1749b
  electronic, *FJ Women* 1242c, *Herts.* 1685b
  ethics, *Nan.Tech.* 1293c, *Panjab* 882a, *SPMV* 924c, *Stell.*
      1395b
  form of, *C'dia.* 343c
  formations (alternative), *Cardiff* 1618a
  freedom, *Cant.* 1088b
  globalisation, *Brun.* 1595c
  governance, *Brun.* 1597b
  history, *C.Qld.* 45a, 45b, *C.Sturt* 51a, *Ebonyi State* 1165b,
      Swansea 1957a, *Wales* 1541b
  impact of, *Karn.* 811b
  in art, *W.Cape* 1407b
  in developing countries, *Islamia, Bahawal.* 1249b,
      W'gong. 209a
  in literature, *W.Cape* 1407b
  institutional context of, *C'dia.* 343c
  interactions, *Brun.* 1597b
  interactive, *Plym.* 1896a
  issues, *Nan.Tech.* 1293c
  literacy, *Wales* 1965b
  management, *Nan.Tech.* 1293c
  mass (in society), *C'dia.* 343c
  mixed, *Chinese HK* 2023b
  mobile, *Swinburne UT* 162a
  new, *Canberra* 42a, 42c, *Cant.* 1088b, *Chinese HK* 2023c,
      Herts. 1685b, *Leic.* 1749b, *Liv.* 1758c, *Lond.*
      1801b, *M.Sund.* 856b, *NU Singapore* 1307a,
      Ulster 1962c

new (applications), *Deakin* 61c
new (development), *Auck.UT* 1084b
new (in language education), *Monash* 127b
new (industry, in Asia), *NU Singapore* 1307a
new (technologies), *S.Cross* 155c
ownership, *Cant.* 1088b
policy, *Brun.* 1597b, *Swinburne UT* 162a
practices (alternative), *Cardiff* 1618a
reception, *Cardiff* 1618a
regulation, *Brun.* 1597b
regulations (in Southeast Asia), *Nan.Tech.* 1293c
relations, *Curtin* 57a, *Swansea* 1957a
representations, *Cant.* 1088b
representations (race, gender, sexuality), *Auck.* 1071c,
      Brun. 1597b
research, *DAV* 726c
risk, *Brun.* 1595c
sociology of, *Glas.* 1668b
streaming, *W.Aust.* 199c
studies, *Adel.* 27a, *Birm.* 1570c, *Botswana* 263c, *C.Qld.*
      45c, *Chinese HK* 2022a, *Lough.* 1834c, *Maur.*
      1052b, *Monash* 124c, 125c, *Montr.* 411c,
      Newcastle(NSW) 145a, *Nott.Trent* 1864b, *Pret.*
      1373c, 1375b, *S.Cross* 155c, *Tas.* 179c,
      Vic.(Aust.) 185b, *W.Cape* 1407b, *W.Laur.*
      557c, *W.Ont.* 543a
studies (critical), *Auck.UT* 1081b, 1084b
systems, *Stir.* 1942b
technoetic, *Plym.* 1896a
technology, *Bath* 1550c, *Canberra* 42a, *Malta* 1045a
telematic, *Plym.* 1896a
theory, *Canberra* 42a, *S.Cross* 155c
traditional, *M'lore.* 843b
violence, *Sheff.* 1924c
western, *Chinese HK* 2023b
mediaeval
  archaeology, *Birm.* 1570a, *Liv.* 1763a
  architecture, *Lond.* 1778a
  art, *Aberd.* 1535c, *Warw.* 1974c
  culture, *Lond.* 1777c, *W.Ont.* 542a
  history, *Belf.* 1559a, *Birm.* 1569b, *Cardiff* 1618a, *Leth.*
      364c, *Liv.* 1763a, *Lond.* 1809a, *MDSU* 835b,
      Manit. 391b, *NE* 135b, *Reading* 1908b,
      Swansea 1956c, *W.Laur.* 558c, *Wales* 1541b,
      1965b
  history (cultural), *Glas.* 1666a
  history (ecclesiastical), *S'ton.* 1935c
  history (economic), *Birm.* 1570a
  history (landscape), *Birm.* 1570a
  history (political), *Glas.* 1666a, *S'ton.* 1935c
  history (religious), *Glas.* 1666a
  history (social), *Birm.* 1570a, *Glas.* 1666a
  language, *Nott.* 1853a
  literature, *Auck.* 1071a, *Bran.* 317a, *Dal.* 352b, *Liv.*
      1763a, *Lond.* 1777c, 1808b, *McG.* 371b, *Nott.*
      1853a, *Reading* 1907c, 1908b, *W.Ont.* 542a
  manuscripts, *W.Laur.* 558c
  monophony (analysis of), *Auck.* 1073c
  music, *Dal.* 353c, *W.Ont.* 544b
  music (chant), *W.Ont.* 544b
  myths, *W.Laur.* 558c
  philosophy, *W.Laur.* 558c
  political thought, *Lond.* 1800a
  studies, *Brist.* 1586b, 1589a, *Gulb.* 754b, *Kent* 1715a,
      McG. 371a, *Monash* 117c, 128a, *Reading*
      1908b, *S'ton.* 1935b, *Sheff.* 1924b, *W.Aust.*
      196a, *Wales* 1541a
  studies (interdisciplinary), *Glas.* 1665c
mediation, *Qu.* 458a, *S.Cross* 156c
medical
  biology, *Lanc.* 1721c
  biotechnology, *Jiw.* 801c
  care, *WI* 2000c
  chemistry, *Melb.* 95c, *R.Gordon* 1911b
  curriculum, *Monash* 121c
  demography, *Ghana* 582c
  education, *KwaZulu-Natal* 1355a, *Leic.* 1749c, *Manit.*
      395c, *McG.* 375b, *Monash* 121b, 123b, *Pret.*
      1384b, *Qu.* 458c, *Stell.* 1398a, *W'gong.* 209c
  education (history of), *Birm.* 1574a
  electronics, *Sheff.* 1923b
  equipment, *Sir Syed UET* 1277c
  ethics, *Glas.* 1666c
  guidelines, *Qu.* 458c
  imaging, *Exe.* 1658a, *ICL* 1701a, *Keele* 1712b, *Kent*
      1715b, *Liv.* 1758b, *Macq.* 91a, *Nan.Tech.*
      1292c, *Nott.Trent* 1863a, *Pret.* 1384b, *W.Ont.*
      549a
  imaging (advanced), *W.Ont.* 553a
  informatics, *Nan.Tech.* 1292c
  physics, *AT Balewa* 1139a, *Cant.* 1092a, *Cardiff* 1617a,
      Colombo 1437c, *Montr.* 421a,
      Newcastle(NSW) 144a, *O.Awolowo* 1200b,
      Qld.UT 152a, 153b, *Qu.* 459b, *Rivers SUST*
      1212a, *Sur.* 1952b, *WI* 2001a, *Waik.* 1121b
  physics (radiation), *McG.* 383b
  practice (development), *Birm.* 1569b
  practice (ethnoveterinary), *Makurdi Ag.* 1144b
  practice (evidence-based), *Keele* 1711b

practice (management), *Stell.* 1398b
professional development, *Newcastle(NSW)* 145b
research, *Birm.* 1572a, *W.Ont.* 553a
risk (information), *Plym.* 1894c
science(s) (basic), *Tor.* 509c
science(s) (clinical), *Tor.* 509c
service(s), *Monash* 121b
statistics, *Ib.* 1176c, *Kent* 1715b, *Reading* 1906b
technology, *Syd.* 177a
technology (in the home), *Tor.* 509b
training, *W.Aust.* 198b
medication
  administering, *Leeds Met.* 1742b
  prescribing, *Leeds Met.* 1742b
  usage, *Bath* 1552c
medicinal
  chemistry, *Chinese HK* 2027a
medicine, *ICL* 1706c, *Ib.* 1176c, *McG.* 380a,
      Newcastle(NSW) 145c
  adverse effects of, *Cape Town* 1340c
  alternative (psychological aspects of), *Plym.* 1894b
  ancient (and health), *Birm.* 1573c
  and society, *Lond.* 1818c
  arts and humanities in, *Durh.* 1635c
  clinical (history of, in Britain), *Glas.* 1671a
  complementary (psychological aspects of), *Plym.* 1894b
  critical care, *Cape Town* 1341a
  environmental, *Manit.* 393a, *Monash* 121c, *S'ton.* 1939a
  essential (use and safety of), *Cape Town* 1340c
  evidence-based, *Qu.* 458c
  experimental, *ICL* 1706c, *Swansea* 1957c
  history of, *Birm.* 1574a, *Cape Town* 1335c, *Durh.* 1635b,
      1636b, *Leeds* 1733c, *Lond.* 1815c, *McG.* 379a,
      Melb. 99a, *Nott.* 1853b
  internal, *Montr.* 416b
  management, *Greenwich* 1678a
  mathematical, *Nott.* 1854b
  molecular, *Colombo* 1439c
  natural, *S.Cross* 156b
  philosophy, *Melb.* 99a
  philosophy of, *Durh.* 1636b
  preventive, *Melb.* 108a, *W.Ont.* 549a
  remote, *W.Aust.* 197b
  sociology of, *McG.* 379a, *Monash* 114b
  statistical applications in, *Belf.* 1560b, *Cant.* 1086b
  traditional, *Cape Town* 1340c, *O.Awolowo* 1200a
  traditional (Sri Lankan), *Kelaniya* 1443c
  use of (risk in), *Lond.* 1818c, *Monash* 124a
meditation
  in the workplace, *Monash* 114b
Mediterranean
  agriculture, *W.Aust.* 199b
  archaeology, *Birm.* 1569c, *Exe.* 1659a
  British writers in, *Malta* 1045a
  cultural studies, *Exe.* 1659a
  economy, *Malta* 1042b
  history, *Birm.* 1569c, *Exe.* 1659a
  history (ancient), *Exe.* 1659a
  history (maritime), *Malta* 1046b
  identity, *Exe.* 1659a
  in early modern times, *Malta* 1042b
  in mediaeval times, *Malta* 1042b
  land use, *Leic.* 1745c
  landscape, *Leic.* 1745c
  politics, *Kingston(UK)* 1720a, *Liv.* 1758b, *Malta* 1042b
  society, *Malta* 1042b
  states (governance in), *Malta* 1046c
  studies, *Birm.* 1569b, *Monash* 120a
  studies (ancient), *La Trobe* 83c
  theatre, *Malta* 1046c
medulloblastoma, *Chinese HK* 2025c
Megalopolis, *Qu.* 452c
megatronics, *Stell.* 1394b
melanoma
  malignant (ocular), *Cape Town* 1341a, *Sheff.* 1928a
membrane
  biology, *Glas.* 1663b, *Panjab* 880c
  equilibria, *Swinburne UT* 163b
  function, *McG.* 374c, *S'ton.* 1933c
  permeability, *Stell.* 1399a
  proteins, *Cape Town* 1339a, *Montr.* 418a, 420c
  structure, *McG.* 374c, *S'ton.* 1933c
  technology, *Dschang* 273a, *Melb.* 97a, *N-W(S.Af.)* 1370a,
      Strath. 1945c
  transport/transporters, *Auck.* 1077a
memory, *Bath* 1552a, *Cape Town* 1335c, *Lanc.* 1724b,
      Liv.J.Moores 1765a, *Melb.* 103a, *Montr.* 420c,
      New Br. 433b, *Portsmouth* 1899a, *W.Laur.* 557a
  abilities (exceptional), *Lond.* 1810c
  and learning, *Aberd.* 1535a
  applications, *Griff.* 75a
  autobiographical, *Hudd.* 1691c, *Lond.* 1810c, *Plym.*
      1895b
  circuits, *Griff.* 75a
  eye-witness, *Plym.* 1895b
  false, *Plym.* 1895b
  inhibitory function, *Plym.* 1895b
  long-term, *Plym.* 1895b
  skills (development), *Lond.* 1810c

moral
  theory (contemporary), *Reading* 1908c
morbidity, *Botswana* 263b, *Montr.* 412b, *WI* 1990c
morphodynamics, *Plym.* 1893c
morphogenesis, *SP* 906c
morphological
  theory, *Cant.* 1087b, *Leeds* 1733a
morphology, *Azad J&K* 1237c, *Calabar* 1160a, *Manit.* 392a,
    McG. 372b, *Pret.* 1382c, *Stell.* 1400c
  functional, *W.Aust.* 191c
mortality, *Botswana* 263b, *Colombo* 1436c, *KwaZulu-Natal*
    1355a, *Montr.* 412b, 421b, *Nott.* 1860a
  causes of, *Auck.* 1077c
  rates (among farmers), *Makurdi Ag.* 1144a
mortgage valuation accuracy, *O.Awolowo* 1198c
mosquito/mosquitoes
  -borne diseases, *Bran.* 318b, *Kwame NUST* 587c
  control, *Bayero* 1149a
  immune systems, *Guy.* 593a
  resistance to insecticides, *Open S.Lanka* 1450c
mother
  and child (health), *J.Hamdard* 791a
motion
  control, *KwaZulu-Natal* 1352b
  devices (incremental), *Makurdi Ag.* 1143c
  processing, *McG.* 383b
  sickness, *McG.* 379c
motivation, *Leth.* 364c
  characterisation of, *Chinese HK* 2028c
  opponent-process models of, *W.Ont.* 546a
motor
  control, *Birm.* 1573b, *Lond.* 1811b, *Manit.* 396a, *McG.*
    369a, *Melb.* 107b, *O.Awolowo* 1200a, *Syd.*
    174a, *W.Aust.* 196b, *Wales* 1548a
  learning, *Botswana* 263a, *Syd.* 174a, *W.Aust.* 196b, *Wales*
    1548a
  memory (acquisition of), *Lond.* 1811a
  perceptual, *Stell.* 1397c
motor neurone disease, *Plym.* 1893b
mountainous regions
  human impact on, *W.Laur.* 560b
  vegetation of, *Plym.* 1897a
movement, *Montr.* 419a
  disorders, *Ib.* 1177b, *S'ton.* 1935c, *Witw.* 1416a
  science, *Oxf.Brookes* 1885c
  science (human), *Pret.* 1374c
  studies, *Pret.* 1375b
MRSA, *S.Ramachandra* 927a
  infections, *S.Ramachandra* 927a
mucorale
  biology, *Stell.* 1396a
mucosal
  immunology, *Glas.* 1670c
mulberry
  agronomy, *SPMV* 925b
  breeding, *SPMV* 925b
  pathology, *SPMV* 925b
  physiology, *SPMV* 925b
multicultural/multiculturalism studies, *Aust.Cath.* 34b, *Birm.*
    1573a, *Cant.* 1089c, *Deakin* 61c, *FJ Women*
    1243b, *Monash* 117b, 120c, 124b, 125a, 127c,
    128c, *Montr.* 416a
multidiscipline(s)/multidisciplinary, *Sheff.* 1930c
multilingualism/multilingual studies, *KwaZulu-Natal* 1353a,
    W.Cape 1408a, 1410a
multimedia, *Curtin* 55c, *Gandh.Rural* 742c, *Ghulam IKIST*
    1245c, *IIT Bombay* 779a, *Manit.* 388b, *Melb.*
    102b, *Monash* 114a, 120a, *Pret.* 1378b, *S'ton.*
    1936c, *Syd.* 169b, *Tas.* 182b
  and education, *Monash* 125b
  applications (development), *Monash* 127b
  communication, *Monash* 127b, *Plym.* 1896b
  content delivery, *W'gong.* 211a
  content protection, *W'gong.* 207b
  data (processing of), *Nan.Tech.* 1294a
  distributed, *Rhodes* 1388c
  educational, *W.Aust.* 199c
  information (indexing), *Monash* 118b
  information (retrieval), *Monash* 118b, *Putra* 1026c
  information (sources), *McG.* 372b
  intelligent, *Ulster* 1961a
  interactive, *Griff.* 69c, *W'gong.* 206c
  interactive (environments), *Montr.* 420a
  interactive (sequencing), *Leth.* 365c
  learning, *G.Caledonian* 1673a
  learning environments, *Plym.* 1894c
  management, *Monash* 127b, *W'gong.* 207b
  mobile, *Monash* 125a
  services, *W'gong.* 211a
  studies, *Vic.(Aust.)* 185b, *Wat.* 529a
  systems, *Brun.* 1594b, *Sur.* 1953a
  technology, *Colombo* 1440a, *Lond.Met.* 1824b, *Putra*
    1026c
  visualisation, *Monash* 117c
multinational
  companies, *Lond.* 1801c
  enterprises, *Maur.* 1051b
  firms, *Montr.* 424a
multiphase
  phenomena, *Newcastle(NSW)* 145c

multiple personality disorder, *KwaZulu-Natal* 1354c
multiple sclerosis, *Brun.* 1597c, *Cardiff* 1619c, *Plym.* 1895a,
    Qu. 459a
  epidemiology of, *Plym.* 1893c
  use of cannabinoids in, *Plym.* 1893c
multiprotocol label switching, *Nan.Tech.* 1294c
multivariate analysis, *Cape Town* 1338b, *Gujar.* 750c, *Lond.*
    1777b, *Manip.* 855a, *Pret.* 1381a
multivitamins
  production (biotechnological processes for), *Ebonyi
    State* 1163c
Munchhausen by proxy syndrome, *Sheff.* 1927a
Mundell-Fleming
  dynamics, *Guy.* 594b
muscle, *Liv.* 1760a
  adaptation, *Wat.* 530c
  artificial, *W'gong.* 210c
  biochemistry, *Stell.* 1397a, *Tas.* 181a
  biology, *Lond.* 1813a
  biophysics, *Macq.* 90b
  cell (biochemistry), *Vic.(Aust.)* 187a
  cells, *Chinese HK* 2025c
  changes, in critical illness, *Liv.* 1761b
  compliance, *Auck.UT* 1083c
  damage and repair, *W.Laur.* 558b
  development, *WI* 1995c
  fatigue, *McG.* 378b, *Syd.* 169c
  fatigue (in clinically impaired patients), *Syd.* 177a
  peripheral, *Monash* 122c
  physiology, *M'lore.* 843c, *Vic.(Aust.)* 185b
  smooth, *Manit.* 397c
  smooth (physiology), *Belf.* 1562c
  smooth (signalling in), *Liv.* 1759a
  spasticity, *Plym.* 1895c
muscular dystrophy, *KwaZulu-Natal* 1355c, *Manit.* 395c,
    Pret. 1383c
musculoskeletal, *La Trobe* 82b, *W.Aust.* 197c
  ageing, *Chinese HK* 2026c
  ailments, *Hull* 1698a
  biology, *Liv.* 1759a
  disease, *Tas.* 181c
  disorders, *Hull* 1698c
  dysfunction, *Plym.* 1894c
  injuries, *Syd.* 174a
  pain, *Plym.* 1894c
  problems, *McG.* 380c, *Ulster* 1962a
  research, *W.Aust.* 199c
  science, *Brist.* 1589b
  tissue (engineering), *NU Singapore* 1318b
museology, *Auck.* 1067c, *Lond.* 1778a
museum(s)
  and First Nations, *C'dia.* 343a
  computing for, *Glas.* 1666b
  national, *C'dia.* 343a
  studies, *Leic.* 1749c, *Monash* 117a, *Montr.* 413b
mushroom
  cultivation, *Dar.* 1480b, *M.Sund.* 856c
  cultures, *O.Awolowo* 1199a
  technology, *Gandh.Rural* 742c
music/musical, *Bath* 1554c, *Cape Coast* 575c, *Lond.* 1778a,
    Melb. 101a, 102b
  aesthetics, *Cardiff* 1621a, *Herts.* 1689b, *W.Laur.* 559a
  aesthetics (nineteenth-century), *Sur.* 1952b
  aesthetics (twentieth-century), *Sur.* 1952b
  allusion, *Wat.* 531c
  analysis, *Auck.* 1073c, *Cant.* 1088a, *Durh.* 1636a, *Hull*
    1696a, 1698c, *Lanc.* 1722a, *Lond.* 1810a
  and community, *Griff.* 74c, *Tas.* 180b
  and language, *Hull* 1699a
  and literature, *Auck.* 1073c
  and Madhwa Bhakthi, *Avina. Women* 685c
  and meaning, *Nipissing* 437a
  and modernism, *Nipissing* 437a
  and multimedia, *S'ton.* 1936c
  and politics, *Cardiff* 1621a
  and popular culture, *W.Laur.* 559a
  and science, *Leeds* 1733a
  and technology, *Portsmouth* 1899c, *Qu.* 453b
  and the Christian church, *Wales* 1547b
  and the network, *Macq.* 90a
  artistic, *Herts.* 1689b
  British, *Brist.* 1588a
  chamber (collaborative performance), *Manit.* 392b
  children's response to, *Winneba* 579b
  civic policies, *Liv.* 1763a
  cognition, *W.Ont.* 544b, 544c
  composition, *Herts.* 1689b, *Hull* 1696a, *Keele* 1712b,
    Sur. 1952b, *Wat.* 531c
  composition (computer-aided), *Plym.* 1893c
  computer, *Glas.* 1667c, *Hudd.* 1694a
  contemporary, *Hudd.* 1694a, *Liv.* 1758a,
    Newcastle(NSW) 142a, *S.Cross* 155c
  contemporary (performance), *Sur.* 1952b
  creative processes in, *Leth.* 365b, *Montr.* 414b
  creativity (psychology of), *Nan.Tech.* 1296a
  critical, *Herts.* 1689b
  cultures (of the world), *Ghana* 583b
  development (in children), *Hull* 1698c
  digital, *Macq.* 88a, *W'gong.* 209c
  early, *Birm.* 1571a, *Glas.* 1667c, *S'ton.* 1936c

early (analysis), *Dal.* 353c
early (performance practice), *Birm.* 1571a
education, *Qu.* 456b, *W.Laur.* 559a
eighteenth-century, *Birm.* 1571a
electro-acoustic, *Hull* 1698c, *W.Ont.* 544c
electronic, *Macq.* 88a
expression, *W'gong.* 209c
folk, *Winneba* 579b
generative, *Plym.* 1893c
hermeneutics, *W.Ont.* 544c
history, *Dal.* 353c
history of, *Lond.* 1810a
improvisation, *Leth.* 365c
in African cultures, *Ghana* 583b
in worship, *Wat.* 531c
industry, *Liv.* 1758a
instrumental studies, *C'dia.* 346b
interaction, *Plym.* 1893c
interactive, *Tas.* 180b
interpretation, *Montr.* 414b
literary values in, *SPMV* 925a
lyrical values in, *SPMV* 925a
modern, *Brun.* 1594c, *Plym.* 1891a
new, *W'gong.* 209c
new (promotion of), *E.Cowan* 66a
nineteenth-century, *W.Laur.* 559a
nineteenth-century (analysis), *Sur.* 1952b
notation (mediaeval), *W.Laur.* 559a
perception, *W.Ont.* 544c
performance, *Brun.* 1596c, *Durh.* 1636a, *Herts.* 1689b,
    Hudd. 1694a, *Leeds* 1733b, *Monash* 120a,
    Putra 1026c, *S'ton.* 1936c, *Tas.* 180b, *W'gong.*
    209c, *W.Laur.* 559a, *W.Ont.* 544c
performance (chamber), *Qu.* 456b
performance (historical), *W.Ont.* 544c
performance practice, *Glas.* 1667c
performance (practice), *Qu.* 456b, *Tas.* 180b, *W.Aust.*
    195a
performance (solo), *Qu.* 456b
performance (studies), *Hull* 1696a
philosophy of, *Brun.* 1596c, *W.Ont.* 544b
popular, *Dal.* 353c, *KwaZulu-Natal* 1353c, *Liv.* 1758a,
    1763a, *Monash* 120a, *S'ton.* 1936c, *Sur.*
    1952b, *W.Ont.* 544b
popular (culture of), *Wales* 1547b
popular (eighteenth-century), *Sheff.* 1925c
popular (nineteenth-century), *Sheff.* 1925c
practical, *SPMV* 925a
production (technology), *Qld.UT* 153a
psychology of, *Hull* 1696a, *Keele* 1712b, *Putra* 1026c,
    Sheff. 1925c
recording, *C'dia.* 346b
robotics and, *Plym.* 1893c
social sciences of, *W.Aust.* 195a
sociology of, *KwaZulu-Natal* 1353c, *Putra* 1026c
software, *Montr.* 414b
studies, *Monash* 117a, 125b
technology, *Bran.* 317c, *C'dia.* 346b, *Durh.* 1636a, *Herts.*
    1689b, *Keele* 1712b, *Pret.* 1379c, *Putra*
    1026c, *Stell.* 1396c, *W.Ont.* 544c
testing, *Cant.* 1086c
theatre (history), *W.Ont.* 544b
theatre (twentieth-century), *Dal.* 355b
theory, *Cape Coast* 575c, *Dal.* 353c, *Durh.* 1636a, *Hull*
    1698c, *Leth.* 365b, *Lond.* 1810a, *Qu.* 456b,
    W.Laur. 559a
theory (history of), *W.Ont.* 544c
theory (philosophy of), *W.Ont.* 544c
theory (pitch-class set theory), *W.Ont.* 544c
theory (post-tonal), *W.Ont.* 544c
theory (Riemanannian transformation theory), *W.Ont.*
    544c
theory (tonal), *W.Ont.* 544c
therapy, *Melb.* 101a, *Pret.* 1379c, *Putra* 1026c, *W.Laur.*
    559a
transcription, *NE* 136c
twentieth-century, *Ghana* 583b, *Hull* 1696a
twentieth-century (analysis), *Qu.* 456b, *Sur.* 1952b
vocal studies, *C'dia.* 346b
world music, *Griff.* 74c
musicians
  injuries of, *W.Ont.* 544c
  injuries of (prevention and rehabilitation), *W.Ont.* 544c
musicology, *Brun.* 1596c, *Durh.* 1636a, *Glas.* 1667c, *Keele*
    1712b, *Leeds* 1733b, *Qu.* 456b, *W.Laur.* 559a
  critical, *Sur.* 1952b
  editorial, *Wales* 1547b
  historical, *Cant.* 1088b, *Leeds* 1733b, *Stell.* 1396c, *Wales*
    1547b
  indigenous, *Adel.* 30b
  sixteenth- to twentieth-, *Chinese HK* 2024b
  systematic, *Stell.* 1396c
Muslim
  history, *Sindh* 1274b
  in Australia, *Griff.* 74b
  societies, *Monash* 125c, 127b
  world (contemporary), *J.Hamdard* 791b
mutual funds, *Panjab* 883a
mycobacterial
  infections, *O.Awolowo* 1201a

Pentateuch
  Samaritan, *Pret.* 1379c
  studies, *C.Sturt* 52b
Pentecostal studies, *Birm.* 1570a
people, creativity and technology, *Wat.* 535a
pepsin
  function, *Liv.* 1759c
  structure, *Liv.* 1759c
peptide(s)
  antimicrobial, *Stell.* 1393a
  chemistry, *M'lore.* 843a
  synthesis, *IIT Bombay* 777a, *McG.* 384c
  therapeutic, *Lond.* 1818c
perception/perceptual systems, *Adel.* 30b, *Birm.* 1572a,
        Cardiff 1622a, *Glas.* 1668b, *Lond.* 1810b, *Montr.*
        415c, *S.Cross* 156c, *Stir.* 1943a, *Sur.* 1952c, *Tor.*
        500b
  categorical, *Plym.* 1893a
  development, *Lond.* 1779a
  processes, *C'dia.* 347a
performance, *Botswana* 263a, *C.Sturt* 52b, *Hull* 1699a,
        Melb. 96a, *Nott.Trent* 1866c, *Plym.* 1888c,
        W.Laur. 557a
  actor and character in, *Exe.* 1655c
  analysis, *Glas.* 1668c
  analysis (methodology), *Reading* 1906a
  analysis (twentieth-century), *Warw.* 1976c
  and body, *Newcastle(NSW)* 142a
  and gender, *Exe.* 1655c, *Newcastle(NSW)* 142a
  and institutional practice (site based), *Hull* 1699a
  and media, *Hull* 1699a
  and ritual, *Adel.* 29b
  and social meaning, *La Trobe* 79b
  and voice, *Newcastle(NSW)* 142a
  anxiety, *Tas.* 183a
  anxiety (muscle relaxation for), *Plym.* 1893c
  cross-artform, *Plym.* 1897c
  cultural identities in, *Plym.* 1897b
  enhancement, *W.Laur.* 558b
  evaluation (in IT industry), *McG.* 382c
  improvement, *Sur.* 1953a
  indicators, *Montr.* 425a
  individual, *Nan.Tech.* 1301c
  innovation, *Qld.UT* 153a
  interdisciplinary, *Plym.* 1897b
  investigation(s), *Kent* 1714a
  management, *Guy.* 593b, *Melb.* 94b
  measurement, *Plym.* 1896c
  media, *Auck.UT* 1081b
  neurology, *E.Cowan* 66a
  place/space, *Kent* 1714a
  post-colonial, *Cant.* 1088b
  practice, *Dal.* 353c
  studies, *Lond.* 1810a, *Monash* 125b, *Plym.* 1897b, *Rhodes*
        1388c, *Vic.(Aust.)* 186b
  studies (practice), *Well.* 1117a
  studies (Welsh-medium), *Wales* 1542b
  texts, *Plym.* 1897b
  the body in, *Plym.* 1897b
  theory, *Glas.* 1668c
  theory (twentieth-century), *Warw.* 1976c
performing arts, *Ghana* 583b, *Greenwich* 1677c, *Ib.* 1176a,
        Leeds Met. 1740c, *Lond.Met.* 1824b, *Melb.* 102b,
        NE Hill 871b, *Wat.* 526b
  education, *Cant.* 1089c
perinatal/perinatology, *La Trobe* 84b, *Pret.* 1383b
  death, *Plym.* 1893b
  health care, *Pret.* 1383b
  medicine, *Liv.* 1761b
  mortality, *Stell.* 1399a
  pathology, *Colombo* 1439b
periodontal/periodontology
  disease, *Peradeniya* 1455c
  disease (and diabetes mellitus), *Malta* 1041c
  disease (juvenile), *Lagos* 1186b
  ligaments, *Manit.* 394c
  medicine, *Manit.* 394c
  therapy (non-surgical), *Kelaniya* 1443b
peritoneal host defence, *Cardiff* 1620c
permafrost, *McG.* 382c, 383a
Persian
  language, *VB* 949c
  literature, *VB* 949c
  literature (mediaeval), *Gulb.* 755a
  literature (modern), *Gulb.* 755a
  studies, *Lond.* 1816a
personal
  name(s) (social and cultural significance), *Leic.* 1750b
personality, *Chinese HK* 2024c, *Gujar.* 750b, *Islamia,*
        Bahawal. 1249c, *Montr.* 425a, *Punjabi* 892c, *Tor.*
        500b
  and individual differences, *C.Qld.* 46a
  areas of, *Panjab* 882b
  assessment, *Wat.* 533c
  development, *Aust.Cath.* 33c
  disorders, *Sheff.* 1927a
  ideas of (in the ancient world), *Exe.* 1655c
  in religion, *Wales* 1548c
  social, *McG.* 373c

personnel
  management, *Dib.* 728c
  psychology, *Ib.* 1174b
  selection, *FJ Women* 1243b
Peru/Peruvian
  studies, *Sheff.* 1924b
  well-being in, *Bath* 1555c
pesticide(s)
  -soil interaction, *Makurdi Ag.* 1143b
  -water interaction, *Makurdi Ag.* 1143b
  agricultural (ecotoxicology of), *Griff.* 74a
  bio-, *S.Pac.* 1423a, *WI* 1997b
  biochemistry, *Jiw.* 801c, *Putra* 1022a
  biodegradable, *GND* 764c
  botanical, *N.Maharashtra* 868c
  degradation of (in soil), *Makurdi Ag.* 1143b
  degradation of (in water), *Makurdi Ag.* 1143b
  eco-friendly, *GND* 764c
  environmental toxicology of, *BSMR Ag.* 218b
  fate, *WI* 1995c
  impact, *WI* 1995c
  residues, *Syd.* 166a
  synthesis and formulation of, *N.Maharashtra* 868b
pest(s), *C.Sturt* 52a, 52c
  control, *Calabar* 1159a, *Maur.* 1050c
  control (alternative), *McG.* 381c
  control (of introduced species), *Canberra* 43a
  control (using phytochemicals), *Gandh.Rural* 742c
  introduced species (ecology of), *Canberra* 43a
  management, *BSMR Ag.* 218b, *Dar.* 1477c, *Lincoln(NZ)*
        1094b, *Manit.* 393b, *Stell.* 1394c, *WI* 1995c
  management (agricultural), *Kelaniya* 1446c
  management (integrated), *Guy.* 593a
  risk analyses, *Griff.* 74c
petrochemicals, *IIT Bombay* 777c
petrogenesis, *Aberd.* 1536b
petroleum, *Plym.* 1896a
  and porous media, *Wat.* 535a
  biotechnology, *Tezpur* 940b
  drilling, *Dib.* 729a, *H-W* 1680b
  engineering, *Curtin* 56a, *Dib.* 729a, *ICL* 1702c,
        NUST(P'stan.) 1265c
  geochemistry, *Curtin* 55c, *O.Awolowo* 1199a, *Plym.* 1889c
  geology, *Dib.* 729a, *Durh.* 1634b, *IIT Bombay* 777b
  geoscience, *Aberd.* 1536b, *ICL* 1702c
  hydrocarbons, *Malta* 1041b
  hydrocarbons (environmental toxicology of), *Plym.*
        1896a
  production, *H-W* 1680b
  refining, *BITS* 710a
  reservoirs, *H-W* 1680b, *Stell.* 1395a
petrology, *Jiw.* 802a, *Macq.* 88b, *Manit.* 391b, *O.Awolowo*
        1199a, *Open S.Lanka* 1450b, *Panjab* 881c, *Tas.*
        179b
  carbonate, *Macq.* 91b
  igneous, *Cape Town* 1335c, *Lond.* 1777b, *McG.* 369b,
        Melb. 96b, *Rhodes* 1389b, *S.Leone* 1287a,
        Waik. 1120c
  metamorphic, *Cape Town* 1335c, *Gauh.* 746a, *Melb.* 96b
pharmaceutical
  analysis, *Ib.* 1175a, *Jos* 1181b, *Lond.* 1819a, *MJP Rohil.*
        840c
  bioavailability, *Lagos* 1187a
  bioequivalence, *Lagos* 1187a
  biology, *Bath* 1552c
  biotechnology, *Monash* 124a
  care, *Bath* 1552c, *R.Gordon* 1911c
  chemistry, *Chinese HK* 2027a, *La Trobe* 82b, *Punjabi*
        892c, *SPMV* 925b, *Syd.* 173b, *Wat.* 525a
  development, of, *W'gong.* 210c
  dosage (forms), *J.Hamdard* 791c
  engineering, *Birm.* 1568b, *Nan.Tech.* 1292c
  industry (history), *Lond.* 1801c
  marketing, *C'dia.* 346a
  policy, *Dal.* 354c
  practice (professionalism in), *Belf.* 1563c
  products (starch in), *Jamaica UT* 956c
  professional development, *Belf.* 1563c
  public health, *R.Gordon* 1911c
  quality assurance, *Lagos* 1187a
  quality control, *Lagos* 1187a
  science, *CSJ Maharaj* 718b, *Kingston(UK)* 1719c, *Tas.*
        180b
  services (district), *KwaZulu-Natal* 1356a
  surface science, *Bath* 1552c
  techniques, *Lond.* 1819a
  technology, *Bath* 1552c, *Chinese HK* 2027a, *Greenwich*
        1678a, *Lond.* 1818c, *Montr.* 414c
  training, *Lond.* 1819a
  utilisation management, *Dal.* 354b
pharmaceutics, *C.Sturt* 50c, *Chinese HK* 2027a, *Dib.* 729a,
        Panjab 882a, *Punjabi* 892c, *Syd.* 173b
  natural products, *Jos* 1181b, 1181c
  natural products (extraction), *Well.* 1114a
pharmaco-economics, *Malta* 1044c, *Pret.* 1384a, 1385c
pharmaco-epidemiology, *Adel.* 27c, *Cardiff* 1620a, *Keele*
        1711b, *McG.* 380c
pharmacodynamics, *Chinese HK* 2026b, 2027a, *Plym.*
        1893a

pharmacogenetics, *Adel.* 28c, *Chinese HK* 2027a, *Ghana*
        584b, 584c, *NU Singapore* 1317c
pharmacogenomics, *Chinese HK* 2027a, *Syd.* 173b
pharmacognosy, *Chinese HK* 2027a, *Dib.* 729a, *Panjab*
        882a, *S.Cross* 156b
  marine, *Lagos* 1187a
pharmacokinetics, *Adel.* 27c, 28c, *Chinese HK* 2026b,
        2027a, *Ghana* 584c, *Ib.* 1175a, *Lagos* 1187a,
        Manit. 395a, *McG.* 374b, 380c, *NU Singapore*
        1317c, *Plym.* 1893a, *Stell.* 1398a, *Tas.* 180b
  clinical, *Ib.* 1175b, *KwaZulu-Natal* 1356a, *Oxf.* 1880b
  population analysis, *KwaZulu-Natal* 1355a
pharmacology, *Adel.* 27c, *C.Qld.* 45a, *Calabar* 1161b, *Dib.*
        729a, *Herts.* 1686c, *Leic.* 1746c, *Melb.* 106a,
        Montr. 414c, 416c, *NU Singapore* 1317a,
        Nott.Trent 1862b, *Panjab* 882a, *Punjabi* 892c,
        SPMV 925b, *Syd.* 172a, *W'gong.* 209c, *W.Aust.*
        196c, 200a, *W.Ont.* 551c, *WI* 2001a, 2001b
  and ethics, *Colombo* 1439b
  and new drug development, *Glas.* 1669c
  anti-cancer, *Auck.* 1077a
  anti-emetic, *Chinese HK* 2026c
  anti-inflammatory, *Chinese HK* 2027a
  applied, *Tor.* 504b
  behavioural, *NE* 137a
  cancer, *McG.* 383b, 383c
  cardiovascular, *Chinese HK* 2027a
  clinical, *Adel.* 28c, *Manit.* 397b, *NU Singapore* 1316c,
        Sheff. 1927c, *Tas.* 180b, 181a
  developmental, *McG.* 378a
  gastro-intestinal, *Chinese HK* 2026c
  molecular, *McG.* 378a, *Monash* 122b
  receptor, *S'ton.* 1933c
  systematic, *Auck.* 1077a
  targets, *Montr.* 420c
  veterinary, *Ib.* 1178a
pharmacotherapeutics, *Ib.* 1175b, *Maur.* 1051c
pharmacovigilance, *Colombo* 1439b
pharmacy, *C.Sturt* 50c, *Kingston(UK)* 1719c
  administration, *O.Awolowo* 1200a
  bio-equivalence studies, *Malta* 1044c
  clinical, *Bath* 1552c, *Chinese HK* 2027a, *Syd.* 173b
  clinical practice, *Belf.* 1560c
  community, *BITS* 711a, *Malta* 1044c
  practice, *Bath* 1552c, *Chinese HK* 2027a, *La Trobe* 82b,
        Portsmouth 1902a, *Syd.* 173b, *Tas.* 180b
  prescribing, *Belf.* 1563c
  professional practice, *Belf.* 1560c
pharyngeal
  tumours, *Hull* 1698b
phase transformation, *Ghulam IKIST* 1246a
phase transitions, *Swinburne UT* 163b
phenomenology, *C'dia.* 346b, *Chinese HK* 2024c, *Durh.*
        1636b, *Lagos* 1186a, *VB* 950c
phenylketonuria, *Malta* 1044c
philanthropy, *Deakin* 62b, *Qld.UT* 153b
  and non-profit studies, *Qld.UT* 149b
Philippines
  anthropology in, *W.Aust.* 195c
  music of, *Malaya* 1011c
  sociology in, *W.Aust.* 195c
philology, *Montr.* 414a, *Reading* 1908b
  Semitic (comparative), *Malta* 1040c
philosophy, *Aust.Cath.* 34a, 35c, *Avina. Women* 685c, *Birm.*
        1572a, *C.Sturt* 51b, *Cyprus* 564b, *Herts.* 1685b,
        1686a, *M.Gandhi* 837c, *MJP Rohil.* 840b, *McG.*
        384a, *Montr.* 420b, *Oxf.Brookes* 1885b, *Rivers*
        SUST 1212b, *Sheff.* 1930a
  analytical, *Cape Town* 1337b, *Gauh.* 746b, *Karn.* 811b,
        NU Singapore 1313b
  ancient, *Glas.* 1667c, *Leeds* 1727c, *Liv.* 1758a, *Lond.*
        1778c
  and medicine, *W.Aust.* 198c
  and science, *W.Aust.* 198c
  applied, *Hull* 1697a, *Rhodes* 1390b, *Tas.* 180b, *Wales*
        1970b
  classical, *Montr.* 415a
  comparative, *Chinese HK* 2024c
  complexity, *Stell.* 1396c
  contemporary, *Gauh.* 746b
  continental, *Montr.* 415a
  early modern, *Reading* 1908c
  environmental, *W.Aust.* 194b
  ethical (applied), *Griff.* 72a
  European/continental, *Durh.* 1636b, *Macq.* 90b
  history of, *Aberd.* 1535c, *Dschang* 274a, *Glas.* 1667c, *Hull*
        1697a, *Leth.* 365c, *Manit.* 392c, *Melb.* 101b,
        Monash 120b, *Stir.* 1943a, *W.Aust.* 194b,
        W.Ont. 545a, *Wat.* 532a
  in literature, *Warw.* 1975c
  issues (in contemporary African experience), *Ghana*
        583c
  legal, *Hull* 1697a, *Stir.* 1943a, *W.Ont.* 545a
  legal (applied), *Griff.* 72a
  mediaeval, *Liv.* 1758a, *Montr.* 415a
  meta-, *C'dia.* 346b
  modern, *Montr.* 415a
  modern (European), *Middx.* 1842c
  modern (history of), *Leeds* 1733c, *W.Laur.* 559a

health (-related), Adel. 29a
health (care), Leeds 1737b
historical, Lanc. 1724b
history of, Lond. 1801b
human, Lough. 1833b
human factors, Liv.J.Moores 1766c
humanistic, Gulb. 754c
industrial, Cape Coast 575c, Melb. 101a, Wat. 533b
industrial-organisational, Chinese HK 2024c
investigative, Liv. 1758c
medical, Ib. 1175b
mental health, C.Sturt 51c
moral, Nott. 1853c
occupational, Cape Town 1336c, Lond.Met. 1824c, Sheff.
        1926a, Stell. 1395b, Swansea 1957b
of vision and action, Plym. 1892c
organisational, Exe. 1658a, Griff. 73b, Macq. 90c, Melb.
        101a, Montr. 425a, Syd. 167a, Waik. 1123b,
        Wat. 533b
personal construct, Hudd. 1691c
philosophy of, Warw. 1976a
physiological, Macq. 90c
positive, Pret. 1376a
professional, Cant. 1092b, Lond.Met. 1824c
psychosocial, Open(UK) 1871b
psychotherapeutic, Sur. 1952c
qualitative, Leeds 1737b
social, Auck. 1074c, C.Qld. 46a, Cant. 1092b, Cardiff
        1622a, Chinese HK 2024c, Dib. 729b, Durh.
        1636c, E.Cowan 66c, Exe. 1658a, Gauh. 746c,
        Griff. 73b, Gulb. 754c, Kingston(UK) 1720a, La
        Trobe 82c, Lanc. 1724b, Leeds 1737b, Lond.
        1810b, Lough. 1834c, Macq. 90c, NE 137a,
        NU Singapore 1314a, Oxf. 1880c, Qu. 457b,
        S'ton. 1937c, Sheff. 1926a, Stell. 1397b, Sur.
        1952c, Syd. 174b, Tor. 500b, Vic.(Aust.) 187a,
        W.Laur. 559c, WI 1998c, 2001c, Waik. 1123b
social (applied), Birm. 1572a, Liv. 1758c, Plym. 1896c,
        Strath. 1948a, Swansea 1957b
social (discursive), Plym. 1896c
social (experimental), Punjabi 892c
theoretical, Cant. 1092b
transpersonal, Liv.J.Moores 1766c, Rhodes 1390c
vocational, Stell. 1397b
psychometric(s), Ghana 583c, Macq. 90c, Stell. 1395b,
        W.Cape 1407c
and assessment, Pret. 1378a
methodology, Macq. 88b
psychoneuroimmunology, Hull 1698a, Pret. 1384a
psychopathology, Ghana 583c, Liv. 1761a, Panjab 882b,
        Wat. 533c
psychopedagogy, Montr. 415c, 421c
psychopharmacology, G.Jamb. 761a, Herts. 1688b,
        J.Hamdard 791c, Stell. 1399c, Tor. 507b
human, Liv. 1758c
psychophysical investigations, Lond. 1811c
psychophysics
visual, Reading 1909c
psychophysiology, Griff. 73c
and emotion, S.Cross 156c
cognitive, Lond. 1779a
psychosis, Camb. 1608c, Hull 1698b, Liv. 1761a
first-episode, Stell. 1399c
manic depressive, Cape Town 1339a
psychopharmacology of, Belf. 1562c
psychosocial
adaptation, Montr. 415b
development, Nan.Tech. 1296a
intervention, Montr. 416a
interventions, QM Edin. 1904b
rehabilitation, KwaZulu-Natal 1353c
sciences, E.Anglia 1641a
studies, La Trobe 84a
wellbeing, N-W(S.Af.) 1370b
psychosomatics, Tor. 507b
psychotherapy, Kent 1715b, Leic. 1749a, NE 137a
cognitive, Rhodes 1390c
group, Auck.UT 1083b
integrative, Auck.UT 1083b
outcomes, Auck.UT 1083b
psychotic
illness, Monash 123a
public
-private partnerships, Nott. 1860a
address, Wat. 526b
administration, Dib. 729b, Exe. 1657a, Ghana 583c, Gulb.
        754c, Lond. 1810b, Manit. 393b, Open HK
        2038a, Punjabi 892c, Tas. 180a, W.Ont. 545b,
        WI 1998c
administration (training, Web-based), Pret. 1380c
choice, Monash 115b
enterprise, Dib. 728c
enterprise (problems of), Wat. 531a
finance, Gujar. 749c, Gulb. 754a, Islamia, Bahawal. 1249a,
        Karn. 810c, Lahore MS 1255c, MDSU 835b,
        Nair. 976c, New Br. 430b
governance, Birm. 1572a, Lond. 1810b, NU Singapore
        1314a
health, Bath 1552a, Birm. 1575a, C.Qld. 45b, Calabar
        1161a, Deakin 62a, Durh. 1635b, Ebonyi State

1165b, 1165c, Gandh.Rural 743c, Glas. 1669a,
        Griff. 74a, Leeds 1735a, Liv. 1763a, Lond.
        1802c, Melb. 104a, 105c, 107b, 109b,
        Monash 121b, Montr. 412b, 416b,
        Newcastle(NSW) 145b, Sheff. 1929a, Sur.
        1951c, WI 2000c, 2001a, 2001b
health (and community development), Aust.Cath. 33c
health (and inequality), Lanc. 1723a
health (and vision), Syd. 166b
health (dental), W.Aust. 193a, WI 2001a
health (evidence-based), Plym. 1894b
health (international), Syd. 172a
health (medicine), E.Anglia 1640c
health (nursing), Melb. 107b
health (nutrition), Auck. 1077c
health (planning), Ib. 1174c
health (policy), Ib. 1174c
health (promotion), Sheff. 1927a
leadership, Birm. 1572a
management, Birm. 1572a, NU Singapore 1314a, Stell.
        1397b, Strath. 1946c
management (reform), Birm. 1572b
offerings (initial), Deakin 61c
opinion, FJ Women 1243b, Glas. 1668a, Kelaniya 1445a,
        Macq. 90b
opinion (measurement of), W.Laur. 560b
policy, Auck.UT 1083c, 1084c, Cant. 1088c, Cape Coast
        575a, Exe. 1657a, Glas. 1668c, Melb. 101c,
        Montr. 421a, NE 137c, New Br. 430b, 433a,
        Panjab 882c, Pret. 1380c, Qu. 457a, 460b,
        R.Gordon 1911a, Sheff. 1926a, Strath. 1946b,
        1946c, Sur. 1953c, Syd. 170a, Tas. 180a,
        Uganda Christian 1503c, WI 1998c
policy (analysis), Ghana 583c
policy (and ethics), Qld.UT 153b
policy (and interest groups), Aberd. 1537a
policy (and management), Durh. 1634a
policy (comparative), Lond. 1779a
policy (democratisation of), Brun. 1596b
policy (ideological framework), Sheff. 1931a
policy (management), W.Cape 1407b
policy (studies), Pret. 1380b
relations, Curtin 57a, Deakin 61c, Ebonyi State 1165b,
        Ghana 582a, Panjab 882a, Punjabi 892b,
        Swansea 1957a
relations (organisational), Qld.UT 149a
sector, Vic.(Aust.) 185a
sector (accountability), Vic.(Aust.) 185a
sector (administration), Liv. 1757c
sector (change), Warw. 1978b
sector (competitive tendering), Vic.(Aust.) 185a
sector (computing), Lond. 1801a
sector (governance), Plym. 1894b
sector (information technology), Botswana 262c, Dal.
        355a, Nan.Tech. 1301a
sector (management), Botswana 263b, Liv. 1757c, Lond.
        1801a, Monash 119c, Stir. 1942c, Vic.(Aust.)
        186c, WI 1995a, 1995b
sector (middle managers in), Nott. 1860a
sector (performance measurement), S.Pac. 1421b
sector (records management), Botswana 262c
sector (reform), S.Leone 1287c, Syd. 175a
sector (restructuring), Well. 1115b
services (management), Aston 1544b, Birm. 1572a, Lond.
        1809b
transport, Leeds 1734c
publication(s), Monash 124c
control, Monash 114b
publishing, Ib. 1173b, 1174c
culture of, Oxf.Brookes 1886b, 1886c
development, Oxf.Brookes 1886c
electronic, New Br. 433c, W'gong. 208b
history of, Oxf.Brookes 1886b, 1886c, S.Fraser 487b
international, Oxf.Brookes 1886c
management, S.Fraser 487b
policy, Oxf.Brookes 1886c, S.Fraser 487b
strategy, Oxf.Brookes 1886c
pulmonary
disease, Qu. 459a
disease (chronic obstructive), Belf. 1562a,
        S.Ramachandra 926c
hypertension, S.Ramachandra 927c
medicine, Adel. 28c
pathology, Stell. 1399c
surgery, Stell. 1398a
pulp and paper, Auck. 1070b, New Br. 433c, Tor. 502a
chemistry, New Br. 430c, Well. 1114a
manufacture, Wales 1548b
technology, Ib. 1173a
waste products (treatment), G.Jamb. 760c
pumps, Bath 1555a
Punchayati Raj system, MDSU 835c
punishment, Well. 1117c
corporal, Winneba 579b
Punjab
history, Punjabi 892a
state politics, GND 763c
Punjabi
drama, Punjabi 893a
fiction, Punjabi 893a

grammar, Punjabi 891a
languages, Punjabi 891a
theatre, Punjabi 893a
pupil(s)
progress (measurement of), Cant. 1086b
puppetry, E.Cowan 66a
Puranas, Gujar. 750c, SP 907c
pychology
forensic, C.Sturt 52a
pyloric
drainage, S.Ramachandra 927a
pyrometallurgy, Pret. 1376c, Stell. 1394c, W'gong. 210b

qualitative
methodology/ies, S'ton. 1938b
research, Lond. 1803a
quality
control, Manit. 394b
management, Auck. 1072c, Avina. Women 685a, Cape
        Town 1335a, E.Cowan 65b, Kingston(UK)
        1718c, MDSU 835b, Melb. 100b, Montr. 424a,
        O.Awolowo 1200c, Portsmouth 1903a
management (in information systems), Well. 1116a
management (in the developing world), Nott. 1860a
management (systems), Maur. 1051a, WI 2001b
of life, N-W(S.Af.) 1370b
purchasing practices, Nipissing 437a
theory, Gulb. 755a
quantitative
methods, Lond.Met. 1824a
research (design), Aust.Cath. 33c
quantum, GND 763b
chaos, Lond. 1811b
chromodynamics, Plym. 1895c
dynamics, W.Aust. 195b
electrodynamics, Ghana 583c
field theory, BITS 711a, Stell. 1396c, 1401b, W.Aust.
        195b
information, Belf. 1560b, Chinese HK 2024c, Pret. 1380a,
        Swinburne UT 162b
interactive systems, Exe. 1658a
mechanics, Dib. 729b, Ghana 583c, Kelaniya 1445b,
        Kwame NUST 589a, Open(UK) 1871a, VB
        950c
mechanics (geometrical methods in), C'dia. 346c
mechanics (probability in), Lond. 1811b
mechanics (stochastic), C'dia. 346c
state diffusion, Lond. 1811b
theory, Pret. 1380a, Wat. 531b
trajectory methods, Lond. 1811b
quaternary
dating, Glas. 1671b
studies, Durh. 1635a, Lond. 1808a, Rhodes 1389b
Quebec/Quebecois, Glas. 1667b
art, Leic. 1750c
cultural groups in, McG. 384c
culture, Leic. 1750c
history of, McG. 384c
literature, Leic. 1750c, Qu. 455a
study of (interdisciplinary approaches to), McG. 384c
queueing
related networks, Well. 1117a
theory, M.Sund. 857a
Quran, the, Lond. 1817a
interpretation, Peradeniya 1452b
Quranic
exegesis, Bayero 1150a
schools, Bayero 1150a

r-DNA
technology, MJP Rohil. 840b
rabbits
diet of, Makurdi Ag. 1143a
nutrition of, Makurdi Ag. 1143a
Rabelais, François, Belf. 1559b
rabies, Colombo 1439c
rabies/rabies related viruses
epidemiology, Makurdi Ag. 1144b
Rabindranath, VB 949c
race, Jo'burg. 1349a, KwaZulu-Natal 1354b, Liv. 1756a,
        Nott. 1850c, W.Laur. 557a
and identity, Aust.Cath. 35b
and immigration, Wat. 530b
discrimination (in industrial tribunal system), Strath.
        1946c
in sport, C.Sturt 51b
politics (in dance), Hull 1699a
relations, Stell. 1397b, W.Aust. 194b
studies, Cape Town 1334c, Open(UK) 1871c
racial
discrimination, Cape Town 1336b, Warw. 1978c
racism, Bran. 317c, Lond. 1801c, Montr. 419c
and Lebanese youth, Syd. 176c
combating, Birm. 1572a
history of (in South Africa), Rhodes 1389b
sociology of, Glas. 1668b
radar, Birm. 1568c, Sheff. 1923b
synthetic aperture (applications), NU Singapore 1318c
systems, Nan.Tech. 1296b

groups (impact of federating), *Gandh.Rural* 742b
health, *Aust.Cath.* 35a, *Bath* 1555c, *Botswana* 263a,
    Chinese HK 2026a, *Dal.* 360a, *Edin.* 1647b,
    Kelaniya 1443b, *Manit.* 395b, *Monash* 127a,
    Northumbria 1849a, *Qu.* 458c, 459a,
    Vic.(Aust.) 187b, *Wat.* 534c, *Witw.* 1418a
health (reproductive), *Gandh.Rural* 742c, *SPMV* 925c
health (services), *R.Gordon* 1911b
history, *Birm.* 1571a, *Hudd.* 1694b, *Liv.* 1756a, *Macq.*
    89b, *Manc.Met.* 1840b, *New Br.* 432a, *W.Aust.*
    194b
history (mediaeval), *Hudd.* 1694b
history (South Africa, Zimbabwe, Africa), *Rhodes* 1389b
literacy, *Pondicherry* 887c
literature, *Avina. Women* 685a, *Wat.* 529c
psychology, *Bath* 1555c, *Malta* 1043c
rights, *Bayero* 1150b, *Birm.* 1572a, *Ebonyi State* 1164a,
    Lagos 1185c, *Rhodes* 1390a
spirituality (contemporary), *Bran.* 318a
studies, *Birm.* 1570c, *Cape Town* 1337a, *Cyprus* 564a, *Dr
    BRA Open* 730c, *Gauh.* 746c, *Gujar.* 750c, *Ib.*
    1174a, *Kent* 1716a, *Leic.* 1749c, *M.Sund.*
    856c, 857a, *McG.* 371c, *Nipissing* 437b,
    O.Awolowo 1198a, *Portsmouth* 1902c, *Punjabi*
    893a, *SP* 907c, *Tas.* 180b, *Ulster* 1963a,
    Vic.(Aust.) 185b, *W.Aust.* 200c, *W.Laur.* 558c
theatre, *Lond.* 1808a, *Plym.* 1897b
welfare, *Karn.* 811c
well-being, *Dal.* 360a
writing, *Gujar.* 750a, *Hull* 1697a, *Leeds Met.* 1741b,
    Macq. 88c
writing (nineteenth-century), *Kingston(UK)* 1719a
writing (seventeenth-century), *Lough.* 1833b
writing (sixteenth-century), *McG.* 371b
writing (twentieth-century), *Cape Town* 1337a,
    Kingston(UK) 1719a, *Lough.* 1833b
wood, *AT Balewa* 1138b
  -based panels, *Wales* 1548b
  anatomy, *Cant.* 1087a
  and log quality, *Cant.* 1087a
  bark harvesting, *Copperbelt* 2005c
  bioenergy, *Cant.* 1090b
  cell-wall structure, *Cant.* 1087a
  chemistry, *McG.* 369a, *New Br.* 434b
  drying technology, *Cant.* 1090b
  engineering, *New Br.* 434b
  manufacture (innovative), *Swinburne UT* 161b
  preservation, *Bindura* 2044c
  processing, *Cant.* 1087a, 1090b
  product development, *New Br.* 434b
  production and marketing, *Kwame NUST* 590c, *New Br.*
    431c
  products (processing), *Cant.* 1087a
  properties, *Cant.* 1087a
  science, *KwaZulu-Natal* 1356c, *New Br.* 431c, 434b,
    Wales 1546c
  technology, *Cant.* 1091a, *Dschang* 273b, *New Br.* 434b
woodlands
  biodiversity, *Plym.* 1897a
  community, *Kwame NUST* 589c
  conservation, *Plym.* 1897a
  management of, *Copperbelt* 2005c
  management (sustainable), *Plym.* 1897a
wool
  biology, *Adel.* 24c
  fabric (plasma treatment of), *H-W* 1681b
word processor(s)
  development, *Copperbelt* 2005b
word recognition, *C'dia.* 348a
worker(s)
  industrial, *Karn.* 811c
  participation, *Malta* 1046a
workflow(s)
  management, *Tezpur* 940a
workforce
  future (preparing), *Plym.* 1896b
  older, *Sur.* 1953c
  practices (in southern Africa), *Cape Town* 1341c
work(ing), *Aberd.* 1535b, *Bath* 1553c, *Herts.* 1688c, *Lanc.*
    1723c, *Maur.* 1052b, *Melb.* 111b,
    Newcastle(NSW) 144c

analysis of, *La Trobe* 84a
and emotional intelligence, *Montr.* 425a
and globalisation, *Chinese HK* 2025a
and health, *C.Sturt* 51a
and leisure, *C.Sturt* 51a, *Cant.* 1088c
and mental health, *Montr.* 425a, *Sheff.* 1931b
and quality of life, *Griff.* 75a
and the public sector, *S'ton.* 1938b
attitudes to, *W.Aust.* 200a
behaviour at, *W.Aust.* 200a
conditions, *Montr.* 421c
design, *Montr.* 424b
effectiveness, *Qld.UT* 151b, 152c, *Sheff.* 1931b
environments, *Manit.* 391c
future of, *Qld.UT* 151b
meaning of, *Montr.* 425a
networked, *Sheff.* 1924c
organisation of, *Montr.* 425a, *W.Cape* 1408b
performance management, *Qld.UT* 152c
policy, *Monash* 125c
producer co-operation, *C.Sturt* 50c
psychology, *Montr.* 425a
role of, *Plym.* 1896c
safety at, *W.Aust.* 200a
sickness absence reduction, *Sur.* 1953a
sociology of, *Witw.* 1415a
spaces, *Montr.* 413b
stress (and managerial support), *Nipissing* 437b
systems, *Plym.* 1894c
teams, *Montr.* 425a
well-being at, *W.Aust.* 200a
world of, *Syd.* 177b
workplace
  change, *Belf.* 1560a, *McG.* 374a, *Monash* 126b
  diversity (management of), *Hudd.* 1691b
  health, *Montr.* 413b, *Qld.UT* 152b, *Sur.* 1953a
  injury, *Manit.* 396a
  language, *NE* 138b
  learning, *Manit.* 398c, *Napier* 1845a
  literacy, *NE* 138b, *Qld.UT* 149b
  restructuring, *Cape Town* 1338b
  safety, *Montr.* 413b, *Qld.UT* 152c
  studies, *Syd.* 174c
  training, *Botswana* 260c
  trust in, *Newcastle(NSW)* 141c
World Trade Organisation, *Lahore MS* 1255c
  impact on agriculture, *Gandh.Rural* 743a
World Wide Web
  accessibility, *Plym.* 1893c
  applications, *Plym.* 1895c
  development (techniques), *Azad J&K* 1237b
  engineering, *Swinburne UT* 163b
  in learning, *E.Cowan* 67a, *Liv.* 1763a
  in teaching, *E.Cowan* 67a, *Liv.* 1763a
  multilingual information on, *Dal.* 353a
  technology, *Plym.* 1895c
wound
  healing, *Cardiff* 1616b, 1620c, *Glas.* 1669c, *Hull* 1698a,
    KwaZulu-Natal 1355a, 1356a, 1356b, *Pret.*
    1384b, *Tas.* 181b
  healing (foetal), *Qu.* 459b
  healing (theoretical modelling), *H-W* 1682a
  management, *Monash* 124a
  models, *Cardiff* 1620c
  repair (ophthalmic), *Liv.* 1759b
writing
  academic, *Syd.* 176a
  at tertiary level, *KwaZulu-Natal* 1358a
  creative, *Adel.* 27a, *Belf.* 1558c, *Brun.* 1594c, *C'dia.* 345a,
    Dschang 272c, *Exe.* 1656b, *Hull* 1697a, *Lanc.*
    1722c, *Leth.* 364b, *Lough.* 1833b, *Macq.* 88c,
    New Br. 431b, *Newcastle(NSW)* 143c, *Plym.*
    1891a, *S.Cross* 155c, *S.Pac.* 1422b, *Strath.*
    1946b, *Sunshine Coast* 159a, *W'gong.* 209a,
    W.Aust. 200c, *Well.* 1118c
  fiction, *W'gong.* 209a
  in a foreign language, *S'ton.* 1936c
  interactive, *Canberra* 42a
  life, *WI* 2000a
  modern, *Stir.* 1942b
  professional, *Deakin* 61c

scripts, *Ib.* 1176a

X-linked disease, *Camb.* 1608a
X-ray
  diffraction, *Stell.* 1401c
  fluorescence spectrometry, *Stell.* 1401c
  imaging, *Monash* 128b, *Sur.* 1952b
  physics (fundamental), *Monash* 120b
  science, *La Trobe* 80a
  topography, *Lond.* 1810c
X-rays
  detection of foreign bodies, *Lond.* 1811c
Xhosa, *Rhodes* 1389c
  literature, *Stell.* 1392c

yams
  properties of, *Ebonyi State* 1164c
  storage, *Eastern(S.Lanka)* 1441b
yeast(s)
  biotechnology, *Abertay* 1539a
  cations in, *Panjab* 880c
  genetic manipulation of, *Stell.* 1396a
  saccharomyces cerevisae, *Ebonyi State* 1163c
Yiddish
  language, *Lond.* 1816a, 1817b
  literature, *Lond.* 1817b, *McG.* 372a
Yoruba
  arts and culture, *O.Awolowo* 1198c
  colour symbolism, *O.Awolowo* 1198c
  ritual poetry, *O.Awolowo* 1198c
  studies, *O.Awolowo* 1198c
young adults, *Montr.* 415b
young people, *Bath* 1553c, *La Trobe* 83b, 84c
  and crime, *Cant.* 1088c
  and social identity, *Melb.* 111b
  disabilities in, *Belf.* 1563b
  health of, *Melb.* 111b
  in employment, *C.Sturt* 51c
  in training, *C.Sturt* 51c
  mental health of, *Belf.* 1563b
  well-being of, *Melb.* 111b
Yourcenar, Marguerite, *Jo'burg.* 1347b
youth, *Aust.Cath.* 33a
  affairs, *Lagos* 1185b
  and school (deviance), *WI* 2001c
  behaviour, *Bayero* 1148b
  behaviour (social), *Belf.* 1563b
  crime, *WI* 2001c
  development, *Belf.* 1563b, *WI* 1990b
  education, *Dar.* 1478b, *Glas.* 1668b
  employment, *Glas.* 1668b
  gambling, *McG.* 385b
  gambling (prevention of), *McG.* 385b
  issues, *NU Singapore* 1314b
  justice, *Herts.* 1688c
  lifestyle, *Belf.* 1563b
  ministry, *Stell.* 1397a
  movements, *Jo'burg.* 1349a
  nursing, *Newcastle(NSW)* 144c, *Qld.UT* 151c
  offenders, *Open(UK)* 1870c
  out-of-school, education and development of, *KwaZulu-
    Natal* 1352a
  psychological capital, *WI* 2001c
  risk-taking behaviours, *McG.* 385b
  studies, *Botswana* 263b, *Herts.* 1688c, *Ulster* 1963a
  values of, *Jos* 1180c
  welfare, *Chinese HK* 2025a, *Warw.* 1974b

Zimbabwe
  privatisation in, *Midlands State* 2046c
zinc, *Deakin* 62b
zoology, *MP Bhoj* 824b, *Melb.* 102c, *Reading* 1906b
zoonoses, *Nair.* 972a
zoonotic diseases, *Ghana* 584a, *Peradeniya* 1456b
Zulu
  linguistics, *KwaZulu-Natal* 1352c
  literature, *KwaZulu-Natal* 1352c, *Stell.* 1392c
  literature (traditional), *KwaZulu-Natal* 1352c
  onomastics, *KwaZulu-Natal* 1352c

INDEX TO PERSONAL NAMES

Names, in 3-column setting, in university chapters are indexed by page number and column reference (a, b or c) plus abbreviation for the chapter in which they appear (*example*: Gagnon, Anita J., *Montr.*, 440b). Names in page-wide setting do not include column references. *Note*—Names appearing in the preliminary pages are not indexed.

Finding names. All personal names are indexed under the first letter of the main/surname element as set out first in entries throughout the book.

Example: Abd-El-Malek, *Sask.*, 541a
Chan Lok Shun, *HK*, 2090b
Jackson, Richard A., *Sus.*, 1976b
Onwuka, Arize, *Enugu SUST*, 1155c
Van Rhyn, Dianne J., *Murd.*, 123b
Zuraidah Mohd Don, *Malaya*, 1022b

Identical names. Names that are identical are indexed in the following ways *irrespective of whether or not they relate to the same person*. If within the same

chapter: as a single name entry. *Example*: Sharma, D. C., *Jiw.*, 818b, 818c, 819b. If in *different* chapters, as two or more name entries in alphabetical order of universities.
Example: Smith, A. J., *Edin.*, 1599a
A. J., *Syd.*, 252b

One element names. Names which consist of one element only (*example*: Mohamad) come before people with the same main element.

Alphabetical order. Names are listed alphabetically in word-by-word order by main/

surname element. Hyphenated names follow two-element unhyphenated names in the alphabetical sort.
Example: El Ansari, Wahid
El Toukhy, M. M.
El-Ashker, Ahmed
Elaigwu, J. J.
Elam, Diane M.

Notes. (i) Names beginning Mac or Mc are listed together under Mac, the next letter of each name determining its position in the sequence.

(ii) Names beginning Saint, St. or St- are listed together under Saint.

A. Aziz Saim, *Tech.U.Malaysia* 1033b
A Hamid bin A Hadi, *Malaya* 1011b
A S Md Abdul Haseeb, *Malaya* 1007a
A-Khavari, Afshin, *Griff.* 72a
Aadil, N., *Lahore UET* 1241b
Aagaard, M. D., *Wat.* 525c, 527b, 528c
Aalbersberg, William, *S.Pac.* 1423a
Aaron, S. L., *Alta.* 311b
Shawn, *Ott.* 444c
Aaronson, Philip I., *Lond.* 1788b, 1794c
Aarssen, L. W., *Qu.* 452a
Aashikpelokhai, U. S. U., *Ambrose Alli* 1146c
Aaskov, John G., *Qld.UT* 151a
Ab Aziz Mohd Zin, *Malaya* 1012a
Ab. Aziz Othman, *NU Malaya* 1014, 1020c
Ab Aziz Shuaib, *Putra* 1022a
Ab Mumin Ab Ghani, *Malaya* 1012b
Ab Rahim Bakar, *Putra* 1023c
Ab Rahim Ismail, *IIU Malaysia* 999a
Ab Rahman Ahmad, *Tech.U.Malaysia* 1031b
Ab Razak bin Ab Karim, *Malaya* 1012c
Ab Saman Abd Kader, *Tech.U.Malaysia* 1034b
Ababio, E. P., *N-W(S.Af.)* 1371b
Abachi, Hamid R., *Monash* 116b
Abadir, Karim M., *ICL* 1705a
Abadjieva, T., *Botswana* 261c
Abah, J. O., *Maid.* 1191b
Abaidoo, Chrissie, *Kwame NUST* 589c
R. C., *Kwame NUST* 587c
Abaitey, A. K., *Kwame NUST* 589b
Abaka, E. N., *Winneba* 579a
Abam, D. P. S., *P.Harcourt* 1207c
Abama, E. A., *Jos* 1181c, 1182a
Abane, A. M., *Cape Coast* 575b
Abang, Moses O., *Calabar* 1158b
Sylvanus O. M., *Calabar* 1158c
T. B., *Jos* 1181a
Abang Abdullah Abang Ali, *Putra* 1024b
Abantanga, F. A., *Kwame NUST* 590b
Abara, Isaac O. C., *Ebonyi State* 1164a
Abari, A. O., *Lagos State* 1189c
Abaru, E. D., *Mak.* 1498c
Abasi, A. H. K., *Devel.Studies(Ghana)* 578a, 578b
Abasiatti, M. B., *Uyo* 1215c, 1216c

Abasiekong, Solomon F., *M.Okpara, Umudike* 1193c
Abasiubong, F., *Uyo* 1216b
Abass, Ademola, *Brun.* 1595a, 1597b
Olayide, *Lagos* 1184a
Abatan, M. O., *Ib.* 1178a
Abate, A. L., *Namibia* 1056a
Abayadeera, Anuja, *Colombo* 1439c
N., *Sri Jay.* 1462b
Abayakoon, S. B. S., *Peradeniya* 1451b, 1453b
Abayarathne, A. H. M. H., *Kelaniya* 1444c
Abayasekara, D. Robert E., *Camb.* 1610b
Robert, *Lond.* 1812c
Abayasekera, C. R., *Peradeniya* 1452c
Abayasundere, A. P. N. de S., *Sri Jay.* 1464a
Abayawardhana, D. L., *Sri Jay.* 1463b
Abayeh, O. J., *AT Balewa* 1138b
Abaza, Mahmoud, *Athab.* 314b
Abba, Abdullahi, *Bayero* 1151c
Isa A., *Bayero* 1150a
S. B., *Maid.* 1191b
Abbas, Asad, *NUST(P'stan.)* 1265a
Farhat, *Aga Khan(P'stan.)* 1232c
G., *Islamia, Bahawal.* 1249b
Ghulam, *Bhutto IST* 1272b
Nadeem, *Foundation(P'stan.)* 1244c
Sagir A., *Bayero* 1149b
Syed Hasan, *Ban.* 692b
Tahir, *Birm.* 1576a
Tanveer, *Karachi* 1252a
Abbas Ali, *Osm.* 876b
Abbas b Hassan, *IIU Malaysia* 1003b
Abbas Khan, A. A., *Maulana Azad Natnl.Urdu* 858, 858c
Abbasi, A. F., *Mehran* 1258a
A. W. M., *Azad J&K* 1237c
Abdul R., *Sindh* 1274c
Aitbar A., *Mehran* 1258a
Atiya, *Karachi* 1253b
G. Q., *Islamia, Bahawal.* 1249b
Hafeez, *Bhutto IST* 1272a
Hina Q., *Islamia, Bahawal.* 1249c
Khurshid, *Karachi* 1253a
M. K., *Azad J&K* 1236c
Nadeem Akhtar, *Arid Ag.* 1235c
S. A., *Osm.* 875c
S. A., *Pondicherry* 886b
Shahid, *Foundation(P'stan.)* 1244b
Siraj A., *Mehran* 1258a
Ubedullah M., *Sindh* 1274b

Uzma Tariq, *NUST(P'stan.)* 1264b
Zarin, *Sindh* 1275a
Abbass, Allan, *Dal.* 358b
Abbasy, Hafsa, *Bhutto IST* 1272c
Abbatt, Jonathan, *Tor.* 491a
Abbe, Hon. Patrick, *Ambrose Alli* 1145
Abbey, Bene W., *P.Harcourt* 1206c
J., *Qld.UT* 151c
Ruth, *Kent* 1715c
Sam, *Rivers SUST* 1210b, 1210c, 1212a
Sharon M., *Brock* 321b
Susan E., *Tor.* 507b
T. M., *P.Harcourt* 1208b
Abbinnett, R., *Birm.* 1573b
Ross, *Leeds Met.* 1741a
Abbiss, J. C., *Nott.Trent* 1864a
Jane E., *Cant.* 1089c
Abbiyesuku, F. M., *Ib.* 1176b
Abbo, Andrew J., *Newcastle(NSW)* 142b
Abbo Jimeta, U. S., *Maid.* 1191c
Abbot, N. Joan, *Lond.* 1788b
Abbott, Andrew J., *Bath* 1550c, 1554b
Andrew P., *Leic.* 1746c
Cathy, *Edin.* 1652b
Chris D., *Lond.* 1793b
Christine, *Birm.* 1577b
Derek Z., *Adel.* 26b, 30a
Elizabeth, *Trin.Coll.(Tor.)* 512
F. J., *Nott.Trent* 1866c
Frances V., *McG.* 378b
Ian D., *Warw.* 1973a
Justine, *Open(UK)* 1867b
K. A., *Lond.* 1813a
Kim A., *C.Sturt* 50b
Lesley, *Manc.Met.* 1838c
Lynette K., *W.Aust.* 193a, 199b
M. G., *Qu.* 453a
Max, *Auck.UT* 1080b, 1080, 1084c
Paul C., *W.Aust.* 195a
Paul V., *W.Aust.* 193a
R. J., *St And.* 1913b
Steven J., *Leeds* 1729c
V. J., *Plym.* 1889b
Abbulu, Y., *And.* 671a
Abd Azim Abd Ghani, *Putra* 1021a
Abd Aziz Abd Muti, *Tech.U.Malaysia* 1032c
Abd Aziz Jemain, *NU Malaysia* 1018a
Abd El Halim, A. O., *Car.* 337b
Abd El-Fattah Anwar Ahmed Rezk, *IIU Malaysia* 1000a
Abd Ghafar Ismail, *NU Malaysia* 1016a
Abd Ghani bin Khalid, *Tech.U.Malaysia* 1035a

Abd Ghani Mohd Rafek, *NU Malaysia* 1016c
Abd Hafidz Omar, *Tech.U.Malaysia* 1031c
Abd Halim Shaari, *Putra* 1026c
Abd Halim Shamsuddin, *NU Malaysia* 1016c
Abd Hamid Ahmad, *Tech.U.Malaysia* 1032b
Abd Hamid Rahman, *NU Malaysia* 1020a
Abd Kadir Marsono, *Tech.U.Malaysia* 1033b
Abd Latif Saleh, *Tech.U.Malaysia* 1033b
Abd Majid bin A Kadir, *Tech.U.Malaysia* 1032b
Abd Malek Abdul Ghani, *Tech.U.Malaysia* 1036b
Abd Manan Ahmad, *Tech.U.Malaysia* 1031a
Abd Rahim Hamdan, *Tech.U.Malaysia* 1031b
Abd Rahim Md Yunus, *Tech.U.Malaysia* 1035a
Abd Rahim Samsudin, *NU Malaysia* 1016c
Abd Rahman bin Abdul Rahim, *Tech.U.Malaysia* 1034b
Abd Rahman Ramli, *Putra* 1024b
Abd Rani Abd Hamid, *Tech.U.Malaysia* 1034c
Abd Razak Daud, *NU Malaysia* 1015b
Abd Wahab Md Salleh, *NU Malaysia* 1018a
Abd Wahid Haron, *Putra* 1027c
Abd Wahid Mukhari, *Tech.U.Malaysia* 1031c
Abd-El Aziem Farouk Abd-El Aziem Gad, *IIU Malaysia* 1000a
Abdalla, Mohamad, *Griff.* 74b
Abdalla A A Abusam, *IIU Malaysia* 1000a
Abdallah, Ali, *Lond.S.Bank* 1829a
Abdel Galil, K. A., *W.Ont.* 548a
Abdel Haleem, Muhammad A. S., *Lond.* 1817a
Abdel Hamed Hamad Md Mahmud El-Zawiei, *IIU Malaysia* 999a
Abdel Magid Saleem Hamouda, *Putra* 1024c
Abdel-Gayed, R., *Coventry* 1626b
Abdel-Haleem, Muhammad A. S., *Lond.* 1816a
Abdel-Kader, Magdy, *Brun.* 1593c
Abdel-Moteleb, Abou-Bakr, *Middx.* 1843a
Abdel-Shaheed, Wagih K., *W.Ont.* 550c
Abdel-Wahab, Yasser, *Ulster* 1960a
Abdella, K., *Trent* 514b

K., *W.Ont.* 543c
Abdelmessih, Abdo H., *Tor.* 503a
Abdelrahman, Tarek S., *Tor.* 502b
Abder, Clyde, *WI* 1999a
Abdi, A. A., *Alta.* 305a
M. A., *Nfld.* 403a, 403b
Abdi Omar Shuriye, *IIU Malaysia* 1000a
Abdin, M. Z., *J.Hamdard* 790c, 792b
Z., *Azad J&K* 1238c
Abdo, H., *Nott.Trent* 1861c
Nahla, *Car.* 341a
Abdoh, A. A., *Manit.* 398a
Abdollah, H., *Qu.* 458c
Abdool, A. D., *N-W(S.Af.)* 1367c
Abdool Karim, Salim, *KwaZulu-Natal* 1350, 1356b
Abdu'Allah, Faisal, *E.Lond.* 1642a
Abdul, Abdulrahman, *Bayero* 1149a
Abdul Amir Hassan Kadhum, *NU Malaysia* 1016b
Abdul Azeez Kadar Hamsa, *IIU Malaysia* 999a
Abdul Azim Abd Ghani, *Putra* 1026a
Abdul Azis, P. K., *Alig.* 668
Abdul Azis Ariffin, *Putra* 1025b
Abdul Aziz Abd Ghani, *Tech.U.Malaysia* 1034b
Abdul Aziz Abdul Kadir, *Tech.U.Malaysia* 1033a
Abdul Aziz Aby Bakar, *NU Malaysia* 1020c
Abdul Aziz Bari, *IIU Malaysia* 1001a
Abdul Aziz Bergout, *IIU Malaysia* 1000c
Abdul Aziz bin Abdul Raman, *Malaya* 1006c
Abdul Aziz bin Abdul Razak, *Malaya* 1009b
Abdul Aziz bin Buang, *Tech.U.Malaysia* 1034a
Abdul Aziz bin Hussin, *Tech.U.Malaysia* 1033a
Abdul Aziz Chik, *Tech.U.Malaysia* 1032c
Abdul Aziz Jaafar, *Putra* 1024a
Abdul Aziz Mohd Amin, *Tech.U.Malaysia* 1034a
Abdul Aziz Saharee, *Putra* 1027c, 1028a
Abdul Barie, M. S., *Peradeniya* 1452a
Abdul Basith, S., *TN Vet.* 936c
Abdul Ghafar Don, *NU Malaysia* 1016a
Abdul Ghaffar bin Hj Abdul Rahman, *Malaya* 1007a
Abdul Ghani Hashim, Hj, *Putra* 1028b
Abdul Ghani Liew Abdullah, *Putra* 1024a

Nicholas D., *Lond.* 1818c
P. Alan, *Auck.* 1075b
P. C., *Birm.* 1573c
S. M., *Sask.* 475a
Sarah, *Lanc.* 1723a
Stephen, *Kingston(UK)* 1719a, 1720a
Zoe H., *Camb.* 1605a
Barberio, Elisabetta, *Melb.* 101b
Barberis, J. P., *Manc.Met.* 1841a
Barbetti, Martin J., *W.Aust.* 195b
Barbieri, Bryan, *C'dia.* 346a
Barbiero, T. P., *Ryerson* 463b
Barblett, Lennie, *E.Cowan* 64c
Barbora, M., *Tezpur* 940b
Barbour, Angela H., *Adel.* 28c
D. F., *Alta.* 306a
Kay, *Napier* 1845b
Len J., *Stell.* 1393b, 1401b
S. L., *Sask.* 473c
Barby, J. A., *Wat.* 527c
Barchanski, Jerzy A., *Brock* 320c
Barclay, A. Neil, *Oxf.* 1880a
Christopher J., *Griff.* 73a
D. W., *W.Ont.* 538c
David W., *New Br.* 432b
Elaine, *NE* 138c
G., *Lond.* 1803c
George, *Vic.(Aust.)* 188b
Ian, *Liv.J.Moores* 1765c
J., *E.Anglia* 1639b
Jean, *G.Caledonian* 1673a
John, *Aust.Cath.* 36a, 36b, 36c
John M. G., *Durh.* 1636c
K. A., *Napier* 1844b
L., *Curtin* 56c
Lyn, *Qu.* 451c
M., *Wales* 1968a
Olivia, *Nelson Mandela Met.* 1360b
R. M. R., *Calg.* 324a
Bard, E. G., *Edin.* 1649c
Harry, *Montr.* 417c
Jonathan, *Edin.* 1650c
Kim A., *Portsmouth* 1902b
Bardakjian, Berj L., *Tor.* 502b
Bardecki, M., *Ryerson* 464b
Barden, Dennis, *Camb.* 1610c
M., *Manc.Met.* 1840c
Miceal, *Open(UK)* 1870a
Nicola, *Portsmouth* 1903c
Bardgett, Richard D., *Lanc.* 1721c
Bardien, Soraya, *Stell.* 1398a
Bardill, John, *W.Cape* 1407b
Bardini, Thierry, *Montr.* 411c
Bardoel, E. A., *Monash* 119b
Bardouille, Deborah, *Nott.Trent* 1866b
Bardsley, Peter, *Melb.* 96b, 108c
R. G., *Nott.* 1851a
W. Earl, *Waik.* 1120c
Baré, Elizabeth, *Melb.* 93, 111b
Baree, Md. Sadiqul, *B'desh.Engin.* 225b
Bareeba, F. B., *Mak.* 1496a
Barefoot, Helen C., *Herts.* 1686b
Baregu, M. L., *Dar.* 1480b
Bareham, Gerard E., *Hudd.* 1691b
Bareil, Céline, *Montr.* 424a
Barendregt, Renè W., *Leth.* 364b
Barer, Michael R., *Leic.* 1748c
Barford, D., *Lond.* 1786a
Bargate, K., *KwaZulu-Natal* 1356c
Bargiela, A., *Nott.Trent* 1863a
Bargman, Joanne, *Tor.* 505b
Barhai, P. K., *BIT(Ranchi)* 708
Barham, D., *Tor.* 501c
G., *Wales* 1968b
Lawrence S., *Liv.* 1755a
P. J., *Brist.* 1588a
Bari, A. J., *Lahore UET* 1241b, 1241c
A. K. M. Abdul, *Rajsh.* 253b
A. Z., *NED Eng.* 1260b
Abdul, *Riphah Internat.* 1271a
Faisal, *Lahore MS* 1255c
George G., *Jomo K.* 967c
M. A., *Rajsh.* 253c, 254c
M. Abdul, *B'desh.Ag.* 222a
M. E., *Dhaka* 236a
M. Ehsan, *Aga Khan(P'stan.)* 1232c
M. Fazlul, *B'desh.Engin.* 225b
M. Shafiul, *B'desh.Engin.* 224b
Md. Abdul, *Rajsh.* 253b
Md. Nasimul, *BSMR Ag.* 218a
Rehana, *Dhaka* 236c
S. A., *JMI* 794b
S. S., *Panjab* 880, 881a, 884b
Vaqar, *Aga Khan(P'stan.)* 1232c
W., *Dhaka* 239a
Bari Jafri, M. Inam, *Karachi* 1252a
Baridam, Don M., *P.Harcourt* 1206, 1208a
Baride, M. V., *N.Maharashtra* 868, 869a
Baridoma, M. B., *Rivers SUST* 1211c
Barifaijo, E., *Mak.* 1497a
Barigou, M., *Birm.* 1568a
Barik, A., *Manc.Met.* 1841a
Arun K., *VB* 949b
B. C., *SRT Marath.* 931b
Kaustuva, *I.Gandhi Nat.Open* 785c
P. C., *Utkal* 945b
S. K., *NE Hill* 871a
Barikor, C. N., *P.Harcourt* 1207a
Barikzai, Safia, *Lond.S.Bank* 1828a
Barimalaa, I. S., *Rivers SUST* 1211c
Bark, Anthony, *Lond.* 1793c
Barkakati, Indira, *Gauh.* 745b
Barkakoty, A., *Gauh.* 745b
Barkat, Captain (Retd.) K., *Dhaka* 240a
M. A., *Dhaka* 234b
Barkati, Sohail, *Karachi* 1253b
Barkatullah, Md. Al-Baki, *Rajsh.* 253b
Barkawi, Tarak K., *Camb.* 1609b
Barkawi Sahari, *Putra* 1024c
Barke, Andrew J., *Well.* 1113c
Barkehall-Thomas, Susan, *Monash* 119a
Barker, A. D., *Birm.* 1569c
A. Tansu, *Brock* 320b
Andrew W., *Edin.* 1648c
Beverly, *Lond.S.Bank* 1828a
Chris, *Kingston(UK)* 1719c
Chris, *W'gong.* 210a
D., *Napier* 1844c
David, *Leeds Met.* 1744a
David, *WI* 1995a
G. W., *Rhodes* 1390a
Gareth J., *Lond.* 1792a, 1792b
Graeme W. W., *Camb.* 1599b
H., *Coventry* 1627a
I., *Nott.Trent* 1861c
Ian, *Birm.* 1576c
J., *Qld.UT* 152c
J. F., *Wat.* 526b, 528a
J. Stuart F., *NE* 137b
James, *Waik.* 1123c
Janet, *Nott.* 1858b
John R., *Glas.* 1665b
Jonathan N. W. N., *Lond.* 1795a
Jonathan S., *Tor.* 499b
K. E., *Calg.* 325a
M., *Lond.* 1803b
M. B., *Napier* 1844c
Martin, *Wales* 1542b
Matthew, *Auck.UT* 1083c
Meg, *Lond.S.Bank* 1828c
Michael F., *Otago* 1106b
Michelle C., *Griff.* 72a
N. P., *Rhodes* 1388b
P., *Coventry* 1625b
P., *W.Ont.* 553c
Paul H., *Auck.* 1074a
Philip A., *Lanc.* 1723a
Philip A., *McG.* 374b, 376c
R., *Dal.* 355b
R., *Nfld.* 409c
R. S., *Lond.* 1800a
Richard G., *Camb.* 1600a
Richard J., *Otago* 1106c
Roger A., *Camb.* 1608b
S., *Alta.* 304c
S., *E.Anglia* 1638c
Sue, *Bourne.* 1580a
Susan J., *W.Aust.* 195b
Trevor, *Herts.* 1684a
William, *Dal.* 352a
William, *KCNS* 362
Barker-Collo, Suzanne, *Auck.* 1074b
Barker-Read, Geoff, *Leeds* 1739c
Barkham, Michael, *Leeds* 1737a, 1739a
Barkhuizen, Gary, *Auck.* 1067b
Barki, Henri, *Montr.* 423c
Barkley, D., *Warw.* 1975a
Barkoczy, Stephen L., *Monash* 114b, 119a
Barkow, J. H., *Dal.* 355b
Barkun, Alan N. G., *McG.* 375b
Jeffrey S. T., *McG.* 379a
Barlex, David, *Brun.* 1595c
Barley, G., *Nott.Trent* 1866b
Mark E., *W.Aust.* 193a, 199a
Michael W., *Auck.* 1068c
Robert W., *Exe.* 1656c
Barling, C., *Swinburne UT* 161b
J. I., *Qu.* 452b
Barlow, Alison, *Salf.* 1919b
Ann, *Wales* 1967b
C. A., *Calg.* 329c
Claire, *Camb.* 1602b
D. H., *Glas.* 1662c
David, *Lond.* 1788b
Delma, *Manc.Met.* 1838a
Edward W. R. (Snow), *Melb.* 94b
G. N. D., *Plym.* 1889a
I. M., *Plym.* 1889a
J., *Warw.* 1977c
J. H., *Coventry* 1627b
J. W., *Plym.* 1890b
James G., *ICL* 1705b
Joanne, *La Trobe* 85c
M. J., *Plym.* 1889b
Michael, *Auck.* 1067b
Neil, *Liv.J.Moores* 1765b
Paul N., *Edin.* 1645b, 1645c
Barlow-Brown, Fiona, *Kingston(UK)* 1719c
Barltrop, Nigel, *Glas.* 1667c
Nigel, *Strath.* 1947b
Barman, Anup, *VB* 950c
D. C., *Dhaka* 237b
Deepak, *Ban.* 690a, 692a
K. K., *Gauh.* 746a
Kandarpa K., *Gauh.* 745b
Kiran, *Ban.* 690c
Rajani K., *Gauh.* 746b
Ramani, *Gauh.* 747a, 747b
Ratneswar, *Gauh.* 746a
Barmasse, P. C. K., *Moi* 969c
Barmby, John, *Vic.(Aust.)* 188a
Tim, *Aberd.* 1535a
Barminas, J. T., *Yola* 1170b
Barmuta, Leon A., *Tas.* 180c
Barn, Ravinder, *Lond.* 1808c
Barnard, A., *Qld.UT* 151c
Adam, *Nott.Trent* 1866b
Alan J., *Edin.* 1650a
Barnie W. S., *Stell.* 1395a
C. J., *Nott.* 1856a
Catherine S., *Camb.* 1604c
David T., *Manit.* 387
E., *Pret.* 1376b
Etienne, *Jo'burg.* 1347b
F. M., *W.Ont.* 545b
Henry G., *Massey* 1100a
J., *Greenwich* 1676b
J. G. (Sthinus), *Stell.* 1397b
J. J., *Nelson Mandela Met.* 1363b
Jaco, *Nelson Mandela Met.* 1360c
John, *Auck.* 1078b
L., *Nelson Mandela Met.* 1361b
Maria, *Jo'burg.* 1346b
Peter, *S.Cross* 157b
R. J. J., *N-W(S.Af.)* 1366c
Roger, *Waik.* 1122b
Timothy, *NU Singapore* 1311a
Barnatt, C. J., *Nott.* 1854c
Barnbaum, Marc, *C.Qld.* 46c
Barnbrook, Geoff, *Birm.* 1570b
Barnden, John, *Birm.* 1567b
Barnes, A., *Nott.Trent* 1863b
A., *Warw.* 1973a
A. C., *Brist.* 1588a
Anna R., *Ghana* 581b
Anne, *Murd.* 132a
Bradley R., *Leeds* 1731c
C., *Swinburne UT* 161b
Celia, *Hudd.* 1692a
Chris, *Dal.* 357a
Christopher, *Dal.* 359c
Christopher J., *Tor.* 500b
Christopher R., *Vic.(BC)* 518a
Colin, *Leeds* 1734a, 1738a
Crispin H. W., *Camb.* 1610c
Dave P., *Wales* 1540c
David, *Dal.* 358b
David, *Lond.* 1809a
Delva, *Jamaica UT* 956a
Gareth, *Aston* 1544c
Geoffrey R. G., *Massey* 1098a
Geraldine R., *Syd.* 169b
Gordon, *Vic.(BC)* 517c
Graeme L., *Melb.* 105b
Hazel S., *KwaZulu-Natal* 1358a
Howard A., *Wales* 1542a
Hugh, *Kingston(UK)* 1719a
Ian, *Lincoln(UK)* 1752b
J. G., *Nfld.* 401c
Jacqueline, *Lond.* 1779a
Jacqueline A., *Lond.* 1779c
Jayne, *Leeds Met.* 1743b
Jayne, *Manc.Met.* 1838c
Jeffrey W., *La Trobe* 80c
Jennifer, *Camb.* 1611b, 1613b
Jo, *Waik.* 1123b, 1123c
Joanne, *Auck.* 1077b
K. J., *S'ton.* 1937b
K. V., *Coventry* 1627b
Karen, *Cape Town* 1340b
Liz, *Manc.Met.* 1838a
M., *Birm.* 1572c
Margaret, *Sunshine Coast* 159a
Melanie, *Massey* 1102b
Michael R., *Bath* 1550a
Nicholas M., *Birm.* 1574c
Pam, *Lincoln(UK)* 1753a, 1753c
Paul, *Lond.* 1776, 1777a
Paul H., *Qld.UT* 151a
Penelope, *Dal.* 357c
Peter J., *ICL* 1706c
Peter R. W., *Open(UK)* 1869a
Philip, *Lond.* 1793c
Philip A., *Hudd.* 1691a
R. F., *Manc.Met.* 1838c
R. W., *R.Gordon* 1911a
Richard D., *Cape Town* 1341a
Richard J., *Camb.* 1606c, 1610a
Richard S. K., *Camb.* 1607c
Robert H., *Oxf.* 1873a
Rosemary A., *Cardiff* 1619b
S., *E.Anglia* 1640a
S., *Warw.* 1973b
S. B., *Brist.* 1585a
S. Barry, *Exe.* 1657b, 1658c
Steven, *Dal.* 357b, 358a
Theresa, *W.Cape* 1407c
Thomas H., *Auck.* 1074a
Thomas R., *ICL* 1707b
Timothy D., *Tor.* 491b
W. R., *Auck.* 1068b
William L., *Exe.* 1657c
Barnes-September, R. L., *W.Cape* 1409c
Barnet, D., *Alta.* 304a
Marie-Claire, *Durh.* 1635c
Barnett, A. H., *Birm.* 1574b
Ann, *Manc.Met.* 1837b
Anthony P., *Monash* 122a
Christopher, *ICL* 1704a
David B., *Leic.* 1746b
Ian S., *Herts.* 1686a
J. J., *Wat.* 523b
Jeremy, *Leeds* 1728a
John J., *Oxf.* 1877c
K., *Hull* 1699b
Ken, *Vic.(Aust.)* 188a
Neil, *Leeds Met.* 1741c
Neil B., *Deakin* 62b
Neil S., *Vic.(Aust.)* 185c
Paul, *Tas.* 178, 183c
Pauline S., *Otago* 1107b
Pennina, *Lond.* 1782c
Richard R., *Ulster* 1959
Ross, *Cant.* 1091c
Stephen M., *Strath.* 1947c
Susan, *R.Gordon* 1911a
Susan C., *Glas.* 1670c
Tony, *Lond.* 1802a
V., *Nott.Trent* 1865b
W. H., *W.Ont.* 549b
Yvonne, *Nott.Trent* 1861
Barney, A., *S'ton.* 1938b
Darin D., *McG.* 368b
H., *Swansea* 1957c
Rachel, *Tor.* 491b
Robert K., *W.Ont.* 546c, 553a
Barnfield, A., *W.Ont.* 553c
Barnhill, Tony, *Ulster* 1964a
Barnit, Rosemary, *S'ton.* 1935c
Barns, Ian, *Murd.* 131c
Barnsley, Janet, *Tor.* 505a
M. J., *Swansea* 1955a, 1956b
Roger H., *T.Rivers* 488
Barnstead, John A., *Dal.* 355a
Martha, *Dal.* 349c
Barnwell, Harry, *Birm.* 1570c
S., *Ryerson* 464a
Barolia, Rubina, *Aga Khan(P'stan.)* 1231c
Baron, Adam, *Kingston(UK)* 1719a
Britta, *Keele* 1710c
J. Steven, *Liv.* 1757c
Jean-Claude, *Camb.* 1608b
John K., *Hudd.* 1692b
Lois J., *C'dia.* 344b
Luc, *Montr.* 422a
Mark, *Lincoln(UK)* 1752a
Michael, *Lond.* 1777b, 1821
Paula, *Griff.* 69a
Paula D., *Well.* 1116a
Stephen, *Qu.* 457c
Stephen, *Strath.* 1945b
Baron-Cohen, Simon, *Camb.* 1608c
Barongo, J. O., *Nair.* 973b
Baroota, Aruna, *Delhi* 724b
Baross, Zsuzsa, *Trent* 515a
Barot, S. H., *Dr BA Open* 734
Barpatra Gohain, R. C., *Gauh.* 746a
Barr, A., *Glas.* 1668b
A. R. S., *Brist.* 1589c
Alan R., *Edin.* 1648b
Andrew R., *Adel.* 24c
David G., *Durh.* 1634a
F. J., *Brist.* 1589c
Francis A., *Liv.* 1759b
Giles D., *Oxf.* 1877c
Graham D. I., *Cape Town* 1338b
Hugh, *Cran.* 1629a
Jean L., *Glas.* 1663a
N., *Lond.* 1799c, 1802b
Niall, *Lond.* 1793b
Owen G., *Ulster* 1962c
R. M., *W.Ont.* 549b
Stephen, *G.Caledonian* 1672c
T., *Swinburne UT* 162a
Warren, *Liv.* 1757b
Barra, M., *Wat.* 524c
Barraclough, Barry R., *Liv.* 1755a
John H., *Liv.J.Moores* 1764c
Simon D., *La Trobe* 82c
Timothy G., *ICL* 1701a
Barralet, Jake, *McG.* 369a, 379b
Barrand, Margery A., *Camb.* 1606a, 1610a
Barrans, Simon M., *Hudd.* 1692b
Barrar, Wayne, *Massey* 1097b
Barras, Judith, *Leeds Met.* 1741c
Barratt, Alexandra, *Waik.* 1122a
Jonathan, *Leic.* 1748c
Julian, *Lond.S.Bank* 1828b
Rod S., *Open(UK)* 1868c
Barratt-Pugh, Caroline H., *E.Cowan* 64c
Barre, Paul E., *McG.* 380a
Barrell, B., *Nfld.* 402c
Graham K., *Lincoln(NZ)* 1094a
Howard, *Cardiff* 1618a
Barresi, John, *Dal.* 354c
Barretino, Diego R., *Glas.* 1665b
Barrett, Ann, *E.Anglia* 1640b
Anne, *ICL* 1708b
Anthony G. M., *ICL* 1701c
B. J., *Nfld.* 407a
Brenda, *Middx.* 1842c
Chris, *S'ton.* 1939c
D. A., *Nott.* 1855b
D. S., *S'ton.* 1935a
David C., *Glas.* 1669a
F. Michael, *Tor.* 501b
Francis, *Leeds Met.* 1744a
Geraldine, *Brun.* 1594c, 1597a
Graham L., *Melb.* 106a
Hazel, *Coventry* 1625c
J. C., *Sheff.* 1922a
J. David, *Portsmouth* 1901c
J. W., *Nott.* 1854a
Jennifer, *Syd.* 172b
John, *Wales* 1540b, 1542b
John W., *ICL* 1704a
Jon, *Tor.* 506c
L. A., *Curtin* 57b
L. Gene, *St Mary's(Can.)* 469c
Lindsay, *W.Syd.* 203b
Louise, *Leth.* 365c
Margaret, *Tas.* 182c
Martin, *E.Lond.* 1642a
Martyn D., *Sur.* 1952b
Mary, *W'gong.* 209b
Megan, *C.Qld.* 47a
Michael I., *Camb.* 1600a
Michael P., *Glas.* 1663c
Neville, *Tas.* 182a
P. Hugh R., *W.Aust.* 196b
Patrick, *Waik.* 1122c
Peter J., *Well.* 1114c, 1118a
Peter S., *Salf.* 1918, 1919a, 1920c
Richard, *Brun.* 1594c
Robert J., *Adel.* 28c
Rodney, *Griff.* 73a
Rowena, *Monash* 119b
S., *Manc.Met.* 1841b

Lise, *Ott.* 444c
DuBois, Thomas, *NU Singapore* 1311a
Dubreuil, Daniel, *Montr.* 416b
Nicole, *Montr.* 411b
Pascal, *Montr.* 416a
Dubrova, Yuri, *Leic.* 1747c
Dubrovsky, Bernardo O., *McG.* 378c
Dubrow-Marshall, Rod, *Glam.* 1660c
Ducas, J., *Manit.* 396b
Ducatenzeiler, Graciela, *Montr.* 415a
Duce, I. R., *Nott.* 1856b
Duch, Raymond M., *Oxf.* 1878b
Ducharme, Al, *Regina* 361
Francine, *McG.* 377c
Francine, *Montr.* 414b
Joseph, *Tor.* 504a
Duchemin, H. Parker, *Car.* 338a
Duchesne, Gillian, *Melb.* 105c
Jean-Pierre, *C'dia.* 342c
Lloyd, *Ott.* 445a
Pierre, *Montr.* 414a
Ricardo, *New Br.* 435b
Duchesneau, François, *Montr.* 415a
Michel, *Montr.* 420c
Duck, Francis A., *Bath* 1553a
N. W., *Brist.* 1585a
T. J., *Dal.* 354c
Ducker, William, *Melb.* 96c
Duckers, L., *Coventry* 1625c
Duckett, David C., *Stir.* 1943c
Jane, *Glas.* 1668a
Duckitt, John, *Auck.* 1074c
Duckworth, Colin R., *Melb.* 99b
H. E., *Manit.* 393a
H. W., *Manit.* 389a
K., *Calg.* 327b
M., *Manit.* 397b
Duclaud-Williams, R. H., *Warw.* 1976a
Duda, J. L., *Birm.* 1573b
Dudas, M. J., *Alta.* 309b
Dudbridge, G., *Chinese HK* 2021c, 2027c, 2028b
Dudchenko, P., *Stir.* 1943a
Duddell, David, *Leeds Met.* 1742c
Dudding, Peter, *Montr.* 419b
Dudek, Debra, *W'gong.* 208b
Gregory, *McG.* 369a, 382a
Duden, Rainer, *Lond.* 1807b
Dudgeon, D., *HK* 2031c
D., *Qu.* 458c
Dudley, Christine J., *Macq.* 89b
E. H., *Plym.* 1888c
Grahame H., *Adel.* 29b
Léonard, *Montr.* 412c
Dudley-McEvoy, Sandra, *Lond.S.Bank* 1827c
Dudul, S. V., *SGB Amravati* 904a
Dudycha, D. J., *Wat.* 529c
Dueck, G. D., *Bran.* 317b
Gerhard, *New Br.* 430a
Peter, *Manit.* 399c, 400a
Duedu, C. B., *Cape Coast* 574c
Duer, Melinda J., *Camb.* 1600b
Duerden, B. I., *Cardiff* 1619c
F., *Ryerson* 464b
Tim, *Salf.* 1918b
Duerksen, F., *Manit.* 398a
Duerr, Eveline, *Auck.UT* 1083c
Duever, T. A., *Wat.* 527a, 528a
Dufey, Gunter, *Nan.Tech.* 1300c
Duff, C., *Car.* 338c
Charles, *Sur.* 1953a
David G., *Tor.* 496a
Sir G. W., *Sheff.* 1928b
Gordon, *C.Darwin* 48c
H. J., *Calg.* 330b, 331c
J. H., *W.Ont.* 547a
Michael J., *ICL* 1704c
P. R., *Aberd.* 1536c
R. A., *Stir.* 1943a
T. E., *Reading* 1908b
Wendy, *Tor.* 495c
Duffell, Annette, *Oxf.* 1881c
Duffett-Smith, Peter J., *Camb.* 1606b
Duffield, Colin F., *Melb.* 97a
John, *W.England* 1980a, 1980c
M. R., *Brist.* 1588c
M. S., *Cape Town* 1338c
N. G., *Sheff.* 1923c
Duffin, J. M., *Qu.* 458a
James, *Tor.* 504a
Duffull, Stephen B., *Otago* 1109c
Duffus, David, *Vic.(BC)* 519b

Gail, *Ryerson* 462b
W. P. H., *Brist.* 1589c
Duffy, Alexander H. B., *Strath.* 1945b
Ann, *Brock* 322b
Anne C., *McG.* 378c
Brian, *Strath.* 1947a
Eamon, *Camb.* 1601b
Geoffrey G., *Auck.* 1070a
J., *Nfld.* 409a
J. F., *Dal.* 350b
Jean H., *Edin.* 1648c
John, *Lond.* 1813, 1814b
Karen, *Manc.Met.* 1838c
Lynne, *New Br.* 432c
Mary Elaine, *C.Sturt* 51c
Michael D., *Exe.* 1657a, 1659a
Patricia D., *Otago* 1106a
Sandra P., *Liv.J.Moores* 1765b
Sean G., *Leeds* 1736c
Stephen, *Mt.All.* 426b
Dufour, Jean-Marie, *Montr.* 412c
Yvon, *Macq.* 89c
Dufournaud, C., *Wat.* 529c
Dufresne, André, *McG.* 375a
Aude, *Montr.* 411c
Claude, *Montr.* 447b
Daniel, *Melb.* 108a
Dufresne-Tassé, Colette, *Montr.* 415c
Dufton, Mark, *Strath.* 1944c
Philip L., *Belf.* 1560b
Dugal, Paul, *Manit.* 400a
Dugan, H. S., *Calg.* 324b
J. S., *Calg.* 325b
Robert, *Well.* 1116a
Dugar, Milap, *Inst.Adv.Studies in Educn.* 788
P. C., *Dhaka* 235c
Dugard, C. J. R., *Pret.* 1386b
Dugas, Michel, *C'dia.* 346c
Dugdale, Alexandra H. A., *Liv.* 1761b
Anni, *Canberra* 41c
Anthony M., *Keele* 1710c
D., *Brist.* 1583c
R. E., *Nott.* 1853a
S. B., *Brist.* 1588b
Dugdill, Lindsey, *Salf.* 1918b
Duggal, C. L., *Panjab* 883a
Kamlesh S., *GND* 764b
Monty S., *Leeds* 1736a
N., *W.Ont.* 548b
Duggan, Anthony, *Tor.* 496a
B. J., *HK* 2032b
Barbara, *Kwantlen* 362a
C., *Nott.* 1857a
C. J. H., *Reading* 1908c
Evan, *WI* 1997a
Laurence, *Griff.* 69c
M. A., *Calg.* 332c, 333b
Paul M., *Adel.* 28b
Sarah, *Wales* 1968a
T. D., *Alta.* 311b
Duggin, John A., *NE* 136a
Duggleby, W. D., *Sask.* 476a
Dugmore, Andrew J., *Edin.* 1647a
Duguid, N., *Nfld.* 407b
Stephen, *S.Fraser* 484c, 487c
Dugwell, Denis R., *ICL* 1702c
Duhaime, Carole, *Montr.* 424b
Jean, *Montr.* 411a, 416a
Duhamel, Fabie, *Montr.* 414b
J., *Wat.* 524c, 527a
Luc, *Montr.* 415a
Duhan, Manoj, *G.Jamb.* 760c, 761c
Stephen, *Oxf.Brookes* 1885a
Duhlinska, D. D., *Jos* 1181a
Duignan, Patrick A., *Aust.Cath.* 32c
Duinker, P., *Dal.* 355a
Duivenvoorden, Leo, *C.Qld.* 45a
D'ujanga, F. M., *Mak.* 1497c
Duke, Alison, *Camb.* 1600b
Colin C., *Syd.* 173b, 175c
David J., *Leeds* 1728a
Jan, *Well.* 1117a
Mike, *Well.* 1121b
Mikel, *Vic.(Aust.)* 187c
N. A., *W.Ont.* 540a
P., *Nfld.* 407a
P. C., *Manit.* 395a
R., *Calabar* 1161b
Richard M., *Cant.* 1086b, 1090c
Sue, *S'ton.* 1939c
T., *Sask.* 477c
Trevor D., *Melb.* 105c

Duke-Williams, Emma, *Portsmouth* 1899b
Duker, A. A., *Kwame NUST* 588b
G. Mary A., *Nelson Mandela Met.* 1361a
Dukes-McEwan, Joanna, *Liv.* 1761c
Dukku, Muhammed I., *Maid.* 1190c
Dulawat, M. S., *M.Sukh.* 859c
Dulay, Naranker, *ICL* 1702a
Duldig, Paul, *Adel.* 24
Duley, W. W., *Wat.* 532b
Dulla, J. R., *Manc.Met.* 1839c
Dullabh, Hemant D., *Pret.* 1382b
Dullar, Pushpa, *Banasth.* 699c
Dulle, F. W., *Sokoine Ag.* 1487c
Duller, Geoffrey A. T., *Wales* 1541a
Dullien, F. A. L., *Wat.* 527a
Dullin, Holger R., *Lough.* 1833c
Duma, Sinegugu L., *Cape Town* 1340a
Dumas, G. A., *Qu.* 454b
M., *Qld.UT* 152b
McD., *WI* 1999c
Dumbrell, John, *Durh.* 1635a
John, *Leic.* 1750a, 1750b
Dumbroff, E. B., *Wat.* 524a
Dumbuya, M. E. M., *S.Leone* 1286
S. N., *S.Leone* 1286, 1287c
Dummalod, C. B., *Dr BA Marath.* 733a
Dummawad, S. D., *Karn.* 812b
Dummer, P. M. H., *Cardiff* 1616a
Dummigan, N. P., *Sheff.* 1925b
Dumont, Alexandre, *Montr.* 417b
Florent (Frank) R., *McG.* 370a
Hélène, *Montr.* 413c
Louis, *Montr.* 418a
Marie, *Montr.* 418b
Dumontier, M., *Car.* 336b
Dumouchel, Daniel, *Montr.* 415a
Dumper, Michael, *Exe.* 1657a
Dumville, David, *Aberd.* 1535c, 1536b
Dunai, T. J., *Edin.* 1647a
Dunaiski, Peter E., *Stell.* 1394a
Dunbar, C. G., *W.Ont.* 539a
Carol A., *Belf.* 1565a
D. C., *Swansea* 1957a
David, *Cran.* 1630c
G., *Warw.* 1976a
Michael, *Dal.* 358c
P. Roderick, *Auck.* 1068a
R., *Aberd.* 1536b, 1536c
Rebekah, *Cant.* 1086b
Robin I. M., *Liv.* 1755a
T., *Manc.Met.* 1837b
Dunbar-Hall, Peter, *Syd.* 172c
Dunbrack, R., *Nfld.* 401b
Duncan, A. B., *Stir.* 1942b
A. G., *Aberd.* 1535c
A. J., *Curtin* 56c
A. S., *Nott.* 1851c
Alan, *Melb.* 94c
Carol, *W.Laur.* 559c
Colin, *Edin.* 1649a, 1651c
D. E., *Brist.* 1587b
David, *Dund.* 1632
E. E., *Mines & Technol., Tarkwa* 591b
E. Madeleine, *Cape Town* 1340b
F. D., *Witw.* 1411b
Garry, *Montr.* 412b
Graham A., *Pret.* 1375a
Henry, *Auck.UT* 1084a
J., *WI* 2000a
J. E., *R.Gordon* 1911a
J. R., *Rhodes* 1388b, 1391b
James S., *Camb.* 1603c
John, *Cant.* 1092c
John, *Wales* 1547b
Karen, *Manit.* 390c
Keith, *Bond* 38c
L. Grant, *Massey* 1100c
M. J., *Qu.* 456c
N. A., *Calg.* 326a
N. T. F., *Witw.* 1414c
Neil M., *Pret.* 1384c
Neville, *WI* 1990c
Newton D., *WI* 1996c
Patricia, *Glas.* 1662c
Peter, *Lond.* 1793c
R., *Rhodes* 1388c
Richard, *Montr.* 414a
Richard P., *Lincoln(NZ)* 1094a
Ronald, *S.Pac.* 1423a

Roy, *Dal.* 357a
Ruth, *Cardiff* 1621b
Ruth, *Keele* 1711a
Stephen R., *Oxf.* 1875a
Warwick J., *Otago* 1104c
William D., *Qld.UT* 150c
Duncan-Brown, Althea S., *KwaZulu-Natal* 1351a
Dunch, R., *Alta.* 306b
Duncker-Gassen, Elke, *Middx.* 1843a
Duncombe, Caroline, *Herts.* 1687b
Duncum, Ken, *Well.* 1118c
Dundas, Paul, *Edin.* 1648c
Dunford, Richard W., *Macq.* 90a
Dung-Gwom, J. Y., *Jos* 1180b
Dungar, Rachel, *Bourne.* 1579c
Dunger, David B., *Camb.* 1608c
Dunham, C. B., *W.Ont.* 539c
David W., *Tor.* 501b
P. J., *Coventry* 1625c
Dunhill, Andrea J., *Kingston(UK)* 1717c
Dunk, Alan, *Canberra* 41c
Dunkeld, Malcolm, *Lond.S.Bank* 1828c
Dunkerley, James, *Lond.* 1821a
Dunkin, Ian R., *Strath.* 1944c
Dunkley, J., *Aberd.* 1536b
M., *Swinburne UT* 161a, 162c
Peter R., *Newcastle(NSW)* 141b
R. G., *Wat.* 535c
Raymond, *Jamaica UT* 956c
Dunlap, R. A., *Dal.* 354b
Dunleavy, Houston, *W'gong.* 209c
P. J., *Lond.* 1800a
P. J., *Manc.Met.* 1839c
Trisha, *Well.* 1115a
Dunlevey, J. N., *KwaZulu-Natal* 1352c
Dunlop, Aline-Wendy, *Strath.* 1945a
D. J., *Tor.* 499a
Ian A., *W.Aust.* 192b
J. Bruce, *Tor.* 496a
James S., *Edin.* 1650a
John, *Strath.* 1945c
M. G., *Edin.* 1652b
Mark, *Strath.* 1945a
Nancy, *Auck.UT* 1085a
Sarah A., *W.Aust.* 191b
Dunmill, Merryn, *Cant.* 1086c
Dunmore, Paul, *Massey* 1096b
Dunn, Alan, *Lond.S.Bank* 1827c
Alison, *Leeds* 1726c
Anne, *Syd.* 171c
Ashley, *Melb.* 107a
C., *Coventry* 1626a
C., *Nfld.* 405c
Christine E., *Durh.* 1635a
D., *Reading* 1909b
D. E., *St And.* 1914c, 1917a
D. H., *Birm.* 1573a
David, *QM Edin.* 1904b
David, *S'ton.* 1935b
Dennis, *Manc.Met.* 1837a
Gregory, *Melb.* 94b
Hamish, *Lincoln(NZ)* 1095c
Hilarie, *Griff.* 75c
Hopeton, *WI* 1995c, 1997a
I. K., *Coventry* 1626c
J., *Warw.* 1977c
J. F., *Calg.* 333c, 334a
J. G., *Curtin* 55b
J. G. H., *Alta.* 308b
J. L., *Nott.* 1855b
Jay, *Athab.* 314c
Jill E., *Belf.* 1565a
Joanna, *Manc.Met.* 1840a
John A., *KwaZulu-Natal* 1356b
John M., *Camb.* 1607b
Judith F., *Lond.* 1793b
Julie, *Griff.* 70b
L., *Swinburne UT* 163a
Leith, *WI* 1990c, 1992b
Leith L., *WI* 1997b
Leone, *W'gong.* 208c
M. H., *St And.* 1916a, 1917a
Marilyn, *Glas.* 1666a
Marilyn, *Montr.* 416a
N., *S'ton.* 1939a, 1939c
O., *Coventry* 1627b
Paul, *Brock* 320a
Peter A., *W.Laur.* 559c
Robert B., *Leeds* 1730a
Robert J., *McG.* 375c, 376c

Roderick W., *Bath* 1551b, 1555c
Roger C. M., *Auck.* 1070b
S. D., *W.Ont.* 548a
S. M. J., *Alta.* 312b
Victor, *Portsmouth* 1900b
W., *Coventry* 1626c
W. J., *W.Ont.* 547c
W. R., *Nott.* 1856b
Wendell E., III, *Auck.* 1073a
Dunn-Walters, Deborah K., *Lond.* 1795b
Dunnage, J. M., *Swansea* 1956c
Dunne, Christopher, *Lincoln(UK)* 1752b
David W., *Camb.* 1606a
Druce, *W'gong.* 208a
Fionn P. E., *Oxf.* 1875a
G. A., *Plym.* 1892c
J. T., *Nfld.* 407b
Jackie, *Leic.* 1749a
John, *Greenwich* 1677c
Kerry, *NE* 136a
L., *Lond.S.Bank* 1827a
M. P., *Qld.UT* 152a
Paul E., *Liv.* 1755c
Stephen M., *Lond.* 1789b
Tim, *Exe.* 1657a
Timothy T., *Cape Town* 1338b
Dunnell, K., *Lond.* 1804a
Dunnett, N. P., *Sheff.* 1924c
Stephen B., *Cardiff* 1614c
Dunnigan, M. W., *H-W* 1680a
Dunnill, John, *Murd.* 131c
Dunning, G. R., *Nfld.* 402b
Gerald, *Glam.* 1661a
Thomas P., *Tas.* 180a
Trisha, *Melb.* 107b
Dunning-Davies, J., *Hull* 1697c
Dunns-Lowe, Angela, *Vic.(Aust.)* 188b
Dunphy, Bruce C., *Dal.* 349, 357b
Gary B., *McG.* 385c
Duns, John, *Monash* 119a
Dunsby, Peter K. S., *Cape Town* 1336c
Dunscombe, P. B., *Calg.* 332c
Dunse, N. A., *H-W* 1679b
Dunshea, Frank R., *Melb.* 94b
Dunsmore, D. A., *Nfld.* 405a
Dunstall, Graeme C., *Cant.* 1087c
Dunstan, David E., *Melb.* 96c
F. D., *Cardiff* 1620a
Helen, *Syd.* 168a
Keitha, *Well.* 1113a
Neil, *NE* 136c
P., *Camb.* 1612a
R. Hugh, *Newcastle(NSW)* 143a
W. David, *Monash* 124c
Dunster, David, *Liv.* 1755a
Dunt, David, *Melb.* 107c, 109c
Dunthorne, Al, *Bran.* 318b
H. L. A., *Swansea* 1956c
Dunton, C., *NUL* 980c
Düntsch, Ivo, *Brock* 320c
Dunukewatte Gunarathna, Ven., *B&P SLanka* 1435b
Dunwell, J. M., *Reading* 1906a
Dunwoodie, P., *Lond.* 1782a
Dunworth, K., *Curtin* 56a
Teresa, *Auck.* 1072c
Duodu, K. G., *Pret.* 1377b
Duperray, Catherine, *Lond.* 1820c
Duplain, Nicole G. M., *Herts.* 1684a
DuPlessis, Dorothy, *New Br.* 429b
Duplessis, Isabelle, *Montr.* 413c
Yvon, *Ott.* 442c
Duplisea, K., *Ryerson* 466a
Dupont, Alan, *Syd.* 176a
Benoit, *Montr.* 412a, 419b
Diane, *Brock* 321a
Stéphane, *Montr.* 419a
Valerie A., *Leeds* 1730a
Dupper, Ockie C., *Stell.* 1395b
Dupraz, J. Y., *W.Ont.* 542b
Dupre, John A., *Exe.* 1657b, 1658c
Dupré, John A., *Lond.* 1778c
Ruth, *Montr.* 423b
Dupree, Marguerite W., *Glas.* 1666b, 1671a
Paul, *Camb.* 1600a, 1611a
Duprex, W. Paul, *Belf.* 1563a
Dupuis, Ann, *Massey* 1100c

O. A., *O.Awolowo* 1197a, 1202a
Faubert, Gaétan M., *McG.* 386b
  Jocelyn, *Montr.* 414c
Faucher, Guy, *Montr.* 422b
  Philippe, *Montr.* 415a
Faudziah Abdul Manan, *NU Malaysia* 1018c
Faudzinaim Badaruddin, *NU Malaysia* 1018b
Faught, Brent, *Brock* 319b
  J. W., *Alta.* 311c
Faujan Ahmad alias Hj Amat, *Putra* 1022c
Faul, C. F. J., *Brist.* 1584b
Faulkes, C. G., *Pret.* 1381b
Faulkner, Christine, *Lond.S.Bank* 1829a
  Christopher G., *Car.* 336a, 336c
  David, *Lond.* 1809a
  Dorothy, *Open(UK)* 1869a
  Gary, *Dal.* 357a
  M. G., *Alta.* 305c
  Michael, *Vic.(Aust.)* 186a, 187c
  R. A. (Bob), *Sask.* 475a
  Richard, *NE* 136a
  Roy, *Lough.* 1834b
  S., *Manc.Met.* 1840b
  T. R., *Nott.* 1854c
  Tom, *Alta.* 313c
  Wendy, *Edin.* 1650a
Faull, C. M., *Nott.* 1856c
  Norman H. B., *Cape Town* 1333c
  Richard L. M., *Auck.* 1076b
Faundez, Julio, *Warw.* 1975a
Fauntleroy, Roy, *C.Darwin* 49b
Faure, A. P., *Fort Hare* 1343c
  A. P., *Rhodes* 1388c
  D. W., *Chinese HK* 2023c
  M. R., *Stell.* 1398b
Faure-Grimaud, A., *Lond.* 1799b
Faust, S., *S'ton.* 1939b
Fausten, Dietrich K., *Monash* 115b
Faux, David A., *Sur.* 1952b
  Jeffrey, *Vic.(Aust.)* 185a
Fauza binti Abdul Ghaffar, *Malaya* 1007c
Fauzan Nordin, *IIU Malaysia* 1001a
Fauzi alias Fauri Ahmad, *IIU Malaysia* 999a
Fauzi Daud, *NU Malaysia* 1015c
Fauzi Deraman, *Malaya* 1012a
Fauziah binti Abdullah, *Malaya* 1005b
Fauziah binti Shahul Hamid Ijazah, *Malaya* 1005b
Fauziah bt Kasim, *Tech.U.Malaysia* 1032c
Fauziah Mohd Noor, *IIU Malaysia* 1001a
Fauziah Othman, *Putra* 1022b
Fauzias Mat Nor, *NU Malaysia* 1017a, 1017c
Favareau, Donald F., *NU Singapore* 1315b
Favelukis, M., *NU Singapore* 1308a
Favis, Basil, *Montr.* 422b
Favretto, Ilaria, *Kingston(UK)* 1719c
Fawaz, Z., *Ryerson* 463b
Fawbert, Jack, *Leeds Met.* 1741b
Fawcett, Barbara, *Syd.* 168c
  J. J., *Nott.* 1854a
  J. Paul, *Otago* 1109c
  James W., *Camb.* 1608b
  Jeff J., *Tor.* 494c
  R., *St And.* 1913b
  S. Lyn, *Ulster* 1962a
  Tonks, *Edin.* 1647b
Fawcus, Susan R., *Cape Town* 1340a
Fawehinmi, H. B., *P.Harcourt* 1209a
Fawkes, Johanna, *Leeds Met.* 1741c
  M. L., *C.Sturt* 53b
Fawn, R., *St And.* 1915a
Fawns, Alan R., *Melb.* 102a
Fawole, A. O., *Ib.* 1177a
  Alla P., *Ib.* 1174a
  B., *Ib.* 1173c
  I., *Ib.* 1173c
  O. I., *Ib.* 1176b
  W. A., *O.Awolowo* 1199b
Fay, Doris, *Aston* 1544a
  Roger, *Tas.* 182b

Fayaz Ahmad, *Kashmir* 816b
Faye, Cathy, *Ryerson* 462b, 466b
Fayek-uz-Zaman, M., *Rajsh.* 254c
Fayemi, O., *Ib.* 1178a
Faynan, R. I., *JMI* 793a
Fayoade, A. L., *O.Awolowo* 1202c
Fayorsey, Clara K., *Ghana* 584a
Faysal, Abdullah, *Bhutto IST* 1272b
Fayyaz, Shahina, *Karachi* 1253c
Fayyaz-ul-Hassan, *Arid Ag.* 1235a
Fazackerley, F., *Manc.Met.* 1839c
  Pauline L., *Nott.Trent* 1861c, 1863a
Fazakarley, Louise, *Bourne.* 1580a
Fazakerley, John K., *Edin.* 1653a
Fazal Rahim Khan, *IIU Malaysia* 999b
Fazal ur Rehman, *MA Jinnah* 1259c
Fazeel, M. J. M., *Colombo* 1436b
Fazidah Bakhtiar, *IIU Malaysia* 1003c
Fazil, Taskeen, *Kashmir* 816b
Fazili, K. Majeed, *Kashmir* 815b
Fazio, Paul P., *C'dia.* 344c
Fazli, Fakhre A., *Bhutto IST* 1272b
Fazlina Othman, *IIU Malaysia* 998c
Fazuliati Fauzi, *IIU Malaysia* 1001c
Feagan, B. G., *W.Ont.* 548c, 549b
Fear, A. D., *Wales* 1970a
  E. C., *Calg.* 326b
  Nicola, *Lond.* 1792c
Fear-Segal, J., *E.Anglia* 1638b
Fearick, Roger W., *Cape Town* 1337c
Fearn, David R., *Glas.* 1662c
Fearnhead, Paul, *Lanc.* 1723c
Fearnley, Stella, *Bourne.* 1578c, 1581a
Fearns, Debra, *Herts.* 1687b
  P., *Curtin* 56c
Fearon, Doug T., *Camb.* 1608b
  K. C. H., *Edin.* 1651a
  P., *Reading* 1909c
  Paul, *Lond.* 1792c
Feasby, T., *Alta.* 311b
Feasey, M., *Lond.* 1786b
  Ron, *Auck.UT* 1080c
Feast, Michael W., *Cape Town* 1333b
Feather, John P., *Lough.* 1833c
Featherston, Carol A., *Cardiff* 1616c
Featherstone, Brigid, *Hudd.* 1694b
  K., *Lond.* 1802b
  Katie, *Cardiff* 1621a
  Mark S., *McG.* 377b
  Mark S., *Nan.Tech.* 1292b
  W. E., *Curtin* 59a
Featherstone-Witty, Mark, *Liv.J.Moores* 1767c
Feaver, D., *Qld.UT* 150c
  Sally, *Oxf.Brookes* 1885c
Febbraio, Mark, *Monash* 120c
Feber, Janusz, *Ott.* 445c
February, Ed C., *Cape Town* 1333b
Fecteau, Gilles, *Montr.* 416a
Fedak, M. A., *St And.* 1913c, 1916c
Fedderke, Johann, *Cape Town* 1334b
Feddes, J., Jr., *Alta.* 303a
Federici, Corrado J. A., *Brock* 321c
Federoff, Paul, *Ott.* 446a
Fedigan, L. M., *Calg.* 323b
Fedorak, P. M., *Alta.* 303b
  R. N., *Alta.* 311b
Fedorec, A. M., *Greenwich* 1676a
Fedosejevs, R., *Alta.* 305c
Fedotova, T., *Witw.* 1412c
Feduniw, L., *Manit.* 390c, 391c
Fedyk, N., *W.Ont.* 538c
Fee, Conan, *Cant.* 1090a
  E. Jane, *S.Fraser* 485a
  J. P. Howard, *Belf.* 1562c
  Mariann, *Melb.* 94a
  Ruth, *Ulster* 1963a
Feehally, John, *Leic.* 1748c
Feehan, J. P., *Nfld.* 402b
Feeley, Marc, *Montr.* 411c
Feelisch, M., *Warw.* 1977c
Feenberg, A., *S.Fraser* 483a
Feenberg-Dibon, A. M., *S.Fraser* 484c, 485a, 487a

Feener, Michael, *NU Singapore* 1311a
Feeney, Aidan, *Durh.* 1636c
  Brian J., *Belf.* 1564b
  Catherine, *Manc.Met.* 1840a
  Dennis, *Oxf.* 1874a
Feeny, D. H., *Alta.* 304b
Feeroz, M. M., *Jahang.* 247b
Fehervari, Joanne, *Bond* 40c
Fehintola, F. A., *Ib.* 1175a
Fehl, P., *Auck.* 1079c
Fehlberg, Belinda L., *Melb.* 99c
Fehlings, Michael G., *Tor.* 507c
Feibel, Robert J., *Ott.* 446b
Feightner, John W., *W.Ont.* 548c
Feil, Daryl K., *Syd.* 166b
Feiler, A. C., *Brist.* 1585b
Feinauer, A. E. (Ilse), *Stell.* 1392c
Fenna, A., *Curtin* 57b, 59b
Feindel, Christopher M., *Tor.* 507c
Feindt, Peter H., *Cardiff* 1615c
Feine, Jocelyne S., *McG.* 369a
Feinstein, J. F., *Nott.* 1854b
Feintuck, M. J., *Hull* 1697a, 1699b
Fejer, Rene, *Murd.* 130b
Fekarurhobo, G. K., *Rivers SUST* 1211a
Fekete, Alan, *Syd.* 170c
  J. A., *Trent* 514a, 515b
Fekken, Cynthia, *Qu.* 457b
Fekri Abidian Hassan, *IIU Malaysia* 1003a
Felce, D., *Cardiff* 1620b
Felcy, H., *Manc.Met.* 1838b
Felderhof, M. C., *Birm.* 1570a
Feldman, Anatol G., *Montr.* 418a
  C., *Witw.* 1416b
  David J., *Camb.* 1604c
  David M., *Lond.* 1777c
  M., *Qu.* 457b
  Maurice, *Brock* 320c
  R. D., *W.Ont.* 549b
  Rayah, *Lond.S.Bank* 1829a
  William, *Tor.* 507b
Feldman-Stewart, D., *Qu.* 459b
Feldmann, J., *Aberd.* 1535b
  Marc, *ICL* 1707c
Feldthusen, Bruce P., *Ott.* 440, 442c
Feletti, Grahame I., *Newcastle(NSW)* 143b
Felice, Alex, *Malta* 1044c
  Arthur, *Malta* 1045a
  Donald, *Malta* 1044b
Felicia Lim Siew Kiau, *NU Malaysia* 1019a
Félix, J. M., *Reading* 1908c
Felix, N., *TN Vet.* 936a
  Robert, *Leeds Met.* 1740b
  S., *TN Vet.* 936a
Fell, A. P., *Qu.* 456b
  John D., *W.England* 1981b
  Kevin, *Melb.* 100a
Felli, L., *Lond.* 1799c
Fellman, M. D., *S.Fraser* 485b
Fellowes, Melanie G., *Hudd.* 1693c
Fellows, Michael R., *Newcastle(NSW)* 142c
  R. F., *HK* 2033a
  Richard A., *Hudd.* 1691b
Fells, Nick, *Glas.* 1667b
  Ray E., *W.Aust.* 192b
Felmingham, Bruce S., *Tas.* 179b
Fels, Allan H. M., *Melb.* 101c
  D., *Ryerson* 464c, 466b
  M., *Dal.* 351b
Felstead, Alan, *Cardiff* 1622b
  Cathie, *Herts.* 1683c
Felt, L. F., *Nfld.* 406a
Feltham, Mark J., *Liv.J.Moores* 1765a
Feltoe, G., *Z'bwe.* 2051a
Felton, Sandra, *Brock* 320a
Felty, Amy P., *Ott.* 442b
Femi-Oyewo, M. N., *Olabisi Onabanjo* 1205c
Femia, Joseph V., *Liv.* 1758b
Fenby, J., *Manc.Met.* 1840a
Fend, Michael, *Lond.* 1790b
Fender, J., *Birm.* 1572c
  R., *S'ton.* 1937b
Fenech, Albert, *Malta* 1044b
  Dominic, *Malta* 1040b, 1042b
  Joseph, *Malta* 1041c
  Thomas, *Malta* 1045a
  Tino O., *Griff.* 72b
Fenemore, M., *Manc.Met.* 1840b
Feng, Dagan, *Syd.* 170c
  Gang, *Nan.Tech.* 1296c

H. Y., *W.Ont.* 541c
J., *Warw.* 1972b
Qingping, *W.Ont.* 549b, 551c
S., *NU Singapore* 1308a
S. S., *NU Singapore* 1305b
W., *Trent* 514b, 515a
X., *Wat.* 527a
Y., *Alta.* 309b
Y., *Swansea* 1955c
Y. P., *NU Singapore* 1313b
Fenge, Lee A., *Bourne.* 1580a
Fenlon, Iain A., *Camb.* 1605c, 1611a
  J., *Warw.* 1979b
  Michael, *Lond.* 1789a
Fenn, B., *Qld.UT* 153c
  P. T., *Nott.* 1855a, 1860a
Fenna, Alan, *ICL* 1705c
  Colin, *Melb.* 99c, 109a
  Gillian, *Tor.* 493b
  Helen M., *Durh.* 1635b
  J., *Curtin* 58a
  Stanley, *Murd.* 132a
  T. J. A., *Alta.* 305a
Fenyes, Lorand, *Tor.* 497b
  Tommy I., *Pret.* 1375c
Feradah Hassan, *Tech.U.Malaysia* 1030b, 1030c
Feramez, Michael, *La Trobe* 79c
Ferapontov, Eugene V., *Lough.* 1833c
Ferdinand, C. I. P., *Warw.* 1976a
Ferdous, Farhana, *B'desh.Engin.* 223b
  M. J., *Rajsh.* 256c
  M. R., *Dhaka* 236c
  Nasima, *Dhaka* 237c
  Razina, *Dhaka* 239a
  S., *Jahang.* 244c
  Tahmina, *Jahang.* 246c
Ferdouse, M. G. K., *Rajsh.* 256c
Ferdousi, H., *Rajsh.* 255b
  M. S. A., *Dhaka* 233c
  Razina, *Dhaka* 236c
  Z., *Rajsh.* 254a
Ferdus, N., *Islamic(B'desh.)* 243a
Fereday, R. J., *Brunei* 267a
Ferenc, Anna, *W.Laur.* 558c
Ferenczi, Michael A., *ICL* 1707a
Feresidis, Alexandros, *Lough.* 1832b
Feresu, Sarah, *Z'bwe.* 2050b
Ferg, E., *Nelson Mandela Met.* 1361a
Fergie, Deane J., *Adel.* 29b
Fergus, Suzanne, *Herts.* 1687b
Ferguson, A. W., *HK* 2030, 2037b
  Alastair V., *Qu.* 459c
  Alison J., *Newcastle(NSW)* 143b
  Allister I., *Strath.* 1944, 1947c
  B., *Sask.* 480c
  B. G., *Manit.* 391b
  Barbara I., *Otago* 1105a
  C. A., *Manit.* 397a
  Colin, *Melb.* 94a

Danise, *Mt.All.* 427a
David J. P., *Oxf.* 1879b
Donald G., *Vic.(BC)* 518b
Dorothy, *G.Caledonian* 1673b
E., *Nott.* 1855c
E. Brendan, *G.Caledonian* 1672
Elaine L., *Otago* 1105c
Evelyn, *Manit.* 394a
G., *St And.* 1914a
Gerard A., *Vic.(BC)* 520a
Greg C., *St Mary's(Can.)* 470a, 470c
H. W., *Stir.* 1941c
Harvie, *Glas.* 1668b
I., *Stir.* 1941b
I. J., *Manit.* 391a
J. D., *Belf.* 1561a
J. Willem H., *Pret.* 1381b, 1386a
James, *Bond* 39c
James B., *Belf.* 1565a
John D., *Strath.* 1945a
K., *S.Fraser* 484c
Kathleen A. A., *W.Ont.* 549b
Kerry, *La Trobe* 77, 85a, 85b, 85c
L. M., *Sask.* 476a
Lorraine, *W.Syd.* 204a
Lynnette B., *Auck.* 1076b, 1076c
M., *Lond.* 1803b
Mary, *W.Ont.* 553c
N. S., *S'ton.* 1938b
Neil M., *ICL* 1705c
R., *Belf.* 1565b
R. G., *St And.* 1915c
R. Stuart, *Auck.* 1076a
Richard, *Lough.* 1834c
Robert I., *Durh.* 1635a
Robyn, *Bond* 40c
Ronald, *C'dia.* 346a
Roy, *Vic.(BC)* 517c
S. G., *W.Ont.* 551c
Sherry D. L., *Ott.* 441b
Stuart J., *Oxf.* 1873b, 1882b
W. C., *Qu.* 454c
W. George, *Auck.* 1070a
Ferguson-Smith, Anne C., *Camb.* 1606c
Fergusson, Barbara, *Flin.* 67
  Christopher L., *W'gong.* 207b
  David, *Edin.* 1646a
  David M., *Otago* 1107b
  J., *Manit.* 393b, 398c
  Jennifer A., *Macq.* 92a
Fergy, Susan P., *Kingston(UK)* 1719b
Feris, Loretta A., *Pret.* 1378c
Ferland, Francine, *Montr.* 418c
  Guylaine, *Montr.* 417b
  Jacques A., *Montr.* 411c
Ferlie, Ewan, *Lond.* 1809a, 1811b
Fern, Robert E., *Leic.* 1746c
Fernandes, Bernard, *Tor.* 505a
  F. A., *Padmashree Dr DYP* 879
  Jenny, *Aberd.* 1538a, 1538c
  Julio C., *Montr.* 418c
  Leta, *Ott.* 441c
  Lynette B., *W.Aust.* 196b
  T., *Napier* 1845a
  T. R. C., *Z'bwe.* 2052c
Fernández, A. C., *SC Tirunal* 922b
  Ann, *Bourne.* 1582a
  B., *Nfld.* 407a, 407b
  Conrad, *Dal.* 357c
  Karen, *Auck.* 1073b
  Louis A. V., *Dal.* 356c
  Lovell D., *W.Cape* 1408a
Fernández, Maribel, *Lond.* 1791b
Fernandes, R., *Lond.* 1799c
Fernandez-Kennedy, Vanessa, *Murd.* 133c
Fernandez-Mateo, Isabel, *Lond.* 1798a
Fernando, A. Dinithi A., *Colombo* 1439b
  A. I., *Ruhuna* 1460b
  Anthony T., III, *Auck.* 1076a
  Aswini D., *Kelaniya* 1445c
  C. A. N., *Ruhuna* 1459b
  C. A. Nandana, *Wayamba* 1467b
  C. H., *Wat.* 524a
  Chandrika, *IIT S.Lanka* 1465c
  D. M. S., *Sri Jay.* 1464c
  Darrel A., *W.Syd.* 204b
  Deepika, *Colombo* 1439b
  Dhammika, *Vic.(Aust.)* 188b
  Dulitha N., *Colombo* 1436a, 1439a

F. R., Kelaniya 1446c
G., Birm. 1569a
G. H., Sri Jay. 1464c
G. M. D., Peradeniya 1454a
G. W. A. R., Open S.Lanka 1450b
G. W. J. S., Kelaniya 1444a
H. A. C., Sri Jay. 1463c
I. M. K., Colombo 1437c
I. V. S., Kelaniya 1446c
J. N. O., Open S.Lanka 1449b
K. M. E. P., Sri Jay. 1462b
K. R., Brunei 267a
L. N. A., Peradeniya 1453c
L. P., Colombo 1438a
Lakshman M. L., W.Ont. 552a
M. A. R. M., Peradeniya 1453b
M. P. W. S., Open S.Lanka 1450b
M. S. J. S. K. D., Sri Jay. 1462b
M. Siromani, Colombo 1437a
Mario, W'gong. 209b
P. H. P., Peradeniya 1456a
P. R., Colombo 1439a
P. R. N., Colombo 1438b
R. L. S., Sri Jay. 1463c
Rajulton, W.Ont. 546a
S., Sri Jay. 1464b
S. A., Colombo 1436b
S. L. J., Ruhuna 1459a
S. S. D., Colombo 1438c
S. S. N., Sri Jay. 1464b
T. A. N., Sri Jay. 1464b
Terence, Salf. 1919a, 1920c
Tyrone L., W.Aust. 193c, 199b
W. C. D. K., Kotelawala Defence 1448a
W. G., Peradeniya 1454a
W. G. D., Manit. 393b
W. M. Clare, Wayamba 1467c
W. S., Kelaniya 1445c
W. S., Sri Jay. 1462c
X., Ryerson 463c
Fernandopulle, B. L. Rohini, Colombo 1439b
M. N. D., Wayamba 1467c
R. C., Sri Jay. 1464b
Ferneley, Elaine H., Salf. 1920a
Fernhout, Harry, King's(Alta.) 361
Fernie, Ewan, Lond. 1808b
Geoffrey R., Tor. 507c
J., H-W 1680c
J. D. Donald, Tor. 490b
Fernig, David G., Liv. 1755b
Ferns, P. N., Cardiff 1614c
Terry, Greenwich 1677a
Fernyhough, Charles P., Durh. 1636c
Liam J., Otago 1107b
Feroz, Chowdhury Md., B'desh.Engin. 225a
Rubina, Karachi 1252c
Feroze, N., Lahore UET 1240c
Ferrall, Charles, Well. 1115a
Christopher, Qu. 453a
Ferran, Anne, Syd. 167a
Eilis V., Camb. 1604c
Ferrari, Michel, Tor. 504b
Ferraro, Pasquale, Montr. 418c
Ferreira, Elizabeth, Nelson Mandela Met. 1363b
Fernanda, Edin. 1649c
G. M., N-W(S.Af.) 1368c
H. C., Jo'burg. 1347a
J. T., Jo'burg. 1348b
L., Qld.UT 152b, 153b
O. J. O., Pret. 1377c
Pedro G., Oxf. 1877c
S. E. S., N-W(S.Af.) 1369b
Sanet L., Stell. 1395a
Ferreira-Meyers, Karren A. F., Swazi. 1471c
Ferrell, Robyn, Melb. 96a
William R., Glas. 1663c
Ferrero, Richard, Monash 122a
Ferres, L. Kay, Griff. 69a, 69c
Ferretti, Todd, W.Laur. 559b
Ferrie, Frank, McG. 370b
John, Warw. 1973b
Ferris, F. Grant, Tor. 494c
G., Nott.Trent 1865c
Ina, Ott. 442a
J. R., Calg. 327c
J. Stephen, Car. 337b
Lorraine E., Tor. 507b
Malcolm, Herts. 1685b, 1688c
Shauna D., Macq. 87a
Ferrito, Victor, Malta 1045c
Ferro, Albert, Lond. 1794c
Ferron, André, Montr. 418a
Jean-Paul, Montr. 417a
Ferroni, P. A., Curtin 59b
Ferry, Brian, W'gong. 207c
David, S'ton. 1933b
Doug, Well. 1117b
Ferryman, J. M., Reading 1907c
Fersht, Sir Alan R., Camb. 1600b
Fertuck, Len, Tor. 496b
Ferworn, A., Ryerson 463a
Ferzacca, Steven, Leth. 363c
Ferzoco, George P., Leic. 1750c
Fesenko, I. B., Nott. 1854b
Festenstein, Richard J., ICL 1706b
Fester, Ferdinand, Jo'burg. 1346c
Feszty, D., Car. 337c
Fetherston, Anthony, E.Cowan 64c
Fethi Ben Jomaa Ahmed, IIU Malaysia 1000a
Fettiplace, Robert, Camb. 1606c
Robert, Keele 1711a
Feuerverger, Andrey, Tor. 501b
Grace, Tor. 503c
Fevre, R. W., Cardiff 1622b
Fewell, J. E., Calg. 333c
Fewer, D., Manit. 398a
Fewkes, A., Nott.Trent 1862b
Fewster, Caroline, Bond 39b
Rachel M., Auck. 1075a
Fey, Martin, Stell. 1397b
Feyisetan, S. O. O., Lagos 1183, 1187c
Feyles, Valter, W.Ont. 550b
Ffolkes David, Paul, Camb. 1612b
ffrench, R. Patrick, Lond. 1790a
Ffrench-Constant, Charles, Edin. 1652b
Charles K., Camb. 1608a
Ffytche, Dominic H., Lond. 1792a
Fiaderio, Jose L., Leic. 1749b
Fiadjoe, Albert, WI 1993a
Fiagbe, N. I. Y., Kwame NUST 589b
Fialor, Sc., Kwame NUST 587a
Fianu, D. A. G., Ghana 581c
Fiarhurst, Stephen, Cardiff 1621b
Fiatarone Singh, Monica, Syd. 169c
Fice, Graham, Sur. 1954b
Fich, Faith E., Tor. 491c
M., Wat. 532b
Fichtinger, Gabor, Qu. 453a
Fick, A. C., Rhodes 1389c
Carolyn, C'dia. 345c
G. C., Witw. 1413c
G. H., Calg. 331a
J. I. J., N-W(S.Af.) 1365a, 1369c
P. H., N-W(S.Af.) 1367a
Wilma C., Pret. 1377b
Fida, Mubassar, Aga Khan(P'stan.) 1232c
Fiddes, Rev. Paul S., Oxf. 1878c
Fiddian, Nicholas J., Cardiff 1616a
Robin W., Oxf. 1877a
Fiddis, Clive, Ulster 1960a
Fiddler, Allyson, Lanc. 1722c
Wayne, Hudd. 1693b
Fiddo, S., Rivers SUST 1212b
Fiddy Davis, J., Manipal 849b
Fidge, C. J., Qld.UT 152b
Noel H., Monash 120c
Fidler, F. B., Reading 1907b
G., C'dia. 344b
Peter, Sund. 1949
Fidrmuc, Jan, Brun. 1594a
Fiech, A., Nfld. 402a
Fieggen, Graham, Cape Town 1340a
Fieguth, P. W., Wat. 527c
Fiehn, J., Warw. 1978b
Field, Andrew J., Monash 114c
Anthony J., ICL 1702a
Bruce W., Monash 116c
C., Wolv. 1983b
C. C., Dal. 353c
C. J., Alta. 303a
David, Bond 40a
David J., Leic. 1748a
Hugh J., Camb. 1607c
J., S'ton. 1939c
J., Stir. 1942a, 1943b
J. C., Calg. 325c
J. R., Nott.Trent 1865c
Jeff, Cant. 1085, 1092c
Jennifer, Greenwich 1676b
Johannes G., Cape Town 1338b
John, Adel. 28a
John, Liv. 1759b
John S., KwaZulu-Natal 1357b
M. C., Camb. 1606a
Max, Glas. 1670c
Michael J., Syd. 172a
Penelope A., Otago 1105c
Peter J. C., Wales 1546c
Peter S., Cant. 1087c
R., Qld.UT 150c
R. A., E.Anglia 1638c
R. H., Alta. 310a
Robert W., Oxf. 1875a
Roger J., Lincoln(NZ) 1093
Rosalind, Lond. 1808b
S., Warw. 1977c
S. A., Cardiff 1618b
S. K., Calg. 331c
Sean, Cape Town 1335c
Fieldes, Mary Ann, W.Laur. 557a
Fieldhouse, John D., Hudd. 1692b
Liliane S., Manc.Met. 1840c
Wes, Auck.UT 1081a
Fielding, A., Birm. 1572c
A., Curtin 56a
A., Manc.Met. 1837b
Bertram C., W.Cape 1408b
David, Otago 1104c
Dorothy M., Leeds 1737a
Helen, W.Ont. 544c
Jane L., Sur. 1952c
John P., Cran. 1629c
K. L., Lond. 1804a
Karyn J., Otago 1105a
Louise M., Wales 1966c
Nigel G., Sur. 1952c
Penny, Edin. 1648c
R., HK 2034a
Stephen J., Salf. 1919a
Susan, Lond. 1812b
Trefor J., Wales 1548b
Fielding-Barnsley, R., Qld.UT 150c
Fieldler, K., Malawi 987b
Fieldon, Jann, Massey 1098a
Fields, A. L. A., Alta. 312a
Bob, Middx. 1843a
Fieller, N. R. J., Sheff. 1925b
Fierke, K., St And. 1915a
Fierlbeck, K., Dal. 354c
Fiertel, N. O., Alta. 303b
Fife, Edward H., Tor. 490b
W., Nfld. 401a
Fife-Schaw, Christopher R., Sur. 1952c
Fifita, Filimone, S.Pac. 1423c, 1424b, 1424c
Figes, Orlando, Lond. 1777c
Figeys, Daniel, Ott. 444b
Figgess, Hugh, Leeds Met. 1744a
Figgins, Elaine, Strath. 1947c
Figgis, Sean, Northumbria 1849b
Figueroa, Mark, WI 1994b, 1994c, 1995b
Figueroa-O'Farrill, Jose, Edin. 1649b
Fihla, P. M., Fort Hare 1343c
Filali-Ansary, Abdou, Aga Khan(P'stan.) 1231c
Filani, M. O., Ib. 1174b
Filanovsky, I., Alta. 305c
Fildes, Robert A., Lanc. 1723b, 1724c
Filek, Donna, St Mary's(Can.) 467c
Filep, Janos G., Montr. 417c
Filewod, G., Ryerson 464c
Filgueira, Luis, W.Aust. 191b
Filiaggi, Mark, Dal. 350a, 355b
Filion, Lionel, Ott. 444b
Louis Jacques, Montr. 424a
P., Wat. 524c, 532c
Filiou, D., Manc.Met. 1841b
Filip, Miodrag, Portsmouth 1900b
Filipovic, Miroslav, W.Syd. 202b
Filippi, V., Lond. 1804a
Filippucci, Paola, Camb. 1611b
Fill, Christopher Y., Portsmouth 1901b
Filler, G., W.Ont. 551a, 551b
Guido, Ott. 445c
Fillery, Edward D., Tor. 492a
Fillion, Michelle, Vic.(BC) 520c
Fillis, I. R., Stir. 1942c
Fillmore, P. A., Dal. 353c
Filloux, Alain A. M., ICL 1701b
Filmer, Paul A., Lond. 1782c
Filmore, P. R., Plym. 1889a
Filoseta, Roberto, Herts. 1685b
Filosof, Jana, Herts. 1686c
Filteau, S., Lond. 1804a
Finamore, Rev. Stephen, Brist. 1592c
Finau, Kisione, S.Pac. 1423c
Finbow, Arthur S., St Mary's(Can.) 469b
M. E., G.Caledonian 1672c
R., Dal. 354c
Finch, Alan D., Bond 38, 40c, 41b
Brian, Massey 1097a
E. F., H-W 1679b
James A., McG. 370c
Dame Janet, Keele 1709
John, Strath. 1947a
John H., Aberd. 1535a
Lester, Waik. 1121b, 1122a
Lynette, Sunshine Coast 159c
Pat, Worcester 1984, 1985c
Patrick, Bath 1556b
R. G., Nott. 1858a
Susan E., Wales 1967c
V. M. I., Lond. 1800c
Fincham, Gail, Cape Town 1335b
Kenneth C., Kent 1714c
R., Stir. 1942c
R. J., KwaZulu-Natal 1357c, 1358c
Fincher, Geoffrey B., Adel. 24c, 31a, 31c
Ruth, Melb. 94c
Findeli, Alain, Montr. 413b
Finden, Walter, St Mary's(Can.) 469b
Findlater, Gordon S., Edin. 1650b
Findlay, Alison G., Lanc. 1722c
B., Alta. 302c
B. M., Swinburne UT 162a
C. Scott, Ott. 447a
David M., Adel. 28b
Hilary, Brock 319c
I., Sask. 475b
Ian, Griff. 70a
Ian, Hudd. 1692c
Jacqueline Y., Leeds 1739b, 1739c
Jeanette, Glas. 1664c
John A., New Br. 429c
John B. C., Leeds 1726c
John M., Durh. 1636c
L. M., Sask. 474a, 479b
M. M., Plym. 1889b
Mark J., Syd. 171a, 175b
Michael, Auck. 1076c
Patricia, Edin. 1649a
Roy, Open(UK) 1867c
T., Car. 339a
Findon, J., Trent 514a
Findsen, Brian, Glas. 1663a, 1671b
Fine, A., Manit. 396b
Alan M., Dal. 358a
Ben J., Lond. 1815b
C., Ryerson 465a
Marshall, W.Laur. 559c
Michael D., Macq. 90c
P. E. M., Lond. 1804a
Robert D., Warw. 1976b
Finegan, Andrew, C.Darwin 48b
B. A., Alta. 310b
Joan E., W.Ont. 545c
Finegood, Diane T., S.Fraser 485a
Fineman, Stephen, Bath 1552a, 1554b
Finestone, Hillel M., Ott. 445a
Finger, Glenn D., Griff. 70b
Fingleton, Bernard, Camb. 1604b
Bernard, Strath. 1945b
Finigan, Alison, Otago 1111b
Fink, Howard, C'dia. 347c
Janet, Open(UK) 1871b
John N., Otago 1107a
Finkel, Alvin, Athab. 315a
Finkenstadt, B. F., Warw. 1976b
Finlay, A. Y., Cardiff 1619a
Alison, Lond. 1777c
D. C., Coventry 1626a
David C., La Trobe 78a
Graeme J., Auck. 1076c
Ian, Strath. 1945b
J., Ryerson 463a
J. L., Manit. 391b
Janet, Leeds Met. 1742c
John, Glas. 1666b
R. J., Manc.Met. 1838b
Richard J., Strath. 1946b
Rosalind, McG. 368a
W. H., Alta. 305c
Finlay-Jones, John, E.Cowan 63, 67c
Finlayson, A., Swansea 1957a
Brian L., Melb. 109a
Bruce, E.Cowan 65c
G. D., E.Anglia 1639a
J., Qu. 454c
Mary, Auck. 1077a
Michael, Tor. 495b
Finley, Allen, Dal. 355c
John P., Dal. 357c
Rhonda, C.Qld. 46c
Finn, A., Alta. 307a
A. H. R., Brist. 1589b, 1590c
Chris, Adel. 27a
Daniel, Portsmouth 1902c
Geraldine M., Car. 336a, 339c
Gerard P. T., Strath. 1945b
Gregory C., Brock 321a
Jeremy, Cant. 1092b
Judith C., W.Aust. 197a
M. C., Warw. 1974b
M. P., Curtin 54c
Mickey, Lincoln(UK) 1752b
Peter B., Belf. 1564c, 1565c
Prema, Melb. 105b
Rev. Richard, Oxf. 1881b, 1883b
Vincent, Hudd. 1690c
Finnane, Antonia, Melb. 98b
Finnegan, David J., Edin. 1645b
Patrick M., W.Aust. 195b
R. E., Manit. 390b
Ruth, Open(UK) 1871b
Tom, G.Caledonian 1674c
Finnerty, Gerald T., Lond. 1792a, 1792b
Finney, Joe, Lanc. 1722a
Kate, Greenwich 1676a
Stephen, Strath. 1945c
Finney-Crawley, J. R., Nfld. 401b
Finnie, Gavin, Bond 40a
Jeff F., KwaZulu-Natal 1357b
K. J. C., W.Ont. 549b
Wilson, Edin. 1648b
Finnigan, John, Edin. 1647a
Timothy, Syd. 169a
Valerie, Leeds Met. 1741c
Finnin, Barrie C., Monash 124a
Finnis, John M., Oxf. 1876a
Michael W., ICL 1704a
Finnissy, Michael, S'ton. 1936c
Finshilescu, G., Witw. 1414c
Finsterwalder, Joerg, Cant. 1089b
Finucane, B. T., Alta. 310b
Lisa, Waik. 1125a
Finzi-Smith, Robert, Jamaica UT 957c
Fionda, J. A., S'ton. 1935c
Fiore, Benjamin, Regina 335
Marcelo P., Camb. 1601a
Fiorini, Anthony, Malta 1044b, 1045b
Stanley, Malta 1043a
Fiott, Antoine, Malta 1042c
Firbank, Oscar E., Montr. 415c
Firby, Patricia A., Liv.J.Moores 1766b
Firdaus Ahmad Azzam, IIU Malaysia 999b
Firdausi Razali, Tech.U.Malaysia 1031c
Firdous, Akhtar, Foundation(P'stan.) 1244c
Nilofer, Sindh 1276b
Rehana, Karachi 1252a
Sadiqa, Karachi 1251a
Tanzeemul, Karachi 1253a
Firer, S., Witw. 1411a
Firestone, Philip, Ott. 443c
Firman, Keith, Portsmouth 1899a
Firmin, David N., ICL 1707a
Firoz Akhtar Ansari, Putra 1025a
Firth, A. Y., Sheff. 1928a
Amanda L., Keele 1713a
Anthony J., ICL 1708a
Bruce T., Adel. 27c
C. G., Sheff. 1924c
D., Warw. 1976b
Dianne F., Canberra 42a
E. C., Lond. 1813a
Elwyn C., Massey 1101a, 1101c
Hilda M., Otago 1109b
Janet E., Hudd. 1693a
Neville, Syd. 167b
Norman A., Otago 1104b
Fisa, Bohuslav, Montr. 422b
Fischbacher, Moira, Glas. 1666c
Fischer, B., S'ton. 1934b
Benedikt, Vic.(BC) 522a
C. L., Rhodes 1388a
Conan, Strath. 1946b
Denise, Syd. 165b
I., H-W 1680a
J. L., Jo'burg. 1346b
Jan, Swinburne UT 164a

Gennard, Dorothy, *Lincoln(UK)* 1752b
John, *Strath.* 1946c
Genno, C., *Tor.* 495a
Genoe, Murray, *Trent* 513, 515c
Genoni, P., *Curtin* 57b
Genovesi, P., *La Trobe* 80c
Gent, I., *St And.* 1914b
Gentil, G., *Car.* 339b
Gentilcore, David C., *Leic.* 1748b
Gentle, Alex, *Melb.* 101a
C. R., *Nott.Trent* 1864b
Louise, *Nott.Trent* 1862a
Gentleman, M., *Dal.* 351a
Morven, *Dal.* 359b
Stephen M., *ICL* 1707b
Gentry, Charles B., *Camb.* 1609c
Gentz, Natascha, *Edin.* 1648c
Geoghegan, M., *Sheff.* 1925c
V., *Belf.* 1561a
Geok Yuan Annie Tan, *Malaya* 1005b
Georgakapoulou, Alexandra, *Lond.* 1789c
Georgala, Douglas L., *Leeds* 1731a
Georganas, Nicolas D., *Ott.* 440
George, A., *WI* 1998b
A. O., *Ib.* 1176c
A. V., *SC Tirunal* 922, 923b
Adrian V., *Syd.* 167c
Andrew J. T., *ICL* 1706b
Andrew R., *Lond.* 1816a
Annette D., *W.Aust.* 193a
B. W., *Nott.Trent* 1862c
C. F. P., *W.Ont.* 549b
Carlisle, *Middx.* 1843a
Cherian, *Nan.Tech.* 1293c
Christeen, *Herts.* 1688a
D. Ian, *Wales* 1964, 1964c
D. J., *Swansea* 1956c
Donald A. R., *Edin.* 1649a
E. O., *Olabisi Onabanjo* 1204b
Elizabeth, *Putra* 1022c
G. H., *Nfld.* 403a
G. N., *Sask.* 474c
Gerard, *ICL* 1705b
Gwyneth, *Guy.* 592, 594c
Helen, *Lond.S.Bank* 1828a
J., *WI* 1999a
J. A., *Wat.* 523b, 525c, 528c, 531b
J. A., *Witw.* 1416a
Jessie-Ann, *WI* 1991b, 2002c
John, *E.Lond.* 1643a
Keith, *Liv.J.Moores* 1766c
Linu S., *Manipal* 850b
M. W., *Nott.* 1851b
Mathew, *Manipal* 846c
Mildred E. R., *Greenwich* 1677a
P. M., *W.Ont.* 546a
Peter J., *McM.* 386
R., *Qu.* 460a
R. M. J., *Open S.Lanka* 1450b
Ron, *Bath Spa* 1556b
Rosalyn P., *Lond.* 1782a
S., *Wales* 1970a
S. G., *Stir.* 1941c
S. J., *Brist.* 1590c
S. L., *S'ton.* 1939a
Susan R., *Tor.* 505c
Thomas, *Manipal* 850a
Usha, *Ryerson* 462b
Usha, *Tor.* 500c
V. I., *Manipal* 851c
Vinu T., *Manipal* 850a
W. D., *Glas.* 1669c
George Tharkan, C., *Hyd.* 769b
Georgellis, Yannis, *Brun.* 1594a
Georgen, M., *Sheff.* 1925a
Georges, Arthur, *Canberra* 42c
Elias, *McG.* 386b
Jo-Ann, *WI* 1991a, 2002b
Michael, *Tor.* 491a
Georgeson, M., *E.Lond.* 1642a
M. A., *Aston* 1544c
Georgewill, Justina W., *Rivers SUST* 1211b, 1212b
O. A., *P.Harcourt* 1209a
Georghiades, P., *Wales* 1967b
Georghiou, P. E., *Nfld.* 402a
Georghis, Georghios, *Cyprus* 564b
Georgiades, Pantelis, *Cyprus* 563a
Georgiadou, Elli, *Middx.* 1843a
Georgiou, D., *Coventry* 1625b
George, *Birm.* 1567a
George, *Cyprus* 564a
Georgios, *Cyprus* 564c
Harry M., *Melb.* 105a
Stelios, *Cyprus* 564c
Georgiou-Karistianis, Nellie, *Monash* 123a
Gephart, R. P., *Alta.* 310a
Gera, S. C., *G.Jamb.* 761c
Gerace, R. V., *W.Ont.* 549b
Geraghty, Christine, *Glas.* 1668c
Dominic P., *Tas.* 182c
Lincoln, *Portsmouth* 1899c
Micheal, *Ott.* 445c
Paul, *S.Pac.* 1422b
Geraldo, P. K., *Winneba* 578b, 579a
Geramita, A. V., *Qu.* 456a
Joan, *Qu.* 456a
Gerard, Karen, *S'ton.* 1939c
Gerasimenko, O. V., *Liv.* 1759a, 1759c
Gerbé, Olivier, *Montr.* 423c
Gerber, A. M., *N-W(S.Af.)* 1367b
Andrew, *New Br.* 431b
C., *St And.* 1914a
D. E., *W.Ont.* 539c
J. J., *N-W(S.Af.)* 1369a
L., *Manc.Met.* 1838a
Matthys, *Syd.* 167a
Mickey F., *Stell.* 1399c
Paula, *Monash* 119a, 126a
S., *Nelson Mandela Met.* 1361a
Thinus C., *Pret.* 1373b
Thomas, *Nelson Mandela Met.* 1361a
Gerbic, Phillippa, *Auck.UT* 1081c
Gerdsen, Trevor J., *Newcastle(NSW)* 146c, 147a
Gerdts, Donna B., *S.Fraser* 485b
Gere, Charles E., *Lanc.* 1722a
Gergely, Laszlo, *Lond.S.Bank* 1827a
Gerhard, J. A., *Manit.* 392a
Gericke, D. H., *N-W(S.Af.)* 1365a
Gertruida J., *Pret.* 1386a
J. S., *N-W(S.Af.)* 1366c
Gérin, Michel, *Montr.* 417b
Gérin-Lajoie, Diane, *Tor.* 503c
Gerlach, Heiko A., *Auck.* 1069a
N., *Car.* 338a, 341a
Richard, *Syd.* 168b
Germain, Josée, *Laval* 363
Randall, *Car.* 340b
German, A. J., *Liv.* 1761c
C. R., *S'ton.* 1936c
Karl, *Malta* 1045a
Germany, David A., *Herts.* 1685a
Germida, J. J., *Sask.* 478a
Germon, R. K., *Nott.Trent* 1864a
Germond, P. A., *Witw.* 1415a
Germov, John B., *Newcastle(NSW)* 143b
Gero, John S., *Syd.* 166c
Geroimenko, V. A., *Plym.* 1889a
Gerolymatos, Andre, *S.Fraser* 484c
Gerrans, Paul A., *E.Cowan* 64b
Philip S., *Adel.* 27a
Gerrard, Anthea J., *Bond* 40a
Christopher M., *Durh.* 1633b
David F., *Otago* 1108c
J., *Manit.* 397a
Juliet A., *Cant.* 1091b
Michael J., *Adel.* 25b
Piera, *Salf.* 1920c, 1921b
Sarah, *Lond.* 1807, 1811c, 1812a
William J., *Leeds* 1732a
Gerridzen, Ronald G., *Ott.* 446b
Gerrish, K., *Sheff.* 1929a
Gerritsen, A., *Warw.* 1974b
Gerrow, J. D., *Dal.* 355c
Gersch, Irvine, *E.Lond.* 1643b
Gershuny, Jonathan, *Oxf.* 1878c
Gerson, Carole, *S.Fraser* 484b
Lloyd, *Tor.* 498b
Gerstenberg, Oliver, *Leeds* 1731c
Gerster, Robin C., *Monash* 117a
Gerstle, Andrew, *Lond.* 1815c
Gerstner, Eitan, *Lough.* 1830c
Gertler, L. O., *Wat.* 532c
M. E., *Sask.* 478a
Meric S., *Tor.* 494c
Gerty, David, *Lough.* 1836c
Gerus, O. W., *Manit.* 391b, 399c
Gervais, Colette, *Montr.* 415c
Daniel, *Ott.* 440c, 442c
Flore, *Montr.* 421c
Lynne B., *McG.* 367
M., *S'ton.* 1937c
P. L., *Alta.* 308b
Stéphan, *McG.* 384b
Gervais-Le Garff, M., *Plym.* 1892b
Gervers, Michael, *Tor.* 495a, 510b
Gervis, Misia, *Brun.* 1595c
Gerwel, Gert J., *Pret.* 1373c
Gerzina, Tania M., *Syd.* 168a
Gesch, Fr. Patrick, *D.Word* 1281
Gescher, Andreas J., *Leic.* 1745c, 1746a
Gesser, H. D., *Manit.* 389a
Gessner, Klaus, *W.Aust.* 199a
Getao, K. W., *Nair.* 970b, 973a
Gethin, D. T., *Swansea* 1955c
Rupert M. L., *Brist.* 1589a
Gething, Fleure, *Leeds Met.* 1740b
Linda, *Hudd.* 1693b
Mary-Jane, *Melb.* 103c
William, *Bath* 1554a
Getliffe, Kathy, *S'ton.* 1939c
Getta, Janusz, *W'gong.* 207a
Gettinby, George C., *Strath.* 1948a
Getty, Grace, *New Br.* 432c
Louise, *Montr.* 418c
Getz, D. P., *Calg.* 324b
Wayne M., *Pret.* 1381b
Getzler, Joshua S., *Oxf.* 1876a
Geurkov, V., *Ryerson* 463c
Geursen, Gus, *C.Qld.* 44, 44c
Geurts, Marie-Anne, *Ott.* 442a
Geuss, Raymond, *Camb.* 1606a
Geva, Esther, *Tor.* 504a
S., *Qld.UT* 152b
Geva-May, Iris, *S.Fraser* 483c
Gevers, Wim R., *Stell.* 1393b
Gewirtz, Sharon, *Lond.* 1793c
Geyer, H. S., *N-W(S.Af.)* 1370b, 1370c
Hendrik B., *Stell.* 1396c, 1401b
Robert R., *Lanc.* 1724a
Geyser, M. M., *Pret.* 1382b
Mariëtte, *Pret.* 1373c
Geyssen, John, *New Br.* 429c
Gfellner, Barbara M., *Bran.* 318a
Ghabriel, Mounir N., *Adel.* 27c
Ghadially, Rehana, *IIT Bombay* 778c
Ghadiri, Hossein, *Griff.* 71a
Mojtaba, *Leeds* 1730b
Ghadirian, Parviz, *Montr.* 417b
Ghadouani, Anas, *W.Aust.* 193c
Ghaffar, Q., *JMI* 794a
Sayeeda, *Dhaka* 237b
Ghafoor, Abdul, *NUST(P'stan.)* 1263c, 1264b
F. H., *NED Eng.* 1262a, 1262b
Ghafouri-Shiraz, H., *Birm.* 1568c
Ghafur, T., *Dhaka* 238a
Ghahary, A., *Alta.* 312c
Ghahramani, F., *Manit.* 392a
Zoubin, *Camb.* 1602b
Ghahreman, Shahzad, *Auck.UT* 1085a
Ghai, Raji, *Jammu* 796c
Ghali, W. A., *Calg.* 331a, 332a
Ghalib, M. A., *Rajsh.* 252c
Ghaloo, Raza H., *Sindh* 1276b
Ghaly, A. E., *Dal.* 351b
Wahid S., *C'dia.* 345a
Ghambi, Roosevelt T., *Mzuzu* 990a
Ghanashyam Krishna, M., *Hyd.* 770c
Ghanasyam, Kishore, *Manipal* 850c
Ghandar, Ann, *NE* 136c
Ghandhi, Leela, *La Trobe* 79a
P. R., *Reading* 1908c
Ghandhi Krishna, B., *Nehru Tech.* 799c
Ghaneh, Paula, *Liv.* 1759b
Ghanei, M., *Greenwich* 1675c
Ghanem, A., *Dal.* 351b
Ghanghro, A. B., *Sindh* 1274a
Abdul R., *Mehran* 1257b
Ghani, A., *Lond.* 1804a
Farooq, *Aga Khan(P'stan.)* 1232b
Imtiaz, *NUST(P'stan.)* 1263c
Jawaid, *Lahore MS* 1255b
M. A., *Rajsh.* 256b
Naheed, *Riphah Internat.* 1271a
Naseem A., *Karachi* 1253b
Ghannouchi, F., *Calg.* 326b
Fadhel M., *Montr.* 422b
Ghanshayam Singh, *NALSAR* 863c
Ghanshyam Das, O., *Kakatiya* 804a
Ghanta, K. C., *Dr BAT* 735a
Ghany, Hamid, *WI* 1998b, 1998c
Gharib Subhi Mahmoud, *IIU Malaysia* 1002c
Gharoro, Etedafe P., *Benin* 1156c
Ghartey, Edward E., *WI* 1994c
Ghasempoor, A., *Ryerson* 464a
Ghasi, Samuel I., *Ebonyi State* 1165c
Ghassan Taha Yassen, *IIU Malaysia* 1000c
Ghatage, P., *Calg.* 332c
Ghatak, K., *Kal.* 807a
Kalyani S., *Kal.* 807a
M., *Lond.* 1799c
Ghatei, Mohammad A., *ICL* 1706a
Ghatol, Ashok A., *Dr BAT* 734
Ghatul, Arjun P., *Bharati V.* 707b
Ghauri, K. M., *Lahore UET* 1241b
Ghavami, Mohammad, *Lond.* 1791c
Ghayas Uddin, *Bhutto IST* 1272b
Ghazal, Peter, *Edin.* 1651a
Ghazala, S., *Nfld.* 401a
Ghazali bin Musa, *Malaya* 1008c
Ghazali bin Sulong, *Tech.U.Malaysia* 1031a
Ghazali Desa, *Tech.U.Malaysia* 1033c
Ghazali Mat Nor, *NU Malaysia* 1015a
Ghazali Mayudin, *NU Malaysia* 1017a
Ghazi, Mahmood A., *IIU(P'stan.)* 1248
Shehnaz, *Karachi* 1253a
Ghaznavi, Dawood, *Lahore MS* 1255b
Mehmood, *Karachi* 1252a
Ghenniwa, H. H., *W.Ont.* 541b
Ghent, E. D., *Calg.* 327b
Gheorge, M., *Sheff.* 1922b
Ghergori, Elena, *W.Aust.* 197b
Gheyara, Kelly F., *C'dia.* 342c
Gheyas, A. R., *B'desh.Ag.* 221a
Ghezelbash, A. M., *Wat.* 532b
Ghiggino, Kenneth P., *Melb.* 95c
Ghilaine, Roquet, *Montr.* 425b
Ghildyal, Sushma, *Ban.* 692b
Ghinea, George, *Brun.* 1595a, 1597b
Ghirlando, Robert, *Malta* 1040b, 1042a
Ghisalberti, Emilio L., *W.Aust.* 192a
Ghitescu, Dorin L., *Montr.* 417c
Ghizan Saleh, *Putra* 1021a, 1023a
Ghobadian, Abby, *Middx.* 1842c
Ghodse, Abdon-Hamid, *Keele* 1711a
Ghogomu, Julius, *Dschang* 273a
Ghogomu Tamouh, Richard, *Dschang* 274a
Ghojel, Jamil T., *Monash* 116c
GholamHosseini, Hamid, *Auck.UT* 1081c
Ghomeshi, J., *Manit.* 391c
Ghorai, Santosh K., *R.Bhar.* 894, 895c
Ghorbani, Ali A., *New Br.* 430a
Ghorpade, S. R., *IIT Bombay* 779b
S. R., *Shiv.* 915b, 915c
Ghos, S. N., *Dhaka* 232c
Ghosal, Goutam, *VB* 950b
Satyabrata, *R.Bhar.* 894, 895c
Sayantan, *Warw.* 1972c
Ghose, A. K., *B'desh.Ag.* 220c
A. K., *Ban.* 696b
Aditya, *W'gong.* 207a
G., *Rajsh.* 253a
Kamal, *Lincoln(NZ)* 1094c
Katie, *Lond.* 1796a
L., *Rajsh.* 253a
Tarun, *Dal.* 357c
Ghosh, A., *I.Sch.Mines* 783a
A., *Qld.UT* 149c
A., *R.Bhar.* 895b
A. K., *Ban.* 694a
A. L., *Assam* 682b
Anup K., *Ban.* 692c
Atanu, *IIT Bombay* 779a
B., *Dhaka* 233a
Banhisikha, *Kal.* 807b
C. K., *I.Gandhi Nat.Open* 787a
Chaitali, *R.Bhar.* 895a
D., *Stir.* 1942a
D., *Tripura* 943a
D., *WI* 2000b
D. C., *Kal.* 807b
D. K., *Saur.* 910b
Dipan K., *IIT Bombay* 776, 779b
Dulal C., *VB* 949b
G., *PNG Tech.* 1282c
Goutam, *R.Bhar.* 895b
Idrani, *R.Bhar.* 895a
Indrani, *R.Bhar.* 895b
K, *Kal.* 807b
Kalyan, *Montr.* 422b
M. C., *R.Bhar.* 895c
M. K., *Ban.* 696b
Brig. M. K., *Sikkim-Manipal* 921b
Madhusudan, *VB* 950a
Mihir K., *VB* 951a
Mrinal K., *IISc.* 774c
Nanda K., *Kal.* 808a
Narendra N., *BITS* 709b
P. D., *Kal.* 807b
P. K., *Delhi* 722a
P. K., *Lucknow* 823a
Pradip N., *Jad.* 788
Pradyumn, *Ban.* 696b
Prahlad C., *Delhi* 722a, 722b
Prasanta K., *VB* 951b
Prasenjit, *IIT Bombay* 776c
R., *Kal.* 807a
R. K., *W.Bengal AFS* 952
R. N., *Rajsh.* 256a
Ranjana, *Ban.* 695b
Ratna, *McG.* 369c
S. B., *I.Gandhi Nat.Open* 786b
S. K., *Chitt.* 230a
S. K., *Dib.* 729a
Sanat K., *R.Bhar.* 895a
Saroj, *Panjab* 882a
Shukla, *Delhi* 724c
Sid, *Bourne.* 1579b
Siddhartha, *IIT Bombay* 777c
Soumya, *W.Aust.* 199c
Subhendu, *Delhi* 722b
Subhendu, *Hyd.* 769b
Subrata, *ICL* 1706b
Sugata, *Brun.* 1594a, 1596b
Sujoy, *Manipal* 849c
Sushant G., *BITS* 710c
Swapan K., *VB* 950c
Swati, *R.Bhar.* 895a
T., *VB* 951c
T. K., *BN Mandal* 687
Ghosh Roy, H. J., *MDU* 833a
Ghoshal, Nandita, *Ban.* 690b
Subhasis, *McG.* 370a
Subrata, *Sikkim-Manipal* 921c
Swapna, *R.Bhar.* 895b
Ghotb, F., *Swinburne UT* 161c
Ghouri, M. S., *Islamia, Bahawal.* 1249a
Ghous, Ghaulam, *Azad J&K* 1237a
Ghulam, *Azad J&K* 1236, 1238b, 1238c
Khalida, *Karachi* 1251c
Muhammad Ali, *NED Eng.* 1261c
Ghufran bin Redzwan, *Malaya* 1005b
Ghugal, A. M., *Dr BAT* 734c
Ghulam, Yaseen, *Portsmouth* 1900a
Ghulam Jilani, *Arid Ag.* 1235c
Ghulam Mustafa, *Kashmir* 815b
Ghulam Nabi, *Sir Syed UET* 1278b
Ghulam Sarwar, Major (Retd.), *Arid Ag.* 1236b, 1236c
Ghulam Sarwar Yousof, *Malaya* 1011c
Ghuman, Abid Parvez, *NUST(P'stan.)* 1265c
B. S., *Panjab* 882b
I. S., *Panjab* 883b
R. S., *Punjabi* 891b
Ghumbo, A. Mhike, *Africa(Z'bwe.)* 2043c
Giacca, Adria, *Tor.* 507a
Giachino, Alan A., *Ott.* 446b
Giacomantonio, Carman, *Dal.* 358c
Michael, *Dal.* 358c
Nicholas B., *Dal.* 356c
Giacomin, Joseph A., *Brun.* 1594a, 1597a
Giaid, Adel, *McG.* 375c
Giami, Y., *Rivers SUST* 1211c
Giannachi, Gabriella, *Exe.* 1655c
Giannakopoulos, Apostolos, *Jo'burg.* 1348b
Giannasi, F. J., *Coventry* 1626c
Gianni, Benjamin, *Car.* 336a

Peter M., *Birm.* 1574a
Hawkin, D. J., *Nfld.* 406a
Wendy, *Leeds Met.* 1743c
Hawking, Paul, *Vic.(Aust.)* 186c
Stephen W., *Camb.* 1605b
Hawkins, Angus B., *Oxf.* 1881c
Barbara J., *Vic.(BC)* 517a
Clive, *Keele* 1711a
Gillian, *Portsmouth* 1900a
John, *Tor.* 497b
John A., *Camb.* 1603a, 1609b
Lawrence E., *S'ton.* 1937a
Leslie H., *Sur.* 1951b
Mary, *Portsmouth* 1903c
Mary, *W.Syd.* 202a
Mike, *Birm.* 1575a
Mike J., *Kingston(UK)* 1719c
P. R., *Nott.Trent* 1866c
Peter G., *Brist.* 1586c
R. K., *Nott.Trent* 1864a
R. W., *Calg.* 324c
Rhonda, *W.Syd.* 201, 205a
Sarah, *Camb.* 1605a
Scott A., *Tor.* 496b
Sean, *Tor.* 495b
Simon, *Canberra* 42b
Stanley A., *Belf.* 1562b
Stephen, *Ryerson* 466b
Wayne, *Canberra* 42a
Hawkridge, S., *Cape Town* 1340c
Hawks, D., *Curtin* 59b
Hawksley, Charles, *W'gong.* 208c
Christopher, *Keele* 1709b
F., *Nfld.* 402c
Hawksworth, Gabrielle M., *Aberd.* 1535a
Hawley, J. Gary, *Bath* 1551b, 1555a
Judith V., *Lond.* 1808b
K., *St And.* 1915c
R. J., *Plym.* 1889a
Richard, *Lond.* 1807c
S., *Manc.Met.* 1837b
Haworth, A., *Zambia* 2008c
Annette E., *Reading* 1905
Avril, *Manc.Met.* 1838c
Barry, *Lough.* 1834b
Christa, *Wales* 1968b
J. C., *Manit.* 397a
L. I., *Edin.* 1646c
L. L., *Wat.* 532a
N., *Qld.UT* 152c
Nigel A. F., *Auck.* 1073a
Penny, *Massey* 1097a
Robert J., *NE* 136b
William J., *Liv.J.Moores* 1766a
Hawranik, Pamela, *Manit.* 392c
Hawrylowicz, Catherine M., *Lond.* 1794b
Hawthorn, Geoffrey P., *Camb.* 1609c
Ian J., *Waik.* 1122c
W. R., *Wat.* 524b
Hawthorne, F. C., *Manit.* 391a
Fiona, *Bond* 39b
Graeme E., *Melb.* 106b
John, *Oxf.* 1877c
K., *Cardiff* 1620a
Sian, *Lond.* 1817a
Wendy F., *Newcastle(NSW)* 142b
Hawtin, Murray, *Leeds Met.* 1742a
Hawting, Gerald R., *Lond.* 1815c
Hawton, Keith E., *Oxf.* 1880c
Hawtrey, K. M., *Macq.* 88b
Haxell, Ailsa, *Auck.UT* 1082a, 1083b
P., *Wat.* 525b
Hay, A., *Dal.* 354a
A., *Nott.Trent* 1865a
A. D., *Brist.* 1591a
Alastair, *Leeds* 1734c
C. S., *Birm.* 1573a
Chris, *Lincoln(UK)* 1752a
D. A., *Curtin* 58b
Dale F., *Cardiff* 1622a
David, *Auck.* 1067a
David, *Lond.* 1796a
Dennis C., *Lanc.* 1724a
Diane, *Bath* 1556a
Elaine, *Keele* 1711a
G. C., *W.Ont.* 540c
Hulme, *Monash* 123b
I., *E.Lond.* 1642a
J. N., *Birm.* 1569a
Jennifer, *Cant.* 1087a
John, *Brock* 319b
John B., *Tor.* 505a
John N., *Sur.* 1950b
Kenneth G., *Leeds* 1728b
Michael, *Lond.* 1797b
N. C., *Napier* 1844c
Peter R., *Tas.* 179c
Philippa, *Well.* 1119b
R., *Lond.* 1804c
Trevor T., *Melb.* 100a
W. T., *Plym.* 1888b
Hay-Smith, E. Jean C., *Otago* 1107c
Hayashi, M., *Calg.* 327b
Hayat, Amir, *NUST(P'stan.)* 1264b
K., *Lahore UET* 1240b, 1241a
Mohd S., *Hyd.* 771b
N., *Lahore UET* 1241a
Zartaj, *Foundation(P'stan.)* 1244b
Hayati Abdul Rahman, *NU Malaysia* 1019c
Hayati bt Abdullah, *Tech.U.Malaysia* 1033c
Hayatsu, A., *W.Ont.* 540a
Hayavadana, J., *Osm.* 877c
Hayburn, G., *Wales* 1966c
Haycock, C. G., *Coventry* 1627c
J. W., *Sheff.* 1923b
Marged, *Wales* 1542b
Haycox, Alan R., *Liv.* 1759a
Hayday, Adrian C., *Lond.* 1795b
Hayden, B. D., *S.Fraser* 482a
Brian E., *S'ton.* 1933c
Carol, *Portsmouth* 1903a
D. B., *W.Ont.* 538b
J. P., *St And.* 1915a
Jacqueline, *W.Syd.* 202a
M., *S.Fraser* 485c
Martin, *S.Cross* 156a
Mary C., *Bath* 1551a, 1554a
S. M., *Brist.* 1588b
Hayder, S., *Lahore UET* 1241c
Haydon, Daniel, *Glas.* 1663b
J. C., *Plym.* 1891c
Richard G., *Oxf.* 1876c
Hayduk, L. A., *Alta.* 309c
M., *E.Lond.* 1642a
Haye, A. H. M. A., *Dhaka* 237a
M. O., *Car.* 339c
Hayee, Sobia, *NUST(P'stan.)* 1264a
Hayek, R., *Macq.* 89a
Hayes, A., *HK* 2033a, 2035b
A., *Wales* 1970b
Alan, *Vic.(Aust.)* 185b
Alan J., *Macq.* 88a
B., *Aberd.* 1537a
C. J., *Nott.* 1851b
C. R., *Swansea* 1955c
D., *Manc.Met.* 1840a
D., *Plym.* 1890a
D. L., *W.Ont.* 546c
G., *KwaZulu-Natal* 1354a
G. M., *Edin.* 1648a
G. W., *Wat.* 530b, 535b
Helen, *Edin.* 1653c
Helen, *Salf.* 1920a
Hennessey, *Griff.* 70b
J., *Namibia* 1056a
J., *Qld.UT* 152b
James C., *C'dia.* 346b
Jennie, *Monash* 129a
Jennifer A., *Melb.* 103b
John, *Herts.* 1685a
John, *Leeds* 1732a
John F., *McG.* 385b
Keith C., *W.Ont.* 551b, 551c
Lillian J., *Syd.* 172c
M., *Manc.Met.* 1837b
M. J. D., *Car.* 337c
Michael, *Pret.* 1380a
Michael P., *Cant.* 1090c
Nick J., *Nott.Trent* 1864c
P. K., *Brist.* 1584a
Patricia, *W.Cape* 1407c
Peter C., *Edin.* 1651a
R. E., *Alta.* 305b
R. J., *Lond.* 1804a
Robert, *Lough.* 1833c
Robert, *W.Syd.* 203c
S. G., *Manc.Met.* 1838a
S. J., *Sask.* 476a
Virginia, *Vic.(BC)* 521a
Vonda, *Dal.* 356b
W. C., *Reading* 1907a
Hayes-Gill, B. R., *Nott.* 1852c
Hayford, B. B., *Winneba* 580a
S., *Winneba* 579c
Hayfron-Acquah, J. B., *Kwame NUST* 587c
HayGlass, K. T., *Manit.* 395c, 397a
Hayhoe, Ruth, *Tor.* 504a
Haykowsky, M. J., *Alta.* 308c
Hayles, Julie, *Vic.(Aust.)* 188a
Michelle, *Hudd.* 1693b
Hayley, S. P., *Car.* 340c
Haylor, J., *Sheff.* 1927b
L. R., *W.Ont.* 546c
Hayman, Alan R., *Otago* 1104a
Gregory, *Camb.* 1612c
Jeremy, *Auck.UT* 1083a
Keith, *Bourne.* 1580c
Simon N., *Syd.* 166c
Stephanie, *Kingston(UK)* 1719c
Hayne, B. S., *Tor.* 493b
Harlene, *Otago* 1110c
Haynes, A., *Sheff.* 1922b
Barry P., *Portsmouth* 1900b
Brian S., *Syd.* 169a
Douglas L., *Liv.J.Moores* 1765b
John M., *Monash* 124a
Kenneth, *ICL* 1706a
M. L., *Nott.* 1855a
Peter D., *ICL* 1704a
Peter H., *Camb.* 1605b
R. M., *E.Anglia* 1639b
Richard J., *KwaZulu-Natal* 1357c
Hayry, P., *Calg.* 333b, 334b
Hays, G. C., *Swansea* 1955b
Richard B., *Keele* 1711a
Hayter, M., *Sheff.* 1929a
Roger, *S.Fraser* 484c
Scott, *W.Laur.* 556, 560c
Hayton, Clive, *Lond.S.Bank* 1829b
D. W., *Belf.* 1559a
Hayward, A., *Wales* 1966c
Annette M., *Qu.* 455a
C. T. Robert, *Durh.* 1636c
D., *Swinburne UT* 160c, 161a, 162c
David J., *Auck.* 1072a
Gordon, *Strath.* 1946a
Janine, *Otago* 1110b
Joel, *Lond.* 1793b
Maria, *Auck.UT* 1082c
Maria, *S'ton.* 1933b
P. J., *Swansea* 1955b
Philip R., *Macq.* 88a
R., *Greenwich* 1675b
R. B., *Alta.* 304a
R. S. A., *Alta.* 311b
Ray, *Waik.* 1125b
Richard L., *Edin.* 1652a
Robert, *Leeds Met.* 1743c
S. J., *E.Anglia* 1638c, 1639a
Susan, *Exe.* 1657b
Tim, *Edin.* 1650b
Vincent, *McG.* 370b
Haywood, Alison, *Griff.* 73a
Helen, *Bourne.* 1579a
J., *Edin.* 1644, 1646a, 1653c
John, *Well.* 1117a
Louise M., *Camb.* 1607b
P. G., *Lond.S.Bank* 1828c
Stephanie K., *Hull* 1696b
Susanne, *Melb.* 111c
Haywood-Farmer, J. S., *W.Ont.* 539a
Hayworth, Roger, *Portsmouth* 1898c
Hazar Bebe bte Mohd Ismail, *Malaya* 1011c
Hazari, S. K. S., *Chitt.* 228b
Hazarika, G. C., *Dib.* 729a, 729c
Indra M., *Gauh.* 746a
M., *Dib.* 728c
Niru, *Gauh.* 746c
P., *Manipal* 847b
Padmolochan, *Gauh.* 744b, 745b
Prasanna, *Dib.* 729b
Rani K., *Gauh.* 745a
Hazell, Paul J., *Cran.* 1630c
Rebecca, *W.Syd.* 205a
Hazelton, M. L., *Massey* 1098c
Michael J., *Newcastle(NSW)* 144b
Hazimah Abdul Hamid, *Tech.U.Malaysia* 1034b
Hazita Azman, *NU Malaysia* 1017b
Hazizan Md Noon, *IIU Malaysia* 998b, 1002c
Hazledine, Tim, *Auck.* 1069a
Hazlehurst, Frances A., *Camb.* 1611b
S. E., *Witw.* 1412a
Hazlett, C. B., *Chinese HK* 2025b
Diane, *Ulster* 1960c
Mark, *New Br.* 435c
Rev. William I., *Glas.* 1668c
Hazlina Hamdan, *Putra* 1023a
Hazon, N., *St And.* 1913c
Hazra, C. R., *IGKVV* 784
P. K., *Delhi* 722c
R., *IIT Bombay* 779a
Swapan, *VB* 951b
Hazrani Awang Basri, *IIU Malaysia* 998b
He, Beiping, *NU Singapore* 1316a
F., *Alta.* 309b
G. W., *Chinese HK* 2027b
J., *Chinese HK* 2023b
J., *NU Singapore* 1309b
Jie, *Nan.Tech.* 1295b
Li, *Durh.* 1634c
Qinglin, *Newcastle(NSW)* 142b
Quming, *Dal.* 352a
Shiusheng, *Aberd.* 1536a
Y., *NU Singapore* 1305c
Yaping, *W.Syd.* 202b
Head, Allen, *Qu.* 453a
D., *Nott.* 1853a
D. W., *Plym.* 1892b
Dianne, *Auck.* 1079c
Judith, *Cape Town* 1338a
Katie M., *Nott.Trent* 1863c
Lesley M., *W'gong.* 207b
Lyndsay F., *Cant.* 1088a
Martin, *Brock* 321a
Michael, *W.Syd.* 203c
Rob, *Liv.* 1763c
Headington, Rita, *Greenwich* 1676b
Headley, Bernard, *WI* 1996c
Betty, *Bond* 40a
Greig, *Leeds Met.* 1743c
P. M., *Brist.* 1590a
Headrick, John P., *Griff.* 72b, 74b
Heady, C., *Bath* 1550c
Heal, Ann, *Portsmouth* 1901c
Barbara J., *Camb.* 1606a
Brian W., *Portsmouth* 1899c
David J., *Bath* 1552c
Kate, *Edin.* 1645c
Matthew R., *Edin.* 1645c
O. W., *Edin.* 1647a
Heald, D. E. A., *Sheff.* 1925a
G. R., *Witw.* 1411c
S., *Manit.* 394b
Heale, E. M., *Reading* 1907c
Healey, Antonette D. P., *Tor.* 493b, 509c
D., *Swansea* 1956c
David L., *Otago* 1104c
John R., *Wales* 1546c
Johnathan J., *Keele* 1709b
Michael, *Lincoln(UK)* 1752b
Nigel, *Cant.* 1085, 1086a
Richard G., *Portsmouth* 1901a
Suzanne M., *Greenwich* 1677c
Terry, *R.Gordon* 1911c
Healy, A., *Qld.UT* 149b
Christopher, *Melb.* 96a
D. T., *Cardiff* 1620b
Dana, *Lond.* 1816b
David L., *Monash* 122b
E., *Nott.* 1857a
E., *S'ton.* 1939b
Linda, *C'dia.* 348b
P. J., *Swinburne UT* 162a
Patrick, *McG.* 372a
Paul, *NE* 137b
Paul, *Trent* 513b
Peter C., *Griff.* 70a
Sarah, *Monash* 121b
Sue, *Edin.* 1645b
T. R., *Waik.* 1120c
Thomas F., *Lond.* 1777c
Thomas W., *Melb.* 96c
Zara, *Lincoln(UK)* 1753b
Heaman, Elsbeth Anne, *McG.* 371b
L. M., *Alta.* 304b
Heames, Ruth, *Coventry* 1627c
Hean, Sarah, *Bourne.* 1581b
Heaney, George, *Ulster* 1960b
Harry, *Lough.* 1831a
John W., *S.Fraser* 482b
Liam, *Belf.* 1562b
Heap, A. R., *Manc.Met.* 1839c
D., *W.Ont.* 542b
James, *Brock* 319b, 321b
Nick W., *Open(UK)* 1868b
Ruby, *Ott.* 442b
Heapy, Nelson, *W.Ont.* 554c
Heard, Alan, *W.Ont.* 544c
Andrew, *S.Fraser* 486a
C. D., *Wales* 1970a
Dwayne E., *Leeds* 1727c
Robert C., *Syd.* 166b, 167a
Stephen, *New Br.* 429b
Hearing, Trevor, *Bourne.* 1579c
Hearle, D., *Cardiff* 1617c
Hearn, Donald, *Camb.* 1609c
G. E., *S'ton.* 1935a
G. N., *Qld.UT* 152c
J., *Nott.Trent* 1862b, 1863a
Jeff, *Hudd.* 1692a
John P., *Syd.* 164, 177c
Jonathan S., *Edin.* 1650b
Milton T. W., *Monash* 114c, 125c
Hearne, G. R., *Witw.* 1414b
W., *Greenwich* 1675c
Hearnshaw, John B., *Cant.* 1092a
Hearty, Paul, *Ryerson* 466b
Heasell, S. L., *Nott.Trent* 1863c
Heaslett, Anne, *Belf.* 1565c
Heaslip, Vanessa, *Bourne.* 1579c
Heasman, Fraser, *Herts.* 1685c
Heath, A. W., *Sheff.* 1928b
Anne-Louise M., *Otago* 1105c
Anthony F., *Oxf.* 1878c
Bernadette, *Portsmouth* 1903a
Christian, *Lond.* 1794a
Ernie T., *Pret.* 1381a
Glyn, *Salf.* 1919b
Gregory P., *Brist.* 1588b
H. F., *Brist.* 1588b
J., *Massey* 1100c
J. K., *Birm.* 1566c
Joan, *Melb.* 107a
Joseph, *Tor.* 498b
Malcolm F., *Leeds* 1727c
Margaret, *E.Lond.* 1642b
Michele, *Tor.* 490c
Nancy L., *McG.* 370a
Natalie, *Northumbria* 1849b
P. R., *Nfld.* 404c
Richard, *Lough.* 1834b
S. J., *S'ton.* 1938b
Stephen, *Salf.* 1919b
Stephen C., *Camb.* 1603a
T. P., *Nott.* 1851b
Terry, *Syd.* 165b
V. A., *Plym.* 1888b
Heath-Brown, D. Roger, *Oxf.* 1876c
Heath-Davies, Rachel, *Cardiff* 1623a
Heathcote, Adrian B., *Syd.* 173b
Andrew J., *Newcastle(NSW)* 144c
David, *Bourne.* 1580a
Elizabeth, *Tor.* 505c
J. Godfrey, *Dal.* 357c
John, *Leeds Met.* 1741a
Krysta, *Jo'burg.* 1345c
Z., *S'ton.* 1940a
Heather, Ken F., *Portsmouth* 1900a
Heatherbell, David A., *Lincoln(NZ)* 1094b
Heatley, Richard V., *Leeds* 1736b
Susan, *Kingston(UK)* 1719b
Heatlie, D. J., *Witw.* 1411c
Heaton, A. J., *Wales* 1549b
C. Alan, *Liv.J.Moores* 1766b
D., *Manc.Met.* 1838c
Garry W., *Otago* 1103c
James, *Lond.* 1783b
Margaret, *Hudd.* 1693a
Norma, *Ulster* 1960c
Pam, *Lond.* 1782b
Sharyn, *Auck.* 1069c
Heaven, Patrick, *W'gong.* 210a
Heavens, Alan F., *Edin.* 1650a
Hebb, Gregory M., *Dal.* 350b, 359b
Hebbar, Harischandra, *Manipal* 849b, 853a
P. S., *Rashtriya SV* 899b
Shripad S., *Manipal* 848a
Hebbditch, N., *Nott.Trent* 1863b
Hebbes, Tim, *Portsmouth* 1899a
Hebdon, Robert, *McG.* 372b
Hebenstreit, Sally, *Adel.* 31c
Heberstein, Marie E., *Macq.* 87b
Hébert, Alain, *Montr.* 422b
Jean, *Montr.* 418b
Louis, *Montr.* 424a
Marie-Josée, *Montr.* 417a
Paul, *Ott.* 445a, 446c
Richard L., *Ott.* 444b
Sylvie, *Montr.* 418c
Hebert, Terence E., *McG.* 378a
Hébert, Y. M., *Calg.* 325c

Hentschel, C. E., *N-W(S.Af.)* 1368b
Henwood, Karen, *Cardiff* 1622b
Murray J., *Syd.* 167b
Henz, M., *NU Singapore* 1307a
Henzi, S. Peter, *Leth.* 365c
Heon, Elise, *Tor.* 506c
Hepburn, Alexa, *Lough.* 1834c
H. R., *Rhodes* 1390c
J. W., *Wat.* 535c
Mary, *Glas.* 1670b
S., *Trent* 513b
William A., *McG.* 371a
Heppell, Steven, *Bourne.* 1581a
T., *Nott.Trent* 1866a
Hepper, P. G., *Belf.* 1561b
Hepple, M., *Sheff.* 1922b
R. T., *Calg.* 328a, 333c
Heppler, G. R., *Wat.* 528b, 528c
Heppner, Robin D., *Alta.* 313c
Heptinstall, J., *Coventry* 1627c
S., *Nott.* 1857b
Tina, *Greenwich* 1677a
Hepworth, Frances A., *Manc.Met.* 1841b
G., *Curtin* 57c
Graham, *Melb.* 100b
Linda, *Leeds Met.* 1740b
Mark, *Lond.* 1777c
Mark, *Lough.* 1833c
S., *Car.* 336b
Sylvia, *Hudd.* 1693a
Heracleous, L., *Warw.* 1977a
Herat, Sunil, *Griff.* 70c
Herath, Chandra, *Monash* 123b
G. B. B., *Peradeniya* 1453b
H. M. A., *Sri Jay.* 1463c
H. M. A., *Wayamba* 1467b
H. M. C., *Peradeniya* 1454c
H. M. D. R., *Peradeniya* 1455a
H. M. R. P., *Kelaniya* 1445c
H. M. S., *Colombo* 1437b
H. M. T. D. K., *Peradeniya* 1455c
H. M. T. N. R., *Sri Jay.* 1463a
H. M. Y. V. K., *B&P SLanka* 1435a
Hemantha, *Brock* 320a
I. H. M. N. N., *Kotelawala Defence* 1448c
K. R. B., *Peradeniya* 1453b
P. K., *Peradeniya* 1451c
R., *Peradeniya* 1453c
S. M. K., *Colombo* 1438b
Heravi, Saeed, *Cardiff* 1615b
Herberg, Paula, *Aga Khan(P'stan.)* 1231c
Herbert, Carol P., *W.Ont.* 538a, 548c
Karl E., *Leic.* 1746b
M., *St And.* 1914c
Richard D., *Newcastle(NSW)* 141c
Robert, *Worcester* 1984b
Robert D., *Syd.* 174a
Herbinger, C., *Dal.* 353c
C. M., *Dal.* 350b
Herbison, Allan E., *Otago* 1110b
Herborn, Peter J., *W.Syd.* 202a
Herbst, A. G., *N-W(S.Af.)* 1370a
Anri, *Cape Town* 1337b
Ben M., *Stell.* 1396a
Frederick, *Jo'burg.* 1348a
Frikkie J., *Stell.* 1393b
G., *Fort Hare* 1343c
R. O., *Nelson Mandela Met.* 1363b
Theo, *Stell.* 1396b
Herbut, I., *S.Fraser* 485c
Herchandani, Pardeep K., *Mehran* 1257b
Hercz, Gavril, *Tor.* 505c
Herd, David, *Kent* 1714b, 1716b
Ian R., *Camb.* 1610c
Herda, Phyllis, *Auck.* 1067a
Herdman, Chris M., *Car.* 336c, 340c
Hergt, Janet M., *Melb.* 96a
Herhoffer, B. L., *Manc.Met.* 1840c
Herholdt, A. D., *Nelson Mandela Met.* 1360c
Herington, Adrian C., *Qld.UT* 151a
Carmel A., *Griff.* 72b
Heristchi, C., *Plym.* 1892c
Heritage, George, *Salf.* 1919b
John, *Leeds* 1727a
Herle, Anita C., *Camb.* 1599c
Ramadev, *Manipal* 852a
Herlekar, S. S., *Karn.* 812a
Herman, Andrew, *W.Laur.* 557c
C., *Pret.* 1375c
C. Peter, *Tor.* 500a
Carl, *Cape Town* 1341c
Didi, *Kent* 1715a
Donna, *Alta.* 313b
Harold D., *W.Cape* 1407a
Mike J., *Herts.* 1686c
Pam, *Monash* 128c
Peter R., *Tor.* 502b
R. J., *Calg.* 332a
Ruth, *Herts.* 1687a
Vimala V., *Nott.* 1853a
Hermann, D. J., *Swansea* 1957b
Hermanutz, L., *Nfld.* 401b, 408a
Hermo, Louis, *McG.* 374b
Hern, T., *W.Ont.* 553b
Hernández, Francisco J., *Car.* 337a, 338c
Hernandez, J. A., *Ryerson* 464b, 466a
Lennox, *Guy.* 593a
Paul, *Dal.* 356c
Hernandez Fuentes, Maria, *Lond.* 1795b
Hernandez-Martin, L., *Lond.* 1802c
Hernandez-Saenz, Luz M., *W.Ont.* 542c
Herndon, Mark, *Macq.* 92b
Hero, Jean-Marc, *Griff.* 71a
Herodotou, Maria, *La Trobe* 80b
Heron, Alastair, *Melb.* 103a
Angela, *WI* 1991a
B. Mark, *Leeds* 1727c
Gordon, *G.Caledonian* 1674a
Judith, *Melb.* 111c
Peter, *Auck.* 1078b
Heroux, Paul, *McG.* 375a
Herr, Richard A., *Tas.* 180a
Herremans, I. M., *Calg.* 324b
Herrera, David, *Malta* 1047b
Herrero, C., *Manc.Met.* 1840c
Herrick, I. A., *W.Ont.* 547c
Herrin, J. E., *Lond.* 1789c
Herring, E., *Brist.* 1588c
Rodney A., *Vic.(BC)* 518c
Herrington, Jan, *W'gong.* 207c
Muriel B., *C'dia.* 343a
Neil, *E.Lond.* 1642c
Paul, *Wales* 1967c
Tony, *W'gong.* 207c
Herrman, Helen E., *Melb.* 107c
Herrmann, F.-G., *Swansea* 1955b
Randy, *Manit.* 389c
Herron, Rebecca, *Lincoln(UK)* 1752b
Tom, *Leeds Met.* 1741a
Herrtage, Michael E., *Camb.* 1607c, 1612a
Herry, Yves, *Ott.* 441c
Herscovics, Annette, *McG.* 374c, 375c
Herscovitch, Daniel, *Syd.* 172c
Hersh, Marion, *Glas.* 1665b
Hershberg, E., *S.Fraser* 485a, 486a
Hershfield, E. S., *Manit.* 395b, 396b
N. B., *Calg.* 332a
Herson, John D., *Liv.J.Moores* 1766c
Herst, Patricia M., *Otago* 1107c
Hertel, Kristina, *E.Lond.* 1642a
Hertz, Alain, *Montr.* 422b
P. B., *Sask.* 474a
Hertzler, Gregory L., *W.Aust.* 191b
Hertzog, Paul J., *Monash* 127a
Hervey, T. K., *Nott.* 1854a
Herwig, H. H., *Calg.* 327c
Heryanto, Ariel, *Melb.* 95b
Herz, Judith S., *C'dia.* 345a
Herzberg, Abe, *Monash* 114c
Agnes, *Qu.* 456a
G. R., *Nfld.* 401a
Rolf-Dietmar, *Liv.* 1758b
Herzberger, Hans G., *Tor.* 498b
Herzig, Edmund, *Oxf.* 1877b
Herzog, W., *Calg.* 326c, 328a
Herzyk, Pawel, *Glas.* 1663b
Heseltine, Richard G., *Hull* 1695, 1699c, 1700a
Hesk, J., *St And.* 1914a
Hesketh, J., *KwaZulu-Natal* 1356c
T. R., *Camb.* 1600a
Heslop, James D., *Massey* 1096b
Joanne, *Leeds Met.* 1744c
Joe, *Lincoln(UK)* 1753b
Karl, *W.Cape* 1407c
Louise A., *Car.* 336b
T. A., *E.Anglia* 1641a
Heslop-Harrison, J. S. (Pat), *Leic.* 1746a
Hesp, S., *Qu.* 452c
Hess, G. C., *Alta.* 305a
G. H., *W.Ont.* 544a
John, *W.Ont.* 544b
Michael, *Tas.* 181c, 182c
Ortwin, *Sur.* 1952b
Peter, *Tor.* 498b
Robert F., *McG.* 377b, 383b
Tim M., *Cran.* 1629b
Hessami, Mir-Akbar, *Monash* 116c
Hesse, I. F. A., *Ghana* 585a
Paul P., *Macq.* 89a
Hesselbo, Stephen P., *Oxf.* 1874b
Hesseling, Pieter B., *Stell.* 1399a
Hesseln, H. F., *Sask.* 472a, 478c
Hesson, I., *Nfld.* 404a
Hestekin, K., *Nfld.* 405a
Hester, David A., *Adel.* 27a
M., *Brist.* 1588b
Stephen, *Wales* 1547c
Hesterman, Dianne C., *W.Aust.* 194a, 198a
Heth, D. C., *Alta.* 309a
Hetherington, A. M., *Brist.* 1584a
Janice I., *Cran.* 1630c
John G., *Cran.* 1630c
Kevin, *Open(UK)* 1869c
Marion, *G.Caledonian* 1673c
Hett, Geoffrey G., *Vic.(BC)* 518b
Hettiarachchi, *IIT S.Lanka* 1466c
Hettiarachchi, G. H. C. Madhu, *Colombo* 1436b
M., *Kelaniya* 1446c
N. F., *Peradeniya* 1454c
P., *Sri Jay.* 1464c
P. L., *Sri Jay.* 1462b
R., *Peradeniya* 1454b
S., *Ruhuna* 1458b
S. R., *Open S.Lanka* 1449b
U., *Kelaniya* 1444b
Hettiarachchy, Tilak, *Colombo* 1438b
Hettiaratchi, J. P. A., *Calg.* 326a
K., *Greenwich* 1676c
Hettiarchchi, L. M., *Ruhuna* 1460b
Hettiarichchi, M. P., *Ruhuna* 1458c
Hettige, Anula M., *Colombo* 1438b
S. T., *Colombo* 1438b
U., *Kelaniya* 1443c
Hettihewa, Samanthala, *W.Syd.* 202c
Hettirachchi, J. N., *Sri Jay.* 1463a
Hétu, Jean, *Montr.* 413c
Heuer, Cord, *Massey* 1101a
Norbert, *Brun.* 1595b
Heughan, C., *Nfld.* 408a
Heukaufer, Margaretha, *St Mary's(Can.)* 469b
Heuman, Gad J., *Warw.* 1974b, 1978b
Heun, Richard, *Birm.* 1574c
Heunis, A. J., *Wat.* 527c, 534b
D., *Rhodes* 1390a
Heuser, D. G. B., *Reading* 1909b
Heuzey, Marie-Claude, *Montr.* 422b
Hevi-Yiboe, L., *Ghana* 581c
Hew, C. L., *NU Singapore* 1305c
Hewabowala, E. M. J., *Kelaniya* 1444b
Hewagamage, Champa, *Sri Jay.* 1463b
K. P., *Colombo* 1439c
Hewage, N. W., *Colombo* 1440c
P., *Ruhuna* 1459a, 1460c
Sujatha, *Colombo* 1436b
T. U., *Colombo* 1437c
U. C. L., *Sri Jay.* 1464b
Hewageegana, P. S., *Kelaniya* 1446a
Hewak, D., *S'ton.* 1937b
Hewamanna, Rohini, *Colombo* 1437c
Hewamanne, Sandya K., *Colombo* 1438b
Hewapathirana, I. S., *Peradeniya* 1455c
T. K., *Kelaniya* 1446c
Hewavithanagamage, U. R., *Kelaniya* 1444c
Hewawasam, Lakshman J., *IIT S.Lanka* 1465, 1466a
Hewawisenthi, S. J. de S., *Kelaniya* 1446a
Hewawitharana, P. B., *Peradeniya* 1456a
Hewer, Paul, *Strath.* 1947a
Hewett, Errol W., *Massey* 1097c
Paul C., *Camb.* 1599c
Hewgill, Denton E., *Vic.(BC)* 520b
Hewings, Ann, *Open(UK)* 1869b
M. J., *Birm.* 1575c
Martin, *Birm.* 1570b
Hewison, A., *Birm.* 1569b
Frances M., *Liv.* 1763c
Jenny, *Leeds* 1735a, 1737a
Hewitson, Bruce C., *Cape Town* 1335b
Hewitt, Alan, *Portsmouth* 1900b
Allan, *Strath.* 1945a
B. George, *Lond.* 1816a
C. G., *Wat.* 531b
C. J., *Birm.* 1568b
C. Nicholas, *Lanc.* 1722c
Carol M., *Strath.* 1945c
Chad, *Tas.* 181c
Chris, *Lough.* 1831c
D. P., *Birm.* 1567c
D. S., *Aberd.* 1536b
Gerald, *Auck.UT* 1082b
Hermi H., *WI* 1996b
I., *Nott.Trent* 1864b
J., *Manc.Met.* 1838b, 1841c
J. E., *Nott.* 1856b, 1859b
James, *Tor.* 504b
Jill A., *Herts.* 1684b
K. C., *Dal.* 354b
Kenneth, *W.Laur.* 560a
Lia, *Jo'burg.* 1348c
Neil J., *Ulster* 1960b
Nicholas, *Nott.* 1854b, 1860a
Robert E., *NU Singapore* 1317b
Roger L., *Lond.* 1783a
Ted, *W.Ont.* 537, 546a
V. M., *Brist.* 1588c
Hewitt-Dundas, N., *Belf.* 1560a
Hewlett, N. P., *Warw.* 1974b
Hewson, Alan, *Newcastle(NSW)* 145b
Daphne M., *Macq.* 90c
J., *Nfld.* 404c
Peter, *Hudd.* 1692b
Hexel, Rene, *Griff.* 71c
Hexham, I. R., *Calg.* 329b
Hey, John D., *KwaZulu-Natal* 1354a
M. H., *W.Ont.* 540c
M. J., *Nott.* 1851b
Tony J. G., *S'ton.* 1934b
Heycock, Caroline, *Edin.* 1649c
Mary, *Leeds Met.* 1740b
Heyd, D. V., *Ryerson* 463a
Heydenrych, Mike D., *Pret.* 1376b
Heyderman, Robert S., *Brist.* 1589b
Heyer, Paul, *W.Laur.* 557c
Heyes, Andrew L., *ICL* 1703b
Anthony, *Lond.* 1808a
C. J., *Alta.* 308b
David M., *Sur.* 1950b
Mary J., *Herts.* 1687b
Heyl, Jeff E., *Lincoln(NZ)* 1094a
Heyland, D. K., *Qu.* 458c
Heylings, David, *E.Anglia* 1640b
Heyman, R. D., *Calg.* 325c
Heymann, Gerhard, *Pret.* 1376b
Heyns, Chris F., *Stell.* 1400a
Christoffel H., *Pret.* 1373b
M. F., *N-W(S.Af.)* 1369b
Philippus S., *Pret.* 1377a
Heys, H. M., *Nfld.* 403a
Heystek, Marthinus J., *Pret.* 1382b
Heyward, Paul, *Auck.* 1070a
Heywood, Brigid, *Open(UK)* 1867
C. M., *Nott.* 1853b
Charles A., *Durh.* 1636c
D. S., *Manc.Met.* 1838c
Ian, *Leeds Met.* 1740b
J. C., *Qu.* 452a
K. J., *E.Anglia* 1639b
M., *Dal.* 351a
M. S., *Manit.* 396c
P., *Qld.UT* 152b
P. M., *Nott.* 1850b, 1855c
Paul, *Malta* 1047a
Philip L., *Leeds* 1735a
Heyworth, H. Lee, *Leeds Met.* 1743a
Jane S., *W.Aust.* 197a
Hezser, Catherine, *Lond.* 1816b
Hiader, Fouzia, *Karachi* 1252a
Hibathul Careem, M. F., *SE(S.Lanka)* 1461, 1461c
Hibberd, Julian, *Camb.* 1607a
R. B., *Nott.Trent* 1863a
S., *Nott.* 1854b
Hibbert, Alan, *Belf.* 1560a
Liesel, *W.Cape* 1407a
S. A., *Nott.* 1855a
Hibbins, Ray T., *Griff.* 73c
Hibbits, Pat M., *S.Fraser* 481, 488a
Hibble, S. J., *Reading* 1907a
Hibbs, M., *Lond.S.Bank* 1827a
Margaret, *Melb.* 107a
Hick, Steven, *Car.* 341a
V., *Manc.Met.* 1837b
Hicken, Robert J., *Exe.* 1657c
Hickey, Bryan J., *Leeds* 1733c
D., *C'dia.* 343a
Don, *Alta.* 302
E., *Dal.* 353a
Ivor G., *Belf.* 1564c
Martha, *W.Aust.* 197c
Philip, *C.Darwin* 48b
Hickford, Jonathan G. H., *Lincoln(NZ)* 1094a
Hickin, Edward J., *S.Fraser* 484c
Hicking, P., *Nott.Trent* 1864b
Hickling, Frederick W., *WI* 1994b
Keith, *Hudd.* 1692a
Marcia, *E.Lond.* 1643c
Hickman, C. L., *Plym.* 1888b
Jon, *Vic.(Aust.)* 184
M., *Alta.* 312c
M., *Brist.* 1591b
Mark S., *Cant.* 1091a
Mary J., *Lond.Met.* 1825a, 1825b
Miranda, *McG.* 371a
Richard D., *Camb.* 1602a
S. P., *Greenwich* 1675c
Hicks, Anna, *Middx.* 1843c
B. J., *Waik.* 1120b, 1124c
C. M., *Birm.* 1569b
F. E., *Alta.* 305b
G., *Manit.* 395a
Helen C., *Manc.Met.* 1838a
James R., *Portsmouth* 1898b
Jarra, *Newcastle(NSW)* 147b
John, *C.Sturt* 50b, 53c
Keith, *W.England* 1891c
Kelvin, *Auck.UT* 1081b
Neville D., *Adel.* 29a
Peter, *Portsmouth* 1900c
R. B., *Calg.* 329a
Richard, *Bond* 40a
Robin G., *Vic.(BC)* 517b
Rodney, *Melb.* 104c
S., *Nfld.* 400c
Sally, *Wales* 1966c
Stephen, *Salf.* 1918b
Stephen, *Wolv.* 1983c
Hickson, C., *Belf.* 1559c
Hicock, S. R., *W.Ont.* 540a
Hidajat, K., *NU Singapore* 1308a
Hidalgo, A., *Birm.* 1566c
F. J., *Lond.* 1799c
Hide, Colin P., *Leic.* 1751c
G., *Salf.* 1919b
K. M., *Plym.* 1891c
P., *Alta.* 303b
Winston, *W.Cape* 1410a
Hider, Philip M., *C.Sturt* 51c
Philip N., *Otago* 1107b, 1109b
Robert C., *Lond.* 1788b
Hides, D. S., *Coventry* 1625b
Hidi, Suzanne E., *Tor.* 503c
Hieatt, A. K., *W.Ont.* 541c
C. B., *W.Ont.* 541c
Hiebert, B. A., *Calg.* 325c
J., *Qu.* 457a
L. M., *Sask.* 478b
Hiebert-Murphy, D., *Manit.* 394a
Hierons, Robert, *Brun.* 1595a, 1597a
Hiesley, Erin, *W'gong.* 211c
Hift, Richard J., *Cape Town* 1339c
Higashitani, Ko, *Leeds* 1730a
Higate, P. R., *Brist.* 1588c
Higginbotham, H. Nicholas, *Newcastle(NSW)* 144a
Higginbottom, G., *Sheff.* 1929a
Higgins, Andrew J., *McG.* 370b
Anne, *S.Fraser* 484b
B. J., *Birm.* 1577a
Bernard, *Portsmouth* 1901c

Ingbian, E. K., *Makurdi Ag.* 1143c
Inger, Simon, *Bath* 1556c
Ingersoll, S., *Nfld.* 403c
Inggs, J. A., *Witw.* 1414a
Michael R., *Cape Town* 1335a
Stephen C., *Cape Town* 1335c, 1341b
Ingham, Barbara M., *Salf.* 1920a
Bruce, *Lond.* 1815c, 1816a
Cali A., *Edin.* 1653a
Derek B., *Leeds* 1732b
Eileen, *Leeds* 1727a
Geoffrey K., *Camb.* 1607b
Hilary, *Lanc.* 1722b
Jason M., *Auck.* 1070b
John, *Tor.* 495b
Malcolm R., *Well.* 1114a, 1114c
P. W., *Sheff.* 1927b, 1930a
Patrick, *Leeds Met.* 1742c
Roger, *S'ton.* 1937c
Stephen, *W'gong.* 209c
Inginshetty, Sujatha S., *Gulb.* 755a
Ingle, Alan, *E.Lond.* 1641, 1643c
S., *Stir.* 1943a
V. V., *Dr BAT* 735a
Ingledew, David K., *Wales* 1547c
W. J., *St And.* 1913c, 1916b
Inglehearn, Christopher, *Leeds* 1736b
Ingles, C. James, *Tor.* 505b
Ernest B., *Alta.* 313b
Inglesfield, Robert, *Lond.* 1777c
Ingleton, C., *Sheff.* 1929a
Ingley, Carol, *Auck.UT* 1083a
Inglis, Alison, *Melb.* 96a
Alistair, *Vic.(Aust.)* 189c
Andy, *Lond.Met.* 1824c
Barry, *La Trobe* 85a
Caroline, *Aberd.* 1538b
D., *Aberd.* 1537a
Debra L., *Brock* 320a
Lesley, *Massey* 1097a
M., *Ryerson* 462c
Tom A., *H-W* 1682b
Ingo Singh, S., *Manip.* 855b
Ingold, T., *Aberd.* 1537a
Ingolfsson, A., *Alta.* 306b
Ingram, A. J., *Witw.* 1413a
C. D., *Newcastle(UK)* 1847a, 1847b
D. W., *Nfld.* 407b
David, *Edin.* 1646c
David M., *Camb.* 1611a
E. L., *Alta.* 303b
Gabrielle, *Griff.* 75b
George A., *Salf.* 1919b
H., *Pret.* 1381c
N., *C'dia.* 343a
Norman, *C'dia.* 345c
Peter, *Plym.* 1897b, 1897c
Peter, *Sur.* 1950c
T., *Nott.Trent* 1866c
Ingrouille, Martin, *Lond.* 1776b
Ings, Welby, *Auck.UT* 1081a
Iniama, E. B., *Calabar* 1162a, 1162c
Iniewski, K., *Alta.* 305c
Ininda, J. M., *Nair.* 973b
Init a/p Ithoi, *Malaya* 1010c
Injendi, Moses M., *CUE Af.* 962, 963a
Inko-Tariah, M. B., *Rivers SUST* 1211c
Inkpen, Robert, *Portsmouth* 1901a
Inkson, B. J., *Sheff.* 1923b
John C., *Exe.* 1658a
Inman, Dave, *Lond.S.Bank* 1828a
Robert D., *Tor.* 506a
Sally, *Lond.S.Bank* 1827b
Inmozhi Sivagama Sundari, R., *Annam.* 679a
Innes, A., *Stir.* 1941b
D., *Nfld.* 401b
Eveline J., *Syd.* 173a
John F., *Liv.* 1761c
Kerry, *Syd.* 175a
Lyn, *Kent* 1716a
Martin, *Cardiff* 1622b
Martin, *Sur.* 1952c
Matthew, *Lond.* 1778a
Mike, *Adel.* 24b
Peter, *Sunshine Coast* 159c
Innes-Brown, M., *Curtin* 57a
Innis, Brian, *W.Syd.* 204a
Matthew, *Lond.* 1776b
Innocent, Troy, *Monash* 120a
Inoka, V. D. B., *P.Harcourt* 1208b
Inoti, Isaac K., *Jomo K.* 966a
Insall, R. H., *Birm.* 1566c
Insull, J., *E.Lond.* 1642a
Intriligator, J., *Wales* 1547c
Introna, Lucas D., *Lanc.* 1723c
Inwood, Brad C., *Tor.* 491b
G., *Ryerson* 465b
Inya-Abam, Eteng, *Ebonyi State* 1166b
Inyang, C. U., *Uyo* 1216a
Domingo D., *Calabar* 1160b
I. B., *Uyo* 1215c
I. J., *Uyo* 1214b
J. D., *Uyo* 1216c
N. E. U., *Uyo* 1216b
O. E., *Uyo* 1217a
U. E., *Uyo* 1215b
Inyang-Abia, M. E., *Calabar* 1161c
Inyiama, Hyacinth C., *Ebonyi State* 1164b
Ioannidis, Christos, *Bath* 1552a
M., *Wat.* 526b, 527a
Ioannidou-Koutselini, Mary, *Cyprus* 563c
Ioannou, Constantinos, *E.Lond.* 1642c
Yiannis, *Cyprus* 564b
Ion, R., *Abertay* 1539a
William J., *Strath.* 1945b
Ionescu, Dan, *Ott.* 442b
Dorina, *Jo'burg.* 1347a
Ioppolo, G. J., *Reading* 1907c
Ioratim-Uba, G. A., *Jos* 1180b
Iordanova, D., *St And.* 1915c, 1916c
Iorns, Catherine, *Well.* 1116a
Iossa, Elisabetta, *Brun.* 1594a
Iovenitti, P., *Swinburne UT* 163a
Iovita, A., *C'dia.* 346b
Ip, Manying, *Auck.* 1067c
Margaret, *Chinese HK* 2026b
Mary S. M., *HK* 2034a, 2036b
Y. K., *NU Singapore* 1305c
Y. K., *Open HK* 2037c
Iphofen, R., *Wales* 1546c
Ipinjolu, J. K., *Yola* 1170c
Ipinmoroti, Kolade O., *Akure* 1167, 1168a
Ipperciel, D. B., *Alta.* 309c
Ipson, Nila M., *Dal.* 352c
Iqbal, A., *Azad J&K* 1238a
A., *St And.* 1914a
Brig. (Retd.) Amjad, *Foundation(P'stan.)* 1244c
Anila, *Inst.Bus.Man.(P'stan.)* 1248c
Asif, *Inst.Bus.Man.(P'stan.)* 1248a
B. M., *Chitt.* 228a
Bilal, *Aga Khan(P'stan.)* 1230c
Ch. Muhammad, *Arid Ag.* 1236a
Farah, *Karachi* 1252c
Hussain, *Islamia, Bahawal.* 1250b
J., *Azad J&K* 1238b
J., *Lahore UET* 1241a, 1241b
Javaid, *NUST(P'stan.)* 1264a
Javed, *N-WFP Eng.* 1266b
Javed, *Sir Syed UET* 1277c
M., *Azad J&K* 1237a
M., *Lahore UET* 1241b
M. Ashraf, *Lahore MS* 1255c
M. M., *Lahore UET* 1241b
M. R., *Jahang.* 246c
M. S., *Rajsh.* 252c
M. T., *Nfld.* 403a
M. T., *Rajsh.* 254a
M. Zafar, *B'desh.Ag.* 221b
M. Zafar, *Karachi* 1251a
Maryam, *Bhutto IST* 1272b
Mohammad Perwaiz, *Aga Khan(P'stan.)* 1230b
Mohd., *JMI* 794a
Muhammad, *J.Hamdard* 791a
Muhammad, *NUST(P'stan.)* 1263c, 1265a, 1265b
Muhammad J., *Karachi* 1252a
Muhammad Naveed, *NUST(P'stan.)* 1265b
Mussarat, *Karachi* 1253a
Najeeb, *NUST(P'stan.)* 1264c
R. M., *Islamia, Bahawal.* 1249c
Raja, *NUST(P'stan.)* 1265b
S. A., *NED Eng.* 1261b
S. M., *And.* 670b
S. M., *NED Eng.* 1261b
S. S., *Open S.Lanka* 1449c
Salim, *Ghulam IKIST* 1246c
Shahzada, *NUST(P'stan.)* 1263b
Tauseef, *NUST(P'stan.)* 1264a
Waseem, *Riphah Internat.* 1271a
Yasir, *Arid Ag.* 1235b
Z., *Azad J&K* 1238c
Zafar, *Karachi* 1253b
Iqbal Ahmed, K. R., *Maulana Azad Natnl.Urdu* 858, 858c
Ir Shaffei Mohamed, *IIU Malaysia* 1003c
Irabanta Singh, N., *Manip.* 854b
Irabor, D. O., *Ib.* 1177b
Iralu, T., *I.Gandhi Nat.Open* 787c
Irandu, E. N., *Nair.* 975c
Irani, Zahir, *Brun.* 1593b, 1594a
Iranloye, T. A., *Jos* 1181b
Iraqi, Khalid M., *Karachi* 1253a
Iravani, Mohammed R., *Tor.* 502b
Ircha, Michael C., *New Br.* 430c
Irchhaiya, Raghuveer, *Bundel.* 713b
Iredale, Ian D., *W.Syd.* 203c
John, *Edin.* 1651a
John P. I., *S'ton.* 1938c
Irefin, D., *Maid.* 1191a
Ireland, A., *H-W* 1681a
David G., *Glas.* 1667c
J. D., *Cape Town* 1339b
Malcolm, *Newcastle(NSW)* 144b
Norman J., *Warw.* 1972c
Paddy W., *Kent* 1715a
Peter, *Salf.* 1920c
Peter T., *Oxf.* 1875a
Richard W., *Wales* 1541c
Robert J., *Mt.All.* 426b
Stanley, *Warw.* 1972b
Irele, J. O., *Ib.* 1175b
Iremiren, Gerald O., *Benin* 1153b
Iremonger, Michael J., *Cran.* 1630c
Irene Singh, S., *Manip.* 854b
Irene Tan Kit Ping, *Malaya* 1005b
Ireson, Gren, *Lough.* 1831b, 1835c
Ireton, E., *Nott.Trent* 1866a
Irfan, Arain N., *Mehran* 1257b
Ghazala, *Lahore MS* 1256a
M., *Lahore UET* 1241c
Seema, *Aga Khan(P'stan.)* 1232b
Syed M., *NED Eng.* 1261b
Irfan Abd Al Hameed Fattah, *IIU Malaysia* 1003a
Irfan Anjum Magami, *Malaya* 1007a
Irfan Mufti, M. A. A., *N-WFP Eng.* 1267b
Irfan-Ul-Haque, *Arid Ag.* 1235c
Irfanullah, *N-WFP Eng.* 1267b
, *Riphah Internat.* 1270c
Irgaziev, Bakhadir F., *Ghulam IKIST* 1246a
Iribarne, Louis, *Tor.* 500b
Iribhogbe, Pius I., *Benin* 1156c
Irina, C. L., *Moi* 969c
Irinoye, O. O., *O.Awolowo* 1201b
Irish, Jonathan, *Tor.* 507a
Irmawati bte Ramli, *Putra* 1022c
Iro, P. C. E., *P.Harcourt* 1209b
Iroegbu, T. O., *Ib.* 1176a
Iroha, E. O., *Lagos* 1187a
Ironmonger, Duncan, *Melb.* 96b
Irons, C. J., *Qld.UT* 151b
Diedre, *Well.* 1117a
Glenwood H., *Brock* 320a
Peter C., *Pret.* 1385a
Ironside, Charles N., *Glas.* 1665b
James W., *Edin.* 1652c
Michael D., *Keele* 1710b
Iroume, Roger N., *Dschang* 273a
Irshad, Asequa, *Dhaka* 236a
Muhammad, *NUST(P'stan.)* 1265b
Irtwange, S. V., *Makurdi Ag.* 1143a
Irudayaraj, A. N. J., *B'thidasan.* 705a
Irune, Stephen O., *Benin* 1157b
Irungu, L. W., *Nair.* 972c, 977c
Irurah, D. K., *Witw.* 1411b
Irusen, E. M., *Stell.* 1398c
Irvin, R. T., *Alta.* 311a
Irvine, Fr. Christopher, *Leeds* 1739c
D., *Dal.* 352b
Dexter R. F., *Monash* 123a
Ian J., *C'dia.* 344b
Irene, *Deakin* 61, 63a, 63b
J. C., *Manit.* 391c
J. D., *Sask.* 474b
James, *Strath.* 1946a
Jill C. A., *Otago* 1105a
John T. S., *St And.* 1914a, 1916a
L., *Napier* 1845a
Robin F., *Camb.* 1606a
Rodney J., *Adel.* 28c
Stuart J. C., *Wales* 1546b
Irvine-Halliday, D., *Calg.* 326b
Irving, Alan, *W.Ont.* 555c
Alan C., *Liv.* 1758a
David O., *Melb.* 108c
E. L., *Wat.* 531c
Greg, *W.Laur.* 557b
Helen, *Syd.* 171b, 176a
Helen R., *Monash* 124a
Howard H., *Tor.* 500c
John A., *Brist.* 1588a
Malcolm, *Brun.* 1594b
Malcolm, *Lond.* 1788a
Pauline, *Ulster* 1960c
Philip, *Cran.* 1629b
Robert W., *Glas.* 1664b
W. L., *Nott.* 1858a
Irving-Bell, Linda, *Oxf.* 1882a
Irwandi Jaswir, *IIU Malaysia* 1002c
Irwin, B. V. W., *Rhodes* 1388c
C. R., *Belf.* 1561c
David M., *Tor.* 505a
F. G. E., *Birm.* 1568a
G., *Wales* 1968b
G. W., *Belf.* 1558a
Geoffrey J., *Auck.* 1067a
J., *W.Ont.* 546c
J. A., *Qu.* 456c
Jude L., *Syd.* 168c
Lyn, *NE* 136b
M. G., *HK* 2033c
Michael, *Kent* 1714b
Michael, *Massey* 1097a
Michael J., *Camb.* 1600a
P. R., *Rhodes* 1389a
Patrick G. J., *Oxf.* 1878a
Peter J., *Murd.* 132a, 132b
Sarah, *Leeds* 1734a
Terence H., *Oxf.* 1877c
Irwin-Zarecka, Iwona, *W.Laur.* 557c
Isa, Mohammed, *B'desh.Engin.* 225c
Mukhtar, *Bayero* 1150c
Mustapha A., *Bayero* 1149c
N., *Nfld.* 407c
Isa Abdullahi, *Maid.* 1192b
Isa Daud, *Putra* 1026b
Isa Mohamad Rose, *NU Malaysia* 1019c
Isaac, A. D., *Sheff.* 1921b
D. H., *Swansea* 1955c
D. W. L., *Greenwich* 1675b
G. E., *Sask.* 471c, 475c
Graham H., *Leeds* 1729c
Joseph E., *Melb.* 100b
K. K., *IIT Bombay* 778b
Mohan K., *W.Aust.* 197b
R. Elwyn, *Leeds* 1727a
Winston, *Ryerson* 464b
Isaacs, Edward, *Lond.S.Bank* 1829b
Enslin B. H., *W.Cape* 1408b
Neil W., *Glas.* 1664a
P. J., *Qld.UT* 150b
Tracy L., *W.Ont.* 544c, 553a
W. J., *Pret.* 1387b, 1387c
Isaacs-Brown, Angella, *Jamaica UT* 957a
Isaak, A., *Qld.UT* 153c
P. J., *Namibia* 1057b
Isaaks, C. M., *Nott.Trent* 1861c
Isabirye, D. A., *N-W(S.Af.)* 1365b
Isacke, C. M., *Lond.* 1785a
Isah, Ambrose O., *Benin* 1152b, 1156b
Essy C., *Benin* 1156b
Isajiw, Wsevolod, *Tor.* 501a
Isamade, E. S., *Jos* 1181a
Isamah, A. N., *Ib.* 1175c
Isangedighi, A. J., *Calabar* 1159b
Isani, Muzaffar A., *Bhutto IST* 1272b
Isarji bin Hj Sarudin, *IIU Malaysia* 1003a
Isawa, Yumiko, *Monash* 118b
Iscan, T., *Dal.* 351b
Iscoe, Steve D., *Qu.* 459c
Iseguan, A. I., *Ambrose Alli* 1146b
Isehunwa, S. O., *Ib.* 1174a
Iseke-Barnes, Judy, *Tor.* 504b
Iselin, Errol, *Bond* 38c
Isemila, Patience A., *Benin* 1152b
Isenman, David E., *Tor.* 504c
Iserles, Arieh, *Camb.* 1605b
Isgor, O. B., *Car.* 337b
Ish, Dan, *Sask.* 475b
Ishak Abdul Razak, *Malaya* 1004b, 1009b
Ishak Aris, *Putra* 1024c
Ishak bin Ismail, *Tech.U.Malaysia* 1033a
Ishak Hashim, *NU Malaysia* 1018a
Ishak Hj Arshad, *NU Malaysia* 1020c
Ishak Hj Suliaman, *Malaya* 1012a
Ishak Yussof, *NU Malaysia* 1016a
Ishaku, M., *AT Balewa* 1138a
Isham, Christopher J., *ICL* 1704c
Isham Pawan Ahmad, *IIU Malaysia* 1003a
Ishaq, K., *SE(S.Lanka)* 1461a
Mazhar, *NUST(P'stan.)* 1265a
Muhammad, *Karachi* 1250b
Ishaque, Qasim, *Bhutto IST* 1272b
Ishar, M. P. S., *GND* 763b
Isharaza, W. K., *Mbarara* 1500c
Ishemo, Amani, *Jamaica UT* 956a
Ishengoma, R. C., *Sokoine Ag.* 1486c
Isherwood, David P., *ICL* 1703b
Ishmael, Kalam, *Lond.* 1783c
Ishola, O. O., *Ib.* 1178a
Ishtiaq Hossain, *IIU Malaysia* 1002b
Ishtiaque, Mohd., *JMI* 793c
Ishumi, A. G., *Dar.* 1478a
Ishwara Bhat, J., *M'lore.* 843a
Isibor, J. O., *Ambrose Alli* 1146c
Isichei, A. O., *O.Awolowo* 1197c
C., *Jos* 1181b
H. U., *Jos* 1181c
Isiekwe, M. C., *Lagos* 1186b
Isife, B. I., *Rivers SUST* 1210b
Isika, Andor M., *Calabar* 1158c
Isikveren, A. T., *Brist.* 1585b
Isinger, Russell, *Sask.* 480b
Isinika, A. C., *Sokoine Ag.* 1487b
Isiramen, C. O., *Ambrose Alli* 1147c
Isirimah, E. U., *Rivers SUST* 1212c
N. O., *Rivers SUST* 1211a, 1212b
Isitor, G. N., *WI* 2001a
Isiugo-Abanihe, U. O., *Ib.* 1175c
Isiyaku, Yakubu M., *AT Balewa* 1139b
Iskander, Magdy N., *Monash* 123c
Iskander Idris bin Yaacob, *Malaya* 1007a
Islam, A., *Chitt.* 228c
A., *Dhaka* 232c, 237c
A. B. M. O., *Dhaka* 237c
A. B. M. S., *Dhaka* 236c
A. F. M. M., *Dhaka* 233c
A. F. M. T., *Chitt.* 228a
A. H. M. A., *Islamic(B'desh.)* 243b
A. H. M. H., *Rajsh.* 254b
A. H. M. N., *Islamic(B'desh.)* 242b
A. I. M. M., *Dhaka* 240b
A. K. M. A., *Rajsh.* 256a
A. K. M. Aminul, *BSMR Ag.* 218b
A. K. M. K., *Chitt.* 230b
A. K. M. Kamrul, *Khulna* 250c
A. K. M. Kausarul, *Khulna* 248b
A. K. M. M., *Islamic(B'desh.)* 242c
A. K. M. N., *Chitt.* 228a
A. K. M. N., *Dhaka* 233b
A. K. M. R., *Rajsh.* 253a
A. K. M. S., *Rajsh.* 256c
A. K. M. Sadrul, *B'desh.Engin.* 225a
A. K. M. Saiful, *B'desh.Engin.* 226b
A. K. M. W., *Dhaka* 237a
A. N. M., *Chitt.* 228c
A. Nahar, *Dhaka* 237c
A. S. M. N., *Rajsh.* 256c
A. S. M. T., *Islamic(B'desh.)* 243a
Ainul, *Massey* 1096b
Anwar, *Car.* 341a
D. M. S., *Jahang.* 245b
Deen, *B'desh.Ag.* 221c
E., *Dhaka* 232c
F. N., *Rajsh.* 256a
Fakhrul, *J.Hamdard* 791b

Gerald C., *Dal.* 357a
Gordon, *Leeds Met.* 1741a
Grace, *Dal.* 352c
Graham A. R., *Syd.* 173a, 175c
Greg, *Tor.* 497b
H., *Bran.* 316c
H. T., *Belf.* 1561a
I., *Alta.* 304c
I. A., *St And.* 1913c, 1916b, 1916c
Ian, *Jo'burg.* 1347c
J., *Manit.* 396b, 398b
J. P., *Alta.* 309a
James A., *Belf.* 1563a
Jane L., *Griff.* 69c
Jessica R., *Cant.* 1087b
Jim H., *Well.* 1114a
Judith E., *W.Aust.* 196a
K. Wayne, *Tor.* 507c
Kate, *Liv.J.Moores* 1765c
Kevin, *Cape Town* 1336a
Kristin, *Aust.Cath.* 35b
L. J. G., *Belf.* 1560c
Les, *Portsmouth* 1903b
Leslie J., *Salf.* 1918c
Linda, *Melb.* 107b
Lindsay C., *Well.* 1117a
Lindsay N., *Newcastle(NSW)* 141a
Lucy C., *Cant.* 1092a
Lynda, *Waik.* 1121c
M., *Aberd.* 1537a
M., *Dal.* 350b
Michael, *Dal.* 358c
Michael R., *Tor.* 507c
Miles G., *Tor.* 505a
Nigel D., *Bath* 1551b, 1555a
Pamela, *Bourne.* 1582b
Pamela, *Glas.* 1669b
Patrick G., *Belf.* 1562a, 1563a
Peter, *Griff.* 70a
R., *Wales* 1970a
R., *Warw.* 1977a
R. H., *Calg.* 326b
R. J., *Brist.* 1586c
R. N., *Calg.* 330a, 332c
R. S., *Hull* 1698c
Rankin F., *La Trobe* 78b
Rebecca, *Wales* 1967b
Robert, *Melb.* 99a, 100c
Robert E., *Monash* 116a
Ron, *Syd.* 176a
Roy L., *Birm.* 1567b, 1575c
Russell, *Brock* 320c
S. L., *Qu.* 459a
Sean F., *Glas.* 1664c
Sebastian L., *ICL* 1707a
Stephen, *Vic.(BC)* 518a
Stewart, *Melb.* 100b
Tammy, *Bond* 40b
Thomas R. R., *Leth.* 364c
V. S., *Newcastle(UK)* 1847c
W., *Alta.* 311b
W. A., *Alta.* 309c
Wendy, *Lond.* 1780b
Johnston-Wilder, P. J., *Warw.* 1973a
S., *Warw.* 1973a
Johnstone, Adrian I. C., *Lond.* 1807c
Alastair C., *Massey* 1101a
Cameron M., *Strath.* 1946a
David, *Syd.* 169c
Eve C., *Edin.* 1652c
I. P., *Qu.* 456c
Iain L., *Glas.* 1663c
J. G., *Hull* 1697a
James, *E.Lond.* 1643a
Keith, *Camb.* 1607a
L. C., *Plym.* 1888b
Lorna, *Auck.* 1068a
Peter T., *Camb.* 1605c
Richard, *Griff.* 72a, 75a
Rufus A., *Camb.* 1607c
S. E., *Qld.UT* 153c
Walter, *Strath.* 1946a
Johri, Mira, *Montr.* 417a
Joice, P. Ann, *Wales* 1967b
Joiner, Duncan, *Massey* 1097a
Richard, *Bath* 1553a, 1555b
T. A., *La Trobe* 78c
Joinson, Adam, *Bath* 1552a, 1554c
Adam N., *Open(UK)* 1871c
Jois, M., *La Trobe* 81a
Joisa, Ganapathi, *Manipal* 849b
Joji Saleh Mohammed, *Maid.* 1191a
Jojich, Danica, *C'dia.* 347b
Jojo, Bipin, *Tata Inst.Soc.Scis.* 938b

Jokhan, Anjeela, *S.Pac.* 1421b
Jokhio, Abdul Hakeem, *Aga Khan(P'stan.)* 1230c, 1232a
M. H., *Mehran* 1257b, 1258b
Rukhsana, *Sindh* 1275c
Sirajuddin, *Quaid-e-Awam UEST* 1269b
Jolaoso, A. O., *Abeokuta Ag.* 1141b
Joldersma, H., *Calg.* 327c
Jolicoeur, Mario, *Montr.* 422b
Pierre, *Montr.* 415b
Joll, C. A., *Curtin* 55b
Jollands, Nigel A., *Massey* 1100a
Jolley, David, *Aberd.* 1536b
Dianne F., *W'gong.* 207a
Kenneth W., *Massey* 1098a
Rowena D., *Manc.Met.* 1839a
Jolly, Brian, *Monash* 126c
Colin K., *Cran.* 1630c
Jatinder Singh, *GND* 763c
Kate, *Birm.* 1575a
M., *Birm.* 1568c
Margaretta, *Exe.* 1656b
Neryla, *Syd.* 166b
Paul D., *Griff.* 69b
Rosemary, *Qu.* 454c
Stephen, *Camb.* 1612c
Wayne T., *Brock* 321a
Jollymore, Gloria, *Mt.All.* 427c
Joly, Allain, *Montr.* 424a
Daniele, *Warw.* 1974b, 1978c
Jona, I. N., *Uyo* 1214c, 1217c
Jonah, K., *Ghana* 583c
Jonas, A. E., *Hull* 1696b
J. L., *Rhodes* 1390b
M., *Sask.* 479c
Jonathan, L. T., *NUL* 980b
Raymond, *Trin.W.* 516
Jonathan-Ibeagha, E. I., *Ib.* 1178b
Jonck, E., *Jo'burg.* 1348a
Joneja, M. G., *Qu.* 458a
Jones, A., *Manc.Met.* 1837b, 1839a
A., *Wales* 1970b
A. B., *Alta.* 312a
A. L., *Cardiff* 1619b, 1620b
A. M., *Swansea* 1958c
A. P., *E.Anglia* 1639b
A. R., *Calg.* 332a, 332c
A. R., *Nott.Trent* 1864b
Adrian N., *La Trobe* 80b
Alan, *Glam.* 1661a
Alan S., *Syd.* 167b
Aled G., *Wales* 1540, 1541b
Alexander R., *Tor.* 491b
Alison, *Auck.* 1069c
Alison, *Lond.* 1791a
Alister T., *Waik.* 1120a, 1124b
Allan S., *Syd.* 176b
Andrew, *Exe.* 1658a
Andrew, *Lond.* 1777c, 1791b
Andrew C., *Cardiff* 1616a
Andrew V., *Camb.* 1605c
Anita C., *Edin.* 1645c
Ann, *H-W* 1682b
Ann C., *Open(UK)* 1871c
Anna, *Middx.* 1842b
Anne, *Vic.(Aust.)* 184
Anne M., *Hudd.* 1691b
Anthony C., *Liv.* 1755c
Anthony H., *Salf.* 1918c
Arwyn T., *Cardiff* 1621b
B., *Alta.* 304b
B., *Lond.* 1804a
B. B., *S.Leone* 1286c
B. L., *W.Ont.* 546b
Barbara E., *McG.* 376c, 381a
Barrie W., *Open(UK)* 1871a
Barry T., *Glas.* 1668a
Bob, *Exe.* 1658a
Bob M., *Wales* 1540c
Brian, *Wales* 1541c
Brian G., *W'gong.* 207b
Bronwyn, *Melb.* 111c
Bryn, *Bath* 1553b
Byron, *Cardiff* 1623a
C., *Lond.* 1785c
C., *Manc.Met.* 1837b, 1840c
C., *St And.* 1914c
C., *W.Ont.* 545b
C., *Wales* 1970b
C., *Warw.* 1976b, 1978b
C. A., *Calg.* 331a, 332a
C. A., *Greenwich* 1675c
C. A., *H-W* 1679b
C. A., *Nott.Trent* 1864c, 1866c
C. B., *Cardiff* 1616a
C. F., *Herts.* 1684c
C. J., *Cardiff* 1620a

C. J., *Manc.Met.* 1837b
C. J. C., *S'ton.* 1938b
C. M., *Wales* 1965c
Cameron, *Cardiff* 1615c
Cameron, *Monash* 114c
Campbell A., *Leic.* 1749a
Caroline, *W'gong.* 207c
Caroline, *Wales* 1967b
Carolyn, *Herts.* 1685c
Caron, *Greenwich* 1678c
Carwyn, *Wales* 1968b
Cath, *Glam.* 1660c
Catherine M., *Liv.* 1754, 1763b
Charles A., *Camb.* 1609b
Charles L., *Tor.* 501a
Chris, *Deakin* 63b
Christian, *Sunshine Coast* 159b
Christine, *Brock* 322c
Christopher, *Leeds Met.* 1741c
Christopher A., *Leeds* 1732b
Clive A., *Leeds* 1734a
Colin, *Liv.J.Moores* 1766b
Cynthia, *Kingston(UK)* 1718c
D., *Coventry* 1626a
D., *H-W* 1682a
D., *Manc.Met.* 1839c, 1841b
D., *Newcastle(UK)* 1847a
D., *Sheff.* 1929a
D. A., *Birm.* 1573b
D. C., *Calg.* 325c
D. F., *W.Ont.* 542b
D. Gareth, *Otago* 1103, 1108b
D. H., *Swansea* 1955b
D. L., *W.Ont.* 549c
D. R. Timothy, *Liv.* 1758a
D. S., *Belf.* 1560c
D. S., *Brunei* 268a
D. W., *Manc.Met.* 1840c
Darryl N., *Griff.* 71a, 74b
David, *C.Qld.* 45c
David, *E.Lond.* 1643c
David A., *Nelson Mandela Met.* 1363b
David H., *Herts.* 1686b
David L., *Wales* 1546c
David R., *Leic.* 1748a
David S., *Adel.* 25a
David T., *Otago* 1109c
David T., *Wales* 1547c
David W., *Cardiff* 1621a
Debbie, *W.Ont.* 553b
Deborah, *Brun.* 1595c
Deborah, *Well.* 1116b
Denis, *Wales* 1969, 1970c
Denise, *W.Cape* 1409b
Derek, *Cardiff* 1622a
Derek, *Dal.* 355c
Dewi I., *Wales* 1546c
Dick P., *Liv.J.Moores* 1766a
Don, *Vic.(BC)* 522c
Dylan, *Portsmouth* 1901c
Dylan M., *Cardiff* 1622a
E., *Wales* 1970a
E. B., *Wales* 1970b
E. L., *Birm.* 1573c
E. T., *Brist.* 1587a
E. Trevor, *Herts.* 1684c
E. Yvonne, *Oxf.* 1879b
Edgar, *Lond.* 1792c
Edwin S., *WI* 1995a
Eileen, *Hudd.* 1694b
Elizabeth, *Brun.* 1593b
Elizabeth, *Manc.Met.* 1839a
Elizabeth A., *Warw.* 1971c
Elspeth, *Leeds Met.* 1740b, 1743b, 1744c
Emily, *Nott.Trent* 1861b, 1861c
Eric, *Melb.* 100c
Eslyn, *Jamaica UT* 957c
F. R., *Sheff.* 1923b
Fiona A., *Leeds* 1737a
Frank R., *Leeds* 1739a
Fred M. A., *Liv.* 1755a
G., *Brist.* 1584a
G., *Massey* 1098c
G. A., *Kingston(UK)* 1718a
G. A., *Lond.* 1800a
G. E., *Keele* 1710a
G. E., *Plym.* 1889b
G. E. M., *Sheff.* 1922a
G. H., *Birm.* 1566c
G. P., *Nfld.* 403c
Gail M., *W.Aust.* 196a
Gar, *W.Syd.* 205b
Gareth A., *S'ton.* 1936b
Gareth E., *Lond.* 1787c
Gareth R., *Wales* 1967b
Gareth W., *Wales* 1549c
Garry, *W.Aust.* 201b
Gary, *Canberra* 42c

Gary J., *Canberra* 43a
Gavin W., *NU Singapore* 1314c
George D. D., *Leic.* 1746a
Geraint A. C., *Camb.* 1606b, 1611c
Geraint W., *Cardiff* 1623b, 1623c
Glen A., *Tor.* 504a
Glenn S., *Macq.* 88b
Glenville, *Qu.* 458b
Glyn, *Glam.* 1661c
Glyn, *Kingston(UK)* 1720c
Glynis, *Hudd.* 1694a
Gordon, *Dal.* 358b
Gordon, *Qu.* 458c
Graeme, *Tas.* 181c
Graeme R, *Keele* 1711c
Graham B., *S.Cross* 156a
Graham L., *NE* 135b
Graham P., *Adel.* 24c
Gregory T., *Otago* 1109c
Gregory V., *Warw.* 1976a
Greta J., *Ulster* 1962a
Gurnos, *Keele* 1711c
Gwynne, *Ott.* 445a
H., *Manc.Met.* 1837b, 1841b
Heddwyn, *Herts.* 1686b
Helen, *Lond.* 1782a
Helen M. F., *Hudd.* 1692c
Hilary A., *Hull* 1700b
Howard, *Lough.* 1835c
Hugh, *Herts.* 1688a
Hugh, *Lond.* 1781, 1783b, 1813
Huw, *Middx.* 1842b
I. A., *Nott.* 1852c
I. L., *Nfld.* 401b
I. M., *Reading* 1906a
Ian, *Bourne.* 1580c, 1581a
Ian, *Lond.* 1814a
Ian, *Macq.* 86c
Ian P., *Birm.* 1569a, 1575c
Ian S., *Liv.J.Moores* 1765c
J., *W.Ont.* 545a
J., *Wales* 1970b
J. Anthony A., *Wales* 1541a
J. Bryan, *Tor.* 491a
J. Clifford, *Aberd.* 1536a
J. D. C., *H-W* 1679, 1680a, 1682a
J. D. G., *E.Anglia* 1638c
J. Edward, *Cardiff* 1618c
J. Mary, *Keele* 1709b
J. R., *Massey* 1100c
Jacqueline L., *Manc.Met.* 1838a
James, *Hudd.* 1693b
Jane, *Lond.* 1793c
Jennifer, *Lough.* 1836a
Jenny M., *Leeds* 1730b
Jeremy, *Canberra* 42b
John, *Portsmouth* 1903b
John D., *S.Fraser* 484a
John D. S., *Warw.* 1975a, 1979c
John R., *Sur.* 1950b
Jonathan A., *Oxf.* 1878a
Judith, *Liv.J.Moores* 1766a
Julie, *Salf.* 1918b
K., *Brist.* 1586c
K., *Lond.* 1785a
K., *Nfld.* 408c
K. D., *Manit.* 397c
K. G., *Greenwich* 1675b
Karen, *Melb.* 101b
Karin E., *Wales* 1966c
Karl O., *Liv.J.Moores* 1765c
Kathleen R., *Greenwich* 1677c
Keith, *Lanc.* 1721c
Keith, *S'ton.* 1934a
Kelvin, *Lincoln(UK)* 1753b
Ken G., *Ryerson* 462b, 465c
Ken P., *Wales* 1966c
Kenneth V., *Monash* 122c
Kenneth W., *Keele* 1710a
Kevin C., *Lanc.* 1722c
Kip, *Bourne.* 1581b
L., *Manc.Met.* 1837c
L., *Wales* 1970a
L., *Wat.* 527a, 531c, 532b
Lawrence J., *Wales* 1967b
Lee, *Glam.* 1660b
Lewis, *Lond.Met.* 1825c
Linda M., *Massey* 1100b
Lisa, *Birm.* 1574c
Liz, *Griff.* 73b
Louise, *Worcester* 1985a
Lucy, *Kingston(UK)* 1719a
Lynda A., *Manc.Met.* 1840c
M., *Nott.Trent* 1861c
M., *Swansea* 1958b

M. B., *Plym.* 1889a
M. C., *Nott.* 1850b
M. C., *Qu.* 454c
M. Chris, *Open(UK)* 1871a
M. H., *Sheff.* 1923c
M. J., *Manc.Met.* 1837b
M. L, *Botswana* 262c
M. L., *Cardiff* 1614, 1616b
M. R., *Brist.* 1589b
M. S., *Waik.* 1123b
Mairwen, *Syd.* 167a
Mandy, *Lincoln(UK)* 1753b
Manina, *W.Ont.* 542a
Marc, *Macq.* 87b
Margaret, *Murd.* 129, 134a
Margaret, *Salf.* 1920a
Mari C., *Camb.* 1603b
Marian V., *Glas.* 1666c
Marilyn, *Bond* 39a
Marion, *Auck.UT* 1082a
Mark, *Auck.UT* 1084a
Mark G., *Newcastle(NSW)* 142b, 145a
Martin, *Lond.* 1790a
Martin K., *Camb.* 1599b
Martin R., *Wales* 1541a
Martyn, *Kent* 1715a
Martyn, *Kingston(UK)* 1717, 1720b
Martyn H., *Herts.* 1687a
Matthew R., *Camb.* 1610a
Melanie J. T., *Cardiff* 1621c
Meriel G., *Liv.* 1755b
Mervyn, *ICL* 1708b
Michael, *Bourne.* 1580b
Michael, *Murd.* 134c
Michael A., *Liv.* 1757b
Michael D., *ICL* 1706a
Michael E., *Oxf.* 1878a
Michael G. K., *Murd.* 130a, 133a, 133b, 133c
Michael J., *Cardiff* 1615b
Miriam, *New Br.* 435a
Hon. Mr. Justice R. J. W., *Rhodes* 1387
N., *Wales* 1967b
N. Barrie, *Leic.* 1747b
N. J., *Liv.* 1755b
Neil G., *Camb.* 1604c
Nigel R., *Adel.* 29b
O. E., *Manc.Met.* 1841c
Owen, *Melb.* 100c
P., *E.Anglia* 1641a
P., *Plym.* 1889b
P. C., *Plym.* 1888c
P. S. G., *Manc.Met.* 1839a
Pamela, *Leeds* 1736b
Patricia A., *Hudd.* 1692a
Paul, *Glam.* 1660b
Peris, *Lond.* 1821c
Peter, *Auck.* 1078b
Peter, *Greenwich* 1677c
Peter, *Herts.* 1686b
Peter, *Nott.Trent* 1861
Peter B., *Camb.* 1608c
Peter D., *Newcastle(NSW)* 146a
Peter J. H., *McG.* 385c
Peter L. M., *Sur.* 1951c
Peter M., *Birm.* 1570a, 1576b
Peter M., *Camb.* 1611a
Peter M., *Lond.* 1788c
Peter W., *Keele* 1709, 1709c, 1712c
Phil, *Leeds Met.* 1743c
Philip A., *Sheff.Hallam* 1932
Philip R., *Bath* 1550c, 1553c
Phillip J., *Cardiff* 1614b
Phillip W., *Syd.* 168c, 175b, 175c
R., *Curtin* 57b
R., *Manc.Met.* 1840a
R., *Nott.Trent* 1863c
R., *Swinburne UT* 161a
R. A. C., *Greenwich* 1676a
R. A. L., *Sheff.* 1925c
R. C., *Birm.* 1571c
R. E., *Alta.* 306a
R. F., *W.Ont.* 542b
R. G., *Nott.* 1851b, 1857a
R. H., *Birm.* 1567a
R. H., *Brist.* 1589b
R. J., *Manc.Met.* 1839a
R. L., *Alta.* 311b
R. L., *Chinese HK* 2026c
R. L., *Curtin* 55b
R. M., *Coventry* 1626a
R. McL., *Melb.* 106c
R. Merfyn, *Wales* 1545
R. Peter, *Warw.* 1973b

McKenna-Black, Margaret A., Ulster 1962a
McKennan, G. T., Manc.Met. 1837b
MacKenny, Virginia, Cape Town 1335c
Mackenzie, A. F. D., Car. 338c, 340a
MacKenzie, A. L., Wat. 537b
A. P., St And. 1916a
A. Robert, Lanc. 1722c
Alexander E., Ott. 446a, 446c
Mackenzie, Angus B., Glas. 1671b
McKenzie, Anne, Tas. 183b
B., Manit. 394a
Mackenzie, B. W., Qu. 455b
McKenzie, Barbra, W'gong. 207c
Bruce A., Lincoln(NZ) 1093c
C. A., W.Ont. 549a
MacKenzie, C. H., Jo'burg. 1347a
Catherine, C'dia. 343a
Mackenzie, Catherine, Strath. 1945c
Catriona A., Macq. 90b
MacKenzie, Christine L., S.Fraser 485a
Clare, Cant. 1086a
McKenzie, Dan P., Camb. 1601c
David R., Syd. 173c
Mackenzie, Donald, Strath. 1946a
MacKenzie, Donald A., Edin. 1650b
Mackenzie, Duncan D. S., Massey 1097c
McKenzie, Edward, Strath. 1948a
Eric, Edin. 1648a
F., W.Ont. 542c
F. N., W.Ont. 552b
Mackenzie, G., Hull 1695c
Geraldine I., Qld.UT 150c
McKenzie, Glenda, Waik. 1124c
Haslam, Curtin 59b
Heather, Syd. 172c
Mackenzie, Herbert, Brock 320b
Ian Z., Oxf. 1880a
MacKenzie, J., St And. 1915a
Mackenzie, J. J., Qu. 459b
J. M., R.Gordon 1911c
James D., Syd. 168c
McKenzie, Janice M., Otago 1107b
John, Melb. 93, 111c
MacKenzie, John A., Strath. 1947a
McKenzie, John L., Cant. 1089c
Mackenzie, K. C. H., Sheff. 1925b
McKenzie, K. J., Calg. 325b
Mackenzie, Kenneth J. D., Well. 1114a
L. W., Qu. 458a
Lewis M., Glas. 1664b
McKenzie, Lisa R., Belf. 1565a
Mackenzie, Lynette A., Newcastle(NSW) 143b
MacKenzie, M. E., Nfld. 404c
McKenzie, Mary L., W.Ont. 553a
MacKenzie, Mhairi F., Glas. 1668c
Murray, Auck.UT 1082b
Mackenzie, N. K., Manc.Met. 1838b
McKenzie, N. L., Nott.Trent 1863a
Mackenzie, Orysia, Hudd. 1693b
MacKenzie, Patricia, Vic.(BC) 522a
Mackenzie, Peter, Strath. 1946a
McKenzie, Pierre, Montr. 412a
R. C., Edin. 1651a
MacKenzie, R. N., Plym. 1890a
Mackenzie, Richard, Montr. 415a
MacKenzie, Robert E., McG. 374c
Mackenzie, Robert F., Leeds 1732a
Robin, Napier 1844
MacKenzie, Roddy, Strath. 1949a
McKenzie, Sati, Greenwich 1676a
Mackenzie, Susan, W.Laur. 560c
Mackenzie Davey, Kate, Lond. 1778c
McKenzie Skene, D., Aberd. 1536c
McKenzie-Davidson, Margaret J., Otago 1110c
McKenzie-Leiper, Jean, W.Ont. 555c
McKeogh, Colm, Waik. 1122c
McKeon, D. G., W.Ont. 545a
D. G. C., W.Ont. 544a
P., Manc.Met. 1837a
R. C., Manc.Met. 1841a
McKeough, A. M., Calg. 325c
McKeown, G. P., E.Anglia 1639a
J. Denis, Leeds 1737a
M. M. Olive, Greenwich 1677a
Neil B., Cardiff 1615c
Pascal P., Belf. 1562b
Robert, Ulster 1961c
Stephanie R., Ulster 1960b
McKercher, Catherine, Car. 339a, 340a
W. R., W.Ont. 555a
McKerlie, D. E., Calg. 329a
McKernan, John F., Glas. 1662c
McKerr, George, Ulster 1960b
MacKerrell, S. O., Birm. 1571b
MacKerron, G., Napier 1845a
McKerrow, P., Curtin 59b
Phillip J., W'gong. 207a
McKessock, Douglas J. R., Ryerson 463a
McKevitt, Paul, Ulster 1961a
Mackey, B. M., Reading 1907a
C., Qu. 455a
J. R., Alta. 312a
Julie K., Cant. 1089c
M., Alta. 307a
M. D., Nfld. 402a
Michael C., McG. 378b, 380b, 384b
McKibbin, Robert, Massey 1098b, 1102a
McKie, Andrew, Lond. 1788a
Mackie, Christopher J., Melb. 98c, 108c
McKie, David, Waik. 1122b
Mackie, Dugald, Manc. 1836
E., Coventry 1625b
Eleanor J., Melb. 102a
Kenneth F., Tas. 180a
M. M., Plym. 1888b
Peter J., Leeds 1726b, 1732a, 1734b
Robert, G.Caledonian 1673b
Robin D. A., KwaZulu-Natal 1351a
Vera, Melb. 98c
McKiel, R. E., Calg. 328c
McKiernan, Kate, Lond. 1806c
P., St And. 1915b
McKillop, A. Brian, Car. 338c
Aine, Ulster 1960b
Ann, Auck. 1077a
D., Greenwich 1676c
D. G., Belf. 1560a
I., Wat. 526a, 530a
James H., Glas. 1670a, 1670c
Mackillop, W. J., Qu. 458b, 459b
McKim, Anne M., Waik. 1122a
Douglas A., Ott. 445b
W. A., Nfld. 405c
McKimm, Jody, Auck. 1076b
McKinlay, A., St And. 1915b
Andy, Edin. 1649c
Ann, G.Caledonian 1672b
MacKinlay, Elizabeth, C.Sturt 52b
Gordon A., Edin. 1652a
Marna E., Edin. 1651a
McKinlay, Robert D., Lanc. 1721
McKinley, Allan J., W.Aust. 192a
Eileen, Otago 1108a
Elizabeth, Auck. 1069c
Michael, Melb. 106a
Patricia, McG. 378b
R. S., Wat. 536a
Robert K., Leic. 1748a
Terry, Lond. 1816c
McKinnell, John S., Durh. 1634c
K. G., HK 2033b
L.-A., Rhodes 1390b
McKinney, Caroline, Auck.UT 1082a
Martin E. T., Ulster 1960c
Patricia A., Leeds 1734c
R. Anne, McG. 378a
T., Belf. 1565b
MacKinnnon, Sue, Swinburne UT 164b
McKinnon, A. C., H-W 1680c, 1681c
Alan E., Lincoln(NZ) 1094a
MacKinnon, Alexander L., Glas. 1663a
Allan M., S.Fraser 484a
McKinnon, Andrew, Waik. 1124c
Mackinnon, Angus, ICL 1704c
McKinnon, C., Reading 1909c
Christine F., Trent 513, 514c, 515c
David H., C.Sturt 52b
MacKinnon, Doug, W'gong. 209a
McKinnon, Gary, Aberd. 1538b
MacKinnon, Gregory, St Mary's(Can.) 468c
McKinnon, Ian R., Monash 114c
MacKinnon, J., Nfld. 409c
J. C., Sask. 474c
McKinnon, J. G., Calg. 333a, 334b
MacKinnon, J. G., Qu. 453b
McKinnon, J. J., Sask. 472b
Mackinnon, Jacquelin, Waik. 1122a
McKinnon, Jennifer, C.Sturt 51b
Jill L., Macq. 87a
MacKinnon, John, St Mary's(Can.) 469b
McKinnon, John, Well. 1118b
MacKinnon, K. M., Herts. 1686a
McKinnon, Ken, Edin. 1649b
Mackinnon, Ken A. B., Waik. 1122a
MacKinnon, Kenneth A., St Mary's(Can.) 468c
Lachlan, Abertay 1538c
Mackinnon, Mary E., McG. 369b
MacKinnon, Neil, Dal. 352c, 354a
Mackinnon, P. A., Belf. 1561a
MacKinnon, R. Peter, Sask. 471
Robert A., New Br. 428c, 435b
S., Nfld. 404c
McKinnon, S. D., Qu. 454c
McKinstry, L. J., Sask. 472a
R., Stir. 1943b
Mackintosh, Andrew, Well. 1114c
B., E.Anglia 1640b
C., Nott.Trent 1865a, 1865c
David, Kingston(UK) 1717c
J. Bruce, W.Aust. 201a
Maureen, Open(UK) 1869a
Raymond S., Open(UK) 1871a
McKinven, Theresa, Durh. 1637b
McKirdy, David M., Adel. 25c, 26a, 30c
Simon, Murd. 133b
McKitrick, Douglas J., W.Aust. 196c
McKitterick, David J., Camb. 1612b
Rosamond D., Camb. 1604a
Macklem, M. Patrick, Tor. 496a
Timothy, Lond. 1791a
Mackley, Malcolm R., Camb. 1603a
Macklin, Audrey, Tor. 496a
Gerald M., Ulster 1962b
John, E.Lond. 1642c
John, Strath. 1947b
Mark G., Wales 1541a
Michael J., NE 135a
Robert B., C.Sturt 50c
MacKnight, Christopher R., Dal. 356c
McKnight, Cliff, Lough. 1833c
David J., Tor. 504b
George, Car. 336a
Jim, W.Syd. 204a
Macknight, Richard C., Otago 1103c
McKnight, Sue, Nott.Trent 1861, 1867c
McKoy, Derrick V., WI 1995b
Mackraj, I., KwaZulu-Natal 1355a
Mackrory, V. A., KwaZulu-Natal 1350c
Macky, Keith, Auck.UT 1083a
Keith, Massey 1099b
McKyes, Edward, McG. 385c
MacLabhrai, Sean, Belf. 1564b
McLachlan, Andrew J., Syd. 173b, 175c
MacLachlan, Bonnie C., W.Ont. 539c
C. J. M., St And. 1914c
McLachlan, Campbell, Well. 1116a
Claire, Massey 1096b
MacLachlan, D., S.Fraser 488b
Maclachlan, D. L. C., Qu. 456b
McLachlan, E. B., Manit. 390c, 391c
Maclachlan, Elizabeth, NU Singapore 1311b
McLachlan, Fiona, Edin. 1645a
G., Nelson Mandela Met. 1360c
H., La Trobe 81c
MacLachlan, Ian, Leth. 364c
John, G.Caledonian 1673a
McLachlan, John C., Durh. 1635b
MacLachlan, Kathleen E., Glas. 1663a
McLachlan, Neil, Melb. 103a
MacLachlan, Richard, Dal. 356b
McLachlan, Richard S., W.Ont. 548b
Robert I., Massey 1098a
Maclachlan, S., Manc.Met. 1839b
McLachlin, C. M., W.Ont. 550b, 551b
Maclagan, D., Warw. 1975b
Margaret A., Cant. 1091c
Robert G. A. R., Cant. 1091b
Mclain, Linda, E.Cowan 67c
Maclaine, Katrina, Lond.S.Bank 1828c
McLaran, Pauline E., Keele 1710b
Mclaren, Andrew J., Strath. 1946a
McLaren, Angus G., Vic.(BC) 519c
Anne, Liv. 1757a
Anne, Melb. 95b, 102c
Arlene T., S.Fraser 486b
David, Strath. 1945c
MacLaren, Donald, Melb. 96b
Donald P. M., Liv.J.Moores 1766c
McLaren, I. A., Dal. 350b
MacLaren, I. S., Alta. 306c
McLaren, James S., Aust.Cath. 34c
John, Vic.(Aust.) 185b
John P. S., Vic.(BC) 520b
Kathryn M., Edin. 1652a
Keith R., Monash 115a, 127a
MacLaren, Leslie P., Nova Scotia Ag. 438
McLaren, Linda, Jo'burg. 1348a
Mary-Rose, Vic.(Aust.) 185c
Paula, Herts. 1687b
Richard H., W.Ont. 543b
Ronald G., Lincoln(NZ) 1095a
S. Glen, Cape Town 1335a
Stuart J., Massey 1097c
Sue, Massey 1096a
Sue J., Leic. 1747c
Mclaren, Susan V., Strath. 1945b
McLaren, T., Ryerson 464c
Maclaren, Virginia W., Tor. 494c
McLarney, C., Dal. 350c
McLarnon, R. Duncan, Ulster 1961a
McLarty, Jane, Camb. 1611a
Lianne M., Vic.(BC) 520a
Marion M., Strath. 1945c
R. W., E.Anglia 1640a
McLatchie, William, Qu. 456c
Maclatchy, Deborah, W.Laur. 556c, 557a
MacLatchy, Deborah L., New Br. 429a
McLauchlan, David, Well. 1116a
Debra, Brock 321b
MacLauchlan, H. Wade, PEI 448
McLauchlin, Alison K., Herts. 1684c
McLaughlin, Andrew, Glas. 1664c
Cahal, Ulster 1962c
Colleen, Camb. 1602a
D. P., Nott. 1856b
Denis G., Aust.Cath. 33c
Eileen A., Newcastle(NSW) 143a, 144c
Elaine, Belf. 1564b
Gregory, Ulster 1962c
Helen, Melb. 111b
Hugh, Salf. 1918b
J. Daniel, C'dia. 343a
J. P., W.Ont. 542c
James A., Ulster 1961c, 1963c
John D., New Br. 428, 431a
Judith A., Belf. 1564c
K. J., Calg. 332a
K. M., Wat. 524c, 530b, 534c
Kenneth, Manc.Met. 1840a
M. L., Oxf. 1877a
Mark, Bishop's 315
N. J., Manc.Met. 1837b
Patricia B., Ulster 1960a
Patrick, Vic.(Aust.) 185b
Peter, Tor. 506a
Philomena, Herts. 1688a
S., Nott.Trent 1866a
Steve, Edin. 1646c
Wayne A., WI 1996a, 1997a
McLaurin, Allen, Lincoln(UK) 1752a, 1753a
Maclaurin, James B., Otago 1110a
McLaurin, Joanne, Tor. 509c
McLaverty, James, Keele 1710b
McLay, D. B., Qu. 456c
Geoffrey, Well. 1116a
MacLayton, D. W., Rivers SUST 1210a, 1210c
McLean, A. B., Qu. 456c
A. Jack, Adel. 30a
MacLean, Alistair W., Qu. 451b, 457b
McLean, Angela R., Oxf. 1879a
Anthony P., Cant. 1092b
Arlene, Guy. 594c
Arnold G., W'gong. 208a
MacLean, C., Dal. 351a
McLean, C. A., W.Ont. 551b
Cassandra, Melb. 102a
David, Ballarat 37c
David, C.Sturt 51b
David, Lond. 1790a
MacLean, David, New Br. 429a, 431c
McLean, David D., Ott. 441c
MacLean, Derryl, S.Fraser 484c
Donald, Glas. 1666c
McLean, Donald, McG. 368a, 373a
MacLean, G., Manit. 393b, 398c
McLean, Graeme R., C.Sturt 51b
Hugh J., W.Ont. 544b
Iain S., Oxf. 1878b
MacLean, Ian, Canberra 41c
McLean, Ian A., W.Aust. 191c
Ian W., Adel. 26a, 30c
Maclean, Ian W. F., Oxf. 1875c
McLean, J., Manc.Met. 1837c
MacLean, J., Nfld. 404a
McLean, J., Nfld. 406b
MacLean, J. Dick, McG. 385a
McLean, Jeffrey J., Monash 119b
Jennifer, Dal. 357c
Jennifer L., Ott. 446a
Maclean, Joan, Leeds 1735b
MacLean, Joanne, Brock 319c
McLean, John, Greenwich 1677c
Maclean, Kevin, Jo'burg. 1346b
MacLean, L. C., Dal. 350b
McLean, Linda, Qu. 460a
Mclean, M., KwaZulu-Natal 1355a
McLean, Margaret, Auck. 1069c
MacLean, Margaret, Glas. 1663c
McLean, Megan M., Manc.Met. 1838a
Morag, G.Caledonian 1673a
Maclean, N., S'ton. 1933c
McLean, Naomi J., Newcastle(NSW) 141a
Maclean, Neil, Syd. 166b
McLean, Patricia S., H-W 1682b
R., Manc.Met. 1837c
R. J., Swinburne UT 162b
Robert, Strath. 1946a
Robert S., Tor. 503c
S. D., Calg. 323a, 325a, 330a
MacLean, S. J., S.Fraser 486a
McLean, S. Vianne, Qld.UT 148
Sheila A. M., Glas. 1666c
Stewart, Tor. 491a
Stuart W., Tas. 180b
T., R.Gordon 1911a
MacLeary, A. R., H-W 1679c
McLeay, Colin, Waik. 1121c
Elizabeth M., Well. 1115c
Lance M., Waik. 1120b
Stuart J., Wales 1546a
McLeish, D. L., Wat. 534b
Thomas C. B., Leeds 1733c, 1739a
McLellan, A. A., Alta. 307a
Alexander D., Otago 1109c
MacLellan, Euphemia M., Strath. 1945c
McLellan, J., Brist. 1587a
Janet, W.Laur. 559c
Ken, Nipissing 438b
MacLellan, Lachlan R., Strath. 1946c
Lorna I., Newcastle(NSW) 144c
McLellan, P. J., Qu. 454a, 456a
T., Witw. 1411c
McLelland, Mark, W'gong. 210a
McLemore, Kathy, Abertay 1539c
McLenaghan, R. G., Wat. 531b, 532b
McLennan, A. C., Witw. 1414c
A. M., R.Gordon 1911c
MacLennan, Alastair H., Adel. 28b
Alastair M., Ulster 1960a
McLennan, Alexander G. (Sandy), Liv. 1755b
Andrew, Syd. 168b
B. D., Sask. 472c
Belinda, Vic.(Aust.) 184
Chris, Bond 39b
MacLennan, David H., Tor. 505b
McLennan, Deborah, Tor. 501b

Maclennan, G., *Qld.UT* 150a
McLennan, Gregor, *Brist.* 1589a
Maclennan, Ian, *Birm.* 1574a, 1576b
McLennan, Ian S., *Otago* 1108b
Jane, *Nott.Trent* 1863b
Jane, *Vic.(Aust.)* 188c
John, *Monash* 123b
MacLennan, Ken A., *Leeds* 1736c, 1737a
McLennan, Nicole, *NE* 139a
Peter L., *W'gong.* 209c
Theresa J., *Lincoln(NZ)* 1094a
McLeod, A. I., *W.Ont.* 546b
Macleod, A. M., *Abertay* 1538c
McLeod, Adele, *Stell.* 1397a
Macleod, Alistair M., *Qu.* 456b
MacLeod, Andrew, *Lond.* 1810b, 1810c
McLeod, Andy, *Edin.* 1647a
MacLeod, C., *Napier* 1844c
Macleod, C. M., *Wat.* 533a
C. T., *Rhodes* 1390c
McLeod, C. W., *Sheff.* 1922b
Mcleod, Carolyn, *W.Ont.* 545a
Macleod, Catriona, *Tas.* 182b
MacLeod, Christine, *Brist.* 1587a
Christopher J., *Cardiff* 1616c
Macleod, Colin, *Vic.(BC)* 520a, 521a
MacLeod, Colin, *W.Aust.* 195c
McLeod, D. H., *Birm.* 1570a
D. R., *Calg.* 331c, 333a
Macleod, Donald, *Glas.* 1664c
MacLeod, Donald G., *Durh.* 1635a
McLeod, E., *Warw.* 1974b
Elizabeth J., *Monash* 123c
MacLeod, Flora J., *Exe.* 1656a
Mcleod, G., *Sask.* 480b
MacLeod, Gordon, *Aga Khan(P'stan.)* 1231a
Macleod, Hamish, *Edin.* 1646b, 1653b
MacLeod, Heather, *Dal.* 350a
McLeod, I., *Napier* 1844c
J., *Abertay* 1539a
Macleod, J. Peter, *Ott.* 445b
McLeod, Jack T., *Tor.* 499c
Jane A., *Brock* 321c
Jen, *Massey* 1099b
Jim, *Athab.* 315b
John, *Leeds* 1730c
MacLeod, John, *Montr.* 410c, 413b
McLeod, John, *Vic.(Aust.)* 188a
Julie C., *Newcastle(NSW)* 142b
Macleod, K., *Plym.* 1892a
K. A., *Plym.* 1888c
McLeod, Keith A., *Tor.* 503b
MacLeod, Kenneth, *Exe.* 1657c
Macleod, Kenneth T., *ICL* 1707a
MacLeod, M., *St And.* 1916a
M. D., *W.Ont.* 552b
M. K., *Nfld.* 404b
M. M., *Sask.* 476b
McLeod, Malcolm D., *Syd.* 167c
MacLeod, Marie, *Keele* 1712c
McLeod, Mary, *C.Qld.* 46c, 47a
Macleod, N., *Greenwich* 1675c
McLeod, N., *Trent* 514b
MacLeod, N. Jock, *Griff.* 69c
McLeod, Neil, *Murd.* 131a
MacLeod, Nikki, *Edin.* 1650c
McLeod, Paul B., *W.Aust.* 192b
Peter J., *McG.* 376a, 378a, 383b
R., *Dal.* 356a
Macleod, R. C., *Alta.* 306c
McLeod, Randall R., *Tor.* 493b
Robert D., *Manit.* 390a
Robin S., *Tor.* 508a
MacLeod, Roderick D., *Otago* 1108c
Macleod, Sarah, *Lond.* 1812c
McLeod, Sharynne L., *C.Sturt* 52b
Warwick, *Well.* 1114b
Wilson, *Edin.* 1648c
Macleod Clark, Jill, *S'ton.* 1939c
Macleod Higgins, Iain, *Vic.(BC)* 520c
Macleod-Johnstone, E. E., *Plym.* 1890a
McLernon, Desmond C., *Leeds* 1729b
Timothy, *Ulster* 1960b
McLigeyo, S. O., *Nair.* 974b
Mclinden, Maggie, *E.Lond.* 1643c
McLinden, Mike, *Birm.* 1568a
McLintock, Claire, *Auck.* 1075c
McLister, Brendan, *Auck.UT* 1083b
McLoone, J. Martin, *Ulster* 1962c
McLoughlin, Catherine, *Aust.Cath.* 34a
Declan M., *Lond.* 1793a
Dominic, *Lond.* 1784c
Ian V., *Nan.Tech.* 1294b
Moira, *Salf.* 1920a
Seán, *Leeds* 1734b
MacLullich, Alasdair M. J., *Edin.* 1651a
Maclure, Maggie, *Manc.Met.* 1839a
McLure, Michael, *W.Aust.* 192b
McLuskie, Kate, *Birm.* 1570b, 1571b
MacLusky, Ian B., *Tor.* 507a
McMahon, April, *Edin.* 1649c
Carmel, *Open(UK)* 1870b
Catherine M., *Macq.* 86c
Christopher A., *Bath* 1551c
K., *Warw.* 1975a
Maeve W., *Car.* 339b, 341b
Malcolm, *Edin.* 1650a
Marilyn, *La Trobe* 81a
Mark, *E.Cowan* 64b
Martha, *Vic.(BC)* 522a
Maureen, *Salf.* 1920a
Michael J., *Leeds* 1736b
MacMahon, Michael K. C., *Glas.* 1665c
McMahon, P., *W.Ont.* 555c
MacMahon, R., *Manit.* 398b
McMahon, Richard A., *Camb.* 1602c
Richard G., *Camb.* 1600a
Samantha, *Hudd.* 1692c
Stephen B., *Lond.* 1788c
T. B., *Wat.* 525a
Teresa, *Greenwich* 1677a
Thomas A., *Melb.* 97a
McMahon-Beattie, Una, *Ulster* 1962b
MacManaway, Norma, *Oxf.* 1882b
McManus, A., *Curtin* 59b
Davina, *Glas.* 1671c
Dennis, *S'ton.* 1937b
F., *Napier* 1845a
J., *St And.* 1914c
K., *Greenwich* 1676a
Lisa A., *Griff.* 69b
MacManus, Mary, *Auck.UT* 1082a
McManus, Michael, *Leeds Met.* 1743c
Michael T., *Massey* 1099c
Philip, *Syd.* 170a
R. M., *W.Ont.* 549c
Richard J., *Birm.* 1575a
Macmanus, S. M., *R.Gordon* 1911c
McManus, Sheila, *Leth.* 364c
McMaster, C. R., *Dal.* 356a
Catherine, *Ryerson* 466b
Christopher, *Dal.* 357c
MacMaster, Elsie, *W.Ont.* 547a
McMaster, G. E., *Bran.* 317c
Maddy, *RMIT* 154
R., *Aberd.* 1535a
Robert, *Glas.* 1666c
T. Brian M., *Belf.* 1560c
T. J., *Brist.* 1588b
McMaster-Kirkwood, Janine, *Griff.* 72a
McMath, Gaye, *W.Aust.* 190
MacMathuna, Seamus, *Ulster* 1962b, 1963b
McMeeken, Joan M., *Melb.* 107b, 108a
McMeekin, Alan, *Monash* 128c
J. D., *Calg.* 330b, 332a
Thomas A., *Tas.* 179a
McMeel, G. P., *Brist.* 1587b
McMenamin, Christine, *W.Aust.* 197b
Patricia R., *Cant.* 1089b
Paul G., *W.Aust.* 191b
McMeniman, Marilyn M., *Griff.* 68
McMichael, Andrew J., *Oxf.* 1879c
MacMillan, A. F., *Dal.* 351c
Macmillan, A. M., *Alta.* 310c
McMillan, A. S., *HK* 2033c
Andrea H., *Otago* 1111c
Blair, *Lincoln(NZ)* 1095c
MacMillan, Carrie, *Mt.All.* 426c
McMillan, D., *St And.* 1915b
D. B., *W.Ont.* 538c
D. S., *Manit.* 388b
Macmillan, David L., *Melb.* 102c
McMillan, Dorothy A., *Glas.* 1665c
Dorothy J., *Belf.* 1564c
Douglas, *Dal.* 357c
Macmillan, Douglas C., *Aberd.* 1536a
MacMillan, F. J., *E.Anglia* 1638c
Macmillan, Fiona, *Lond.* 1776, 1778b
MacMillan, J. A., *Manit.* 388a
J. B., *W.Ont.* 550b
McMillan, James F., *Edin.* 1647c
MacMillan, John, *Brun.* 1595b
McMillan, John, *Ulster* 1960a
Macmillan, Keith L., *Melb.* 94b, 102a
MacMillan, Lamont, *Dal.* 358b
M., *Napier* 1845b
M. G. M., *Calg.* 329b
McMillan, M. L., *Alta.* 304b
Mcmillan, Malcolm, *Melb.* 103a
MacMillan, Margaret, *Oxf.* 1882b, 1883c
Macmillan, Robert B., *W.Ont.* 540c
McMillan, Thomas M., *Glas.* 1670a
Trevor J., *Lanc.* 1721, 1721c
Macmillan, William D., *E.Anglia* 1638
McMillen, Caroline, *S.Aust.* 154
Isabella C., *Adel.* 28a, 28c
MacMillen, Malcolm J. J., *Exe.* 1655b
McMinn, Andrew, *Tas.* 181c
Jean, *Belf.* 1565c
Joseph M., *Ulster* 1962b
McMorran, Pat, *Herts.* 1687b
McMullan, Anna, *Belf.* 1559b
D., *Plym.* 1891b, 1895c
Geoffrey, *Ulster* 1960b
Gordon, *Lond.* 1789c
Iain, *Bourne.* 1581c
John, *St Mary's(Can.)* 469c
Lorraine, *Wales* 1966b
Niall M., *Herts.* 1686c
T. P. S., *Belf.* 1559b
W. E., *Calg.* 324b
McMullen, Gabrielle, *Aust.Cath.* 32, 35c
Jean-Norbert, *Montr.* 414c
John, *Leeds* 1731c
L. M., *Alta.* 303a
L. M., *Sask.* 477c
MacMullen, Lori, *New Br.* 428, 435c
McMullen, P., *Dal.* 354c
McMullin, J. N., *Alta.* 305c
Julie, *W.Ont.* 546a
Mary F., *Belf.* 1562b, 1563a
Neil, *Tor.* 500b
Ross, *Melb.* 98c
McMurchie, Colin, *Liv.J.Moores* 1766b
McMurchy-Pilkington, Colleen, *Auck.* 1069c
McMurray, Anne, *Murd.* 131b
Frances, *Belf.* 1562c
H. N., *Swansea* 1955c
J. G., *W.Ont.* 540c
John J., *Glas.* 1670a
Nancy E., *Melb.* 103a
Sharon, *Belf.* 1565a
McMurry, A., *Wat.* 529a
McMurtary, Jennifer, *Kingston(UK)* 1718c
McMurtry, Mervyn E., *KwaZulu-Natal* 1353b
McNab, Hamish, *Edin.* 1645c
McNabb, Robert, *Cardiff* 1615b
S., *Nott.Trent* 1864c
McNabney, Douglas, *McG.* 373a
Macnaghten, Philip, *Durh.* 1635a
McNair, Brian, *Strath.* 1946b
Macnair, Mark R., *Exe.* 1654c, 1655a
McNair, Peter, *Auck.UT* 1083c, 1084b
Ruth, *Melb.* 104a
Stephen, *Sur.* 1953c
Susan M., *W.Ont.* 548c
Victor, *Ulster* 1961b
McNally, D. S., *Nott.* 1852c
Gerard M. P., *Belf.* 1563c
J. G., *Stir.* 1942a
Mary, *Dal.* 355c
Paddy, *Worcester* 1984b
Peter F., *McG.* 372b
MacNally, Ralph C., *Monash* 114b, 124c
McNally, William, *W.Laur.* 557b, 560b
Mcnamara, A., *Qld.UT* 152c
McNamara, Beverley A., *W.Aust.* 195c
Derek A., *Ott.* 442b
J. M., *Brist.* 1587c
James, *Cape Town* 1332, 1341c, 1342a
John, *Brock* 320c
L., *Reading* 1909a
Lawrence J., *Macq.* 89c
Luke, *W'gong.* 206b
M., *Nott.* 1850
MacNamara, Oisin, *Northumbria* 1849c
McNamara, Ray P., *Bond* 38c
Sue, *Aust.Cath.* 33b, 34b
Timothy F., *Melb.* 99b
Mcnamee, M. J., *Swansea* 1956b
McNamee, Patrick B., *Ulster* 1962b
McNatty, Kenneth, *Well.* 1114a
McNaught, Allan G., *Greenwich* 1677a
C. M., *Chinese HK* 2028c
Macnaughton, A., *Wat.* 523c
McNaughton, David A., *Keele* 1710b
Donald, *Monash* 114c
MacNaughton, Glenda, *Melb.* 100a, 109a
McNaughton, Howard D., *Cant.* 1087b
L. R., *Hull* 1699a
Marie-Jeanne, *Strath.* 1945a
Neal J., *W.Aust.* 193b, 199a, 200c
Neil, *Otago* 1110c, 1111b
Peter A., *Camb.* 1606a
R., *Wat.* 531a
MacNaughton, R. F., *Ryerson* 464c
Macnaughton, R. Jane, *Durh.* 1635b
McNaughton, Stuart S., *Auck.* 1069b, 1079b
Trudie, *Auck.* 1066
MacNaughton, W. K., *Calg.* 333c
McNaull, Philip G., *H-W* 1679, 1682b
McNay, Iain, *Greenwich* 1676b
Lois, *Oxf.* 1878b
Margaret L., *W.Ont.* 540c
MacNee, William, *Edin.* 1651c
McNeely, David J., *Tor.* 506a
McNeil, A. J., *H-W* 1681a
Brian, *Strath.* 1947c
MacNeil, C., *Kingston(UK)* 1718c
McNeil, D., *Dal.* 352b
D. A., *H-W* 1680a
Iain C., *Glas.* 1662c
MacNeil, Iain G., *Glas.* 1666c
McNeil, J. N., *W.Ont.* 538c
John J., *Monash* 121b
Julian D., *Adel.* 27c
Shelley, *Dal.* 357a
MacNeil, William, *Griff.* 72a
McNeilage, A., *Mbarara* 1501c
McNeill, A. M., *Manit.* 395a
D., *Sask.* 476a
Fergus E., *Glas.* 1668b
Hinematau, *Auck.UT* 1084a
MacNeill, I. B., *W.Ont.* 546b
McNeill, J. B., *Rhodes* 1389b
J. N. Chris, *Tor.* 511a
Kenneth G., *Tor.* 499a
Lisa S., *Otago* 1106c
MacNeill, Margaret, *Tor.* 499a
McNeill, Michael, *W.Syd.* 203b
Michael C., *Nan.Tech.* 1295c
T. E., *Belf.* 1558c
McNeilly, Alan S., *Edin.* 1652a
McNeney, W. B., *S.Fraser* 486c
McNerney, R., *Lond.* 1804c
McNess, E. M., *Brist.* 1585b
McNichol, Elaine, *Leeds* 1735b
John, *Hudd.* 1692c
McNickle, Don C., *Cant.* 1089b
Raymond, *Waik.* 1119
McNicol, Annette, *Waik.* 1125a
Archibald, *Manit.* 394c
MacNish, Cara K., *W.Aust.* 192c
McNiven, Ian J., *Monash* 117b
McNorton, J. A., *Wales* 1967a
Maggy, *Glam.* 1661a
McNulty, Eugene, *Portsmouth* 1902c
Helene M., *Ulster* 1960b
Sir Roy, *Warw.* 1973b
S., *Manc.Met.* 1838c
Terence H., *Leeds* 1732a
Terence H., *Liv.* 1757c
Macoco, D. K., *Nair.* 972b
McOliver, Prince F. O., *Benin* 1153a, 1157a
Maconachie, G., *Qld.UT* 151b
Maconochie, N. E. S., *Lond.* 1804a
McPake, B., *Lond.* 1805b
Barbara, *QM Edin.* 1904b
J. M., *Stir.* 1943b
McParland, Columba P., *Dal.* 357a
John, *Lond.Met.* 1824
Penelope C., *Leic.* 1746a
McParlin, David F., *Wales* 1542c
McPaul, Susan, *Griff.* 75b
McPeake, J. C., *Manc.Met.* 1839a
McPeck, J. E., *W.Ont.* 540c
MacPhail, A. P., *Witw.* 1415c
McPhail, Alan, *W.Syd.* 204c
David S., *ICL* 1704a
Kenneth J., *Glas.* 1662c
McPhedran, Ross C., *Syd.* 173c
McPhee, Alastair D., *Glas.* 1665a
MacPhee, Cait, *Edin.* 1650a
Macphee, D. E., *Aberd.* 1535b
McPhee, Hilary, *Melb.* 98c
Ian D., *La Trobe* 83c
J. J., *Wat.* 528b, 528c
Peter B., *Melb.* 93, 98c
Wendy J., *Monash* 126a
McPherran, M., *S.Fraser* 485c
Macpherson, A. G., *Nfld.* 404a
MacPherson, Allan M., *Liv.* 1757c
Macpherson, B. D., *Manit.* 394b
McPherson, C. G., *G.Caledonian* 1673b
MacPherson, Cluny, *Massey* 1100c
Macpherson, Colin G., *Durh.* 1634b
Craig, *Syd.* 174b
McPherson, D. B., *HK* 2035c
David, *Waik.* 1123a, 1124b
MacPherson, E. D., *Manit.* 389b
McPherson, Elsworth A., *W.Cape* 1407b
Macpherson, Ewen, *Edin.* 1646c
McPherson, F., *Abertay* 1539b
MacPherson, Fergus, *G.Caledonian* 1674c
G. R. Ian, *Vic.(BC)* 519c
George G., *Oxf.* 1882a
Gordon G., *Oxf.* 1880b
H. Dugald, *Leeds* 1732c
Macpherson, J. C., *Nfld.* 404b
McPherson, K., *Lond.* 1804b
Macpherson, Karen, *Canberra* 42c
McPherson, Kathryn, *Auck.UT* 1083c
MacPherson, Kerrie L., *HK* 2036c
Macpherson, Lorna M., *Glas.* 1670b
McPherson, M., *N-W(S.Af.)* 1364c
Michael J., *Leeds* 1727a
Peter S., *McG.* 374b, 376c
Mcpherson, Phyllis, *Ott.* 445b
MacPherson, R., *Napier* 1844c
McPherson, Ruth, *Ott.* 445b
MacPherson, Stuart G., *Edin.* 1652a
McPherson, Valerie, *Nott.Trent* 1862a
McPhie, Jocelyn, *Tas.* 179b, 182a
McPhillips, Kath, *W.Syd.* 203b
McPolin, Peter, *Belf.* 1564b
McQuaid, C. D., *Rhodes* 1390c
MacQuarrie, Kerry T., *New Br.* 430c
McQuarrie, S. A., *Alta.* 308b
McQuater, R., *Manc.Met.* 1837c
McQuay, Henry J., *Oxf.* 1879a
McQueen, Anne, *Edin.* 1647b
Daniel S., *Edin.* 1650c
Fiona M., *Auck.* 1075b, 1076c
H., *C'dia.* 345a
MacQueen, Hector L., *Edin.* 1648b
Hilary, *Open(UK)* 1868a
McQueen, Ken G., *Canberra* 42c
M., *Reading* 1906b
Maureen, *Athab.* 315a
Rob, *Griff.* 72a
Robert J., *Waik.* 1122b
T. J., *Plym.* 1890a

M. A., Chitt. 228b, 230b
M. A., Dhaka 236b, 239c, 240a
M. A., Jahang. 246b
M. A., Rajsh. 257a
Md. Abdul, Khulna 248b
S. M., Dhaka 235c
Samjid, Lond. 1791c
Sayyad A., Dr BA Marath. 732b
Mannar Jawahar, P., Anna 675
Manne, Robert, La Trobe 83a
Mannell, R. C., Wat. 530a, 533b
Robert H., Macq. 89c, 92b
Steven, Dal. 350a
Manners, I., Brist. 1584b
Ian, Tor. 491a
John M., Leeds Met. 1741c
Prudence J., W.Aust. 196c
William, Leic. 1747b
Mannila, P. N., P.Harcourt 1207a
Mannin, Michael L., Liv.J.Moores 1766c
Manning, A., Lond. 1799c
Anthony K., Warw. 1975b
Carl D., Lough. 1832b
Christine J., Liv. 1760a
Eric G., Vic.(BC) 517c, 518c
G., Nott. 1858a
Gemma, Hudd. 1693c
J., Wales 1965b, 1969b
Joanna M., Auck. 1072c
Karen, Vic.(Aust.) 186c
Nick P., Nott. 1856a
P., Trent 513b
Paul L., W'gong. 211c
Peter D., Durh. 1636a
R., Nott.Trent 1866a
Richard, Car. 339c
S. T., Sask. 475b
Susan, Edin. 1648c
W., Manc.Met. 1839b
Mannion, J., Qld.UT 153c
Mike, G.Caledonian 1672b, 1672c
Mannocci, Francesco, Lond. 1788c
Manns, Katy J., Leeds 1739c
Mannsaker, Frances, Lincoln(UK) 1751
Manocha, L. M., SP 907b
S., SP 907b
Manogue, Michael, Leeds 1735c
Manohar, C. S., IISc. 774b
Chethan, Manipal 848b
N., Madr. 826b
N., TN Law 932a, 932b, 932c
Rajiv, Lucknow 823b
T., Kakatiya 804b
U., Annam. 679b
Manohar Rao, D., Osm. 877a
J., Hyd. 770a
P., Kakatiya 805a
Manohara Pai, M. M., Manipal 852a
Manoharan, A., Annam. 677a
C., Annam. 680a
K., Madurai K. 828b
P., Annam. 678c
S., Annam. 676a
S., Auck. 1068c
T., Peradeniya 1455b
T. R., Annam. 677c
Manokaran, V., Annam. 681b
Manolopoulos, David E., Oxf. 1873c
Manomohanan, O. C., Kannur 809b
Manonmani, V., Bharati V. 707c
Manoochehri, Jamileh, Lincoln(UK) 1752a
Manor, James, Lond. 1821c
Manoranjitham, P. V., M.Teresa Women's 861b
Manormani, T., Madurai K. 829a
Manormoney, N., Madurai K. 829a
Mans, Bernard P., Macq. 87c
Mansel, R. E., Cardiff 1620c
Mansell, Heather L., Waik. 1123a, 1124b
Jim M., Kent 1716a
Lesley, Lough. 1836a, 1836b
Mervyn W., Pret. 1381b
Peter D., Melb. 102b
Phil, Wales 1971b
R., Lond. 1801a
Wade, Kent 1715a
Mansey, P. Anne, Herts. 1684c
Mansfield, Elizabeth, Kent 1715b
John, ICL 1701b
John, Nott.Trent 1866c
Neil, Lough. 1833b
Nicholas J., Macq. 88a
P., E.Cowan 64b
Paul, Durh. 1635c
R., Coventry 1626c
Roger, Cardiff 1617c
Mansi, Omaima, McG. 377a
Mansinha, L., W.Ont. 540a
Manson, A. H., Sask. 477a, 480a
A. S., Qu. 455c
Doreen E., Manc.Met. 1840a
G. A., Sheff. 1922c
J., Wat. 536c
Jean C., Edin. 1652c
Margaret M., Leic. 1746a
Morna, Wales 1970c
Neil, Lanc. 1724a
Mansoor, A. C. A. M., SE(S.Lanka) 1461c
A. Jalil, NU Singapore 1309a
Atif Bin, NUST(P'stan.) 1263b
R., WI 2000a
Simeen, Karachi 1251c
Mansoor Imam, Sir Syed UET 1278a
Mansoor-ul-Haq, Foundation(P'stan.) 1244a
Mansoori, Hissamuddin, Karachi 1253b
Mansor, M. N., Jahang. 246c
Mansor Abu Talib, Putra 1025c
Mansor Ahmad, Putra 1022c
Mansor bin Md Isa, Malaya 1007c
Mansor Hashim, Putra 1026c
Mansor Hj Ibrahim, IIU Malaysia 998b, 999c
Mansor Ibrahim, IIU Malaysia 998b, 999a
Mansor Jusoh, NU Malaysia 1016a
Mansour, R. R., Wat. 527c
Manstead, Antony, Cardiff 1622a
Mansuetus, A. B., Swazi. 1470c
Mansur, A., Chitt. 229a
S. S., W.Ont. 545b
Sale K., Bayero 1149b
Taslima, Dhaka 236b
Mansvelt, Erna P. G., Stell. 1399c
Juliana R., Massey 1100a
Mant, David, Oxf. 1881a
Jonathan W. F., Birm. 1575a
M. J., Alta. 311c
Mantalaris, Athanasios, ICL 1702c
Mantamadiotis, Theo, Monash 124a
Manteau, Kojo A., Kwame NUST 587c
Manthappa, M., Manipal 847b
Manthei, Bob J., Cant. 1089b
Manthorpe, Jill, Lond. 1792b, 1796b
Manthriratna, M. A. S. R. S., Sri Jay. 1463b
Mantle, Peter G., Lond. 1776c
Mantler, J., Car. 340c
Manton, Jonathan H., Melb. 97b
Nicholas S., Camb. 1605b
Mantrala, Murali, Lough. 1830c
Mantyka, S., Nfld. 404c
Mantzaris, E., KwaZulu-Natal 1354b
Manu, Dschang 273b
Manu, J., Ghana 582c
Patrick, Bugema 1493
Yayo A., Bayero 1151b
Manu Mohan, K., Manipal 849a
Manu'atu, Linita, Auck.UT 1081c
Manuel, H., Nfld. 403c
Jacqueline, Syd. 168c
P., Dal. 354c
Manuh, T., Ghana 585b
Manuja Devi, K., Kakatiya 804a
Manuratne, M. G., Peradeniya 1455a
Manus, C. U., O.Awolowo 1200c
Manuwa, S. I., Akure 1167c
Manwa, H. A., Botswana 262c
Manwar, M. A. M., Islamic(B'desh.) 243a
Manwaring, John A., Ott. 442c
Manyahi, M. J., Dar. 1478c
Manyaka, Johannes, Jo'burg. 1349a
Manyala, N., NUL 981b
Manyam, Joel, Waik. 1122a
Manyane, R. M., N-W(S.Af.) 1365c
Manyatsi, A. M., Swazi. 1471b
Manyeh, A. J., Njala 1285
M. K., Njala 1285c
Manyele, S. V., Dar. 1478b
Manyire, H., Mak. 1497a
Manz, Stefan, Greenwich 1677c
Manzar, Mehtab, JMI 794b
Manzie, Christopher, Melb. 97c
Manzoor, Manzoor Ahmed, NUST(P'stan.) 1265a
Raja A., Bhutto IST 1272c
Sadia, Karachi 1252c
Shahid, Riphah Internat. 1271b
Tasnim, Leeds Met. 1742a
Manzur, M., Curtin 55c
Mao, K., Warw. 1973b
Kezhi, Nan.Tech. 1296c
Lingling, Nott.Trent 1865b
Xeurong, Strath. 1948a
Maogoto, Jackson N., Newcastle(NSW) 143c
Maor, Dorit, Murd. 130c
Mapa, R. B., Peradeniya 1455b
Mapanga, K. G., Z'bwe. 2052a
Mapani, B., Z'bwe. 2051a
B. S., Namibia 1056c
Mapanje, Jack, Leeds 1730c
Mapara, Shakeel, Bhutto IST 1272c
Mapaure, I., Namibia 1056b
Maphisa, G. S., Zululand 1419
Maphosa, F., Z'bwe. 2051c
M., NUST Bulawayo 2048c
Norman, Solusi 2049
Maphumulo, Abednego M., KwaZulu-Natal 1358a
Mapitse, R., Botswana 261a
Mapiye, C., Bindura 2044b
Maples, Andrew J., Cant. 1089a
Mapletoft, R. J., Sask. 475b
Mapolelo, D., Botswana 261b
Mapolie, Selwyn F., W.Cape 1406b
Maponya, Simon, Cape Town 1332b
Mapopa, M., Zambia 2008c
Mapp, Katherine N., Leeds 1739b
Richard, Massey 1099c
Richard, Well. 1117a
Mappin, D., Alta. 305a
Mapps, D. J., Plym. 1894c
Mapstone, Bruce, Tas. 181c
Sally L., Oxf. 1875b
Mapunda, A. M., Dar. 1480a
B., Dar. 1479c
B. T., Dar. 1480a
Maqagi, S., Nelson Mandela Met. 1362b
Maqbool, Col., FJ Women 1242
M. A., Osm. 873c
Nauman, Foundation(P'stan.) 1244c
Maqbool Ahamed, TN Vet. 935c
Maqbool ur Rehman, Syed, Inst.Bus.Man.(P'stan.) 1247b
Maqddus, Khudija, Al-Khair 1234
Maqelepo, S. K., NUL 981b
Maqsood, Azra, Bhutto IST 1272c, 1273a, 1273c
Haris B., Bhutto IST 1273a
Shahid, N-WFP Eng. 1267a
Tariq, NUST(P'stan.) 1265b, 1265c
Zahida, Karachi 1251a
Maqutu, D., NUL 981b
Mar, A., Alta. 303c
Mar Molinero, Cecilio, Kent 1715a
Mar Yah Said, Putra 1026a
Mar-Molinero, F. C., S'ton. 1936c
Mara, Duncan D., Leeds 1729a
Thomas, W.Ont. 547b
Maradithaya, Laxminarayana, Manipal 851c
Maradufu, Asaph, E.Af.Baraton 964b
Marais, A., N-W(S.Af.) 1371a
A. F., N-W(S.Af.) 1369a
Adrian D., Cape Town 1339c
D. D., Pret. 1387a, 1387b
E., Jo'burg. 1347c
G. Frans, Stell. 1395a
Hendrik J., Pret. 1384c
M. J., Rhodes 1389a
Margaret R., W.Cape 1409a
Marialda, Jo'burg. 1347b
Nicholas J., Cape Town 1334c
Patrick C., Cape Town 1334a
R. M., Lond. 1785b
Renee, Pret. 1385b
Maraj, B., Alta. 308b
Marak, C. R., NE Hill 872b
Marake, Makoala V., NUL 980
Marala, K., Fort Hare 1344c
Marama, Ada, Auck. 1066c
Marambe, P. W. M. B., Peradeniya 1451b, 1452c
Marambos, P., Herts. 1683c
Marandu, E. E., Botswana 262c
Maranga, Japheth, E.Af.Baraton 964a
Rosebella O., Jomo K. 966c
S. Moffat, Jomo K. 966b
Marangos, Jonathan P., ICL 1704c
Maras, Pamela F., Greenwich 1677a
Marasas, Walter F. O., Pret. 1386a
Maraschin, Donatella, Lond.S.Bank 1827a
Marathe, A. G., IIT Bombay 777b
R. A., Bharati V. 707c
Vigneswar, Manipal 849b
Maraun, Michael D., S.Fraser 486a
Maravanyika, O. E., Masvingo 2046
O. E., Z'bwe. 2050b
Maraveyas, A., Hull 1698b
Marazi, Hamidullah, Kashmir 815c
Marber, Michael S., Lond. 1794c
Marble, A. E., Dal. 351c
Marc, Jan, Syd. 167b
Marcean, D. J., Calg. 326c
Marceau, Lawrence, Auck. 1067c
Marcell, A. T., Herts. 1688b
Marcella, Rita C., R.Gordon 1910c, 1911a
March, C., Coventry 1626c
Caty, Lond.S.Bank 1827b
Karen R., Car. 341b
Luke, Edin. 1650b
Peter, St Mary's(Can.) 469b
March-Russell, John, Oxf. 1878a
Marchand, Luc, Montr. 422c
R., Alta. 308c
Trevor M. J., Lond. 1815a
Marchant, Alan, Lincoln(UK) 1752b
Ali Imran, NUST(P'stan.) 1264c
Daryl, Vic.(Aust.) 186b
G. C., Witw. 1412b
Garry, Bond 38b, 38
Harvey, Melb. 102c
John, Lond.S.Bank 1829c
Roger, Ulster 1960a
T. A., Sask. 472c
Tim R., W'gong. 209b
Marchbank, J., S.Fraser 486c
Marche, Claude, Montr. 422c
S., Dal. 350c
T., Sask. 477c
Marchessault, Robert H., McG. 368c
Marchetti, Elena M., Griff. 72a
Marchetti-Mercer, Maria C., Pret. 1380b
Marchie, Tobechukwu T., Benin 1156c
Marchment, Wendy, Griff. 75c
Marchon, Maurice N., Montr. 423b
Marciniuk, D. D., Sask. 476a
Marcolin, B. L., Calg. 324b
Marcombe, D., Nott. 1852a
Marcora, S., Wales 1548a
Marcotte, Denis, Montr. 422c
Patrice, Montr. 412a
Marcoux, L. W., Wat. 531b
Marcel, Montr. 416b
Yves, Montr. 413c
Marcus, B. T., Open S.Lanka 1451b
Donna, Griff. 69b
Nizar, W.Cape 1408b
Marczyk, Alexandra A., Herts. 1684b
Marczynski, Gregory T., McG. 376b
Marden, Adrian, Herts. 1685b
Marder, Todd B., Durh. 1633c
Mardia, Kanti V., Leeds 1734b
Mardiana binti Nordin, Malaya 1008a
Mardikar, U. B., Bharati V. 707a
Mardling, Rosemary A., Monash 120a, 128a
Mardon, Helen J., Oxf. 1880a
Maré, Eben, Pret. 1379a
P. Gerhard, KwaZulu-Natal 1354b
Maree, Adele, Pret. 1377b
D., Fort Hare 1344a
David J. F., Pret. 1380b
H. B., Mehran 1258a
J. G., Pret. 1375b
Johannes J., Cape Town 1338a
K. W., Rhodes 1388a
Leon, Pret. 1376b
M., Namibia 1057b
M. Rehman, Sindh 1275b
Mareels, Iven M. Y., Melb. 93c, 97b
Marek, S. A., Napier 1844b
Marelli-Berg, Federica M., ICL 1706b
Marentette, P. F., Alta. 310b
Mares, Daryl J., Adel. 24c
Edwin D., Well. 1115c
Mareschal, Denis, Lond. 1779a
Marett, Allan, Syd. 172b
Mareya, L., Africa(Z'bwe.) 2043c
Marfany, Joan-Luis, Liv. 1756a
Marfo-Yiadom, E., Cape Coast 574b
Margaritis, Dimitri, Auck.UT 1080c
Margaroni, Maria, Cyprus 564b
Margerison, J. K., Plym. 1889a
Jean K., Massey 1097c
Margetts, Anna, Monash 118c
B. M., S'ton. 1939a
Helena Z., Oxf. 1877c
Kay, Melb. 100a
Marggraf Turley, Richard, Wales 1541a
Margham, J. Phil, Liv.J.Moores 1767a, 1767b
Marginson, David, Cardiff 1615b
Paul, Warw. 1977b, 1979a
Simon, Melb. 98b
Simon W., Monash 126b
Margison, Jennifer, Vic.(BC) 522c
Margolese, Richard G., McG. 377b, 379a, 383c
Margolin, U., Alta. 307c
Margolis, Harriet, Well. 1115a
Judith, Open(UK) 1870c
Margot, Jöelle, Montr. 415a
Margrain, T., Cardiff 1621a
Margrave, Frank, Portsmouth 1900b
G. F., Calg. 327b, 328b
Margret, J., La Trobe 78c
Marh, B. S., HP 767c
Mari-Beffa, Paloma, Wales 1547c
Maria Das, M., And. 671c
Maria John, B., M.Sund. 856c
Mariam Ali, Brunei 268b
Mariam binti Abdullah, Malaya 1009b
Mariana Nor Shamsudin, Putra 1022c
Mariani, John A., Lanc. 1722a
Mariani binti Md Nor, Malaya 1006b
Mariani Idraos, Tech.U.Malaysia 1032b
Mariani Mansor, Putra 1025c
Mariappan, A., Delhi 723c
R., Annam. 679a
Mariappandar, Sugumar, Aust.Cath. 34b
Mariayanayagam, David, Manipal 849c
Mariba, Thanyani J., Pret. 1373a, 1382c
Maribei, J. M., Nair. 971c
Marie Stanislas Ashok, Pondicherry 887c
Marikkar, Faiz, IIT S.Lanka 1465c, 1466c
Marima-Matarira, Hilda T., Great Z'bwe. 2045
Marimuthu, G., Madurai K. 828b
T., Annam. 681a
Marin, A. M., Lond. 1799c
Marina binti Mohd Bakri, Malaya 1009c
Marindo, R., Z'bwe. 2052c
Marinelli, M., Brist. 1588b
Mariney binti Mohd Yusoff, Malaya 1007c
Marini, A. E., Calg. 325c
Zopito A., Brock 320c
Mariniello, Silvestra, Montr. 411b, 420a
Marino, Frank, C.Sturt 51b
P., Nfld. 401b
R., W.Ont. 555c
Marinova, Dora, Murd. 131c
S. T., Birm. 1567b
Maripe, B., Botswana 262b

Mkony, Charles, *Aga Khan(P'stan.)* 1232b
Mkpa, A. Mkpa, *Abia State* 1136
M. A., *Abia State* 1136c
N. D., *Abia State* 1136c, 1137b
Mkposong, E. O., *Calabar* 1161c
Mkuchu, S. G. V., *Open Tanz.* 1484b
Mkude, D. J., *Dar.* 1479c
Mkumbwa, M. H., *Dar.* 1478c
Mkusa, E. L., *Namibia* 1056b
Mkwananzi, T. N., *Midlands State* 2046
Mkwara, B., *Malawi* 988a
Mladenova, O. M., *Calg.* 327c
Mladenovic, Nenad, *Brun.* 1595b
Rosalina, *Syd.* 165c
Mlama, Penina O. P., *Dar.* 1479b
Mlambiti, M. E., *Sokoine Ag.* 1485b
Mlambo, A. S., *Z'bwe.* 2050c
Alois S., *Pret.* 1377c
E. T., *Midlands State* 2046b
N., *Bindura* 2044b
Mlangwa, J. E. D., *Sokoine Ag.* 1486c
Mlawa, H. M., *Dar.* 1481a
Mlay, P. S., *Sokoine Ag.* 1487a
Mle, T. R., *Fort Hare* 1344c
Mlekwa, V. M., *Dar.* 1477b
Mlilo, T., *N-W(S.Af.)* 1365b
Mlimuka, A. K. L. J., *Dar.* 1479c
Mlipha, M., *Swazi.* 1471b
Mloza-Banda, H. R., *Malawi* 986a
Mlozi, M. R. S., *Sokoine Ag.* 1485c
Mmadike, B. I., *Abia State* 1137a
B. I., *N.Azikiwe* 1196a
Mmereki, T. T., *Botswana* 261a
Mmope, P., *N-W(S.Af.)* 1364
Mmuya, M., *Dar.* 1480b
Mndebele, C. B., *Swazi.* 1470c, 1472a
Mnembuka, B. V., *Sokoine Ag.* 1485c
Mneney, Edith, *KwaZulu-Natal* 1350
Stanley H., *KwaZulu-Natal* 1352b
Mnjama, N. M., *Botswana* 262c
Mnkandla, V. A., *NUST Bulawayo* 2047c
Mnkeni, A. P., *Sokoine Ag.* 1486a
P. N. S., *Fort Hare* 1343b
Mntambo, N., *Fort Hare* 1344c
Mnthali, F. W. J., *Botswana* 261c
Mnukhin, Valeriy, *S.Pac.* 1422c
Moahi, K. H. N., *Botswana* 262c
Moala, Emily, *S.Pac.* 1423a
Moallem, M., *S.Fraser* 484a
M., *W.Ont.* 541b
Moatter, Tariq, *Aga Khan(P'stan.)* 1232b
Moav, Omer, *Lond.* 1808a
Moazzam, M., *Islamia, Bahawal.* 1249a
M. G., *Jahang.* 245c
Moazzen-Ahmadi, N., *Calg.* 329a
Mobarak, A., *Dhaka* 233a
Mobarek, A., *Botswana* 260b
Mobbs, Ian G., *Dal.* 356a, 356b, 358c
Kenneth L., *Leeds Met.* 1741b
Stephen D., *Leeds* 1728b
Moberly, Rev. R. Walter L., *Durh.* 1636c
Mobin, Sajjad, *Lahore UET* 1240c
Mocerino, M., *Curtin* 55b
Mochaba, B. M., *NUL* 980a
Mochiwa, Z., *Dar.* 1479c
Mochnacki, Stefan W., *Tor.* 490c
Mochrie, R. I., *H-W* 1680c
Mock, David, *Tor.* 489b, 492a
Dennis R., *Nipissing* 436, 438a, 438b
Mockaitis, Audra, *Well.* 1116c
Mockett, S. P., *Nott.* 1856c
Mockler, Gary M., *W'gong.* 207a
Mocquais, P. Y. A., *Calg.* 327b
Modak, B., *Kal.* 808a
Jayant M., *IISc.* 774a
P. C., *B'desh.Ag.* 220a
Sharmila B., *Delhi* 722c
Moddeman, Diane, *Manit.* 397a
Modebe, Onyechi, *Ebonyi State* 1165c
Modeen, T., *E.Lond.* 1642a
Modi, A. K., *G.Jamb.* 761c
Albert T., *KwaZulu-Natal* 1357a
D., *Witw.* 1415c
G., *Witw.* 1416a
K. B., *Saur.* 910a
Monica, *Herts.* 1683c
Neena, *ICL* 1706b
P. C., *Witw.* 1416b
Modiba, M. M., *Witw.* 1412b
Modise, M. R., *N-W(S.Af.)* 1371b
Modisi, M. P., *Botswana* 262a
Modo, I. V. O., *Uyo* 1216c
Modood, T., *Brist.* 1589a
Modu, S., *Maid.* 1192b
Modu Babagana Alhaji, *Maid.* 1191c
Mody, C. H., *Calg.* 332a, 332b
Girish M., *KwaZulu-Natal* 1355b, 1355c
Moe, Gordon, *Tor.* 506a
Moebus, G., *Sheff.* 1923c
Moeed, Azra, *Well.* 1117b
Moehr, Jochen R., *Vic.(BC)* 519c
Moeller, Hans-Georg, *Brock* 322a
Moeno, Sylvia, *Jo'burg.* 1348c
Moens, Alexander, *S.Fraser* 486a
Gabriel, *Murd.* 131a
Moerdijk, I., *Sheff.* 1925b
Moeti, L. D., *NUL* 980c
N., *Botswana* 262c
Moewes, A., *Sask.* 477a
Mofammere, M., *NUL* 980b
Moffat, Alistair M., *Melb.* 97b
Anthony, *Montr.* 415a
Barb A., *Wat.* 524b
J. B., *Wat.* 525a
John W., *Tor.* 499a
K., *Ryerson* 466a
K. G., *Warw.* 1972a
Miriam F., *ICL* 1707a
S. M., *Nfld.* 407a
Tony, *Lond.* 1819a
Moffatt, G., *Warw.* 1975a
I., *Stir.* 1941c
M. E. K., *Manit.* 395b, 397a
P., *Nott.Trent* 1866a
P. G., *E.Anglia* 1639b
Susan L., *Qu.* 458c
Moffett, Ashley, *Camb.* 1606a
Bruce, *E.Lond.* 1643a
J., *Hull* 1698c
Pamela V., *Belf.* 1565a
Moffitt, Emerson, *Dal.* 357a
Terrie E., *Lond.* 1793b
Mofizuddin, Mirza, *Jahang.* 246a, 247c
Mofuoa, K. V., *NUL* 981b
Mogadime, Y. M., *Venda* 1404c, 1405a
Mogalakwe, M., *Botswana* 263c
Mogale, T. M., *Witw.* 1414c
Mogali, B. C., *Karn.* 812b
Mogariya, V. D., *SP* 907a
Mogbo, O., *N.Azikiwe* 1195b
Mogella, Fr. C. A., *Dar.* 1480b
Mogg, Karin, *S'ton.* 1937c
Tony D., *Syd.* 174c
Moggach, Douglas A., *Ott.* 443c
Moggridge, Donald E., *Tor.* 492c
Geoff D., *Camb.* 1603a, 1611a
Moghtaderi, Behdad, *Newcastle(NSW)* 142c
Mogiba, A., *Fort Hare* 1344c
Mogie, Michael, *Bath* 1550b, 1554c
Mogil, Jeffrey S., *McG.* 373c
Mogilaiah, K., *Kakatiya* 803c
Mogin, Pavle, *Well.* 1116c
Mogoa, E. G., *Nair.* 971c
Mogobe, K. D., *Botswana* 263a
Mogobjwa, D., *Botswana* 261b
Mogorosi, L. D., *Venda* 1404b
Mogotlane, R. A., *Pret.* 1372
Mogotsi, I., *Botswana* 261a
Mogra, Subraya, *Manipal* 850a
Mohad Anizu Mohd Nor, *Tech.U.Malaysia* 1031c
Mohal, Ferdosi, *Rajsh.* 253a
Mohamad, A. A., *Calg.* 326c
Mohamad Abu Bakar, *IIU Malaysia* 999a
Mohamad Afifi Abdul Mukti, *Tech.U.Malaysia* 1034b
Mohamad Ali Abdul Hamid, *Putra* 1021c
Mohamad alias Md Som Sujimon, *IIU Malaysia* 1000c
Mohamad Amran Mohd Salleh, *Putra* 1024b
Mohamad Aslam Haneef, *IIU Malaysia* 999c
Mohamad Asri Basil, *IIU Malaysia* 1003b
Mohamad b Bilal Ali, *Tech.U.Malaysia* 1031c
Mohamad Bakhir Hj Abdullah, *IIU Malaysia* 999a
Mohamad bin Abd Razak, *NU Malaysia* 1019c
Mohamad bin Abu Bakar, *Malaya* 1008b
Mohamad Deraman, *NU Malaysia* 1015b
Mohamad Fazli Sabri, *Putra* 1027a
Mohamad Hilmi Abdullah, *Putra* 1022a
Mohamad Hussain bin Habil, *Malaya* 1011b
Mohamad Iskandr bin Mohamad Nor, *Malaya* 1006c
Mohamad Ismail b Yaziz, *Putra* 1025a
Mohamad Ismail Mohamad Yunus, *IIU Malaysia* 1001b
Mohamad Johdi Salleh, *IIU Malaysia* 999c
Mohamad Kamal A Rahim, *Tech.U.Malaysia* 1032a
Mohamad Kamil Haji Abdul Majid, *Malaya* 1012a
Mohamad Khairi Saidin, *Tech.U.Malaysia* 1034c
Mohamad Khazani Abdullah, *Putra* 1024b
Mohamad Md Tan, *NU Malaysia* 1017a
Mohamad Mokhtar bin Abu Hassan, *Malaya* 1012c
Mohamad Ngasri Dimon, *Tech.U.Malaysia* 1033b
Mohamad Noh Ahmad, *Tech.U.Malaysia* 1033a
Mohamad Nor bin Said, *Tech.U.Malaysia* 1033c
Mohamad Osman, *NU Malaysia* 1017a
Mohamad Pauzi b Zakaria, *Putra* 1025a
Mohamad Ragab Abd El-Hady Shalaby, *Malaya* 1007c
Mohamad Ramlan Mohamed Salleh, *IIU Malaysia* 1000a
Mohamad Rom bin Tamjis, *Malaya* 1007a
Mohamad Rushdan Md Said, *Putra* 1026b
Mohamad Sahari Nordin, *IIU Malaysia* 999c
Mohamad Saleeh bin Rahamad @ Ahamad, *Malaya* 1009a
Mohamad Shanudin Zakaria, *NU Malaysia* 1018b
Mohamad Som bin Sujimon, Hj, *Brunei* 266b
Mohamad Suffian bin Mohamad Annuar, *Malaya* 1005b
Mohamad Yasim bin Mohamad Yusof, *Malaya* 1010a
Mohamad Zaidi Abdul Rahman, *Malaya* 1012b
Mohamad Zakaria Hussin, *Putra* 1027a
Mohamed, A., *Sask.* 472b
Azhar, *Massey* 1097a
P. P., *Calicut* 715
Sherif, *Griff.* 70c, 74b
Yasien, *W.Cape* 1407b
Mohamed Abdeal Aziem Sayed, *Brunei* 268a
Mohamed Abdullah, *Tech.U.Malaysia* 1030
Mohamed Afendi Mohamed Piah, *Tech.U.Malaysia* 1033b
Mohamed Ali, Sitty K., *Ruhuna* 1459a
Mohamed Ali Rajion, *Putra* 1027c
Mohamed Amin b Alias, *Tech.U.Malaysia* 1032b
Mohamed Amin Embi, *NU Malaysia* 1016b
Mohamed Aris Hj Osman, *IIU Malaysia* 1002c
Mohamed Awang, *IIU Malaysia* 1002a
Mohamed Azharashid bin Mohamed Tahir, *NU Singapore* 1315c
Mohamed Aziz Dollah, *Putra* 1022b
Mohamed Azlan bin Hussain, *Malaya* 1006c
Mohamed Azril Mohamed Amin, *IIU Malaysia* 1001c
Mohamed Azwan Mohamed Zawawi, *Putra* 1024a
Mohamed Baha'addin H Ahmed, *IIU Malaysia* 1002b
Mohamed bin Abdul Majid, *Malaya* 1005b
Mohamed Daud, *Putra* 1024a
Mohamed El Tahir Abu Elgasim El Mesawie, *IIU Malaysia* 1000c
Mohamed Esmail, S., *Annam.* 678b
Mohamed Fadzil Che Din, *Putra* 1023b
Mohamed Hassan Mohamed Hassan, *IIU Malaysia* 1000b
Mohamed Ibrahim bin Noordin, *Malaya* 1011a
Mohamed Ibrahim Mohamed Tahir, *Putra* 1022c
Mohamed Ismail Abdul Karim, *IIU Malaysia* 1000b
Mohamed Ismail Ahamed Shah, *IIU Malaysia* 1003a
Mohamed Kamel Abd Ghani, *NU Malaysia* 1018c
Mohamed Khalil Mohd Hani, *Tech.U.Malaysia* 1032b, 1033a
Mohamed Kheireddine bin Taieb Aroua, *Malaya* 1006c
Mohamed Konneh, *IIU Malaysia* 1000b
Mohamed Magdi El Sersi, *IIU Malaysia* 1001c
Mohamed Mahmoud El-Sayed Nasef, *Tech.U.Malaysia* 1032a
Mohamed Mustafa Ishak, *Utara* 1037
Mohamed Najib b Abdul Ghafar, *Tech.U.Malaysia* 1031b
Mohamed Noor Hasan, *Tech.U.Malaysia* 1031a
Mohamed Othman, *Putra* 1022c
Mohamed Rashid Embi, *Tech.U.Malaysia* 1030c
Mohamed Rehan bin Karim, *Malaya* 1006c
Mohamed Roji Samidi, *Tech.U.Malaysia* 1032a
Mohamed Saeed, *IIU Malaysia* 1002a
Mohamed Safiullah, A., *TN Vet.* 936c
Mohamed Salleh Mohamed Yasin, *NU Malaysia* 1018c
Mohamed Sharif Mustaffa, *Tech.U.Malaysia* 1031b
Mohamed Shariff Mohamed Din, Dato, *Putra* 1027c, 1028a
Mohamed Shariff Nabi Baksh, *Tech.U.Malaysia* 1034b
Mohamed Suleiman, *Putra* 1026b
Mohamed Tarmizi Ahmad, Lt.-Col., *Putra* 1024a
Mohamed Thameem Ansari, *Annam.* 677b
Mohamed Wijayanuddin Ali, *Tech.U.Malaysia* 1032a
Mohamed Yusoff Ismail, *NU Malaysia* 1018b
Mohamedali, Ownali N., *WI* 1995b
Mohammad, Jawed, *I.Sch.Mines* 782b
Jigar, *Jammu* 796a
Magana A., *Bayero* 1149b
N., *Islamic(B'desh.)* 242c
Razia Fakir, *Aga Khan(P'stan.)* 1231a
Mohammad Abdul Mohit, *IIU Malaysia* 999b
Mohammad Abdul Quayum Abdus Salam, *IIU Malaysia* 1000b
Mohammad Abdur Rashid, *IIU Malaysia* 1002b
Mohammad Agus Yusoff, *NU Malaysia* 1017b
Mohammad Akram, *IIU Malaysia* 1001b
Mohammad Al-Amin, *Jahang.* 246a
Mohammad Azram, *IIU Malaysia* 1000b
Mohammad Fuad Rahman, *Putra* 1023a
Mohammad Hashim Kamali, *IIU Malaysia* 1001b
Mohammad Hassan Zakaria, *Tech.U.Malaysia* 1034c
Mohammad Ibrahim Mohamad, *Tech.U.Malaysia* 1033c
Mohammad Ishak Desa, *Tech.U.Malaysia* 1031b
Mohammad Ismail, *Tech.U.Malaysia* 1033c
Mohammad Lutfi Othman, *Putra* 1024c
Mohammad Mohd Lassim, *Putra* 1023a
Mohammad Nabil Al-Munawar, *Brunei* 267a
Mohammad Naqib s/o Ishan Jan, *IIU Malaysia* 1001b
Mohammad Nazri Mohd Ja'afar, *Tech.U.Malaysia* 1031c
Mohammad Niyaz Khan, *Malaya* 1011c
Mohammad Nizam Filipski Abdullah, *Putra* 1024a
Mohammad Raduan Mohd Ariff, *Malaya* 1009a
Mohammad Radzi Sudin, *Tech.U.Malaysia* 1034c
Mohammad Razali Abdul Kadir, *Putra* 1024b
Mohammad Redzuan Othman, *Malaya* 1008a
Mohammad Sadegh Bazaz, *Malaya* 1007c
Mohammad Saleem, *Putra* 1024a
Mohammad Shatar bin Sabran, *Putra* 1027b
Mohammad Yeakub Ali, *IIU Malaysia* 1000b
Mohammad Yousuf Rathor, *IIU Malaysia* 1001c
Mohammad Yusof bin Arshad, *Tech.U.Malaysia* 1031b
Mohammad Yusri Hassan, *Tech.U.Malaysia* 1033b
Mohammadullah, S., *Dhaka* 238c
Mohammed, A., *Maid.* 1192b
Ahmed R., *Bayero* 1150a
Ahmed T., *Maid.* 1192c
Aminu F., *Bayero* 1151a
Ashfaque, *Manipal* 845b
I., *AT Balewa* 1138b
I. S., *Malawi* 987b
J., *NUL* 980b
M., *WI* 1999c
Mustapha, *Bayero* 1149c
Nizam I., *Kingston(UK)* 1719b
Noor, *Delhi* 723b
Patricia, *WI* 1990c
Yusuf, *W.Cape* 1406a
Zango I., *Bayero* 1151a
Mohammed Abul Lais, *IIU Malaysia* 1002b
Mohammed Akram Laldin, *IIU Malaysia* 1000c
Mohammed Al-Habib Abu Ya'arub Al-Marzougui, *IIU Malaysia* 1003a
Mohammed Ali Berawi, *Malaya* 1009a
Mohammed Fauzi Abdul Rani, *IIU Malaysia* 1001c
Mohammed Imad Al-Deen Mustafa, *IIU Malaysia* 1001c
Mohammed Nor Che' Noh, *Malaya* 1013c
Mohammed Rizman bin Idid, *Malaya* 1005b
Mohammed Yusoff, *IIU Malaysia* 999c
Mohamod Ismail, *NU Malaysia* 1016c
Mohan, Alladi, *S.Venkat.IMS* 930b
Anand, *Ban.* 691b, 696a
Arvind, *Lucknow* 822c
B., *TN Vet.* 935a
Devender, *G.Jamb.* 761a
G., *Annam.* 677b
G., *IIT Bombay* 777a
G., *NU Singapore* 1309a
G. Krishna, *Kakatiya* 805b
Giles, *Open(UK)* 1868c
Harsh, *Lucknow* 822c
J., *S'ton.* 1938b
J. S. S., *SP* 906c
Jayanthi, *S.Ramachandra* 927b
K., *Pondicherry* 886c
K., *Z'bwe.* 2052b
K. H., *Manipal* 849a
K. S., *SRT Marath.* 931a
K. T. Ram, *M.Gandhi* 838a
Krishna, *Panjab* 881b

2377 INDEX TO PERSONAL NAMES Naya...Nels

Jagadish H., Manipal 852c
Krishnamurthy, Manipal 851c
L., Berh. 702c
L. T., Karn. 812b
Laxman, Birm. 1574b
M. S., Karn. 812c
Nitin D., Bharati V. 707b
P., I.Gandhi Nat.Open 786b
P., NE Hill 871b
P., Samb. 901c
P. K., Samb. 901b
P. K., Utkal 944a, 945b
Pulin B., Delhi 722c
R., Qld.UT 150b
R. B. K., Shiv. 915a
R. C., Berh. 702c
Rajesh, Manipal 852a
Rajesh R., Manipal 846a
S., Utkal 945a
S. Radhakrishna, Manipal 846a
S. S., Gulb. 755a
Sadananda, Berh. 702c
Sailendra K., Berh. 702c
Santanu K., Berh. 702b
Sathisha, Manipal 848a
Subramanya, Manipal 851c
Sudhakar, Manipal 847a, 847b
Suresh P., M'lore. 843a
Udaya B., Manipal 845c
Vinod C., Manipal 847b
Nayak Govinda, N., M'lore. 843c
Nayak Kishori, M'lore. 843a
Nayanapriya, T. W. K. O., Kelaniya 1444b
Nayar, A., Saur. 909c
C. V., Curtin 56b
N. K., Thapar 941b
R. J., Warw. 1975a
Rana, Panjab 881b
Usha S., Tata Inst.Soc.Scis. 937, 939b, 939c
Nayar M. Azim, Kashmir 816b
Nayeem, A. I., Dhaka 235c
Nayer, Bhaskaran, Lincoln(UK) 1753a
Nayler, S. J., Witw. 1417a
Naylor, A. Ross, Leic. 1746b
Beth, Liv. 1763c
Bronwyn G., Monash 119a
C. David, Tor. 489, 504b, 506a
Carole, Leeds Met. 1741c
D., Ryerson 464a
D., W.Ont. 544a
David A., Leth. 365c
E., Wales 1547b
Elaine, Mt.All. 427a
J., Bran. 317b
Jeff, Lond.Met. 1824b
John B., Liv.J.Moores 1766a
Maxine, Lincoln(UK) 1752b
Michael, Massey 1097b
Patrick A., ICL 1703b
R. Thomas, McG. 369b
Robin A., Warw. 1972c
Sandra, Brun. 1595a
Tim, Exe. 1658a
Naysmith, John, Portsmouth 1901c
Nayyar, A. Q., Azad J&K 1238b
Harsh, Panjab 881a
S., Azad J&K 1237c
S. K., Panjab 883a
Nayyer, S., Azad J&K 1236c
Naz, Farah, Bhutto IST 1273a
Fouzia, Karachi 1252a
Hajra, Karachi 1250c
Neelum, Lahore UET 1240b
Sabrina, Rajsh. 253a
Shahina, Karachi 1251b
Nazamid Saari, Putra 1025b
Nazar, L. F., Wat. 525a, 532b
Nazarali, A. J., Sask. 476c
Nazarenko, S. V., Warw. 1975b
Nazarina binti Abdul Rahman, Malaya 1011a
Nazatul Shiha binti Bachtiar, Malaya 1011a
Nazeer, H. M., Peradeniya 1454b
Nazeer Ahamad, R., Karn. 811c
Nazeeruddin Yaacob, Tech.U.Malaysia 1034b
Nazib, M., Dhaka 235b
Nazifa Yaswi, Kashmir 816b
Naziha Ahmad Azli, Tech.U.Malaysia 1032b
Nazimah Sheikh Abdul Hamid, Putra 1025b
Nazimuddin, M., Chitt. 228b
S. M., Khulna 248b
Nazir, Arshad, NUST(P'stan.) 1264b
Imran, NUST(P'stan.) 1264c
Muhammad, Riphah Internat. 1271b
Nazir A., Kashmir 815b
Zafar, Aga Khan(P'stan.) 1233a
Nazira, S., S.Ramachandra 927b
Nazirah binti Hasnan, Malaya 1009c
Naziruddin Abdullah, IIU Malaysia 999c
Nazli Anum Mohd Ghazali, IIU Malaysia 998c
Nazneen, D. R. Zinnatara, Dhaka 237b
S., Chitt. 229a
Naznin, M. Hushna A., B'desh.Ag. 222a
Nazreen, S., Dhaka 236a
Nazri Mohd Yusof, IIU Malaysia 1002a
Nazzini, R., S'ton. 1936a
Ncala, N., N-W(S.Af.) 1366b
Ncayiyana, D. J., KwaZulu-Natal 1355b
Daniel J. M., Cape Town 1340a
Nchai, N., NUL 981a
Nchimbi, M. I., Dar. 1477b
Nchimbi-Msolla, S., Sokoine Ag. 1486a
Nchimi, Mebu J. C., Yaounde II 277c
Ncube, Cornelius, Bourne. 1580b
F., Z'bwe. 2053a
M., Fort Hare 1343c
M., Witw. 1411c
Ndabezinhle J., Z'bwe.Open 2054b
P. Z., N-W(S.Af.) 1365c
W., Z'bwe. 2051a
Ndabandaba, G., Swazi. 1470a
Ndaeyo, N. U., Uyo 1214c
Ndagana, J. M., Yola 1171b
Ndagi, M. A., Islamic Uganda 1494b
Ndaguatha, P. L. W., Nair. 975a
Ndahi, Kujara S., Maid. 1191b
N. P., Maid. 1191a
Ndalianis, Angela, Melb. 96a
Ndalichako, J., Dar. 1478b
Ndaliman, Umaru, Bayero 1151c
Ndalut, P. K., Moi 968c
Ndambuki, J. M., Moi 969a
Ndanshau, M. O. A., Dar. 1478a
N. O., Dar. 1478a
Ndavi, P. M., Nair. 974c
Ndawi, O., Midlands State 2046a
Ndayiragije, Juvenal, Tor. 494b
Ndebbio, John E. U., Calabar 1159a
Ndee, H. S., Dar. 1480b
Ndeezi, G., Mak. 1499a
Ndege, M., KwaZulu-Natal 1352a
Peter O., Moi 968a
Ndegwa, E. N. W., Nair. 972c
George M., Jomo K. 966a
P. N., Nair. 972c
Ndekha, M. J., Malawi 987b
Ndekwere, Perpetual, Z'bwe.Open 2053
Ndekwu, O. S., Ib. 1178b
Ndele, J. K., Nair. 974b
Ndem, U. D., Uyo 1215a
Ndemanisho, E., Sokoine Ag. 1486a
Ndembiyembe, Bakoume P. C., Yaounde II 276b
Ndemo, E. B., Nair. 975c
F. A., Nair. 975b
Ndengu, Dominic M., Mzuzu 989c, 990a, 990b
Nder, M. O., Makurdi Ag. 1143c
Nderitu, J. H., Nair. 970b, 971b
Ndetei, D., Nair. 975a
Ndhlovu, B. J., Copperbelt 2006a, 2006b
C. E., Z'bwe. 2052a
S. N., Midlands State 2046
T. P., Manc.Met. 1838c
Ndi, George, Hudd. 1693c
Ndiaye, Christiane, Montr. 413a
Ndiema, Moses, Moi 968b
Ndieyira, Joseph W., Jomo K. 966a
Ndifon, C. O., Calabar 1160a
Henry M., Calabar 1158c
Ndikuwera, J., Mak. 1499b
Ndima, D. D., N-W(S.Af.) 1366a
Ndimande, N. P., KwaZulu-Natal 1352c
Ndimele, O. M., P.Harcourt 1208a
Ndinechi, Gabriel I., Ebonyi State 1164a
Ndinya-Achola, J. O., Nair. 974c
Ndiokwere, Chinaka L., Benin 1153b
Ndiritu, E. M., Nair. 976a
Emilius, CUE Af. 962b
J. G., Witw. 1412c
Nditi, N. N. N., Dar. 1480a
Ndiweni, Nomathemba, NUST Bulawayo 2047c
Ndiyo, N. A., Calabar 1159a
Ndjanyou, Laurent, Dschang 273c
Ndjieunde, Germain, Yaounde II 276b, 276c
Ndjiojip, Robert, Yaounde II 277a
Ndjountche Njiki, G. A., Dschang 273b
Ndlalane, Thembe C., Pret. 1386c
Ndlovu, Hebron L., Swazi. 1470b, 1471c
Lindela R., NUST Bulawayo 2047
M., Fort Hare 1343a
M. W., NUST Bulawayo 2048a
Ndogmo, Jean-Claude, W.Cape 1408b
Ndoko, Nicole C., Yaounde II 276a
Ndoleriire, O., Mak. 1497b
Ndoloi, D. B., Dar. 1479b
Ndoma, H., Z'bwe. 2053b
Ndoma-Egba, Roland, Calabar 1161c
Ndomahina, Ernest T., S.Leone 1286b, 1287c
Ndombi, S. J., Nair. 974c
Ndome, C. B., Calabar 1160c
Ndomi, Benjamin M., Yola 1171b
Ndon, B. A., Uyo 1214c
Ndongbou, Gabriel, Dschang 274b
Ndongo, Barthelemy, Dschang 273a
Ndou, R. V., N-W(S.Af.) 1365b
Ndu, E. C., P.Harcourt 1208c
Umeche, Ebonyi State 1163b
Nduanya, Maurice O., Ebonyi State 1164b
Nduati, Ruth W. K., Nair. 974c
Ndubani, P., Zambia 2009a
Ndubisi, O. L., Ambrose Alli 1146b
Ndububa, D., O.Awolowo 1201b
Ndubuisi, Friday N., Lagos 1185c
W. C., Maid. 1191a
Nduji, Alex A., Ebonyi State 1164a
Nduka, Dennis M., Ebonyi State 1164b
E. C., P.Harcourt 1208a
F. O., Abia State 1136b, 1137c
Ndukuba, P. I., Abia State 1137b
Ndukwe, K. C., O.Awolowo 1202a
Ndukwu, B. C., P.Harcourt 1208b
Ndulo, M., Zambia 2007a
Ndumbaro, L., Dar. 1480b
P., Dar. 1479a
Ndumbe, Peter Martins, Yaounde I 275b
Ndung'u, C. Kamande, Jomo K. 966c
E. Ng'ang'a, Jomo K. 966b
Ndungu, N. S., Nair. 975c
N. W., Nair. 976b
Ndungutse, D., Mak. 1498c
Nduru, Gilbert, Moi 969a
Ndurumo, M., Moi 969a
Ndyabahika, J. F., Africa(Z'bwe.) 2043c
Ndzi, David, Portsmouth 1900b
Ndzie, Otabela, Yaounde II 275c
Ndzinge, S. E., Botswana 260b
Nead, Lynda, Lond. 1778a
Neades, B., Napier 1845b
Neailey, K., Warw. 1973c
Neal, A., Warw. 1975a
Andrew C., Lanc. 1721, 1725b
D. B., Nott.Trent 1862b, 1863a
David, Herts. 1688b
David E., Camb. 1608c, 1609a
Debbie, Leeds Met. 1742b
Derrick J., Cran. 1629a, 1630c
J. W., Cardiff 1620a
Leo, Auck.UT 1081c
Maureen, Manc.Met. 1837a
Nicholas C., Keele 1711b
Radford M., Tor. 501b
Neal-Sturgess, C. E., Birm. 1568c
Neale, Jenny, Well. 1117c
Jim, Dal. 360c
Michael R., Adel. 31c
Ray, W.Syd. 203c
Stephen B. M., Exe. 1656b
Neall, V. E., Massey 1100a
Neame, Charles, Cran. 1629b
Neanon, Chris, Portsmouth 1900a
Nearey, T. M., Alta. 307a
Neary, J. Peter, Oxf. 1874c
Jane, ICL 1708b
Peter F., W.Ont. 542c
Neath, I., Nfld. 405c
Nebauer, Monica L., Aust.Cath. 33c
Nebe, W. A., Witw. 1411b
Nebebe, Fassil, C'dia. 344a
Nebhwani, M., Mehran 1258a
Nebo, Chinedu O., Nigeria 1194
Nebot, Eduardo M., Syd. 169a, 175c
Nebuwa, Ikechukwu J., Ebonyi State 1166a
Necsulescu, Dan S., Ott. 441c
Nectoux, François, Kingston(UK) 1719a, 1720a
Nedelcu, Aurora, New Br. 429b
Nedeljkovic, V., Witw. 1415c
Nedelsky, Jennifer, Tor. 496a
Nediger, W. G., W.Ont. 540c
Nedimovic, M., Dal. 351b
Nedzela, Michel, Ott. 443a
Nee, Andrew Y. C., NU Singapore 1310a, 1319c
Claire, Portsmouth 1902b
S., Edin. 1645b
Needham, Alan, E.Cowan 65c
D., Nott.Trent 1862c
David J., Reading 1909a
Gary W., Nott.Trent 1863a
Joy, E.Lond. 1643a
Ted, New Br. 431c
W. R., Wat. 526c
Needs, Adrian, Portsmouth 1902b
Richard J., Camb. 1606b
Neela, R., Annam. 677b
Neelagund, Y. F., Gulb. 753b, 754c
Neelakantan Nair, O. S., SC Tirunal 922a
Neelakantham, K., Osm. 875b
Neelakanthan, Kusuma, Karn. 812a
Neelakrishnan, R., Annam. 679b
Neelam, Ban. 695a
, Kuruk. 819b
Neelam Pandey, Annam. 680a
Neelands, J., Warw. 1973a
Rev. W. David, Trin.Coll.(Tor.) 512
Neelasiddaiah, B., Gulb. 755b
Neelavathi, B., Avina. Women 685c
Neelima, B. N., SPMV 924c
Neels, J. L., Jo'burg. 1348a
Neely, Andrew D., Cran. 1630b
Donald, W.Syd. 204b
Neema, P. K., SC Tirunal 922b
Stella, Mak. 1498a
Neemia, Ueantabo, S.Pac. 1423b
Neequaye, A. R., Ghana 584c
J. E., Ghana 584b
Neeraja, M., SPMV 924c
Neeru, Panjab 883b
Neethling, Jan, Nelson Mandela Met. 1363a
Siebert J., W.Cape 1409c
Stephen, ICL 1702b
Neetling, A., Stell. 1396b
Neeves, Ramona, E.Lond. 1642c
Neff, B. D., W.Ont. 538c
Stephen C., Edin. 1648b
Neftci, S., Reading 1906c
Negash, M. M., Witw. 1411a
Negbenebor, C. A., Maid. 1191b
Negi, Atul, Hyd. 770a
D. B., I.Gandhi Nat.Open 787c
Jita S., CIHTS 716b
S. S., Dr HGV 737b
S. S., Forest RI 742
Sudesh, HP 768b
Vidya S., HP 767b
W. D., CIHTS 716a
Neglia, Erminio, Tor. 501a
Negnevitsky, Michael, Tas. 179c
Negra, D., E.Anglia 1639c
Negrin, Llewellyn, Tas. 179a
Negrine, R., Sheff. 1924c
Negro, Giacomo, Durh. 1634a
Negus, Keith, Lond. 1782b, 1783a
Nehaniv, Christopher L., Herts. 1684b
Nehdi, M., W.Ont. 541b
Neher, Erhard, Ott. 443a
Nehru, Bimla, Panjab 880c
Joginder S., Panjab 882a
Nehru Dutt, N., A.Nagar. 664a
Nehru Kumar, V., Annam. 677a
Nehusi, Kimani, E.Lond. 1642c
Nehvi, B. Ahmad, Kashmir 815c, 816b
Neidhart, Helga, Aust.Cath. 34b
Neidle, Stephen, Lond. 1818b
Neihart, Maureen F., Nan.Tech. 1296a
Neil, Amanda, Newcastle(NSW) 144b
David, W'gong. 208b
Douglas M., Glas. 1663b
E. C., E.Anglia 1640c
H. Andrew W., Oxf. 1881a
James C., Glas. 1669b
Mark A. A., ICL 1705a
Peter S., Wales 1541a
Stuart, Wales 1967a, 1967b
Neill, Alex, S'ton. 1937b
Alister M., Otago 1107c
Leonie, Adel. 31b
Lindsay, Auck.UT 1082b
Michael A. F., Auck. 1071a
S., W.England 1981b
Sean R. St. J., Warw. 1973a
Neilsen, P. M., Qld.UT 149b
Neilson, Alan M., Waik. 1125c
Brett, W.Syd. 203b
David J. M., Waik. 1123b
J. E., Curtin 54c
James P., Liv. 1761b
Marion B., Glas. 1664c
Patrick, McG. 371a
Richard D., Aberd. 1536a
William A. W., Vic.(BC) 520b
Neis, B., Nfld. 406a
Neishtadt, Anatoly, Lough. 1833c
Neitz, Albert W. H., Pret. 1374b
Nejad, L., Manc.Met. 1838a
Neke, S. M., Sokoine Ag. 1486b
Nel, A., N-W(S.Af.) 1370c
A. L., Jo'burg. 1347a
A. L., N-W(S.Af.) 1366c
C., N-W(S.Af.) 1367c
Daan G., Stell. 1397c, 1401b
Etienne, Otago 1105b
Etienne D., Stell. 1399b
G. F., Stell. 1392c
H., Rhodes 1388c
Hannelie, Jo'burg. 1347c
I., N-W(S.Af.) 1369c
J. B. S., Jo'burg. 1348c
J. Hannelie, Stell. 1395c
J. S. J., Pret. 1372
Jeanne, Monash 113c, 114c
Louis H., Pret. 1379b
M., N-W(S.Af.) 1371a
Lt.-Col. M., Stell. 1396b
Marius S., Pret. 1381c
Mary, Stell. 1395c
P. J., Pret. 1381a
Philip R., Otago 1110b
Stephanus J. P., Pret. 1382b
Wanda E., Jo'burg. 1348b
Neligan, Peter C., Tor. 508a
Nelken, David, Cardiff 1618b
Nell, H. W., N-W(S.Af.) 1371b
Nellaiyapen, N. O., Annam. 677a
Nellaiyappan, T., Annam. 681b
Neller, Anne, Sunshine Coast 159b
Ronald J., Sunshine Coast 159b
Nelles, P. N., Car. 338c
Nellis, Joe G., Cran. 1628, 1630b
Mike, Glas. 1668b
Mike, Strath. 1948a
Nelmes, P., Plym. 1891c
R. J., Edin. 1650a
Nelson, A. J., W.Ont. 538b
Adam, Leeds 1727c
Andrea, Leeds 1735b
Anna, Lond.S.Bank 1828c
Brian, Monash 118c
C., Nfld. 408c
C. S., Waik. 1120c
Cordel, WI 1991b, 1997c
D. Bruce, Edin. 1644, 1653b
D. Erle, S.Fraser 482a
D. R., Nott. 1851c

Paudyal, Krishna, *Durh.* 1634a
Paul, A., *Chitt.* 229b
A. B., *Jahang.* 245a
A. C., *Rajsh.* 255b
A. S., *Calabar* 1162c
B. A., *Plym.* 1891a
Beaulé, *Ott.* 446c
Charlotte E., *Otago* 1109b
Christine L., *Newcastle(NSW)* 144b, 145b
D. P., *Chitt.* 230b
David, *W.Aust.* 197b
Diane, *Montr.* 423b
Douglas J., *Glas.* 1665b
G. C., *Rajsh.* 255b
J. C., *Chitt.* 231a
James J., *Maur.* 1053a
Krishna, *IIT Bombay* 779a
Kumar S., *Rajsh.* 254b
Lorna, *Glas.* 1671a
M., *Nfld.* 407b
M. A., *H-W* 1680b
M. E., *Massey* 1100c
Meenu, *Panjab* 881c
N. K., *Rajsh.* 253a
Natalie, *Griff.* 69a
Neelam, *Panjab* 882a
Nigel, *Edin.* 1653c
Nigel D., *Lanc.* 1721c
P., *Alta.* 308a
P. J., *IISc.* 774a
Paulette, *Guy.* 594c
Priyabrata, *Rajsh.* 252b
R., *Calg.* 324c
Ravindra, *Gulb.* 755a
S., *Banasth.* 698c
S. B., *Assam* 682, 683c
S. C., *Rajsh.* 253a
S. K., *I.Sch.Mines* 782b
Satya, *W.Syd.* 202c
Solomon F. D., *S.Ramachandra* 928a, 929a
Stephen, *Leeds Met.* 1741b
T. V., *McG.* 373c, 382a
Tomlin, *WI* 1994c
V. I., *Annam.* 680b
V. K., *SPA Delhi* 912b
W. J., *Calg.* 325c
Paul Douglas, S., *And.* 671b
Pauleen, David, *Well.* 1115c
Paulin, Michael G., *Otago* 1111a
Paull, Stephen, *Vic.(Aust.)* 186c
Paulo, Stanley B. S., *Lincoln(NZ)* 1094b
Paulraj Joseph, J., *M.Sund.* 856, 857a, 857b
Paulraja, P., *Annam.* 678c
Paulson, Allan T., *Dal.* 352b, 359b
B. L., *Alta.* 305a
Lawrence C., *Camb.* 1601a
Pauly, Louis W., *Tor.* 499c, 509b
Peter H., *Tor.* 496c
Paunescu, Laurentiu, *Syd.* 171c
Paunonen, S., *W.Ont.* 545c
Paunov, V. N., *Hull* 1695c
Paus, T., *Nott.* 1855c
Pausch, H. A., *Alta.* 307c
Pause, Arnim, *McG.* 374c
Pauw, Henk, *Nelson Mandela Met.* 1363b
Niel E., *Stell.* 1396b
Pauwels, Anne, *W.Aust.* 191a
Frederick E. T., *Massey* 1101b
Pauzer, I., *Ryerson* 466a
Pavamani, Joseph, *Manipal* 851a
Pavan, M. R., *Manipal* 845c
S. Nuggehalli, *IISc.* 775b
Pavan Kumar, P., *Hyd.* 771a
Pavanguau, R., *Osm.* 877b
Pavarala, Vinod, *Hyd.* 769b, 770b
Pavel, S., *Dhaka* 234c
Pavelin, S., *Reading* 1906b
Pavelka, M. S., *Calg.* 323b
Pavendan, A., *S.Ramachandra* 926a
Paver, Chloe E. M., *Exe.* 1657b
Graham, *Newcastle(NSW)* 141a
Heather, *Birm.* 1576c, 1577a
Pavic, A., *Sheff.* 1923b
Pavier, Martyn J., *Brist.* 1586a
Pavithran, Pallavi, *Manipal* 847b
Pavithranand, A., *Annam.* 676c
Pavkovic, Aleksandar, *Macq.* 90b
Pavlich, G. C., *Alta.* 309c
Pavliuc, Nicolae, *Tor.* 500b
Pavlosky, W. F., *W.Ont.* 548b
Pavlou, George, *Sur.* 1953a
Pavlos, *Cyprus* 564b
Pavlov, A. D., *S.Fraser* 482b
Evgeny, *Cant.* 1087c, 1088a
Pavlova, Anna, *Lond.* 1797c
Margarita, *Griff.* 70c
Pavlovic, Milija N., *ICL* 1703a
Pavlovich, Kathryn, *Waik.* 1124a
Pavlyshyn, Marko J., *Monash* 118c
Pawar, B. H., *SGB Amravati* 904b
B. V., *N.Maharashtra* 868b, 868c
D. V., *Dr BA Marath.* 732b
H. K. K., *Karn.* 813a
K., *Nott.* 1855a
M. C., *Dr BA Marath.* 733a
Manohar S., *C.Sturt* 51b
Nisha H., *Shiv.* 915a
Pankaj, *VB* 951a
S. S., *DAV* 727a
Yashashri S., *Shiv.* 915b
Pawate, Channambika, *Karn.* 811a
P. P., *Karn.* 810b
Pawlaczek, Zofia, *Monash* 115c
Pawlak, Miroslaw, *Manit.* 390a
Pawliez, Myreille, *Well.* 1113c
Pawlikowski, Krzysztof, *Cant.* 1090a
Pawliszyn, J., *Wat.* 525a
Pawlowska, Chrisoulla, *Greenwich* 1677c
Pawlowski, Mark, *Greenwich* 1677c
Michael K., *Lakehead* 362
Pawluch, D. C. T., *Nott.Trent* 1865c
Pawson, Chris, *E.Lond.* 1643b
Eric J., *Cant.* 1091c
H., *H-W* 1679c
Patricia, *Auck.UT* 1082c
R. D., *Leeds* 1734b
Paxton, Anthony T., *Belf.* 1560b
Catherine, *Oxf.* 1882a
James W., *Auck.* 1077a
Patsy, *Auck.UT* 1085c
R., *Belf.* 1557c
R. A., *H-W* 1679c
Richard, *Sur.* 1953c
Susan J., *La Trobe* 82b
Pay, Levi, *Leeds* 1739b, 1739c
P. R., *Plym.* 1888c
Paya, Ivan, *Lanc.* 1722b
Payandeh, Shahram, *S.Fraser* 484a
Payenberg, Tobias, *Adel.* 29b
Paylor, Ian, *Lanc.* 1721b
Payn, Elaine, *Leeds Met.* 1741c
Payne, A. J., *Brist.* 1586c, 1591b
A. J., *Sheff.* 1926a
Alan G. T., *Otago* 1104b
Anthony P., *Glas.* 1664a
B., *Manit.* 394a
B. J., *Nott.Trent* 1865c
C., *Car.* 336a
Craig, *La Trobe* 78b
David N., *S'ton.* 1934c, 1937b
Deborah, *Auck.UT* 1082a, 1084c
Donald, *W.Aust.* 196c
Elizabeth H., *Cardiff* 1618c
Geoffrey S., *Camb.* 1609c
Helen L., *Herts.* 1688b
Julie A., *Greenwich* 1677b
Kate, *Auck.UT* 1082b
L. C., *Herts.* 1685c
Lisa, *Coventry* 1627a
Malcolm J., *Cape Town* 1335c, 1341c
Martin J., *Syd.* 176c
Michael C., *Camb.* 1606b
Monica, *Waik.* 1121c
N. C., *W.Ont.* 539b
Philip, *Lond.* 1776, 1780a
Phillip, *Monash* 115c
R., *Brist.* 1583c
S., *Brist.* 1588b
S., *Sheff.* 1929a
S. J., *Plym.* 1893a
Tony, *Tas.* 183c
V. F., *Ib.* 1175a
Vincent K., *Dschang* 272b
Payton, B. W., *Nfld.* 408a
C., *Manc.Met.* 1839c
K. B., *W.Ont.* 549c, 551a
Philip J., *Exe.* 1658b
Payzant, G. B., *Tor.* 498c
Pazderka, B., *Qu.* 452b
Pazhamalai, S., *Annam.* 680c
Pazhamaneri Subramanian, Thiagarajan, *NU Singapore* 1307b
Pazhani, V. C., *Annam.* 677b
Pazhani Bala Murugan, S., *Annam.* 678a
Pazienza, Jennifer, *New Br.* 430b
Pazim alias Fadzim bin Othman, *Malaya* 1006a
Pazner, Micha, *W.Ont.* 542b
Pe-Piper, Georgia, *St Mary's(Can.)* 469a
Peabody, N., *Lond.* 1799b
Peace, Adrian J., *Adel.* 29b
Robin, *Massey* 1100b
Sheila M., *Open(UK)* 1869c
Peach, Jeremy, *Nott.Trent* 1866b
Ken, *Oxf.* 1878a
Peacham, C. E., *Plym.* 1888b
Peachell, P. T., *Sheff.* 1927c
Peachey, Linda, *Leeds Met.* 1740
Tom, *Monash* 118a
Peacock, Sir Alan, *H-W* 1679c
Alan D., *Herts.* 1685b
Briton R., *Leeds Met.* 1740c
Christine, *W'gong.* 206b
D. K., *Hull* 1696a
David P. S., *S'ton.* 1933a
G. S., *Alta.* 303b
J. A., *Edin.* 1650a
Janet, *Brun.* 1595a, 1597a
John, *S'ton.* 1935b
Kent, *Leth.* 365c
Noel A., *Glas.* 1667a
Pead, John, *Melb.* 106b
M. J., *Lond.* 1813a
Peak, Ian, *Griff.* 72b
Peake, Barrie M., *Otago* 1104a
Helen, *W.Aust.* 198a
I. R., *Sheff.* 1928b
Nigel, *Camb.* 1602c, 1605b
Sheila, *Sunshine Coast* 159a
Peakman, Mark, *Lond.* 1795b
Pear, J. J., *Manit.* 393c, 399b
Pearce, Adrian J., *Nott.Trent* 1864c
Adrian R., *Melb.* 97b
Brian, *Lond.* 1818c
C M., *W.Ont.* 539a
C. W., *Brist.* 1586c
Catherine, *Manc.Met.* 1839a
Charles E. M., *Adel.* 27b
Cheryl M., *W.Ont.* 542c
Christopher J., *Glas.* 1665a
Dave M., *Herts.* 1685a
David, *Lond.S.Bank* 1829c
David G., *Leeds Met.* 1741a
Douglas, *Well.* 1116b
Elizabeth H., *Well.* 1116b
F., *Qu.* 457c
Glenn, *W.Syd.* 204a
Graham, *Aston* 1544a
Howard T., *Cape Town* 1335a, 1341b
J., *Plym.* 1889a
Jamie, *Cant.* 1091c
John M., *Cardiff* 1622a
Jon, *Melb.* 99a
Julian A., *Cardiff* 1616c
Lynne, *Lanc.* 1722c
M. J., *Nott.* 1853b
Martin L., *Portsmouth* 1898c
Nadine, *E.Cowan* 67c
Neil, *Massey* 1102b
Nicholas J., *Glas.* 1666b
Nicholas J. G., *Wales* 1541a
P. Jim, *Well.* 1114a
Patricia, *Syd.* 177b
Paul A., *Melb.* 100c
R. D., *Reading* 1906b
R. J., *W.Ont.* 538b
Robert A., *Wales* 1965
S., *Qld.UT* 149b
Sarah J., *S'ton.* 1935c
Shirley, *Lough.* 1830
Susan M., *Leic.* 1749c
T. C., *Leic.* 1747b
T. H., *Qu.* 455b
T. W., *Car.* 338a
Pearcy, M. J., *Qld.UT* 150a
Pearl, Daniel, *Montr.* 411a
Jonathan L., *Tor.* 495b
L. H., *Lond.* 1786b
Robert G., *KwaZulu-Natal* 1352a
Pearlman, Michael, *Vic.(Aust.)* 186b
Pearlman-Houghie, Deborah, *Herts.* 1686c
Pearman, Alan D., *Leeds* 1732a
Geoff, *Syd.* 177b
Pears, Russel, *Auck.UT* 1082b
Pearsall, David J., *McG.* 372a, 384c
Pearse, Edwin J., *W'gong.* 210b
John R., *Cant.* 1090c
N. J., *Rhodes* 1388b
Pearson, A., *Lond.* 1785c
Alan, *Adel.* 30c
Alastair, *Portsmouth* 1901a
Allen T., *W.Ont.* 538a, 541a
Andrew, *WI* 1996a
Bronwyn, *NE* 139b, 139c
Catherine, *Leeds Met.* 1743c
D. Graham, *Durh.* 1634b
David, *Lond.* 1768c
David G., *Well.* 1118a
E., *Plym.* 1892b
G., *Lond.* 1782b
G. R., *Brist.* 1590a
G. T., *Edin.* 1653a
Gail, *Syd.* 167c
Hugh, *Leeds* 1727a
Ingrid, *Kingston(UK)* 1719b
J., *Herts.* 1686c
J. Alan, *Durh.* 1637a
J. M., *Nott.Trent* 1861c
J. R. A., *Birm.* 1571c
J. R. Anthony, *Wales* 1542a
Jeremy D., *Lond.* 1788c, 1794c
Joanne, *Herts.* 1685c
Joanne, *Hudd.* 1693a
John, *S.Qld.* 158
John S., *Hudd.* 1691c
K. G., *Alta.* 312b
Ken, *Monash* 127c
Lesley, *Hudd.* 1693a
M., *Aberd.* 1535c
Marcus, *Auck.UT* 1082b
Margaret, *Keele* 1709
Mark, *Bond* 40a
Michael, *Wales* 1542b
Michael N., *Auck.* 1068a
Murray, *Waik.* 1120c
N. A., *Swansea* 1956c
Paul N., *Cardiff* 1616c
Peter J. G., *ICL* 1703c
R., *Hull* 1696c
R. E., *Nott.* 1850b, 1859a
Richard, *Worcester* 1984c
Roger A. G., *Oxf.* 1877a
Russell, *Middx.* 1843a
Russell, *W'gong.* 209c
Ruth, *Leeds* 1734a, 1738a
Sarina, *Auck.* 1071c
Steve H., *Lond.S.Bank* 1828c
Terry W., *Vic.(BC)* 517a
Tony, *Wales* 1549b
W. B., *Wat.* 525a, 532b
Peart, Amanda, *Portsmouth* 1899b
Joseph, *Auck.UT* 1081b
M. R., *HK* 2032b
Nicola S., *Otago* 1106a
R., *Manc.Met.* 1840c
S., *Nott.Trent* 1863c
Pease, James E., *ICL* 1707a
Ken, *Lough.* 1835a
Peasnell, Kenneth V., *Lanc.* 1721b
Peat, Briar, *Auck.* 1075b, 1078a
George M., *Keele* 1711b
Keith S., *Lough.* 1831c
Maurice, *Syd.* 169c
Peate, Ian G., *Herts.* 1687c
Peattie, Kenneth J., *Cardiff* 1622c
Peay, J. V., *Lond.* 1800c
Peccei, Riccardo, *Lond.* 1794a
Pech, Richard, *La Trobe* 81b
Peck, Chris, *Syd.* 168a
E., *Birm.* 1572b
Helen L., *Cran.* 1630c
Martyn M., *Massey* 1101b
Stewart, *Car.* 336b
Peckham, Michelle, *Leeds* 1727a
S., *Lond.* 1805b
Pecl, Gretta, *Tas.* 182b
Pecorino, Lauren, *Greenwich* 1678b
Pecotich, Anthony, *W.Aust.* 192c
Peda Raju, D., *And.* 670a
Peddle, D., *Nfld.* 408b
Derek R., *Leth.* 364c
Peden, Elisabeth, *Syd.* 171b
G. C., *Stir.* 1942b
Peden-Smith, Andrew, *Northumbria* 1849c
Pedersen, Evelyn, *Auck.UT* 1081b
Georg, *Syd.* 172c
Paul R., *Tor.* 497c
R. A. L., *Camb.* 1609a
Thomas F., *Vic.(BC)* 516c, 518b
Pederson, D. R., *W.Ont.* 545c
Pedicoil, Abraham, *TN Med.* 933b
Pedigo, K., *Curtin* 59b
Pedlar, A. M., *Wat.* 530a, 533b
Jonathan, *Leeds* 1736a
Pedler, Daryl, *Monash* 121c, 123b
Pedley, Rev. Christopher, *Lond.* 1783, 1784c
Gillian, *Kingston(UK)* 1719b
H. M., *Hull* 1696b
Kevin C., *Massey* 1097c
M. C., *Manc.Met.* 1841b
S., *Sur.* 1953a
Timothy J., *Camb.* 1605b
Timothy J., *Leeds* 1732b
Pedras, M. S. C., *Sask.* 472c
Pedreschi, Remo, *Edin.* 1645a
Pedretti, Erminia, *Tor.* 503c
Pedriali, Federica G., *Edin.* 1648c
Pedro, Isiaka A., *Bayero* 1149b
J. O., *Witw.* 1413a
Pedrotti, Mark, *Montr.* 414b
Pedrycz, W., *Alta.* 305c
Peebles, David, *Hudd.* 1692a
Peehal, Dharampal, *Osm.* 874c
Peek, Andrew, *Tas.* 179c
Michael J., *Syd.* 172a
Peeks, David, *Lanc.* 1725b
Peel, David, *Lanc.* 1722b
Jacqueline, *Melb.* 99c
Jennifer, *Liv.J.Moores* 1765c
John D. Y., *Lond.* 1815a
Mark, *Monash* 117c
Michael J., *Cardiff* 1615b
R. J., *Manc.Met.* 1840a
R. W., *Plym.* 1891a
Roger, *Sur.* 1950c
Peele, A. G., *La Trobe* 80a
Peeling, J., *Manit.* 397b
W. J., *Manit.* 398a
Peemoeller, H., *Wat.* 532b
Peens, A., *N-W(S.Af.)* 1367a
Peer, Abdool, *Jo'burg.* 1346a
M., *M'lore.* 843c
Mushtaq A., *Kashmir* 816b, 816c
Showkat S., *Kashmir* 816c
Peers, Angela C., *Manc.Met.* 1838a
Christopher S., *Leeds* 1734c, 1737c
Doug M., *Calg.* 323b, 327c
Peerzada, Bashir A., *Kashmir* 815b
Naseem, *C.Darwin* 48c
Sharief-ud-Din, *Kashmir* 816a
Peet, S. T., *Manc.Met.* 1837c
Peeters, Bert, *Tas.* 179c
Petra H. M., *ICL* 1705c
Peetz, David R., *Griff.* 71b
Pefanis, A. Julian, *Syd.* 166c
Pegg, Beverley, *W.Syd.* 204a
David T., *Griff.* 70a
J., *E.Lond.* 1642a
John E., *NE* 135c, 138c
M. J., *Dal.* 351c
S., *Nott.Trent* 1866a
Peggs, Kay, *Portsmouth* 1902c
Pegna, Joseph, *Montr.* 422c
Pegoraro, Rosemary J., *KwaZulu-Natal* 1354c
Pegram, Robert S., *Adel.* 27c
Pegum, Roger H., *Liv.J.Moores* 1764c
Peh Suat Cheng, *Malaya* 1011a
Pehkonen, S. O., *NU Singapore* 1309b, 1315b
Pehm, Stephen, *Vic.(Aust.)* 188c
Pehowich, D. J., *Alta.* 310c
Pei, Likun, *La Trobe* 82c
Peile, Ed, *Warw.* 1978a
Peirce, Christine, *Durh.* 1634b
Susan N., *Alta.* 313b
Peiris, B. C. N., *Peradeniya* 1452c
B. D., *Kelaniya* 1443c
B. L., *Peradeniya* 1452c
Harsha, *IIT S.Lanka* 1466b
Hemantha, *Sri Jay.* 1464b
J. S. M., *HK* 2034b
John R. J., *Sri Jay.* 1464c
L. Dinithi C., *Colombo* 1438c
M. D. P., *Kelaniya* 1444c
M. G. C., *Sri Jay.* 1463c
Paul, *W.Syd.* 204b
R. Grace X., *Colombo* 1440b
S. E., *Peradeniya* 1452c
Peiro, Joaquim, *ICL* 1701a
Peirson, John, *Kent* 1714a
Pejovic-Milic, A., *Ryerson* 465b
Pek, Siok Ching, *Nan.Tech.* 1291
Pekacz, J., *Dal.* 353a

Shaji, S., *Gandh.Rural* 743b
Shajjath Hussain, A., *TN Law* 932, 932c
Shaka, Femi O., *P.Harcourt* 1208c
Shakaib, M., *NED Eng.* 1261b
Shakantu, Winston, *Cape Town* 1334a
Shakeel, Mohd., *JMI* 793c
Muhammad, *NUST(P'stan.)* 1264c
Rehana, *Karachi* 1252a
Shakeela Khanam, *Dr BRA Open* 730c
Shaker, P., *S.Fraser* 482a, 484a
Shakesby, R. A., *Swansea* 1956b
Shakesheff, K., *Nott.* 1855b
Shakespeare, Anthony S., *Pret.* 1385a
Pam, *Open(UK)* 1870a
Shaketange, L., *Namibia* 1056b
Shakib, F., *Nott.* 1858b
Shakila Banu, M., *Avina. Women* 685a
Shakila Parween binti Yacob, *Malaya* 1008a
Shakinovsky, Lynn, *W.Laur.* 558a
Shakir, A. S., *Lahore UET* 1240c
Hina, *Bhutto IST* 1272b
Huma, *Karachi* 1251b
S. M., *Rajsh.* 256a
Shakoor, Abdul, *N-WFP Eng.* 1267b
Abdul, *NUST(P'stan.)* 1264c
Abdush, *Arid Ag.* 1235c
Farzana, *NED Eng.* 1261c
Nuzhat, *Riphah Internat.* 1270b
Shakur, A., *Dhaka* 240c
Shalabi, Badrudin, *Islamic Uganda* 1494a
Shalaby, Ahmed, *Manit.* 390a
N. A. I., *Nfld.* 404c
Shale, Dennis J., *Cardiff* 1619c, 1620c
E. A., *Warw.* 1977b
Shalem, Y. T., *Witw.* 1412b
Shalini, H. J., *M'lore.* 844a
Shalivahan, *I.Sch.Mines* 782c
Shaliza binti Ibrahim, *Malaya* 1006c
Shallcross, A. G., *Manc.Met.* 1839a
D. E., *Brist.* 1584b
David C., *Melb.* 96c
Shalliker, R. Andrew, *W.Syd.* 204c
Shallit, J. O., *Wat.* 526a
Shalyefu-Shimopileni, R. K., *Namibia* 1056b
Sham, M. H., *HK* 2033c
T. K., *W.Ont.* 539b
Sham Bhat, A., *Pondicherry* 886c
Sham Sunder, *Manipal* 846c
Sham Sunder, R. S., *Hyd.* 770b
Shama, Gilbert, *Lough.* 1831c
Kumara, *Manipal* 851c
Shamail, Shafay, *Lahore MS* 1255c
Shamal, S. N., *Ban.* 694a
Shamala, M., *Osm.* 876c
N., *IISc.* 775a
Shamala Devi a/p K C Sekaran, *Malaya* 1010a
Shambe, T., *Jos* 1180b
Shamdasani, Prem, *NU Singapore* 1312b
Shameel, Suraiya, *Karachi* 1253b
Shameem, A., *And.* 672c
V. P. A., *Manipal* 846a
Shami, Muiz ud Din, *NUST(P'stan.)* 1263b
U. T., *Lahore UET* 1241a
Shamila Abu Hasan, *IIU Malaysia* 1003c
Shamim, Ishrat, *Dhaka* 238c
Shakur, *Massey* 1097a
Shamim bt Abdul Samad, *NU Malaysia* 1019b
Shamji, Farid M., *Ott.* 446c
Shammakhi, Nureddin, *Keele* 1711b
Shampa, Anupurba, *Ban.* 694c
Shams, M., *Car.* 337c
M. N. A., *Jahang.* 245c
Md. Iftekhar, *Khulna* 249c
Muniba, *NUST(P'stan.)* 1264b
N. A., *Rajsh.* 256c
Shams-Ud-Din, Md., *B'desh.Ag.* 221b
Shamsad, Sadah, *Khulna* 248c
Shamsavari, Ali, *Kingston(UK)* 1718b

Shamseldin, Asaad Y., *Auck.* 1070b
Shamsher Mohamad Ramadilli, *Putra* 1021c
Shamshuddin bin Jusop, *Putra* 1027b
Shamsi, Shamim, *Dhaka* 233c
Shamsiah Mohamad, *Malaya* 1012b
Shamsuddin, *Ban.* 696b
Shamsuddin, A. K. M., *B'desh.Ag.* 221b
Abdul F. M., *Newcastle(NSW)* 141c
M., *B'desh.Ag.* 222b
M., *Karachi* 1250a, 1252a, 1253b, 1253c
M., *Rajsh.* 255b, 256a
Mohammed, *Chitt.* 230c
Muhammad, *Islamia, Bahawal.* 1249b
S., *Dhaka* 235a
S. D., *Jahang.* 246a
S. M., *Dhaka* 234a
Shamsuddin Ahmed Mohammed Shahadat, *Malaya* 1007a
Shamsuddin Mohd Noor, *IIU Malaysia* 1003b
Shamsuddin Suhor, *NU Malaysia* 1017c
Shamsuddin Sulaiman, *Putra* 1025a
Shamsuddoha, A. K., *Rajsh.* 255b
M., *Chitt.* 230a
Shamsudin Ahmad, *Tech.U.Malaysia* 1034b
Shamsudin b Hj Mohd Amin, *Tech.U.Malaysia* 1033a
Shamsul Amri Baharuddin, Dato', *NU Malaysia* 1018b, 1020b
Shamsul Azahari Zainal Badari, *Putra* 1027a
Shamsul Azhar Mohd. Yusof, *IIU Malaysia* 1003c
Shamsul Bahri bin Zakaria, *Malaya* 1008c
Shamsul bin Sahibuddin, *Tech.U.Malaysia* 1031b, 1035a
Shamsul Haque, S. M., *IIU Malaysia* 1002b
Shamugam, V. U., *Annam.* 679a
Shan, Gongbing, *Leth.* 364c
Jordan, *Vic.(Aust.)* 185a
Shanabhag, Bhagyasri A., *Karn.* 811c
Shanahan, Catherine M., *Lond.* 1794c
Cathie, *Newcastle(NSW)* 146c
Murray P., *ICL* 1702a
Paul E., *KwaZulu-Natal* 1357a
Steve T., *C.Darwin* 48a
Yvonne P., *Cant.* 1089a
Shanaz Bahatul, *Nehru Tech.* 798c
Shanbhag, Col. M. M., *Manipal* 851a, 853b
Ravindranath, *Manipal* 850c
Shanbhogue, Krishnayya K., *Manipal* 845c
Vikram V., *Manipal* 847c
Shand, P. J., *Sask.* 474b
Patricia, *Tor.* 497c
Peter, *Auck.* 1071c
Shandil, R. G., *HP* 768a
Shandilya, Arun K., *Dr HGV* 736, 737a, 737c
Shandling, Maureen, *Tor.* 506a
Shane, Phil, *Auck.* 1072a
Shang, Angela L. P., *Nan.Tech.* 1303a
Huai Min, *Nan.Tech.* 1299a, 1303a
Julie Q., *W.Ont.* 541b
Shangasi, Sindiswe L., *Pret.* 1382b
Shani, N., *Manc.Met.* 1838b
Shank, R. James, *Kent* 1715b
Shankanga, A., *Africa(Z'bwe.)* 2043c
Shankar, Anoop, *NU Singapore* 1316b
Avi, *Bath* 1552b, 1553b, 1554b
B., *Osm.* 875b
B., *Reading* 1905c
H., *Annam.* 676b
N., *Manipal* 845c
Priti, *IISc.* 774a
R., *B'thidasan.* 705b
R., *M'lore.* 843b
Ravi K., *I.Gandhi Nat.Open* 786b

T. Gowri, *Potti ST* 888
Uma, *NE Hill* 871a
V., *Nehru Tech.* 798b
V., *S.Ramachandra* 927b
Shankar Jogan, *M'lore.* 843c
Shankar Ram, B. V., *Nehru Tech.* 798c
Shankar Reddy, M., *Potti ST* 889c
Shankaraiah, K., *Osm.* 876b
Shankaranarayana, K., *Manipal* 851c
Shankarnarayanan, L., *S.Ramachandra* 927b
Shanker, Lattia, *C'dia.* 345b
M. J. A., *Rajsh.* 257c
R., *Ban.* 692c
Shankland, C. E., *Stir.* 1942a
D. P., *Brist.* 1583c
Shanks, Brenda M., *Otago* 1105a
Gavin. L., *Qu.* 459c
Graeme, *Melb.* 99a
J., *Sask.* 479c
John A., *Otago* 1106c
Thomas, *Durh.* 1636b
Shanley, Liz, *Newcastle(NSW)* 147c
Paul, *Lond.* 1805c
Shanmuga Vadivel, T., *Annam.* 677c
Shanmugalingam, Nagalingam, *Jaffna* 1442
Shanmugam, A., *Annam.* 678c
Bala, *Monash* 113c
G., *Madr.* 825c
K., *Annam.* 678b
Shanmugaratnam, K., *NU Singapore* 1317c
Shanmugasamy, R., *Madr.* 826b
Shanmugasundaram, S., *Madurai K.* 828c
Shanmugham, M., *S.Ramachandra* 928c, 929c
Shanmugiah, S., *Madurai K.* 829c
Shann, Frank A., *Melb.* 105c
Shanner, L., *Alta.* 312c
Shannon, Catherine, *Canberra* 43c
J. T., *Coventry* 1627c
John, *La Trobe* 78c
John M., *Sur.* 1953b
L. Vere, *Cape Town* 1337b
Patrick T., *Otago* 1110c
Robert, *NE* 137a
Susan, *Adel.* 25a
Shanta, P., *BITS* 709c, 711a
S. S., *Rajsh.* 255c
Shanta Nair-Venugopal, *NU Malaysia* 1017c
Shantha Kumari, B. R., *Pondicherry* 887a
Shanthala Kamath, M., *Manipal* 852a
Shanthawimala, Rev. B., *Peradeniya* 1454c
Shanthi, B., *Annam.* 681b
G., *Annam.* 679a
J., *Avina. Women* 685c
K., *Madr.* 826a
M., *Annam.* 676b
P., *Madr.* 825b
R. K., *Annam.* 677b
S., *Annam.* 677c
S., *S.Ramachandra* 927b, 928b
Shanthi Ganabadi, *Putra* 1027c
Shanthini, R., *Peradeniya* 1453b
Shantibala Devi, G. A., *Manip.* 854b
Shantidevi, K. C. N., *Ruhuna* 1459a
Shantinath Dibbad, *Gulb.* 754b
Shantz, D. H., *Calg.* 329c
S. D., *Sask.* 472b
Shao, I., *Dar.* 1481a
Jianhua, *Cardiff* 1616a
John, *Tumaini* 1488
L., *Nott.* 1851b
Yixin B. S., *McG.* 370a
Shao Ying, *Malaya* 1012c
Shapcott, Alison, *Sunshine Coast* 159b
C. Mary, *Ulster* 1961a
Thomas W., *Adel.* 27a
Shapiro, A. M. J., *Alta.* 312c
B. L., *Calg.* 325c
Ben Z., *Tor.* 500c
Colin, *Tor.* 507b
Daniel M., *S.Fraser* 482c
Daniel Z., *Lanc.* 1724b
David A., *Leeds* 1737a
Faydra, *W.Laur.* 559c

G. I., *Plym.* 1889c
Henry P., *Pret.* 1383b
I., *Ryerson* 465a
Kimron L., *Wales* 1547c
L., *S.Fraser* 485c
L. J., *Manit.* 393c
S., *St And.* 1915c, 1916c
S., *Warw.* 1974a
Stanley H., *McG.* 375a
Shapland, J. M., *Sheff.* 1924c, 1930a
Shapley, M. J., *Nott.Trent* 1864a
Shar, B. K., *Mehran* 1257b
Sharada, L. N., *Osm.* 875a
V., *Karn.* 812a
Y. S., *SPMV* 924c
Sharada Devi, A., *ANG Ranga Ag.* 663b
Sharaf, Adel M. M., *New Br.* 431a
Sharaf Ibrahim, *NU Malaysia* 1019c
Sharan, A. M., *Nfld.* 403b
P., *JMI* 794a
R. N., *NE Hill* 871a
Sharanabasappa, M., *Manipal* 847a
Sharanjeet Kaur, *NU Malaysia* 1018c
Sharankumar, Limbale, *YCM Open* 953c
Sharatbabu, I., *Karn.* 811a
Sharath Kumar Rao, K., *Manipal* 848c
Sharavanan, P. S., *Annam.* 676b
Sharda, N. K., *HP* 768b
Nalin, *Vic.(Aust.)* 185c
Parveen, *Panjab* 883b
Vidya, *HP* 767a, 768a
Shareef, A., *Osm.* 877b
Mohd M., *Osm.* 875c
Sharf, Inna, *McG.* 370c
Shargorodsky, Eugene, *Lond.* 1791c
Sharief, Khalid, *NUST(P'stan.)* 1264a
Mohammed, *Lond.* 1795c
Sharif, A. H., *Jahang.* 246b
A. H. M. R., *Jahang.* 246a
Adel, *Sur.* 1951a
Ahmed, *B'desh.Engin.* 225a
Amir, *Brun.* 1594a
B. S., *Newcastle(UK)* 1846c
Dilara I., *Khulna* 248c
Hasanat, *Aga Khan(P'stan.)* 1233a
M., *Brist.* 1589a
M. B., *Lahore UET* 1240c
M. R. I., *Dhaka* 238a
Mohd., *JMI* 793c
Muhammad, *Sir Syed UET* 1278a
N., *St Mary's(Can.)* 468b
Sharif Hossain, A. B. M., *Malaya* 1005c
Sharif-Ar-Raffi, *B'desh.Ag.* 221b
Sharif-uz-Zaman, *Riphah Internat.* 1271a
Sharifah Azizah Haron, *Putra* 1027a
Sharifah Bee binti O A Abd Hamid, *Malaya* 1011c
Sharifah bt Mohd Nor, Datin, *Putra* 1023c
Sharifah Eliza E. binti Syed Hj Hashim, *Brunei* 266c
Sharifah Faridah binti Syed Alwi, *Malaya* 1008c
Sharifah Hapsah Syed Hasan Shahabudin, Dato', *NU Malaysia* 1014
Sharifah Hayaati Syed Ismail, *Malaya* 1012b
Sharifah Kamilah Syed Yusof, *Tech.U.Malaysia* 1033a
Sharifah Kharidah Syed Muhammad, *Putra* 1025b
Sharifah Latifah binti Syed A Kadir, *Malaya* 1007c
Sharifah Maimunah Syed Zin, *Malaya* 1006a
Sharifah Mastura Syed Abdullah, *NU Malaysia* 1015b, 1018b
Sharifah Md Yasin, *Putra* 1023a
Sharifah Noor Akmal Syed Hussain, *NU Malaysia* 1019c
Sharifah Norazizan Syed Abd Rashid, *Putra* 1027b
Sharifah Norul Akmar binti Syed Zamri, *Malaya* 1006b

Sharifah Raihan Syed Mohd Zain, *IIU Malaysia* 999b
Sharifah Suhanah binti Syed Ahmad, *Malaya* 1008b
Sharifah Zainiyah Syed Yahya, *Putra* 1023a
Sharifah Zaleha Syed Hassan, *NU Malaysia* 1018b
Sharifah Zubaidah Syed Abdul Kader, *IIU Malaysia* 1001b
Sharifi, F. J., *Ryerson* 464a
Sedigheh, *Salf.* 1920b
V. N., *Sheff.* 1931a
Sharifian, Farzad, *Monash* 118c
Sharifuddin, M., *Dhaka* 240a
M., *Jahang.* 246b
Sharifuddin bin Hj Abdul Hamid, *Putra* 1027b
Sharifuddin bin Mohd Zain, *Malaya* 1011c
Sharifuddin bin Zainuddin, *Malaya* 1005a
Sharih, Saba, *Bhutto IST* 1273a
Shariq, Ahmad, *NUST(P'stan.)* 1265c
Sharir, S. D., *Alta.* 304b
Shariv, Isaac, *Syd.* 177b
Sharker, M. M., *Rajsh.* 257b
Sharkey, A. J. C., *Sheff.* 1922c
G., *Napier* 1845a
K. A., *Calg.* 332b, 334a
Michael F., *NE* 136a
N., *Sheff.* 1922c
P. M., *Reading* 1907c
Ronald, *Newcastle(NSW)* 144c
S., *Stir.* 1942c
Sharkh, S. M., *S'ton.* 1935a
Sharland, S., *KwaZulu-Natal* 1353b
Sharma, A., *Qld.UT* 148
A., *Ryerson* 464b
A., *S.Pac.* 1422a
A., *Sask.* 477c
A. B., *I.Gandhi Nat.Open* 786a
A. D., *Dr HGV* 737b
A. K., *MJP Rohil.* 840c
A. K., *SPA Delhi* 912c, 913a
A. K., *Shiv.* 915b
A. L., *DAV* 726b
A. M., *Sikkim-Manipal* 921a
A. N., *Dr HGV* 736b
Akhilesh, *B'tullah.V.* 701a
Alka, *Banasth.* 699b
Alka, *G.Jamb.* 760c
Anand, *NI Pharm.Ed.* 864b
Anil, *DAV* 726c
Anita, *Delhi* 722c
Anupam, *Panjab* 882a
Anupama, *Panjab* 881a
Arati, *R.Bhar.* 895c
Arun Kumar, *Delhi* 724a
Aruna, *Kuruk.* 819c
Arvind, *McG.* 374a, 380a
Arvind K., *BITS* 710a
Arvind Kumar, *Panjab* 882a
Asha, *MDU* 833a
Ashima, *HP* 768b
Ashok K., *G.Jamb.* 760b
Ashwani, *E.Lond.* 1643b
Atul, *IIT Bombay* 778b
B., *JMI* 794b
B., *Plym.* 1890b
B. A. G., *IISc.* 773, 776a
B. B., *HP* 767c
B. C., *Jammu* 796a
B. C., *SMVD* 920b
B. K., *Chitt.* 227c
B. K., *NE Hill* 872b
B. L., *M.Sukh.* 860b
B. L., *Saur.* 910a
B. R., *Delhi* 729a
B. R., *HP* 768a
B. V., *Hyd.* 769c
Baldev, *Jammu* 796b
Bansi L., *Jammu* 795b
Barnali, *Gauh.* 746a
Basu D., *New Br.* 429c
Bharat, *Hyd.* 770b
Bharti, *MDU* 833a
Bhuvnesh, *MMYVV* 832
Bishnu, *Sunshine Coast* 159b
C., *WI* 1996b
C. B., *I.Gandhi Nat.Open* 786a
C. K., *APS* 687a
C. P., *SC Tirunal* 922a
Chanchal, *HP* 767a
D., *CSJ Maharaj* 718a
D. B., *SMVD* 920c
D. C., *Dr HGV* 737a
D. K., *Ban.* 691c

Sousa, Antonio C. M., *New Br.* 431b
Cristina, *Salf.* 1920c
Elvino S., *Tor.* 502c
Paulo, *Belf.* 1563b
Soutar, Geoffrey N., *W.Aust.* 192c
Souter, Kay M., *La Trobe* 79a
Nicholas T., *Strath.* 1945b
South, G. E., *Manc.Met.* 1839b
M., *Melb.* 105c
S. L., *Sheff.* 1931c
Tim, *Leeds Met.* 1742c
Southall, D., *Manc.Met.* 1839b
Humphrey, *Portsmouth* 1901a
Southam, G., *W.Ont.* 540a
J. V., *Plym.* 1891b
Southan, John M., *Salf.* 1920b
Southby, Richard F., *Monash* 121b
Southcombe, Mark, *Well.* 1113a
Southcott, Jane E., *Monash* 115c
Southern, Alan, *Liv.* 1757c
B. W., *Manit.* 393a
Geoffrey, *Glas.* 1666c
Jennifer A., *Hudd.* 1691b
Kevin W., *Liv.* 1761b
Richard, *Herts.* 1686c
Southey, Melissa C., *Melb.* 106a
P., *Coventry* 1627a
Southway, Colin, *KwaZulu-Natal* 1357c
Southwell, Beth, *W.Syd.* 202c
D., *Qld.UT* 153c
Rev. Peter J. M., *Oxf.* 1883a
Southwood, David J., *ICL* 1705a
Frenette, *Stell.* 1395c
M. Helen, *Massey* 1097a
S. L., *Rhodes* 1389a
Taunton R., *Birm.* 1575b, 1575c
Southworth, Eric, *Oxf.* 1882c
Soutis, C., *Sheff.* 1923c
Soutsos, Marios N., *Liv.* 1756b
Soutter, David, *Coventry* 1625, 1628c
Souvik Mahapatra, *IIT Bombay* 778c
Sow, C. H., *NU Singapore* 1313b
Sowande, O. A., *O.Awolowo* 1201c
Soward, Andrew M., *Exe.* 1656b
Sowden, C., *Wales* 1968a
Paul T., *Sur.* 1952c
Sowemimo, G. O. A., *Lagos* 1187b
Sowerby, Kevin W., *Auck.* 1070c
R. E., *Stir.* 1942a
Sowerwine, Charles O., *Melb.* 98c
Sowter, Julie R., *Leeds* 1735c
Martin, *Auck.* 1075c
Sowunmi, A., *Ib.* 1175a
Soyannwo, Olaitan A., *Ib.* 1176b
Soyanwo, O. A., *Olabisi Onabanjo* 1204a
Soyebi, K. O., *Lagos* 1187b
Soyer, B., *Swansea* 1956c
Soyibo, A., *Ib.* 1173c
Kolawole, *WI* 1994c
Soyjaudah, Krishnaraj M. S., *Maur.* 1051b
Soyode, A., *Ib.* 1173c
Soyombo, Omolulu, *Lagos* 1186a, 1187c
Soyoye, F. A., *O.Awolowo* 1199a
Soysa, S. S. B. D. Preethi, *Colombo* 1438c
Spackman, Mark A., *W.Aust.* 192a
Spada, Nina, *Tor.* 503c
Spadaccini, Nick, *W.Aust.* 193a
Spadafora, S. M., *W.Ont.* 547c
Spady, D. W., *Alta.* 312a
Spaeth, Donald A., *Glas.* 1666a
Spafford, M. M., *Wat.* 531c
Spagat, Michael, *Lond.* 1808a
Spagnolo, Fabio, *Brun.* 1594b
Nicola, *Brun.* 1594b
Spahic Omer, *IIU Malaysia* 999b
Spalding, K., *Ryerson* 465b
N., *E.Anglia* 1638b
T. L., *Alta.* 309a
Spalinger, Anthony J., *Auck.* 1068b
Spamer, E. J., *N-W(S.Af.)* 1370c
Spanbroek, N. W., *Curtin* 55a
Spanel, Patrick, *Keele* 1711b
Spaner, D. M., *Alta.* 303a
Spanier, Noel, *Auck.UT* 1083b
Spanjers, Willy, *Kingston(UK)* 1718b
Spann, D., *Qld.UT* 154c
M., *Birm.* 1568c
Spanos, T. J., *Alta.* 308c
Spanswick, David C., *Warw.* 1978a
Spanu, Pietro D., *ICL* 1701b
Spargo, P., *Cape Town* 1337c
Tamsin E. M., *Liv.J.Moores* 1766b
Spark, Andi, *Griff.* 71b
David, *Auck.UT* 1082a
Kate, *Liv.* 1763c
M., *Swinburne UT* 162b
Sparke, Penny, *Kingston(UK)* 1717
Sparkes, Andrew C., *Exe.* 1658b
B. M., *Nott.Trent* 1864c
Brian A., *S'ton.* 1933a
P., *S'ton.* 1936a
Sparks, B. L. W., *Witw.* 1415c
Beverley A., *Griff.* 73c
Daniel L., *Ott.* 446a
G. A., *Sask.* 473c
Geoffrey H., *Hudd.* 1691c
J. M., *Wales* 1970a
R. S. J., *Brist.* 1585a
Richard, *Edin.* 1648b
Sparling, B. F., *Sask.* 473c
R. R. M., *Manit.* 392b
Sparrow, C., *Nfld.* 406c
C., *Warw.* 1975b
Claire, *Portsmouth* 1898c
Heather, *E.Cowan* 65a
Keith, *W.Ont.* 548b
Paul, *Nott.Trent* 1863b
R. L., *Curtin* 56a
Sparrowhawk, John, *E.Lond.* 1642b
Sparshott, F. E., *Tor.* 498c
Ingrid, *Portsmouth* 1899a
Spash, Clive, *Aberd.* 1536a
Spatcher, Pat, *Lond.S.Bank* 1828c
Spathopoulos, Michael, *Strath.* 1946a
Spaulding, S. J., *W.Ont.* 547a
Spaventa, Eleanor, *Durh.* 1635c
Spavin, S., *Nott.Trent* 1862a
Speake, C. C., *Birm.* 1571c
Speakman, J. R., *Aberd.* 1537b
Spear, Nasser, *Melb.* 94b
R., *Open(UK)* 1868b
Speare, Jane, *Greenwich* 1676c
Spearey, Susan, *Brock* 321b
Spearing, F. E., *Nott.Trent* 1866a
S. Mark, *S'ton.* 1935a
Spearman, L., *Manit.* 394a
Wendy, *Cape Town* 1340a
Spearpoint, Michael J., *Cant.* 1090b
Spears, K., *Lond.S.Bank* 1827a
Norah, *Edin.* 1650c
Russell, *Cardiff* 1622a
Specht, Alison, *S.Cross* 156b
J. A., *W.Ont.* 541a
Speck, Catherine, *Adel.* 26c
Speckman, M. T., *Pret.* 1387b, 1387c
Spector, Timothy D., *Lond.* 1795a
Spedding, Paul, *Salf.* 1920b
Susan F., *Newcastle(NSW)* 142b, 145a
Trevor, *W'gong.* 209b
Speechley, Kathy N., *W.Ont.* 548c, 551a
Mark R., *W.Ont.* 548c, 552c
Speed, C. J., *Plym.* 1889b
Diane P., *Syd.* 169b
Harriet, *Vic.(Aust.)* 186b
Mike P., *Liv.* 1755b
Richard, *Melb.* 101a
Roy, *Auck.UT* 1081c
Terence, *Melb.* 100c
Terrence, *Melb.* 104a
Speedy, J., *Brist.* 1585b
Speelman, Craig, *E.Cowan* 66a
Speers, R. Alexander, *Dal.* 352b, 359b
Speicher, R., *Qu.* 456a
Speidel, Ulrich, *Auck.* 1068c
Speight, A. E. H., *Swansea* 1955c
Martin R., *Oxf.* 1879a
P. M., *Sheff.* 1926c
S. J., *Nott.* 1852a
Speirs, Alastair F., *Leeds* 1735c
R. C., *Birm.* 1571a
Valerie, *Leeds* 1736b
Speller, Martin, *G.Caledonian* 1673b
Spellerberg, Ian F., *Lincoln(NZ)* 1094b, 1095a
Spelman Miller, K. E., *Reading* 1908c
Spelt, Jan K., *Tor.* 503b
Spence, A. K., *W.Ont.* 549a
Alastair, *Bath* 1552c
Andrew M., *Tor.* 505b
Charles J., *Oxf.* 1880c
Deb, *Auck.UT* 1082a
George D., *Vic.(BC)* 518b
I. T. A., *Belf.* 1558b
Iain G., *NE* 135b
Ian, *Syd.* 173b
Ian, *Tor.* 500a
J. A., *WI* 2000a
J. C., *Alta.* 308c
J. David, *W.Ont.* 548b
J. R., *Alta.* 309b
Laura, *Brun.* 1594a
M. W., *W.Ont.* 538b
Mark, *Bond* 39a
Michael, *Syd.* 164
Rebecca D., *NE* 137a, 138c
Robin J. S., *Camb.* 1599c
Roy A. J., *Belf.* 1563a
S. A., *Sheff.* 1928b
Susan, *Macq.* 86c
Spence-Brown, Robyn L., *Monash* 118c
Spence-Sales, J., *Ryerson* 462c
Spencer, A. John, *Adel.* 25c, 30a
A. N., *Alta.* 303c
B. R., *Manc.Met.* 1837b
Brian J., *Macq.* 86, 92b
Brian T., *Pret.* 1385a
Bruce, *Athab.* 315b
C. A., *Alta.* 312a
D. R., *W.Ont.* 543a
David A., *Leeds* 1732a
David L., *Macq.* 89c
Elizabeth C., *Bond* 40b
Gaynor, *Brock* 320a
H., *W.Ont.* 544a
Hamish, *Otago* 1111a
Howard W., *WI* 1996c
J., *Greenwich* 1678b
J. O., *Alta.* 310a
J. P., *Venda* 1404b
Jane, *Exe.* 1656b
Jennifer, *Nott.Trent* 1867c
Jo M., *Lond.* 1795c
John, *Well.* 1114a
John H., *Qu.* 458b
John R., *Camb.* 1604c
Jonathan, *Edin.* 1650b
Jonathan B., *Camb.* 1600c, 1612b
Joseph W., *Liv.* 1756c, 1762c
K. M., *Birm.* 1572b
L., *Wales* 1970b
Laurence C., *W.Aust.* 194a
Marcus P., *Monash* 113b
Michael S., *Cardiff* 1615c
Neil H., *Herts.* 1687a
Paul S., *Wales* 1546b, 1548c
Peter, *Murd.* 130a
R. J., *Calg.* 327c
Rachel, *Lincoln(UK)* 1752c
Robert E., *Athab.* 314b
S. Andrew, *Keele* 1711b
S. J., *Wat.* 533b
Sarah, *Wales* 1968c
Sheila M., *Nott.Trent* 1863c
Terence, *Lincoln(UK)* 1753b
Tom, *Brun.* 1595b
Tom, *Camb.* 1603c, 1611a
Spencer-Oatey, H., *Warw.* 1974a
Spencer-Wood, J. E., *Greenwich* 1676a
Spender, John-Christopher, *Leeds* 1732a
Linda, *Greenwich* 1677b
Spenneman, Dirk H. R., *C.Sturt* 51b
Spensley, M. Fiona, *Oxf.* 1881c
Spentzou, Efi, *Lond.* 1807c
Sperkados, Paula, *Tor.* 510b
Sperl, Stefan, *Lond.* 1816a
Sperling, F. A. H., *Alta.* 303c
Spero, Lawrence, *Tor.* 506b, 510a
Sperring, Anthony, *Syd.* 168c
Spetch, M. L., *Alta.* 309b
Speth, Linda, *WI* 1992a, 1997c
Spettigue, D. O., *Qu.* 454c
Spiccia, Leone, *Monash* 114c
Spicer, A., *Warw.* 1977b
Barry H., *Auck.* 1066c, 1067a
J. I., *Plym.* 1889a
James, *Lond.* 1794c
Mark D., *Strath.* 1945a
Robert A., *Open(UK)* 1869a, 1871c
Spickett, Corinne, *Strath.* 1948b
J. T., *Curtin* 58c
Spiece, Sharon, *Brock* 319b
Spiegel, Andrew D., *Cape Town* 1338a
Spier, S., *Calg.* 333b
Spiers, A. J., *Abertay* 1538c
Colin, *Newcastle(NSW)* 142a
Edward M., *Leeds* 1731b
Lisa, *Murd.* 133c
Spies, Gloudien M., *Pret.* 1380c
Spiethenner, G., *Zambia* 2008a
Spiewak, S. A., *Calg.* 326c
Spiff, A. I., *P.Harcourt* 1207a
Spigelblatt, Linda, *Montr.* 417c
Spike, Neil, *Monash* 121b
Spikes, Hugh A., *ICL* 1703c
Spilberg, Rose, *Lincoln(UK)* 1753b
Spillane, Robert M., *Macq.* 90a
Spillantini, Maria-Grazia, *Camb.* 1608b
Spiller, Dorothy, *Waik.* 1124c
O. Bradley, *Cardiff* 1618c
Peter, *Waik.* 1122a
R. C., *Nott.* 1858a
Spilsbury, Hilary, *Hudd.* 1691a
S., *Manc.Met.* 1841a
Spina, Domenico, *Lond.* 1788b, 1794b
Sandra, *C'dia.* 348c
Spindler, John, *York St John* 1985c
Spink, E., *Manc.Met.* 1839a
Irene, *Hudd.* 1691c
John, *Leeds Met.* 1744b
K. S., *Sask.* 475a
Spinks, Anthony, *Canberra* 42a
Geoffrey M., *W'gong.* 208a, 210b
J. A., *HK* 2033a
Lee, *Edin.* 1648c
Will, *Lough.* 1830
Spinner, Barry, *New Br.* 433a
I. H., *Tor.* 502a
Spira, Laura, *Oxf.Brookes* 1885a
Spirydowicz, Krystyna, *Qu.* 452a
Spiteri, Anthony, *Malta* 1043b
Chris, *Malta* 1046c, 1047b
Doreen, *Malta* 1041a
Joseph H., *Malta* 1040c
Louise, *Dal.* 353a
Monica, *Keele* 1711b
R. J., *Sask.* 473a
Richard, *Malta* 1042b
Spiteri Staines, Cyril, *Malta* 1042a
Spithill, Terrence W., *McG.* 381c, 386b
Spittle, J. A., *Swansea* 1956a
Spittles, Heather A., *Greenwich* 1677b
Spitzer, Michael, *Durh.* 1636a
Spivack, Orsola, *Camb.* 1611a
Spivey, Alan C., *ICL* 1702a
Spoehr, John, *Adel.* 30c
Spoelstra, J., *N-W(S.Af.)* 1368c
Spong, S., *Wales* 1970b
Spongberg, Mary L., *Macq.* 89b
Spooner, Catherine L., *Lanc.* 1722c
Cheri, *Sask.* 480b
Edward T. C., *Tor.* 495a
G. R., *Alta.* 311a
N. J. C., *Sheff.* 1925c, 1931b
Spooner-Hart, Robert, *W.Syd.* 204c
Spoor, Christopher, *Leeds Met.* 1741b, 1742a
Sporns, P., *Alta.* 303a
Sporton, D. S., *Sheff.* 1924a
Spotar, Sergei Y., *Putra* 1025a
Spouge, Alison R. I., *W.Ont.* 548b
Spowage, R., *Manc.Met.* 1837c
Spracklen, C. Tim, *Aberd.* 1536a
Spragg, Melanie, *E.Lond.* 1643b
Sprague, T. J., *Macq.* 92c
Spratt, B. G., *Lond.* 1805a
Brian, *Kent* 1714a
Brian G., *ICL* 1705c
D. A., *Calg.* 327c
T., *Belf.* 1561c
Sprawson, D. H., *Nott.Trent* 1866c
Spray, Christopher, *Lough.* 1835a
John G., *New Br.* 432a, 434a
Sprenglemeyer, R., *St And.* 1916a
Sprik, Michiel, *Camb.* 1600c
Spring, Martin, *Lanc.* 1723c
William, *Herts.* 1684b
Springborg, Robert, *Lond.* 1816a, 1817b
Springer, C. J., *Lond.* 1785a
J. H., *Ryerson* 466a, 466b
Kimberley, *Lond.* 1789c
Springett, B. P., *Massey* 1100a
Mark, *Middx.* 1843a
Rosemary J., *Liv.J.Moores* 1766c
Springham, Stuart V., *Nan.Tech.* 1295b
Spronken-Smith, Rachel A., *Otago* 1111b
Sproston, G. S., *Wolv.* 1983
Kenneth B. G., *Staffs.* 1940
Sprott, D. A., *Wat.* 534b
S. E., *Dal.* 352b
Sproule, Catherine, *Trent* 514c
John S., *Edin.* 1646b
Spruce, Austen E., *Birm.* 1574c
Sprumont, Yves, *Montr.* 412c
Spry, V. Gayle, *Aust.Cath.* 33c
Spunta, M., *Leic.* 1749c
Spurgeon, Anne, *Birm.* 1573c
P., *Warw.* 1978a
P. C., *Birm.* 1572b
Sarah K., *Leic.* 1747b
Spurr, Barry, *Syd.* 169b
Ian G., *Herts.* 1687a
J., *Swansea* 1956c
Michael W., *Tas.* 183c
Nigel K., *Leeds* 1737a
Spurrett, David, *KwaZulu-Natal* 1353c
Spurway, Maggie, *Kingston(UK)* 1719b
Spuzic, S., *Massey* 1101a
Spyer, K. Michael, *Lond.* 1819
Spyrou, Nicholas M., *Sur.* 1952b
Spyt, Tom, *Lough.* 1832b
Square, Paula A., *Tor.* 506b
Sque, Magaret, *S'ton.* 1940a
Squelch, J., *Curtin* 55b
Squire, C., *S.Leone* 1287a
Corinne, *E.Lond.* 1643b
David M., *Monash* 118b
Iain B., *Leic.* 1746b
M. L., *Plym.* 1889b
Patrick J., *Edin.* 1646b
Paul, *Lincoln(UK)* 1752a
Sarah, *Camb.* 1610c, 1613b
Vernon A., *Otago* 1103b
Squires, Graham, *Newcastle(NSW)* 143c
J. A., *Brist.* 1588c
Rev. John, *C.Sturt* 52b
Kim, *St Mary's(Can.)* 470c
N., *Coventry* 1626b
P. E., *Warw.* 1972a
Paul L., *Hudd.* 1691c
Richard, *Herts.* 1685b
Richard A., *Massey* 1101b
T. M., *Manc.Met.* 1838c
Sreberny, Annabelle, *Lond.* 1817b
Srebrnik, P. T., *Calg.* 327a
Sree Kumar, P., *Drav.* 739c
Sree Lakshmi, K. N., *Manipal* 848a
Sreedevi, K., *Annam.* 679a
S., *SPMV* 925b
Sreedhar, G., *Rashtriya SV* 899b
K., *Annam.* 680a
Sreedhar Babu, K. V., *S.Venkat.IMS* 930c
Sreedhar Ranganath Pai, K., *Manipal* 850c
Sreedhar Reddy, C. P., *Manipal* 849c
Sreedhara, T. N., *M'lore.* 843a
Sreedhara Murthy, T. R., *M'lore.* 843b
Sreedharan, Suja S., *Manipal* 845b
Sreejith, K., *Kannur* 809a
Sreekantha, *Manipal* 845b
Sreekumar, G. V., *IIT Bombay* 779a
K. S., *M.Gandhi* 838a
Sharmila, *IIT Bombay* 779a
T. T., *NU Singapore* 1307a
Sreenivas, Kondapudy, *Delhi* 724a
T. V., *IISc.* 774b
Sreenivas Reddy, G., *Kakatiya* 804c
Sreenivasa Raju, A., *ANG Ranga Ag.* 663a
Sreenivasa Rao, K., *And.* 673a

Subbaratnam, G. V., *ANG Ranga Ag.* 662b
Subbarayan, P., *Rashtriya SV* 899c
Subbarayudu, T., *And.* 670b
Subbayamma, G., *I.Gandhi Nat.Open* 786b
Subbayya Sastry, P., *IISc.* 774b
Subbiah, A., *Annam.* 680b
G., *Madurai K.* 829b
S., *Annam.* 681a
Subbotsky, Eugene V., *Lanc.* 1724b
Subbulakshmi, B., *Madurai K.* 829c
C. V., *Avina. Women* 684c
Subburaj, B., *Gandh.Rural* 743a
Subburaman, B. K., *IISc.* 776b
Subedi, Surya P., *Leeds* 1731c
Suberu, R. T., *Ib.* 1175b
Subhadra, K. G., *Kakatiya* 804c
Subhan, K. M. A., *Islamic(B'desh.)* 243b
Syed A., *Karachi* 1252b
Subhas, M. S., *Karn.* 810a, 811b
Subhash, Abel M., *Gulb.* 754c
Anitha, *Avina. Women* 684b
K., *Kakatiya* 803c, 805b
Rema, *SP* 906b, 907b
Subhash Babu, A., *IIT Bombay* 778b, 780a
Subhash Reddy, R., *ANG Ranga Ag.* 662c
Subhashini, A. S., *S.Ramachandra* 927c
Subhashini Devi, P., *And.* 672a
Subodh, Sanjay, *Hyd.* 770b
Subodh Mhaisalkar, *Nan.Tech.* 1301c
Subotincic, N., *Manit.* 388b, 390c
Subrahmanya Sarma, N., *And.* 672b
Subrahmanya Sharma, M. S. R., *Rashtriya SV* 899b
Subrahmanyam, A., *A.Nagar.* 664a
A., *And.* 669b
Ch., *And.* 670a
Ch. V. B., *Potti ST* 889a, 889b
G., *IIT Bombay* 776c
K., *Hyd.* 771b
Sripada, *Potti ST* 889b
T., *And.* 671c
V., *And.* 669c
V., *Potti ST* 889b, 889c
Subramani, *S.Pac.* 1422b
Subramani, P., *Annam.* 677a
Subramaniam, C., *B'thiar.* 704
C., *S.Ramachandra* 927b
D. R., *S.Ramachandra* 927c
E., *M.Sund.* 856a
Nava, *Griff.* 69b, 74c
P., *Manipal* 851a
P. K., *Pondicherry* 887a, 887c
P. R., *Plym.* 1889b
R., *Annam.* 678a
Ramanathan, *Nan.Tech.* 1295b, 1303a
Shamala K., *Putra* 1022c
Velusamy, *NU Singapore* 1310a
Subramaniam Govindasamy, *IIU Malaysia* 1000b
Subramaniam Krishnan, *Malaya* 1010a
Subramanian, A., *Annam.* 680a, 681b, 681c
A., *TN Vet.* 935a, 936c
C., *Annam.* 680b, 681b
C. S., *Annam.* 679c
K. Venkat, *Bharati V.* 707b
M., *Annam.* 679b, 681a
M., *S.Ramachandra* 927a, 927b
M., *TN Vet.* 937a
N., *Annam.* 681b
Narendra, *McG.* 373c
Nathan, *W.Syd.* 204a
P., *Annam.* 676a
P., *B'thidasan.* 704b
P., *Gandh.Rural* 743b
P. R., *Madr.* 826b
R., *Pondicherry* 886b
R. B., *SP* 906c
Raja K., *Maur.* 1051a
S., *Annam.* 676b, 677b
S., *IISc.* 775a
S. P., *Annam.* 678a
T. V., *I.Gandhi IDR* 784
V. S., *TN Vet.* 936b
Vasanta, *Bath* 1550b
Subramaniayan, G., *Madurai K.* 828, 829a
Subramaniyam, Ramesh Kumar, *S.Ramachandra* 926b
Subramaniyan, Arunachalam, *S.Ramachandra* 926, 928c
J., *Annam.* 680a
Subramanya Sharma, V. V., *Kakatiya* 804a
Subramanyam, A., *IIT Bombay* 779b
B., *S.Venkat.IMS* 930b
C., *Osm.* 877a
G., *S.Venkat.IMS* 929, 930a
S., *S.Venkat.IMS* 930c
S. V., *IISc.* 775a
V. M., *Manipal* 850c
Subramanyam Naidu, T. S., *Pondicherry* 886a
Subratty, Anwar H., *Maur.* 1051c
Subraya Bhat, G., *Manipal* 850a
Subraya Kamath, K., *Manipal* 845c
Subrina, Samia, *B'desh.Engin.* 224c
Subrmanya Sharma, M., *Kakatiya* 804a
Subtelny, Maria E., *Tor.* 498a
Subuddhi, Karunamay, *IIT Bombay* 779a
Subuddi, Lakkarajula, *ANG Ranga Ag.* 662, 663b
Subudhi, Bhagaban, *Gauh.* 745c
Sucharita, J., *Osm.* 875b
Sucharov, M., *Car.* 340b
Suchithra, M. M., *S.Venkat.IMS* 930a
Suchitra, J., *Osm.* 875a
U., *Manipal* 846a
Suchman, Lucy A., *Lanc.* 1724b
Suchowersky, O., *Calg.* 331a, 331c
Suckling, Colin J., *Strath.* 1945a
Roger, *Lincoln(UK)* 1752b
Sud, K. K., *M.Sukh.* 860a
Suda, Colletta, *Nair.* 976c, 977a
Sudalaimuthu, S., *Alagappa* 667b, 667c
Sudan, C. S., *Jammu* 796a
F. Kumar, *Jammu* 795c
O. S., *Jammu* 795, 796c
Sudan Paulraj, R. L., *Annam.* 680a
Sudarmawathi, J. M., *Kelaniya* 1444c
Sudarsana Raju, K., *And.* 670c
Sudarsana Rao, G., *And.* 669c, 673a
R., *And.* 670a
Sudarsanakumar, C., *M.Gandhi* 838a
Sudarsanam, P. Sudi., *Cran.* 1630b
Sudarsanasarma, S., *Rashtriya SV* 900a
Sudarshan, S., *IIT Bombay* 777a
T. S. B., *BITS* 709c
Sudarshan Rao, H., *Nehru Tech.* 798b
Sudarshan Reddy, M., *ANG Ranga Ag.* 662a
Sudarshanam, G., *Hyd.* 770c, 771b
Sudbery, John, *Salf.* 1918c
P. E., *Sheff.* 1929a
Sudbury, Aidan W., *Monash* 120a, 127a
Suddaby, Andrew, *Lincoln(UK)* 1753c
Gordon, *Massey* 1102c
Suddes, M., *Newcastle(UK)* 1847c
Sudeep Kumar, N. K., *TN Vet.* 936b
Sudeept Mohan, *BITS* 709c
Sudershan, G., *Kakatiya* 804a
R., *Kakatiya* 804a
V., *Osm.* 877b
Sudershanam, M., *Dr BRA Open* 730
Sudesh, *Kuruk.* 819a
Sudha, K., *Manipal* 845b
L. R., *Annam.* 677b
P., *Manipal* 850a
R., *S.Ramachandra* 926c
S., *Madr.* 827a
T., *Annam.* 677a
T., *SPMV* 924c
Sudha Bhat, S., *Manipal* 848b
Sudha Rani, E., *Dr BRA Open* 730c
Sudhakar, A., *Dr BRA Open* 730c
G., *And.* 672c
G., *Kakatiya* 805a
G. K., *Manipal* 846b
K., *IIT Bombay* 777b, 779c
K., *Kakatiya* 804b
M. K., *S.Ramachandra* 927a
P., *Annam.* 677b
S., *Osm.* 875a
S. V., *And.* 670c
V., *Osm.* 873a, 876b
Yedla, *I.Gandhi IDR* 784c
Sudhakar Babu, L. D., *And.* 670a
Sudhakar Bhat, G., *Manipal* 850b
Sudhakar Rao, M., *IISc.* 774b
N., *Hyd.* 769c
Sudhakar Reddy, Y., *Osm.* 877b
Y. A., *Hyd.* 771b
Sudhakara Rao, A., *A.Nagar.* 663
N., *A.Nagar.* 663c
Y., *Potti ST* 889c
Sudhakara Reddy, B., *And.* 670a
T., *And.* 670b
Sudhakarswamy, P., *Madurai K.* 828b
Sudhaker, Christopher, *Manipal* 850b
Sudhamma, Ven. Wegama, *Buddha SK* 1434c
Sudhanshu Shekhar Jamuar, *Putra* 1024c
Sudharani, P., *S.Venkat.IMS* 929c
Sudharma, A., *M.Gandhi* 838a
Sudharsan, S., *Annam.* 679a
Sudheer, V. C., *And.* 670a
Sudheer Prem Kumar, B., *Nehru Tech.* 798c
Sudhindra, B. S., *I.Gandhi Nat.Open* 787c
Sudhir, M. A., *Gandh.Rural* 742c, 743a, 744a
Sudhir Kumar, K., *Potti ST* 889b
Sudicky, E. A., *Wat.* 526b
Sudish Kumar, *M.Sukh.* 860a
Sudlow, Catherine L. M., *Edin.* 1652b
Sudmalis, David, *Tas.* 183a
Sudweeks, Fay, *Murd.* 131a
Sue, R. E., *Greenwich* 1676b
Sueli, Endre E., *Oxf.* 1874b
Suen, Ching Yee, *C'dia.* 344a, 348a
Sufean bin Hussin, *Malaya* 1006b
Suffling, R. C., *Wat.* 529b, 529c, 532c
Suffolk, John A., *Brunei* 268b
Sufi, S. A., *Bayero* 1148b
Sufi Begum, Gulroo, *Dhaka* 239b
Sufrin, Brenda E., *Brist.* 1587c
Sugaman, J. H., *S.Fraser* 484a
Suganami, Hidemi, *Wales* 1541c
Suganthan, Ponnuthurai N., *Nan.Tech.* 1296c
Sugar, Nicky, *Lond.* 1811c
Sugarman, David, *Lanc.* 1723b, 1724c
I., *Manc.Met.* 1839a
Sugathan, Venu, *Manipal* 852b
Sugathapala, P. D., *Ruhuna* 1459b
R. D., *Peradeniya* 1453a
Sugatharatana, Ven. K., *Kelaniya* 1446b
Sugden, D. E., *Edin.* 1647b
David, *Lond.* 1788c
David A., *Leeds* 1729a, 1739a
Peter H., *ICL* 1707b
R., *Birm.* 1567b
R., *E.Anglia* 1639b
Stephen, *Bond* 40a
Sugianto, LyFie, *Monash* 118b
Sugimoto, A., *W.Ont.* 550b, 550c
Sugirtharajah, R. S., *Birm.* 1570a
Suglo, R. S., *Mines & Technol., Tarkwa* 591b
Sugo, Heber O., *Newcastle(NSW)* 142c
Sugrue, Ciaran, *Camb.* 1602a
Richard J., *Nan.Tech.* 1292b
Sugumar, B., *Eastern(S.Lanka)* 1441a, 1441c
G., *TN Vet.* 936a
Sugumaran, D. K., *Annam.* 676c
Sugumaran a/l Manickam, *Malaya* 1005c
Suguna, K., *Annam.* 678a
K., *IISc.* 775a
Suguna Kumari, S. C., *And.* 670b
Sugunamma, B., *SPMV* 924, 925c
Suhag, Asif A., *Sindh* 1274c
Riaz A., *Mehran* 1257a
Suhail, Anwar, *Aga Khan(P'stan.)* 1233a
Suhaila Mohammed, *Putra* 1025b
Suhaimi bin Hj Abdul Karim, *Brunei* 268c
Suhaimi Ibrahim, *Tech.U.Malaysia* 1031b
Suhaimi Napis, *Putra* 1022b, 1028a, 1028b
Suhan, *Manipal* 851a
Suhana binti Mohd Said, *Malaya* 1007a
Suhov, Yuri M., *Camb.* 1605c
Suissa, Samy, *McG.* 375a, 376b
Suits, B. H., *Wat.* 532a
Sujan, D. K., *Ban.* 693c
Sujatha, B., *And.* 672a
G., *Dr BRA Open* 731c
K., *And.* 672c
K., *Annam.* 676b
S., *S.Ramachandra* 927a
V., *And.* 671a
V., *Rashtriya SV* 899c
Sujatha Kumari, T. V., *Kakatiya* 804c
Sujathamma, P., *SPMV* 925b
Sujet, K. M., *Islamic(B'desh.)* 243a
Sujir, Leila, *C'dia.* 347b
Premjit R., *Manipal* 848b
Sujit, Ghosh, *I.Gandhi Nat.Open* 787a
Sukati, C. Walter S., *Swazi.* 1472a, 1472b
Nonhlanhla A., *Swazi.* 1471a
Sukava, A. J., *W.Ont.* 539b
Sukerman, S., *W.Ont.* 550c
Sukhdev, *Bundel.* 712c
Sukhdev, R. D., *Osm.* 874a
Sukhdev Nanda, *Samb.* 901c
Sukiman Sarmani, Datuk, *NU Malaysia* 1014
Sukiman Sarmani, *NU Malaysia* 1016a
Sukkarieh, Salah, *Syd.* 169a
Sukumar, D., *TN Vet.* 936a
R., *IISc.* 775b
R. G., *TN Med.* 933b
Sarojini, *Avina. Women* 686a
Sukumaran, C. R., *ANG Ranga Ag.* 662b
N., *M.Sund.* 856c
Sul, Donggyu, *Auck.* 1069a
Sulaiha Beevi, M. A. C., *SE(S.Lanka)* 1461b
Sulaiman, Dije M., *Bayero* 1148b
Hamza A., *Bayero* 1150a
Mubarak A., *W.Cape* 1408a
Nabil, *Melb.* 104a
Sulaiman b Yamin, *Tech.U.Malaysia* 1031c
Sulaiman Mohd Nor, *Tech.U.Malaysia* 1033a
Sulaiman Wadi Harun, *Malaya* 1007a
Sulakhe, M. V., *Bharati V.* 707a
P. V., *Sask.* 477a
Sulcas, P., *Cape Town* 1333c
Sule, A. Z., *Jos* 1181c
Mohammed S., *Bayero* 1151a
Richard A. O., *Calabar* 1159c
V. R., *IIT Bombay* 778a
Sule-Odu, A. O., *Olabisi Onabanjo* 1205b
Suleiman, Abubakar G., *Bayero* 1150c
Dahiru M., *Bayero* 1148a
Idris D., *AT Balewa* 1139a
K. G., *AT Balewa* 1139c
M.-S., *Brist.* 1590c
Maryam, *AT Balewa* 1138a
Mohammed D., *Bayero* 1150a
Salihu, *AT Balewa* 1138c
Yasir, *Camb.* 1599c, 1609b
Sulem, Catherine, *Tor.* 497b
Suleman, Afzal, *Vic.(BC)* 519a
Hussein, *Cape Town* 1334a
M., *Lahore UET* 1241a
Suleyman Aremu Muyibi, *IIU Malaysia* 1000b
Suliman, Rosemary, *W.Syd.* 203b
Sulistiyanto, Priyambudi, *NU Singapore* 1315a
Sull, Don, *Lond.* 1798b
Sullenger, Karen, *New Br.* 430b
Sullivan, Ann, *Auck.* 1073b
Ceri, *Wales* 1546c
Denis J., *Well.* 1114b
Gerard, *Syd.* 168c
John, *Aston* 1544b
John, *C.Darwin* 49b
John A., *Dal.* 358c
John T., *Brunei* 267b
K. A., *Qld.UT* 152a
Leigh A., *S.Cross* 156b
M., *Manc.Met.* 1837c
M., *Nott.Trent* 1865b
M. J., *Swansea* 1957b, 1957c
Mark H. F., *ICL* 1708b
Martin, *Glas.* 1669a
Martin, *Massey* 1100c
Michael J., *Otago* 1107a
Michael J. L., *Montr.* 415c
N., *Nfld.* 406a
N. K., *Macq.* 88a
Nancy J., *Guelph* 361
P., *Wat.* 528b
P. A., *Tor.* 508b
P. J., *W.Ont.* 544a
P. L., *HK* 2034b
P. L., *KwaZulu-Natal* 1350c
P. M., *Stir.* 1943a
Patricia L., *Dal.* 353c
Peter, *Monash* 115c
Peter D., *Oxf.* 1877b
Philip, *Brock* 319c
Pierre E., *Tor.* 503b
R., *Calg.* 325a
Ros, *Auck.* 1069c
Rosemary, *Tor.* 493c
Ruth, *Ott.* 442c
S. John, *Otago* 1110b
Terry J., *Kingston(UK)* 1720a
Tim, *Car.* 341c
Sullman, Mark, *Herts.* 1688b
Mark J. M., *Massey* 1098b
Sully, Max, *Murd.* 131b
Sulman, Nasir, *Karachi* 1253a
Sulochana, C., *Gulb.* 754c
M., *Osm.* 876b
Sulochana Nair a/p Kutiri Raman Nair, *Malaya* 1006a
Sulong Mohammad, *NU Malaysia* 1018b
Sulsky, Lorne, *W.Laur.* 557b
Sultan, Fateh Ali Tipoo, *Aga Khan(P'stan.)* 1231c
M. Sarwar, *NED Eng.* 1261b
N., *Jahang.* 246b
Sheikh R., *Khulna* 248c
Saba Rana, *Karachi* 1253a
Shahab, *Bhutto IST* 1272c
U., *NED Eng.* 1261a
Sultan Nazar, A., *Madr.* 826b
Sultana, *Jahang.* 246b
Sultana, A., *Dhaka* 238a
A., *Jahang.* 246b
Abida, *NUST(P'stan.)* 1265a
Akhter, *Dhaka* 236c
Arifa, *B'desh.Engin.* 225a
Aysha, *Dhaka* 237c
D., *Pondicherry* 887a
F., *Rajsh.* 257b
Fowzia, *B'desh.Ag.* 222b
K. S., *Dhaka* 234a
Kazi S., *Chitt.* 230b
Khanam N., *B'desh.Engin.* 225c
M., *Dhaka* 238b
M. A., *Islamic(B'desh.)* 243b
M. S., *Jahang.* 246a
M. T., *Jahang.* 244c
N., *Rajsh.* 255c, 256c
Najma, *Karachi* 1250b, 1252b, 1253c
Nasima, *Dhaka* 233a
Nasreen, *BSMR Ag.* 218c
Pervin, *Chitt.* 230c
Q. S., *Rajsh.* 255c
R., *Dhaka* 235b
Rabeya, *Khulna* 249a
Razia, *Dhaka* 239b
Razia, *Jahang.* 246a
Robert, *Malta* 1046c
Ronald, *Malta* 1041c, 1045b
S., *Chitt.* 228c
S., *Dhaka* 237a
S., *Jahang.* 245a, 246c
S., *Rajsh.* 254c, 256c
Sabiha, *Jahang.* 246a
Saleha, *Kakatiya* 804c
Sarwat, *J.Hamdard* 791b
Shamima, *Rajsh.* 255c
Summer, *Karachi* 1252c
T., *Chitt.* 230a
Taranum, *Aga Khan(P'stan.)* 1230c
Viqar, *Karachi* 1251a
Sultanuddin, S. K., *Osm.* 878a
Sultata Rahat, *Karachi* 1251a
Sulzmann, Martin, *NU Singapore* 1307b
Sum, Chee Chuong, *NU Singapore* 1307b
Ngai-Ling, *Lanc.* 1724a
Suma, D., *Manipal* 851b
Suma Devi, D., *And.* 670c

Teelock, Vijayalakshmi, *Maur.* 1051c
Teelucksingh, S., *WI* 2000c
Teeple, Gary B., *S.Fraser* 486b
L. E., *W.Ont.* 550a
Teer-Tomaselli, Ruth E., *KwaZulu-Natal* 1353b
Teesdale-Spittle, Paul, *Well.* 1114a
Teese, Richard V., *Melb.* 110c
Teeuw, Richard, *Portsmouth* 1900a
Teevan, James J., *W.Ont.* 546a
Teferra, Y., *NUL* 981b
Teffeteller, Annette, *C'dia.* 343b
Tefft, B. M., *Manit.* 393c, 399b
Tegerdine, E., *Nott.Trent* 1866a
Tegg, Amy, *Bran.* 318c
Teghe, Daniel, *C.Qld.* 46a
Teguia, Alexis, *Dschang* 272c
Teh, Cee Ing, *Nan.Tech.* 1292a, 1293a, 1293b
H. C., *NU Singapore* 1307b
K. K., *Curtin* 56b
Kah Chan, *Nan.Tech.* 1296b
Kem Jin, *NU Singapore* 1305b
Ming, *NU Singapore* 1317c
Teh Guan Hoe, *Malaya* 1008a
Teh Ying Wah, *Malaya* 1008a
Tehami, Ahmad Waqar, *NUST(P'stan.)* 1263b
Tehan, Maureen F., *Melb.* 100a
Tehrani, A. D. H., *H-W* 1680b
Teicher, Julian, *Monash* 119c
Teichman, Judith, *Tor.* 499c
Teilanyo, Dirikon I., *Benin* 1154b
Teillet, Philippe M., *Leth.* 365c
Teitel, Jerome M., *Tor.* 506b
Teitelbaum, Heshel, *Ott.* 441a
Teixeira-Dias, Pedro, *Lond.* 1810a
Teja, M. K., *Panjab* 882c, 884a
Tejmani Singh, N., *Manip.* 854a
Teke, G. T., *Jos* 1180b
Tekounegning, *Dschang* 273a
Telang, M., *G.Ghasidas* 757b
Vijaya, *Gulb.* 754b
Telefo, Phelix B., *Dschang* 272c
Teleman, Constantin, *Edin.* 1649b
Telfer, David, *Brock* 322b
Evelyn, *Edin.* 1645c
Lesley, *QM Edin.* 1904b, 1904c
T., *W.Ont.* 543b
T. C., *Stir.* 1941c
Telford, Barry, *Swinburne UT* 160, 163c
G. M., *Tor.* 501c
Mike, *R.Gordon* 1912b
R. William, *Durh.* 1636c
Tella, I. O., *Yola* 1170c
S. A., *Olabisi Onabanjo* 1203c, 1204b
Tellam, J. H., *Birm.* 1569a
Tellambura, C., *Alta.* 305c
Telle, H. H., *Swansea* 1957a
Teller, J. T., *Manit.* 391b
Tellier, Christine, *Montr.* 414a
Telmer, Kevin, *Vic.(BC)* 518b
Telue, Y. K., *PNG Tech.* 1282b
Temane, Q. M., *N-W(S.Af.)* 1369c
Temara, Pou, *Waik.* 1124a
Temarel, P., *S'ton.* 1935b
Tematio, Paul, *Dschang* 273b
Temba, Sr. Auxilia, *CUE Af.* 963a
Tembe, B. L., *IIT Bombay* 777a
Tembo, F., *Zambia* 2007b
Teme, S. C., *Rivers SUST* 1212b
Temelli, F., *Alta.* 303a
Temeng, V. A., *Mines & Technol., Tarkwa* 591c
Temlett, James A., *Adel.* 28a
Temov, Lewis, *E.Cowan* 66b, 66c
Tempelhoff, J. W. N., *N-W(S.Af.)* 1371a
Temperley, John, *Leeds Met.* 1741c
Tempero, Ewan, *Auck.* 1068c
Tempest, S., *Nott.* 1855a
Tempier, R., *Sask.* 477b
Temple, Bryan K., *G.Caledonian* 1673a
I. K., *S'ton.* 1939b
J. A., *Plym.* 1891c
J. R. W., *Brist.* 1585a
John, *Deakin* 62c, 63c
John T., *Lond.* 1777b
Norman, *Athab.* 315a
P. A., *Sur.* 1950c
Richard, *Lond.* 1768c

Ruth, *Auck.UT* 1080b
Viviene A., *Vic.(BC)* 521b
W. J., *Calg.* 333a, 334b
William, *Waik.* 1123b
Temple-Smith, Peter D., *Monash* 127a
Peter D. McN., *Melb.* 102c
Templer, Klaus-Jurgen, *Nan.Tech.* 1301b
Richard, *ICL* 1702a
Templeton, Brian C., *Glas.* 1664c
Douglas M., *Tor.* 505a
J. F., *Manit.* 392c
John R., *Keele* 1711b
Tempone, I., *Swinburne UT* 161a, 163a
Temtime, Z. T., *Botswana* 262c
Temu, A. A., *Sokoine Ag.* 1485b
A. E., *Sokoine Ag.* 1485b
A. K., *Dar.* 1478b, 1479a
Elisei B., *Open Tanz.* 1483, 1483c
R. P. C., *Sokoine Ag.* 1486b
S., *Dar.* 1477b
S. S, *Dar.* 1481b
Ten, Chin Liew, *NU Singapore* 1313b
Ten Eyck, Joanne, *McG.* 367c
ten Hove, M., *Qu.* 459b
ten Kortenaar, Neil, *Tor.* 510b
Tenanakon, F. L., *Brunei* 267a
Tenbensel, Timothy G. T., *Auck.* 1077c
Tench, Ralph, *Leeds Met.* 1741c
Tendler, S. J. B., *Nott.* 1855b
Tene, Mathieu, *Dschang* 273a
Tenebe, V. T., *AT Balewa* 1138b
Tenenbaum, Harriett, *Kingston(UK)* 1720a
Howard C., *Tor.* 492b
Jerry, *Tor.* 506b
Sergio, *Tor.* 498c
Tenenbein, M., *Manit.* 395b, 396b, 397a, 397b
Teng, Piang-Siong (Paul), *Nan.Tech.* 1295c
Susanto, *Nan.Tech.* 1293b
W., *Nott.Trent* 1866c
Tenga, R. W., *Dar.* 1480a
Tengbeh, Paul B., *S.Leone* 1287a
Tengku Ahmad Shahrizal bin Tengku Dato' Omar, *Malaya* 1010c
Tengku Aizan Tengku Abd Hamid, *Putra* 1025c, 1028a
Tengku Azmi Tengku Ibrahim, *Putra* 1027c
Tengku Ghani Tengku Jusoh, *NU Malaysia* 1015b
Tengku Mohd Tengku Sembok, *NU Malaysia* 1017b
Tengse, A. A., *SRT Marath.* 930
Tennakoon, K. U., *Peradeniya* 1452b
K. U. A., *Kelaniya* 1444b
T. M. Kamani P., *Colombo* 1437a
T. M. S. P. K., *Sri Jay.* 1463b
Tennant, A., *Sheff.* 1923a
Alan, *Leeds* 1736c
C., *Warw.* 1973c
D., *Wales* 1970a
Howard E., *Leth.* 365a
J., *W.Ont.* 542b
M., *Sask.* 475a
Marc, *W.Aust.* 193a, 197b
Peter M. W., *KwaZulu-Natal* 1358a
Tennekoon, D. T. B., *Peradeniya* 1452b
Kamani H., *Colombo* 1439b, 1439c
Tennent, C. F., *Sask.* 471, 480b
D. A., *Nfld.* 407c
Robert T., *Qu.* 453a
Tennison, B. R., *Lond.* 1805c
Stephen, *Bath* 1551a
Tennyson, Roderick C., *Tor.* 508b
Tenorio, Rosangela, *Auck.* 1067c
Tenove Brummitt, S. C., *Calg.* 328c
Tensingh Gnanaraj, P., *TN Vet.* 936b
Tenti, G., *Wat.* 528a, 531b
Tenywa, J. S., *Mak.* 1498b
Tenywa-Makooma, M., *Mak.* 1498b
Tenza, T. B., *KwaZulu-Natal* 1351c

Tenzin, Lobsang, *CIHTS* 715, 716a, 716b, 716c
Teo, Albert C. Y., *NU Singapore* 1312a, 1315b
Anthony, *Nan.Tech.* 1291
Beng Chong, *Nan.Tech.* 1295b
C. C. (Jack), *Nan.Tech.* 1301a
C. L., *NU Singapore* 1310a
Chin Kwei (Jimmy), *Nan.Tech.* 1303b
Choo Soo, *NU Singapore* 1315c, 1319b
Chung Piaw, *NU Singapore* 1307c, 1318b
E. H. K., *NU Singapore* 1313b
Ee Chon, *Nan.Tech.* 1299a
Eu-Jin, *Melb.* 94b
Evelyn A. L., *NU Singapore* 1306a
H. H., *NU Singapore* 1311b
K. L., *Curtin* 57b
K. L., *NU Singapore* 1309a
Keang Sood, *NU Singapore* 1312a
Kee L., *Massey* 1098a
Khay Chuan, *Nan.Tech.* 1295c
Thompson S. H., *NU Singapore* 1307c, 1318b
Tian Seng, *NU Singapore* 1316a
Y. M., *NU Singapore* 1307b
Teo Cheok Chin, Peggy, *NU Singapore* 1311a
Teo Kok Seong, *NU Malaysia* 1017c
Teo Lay Teen, *Malaya* 1006a
Teo-Koh, Sock Miang, *Nan.Tech.* 1295c
Teoh, Eam Khwang, *Nan.Tech.* 1296c
Kok Soo, *Monash* 117a
L. K., *Coventry* 1626b
S. H., *NU Singapore* 1310a
Teorongonui, Keelan, *Auck.UT* 1084a
Teotia, S. S., *Kuruk.* 819a
Teow, See Heng, *NU Singapore* 1311a
Tepass, Ulrich, *Tor.* 501c
Teperek, R. J., *R.Gordon* 1911b
Tepi, Samuel, *Dschang* 273c
Tepikin, Alexey, *Liv.* 1759a
Teplitsky, P. E., *Sask.* 473b
Tepperman, Lorne, *Tor.* 501a
Ter, Kah Leng, *NU Singapore* 1306b
ter Haar, G. R., *Lond.* 1785c
ter Keurs, H. E. D. J., *Calg.* 330b, 332b, 334a
ter Meulen, R. H. J., *Brist.* 1591c
Terada, Takashi, *NU Singapore* 1311b
Teram, Eli, *W.Laur.* 559c
Terblanche, Andries B., *Pret.* 1373b
Elmarie, *Stell.* 1397c
J. E., *N-W(S.Af.)* 1368b
John, *Cape Town* 1341a
Lourens S., *Pret.* 1380c
Nic S., *Stell.* 1393b
Otto, *Nelson Mandela Met.* 1363b
Petro, *Pret.* 1377c
Terblanché, Stephanus E., *Pret.* 1373c
Terblanche, Stephanus E., *Pret.* 1385b
Susan S., *W.Cape* 1409b
Terentjev, Eugene M., *Camb.* 1606b
Terhune, John M., *New Br.* 434c
Terjesen, Siri, *Qld.UT* 151b
Terlet, John, *Adel.* 29c
Termezy, Syed M., *Bhutto IST* 1272c
Ternan, J. L., *Plym.* 1890c
Terpstra, C. Nicholas, *Tor.* 495b
Terracciano, Cesare M. N., *ICL* 1707b
Terrazzini, Nadia, *E.Lond.* 1643a
Terreblanche, G., *N-W(S.Af.)* 1369a
Sampie J., *Stell.* 1394a
Terrell-Nield, C. E., *Nott.Trent* 1862b
Terrett, J., *Herts.* 1685c
Terrier, Jean-Marc, *Montr.* 414a
Terriff, T. R., *Birm.* 1573a
Terry, A. V., *Lond.S.Bank* 1827c
E., *Ryerson* 463a

J., *Newcastle(UK)* 1847c, 1848c
J. R., *Brist.* 1586a
James, *S.Pac.* 1422a
Jill, *Worcester* 1984c
Leslie, *Vic.(Aust.)* 187a
Matthew J., *S'ton.* 1933b
Michael A., *Warw.* 1977b
Nicholas, *Abertay* 1538, 1539c, 1540a
P., *Birm.* 1572a
P. D., *Rhodes* 1388a, 1388c
Terstappen, Claudia, *Monash* 117b
Tervo, Richard J., *New Br.* 431a
Terziovski, Milé, *Melb.* 100b, 109a
Terzopoulos, Demetri, *Tor.* 491c
Teschendorff, J., *Curtin* 55a
Tesha, J. V., *Dar.* 1478c
Teskey, G. C., *Calg.* 329b
John, *New Br.* 428, 435c
W. F., *Calg.* 326c
Tesner, Hermanus E. C., *Pret.* 1375a
Tessema, L. S., *Venda* 1404a
Tester, Keith, *Portsmouth* 1899c
Mark, *Adel.* 24c
Richard, *G.Caledonian* 1672c
Tetenta, Ash, *Abia State* 1137b
Tether, Bruce S., *ICL* 1705b
Philip, *Lincoln(UK)* 1752b
Tetley, Teresa D., *ICL* 1707b
Tetreault, R. G., *Dal.* 352b
Tetsell, Margot M., *Herts.* 1683b
Tett, Lyn, *Edin.* 1646b
P., *Napier* 1845a
Simon F. B., *Edin.* 1647b
Tetteh, Antonia, *Kwame NUST* 587b
G. K., *Ghana* 583c
Godwin, *Lond.S.Bank* 1827b
Tettenborn, Andrew M., *Exe.* 1657b
Tettey, Justice N. A., *Strath.* 1948b
W. J., *Calg.* 325a
Y., *Ghana* 584c
Teubert, W., *Birm.* 1570c
Teubner, Michael D., *Adel.* 27b, 29c
Teufel, Simone H., *Camb.* 1601a
Teulon, Paul, *Oxf.* 1883a
Teunter, Ruud, *Lanc.* 1723c
Tevar Terol, Esperanza, *Wales* 1967b
Tevera, D. S., *Swazi.* 1471b
D. S., *Z'bwe.* 2051a
Teverson, Andrew, *Kingston(UK)* 1719a
Teviotdale, Wilma W., *Hudd.* 1693b
Tew, Graham, *Monash* 128a
Philip, *Brun.* 1594c, 1596c
R. E., *Nott.Trent* 1867c
R. H., *Nott.* 1854b
Tewari, B. K., *Lucknow* 823b
D. P., *Lucknow* 822b
Indu, *Panjab* 883c
P. K., *Panjab* 883a
R. K., *Lucknow* 822c
Ram P., *Panjab* 882a
Rupinder, *Panjab* 883a
S. C., *Panjab* 884b
S. P., *Delhi* 724b
S. P., *Hyd.* 770c
Sanjiv, *Panjab* 884b
V. K., *Sikkim-Manipal* 921c
Tewarie, Bhoendradatt, *WI* 1990, 1992c, 1998
Tewe, O. O., *Ib.* 1173a
Tey Beng Ti, *Putra* 1024b
Teye, Gabriel A., *Devel.Studies(Ghana)* 577b
Teys, Pam, *Bond* 39b
Teyssedou, Alberto, *Montr.* 423a
Tezel, F. Handan, *Ott.* 440c, 441c
Thabane, M., *NUL* 981a
Thabede, D. G., *Venda* 1404b
Thabkhe, Yeshe, *CIHTS* 716a
Thabrew, M. I., *Kelaniya* 1443c
Thacker, A. T., *Lond.* 1822c
Julie, *Vic.(Aust.)* 185b
P. A., *Sask.* 472b
Thackeray, J. F., *Pret.* 1381c
Thackray, John, *Leeds Met.* 1742a
Thadikkaran Raju, K., *M.Gandhi* 837c
Thagard, P., *Wat.* 525b, 526a, 530b, 532a, 533b
Thaheem, Nagina P., *Sindh* 1275c

Thai, Ah Chuan, *NU Singapore* 1316c
Binh, *W.Syd.* 202b
Thain, Colin, *Ulster* 1961b
Marion, *Birm.* 1570c
Thaine, Francisco, *C'dia.* 346b
Thairu, Kihumbu, *Moi* 969c
Wanju, *Moi* 969a
Thajuddeen, K., *Manipal* 845c
Thajuddin, *B'thidasan.* 705a
Thakar, H. M., *Shiv.* 915b
P. H., *HN.Guj.* 766a
S. B., *Guj.Vid.* 753b
S. H., *N.Maharashtra* 868c
S. H., *Shiv.* 915b
V. S., *Saur.* 909b
Thakare, S. D., *YCM Open* 953a
Thake, C. D., *Coventry* 1628a
Thake Vassallo, Clare, *Malta* 1044a
Thaker, U. A., *SP* 907b
Thakkar, Ajit, *New Br.* 429c
D. K., *Saur.* 910a
Thakker, Jo, *Waik.* 1123b
Rajesh V., *Oxf.* 1879c
Thakor, A. L., *SP* 907c
Mrugank, *C'dia.* 346a
Thakore, B. Y., *SP* 907c
Thakran, R. C., *Delhi* 723b
Thakur, A. K., *NE Hill* 871c
B. B., *Dr BA Marath.* 732c
Baleshwar, *Delhi* 723b
D. G., *Dr BAT* 735a
Dalip S., *HP* 767b, 767c
Harshad B., *Tata Inst.Soc.Scis.* 938a
Jawahar, *Rajendra Ag.* 896
K. S., *Jiw.* 802a
Laxmi, *MDSU* 835c
M. K., *Ban.* 693b
Manjula, *HP* 768b
Nalini M., *SPA Delhi* 912a, 912c
Parsram, *Guy.* 594c
Prem L., *HP* 768a
R. N., *Shiv.* 915b
Radhakanth, *Rashtriya SV* 899b, 899c
S. K., *HP* 768b
Shori, *Herts.* 1686c
V. M., *Bharati V.* 707c
Yashwant S., *Dr HGV* 736b, 737a
Thakurpersad, A. R. (Ronal), *KwaZulu-Natal* 1350b
Thakurta, M. G., *Dhaka* 236a
Thalagune, T. K. W. T., *Sab.* 1460
Thalak, Sitharam G., *IISc.* 774b
Thalathoti, Vijay, *Vic.(Aust.)* 185c
Thaler, Danielle, *Vic.(BC)* 519b
Tham, C. K., *NU Singapore* 1309a
Clement C. Y., *Chinese HK* 2026b
Foong Yee, *Nan.Tech.* 1295c
Joo-Cheong, *Melb.* 100a
K. D., *Ryerson* 464a
Kwok Wai, *NU Singapore* 1306a, 1319a
L. G., *HK* 2032a
Tham Siew Yean, *NU Malaysia* 1020b
Thamae, Z. L., *NUL* 981b
Thaman, Konai H., *S.Pac.* 1422a
R. R., *S.Pac.* 1422a
Thambi Dorai, C. R., *NU Malaysia* 1020a
Thambipillai, Pushpa, *Brunei* 268a
Thambirasah, Sukantheni, *Colombo* 1436a
Thambiratnam, D. P., *Qld.UT* 152b
Thamboo, Thomas P., *NU Singapore* 1317c
Thamburaja, P., *NU Singapore* 1310a
Thame, Miverva, *WI* 1996b
Thameem Ushama, *IIU Malaysia* 1003a
Thamilamaran, V. T., *Colombo* 1437b
Thamizhselvan, K., *Annam.* 680c
Thampapillai, Jesuthason, *Macq.* 88c
Jesuthason, *NU Singapore* 1314a
Than, Cheok Fah, *Monash* 117a
Thanaraj, T., *Eastern(S.Lanka)* 1441a

Michael J., *Reading* 1906b
Michael J., *Wales* 1540c
Mike, *Lond.S.Bank* 1826
Myra, *Portsmouth* 1902a
P., *Lond.* 1805c
P., *St And.* 1917b
Peter B., *Cape Town* 1333b, 1341c
R., *Coventry* 1626b
R. G., *Nott.* 1856c
R. M., *HK* 2033a
Ray, *Herts.* 1685a
Robert J., *ICL* 1706c
Sally-Anne, *Vic.(Aust.)* 189c
Stephen, *Keele* 1710c
Stephen, *Tas.* 181b
Stephen P., *Leeds Met.* 1743b
Susan, *Lough.* 1834c
Suzanne, *Griff.* 75c
Suzanne J., *Auck.* 1070b
Timothy D., *Camb.* 1602c, 1611a
Timothy J., *Otago* 1107a
Tony, *Durh.* 1633b
W., *Namibia* 1057c
Wilks, Barry, *S.Cross* 156a
Clarissa F., *Kingston(UK)* 1719a
Graham, *Keele* 1709c
Rainford, *WI* 1991a
Rainford J., *WI* 1997b
S. P., *Swansea* 1956a
Stephen R. M., *Exe.* 1657a
Tom, *Lond.S.Bank* 1828c
Y., *Sheff.* 1930c
Wilkshire, M. A., *Nfld.* 404a
Will, C. Renee, *Bran.* 317b
Hartmut J., *Vic.(BC)* 521c
James, *Melb.* 102a
R. G., *Edin.* 1652b
Willan, J. E. A., *Plym.* 1890b
Willans, Julie, *C.Qld.* 46b
Willard, James, *Herts.* 1687a
Jill C., *Trin.Coll.(Tor.)* 512
R. D., *Wat.* 531c
Willars, Gary, *Leic.* 1746c
Willat, Philip, *Lond.* 1798c
Willby, N. J., *Stir.* 1941c
Willcock, Hiroko, *Griff.* 72a
Pamela H., *Manc.Met.* 1839a
Willcocks, Dianne, *York St John* 1985
G., *Coventry* 1625c
Geoff, *Bourne.* 1578c
L., *Lond.* 1801a
Willcox, H. Nick A., *Oxf.* 1879c
J., *Manc.Met.* 1837c
Paul A., *Cape Town* 1340a
Willeboordse, H. F., *NU Singapore* 1313c
Willemen, Paul, *Ulster* 1962c
Willems, Bernard, *Montr.* 417b
Gerard, *Syd.* 172c
Willemse, Barend, *Jo'burg.* 1346b
D., *Namibia* 1058c
Heinrich S. S., *Pret.* 1373c
Naudine, *Pret.* 1384a
Willes, Heather A., *Lanc.* 1725b
Willett, Brian J., *Glas.* 1669b
Caroline, *Portsmouth* 1898c
Keith M., *Oxf.* 1880a
P., *Sheff.* 1924c
T. C., *Qu.* 457c
Willey, D. S., *Plym.* 1888b
David, *Bourne.* 1578
Willgoose, Garry R., *Newcastle(NSW)* 142c
Willi, Andreas J., *Oxf.* 1874a
William, Robins, *Tor.* 493c
William Baskaran, M., *Gandh.Rural* 743b
Williams, A., *Nfld.* 401a
A., *Warw.* 1975a
A. A., *Nott.Trent* 1864a
A. C., *Brist.* 1589c
A. C., *Reading* 1907b
A. D., *Warw.* 1975c
A. E., *Lond.* 1812b
A. G., *Manc.Met.* 1839c
A. G., *Plym.* 1890c
A. J., *Cardiff* 1618c
A. J., *St And.* 1915a
A. M., *Swansea* 1956c
A. Paul, *Tor.* 505a
Alan, *Leeds* 1730b
Alan, *Salf.* 1919c
Alan, *Wales* 1967b
Alastair, *Keele* 1710c
Alex J., *Salf.* 1918b
Alistair R. W., *Edin.* 1652c
Allan R., *Keele* 1712c

Andrew, *Portsmouth* 1901a, 1903b
Andrew J., *Kent* 1715c
Andrew M., *Liv.J.Moores* 1767a
Angela M., *Cardiff* 1617b
Anne, *Cardiff* 1621a
Anthony G., *Adel.* 25b, 31a
Anthony P., *Newcastle(NSW)* 141a
Anwen S., *Cardiff* 1620c
B. C., *E.Anglia* 1640b
B. E., *Coventry* 1628a
Barbara, *Leth.* 366c
Barry, *Bond* 39a
Barry, *Strath.* 1946a
Bernard E., *Leth.* 365a
Bill R. S., *Auck.* 1079c
Brenda P., *Lond.* 1792c
Brian D., *Adel.* 26a
Bronwyn, *E.Cowan* 67c
Bryan, *Leic.* 1746c, 1750b
Bryan R. G., *Monash* 127a
C., *Sheff.* 1924c
C. A., *Brist.* 1587a
C. C., *Sheff.* 1925a
C. M., *Swansea* 1956c
Carolyn, *W.Aust.* 198a
Catrin H., *Wales* 1548a
Charles D. H., *Exe.* 1658a
Charles R., *Monash* 119b
Charlotte, *Keele* 1709c
Charlotte K., *ICL* 1702a
Chris, *Auck.* 1073a
Chris, *Melb.* 107b
Christine M., *Reading* 1905b, 1907a
Christopher J., *Bath* 1550b
Christopher K. I., *Edin.* 1648a
Claire, *Lond.* 1795c
Clare, *Lond.* 1791b
Clarence G., *W.Cape* 1407a
Claudette, *WI* 1996b
Clyde, *Lough.* 1835a
Colin H., *Cardiff* 1622c
Craig A., *Exe.* 1658b
D., *Cardiff* 1616b
D., *Swansea* 1957a
D. A., *Hull* 1697b
D. A. F., *Witw.* 1412c
D. B. G., *Jo'burg.* 1346c
D. Dudley, *Tor.* 501c
D. E., *Greenwich* 1676a
D. E., *Sask.* 475c
D. G., *Swansea* 1958a, 1958b
Sir D. G. T., *Chinese HK* 2024a
D. I., *Hull* 1698c
D. L., *Manit.* 390b
D. T., *Wales* 1967c
Daryl R., *ICL* 1702c
David, *Cardiff* 1615b
David, *La Trobe* 78a
David, *Liv.J.Moores* 1765c
David, *Portsmouth* 1901b
David, *WI* 1995c
David A., *Melb.* 106a
David B., *Tor.* 504c
David E., *Auck.* 1068b
David F., *Liv.* 1759c
David G., *Canberra* 43a
David J., *Lough.* 1833a
David M., *Lond.* 1805
David M., *S'ton.* 1933a
David R., *Cardiff* 1615c
David S., *Brun.* 1595a
David V., *Auck.* 1072c
Deane M., *Monash* 117a
Delyth W., *Liv.J.Moores* 1765b
Denise, *Glam.* 1661b
Diana J. L., *Liv.* 1762a
Dudley D., *Wales* 1546a
E., *Wales* 1547a
E. J., *Nott.* 1853a
E. N., *Plym.* 1889a
Edward W., *Keele* 1712a
Eka, *Calabar* 1160a
Elaine E., *WI* 1996c
Elizabeth N., *Melb.* 107b
Esther, *S.Pac.* 1421, 1423c
Evan, *Melb.* 100c
Evelyn M. I., *Liv.* 1761a
Fiona, *Leeds* 1734a
Fred W., *Cardiff* 1617a
G., *Car.* 338b
G., *Manit.* 393a
G. A., *HK* 2031b, 2036b
G. A. P., *Lagos* 1183c
G. D., *Reading* 1909a
G. J., *Manit.* 395b, 397b
G. O., *Lagos* 1184a
G. Ronald, *Tor.* 504c

G. T., *Cardiff* 1620a
Gail, *Cardiff* 1621a
Gail, *Otago* 1109a
Gareth, *Brist.* 1583b
Gareth, *Leeds Met.* 1741c
Gareth H., *Cardiff* 1622c
George, *Cran.* 1630a
Gill L., *Wales* 1967c
Glen S., *Car.* 340b
Godfried, *E.Lond.* 1642c
Graham D., *Keele* 1711c
Graham H., *W'gong.* 209c
Graham R., *ICL* 1706c
Granville, *Hudd.* 1694b
Gruffydd A., *Wales* 1542b
Gwyn T., *Keele* 1711a
H., *Nfld.* 402b
H., *Nott.Trent* 1865a
H. C., *Calg.* 328b
H. C., *Nott.* 1857c
H. C., *Nott.Trent* 1865c
H. E., *WI* 1999c
H. J., *N-W(S.Af.)* 1371b
H. P., *Lond.* 1801a
H. S. A., *Kelaniya* 1446a
Heather K., *W.Aust.* 201b
Howard Ll., *Wales* 1541c
Howe B., *McG.* 378a
Huw D., *ICL* 1701b
Huw R., *Glam.* 1660, 1661b
I. D., *S'ton.* 1934a
I. D., *Wat.* 530c
I. W., *Wales* 1546b
Ian D., *Belf.* 1560b
Ian H., *Bath* 1550c
Ian H., *W.Aust.* 191c
Ioan M., *Wales* 1540b, 1542b
J., *Cardiff* 1620b
J., *Coventry* 1628a
J., *Wales* 1970a
J. A., *Manc.Met.* 1837c
J. A., *Rhodes* 1390b
J. A. Gareth, *Durh.* 1633a
J. D., *Cardiff* 1619c
J. E. M., *Plym.* 1892c
J. H., *Rhodes* 1388b
J. J., *Manit.* 392a
J. J., *Plym.* 1890c
J. L., *Wat.* 536c, 537b
J. L. H., *Fort Hare* 1343b
J. Mark G., *Wales* 1547c
James, *Lond.* 1809c
James E., *Otago* 1106b
James F., *W.Aust.* 195b
James S., *Kent* 1714c
Jan, *Middx.* 1843b
Jane, *Hudd.* 1691a, 1693a
Janet, *Auck.UT* 1082a
Janet E., *Cardiff* 1618c
Jenny, *Melb.* 96c
John, *Adel.* 27b
John, *Aston* 1544b
John, *Auck.UT* 1080
John, *E.Cowan* 65a
John, *Leic.* 1750b, 1750c
John, *Portsmouth* 1900b
John, *S'ton.* 1937a
John, *W.Cape* 1407b
John A., *Camb.* 1602c
John C., *Durh.* 1635a
John F., *Melb.* 97c
John P., *Tor.* 491a
John R., *Greenwich* 1677c
John R., *Wales* 1541c
Jonathan, *Wales* 1542c, 1546a
Jonathan M. J., *Bath* 1550c
Julia, *Herts.* 1685c
June H., *Pret.* 1384c
K. E., *Sask.* 476a
K. L., *Swansea* 1957c, 1958b
K. M., *Swansea* 1955a, 1957a
Kate E., *Herts.* 1685b
Katherine E., *Leic.* 1745, 1751a
Kathryn J., *Melb.* 102a
Katie, *W.England* 1981a
Katrina, *Bond* 38c
Keith P., *Cardiff* 1617c
Kim, *Vic.(Aust.)* 188b
L., *Sask.* 479c
Lauren T., *Newcastle(NSW)* 143b
Laurie E., *Herts.* 1685c
Leonard T., *Leeds Met.* 1743a
Leonie, *Sunshine Coast* 159b
Les, *Auck.UT* 1081c
Linda, *S'ton.* 1935b
Lorraine E., *S'ton.* 1933c
M., *Plym.* 1893a
M., *Wales* 1970a
M. A., *Witw.* 1414a

M. C., *Calg.* 329c
M. D., *Swansea* 1956a
M. H., *H-W* 1681a
M. J. S., *N-W(S.Af.)* 1369a
M. L., *Swansea* 1956c
M. P., *Dal.* 351a
M. R., *E.Anglia* 1638c
M. T., *Coventry* 1626b
Marian, *Bond* 39c
Mark, *Cant.* 1087b
Mark B., *Leeds* 1732c
Mark C., *Pret.* 1384c
Martin A., *Adel.* 29c, 30c
Martin A. K., *Massey* 1098a
Martin S., *Oxf.* 1875a
Mat, *Edin.* 1647b
Melissa S., *Tor.* 499c
Michael, *Griff.* 70a
Michael, *Liv.* 1760b
Michael, *Wales* 1541c
Michael D., *Nan.Tech.* 1295a
Miriam, *Lond.S.Bank* 1826c
Murray, *Well.* 1114a
N., *Greenwich* 1676a
N. A., *Coventry* 1628a
N. H., *Sheff.* 1922b
Nadia P., *WI* 1996c
Natalie, *Vic.(Aust.)* 188c
Neil, *Kingston(UK)* 1719c
Neil A., *Brist.* 1589c
Nigel M., *Cardiff* 1620b
P., *Nott.* 1859c
P., *Wales* 1546c
P. D., *Warw.* 1976a
P. M., *Nott.* 1855b
P. R., *Swansea* 1956a
Pamela, *Hudd.* 1692a
Pamela A., *Hull* 1697c
Patrick, *Jamaica UT* 956c
Patrick, *Portsmouth* 1901c
Paul, *Birm.* 1573a
Paul F., *New Br.* 432a
Paul M., *Brist.* 1589a
Paul T., *Leeds* 1730a
Paul W., *Auck.* 1072a
Peter, *W'gong.* 208c, 210c
Peter, *W.Syd.* 204c
Peter H., *Leic.* 1747c
Peter H. M., *Melb.* 95a
Peter J. leB., *Wales* 1547b
Peter N., *Liv.J.Moores* 1765b
Peter T., *Manit.* 395a
Peter W., *S.Fraser* 486b, 487c
Philip, *Hudd.* 1694c
Philip F., *Massey* 1099a
Philip L., *Melb.* 101a
Philip R., *Griff.* 71a
Phillip, *Keele* 1712c
R., *Aberd.* 1535c
R. J., *Plym.* 1891a
R. J., *Wat.* 533a, 535b
R. W., *Swansea* 1954, 1956b
Rachel L., *Liv.* 1760a
Raymond N., *Tas.* 182b
Rhys, *Wales* 1542c
Richard, *Bourne.* 1580a
Richard, *ICL* 1707c
Richard, *Swinburne UT* 163c, 164a, 164b, 164c
Richard A., *Leeds* 1726, 1730b, 1738b, 1738c
Richard A., *Melb.* 106a
Richard G., *Liv.* 1756b
Robert, *Leth.* 364c
Robert, *Lond.* 1788a
Robert C., *KwaZulu-Natal* 1358a
Robert G., *Wales* 1967c
Robert J., *Wales* 1968a
Robert L., *McG.* 378a
Robin, *Durh.* 1633a
Robin A., *Edin.* 1650b
Roger H., *Wolv.* 1983c
Roger J., *Wolv.* 1984a
Ronald J. H., *Wales* 1967a
Ross, *NE* 139c
Ross A., *Melb.* 94c
Roy, *Portsmouth* 1903b
Ruth, *Auck.* 1070a
Ruth M., *Camb.* 1605b
S., *Cardiff* 1621c
S., *Warw.* 1978a
S. A., *Reading* 1907c
S. B., *O.Awolowo* 1197b
S. D., *Plym.* 1888b
S. J., *Warw.* 1976b
S. S., *Kelaniya* 1446b
Sandy, *Murd.* 131b
Sarah, *Bourne.* 1580a

Sian R., *Wales* 1967c
Sonia A., *Leeds* 1736a
Stefan, *Syd.* 169a
Stephanie, *Glam.* 1661b
Stephanie, *Trent* 513, 515c
Stephen, *Portsmouth* 1901b
Steve, *Lond.S.Bank* 1826b
Steven C. R., *Lond.* 1792c
Stewart W., *Cran.* 1629c
Sue, *Bath* 1556b
Sue, *Syd.* 167c
Terry M., *S'ton.* 1936a
Thomas, *McG.* 373a
Thomas R., *Qu.* 451, 457a
Timothy J., *ICL* 1707b
Tony D., *S.Fraser* 482b
Trefor, *Glam.* 1660b
V. A., *Nott.Trent* 1862c, 1865a
V. E., *Lagos* 1187c
V. P., *Nott.* 1861a
Val, *Keele* 1711b
Vaughan, *Lond.* 1814b, 1814c
Vincent J., *Liv.J.Moores* 1765c
W., *Edin.* 1647b
W. Huw, *Exe.* 1658a
W. Tudor, *Glam.* 1661c
William, *Ott.* 445b
Winston, *WI* 1996a
Williams-Ashman, P. F., *Cape Town* 1340c
Williams-Bovell, Bernice, *Guy.* 594b
Williams-Findlay, Cindy, *Wolv.* 1984c
Williams-Jones, Anthony E., *McG.* 369b
Williams-Myers, Claudette, *Jamaica UT* 956b
Williams-Wynn, D. E. A., *KwaZulu-Natal* 1351b
Williamson, Alan G., *Auck.* 1070c
Andy, *E.Lond.* 1643a
Arthur P., *Ulster* 1963a
B., *S.Fraser* 487c
B. A., *Brist.* 1587b
Bryce E., *Cant.* 1091b
C. L., *Calg.* 325a
Catherine, *ICL* 1708b
Christina M., *C.Sturt* 51c
Christopher J., *Cant.* 1090b
Craig, *Strath.* 1948c
D. C., *Nott.Trent* 1865c
D. L., *Alta.* 306c
David R., *W.Ont.* 554a
Dianne B., *La Trobe* 82c
Dugald, *NE* 136a
E., *Lond.* 1822c
E. M., *Reading* 1907b
Eddy, *Vic.(Aust.)* 188b
Edwin H., *Oxf.* 1877b
Elaine, *Lond.* 1820c
Elizabeth, *G.Caledonian* 1672c
G. M., *Plym.* 1888b, 1891c
Geoffrey H., *G.Caledonian* 1673b
Hugh G. M., *Oxf.* 1877b
I. G., *Plym.* 1939a
Ian P., *Melb.* 98b, 111a
J., *Alta.* 306b
J., *Coventry* 1627a
J., *Qld.UT* 150b
J. G. (Ian), *Liv.* 1758a
J. H., *Warw.* 1973a
John, *Tas.* 182c
John G., *Glas.* 1665b
John R., *New Br.* 432a
Kathleen, *Belf.* 1563a
Kirsty M., *Monash* 118a
L. M., *Camb.* 1608b
M. P., *Sheff.* 1929a
Malcolm, *Lincoln(UK)* 1753b
Martyn I., *Otago* 1108c
Norman B., *Massey* 1101b
Owen, *Monash* 121b
P., *Greenwich* 1676a
P. C., *W.Ont.* 548c, 552a
Paul, *Liv.* 1757a
Paula N., *Liv.* 1760b
Peter M., *Liv.J.Moores* 1766a
Philip, *Leeds Met.* 1743c
Philip A., *Durh.* 1635b
R., *Plym.* 1888a
Raymond A., *W.Aust.* 193a
Robert, *Melb.* 105c
Rodney, *Ott.* 443b
Ronald, *KwaZulu-Natal* 1354c
S., *Wales* 1970b
T., *E.Anglia* 1639c
T., *Manc.Met.* 1837a
Terry, *Adel.* 25a

Robert J., *Wales* 1540c
S., *Nott.Trent* 1866b
S. A., *S'ton* 1939b
Worbec, E. A., *Manit.* 392b
Worboys, Jenny, *Monash* 123b
Worden, Blair, *Lond.* 1809a
K., *Sheff.* 1923c
Lee, *Durh.* 1637c
Nigel A., *Cape Town* 1335c
Richard, *Liv.* 1756b
S. A., *Curtin* 55a
Wordley, John, *Trent* 515c
Wordsworth, B. Paul, *Oxf.* 1879c
Wordu, H., *Rivers SUST* 1211b
Worika, I. L., *Rivers SUST* 1211a, 1211c
Workentin, M. S., *W.Ont.* 539b
Workman, Barbara, *Monash* 122a, 126a
Helen M., *Oxf.Brookes* 1884, 1887a
P., *Lond.* 1785a
Paul, *Leeds* 1737a
Stephen R., *Dal.* 357a
W. Thom, *New Br.* 433a
Workman-Davies, C. L., *Curtin* 57c
Worley, Jonathan, *Belf.* 1564c
Wormald, M. R., *Camb.* 1611c
Michael P., *Cape Town* 1333a
N., *Wat.* 525b
P., *Manc.Met.* 1839b
Paul, *Lough.* 1831b
Peter J., *Adel.* 29b
Wormell, Paul, *W.Syd.* 204c
Wormith, J. S., *Sask.* 477c
Worner, Susan P. M., *Lincoln(NZ)* 1094a
Worobetz, L. J., *Sask.* 476a
Worrall, Ann J., *Keele* 1709c
D. M., *Brist.* 1588b
Fred, *Durh.* 1634b
G., *Nfld.* 407a
J., *Lond.* 1801b
Timothy S., *Keele* 1710a
Worrall-Davies, Anne, *Leeds* 1735b
Worrell, Gary L., *New Br.* 435b
Worringham, C., *Qld.UT* 150a
Worsdale, Graham J., *Hudd.* 1694a
Worsfold, A., *Nott.Trent* 1866b
P. J., *Plym.* 1889c
Worsley, D. A., *Swansea* 1956a
Keith J., *McG.* 373a
Worster, M. Grae, *Camb.* 1605b
Worswick, Christopher, *Car.* 337b
M. J., *Wat.* 528b
Worth, Andrew J., *Massey* 1101a
Christopher G., *Monash* 117a, 119a
S. G., *Manc.Met.* 1838c
S. H., *KwaZulu-Natal* 1357c
Worthington, David J., *Lanc.* 1723c
F. T., *Liv.* 1757c
P., *Brun.* 1593b
S. E., *Lond.* 1799, 1800c
Stephen, *Monash* 119c
Worthley, Stephen, *Adel.* 28a
Worthy, Annette L., *W'gong.* 209c
Wortley, J. T., *Manit.* 391b
N. Scot, *Tor.* 508c
Richard K., *Griff.* 70b
Wortman, David J., *Lanc.* 1723c
Worton, Michael J., *Lond.* 1819
Ronald, *Ott.* 445c, 447b
Worugji, Israel N. C., *Calabar* 1160a
Worwood, M., *Cardiff* 1619b
Woscholski, Rudiger, *ICL* 1701c
Wossler, Theresa C., *Stell.* 1393b
Wosu, Desmond I., *Rivers SUST* 1212c
L. O., *Makurdi Ag.* 1144b
Woszczyk, Wieslaw, *McG.* 373a, 383c
Wotherspoon, Simon, *Tas.* 180b
T. L., *Sask.* 478a
Wotshela, L., *Fort Hare* 1344a
Wotton, Paul R., *Glas.* 1669a
Wouatong, Armand S. L., *Dschang* 273b
Woudsma, C. G., *Wat.* 532a
Woudstra, J., *Sheff.* 1924c
Woudt, Patrick A., *Cape Town* 1333b
Wouk, Fay, *Auck.* 1067b

Would, Joan, *Nott.Trent* 1862a
Wouldes, Trecia, *Auck.* 1076a
Wowk, Maria T., *Manc.Met.* 1841b
Wozniak, D., *Birm.* 1576b
J., *Nelson Mandela Met.* 1362b
R. W., *Alta.* 310c
Wraith, David C., *Brist.* 1589c
Peter C., *Hudd.* 1693c
Wranz, Peter A. B., *Stell.* 1399b
Wrathall, Jeffrey P., *Monash* 119c
Wratten, Stephen D., *Lincoln(NZ)* 1094a
Wray, Alison M., *Cardiff* 1617b
D. S., *Greenwich* 1678b
David, *Glas.* 1670b
David J., *Warw.* 1973a
Dennis A., *Leeds* 1727b
Elizabeth, *Herts.* 1684a
J. L., *St And.* 1914a
Sharon, *Hudd.* 1692a
Susan C., *Liv.* 1759a
Wreford, Nigel G. M., *Monash* 120c
Wren, B. W., *Lond.* 1805a
Wren-Lewis, Simon, *Exe.* 1655b
Wrenn, Phyllis, *S.Fraser* 484b
Wrennall, Mike, *G.Caledonian* 1673c
Wrigg, James, *Lond.* 1796c
Wrigglesworth, John, *Portsmouth* 1901c
Wright, A., *Curtin* 58c
A. C., *Massey* 1101a
A. C., *Reading* 1909b
A. E., *Witw.* 1415c
A. N., *St And.* 1915b
Alan F., *Edin.* 1652b
Alexis, *Open(UK)* 1870c
Andrew, *Lond.* 1793c
Anthony D., *Leeds* 1731b
Astri, *Vic.(BC)* 520a
B. J., *Calg.* 331b
Barry, *Brock* 320b
Bianca M., *Nelson Mandela Met.* 1362a
Bronwyn, *C.Darwin* 48a
Bruce, *Dal.* 358a
C., *Aberd.* 1537a
C., *W.Ont.* 543b
C., *Warw.* 1976a
C. A., *Stell.* 1399b
C. J., *Witw.* 1412a
C. J. G., *St And.* 1915c, 1916b
Cecile, *Nott.Trent* 1866b
Charlotte M., *Glas.* 1670b
Chris, *Lincoln(NZ)* 1093c
Chris, *Middx.* 1843a
Christine, *Melb.* 106a
D., *E.Anglia* 1639a
D., *Manc.Met.* 1837c
D., *Nott.Trent* 1864a
D. E., *Plym.* 1891b
D. G., *Auck.* 1071b
D. L., *Plym.* 1890b
D. M., *Nott.* 1855a, 1859c
David, *W.Syd.* 202c
David, *Wales* 1545c, 1546c
David C., *Exe.* 1656a
David J., *Ott.* 443a
David K., *Brun.* 1594a
David M., *Adel.* 27b
Deborah, *Lond.S.Bank* 1826c
Denis A., *NE* 135b
Denis J., *ICL* 1701b
Dominic S., *Camb.* 1600c
Donald, *New Br.* 433a
Donald, *Syd.* 168b
Dorothy, *QM Edin.* 1904c
E. M., *Plym.* 1892a
Edmund W., *Newcastle(NSW)* 143c, 145c
Fiona, *S.Cross* 157b
Frederick A. C., *Melb.* 103b
George, *Durh.* 1634a
Graeme L., *Curtin* 54c
Graham, *E.Lond.* 1642b
H., *Hull* 1696a
H. H., *N-W(S.Af.)* 1369b
Helen, *Griff.* 69a
Helen M., *W.Aust.* 197a
I. M., *Manc.Met.* 1838c
Ian P., *Open(UK)* 1872a
J., *Manit.* 395b
J., *NU Singapore* 1307c
J. A., *Coventry* 1627a
J. A., *Manit.* 392b
J. A., *Nfld.* 402b
J. Barry, *Car.* 339b
J. K., *Car.* 336a

J. L., *Wat.* 528b
J. M., *Dal.* 350b
J. R., *Calg.* 333c
James, *Edin.* 1649b
James S., *Car.* 336c
Janet, *Bran.* 316, 318b, 318c
Janice E., *W'gong.* 207c
Jeannie, *Massey* 1096a
Joanne, *Lond.* 1808b
Joanne, *New Br.* 433a
John, *Aberd.* 1536c
John, *E.Lond.* 1643a
John, *Montr.* 415c, 421b
John G., *Tor.* 506b
John N., *Newcastle(NSW)* 143c
John W., *Sur.* 1950a
Jonathan, *Lough.* 1832a
Jonathan R. C., *Oxf.* 1878b
Judith, *Worcester* 1985a
K., *Curtin* 55b
K. E., *Sask.* 476b
K. Marcella, *Herts.* 1689c, 1690b, 1690c
Kathryn E., *Ott.* 444b
Kenneth, *Melb.* 94b
Kerri, *Greenwich* 1677b
L., *Plym.* 1891a
L. James, *Auck.* 1068b
Laura C., *Camb.* 1603b
Linda P., *Liv.J.Moores* 1765b
Lynne, *W'gong.* 211b, 211c
M. C. M., *S'ton.* 1938b
M. E., *Calg.* 324c
M. K., *Rhodes* 1388c
Mac, *Vic.(Aust.)* 185c
Mary J., *W.Ont.* 546a
Michael, *Brun.* 1595c, 1596b
Michael, *Cant.CC* 1613
Michael B., *Lanc.* 1723c
Michael J., *Herts.* 1684a
N., *Coventry* 1627a
Sir N. A., *Lond.* 1805
N. G., *Hull* 1697b
N. G., *Nott.* 1852b
Nancy, *Auck.UT* 1083a
Nancy, *W.Syd.* 203b
Nevan, *Auck.UT* 1083a
Nicholas R. M., *Camb.* 1611b
Noeline, *Waik.* 1123a
Owen, *Lond.* 1816a
P. A., *Nott.* 1853c
P. A., *St And.* 1914a, 1916a
P. C., *Sheff.* 1923a
P. G., *Plym.* 1892c
P. W., *Alta.* 305a
P. W., *Nott.* 1852a
P. W., *Sheff.* 1925a
Patricia, *Cardiff* 1622a
Patrick, *Adel.* 30c
Paul, *Lough.* 1833a
Paul, *W.Aust.* 195a
Peter, *Edin.* 1649c
Peter, *Murd.* 130c
Peter J., *Monash* 122a
Peter M., *Tor.* 502b
R. A., *Trent* 514a
R. E., *Ryerson* 463b
R. J., *S.Cross* 156a
Richard, *Lincoln(UK)* 1752a
Richard D., *S.Fraser* 486a
Rob, *Herts.* 1685b
Robert, *Aberd.* 1536a
Robert, *Portsmouth* 1899a
Robert, *Strath.* 1945b
Robert M., *Tor.* 490b
Robin, *Lincoln(UK)* 1753c
Roger H. P., *Liv.* 1756a
Russell, *Vic.(Aust.)* 187b
S., *Nfld.* 409c
S., *Nott.Trent* 1864a
S., *Sask.* 479a
S. C., *S.Fraser* 486a
S. L., *Nfld.* 409a
Sarah, *Lond.* 1809c
Shane D. T., *Auck.* 1068b
Stephanie C., *Leeds* 1727b
Stephen, *Lond.* 1777b
Sue, *Manc.Met.* 1839a
Sue, *Portsmouth* 1901c
Sue J., *Macq.* 87a
Susan K., *Nan.Tech.* 1294c
T., *Sheff.* 1922c
T. G., *Nott.* 1851b
Terence V., *Ulster* 1960a
Timothy E., *Edin.* 1654b
Tony, *E.Lond.* 1643c
V. M., *S'ton.* 1936c
Victor P., *Cardiff* 1616c
Warren, *Worcester* 1985c
Wendy, *Monash* 114a

Zane, *Strath.* 1948c, 1949b
Wright-Neville, David, *Monash* 120b, 125c
Wright-Pascoe, Rosemarie A., *WI* 1996a
Wright-St Clair, Valerie, *Auck.UT* 1083c
Wrightson, Jim, *Liv.J.Moores* 1767b
P. A., *Birm.* 1569b
Wrigley, C. J., *Nott.* 1853b
Jack, *Qld.UT* 151b
L., *Manc.Met.* 1841a
M. P., *Massey* 1100a
Neil, *S'ton.* 1935b
Roger, *Melb.* 94b
Wring, Dominic, *Lough.* 1834c
Wrobel, Luiz, *Brun.* 1594a
Wróbel, Piotr, *Tor.* 495b
Wroblewski, J. S., *Nfld.* 401c, 405b, 408b
Michael, *Leeds* 1729c
Wrogemann, K., *Manit.* 395b
Wronski, Ian, *James Cook* 76c
Wroot, Andrew J., *Herts.* 1689c
Ian, *Liv.J.Moores* 1765a
Wu, B., *Ryerson* 464a
C., *Chinese HK* 2021b, 2028c
Christine, *Manit.* 390b
Chung-Tong, *W.Syd.* 201
Duncan, *Oxf.* 1875b
Fei, *Massey* 1097b
Felix F., *HK* 2032a
Fulong, *Cardiff* 1616a
G., *Qu.* 452c
Gabriel Y. C., *NU Singapore* 1306c
Guo, *W.Syd.* 203b
Guoguang, *Vic.(BC)* 520a, 521b
H., *Coventry* 1627a
H., *Curtin* 56a
Houzheng, *Lough.* 1834b
J., *NU Singapore* 1313a
J., *Ryerson* 463c
Jesse, *C.Darwin* 48b
K. L., *Chinese HK* 2022c
Ke, *Montr.* 423a
L., *Sask.* 476c
Mao See, *Nan.Tech.* 1299b
P. P. C., *Calg.* 327c
Pei Chuan, *NU Singapore* 1312a
Qing-Hua (Henry), *Liv.* 1756c
R., *Greenwich* 1676c
Shu Hui, *Car.* 340c
Shuyuan, *Auck.UT* 1083a
Tai-Wing, *Tor.* 505a
Thomas W. O., *Chinese HK* 2029b, 2029c
W., *Chinese HK* 2028c
W. Y., *Chinese HK* 2021a
Wenbo, *NU Singapore* 1314a
Wendy, *Middx.* 1843b
Xiao Yu, *Tor.* 498b
Xiaoming, *Cant.* 1087c
Xuesong, *ICL* 1704b
Xun, *NU Singapore* 1314a
Y., *Ryerson* 464a
Y. H., *Curtin* 57b
Y. H., *NU Singapore* 1309a
Y. L., *Chinese HK* 2022c
Yanrui, *W.Aust.* 192c
Z., *Nott.Trent* 1863c
Zhang, *Nan.Tech.* 1300a
Zheng, *Vic.(BC)* 522a
Zheng da, *Bond* 40a
Wu Loo Ling, *NU Malaysia* 1019c
Wu Yunji, *Melb.* 95b
Wuensche, Burkhard, *Auck.* 1069a
Wuerger, Sophie M., *Liv.* 1758c
Wuest, James D., *Montr.* 411c, 421a
Judith, *New Br.* 432c
Wulff, Lydia, *Wales* 1968c
Rodney, *Melb.* 95a
Wulfu, Rabi, *Maid.* 1190b
Wunder, Jay, *Tor.* 508a
Wurapa, F. K., *Ghana* 585a
Wurtele, Susan E., *Trent* 514a
Wurzel, R. K., *Hull* 1697c
Wuta, M., *Z'bwe.* 2051c
Wuthnow, Julie, *Cant.* 1087c
Wuthrich, K., *Chinese HK* 2025a
Wuttunee, Wanda, *Manit.* 392b
Wuyep, S. N., *Jos* 1181a
Wyatt, A. K. J., *Brist.* 1588c
Adrian F. G., *Exe.* 1658a
Andrea, *Monash* 121a
Derrick A., *Oxf.* 1876b

Di, *Monash* 123b
Earl, *Auck.* 1079c
G. J., *H-W* 1680c
Jeremy, *Birm.* 1567c
Joan C., *Vic.(Tor.)* 512b
Kim J., *Monash* 114a
L. R., *Sheff.* 1925b
P. J., *Brist.* 1584b
Rev. Peter S., *Tor.* 511b
Ray, *Melb.* 109a
S., *Cardiff* 1615a
S. Peter, *Vic.(Tor.)* 512, 513b
Victoria, *Vic.(BC)* 520a
Wyatt-Smith, Claire, *Griff.* 69a
Wycliffe-Jones, K. W. J., *Calg.* 331c
Wydell, Taeko, *Brun.* 1595c, 1596b
Wyer, N. A., *Plym.* 1892c
S., *Herts.* 1685c
Wyeth, Paul, *S'ton.* 1933b
Wygant, Amy, *Glas.* 1667b
Wyke, S., *Stir.* 1942c, 1943b
T. J., *Manc.Met.* 1840b
Wykes, Catherine, *Nott.* 1853a
Linda J., *McG.* 385c
M., *Sheff.* 1924c
Til I. R., *Lond.* 1792b
Wylde, Charmain, *E.Lond.* 1643a
Wylie, D., *Rhodes* 1389a
John C. W., *Cardiff* 1618b
Kenneth W., *Belf.* 1565a
O. Philip, *Cardiff* 1618b
R. S., *Ryerson* 463a
Wyllie, Andrew H., *Camb.* 1606a
David J. A., *Edin.* 1651a
J. H., *Aberd.* 1537a
Wyman, M., *Stir.* 1941c
Matthew D., *Keele* 1712a
Wymer, Walter W. (Jr.), *Leth.* 365a
Wyn, Johanna G., *Melb.* 111b
Wyn Jones, Richard, *Wales* 1541c
Wyn-Jones, R. Gareth, *Wales* 1546c, 1548b
Wynaden, D. G., *Curtin* 58a
Wynant, L., *W.Ont.* 539a
Wynder, Monte, *Sunshine Coast* 159a
Wyness, M., *Warw.* 1973a
Wynford-Thomas, D., *Cardiff* 1618c, 1620a
Wynick, David, *Brist.* 1592a
Wynn, Graham A., *Leic.* 1750a
H., *Lond.* 1801c
M., *Kingston(UK)* 1719a
Mark, *Exe.* 1655c
Peter C., *Syd.* 174c
Wynn-Williams, Katharine L. H., *Otago* 1103c
Wynne, Brian E., *Lanc.* 1724c
J., *Manc.Met.* 1837a
Klaas, *Strath.* 1947c
Wynne-Edwards, Katherine, *Qu.* 452b
Wynne-Jones, M., *Nott.* 1860c
Wynyard, Hilary, *Auck.UT* 1081c
Wypych, Peter W., *W'gong.* 208a
Wyrwoll, Karl-Heinz, *W.Aust.* 193b
Wyse, D. G., *Calg.* 330b, 332b
Dominic, *Camb.* 1602a
J. E., *Nfld.* 401c
Wysling, G. Dave, *Herts.* 1688b
Wysocki, Tadeusz, *W'gong.* 208a
Wyszynski, M. L., *Birm.* 1568c
Wyver, John, *Lond.* 1778a
Shirley R., *Macq.* 88a
Wyvill, B. L. M., *Calg.* 325a
Brian, *Vic.(BC)* 518a
Geoff, *Otago* 1104b

Xaba, M. I., *N-W(S.Af.)* 1371a
Thokozani, *KwaZulu-Natal* 1354b
Xanthaki, Alexandra, *Brun.* 1597b
H., *Lond.* 1821b
Xavier, P., *Swinburne UT* 161a, 163a
R., *Qld.UT* 149a
Xaxa, Virginius, *Delhi* 724c
Xenis, Georgios, *Cyprus* 563b
Xenophontos, Christos, *Cyprus* 564c
Xi, F., *Ryerson* 463b
Jiangtao, *W'gong.* 208a
Xia, Aihua, *Melb.* 100c
K., *Chinese HK* 2024c
Kenong, *Melb.* 97c

NOTES

NOTES

NOTES

NOTES